Peterson's Four-Year Colleges 2014

WITHDRAWN

PETERSON'S

About Peterson's

Peterson's provides the accurate, dependable, high-quality education content and guidance you need to succeed. No matter where you are on your academic or professional path, you can rely on Peterson's print and digital publications for the most up-to-date education exploration data, expert test-prep tools, and top-notch career success resources—everything you need to achieve your goals.

Visit us online at **www.petersonsbooks.com** and let Peterson's help you achieve your goals.

For more information, contact Peterson's, 3 Columbia Circle, Suite 205, Albany, NY 12203-5158; 800-338-3282 Ext. 54229; or find us on the World Wide Web at www.petersonspublishing.com.

Bernadette Webster, Managing Editor; Jill C. Schwartz, Editor; John Wells, Research Project Manager; Jim Bonar, Research Operations Data Analyst; Amanda Ortiz, Research Associate; Phyllis Johnson, Software Engineer; Ray Golaszewski, Publishing Operations Manager; Linda M. Williams, Composition Manager; Carrie Hansen, Christine Lucht, Kiele Nowak, Bailey Williams, Fulfillment Coordinators; Charlotte Thomas, Richard Woodland, Contributing Authors

ISSN 1544-2330
ISBN-13: 978-0-7689-3753-4

Printed in the United States of America

10 9 8 7 6 5 4 3 2 1   15 14 13

Forty-fourth Edition

Contents

A Note from the Peterson's Editors

For nearly fifty years, Peterson's has given students and parents the most comprehensive, up-to-date information on undergraduate institutions in the United States and Canada. *Peterson's Four-Year Colleges 2014* features advice and tips on the college search and selection process, such as how to consider the factors that truly make a difference during your search, how to understand the application process, and how to get financial aid. Each year, Peterson's researches the data published in *Peterson's Four-Year Colleges*. The information is furnished by the colleges and is accurate at the time of publishing.

Opportunities abound for students, and this guide can help you find what you want in a number of ways:

- For application and admissions advice and guidance, just head to **THE ADVICE CENTER**. Within the **Search, Find, Select** section, the "College Admissions Countdown Calendar" outlines pertinent month-by-month milestones. "Choosing Your Top Ten Colleges" gets you started on putting together the most important top ten list you have ever made. "Surviving Standardized Tests" describes frequently used tests and what you need to know to succeed on them. Of course, part of the college selection process involves visiting the schools themselves, and "The Whys and Whats of College Visits" is just the planner you need to make those trips well worth your while. Next, "Applying 101" provides advice on how best to approach the application phase of the process. If you can't make sense out of the early decision/ early action conundrum, "The Early Decision Decision" can help clarify it for you. Finally, "What International Students Need to Know About Admission to U.S. Colleges and Universities" has tips on college admissions for non–U.S. citizens and can also be useful to U.S. citizens. Up next is the **Money, Money, Money** section, which provides all the essential information on how to meet your education expenses, starting with the "Financial Aid Countdown Calendar" and followed by articles covering "Who's Paying for This? Financial Aid Basics" and "Middle Income Families: Making the Financial Aid Process Work." And be sure to check out our **Options, Options, Options** section for some sneak peeks into specific institutions and programs that may be just right for you, including the latest on honors programs, public versus private colleges, women's colleges, and online learning. Finally, you'll want to read through the **How to Use This Guide** section, which explains the information presented for each individual college, how Peterson's collects its data, and how Peterson's determines eligibility for inclusion in this guide.

- Next up is the **PROFILES** section. Here you'll find our unparalleled college profiles, arranged alphabetically by state. They provide need-to-know information about accredited four-year colleges—including entrance difficulty, campus setting, total enrollment, student-faculty ratio, application deadlines, expenses, most frequently chosen baccalaureate fields, and academic programs. All the information you need to apply is placed together at the conclusion of each college profile. Display ads, which appear near some of the institutions' profiles, have been provided and paid for by those colleges or universities that wished to supplement their profile data with additional information about their institution.

- And if you still thirst for even more information, over 300 two-page narrative descriptions appear as **COLLEGE CLOSE-UPS**—descriptions written by admissions or college officials that provide great detail about each school. They are edited to provide a consistent format across entries for your ease of comparison.

- If you already have specifics in mind, such as a particular major or institution, turn to the **INDEXES** section. Here you can search for a school based on major, entrance difficulty, cost ranges, and geography. If you already have colleges in mind that pique your interest, you can use the "Alphabetical Listing of Colleges and Universities" to search for these schools. Page numbers referring to all information presented about a college are conveniently referenced.

Peterson's publishes a full line of books—college and grad guides, education exploration, test preparation, financial aid, and career preparation. Peterson's publications can be found at high school guidance offices, college libraries and career centers, and your local bookstore and library. Peterson's books are now also available as eBooks and online at www.petersonsbooks.com..

We welcome any comments or suggestions you may have about this publication. Your feedback will help us make educational dreams possible for you—and others like you.

Colleges will be pleased to know that Peterson's helped you in your selection. Admissions staff members are more than happy to answer questions, address specific problems, and help in any way they can. The editors at Peterson's wish you great success in your college search!

The Advice Center

College Admissions Countdown Calendar

This practical month-by-month calendar is designed to help you stay on top of the process of applying to college. For most students, the process begins in September of the junior year of high school and ends in June of the senior year. You may want to begin considering financial aid options, reviewing your academic schedule, and attending college fairs before your junior year.

JUNIOR YEAR

September
- Check with your counselor to make sure your course credits will meet college requirements.
- Be sure you are involved in one or two extracurricular activities.
- Begin building your personal list of colleges.

October
- Register for and take the PSAT/NMSQT®.

November
- Strive to get the best grades you can. A serious effort will provide you with the most options during the application process.

December
- Get involved in a community service activity.
- Begin to read newspapers and a weekly news magazine.
- Buy *Peterson's Master the SAT,* or *The Real ACT* and begin to study for the tests.

January
- With your school counselor, decide when to take the ACT®, SAT®, and SAT Subject Tests™ (and which Subject Tests to take). If English is not your primary language and you are planning on attending a college in North America, decide when to take the TOEFL®.
- Keep your grades up!

February
- Plan a challenging schedule of classes for your senior year.
- Think about which teachers you will ask to write recommendations.
- Check http://www.nacacnet.org/ and click on "College Fairs" for up-to-date schedules and locations of college fairs.

March
- Register for the tests you will take in the spring (ACT, SAT, SAT Subject Tests, or the TOEFL).
- Meet with your school counselor to discuss college choices.
- Review your transcript and test scores with your counselor to determine how competitive your range of choices should be.
- Develop a preliminary list of fifteen to twenty colleges and universities.
- Start scheduling campus visits. The best time is when school is in session (but never during final exams). Summers are OK but will not show you what the college is really like. If possible, save your top college choices for the fall. Be aware, however, that fall is the busiest visit season, and you will need advance planning. Don't forget to write thank you letters to your interviewers.

April
- Take any standardized tests for which you have registered.
- Create a list of your potential college choices and begin to record personal and academic information that can be transferred later to your college applications.

May
- Plan college visits and make appointments.
- Structure your summer plans to include advanced academic work, travel, volunteer work, or a job.
- Confirm your academic schedule for the fall.

Summer
- Write to any colleges on your list that do not accept the Common Application to request application forms.
- Begin working on your application essays

SENIOR YEAR

September

- ☐ Register for the ACT, SAT, SAT Subject Tests, or TOEFL, as necessary.
- ☐ Check with your school counselor for the fall visiting schedule of college reps.
- ☐ Ask appropriate teachers if they would write recommendations for you. Don't forget to write thank you letters when they accept.
- ☐ Meet with your counselor to compile your final list of colleges.

October

- ☐ Mail or send early applications electronically after carefully checking them to be sure they are completely filled out.
- ☐ Photocopy or print extra copies of your applications to use as a backup.
- ☐ Take the tests for which you have registered.
- ☐ Don't be late! Keep track of all deadlines for transcripts, recommendations, financial aid, etc.

November

- ☐ Be sure that you have requested your ACT and SAT scores be sent to your colleges of choice.
- ☐ Complete and submit all applications. Print or photocopy an extra copy for your records.

December

- ☐ Take any necessary tests: ACT, SAT, SAT Subject Tests, or TOEFL.
- ☐ Meet with your counselor to verify that all is in order and that transcripts are out to colleges.

January

- ☐ Prepare the Free Application for Federal Student Aid (FAFSA), available at www.fafsa.ed.gov or through your school counseling office. An estimated income tax statement (which can be corrected later) can be used. The sooner you apply for financial aid, the better your chances.

February

- ☐ Submit your FAFSA either online or via U.S. mail.
- ☐ Be sure your midyear report has gone out to the colleges to which you've applied.
- ☐ Let colleges know of any new honors or accomplishments that were not in your original application.

March

- ☐ Register for any Advanced Placement (AP) tests you might take.
- ☐ Be sure you have received a FAFSA acknowledgment.

April

- ☐ Review the acceptances and financial aid offers you receive.
- ☐ Go back to visit one or two of your top-choice colleges.
- ☐ Notify your college of choice that you have accepted its offer (and send in a deposit by May 1).
- ☐ Notify the colleges you have chosen not to attend of your decision.

May

- ☐ Take AP tests.

June

- ☐ Graduate! Congratulations and best of luck.

Choosing Your Top Ten Colleges

By using all the information in the various sections of this guide, you will find colleges worthy of the most important top-ten list on the planet—yours.

The first thing you will need to do is decide what type of institution of higher learning you want to attend. Each of the thousands of four-year colleges and universities in the United States is as unique as the people applying to it. Although listening to the voices and media hype around you can make it sound as though there are only a few elite schools worth attending, this simply is not true. By considering some of the following criteria, you will soon find that the large pool of interesting colleges can be narrowed down to a more reasonable number.

SIZE AND CATEGORY

Schools come in all shapes and sizes, from tiny rural colleges of 400 students to massive state university systems serving 100,000 students or more. If you are coming from a small high school, a college with 3,500 students may seem large to you. If you are currently attending a high school with 3,000 students, selecting a college of a similar size may not feel like a new enough experience. Some students coming from very large impersonal high schools are looking for a place where they will be recognized from the beginning and offered a more personal approach. If you don't have a clue about what size might feel right to you, try visiting a couple of nearby colleges of varying sizes. You do not have to be seriously interested in them; just feel what impact the number of students on campus has on you.

Large Universities

Large universities offer a wide range of educational, athletic, and social experiences. Universities offer a full scope of undergraduate majors and award master's and doctoral degrees as well. Universities are usually composed of several smaller colleges. Depending on your interest in a major field or area of study, you would likely apply to a specific college within the university. Each college has the flexibility to set its own standards for admission, which may differ from the overall average of the university. The colleges within a university system also set their own course requirements for earning a degree.

Universities may be public or private. Some large private universities, such as Harvard, Yale, Princeton, University of Pennsylvania, New York University, Northwestern, and Stanford, are well-known for their high entrance standards, the excellence of their education, and the success rates of their graduates. These institutions place a great deal of emphasis on research and compete aggressively for grants from the federal government to fund these projects. Large public universities,

such as the State University of New York (SUNY) System, University of Michigan, University of Texas, University of Illinois, University of Washington, and University of North Carolina, also support excellent educational programs, compete for and win research funding, and have successful graduates. Public universities usually offer substantially lower tuition rates to in-state students, although their tuition rates for out-of-state residents are often comparable to those of private institutions.

At many large universities, sports play a major role on campus. Athletics can dominate the calendar and set the tone year-round at some schools. Alumni travel from far and wide to attend their alma mater's football or basketball games, and the campus—and frequently the entire town—grinds to a halt when there is a home game. Athletes are heroes and dominate campus social life.

What are some other features of life on a university campus? Every kind of club imaginable, from literature to bioengineering and chorus to politics, can be found on most college campuses. You will be able to play the intramural version of almost every sport in which the university fields interscholastic teams and join fraternities, sororities, and groups dedicated to social action. You can become a member of a band, an orchestra, or perhaps a chamber music group or work on the newspaper, the literary magazine, or the website. The list can go on and on. You may want to try out a new interest or two or pursue what you have always been interested in and make like-minded friends along the way.

Take a look at the size of the classrooms in the larger universities and envision yourself sitting in that atmosphere. Would this offer a learning environment that would benefit you?

Liberal Arts Colleges

If you have considered large universities and come to the conclusion that all that action could be a distraction, a small liberal arts college might be right for you. Ideally tucked away on a picture-perfect campus, a liberal arts college generally has fewer than 5,000 students. The mission of most liberal arts schools is learning for the sake of learning, with a strong emphasis on creating lifelong learners who will be able to apply their education to any number of careers. This contrasts with objectives of the profession-based preparation of specialized colleges.

Liberal arts colleges cannot offer the breadth of courses provided by the large universities. As a result, liberal arts colleges try to create a niche for themselves. For instance, a college may place its emphasis on its humanities departments, whose professors are all well-known published authors and international presenters in their areas of expertise. A college may

Surviving Standardized Tests

WHAT ARE STANDARDIZED TESTS?

Colleges and universities in the United States use tests to help evaluate applicants' readiness for admission or to place them in appropriate courses. The tests that are most frequently used by colleges are the ACT® of American College Testing, Inc., and the College Board's SAT®. In addition, the Educational Testing Service (ETS) offers the TOEFL® test, which evaluates the English-language proficiency of nonnative speakers. The tests are offered at designated testing centers located at high schools and colleges throughout the United States and U.S. territories and at testing centers in various countries throughout the world.

Upon request, special accommodations for students with documented visual, hearing, physical, or learning disabilities are available. Examples of special accommodations include tests in Braille or large print and such aids as a reader, recorder, magnifying glass, or sign language interpreter. Additional testing time may be allowed in some instances. Contact the appropriate testing program or your guidance counselor for details on how to request special accommodations.

THE ACT

The ACT is a standardized college entrance examination that measures knowledge and skills in English, mathematics, reading, and science reasoning and the application of these skills to future academic tasks. The ACT consists of four multiple-choice tests.

Test 1: English
- 75 questions, 45 minutes
- Usage and mechanics
- Rhetorical skills

Test 2: Mathematics
- 60 questions, 60 minutes
- Pre-algebra
- Elementary algebra
- Intermediate algebra
- Coordinate geometry
- Plane geometry
- Trigonometry

Test 3: Reading
- 40 questions, 35 minutes
- Prose fiction
- Humanities
- Social studies
- Natural sciences

Test 4: Science
- 40 questions, 35 minutes
- Data representation
- Research summary
- Conflicting viewpoints

Each section is scored from 1 to 36 and is scaled for slight variations in difficulty. Students are not penalized for incorrect responses. The composite score is the average of the four scaled scores. The ACT Plus Writing includes the four multiple-choice tests and a writing test, which measures writing skills emphasized in high school English classes and in entry-level college composition courses.

- To prepare for the ACT, ask your guidance counselor for a free guidebook called "Preparing for the ACT." Besides providing general test-preparation information and additional test-taking strategies, this guidebook describes the content and format of the four ACT subject area tests, summarizes test administration procedures followed at ACT test centers, and includes a practice test. Peterson's publishes *The Real ACT* that includes five official ACT tests.

DON'T FORGET TO . . .

- ❑ Take the SAT or ACT before application deadlines.
- ❑ Note that test registration deadlines precede test dates by about six weeks.
- ❑ Register to take the TOEFL test if English is not your native language and you are planning on studying at a North American college.
- ❑ Practice your test-taking skills with *Peterson's Master the SAT* and *The Real ACT*
- ❑ Contact the College Board or American College Testing, Inc., in advance if you need special accommodations when taking tests.

THE SAT

The SAT measures developed critical reading and mathematical reasoning abilities as they relate to successful performance in college. It is intended to supplement the secondary school record and other information about the student in assessing readiness for college. There is one unscored, experimental section on the exam, which is used for equating and/or pretesting purposes and can cover either the mathematics or critical reading area.

Critical Reading
- 67 questions, 70 minutes
- Sentence completion
- Passage-based reading

Mathematics
- 54 questions, 70 minutes
- Multiple-choice
- Student-produced response (grid-ins)

Writing

- 49 questions plus essay, 60 minutes
- Identifying sentence errors
- Improving paragraphs
- Improving sentences
- Essay

Students receive one point for each correct response and lose a fraction of a point for each incorrect response (except for student-produced responses). These points are totaled to produce the raw scores, which are then scaled to equalize the scores for slight variations in difficulty for various editions of the test. The critical reading, writing, and mathematics scaled scores range from 200–800 per section. The total scaled score range is from 600–2400.

Top 10 Ways Not to Take the Test

10. Cramming the night before the test.

9. Not becoming familiar with the directions before you take the test.

8. Not becoming familiar with the format of the test before you take it.

7. Not knowing how the test is graded.

6. Spending too much time on any one question.

5. Second-guessing yourself.

4. Not checking spelling, grammar, and sentence structure in essays.

3. Writing a one-paragraph essay.

2. Forgetting to take a deep breath to keep from—

1. Losing It!

SAT SUBJECT TESTS

Subject Tests are required by some institutions for admission and/or placement in freshman-level courses. Each Subject Test measures one's knowledge of a specific subject and the ability to apply that knowledge. Students should check with each institution for its specific requirements. In general, students are required to take three Subject Tests (one English, one mathematics, and one of their choice).

Subject Tests are given in the following areas: biology, chemistry, Chinese, French, German, Italian, Japanese, Korean, Latin, literature, mathematics, modern Hebrew, physics, Spanish, U.S. history, and world history. These tests are 1 hour long and are primarily multiple-choice tests. Three Subject Tests may be taken on one test date.

Scored like the SAT, students gain a point for each correct answer and lose a fraction of a point for each incorrect answer. The raw scores are then converted to scaled scores that range from 200 to 800.

THE TOEFL INTERNET-BASED TEST (IBT)

The Test of English as a Foreign Language Internet-Based Test (TOEFL iBT) is designed to help assess a student's grasp of English if it is not the student's first language. Performance on the TOEFL test may help interpret scores on the critical reading sections of the SAT. The test consists of four integrated sections: speaking, listening, reading, and writing. The TOEFL iBT emphasizes integrated skills. The paper-based versions of the TOEFL will continue to be administered in certain countries where the Internet-based version has not yet been introduced. For further information, visit www.toefl.org.

WHAT OTHER TESTS SHOULD I KNOW ABOUT?

The AP Program

This program allows high school students to try college-level work and build valuable skills and study habits in the process. Subject matter is explored in more depth in AP courses than in other high school classes. A qualifying score on an AP test—which varies from school to school—can earn you college credit or advanced placement. Getting qualifying grades on enough exams can even earn you a full year's credit and sophomore standing at more than 1,500 higher-education institutions. There are more than thirty AP courses across multiple subject areas, including art history, biology, and computer science. Speak to your guidance counselor for information about your school's offerings.

College-Level Examination Program (CLEP)

The CLEP enables students to earn college credit for what they already know, whether it was learned in school, through independent study, or through other experiences outside of the classroom. More than 2,900 colleges and universities now award credit for qualifying scores on one or more of the 33 CLEP exams. The exams, which are 90 minutes in length and are primarily multiple choice, are administered at participating colleges and universities. For more information, check out the website at www.collegeboard.com/clep.

WHAT CAN I DO TO PREPARE FOR THESE TESTS?

Know what to expect. Get familiar with how the tests are structured, how much time is allowed, and the directions for each type of question. Get plenty of rest the night before the test and eat breakfast that morning.

There are a variety of products, from books to software to videos, available to help you prepare for most standardized tests. Find the learning style that suits you best. As for which products to buy, there are two major categories— those created by the test-makers and those created by private companies. The best approach is to talk to someone who has been through the process and find out which product or products he or she recommends.

Some students report significant increases in scores after participating in coaching programs. Longer-term programs (40 hours) seem to raise scores more than short-term programs (20 hours), but beyond 40 hours, score gains are minor. Math scores appear to benefit more from coaching than critical reading scores.

Resources

There is a variety of ways to prepare for standardized tests—find a method that fits your schedule and your budget. But you should definitely prepare. Far too many students walk into these tests cold, either because they find standardized tests frightening or annoying or they just haven't found the time to study. The key is that these exams are standardized. That means these tests are largely the same from administration to administration; they always test the same concepts. They have to, or else you couldn't compare the scores of people who took the tests on different dates. The numbers or words may change, but the underlying content doesn't.

So how do you prepare? At the very least, you should review relevant material, such as math formulas and commonly used vocabulary words, and know the directions for each question type or test section. You should take at least one practice test and review your mistakes so you don't make them again on the test day. Beyond that, you know best how much preparation you need. You'll also find lots of material in libraries or bookstores to help you: books and software from the test-makers and from other publishers (including Peterson's) or live courses that range from national test-preparation companies to teachers at your high school who offer classes.

The Whys and Whats of College Visits

Dawn B. Sova, Ph.D.

The campus visit should not be a passive activity for you and your parents. Take the initiative and gather information beyond that provided in the official tour. You will see many important indicators during your visit that will tell you more about the true character of a college and its students than the tour guide will reveal. Know what to look for and how to assess the importance of such indicators.

WHAT SHOULD YOU ASK AND WHAT SHOULD YOU LOOK FOR?

Your first stop on a campus visit is the visitor center or admissions office, where you will probably have to wait to meet with a counselor. Colleges usually plan to greet visitors later than the appointed time in order to give them the opportunity to review some of the campus information that is liberally scattered throughout the visitor waiting room. Take advantage of the time to become even more familiar with the college by arriving 15 to 30 minutes before your appointment to observe the behavior of staff members and to browse through the yearbooks and student newspapers that will be available.

If you prepare in advance, you will have already reviewed the college catalog and map of the campus. These materials familiarize you with the academic offerings and the physical layout of the campus, but the true character of the college and its students emerges in other ways.

Begin your investigation with the visitor center staff members. As a student's first official contact with the college, they should make every effort to welcome prospective students and project a friendly image.

- How do they treat you and other prospective students who are waiting? Are they friendly and willing to speak with you, or do they try their hardest to avoid eye contact and conversation?

- Are they friendly with each other and with students who enter the office, or are they curt and unwilling to help?

- Does the waiting room have a friendly feeling or is it cold and sterile?

If the visitor center staff members seem indifferent to prospective students, there is little reason to believe that they will be warm and welcoming to current students. View such behavior as a warning to watch very carefully the interaction of others with you during the tour. An indifferent or unfriendly reception in the admissions office may be simply the first of

many signs that attending this college will not be a pleasant experience.

Look through several yearbooks and see the types of activities that are actually photographed, as opposed to the activities that colleges promise in their promotional literature. Some questions are impossible to answer if the college is very large, but for small and moderately sized colleges the yearbook is a good indicator of campus activity.

- Has the number of clubs and organizations increased or decreased in the past five years?

- Do the same students appear repeatedly in activities?

- Do sororities and fraternities dominate campus activities?

- Are participants limited to one sex or one ethnic group, or is there diversity?

- Are all activities limited to the campus, or are students involved in activities in the community?

Use what you observe in the yearbooks as a means of forming a more complete understanding of the college, but don't base your entire impression on just one facet. If time permits, look through several copies of the school newspaper, which should reflect the major concerns and interests of the students. The paper is also a good way to learn about the campus social life.

- Does the paper contain a mix of national and local news?

- What products or services are advertised?

- How assertive are the editorials?

- With what topics are the columnists concerned?

- Are movies and concerts that meet your tastes advertised or reviewed?

- What types of ads appear in the classified section?

The newspaper should be a public forum for students, and, as such, should reflect the character of the campus and of the student body. A paper that deals only with seemingly safe and well-edited topics on the editorial page and in regular feature columns might indicate administrative censorship. A lack of ads for restaurants might indicate either a lack of good places to eat or that area restaurants do not welcome student business. A limited mention of movies, concerts, or other entertainment might reveal a severely limited campus social life. Even if ads and reviews are included, you should still balance how such activities reflect your tastes.

You will have only a limited amount of time to ask questions during your initial meeting with the admissions counselor, for very few schools include a formal interview in the initial campus visit or tour. Instead, this brief meeting is often just a nicety that allows the admissions office to begin a file for the student and to record some initial impressions. Save your questions for the tour guide and for students on campus you meet along the way.

HOW CAN YOU ASSESS THE TRUE CHARACTER OF A COLLEGE AND ITS STUDENTS?

Colleges do not train their tour guides to deceive prospective students, but they do caution guides to avoid unflattering topics and campus sites. Does this mean that you will see only a sugarcoated version of life on a particular college campus? Not at all, especially not if you are observant.

Most organized campus visits include such campus facilities as dormitories, dining halls, libraries, student activity and recreation centers, and the health and student services centers. Some may only be pointed out, while you will walk through others. Either way, you will find that many signs of the true character of the college emerge if you keep your eyes open.

Bulletin boards in dormitories and student centers contain a wealth of information about campus activities, student concerns, and campus groups. Read the posters, notices, and messages to learn what *really* interests students. Unlike ads in the school newspaper, posters put up by students advertise both on-and off-campus events, so they will give you an idea of what is also available in the surrounding community.

Review the notices, which may cover either campuswide events or events that concern only small groups of students. The catalog may not mention a performance group, but an individual dormitory with its own small theater may offer regular productions. Poetry readings, jam sessions, writers' groups, and other activities may be announced and show diversity of student interests.

Even the brief bulletin board messages offering objects for sale and noting objects that people want to purchase reveal a lot about a campus. Are most of the items computer related? Or do the messages specify audio equipment or musical instruments? Are offers to trade goods or services posted? Don't ignore the "ride wanted" messages. Students who want to share rides home during a break may specify widely diverse geographical locations. If so, then you know that the student body is not limited to only the immediate area or one locale. Other messages can also enhance your knowledge of the true character of the campus and its students.

As you walk through various buildings, examine their condition carefully.

- Is the paint peeling, and do the exteriors look worn?

- Are the exteriors and interiors of the building clean?

- Is the equipment in the classrooms up-to-date or outdated?

Pay particular attention to the dormitories, especially to factors that might affect your safety. Observe the appearance of the structure, and ask about the security measures in and around the dormitories.

- Are the dormitories noisy or quiet?

- Do they seem crowded?

- How good is the lighting around each dormitory?

- Are the dormitories spread throughout the campus or are they clustered in one main area?

- Who has access to the dormitories in addition to students?

- How secure are the means by which students enter and leave the dormitory?

While you are on the subject of dormitory safety, you should also ask about campus safety. Don't expect that the guide will rattle off a list of crimes that have been committed in the past year. To obtain that information, access the recent year of issues of *The Chronicle of Higher Education* and locate its yearly report on campus crime. Also ask the guide about safety measures that the campus police take and those that students have initiated.

- Can students request escorts to their residences late at night?

- Do campus shuttle buses run at frequent intervals all night?

- Are "blue-light" telephones liberally placed throughout the campus for students to use to call for help?

- Do the campus police patrol the campus regularly?

If the guide does not answer your questions satisfactorily, wait until after the tour to contact the campus police or traffic office for answers.

Campus tours usually just point out the health services center without taking the time to walk through. Even if you don't see the inside of the building, you should take a close look at the location of the health services center and ask the guide questions about services.

- How far is the health center from the dormitories?

- Is a doctor always on call?

- Does the campus transport sick students from their dormitories or must they walk?

- What are the operating hours of the health center?

- Does the health center refer students to a nearby hospital?

If the guide can't answer your questions, visit the health center later and ask someone there.

Most campus tours take pride in showing students their activities centers, which may contain snack bars, game rooms, workout facilities, and other means of entertainment. Should you scrutinize this building as carefully as the rest? Of course. Outdated and poorly maintained activity equipment contributes to your total impression of the college. You should also ask about the hours, availability, and cost (no, the activities are usually not free) of using the bowling alleys, pool tables, air hockey tables, and other amenities.

As you walk through campus with the tour, also look carefully at the appearance of the students who pass. The way in which both men and women groom themselves, the way they dress, and even their physical bearing communicate a lot more than any guidebook can. If everyone seems to conform to the same look, you might feel that you would be uncomfortable at the college, however nonconformist that look might be. On the other hand, you might not feel comfortable on a campus that stresses diversity of dress and behavior, and your observations now can save you discomfort later.

- Does every student seem to wear a sorority or fraternity t-shirt or jacket?

- Is everyone of your sex sporting the latest fad haircut?

- Do all of the men or the women seem to be wearing expensive name-brand clothes?

- Do most of the students seem to be working hard to look outrageous with regards to clothing, hair color, and body art?

- Would you feel uncomfortable in a room full of these students?

Is appearance important to you? If it is, then you should consider very seriously if you answer yes to any of the above questions. You don't have to be the same as everyone else on campus, but standing out too much may make you unhappy.

As you observe the physical appearance of the students, also listen to their conversations as you pass them. What are they talking about? How are they speaking? Are their voices and accents all the same, or do you hear diversity in their speech? Are you offended by their language? Think how you will feel if surrounded by the same speech habits and patterns for four years.

WHERE SHOULD YOU VISIT ON YOUR OWN?

Your campus visit is not over when the tour ends because you will probably have many questions yet to be answered and many places to still be seen. Where you go depends upon the extent to which the organized tour covers the campus. Your tour should take you to view residential halls, health and student services centers, the gymnasium or field house, dining halls, the library, and recreational centers. If any of the facilities on this list have been omitted, visit them on your own and ask questions of the students and staff members you meet. In addition, you should step off campus and gain an impression of the surrounding community. You will probably become bored with life on campus and spend at least some time off campus. Make certain that you know what the surrounding area is like.

The campus tour leaves little time to ask impromptu questions of current students, but you can do so after the tour. Eat lunch in one of the dining halls. Most will allow visitors to pay cash to experience a typical student meal. Food may not be important to you now while you are living at home and can

simply take anything you want from the refrigerator at any time, but it will be when you are away at college with only a meal ticket to feed you.

- How clean is the dining hall? Consider serving tables, floors, and seating.

- What is the quality of the food?

- How big are the portions?

- How much variety do students have at each meal?

- How healthy are the food choices?

While you are eating, try to strike up a conversation with students and tell them that you are considering attending their college. Their reactions and advice can be eye-opening. Ask them questions about the academic atmosphere and the professors.

- Are the classes large or small?

- Do the majority of the professors only lecture or are tutorials and seminars common?

- Is the emphasis of the faculty career-oriented or abstract?

- Are the teaching methods innovative and stimulating or boring and dull?

- Is the academic atmosphere pressured, lax, or somewhere in between?

- Which are the strong majors? The weak majors?

- Is the emphasis on grades or social life or a mix of both at the college?

- How hard do students have to work to receive high grades?

Current students can also give you the inside line on the true nature of the college social life. You may gain some idea through looking in the yearbook, in the newspaper, and on the bulletin boards, but students will reveal the true highs and lows of campus life. Ask them about drug use, partying, dating, drinking, and anything else that may affect your life as a student.

- Which are the most popular club activities?

- What do students do on weekends? Do most go home?

- How frequently do concerts occur on campus? Who has recently performed?

- How can you become involved in specific activities (name them)?

- How strictly are campus rules enforced and how severe are penalties?

- What counseling services are available?

- Are academic tutoring services available?

- Do they feel that the faculty really cares about students, especially freshmen?

You will receive the most valuable information from current students, but you will only be able to speak with them after the tour is over. And you might have to risk rejection as you try to initiate conversations with students who might not want to reveal how they feel about the campus. Still, the value of this information is worth the chance.

If you have the time, you should also visit the library to see just how accessible research materials are and to observe the physical layout. The catalog usually specifies the days and hours of operation, as well as the number of volumes contained in the library and the number of periodicals to which it subscribes. A library also requires accessibility, good lighting, an adequate number of study carrels, and lounge areas for students. Many colleges have created 24-hour study lounges for students who find the residence halls too noisy for studying, although most colleges claim that they designate areas of the residences as "quiet study" areas. You may not be interested in any of this information, but when you are a student you will have to make frequent use of the campus library so you should know what is available. You should at least ask how extensive their holdings are in your proposed major area. If they have virtually nothing, you will have to spend a lot of time ordering items via interlibrary loan or making copies, which can become expensive. The ready answer of students that they will obtain their information from the Internet is unpleasantly countered by professors who demand journal articles with documentation.

Make a point of at least driving through the community surrounding the college because you will be spending time there shopping, dining, working in a part-time job, or attending events. Even the largest and best-stocked campus will not meet all of your social and personal needs. If you can spare the time, stop in several stores to see if they welcome college students.

- Is the surrounding community suburban, urban, or rural?

- Does the community offer stores of interest, such as bookstores, craft shops, and boutiques?

- Do the businesses employ college students?

- Does the community have a movie or stage theater?

- Are there several types of interesting restaurants?

- Do there seem to be any clubs that court a college clientele?

- Is the center of activity easy to walk to, or do you need other transportation?

You might feel that a day is not enough to answer all of your questions, but even answering some questions will provide you with a stronger basis for choosing a college. Many students visit a college campus several times before making their decision. Keep in mind that for the rest of your life you will be associated with the college that you attend. You will spend four years of your life at this college. The effort of spending several days to obtain the information to make your decision is worthwhile.

———————

Dawn B. Sova, Ph.D., is a former newspaper reporter and columnist, as well as the author of more than eight books and numerous magazine articles. She teaches creative and research writing, as well as scientific and technical writing, newswriting, and journalism.

Applying 101

The words "applying yourself" have several important meanings in the college application process. One meaning refers to the fact that you need to keep focused during this important time in your life, keep your priorities straight, and know the dates that your applications are due so you can apply on time. The phrase might also refer to the person who is really responsible for your application—you.

You are the only person who should compile your college application. You need to take ownership of this process. The guidance counselor is not responsible for completing your applications, and neither are your parents. College applications must be completed in addition to your normal workload at school, college visits, and SAT, ACT, or TOEFL testing.

THE APPLICATION

The application is your way of introducing yourself to a college admissions office. As with any introduction, you want to make a good first impression. The first thing you should do in presenting your application is to find out what the college or university needs from you. Read the application carefully to find out the application fee and deadline, required standardized tests, number of essays, interview requirements, and anything else you can do or submit to help improve your chances for acceptance.

Completing college applications yourself helps you learn more about the schools to which you are applying. The information a college asks for in its application can tell you much about the school. State university applications often tell you how they are going to view their applicants. Usually, they select students based on GPAs and test scores. Colleges that request an interview, ask you to respond to a few open-ended questions, or require an essay are interested in a more personal approach to the application process and may be looking for different types of students than those sought by a state school.

In addition to submitting the actual application, there are several other items that are commonly required. You will be responsible for ensuring that your standardized test scores and your high school transcript arrive at the colleges to which you apply. Most colleges will ask that you submit teacher recommendations as well. Select teachers who know you and your abilities well and allow them plenty of time to complete the recommendations. When all portions of the application have been completed and sent in, whether electronically or by mail, make sure you follow up with the college to ensure their receipt.

FOLLOW THESE TIPS WHEN FILLING OUT YOUR APPLICATIONS

- **Follow the directions to the letter.** You don't want to be in a position to ask an admissions officer for exceptions due to your inattentiveness.
- **Proofread all parts of your application,** including your essay. Again, the final product indicates to the admissions staff how meticulous and careful you are in your work.
- **Submit your application as early as possible,** provided all of the pieces are available. If there is a problem with your application, this will allow you to work through it with the admissions staff in plenty of time. If you wait until the last minute, it not only takes away that cushion but also reflects poorly on your sense of priorities.
- **Keep a copy of the completed application,** whether it is a photocopy or a copy saved on your computer.

THE APPLICATION ESSAY

Whereas the other portions of your application—your transcript, test scores, and involvement in extracurricular activities—are a reflection of what you've accomplished up to this point, your application essay is an opportunity to present yourself in the here and now. The essay shows your originality and verbal skills and how you approach a topic or problem and express your opinion.

Some colleges may request one essay or a combination of essays and short-answer topics to learn more about who you are and how well you can communicate your thoughts. Common essay topics cover such simple themes as writing about yourself and your experiences or why you want to attend that particular school. Other colleges will ask that you show your imaginative or creative side by writing about a favorite author, for instance, or commenting on a hypothetical situation. In such cases, they will be looking at your thought processes and level of creativity.

Admissions officers, particularly those at small or mid-size colleges, use the essay to determine how you, as a student, will fit into life at that college. The essay, therefore, is a critical component of the application process. Here are some tips for writing a winning essay:

- Colleges are looking for an honest representation of who you are and what you think. Make sure that the tone of the essay reflects enthusiasm, maturity, creativity, the ability to communicate, talent, and your leadership skills.

- Be sure you set aside enough time to write the essay, revise it, and revise it *again*. Running "spell check" will only detect a fraction of the errors you probably made on your first pass at writing it. Take a break and then come back to it and reread it. You will probably notice other style, content, and grammar problems—and ways that you can improve the essay overall.

- Always answer the question that is being asked, making sure that you are specific, clear, and true to your personality.

- Enlist the help of reviewers who know you well— friends, parents, teachers—since they are likely to be the most honest and will keep you on track in the presentation of your true self.

THE PERSONAL INTERVIEW

Although it is relatively rare that a personal interview is required, many colleges recommend that you take this opportunity for a face-to-face discussion with a member of the admissions staff. Read through the application materials to determine whether or not a college places great emphasis on the interview. If they strongly recommend that you have one, it may work against you to forego it.

In contrast to a group interview and some alumni interviews, which are intended to provide information about a college, the personal interview is viewed both as an information session and as further evaluation of your skills and strengths. You will meet with a member of the admissions staff who will be assessing your personal qualities, high school preparation, and your capacity to contribute to undergraduate life at the institution. On average, these meetings last about 45 minutes—a relatively short amount of time in which to gather information and leave the desired impression—so here are some suggestions on how to make the most of it.

Scheduling Your Visit

Generally, students choose to visit campuses in the summer or fall of their senior year. Both times have their advantages. A summer visit, when the campus is not in session, generally allows for a less hectic visit and interview. Visiting in the fall, on the other hand, provides the opportunity to see what campus life is like in full swing. If you choose the fall, consider arranging an overnight trip so that you can stay in one of the college dormitories. At the very least, you should make your way around campus to take part in classes, athletic events, and social activities. Always make an appointment and avoid scheduling more than two college interviews on any given day. Multiple interviews in a single day hinder your chances of making a good impression, and your impressions of the colleges will blur into each other as you hurriedly make your way from place to place.

Preparation

Know the basics about the college before going for your interview. Read the college catalog and website in addition to this guide. You will be better prepared to ask questions that are not answered in the literature and that will give you a better understanding of what the college has to offer. You should also spend some time thinking about your strengths and weaknesses and, in particular, what you are looking for in a college education. You will find that as you get a few interviews under your belt, they will get easier. You might consider starting with a college that is not a top contender on your list, so that the stakes are not as high.

Asking Questions

Inevitably, your interviewer will ask you, "Do you have any questions?" Not having one may suggest that you're unprepared or, even worse, not interested. When you do ask questions, make sure that they are ones that matter to you and that have a bearing on your decision about whether or not to attend that college. The questions that you ask will give the interviewer some insight into your personality and priorities. Avoid asking questions that are answered in the college literature—again, a sign of unpreparedness. Although the interviewer will undoubtedly pose questions to you, the interview should not be viewed merely as a question-and-answer session. If a conversation evolves out of a particular question, so much the better. Your interviewer can learn a great deal about you from how you sustain a conversation. Similarly, you will be able to learn a great deal about the college in a conversational format.

Separate the Interview from the Interviewer

Many students base their feelings about a college solely on their impressions of the interviewer. Try not to characterize a college based only on your personal reaction, however, since your impressions can be skewed by whether you and your interviewer hit it off. Pay lots of attention to everything else that you see, hear, and learn about a college. Once on campus, you may never see your interviewer again.

In the end, remember to relax and be yourself. Your interviewer will expect you to be somewhat nervous, which will relieve some of the pressure. Don't drink jitters-producing caffeinated beverages prior to the interview, and suppress nervous fidgets like leg-wagging, finger-drumming, or bracelet jangling. Consider your interview an opportunity to put forth your best effort and to enhance everything that the college knows about you up to this point.

THE FINAL DECISION

Once you have received your acceptance letters, it is time to go back and look at the whole picture. Provided you received more than one acceptance, you are now in a position to compare your options. The best way to do this is to compare your original list of important college-ranking criteria with what you've discovered about each college along the way. In addition, you and your family will need to factor in the financial aid component. You will need to look beyond these cost issues and the quantifiable pros and cons of each college, however, and know that you have a good feeling about your final choice. Before sending off your acceptance letter, you need to feel confident that the college will feel like home for the next four years. Once the choice is made, the only hard part will be waiting for an entire summer before heading off to college!

The Early Decision

Maybe a senior you knew last year didn't get into the college he wanted. He said it was because he didn't apply early decision. Maybe your friend's mom told your mom that unless students apply early decision, their chances of getting into top schools are slim to none, even though they have great grades and spectacular essays. Maybe you figure you'd better get in on the early decision action.

All of the above are true—well, sort of—because many students applying to college get the term "early decision" backwards. High school guidance and college counselors run into this kind of thinking all the time and suggest putting "decision" before "early"—as in making a wise decision about committing to a college before applying early. For some students, early decision is a great option. For others, early decision is loaded with pitfalls and dangers.

"When students come back in the fall of their senior year, I often hear 'I know I want to apply early. Can you help me choose the school?'" says Kathy Cleaver, Co-Director of College Counseling at Durham Academy in Durham, North Carolina. She compares that to saying, "I know I want to get married, please help me pick the man." Continues Cleaver, "First you have to fall in love with the school and know it's your first choice and then join the circus for early decision." She's referring to the media hype flying around high school halls about early decision—it's easy to fall prey to the early decision madness. Hot competition to get into "top" schools creates early decision anxiety. Michael "Mickey" Gilbert, Guidance Counselor at Passaic High School in Passaic, New Jersey, throws out some scary numbers that confirm that, yes, the competition for admittance to top schools is white-hot. There are about 30,000 high schools in the United States, and although the majority of high school seniors apply to institutions in their own states, there are still limited spaces in the "top" schools and the eight Ivy League schools. "No wonder kids think that early decision is the way to go," speculates Gilbert. Early decision panic sets in because students are convinced that if they get their applications in early, they have an edge. Sometimes early decision might make the difference, but there are many issues to consider before taking the early decision leap.

EARLY THIS, EARLY THAT

With all the buzz about early decision, do you really know what it means along with all the other early options, such as early action and early notification? And what about the variations of early decision? Each institution can have its own version of early decision, meaning that deadlines and criteria are different. There's the early decision that notifies students by December, there's the early decision round two, and then there is the early action/single choice.

Seeing the confusion, the National Association for College Admission Counseling (NACAC) developed a standard set of definitions. NACAC is an education association of secondary school counselors, college and university admissions and financial aid officers, counselors, and other individuals who work with students as they transition from high school to college. While each institution has its own variations of each early option, an understanding of the basic differences can help. The list that follows was adapted from the definitions found on the NACAC website (www.nacacnet.org).

Early Decision

- Early decision is the application process in which students make a commitment to a first-choice institution where, if admitted, they definitely will enroll. Should a student who applies for financial aid not be offered an award that makes attendance possible, the student may decline the offer of admission and be released from the early decision commitment.

- While pursuing admission under an early decision plan, students may apply to other institutions, but may have only one early decision application pending at any time.

- The institution must notify the applicant of the decision within a reasonable and clearly stated period of time after the early decision deadline. Usually, a nonrefundable deposit must be made well in advance of May 1.

- A student applying for financial aid must adhere to institutional early decision aid application deadlines.

- The institution will respond to an application for financial aid at or near the time of an offer of admission.

- The early decision application supercedes all other applications. Immediately upon acceptance of an offer of admission, a student must withdraw all other applications and make no subsequent applications.

- The application form will include a request for a parent and a counselor signature, in addition to the student's signature, indicating an understanding of the early decision commitment and agreement to abide by its terms.

Early Action

- Early action is the application process in which students make application to an institution of preference and receive a decision well in advance of the institution's regular response date. Students who are admitted under early action are not obligated to accept the institution's offer of admission or to submit a deposit until the regular reply date (not prior to May 1).

- A student may apply to other colleges without restriction.

- The institution must notify the applicant of the decision within a reasonable and clearly stated period of time after the early action deadline.

- A student applying for financial aid must adhere to institutional aid application deadlines.

- A student admitted under an early action plan may not be required to make a commitment prior to May 1, but may be encouraged to do so as soon as a final college choice is made. Colleges that solicit commitments to offers of early action admission and/or financial assistance prior to May 1 may do so provided those offers include a clear statement that written requests for extensions until May 1 will be granted, and that such requests will not jeopardize a student's status for admission or financial aid.

Regular Decision

- Regular decision is the application process in which a student submits an application to an institution by a specified date and receives a decision within a reasonable and clearly stated period of time, but not later than April 15.

- A student may apply to other colleges without restriction.

- The institution will state a deadline for completion of applications and will respond to completed applications by a specified date.

- A student applying for financial aid must adhere to institutional aid application deadlines.

- A student admitted under a regular decision plan may not be required to make a commitment prior to May 1, but may be encouraged to do so as soon as a final college choice is made. Colleges that solicit commitments to offers of admission and/or financial assistance prior to May 1 may do so provided those offers include a clear statement that written requests for extensions until May 1 will be granted, and that such requests will not jeopardize a student's status for admission or financial aid.

Rolling Admission

- Rolling admission is the application process in which an institution reviews applications as they are completed and renders admission decisions to students throughout the admission cycle.

- A student may apply to other colleges without restriction.

- The institution will respond to completed applications in a timely manner.

- A student applying for financial aid must adhere to institutional aid application deadlines.

- A student admitted under a rolling admission plan may not be required to make a commitment prior to May 1, but may be encouraged to do so as soon as a final college choice is made. Colleges that solicit commitments to offers of admission and/or financial assistance prior to May 1 may do so provided those offers include a clear statement that written requests for extensions until May 1 will be granted, and that such requests will not jeopardize a student's status for admission or financial aid.

Wait List

- Wait list is an admission decision option utilized by institutions to protect against shortfalls in enrollment. Wait lists are sometimes made necessary because of the uncertainty of the admission process, as students submit applications for admission to multiple institutions and may receive several offers of admission. By placing a student on the wait list, an institution does not initially offer or deny admission, but extends to a candidate the possibility of admission in the future before the institution's admission cycle is concluded.

- The institution will ensure that a wait list, if necessary, is of reasonable length and is maintained for a reasonable period of time, but never later than August 1.

- In the letter offering a wait list position, the institution should provide a past wait list history, which describes the number of students placed on the wait list(s), the number offered admission from the wait list, and the availability of financial aid. Students should be given an indication of when they can expect to be notified of a final admission decision.

- An institution must resolve final status and notify wait list candidates as soon after May 1 as possible.

- The institution will not require students to submit deposits to remain on a wait list or pressure students for a commitment to enroll prior to sending an official offer of admission in writing.

There is one more option, called early action/single choice (EASC), that some highly selective schools such as Harvard, Yale, and Stanford have begun using. Early action/single choice is a nonbinding early admission option for freshman applicants that replaces early decision. With this change, students learn about their admission decision in December without being required to reply until May 1. This option allows students to apply to as many colleges as they want under a regular admission time frame. The difference is that the early action/single choice option does not allow a candidate to apply to other schools under any type of early action, early decision, or early notification program. Students are asked to sign a statement in their application agreeing to file only one early application.

Each of these options has variations, depending on the institution using them. Some schools have a November 1 deadline for early decision round one. Smaller schools have a deadline of November 15, while others have a December 1 deadline. Then there's an early decision round two. To make matters even more complicated, some schools with early decision say that students can't apply to other institutions if they've sent in an early decision application to their admissions office. Others say it's okay to apply to other schools at the same time you're applying early decision to them, but if they send you an acceptance, you must withdraw the other applications.

Just because two institutions have an application process called early decision or early action doesn't mean that their policies are identical. "There is no common terminology, even among the colleges that have early decision," says Christoph Guttentag, Dean of Undergraduate Admissions at Duke University in Durham, North Carolina. He also points out that just when you think you've got the definitions figured out, institu-

PARENTS, SOME ADVICE FOR YOU

Though guidance counselors stress that high school students should make the final decision about which college to attend, they also say that parents are a very important part of the decision equation. Parents can help as organizers of all the information and provide the support needed to make a good choice. "Little things like setting up file folders and keeping track of deadlines can keep a student on track," advises David Gibson, College Advisor at St. Mary's Parish in Annapolis, Maryland.

Along with their children, parents also need to understand the basics of early option terminology as it applies to each institution being considered. Five different colleges might have five different early decision criteria. Read the fine print, and make note of deadlines.

What really will help—you, your child, and your wallet—is to understand the basics about financial aid. Says Shawn Leftwich, Director of Undergraduate Admissions at Wheaton College in Illinois, "Have an in-depth discussion with the financial aid officer so that you are aware of the ramifications, restrictions, and implications of the financial aid offer."

If possible, make an appointment to visit with a financial aid officer at the college while your child is visiting the campus. Bring your tax forms and discuss the prospects of financial aid. "Financial aid people are straight shooters. It's not in their best interest to tell you one thing to get your foot in the door and then turn around and pull the rug out from under you," says Bill McClintick, Director of College Counseling at Mercerburg Academy. "Parents might not like the answer they get from the financial aid officer, but they will get a candid assessment of their eligibility for financial aid."

Leftwich suggests having an honest discussion with your child early in the college selection process. Talk about what you can realistically afford, what colleges will appropriately challenge him or her, if location is a factor, and what kind of environment best suits your child. Whichever option your child uses to apply, you both will know the decision is an informed one.

tions change them. "Colleges are always balancing the needs of their institution and the needs of students," he comments.

EARLY DECISION: A MATCHMAKING TOOL OR A CLEVER STRATEGY?

Despite the differences in what actually constitutes early decision, it has become more of a strategy than a matchmaking tool, according to Bill McClintick, Director of College Counseling at Mercersburg Academy in Mercersburg, Pennsylvania. He also chairs the national steering committee on admissions standards for NACAC. The focus of early decision used to be on matching the student with the college and letting the admissions office know that that institution is where the student wants to be above all others. Today, early decision is

misunderstood and misused. High school seniors think that they must use the early decision tactic to get an edge. The result, says McClintick is "at many of the top places, early decision applications have gone through the roof."

Though high school students may have exaggerated ideas of how much early decision can really help them, it is true that it does give a small segment of students applying at highly selective schools an advantage. Generally, the more selective the institution, the more small differences matter. "Even if it's a small increase, you need everything you can get," states John Latting, Dean of Undergraduate Admissions at Emory University in Atlanta, Georgia.

"Remember," cautions McClintick, "we're only talking about a small slice of kids in the grand scheme of things." He mentions 5 percent of high school seniors nationally who aspire to the "top" institutions. State colleges and universities fill a much lower percentage of their freshman class with early decision applications. "I don't believe that more kids are chasing the same number of spots," says Jon Reider, Director of College Counseling at San Francisco University High School in San Francisco, California. "Students are applying to more and more schools, even with the early decision option on the side. This is inflating the selectivity of some colleges beyond what it used to be." In reality, 90 percent of students apply regular admission. Interest in early decision comes from a relatively small segment of the college applicant pool.

THE BENEFITS OF EARLY DECISION

There are clear benefits for students who apply for early decision. Aside from the fact that early decision does play a role in acceptance rates for a relatively small percentage of students at a small number of schools, early decision is a good option. The caveat is that students must know, without a shred of doubt, that one institution, above all others, is the best match for their goals and their likes and dislikes, and that based on grades and test scores, they solidly match the institution's criteria for admission. The option to go early decision should be taken after extensive research, multiple visits to the campus, and talking to a lot of people. "Early decision is for those who can put their hearts and souls into one application," advises Cleaver.

There are other advantages. You have to make only one choice, and you will know by December if you've been accepted. You have to fill out only one application. You are not chewing your nails over your list of possibilities during the Christmas holiday. Instead, you know where you're going and can sit back and enjoy the rest of your senior year, while others in your class are madly filling out applications, writing essays, and agonizing over the thin envelopes that arrive in the mail. Says Guttentag, "The advantage of having that challenging process over with is not insignificant."

Early decision is helpful for admissions officers at selective colleges because it allows them to make decisions between well-qualified students and select those who really want to be at their institution. As Shawn Leftwich, Director of Undergraduate Admissions at Wheaton College in Illinois, points out, early decision is for the students who are strongly committed. "We like you. You like us. We know you're coming, and we can fill our freshman class." However, on the flip side, she adds that some students aren't so sure about which college they want to attend, and early decision only makes the process more stressful.

Before you decide to go with early decision, consider early action. Many high school counselors lean toward early action, which is another good option. With early action you're able to apply later in the process. This means you will be able to take the SATs again. Your first-semester grades and AP classes taken in the first semester of your senior year can be used to evaluate your eligibility. You have September and October to visit several campuses while they are in session and plenty of time to do the research to put more than one school on your list.

THE PITFALLS OF EARLY DECISION

Though early decision has benefits, before you jump into it, look at the ramifications of that option. Advises Gilbert, "Early decision might give you an edge, but the tradeoff is not so great."

Perhaps the most compelling reason why students should seriously examine early decision before jumping at it is because they are bound by an agreement to attend that school if accepted. Students sign a pledge to attend that institution and are required to withdraw applications from all other schools. They also are obligated to accept the financial aid award that the institution gives them. An early decision is a binding decision. "Regardless," advises David Gibson, College Advisor at St. Mary's Parish in Annapolis, Maryland, "students don't learn about their financial aid awards until March or April, and if the award funding is not at all acceptable because the family's financial need was not met, they need to decline the offer and begin searching for a new college. March or April is not a good time to start applying to new colleges."

How binding is binding? Though no school can force a student to attend if they've signed an early decision agreement, students who decide not to attend that school hurt others with that decision. High school counselors have to sign the binding agreement, along with parents, and must state that they will not send out transcripts to other institutions. Many institutions will not accept the application of a student who applied early decision elsewhere and backed out of the agreement. Admissions officers may find out in May that an early decision student is not coming, so they'll call the counselor and ask if the student applied to another school. If so, often a phone call to the other institution is made and acceptance denied. Sometimes the counselor loses a good reputation with that institution, putting applicants who follow in subsequent years at a disadvantage.

After the consequences of signing a binding agreement, the financial aspect of early decision is the next biggest pitfall. "You can't compare financial aid offers," says Latting. "You have only one offer." Students won't know if they're eligible for Pell grants or merit scholarships. Government FAFSA forms are not submitted until January, and students might not find out how much aid they can get until March or April, long

QUESTIONS TO ASK YOURSELF BEFORE APPLYING EARLY DECISION

What if you don't get accepted early decision—then what? Speaking from the experience of seeing students deal with early decision rejection letters, Reider says, "Some of your friends are getting acceptance letters, and you get one thin envelope and the pain of rejection. You've given the early decision institution your best shot and you lost." Cleaver has seen kids in her high school end up thinking they won't get in anywhere. "This is the first time they've faced a big rejection and news they don't want to hear," she says, noting that because of the timetable of early decision, letters often come right around exam time in December.

When students apply regular decision, meaning they wait until well into their senior year and apply to several different institutions, it's "all or some," quips Latting. "With early decision, it's all or nothing." Many application deadlines for regular decision are in January. If you get that rejection letter from the school you were counting on, that doesn't give you much time to apply to other schools, much less visit them.

Are you ready to make such a drastic decision so early in your senior year? A lot can change in how you think about your future between the beginning of your senior year and graduation. With six or seven months behind you as a senior, you might be in a better position to compare colleges in April than you were back in September. Think about it—you're making the decision about where you want to spend the next four years of your life in early October of your senior year!

Have you given yourself enough time to pick one college above all others? If you want to apply early decision, you should start making plans to do so in your junior year. In order to apply early decision, you must have your ACTs or SATs taken, campus visits done, a final choice made, a dynamite essay written, a stellar application filled out, and teacher recommendation letters collected. That's a lot to cram into the end of your junior year and a few months into your senior year.

Have you given an admissions office enough information to make a decision about you? The more information the admissions office has about grades and classes you took and activities and leadership positions you held, the better they can decide if you're a good match for them. Do you really want decisions being made about you based on sophomore and junior grades and activities? What happens to that AP English class you finally felt ready to take the beginning of your senior year? What about that calculus class you aced in the first semester of your senior year? Admissions won't be able to assess that on an early decision application.

after the early decision agreement was signed and sealed. "This means that if they are accepted, they are then obligated to a college that might not fund them to the level of their financial need," says Gibson. Students who apply early action or regular decision are in a better position to negotiate financial aid packages.

EARLY DECISION REJECTION

In case you haven't heard, fat is good, thin is bad. Thin envelopes from college admissions offices usually mean a single-page letter saying good luck, we wish you the best, but you're not going to be attending our school next fall. However stated, it's hard to be rejected, especially when you've applied early decision, which states to the college and to yourself that this is the college you've decided is the only one you really, really want to attend above all others.

But thin envelopes don't mean the end of the world. Cleaver advises to not let early decision get control of you. "There are too many choices of colleges for you not to get into college. You might not get into Princeton, but there are many other wonderful schools if you do the research to look for a good match. Early decision is a tool to use to apply, but it is not always the best tool."

Objecting to the term "perfect match," Reider asks, "Does it really matter what kind of car you drive? There are twenty different colleges that can get you where you want to go. You'll be successful in most places."

HOW TO DO EARLY DECISION THE RIGHT WAY

Taking the early decision option requires more than gathering information, filling out an application, writing an essay, and waiting for an envelope to come in the mail or an e-mail to hit your Inbox. If you're going to be serious about early decision, the time to start is in your junior year.

Research the institutions at the top of your list. Think through what you want out of college—not just in terms of a future career, but also factors such as location, size, distance from home, sports, and other activities. Think about who you want to be. "It has to be a love connection," says Cleaver. Tune out all the early decision talk and do your homework about each college. Then ask yourself if one stands out above all the others you've researched. Is this the one to which you can

commit to a binding agreement? Are you in the competition to be admitted? Will you have the funds to attend this college?

"Admissions can tell if your application is from the heart," Cleaver cautions. Students ask her how to make their applications "look like they want to go there." She replies that what they put on an application and in an essay has to pour out of their hearts. Students who visit the campus and sit in on a class or a campus organization have the edge if something really clicked with them. They will write a convincing application. Perhaps they'll tell about how exciting the professor they heard was or how wonderful it is that the college has a chess club. Cleaver observes that kids usually write about an institution's sports team or about the ivy-covered walls of the campus on their application essay instead of writing about some interesting aspect of the university that spoke to them, which takes research, time, and reflection. "Don't make the mistake of chasing a name and not being a good consumer," cautions McClintick. Part of being a good consumer is to make sure you are a reasonably competitive applicant. This means looking at the school's admission criteria and statistics. What percentage of the freshman class is filled with early decision and early action students? If it's a high percentage, then you might want to reconsider where that school falls on your wish list. How many students return for their sophomore year? If more than 10 percent leave after their freshman year, that should tell you something about student satisfaction—and ultimately yours.

One of the most important ways to choose the right school is to visit the campus, perhaps multiple times and preferably with students on campus. "Campus visits are a critical time to talk with undergraduates and to find out what the academic, social, and physical climate is like," advises Guttentag. If you're staying in a dorm on Tuesday night during a visit, you can tell how serious kids are about their work. What kinds of conversations are they having? "Are these the kind of kids you want to spend four years of your life with?" asks McClintick.

After you've thoroughly investigated all the aspects of a college and decided it's at the absolute top of your list, after you are familiar with the early decision requirements at that institution, and after you've determined that you have a good chance of getting into that institution, then you can say early decision is for you. For those who are not so sure, fortunately, colleges and universities have plenty of other options for admission.

What International Students Need to Know About Admission to U.S. Colleges and Universities

Kitty M. Villa

There are two principles to remember about admission to a university in the United States. First, applying is almost never a one-time request for admission but an ongoing process that may involve several exchanges of information between applicant and institution. "Admission process" or "application process" means that a "yes" or "no" is usually not immediate, and requests for additional information are to be expected. To successfully manage this process, you must be prepared to send additional information when requested and then wait for replies. You need a thoughtful balance of persistence to communicate regularly and effectively with your selected universities and patience to endure what can be a very long process.

The second principle involves a marketplace analogy. The most successful applicants are alert to opportunities to create a positive impression that sets them apart from other applicants. They are able to market themselves to their target institution. Institutions are also trying to attract the highest-quality student that they can. The admissions process presents you with the opportunity to analyze your strengths and weaknesses as a student and to look for ways to present yourself in the most marketable manner.

FIRST STEP—SELECTING INSTITUTIONS

With thousands of institutions of higher education in the United States, how do you begin to narrow your choices down to the institutions that are best for you? There are many factors to consider, and you must ultimately decide which factors are most important to you.

Location

You may spend several years studying in the United States. Do you prefer an urban or rural campus? Large or small metropolitan area? If you need to live on campus, will you be unhappy at a university where most students commute from off-campus housing? How do you feel about extremely hot summers or cold winters? Eliminating institutions that do not match your preferences in terms of location will narrow your choices.

Recommendations from Friends, Professors, or Others

There are valid academic reasons to consider the recommendations of people who know you well and have firsthand knowledge about particular institutions. Friends and contacts may be able to provide you with "inside information" about the campus or its academic programs to which published sources have no access. You should carefully balance anecdotal information with your own research and your own impressions. However, current and former students, professors, and others may provide excellent information during the application process.

Your Own Academic and Career Goals

Consideration of your academic goals is more complex than it may seem at first glance. All institutions do not offer the same academic programs. The application form usually provides a definitive listing of the academic programs offered by an institution. A course catalog describes the degree program and all the courses offered. In addition to printed sources, there is a tremendous amount of institutional information available on the Web. Program descriptions, even course descriptions and course syllabi, are often available to peruse online.

You may be interested in the rankings of either the university or of a program of study. Keep in mind, however, that rankings usually assume that quality is quantifiable. Rankings are usually based on presumptions about how data relate to quality and are likely to be unproven. It is important to carefully consider the source and the criteria of any ranking information before believing and acting upon it.

Your Own Educational Background

You may be concerned about the interpretation of your educational credentials, since your country's degree nomenclature and the grading scale may differ from those in the United States. Universities use reference books about the educational systems of other countries to help them understand specific educational credentials. Generally, these credentials are interpreted by each institution; there is not a single interpretation that applies to every institution. The lack of uniformity is good news for most students, since it means that students from a wide variety of educational backgrounds can find a U.S. university that is appropriate to their needs.

To choose an appropriate institution, you can and should do an informal self-evaluation of your educational background. This self-analysis involves three important questions:

1. How Many Years of Study Have You Completed?

Completion of secondary school with at least twelve total years of education usually qualifies students to apply for undergraduate (bachelor's) degree programs. Completion of a university degree program that involves at least sixteen years of total education qualifies one to apply for admission to graduate (master's) degree programs in the United States.

2. Does the Education That You Have Completed in Your Country Provide Access to Further Study in the United States?

Consider the kind of institution where you completed your previous studies. If educational opportunities in your country are limited, it may be necessary to investigate many U.S. institutions and programs in order to find a match.

3. Are Your Previous Marks or Grades Excellent, Average, or Poor?

Your educational record influences your choice of U.S. institutions. If your grades are average or poor, it may be advisable to apply to several institutions with minimally difficult or non-competitive entrance levels.

YOU are one of the best sources of information about the level and quality of your previous studies. Awareness of your educational assets and liabilities will serve you well throughout the application process.

SECOND STEP—PLANNING AND ASSEMBLING THE APPLICATION

Planning and assembling a university application can be compared to the construction of a building. First, you must start with a solid foundation, which is the application form itself. The application, often available online as well as in paper form, usually contains a wealth of useful information, such as deadlines, fees, and degree programs available at that institution. To build a solid application, it is best to begin well in advance of the application deadline.

How to Obtain the Application Form

Application forms and links to institutional websites may also be available at a U.S. educational advising center associated with the American Embassy or Consulate in your country. These centers are excellent resources for international students and provide information about standardized test administration, scholarships, and other matters to students who are interested in studying in the United States. Your local U.S. Embassy or Consulate can guide you to the nearest educational advising center.

What Are the Key Components of a Complete Application?

Institutional requirements vary, but the standard components of a complete application include the following:

- Transcript
- Required standardized examination scores
- Evidence of financial support
- Letters of recommendation
- Application fee

Transcript

A complete academic record or transcript includes all courses completed, grades earned, and degrees awarded. Most universities require an official transcript to be sent directly from the school or university. In many other countries, however, the practice is to issue official transcripts and degree certificates directly to the student. If you have only one official copy of your transcript, it may be a challenge to get additional certified copies that are acceptable to U.S. universities. Some institutions will issue additional official copies for application purposes.

If your institution does not provide this service, you may have to seek an alternate source of certification. As a last resort, you may send a photocopy of your official transcript, explain that you have only one original, and ask the university for advice on how to deal with this situation.

Required Standardized Examination Scores

Arranging to take standardized examinations and earning the required scores seem to cause the most anxiety for international students.

The university application form usually indicates which examinations are required. The standardized examination required most often for undergraduate admission is the Test of English as a Foreign Language (TOEFL). Institutions may also require the SAT of undergraduate applicants. These standardized examinations are administered by the Educational Testing Service (ETS).

These examinations are offered in almost every country of the world. It is advisable to begin planning for standardized examinations at least six months prior to the application deadline of your desired institutions. Test centers fill up quickly, so it is important to register as soon as possible. Information about the examinations is available at U.S. educational advising centers associated with embassies or consulates.

Most universities require that the original test scores, not a student copy, be sent directly by the testing service. When you register for the test, be sure to indicate that the testing service should send the test scores directly to the universities.

You should begin your application process before you receive your test scores. Delaying submission of your application until the test scores arrive may cause you to miss deadlines and negatively affect the outcome of your application. If you want to know your scores in order to assess your chances of admission to an institution with rigorous admission standards, you should take the tests early.

Many universities in the United States set minimum required scores on the TOEFL or other standardized examinations. Test scores are an important factor, but most institutions also look at a number of other factors in their consideration of a candidate for admission.

For More Information

Questions about test formats, locations, dates, and registration may be addressed to:

ETS Corporate Headquarters
Rosedale Road
Princeton, New Jersey 08541
Websites: http://www.ets.org
                 http://www.ets.org/toefl/
Phone: 609-921-9000
Fax: 609-734-5410

Evidence of Financial Support

Evidence of financial support is required to issue immigration documents to admitted students. This is part of a complete application package but usually plays no role in determining admission. Most institutions make admissions decisions without regard to the source and amount of financial support.

Letters of Recommendation

Most institutions require one or more letters of recommendation. The best letters are written by former professors, employers, or others who can comment on your academic achievements or professional potential.

Some universities provide a special form for the letters of recommendation. If possible, use the forms provided. If you are applying to a large number of universities, however, or if your recommenders are not available to complete several forms, it may be necessary for you to duplicate a general recommendation letter.

Application Fee

Most universities also require an application fee, ranging from $25 to $100, which must be paid to initiate consideration of the application.

Completing the Application Form

Whether sent by mail or electronically, the application form must be neat and thoroughly filled out. Although parts of the application may not seem to apply to you or your situation, do your best to answer all the questions.

Remember that this is a process. You provide information, and your proposed university then may request clarification and further information. If you have questions, it is better to initiate the entire process by submitting the application form rather than asking questions before you apply. The university will be better able to respond to you after it has your application. Always complete as much as you can. Do not permit uncertainty about the completion of the application form to cause unnecessary delays.

THIRD STEP—DISTINGUISH YOUR APPLICATION

To distinguish your application—to market yourself successfully—is ultimately the most important part of the application process. As you select your prospective universities, begin to analyze your strengths and weaknesses as a prospective student. As you complete your application, you should strive to create a positive impression and set yourself apart from other applicants, to highlight your assets and bring these qualities to the attention of the appropriate university administrators and professors. Applying early is a very easy way to distinguish your application.

Deadline or Guideline?

The application deadline is the last date that an application for a given semester will be accepted. Often, the application will specify that all required documents and information be submitted before the deadline date. To meet the deadlines, start the application process early. This also gives you more time to take—and perhaps retake and improve—the required standardized tests.

Admissions deliberations may take several weeks or months. In the meantime, most institutions accept additional information, including improved test scores, after the posted deadline.

Even if your application is initially rejected, you may be able to provide additional information to change the decision. You can request reconsideration based on additional information, such as improved test scores, strong letters of recommendation, or information about your class rank. Applying early allows more time to improve your application. Also, some students may decide not to accept their offers of admission, leaving room for offers to students on a waiting list. Reconsideration of the admission decisions can occur well beyond the application deadline.

Think of the deadline as a guideline rather than an impermeable barrier. Many factors—the strength of the application, your research interests, the number of spaces available at the proposed institution—can override the enforcement of an application deadline. So, if you lack a test score or transcript by the official deadline, you may still be able to apply and be accepted.

Statement of Purpose

The statement of purpose is your first and perhaps best opportunity to present yourself as an excellent candidate for admission. Whether or not a personal history essay or statement of purpose is required, always include a carefully written statement of purpose with your applications. A compelling statement of purpose does not have to be lengthy, but it should include some basic components:

- Part One—Introduce yourself and describe your educational background. This is your opportunity to describe any facet of your educational experience that you wish to emphasize. Perhaps you attended a highly ranked secondary school or university in your home country. Mention the name and any noteworthy characteristics of the secondary school or university from which you graduated. Explain the grading scale used at your university. Do not forget to mention your rank in your graduating class and any honors you may have received. This is not the time to be modest.
- Part Two—Describe your current academic and career interests and goals. Think about how these will fit into

those of the institution to which you are applying, and mention the reasons why you have selected that institution.

- Part Three—Describe your long-term goals. When you finish your program of study, what do you plan to do next? If you already have a job offer or a career plan, describe it. Give some thought to how you'll demonstrate that studying in the United States. will ultimately benefit others.

Use Personal Contacts When Possible

Appropriate and judicious use of your own network of contacts can be very helpful. Friends, former professors, former students of your selected institutions, and others may be willing to advise you during the application process and provide you with introductions to key administrators or professors. If suggested, you may wish to contact certain professors or administrators by mail, phone, or e-mail. A personal

visit to discuss your interest in the institution may be appropriate. Whatever your choice of communication, try to make the encounter pleasant and personal. Your goal is to make a positive impression, not to rush the admission decision.

There is no single right way to be admitted to U.S. universities. The same characteristics that make the educational choice in the United States so difficult—the number of institutions and the variety of programs of study—are the same attributes that allow so many international students to find the institution that's right for them.

Kitty M. Villa is the former Assistant Director, International Office, at the University of Texas at Austin.

Financial Aid Countdown Calendar

JUNIOR YEAR

Fall

Now is the time to get serious about the colleges in which you are interested. Meet with your guidance counselor to help you narrow down your choices. Hopefully by the spring, your list will have five to ten solid choices. College visits are always a great idea—remember this will be the place you will call home for four years, so start your campus visits soon!

❑ Register for the PSAT/NMSQT.

❑ Check out local financial aid nights in the area. Be sure to attend these valuable sessions, especially if this is the first time your family is sending someone off to college. Try to become familiar with common financial aid terms. Start reviewing the literature available and begin to familiarize yourself with the various programs. A good booklet is published by the U.S. Department of Education, "Funding Your Education: The Guide to Federal Student Aid" and is available at any financial aid office or on the web at https://studentaid.ed.gov/sites/default/files/2012-13-funding-your-education.pdf

❑ In October, take the PSAT/NMSQT.

❑ Do some web browsing! There are many free scholarship search engines, such as Petersons.com. Also, head to the bookstore or library and pick up a copy of *Peterson's Scholarships, Grants & Prizes,* which features details on billions of dollars of aid from private sources, or *Best Scholarships for the Best Students,* which offers great info on scholarships, fellowships, and experiential learning programs for top students.

❑ Ask your parents to contact their employers, unions, and any religious and fraternal organizations with which they have a connection to learn about possible scholarship opportunities.

❑ Check with your high school guidance counselor for the qualifications and deadlines of local scholarship awards. Many guidance counselors report that there are few applicants for these awards.

Winter

❑ Keep checking for scholarships! Remember that this is the one area over which you have control. The harder you work, the better your chances for success!

❑ Register and study for the ACT or SAT and SAT Subject Tests.

Spring

❑ Spring Break—a great time to visit colleges. Remember your top ten list? Time to start narrowing it down.

❑ Review the requirements for local scholarships. What can you do now and over the summer to improve your chances?

❑ Take the ACT or SAT. Good luck!

❑ Look for a summer job, especially one that ties in with your college plans. For example, if you want to major in premed, why not try to get a job at a hospital or with a laboratory?

Summer

❑ College visit time! Ask: Is this where I see myself getting my undergraduate degree? Can I adjust to the seasons, the town surrounding the campus, the distance from home, the college size? Does this school feel right for me?

❑ Why not get a jump on college (and maybe save some money!) and enroll for a college course at the local community college? Or, better yet, do some extra prep work for the ACT or SAT!

SENIOR YEAR

Fall

How's the college list coming? Can you get your list down to five or six choices? Your guidance counselor can help with this process. Once you have your top choices, make a list of what each college requires for admission and financial aid. Be sure your list includes all deadlines. Attend a financial aid night presentation with your parents. Some of these sessions offer help in completing forms; others offer a broader view of the process. Contact the presenter (usually a local college financial aid professional) to be sure you are getting the information you need.

❑ Do any of these colleges require the CSS/Financial Aid PROFILE® financial aid application? Many private colleges use this form for institutional aid. You need to file this comprehensive form in late September or early October. For more information or to find out which colleges use this supplemental form, go to http://profileonline.collegeboard.com/index.jsp. (Website registration is free; however, PROFILE is a fee-based application).

❑ Don't falter now in your scholarship search. Get the applications filed by the published deadlines.

❑ Register now if you are planning to retake the SAT.

❑ Most important, start completing your college applications—the earlier, the better! If you are interested in early decision or early action, now is the time! Remember, accuracy and completeness are a must!

Winter

❑ Ensure all college applications are completed.

❑ Get the Free Application for Federal Student Aid (FAFSA). This is the key form for financial aid for every school across the country. Remember, watch your deadlines, but do not file until after January 1. Be sure to keep a copy of the form, whether you file electronically or with the paper application. Do you have some questions? Call the local financial aid office. Many states have special toll-free call-in programs in

January and February, Financial Aid Awareness Month. Be sure that you have completed each school's required forms.

❑ As the letters of admission start to arrive, the financial aid award letters should be right behind them. Important question for parents: What is the bottom line? Remember, aid at a lower-cost state school will be less than a higher-cost private college. But what will you be required to pay? This can be confusing, so consider gift aid (scholarships and grants), student loans, and parent loans. The school with the lowest sticker price (tuition, fees, and room and board) might not be the best bargain when you look at the overall financial aid package.

Spring

❑ Still not sure where to go? The financial aid package at your top choice just not enough? Call the financial aid office and the admissions office. Talk it over. While schools don't like to bargain, they are usually willing to take a second look. Is there something unusual about your family's financial situation that might impact your parents' ability to pay?

❑ By May 1, you must make your final decision. Notify your chosen college and find out what you need to do next. Tell the other colleges you are not accepting their offers of admission and financial aid.

Summer

❑ Time to crunch the numbers. Parents, get information from the college on the total charges for the coming fall term. Deduct the aid package and then plan for how the balance will be paid. Contact the college financial aid office for the best parental loan program. If you want to arrange for a payment plan, contact the business office for further information. Most schools have deferred payment plans available for a nominal fee.

Congratulations! Remember that you need to reapply for aid every year!

Who's Paying for This?
Financial Aid Basics

A college education can be expensive—costing more than $150,000 for four years at some of the higher priced private colleges and universities. Even at the lower-cost state colleges and universities, the cost of a four-year education can approach $60,000. Determining how you and your family will come up with the necessary funds to pay for your education requires planning, perseverance, and learning as much as you can about the options that are available to you. But before you get discouraged, College Board statistics show that 53 percent of full-time students attend four-year public and private colleges with tuition and fees less than $9000, while 20 percent attend colleges that have tuition and fees more than $36,000. College costs tend to be less in the western states and higher in New England.

Paying for college should not be looked at as a four-year financial commitment. For many families, paying the total cost of a student's college education out of current income and savings is usually not realistic. For families that have planned ahead and have financial savings established for higher education, the burden is a lot easier. But for most, meeting the cost of college requires the pooling of current income and assets and investing in longer-term loan options. These family resources, together with financial assistance from state, federal, and institutional sources, enable millions of students each year to attend the institution of their choice.

FINANCIAL AID PROGRAMS

There are three types of financial aid:

1. Gift-aid—Scholarships and grants are funds that do not have to be repaid.

2. Loans—Loans must be repaid, usually after graduation; the amount you have to pay back is the total you've borrowed plus any accrued interest. This is considered a source of self-help aid.

3. Student employment—Student employment is a job arranged for you by the financial aid office. This is another source of self-help aid.

The federal government has four major grant programs—the Federal Pell Grant, the Federal Supplemental Educational Opportunity Grant, Academic Competitiveness Grants (ACG), and SMART grants. ACG and SMART grants are limited to students who qualify for a Pell grant and are awarded to a select group of students. Overall, these grants are targeted to low-to-moderate income families with significant financial need. The federal government also sponsors a student employment program called the Federal Work-Study Program, which offers jobs both on and off campus, and several loan programs, including those for students and for parents of undergraduate students.

There are two types of student loan programs: subsidized and unsubsidized. The subsidized Federal Direct Loan and the Federal Perkins Loan are need-based, government-subsidized loans. Students who borrow through these programs do not have to pay interest on the loan until after they graduate or leave school. The unsubsidized Federal Direct Loan and the Federal Direct PLUS Loan Program are not based on need, and borrowers are responsible for the interest while the student is in school. These loans are administered by different methods. Once you choose your college, the financial aid office will guide you through this process.

After you've submitted your financial aid application and you've been accepted for admission, each college will send you a letter describing your financial aid award. Most award letters show estimated college costs, how much you and your family are expected to contribute, and the amount and types of aid you have been awarded. Most students are awarded aid from a combination of sources and programs. Hence, your award is often called a financial aid "package."

SOURCES OF FINANCIAL AID

Millions of students and families apply for financial aid each year. Financial aid from all sources exceeds $143 billion per year. The largest single source of aid is the federal government, which will award more than $100 billion this year.

The next largest source of financial aid is found in the college and university community. Most of this aid is awarded to students who have a demonstrated need based on the Federal Methodology. Some institutions use a different formula, the Institutional Methodology (IM), to award their own funds in conjunction with other forms of aid. Institutional aid may be either need-based or non-need based. Aid that is not based on need is usually awarded for a student's academic performance (merit awards), specific talents or abilities, or to attract the type of students a college seeks to enroll.

Another source of financial aid is from state government. All states offer grant and/or scholarship aid, most of which is need-based. However, more and more states are offering substantial merit-based aid programs. Most state programs award aid only to students attending college in their home state.

Other sources of financial aid include:

- Private agencies
- Foundations
- Corporations
- Clubs
- Fraternal and service organizations

- Civic associations
- Unions
- Religious groups that award grants, scholarships, and low-interest loans
- Employers that provide tuition reimbursement benefits for employees and their children

More information about these different sources of aid is available from high school guidance offices, public libraries, college financial aid offices, directly from the sponsoring organizations, and on the Web at www.petersons.com and www.finaid.org.

HOW NEED-BASED FINANCIAL AID IS AWARDED

When you apply for aid, your family's financial situation is analyzed using a government-approved formula called the Federal Methodology. This formula looks at five items:

1. Demographic information of the family
2. Income of the parents
3. Assets of the parents
4. Income of the student
5. Assets of the student

This analysis determines the amount you and your family are expected to contribute toward your college expenses, called your Expected Family Contribution, or EFC. If the EFC is equal to or more than the cost of attendance at a particular college, then you do not demonstrate financial need. However, even if you don't have financial need, you may still qualify for aid, as there are grants, scholarships, and loan programs that are not need-based.

If the cost of your education is greater than your EFC, then you do demonstrate financial need and qualify for assistance. The amount of your financial need that can be met varies from school to school. Some are able to meet your full need, while others can only cover a certain percentage of need. Here's the formula:

$$\begin{array}{r} \text{Cost of Attendance} \\ - \underline{\text{Expected Family Contribution}} \\ = \text{Financial Need} \end{array}$$

The EFC remains constant, but your need will vary according to the costs of attendance at a particular college. In general, the higher the tuition and fees at a particular college, the higher the cost of attendance will be. Expenses for books and supplies, room and board, transportation, and other miscellaneous items are included in the overall cost of attendance. It is important to remember that you do not have to be "needy" to qualify for financial aid. Many middle and upper-middle income families qualify for need-based financial aid.

APPLYING FOR FINANCIAL AID

Every student must complete the Free Application for Federal Student Aid (FAFSA) to be considered for financial aid. The FAFSA is available from your high school guidance office, many public libraries, colleges in your area, or directly from the U.S. Department of Education.

Students are encouraged to apply for federal student aid on the Web. The electronic version of the FAFSA can be accessed at http://www.fafsa.ed.gov. Both the student and at least one parent must apply for a federal PIN at http:// www.pin.ed.gov. The PIN serves as your electronic signature when applying for aid on the Web.

To award their own funds, some colleges require an additional application, the CSS/Financial Aid PROFILE® form. The PROFILE asks supplemental questions that some colleges and awarding agencies feel provide a more accurate assessment of the family's ability to pay for college. It is up to the college to decide whether it will use only the FAFSA or both the FAFSA and the PROFILE. PROFILE applications are available from the high school guidance office and on the Web. Both the paper application and the website list those colleges and programs that require the PROFILE application.

If Every College You're Applying to for Fall 2013 Requires the FAFSA

. . . then it's pretty simple: Complete the FAFSA after January 1, 2014, being certain to send it in before any college-imposed deadlines. (You are not permitted to send in the 2014–15 FAFSA before January 1, 2014.) Most college FAFSA application deadlines are in February or early March. It is easier if you have all your financial records for the previous year available, but if that is not possible, you are strongly encouraged to use estimated figures.

After you send in your FAFSA, either with the paper application or electronically, you'll receive a Student Aid Report (SAR) that includes all of the information you reported and shows your EFC. If you provided an e-mail address, the SAR is sent to you electronically; otherwise, you will receive a paper copy in the mail. Be sure to review the SAR, checking to see if the information you reported is accurately represented. If you used estimated numbers to complete the FAFSA, you may have to resubmit the SAR with any corrections to the data. The college(s) you have designated on the FAFSA will receive the information you reported and will use that data to make their decision. In many instances, the colleges to which you've applied will ask you to send copies of your and your parents' federal income tax returns for 2012, plus any other documents needed to verify the information you reported.

If a College Requires the PROFILE

Step 1: Register for the CSS/Financial Aid PROFILE in the fall of your senior year in high school. You can apply for the PROFILE online at http://profileonline.collegeboard.com/prf/index.jsp. Registration information with a list of the colleges that require the PROFILE is available in most high school guidance offices. There is a fee for using the Financial Aid PROFILE application ($25 for the first college, which includes the $9 application fee, and $16 for each additional college). You must pay for the service by credit card when you register. If you do not have a credit card, you will be billed. A limited number of fee waivers are automatically granted to first-time applicants based on the financial information provided on the PROFILE.

Step 2: Fill out your customized CSS/Financial Aid PROFILE. Once you register, your application will be immediately available online and will have questions that all students must complete, questions which must be completed by the student's parents (unless the student is independent and the colleges or programs selected do not require parental information), and *may* have supplemental questions needed by one or more of your schools or programs. If required, those will be found in Section Q of the application.

In addition to the PROFILE application you complete online, you may also be required to complete a Business/ Farm Supplement via traditional paper format. Completion of this form is not a part of the online process. If this form is required, instructions on how to download and print the supplemental form are provided. If your biological or adoptive parents are separated or divorced and your colleges and programs require it, your noncustodial parent may be asked to complete the Noncustodial PROFILE.

Once you complete and submit your PROFILE application, it will be processed and sent directly to your requested colleges and programs.

IF YOU DON'T QUALIFY FOR NEED-BASED AID

If you are not eligible for need-based aid, you can still find ways to lessen your burden.

Here are some suggestions:

- Search for merit scholarships. You can start at the initial stages of your application process. College merit awards are increasingly important as more and more colleges award these to students they especially want to attract. As a result, applying to a college at which your qualifications put you at the top of the entering class may give you a larger merit award. Another source of aid to look for is private scholarships that are given for special skills and talents. Additional information can be found at www.finaid.org.

- Seek employment during the summer and the academic year. The student employment office at your college can help you locate a school-year job. Many colleges and local businesses have vacancies remaining after they have hired students who are receiving Federal Work-Study Program financial aid.

- Borrow through the unsubsidized Federal Direct Loan program. This is generally available to all students. The terms and conditions are similar to the subsidized loans. The biggest difference is that the borrower is responsible for the interest while still in college, although the government permits students to delay paying the interest right away and add the accrued interest to the total amount owed. You must file the FAFSA to be considered.

- After you've secured what you can through scholarships, working, and borrowing, you and your parents will be expected to meet your share of the college bill (the Expected Family Contribution). Many colleges offer monthly payment plans that spread the cost over the academic year. If the monthly payments are too high, parents can borrow through the Federal Direct PLUS Loan Program, through one of the many private education loan programs available, or through home equity loans and lines of credit. Families seeking assistance in financing college expenses should inquire at the financial aid office about what programs are available at the college. Some families seek the advice of professional financial advisers and tax consultants.

Middle-Income Families: Making the Financial Aid Process Work

Richard Woodland

A report from the U.S. Department of Education's National Center for Education Statistics took a close look at how middle-income families finance a college education. The report, *Middle Income Undergraduates: Where They Enroll and How They Pay for Their Education,* was one of the first detailed studies of these families. Even though 31 percent of middle-income families have the entire cost of attendance covered by financial aid, there is widespread angst among middle-income families that, while they earn too much to qualify for grant assistance, they are financially unable to pay the spiraling costs of higher education.

First, we have to agree on what constitutes a "middle-income" family. For the purposes of the federal study, middle income is defined as those families with incomes between $35,000 and $70,000. The good news is that 52 percent of these families received grants, while the balance received loans. Other sources of aid, including work-study, also helped close the gap.

So how do these families do it? Is there a magic key that will open the door to significant amounts of grants and scholarships?

The report found some interesting trends. One way families can make college more affordable is by choosing a less expensive college. In fact, in this income group, 29 percent choose to enroll in low- to moderate-cost schools. These include schools where the total cost is less than $8,500 per year. In this sector, we find the community colleges and lower-priced state colleges and universities. But almost half of these middle-income families choose schools in the upper-level tier, with costs ranging from $8,500 to $16,000. The remaining 23 percent enrolled at the highest-tier schools, with costs above $16,000. Clearly, while cost is a factor, middle-income families are not limiting their choices based on costs alone.

The report shows that families pay these higher costs with a combination of family assets, current income, and long-term borrowing. This is often referred to as the "past-present-future" model of financing. In fact, just by looking at the Expected Family Contributions, it is clear that there is a significant gap in what families need and what the financial aid process can provide. Families are closing this gap by making the financial sacrifices necessary to pay the price at higher-cost schools, especially if they think their child is academically strong. The report concludes that parents are more likely to pay for a higher-priced education if their child scores high on the SAT.

The best place for middle-income families to start is with the high school guidance office. This office has information on financial aid and valuable leads on local scholarships. Most guidance officers report that there are far fewer applicants for these locally based scholarships than one would expect. So read the information they send home and check on the application process. A few of those $500–$1000 scholarships can add up!

Plan to attend a financial aid awareness program. If your school does not offer one, contact your local college financial aid office and see when and where they will be speaking. You can get a lot of "inside" information on how the financial aid process works.

Next, be sure to file the correct applications for aid. Remember, each school can have a different set of requirements. For example, many higher-cost private colleges will require the CSS/Financial Aid PROFILE® application, filed in September or October of the senior year. Other schools may have their own institutional aid application. All schools will require the Free Application for Federal Student Aid (FAFSA). Watch the deadlines! It is imperative that you meet the school's published application deadline. Generally, schools are not flexible about this, so be sure to double-check the due date of all applications.

Finally, become a smart educational consumer. Peterson's has a wide range of resources available to help you understand the process. Be sure to also check your local library, bookstore, and of course, the Internet. A great website to check is www.finaid.org.

Once admitted to the various colleges and universities, you will receive an award notice outlining the aid you are eligible to receive. If you feel the offer is not sufficient, or if you have some unique financial circumstances, call the school's financial aid office to see if you can have your application reviewed again. The financial aid office is your best source for putting the pieces together and finding financial solutions.

The financial aid office will help you determine the "net price." This is the actual out-of-pocket cost that you will need to cover. Through a combination of student and parent loans, most families are able to meet these expenses with other forms of financial aid and family resources.

Many students help meet their educational expenses by working while in school. While this works for many students, research shows that too many hours spent away from your studies will negatively impact your academic success. Most experts feel that working 10 to 15 hours a week is optimal.

An overlooked source of aid is the tax credits given to middle-income families. Rather than extending eligibility for traditional sources of grant assistance to middle-income families, the federal tax system has built in a number of significant tax benefits, known as the Hope Scholarship and Lifetime Learning tax credit, for middle-income families. While it may be seven or eight months before you see the tax credit, most families in this income group can count on this benefit, usually between $1500 to $2000 per student. This is real money in your pocket. You do not need to itemize your deductions to qualify for this tax credit.

A tool to help families get a handle on the ever-rising costs of college is to assume that you can pay one third of the "net charges" from savings, another third from available (non-retirement) assets, and the rest from parent borrowing. If any one of these "thirds" is not available, shift that amount to one of the other resources. However, if it looks like you will be financing most or all of the costs from future income (borrowing), it may be wise to consider a lower-cost college.

Millions of middle-income families send their children to colleges and universities every year. Only 8 percent attend the lowest-priced schools. By using the concept of past-present-future financing, institutional assistance, federal and state aid, meaningful targeted tax relief, and student earnings, you can afford even the highest-cost schools.

Richard Woodland is the former Director of Financial Aid at Rutgers University–Camden.

Honors Programs and Colleges: Smart Choices for an Undergraduate Education

Dr. Joan Digby

In general, students and their parents are guided toward a narrow selection of colleges and universities based on reputation, conversations with friends, or promotional material. Few people think to approach the college search focused on honors opportunities. As a result, students with extraordinary talents and interests miss out on a rich variety of untapped financial resources and exciting college experiences.

The smarter approach is to seek out a distinctive education that caters to students' great diversity of intellectual and creative strengths. If you are a strong student filled with ideas, longing for creative expression and ready to take on career-shaping challenges, then an honors education is just for you. Honors programs and colleges offer some of the finest undergraduate degrees available at U.S. colleges and do it with students in mind. The essence of honors is personal attention, top faculty, enlightening seminars, illuminating study-travel experiences, research options, and career-building internships—all designed to enhance a classic education and prepare you for life achievements. And here is an eye-opening bonus: Honors programs and colleges may reward your past academic performance by giving you scholarships that will help you pay for your higher education!

Take your choice of institutions: community college, state or private, two- or four-year, college or large research university. There are honors opportunities in each. What they share is an unqualified commitment to academic excellence. Honors education teaches students to think and write clearly, be excited by ideas, and become independent, creative, self-confident learners. It prepares exceptional students for professional choices in every imaginable sphere of life: arts and sciences, engineering, business, health, education, medicine, theater, music, film, journalism, media, law, politics—invent your own professional goal and honors will guide you to it! Whichever honors program or college you choose, you can be sure to enjoy an extraordinarily fulfilling undergraduate education.

WHO ARE HONORS STUDENTS?

Who are you? Perhaps a high school junior filling out your first college application, a community college student seeking to transfer to a four-year college, or possibly a four-year college student doing better than you had expected. You might

be an international student, a varsity athlete, captain of the debate team, or second violin in the orchestra. Whether you are the first person in your family to attend college or an adult with a grown family seeking a new career, honors might well be right for you. Honors programs admit students with every imaginable background and educational goal.

How does honors satisfy students and give them something special? Read what students in some honors programs and colleges say. Although they refer to particular honors colleges or programs, their experiences are typical of what students find exciting about honors education on hundreds of campuses around the country.

"Being an honors program student has been a life-changing experience for me. I have gained tremendously in knowledge, experience, and self-esteem. I have learned so much more in the program than any textbook could teach about the value of encouraging support and positive thinking."

—*Cheri Becker, Mount Wachusett Community College*

"I've been in a healing ceremony in Ecuador and have performed music on stage. I've guided my peers and Navajo children, hiked the Grand Canyon, and so much more. Sometimes, experience speaks for itself; always, it creates paths, opens eyes, and helps us find our places. Thanks to my honors program, I've experienced these wonders and accomplishments. Now I know that there are no greater lessons than how to learn and love discovery."

—*April Fisher, University of North Florida*

"The Honors College has been my home away from home. In the midst of a diverse, fairly large university, it has provided me with the intimacy that I needed... My freshman-year living situation on the honors floor... allowed me to find like-minded students early in my college career."

—*Brian Leech, Davidson Honors College, University of Montana*

"I was able to transition from an honors program at a two-year institution into an honors program at a four-year institution without any reservations or tribulations."

—*Rachel Jones Williams, Harrisburg Area Community College*

"Every single professor is in love with what they do and it shows in their research, their amazing teaching, and their interaction with students outside of the classroom. The undergraduate journey can be very difficult at times, but as an Honors College student, you're sure to have plenty of support every step of the way."

—*Walteria Tucker, Wilkes Honors College, Florida Atlantic University*

"The class size is perfect and I've been able to make some of my closest relationships with students and teachers through the program. The majority of honors faculty I have encountered have been overwhelmingly helpful... and my favorite courses have been honors classes."

—*Ellen Daschler, Eastern Illinois University*

"Our professor met us at a local restaurant the last evening of class, and we shared a wonderful dinner. It had such a familiar feel to it because these are students I have known throughout my four years in the program."

—*Betsy Porter, University of La Verne*

"For the last two years, I have investigated new synthetic methods under the direction of a professor emeritus. Through the University Honors College, I am able to pursue this interest in chemistry and other academic endeavors... that have allowed me to develop my academic potential and contribute to the scientific body of knowledge."

—*Justin Chalker, University of Pittsburgh*

"The most rewarding part of being a member of the honors program is the joy of doing creative, meaningful projects with faculty I love."

—*Meleia Egger, Hartwick College*

"I would... like to add a word of praise for the way the curriculum is structured. It has deepened and enriched my thinking and helped me develop tools to negotiate the complex world we live in."

—*Monideepa Talukdar, Southeastern Louisiana University*

"We have a better time... our discussions get rather heated. In a lot of classes, only one or two students will speak up, but in the honors classes, it's a free-for-all."

—*Jonathan Post, Reinhardt College*

"My internship at a major international bank gave me an in-depth look into the world of investment and accounting. Funded by the Honors College, I was able to study business and culture in Shanghai, China, for a month. These valuable experiences are helping me to develop professionally, academically, and personally."

—*Jenny Lam, Honors College, The College of Staten Island, CUNY*

"The honors thesis was the key factor during the selection process at my future employer.... It helped me to get the job and have an advantage over others. It is a lot of work but, in the end, it is worth it."

—*Olgierd Hinz, Lee Honors College, Western Michigan University*

These portraits don't tell the whole story, but they should give you a sense of what it means to be part of an honors program or college. One of the great strengths of honors programs and colleges is that they are nurturing environments that encourage students to be well-rounded and help students make life choices.

WHAT IS AN HONORS PROGRAM?

An honors program is a sequence of courses designed specifically to encourage independent and creative learning. For more than half a century, honors education—given definition by the National Collegiate Honors Council—has been an institution on U.S. campuses. Although honors programs have many different designs, there are typical components. At two-year colleges, the programs often concentrate on special versions of general education courses and may have individual capstone projects that come out of students' special interests. At four-year colleges and universities, honors programs are generally designed for students of almost every major in every college on campus. In growing numbers, they are given additional prominence as honors colleges. Whether a program or a college, honors often includes a general education or "core" component followed by advanced courses (often called colloquia or seminars). Some programs have honors contracts that shape existing courses into honors components to suit the needs of individual students. Many have interdisciplinary or collaborative seminars that bring students of different majors together to discuss a complex topic with faculty members from different disciplines. A good number have final thesis, capstone, or creative projects, which may or may not be in the departmental major. Almost always, honors curriculum is incorporated within whatever number of credits is required of every student for graduation. Honors very rarely requires students to take additional credits. Students who complete an honors program or honors college curriculum frequently receive transcript and diploma notations as well as certificates, medallions, or other citations at graduation ceremonies.

In every case, catering to the student as an individual plays a central role in honors course design. Most honors classes are small (fewer than 20 students); most are discussion-oriented, giving students a chance to present their own interpretations of ideas and even teach a part of the course. Many classes are interdisciplinary, which means they are taught by faculty members from two or more departments, providing different perspectives on a subject. All honors classes help students develop and articulate their own perspectives by cultivating both verbal and written style. They help students mature intel-

SEARCH, FIND, SELECT

lectually, preparing them to engage in their own explorations and research. Some programs even extend the options for self-growth to study abroad and internships in science, government, the arts, or business related to the major. Other programs encourage or require community service as part of the honors experience. In every case, honors is an experiential education that deepens classroom learning and extends far beyond.

Despite their individual differences, all honors programs and honors colleges rely on faculty members who enjoy working with bright, independent students. The ideal honors faculty members are open-minded, encouraging master teachers. They want to see their students achieve at their highest capacity and are glad to spend time with students in discussions and laboratories, on field trips and at conferences, or online in e-mail. They often influence career decisions, are inspiring role models, and remain friends long after they have served as thesis advisers.

WHERE ARE HONORS PROGRAMS AND HONORS COLLEGES LOCATED?

Because honors programs and honors colleges include students from many different departments or colleges, they usually have their own offices and space on campus. Some have their own buildings. Most programs have honors centers or lounges, where students gather together for informal conversations, luncheons, discussions, lectures, and special projects.

Many honors students have cultivated strong personal interests that have nothing to do with classes. They may be multilingual; they may be fine artists or poets, musicians or racing car enthusiasts, mothers or fathers. Some volunteer in hospitals or do landscape gardening to pay for college. Many work in retail stores and catering. Some are avid sports enthusiasts, while others collect antiques. When they get together in honors lounges, there is always an interesting mixture of ideas!

In the honors center, you will also find the honors director or dean. The honors director often serves as a personal adviser to all of the students in the program. Many programs also have peer counselors and mentors who are upperclass honors students and know the ropes from a student's perspective and experience. Some have specially assigned honors advisers who guide honors students through their degrees, assist in registration, and answer every imaginable question. The honors office area usually is a good place to meet people, ask questions, and solve problems.

In general, honors provides an environment in which students feel free to talk about their passionate interests and ideas knowing that they will find good listeners and, sometimes, even arguers. There is no end to conversations among honors students. Like many students in honors, you may feel a great relief in finding a sympathetic group that respects your intelligence and creativity. In honors, you can be eccentric; you can be yourself! Some lifelong friendships, even marriages, are the result of social relationships developed in honors programs.

ARE YOU READY FOR HONORS?

Admission to honors programs and honors colleges is generally based on a combination of several factors: high school or previous college grades, experience taking AP or IB courses, SAT or ACT scores, personal essay, and extracurricular achievements. To stay in honors, students need to maintain a certain grade point average (GPA) and show progress toward the completion of the specific honors program or college requirements. Since you have probably exceeded admissions standards all along, maintaining your GPA will not be as big a problem as it sounds. Your professors and your honors director are there to help you succeed in the program. Most honors programs have very low attrition rates because students enjoy classes and do well.

Of course, you must be careful about how you budget your time for studying. Honors encourages well-rounded, diversified students, so you should play a sport, work at the radio station, join clubs of interest, or pledge a sorority or fraternity. You might find a job in the student center or library that will help you pay for your car expenses and that also is reasonable. But remember, each activity takes time, and you must strike the balance that leaves you enough time to do your homework, write papers, prepare for seminar discussions, do your research, and do well on exams. Choose the jobs and activities that attract you, but never let them overshadow your primary purpose—which is to be a student.

Sometimes even the very best students who apply for admission into an honors program or college are frightened by the thought of speaking in front of a group, giving seminar papers, or writing a thesis. But if you understand how the programs work, you will see that there is nothing to fear. The basis of honors is confidence in the student and building the student's self-confidence. Admittance to an honors program means you have already demonstrated your academic achievement in high school or college classes. Once in the honors environment, you learn how to formulate and structure ideas so that you can apply critical judgment to sets of facts and opinions. In small seminar classes, you practice discussion and arguments, so by the time you come to the senior thesis or project, the method is second nature. For most honors students, the senior thesis, performance, or portfolio presentation is the project that gives them the greatest fulfillment and pride. In many honors programs and colleges, students present their work either to other students or to faculty members in their major departments. Students often present their work at regional and national honors conferences. Some students even publish their work jointly with their faculty mentors. These are great achievements, and they come naturally with the training. There is nothing to fear. Honors will prepare you for life.

Dr. Joan Digby is Director of the Honors Program and Merit Fellowship at Long Island University, C.W. Post Campus. She was also President of the National Collegiate Honors Council from 1999 to 2000.

Public and Private Colleges and Universities— How to Choose

Debra Humphreys

As you survey the thousands of four-year colleges in the country and weigh the options before you, it is important to be aware of how colleges differ and what kind of educational experience each college offers you. In every state in the country, you will find both public and private colleges and universities. What are the differences between public and private colleges, and how should you approach the decision to attend one or the other? What are some common misconceptions regarding both public and private colleges that you should know about before you eliminate an entire category of institution from your list of prospective schools?

WHAT ARE THE BASIC CHARACTERISTICS OF PUBLIC AND PRIVATE INSTITUTIONS?

Over the course of the nation's history, what began as a small group of mostly church-affiliated colleges has grown in both size and complexity. Over the years, education in the United States became increasingly democratized, and more and more state-sponsored institutions and state systems of higher education emerged. These included small colleges, sometimes called "normal schools," designed to train school teachers for the expanding public school system; land-grant colleges and universities brought into existence with federal support in the mid-nineteenth century in order to prepare workers to expand the nation's agricultural and technological capacity; and large state systems that evolved in the twentieth century and now include two-year colleges, basic four-year institutions, and large research universities, all supported at least in part by state revenues.

While there are some clear distinctions to be made, even some of the core characteristics of public and private colleges vary from state to state. In general, a public institution receives at least part of its operating budget from state tax revenues, operates with a mandate and mission from the state where it is located, and is accountable to the elected officials of that state. Most private colleges and universities are independent, not-for-profit institutions. They operate with revenues from tuition; income from endowments; private gifts and bequests; and federal, private, or corporate foundation grants. These institutions are primarily accountable to a board of trustees,

usually made up of local or national business and community leaders and esteemed alumni.

There are also a small but growing number of for-profit colleges whose operating revenues include tuition dollars but also might include investor financing. Some of these colleges are owned and operated by publicly traded corporations. Most of the following generalizations about private institutions however refer to the more familiar not-for-profit independent college previously described.

While the distinction between public and private institutions might seem clear at first, these two kinds of colleges and universities actually share many characteristics. All accredited colleges and universities in the country—whether public or private, for profit or not—are entitled to receive public funds from the federal government in the form of direct grants and loans for eligible students, support for student work-study programs, and competitive grants to support research or campus programs. In exchange for this federal support, all schools undergo a peer-reviewed accreditation process by a regional accreditor authorized by the federal government's Department of Education.

Whether a college is public or private, you should know if it is accredited and therefore an institution whose students are eligible for all available federal financial aid. Accreditation status also provides you with assurance that the school operates in a fiscally responsible manner and that its academic programs have been deemed sound by an outside group of educators from its peer institutions.

HOW ARE PUBLIC AND PRIVATE COLLEGES AND UNIVERSITIES RUN?

In many ways, your experience as a student will not differ significantly based on what type of governance system a college or university uses. However, some knowledge of this might be useful in making choices among the various options. Private colleges and universities tend to have more independence and autonomy in how they are run, with boards of trustees that oversee financial and other program and life on campus at these schools. Public colleges and universities often have more complex governing structures with boards of regents or other types of oversight committees made up of politically appointed or elected officials exercising more or less oversight and intrusion into their day-to-day operations. New York, for instance, has a board of regents that oversees the system's campuses and is more actively involved in reviewing and revising curricular requirements that apply to institutions throughout the system. Other states have multiple public colleges, each with its own board overseeing each campus' operations with more or less intrusion into day-to-day operations.

Whether an institution is public or private, you will want to ask lots of questions about campus climate and academic programs in order to help you determine if a school is right for you. Being aware of some facts about public and private institutions will help you frame these questions to get truly useful answers.

ARE ALL PUBLIC COLLEGES AND UNIVERSITIES BIG AND IMPERSONAL?

Like private institutions, public colleges come in all shapes and sizes. Some are large institutions offering multiple degrees and majors to both undergraduate and graduate students alike. These institutions offer students many curricular options as well as access to leading scholars and an environment where cutting-edge academic research is conducted. While an institution of this size and scope might seem intimidating at first, remember that there are large institutions that do take very seriously their undergraduate programs. While you may receive less customized attention at a larger institution, many large public and private research universities offer options such as smaller honors programs, academic learning communities with smaller cohorts of students, or theme residence halls that can minimize the potential that you will get lost in the crowd.

If you are considering a large research institution— whether it is public or private—you should ask questions about the undergraduate program. What is the student-faculty ratio for undergraduates? What is the average class size, especially for introductory first-year courses? How many courses are taught by graduate students, and what sort of teacher training do those students receive? Are there opportunities for undergraduate students to participate in research projects with university faculty members?

In addition to the large, public research universities, there are many other smaller, state-funded regional institutions that still offer a wide range of both liberal arts and sciences fields as well as professional fields of study. Many states also offer small, public liberal arts colleges that share many of the defining characteristics of traditional, private liberal arts colleges. In 1987, some of these institutions formed the Council of Public Liberal Arts Colleges (COPLAC). COPLAC schools pride themselves on providing students of high ability and from all backgrounds access to a quality liberal education. These colleges and universities have been nationally recognized as outstanding in many ways. They offer small classes, innovations in teaching, personal interactions with faculty members, opportunities for faculty-supervised research, and supportive atmospheres. Most of them are located on campuses in rural or small-town settings. In addition to offering rigorous and well-integrated undergraduate programs, these

institutions often charge far less tuition than many private colleges do. More information can be found at http://www.coplac.org.

These public liberal arts colleges, along with more traditional private liberal arts institutions, do offer unique learning environments that research suggests often lead to higher levels of student achievement. Liberal arts colleges tend to offer a high degree of student-faculty interaction, high levels of student engagement with both in-class and out-of-class experiences, and lots of opportunities for collaborative and innovative learning practices. Businesses are also increasingly asking for exactly the set of skills and capacities that a liberal education provides, whether offered in a traditional liberal arts college setting or within a larger university that grants degrees in both liberal arts and other fields. Many public liberal arts and more comprehensive colleges and universities also now offer students a rigorous liberal education while integrating liberal learning into professional degree programs, for instance in health sciences, engineering, or education.

ARE PUBLIC COLLEGES CHEAPER THAN PRIVATE COLLEGES?

The cost of college is not easy to calculate and is not limited simply to the advertised price of tuition. It is absolutely not the case that attending a public college will always cost a student less money than attending a private institution. It is true that the basic tuition for in-state or out-of-state students attending public colleges is on average less expensive than the advertised tuition rate at private institutions. It is very important, however, to note that many private colleges and universities offer significant amounts of financial aid—often beyond the basic federal loans and grants available to all students. Many, but not all, private colleges have large endowments that allow them to effectively discount the standard, published tuition rates for a great number of their students. The National Association of College and University Business Officers sampled a small group of private colleges and discovered that only 10 percent of entering students were paying the full, advertised tuition. Ninety percent of their students received price discounts in the form of scholarships or financial aid. In other words, don't write off a college simply because its tuition looks extremely high relative to other institutions.

Both private and public institutions, however, have been fiscally stressed in recent years because of declining values of stock portfolios in endowments or because of declining state revenues resulting from the deteriorating economy. It is safe to say that for many students in the coming years, it will become increasingly difficult to get large amounts of financial aid. Many institutions, however, remain committed to widening access to more students from less economically privileged backgrounds. In addition, students demonstrating high levels of academic achievement are being rewarded at both private and public institutions—both in terms of admission and financial aid.

It is important to look carefully at the tuition and the financial aid requirements and availability at each school you are considering, private or public. In-state and out-of-state tuitions and the difference between them varies substantially from state to state. Out-of-state tuition also varies from state to state but still tends to be lower than average private tuition levels.

Policies vary as well for determining state residency status. In many states, the policy for dependent students requires that their parents must have lived in the state for at least twelve months prior to attendance in order to qualify for in-state tuition. For independent students, the requirement of twelve months residence prior to enrollment applies to the student. Independent status must be verified and generally entails proof that a student receives no support from parents or other relatives living in or out of the state in question. As budgets have increasingly tightened, states have over the past several years made it increasingly difficult to establish in-state residence after matriculating at a school. Exceptions are sometimes made, however, for students from migrant, refugee, or military families.

IS IT EASIER TO GAIN ADMISSION TO A PUBLIC INSTITUTION ESPECIALLY AS A STATE RESIDENT?

Few public colleges and universities automatically admit students who graduate from a public high school in their state. Many, however, give preference in admissions and financial assistance to in-state residents. Moreover, some states have implemented policies that guarantee admission to at least one of the state's public institutions for all students graduating in a top percentage of their high school classes.

There are, indeed, more highly selective private than public institutions. Many public colleges and universities, however, do admit very few applicants. These highly selective institutions might draw their students from a national pool of applicants and can be among the most selective in the country. However, the national universities and liberal arts colleges with the lowest acceptance rates in the country are mostly all private institutions.

While some public institutions offer virtually open admissions to state residents, it is important for all prospective students to realize that even an open-admission institution will require incoming students to meet certain academic standards before being admitted to credit-bearing courses. In most cases, public and private institutions give incoming students a series of placement exams that determines at what level the student can begin his or her course work. Depending on the results of these exams, a student may be required to take and pass one or more remedial courses before being admitted to courses that will actually count towards a degree.

Since each state's requirements are different and shift often, you should not assume that, regardless of your academic background, admission is automatic to your local state college. In the current climate—with costs rising and competition across systems tightening—admission rates are dropping at many public institutions.

IS THE CLIMATE ON A PUBLIC COLLEGE CAMPUS SIGNIFICANTLY DIFFERENT THAN THAT ON A PRIVATE COLLEGE CAMPUS?

The social and academic climate at colleges and universities varies substantially, and public institutions do not necessarily offer a distinctively different climate than private institutions do. You can find, at some public institutions, the small, residential environment traditionally associated with private liberal arts colleges. You will also find the presence of fraternities and sororities at both public and private institutions. You should look carefully at whether a school in which you are interested has fraternities and sororities and how much influence the Greek system has on college life. At some institutions, fraternities and sororities dominate the entire social life of the campus.

One campus environment that can only be found at a private institution is a highly religious environment. Many early colleges and universities were founded by churches or religious orders. Some of these institutions no longer retain a strong affiliation with one church or denomination. Others do retain a strong affiliation, and church traditions can heavily influence the climate of these institutions. Usually, these campuses will admit a student from any religious background, but they may require students to attend chapel services and/or take religion or theology courses to graduate. In addition, some college missions and curricula are influenced by their religious affiliations. For instance, many Catholic institutions have a strong commitment to community service and social justice. Students may find, at these institutions, curricula related to social justice issues and requirements that they complete a community-service learning activity or course to graduate. Institutions with a strong mission are also often able to develop more coherent, cohesive, and innovative curricula for their students.

Finally, other important climate factors to consider include whether a college or university is in an urban or rural setting; what the diversity of the student body is in terms of geographic, religious, or racial/ethnic background; if most students live on campus or commute from home; and finally if the college dominates the life of the community in which it is located. Each of these options has advantages and disadvantages you will want to weigh in making your decisions.

ARE PRIVATE COLLEGES MORE ACADEMICALLY RIGOROUS THAN PUBLIC COLLEGES?

Private colleges and universities are not necessarily more academically rigorous than public institutions. You will find rigorous, intellectually challenging, and innovative academic programs at both private and public institutions. There is also a common misconception that schools that are more highly selective have the most effective or engaging academic programs. Research suggests that there is no connection between the selectivity of an institution and the presence of effective or innovative teaching and learning practices. There is, however,

Questions to Ask as You Evaluate Prospective Colleges and Universities

- Does the college offer a distinctive first-year experience?
- Does the college offer a small-size freshman seminar for all students?
- Are all students required to complete a senior project or assignment that allows them to integrate all that they have learned and demonstrate acquired skills and knowledge?
- Are students encouraged or required to complete internships and/or service learning courses?
- Are students encouraged to study abroad? Is support for study abroad provided to all students and are study abroad experiences integrated into a student's overall curricula?
- Does the college offer learning communities, especially in the student's early years?
- Are students required to complete rigorous writing courses not only in the freshman year but also across the curriculum in whatever major he or she chooses to pursue?
- Are there opportunities for students to pursue independent research or creative projects under the supervision of a senior faculty member?

preliminary research that suggests that the academic quality of one's peers does seem to have an impact on the grade point averages of fellow students.

Nothing could be more important in your decision-making process than evaluating the nature of academic programs at prospective colleges or universities. Across both public and private institutions, there have been exciting and important changes in how colleges and universities are organizing undergraduate curricula. Many promising programs have been proven to result in higher levels of student retention, graduation, satisfaction, and academic achievement.

Many colleges and universities also now participate in the National Survey of Student Engagement. This survey asks students in both their first and last years about a series of effective educational practices and the degree to which they are engaged in the academic life of their school. Issues that are examined in the survey include the level of academic challenge, active and collaborative learning opportunities, the nature of student-faculty interactions, the number of enriching educational experiences available, and the supportive nature of the campus environment. Ask if the school you are considering participates in this survey and if you can see the results from recent classes of students.

THE PRIVATE/PUBLIC CHOICE

While there are distinct differences between public and private colleges and universities you should not limit your choice—whatever your background—to only one type of institution. There are wonderful opportunities at many different kinds of schools. The availability of many kinds of financial aid may bring private institutions with high-tuition levels within reach for you, whatever your financial background. Whether a school is highly selective or has open admissions, you should also be able to find a college or university that will challenge you academically and provide you with a supportive environment in which to live, learn, and pursue a college degree of lasting value.

Debra Humphreys is Vice President for Communications and Public Affairs for the Association of American Colleges and Universities.

Distance Education— It's Closer Than You Think

You may not realize it, but as an incoming college student, you are joining a revolution that is radically changing education. It's called distance learning. From kindergarten up to postgraduate degrees, distance learning is fast becoming an essential teaching tool. Most of the colleges and universities you are considering for a bachelor's degree offer distance learning in one form or another. Most likely you will be a distance learner at some point, whether during college or graduate school or throughout your career.

In case you're not familiar with distance learning—or asynchronous learning, online learning, or distance education—it means you don't sit in a classroom facing a teacher. You can be hundreds of miles or minutes from the teacher and other students. Most often you connect through the Internet to the teacher, fellow students, and study materials. However, increasingly sophisticated technologies, such as virtual laboratories, simulations, and interactive multimedia, are also used. You may run across the term "blended learning." Many institutions incorporate online learning into their face-to-face classes. In fact, a number of colleges require that a part of all classes is online.

FROM SNAIL-MAIL COURSES TO LEADING-EDGE TECHNOLOGY

Talk about change. Distance education began in the late 1800s, when schools mailed correspondence courses to farmers who wanted to learn how to grow better crops. Since technology came along, distance learning has become accessible and widespread. At first educators were skeptical, but as name-plate universities began to incorporate it into their teaching methodology, distance education became accepted.

When brick-and-mortar colleges and universities first considered distance education, the goal was to make it as good as face-to-face education. Now, says Ray Schroeder, Professor Emeritus of Communication and Director of the Center for Online Learning, Research, and Service (COLRS), at the University of Illinois at Springfield, "Field research shows that online learning technologies are better than face-to-face learning in a number of ways." Having taught online, he has seen firsthand how students participate more in discussions and learn from one another. Peg Miller, Ph.D., former Coordinator of Academic Support for Distributed Learning, University of Central Florida, cites a survey she conducted every other semester that compares face-to-face and distance learners at her institution. She has found that students from face-to-face and online classes were almost identical in the grades they earned and in their satisfaction with the classes.

ON THE UPSWING

Many reasons have caused the phenomenal growth of distance education. It's convenient and user-friendly, plus the scope of classes is stunning. Not that you'll likely begin your college years with classes in forensics or grading diamonds, but they are offered and indicate the enormous variety of courses. Along with many others in education, Michael P. Lambert, Secretary and Executive Director of the Distance Education Training Council, feels that online learning has transformed how people learn. "You no longer sit in a box with 35 other people where you might never raise your hand," he says. Adds Gerald Heeger, former President of the University of Maryland University College (UMUC), "Online learning gets rid of the limitations of geography and time. And as bandwidth increases, we will do more and more."

PROCEED WITH CAUTION

Now that you're convinced that distance education sounds great, sign me up, it's only fair to warn you that perhaps you shouldn't start your bachelor's degree totally online. Distance learning changes how you study, respond to your teachers, participate in class discussions, and take exams. If you're not prepared for the differences, you can easily fall behind and even fail. Though the age of online students continues to drop, most are older, have had some life experience since graduating from high school, and have the self-discipline, maturity, and self-motivation, that distance education demands. The average age of distance students is in the mid-30s, and 95 percent of them work full-time. They know what they want from college and are willing to meet the rigors of online learning, which are considerable.

Of course, some students straight from high school do successfully start college as distance learners because they've already had some online learning experience. Some take online classes in high school or advanced-placement and college courses. At Stevens Institute of Technology's Web Campus, incoming freshmen brush up on math and precalculus online before their first fall semester. At first, Nathan Kahl, former instructor for the Euclid Program at Stevens Institute of Technology Web Campus, was skeptical that high school graduates could succeed in the online courses he taught, but he saw that "everyone quickly got into the swing of things." He admits that he underestimated the students' ability to learn online. Heeger agrees "There's no reason why a bright junior in high school who is ready to take college freshmen courses can't do it."

The University of Phoenix Online (parent company: Apollo Group, Inc.) has developed a bachelor's degree program specifically for incoming freshmen of any age—including those just out of high school. In today's job market, a college education is a necessity, yet many students have life situations that prevent them from attending. Notes former president of Apollo Group, Inc., Brian Mueller about the accommodations their program makes for students who are new to higher education, "It is our experience that if you create an online classroom, it must have all the features that incoming students need, which are small, highly interactive, and collaborative classes." Their freshman classes average 15 and require that the instructor has consistent contact with the students. New freshmen also get a tremendous amount of support in writing, math, and online research skills and have the help of an academic counselor who closely tracks them for ten weeks into their first semester. "We think there are more students coming out of high school who must have jobs, so we took the model for working adults and created an environment for traditional students that combines education and work," says Mueller.

However, not all educators have the same experience with incoming freshmen. Jimmy Reeves, Ph.D., Professor and Chair, Department of Chemistry and Biochemistry at the University of North Carolina at Wilmington, teaches both online and face-to-face classes and knows how students can react. Freshmen who fail his face-to-face class sometimes ask to take his class online. He says no because the discipline required is rare among 19-year-old students. "Junior and senior college students do well, but it has more to do with their level of maturity and the reasons why they're in college," he says, referring to the fact that many incoming college students want to experiment or come because their parents demand it. "Without any real desire to learn or sense of why they're in college, it's easy to get distracted in online classes," he notes. You can't hide in the back of a lecture hall half asleep on Monday morning and hope for the best on multiple-choice questions. In online classes, your active participation is noticed and taken into account for final grades.

Attending college isn't just about acquiring knowledge in a particular field in order to get a job. It's also about learning social skills and meeting people with different ideas from diverse backgrounds. "If you want to live in a dorm and have bull sessions on the meaning of life with the kids down the hall, then being a fully online freshman student isn't for you," advises Cynthia Davis, Associate Dean of Academic Affairs in the School of Undergraduate Studies at the University of Maryland University College (UMUC). She adds that sometimes students mistakenly think getting a bachelor's degree online will take less time than physically attending classes or won't require as much work. But as she points out, online classes demand the same amount of effort, if not more, than face-to-face classes.

WHAT'S IT GOING TO BE LIKE?

Blended learning or mixed-mode classes, combining face-to-face and online instruction, are becoming a permanent fixture in higher education. Students might sit in a classroom on Monday but take the remaining two classes for that week online. Professors routinely post the syllabus, class calendar, or PowerPoint lectures. Reeves says that it's rare to see college classes without some Web-based materials. Davis

comments that UMUC routinely Web-enhances all of its face-to-face classes with companion Web classrooms. Students can have optional online discussions or print copies of class materials.

"We find more students use online technology to enhance their studies and get better grades," comments Schroeder. Educators see a trend of students enrolling in one university and taking courses from other institutions. For instance, say you're in an art class but want to study German cathedral architecture, which your university doesn't have but another one offers online. It's only a matter of time before this will be a standard option for college students.

LOTS TO LOOK FOR, LOTS TO AVOID, LOTS TO ASK

Though much of distance education depends on the Internet, you can't just type in "distance education" and see what comes up in a search for a college. You must seriously research and do background checks to make sure a diploma mill doesn't hand you a bachelor's degree that isn't credible. There are plenty of places to get information. Petersons.com offers a database of colleges and universities that have online courses, as well as totally online distance education providers. "You have to be a good consumer," recommends Heeger. "It's no different from getting a loan. You don't borrow money from people you never heard of. You shouldn't get degrees from people you never heard of." Schroeder suggests checking the course completion of online programs, their enrollment, and growth of programs. "Just as one checks with friends and colleagues about the quality of consumer services, such as computers and cars, one should check with students who are enrolled in online programs," he advises.

Is the Institution Accredited by a Valid Accrediting Body?

There are several kinds of accrediting organizations:

- The six regional accrediting agencies recognized by the U.S. Department of Education
- The Council for Higher Education Accreditation (www.chea.org)
- Other institutional accrediting agencies, such as the Accrediting Council for Independent Colleges and Schools and the Distance Education and Training Council
- Specialized accrediting agencies that cover schools offering everything from acupuncture to veterinary medicine
- Other discipline-based accrediting organizations, such as those for law and business schools

Can You Transfer Credits Received Online from One Institution to Another?

Policies vary greatly among universities and colleges. Though distance education is widely accepted, there are so many places where students can take bogus online courses that institutions are justifiably cautious. If students do decide they want to get a bachelor's degree completely online, they need to be sure the campus-based program and distance education program offer the same degree. At most institutions, both on-campus and online degrees are the same, but others do differ-

Test-Drive an Online Class

Just like face-to-face instruction, online classes are different, depending on the course material and how each teacher chooses to structure the course, but here's a typical scenario of what it's like to be a distance learner.

Getting started. First you'll want to get to the general information page for the class, which you'll visit often. The professor's contact information, the class calendar, the syllabus, and announcements on quizzes and tests or links to other pages on which you'll find posted discussion questions may be found here. Some teachers will ask you to tell something about yourself to the other students in the class. Be sure to read the syllabus, which will outline the course and tell you when assignments are due and how grades are determined.

Responding to discussion questions. Those students who never raised their hands will get a shock in online courses. Responding with thoughtful answers to online discussion groups is mandatory. Usually the teacher will assign reading material and then post a discussion question. The material might be from your textbook or websites. You must respond to the question and possibly to the postings of other students in the class. Teachers will gauge your participation in the class and how well you learn the material.

Interacting with fellow students and your teacher. Ray Schroeder, Professor Emeritus of Communication and Director of the Center for Online Learning, Research, and Service (COLRS) at the University of Illinois at Springfield, gives talks about distance education. Often he'll ask his audience to recall their favorite class from elementary school up to college and what made it so memorable. Was it the textbook? The actual classroom? The view out the window? When he asks if it was the interaction among students and with the teacher, the audience realizes that's what made the class good. "Both in person and online, learning takes place in the interaction," says Schroeder. "Otherwise, we would do just as well to read a book or watch a video to learn." In online classes, interaction between you and the professor and other students is an enormous part of your success.

Nathan Kahl, former instructor for the Euclid Program at Stevens Institute of Technology Web Campus, explains, "Distance students expect that their teachers will be online

at least as much as they are." The level of interaction expected from you will vary by school and course, but you should know that in online courses, you must be an active participant. On the flip side, teachers carefully monitor discussions to make sure the more talkative students don't dominate. Keith W. Miller, Professor of Computer Science at the University of Illinois at Springfield, interacts with his students in a variety of ways. "I make announcements to the whole class on the homepage. I send e-mails to the whole class. I enter into the electronic discussions on the bulletin board forums, and post daily reminders and assignments to the course calendar. The students interact with me using e-mail, notes in their assignments, and via the bulletin boards. Now and then someone calls me at my office on the phone, but that's rare." He likes to answer his e-mails at least once a day, which means that his students get much more feedback than they would if he were physically in a classroom with them.

As do most online teachers, Cynthia Davis, Associate Dean of Academic Affairs in the School of Undergraduate Studies at the University of Maryland University College, gets students to participate with a weekly discussion topic. "If we're reading a novel," she says, "I ask them to discuss the role of the narrator or analyze a passage. The students respond individually and then respond to other students' comments."

Attending virtual lectures. Some online courses allow you to hear and see the professor or other guest speakers who are also online. If you want to ask a question, there's a button to indicate you want to speak. Everyone else can hear you as if you all were in the same room. Other professors add voice to PowerPoint lectures, which you can view when you want to, not at some prearranged time.

Taking quizzes and tests. No more waiting weeks to get your tests back. Online technology in some courses instantly zaps back the corrected test and notes that you missed question six and need to study page 54 of the textbook. Just like in face-to-face classes, you have an allotted amount of time to take the quiz. Some online courses may have automated components, such as instant quizzes and animated and interactive practice sessions. Others have mandatory proctored exams at a nearby community college or learning center for students who are off campus.

entiate in the degrees conferred, and it will show up on your diploma.

What Kind of Refund Policy Does the University Have for Distance Learners?

It might become painfully apparent for students that online learning is not for them, and they want to drop out. Find out ahead of time about the refund policy for online classes. What happens if you're ill during an online class? How can you make up the work? Even before taking any classes, you should

find out if you're suited for online learning. Many institutions offer self-assessment tests on their websites.

What Online Services Does the College Provide?

Is the dorm wired? Can you get an e-mail address from the university? What about browsers and computer compatibility? Ask how the Internet is part of face-to-face classes. To what extent is the library online, and is it available 24/7 for research? Ask about writing and math labs and help-desk support. Look for online tutorials that show students how to use the school's specific software. Is there a tech fee?

IF YOU'RE LEARNING ONLINE, YOU BETTER HAVE THESE

Since online learning is part of college, it's helpful to know what to expect ahead of time, rather than three weeks into the class, when you feel like throwing your laptop out the window and would happily settle for sitting in the back row of the nearest classroom. Here are the five skills and abilities that successful online students must have:

1. You must have the self-discipline to do things you don't want to do when you don't want to do them.

If you're a procrastinator, you'll find the catch-up tactics that served you well in face-to-face classes won't work online. "Students get the idea they can whiz by without studying, or they came from high schools where they weren't pushed," cautions Heeger. "Maybe they never got Fs in high school, but they do here." That's because they don't realize they're responsible for learning the material on their own. The burden is on you to keep up with the homework. It doesn't take long to fall far behind in online classes.

Typically, students in face-to-face and online classes need 2 hours for work outside of class for every hour in class. But online students often forget to add that hour. For every hour they would have to sit in a traditional classroom, they should be listening, studying, thinking, writing, responding to discussions, and getting ready for tests, plus the 2 hours outside of class. Three classes a week—that's 9 to 10 hours for one class. Online teachers keep students on track with weekly quizzes and homework assignments. If students start lagging, they're likely to get an e-mail from the professor asking what's going on. Claudine SchWeber, Ph.D., Chair of the Doctor of Management Program at the University of Maryland University College, has taught online for years and states, "My classes are structured by weekly readings, activities, and discussions. Students can't decide to get around to doing the work when they feel like it. It must be done at the instructor's pace. The first shot of online can be a shock to their system."

2. You must have the ability to manage your time without anyone telling you do your homework NOW.

In high school, students usually can put off studying until the weekend. "That doesn't work in college. You can't write complex papers the night before," says Karen L. Kirkendall, Ph.D., Associate Professor of Liberal and Integrative Studies and Director of the Capitol Scholars Honors Program at the University of Illinois at Springfield. She teaches both online and face-to-face classes and has seen first-time online students who have never failed before start to slip and suddenly realize they are in big trouble. "My online classes are extraordinarily structured so I pretty much know when students aren't engaged, which I monitor by seeing how much they participate in online discussions," she notes.

Distance Learning Myths

As distance education becomes more accepted, people will readily discard some of the myths on this list. But for now, they persist.

Distance learning is for people on ranches 200 miles from the nearest freeway. Geography is not a factor. Many distance learners who are located across the campus or a few miles away just don't want to deal with the commute or have a work schedule that conflicts with being in a class at a certain time. They appreciate the flexibility that distance education gives them.

Distance learning is easier than face-to-face classes. Once you start an online class, you'll knock that myth off the list. Still, some students think it will be easier. When they realize they must not only respond to discussion questions but also comment on the responses from other students, they wonder why they ever thought distance education was going to be easy. Online teachers normally keep track of how their students progress with frequent monitoring and quizzes.

I'll get a better education in face-to-face classes. Much research has been conducted comparing the two and consistently, online learning is equivalent or better. Teachers of online courses now have plenty of precedents to follow, training and research to help them teach better, and technology to prepare for classes and keep up with their students' progress.

I'll talk to a computer all day. Yes, you are in front of a computer as a distance learner, but you also interact with professors and other students much more than you ever would in a core freshman class of 200. Teachers have sophisticated software to facilitate interaction. Even though you don't physically see your teachers, they put a great deal of effort into class preparation and reading e-mails. Some get as many as 3,000 e-mails in a ten-week class. Distance learners often get to know fellow students much more easily online than they would walking in and out of a class.

I need to be a computer geek. If you can handle the simplest maneuvers around a computer, such as attaching documents to e-mails or going to a specified Web address, you can be a distance learner. And you'll have tech support to help out if you run into problems.

Distance education is cheaper than face-to-face. Too bad this is a myth. It costs the same as a traditional college if you attend a recognized institution. Most students pay for distance education through student loans.

3. You must have the skills to communicate your thoughts in writing.

"Online participation in class discussions isn't instant messaging. You are what you write in online classes," advises SchWeber. Most of the work in online classes is written, whether it's participation in discussions, homework, quizzes, papers, or tests.

Since you'll communicate by e-mail and post your thoughts, netiquette is essential. You need to think differently online than when speaking on the phone or face-to-face. "You can't write a report that sounds like you are hanging out with friends," advises SchWeber. "When you are totally online, the only image people (including your professor) have of you is how you write." Kirkendall has reprimanded students who sent e-mails showing disrespect to the teacher because they were upset about something. Probably they would never respond that way if face-to-face. "Never hit the submit button when you're angry," Kirkendall cautions.

4. You must have the ability to research worthwhile information on the Web.

You need to know what's junk and what's reliable. In addition, professors take plagiarism very seriously, especially because it's so easy to do.

5. You must have some computer skills and know some computer-speak.

Those who design the software and set up how a distance learning class is taught are careful to make sure the technology doesn't get in the way of learning; however, you should know the basics. "In some classes, certain downloads are required, such as Adobe Acrobat, but in general, the skills are not beyond the abilities used daily by most elementary school children," says Schroeder, pointing out that if distance programs use expensive or exotic technology, they defeat the purpose. He reports that most computers that are five years old have the speed, memory, and capability to support online learning. Some classes might require a microphone. You should be familiar with some of the computer jargon so that if you're asked to post something or use a drop box, add an attachment, or take part in a threaded discussion, you'll know what you need to do. Just about every distance learning provider has online tutorials to familiarize you with their particular online software. If you run into technical problems, help-desk support is available.

Why Not Women's Colleges?

Before we start talking about the many advantages that women's colleges offer, let's get some myths out of the way. It is almost certain that the minute you hear "women's colleges" in the same sentence with "choosing colleges" you immediately think: no boys, no fun, no way!

Maybe that is why some girls who visit Joan Jaffe's office at Mills College in San Francisco, California, rush in to tell her that they just saw some guys on the campus of this women's college. Jaffe, Associate Dean of Admission, frequently gets this reaction from the young women who visit the campus. That's because many think that if they go to a women's college they are never going to see a guy within 2 miles of the campus gates, which, by the way, will clang shut behind them, leaving them secluded inside a heavily guarded male-free zone.

KISS MYTH NUMBER ONE GOOD-BYE

Forget iron gates. The first myth to get rid of is the one that assumes attending a women's college means kissing your social life good-bye. In fact, as Patricia Gibbs, Vice President for Student Affairs, Dean of Students at Wesleyan College in Macon, Georgia, points out, "If you were a guy looking for a date, where would you go?" Not only that, the majority of women's colleges are near, if not next to, coed campuses. Most share activities with other colleges and universities, and many have reciprocal agreements so that guys can take classes at the women's college and vice versa.

When it comes to dating, women's colleges offer the best of both worlds. You can hang out with guys when you want to and then retreat to your own lovely environment (women's dorms usually are beautiful) and hang out with the girls. Julie Binder, who transferred from the University of Wisconsin to all-women's Barnard College in New York City, notes that there is open registration with Columbia University, which just happens to be right next door. "Campus life is shared. Sports are shared," she says.

As you dig deeper into this myth, you will find that attending a women's college is not about isolation, it's about options. You get to choose if you want to be in classes, clubs, and organizations only with women or mingle with the men.

SCRATCH MYTH NUMBER TWO

Myth Number Two: Women's colleges are just a bunch of catty, competitive females waiting for the right moment to scratch each other's eyes out. Scratch that myth, too. Instead, women's colleges cultivate an environment of sisterhood— women who look out for one another. Most women's colleges encourage women in the upper-level classes to help their younger classmates. Talking to their "big sisters," newcomers can find out what classes to take and which professors are best, and they find a sympathetic ear for the problems that most first-year college students face.

The Rich Traditions in Women's Colleges

Tradition plays an important part of the experience women have in women's colleges. They run the gamut from solemn ceremonies of passing along the bond of sisterhood to the fun of secret surprises. "Women's colleges have a strong sense of tradition," says Amy Shaver, former Academic Dean at Stephens College in Columbia, Missouri. It's also a wonderful way to help women from all social, economic, religious, and ethnic backgrounds to share a common experience and pass it on to the next generation of students. "Traditions bond women over the generations," says Jennifer Rickard, Dean of Admissions and Financial Aid at Bryn Mawr College, who notes that it's not unusual at all to have students today singing songs and participating in ceremonies that the class of 1945 did and which will be the same when today's students have their twenty-year reunion.

Here's a sampling of the many traditions you'll find on women's college campuses:

Lantern Night At Bryn Mawr's Lantern Night, women gather around a fountain on campus. Each woman is given a lantern as a symbol of knowledge and learning. Each class has a color, and as the lanterns are passed from the sophomores to the first-year students, songs are sung in Greek that are the same as the ones sung 100 years ago around the same fountain.

Senior Paint Night Mills College seniors get the okay to paint the campus in their class color. Along with brushes and cans of paint, they are given a few guidelines as to what can and cannot be painted, but the rest is up to them.

The Crossing of the Bridge As women students come to Stephens to begin their college education, they cross over a bridge on campus in a ceremony symbolizing their entrance into the world of academia. At graduation, they cross over another bridge on campus and are welcomed into the alumnae society.

Candlelight Induction Ceremony Spelman students dressed in white dresses and black shoes light candles and hear the charge to be the best they can be. While the candles are still lit, they sing the Spelman hymn.

Midnight Breakfast At Barnard, the night before finals, the president of the college, deans, and professors make breakfast for the students.

"The sense of community is very strong at women's colleges," observes Fran Samuels, former Director of College Counseling at The Master's School in Dobbs Ferry, New York. "The myth is that a women's college will be cliquish. In truth, the women are supportive of each other." The strong bonds of sisterhood that naturally develop connect students to their college, its history, and its students—past, present, and future. Many women's colleges designate a rotating color for each incoming class. For example, if the freshman class you enter is dubbed the golden hearts, by the time you graduate, you are connected to all the golden hearts who graduated ahead of you and all the golden hearts who will graduate after you.

TOSS MYTH NUMBER THREE

Another myth that should be tossed out is that women's colleges don't prepare you for the "real world." Well, try saying that to the 12 women members of Congress who graduated from women's colleges. Or to the 15 women on *Business Week*'s list of the rising stars in corporate America. Although you are not in a totally coed situation, on the other hand you are in an environment in which you can gain skills to think critically and learn to meet challenges. Becky Marsh, Director of Advancement at Whitfield School, in St. Louis, Missouri, points out that when you first ride a bike, training wheels allow you to learn how to balance. Once you are ready to race down the street, you take them off. Same with women's colleges. The focus is on your education and your strengths, and who you are. You graduate ready to take on the obstacles of the real world. "In high school, I had the feeling that boys were given more opportunities to share their knowledge. It was harder and more intimidating for me to share my opinions in a coed class," says Brittany Johnson, from Spelman College in Atlanta, Georgia. "Now I feel like I can do anything."

Graduates of women's colleges feel empowered and willing to confront any limits to their abilities. While in college, they have many opportunities to assume leadership roles and see women in leadership positions as professors and deans. "They don't doubt whether they can do anything. Instead, they ask, 'Why can't I do it now?'" reports Amy Shaver, former Academic Dean at Stephens College in Columbia, Missouri. Women can find their own voices and establish their own ways of approaching things that will ultimately make them successful in a male-dominated world. They learn from seeing other women students and professors engaged in the intellectual process.

THE ADVANTAGES

As more young women find out about the advantages that women's colleges offer them, they like what they see. Maybe that is why attendance at women's colleges is growing. Learning leadership skills tops the list of advantages. Says Shaver, "Women in a same-sex environment are more likely to take risks and speak up in class. They are more willing to stand up and voice an opinion." If you think about it, students get plenty of practice at a women's college because all the leadership roles go to women. From day one on a women's campus, you will see women leading the entire college or involved in interesting and significant research. You get more exposure to what leadership is and what to expect as a leader. "Leadership becomes ingrained," notes Jennifer Fondiller, Dean of Admissions and Financial Aid at Barnard College in New York City.

You might not realize it, but women react differently in classrooms with all women. They tend to speak up with confidence and test their ideas more readily when they are not competing with men. Researchers find that even as early as the fifth grade, girls are taught differently than boys. Teachers call on boys more frequently and don't ask girls the more thought-provoking questions or to critically analyze problems. In coed situations, the more aggressive and competitive guys take over, whereas in all-female classes, research indicates there is much more give-and-take and exchange of ideas.

Coming from a coed public school, Johnson realized that more attention was given to the guys in her classes, but at Spelman, she says, "Everyone is on the same path." Arlene Cash, Vice President for Enrollment Management at Spelman, notes that women don't have to vie for attention or retreat into the intellectual background in all-women classes. In a coed class, the environment becomes more adversarial. "Women feel they have to perform. In women's colleges they become more academically involved and interact with faculty members more frequently," says Debbie Greenberg, former College Counselor at Whitfield School. Speaking of the rich interaction that occurs in her classes at Barnard, Binder says, "The diversity of experience around the discussion table is unparalleled."

YOU CAN SUCCEED

Shaver characterizes the environment in women's colleges as one in which there is no fear of failing when the social pressures and dynamics of men and women are removed from the classroom. Women's colleges give women the opportunity to explore different avenues without the fear of failing. "We challenge them to become what they want to become," says Gibbs from Wesleyan. "No one says, 'You can't do that because you are a woman.'" At the same time, you are interacting with other women who have the same goals as you, which reinforces who you are. Or, as Jennifer Rickard, Dean of Admissions and Financial Aid at Bryn Mawr College, in Bryn Mawr, Pennsylvania, points out, women are not just sitting in classes to do well on exams and get good grades. They also are figuring out what they want to do with their education. "There's less expectation to conform to an external measure," she says.

Many women's colleges foster self-government and give their students responsibilities they might not find in a coed institution. At Bryn Mawr, for instance, students pay a self-government association fee as part of their tuition. This is put into a fund that is controlled by a student government that takes ownership of how the students want to govern themselves. "This isn't student government making only recommendations to the administration as to how to allocate the budget to the different student groups vying for funds," notes Rickard. "You have students dealing with real-world management issues, such as resource allocation."

Since women's colleges are smaller than big coed universities, women receive all the benefits that students get from a small liberal arts college in addition to the advantages that only a women's college offers. A big plus is interaction with professors and staff, which is hard to achieve when you are one of

What Made You Choose a Women's College?

When she got to the point of choosing which college to attend, Wisambi Loundu had plenty of options. Coming from San Diego, the California universities were a logical choice. Women's colleges were not on her list. In fact, she hardly knew they existed. Her first thought when someone suggested a women's college to her was, "I'm not going to a school full of girls minus boys." Her second thought was just as negative. "If it's all girls, they will always be fighting." The third and fourth thoughts assumed that a women's college wouldn't prepare her for the real world, plus she would be isolated.

But then her math teacher's daughter told her about Bryn Mawr, and as Wisambi started exploring the possibility, the advantages of a women's college started lining up. However, it wasn't until she visited Bryn Mawr that she really began to see herself there. "I fell in love with the campus," says Wisambi. "It was like nothing I'd ever seen before." Her stay in the dorm added to her steadily growing thoughts that Bryn Mawr might be it. "The girls I stayed with in the dorm were so friendly. At first I was suspicious, but I saw it was not a front. Plus, there were girls from all over the world."

But Wisambi didn't make her final decision just yet. She decided to look at other schools, like Wellesley and the University of California schools, as well as Stanford. Meanwhile, her friend told her more about Bryn Mawr. "She said I'd make lasting friends and she talked about how the academics would train me for the outside world even if there were no men on campus. Bryn Mawr would build my identity as a woman."

She still wasn't convinced and made a second visit, along with visits to Wellesley and Stanford, which she says were nice, but too big. It would be too hard to make friends there, she thought. When the time came to make her final selection, she chose Bryn Mawr.

Now at Bryn Mawr, how does Wisambi feel about her choice? The academics are more challenging than she anticipated but doable, and she is excited about the internships she will be able to access. She also finds that the staff and teachers at Bryn Mawr go out of their way to make her feel at home. "They match us up with a mentor and professor," she says.

How about dating? Since Bryn Mawr is part of a tri-college community, guys are around, though Wisambi says you have to make an effort to meet people on other campuses.

Talking to seniors who are getting ready to head out to the "real world," Wisambi can see that they are full of confidence and don't think for a minute that they won't do well. "And that's a positive," she says.

200 students in a lecture hall taught by a graduate student. Women's colleges tend to foster seminar-style classes taught by full professors, many of them women. "You have an expert teaching you," says Gibbs. Faculty members get to know their students and can challenge them intellectually on an individual basis. "Within two days, all my teachers knew my name," recalls Johnson, who says she was given each professor's e-mail address, home phone number, and all the contact information she needed and was encouraged to reach out to them.

Women are encouraged to achieve their intellectual goals. Professors often will point out specific programs that they know suit the student's interests. Add to this the opportunities to conduct research with a professor, and in many cases actually present research findings to a professional society, and you can see why women graduate with a terrific resume before they even start their careers. Rickard mentions the opportunity that Bryn Mawr students have to work on funded projects with professors during the summer and then present the results along with them at conferences. "It's a window into the academic world and the world of the intellectual," she notes. It's no surprise that women in women's colleges major in math and science at a higher national average than women in coed institutions.

Paid and unpaid internships, too, are more available for women at women's colleges, mainly because of the network of women graduates in business and industry who want to help their "sisters" at their alma maters. "I'm getting my professional edge now," says Binder, who is interested in TV production and had a paid internship as a production assistant while a sophomore at Barnard. "You will have an amazing resume by the time you graduate," she says.

Peggy Hock, Ph.D., former College Counselor at Notre Dame High School in San Jose, California, points out that colleges naturally rely on their alumni to come forward with networking opportunities for students; however, the alumnae of women's colleges tend to be more loyal and willing to give of their time. This translates into many more opportunities for internships, mentoring, and job possibilities. At Barnard, for example, the career office has an alumna mentor network. Students can call, ask questions, and get advice about career choices. At alumnae events, current students mix with the graduates. Binder takes full advantage of the Web log of women who are working all over the world and willing to spend time online with Barnard students. She applied for a job at a public relations firm in New York after contacting a fellow Barnard graduate working there. She met with her and subsequently got a letter of recommendation.

HOW TO CHOOSE

Choosing a women's college isn't any different from choosing a coed college. You should definitely visit the campus and don't be afraid to ask lots of questions—even the ones that might make you uncomfortable. Because women's colleges are similar to small coed liberal arts colleges, make sure that you don't compare a women's campus to a big university.

Janet Ashley, former Interim Director for Admissions at Spelman College, advises high school women to ask what a women's college can give them academically. "Their choice depends on what their goals are," she says.

If you're worried about the dating scene, ask about the levels of interaction with guys and how close the relationships are with neighboring institutions.

"Look at the individuality of each women's college," suggests Rickard, "because each has its own personality."

Look at the school before looking at the fact that it's a women's college, and on the flip side, don't rule out a school just because it is a women's college. "So many students make quick decisions about where to apply," warns Fondiller, noting that sometimes the decision hinges on what schools a friend is applying to rather than if that institution really fits the student. Many women's colleges specialize in certain fields like science, math, or theater.

Famous Firsts from Women's Colleges

Quick, from which college did the first woman to be named Secretary of State graduate? Or the woman scientist who identified the Hong Kong flu? Or the first woman executive vice president of the American Stock Exchange? Here's a big clue. They were all graduates of women's colleges.

SENATOR
- Barbara Mikulski (MD)—Mount Saint Agnes College

REPRESENTATIVES
- Tammy Baldwin (WI)—Smith College
- Donna Christian-Christensen (VI)—St. Mary's College
- Rosa DeLauro (CT)—Marymount College
- Jane Harman (CA)—Smith College
- Gabrielle Giffords (AZ)—Scripps College
- Eddie Bernice Johnson (TX)—Saint Mary's College
- Barbara Lee (CA)—Mills College
- Nita Lowey (NY)—Mount Holyoke College
- Betty McCollum (MN)—College of Saint Catherine
- Nancy Pelosi (CA), first woman elected as Speaker of the House of Representatives—Trinity College
- Allyson Schwartz (PA)—Simmons College

SECRETARY OF STATE
- Hillary Rodham Clinton (NY)—Wellesley College

OTHER FAMOUS WOMEN FIRSTS
- Madeleine Albright, first woman to be named Secretary of State in the United States, appointed in 1997—Wellesley College
- Jane Amsterdam, first woman editor, the New York Post—Cedar Crest College
- Emily Green Balch, first woman to receive the Nobel Peace Prize in 1946—Bryn Mawr College
- Catherine Brewer Benson, first woman to receive a college bachelor's degree—Wesleyan College
- Earla Biekert, first scientist to identify the Hong Kong flu virus—Wesleyan College
- Cathleen Black, first woman leader of the American Newspaper Publishers Association—Trinity Washington University
- Sarah Porter Boehmler, first woman executive vice president of American Stock Exchange—Sweet Briar College
- Jane Matilda Bolin, first African American woman judge in the United States—Wellesley College
- Dorothy L. Brown, first African American woman general surgeon in the South—Bennett College for Women
- Pearl S. Buck, first American woman to win the Nobel Prize in Literature—Randolph-Macon Woman's College
- Ila Burdett, Georgia's first female Rhodes Scholar—Agnes Scott College
- Dorothy Vredenburgh Bush, first woman secretary of the Democratic National Party—Mississippi University for Women
- Hon. Audrey J. S. Carrion, first Hispanic woman judge Circuit Court for Baltimore City—College of Notre Dame of Maryland
- Rachel Carson, first environmentalist who awakened public consciousness through her book, *Silent Spring*—Chatham University
- Barbara Cassani, first woman CEO of a commercial airline—Mount Holyoke College
- Elaine L. Chao, U.S. Secretary of Labor, 2001; First Asian American woman appointed to a President's cabinet—Mount Holyoke College

Adapted from the website of the Women's College Coalition at http://www.womenscolleges.org.

How to Use This Guide

PROFILES

The **PROFILES** section contains basic data in capsule form for quick review and comparison. The following outline of the format shows the section headings and the items that each section covers. Any item that does not apply to a particular college or for which no information was supplied is omitted from that college's listing. Display ads, which appear near some of the institutions' profiles, have been provided and paid for by those colleges and universities that chose to supplement their profile with additional information.

Category Overviews

Type of Institution

Private institutions are designated as *independent* (nonprofit), *proprietary* (profit-making), or *independent with a specific religious denomination or affiliation*. Nondenominational or interdenominational religious orientation is possible and would be indicated. Public institutions are designated by the source of funding. Designations include *federal, state, province, commonwealth* (Puerto Rico), *territory* (U.S. territories), *county, district* (an educational administrative unit often having boundaries different from units of local government), *city, state and local* (local may refer to county, district, or city), or *state-related* (funded primarily by the state but administratively autonomous). *Religious affiliation* may follow, along with year founded. Each institution is classified as one of the following:

- Primarily two-year: Awards baccalaureate degrees but majority of students are enrolled in two-year programs.

- Four-year: Awards baccalaureate degrees; may also award associate degrees; does not award graduate (postbaccalaureate) degrees.

- Five-year: Awards a five-year baccalaureate in a professional field such as architecture or pharmacy; does not award graduate degrees.

- Upper-level: Awards baccalaureate degrees, but entering students must have at least two years of previous college-level credit; may also offer graduate degrees.

- Comprehensive: Awards baccalaureate degrees; may also award associate degrees; offers graduate degree programs, primarily at the master's, specialist's, or professional level, although one or two doctoral programs may be offered.

- University: Offers four years of undergraduate work, plus graduate degrees through the doctorate in more than two academic or professional fields.

Setting

Designated as *urban* (located within a major city), *suburban* (a residential area within commuting distance of a major city), *small town* (a small but compactly settled area not within commuting distance of a major city), or *rural* (a remote and sparsely populated area).

Endowment

The total dollar value of funds and/or property donated to the institution or the multicampus educational system of which the institution is a part.

Student body

An institution is *coed* (coeducational—admits men and women), *primarily* (80 percent or more) *women, primarily men, women only,* or *men only*. A few schools are designated as *undergraduate: women only; graduate: coed* or *undergraduate: men only; graduate: coed.*

Entrance

The five levels of entrance difficulty *(most difficult, very difficult, moderately difficult, minimally difficult,* and *noncompetitive)* are based on the percentage of applicants who were accepted for fall 2012 freshman admission (or, in the case of upper-level schools, for entering-class admission) and on the high school class rank and standardized test scores of the accepted freshmen who actually enrolled in fall 2012. The colleges were asked to select the level that most closely corresponds to their entrance difficulty, according to these guidelines.

Undergraduates

Percentages of undergraduates who are part-time or full-time students; transfers in; live on campus; out-of-state; Black or African American, non-Hispanic/Latino; Hispanic/Latino; Asian, non-Hispanic/Latino; Native Hawaiian or other Pacific Islander, non-Hispanic/Latino; American Indian or Alaska Native, non-Hispanic/Latino are given. *Retention:* The percentage of freshmen (or, for upper-level institutions, entering students) who returned the following year for the fall term.

Freshmen

Admission: Figures are given for the number of students who applied for fall 2012 admission, the number of those who were admitted, and the number who enrolled. *Average high school GPA:* Freshman statistics include the average high school GPA. *Test scores:* Percentage of freshmen who took the SAT and received critical reading, math, and writing scores above 500, above 600, and above 700; as well as percentage of freshmen taking the ACT who received a composite score of 18 or higher, 24 or higher, and 30 or higher.

Faculty

Total: The total number of faculty members; percentage of full-time faculty members as of fall 2012; and percentage of total faculty members who hold terminal degrees. *Student/faculty ratio:* School's estimate of the ratio of matriculated undergraduate students to faculty members teaching undergraduate courses.

Academics

Calendar: Most colleges indicate one of the following: 4-1-4, 4-4-1, or a similar arrangement (two terms of equal length plus an abbreviated winter or spring term, with the numbers referring to months); semesters; trimesters; quarters; 3-3 (three courses for each of three terms); modular (the academic year is divided into small blocks of time; courses of varying lengths are assembled according to individual programs); or standard year (for most Canadian institutions). *Degrees:* This names the full range of levels of certificates, diplomas, and degrees, including prebaccalaureate, baccalaureate, graduate, and professional, that are offered by this institution. *Special study options:* Details on study options available at each college, such as accelerated degree program, academic remediation for entering students, Advanced Placement credit, cooperative education programs, distance learning, double majors, English as a second language (ESL), and external degree programs. *ROTC:* Army, Naval, or Air Force Reserve Officers' Training Corps programs offered either on campus, at a branch campus [designated by a (b)], or at a cooperating host institution [designated by (c)].

Computers on Campus

Information is provided on the numbers of computers/terminals available on campus for general student use, what computer technology is accessible to students, and availability of a campuswide network and wireless campus network.

Student Life

Housing options: Institution's policy about whether students are permitted to live off-campus or are required to live on campus for a specified period; whether freshmen only, coed, single-sex, cooperative, and disabled student housing options are available; whether campus housing is leased by the school and/or provided by a third party; whether freshman applicants are given priority for college housing. "College housing not available" indicates that no college-owned or -operated housing facilities are provided for undergraduates and that noncommuting students must arrange for their own accommodations. *Activities and organizations:* Information on clubs and organizations, including sororities and fraternities. *Campus security:* Campus safety measures including 24-hour emergency response devices (phones and alarms) and patrols by trained security personnel, student patrols, late-night transport-escort service, and controlled dormitory access (key, security card, etc.). *Student services:* Information indicates services offered to students by the college, such as legal services, health clinics, personal-psychological counseling, and women's centers.

Athletics

Membership in one or more of the following athletic associations is indicated by initials: NCAA: National Collegiate Athletic Association; NAIA: National Association of Intercollegiate Athletics; NCCAA: National Christian College Athletic Association; USCAA: United States Collegiate Athletic Association; and CIS: Canadian Interuniversity Sport. The overall NCAA division in which all or most intercollegiate teams compete is designated by I, II, or III. All teams that do not compete in this division are listed as exceptions.

Sports offered by the college are divided into two groups: *Intercollegiate* ("M" or "W" following the name of each sport indicates that it is offered for men or women) and *Intramural.* An "s" in parentheses following an "M" or "W" for an intercollegiate sport indicates that athletic scholarships (or grants-in-aid) are offered for men or women in that sport, and a "c" indicates a club team as opposed to a varsity team.

Standardized Tests

The most commonly required standardized tests are the ACT, SAT, and SAT Subject Tests. These and other standardized tests may be used for selective admission, as a basis for counseling or course placement, or for both purposes. This section notes if a test is used for admission or placement and whether it is required, required for some, or recommended. In addition to the ACT and SAT, the following standardized entrance and placement examinations are referred to by their initials: ABLE (Adult Basic Learning Examination); ACT ASSET (ACT Assessment of Skills for Successful Entry and Transfer); ACT PEP (ACT Proficiency Examination Program); CAT (California Achievement Tests); CELT (Comprehensive English Language Test); CPAt (Career Programs Assessment); CPT (Computerized Placement Test); DAT (Differential Aptitude Test); LSAT (Law School Admission Test); MAPS (Multiple Assessment Program Service); MCAT (Medical College Admission Test); MMPI (Minnesota Multiphasic Personality Inventory); OAT (Optometry Admission Test); PAA (Prueba de Aptitud Académica—Spanish-language version of SAT); PCAT (Pharmacy College Admission Test); PSAT/NMSQT (Preliminary SAT/National Merit Scholarship Qualifying Test); SCAT (Scholastic College Aptitude Test); TABE (Test of Adult Basic Education); TASP (Texas Academic Skills Program); TOEFL (Test of English as a Foreign Language); WPCT (Washington Pre-College Test).

Costs

Costs are given for the 2013–14 academic year or for the 2012–13 academic year if 2013–14 figures were not yet available. Annual expenses may be expressed as a comprehensive fee (including full-time tuition, mandatory fees, and college room and board) or as separate figures for full-time tuition, fees, room and board, or room only. For public institutions where tuition differs according to residence, separate figures are given for area or state residents and for nonresidents. Part-time tuition is expressed in terms of a per-unit rate (per credit, per semester hour, etc.).

The tuition structure at some institutions is complex in that freshmen and sophomores may be charged a different rate from that for juniors and seniors, a professional or vocational division may have a different fee structure from the liberal arts division of the same institution, or part-time tuition may be prorated on a sliding scale according to the number of credit hours taken. Tuition and fees may vary according to academic program, campus/location, class time (day, evening, weekend), course/credit load, course level, degree level, reciprocity agreements, and student level. *Room and board* charges are reported as an average for one academic year and may vary according to the board plan selected, campus/location, type of housing facility, or student level. *Payment plans* may include tuition prepayment, installment payments, and deferred payment. A tuition prepayment plan gives a student the option of locking in the current tuition rate for the entire term of enrollment by paying the full amount in advance rather than year by year. *Waivers:* availability of full or partial undergraduate tuition waivers to minority students, children of alumni, employees or their children, adult students, and senior citizens may be listed.

Financial Aid

This information represents aid awarded to undergraduates for the available academic year. Figures are given for the number of undergraduates who applied for aid, the number who were judged to have need, and the number who had their need met. The number of Federal Work-Study Programs and/or part-time jobs and average earnings are listed, as well as the number of non-need-based awards. The *Average percent of need met* for those determined to have need, *Average financial aid package* awarded to undergraduates (the amount of scholarships, grants, work-study payments, or loans in the institutionally administered financial aid package divided by the number of students who received any financial aid-amounts used to pay the officially designated Expected Family Contribution (EFC), *Average need-based loan, Average need-based gift aid,* and *Average non-need-based aid* are given. *Average indebtedness upon graduation,* which is the average per-borrower indebtedness of the last graduating undergraduate class from amounts borrowed at this institution through any loan programs, excluding parent loans, is listed last.

Applying

Application and admission options include the following: Early admission—(highly qualified students may matriculate before graduating from high school); Early action—admission plan that allows students to apply and be notified of an admission decision well in advance of the regular notification dates (if accepted, the candidate is not committed to enroll; students may reply to the offer under the college's regular reply policy); Deferred entrance—practice of permitting accepted students to postpone enrollment, usually for a period of one academic term or year; Early decision deadline—plan that permits students to apply and be notified of an admission decision (and financial aid offer, if applicable) well in advance of the regular notification date, and applicants agree to accept an offer of admission and to withdraw their applications from other colleges. *Application fee:* The fee required with an application is noted. *Required, Required for some,* and *Recommended:* Other application requirements are grouped into three categories and may include an essay, standardized test scores, a high school transcript, a minimum high school grade point average (expressed as a number on a scale of 0 to 4.0, where 4.0 equals A, 3.0 equals B, etc.), letters of recommendation, an interview on campus or with local alumni, and, for certain types of schools or programs, special requirements such as a musical audition or an art portfolio. *Application deadlines and notification:* Admission application deadlines and dates for notification of acceptance or rejection are given either as specific dates or as rolling and continuous. Rolling means that applications are processed as they are received, and qualified students are accepted as long as there are openings. Continuous means that applicants are notified of acceptance or rejection as applications are processed up until the date indicated or the actual beginning of classes. The application deadline and the notification date for transfers are given if they differ from the dates for freshmen. Early decision and early action application deadlines and notification dates are also indicated when relevant.

Freshman Application Contact

The name, title, mailing address, and phone number of the person to contact for further information are given at the end of the profile. The fax number, e-mail address, and website may also be provided.

Additional Information

Each school that has a College Close-Up and a half-page display in this guide will have a cross-reference with the page numbers of the half-page display and Close-Up..

COLLEGE CLOSE-UPS

The over 300 two-page descriptions provide an inside look at colleges and universities. The descriptions provide a wealth of information that is crucial in the college decision-making process—components such as tuition, financial aid, and major fields of study. Prepared exclusively by college officials, the descriptions are designed to help give students a better sense of the individuality of each institution, in terms that include campus environment, student activities, and lifestyle. The absence of any college or university does not constitute an editorial decision on the part of Peterson's. In essence, these descriptions are an open forum for colleges and universities, on a voluntary basis, to communicate their particular message to prospective college students. The colleges included have paid a fee to Peterson's to provide this information. The College Close-Ups are edited to provide a consistent format across entries for your ease of comparison.

INDEXES

Here you'll find easy-to-use breakdowns of schools' majors, entrance difficulty, and cost ranges. We've also provided an "Advertisers Index," a "Geographical Listing of College Close-Ups," and an "Alphabetical Listing of Colleges and Universities."

Majors

This listing presents hundreds of undergraduate fields of study that are currently offered, according to the colleges' responses on *Peterson's Annual Survey of Undergraduate Institutions.* The majors appear in alphabetical order, each followed by an alphabetical list of the schools that offer a bachelor's-level program in that particular field. Liberal Arts and Studies indicates a general program with no specified major.

The terms used are those of the U.S. Department of Education Classification of Instructional Programs (CIP). Many institutions, however, use different terms. Although the term major is used in this guide, some colleges may use other terms, such as concentration, program of study, or field.

Entrance Difficulty

This listing groups colleges by their own assessment of their entrance difficulty level. The colleges were asked to select the level that most closely corresponds to their entrance difficulty. Institutions for which high school class rank and/or standardized test scores do not apply as admission criteria were asked to select the level that best indicates their entrance difficulty as compared to other institutions.

Cost Ranges

Colleges are grouped into thirteen price ranges, from under $2000 to $30,000 and over.

Institutional Changes Since Peterson's Four-Year Colleges 2013

The following is an alphabetical listing of institutions that have closed, merged with other institutions, or changed their names or status since *Peterson's Four-Year Colleges 2013*.

Adams State College (Alamosa, CO): *name changed to Adams State University.*

The Art Institute of Boston at Lesley University (Boston, MA): *merged into a single entry for Lesley University (Cambridge, MA).*

The Art Institute of California, a college of Argosy University, Sunnyvale (Sunnyvale, CA): *name changed to The Art Institute of California–Silicon Valley, a campus of Argosy University.*

Atlantic College (Guaynabo, PR): *name changed to Atlantic University College.*

Auburn University Montgomery (Montgomery, AL): *name changed to Auburn University at Montgomery.*

Augusta State University (Augusta, GA): *merged into a single entry for the new Georgia Regents University (Augusta, GA).*

Baldwin-Wallace College (Berea, OH): *name changed to Baldwin Wallace University.*

Bennett College for Women (Greensboro, NC): *name changed to Bennett College.*

Bernard M. Baruch College of the City University of New York (New York, NY): *name changed to Baruch College of the City University of New York.*

Broadview University (West Jordan, UT): *name changed to Broadview University–West Jordan.*

Carson-Newman College (Jefferson City, TN): *name changed to Carson-Newman University.*

Carver Bible College (Atlanta, GA): *name changed to Carver College.*

Chester College of New England (Chester, NH): *closed.*

The Cleveland Institute of Art (Cleveland, OH): *name changed to Cleveland Institute of Art.*

College of the Humanities and Sciences, Harrison Middleton University (Tempe, AZ): *name changed to Harrison Middleton University.*

College of Visual Arts (St. Paul, MN): *closed.*

Collins College (Tempe, AZ): *closed.*

Concordia College (Selma, AL): *name changed to Concordia College Alabama.*

Concordia University (Ann Arbor, MI): *name changed to Concordia University Ann Arbor.*

Florida Hospital College of Health Sciences (Orlando, FL): *name changed to Adventist University of Health Sciences.*

Florida National College (Hialeah, FL): *name changed to Florida National University.*

Free Will Baptist Bible College (Nashville, TN): *name changed to Welch College.*

Georgia Health Sciences University (Augusta, GA): *merged into a single entry for the new Georgia Regents University (Augusta, GA).*

Gratz College (Melrose Park, PA): *primarily offers graduate degrees.*

Hebrew College (Newton Centre, MA): *primarily offers graduate degrees.*

International Technological University (Santa Clara, CA): *no longer offers undergraduate degrees.*

Kettering College of Medical Arts (Kettering, OH): *name changed to Kettering College.*

Kwantlen Polytechnic University (Surrey, BC): *omitted by request from the institution.*

LA College International (Los Angeles, CA): *closed.*

Laura and Alvin Siegal College of Judaic Studies (Beachwood, OH): *merged into a single entry for Case Western Reserve University.*

Macon State College (Macon, GA): *merged into a single entry for new Middle Georgia State College (Cochran, GA).*

Manchester College (North Manchester, IN): *name changed to Manchester University.*

Medcenter One College of Nursing (Bismarck, ND): *name changed to Sanford College of Nursing.*

Mercyhurst College (Erie, PA): *name changed to Mercyhurst University.*

Metropolitan State College of Denver (Denver, CO): *name changed to Metropolitan State University of Denver.*

Mountain State University (Beckley, WV): *closed.*

National-Louis University (Chicago, IL): *name changed to National Louis University.*

The New School for General Studies (New York, NY): *name changed to The New School for Public Engagement.*

The Nigerian Baptist Theological Seminary (Ogbomoso): *not accredited by an agency recognized by USDE or CHEA at the time of publication.*

North Georgia College & State University (Dahlonega, GA): *merged into a single entry for new University of North Georgia.*

Nova Scotia Agricultural College (Truro, NS): *merged into a single entry for Dalhousie University (Halifax, NS).*

Parsons Paris School of Art + Design (Paris): *name changed to Paris College of Art.*

Philadelphia Biblical University (Langhorne, PA): *name changed to Cairn University.*

Polytechnic Institute of NYU (Brooklyn, NY): *name changed to Polytechnic Institute of New York University.*

Providence College and Theological Seminary (Otterburne, MB): *name changed to Providence University College & Theological Seminary.*

Rivier College (Nashua, NH): *name changed to Rivier University.*

Saint Peter's College (Jersey City, NJ): *name changed to Saint Peter's University.*

Silver Lake College (Manitowoc, WI): *name changed to Silver Lake College of the Holy Family.*

Somerset Christian College (Zarephath, NJ): *name changed to Pillar College.*

State University of New York at Binghamton (Binghamton, NY): *name changed to Binghamton University, State University of New York.*

Stevens-Henager College (Boise, ID): *name changed to Stevens-Henager College–Boise.*

Stevens-Henager College (Ogden, UT): *name changed to Stevens-Henager College–Ogden/West Haven.*

Strayer University—Cranberry Woods Campus (Cranberry Township, PA): *name changed to Strayer University—Warrendale Campus.*

Strayer University—Salt Lake Campus (Sandy, UT): *name changed to Strayer University—Sandy Campus.*

Strayer University—Shelby Oaks Campus (Memphis, TN): *name changed to Strayer University—Shelby Campus.*

Temple Baptist College (Cincinnati, OH): *name changed to Ohio Mid-Western College.*

Universidad de las Américas–Puebla (Puebla): *name changed to Universidad de las Américas Puebla.*

University of Colorado at Colorado Springs (Colorado Springs, CO): *name changed to University of Colorado Colorado Springs.*

The University of North Carolina at Asheville (Asheville, NC): *name changed to University of North Carolina at Asheville.*

University of Phoenix (Phoenix, AZ): *name changed to University of Phoenix–Online Campus.*

University of Phoenix–Phoenix Hohokam Campus (Phoenix, AZ): *name changed to University of Phoenix–Phoenix Main Campus.*

University of Phoenix–Vancouver Campus (Burnaby, BC): *closed.*

University of the Sciences in Philadelphia (Philadelphia, PA): *name changed to University of the Sciences.*

Virginia College at Birmingham (Birmingham, AL): *name changed to Virginia College in Birmingham.*

Virginia College at Huntsville (Huntsville, AL): *name changed to Virginia College in Huntsville.*

Western Christian College (Regina, SK): *closed.*

Western State College of Colorado (Gunnison, CO): *ame changed to Western State Colorado University.*

Westwood College–Dallas (Dallas, TX): *closed.*

Westwood College–Fort Worth (Fort Worth, TX): *closed.*

Yorktown University (Denver, CO): *no longer offers undergraduate degrees.*

Zion Bible College (Haverhill, MA): *name changed to Northpoint Bible College.*

DATA COLLECTION PROCEDURES

The data contained in the **PROFILES** and **INDEXES** sections were researched between winter 2012 and spring 2013 through *Peterson's Annual Survey of Undergraduate Institutions.* Questionnaires were sent to the more than 2,700 colleges and universities that met the outlined inclusion criteria. All data included in this edition have been submitted by officials (usually admissions and financial aid officers, registrars, or institutional research personnel) at the colleges. Some of the institutions that submitted data were contacted directly by the Peterson's research staff to verify unusual figures, resolve discrepancies, or obtain additional data. All usable information received in time for publication has been included. The omission of any particular item from the **PROFILES** and **INDEXES** sections signifies that the information is either not applicable to that institution or not available. Because of Peterson's comprehensive editorial review and because all material comes directly from college officials, we believe that the information presented is accurate. You should check with a specific college or university at the time of application to verify such figures as tuition and fees, which may have changed since this guide's publication.

CRITERIA FOR INCLUSION IN THIS BOOK

The term "four-year college" is the commonly used designation for institutions that grant the baccalaureate degree. Four years is the expected amount of time required to earn this degree, although some bachelor's degree programs may be completed in three years, others require five years, and part-time programs may take considerably longer. Upper-level institutions offer only the junior and senior years and accept only students with two years of college-level credit. Therefore, "four-year college" is a conventional term that accurately describes most of the institutions included in this guide, but should not be taken literally in all cases.

To be included in this guide, an institution must have full accreditation or be a candidate for accreditation (preaccreditation) status by an institutional or specialized accrediting body recognized by the U.S. Department of Education or the Council for Higher Education Accreditation (CHEA). Institutional accrediting bodies, which review each institution as a whole, include the six regional associations of schools and colleges (Middle States, New England, North Central, Northwest, Southern, and Western), each of which is responsible for a specified portion of the United States and its territories. Other institutional accrediting bodies are national in scope and accredit specific kinds of institutions (e.g., Bible colleges, independent colleges, and rabbinical and Talmudic schools). Program registration by the New York State Board of Regents is considered to be the equivalent of institutional accreditation, since the board requires that all programs offered by an institution meet its standards before recognition is granted. A Canadian institution must be chartered and authorized to grant degrees by the provincial government, affiliated with a chartered institution, or accredited by a recognized U.S. accrediting body. This guide also includes institutions outside the United States that are accredited by these U.S. accrediting bodies. There are recognized specialized or professional accrediting bodies in more than forty different fields, each of which is authorized to accredit institutions or specific programs in its particular field. For specialized institutions that offer programs in one field only, we designate this to be the equivalent of institutional accreditation. A full explanation of the accrediting process and complete information on recognized, institutional (regional and national) and specialized accrediting bodies can be found online at www.chea.org or at www2.ed.gov/admins/finaid/accred/index.html.

NOTICE: Certain portions of or information contained in this book have been submitted and paid for by the educational institution identified, and such institutions take full responsibility for the accuracy, timeliness, completeness and functionality of such content. Such portions or information include (i) each display ad in the "Profiles" section from pages 55 through 1032 that comprises a half or full page of information covering a single educational institution, and (ii) each two-page description in the "College Close-Up" section from pages 1034 through 1657.

Profiles

Creativity is all around you, and so is opportunity. We can help you prepare for it with a focused education in programs in the areas of design, media arts, fashion, or culinary. We'll guide your learning as you prepare to enter the job market with a strong set of professional skills and the portfolio to prove it to employers. The world is your canvas. Together, we can fill it in.

create.artinstitutes.edu
1.800.894.5793

Ai The Art Institutes SM

CREATE TOMORROW

DESIGN · MEDIA ARTS · FASHION · CULINARY

ALABAMA

Alabama Agricultural and Mechanical University
Huntsville, Alabama

Freshman Application Contact Dr. Evelyn Ellis, Interim Director of Admissions, Alabama Agricultural and Mechanical University, 4900 Meridian Street, Huntsville, AL 35811. *Phone:* 256-372-5245. *Toll-free phone:* 800-553-0816. *Fax:* 256-851-9747.
Website: http://www.aamu.edu/.

Alabama State University
Montgomery, Alabama

- **State-supported** comprehensive, founded 1867, part of Alabama Commission on Higher Education
- **Urban** 172-acre campus
- **Coed** 5,130 undergraduate students, 91% full-time, 60% women, 40% men
- **Minimally difficult** entrance level, 52% of applicants were admitted

Undergraduates 4,683 full-time, 447 part-time. 28% are from out of state; 95% Black or African American, non-Hispanic/Latino; 1% Hispanic/Latino; 0.1% Asian, non-Hispanic/Latino; 0.1% Native Hawaiian or other Pacific Islander, non-Hispanic/Latino; 0.1% American Indian or Alaska Native, non-Hispanic/Latino; 0.4% Two or more races, non-Hispanic/Latino; 2% Race/ethnicity unknown; 0.8% international; 4% transferred in. *Retention:* 62% of full-time freshmen returned.
Freshmen *Admission:* 10,284 applied, 5,327 admitted, 1,414 enrolled. *Average high school GPA:* 2.8. *Test scores:* SAT critical reading scores over 500: 19%; SAT math scores over 500: 21%; ACT scores over 18: 43%; SAT critical reading scores over 600: 2%; SAT math scores over 600: 5%; ACT scores over 24: 6%.
Faculty *Total:* 430, 64% full-time, 52% with terminal degrees. *Student/faculty ratio:* 16:1.
Academics *Calendar:* semesters. *Degrees:* bachelor's, master's, doctoral, post-master's, and postbachelor's certificates. *Special study options:* academic remediation for entering students, advanced placement credit, cooperative education, distance learning, double majors, freshman honors college, honors programs, independent study, internships, part-time degree program, student-designed majors, summer session for credit. *ROTC:* Army (c), Air Force (b).
Computers on Campus 541 computers/terminals and 1,082 ports are available on campus for general student use. Students can access the following: computer help desk, free student e-mail accounts, online (class) grades, online (class) registration, online (class) schedules. Campuswide network is available. Wireless service is available via entire campus.
Student Life *Housing options:* men-only, women-only, disabled students. Campus housing is university owned. *Activities and organizations:* drama/theater group, student-run newspaper, radio station, choral group, marching band, Alpha Kappa Alpha Sorority Inc., Empower Ministry, Nu Alpha Nu Service Fraternity Inc., Gamma Sigma Sigma National Service Sorority Inc., Delta Sigma Theta Sorority Inc, national fraternities, national sororities. *Campus security:* 24-hour emergency response devices and patrols, late-night transport/escort service, self-defense education, well-lit campus. *Student services:* health clinic, personal/psychological counseling.
Athletics Member NCAA. All Division I. *Intercollegiate sports:* baseball M(s), basketball M(s)/W(s), bowling W(s), cheerleading M(s)/W(s), cross-country running M(s)/W(s), football M(s), golf M(s)/W(s), soccer W(s), softball W(s), tennis M(s)/W(s), track and field M(s)/W(s), volleyball W(s). *Intramural sports:* basketball M, football M.
Standardized Tests *Required:* SAT or ACT (for admission).
Costs (2013–14) *One-time required fee:* $150. *Tuition:* state resident $6312 full-time, $263 per credit hour part-time; nonresident $12,624 full-time, $526 per credit hour part-time. *Required fees:* $213 per term part-time. *Room and board:* $5366. Room and board charges vary according to board plan and housing facility. *Payment plan:* deferred payment. *Waivers:* employees or children of employees.
Financial Aid Of all full-time matriculated undergraduates who enrolled in 2012, 4,586 applied for aid, 4,572 were judged to have need, 1,766 had their need fully met. In 2012, 55 non-need-based awards were made. *Average percent of need met:* 84%. *Average financial aid package:* $17,887. *Average need-based loan:* $3791. *Average need-based gift aid:* $4897. *Average non-need-based aid:* $9552. *Average indebtedness upon graduation:* $29,795.

Applying *Options:* electronic application, early admission, deferred entrance. *Application fee:* $25. *Required:* high school transcript, minimum 2.0 GPA. *Recommended:* essay or personal statement, interview. *Application deadlines:* 7/31 (freshmen), 7/31 (transfers). *Notification:* continuous (freshmen), continuous (transfers).
Freshman Application Contact Mr. Freddie Williams, Director of Admissions and Recruitment, Alabama State University, 915 South Jackson Street, Montgomery, AL 36101-0271. *Phone:* 334-229-4291. *Toll-free phone:* 800-253-5037. *Fax:* 334-229-4984. *E-mail:* admissions@alasu.edu. *Website:* http://www.alasu.edu/.

Amridge University
Montgomery, Alabama

- **Independent** university, founded 1967, affiliated with Church of Christ
- **Urban** 9-acre campus
- **Endowment** $2.5 million
- **Coed**
- **Minimally difficult** entrance level

Undergraduates Students come from 48 states and territories; 75% are from out of state. *Retention:* 75% of full-time freshmen returned.
Faculty *Student/faculty ratio:* 11:1.
Academics *Calendar:* semesters. *Degrees:* associate, bachelor's, master's, and doctoral. *Special study options:* accelerated degree program, adult/continuing education programs, advanced placement credit, distance learning, double majors, external degree program, internships, part-time degree program, services for LD students, summer session for credit.
Computers on Campus 5 computers/terminals are available on campus for general student use. Students can access the following: online (class) registration, access to over 20 million monographs and journals online. Campuswide network is available.
Student Life *Housing:* college housing not available.
Costs (2012–13) *Tuition:* $6000 full-time, $365 per semester hour part-time. Full-time tuition and fees vary according to course load and student level. Part-time tuition and fees vary according to course load and student level. *Required fees:* $400 per term part-time. *Waivers:* employees or children of employees.
Financial Aid Of all full-time matriculated undergraduates who enrolled in 2012, 364 applied for aid, 364 were judged to have need, 364 had their need fully met. In 2012, 18 non-need-based awards were made. *Average percent of need met:* 90%. *Average financial aid package:* $9260. *Average need-based loan:* $8260. *Average need-based gift aid:* $6831. *Average non-need-based aid:* $4200.
Applying *Options:* electronic application. *Application fee:* $50. *Required:* high school transcript, minimum 2.0 GPA. *Application deadlines:* rolling (freshmen), rolling (out-of-state freshmen), rolling (transfers).
Freshman Application Contact Mrs. Ora Davis, Admissions Officer, Amridge University, 1200 Taylor Road, Montgomery, AL 36117. *Phone:* 334-387-3877 Ext. 7524. *Toll-free phone:* 888-790-8080. *Fax:* 334-387-3878. *E-mail:* oradavis@amridgeuniversity.edu. *Website:* http://www.amridgeuniversity.edu/.

See next page for display ad and page 1042 for the College Close-Up.

Athens State University
Athens, Alabama

- **State-supported** upper-level, founded 1822
- **Small-town** 45-acre campus
- **Coed** 3,415 undergraduate students, 45% full-time, 65% women, 35% men
- **Noncompetitive** entrance level

Undergraduates 1,533 full-time, 1,882 part-time. Students come from 18 states and territories; 4% are from out of state; 12% Black or African American, non-Hispanic/Latino; 2% Hispanic/Latino; 0.6% Asian, non-Hispanic/Latino; 2% American Indian or Alaska Native, non-Hispanic/Latino; 1% Two or more races, non-Hispanic/Latino; 3% Race/ethnicity unknown; 0.9% international; 25% transferred in.
Faculty *Total:* 218, 40% full-time, 41% with terminal degrees. *Student/faculty ratio:* 17:1.
Academics *Calendar:* semesters. *Degree:* certificates and bachelor's. *Special study options:* adult/continuing education programs, advanced placement credit, cooperative education, distance learning, double majors, independent study, internships, off-campus study, part-time degree program, study abroad, summer session for credit.

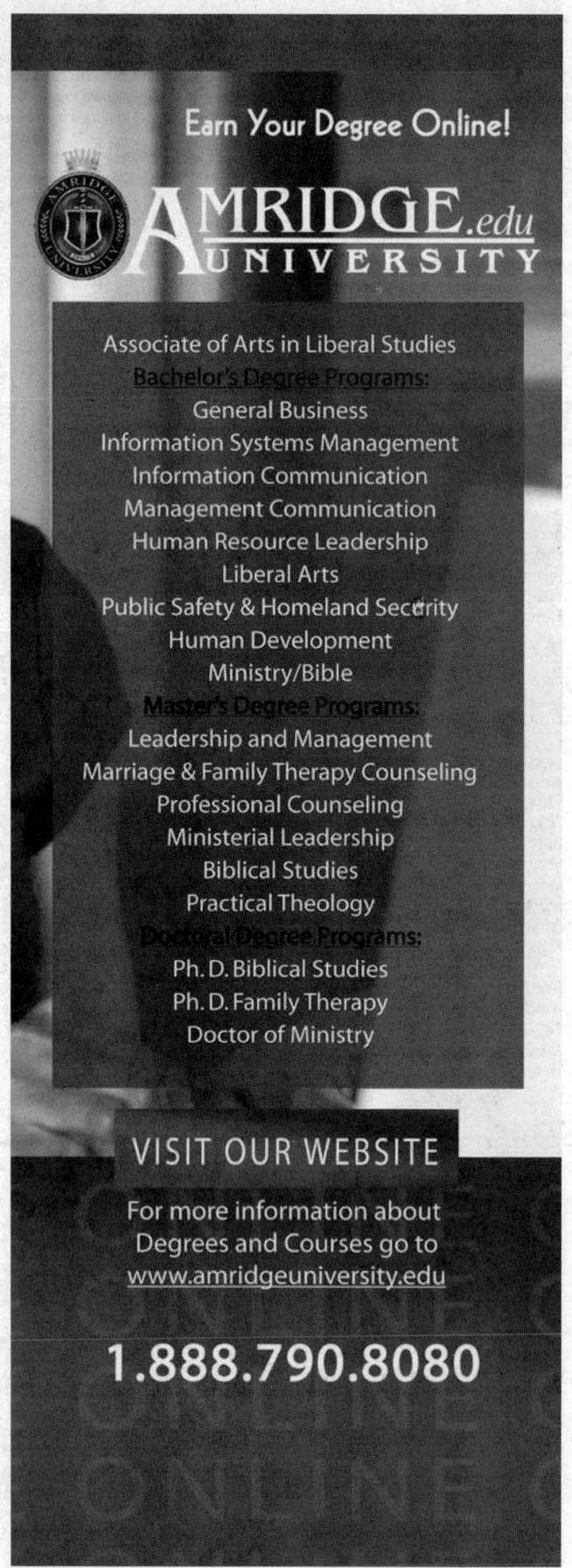

Computers on Campus 210 computers/terminals are available on campus for general student use. Students can access the following: online (class) registration, grades, transcripts, schedules, e-mail. Campuswide network is available.
Student Life *Housing:* college housing not available. *Activities and organizations:* drama/theater group, student-run newspaper, national sororities. *Student services:* personal/psychological counseling.
Athletics *Intramural sports:* table tennis M/W, volleyball M/W.
Costs (2012–13) *Tuition:* state resident $4590 full-time; nonresident $9180 full-time. *Required fees:* $750 full-time. *Waivers:* senior citizens and employees or children of employees.
Financial Aid Of all full-time matriculated undergraduates who enrolled in 2011, 1,046 applied for aid. *Average financial aid package:* $12,815.
Applying *Options:* electronic application, deferred entrance. *Application fee:* $30. *Application deadline:* rolling (transfers). *Notification:* continuous (transfers).
Application Contact Athens State University, 300 North Beaty Street, Athens, AL 35611. *Phone:* 256-233-8151. *Toll-free phone:* 800-522-0272. *Website:* http://www.athens.edu/.

Auburn University
Auburn University, Alabama

- **State-supported** university, founded 1856
- **Small-town** 1875-acre campus with easy access to Atlanta, Birmingham
- **Endowment** $498.8 million
- **Coed** 20,175 undergraduate students, 91% full-time, 49% women, 51% men
- **Moderately difficult** entrance level, 77% of applicants were admitted

Undergraduates 18,449 full-time, 1,726 part-time. Students come from 53 states and territories; 44 other countries; 38% are from out of state; 7% Black or African American, non-Hispanic/Latino; 3% Hispanic/Latino; 2% Asian, non-Hispanic/Latino; 0.7% American Indian or Alaska Native, non-Hispanic/Latino; 1% Race/ethnicity unknown; 0.7% international; 6% transferred in; 20% live on campus. *Retention:* 90% of full-time freshmen returned.
Freshmen *Admission:* 17,463 applied, 13,486 admitted, 3,852 enrolled. *Average high school GPA:* 3.78. *Test scores:* SAT critical reading scores over 500: 88%; SAT math scores over 500: 94%; SAT writing scores over 500: 85%; ACT scores over 18: 100%; SAT critical reading scores over 600: 41%; SAT math scores over 600: 54%; SAT writing scores over 600: 34%; ACT scores over 24: 82%; SAT critical reading scores over 700: 9%; SAT math scores over 700: 13%; SAT writing scores over 700: 5%; ACT scores over 30: 28%.
Faculty *Total:* 1,368, 87% full-time, 84% with terminal degrees. *Student/faculty ratio:* 18:1.
Academics *Calendar:* semesters. *Degrees:* bachelor's, master's, doctoral, post-master's, and postbachelor's certificates. *Special study options:* accelerated degree program, adult/continuing education programs, advanced placement credit, cooperative education, distance learning, double majors, English as a second language, freshman honors college, honors programs, independent study, internships, off-campus study, part-time degree program, services for LD students, study abroad, summer session for credit. *ROTC:* Army (b), Navy (b), Air Force (b). *Unusual degree programs:* 3-2 engineering.
Computers on Campus 1,722 computers/terminals are available on campus for general student use. Students can access the following: computer help desk, free student e-mail accounts, online (class) grades, online (class) registration, pay Bursar online, course materials available online. Campuswide network is available. 100% of college-owned or -operated housing units are wired for high-speed Internet access. Wireless service is available via entire campus.
Student Life *Housing options:* coed, men-only, women-only, disabled students. Campus housing is university owned. *Activities and organizations:* drama/theater group, student-run newspaper, radio and television station, choral group, marching band, Student Government Association, University Program Council, IMPACT (volunteer opportunities), International Student Organization, student media (AU Plainsman newspaper, WEGL radio, Glomerata yearbook, Eagle Eye television, AU Circle literary journal), national fraternities, national sororities. *Campus security:* 24-hour emergency response devices and patrols, late-night transport/escort service, controlled dormitory access. *Student services:* health clinic, personal/psychological counseling.
Athletics Member NCAA. All Division I except football (Division I-A). *Intercollegiate sports:* baseball M(s), basketball M(s)/W(s), cross-country running M(s)/W(s), equestrian sports W(s), golf M(s)/W(s), gymnastics W(s), soccer W(s), softball W(s), swimming and diving M(s)/W(s), tennis M(s)/W(s), track and field M(s)/W(s), volleyball W(s). *Intramural sports:* badminton M/W, basketball M/W, bowling M/W, crew M(c)/W(c), football M/W, golf M/W, ice hockey M(c), lacrosse M(c)/W(c), racquetball M/W, rugby M(c)/W(c), sailing M(c)/W(c), soccer M/W, softball M/W, swimming and diving M/W, table tennis M/W, tennis M/W, track and field M/W, ultimate Frisbee M/W, volleyball M/W, water polo M(c)/W(c), wrestling M(c)/W(c).
Standardized Tests *Required:* SAT or ACT (for admission).

Costs (2012–13) *Tuition:* state resident $7872 full-time, $328 per semester hour part-time; nonresident $23,616 full-time, $984 per semester hour part-time. Full-time tuition and fees vary according to program and reciprocity agreements. Part-time tuition and fees vary according to course load, program, and reciprocity- agreements. *Required fees:* $1574 full-time, $787 per term part-time. *Room and board:* $10,606; room only: $5500. Room and board charges vary according to board plan and housing facility. *Payment plan:* installment. *Waivers:* employees or children of employees.

Financial Aid Of all full-time matriculated undergraduates who enrolled in 2011, 11,837 applied for aid, 7,117 were judged to have need, 1,100 had their need fully met. 223 Federal Work-Study jobs (averaging $3862). In 2011, 1698 non-need-based awards were made. *Average percent of need met:* 48%. *Average financial aid package:* $10,502. *Average need-based loan:* $4545. *Average need-based gift aid:* $6735. *Average non-need-based aid:* $2893. *Average indebtedness upon graduation:* $24,903.

Applying *Options:* electronic application, early admission, early action, deferred entrance. *Application fee:* $50. *Required:* essay or personal statement, high school transcript, minimum 2.0 GPA. *Required for some:* minimum 3.0 GPA. *Recommended:* minimum 3.0 GPA. *Application deadlines:* 2/1 (freshmen), 2/1 (out-of-state freshmen), rolling (transfers), 10/1 (early action). *Notification:* 2/15 (freshmen), 2/15 (out-of-state freshmen), continuous (transfers), 10/15 (early action).

Freshman Application Contact Ms. Cindy Singley, Director, University Recruitment, Auburn University, Auburn University, AL 36849. *Phone:* 334-844-4080. *Toll-free phone:* 800-AUBURN9. *E-mail:* admissions@auburn.edu. *Website:* http://www.auburn.edu/.

Auburn University at Montgomery
Montgomery, Alabama

- **State-supported** comprehensive, founded 1967, part of Auburn University
- **Suburban** 500-acre campus
- **Endowment** $40.6 million
- **Coed** 4,225 undergraduate students, 69% full-time, 60% women, 40% men
- **Moderately difficult** entrance level, 72% of applicants were admitted

Undergraduates 2,906 full-time, 1,319 part-time. 6% are from out of state; 28% Black or African American, non-Hispanic/Latino; 0.4% Hispanic/Latino; 2% Asian, non-Hispanic/Latino; 1% American Indian or Alaska Native, non-Hispanic/Latino; 2% Two or more races, non-Hispanic/Latino; 7% Race/ethnicity unknown; 4% international; 6% transferred in; 12% live on campus. *Retention:* 58% of full-time freshmen returned.

Freshmen *Admission:* 2,386 applied, 1,723 admitted, 785 enrolled. *Average high school GPA:* 3.21. *Test scores:* ACT scores over 18: 98%; ACT scores over 24: 24%; ACT scores over 30: 2%.

Faculty *Total:* 333, 67% full-time. *Student/faculty ratio:* 15:1.

Academics *Calendar:* semesters. *Degrees:* bachelor's, master's, doctoral, and post-master's certificates. *Special study options:* academic remediation for entering students, adult/continuing education programs, advanced placement credit, cooperative education, distance learning, double majors, English as a second language, honors programs, independent study, internships, off-campus study, part-time degree program, services for LD students, study abroad, summer session for credit. *ROTC:* Army (b), Air Force (c).

Computers on Campus 705 computers/terminals are available on campus for general student use. Students can access the following: campus intranet, computer help desk, free student e-mail accounts, online (class) grades, online (class) registration, online (class) schedules. Campuswide network is available. 100% of college-owned or -operated housing units are wired for high-speed Internet access. Wireless service is available via classrooms, computer labs, libraries, student centers.

Student Life *Housing options:* coed, disabled students. Campus housing is university owned. *Activities and organizations:* drama/theater group, student-run newspaper, choral group, national fraternities, national sororities. *Campus security:* 24-hour emergency response devices and patrols, student patrols, late-night transport/escort service, controlled dormitory access. *Student services:* health clinic, personal/psychological counseling.

Athletics Member NAIA. *Intercollegiate sports:* baseball M(s), basketball M(s)/W(s), cheerleading M(s)/W(s), cross-country running M(s)/W(s), soccer M(s)/W(s), softball W(s), tennis M(s)/W(s). *Intramural sports:* badminton M/W, basketball M/W, bowling M/W, football M/W, soccer M/W, softball W, table tennis M/W, tennis M/W, volleyball M/W, wrestling M.

Standardized Tests *Required:* ACT (for admission). *Recommended:* SAT (for admission).

Costs (2013–14) *Tuition:* state resident $7500 full-time, $250 per credit hour part-time; nonresident $22,500 full-time, $750 per credit hour part-time. Full-time tuition and fees vary according to course load. Part-time tuition and fees vary according to course load. *Required fees:* $650 full-time. *Room only:*

$3270. Room and board charges vary according to housing facility. *Payment plan:* installment. *Waivers:* employees or children of employees.

Financial Aid Of all full-time matriculated undergraduates who enrolled in 2012, 2,102 applied for aid, 421 had their need fully met. *Average need-based loan:* $4110. *Average need-based gift aid:* $4631.

Applying *Options:* electronic application, deferred entrance. *Required:* high school transcript. *Application deadlines:* rolling (freshmen), rolling (transfers). *Notification:* continuous (freshmen), continuous (transfers).

Freshman Application Contact Mr. Ronnie McKinney, Director of Recruitment, Auburn University at Montgomery, PO Box 244023, Montgomery, AL 36124-4023. *Phone:* 334-244-3615. *Toll-free phone:* 800-227-2649. *Fax:* 334-244-3795. *E-mail:* rmckinne@aum.edu. *Website:* http://www.aum.edu/.

Birmingham-Southern College
Birmingham, Alabama

- **Independent Methodist** 4-year, founded 1856
- **Urban** 196-acre campus with easy access to Birmingham
- **Endowment** $56.6 million
- **Coed**
- **Moderately difficult** entrance level

Faculty *Student/faculty ratio:* 13:1.

Academics *Calendar:* 4-1-4. *Degree:* bachelor's.

Student Life *Campus security:* 24-hour emergency response devices and patrols, late-night transport/escort service, controlled dormitory access, vehicle safety inspections for students, emergency phone stations throughout campus.

Athletics Member NCAA. All Division III.

Standardized Tests *Required:* SAT or ACT (for admission).

Costs (2012–13) *Comprehensive fee:* $40,910 includes full-time tuition ($29,600), mandatory fees ($1090), and room and board ($10,220). Full-time tuition and fees vary according to program and reciprocity agreements. Part-time tuition and fees vary according to course load, program, and reciprocity agreements. *College room only:* $5900. Room and board charges vary according to board plan, housing facility, and location.

Financial Aid *Of all full-time matriculated undergraduates who enrolled in 2010,* 994 applied for aid, 841 were judged to have need, 227 had their need fully met. 178 Federal Work-Study jobs (averaging $1351). 281 state and other part-time jobs (averaging $1213). *In 2010,* 598 non-need-based awards were made. *Average percent of need met:* 82. *Average financial aid package:* $27,468. *Average need-based loan:* $3935. *Average need-based gift aid:* $5341. *Average non-need-based aid:* $9987. *Average indebtedness upon graduation:* $28,157.

Applying *Options:* electronic application, deferred entrance. *Application fee:* $40. *Required:* essay or personal statement, high school transcript, minimum 2.0 GPA, 1 letter of recommendation. *Required for some:* interview. *Recommended:* interview.

Freshman Application Contact Ms. Jennifer Waters, Director of Admission, Birmingham-Southern College, Box 549008, Birmingham, AL 35254. *Phone:* 205-226-4696. *Toll-free phone:* 800-523-5793. *Fax:* 205-226-3074. *E-mail:* jwaters@bsc.edu. *Website:* http://www.bsc.edu/.

Brown Mackie College–Birmingham
Birmingham, Alabama

Freshman Application Contact Brown Mackie College–Birmingham, 105 Vulcan Road, Suite 400, Birmingham, AL 35209. *Phone:* 205-909-1500. *Toll-free phone:* 888-299-4699. *Website:* http://www.brownmackie.edu/birmingham.

See next page for display ad and page 1172 for the College Close-Up.

Columbia Southern University
Orange Beach, Alabama

- **Proprietary** comprehensive, founded 1993
- **Small-town** campus
- **Coed**
- **Noncompetitive** entrance level

Faculty *Student/faculty ratio:* 67:1.

Academics *Calendar:* modular. *Degrees:* certificates, associate, bachelor's, master's, doctoral, and postbachelor's certificates (offers only distance learning degree programs).

Costs (2012–13) *Tuition:* $4800 full-time, $200 per credit hour part-time. Full-time tuition and fees vary according to course load and degree level. Part-time tuition and fees vary according to course load and degree level. *Required fees:* $95 full-time.

Applying *Options:* electronic application. *Application fee:* $25. *Required for some:* high school transcript.

Freshman Application Contact Director of Admissions, Columbia Southern University, 21982 University Lane, Orange Beach, AL 36561. *Phone:* 251-981-3771. *Toll-free phone:* 800-977-8449. *Fax:* 251-224-0540. *E-mail:* admissions@columbiasouthern.edu.

Website: http://www.columbiasouthern.edu/.

Concordia College Alabama
Selma, Alabama

- **Independent Lutheran** 4-year, founded 1922, part of Concordia University System
- **Small-town** 59-acre campus with easy access to Birmingham
- **Coed** 611 undergraduate students, 92% full-time, 42% women, 58% men
- **Moderately difficult** entrance level

Undergraduates 565 full-time, 46 part-time. Students come from 21 states and territories; 5 other countries; 23% are from out of state; 86% Black or African American, non-Hispanic/Latino; 0.8% Hispanic/Latino; 3% Race/ethnicity unknown; 2% international; 12% transferred in. *Retention:* 50% of full-time freshmen returned.

Freshmen *Admission:* 2,377 applied, 157 enrolled.

Faculty *Total:* 46, 48% full-time. *Student/faculty ratio:* 19:1.

Academics *Calendar:* semesters. *Degrees:* associate and bachelor's. *Special study options:* academic remediation for entering students, adult/continuing education programs, advanced placement credit, double majors, honors programs, independent study, internships, part-time degree program, services for LD students, study abroad, summer session for credit. *ROTC:* Army (b).

Computers on Campus 90 computers/terminals and 2 ports are available on campus for general student use. Students can access the following: campus intranet, computer help desk, free student e-mail accounts, online (class) grades, online (class) schedules. Campuswide network is available. 100% of college-owned or -operated housing units are wired for high-speed Internet access. Wireless service is available via entire campus.

Student Life *Housing options:* coed. Campus housing is university owned. Freshman applicants given priority for college housing. *Activities and organizations:* drama/theater group, student-run newspaper, choral group, marching band, Music Ensemble, Rotaract, Phi Theta Kappa, Spiritual Life, Red Cross, national fraternities. *Campus security:* 24-hour patrols. *Student services:* personal/psychological counseling.

Athletics *Intercollegiate sports:* baseball M(s), basketball M(s)/W(s), cheerleading M(s), football M(s), soccer M(s), softball W(s), track and field M(s)/W(s), volleyball M(s)/W(s).

Standardized Tests *Recommended:* SAT or ACT (for admission).

Costs (2013–14) *Comprehensive fee:* $12,930 includes full-time tuition ($7920), mandatory fees ($670), and room and board ($4340). Full-time tuition and fees vary according to course load. Part-time tuition: $330 per credit hour. Part-time tuition and fees vary according to course load. *Required fees:* $170 per term part-time. *College room only:* $1800. Room and board charges vary according to board plan and housing facility. *Payment plan:* installment. *Waivers:* employees or children of employees.

Financial Aid Of all full-time matriculated undergraduates who enrolled in 2008, 800 applied for aid, 782 were judged to have need, 487 had their need fully met. 86 Federal Work-Study jobs (averaging $600). In 2008, 22 non-need-based awards were made. *Average percent of need met:* 92%. *Average financial aid package:* $4410. *Average need-based gift aid:* $1500. *Average non-need-based aid:* $500. *Average indebtedness upon graduation:* $5500.

Applying *Options:* electronic application, deferred entrance. *Application fee:* $10. *Required:* high school transcript, minimum 2.0 GPA. *Application deadlines:* 8/15 (freshmen), 8/15 (transfers). *Notification:* continuous (freshmen), continuous (transfers).

Freshman Application Contact Ms. Phyllis Richardson, Director, STARRS, Concordia College Alabama, 1712 Broad Street, PO Box 2470-36702, Selma, AL 36701. *Phone:* 334-874-5700 Ext. 102. *Fax:* 334-874-5755. *E-mail:* prichardson@ccal.edu.

Website: http://www.ccal.edu/.

Faulkner University
Montgomery, Alabama

- **Independent** comprehensive, founded 1942, affiliated with Church of Christ
- **Urban** 75-acre campus
- **Endowment** $18.3 million
- **Coed** 2,763 undergraduate students, 72% full-time, 63% women, 37% men
- **Minimally difficult** entrance level, 60% of applicants were admitted

Undergraduates 1,993 full-time, 770 part-time. Students come from 35 states and territories; 27 other countries; 14% are from out of state; 47% Black or African American, non-Hispanic/Latino; 1% Hispanic/Latino; 0.7% Asian, non-Hispanic/Latino; 0.3% Native Hawaiian or other Pacific Islander, non-Hispanic/Latino; 0.6% American Indian or Alaska Native, non-Hispanic/Latino; 0.8% Two or more races, non-Hispanic/Latino; 3% Race/ethnicity unknown; 2% international; 20% transferred in; 19% live on campus. *Retention:* 54% of full-time freshmen returned.

Freshmen *Admission:* 1,305 applied, 788 admitted, 388 enrolled. *Average high school GPA:* 3.13. *Test scores:* SAT writing scores over 500: 21%; ACT scores over 18: 77%; SAT writing scores over 600: 5%; ACT scores over 24: 21%; ACT scores over 30: 2%.

Faculty *Total:* 349, 34% full-time, 44% with terminal degrees. *Student/faculty ratio:* 15:1.

Academics *Calendar:* semesters. *Degrees:* associate, bachelor's, master's, and doctoral. *Special study options:* academic remediation for entering students, accelerated degree program, adult/continuing education programs, advanced placement credit, distance learning, double majors, English as a second language, freshman honors college, honors programs, independent study, internships, off-campus study, part-time degree program, services for LD students, study abroad, summer session for credit. *ROTC:* Army (c), Air Force (c).

Computers on Campus 480 computers/terminals and 150 ports are available on campus for general student use. Students can access the following: campus intranet, computer help desk, free student e-mail accounts, online (class) grades, online (class) registration, online (class) schedules, student account access. Campuswide network is available. 100% of college-owned or -operated housing units are wired for high-speed Internet access. Wireless service is available via entire campus.

Student Life *Housing:* on-campus residence required through junior year. *Options:* men-only, women-only, disabled students. Campus housing is university owned. Freshman campus housing is guaranteed. *Activities and organizations:* drama/theater group, student-run newspaper, choral group, marching band, Student Government, Marching Band, Dinner Theatre, Acappella Chorus, Phi Lambda/Kappa Social Clubs. *Campus security:* 24-hour emergency response devices and patrols, late-night transport/escort service. *Student services:* health clinic, personal/psychological counseling.

Athletics Member NAIA. *Intercollegiate sports:* baseball M(s), basketball M(s)/W(s), cheerleading M(s)(c)/W(s)(c), football M(s), golf M(s)/W(s), soccer M(s)/W(s), softball W(s), volleyball W(s). *Intramural sports:* basketball M/W, bowling M/W, golf M/W, racquetball M/W, soccer M/W, softball M/W, table tennis M/W, ultimate Frisbee M/W, volleyball M/W.

Standardized Tests *Required:* SAT or ACT (for admission).

Costs (2012–13) *Comprehensive fee:* $24,030 includes full-time tuition ($15,730), mandatory fees ($1650), and room and board ($6650). Full-time tuition and fees vary according to class time, course load, degree level, location, and program. Part-time tuition: $530 per semester hour. Part-time tuition and fees vary according to class time, degree level, and location. *Required fees:* $415 per semester part-time. *College room only:* $3250. Room and board charges vary according to board plan and housing facility. *Payment plan:* installment. *Waivers:* adult students, senior citizens, and employees or children of employees.

Financial Aid Of all full-time matriculated undergraduates who enrolled in 2011, 1,748 applied for aid, 1,486 were judged to have need, 506 had their need fully met. In 2011, 308 non-need-based awards were made. *Average percent of need met:* 60%. *Average financial aid package:* $5600. *Average need-based loan:* $5000. *Average need-based gift aid:* $5100. *Average non-need-based aid:* $1700. *Average indebtedness upon graduation:* $9500.

Applying *Options:* electronic application, early admission, deferred entrance. *Application fee:* $25. *Required:* high school transcript, minimum 2.0 GPA. *Recommended:* essay or personal statement, 2 letters of recommendation, interview. *Application deadlines:* rolling (freshmen), rolling (out-of-state freshmen), rolling (transfers). *Notification:* continuous (freshmen), continuous (out-of-state freshmen), continuous (transfers).

Freshman Application Contact Mr. Neil Scott, Director of Admissions, Faulkner University, 5345 Atlanta Highway, Montgomery, AL 36109-3398. *Phone:* 334-386-7200. *Toll-free phone:* 800-879-9816. *Fax:* 334-386-7137. *E-mail:* nscott@faulkner.edu. *Website:* http://www.faulkner.edu/.

Heritage Christian University
Florence, Alabama

- **Independent** comprehensive, founded 1971, affiliated with Church of Christ
- **Small-town** 43-acre campus
- **Endowment** $6.0 million
- **Coed, primarily men**
- **Noncompetitive** entrance level

Faculty *Student/faculty ratio:* 5:1.

Academics *Calendar:* semesters. *Degrees:* associate, bachelor's, and master's.

Standardized Tests *Required for some:* TOEFL (Test of English as a Foreign Language) for international students.

Costs (2012–13) *One-time required fee:* $300. *Comprehensive fee:* $18,202 includes full-time tuition ($11,936), mandatory fees ($840), and room and board ($5426). Part-time tuition: $373 per credit hour. *Required fees:* $35 per credit hour part-time. *College room only:* $3000. Room and board charges vary according to housing facility.

Financial Aid Of all full-time matriculated undergraduates who enrolled in 2011, 21 applied for aid, 21 were judged to have need, 6 had their need fully met. 8 Federal Work-Study jobs (averaging $1500). *Average percent of need met:* 93. *Average financial aid package:* $13,500. *Average need-based loan:* $4500. *Average need-based gift aid:* $6550. *Average indebtedness upon graduation:* $18,950.

Applying *Options:* electronic application, early admission, deferred entrance. *Application fee:* $25. *Required:* high school transcript, minimum 2.0 GPA, 3 letters of recommendation. *Recommended:* interview.

Freshman Application Contact Mr. Brad McKinnon, Dean of Students, Heritage Christian University, PO Box HCU, Florence, AL 35630. *Phone:* 256-766-6610 Ext. 305. *Toll-free phone:* 800-367-3565. *Fax:* 256-766-9289. *E-mail:* bmckinnon@hcu.edu. *Website:* http://www.hcu.edu/.

Herzing University
Birmingham, Alabama

Director of Admissions Ms. Tess Anderson, Admissions Coordinator, Herzing University, 280 West Valley Avenue, Birmingham, AL 35209. *Phone:* 205-916-2800. *Toll-free phone:* 800-596-0724. *E-mail:* admiss@bhm.herzing.edu. *Website:* http://www.herzing.edu/birmingham/.

Huntingdon College
Montgomery, Alabama

- **Independent United Methodist** 4-year, founded 1854
- **Suburban** 71-acre campus with easy access to Birmingham
- **Endowment** $40.1 million
- **Coed** 1,118 undergraduate students, 80% full-time, 50% women, 50% men

Undergraduates 896 full-time, 222 part-time. Students come from 27 states and territories; 3 other countries; 17% are from out of state; 19% Black or African American, non-Hispanic/Latino; 2% Hispanic/Latino; 0.6% Asian, non-Hispanic/Latino; 0.2% Native Hawaiian or other Pacific Islander, non-Hispanic/Latino; 0.4% American Indian or Alaska Native, non-Hispanic/Latino; 2% Two or more races, non-Hispanic/Latino; 23% Race/ethnicity unknown; 0.4% international; 9% transferred in; 47% live on campus. *Retention:* 55% of full-time freshmen returned.

Freshmen *Admission:* 276 enrolled. *Average high school GPA:* 3.3. *Test scores:* SAT critical reading scores over 500: 37%; SAT math scores over 500: 39%; ACT scores over 18: 92%; SAT critical reading scores over 600: 2%; SAT math scores over 600: 6%; ACT scores over 24: 26%; ACT scores over 30: 1%.

Faculty *Total:* 120, 43% full-time, 62% with terminal degrees. *Student/faculty ratio:* 13:1.

Academics *Calendar:* semesters. *Degree:* bachelor's. *Special study options:* accelerated degree program, adult/continuing education programs, advanced placement credit, distance learning, double majors, freshman honors college, honors programs, independent study, internships, off-campus study, part-time degree program, services for LD students, student-designed majors, study abroad, summer session for credit. *ROTC:* Army (c), Air Force (c). *Unusual degree programs:* 3-2 engineering with Auburn University.

Computers on Campus 13 computers/terminals are available on campus for general student use. Students can access the following: campus intranet, free student e-mail accounts, online (class) grades, online (class) registration, online (class) schedules, online library, student web hosting. Campuswide network is available. 100% of college-owned or -operated housing units are wired for high-speed Internet access. Wireless service is available via classrooms, dorm rooms, learning centers, libraries.

Student Life *Housing:* on-campus residence required through junior year. *Options:* coed, disabled students. Campus housing is university owned. Freshman campus housing is guaranteed. *Activities and organizations:* drama/theater group, student-run newspaper, choral group, marching band, Student Government Association, Campus Activities Board, Voice of Justice, Freshman Forum, Exchange Club, national fraternities, national sororities. *Campus security:* 24-hour emergency response devices and patrols, student patrols, late-night transport/escort service, controlled dormitory access, electronic video surveillance. *Student services:* health clinic, personal/psychological counseling.

Athletics Member NCAA. All Division III. *Intercollegiate sports:* baseball M, basketball M/W, cross-country running M/W, football M, golf M/W, lacrosse M/W, soccer M/W, softball W, tennis M/W, volleyball W. *Intramural sports:* baseball M/W, basketball M/W, cheerleading M(c)/W(c), soccer M/W, softball M/W, table tennis M/W, tennis M/W, volleyball M/W.

Standardized Tests *Required:* SAT or ACT (for admission).

Costs (2012–13) *Comprehensive fee:* $30,750 includes full-time tuition ($21,500), mandatory fees ($1000), and room and board ($8250). Full-time tuition and fees vary according to course load, program, and student level. Part-time tuition: $900 per credit hour. Part-time tuition and fees vary according to course load and program. No tuition increase for student's term of enrollment. *Room and board:* Room and board charges vary according to housing facility. *Payment plan:* deferred payment. *Waivers:* children of alumni and employees or children of employees.

Financial Aid Of all full-time matriculated undergraduates who enrolled in 2012, 783 applied for aid, 698 were judged to have need, 134 had their need fully met. 200 Federal Work-Study jobs (averaging $1142). In 2012, 192 non-need-based awards were made. *Average percent of need met:* 68%. *Average financial aid package:* $16,177. *Average need-based loan:* $4047. *Average need-based gift aid:* $13,015. *Average non-need-based aid:* $9808. *Average indebtedness upon graduation:* $21,034.

Applying *Required:* high school transcript. *Required for some:* essay or personal statement, 3 letters of recommendation, interview, auditions for music students; portfolios for art.

Freshman Application Contact Office of Admission, Huntingdon College, 1500 East Fairview Avenue, Montgomery, AL 36106-2148. *Phone:* 334-833-4497. *Toll-free phone:* 800-763-0313. *Fax:* 334-833-4347. *E-mail:* admiss@huntingdon.edu.
Website: http://www.huntingdon.edu/.

ITT Technical Institute

Bessemer, Alabama

- **Proprietary** primarily 2-year, founded 1994, part of ITT Educational Services, Inc.
- **Suburban** campus
- **Coed**
- **Minimally difficult** entrance level

Academics *Calendar:* quarters. *Degrees:* associate and bachelor's.

Student Life *Campus security:* 24-hour emergency response devices.

Freshman Application Contact Director of Recruitment, ITT Technical Institute, 6270 Park South Drive, Bessemer, AL 35022. *Phone:* 205-497-5700. *Toll-free phone:* 800-488-7033.
Website: http://www.itt-tech.edu/.

ITT Technical Institute

Madison, Alabama

- **Proprietary** primarily 2-year, part of ITT Educational Services, Inc.
- **Coed**
- **Minimally difficult** entrance level

Academics *Degrees:* associate and bachelor's.

Freshman Application Contact Director of Recruitment, ITT Technical Institute, 9238 Madison Boulevard, Suite 500, Madison, AL 35758. *Phone:* 256-542-2900. *Toll-free phone:* 877-628-5960.
Website: http://www.itt-tech.edu/.

ITT Technical Institute

Mobile, Alabama

- **Proprietary** primarily 2-year, part of ITT Educational Services, Inc.
- **Coed**
- **Minimally difficult** entrance level

Academics *Degrees:* associate and bachelor's.

Freshman Application Contact Director of Recruitment, ITT Technical Institute, Office Mall South, 3100 Cottage Hill Road, Building 3, Mobile, AL 36606. *Phone:* 251-472-4760. *Toll-free phone:* 877-327-1013.
Website: http://www.itt-tech.edu/.

Jacksonville State University

Jacksonville, Alabama

- **State-supported** comprehensive, founded 1883
- **Small-town** 459-acre campus with easy access to Birmingham
- **Coed** 7,991 undergraduate students, 76% full-time, 58% women, 42% men
- **Minimally difficult** entrance level, 82% of applicants were admitted

Undergraduates 6,044 full-time, 1,947 part-time. 20% are from out of state; 28% Black or African American, non-Hispanic/Latino; 1% Hispanic/Latino; 0.5% Asian, non-Hispanic/Latino; 0.1% Native Hawaiian or other Pacific Islander, non-Hispanic/Latino; 0.4% American Indian or Alaska Native, non-Hispanic/Latino; 3% Race/ethnicity unknown; 2% international; 8% transferred in; 25% live on campus. *Retention:* 67% of full-time freshmen returned.

Freshmen *Admission:* 3,161 applied, 2,604 admitted, 1,332 enrolled. *Average high school GPA:* 3.16. *Test scores:* SAT critical reading scores over 500: 40%; SAT math scores over 500: 42%; ACT scores over 18: 88%; SAT critical reading scores over 600: 12%; SAT math scores over 600: 10%; ACT scores over 24: 38%; SAT critical reading scores over 700: 2%; ACT scores over 30: 4%.

Faculty *Total:* 497, 64% full-time. *Student/faculty ratio:* 18:1.

Academics *Calendar:* semesters. *Degrees:* bachelor's, master's, doctoral, post-master's, and postbachelor's certificates. *Special study options:* academic remediation for entering students, accelerated degree program, adult/continuing education programs, advanced placement credit, cooperative education, distance learning, double majors, honors programs, independent study, internships, part-time degree program, services for LD students, summer session for credit. *ROTC:* Army (b).

Computers on Campus 350 computers/terminals are available on campus for general student use. Students can access the following: computer help desk, free student e-mail accounts, online (class) grades, online (class) registration, online (class) schedules. Campuswide network is available.

Student Life *Housing options:* coed, men-only, women-only, disabled students. Campus housing is university owned. *Activities and organizations:* drama/theater group, student-run newspaper, radio and television station, choral group, marching band, Student Government Association, Archaeology Club, Campus Fellowship Clubs, Computer Science Club, Biology Club, national fraternities, national sororities. *Campus security:* 24-hour emergency response devices and patrols, student patrols, late-night transport/escort service, controlled dormitory access, night security officer in female residence halls. *Student services:* health clinic, personal/psychological counseling.

Athletics Member NCAA. All Division I except football (Division I-AA). *Intercollegiate sports:* baseball M(s), basketball M(s)/W(s), cross-country running M(s)/W(s), golf M(s)/W(s), riflery M(s)/W(s), soccer W(s), softball W(s), tennis M(s)/W(s), volleyball W(s). *Intramural sports:* badminton M(c)/W(c), basketball M(c)/W(c), bowling M(c)/W(c), football M(c), golf M(c)/W(c), racquetball M(c)/W(c), soccer M(c)/W(c), softball M(c)/W(c), table tennis M(c)/W(c), tennis M(c)/W(c), volleyball M(c)/W(c).

Standardized Tests *Required:* SAT or ACT (for admission).

Costs (2012–13) *Tuition:* state resident $7950 full-time; nonresident $15,900 full-time. *Room and board:* $6300; room only: $3550. Room and board charges vary according to board plan and housing facility. *Payment plan:* installment. *Waivers:* employees or children of employees.

Financial Aid Of all full-time matriculated undergraduates who enrolled in 2011, 5,377 applied for aid, 5,293 were judged to have need. 161 Federal Work-Study jobs (averaging $1235). *Average financial aid package:* $8643. *Average need-based loan:* $970. *Average need-based gift aid:* $4415.

Applying *Options:* electronic application, early admission, deferred entrance. *Application fee:* $30. *Required:* high school transcript. *Application deadlines:* rolling (freshmen), rolling (out-of-state freshmen), rolling (transfers). *Notification:* continuous (freshmen), continuous (out-of-state freshmen), continuous (transfers).

Freshman Application Contact Mr. Andrew Green, Director of Admission, Jacksonville State University, 700 Pelham Road North, Jacksonville, AL 36265. *Phone:* 256-782-5363. *Toll-free phone:* 800-231-5291. *Fax:* 256-782-5291. *E-mail:* info@jsu.edu.
Website: http://www.jsu.edu/.

Judson College

Marion, Alabama

- **Independent Baptist** 4-year, founded 1838
- **Rural** 118-acre campus with easy access to Birmingham
- **Endowment** $14.1 million
- **Coed, primarily women** 357 undergraduate students, 82% full-time, 97% women, 3% men
- **Moderately difficult** entrance level, 82% of applicants were admitted

Undergraduates 293 full-time, 64 part-time. Students come from 21 states and territories; 1 other country; 19% are from out of state; 21% Black or African American, non-Hispanic/Latino; 1% Hispanic/Latino; 0.8% Asian, non-Hispanic/Latino; 0.3% American Indian or Alaska Native, non-Hispanic/Latino; 0.6% Two or more races, non-Hispanic/Latino; 4% Race/ethnicity unknown; 0.6% international; 14% transferred in; 63% live on campus. *Retention:* 72% of full-time freshmen returned.

Freshmen *Admission:* 309 applied, 252 admitted, 77 enrolled. *Average high school GPA:* 3.31. *Test scores:* SAT critical reading scores over 500: 50%; SAT writing scores over 500: 50%; ACT scores over 18: 80%; SAT critical reading scores over 600: 17%; SAT writing scores over 600: 33%; ACT scores over 24: 25%; ACT scores over 30: 4%.

Faculty *Total:* 40, 73% full-time, 63% with terminal degrees. *Student/faculty ratio:* 9:1.

Academics *Calendar:* semesters plus 2-month term. *Degrees:* associate and bachelor's. *Special study options:* academic remediation for entering students, accelerated degree program, adult/continuing education programs, advanced placement credit, distance learning, double majors, external degree program, honors programs, independent study, internships, off-campus study, part-time degree program, services for LD students, student-designed majors, study abroad, summer session for credit. *ROTC:* Army (c).

Computers on Campus 50 computers/terminals and 50 ports are available on campus for general student use. Students can access the following: computer help desk, free student e-mail accounts, online (class) grades, online (class) schedules. Campuswide network is available. 100% of college-owned or -operated housing units are wired for high-speed Internet access. Wireless service is available via classrooms, computer labs, dorm rooms, libraries, student centers.

Student Life *Housing:* on-campus residence required through senior year. *Options:* women-only. Campus housing is university owned. Freshman campus housing is guaranteed. *Activities and organizations:* drama/theater group, student-run newspaper, choral group, marching band, Student Government Association, Campus Ministries, Faith-Based Service Learning Activities, Ambassadors, Science Club. *Campus security:* 24-hour emergency response devices and patrols, late-night transport/escort service, controlled dormitory access. *Student services:* personal/psychological counseling.

Athletics Member USCAA. *Intercollegiate sports:* basketball W(s), equestrian sports W, soccer W(s), softball W(s), tennis W(s)(c), volleyball W(s). *Intramural sports:* basketball W, field hockey W, softball W, swimming and diving W, tennis W, volleyball W.

Standardized Tests *Required:* SAT or ACT (for admission).

Costs (2013–14) *Comprehensive fee:* $24,940 includes full-time tuition ($14,800), mandatory fees ($940), and room and board ($9200). Full-time tuition and fees vary according to degree level. Part-time tuition: $500 per hour. Part-time tuition and fees vary according to degree level. *Required fees:* $470 per term part-time. *College room only:* $5150. *Payment plans:* installment, deferred payment. *Waivers:* employees or children of employees.

Financial Aid Of all full-time matriculated undergraduates who enrolled in 2009, 209 applied for aid, 196 were judged to have need, 25 had their need fully met. In 2009, 18 non-need-based awards were made. *Average percent of need met:* 76%. *Average financial aid package:* $13,259. *Average need-based loan:* $3926. *Average need-based gift aid:* $9855. *Average non-need-based aid:* $8859. *Average indebtedness upon graduation:* $17,563.

Applying *Options:* electronic application, early admission, deferred entrance. *Application fee:* $35. *Required:* high school transcript, minimum 2.0 GPA. *Application deadlines:* rolling (freshmen), rolling (out-of-state freshmen), rolling (transfers). *Notification:* continuous (freshmen), continuous (out-of-state freshmen), continuous (transfers).

Freshman Application Contact Ms. Layne Calhoun, Executive Director of Enrollment Services, Judson College, 302 Bibb Street, Marion, AL 36756. *Phone:* 334-683-5110. *Toll-free phone:* 800-447-9472. *Fax:* 334-683-5282. *E-mail:* admissions@judson.edu. *Website:* http://www.judson.edu/.

Miles College
Fairfield, Alabama

Freshman Application Contact Mr. Christopher Robertson, Director of Admissions and Recruitment, Miles College, 5500 Myron Massey Boulevard, Bell Building, Fairfield, AL 35064. *Phone:* 205-929-1657. *Toll-free phone:* 800-445-0708. *Fax:* 205-929-1627. *E-mail:* admissions@miles.edu. *Website:* http://www.miles.edu/.

Oakwood University
Huntsville, Alabama

Freshman Application Contact Mr. Jason McCracken, Director of Enrollment Management, Oakwood University, 7000 Adventist Boulevard, NW, Huntsville, AL 35896. *Phone:* 256-726-7354. *Toll-free phone:* 800-824-5312. *Fax:* 256-726-7154. *E-mail:* admission@oakwood.edu. *Website:* http://www.oakwood.edu/.

Remington College–Mobile Campus
Mobile, Alabama

Freshman Application Contact Remington College–Mobile Campus, 828 Downtowner Loop West, Mobile, AL 36609-5404. *Phone:* 251-343-8200. *Toll-free phone:* 800-560-6192. *Website:* http://www.remingtoncollege.edu/.

Samford University
Birmingham, Alabama

- **Independent Baptist** university, founded 1841
- **Suburban** 212-acre campus
- **Endowment** $241.2 million
- **Coed** 2,965 undergraduate students, 93% full-time, 65% women, 35% men
- **Moderately difficult** entrance level, 76% of applicants were admitted

Undergraduates 2,769 full-time, 196 part-time. Students come from 38 states and territories; 12 other countries; 62% are from out of state; 7% Black or African American, non-Hispanic/Latino; 5% Hispanic/Latino; 0.7% Asian, non-Hispanic/Latino; 0.1% Native Hawaiian or other Pacific Islander, non-Hispanic/Latino; 0.3% American Indian or Alaska Native, non-Hispanic/Latino; 1% Two or more races, non-Hispanic/Latino; 2% Race/ethnicity unknown; 2% international; 4% transferred in; 68% live on campus. *Retention:* 87% of full-time freshmen returned.

Freshmen *Admission:* 3,234 applied, 2,443 admitted, 708 enrolled. *Average high school GPA:* 3.67. *Test scores:* SAT critical reading scores over 500: 84%; SAT math scores over 500: 82%; SAT writing scores over 500: 100%; ACT scores over 18: 100%; SAT critical reading scores over 600: 42%; SAT math scores over 600: 36%; SAT writing scores over 600: 67%; ACT scores over 24: 67%; SAT critical reading scores over 700: 8%; SAT math scores over 700: 5%; SAT writing scores over 700: 19%; ACT scores over 30: 19%.

Faculty *Total:* 487, 62% full-time, 69% with terminal degrees. *Student/faculty ratio:* 12:1.

Academics *Calendar:* 4-1-4. *Degrees:* certificates, bachelor's, master's, doctoral, and post-master's certificates. *Special study options:* accelerated degree program, adult/continuing education programs, cooperative education, distance learning, double majors, English as a second language, honors programs, independent study, internships, off-campus study, part-time degree program, services for LD students, study abroad, summer session for credit. *ROTC:* Army (c), Air Force (b). *Unusual degree programs:* 3-2 engineering with The University of Alabama at Birmingham, Auburn University, and Mercer University (Georgia).

Computers on Campus 330 computers/terminals and 400 ports are available on campus for general student use. Students can access the following: campus intranet, computer help desk, free student e-mail accounts, online (class) grades, online (class) registration, online (class) schedules, free online storage and tech support. Campuswide network is available. 100% of college-owned or -operated housing units are wired for high-speed Internet access. Wireless service is available via entire campus.

Student Life *Housing:* on-campus residence required through sophomore year. *Options:* men-only, women-only, disabled students. Campus housing is university owned. Freshman campus housing is guaranteed. *Activities and organizations:* drama/theater group, student-run newspaper, radio station, choral group, marching band, Alpha Delta Pi sorority, Chi Omega sorority, Phi Mu Sorority, Zeta Tau Alpha sorority, Alpha Omicron Pi sorority, national fraternities, national sororities. *Campus security:* 24-hour emergency response devices and patrols, late-night transport/escort service, self defense education, security escort services, and lighted pathways/sidewalks. *Student services:* health clinic, personal/psychological counseling.

Athletics Member NCAA. All Division I except football (Division I-AA). *Intercollegiate sports:* baseball M(s), basketball M(s)/W(s), cross-country running M(s)/W(s), golf M(s)/W(s), soccer M(s)/W(s), softball W(s), tennis M(s)/W(s), track and field M(s)/W(s), volleyball W(s). *Intramural sports:* basketball M/W, football M/W, soccer M/W, softball M/W, ultimate Frisbee M(c)/W(c), volleyball M/W.

Standardized Tests *Required:* SAT or ACT (for admission).

Costs (2012–13) *Comprehensive fee:* $33,400 includes full-time tuition ($24,570), mandatory fees ($580), and room and board ($8250). Full-time tuition and fees vary according to course load, location, and program. Part-time tuition: $821 per credit hour. Part-time tuition and fees vary according to course load and program. *Required fees:* $210 per term part-time. *College room only:* $4250. Room and board charges vary according to board plan, housing facility, and location. *Waivers:* employees or children of employees.

Financial Aid Of all full-time matriculated undergraduates who enrolled in 2011, 1,639 applied for aid, 1,251 were judged to have need, 258 had their need fully met. 308 Federal Work-Study jobs (averaging $2151). 587 state and other part-time jobs (averaging $1599). In 2011, 1015 non-need-based awards

were made. *Average percent of need met:* 68%. *Average financial aid package:* $16,804. *Average need-based loan:* $3600. *Average need-based gift aid:* $12,884. *Average non-need-based aid:* $8475. *Average indebtedness upon graduation:* $25,252.

Applying *Options:* electronic application, early admission, deferred entrance. *Application fee:* $35. *Required:* essay or personal statement, high school transcript, 1 letter of recommendation. *Required for some:* interview. *Application deadlines:* rolling (freshmen), rolling (out-of-state freshmen), 8/1 (transfers). *Notification:* continuous (freshmen), continuous (out-of-state freshmen).

Freshman Application Contact Mr. Brian L. Kennedy, Associate Director, Communications, Samford University, 800 Lakeshore Drive, Samford Hall, Birmingham, AL 35229-0002. *Phone:* 205-726-4176. *Toll-free phone:* 800-888-7218. *Fax:* 205-726-2171. *E-mail:* blkenned@samford.edu. *Website:* http://www.samford.edu/.

Selma University
Selma, Alabama

Director of Admissions Mrs. Estella Davis-Baynes, Director of Admissions and Records, Selma University, 1501 Lapsley Street, Selma, AL 36701-5299. *Phone:* 334-872-2533.
Website: http://www.selmauniversity.org/.

Southeastern Bible College
Birmingham, Alabama

- **Independent nondenominational** 4-year, founded 1935
- **Suburban** 22-acre campus
- **Coed** 179 undergraduate students, 82% full-time, 41% women, 59% men
- **Noncompetitive** entrance level, 100% of applicants were admitted

Undergraduates 146 full-time, 33 part-time. Students come from 9 states and territories; 1 other country; 8% are from out of state; 33% Black or African American, non-Hispanic/Latino; 1% Hispanic/Latino; 0.6% American Indian or Alaska Native, non-Hispanic/Latino; 7% Race/ethnicity unknown; 0.6% international; 25% transferred in; 33% live on campus. *Retention:* 67% of full-time freshmen returned.

Freshmen *Admission:* 22 applied, 22 admitted, 16 enrolled. *Average high school GPA:* 3.34. *Test scores:* ACT scores over 18: 58%; ACT scores over 24: 8%.

Faculty *Total:* 27, 26% full-time, 33% with terminal degrees. *Student/faculty ratio:* 11:1.

Academics *Calendar:* semesters. *Degrees:* diplomas, associate, and bachelor's. *Special study options:* academic remediation for entering students, adult/continuing education programs, advanced placement credit, distance learning, double majors, independent study, internships, part-time degree program, services for LD students, summer session for credit.

Computers on Campus 30 computers/terminals are available on campus for general student use. Students can access the following: free student e-mail accounts. Wireless service is available via entire campus.

Student Life *Housing options:* men-only, women-only. Campus housing is university owned. *Activities and organizations:* choral group, Student Council, Student Missions Fellowship, chorale. *Campus security:* controlled dormitory access.

Standardized Tests *Required:* SAT or ACT (for admission).

Applying *Options:* electronic application, deferred entrance. *Application fee:* $30. *Required:* essay or personal statement, high school transcript, minimum 1.5 GPA, 2 letters of recommendation.

Freshman Application Contact Ms. Deidra Whitfield, Admissions Counselor, Southeastern Bible College, 2545 Valleydale Road, Birmingham, AL 35244. *Phone:* 205-970-9210. *Toll-free phone:* 800-749-8878. *Fax:* 205-970-9207. *E-mail:* deidra.whitfield@sebc.edu. *Website:* http://www.sebc.edu/.

South University
Montgomery, Alabama

- **Proprietary** comprehensive, founded 1887, part of Education Management Corporation
- **Coed**

Academics *Calendar:* quarters. *Degrees:* associate, bachelor's, and master's.

Freshman Application Contact South University, 5355 Vaughn Road, Montgomery, AL 36116-1120. *Phone:* 334-395-8800. *Toll-free phone:* 866-629-2962.
Website: http://www.southuniversity.edu/montgomery/.

Spring Hill College
Mobile, Alabama

- **Independent Roman Catholic (Jesuit)** comprehensive, founded 1830
- **Suburban** 450-acre campus
- **Coed** 1,202 undergraduate students, 93% full-time, 61% women, 39% men
- **Moderately difficult** entrance level, 47% of applicants were admitted

Undergraduates 1,119 full-time, 83 part-time. Students come from 39 states and territories; 12 other countries; 60% are from out of state; 17% Black or African American, non-Hispanic/Latino; 8% Hispanic/Latino; 0.9% Asian, non-Hispanic/Latino; 0.1% Native Hawaiian or other Pacific Islander, non-Hispanic/Latino; 0.9% American Indian or Alaska Native, non-Hispanic/Latino; 2% Two or more races, non-Hispanic/Latino; 4% Race/ethnicity unknown; 1% international; 3% transferred in; 80% live on campus. *Retention:* 74% of full-time freshmen returned.

Freshmen *Admission:* 2,817 applied, 1,337 admitted, 299 enrolled. *Average high school GPA:* 3.44. *Test scores:* SAT critical reading scores over 500: 69%; SAT math scores over 500: 70%; SAT writing scores over 500: 66%; ACT scores over 18: 99%; SAT critical reading scores over 600: 29%; SAT math scores over 600: 26%; SAT writing scores over 600: 24%; ACT scores over 24: 49%; SAT critical reading scores over 700: 4%; SAT math scores over 700: 1%; SAT writing scores over 700: 2%; ACT scores over 30: 7%.

Faculty *Total:* 134, 58% full-time, 67% with terminal degrees. *Student/faculty ratio:* 12:1.

Academics *Calendar:* semesters. *Degrees:* certificates, bachelor's, master's, post-master's, and postbachelor's certificates. *Special study options:* academic remediation for entering students, accelerated degree program, adult/continuing education programs, advanced placement credit, distance learning, double majors, honors programs, independent study, internships, off-campus study, part-time degree program, services for LD students, student-designed majors, study abroad, summer session for credit. *ROTC:* Army (c), Air Force (c). *Unusual degree programs:* 3-2 engineering with Marquette University, University of Alabama at Birmingham, University of Florida, Auburn University, Texas A&M University, University of South Alabama.

Computers on Campus 194 computers/terminals and 250 ports are available on campus for general student use. Students can access the following: campus intranet, computer help desk, free student e-mail accounts, online (class) grades, online (class) registration, online (class) schedules. Campuswide network is available. 100% of college-owned or -operated housing units are wired for high-speed Internet access. Wireless service is available via computer centers, computer labs, dorm rooms, libraries, student centers.

Student Life *Housing:* on-campus residence required through senior year. *Options:* coed. Campus housing is university owned. Freshman campus housing is guaranteed. *Activities and organizations:* drama/theater group, student-run newspaper, choral group, Fraternities and sororities, SHAPe, National Society of Leadership and Success, Peer One Project, Chemistry Club, national fraternities, national sororities. *Campus security:* 24-hour emergency response devices and patrols, late-night transport/escort service, controlled dormitory access. *Student services:* health clinic, personal/psychological counseling.

Athletics Member NAIA. *Intercollegiate sports:* baseball M(s), basketball M(s)/W(s), cross-country running M(s)/W(s), golf M(s)/W(s), soccer M(s)/W(s), softball W(s), tennis M(s)/W(s), track and field M(s)/W(s), volleyball W(s). *Intramural sports:* basketball M/W, cheerleading W(c), football M/W, racquetball M/W, rugby M(c), soccer M/W, softball M/W, ultimate Frisbee M/W, volleyball M/W.

Standardized Tests *Required:* SAT or ACT (for admission).

Costs (2012–13) *Comprehensive fee:* $40,746 includes full-time tuition ($27,670), mandatory fees ($1780), and room and board ($11,296). Part-time tuition: $975 per credit hour. *Required fees:* $50 per credit hour part-time. *College room only:* $5900. Room and board charges vary according to housing facility. *Payment plan:* installment. *Waivers:* employees or children of employees.

Financial Aid Of all full-time matriculated undergraduates who enrolled in 2012, 893 applied for aid, 758 were judged to have need, 164 had their need fully met. In 2012, 313 non-need-based awards were made. *Average percent of need met:* 86%. *Average financial aid package:* $28,744. *Average need-based loan:* $4767. *Average need-based gift aid:* $9454. *Average non-need-based aid:* $14,993. *Average indebtedness upon graduation:* $30,356.

Applying *Options:* electronic application, early admission, deferred entrance. *Application fee:* $25. *Required:* essay or personal statement, high school transcript, 1 letter of recommendation. *Recommended:* minimum 2.5 GPA, interview. *Application deadlines:* 7/15 (freshmen), 7/15 (out-of-state freshmen), rolling (transfers). *Notification:* continuous (freshmen), continuous (out-of-state freshmen), continuous (transfers).

Freshman Application Contact Ms. Elisabeth Ruscin, Front Office Operations, Campus Visit Coordinator, Spring Hill College, 4000 Dauphin

Street, Mobile, AL 36608-1791. *Phone:* 251-380-3030. *Toll-free phone:* 800-SHC-6704. *Fax:* 251-460-2186. *E-mail:* eruscin@shc.edu. *Website:* http://www.shc.edu/.

Stillman College
Tuscaloosa, Alabama
- **Independent** 4-year, founded 1876, affiliated with Presbyterian Church (U.S.A.)
- **Urban** 100-acre campus with easy access to Birmingham
- **Endowment** $18.2 million
- **Coed**
- **Minimally difficult** entrance level

Faculty *Student/faculty ratio:* 18:1.
Academics *Calendar:* semesters. *Degree:* bachelor's.
Student Life *Campus security:* 24-hour patrols, 24-hour patrols by trained campus police.
Athletics Member NCAA. All Division II.
Standardized Tests *Required:* SAT or ACT (for admission), SAT and SAT Subject Tests or ACT (for admission). *Recommended:* SAT (for admission), ACT (for admission), SAT Subject Tests (for admission).
Costs (2012–13) *Comprehensive fee:* $22,721 includes full-time tuition ($13,548), mandatory fees ($2117), and room and board ($7056). Part-time tuition: $534 per credit. No tuition increase for student's term of enrollment. *Required fees:* $2117 per term part-time. *College room only:* $3404. Room and board charges vary according to housing facility.
Financial Aid *Of all full-time matriculated undergraduates who enrolled in 2011,* 980 applied for aid, 980 were judged to have need, 568 had their need fully met. 169 Federal Work-Study jobs (averaging $1056). *In 2011,* 16 non-need-based awards were made. *Average percent of need met:* 80. *Average financial aid package:* $24,300. *Average need-based loan:* $5500. *Average need-based gift aid:* $7250. *Average non-need-based aid:* $12,250. *Average indebtedness upon graduation:* $30,429. *Financial aid deadline:* 6/1.
Applying *Options:* electronic application, early admission, early decision, deferred entrance. *Application fee:* $15. *Required:* high school transcript, minimum 2.5 GPA. *Recommended:* essay or personal statement, interview.
Freshman Application Contact Stillman College, PO Drawer 1430, 3600 Stillman Boulevard, Tuscaloosa, AL 35403-9990. *Phone:* 205-366-8837. *Toll-free phone:* 800-841-5722.
Website: http://www.stillman.edu/.

Strayer University—Birmingham Campus
Birmingham, Alabama
Freshman Application Contact Strayer University—Birmingham Campus, 3570 Grandview Parkway, Suite 200, Birmingham, AL 35243.
Website: http://www.strayer.edu/campus/birmingham/.

Strayer University—Huntsville Campus
Huntsville, Alabama
Freshman Application Contact Strayer University—Huntsville Campus, 4955 Corporate Drive, NW, Suite 200, Huntsville, AL 35805.
Website: http://www.strayer.edu/campus/huntsville/.

Talladega College
Talladega, Alabama
Freshman Application Contact Talladega College, 627 West Battle Street, Talladega, AL 35160-2354. *Phone:* 256-761-6415. *Toll-free phone:* 866-540-3956.
Website: http://www.talladega.edu/.

Troy University
Troy, Alabama
- **State-supported** comprehensive, founded 1887, part of Troy University System
- **Small-town** 906-acre campus
- **Endowment** $32.9 million
- **Coed** 17,915 undergraduate students, 54% full-time, 63% women, 37% men
- **Moderately difficult** entrance level, 72% of applicants were admitted

Undergraduates 9,634 full-time, 8,281 part-time. Students come from 52 states and territories; 52 other countries; 40% are from out of state; 39% Black or African American, non-Hispanic/Latino; 3% Hispanic/Latino; 0.8% Asian, non-Hispanic/Latino; 0.1% Native Hawaiian or other Pacific Islander, non-Hispanic/Latino; 1% American Indian or Alaska Native, non-Hispanic/Latino; 1% Two or more races, non-Hispanic/Latino; 5% Race/ethnicity unknown; 2% international; 8% transferred in; 29% live on campus. *Retention:* 71% of full-time freshmen returned.
Freshmen *Admission:* 5,646 applied, 4,056 admitted, 2,087 enrolled. *Test scores:* ACT scores over 18: 79%; ACT scores over 24: 35%; ACT scores over 30: 8%.
Faculty *Total:* 1,284, 43% full-time, 56% with terminal degrees. *Student/faculty ratio:* 19:1.
Academics *Calendar:* semesters. *Degrees:* associate, bachelor's, master's, doctoral, and post-master's certificates. *Special study options:* academic remediation for entering students, accelerated degree program, advanced placement credit, distance learning, double majors, English as a second language, honors programs, independent study, internships, part-time degree program, services for LD students, summer session for credit. *ROTC:* Army (b), Air Force (b).
Computers on Campus 12,792 computers/terminals and 18,117 ports are available on campus for general student use. Students can access the following: campus intranet, computer help desk, free student e-mail accounts, online (class) grades, online (class) registration, online (class) schedules. Campus-wide network is available. Wireless service is available via classrooms, dorm rooms, libraries.
Student Life *Housing:* on-campus residence required for freshman year. *Options:* coed, men-only, women-only. Campus housing is university owned. Freshman campus housing is guaranteed. *Activities and organizations:* drama/theater group, student-run newspaper, television station, choral group, marching band, T-Day/Athletic Events (Homecoming), Activities Council, Pep Rallies, national fraternities, national sororities. *Campus security:* 24-hour emergency response devices and patrols, student patrols, late-night transport/escort service, controlled dormitory access. *Student services:* health clinic, personal/psychological counseling.
Athletics Member NCAA. All Division I except football (Division I-A). *Intercollegiate sports:* baseball M(s), basketball M(s)/W(s), cross-country running M(s)/W(s), golf M(s)/W(s), soccer W(s), softball W(s), tennis M(s)/W(s), track and field M(s)/W(s), volleyball W(s). *Intramural sports:* basketball M/W, bowling M/W, cross-country running M/W, football M, golf M/W, soccer W, softball W, tennis M/W, track and field M/W, volleyball W.
Standardized Tests *Required:* SAT or ACT (for admission).
Costs (2012–13) *Tuition:* state resident $7470 full-time, $249 per credit hour part-time; nonresident $14,940 full-time, $498 per credit hour part-time. Full-time tuition and fees vary according to location and program. Part-time tuition and fees vary according to location and program. *Required fees:* $1600 full-time, $32 per credit hour part-time, $50 per term part-time. *Room and board:* $7071; room only: $3686. Room and board charges vary according to board plan and housing facility. *Payment plan:* installment. *Waivers:* employees or children of employees.
Financial Aid *Of all full-time matriculated undergraduates who enrolled in 2012,* 6,822 applied for aid, 6,793 were judged to have need. In 2012, 2079 non-need-based awards were made. *Average financial aid package:* $4528. *Average need-based loan:* $4586. *Average need-based gift aid:* $4485. *Average non-need-based aid:* $5259.
Applying *Options:* electronic application, deferred entrance. *Application fee:* $30. *Required:* high school transcript. *Recommended:* interview. *Application deadlines:* rolling (freshmen), rolling (transfers).
Freshman Application Contact Mr. Buddy Starling, Dean of Enrollment Management, Troy University, University Avenue, Troy, AL 36082. *Phone:* 334-670-3243. *Toll-free phone:* 800-551-9716. *Fax:* 334-670-3733. *E-mail:* bstar@troy.edu.
Website: http://www.troy.edu/.

Tuskegee University
Tuskegee, Alabama
- **Independent** comprehensive, founded 1881
- **Small-town** 5000-acre campus
- **Endowment** $113.7 million
- **Coed** 2,684 undergraduate students, 97% full-time, 57% women, 43% men
- **Moderately difficult** entrance level, 65% of applicants were admitted

Undergraduates 2,614 full-time, 70 part-time. Students come from 44 states and territories; 19 other countries; 72% are from out of state; 87% Black or African American, non-Hispanic/Latino; 0.1% Hispanic/Latino; 0.1% American Indian or Alaska Native, non-Hispanic/Latino; 12% Race/ethnicity unknown; 1% international; 6% transferred in; 63% live on campus. *Retention:* 71% of full-time freshmen returned.

Freshmen *Admission:* 2,815 applied, 1,816 admitted, 819 enrolled. *Average high school GPA:* 3.2. *Test scores:* SAT critical reading scores over 500: 25%; SAT math scores over 500: 29%; SAT critical reading scores over 600: 6%; SAT math scores over 600: 6%; SAT math scores over 700: 2%.
Faculty *Total:* 297, 91% full-time, 74% with terminal degrees. *Student/faculty ratio:* 12:1.
Academics *Calendar:* semesters. *Degrees:* bachelor's, master's, and doctoral. *Special study options:* academic remediation for entering students, cooperative education, English as a second language, honors programs, internships, off-campus study, part-time degree program, summer session for credit. *ROTC:* Army (b), Air Force (b). *Unusual degree programs:* 3-2 forestry with Auburn University, Iowa State University of Science and Technology, University of Michigan, Idaho State University.
Computers on Campus 1,000 computers/terminals are available on campus for general student use. Students can access the following: online (class) registration. Campuswide network is available. 91% of college-owned or -operated housing units are wired for high-speed Internet access.
Student Life *Housing:* on-campus residence required through sophomore year. *Options:* coed, men-only, women-only. Freshman applicants given priority for college housing. *Activities and organizations:* drama/theater group, student-run newspaper, choral group, marching band, Student Government, Marching Band, State Clubs, Fraternities, Sororities, national fraternities, national sororities. *Campus security:* 24-hour emergency response devices and patrols, late-night transport/escort service. *Student services:* health clinic, personal/psychological counseling.
Athletics Member NCAA. All Division II. *Intercollegiate sports:* baseball M(s), basketball M(s)/W(s), cross-country running M/W, football M(s), golf M(s), riflery M/W, soccer M, tennis M(s)/W(s), track and field M(s)/W(s), volleyball W(s). *Intramural sports:* badminton M/W, basketball M/W, football M, golf M, gymnastics M/W, riflery M/W, soccer M, swimming and diving M/W, tennis M/W, track and field M/W, volleyball M/W.
Standardized Tests *Required:* SAT or ACT (for admission).
Costs (2013–14) *One-time required fee:* $500. *Comprehensive fee:* $27,350 includes full-time tuition ($18,100), mandatory fees ($800), and room and board ($8450). Full-time tuition and fees vary according to course level, course load, degree level, and program. Part-time tuition: $750 per hour. Part-time tuition and fees vary according to course level, course load, degree level, and program. *Required fees:* $800 per year part-time. *College room only:* $4190. Room and board charges vary according to housing facility. *Payment plan:* installment. *Waivers:* employees or children of employees.
Financial Aid Of all full-time matriculated undergraduates who enrolled in 2010, 2,519 applied for aid, 2,147 were judged to have need, 1,379 had their need fully met. 525 Federal Work-Study jobs (averaging $1879). 424 state and other part-time jobs (averaging $4628). In 2010, 597 non-need-based awards were made. *Average percent of need met:* 85%. *Average financial aid package:* $19,250. *Average need-based loan:* $6006. *Average need-based gift aid:* $8000. *Average non-need-based aid:* $6000. *Average indebtedness upon graduation:* $28,575.
Applying *Options:* electronic application, early admission. *Application fee:* $25. *Required:* high school transcript, minimum 3.0 GPA. *Application deadlines:* 4/15 (freshmen), 4/15 (transfers).
Freshman Application Contact Tuskegee University, Tuskegee, AL 36088. *Phone:* 334-727-8500. *Toll-free phone:* 800-622-6531. *Website:* http://www.tuskegee.edu/.

United States Sports Academy
Daphne, Alabama

Application Contact United States Sports Academy, One Academy Drive, Daphne, AL 36526-7055. *Toll-free phone:* 800-223-2668. *Website:* http://www.ussa.edu/.

The University of Alabama
Tuscaloosa, Alabama

- **State-supported** university, founded 1831, part of University of Alabama System
- **Suburban** 1000-acre campus with easy access to Birmingham
- **Endowment** $616.9 million
- **Coed** 28,026 undergraduate students, 91% full-time, 54% women, 46% men
- **Moderately difficult** entrance level, 53% of applicants were admitted

Undergraduates 25,430 full-time, 2,596 part-time. Students come from 52 states and territories; 47 other countries; 40% are from out of state; 12% Black or African American, non-Hispanic/Latino; 3% Hispanic/Latino; 1% Asian, non-Hispanic/Latino; 0.1% Native Hawaiian or other Pacific Islander, non-Hispanic/Latino; 0.4% American Indian or Alaska Native, non-Hispanic/Latino; 2% Two or more races, non-Hispanic/Latino; 0.3% Race/ethnicity unknown; 2% international; 5% transferred in; 27% live on campus. *Retention:* 85% of full-time freshmen returned.
Freshmen *Admission:* 26,409 applied, 14,019 admitted, 6,371 enrolled. *Average high school GPA:* 3.57. *Test scores:* SAT critical reading scores over 500: 77%; SAT math scores over 500: 81%; SAT writing scores over 500: 72%; ACT scores over 18: 100%; SAT critical reading scores over 600: 31%; SAT math scores over 600: 38%; SAT writing scores over 600: 28%; ACT scores over 24: 63%; SAT critical reading scores over 700: 12%; SAT math scores over 700: 15%; SAT writing scores over 700: 9%; ACT scores over 30: 27%.
Faculty *Total:* 1,663, 72% full-time, 76% with terminal degrees. *Student/faculty ratio:* 20:1.
Academics *Calendar:* semesters. *Degrees:* bachelor's, master's, doctoral, and post-master's certificates. *Special study options:* academic remediation for entering students, accelerated degree program, adult/continuing education programs, advanced placement credit, cooperative education, distance learning, double majors, English as a second language, external degree program, freshman honors college, honors programs, independent study, internships, off-campus study, part-time degree program, services for LD students, student-designed majors, study abroad, summer session for credit. *ROTC:* Army (b), Air Force (b).
Computers on Campus 1,500 computers/terminals are available on campus for general student use. Students can access the following: campus intranet, computer help desk, free student e-mail accounts, online (class) grades, online (class) registration, online (class) schedules. Campuswide network is available. 100% of college-owned or -operated housing units are wired for high-speed Internet access. Wireless service is available via entire campus.
Student Life *Housing:* on-campus residence required for freshman year. *Options:* coed, men-only, women-only, disabled students. Campus housing is university owned and leased by the school. Freshman campus housing is guaranteed. *Activities and organizations:* drama/theater group, student-run newspaper, radio station, choral group, marching band, SOURCE Board of Governors, Association of Residence Communities, International Student Association, Student Government Association, Black Student Union, national fraternities, national sororities. *Campus security:* 24-hour emergency response devices and patrols, late-night transport/escort service, controlled dormitory access, 24-hour patrols by University of Alabama Police (UAPD), certified law enforcement personnel. *Student services:* health clinic, personal/psychological counseling, women's center, legal services.
Athletics Member NCAA. All Division I except football (Division I-A), golf (Division III). *Intercollegiate sports:* badminton M(c)/W(c), baseball M(s), basketball M(s)/W(s), bowling M(c), cheerleading M(s)/W(s), crew M(c)/W(s), cross-country running M(s)/W(s), equestrian sports W(c), golf M(s)/W(s), gymnastics W(s), ice hockey M(c), lacrosse M(c)/W(c), racquetball M(c)/W(c), rock climbing M(c)/W(c), rugby M(c)/W(c), soccer M(c)/W(s), softball W(s), swimming and diving M(s)/W(s), table tennis M(c)/W(c), tennis M(s)/W(s), track and field M(s)/W(s), ultimate Frisbee M(c)/W(c), volleyball M(c)/W(c), water polo M(c), weight lifting M(c)/W(c), wrestling M(c). *Intramural sports:* badminton M/W, basketball M/W, bowling M/W, golf M/W, racquetball M/W, soccer M/W, swimming and diving M/W, table tennis M/W, tennis M/W, ultimate Frisbee M/W, volleyball M/W.
Standardized Tests *Required:* SAT or ACT (for admission).
Costs (2012–13) *Tuition:* state resident $9200 full-time; nonresident $22,950 full-time. Full-time tuition and fees vary according to course load. Part-time tuition and fees vary according to course load. *Room and board:* $8650; room only: $5600. Room and board charges vary according to board plan and housing facility. *Payment plans:* installment, deferred payment. *Waivers:* employees or children of employees.
Financial Aid Of all full-time matriculated undergraduates who enrolled in 2011, 12,947 applied for aid, 10,129 were judged to have need, 1,469 had their need fully met. 430 Federal Work-Study jobs (averaging $3014). In 2011, 4967 non-need-based awards were made. *Average percent of need met:* 52%. *Average financial aid package:* $10,485. *Average need-based loan:* $4313. *Average need-based gift aid:* $7619. *Average non-need-based aid:* $9291. *Average indebtedness upon graduation:* $27,639.
Applying *Options:* electronic application, early admission. *Application fee:* $40. *Required:* high school transcript, minimum 3.0 GPA. *Required for some:* essay or personal statement, 2 letters of recommendation. *Application deadlines:* 5/1 (freshmen), 5/1 (out-of-state freshmen), 3/1 (transfers). *Notification:* continuous (freshmen), continuous (out-of-state freshmen), continuous (transfers).
Freshman Application Contact Ms. Mary K. Spiegel, Executive Director of Undergraduate Admissions, The University of Alabama, Box 870132, Tuscaloosa, AL 35487. *Phone:* 205-348-5666. *Toll-free phone:* 800-933-BAMA. *Fax:* 205-348-9046. *E-mail:* admissions@ua.edu. *Website:* http://www.ua.edu/.

The University of Alabama at Birmingham

Birmingham, Alabama

- **State-supported** university, founded 1969, part of University of Alabama System
- **Urban** 323-acre campus with easy access to Birmingham
- **Coed** 11,291 undergraduate students, 73% full-time, 58% women, 42% men
- **Moderately difficult** entrance level, 74% of applicants were admitted

Undergraduates 8,295 full-time, 2,996 part-time. Students come from 47 states and territories; 52 other countries; 7% are from out of state; 27% Black or African American, non-Hispanic/Latino; 2% Hispanic/Latino; 5% Asian, non-Hispanic/Latino; 0.1% Native Hawaiian or other Pacific Islander, non-Hispanic/Latino; 0.3% American Indian or Alaska Native, non-Hispanic/Latino; 3% Two or more races, non-Hispanic/Latino; 2% Race/ethnicity unknown; 2% international; 11% transferred in; 21% live on campus. *Retention:* 80% of full-time freshmen returned.

Freshmen *Admission:* 6,026 applied, 4,438 admitted, 1,676 enrolled. *Average high school GPA:* 3.54. *Test scores:* ACT scores over 18: 100%; ACT scores over 24: 58%; ACT scores over 30: 10%.

Faculty *Total:* 943, 91% full-time, 85% with terminal degrees. *Student/faculty ratio:* 18:1.

Academics *Calendar:* semesters. *Degrees:* certificates, bachelor's, master's, doctoral, post-master's, and postbachelor's certificates. *Special study options:* academic remediation for entering students, accelerated degree program, adult/continuing education programs, advanced placement credit, cooperative education, distance learning, double majors, English as a second language, freshman honors college, honors programs, independent study, internships, off-campus study, part-time degree program, services for LD students, student-designed majors, study abroad, summer session for credit. *ROTC:* Army (b), Air Force (c). *Unusual degree programs:* 3-2 engineering with Biomedical Engineering 5th Year Master's Program; Fast-Track Program—Civil Engineering, Electrical Engineering, Materials Engineering, and Mechanical Engineering; BS/MS in Biology; BS/MS in Computer Science; Public Health Fifth Year Master's Program.

Computers on Campus Students can access the following: campus intranet, computer help desk, free student e-mail accounts, online (class) grades, online (class) registration, online (class) schedules, transcript requests. Campuswide network is available. 100% of college-owned or -operated housing units are wired for high-speed Internet access. Wireless service is available via classrooms, computer labs, dorm rooms, learning centers, libraries, student centers.

Student Life *Housing options:* coed, disabled students. Campus housing is university owned and is provided by a third party. Freshman applicants given priority for college housing. *Activities and organizations:* drama/theater group, student-run newspaper, radio station, choral group, marching band, campus ministries, service-oriented groups, sports-affiliated groups, national fraternities, national sororities. *Campus security:* 24-hour emergency response devices and patrols, late-night transport/escort service, controlled dormitory access. *Student services:* health clinic, personal/psychological counseling, women's center.

Athletics Member NCAA. All Division I except football (Division I-A). *Intercollegiate sports:* baseball M(s), basketball M(s)/W(s), bowling W, cross-country running W(s), golf M(s)/W(s), riflery W, soccer M(s)/W(s), softball W(s), tennis M(s)/W(s), track and field W(s), volleyball W(s). *Intramural sports:* badminton M/W, basketball M/W, bowling M/W, football M/W, racquetball M/W, skiing (downhill) M/W, soccer M/W, softball M/W, swimming and diving M/W, table tennis M/W, tennis M/W, track and field M/W, ultimate Frisbee M/W, volleyball M/W, water polo M/W, wrestling M.

Standardized Tests *Required:* SAT or ACT (for admission).

Costs (2012–13) *Tuition:* state resident $8400 full-time, $267 per credit hour part-time; nonresident $19,230 full-time, $628 per credit hour part-time. Full-time tuition and fees vary according to program. Part-time tuition and fees vary according to program. *Room only:* $5400. Room and board charges vary according to board plan and housing facility. *Payment plan:* installment. *Waivers:* employees or children of employees.

Financial Aid Of all full-time matriculated undergraduates who enrolled in 2011, 5,805 applied for aid, 4,899 were judged to have need, 512 had their need fully met. In 2011, 1256 non-need-based awards were made. *Average percent of need met:* 44%. *Average financial aid package:* $9420. *Average need-based loan:* $4511. *Average need-based gift aid:* $4709. *Average non-need-based aid:* $6094. *Average indebtedness upon graduation:* $21,503.

Applying *Options:* electronic application, early admission, deferred entrance. *Application fee:* $30. *Required:* high school transcript. *Application deadlines:* 5/1 (freshmen), 5/1 (transfers). *Notification:* continuous (freshmen), continuous (transfers).

Freshman Application Contact Mr. Kirk Kluver, Director of Undergraduate Admissions, The University of Alabama at Birmingham, 1530 3rd Avenue South, HUC 260, Birmingham, AL 35294-1150. *Phone:* 205-934-8221. *Toll-free phone:* 800-421-8743. *Fax:* 205-975-7114. *E-mail:* undergradadmit@uab.edu.
Website: http://www.uab.edu/.

The University of Alabama in Huntsville

Huntsville, Alabama

- **State-supported** university, founded 1950, part of University of Alabama System
- **Suburban** 400-acre campus
- **Endowment** $56.4 million
- **Coed**
- **Moderately difficult** entrance level

Faculty *Student/faculty ratio:* 15:1.

Academics *Calendar:* semesters. *Degrees:* bachelor's, master's, doctoral, post-master's, and postbachelor's certificates.

Student Life *Campus security:* 24-hour emergency response devices and patrols, late-night transport/escort service, controlled dormitory access, Sworn Police Department with state certified police officers; 24/7 dispatch center; community policing efforts.

Athletics Member NCAA. All Division II except ice hockey (Division I).

Standardized Tests *Required:* SAT or ACT (for admission).

Costs (2012–13) *Tuition:* state resident $8794 full-time, $339 per credit hour part-time; nonresident $21,108 full-time, $815 per credit hour part-time. Full-time tuition and fees vary according to course load. Part-time tuition and fees vary according to course load. *Room and board:* $8070; room only: $5480. Room and board charges vary according to board plan and housing facility.

Financial Aid *Of all full-time matriculated undergraduates who enrolled in 2012,* 3,582 applied for aid, 2,448 were judged to have need, 252 had their need fully met. 72 Federal Work-Study jobs (averaging $4869). *In 2012,* 669 non-need-based awards were made. *Average percent of need met:* 53. *Average financial aid package:* $9394. *Average need-based loan:* $7912. *Average need-based gift aid:* $6311. *Average non-need-based aid:* $7798. *Average indebtedness upon graduation:* $25,437. *Financial aid deadline:* 7/31.

Applying *Options:* electronic application, deferred entrance. *Application fee:* $30. *Required:* high school transcript.

Freshman Application Contact Ms. Sandra Ranae Barinowski, Director of Admissions, The University of Alabama in Huntsville, Enrollment Services, 301 Sparkman Drive, Huntsville, AL 35899. *Phone:* 256-824-2773. *Toll-free phone:* 800-UAH-CALL. *Fax:* 256-824-4539. *E-mail:* admitme@email.uah.edu.
Website: http://www.uah.edu/.

University of Mobile

Mobile, Alabama

- **Independent Southern Baptist** comprehensive, founded 1961
- **Suburban** 830-acre campus
- **Endowment** $18.9 million
- **Coed** 1,552 undergraduate students, 82% full-time, 69% women, 31% men
- **Moderately difficult** entrance level, 80% of applicants were admitted

Undergraduates 1,274 full-time, 278 part-time. Students come from 31 states and territories; 26 other countries; 18% are from out of state; 24% Black or African American, non-Hispanic/Latino; 1% Hispanic/Latino; 0.9% Asian, non-Hispanic/Latino; 0.1% Native Hawaiian or other Pacific Islander, non-Hispanic/Latino; 2% American Indian or Alaska Native, non-Hispanic/Latino; 1% Two or more races, non-Hispanic/Latino; 7% Race/ethnicity unknown; 2% international; 11% transferred in; 38% live on campus. *Retention:* 73% of full-time freshmen returned.

Freshmen *Admission:* 789 applied, 634 admitted, 230 enrolled. *Average high school GPA:* 3.45. *Test scores:* SAT critical reading scores over 500: 59%; SAT math scores over 500: 59%; ACT scores over 18: 93%; SAT critical reading scores over 600: 29%; SAT math scores over 600: 29%; ACT scores over 24: 30%; ACT scores over 30: 1%.

Faculty *Total:* 178, 49% full-time, 39% with terminal degrees. *Student/faculty ratio:* 12:1.

Academics *Calendar:* semesters. *Degrees:* associate, bachelor's, and master's. *Special study options:* academic remediation for entering students, accelerated degree program, adult/continuing education programs, advanced placement credit, double majors, honors programs, independent study, internships, part-time degree program, services for LD students, summer session for credit. *ROTC:* Army (c), Air Force (c). *Unusual degree programs:* 3-2 engineering with Auburn University and University of South Alabama.

Computers on Campus 120 computers/terminals are available on campus for general student use. Students can access the following: campus intranet, computer help desk, free student e-mail accounts, online (class) grades, online (class) registration, online (class) schedules. Campuswide network is available. 100% of college-owned or -operated housing units are wired for high-speed Internet access. Wireless service is available via classrooms, computer centers, computer labs, dorm rooms, learning centers, libraries, student centers.

Student Life *Housing:* on-campus residence required for freshman year. *Options:* men-only, women-only. Campus housing is university owned. Freshman campus housing is guaranteed. *Activities and organizations:* drama/theater group, choral group, Campus Activity Board, Baptist Campus Ministry, Student Government Association, Fellowship of Christian Athletes. *Campus security:* 24-hour emergency response devices and patrols, controlled dormitory access, text alerts. *Student services:* health clinic, personal/psychological counseling.

Athletics Member NAIA. *Intercollegiate sports:* baseball M(s), basketball M(s)/W(s), cheerleading W(s), cross-country running M(s)/W(s), golf M(s)/W(s), soccer M(s)/W(s), softball W(s), tennis M(s)/W(s), track and field M(s)/W(s), volleyball W(s). *Intramural sports:* basketball M/W, golf M/W, soccer M/W, softball M/W, tennis M/W, track and field M/W, volleyball M/W.

Standardized Tests *Required:* SAT or ACT (for admission). *Recommended:* SAT and SAT Subject Tests or ACT (for admission), SAT Subject Tests (for admission).

Costs (2012–13) *Comprehensive fee:* $26,330 includes full-time tuition ($17,110), mandatory fees ($570), and room and board ($8650). Full-time tuition and fees vary according to course load. Part-time tuition: $609 per credit hour. Part-time tuition and fees vary according to course load. *Required fees:* $346 per year part-time. *College room only:* $5100. Room and board charges vary according to housing facility. *Payment plan:* installment. *Waivers:* employees or children of employees.

Financial Aid Of all full-time matriculated undergraduates who enrolled in 2012, 902 applied for aid, 816 were judged to have need, 142 had their need fully met. 63 Federal Work-Study jobs (averaging $2175). In 2012, 86 non-need-based awards were made. *Average percent of need met:* 54%. *Average financial aid package:* $15,931. *Average need-based loan:* $4642. *Average need-based gift aid:* $5189. *Average non-need-based aid:* $5200. *Average indebtedness upon graduation:* $29,474.

Applying *Options:* electronic application, deferred entrance. *Application fee:* $50. *Required:* high school transcript, minimum 2.8 GPA. *Required for some:* interview. *Application deadlines:* rolling (freshmen), rolling (transfers). *Notification:* continuous (freshmen), continuous (transfers).

Freshman Application Contact Mrs. Charity Wittner, Director of Enrollment Services, University of Mobile, 5735 College Parkway, Mobile, AL 36613-2842. *Phone:* 251-442-2507. *Toll-free phone:* 800-946-7267. *Fax:* 251-442-2498. *E-mail:* cwittner@umobile.edu. *Website:* http://www.umobile.edu/.

University of Montevallo
Montevallo, Alabama

- **State-supported** comprehensive, founded 1896
- **Small-town** 160-acre campus with easy access to Birmingham
- **Coed** 2,598 undergraduate students, 89% full-time, 65% women, 35% men
- **Moderately difficult** entrance level, 87% of applicants were admitted

Undergraduates 2,319 full-time, 279 part-time. Students come from 20 other countries; 5% are from out of state; 14% Black or African American, non-Hispanic/Latino; 3% Hispanic/Latino; 0.5% Asian, non-Hispanic/Latino; 0.5% American Indian or Alaska Native, non-Hispanic/Latino; 2% Two or more races, non-Hispanic/Latino; 7% Race/ethnicity unknown; 2% international; 7% transferred in; 47% live on campus. *Retention:* 78% of full-time freshmen returned.

Freshmen *Admission:* 1,385 applied, 1,209 admitted, 552 enrolled. *Average high school GPA:* 3.32. *Test scores:* ACT scores over 18: 98%; ACT scores over 24: 46%; ACT scores over 30: 5%.

Faculty *Total:* 223, 64% full-time. *Student/faculty ratio:* 16:1.

Academics *Calendar:* semesters. *Degrees:* bachelor's, master's, and post-master's certificates. *Special study options:* academic remediation for entering students, accelerated degree program, advanced placement credit, distance learning, double majors, honors programs, independent study, internships, part-time degree program, services for LD students, study abroad, summer session for credit. *ROTC:* Army (c), Air Force (c). *Unusual degree programs:* 3-2 engineering with Auburn University, University of Alabama at Birmingham.

Computers on Campus 340 computers/terminals are available on campus for general student use. Students can access the following: campus intranet, computer help desk, free student e-mail accounts, online (class) grades, online (class) registration, online (class) schedules. Campuswide network is available. 100% of college-owned or -operated housing units are wired for high-speed

Internet access. Wireless service is available via classrooms, computer centers, computer labs, dorm rooms, libraries, student centers.

Student Life *Housing:* on-campus residence required for freshman year. *Options:* coed, men-only, women-only. Campus housing is university owned. Freshman campus housing is guaranteed. *Activities and organizations:* drama/theater group, student-run newspaper, television station, choral group, Student Government Association, University Programming Council, Campus Ministries, Greek Life, Environmental Club, national fraternities, national sororities. *Campus security:* 24-hour emergency response devices and patrols, late-night transport/escort service, controlled dormitory access. *Student services:* health clinic, personal/psychological counseling.

Athletics Member NCAA. All Division II. *Intercollegiate sports:* baseball M(s), basketball M(s)/W(s), cross-country running M/W, golf M(s)/W(s), soccer M(s)/W(s), tennis W(s), track and field W, volleyball W(s). *Intramural sports:* basketball M/W, bowling M, football M, golf M, tennis M/W, volleyball M/W.

Standardized Tests *Required:* SAT or ACT (for admission). *Recommended:* ACT (for admission).

Costs (2012–13) *Tuition:* state resident $8790 full-time, $293 per credit hour part-time; nonresident $17,580 full-time, $586 per credit hour part-time. *Required fees:* $490 full-time. *Room and board:* $5522. Room and board charges vary according to housing facility. *Waivers:* employees or children of employees.

Financial Aid Of all full-time matriculated undergraduates who enrolled in 2012, 1,713 applied for aid, 1,458 were judged to have need, 241 had their need fully met. 108 Federal Work-Study jobs (averaging $1550). In 2012, 517 non-need-based awards were made. *Average percent of need met:* 58%. *Average financial aid package:* $9488. *Average need-based loan:* $4215. *Average need-based gift aid:* $6447. *Average non-need-based aid:* $8036. *Average indebtedness upon graduation:* $24,723.

Applying *Options:* electronic application, early admission, deferred entrance. *Application fee:* $30. *Required:* high school transcript, minimum 2.0 GPA. *Recommended:* interview. *Application deadlines:* 8/1 (freshmen), rolling (transfers). *Notification:* 9/1 (freshmen).

Freshman Application Contact Mr. Greg Embry, Director of Admissions, University of Montevallo, University of Montevallo, Office of Admissions, Station 6030, Montevallo, AL 35115-6030. *Phone:* 205-665-6030. *Toll-free phone:* 800-292-4349. *Fax:* 205-665-6032. *E-mail:* admissions@montevallo.edu. *Website:* http://www.montevallo.edu/.

University of North Alabama
Florence, Alabama

- **State-supported** comprehensive, founded 1830
- **Urban** 200-acre campus with easy access to Huntsville, AL
- **Endowment** $23.6 million
- **Coed** 6,082 undergraduate students, 81% full-time, 58% women, 42% men
- **Minimally difficult** entrance level, 88% of applicants were admitted

Undergraduates 4,941 full-time, 1,141 part-time. Students come from 38 states and territories; 34 other countries; 15% are from out of state; 13% Black or African American, non-Hispanic/Latino; 2% Hispanic/Latino; 0.5% Asian, non-Hispanic/Latino; 0.1% Native Hawaiian or other Pacific Islander, non-Hispanic/Latino; 0.9% American Indian or Alaska Native, non-Hispanic/Latino; 1% Two or more races, non-Hispanic/Latino; 3% Race/ethnicity unknown; 4% international; 10% transferred in; 23% live on campus. *Retention:* 69% of full-time freshmen returned.

Freshmen *Admission:* 2,419 applied, 2,140 admitted, 1,078 enrolled. *Average high school GPA:* 3.07. *Test scores:* SAT critical reading scores over 500: 39%; SAT math scores over 500: 36%; ACT scores over 18: 85%; SAT critical reading scores over 600: 10%; SAT math scores over 600: 6%; ACT scores over 24: 29%; SAT math scores over 700: 3%; ACT scores over 30: 3%.

Faculty *Total:* 331, 72% full-time, 63% with terminal degrees. *Student/faculty ratio:* 21:1.

Academics *Calendar:* semesters. *Degrees:* bachelor's, master's, post-master's, and postbachelor's certificates. *Special study options:* academic remediation for entering students, accelerated degree program, advanced placement credit, cooperative education, distance learning, double majors, English as a second language, freshman honors college, honors programs, independent study, internships, off-campus study, part-time degree program, services for LD students, student-designed majors, study abroad, summer session for credit. *ROTC:* Army (b).

Computers on Campus 1,000 computers/terminals are available on campus for general student use. Students can access the following: campus intranet, computer help desk, free student e-mail accounts, online (class) grades, online (class) registration, online (class) schedules. Campuswide network is available. Wireless service is available via entire campus.

Student Life *Housing options:* coed, men-only, women-only. Campus housing is university owned. *Activities and organizations:* drama/theater group, student-run newspaper, radio station, choral group, marching band, Student Government Association, University Program Council, Baptist campus ministries, Physical Education Majors Club, Residence Hall Association, national fraternities, national sororities. *Campus security:* 24-hour emergency response devices and patrols, student patrols, late-night transport/escort service, controlled dormitory access. *Student services:* health clinic, personal/psychological counseling, women's center.

Athletics Member NCAA. All Division II. *Intercollegiate sports:* baseball M(s), basketball M(s)/W(s), cheerleading M(s)/W(s), cross-country running M(s)/W(s), football M(s), golf M(s), soccer W(s), softball W(s), tennis M(s)/W(s), volleyball W(s). *Intramural sports:* badminton M/W, baseball M, basketball M/W, bowling M/W, cross-country running M/W, football M/W, golf M, racquetball M/W, rugby M, softball W, swimming and diving M/W, table tennis M/W, tennis M/W, volleyball M/W, weight lifting M/W.

Standardized Tests *Required:* SAT or ACT (for admission).

Costs (2012–13) *Tuition:* state resident $6660 full-time, $222 per credit hour part-time; nonresident $13,320 full-time, $444 per credit hour part-time. Full-time tuition and fees vary according to course load and program. Part-time tuition and fees vary according to course load and program. *Required fees:* $1488 full-time. *Room and board:* $5678. Room and board charges vary according to board plan and housing facility. *Payment plan:* installment. *Waivers:* senior citizens and employees or children of employees.

Financial Aid Of all full-time matriculated undergraduates who enrolled in 2011, 3,623 applied for aid, 3,323 were judged to have need, 1,636 had their need fully met. 163 Federal Work-Study jobs (averaging $1604). 382 state and other part-time jobs (averaging $1413). In 2011, 101 non-need-based awards were made. *Average percent of need met:* 62%. *Average financial aid package:* $7457. *Average need-based loan:* $3825. *Average need-based gift aid:* $4715. *Average non-need-based aid:* $2061. *Average indebtedness upon graduation:* $34,100.

Applying *Options:* electronic application, early admission, deferred entrance. *Application fee:* $25. *Required:* high school transcript. *Application deadlines:* rolling (freshmen), rolling (out-of-state freshmen), rolling (transfers).

Freshman Application Contact Mrs. Kim O. Mauldin, Director of Admissions, University of North Alabama, One Harrison Plaza, Florence, AL 35632-0001. *Phone:* 256-765-4680. *Toll-free phone:* 800-TALK-UNA. *Fax:* 256-765-4329. *E-mail:* admissions@una.edu. *Website:* http://www.una.edu/.

University of Phoenix–Birmingham Campus

Birmingham, Alabama

Admissions Office Contact University of Phoenix–Birmingham Campus, One Corporate Center, Suite 400, Birmingham, AL 35244. *Toll-free phone:* 866-766-0766.
Website: http://www.phoenix.edu/.

University of South Alabama

Mobile, Alabama

- **State-supported** university, founded 1963
- **Suburban** 1225-acre campus
- **Endowment** $126.7 million
- **Coed** 11,315 undergraduate students, 77% full-time, 56% women, 44% men
- **Moderately difficult** entrance level, 87% of applicants were admitted

Undergraduates 8,708 full-time, 2,607 part-time. Students come from 54 states and territories; 87 other countries; 18% are from out of state; 22% Black or African American, non-Hispanic/Latino; 3% Hispanic/Latino; 3% Asian, non-Hispanic/Latino; 0.2% Native Hawaiian or other Pacific Islander, non-Hispanic/Latino; 0.9% American Indian or Alaska Native, non-Hispanic/Latino; 2% Two or more races, non-Hispanic/Latino; 1% Race/ethnicity unknown; 4% international; 9% transferred in; 25% live on campus. *Retention:* 66% of full-time freshmen returned.

Freshmen *Admission:* 4,770 applied, 4,159 admitted, 1,944 enrolled. *Average high school GPA:* 3.38. *Test scores:* SAT critical reading scores over 500: 55%; SAT math scores over 500: 59%; SAT writing scores over 500: 51%; ACT scores over 18: 93%; SAT critical reading scores over 600: 17%; SAT math scores over 600: 21%; SAT writing scores over 600: 11%; ACT scores over 24: 41%; SAT critical reading scores over 700: 3%; SAT math scores over 700: 2%; SAT writing scores over 700: 4%; ACT scores over 30: 6%.

Faculty *Total:* 858, 62% full-time. *Student/faculty ratio:* 21:1.

Academics *Calendar:* semesters. *Degrees:* certificates, bachelor's, master's, doctoral, post-master's, and postbachelor's certificates. *Special study options:*

academic remediation for entering students, accelerated degree program, adult/continuing education programs, advanced placement credit, cooperative education, distance learning, double majors, English as a second language, freshman honors college, honors programs, part-time degree program, services for LD students, study abroad, summer session for credit. *ROTC:* Army (b), Air Force (b).

Computers on Campus 500 computers/terminals are available on campus for general student use. Students can access the following: campus intranet, computer help desk, free student e-mail accounts, online (class) grades, online (class) registration, online (class) schedules. Campuswide network is available. 100% of college-owned or -operated housing units are wired for high-speed Internet access. Wireless service is available via entire campus.

Student Life *Housing options:* coed, disabled students. Campus housing is university owned and is provided by a third party. *Activities and organizations:* drama/theater group, student-run newspaper, television station, choral group, marching band, Student Government Association, African American Student Association, Council of International Student Organizations, Alpha Epsilon Delta Pre-Health Professions, Panhellenic Council, national fraternities, national sororities. *Campus security:* 24-hour emergency response devices and patrols, late-night transport/escort service. *Student services:* health clinic, personal/psychological counseling, legal services.

Athletics Member NCAA. All Division I. *Intercollegiate sports:* baseball M(s), basketball M(s)/W(s), cross-country running M(s)/W(s), fencing M(c)/W(c), football M(s)(c), golf M/W, soccer W(s), tennis M(s)/W(s), track and field M(s)/W(s), volleyball W(s). *Intramural sports:* badminton M/W, basketball M/W, bowling M/W, cheerleading M(c)/W(c), golf M/W, racquetball M/W, sailing M(c)/W(c), soccer M/W, softball M/W, table tennis M/W, tennis M/W, volleyball M/W, water polo M/W.

Standardized Tests *Required for some:* SAT or ACT (for admission).

Costs (2013–14) *Tuition:* state resident $7950 full-time, $265 per hour part-time; nonresident $15,900 full-time, $530 per hour part-time. Full-time tuition and fees vary according to course load and program. Part-time tuition and fees vary according to course load and program. *Room and board:* $7150; room only: $3900. Room and board charges vary according to board plan and housing facility. *Payment plan:* installment. *Waivers:* employees or children of employees.

Financial Aid Of all full-time matriculated undergraduates who enrolled in 2011, 6,038 applied for aid, 4,976 were judged to have need, 513 had their need fully met. In 2011, 849 non-need-based awards were made. *Average percent of need met:* 57%. *Average financial aid package:* $9155. *Average need-based loan:* $4282. *Average need-based gift aid:* $6223. *Average non-need-based aid:* $4350.

Applying *Options:* electronic application, early admission. *Application fee:* $35. *Required:* high school transcript. *Required for some:* 1 letter of recommendation. *Recommended:* minimum 2.0 GPA. *Application deadlines:* 7/15 (freshmen), 7/15 (out-of-state freshmen), 8/10 (transfers). *Notification:* continuous until 8/18 (freshmen), continuous until 8/18 (out-of-state freshmen), continuous until 8/18 (transfers).

Freshman Application Contact Mr. Christopher A. Lynch, Director, New Student Recruitment, University of South Alabama, Mobile, AL 36688-0002. *Phone:* 251-460-6141. *Toll-free phone:* 800-872-5247. *E-mail:* admiss@usouthal.edu.
Website: http://www.southalabama.edu/.

The University of West Alabama

Livingston, Alabama

- **State-supported** comprehensive, founded 1835
- **Small-town** 514-acre campus
- **Coed** 2,108 undergraduate students, 85% full-time, 60% women, 40% men
- **Minimally difficult** entrance level, 97% of applicants were admitted

Undergraduates 1,793 full-time, 315 part-time. Students come from 37 states and territories; 18 other countries; 21% are from out of state; 44% Black or African American, non-Hispanic/Latino; 1% Hispanic/Latino; 0.5% Asian, non-Hispanic/Latino; 0.3% Native Hawaiian or other Pacific Islander, non-Hispanic/Latino; 0.5% American Indian or Alaska Native, non-Hispanic/Latino; 0.6% Two or more races, non-Hispanic/Latino; 6% Race/ethnicity unknown; 5% international; 14% transferred in; 39% live on campus. *Retention:* 56% of full-time freshmen returned.

Freshmen *Admission:* 467 applied, 455 admitted, 207 enrolled. *Test scores:* ACT scores over 18: 80%; ACT scores over 24: 13%; ACT scores over 30: 1%.

Faculty *Total:* 268, 47% full-time, 66% with terminal degrees. *Student/faculty ratio:* 26:1.

Academics *Calendar:* semesters. *Degrees:* associate, bachelor's, master's, and post-master's certificates. *Special study options:* academic remediation for entering students, accelerated degree program, advanced placement credit, cooperative education, distance learning, double majors, honors programs, independent study, internships, off-campus study, part-time degree program, services for LD students, summer session for credit. *ROTC:* Army (c), Air Force (c). *Unusual degree programs:* 3-2 engineering with Auburn University, The University of Alabama at Birmingham, Mississippi State University, The University of Alabama; forestry with Auburn University; nursing with University of Alabama.

Computers on Campus 400 computers/terminals are available on campus for general student use. Students can access the following: computer help desk, free student e-mail accounts, online (class) grades, online (class) registration, online (class) schedules, Wireless intranet is available campus wide for all students to use. Campuswide network is available. 100% of college-owned or -operated housing units are wired for high-speed Internet access. Wireless service is available via entire campus.

Student Life *Housing:* on-campus residence required through sophomore year. *Options:* coed. Campus housing is university owned. *Activities and organizations:* drama/theater group, student-run newspaper, television station, choral group, marching band, The Student Government Association, The UWA Band, The UWA Choir, Fellowship of Christian Athletes (FCA), Livingston's Early Alumni Development (LEAD), national fraternities, national sororities. *Campus security:* 24-hour patrols, late-night transport/escort service. *Student services:* health clinic, personal/psychological counseling.

Athletics Member NCAA. All Division II. *Intercollegiate sports:* baseball M(s), basketball M(s)/W(s), cross-country running M(s)/W(s), football M(s), soccer M(s)/W(s), softball W(s), tennis M(s)/W(s), volleyball W(s). *Intramural sports:* archery M/W, basketball M/W, football M/W, golf M/W, soccer M/W, softball M/W, table tennis M/W, tennis M/W, ultimate Frisbee M/W, volleyball M/W, water polo M/W, weight lifting M/W.

Standardized Tests *Required:* SAT or ACT (for admission).

Costs (2013–14) *Tuition:* state resident $6170 full-time, $263 per credit part-time; nonresident $12,340 full-time, $526 per credit part-time. Full-time tuition and fees vary according to course load, degree level, and program. Part-time tuition and fees vary according to course load, degree level, and program. *Required fees:* $1150 full-time. *Room and board:* $5920; room only: $3640. Room and board charges vary according to board plan and housing facility. *Payment plan:* installment. *Waivers:* employees or children of employees.

Financial Aid Of all full-time matriculated undergraduates who enrolled in 2012, 1,585 applied for aid, 1,393 were judged to have need, 14 had their need fully met. 132 Federal Work-Study jobs (averaging $3400). In 2012, 77 non-need-based awards were made. *Average percent of need met:* 28%. *Average financial aid package:* $9610. *Average need-based gift aid:* $4912. *Average non-need-based aid:* $3750. *Average indebtedness upon graduation:* $27,815.

Applying *Options:* electronic application, early admission, deferred entrance. *Application fee:* $35. *Required:* high school transcript, minimum 2.0 GPA. *Application deadlines:* rolling (freshmen), rolling (transfers). *Notification:* continuous (freshmen), continuous (transfers).

Freshman Application Contact Mr. Danny Buckalew, Vice President of Student Affairs, The University of West Alabama, Station 4, Livingston, AL 35470. *Phone:* 205-652-3581. *Toll-free phone:* 800-621-8044. *Fax:* 205-652-3881. *E-mail:* dbuckalew@uwa.edu.
Website: http://www.uwa.edu/.

Virginia College in Birmingham

Birmingham, Alabama

Director of Admissions Director of Admissions, Virginia College in Birmingham, 488 Palisades Boulevard, Birmingham, AL 35209. *Phone:* 205-802-1200.
Website: http://www.vc.edu/.

Virginia College in Huntsville

Huntsville, Alabama

Freshman Application Contact Director of Admission, Virginia College in Huntsville, 2021 Drake Avenue SW, Huntsville, AL 35801. *Phone:* 256-533-7387. *Fax:* 256-533-7785.
Website: http://www.vc.edu/.

ALASKA

Alaska Bible College

Glennallen, Alaska

- **Independent nondenominational** 4-year, founded 1966
- **Rural** 97-acre campus
- **Endowment** $46,833
- **Coed** 34 undergraduate students, 82% full-time, 44% women, 56% men
- **Minimally difficult** entrance level

Undergraduates 28 full-time, 6 part-time. Students come from 14 states and territories; 57% are from out of state; 3% Black or African American, non-Hispanic/Latino; 3% Hispanic/Latino; 15% American Indian or Alaska Native, non-Hispanic/Latino; 93% live on campus. *Retention:* 20% of full-time freshmen returned.

Freshmen *Admission:* 11 enrolled.

Faculty *Total:* 11, 73% full-time, 9% with terminal degrees. *Student/faculty ratio:* 3:1.

Academics *Calendar:* semesters. *Degrees:* certificates, associate, and bachelor's. *Special study options:* academic remediation for entering students, advanced placement credit, distance learning, double majors, independent study, internships, off-campus study, part-time degree program.

Computers on Campus 8 computers/terminals are available on campus for general student use. Students can access the following: campus intranet, computer help desk, free student e-mail accounts, online (class) grades, online (class) registration, online (class) schedules. Campuswide network is available. 100% of college-owned or -operated housing units are wired for high-speed Internet access. Wireless service is available via entire campus.

Student Life *Housing:* on-campus residence required through sophomore year. *Options:* men-only, women-only. Campus housing is university owned. Freshman campus housing is guaranteed. *Activities and organizations:* student-run radio station. *Campus security:* 24-hour emergency response devices.

Standardized Tests *Required:* SAT or ACT (for admission).

Costs (2013–14) *Comprehensive fee:* $14,790 includes full-time tuition ($9000), mandatory fees ($390), and room and board ($5400). Part-time tuition: $375 per credit. *Room and board:* Room and board charges vary according to housing facility. *Payment plan:* installment. *Waivers:* employees or children of employees.

Financial Aid Of all full-time matriculated undergraduates who enrolled in 2009, 8 applied for aid, 8 were judged to have need. 20 state and other part-time jobs (averaging $842). *Average need-based gift aid:* $850. *Average indebtedness upon graduation:* $8075. *Financial aid deadline:* 7/1.

Applying *Options:* electronic application, deferred entrance. *Application fee:* $35. *Required:* essay or personal statement, high school transcript, minimum 2.0 GPA, interview, 3 reference forms. *Application deadlines:* 7/1 (freshmen), 7/1 (transfers). *Notification:* continuous until 7/15 (freshmen), continuous until 7/15 (transfers).

Freshman Application Contact Nikki Palmer, Director of Admissions, Alaska Bible College, PO Box 289, Glennallen, AK 99588. *Phone:* 907-822-3201 Ext. 224. *Toll-free phone:* 800-478-7884. *Fax:* 907-822-5027. *E-mail:* npalmer@akbible.edu.
Website: http://www.akbible.edu/.

Alaska Pacific University

Anchorage, Alaska

- **Independent** comprehensive, founded 1959
- **Urban** 170-acre campus
- **Endowment** $42.7 million
- **Coed** 436 undergraduate students, 64% full-time, 64% women, 36% men
- **Moderately difficult** entrance level, 62% of applicants were admitted

Undergraduates 277 full-time, 159 part-time. Students come from 15 states and territories; 31% are from out of state; 2% Black or African American, non-Hispanic/Latino; 3% Hispanic/Latino; 2% Asian, non-Hispanic/Latino; 0.9% Native Hawaiian or other Pacific Islander, non-Hispanic/Latino; 12% American Indian or Alaska Native, non-Hispanic/Latino; 14% Two or more races, non-Hispanic/Latino; 14% Race/ethnicity unknown; 6% transferred in; 26% live on campus. *Retention:* 65% of full-time freshmen returned.

Freshmen *Admission:* 180 applied, 112 admitted, 29 enrolled. *Average high school GPA:* 3.32. *Test scores:* SAT critical reading scores over 500: 55%; SAT math scores over 500: 50%; SAT writing scores over 500: 50%; ACT scores over 18: 89%; SAT critical reading scores over 600: 30%; SAT math scores over 600: 15%; SAT writing scores over 600: 25%; ACT scores over 24: 22%; SAT critical reading scores over 700: 10%; SAT math scores over 700: 5%; SAT writing scores over 700: 10%; ACT scores over 30: 11%.

Faculty *Total:* 115, 43% full-time. *Student/faculty ratio:* 17:1.

Academics *Calendar:* semesters. *Degrees:* certificates, associate, bachelor's, master's, doctoral, and postbachelor's certificates. *Special study options:* academic remediation for entering students, adult/continuing education programs, advanced placement credit, distance learning, double majors, independent study, internships, part-time degree program, services for LD students, student-designed majors, study abroad, summer session for credit. *ROTC:* Army (c), Air Force (c). *Unusual degree programs:* 3-2 business administration.

Computers on Campus 105 computers/terminals and 480 ports are available on campus for general student use. Students can access the following: campus intranet, computer help desk, free student e-mail accounts, online (class) grades, online (class) registration, online (class) schedules. Campuswide network is available. 100% of college-owned or -operated housing units are wired for high-speed Internet access. Wireless service is available via entire campus.

Student Life *Housing:* on-campus residence required for freshman year. *Options:* coed. Campus housing is university owned. Freshman campus housing is guaranteed. *Activities and organizations:* drama/theater group, student-run newspaper, choral group, ASAPU (Associated Students of Alaska Pacific University), Photography Club, Dive Club, basketball club, Spectrum Club. *Campus security:* 24-hour emergency response devices, student patrols, late-night transport/escort service, controlled dormitory access. *Student services:* personal/psychological counseling.

Athletics *Intramural sports:* basketball M/W, skiing (cross-country) M/W, soccer M/W, volleyball M/W.

Standardized Tests *Required:* SAT or ACT (for admission).

Costs (2013–14) *Comprehensive fee:* $39,180 includes full-time tuition ($29,700), mandatory fees ($180), and room and board ($9300). Full-time tuition and fees vary according to course load, degree level, program, and reciprocity agreements. Part-time tuition: $1240 per semester hour. Part-time tuition and fees vary according to course load, degree level, and program. *College room only:* $4400. Room and board charges vary according to board plan and housing facility. *Payment plans:* installment, deferred payment. *Waivers:* employees or children of employees.

Financial Aid Of all full-time matriculated undergraduates who enrolled in 2011, 185 applied for aid, 118 were judged to have need, 57 had their need fully met. 41 Federal Work-Study jobs (averaging $1010). In 2011, 57 non-need-based awards were made. *Average percent of need met:* 40%. *Average financial aid package:* $17,524. *Average need-based loan:* $3175. *Average need-based gift aid:* $6414. *Average non-need-based aid:* $16,500. *Average indebtedness upon graduation:* $28,000.

Applying *Options:* electronic application, deferred entrance. *Application fee:* $25. *Required:* essay or personal statement, high school transcript, minimum 2.5 GPA, 2 letters of recommendation. *Required for some:* interview. *Application deadlines:* 8/15 (freshmen), 8/15 (transfers).

Freshman Application Contact Mr. Barclay Roeder, Director of Admissions, Alaska Pacific University, 4101 University Drive, Anchorage, AK 99508. *Phone:* 907-564-8248. *Toll-free phone:* 800-252-7528. *Fax:* 907-564-8317. *E-mail:* admissions@alaskapacific.edu. *Website:* http://www.alaskapacific.edu/.

Charter College
Anchorage, Alaska

Director of Admissions Ms. Lily Sirianni, Vice President, Charter College, 2221 East Northern Lights Boulevard, Suite 120, Anchorage, AK 99508. *Phone:* 907-277-1000. *Toll-free phone:* 888-200-9942. *Website:* http://www.chartercollege.edu/.

University of Alaska Anchorage
Anchorage, Alaska

- **State-supported** comprehensive, founded 1954, part of University of Alaska System
- **Urban** 428-acre campus
- **Coed** 17,129 undergraduate students, 46% full-time, 58% women, 42% men
- **Noncompetitive** entrance level, 76% of applicants were admitted

Undergraduates 7,936 full-time, 9,193 part-time. 10% are from out of state; 4% Black or African American, non-Hispanic/Latino; 7% Hispanic/Latino; 7% Asian, non-Hispanic/Latino; 0.9% Native Hawaiian or other Pacific Islander, non-Hispanic/Latino; 12% American Indian or Alaska Native, non-Hispanic/Latino; 3% Two or more races, non-Hispanic/Latino; 8% Race/ethnicity unknown; 0.6% international; 4% transferred in. *Retention:* 73% of full-time freshmen returned.

Freshmen *Admission:* 3,924 applied, 2,967 admitted, 1,997 enrolled. *Average high school GPA:* 3.0. *Test scores:* SAT critical reading scores over 500: 59%; ACT scores over 18: 80%; SAT critical reading scores over 600: 21%; ACT scores over 24: 32%; SAT critical reading scores over 700: 8%; ACT scores over 30: 3%.

Faculty *Total:* 1,390, 49% full-time, 27% with terminal degrees. *Student/faculty ratio:* 12:1.

Academics *Calendar:* semesters. *Degrees:* certificates, associate, bachelor's, master's, doctoral, post-master's, and postbachelor's certificates. *Special study options:* academic remediation for entering students, adult/continuing education programs, advanced placement credit, cooperative education, distance learning, double majors, English as a second language, honors programs, independent study, internships, off-campus study, part-time degree program, services for LD students, student-designed majors, study abroad, summer session for credit. *ROTC:* Army (b), Air Force (b).

Computers on Campus Students can access the following: campus intranet, computer help desk, free student e-mail accounts, online (class) registration. Campuswide network is available. Wireless service is available via entire campus.

Student Life *Housing options:* coed, disabled students. *Activities and organizations:* drama/theater group, student-run newspaper, radio station, choral group, Accounting Club, African-American Students Association, Association of Latin-American Spanish Students, Inter-Varsity Christian Fellowship, Student Nurses Association, national fraternities, national sororities. *Campus security:* 24-hour emergency response devices and patrols, student patrols, late-night transport/escort service, controlled dormitory access. *Student services:* health clinic, personal/psychological counseling, women's center.

Athletics Member NCAA. All Division II. *Intercollegiate sports:* basketball M(s)/W(s), cross-country running M(s)/W, gymnastics W(s), ice hockey M(s), skiing (cross-country) M(s)/W(s), skiing (downhill) M(s)/W(s), track and field M/W, volleyball W(s). *Intramural sports:* basketball M/W, cheerleading M/W, ice hockey M/W, soccer M/W, volleyball M/W, water polo M/W.

Standardized Tests *Required:* SAT or ACT (for admission), Completion of either SAT, ACT or a UAA approved test required (for admission).

Costs (2012–13) *Tuition:* state resident $4950 full-time; nonresident $17,400 full-time. Full-time tuition and fees vary according to course level and location. Part-time tuition and fees vary according to course level and location. *Room and board:* $9780; room only: $5980. Room and board charges vary according to board plan and housing facility.

Financial Aid Of all full-time matriculated undergraduates who enrolled in 2012, 3,827 applied for aid, 3,070 were judged to have need, 682 had their need fully met. In 2012, 374 non-need-based awards were made. *Average percent of need met:* 69%. *Average financial aid package:* $8188. *Average need-based loan:* $4286. *Average need-based gift aid:* $2810. *Average non-need-based aid:* $2392. *Average indebtedness upon graduation:* $30,363.

Applying *Options:* electronic application, deferred entrance. *Application fee:* $50. *Required:* minimum 2.0 GPA. *Required for some:* high school transcript. *Application deadlines:* 6/15 (freshmen), rolling (transfers). *Notification:* continuous (freshmen), continuous (transfers).

Freshman Application Contact Enrollment Services, University of Alaska Anchorage, PO Box 141629, 3901 Old Seward Highway, Anchorage, AK 99508-8046. *Phone:* 907-786-1480. *Fax:* 907-786-4888. *E-mail:* enroll@uaa.alaska.edu. *Website:* http://www.uaa.alaska.edu/.

University of Alaska Anchorage, Kenai Peninsula College
Soldotna, Alaska

- **State-supported** primarily 2-year, founded 1964, part of University of Alaska System
- **Rural** 360-acre campus
- **Coed** 2,733 undergraduate students
- **Noncompetitive** entrance level

Academics *Calendar:* semesters. *Degrees:* certificates, associate, and bachelor's. *Special study options:* academic remediation for entering students, adult/continuing education programs, advanced placement credit, cooperative education, distance learning, English as a second language, part-time degree program, services for LD students.

Computers on Campus Campuswide network is available.

Student Life *Housing options:* coed. *Campus security:* 24-hour emergency response devices. *Student services:* health clinic.

Standardized Tests *Required:* ACT, SAT or ACCUPLACER scores (for admission).

Financial Aid Of all full-time matriculated undergraduates who enrolled in 2011, 50 Federal Work-Study jobs (averaging $3000). 50 state and other part-time jobs (averaging $3000).

Applying *Options:* electronic application. *Application fee:* $40. *Required:* high school transcript. *Application deadlines:* rolling (freshmen), rolling (transfers).

Freshman Application Contact Ms. Shelly Love Blatchford, Admission and Registration Coordinator, University of Alaska Anchorage, Kenai Peninsula

College, 156 College Road, Soldotna, AK 99669-9798. *Phone:* 907-262-0311. *Toll-free phone:* 877-262-0330.
Website: http://www.kpc.alaska.edu/.

University of Alaska Fairbanks
Fairbanks, Alaska

- **State-supported** university, founded 1917, part of University of Alaska System
- **Small-town** 2250-acre campus
- **Endowment** $74.1 million
- **Coed** 8,131 undergraduate students, 46% full-time, 58% women, 42% men
- **Minimally difficult** entrance level, 75% of applicants were admitted

Undergraduates 3,727 full-time, 4,404 part-time. Students come from 49 states and territories; 49 other countries; 12% are from out of state; 3% Black or African American, non-Hispanic/Latino; 5% Hispanic/Latino; 1% Asian, non-Hispanic/Latino; 0.2% Native Hawaiian or other Pacific Islander, non-Hispanic/Latino; 14% American Indian or Alaska Native, non-Hispanic/Latino; 4% Two or more races, non-Hispanic/Latino; 24% Race/ethnicity unknown; 1% international; 6% transferred in; 24% live on campus. *Retention:* 74% of full-time freshmen returned.
Freshmen *Admission:* 1,541 applied, 1,163 admitted, 945 enrolled. *Average high school GPA:* 3.15. *Test scores:* SAT critical reading scores over 500: 64%; SAT math scores over 500: 60%; SAT writing scores over 500: 53%; ACT scores over 18: 79%; SAT critical reading scores over 600: 24%; SAT math scores over 600: 23%; SAT writing scores over 600: 15%; ACT scores over 24: 37%; SAT critical reading scores over 700: 5%; SAT math scores over 700: 4%; SAT writing scores over 700: 2%; ACT scores over 30: 5%.
Faculty *Total:* 1,060, 32% full-time, 47% with terminal degrees. *Student/faculty ratio:* 11:1.
Academics *Calendar:* semesters. *Degrees:* certificates, associate, bachelor's, master's, doctoral, and postbachelor's certificates. *Special study options:* academic remediation for entering students, accelerated degree program, advanced placement credit, cooperative education, distance learning, double majors, English as a second language, external degree program, honors programs, independent study, internships, off-campus study, part-time degree program, services for LD students, student-designed majors, study abroad, summer session for credit. *ROTC:* Army (b). *Unusual degree programs:* 3-2 engineering; computer science.
Computers on Campus 125 computers/terminals and 22 ports are available on campus for general student use. Students can access the following: campus intranet, computer help desk, free student e-mail accounts, online (class) grades, online (class) registration, online (class) schedules, university portal, campus wireless access. Campuswide network is available. 100% of college-owned or -operated housing units are wired for high-speed Internet access. Wireless service is available via entire campus.
Student Life *Housing options:* coed, disabled students. Campus housing is university owned. Freshman applicants given priority for college housing. *Activities and organizations:* drama/theater group, student-run newspaper, radio and television station, choral group, Alpha Phi Omega, Festival of Native Arts, Socratic Society, Parkour and Free Running Club, Gay-Straight Alliance, national fraternities, national sororities. *Campus security:* 24-hour emergency response devices and patrols, student patrols, late-night transport/escort service, controlled dormitory access, ID check at door of residence halls, crime prevention and safety workshops. *Student services:* health clinic, personal/psychological counseling, women's center, legal services.
Athletics Member NCAA. All Division II except ice hockey (Division I). *Intercollegiate sports:* basketball M(s)/W(s), cross-country running M(s)/W(s), ice hockey M(s), riflery M(s)/W(s), skiing (cross-country) M(s)/W(s), swimming and diving W(s), volleyball W(s). *Intramural sports:* archery M/W, badminton M(c)/W(c), basketball M/W, cross-country running M/W, fencing M(c)/W(c), ice hockey M/W(c), riflery M/W, rugby M(c)/W(c), skiing (cross-country) M(c)/W(c), skiing (downhill) M(c)/W(c), soccer M(c)/W(c), swimming and diving M/W, tennis M(c)/W(c), volleyball W.
Standardized Tests *Required:* SAT or ACT (for admission).
Costs (2013–14) *Tuition:* state resident $5580 full-time, $168 per credit part-time; nonresident $18,270 full-time, $591 per credit part-time. Full-time tuition and fees vary according to course level, course load, location, and reciprocity agreements. Part-time tuition and fees vary according to course level, course load, location, and reciprocity agreements. *Room and board:* $7200; room only: $3680. Room and board charges vary according to board plan and housing facility. *Payment plans:* installment, deferred payment. *Waivers:* children of alumni, senior citizens, and employees or children of employees.
Financial Aid Of all full-time matriculated undergraduates who enrolled in 2011, 2,753 applied for aid, 1,977 were judged to have need, 443 had their need fully met. 17 Federal Work-Study jobs (averaging $4317). In 2011, 552 non-need-based awards were made. *Average percent of need met:* 66%. *Aver-*

age financial aid package: $9615. *Average need-based loan:* $7872. *Average need-based gift aid:* $6001. *Average non-need-based aid:* $3727. *Average indebtedness upon graduation:* $29,762. *Financial aid deadline:* 7/1.
Applying *Options:* electronic application, deferred entrance. *Application fee:* $50. *Required:* high school transcript, minimum 2.5 GPA. *Application deadlines:* 7/1 (freshmen), 7/1 (out-of-state freshmen), 7/1 (transfers). *Notification:* continuous (freshmen), continuous (out-of-state freshmen), continuous (transfers).
Freshman Application Contact Ms. Libby Eddy, Registrar and Director of Admissions, University of Alaska Fairbanks, PO Box 757480, Fairbanks, AK 99775-7480. *Phone:* 907-474-7500. *Toll-free phone:* 800-478-1823. *Fax:* 907-474-7097. *E-mail:* admissions@uaf.edu.
Website: http://www.uaf.edu/.

See next page for display ad and page 1552 for the College Close-Up.

University of Alaska Southeast
Juneau, Alaska

Freshman Application Contact Ms. Deema Ferguson, Admissions Clerk, University of Alaska Southeast, 11120 Glacier Highway, Juneau, AK 99801-8625. *Phone:* 907-796-6294 Ext. 6100. *Toll-free phone:* 877-465-4827. *Fax:* 907-796-6365. *E-mail:* admissions@uas.alaska.edu.
Website: http://www.uas.alaska.edu/.

ARIZONA

American Indian College of the Assemblies of God, Inc.
Phoenix, Arizona

Director of Admissions Sandra Gonzales, Director of Enrollment Management, American Indian College of the Assemblies of God, Inc., 10020 North Fifteenth Avenue, Phoenix, AZ 85021-2199. *Phone:* 602-944-3335 Ext. 226. *E-mail:* sgonzales@aicag.edu.
Website: http://www.aicag.edu/.

Anthem College–Phoenix
Phoenix, Arizona

Freshman Application Contact Mr. Glen Husband, Vice President of Admissions, Anthem College–Phoenix, 1515 East Indian School Road, Phoenix, AZ 85014-4901. *Phone:* 602-279-9700. *Toll-free phone:* 855-331-7767.
Website: http://anthem.edu/phoenix-arizona/.

Argosy University, Phoenix
Phoenix, Arizona

Freshman Application Contact Argosy University, Phoenix, 2233 West Dunlap Avenue, Phoenix, AZ 85021. *Phone:* 602-216-2600. *Toll-free phone:* 866-216-2777.
Website: http://www.argosy.edu/phoenix/.

Arizona Christian University
Phoenix, Arizona

- **Independent Conservative Baptist** 4-year, founded 1960
- **Urban** 19-acre campus with easy access to Phoenix
- **Coed** 683 undergraduate students, 75% full-time, 48% women, 52% men
- **Minimally difficult** entrance level, 71% of applicants were admitted

Undergraduates 509 full-time, 174 part-time. Students come from 31 states and territories; 5 other countries; 17% are from out of state; 5% Black or African American, non-Hispanic/Latino; 6% Hispanic/Latino; 1% Asian, non-Hispanic/Latino; 0.7% Native Hawaiian or other Pacific Islander, non-Hispanic/Latino; 0.7% American Indian or Alaska Native, non-Hispanic/Latino; 27% Race/ethnicity unknown; 0.9% international; 17% transferred in. *Retention:* 68% of full-time freshmen returned.
Freshmen *Admission:* 310 applied, 221 admitted, 97 enrolled.
Academics *Calendar:* 4-4-1. *Degrees:* associate and bachelor's. *Special study options:* academic remediation for entering students, adult/continuing education programs, advanced placement credit, cooperative education, double majors, independent study, internships, services for LD students, study abroad, summer session for credit. *ROTC:* Air Force (c).

Computers on Campus 44 computers/terminals are available on campus for general student use. Students can access the following: free student e-mail accounts, online (class) grades. Campuswide network is available. 100% of college-owned or -operated housing units are wired for high-speed Internet access. Wireless service is available via entire campus.

Student Life *Housing options:* men-only, women-only, disabled students. Campus housing is university owned. Freshman campus housing is guaranteed. *Activities and organizations:* drama/theater group, student-run newspaper, choral group, Student Leadership Council. *Campus security:* student patrols, controlled dormitory access. *Student services:* personal/psychological counseling.

Athletics Member NAIA, NCCAA. *Intercollegiate sports:* baseball M(s), basketball M(s)/W(s), cross-country running M(s)/W(s), golf M(s)/W(s), soccer M(s)/W(s), softball W(s), tennis M(s)/W(s), track and field M(s)/W(s), volleyball W(s). *Intramural sports:* basketball M/W, bowling M/W, football M/W, soccer M/W, table tennis M/W, volleyball M/W.

Standardized Tests *Required:* SAT or ACT (for admission).

Financial Aid Of all full-time matriculated undergraduates who enrolled in 2009, 377 applied for aid, 377 were judged to have need. 32 Federal Work-Study jobs (averaging $1333). *Average financial aid package:* $10,878. *Average need-based loan:* $4013. *Average need-based gift aid:* $8327. *Average indebtedness upon graduation:* $21,801.

Applying *Options:* electronic application, deferred entrance. *Application fee:* $30. *Required:* essay or personal statement, high school transcript, minimum 2.0 GPA, 1 letter of recommendation. *Required for some:* interview. *Application deadlines:* 8/1 (freshmen), 8/1 (transfers). *Notification:* continuous (freshmen), continuous (transfers).

Freshman Application Contact Arizona Christian University, 2625 East Cactus Road, Phoenix, AZ 85032-7042. Phone: 602-386-4154. *Toll-free phone:* 800-247-2697.

Website: http://arizonachristian.edu/.

Arizona State University

Tempe, Arizona

- **State-supported** university, founded 1885, part of Arizona State University System
- **Urban** 1952-acre campus with easy access to Phoenix
- **Coed** 59,382 undergraduate students, 84% full-time, 50% women, 50% men
- **Moderately difficult** entrance level, 88% of applicants were admitted

Undergraduates 49,945 full-time, 9,437 part-time. Students come from 54 states and territories; 93 other countries; 25% are from out of state; 5% Black or African American, non-Hispanic/Latino; 19% Hispanic/Latino; 6% Asian, non-Hispanic/Latino; 0.3% Native Hawaiian or other Pacific Islander, non-Hispanic/Latino; 2% American Indian or Alaska Native, non-Hispanic/Latino; 3% Two or more races, non-Hispanic/Latino; 1% Race/ethnicity unknown; 4% international; 12% transferred in; 20% live on campus. *Retention:* 80% of full-time freshmen returned.

Freshmen *Admission:* 30,696 applied, 26,986 admitted, 9,265 enrolled. *Average high school GPA:* 3.42. *Test scores:* SAT critical reading scores over 500: 72%; SAT math scores over 500: 77%; ACT scores over 18: 95%; SAT critical reading scores over 600: 30%; SAT math scores over 600: 38%; ACT scores over 24: 55%; SAT critical reading scores over 700: 6%; SAT math scores over 700: 9%; ACT scores over 30: 11%.

Faculty *Total:* 2,762, 92% full-time, 85% with terminal degrees. *Student/faculty ratio:* 23:1.

Academics *Calendar:* semesters. *Degrees:* certificates, bachelor's, master's, doctoral, post-master's, and postbachelor's certificates (profile includes data for the West, Polytechnic and Downtown Phoenix campuses). *Special study options:* accelerated degree program, adult/continuing education programs, advanced placement credit, cooperative education, distance learning, double majors, English as a second language, freshman honors college, honors programs, independent study, internships, off-campus study, part-time degree program, services for LD students, student-designed majors, study abroad, summer session for credit. *ROTC:* Army (b), Navy (b), Air Force (b). *Unusual degree programs:* 3-2 Global Health (BA/MA); Political Science (BA/MA); Biological Science; Biology (BS./MS); Urban Planning/Urban and Environmental Planning (BSP./MUEP); American Studies/ Interdisciplinary Studies (BA/MA) Biochemistry/Emphasis in Medicinal Chemistry (BS/MS); Communication Studies (BA or BS/MA).

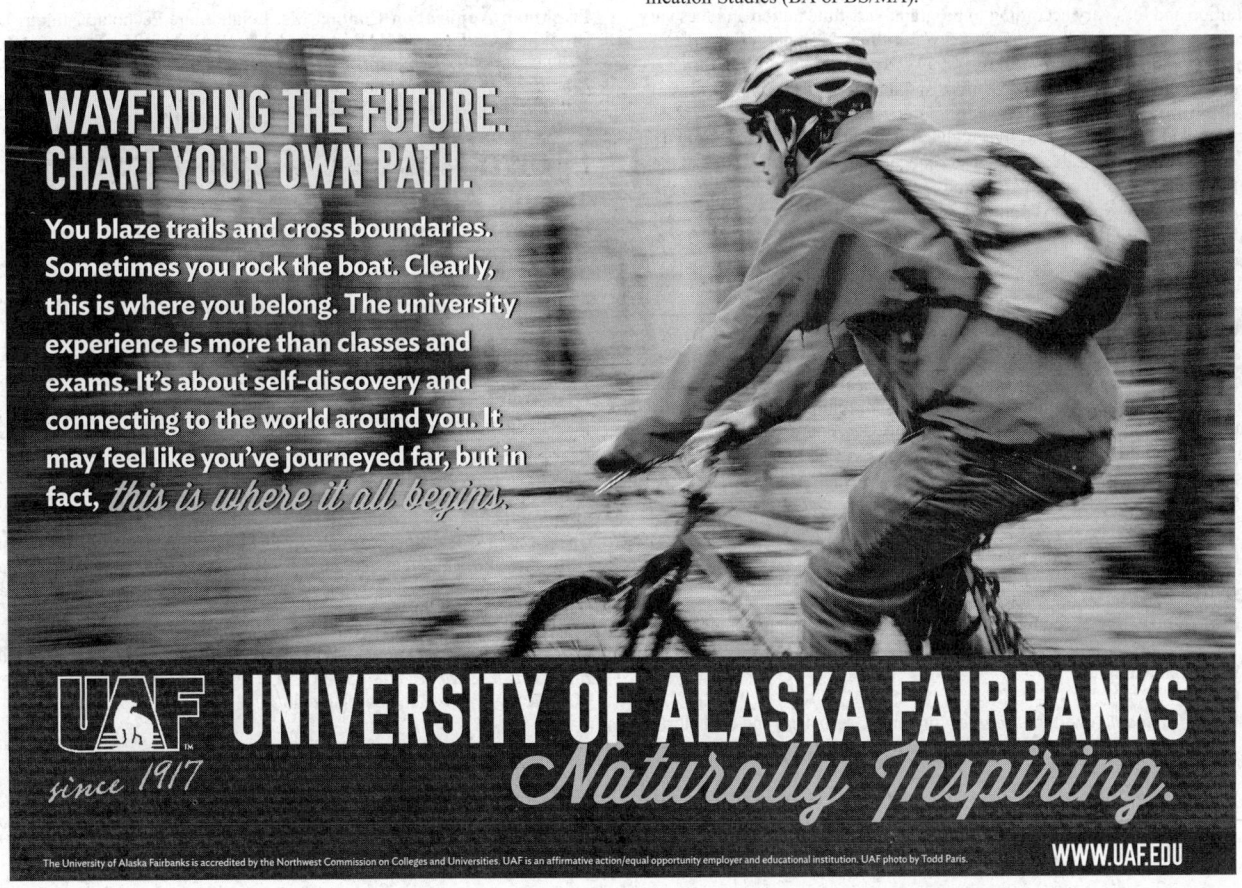

COLLEGES AT-A-GLANCE

Computers on Campus 4,500 computers/terminals and 1,000 ports are available on campus for general student use. Students can access the following: campus intranet, computer help desk, free student e-mail accounts, online (class) grades, online (class) registration, online (class) schedules, My Apps offers enrolled students, faculty and staff access to software applications for use online, in the classroom, by download, or for purchase. My Apps is free of charge and is accessible from any computer using your ASURITE UserID and password. Campuswide network is available. 100% of college-owned or -operated housing units are wired for high-speed Internet access. Wireless service is available via classrooms, computer centers, computer labs, dorm rooms, learning centers, libraries, student centers.

Student Life *Housing:* on-campus residence required for freshman year. *Options:* coed. Campus housing is university owned and leased by the school. Freshman applicants given priority for college housing. *Activities and organizations:* drama/theater group, student-run newspaper, radio and television station, choral group, marching band, Interfraternity Council, Panhellenic Council, Undergraduate Student Government, Business School Council, Residence Hall Association, national fraternities, national sororities. *Campus security:* 24-hour emergency response devices and patrols, late-night transport/escort service. *Student services:* health clinic, personal/psychological counseling, legal services.

Athletics Member NCAA. All Division I except football (Division I-A). *Intercollegiate sports:* baseball M(s), basketball M(s)/W(s), cross-country running M(s)/W(s), golf M(s)/W(s), gymnastics W(s), soccer W(s), softball W(s), swimming and diving M(s)/W(s), tennis W(s), track and field M(s)/W(s), volleyball W(s), water polo W(s), wrestling M(s). *Intramural sports:* badminton M/W, baseball M(c), basketball M(c)/W, bowling M/W, cheerleading M(c)/W(c), crew M(c)/W(c), equestrian sports M(c)/W(c), fencing M(c)/W(c), field hockey M(c)/W(c), gymnastics M(c), ice hockey M(c), lacrosse M(c)/W(c), racquetball M(c)/W(c), rugby M(c)/W(c), sailing M(c)/W(c), soccer M(c)/W(c), softball M(c)/W(c), table tennis M/W, tennis M(c)/W(c), ultimate Frisbee M(c)/W(c), volleyball M(c)/W(c), water polo M(c)/W(c), weight lifting M(c)/W(c).

Standardized Tests *Required for some:* SAT or ACT (for admission), SAT and SAT Subject Tests or ACT (for admission). *Recommended:* SAT or ACT (for admission).

Costs (2012–13) *Tuition:* state resident $9208 full-time, $658 per credit hour part-time; nonresident $22,461 full-time, $936 per credit hour part-time. Full-time tuition and fees vary according to program. Part-time tuition and fees vary according to program. *Required fees:* $516 full-time, $154 per term part-time. *Room and board:* $9094; room only: $5998. Room and board charges vary according to board plan, housing facility, and location. *Payment plan:* installment. *Waivers:* employees or children of employees.

Financial Aid Of all full-time matriculated undergraduates who enrolled in 2011, 37,125 applied for aid, 32,301 were judged to have need, 4,926 had their need fully met. 1,363 Federal Work-Study jobs (averaging $2526). 6,866 state and other part-time jobs (averaging $3354). In 2011, 6156 non-need-based awards were made. *Average percent of need met:* 56%. *Average financial aid package:* $12,011. *Average need-based loan:* $4209. *Average need-based gift aid:* $8182. *Average non-need-based aid:* $7884. *Average indebtedness upon graduation:* $18,615.

Applying *Options:* electronic application. *Application fee:* $50. *Required:* high school transcript, minimum 3.0 GPA. *Required for some:* application fee is $65 for nonresidents. *Application deadlines:* rolling (freshmen), rolling (transfers). *Notification:* continuous (freshmen), continuous (transfers).

Freshman Application Contact Arizona State University, PO Box 870112, Tempe, AZ 85287-0112. *Phone:* 480-965-7788. *Fax:* 480-965-3610. *E-mail:* admissions@asu.edu.

Website: http://www.asu.edu/.

The Art Institute of Phoenix

Phoenix, Arizona

- **Proprietary** 4-year, founded 1995, part of Education Management Corporation
- **Suburban** campus
- **Coed**

Academics *Calendar:* quarters. *Degrees:* diplomas, associate, and bachelor's.

Freshman Application Contact The Art Institute of Phoenix, 2233 West Dunlap Avenue, Phoenix, AZ 85021-2859. *Phone:* 602-331-7500. *Toll-free phone:* 800-474-2479.

Website: http://www.artinstitutes.edu/phoenix/.

See full-page ad on page 54 and page 1102 for the College Close-Up.

The Art Institute of Tucson

Tucson, Arizona

- **Proprietary** 4-year, founded 2007
- **Coed**

Academics *Degrees:* diplomas, associate, and bachelor's.

Freshman Application Contact The Art Institute of Tucson, 5099 East Grant Road, Suite 100, Tucson, AZ 85712. *Phone:* 520-318-2700. *Toll-free phone:* 866-690-8850.

Website: http://www.artinstitutes.edu/tucson/.

See full-page ad on page 54 and page 1122 for the College Close-Up.

Brookline College

Phoenix, Arizona

Freshman Application Contact Ms. Theresa Dean, Director of Admissions, Brookline College, 2445 West Dunlap Avenue, Suite 100, Phoenix, AZ 85021. *Phone:* 602-242-6265. *Toll-free phone:* 800-793-2428. *Fax:* 602-973-2572. *E-mail:* tdean@brooklinecollege.edu.

Website: http://brooklinecollege.edu/.

Brookline College

Tempe, Arizona

Freshman Application Contact Ms. Cheryl Kindred, Campus Director, Brookline College, 1140-1150 South Priest Drive, Tempe, AZ 85281. *Phone:* 480-545-8755. *Toll-free phone:* 888-886-2428. *Fax:* 480-926-1371. *E-mail:* ckindred@brooklinecollege.edu.

Website: http://brooklinecollege.edu/.

Brookline College

Tucson, Arizona

Freshman Application Contact Ms. Leigh Anne Pechota, Campus Director, Brookline College, 5441 East 22nd Street, Suite 125, Tucson, AZ 85711. *Phone:* 520-748-9799. *Toll-free phone:* 888-292-2428. *Fax:* 520-748-9355. *E-mail:* lpechota@brooklinecollege.edu.

Website: http://brooklinecollege.edu/.

Brown Mackie College–Tucson

Tucson, Arizona

Freshman Application Contact Brown Mackie College–Tucson, 4585 East Speedway, Suite 204, Tucson, AZ 85712. *Phone:* 520-319-3300.

Website: http://www.brownmackie.edu/tucson/.

See next page for display ad and page 1212 for the College Close-Up.

Chamberlain College of Nursing

Phoenix, Arizona

- **Proprietary** 4-year
- **Coed**

Faculty *Student/faculty ratio:* 14:1.

Academics *Calendar:* semesters. *Degree:* bachelor's.

Standardized Tests *Required:* SAT or ACT (for admission).

Costs (2013–14) *Tuition:* $16,360 full-time, $665 per credit hour part-time. Full-time tuition and fees vary according to course load and program. Part-time tuition and fees vary according to course load and program. *Required fees:* $600 full-time.

Freshman Application Contact Admissions, Chamberlain College of Nursing, 2149 West Dunlap Avenue, Phoenix, AZ 85021. *Phone:* 602-331-2720. *Toll-free phone:* 888-556-8CCN.

Website: http://www.chamberlain.edu/.

CollegeAmerica–Flagstaff

Flagstaff, Arizona

Freshman Application Contact CollegeAmerica–Flagstaff, 3012 East Route 66, Flagstaff, AZ 86004. *Phone:* 928-213-6060. *Toll-free phone:* 800-622-2894.

Website: http://www.collegeamerica.edu/.

DeVry University

Mesa, Arizona

Admissions Office Contact DeVry University, 1201 South Alma School Road, Mesa, AZ 85210-2011. *Toll-free phone:* 866-338-7941.

Website: http://www.devry.edu/.

DeVry University

Phoenix, Arizona

- **Proprietary** comprehensive, founded 1967, part of DeVry University
- **Urban** campus
- **Coed** 1,111 undergraduate students, 47% full-time, 31% women, 69% men
- **Minimally difficult** entrance level

Undergraduates 521 full-time, 590 part-time. 17% are from out of state; 6% Black or African American, non-Hispanic/Latino; 24% Hispanic/Latino; 3% Asian, non-Hispanic/Latino; 0.4% Native Hawaiian or other Pacific Islander, non-Hispanic/Latino; 4% American Indian or Alaska Native, non-Hispanic/Latino; 1% Two or more races, non-Hispanic/Latino; 16% Race/ethnicity unknown; 0.5% international; 19% transferred in.

Freshmen *Admission:* 98 enrolled.

Faculty *Total:* 157, 20% full-time. *Student/faculty ratio:* 11:1.

Academics *Calendar:* semesters. *Degrees:* associate, bachelor's, master's, and postbachelor's certificates. *Special study options:* adult/continuing education programs, part-time degree program.

Computers on Campus Students can access the following: online (class) registration.

Student Life *Housing:* college housing not available.

Costs (2013–14) *Tuition:* $16,076 full-time, $609 per credit hour part-time. *Required fees:* $80 full-time.

Financial Aid Of all full-time matriculated undergraduates who enrolled in 2007, 435 applied for aid, 414 were judged to have need, 32 had their need fully met. In 2007, 34 non-need-based awards were made. *Average percent of need met:* 43%. *Average financial aid package:* $13,557. *Average need-based loan:* $8565. *Average need-based gift aid:* $6253. *Average non-need-based aid:* $15,538. *Average indebtedness upon graduation:* $20,667.

Applying *Application fee:* $40. *Required:* high school transcript, interview. *Application deadlines:* rolling (freshmen), rolling (transfers). *Notification:* continuous (freshmen), continuous (transfers).

Freshman Application Contact DeVry University, 2149 West Dunlap Avenue, Phoenix, AZ 85021-2995. *Phone:* 602-870-9222. *Toll-free phone:* 866-338-7941.

Website: http://www.devry.edu/.

Dunlap-Stone University

Phoenix, Arizona

Freshman Application Contact Dunlap-Stone University, 19820 North 7th Street, Suite #100, Phoenix, AZ 85024. *Phone:* 602-648-5750. *Toll-free phone:* 800-474-8013.

Website: http://www.dunlap-stone.edu/.

Embry-Riddle Aeronautical University–Prescott

Prescott, Arizona

- **Independent** comprehensive, founded 1978
- **Small-town** 547-acre campus with easy access to Phoenix
- **Endowment** $80.9 million
- **Coed** 1,678 undergraduate students, 94% full-time, 18% women, 82% men
- **Moderately difficult** entrance level

Undergraduates 1,576 full-time, 102 part-time. Students come from 48 states and territories; 25 other countries; 72% are from out of state; 2% Black or African American, non-Hispanic/Latino; 10% Hispanic/Latino; 5% Asian, non-Hispanic/Latino; 0.4% Native Hawaiian or other Pacific Islander, non-Hispanic/Latino; 0.7% American Indian or Alaska Native, non-Hispanic/Latino; 6% Two or more races, non-Hispanic/Latino; 9% Race/ethnicity unknown; 6%

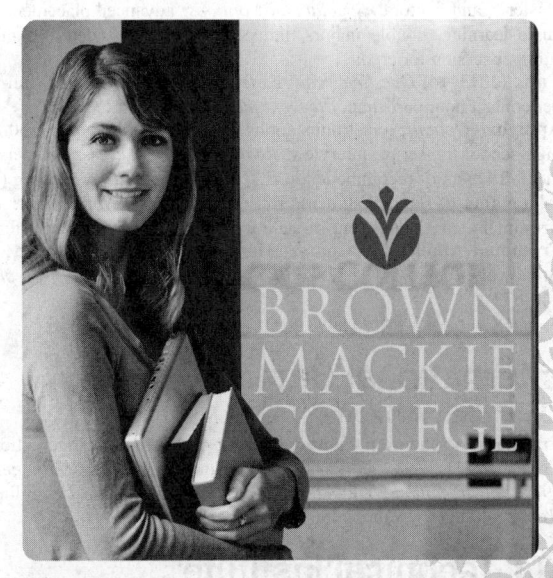

international; 6% transferred in; 47% live on campus. *Retention:* 76% of full-time freshmen returned.

Freshmen *Admission:* 375 enrolled. *Average high school GPA:* 3.63. *Test scores:* SAT critical reading scores over 500: 77%; SAT math scores over 500: 86%; ACT scores over 18: 97%; SAT critical reading scores over 600: 35%; SAT math scores over 600: 54%; ACT scores over 24: 75%; SAT critical reading scores over 700: 8%; SAT math scores over 700: 12%; ACT scores over 30: 22%.

Faculty *Total:* 136, 71% full-time, 52% with terminal degrees. *Student/faculty ratio:* 15:1.

Academics *Calendar:* semesters. *Degrees:* bachelor's and master's. *Special study options:* academic remediation for entering students, accelerated degree program, adult/continuing education programs, advanced placement credit, cooperative education, distance learning, double majors, honors programs, independent study, internships, part-time degree program, services for LD students, student-designed majors, study abroad, summer session for credit. *ROTC:* Army (b), Air Force (b).

Computers on Campus 470 computers/terminals are available on campus for general student use. Students can access the following: campus intranet, computer help desk, free student e-mail accounts, online (class) grades, online (class) registration, online (class) schedules. Campuswide network is available. 100% of college-owned or -operated housing units are wired for high-speed Internet access. Wireless service is available via entire campus.

Student Life *Housing:* on-campus residence required for freshman year. *Options:* coed. Campus housing is university owned. Freshman campus housing is guaranteed. *Activities and organizations:* student-run newspaper, radio station, Hawaii Club, Strike Eagles, Theta XI, American Institute of Aeronautics and Astronautics (AIAA), Arnold Air Society, national fraternities, national sororities. *Campus security:* 24-hour emergency response devices and patrols, student patrols, late-night transport/escort service. *Student services:* health clinic, personal/psychological counseling.

Athletics Member NAIA. *Intercollegiate sports:* cross-country running M(s)/W(s), golf M(s)/W(s), soccer M(s)/W(s), softball W(s), volleyball W(s), wrestling M(s). *Intramural sports:* basketball M/W, bowling M(c)/W(c), football M/W, racquetball M/W, rock climbing M/W, soccer M/W, softball M/W, table tennis M/W, tennis M/W, ultimate Frisbee M(c)/W(c), volleyball M/W.

Standardized Tests *Recommended:* SAT or ACT (for admission).

Costs (2013–14) *Comprehensive fee:* $40,584 includes full-time tuition ($30,120), mandatory fees ($914), and room and board ($9550). Part-time tuition: $1255 per credit hour. *College room only:* $5600. Room and board charges vary according to board plan and housing facility. *Payment plans:* installment, deferred payment. *Waivers:* employees or children of employees.

Financial Aid Of all full-time matriculated undergraduates who enrolled in 2011, 1,205 applied for aid, 1,102 were judged to have need. 28 Federal Work-Study jobs (averaging $1527). 454 state and other part-time jobs (averaging $1419). *Average financial aid package:* $16,521. *Average need-based loan:* $5189. *Average need-based gift aid:* $10,661.

Applying *Options:* electronic application, deferred entrance. *Application fee:* $50. *Required:* high school transcript, minimum 2.0 GPA, 2 letters of recommendation, medical examination for flight students. *Required for some:* minimum 3.0 GPA. *Recommended:* essay or personal statement, interview. *Application deadlines:* rolling (freshmen), rolling (out-of-state freshmen), rolling (transfers). *Notification:* continuous (freshmen), continuous (out-of-state freshmen), continuous (transfers).

Freshman Application Contact Bryan Dougherty, Director of Admissions, Embry-Riddle Aeronautical University–Prescott, 3700 Willow Creek Road, Prescott, AZ 863013720. *Phone:* 928-777-6600. *Toll-free phone:* 800-888-3728. *Fax:* 928-777-6606. *E-mail:* pradmit@erau.edu.
Website: http://www.embryriddle.edu/.

Everest College
Phoenix, Arizona

Freshman Application Contact Mr. Jim Askins, Director of Admissions, Everest College, 10400 North 25th Avenue, Suite 190, Phoenix, AZ 85021. *Phone:* 602-942-4141. *Toll-free phone:* 888-741-4270. *Fax:* 602-943-0960. *E-mail:* jaskins@cci.edu.
Website: http://www.everest.edu/.

Everest Online
Tempe, Arizona

Admissions Office Contact Everest Online, 8150 South Hardy Drive #102, Tempe, AZ 85284-1117.
Website: http://www.everestonline.edu/.

Grand Canyon University
Phoenix, Arizona

- **Independent Southern Baptist** comprehensive, founded 1949
- **Urban** 100-acre campus with easy access to Phoenix
- **Coed**
- **Moderately difficult** entrance level

Academics *Calendar:* semesters. *Degrees:* bachelor's, master's, doctoral, and post-master's certificates.

Student Life *Campus security:* 24-hour emergency response devices and patrols, late-night transport/escort service, controlled dormitory access, staffed gates to enter campus after non-business hours.

Athletics Member NCAA. All Division II.

Standardized Tests *Recommended:* SAT or ACT (for admission).

Costs (2012–13) *Comprehensive fee:* $27,100 includes full-time tuition ($16,500), mandatory fees ($2500), and room and board ($8100). Full-time tuition and fees vary according to course load. Part-time tuition: $688 per credit. Part-time tuition and fees vary according to course load. *College room only:* $4000. Room and board charges vary according to board plan and housing facility.

Financial Aid *Of all full-time matriculated undergraduates who enrolled in 2007,* 1,102 applied for aid, 942 were judged to have need, 155 had their need fully met. *Average financial aid package:* $3371. *Average need-based loan:* $3701. *Average need-based gift aid:* $3360.

Applying *Options:* electronic application, early admission, deferred entrance. *Required:* high school transcript, minimum 2.8 GPA.

Freshman Application Contact Enrollment, Grand Canyon University, 3300 West Camelback Road, PO Box 11097, Phoenix, AZ 86017-3030. *Phone:* 800-486-7085. *Toll-free phone:* 800-800-9776. *E-mail:* admissionsonline@gcu.edu.
Website: http://www.gcu.edu/.

Harrison Middleton University
Tempe, Arizona

- **Independent** comprehensive, founded 1998
- **Suburban** campus with easy access to Phoenix
- **Coed** 79 undergraduate students, 100% full-time, 47% women, 53% men

Undergraduates 79 full-time.

Faculty *Total:* 23, 74% full-time, 43% with terminal degrees.

Academics *Calendar:* continuous. *Degrees:* diplomas, associate, bachelor's, master's, and doctoral. *Special study options:* advanced placement credit, distance learning, double majors, independent study, student-designed majors, summer session for credit.

Costs (2013–14) *One-time required fee:* $400. *Tuition:* $6000 full-time, $250 per contact hour part-time. *Payment plan:* installment.

Applying *Options:* electronic application. *Application fee:* $50. *Required:* high school transcript, interview. *Required for some:* essay or personal statement, 2 letters of recommendation. *Application deadlines:* rolling (freshmen), rolling (out-of-state freshmen), rolling (transfers). *Notification:* continuous (freshmen), continuous (out-of-state freshmen), continuous (transfers).

Freshman Application Contact Harrison Middleton University, 1105 East Broadway, Tempe, AZ 85282. *Phone:* 877-248.6724. *Toll-free phone:* 877-248-6724.
Website: http://www.hmu.edu/.

International Baptist College
Chandler, Arizona

Freshman Application Contact Director of Admissions, International Baptist College, 2211 West Germann Road, Chandler, AZ 85286. *Phone:* 480-245-7970. *Toll-free phone:* 800-422-4858. *E-mail:* admissions@ibconline.edu.
Website: http://www.ibcs.edu/.

ITT Technical Institute
Phoenix, Arizona

- **Proprietary** primarily 2-year, founded 1972, part of ITT Educational Services, Inc.
- **Urban** campus
- **Coed**
- **Minimally difficult** entrance level

Academics *Calendar:* quarters. *Degrees:* associate and bachelor's.

Financial Aid *Of all full-time matriculated undergraduates who enrolled in 2011,* 10 Federal Work-Study jobs (averaging $4000).

Freshman Application Contact Director of Recruitment, ITT Technical Institute, 10220 North 25th Avenue, Suite 100, Phoenix, AZ 85021. *Phone:* 602-749-7900. *Toll-free phone:* 877-221-1132. *Website:* http://www.itt-tech.edu/.

ITT Technical Institute

Phoenix, Arizona

- **Proprietary** primarily 2-year, part of ITT Educational Services, Inc.
- **Coed**

Academics *Calendar:* quarters. *Degrees:* associate and bachelor's.

Freshman Application Contact Director of Recruitment, ITT Technical Institute, 1840 N. 95th Avenue, Suite 132, Phoenix, AZ 85037. *Phone:* 623-474-7900. *Toll-free phone:* 800-210-1178. *Website:* http://www.itt-tech.edu/.

ITT Technical Institute

Tempe, Arizona

- **Proprietary** 4-year, founded 1963, part of ITT Educational Services, Inc.
- **Coed**
- **Minimally difficult** entrance level

Academics *Degrees:* associate and bachelor's.

Freshman Application Contact Director of Recruitment, ITT Technical Institute, 5005 S. Wendler Drive, Tempe, AZ 85282. *Phone:* 602-437-7500. *Toll-free phone:* 800-879-4881. *Website:* http://www.itt-tech.edu/.

ITT Technical Institute

Tucson, Arizona

- **Proprietary** primarily 2-year, founded 1984, part of ITT Educational Services, Inc.
- **Urban** campus
- **Coed**
- **Minimally difficult** entrance level

Academics *Calendar:* quarters. *Degrees:* associate and bachelor's.

Freshman Application Contact Director of Recruitment, ITT Technical Institute, 1455 West River Road, Tucson, AZ 85704. *Phone:* 520-408-7488. *Toll-free phone:* 800-870-9730. *Website:* http://www.itt-tech.edu/.

Le Cordon Bleu College of Culinary Arts in Scottsdale

Scottsdale, Arizona

Director of Admissions Le Cordon Bleu College of Culinary Arts in Scottsdale, 8100 East Camelback Road, Suite 1001, Scottsdale, AZ 85251-3940. *Toll-free phone:* 888-557-4222. *Website:* http://www.chefs.edu/SCOTTSDALE.

National Paralegal College

Phoenix, Arizona

Freshman Application Contact Admissions Office, National Paralegal College, 6516 N 7th Street, Suite 103, Phoenix, AZ 85014. *Phone:* 845-371-9101. *Toll-free phone:* 800-371-6105. *Fax:* 866-347-2744. *E-mail:* info@nationalparalegal.edu. *Website:* http://nationalparalegal.edu/.

Northcentral University

Prescott Valley, Arizona

- **Proprietary** upper-level
- **Coed** 329 undergraduate students, 24% full-time, 64% women, 36% men
- **Minimally difficult** entrance level

Undergraduates 78 full-time, 251 part-time. Students come from 45 states and territories; 2 other countries; 11% Black or African American, non-Hispanic/Latino; 4% Hispanic/Latino; 2% Asian, non-Hispanic/Latino; 0.3% Native Hawaiian or other Pacific Islander, non-Hispanic/Latino; 0.3% American Indian or Alaska Native, non-Hispanic/Latino; 1% Two or more races, non-Hispanic/Latino; 53% Race/ethnicity unknown; 100% transferred in.

Faculty *Total:* 481, 9% full-time, 100% with terminal degrees. *Student/faculty ratio:* 9:1.

Academics *Calendar:* continuous. *Degrees:* bachelor's, master's, doctoral, post-master's, and postbachelor's certificates (offers only distance learning programs). *Special study options:* accelerated degree program, distance learning, services for LD students.

Costs (2013–14) *Tuition:* $9760 full-time. *Payment plans:* tuition prepayment, installment. *Waivers:* employees or children of employees.

Applying *Options:* electronic application. *Application deadline:* rolling (transfers). *Notification:* continuous (transfers).

Application Contact Northcentral University, 10000 East University Drive, Prescott Valley, AZ 86314. *Phone:* 480-253-3535. *Toll-free phone:* 866-776-0331. *Website:* http://www.ncu.edu/.

Northern Arizona University

Flagstaff, Arizona

- **State-supported** university, founded 1899, part of Arizona University System, under the Arizona Board of Regents
- **Small-town** 740-acre campus
- **Endowment** $108.3 million
- **Coed** 21,774 undergraduate students, 84% full-time, 58% women, 42% men
- **Moderately difficult** entrance level, 76% of applicants were admitted

Undergraduates 18,386 full-time, 3,388 part-time. Students come from 51 states and territories; 42 other countries; 26% are from out of state; 3% Black or African American, non-Hispanic/Latino; 18% Hispanic/Latino; 1% Asian, non-Hispanic/Latino; 0.3% Native Hawaiian or other Pacific Islander, non-Hispanic/Latino; 4% American Indian or Alaska Native, non-Hispanic/Latino; 4% Two or more races, non-Hispanic/Latino; 0.7% Race/ethnicity unknown; 4% international; 11% transferred in; 33% live on campus. *Retention:* 76% of full-time freshmen returned.

Freshmen *Admission:* 34,461 applied, 26,299 admitted, 4,254 enrolled. *Average high school GPA:* 3.4. *Test scores:* SAT critical reading scores over 500: 63%; SAT math scores over 500: 67%; SAT writing scores over 500: 58%; ACT scores over 18: 90%; SAT critical reading scores over 600: 20%; SAT math scores over 600: 23%; SAT writing scores over 600: 16%; ACT scores over 24: 42%; SAT critical reading scores over 700: 2%; SAT math scores over 700: 3%; SAT writing scores over 700: 1%; ACT scores over 30: 4%.

Faculty *Total:* 1,539, 58% full-time. *Student/faculty ratio:* 20:1.

Academics *Calendar:* semesters. *Degrees:* certificates, bachelor's, master's, doctoral, and postbachelor's certificates. *Special study options:* accelerated degree program, advanced placement credit, cooperative education, distance learning, double majors, English as a second language, freshman honors college, honors programs, independent study, internships, off-campus study, part-time degree program, services for LD students, study abroad, summer session for credit. *ROTC:* Army (b), Air Force (b).

Computers on Campus 400 computers/terminals are available on campus for general student use. Students can access the following: campus intranet, computer help desk, free student e-mail accounts, online (class) grades, online (class) registration, online (class) schedules. Campuswide network is available. 100% of college-owned or -operated housing units are wired for high-speed Internet access. Wireless service is available via entire campus.

Student Life *Housing options:* coed, men-only, women-only, disabled students. Campus housing is university owned. Freshman campus housing is guaranteed. *Activities and organizations:* drama/theater group, student-run newspaper, radio and television station, choral group, marching band, Northern Arizona Snow Association, Golden Key Honor Society, Younglife, Astronomy/Astrobiology Club, IEEE Student Chapter, national fraternities, national sororities. *Campus security:* 24-hour emergency response devices and patrols, late-night transport/escort service, controlled dormitory access. *Student services:* health clinic, personal/psychological counseling, legal services.

Athletics Member NCAA. All Division I. *Intercollegiate sports:* basketball M(s)/W(s), cheerleading M/W, cross-country running M(s)/W(s), football M(s), golf W(s), soccer W(s), swimming and diving W(s), tennis M(s)/W(s), track and field M(s)/W(s), volleyball W(s). *Intramural sports:* archery M(c)/W(c), badminton M/W, baseball M(c)/W(c), basketball M/W, equestrian sports M(c)/W(c), fencing M(c)/W(c), football M(c), gymnastics M(c)/W(c), ice hockey M(c)/W(c), lacrosse M(c)/W(c), racquetball M(c)/W(c), rugby M(c)/W(c), skiing (downhill) M(c)/W(c), soccer M/W, softball M(c)/W(c), tennis M(c)/W(c), ultimate Frisbee M(c)/W(c), volleyball M/W, water polo M(c)/W(c), wrestling M(c)/W(c).

Standardized Tests *Required for some:* SAT (for admission), ACT (for admission), SAT or ACT (for admission), SAT and SAT Subject Tests or ACT (for admission), SAT Subject Tests (for admission), ACT/SAT test scores required for home-schooled students.

Costs (2012–13) *Tuition:* state resident $8453 full-time, $363 per credit hour part-time; nonresident $20,808 full-time, $749 per credit hour part-time. Full-time tuition and fees vary according to degree level, location, and program.

Part-time tuition and fees vary according to course load, degree level, location, and program. No tuition increase for student's term of enrollment. *Required fees:* $818 full-time, $6 per credit hour part-time, $322 per term part-time. *Room and board:* $8784; room only: $4824. Room and board charges vary according to board plan and housing facility. *Payment plan:* installment. *Waivers:* employees or children of employees.

Financial Aid Of all full-time matriculated undergraduates who enrolled in 2011, 13,629 applied for aid, 11,448 were judged to have need, 986 had their need fully met. In 2011, 1934 non-need-based awards were made. *Average percent of need met:* 58%. *Average financial aid package:* $9810. *Average need-based loan:* $4131. *Average need-based gift aid:* $6019. *Average non-need-based aid:* $4601. *Average indebtedness upon graduation:* $22,621.

Applying *Options:* electronic application, deferred entrance. *Application fee:* $25. *Required:* high school transcript, minimum 3.0 GPA, Completion of 16 required college preparatory courses with minimum 2.0 in each subject area. *Application deadlines:* rolling (freshmen), rolling (out-of-state freshmen), rolling (transfers). *Notification:* continuous (freshmen), continuous (out-of-state freshmen), continuous (transfers).

Freshman Application Contact Undergraduate Admissions, Northern Arizona University, Box 4084, Flagstaff, AZ 86011. *Phone:* 928-523-5511. *Toll-free phone:* 888-MORE-NAU. *Fax:* 928-523-0226. *E-mail:* Admissions@nau.edu.
Website: http://www.nau.edu/.

Northern Arizona University–Yuma
Yuma, Arizona

Director of Admissions Eileen Knight, Associate Director of Admissions, Northern Arizona University–Yuma, 2020 South Avenue 8E, PO Box 6236, Yuma, AZ 85365. *Phone:* 928-317-6431. *Toll-free phone:* 888-NAU-Yuma. *E-mail:* eileen.knight@nau.edu.
Website: http://www.yuma.nau.edu/.

Penn Foster College
Scottsdale, Arizona

Freshman Application Contact Admissions, Penn Foster College, 14300 North Northsight Boulevard, Suite 120, Scottsdale, AZ 85260. *Phone:* 480-315-4950. *Toll-free phone:* 800-471-3232.
Website: http://www.pennfostercollege.edu/.

Pima Medical Institute
Mesa, Arizona

Freshman Application Contact Admissions Office, Pima Medical Institute, 957 South Dobson Road, Mesa, AZ 85202. *Phone:* 480-644-0267 Ext. 225. *Toll-free phone:* 800-477-PIMA (in-state); 888-477-PIMA (out-of-state). *Website:* http://www.pmi.edu/.

Pima Medical Institute
Tucson, Arizona

Freshman Application Contact Admissions Office, Pima Medical Institute, 3350 East Grant Road, Tucson, AZ 85716. *Phone:* 520-326-1600 Ext. 5112. *Toll-free phone:* 800-477-PIMA (in-state); 888-477-PIMA (out-of-state). *Website:* http://www.pmi.edu/.

Prescott College
Prescott, Arizona

- **Independent** comprehensive, founded 1966
- **Small-town** 13-acre campus
- **Endowment** $1.1 million
- **Coed** 673 undergraduate students, 80% full-time, 57% women, 43% men
- **Moderately difficult** entrance level, 73% of applicants were admitted

Undergraduates 541 full-time, 132 part-time. Students come from 45 states and territories; 11 other countries; 75% are from out of state; 2% Black or African American, non-Hispanic/Latino; 7% Hispanic/Latino; 0.7% Asian, non-Hispanic/Latino; 0.1% Native Hawaiian or other Pacific Islander, non-Hispanic/Latino; 3% American Indian or Alaska Native, non-Hispanic/Latino; 4% Two or more races, non-Hispanic/Latino; 7% Race/ethnicity unknown; 2% international; 23% transferred in; 17% live on campus. *Retention:* 73% of full-time freshmen returned.

Freshmen *Admission:* 551 applied, 400 admitted, 64 enrolled. *Average high school GPA:* 3.13. *Test scores:* SAT critical reading scores over 500: 77%; SAT math scores over 500: 64%; SAT writing scores over 500: 64%; SAT critical reading scores over 600: 39%; SAT math scores over 600: 21%; SAT writing scores over 600: 33%; SAT critical reading scores over 700: 2%; SAT math scores over 700: 2%; SAT writing scores over 700: 7%.

Faculty *Total:* 149, 48% full-time, 38% with terminal degrees. *Student/faculty ratio:* 8:1.

Academics *Calendar:* quarters (4-week blocks followed by 10-week terms for each quarter). *Degrees:* bachelor's, master's, doctoral, post-master's, and post-bachelor's certificates. *Special study options:* adult/continuing education programs, advanced placement credit, distance learning, double majors, external degree program, independent study, internships, off-campus study, services for LD students, student-designed majors, study abroad, summer session for credit.

Computers on Campus 80 computers/terminals and 20 ports are available on campus for general student use. Students can access the following: computer help desk, free student e-mail accounts, online (class) grades, online (class) schedules, Learning Management System (Moodle), free E-portfolios. Campuswide network is available. 100% of college-owned or -operated housing units are wired for high-speed Internet access. Wireless service is available via entire campus.

Student Life *Housing:* on-campus residence required for freshman year. *Options:* coed. Campus housing is university owned. Freshman campus housing is guaranteed. *Activities and organizations:* drama/theater group, student-run newspaper, choral group, Student Union, Catalyst, WEB (Women's Empowerment Breakthrough), HUB (Helping Understand Bikes), Aztlan Center. *Campus security:* 24-hour emergency response devices, late-night transport/escort service, controlled dormitory access. *Student services:* personal/psychological counseling.

Standardized Tests *Required:* SAT or ACT (for admission).

Costs (2012–13) *Comprehensive fee:* $33,919 includes full-time tuition ($27,408), mandatory fees ($611), and room and board ($5900). Full-time tuition and fees vary according to course load, degree level, and reciprocity agreements. Part-time tuition: $1142 per credit. Part-time tuition and fees vary according to course load, degree level, and reciprocity agreements. *Required fees:* $306 per term part-time. *College room only:* $4230. Room and board charges vary according to board plan and housing facility. *Payment plans:* installment, deferred payment. *Waivers:* employees or children of employees.

Financial Aid Of all full-time matriculated undergraduates who enrolled in 2012, 410 applied for aid, 378 were judged to have need, 33 had their need fully met. 92 Federal Work-Study jobs (averaging $1500). 141 state and other part-time jobs (averaging $660). In 2012, 110 non-need-based awards were made. *Average percent of need met:* 58%. *Average financial aid package:* $18,738. *Average need-based loan:* $5278. *Average need-based gift aid:* $13,497. *Average non-need-based aid:* $8232. *Average indebtedness upon graduation:* $23,476.

Applying *Options:* electronic application, early decision, deferred entrance. *Application fee:* $25. *Required:* essay or personal statement, high school transcript, 1 letter of recommendation. *Required for some:* interview. *Application deadlines:* 8/15 (freshmen), 8/15 (out-of-state freshmen), 8/15 (transfers). *Early decision deadline:* 12/1. *Notification:* continuous (freshmen), continuous (out-of-state freshmen), continuous (transfers), 12/15 (early decision).

Freshman Application Contact Nancy Simmons, Receptionist, Prescott College, 220 Grove Avenue, Prescott, AZ 86301. *Phone:* 928-350-2100. *Toll-free phone:* 877-350-2100. *Fax:* 928-776-5242. *E-mail:* admissions@prescott.edu.
Website: http://www.prescott.edu/.

Southwest University of Visual Arts
Tucson, Arizona

Freshman Application Contact Sarah LaVetter, Director of Admissions, Southwest University of Visual Arts, 2525 North Country Club Road, Tucson, AZ 85716-2505. *Phone:* 520-325-0123. *Toll-free phone:* 800-825-8753. *Fax:* 520-325-5535.
Website: http://www.suva.edu/.

University of Advancing Technology
Tempe, Arizona

Freshman Application Contact Admissions Office, University of Advancing Technology, 2625 West Baseline Road, Tempe, AZ 85283-1042. *Phone:* 602-383-8228. *Toll-free phone:* 800-658-5744. *Fax:* 602-383-8222. *E-mail:* admissions@uat.edu.
Website: http://www.uat.edu/.

The University of Arizona

Tucson, Arizona

- **State-supported** university, founded 1885, part of Arizona Board of Regents
- **Urban** 391-acre campus
- **Endowment** $563.7 million
- **Coed** 31,565 undergraduate students, 89% full-time, 52% women, 48% men
- **Moderately difficult** entrance level, 77% of applicants were admitted

Undergraduates 28,210 full-time, 3,355 part-time. Students come from 116 other countries; 29% are from out of state; 3% Black or African American, non-Hispanic/Latino; 23% Hispanic/Latino; 6% Asian, non-Hispanic/Latino; 0.2% Native Hawaiian or other Pacific Islander, non-Hispanic/Latino; 1% American Indian or Alaska Native, non-Hispanic/Latino; 4% Two or more races, non-Hispanic/Latino; 1% Race/ethnicity unknown; 5% international; 6% transferred in; 21% live on campus. *Retention:* 80% of full-time freshmen returned.

Freshmen *Admission:* 26,329 applied, 20,251 admitted, 7,401 enrolled. *Average high school GPA:* 3.42. *Test scores:* SAT critical reading scores over 500: 72%; SAT math scores over 500: 76%; SAT writing scores over 500: 68%; ACT scores over 18: 93%; SAT critical reading scores over 600: 28%; SAT math scores over 600: 37%; SAT writing scores over 600: 25%; ACT scores over 24: 54%; SAT critical reading scores over 700: 6%; SAT math scores over 700: 8%; SAT writing scores over 700: 4%; ACT scores over 30: 11%.

Faculty *Student/faculty ratio:* 22:1.

Academics *Calendar:* semesters. *Degrees:* bachelor's, master's, doctoral, post-master's, and postbachelor's certificates. *Special study options:* accelerated degree program, adult/continuing education programs, advanced placement credit, cooperative education, distance learning, double majors, English as a second language, external degree program, freshman honors college, honors programs, independent study, internships, off-campus study, part-time degree program, services for LD students, student-designed majors, study abroad, summer session for credit. *ROTC:* Army (b), Navy (b), Air Force (b). *Unusual degree programs:* 3-2 business administration with American Graduate School of International Management; engineering; sciences.

Computers on Campus Students can access the following: campus intranet, computer help desk, free student e-mail accounts, online (class) grades, online (class) registration, online (class) schedules. Campuswide network is available. Wireless service is available via classrooms, computer centers, computer labs, dorm rooms, learning centers, libraries, student centers.

Student Life *Housing options:* coed, women-only, disabled students. Campus housing is university owned and leased by the school. Freshman applicants given priority for college housing. *Activities and organizations:* drama/theater group, student-run newspaper, radio and television station, choral group, marching band, national fraternities, national sororities. *Campus security:* 24-hour patrols, student patrols, late-night transport/escort service, emergency telephones. *Student services:* health clinic, personal/psychological counseling, women's center, legal services.

Athletics Member NCAA. All Division I except football (Division I-A). *Intercollegiate sports:* badminton M(c)/W(c), baseball M(s), basketball M(s)/W(s), cheerleading M(c)/W(c), cross-country running M(s)/W(s), fencing M(c)/W(c), golf M(s)/W(s), gymnastics W(s), ice hockey M(c)/W(c), lacrosse M(c)/W(c), racquetball M(c)/W(c), rugby M(c)/W(c), soccer M(c)/W(s), softball W(s), swimming and diving M(s)/W(s), table tennis M(c)/W(c), tennis M(s)/W(s), track and field M(s)/W(s), ultimate Frisbee M(c)/W(c), volleyball M(c)/W(s), water polo M(c)/W(c). *Intramural sports:* basketball M/W, football M/W, racquetball M/W, soccer M/W, table tennis M/W, tennis M/W, ultimate Frisbee M/W, volleyball M/W, water polo M/W.

Standardized Tests *Recommended:* SAT or ACT (for admission).

Costs (2013–14) *Tuition:* state resident $9114 full-time, $651 per credit hour part-time; nonresident $25,310 full-time, $1055 per credit hour part-time. Full-time tuition and fees vary according to course level, course load, degree level, location, program, reciprocity agreements, and student level. Part-time tuition and fees vary according to course level, course load, degree level, location, program, reciprocity agreements, and student level. *Required fees:* $921 full-time, $80 per credit hour part-time. *Room and board:* $9714; room only: $6784. Room and board charges vary according to board plan and housing facility. *Payment plan:* installment. *Waivers:* employees or children of employees.

Financial Aid Of all full-time matriculated undergraduates who enrolled in 2011, 17,357 applied for aid, 14,257 were judged to have need, 1,563 had their need fully met. In 2011, 5470 non-need-based awards were made. *Average percent of need met:* 61%. *Average financial aid package:* $12,059. *Average need-based loan:* $4196. *Average need-based gift aid:* $10,090. *Average non-need-based aid:* $7160. *Average indebtedness upon graduation:* $22,269.

Applying *Options:* electronic application, early admission. *Application fee:* $50. *Required:* essay or personal statement, high school transcript. *Required for some:* minimum 3.0 GPA, interview. *Application deadlines:* 5/1 (freshmen), rolling (transfers). *Notification:* continuous (freshmen).

Freshman Application Contact The University of Arizona, Tucson, AZ 85721. *Phone:* 520-621-3087.

Website: http://www.arizona.edu/.

University of Phoenix–Online Campus

Phoenix, Arizona

Freshman Application Contact Marc Booker, Sr. Director, Office of Admissions and Evaluation, University of Phoenix–Online Campus, 4035 South Riverpoint Parkway, Mail Stop CF-L101, Phoenix, AZ 85040. *Phone:* 602-557-4609. *Toll-free phone:* 866-766-0766. *Fax:* 480-643-1156.

Website: http://www.uopxonline.com/.

University of Phoenix–Phoenix Main Campus

Tempe, Arizona

Freshman Application Contact Marc Booker, Sr. Director, Office of Admissions and Evaluation, University of Phoenix–Phoenix Main Campus, 4035 South Riverpoint Parkway, Mail Stop CF-L101, Phoenix, AZ 85040. *Phone:* 602-557-4609. *Toll-free phone:* 866-766-0766. *Fax:* 480-643-1156.

Website: http://www.phoenix.edu/.

University of Phoenix–Southern Arizona Campus

Tucson, Arizona

Freshman Application Contact Marc Booker, Sr. Director, Office of Admissions and Evaluation, University of Phoenix–Southern Arizona Campus, 4035 South Riverpoint Parkway, Mail Stop CF-L101, Phoenix, AZ 85040-1958. *Phone:* 602-557-4609. *Toll-free phone:* 866-766-0766. *Fax:* 480-643-1156.

Website: http://www.phoenix.edu/.

Western International University

Phoenix, Arizona

- **Proprietary** comprehensive, founded 1978, part of Apollo Global and Apollo Group
- **Urban** 4-acre campus with easy access to Phoenix
- **Coed**
- **Moderately difficult** entrance level

Faculty *Student/faculty ratio:* 24:1.

Academics *Calendar:* continuous. *Degrees:* associate, bachelor's, master's, and postbachelor's certificates.

Student Life *Campus security:* 24-hour emergency response devices and patrols, late-night transport/escort service.

Financial Aid *Average financial aid package:* $3321. *Average indebtedness upon graduation:* $5285.

Applying *Options:* electronic application, deferred entrance. *Application fee:* $25. *Required:* high school transcript, minimum 2.5 GPA.

Freshman Application Contact Ms. Melissa Machuca, Director of Enrollment, Western International University, 9215 North Black Canyon Highway, Phoenix, AZ 85021-2718. *Phone:* 602-943-2311. *E-mail:* Melissa.Machuca@west.edu.

Website: http://www.west.edu/.

ARKANSAS

Arkansas Baptist College

Little Rock, Arkansas

Freshman Application Contact Arkansas Baptist College, 1621 Dr. Martin Luther King, Jr. Drive, Little Rock, AR 72202-6067. *Phone:* 501-244-5104 Ext. 5124.

Website: http://www.arkansasbaptist.edu/.

Arkansas State University

Jonesboro, Arkansas

- **State-supported** comprehensive, founded 1909, part of Arkansas State University System
- **Small-town** 1376-acre campus with easy access to Memphis
- **Endowment** $39.4 million
- **Coed** 10,168 undergraduate students, 77% full-time, 57% women, 43% men
- **Moderately difficult** entrance level, 71% of applicants were admitted

Undergraduates 7,822 full-time, 2,346 part-time. Students come from 40 states and territories; 48 other countries; 11% are from out of state; 16% Black or African American, non-Hispanic/Latino; 2% Hispanic/Latino; 0.7% Asian, non-Hispanic/Latino; 0.1% Native Hawaiian or other Pacific Islander, non-Hispanic/Latino; 0.4% American Indian or Alaska Native, non-Hispanic/Latino; 1% Two or more races, non-Hispanic/Latino; 2% Race/ethnicity unknown; 6% international; 10% transferred in; 27% live on campus. *Retention:* 70% of full-time freshmen returned.
Freshmen *Admission:* 5,289 applied, 3,732 admitted, 1,671 enrolled. *Average high school GPA:* 3.37. *Test scores:* SAT critical reading scores over 500: 19%; SAT math scores over 500: 37%; SAT writing scores over 500: 30%; ACT scores over 18: 97%; SAT math scores over 600: 11%; ACT scores over 24: 42%; ACT scores over 30: 4%.
Faculty *Total:* 660, 74% full-time, 61% with terminal degrees. *Student/faculty ratio:* 19:1.
Academics *Calendar:* semesters. *Degrees:* certificates, associate, bachelor's, master's, doctoral, post-master's, and postbachelor's certificates. *Special study options:* academic remediation for entering students, accelerated degree program, advanced placement credit, distance learning, double majors, English as a second language, honors programs, independent study, internships, off-campus study, part-time degree program, services for LD students, study abroad, summer session for credit. *ROTC:* Army (b).
Computers on Campus 600 computers/terminals and 5,304 ports are available on campus for general student use. Students can access the following: campus intranet, computer help desk, free student e-mail accounts, online (class) grades, online (class) registration, online (class) schedules. Campuswide network is available. 99% of college-owned or -operated housing units are wired for high-speed Internet access. Wireless service is available via entire campus.
Student Life *Housing:* on-campus residence required for freshman year. *Options:* coed, men-only, women-only. Campus housing is university owned. *Activities and organizations:* drama/theater group, student-run newspaper, radio and television station, choral group, marching band, ASU Rugby, Black Student Association, Student Activities Board, Honors College Association, Student Government Association, national fraternities, national sororities. *Campus security:* 24-hour emergency response devices and patrols, student patrols, late-night transport/escort service, controlled dormitory access, check-in desk; video surveillance cameras. *Student services:* health clinic, personal/psychological counseling.
Athletics Member NCAA. All Division I except football (Division I-A). *Intercollegiate sports:* baseball M(s), basketball M(s)/W(s), bowling W(s), cross-country running M(s)/W(s), golf M(s)/W(s), soccer W(s), tennis W(s), track and field M(s)/W(s), volleyball W(s). *Intramural sports:* badminton M/W, basketball M/W, bowling M/W, football M/W, golf M/W, rugby M(c), soccer M/W, softball M/W, table tennis M/W, tennis M/W, ultimate Frisbee M/W, volleyball M/W.
Standardized Tests *Required:* SAT or ACT (for admission). *Required for some:* ACT ASSET; ACT COMPASS; TOEFL, IELTS, PTE or Proof of English Proficiency for international students. *Recommended:* ACT (for admission).
Costs (2012–13) *Tuition:* state resident $5430 full-time, $181 per credit hour part-time; nonresident $10,860 full-time, $362 per credit hour part-time. Full-time tuition and fees vary according to course load, location, and program. Part-time tuition and fees vary according to course load, location, and program. *Required fees:* $1750 full-time, $56 per credit hour part-time, $25 per term part-time. *Room and board:* $7150. Room and board charges vary according to board plan, housing facility, and student level. *Payment plan:* installment. *Waivers:* senior citizens and employees or children of employees.
Financial Aid Of all full-time matriculated undergraduates who enrolled in 2012, 7,797 applied for aid, 6,851 were judged to have need, 2,316 had their need fully met. 155 Federal Work-Study jobs (averaging $3179). 310 state and other part-time jobs (averaging $3550). In 2012, 627 non-need-based awards were made. *Average percent of need met:* 45%. *Average financial aid package:* $8500. *Average need-based loan:* $8000. *Average need-based gift aid:* $8000. *Average non-need-based aid:* $5550. *Average indebtedness upon graduation:* $21,000. *Financial aid deadline:* 7/1.
Applying *Options:* electronic application, early admission. *Application fee:* $15. *Required:* high school transcript, minimum 2.8 GPA, For Fall 2013, ACT

composite score of 21 plus a 2.75 high school GPA, immunization, selective service. *Application deadlines:* rolling (freshmen), rolling (transfers). *Notification:* continuous (freshmen), continuous (transfers).
Freshman Application Contact Ms. Tracy Finch, Director of Admissions, Records, and Registration, Arkansas State University, PO Box 1570, State University, AR 72467. *Phone:* 870-972-3024. *Toll-free phone:* 800-382-3030. *Fax:* 870-972-3406. *E-mail:* admissions@astate.edu. *Website:* http://www.astate.edu/.

Arkansas Tech University

Russellville, Arkansas

- **State-supported** comprehensive, founded 1909
- **Small-town** 559-acre campus
- **Endowment** $17.0 million
- **Coed** 10,089 undergraduate students, 70% full-time, 55% women, 45% men
- **Moderately difficult** entrance level, 88% of applicants were admitted

Undergraduates 7,068 full-time, 3,021 part-time. Students come from 41 states and territories; 32 other countries; 4% are from out of state; 7% Black or African American, non-Hispanic/Latino; 5% Hispanic/Latino; 2% Asian, non-Hispanic/Latino; 0.0% Native Hawaiian or other Pacific Islander, non-Hispanic/Latino; 2% American Indian or Alaska Native, non-Hispanic/Latino; 1% Two or more races, non-Hispanic/Latino; 2% international; 6% transferred in; 30% live on campus. *Retention:* 67% of full-time freshmen returned.
Freshmen *Admission:* 3,857 applied, 3,394 admitted, 1,787 enrolled. *Average high school GPA:* 3.16. *Test scores:* SAT critical reading scores over 500: 55%; SAT math scores over 500: 64%; ACT scores over 18: 81%; SAT math scores over 600: 9%; ACT scores over 24: 34%; SAT math scores over 700: 9%; ACT scores over 30: 4%.
Faculty *Total:* 519, 64% full-time, 42% with terminal degrees. *Student/faculty ratio:* 20:1.
Academics *Calendar:* semesters. *Degrees:* certificates, associate, bachelor's, master's, and post-master's certificates. *Special study options:* academic remediation for entering students, accelerated degree program, adult/continuing education programs, advanced placement credit, distance learning, double majors, English as a second language, honors programs, independent study, internships, off-campus study, part-time degree program, services for LD students, study abroad, summer session for credit. *ROTC:* Army (c).
Computers on Campus 1,124 computers/terminals are available on campus for general student use. Students can access the following: campus intranet, computer help desk, free student e-mail accounts, online (class) grades, online (class) registration, online (class) schedules. Campuswide network is available. 100% of college-owned or -operated housing units are wired for high-speed Internet access. Wireless service is available via classrooms, computer centers, computer labs, dorm rooms, learning centers, libraries, student centers.
Student Life *Housing:* on-campus residence required through sophomore year. *Options:* coed, men-only, women-only, cooperative, disabled students. Campus housing is university owned. Freshman campus housing is guaranteed. *Activities and organizations:* drama/theater group, student-run newspaper, radio and television station, choral group, marching band, national fraternities, national sororities. *Campus security:* 24-hour emergency response devices and patrols, student patrols, late-night transport/escort service, controlled dormitory access. *Student services:* health clinic, personal/psychological counseling.
Athletics Member NCAA. All Division II. *Intercollegiate sports:* baseball M(s), basketball M(s)/W(s), cheerleading M(s)/W(s), cross-country running W(s), football M(s), golf M(s)/W(s), softball W(s), tennis W(s), volleyball W(s). *Intramural sports:* basketball M/W, bowling M/W, football M/W, racquetball M/W, soccer M/W, softball M/W, table tennis M/W, tennis M/W, ultimate Frisbee M/W, volleyball M/W.
Standardized Tests *Required:* SAT or ACT (for admission).
Costs (2012–13) *Tuition:* state resident $5610 full-time, $187 per credit hour part-time; nonresident $11,220 full-time, $374 per credit hour part-time. Full-time tuition and fees vary according to course load and location. Part-time tuition and fees vary according to course load and location. *Required fees:* $1188 full-time, $20 per credit hour part-time, $159 per term part-time. *Room and board:* $5846; room only: $3582. Room and board charges vary according to board plan, housing facility, and location. *Payment plans:* installment, deferred payment. *Waivers:* senior citizens and employees or children of employees.
Financial Aid Of all full-time matriculated undergraduates who enrolled in 2011, 6,418 applied for aid, 4,770 were judged to have need, 768 had their need fully met. In 2011, 878 non-need-based awards were made. *Average percent of need met:* 68%. *Average financial aid package:* $9044. *Average need-based loan:* $3696. *Average need-based gift aid:* $4688. *Average non-need-based aid:* $6606. *Average indebtedness upon graduation:* $22,649.

Applying *Options:* electronic application, early action, deferred entrance. *Required:* high school transcript, minimum 2.0 GPA. *Notification:* continuous (freshmen), continuous (transfers).

Freshman Application Contact Ms. Shauna Donnell, Director of Enrollment Management, Arkansas Tech University, Doc Bryan Student Services Building, Suite 141, Russellville, AR 72801. *Phone:* 479-968-0343. *Toll-free phone:* 800-582-6953. *Fax:* 479-964-0522. *E-mail:* tech.enroll@atu.edu. *Website:* http://www.atu.edu/.

Central Baptist College

Conway, Arkansas

- **Independent Baptist** 4-year, founded 1952
- **Small-town** 11-acre campus
- **Endowment** $1.5 million
- **Coed** 833 undergraduate students, 82% full-time, 48% women, 52% men
- **Minimally difficult** entrance level

Undergraduates 686 full-time, 147 part-time. Students come from 19 states and territories; 13 other countries; 13% are from out of state; 21% Black or African American, non-Hispanic/Latino; 2% Hispanic/Latino; 0.7% Asian, non-Hispanic/Latino; 0.2% Native Hawaiian or other Pacific Islander, non-Hispanic/Latino; 0.8% American Indian or Alaska Native, non-Hispanic/Latino; 0.7% Two or more races, non-Hispanic/Latino; 3% international; 14% transferred in. *Retention:* 50% of full-time freshmen returned.

Freshmen *Admission:* 108 enrolled. *Average high school GPA:* 3.14.

Faculty *Total:* 70, 37% full-time, 27% with terminal degrees. *Student/faculty ratio:* 20:1.

Academics *Calendar:* semesters. *Degrees:* associate and bachelor's. *Special study options:* academic remediation for entering students, adult/continuing education programs, advanced placement credit, internships, part-time degree program, summer session for credit. *ROTC:* Army (c).

Computers on Campus 70 computers/terminals are available on campus for general student use. Campuswide network is available.

Student Life *Housing:* on-campus residence required through senior year. *Activities and organizations:* drama/theater group, choral group. *Student services:* personal/psychological counseling.

Athletics Member NCCAA. *Intercollegiate sports:* baseball M/W, basketball M/W, cross-country running M/W, golf M/W, softball W, volleyball W. *Intramural sports:* badminton M/W, basketball M, bowling M/W, football M, softball M/W, table tennis M/W, tennis M/W, volleyball M/W.

Standardized Tests *Required:* ACT (for admission).

Applying *Options:* electronic application, early admission. *Required:* high school transcript, minimum 2.5 GPA, . *Application deadlines:* 8/15 (freshmen), 8/15 (transfers).

Freshman Application Contact Mr. Thomas Mobly, Admissions Counselor, Central Baptist College, 1501 College Avenue, Conway, AR 72034. *Phone:* 501-2058875 Ext.. *Toll-free phone:* 800-205-6872. *Fax:* 501-329-2941. *E-mail:* tmobly@cbc.edu. *Website:* http://www.cbc.edu/.

Ecclesia College

Springdale, Arkansas

Freshman Application Contact Ecclesia College, 9653 Nations Drive, Springdale, AR 72762. *Phone:* 479-248-7236 Ext. 223. *Website:* http://www.ecollege.edu/.

Harding University

Searcy, Arkansas

- **Independent** university, founded 1924, affiliated with Church of Christ
- **Small-town** 350-acre campus with easy access to Little Rock
- **Endowment** $99.3 million
- **Coed** 4,293 undergraduate students, 93% full-time, 54% women, 46% men
- **Moderately difficult** entrance level, 75% of applicants were admitted

Undergraduates 4,007 full-time, 286 part-time. Students come from 49 states and territories; 53 other countries; 71% are from out of state; 4% Black or African American, non-Hispanic/Latino; 3% Hispanic/Latino; 0.8% Asian, non-Hispanic/Latino; 0.5% American Indian or Alaska Native, non-Hispanic/Latino; 1% Two or more races, non-Hispanic/Latino; 0.3% Race/ethnicity unknown; 7% international; 5% transferred in; 72% live on campus. *Retention:* 81% of full-time freshmen returned.

Freshmen *Admission:* 2,477 applied, 1,849 admitted, 1,022 enrolled. *Average high school GPA:* 3.57. *Test scores:* SAT critical reading scores over 500: 75%; SAT math scores over 500: 72%; ACT scores over 18: 96%; SAT critical reading scores over 600: 35%; SAT math scores over 600: 30%; ACT scores over

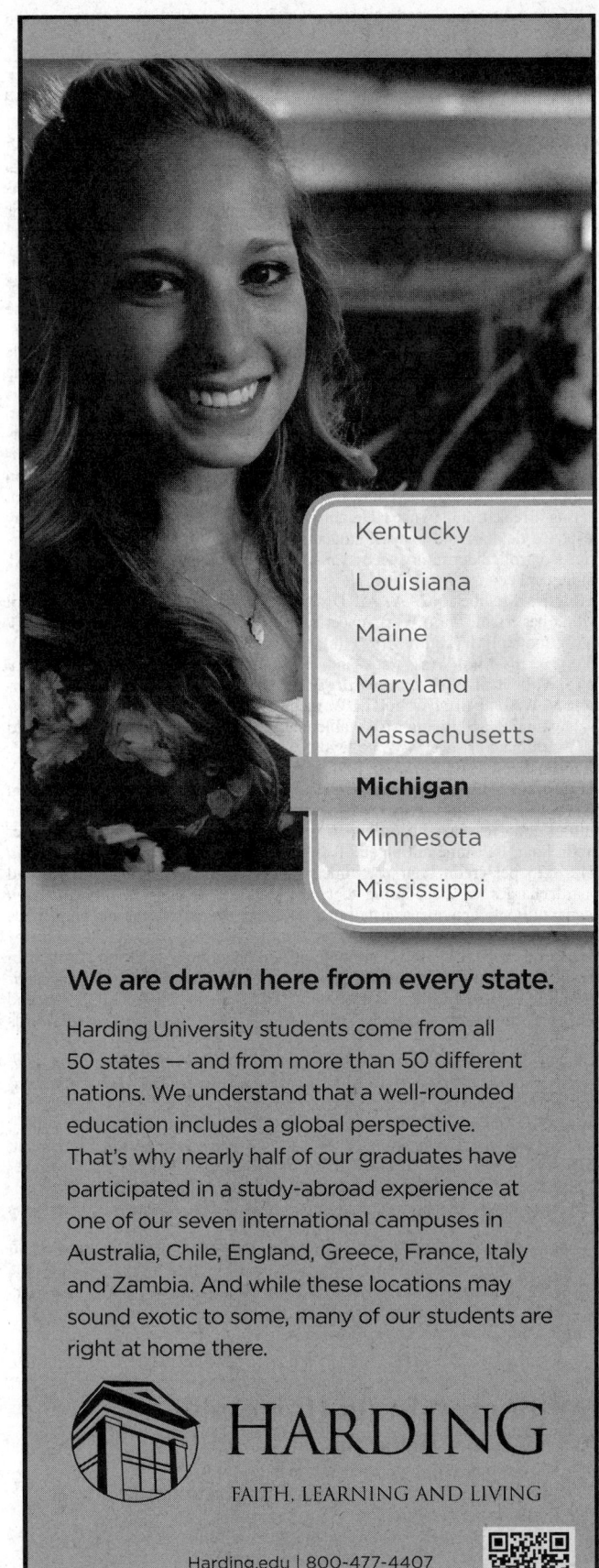

24: 63%; SAT critical reading scores over 700: 9%; SAT math scores over 700: 4%; ACT scores over 30: 16%.

Faculty *Total:* 585, 49% full-time, 45% with terminal degrees. *Student/faculty ratio:* 17:1.

Academics *Calendar:* semesters. *Degrees:* bachelor's, master's, doctoral, and post-master's certificates. *Special study options:* academic remediation for entering students, accelerated degree program, adult/continuing education programs, advanced placement credit, cooperative education, distance learning, double majors, English as a second language, freshman honors college, honors programs, independent study, internships, part-time degree program, services for LD students, student-designed majors, study abroad, summer session for credit.

Computers on Campus 482 computers/terminals and 2,400 ports are available on campus for general student use. Students can access the following: campus intranet, computer help desk, free student e-mail accounts, online (class) grades, online (class) registration, online (class) schedules. Campus-wide network is available. 100% of college-owned or -operated housing units are wired for high-speed Internet access. Wireless service is available via entire campus.

Student Life *Housing:* on-campus residence required through senior year. *Options:* men-only, women-only, disabled students. Campus housing is university owned. Freshman campus housing is guaranteed. *Activities and organizations:* drama/theater group, student-run newspaper, radio and television station, choral group, marching band, Bisons for Christ, Harding in Action, Spring Break Campaigns, HUmanity. *Campus security:* 24-hour emergency response devices and patrols, student patrols, late-night transport/escort service, controlled dormitory access. *Student services:* health clinic, personal/psychological counseling.

Athletics Member NCAA. All Division II. *Intercollegiate sports:* baseball M(s), basketball M(s)/W(s), cheerleading W, cross-country running M(s)/W(s), football M(s), golf M(s)/W(s), lacrosse M(c), rugby M(c), soccer M(s)/W(s), tennis M(s)/W(s), track and field M(s)/W(s), ultimate Frisbee M(c)/W(c), volleyball W(s). *Intramural sports:* basketball M/W, cross-country running M/W, football M/W, golf M/W, racquetball M/W, soccer M/W, softball M/W, swimming and diving M/W, table tennis M/W, tennis M/W, track and field M/W, ultimate Frisbee M/W, volleyball M/W, weight lifting M/W.

Standardized Tests *Required:* SAT or ACT (for admission).

Costs (2012–13) *Comprehensive fee:* $21,432 includes full-time tuition ($14,790), mandatory fees ($450), and room and board ($6192). Full-time tuition and fees vary according to course load. Part-time tuition: $493 per credit hour. Part-time tuition and fees vary according to course load. *Required fees:* $25 per credit hour part-time. *College room only:* $3094. Room and board charges vary according to board plan and housing facility. *Payment plans:* tuition prepayment, installment. *Waivers:* senior citizens and employees or children of employees.

Financial Aid Of all full-time matriculated undergraduates who enrolled in 2011, 3,136 applied for aid, 2,431 were judged to have need, 636 had their need fully met. 424 Federal Work-Study jobs (averaging $807). 1,398 state and other part-time jobs (averaging $1677). In 2011, 1285 non-need-based awards were made. *Average percent of need met:* 71%. *Average financial aid package:* $13,114. *Average need-based loan:* $4853. *Average need-based gift aid:* $8510. *Average non-need-based aid:* $7136. *Average indebtedness upon graduation:* $32,752.

Applying *Options:* electronic application, early admission, early action, deferred entrance. *Application fee:* $40. *Required:* essay or personal statement, high school transcript, 2 letters of recommendation. *Application deadlines:* rolling (freshmen), rolling (out-of-state freshmen), rolling (transfers). *Notification:* continuous (freshmen), continuous (out-of-state freshmen), continuous (transfers).

Freshman Application Contact Mr. Glenn Dillard, Assistant Vice President for Enrollment Management, Harding University, Box 12255, Searcy, AR 72149-2255. *Phone:* 501-279-4407. *Toll-free phone:* 800-477-4407. *Fax:* 501-279-4129. *E-mail:* admissions@harding.edu.
Website: http://www.harding.edu/.

See display ad on previous page and page 1314 for the College Close-Up.

Henderson State University
Arkadelphia, Arkansas
- **State-supported** comprehensive, founded 1890
- **Small-town** 151-acre campus with easy access to Little Rock
- **Endowment** $12.3 million
- **Coed** 3,363 undergraduate students, 90% full-time, 56% women, 44% men
- **Moderately difficult** entrance level, 61% of applicants were admitted

Undergraduates 3,017 full-time, 346 part-time. Students come from 25 states and territories; 15 other countries; 13% are from out of state; 23% Black or African American, non-Hispanic/Latino; 3% Hispanic/Latino; 0.7% Asian,

non-Hispanic/Latino; 0.3% American Indian or Alaska Native, non-Hispanic/Latino; 5% Two or more races, non-Hispanic/Latino; 0.8% international; 10% transferred in; 41% live on campus. *Retention:* 59% of full-time freshmen returned.

Freshmen *Admission:* 3,383 applied, 2,067 admitted, 781 enrolled. *Average high school GPA:* 3.2. *Test scores:* SAT critical reading scores over 500: 37%; SAT math scores over 500: 63%; ACT scores over 18: 84%; SAT critical reading scores over 600: 13%; SAT math scores over 600: 17%; ACT scores over 24: 29%; SAT critical reading scores over 700: 3%; ACT scores over 30: 2%.

Faculty *Total:* 259, 67% full-time, 53% with terminal degrees. *Student/faculty ratio:* 16:1.

Academics *Calendar:* semesters. *Degrees:* certificates, bachelor's, master's, post-master's, and postbachelor's certificates. *Special study options:* academic remediation for entering students, advanced placement credit, distance learning, English as a second language, freshman honors college, honors programs, internships, off-campus study, part-time degree program, services for LD students, summer session for credit. *ROTC:* Army (c).

Computers on Campus 125 computers/terminals are available on campus for general student use. Students can access the following: campus intranet, computer help desk, free student e-mail accounts, online (class) grades, online (class) registration, online (class) schedules. Campuswide network is available. 100% of college-owned or -operated housing units are wired for high-speed Internet access. Wireless service is available via classrooms, computer centers, computer labs, dorm rooms, libraries, student centers.

Student Life *Housing:* on-campus residence required for freshman year. *Options:* coed, men-only, women-only, cooperative. Campus housing is university owned and is provided by a third party. Freshman applicants given priority for college housing. *Activities and organizations:* drama/theater group, student-run newspaper, radio and television station, choral group, marching band, Heart and Key, Student Government Association, Residence Hall Association, national fraternities, national sororities. *Campus security:* 24-hour emergency response devices and patrols, late-night transport/escort service, controlled dormitory access. *Student services:* health clinic, personal/psychological counseling.

Athletics Member NCAA. All Division II. *Intercollegiate sports:* baseball M(s), basketball M(s)/W(s), cross-country running W(s), football M(s), golf M(s)/W(s), softball W(s), swimming and diving M(s)/W(s), tennis M(s)/W(s), volleyball W(s). *Intramural sports:* basketball M/W, football M, golf M/W, soccer M, softball W, swimming and diving M/W, tennis M/W.

Standardized Tests *Required:* SAT or ACT (for admission). *Recommended:* ACT (for admission).

Costs (2012–13) *Tuition:* state resident $5880 full-time, $196 per credit hour part-time; nonresident $11,760 full-time, $392 per credit hour part-time. Full-time tuition and fees vary according to course load, degree level, and student level. Part-time tuition and fees vary according to course load, degree level, and student level. *Required fees:* $1104 full-time. *Room and board:* $5332. Room and board charges vary according to board plan and housing facility. *Waivers:* children of alumni, senior citizens, and employees or children of employees.

Financial Aid Of all full-time matriculated undergraduates who enrolled in 2009, 3,026 applied for aid, 2,535 were judged to have need, 24 had their need fully met. In 2009, 95 non-need-based awards were made. *Average percent of need met:* 83%. *Average financial aid package:* $10,648. *Average need-based loan:* $3984. *Average need-based gift aid:* $11,908. *Average non-need-based aid:* $9096. *Average indebtedness upon graduation:* $16,529.

Applying *Options:* electronic application, deferred entrance. *Required:* high school transcript. *Required for some:* essay or personal statement, 3 letters of recommendation. *Recommended:* minimum 2.5 GPA. *Application deadlines:* 7/15 (freshmen), rolling (transfers). *Notification:* continuous (freshmen), continuous (transfers).

Freshman Application Contact Ms. Vikita Hardwrick, Director of University Relations/Admissions, Henderson State University, 1100 Henderson Street, PO Box 7560, Arkadelphia, AR 71999-0001. *Phone:* 870-230-5028. *Toll-free phone:* 800-228-7333. *Fax:* 870-230-5066. *E-mail:* hardwrv@hsu.edu.
Website: http://www.hsu.edu/.

Hendrix College
Conway, Arkansas
- **Independent United Methodist** comprehensive, founded 1876
- **Suburban** 180-acre campus with easy access to Little Rock
- **Endowment** $158.0 million
- **Coed** 1,373 undergraduate students, 99% full-time, 57% women, 43% men
- **Very difficult** entrance level, 83% of applicants were admitted

Undergraduates 1,356 full-time, 17 part-time. Students come from 45 states and territories; 11 other countries; 55% are from out of state; 3% Black or African American, non-Hispanic/Latino; 5% Hispanic/Latino; 3% Asian, non-His-

panic/Latino; 0.5% American Indian or Alaska Native, non-Hispanic/Latino; 3% Two or more races, non-Hispanic/Latino; 7% Race/ethnicity unknown; 5% international; 0.9% transferred in; 91% live on campus. *Retention:* 86% of full-time freshmen returned.

Freshmen *Admission:* 1,656 applied, 1,374 admitted, 369 enrolled. *Average high school GPA:* 3.9. *Test scores:* SAT critical reading scores over 500: 90%; SAT math scores over 500: 92%; ACT scores over 18: 100%; SAT critical reading scores over 600: 57%; SAT math scores over 600: 56%; ACT scores over 24: 90%; SAT critical reading scores over 700: 22%; SAT math scores over 700: 16%; ACT scores over 30: 46%.

Faculty *Total:* 142, 76% full-time, 80% with terminal degrees. *Student/faculty ratio:* 11:1.

Academics *Calendar:* semesters. *Degrees:* bachelor's and master's. *Special study options:* advanced placement credit, cooperative education, double majors, English as a second language, external degree program, independent study, internships, off-campus study, services for LD students, student-designed majors, study abroad. *ROTC:* Army (c). *Unusual degree programs:* 3-2 engineering with Columbia University, Vanderbilt University, Washington University in St. Louis; Public Health BA/MPH with University of Arkansas Medical School.

Computers on Campus 75 computers/terminals are available on campus for general student use. Students can access the following: campus intranet, computer help desk, free student e-mail accounts, online (class) grades, online (class) registration, online (class) schedules. Campuswide network is available. 100% of college-owned or -operated housing units are wired for high-speed Internet access. Wireless service is available via entire campus.

Student Life *Housing:* on-campus residence required through senior year. *Options:* coed, men-only, women-only. Campus housing is university owned. Freshman campus housing is guaranteed. *Activities and organizations:* drama/theater group, student-run newspaper, radio station, choral group, Volunteer Action Center, student government, Music ensembles, Unity, Social Committee. *Campus security:* 24-hour emergency response devices and patrols, late-night transport/escort service, controlled dormitory access. *Student services:* health clinic, personal/psychological counseling.

Athletics Member NCAA. All Division III. *Intercollegiate sports:* baseball M, basketball M/W, cross-country running M/W, field hockey W, football M, golf M/W, lacrosse M/W, soccer M/W, softball W, swimming and diving M/W, tennis M/W, track and field M/W, volleyball W. *Intramural sports:* basketball M/W, cheerleading M/W, football M/W, racquetball M/W, soccer M/W, softball M/W, table tennis M/W, tennis M/W, ultimate Frisbee M/W.

Standardized Tests *Required:* SAT or ACT (for admission).

Costs (2013–14) *Comprehensive fee:* $48,436 includes full-time tuition ($37,516), mandatory fees ($300), and room and board ($10,620). Full-time tuition and fees vary according to course load and student level. Part-time tuition and fees vary according to course load and student level. *College room only:* $5480. Room and board charges vary according to board plan and housing facility. *Payment plan:* installment. *Waivers:* employees or children of employees.

Financial Aid Of all full-time matriculated undergraduates who enrolled in 2012, 1,071 applied for aid, 815 were judged to have need, 330 had their need fully met. 504 Federal Work-Study jobs (averaging $1421). 301 state and other part-time jobs (averaging $1407). In 2012, 529 non-need-based awards were made. *Average percent of need met:* 83%. *Average financial aid package:* $28,189. *Average need-based loan:* $4252. *Average need-based gift aid:* $24,498. *Average non-need-based aid:* $21,174. *Average indebtedness upon graduation:* $24,492.

Applying *Options:* electronic application, early action. *Application fee:* $40. *Required:* essay or personal statement, high school transcript. *Required for some:* interview. *Recommended:* 1 letter of recommendation. *Application deadlines:* 6/1 (freshmen), 7/1 (transfers). *Notification:* continuous (freshmen), 4/30 (out-of-state freshmen), continuous (transfers).

Freshman Application Contact Mr. Fred Baker, Director of Admission, Hendrix College, 1600 Washington Avenue, Conway, AR 72032. *Phone:* 501-450-1362. *Toll-free phone:* 800-277-9017. *Fax:* 501-450-3843. *E-mail:* baker@hendrix.edu. *Website:* http://www.hendrix.edu/.

ITT Technical Institute
Little Rock, Arkansas

- **Proprietary** primarily 2-year, founded 1993, part of ITT Educational Services, Inc.
- **Urban** campus
- **Coed**
- **Minimally difficult** entrance level

Academics *Calendar:* quarters. *Degrees:* associate and bachelor's.

Freshman Application Contact Director of Recruitment, ITT Technical Institute, 12200 Westhaven Drive, Little Rock, AR 72211. *Phone:* 501-565-5550. *Toll-free phone:* 800-359-4429. *Website:* http://www.itt-tech.edu/.

John Brown University
Siloam Springs, Arkansas

- **Independent interdenominational** comprehensive, founded 1919
- **Small-town** 200-acre campus
- **Coed** 1,779 undergraduate students, 88% full-time, 56% women, 44% men
- **Moderately difficult** entrance level, 66% of applicants were admitted

Undergraduates 1,563 full-time, 216 part-time. Students come from 40 states and territories; 39 other countries; 62% are from out of state; 2% Black or African American, non-Hispanic/Latino; 8% Hispanic/Latino; 0.7% Asian, non-Hispanic/Latino; 0.1% Native Hawaiian or other Pacific Islander, non-Hispanic/Latino; 1% American Indian or Alaska Native, non-Hispanic/Latino; 1% Race/ethnicity unknown; 6% international; 4% transferred in; 74% live on campus. *Retention:* 84% of full-time freshmen returned.

Freshmen *Admission:* 1,170 applied, 777 admitted, 318 enrolled. *Average high school GPA:* 3.59. *Test scores:* SAT critical reading scores over 500: 77%; SAT math scores over 500: 83%; SAT writing scores over 500: 76%; ACT scores over 18: 99%; SAT critical reading scores over 600: 42%; SAT math scores over 600: 37%; SAT writing scores over 600: 32%; ACT scores over 24: 60%; SAT critical reading scores over 700: 4%; SAT math scores over 700: 5%; SAT writing scores over 700: 4%; ACT scores over 30: 17%.

Faculty *Total:* 156, 54% full-time, 54% with terminal degrees. *Student/faculty ratio:* 14:1.

Academics *Calendar:* semesters. *Degrees:* associate, bachelor's, and master's. *Special study options:* accelerated degree program, adult/continuing education programs, distance learning, double majors, English as a second language, external degree program, honors programs, independent study, internships, services for LD students, study abroad. *ROTC:* Army (c), Air Force (c).

Computers on Campus 100 computers/terminals are available on campus for general student use. Students can access the following: campus intranet, computer help desk, free student e-mail accounts, online (class) grades, online (class) registration, online (class) schedules. Campuswide network is available. 100% of college-owned or -operated housing units are wired for high-speed Internet access. Wireless service is available via classrooms, dorm rooms, learning centers, libraries, student centers.

Student Life *Housing:* on-campus residence required through junior year. *Options:* coed, men-only, women-only, disabled students. Campus housing is university owned. Freshman campus housing is guaranteed. *Activities and organizations:* drama/theater group, student-run newspaper, radio station, choral group, Student Government Association, Student Ministries Organization, Student Activities Club, Student Missionary Fellowship. *Campus security:* 24-hour emergency response devices and patrols, late-night transport/escort service, controlled dormitory access. *Student services:* health clinic, personal/psychological counseling.

Athletics Member NAIA. *Intercollegiate sports:* basketball M(s)/W(s), cheerleading M(s)/W(s), cross-country running M(s)/W(s), golf M(s), soccer M(s)/W(s), tennis M(s)/W(s), volleyball W(s). *Intramural sports:* baseball M, basketball M/W, football M/W, golf M, racquetball M/W, rugby M, soccer M/W, softball M/W, table tennis M/W, tennis M/W, ultimate Frisbee M/W, volleyball M/W.

Standardized Tests *Required:* SAT or ACT (for admission).

Costs (2013–14) *Comprehensive fee:* $30,996 includes full-time tuition ($21,736), mandatory fees ($998), and room and board ($8262). Full-time tuition and fees vary according to course load. Part-time tuition: $694 per credit. Part-time tuition and fees vary according to course load. *Room and board:* Room and board charges vary according to board plan and housing facility. *Payment plan:* installment. *Waivers:* employees or children of employees.

Financial Aid Of all full-time matriculated undergraduates who enrolled in 2012, 1,033 applied for aid, 897 were judged to have need, 141 had their need fully met. In 2012, 348 non-need-based awards were made. *Average percent of need met:* 83%. *Average financial aid package:* $19,072. *Average need-based loan:* $3231. *Average need-based gift aid:* $14,709. *Average non-need-based aid:* $13,752. *Average indebtedness upon graduation:* $24,160.

Applying *Options:* electronic application, deferred entrance. *Application fee:* $25. *Required:* essay or personal statement, high school transcript, minimum 2.5 GPA, 2 letters of recommendation. *Recommended:* interview. *Application deadlines:* rolling (freshmen), rolling (transfers). *Notification:* continuous (freshmen), continuous (transfers).

Freshman Application Contact Mr. Jared Burgess, Director of Visitation Program, John Brown University, 2000 West University, Siloam Springs, AR

72761. *Phone:* 479-524-7190. *Toll-free phone:* 877-JBU-INFO. *Fax:* 479-524-4196. *E-mail:* JBurgess@jbu.edu.
Website: http://www.jbu.edu/.

Lyon College
Batesville, Arkansas

- **Independent Presbyterian** 4-year, founded 1872
- **Small-town** 136-acre campus
- **Endowment** $37.1 million
- **Coed** 600 undergraduate students, 96% full-time, 53% women, 47% men
- **Moderately difficult** entrance level, 98% of applicants were admitted

Undergraduates 573 full-time, 27 part-time. Students come from 21 states and territories; 13 other countries; 24% are from out of state; 4% Black or African American, non-Hispanic/Latino; 5% Hispanic/Latino; 1% Asian, non-Hispanic/Latino; 1% American Indian or Alaska Native, non-Hispanic/Latino; 7% Race/ethnicity unknown; 4% international; 9% transferred in; 78% live on campus. *Retention:* 72% of full-time freshmen returned.

Freshmen *Admission:* 500 applied, 488 admitted, 160 enrolled. *Average high school GPA:* 3.6. *Test scores:* SAT critical reading scores over 500: 59%; SAT math scores over 500: 71%; SAT writing scores over 500: 41%; ACT scores over 18: 100%; SAT critical reading scores over 600: 18%; SAT math scores over 600: 18%; SAT writing scores over 600: 17%; ACT scores over 24: 64%; SAT math scores over 700: 6%; ACT scores over 30: 12%.

Faculty *Total:* 75, 55% full-time. *Student/faculty ratio:* 11:1.

Academics *Calendar:* semesters. *Degree:* bachelor's. *Special study options:* accelerated degree program, advanced placement credit, double majors, independent study, internships, off-campus study, part-time degree program, student-designed majors, study abroad, summer session for credit. *Unusual degree programs:* 3-2 engineering with University of Missouri-Rolla, University of Arkansas, University of Minnesota.

Computers on Campus 101 computers/terminals are available on campus for general student use. Students can access the following: campus intranet, computer help desk, free student e-mail accounts, online (class) grades, online (class) registration, online (class) schedules. Campuswide network is available. 100% of college-owned or -operated housing units are wired for high-speed Internet access. Wireless service is available via entire campus.

Student Life *Housing:* on-campus residence required through junior year. *Options:* coed, men-only, women-only. Campus housing is university owned. Freshman campus housing is guaranteed. *Activities and organizations:* drama/theater group, student-run newspaper, choral group, Wesley Fellowship, Gay-Straight Alliance, Alpha Xi Delta Sorority, Fellowship of Christian Athletes, Young Democrats/Japanese Culture Club, national fraternities, national sororities. *Campus security:* 24-hour patrols, late-night transport/escort service, controlled dormitory access. *Student services:* health clinic, personal/psychological counseling.

Athletics Member NAIA. *Intercollegiate sports:* baseball M(s), basketball M(s)/W(s), cross-country running M(s)/W(s), golf M(s)/W(s), soccer M(s)/W(s), softball W(s), volleyball W(s). *Intramural sports:* badminton M/W, basketball M/W, football M/W, softball M/W, table tennis M/W, tennis M/W, ultimate Frisbee M/W, volleyball M/W.

Standardized Tests *Required:* SAT or ACT (for admission).

Costs (2012–13) *Comprehensive fee:* $31,154 includes full-time tuition ($23,370), mandatory fees ($224), and room and board ($7560). Part-time tuition: $780 per credit hour. *Room and board:* Room and board charges vary according to board plan and housing facility. *Payment plan:* installment. *Waivers:* employees or children of employees.

Financial Aid Of all full-time matriculated undergraduates who enrolled in 2012, 506 applied for aid, 452 were judged to have need, 109 had their need fully met. 157 Federal Work-Study jobs (averaging $921). 4 state and other part-time jobs (averaging $1000). In 2012, 71 non-need-based awards were made. *Average percent of need met:* 81%. *Average financial aid package:* $21,897. *Average need-based loan:* $4506. *Average need-based gift aid:* $18,274. *Average non-need-based aid:* $13,164. *Average indebtedness upon graduation:* $17,179.

Applying *Options:* electronic application, early admission, early action, deferred entrance. *Application fee:* $25. *Required:* high school transcript, minimum 2.5 GPA. *Required for some:* essay or personal statement, 2 letters of recommendation. *Application deadlines:* rolling (freshmen), rolling (transfers). *Notification:* continuous (freshmen), continuous (transfers).

Freshman Application Contact Office of Enrollment Services, Lyon College, 2300 Highland Road, Batesville, AR 72501. *Phone:* 870-307-7250. *Toll-free phone:* 800-423-2542. *Fax:* 870-307-7542. *E-mail:* admissions@lyon.edu. *Website:* http://www.lyon.edu/.

Ouachita Baptist University
Arkadelphia, Arkansas

- **Independent Baptist** 4-year, founded 1886
- **Small-town** 200-acre campus with easy access to Little Rock
- **Endowment** $81.3 million
- **Coed** 1,532 undergraduate students, 98% full-time, 54% women, 46% men
- **Moderately difficult** entrance level, 69% of applicants were admitted

Undergraduates 1,496 full-time, 36 part-time. Students come from 29 states and territories; 36 other countries; 40% are from out of state; 7% Black or African American, non-Hispanic/Latino; 3% Hispanic/Latino; 0.7% Asian, non-Hispanic/Latino; 0.1% Native Hawaiian or other Pacific Islander, non-Hispanic/Latino; 1% American Indian or Alaska Native, non-Hispanic/Latino; 0.1% Two or more races, non-Hispanic/Latino; 2% international; 3% transferred in; 96% live on campus. *Retention:* 76% of full-time freshmen returned.

Freshmen *Admission:* 1,822 applied, 1,259 admitted, 363 enrolled. *Average high school GPA:* 3.56. *Test scores:* SAT critical reading scores over 500: 67%; SAT math scores over 500: 64%; ACT scores over 18: 97%; SAT critical reading scores over 600: 24%; SAT math scores over 600: 25%; ACT scores over 24: 59%; SAT critical reading scores over 700: 4%; SAT math scores over 700: 7%; ACT scores over 30: 15%.

Faculty *Total:* 155, 71% full-time, 63% with terminal degrees. *Student/faculty ratio:* 12:1.

Academics *Calendar:* semesters. *Degree:* bachelor's. *Special study options:* academic remediation for entering students, accelerated degree program, advanced placement credit, cooperative education, distance learning, double majors, English as a second language, honors programs, independent study, internships, off-campus study, part-time degree program, study abroad, summer session for credit. *ROTC:* Army (b). *Unusual degree programs:* 3-2 engineering with University of Arkansas at Fayetteville.

Computers on Campus 275 computers/terminals and 1,350 ports are available on campus for general student use. Students can access the following: campus intranet, computer help desk, free student e-mail accounts, online (class) grades, online (class) schedules, student Web portal. Campuswide network is available. 100% of college-owned or -operated housing units are wired for high-speed Internet access. Wireless service is available via entire campus.

Student Life *Housing:* on-campus residence required through senior year. *Options:* men-only, women-only, disabled students. Campus housing is university owned and leased by the school. Freshman campus housing is guaranteed. *Activities and organizations:* drama/theater group, student-run newspaper, television station, choral group, marching band, Phi Beta Lambda, Campus Activities Board, Student Education Association, Student Foundation, International Club. *Campus security:* 24-hour emergency response devices and patrols, controlled dormitory access. *Student services:* health clinic, personal/psychological counseling.

Athletics Member NCAA. All Division II. *Intercollegiate sports:* baseball M(s), basketball M(s)/W(s), cheerleading M/W, cross-country running W(s), football M(s), golf M(s)/W(s), soccer M(s)/W(s), softball W(s), swimming and diving M(s)/W(s), tennis M(s)/W(s), volleyball W(s), wrestling M(s). *Intramural sports:* basketball M/W, football M/W, soccer M, softball M/W, table tennis M/W.

Standardized Tests *Required:* SAT or ACT (for admission).

Costs (2013–14) *Comprehensive fee:* $28,980 includes full-time tuition ($21,860), mandatory fees ($480), and room and board ($6640). Part-time tuition: $605 per semester hour. *Room and board:* Room and board charges vary according to housing facility. *Payment plans:* installment, deferred payment. *Waivers:* employees or children of employees.

Financial Aid Of all full-time matriculated undergraduates who enrolled in 2012, 1,128 applied for aid, 923 were judged to have need, 314 had their need fully met. 303 Federal Work-Study jobs (averaging $1800). 154 state and other part-time jobs (averaging $1730). In 2012, 522 non-need-based awards were made. *Average percent of need met:* 84%. *Average financial aid package:* $19,727. *Average need-based loan:* $4191. *Average need-based gift aid:* $13,534. *Average non-need-based aid:* $9643. *Average indebtedness upon graduation:* $24,367. *Financial aid deadline:* 6/1.

Applying *Options:* deferred entrance. *Required:* high school transcript, minimum 2.8 GPA. *Recommended:* interview. *Application deadlines:* 8/15 (freshmen), 8/15 (transfers). *Notification:* continuous (freshmen), continuous (transfers).

Freshman Application Contact Mrs. Lori Motl, Director of Admissions Counseling, Ouachita Baptist University, OBU Box 3776, Arkadelphia, AR 71998-0001. *Phone:* 870-245-5110. *Toll-free phone:* 800-342-5628. *Fax:* 870-245-5500. *E-mail:* motll@obu.edu. *Website:* http://www.obu.edu/.

Philander Smith College

Little Rock, Arkansas

- **Independent United Methodist** 4-year, founded 1877
- **Urban** 25-acre campus
- **Coed**
- **Minimally difficult** entrance level

Faculty *Student/faculty ratio:* 13:1.

Academics *Calendar:* semesters. *Degree:* bachelor's.

Student Life *Campus security:* 24-hour emergency response devices and patrols, student patrols, controlled dormitory access.

Standardized Tests *Required:* SAT or ACT (for admission).

Costs (2012–13) *Comprehensive fee:* $19,510 includes full-time tuition ($11,350), mandatory fees ($560), and room and board ($7600). Full-time tuition and fees vary according to course load, program, and student level. Part-time tuition: $400 per credit hour. Part-time tuition and fees vary according to course load, program, and student level. *Room and board:* Room and board charges vary according to housing facility. *Payment plans:* installment, deferred payment.

Financial Aid *Of all full-time matriculated undergraduates who enrolled in 2011,* 690 applied for aid, 668 were judged to have need, 36 had their need fully met. 76 Federal Work-Study jobs (averaging $2600). *In 2011,* 37 non-need-based awards were made. *Average percent of need met:* 54. *Average financial aid package:* $11,336. *Average need-based loan:* $3618. *Average need-based gift aid:* $8165. *Average non-need-based aid:* $11,012. *Average indebtedness upon graduation:* $35,000.

Applying *Options:* deferred entrance. *Application fee:* $25. *Required:* high school transcript, minimum 2.0 GPA. *Required for some:* essay or personal statement, interview.

Freshman Application Contact Mr. George Gray, Director of Recruitment and Admissions, Philander Smith College, 812 West 13th Street, Little Rock, AR 72202-3799. *Phone:* 501-370-5310. *Toll-free phone:* 800-446-6772. *Fax:* 501-370-5225. *E-mail:* ggray@philander.edu.

Website: http://www.philander.edu/.

Southern Arkansas University–Magnolia

Magnolia, Arkansas

- **State-supported** comprehensive, founded 1909, part of Southern Arkansas University System
- **Small-town** 781-acre campus
- **Endowment** $22.2 million
- **Coed** 2,918 undergraduate students, 84% full-time, 58% women, 42% men
- **Moderately difficult** entrance level, 65% of applicants were admitted

Undergraduates 2,457 full-time, 461 part-time. Students come from 26 states and territories; 25 other countries; 23% are from out of state; 29% Black or African American, non-Hispanic/Latino; 3% Hispanic/Latino; 0.7% Asian, non-Hispanic/Latino; 0.7% Native Hawaiian or other Pacific Islander, non-Hispanic/Latino; 0.5% American Indian or Alaska Native, non-Hispanic/Latino; 3% international; 8% transferred in; 46% live on campus. *Retention:* 60% of full-time freshmen returned.

Freshmen *Admission:* 2,631 applied, 1,699 admitted, 598 enrolled. *Average high school GPA:* 3.2. *Test scores:* SAT critical reading scores over 500: 35%; SAT math scores over 500: 45%; ACT scores over 18: 81%; SAT critical reading scores over 600: 10%; SAT math scores over 600: 17%; ACT scores over 24: 29%; SAT math scores over 700: 5%; ACT scores over 30: 2%.

Faculty *Total:* 174, 100% full-time, 56% with terminal degrees. *Student/faculty ratio:* 16:1.

Academics *Calendar:* semesters. *Degrees:* certificates, associate, bachelor's, and master's. *Special study options:* academic remediation for entering students, accelerated degree program, adult/continuing education programs, advanced placement credit, distance learning, double majors, English as a second language, freshman honors college, honors programs, independent study, internships, part-time degree program, services for LD students, study abroad, summer session for credit.

Computers on Campus 199 computers/terminals and 199 ports are available on campus for general student use. Students can access the following: campus intranet, computer help desk, free student e-mail accounts, online (class) grades, online (class) registration, online (class) schedules. Campuswide network is available. 100% of college-owned or -operated housing units are wired for high-speed Internet access. Wireless service is available via computer centers, computer labs, dorm rooms, libraries, student centers.

Student Life *Housing:* on-campus residence required through sophomore year. *Options:* coed, men-only, women-only. Campus housing is university owned and is provided by a third party. Freshman campus housing is guaranteed.

Activities and organizations: drama/theater group, student-run newspaper, radio station, choral group, marching band, Student Government Association, Student Activities Board, Resident Hall Association, Residential College, International Student Association, national fraternities, national sororities. *Campus security:* 24-hour emergency response devices, student patrols, late-night transport/escort service, controlled dormitory access. *Student services:* health clinic, personal/psychological counseling.

Athletics Member NCAA. All Division II. *Intercollegiate sports:* baseball M(s), basketball M(s)/W(s), cheerleading M(s)(c)/W(s)(c), cross-country running M(s)/W(s), football M(s), golf M/W, softball W(s), tennis W(s), track and field M(s)/W(s), volleyball W(s). *Intramural sports:* badminton M/W, basketball M/W, football M, golf M/W, soccer M/W, softball M/W, swimming and diving M/W, table tennis M/W, tennis M/W, ultimate Frisbee M/W, volleyball M/W.

Standardized Tests *Required:* SAT or ACT (for admission). *Recommended:* ACT (for admission).

Costs (2012–13) *Tuition:* state resident $5880 full-time, $196 per hour part-time; nonresident $8910 full-time, $297 per hour part-time. Full-time tuition and fees vary according to course load. Part-time tuition and fees vary according to course load. *Required fees:* $1466 full-time, $39 per hour part-time, $18 per term part-time. *Room and board:* $4974; room only: $2440. Room and board charges vary according to board plan and housing facility. *Payment plan:* installment. *Waivers:* children of alumni, senior citizens, and employees or children of employees.

Financial Aid *Of all full-time matriculated undergraduates who enrolled in 2009,* 1,959 applied for aid, 1,766 were judged to have need, 1,187 had their need fully met. 1,250 Federal Work-Study jobs (averaging $3097). 303 state and other part-time jobs (averaging $4268). *In 2009,* 284 non-need-based awards were made. *Average percent of need met:* 100%. *Average financial aid package:* $7679. *Average need-based loan:* $3692. *Average need-based gift aid:* $4106. *Average non-need-based aid:* $5891. *Average indebtedness upon graduation:* $15,672.

Applying *Options:* electronic application, early admission, deferred entrance. *Required:* high school transcript. *Required for some:* interview. *Application deadlines:* 8/27 (freshmen), 8/27 (transfers).

Freshman Application Contact Southern Arkansas University–Magnolia, 100 East University, Magnolia, AR 71753. *Phone:* 870-235-4040. *Toll-free phone:* 800-332-7286.

Website: http://www.saumag.edu/.

Strayer University—Little Rock Campus

Little Rock, Arkansas

Freshman Application Contact Strayer University—Little Rock Campus, 10825 Financial Centre Parkway, Suite 131, Little Rock, AR 72211. *Website:* http://www.strayer.edu/campus/little-rock.

University of Arkansas

Fayetteville, Arkansas

- **State-supported** university, founded 1871, part of University of Arkansas System
- **Suburban** 410-acre campus
- **Endowment** $673.1 million
- **Coed**
- **Moderately difficult** entrance level

Faculty *Student/faculty ratio:* 18:1.

Academics *Calendar:* semesters. *Degrees:* bachelor's, master's, doctoral, post-master's, and postbachelor's certificates.

Student Life *Campus security:* 24-hour emergency response devices and patrols, student patrols, late-night transport/escort service, controlled dormitory access, RAD (Rape Aggression Defense program).

Athletics Member NCAA. All Division I except football (Division I-A).

Standardized Tests *Required:* SAT or ACT (for admission).

Costs (2012–13) *Tuition:* state resident $6141 full-time; nonresident $17,022 full-time. Full-time tuition and fees vary according to course load and program. Part-time tuition and fees vary according to course load and program. *Required fees:* $1412 full-time. *Room and board:* $8672; room only: $5494. Room and board charges vary according to board plan and housing facility.

Financial Aid *Of all full-time matriculated undergraduates who enrolled in 2010,* 11,311 applied for aid, 7,954 were judged to have need, 1,500 had their need fully met. *In 2010,* 2248 non-need-based awards were made. *Average percent of need met:* 63. *Average financial aid package:* $9691. *Average need-based loan:* $4310. *Average need-based gift aid:* $6896. *Average non-need-based aid:* $5301. *Average indebtedness upon graduation:* $23,111.

Applying *Options:* electronic application, early admission, early action. *Application fee:* $40. *Required:* high school transcript. *Recommended:* minimum 3.0 GPA.

Freshman Application Contact University of Arkansas, 232 Silas H. Hunt Hall, Office of Admissions, Fayetteville, AR 72701-1201. *Phone:* 479-575-5346. *Toll-free phone:* 800-377-8632. *Fax:* 479-575-7515. *E-mail:* uofa@uark.edu.
Website: http://www.uark.edu/.

University of Arkansas at Little Rock
Little Rock, Arkansas

- **State-supported** university, founded 1927, part of University of Arkansas System
- **Urban** 229-acre campus
- **Endowment** $70.1 million
- **Coed** 10,311 undergraduate students, 56% full-time, 59% women, 41% men
- **Minimally difficult** entrance level, 97% of applicants were admitted

Undergraduates 5,749 full-time, 4,562 part-time. Students come from 45 states and territories; 50 other countries; 3% are from out of state; 26% Black or African American, non-Hispanic/Latino; 5% Hispanic/Latino; 2% Asian, non-Hispanic/Latino; 0.4% American Indian or Alaska Native, non-Hispanic/Latino; 5% Two or more races, non-Hispanic/Latino; 0.1% Race/ethnicity unknown; 3% international; 12% transferred in; 10% live on campus. *Retention:* 67% of full-time freshmen returned.
Freshmen *Admission:* 923 applied, 893 admitted, 836 enrolled. *Test scores:* SAT critical reading scores over 500: 30%; SAT math scores over 500: 57%; ACT scores over 18: 88%; SAT critical reading scores over 600: 6%; SAT math scores over 600: 19%; ACT scores over 24: 37%; SAT critical reading scores over 700: 1%; SAT math scores over 700: 5%; ACT scores over 30: 6%.
Faculty *Total:* 804, 61% full-time, 55% with terminal degrees. *Student/faculty ratio:* 14:1.
Academics *Calendar:* semesters. *Degrees:* certificates, associate, bachelor's, master's, doctoral, post-master's, and postbachelor's certificates. *Special study options:* academic remediation for entering students, accelerated degree program, adult/continuing education programs, advanced placement credit, cooperative education, distance learning, double majors, English as a second language, freshman honors college, honors programs, independent study, internships, part-time degree program, student-designed majors, study abroad, summer session for credit. *ROTC:* Army (b).
Computers on Campus 3,500 computers/terminals and 1,200 ports are available on campus for general student use. Students can access the following: campus intranet, computer help desk, free student e-mail accounts, online (class) grades, online (class) registration, online (class) schedules. Campus-wide network is available. 100% of college-owned or -operated housing units are wired for high-speed Internet access. Wireless service is available via entire campus.
Student Life *Housing:* on-campus residence required for freshman year. *Options:* coed. Freshman applicants given priority for college housing. *Activities and organizations:* drama/theater group, student-run newspaper, radio and television station, Student Government, University Program Council, Housing Activities Council, International Student Organization, Panhellenic Council, national fraternities, national sororities. *Campus security:* 24-hour emergency response devices and patrols, student patrols, late-night transport/escort service, controlled dormitory access. *Student services:* health clinic.
Athletics Member NCAA. All Division I. *Intercollegiate sports:* baseball M(s), basketball M(s)/W, cross-country running M(s)/W(s), golf M(s)/W(s), soccer M/W(s), swimming and diving W, track and field M/W(s), volleyball W(s). *Intramural sports:* archery M/W, badminton M/W, basketball M, bowling M/W, football M/W, golf M/W, swimming and diving M/W, table tennis M/W, tennis M/W, volleyball M/W.
Standardized Tests *Required:* SAT or ACT (for admission).
Costs (2013–14) *One-time required fee:* $40. *Tuition:* state resident $5348 full-time, $191 per credit part-time; nonresident $14,560 full-time, $520 per credit part-time. Full-time tuition and fees vary according to degree level and program. Part-time tuition and fees vary according to degree level and program. *Required fees:* $1506 full-time, $807 per term part-time. *Room and board:* $8989. Room and board charges vary according to board plan and housing facility. *Payment plan:* deferred payment. *Waivers:* senior citizens and employees or children of employees.
Applying *Options:* electronic application, early admission, deferred entrance. *Application fee:* $40. *Required:* high school transcript, minimum 2.5 GPA, proof of immunization. *Application deadlines:* rolling (freshmen), rolling (transfers). *Notification:* continuous (freshmen), continuous (transfers).
Freshman Application Contact Ms. Tammy Harrison, Director of Admissions, University of Arkansas at Little Rock, 2801 South University

Avenue, Little Rock, AR 72204-1099. *Phone:* 501-569-3127. *Toll-free phone:* 800-482-8892. *Fax:* 501-569-8956. *E-mail:* twharrison@ualn.edu.
Website: http://www.ualr.edu/.

University of Arkansas at Monticello
Monticello, Arkansas

- **State-supported** comprehensive, founded 1909, part of University of Arkansas System
- **Small-town** 1600-acre campus
- **Endowment** $2.5 million
- **Coed**
- **Noncompetitive** entrance level

Faculty *Student/faculty ratio:* 16:1.
Academics *Calendar:* semesters. *Degrees:* certificates, associate, bachelor's, master's, and postbachelor's certificates.
Student Life *Campus security:* 24-hour emergency response devices and patrols.
Athletics Member NCAA. All Division II.
Standardized Tests *Recommended:* used for placement.
Costs (2012–13) *Tuition:* state resident $3960 full-time, $132 per semester hour part-time; nonresident $9450 full-time, $315 per semester hour part-time. Full-time tuition and fees vary according to location and program. Part-time tuition and fees vary according to location and program. *Required fees:* $1740 full-time, $58 per semester hour part-time. *Room and board:* $4880. Room and board charges vary according to board plan and housing facility.
Financial Aid *Of all full-time matriculated undergraduates who enrolled in 2006,* 166 Federal Work-Study jobs (averaging $1159). 292 state and other part-time jobs (averaging $1388).
Applying *Options:* early admission, deferred entrance. *Required:* high school transcript, proof of immunization.
Freshman Application Contact Ms. Mary Whiting, Director of Admissions, University of Arkansas at Monticello, Monticello, AR 71656. *Phone:* 870-460-1026. *Toll-free phone:* 800-844-1826. *E-mail:* admissions@uamont.edu.
Website: http://www.uamont.edu/.

University of Arkansas at Pine Bluff
Pine Bluff, Arkansas

Freshman Application Contact University of Arkansas at Pine Bluff, 1200 North University Drive, Pine Bluff, AR 71601-2799. *Phone:* 870-575-8461. *Toll-free phone:* 800-621-7440.
Website: http://www.uapb.edu/.

University of Arkansas for Medical Sciences
Little Rock, Arkansas

- **State-supported** university, founded 1879, part of University of Arkansas System
- **Urban** 5-acre campus with easy access to Little Rock
- **Endowment** $27.4 million
- **Coed** 821 undergraduate students, 70% full-time, 79% women, 21% men
- **31%** of applicants were admitted

Undergraduates 575 full-time, 246 part-time. 8% are from out of state; 12% Black or African American, non-Hispanic/Latino; 3% Hispanic/Latino; 2% Asian, non-Hispanic/Latino; 1% American Indian or Alaska Native, non-Hispanic/Latino; 2% Two or more races, non-Hispanic/Latino; 0.2% Race/ethnicity unknown; 0.5% international.
Freshmen *Admission:* 3,854 applied, 1,210 admitted.
Faculty *Total:* 1,271. *Student/faculty ratio:* 2:1.
Academics *Calendar:* semesters. *Degrees:* certificates, associate, bachelor's, master's, doctoral, and postbachelor's certificates (bachelor's degree is upper-level). *Special study options:* part-time degree program, services for LD students. *ROTC:* Army (c).
Computers on Campus Students can access the following: campus intranet, computer help desk, free student e-mail accounts, online (class) grades. Campus-wide network is available. 100% of college-owned or -operated housing units are wired for high-speed Internet access. Wireless service is available via entire campus.
Student Life *Housing options:* coed. Campus housing is university owned. *Campus security:* 24-hour emergency response devices and patrols, late-night transport/escort service, controlled dormitory access. *Student services:* health clinic, personal/psychological counseling.

Athletics *Intercollegiate sports:* ultimate Frisbee M/W, volleyball M/W. *Intramural sports:* basketball M/W, football M, golf M, ultimate Frisbee M/W, volleyball M/W.

Financial Aid Of all full-time matriculated undergraduates who enrolled in 2005, 734 applied for aid, 686 were judged to have need. 9 Federal Work-Study jobs (averaging $1201). *Average percent of need met:* 62%. *Average financial aid package:* $3000. *Average need-based loan:* $4000. *Average need-based gift aid:* $500. *Average indebtedness upon graduation:* $7000.

Freshman Application Contact University of Arkansas for Medical Sciences, 4301 West Markham, Little Rock, AR 72205-7199. *Phone:* 501-686-5730. *Website:* http://www.uams.edu/.

University of Arkansas–Fort Smith
Fort Smith, Arkansas

- **State and locally supported** 4-year, founded 1928, part of University of Arkansas System
- **Suburban** 120-acre campus
- **Endowment** $63.3 million
- **Coed** 7,352 undergraduate students, 70% full-time, 58% women, 42% men
- **Minimally difficult** entrance level, 54% of applicants were admitted

Undergraduates 5,136 full-time, 2,216 part-time. Students come from 33 states and territories; 17 other countries; 9% are from out of state; 4% Black or African American, non-Hispanic/Latino; 7% Hispanic/Latino; 4% Asian, non-Hispanic/Latino; 0.1% Native Hawaiian or other Pacific Islander, non-Hispanic/Latino; 3% American Indian or Alaska Native, non-Hispanic/Latino; 5% Two or more races, non-Hispanic/Latino; 0.9% Race/ethnicity unknown; 0.9% international; 6% transferred in; 12% live on campus. *Retention:* 64% of full-time freshmen returned.

Freshmen *Admission:* 4,126 applied, 2,242 admitted, 1,358 enrolled. *Average high school GPA:* 3.19. *Test scores:* ACT scores over 18: 87%; ACT scores over 24: 30%; ACT scores over 30: 2%.

Faculty *Total:* 449, 55% full-time, 40% with terminal degrees. *Student/faculty ratio:* 19:1.

Academics *Calendar:* semesters. *Degrees:* certificates, associate, and bachelor's. *Special study options:* academic remediation for entering students, accelerated degree program, adult/continuing education programs, advanced placement credit, cooperative education, distance learning, double majors, English as a second language, external degree program, honors programs, internships, off-campus study, part-time degree program, services for LD students, study abroad, summer session for credit. *ROTC:* Army (b), Air Force (c).

Computers on Campus 1,553 computers/terminals and 2,000 ports are available on campus for general student use. Students can access the following: campus intranet, computer help desk, free student e-mail accounts, online (class) grades, online (class) registration, online (class) schedules, online subscription databases, information portal, online course management system and online courses. Campuswide network is available. 100% of college-owned or operated housing units are wired for high-speed Internet access. Wireless service is available via classrooms, computer centers, computer labs, dorm rooms, learning centers, libraries, student centers.

Student Life *Housing options:* coed, disabled students. Campus housing is university owned. *Activities and organizations:* drama/theater group, student-run newspaper, choral group, Campus Activities Board, Phi Beta Lambda, Student Alumni Association, Non-Traditional Students, Baptist Collegiate Ministry, national fraternities, national sororities. *Campus security:* 24-hour emergency response devices and patrols, student patrols, late-night transport/escort service, controlled dormitory access, student patrols; new dormitory facilities have electronic card readers entrances. *Student services:* health clinic, personal/psychological counseling.

Athletics Member NCAA. All Division II. *Intercollegiate sports:* baseball M(s), basketball M(s)/W(s), cross-country running M(s)/W(s), golf M(s)/W(s), tennis M(s)/W(s), volleyball W(s). *Intramural sports:* badminton M/W, basketball M/W, bowling M/W, cheerleading M/W, football M/W, riflery M(c)/W(c), soccer M/W, softball M/W, table tennis M/W, ultimate Frisbee M/W, volleyball M/W.

Standardized Tests *Required:* SAT or ACT (for admission), COMPASS (in lieu of SAT or ACT) (for admission).

Costs (2013–14) *Tuition:* state resident $3900 full-time, $130 per credit hour part-time; nonresident $10,650 full-time, $355 per credit hour part-time. Full-time tuition and fees vary according to course load and program. Part-time tuition and fees vary according to course load and program. *Required fees:* $1536 full-time, $45 per credit hour part-time, $93 per credit hour part-time. *Room and board:* $7828; room only: $4848. Room and board charges vary according to board plan and housing facility. *Payment plan:* installment. *Waivers:* senior citizens and employees or children of employees.

Financial Aid Of all full-time matriculated undergraduates who enrolled in 2004, 2,564 applied for aid, 2,232 were judged to have need, 215 had their need fully met. 110 Federal Work-Study jobs (averaging $3000). 94 state and other part-time jobs (averaging $3000). In 2004, 350 non-need-based awards were made. *Average percent of need met:* 62%. *Average financial aid package:* $5568. *Average need-based loan:* $3183. *Average need-based gift aid:* $3504. *Average non-need-based aid:* $2643. *Average indebtedness upon graduation:* $7339.

Applying *Options:* electronic application, early admission, deferred entrance. *Required:* high school transcript. *Application deadlines:* rolling (freshmen), rolling (transfers).

Freshman Application Contact Mr. Mark Lloyd, Office of Admissions and School Relations, University of Arkansas–Fort Smith, 5210 Grand Avenue, PO Box 3649, Fort Smith, AR 72913-3649. *Phone:* 479-788-7120. *Toll-free phone:* 888-512-5466. *Fax:* 479-424-6120. *E-mail:* information@uafortsmith.edu. *Website:* http://www.uafortsmith.edu/.

University of Central Arkansas
Conway, Arkansas

- **State-supported** university, founded 1907
- **Small-town** 365-acre campus
- **Coed** 9,604 undergraduate students, 85% full-time, 58% women, 42% men
- **Moderately difficult** entrance level, 90% of applicants were admitted

Undergraduates 8,136 full-time, 1,468 part-time. Students come from 43 states and territories; 60 other countries; 8% are from out of state; 18% Black or African American, non-Hispanic/Latino; 3% Hispanic/Latino; 2% Asian, non-Hispanic/Latino; 0.1% Native Hawaiian or other Pacific Islander, non-Hispanic/Latino; 0.6% American Indian or Alaska Native, non-Hispanic/Latino; 2% Two or more races, non-Hispanic/Latino; 3% Race/ethnicity unknown; 3% international; 6% transferred in. *Retention:* 70% of full-time freshmen returned.

Freshmen *Admission:* 3,659 applied, 3,292 admitted, 2,157 enrolled. *Average high school GPA:* 3.3. *Test scores:* ACT scores over 18: 92%; ACT scores over 24: 44%; ACT scores over 30: 9%.

Faculty *Total:* 726, 75% full-time. *Student/faculty ratio:* 16:1.

Academics *Calendar:* semesters. *Degrees:* certificates, bachelor's, master's, doctoral, post-master's, and postbachelor's certificates. *Special study options:* academic remediation for entering students, accelerated degree program, advanced placement credit, cooperative education, distance learning, double majors, English as a second language, freshman honors college, honors programs, independent study, internships, part-time degree program, services for LD students, summer session for credit. *ROTC:* Army (b). *Unusual degree programs:* 3-2 engineering with Arkansas Tech University in Russellville.

Computers on Campus 608 computers/terminals are available on campus for general student use. Students can access the following: campus intranet, computer help desk, free student e-mail accounts, online (class) grades, online (class) registration, online (class) schedules. Campuswide network is available. Wireless service is available via entire campus.

Student Life *Housing:* on-campus residence required for freshman year. *Options:* coed, men-only, women-only, disabled students. Campus housing is university owned and leased by the school. Freshman campus housing is guaranteed. *Activities and organizations:* drama/theater group, student-run newspaper, radio and television station, choral group, marching band, Student Government Association, national fraternities, national sororities. *Campus security:* 24-hour emergency response devices and patrols, student patrols, late-night transport/escort service, controlled dormitory access. *Student services:* health clinic, personal/psychological counseling, women's center.

Athletics Member NCAA. All Division I. *Intercollegiate sports:* baseball M(s), basketball M(s)/W(s), cheerleading M(s)(c)/W(s)(c), cross-country running M(s)/W(s), football M(s), golf M(s)/W(s), soccer M(s)/W(s), softball W(s), tennis W(s), track and field M(s)/W(s), volleyball W(s). *Intramural sports:* basketball M/W, bowling M/W, soccer M/W, softball M/W, table tennis M, tennis W, track and field M/W, volleyball M/W.

Standardized Tests *Required:* SAT or ACT (for admission).

Costs (2012–13) *Tuition:* state resident $5498 full-time, $183 per credit hour part-time; nonresident $10,995 full-time, $367 per credit hour part-time. Full-time tuition and fees vary according to course load. Part-time tuition and fees vary according to course load. *Required fees:* $1835 full-time, $53 per credit hour part-time, $127 per term part-time. *Room and board:* $5270; room only: $3030. Room and board charges vary according to board plan and housing facility. *Payment plan:* installment. *Waivers:* senior citizens and employees or children of employees.

Financial Aid *Financial aid deadline:* 7/1.

Applying *Options:* electronic application, early admission, deferred entrance. *Application fee:* $25. *Required:* high school transcript. *Application deadlines:*

rolling (freshmen), rolling (transfers). *Notification:* continuous (freshmen), continuous (transfers).

Freshman Application Contact Mr. Ron Patterson, Director of Admissions, University of Central Arkansas, 201 Donaghey Avenue, Bernard 100, Conway, AR 72035. *Phone:* 501-450-3128. *Toll-free phone:* 800-243-8245. *Fax:* 501-450-5228. *E-mail:* rpatterson@uca.edu. *Website:* http://www.uca.edu/.

University of Phoenix–Little Rock Campus
Little Rock, Arkansas

Freshman Application Contact Marc Booker, Sr. Director, Office of Admissions and Evaluation, University of Phoenix–Little Rock Campus, 4035 South Riverpoint Parkway, Mail Stop CF-L101, Phoenix, AZ 85040. *Phone:* 602-557-4609. *Toll-free phone:* 866-766-0766. *Fax:* 480-643-1156. *Website:* http://www.phoenix.edu/.

University of Phoenix–Northwest Arkansas Campus
Rogers, Arkansas

Admissions Office Contact University of Phoenix–Northwest Arkansas Campus, 903 North 47th Street—Barrington Centre 2, Rogers, AR 72756-9615. *Toll-free phone:* 866-766-0766. *Website:* http://www.phoenix.edu/.

University of the Ozarks
Clarksville, Arkansas

- **Independent Presbyterian** 4-year, founded 1834
- **Small-town** campus
- **Coed** 630 undergraduate students, 94% full-time, 52% women, 48% men
- **Moderately difficult** entrance level, 85% of applicants were admitted

Undergraduates 595 full-time, 35 part-time. 32% are from out of state; 5% Black or African American, non-Hispanic/Latino; 8% Hispanic/Latino; 0.3% Asian, non-Hispanic/Latino; 1% American Indian or Alaska Native, non-Hispanic/Latino; 3% Two or more races, non-Hispanic/Latino; 0.7% Race/ethnicity unknown; 11% international; 3% transferred in; 70% live on campus. *Retention:* 59% of full-time freshmen returned.

Freshmen *Admission:* 929 applied, 791 admitted, 186 enrolled. *Average high school GPA:* 3.39. *Test scores:* SAT critical reading scores over 500: 46%; SAT math scores over 500: 66%; ACT scores over 18: 94%; SAT critical reading scores over 600: 9%; SAT math scores over 600: 20%; ACT scores over 24: 42%; SAT critical reading scores over 700: 3%; SAT math scores over 700: 3%; ACT scores over 30: 9%.

Faculty *Total:* 79, 61% full-time, 42% with terminal degrees. *Student/faculty ratio:* 11:1.

Academics *Calendar:* semesters. *Degree:* bachelor's. *Special study options:* part-time degree program.

Computers on Campus Students can access the following: campus intranet, computer help desk, free student e-mail accounts. Campuswide network is available. 100% of college-owned or -operated housing units are wired for high-speed Internet access. Wireless service is available via libraries.

Student Life *Housing:* on-campus residence required through sophomore year. *Options:* coed, women-only. Campus housing is university owned. Freshman campus housing is guaranteed. *Campus security:* 24-hour emergency response devices and patrols, late-night transport/escort service.

Athletics Member NCAA. All Division III. *Intercollegiate sports:* baseball M, basketball M/W, cheerleading M/W, cross-country running M/W, soccer M/W, softball W, tennis M/W. *Intramural sports:* badminton M/W, basketball M/W, bowling M/W, football M/W, racquetball M/W, soccer M, softball M/W, table tennis M/W, tennis M/W, ultimate Frisbee M/W, volleyball M/W, weight lifting M/W.

Standardized Tests *Required:* SAT or ACT (for admission).

Costs (2012–13) *Comprehensive fee:* $29,950 includes full-time tuition ($22,650), mandatory fees ($600), and room and board ($6700). Part-time tuition: $950 per credit hour. *College room only:* $3100. Room and board charges vary according to board plan and housing facility. *Payment plan:* installment. *Waivers:* children of alumni and employees or children of employees.

Applying *Options:* deferred entrance. *Application fee:* $30. *Required:* minimum 2.0 GPA. *Required for some:* essay or personal statement, high school transcript, interview. *Application deadlines:* rolling (freshmen), rolling (transfers). *Notification:* continuous (freshmen), continuous (transfers).

Freshman Application Contact Ms. Kim Myrick, Vice President for Enrollment Management, University of the Ozarks, 415 North College Avenue, Clarksville, AR 72830-2880. *Phone:* 479-979-1227. *Toll-free phone:* 800-264-8636. *Fax:* 479-979-1417. *E-mail:* admiss@ozarks.edu. *Website:* http://www.ozarks.edu/.

Williams Baptist College
Walnut Ridge, Arkansas

- **Independent Southern Baptist** 4-year, founded 1941
- **Rural** 180-acre campus
- **Coed**
- **Minimally difficult** entrance level

Faculty *Student/faculty ratio:* 13:1.

Academics *Calendar:* semesters. *Degrees:* associate and bachelor's.

Student Life *Campus security:* 24-hour emergency response devices, student patrols.

Athletics Member NAIA, NCCAA.

Standardized Tests *Required:* SAT or ACT (for admission).

Financial Aid *Of all full-time matriculated undergraduates who enrolled in 2011,* 433 applied for aid, 373 were judged to have need. 188 Federal Work-Study jobs (averaging $1329). 32 state and other part-time jobs (averaging $1438). *Average financial aid package:* $14,541. *Average need-based loan:* $3664. *Average need-based gift aid:* $4491. *Average indebtedness upon graduation:* $18,720.

Applying *Options:* electronic application. *Application fee:* $20. *Required:* high school transcript, minimum 2.5 GPA. *Required for some:* essay or personal statement. *Recommended:* interview.

Freshman Application Contact Mrs. Angela Flippo, Vice President for Enrollment, Williams Baptist College, 60 West Fulbright Avenue, Walnut Ridge, AR 72476. *Phone:* 870-759-4120. *Toll-free phone:* 800-722-4434. *Fax:* 870-759-4163. *E-mail:* admissions@wbcoll.edu. *Website:* http://www.wbcoll.edu/.

CALIFORNIA

Academy of Art University
San Francisco, California

- **Proprietary** comprehensive, founded 1929
- **Urban** 3-acre campus
- **Coed** 11,992 undergraduate students, 55% full-time, 56% women, 44% men
- **Noncompetitive** entrance level, 100% of applicants were admitted

Undergraduates 6,623 full-time, 5,369 part-time. Students come from 55 states and territories; 118 other countries; 41% are from out of state; 6% Black or African American, non-Hispanic/Latino; 9% Hispanic/Latino; 8% Asian, non-Hispanic/Latino; 0.3% Native Hawaiian or other Pacific Islander, non-Hispanic/Latino; 0.6% American Indian or Alaska Native, non-Hispanic/Latino; 2% Two or more races, non-Hispanic/Latino; 27% Race/ethnicity unknown; 20% international; 9% transferred in; 13% live on campus. *Retention:* 71% of full-time freshmen returned.

Freshmen *Admission:* 3,055 applied, 3,055 admitted, 1,240 enrolled.

Faculty *Total:* 1,468, 18% full-time. *Student/faculty ratio:* 19:1.

Academics *Calendar:* semesters. *Degrees:* certificates, bachelor's, and master's. *Special study options:* academic remediation for entering students, adult/continuing education programs, distance learning, English as a second language, independent study, internships, part-time degree program, services for LD students, summer session for credit.

Computers on Campus 1,720 computers/terminals are available on campus for general student use. Students can access the following: free student e-mail accounts, online (class) grades, online (class) registration, online (class) schedules, Provide support for students taking online courses. Campuswide network is available. 100% of college-owned or -operated housing units are wired for high-speed Internet access. Wireless service is available via classrooms, computer labs, dorm rooms, libraries.

Student Life *Housing options:* coed, men-only, women-only, disabled students. Campus housing is university owned and leased by the school. Freshman campus housing is guaranteed. *Activities and organizations:* drama/theater group, student-run radio and television station, Tea Time Animation, Beyond the Front Row, Children's Book Club, Comic Book Club, Ideation Club, national fraternities, national sororities. *Campus security:* 24-hour emergency response devices and patrols, late-night transport/escort service, controlled dormitory access, ID check at all buildings.

Athletics Member NCAA. All Division II. *Intercollegiate sports:* baseball M(s), basketball M(s)/W(s), cross-country running M(s)/W(s), golf M(s)/W(s), soccer M(s)/W(s), softball W(s), tennis W(s), track and field M(s)/W(s), volleyball W(s).

Costs (2013–14) *Comprehensive fee:* $37,240 includes full-time tuition ($23,550), mandatory fees ($290), and room and board ($13,400). Full-time tuition and fees vary according to course load. Part-time tuition: $785 per credit. Part-time tuition and fees vary according to course load. *Room and board:* Room and board charges vary according to board plan and housing facility. *Payment plan:* installment.

Financial Aid Of all full-time matriculated undergraduates who enrolled in 2011, 4,028 applied for aid, 3,680 were judged to have need, 1 had their need fully met. 128 Federal Work-Study jobs (averaging $3111). In 2011, 5 non-need-based awards were made. *Average percent of need met:* 35%. *Average financial aid package:* $9183. *Average need-based loan:* $3936. *Average need-based gift aid:* $5464. *Average non-need-based aid:* $3996. *Average indebtedness upon graduation:* $46,726.

Applying *Options:* electronic application, early admission, deferred entrance. *Application fee:* $100. *Required:* high school transcript. *Recommended:* minimum 2.0 GPA, interview, Undergraduate applicants are not required to submit a portfolio, but may do so for possible waiver of foundation or major classes for graduate admissions. *Application deadlines:* rolling (freshmen), rolling (transfers).

Freshman Application Contact Admissions, Academy of Art University, 79 New Montgomery Street, San Francisco, CA 94105. *Phone:* 800-544-2787. *Toll-free phone:* 800-544-ARTS. *Fax:* 415-618-6287. *E-mail:* info@academyart.edu.
Website: http://www.academyart.edu/.

See below for display ad and page 1034 for the College Close-Up.

Academy of Couture Art
West Hollywood, California

Admissions Office Contact Academy of Couture Art, Pacific Design Center, 8687 Melrose Avenue, Suite G520, West Hollywood, CA 90069.
Website: http://www.academyofcoutureart.edu/.

Alliant International University
San Diego, California

- **Independent** university, founded 1952, part of Alliant International University
- **Suburban** 60-acre campus with easy access to San Diego
- **Coed** 132 undergraduate students, 70% full-time, 61% women, 39% men

Undergraduates 93 full-time, 39 part-time. Students come from 8 states and territories; 17 other countries; 5% are from out of state; 8% Black or African American, non-Hispanic/Latino; 20% Hispanic/Latino; 4% Asian, non-Hispanic/Latino; 3% Two or more races, non-Hispanic/Latino; 5% Race/ethnicity unknown; 27% international; 40% live on campus.

Faculty *Total:* 670, 35% full-time, 93% with terminal degrees. *Student/faculty ratio:* 9:1.

Academics *Calendar:* semesters. *Degrees:* certificates, bachelor's, master's, doctoral, and postbachelor's certificates. *Special study options:* academic remediation for entering students, advanced placement credit, distance learning, English as a second language, honors programs, independent study, internships, part-time degree program, services for LD students, summer session for credit.

Computers on Campus 100 computers/terminals are available on campus for general student use. Students can access the following: campus intranet, computer help desk, free student e-mail accounts, online (class) grades, online (class) registration, online (class) schedules. Campuswide network is available. Wireless service is available via entire campus.

Student Life *Housing options:* coed. Campus housing is university owned. *Activities and organizations:* student-run newspaper, Residence Hall Association, Latino Students Association, Finance Club, student government, Sigma Iota Epsilon. *Campus security:* 24-hour emergency response devices and patrols, student patrols, late-night transport/escort service. *Student services:* health clinic, personal/psychological counseling.

Athletics *Intramural sports:* basketball M/W, cross-country running M/W, football M/W, soccer M/W, softball M/W, table tennis M/W, tennis M/W, volleyball M/W.

Costs (2012–13) *Comprehensive fee:* $24,270 includes full-time tuition ($16,740), mandatory fees ($190), and room and board ($7340). Full-time tuition and fees vary according to course load and location. Part-time tuition: $620 per unit. Part-time tuition and fees vary according to course load and location. *Room and board:* Room and board charges vary according to board

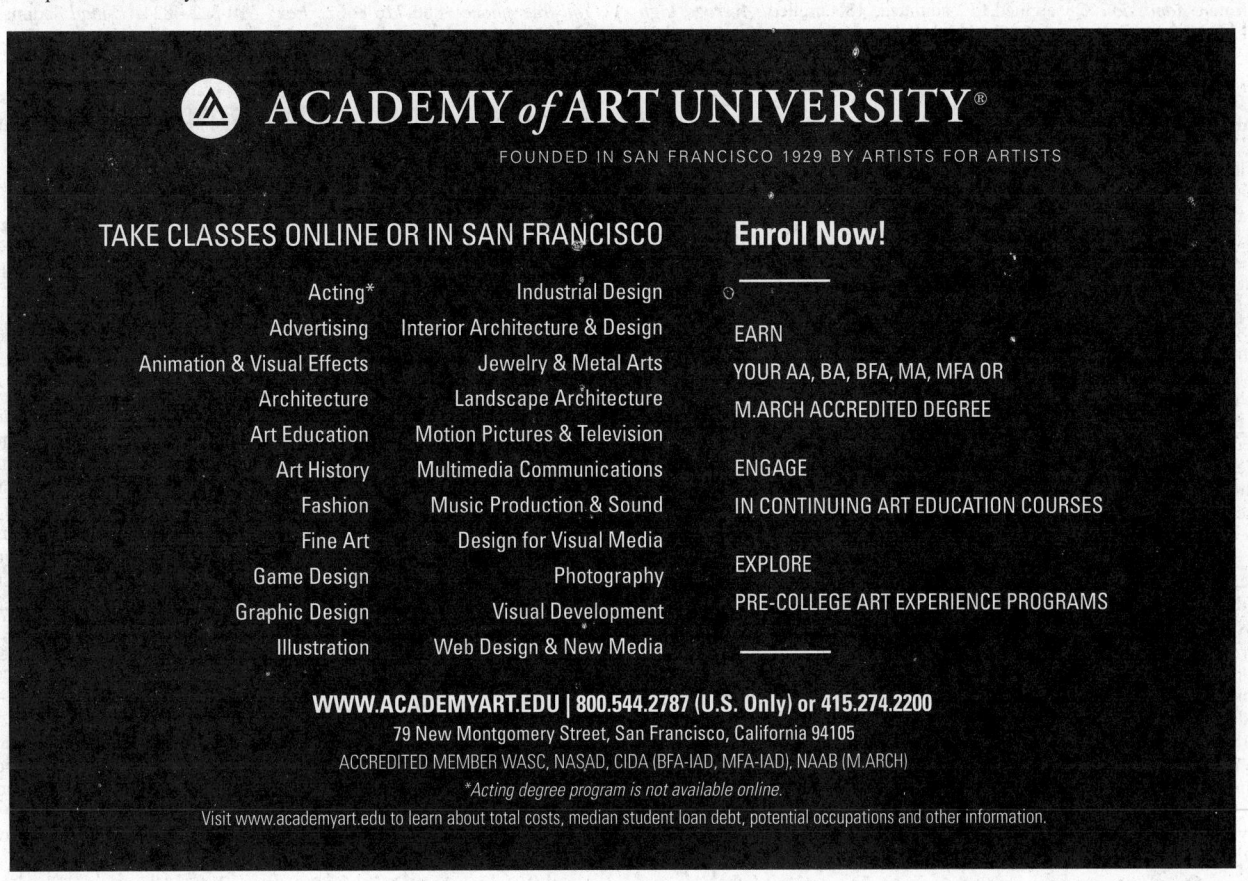

plan. *Payment plan:* installment. *Waivers:* employees or children of employees.

Financial Aid Of all full-time matriculated undergraduates who enrolled in 2012, 77 applied for aid, 75 were judged to have need. 13 Federal Work-Study jobs (averaging $4000). 2 state and other part-time jobs (averaging $3000). In 2012, 9 non-need-based awards were made. *Average percent of need met:* 67%. *Average financial aid package:* $13,650. *Average need-based loan:* $5500. *Average need-based gift aid:* $6750. *Average non-need-based aid:* $4000.

Applying *Options:* electronic application, deferred entrance. *Application fee:* $45. *Required:* high school transcript, minimum 2.0 GPA. *Application deadline:* rolling (transfers). *Notification:* continuous (transfers).

Freshman Application Contact Alliant International University, 10455 Pomerado Road, San Diego, CA 92131-1799. *Phone:* 858-635-4772. *Toll-free phone:* 866-825-5426.
Website: http://www.alliant.edu/.

Allied American University

Laguna Hills, California

Director of Admissions Lindsay Oglesby, Admissions Director, Allied American University, 22952 Alcade Drive, Laguna Hills, CA 92653. *Phone:* 888-384-0849. *Toll-free phone:* 888-384-0849. *Fax:* 949-707-2978. *E-mail:* info@allied.edu.
Website: http://allied.edu/.

American Jewish University

Bel Air, California

- **Independent Jewish** comprehensive, founded 1947
- **Suburban** 28-acre campus with easy access to Los Angeles
- **Endowment** $21.6 million
- **Coed** 125 undergraduate students, 91% full-time, 50% women, 50% men
- **Moderately difficult** entrance level, 96% of applicants were admitted

Undergraduates 114 full-time, 11 part-time. Students come from 7 states and territories; 5 other countries; 15% are from out of state; 2% Black or African American, non-Hispanic/Latino; 3% Hispanic/Latino; 2% Asian, non-Hispanic/Latino; 2% American Indian or Alaska Native, non-Hispanic/Latino; 37% Race/ethnicity unknown; 5% international; 24% transferred in; 34% live on campus. *Retention:* 58% of full-time freshmen returned.

Freshmen *Admission:* 28 applied, 27 admitted, 13 enrolled. *Average high school GPA:* 3.11. *Test scores:* SAT critical reading scores over 500: 71%; SAT math scores over 500: 72%; SAT writing scores over 500: 71%; ACT scores over 18: 67%; SAT critical reading scores over 600: 14%; SAT math scores over 600: 29%; SAT writing scores over 600: 14%; ACT scores over 24: 34%.

Faculty *Total:* 38, 21% full-time, 50% with terminal degrees. *Student/faculty ratio:* 7:1.

Academics *Calendar:* semesters. *Degrees:* bachelor's and master's. *Special study options:* academic remediation for entering students, adult/continuing education programs, advanced placement credit, cooperative education, double majors, independent study, internships, part-time degree program, services for LD students, student-designed majors, study abroad, summer session for credit. *Unusual degree programs:* 3-2 business administration; education.

Computers on Campus 38 computers/terminals and 10 ports are available on campus for general student use. Students can access the following: campus intranet, free student e-mail accounts, online (class) grades, online (class) schedules. Campuswide network is available. 100% of college-owned or -operated housing units are wired for high-speed Internet access. Wireless service is available via computer centers, computer labs, dorm rooms, libraries, student centers.

Student Life *Housing options:* coed. Campus housing is university owned. Freshman campus housing is guaranteed. *Activities and organizations:* drama/theater group, student-run newspaper, Investment Club, Hiking Club, Film Club, AJU Sangha, Social Action Committee. *Campus security:* 24-hour emergency response devices, controlled dormitory access. *Student services:* health clinic, personal/psychological counseling.

Standardized Tests *Required:* SAT or ACT (for admission).

Costs (2013–14) *Comprehensive fee:* $42,578 includes full-time tuition ($26,784), mandatory fees ($1712), and room and board ($14,082). Full-time tuition and fees vary according to course load and degree level. Part-time tuition: $1116 per unit. Part-time tuition and fees vary according to course load and degree level. *College room only:* $7098. Room and board charges vary according to board plan and housing facility. *Payment plan:* installment. *Waivers:* employees or children of employees.

Financial Aid Of all full-time matriculated undergraduates who enrolled in 2011, 129 applied for aid, 129 were judged to have need. 27 Federal Work-Study jobs (averaging $889). In 2011, 47 non-need-based awards were made. *Average percent of need met:* 95%. *Average financial aid package:* $27,500.

Average need-based loan: $4500. *Average need-based gift aid:* $10,000. *Average non-need-based aid:* $2500. *Average indebtedness upon graduation:* $29,500.

Applying *Options:* electronic application, deferred entrance. *Application fee:* $35. *Required:* essay or personal statement, high school transcript, 2 letters of recommendation. *Recommended:* interview. *Application deadlines:* 5/31 (freshmen), 5/31 (out-of-state freshmen), 5/31 (transfers). *Notification:* continuous (freshmen), continuous (out-of-state freshmen), continuous (transfers).

Freshman Application Contact Mr. Matt Spooner, Director of Undergraduate Admissions, American Jewish University, Familian Campus, 15600 Mulholland Drive, Los Angeles, CA 90077-1599. *Phone:* 310-440-1250. *Toll-free phone:* 888-853-6763. *Fax:* 310-471-3657. *E-mail:* admissions@ajula.edu.
Website: http://www.ajula.edu/.

American Musical and Dramatic Academy, Los Angeles

Los Angeles, California

Freshman Application Contact Karen Jackson, Director of Admission, American Musical and Dramatic Academy, Los Angeles, 6305 Yucca Street, Los Angeles, CA 90028. *Phone:* 323-469-3300. *Toll-free phone:* 888-474-9444. *Fax:* 323-469-5246. *E-mail:* kjackson@amda.edu.
Website: http://www.amda.edu/.

American University of Health Sciences

Signal Hill, California

Admissions Office Contact American University of Health Sciences, 1600 East Hill Street, Building #1, Signal Hill, CA 90755.
Website: http://www.auhs.edu/.

Antioch University Los Angeles

Culver City, California

Application Contact Admissions, Antioch University Los Angeles, 400 Corporate Pointe, Culver City, CA 90230. *Phone:* 310-578-1080 Ext. 100. *Toll-free phone:* 800-726-8462. *Fax:* 310-822-4824. *E-mail:* admissions@antiochla.edu.
Website: http://www.antiochla.edu/.

Antioch University Santa Barbara

Santa Barbara, California

- **Independent** upper-level, founded 1977, part of Antioch University
- **Small-town** campus
- **Coed** 148 undergraduate students, 43% full-time, 72% women, 28% men
- **Moderately difficult** entrance level

Undergraduates 64 full-time, 84 part-time. Students come from 3 other countries; 3% Black or African American, non-Hispanic/Latino; 33% Hispanic/Latino; 2% Asian, non-Hispanic/Latino; 0.7% Native Hawaiian or other Pacific Islander, non-Hispanic/Latino; 2% American Indian or Alaska Native, non-Hispanic/Latino; 1% Race/ethnicity unknown; 3% international.

Faculty *Total:* 75, 16% full-time. *Student/faculty ratio:* 9:1.

Academics *Calendar:* quarters. *Degrees:* certificates, bachelor's, master's, and doctoral. *Special study options:* academic remediation for entering students, accelerated degree program, distance learning, external degree program, independent study, internships, off-campus study, part-time degree program, student-designed majors, summer session for credit.

Computers on Campus 16 computers/terminals are available on campus for general student use. Students can access the following: computer help desk, free student e-mail accounts, online (class) grades, online (class) registration, online (class) schedules. Campuswide network is available. Wireless service is available via entire campus.

Student Life *Housing:* college housing not available. *Activities and organizations:* student-run newspaper. *Campus security:* late-night transport/escort service.

Standardized Tests *Required for some:* TOFFL.

Costs (2012–13) *Tuition:* $453 per unit part-time. Full-time tuition and fees vary according to degree level. Part-time tuition and fees vary according to degree level. *Payment plan:* installment. *Waivers:* employees or children of employees.

Financial Aid Of all full-time matriculated undergraduates who enrolled in 2003, 23 Federal Work-Study jobs (averaging $2120).

Applying *Options:* electronic application, deferred entrance. *Application fee:* $60. *Application deadline:* rolling (transfers). *Notification:* continuous (transfers).
Application Contact Mrs. Sharisse Estomo, Assistant Director of Admissions, Antioch University Santa Barbara, 602 Anacapa Street, Santa Barbara, CA 93101. *Phone:* 805-962-8179 Ext. 5113. *Toll-free phone:* 866-526-8462. *Fax:* 805-962-4786. *E-mail:* sestomo@antioch.edu.
Website: http://www.antiochsb.edu/.

Argosy University, Inland Empire
Ontario, California

Freshman Application Contact Argosy University, Inland Empire, 3401 Centre Lake Drive, Suite 200, Ontario, CA 91761. *Phone:* 909-915-3800. *Toll-free phone:* 866-217-9075.
Website: http://www.argosy.edu/inland-empire/.

Argosy University, Los Angeles
Santa Monica, California

Freshman Application Contact Argosy University, Los Angeles, 5230 Pacific Concourse, Suite 200, Santa Monica, CA 90045. *Phone:* 310-866-4000. *Toll-free phone:* 866-505-0332.
Website: http://www.argosy.edu/los-angeles/.

Argosy University, Orange County
Orange, California

Freshman Application Contact Argosy University, Orange County, 601 South Lewis Street, Orange, CA 92868. *Phone:* 714-620-3700. *Toll-free phone:* 800-716-9598.
Website: http://www.argosy.edu/locations/los-angeles-orange-county/.

Argosy University, San Diego
San Diego, California

Freshman Application Contact Argosy University, San Diego, 1615 Murray Canyon Road, Suite 100, San Diego, CA 92108. *Phone:* 619-321-3000. *Toll-free phone:* 866-505-0333.
Website: http://www.argosy.edu/sandiego/.

Argosy University, San Francisco Bay Area
Alameda, California

Freshman Application Contact Argosy University, San Francisco Bay Area, 1005 Atlantic Avenue, Alameda, CA 94501. *Phone:* 510-217-4700. *Toll-free phone:* 866-215-2777.
Website: http://www.argosy.edu/sanfrancisco/.

Art Center College of Design
Pasadena, California

- **Independent** comprehensive, founded 1930
- **Suburban** 175-acre campus with easy access to Los Angeles
- **Coed** 1,657 undergraduate students, 87% full-time, 49% women, 51% men
- **Very difficult** entrance level, 81% of applicants were admitted

Undergraduates 1,443 full-time, 214 part-time. 1% Black or African American, non-Hispanic/Latino; 10% Hispanic/Latino; 36% Asian, non-Hispanic/Latino; 0.5% Native Hawaiian or other Pacific Islander, non-Hispanic/Latino; 0.1% American Indian or Alaska Native, non-Hispanic/Latino; 3% Two or more races, non-Hispanic/Latino; 3% Race/ethnicity unknown; 21% international; 11% transferred in. *Retention:* 83% of full-time freshmen returned.
Freshmen *Admission:* 450 applied, 365 admitted, 159 enrolled. *Average high school GPA:* 3.25.
Faculty *Total:* 431, 22% full-time. *Student/faculty ratio:* 9:1.
Academics *Calendar:* trimesters. *Degrees:* bachelor's and master's.
Computers on Campus Students can access the following: campus intranet, computer help desk, free student e-mail accounts, online (class) grades, online (class) registration, online (class) schedules. Campuswide network is available. Wireless service is available via entire campus.
Student Life *Housing:* college housing not available. *Campus security:* 24-hour emergency response devices and patrols.
Standardized Tests *Required for some:* SAT (for admission), ACT (for admission), SAT or ACT (for admission).

Costs (2012–13) *Tuition:* $35,052 full-time. *Required fees:* $500 full-time. *Payment plan:* installment. *Waivers:* employees or children of employees.
Financial Aid *Average financial aid package:* $17,803. *Average need-based loan:* $10,169. *Average need-based gift aid:* $14,627.
Applying *Options:* electronic application, deferred entrance. *Application fee:* $50. *Required:* essay or personal statement, high school transcript, portfolio. *Recommended:* interview. *Application deadlines:* rolling (freshmen), rolling (transfers). *Notification:* continuous (freshmen), continuous (transfers).
Freshman Application Contact Ms. Kit Baron, Vice President, Admissions and Enrollment Management, Art Center College of Design, 1700 Lida Street, Pasadena, CA 91103. *Phone:* 626-396-2322. *Fax:* 626-795-0578. *E-mail:* kit.baron@artcenter.edu.
Website: http://www.artcenter.edu/.

The Art Institute of California–Hollywood, a campus of Argosy University
North Hollywood, California

- **Proprietary** 4-year, founded 1992, part of Education Management Corporation
- **Urban** campus
- **Coed**

Academics *Calendar:* quarters. *Degrees:* associate and bachelor's.
Freshman Application Contact The Art Institute of California–Hollywood, a campus of Argosy University, 5250 Lankershim Boulevard, North Hollywood, CA 91601. *Phone:* 818-299-5100. *Toll-free phone:* 877-468-6232.
Website: http://www.artinstitutes.edu/hollywood/.

See full-page ad on page 54 and page 1056 for the College Close-Up.

The Art Institute of California–Inland Empire, a campus of Argosy University
San Bernardino, California

- **Proprietary** 4-year, part of Education Management Corporation
- **Suburban** campus
- **Coed**

Academics *Degrees:* associate and bachelor's.
Freshman Application Contact The Art Institute of California–Inland Empire, a campus of Argosy University, 674 East Brier Drive, San Bernardino, CA 92408. *Phone:* 909-915-2100. *Toll-free phone:* 800-353-0812.
Website: http://www.artinstitutes.edu/inlandempire/.

See full-page ad on page 54 and page 1058 for the College Close-Up.

The Art Institute of California–Los Angeles, a campus of Argosy University
Santa Monica, California

- **Proprietary** 4-year, part of Education Management Corporation
- **Urban** campus
- **Coed**

Academics *Calendar:* quarters. *Degrees:* diplomas, associate, and bachelor's.
Freshman Application Contact The Art Institute of California–Los Angeles, a campus of Argosy University, 2900 31st Street, Santa Monica, CA 90405-3035. *Phone:* 310-752-4700. *Toll-free phone:* 888-646-4610.
Website: http://www.artinstitutes.edu/losangeles/.

See full-page ad on page 54 and page 1060 for the College Close-Up.

The Art Institute of California–Orange County, a campus of Argosy University
Santa Ana, California

- **Proprietary** 4-year, founded 2000, part of Education Management Corporation
- **Urban** campus with easy access to Orange County
- **Coed**

Academics *Calendar:* quarters. *Degrees:* diplomas, associate, and bachelor's.

Freshman Application Contact The Art Institute of California–Orange County, a campus of Argosy University, 3601 West Sunflower Avenue, Santa Ana, CA 92704. *Phone:* 714-830-0200. *Toll-free phone:* 888-549-3055. *Website:* http://www.artinstitutes.edu/orangecounty/.

See full-page ad on page 54 and page 1062 for the College Close-Up.

The Art Institute of California–Sacramento, a campus of Argosy University
Sacramento, California

- **Proprietary** 4-year
- **Coed**

Academics *Degrees:* diplomas, associate, and bachelor's.
Freshman Application Contact The Art Institute of California–Sacramento, a campus of Argosy University, 2850 Gateway Oaks Drive, Suite 100, Sacramento, CA 95833. *Phone:* 916-830-6320. *Toll-free phone:* 800-477-1957.
Website: http://www.artinstitutes.edu/sacramento/.

See full-page ad on page 54 and page 1064 for the College Close-Up.

The Art Institute of California–San Diego, a campus of Argosy University
San Diego, California

- **Proprietary** 4-year, founded 1981, part of Education Management Corporation
- **Urban** campus
- **Coed**

Academics *Calendar:* quarters. *Degrees:* associate and bachelor's.
Freshman Application Contact The Art Institute of California–San Diego, a campus of Argosy University, 7650 Mission Valley Road, San Diego, CA 92108. *Phone:* 858-598-1200. *Toll-free phone:* 866-275-2422.
Website: http://www.artinstitutes.edu/sandiego/.

See full-page ad on page 54 and page 1066 for the College Close-Up.

The Art Institute of California–San Francisco, a campus of Argosy University
San Francisco, California

- **Proprietary** comprehensive, founded 1939, part of Education Management Corporation
- **Urban** campus
- **Coed**

Academics *Calendar:* quarters. *Degrees:* diplomas, associate, bachelor's, and master's.
Freshman Application Contact The Art Institute of California–San Francisco, a campus of Argosy University, 1170 Market Street, San Francisco, CA 94102. *Phone:* 415-865-0198. *Toll-free phone:* 888-493-3261.
Website: http://www.artinstitutes.edu/sanfrancisco/.

See full-page ad on page 54 and page 1068 for the College Close-Up.

The Art Institute of California–Silicon Valley, a campus of Argosy University
Sunnyvale, California

- **Proprietary** 4-year
- **Coed**

Academics *Degrees:* associate and bachelor's.
Freshman Application Contact The Art Institute of California–Silicon Valley, a campus of Argosy University, 1120 Kifer Road, Sunnyvale, CA 94086. *Phone:* 408-962-6400. *Toll-free phone:* 866-583-7961.
Website: http://www.artinstitutes.edu/silicon-valley/.

See full-page ad on page 54 and page 1070 for the College Close-Up.

Azusa Pacific University
Azusa, California

- **Independent nondenominational** university, founded 1899
- **Suburban** 60-acre campus with easy access to Los Angeles
- **Coed** 6,224 undergraduate students, 87% full-time, 64% women, 36% men
- **Moderately difficult** entrance level, 52% of applicants were admitted

Undergraduates 5,412 full-time, 812 part-time. 5% Black or African American, non-Hispanic/Latino; 20% Hispanic/Latino; 8% Asian, non-Hispanic/Latino; 0.8% Native Hawaiian or other Pacific Islander, non-Hispanic/Latino; 0.3% American Indian or Alaska Native, non-Hispanic/Latino; 5% Two or more races, non-Hispanic/Latino; 8% Race/ethnicity unknown; 2% international; 58% live on campus. *Retention:* 83% of full-time freshmen returned.
Freshmen *Admission:* 8,515 applied, 4,453 admitted, 1,250 enrolled. *Average high school GPA:* 3.61. *Test scores:* SAT critical reading scores over 500: 74%; SAT math scores over 500: 72%; SAT writing scores over 500: 72%; ACT scores over 18: 97%; SAT critical reading scores over 600: 27%; SAT math scores over 600: 31%; SAT writing scores over 600: 28%; ACT scores over 24: 53%; SAT critical reading scores over 700: 4%; SAT math scores over 700: 4%; SAT writing scores over 700: 4%; ACT scores over 30: 9%.
Faculty *Total:* 1,020, 40% full-time, 29% with terminal degrees. *Student/faculty ratio:* 14:1.
Academics *Calendar:* semesters. *Degrees:* bachelor's, master's, doctoral, post-master's, and postbachelor's certificates. *Special study options:* academic remediation for entering students, accelerated degree program, adult/continuing education programs, advanced placement credit, cooperative education, distance learning, double majors, English as a second language, honors programs, independent study, internships, off-campus study, part-time degree program, services for LD students, study abroad, summer session for credit. *ROTC:* Army (b), Air Force (c).
Computers on Campus Students can access the following: campus intranet, computer help desk, free student e-mail accounts, online (class) grades, online (class) registration, online (class) schedules. Campuswide network is available. Wireless service is available via entire campus.
Student Life *Housing:* on-campus residence required through sophomore year. *Options:* coed, men-only, women-only. Campus housing is university owned and leased by the school. Freshman applicants given priority for college housing. *Activities and organizations:* drama/theater group, student-run newspaper, radio and television station, choral group, marching band, community service groups, choir, outreach ministries groups, Habitat for Humanity, Multi-Ethnic Student Alliance (MESA). *Campus security:* 24-hour emergency response devices and patrols, student patrols, late-night transport/escort service, controlled dormitory access. *Student services:* health clinic, personal/psychological counseling.
Athletics Member NCAA, NAIA. All NCAA Division II. *Intercollegiate sports:* baseball M(s), basketball M(s)/W(s), cross-country running M(s)/W(s), football M(s), gymnastics W(s), soccer M(s)/W(s), softball W(s), swimming and diving M(s)/W(s), tennis M(s)/W(s), track and field M(s)/W(s), volleyball W(s). *Intramural sports:* basketball M/W, cheerleading W(c), football M/W, rugby M(c), skiing (downhill) M/W, soccer M/W, softball M/W, tennis M/W, volleyball M/W.
Standardized Tests *Required:* SAT or ACT (for admission).
Costs (2012–13) *Tuition:* $30,236 full-time, $1261 per credit part-time. *Required fees:* $840 full-time. *Room only:* $4242. Room and board charges vary according to board plan and housing facility. *Payment plan:* installment.
Financial Aid Of all full-time matriculated undergraduates who enrolled in 2011, 4,366 applied for aid, 3,707 were judged to have need, 147 had their need fully met. 1,172 Federal Work-Study jobs (averaging $931). In 2011, 967 non-need-based awards were made. *Average percent of need met:* 63%. *Average financial aid package:* $18,005. *Average need-based loan:* $4586. *Average need-based gift aid:* $9824. *Average non-need-based aid:* $7670. *Average indebtedness upon graduation:* $23,070. *Financial aid deadline:* 7/1.
Applying *Options:* electronic application, early admission, early action. *Application fee:* $45. *Required:* essay or personal statement, high school transcript, 1 letter of recommendation. *Required for some:* interview. *Application deadlines:* 6/1 (freshmen), 6/1 (transfers), 11/15 (early action). *Notification:* continuous until 10/1 (freshmen), continuous (transfers), 1/15 (early action).
Freshman Application Contact Ms. Lynnette Barnes, Processing Coordinator, Azusa Pacific University, 901 East Alosta Avenue, PO Box 7000, Undergraduate Admissions, 7221, Azusa, CA 91702-7000. *Phone:* 626-815-6000 Ext. 3419. *Toll-free phone:* 800-TALK-APU. *E-mail:* admissions@apu.edu.
Website: http://www.apu.edu/.

Bergin University of Canine Studies
Rohnert Park, California

Admissions Office Contact Bergin University of Canine Studies, 5860 Labath Avenue, Rohnert Park, CA 94928.
Website: http://www.berginu.edu/.

Bethesda University of California
Anaheim, California

Director of Admissions Jacquie Ha, Director of Admission, Bethesda University of California, 730 North Euclid Street, Anaheim, CA 92801. *Phone:* 714-517-1945. *Fax:* 714-517-1948. *E-mail:* admission@bcu.edu. *Website:* http://www.buc.edu/.

Biola University
La Mirada, California

- **Independent interdenominational** university, founded 1908
- **Suburban** 95-acre campus with easy access to Los Angeles
- **Endowment** $74.6 million
- **Coed**
- **Moderately difficult** entrance level

Faculty *Student/faculty ratio:* 14:1.
Academics *Calendar:* 4-1-4. *Degrees:* certificates, bachelor's, master's, doctoral, post-master's, and postbachelor's certificates.
Student Life *Campus security:* 24-hour emergency response devices and patrols, late-night transport/escort service, controlled dormitory access.
Athletics Member NAIA.
Standardized Tests *Required:* SAT or ACT (for admission).
Costs (2012–13) *Comprehensive fee:* $38,916 includes full-time tuition ($31,004) and room and board ($7912). Full-time tuition and fees vary according to course load. Part-time tuition: $1292 per unit. Part-time tuition and fees vary according to course load. *College room only:* $4732. Room and board charges vary according to board plan and housing facility.
Financial Aid *Of all full-time matriculated undergraduates who enrolled in 2011,* 3,200 applied for aid, 2,784 were judged to have need, 128 had their need fully met. 501 Federal Work-Study jobs (averaging $1106). *In 2011,* 775 non-need-based awards were made. *Average percent of need met:* 50. *Average financial aid package:* $17,348. *Average need-based loan:* $3509. *Average need-based gift aid:* $12,496. *Average non-need-based aid:* $6009. *Average indebtedness upon graduation:* $34,587.
Applying *Options:* electronic application, early action, deferred entrance. *Application fee:* $45. *Required:* essay or personal statement, high school transcript, minimum 3.0 GPA, 1 letter of recommendation, evangelical believer in the Christian faith. *Required for some:* interview.
Freshman Application Contact Andrea Helmuth, Associate Director of Undergraduate Admissions, Biola University, 13800 Biola Avenue, La Mirada, CA 90639. *Phone:* 562-903-4752. *Toll-free phone:* 800-652-4652. *E-mail:* admissions@biola.edu.
Website: http://www.biola.edu/.

Brandman University
Irvine, California

Admissions Office Contact Brandman University, 16355 Laguna Canyon Road, Irvine, CA 92618. *Toll-free phone:* 800-746-0082.
Website: http://www.brandman.edu/irvine/.

Brooks Institute
Santa Barbara, California

Freshman Application Contact Admissions Office, Brooks Institute, 27 East Cota Street, Santa Barbara, CA 93101. *Phone:* 805-966-3888. *Toll-free phone:* 888-276-4999. *Fax:* 805-565-1386. *E-mail:* admissions@brooks.edu.
Website: http://www.brooks.edu/.

California Baptist University
Riverside, California

- **Independent Southern Baptist** comprehensive, founded 1950
- **Suburban** 131-acre campus with easy access to Los Angeles
- **Endowment** $12.3 million
- **Coed** 4,954 undergraduate students, 88% full-time, 63% women, 37% men
- **Minimally difficult** entrance level, 73% of applicants were admitted

Undergraduates 4,342 full-time, 612 part-time. Students come from 43 states and territories; 29 other countries; 6% are from out of state; 9% Black or African American, non-Hispanic/Latino; 27% Hispanic/Latino; 5% Asian, non-Hispanic/Latino; 0.4% Native Hawaiian or other Pacific Islander, non-Hispanic/Latino; 0.7% American Indian or Alaska Native, non-Hispanic/Latino; 2% Two or more races, non-Hispanic/Latino; 6% Race/ethnicity unknown; 2% international; 14% transferred in; 44% live on campus. *Retention:* 78% of full-time freshmen returned.
Freshmen *Admission:* 2,916 applied, 2,137 admitted, 909 enrolled. *Average high school GPA:* 3.28. *Test scores:* SAT critical reading scores over 500: 44%; SAT math scores over 500: 46%; SAT writing scores over 500: 42%; ACT scores over 18: 78%; SAT critical reading scores over 600: 10%; SAT math scores over 600: 13%; SAT writing scores over 600: 10%; ACT scores over 24: 25%; SAT critical reading scores over 700: 1%; SAT math scores over 700: 1%; SAT writing scores over 700: 1%; ACT scores over 30: 2%.
Faculty *Total:* 531, 43% full-time, 45% with terminal degrees. *Student/faculty ratio:* 17:1.
Academics *Calendar:* 2-4-4-2. *Degrees:* bachelor's and master's. *Special study options:* accelerated degree program, adult/continuing education programs, advanced placement credit, distance learning, double majors, English as a second language, honors programs, independent study, internships, off-campus study, part-time degree program, services for LD students, study abroad, summer session for credit. *ROTC:* Army (b), Air Force (c).
Computers on Campus 279 computers/terminals are available on campus for general student use. Students can access the following: campus intranet, computer help desk, free student e-mail accounts, online (class) grades, online (class) registration, online (class) schedules. Campuswide network is available. 70% of college-owned or -operated housing units are wired for high-speed Internet access. Wireless service is available via entire campus.
Student Life *Housing:* on-campus residence required for freshman year. *Options:* men-only, women-only. Campus housing is university owned. Freshman applicants given priority for college housing. *Activities and organizations:* drama/theater group, student-run newspaper, choral group, International Service Projects, United States Service Projects and Summer of Service, CBU Crazies (Campus Spirit), Associated Students of California Baptist University (government and leadership), Students of Nursing Association. *Campus security:* 24-hour emergency response devices and patrols, student patrols, late-night transport/escort service, controlled dormitory access. *Student services:* health clinic, personal/psychological counseling.
Athletics Member NCAA. All Division II. *Intercollegiate sports:* baseball M(s), basketball M(s)/W(s), cheerleading M(s)/W(s), cross-country running M(s)/W(s), golf M(s)/W(s), soccer M(s)/W(s), softball W(s), swimming and diving M(s)/W(s), track and field M(s)/W(s), volleyball M(s)/W(s), water polo M(s)/W(s), wrestling M(s). *Intramural sports:* basketball M/W, bowling M/W, football M/W, softball M/W, table tennis M/W, ultimate Frisbee M/W, volleyball M/W.
Standardized Tests *Required:* SAT or ACT (for admission). *Recommended:* SAT Subject Tests (for admission).
Costs (2012–13) *Comprehensive fee:* $35,890 includes full-time tuition ($25,090), mandatory fees ($1810), and room and board ($8990). Full-time tuition and fees vary according to course load, location, and program. Part-time tuition: $5790 per year. Part-time tuition and fees vary according to course load, location, and program. *Required fees:* $350 per year part-time. *College room only:* $4560. Room and board charges vary according to board plan and housing facility. *Payment plan:* installment. *Waivers:* employees or children of employees.
Financial Aid Of all full-time matriculated undergraduates who enrolled in 2009, 2,576 applied for aid, 1,894 were judged to have need, 1,605 had their need fully met. 178 Federal Work-Study jobs (averaging $888). In 2009, 449 non-need-based awards were made. *Average percent of need met:* 58%. *Average financial aid package:* $8651. *Average need-based loan:* $2298. *Average need-based gift aid:* $4677. *Average non-need-based aid:* $3656. *Average indebtedness upon graduation:* $34,650.
Applying *Options:* electronic application, early action, deferred entrance. *Application fee:* $45. *Required:* essay or personal statement, minimum 2.0 GPA, 2 letters of recommendation. *Required for some:* high school transcript. *Application deadlines:* rolling (freshmen), rolling (out-of-state freshmen), rolling (transfers), 12/15 (early action). *Notification:* continuous until 11/9 (freshmen), continuous (out-of-state freshmen), continuous (transfers), 1/31 (early action).
Freshman Application Contact Mr. Allen Johnson, Director, Undergraduate Admissions, California Baptist University, 8432 Magnolia Avenue, Riverside, CA 92504-3297. *Phone:* 951-343-4212. *Toll-free phone:* 877-228-8866. *Fax:* 951-343-4525. *E-mail:* admissions@calbaptist.edu.
Website: http://www.calbaptist.edu/.

California Christian College
Fresno, California

- **Independent Free Will Baptist** 4-year
- **Urban** 5-acre campus
- **Endowment** $122,093
- **Coed**
- **Noncompetitive** entrance level

Faculty *Student/faculty ratio:* 4:1.

Academics *Calendar:* semesters. *Degrees:* associate and bachelor's.

Standardized Tests *Required:* standardized Bible content tests (for admission). *Recommended:* SAT or ACT (for admission).

Costs (2012–13) *Comprehensive fee:* $12,210 includes full-time tuition ($7440), mandatory fees ($570), and room and board ($4200). Part-time tuition: $310 per credit hour.

Financial Aid *Of all full-time matriculated undergraduates who enrolled in 2011,* 23 applied for aid, 22 were judged to have need, 1 had their need fully met. 10 Federal Work-Study jobs (averaging $1153). *Average percent of need met:* 52. *Average financial aid package:* $9049. *Average need-based loan:* $3484. *Average need-based gift aid:* $4600. *Average indebtedness upon graduation:* $33,595.

Applying *Options:* electronic application. *Application fee:* $40. *Required:* essay or personal statement, high school transcript, minimum 2.0 GPA, 2 letters of recommendation, statement of faith, moral/ethical statement. *Recommended:* interview.

Freshman Application Contact California Christian College, 4881 East University Avenue, Fresno, CA 93703-3533. *Phone:* 559-251-4215. *Website:* http://www.calchristiancollege.edu/.

California Coast University
Santa Ana, California

- **Proprietary** comprehensive, founded 1973
- **Coed**

Academics *Degrees:* associate, bachelor's, master's, and doctoral (distance learning only).

Applying *Application fee:* $75. *Required:* resume, high school transcript or GED equivalent.

Freshman Application Contact California Coast University, 925 North Spurgeon Street, Santa Ana, CA 92701. *Phone:* 714-547-9625. *Toll-free phone:* 888-CCU-UNIV. *Website:* http://www.calcoast.edu/.

California College
San Diego, California

Director of Admissions Tana Sanderson, Director of Admission, California College, 6602 Convoy Court, Suite 100, San Diego, CA 92111. *Phone:* 619-295-5785. *Toll-free phone:* 800-622-3188. *E-mail:* tana.sanderson@cc-sd.edu. *Website:* http://www.cc-sd.edu/.

California College of the Arts
San Francisco, California

- **Independent** comprehensive, founded 1907
- **Urban** 4-acre campus with easy access to San Francisco, Oakland
- **Endowment** $31.1 million
- **Coed**
- **Moderately difficult** entrance level

Faculty *Student/faculty ratio:* 10:1.

Academics *Calendar:* semesters. *Degrees:* bachelor's and master's.

Student Life *Campus security:* 24-hour emergency response devices and patrols, late-night transport/escort service.

Standardized Tests *Recommended:* SAT or ACT (for admission).

Costs (2012–13) *Tuition:* $36,960 full-time, $1540 per unit part-time. Full-time tuition and fees vary according to degree level. Part-time tuition and fees vary according to course load and degree level. *Required fees:* $350 full-time. *Room only:* $7400. Room and board charges vary according to housing facility.

Financial Aid *Of all full-time matriculated undergraduates who enrolled in 2012,* 916 applied for aid, 848 were judged to have need, 31 had their need fully met. 806 Federal Work-Study jobs (averaging $3019). 99 state and other part-time jobs (averaging $2916). *In 2012,* 222 non-need-based awards were made. *Average percent of need met:* 58. *Average financial aid package:* $25,533. *Average need-based loan:* $5035. *Average need-based gift aid:* $20,474. *Average non-need-based aid:* $8635. *Average indebtedness upon graduation:* $36,300.

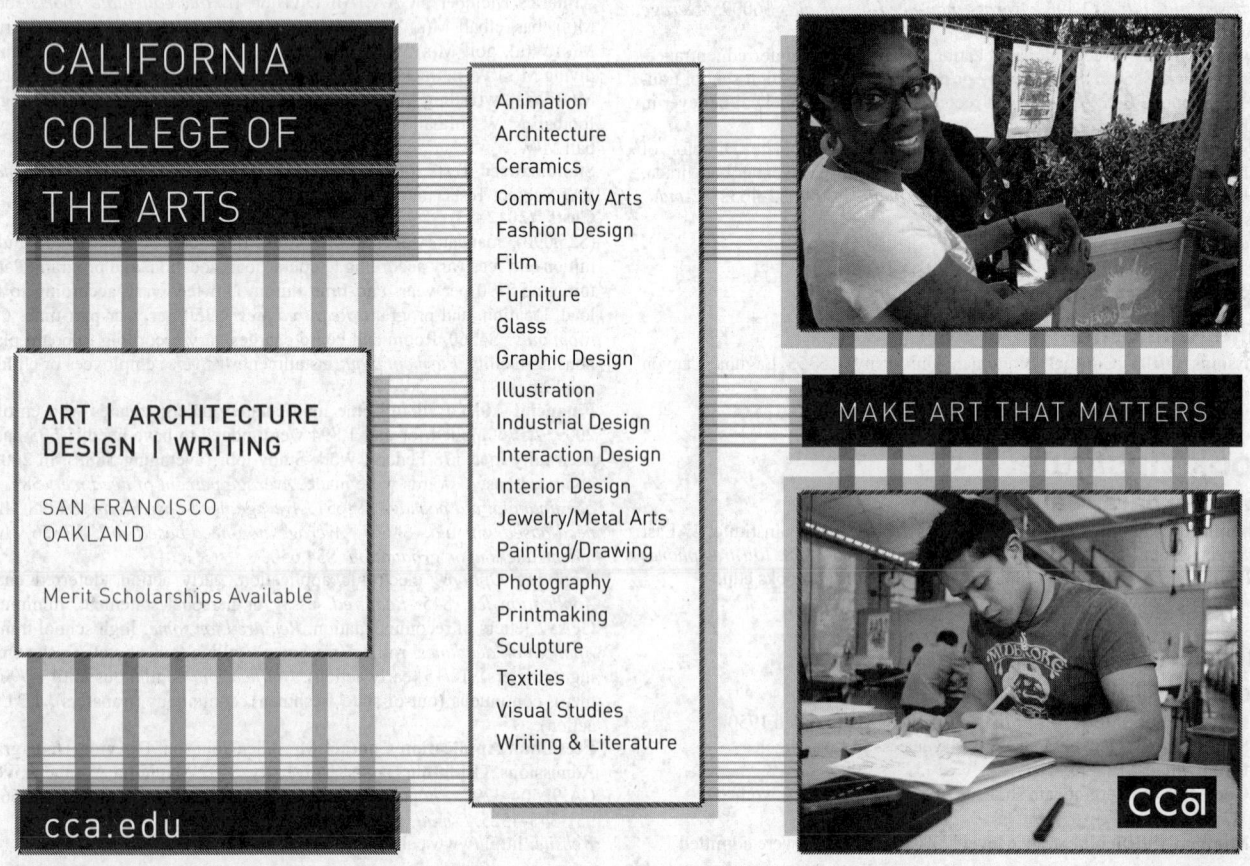

CALIFORNIA COLLEGE OF THE ARTS

ART | ARCHITECTURE
DESIGN | WRITING

SAN FRANCISCO
OAKLAND

Merit Scholarships Available

Animation
Architecture
Ceramics
Community Arts
Fashion Design
Film
Furniture
Glass
Graphic Design
Illustration
Industrial Design
Interaction Design
Interior Design
Jewelry/Metal Arts
Painting/Drawing
Photography
Printmaking
Sculpture
Textiles
Visual Studies
Writing & Literature

MAKE ART THAT MATTERS

CCA

cca.edu

Applying *Options:* electronic application, deferred entrance. *Application fee:* $60. *Required:* essay or personal statement, high school transcript, 2 letters of recommendation, portfolio of creative work and statement of artistic and professional goals required. *Required for some:* interview.

Freshman Application Contact Ms. Robynne Royster, Director of Admissions, California College of the Arts, 1111 Eighth Street, San Francisco, CA 94107. *Phone:* 415-703-9523 Ext. 9532. *Toll-free phone:* 800-447-1ART. *Fax:* 415-703-9539. *E-mail:* enroll@cca.edu. *Website:* http://www.cca.edu/.

See previous page for display ad and page 1218 for the College Close-Up.

California Institute of Integral Studies
San Francisco, California

Application Contact Admissions Department, California Institute of Integral Studies, 1453 Mission Street, San Francisco, CA 94103. *Phone:* 415-575-6156. *Fax:* 415-575-1268. *E-mail:* admissions@ciis.edu. *Website:* http://www.ciis.edu/.

California Institute of Technology
Pasadena, California

- **Independent** university, founded 1891
- **Suburban** 124-acre campus with easy access to Los Angeles
- **Endowment** $1.5 billion
- **Coed**
- **Most difficult** entrance level

Faculty *Student/faculty ratio:* 3:1.

Academics *Calendar:* 3 ten-week terms. *Degrees:* bachelor's, master's, doctoral, and post-master's certificates.

Student Life *Campus security:* 24-hour emergency response devices and patrols, late-night transport/escort service, controlled dormitory access.

Athletics Member NCAA. All Division III.

Standardized Tests *Required:* SAT or ACT (for admission), SAT Subject Tests (for admission).

Costs (2012–13) *One-time required fee:* $500. *Comprehensive fee:* $51,672 includes full-time tuition ($38,085), mandatory fees ($1503), and room and board ($12,084). Full-time tuition and fees vary according to course load. Part-time tuition and fees vary according to course load. *College room only:* $6798. *Payment plans:* installment, deferred payment.

Financial Aid *Of all full-time matriculated undergraduates who enrolled in 2012,* 609 applied for aid, 522 were judged to have need, 522 had their need fully met. 288 Federal Work-Study jobs (averaging $3062). 58 state and other part-time jobs (averaging $2600). *In 2012,* 1 non-need-based awards were made. *Average percent of need met:* 100. *Average financial aid package:* $38,756. *Average need-based loan:* $3978. *Average need-based gift aid:* $34,831. *Average non-need-based aid:* $56,382. *Average indebtedness upon graduation:* $15,090.

Applying *Options:* electronic application, early admission, early action, deferred entrance. *Application fee:* $65. *Required:* essay or personal statement, high school transcript, 2 letters of recommendation.

Freshman Application Contact Mr. Jarrid James Whitney, Director of Admissions, California Institute of Technology, 383 South Hill Avenue, Mail Code 10-90, Pasadena, CA 91125. *Phone:* 626-395-6341. *Fax:* 626-683-3026. *Website:* http://www.caltech.edu/.

California Institute of the Arts
Valencia, California

Freshman Application Contact Molly Ryan, Director of Admissions, California Institute of the Arts, 24700 McBean Parkway, Valencia, CA 91355-2340. *Phone:* 661-255-1050. *Toll-free phone:* 800-545-2787. *Fax:* 661-253-7710. *E-mail:* admiss@calarts.edu. *Website:* http://www.calarts.edu/.

See below for display ad and page 1220 for the College Close-Up.

California Intercontinental University
Diamond Bar, California

Director of Admissions John Ramsay, Director of Admission, California Intercontinental University, 1470 Valley Vista Drive, Suite 150, Diamond Bar, CA 91765. *Phone:* 909-396-6090. *Toll-free phone:* 866-687-2258. *Fax:* 909-804-5151. *E-mail:* admissions@caluniversity.com. *Website:* http://caluniversity.edu/.

California Lutheran University
Thousand Oaks, California

- **Independent Lutheran** comprehensive, founded 1959
- **Suburban** 290-acre campus with easy access to Los Angeles
- **Endowment** $55.5 million
- **Coed** 2,713 undergraduate students, 91% full-time, 56% women, 44% men
- **Moderately difficult** entrance level, 44% of applicants were admitted

Undergraduates 2,480 full-time, 233 part-time. Students come from 38 states and territories; 50 other countries; 15% are from out of state; 4% Black or African American, non-Hispanic/Latino; 20% Hispanic/Latino; 6% Asian, non-Hispanic/Latino; 0.6% Native Hawaiian or other Pacific Islander, non-Hispanic/Latino; 1% American Indian or Alaska Native, non-Hispanic/Latino; 4% Two or more races, non-Hispanic/Latino; 6% Race/ethnicity unknown; 4% international; 9% transferred in; 56% live on campus. *Retention:* 85% of full-time freshmen returned.

Freshmen *Admission:* 7,245 applied, 3,187 admitted, 502 enrolled. *Average high school GPA:* 3.7. *Test scores:* SAT critical reading scores over 500: 79%; SAT math scores over 500: 82%; SAT writing scores over 500: 74%; ACT scores over 18: 99%; SAT critical reading scores over 600: 27%; SAT math scores over 600: 31%; SAT writing scores over 600: 25%; ACT scores over 24: 55%; SAT critical reading scores over 700: 3%; SAT math scores over 700: 4%; SAT writing scores over 700: 2%; ACT scores over 30: 8%.

Faculty *Total:* 373, 44% full-time, 57% with terminal degrees. *Student/faculty ratio:* 15:1.

Academics *Calendar:* semesters. *Degrees:* certificates, bachelor's, master's, doctoral, post-master's, and postbachelor's certificates. *Special study options:* accelerated degree program, adult/continuing education programs, advanced placement credit, cooperative education, double majors, honors programs, independent study, internships, off-campus study, part-time degree program, services for LD students, student-designed majors, study abroad, summer session for credit. *ROTC:* Army (c), Air Force (c). *Unusual degree programs:* 3-2 computer science, political public policy and administration.

Computers on Campus 300 computers/terminals are available on campus for general student use. Students can access the following: campus intranet, computer help desk, free student e-mail accounts, online (class) grades, online (class) registration, online (class) schedules. Campuswide network is available. 100% of college-owned or -operated housing units are wired for high-speed Internet access. Wireless service is available via entire campus.

Student Life *Housing:* on-campus residence required through junior year. *Options:* coed, disabled students. Campus housing is university owned. Freshman campus housing is guaranteed. *Activities and organizations:* drama/theater group, student-run newspaper, radio and television station, choral group, student government, recreation, sports fan, or club sports related, service organizations, campus ministry or other religiously affiliated organization, multicultural organizations. *Campus security:* 24-hour emergency response devices and patrols, late-night transport/escort service, controlled dormitory access, escort service; shuttle service. *Student services:* health clinic, personal/psychological counseling, women's center.

Athletics Member NCAA. All Division III. *Intercollegiate sports:* baseball M, basketball M/W, cheerleading M/W, cross-country running M/W, football M, golf M/W, soccer M/W, softball W, swimming and diving M/W, tennis M/W, track and field M/W, volleyball W, water polo M/W. *Intramural sports:* badminton M(c)/W(c), basketball M(c)/W(c), football M(c)/W(c), lacrosse M(c)/W(c), rugby M(c), soccer M(c)/W(c), softball M(c)/W(c), tennis M(c)/W(c), volleyball M(c)/W(c), water polo M(c)/W(c).

Standardized Tests *Required:* SAT or ACT (for admission).

Costs (2012–13) *Comprehensive fee:* $45,870 includes full-time tuition ($33,910), mandatory fees ($450), and room and board ($11,510). Part-time tuition: $1090 per credit hour. *Required fees:* $225 per term part-time. *College room only:* $6220. Room and board charges vary according to board plan.

Financial Aid Of all full-time matriculated undergraduates who enrolled in 2012, 1,952 applied for aid, 1,748 were judged to have need, 200 had their need fully met. 301 Federal Work-Study jobs (averaging $2500). In 2012, 663 non-need-based awards were made. *Average percent of need met:* 65%. *Average financial aid package:* $22,740. *Average need-based loan:* $4680. *Average need-based gift aid:* $18,880. *Average non-need-based aid:* $13,020. *Average indebtedness upon graduation:* $26,610.

Applying *Options:* electronic application, early action, deferred entrance. *Application fee:* $45. *Required:* essay or personal statement, high school transcript, minimum 2.8 GPA, 1 letter of recommendation. *Recommended:* minimum 3.0 GPA, interview. *Application deadline:* 3/15 (freshmen). *Notification:* 12/1 (freshmen), 5/1 (transfers).

Freshman Application Contact Dr. Michael Elgarico, Dean of Undergraduate Enrollment, California Lutheran University, Office of Admission, #1350, Thousand Oaks, CA 91360. *Phone:* 805-493-3135. *Toll-free phone:* 877-258-3678. *Fax:* 805-493-3114. *E-mail:* cluadm@clunet.edu. *Website:* http://www.callutheran.edu/.

California Maritime Academy
Vallejo, California

- **State-supported** comprehensive, founded 1929, part of California State University System
- **Suburban** 64-acre campus with easy access to San Francisco
- **Coed**
- **Moderately difficult** entrance level

Academics *Calendar:* semesters. *Degrees:* bachelor's and master's.

Student Life *Campus security:* 24-hour patrols, student patrols.

Athletics Member NAIA.

Standardized Tests *Required:* SAT or ACT (for admission).

Applying *Options:* electronic application. *Application fee:* $55. *Required:* high school transcript, minimum 2.0 GPA, health form.

Freshman Application Contact California Maritime Academy, 200 Maritime Academy Drive, Vallejo, CA 94590. *Phone:* 707-654-1330. *Toll-free phone:* 800-561-1945. *Website:* http://www.csum.edu/.

California Miramar University
San Diego, California

Director of Admissions Jean Van Slyke, Director of Admissions, California Miramar University, 9750 Miramar Road, Suite 180, San Diego, CA 92126. *Phone:* 858-653-3000. *Toll-free phone:* 877-570-5678. *Fax:* 858-653-6786. *E-mail:* admissions@calmu.edu. *Website:* http://www.calmu.edu/.

California National University for Advanced Studies
Northridge, California

Freshman Application Contact Ms. Stephanie Smith, Registrar, California National University for Advanced Studies, Admissions, 8550 Balboa Boulevard, Suite 210, Northridge, CA 91325. *Phone:* 818-830-2411. *Toll-free phone:* 800-782-2422. *Fax:* 818-830-2418. *E-mail:* cnuadms@mail.cnuas.edu. *Website:* http://www.cnuas.edu/.

California Polytechnic State University, San Luis Obispo
San Luis Obispo, California

- **State-supported** comprehensive, founded 1901, part of California State University System
- **Suburban** 6000-acre campus
- **Coed** 17,680 undergraduate students, 96% full-time, 45% women, 55% men
- **Moderately difficult** entrance level, 31% of applicants were admitted

Undergraduates 17,027 full-time, 653 part-time. 9% are from out of state; 0.7% Black or African American, non-Hispanic/Latino; 14% Hispanic/Latino; 11% Asian, non-Hispanic/Latino; 0.2% Native Hawaiian or other Pacific Islander, non-Hispanic/Latino; 0.3% American Indian or Alaska Native, non-Hispanic/Latino; 6% Two or more races, non-Hispanic/Latino; 5% Race/ethnicity unknown; 1% international; 5% transferred in; 36% live on campus. *Retention:* 93% of full-time freshmen returned.

Freshmen *Admission:* 36,941 applied, 11,545 admitted, 3,701 enrolled. *Average high school GPA:* 3.87. *Test scores:* SAT critical reading scores over 500: 92%; SAT math scores over 500: 97%; ACT scores over 18: 100%; SAT critical reading scores over 600: 51%; SAT math scores over 600: 72%; ACT scores over 24: 85%; SAT critical reading scores over 700: 10%; SAT math scores over 700: 21%; ACT scores over 30: 27%.

Faculty *Total:* 1,259, 65% full-time, 59% with terminal degrees. *Student/faculty ratio:* 19:1.

Academics *Calendar:* quarters. *Degrees:* bachelor's and master's. *Special study options:* academic remediation for entering students, advanced placement credit, cooperative education, distance learning, double majors, English as a second language, honors programs, internships, off-campus study, part-time degree program, services for LD students, study abroad, summer session for credit. *ROTC:* Army (b).

Computers on Campus Students can access the following: campus intranet, free student e-mail accounts, online (class) grades, online (class) registration, online (class) schedules. Campuswide network is available. Wireless service is available via classrooms, computer centers, computer labs, learning centers, libraries, student centers.

Student Life *Housing options:* coed, disabled students. Campus housing is university owned. *Activities and organizations:* drama/theater group, student-run newspaper, radio and television station, choral group, marching band, national fraternities, national sororities. *Campus security:* 24-hour emergency response devices and patrols, student patrols, late-night transport/escort service, controlled dormitory access. *Student services:* health clinic, personal/psychological counseling, women's center, legal services.

Athletics Member NCAA. All Division I except football (Division I-AA). *Intercollegiate sports:* baseball M(s), basketball M(s)/W(s), cross-country running M(s)/W(s), golf M(s)/W(s), soccer M(s)/W(s), softball W(s), swimming and diving M(s)/W(s), tennis M(s)/W(s), track and field M(s)/W(s), volleyball W(s), wrestling M(s). *Intramural sports:* badminton M/W, basketball M/W, football M/W, racquetball M/W, soccer M/W, softball M/W, table tennis M/W, tennis M/W, volleyball M/W.

Standardized Tests *Required:* SAT or ACT (for admission).

Costs (2013–14) *Tuition:* state resident $5472 full-time; nonresident $16,632 full-time, $248 per unit part-time. Full-time tuition and fees vary according to course load, degree level, and program. Part-time tuition and fees vary according to course load, degree level, and program. *Required fees:* $3051 full-time. *Room and board:* $10,679; room only: $6123. Room and board charges vary according to housing facility. *Payment plan:* installment. *Waivers:* employees or children of employees.

Financial Aid Of all full-time matriculated undergraduates who enrolled in 2011, 10,309 applied for aid, 7,168 were judged to have need, 351 had their need fully met. In 2011, 871 non-need-based awards were made. *Average percent of need met:* 60%. *Average financial aid package:* $10,101. *Average need-based loan:* $3794. *Average need-based gift aid:* $3605. *Average non-need-based aid:* $2416.

Applying *Options:* electronic application, early admission, early decision. *Application fee:* $55. *Required:* high school transcript. *Application deadlines:* 11/30 (freshmen), 11/30 (transfers). *Early decision deadline:* 10/31. *Notification:* 4/1 (freshmen), 4/1 (transfers), 12/15 (early decision).

Freshman Application Contact Mr. James Maraviglia, Associate Vice Provost for Marketing and Enrollment Development, California Polytechnic State University, San Luis Obispo, Admissions Office, 1 Grand Avenue, San Luis Obispo, CA 93407-0031. *Phone:* 805-756-2311. *Fax:* 805-756-5911. *E-mail:* admissions@calpoly.edu. *Website:* http://www.calpoly.edu/.

California State Polytechnic University, Pomona

Pomona, California

- **State-supported** comprehensive, founded 1938, part of California State University System
- **Urban** 1400-acre campus with easy access to Los Angeles
- **Endowment** $55.6 million
- **Coed** 20,542 undergraduate students, 87% full-time, 43% women, 57% men
- **Moderately difficult** entrance level, 54% of applicants were admitted

Undergraduates 17,837 full-time, 2,705 part-time. Students come from 48 states and territories; 35 other countries; 1% are from out of state; 3% Black or African American, non-Hispanic/Latino; 35% Hispanic/Latino; 25% Asian, non-Hispanic/Latino; 0.4% Native Hawaiian or other Pacific Islander, non-Hispanic/Latino; 0.2% American Indian or Alaska Native, non-Hispanic/Latino; 4% Two or more races, non-Hispanic/Latino; 5% Race/ethnicity unknown; 4% international; 10% transferred in; 12% live on campus. *Retention:* 92% of full-time freshmen returned.

Freshmen *Admission:* 40,456 applied, 21,751 admitted, 3,120 enrolled. *Average high school GPA:* 3.41. *Test scores:* SAT critical reading scores over 500: 59%; SAT math scores over 500: 74%; ACT scores over 18: 91%; SAT critical reading scores over 600: 18%; SAT math scores over 600: 36%; ACT scores over 24: 46%; SAT critical reading scores over 700: 2%; SAT math scores over 700: 7%; ACT scores over 30: 7%.

Faculty *Total:* 1,077, 49% full-time, 56% with terminal degrees. *Student/faculty ratio:* 25:1.

Academics *Calendar:* quarters. *Degrees:* bachelor's, master's, and doctoral. *Special study options:* academic remediation for entering students, adult/continuing education programs, advanced placement credit, cooperative education, distance learning, double majors, English as a second language, honors programs, internships, off-campus study, part-time degree program, services for LD students, study abroad, summer session for credit. *ROTC:* Army (b).

Computers on Campus 1,875 computers/terminals are available on campus for general student use. Students can access the following: campus intranet, computer help desk, free student e-mail accounts, online (class) grades, online (class) registration, online (class) schedules. Campuswide network is available. 100% of college-owned or -operated housing units are wired for high-speed Internet access. Wireless service is available via entire campus.

Student Life *Housing:* on-campus residence required for freshman year. *Options:* coed, disabled students. Campus housing is university owned and is provided by a third party. Freshman applicants given priority for college housing. *Activities and organizations:* drama/theater group, student-run newspaper, choral group, Rose Float Club, Ridge Runners Ski Club, Barkada (Asian club), American Marketing Association, Cal Poly Society of Accountants, national fraternities, national sororities. *Campus security:* 24-hour emergency response devices and patrols, student patrols, late-night transport/escort service, controlled dormitory access, video camera surveillance. *Student services:* health clinic, personal/psychological counseling, women's center.

Athletics Member NCAA. All Division II. *Intercollegiate sports:* baseball M(s), basketball M(s)/W(s), cross-country running M(s)/W(s), soccer M(s)/W(s), tennis M(s)/W(s), track and field M(s)/W(s), volleyball W(s). *Intramural sports:* basketball M/W, bowling M/W, football M/W, softball M/W, tennis M/W, volleyball M/W.

Standardized Tests *Required:* SAT or ACT (for admission).

Costs (2013–14) *Tuition:* state resident $5970 full-time; nonresident $17,130 full-time. Full-time tuition and fees vary according to course load, degree level, and program. Part-time tuition and fees vary according to course load, degree level, and program. *Required fees:* $653 full-time, $248 per credit part-time. *Room and board:* $11,615; room only: $6921. Room and board charges vary according to board plan and housing facility. *Payment plans:* installment, deferred payment. *Waivers:* employees or children of employees.

Financial Aid Of all full-time matriculated undergraduates who enrolled in 2012, 13,503 applied for aid, 11,804 were judged to have need, 133 had their need fully met. 323 Federal Work-Study jobs (averaging $2736). In 2012, 12 non-need-based awards were made. *Average percent of need met:* 54%. *Average financial aid package:* $10,005. *Average need-based loan:* $4525. *Average need-based gift aid:* $8772. *Average non-need-based aid:* $2791. *Average indebtedness upon graduation:* $18,805.

Applying *Options:* electronic application. *Application fee:* $55. *Required:* high school transcript, minimum 2.0 GPA. *Application deadlines:* 11/30 (freshmen), 11/30 (transfers). *Notification:* continuous until 10/2 (freshmen), 5/1 (transfers).

Freshman Application Contact Ms. Deborah L. Brandon, Executive Director, Admissions and Outreach, California State Polytechnic University, Pomona, 3801 West Temple Avenue, Pomona, CA 91768-2557. *Phone:* 909-869-3427. *Fax:* 909-869-5315. *E-mail:* admissions@csupomona.edu. *Website:* http://www.csupomona.edu/.

California State University, Bakersfield

Bakersfield, California

- **State-supported** comprehensive, founded 1970, part of California State University System
- **Urban** 575-acre campus
- **Coed**
- **Moderately difficult** entrance level

Faculty *Student/faculty ratio:* 27:1.

Academics *Calendar:* quarters. *Degrees:* bachelor's and master's.

Student Life *Campus security:* 24-hour emergency response devices and patrols, late-night transport/escort service.

Athletics Member NCAA. All Division II except wrestling (Division I).

Standardized Tests *Required for some:* SAT or ACT (for admission).

Costs (2012–13) *Tuition:* state resident $5472 full-time; nonresident $16,632 full-time. Full-time tuition and fees vary according to course load, degree level, and reciprocity agreements. Part-time tuition and fees vary according to course load, degree level, and reciprocity agreements. *Required fees:* $1237 full-time. *Room and board:* $8787. Room and board charges vary according to board plan.

Financial Aid *Of all full-time matriculated undergraduates who enrolled in 2010,* 4,644 applied for aid, 4,353 were judged to have need, 374 had their need fully met. *Average percent of need met:* 9. *Average financial aid package:* $3961. *Average need-based loan:* $1566. *Average need-based gift aid:* $3326. *Average indebtedness upon graduation:* $8892.

Applying *Options:* electronic application, deferred entrance. *Required:* high school transcript.

Freshman Application Contact Debra Blowers, Assistant Director, Admissions and Evaluations, California State University, Bakersfield, 9001 Stockdale Highway, Balersfield, CA 93311-1099. *Phone:* 661-664-3036. *Toll-free phone:* 800-788-2782. *E-mail:* admissions@csub.edu. *Website:* http://www.csub.edu/.

California State University Channel Islands

Camarillo, California

Freshman Application Contact Ms. Ginger Reyes, California State University Channel Islands, One University Drive, Camarillo, CA 93012. *Phone:* 805-437-8520. *Fax:* 805-437-8519. *E-mail:* prospective.student@ csuci.edu.
Website: http://www.csuci.edu/.

California State University, Chico

Chico, California

- **State-supported** comprehensive, founded 1887, part of California State University System
- **Small-town** 119-acre campus
- **Endowment** $43.0 million
- **Coed** 15,316 undergraduate students, 92% full-time, 52% women, 48% men
- **Moderately difficult** entrance level, 79% of applicants were admitted

Undergraduates 14,103 full-time, 1,213 part-time. Students come from 36 states and territories; 39 other countries; 2% are from out of state; 2% Black or African American, non-Hispanic/Latino; 20% Hispanic/Latino; 6% Asian, non-Hispanic/Latino; 0.2% Native Hawaiian or other Pacific Islander, non-Hispanic/Latino; 0.7% American Indian or Alaska Native, non-Hispanic/Latino; 4% Two or more races, non-Hispanic/Latino; 8% Race/ethnicity unknown; 4% international; 9% transferred in; 1% live on campus. *Retention:* 86% of full-time freshmen returned.

Freshmen *Admission:* 15,568 applied, 12,326 admitted, 2,714 enrolled. *Average high school GPA:* 3.21. *Test scores:* SAT critical reading scores over 500: 55%; SAT math scores over 500: 62%; ACT scores over 18: 87%; SAT critical reading scores over 600: 13%; SAT math scores over 600: 19%; ACT scores over 24: 31%; SAT critical reading scores over 700: 1%; SAT math scores over 700: 1%; ACT scores over 30: 2%.

Faculty *Total:* 862, 52% full-time, 58% with terminal degrees. *Student/faculty ratio:* 25:1.

Academics *Calendar:* semesters. *Degrees:* certificates, bachelor's, master's, post-master's, and postbachelor's certificates. *Special study options:* academic remediation for entering students, adult/continuing education programs, advanced placement credit, cooperative education, distance learning, double majors, English as a second language, external degree program, honors programs, independent study, internships, off-campus study, part-time degree program, services for LD students, student-designed majors, study abroad, summer session for credit.

Computers on Campus 1,212 computers/terminals and 1,205 ports are available on campus for general student use. Students can access the following: campus intranet, computer help desk, free student e-mail accounts, online (class) grades, online (class) registration, online (class) schedules, student account information, calendar, transcripts. Campuswide network is available. 100% of college-owned or -operated housing units are wired for high-speed Internet access. Wireless service is available via entire campus.

Student Life *Housing options:* coed, women-only, disabled students. Campus housing is university owned. Freshman applicants given priority for college housing. *Activities and organizations:* drama/theater group, student-run newspaper, radio station, choral group, Scour and Devour, Panhellenic Council, The Edge Campus Christian Fellowship, Golden Key International Honor Society, Music and Entertainment Industry, national fraternities, national sororities. *Campus security:* 24-hour emergency response devices and patrols, student patrols, late-night transport/escort service, controlled dormitory access, crime prevention workshops, RAD self-defense program, Chico Safe Rides, blue light emergency phones, freshmen safety orientation. *Student services:* health clinic, personal/psychological counseling, women's center, legal services.

Athletics Member NCAA. All Division II. *Intercollegiate sports:* baseball M(s), basketball M(s)/W(s), cross-country running M(s)/W(s), field hockey W(c), golf M(s)/W(s), racquetball M(c)/W(c), rugby M(c)/W(c), soccer M(s)/W(s), softball W(s), swimming and diving M(c)/W(c), table tennis M(c)/W(c), tennis M(c)/W(c), track and field M(s)/W(s), ultimate Frisbee M(c)/W(c), volleyball W(s), water polo M(c)/W(c), wrestling M(c). *Intramural sports:* badminton M/W, basketball M/W, bowling M/W, football M/W, soccer M/W, softball M/W, volleyball M/W.

Standardized Tests *Required:* SAT or ACT (for admission).

Costs (2012–13) *Tuition:* state resident $7438 full-time; nonresident $18,598 full-time. Full-time tuition and fees vary according to degree level. Part-time tuition and fees vary according to course load and degree level. *Required fees:* $1468 full-time. *Room and board:* $11,208. Room and board charges vary according to board plan and housing facility. *Payment plans:* installment, deferred payment. *Waivers:* senior citizens and employees or children of employees.

Financial Aid Of all full-time matriculated undergraduates who enrolled in 2011, 9,927 applied for aid, 8,356 were judged to have need, 1,110 had their need fully met. In 2011, 140 non-need-based awards were made. *Average percent of need met:* 84%. *Average financial aid package:* $11,501. *Average need-based loan:* $4427. *Average need-based gift aid:* $9374. *Average non-need-based aid:* $2595.

Applying *Options:* electronic application, deferred entrance. *Application fee:* $55. *Required:* high school transcript, GPA of 10th /11th grade college preparatory courses only. *Required for some:* minimum 2.0 GPA. *Application deadlines:* 11/30 (freshmen), 11/30 (transfers). *Notification:* 3/1 (freshmen), 3/1 (transfers).

Freshman Application Contact California State University, Chico, Chico, CA 95929-0722. *Phone:* 530-898-4428. *Toll-free phone:* 800-542-4426. *Fax:* 530-898-6456.
Website: http://www.csuchico.edu/.

California State University, Dominguez Hills

Carson, California

- **State-supported** comprehensive, founded 1960, part of California State University System
- **Urban** 350-acre campus with easy access to Los Angeles
- **Endowment** $10.2 million
- **Coed** 11,427 undergraduate students, 68% full-time, 64% women, 36% men
- **Moderately difficult** entrance level, 87% of applicants were admitted

Undergraduates 7,800 full-time, 3,627 part-time. Students come from 16 states and territories; 31 other countries; 18% Black or African American, non-Hispanic/Latino; 52% Hispanic/Latino; 9% Asian, non-Hispanic/Latino; 0.5% Native Hawaiian or other Pacific Islander, non-Hispanic/Latino; 0.3% American Indian or Alaska Native, non-Hispanic/Latino; 3% Two or more races, non-Hispanic/Latino; 5% Race/ethnicity unknown; 2% international; 16% transferred in; 6% live on campus. *Retention:* 77% of full-time freshmen returned.

Freshmen *Admission:* 9,358 applied, 8,138 admitted, 1,214 enrolled. *Average high school GPA:* 3.09. *Test scores:* SAT critical reading scores over 500: 16%; SAT math scores over 500: 18%; SAT writing scores over 500: 16%; ACT scores over 18: 46%; SAT critical reading scores over 600: 2%; SAT math scores over 600: 2%; SAT writing scores over 600: 2%; ACT scores over 24: 6%; ACT scores over 30: 1%.

Faculty *Total:* 743, 35% full-time, 51% with terminal degrees. *Student/faculty ratio:* 25:1.

Academics *Calendar:* semesters. *Degrees:* bachelor's, master's, post-master's, and postbachelor's certificates. *Special study options:* academic remediation for entering students, accelerated degree program, advanced placement credit, cooperative education, distance learning, double majors, external degree program, honors programs, independent study, internships, off-campus study, part-time degree program, services for LD students, student-designed majors, study abroad, summer session for credit. *ROTC:* Army (b), Air Force (c).

Computers on Campus 1,100 computers/terminals and 1,100 ports are available on campus for general student use. Students can access the following: campus intranet, computer help desk, free student e-mail accounts, online (class) grades, online (class) registration, online (class) schedules. Campuswide network is available. 100% of college-owned or -operated housing units are wired for high-speed Internet access. Wireless service is available via entire campus.

Student Life *Housing options:* coed, disabled students. Campus housing is university owned. *Activities and organizations:* drama/theater group, student-run newspaper, radio station, choral group, Latino Student Business Association, Espirito de Nuestro Futuro, Organization of African Studies, American Marketing Association, Circle K, national fraternities, national sororities. *Campus security:* 24-hour emergency response devices, student patrols, late-night transport/escort service, Campus Police Patrol Division is staffed 24 hours a day, 7 days a week. Officers are vested with full police powers. *Student services:* health clinic, personal/psychological counseling, women's center.

Athletics Member NCAA. All Division II. *Intercollegiate sports:* baseball M(s), basketball M(s)/W(s), golf M(s), soccer M(s)/W(s), softball W(s), track and field W(s), volleyball W(s). *Intramural sports:* basketball M/W, football M/W, soccer M/W, softball M/W, swimming and diving M/W, tennis M/W, ultimate Frisbee M/W, volleyball M/W, water polo M/W, weight lifting M/W.

Standardized Tests *Required for some:* SAT or ACT (for admission).

Costs (2013–14) *Tuition:* state resident $5472 full-time; nonresident $16,632 full-time, $372 per credit part-time. *Required fees:* $623 full-time. *Room and board:* $10,733. Room and board charges vary according to housing facility.

Payment plan: installment. *Waivers:* senior citizens and employees or children of employees.

Financial Aid Of all full-time matriculated undergraduates who enrolled in 2012, 6,038 applied for aid, 5,834 were judged to have need, 91 had their need fully met. 139 Federal Work-Study jobs (averaging $1861). In 2012, 148 non-need-based awards were made. *Average percent of need met:* 36%. *Average financial aid package:* $6687. *Average need-based loan:* $2400. *Average need-based gift aid:* $5038. *Average non-need-based aid:* $4373. *Average indebtedness upon graduation:* $11,783. *Financial aid deadline:* 5/16.

Applying *Options:* electronic application. *Application fee:* $55. *Required:* high school transcript. *Application deadlines:* rolling (freshmen), rolling (transfers). *Notification:* continuous (freshmen), continuous (transfers).

Freshman Application Contact Information Center, California State University, Dominguez Hills, 1000 East Victoria Street, Carson, CA 90747-0001. *Phone:* 310-243-3696.

Website: http://www.csudh.edu/.

California State University, East Bay
Hayward, California

- **State-supported** comprehensive, founded 1957, part of California State University System
- **Suburban** 343-acre campus with easy access to San Francisco Bay Area
- **Endowment** $9.2 million
- **Coed** 11,450 undergraduate students, 87% full-time, 61% women, 39% men
- **Moderately difficult** entrance level, 58% of applicants were admitted

Undergraduates 9,975 full-time, 1,475 part-time. Students come from 33 states and territories; 62 other countries; 1% are from out of state; 12% Black or African American, non-Hispanic/Latino; 22% Hispanic/Latino; 20% Asian, non-Hispanic/Latino; 3% Native Hawaiian or other Pacific Islander, non-Hispanic/Latino; 0.3% American Indian or Alaska Native, non-Hispanic/Latino; 3% Two or more races, non-Hispanic/Latino; 12% Race/ethnicity unknown; 7% international; 11% transferred in. *Retention:* 75% of full-time freshmen returned.

Freshmen *Admission:* 11,625 applied, 6,779 admitted, 1,572 enrolled. *Average high school GPA:* 3. *Test scores:* SAT critical reading scores over 500: 28%; SAT math scores over 500: 36%; SAT writing scores over 500: 27%; ACT scores over 18: 62%; SAT critical reading scores over 600: 5%; SAT math scores over 600: 7%; SAT writing scores over 600: 4%; ACT scores over 24: 13%; SAT critical reading scores over 700: 1%; SAT math scores over 700: 1%; ACT scores over 30: 1%.

Faculty *Total:* 709, 43% full-time. *Student/faculty ratio:* 31:1.

Academics *Calendar:* quarters. *Degrees:* certificates, bachelor's, master's, doctoral, and postbachelor's certificates. *Special study options:* academic remediation for entering students, accelerated degree program, adult/continuing education programs, advanced placement credit, cooperative education, distance learning, double majors, English as a second language, honors programs, independent study, internships, off-campus study, part-time degree program, services for LD students, student-designed majors, study abroad, summer session for credit.

Computers on Campus 700 computers/terminals are available on campus for general student use. Students can access the following: campus intranet, computer help desk, free student e-mail accounts, online (class) grades, online (class) registration, online (class) schedules. Campuswide network is available. 100% of college-owned or -operated housing units are wired for high-speed Internet access. Wireless service is available via entire campus.

Student Life *Housing options:* coed, disabled students. Campus housing is university owned. *Activities and organizations:* drama/theater group, student-run newspaper, radio and television station, choral group, Vietnamese Student Association, Accounting Association, Filipino-American Students Association, Movimiento Estudiantil Chicano, Hayward Orientation Team, national fraternities, national sororities. *Campus security:* 24-hour emergency response devices and patrols, late-night transport/escort service. *Student services:* health clinic, personal/psychological counseling, legal services.

Athletics Member NCAA, NAIA. All NCAA Division III. *Intercollegiate sports:* baseball M, basketball M/W, cross-country running M/W, soccer M/W, softball W, swimming and diving W, volleyball W, water polo W. *Intramural sports:* badminton M/W, basketball M/W, golf M/W, gymnastics M, racquetball M/W, soccer M/W, softball M/W, swimming and diving M/W, tennis M/W, volleyball M/W, weight lifting M/W.

Standardized Tests *Required for some:* SAT or ACT (for admission).

Costs (2012–13) *Tuition:* state resident $5472 full-time; nonresident $16,632 full-time. *Required fees:* $837 full-time. *Room and board:* $11,321.

Financial Aid Of all full-time matriculated undergraduates who enrolled in 2012, 6,459 applied for aid, 6,326 were judged to have need, 118 had their need fully met. *Average percent of need met:* 54%. *Average financial aid pack-*

age: $11,342. *Average need-based loan:* $7083. *Average need-based gift aid:* $9618. *Average indebtedness upon graduation:* $19,303.

Applying *Options:* electronic application. *Application fee:* $55. *Required:* high school transcript, minimum 2.0 GPA, California State University eligibility index. *Application deadlines:* 11/30 (freshmen), 11/11 (transfers). *Notification:* continuous (freshmen), continuous (transfers).

Freshman Application Contact Greg Smith, Enrollment Development and Management, California State University, East Bay, 25800 Carlos Bee Boulevard, Hayward, CA 94542-3000. *Phone:* 510-885-3249. *E-mail:* admissions@csueastbay.edu.

Website: http://www.csueastbay.edu/.

California State University, Fresno
Fresno, California

- **State-supported** comprehensive, founded 1911, part of California State University System
- **Urban** 1399-acre campus
- **Coed** 19,719 undergraduate students, 87% full-time, 57% women, 43% men
- **Minimally difficult** entrance level, 58% of applicants were admitted

Undergraduates 17,156 full-time, 2,563 part-time. 0.4% are from out of state; 4% Black or African American, non-Hispanic/Latino; 40% Hispanic/Latino; 15% Asian, non-Hispanic/Latino; 0.4% Native Hawaiian or other Pacific Islander, non-Hispanic/Latino; 0.4% American Indian or Alaska Native, non-Hispanic/Latino; 3% Two or more races, non-Hispanic/Latino; 6% Race/ethnicity unknown; 3% international; 8% transferred in; 5% live on campus. *Retention:* 84% of full-time freshmen returned.

Freshmen *Admission:* 16,242 applied, 9,444 admitted, 3,060 enrolled. *Average high school GPA:* 3.3. *Test scores:* SAT critical reading scores over 500: 31%; SAT math scores over 500: 39%; SAT writing scores over 500: 31%; ACT scores over 18: 62%; SAT critical reading scores over 600: 7%; SAT math scores over 600: 9%; SAT writing scores over 600: 6%; ACT scores over 24: 15%; SAT critical reading scores over 700: 1%; SAT math scores over 700: 1%; SAT writing scores over 700: 1%; ACT scores over 30: 2%.

Faculty *Total:* 1,186, 53% full-time. *Student/faculty ratio:* 22:1.

Academics *Calendar:* semesters. *Degrees:* bachelor's, master's, doctoral, post-master's, and postbachelor's certificates. *Special study options:* academic remediation for entering students, accelerated degree program, adult/continuing education programs, advanced placement credit, cooperative education, distance learning, double majors, English as a second language, freshman honors college, honors programs, independent study, internships, off-campus study, part-time degree program, services for LD students, student-designed majors, study abroad, summer session for credit. *ROTC:* Army (b), Air Force (b).

Computers on Campus Students can access the following: campus intranet, computer help desk, free student e-mail accounts, online (class) grades, online (class) registration, online (class) schedules. Campuswide network is available. 100% of college-owned or -operated housing units are wired for high-speed Internet access. Wireless service is available via classrooms, computer centers, computer labs, learning centers, libraries, student centers.

Student Life *Housing options:* coed, men-only, women-only. Campus housing is university owned. *Activities and organizations:* drama/theater group, student-run newspaper, radio station, choral group, marching band, national fraternities, national sororities. *Campus security:* 24-hour emergency response devices and patrols, late-night transport/escort service, controlled dormitory access. *Student services:* health clinic, personal/psychological counseling, women's center.

Athletics Member NCAA. All Division I except football (Division I-A). *Intercollegiate sports:* baseball M(s), basketball M(s)/W(s), cross-country running M(s)/W(s), equestrian sports W(s), golf M(s)/W(s), lacrosse W(s), soccer W(s), softball W(s), swimming and diving W(s), tennis M(s)/W(s), track and field M(s)/W(s), volleyball W(s). *Intramural sports:* archery M/W, badminton M/W, baseball M, basketball M/W, bowling M/W, cross-country running M/W, equestrian sports W, fencing M/W, golf M/W, gymnastics M/W, racquetball M/W, tennis M/W, volleyball M/W.

Standardized Tests *Required:* SAT or ACT (for admission).

Costs (2013–14) *Tuition:* state resident $6274 full-time; nonresident $14,400 full-time, $372 per credit hour part-time. *Room and board:* $10,192. Room and board charges vary according to board plan. *Payment plan:* installment.

Financial Aid Of all full-time matriculated undergraduates who enrolled in 2012, 13,863 applied for aid, 12,840 were judged to have need, 1,656 had their need fully met. 240 Federal Work-Study jobs (averaging $3009). In 2012, 160 non-need-based awards were made. *Average percent of need met:* 69%. *Average financial aid package:* $11,897. *Average need-based loan:* $4202. *Average need-based gift aid:* $9968. *Average non-need-based aid:* $3930. *Average indebtedness upon graduation:* $16,100.

California

Applying *Options:* electronic application. *Application fee:* $55. *Required:* high school transcript, minimum 2.0 GPA. *Application deadlines:* 11/30 (freshmen), 11/30 (transfers). *Notification:* continuous (freshmen).

Freshman Application Contact Mr. Andy Hernandez, Admissions Officer, California State University, Fresno, 5150 North Maple Avenue, M/S JA 57, Fresno, CA 93740-8026. *Phone:* 559-278-6115. *Fax:* 559-278-4812. *E-mail:* andyhe@csufresno.edu.
Website: http://www.csufresno.edu/.

California State University, Fullerton
Fullerton, California

- **State-supported** comprehensive, founded 1957, part of California State University System
- **Suburban** 236-acre campus with easy access to Los Angeles
- **Endowment** $32.3 million
- **Coed** 32,379 undergraduate students, 81% full-time, 56% women, 44% men
- **Moderately difficult** entrance level, 46% of applicants were admitted

Undergraduates 26,079 full-time, 6,300 part-time. Students come from 36 states and territories; 51 other countries; 1% are from out of state; 2% Black or African American, non-Hispanic/Latino; 35% Hispanic/Latino; 22% Asian, non-Hispanic/Latino; 0.3% Native Hawaiian or other Pacific Islander, non-Hispanic/Latino; 0.3% American Indian or Alaska Native, non-Hispanic/Latino; 4% Two or more races, non-Hispanic/Latino; 5% Race/ethnicity unknown; 4% international; 13% transferred in; 6% live on campus. *Retention:* 88% of full-time freshmen returned.
Freshmen *Admission:* 38,909 applied, 17,817 admitted, 4,526 enrolled. *Average high school GPA:* 3.39. *Test scores:* SAT critical reading scores over 500: 54%; SAT math scores over 500: 64%; ACT scores over 18: 86%; SAT critical reading scores over 600: 12%; SAT math scores over 600: 21%; ACT scores over 24: 29%; SAT critical reading scores over 700: 1%; SAT math scores over 700: 2%; ACT scores over 30: 2%.
Faculty *Total:* 1,680, 50% full-time, 77% with terminal degrees. *Student/faculty ratio:* 26:1.
Academics *Calendar:* semesters. *Degrees:* bachelor's, master's, doctoral, post-master's, and postbachelor's certificates. *Special study options:* academic remediation for entering students, adult/continuing education programs, advanced placement credit, cooperative education, distance learning, double majors, honors programs, independent study, internships, off-campus study, part-time degree program, services for LD students, student-designed majors, study abroad, summer session for credit. *ROTC:* Army (b).
Computers on Campus 2,000 computers/terminals are available on campus for general student use. Students can access the following: campus intranet, computer help desk, free student e-mail accounts, online (class) grades, online (class) registration, online (class) schedules. Campuswide network is available. Wireless service is available via entire campus.
Student Life *Housing options:* coed. Campus housing is university owned. Freshman applicants given priority for college housing. *Activities and organizations:* drama/theater group, student-run newspaper, radio station, choral group, Pan-Hellenic Council, American Marketing Association, Lacrosse Club, Samaritans (volunteer service club), Human Services Student Association, national fraternities, national sororities. *Campus security:* 24-hour emergency response devices and patrols, student patrols, late-night transport/escort service, controlled dormitory access. *Student services:* health clinic, personal/psychological counseling, women's center, legal services.
Athletics Member NCAA. All Division I. *Intercollegiate sports:* archery M(c)/W(c), baseball M(s), basketball M(s)/W(s), bowling M(c)/W(c), cross-country running M(s)/W(s), equestrian sports M(c)/W(c), golf M(s)/W(s), gymnastics W(s), ice hockey M(c)/W(c), lacrosse M(c)/W(c), rugby M(c)/W(c), sailing M(c)/W(c), skiing (downhill) M(c)/W(c), soccer M(s)/W(s), softball W(s), tennis W(s), track and field M(s)/W(s), ultimate Frisbee M(c)/W(c), volleyball M(c)/W(s), water polo M(c)/W(c). *Intramural sports:* badminton M/W, basketball M/W, bowling M/W, football M/W, racquetball M/W, rugby M, skiing (downhill) M/W, soccer M, softball M/W, swimming and diving M/W, table tennis M/W, tennis M(c)/W(c), volleyball M/W.
Standardized Tests *Required:* SAT (for admission), SAT or ACT (for admission).
Costs (2013–14) *Tuition:* state resident $0 full-time; nonresident $11,160 full-time, $372 per unit part-time. Full-time tuition and fees vary according to course load. Part-time tuition and fees vary according to course load. *Required fees:* $6182 full-time, $1945 part-time. *Room and board:* $12,096. Room and board charges vary according to board plan and housing facility. *Payment plans:* installment, deferred payment. *Waivers:* senior citizens and employees or children of employees.
Financial Aid Of all full-time matriculated undergraduates who enrolled in 2012, 19,555 applied for aid, 15,850 were judged to have need, 13,471 had their need fully met. 215 Federal Work-Study jobs (averaging $3303). In 2012,

1528 non-need-based awards were made. *Average percent of need met:* 67%. *Average financial aid package:* $11,273. *Average need-based loan:* $6758. *Average need-based gift aid:* $7071. *Average non-need-based aid:* $7826. *Average indebtedness upon graduation:* $14,983.
Applying *Options:* electronic application. *Application fee:* $55. *Required:* high school transcript, minimum 2.0 GPA. *Application deadlines:* 11/30 (freshmen), 11/30 (transfers). *Notification:* continuous (freshmen), continuous (transfers).
Freshman Application Contact Ms. Nancy J. Dority, Assistant Vice President of Enrollment Services, California State University, Fullerton, Office of Admissions and Records, PO Box 34080, Fullerton, CA 92834-9480. *Phone:* 657-278-2370. *Fax:* 657-278-2356. *E-mail:* admissions@fullerton.edu.
Website: http://www.fullerton.edu/.

California State University, Long Beach
Long Beach, California

- **State-supported** comprehensive, founded 1949, part of California State University System
- **Suburban** 320-acre campus with easy access to Los Angeles
- **Endowment** $42.5 million
- **Coed** 30,931 undergraduate students, 84% full-time, 57% women, 43% men
- **Moderately difficult** entrance level, 31% of applicants were admitted

Undergraduates 25,880 full-time, 5,051 part-time. Students come from 40 states and territories; 85 other countries; 1% are from out of state; 4% Black or African American, non-Hispanic/Latino; 35% Hispanic/Latino; 22% Asian, non-Hispanic/Latino; 2% Native Hawaiian or other Pacific Islander, non-Hispanic/Latino; 0.6% American Indian or Alaska Native, non-Hispanic/Latino; 4% Two or more races, non-Hispanic/Latino; 5% Race/ethnicity unknown; 5% international; 13% transferred in; 30% live on campus. *Retention:* 88% of full-time freshmen returned.
Freshmen *Admission:* 54,970 applied, 16,957 admitted, 4,276 enrolled. *Average high school GPA:* 3.43. *Test scores:* SAT critical reading scores over 500: 49%; SAT math scores over 500: 60%; ACT scores over 18: 82%; SAT critical reading scores over 600: 12%; SAT math scores over 600: 22%; ACT scores over 24: 31%; SAT critical reading scores over 700: 1%; SAT math scores over 700: 3%; ACT scores over 30: 4%.
Faculty *Total:* 1,908, 48% full-time, 58% with terminal degrees. *Student/faculty ratio:* 22:1.
Academics *Calendar:* semesters. *Degrees:* bachelor's, master's, doctoral, and postbachelor's certificates. *Special study options:* academic remediation for entering students, accelerated degree program, adult/continuing education programs, advanced placement credit, distance learning, double majors, English as a second language, honors programs, independent study, internships, off-campus study, part-time degree program, services for LD students, student-designed majors, study abroad, summer session for credit. *ROTC:* Army (b).
Computers on Campus 2,000 computers/terminals are available on campus for general student use. Campuswide network is available.
Student Life *Housing options:* coed. *Activities and organizations:* drama/theater group, student-run newspaper, radio and television station, choral group, national fraternities, national sororities. *Campus security:* 24-hour emergency response devices and patrols, student patrols, late-night transport/escort service. *Student services:* health clinic, personal/psychological counseling, women's center, legal services.
Athletics Member NCAA. All Division I. *Intercollegiate sports:* archery M(c)/W(c), badminton M(c)/W(c), basketball M(s)/W(s), bowling M(c)/W(c), crew M(c)/W(c), cross-country running M(s)/W(s), fencing M(c)/W(c), golf M/W, rugby M(c), sailing M(c)/W(c), skiing (downhill) M(c)/W(c), soccer M(c)/W(s), softball W(s), table tennis M(c), tennis W(s), track and field M(s)/W(s), volleyball M(s)/W(s), water polo M(s)/W(s). *Intramural sports:* basketball M/W, gymnastics M/W, racquetball M/W, softball W, swimming and diving M/W, table tennis W(c), tennis W, track and field M(c)/W(c), volleyball M/W.
Standardized Tests *Required:* SAT or ACT (for admission).
Costs (2013–14) *Tuition:* state resident $0 full-time; nonresident $11,160 full-time, $372 per unit part-time. Full-time tuition and fees vary according to degree level and program. Part-time tuition and fees vary according to course load, degree level, and program. *Required fees:* $6240 full-time. *Room and board:* $11,300. Room and board charges vary according to board plan. *Payment plan:* installment. *Waivers:* senior citizens and employees or children of employees.
Financial Aid Of all full-time matriculated undergraduates who enrolled in 2012, 20,755 applied for aid, 19,395 were judged to have need, 9,422 had their need fully met. *Average percent of need met:* 83%. *Average financial aid pack-*

age: $13,678. *Average need-based loan:* $3721. *Average need-based gift aid:* $6554.

Applying *Options:* electronic application. *Application fee:* $55. *Required:* high school transcript. *Required for some:* minimum 2.0 GPA. *Application deadlines:* 11/30 (freshmen), 11/30 (transfers). *Notification:* continuous (freshmen), continuous (transfers).

Freshman Application Contact Mr. Thomas Enders, Director of Enrollment Services, California State University, Long Beach, Brotman Hall, 1250 Bellflower Boulevard, Long Beach, CA 90840. *Phone:* 562-985-4641. *Website:* http://www.csulb.edu/.

California State University, Los Angeles

Los Angeles, California

- **State-supported** comprehensive, founded 1947, part of California State University System
- **Urban** 173-acre campus
- **Endowment** $15.8 million
- **Coed** 18,074 undergraduate students, 83% full-time, 59% women, 41% men
- **Moderately difficult** entrance level, 65% of applicants were admitted

Undergraduates 14,991 full-time, 3,083 part-time. Students come from 50 states and territories; 44 other countries; 0.4% are from out of state; 5% Black or African American, non-Hispanic/Latino; 58% Hispanic/Latino; 17% Asian, non-Hispanic/Latino; 0.4% Native Hawaiian or other Pacific Islander, non-Hispanic/Latino; 0.1% American Indian or Alaska Native, non-Hispanic/Latino; 2% Two or more races, non-Hispanic/Latino; 6% Race/ethnicity unknown; 4% international; 12% transferred in; 5% live on campus. *Retention:* 81% of full-time freshmen returned.

Freshmen *Admission:* 27,321 applied, 17,848 admitted, 2,908 enrolled. *Average high school GPA:* 3.16. *Test scores:* SAT critical reading scores over 500: 19%; SAT math scores over 500: 30%; SAT writing scores over 500: 20%; ACT scores over 18: 47%; SAT critical reading scores over 600: 3%; SAT math scores over 600: 6%; SAT writing scores over 600: 2%; ACT scores over 24: 9%; SAT math scores over 700: 1%; ACT scores over 30: 1%.

Faculty *Total:* 1,117, 48% full-time, 34% with terminal degrees. *Student/faculty ratio:* 25:1.

Academics *Calendar:* quarters. *Degrees:* bachelor's, master's, and doctoral. *Special study options:* academic remediation for entering students, accelerated degree program, adult/continuing education programs, advanced placement credit, cooperative education, distance learning, double majors, English as a second language, honors programs, independent study, internships, off-campus study, part-time degree program, services for LD students, student-designed majors, study abroad, summer session for credit. *ROTC:* Army (c), Air Force (c). *Unusual degree programs:* 3-2 nursing.

Computers on Campus 1,500 computers/terminals are available on campus for general student use. Students can access the following: campus intranet, computer help desk, free student e-mail accounts, online (class) grades, online (class) registration, online (class) schedules. Campuswide network is available. 100% of college-owned or -operated housing units are wired for high-speed Internet access. Wireless service is available via classrooms, computer centers, computer labs, dorm rooms, learning centers, libraries, student centers.

Student Life *Housing options:* coed. Campus housing is university owned. *Activities and organizations:* drama/theater group, student-run newspaper, choral group, Society of Hispanic Engineering and Science Students, Institute of Electrical and Electronics Engineer, Sigma Delta PI, Asian Unified, Society of Automotive Engineers, national fraternities, national sororities. *Campus security:* 24-hour emergency response devices, student patrols, late-night transport/escort service. *Student services:* health clinic, personal/psychological counseling, women's center, legal services.

Athletics Member NCAA. All Division II. *Intercollegiate sports:* baseball M(s), basketball M(s)/W(s), cross-country running W(s), soccer M(s)/W(s), tennis W(s), track and field M(s)/W(s), volleyball W(s). *Intramural sports:* basketball M/W, bowling M/W, gymnastics M/W, racquetball M/W, skiing (cross-country) M/W, soccer M/W, softball M/W, swimming and diving M/W, tennis M/W, track and field M/W, volleyball M/W, water polo M/W, wrestling M.

Standardized Tests *Required for some:* SAT or ACT (for admission).

Costs (2013–14) *Tuition:* state resident $0 full-time; nonresident $15,263 full-time, $248 per unit part-time. Full-time tuition and fees vary according to course level and course load. Part-time tuition and fees vary according to course level and course load. *Room and board:* $9728; room only: $5895. Room and board charges vary according to housing facility. *Payment plan:* installment. *Waivers:* employees or children of employees.

Financial Aid Of all full-time matriculated undergraduates who enrolled in 2008, 9,412 applied for aid, 8,916 were judged to have need, 1,449 had their need fully met. In 2008, 95 non-need-based awards were made. *Average percent of need met:* 66%. *Average financial aid package:* $9484. *Average need-based loan:* $5002. *Average need-based gift aid:* $7561. *Average non-need-based aid:* $4048.

Applying *Options:* electronic application, early admission. *Application fee:* $55. *Required:* high school transcript. *Application deadlines:* 11/30 (freshmen), 11/30 (transfers). *Notification:* 8/30 (freshmen), 8/30 (transfers).

Freshman Application Contact Mr. Vince Lopez, Director of Outreach and Recruitment, California State University, Los Angeles, 5151 State University Drive, Los Angeles, CA 90032-8530. *Phone:* 323-343-3839. *E-mail:* admission@calstatela.edu.

Website: http://www.calstatela.edu/.

California State University, Monterey Bay

Seaside, California

- **State-supported** comprehensive, founded 1994, part of California State University System
- **Small-town** 1387-acre campus with easy access to San Jose
- **Endowment** $13.9 million
- **Coed** 5,194 undergraduate students, 94% full-time, 62% women, 38% men
- **Moderately difficult** entrance level, 44% of applicants were admitted

Undergraduates 4,879 full-time, 315 part-time. Students come from 37 states and territories; 19 other countries; 3% are from out of state; 6% Black or African American, non-Hispanic/Latino; 33% Hispanic/Latino; 5% Asian, non-Hispanic/Latino; 0.9% Native Hawaiian or other Pacific Islander, non-Hispanic/Latino; 0.9% American Indian or Alaska Native, non-Hispanic/Latino; 7% Two or more races, non-Hispanic/Latino; 5% Race/ethnicity unknown; 2% international; 13% transferred in; 60% live on campus. *Retention:* 80% of full-time freshmen returned.

Freshmen *Admission:* 12,562 applied, 5,577 admitted, 902 enrolled. *Average high school GPA:* 3.22. *Test scores:* SAT critical reading scores over 500: 45%; SAT math scores over 500: 46%; SAT writing scores over 500: 42%; ACT scores over 18: 77%; SAT critical reading scores over 600: 8%; SAT math scores over 600: 10%; SAT writing scores over 600: 8%; ACT scores over 24: 26%; ACT scores over 30: 1%.

Faculty *Total:* 383, 32% full-time, 45% with terminal degrees. *Student/faculty ratio:* 26:1.

Academics *Calendar:* semesters. *Degrees:* bachelor's and master's. *Special study options:* academic remediation for entering students, advanced placement credit, cooperative education, distance learning, double majors, independent study, internships, off-campus study, part-time degree program, services for LD students, student-designed majors, study abroad, summer session for credit.

Computers on Campus 994 computers/terminals are available on campus for general student use. Students can access the following: campus intranet, computer help desk, free student e-mail accounts, online (class) grades, online (class) registration, online (class) schedules. Campuswide network is available. 100% of college-owned or -operated housing units are wired for high-speed Internet access. Wireless service is available via entire campus.

Student Life *Housing:* on-campus residence required through sophomore year. *Options:* coed, disabled students. Campus housing is university owned. Freshman applicants given priority for college housing. *Activities and organizations:* student-run newspaper, radio station, National Society for Leadership & Success, Math & Statistics Club, National Association for the Advancement of Colored People (NAACP), Robotics Club, Black Students United, national fraternities, national sororities. *Campus security:* 24-hour emergency response devices and patrols, student patrols, late-night transport/escort service, controlled dormitory access. *Student services:* health clinic, personal/psychological counseling, women's center.

Athletics Member NCAA. All Division II. *Intercollegiate sports:* baseball M(s), basketball M(s)/W(s), cross-country running M(s)/W(s), golf M(s)/W(s), sailing M/W, soccer M(s)/W(s), softball W(s), volleyball W(s), water polo W(s). *Intramural sports:* basketball M/W, bowling M/W, soccer M/W, softball M/W, ultimate Frisbee M/W, volleyball M/W.

Standardized Tests *Required:* SAT or ACT (for admission).

Costs (2013–14) *Tuition:* state resident $0 full-time; nonresident $11,160 full-time, $372 per credit hour part-time. Full-time tuition and fees vary according to course load and degree level. Part-time tuition and fees vary according to course load and degree level. *Required fees:* $5963 full-time. *Room and board:* $9498. Room and board charges vary according to board plan and housing facility. *Payment plan:* installment. *Waivers:* senior citizens and employees or children of employees.

Financial Aid Of all full-time matriculated undergraduates who enrolled in 2011, 3,457 applied for aid, 2,960 were judged to have need, 1,006 had their need fully met. In 2011, 16 non-need-based awards were made. *Average percent of need met:* 78%. *Average financial aid package:* $10,982. *Average need-based loan:* $4315. *Average need-based gift aid:* $9712. *Average non-need-based aid:* $2654. *Average indebtedness upon graduation:* $16,556.

Applying *Options:* electronic application, deferred entrance. *Application fee:* $55. *Required:* high school transcript, minimum 2.0 GPA. *Application deadlines:* 11/30 (freshmen), 11/30 (out-of-state freshmen), 11/30 (transfers). *Notification:* continuous (freshmen), continuous (out-of-state freshmen), continuous (transfers).

Freshman Application Contact Mr. John Larsen, Assistant Director of Recruitment, California State University, Monterey Bay, 100 Campus Center, Seaside, CA 93955. *Phone:* 831-582-3738. *Fax:* 831-582-3783. *E-mail:* admissions@csumb.edu.

Website: http://www.csumb.edu/.

California State University, Northridge

Northridge, California

- **State-supported** comprehensive, founded 1958, part of California State University System
- **Urban** 356-acre campus with easy access to Los Angeles
- **Coed** 31,119 undergraduate students, 82% full-time, 55% women, 45% men
- **Moderately difficult** entrance level, 46% of applicants were admitted

Undergraduates 25,460 full-time, 5,659 part-time. 3% are from out of state; 7% Black or African American, non-Hispanic/Latino; 38% Hispanic/Latino; 11% Asian, non-Hispanic/Latino; 0.3% Native Hawaiian or other Pacific Islander, non-Hispanic/Latino; 0.2% American Indian or Alaska Native, non-Hispanic/Latino; 3% Two or more races, non-Hispanic/Latino; 7% Race/ethnicity unknown; 7% international; 13% transferred in. *Retention:* 75% of full-time freshmen returned.

Freshmen *Admission:* 29,339 applied, 13,566 admitted, 4,149 enrolled. *Average high school GPA:* 3.15. *Test scores:* SAT critical reading scores over 500: 33%; SAT math scores over 500: 38%; SAT critical reading scores over 600: 6%; SAT math scores over 600: 9%; SAT math scores over 700: 1%.

Faculty *Total:* 1,857, 46% full-time. *Student/faculty ratio:* 26:1.

Academics *Calendar:* semesters. *Degrees:* bachelor's and master's. *Special study options:* academic remediation for entering students, adult/continuing education programs, advanced placement credit, distance learning, double majors, English as a second language, independent study, internships, off-campus study, part-time degree program, services for LD students, student-designed majors, study abroad, summer session for credit. *ROTC:* Army (c), Air Force (c).

Computers on Campus Students can access the following: online (class) registration. Campuswide network is available.

Student Life *Activities and organizations:* drama/theater group, student-run newspaper, radio station, choral group, national fraternities, national sororities. *Campus security:* 24-hour emergency response devices, late-night transport/escort service. *Student services:* health clinic, personal/psychological counseling, women's center.

Athletics Member NCAA. All Division I except football (Division II). *Intercollegiate sports:* baseball M(s), basketball M(s)/W(s), cross-country running M(s)/W(s), football M(s), golf M(s), soccer M(s), softball W(s), swimming and diving M(s)/W(s), tennis W(s), track and field M(s)/W(s), volleyball M(s)/W(s). *Intramural sports:* baseball M, basketball M/W, bowling M(c)/W(c), cross-country running M/W, football M/W, golf M, ice hockey M(c), racquetball M/W, rugby M(c), sailing M(c)/W(c), skiing (downhill) M(c)/W(c), soccer M/W, softball W, swimming and diving M/W, table tennis M(c)/W(c), tennis W, track and field M/W, volleyball M/W.

Standardized Tests *Required:* SAT or ACT (for admission).

Costs (2013–14) *Tuition:* state resident $0 full-time; nonresident $11,160 full-time, $372 per credit hour part-time. *Required fees:* $6520 full-time. *Room and board:* $12,404. Room and board charges vary according to board plan and housing facility. *Payment plan:* installment. *Waivers:* senior citizens and employees or children of employees.

Financial Aid Of all full-time matriculated undergraduates who enrolled in 2011, 19,138 applied for aid, 18,092 were judged to have need. In 2011, 926 non-need-based awards were made. *Average financial aid package:* $18,189. *Average need-based loan:* $6076. *Average need-based gift aid:* $15,051. *Average non-need-based aid:* $1608. *Average indebtedness upon graduation:* $17,198.

Applying *Options:* electronic application. *Application fee:* $55. *Required:* high school transcript. *Application deadlines:* 11/30 (freshmen), 11/30 (transfers). *Notification:* continuous (freshmen), continuous (transfers).

Freshman Application Contact Ms. Mary Baxton, Associate Director of Admissions and Records, California State University, Northridge, 18111

Nordhoff Street, Northridge, CA 91330-8207. *Phone:* 818-677-3777. *Fax:* 818-677-3766. *E-mail:* admissions.records@csun.edu.

Website: http://www.csun.edu/.

California State University, Sacramento

Sacramento, California

- **State-supported** comprehensive, founded 1947, part of California State University System
- **Urban** 300-acre campus
- **Coed**
- **Moderately difficult** entrance level

Faculty *Student/faculty ratio:* 26:1.

Academics *Calendar:* semesters. *Degrees:* bachelor's, master's, and doctoral.

Student Life *Campus security:* 24-hour emergency response devices and patrols, student patrols, late-night transport/escort service, controlled dormitory access.

Athletics Member NCAA. All Division I except football (Division I-AA).

Standardized Tests *Required:* SAT or ACT (for admission).

Costs (2012–13) *Tuition:* state resident $5472 full-time; nonresident $16,632 full-time. *Required fees:* $1148 full-time. *Room and board:* $11,724. Room and board charges vary according to board plan and housing facility.

Financial Aid Of all full-time matriculated undergraduates who enrolled in 2011, 16,147 applied for aid, 14,897 were judged to have need, 514 had their need fully met. *In 2011,* 12 non-need-based awards were made. *Average percent of need met:* 58. *Average financial aid package:* $10,925. *Average need-based loan:* $4476. *Average need-based gift aid:* $9608. *Average non-need-based aid:* $927. *Average indebtedness upon graduation:* $4456.

Applying *Options:* electronic application, early action, deferred entrance. *Application fee:* $55. *Required:* minimum 2.0 GPA. *Required for some:* high school transcript.

Freshman Application Contact Mr. Emiliano Diaz, Director of University Outreach Services, California State University, Sacramento, 6000 J Street, Lassen Hall, Sacramento, CA 95819-6048. *Phone:* 916-278-3901. *Fax:* 916-278-5603. *E-mail:* admissions@csus.edu.

Website: http://www.csus.edu/.

California State University, San Bernardino

San Bernardino, California

- **State-supported** comprehensive, founded 1965, part of California State University System
- **Suburban** 430-acre campus with easy access to Los Angeles
- **Coed** 15,885 undergraduate students, 89% full-time, 62% women, 38% men
- **Moderately difficult** entrance level, 58% of applicants were admitted

Undergraduates 14,075 full-time, 1,810 part-time. 8% Black or African American, non-Hispanic/Latino; 53% Hispanic/Latino; 6% Asian, non-Hispanic/Latino; 0.2% Native Hawaiian or other Pacific Islander, non-Hispanic/Latino; 0.3% American Indian or Alaska Native, non-Hispanic/Latino; 3% Two or more races, non-Hispanic/Latino; 5% Race/ethnicity unknown; 5% international. *Retention:* 88% of full-time freshmen returned.

Freshmen *Admission:* 12,241 applied, 7,137 admitted, 2,448 enrolled. *Average high school GPA:* 3.21. *Test scores:* SAT critical reading scores over 500: 24%; SAT math scores over 500: 31%; SAT writing scores over 500: 24%; ACT scores over 18: 52%; SAT critical reading scores over 600: 3%; SAT math scores over 600: 5%; SAT writing scores over 600: 2%; ACT scores over 24: 6%.

Faculty *Total:* 730, 59% full-time, 52% with terminal degrees. *Student/faculty ratio:* 26:1.

Academics *Calendar:* quarters. *Degrees:* bachelor's, master's, and doctoral. *Special study options:* accelerated degree program, cooperative education, distance learning, double majors, honors programs, independent study, internships, off-campus study, part-time degree program, services for LD students, student-designed majors, study abroad, summer session for credit. *ROTC:* Army (b), Air Force (b).

Computers on Campus 1,300 computers/terminals are available on campus for general student use. Students can access the following: computer help desk, free student e-mail accounts, online (class) grades, online (class) registration, online (class) schedules. Campuswide network is available. Wireless service is available via entire campus.

Student Life *Housing options:* coed, women-only. Campus housing is university owned and is provided by a third party. *Activities and organizations:* drama/theater group, student-run newspaper, radio and television station, choral group, national fraternities, national sororities. *Campus security:* 24-hour emergency response devices and patrols, student patrols, late-night transport/escort service, residence staff on call 24 hours. *Student services:* health clinic, personal/psychological counseling, women's center, legal services.

Athletics Member NCAA. All Division II. *Intercollegiate sports:* baseball M(s), basketball M(s)/W(s), cross-country running W, golf M(s), soccer M(s)/W(s), softball W(s), swimming and diving M(s)/W(s), tennis W, volleyball W(s), water polo M/W. *Intramural sports:* basketball M/W, field hockey M/W, football M/W, soccer M/W, softball M, volleyball M/W.

Standardized Tests *Recommended:* SAT or ACT (for admission).

Costs (2013–14) *Tuition:* state resident $5472 full-time; nonresident $11,160 full-time. Part-time tuition and fees vary according to course load. *Required fees:* $6549 full-time. *Room and board:* $9972. Room and board charges vary according to board plan and housing facility. *Payment plan:* installment. *Waivers:* senior citizens and employees or children of employees.

Financial Aid Of all full-time matriculated undergraduates who enrolled in 2012, 12,606 applied for aid, 11,347 were judged to have need, 1,051 had their need fully met. 314 Federal Work-Study jobs (averaging $3795). In 2012, 25 non-need-based awards were made. *Average percent of need met:* 68%. *Average financial aid package:* $11,702. *Average need-based loan:* $4075. *Average need-based gift aid:* $9414. *Average non-need-based aid:* $3242. *Average indebtedness upon graduation:* $21,787.

Applying *Options:* electronic application, early admission, early action. *Application fee:* $55. *Required:* high school transcript, minimum 2.0 GPA. *Application deadlines:* rolling (freshmen), rolling (transfers). *Notification:* continuous (freshmen), continuous (transfers).

Freshman Application Contact Ms. Julie Mellen, Assistant Director of Admissions and Evaluations, California State University, San Bernardino, 5500 University Parkway, University Hall, Room 107, San Bernardino, CA 92407-2397. *Phone:* 909-537-5211. *Fax:* 909-537-7034. *E-mail:* moreinfo@mail.csusb.edu.
Website: http://www.csusb.edu/.

California State University, San Marcos
San Marcos, California

- **State-supported** comprehensive, founded 1990, part of California State University System
- **Suburban** 304-acre campus with easy access to San Diego
- **Coed** 9,928 undergraduate students, 79% full-time, 60% women, 40% men
- **Moderately difficult** entrance level, 62% of applicants were admitted

Undergraduates 7,801 full-time, 2,127 part-time. 2% are from out of state; 3% Black or African American, non-Hispanic/Latino; 32% Hispanic/Latino; 10% Asian, non-Hispanic/Latino; 0.5% American Indian or Alaska Native, non-Hispanic/Latino; 5% Two or more races, non-Hispanic/Latino; 9% Race/ethnicity unknown; 2% international; 14% transferred in. *Retention:* 83% of full-time freshmen returned.

Freshmen *Admission:* 10,848 applied, 6,717 admitted, 1,783 enrolled. *Average high school GPA:* 3.17. *Test scores:* SAT critical reading scores over 500: 40%; SAT math scores over 500: 46%; SAT critical reading scores over 600: 6%; SAT math scores over 600: 10%; SAT critical reading scores over 700: 1%; SAT math scores over 700: 1%.

Faculty *Total:* 609, 39% full-time. *Student/faculty ratio:* 25:1.

Academics *Calendar:* semesters. *Degrees:* bachelor's and master's. *Special study options:* academic remediation for entering students, adult/continuing education programs, advanced placement credit, distance learning, double majors, English as a second language, independent study, internships, off-campus study, part-time degree program, services for LD students, student-designed majors, study abroad, summer session for credit. *ROTC:* Army (c), Navy (c), Air Force (c).

Computers on Campus 1,400 computers/terminals are available on campus for general student use. Students can access the following: computer help desk, free student e-mail accounts, online (class) registration, online (class) schedules. Campuswide network is available.

Student Life *Housing options:* disabled students. Campus housing is provided by a third party. *Activities and organizations:* drama/theater group, student-run newspaper, choral group, Accounting Club, Liberal Studies Club, MECHA, Sigma IOTA Epsilon, national fraternities, national sororities. *Campus security:* 24-hour emergency response devices and patrols, student patrols, late-night transport/escort service. *Student services:* health clinic, personal/psychological counseling, women's center.

Athletics Member NAIA. *Intercollegiate sports:* baseball M, basketball M/W, cross-country running M/W, golf M/W, soccer M/W, softball W, track and field M/W.

Standardized Tests *Recommended:* SAT or ACT (for admission).

Costs (2013–14) *Tuition:* state resident $0 full-time; nonresident $11,762 full-time, $372 per unit part-time. Part-time tuition and fees vary according to course load. *Required fees:* $7298 full-time, $2251 per term part-time. *Room and board:* Room and board charges vary according to housing facility. *Waivers:* senior citizens and employees or children of employees.

Applying *Options:* electronic application. *Application fee:* $55. *Required:* high school transcript, minimum 3.0 GPA. *Application deadlines:* 11/30 (freshmen), 11/30 (transfers). *Notification:* continuous (freshmen), continuous (transfers).

Freshman Application Contact Scott Hagg, Director of Admissions, California State University, San Marcos, 333 South Twin Oaks Valley Road, San Marcos, CA 92096-0001. *Phone:* 760-750-4848. *Fax:* 760-750-3248. *E-mail:* apply@csusm.edu.
Website: http://www.csusm.edu/.

California State University, Stanislaus
Turlock, California

- **State-supported** comprehensive, founded 1957, part of California State University System
- **Small-town** 228-acre campus
- **Endowment** $8.1 million
- **Coed** 7,621 undergraduate students, 83% full-time, 64% women, 36% men
- **Moderately difficult** entrance level, 72% of applicants were admitted

Undergraduates 6,321 full-time, 1,300 part-time. Students come from 18 states and territories; 22 other countries; 1% are from out of state; 3% Black or African American, non-Hispanic/Latino; 42% Hispanic/Latino; 11% Asian, non-Hispanic/Latino; 0.7% Native Hawaiian or other Pacific Islander, non-Hispanic/Latino; 0.4% American Indian or Alaska Native, non-Hispanic/Latino; 4% Two or more races, non-Hispanic/Latino; 8% Race/ethnicity unknown; 1% international; 11% transferred in; 8% live on campus. *Retention:* 83% of full-time freshmen returned.

Freshmen *Admission:* 5,763 applied, 4,158 admitted, 1,109 enrolled. *Average high school GPA:* 3.26. *Test scores:* SAT critical reading scores over 500: 30%; SAT math scores over 500: 36%; SAT writing scores over 500: 29%; ACT scores over 18: 66%; SAT critical reading scores over 600: 6%; SAT math scores over 600: 7%; SAT writing scores over 600: 4%; ACT scores over 24: 13%; SAT critical reading scores over 700: 1%; ACT scores over 30: 1%.

Faculty *Total:* 446, 58% full-time, 61% with terminal degrees. *Student/faculty ratio:* 21:1.

Academics *Calendar:* semesters. *Degrees:* bachelor's, master's, doctoral, post-master's, and postbachelor's certificates. *Special study options:* academic remediation for entering students, adult/continuing education programs, advanced placement credit, cooperative education, distance learning, double majors, English as a second language, honors programs, independent study, internships, off-campus study, part-time degree program, services for LD students, student-designed majors, study abroad, summer session for credit.

Computers on Campus 200 computers/terminals are available on campus for general student use. Students can access the following: computer help desk, free student e-mail accounts, online (class) grades, online (class) registration, online (class) schedules. Campuswide network is available. 100% of college-owned or -operated housing units are wired for high-speed Internet access. Wireless service is available via entire campus.

Student Life *Housing options:* coed. Campus housing is university owned and leased by the school. *Activities and organizations:* drama/theater group, student-run newspaper, radio station, choral group, Alpha Xi Delta, Phi Sigma Sigma, Kappa Sigma, Tau Kappa Epsilon, Theta Chi, national fraternities, national sororities. *Campus security:* 24-hour emergency response devices and patrols, student patrols, late-night transport/escort service, controlled dormitory access. *Student services:* health clinic, personal/psychological counseling, women's center.

Athletics Member NCAA. All Division II. *Intercollegiate sports:* baseball M, basketball M/W, cheerleading M(c)/W(c), cross-country running M/W, golf M, soccer M/W, softball W, tennis W, track and field M/W, volleyball W. *Intramural sports:* basketball M/W, football M/W, soccer M/W, ultimate Frisbee M/W, volleyball M/W.

Standardized Tests *Required for some:* SAT or ACT (for admission).

Costs (2012–13) *Tuition:* state resident $5472 full-time; nonresident $16,632 full-time. Full-time tuition and fees vary according to course load and reciprocity agreements. Part-time tuition and fees vary according to course load and reciprocity agreements. *Required fees:* $1112 full-time. *Room and board:* $9056. Room and board charges vary according to board plan and housing facility.

Financial Aid Of all full-time matriculated undergraduates who enrolled in 2012, 5,235 applied for aid, 4,964 were judged to have need, 945 had their need fully met. 148 Federal Work-Study jobs (averaging $3433). In 2012, 21 non-need-based awards were made. *Average percent of need met:* 70%. *Aver-*

age financial aid package: $14,722. *Average need-based loan:* $5135. *Average need-based gift aid:* $9343. *Average non-need-based aid:* $1976.

Applying *Options:* electronic application. *Application fee:* $55. *Required:* high school transcript. *Required for some:* interview. *Recommended:* minimum 3.0 GPA. *Application deadlines:* 11/30 (freshmen), 11/30 (transfers). *Notification:* continuous (freshmen), continuous (transfers).

Freshman Application Contact Admissions & Outreach Services, California State University, Stanislaus, One University Circle, Turlock, CA 95382. *Phone:* 209-667-3070. *Toll-free phone:* 800-300-7420. *Fax:* 209-667-3788. *E-mail:* outreach_help_desk@csustan.edu.
Website: http://www.csustan.edu/.

California University of Management and Sciences
Anaheim, California

Admissions Office Contact California University of Management and Sciences, 721 North Euclid Street, Anaheim, CA 92801.
Website: http://www.calums.edu/.

Chapman University
Orange, California

- **Independent** comprehensive, founded 1861, affiliated with Christian Church (Disciples of Christ)
- **Suburban** 78-acre campus with easy access to Los Angeles
- **Endowment** $188.1 million
- **Coed** 5,677 undergraduate students, 96% full-time, 57% women, 43% men
- **Very difficult** entrance level, 44% of applicants were admitted

Undergraduates 5,446 full-time, 231 part-time. Students come from 51 states and territories; 60 other countries; 27% are from out of state; 2% Black or African American, non-Hispanic/Latino; 13% Hispanic/Latino; 9% Asian, non-Hispanic/Latino; 0.3% Native Hawaiian or other Pacific Islander, non-Hispanic/Latino; 0.3% American Indian or Alaska Native, non-Hispanic/Latino; 5% Two or more races, non-Hispanic/Latino; 7% Race/ethnicity unknown; 4% international; 7% transferred in; 34% live on campus. *Retention:* 91% of full-time freshmen returned.

Freshmen *Admission:* 10,489 applied, 4,572 admitted, 1,278 enrolled. *Average high school GPA:* 3.65. *Test scores:* SAT critical reading scores over 500: 93%; SAT math scores over 500: 95%; SAT writing scores over 500: 96%; ACT scores over 18: 100%; SAT critical reading scores over 600: 51%; SAT math scores over 600: 60%; SAT writing scores over 600: 62%; ACT scores over 24: 87%; SAT critical reading scores over 700: 9%; SAT math scores over 700: 11%; SAT writing scores over 700: 13%; ACT scores over 30: 19%.

Faculty *Total:* 781, 47% full-time. *Student/faculty ratio:* 14:1.

Academics *Calendar:* 4-1-4. *Degrees:* bachelor's, master's, doctoral, and postbachelor's certificates. *Special study options:* academic remediation for entering students, adult/continuing education programs, advanced placement credit, distance learning, double majors, honors programs, independent study, internships, off-campus study, part-time degree program, services for LD students, student-designed majors, study abroad, summer session for credit. *ROTC:* Army (c), Air Force (c). *Unusual degree programs:* 3-2 business administration; engineering with University of California, Irvine.

Computers on Campus Students can access the following: campus intranet, computer help desk, free student e-mail accounts, online (class) grades, online (class) registration, online (class) schedules. Campuswide network is available. 100% of college-owned or -operated housing units are wired for high-speed Internet access. Wireless service is available via entire campus.

Student Life *Housing options:* coed, disabled students. Campus housing is university owned. Freshman campus housing is guaranteed. *Activities and organizations:* drama/theater group, student-run newspaper, radio station, choral group, Gamma Beta Phi, Alpha Kappa Psi Professional Business Fraternity, Public Relations Student Society of America, Black Student Union, Disciples on Campus, national fraternities, national sororities. *Campus security:* 24-hour emergency response devices and patrols, late-night transport/escort service, controlled dormitory access, full safety education program. *Student services:* health clinic, personal/psychological counseling.

Athletics Member NCAA. All Division III. *Intercollegiate sports:* baseball M, basketball M/W, cheerleading W(c), crew M(c)/W(c), cross-country running M/W, football M, golf M, ice hockey M(c), lacrosse M(c)/W, sailing M(c)/W(c), soccer M/W, softball W, swimming and diving M/W, tennis M/W, track and field W, volleyball M(c)/W, water polo M/W. *Intramural sports:* basketball M/W, soccer M/W, ultimate Frisbee M/W, volleyball M/W.

Standardized Tests *Required:* SAT or ACT (for admission). *Recommended:* SAT Subject Tests (for admission).

Costs (2013–14) *Comprehensive fee:* $55,777 includes full-time tuition ($42,890), mandatory fees ($683), and room and board ($12,204). Part-time tuition: $1330 per credit. *College room only:* $8238. Room and board charges vary according to board plan and housing facility. *Payment plans:* tuition prepayment, installment, deferred payment. *Waivers:* employees or children of employees.

Financial Aid Of all full-time matriculated undergraduates who enrolled in 2012, 3,730 applied for aid, 3,276 were judged to have need, 331 had their need fully met. 2,853 Federal Work-Study jobs (averaging $2907). In 2012, 1150 non-need-based awards were made. *Average percent of need met:* 10%. *Average financial aid package:* $30,655. *Average need-based loan:* $4266. *Average need-based gift aid:* $15,331. *Average non-need-based aid:* $17,053. *Average indebtedness upon graduation:* $29,371.

Applying *Options:* electronic application, early action. *Application fee:* $65. *Required:* essay or personal statement, high school transcript, 1 letter of recommendation. *Required for some:* Audition required for music, dance, and theatre majors. Portfolio required for art and film majors. Supplemental application required for all talent-based majors. *Application deadlines:* 1/15 (freshmen), 3/15 (transfers), 11/1 (early action). *Notification:* 3/15 (freshmen), 4/15 (transfers), 1/10 (early action).

Freshman Application Contact Ms. Marcela Mejia-Martinez, Director of Admission, Chapman University, One University Drive, Orange, CA 92866. *Phone:* 714-997-6711. *Toll-free phone:* 888-CUAPPLY. *Fax:* 714-997-6713. *E-mail:* admit@chapman.edu. *Website:* http://www.chapman.edu/.

See previous page for display ad and page 1236 for the College Close-Up.

Charles Drew University of Medicine and Science

Los Angeles, California

Freshman Application Contact Ms. Yvette Lane, Associate Director, Student Service, Charles Drew University of Medicine and Science, 1731 East 120th Street, Los Angeles, CA 90059. *Phone:* 323-563-4922. *Fax:* 323-563-4923. *E-mail:* yvettelane@cdrewu.edu. *Website:* http://www.cdrewu.edu/.

Claremont McKenna College

Claremont, California

- **Independent** comprehensive, founded 1946
- **Suburban** 69-acre campus with easy access to Los Angeles
- **Endowment** $520.6 million
- **Coed** 1,264 undergraduate students, 100% full-time, 48% women, 52% men
- **Most difficult** entrance level, 14% of applicants were admitted

Undergraduates 1,260 full-time, 4 part-time. Students come from 45 states and territories; 32 other countries; 56% are from out of state; 3% Black or African American, non-Hispanic/Latino; 9% Hispanic/Latino; 11% Asian, non-Hispanic/Latino; 0.2% Native Hawaiian or other Pacific Islander, non-Hispanic/Latino; 0.1% American Indian or Alaska Native, non-Hispanic/Latino; 6% Two or more races, non-Hispanic/Latino; 13% Race/ethnicity unknown; 12% international; 3% transferred in; 94% live on campus. *Retention:* 95% of full-time freshmen returned.

Freshmen *Admission:* 5,058 applied, 688 admitted, 291 enrolled. *Test scores:* SAT critical reading scores over 500: 100%; SAT math scores over 500: 100%; SAT writing scores over 500: 100%; ACT scores over 18: 100%; SAT critical reading scores over 600: 93%; SAT math scores over 600: 97%; SAT writing scores over 600: 93%; ACT scores over 24: 99%; SAT critical reading scores over 700: 51%; SAT math scores over 700: 60%; SAT writing scores over 700: 57%; ACT scores over 30: 68%.

Faculty *Total:* 162, 85% full-time, 96% with terminal degrees. *Student/faculty ratio:* 8:1.

Academics *Calendar:* semesters. *Degrees:* bachelor's and master's. *Special study options:* advanced placement credit, double majors, independent study, internships, off-campus study, services for LD students, student-designed majors, study abroad, summer session for credit. *ROTC:* Army (b), Air Force (c). *Unusual degree programs:* 3-2 engineering with Stanford University, Harvey Mudd College, Columbia University, University of California System schools, University of Southern California.

Computers on Campus 289 computers/terminals are available on campus for general student use. Students can access the following: campus intranet, computer help desk, free student e-mail accounts, online (class) grades, online (class) registration, online (class) schedules. Campuswide network is available. 100% of college-owned or -operated housing units are wired for high-speed Internet access. Wireless service is available via entire campus.

Student Life *Housing:* on-campus residence required for freshman year. *Options:* coed, disabled students. Campus housing is university owned. Freshman campus housing is guaranteed. *Activities and organizations:* drama/theater group, student-run newspaper, radio station, choral group, The Forum—

student newspaper, ASCMC—student government, Debate/Forensics Club, SOURCE, Rotaract. *Campus security:* 24-hour emergency response devices and patrols, student patrols, late-night transport/escort service, controlled dormitory access. *Student services:* health clinic, personal/psychological counseling.

Athletics Member NCAA. All Division III. *Intercollegiate sports:* archery M(c)/W(c), baseball M, basketball M/W, cheerleading M(c)/W(c), cross-country running M/W, equestrian sports M(c)/W(c), fencing M(c)/W(c), field hockey M(c)/W(c), football M, golf M/W, lacrosse M(c)/W, rugby M(c)/W(c), sailing M(c)/W(c), skiing (downhill) M(c)/W(c), soccer M/W, softball W, swimming and diving M/W, tennis M/W, track and field M/W, volleyball M(c)/W, water polo M/W. *Intramural sports:* basketball M/W, bowling M/W, crew M/W, football M, soccer M/W, squash M/W, table tennis M/W, tennis M/W, ultimate Frisbee M/W, volleyball M/W, water polo M/W, weight lifting M/W.

Standardized Tests *Required:* SAT or ACT (for admission). *Required for some:* SAT Subject Tests (for admission).

Costs (2012–13) *Comprehensive fee:* $58,065 includes full-time tuition ($43,840), mandatory fees ($245), and room and board ($13,980). Full-time tuition and fees vary according to course load. Part-time tuition: $7307 per course. Part-time tuition and fees vary according to course load. *College room only:* $7380. Room and board charges vary according to board plan and housing facility. *Payment plan:* installment. *Waivers:* employees or children of employees.

Financial Aid Of all full-time matriculated undergraduates who enrolled in 2012, 575 applied for aid, 518 were judged to have need, 518 had their need fully met. In 2012, 70 non-need-based awards were made. *Average percent of need met:* 100%. *Average financial aid package:* $39,332. *Average need-based gift aid:* $37,778. *Average non-need-based aid:* $16,256. *Average indebtedness upon graduation:* $23,179. *Financial aid deadline:* 2/1.

Applying *Options:* electronic application, early decision, deferred entrance. *Application fee:* $60. *Required:* essay or personal statement, high school transcript, 3 letters of recommendation. *Recommended:* interview. *Application deadlines:* 1/2 (freshmen), 4/1 (transfers). *Early decision deadline:* 11/1 (for plan 1), 1/2 (for plan 2). *Notification:* 4/1 (freshmen), 5/15 (transfers), 12/15 (early decision plan 1), 2/15 (early decision plan 2).

Freshman Application Contact Ms. Jennifer Sandoval-Dancs, Director of Admission, Claremont McKenna College, Office of Admission and Financial Aid, 888 Columbia Avenue, Claremont, CA 91711. *Phone:* 909-621-8088. *Fax:* 909-621-8516. *E-mail:* jennifer.sandoval@cmc.edu. *Website:* http://www.claremontmckenna.edu/.

Cogswell Polytechnical College

Sunnyvale, California

- **Independent** comprehensive, founded 1887
- **Suburban** 2-acre campus with easy access to San Francisco, San Jose
- **Coed, primarily men** 392 undergraduate students, 64% full-time, 21% women, 79% men
- **Moderately difficult** entrance level, 49% of applicants were admitted

Undergraduates 252 full-time, 140 part-time. Students come from 13 states and territories; 3 other countries; 13% are from out of state; 5% Black or African American, non-Hispanic/Latino; 13% Hispanic/Latino; 8% Asian, non-Hispanic/Latino; 3% Native Hawaiian or other Pacific Islander, non-Hispanic/Latino; 0.5% American Indian or Alaska Native, non-Hispanic/Latino; 7% Two or more races, non-Hispanic/Latino; 16% Race/ethnicity unknown; 3% international; 19% transferred in; 29% live on campus. *Retention:* 68% of full-time freshmen returned.

Freshmen *Admission:* 162 applied, 80 admitted, 62 enrolled. *Average high school GPA:* 2.69. *Test scores:* SAT critical reading scores over 500: 73%; SAT math scores over 500: 66%; SAT writing scores over 500: 81%; ACT scores over 18: 100%; SAT critical reading scores over 600: 33%; SAT math scores over 600: 46%; SAT writing scores over 600: 34%; ACT scores over 24: 75%; SAT math scores over 700: 13%; SAT writing scores over 700: 7%; ACT scores over 30: 25%.

Faculty *Total:* 72, 22% full-time, 19% with terminal degrees. *Student/faculty ratio:* 9:1.

Academics *Calendar:* semesters. *Degrees:* bachelor's and master's. *Special study options:* advanced placement credit, distance learning, double majors, internships, part-time degree program, student-designed majors, summer session for credit.

Computers on Campus 224 computers/terminals are available on campus for general student use. Students can access the following: computer help desk, free student e-mail accounts, online (class) grades, online (class) registration, online (class) schedules. Campuswide network is available. Wireless service is available via entire campus.

Student Life *Housing options:* coed. Campus housing is provided by a third party. Freshman campus housing is guaranteed. *Activities and organizations:* choral group, ASB, Game Development club, Audio Production and Engineering club, Comic Club, Women's club. *Campus security:* 24-hour emergency response devices. *Student services:* personal/psychological counseling.

Standardized Tests *Recommended:* SAT or ACT (for admission).

Costs (2013–14) *Tuition:* $19,488 full-time, $812 per credit hour part-time. Full-time tuition and fees vary according to course load and degree level. Part-time tuition and fees vary according to course load and degree level. *Required fees:* $180 full-time. *Room only:* $6000. Room and board charges vary according to housing facility. *Payment plan:* deferred payment. *Waivers:* employees or children of employees.

Financial Aid Of all full-time matriculated undergraduates who enrolled in 2011, 14 Federal Work-Study jobs (averaging $1900).

Applying *Options:* electronic application, deferred entrance. *Required:* essay or personal statement, high school transcript, minimum 2.0 GPA. *Required for some:* portfolio for Digital Art and Animation and Digital Audio Technology majors. *Recommended:* minimum 2.7 GPA, interview. *Application deadlines:* rolling (freshmen), rolling (out-of-state freshmen), rolling (transfers). *Notification:* continuous (freshmen), continuous (out-of-state freshmen), continuous (transfers).

Freshman Application Contact Abraham Chacko, Executive Director of Admissions, Cogswell Polytechnical College, 1175 Bordeaux Drive, Sunnyvale, CA 94089-1299. *Phone:* 408-4985123. *Toll-free phone:* 800-264-7955. *Fax:* 408-747-0764. *E-mail:* achacko@cogswell.edu. *Website:* http://www.cogswell.edu/.

The Colburn School Conservatory of Music

Los Angeles, California

Freshman Application Contact Ms. Kathleen Tesar, Associate Dean, The Colburn School Conservatory of Music, 200 South Grand Avenue, Los Angeles, CA 90012. *Phone:* 213-621-4534. *Fax:* 213-625-0371. *E-mail:* admissions@colburnschool.edu. *Website:* http://www.colburnschool.edu/.

Coleman University

San Diego, California

Freshman Application Contact Admissions Department, Coleman University, 7380 Parkway Drive, La Mesa, CA 91942-1532. *Phone:* 619-465-3990. *Toll-free phone:* 800-430-2030. *E-mail:* jschafer@cts.com. *Website:* http://www.coleman.edu/.

Coleman University

San Marcos, California

Director of Admissions Senior Admissions Officer, Coleman University, 1284 West San Marcos Boulevard, San Marcos, CA 92078. *Phone:* 760-747-3990. *Fax:* 760-752-9808. *Website:* http://www.coleman.edu/.

Columbia College Hollywood

Tarzana, California

- **Independent** 4-year, founded 1952
- **Urban** 1-acre campus with easy access to Los Angeles
- **Coed** 359 undergraduate students, 100% full-time, 33% women, 67% men
- **Minimally difficult** entrance level, 57% of applicants were admitted

Undergraduates 359 full-time. Students come from 5 other countries; 42% are from out of state; 16% Black or African American, non-Hispanic/Latino; 17% Hispanic/Latino; 7% Asian, non-Hispanic/Latino; 8% Race/ethnicity unknown. *Retention:* 81% of full-time freshmen returned.

Freshmen *Admission:* 196 applied, 111 admitted. *Average high school GPA:* 3.2.

Faculty *Total:* 52. *Student/faculty ratio:* 33:1.

Academics *Calendar:* quarters. *Degrees:* associate and bachelor's. *Special study options:* accelerated degree program, adult/continuing education programs, part-time degree program, summer session for credit.

Computers on Campus 12 computers/terminals are available on campus for general student use. Students can access the following: campus intranet, computer help desk, free student e-mail accounts, online (class) grades, online (class) registration, online (class) schedules. Wireless service is available via entire campus.

Student Life *Housing options:* coed. Campus housing is provided by a third party. *Activities and organizations:* drama/theater group. *Campus security:* 24-hour emergency response devices and patrols, late-night transport/escort service. *Student services:* personal/psychological counseling.

Costs (2013–14) *One-time required fee:* $95. *Comprehensive fee:* $48,141 includes full-time tuition ($18,375), mandatory fees ($18,804), and room and board ($10,962). Part-time tuition: $550 per unit. *Room and board:* Room and board charges vary according to housing facility. *Payment plans:* installment, deferred payment.

Financial Aid Of all full-time matriculated undergraduates who enrolled in 2009, 259 applied for aid, 238 were judged to have need. 10 Federal Work-Study jobs (averaging $2000). *Average financial aid package:* $6119. *Average need-based loan:* $1362. *Average need-based gift aid:* $2063.

Applying *Options:* electronic application, deferred entrance. *Application fee:* $50. *Required:* essay or personal statement, high school transcript, minimum 2.0 GPA, 2 letters of recommendation, interview. *Recommended:* portfolio. *Application deadline:* rolling (freshmen). *Notification:* continuous (freshmen), continuous (transfers).

Freshman Application Contact Carmen Munoz, Admissions Director, Columbia College Hollywood, 18618 Oxnard Street, Tarzana, CA 91356. *Phone:* 818-345-8414 Ext. 203. *Toll-free phone:* 800-785-0585. *Fax:* 818-345-9053. *E-mail:* admissions@columbiacollege.edu. *Website:* http://www.columbiacollege.edu/.

Concordia University

Irvine, California

- **Independent** comprehensive, founded 1972, affiliated with Lutheran Church–Missouri Synod, part of The Concordia University System
- **Suburban** 70-acre campus with easy access to Los Angeles
- **Endowment** $12.2 million
- **Coed** 1,738 undergraduate students, 92% full-time, 62% women, 38% men
- **Moderately difficult** entrance level, 69% of applicants were admitted

Undergraduates 1,592 full-time, 146 part-time. Students come from 30 states and territories; 22 other countries; 11% are from out of state; 4% Black or African American, non-Hispanic/Latino; 19% Hispanic/Latino; 6% Asian, non-Hispanic/Latino; 0.3% Native Hawaiian or other Pacific Islander, non-Hispanic/Latino; 0.5% American Indian or Alaska Native, non-Hispanic/Latino; 4% Two or more races, non-Hispanic/Latino; 5% Race/ethnicity unknown; 3% international; 12% transferred in; 50% live on campus. *Retention:* 78% of full-time freshmen returned.

Freshmen *Admission:* 1,808 applied, 1,256 admitted, 301 enrolled. *Average high school GPA:* 3.46. *Test scores:* SAT critical reading scores over 500: 57%; SAT math scores over 500: 61%; SAT writing scores over 500: 60%; ACT scores over 18: 91%; SAT critical reading scores over 600: 17%; SAT math scores over 600: 21%; SAT writing scores over 600: 16%; ACT scores over 24: 43%; SAT critical reading scores over 700: 3%; SAT math scores over 700: 2%; SAT writing scores over 700: 2%; ACT scores over 30: 4%.

Faculty *Total:* 319, 26% full-time, 56% with terminal degrees. *Student/faculty ratio:* 19:1.

Academics *Calendar:* semesters. *Degrees:* associate, bachelor's, and master's (associate's degree for international students only). *Special study options:* academic remediation for entering students, accelerated degree program, adult/continuing education programs, advanced placement credit, distance learning, double majors, honors programs, independent study, internships, off-campus study, part-time degree program, services for LD students, study abroad, summer session for credit.

Computers on Campus 89 computers/terminals are available on campus for general student use. Students can access the following: computer help desk, free student e-mail accounts, online (class) grades, online (class) registration, online (class) schedules. Campuswide network is available. 100% of college-owned or -operated housing units are wired for high-speed Internet access. Wireless service is available via entire campus.

Student Life *Housing options:* coed, disabled students. Campus housing is university owned. Freshman campus housing is guaranteed. *Activities and organizations:* drama/theater group, student-run newspaper, choral group, intramurals, Screaming Eagles, Lacrosse, abbey west, student activities. *Campus security:* 24-hour emergency response devices and patrols, student patrols, late-night transport/escort service, lighted walkways, 24-hour dispatch. *Student services:* health clinic, personal/psychological counseling.

Athletics Member NAIA. *Intercollegiate sports:* baseball M(s), basketball M(s)/W(s), cross-country running M(s)/W(s), lacrosse M(s)(c), soccer M(s)/W(s), softball W(s), swimming and diving M(s)/W(s), tennis M(s)/W(s), track and field M(s)/W(s), volleyball M(s)/W(s), water polo M(s)/W(s). *Intramural sports:* basketball M/W, bowling M/W, cheerleading M(c)/W(c), football M/W, soccer M/W, softball M/W, track and field M/W, ultimate Frisbee M/W, volleyball M/W.

Standardized Tests *Required:* SAT or ACT (for admission).

Costs (2013–14) *Comprehensive fee:* $38,680 includes full-time tuition ($29,000), mandatory fees ($630), and room and board ($9050). Full-time tuition and fees vary according to course load. Part-time tuition: $900 per unit.

Part-time tuition and fees vary according to course load. *Required fees:* $315 per term part-time. *College room only:* $5100. Room and board charges vary according to board plan and housing facility. *Payment plan:* installment. *Waivers:* employees or children of employees.

Financial Aid Of all full-time matriculated undergraduates who enrolled in 2012, 1,296 applied for aid, 1,102 were judged to have need, 138 had their need fully met. 43 Federal Work-Study jobs (averaging $2305). In 2012, 232 non-need-based awards were made. *Average percent of need met:* 60%. *Average financial aid package:* $17,606. *Average need-based loan:* $4542. *Average need-based gift aid:* $14,255. *Average non-need-based aid:* $7578. *Average indebtedness upon graduation:* $29,091. *Financial aid deadline:* 3/2.

Applying *Options:* electronic application, early action, deferred entrance. *Application fee:* $50. *Required:* essay or personal statement, high school transcript, 1 letter of recommendation. *Recommended:* minimum 2.8 GPA, interview. *Application deadlines:* rolling (freshmen), rolling (transfers), 12/1 (early action). *Notification:* continuous (freshmen), continuous (transfers), 12/15 (early action).

Freshman Application Contact Mr. Rick Hardy, Associate Vice President for Enrollment Management, Concordia University, 1530 Concordia West, Irvine, CA 92612-3299. *Phone:* 949-214-3147. *Toll-free phone:* 800-229-1200. *Fax:* 949-854-6894. *E-mail:* admission@cui.edu.
Website: http://www.cui.edu/.

Design Institute of San Diego
San Diego, California

Director of Admissions Ms. Paula Parrish, Director of Admissions, Design Institute of San Diego, 8555 Commerce Avenue, San Diego, CA 92121-2685. *Phone:* 858-566-1200. *Toll-free phone:* 800-619-4337. *Fax:* 858-566-2711. *E-mail:* admissions@disd.edu.
Website: http://www.disd.edu/.

DeVry University
Alhambra, California

Admissions Office Contact DeVry University, Unit 100, Building A-11, First Floor, 1000 South Fremont Avenue, Alhambra, CA 91803. *Toll-free phone:* 866-338-7941.
Website: http://www.devry.edu/.

DeVry University
Anaheim, California

Admissions Office Contact DeVry University, 1900 South State College Boulevard, Suite 150, Anaheim, CA 92806-6136. *Toll-free phone:* 866-338-7941.
Website: http://www.devry.edu/.

DeVry University
Bakersfield, California

Admissions Office Contact DeVry University, 3000 Ming Avenue, Bakersfield, CA 93304-4136. *Toll-free phone:* 866-338-7941.
Website: http://www.devry.edu/.

DeVry University
Daly City, California

Admissions Office Contact DeVry University, 2001 Junipero Serra Boulevard, Suite 161, Daly City, CA 94014-3899. *Toll-free phone:* 866-338-7941.
Website: http://www.devry.edu/.

DeVry University
Elk Grove, California

Admissions Office Contact DeVry University, Sacramento Center, 2216 Kausen Drive, Elk Grove, CA 95758. *Toll-free phone:* 866-338-7941.
Website: http://www.devry.edu/.

DeVry University
Fremont, California

Freshman Application Contact DeVry University, 6600 Dumbarton Circle, Fremont, CA 94555. *Toll-free phone:* 866-338-7941.
Website: http://www.devry.edu/.

DeVry University
Irvine, California

Admissions Office Contact DeVry University, 430 Exchange, Suite 250, Irvine, CA 92602-1303. *Toll-free phone:* 866-338-7941.
Website: http://www.devry.edu/.

DeVry University
Long Beach, California

Freshman Application Contact DeVry University, 3880 Kilroy Airport Way, Long Beach, CA 90806. *Toll-free phone:* 866-338-7941.
Website: http://www.devry.edu/.

DeVry University
Oakland, California

Admissions Office Contact DeVry University, 505 14th Street, Oakland, CA 94612. *Toll-free phone:* 866-338-7941.
Website: http://www.devry.edu/.

DeVry University
Palmdale, California

Director of Admissions Admissions Office, DeVry University, One 39115 Trade Center Drive, Suite 100, Palmdale, CA 93551. *Toll-free phone:* 866-338-7941.
Website: http://www.devry.edu/.

DeVry University
Pomona, California

- **Proprietary** comprehensive, founded 1983, part of DeVry University
- **Urban** campus
- **Coed** 2,323 undergraduate students, 35% full-time, 42% women, 58% men
- **Minimally difficult** entrance level

Undergraduates 812 full-time, 1,511 part-time. 9% are from out of state; 9% Black or African American, non-Hispanic/Latino; 38% Hispanic/Latino; 10% Asian, non-Hispanic/Latino; 2% Native Hawaiian or other Pacific Islander, non-Hispanic/Latino; 0.6% American Indian or Alaska Native, non-Hispanic/Latino; 2% Two or more races, non-Hispanic/Latino; 12% Race/ethnicity unknown; 1% international; 18% transferred in.

Freshmen *Admission:* 151 enrolled.

Faculty *Total:* 98, 21% full-time. *Student/faculty ratio:* 31:1.

Academics *Calendar:* semesters. *Degrees:* associate, bachelor's, master's, and postbachelor's certificates. *Special study options:* adult/continuing education programs, part-time degree program.

Computers on Campus Students can access the following: online (class) registration.

Student Life *Housing:* college housing not available.

Costs (2013–14) *Tuition:* $16,076 full-time, $609 per credit hour part-time. *Required fees:* $80 full-time.

Financial Aid Of all full-time matriculated undergraduates who enrolled in 2007, 414 applied for aid, 394 were judged to have need, 6 had their need fully met. In 2007, 50 non-need-based awards were made. *Average percent of need met:* 36%. *Average financial aid package:* $12,689. *Average need-based loan:* $7876. *Average need-based gift aid:* $8289. *Average non-need-based aid:* $16,971. *Average indebtedness upon graduation:* $33,385.

Applying *Application fee:* $40. *Required:* high school transcript, interview. *Application deadlines:* rolling (freshmen), rolling (transfers). *Notification:* continuous (freshmen), continuous (transfers).

Freshman Application Contact DeVry University, 901 Corporate Center Drive, Pomona, CA 91768-2642. *Phone:* 909-622-8866. *Toll-free phone:* 866-338-7941.
Website: http://www.devry.edu/.

DeVry University
San Diego, California

Admissions Office Contact DeVry University, 2655 Camino Del Rio North, Suite 201, San Diego, CA 92108-1633. *Toll-free phone:* 866-338-7941.
Website: http://www.devry.edu/.

DeVry University
Sherman Oaks, California

Freshman Application Contact DeVry University, 15301 Ventura Boulevard, D-100, Sherman Oaks, CA 91403. *Toll-free phone:* 866-338-7941. *Website:* http://www.devry.edu/.

Dominican University of California
San Rafael, California

- **Independent** comprehensive, founded 1890, affiliated with Roman Catholic Church
- **Suburban** 85-acre campus with easy access to San Francisco
- **Endowment** $26.1 million
- **Coed**
- **Moderately difficult** entrance level

Faculty *Student/faculty ratio:* 11:1.
Academics *Calendar:* semesters. *Degrees:* bachelor's, master's, and postbachelor's certificates.
Student Life *Campus security:* 24-hour emergency response devices and patrols, late-night transport/escort service, controlled dormitory access.
Athletics Member NCAA. All Division II.
Standardized Tests *Required:* SAT or ACT (for admission).
Costs (2012–13) *Comprehensive fee:* $52,990 includes full-time tuition ($38,600), mandatory fees ($450), and room and board ($13,940). Full-time tuition and fees vary according to course load. Part-time tuition: $1560 per credit. *Required fees:* $150 per term part-time. *College room only:* $7880. Room and board charges vary according to board plan.
Financial Aid *Of all full-time matriculated undergraduates who enrolled in 2010,* 1,118 applied for aid, 1,046 were judged to have need, 62 had their need fully met. 213 Federal Work-Study jobs (averaging $1615). 32 state and other part-time jobs (averaging $2910). *In 2010,* 63 non-need-based awards were made. *Average percent of need met:* 58. *Average financial aid package:* $24,466. *Average need-based loan:* $4660. *Average need-based gift aid:* $19,950. *Average non-need-based aid:* $11,032. *Average indebtedness upon graduation:* $41,189.
Applying *Options:* electronic application, deferred entrance. *Application fee:* $40. *Required:* essay or personal statement, high school transcript, 1 letter of recommendation. *Recommended:* interview.
Freshman Application Contact Ms. Rebecca Finn Kenney, Director of Undergraduate Admissions, Dominican University of California, 50 Acacia Avenue, San Rafael, CA 94901-2298. *Phone:* 415-485-3204. *Toll-free phone:* 888-323-6763. *Fax:* 415-485-3214. *E-mail:* enroll@dominican.edu. *Website:* http://www.dominican.edu/.

See below for display ad and page 1270 for the College Close-Up.

Epic Bible College
Sacramento, California

Director of Admissions Ms. Sheila Knoll, Assistant Director of Records, Epic Bible College, 5225 Hillsdale Boulevard, Sacramento, CA 95842. *Phone:* 916-348-4689. *E-mail:* kclarke@tlbc.edu. *Website:* http://epic.edu/.

Everest College
Ontario, California

Freshman Application Contact Admissions Office, Everest College, 1819 South Excise Avenue, Ontario, CA 91761. *Phone:* 909-484-4311. *Toll-free phone:* 888-741-4270. *Fax:* 909-484-1162. *Website:* http://www.everest.edu/.

Ex'pression College for Digital Arts
Emeryville, California

Admissions Office Contact Ex'pression College for Digital Arts, 6601 Shellmound Street, Emeryville, CA 94608. *Toll-free phone:* 877-833-8800. *Website:* http://www.expression.edu/.

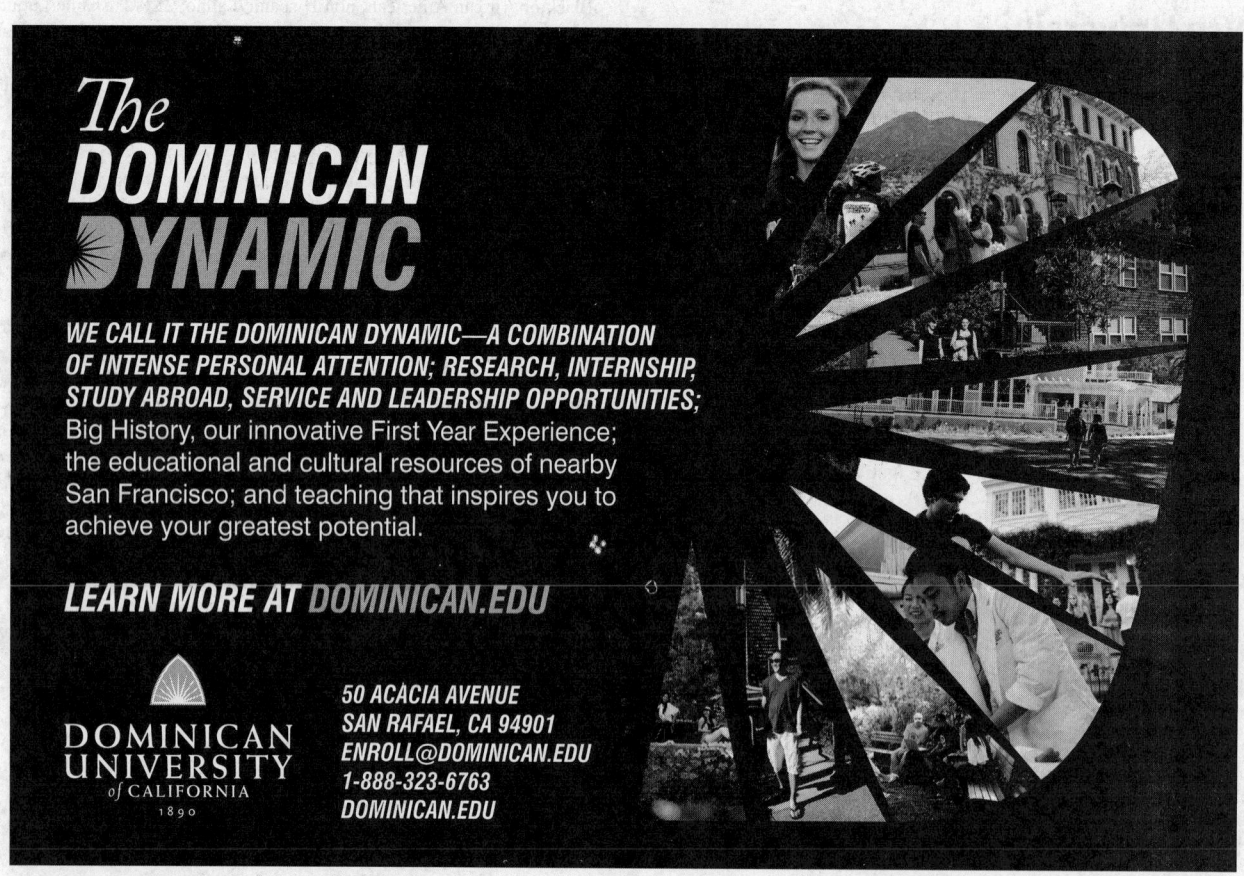

FIDM/The Fashion Institute of Design & Merchandising, Los Angeles Campus

Los Angeles, California

- **Proprietary** primarily 2-year, founded 1969, part of The Fashion Institute of Design and Merchandising/FIDM
- **Urban** campus
- **Coed** 3,743 undergraduate students, 88% full-time, 89% women, 11% men
- **Moderately difficult** entrance level, 57% of applicants were admitted

Undergraduates 3,288 full-time, 455 part-time. 6% Black or African American, non-Hispanic/Latino; 23% Hispanic/Latino; 12% Asian, non-Hispanic/Latino; 1% Native Hawaiian or other Pacific Islander, non-Hispanic/Latino; 0.3% American Indian or Alaska Native, non-Hispanic/Latino; 3% Two or more races, non-Hispanic/Latino; 9% Race/ethnicity unknown; 12% international. *Retention:* 91% of full-time freshmen returned.
Freshmen *Admission:* 1,777 applied, 1,009 admitted, 638 enrolled. *Average high school GPA:* 2.75.
Faculty *Total:* 326, 21% full-time. *Student/faculty ratio:* 21:1.
Academics *Calendar:* quarters. *Degrees:* associate and bachelor's (also includes Orange County Campus). *Special study options:* academic remediation for entering students, adult/continuing education programs, advanced placement credit, cooperative education, distance learning, English as a second language, independent study, internships, part-time degree program, services for LD students, study abroad, summer session for credit.
Computers on Campus Students can access the following: campus intranet, online (class) grades, online (class) registration, online (class) schedules. Campuswide network is available. Wireless service is available via computer centers, learning centers, libraries, student centers.
Student Life *Activities and organizations:* student-run newspaper, ASID (student chapter), Design Council, Phi Theta Kappa Honor Society, Student Council, MODE. *Campus security:* 24-hour emergency response devices and patrols, late-night transport/escort service. *Student services:* personal/psychological counseling.
Standardized Tests *Recommended:* SAT or ACT (for admission).
Costs (2013–14) *Tuition:* $23,965 full-time. Full-time tuition and fees vary according to degree level and program. *Required fees:* $225 full-time.
Financial Aid Of all full-time matriculated undergraduates who enrolled in 2011, 88 Federal Work-Study jobs (averaging $2935).
Applying *Options:* electronic application, deferred entrance. *Application fee:* $225. *Required:* essay or personal statement, high school transcript, minimum 2.0 GPA, 3 letters of recommendation, interview, major-determined project. *Application deadlines:* rolling (freshmen), rolling (out-of-state freshmen), rolling (transfers).
Freshman Application Contact Ms. Susan Aronson, Director of Admissions, FIDM/The Fashion Institute of Design & Merchandising, Los Angeles Campus, Los Angeles, CA 90015. *Phone:* 213-624-1201. *Toll-free phone:* 800-624-1200. *Fax:* 213-624-4799. *E-mail:* saronson@fidm.com. *Website:* http://www.fidm.edu/.

See below for display ad and page 1290 for the College Close-Up.

Fresno Pacific University

Fresno, California

Freshman Application Contact Fresno Pacific University, 1717 South Chestnut Avenue, #2005, Fresno, CA 93727. *Phone:* 800-660-6089. *Toll-free phone:* 800-660-6089. *Fax:* 559-453-2007. *E-mail:* ugadmis@fresno.edu. *Website:* http://www.fresno.edu/.

Golden Gate University

San Francisco, California

Freshman Application Contact Mr. Louis D. Riccardi Jr., Director of Enrollment Services, Golden Gate University, 536 Mission Street, San Francisco, CA 94105-2968. *Phone:* 415-442-7800. *Toll-free phone:* 800-448-3381. *Fax:* 415-442-7807. *E-mail:* info@ggu.edu. *Website:* http://www.ggu.edu/.

Harvey Mudd College
Claremont, California

- **Independent** 4-year, founded 1955, part of The Claremont Colleges Consortium
- **Suburban** 33-acre campus with easy access to Los Angeles
- **Endowment** $225.5 million
- **Coed** 783 undergraduate students, 100% full-time, 44% women, 56% men
- **Most difficult** entrance level, 19% of applicants were admitted

Undergraduates 782 full-time, 1 part-time. Students come from 42 states and territories; 19 other countries; 63% are from out of state; 1% Black or African American, non-Hispanic/Latino; 7% Hispanic/Latino; 22% Asian, non-Hispanic/Latino; 0.4% American Indian or Alaska Native, non-Hispanic/Latino; 2% Two or more races, non-Hispanic/Latino; 5% Race/ethnicity unknown; 8% international; 0.3% transferred in; 98% live on campus. *Retention:* 98% of full-time freshmen returned.

Freshmen *Admission:* 3,336 applied, 642 admitted, 198 enrolled. *Test scores:* SAT critical reading scores over 500: 100%; SAT math scores over 500: 100%; SAT writing scores over 500: 100%; ACT scores over 18: 100%; SAT critical reading scores over 600: 96%; SAT math scores over 600: 100%; SAT writing scores over 600: 98%; ACT scores over 24: 100%; SAT critical reading scores over 700: 67%; SAT math scores over 700: 91%; SAT writing scores over 700: 68%; ACT scores over 30: 94%.

Faculty *Total:* 106, 83% full-time, 100% with terminal degrees. *Student/faculty ratio:* 8:1.

Academics *Calendar:* semesters. *Degree:* bachelor's. *Special study options:* double majors, internships, off-campus study, services for LD students, student-designed majors, study abroad. *ROTC:* Army (c), Air Force (b). *Unusual degree programs:* 3-2 economics/engineering with Claremont McKenna College and /engineering with Scripps College.

Computers on Campus 120 computers/terminals and 860 ports are available on campus for general student use. Students can access the following: campus intranet, computer help desk, free student e-mail accounts, online (class) grades, online (class) registration, online (class) schedules. Campuswide network is available. 100% of college-owned or -operated housing units are wired for high-speed Internet access. Wireless service is available via entire campus.

Student Life *Housing:* on-campus residence required for freshman year. *Options:* coed. Campus housing is university owned. Freshman campus housing is guaranteed. *Activities and organizations:* drama/theater group, student-run newspaper, radio station, choral group, Ballroom Dancing, Delta-H (outdoors club), Intervarsity Christian Fellowship, Science Bus, SWE (Society of Women Engineers). *Campus security:* 24-hour emergency response devices and patrols, late-night transport/escort service. *Student services:* health clinic, personal/psychological counseling, women's center.

Athletics Member NCAA. All Division III. *Intercollegiate sports:* baseball M, basketball M/W, cross-country running M/W, football M, golf M/W, lacrosse W, soccer M/W, softball W, swimming and diving M/W, tennis M/W, track and field M/W, volleyball W, water polo M/W. *Intramural sports:* badminton M(c)/W(c), equestrian sports M(c)/W(c), fencing M(c)/W(c), football M/W, ice hockey M(c), lacrosse M(c), rock climbing M(c)/W(c), rugby M(c)/W(c), sailing M(c)/W(c), soccer M/W, swimming and diving M/W, table tennis M(c)/W(c), tennis M/W, ultimate Frisbee M(c)/W(c), volleyball M/W.

Standardized Tests *Required:* SAT or ACT (for admission), SAT Subject Tests (for admission), SAT or ACT and the SAT Subject Test in Math 2 and a second SAT Subject exam (for admission).

Costs (2012–13) *One-time required fee:* $100. *Comprehensive fee:* $58,913 includes full-time tuition ($44,159), mandatory fees ($283), and room and board ($14,471). *College room only:* $7763. Room and board charges vary according to board plan. *Payment plan:* installment. *Waivers:* employees or children of employees.

Financial Aid Of all full-time matriculated undergraduates who enrolled in 2011, 462 applied for aid, 398 were judged to have need, 398 had their need fully met. 230 Federal Work-Study jobs (averaging $2245). 23 state and other part-time jobs (averaging $6004). In 2011, 171 non-need-based awards were made. *Average percent of need met:* 100%. *Average financial aid package:* $35,122. *Average need-based loan:* $5411. *Average need-based gift aid:* $30,475. *Average non-need-based aid:* $11,087. *Average indebtedness upon graduation:* $25,265. *Financial aid deadline:* 2/1.

Applying *Options:* electronic application, early admission, early decision, deferred entrance. *Application fee:* $70. *Required:* essay or personal statement, high school transcript, 3 letters of recommendation. *Recommended:* interview. *Application deadlines:* 1/1 (freshmen), 4/1 (transfers). *Early decision deadline:* 11/15 (for plan 1), 1/1 (for plan 2). *Notification:* 4/1 (freshmen), 5/15 (transfers), 12/15 (early decision plan 1), 2/15 (early decision plan 2).

Freshman Application Contact Mr. Peter Osgood, Director of Admission, Harvey Mudd College, 301 Platt Boulevard, Claremont, CA 91711. *Phone:* 909-621-8011. *Fax:* 909-607-7046. *E-mail:* admission@hmc.edu. *Website:* http://www.hmc.edu/.

Henley-Putnam University
Santa Clara, California

- **Proprietary** comprehensive, founded 1991
- **Coed**

Academics *Degrees:* certificates, bachelor's, master's, and doctoral (offers only online degree programs). *Special study options:* adult/continuing education programs, external degree program, part-time degree program.

Computers on Campus Students can access the following: campus intranet, computer help desk, free student e-mail accounts, Online courses. Campuswide network is available.

Costs (2012–13) *Tuition:* $264 per unit part-time. Full-time tuition and fees vary according to course level and degree level. Part-time tuition and fees vary according to course level and degree level. No tuition increase for student's term of enrollment. *Payment plan:* installment.

Applying *Options:* electronic application. *Required for some:* essay or personal statement, high school transcript, interview, official transcripts from all colleges and universities attended; background checks. *Application deadlines:* rolling (freshmen), rolling (out-of-state freshmen), rolling (transfers).

Freshman Application Contact Henley-Putnam University, 2804 Mission College Boulevard, Suite 240, Santa Clara, CA 95054. *Phone:* 408-453-9900 Ext. 9928. *Toll-free phone:* 88-852-8746 (in-state); 888-852-8746 (out-of-state). *Website:* http://www.henley-putnam.edu/.

Holy Names University
Oakland, California

- **Independent Roman Catholic** comprehensive, founded 1868
- **Urban** 60-acre campus with easy access to San Francisco
- **Endowment** $10.8 million
- **Coed, primarily women** 887 undergraduate students, 78% full-time, 70% women, 30% men
- **Moderately difficult** entrance level, 51% of applicants were admitted

Undergraduates 695 full-time, 192 part-time. Students come from 24 states and territories; 34 other countries; 6% are from out of state; 23% Black or African American, non-Hispanic/Latino; 24% Hispanic/Latino; 14% Asian, non-Hispanic/Latino; 4% Native Hawaiian or other Pacific Islander, non-Hispanic/Latino; 0.7% American Indian or Alaska Native, non-Hispanic/Latino; 7% Two or more races, non-Hispanic/Latino; 5% Race/ethnicity unknown; 3% international; 16% transferred in; 66% live on campus. *Retention:* 70% of full-time freshmen returned.

Freshmen *Admission:* 742 applied, 379 admitted, 134 enrolled. *Average high school GPA:* 3.2. *Test scores:* SAT critical reading scores over 500: 29%; SAT math scores over 500: 37%; SAT writing scores over 500: 33%; ACT scores over 18: 62%; SAT critical reading scores over 600: 5%; SAT math scores over 600: 4%; SAT writing scores over 600: 4%; ACT scores over 24: 13%.

Faculty *Total:* 209, 26% full-time, 53% with terminal degrees. *Student/faculty ratio:* 14:1.

Academics *Calendar:* semesters. *Degrees:* certificates, bachelor's, master's, post-master's, and postbachelor's certificates. *Special study options:* academic remediation for entering students, accelerated degree program, adult/continuing education programs, advanced placement credit, distance learning, double majors, English as a second language, honors programs, independent study, internships, part-time degree program, services for LD students, student-designed majors, study abroad, summer session for credit. *ROTC:* Army (c), Air Force (c). *Unusual degree programs:* 3-2 business administration.

Computers on Campus 92 computers/terminals are available on campus for general student use. Students can access the following: computer help desk, free student e-mail accounts, online (class) grades, online (class) registration, online (class) schedules. Campuswide network is available. Wireless service is available via entire campus.

Student Life *Housing options:* coed. Campus housing is university owned. Freshman campus housing is guaranteed. *Activities and organizations:* drama/theater group, choral group, Drama Club, Latinos Unidos, Black Student Union, Biology Club, Hiking Club. *Campus security:* 24-hour emergency response devices, late-night transport/escort service, controlled dormitory access, 24-hour security main gate. *Student services:* personal/psychological counseling.

Athletics Member NCAA. All Division II. *Intercollegiate sports:* baseball M, basketball M(s)/W(s), cross-country running M(s)/W(s), golf M(s)/W(s), soccer M(s)/W(s), softball W(s), tennis M/W, volleyball M(s)/W(s).

Standardized Tests *Required:* SAT or ACT (for admission).

Financial Aid Of all full-time matriculated undergraduates who enrolled in 2006, 373 applied for aid, 247 were judged to have need, 58 had their need fully met. 50 Federal Work-Study jobs (averaging $1699). 53 state and other part-time jobs (averaging $1750). In 2006, 77 non-need-based awards were made. *Average percent of need met:* 43%. *Average financial aid package:* $15,554. *Average need-based loan:* $4154. *Average need-based gift aid:* $13,258. *Average non-need-based aid:* $10,557. *Average indebtedness upon graduation:* $10,500. *Financial aid deadline:* 6/30.

Applying *Options:* electronic application, early admission, deferred entrance. *Application fee:* $20. *Required:* essay or personal statement, high school transcript, 1 letter of recommendation, 1 recommendation minimum, 3 maximum. Letters must be in English. *Required for some:* interview. *Application deadlines:* 8/15 (freshmen), 8/15 (out-of-state freshmen), 8/15 (transfers), 3/2 (early action). *Notification:* continuous (freshmen), continuous (out-of-state freshmen), continuous (transfers), rolling (early action).

Freshman Application Contact Holy Names University, 3500 Mountain Boulevard, Oakland, CA 94619-1699. *Phone:* 510-436-1124. *Toll-free phone:* 800-430-1321.
Website: http://www.hnu.edu/.

Hope International University
Fullerton, California

- **Independent** comprehensive, founded 1928, affiliated with Christian Churches and Churches of Christ
- **Suburban** 16-acre campus with easy access to Los Angeles
- **Coed** 1,167 undergraduate students, 68% full-time, 57% women, 43% men
- **Moderately difficult** entrance level, 56% of applicants were admitted

Undergraduates 798 full-time, 369 part-time. 11% are from out of state; 7% Black or African American, non-Hispanic/Latino; 16% Hispanic/Latino; 3% Asian, non-Hispanic/Latino; 1% Native Hawaiian or other Pacific Islander, non-Hispanic/Latino; 0.4% American Indian or Alaska Native, non-Hispanic/Latino; 10% Two or more races, non-Hispanic/Latino; 12% Race/ethnicity unknown; 9% international; 13% transferred in; 25% live on campus. *Retention:* 72% of full-time freshmen returned.

Freshmen *Admission:* 439 applied, 244 admitted, 286 enrolled. *Average high school GPA:* 3.17. *Test scores:* SAT critical reading scores over 500: 42%; SAT math scores over 500: 44%; SAT writing scores over 500: 36%; ACT scores over 18: 72%; SAT critical reading scores over 600: 8%; SAT math scores over 600: 11%; SAT writing scores over 600: 6%; ACT scores over 24: 33%; SAT critical reading scores over 700: 1%.

Faculty *Total:* 208, 19% full-time, 41% with terminal degrees. *Student/faculty ratio:* 10:1.

Academics *Calendar:* 4-1-4. *Degrees:* certificates, associate, bachelor's, master's, and postbachelor's certificates. *Special study options:* academic remediation for entering students, accelerated degree program, adult/continuing education programs, advanced placement credit, distance learning, double majors, English as a second language, independent study, internships, off-campus study, part-time degree program, services for LD students, study abroad. *ROTC:* Army (c).

Computers on Campus 30 computers/terminals are available on campus for general student use. Students can access the following: computer help desk, free student e-mail accounts, online (class) grades, online (class) registration, online (class) schedules. Campuswide network is available. 100% of college-owned or -operated housing units are wired for high-speed Internet access. Wireless service is available via entire campus.

Student Life *Housing:* on-campus residence required through sophomore year. *Options:* men-only, women-only, disabled students. Campus housing is university owned. Freshman campus housing is guaranteed. *Activities and organizations:* drama/theater group, student-run newspaper, choral group, Campus Ministries, International Student Organization, Musical Theater, Student Government, Student Publications. *Campus security:* 24-hour emergency response devices and patrols, student patrols. *Student services:* personal/psychological counseling.

Athletics Member NAIA, NCCAA. *Intercollegiate sports:* basketball M(s)/W(s), cheerleading M/W, cross-country running M(s)/W(s), soccer M(s)/W(s), softball W(s), tennis M(s)/W(s), volleyball M(s)/W(s). *Intramural sports:* ultimate Frisbee M/W, volleyball M/W.

Standardized Tests *Required:* SAT or ACT (for admission).

Costs (2013–14) *One-time required fee:* $160. *Comprehensive fee:* $34,650 includes full-time tuition ($25,550), mandatory fees ($500), and room and board ($8600). Full-time tuition and fees vary according to course level, course load, degree level, location, program, and reciprocity agreements. Part-time tuition: $1075 per unit. Part-time tuition and fees vary according to course level, course load, degree level, location, program, and reciprocity agreements. *Required fees:* $500 per year part-time. *College room only:* $4610. Room and

board charges vary according to board plan and student level. *Payment plan:* installment. *Waivers:* employees or children of employees.

Financial Aid Of all full-time matriculated undergraduates who enrolled in 2012, 620 applied for aid, 596 were judged to have need, 93 had their need fully met. 28 Federal Work-Study jobs (averaging $2000). In 2012, 20 non-need-based awards were made. *Average percent of need met:* 38%. *Average financial aid package:* $12,110. *Average need-based loan:* $4661. *Average need-based gift aid:* $8339. *Average non-need-based aid:* $7550. *Average indebtedness upon graduation:* $20,500.

Applying *Options:* electronic application. *Application fee:* $40. *Required:* essay or personal statement, high school transcript, minimum 2.5 GPA, 2 letters of recommendation, rank in upper 50% of high school class. *Required for some:* interview. *Application deadline:* 2/1 (freshmen).

Freshman Application Contact Ms. Midge Madden, Office Manager, Hope International University, 2500 East Nutwood Avenue, Fullerton, CA 92831-3138. *Phone:* 714-879-3901 Ext. 2240. *Toll-free phone:* 866-722-HOPE. *Fax:* 714-681-7423. *E-mail:* mfmadden@hiu.edu.
Website: http://www.hiu.edu/.

Horizon College San Diego
San Diego, California

Admissions Office Contact Horizon College San Diego, 5331 Mt. Alifan Drive, San Diego, CA 92111.
Website: http://www.horizoncollege.org/.

Humboldt State University
Arcata, California

- **State-supported** comprehensive, founded 1913, part of California State University System
- **Rural** 161-acre campus
- **Coed** 7,597 undergraduate students, 93% full-time, 53% women, 47% men
- **Moderately difficult** entrance level, 80% of applicants were admitted

Undergraduates 7,047 full-time, 550 part-time. Students come from 48 states and territories; 41 other countries; 12% are from out of state; 4% Black or African American, non-Hispanic/Latino; 23% Hispanic/Latino; 3% Asian, non-Hispanic/Latino; 0.3% Native Hawaiian or other Pacific Islander, non-Hispanic/Latino; 1% American Indian or Alaska Native, non-Hispanic/Latino; 6% Two or more races, non-Hispanic/Latino; 9% Race/ethnicity unknown; 1% international; 12% transferred in; 26% live on campus. *Retention:* 73% of full-time freshmen returned.

Freshmen *Admission:* 9,979 applied, 7,953 admitted, 1,237 enrolled. *Average high school GPA:* 3.15. *Test scores:* SAT critical reading scores over 500: 56%; SAT math scores over 500: 52%; SAT writing scores over 500: 51%; ACT scores over 18: 81%; SAT critical reading scores over 600: 18%; SAT math scores over 600: 15%; SAT writing scores over 600: 12%; ACT scores over 24: 31%; SAT critical reading scores over 700: 2%; SAT math scores over 700: 1%; SAT writing scores over 700: 1%; ACT scores over 30: 3%.

Faculty *Total:* 538, 42% full-time, 54% with terminal degrees. *Student/faculty ratio:* 23:1.

Academics *Calendar:* semesters. *Degrees:* bachelor's, master's, post-master's, and postbachelor's certificates. *Special study options:* academic remediation for entering students, adult/continuing education programs, advanced placement credit, cooperative education, distance learning, double majors, English as a second language, honors programs, independent study, internships, off-campus study, part-time degree program, services for LD students, student-designed majors, study abroad, summer session for credit.

Computers on Campus 1,098 computers/terminals are available on campus for general student use. Students can access the following: computer help desk, free student e-mail accounts, online (class) grades, online (class) registration, online (class) schedules. Campuswide network is available. 100% of college-owned or -operated housing units are wired for high-speed Internet access. Wireless service is available via entire campus.

Student Life *Housing options:* coed. Campus housing is university owned. Freshman applicants given priority for college housing. *Activities and organizations:* drama/theater group, student-run newspaper, radio station, choral group, marching band, Bicycle Learning Center, Campus Center for Appropriate Technology (CCAT), Youth Educational Services, HOLA, MECHA, national fraternities, national sororities. *Campus security:* 24-hour emergency response devices and patrols, late-night transport/escort service, controlled dormitory access. *Student services:* health clinic, personal/psychological counseling, women's center.

Athletics Member NCAA. All Division II. *Intercollegiate sports:* basketball M(s)/W(s), cheerleading W(c), crew M(c)/W, cross-country running M(s)/W(s), football M(s), lacrosse M(c), soccer M(s)/W(s), softball W(s), track and field M(s)/W(s), volleyball W(s). *Intramural sports:* baseball M(c), basketball

M/W, fencing M(c)/W(c), rugby M(c)/W(c), soccer M/W, ultimate Frisbee M(c)/W(c), volleyball M(c), water polo M(c).
Standardized Tests *Required for some:* SAT or ACT (for admission).
Costs (2013–14) *Tuition:* state resident $0 full-time; nonresident $11,160 full-time, $372 per credit hour part-time. Full-time tuition and fees vary according to degree level. Part-time tuition and fees vary according to course load and degree level. *Required fees:* $7130 full-time, $2208 per term part-time. *Room and board:* $11,440. Room and board charges vary according to board plan and housing facility. *Payment plan:* installment. *Waivers:* employees or children of employees.
Financial Aid Of all full-time matriculated undergraduates who enrolled in 2010, 4,957 applied for aid, 4,293 were judged to have need, 26 had their need fully met. 308 Federal Work-Study jobs (averaging $2793). In 2010, 21 non-need-based awards were made. *Average percent of need met:* 67%. *Average financial aid package:* $11,339. *Average need-based loan:* $4498. *Average need-based gift aid:* $9356. *Average non-need-based aid:* $1649. *Average indebtedness upon graduation:* $17,889.
Applying *Options:* electronic application. *Application fee:* $55. *Required:* high school transcript, minimum 2.0 GPA. *Application deadlines:* 11/30 (freshmen), 11/30 (out-of-state freshmen), 11/30 (transfers). *Notification:* continuous (freshmen), continuous (out-of-state freshmen), continuous (transfers).
Freshman Application Contact Mr. Steven Ladwig, Interim Director of Admissions, Humboldt State University, 1 Harpst Street, Arcata, CA 95521. *Phone:* 707-826-4402. *Toll-free phone:* 866-850-9556. *Fax:* 707-826-6190. *E-mail:* hsuinfo@humboldt.edu.
Website: http://www.humboldt.edu/.

Humphreys College
Stockton, California

Director of Admissions Director of Admission, Humphreys College, 6650 Inglewood Avenue, Stockton, CA 95207-3896. *Phone:* 209-235-2901. *E-mail:* ugadmission@humphreys.edu.
Website: http://www.humphreys.edu/.

Interior Designers Institute
Newport Beach, California

Freshman Application Contact Interior Designers Institute, 1061 Camelback Road, Newport Beach, CA 92660.
Website: http://www.idi.edu/.

ITT Technical Institute
Clovis, California

- **Proprietary** 4-year, founded 2005, part of ITT Educational Services, Inc.
- **Coed**
- **Minimally difficult** entrance level

Academics *Calendar:* quarters. *Degrees:* associate and bachelor's.
Freshman Application Contact Director of Recruitment, ITT Technical Institute, 362 North Clovis Avenue, Clovis, CA 93612. *Phone:* 559-325-5400. *Toll-free phone:* 800-564-9771.
Website: http://www.itt-tech.edu/.

ITT Technical Institute
Concord, California

- **Proprietary** 4-year, part of ITT Educational Services, Inc.
- **Coed**
- **Minimally difficult** entrance level

Academics *Calendar:* quarters. *Degrees:* associate and bachelor's.
Freshman Application Contact Director of Recruitment, ITT Technical Institute, 1140 Galaxy Way, Suite 400, Concord, CA 94520. *Phone:* 925-674-8200. *Toll-free phone:* 800-211-7062.
Website: http://www.itt-tech.edu/.

ITT Technical Institute
Corona, California

- **Proprietary** 4-year
- **Coed**
- **Minimally difficult** entrance level

Academics *Degrees:* associate and bachelor's.
Freshman Application Contact Director of Recruitment, ITT Technical Institute, 4160 Temescal Canyon Road, Suite 100, Corona, CA 92883. *Phone:* 951-277-5400. *Toll-free phone:* 877-764-9661.
Website: http://www.itt-tech.edu/.

ITT Technical Institute
Culver City, California

- **Proprietary** primarily 2-year, part of ITT Educational Services, Inc.
- **Coed**

Academics *Calendar:* quarters. *Degrees:* associate and bachelor's.
Freshman Application Contact Director of Recruitment, ITT Technical Institute, 6101 W. Centinela Avenue, Suite 180, Culver City, CA 90230. *Phone:* 310-417-5800. *Toll-free phone:* 800-215-6151.
Website: http://www.itt-tech.edu/.

ITT Technical Institute
Lathrop, California

- **Proprietary** primarily 2-year, founded 1997, part of ITT Educational Services, Inc.
- **Coed**
- **Minimally difficult** entrance level

Academics *Calendar:* quarters. *Degrees:* associate and bachelor's.
Freshman Application Contact Director of Recruitment, ITT Technical Institute, 16916 South Harlan Road, Lathrop, CA 95330. *Phone:* 209-858-0077. *Toll-free phone:* 800-346-1786.
Website: http://www.itt-tech.edu/.

ITT Technical Institute
Oakland, California

- **Proprietary** primarily 2-year, part of ITT Educational Services, Inc.
- **Coed**

Academics *Calendar:* quarters. *Degrees:* associate and bachelor's.
Freshman Application Contact Director of Recruitment, ITT Technical Institute, 7901 Oakport Street, Suite 3000, Oakland, CA 94621. *Phone:* 510-553-2800. *Toll-free phone:* 877-442-5833.
Website: http://www.itt-tech.edu/.

ITT Technical Institute
Orange, California

- **Proprietary** primarily 2-year, founded 1982, part of ITT Educational Services, Inc.
- **Suburban** campus
- **Coed**
- **Minimally difficult** entrance level

Academics *Calendar:* quarters. *Degrees:* associate and bachelor's.
Financial Aid *Of all full-time matriculated undergraduates who enrolled in 2011,* 20 Federal Work-Study jobs (averaging $5000).
Freshman Application Contact Director of Recruitment, ITT Technical Institute, 4000 West Metropolitan Drive, Suite 100, Orange, CA 92868. *Phone:* 714-941-2400.
Website: http://www.itt-tech.edu/.

ITT Technical Institute
Oxnard, California

- **Proprietary** primarily 2-year, founded 1993, part of ITT Educational Services, Inc.
- **Urban** campus
- **Coed**
- **Minimally difficult** entrance level

Academics *Calendar:* quarters. *Degrees:* associate and bachelor's.
Freshman Application Contact Director of Recruitment, ITT Technical Institute, 2051 Solar Drive, Suite 150, Oxnard, CA 93036. *Phone:* 805-988-0143. *Toll-free phone:* 800-530-1582.
Website: http://www.itt-tech.edu/.

ITT Technical Institute
Rancho Cordova, California

- **Proprietary** primarily 2-year, founded 1954, part of ITT Educational Services, Inc.
- **Urban** campus
- **Coed**
- **Minimally difficult** entrance level

Academics *Calendar:* quarters. *Degrees:* associate and bachelor's.

COLLEGES AT-A-GLANCE

Freshman Application Contact Director of Recruitment, ITT Technical Institute, 10863 Gold Center Drive, Rancho Cordova, CA 95670-6034. *Phone:* 916-851-3900. *Toll-free phone:* 800-488-8466.
Website: http://www.itt-tech.edu/.

ITT Technical Institute
San Bernardino, California

- **Proprietary** primarily 2-year, founded 1987, part of ITT Educational Services, Inc.
- **Urban** campus
- **Coed**
- **Minimally difficult** entrance level

Academics *Calendar:* quarters. *Degrees:* associate and bachelor's.
Freshman Application Contact Director of Recruitment, ITT Technical Institute, 670 East Carnegie Drive, San Bernardino, CA 92408. *Phone:* 909-806-4600. *Toll-free phone:* 800-888-3801.
Website: http://www.itt-tech.edu/.

ITT Technical Institute
San Diego, California

- **Proprietary** primarily 2-year, founded 1981, part of ITT Educational Services, Inc.
- **Suburban** campus
- **Coed**
- **Minimally difficult** entrance level

Academics *Calendar:* quarters. *Degrees:* associate and bachelor's.
Freshman Application Contact Director of Recruitment, ITT Technical Institute, 9680 Granite Ridge Drive, San Diego, CA 92123. *Phone:* 858-571-8500. *Toll-free phone:* 800-883-0380.
Website: http://www.itt-tech.edu/.

ITT Technical Institute
San Dimas, California

- **Proprietary** primarily 2-year, founded 1982, part of ITT Educational Services, Inc.
- **Suburban** campus
- **Coed**
- **Minimally difficult** entrance level

Academics *Calendar:* quarters. *Degrees:* associate and bachelor's.
Financial Aid *Of all full-time matriculated undergraduates who enrolled in 2011,* 20 Federal Work-Study jobs (averaging $4500).
Freshman Application Contact Director of Recruitment, ITT Technical Institute, 650 West Cienega Avenue, San Dimas, CA 91773. *Phone:* 909-971-2300. *Toll-free phone:* 800-414-6522.
Website: http://www.itt-tech.edu/.

ITT Technical Institute
Sylmar, California

- **Proprietary** primarily 2-year, founded 1982, part of ITT Educational Services, Inc.
- **Urban** campus
- **Coed**
- **Minimally difficult** entrance level

Academics *Calendar:* quarters. *Degrees:* associate and bachelor's.
Freshman Application Contact Director of Recruitment, ITT Technical Institute, 12669 Encinitas Avenue, Sylmar, CA 91342-3664. *Phone:* 818-364-5151. *Toll-free phone:* 800-363-2086 (in-state); 800-636-2086 (out-of-state).
Website: http://www.itt-tech.edu/.

ITT Technical Institute
Torrance, California

- **Proprietary** primarily 2-year, founded 1987, part of ITT Educational Services, Inc.
- **Urban** campus
- **Coed**
- **Minimally difficult** entrance level

Academics *Calendar:* quarters. *Degrees:* associate and bachelor's.
Financial Aid *Of all full-time matriculated undergraduates who enrolled in 2011,* 6 Federal Work-Study jobs (averaging $4000).

Freshman Application Contact Director of Recruitment, ITT Technical Institute, 2555 West 190th Street, Suite 125, Torrance, CA 90504. *Phone:* 310-965-5900.
Website: http://www.itt-tech.edu/.

ITT Technical Institute
West Covina, California

- **Proprietary** primarily 2-year, part of ITT Educational Services, Inc.
- **Coed**

Academics *Calendar:* quarters. *Degrees:* associate and bachelor's.
Freshman Application Contact Director of Recruitment, ITT Technical Institute, 1530 W. Cameron Avenue, West Covina, CA 91790. *Phone:* 626-813-3681. *Toll-free phone:* 877-480-2766.
Website: http://www.itt-tech.edu/.

John F. Kennedy University
Pleasant Hill, California

Director of Admissions Ms. Jen Miller-Hogg, Director of Admissions, John F. Kennedy University, 100 Ellinwood Way, Pleasant Hill, CA 94523-4817. *Phone:* 925-969-3584. *Toll-free phone:* 800-696-JFKU. *E-mail:* jmhogg@jfku.edu.
Website: http://www.jfku.edu/.

John Paul the Great Catholic University
San Diego, California

Admissions Office Contact John Paul the Great Catholic University, 10174 Old Grove Road, Suite 200, San Diego, CA 92131.
Website: http://www.jpcatholic.com/.

King's University
Van Nuys, California

Freshman Application Contact Mrs. Marilyn J. Chappell, Director of Admissions, King's University, 14800 Sherman Way, Van Nuys, CA 91405-8040. *Phone:* 818-779-8040. *Toll-free phone:* 888-779-8040. *Fax:* 818-779-8429. *E-mail:* mchappell@kingscollege.edu.
Website: http://kingsuniversity.edu/.

Laguna College of Art & Design
Laguna Beach, California

Director of Admissions Mike Rivas, Vice President of Enrollment, Laguna College of Art & Design, 2222 Laguna Canyon Road, Laguna Beach, CA 92651-1136. *Phone:* 949-376-6000 Ext. 232. *Toll-free phone:* 800-255-0762.
Website: http://www.lcad.edu/.

La Sierra University
Riverside, California

- **Independent Seventh-day Adventist** comprehensive, founded 1922, part of Seventh-Day Adventist Education System
- **Suburban** 100-acre campus with easy access to Los Angeles
- **Endowment** $15.0 million
- **Coed** 2,048 undergraduate students, 91% full-time, 57% women, 43% men
- **Minimally difficult** entrance level, 48% of applicants were admitted

Undergraduates 1,872 full-time, 176 part-time. Students come from 16 states and territories; 8 other countries; 9% are from out of state; 8% Black or African American, non-Hispanic/Latino; 40% Hispanic/Latino; 15% Asian, non-Hispanic/Latino; 2% Native Hawaiian or other Pacific Islander, non-Hispanic/Latino; 0.0% American Indian or Alaska Native, non-Hispanic/Latino; 5% Two or more races, non-Hispanic/Latino; 0.2% Race/ethnicity unknown; 13% international; 12% transferred in; 31% live on campus. *Retention:* 77% of full-time freshmen returned.
Freshmen *Admission:* 3,208 applied, 1,555 admitted, 506 enrolled. *Average high school GPA:* 3.33. *Test scores:* SAT critical reading scores over 500: 38%; SAT math scores over 500: 40%; ACT scores over 18: 65%; SAT critical reading scores over 600: 10%; SAT math scores over 600: 12%; ACT scores over 24: 16%; SAT critical reading scores over 700: 1%; SAT math scores over 700: 3%; ACT scores over 30: 1%.
Faculty *Total:* 212, 47% full-time, 44% with terminal degrees. *Student/faculty ratio:* 16:1.

Academics *Calendar:* quarters. *Degrees:* certificates, bachelor's, master's, doctoral, post-master's, and postbachelor's certificates. *Special study options:* academic remediation for entering students, accelerated degree program, adult/continuing education programs, advanced placement credit, distance learning, double majors, English as a second language, honors programs, independent study, internships, off-campus study, part-time degree program, services for LD students, student-designed majors, study abroad, summer session for credit. *Unusual degree programs:* business administration with White memorial branch (CA), Riverside branch (CA), Glendale branch (CA), Chino Branch (CA); criminal justice at Corona Branch.

Computers on Campus 300 computers/terminals are available on campus for general student use. Students can access the following: computer help desk, free student e-mail accounts, online (class) grades, online (class) registration, online (class) schedules. Campuswide network is available. Wireless service is available via entire campus.

Student Life *Housing:* on-campus residence required for freshman year. *Options:* men-only, women-only, cooperative. Campus housing is university owned. Freshman campus housing is guaranteed. *Activities and organizations:* drama/theater group, student-run newspaper, choral group, Student Association of LSU, Korean Student Association, Students In Free Enterprise (SIFE), Ol Club, Black Student Association. *Campus security:* 24-hour emergency response devices and patrols, student patrols, late-night transport/escort service. *Student services:* health clinic, personal/psychological counseling, women's center.

Athletics Member NAIA. *Intercollegiate sports:* basketball M/W, golf M, soccer M, softball W, volleyball W. *Intramural sports:* baseball M, basketball M/W, soccer M, softball W, volleyball W.

Standardized Tests *Required:* SAT or ACT (for admission).

Costs (2012–13) *Comprehensive fee:* $35,694 includes full-time tuition ($27,180), mandatory fees ($1134), and room and board ($7380). Full-time tuition and fees vary according to course load, degree level, and location. Part-time tuition: $755 per quarter hour. Part-time tuition and fees vary according to course load, degree level, and location. *Room and board:* Room and board charges vary according to board plan and housing facility. *Payment plan:* installment. *Waivers:* employees or children of employees.

Financial Aid Of all full-time matriculated undergraduates who enrolled in 2011, 1,417 applied for aid, 1,317 were judged to have need, 298 had their need fully met. 217 Federal Work-Study jobs (averaging $1598). In 2011, 89 non-need-based awards were made. *Average percent of need met:* 70%. *Average financial aid package:* $17,847. *Average need-based loan:* $4365. *Average need-based gift aid:* $25,649. *Average non-need-based aid:* $7598. *Average indebtedness upon graduation:* $42,934. *Financial aid deadline:* 8/15.

Applying *Options:* electronic application, deferred entrance. *Application fee:* $30. *Required:* essay or personal statement, high school transcript, minimum 2.0 GPA, 2 letters of recommendation, Eligibility Index Table (combination of GPA and test scores). *Required for some:* interview. *Application deadlines:* 2/1 (freshmen), 2/1 (out-of-state freshmen), 7/1 (transfers). *Notification:* continuous (freshmen), continuous (out-of-state freshmen), continuous (transfers).

Freshman Application Contact Ms. Ivy Teheda, Ass. Director of Admissions, La Sierra University, 4500 Riverwalk Parkway, Riverside, CA 92515. *Phone:* 951-7852957. *Toll-free phone:* 800-874-5587. *Fax:* 951-7852447. *E-mail:* iteheda@lasierra.edu.
Website: http://www.lasierra.edu/.

Life Pacific College
San Dimas, California

Freshman Application Contact Ms. Dorienne Elston, Director of Admissions, Life Pacific College, 1100 Covina Boulevard, San Dimas, CA 91773-3298. *Phone:* 909-599-5433 Ext. 314. *Toll-free phone:* 877-886-5433 Ext. 314. *Fax:* 909-706-3070. *E-mail:* adm@lifepacific.edu.
Website: http://www.lifepacific.edu/.

Lincoln University
Oakland, California

- **Independent** comprehensive, founded 1919
- **Urban** 2-acre campus
- **Coed**
- **Minimally difficult** entrance level

Faculty *Student/faculty ratio:* 20:1.

Academics *Calendar:* semesters. *Degrees:* certificates, associate, bachelor's, master's, and doctoral.

Student Life *Campus security:* 24-hour emergency response devices.

Applying *Options:* electronic application, deferred entrance. *Application fee:* $75. *Required:* high school transcript, minimum 2.0 GPA. *Required for some:* essay or personal statement, interview.

Freshman Application Contact Ms. Reenu Shrestha, Admissions Officer, Lincoln University, 401 15th Street, Oakland, CA 94612. *Phone:* 510-628-8010 Ext. 8030. *Toll-free phone:* 888-810-9998. *Fax:* 510-628-8012. *E-mail:* admissions@lincolnuca.edu.
Website: http://www.lincolnuca.edu/.

Loma Linda University
Loma Linda, California

Freshman Application Contact Admissions Office, Loma Linda University, Loma Linda, CA 92350. *Phone:* 909-558-1000. *Toll-free phone:* 800-422-4558.
Website: http://www.llu.edu/.

Loyola Marymount University
Los Angeles, California

- **Independent Roman Catholic** comprehensive, founded 1911
- **Suburban** 142-acre campus with easy access to Los Angeles
- **Endowment** $358.9 million
- **Coed** 6,085 undergraduate students, 96% full-time, 57% women, 43% men
- **Very difficult** entrance level, 50% of applicants were admitted

Undergraduates 5,834 full-time, 251 part-time. Students come from 48 states and territories; 65 other countries; 24% are from out of state; 6% Black or African American, non-Hispanic/Latino; 22% Hispanic/Latino; 10% Asian, non-Hispanic/Latino; 0.2% Native Hawaiian or other Pacific Islander, non-Hispanic/Latino; 0.3% American Indian or Alaska Native, non-Hispanic/Latino; 7% Two or more races, non-Hispanic/Latino; 0.4% Race/ethnicity unknown; 4% international; 5% transferred in; 52% live on campus. *Retention:* 89% of full-time freshmen returned.

Freshmen *Admission:* 11,913 applied, 5,975 admitted, 1,278 enrolled. *Average high school GPA:* 3.76. *Test scores:* SAT critical reading scores over 500: 91%; SAT math scores over 500: 94%; SAT writing scores over 500: 93%; ACT scores over 18: 100%; SAT critical reading scores over 600: 47%; SAT math scores over 600: 58%; SAT writing scores over 600: 59%; ACT scores over 24: 83%; SAT critical reading scores over 700: 8%; SAT math scores over 700: 12%; SAT writing scores over 700: 12%; ACT scores over 30: 19%.

Faculty *Total:* 1,115, 49% full-time, 47% with terminal degrees. *Student/faculty ratio:* 11:1.

Academics *Calendar:* semesters. *Degrees:* bachelor's, master's, doctoral, post-master's, and postbachelor's certificates. *Special study options:* academic remediation for entering students, accelerated degree program, advanced placement credit, cooperative education, double majors, English as a second language, honors programs, independent study, internships, part-time degree program, services for LD students, student-designed majors, study abroad, summer session for credit. *ROTC:* Army (c), Navy (c), Air Force (b). *Unusual degree programs:* 3-2 engineering.

Computers on Campus 780 computers/terminals and 2,000 ports are available on campus for general student use. Students can access the following: campus intranet, computer help desk, free student e-mail accounts, online (class) grades, online (class) registration, online (class) schedules. Campuswide network is available. 100% of college-owned or -operated housing units are wired for high-speed Internet access. Wireless service is available via entire campus.

Student Life *Housing options:* coed, men-only, women-only, disabled students. Campus housing is university owned. Freshman applicants given priority for college housing. *Activities and organizations:* drama/theater group, student-run newspaper, radio and television station, choral group, Greeks, Christian Life Community, Intramurals, Black Student Union, Na Kolea Hawaii Club, national fraternities, national sororities. *Campus security:* 24-hour emergency response devices and patrols, late-night transport/escort service, controlled dormitory access. *Student services:* health clinic, personal/psychological counseling.

Athletics Member NCAA. All Division I. *Intercollegiate sports:* baseball M(s), basketball M(s)/W(s), cheerleading M/W, crew M/W(s), cross-country running M(s)/W(s), golf M(s), soccer M(s)/W(s), softball W(s), swimming and diving W(s), tennis M(s)/W(s), track and field M/W, volleyball W(s), water polo M(s)/W(s). *Intramural sports:* baseball M(c), basketball M/W(c), football M/W, ice hockey M(c), lacrosse M(c)/W(c), rugby M(c), skiing (downhill) M(c)/W(c), soccer M(c)/W(c), table tennis M/W, tennis M(c)/W(c), volleyball M(c)/W(c), water polo W(c).

Standardized Tests *Required:* SAT or ACT (for admission).

Costs (2012–13) *One-time required fee:* $225. *Comprehensive fee:* $53,295 includes full-time tuition ($38,212), mandatory fees ($688), and room and board ($14,395). Full-time tuition and fees vary according to reciprocity agreements. Part-time tuition: $1594 per credit hour. Part-time tuition and fees vary according to course load. *Required fees:* $8 per credit hour part-time, $64 per

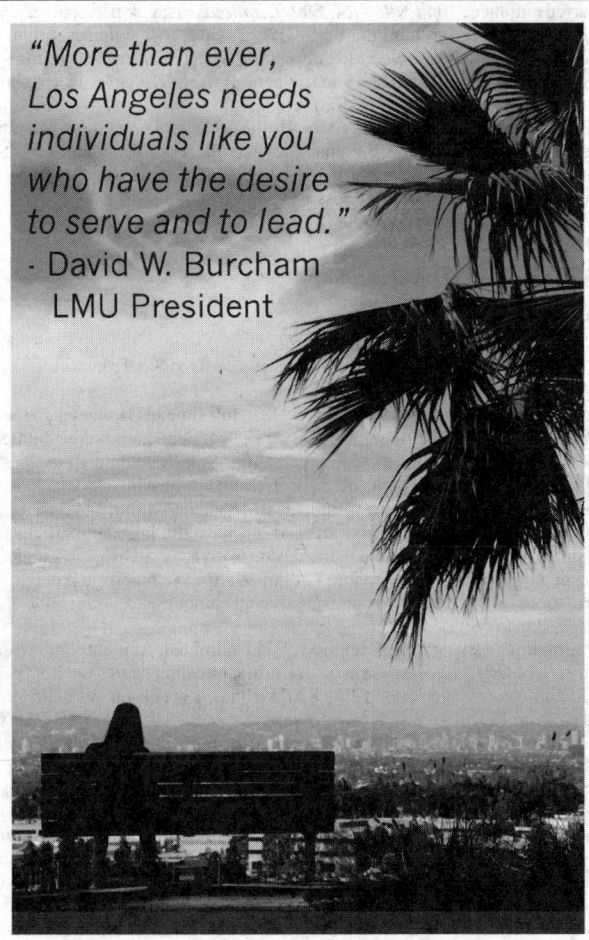

term part-time. *College room only:* $9995. Room and board charges vary according to board plan and housing facility. *Payment plans:* installment, deferred payment. *Waivers:* employees or children of employees.

Financial Aid Of all full-time matriculated undergraduates who enrolled in 2011, 4,374 applied for aid, 3,406 were judged to have need, 526 had their need fully met. 1,651 Federal Work-Study jobs (averaging $1943). 2,183 state and other part-time jobs (averaging $2683). In 2011, 1075 non-need-based awards were made. *Average percent of need met:* 65%. *Average financial aid package:* $26,246. *Average need-based loan:* $5461. *Average need-based gift aid:* $18,962. *Average non-need-based aid:* $9584. *Average indebtedness upon graduation:* $34,629. *Financial aid deadline:* 7/30.

Applying *Options:* electronic application, early admission, early action, deferred entrance. *Application fee:* $60. *Required:* essay or personal statement, high school transcript, 1 letter of recommendation. *Required for some:* portfolios or auditions for animation, dance, music, or theatre arts majors. *Recommended:* interview. *Application deadlines:* 1/15 (freshmen), 3/15 (transfers), 11/1 (early action). *Notification:* continuous (freshmen), continuous (transfers), 12/20 (early action).

Freshman Application Contact Loyola Marymount University, One LMU Drive, Los Angeles, CA 90045-2659. *Phone:* 310-338-2750. *Toll-free phone:* 800-LMU-INFO.

Website: http://www.lmu.edu/.

See display ad on this page and page 1362 for the College Close-Up.

Marymount College, Palos Verdes, California
Rancho Palos Verdes, California

- **Independent Roman Catholic** 4-year, founded 1932
- **Suburban** 26-acre campus with easy access to Los Angeles
- **Endowment** $7.8 million
- **Coed** 1,001 undergraduate students, 96% full-time, 54% women, 46% men
- **Minimally difficult** entrance level, 58% of applicants were admitted

Undergraduates 958 full-time, 43 part-time. Students come from 24 states and territories; 23 other countries; 7% are from out of state; 9% Black or African American, non-Hispanic/Latino; 28% Hispanic/Latino; 4% Asian, non-Hispanic/Latino; 2% Native Hawaiian or other Pacific Islander, non-Hispanic/Latino; 0.2% American Indian or Alaska Native, non-Hispanic/Latino; 4% Two or more races, non-Hispanic/Latino; 16% Race/ethnicity unknown; 8% international; 7% transferred in; 43% live on campus. *Retention:* 66% of full-time freshmen returned.

Freshmen *Admission:* 2,476 applied, 1,447 admitted, 415 enrolled. *Average high school GPA:* 2.94. *Test scores:* SAT math scores over 500: 36%; SAT writing scores over 500: 28%; ACT scores over 18: 55%; SAT math scores over 600: 8%; SAT writing scores over 600: 5%; ACT scores over 24: 23%; SAT math scores over 700: 2%; SAT writing scores over 700: 1%; ACT scores over 30: 2%.

Faculty *Total:* 105, 33% full-time, 53% with terminal degrees. *Student/faculty ratio:* 17:1.

Academics *Calendar:* semesters. *Degrees:* certificates, associate, and bachelor's. *Special study options:* academic remediation for entering students, adult/continuing education programs, advanced placement credit, distance learning, English as a second language, honors programs, independent study, internships, off-campus study, part-time degree program, services for LD students, study abroad, summer session for credit.

Computers on Campus 200 computers/terminals are available on campus for general student use. Students can access the following: campus intranet, computer help desk, free student e-mail accounts, online (class) grades, online (class) registration, online (class) schedules. Campuswide network is available. 100% of college-owned or -operated housing units are wired for high-speed Internet access. Wireless service is available via entire campus.

Student Life *Housing:* on-campus residence required for freshman year. *Options:* coed. Campus housing is university owned. Freshman campus housing is guaranteed. *Activities and organizations:* drama/theater group, student-run newspaper, radio station, choral group. *Campus security:* 24-hour emergency response devices and patrols, late-night transport/escort service, controlled dormitory access. *Student services:* health clinic, personal/psychological counseling.

Athletics Member NAIA. *Intercollegiate sports:* golf M/W, lacrosse M/W, soccer M(s). *Intramural sports:* basketball M/W, golf M/W, lacrosse M/W, soccer M/W, softball M/W, swimming and diving M/W, volleyball M/W.

Standardized Tests *Recommended:* SAT or ACT (for admission).

Costs (2012–13) *Comprehensive fee:* $40,942 includes full-time tuition ($28,217), mandatory fees ($650), and room and board ($12,075). Part-time tuition: $1066 per credit hour. *Room and board:* Room and board charges vary according to board plan and housing facility. *Payment plan:* installment. *Waivers:* senior citizens and employees or children of employees.

Financial Aid Of all full-time matriculated undergraduates who enrolled in 2011, 40 Federal Work-Study jobs (averaging $2000).

Applying *Options:* electronic application, early admission. *Application fee:* $40. *Required:* high school transcript. *Required for some:* essay or personal statement, interview. *Application deadlines:* 7/1 (freshmen), 8/15 (transfers). *Notification:* continuous until 9/1 (freshmen), continuous until 9/1 (transfers). **Freshman Application Contact** Mr. Jeremy Smotherman, Director of Admissions, Marymount College, Palos Verdes, California, 30800 Palos Verdes Drive East, Rancho Palos Verdes, CA 90275-6299. *Phone:* 310-377-5501 Ext. 211. *Fax:* 310-265-0962. *E-mail:* admissions@marymountpv.edu. *Website:* http://www.marymountpv.edu/.

The Master's College and Seminary
Santa Clarita, California

- **Independent nondenominational** comprehensive, founded 1927
- **Suburban** 110-acre campus with easy access to Los Angeles
- **Endowment** $14.4 million
- **Coed** 1,134 undergraduate students, 88% full-time, 47% women, 53% men
- **Moderately difficult** entrance level, 61% of applicants were admitted

Undergraduates 998 full-time, 136 part-time. Students come from 42 states and territories; 25 other countries; 29% are from out of state; 3% Black or African American, non-Hispanic/Latino; 10% Hispanic/Latino; 6% Asian, non-Hispanic/Latino; 0.5% Native Hawaiian or other Pacific Islander, non-Hispanic/Latino; 0.8% American Indian or Alaska Native, non-Hispanic/Latino; 5% Two or more races, non-Hispanic/Latino; 3% Race/ethnicity unknown; 5% international; 8% transferred in; 75% live on campus. *Retention:* 77% of full-time freshmen returned.

Freshmen *Admission:* 849 applied, 521 admitted, 209 enrolled. *Average high school GPA:* 3.67. *Test scores:* SAT critical reading scores over 500: 73%; SAT math scores over 500: 65%; ACT scores over 18: 93%; SAT critical reading scores over 600: 34%; SAT math scores over 600: 28%; ACT scores over 24: 53%; SAT critical reading scores over 700: 6%; SAT math scores over 700: 7%; ACT scores over 30: 8%.

Faculty *Total:* 191, 28% full-time, 25% with terminal degrees. *Student/faculty ratio:* 19:1.

Academics *Calendar:* semesters. *Degrees:* certificates, bachelor's, master's, and doctoral. *Special study options:* academic remediation for entering students, accelerated degree program, adult/continuing education programs, advanced placement credit, cooperative education, distance learning, double majors, external degree program, independent study, internships, part-time degree program, services for LD students, study abroad, summer session for credit.

Computers on Campus 57 computers/terminals are available on campus for general student use. Students can access the following: free student e-mail accounts, online (class) grades, online (class) registration, online (class) schedules. Campuswide network is available. Wireless service is available via entire campus.

Student Life *Housing:* on-campus residence required through junior year. *Options:* men-only, women-only. Campus housing is university owned. Freshman campus housing is guaranteed. *Activities and organizations:* drama/theater group, choral group, College Chorale, Summer Missions, intramurals, Church Ministries, Drama Club. *Campus security:* 24-hour patrols. *Student services:* health clinic, personal/psychological counseling.

Athletics Member NAIA, NCCAA. *Intercollegiate sports:* baseball M(s), basketball M(s)/W(s), cross-country running M(s)/W(s), golf M(s), soccer M(s)/W(s), track and field M(s)/W(s), volleyball W(s). *Intramural sports:* basketball M/W, football M/W, soccer M/W, volleyball M/W.

Standardized Tests *Required:* SAT or ACT (for admission).

Costs (2013–14) *Comprehensive fee:* $38,840 includes full-time tuition ($28,380), mandatory fees ($1100), and room and board ($9360). Full-time tuition and fees vary according to course load, degree level, and program. Part-time tuition: $1190 per credit hour. Part-time tuition and fees vary according to course load, degree level, and program. *Required fees:* $1190 per credit hour part-time. *Room and board:* Room and board charges vary according to board plan. *Payment plan:* installment. *Waivers:* employees or children of employees.

Financial Aid Of all full-time matriculated undergraduates who enrolled in 2011, 847 applied for aid, 761 were judged to have need, 102 had their need fully met. 49 Federal Work-Study jobs (averaging $1740). 183 state and other part-time jobs (averaging $2842). In 2011, 147 non-need-based awards were made. *Average percent of need met:* 69%. *Average financial aid package:* $20,666. *Average need-based loan:* $4935. *Average need-based gift aid:* $15,957. *Average non-need-based aid:* $9193. *Average indebtedness upon graduation:* $20,265.

Applying *Options:* electronic application, early admission, early action, deferred entrance. *Application fee:* $40. *Required:* essay or personal statement, high school transcript, minimum 2.8 GPA, 2 letters of recommendation. *Recommended:* interview. *Application deadlines:* 9/1 (freshmen), 9/1 (out-of-state freshmen), 9/1 (transfers), 11/15 (early action). *Notification:* 3/15 (freshmen), 3/15 (transfers), 12/22 (early action).

Freshman Application Contact Mrs. Hollie Jackson, Director of Admissions, The Master's College and Seminary, 21726 Placerita Canyon Road, Santa Clarita, CA 91321. *Phone:* 661-362-2209. *Toll-free phone:* 800-568-6248. *Fax:* 661-288-1037. *E-mail:* admissions@masters.edu. *Website:* http://www.masters.edu/.

Menlo College
Atherton, California

- **Independent** 4-year, founded 1927
- **Small-town** 45-acre campus with easy access to San Francisco
- **Endowment** $27.2 million
- **Coed** 681 undergraduate students, 98% full-time, 37% women, 63% men
- **Moderately difficult** entrance level, 92% of applicants were admitted

Undergraduates 670 full-time, 11 part-time. Students come from 20 states and territories; 24 other countries; 23% are from out of state; 6% Black or African American, non-Hispanic/Latino; 21% Hispanic/Latino; 6% Asian, non-Hispanic/Latino; 4% Native Hawaiian or other Pacific Islander, non-Hispanic/Latino; 0.4% American Indian or Alaska Native, non-Hispanic/Latino; 6% Two or more races, non-Hispanic/Latino; 9% Race/ethnicity unknown; 12% international; 13% transferred in; 67% live on campus. *Retention:* 74% of full-time freshmen returned.

Freshmen *Admission:* 1,856 applied, 1,711 admitted, 179 enrolled. *Average high school GPA:* 3.2. *Test scores:* SAT critical reading scores over 500: 38%; SAT math scores over 500: 52%; SAT writing scores over 500: 39%; ACT scores over 18: 87%; SAT critical reading scores over 600: 8%; SAT math scores over 600: 15%; SAT writing scores over 600: 7%; ACT scores over 24: 36%; SAT math scores over 700: 1%; ACT scores over 30: 2%.

Faculty *Total:* 78, 40% full-time, 55% with terminal degrees. *Student/faculty ratio:* 15:1.

Academics *Calendar:* semesters. *Degree:* bachelor's. *Special study options:* accelerated degree program, adult/continuing education programs, advanced placement credit, cooperative education, double majors, English as a second language, independent study, internships, part-time degree program, services for LD students, student-designed majors, study abroad, summer session for credit. *ROTC:* Army (c), Air Force (c).

Computers on Campus 200 computers/terminals are available on campus for general student use. Students can access the following: campus intranet, computer help desk, free student e-mail accounts, online (class) grades, online (class) registration, online (class) schedules. Campuswide network is available. 100% of college-owned or -operated housing units are wired for high-speed Internet access. Wireless service is available via classrooms, computer centers, computer labs, dorm rooms, learning centers, libraries, student centers.

Student Life *Housing:* on-campus residence required through sophomore year. *Options:* coed, men-only, women-only. Campus housing is university owned. *Activities and organizations:* choral group, International Club, Student Government, SERV, Finance Club, Hawaiian Club. *Campus security:* 24-hour emergency response devices and patrols, controlled dormitory access. *Student services:* personal/psychological counseling, women's center.

Athletics Member NAIA. *Intercollegiate sports:* baseball M(s), basketball M(s)/W(s), cheerleading M(s)/W(s), cross-country running M(s)/W(s), football M(s), golf M(s)/W(s), soccer M(s)/W(s), softball W(s), volleyball W(s), wrestling M(s)/W(s). *Intramural sports:* basketball M(c)/W(c).

Standardized Tests *Required:* SAT or ACT (for admission).

Costs (2013–14) *Comprehensive fee:* $49,002 includes full-time tuition ($36,500), mandatory fees ($600), and room and board ($11,902). Part-time tuition: $1521 per credit. *Room and board:* Room and board charges vary according to housing facility. *Payment plan:* installment. *Waivers:* employees or children of employees.

Financial Aid Of all full-time matriculated undergraduates who enrolled in 2012, 477 applied for aid, 444 were judged to have need, 35 had their need fully met. 318 Federal Work-Study jobs (averaging $673). In 2012, 194 non-need-based awards were made. *Average percent of need met:* 69%. *Average financial aid package:* $28,606. *Average need-based loan:* $3987. *Average need-based gift aid:* $24,443. *Average non-need-based aid:* $12,410. *Average indebtedness upon graduation:* $25,753.

Applying *Options:* electronic application, early admission, early action, deferred entrance. *Application fee:* $40. *Required:* essay or personal statement, high school transcript, 1 letter of recommendation. *Recommended:* minimum 2.5 GPA, interview. *Application deadlines:* rolling (freshmen), rolling (out-of-state freshmen), rolling (transfers), 12/1 (early action). *Notification:* continuous (freshmen), continuous (out-of-state freshmen), continuous (transfers), 12/15 (early action).

Freshman Application Contact Jadelin Felipe, Director, Enrollment Management Operations, Menlo College, 1000 El Camino Real, Atherton, CA 94027. *Phone:* 650-543-3918. *Toll-free phone:* 800-556-3656. *Fax:* 650-543-4496. *E-mail:* admissions@menlo.edu.
Website: http://www.menlo.edu/.

See display ad on this page and page 1382 for the College Close-Up.

Mills College

Oakland, California

- **Independent** comprehensive, founded 1852
- **Urban** 135-acre campus with easy access to San Francisco
- **Endowment** $165.8 million
- **Undergraduate: women only; graduate: coed** 937 undergraduate students, 95% full-time, 100% women
- **Moderately difficult** entrance level, 63% of applicants were admitted

Undergraduates 894 full-time, 43 part-time. Students come from 34 states and territories; 14 other countries; 19% are from out of state; 6% Black or African American, non-Hispanic/Latino; 21% Hispanic/Latino; 12% Asian, non-Hispanic/Latino; 0.5% Native Hawaiian or other Pacific Islander, non-Hispanic/Latino; 0.1% American Indian or Alaska Native, non-Hispanic/Latino; 11% Two or more races, non-Hispanic/Latino; 1% Race/ethnicity unknown; 2% international; 14% transferred in; 55% live on campus. *Retention:* 77% of full-time freshmen returned.

Freshmen *Admission:* 2,031 applied, 1,273 admitted, 208 enrolled. *Average high school GPA:* 3.59. *Test scores:* SAT critical reading scores over 500: 86%; SAT math scores over 500: 81%; SAT writing scores over 500: 88%; ACT scores over 18: 100%; SAT critical reading scores over 600: 52%; SAT math scores over 600: 37%; SAT writing scores over 600: 41%; ACT scores over 24: 69%; SAT critical reading scores over 700: 16%; SAT math scores over 700: 4%; SAT writing scores over 700: 9%; ACT scores over 30: 12%.

Faculty *Total:* 211, 48% full-time, 79% with terminal degrees. *Student/faculty ratio:* 10:1.

Academics *Calendar:* semesters. *Degrees:* certificates, bachelor's, master's, doctoral, and postbachelor's certificates. *Special study options:* accelerated degree program, adult/continuing education programs, advanced placement credit, double majors, English as a second language, independent study, internships, off-campus study, part-time degree program, services for LD students, student-designed majors, study abroad. *ROTC:* Army (c). *Unusual degree programs:* 3-2 business administration; engineering with University of Southern California; Education; Public Policy; Infant Mental Health.

Computers on Campus 320 computers/terminals and 8 ports are available on campus for general student use. Students can access the following: campus intranet, computer help desk, free student e-mail accounts, online (class) grades, online (class) registration, online (class) schedules, online degree audit. Campuswide network is available. 100% of college-owned or -operated housing units are wired for high-speed Internet access. Wireless service is available via entire campus.

Student Life *Housing options:* coed, women-only, cooperative, disabled students. Campus housing is university owned. Freshman campus housing is guaranteed. *Activities and organizations:* drama/theater group, student-run newspaper, radio station, choral group, Mujeres Unidas, Black Women's Collective, Student Athlete Advisory Committee, Women's Health Resource Center, Phi Alpha Delta Pre-Law Fraternity. *Campus security:* 24-hour emergency response devices and patrols, late-night transport/escort service, controlled dormitory access. *Student services:* health clinic, personal/psychological counseling, women's center.

Athletics Member NCAA, NAIA. All NCAA Division III. *Intercollegiate sports:* crew W, cross-country running W, soccer W, swimming and diving W, tennis W, volleyball W. *Intramural sports:* badminton W, basketball W, soccer W, softball W, tennis W, volleyball W.

Standardized Tests *Required:* SAT or ACT (for admission). *Recommended:* SAT Subject Tests (for admission).

Costs (2013–14) *Comprehensive fee:* $54,119 includes full-time tuition ($40,210), mandatory fees ($1284), and room and board ($12,625). Full-time tuition and fees vary according to course load. Part-time tuition: $6702 per course. Part-time tuition and fees vary according to course load. *Required fees:* $1284 per year part-time. *College room only:* $6495. Room and board charges vary according to board plan and housing facility. *Payment plan:* installment. *Waivers:* employees or children of employees.

Financial Aid Of all full-time matriculated undergraduates who enrolled in 2011, 792 applied for aid, 748 were judged to have need, 123 had their need fully met. In 2011, 105 non-need-based awards were made. *Average percent of need met:* 78%. *Average financial aid package:* $34,160. *Average need-based loan:* $7568. *Average need-based gift aid:* $19,420. *Average non-need-based aid:* $15,464. *Average indebtedness upon graduation:* $27,342.

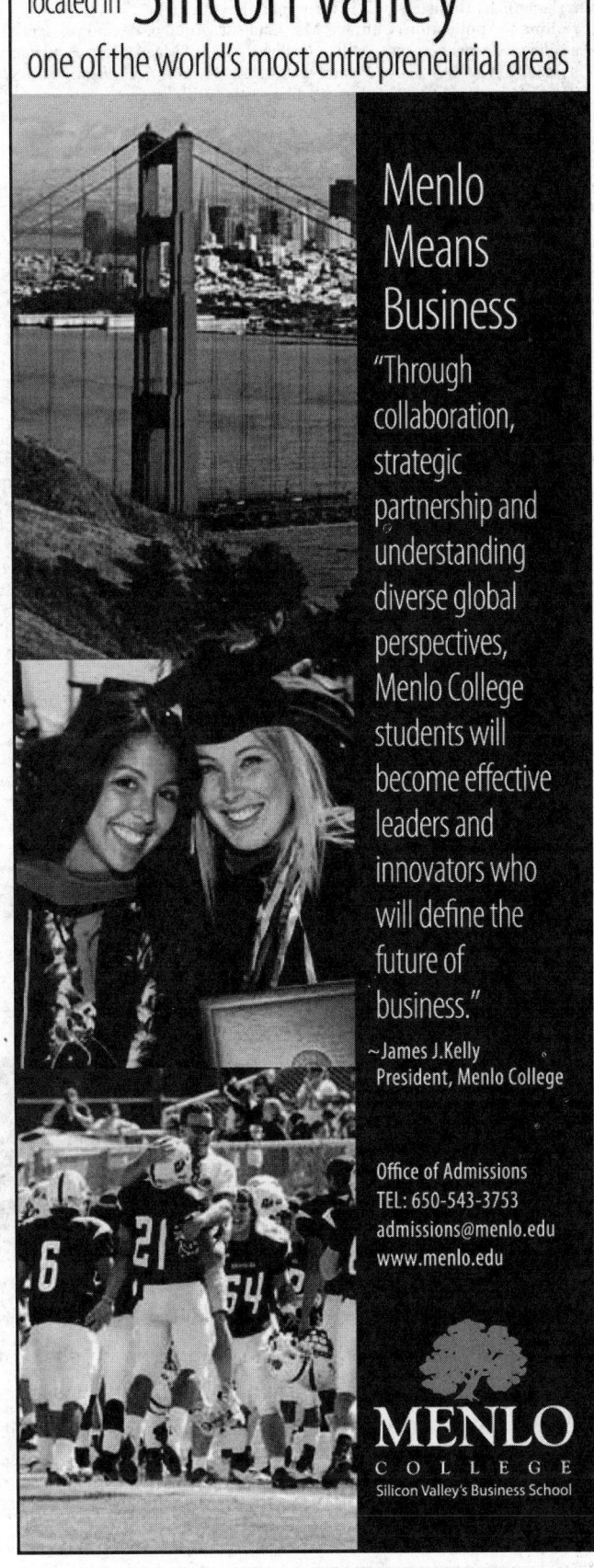

Applying *Options:* electronic application, early action, deferred entrance. *Application fee:* $50. *Required:* high school transcript, 2 letters of recommendation, essay or graded paper. *Recommended:* interview. *Application deadlines:* 2/1 (freshmen), 3/1 (transfers), 11/15 (early action). *Notification:* 3/30 (freshmen), 4/1 (transfers), 12/1 (early action).

Freshman Application Contact Ms. Giulietta Aquino, Vice President of Enrollment Management, Mills College, 5000 MacArthur Boulevard, Oakland, CA 94613-1301. *Phone:* 510-430-2135. *Toll-free phone:* 800-87-MILLS. *Fax:* 510-430-3314. *E-mail:* admission@mills.edu. *Website:* http://www.mills.edu/.

See below for display ad and page 1394 for the College Close-Up.

Mount St. Mary's College
Los Angeles, California

- **Independent Roman Catholic** comprehensive, founded 1925
- **Urban** 49-acre campus with easy access to Los Angeles
- **Endowment** $97.7 million
- **Coed, primarily women** 2,458 undergraduate students, 78% full-time, 93% women, 7% men
- **Moderately difficult** entrance level, 71% of applicants were admitted

Undergraduates 1,919 full-time, 539 part-time. Students come from 18 states and territories; 7 other countries; 2% are from out of state; 8% Black or African American, non-Hispanic/Latino; 55% Hispanic/Latino; 17% Asian, non-Hispanic/Latino; 0.8% Native Hawaiian or other Pacific Islander, non-Hispanic/Latino; 0.5% American Indian or Alaska Native, non-Hispanic/Latino; 3% Two or more races, non-Hispanic/Latino; 5% Race/ethnicity unknown; 0.5% international; 4% transferred in; 20% live on campus. *Retention:* 79% of full-time freshmen returned.

Freshmen *Admission:* 2,244 applied, 1,598 admitted, 535 enrolled. *Average high school GPA:* 3.35. *Test scores:* SAT critical reading scores over 500: 30%; SAT math scores over 500: 32%; SAT writing scores over 500: 36%; ACT scores over 18: 58%; SAT critical reading scores over 600: 4%; SAT math scores over 600: 6%; SAT writing scores over 600: 6%; ACT scores over 24: 8%; SAT math scores over 700: 1%.

Faculty *Total:* 347, 29% full-time, 45% with terminal degrees. *Student/faculty ratio:* 13:1.

Academics *Calendar:* semesters. *Degrees:* associate, bachelor's, master's, doctoral, and post-master's certificates. *Special study options:* academic remediation for entering students, accelerated degree program, advanced placement credit, distance learning, double majors, English as a second language, freshman honors college, honors programs, independent study, internships, off-campus study, part-time degree program, services for LD students, student-designed majors, study abroad, summer session for credit.

Computers on Campus 170 computers/terminals are available on campus for general student use. Students can access the following: campus intranet, computer help desk, free student e-mail accounts, online (class) grades, online (class) registration, online (class) schedules. Campuswide network is available. 100% of college-owned or -operated housing units are wired for high-speed Internet access. Wireless service is available via entire campus.

Student Life *Housing options:* men-only, women-only. Campus housing is university owned. Freshman applicants given priority for college housing. *Activities and organizations:* drama/theater group, student-run newspaper, choral group, Na Pua O Ka Aina, Pangkat Pilipino, Alpha Tau Delta, California Nursing Student Association, Mount Movement. *Campus security:* 24-hour emergency response devices and patrols, late-night transport/escort service, controlled dormitory access. *Student services:* health clinic, personal/psychological counseling, women's center.

Athletics *Intramural sports:* basketball M/W, soccer M/W, softball M/W, swimming and diving M/W, tennis M/W, volleyball M/W.

Standardized Tests *Required:* SAT or ACT (for admission).

Costs (2013–14) *Comprehensive fee:* $44,382 includes full-time tuition ($32,882), mandatory fees ($970), and room and board ($10,530). Full-time tuition and fees vary according to course load, degree level, and program. Part-time tuition: $1370 per unit. Part-time tuition and fees vary according to course load, degree level, and program. *College room only:* $6318. Room and board charges vary according to board plan and housing facility. *Payment plan:* installment. *Waivers:* employees or children of employees.

Financial Aid Of all full-time matriculated undergraduates who enrolled in 2011, 1,825 applied for aid, 1,768 were judged to have need, 44 had their need fully met. In 2011, 45 non-need-based awards were made. *Average percent of need met:* 69%. *Average financial aid package:* $27,635. *Average need-based loan:* $3829. *Average need-based gift aid:* $12,341. *Average non-need-based aid:* $11,911. *Average indebtedness upon graduation:* $34,998.

Applying *Options:* electronic application, early action. *Application fee:* $50. *Required:* essay or personal statement, high school transcript, minimum 2.5 GPA, 1 letter of recommendation. *Recommended:* 2 letters of recommendation, interview. *Application deadlines:* 2/15 (freshmen), 3/15 (transfers), 12/1 (early action). *Notification:* continuous (freshmen), continuous (transfers), 1/1 (early action).

Freshman Application Contact Yvonne Berumen, Director of Admissions, Mount St. Mary's College, 12001 Chalon Road, Los Angeles, CA 90049-1599. *Phone:* 310-954-4250. *Toll-free phone:* 800-999-9893. *Fax:* 310-954-4259. *E-mail:* admissions@msmc.la.edu. *Website:* http://www.msmc.la.edu/.

Mt. Sierra College
Monrovia, California

Freshman Application Contact Mt. Sierra College, 101 East Huntington Drive, Monrovia, CA 91016. *Phone:* 888-486-9818. *Toll-free phone:* 888-828-8000.
Website: http://www.mtsierra.edu/.

Musicians Institute
Hollywood, California

- **Proprietary** 4-year, founded 1976
- **Urban** campus
- **Coed**
- **Minimally difficult** entrance level

Faculty *Student/faculty ratio:* 10:1.
Academics *Calendar:* quarters. *Degrees:* certificates, diplomas, associate, and bachelor's.
Student Life *Campus security:* 24-hour emergency response devices and patrols.
Standardized Tests *Required for some:* SAT or ACT (for admission).
Costs (2012–13) *Tuition:* $24,720 full-time. Full-time tuition and fees vary according to course load, degree level, and program. Part-time tuition and fees vary according to course load and degree level. *Required fees:* $5700 full-time.
Financial Aid *Of all full-time matriculated undergraduates who enrolled in 2002,* 520 applied for aid, 465 were judged to have need. *Average percent of need met:* 40. *Average financial aid package:* $6100. *Average need-based loan:* $3100. *Average indebtedness upon graduation:* $14,000.
Applying *Options:* electronic application, deferred entrance. *Application fee:* $100. *Required:* high school transcript, 1 letter of recommendation. *Required for some:* essay or personal statement, 2 letters of recommendation.
Freshman Application Contact Musicians Institute, 1655 North McCadden Place, Hollywood, CA 90028. *Phone:* 323-860-4345. *Toll-free phone:* 800-255-PLAY.
Website: http://www.mi.edu/.

The National Hispanic University
San Jose, California

Director of Admissions Ms. Pamela Bustillo, Director of Office of Admissions/Registrar, The National Hispanic University, 14271 Story Road, San Jose, CA 95127-3823. *Phone:* 408-273-2772. *E-mail:* chernandez@nhu.edu.
Website: http://www.nhu.edu/.

National University
La Jolla, California

- **Independent** comprehensive, founded 1971, part of National University System
- **Urban** campus
- **Endowment** $403.0 million
- **Coed** 9,482 undergraduate students, 55% full-time, 58% women, 42% men
- **Minimally difficult** entrance level, 100% of applicants were admitted

Undergraduates 5,248 full-time, 4,234 part-time. Students come from 51 states and territories; 43 other countries; 9% are from out of state; 11% Black or African American, non-Hispanic/Latino; 25% Hispanic/Latino; 10% Asian, non-Hispanic/Latino; 2% Native Hawaiian or other Pacific Islander, non-Hispanic/Latino; 0.8% American Indian or Alaska Native, non-Hispanic/Latino; 4% Two or more races, non-Hispanic/Latino; 7% Race/ethnicity unknown; 1% international; 53% transferred in. *Retention:* 58% of full-time freshmen returned.
Freshmen *Admission:* 1,659 applied, 1,659 admitted, 893 enrolled.
Faculty *Total:* 2,756, 9% full-time, 29% with terminal degrees. *Student/faculty ratio:* 11:1.
Academics *Calendar:* continuous. *Degrees:* certificates, associate, bachelor's, master's, doctoral, and postbachelor's certificates. *Special study options:* accelerated degree program, adult/continuing education programs, advanced placement credit, distance learning, double majors, English as a second language, independent study, internships, off-campus study, part-time degree pro-

gram, services for LD students, summer session for credit. *ROTC:* Army (c), Air Force (c).
Computers on Campus 2,800 computers/terminals are available on campus for general student use. Students can access the following: computer help desk, online (class) grades, online (class) registration, online (class) schedules. Campuswide network is available. Wireless service is available via entire campus.
Student Life *Housing:* college housing not available. *Activities and organizations:* student-run television station. *Campus security:* 24-hour emergency response devices and patrols, late-night transport/escort service.
Costs (2013–14) *Tuition:* $14,670 full-time, $326 per quarter hour part-time. Full-time tuition and fees vary according to location and program. Part-time tuition and fees vary according to location and program. *Waivers:* employees or children of employees.
Financial Aid Of all full-time matriculated undergraduates who enrolled in 2010, 5,852 applied for aid, 5,765 were judged to have need, 23 had their need fully met. *Average percent of need met:* 86%. *Average financial aid package:* $7867. *Average need-based loan:* $7912. *Average need-based gift aid:* $4462.
Applying *Options:* electronic application, deferred entrance. *Application fee:* $60. *Required:* high school transcript, minimum 2.0 GPA, interview. *Required for some:* essay or personal statement, TEAS Exam for BSN Students. *Application deadlines:* rolling (freshmen), rolling (transfers). *Notification:* continuous (freshmen), continuous (transfers).
Freshman Application Contact National University, 11255 North Torrey Pines Road, La Jolla, CA 92037-1011. *Phone:* 858-628-8648 Ext. 7701. *Toll-free phone:* 800-NAT-UNIV.
Website: http://www.nu.edu/.

New Charter University
San Francisco, California

Freshman Application Contact Ms. Tammy J. Kassner, Director of Admissions, New Charter University, 2919 John Hawkins Parkway, Birmingham, AL 35244. *Phone:* 205-871-9288 Ext. 107. *Toll-free phone:* 888-639-1388. *Fax:* 800-871-9294. *E-mail:* admissions@aju.edu.
Website: http://www.new.edu/.

NewSchool of Architecture & Design
San Diego, California

Freshman Application Contact Ms. Lexi Rogers, Director of Admissions, NewSchool of Architecture & Design, 1249 F Street, San Diego, CA 92101-6634. *Phone:* 619-235-4100 Ext. 106. *Toll-free phone:* 800-490-7081.
Website: http://www.newschoolarch.edu/.

New York Film Academy
Los Angeles, California

Freshman Application Contact Admissions Office, New York Film Academy, 3801 Barham Boulevard, Los Angeles, CA 90068. *Phone:* 818-733-2600. *Fax:* 818-733-4074. *E-mail:* studios@nyfa.edu.
Website: http://www.nyfa.com/.

Northwestern Polytechnic University
Fremont, California

Freshman Application Contact Mr. Michael Tang, Admission Officer, Northwestern Polytechnic University, 47671 Westinghouse Drive, Fremont, CA 94539. *Phone:* 510-592-9688 Ext. 15. *Fax:* 510-657-8975. *E-mail:* admission@npu.edu.
Website: http://www.npu.edu/.

Notre Dame de Namur University
Belmont, California

- **Independent Roman Catholic** comprehensive, founded 1851
- **Suburban** 50-acre campus with easy access to San Francisco
- **Endowment** $12.1 million
- **Coed** 1,183 undergraduate students, 68% full-time, 66% women, 34% men
- **Moderately difficult** entrance level, 75% of applicants were admitted

Undergraduates 802 full-time, 381 part-time. Students come from 30 states and territories; 29 other countries; 7% are from out of state; 7% Black or African American, non-Hispanic/Latino; 30% Hispanic/Latino; 11% Asian, non-Hispanic/Latino; 3% Native Hawaiian or other Pacific Islander, non-Hispanic/Latino; 0.6% American Indian or Alaska Native, non-Hispanic/Latino; 4% Two or more races, non-Hispanic/Latino; 14% Race/ethnicity unknown; 3%

international; 16% transferred in; 39% live on campus. *Retention:* 81% of full-time freshmen returned.

Freshmen *Admission:* 2,209 applied, 1,652 admitted, 182 enrolled. *Average high school GPA:* 3.11. *Test scores:* SAT critical reading scores over 500: 34%; SAT math scores over 500: 43%; SAT writing scores over 500: 41%; ACT scores over 18: 80%; SAT critical reading scores over 600: 9%; SAT math scores over 600: 11%; SAT writing scores over 600: 8%; ACT scores over 24: 20%; SAT critical reading scores over 700: 1%; SAT math scores over 700: 1%; SAT writing scores over 700: 1%; ACT scores over 30: 2%.

Faculty *Total:* 226, 26% full-time, 54% with terminal degrees. *Student/faculty ratio:* 12:1.

Academics *Calendar:* semesters. *Degrees:* bachelor's, master's, doctoral, and postbachelor's certificates. *Special study options:* academic remediation for entering students, accelerated degree program, adult/continuing education programs, advanced placement credit, cooperative education, double majors, English as a second language, independent study, internships, off-campus study, part-time degree program, services for LD students, student-designed majors, study abroad, summer session for credit. *ROTC:* Air Force (c).

Computers on Campus 80 computers/terminals and 100 ports are available on campus for general student use. Students can access the following: campus intranet, computer help desk, free student e-mail accounts, online (class) grades, online (class) registration, online (class) schedules. Campuswide network is available. Wireless service is available via classrooms, computer centers, computer labs, dorm rooms, learning centers, libraries, student centers.

Student Life *Housing:* on-campus residence required through sophomore year. *Options:* coed. Campus housing is university owned. Freshman campus housing is guaranteed. *Activities and organizations:* drama/theater group, student-run newspaper, choral group, Associated Students of Notre Dame de Namur University, BizCom, Rotaract, Students for Sustainability, International Club. *Campus security:* 24-hour emergency response devices and patrols, late-night transport/escort service, controlled dormitory access. *Student services:* health clinic, personal/psychological counseling.

Athletics Member NCAA. All Division II. *Intercollegiate sports:* basketball M(s)/W(s), cross-country running M(s)/W(s), golf M(s), lacrosse M(s), soccer M(s)/W(s), softball W(s), tennis W(s), volleyball W(s).

Standardized Tests *Required:* SAT or ACT (for admission).

Costs (2013–14) *Comprehensive fee:* $43,358 includes full-time tuition ($30,806), mandatory fees ($400), and room and board ($12,152). Full-time tuition and fees vary according to degree level and program. Part-time tuition: $994 per unit. Part-time tuition and fees vary according to degree level and program. *College room only:* $7878. Room and board charges vary according to board plan and housing facility. *Payment plan:* installment. *Waivers:* senior citizens and employees or children of employees.

Financial Aid Of all full-time matriculated undergraduates who enrolled in 2012, 761 applied for aid, 723 were judged to have need, 29 had their need fully met. 167 Federal Work-Study jobs (averaging $1991). In 2012, 35 non-need-based awards were made. *Average percent of need met:* 53%. *Average financial aid package:* $22,173. *Average need-based loan:* $4767. *Average need-based gift aid:* $18,050. *Average non-need-based aid:* $7189. *Average indebtedness upon graduation:* $31,915.

Applying *Options:* electronic application, early admission, early action, deferred entrance. *Application fee:* $50. *Required:* essay or personal statement, high school transcript, audition is required for music programs. *Required for some:* interview. *Application deadlines:* rolling (freshmen), rolling (transfers). *Notification:* continuous (freshmen), continuous (transfers).

Freshman Application Contact Notre Dame de Namur University, 1500 Ralston Avenue, Belmont, CA 94002-1908. *Phone:* 650-508-3600. *Toll-free phone:* 800-263-0545.

Website: http://www.ndnu.edu/.

Occidental College

Los Angeles, California

- **Independent** comprehensive, founded 1887
- **Urban** 120-acre campus
- **Endowment** $342.4 million
- **Coed**
- **Very difficult** entrance level

Faculty *Student/faculty ratio:* 10:1.

Academics *Calendar:* semesters. *Degrees:* diplomas, bachelor's, and master's.

Student Life *Campus security:* 24-hour emergency response devices and patrols, late-night transport/escort service, controlled dormitory access.

Athletics Member NCAA. All Division III.

Standardized Tests *Required:* SAT or ACT (for admission). *Recommended:* SAT Subject Tests (for admission).

Costs (2012–13) *Comprehensive fee:* $56,990 includes full-time tuition ($43,490), mandatory fees ($1050), and room and board ($12,450). Part-time

tuition: $1810 per credit. Part-time tuition and fees vary according to course load. *College room only:* $7080. Room and board charges vary according to board plan and housing facility.

Financial Aid Of all full-time matriculated undergraduates who enrolled in 2011, 1,386 applied for aid, 1,200 were judged to have need, 1,196 had their need fully met. 601 Federal Work-Study jobs (averaging $1477). 251 state and other part-time jobs (averaging $3254). *In 2011,* 360 non-need-based awards were made. *Average percent of need met:* 100. *Average financial aid package:* $39,160. *Average need-based loan:* $6145. *Average need-based gift aid:* $32,146. *Average non-need-based aid:* $10,619. *Average indebtedness upon graduation:* $28,723. *Financial aid deadline:* 2/1.

Applying *Options:* electronic application, early admission, early decision, deferred entrance. *Application fee:* $60. *Required:* essay or personal statement, high school transcript, 2 letters of recommendation, a statement describing structure and mission for home schoolers. *Recommended:* interview.

Freshman Application Contact Ms. Sally Stone Richmond, Director of Admission, Occidental College, 1600 Campus Road, Los Angeles, CA 90041. *Phone:* 323-259-2700. *Toll-free phone:* 800-825-5262. *Fax:* 323-341-4875. *E-mail:* admission@oxy.edu.

Website: http://www.oxy.edu/.

Otis College of Art and Design

Los Angeles, California

- **Independent** comprehensive, founded 1918
- **Urban** 5-acre campus
- **Coed** 1,105 undergraduate students, 98% full-time, 66% women, 34% men
- **Moderately difficult** entrance level, 55% of applicants were admitted

Undergraduates 1,085 full-time, 20 part-time. Students come from 26 states and territories; 15 other countries; 19% are from out of state; 4% Black or African American, non-Hispanic/Latino; 14% Hispanic/Latino; 33% Asian, non-Hispanic/Latino; 0.4% Native Hawaiian or other Pacific Islander, non-Hispanic/Latino; 0.4% American Indian or Alaska Native, non-Hispanic/Latino; 4% Two or more races, non-Hispanic/Latino; 6% Race/ethnicity unknown; 17% international; 7% transferred in; 9% live on campus. *Retention:* 77% of full-time freshmen returned.

Freshmen *Admission:* 1,493 applied, 820 admitted, 183 enrolled. *Average high school GPA:* 3.2. *Test scores:* SAT critical reading scores over 500: 52%; SAT math scores over 500: 60%; ACT scores over 18: 88%; SAT critical reading scores over 600: 14%; SAT math scores over 600: 25%; ACT scores over 24: 29%; SAT critical reading scores over 700: 2%; SAT math scores over 700: 5%.

Faculty *Total:* 544, 10% full-time, 22% with terminal degrees. *Student/faculty ratio:* 5:1.

Academics *Calendar:* semesters. *Degrees:* bachelor's and master's. *Special study options:* academic remediation for entering students, adult/continuing education programs, advanced placement credit, cooperative education, double majors, freshman honors college, honors programs, independent study, internships, off-campus study, services for LD students, student-designed majors, study abroad, summer session for credit.

Computers on Campus 400 computers/terminals are available on campus for general student use. Students can access the following: campus intranet, computer help desk, free student e-mail accounts, online (class) grades, online (class) registration, online (class) schedules. Campuswide network is available. Wireless service is available via entire campus.

Student Life *Housing options:* Campus housing is provided by a third party. Freshman applicants given priority for college housing. *Activities and organizations:* Student Government Association, international students organization, Otis Students in Service (OASIS), Literary Magazine Club, Campus Crusade. *Campus security:* 24-hour patrols. *Student services:* personal/psychological counseling.

Athletics *Intramural sports:* skiing (downhill) W, soccer M.

Standardized Tests *Required:* SAT or ACT (for admission).

Financial Aid Of all full-time matriculated undergraduates who enrolled in 2012, 803 applied for aid, 770 were judged to have need, 30 had their need fully met. 150 Federal Work-Study jobs (averaging $661). 4 state and other part-time jobs (averaging $309). In 2012, 158 non-need-based awards were made. *Average percent of need met:* 52%. *Average financial aid package:* $21,771. *Average need-based loan:* $4788. *Average need-based gift aid:* $16,717. *Average non-need-based aid:* $10,243. *Average indebtedness upon graduation:* $41,842.

Applying *Options:* electronic application, early admission. *Application fee:* $50. *Required:* essay or personal statement, high school transcript, minimum 2.5 GPA, portfolio. *Recommended:* interview. *Application deadlines:* rolling (freshmen), rolling (transfers). *Notification:* continuous (freshmen), continuous (transfers).

Freshman Application Contact Otis College of Art and Design, 9045 Lincoln Boulevard, Los Angeles, CA 90045-9785. *Phone:* 310-665-6820. *Toll-free phone:* 800-527-OTIS.
Website: http://www.otis.edu/.

Pacific Oaks College

Pasadena, California

Application Contact Ms. Augusta Pickens, Office of Admissions, Pacific Oaks College, 5 Westmoreland Place, Pasadena, CA 91103. *Phone:* 626-397-1349. *Toll-free phone:* 877-314-2380. *Fax:* 626-666-1220. *E-mail:* admissions@pacificoaks.edu.
Website: http://www.pacificoaks.edu/.

Pacific States University

Los Angeles, California

- **Independent** comprehensive, founded 1928
- **Urban** 1-acre campus
- **Coed** 19 undergraduate students, 100% full-time, 37% women, 63% men
- **Noncompetitive** entrance level

Undergraduates 19 full-time. Students come from 1 other state; 6 other countries; 16% Asian, non-Hispanic/Latino; 79% international; 21% transferred in. *Retention:* 90% of full-time freshmen returned.
Freshmen *Admission:* 1 enrolled.
Faculty *Total:* 34, 21% full-time, 35% with terminal degrees. *Student/faculty ratio:* 5:1.
Academics *Calendar:* quarters. *Degrees:* bachelor's, master's, doctoral, and postbachelor's certificates. *Special study options:* academic remediation for entering students, accelerated degree program, adult/continuing education programs, distance learning, double majors, English as a second language, independent study.
Computers on Campus 50 computers/terminals are available on campus for general student use. Students can access the following: online (class) schedules. Campuswide network is available. 90% of college-owned or -operated housing units are wired for high-speed Internet access. Wireless service is available via classrooms, computer labs, dorm rooms, libraries, student centers.
Student Life *Housing options:* coed. Campus housing is university owned. *Campus security:* patrols by trained security personnel during campus hours.
Standardized Tests *Required for some:* TOEFL or IELTS. *Recommended:* SAT or ACT (for admission).
Costs (2013–14) *Tuition:* $14,055 full-time. Full-time tuition and fees vary according to course load, degree level, and program. Part-time tuition and fees vary according to course load, degree level, and program. No tuition increase for student's term of enrollment. *Required fees:* $540 full-time. *Room only:* $7200. Room and board charges vary according to housing facility. *Payment plan:* installment. *Waivers:* employees or children of employees.
Applying *Options:* electronic application, deferred entrance. *Application fee:* $100. *Required:* high school transcript, minimum 2.5 GPA, proof of English proficiency (i.e. TOEFL, IBT, IELTS). *Recommended:* essay or personal statement. *Application deadlines:* rolling (freshmen), rolling (out-of-state freshmen), rolling (transfers). *Notification:* continuous (freshmen), continuous (out-of-state freshmen), continuous (transfers).
Freshman Application Contact Mr. Maawiya Ayeva, Admission officer, Pacific States University, 3450 Wilshire Bjoulevard, #500, Los Angeles, CA 90010. *Phone:* 323-731-2383 Ext. 202. *Toll-free phone:* 888-200-0383. *Fax:* 323-731-7276. *E-mail:* admissions@psuca.edu.
Website: http://www.psuca.edu/.

Pacific Union College

Angwin, California

- **Independent Seventh-day Adventist** comprehensive, founded 1882
- **Rural** 200-acre campus with easy access to San Francisco Bay Area
- **Coed** 1,564 undergraduate students, 87% full-time, 55% women, 45% men
- **Moderately difficult** entrance level, 47% of applicants were admitted

Undergraduates 1,364 full-time, 200 part-time. 18% are from out of state; 7% Black or African American, non-Hispanic/Latino; 23% Hispanic/Latino; 18% Asian, non-Hispanic/Latino; 2% Native Hawaiian or other Pacific Islander, non-Hispanic/Latino; 1% American Indian or Alaska Native, non-Hispanic/Latino; 5% Two or more races, non-Hispanic/Latino; 11% Race/ethnicity unknown; 3% international; 7% transferred in; 71% live on campus. *Retention:* 78% of full-time freshmen returned.
Freshmen *Admission:* 2,105 applied, 995 admitted, 292 enrolled. *Test scores:* SAT critical reading scores over 500: 53%; SAT math scores over 500: 51%; SAT writing scores over 500: 51%; ACT scores over 18: 74%; SAT critical reading scores over 600: 22%; SAT math scores over 600: 21%; SAT writing scores over 600: 18%; ACT scores over 24: 33%; SAT critical reading scores over 700: 3%; SAT math scores over 700: 3%; SAT writing scores over 700: 5%; ACT scores over 30: 6%.
Faculty *Total:* 139, 66% full-time, 42% with terminal degrees. *Student/faculty ratio:* 13:1.
Academics *Calendar:* quarters. *Degrees:* certificates, associate, bachelor's, and master's. *Special study options:* academic remediation for entering students, adult/continuing education programs, advanced placement credit, cooperative education, double majors, honors programs, independent study, internships, off-campus study, part-time degree program, services for LD students, study abroad, summer session for credit.
Computers on Campus 150 computers/terminals and 1,200 ports are available on campus for general student use. Students can access the following: campus intranet, computer help desk, free student e-mail accounts, online (class) grades, online (class) registration, online (class) schedules, student financial information. Campuswide network is available. 100% of college-owned or -operated housing units are wired for high-speed Internet access. Wireless service is available via computer centers, computer labs, learning centers, libraries, student centers.
Student Life *Housing:* on-campus residence required through senior year. *Options:* men-only, women-only. Campus housing is university owned. *Activities and organizations:* drama/theater group, student-run newspaper, choral group, Student Association, Business Club, Asian Student Association, Korean Adventist Student Association, Student Organization of Latinos. *Campus security:* 24-hour emergency response devices and patrols, late-night transport/escort service. *Student services:* health clinic, personal/psychological counseling, women's center.
Athletics Member NAIA. *Intercollegiate sports:* basketball M/W, cross-country running M/W, soccer M, volleyball W. *Intramural sports:* badminton M/W, baseball M/W, basketball M/W, cross-country running M/W, football M/W, golf M/W, soccer M/W, softball M/W, tennis M/W, volleyball M/W.
Standardized Tests *Required:* SAT or ACT (for admission).
Costs (2013–14) *Comprehensive fee:* $34,335 includes full-time tuition ($26,550), mandatory fees ($300), and room and board ($7485). Full-time tuition and fees vary according to course load. Part-time tuition and fees vary according to course load. No tuition increase for student's term of enrollment. *Payment plan:* installment. *Waivers:* senior citizens and employees or children of employees.
Financial Aid Of all full-time matriculated undergraduates who enrolled in 2012, 1,356 applied for aid, 1,083 were judged to have need, 4 had their need fully met. 201 Federal Work-Study jobs (averaging $1964). In 2012, 285 non-need-based awards were made. *Average percent of need met:* 51%. *Average financial aid package:* $21,314. *Average need-based loan:* $4421. *Average need-based gift aid:* $19,477. *Average non-need-based aid:* $5428. *Average indebtedness upon graduation:* $33,662.
Applying *Options:* electronic application, deferred entrance. *Required:* high school transcript, minimum 2.3 GPA, 3 letters of recommendation. *Application deadlines:* rolling (freshmen), rolling (transfers).
Freshman Application Contact Mr. Craig Philpott, Associate Director, Admissions, Pacific Union College, Enrollment Services, One Angwin Avenue, Angwin, CA 94508. *Phone:* 800-862-7080. *Toll-free phone:* 800-862-7080. *Fax:* 707-965-6671. *E-mail:* enroll@puc.edu.
Website: http://www.puc.edu/.

Patten University

Oakland, California

Freshman Application Contact Ms. Kim Guerra, Director of Admissions, Patten University, 2433 Coolidge Avenue, Oakland, CA 94601-2699. *Phone:* 510-261-8500 Ext. 7763. *Toll-free phone:* 877-4PATTEN. *Fax:* 510-534-4344.
Website: http://www.patten.edu/.

Pepperdine University

Malibu, California

- **Independent** university, founded 1937, affiliated with Church of Christ
- **Suburban** 830-acre campus with easy access to Los Angeles
- **Endowment** $583.3 million
- **Coed** 3,488 undergraduate students, 88% full-time, 57% women, 43% men
- **Very difficult** entrance level, 38% of applicants were admitted

Undergraduates 3,086 full-time, 402 part-time. Students come from 50 states and territories; 50 other countries; 38% are from out of state; 7% Black or African American, non-Hispanic/Latino; 15% Hispanic/Latino; 12% Asian, non-Hispanic/Latino; 0.5% Native Hawaiian or other Pacific Islander, non-Hispanic/Latino; 0.6% American Indian or Alaska Native, non-Hispanic/Latino;

5% Two or more races, non-Hispanic/Latino; 6% Race/ethnicity unknown; 8% international; 2% transferred in; 58% live on campus. *Retention:* 91% of full-time freshmen returned.

Freshmen *Admission:* 8,567 applied, 3,294 admitted, 777 enrolled. *Average high school GPA:* 3.55. *Test scores:* SAT critical reading scores over 500: 94%; SAT math scores over 500: 94%; SAT writing scores over 500: 95%; ACT scores over 18: 99%; SAT critical reading scores over 600: 55%; SAT math scores over 600: 67%; SAT writing scores over 600: 62%; ACT scores over 24: 80%; SAT critical reading scores over 700: 13%; SAT math scores over 700: 21%; SAT writing scores over 700: 18%; ACT scores over 30: 25%.

Faculty *Total:* 707, 54% full-time, 72% with terminal degrees. *Student/faculty ratio:* 13:1.

Academics *Calendar:* semesters. *Degrees:* bachelor's, master's, and doctoral. *Special study options:* adult/continuing education programs, advanced placement credit, double majors, honors programs, independent study, internships, part-time degree program, student-designed majors, study abroad, summer session for credit. *ROTC:* Army (c), Air Force (c). *Unusual degree programs:* 3-2 business administration; engineering with University of Southern California School of Engineering, or Washington University School of Engineering in St. Louis; 5-year BS/MBA program -Pepperdine's Graziadio School of Business and Management offers a program that allows Seaver College business majors to earn their bachelor's and MBA or International MBA degrees in just five years.

Computers on Campus 218 computers/terminals and 139 ports are available on campus for general student use. Students can access the following: campus intranet, computer help desk, free student e-mail accounts, online (class) grades, online (class) registration, online (class) schedules. Campuswide network is available. 100% of college-owned or -operated housing units are wired for high-speed Internet access. Wireless service is available via entire campus.

Student Life *Housing:* on-campus residence required through sophomore year. *Options:* men-only, women-only, disabled students. Campus housing is university owned. Freshman campus housing is guaranteed. *Activities and organizations:* drama/theater group, student-run newspaper, radio and television station, choral group, Latino Student Association, Black Student Union, Panhellenic Council, Interfraternity Council, International Justice Mission, national fraternities, national sororities. *Campus security:* 24-hour emergency response devices and patrols, student patrols, late-night transport/escort service, controlled dormitory access, front gate security, 24-hour security in residence halls, controlled access, crime prevention programs. *Student services:* health clinic, personal/psychological counseling.

Athletics Member NCAA. All Division I. *Intercollegiate sports:* baseball M(s), basketball M(s)/W(s), cheerleading M/W, crew M(c)/W(c), cross-country running M(s)/W(s), field hockey W(c), golf M(s)/W(s), lacrosse M(c), rugby M(c), sailing M(c)/W(c), soccer M(c)/W(s), swimming and diving W(s), tennis M(s)/W(s), volleyball M(s)/W(s), water polo M(s)/W(c). *Intramural sports:* badminton M/W, basketball M/W, cross-country running M/W, football M/W, golf M/W, lacrosse M, soccer M/W, softball M/W, swimming and diving M/W, tennis M/W, volleyball M/W.

Standardized Tests *Required:* SAT or ACT (for admission).

Costs (2012–13) *Comprehensive fee:* $55,372 includes full-time tuition ($42,520), mandatory fees ($252), and room and board ($12,600). Part-time tuition: $1330 per credit hour. *College room only:* $9600. Room and board charges vary according to board plan and housing facility. *Payment plan:* installment. *Waivers:* employees or children of employees.

Financial Aid Of all full-time matriculated undergraduates who enrolled in 2012, 2,416 applied for aid, 1,771 were judged to have need, 488 had their need fully met. In 2012, 460 non-need-based awards were made. *Average percent of need met:* 83%. *Average financial aid package:* $39,417. *Average need-based loan:* $4911. *Average need-based gift aid:* $40,830. *Average non-need-based aid:* $19,161. *Average indebtedness upon graduation:* $30,101.

Applying *Options:* electronic application. *Application fee:* $65. *Required:* essay or personal statement, high school transcript, 2 letters of recommendation. *Application deadlines:* 1/5 (freshmen), 1/5 (out-of-state freshmen), 1/5 (transfers). *Notification:* 4/1 (freshmen), 4/1 (out-of-state freshmen), 4/1 (transfers).

Freshman Application Contact Mrs. Laura Kalinkewicz, Director of Admission, Admission, Enrollment Management, Seaver College, Pepperdine University, 24255 Pacific Coast Highway, Malibu, CA 90263. *Phone:* 310-506-4392. *E-mail:* laura.reisert@pepperdine.edu. *Website:* http://www.pepperdine.edu/.

See below for display ad and page 1436 for the College Close-Up.

Perelandra College
La Mesa, California
- **Independent Christian** comprehensive
- **Suburban** campus with easy access to San Diego
- **Coed**
- **Minimally difficult** entrance level

Faculty *Student/faculty ratio:* 3:1.

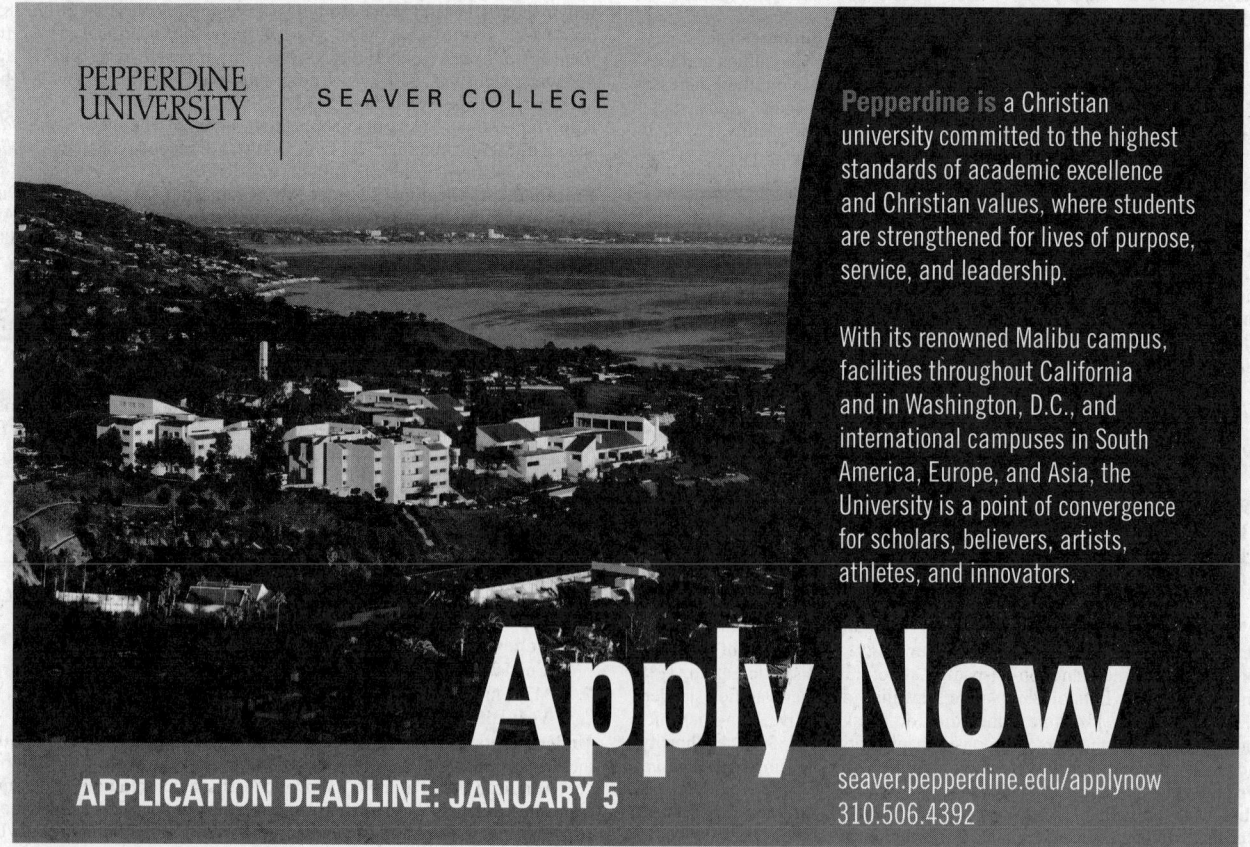

Academics *Degrees:* diplomas, bachelor's, and master's.
Applying *Options:* electronic application. *Application fee:* $50. *Required:* essay or personal statement, minimum 2.5 GPA, 2 letters of recommendation, letter of intent. *Required for some:* high school transcript.
Freshman Application Contact Perelandra College, 8697-C La Mesa Boulevard, PMB 21, La Mesa, CA 91941. *Phone:* 619-335-0441. *Website:* http://www.perelandra.edu/.

Pima Medical Institute
Chula Vista, California

Freshman Application Contact Admissions Office, Pima Medical Institute, 780 Bay Boulevard, Suite 101, Chula Vista, CA 91910. *Phone:* 619-425-3200. *Toll-free phone:* 800-477-PIMA (in-state); 888-477-PIMA (out-of-state). *Website:* http://www.pmi.edu/.

Pitzer College
Claremont, California

- **Independent** 4-year, founded 1963, part of The Claremont Colleges Consortium
- **Suburban** 35-acre campus with easy access to Los Angeles
- **Endowment** $113.7 million
- **Coed** 1,084 undergraduate students, 96% full-time, 61% women, 39% men
- **Very difficult** entrance level, 16% of applicants were admitted

Undergraduates 1,041 full-time, 43 part-time. Students come from 40 states and territories; 17 other countries; 52% are from out of state; 5% Black or African American, non-Hispanic/Latino; 15% Hispanic/Latino; 8% Asian, non-Hispanic/Latino; 0.1% Native Hawaiian or other Pacific Islander, non-Hispanic/Latino; 0.6% American Indian or Alaska Native, non-Hispanic/Latino; 4% Two or more races, non-Hispanic/Latino; 15% Race/ethnicity unknown; 4% international; 1% transferred in; 74% live on campus. *Retention:* 93% of full-time freshmen returned.
Freshmen *Admission:* 4,227 applied, 663 admitted, 273 enrolled. *Average high school GPA:* 3.81. *Test scores:* SAT critical reading scores over 500: 100%; SAT math scores over 500: 99%; SAT critical reading scores over 600: 81%; SAT math scores over 600: 84%; SAT critical reading scores over 700: 33%; SAT math scores over 700: 18%.

Faculty *Total:* 121, 69% full-time, 93% with terminal degrees. *Student/faculty ratio:* 10:1.
Academics *Calendar:* semesters. *Degree:* bachelor's. *Special study options:* adult/continuing education programs, advanced placement credit, cooperative education, double majors, English as a second language, honors programs, independent study, internships, off-campus study, part-time degree program, services for LD students, student-designed majors, study abroad, summer session for credit. *ROTC:* Army (c), Air Force (c). *Unusual degree programs:* 3-2 business administration; public administration, mathematics, psychology with Claremont Graduate University.
Computers on Campus 100 computers/terminals are available on campus for general student use. Students can access the following: campus intranet, computer help desk, free student e-mail accounts, online (class) grades, online (class) registration, online (class) schedules. Campuswide network is available. 100% of college-owned or -operated housing units are wired for high-speed Internet access. Wireless service is available via entire campus.
Student Life *Housing:* on-campus residence required for freshman year. *Options:* coed, women-only, cooperative, disabled students. Campus housing is university owned. Freshman campus housing is guaranteed. *Activities and organizations:* drama/theater group, student-run newspaper, radio station, choral group, Student Senate, The Other Side, Without A Box, Residence Hall Association. *Campus security:* 24-hour emergency response devices and patrols, late-night transport/escort service, controlled dormitory access. *Student services:* health clinic, personal/psychological counseling, women's center.
Athletics Member NCAA. All Division III. *Intercollegiate sports:* baseball M, basketball M/W, cross-country running M/W, football M, golf M, lacrosse W, soccer M/W, softball W, swimming and diving M/W, tennis M/W, track and field M/W, volleyball W, water polo M/W. *Intramural sports:* badminton M/W, baseball M, basketball M/W, fencing M(c)/W(c), football M, lacrosse M(c)/W(c), rugby M(c), sailing M(c)/W(c), skiing (downhill) M(c)/W(c), soccer M/W, softball W, tennis M/W, track and field M/W, ultimate Frisbee M/W, volleyball M(c)/W, water polo M(c)/W(c).
Standardized Tests *Required for some:* SAT or ACT (for admission).
Costs (2012–13) *Comprehensive fee:* $57,266 includes full-time tuition ($43,136), mandatory fees ($266), and room and board ($13,864). Full-time tuition and fees vary according to course load. Part-time tuition: $5392 per course. Part-time tuition and fees vary according to course load. *College room only:* $8028. Room and board charges vary according to board plan. *Payment plans:* installment, deferred payment. *Waivers:* employees or children of employees.

Financial Aid Of all full-time matriculated undergraduates who enrolled in 2011, 491 applied for aid, 422 were judged to have need, 414 had their need fully met. 377 Federal Work-Study jobs (averaging $2486). In 2011, 28 non-need-based awards were made. *Average percent of need met:* 100%. *Average financial aid package:* $38,798. *Average need-based loan:* $4336. *Average need-based gift aid:* $33,775. *Average non-need-based aid:* $4821. *Average indebtedness upon graduation:* $22,568. *Financial aid deadline:* 2/1.

Applying *Options:* electronic application, early decision, deferred entrance. *Application fee:* $60. *Required:* essay or personal statement, high school transcript, minimum 2.0 GPA, 3 letters of recommendation. *Recommended:* interview. *Application deadlines:* 1/1 (freshmen), 4/15 (transfers). *Early decision deadline:* 11/15. *Notification:* 4/1 (freshmen), 5/15 (transfers), 1/1 (early decision).

Freshman Application Contact Mr. Angel Perez, Vice President for Admission and Financial Aid, Pitzer College, 1050 North Mills Avenue, Claremont, CA 91711-6101. *Phone:* 909-621-8129. *Toll-free phone:* 800-748-9371. *Fax:* 909-621-8770. *E-mail:* admission@pitzer.edu. *Website:* http://www.pitzer.edu/.

See previous page for display ad and page 1440 for the College Close-Up.

Platt College
Alhambra, California

Director of Admissions Mr. Detroit Whiteside, Director of Admissions, Platt College, 1000 South Fremont A9W, Alhambra, CA 91803. *Phone:* 323-258-8050. *Toll-free phone:* 888-866-6697 (in-state); 888-80-PLATT (out-of-state). *Website:* http://www.plattcollege.edu/.

Platt College
Ontario, California

Director of Admissions Ms. Jennifer Abandonato, Director of Admissions, Platt College, 3700 Inland Empire Boulevard, Suite 400, Ontario, CA 91764. *Phone:* 909-941-9410. *Toll-free phone:* 888-80-PLATT. *Website:* http://www.plattcollege.edu/.

Platt College San Diego
San Diego, California

Freshman Application Contact Mr. Steve Gallup, Admissions Representative, Platt College San Diego, 6250 El Cajon Boulevard, San Diego, CA 92115-3919. *Phone:* 619-265-0107. *Toll-free phone:* 866-752-8826. *Fax:* 619-265-8655. *E-mail:* sgallup@platt.edu. *Website:* http://www.platt.edu/.

Point Loma Nazarene University
San Diego, California

- **Independent Nazarene** comprehensive, founded 1902
- **Suburban** 93-acre campus with easy access to San Diego
- **Endowment** $35.7 million
- **Coed** 2,415 undergraduate students, 97% full-time, 62% women, 38% men
- **Moderately difficult** entrance level, 56% of applicants were admitted

Undergraduates 2,350 full-time, 65 part-time. 18% are from out of state; 2% Black or African American, non-Hispanic/Latino; 19% Hispanic/Latino; 6% Asian, non-Hispanic/Latino; 0.7% Native Hawaiian or other Pacific Islander, non-Hispanic/Latino; 2% American Indian or Alaska Native, non-Hispanic/Latino; 3% Two or more races, non-Hispanic/Latino; 0.7% Race/ethnicity unknown; 0.4% international; 6% transferred in; 68% live on campus. *Retention:* 83% of full-time freshmen returned.

Freshmen *Admission:* 3,545 applied, 1,983 admitted, 601 enrolled. *Average high school GPA:* 3.78. *Test scores:* SAT critical reading scores over 500: 86%; SAT math scores over 500: 86%; SAT writing scores over 500: 84%; ACT scores over 18: 98%; SAT critical reading scores over 600: 42%; SAT math scores over 600: 44%; SAT writing scores over 600: 37%; ACT scores over 24: 70%; SAT critical reading scores over 700: 7%; SAT math scores over 700: 7%; SAT writing scores over 700: 6%; ACT scores over 30: 10%.

Faculty *Total:* 362, 39% full-time, 37% with terminal degrees. *Student/faculty ratio:* 14:1.

Academics *Calendar:* semesters. *Degrees:* bachelor's, master's, and post-master's certificates. *Special study options:* academic remediation for entering students, advanced placement credit, double majors, honors programs, independent study, internships, off-campus study, part-time degree program, services for LD students, study abroad, summer session for credit. *ROTC:* Army (c), Navy (c), Air Force (c).

Computers on Campus Students can access the following: computer help desk, free student e-mail accounts, online (class) grades, online (class) registration, online (class) schedules. Campuswide network is available. 100% of college-owned or -operated housing units are wired for high-speed Internet access. Wireless service is available via entire campus.

Student Life *Housing:* on-campus residence required through junior year. *Options:* men-only, women-only. Campus housing is university owned. Freshman campus housing is guaranteed. *Activities and organizations:* drama/theater group, student-run newspaper, radio and television station, choral group. *Campus security:* 24-hour patrols, student patrols, late-night transport/escort service. *Student services:* health clinic, personal/psychological counseling, women's center.

Athletics Member NAIA. *Intercollegiate sports:* baseball M(s), basketball M(s)/W(s), cross-country running M(s)/W(s), golf M(s)/W, soccer M(s)/W(s), tennis M(s)/W(s), track and field M(s)/W(s), volleyball W(s). *Intramural sports:* basketball M/W, football M, soccer M/W, volleyball M/W.

Standardized Tests *Required:* SAT or ACT (for admission). *Recommended:* SAT (for admission), ACT (for admission).

Costs (2012–13) *Comprehensive fee:* $39,060 includes full-time tuition ($28,900), mandatory fees ($610), and room and board ($9550). Full-time tuition and fees vary according to course load. Part-time tuition: $1205 per credit hour. Part-time tuition and fees vary according to course load. *College room only:* $5440. Room and board charges vary according to board plan. *Payment plan:* installment. *Waivers:* senior citizens and employees or children of employees.

Financial Aid Of all full-time matriculated undergraduates who enrolled in 2012, 1,925 applied for aid, 1,654 were judged to have need, 279 had their need fully met. In 2012, 334 non-need-based awards were made. *Average percent of need met:* 63%. *Average financial aid package:* $20,225. *Average need-based loan:* $4608. *Average need-based gift aid:* $15,237. *Average non-need-based aid:* $8049. *Average indebtedness upon graduation:* $31,851.

Applying *Options:* electronic application, early action. *Application fee:* $50. *Required:* essay or personal statement, high school transcript, minimum 2.8 GPA, 2 letters of recommendation. *Application deadlines:* 2/15 (freshmen), 11/15 (early action). *Notification:* 4/1 (freshmen), 12/21 (early action).

Freshman Application Contact Eric Groves, Director of Admissions, Point Loma Nazarene University, 3900 Lomaland Drive, San Diego, CA 92106. *Phone:* 619-849-2273. *Toll-free phone:* 800-733-7770. *Fax:* 619-849-2601. *E-mail:* admissions@pointloma.edu. *Website:* http://www.pointloma.edu/.

Pomona College
Claremont, California

- **Independent** 4-year, founded 1887
- **Suburban** 140-acre campus with easy access to Los Angeles
- **Endowment** $1.7 billion
- **Coed** 1,607 undergraduate students, 99% full-time, 52% women, 48% men
- **Most difficult** entrance level, 13% of applicants were admitted

Undergraduates 1,589 full-time, 18 part-time. Students come from 49 states and territories; 24 other countries; 66% are from out of state; 6% Black or African American, non-Hispanic/Latino; 14% Hispanic/Latino; 11% Asian, non-Hispanic/Latino; 0.1% American Indian or Alaska Native, non-Hispanic/Latino; 6% Two or more races, non-Hispanic/Latino; 11% Race/ethnicity unknown; 7% international; 0.7% transferred in; 98% live on campus. *Retention:* 97% of full-time freshmen returned.

Freshmen *Admission:* 7,456 applied, 966 admitted, 399 enrolled. *Test scores:* SAT critical reading scores over 500: 100%; SAT math scores over 500: 100%; SAT writing scores over 500: 100%; ACT scores over 18: 100%; SAT critical reading scores over 600: 95%; SAT math scores over 600: 94%; SAT writing scores over 600: 95%; ACT scores over 24: 99%; SAT critical reading scores over 700: 65%; SAT math scores over 700: 69%; SAT writing scores over 700: 70%; ACT scores over 30: 74%.

Faculty *Total:* 241, 80% full-time, 93% with terminal degrees. *Student/faculty ratio:* 8:1.

Academics *Calendar:* semesters. *Degree:* bachelor's. *Special study options:* advanced placement credit, double majors, independent study, internships, off-campus study, services for LD students, student-designed majors, study abroad. *ROTC:* Army (c), Air Force (c). *Unusual degree programs:* 3-2 engineering with California Institute of Technology, Washington University in St. Louis.

Computers on Campus 180 computers/terminals are available on campus for general student use. Students can access the following: computer help desk, free student e-mail accounts, online (class) grades, online (class) registration, online (class) schedules. Campuswide network is available. 100% of college-owned or -operated housing units are wired for high-speed Internet access. Wireless service is available via entire campus.

Student Life *Housing:* on-campus residence required for freshman year. *Options:* coed. Campus housing is university owned. Freshman campus housing is guaranteed. *Activities and organizations:* drama/theater group, student-run newspaper, radio and television station, choral group, student government, music/choral organizations, service organizations, intramural sports, outdoor activities club. *Campus security:* 24-hour emergency response devices and patrols, late-night transport/escort service, controlled dormitory access. *Student services:* health clinic, personal/psychological counseling, women's center.

Athletics Member NCAA. All Division III. *Intercollegiate sports:* baseball M, basketball M/W, cross-country running M/W, football M, golf M/W, lacrosse W, soccer M/W, softball W, swimming and diving M/W, tennis M/W, track and field M/W, ultimate Frisbee M(c)/W(c), volleyball M(c)/W, water polo M/W. *Intramural sports:* badminton M(c)/W(c), basketball M/W, crew W(c), cross-country running M/W, equestrian sports M(c)/W(c), fencing M/W, field hockey M(c)/W(c), football M, golf M/W, lacrosse M(c), racquetball M/W, rock climbing M/W, skiing (cross-country) M(c)/W(c), skiing (downhill) M(c)/W(c), soccer M/W, softball M/W, squash M/W, swimming and diving M/W, tennis M/W, track and field M/W, ultimate Frisbee M, volleyball M/W, water polo M/W.

Standardized Tests *Required:* SAT and SAT Subject Tests or ACT (for admission).

Costs (2012–13) *Comprehensive fee:* $54,964 includes full-time tuition ($41,120), mandatory fees ($318), and room and board ($13,526). *Room and board:* Room and board charges vary according to board plan. *Payment plan:* installment. *Waivers:* employees or children of employees.

Financial Aid Of all full-time matriculated undergraduates who enrolled in 2011, 1,078 applied for aid, 844 were judged to have need, 844 had their need fully met. 175 Federal Work-Study jobs (averaging $1369). 949 state and other part-time jobs (averaging $1188). *Average percent of need met:* 100%. *Average financial aid package:* $39,506. *Average need-based gift aid:* $37,611. *Average indebtedness upon graduation:* $15,714. *Financial aid deadline:* 2/1.

Applying *Options:* electronic application, early admission, early decision, deferred entrance. *Application fee:* $70. *Required:* essay or personal statement, high school transcript, 3 letters of recommendation. *Recommended:* interview, Supplemental forms for visual and performing arts, athletics, and science research are available. *Application deadlines:* 1/1 (freshmen), 3/15 (transfers). *Early decision deadline:* 11/1 (for plan 1), 1/1 (for plan 2). *Notification:* 4/1 (freshmen), 5/15 (transfers), 12/15 (early decision plan 1), 2/15 (early decision plan 2).

Freshman Application Contact Mr. C. Seth Allen, Vice President for Enrollment and Dean of Admissions and Financial Aid, Pomona College, 333 North College Way, Claremont, CA 91711. *Phone:* 909-621-8134. *Fax:* 909-621-8952. *E-mail:* admissions@pomona.edu. *Website:* http://www.pomona.edu/.

Saint Mary's College of California
Moraga, California

- **Independent Roman Catholic** upper-level, founded 1863
- **Suburban** 420-acre campus with easy access to San Francisco
- **Endowment** $124.2 million
- **Coed** 3,035 undergraduate students, 92% full-time, 60% women, 40% men
- **Moderately difficult** entrance level, 66% of applicants were admitted

Undergraduates 2,781 full-time, 254 part-time. Students come from 40 states and territories; 22 other countries; 10% are from out of state; 4% Black or African American, non-Hispanic/Latino; 25% Hispanic/Latino; 10% Asian, non-Hispanic/Latino; 0.6% Native Hawaiian or other Pacific Islander, non-Hispanic/Latino; 0.5% American Indian or Alaska Native, non-Hispanic/Latino; 5% Two or more races, non-Hispanic/Latino; 5% Race/ethnicity unknown; 2% international; 7% transferred in; 53% live on campus.

Freshmen *Admission:* 5,256 applied, 3,448 admitted.

Faculty *Total:* 458, 42% full-time, 100% with terminal degrees. *Student/faculty ratio:* 13:1.

Academics *Calendar:* 4-1-4. *Degrees:* bachelor's, master's, and doctoral. *Special study options:* adult/continuing education programs, advanced placement credit, double majors, honors programs, independent study, internships, off-campus study, part-time degree program, services for LD students, student-designed majors, study abroad, summer session for credit. *ROTC:* Army (c), Air Force (c). *Unusual degree programs:* 3-2 engineering with Washington University in St. Louis, University of Southern California in Los Angeles.

Computers on Campus 244 computers/terminals and 1,800 ports are available on campus for general student use. Students can access the following: campus intranet, computer help desk, free student e-mail accounts, online (class) grades, online (class) registration, online (class) schedules, student accounts. Campuswide network is available. 100% of college-owned or -operated housing units are wired for high-speed Internet access. Wireless service is available via classrooms, computer centers, computer labs, learning centers, libraries, student centers.

Student Life *Housing options:* coed, men-only, women-only, disabled students. Campus housing is university owned. Freshman campus housing is guaranteed. *Activities and organizations:* drama/theater group, student-run newspaper, radio and television station, choral group, Gael Force, Student Alumni Association, LASA-Latin American Student Association-Black Student Union, Inter-Varsity Christian Fellowship, Asian Pacific America Student Association. *Campus security:* 24-hour emergency response devices and patrols, late-night transport/escort service. *Student services:* health clinic, personal/psychological counseling, women's center.

Athletics Member NCAA. All Division I. *Intercollegiate sports:* baseball M(s), basketball M(s)/W(s), cheerleading W, crew M(c)/W(s), cross-country running M(s)/W(s), golf M(s), lacrosse M(c)/W(s), rugby M(c), soccer M(s)/W(s), softball W(s), tennis M(s)/W(s), track and field M(s)/W(s)(c), volleyball M(c)/W(s), water polo M(c)/W(c). *Intramural sports:* badminton M/W, basketball M/W, football M/W, skiing (cross-country) M/W, skiing (downhill) M/W, soccer M(c)/W(c), softball M/W, tennis M(c)/W(c), volleyball M/W(c).

Standardized Tests *Required:* SAT or ACT (for admission).

Costs (2013–14) *Comprehensive fee:* $53,550 includes full-time tuition ($39,740), mandatory fees ($150), and room and board ($13,660). Part-time tuition: $4972 per course. Part-time tuition and fees vary according to course load and program. *College room only:* $7450. Room and board charges vary according to board plan and housing facility. *Payment plans:* tuition prepayment, installment. *Waivers:* employees or children of employees.

Financial Aid Of all full-time matriculated undergraduates who enrolled in 2012, 2,248 applied for aid, 2,123 were judged to have need, 150 had their need fully met. 342 Federal Work-Study jobs (averaging $1970). In 2012, 223 non-need-based awards were made. *Average percent of need met:* 60%. *Average financial aid package:* $25,521. *Average need-based loan:* $4662. *Average need-based gift aid:* $21,919. *Average non-need-based aid:* $16,868. *Average indebtedness upon graduation:* $31,828.

Applying *Options:* electronic application, early action, deferred entrance. *Application fee:* $55. *Application deadline:* 7/1 (transfers). *Notification:* continuous (transfers).

Application Contact Mr. Michael McKeon, Dean of Admissions, Saint Mary's College of California, PO Box 4800, Moraga, CA 94575-4800. *Phone:* 925-631-4224. *Toll-free phone:* 800-800-4SMC. *Fax:* 925-376-7193. *E-mail:* smcadmit@stmarys-ca.edu. *Website:* http://www.stmarys-ca.edu/.

Samuel Merritt University
Oakland, California

- **Independent** upper-level, founded 1909
- **Urban** 1-acre campus with easy access to San Francisco
- **Endowment** $38.2 million
- **Coed, primarily women** 584 undergraduate students, 88% full-time, 82% women, 18% men
- **Moderately difficult** entrance level

Undergraduates 513 full-time, 71 part-time. Students come from 2 states and territories; 1 other country; 0.8% are from out of state; 4% Black or African American, non-Hispanic/Latino; 13% Hispanic/Latino; 29% Asian, non-Hispanic/Latino; 2% Native Hawaiian or other Pacific Islander, non-Hispanic/Latino; 0.5% American Indian or Alaska Native, non-Hispanic/Latino; 6% Two or more races, non-Hispanic/Latino; 3% Race/ethnicity unknown; 41% transferred in.

Faculty *Total:* 271, 40% full-time, 39% with terminal degrees. *Student/faculty ratio:* 10:1.

Academics *Calendar:* trimesters. *Degrees:* bachelor's, master's, and doctoral (bachelor's degree offered jointly with Saint Mary's College of California). *Special study options:* academic remediation for entering students, accelerated degree program, advanced placement credit, cooperative education, distance learning, independent study, internships, off-campus study, part-time degree program, services for LD students, summer session for credit. *ROTC:* Army (c), Air Force (c).

Computers on Campus 102 computers/terminals are available on campus for general student use. Students can access the following: campus intranet, computer help desk, free student e-mail accounts, online (class) grades, online (class) registration, online (class) schedules. Campuswide network is available. Wireless service is available via entire campus.

Student Life *Housing:* college housing not available. *Activities and organizations:* student-run newspaper, Student Body Association, Green Team, International Health Club, Multicultural Group. *Campus security:* 24-hour emergency response devices and patrols, late-night transport/escort service, controlled dormitory access, 24-hour controlled access. *Student services:* health clinic, personal/psychological counseling.

Costs (2013–14) *Tuition:* $39,456 full-time, $1663 per unit part-time. Full-time tuition and fees vary according to degree level and program. Part-time tuition and fees vary according to degree level and program. *Payment plan:* installment.

Financial Aid Of all full-time matriculated undergraduates who enrolled in 2009, 495 applied for aid, 448 were judged to have need, 20 had their need fully met. 120 Federal Work-Study jobs (averaging $1583). *Average percent of need met:* 69%. *Average financial aid package:* $32,000. *Average need-based loan:* $10,457. *Average need-based gift aid:* $20,000.

Applying *Options:* deferred entrance. *Application fee:* $50. *Application deadline:* 3/1 (transfers). *Notification:* continuous (transfers).

Application Contact Samuel Merritt University, 3100 Telegraph Avenue, Oakland, CA 94609-3108. *Phone:* 510-869-6610. *Toll-free phone:* 800-607-MERRITT.

Website: http://www.samuelmerritt.edu/.

San Diego Christian College

El Cajon, California

- **Independent nondenominational** 4-year, founded 1970
- **Suburban** 55-acre campus with easy access to San Diego
- **Endowment** $532,546
- **Coed** 739 undergraduate students, 88% full-time, 50% women, 50% men
- **Moderately difficult** entrance level, 43% of applicants were admitted

Undergraduates 652 full-time, 87 part-time. Students come from 44 states and territories; 5 other countries; 31% are from out of state; 15% Black or African American, non-Hispanic/Latino; 15% Hispanic/Latino; 2% Asian, non-Hispanic/Latino; 1% Native Hawaiian or other Pacific Islander, non-Hispanic/Latino; 1% American Indian or Alaska Native, non-Hispanic/Latino; 4% Two or more races, non-Hispanic/Latino; 22% Race/ethnicity unknown; 0.5% international; 30% transferred in; 42% live on campus. *Retention:* 66% of full-time freshmen returned.

Freshmen *Admission:* 596 applied, 254 admitted, 101 enrolled. *Average high school GPA:* 3.19. *Test scores:* SAT critical reading scores over 500: 37%; SAT math scores over 500: 41%; SAT writing scores over 500: 35%; ACT scores over 18: 96%; SAT critical reading scores over 600: 7%; SAT math scores over 600: 8%; SAT writing scores over 600: 5%; ACT scores over 24: 24%; ACT scores over 30: 4%.

Faculty *Total:* 94, 17% full-time, 16% with terminal degrees. *Student/faculty ratio:* 17:1.

Academics *Calendar:* semesters. *Degrees:* associate, bachelor's, and postbachelor's certificates. *Special study options:* academic remediation for entering students, accelerated degree program, adult/continuing education programs, advanced placement credit, distance learning, double majors, English as a second language, honors programs, independent study, internships, off-campus study, part-time degree program, services for LD students, student-designed majors, study abroad, summer session for credit. *ROTC:* Army (c), Air Force (c).

Computers on Campus 65 computers/terminals and 200 ports are available on campus for general student use. Students can access the following: computer help desk, free student e-mail accounts, online (class) grades, online (class) registration, online (class) schedules. Campuswide network is available. 100% of college-owned or -operated housing units are wired for high-speed Internet access. Wireless service is available via entire campus.

Student Life *Housing:* on-campus residence required through sophomore year. *Options:* men-only, women-only. Campus housing is leased by the school. Freshman campus housing is guaranteed. *Activities and organizations:* drama/theater group, choral group, ASB—Student Government, Service & Community Engagement, Ministry Teams, Flight team, SALSA. *Campus security:* 24-hour emergency response devices and patrols. *Student services:* health clinic, personal/psychological counseling.

Athletics Member NAIA. *Intercollegiate sports:* baseball M(s), basketball M(s)/W(s), cross-country running M(s)/W(s), soccer M(s)/W(s), volleyball W(s). *Intramural sports:* basketball M/W, soccer M/W, softball M/W, ultimate Frisbee M/W, volleyball M/W.

Standardized Tests *Required for some:* SAT or ACT (for admission).

Costs (2013–14) *Comprehensive fee:* $35,166 includes full-time tuition ($24,540), mandatory fees ($1348), and room and board ($9278). Full-time tuition and fees vary according to class time, course load, location, and program. Part-time tuition and fees vary according to class time, course load, and program. *Room and board:* Room and board charges vary according to location. *Payment plan:* installment. *Waivers:* employees or children of employees.

Financial Aid Of all full-time matriculated undergraduates who enrolled in 2012, 627 applied for aid, 547 were judged to have need, 64 had their need fully met. 28 Federal Work-Study jobs (averaging $2211). 12 state and other part-time jobs (averaging $2233). In 2012, 9 non-need-based awards were made. *Average percent of need met:* 82%. *Average financial aid package:* $14,346. *Average need-based loan:* $4229. *Average need-based gift aid:*

$7114. *Average non-need-based aid:* $3296. *Average indebtedness upon graduation:* $23,868. *Financial aid deadline:* 7/15.

Applying *Options:* electronic application, deferred entrance. *Application fee:* $25. *Required:* essay or personal statement, high school transcript, 2 letters of recommendation. *Recommended:* minimum 2.8 GPA, interview. *Application deadlines:* 7/1 (freshmen), 7/1 (transfers). *Notification:* continuous (freshmen), continuous (transfers).

Freshman Application Contact Candice Del Giudice, Director of Admissions, San Diego Christian College, 2100 Greenfield Drive, El Cajon, CA 92019-1157. *Phone:* 619-201-8741. *Toll-free phone:* 800-676-2242. *Fax:* 619-201-8749. *E-mail:* cdelgiudice@sdcc.edu.

Website: http://www.sdcc.edu/.

San Diego State University

San Diego, California

- **State-supported** university, founded 1897, part of California State University System
- **Urban** 300-acre campus with easy access to San Diego
- **Endowment** $136.4 million
- **Coed** 26,624 undergraduate students, 88% full-time, 56% women, 44% men
- **Moderately difficult** entrance level, 31% of applicants were admitted

Undergraduates 23,473 full-time, 3,151 part-time. Students come from 53 states and territories; 66 other countries; 7% are from out of state; 4% Black or African American, non-Hispanic/Latino; 30% Hispanic/Latino; 7% Asian, non-Hispanic/Latino; 7% Native Hawaiian or other Pacific Islander, non-Hispanic/Latino; 0.3% American Indian or Alaska Native, non-Hispanic/Latino; 5% Two or more races, non-Hispanic/Latino; 6% Race/ethnicity unknown; 4% international; 15% transferred in; 14% live on campus. *Retention:* 89% of full-time freshmen returned.

Freshmen *Admission:* 51,364 applied, 16,092 admitted, 4,240 enrolled. *Average high school GPA:* 3.6. *Test scores:* SAT critical reading scores over 500: 68%; SAT math scores over 500: 75%; ACT scores over 18: 94%; SAT critical reading scores over 600: 21%; SAT math scores over 600: 32%; ACT scores over 24: 53%; SAT critical reading scores over 700: 2%; SAT math scores over 700: 4%; ACT scores over 30: 5%.

Faculty *Total:* 1,370, 54% full-time, 51% with terminal degrees. *Student/faculty ratio:* 23:1.

Academics *Calendar:* semesters. *Degrees:* bachelor's, master's, doctoral, and postbachelor's certificates. *Special study options:* academic remediation for entering students, advanced placement credit, distance learning, double majors, English as a second language, external degree program, honors programs, independent study, internships, off-campus study, part-time degree program, services for LD students, study abroad, summer session for credit. *ROTC:* Army (b), Navy (b), Air Force (b). *Unusual degree programs:* 3-2 business administration; engineering.

Computers on Campus 400 computers/terminals are available on campus for general student use. Students can access the following: computer help desk, free student e-mail accounts, online (class) grades, online (class) registration, online (class) schedules, Blackboard. Campuswide network is available. 100% of college-owned or -operated housing units are wired for high-speed Internet access. Wireless service is available via entire campus.

Student Life *Housing:* on-campus residence required for freshman year. *Options:* coed. Campus housing is university owned. Freshman applicants given priority for college housing. *Activities and organizations:* drama/theater group, student-run newspaper, radio and television station, choral group, marching band, AB Samahan, Asian Pacific Student Alliance, Enviro-Business Society, M.E.Ch.A de SDSU, Social fraternities and Sororities, including both general and culturally based organizations, national fraternities, national sororities. *Campus security:* 24-hour emergency response devices and patrols, student patrols, late-night transport/escort service. *Student services:* health clinic, personal/psychological counseling, women's center.

Athletics Member NCAA. All Division I. *Intercollegiate sports:* baseball M(s), basketball M(s)/W(s), crew W(s), cross-country running W(s), football M(s), golf M(s)/W(s), soccer M(s)/W(s), softball W(s), swimming and diving W(s), tennis M(s)/W(s), track and field W(s), volleyball W(s), water polo W(s). *Intramural sports:* basketball M/W, bowling M/W, cheerleading W(c), crew M(c), football M/W, golf M/W, ice hockey M(c), lacrosse M(c)/W(c), racquetball M/W, rugby M(c), skiing (downhill) M(c)/W(c), soccer M(c)/W(c), softball M/W, swimming and diving M/W, tennis M/W, ultimate Frisbee M(c)/W(c), volleyball M(c)/W(c), water polo M(c)/W(c).

Standardized Tests *Required:* SAT or ACT (for admission).

Costs (2013–14) *Tuition:* state resident $0 full-time; nonresident $11,160 full-time, $372 per unit part-time. Full-time tuition and fees vary according to degree level, location, and program. Part-time tuition and fees vary according to course load, degree level, location, and program. *Required fees:* $6766 full-time, $2140 per term part-time. *Room and board:* $13,812. Room and board charges vary according to board plan and housing facility. *Payment plan:* installment. *Waivers:* employees or children of employees.

Financial Aid Of all full-time matriculated undergraduates who enrolled in 2012, 17,000 applied for aid, 14,200 were judged to have need, 3,100 had their need fully met. 537 Federal Work-Study jobs (averaging $2010). In 2012, 1000 non-need-based awards were made. *Average percent of need met:* 71%. *Average financial aid package:* $11,000. *Average need-based loan:* $3900. *Average need-based gift aid:* $10,100. *Average non-need-based aid:* $1800. *Average indebtedness upon graduation:* $17,600. *Financial aid deadline:* 3/2.

Applying *Options:* electronic application, early action. *Application fee:* $55. *Required:* high school transcript, minimum 2.0 GPA, 2.5 GPA for non-California residents. *Application deadlines:* 11/30 (freshmen), 11/30 (transfers). *Notification:* 3/1 (freshmen), 3/1 (transfers).

Freshman Application Contact Ms. Beverly Arata, Director of Admissions, San Diego State University, 5500 Campanile Drive, San Diego, CA 92182-0771. *Phone:* 619-594-6336. *E-mail:* admissions@sdsu.edu. *Website:* http://www.sdsu.edu/.

San Diego State University–Imperial Valley Campus

Calexico, California

Freshman Application Contact Aracely Bororquez, Admissions Department, San Diego State University–Imperial Valley Campus, 720 Heber Avenue, Calexico, CA 92231. *Phone:* 760-768-5506. *Fax:* 760-768-5589. *E-mail:* transfer@mail.sdsu.edu. *Website:* http://www.ivcampus.sdsu.edu/.

San Francisco Art Institute

San Francisco, California

- **Independent** comprehensive, founded 1871
- **Urban** 3-acre campus with easy access to San Francisco
- **Endowment** $8.2 million
- **Coed** 453 undergraduate students, 92% full-time, 59% women, 41% men
- **Moderately difficult** entrance level, 63% of applicants were admitted

Undergraduates 418 full-time, 35 part-time. Students come from 14 other countries; 2% Black or African American, non-Hispanic/Latino; 14% Hispanic/Latino; 3% Asian, non-Hispanic/Latino; 0.5% Native Hawaiian or other Pacific Islander, non-Hispanic/Latino; 1% American Indian or Alaska Native, non-Hispanic/Latino; 10% Two or more races, non-Hispanic/Latino; 8% Race/ethnicity unknown; 9% international; 22% transferred in; 29% live on campus. *Retention:* 63% of full-time freshmen returned.

Freshmen *Admission:* 511 applied, 321 admitted, 82 enrolled. *Average high school GPA:* 3.03. *Test scores:* SAT critical reading scores over 500: 69%; SAT math scores over 500: 41%; SAT writing scores over 500: 63%; ACT scores over 18: 93%; SAT critical reading scores over 600: 22%; SAT math scores over 600: 19%; SAT writing scores over 600: 16%; ACT scores over 24: 50%; SAT critical reading scores over 700: 6%; SAT math scores over 700: 3%.

Faculty *Total:* 130, 15% full-time, 71% with terminal degrees. *Student/faculty ratio:* 11:1.

Academics *Calendar:* semesters. *Degrees:* bachelor's, master's, and postbachelor's certificates. *Special study options:* academic remediation for entering students, adult/continuing education programs, advanced placement credit, double majors, English as a second language, external degree program, honors programs, independent study, internships, off-campus study, part-time degree program, services for LD students, study abroad, summer session for credit.

Computers on Campus 70 computers/terminals are available on campus for general student use. Students can access the following: computer help desk, free student e-mail accounts, online (class) grades, online (class) registration, online (class) schedules. Campuswide network is available. 100% of college-owned or -operated housing units are wired for high-speed Internet access. Wireless service is available via entire campus.

Student Life *Housing:* on-campus residence required for freshman year. *Options:* coed. Campus housing is leased by the school and is provided by a third party. Freshman applicants given priority for college housing. *Activities and organizations:* student-run newspaper, radio station, Docuphoto, The Tower 102.5 fm, Film Salon, Indigenous Arts Coalition, Chinese Student Association. *Campus security:* 24-hour patrols, security cameras. *Student services:* personal/psychological counseling.

Standardized Tests *Recommended:* SAT or ACT (for admission).

Costs (2012–13) *Comprehensive fee:* $50,462 includes full-time tuition ($35,748), mandatory fees ($870), and room and board ($13,844). Full-time tuition and fees vary according to degree level. Part-time tuition: $1566 per credit. Part-time tuition and fees vary according to degree level. *College room only:* $9974. Room and board charges vary according to housing facility. *Payment plan:* installment. *Waivers:* employees or children of employees.

Financial Aid Of all full-time matriculated undergraduates who enrolled in 2011, 161 applied for aid, 161 were judged to have need. In 2011, 54 non-need-based awards were made. *Average percent of need met:* 47%. *Average financial aid package:* $16,990. *Average need-based loan:* $3720. *Average need-based gift aid:* $7120. *Average non-need-based aid:* $5673. *Average indebtedness upon graduation:* $29,541. *Financial aid deadline:* 5/31.

Applying *Options:* electronic application, deferred entrance. *Application fee:* $65. *Required:* essay or personal statement, high school transcript, portfolio. *Recommended:* minimum 2.0 GPA, 2 letters of recommendation, interview. *Application deadlines:* rolling (freshmen), rolling (out-of-state freshmen), rolling (transfers). *Notification:* continuous (freshmen), continuous (out-of-state freshmen), continuous (transfers).

Freshman Application Contact Office of Admissions, San Francisco Art Institute, 800 Chestnut Street, San Francisco, CA 94133. *Phone:* 415-749-4500. *Toll-free phone:* 800-345-SFAI. *Fax:* 415-749-4592. *E-mail:* admissions@sfai.edu. *Website:* http://www.sfai.edu/.

San Francisco Conservatory of Music

San Francisco, California

- **Independent** comprehensive, founded 1917
- **Urban** 2-acre campus
- **Endowment** $35.2 million
- **Coed** 186 undergraduate students, 98% full-time, 48% women, 52% men

Undergraduates 182 full-time, 4 part-time. Students come from 26 states and territories; 18 other countries; 36% are from out of state; 5% Black or African American, non-Hispanic/Latino; 5% Hispanic/Latino; 8% Asian, non-Hispanic/Latino; 1% American Indian or Alaska Native, non-Hispanic/Latino; 12% Two or more races, non-Hispanic/Latino; 5% Race/ethnicity unknown; 22% international; 8% transferred in; 42% live on campus. *Retention:* 82% of full-time freshmen returned.

Freshmen *Admission:* 37 enrolled. *Average high school GPA:* 3.4.

Faculty *Total:* 121, 26% full-time, 24% with terminal degrees. *Student/faculty ratio:* 7:1.

Academics *Calendar:* semesters. *Degrees:* diplomas, bachelor's, master's, and post-master's certificates. *Special study options:* academic remediation for entering students, advanced placement credit, independent study, internships, part-time degree program.

Computers on Campus 15 computers/terminals and 100 ports are available on campus for general student use. Students can access the following: campus intranet, computer help desk, free student e-mail accounts. Campuswide network is available. Wireless service is available via classrooms, computer centers, computer labs, libraries, student centers.

Student Life *Housing options:* coed. Campus housing is leased by the school and is provided by a third party. *Activities and organizations:* drama/theater group, choral group, Yoga Group, Meditation Group, Conservatory Ball Planning Committee. *Campus security:* 24-hour emergency response devices and patrols, controlled dormitory access, resident assistant on-call for residential hall residents. *Student services:* personal/psychological counseling.

Standardized Tests *Recommended:* SAT or ACT (for admission).

Costs (2012–13) *Tuition:* $37,600 full-time, $1660 per credit part-time. Part-time tuition and fees vary according to course load and program. *Required fees:* $540 full-time, $270 per term part-time. *Payment plan:* installment. *Waivers:* employees or children of employees.

Financial Aid Of all full-time matriculated undergraduates who enrolled in 2009, 127 applied for aid, 112 were judged to have need, 16 had their need fully met. In 2009, 69 non-need-based awards were made. *Average percent of need met:* 66%. *Average financial aid package:* $22,952. *Average need-based loan:* $6127. *Average need-based gift aid:* $17,133. *Average non-need-based aid:* $12,389. *Average indebtedness upon graduation:* $15,454.

Applying *Required:* essay or personal statement, high school transcript, minimum 2.5 GPA, 2 letters of recommendation, audition, pre-screen recording in select areas.

Freshman Application Contact Ms. Melissa Cocco-Mitten, San Francisco Conservatory of Music, 50 Oak Street, San Francisco, CA 94102. *Phone:* 800-899-7326. *Fax:* 415-503-6231. *E-mail:* admit@sfcm.edu. *Website:* http://www.sfcm.edu/.

San Francisco State University
San Francisco, California

- **State-supported** university, founded 1899, part of California State University System
- **Urban** 142-acre campus
- **Endowment** $49.0 million
- **Coed** 26,449 undergraduate students, 85% full-time, 57% women, 43% men
- **Moderately difficult** entrance level, 64% of applicants were admitted

Undergraduates 22,510 full-time, 3,939 part-time. 0.8% are from out of state; 5% Black or African American, non-Hispanic/Latino; 22% Hispanic/Latino; 28% Asian, non-Hispanic/Latino; 0.6% Native Hawaiian or other Pacific Islander, non-Hispanic/Latino; 0.2% American Indian or Alaska Native, non-Hispanic/Latino; 5% Two or more races, non-Hispanic/Latino; 6% Race/ethnicity unknown; 7% international; 13% transferred in; 12% live on campus. *Retention:* 80% of full-time freshmen returned.
Freshmen *Admission:* 31,439 applied, 20,070 admitted, 3,807 enrolled. *Average high school GPA:* 3.14. *Test scores:* SAT critical reading scores over 500: 49%; SAT math scores over 500: 54%; ACT scores over 18: 86%; SAT critical reading scores over 600: 13%; SAT math scores over 600: 15%; ACT scores over 24: 32%; SAT critical reading scores over 700: 1%; SAT math scores over 700: 1%; ACT scores over 30: 2%.
Faculty *Total:* 1,712, 45% full-time, 48% with terminal degrees. *Student/faculty ratio:* 25:1.
Academics *Calendar:* semesters. *Degrees:* certificates, bachelor's, master's, doctoral, post-master's, and postbachelor's certificates. *Special study options:* academic remediation for entering students, adult/continuing education programs, advanced placement credit, cooperative education, distance learning, double majors, English as a second language, honors programs, independent study, internships, off-campus study, part-time degree program, services for LD students, student-designed majors, study abroad, summer session for credit. *ROTC:* Army (c), Air Force (c).
Computers on Campus 2,800 computers/terminals and 800 ports are available on campus for general student use. Students can access the following: campus intranet, computer help desk, free student e-mail accounts, online (class) grades, online (class) registration, online (class) schedules. Campuswide network is available. 100% of college-owned or -operated housing units are wired for high-speed Internet access. Wireless service is available via entire campus.
Student Life *Housing options:* coed, disabled students. Campus housing is university owned. Freshman applicants given priority for college housing. *Activities and organizations:* drama/theater group, student-run newspaper, radio and television station, choral group, International Education Exchange Council, Graduate Students Association, Accounting Students Organization, Improv Nation @ San Francisco State University, Asian Student Union, national fraternities, national sororities. *Campus security:* 24-hour emergency response devices and patrols, student patrols, late-night transport/escort service, controlled dormitory access. *Student services:* health clinic, personal/psychological counseling, women's center, legal services.
Athletics Member NCAA. All Division II. *Intercollegiate sports:* baseball M(s), basketball M(s)/W(s), cross-country running M(s)/W(s), soccer M(s)/W(s), softball W(s), track and field W(s), volleyball W(s), wrestling M(s). *Intramural sports:* basketball M/W, cheerleading M(c)/W(c), rugby M(c)/W(c), soccer M/W, tennis M/W, volleyball M/W, water polo M(c)/W(c).
Standardized Tests *Required:* SAT or ACT (for admission).
Costs (2012–13) *Tuition:* state resident $5472 full-time; nonresident $16,632 full-time, $372 per unit part-time. Full-time tuition and fees vary according to course load. Part-time tuition and fees vary according to course load. *Required fees:* $968 full-time. *Room and board:* $11,576. Room and board charges vary according to board plan and housing facility. *Payment plan:* installment. *Waivers:* employees or children of employees.
Financial Aid Of all full-time matriculated undergraduates who enrolled in 2012, 15,846 applied for aid, 14,249 were judged to have need, 832 had their need fully met. In 2012, 73 non-need-based awards were made. *Average percent of need met:* 60%. *Average financial aid package:* $11,652. *Average need-based loan:* $3243. *Average need-based gift aid:* $9436. *Average non-need-based aid:* $2526. *Average indebtedness upon graduation:* $20,493.
Applying *Options:* electronic application. *Application fee:* $55. *Required:* high school transcript. *Application deadlines:* 11/30 (freshmen), 8/31 (transfers). *Notification:* 10/1 (freshmen).
Freshman Application Contact Admissions Officer, San Francisco State University, 1600 Holloway Avenue, San Francisco, CA 94132-1722. *Phone:* 415-338-1113. *Fax:* 415-338-7196. *E-mail:* ugadmit@sfsu.edu. *Website:* http://www.sfsu.edu/.

San Jose State University
San Jose, California

- **State-supported** comprehensive, founded 1857, part of California State University System
- **Urban** 152-acre campus
- **Coed** 25,157 undergraduate students, 81% full-time, 50% women, 50% men
- **Very difficult** entrance level, 63% of applicants were admitted

Undergraduates 20,320 full-time, 4,837 part-time. 4% Black or African American, non-Hispanic/Latino; 23% Hispanic/Latino; 35% Asian, non-Hispanic/Latino; 0.9% Native Hawaiian or other Pacific Islander, non-Hispanic/Latino; 0.2% American Indian or Alaska Native, non-Hispanic/Latino; 5% Two or more races, non-Hispanic/Latino; 4% Race/ethnicity unknown; 4% international; 12% transferred in; 14% live on campus. *Retention:* 83% of full-time freshmen returned.
Freshmen *Admission:* 25,155 applied, 15,967 admitted, 3,384 enrolled. *Average high school GPA:* 3.29. *Test scores:* SAT critical reading scores over 500: 52%; SAT math scores over 500: 68%; SAT writing scores over 500: 53%; SAT critical reading scores over 600: 15%; SAT math scores over 600: 28%; SAT writing scores over 600: 13%; SAT critical reading scores over 700: 1%; SAT math scores over 700: 5%; SAT writing scores over 700: 1%.
Faculty *Total:* 1,656, 37% full-time. *Student/faculty ratio:* 27:1.
Academics *Calendar:* semesters. *Degrees:* bachelor's and master's. *Special study options:* academic remediation for entering students, adult/continuing education programs, advanced placement credit, distance learning, double majors, honors programs, independent study, internships, off-campus study, part-time degree program, services for LD students, student-designed majors, study abroad, summer session for credit. *ROTC:* Army (b), Air Force (b).
Computers on Campus Students can access the following: computer help desk, online (class) registration. Campuswide network is available. Wireless service is available via entire campus.
Student Life *Housing options:* coed, men-only, women-only, cooperative, disabled students. *Activities and organizations:* drama/theater group, student-run newspaper, radio and television station, choral group, marching band, national fraternities, national sororities. *Campus security:* 24-hour emergency response devices and patrols, student patrols, late-night transport/escort service. *Student services:* health clinic, personal/psychological counseling, women's center.
Athletics Member NCAA. All Division I except football (Division I-A). *Intercollegiate sports:* badminton M(c)/W(c), baseball M(s), basketball M(s)/W(s), bowling M(c)/W(c), cheerleading M(c)/W(c), cross-country running M(s)/W(s), golf M(s)/W(s), gymnastics W(s), ice hockey M(c)/W(c), rugby M(c), sailing M(c)/W(c), soccer M(s)/W(s), softball W, swimming and diving W(s), tennis W(s), volleyball M(c)/W(s), water polo M(c)/W(c), wrestling M(c)/W(c). *Intramural sports:* archery M(c)/W(c), badminton M/W, baseball M, basketball M/W, bowling M/W, cross-country running M(c)/W(c), fencing M(c)/W(c), field hockey W(c), football M/W, ice hockey M(c), lacrosse M(c)/W(c), racquetball M/W, rugby W(c), soccer M/W, softball M/W, table tennis M(c)/W(c), tennis M/W, track and field M(c)/W(c), volleyball M(c)/W, water polo M/W, wrestling M(c)/W(c).
Standardized Tests *Required for some:* SAT or ACT (for admission).
Costs (2013–14) *Tuition:* state resident $6852 full-time; nonresident $11,160 full-time. *Required fees:* $6852 full-time. *Room and board:* $11,733; room only: $6633.
Financial Aid Of all full-time matriculated undergraduates who enrolled in 2011, 14,829 applied for aid, 13,514 were judged to have need, 7,051 had their need fully met. In 2011, 81 non-need-based awards were made. *Average percent of need met:* 87%. *Average financial aid package:* $16,323. *Average need-based loan:* $3823. *Average need-based gift aid:* $7142. *Average non-need-based aid:* $1948. *Average indebtedness upon graduation:* $16,519. *Financial aid deadline:* 6/15.
Applying *Options:* electronic application. *Application fee:* $55. *Required:* high school transcript. *Application deadlines:* 11/30 (freshmen), 11/30 (transfers). *Notification:* continuous (freshmen), continuous (transfers).
Freshman Application Contact Admissions Office, San Jose State University, One Washington Square, San Jose, CA 95192-0001. *Phone:* 408-283-7500. *Fax:* 408-924-2050. *E-mail:* admissions@sjsu.edu. *Website:* http://www.sjsu.edu/.

Santa Clara University
Santa Clara, California

- **Independent Roman Catholic (Jesuit)** university, founded 1851
- **Suburban** 106-acre campus with easy access to San Francisco, San Jose
- **Endowment** $716.8 million
- **Coed**
- **Moderately difficult** entrance level

Faculty *Student/faculty ratio:* 13:1.

Academics *Calendar:* quarters. *Degrees:* bachelor's, master's, doctoral, post-master's, and postbachelor's certificates.
Student Life *Campus security:* 24-hour emergency response devices and patrols, late-night transport/escort service, controlled dormitory access.
Athletics Member NCAA. All Division I.
Standardized Tests *Required:* SAT or ACT (for admission).
Costs (2012–13) *Comprehensive fee:* $52,848 includes full-time tuition ($40,572) and room and board ($12,276). Part-time tuition: $1127 per unit. Part-time tuition and fees vary according to course load. *Room and board:* Room and board charges vary according to board plan, housing facility, location, and student level.
Financial Aid *Of all full-time matriculated undergraduates who enrolled in 2012,* 3,400 applied for aid, 2,654 were judged to have need, 820 had their need fully met. 407 Federal Work-Study jobs (averaging $3015). *In 2012,* 1408 non-need-based awards were made. *Average percent of need met:* 68. *Average financial aid package:* $27,067. *Average need-based loan:* $4971. *Average need-based gift aid:* $19,985. *Average non-need-based aid:* $12,228. *Average indebtedness upon graduation:* $28,672.
Applying *Options:* electronic application, early decision, early action, deferred entrance. *Application fee:* $55. *Required:* essay or personal statement, high school transcript, 1 letter of recommendation.
Freshman Application Contact Ms. Sandra Hayes, Dean of Undergraduate Admissions, Santa Clara University, 500 El Camino Real, Santa Clara, CA 95053. *Phone:* 408-554-4700. *Fax:* 408-554-5255. *E-mail:* ugadmissions@scu.edu.
Website: http://www.scu.edu/.

School of Urban Missions
Oakland, California

Freshman Application Contact Admissions, School of Urban Missions, 735 105th Avenue, Oakland, CA 94603. *Phone:* 510-567-6174. *Toll-free phone:* 888-567-6174. *Fax:* 510-568-1024.
Website: http://www.sum.edu/.

Scripps College
Claremont, California

- **Independent** 4-year, founded 1926
- **Suburban** 37-acre campus with easy access to Los Angeles
- **Endowment** $258.7 million
- **Women only** 945 undergraduate students, 99% full-time
- **Very difficult** entrance level, 32% of applicants were admitted

Undergraduates 940 full-time, 5 part-time. Students come from 47 states and territories; 19 other countries; 52% are from out of state; 4% Black or African American, non-Hispanic/Latino; 9% Hispanic/Latino; 18% Asian, non-Hispanic/Latino; 0.3% Native Hawaiian or other Pacific Islander, non-Hispanic/Latino; 0.2% American Indian or Alaska Native, non-Hispanic/Latino; 3% Two or more races, non-Hispanic/Latino; 9% Race/ethnicity unknown; 5% international; 1% transferred in; 95% live on campus. *Retention:* 92% of full-time freshmen returned.
Freshmen *Admission:* 2,373 applied, 769 admitted, 235 enrolled. *Average high school GPA:* 4.11. *Test scores:* SAT critical reading scores over 500: 100%; SAT math scores over 500: 100%; SAT writing scores over 500: 100%; ACT scores over 18: 100%; SAT critical reading scores over 600: 90%; SAT math scores over 600: 88%; SAT writing scores over 600: 95%; ACT scores over 24: 100%; SAT critical reading scores over 700: 44%; SAT math scores over 700: 29%; SAT writing scores over 700: 50%; ACT scores over 30: 57%.
Faculty *Total:* 115, 70% full-time, 98% with terminal degrees. *Student/faculty ratio:* 10:1.
Academics *Calendar:* semesters. *Degrees:* bachelor's and postbachelor's certificates. *Special study options:* accelerated degree program, advanced placement credit, double majors, independent study, internships, off-campus study, part-time degree program, student-designed majors, study abroad. *ROTC:* Army (c), Air Force (c). *Unusual degree programs:* 3-2 business administration with Claremont Graduate University; engineering with Stanford University, University of Southern California, Harvey Mudd College, University of California, Berkeley, Washington University in St. Louis, Columbia University, Rensselaer and Boston University; American politics, economics, philosophy, public policy, international studies, or religion with Claremont Graduate University.
Computers on Campus 151 computers/terminals are available on campus for general student use. Students can access the following: campus intranet, computer help desk, free student e-mail accounts, online (class) grades, online (class) registration, online (class) schedules, 2 ports per dorm room. Campus-wide network is available. 100% of college-owned or -operated housing units are wired for high-speed Internet access. Wireless service is available via entire campus.

Student Life *Housing:* on-campus residence required for freshman year. *Options:* women-only, disabled students. Campus housing is university owned. Freshman campus housing is guaranteed. *Activities and organizations:* drama/theater group, student-run newspaper, radio station, choral group, Scripps Associated Students, Asian/Black/Latina clubs, National Organization for Women, Sexual Assault Task Force. *Campus security:* 24-hour emergency response devices and patrols, late-night transport/escort service, controlled dormitory access. *Student services:* health clinic, personal/psychological counseling, women's center.
Athletics Member NCAA. All Division III. *Intercollegiate sports:* badminton W(c), basketball W, cross-country running W, fencing W(c), golf W, lacrosse W, rock climbing W(c), rugby W(c), skiing (downhill) W(c), soccer W, softball W, swimming and diving W, tennis W, track and field W, ultimate Frisbee W(c), volleyball W, water polo W. *Intramural sports:* basketball W, cheerleading W, football W, soccer W, softball W, volleyball W, water polo W.
Standardized Tests *Required:* SAT or ACT (for admission).
Costs (2012–13) *Comprehensive fee:* $57,088 includes full-time tuition ($43,406), mandatory fees ($214), and room and board ($13,468). Full-time tuition and fees vary according to course load. Part-time tuition: $5426 per course. Part-time tuition and fees vary according to course load. *College room only:* $7280. Room and board charges vary according to board plan. *Payment plans:* tuition prepayment, installment. *Waivers:* employees or children of employees.
Financial Aid Of all full-time matriculated undergraduates who enrolled in 2011, 509 applied for aid, 397 were judged to have need, 397 had their need fully met. 307 Federal Work-Study jobs (averaging $1899). 28 state and other part-time jobs (averaging $1899). In 2011, 98 non-need-based awards were made. *Average percent of need met:* 100%. *Average financial aid package:* $36,673. *Average need-based loan:* $3506. *Average need-based gift aid:* $33,988. *Average non-need-based aid:* $22,621. *Average indebtedness upon graduation:* $13,121. *Financial aid deadline:* 5/1.
Applying *Options:* early admission, early decision, deferred entrance. *Application fee:* $60. *Required:* essay or personal statement, high school transcript, interview, graded writing sample. *Recommended:* minimum 3.0 GPA. *Application deadlines:* 1/2 (freshmen), 1/2 (out-of-state freshmen), 4/1 (transfers). *Early decision deadline:* 11/15 (for plan 1), 1/2 (for plan 2). *Notification:* 4/1 (freshmen), 4/1 (out-of-state freshmen), 5/15 (transfers), 12/15 (early decision plan 1), 2/15 (early decision plan 2).
Freshman Application Contact Ms. Laura Stratton, Director of Admission, Scripps College, 1030 Columbia Avenue, Claremont, CA 91711. *Phone:* 909-621-8149. *Toll-free phone:* 800-770-1333. *Fax:* 909-607-7508. *E-mail:* admission@scrippscollege.edu.
Website: http://www.scrippscollege.edu/.

Shasta Bible College
Redding, California

Freshman Application Contact Connie Barton, Registrar, Shasta Bible College, 2951 Goodwater Avenue, Redding, CA 96002. *Phone:* 530-221-4275 Ext. 26. *Toll-free phone:* 800-800-4SBC. *Fax:* 530-221-6929. *E-mail:* registrar@shasta.edu.
Website: http://www.shasta.edu/.

Silicon Valley University
San Jose, California

Freshman Application Contact Admissions Office, Silicon Valley University, 2160 Lundy Avenue, Suite 110, San Jose, CA 95131. *Phone:* 408-435-8989 Ext. 109. *E-mail:* admission-office@svuca.edu.
Website: http://www.svuca.edu/.

Simpson University
Redding, California

- **Independent** comprehensive, founded 1921, affiliated with The Christian and Missionary Alliance
- **Suburban** 100-acre campus
- **Endowment** $5.0 million
- **Coed** 1,033 undergraduate students, 97% full-time, 66% women, 34% men
- **Moderately difficult** entrance level, 62% of applicants were admitted

Undergraduates 1,007 full-time, 26 part-time. Students come from 31 states and territories; 6 other countries; 15% are from out of state; 3% Black or African American, non-Hispanic/Latino; 12% Hispanic/Latino; 6% Asian, non-Hispanic/Latino; 0.6% Native Hawaiian or other Pacific Islander, non-Hispanic/Latino; 2% American Indian or Alaska Native, non-Hispanic/Latino; 0.6% Two or more races, non-Hispanic/Latino; 17% Race/ethnicity unknown;

0.1% international; 12% transferred in; 61% live on campus. *Retention:* 63% of full-time freshmen returned.

Freshmen *Admission:* 544 applied, 337 admitted, 147 enrolled. *Average high school GPA:* 3.45. *Test scores:* SAT critical reading scores over 500: 58%; SAT math scores over 500: 56%; SAT writing scores over 500: 48%; ACT scores over 18: 87%; SAT critical reading scores over 600: 13%; SAT math scores over 600: 16%; SAT writing scores over 600: 11%; ACT scores over 24: 28%; SAT critical reading scores over 700: 1%; SAT math scores over 700: 1%.

Faculty *Total:* 154, 34% full-time, 40% with terminal degrees. *Student/faculty ratio:* 14:1.

Academics *Calendar:* semesters. *Degrees:* certificates, associate, bachelor's, and master's. *Special study options:* academic remediation for entering students, accelerated degree program, adult/continuing education programs, advanced placement credit, distance learning, double majors, honors programs, independent study, internships, off-campus study, part-time degree program, services for LD students, student-designed majors, study abroad, summer session for credit. *ROTC:* Army (b).

Computers on Campus 50 computers/terminals are available on campus for general student use. Students can access the following: campus intranet, computer help desk, free student e-mail accounts, online (class) grades, online (class) registration, online (class) schedules. Campuswide network is available. 100% of college-owned or -operated housing units are wired for high-speed Internet access. Wireless service is available via entire campus.

Student Life *Housing:* on-campus residence required through junior year. *Options:* men-only, women-only, disabled students. Campus housing is university owned. Freshman campus housing is guaranteed. *Activities and organizations:* drama/theater group, student-run newspaper, choral group, Summer Missions Trips, Social Action Committee, Asian Fellowship, Vida, Psychology Club. *Campus security:* 24-hour emergency response devices and patrols, student patrols, late-night transport/escort service, controlled dormitory access, emergency whistle program and monthly campus safety meetings. *Student services:* health clinic, personal/psychological counseling.

Athletics Member NAIA, NCCAA. *Intercollegiate sports:* baseball M(s), basketball M(s)/W(s), cross-country running M(s)/W(s), golf M(s)/W(s), soccer M(s)/W(s), softball W(s), volleyball W(s), wrestling M(s). *Intramural sports:* basketball M/W, volleyball M(c).

Standardized Tests *Required:* SAT or ACT (for admission). *Recommended:* SAT Subject Tests (for admission).

Costs (2013–14) *Comprehensive fee:* $30,800 includes full-time tuition ($23,300) and room and board ($7500). Full-time tuition and fees vary according to course load. Part-time tuition: $975 per credit. Part-time tuition and fees vary according to course load. *College room only:* $4200. Room and board charges vary according to board plan. *Payment plan:* deferred payment. *Waivers:* employees or children of employees.

Financial Aid Of all full-time matriculated undergraduates who enrolled in 2012, 728 applied for aid, 673 were judged to have need, 20 had their need fully met. 184 Federal Work-Study jobs (averaging $549). In 2012, 40 non-need-based awards were made. *Average percent of need met:* 68%. *Average financial aid package:* $19,272. *Average need-based loan:* $4559. *Average need-based gift aid:* $12,752. *Average non-need-based aid:* $7646. *Average indebtedness upon graduation:* $28,196.

Applying *Options:* electronic application, deferred entrance. *Application fee:* $25. *Required:* essay or personal statement, high school transcript, 2 letters of recommendation, Christian commitment. *Required for some:* interview. *Application deadlines:* rolling (freshmen), rolling (transfers). *Notification:* continuous (freshmen), continuous (transfers).

Freshman Application Contact Mrs. Kendell Kluttz, Director of Undergraduate Admissions, Simpson University, 2211 College View Drive, Redding, CA 96003-8606. *Phone:* 530-226-5600. *Toll-free phone:* 888-9-SIMPSON. *Fax:* 530-226-4861. *E-mail:* admissions@simpsonu.edu. *Website:* http://www.simpsonu.edu/.

Soka University of America

Aliso Viejo, California

- **Independent** comprehensive, founded 2001
- **Suburban** 103-acre campus with easy access to Los Angeles, San Diego
- **Endowment** $950.0 million
- **Coed** 436 undergraduate students, 100% full-time, 65% women, 35% men
- **Very difficult** entrance level, 46% of applicants were admitted

Undergraduates 435 full-time, 1 part-time. Students come from 32 states and territories; 27 other countries; 33% are from out of state; 3% Black or African American, non-Hispanic/Latino; 9% Hispanic/Latino; 21% Asian, non-Hispanic/Latino; 0.2% Native Hawaiian or other Pacific Islander, non-Hispanic/Latino; 0.5% American Indian or Alaska Native, non-Hispanic/Latino; 3% Two or more races, non-Hispanic/Latino; 5% Race/ethnicity unknown; 39% international; 99% live on campus. *Retention:* 99% of full-time freshmen returned.

Freshmen *Admission:* 345 applied, 158 admitted, 103 enrolled. *Average high school GPA:* 3.73. *Test scores:* SAT critical reading scores over 500: 74%; SAT math scores over 500: 94%; SAT writing scores over 500: 97%; ACT scores over 18: 100%; SAT critical reading scores over 600: 37%; SAT math scores over 600: 75%; SAT writing scores over 600: 38%; ACT scores over 24: 73%; SAT critical reading scores over 700: 11%; SAT math scores over 700: 31%; SAT writing scores over 700: 6%; ACT scores over 30: 11%.

Faculty *Total:* 65, 63% full-time, 83% with terminal degrees. *Student/faculty ratio:* 9:1.

Academics *Calendar:* semesters. *Degrees:* bachelor's and master's. *Special study options:* cooperative education, double majors, English as a second language, honors programs, independent study, internships, off-campus study, services for LD students, study abroad.

Computers on Campus 100 computers/terminals and 100 ports are available on campus for general student use. Students can access the following: campus intranet, computer help desk, free student e-mail accounts, online (class) grades, online (class) registration, online (class) schedules, Angel courseware/PeopleSoft Portal. Campuswide network is available. 100% of college-owned or -operated housing units are wired for high-speed Internet access. Wireless service is available via entire campus.

Student Life *Housing:* on-campus residence required through senior year. *Options:* coed, men-only, women-only, cooperative, disabled students. Campus housing is university owned. Freshman campus housing is guaranteed. *Activities and organizations:* student-run newspaper, choral group, Josho Daiko (Japanese Drum Club), Rhythmission (Hip Hop Dance Club), Sualseros (Salsa Dance Club), Ka Pilina Ho'olokahi (Hawaiian Dance Club), Soul Wings (Choir). *Campus security:* 24-hour emergency response devices and patrols, student patrols, late-night transport/escort service, controlled dormitory access. *Student services:* health clinic, personal/psychological counseling.

Athletics Member NAIA. *Intercollegiate sports:* cross-country running M(s)/W(s), soccer M(s)/W(s), swimming and diving M(s)/W(s), track and field M(s)/W(s). *Intramural sports:* badminton M/W, baseball M/W, basketball M/W, cheerleading M(c)/W(c), football M/W, racquetball M(c)/W(c), soccer M(c)/W(c), softball M/W, table tennis M(c)/W(c), tennis M/W, volleyball M(c)/W(c), water polo M/W, weight lifting M/W.

Standardized Tests *Required:* SAT or ACT (for admission). *Recommended:* SAT Subject Tests (for admission).

Costs (2013–14) *Comprehensive fee:* $39,724 includes full-time tuition ($27,950), mandatory fees ($858), and room and board ($10,916). Full-time tuition and fees vary according to class time, course load, and program. Part-time tuition: $1164 per credit. Part-time tuition and fees vary according to class time, course load, and program. *Room and board:* Room and board charges vary according to board plan. *Payment plans:* installment, deferred payment. *Waivers:* employees or children of employees.

Financial Aid Of all full-time matriculated undergraduates who enrolled in 2012, 409 applied for aid, 395 were judged to have need, 33 had their need fully met. 15 Federal Work-Study jobs (averaging $1114). 10 state and other part-time jobs (averaging $10,628). In 2012, 32 non-need-based awards were made. *Average percent of need met:* 83%. *Average financial aid package:* $34,091. *Average need-based loan:* $5718. *Average need-based gift aid:* $23,032. *Average non-need-based aid:* $13,833. *Average indebtedness upon graduation:* $22,387. *Financial aid deadline:* 3/2.

Applying *Options:* electronic application, early admission, early action, deferred entrance. *Application fee:* $30. *Required:* essay or personal statement, high school transcript, 2 letters of recommendation, Applications will be evaluated only when all required materials have been received. It is the students responsibility to ensure that all of the required documents have been requested of the school they are attending and submitted. *Recommended:* interview. *Application deadlines:* 1/15 (freshmen), 1/15 (out-of-state freshmen), 10/15 (early action). *Notification:* 3/1 (freshmen), 3/1 (out-of-state freshmen), 12/1 (early action).

Freshman Application Contact Jennifer Serna, Admissions Operations Data Specialist, Soka University of America, Enrollment Services, 1 University Drive, Aliso Viejo, CA 92656. *Phone:* 949-480-4151 Ext. 4151. *Toll-free phone:* 888-600-SOKA. *Fax:* 949-480-4151. *E-mail:* jserna@soka.edu. *Website:* http://www.soka.edu/.

Sonoma State University

Rohnert Park, California

- **State-supported** comprehensive, founded 1960, part of California State University System
- **Small-town** 280-acre campus with easy access to San Francisco
- **Endowment** $28.0 million
- **Coed** 8,122 undergraduate students, 90% full-time, 60% women, 40% men
- **Moderately difficult** entrance level, 82% of applicants were admitted

Undergraduates 7,288 full-time, 834 part-time. Students come from 28 states and territories; 20 other countries; 1% are from out of state; 2% Black or African American, non-Hispanic/Latino; 17% Hispanic/Latino; 5% Asian, non-Hispanic/Latino; 0.6% Native Hawaiian or other Pacific Islander, non-Hispanic/Latino; 0.9% American Indian or Alaska Native, non-Hispanic/Latino; 7% Two or more races, non-Hispanic/Latino; 3% Race/ethnicity unknown; 1% international; 10% transferred in; 37% live on campus. *Retention:* 79% of full-time freshmen returned.
Freshmen *Admission:* 13,142 applied, 10,758 admitted, 1,749 enrolled. *Average high school GPA:* 2.93. *Test scores:* SAT critical reading scores over 500: 54%; SAT math scores over 500: 57%; ACT scores over 18: 85%; SAT critical reading scores over 600: 12%; SAT math scores over 600: 14%; ACT scores over 24: 30%; SAT critical reading scores over 700: 1%; SAT math scores over 700: 1%; ACT scores over 30: 1%.
Faculty *Total:* 514, 47% full-time, 59% with terminal degrees. *Student/faculty ratio:* 25:1.
Academics *Calendar:* semesters. *Degrees:* bachelor's and master's. *Special study options:* academic remediation for entering students, accelerated degree program, adult/continuing education programs, advanced placement credit, cooperative education, distance learning, double majors, English as a second language, honors programs, independent study, internships, off-campus study, part-time degree program, services for LD students, student-designed majors, study abroad, summer session for credit. *ROTC:* Army (c), Air Force (c).
Computers on Campus 400 computers/terminals are available on campus for general student use. Students can access the following: computer help desk, free student e-mail accounts, online (class) grades, online (class) registration, online (class) schedules. Campuswide network is available. 100% of college-owned or -operated housing units are wired for high-speed Internet access. Wireless service is available via entire campus.
Student Life *Housing options:* coed, women-only, disabled students. Campus housing is university owned. Freshman applicants given priority for college housing. *Activities and organizations:* drama/theater group, student-run newspaper, radio station, choral group, Accounting Forum, Sonoma Earth Action, Re-Entry Student Association, Lacrosse Club, Inter-Varsity Christian Fellowship, national fraternities, national sororities. *Campus security:* 24-hour emergency response devices and patrols, student patrols, late-night transport/escort service, controlled dormitory access. *Student services:* health clinic, personal/psychological counseling, women's center, legal services.
Athletics Member NCAA. All Division II. *Intercollegiate sports:* baseball M(s), basketball M(s)/W(s), cross-country running M(s), golf M/W, soccer M(s)/W(s), softball W(s), tennis M(s)/W(s), volleyball W(s), water polo W. *Intramural sports:* baseball M, basketball M/W, cheerleading M/W, crew M/W, cross-country running M, fencing M/W, lacrosse M/W, rock climbing M/W, soccer M/W, softball M/W, swimming and diving M/W, volleyball M/W.
Standardized Tests *Required:* SAT or ACT (for admission).
Costs (2012–13) *Tuition:* state resident $5970 full-time; nonresident $10,434 full-time, $372 per unit part-time. Full-time tuition and fees vary according to course load and degree level. Part-time tuition and fees vary according to course load and degree level. *Required fees:* $1426 full-time. *Room and board:* $11,241. Room and board charges vary according to housing facility. *Payment plan:* installment. *Waivers:* employees or children of employees.
Financial Aid Of all full-time matriculated undergraduates who enrolled in 2012, 5,368 applied for aid, 4,373 were judged to have need, 280 had their need fully met. 188 Federal Work-Study jobs (averaging $2922). 620 state and other part-time jobs (averaging $2580). In 2012, 90 non-need-based awards were made. *Average percent of need met:* 79%. *Average financial aid package:* $12,196. *Average need-based loan:* $4268. *Average need-based gift aid:* $9250. *Average non-need-based aid:* $4268. *Average indebtedness upon graduation:* $21,206.
Applying *Options:* electronic application, early admission. *Application fee:* $55. *Required:* high school transcript. *Application deadlines:* rolling (freshmen), rolling (transfers). *Notification:* continuous (freshmen), continuous (transfers).
Freshman Application Contact Mr. Gustavo Flores, Director of Admissions, Sonoma State University, 1801 East Cotati Avenue, Rohnert Park, CA 94928-3609. *Phone:* 707-664-2778. *E-mail:* gustavo.flores@sonoma.edu. *Website:* http://www.sonoma.edu/.

Southern California Institute of Architecture

Los Angeles, California

- **Independent** comprehensive, founded 1972
- **Urban** campus with easy access to Los Angeles
- **Coed** 278 undergraduate students, 94% full-time, 33% women, 67% men
- **Moderately difficult** entrance level, 70% of applicants were admitted

Undergraduates 261 full-time, 17 part-time. Students come from 21 other countries; 10% are from out of state; 0.7% Black or African American, non-Hispanic/Latino; 23% Hispanic/Latino; 26% Asian, non-Hispanic/Latino; 1% Native Hawaiian or other Pacific Islander, non-Hispanic/Latino; 2% Two or more races, non-Hispanic/Latino; 0.4% Race/ethnicity unknown; 28% international; 9% transferred in. *Retention:* 78% of full-time freshmen returned.
Freshmen *Admission:* 227 applied, 160 admitted, 32 enrolled. *Average high school GPA:* 3.2. *Test scores:* SAT critical reading scores over 500: 63%; SAT math scores over 500: 97%; SAT writing scores over 500: 63%; ACT scores over 18: 100%; SAT critical reading scores over 600: 38%; SAT math scores over 600: 59%; SAT writing scores over 600: 29%; ACT scores over 24: 40%; SAT critical reading scores over 700: 7%; SAT math scores over 700: 25%; SAT writing scores over 700: 13%; ACT scores over 30: 20%.
Faculty *Total:* 75, 37% full-time. *Student/faculty ratio:* 15:1.
Academics *Calendar:* semesters. *Degrees:* bachelor's and master's. *Special study options:* academic remediation for entering students, advanced placement credit, cooperative education, English as a second language, internships, study abroad, summer session for credit.
Computers on Campus 85 computers/terminals and 1,000 ports are available on campus for general student use. Students can access the following: campus intranet, computer help desk, free student e-mail accounts, online (class) grades, online (class) registration, online (class) schedules. Campuswide network is available. Wireless service is available via entire campus.
Student Life *Housing:* college housing not available. *Activities and organizations:* Student Union. *Campus security:* 24-hour emergency response devices and patrols, Electronically operated school entrances (e.g., access only with key/security card available to students 24/7). *Student services:* personal/psychological counseling.
Standardized Tests *Required:* SAT or ACT (for admission).
Costs (2013–14) *Tuition:* $36,600 full-time. Full-time tuition and fees vary according to course load. *Required fees:* $700 full-time.
Financial Aid Of all full-time matriculated undergraduates who enrolled in 2005, 173 applied for aid, 147 were judged to have need. In 2005, 12 non-need-based awards were made. *Average percent of need met:* 19%. *Average financial aid package:* $11,946. *Average need-based loan:* $4589. *Average need-based gift aid:* $4271. *Average non-need-based aid:* $2239. *Average indebtedness upon graduation:* $33,000.
Applying *Options:* electronic application, deferred entrance. *Application fee:* $85. *Required:* essay or personal statement, high school transcript, 3 letters of recommendation, portfolio of creative visual work, resume, statement of purpose, application, application fee, test score (SAT/ACT and TOEFL/IELTS for international students). *Required for some:* interview. *Recommended:* minimum 3.0 GPA. *Application deadlines:* 1/15 (freshmen), 5/1 (transfers). *Notification:* continuous until 4/1 (freshmen), continuous until 6/1 (transfers).
Freshman Application Contact Sandy Frigo, Associate Director of Admissions, Southern California Institute of Architecture, 960 East Third Street, Los Angeles, CA 90013. *Phone:* 213-613-2200 Ext. 320. *Fax:* 213-613-2260. *E-mail:* admissions@sciarc.edu.
Website: http://www.sciarc.edu/.

Southern California Institute of Technology

Anaheim, California

- **Proprietary** 4-year, founded 1987
- **Urban** campus with easy access to Anaheim, Los Angeles
- **Coed** 538 undergraduate students, 100% full-time, 7% women, 93% men

Undergraduates 538 full-time. 8% Black or African American, non-Hispanic/Latino; 46% Hispanic/Latino; 15% Asian, non-Hispanic/Latino; 1% Native Hawaiian or other Pacific Islander, non-Hispanic/Latino; 0.2% American Indian or Alaska Native, non-Hispanic/Latino; 4% Two or more races, non-Hispanic/Latino; 0.7% Race/ethnicity unknown. *Retention:* 86% of full-time freshmen returned.
Freshmen *Admission:* 538 enrolled.
Academics *Degrees:* diplomas, associate, and bachelor's. *Special study options:* accelerated degree program, adult/continuing education programs, double majors, English as a second language.

Computers on Campus 300 computers/terminals are available on campus for general student use. Students can access the following: campus intranet. Campuswide network is available. Wireless service is available via entire campus.
Student Life *Housing:* college housing not available.
Standardized Tests *Required:* entrance exam (for admission).
Financial Aid Of all full-time matriculated undergraduates who enrolled in 2011, 8 Federal Work-Study jobs (averaging $2800).
Applying *Application fee:* $100. *Required:* interview. *Required for some:* high school transcript.
Freshman Application Contact Mrs. Olivia Malone, Southern California Institute of Technology, 525 N Muller St, Anaheim, CA 92801. *Phone:* 714-300-0300 Ext. 216. *Fax:* 714-300-0311. *E-mail:* admissions@scitech.edu. *Website:* http://www.scitech.edu/.

Southern California Seminary

El Cajon, California

Freshman Application Contact Thomas Pittman, Director of Admissions, Southern California Seminary, 2075 East Madison Avenue, El Cajon, CA 92019. *Phone:* 888-389-7244. *E-mail:* thpittman@socalsem.edu. *Website:* http://www.socalsem.edu/.

Stanford University

Stanford, California

- **Independent** university, founded 1891
- **Suburban** 8180-acre campus with easy access to San Francisco, San Jose
- **Endowment** $17.0 billion
- **Coed** 7,063 undergraduate students, 99% full-time, 48% women, 52% men
- **Most difficult** entrance level, 7% of applicants were admitted

Undergraduates 7,003 full-time, 60 part-time. Students come from 52 states and territories; 89 other countries; 53% are from out of state; 6% Black or African American, non-Hispanic/Latino; 17% Hispanic/Latino; 19% Asian, non-Hispanic/Latino; 0.4% Native Hawaiian or other Pacific Islander, non-Hispanic/Latino; 1% American Indian or Alaska Native, non-Hispanic/Latino; 11% Two or more races, non-Hispanic/Latino; 0.7% Race/ethnicity unknown; 7% international; 0.4% transferred in; 91% live on campus. *Retention:* 98% of full-time freshmen returned.
Freshmen *Admission:* 36,632 applied, 2,423 admitted, 1,762 enrolled. *Test scores:* SAT critical reading scores over 500: 100%; SAT math scores over 500: 100%; SAT writing scores over 500: 100%; ACT scores over 18: 100%; SAT critical reading scores over 600: 96%; SAT math scores over 600: 97%; SAT writing scores over 600: 97%; ACT scores over 24: 99%; SAT critical reading scores over 700: 69%; SAT math scores over 700: 77%; SAT writing scores over 700: 76%; ACT scores over 30: 87%.
Faculty *Total:* 1,508, 99% full-time, 99% with terminal degrees. *Student/faculty ratio:* 5:1.
Academics *Calendar:* quarters. *Degrees:* bachelor's, master's, doctoral, and post-master's certificates. *Special study options:* advanced placement credit, distance learning, double majors, English as a second language, honors programs, independent study, internships, off-campus study, services for LD students, student-designed majors, study abroad, summer session for credit. *ROTC:* Army (c), Navy (c), Air Force (c).
Computers on Campus 1,000 computers/terminals and 22,000 ports are available on campus for general student use. Students can access the following: campus intranet, computer help desk, free student e-mail accounts, online (class) grades, online (class) registration, online (class) schedules. Campuswide network is available. 100% of college-owned or -operated housing units are wired for high-speed Internet access. Wireless service is available via entire campus.
Student Life *Housing:* on-campus residence required for freshman year. *Options:* coed, women-only, cooperative, disabled students. Campus housing is university owned. Freshman campus housing is guaranteed. *Activities and organizations:* drama/theater group, student-run newspaper, radio and television station, choral group, marching band, Ram's Head (theatre club), Axe Committee (athletic support), Business Association of Engineering Students, Asian-American Student Association, Stanford Daily, national fraternities, national sororities. *Campus security:* 24-hour emergency response devices and patrols, late-night transport/escort service, controlled dormitory access. *Student services:* health clinic, personal/psychological counseling, women's center, legal services.
Athletics Member NCAA, NAIA. All NCAA Division I. *Intercollegiate sports:* archery M(c)/W(c), baseball M(s), basketball M(s)/W(s), cheerleading M(c)/W(c), crew M(s)/W(s), cross-country running M(s)/W(s), equestrian sports M(c)/W(c), fencing M(s)/W(s), field hockey W(s), football M(s), golf M(s)/W(s), gymnastics M(s)/W(s), ice hockey M(c), lacrosse M(c)/W(s), racquetball M(c)/W(c), rock climbing M(c)/W(c), rugby M(c)/W(c), sailing M/W,

skiing (downhill) M(c)/W(c), soccer M(s)/W(s), softball W(s), squash M(c)/W, swimming and diving M(s)/W(s), tennis M(s)/W(s), track and field M(s)/W(s), ultimate Frisbee M(c)/W(c), volleyball M(s)/W(s), water polo M(s)/W(s), wrestling M(s). *Intramural sports:* badminton M/W, baseball M, basketball M/W, bowling M/W, cross-country running M/W, field hockey W, football M/W, golf M/W, lacrosse W(c), soccer M(c)/W(c), softball M/W, table tennis M(c)/W(c), tennis M(c)/W(c), track and field M/W, volleyball M/W, water polo M/W.
Standardized Tests *Required:* SAT or ACT (for admission). *Recommended:* SAT Subject Tests (for admission).
Costs (2013–14) *Comprehensive fee:* $55,856 includes full-time tuition ($42,690) and room and board ($13,166). *Room and board:* Room and board charges vary according to board plan. *Waivers:* employees or children of employees.
Financial Aid Of all full-time matriculated undergraduates who enrolled in 2011, 4,008 applied for aid, 3,692 were judged to have need, 3,217 had their need fully met. 707 Federal Work-Study jobs (averaging $2322). 1,780 state and other part-time jobs (averaging $2212). In 2011, 13 non-need-based awards were made. *Average percent of need met:* 100%. *Average financial aid package:* $42,354. *Average need-based loan:* $2945. *Average need-based gift aid:* $39,897. *Average non-need-based aid:* $14,010. *Average indebtedness upon graduation:* $18,833.
Applying *Options:* electronic application, early action, deferred entrance. *Application fee:* $90. *Required:* essay or personal statement, high school transcript, 2 letters of recommendation. *Application deadlines:* 1/1 (freshmen), 3/15 (transfers), 11/1 (early action). *Notification:* 4/1 (freshmen), 5/15 (transfers), 12/15 (early action).
Freshman Application Contact Rick Shaw, Dean of Undergraduate Admission and Financial Aid, Stanford University, Montag Hall, 355 Galvez Street, Stanford, CA 94305-3020. *Phone:* 650-723-2091. *Fax:* 650-725-2846. *E-mail:* admission@stanford.edu.
Website: http://www.stanford.edu/.

Thomas Aquinas College

Santa Paula, California

- **Independent Roman Catholic** 4-year, founded 1971
- **Rural** 131-acre campus with easy access to Los Angeles
- **Endowment** $13.9 million
- **Coed** 370 undergraduate students, 100% full-time, 51% women, 49% men
- **Very difficult** entrance level, 81% of applicants were admitted

Undergraduates 370 full-time. Students come from 39 states and territories; 5 other countries; 60% are from out of state; 12% Hispanic/Latino; 1% Asian, non-Hispanic/Latino; 0.3% American Indian or Alaska Native, non-Hispanic/Latino; 4% Two or more races, non-Hispanic/Latino; 4% Race/ethnicity unknown; 4% international; 99% live on campus. *Retention:* 85% of full-time freshmen returned.
Freshmen *Admission:* 165 applied, 133 admitted, 84 enrolled. *Average high school GPA:* 3.77. *Test scores:* SAT critical reading scores over 500: 100%; SAT math scores over 500: 97%; SAT writing scores over 500: 97%; ACT scores over 18: 100%; SAT critical reading scores over 600: 87%; SAT math scores over 600: 57%; SAT writing scores over 600: 71%; ACT scores over 24: 87%; SAT critical reading scores over 700: 27%; SAT math scores over 700: 12%; SAT writing scores over 700: 22%; ACT scores over 30: 17%.
Faculty *Total:* 36, 83% full-time, 75% with terminal degrees. *Student/faculty ratio:* 12:1.
Academics *Calendar:* semesters. *Degree:* bachelor's. *Special study options:* cooperative education.
Computers on Campus 20 computers/terminals and 24 ports are available on campus for general student use. Students can access the following: free student e-mail accounts. Campuswide network is available.
Student Life *Housing:* on-campus residence required through senior year. *Options:* men-only, women-only. Campus housing is university owned. Freshman campus housing is guaranteed. *Activities and organizations:* drama/theater group, choral group, Musical Groups (Choir, Chamber Orchestra), Theatre Groups, Language Clubs, Pro-Life Ministry, religious groups. *Campus security:* daily security patrol. *Student services:* personal/psychological counseling.
Athletics *Intramural sports:* basketball M/W, football M, soccer M/W, softball M/W, table tennis M/W, tennis M/W, ultimate Frisbee M/W, volleyball M/W.
Standardized Tests *Required:* SAT or ACT (for admission).
Costs (2013–14) *Comprehensive fee:* $32,450 includes full-time tuition ($24,500) and room and board ($7950). *Payment plan:* installment.
Financial Aid Of all full-time matriculated undergraduates who enrolled in 2012, 302 applied for aid, 299 were judged to have need, 299 had their need fully met. 265 state and other part-time jobs (averaging $3814). *Average percent of need met:* 100%. *Average financial aid package:* $21,556. *Average*

need-based loan: $3973. *Average need-based gift aid:* $15,498. *Average indebtedness upon graduation:* $17,820. *Financial aid deadline:* 3/2.

Applying *Options:* electronic application. *Required:* essay or personal statement, high school transcript, 3 letters of recommendation. *Required for some:* interview. *Recommended:* minimum 3.0 GPA. *Application deadlines:* rolling (freshmen), rolling (out-of-state freshmen). *Notification:* continuous (freshmen), continuous (out-of-state freshmen).

Freshman Application Contact Mr. Jonathan P. Daly, Director of Admissions, Thomas Aquinas College, 10000 Ojai Road, Santa Paula, CA 93060-9621. *Phone:* 805-525-4417 Ext. 5901. *Toll-free phone:* 800-634-9797. *Fax:* 805-421-5905. *E-mail:* admissions@thomasaquinas.edu. *Website:* http://www.thomasaquinas.edu/.

Touro College Los Angeles

West Hollywood, California

Admissions Office Contact Touro College Los Angeles, 1317 North Crescent Heights Boulevard, West Hollywood, CA 90046.
Website: http://www.touro.edu/losangeles/.

Trident University International

Cypress, California

- **Independent** university
- **Urban** campus
- **Coed**
- **Minimally difficult** entrance level

Faculty *Student/faculty ratio:* 25:1.

Academics *Calendar:* four 12 week sessions per year. *Degrees:* certificates, diplomas, bachelor's, master's, doctoral, post-master's, and postbachelor's certificates (offers only online degree programs). *Special study options:* accelerated degree program, adult/continuing education programs, distance learning, double majors, honors programs, part-time degree program, summer session for credit.

Computers on Campus Students can access the following: computer help desk, free student e-mail accounts, online (class) grades, online (class) registration, online (class) schedules. Campuswide network is available.

Student Life *Housing:* college housing not available.

Financial Aid Of all full-time matriculated undergraduates who enrolled in 2009, 650 applied for aid, 650 were judged to have need, 552 had their need fully met. In 2009, 55 non-need-based awards were made. *Average percent of need met:* 98%. *Average financial aid package:* $4415. *Average need-based gift aid:* $3293. *Average non-need-based aid:* $5898. *Average indebtedness upon graduation:* $38,298.

Applying *Options:* electronic application. *Required:* high school transcript. *Required for some:* essay or personal statement. *Application deadlines:* rolling (freshmen), rolling (out-of-state freshmen), rolling (transfers). *Notification:* continuous (freshmen), continuous (out-of-state freshmen), continuous (transfers).

Freshman Application Contact Trident University International, 5757 Plaza Drive, Suite 100, Cypress, CA 90630. *Phone:* 800-579-3197.
Website: http://www.trident.edu/.

United States University

Chula Vista, California

Freshman Application Contact Admissions, United States University, 830 Bay Boulevard, Chula Vista, CA 91911. *Phone:* 619-477-6310. *Toll-free phone:* 888-422-3381. *Fax:* 619-477-7340.
Website: http://www.usuniversity.edu/sd/.

United States University

Cypress, California

Freshman Application Contact Admissions, United States University, 6251 Katella Avenue, Cypress, CA 90630. *Phone:* 714-252-8592. *Toll-free phone:* 888-422-3381.
Website: http://www.usuniversity.edu/oc/.

University of Antelope Valley

Lancaster, California

Admissions Office Contact University of Antelope Valley, 44055 North Sierra Highway, Lancaster, CA 93534.
Website: http://www.uav.edu/.

University of California, Berkeley

Berkeley, California

- **State-supported** university, founded 1868, part of University of California
- **Urban** 1232-acre campus with easy access to San Francisco
- **Endowment** $3.0 billion
- **Coed** 25,774 undergraduate students
- 18% of applicants were admitted

Undergraduates 11% are from out of state; 3% Black or African American, non-Hispanic/Latino; 13% Hispanic/Latino; 39% Asian, non-Hispanic/Latino; 0.2% Native Hawaiian or other Pacific Islander, non-Hispanic/Latino; 0.8% American Indian or Alaska Native, non-Hispanic/Latino; 5% Race/ethnicity unknown; 10% international; 26% live on campus. *Retention:* 96% of full-time freshmen returned.

Freshmen *Admission:* 61,731 applied, 11,130 admitted. *Average high school GPA:* 3.84. *Test scores:* SAT critical reading scores over 500: 93%; SAT math scores over 500: 96%; SAT writing scores over 500: 94%; ACT scores over 18: 99%; SAT critical reading scores over 600: 74%; SAT math scores over 600: 84%; SAT writing scores over 600: 80%; ACT scores over 24: 89%; SAT critical reading scores over 700: 36%; SAT math scores over 700: 56%; SAT writing scores over 700: 46%; ACT scores over 30: 60%.

Faculty *Student/faculty ratio:* 17:1.

Academics *Calendar:* semesters. *Degrees:* bachelor's, master's, and doctoral. *Special study options:* accelerated degree program, adult/continuing education programs, advanced placement credit, double majors, English as a second language, honors programs, independent study, internships, off-campus study, services for LD students, student-designed majors, study abroad, summer session for credit. *ROTC:* Army (b), Navy (b), Air Force (b).

Computers on Campus Students can access the following: computer help desk, free student e-mail accounts, online (class) grades, online (class) registration, online (class) schedules. Campuswide network is available. Wireless service is available via classrooms, computer centers, computer labs, dorm rooms, learning centers, libraries, student centers.

Student Life *Housing options:* coed, men-only, women-only, cooperative, disabled students. Campus housing is university owned and is provided by a third party. Freshman campus housing is guaranteed. *Activities and organizations:* drama/theater group, student-run newspaper, radio and television station, choral group, marching band, national fraternities, national sororities. *Campus security:* 24-hour emergency response devices and patrols, late-night transport/escort service, controlled dormitory access, Office of Emergency Preparedness. *Student services:* health clinic, personal/psychological counseling, women's center, legal services.

Athletics Member NCAA. All Division I. *Intercollegiate sports:* baseball M, basketball M/W, crew M/W, cross-country running M/W, field hockey W, football M, golf M/W, gymnastics M/W, lacrosse M/W, rugby M, soccer M/W, softball W, swimming and diving M/W, tennis M/W, track and field M/W, volleyball W, water polo M/W. *Intramural sports:* basketball M/W, soccer M/W, softball M/W, tennis M/W, ultimate Frisbee M/W, volleyball M/W.

Standardized Tests *Required:* SAT or ACT (for admission). *Recommended:* SAT Subject Tests (for admission).

Costs (2012–13) *Tuition:* state resident $11,220 full-time; nonresident $34,098 full-time. *Required fees:* $1654 full-time. *Room and board:* $15,000. Room and board charges vary according to board plan and housing facility. *Payment plan:* installment.

Financial Aid Of all full-time matriculated undergraduates who enrolled in 2011, 17,065 applied for aid, 14,421 were judged to have need, 2,762 had their need fully met. In 2011, 1225 non-need-based awards were made. *Average percent of need met:* 83%. *Average financial aid package:* $20,471. *Average need-based loan:* $4329. *Average need-based gift aid:* $16,214. *Average non-need-based aid:* $8371. *Average indebtedness upon graduation:* $17,116. *Financial aid deadline:* 3/2.

Applying *Options:* electronic application. *Application fee:* $70. *Required:* essay or personal statement. *Application deadlines:* 11/30 (freshmen), 11/30 (transfers). *Notification:* 3/31 (freshmen), 4/30 (transfers).

Freshman Application Contact University of California, Berkeley, Berkeley, CA 94720-1500.
Website: http://www.berkeley.edu/.

University of California, Davis

Davis, California

- **State-supported** university, founded 1905, part of University of California System
- **Suburban** 5993-acre campus with easy access to San Francisco
- **Coed** 25,759 undergraduate students, 99% full-time, 55% women, 45% men
- **Very difficult** entrance level, 46% of applicants were admitted

Undergraduates 25,446 full-time, 313 part-time. 2% are from out of state; 2% Black or African American, non-Hispanic/Latino; 16% Hispanic/Latino; 37% Asian, non-Hispanic/Latino; 0.5% Native Hawaiian or other Pacific Islander, non-Hispanic/Latino; 0.3% American Indian or Alaska Native, non-Hispanic/Latino; 4% Two or more races, non-Hispanic/Latino; 3% Race/ethnicity unknown; 4% international; 11% transferred in; 25% live on campus. *Retention:* 92% of full-time freshmen returned.

Freshmen *Admission:* 49,333 applied, 22,521 admitted, 5,208 enrolled. *Average high school GPA:* 3.96. *Test scores:* SAT critical reading scores over 500: 83%; SAT math scores over 500: 92%; SAT writing scores over 500: 88%; SAT critical reading scores over 600: 46%; SAT math scores over 600: 68%; SAT writing scores over 600: 54%; SAT critical reading scores over 700: 11%; SAT math scores over 700: 23%; SAT writing scores over 700: 15%.

Faculty *Total:* 1,620, 91% full-time, 98% with terminal degrees. *Student/faculty ratio:* 17:1.

Academics *Calendar:* quarters. *Degrees:* bachelor's, master's, doctoral, post-master's, and postbachelor's certificates. *Special study options:* academic remediation for entering students, adult/continuing education programs, advanced placement credit, double majors, English as a second language, freshman honors college, honors programs, independent study, internships, part-time degree program, services for LD students, student-designed majors, study abroad, summer session for credit. *ROTC:* Army (b), Navy (c), Air Force (c).

Computers on Campus Students can access the following: campus intranet, computer help desk, free student e-mail accounts, online (class) grades, online (class) registration, online (class) schedules, software packages. Campuswide network is available. 100% of college-owned or -operated housing units are wired for high-speed Internet access. Wireless service is available via classrooms, libraries.

Student Life *Housing options:* coed, women-only, cooperative, disabled students. Campus housing is university owned, leased by the school and is provided by a third party. Freshman campus housing is guaranteed. *Activities and organizations:* drama/theater group, student-run newspaper, radio and television station, choral group, marching band, Filipino Student Organization, Vietnamese Student Association, Jewish Student Union, Alpha Phi Omega, national fraternities, national sororities. *Campus security:* 24-hour emergency response devices and patrols, student patrols, late-night transport/escort service, controlled dormitory access, Campus Violence Prevention Program (CVPP). *Student services:* health clinic, personal/psychological counseling, women's center, legal services.

Athletics Member NCAA. All Division I except football (Division I-AA). *Intercollegiate sports:* baseball M(s), basketball M(s)/W(s), cross-country running M(s)/W(s), field hockey W(s), golf M(s)/W(s), gymnastics W(s), lacrosse W(s), soccer M(s)/W(s), softball W(s), swimming and diving W(s), tennis M(s)/W(s), track and field M(s)/W(s), volleyball W(s), water polo M(s)/W(s). *Intramural sports:* archery M(c)/W(c), badminton M(c)/W(c), basketball M/W, crew M(c)/W(c), equestrian sports M(c)/W(c), fencing M(c)/W(c), football M/W, golf M/W, gymnastics M(c), ice hockey M(c)/W, lacrosse M(c)/W(c), racquetball M(c)/W(c), riflery M(c)/W(c), rugby M(c), sailing M(c)/W(c), skiing (cross-country) M(c)/W(c), skiing (downhill) M(c)/W(c), soccer M/W, softball M/W, swimming and diving W(c), table tennis M/W, tennis M/W, volleyball M(c)/W, water polo W(c).

Standardized Tests *Required:* SAT or ACT (for admission), SAT Subject Tests (for admission).

Costs (2013–14) *Tuition:* state resident $15,727 full-time; nonresident $38,605 full-time. *Room and board:* Room and board charges vary according to board plan. *Payment plan:* deferred payment.

Financial Aid Of all full-time matriculated undergraduates who enrolled in 2012, 18,969 applied for aid, 16,513 were judged to have need, 2,517 had their need fully met. In 2012, 869 non-need-based awards were made. *Average percent of need met:* 80%. *Average financial aid package:* $19,658. *Average need-based loan:* $5625. *Average need-based gift aid:* $16,313. *Average non-need-based aid:* $5675. *Average indebtedness upon graduation:* $19,285.

Applying *Options:* electronic application. *Application fee:* $70. *Required:* essay or personal statement, high school transcript, minimum 2.8 GPA, high school subject requirements. *Application deadlines:* 11/30 (freshmen), 11/30 (transfers). *Notification:* 3/15 (freshmen), continuous until 3/15 (transfers).

Freshman Application Contact University of California, Davis, CA. *E-mail:* undergraduateadmissions@ucdavis.edu. *Website:* http://www.ucdavis.edu/.

University of California, Irvine
Irvine, California

- **State-supported** university, founded 1965, part of University of California System
- **Suburban** 1477-acre campus with easy access to Los Angeles
- **Coed** 22,216 undergraduate students, 98% full-time, 54% women, 46% men
- **Very difficult** entrance level, 42% of applicants were admitted

Undergraduates 21,878 full-time, 338 part-time. Students come from 43 states and territories; 70 other countries; 1% are from out of state; 2% Black or African American, non-Hispanic/Latino; 20% Hispanic/Latino; 47% Asian, non-Hispanic/Latino; 0.1% Native Hawaiian or other Pacific Islander, non-Hispanic/Latino; 0.2% American Indian or Alaska Native, non-Hispanic/Latino; 4% Two or more races, non-Hispanic/Latino; 3% Race/ethnicity unknown; 6% international; 8% transferred in; 38% live on campus. *Retention:* 93% of full-time freshmen returned.

Freshmen *Admission:* 56,508 applied, 23,956 admitted, 5,077 enrolled. *Average high school GPA:* 3.89. *Test scores:* SAT critical reading scores over 500: 66%; SAT math scores over 500: 85%; SAT writing scores over 500: 73%; SAT critical reading scores over 600: 29%; SAT math scores over 600: 54%; SAT writing scores over 600: 33%; SAT critical reading scores over 700: 6%; SAT math scores over 700: 17%; SAT writing scores over 700: 6%.

Faculty *Total:* 1,906, 77% full-time, 98% with terminal degrees. *Student/faculty ratio:* 19:1.

Academics *Calendar:* quarters. *Degrees:* bachelor's, master's, doctoral, and postbachelor's certificates. *Special study options:* accelerated degree program, advanced placement credit, distance learning, double majors, English as a second language, honors programs, independent study, internships, off-campus study, services for LD students, study abroad, summer session for credit. *ROTC:* Army (b), Air Force (c).

Computers on Campus 1,500 computers/terminals are available on campus for general student use. Students can access the following: campus intranet, computer help desk, free student e-mail accounts, online (class) grades, online (class) registration, online (class) schedules. Campuswide network is available. Wireless service is available via entire campus.

Student Life *Housing options:* coed, men-only, women-only, disabled students. Campus housing is university owned and is provided by a third party. Freshman campus housing is guaranteed. *Activities and organizations:* drama/theater group, student-run newspaper, radio station, choral group, marching band, national fraternities, national sororities. *Campus security:* 24-hour emergency response devices and patrols, student patrols, late-night transport/escort service, controlled dormitory access. *Student services:* health clinic, personal/psychological counseling.

Athletics Member NCAA. All Division I. *Intercollegiate sports:* archery M(c)/W(c), badminton M(c)/W(c), baseball M(s), basketball M(s)/W(s), crew M(c)/W(c), cross-country running M(s)/W(s), equestrian sports M(c)/W(c), fencing M(c)/W(c), golf M(s)/W(s), lacrosse M(c)/W(c), rugby M(c)/W(c), sailing M(c)/W(c), soccer M(s)/W(s), table tennis M(c)/W(c), tennis M(s)/W(s), track and field M(s)/W(s), ultimate Frisbee M(c)/W(c), volleyball M(s)/W(s), water polo M(s)/W(s), wrestling M(c)/W(c). *Intramural sports:* badminton M/W, basketball M/W, bowling M/W, football M/W, racquetball M/W, soccer M/W, softball M/W, swimming and diving M/W, table tennis M/W, tennis M/W, track and field M/W, ultimate Frisbee M/W, volleyball M/W, water polo M/W, wrestling M/W.

Standardized Tests *Required:* SAT or ACT (for admission). *Recommended:* SAT Subject Tests (for admission).

Costs (2012–13) *Tuition:* state resident $11,220 full-time; nonresident $34,098 full-time. *Required fees:* $3006 full-time. *Room and board:* $11,735. Room and board charges vary according to board plan and housing facility. *Payment plan:* installment. *Waivers:* employees or children of employees.

Financial Aid Of all full-time matriculated undergraduates who enrolled in 2012, 16,988 applied for aid, 14,893 were judged to have need, 4,457 had their need fully met. 2,605 Federal Work-Study jobs (averaging $1425). 2,305 state and other part-time jobs (averaging $1781). In 2012, 553 non-need-based awards were made. *Average percent of need met:* 84%. *Average financial aid package:* $20,510. *Average need-based loan:* $6420. *Average need-based gift aid:* $16,918. *Average non-need-based aid:* $10,007. *Average indebtedness upon graduation:* $19,828. *Financial aid deadline:* 6/28.

Applying *Options:* electronic application. *Application fee:* $70. *Required:* essay or personal statement, high school transcript. *Application deadlines:* 11/30 (freshmen), 11/30 (transfers). *Notification:* 3/31 (freshmen), 4/30 (transfers).

Freshman Application Contact University of California, Irvine, UC IRVINE Office of Admissions and Relations with Schools, 260 Aldrich Hall, Irvine, CA 92697-1075. *Phone:* 949-824-6703. *Fax:* 949-824-2951. *E-mail:* admissions@uci.edu. *Website:* http://www.uci.edu/.

University of California, Los Angeles
Los Angeles, California

- **State-supported** university, founded 1919, part of University of California System
- **Urban** 419-acre campus with easy access to Los Angeles
- **Coed** 27,948 undergraduate students, 98% full-time, 55% women, 45% men
- **Very difficult** entrance level, 22% of applicants were admitted

Undergraduates 27,365 full-time, 583 part-time. Students come from 51 states and territories; 119 other countries; 7% are from out of state; 3% Black or African American, non-Hispanic/Latino; 18% Hispanic/Latino; 32% Asian, non-Hispanic/Latino; 0.3% Native Hawaiian or other Pacific Islander, non-Hispanic/Latino; 0.2% American Indian or Alaska Native, non-Hispanic/Latino; 4% Two or more races, non-Hispanic/Latino; 3% Race/ethnicity unknown; 10% international; 11% transferred in; 45% live on campus. *Retention:* 96% of full-time freshmen returned.

Freshmen *Admission:* 72,697 applied, 15,982 admitted, 5,621 enrolled. *Average high school GPA:* 4.21. *Test scores:* SAT critical reading scores over 500: 91%; SAT math scores over 500: 94%; SAT writing scores over 500: 92%; ACT scores over 18: 98%; SAT critical reading scores over 600: 61%; SAT math scores over 600: 78%; SAT writing scores over 600: 73%; ACT scores over 24: 78%; SAT critical reading scores over 700: 21%; SAT math scores over 700: 47%; SAT writing scores over 700: 31%; ACT scores over 30: 40%.

Faculty *Total:* 2,553, 78% full-time, 98% with terminal degrees. *Student/faculty ratio:* 17:1.

Academics *Calendar:* quarters. *Degrees:* bachelor's, master's, and doctoral. *Special study options:* accelerated degree program, advanced placement credit, double majors, freshman honors college, honors programs, independent study, internships, off-campus study, services for LD students, student-designed majors, study abroad, summer session for credit. *ROTC:* Army (b), Navy (b), Air Force (b).

Computers on Campus 3,930 computers/terminals are available on campus for general student use. Students can access the following: campus intranet, computer help desk, free student e-mail accounts, online (class) grades, online (class) registration, online (class) schedules. Campuswide network is available. 100% of college-owned or -operated housing units are wired for high-speed Internet access. Wireless service is available via entire campus.

Student Life *Housing options:* coed, disabled students. Campus housing is university owned. Freshman campus housing is guaranteed. *Activities and organizations:* drama/theater group, student-run newspaper, radio and television station, choral group, marching band, national fraternities, national sororities. *Campus security:* 24-hour emergency response devices and patrols, student patrols, late-night transport/escort service, controlled dormitory access. *Student services:* health clinic, personal/psychological counseling, women's center, legal services.

Athletics Member NCAA. All Division I except football (Division I-A). *Intercollegiate sports:* baseball M(s), basketball M(s)/W(s), crew W(s), cross-country running M(s)/W(s), golf M(s)/W(s), gymnastics W(s), soccer M(s)/W(s), softball W(s), swimming and diving W(s), tennis M(s)/W(s), track and field M(s)/W(s), volleyball M(s)/W(s), water polo M(s)/W(s). *Intramural sports:* archery M/W, badminton M/W, basketball M/W, bowling M/W, crew M/W, cross-country running M/W, fencing M/W, field hockey W, football M/W, golf M/W, gymnastics M/W, ice hockey M/W, lacrosse M/W, racquetball M/W, riflery M/W, rugby M/W, sailing M/W, skiing (cross-country) M/W, skiing (downhill) M/W, soccer M/W, softball M/W, squash M/W, swimming and diving M/W, table tennis M/W, tennis M/W, track and field M/W, ultimate Frisbee M/W, volleyball M/W, water polo M/W.

Standardized Tests *Required:* SAT or ACT (for admission).

Costs (2013–14) *Tuition:* area resident $11,220 full-time; state resident $11,220 full-time; nonresident $34,098 full-time. *Required fees:* $1472 full-time. *Room and board:* $12,675. Room and board charges vary according to board plan and housing facility.

Financial Aid Of all full-time matriculated undergraduates who enrolled in 2011, 16,196 applied for aid, 14,846 were judged to have need, 3,955 had their need fully met. 2,388 Federal Work-Study jobs (averaging $1969). 1,022 state and other part-time jobs (averaging $1203). In 2011, 924 non-need-based awards were made. *Average percent of need met:* 84%. *Average financial aid package:* $20,362. *Average need-based loan:* $6606. *Average need-based gift aid:* $16,659. *Average non-need-based aid:* $5736. *Average indebtedness upon graduation:* $18,814.

Applying *Options:* electronic application. *Application fee:* $70. *Required:* essay or personal statement, high school transcript. *Application deadlines:* 11/30 (freshmen), 11/30 (out-of-state freshmen), 11/30 (transfers). *Notification:* 3/31 (freshmen), 3/31 (out-of-state freshmen), 4/30 (transfers).

Freshman Application Contact Sue Wilbur, Director of Undergraduate Admissions, University of California, Los Angeles, 405 Hilgard Avenue, Box 951436, Los Angeles, CA 90095-1436. *Phone:* 310-825-3101. *E-mail:* ugadm@saonet.ucla.edu.
Website: http://www.ucla.edu/.

University of California, Merced
Merced, California

- **State-supported** university, part of University of California System
- **Small-town** 815-acre campus with easy access to Fresno, CA
- **Endowment** $26.8 million
- **Coed** 5,431 undergraduate students, 99% full-time, 50% women, 50% men
- **Moderately difficult** entrance level, 76% of applicants were admitted

Undergraduates 5,363 full-time, 68 part-time. Students come from 19 states and territories; 17 other countries; 1% are from out of state; 7% Black or African American, non-Hispanic/Latino; 40% Hispanic/Latino; 28% Asian, non-Hispanic/Latino; 0.7% Native Hawaiian or other Pacific Islander, non-Hispanic/Latino; 0.3% American Indian or Alaska Native, non-Hispanic/Latino; 4% Two or more races, non-Hispanic/Latino; 2% Race/ethnicity unknown; 2% international; 2% transferred in; 29% live on campus. *Retention:* 83% of full-time freshmen returned.

Freshmen *Admission:* 13,959 applied, 10,551 admitted, 1,495 enrolled. *Average high school GPA:* 3.47. *Test scores:* SAT critical reading scores over 500: 47%; SAT math scores over 500: 61%; SAT writing scores over 500: 49%; ACT scores over 18: 85%; SAT critical reading scores over 600: 13%; SAT math scores over 600: 23%; SAT writing scores over 600: 11%; ACT scores over 24: 30%; SAT critical reading scores over 700: 2%; SAT math scores over 700: 4%; SAT writing scores over 700: 1%; ACT scores over 30: 3%.

Faculty *Total:* 306, 85% full-time, 72% with terminal degrees. *Student/faculty ratio:* 20:1.

Academics *Degrees:* bachelor's, master's, and doctoral. *Special study options:* academic remediation for entering students, advanced placement credit, double majors, independent study, internships, off-campus study, part-time degree program, services for LD students, study abroad, summer session for credit.

Computers on Campus 220 computers/terminals are available on campus for general student use. Students can access the following: campus intranet, computer help desk, free student e-mail accounts, online (class) grades, online (class) registration, online (class) schedules. Campuswide network is available. 100% of college-owned or -operated housing units are wired for high-speed Internet access. Wireless service is available via entire campus.

Student Life *Housing options:* coed, disabled students. Campus housing is university owned. Freshman campus housing is guaranteed. *Activities and organizations:* drama/theater group, student-run newspaper, radio station, choral group, marching band, Philipino American Alliance, Vietnamese Student Association, Intervarsity Christian Fellowship, Latino Associated Students, Hip Hop Movement, national fraternities, national sororities. *Campus security:* 24-hour emergency response devices and patrols, student patrols, late-night transport/escort service, controlled dormitory access. *Student services:* health clinic, personal/psychological counseling, women's center, legal services.

Athletics Member NAIA. *Intercollegiate sports:* basketball M/W, cross-country running M/W, soccer M/W, volleyball M/W. *Intramural sports:* baseball M(c), basketball M/W, cheerleading M(c)/W(c), football M/W, lacrosse M(c), soccer M/W, softball M/W, table tennis M(c)/W(c), ultimate Frisbee M/W, volleyball M/W.

Standardized Tests *Required:* SAT or ACT (for admission).

Costs (2013–14) *Tuition:* state resident $13,070 full-time; nonresident $35,948 full-time. *Room and board:* $14,272.

Financial Aid Of all full-time matriculated undergraduates who enrolled in 2011, 4,390 applied for aid, 4,040 were judged to have need, 1,544 had their need fully met. In 2011, 82 non-need-based awards were made. *Average percent of need met:* 88%. *Average financial aid package:* $20,921. *Average need-based loan:* $5268. *Average need-based gift aid:* $16,550. *Average non-need-based aid:* $11,190. *Average indebtedness upon graduation:* $16,982.

Applying *Options:* electronic application. *Application fee:* $70. *Required:* essay or personal statement, high school transcript, minimum 3.0 high school GPA for California residents. *Application deadlines:* 11/30 (freshmen), 12/15 (transfers). *Notification:* 3/1 (freshmen), 4/30 (transfers).

Freshman Application Contact Ms. Susan Fauroat, Associate Director of Admissions and Outreach, University of California, Merced, 5200 North Lake Road, Merced, CA 95343. *Phone:* 209-228-4779. *E-mail:* admissions@ucmerced.edu.
Website: http://www.ucmerced.edu/.

University of California, Riverside
Riverside, California

- **State-supported** university, founded 1954, part of University of California System
- **Urban** 1200-acre campus with easy access to Los Angeles
- **Endowment** $138.8 million
- **Coed** 18,539 undergraduate students, 97% full-time, 52% women, 48% men
- **Very difficult** entrance level, 63% of applicants were admitted

Undergraduates 18,054 full-time, 485 part-time. Students come from 35 states and territories; 43 other countries; 0.6% are from out of state; 6% Black or African American, non-Hispanic/Latino; 35% Hispanic/Latino; 36% Asian, non-Hispanic/Latino; 0.4% Native Hawaiian or other Pacific Islander, non-Hispanic/Latino; 0.2% American Indian or Alaska Native, non-Hispanic/Latino; 3% Two or more races, non-Hispanic/Latino; 2% Race/ethnicity unknown; 2% international; 7% transferred in; 31% live on campus. *Retention:* 88% of full-time freshmen returned.

Freshmen *Admission:* 30,395 applied, 19,062 admitted, 4,034 enrolled. *Average high school GPA:* 3.58. *Test scores:* SAT critical reading scores over 500: 64%; SAT math scores over 500: 77%; SAT writing scores over 500: 69%; ACT scores over 18: 92%; SAT critical reading scores over 600: 19%; SAT math scores over 600: 40%; SAT writing scores over 600: 23%; ACT scores over 24: 42%; SAT critical reading scores over 700: 2%; SAT math scores over 700: 8%; SAT writing scores over 700: 2%; ACT scores over 30: 5%.

Faculty *Total:* 902, 83% full-time, 98% with terminal degrees. *Student/faculty ratio:* 22:1.

Academics *Calendar:* quarters. *Degrees:* bachelor's, master's, doctoral, and postbachelor's certificates. *Special study options:* accelerated degree program, adult/continuing education programs, advanced placement credit, distance learning, double majors, honors programs, independent study, internships, off-campus study, services for LD students, summer session for credit. *ROTC:* Army (c), Air Force (c). *Unusual degree programs:* 3-2 engineering with five-year joint BS/MS programs in chemical and environmental engineering, computer science and engineering, electrical engineering, mechanical engineering.

Computers on Campus 556 computers/terminals are available on campus for general student use. Students can access the following: campus intranet, computer help desk, free student e-mail accounts, online (class) grades, online (class) registration, online (class) schedules, online viewing of financial information. Campuswide network is available. 100% of college-owned or -operated housing units are wired for high-speed Internet access. Wireless service is available via entire campus.

Student Life *Housing options:* coed. Campus housing is university owned and is provided by a third party. Freshman campus housing is guaranteed. *Activities and organizations:* drama/theater group, student-run newspaper, radio station, choral group, Associated Students, Student Alumni Association, Health Careers Organization, national fraternities, national sororities. *Campus security:* 24-hour emergency response devices and patrols, student patrols, late-night transport/escort service, controlled dormitory access. *Student services:* health clinic, personal/psychological counseling, women's center, legal services.

Athletics Member NCAA. All Division I. *Intercollegiate sports:* baseball M(s), basketball M(s)/W(s), cross-country running M(s)/W(s), golf M(s), soccer M(s)/W(s), softball W(s), tennis M/W, volleyball W(s). *Intramural sports:* badminton M/W, basketball M/W, racquetball M/W, rugby M(c)/W(c), soccer M/W, softball M/W, table tennis M(c)/W(c), tennis M/W, volleyball M/W, wrestling M(c).

Standardized Tests *Required:* SAT or ACT (for admission). *Recommended:* SAT Subject Tests (for admission).

Costs (2013–14) *Tuition:* state resident $11,220 full-time; nonresident $34,098 full-time. Full-time tuition and fees vary according to course load. Part-time tuition and fees vary according to course load. *Required fees:* $1740 full-time. *Room and board:* $13,200. Room and board charges vary according to board plan and housing facility. *Payment plan:* deferred payment.

Financial Aid Of all full-time matriculated undergraduates who enrolled in 2011, 15,238 applied for aid, 14,030 were judged to have need, 4,295 had their need fully met. 3,511 Federal Work-Study jobs (averaging $1650). In 2011, 120 non-need-based awards were made. *Average percent of need met:* 85%. *Average financial aid package:* $20,428. *Average need-based loan:* $6217. *Average need-based gift aid:* $16,391. *Average non-need-based aid:* $5808. *Average indebtedness upon graduation:* $21,828. *Financial aid deadline:* 3/2.

Applying *Options:* electronic application. *Application fee:* $70. *Required:* essay or personal statement, high school transcript, minimum 3.0 GPA. *Application deadlines:* 11/30 (freshmen), 11/30 (transfers). *Notification:* continuous until 2/1 (freshmen), continuous until 3/1 (transfers).

Freshman Application Contact Ms. Emily D Engelschall, Director, Undergraduate Recruitment, University of California, Riverside, 3221 Student Services, 900 University Avenue, Riverside, CA 92521. *Phone:* 951-827-3986. *Fax:* 951-827-6346. *E-mail:* discover@ucr.edu. *Website:* http://www.ucr.edu/.

University of California, San Diego
La Jolla, California

Freshman Application Contact Ms. Mae Brown, Assistant Vice Chancellor, Admissions and Relations with Schools, University of California, San Diego, 9500 Gilman Drive, 0021, La Jolla, CA 92093-0021. *Phone:* 858-534-4831. *E-mail:* admissionsreply@ucsd.edu. *Website:* http://www.ucsd.edu/.

University of California, Santa Barbara
Santa Barbara, California

- **State-supported** university, founded 1909, part of University of California System
- **Suburban** 989-acre campus
- **Endowment** $109.0 million
- **Coed** 18,977 undergraduate students, 99% full-time, 53% women, 47% men
- **Very difficult** entrance level, 44% of applicants were admitted

Undergraduates 18,715 full-time, 262 part-time. Students come from 50 states and territories; 76 other countries; 3% are from out of state; 4% Black or African American, non-Hispanic/Latino; 24% Hispanic/Latino; 23% Asian, non-Hispanic/Latino; 0.2% Native Hawaiian or other Pacific Islander, non-Hispanic/Latino; 1% American Indian or Alaska Native, non-Hispanic/Latino; 4% Race/ethnicity unknown; 3% international; 9% transferred in; 37% live on campus. *Retention:* 91% of full-time freshmen returned.

Freshmen *Admission:* 54,762 applied, 24,116 admitted, 4,736 enrolled. *Average high school GPA:* 3.91. *Test scores:* SAT critical reading scores over 500: 89%; SAT math scores over 500: 95%; ACT scores over 18: 98%; SAT critical reading scores over 600: 54%; SAT math scores over 600: 71%; ACT scores over 24: 78%; SAT critical reading scores over 700: 13%; SAT math scores over 700: 24%; ACT scores over 30: 24%.

Faculty *Total:* 1,050, 84% full-time, 100% with terminal degrees. *Student/faculty ratio:* 17:1.

Academics *Calendar:* quarters plus 6-week summer term. *Degrees:* bachelor's, master's, doctoral, post-master's, and postbachelor's certificates. *Special study options:* accelerated degree program, advanced placement credit, cooperative education, double majors, English as a second language, honors programs, independent study, internships, off-campus study, services for LD students, student-designed majors, study abroad, summer session for credit. *ROTC:* Army (b), Air Force (c).

Computers on Campus 700 computers/terminals are available on campus for general student use. Students can access the following: computer help desk, free student e-mail accounts, online (class) grades, online (class) registration, online (class) schedules. Campuswide network is available. 100% of college-owned or -operated housing units are wired for high-speed Internet access. Wireless service is available via classrooms, computer labs, dorm rooms, libraries, student centers.

Student Life *Housing:* on-campus residence required for freshman year. *Options:* coed, cooperative. Campus housing is university owned and is provided by a third party. Freshman applicants given priority for college housing. *Activities and organizations:* drama/theater group, student-run newspaper, radio and television station, choral group, national fraternities, national sororities. *Campus security:* 24-hour emergency response devices and patrols, student patrols, late-night transport/escort service, controlled dormitory access. *Student services:* health clinic, personal/psychological counseling, women's center, legal services.

Athletics Member NCAA. All Division I. *Intercollegiate sports:* baseball M(s), basketball M(s)/W(s), bowling M(c)/W(c), crew M(c)/W(c), cross-country running M(s)/W(s), equestrian sports M(c)/W(c), fencing M(c)/W(c), field hockey W(c), golf M(s), gymnastics M(s)/W(s), lacrosse M(c)/W(c), rugby M(c), sailing M(c)/W(c), skiing (downhill) M(c)/W(c), soccer M(s)/W(s), softball W(s), swimming and diving M(s)/W(s), tennis M(s)/W(s), track and field M(s)/W(s), ultimate Frisbee M(c)/W(c), volleyball M(s)/W(s), water polo M(s)/W(s). *Intramural sports:* badminton M/W, basketball M/W, bowling M/W, cross-country running M/W, football M/W, golf M/W, gymnastics M/W, racquetball M/W, soccer M/W, softball M/W, squash M/W, tennis M/W, ultimate Frisbee M/W, volleyball M/W, water polo M/W.

Standardized Tests *Required:* SAT or ACT (for admission). *Recommended:* SAT Subject Tests (for admission).

Costs (2013–14) *Tuition:* state resident $12,192 full-time; nonresident $34,213 full-time. *Required fees:* $2844 full-time. *Room and board:* $13,275. Room and board charges vary according to board plan and housing facility. *Payment plan:* installment.

Financial Aid Of all full-time matriculated undergraduates who enrolled in 2011, 13,071 applied for aid, 11,138 were judged to have need, 3,927 had their need fully met. In 2011, 343 non-need-based awards were made. *Average percent of need met:* 86%. *Average financial aid package:* $21,398. *Average need-based loan:* $6408. *Average need-based gift aid:* $17,223. *Average non-need-based aid:* $8653. *Average indebtedness upon graduation:* $18,627.

Applying *Options:* electronic application. *Application fee:* $70. *Required:* essay or personal statement, high school transcript. *Required for some:* interview. *Application deadlines:* 11/30 (freshmen), 11/30 (transfers). *Notification:* 3/15 (freshmen), 5/1 (transfers).

Freshman Application Contact Office of Admissions, University of California, Santa Barbara, 1210 Cheadle Hall, Santa Barbara, CA 93106-2014. *Phone:* 805-893-2881. *Fax:* 805-893-2676. *E-mail:* admissions@sa.ucsb.edu. *Website:* http://www.ucsb.edu/.

University of California, Santa Cruz
Santa Cruz, California

- **State-supported** university, founded 1965, part of University of California System
- **Small-town** 2000-acre campus with easy access to San Francisco, San Jose
- **Endowment** $121.9 million
- **Coed** 15,978 undergraduate students, 98% full-time, 53% women, 47% men
- **Very difficult** entrance level, 61% of applicants were admitted

Undergraduates 15,721 full-time, 257 part-time. Students come from 41 states and territories; 14 other countries; 2% are from out of state; 2% Black or African American, non-Hispanic/Latino; 28% Hispanic/Latino; 21% Asian, non-Hispanic/Latino; 0.2% Native Hawaiian or other Pacific Islander, non-Hispanic/Latino; 0.3% American Indian or Alaska Native, non-Hispanic/Latino; 6% Two or more races, non-Hispanic/Latino; 4% Race/ethnicity unknown; 0.3% international; 7% transferred in; 45% live on campus. *Retention:* 89% of full-time freshmen returned.

Freshmen *Admission:* 33,142 applied, 20,178 admitted, 3,828 enrolled. *Average high school GPA:* 3.62. *Test scores:* SAT critical reading scores over 500: 68%; SAT math scores over 500: 75%; SAT writing scores over 500: 70%; ACT scores over 18: 91%; SAT critical reading scores over 600: 32%; SAT math scores over 600: 38%; SAT writing scores over 600: 31%; ACT scores over 24: 52%; SAT critical reading scores over 700: 6%; SAT math scores over 700: 7%; SAT writing scores over 700: 7%; ACT scores over 30: 11%.

Faculty *Total:* 804, 68% full-time, 98% with terminal degrees. *Student/faculty ratio:* 18:1.

Academics *Calendar:* quarters. *Degrees:* bachelor's, master's, doctoral, and postbachelor's certificates. *Special study options:* accelerated degree program, advanced placement credit, cooperative education, double majors, freshman honors college, honors programs, independent study, internships, off-campus study, services for LD students, student-designed majors, study abroad, summer session for credit. *ROTC:* Army (c), Navy (c), Air Force (c).

Computers on Campus Students can access the following: campus intranet, computer help desk, free student e-mail accounts, online (class) grades, online (class) registration, online (class) schedules. Campuswide network is available. 100% of college-owned or -operated housing units are wired for high-speed Internet access. Wireless service is available via entire campus.

Student Life *Housing options:* coed, men-only, women-only, cooperative. Campus housing is university owned. Freshman campus housing is guaranteed. *Activities and organizations:* drama/theater group, student-run newspaper, radio and television station, choral group, Filipino Student Association, Movimiento Estudiantil Chicano de Aztlan, CSA (Chinese Student Association), A/BSA (African/Black Student Alliance), SEC (Student Environmental Center), national fraternities, national sororities. *Campus security:* 24-hour emergency response devices and patrols, late-night transport/escort service, controlled dormitory access, evening main gate security, campus police force and fire station. *Student services:* health clinic, personal/psychological counseling, women's center.

Athletics Member NCAA. All Division III. *Intercollegiate sports:* badminton M(c)/W(c), baseball M(c)/W(c), basketball M/W, cheerleading M(c)/W(c), cross-country running M(c)/W, equestrian sports M(c)/W(c), fencing M(c)/W(c), golf W, lacrosse M(c), racquetball M(c)/W(c), rugby M(c)/W(c), soccer M/W, swimming and diving M/W, table tennis M(c)/W(c), tennis M/W, track and field M(c)/W(c), ultimate Frisbee M(c)/W(c), volleyball M/W, water polo M(c)/W(c). *Intramural sports:* basketball M/W, soccer M/W, softball M/W, ultimate Frisbee M/W, volleyball M/W, water polo M/W.

Standardized Tests *Required:* SAT or ACT (for admission), (for admission).

Costs (2013–14) *Tuition:* state resident $12,192 full-time; nonresident $35,070 full-time. Part-time tuition and fees vary according to course load. *Required*

fees: $1225 full-time. *Room and board:* $14,856. Room and board charges vary according to board plan and housing facility. *Payment plan:* installment.

Financial Aid Of all full-time matriculated undergraduates who enrolled in 2011, 12,027 applied for aid, 10,222 were judged to have need, 3,739 had their need fully met. 7,625 Federal Work-Study jobs (averaging $1936). In 2011, 290 non-need-based awards were made. *Average percent of need met:* 88%. *Average financial aid package:* $21,922. *Average need-based loan:* $6248. *Average need-based gift aid:* $16,591. *Average non-need-based aid:* $10,016. *Average indebtedness upon graduation:* $19,851. *Financial aid deadline:* 6/1.

Applying *Options:* electronic application. *Application fee:* $70. *Required:* essay or personal statement, high school transcript, minimum high school GPA of 3.0 for California residents, 3.4 for non-residents. *Application deadlines:* 11/30 (freshmen), 11/30 (transfers). *Notification:* 3/31 (freshmen), 4/30 (transfers).

Freshman Application Contact Michael McCawley, Director, Admissions, University of California, Santa Cruz, 1156 High Street, Santa Cruz, CA 95064. *Phone:* 831-459-2374. *Fax:* 831-459-4163. *E-mail:* admissions@ucsc.edu. *Website:* http://www.ucsc.edu/.

University of La Verne
La Verne, California

- **Independent** university, founded 1891
- **Suburban** 38-acre campus with easy access to Los Angeles
- **Endowment** $37.6 million
- **Coed** 2,499 undergraduate students, 97% full-time, 60% women, 40% men
- **Moderately difficult** entrance level, 39% of applicants were admitted

Undergraduates 2,413 full-time, 86 part-time. Students come from 18 states and territories; 9 other countries; 4% are from out of state; 5% Black or African American, non-Hispanic/Latino; 50% Hispanic/Latino; 6% Asian, non-Hispanic/Latino; 0.4% Native Hawaiian or other Pacific Islander, non-Hispanic/Latino; 0.3% American Indian or Alaska Native, non-Hispanic/Latino; 4% Two or more races, non-Hispanic/Latino; 3% Race/ethnicity unknown; 4% international; 9% transferred in; 33% live on campus. *Retention:* 85% of full-time freshmen returned.

Freshmen *Admission:* 6,989 applied, 2,722 admitted, 621 enrolled. *Average high school GPA:* 3.52. *Test scores:* SAT critical reading scores over 500: 56%; SAT math scores over 500: 64%; SAT writing scores over 500: 57%; ACT scores over 18: 95%; SAT critical reading scores over 600: 13%; SAT math scores over 600: 19%; SAT writing scores over 600: 12%; ACT scores over 24: 35%; SAT critical reading scores over 700: 2%; SAT math scores over 700: 1%; SAT writing scores over 700: 1%; ACT scores over 30: 2%.

Faculty *Total:* 665, 34% full-time. *Student/faculty ratio:* 12:1.

Academics *Calendar:* 4-1-4. *Degrees:* certificates, associate, bachelor's, master's, doctoral, and postbachelor's certificates (also offers continuing education program with significant enrollment not reflected in profile). *Special study options:* academic remediation for entering students, accelerated degree program, adult/continuing education programs, advanced placement credit, distance learning, double majors, English as a second language, freshman honors college, honors programs, independent study, internships, off-campus study, part-time degree program, services for LD students, student-designed majors, study abroad, summer session for credit. *ROTC:* Army (c).

Computers on Campus 520 computers/terminals and 520 ports are available on campus for general student use. Students can access the following: computer help desk, free student e-mail accounts, online (class) grades, online (class) registration, online (class) schedules, MyLaVerne (online). Campuswide network is available. 100% of college-owned or -operated housing units are wired for high-speed Internet access. Wireless service is available via entire campus.

Student Life *Housing options:* coed, men-only, women-only, disabled students. Campus housing is university owned. Freshman campus housing is guaranteed. *Activities and organizations:* drama/theater group, student-run newspaper, radio and television station, choral group, Latino Student Forum, Black Student Union, Associated Students of La Verne, Alpha Kappa Psi, Voices in Action, national fraternities, national sororities. *Campus security:* 24-hour emergency response devices and patrols, late-night transport/escort service, controlled dormitory access. *Student services:* health clinic, personal/psychological counseling.

Athletics Member NCAA. All Division III. *Intercollegiate sports:* baseball M, basketball M/W, cross-country running M/W, football M, golf M, soccer M/W, softball W, swimming and diving M/W, tennis M/W, track and field M/W, volleyball W, water polo M/W.

Standardized Tests *Required:* SAT or ACT (for admission).

Costs (2013–14) *Comprehensive fee:* $46,910 includes full-time tuition ($33,628), mandatory fees ($1372), and room and board ($11,910). Full-time tuition and fees vary according to degree level and location. Part-time tuition: $979 per unit. Part-time tuition and fees vary according to degree level and location. *College room only:* $6100. Room and board charges vary according to board plan and housing facility. *Payment plans:* installment, deferred payment. *Waivers:* employees or children of employees.

Financial Aid Of all full-time matriculated undergraduates who enrolled in 2012, 2,164 applied for aid, 2,061 were judged to have need, 215 had their need fully met. In 2012, 264 non-need-based awards were made. *Average percent of need met:* 49%. *Average financial aid package:* $27,750. *Average need-based loan:* $4659. *Average need-based gift aid:* $11,716. *Average non-need-based aid:* $18,970. *Average indebtedness upon graduation:* $30,566.

Applying *Options:* electronic application, deferred entrance. *Application fee:* $50. *Required:* essay or personal statement, high school transcript, 2 letters of recommendation. *Recommended:* interview. *Application deadlines:* 2/1 (freshmen), 4/1 (transfers). *Notification:* continuous (freshmen), continuous (transfers).

Freshman Application Contact Ms. Ana Liza V. Zell, Associate Dean of Undergraduate Admissions, University of La Verne, 1950 Third Street, La Verne, CA 91750. *Phone:* 909-593-3511 Ext. 4035. *Toll-free phone:* 800-876-4858. *Fax:* 909-392-2714. *E-mail:* admissions@ulv.edu. *Website:* http://www.laverne.edu/.

University of Phoenix–Bay Area Campus
San Jose, California

Freshman Application Contact Marc Booker, Sr. Director, Office of Admissions and Evaluation, University of Phoenix–Bay Area Campus, 4035 South Riverpoint Parkway, Mail Stop CF-L101, Phoenix, AZ 85040-1958. *Phone:* 602-557-4609. *Toll-free phone:* 866-766-0766. *Fax:* 480-643-1156. *Website:* http://www.phoenix.edu/.

University of Phoenix–Central Valley Campus
Fresno, California

Freshman Application Contact Marc Booker, Sr. Director, Office of Admissions and Evaluation, University of Phoenix–Central Valley Campus, 4035 South Riverpoint Parkway, Mail Stop CF-L101, Phoenix, AZ 85040. *Phone:* 602-557-4609. *Toll-free phone:* 866-766-0766. *Fax:* 480-643-1156. *Website:* http://www.phoenix.edu/.

University of Phoenix–Sacramento Valley Campus
Sacramento, California

Freshman Application Contact Marc Booker, Sr. Director, Office of Admissions and Evaluation, University of Phoenix–Sacramento Valley Campus, 4035 South Riverpoint Parkway, Mail Stop CF-L101, Phoenix, AZ 85040. *Phone:* 602-557-4609. *Toll-free phone:* 866-766-0766. *Fax:* 480-643-1156. *Website:* http://www.phoenix.edu/.

University of Phoenix–San Diego Campus
San Diego, California

Freshman Application Contact Marc Booker, Sr. Director, Office of Admissions and Evaluation, University of Phoenix–San Diego Campus, 4035 South Riverpoint Parkway, Mail Stop CF-L101, Phoenix, AZ 85040. *Phone:* 602-557-4609. *Toll-free phone:* 866-766-0766. *Fax:* 480-643-1156. *Website:* http://www.phoenix.edu/.

University of Phoenix–Southern California Campus
Costa Mesa, California

Freshman Application Contact Marc Booker, Sr. Director, Office of Admissions and Evaluation, University of Phoenix–Southern California Campus, 4035 South Riverpoint Parkway, Mail Stop CF-L101, Phoenix, AZ 85040. *Phone:* 602-557-4609. *Toll-free phone:* 866-766-0766. *Fax:* 480-643-1156. *Website:* http://www.phoenix.edu/.

University of Redlands
Redlands, California

- **Independent** comprehensive, founded 1907
- **Small-town** 140-acre campus with easy access to Los Angeles
- **Endowment** $103.8 million
- **Coed** 3,360 undergraduate students, 78% full-time, 56% women, 44% men
- **Moderately difficult** entrance level, 69% of applicants were admitted

Undergraduates 2,611 full-time, 749 part-time. Students come from 43 states and territories; 8 other countries; 24% are from out of state; 5% Black or African American, non-Hispanic/Latino; 25% Hispanic/Latino; 4% Asian, non-Hispanic/Latino; 0.6% Native Hawaiian or other Pacific Islander, non-Hispanic/Latino; 0.6% American Indian or Alaska Native, non-Hispanic/Latino; 3% Two or more races, non-Hispanic/Latino; 12% Race/ethnicity unknown; 0.7% international; 2% transferred in; 69% live on campus. *Retention:* 91% of full-time freshmen returned.

Freshmen *Admission:* 4,501 applied, 3,099 admitted, 724 enrolled. *Average high school GPA:* 3.58. *Test scores:* SAT critical reading scores over 500: 87%; SAT math scores over 500: 87%; SAT writing scores over 500: 79%; ACT scores over 18: 98%; SAT critical reading scores over 600: 35%; SAT math scores over 600: 39%; SAT writing scores over 600: 31%; ACT scores over 24: 52%; SAT critical reading scores over 700: 5%; SAT math scores over 700: 4%; SAT writing scores over 700: 4%; ACT scores over 30: 5%.

Faculty *Total:* 492, 40% full-time. *Student/faculty ratio:* 14:1.

Academics *Calendar:* 4-4-1. *Degrees:* bachelor's, master's, doctoral, post-master's, and postbachelor's certificates. *Special study options:* academic remediation for entering students, adult/continuing education programs, advanced placement credit, double majors, freshman honors college, honors programs, independent study, internships, off-campus study, part-time degree program, services for LD students, student-designed majors, study abroad. *ROTC:* Army (c), Air Force (c). *Unusual degree programs:* engineering.

Computers on Campus 804 computers/terminals and 1,500 ports are available on campus for general student use. Students can access the following: campus intranet, computer help desk, free student e-mail accounts, online (class) grades, online (class) registration, online (class) schedules. Campus-wide network is available. 100% of college-owned or -operated housing units are wired for high-speed Internet access. Wireless service is available via entire campus.

Student Life *Housing:* on-campus residence required through senior year. *Options:* coed, men-only, women-only, cooperative, disabled students. Campus housing is university owned. Freshman campus housing is guaranteed. *Activities and organizations:* drama/theater group, student-run newspaper, radio station, choral group, Associated Students, service organizations, cultural organizations, social awareness groups. *Campus security:* 24-hour emergency response devices and patrols, student patrols, late-night transport/escort service, controlled dormitory access. *Student services:* health clinic, personal/psychological counseling, women's center.

Athletics Member NCAA. All Division III. *Intercollegiate sports:* baseball M, basketball M/W, cross-country running M/W, football M, golf M/W, lacrosse W, soccer M/W, softball W, swimming and diving M/W, tennis M/W, track and field M/W, volleyball W, water polo M/W. *Intramural sports:* basketball M/W, cheerleading W, football M, racquetball M/W, soccer M/W, softball M/W, table tennis M/W, volleyball W, water polo M/W.

Standardized Tests *Required:* SAT or ACT (for admission).

Costs (2012–13) *Comprehensive fee:* $51,262 includes full-time tuition ($39,038), mandatory fees ($300), and room and board ($11,924). Full-time tuition and fees vary according to program. Part-time tuition and fees vary according to course load and program. *Required fees:* $150 per term part-time. *Room and board:* Room and board charges vary according to board plan and housing facility. *Payment plan:* installment. *Waivers:* employees or children of employees.

Financial Aid Of all full-time matriculated undergraduates who enrolled in 2012, 2,406 applied for aid, 2,141 were judged to have need, 987 had their need fully met. In 2012, 257 non-need-based awards were made. *Average percent of need met:* 87%. *Average financial aid package:* $32,719. *Average need-based loan:* $5027. *Average need-based gift aid:* $27,088. *Average non-need-based aid:* $14,914. *Average indebtedness upon graduation:* $32,035.

Applying *Options:* electronic application, deferred entrance. *Application fee:* $30. *Required:* essay or personal statement, high school transcript, 2 letters of recommendation. *Recommended:* interview. *Application deadlines:* rolling (freshmen), rolling (transfers). *Notification:* continuous until 12/1 (freshmen), continuous (transfers).

UR Unique
UR Connected
UR Bold

UR Home.

UNIVERSITY OF REDLANDS

Freshman Application Contact University of Redlands, 1200 East Colton Avenue, PO Box 3080, Redlands, CA 92373-0999. *Phone:* 909-748-8159. *Toll-free phone:* 800-455-5064.
Website: http://www.redlands.edu/.

See display ad on this page and page 1596 for the College Close-Up.

University of San Diego

San Diego, California

- **Independent Roman Catholic** university, founded 1949
- **Urban** 180-acre campus with easy access to San Diego
- **Endowment** $345.6 million
- **Coed** 5,457 undergraduate students, 97% full-time, 55% women, 45% men
- **Very difficult** entrance level, 43% of applicants were admitted

Undergraduates 5,269 full-time, 188 part-time. Students come from 52 states and territories; 58 other countries; 38% are from out of state; 3% Black or African American, non-Hispanic/Latino; 18% Hispanic/Latino; 6% Asian, non-Hispanic/Latino; 0.3% Native Hawaiian or other Pacific Islander, non-Hispanic/Latino; 0.3% American Indian or Alaska Native, non-Hispanic/Latino; 5% Two or more races, non-Hispanic/Latino; 5% Race/ethnicity unknown; 6% international; 7% transferred in; 45% live on campus. *Retention:* 90% of full-time freshmen returned.

Freshmen *Admission:* 16,578 applied, 7,060 admitted, 1,074 enrolled. *Average high school GPA:* 3.86. *Test scores:* SAT critical reading scores over 500: 93%; SAT math scores over 500: 93%; SAT writing scores over 500: 94%; ACT scores over 18: 100%; SAT critical reading scores over 600: 55%; SAT math scores over 600: 65%; SAT writing scores over 600: 59%; ACT scores over 24: 89%; SAT critical reading scores over 700: 9%; SAT math scores over 700: 14%; SAT writing scores over 700: 10%; ACT scores over 30: 27%.

Faculty *Total:* 875, 46% full-time, 76% with terminal degrees. *Student/faculty ratio:* 16:1.

Academics *Calendar:* 4-1-4. *Degrees:* bachelor's, master's, doctoral, post-master's, and postbachelor's certificates. *Special study options:* advanced placement credit, double majors, English as a second language, honors programs, independent study, internships, part-time degree program, services for LD students, study abroad, summer session for credit. *ROTC:* Army (c), Navy (b), Air Force (c).

Computers on Campus 946 computers/terminals and 4,250 ports are available on campus for general student use. Students can access the following: campus intranet, computer help desk, free student e-mail accounts, online (class) grades, online (class) registration, online (class) schedules. Campus-wide network is available. 100% of college-owned or -operated housing units are wired for high-speed Internet access. Wireless service is available via entire campus.

Student Life *Housing:* on-campus residence required for freshman year. *Options:* coed, men-only, women-only, disabled students. Campus housing is university owned. Freshman campus housing is guaranteed. *Activities and organizations:* drama/theater group, student-run newspaper, radio and television station, choral group, Panhellenic Council, Interfraternity Council, Residence Hall Association, Kappa Kappa Gamma Sorority, Accounting Society, national fraternities, national sororities. *Campus security:* 24-hour emergency response devices and patrols, late-night transport/escort service, controlled dormitory access. *Student services:* health clinic, personal/psychological counseling, women's center, legal services.

Athletics Member NCAA. All Division I except football (Division I-AA). *Intercollegiate sports:* baseball M(s), basketball M(s)/W(s), crew M/W(s), cross-country running M(s)/W(s), equestrian sports W(c), golf M(s), lacrosse M(c)/W(c), rock climbing M(c)/W(c), rugby M(c), soccer M(s)/W(s), softball W(s), swimming and diving W(s), tennis M(s)/W(s), track and field W(s), ultimate Frisbee M(c)/W(c), volleyball M(c)/W(s). *Intramural sports:* baseball M(c), basketball M/W, football M/W, golf M(c)/W(c), skiing (downhill) M(c)/W(c), soccer M(c)/W(c), softball M/W, tennis M/W, ultimate Frisbee M/W, volleyball M/W(c), water polo M(c)/W(c).

Standardized Tests *Required:* SAT or ACT (for admission).

Costs (2013–14) *Comprehensive fee:* $53,302 includes full-time tuition ($40,900), mandatory fees ($492), and room and board ($11,910). Part-time tuition: $1410 per unit. Part-time tuition and fees vary according to course load. *Room and board:* Room and board charges vary according to board plan and housing facility. *Payment plan:* installment. *Waivers:* employees or children of employees.

Financial Aid Of all full-time matriculated undergraduates who enrolled in 2011, 3,263 applied for aid, 2,856 were judged to have need, 426 had their need fully met. 563 Federal Work-Study jobs (averaging $2008). In 2011, 763 non-need-based awards were made. *Average percent of need met:* 71%. *Average financial aid package:* $29,830. *Average need-based loan:* $8109. *Average need-based gift aid:* $22,914. *Average non-need-based aid:* $13,522. *Average indebtedness upon graduation:* $29,874.

Applying *Options:* electronic application, deferred entrance. *Application fee:* $55. *Required:* essay or personal statement, high school transcript, 1 letter of recommendation. *Application deadlines:* 12/15 (freshmen), 3/1 (transfers). *Notification:* 4/1 (freshmen), continuous until 6/30 (transfers).

Freshman Application Contact Ms. Minh-Ha Hoang, Director of Admission, University of San Diego, 5998 Alcala Park, San Diego, CA 92110. *Phone:* 619-260-4506. *Toll-free phone:* 800-248-4873. *Fax:* 619-260-6836. *E-mail:* admissions@sandiego.edu.
Website: http://www.sandiego.edu/.

University of San Francisco
San Francisco, California

Freshman Application Contact Mr. Michael Hughes, Director, University of San Francisco, 2130 Fulton Street, San Francisco, CA 94117-1080. *Phone:* 415-422-6563. *Toll-free phone:* 800-CALL-USF. *Fax:* 415-422-2217. *E-mail:* admissions@usfca.edu.
Website: http://www.usfca.edu/.

See below for display ad and page 1602 for the College Close-Up.

University of Southern California
Los Angeles, California

- **Independent** university, founded 1880
- **Urban** 229-acre campus with easy access to Los Angeles
- **Endowment** $3.5 billion
- **Coed** 18,316 undergraduate students, 96% full-time, 51% women, 49% men
- **Most difficult** entrance level, 20% of applicants were admitted

Undergraduates 17,619 full-time, 697 part-time. Students come from 56 states and territories; 95 other countries; 32% are from out of state; 4% Black or African American, non-Hispanic/Latino; 13% Hispanic/Latino; 23% Asian, non-Hispanic/Latino; 0.2% Native Hawaiian or other Pacific Islander, non-Hispanic/Latino; 0.2% American Indian or Alaska Native, non-Hispanic/Latino; 4% Two or more races, non-Hispanic/Latino; 2% Race/ethnicity unknown; 12% international; 9% transferred in; 38% live on campus. *Retention:* 97% of full-time freshmen returned.

Freshmen *Admission:* 46,104 applied, 9,187 admitted, 3,021 enrolled. *Average high school GPA:* 3.7. *Test scores:* SAT critical reading scores over 500: 97%; SAT math scores over 500: 98%; SAT writing scores over 500: 98%; ACT scores over 18: 100%; SAT critical reading scores over 600: 83%; SAT math scores over 600: 90%; SAT writing scores over 600: 89%; ACT scores over 24: 97%; SAT critical reading scores over 700: 36%; SAT math scores over 700: 57%; SAT writing scores over 700: 50%; ACT scores over 30: 68%.

Faculty *Total:* 3,264, 54% full-time, 78% with terminal degrees. *Student/faculty ratio:* 9:1.

Academics *Calendar:* semesters. *Degrees:* bachelor's, master's, doctoral, post-master's, and postbachelor's certificates. *Special study options:* accelerated degree program, advanced placement credit, cooperative education, distance learning, double majors, English as a second language, freshman honors college, honors programs, independent study, internships, off-campus study, part-time degree program, services for LD students, student-designed majors, study abroad, summer session for credit. *ROTC:* Army (b), Navy (b), Air Force (b). *Unusual degree programs:* 3-2 engineering with more than 20 liberal art colleges nationwide.

Computers on Campus 2,000 computers/terminals and 6,000 ports are available on campus for general student use. Students can access the following: campus intranet, computer help desk, free student e-mail accounts, online (class) grades, online (class) registration, online (class) schedules, online degree progress, financial aid applications, document sharing, calendars, personal Web space, customizable Web portal, course management systems (including data and video). Campuswide network is available. 100% of college-owned or -operated housing units are wired for high-speed Internet access. Wireless service is available via entire campus.

Student Life *Housing options:* coed, disabled students. Campus housing is university owned and is provided by a third party. Freshman campus housing is guaranteed. *Activities and organizations:* drama/theater group, student-run newspaper, radio and television station, choral group, marching band, Troy Camp, USC Helenes, Alpha Phi Omega, Student Bar Association, USC Accounting Society, national fraternities, national sororities. *Campus security:* 24-hour emergency response devices and patrols, student patrols, late-night transport/escort service, controlled dormitory access. *Student services:* health clinic, personal/psychological counseling, women's center, legal services.

Athletics Member NCAA. All Division I except football (Division I-A). *Intercollegiate sports:* archery M(c)/W(c), badminton M(c)/W(c), baseball M(s), basketball M(s)/W(s), cheerleading M(c)/W(c), crew M(c)/W(s), cross-country running M(c)/W(s), equestrian sports W(c), fencing W(c), field hockey W(c), golf M(s)/W(s), gymnastics W(c), ice hockey M(c)/W(c), lacrosse M(c)/W, racquetball M(c)/W(c), rock climbing M(c)/W(c), rugby M(c)/W(c), sailing W(c), skiing (downhill) M(c)/W(c), soccer M(c)/W(s), softball W(c), squash

M(c)/W(c), swimming and diving M(s)/W(s), tennis M(s)/W(s), track and field M(s)/W(s), ultimate Frisbee M(c)/W(c), volleyball M(s)/W(s), water polo M(s)/W(s). *Intramural sports:* badminton M/W, basketball M/W, cross-country running M/W, football M/W, golf M/W, racquetball M/W, soccer M/W, softball M/W, tennis M/W, ultimate Frisbee M/W, volleyball M/W.

Standardized Tests *Required:* SAT or ACT (for admission).

Costs (2012–13) *One-time required fee:* $150. *Comprehensive fee:* $56,903 includes full-time tuition ($43,722), mandatory fees ($741), and room and board ($12,440). Full-time tuition and fees vary according to program. Part-time tuition: $1473 per unit. Part-time tuition and fees vary according to course load and program. *College room only:* $7340. Room and board charges vary according to board plan and housing facility. *Payment plans:* tuition prepayment, installment. *Waivers:* employees or children of employees.

Financial Aid Of all full-time matriculated undergraduates who enrolled in 2009, 8,671 applied for aid, 6,400 were judged to have need, 5,931 had their need fully met. 4,945 Federal Work-Study jobs (averaging $2681). In 2009, 2769 non-need-based awards were made. *Average percent of need met:* 100%. *Average financial aid package:* $35,906. *Average need-based loan:* $5873. *Average need-based gift aid:* $24,777. *Average non-need-based aid:* $15,639. *Average indebtedness upon graduation:* $30,090.

Applying *Options:* electronic application, deferred entrance. *Application fee:* $80. *Required:* essay or personal statement, high school transcript. *Application deadlines:* 1/10 (freshmen), 1/10 (out-of-state freshmen), 2/1 (transfers). *Notification:* 4/1 (freshmen), 4/1 (out-of-state freshmen), 6/1 (transfers).

Freshman Application Contact Timothy Brunold, Dean of Admission, University of Southern California, University Park Campus, Los Angeles, CA 90089. *Phone:* 213-740-1111. *Fax:* 213-821-0200. *E-mail:* admitusc@usc.edu. *Website:* http://www.usc.edu/.

University of the Pacific
Stockton, California

- **Independent** university, founded 1851
- **Suburban** 175-acre campus with easy access to Sacramento
- **Coed**
- **Moderately difficult** entrance level

Faculty *Student/faculty ratio:* 13:1.

Academics *Calendar:* semesters. *Degrees:* bachelor's, master's, and doctoral.

Student Life *Campus security:* 24-hour emergency response devices and patrols, late-night transport/escort service, controlled dormitory access.

Athletics Member NCAA. All Division I.

Standardized Tests *Required:* SAT or ACT (for admission). *Recommended:* SAT Subject Tests (for admission).

Costs (2012–13) *Comprehensive fee:* $50,358 includes full-time tuition ($37,800), mandatory fees ($520), and room and board ($12,038). Part-time tuition and fees vary according to course load. *Room and board:* Room and board charges vary according to board plan and housing facility.

Financial Aid Of all full-time matriculated undergraduates who enrolled in 2012, 3,010 applied for aid, 2,771 were judged to have need, 229 had their need fully met. In 2012, 420 non-need-based awards were made. *Average financial aid package:* $29,279. *Average need-based loan:* $7561. *Average need-based gift aid:* $21,896. *Average non-need-based aid:* $9074.

Applying *Options:* electronic application, early action. *Application fee:* $60. *Required:* essay or personal statement, high school transcript, minimum 2.5 GPA, 1 letter of recommendation. *Required for some:* audition for music program. *Recommended:* minimum 3.0 GPA.

Freshman Application Contact Mr. Rich Toledo, Director of Admissions, University of the Pacific, 3601 Pacific Avenue, Stockton, CA 95211-0197. *Phone:* 209-946-2211. *Fax:* 209-946-2413. *E-mail:* admissions@pacific.edu. *Website:* http://www.pacific.edu/.

University of the West
Rosemead, California

Freshman Application Contact University of the West, 1409 North Walnut Grove Avenue, Rosemead, CA 91770. *Phone:* 626-571-8811 Ext. 120. *Website:* http://www.uwest.edu/.

Vanguard University of Southern California
Costa Mesa, California

- **Independent** comprehensive, founded 1920, affiliated with Assemblies of God
- **Suburban** 38-acre campus with easy access to Los Angeles
- **Endowment** $5.0 million
- **Coed**
- **Moderately difficult** entrance level

Faculty *Student/faculty ratio:* 17:1.

Academics *Calendar:* semesters. *Degrees:* bachelor's and master's.

Student Life *Campus security:* 24-hour emergency response devices and patrols, student patrols, late-night transport/escort service.

Athletics Member NAIA.

Standardized Tests *Required:* SAT or ACT (for admission).

Costs (2012–13) *Comprehensive fee:* $37,200 includes full-time tuition ($28,500) and room and board ($8700). Full-time tuition and fees vary according to course load. Part-time tuition and fees vary according to course load. *Room and board:* Room and board charges vary according to board plan and housing facility.

Financial Aid Of all full-time matriculated undergraduates who enrolled in 2010, 1,183 applied for aid, 1,110 were judged to have need, 135 had their need fully met. 94 Federal Work-Study jobs (averaging $2386). In 2010, 196 non-need-based awards were made. *Average percent of need met:* 67. *Average financial aid package:* $19,230. *Average need-based loan:* $4683. *Average need-based gift aid:* $8695. *Average non-need-based aid:* $12,957. *Average indebtedness upon graduation:* $28,256.

Applying *Options:* electronic application, early admission, early action, deferred entrance. *Application fee:* $45. *Required:* essay or personal statement, high school transcript, minimum 2.8 GPA, 2 letters of recommendation. *Required for some:* interview.

Freshman Application Contact Kristi Pruett, Undergraduate Inquiry Data Coordinator, Vanguard University of Southern California, 55 Fair Drive, Costa Mesa, CA 92626. *Phone:* 800-722-6279 Ext. 4107. *Toll-free phone:* 800-722-6279. *Fax:* 714-966-5471. *E-mail:* admissions@vanguard.edu. *Website:* http://www.vanguard.edu/.

West Coast University
Anaheim, California

Admissions Office Contact West Coast University, 1477 S. Manchester Avenue, Anaheim, CA 92802. *Website:* http://westcoastuniversity.edu/.

West Coast University
North Hollywood, California

Director of Admissions Mr. Roger A. Miller, Dean of Admissions and Registrar, West Coast University, 12215 Victory Boulevard, North Hollywood, CA 91606. *Phone:* 213-427-4400. *Toll-free phone:* 866-508-2684. *E-mail:* info@katz.wcula.edu. *Website:* http://www.westcoastuniversity.edu/.

West Coast University
Ontario, California

Admissions Office Contact West Coast University, 2855 E. Guasti Road, Ontario, CA 91761. *Website:* http://westcoastuniversity.edu/.

Westmont College
Santa Barbara, California

Freshman Application Contact Mrs. Joyce Luy, Dean of Admission, Westmont College, 955 La Paz Road, Santa Barbara, CA 93108. *Phone:* 805-565-6200. *Toll-free phone:* 800-777-9011. *Fax:* 805-565-6234. *E-mail:* admissions@westmont.edu. *Website:* http://www.westmont.edu/.

See next page for display ad and page 1642 for the College Close-Up.

Westwood College–Anaheim

Anaheim, California

Freshman Application Contact Westwood College–Anaheim, 1551 South Douglass Road, Anaheim, CA 92806. *Phone:* 714-704-2721. *Toll-free phone:* 877-840-8999.
Website: http://www.westwood.edu/.

Westwood College–Inland Empire

Upland, California

Freshman Application Contact Westwood College–Inland Empire, 20 West 7th Street, Upland, CA 91786. *Phone:* 909-931-7599. *Toll-free phone:* 866-221-5632.
Website: http://www.westwood.edu/.

Westwood College–Los Angeles

Los Angeles, California

Freshman Application Contact Westwood College–Los Angeles, 3250 Wilshire Boulevard, 4th Floor, Los Angeles, CA 90010. *Phone:* 213-382-2328. *Toll-free phone:* 866-930-9256.
Website: http://www.westwood.edu/.

Westwood College–South Bay Campus

Torrance, California

Freshman Application Contact Westwood College–South Bay Campus, 19700 South Vermont Avenue, Suite 100, Torrance, CA 90502. *Phone:* 310-965-0877. *Toll-free phone:* 888-403-3308.
Website: http://www.westwood.edu/.

Whittier College

Whittier, California

- **Independent** comprehensive, founded 1887
- **Suburban** 95-acre campus with easy access to Los Angeles
- **Coed**
- **Moderately difficult** entrance level

Faculty *Student/faculty ratio:* 13:1.
Academics *Calendar:* 4-1-4. *Degrees:* bachelor's, master's, and doctoral.
Student Life *Campus security:* 24-hour emergency response devices and patrols, late-night transport/escort service, controlled dormitory access.
Athletics Member NCAA. All Division III.
Standardized Tests *Required:* SAT or ACT (for admission). *Recommended:* SAT Subject Tests (for admission).
Costs (2012–13) *One-time required fee:* $200. *Comprehensive fee:* $50,058 includes full-time tuition ($38,280), mandatory fees ($390), and room and board ($11,388). Part-time tuition: $1610 per unit. *College room only:* $6108. Room and board charges vary according to board plan.
Financial Aid *Of all full-time matriculated undergraduates who enrolled in 2011,* 1,361 applied for aid, 1,243 were judged to have need, 144 had their need fully met. *In 2011,* 275 non-need-based awards were made. *Average percent of need met:* 73. *Average financial aid package:* $31,261. *Average need-based loan:* $6905. *Average need-based gift aid:* $26,632. *Average non-need-based aid:* $17,658. *Average indebtedness upon graduation:* $26,541. *Financial aid deadline:* 6/30.
Applying *Options:* electronic application, early action, deferred entrance. *Application fee:* $50. *Required:* essay or personal statement, high school transcript, minimum 2.0 GPA, 2 letters of recommendation. *Required for some:* minimum 3.5 GPA. *Recommended:* minimum 2.5 GPA, interview.
Freshman Application Contact Mr. Kieron Miller, Director of Admission, Whittier College, Office of Admission, 13406 East Philadelphia Street, Whittier, CA 90608-0634. *Phone:* 562-907-4238. *Fax:* 562-907-4870. *E-mail:* admission@whittier.edu.
Website: http://www.whittier.edu/.

William Jessup University
Rocklin, California

- **Independent nondenominational** 4-year, founded 1939
- **Suburban** 126-acre campus with easy access to Sacramento
- **Coed**
- **Moderately difficult** entrance level

Faculty *Student/faculty ratio:* 13:1.

Academics *Calendar:* semesters. *Degrees:* certificates, associate, bachelor's, and postbachelor's certificates.

Student Life *Campus security:* student patrols, late-night transport/escort service, controlled dormitory access, day and evening patrols by trained security personnel.

Athletics Member NAIA.

Standardized Tests *Required:* SAT or ACT (for admission).

Costs (2012–13) *Comprehensive fee:* $31,970 includes full-time tuition ($22,900) and room and board ($9070). Full-time tuition and fees vary according to course load. Part-time tuition: $970 per credit hour. Part-time tuition and fees vary according to course load. *Room and board:* Room and board charges vary according to board plan and housing facility.

Financial Aid *Of all full-time matriculated undergraduates who enrolled in 2012,* 724 applied for aid, 667 were judged to have need, 71 had their need fully met. 65 Federal Work-Study jobs (averaging $2591). 30 state and other part-time jobs (averaging $1580). *In 2012,* 99 non-need-based awards were made. *Average percent of need met:* 66. *Average financial aid package:* $18,852. *Average need-based loan:* $4527. *Average need-based gift aid:* $15,258. *Average non-need-based aid:* $5775. *Average indebtedness upon graduation:* $21,057.

Applying *Options:* electronic application. *Application fee:* $45. *Required:* essay or personal statement, high school transcript, minimum 2.5 GPA. *Required for some:* 1 letter of recommendation, interview. *Recommended:* 1 letter of recommendation, interview.

Freshman Application Contact Mr. Vance Pascua, Director of Admission, William Jessup University, 333 Sunset Boulevard, Rocklin, CA 95765. *Phone:* 916-577-2222. *Toll-free phone:* 800-355-7522. *Fax:* 916-577-2220. *E-mail:* admissions@jessup.edu.

Website: http://www.jessup.edu/.

Woodbury University
Burbank, California

- **Independent** comprehensive, founded 1884
- **Suburban** 22-acre campus with easy access to Los Angeles
- **Endowment** $16.9 million
- **Coed** 1,488 undergraduate students, 83% full-time, 50% women, 50% men
- **Moderately difficult** entrance level, 65% of applicants were admitted

Undergraduates 1,236 full-time, 252 part-time. Students come from 30 states and territories; 9 other countries; 4% Black or African American, non-Hispanic/Latino; 30% Hispanic/Latino; 9% Asian, non-Hispanic/Latino; 0.9% Native Hawaiian or other Pacific Islander, non-Hispanic/Latino; 0.5% American Indian or Alaska Native, non-Hispanic/Latino; 2% Two or more races, non-Hispanic/Latino; 0.5% Race/ethnicity unknown; 15% international; 61% transferred in; 16% live on campus. *Retention:* 83% of full-time freshmen returned.

Freshmen *Admission:* 661 applied, 432 admitted, 180 enrolled. *Average high school GPA:* 3.24. *Test scores:* SAT critical reading scores over 500: 40%; SAT math scores over 500: 49%; ACT scores over 18: 100%; SAT critical reading scores over 600: 10%; SAT math scores over 600: 11%; ACT scores over 24: 36%; SAT math scores over 700: 1%.

Faculty *Total:* 315, 26% full-time. *Student/faculty ratio:* 10:1.

Academics *Calendar:* semesters. *Degrees:* bachelor's and master's. *Special study options:* academic remediation for entering students, accelerated degree program, adult/continuing education programs, advanced placement credit, double majors, English as a second language, independent study, internships, part-time degree program, services for LD students, student-designed majors, study abroad, summer session for credit.

Computers on Campus 225 computers/terminals are available on campus for general student use. Students can access the following: campus intranet, computer help desk, free student e-mail accounts, online (class) grades, online (class) registration, online (class) schedules. Campuswide network is available. 100% of college-owned or -operated housing units are wired for high-speed Internet access. Wireless service is available via classrooms, computer centers, computer labs, learning centers, libraries, student centers.

Student Life *Housing options:* coed. Campus housing is university owned and is provided by a third party. Freshman applicants given priority for college housing. *Activities and organizations:* Associated Student Government, American Institute of Architecture Students, Armenian Student Association, La Voz

Unida, Collegiate Entrepreneurs' Organization (CEO), national fraternities, national sororities. *Campus security:* 24-hour patrols, late-night transport/escort service, controlled dormitory access. *Student services:* health clinic, personal/psychological counseling.

Athletics *Intramural sports:* basketball M/W, soccer M/W.

Standardized Tests *Required:* SAT or ACT (for admission).

Costs (2012–13) *Comprehensive fee:* $41,396 includes full-time tuition ($31,054), mandatory fees ($390), and room and board ($9952). Full-time tuition and fees vary according to course load, degree level, and program. Part-time tuition and fees vary according to course load, degree level, and program. *College room only:* $6200. Room and board charges vary according to board plan, housing facility, and location. *Payment plan:* deferred payment. *Waivers:* employees or children of employees.

Financial Aid Of all full-time matriculated undergraduates who enrolled in 2012, 984 applied for aid, 939 were judged to have need, 22 had their need fully met. In 2012, 91 non-need-based awards were made. *Average percent of need met:* 51%. *Average financial aid package:* $20,007. *Average need-based loan:* $4469. *Average need-based gift aid:* $15,923. *Average non-need-based aid:* $9706. *Average indebtedness upon graduation:* $37,856.

Applying *Options:* electronic application, deferred entrance. *Application fee:* $50. *Required:* minimum 2.0 GPA. *Required for some:* high school transcript. *Recommended:* essay or personal statement, minimum 3.0 GPA, 2 letters of recommendation. *Application deadlines:* rolling (freshmen), rolling (transfers). *Notification:* continuous (freshmen), continuous (transfers).

Freshman Application Contact Sabrina Taylor, Woodbury University, 7500 Glenoaks Boulevard, Burbank, CA 91510-7846. *Phone:* 800-784-9663. *Toll-free phone:* 800-784-WOOD. *Fax:* 818-767-0032. *E-mail:* admissions@woodbury.edu.

Website: http://www.woodbury.edu/.

Yeshiva Ohr Elchonon Chabad/West Coast Talmudical Seminary
Los Angeles, California

Director of Admissions Rabbi Ezra Binyomin Schochet, Dean, Yeshiva Ohr Elchonon Chabad/West Coast Talmudical Seminary, 7215 Waring Avenue, Los Angeles, CA 90046-7660. *Phone:* 323-937-3763. *E-mail:* roshyeshiva@yoec.edu.

Website: http://www.yoec.edu/.

COLORADO

Adams State University
Alamosa, Colorado

- **State-supported** comprehensive, founded 1921
- **Small-town** 90-acre campus with easy access to Pueblo
- **Endowment** $643,931
- **Coed** 2,431 undergraduate students, 79% full-time, 52% women, 48% men
- **Moderately difficult** entrance level, 66% of applicants were admitted

Undergraduates 1,909 full-time, 522 part-time. Students come from 52 states and territories; 12 other countries; 20% are from out of state; 6% Black or African American, non-Hispanic/Latino; 31% Hispanic/Latino; 1% Asian, non-Hispanic/Latino; 0.4% Native Hawaiian or other Pacific Islander, non-Hispanic/Latino; 1% American Indian or Alaska Native, non-Hispanic/Latino; 3% Two or more races, non-Hispanic/Latino; 5% Race/ethnicity unknown; 9% transferred in; 47% live on campus. *Retention:* 55% of full-time freshmen returned.

Freshmen *Admission:* 2,569 applied, 1,701 admitted, 514 enrolled. *Average high school GPA:* 3.02. *Test scores:* SAT critical reading scores over 500: 40%; SAT math scores over 500: 37%; SAT writing scores over 500: 31%; ACT scores over 18: 76%; SAT critical reading scores over 600: 8%; SAT math scores over 600: 15%; SAT writing scores over 600: 4%; ACT scores over 24: 17%; SAT critical reading scores over 700: 1%; SAT writing scores over 700: 1%.

Faculty *Total:* 177, 63% full-time, 42% with terminal degrees. *Student/faculty ratio:* 15:1.

Academics *Calendar:* semesters. *Degrees:* associate, bachelor's, and master's. *Special study options:* academic remediation for entering students, accelerated degree program, adult/continuing education programs, advanced placement credit, distance learning, double majors, independent study, internships, off-campus study, part-time degree program, services for LD students, student-designed majors, study abroad, summer session for credit.

Computers on Campus 326 computers/terminals are available on campus for general student use. Students can access the following: campus intranet, computer help desk, free student e-mail accounts, online (class) grades, online (class) registration, online (class) schedules. Campuswide network is available. 100% of college-owned or -operated housing units are wired for high-speed Internet access. Wireless service is available via classrooms, computer centers, computer labs, dorm rooms, learning centers, libraries, student centers.
Student Life *Housing:* on-campus residence required through sophomore year. *Options:* coed, men-only, women-only. Campus housing is university owned. Freshman campus housing is guaranteed. *Activities and organizations:* drama/theater group, student-run newspaper, radio station, choral group, marching band, Student Programming Board, Student Government, Semillas de la Tierra, Newman Club, Fellowship of Christian Athletes. *Campus security:* 24-hour emergency response devices and patrols, student patrols, late-night transport/escort service, controlled dormitory access. *Student services:* personal/psychological counseling.
Athletics Member NCAA. All Division II. *Intercollegiate sports:* baseball M(s), basketball M(s)/W(s), cross-country running M(s)/W(s), football M(s), golf M(s)/W(s), lacrosse M(s)/W(s), soccer M(s)/W(s), softball W(s), swimming and diving M(s)/W(s), track and field M(s)/W(s), volleyball W(s), wrestling M(s). *Intramural sports:* basketball M/W, bowling M/W, cheerleading M(c)/W(c), football M/W, golf M(c)/W(c), racquetball M/W, rock climbing M/W, rugby M(c)/W(c), skiing (cross-country) M/W, skiing (downhill) M/W, soccer M/W, softball M/W, swimming and diving M/W, volleyball M/W, water polo M/W.
Standardized Tests *Required:* SAT or ACT (for admission).
Costs (2012–13) *Tuition:* state resident $3816 full-time; nonresident $14,784 full-time. Full-time tuition and fees vary according to course load. Part-time tuition and fees vary according to course load. *Required fees:* $2632 full-time. *Room and board:* $7900; room only: $4200. Room and board charges vary according to board plan and housing facility. *Payment plans:* installment, deferred payment. *Waivers:* senior citizens and employees or children of employees.
Financial Aid Of all full-time matriculated undergraduates who enrolled in 2011, 1,878 applied for aid, 1,640 were judged to have need, 13 had their need fully met. 241 Federal Work-Study jobs (averaging $993). 408 state and other part-time jobs (averaging $2025). *Average percent of need met:* 59%. *Average financial aid package:* $12,079. *Average need-based loan:* $3764. *Average need-based gift aid:* $7717. *Average indebtedness upon graduation:* $27,785.
Applying *Options:* electronic application, early admission, deferred entrance. *Application fee:* $30. *Required:* high school transcript, minimum 2.0 GPA. *Required for some:* essay or personal statement, interview, audition for music majors, portfolio for art majors. *Application deadlines:* 8/1 (freshmen), 8/10 (out-of-state freshmen), 8/1 (transfers). *Notification:* continuous (freshmen), continuous (out-of-state freshmen), continuous (transfers).
Freshman Application Contact Miss Michelle Romero, Associate Director of Admissions, Adams State University, 208 Edgemont Boulevard, Alamosa, CO 81101. *Phone:* 719-587-7712. *Toll-free phone:* 800-824-6494. *Fax:* 719-587-7522. *E-mail:* admissions@adams.edu.
Website: http://www.adams.edu/.

American Sentinel University
Aurora, Colorado
Director of Admissions Natalie Nixon, Vice President of Admission, American Sentinel University, 2260 South Xanadu Way, Suite 310, Aurora, CO 80014. *Phone:* 800-729-2427. *Toll-free phone:* 800-729-2427. *Fax:* 866-505-2450. *E-mail:* natalie.nixon@AmericanSentinel.edu.
Website: http://www.americansentinel.edu/.

Argosy University, Denver
Denver, Colorado
Freshman Application Contact Argosy University, Denver, 7600 East Eastman Avenue, Denver, CO 80231. *Phone:* 303-248-2700. *Toll-free phone:* 866-431-5981.
Website: http://www.argosy.edu/denver/.

The Art Institute of Colorado
Denver, Colorado
- **Proprietary** 4-year, founded 1952, part of Education Management Corporation
- **Urban** campus
- **Coed**
Academics *Calendar:* quarters. *Degrees:* diplomas, associate, and bachelor's.

Freshman Application Contact The Art Institute of Colorado, 1200 Lincoln Street, Denver, CO 80203. *Phone:* 303-837-0825. *Toll-free phone:* 800-275-2420.
Website: http://www.artinstitutes.edu/denver/.
See full-page ad on page 54 and page 1076 for the College Close-Up.

Aspen University
Denver, Colorado
Director of Admissions Admissions, Aspen University, 501 South Cherry Street, Suite 350, Denver, CO 80246. *Phone:* 303-333-4224. *Toll-free phone:* 800-441-4746. *Fax:* 303-336-1144. *E-mail:* admissions@aspen.edu.
Website: http://www.aspen.edu/.

CollegeAmerica–Colorado Springs
Colorado Springs, Colorado
Freshman Application Contact CollegeAmerica–Colorado Springs, 3645 Citadel Drive South, Colorado Springs, CO 80909. *Phone:* 719-637-0600. *Toll-free phone:* 800-622-2894.
Website: http://www.collegeamerica.edu/.

CollegeAmerica–Denver
Denver, Colorado
Freshman Application Contact Admissions Office, CollegeAmerica–Denver, 1385 South Colorado Boulevard, Denver, CO 80222. *Phone:* 303-300-8740. *Toll-free phone:* 800-622-2894.
Website: http://www.collegeamerica.edu/.

CollegeAmerica–Fort Collins
Fort Collins, Colorado
Director of Admissions Ms. Anna DiTorrice-Mull, Director of Admissions, CollegeAmerica–Fort Collins, 4601 South Mason Street, Fort Collins, CO 80525-3740. *Phone:* 970-223-6060 Ext. 8002. *Toll-free phone:* 800-622-2894.
Website: http://www.collegeamerica.edu/.

Colorado Christian University
Lakewood, Colorado
Freshman Application Contact Jo Leda Martin, Associate Director of Admissions, Colorado Christian University, 8787 W Alameda Avenue. *Phone:* 303-963-3000. *Toll-free phone:* 800-44-FAITH. *Fax:* 303-963-3201. *E-mail:* jomartin@ccu.edu.
Website: http://www.ccu.edu/.

The Colorado College
Colorado Springs, Colorado
- **Independent** comprehensive, founded 1874
- **Urban** 90-acre campus with easy access to Denver
- **Endowment** $507.0 million
- **Coed** 2,008 undergraduate students, 99% full-time, 54% women, 46% men
- **Very difficult** entrance level, 23% of applicants were admitted
Undergraduates 1,983 full-time, 25 part-time. Students come from 51 states and territories; 58 other countries; 80% are from out of state; 2% Black or African American, non-Hispanic/Latino; 7% Hispanic/Latino; 4% Asian, non-Hispanic/Latino; 0.3% American Indian or Alaska Native, non-Hispanic/Latino; 7% Two or more races, non-Hispanic/Latino; 1% Race/ethnicity unknown; 5% international; 2% transferred in; 78% live on campus. *Retention:* 95% of full-time freshmen returned.
Freshmen *Admission:* 5,606 applied, 1,289 admitted, 510 enrolled. *Test scores:* SAT critical reading scores over 500: 99%; SAT math scores over 500: 99%; SAT writing scores over 500: 99%; ACT scores over 18: 100%; SAT critical reading scores over 600: 87%; SAT math scores over 600: 89%; SAT writing scores over 600: 88%; ACT scores over 24: 95%; SAT critical reading scores over 700: 40%; SAT math scores over 700: 35%; SAT writing scores over 700: 33%; ACT scores over 30: 53%.
Faculty *Total:* 198, 84% full-time. *Student/faculty ratio:* 10:1.
Academics *Calendar:* modular. *Degrees:* bachelor's and master's (master's degree in education only). *Special study options:* advanced placement credit, double majors, English as a second language, independent study, off-campus study, services for LD students, student-designed majors, study abroad, summer session for credit. *ROTC:* Army (c). *Unusual degree programs:* 3-2 engi-

neering with Rensselaer Polytechnic Institute, Washington University in St. Louis, University of Southern California, Columbia University.

Computers on Campus 396 computers/terminals are available on campus for general student use. Students can access the following: campus intranet, computer help desk, free student e-mail accounts, online (class) grades, online (class) registration, online (class) schedules. Campuswide network is available. 100% of college-owned or -operated housing units are wired for high-speed Internet access. Wireless service is available via entire campus.

Student Life *Housing:* on-campus residence required through junior year. *Options:* coed, men-only, women-only. Campus housing is university owned. Freshman campus housing is guaranteed. *Activities and organizations:* drama/theater group, student-run newspaper, choral group, national fraternities, national sororities. *Campus security:* 24-hour emergency response devices and patrols, late-night transport/escort service, controlled dormitory access, whistle program, student escort service, good campus lighting. *Student services:* health clinic, personal/psychological counseling.

Athletics Member NCAA. All Division III except ice hockey (Division I), soccer (Division I). *Intercollegiate sports:* baseball M(c), basketball M/W, cross-country running M/W, equestrian sports M(c)/W(c), ice hockey M(s)/W(c), lacrosse M/W, rugby M(c)/W(c), skiing (downhill) M(c)/W(c), soccer M/W(s), softball W(c), swimming and diving M/W, tennis M/W, track and field M/W, ultimate Frisbee M(c)/W(c), volleyball W, water polo W(c). *Intramural sports:* basketball M/W, football M/W, ice hockey M/W, racquetball M/W, soccer M/W, softball M/W, table tennis M/W, ultimate Frisbee M/W, volleyball M/W.

Standardized Tests *Required for some:* SAT and SAT Subject Tests or ACT (for admission).

Costs (2012–13) *One-time required fee:* $150. *Comprehensive fee:* $51,670 includes full-time tuition ($41,742), mandatory fees ($200), and room and board ($9728). Part-time tuition: $6957 per course. Part-time tuition and fees vary according to course load. *College room only:* $5496. Room and board charges vary according to board plan and housing facility. *Payment plan:* installment. *Waivers:* employees or children of employees.

Financial Aid Of all full-time matriculated undergraduates who enrolled in 2010, 888 applied for aid, 750 were judged to have need, 469 had their need fully met. 225 Federal Work-Study jobs (averaging $1750). 128 state and other part-time jobs (averaging $1664). In 2010, 158 non-need-based awards were made. *Average percent of need met:* 92%. *Average financial aid package:* $33,298. *Average need-based loan:* $4355. *Average need-based gift aid:* $30,672. *Average non-need-based aid:* $13,573. *Average indebtedness upon graduation:* $18,349. *Financial aid deadline:* 2/15.

Applying *Options:* electronic application, early decision, early action, deferred entrance. *Application fee:* $60. *Required:* essay or personal statement, high school transcript, 2 letters of recommendation. *Recommended:* interview. *Application deadlines:* 1/15 (freshmen), 3/1 (transfers), 11/15 (early action). *Early decision deadline:* 11/15 (for plan 1), 1/1 (for plan 2). *Notification:* 4/1 (freshmen), 5/1 (transfers), 12/15 (early decision plan 1), 2/10 (early decision plan 2), 12/20 (early action).

Freshman Application Contact Mr. Matthew Bonser, Associate Director of Admission, The Colorado College, 14 East Cache La Poudre, Colorado Springs, CO 80903-3294. *Phone:* 719-389-6344. *Toll-free phone:* 800-542-7214. *Fax:* 719-389-6816. *E-mail:* admission@coloradocollege.edu. *Website:* http://www.coloradocollege.edu/.

Colorado Heights University

Denver, Colorado

Director of Admissions Ashley Henderson, Admissions Coordinator, Colorado Heights University, 3001 South Federal Boulevard, Denver, CO 80236-2711. *Phone:* 303-937-4221. *E-mail:* admissions@tlhu.edu. *Website:* http://www.chu.edu/.

Colorado Mesa University

Grand Junction, Colorado

- **State-supported** comprehensive, founded 1925
- **Small-town** 78-acre campus
- **Coed** 10,393 undergraduate students, 77% full-time, 49% women, 51% men
- **Minimally difficult** entrance level, 82% of applicants were admitted

Undergraduates 8,017 full-time, 2,376 part-time. Students come from 43 states and territories; 14 other countries; 12% are from out of state; 2% Black or African American, non-Hispanic/Latino; 13% Hispanic/Latino; 1% Asian, non-Hispanic/Latino; 0.6% Native Hawaiian or other Pacific Islander, non-Hispanic/Latino; 1% American Indian or Alaska Native, non-Hispanic/Latino; 3% Two or more races, non-Hispanic/Latino; 46% Race/ethnicity unknown; 0.6% international; 6% transferred in; 21% live on campus. *Retention:* 64% of full-time freshmen returned.

Freshmen *Admission:* 5,840 applied, 4,812 admitted, 3,094 enrolled. *Average high school GPA:* 3. *Test scores:* SAT critical reading scores over 500: 40%; SAT math scores over 500: 47%; ACT scores over 18: 75%; SAT critical reading scores over 600: 11%; SAT math scores over 600: 13%; ACT scores over 24: 23%; SAT critical reading scores over 700: 2%; SAT math scores over 700: 2%; ACT scores over 30: 2%.

Faculty *Total:* 607, 44% full-time. *Student/faculty ratio:* 22:1.

Academics *Calendar:* semesters. *Degrees:* certificates, associate, bachelor's, master's, and doctoral. *Special study options:* academic remediation for entering students, accelerated degree program, adult/continuing education programs, advanced placement credit, distance learning, double majors, honors programs, independent study, internships, off-campus study, part-time degree program, services for LD students, study abroad, summer session for credit.

Computers on Campus 525 computers/terminals are available on campus for general student use. Students can access the following: campus intranet, computer help desk, free student e-mail accounts, online (class) grades, online (class) registration, online (class) schedules. Campuswide network is available. 100% of college-owned or -operated housing units are wired for high-speed Internet access. Wireless service is available via entire campus.

Student Life *Housing:* on-campus residence required through sophomore year. *Options:* coed, women-only, disabled students. Campus housing is university owned. Freshman applicants given priority for college housing. *Activities and organizations:* drama/theater group, student-run newspaper, radio and television station, choral group, marching band, Environmental Club, Student Body Association, KMSA radio station, Rodeo Club, Campus Residents Association. *Campus security:* 24-hour emergency response devices and patrols, late-night transport/escort service, controlled dormitory access. *Student services:* health clinic, personal/psychological counseling, legal services.

Athletics Member NCAA. All Division II. *Intercollegiate sports:* baseball M(s), basketball M(s)/W(s), cross-country running M(s)/W(s), football M(s), golf M(s)/W(s), lacrosse M(s)/W(s), rugby M(c)/W(c), skiing (cross-country) M(c)/W(c), skiing (downhill) M(c)/W(c), soccer M(s)/W(s), softball W(s), swimming and diving M(s)/W(s), tennis M(s)/W(s), track and field M(s)/W(s), volleyball W(s), wrestling M(s). *Intramural sports:* badminton M/W, basketball M/W, equestrian sports M/W, football M/W, racquetball M/W, soccer M/W, softball M/W, tennis M/W, ultimate Frisbee M/W, volleyball M/W, water polo M/W.

Standardized Tests *Required:* SAT or ACT (for admission).

Costs (2012–13) *Tuition:* state resident $6102 full-time, $203 per credit hour part-time; nonresident $16,280 full-time, $543 per credit hour part-time. Full-time tuition and fees vary according to course load. Part-time tuition and fees vary according to course load. *Required fees:* $768 full-time, $26 per credit hour part-time. *Room and board:* $9103. Room and board charges vary according to board plan and housing facility. *Payment plan:* installment. *Waivers:* employees or children of employees.

Financial Aid Of all full-time matriculated undergraduates who enrolled in 2011, 5,563 applied for aid, 4,717 were judged to have need, 539 had their need fully met. In 2011, 274 non-need-based awards were made. *Average percent of need met:* 56%. *Average financial aid package:* $7857. *Average need-based loan:* $3727. *Average need-based gift aid:* $4787. *Average non-need-based aid:* $2230. *Average indebtedness upon graduation:* $24,714.

Applying *Options:* electronic application, deferred entrance. *Application fee:* $30. *Required:* high school transcript. *Recommended:* essay or personal statement, 2 letters of recommendation. *Application deadlines:* rolling (freshmen), rolling (out-of-state freshmen), rolling (transfers). *Notification:* continuous (freshmen), continuous (out-of-state freshmen), continuous (transfers).

Freshman Application Contact Admissions, Colorado Mesa University, 1100 North Avenue, Grand Junction, CO 81501. *Phone:* 970-248-1875. *Toll-free phone:* 800-982-MESA. *Fax:* 970-248-1973. *E-mail:* admissions@coloradomeas.edu. *Website:* http://www.coloradomesa.edu/.

Colorado Mountain College

Glenwood Springs, Colorado

- **District-supported** 4-year, founded 1965, part of Colorado Mountain College District System
- **Rural** 680-acre campus
- **Coed** 2,465 undergraduate students
- **Noncompetitive** entrance level

Undergraduates 44% live on campus.

Freshmen *Average high school GPA:* 2.4.

Faculty *Total:* 28. *Student/faculty ratio:* 12:1.

Academics *Calendar:* semesters. *Degrees:* certificates, associate, and bachelor's. *Special study options:* academic remediation for entering students, adult/continuing education programs, advanced placement credit, cooperative education, distance learning, double majors, English as a second language, honors programs, independent study, internships, part-time degree program, services for LD students, study abroad, summer session for credit.

Computers on Campus 65 computers/terminals are available on campus for general student use. Students can access the following: campus intranet, computer help desk, free student e-mail accounts, online (class) grades, online (class) registration, online (class) schedules. Campuswide network is available. Wireless service is available via entire campus.

Student Life *Housing:* on-campus residence required for freshman year. *Options:* coed, disabled students. Campus housing is university owned. Freshman applicants given priority for college housing. *Activities and organizations:* drama/theater group, student-run newspaper, student government, Outdoor activities, World Awareness Society, Peer Mentors, Student Activities Board. *Campus security:* 24-hour emergency response devices, student patrols, controlled dormitory access. *Student services:* health clinic, personal/psychological counseling.

Athletics Member NCAA, NJCAA. All NCAA Division I. *Intercollegiate sports:* skiing (downhill) M/W. *Intramural sports:* basketball M/W, rock climbing M/W, skiing (cross-country) M/W, skiing (downhill) M/W, ultimate Frisbee M/W, volleyball M/W.

Standardized Tests *Recommended:* SAT or ACT (for admission).

Costs (2013–14) *Tuition:* area resident $1680 full-time, $56 per credit part-time; state resident $2850 full-time, $95 per credit part-time; nonresident $9970 full-time, $299 per credit part-time. Full-time tuition and fees vary according to course level. Part-time tuition and fees vary according to course level. *Required fees:* $180 full-time. *Room and board:* $8164. *Payment plan:* installment. *Waivers:* senior citizens.

Applying *Options:* electronic application, early admission, deferred entrance. *Required:* high school transcript. *Application deadlines:* rolling (freshmen), rolling (out-of-state freshmen), rolling (transfers).

Freshman Application Contact Vicky Butler, Admissions Assistant, Colorado Mountain College, 3000 CR 114, Glenwood Springs, CO 81601. *Phone:* 970-947-8276. *Toll-free phone:* 800-621-8559. *E-mail:* Vvalentine@coloradomtn.edu.
Website: http://www.coloradomtn.edu/.

Colorado Mountain College, Alpine Campus

Steamboat Springs, Colorado

- **District-supported** 4-year, founded 1965, part of Colorado Mountain College District System
- **Small-town** 10-acre campus
- **Coed** 1,550 undergraduate students
- **Noncompetitive** entrance level

Undergraduates 44% live on campus.
Freshmen *Average high school GPA:* 2.4.
Faculty *Total:* 25. *Student/faculty ratio:* 12:1.
Academics *Calendar:* semesters. *Degrees:* certificates, associate, and bachelor's. *Special study options:* academic remediation for entering students, adult/continuing education programs, advanced placement credit, cooperative education, distance learning, double majors, English as a second language, honors programs, independent study, internships, off-campus study, part-time degree program, services for LD students, study abroad, summer session for credit.

Computers on Campus 60 computers/terminals are available on campus for general student use. Students can access the following: campus intranet, computer help desk, free student e-mail accounts, online (class) grades, online (class) registration, online (class) schedules. Campuswide network is available. 100% of college-owned or -operated housing units are wired for high-speed Internet access. Wireless service is available via entire campus.

Student Life *Housing:* on-campus residence required for freshman year. *Options:* coed, disabled students. Campus housing is university owned. *Activities and organizations:* student-run newspaper, student government, Sky Club, Ski Club, International Club, Phi Theta Kappa. *Campus security:* 24-hour emergency response devices, student patrols, controlled dormitory access. *Student services:* health clinic, personal/psychological counseling.

Athletics Member NCAA, NJCAA. All NCAA Division I. *Intercollegiate sports:* skiing (downhill) M/W. *Intramural sports:* basketball M/W, skiing (cross-country) M/W, skiing (downhill) M/W, soccer M/W, ultimate Frisbee M/W, volleyball M/W.

Standardized Tests *Recommended:* SAT or ACT (for admission).

Costs (2013–14) *Tuition:* area resident $1680 full-time, $56 per credit part-time; state resident $2850 full-time, $95 per quarter hour part-time; nonresident $8970 full-time, $299 per credit part-time. Full-time tuition and fees vary according to course level. Part-time tuition and fees vary according to course level. *Required fees:* $180 full-time. *Room and board:* $8164. Room and board charges vary according to board plan. *Payment plan:* installment. *Waivers:* senior citizens.

Financial Aid Of all full-time matriculated undergraduates who enrolled in 2011, 40 Federal Work-Study jobs (averaging $1173). 62 state and other part-time jobs (averaging $1060).

Applying *Options:* electronic application, early admission, deferred entrance. *Required:* high school transcript. *Application deadlines:* rolling (freshmen), rolling (out-of-state freshmen), rolling (transfers).

Freshman Application Contact Ms. Stephanie Fletcher, Admissions Assistant, Colorado Mountain College, Alpine Campus, 1330 Bob Adams Drive, Steamboat Springs, CO 80487. *Phone:* 970-870-4417 Ext. 4417. *Toll-free phone:* 800-621-8559. *E-mail:* stephaniefletcher@coloradomtn.edu.
Website: http://www.coloradomtn.edu/.

Colorado Mountain College, Timberline Campus

Leadville, Colorado

- **District-supported** 4-year, founded 1965, part of Colorado Mountain College District System
- **Rural** 200-acre campus
- **Coed** 1,209 undergraduate students
- **Noncompetitive** entrance level

Undergraduates 30% live on campus.
Freshmen *Average high school GPA:* 2.4.
Faculty *Total:* 16. *Student/faculty ratio:* 12:1.
Academics *Calendar:* semesters. *Degrees:* certificates, associate, and bachelor's. *Special study options:* academic remediation for entering students, adult/continuing education programs, advanced placement credit, cooperative education, distance learning, double majors, English as a second language, honors programs, independent study, internships, off-campus study, part-time degree program, services for LD students, student-designed majors, study abroad, summer session for credit.

Computers on Campus 30 computers/terminals are available on campus for general student use. Students can access the following: free student e-mail accounts, online (class) grades, online (class) registration, online (class) schedules. Campuswide network is available. 100% of college-owned or -operated housing units are wired for high-speed Internet access. Wireless service is available via entire campus.

Student Life *Housing:* on-campus residence required for freshman year. *Options:* coed, disabled students. Campus housing is university owned. Freshman applicants given priority for college housing. *Activities and organizations:* Environmental Club, Outdoor Club, Student Activities Board. *Campus security:* 24-hour emergency response devices, student patrols, controlled dormitory access. *Student services:* health clinic, personal/psychological counseling.

Athletics Member NCAA, NJCAA. All NCAA Division I. *Intercollegiate sports:* skiing (downhill) M/W. *Intramural sports:* basketball M, rock climbing M/W, skiing (cross-country) M/W, skiing (downhill) M/W, soccer M/W, volleyball M/W.

Standardized Tests *Recommended:* SAT or ACT (for admission).

Costs (2013–14) *Tuition:* area resident $1680 full-time, $56 per credit part-time; state resident $2850 full-time, $95 per credit part-time; nonresident $8970 full-time, $299 per credit part-time. Full-time tuition and fees vary according to course level. Part-time tuition and fees vary according to course level. *Required fees:* $180 full-time. *Room and board:* $8164. Room and board charges vary according to board plan. *Payment plan:* installment. *Waivers:* senior citizens.

Applying *Options:* electronic application, early admission, deferred entrance. *Required:* high school transcript. *Application deadlines:* rolling (freshmen), rolling (out-of-state freshmen), rolling (transfers).

Freshman Application Contact Ms. Mary Laing, Admissions Assistant, Colorado Mountain College, Timberline Campus, 901 South Highway 24, Leadville, CO 80461. *Phone:* 719-486-4292. *Toll-free phone:* 800-621-8559. *E-mail:* joinus@coloradomtn.edu.
Website: http://www.coloradomtn.edu/.

Colorado School of Mines

Golden, Colorado

- **State-supported** university, founded 1874
- **Small-town** 491-acre campus with easy access to Denver, Boulder, Colorado Springs
- **Endowment** $196.0 million
- **Coed** 4,169 undergraduate students, 95% full-time, 26% women, 74% men
- **Very difficult** entrance level, 37% of applicants were admitted

Undergraduates 3,953 full-time, 216 part-time. Students come from 55 states and territories; 54 other countries; 38% are from out of state; 1% Black or Afri-

can American, non-Hispanic/Latino; 7% Hispanic/Latino; 5% Asian, non-Hispanic/Latino; 0.3% American Indian or Alaska Native, non-Hispanic/Latino; 3% Two or more races, non-Hispanic/Latino; 4% Race/ethnicity unknown; 6% international; 3% transferred in; 43% live on campus. *Retention:* 89% of full-time freshmen returned.

Freshmen *Admission:* 11,682 applied, 4,373 admitted, 949 enrolled. *Average high school GPA:* 3.8. *Test scores:* SAT critical reading scores over 500: 97%; SAT math scores over 500: 100%; SAT writing scores over 500: 91%; ACT scores over 18: 100%; SAT critical reading scores over 600: 65%; SAT math scores over 600: 91%; SAT writing scores over 600: 51%; ACT scores over 24: 98%; SAT critical reading scores over 700: 17%; SAT math scores over 700: 39%; SAT writing scores over 700: 9%; ACT scores over 30: 46%.

Faculty *Total:* 368, 68% full-time, 72% with terminal degrees. *Student/faculty ratio:* 16:1.

Academics *Calendar:* semesters. *Degrees:* bachelor's, master's, doctoral, and post-master's certificates. *Special study options:* accelerated degree program, advanced placement credit, cooperative education, double majors, honors programs, independent study, internships, off-campus study, services for LD students, study abroad, summer session for credit. *ROTC:* Army (b), Air Force (b).

Computers on Campus 508 computers/terminals are available on campus for general student use. Students can access the following: campus intranet, computer help desk, free student e-mail accounts, online (class) grades, online (class) registration, online (class) schedules. Campuswide network is available. 100% of college-owned or -operated housing units are wired for high-speed Internet access. Wireless service is available via entire campus.

Student Life *Housing:* on-campus residence required for freshman year. *Options:* coed, men-only. Campus housing is university owned and is provided by a third party. Freshman campus housing is guaranteed. *Activities and organizations:* drama/theater group, student-run newspaper, radio station, choral group, marching band, Society of Women Engineers, Residence Hall Association, Associated Students of Colorado School of Mines, Student Professional Societies/ and/ Religious Organizations, Multicultural Engineering Program, national fraternities, national sororities. *Campus security:* 24-hour emergency response devices and patrols, late-night transport/escort service, controlled dormitory access, full service, community oriented law enforcement agency employing fully trained police officers. *Student services:* health clinic, personal/psychological counseling, women's center.

Athletics Member NCAA. All Division II. *Intercollegiate sports:* baseball M(s), basketball M(s)/W(s), bowling M(c)/W(c), cross-country running M(s)/W(s), football M(s), golf M, ice hockey M(c)/W(c), lacrosse M(c)/W(c), rugby M(c)/W(c), soccer M(s)/W(s), softball W(s), swimming and diving M/W, track and field M(s)/W(s), volleyball W(s), wrestling M(s). *Intramural sports:* badminton M/W, basketball M/W, bowling M/W, cross-country running M/W, equestrian sports M/W, field hockey M/W, football M/W, golf M/W, lacrosse M, racquetball M/W, skiing (downhill) M/W, soccer M/W, softball M/W, swimming and diving M/W, table tennis M/W, tennis M/W, track and field M/W, ultimate Frisbee M/W, volleyball M/W, wrestling M.

Standardized Tests *Required:* SAT or ACT (for admission).

Financial Aid Of all full-time matriculated undergraduates who enrolled in 2011, 2,622 applied for aid, 1,997 were judged to have need, 395 had their need fully met. 193 Federal Work-Study jobs (averaging $1065). 1,234 state and other part-time jobs (averaging $1987). In 2011, 821 non-need-based awards were made. *Average percent of need met:* 61%. *Average financial aid package:* $12,214. *Average need-based loan:* $4614. *Average need-based gift aid:* $5859. *Average non-need-based aid:* $6032. *Average indebtedness upon graduation:* $33,209.

Applying *Options:* electronic application, deferred entrance. *Application fee:* $45. *Required:* high school transcript. *Required for some:* essay or personal statement, interview. *Recommended:* minimum 3.8 GPA, rank in upper quartile of high school class. *Application deadlines:* 5/1 (freshmen), 5/1 (transfers). *Notification:* continuous until 10/1 (freshmen), continuous until 10/1 (transfers).

Freshman Application Contact Mrs. Joanne Lambert, Assistant Director of Enrollment Management, Colorado School of Mines, Student Center, 1600 Maple Street, Golden, CO 80401. *Phone:* 303-273-3220. *Toll-free phone:* 800-446-9488 Ext. 3220. *Fax:* 303-273-3509. *E-mail:* admit@mines.edu. *Website:* http://www.mines.edu/.

Colorado State University
Fort Collins, Colorado

- **State-supported** university, founded 1870, part of Colorado State University System
- **Urban** 582-acre campus with easy access to Denver
- **Endowment** $225.4 million
- **Coed** 23,479 undergraduate students, 90% full-time, 51% women, 49% men
- **Moderately difficult** entrance level, 75% of applicants were admitted

Undergraduates 21,193 full-time, 2,286 part-time. Students come from 57 states and territories; 55 other countries; 18% are from out of state; 2% Black or African American, non-Hispanic/Latino; 9% Hispanic/Latino; 2% Asian, non-Hispanic/Latino; 0.2% Native Hawaiian or other Pacific Islander, non-Hispanic/Latino; 0.4% American Indian or Alaska Native, non-Hispanic/Latino; 3% Two or more races, non-Hispanic/Latino; 6% Race/ethnicity unknown; 2% international; 6% transferred in; 25% live on campus. *Retention:* 84% of full-time freshmen returned.

Freshmen *Admission:* 17,929 applied, 13,394 admitted, 4,544 enrolled. *Average high school GPA:* 3.57. *Test scores:* SAT critical reading scores over 500: 79%; SAT math scores over 500: 84%; ACT scores over 18: 98%; SAT critical reading scores over 600: 36%; SAT math scores over 600: 44%; ACT scores over 24: 62%; SAT critical reading scores over 700: 8%; SAT math scores over 700: 8%; ACT scores over 30: 11%.

Faculty *Total:* 966, 97% full-time, 99% with terminal degrees. *Student/faculty ratio:* 19:1.

Academics *Calendar:* semesters. *Degrees:* bachelor's, master's, and doctoral. *Special study options:* accelerated degree program, advanced placement credit, cooperative education, distance learning, double majors, English as a second language, honors programs, independent study, internships, off-campus study, part-time degree program, services for LD students, study abroad, summer session for credit. *ROTC:* Army (b), Air Force (b). *Unusual degree programs:* 3-2 engineering.

Computers on Campus 2,700 computers/terminals and 2,800 ports are available on campus for general student use. Students can access the following: campus intranet, computer help desk, free student e-mail accounts, online (class) grades, online (class) registration, online (class) schedules, personalized portal services including transcripts and financials (billing, financial aid). Campuswide network is available. 100% of college-owned or -operated housing units are wired for high-speed Internet access. Wireless service is available via classrooms, computer centers, computer labs, dorm rooms, libraries, student centers.

Student Life *Housing:* on-campus residence required for freshman year. *Options:* coed, disabled students. Campus housing is university owned. Freshman campus housing is guaranteed. *Activities and organizations:* drama/theater group, student-run newspaper, radio and television station, choral group, marching band, Golden Key International Honor Society, Council of International Student Affairs, Campus Crusade for Christ, Associated Students of CSU (ASCSU Student Government), Snowriders, national fraternities, national sororities. *Campus security:* 24-hour emergency response devices and patrols, student patrols, late-night transport/escort service, controlled dormitory access. *Student services:* health clinic, personal/psychological counseling, women's center, legal services.

Athletics Member NCAA. All Division I except football (Division I-A). *Intercollegiate sports:* baseball M(c), basketball M(s)/W(s), crew M(c)/W(c), cross-country running M(s)/W(s), field hockey M(c)/W(c), golf M(s)/W(s), ice hockey M(c)/W(c), lacrosse M(c)/W(c), rugby M(c)/W(c), skiing (downhill) M(c)/W(c), soccer M(c)/W(s), softball W(s), swimming and diving M(c)/W(s), tennis M(c)/W(s), track and field M(s)/W(s), ultimate Frisbee M(c)/W(c), volleyball W(s), water polo M(c)/W(c), wrestling M(c)/W(c). *Intramural sports:* basketball M/W, bowling M/W, golf M/W, racquetball M/W, soccer M/W, softball M/W, ultimate Frisbee M/W, volleyball M/W.

Standardized Tests *Required:* SAT or ACT (for admission).

Costs (2012–13) *Tuition:* state resident $6875 full-time, $312 per credit hour part-time; nonresident $22,667 full-time, $1133 per credit hour part-time. Full-time tuition and fees vary according to course load, program, and student level. Part-time tuition and fees vary according to course load, program, and student level. *Required fees:* $1774 full-time, $30 per credit hour part-time, $149 per term part-time. *Room and board:* $10,278; room only: $4720. Room and board charges vary according to board plan and housing facility. *Waivers:* employees or children of employees.

Financial Aid Of all full-time matriculated undergraduates who enrolled in 2011, 15,032 applied for aid, 11,049 were judged to have need, 2,007 had their need fully met. 454 Federal Work-Study jobs (averaging $1983). 1,198 state and other part-time jobs (averaging $1860). In 2011, 2208 non-need-based awards were made. *Average percent of need met:* 69%. *Average financial aid package:* $15,195. *Average need-based loan:* $6925. *Average need-based gift*

COLLEGES AT-A-GLANCE

aid: $9360. *Average non-need-based aid:* $4306. *Average indebtedness upon graduation:* $22,131.
Applying *Options:* electronic application, early action, deferred entrance. *Application fee:* $50. *Required:* essay or personal statement, high school transcript, 1 letter of recommendation. *Application deadlines:* 2/1 (freshmen), 6/1 (transfers). *Notification:* continuous (freshmen), continuous (transfers).
Freshman Application Contact Mr. Jim Rawlins, Executive Director of Admissions, Colorado State University, Ammons Hall, Fort Collins, CO 80523-1062. *Phone:* 970-491-6909. *Fax:* 970-491-7799. *E-mail:* admissions@colostate.edu.
Website: http://www.colostate.edu/.

Colorado State University–Pueblo

Pueblo, Colorado

Freshman Application Contact Mrs. Dana Trujillo, Director of Admissions, Colorado State University–Pueblo, 2200 Bonforte Boulevard, Pueblo, CO 81001-4901. *Phone:* 719-549-2391. *Fax:* 719-549-2419. *E-mail:* dana.trujillo@colostate-pueblo.edu.
Website: http://www.colostate-pueblo.edu/.

Colorado Technical University Colorado Springs

Colorado Springs, Colorado

Director of Admissions Beth Braaten, Vice President of Admissions, Colorado Technical University Colorado Springs, 4435 North Chestnut Street, Colorado Springs, CO 80907-3896. *Phone:* 888-404-7555. *Toll-free phone:* 866-942-6555. *E-mail:* bbraaten@coloradotech.edu.
Website: http://www.coloradotech.edu/.

Colorado Technical University Denver South

Aurora, Colorado

Director of Admissions Rosaland Giboney, Associate Director of Admissions, Colorado Technical University Denver South, 3151 South Vaughn Way, Aurora, CO 80014. *Phone:* 888-404-7555. *Toll-free phone:* 888-309-6555. *E-mail:* rgiboney@coloradotech.edu.
Website: http://www.coloradotech.edu/.

Colorado Technical University Online

Colorado Springs, Colorado

Director of Admissions William Beckley, Chief Admission Officer, Colorado Technical University Online, 4435 North Chestnut Street, Suite E, Colorado Springs, CO 80907. *Phone:* 888-404-7555.
Website: http://www.coloradotech.edu/.

Denver School of Nursing

Denver, Colorado

Admissions Office Contact Denver School of Nursing, 1401 19th Street, Denver, CO 80202. *Toll-free phone:* 888-479-5550.
Website: http://www.denverschoolofnursing.edu/.

DeVry University

Colorado Springs, Colorado

Director of Admissions Admissions Office, DeVry University, 1175 Kelly Johnson Boulevard, Colorado Springs, CO 80920. *Toll-free phone:* 866-338-7941.
Website: http://www.devry.edu/.

DeVry University

Westminster, Colorado

- **Proprietary** comprehensive, founded 1945
- **Urban** campus
- **Coed** 613 undergraduate students, 31% full-time, 36% women, 64% men
- **Noncompetitive** entrance level

Undergraduates 188 full-time, 425 part-time. 14% are from out of state; 6% Black or African American, non-Hispanic/Latino; 14% Hispanic/Latino; 4% Asian, non-Hispanic/Latino; 0.5% Native Hawaiian or other Pacific Islander, non-Hispanic/Latino; 0.7% American Indian or Alaska Native, non-Hispanic/

Latino; 2% Two or more races, non-Hispanic/Latino; 11% Race/ethnicity unknown; 0.2% international; 17% transferred in.
Freshmen *Admission:* 41 enrolled.
Faculty *Total:* 72, 17% full-time. *Student/faculty ratio:* 12:1.
Academics *Calendar:* semesters. *Degrees:* associate, bachelor's, master's, and postbachelor's certificates. *Special study options:* adult/continuing education programs.
Student Life *Housing:* college housing not available.
Costs (2013–14) *Tuition:* $16,076 full-time, $609 per credit hour part-time. *Required fees:* $80 full-time.
Financial Aid Of all full-time matriculated undergraduates who enrolled in 2007, 148 applied for aid, 136 were judged to have need, 6 had their need fully met. In 2007, 17 non-need-based awards were made. *Average percent of need met:* 37%. *Average financial aid package:* $11,971. *Average need-based loan:* $8024. *Average need-based gift aid:* $6094. *Average non-need-based aid:* $13,350. *Average indebtedness upon graduation:* $11,071.
Applying *Application fee:* $40. *Required:* high school transcript. *Required for some:* essay or personal statement, interview. *Application deadlines:* rolling (freshmen), rolling (transfers). *Notification:* continuous (freshmen), continuous (transfers).
Freshman Application Contact Admissions Office, DeVry University, 1870 West 122nd Avenue, Westminster, CO 80234-2010. *Phone:* 303-280-7400. *Toll-free phone:* 866-338-7941.
Website: http://www.devry.edu/.

Fort Lewis College

Durango, Colorado

- **State-supported** 4-year, founded 1911
- **Small-town** 350-acre campus
- **Endowment** $4.7 million
- **Coed** 3,891 undergraduate students, 92% full-time, 49% women, 51% men
- **Moderately difficult** entrance level, 87% of applicants were admitted

Undergraduates 3,565 full-time, 326 part-time. Students come from 47 states and territories; 19 other countries; 41% are from out of state; 0.8% Black or African American, non-Hispanic/Latino; 9% Hispanic/Latino; 0.4% Asian, non-Hispanic/Latino; 0.3% Native Hawaiian or other Pacific Islander, non-Hispanic/Latino; 20% American Indian or Alaska Native, non-Hispanic/Latino; 5% Two or more races, non-Hispanic/Latino; 2% Race/ethnicity unknown; 2% international; 10% transferred in; 37% live on campus. *Retention:* 62% of full-time freshmen returned.
Freshmen *Admission:* 2,417 applied, 2,111 admitted, 857 enrolled. *Average high school GPA:* 3.2. *Test scores:* ACT scores over 18: 89%; ACT scores over 24: 32%; ACT scores over 30: 3%.
Faculty *Total:* 205, 78% full-time, 79% with terminal degrees. *Student/faculty ratio:* 19:1.
Academics *Calendar:* modified trimesters. *Degree:* bachelor's. *Special study options:* academic remediation for entering students, advanced placement credit, double majors, honors programs, independent study, internships, services for LD students, student-designed majors, study abroad, summer session for credit. *Unusual degree programs:* 3-2 social work with Psychology or Sociology majors may be able to complete both their Bachelor's degree and their Master of Social Work degrees in a total of five years through the Fort Lewis College and University of Denver Graduate Degree Program.
Computers on Campus 786 computers/terminals are available on campus for general student use. Students can access the following: campus intranet, computer help desk, free student e-mail accounts, online (class) grades, online (class) registration, online (class) schedules. Campuswide network is available. 100% of college-owned or -operated housing units are wired for high-speed Internet access. Wireless service is available via entire campus.
Student Life *Housing:* on-campus residence required for freshman year. *Options:* coed, disabled students. Campus housing is university owned. Freshman applicants given priority for college housing. *Activities and organizations:* drama/theater group, student-run newspaper, radio station. *Campus security:* 24-hour emergency response devices and patrols, late-night transport/escort service, controlled dormitory access. *Student services:* health clinic, personal/psychological counseling.
Athletics Member NCAA. All Division II. *Intercollegiate sports:* baseball M(c), basketball M(s)/W(s), cheerleading M(c)/W(c), cross-country running M(s)/W(s), fencing M(c)/W(c), football M(s), golf M(s), ice hockey M(c)/W(c), lacrosse M(c)/W(s), rock climbing M(c)/W(c), rugby M(c)/W(c), skiing (cross-country) M(c)/W(c), skiing (downhill) M(c)/W(c), soccer M(s)/W(s), softball W(s), ultimate Frisbee M(c)/W(c), volleyball W(s), wrestling M(c)/W(c). *Intramural sports:* badminton M/W, basketball M/W, football M/W, golf M/W, racquetball M/W, soccer M/W, softball M/W, ultimate Frisbee M/W, volleyball M/W.
Standardized Tests *Required:* SAT or ACT (for admission).

Costs (2013–14) *Tuition:* state resident $5232 full-time, $218 per credit hour part-time; nonresident $16,072 full-time, $670 per credit hour part-time. Full-time tuition and fees vary according to course load and reciprocity agreements. Part-time tuition and fees vary according to course load and reciprocity agreements. *Required fees:* $1691 full-time. *Room and board:* $8590; room only: $4270. Room and board charges vary according to board plan and housing facility. *Payment plan:* installment. *Waivers:* minority students and employees or children of employees.

Financial Aid Of all full-time matriculated undergraduates who enrolled in 2011, 2,521 applied for aid, 2,094 were judged to have need, 105 had their need fully met. In 2011, 635 non-need-based awards were made. *Average percent of need met:* 90%. *Average financial aid package:* $12,120. *Average need-based loan:* $3828. *Average need-based gift aid:* $4920. *Average non-need-based aid:* $3152. *Average indebtedness upon graduation:* $19,811.

Applying *Options:* early action, deferred entrance. *Application fee:* $40. *Required:* high school transcript. *Required for some:* interview. *Recommended:* essay or personal statement, 2 letters of recommendation. *Application deadline:* 8/1 (freshmen).

Freshman Application Contact Fort Lewis College, 1000 Rim Drive, Durango, CO 81301-3999. *Phone:* 970-247-7184. *Toll-free phone:* 877-FLC-COLO.
Website: http://www.fortlewis.edu/.

ITT Technical Institute

Aurora, Colorado

- **Proprietary** primarily 2-year
- **Coed**
- **Minimally difficult** entrance level

Academics *Degrees:* associate and bachelor's.
Freshman Application Contact Director of Recruitment, ITT Technical Institute, 12500 East Iliff Avenue, Suite 100, Aurora, CO 80014. *Phone:* 303-695-6317. *Toll-free phone:* 877-832-8460.
Website: http://www.itt-tech.edu/.

ITT Technical Institute

Westminster, Colorado

- **Proprietary** primarily 2-year, founded 1984, part of ITT Educational Services, Inc.
- **Suburban** campus
- **Coed**
- **Minimally difficult** entrance level

Academics *Calendar:* quarters. *Degrees:* associate and bachelor's.
Freshman Application Contact Director of Recruitment, ITT Technical Institute, 8620 Wolff Court, Suite 100, Westminster, CO 80031. *Phone:* 303-288-4488. *Toll-free phone:* 800-395-4488.
Website: http://www.itt-tech.edu/.

Johnson & Wales University

Denver, Colorado

Freshman Application Contact Kim Ostrowski, Director of Admissions, Johnson & Wales University, 7150 Montview Boulevard, Denver, CO 80220. *Phone:* 303-256-9300. *Toll-free phone:* 877-598-3368. *Fax:* 303-598-3368. *E-mail:* den@admissions.jwu.edu.
Website: http://www.jwu.edu/denver/.

Jones International University

Centennial, Colorado

- **Proprietary** university, founded 1995
- **Suburban** campus
- **Coed** 1,730 undergraduate students, 37% full-time, 62% women, 38% men
- **Noncompetitive** entrance level

Undergraduates 638 full-time, 1,092 part-time. Students come from 54 states and territories; 20 other countries; 95% are from out of state; 32% Black or African American, non-Hispanic/Latino; 4% Hispanic/Latino; 0.7% Asian, non-Hispanic/Latino; 0.1% Native Hawaiian or other Pacific Islander, non-Hispanic/Latino; 0.8% American Indian or Alaska Native, non-Hispanic/Latino; 8% Two or more races, non-Hispanic/Latino; 20% Race/ethnicity unknown.
Freshmen *Admission:* 322 enrolled.
Faculty *Total:* 111, 11% full-time, 81% with terminal degrees.
Academics *Calendar:* continuous. *Degrees:* certificates, associate, bachelor's, master's, doctoral, and postbachelor's certificates (offers only online degree programs). *Special study options:* academic remediation for entering students, advanced placement credit, distance learning, independent study, internships, part-time degree program, services for LD students.

Computers on Campus Students can access the following: computer help desk, free student e-mail accounts, online (class) grades, online (class) registration, online (class) schedules.

Costs (2013–14) *Tuition:* $12,720 full-time, $530 per credit hour part-time. Full-time tuition and fees vary according to course level, course load, degree level, and program. Part-time tuition and fees vary according to course level, course load, degree level, and program. *Payment plan:* installment. *Waivers:* employees or children of employees.

Financial Aid Of all full-time matriculated undergraduates who enrolled in 2009, 469 applied for aid, 368 were judged to have need. *Average percent of need met:* 80%. *Average financial aid package:* $7020. *Average need-based loan:* $3450. *Average need-based gift aid:* $3570.

Applying *Options:* electronic application, early admission, deferred entrance. *Required:* high school transcript, minimum 2.0 GPA. *Application deadlines:* rolling (freshmen), rolling (out-of-state freshmen), rolling (transfers). *Notification:* continuous (freshmen), continuous (out-of-state freshmen), continuous (transfers).

Freshman Application Contact Admissions Center, Jones International University, 9697 East Mineral Avenue, Centennial, CO 80112. *Phone:* 800-811-5663 Ext. 2. *Toll-free phone:* 800-811-5663. *Fax:* 303-799-0966.
Website: http://www.jiu.edu/.

Metropolitan State University of Denver

Denver, Colorado

- **State-supported** comprehensive, founded 1963
- **Urban** 175-acre campus with easy access to Denver
- **Coed** 23,019 undergraduate students, 58% full-time, 54% women, 46% men
- **Minimally difficult** entrance level, 71% of applicants were admitted

Undergraduates 13,335 full-time, 9,684 part-time. 4% are from out of state; 6% Black or African American, non-Hispanic/Latino; 20% Hispanic/Latino; 3% Asian, non-Hispanic/Latino; 0.3% Native Hawaiian or other Pacific Islander, non-Hispanic/Latino; 0.7% American Indian or Alaska Native, non-Hispanic/Latino; 3% Two or more races, non-Hispanic/Latino; 4% Race/ethnicity unknown; 0.5% international; 9% transferred in. *Retention:* 66% of full-time freshmen returned.

Freshmen *Admission:* 5,867 applied, 4,175 admitted, 2,306 enrolled. *Average high school GPA:* 2.94. *Test scores:* SAT critical reading scores over 500: 69%; SAT math scores over 500: 64%; ACT scores over 18: 83%; SAT critical reading scores over 600: 25%; SAT math scores over 600: 32%; ACT scores over 24: 24%; SAT critical reading scores over 700: 6%; ACT scores over 30: 2%.
Faculty *Total:* 1,494, 36% full-time. *Student/faculty ratio:* 20:1.
Academics *Calendar:* semesters. *Degrees:* bachelor's, master's, and post-master's certificates. *Special study options:* accelerated degree program, adult/continuing education programs, advanced placement credit, cooperative education, distance learning, double majors, external degree program, honors programs, independent study, internships, off-campus study, part-time degree program, services for LD students, student-designed majors, study abroad, summer session for credit. *ROTC:* Army (c), Air Force (c).

Computers on Campus 808 computers/terminals are available on campus for general student use. Students can access the following: computer help desk, free student e-mail accounts, online (class) grades, online (class) registration, online (class) schedules. Campuswide network is available. Wireless service is available via entire campus.

Student Life *Housing:* college housing not available. *Activities and organizations:* drama/theater group, student-run newspaper, radio and television station, choral group, national fraternities, national sororities. *Campus security:* 24-hour emergency response devices and patrols, late-night transport/escort service. *Student services:* health clinic, personal/psychological counseling, women's center, legal services.

Athletics Member NCAA. All Division II. *Intercollegiate sports:* baseball M(s), basketball M(s)/W(s), cross-country running M/W, soccer M(s)/W(s), softball W(s), tennis M(s)/W(s), track and field M/W, volleyball W(s). *Intramural sports:* baseball M(c)/W(c), cheerleading M(c)/W(c), fencing M(c)/W(c), football M(c), ice hockey M(c), lacrosse M(c), rugby M(c), soccer M(c), squash M(c)/W, swimming and diving M(c)/W(c), ultimate Frisbee M(c)/W(c), volleyball M(c)/W(c).

Standardized Tests *Required:* SAT or ACT (for admission). *Required for some:* SAT (for admission), ACT (for admission).

Financial Aid Of all full-time matriculated undergraduates who enrolled in 2011, 10,533 applied for aid, 8,981 were judged to have need, 144 had their need fully met. 4 Federal Work-Study jobs (averaging $4119). 16 state and other part-time jobs (averaging $3460). In 2011, 2384 non-need-based awards

were made. *Average percent of need met:* 53%. *Average financial aid package:* $7569. *Average need-based loan:* $3884. *Average need-based gift aid:* $4792. *Average non-need-based aid:* $1706. *Average indebtedness upon graduation:* $31,427.

Applying *Options:* electronic application, deferred entrance. *Application fee:* $25. *Required:* high school transcript. *Recommended:* minimum 2.0 GPA. *Application deadline:* rolling (transfers). *Notification:* continuous (freshmen), continuous (transfers).

Freshman Application Contact Ms. Michelle Brown, Associate Director of Admissions, Metropolitan State University of Denver, PO Box 173362, Denver, CO 80217-3362. *Phone:* 303-556-2615.
Website: http://www.msudenver.edu/.

Naropa University
Boulder, Colorado

- **Independent** comprehensive, founded 1974
- **Urban** 12-acre campus with easy access to Denver
- **Endowment** $5.6 million
- **Coed** 403 undergraduate students, 90% full-time, 61% women, 39% men
- **Moderately difficult** entrance level, 83% of applicants were admitted

Undergraduates 361 full-time, 42 part-time. Students come from 47 states and territories; 8 other countries; 64% are from out of state; 0.7% Black or African American, non-Hispanic/Latino; 8% Hispanic/Latino; 1% Asian, non-Hispanic/Latino; 4% Two or more races, non-Hispanic/Latino; 19% Race/ethnicity unknown; 1% international; 24% transferred in; 18% live on campus. *Retention:* 50% of full-time freshmen returned.
Freshmen *Admission:* 93 applied, 77 admitted, 27 enrolled.
Faculty *Total:* 164, 26% full-time, 33% with terminal degrees. *Student/faculty ratio:* 9:1.
Academics *Calendar:* semesters. *Degrees:* bachelor's and master's. *Special study options:* advanced placement credit, cooperative education, double majors, independent study, internships, part-time degree program, services for LD students, student-designed majors, study abroad, summer session for credit.
Computers on Campus 37 computers/terminals are available on campus for general student use. Students can access the following: computer help desk, free student e-mail accounts, online (class) grades, online (class) registration, online (class) schedules. Campuswide network is available. 100% of college-owned or -operated housing units are wired for high-speed Internet access. Wireless service is available via entire campus.
Student Life *Housing:* on-campus residence required for freshman year. *Options:* coed. Campus housing is university owned. Freshman campus housing is guaranteed. *Activities and organizations:* drama/theater group, student-run newspaper, choral group, Team Asana, ROOT: Reconnecting on Outdoor Terrain, United Naropa. *Campus security:* late-night transport/escort service, controlled dormitory access, foot and vehicle patrol 4:30 pm to midnight, 24 hour on-call Safety and Security Manager. *Student services:* personal/psychological counseling.
Costs (2013–14) *Comprehensive fee:* $37,770 includes full-time tuition ($28,620), mandatory fees ($170), and room and board ($8980). Full-time tuition and fees vary according to course load. Part-time tuition: $936 per hour. Part-time tuition and fees vary according to course load. *Required fees:* $335 per term part-time. *Payment plan:* installment. *Waivers:* employees or children of employees.
Financial Aid Of all full-time matriculated undergraduates who enrolled in 2012, 250 applied for aid, 239 were judged to have need, 6 had their need fully met. 177 Federal Work-Study jobs (averaging $3156). 17 state and other part-time jobs (averaging $2000). In 2012, 4 non-need-based awards were made. *Average percent of need met:* 86%. *Average financial aid package:* $33,744. *Average need-based loan:* $10,412. *Average need-based gift aid:* $21,331. *Average non-need-based aid:* $4000. *Average indebtedness upon graduation:* $26,511.
Applying *Options:* electronic application, deferred entrance. *Application fee:* $50. *Required:* essay or personal statement, high school transcript, 2 letters of recommendation, interview. *Required for some:* supplemental application and/or art samples required for applicants to performance, environmental studies, INTD studies, music, visual arts and writing and literature programs. *Application deadlines:* 1/15 (freshmen), 1/15 (out-of-state freshmen), 1/15 (transfers). *Notification:* continuous (freshmen), continuous (out-of-state freshmen), continuous (transfers).
Freshman Application Contact Mr. Jason Makowsky, Associate Director of Undergraduate Admissions, Naropa University, 2130 Arapahoe Avenue, Boulder, CO 80302. *Phone:* 303-245-4693. *Toll-free phone:* 800-772-6951. *Fax:* 303-546-3583. *E-mail:* jmakowsky@naropa.edu.
Website: http://www.naropa.edu/.

National American University
Colorado Springs, Colorado

Director of Admissions Director of Admissions, National American University, 5125 North Academy Boulevard, Colorado Springs, CO 80918. *Phone:* 719-590-8300. *E-mail:* csadmissions@national.edu.
Website: http://www.national.edu/.

National American University
Denver, Colorado

Freshman Application Contact National American University, 1325 South Colorado Blvd, Suite 100, Denver, CO 80222. *Phone:* 303-876-7112.
Website: http://www.national.edu/.

Nazarene Bible College
Colorado Springs, Colorado

Freshman Application Contact Dr. Laurel Matson, Director of Admissions/Public Relations, Nazarene Bible College, 1111 Academy Park Loop, Colorado Springs, CO 80910-3704. *Phone:* 719-884-5061. *Toll-free phone:* 800-873-3873. *Fax:* 719-884-5199.
Website: http://www.nbc.edu/.

Pima Medical Institute
Denver, Colorado

Freshman Application Contact Admissions Office, Pima Medical Institute, 7475 Dakin Street, Denver, CO 80221. *Phone:* 303-426-1800. *Toll-free phone:* 800-477-PIMA (in-state); 888-477-PIMA (out-of-state).
Website: http://www.pmi.edu/.

Platt College
Aurora, Colorado

Freshman Application Contact Admissions Office, Platt College, 3100 South Parker Road, Suite 200, Aurora, CO 80014-3141. *Phone:* 303-369-5151.
Website: http://www.plattcolorado.edu/.

Regis University
Denver, Colorado

- **Independent Roman Catholic (Jesuit)** comprehensive, founded 1877
- **Suburban** 90-acre campus with easy access to Denver
- **Coed** 5,750 undergraduate students, 44% full-time, 63% women, 37% men
- **Moderately difficult** entrance level, 90% of applicants were admitted

Undergraduates 2,555 full-time, 3,195 part-time. 33% are from out of state; 6% Black or African American, non-Hispanic/Latino; 16% Hispanic/Latino; 4% Asian, non-Hispanic/Latino; 0.1% Native Hawaiian or other Pacific Islander, non-Hispanic/Latino; 0.6% American Indian or Alaska Native, non-Hispanic/Latino; 2% Two or more races, non-Hispanic/Latino; 8% Race/ethnicity unknown; 0.7% international; 6% transferred in; 8% live on campus. *Retention:* 88% of full-time freshmen returned.
Freshmen *Admission:* 2,531 applied, 2,289 admitted, 490 enrolled. *Average high school GPA:* 3.49. *Test scores:* SAT critical reading scores over 500: 73%; SAT math scores over 500: 76%; SAT writing scores over 500: 76%; ACT scores over 18: 99%; SAT critical reading scores over 600: 28%; SAT math scores over 600: 29%; SAT writing scores over 600: 22%; ACT scores over 24: 61%; SAT critical reading scores over 700: 4%; SAT math scores over 700: 1%; SAT writing scores over 700: 3%; ACT scores over 30: 9%.
Faculty *Total:* 1,181, 24% full-time. *Student/faculty ratio:* 12:1.
Academics *Calendar:* semesters. *Degrees:* certificates, bachelor's, master's, doctoral, post-master's, and postbachelor's certificates. *Special study options:* academic remediation for entering students, accelerated degree program, adult/continuing education programs, advanced placement credit, cooperative education, distance learning, double majors, external degree program, freshman honors college, honors programs, independent study, internships, off-campus study, part-time degree program, services for LD students, student-designed majors, study abroad, summer session for credit. *ROTC:* Army (c), Navy (c), Air Force (c). *Unusual degree programs:* 3-2 engineering with Washington University in St. Louis.
Computers on Campus 450 computers/terminals and 1,000 ports are available on campus for general student use. Students can access the following: campus intranet, computer help desk, free student e-mail accounts, online (class) grades, online (class) registration, online (class) schedules. Campuswide network is available. 100% of college-owned or -operated housing units

are wired for high-speed Internet access. Wireless service is available via entire campus.

Student Life *Housing:* on-campus residence required through sophomore year. *Options:* coed, disabled students. Campus housing is university owned. Freshman applicants given priority for college housing. *Activities and organizations:* drama/theater group, student-run newspaper, radio station, choral group, Musical Theater Club, Student government, Club Sports, Outdoor Adventure, Black Student Association. *Campus security:* 24-hour emergency response devices and patrols, student patrols, late-night transport/escort service, controlled dormitory access. *Student services:* health clinic, personal/psychological counseling.

Athletics Member NCAA. All Division II. *Intercollegiate sports:* baseball M(s), basketball M(s)/W(s), cross-country running M(s)/W(s), golf M(s)/W(s), lacrosse W(s), soccer M(s)/W(s), softball W(s), volleyball W(s). *Intramural sports:* basketball M/W, bowling M/W, cheerleading M/W, football M/W, ice hockey M, lacrosse M, rugby M, soccer M/W, softball W, tennis M/W, ultimate Frisbee M/W, volleyball M/W.

Standardized Tests *Required:* SAT or ACT (for admission).

Costs (2013–14) *Comprehensive fee:* $41,804 includes full-time tuition ($31,824), mandatory fees ($600), and room and board ($9380). Full-time tuition and fees vary according to course load, location, program, and reciprocity agreements. *Part-time tuition:* $995 per credit hour. Part-time tuition and fees vary according to location, program, and reciprocity agreements. *College room only:* $5200. Room and board charges vary according to board plan and housing facility. *Payment plans:* installment, deferred payment. *Waivers:* employees or children of employees.

Financial Aid Of all full-time matriculated undergraduates who enrolled in 2011, 2,244 applied for aid, 1,736 were judged to have need, 621 had their need fully met. 351 Federal Work-Study jobs (averaging $1501). 554 state and other part-time jobs (averaging $1795). In 2011, 438 non-need-based awards were made. *Average percent of need met:* 63%. *Average financial aid package:* $18,947. *Average need-based loan:* $4328. *Average need-based gift aid:* $12,565. *Average non-need-based aid:* $12,561. *Average indebtedness upon graduation:* $28,127.

Applying *Options:* electronic application, deferred entrance. *Application fee:* $40. *Required:* essay or personal statement, high school transcript, minimum 2.5 GPA. *Required for some:* 1 letter of recommendation, interview. *Application deadlines:* rolling (freshmen), rolling (out-of-state freshmen), rolling (transfers). *Notification:* continuous (freshmen), continuous (transfers).

Freshman Application Contact Mr. Vic Davolt, Director of Admission, Regis University, 3333 Regis Boulevard, Denver, CO 80221-1099. *Phone:* 303-458-4905. *Toll-free phone:* 800-388-2366 Ext. 4900. *Fax:* 303-964-5534. *E-mail:* regisadm@regis.edu.
Website: http://www.regis.edu/.

Rocky Mountain College of Art + Design
Lakewood, Colorado

- **Proprietary** comprehensive, founded 1963
- **Suburban** 23-acre campus with easy access to Denver
- **Coed** 623 undergraduate students, 92% full-time, 64% women, 36% men
- **Moderately difficult** entrance level, 50% of applicants were admitted

Undergraduates 573 full-time, 50 part-time. Students come from 44 states and territories; 5 other countries; 23% are from out of state; 2% Black or African American, non-Hispanic/Latino; 9% Hispanic/Latino; 3% Asian, non-Hispanic/Latino; 1% American Indian or Alaska Native, non-Hispanic/Latino; 1% Two or more races, non-Hispanic/Latino; 13% Race/ethnicity unknown; 1% international; 14% transferred in. *Retention:* 100% of full-time freshmen returned.

Freshmen *Admission:* 171 applied, 85 admitted, 111 enrolled. *Test scores:* ACT scores over 18: 78%; ACT scores over 24: 29%; ACT scores over 30: 3%.

Faculty *Total:* 119, 43% full-time, 3% with terminal degrees. *Student/faculty ratio:* 8:1.

Academics *Calendar:* trimesters. *Degrees:* bachelor's and master's. *Special study options:* academic remediation for entering students, accelerated degree program, advanced placement credit, cooperative education, distance learning, double majors, honors programs, independent study, internships, off-campus study, part-time degree program, services for LD students, study abroad, summer session for credit.

Computers on Campus 300 computers/terminals are available on campus for general student use. Students can access the following: campus intranet, computer help desk, free student e-mail accounts, online (class) grades, online (class) registration, online (class) schedules, computer assistance, online library, wireless network, discounted software/hardware. Campuswide network is available. Wireless service is available via entire campus.

Student Life *Housing:* college housing not available. *Activities and organizations:* The American Institute of Graphic Arts, The American Society of Interior Designers. *Campus security:* 24-hour emergency response devices, late-night transport/escort service. *Student services:* personal/psychological counseling.

Standardized Tests *Required:* SAT or ACT (for admission).

Costs (2013–14) *Tuition:* $27,648 full-time, $1152 per credit hour part-time. Full-time tuition and fees vary according to degree level and location. Part-time tuition and fees vary according to course load, degree level, and location. No tuition increase for student's term of enrollment. *Payment plan:* installment. *Waivers:* employees or children of employees.

Financial Aid Of all full-time matriculated undergraduates who enrolled in 2012, 439 applied for aid, 394 were judged to have need, 40 had their need fully met. 29 Federal Work-Study jobs (averaging $2417). 40 state and other part-time jobs (averaging $2767). In 2012, 101 non-need-based awards were made. *Average percent of need met:* 73%. *Average financial aid package:* $20,977. *Average need-based loan:* $4346. *Average need-based gift aid:* $4682. *Average non-need-based aid:* $7142. *Average indebtedness upon graduation:* $30,067.

Applying *Options:* electronic application. *Application fee:* $50. *Required:* minimum 2.0 GPA, interview, portfolio. *Required for some:* essay or personal statement, high school transcript. *Application deadlines:* rolling (freshmen), rolling (transfers). *Notification:* continuous (freshmen), continuous (transfers).

Freshman Application Contact Ms. Amber Atkins, Director of Outreach, Rocky Mountain College of Art + Design, 1600 Pierce Street, Lakewood, CO 80214. *Phone:* 303-753-6046. *Toll-free phone:* 800-888-ARTS. *Fax:* 303-759-4970. *E-mail:* alatkins@rmcad.edu.
Website: http://www.rmcad.edu/.

United States Air Force Academy
Colorado Springs, Colorado

- **Federally supported** 4-year, founded 1954
- **Suburban** 18,000-acre campus with easy access to Colorado Springs, Denver
- **Coed, primarily men** 4,120 undergraduate students, 100% full-time, 22% women, 78% men
- **Most difficult** entrance level, 8% of applicants were admitted

Undergraduates 4,120 full-time. Students come from 54 states and territories; 38 other countries; 91% are from out of state; 7% Black or African American, non-Hispanic/Latino; 9% Hispanic/Latino; 7% Asian, non-Hispanic/Latino; 1% Native Hawaiian or other Pacific Islander, non-Hispanic/Latino; 1% American Indian or Alaska Native, non-Hispanic/Latino; 7% Two or more races, non-Hispanic/Latino; 1% Race/ethnicity unknown; 1% international; 100% live on campus. *Retention:* 93% of full-time freshmen returned.

Freshmen *Admission:* 12,274 applied, 1,023 admitted, 981 enrolled. *Average high school GPA:* 3.86. *Test scores:* SAT critical reading scores over 500: 97%; SAT math scores over 500: 100%; ACT scores over 18: 100%; SAT critical reading scores over 600: 76%; SAT math scores over 600: 90%; ACT scores over 24: 99%; SAT critical reading scores over 700: 23%; SAT math scores over 700: 37%; ACT scores over 30: 57%.

Faculty *Total:* 523, 99% full-time, 55% with terminal degrees. *Student/faculty ratio:* 8:1.

Academics *Calendar:* semesters. *Degree:* bachelor's. *Special study options:* academic remediation for entering students, advanced placement credit, double majors, English as a second language, honors programs, independent study, internships, off-campus study, study abroad, summer session for credit.

Computers on Campus 400 computers/terminals and 100 ports are available on campus for general student use. Students can access the following: campus intranet, computer help desk, free student e-mail accounts, online (class) grades, online (class) registration, online (class) schedules. Campuswide network is available. 100% of college-owned or -operated housing units are wired for high-speed Internet access. Wireless service is available via classrooms, computer centers, computer labs, learning centers, libraries, student centers.

Student Life *Housing:* on-campus residence required through senior year. *Options:* coed. Campus housing is university owned. Freshman campus housing is guaranteed. *Activities and organizations:* drama/theater group, student-run radio station, choral group, marching band, Cadet Ski Club, Men's and Women's Rugby Club, Cadet Cycling Club, Aviation Club, Drum and Bugle Corps. *Campus security:* 24-hour emergency response devices and patrols, late-night transport/escort service, controlled dormitory access, self-defense education, well-lit campus. *Student services:* health clinic, personal/psychological counseling, women's center, legal services.

Athletics Member NCAA. All Division I. *Intercollegiate sports:* archery M(c)/W(c), baseball M, basketball M/W, cheerleading M/W, cross-country running M/W, equestrian sports M(c)/W(c), fencing M/W, football M, golf M(c)/W(c), gymnastics M/W, ice hockey M/W(c), lacrosse M/W(c), racquetball M(c)/W(c), riflery M/W, rock climbing M(c)/W(c), rugby M(c)/W(c), skiing (cross-country) M(c)/W(c), skiing (downhill) M(c)/W(c), soccer M/W, softball W(c), swimming and diving M/W, tennis M/W, track and field M/W, ultimate Frisbee M(c)/W(c), volleyball M(c)/W, water polo M/W(c), weight lifting M(c)/W(c), wrestling M. *Intramural sports:* basketball M/W, cross-country running M/W, racquetball M/W, rugby M/W, soccer M/W, softball M/W, ultimate Frisbee M/W, volleyball M/W, wrestling M.

Standardized Tests *Required:* SAT or ACT (for admission).

Costs (2012–13) *Comprehensive fee:* Tuition, room and board, and medical and dental care are provided by the U.S. government. Each cadet receives a salary from which to pay for uniforms, supplies, and personal expenses.

Applying *Options:* electronic application. *Required:* essay or personal statement, high school transcript, minimum 2.0 GPA, interview, authorized nomination. *Recommended:* 3 letters of recommendation. *Application deadlines:* 12/31 (freshmen), 12/31 (transfers). *Notification:* 10/15 (freshmen), 10/15 (transfers).

Freshman Application Contact Selections Division Admission Counselor, United States Air Force Academy, HQ USAFA/RR, 2304 Cadet Drive, Suite 2400, USAF Academy, CO 80840-5025. *Phone:* 800-443-9266. *Toll-free phone:* 800-443-9266. *Fax:* 719-333-3012.
Website: http://www.usafa.edu/.

See below for display ad and page 1548 for the College Close-Up.

University of Colorado Boulder
Boulder, Colorado

- **State-supported** university, founded 1876, part of University of Colorado System
- **Suburban** 600-acre campus with easy access to Denver
- **Endowment** $385.7 million
- **Coed** 25,805 undergraduate students, 91% full-time, 46% women, 54% men
- **Moderately difficult** entrance level, 84% of applicants were admitted

Undergraduates 23,582 full-time, 2,223 part-time. Students come from 53 states and territories; 94 other countries; 37% are from out of state; 2% Black or African American, non-Hispanic/Latino; 9% Hispanic/Latino; 5% Asian, non-Hispanic/Latino; 0.5% American Indian or Alaska Native, non-Hispanic/Latino; 3% Two or more races, non-Hispanic/Latino; 3% Race/ethnicity unknown; 3% international; 4% transferred in; 28% live on campus. *Retention:* 84% of full-time freshmen returned.

Freshmen *Admission:* 21,744 applied, 18,172 admitted, 5,472 enrolled. *Average high school GPA:* 3.57. *Test scores:* SAT critical reading scores over 500: 86%; SAT math scores over 500: 90%; ACT scores over 18: 99%; SAT critical reading scores over 600: 42%; SAT math scores over 600: 52%; ACT scores over 24: 74%; SAT critical reading scores over 700: 8%; SAT math scores over 700: 12%; ACT scores over 30: 17%.

Faculty *Total:* 1,899, 73% full-time, 75% with terminal degrees. *Student/faculty ratio:* 18:1.

Academics *Calendar:* semesters. *Degrees:* bachelor's, master's, doctoral, and post-master's certificates. *Special study options:* accelerated degree program, adult/continuing education programs, advanced placement credit, cooperative education, distance learning, double majors, English as a second language, freshman honors college, honors programs, independent study, internships, off-campus study, part-time degree program, services for LD students, student-designed majors, study abroad, summer session for credit. *ROTC:* Army (b), Navy (b), Air Force (b).

Computers on Campus 2,800 computers/terminals are available on campus for general student use. Students can access the following: campus intranet, computer help desk, free student e-mail accounts, online (class) grades, online (class) registration, online (class) schedules, training, tutorials, workshops, and seminars; standard and academic software; student government voting. Campuswide network is available. 100% of college-owned or -operated housing units are wired for high-speed Internet access. Wireless service is available via entire campus.

Student Life *Housing:* on-campus residence required for freshman year. *Options:* coed, disabled students. Campus housing is university owned and is provided by a third party. Freshman campus housing is guaranteed. *Activities and organizations:* drama/theater group, student-run newspaper, radio station, choral group, marching band, student government, Environmental Center, Ski and Snowboard Club, AIESEC (international leadership organization), Program Council, national fraternities, national sororities. *Campus security:* 24-hour emergency response devices and patrols, student patrols, late-night transport/escort service, controlled dormitory access, University police department. *Student services:* health clinic, personal/psychological counseling, women's center, legal services.

Athletics Member NCAA. All Division I except football (Division I-A). *Intercollegiate sports:* baseball M(c), basketball M(s)/W(s), crew M(c)/W(c), cross-country running M(s)/W(s), equestrian sports M(c)/W(c), fencing M(c)/W(c), field hockey M(c)/W(c), golf M(s)/W(s), ice hockey M(c)/W(c), lacrosse M(c)/W(s), racquetball M(c)/W(c), rugby M(c)/W(c), skiing (cross-country) M(s)/W(s), skiing (downhill) M(s)/W(s), soccer M(c)/W(s), softball W(c),

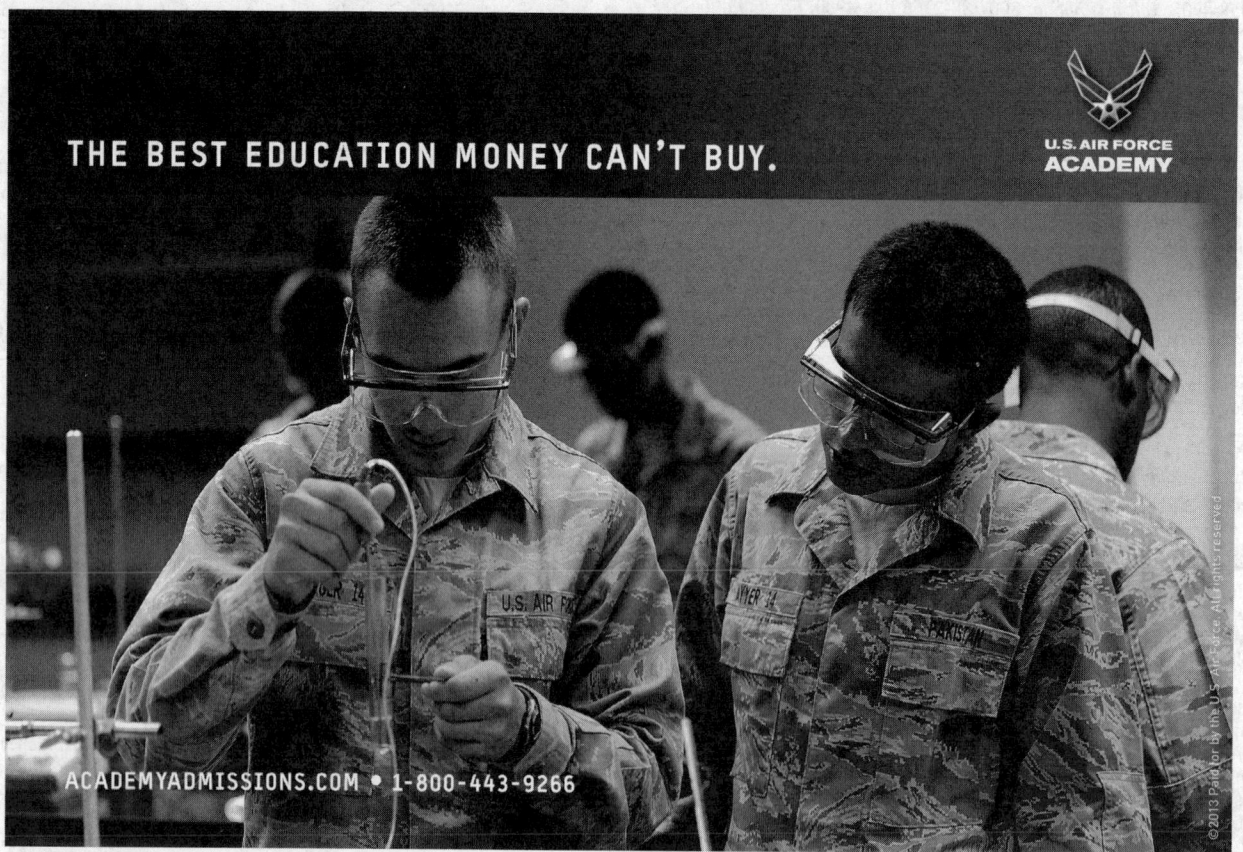

swimming and diving M(c)/W(c), tennis M(c)/W(s), track and field M(s)/W(s), ultimate Frisbee M(c)/W(c), volleyball M(c)/W(s), water polo M(c)/W(c), wrestling M(c). *Intramural sports:* badminton M/W, basketball M/W, ice hockey M/W, soccer M/W, table tennis M/W, tennis M/W, ultimate Frisbee M/W, volleyball M/W, water polo M/W.

Standardized Tests *Required:* SAT or ACT (for admission).

Costs (2012–13) *One-time required fee:* $182. *Tuition:* state resident $8056 full-time; nonresident $29,952 full-time. Full-time tuition and fees vary according to program. Part-time tuition and fees vary according to course load and program. *Required fees:* $1426 full-time. *Room and board:* $11,730. Room and board charges vary according to board plan, housing facility, and location. *Payment plan:* deferred payment. *Waivers:* senior citizens and employees or children of employees.

Financial Aid Of all full-time matriculated undergraduates who enrolled in 2012, 12,362 applied for aid, 9,317 were judged to have need, 5,160 had their need fully met. 778 Federal Work-Study jobs (averaging $1140). 605 state and other part-time jobs (averaging $1113). In 2012, 4940 non-need-based awards were made. *Average percent of need met:* 87%. *Average financial aid package:* $13,912. *Average need-based loan:* $6476. *Average need-based gift aid:* $7994. *Average non-need-based aid:* $7736. *Average indebtedness upon graduation:* $23,413.

Applying *Options:* electronic application, early action, deferred entrance. *Application fee:* $50. *Required:* essay or personal statement, high school transcript. *Required for some:* audition for music program. *Recommended:* minimum 3.0 GPA, 2 letters of recommendation. *Application deadlines:* 1/15 (freshmen), 4/1 (transfers), 12/1 (early action). *Notification:* 4/1 (freshmen), continuous (transfers), 1/15 (early action).

Freshman Application Contact Admissions Office, University of Colorado Boulder, Regent Administrative Center 125, 552 UCB, Boulder, CO 80309. *Phone:* 303-492-6301. *Fax:* 303-735-2501. *E-mail:* apply@colorado.edu. *Website:* http://www.colorado.edu/.

University of Colorado Colorado Springs

Colorado Springs, Colorado

- **State-supported** university, founded 1965, part of University of Colorado System
- **Urban** 532-acre campus with easy access to Colorado Springs
- **Endowment** $31.3 million
- **Coed** 8,354 undergraduate students, 77% full-time, 54% women, 46% men
- **Moderately difficult** entrance level, 92% of applicants were admitted

Undergraduates 6,439 full-time, 1,915 part-time. Students come from 48 states and territories; 18 other countries; 11% are from out of state; 4% Black or African American, non-Hispanic/Latino; 13% Hispanic/Latino; 4% Asian, non-Hispanic/Latino; 0.2% Native Hawaiian or other Pacific Islander, non-Hispanic/Latino; 0.6% American Indian or Alaska Native, non-Hispanic/Latino; 5% Two or more races, non-Hispanic/Latino; 4% Race/ethnicity unknown; 0.5% international; 13% transferred in; 13% live on campus. *Retention:* 66% of full-time freshmen returned.

Freshmen *Admission:* 5,612 applied, 5,183 admitted, 1,442 enrolled. *Average high school GPA:* 3.26. *Test scores:* SAT critical reading scores over 500: 71%; SAT math scores over 500: 73%; ACT scores over 18: 98%; SAT critical reading scores over 600: 23%; SAT math scores over 600: 28%; ACT scores over 24: 45%; SAT critical reading scores over 700: 3%; SAT math scores over 700: 4%; ACT scores over 30: 5%.

Faculty *Total:* 712, 50% full-time, 49% with terminal degrees. *Student/faculty ratio:* 18:1.

Academics *Calendar:* semesters. *Degrees:* bachelor's, master's, and doctoral. *Special study options:* academic remediation for entering students, accelerated degree program, adult/continuing education programs, advanced placement credit, cooperative education, distance learning, double majors, English as a second language, honors programs, independent study, internships, off-campus study, part-time degree program, services for LD students, student-designed majors, study abroad, summer session for credit. *ROTC:* Army (b). *Unusual degree programs:* 3-2 business administration; engineering; nursing; Chemistry, Criminal Justice.

Computers on Campus 672 computers/terminals and 11,414 ports are available on campus for general student use. Students can access the following: campus intranet, computer help desk, free student e-mail accounts, online (class) grades, online (class) registration, online (class) schedules, wireless network, student portal, learning management system. Campuswide network is available. 100% of college-owned or -operated housing units are wired for high-speed Internet access. Wireless service is available via entire campus.

Student Life *Housing options:* coed, men-only, women-only, disabled students. Campus housing is university owned. Freshman applicants given prior-

ity for college housing. *Activities and organizations:* drama/theater group, student-run newspaper, radio and television station, choral group, Fans Initiating Growth Honor and Tradition (spirit club), Pi Beta Phi, Sustainability Club, Gamers (computing), El Circulo, national fraternities, national sororities. *Campus security:* 24-hour emergency response devices and patrols, student patrols, late-night transport/escort service, controlled dormitory access, emergency text messaging. *Student services:* health clinic, personal/psychological counseling.

Athletics Member NCAA. All Division II. *Intercollegiate sports:* baseball M(c), basketball M(s)/W(s), cross-country running M(s)/W(s), golf M(s), ice hockey M(c), lacrosse M(c), rock climbing M(c)/W(c), soccer M(s)/W(s), softball W(s), tennis M(c)/W(c), track and field M(s)/W(s), volleyball M(c)/W(s). *Intramural sports:* badminton M/W, basketball M/W, bowling M/W, soccer M/W, softball M/W, table tennis M/W, ultimate Frisbee M/W, volleyball M/W, water polo M/W.

Standardized Tests *Required:* SAT or ACT (for admission).

Costs (2013–14) *Tuition:* state resident $7051 full-time, $297 per credit hour part-time; nonresident $16,720 full-time, $848 per credit hour part-time. Full-time tuition and fees vary according to course level, course load, degree level, location, program, reciprocity agreements, and student level. Part-time tuition and fees vary according to course level, course load, degree level, location, program, reciprocity agreements, and student level. *Required fees:* $1288 full-time, $28 per contact hour part-time, $243 per term part-time. *Room and board:* $8300; room only: $7250. Room and board charges vary according to board plan and housing facility. *Payment plan:* installment. *Waivers:* employees or children of employees.

Financial Aid Of all full-time matriculated undergraduates who enrolled in 2011, 4,647 applied for aid, 3,455 were judged to have need, 179 had their need fully met. In 2011, 279 non-need-based awards were made. *Average percent of need met:* 47%. *Average financial aid package:* $7907. *Average need-based loan:* $4185. *Average need-based gift aid:* $5515. *Average non-need-based aid:* $3638. *Average indebtedness upon graduation:* $15,447.

Applying *Options:* electronic application, deferred entrance. *Application fee:* $50. *Required:* high school transcript. *Required for some:* minimum 2.0 GPA, GED certificate in lieu of high school transcript; SAT or ACT test scores are required for most new students. *Application deadlines:* rolling (freshmen), rolling (out-of-state freshmen), rolling (transfers). *Notification:* continuous (freshmen), continuous (out-of-state freshmen), continuous (transfers).

Freshman Application Contact Mr. Chris Beiswanger, Director of Student Recruitment and Admissions Counseling, University of Colorado Colorado Springs, 1420 Austin Bluffs Parkway, Colorado Springs, CO 80918. *Phone:* 719-255-3088. *Toll-free phone:* 800-990-8227 Ext. 3383. *E-mail:* cbeiswan@uccs.edu. *Website:* http://www.uccs.edu/.

University of Colorado Denver

Denver, Colorado

- **State-supported** university, founded 1912, part of University of Colorado System
- **Urban** 171-acre campus with easy access to Denver
- **Endowment** $282.8 million
- **Coed** 13,103 undergraduate students, 59% full-time, 54% women, 46% men
- **Moderately difficult** entrance level, 76% of applicants were admitted

Undergraduates 7,741 full-time, 5,362 part-time. Students come from 49 states and territories; 66 other countries; 7% are from out of state; 5% Black or African American, non-Hispanic/Latino; 15% Hispanic/Latino; 10% Asian, non-Hispanic/Latino; 0.1% Native Hawaiian or other Pacific Islander, non-Hispanic/Latino; 0.5% American Indian or Alaska Native, non-Hispanic/Latino; 3% Two or more races, non-Hispanic/Latino; 5% Race/ethnicity unknown; 9% international; 12% transferred in; 5% live on campus. *Retention:* 76% of full-time freshmen returned.

Freshmen *Admission:* 3,075 applied, 2,333 admitted, 1,030 enrolled. *Average high school GPA:* 3.4. *Test scores:* SAT critical reading scores over 500: 74%; SAT math scores over 500: 70%; ACT scores over 18: 94%; SAT critical reading scores over 600: 27%; SAT math scores over 600: 30%; ACT scores over 24: 43%; SAT critical reading scores over 700: 6%; SAT math scores over 700: 7%; ACT scores over 30: 6%.

Faculty *Total:* 3,417, 84% full-time, 72% with terminal degrees. *Student/faculty ratio:* 17:1.

Academics *Calendar:* semesters. *Degrees:* bachelor's, master's, doctoral, and post-master's certificates. *Special study options:* accelerated degree program, adult/continuing education programs, advanced placement credit, cooperative education, distance learning, double majors, English as a second language, honors programs, independent study, internships, off-campus study, part-time degree program, services for LD students, student-designed majors, study abroad, summer session for credit. *ROTC:* Army (c), Air Force (c). *Unusual degree programs:* 3-2 Criminal Justice (BACJ/MCJ).

Computers on Campus 750 computers/terminals are available on campus for general student use. Students can access the following: campus intranet, computer help desk, free student e-mail accounts, online (class) grades, online (class) registration, online (class) schedules. Campuswide network is available. 100% of college-owned or -operated housing units are wired for high-speed Internet access. Wireless service is available via entire campus.

Student Life *Housing:* on-campus residence required for freshman year. *Options:* coed. Campus housing is provided by a third party. Freshman applicants given priority for college housing. *Activities and organizations:* drama/theater group, student-run newspaper, choral group, Veterans Student Organization (Service), Golden Key Honor Society (Academic), Minority Association for Pre-Health Students (Health), Future Doctors of Denver, Intercultural Club Beijing (Cultural and Social). *Campus security:* 24-hour emergency response devices and patrols, student patrols, late-night transport/escort service. *Student services:* health clinic, personal/psychological counseling.

Athletics *Intramural sports:* basketball M/W, cheerleading W(c), football M(c)/W(c), ice hockey M(c)/W(c), soccer M(c)/W(c), tennis M(c)/W(c), ultimate Frisbee M(c)/W(c), volleyball M(c)/W(c).

Standardized Tests *Required:* SAT or ACT (for admission).

Costs (2013–14) *Tuition:* area resident $6384 full-time, $266 per credit hour part-time; state resident $6384 full-time, $266 per credit hour part-time; nonresident $19,896 full-time, $829 per credit hour part-time. Full-time tuition and fees vary according to course level, course load, degree level, location, program, reciprocity agreements, and student level. Part-time tuition and fees vary according to course level, course load, degree level, location, program, reciprocity agreements, and student level. *Required fees:* $1110 full-time, $266 per credit hour part-time, $550 per term part-time. *Room and board:* $10,410; room only: $7110. Room and board charges vary according to board plan. *Payment plans:* installment, deferred payment. *Waivers:* employees or children of employees.

Financial Aid Of all full-time matriculated undergraduates who enrolled in 2011, 5,205 applied for aid, 4,521 were judged to have need, 209 had their need fully met. 223 Federal Work-Study jobs (averaging $3221). 199 state and other part-time jobs (averaging $3699). In 2011, 191 non-need-based awards were made. *Average percent of need met:* 48%. *Average financial aid package:* $8529. *Average need-based loan:* $4427. *Average need-based gift aid:* $6694. *Average non-need-based aid:* $2525. *Average indebtedness upon graduation:* $21,285.

Applying *Options:* electronic application, deferred entrance. *Application fee:* $50. *Required:* high school transcript, minimum 2.5 GPA. *Required for some:* essay or personal statement, minimum 3.0 GPA, audition, portfolio, entrance exam for some programs. *Recommended:* essay or personal statement. *Application deadlines:* 7/22 (freshmen), 7/22 (out-of-state freshmen), 7/22 (transfers). *Notification:* continuous (freshmen), continuous (out-of-state freshmen), continuous (transfers).

Freshman Application Contact Office of Admissions, University of Colorado Denver, PO Box 173364, Campus Box 167, Denver, CO 80217. *Phone:* 303-556-2704. *E-mail:* admissions@ucdenver.edu. *Website:* http://www.ucdenver.edu/.

University of Denver

Denver, Colorado

- **Independent** university, founded 1864
- **Urban** 125-acre campus with easy access to Denver
- **Endowment** $373.4 million
- **Coed** 5,394 undergraduate students, 92% full-time, 56% women, 44% men
- **Moderately difficult** entrance level, 68% of applicants were admitted

Undergraduates 4,965 full-time, 429 part-time. Students come from 50 states and territories; 54 other countries; 50% are from out of state; 3% Black or African American, non-Hispanic/Latino; 8% Hispanic/Latino; 4% Asian, non-Hispanic/Latino; 0.1% Native Hawaiian or other Pacific Islander, non-Hispanic/Latino; 0.5% American Indian or Alaska Native, non-Hispanic/Latino; 3% Two or more races, non-Hispanic/Latino; 4% Race/ethnicity unknown; 9% international; 3% transferred in; 44% live on campus. *Retention:* 86% of full-time freshmen returned.

Freshmen *Admission:* 11,448 applied, 7,740 admitted, 1,213 enrolled. *Average high school GPA:* 3.7. *Test scores:* SAT critical reading scores over 500: 91%; SAT math scores over 500: 93%; SAT writing scores over 500: 86%; ACT scores over 18: 100%; SAT critical reading scores over 600: 53%; SAT math scores over 600: 59%; SAT writing scores over 600: 44%; ACT scores over 24: 87%; SAT critical reading scores over 700: 11%; SAT math scores over 700: 13%; SAT writing scores over 700: 9%; ACT scores over 30: 30%.

Faculty *Total:* 1,349, 50% full-time, 60% with terminal degrees. *Student/faculty ratio:* 11:1.

Academics *Calendar:* quarters; semesters for law school. *Degrees:* certificates, bachelor's, master's, doctoral, post-master's, and postbachelor's certifi-

cates. *Special study options:* accelerated degree program, adult/continuing education programs, advanced placement credit, cooperative education, distance learning, double majors, English as a second language, freshman honors college, honors programs, independent study, internships, off-campus study, part-time degree program, services for LD students, student-designed majors, study abroad, summer session for credit. *ROTC:* Army (c), Air Force (c). *Unusual degree programs:* 3-2 business administration; engineering; social work; art history; public policy; accounting; international studies; education; environmental science; and geography.

Computers on Campus 150 computers/terminals and 35,000 ports are available on campus for general student use. Students can access the following: campus intranet, computer help desk, free student e-mail accounts, online (class) grades, online (class) registration, online (class) schedules. Campuswide network is available. 95% of college-owned or -operated housing units are wired for high-speed Internet access. Wireless service is available via entire campus.

Student Life *Housing:* on-campus residence required through sophomore year. *Options:* coed, men-only, women-only, cooperative. Campus housing is university owned. Freshman campus housing is guaranteed. *Activities and organizations:* drama/theater group, student-run newspaper, radio station, choral group, Club Sports Council, Alpine Club, DU Programs Board, Greek Life Council, Residence Hall Association, national fraternities, national sororities. *Campus security:* 24-hour emergency response devices and patrols, late-night transport/escort service, controlled dormitory access, 24-hour locked residence hall entrances. *Student services:* health clinic, personal/psychological counseling, women's center.

Athletics Member NCAA. All Division I. *Intercollegiate sports:* baseball M(c), basketball M(s)/W(s), cross-country running M(c)/W(c), equestrian sports M(c)/W(c), golf M(s)/W(s), gymnastics W(s), ice hockey M(s)/W(c), lacrosse M(s)/W(s), racquetball M(c)/W(c), skiing (cross-country) M(s)/W(s), skiing (downhill) M(s)/W(s), soccer M(s)/W(s), softball W(c), swimming and diving M(s)/W(s), tennis M(s)/W(s), volleyball W(s), water polo M(c)/W(c). *Intramural sports:* basketball M/W, field hockey M(c)/W(c), football M/W, golf M(c)/W(c), ice hockey M(c), lacrosse M(c)/W(c), racquetball M(c)/W(c), rock climbing M(c)/W(c), rugby M(c), skiing (downhill) M(c)/W(c), soccer M(c)/W(c), softball M/W, tennis M(c)/W(c), ultimate Frisbee M(c)/W(c), volleyball M(c)/W(c).

Standardized Tests *Required:* SAT or ACT (for admission).

Costs (2013–14) *Comprehensive fee:* $51,787 includes full-time tuition ($39,744), mandatory fees ($963), and room and board ($11,080). Full-time tuition and fees vary according to class time, course load, and program. Part-time tuition: $1104 per quarter hour. Part-time tuition and fees vary according to class time, course load, and program. *College room only:* $6780. Room and board charges vary according to board plan and housing facility. *Payment plans:* installment, deferred payment. *Waivers:* senior citizens and employees or children of employees.

Financial Aid Of all full-time matriculated undergraduates who enrolled in 2012, 2,660 applied for aid, 2,134 were judged to have need, 698 had their need fully met. 377 Federal Work-Study jobs (averaging $2763). 177 state and other part-time jobs (averaging $2919). In 2012, 1858 non-need-based awards were made. *Average percent of need met:* 83%. *Average financial aid package:* $31,160. *Average need-based loan:* $4220. *Average need-based gift aid:* $25,917. *Average non-need-based aid:* $13,708. *Average indebtedness upon graduation:* $30,268. *Financial aid deadline:* 5/1.

Applying *Options:* electronic application, early admission, early action, deferred entrance. *Application fee:* $60. *Required:* essay or personal statement, high school transcript, 2 letters of recommendation. *Required for some:* minimum 2.0 GPA. *Recommended:* interview. *Application deadlines:* 1/15 (freshmen), rolling (transfers), 11/1 (early action). *Notification:* 3/15 (freshmen), continuous (transfers), 1/15 (early action).

Freshman Application Contact Mr. Todd R. Rinehart, Assistant Vice Chancellor for Enrollment, University of Denver, 2197 South University Boulevard, Denver, CO 80208. *Phone:* 303-871-3125. *Toll-free phone:* 800-525-9495. *Fax:* 303-871-3301. *E-mail:* admission@du.edu. *Website:* http://www.du.edu/.

See next page for display ad and page 1558 for the College Close-Up.

University of Northern Colorado

Greeley, Colorado

- **State-supported** university, founded 1890
- **Suburban** 240-acre campus with easy access to Denver
- **Endowment** $71.5 million
- **Coed** 10,102 undergraduate students, 90% full-time, 62% women, 38% men
- **Moderately difficult** entrance level, 89% of applicants were admitted

Undergraduates 9,110 full-time, 992 part-time. Students come from 50 states and territories; 37 other countries; 12% are from out of state; 4% Black or Afri-

can American, non-Hispanic/Latino; 15% Hispanic/Latino; 1% Asian, non-Hispanic/Latino; 0.3% Native Hawaiian or other Pacific Islander, non-Hispanic/Latino; 0.4% American Indian or Alaska Native, non-Hispanic/Latino; 3% Two or more races, non-Hispanic/Latino; 17% Race/ethnicity unknown; 0.9% international; 8% transferred in; 30% live on campus. *Retention:* 65% of full-time freshmen returned.

Freshmen *Admission:* 6,823 applied, 6,077 admitted, 2,218 enrolled. *Average high school GPA:* 3.18. *Test scores:* SAT critical reading scores over 500: 66%; SAT math scores over 500: 64%; ACT scores over 18: 91%; SAT critical reading scores over 600: 19%; SAT math scores over 600: 18%; ACT scores over 24: 34%; SAT critical reading scores over 700: 4%; SAT math scores over 700: 2%; ACT scores over 30: 4%.

Faculty *Total:* 737, 66% full-time. *Student/faculty ratio:* 19:1.

Academics *Calendar:* semesters. *Degrees:* bachelor's, master's, and doctoral. *Special study options:* academic remediation for entering students, accelerated degree program, adult/continuing education programs, advanced placement credit, cooperative education, distance learning, double majors, English as a second language, external degree program, honors programs, independent study, internships, off-campus study, part-time degree program, services for LD students, student-designed majors, study abroad, summer session for credit. *ROTC:* Army (b), Air Force (b).

Computers on Campus 1,736 computers/terminals and 800 ports are available on campus for general student use. Students can access the following: computer help desk, free student e-mail accounts, online (class) grades, online (class) registration, online (class) schedules. Campuswide network is available. 100% of college-owned or -operated housing units are wired for high-speed Internet access. Wireless service is available via entire campus.

Student Life *Housing:* on-campus residence required for freshman year. *Options:* coed, women-only, disabled students. Campus housing is university owned. Freshman campus housing is guaranteed. *Activities and organizations:* drama/theater group, student-run newspaper, radio and television station, choral group, marching band, Fraternities and Sororities, Club Sports, Campus Religious/Spiritual Organizations, Academic Clubs, Services Clubs, national fraternities, national sororities. *Campus security:* 24-hour emergency response

devices and patrols, student patrols, late-night transport/escort service, controlled dormitory access. *Student services:* health clinic, personal/psychological counseling, women's center, legal services.

Athletics Member NCAA. All Division I. *Intercollegiate sports:* baseball M(s), basketball M(s)/W(s), cross-country running W(s), football M(s), golf M(s)/W(s), ice hockey M(c), lacrosse M(c), rugby M(c)/W(c), soccer M(c)/W(s), softball W(s), swimming and diving W(s), tennis M(s)/W(s), track and field M(s)/W(s), volleyball W(s), wrestling M(s). *Intramural sports:* basketball M/W, football M/W, soccer M/W, softball M/W, volleyball M/W, water polo M/W.

Standardized Tests *Required:* SAT or ACT (for admission).

Costs (2012–13) *One-time required fee:* $225. *Tuition:* state resident $5214 full-time, $217 per credit hour part-time; nonresident $16,488 full-time, $687 per credit hour part-time. Full-time tuition and fees vary according to course load and program. Part-time tuition and fees vary according to course load and program. *Required fees:* $1300 full-time, $63 per credit hour part-time. *Room and board:* $10,040; room only: $4914. Room and board charges vary according to board plan, housing facility, and student level. *Payment plan:* deferred payment. *Waivers:* employees or children of employees.

Financial Aid Of all full-time matriculated undergraduates who enrolled in 2010, 6,739 applied for aid, 5,781 were judged to have need, 2,290 had their need fully met. In 2010, 1153 non-need-based awards were made. *Average percent of need met:* 79%. *Average financial aid package:* $6174. *Average need-based loan:* $3829. *Average need-based gift aid:* $3724. *Average non-need-based aid:* $314.

Applying *Options:* electronic application, deferred entrance. *Application fee:* $45. *Required:* high school transcript, minimum 2.9 GPA. *Application deadlines:* 8/1 (freshmen), 8/1 (out-of-state freshmen), rolling (transfers). *Notification:* continuous (freshmen), continuous (transfers).

Freshman Application Contact Sean Broghammer, Director of Admissions, University of Northern Colorado, Campus Box 10, Carter Hall 3006, Greeley, CO 80639. *Phone:* 970-351-2881. *Toll-free phone:* 888-700-4UNC. *Fax:* 970-351-2984. *E-mail:* admissions@unco.edu. *Website:* http://www.unco.edu/.

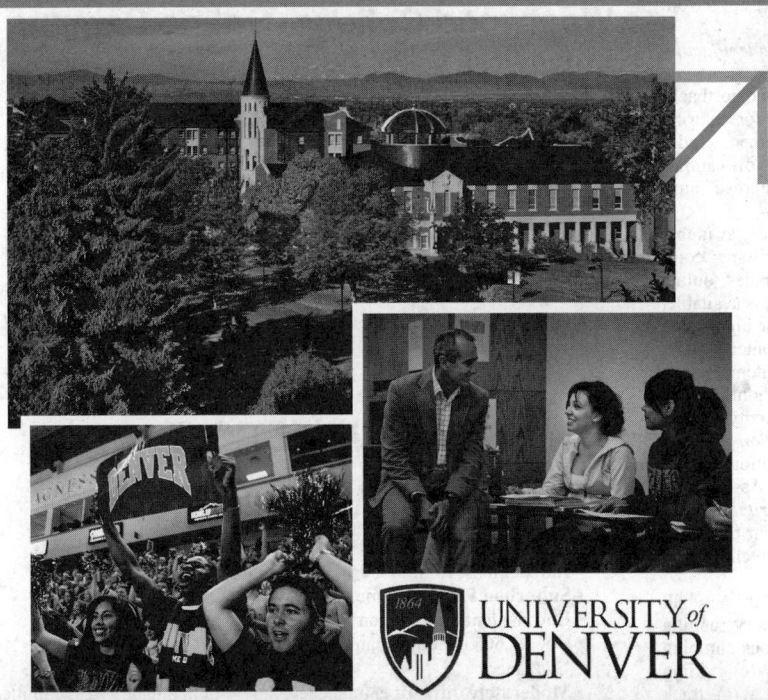

University of Phoenix–Denver Campus

Lone Tree, Colorado

Freshman Application Contact Marc Booker, Sr. Director, Office of Admissions and Evaluation, University of Phoenix–Denver Campus, 4035 South Riverpoint Parkway, Mail Stop CF-L101, Phoenix, AZ 85040. *Phone:* 602-557-4609. *Toll-free phone:* 866-766-0766. *Fax:* 480-643-1156. *Website:* http://www.phoenix.edu/.

University of Phoenix–Southern Colorado Campus

Colorado Springs, Colorado

Freshman Application Contact Marc Booker, Sr. Director, Office of Admissions and Evaluation, University of Phoenix–Southern Colorado Campus, 4035 South Riverpoint Parkway, Mail Stop CF-L101, Phoenix, AZ 85040. *Phone:* 602-557-4609. *Toll-free phone:* 866-766-0766. *Fax:* 480-643-1156. *Website:* http://www.phoenix.edu/.

Western State Colorado University

Gunnison, Colorado

- **State-supported** comprehensive, founded 1901
- **Rural** 381-acre campus
- **Coed** 2,105 undergraduate students, 88% full-time, 39% women, 61% men
- **Moderately difficult** entrance level, 96% of applicants were admitted

Undergraduates 1,853 full-time, 252 part-time. Students come from 50 states and territories; 8 other countries; 25% are from out of state; 2% Black or African American, non-Hispanic/Latino; 7% Hispanic/Latino; 0.7% Asian, non-Hispanic/Latino; 0.5% Native Hawaiian or other Pacific Islander, non-Hispanic/Latino; 0.3% American Indian or Alaska Native, non-Hispanic/Latino; 2% Two or more races, non-Hispanic/Latino; 18% Race/ethnicity unknown; 0.7% international; 8% transferred in; 37% live on campus. *Retention:* 64% of full-time freshmen returned.

Freshmen *Admission:* 1,515 applied, 1,448 admitted, 450 enrolled. *Average high school GPA:* 3.11. *Test scores:* SAT critical reading scores over 500: 52%; SAT math scores over 500: 47%; ACT scores over 18: 87%; SAT critical reading scores over 600: 12%; SAT math scores over 600: 17%; ACT scores over 24: 29%; SAT critical reading scores over 700: 1%; SAT math scores over 700: 3%; ACT scores over 30: 2%.

Faculty *Total:* 163, 69% full-time, 95% with terminal degrees. *Student/faculty ratio:* 15:1.

Academics *Calendar:* semesters. *Degrees:* bachelor's, master's, and postbachelor's certificates. *Special study options:* academic remediation for entering students, adult/continuing education programs, advanced placement credit, double majors, honors programs, independent study, internships, off-campus study, part-time degree program, services for LD students, study abroad, summer session for credit.

Computers on Campus 181 computers/terminals and 600 ports are available on campus for general student use. Students can access the following: computer help desk, free student e-mail accounts, online (class) grades, online (class) registration, online (class) schedules. Campuswide network is available. 100% of college-owned or -operated housing units are wired for high-speed Internet access. Wireless service is available via classrooms, computer centers, computer labs, dorm rooms, learning centers, libraries, student centers.

Student Life *Housing:* on-campus residence required through sophomore year. *Options:* coed, men-only, women-only. Campus housing is university owned. Freshman campus housing is guaranteed. *Activities and organizations:* drama/theater group, student-run newspaper, radio and television station, choral group, Mountain Search and Rescue Team, Student Government Association, Rodeo Club, wilderness pursuits, Peak Productions. *Campus security:* 24-hour emergency response devices and patrols, student patrols, late-night transport/escort service, controlled dormitory access. *Student services:* health clinic, personal/psychological counseling.

Athletics Member NCAA. All Division II. *Intercollegiate sports:* baseball M(c), basketball M(s)/W(s), cheerleading M(c)/W(c), cross-country running M(s)/W(s), football M(s), ice hockey M(c), lacrosse M(c)/W(c), rock climbing M(c)/W(c), rugby M(c)/W(c), skiing (cross-country) M(c)/W(c), skiing (downhill) M(c)/W(c), soccer M(c)/W(s), swimming and diving W(s), track and field M(s)/W(s), volleyball M(c)/W(s), wrestling M(s)/W(c). *Intramural sports:* basketball M/W, football M/W, golf M/W, soccer M/W, softball M/W, table tennis M/W, tennis M/W, ultimate Frisbee M/W, volleyball M/W.

Standardized Tests *Required:* SAT or ACT (for admission).

Costs (2013–14) *Tuition:* state resident $5275 full-time, $220 per credit hour part-time; nonresident $15,216 full-time, $634 per credit hour part-time. Full-time tuition and fees vary according to course load and reciprocity agreements. Part-time tuition and fees vary according to course load and reciprocity agreements. *Required fees:* $2068 full-time. *Room and board:* $8792; room only: $4700. Room and board charges vary according to board plan and housing facility. *Payment plans:* installment, deferred payment. *Waivers:* senior citizens.

Financial Aid Of all full-time matriculated undergraduates who enrolled in 2012, 1,367 applied for aid, 1,086 were judged to have need, 173 had their need fully met. 222 Federal Work-Study jobs (averaging $709). 245 state and other part-time jobs (averaging $707). In 2012, 763 non-need-based awards were made. *Average percent of need met:* 50%. *Average financial aid package:* $9437. *Average need-based loan:* $3720. *Average need-based gift aid:* $5113. *Average non-need-based aid:* $1209. *Average indebtedness upon graduation:* $18,558.

Applying *Options:* electronic application, deferred entrance. *Application fee:* $30. *Required:* high school transcript. *Required for some:* essay or personal statement, interview. *Recommended:* minimum 2.5 GPA. *Notification:* continuous until 11/15 (freshmen), continuous until 11/15 (out-of-state freshmen), continuous (transfers).

Freshman Application Contact Ms. Lisa Garcia-Hanson, Director of Admissions, Western State Colorado University, 600 North Adams Street, Gunnison, CO 81231. *Phone:* 970-943-2119. *Toll-free phone:* 800-876-5309. *Fax:* 970-943-2212. *E-mail:* admissions@western.edu. *Website:* http://www.western.edu/.

Westwood College–Denver North

Denver, Colorado

Freshman Application Contact Westwood College–Denver North, 7350 North Broadway, Denver, CO 80221-3653. *Phone:* 303-426-7000. *Toll-free phone:* 800-281-2978. *Website:* http://www.westwood.edu/.

Westwood College–Denver South

Denver, Colorado

Freshman Application Contact Westwood College–Denver South, 3150 South Sheridan Boulevard, Denver, CO 80227. *Phone:* 303-934-1122. *Toll-free phone:* 800-281-2978. *Website:* http://www.westwood.edu/.

Westwood College–Online Campus

Broomfield, Colorado

Freshman Application Contact Westwood College–Online Campus, 10249 Church Ranch Way, Broomfield, CO 80021. *Phone:* 720-887-8888. *Website:* http://www.westwood.edu/.

Yeshiva Toras Chaim Talmudical Seminary

Denver, Colorado

Director of Admissions Rabbi Israel Kagan, Dean, Yeshiva Toras Chaim Talmudical Seminary, 1555 Stuart Street, Denver, CO 80204-1415. *Phone:* 303-629-8200. *Fax:* 303-623-5949.

CONNECTICUT

Albertus Magnus College

New Haven, Connecticut

- **Independent Roman Catholic** comprehensive, founded 1925
- **Suburban** 55-acre campus
- **Endowment** $6.1 million
- **Coed** 1,604 undergraduate students, 86% full-time, 66% women, 34% men
- **Moderately difficult** entrance level, 67% of applicants were admitted

Undergraduates 1,376 full-time, 228 part-time. Students come from 7 states and territories; 2 other countries; 17% are from out of state; 22% Black or African American, non-Hispanic/Latino; 11% Hispanic/Latino; 1% Asian, non-Hispanic/Latino; 0.1% Native Hawaiian or other Pacific Islander, non-Hispanic/Latino; 1% American Indian or Alaska Native, non-Hispanic/Latino; 21% Race/ethnicity unknown; 0.1% international; 9% transferred in; 46% live on campus. *Retention:* 76% of full-time freshmen returned.

Freshmen *Admission:* 722 applied, 485 admitted, 151 enrolled. *Average high school GPA:* 2.8. *Test scores:* SAT critical reading scores over 500: 37%; SAT writing scores over 500: 40%; SAT critical reading scores over 600: 8%; SAT writing scores over 600: 5%.

Faculty *Total:* 76, 55% full-time, 54% with terminal degrees. *Student/faculty ratio:* 15:1.

Academics *Calendar:* semesters. *Degrees:* associate, bachelor's, and master's. *Special study options:* academic remediation for entering students, accelerated degree program, advanced placement credit, distance learning, double majors, English as a second language, freshman honors college, honors programs, independent study, internships, part-time degree program, services for LD students, student-designed majors, summer session for credit. *Unusual degree programs:* 3-2 business administration.

Computers on Campus 146 computers/terminals are available on campus for general student use. Students can access the following: campus intranet, computer help desk, free student e-mail accounts, online (class) grades, online (class) registration, online (class) schedules, online class sessions—Moodle. Campuswide network is available. 100% of college-owned or -operated housing units are wired for high-speed Internet access. Wireless service is available via entire campus.

Student Life *Housing options:* coed, women-only. Campus housing is university owned. Freshman applicants given priority for college housing. *Activities and organizations:* drama/theater group, choral group, Student Government Association, College Drama, Campus ministry. *Campus security:* 24-hour emergency response devices and patrols, late-night transport/escort service, controlled dormitory access. *Student services:* health clinic, personal/psychological counseling.

Athletics Member NCAA. All Division III. *Intercollegiate sports:* baseball M, basketball M/W, cross-country running M/W, lacrosse M/W, soccer M/W, softball W, tennis M/W, volleyball M/W. *Intramural sports:* basketball M/W, racquetball M/W, soccer M/W, squash M/W, table tennis M/W.

Standardized Tests *Required:* SAT or ACT (for admission). *Recommended:* SAT Subject Tests (for admission).

Costs (2012–13) *Comprehensive fee:* $40,112 includes full-time tuition ($27,888), mandatory fees ($470), and room and board ($11,754). Full-time tuition and fees vary according to program. Part-time tuition and fees vary according to program. *Payment plan:* installment. *Waivers:* senior citizens and employees or children of employees.

Financial Aid Of all full-time matriculated undergraduates who enrolled in 2008, 1,442 applied for aid, 1,307 were judged to have need, 90 had their need fully met. 78 Federal Work-Study jobs (averaging $1583). 34 state and other part-time jobs (averaging $3400). In 2008, 32 non-need-based awards were made. *Average percent of need met:* 53%. *Average financial aid package:* $9074. *Average need-based loan:* $4398. *Average need-based gift aid:* $5739. *Average non-need-based aid:* $3537. *Average indebtedness upon graduation:* $26,404.

Applying *Options:* electronic application, deferred entrance. *Application fee:* $35. *Required:* high school transcript, 1 letter of recommendation. *Required for some:* minimum 2.5 GPA. *Recommended:* essay or personal statement, minimum 2.5 GPA, interview. *Application deadlines:* 8/30 (freshmen), rolling (transfers). *Notification:* continuous (freshmen), continuous (transfers).

Freshman Application Contact Mr. Nilvio Perez, Director of Admission, Albertus Magnus College, 700 Prospect Street, New Haven, CT 06511-1189. *Phone:* 203-773-8501. *Toll-free phone:* 800-578-9160. *Fax:* 203-773-5248. *E-mail:* admissions@albertus.edu. *Website:* http://www.albertus.edu/.

Bais Binyomin Academy

Stamford, Connecticut

Director of Admissions Director of Admissions, Bais Binyomin Academy, 132 Prospect Street, Stamford, CT 06901-1202. *Phone:* 203-325-4351.

Central Connecticut State University

New Britain, Connecticut

- **State-supported** comprehensive, founded 1849, part of Connecticut State University System
- **Suburban** 294-acre campus
- **Endowment** $38.2 million
- **Coed** 10,092 undergraduate students, 78% full-time, 48% women, 52% men
- **Moderately difficult** entrance level, 64% of applicants were admitted

Undergraduates 7,823 full-time, 2,269 part-time. Students come from 29 states and territories; 41 other countries; 3% are from out of state; 10% Black

or African American, non-Hispanic/Latino; 9% Hispanic/Latino; 3% Asian, non-Hispanic/Latino; 0.1% Native Hawaiian or other Pacific Islander, non-Hispanic/Latino; 0.2% American Indian or Alaska Native, non-Hispanic/Latino; 2% Two or more races, non-Hispanic/Latino; 3% Race/ethnicity unknown; 1% international; 11% transferred in; 23% live on campus. *Retention:* 76% of full-time freshmen returned.

Freshmen *Admission:* 5,699 applied, 3,645 admitted, 1,387 enrolled. *Average high school GPA:* 2.97. *Test scores:* SAT critical reading scores over 500: 53%; SAT math scores over 500: 57%; SAT writing scores over 500: 54%; SAT critical reading scores over 600: 9%; SAT math scores over 600: 11%; SAT writing scores over 600: 10%; SAT critical reading scores over 700: 1%; SAT writing scores over 700: 1%.

Faculty *Total:* 968, 45% full-time, 45% with terminal degrees. *Student/faculty ratio:* 16:1.

Academics *Calendar:* semesters. *Degrees:* bachelor's, master's, doctoral, post-master's, and postbachelor's certificates. *Special study options:* academic remediation for entering students, adult/continuing education programs, advanced placement credit, cooperative education, distance learning, English as a second language, honors programs, independent study, internships, off-campus study, part-time degree program, services for LD students, student-designed majors, study abroad, summer session for credit. *ROTC:* Army (c), Air Force (c).

Computers on Campus 750 computers/terminals are available on campus for general student use. Students can access the following: campus intranet, computer help desk, free student e-mail accounts, online (class) grades, online (class) registration, online (class) schedules. Campuswide network is available. 97% of college-owned or -operated housing units are wired for high-speed Internet access. Wireless service is available via entire campus.

Student Life *Housing options:* coed, women-only. Campus housing is university owned. *Activities and organizations:* drama/theater group, student-run newspaper, radio and television station, choral group, Inter-Residence Council, student radio station, Program Council, Outing Club, NAACP, national fraternities, national sororities. *Campus security:* 24-hour emergency response devices and patrols, student patrols, late-night transport/escort service, controlled dormitory access. *Student services:* health clinic, personal/psychological counseling, women's center.

Athletics Member NCAA. All Division I except football (Division I-AA). *Intercollegiate sports:* baseball M(s), basketball M(s)/W(s), cross-country running M(s)/W(s), fencing M(c)/W(c), golf M(s)/W(s), lacrosse M(c)/W(s), soccer M(s)/W(s), softball W(s), swimming and diving W(s), track and field M(s)/W(s), volleyball W(s). *Intramural sports:* basketball M/W, field hockey W(c), football M, rugby M(c)/W(c), soccer M/W, softball M/W, volleyball M/W.

Standardized Tests *Required:* SAT (for admission).

Costs (2012–13) *Tuition:* state resident $4285 full-time, $179 per credit part-time; nonresident $13,866 full-time, $182 per credit part-time. Full-time tuition and fees vary according to course level, course load, program, and reciprocity agreements. Part-time tuition and fees vary according to course level, course load, and program. *Required fees:* $4036 full-time, $218 per credit part-time, $223 per credit part-time. *Room and board:* $10,056; room only: $5850. Room and board charges vary according to board plan. *Payment plan:* installment. *Waivers:* senior citizens and employees or children of employees.

Financial Aid Of all full-time matriculated undergraduates who enrolled in 2010, 6,898 applied for aid, 5,295 were judged to have need, 478 had their need fully met. In 2010, 147 non-need-based awards were made. *Average percent of need met:* 62%. *Average financial aid package:* $7759. *Average need-based loan:* $4181. *Average need-based gift aid:* $4007. *Average non-need-based aid:* $3615. *Average indebtedness upon graduation:* $19,086.

Applying *Options:* electronic application. *Application fee:* $50. *Required:* essay or personal statement, high school transcript, minimum 2.0 GPA. *Required for some:* interview. *Recommended:* minimum 3.0 GPA, 1 letter of recommendation. *Application deadlines:* 5/1 (freshmen), 6/1 (transfers). *Notification:* continuous until 10/15 (freshmen), continuous until 10/15 (transfers).

Freshman Application Contact Central Connecticut State University, 1615 Stanley Street, New Britain, CT 06050. *Phone:* 860-832-2285. *Fax:* 860-832-2522. *E-mail:* admissions@ccsu.edu. *Website:* http://www.ccsu.edu/.

Charter Oak State College

New Britain, Connecticut

- **State-supported** 4-year, founded 1973
- **Small-town** campus
- **Coed** 1,644 undergraduate students, 17% full-time, 67% women, 33% men
- **Noncompetitive** entrance level

Undergraduates 276 full-time, 1,368 part-time. Students come from 43 states and territories; 25% are from out of state; 17% Black or African American, non-Hispanic/Latino; 11% Hispanic/Latino; 2% Asian, non-Hispanic/Latino;

0.1% Native Hawaiian or other Pacific Islander, non-Hispanic/Latino; 0.1% American Indian or Alaska Native, non-Hispanic/Latino; 1% Two or more races, non-Hispanic/Latino; 5% Race/ethnicity unknown; 0.3% international; 28% transferred in.
Faculty *Total:* 153. *Student/faculty ratio:* 14:1.
Academics *Calendar:* continuous. *Degrees:* certificates, associate, and bachelor's (offers only external degree programs). *Special study options:* accelerated degree program, adult/continuing education programs, advanced placement credit, distance learning, external degree program, independent study, part-time degree program, services for LD students, student-designed majors, summer session for credit.
Student Life *Housing:* college housing not available.
Costs (2012–13) *Tuition:* state resident $7350 full-time, $245 per credit hour part-time; nonresident $9660 full-time, $322 per credit hour part-time. *Required fees:* $342 full-time, $171 per term part-time.
Financial Aid Of all full-time matriculated undergraduates who enrolled in 2003, 355 applied for aid, 226 were judged to have need, 25 had their need fully met. *Average percent of need met:* 75%. *Average financial aid package:* $4464. *Average need-based loan:* $1800.
Applying *Options:* electronic application, deferred entrance. *Application fee:* $75. *Application deadline:* rolling (transfers). *Notification:* continuous (transfers).
Freshman Application Contact Lori Pendleton, Director of Admissions, Charter Oak State College, 55 Paul Manafort Drive, New Britain, CT 06053-2150. *Phone:* 860-515-3858. *E-mail:* admissions@charteroak.edu. *Website:* http://www.charteroak.edu/.

Connecticut College

New London, Connecticut

- **Independent** comprehensive, founded 1911
- **Small-town** 702-acre campus
- **Endowment** $211.2 million
- **Coed** 1,926 undergraduate students, 98% full-time, 60% women, 40% men
- **Very difficult** entrance level, 36% of applicants were admitted

Undergraduates 1,884 full-time, 42 part-time. Students come from 42 states and territories; 74 other countries; 83% are from out of state; 4% Black or African American, non-Hispanic/Latino; 7% Hispanic/Latino; 3% Asian, non-Hispanic/Latino; 0.1% American Indian or Alaska Native, non-Hispanic/Latino; 2% Two or more races, non-Hispanic/Latino; 7% Race/ethnicity unknown; 4% international; 0.9% transferred in; 99% live on campus. *Retention:* 92% of full-time freshmen returned.
Freshmen *Admission:* 4,837 applied, 1,734 admitted, 503 enrolled. *Test scores:* SAT critical reading scores over 500: 99%; SAT math scores over 500: 99%; SAT writing scores over 500: 99%; ACT scores over 18: 100%; SAT critical reading scores over 600: 85%; SAT math scores over 600: 85%; SAT writing scores over 600: 93%; ACT scores over 24: 96%; SAT critical reading scores over 700: 36%; SAT math scores over 700: 26%; SAT writing scores over 700: 44%; ACT scores over 30: 53%.
Faculty *Total:* 249, 72% full-time, 71% with terminal degrees. *Student/faculty ratio:* 9:1.
Academics *Calendar:* semesters. *Degrees:* bachelor's and master's. *Special study options:* accelerated degree program, adult/continuing education programs, advanced placement credit, double majors, independent study, internships, off-campus study, part-time degree program, services for LD students, student-designed majors, study abroad. *Unusual degree programs:* 3-2 engineering with Washington University in St. Louis.
Computers on Campus Students can access the following: campus intranet, computer help desk, free student e-mail accounts, online (class) grades, online (class) registration, online (class) schedules, Moodle course web pages. Campuswide network is available. 100% of college-owned or -operated housing units are wired for high-speed Internet access. Wireless service is available via classrooms, computer centers, computer labs, dorm rooms, learning centers, libraries, student centers.
Student Life *Housing:* on-campus residence required through sophomore year. *Options:* coed. Campus housing is university owned. Freshman campus housing is guaranteed. *Activities and organizations:* drama/theater group, student-run newspaper, radio station, choral group, Student Government Association, Student Activity Council, Unity House organizations, sports clubs, student radio station. *Campus security:* 24-hour emergency response devices and patrols, late-night transport/escort service, controlled dormitory access. *Student services:* health clinic, personal/psychological counseling, women's center.
Athletics Member NCAA. All Division III. *Intercollegiate sports:* baseball M(c), basketball M/W, crew M/W, cross-country running M/W, equestrian sports M(c)/W(c), field hockey W, ice hockey M/W, lacrosse M/W, rugby W(c), sailing M/W, skiing (cross-country) M(c)/W(c), skiing (downhill) M(c)/

W(c), soccer M/W, squash M/W, swimming and diving M/W, tennis M/W, track and field M/W, ultimate Frisbee M(c)/W(c), volleyball M/W, water polo M/W. *Intramural sports:* basketball M/W, football M, golf M/W, ice hockey M/W, lacrosse M, soccer M/W, softball M/W, tennis M/W, volleyball M/W.
Costs (2013–14) *Comprehensive fee:* $58,780 includes full-time tuition ($45,765), mandatory fees ($320), and room and board ($12,695). Part-time tuition: $1364 per credit hour. *College room only:* $7325. *Payment plan:* installment. *Waivers:* senior citizens and employees or children of employees.
Financial Aid Of all full-time matriculated undergraduates who enrolled in 2010, 983 applied for aid, 866 were judged to have need, 866 had their need fully met. *Average percent of need met:* 100%. *Average financial aid package:* $32,873. *Average need-based loan:* $4401. *Average need-based gift aid:* $30,926. *Average indebtedness upon graduation:* $26,545.
Applying *Options:* electronic application, early decision, deferred entrance. *Application fee:* $60. *Required:* essay or personal statement, high school transcript, minimum 2.0 GPA, 1 letter of recommendation, Supplement to Common Application. *Recommended:* interview. *Application deadlines:* 1/1 (freshmen), 4/1 (transfers). *Early decision deadline:* 11/15 (for plan 1), 1/1 (for plan 2). *Notification:* 3/31 (freshmen), 5/15 (transfers), 12/15 (early decision plan 1), 2/15 (early decision plan 2).
Freshman Application Contact Ms. Martha C. Merrill, Dean of Admissions and Financial Aid, Connecticut College, 270 Mohegan Avenue, New London, CT 06320-4196. *Phone:* 860-439-2200. *Fax:* 860-439-4301. *E-mail:* admission@conncoll.edu.
Website: http://www.connecticutcollege.edu/.

Eastern Connecticut State University

Willimantic, Connecticut

- **State-supported** comprehensive, founded 1889, part of Connecticut State Colleges and Universities
- **Small-town** 182-acre campus with easy access to Hartford
- **Coed**
- **Moderately difficult** entrance level

Faculty *Student/faculty ratio:* 16:1.
Academics *Calendar:* semesters. *Degrees:* associate, bachelor's, and master's.
Student Life *Campus security:* 24-hour emergency response devices and patrols, student patrols, late-night transport/escort service, controlled dormitory access.
Athletics Member NCAA. All Division III.
Standardized Tests *Required:* SAT or ACT (for admission).
Costs (2012–13) *Tuition:* state resident $4285 full-time; nonresident $15,317 full-time. Full-time tuition and fees vary according to reciprocity agreements. *Required fees:* $4626 full-time. *Room and board:* $10,634; room only: $6067. Room and board charges vary according to board plan.
Financial Aid Of all full-time matriculated undergraduates who enrolled in 2010, 3,506 applied for aid, 2,869 were judged to have need, 239 had their need fully met. *In 2010,* 91 non-need-based awards were made. *Average percent of need met:* 52. *Average financial aid package:* $8677. *Average need-based loan:* $4634. *Average need-based gift aid:* $6657. *Average non-need-based aid:* $2694. *Average indebtedness upon graduation:* $26,192.
Applying *Options:* electronic application, early admission, deferred entrance. *Application fee:* $50. *Required:* high school transcript. *Required for some:* interview. *Recommended:* essay or personal statement, rank in upper 50% of high school class.
Freshman Application Contact Christopher Dorsey, Interim Director of Admissions and Enrollment Management, Eastern Connecticut State University, 83 Windham Street, Willimantic, CT 06226. *Phone:* 860-465-5286. *Fax:* 860-465-5544. *E-mail:* admissions@easternct.edu.
Website: http://www.easternct.edu/.

Fairfield University

Fairfield, Connecticut

- **Independent Roman Catholic (Jesuit)** comprehensive, founded 1942
- **Suburban** 200-acre campus with easy access to New York City
- **Endowment** $245.3 million
- **Coed** 3,879 undergraduate students, 89% full-time, 59% women, 41% men
- **Moderately difficult** entrance level, 71% of applicants were admitted

Undergraduates 3,471 full-time, 408 part-time. Students come from 31 states and territories; 24 other countries; 64% are from out of state; 3% Black or African American, non-Hispanic/Latino; 8% Hispanic/Latino; 2% Asian, non-Hispanic/Latino; 0.1% Native Hawaiian or other Pacific Islander, non-Hispanic/Latino; 0.1% American Indian or Alaska Native, non-Hispanic/Latino; 1% Two or more races, non-Hispanic/Latino; 15% Race/ethnicity unknown; 1% international; 1% transferred in; 82% live on campus. *Retention:* 87% of full-time freshmen returned.

Freshmen *Admission:* 9,254 applied, 6,585 admitted, 990 enrolled. *Average high school GPA:* 3.36. *Test scores:* SAT critical reading scores over 500: 93%; SAT math scores over 500: 94%; SAT writing scores over 500: 92%; ACT scores over 18: 100%; SAT critical reading scores over 600: 39%; SAT math scores over 600: 53%; SAT writing scores over 600: 44%; ACT scores over 24: 80%; SAT critical reading scores over 700: 6%; SAT math scores over 700: 6%; SAT writing scores over 700: 5%; ACT scores over 30: 9%.

Faculty *Total:* 587, 45% full-time, 65% with terminal degrees. *Student/faculty ratio:* 11:1.

Academics *Calendar:* semesters. *Degrees:* bachelor's, master's, doctoral, and post-master's certificates. *Special study options:* adult/continuing education programs, advanced placement credit, distance learning, double majors, honors programs, independent study, internships, off-campus study, part-time degree program, services for LD students, student-designed majors, study abroad, summer session for credit. *ROTC:* Army (c), Air Force (c). *Unusual degree programs:* 3-2 engineering with University of Connecticut, Rensselaer Polytechnic Institute, Columbia University, Stevens Institute of Technology.

Computers on Campus 101 computers/terminals and 150 ports are available on campus for general student use. Students can access the following: campus intranet, computer help desk, free student e-mail accounts, online (class) grades, online (class) registration, online (class) schedules. Campuswide network is available. 100% of college-owned or -operated housing units are wired for high-speed Internet access. Wireless service is available via classrooms, computer labs, dorm rooms, libraries, student centers.

Student Life *Housing:* on-campus residence required through senior year. *Options:* coed, disabled students. Campus housing is university owned. Freshman campus housing is guaranteed. *Activities and organizations:* drama/theater group, student-run newspaper, radio and television station, choral group, Student government, Glee Club, Residence Hall Council, Stags in the Stands, Campus Ministry. *Campus security:* 24-hour emergency response devices and patrols, late-night transport/escort service, controlled dormitory access, bicycle patrols. *Student services:* health clinic, personal/psychological counseling, women's center.

Athletics Member NCAA. All Division I. *Intercollegiate sports:* baseball M(s), basketball M(s)/W(s), crew M(s)/W(s), cross-country running M(s)/W(s), equestrian sports W(c), field hockey W(s), golf M(s)/W(s), ice hockey M(c)/W(c), lacrosse M(s)/W(s), soccer M(s)/W(s), softball W(s), swimming and diving M(s)/W(s), tennis M(s)/W(s), volleyball M(c)/W(s). *Intramural sports:* basketball M/W, field hockey W, golf M/W, lacrosse W, rugby M(c)/W(c), sailing M(c)/W(c), skiing (downhill) M(c)/W(c), soccer M/W, softball M/W, tennis M/W, volleyball M/W.

Costs (2012–13) *One-time required fee:* $230. *Comprehensive fee:* $54,240 includes full-time tuition ($41,090), mandatory fees ($600), and room and board ($12,550). Part-time tuition: $700 per credit hour. Part-time tuition and fees vary according to course load. *Required fees:* $60 per term part-time. *College room only:* $7690. Room and board charges vary according to board plan and housing facility. *Payment plan:* installment. *Waivers:* employees or children of employees.

Financial Aid Of all full-time matriculated undergraduates who enrolled in 2012, 2,414 applied for aid, 1,835 were judged to have need, 231 had their need fully met. 422 Federal Work-Study jobs (averaging $997). In 2012, 719 non-need-based awards were made. *Average percent of need met:* 88%. *Average financial aid package:* $29,491. *Average need-based loan:* $4839. *Average need-based gift aid:* $19,098. *Average non-need-based aid:* $16,105. *Average indebtedness upon graduation:* $28,507. *Financial aid deadline:* 2/15.

Applying *Options:* electronic application, early admission, early decision, early action, deferred entrance. *Application fee:* $60. *Required:* essay or personal statement, high school transcript, 1 letter of recommendation. *Recommended:* interview. *Application deadlines:* 1/15 (freshmen), 5/1 (transfers), 11/1 (early action). *Early decision deadline:* 1/1. *Notification:* 4/1 (freshmen), continuous (transfers), 2/1 (early decision), 1/1 (early action).

Freshman Application Contact Ms. Karen Pellegrino, Dean of Enrollment, Fairfield University, 1073 North Benson Road, Fairfield, CT 06824-5195. *Phone:* 203-254-4100. *Fax:* 203-254-4199. *E-mail:* admis@fairfield.edu. *Website:* http://www.fairfield.edu/.

Goodwin College
East Hartford, Connecticut

- **Independent** primarily 2-year, founded 1999
- **Suburban** 660-acre campus with easy access to Hartford
- **Endowment** $3.4 million
- **Coed** 3,317 undergraduate students, 15% full-time, 83% women, 17% men
- **Minimally difficult** entrance level, 100% of applicants were admitted

Undergraduates 495 full-time, 2,822 part-time. 2% are from out of state; 22% Black or African American, non-Hispanic/Latino; 19% Hispanic/Latino; 2% Asian, non-Hispanic/Latino; 0.4% American Indian or Alaska Native, non-Hispanic/Latino; 3% Two or more races, non-Hispanic/Latino; 0.2% Race/ethnicity unknown; 0.1% international; 15% transferred in. *Retention:* 57% of full-time freshmen returned.

Freshmen *Admission:* 604 applied, 604 admitted, 370 enrolled.

Faculty *Total:* 275, 23% full-time. *Student/faculty ratio:* 11:1.

Academics *Calendar:* semesters. *Degrees:* certificates, associate, and bachelor's. *Special study options:* academic remediation for entering students, adult/continuing education programs, advanced placement credit, distance learning, double majors, English as a second language, internships, off-campus study, part-time degree program, services for LD students, summer session for credit.

Computers on Campus 204 computers/terminals are available on campus for general student use. Students can access the following: campus intranet, computer help desk, free student e-mail accounts, online (class) grades, online (class) registration, online (class) schedules. Campuswide network is available. Wireless service is available via entire campus.

Student Life *Housing:* college housing not available. *Activities and organizations:* student-run newspaper, choral group. *Campus security:* 24-hour emergency response devices, evening security patrolman. *Student services:* personal/psychological counseling.

Athletics *Intramural sports:* basketball M, football M/W, soccer M/W, softball M/W.

Costs (2013–14) *Tuition:* $18,900 full-time, $590 per credit hour part-time. Full-time tuition and fees vary according to course load and program. Part-time tuition and fees vary according to course load and program. *Required fees:* $500 full-time. *Payment plan:* installment. *Waivers:* employees or children of employees.

Financial Aid Of all full-time matriculated undergraduates who enrolled in 2010, 662 applied for aid, 644 were judged to have need. 74 Federal Work-Study jobs (averaging $2745). In 2010, 11 non-need-based awards were made. *Average percent of need met:* 25%. *Average financial aid package:* $8029. *Average need-based loan:* $3231. *Average need-based gift aid:* $5404. *Average non-need-based aid:* $3333.

Applying *Options:* electronic application, early admission, early decision, early action, deferred entrance. *Application fee:* $50. *Required:* essay or personal statement, high school transcript, minimum 2.0 GPA, medical exam. *Recommended:* 2 letters of recommendation, interview. *Application deadlines:* rolling (freshmen), rolling (transfers), 6/1 (early action). *Early decision deadline:* 3/1. *Notification:* continuous (freshmen), continuous (transfers), 3/15 (early decision), 6/15 (early action).

Freshman Application Contact Mr. Nicholas Lentino, Director of Admissions, Goodwin College, One Riverside Drive, East Hartford, CT 06118. *Phone:* 860-727-6765. *Toll-free phone:* 800-889-3282. *Fax:* 860-291-9550. *E-mail:* nlantino@goodwin.edu. *Website:* http://www.goodwin.edu/.

Holy Apostles College and Seminary
Cromwell, Connecticut

- **Independent Roman Catholic** comprehensive, founded 1956
- **Suburban** 17-acre campus with easy access to Hartford, New Haven
- **Endowment** $657,367
- **Coed** 58 undergraduate students, 45% full-time, 55% women, 45% men
- **Noncompetitive** entrance level, 100% of applicants were admitted

Undergraduates 26 full-time, 32 part-time. 9% transferred in. *Retention:* 60% of full-time freshmen returned.

Freshmen *Admission:* 10 applied, 10 admitted, 3 enrolled.

Faculty *Total:* 30, 57% full-time, 67% with terminal degrees. *Student/faculty ratio:* 2:1.

Academics *Calendar:* semesters. *Degrees:* certificates, associate, bachelor's, master's, post-master's, and postbachelor's certificates. *Special study options:* academic remediation for entering students, adult/continuing education programs, English as a second language, external degree program, independent study, part-time degree program, services for LD students, summer session for credit.

Computers on Campus 10 computers/terminals are available on campus for general student use. Students can access the following: free student e-mail accounts, online (class) grades. Campuswide network is available. 100% of college-owned or -operated housing units are wired for high-speed Internet access. Wireless service is available via libraries.

Student Life *Housing:* college housing not available. *Activities and organizations:* Toastmasters, Pro-Life Organization, Student Council, Schola Choir. *Student services:* personal/psychological counseling.

Standardized Tests *Recommended:* SAT (for admission).

Costs (2012–13) *Tuition:* $10,080 full-time, $420 per credit part-time. Full-time tuition and fees vary according to course load and degree level. Part-time tuition and fees vary according to degree level. *Required fees:* $35 full-time. *Payment plan:* installment. *Waivers:* employees or children of employees.

Applying *Options:* deferred entrance. *Application fee:* $50. *Required:* high school transcript. *Required for some:* interview. *Application deadlines:* rolling (freshmen), rolling (out-of-state freshmen), rolling (transfers).
Freshman Application Contact Holy Apostles College and Seminary, 33 Prospect Hill Road, Cromwell, CT 06416-2005. *Phone:* 860-632-3010. *Website:* http://www.holyapostles.edu/.

Lincoln College of New England
Southington, Connecticut

Freshman Application Contact Anthony Reich, Vice President of Admissions, Lincoln College of New England, 2279 Mount Vernon Road, Southington, CT 06489. *Phone:* 860-628-4751 Ext. 40904. *Toll-free phone:* 800-825-0087. *Fax:* 860-628-6444. *E-mail:* areich@lincolncollegene.edu. *Website:* http://www.lincolncollegene.edu/.

Lyme Academy College of Fine Arts
Old Lyme, Connecticut

- **Independent** 4-year, founded 1976
- **Rural** 47-acre campus with easy access to New Haven, Hartford
- **Endowment** $4.0 million
- **Coed**
- **Moderately difficult** entrance level

Faculty *Student/faculty ratio:* 4:1.
Academics *Calendar:* semesters. *Degrees:* bachelor's and postbachelor's certificates.
Student Life *Campus security:* student patrols.
Standardized Tests *Required:* SAT or ACT (for admission).
Costs (2012–13) *Comprehensive fee:* $39,336 includes full-time tuition ($26,904), mandatory fees ($1632), and room and board ($10,800). Part-time tuition: $1121 per credit. Part-time tuition and fees vary according to course load. *Required fees:* $68 per credit part-time. *College room only:* $7200.
Financial Aid *Of all full-time matriculated undergraduates who enrolled in 2011,* 64 applied for aid, 64 were judged to have need. 9 Federal Work-Study jobs (averaging $839). 2 state and other part-time jobs (averaging $1345). *In 2011,* 16 non-need-based awards were made. *Average need-based loan:* $3953. *Average need-based gift aid:* $7801. *Average non-need-based aid:* $6539. *Average indebtedness upon graduation:* $31,000.
Applying *Options:* electronic application, early admission, early decision, deferred entrance. *Application fee:* $55. *Required:* high school transcript, art portfolio of at least 5 pieces but recommend 10-12 pieces. *Recommended:* essay or personal statement, 2 letters of recommendation, interview.
Freshman Application Contact Mr. Karl Holzenthal, Admissions Representative, Lyme Academy College of Fine Arts, 84 Lyme Street, Old Lyme, CT 06371. *Phone:* 860-434-3571 Ext. 127. *Fax:* 860-434-8725. *E-mail:* kholzenthal@lymeacademy.edu. *Website:* http://www.lymeacademy.edu/.

Mitchell College
New London, Connecticut

- **Independent** 4-year, founded 1938
- **Suburban** 67-acre campus with easy access to Hartford (CT), Providence (RI)
- **Coed** 858 undergraduate students, 85% full-time, 47% women, 53% men
- **Moderately difficult** entrance level, 60% of applicants were admitted

Undergraduates 731 full-time, 127 part-time. 43% are from out of state; 10% Black or African American, non-Hispanic/Latino; 12% Hispanic/Latino; 2% Asian, non-Hispanic/Latino; 0.1% Native Hawaiian or other Pacific Islander, non-Hispanic/Latino; 2% American Indian or Alaska Native, non-Hispanic/Latino; 4% Two or more races, non-Hispanic/Latino; 5% Race/ethnicity unknown; 0.3% international; 9% transferred in; 56% live on campus. *Retention:* 56% of full-time freshmen returned.
Freshmen *Admission:* 1,041 applied, 621 admitted, 150 enrolled. *Average high school GPA:* 2.68.
Faculty *Total:* 94, 37% full-time, 43% with terminal degrees. *Student/faculty ratio:* 14:1.
Academics *Calendar:* semesters. *Degrees:* associate and bachelor's. *Special study options:* advanced placement credit, cooperative education, double majors, independent study, internships, part-time degree program, services for LD students, student-designed majors, summer session for credit.
Computers on Campus 176 computers/terminals are available on campus for general student use. Students can access the following: campus intranet, computer help desk, free student e-mail accounts, online (class) grades, online (class) schedules, online student portfolios, online course requests. Campus-wide network is available. 100% of college-owned or -operated housing units

are wired for high-speed Internet access. Wireless service is available via entire campus.
Student Life *Housing:* on-campus residence required through senior year. *Options:* coed, men-only, women-only. Campus housing is university owned. Freshman applicants given priority for college housing. *Activities and organizations:* drama/theater group, student-run radio station, choral group, Mitchell College Drama Society, Sigma Alpha Pi Leadership Society, Behavioral Science, Early Childhood, Gaming Club. *Campus security:* 24-hour emergency response devices and patrols, student patrols, late-night transport/escort service, controlled dormitory access. *Student services:* health clinic, personal/psychological counseling.
Athletics Member NCAA. All Division III. *Intercollegiate sports:* baseball M, basketball M/W, cross-country running M/W, golf M, lacrosse M, sailing M/W, soccer M/W, softball W, tennis M/W, volleyball W. *Intramural sports:* basketball M/W, cheerleading M/W, rugby M/W, sailing M/W, soccer M/W, softball M/W, tennis M/W, volleyball M/W.
Costs (2013–14) *Comprehensive fee:* $40,986 includes full-time tuition ($26,774), mandatory fees ($1720), and room and board ($12,492). Part-time tuition and fees vary according to course load. *Required fees:* $300 per credit part-time. *College room only:* $6496. *Payment plan:* installment. *Waivers:* employees or children of employees.
Financial Aid Of all full-time matriculated undergraduates who enrolled in 2004, 491 applied for aid, 414 were judged to have need. 44 Federal Work-Study jobs (averaging $1000). In 2004, 70 non-need-based awards were made. *Average percent of need met:* 89%. *Average financial aid package:* $16,357. *Average need-based loan:* $2904. *Average need-based gift aid:* $8058. *Average non-need-based aid:* $2890.
Applying *Options:* electronic application, early admission, early decision, deferred entrance. *Application fee:* $30. *Required:* essay or personal statement, high school transcript, minimum 2.0 GPA, 1 letter of recommendation. *Recommended:* interview. *Application deadlines:* rolling (freshmen), rolling (out-of-state freshmen), rolling (transfers). *Early decision deadline:* 11/15. *Notification:* continuous (freshmen), continuous (out-of-state freshmen), continuous (transfers), 12/1 (early decision).
Freshman Application Contact Ms. Susan Bibeau, Vice President of Enrollment Management, Mitchell College, 437 Pequot Avenue, New London, CT 06320. *Phone:* 860-701-5039. *Toll-free phone:* 800-443-2811. *Fax:* 860-444-1209. *E-mail:* admissions@mitchell.edu. *Website:* http://www.mitchell.edu/.

Paier College of Art, Inc.
Hamden, Connecticut

- **Proprietary** 4-year, founded 1946
- **Suburban** 3-acre campus with easy access to New York City
- **Coed** 192 undergraduate students, 73% full-time, 60% women, 40% men

Undergraduates 141 full-time, 51 part-time. Students come from 5 states and territories; 1 other country; 5% Black or African American, non-Hispanic/Latino; 8% Hispanic/Latino; 0.5% Asian, non-Hispanic/Latino; 0.5% Two or more races, non-Hispanic/Latino; 0.5% Race/ethnicity unknown; 9% transferred in. *Retention:* 89% of full-time freshmen returned.
Freshmen *Admission:* 16 enrolled. *Average high school GPA:* 3. *Test scores:* SAT critical reading scores over 500: 32%; SAT math scores over 500: 27%.
Faculty *Total:* 39, 26% full-time, 56% with terminal degrees. *Student/faculty ratio:* 5:1.
Academics *Calendar:* semesters plus 1 summer session. *Degree:* certificates, diplomas, and bachelor's. *Special study options:* academic remediation for entering students, advanced placement credit, independent study, part-time degree program, services for LD students, study abroad.
Computers on Campus 48 computers/terminals are available on campus for general student use. Wireless service is available via entire campus.
Student Life *Housing:* college housing not available. *Activities and organizations:* student-run newspaper, Student Council, School Newspaper. *Campus security:* evening patrols by security.
Standardized Tests *Required:* SAT or ACT (for admission).
Costs (2013–14) *Tuition:* $12,000 full-time, $400 per credit part-time. Full-time tuition and fees vary according to degree level. Part-time tuition and fees vary according to course load. *Required fees:* $360 full-time, $400 per credit part-time, $125 per semester part-time. *Payment plan:* installment.
Financial Aid Of all full-time matriculated undergraduates who enrolled in 1999, 102 applied for aid, 92 were judged to have need, 1 had their need fully met. *Average percent of need met:* 62%. *Average financial aid package:* $6717. *Average need-based loan:* $3446. *Average need-based gift aid:* $3460. *Average indebtedness upon graduation:* $13,536.
Applying *Required:* high school transcript, minimum 2.0 GPA, 2 letters of recommendation, interview, Portfolio Interview. *Recommended:* essay or personal statement.

Freshman Application Contact Ms. Lynn Pascale, Admissions Secretary, Paier College of Art, Inc., 20 Gorham Avenue, Hamden, CT 06514 . *Phone:* 203-287-3031. *Fax:* 203-287-3021. *E-mail:* paier.admission@snet.net. *Website:* http://www.paiercollegeofart.edu/.

Post University
Waterbury, Connecticut

- **Independent** comprehensive, founded 1890
- **Suburban** 70-acre campus with easy access to Hartford
- **Coed** 722 undergraduate students, 97% full-time, 50% women, 50% men
- **Moderately difficult** entrance level, 13% of applicants were admitted

Undergraduates 700 full-time, 22 part-time. Students come from 26 states and territories; 11 other countries; 31% are from out of state; 28% Black or African American, non-Hispanic/Latino; 12% Hispanic/Latino; 2% Asian, non-Hispanic/Latino; 0.1% Native Hawaiian or other Pacific Islander, non-Hispanic/Latino; 1% American Indian or Alaska Native, non-Hispanic/Latino; 2% Two or more races, non-Hispanic/Latino; 12% Race/ethnicity unknown; 2% international; 11% transferred in; 52% live on campus. *Retention:* 58% of full-time freshmen returned.

Freshmen *Admission:* 1,861 applied, 239 admitted, 208 enrolled. *Average high school GPA:* 2.63. *Test scores:* SAT critical reading scores over 500: 15%; SAT math scores over 500: 56%; SAT writing scores over 500: 12%; ACT scores over 18: 3%; SAT critical reading scores over 600: 1%; SAT math scores over 600: 14%; ACT scores over 24: 1%; SAT math scores over 700: 2%.

Faculty *Total:* 165, 26% full-time, 22% with terminal degrees. *Student/faculty ratio:* 9:1.

Academics *Calendar:* semesters (modular courses offered in the evening). *Degrees:* certificates, associate, bachelor's, and master's. *Special study options:* accelerated degree program, adult/continuing education programs, advanced placement credit, cooperative education, distance learning, double majors, English as a second language, freshman honors college, honors programs, independent study, internships, part-time degree program, services for LD students, study abroad, summer session for credit.

Computers on Campus 150 computers/terminals and 150 ports are available on campus for general student use. Students can access the following: campus intranet, computer help desk, free student e-mail accounts, online (class) grades, online (class) registration, online (class) schedules, software applications. Campuswide network is available. 100% of college-owned or -operated housing units are wired for high-speed Internet access. Wireless service is available via entire campus.

Student Life *Housing options:* coed. Campus housing is university owned. Freshman campus housing is guaranteed. *Activities and organizations:* drama/theater group, choral group, Equine Club, Newman Club, GSA, Accounting Club, Choir. *Campus security:* 24-hour emergency response devices and patrols, late-night transport/escort service, controlled dormitory access. *Student services:* health clinic, personal/psychological counseling.

Athletics Member NCAA. All Division II. *Intercollegiate sports:* baseball M(s), basketball M(s)/W(s), cross-country running M(s)/W(s), equestrian sports M(s)/W(s), football M, golf M(s), lacrosse M(s)/W(s), soccer M(s)/W(s), softball W(s), swimming and diving M(s)/W(s), tennis M(s)/W(s), volleyball W(s). *Intramural sports:* basketball M/W, lacrosse M/W, soccer M/W, swimming and diving M/W, tennis M/W.

Standardized Tests *Required:* SAT or ACT (for admission).

Costs (2012–13) *Comprehensive fee:* $37,880 includes full-time tuition ($26,250), mandatory fees ($1200), and room and board ($10,430). Full-time tuition and fees vary according to degree level and program. Part-time tuition: $875 per credit. Part-time tuition and fees vary according to class time, course load, degree level, and program. *Room and board:* Room and board charges vary according to housing facility. *Payment plan:* installment. *Waivers:* senior citizens and employees or children of employees.

Financial Aid Of all full-time matriculated undergraduates who enrolled in 2011, 626 applied for aid, 597 were judged to have need, 79 had their need fully met. In 2011, 13 non-need-based awards were made. *Average percent of need met:* 54%. *Average financial aid package:* $19,550. *Average need-based loan:* $4245. *Average need-based gift aid:* $15,408. *Average non-need-based aid:* $8769. *Average indebtedness upon graduation:* $16,499.

Applying *Options:* electronic application, deferred entrance. *Application fee:* $40. *Required:* high school transcript, 1 letter of recommendation. *Recommended:* essay or personal statement, minimum 2.0 GPA, interview. *Application deadlines:* rolling (freshmen), rolling (transfers). *Notification:* continuous (freshmen), continuous (transfers).

Freshman Application Contact Ms. Elizabeth Johnson, Acting Director of Admissions, Post University, PO Box 2540, Waterbury, CT 06723. *Phone:* 203-596-4500. *Toll-free phone:* 800-345-2562. *Fax:* 203-756-5810. *E-mail:* admiss@post.edu. *Website:* http://www.post.edu/.

Quinnipiac University
Hamden, Connecticut

- **Independent** comprehensive, founded 1929
- **Suburban** 600-acre campus with easy access to New Haven, Hartford
- **Endowment** $275.5 million
- **Coed** 6,430 undergraduate students, 97% full-time, 62% women, 38% men
- **Moderately difficult** entrance level, 69% of applicants were admitted

Undergraduates 6,231 full-time, 199 part-time. Students come from 28 states and territories; 22 other countries; 73% are from out of state; 4% Black or African American, non-Hispanic/Latino; 8% Hispanic/Latino; 2% Asian, non-Hispanic/Latino; 0.1% Native Hawaiian or other Pacific Islander, non-Hispanic/Latino; 0.3% American Indian or Alaska Native, non-Hispanic/Latino; 1% Two or more races, non-Hispanic/Latino; 4% Race/ethnicity unknown; 1% international; 3% transferred in; 78% live on campus. *Retention:* 85% of full-time freshmen returned.

Freshmen *Admission:* 18,825 applied, 12,924 admitted, 1,781 enrolled. *Average high school GPA:* 3.4. *Test scores:* SAT critical reading scores over 500: 78%; SAT math scores over 500: 82%; ACT scores over 18: 98%; SAT critical reading scores over 600: 20%; SAT math scores over 600: 30%; ACT scores over 24: 69%; SAT critical reading scores over 700: 2%; SAT math scores over 700: 3%; ACT scores over 30: 10%.

Faculty *Total:* 942, 39% full-time, 65% with terminal degrees. *Student/faculty ratio:* 12:1.

Academics *Calendar:* semesters. *Degrees:* bachelor's, master's, doctoral, post-master's, and postbachelor's certificates. *Special study options:* accelerated degree program, advanced placement credit, distance learning, double majors, honors programs, independent study, internships, part-time degree program, services for LD students, student-designed majors, study abroad, summer session for credit. *ROTC:* Army (c), Navy (c), Air Force (c).

Computers on Campus 600 computers/terminals and 2,500 ports are available on campus for general student use. Students can access the following: campus intranet, computer help desk, free student e-mail accounts, online (class) grades, online (class) registration, online (class) schedules, e-commerce 'Q' card for local merchants, food service, dorm card access. Campuswide network is available. 100% of college-owned or -operated housing units are wired for high-speed Internet access. Wireless service is available via entire campus.

Student Life *Housing options:* coed. Campus housing is university owned. Freshman campus housing is guaranteed. *Activities and organizations:* drama/theater group, student-run newspaper, radio and television station, choral group, student government, Social Programming Board, Drama Club, Chronicle (student newspaper), dance company, national fraternities, national sororities. *Campus security:* 24-hour emergency response devices and patrols, late-night transport/escort service, controlled dormitory access, text message emergency notification system. *Student services:* health clinic, personal/psychological counseling.

Athletics Member NCAA. All Division I. *Intercollegiate sports:* baseball M(s), basketball M(s)/W(s), cross-country running M(s)/W(s), field hockey W(s), golf W(s), gymnastics W(s), ice hockey M(s)/W(s), lacrosse M(s)/W(s), rugby M(s), soccer M(s)/W(s), softball W(s), tennis M(s)/W(s), track and field W(s), volleyball W(s). *Intramural sports:* baseball M, basketball M/W, bowling M/W, field hockey W, soccer M/W, softball W, tennis M/W, volleyball M/W.

Standardized Tests *Required:* SAT or ACT (for admission).

Costs (2013–14) *Comprehensive fee:* $53,580 includes full-time tuition ($37,830), mandatory fees ($1500), and room and board ($14,250). Part-time tuition: $900 per credit. Part-time tuition and fees vary according to class time and course load. *Required fees:* $37 per credit part-time. *Room and board:* Room and board charges vary according to housing facility. *Payment plan:* installment. *Waivers:* employees or children of employees.

Financial Aid Of all full-time matriculated undergraduates who enrolled in 2012, 4,658 applied for aid, 3,986 were judged to have need, 489 had their need fully met. 1,829 Federal Work-Study jobs (averaging $2032). 27 state and other part-time jobs (averaging $1686). In 2012, 973 non-need-based awards were made. *Average percent of need met:* 64%. *Average financial aid package:* $22,679. *Average need-based loan:* $4593. *Average need-based gift aid:* $17,162. *Average non-need-based aid:* $12,053. *Average indebtedness upon graduation:* $42,730.

Applying *Options:* electronic application, early decision, deferred entrance. *Application fee:* $45. *Required:* essay or personal statement, high school transcript, 1 letter of recommendation. *Required for some:* minimum 3.0 GPA. *Recommended:* minimum 3.0 GPA, interview. *Application deadlines:* 2/1 (freshmen), 2/1 (out-of-state freshmen), 4/1 (transfers). *Early decision deadline:* 11/1. *Notification:* continuous (freshmen), continuous (out-of-state freshmen), continuous (transfers), rolling (early decision).

Freshman Application Contact Ms. Joan Isaac-Mohr, Vice President for Admissions and Financial Aid, Quinnipiac University, 275 Mount Carmel

Avenue, Hamden, CT 06518. *Phone:* 203-582-8600. *Toll-free phone:* 800-462-1944. *Fax:* 203-582-8906. *E-mail:* admissions@quinnipiac.edu. *Website:* http://www.quinnipiac.edu/.

See below for display ad and page 1446 for the College Close-Up.

Sacred Heart University
Fairfield, Connecticut

- **Independent Roman Catholic** comprehensive, founded 1963
- **Suburban** 71-acre campus with easy access to New York City
- **Endowment** $112.7 million
- **Coed** 4,092 undergraduate students, 83% full-time, 63% women, 37% men
- **Moderately difficult** entrance level, 76% of applicants were admitted

Undergraduates 3,399 full-time, 693 part-time. Students come from 35 states and territories; 14 other countries; 59% are from out of state; 4% Black or African American, non-Hispanic/Latino; 6% Hispanic/Latino; 2% Asian, non-Hispanic/Latino; 0.1% Native Hawaiian or other Pacific Islander, non-Hispanic/Latino; 0.3% American Indian or Alaska Native, non-Hispanic/Latino; 0.1% Two or more races, non-Hispanic/Latino; 21% Race/ethnicity unknown; 1% international; 51% live on campus. *Retention:* 83% of full-time freshmen returned.

Freshmen *Admission:* 8,221 applied, 6,272 admitted, 865 enrolled. *Average high school GPA:* 3.3. *Test scores:* SAT critical reading scores over 500: 76%; SAT math scores over 500: 83%; SAT writing scores over 500: 75%; ACT scores over 18: 100%; SAT critical reading scores over 600: 19%; SAT math scores over 600: 26%; SAT writing scores over 600: 21%; ACT scores over 24: 49%; SAT critical reading scores over 700: 2%; SAT math scores over 700: 2%; SAT writing scores over 700: 2%; ACT scores over 30: 4%.

Faculty *Total:* 634, 37% full-time, 46% with terminal degrees. *Student/faculty ratio:* 13:1.

Academics *Calendar:* semesters. *Degrees:* bachelor's, master's, doctoral, post-master's, and postbachelor's certificates (also offers part-time program with significant enrollment not reflected in profile). *Special study options:* academic remediation for entering students, accelerated degree program, adult/continuing education programs, advanced placement credit, cooperative education, distance learning, double majors, English as a second language, honors programs, independent study, internships, off-campus study, part-time degree program, services for LD students, student-designed majors, study abroad,

summer session for credit. *ROTC:* Army (c). *Unusual degree programs:* 3-2 business administration.

Computers on Campus 111 computers/terminals and 3,100 ports are available on campus for general student use. Students can access the following: campus intranet, computer help desk, free student e-mail accounts, online (class) grades, online (class) registration, online (class) schedules. Campus-wide network is available. 100% of college-owned or -operated housing units are wired for high-speed Internet access. Wireless service is available via entire campus.

Student Life *Housing:* on-campus residence required through sophomore year. *Options:* coed, men-only, women-only, disabled students. Campus housing is university owned and leased by the school. Freshman campus housing is guaranteed. *Activities and organizations:* drama/theater group, student-run newspaper, radio and television station, choral group, marching band, Habitat for Humanity, Student Government, Performing Arts Program, Student Athletic Training Organization, Student Nurses Association, national fraternities, national sororities. *Campus security:* 24-hour emergency response devices and patrols, late-night transport/escort service, controlled dormitory access, Campus Emergency Plan, Personal Safety Escort Program, Security Alarm Systems, Crime Prevention Announcements, Security Surveys. *Student services:* health clinic, personal/psychological counseling.

Athletics Member NCAA. All Division I except football (Division I-AA). *Intercollegiate sports:* baseball M(s), basketball M(s)/W(s), bowling W(s), cheerleading W(c), crew W, cross-country running M(s)/W(s), equestrian sports W, fencing M/W, field hockey W(s), golf M(s)/W(s), ice hockey M(s)/W(s), lacrosse M(s)/W(s), soccer M(s)/W(s), softball W(s), swimming and diving W(s), tennis M(s)/W(s), track and field M(s)/W(s), volleyball M/W(s), wrestling M(s). *Intramural sports:* baseball M(c), basketball M(c)/W(c), cross-country running M(c)/W(c), field hockey W(c), football M/W, golf M(c)/W(c), gymnastics W(c), ice hockey M(c), lacrosse M(c)/W(c), rugby M(c)/W(c), sailing M(c)/W(c), soccer M(c)/W(c), softball M/W, tennis M(c)/W(c), ultimate Frisbee M(c)/W(c), volleyball M(c)/W(c), weight lifting W(c).

Standardized Tests *Recommended:* Test-Optional Admissions Policy, SAT/ACT scores will be considered if submitted.

Costs (2012–13) *Comprehensive fee:* $47,260 includes full-time tuition ($33,780), mandatory fees ($250), and room and board ($13,230). Full-time tuition and fees vary according to course load, location, and program. Part-time tuition: $515 per credit. Part-time tuition and fees vary according to location and program. *Required fees:* $90 per term part-time. *College room only:* $9380. Room and board charges vary according to board plan, housing facility,

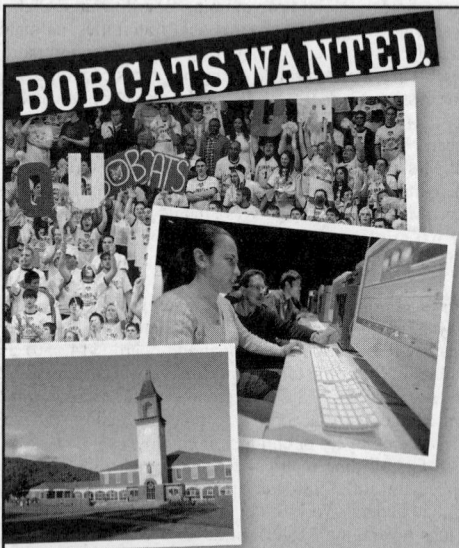

and student level. *Payment plan:* installment. *Waivers:* minority students, adult students, senior citizens, and employees or children of employees.

Financial Aid Of all full-time matriculated undergraduates who enrolled in 2011, 3,101 applied for aid, 2,574 were judged to have need, 308 had their need fully met. 944 Federal Work-Study jobs (averaging $668). 858 state and other part-time jobs (averaging $832). In 2011, 494 non-need-based awards were made. *Average percent of need met:* 58%. *Average financial aid package:* $18,184. *Average need-based loan:* $5087. *Average need-based gift aid:* $13,958. *Average non-need-based aid:* $5652. *Average indebtedness upon graduation:* $42,779.

Applying *Options:* electronic application, early admission, early decision. *Application fee:* $70. *Required:* essay or personal statement, high school transcript, 1 letter of recommendation. *Required for some:* interview, interview required for Early Decision candidates. *Recommended:* minimum 3.2 GPA, interview. *Early decision deadline:* 12/1. *Notification:* continuous (freshmen), continuous (transfers), 12/15 (early decision).

Freshman Application Contact Mr. Kenneth Higgins, Director of Undergraduate Admissions, Sacred Heart University, 5151 Park Avenue, Fairfield, CT 06825-1000. *Phone:* 203-610-9388. *Fax:* 203-365-7607. *E-mail:* higginsk2288@sacredheart.edu.
Website: http://www.sacredheart.edu/.

Southern Connecticut State University

New Haven, Connecticut

- **State-supported** comprehensive, founded 1893, part of Connecticut State Colleges and Universities (ConnSCU)
- **Suburban** 168-acre campus with easy access to New York City
- **Endowment** $14.7 million
- **Coed** 8,525 undergraduate students, 86% full-time, 60% women, 40% men
- **Moderately difficult** entrance level, 75% of applicants were admitted

Undergraduates 7,289 full-time, 1,236 part-time. Students come from 27 states and territories; 10 other countries; 4% are from out of state; 16% Black or African American, non-Hispanic/Latino; 10% Hispanic/Latino; 3% Asian, non-Hispanic/Latino; 0.1% Native Hawaiian or other Pacific Islander, non-Hispanic/Latino; 0.3% American Indian or Alaska Native, non-Hispanic/Latino; 2% Two or more races, non-Hispanic/Latino; 6% Race/ethnicity unknown; 0.4% international; 10% transferred in; 31% live on campus. *Retention:* 73% of full-time freshmen returned.

Freshmen *Admission:* 4,978 applied, 3,756 admitted, 1,382 enrolled. *Average high school GPA:* 2.83. *Test scores:* SAT math scores over 500: 32%; ACT scores over 18: 72%; SAT math scores over 600: 5%; ACT scores over 24: 19%.

Faculty *Total:* 1,055, 41% full-time, 34% with terminal degrees. *Student/faculty ratio:* 14:1.

Academics *Calendar:* semesters. *Degrees:* bachelor's, master's, doctoral, post-master's, and postbachelor's certificates. *Special study options:* academic remediation for entering students, accelerated degree program, advanced placement credit, cooperative education, distance learning, double majors, freshman honors college, honors programs, independent study, internships, off-campus study, part-time degree program, services for LD students, student-designed majors, study abroad, summer session for credit. *ROTC:* Army (c), Air Force (c).

Computers on Campus 800 computers/terminals are available on campus for general student use. Students can access the following: computer help desk, free student e-mail accounts, online (class) grades, online (class) registration, online (class) schedules. Campuswide network is available. 100% of college-owned or -operated housing units are wired for high-speed Internet access. Wireless service is available via entire campus.

Student Life *Housing options:* coed, disabled students. Campus housing is university owned. Freshman campus housing is guaranteed. *Activities and organizations:* drama/theater group, student-run newspaper, radio and television station, choral group, marching band, Student Government Association, Psychology Club, Habitat for Humanity, Crescent Players, Black Student Union, national fraternities, national sororities. *Campus security:* 24-hour emergency response devices and patrols, late-night transport/escort service, controlled dormitory access. *Student services:* health clinic, personal/psychological counseling, women's center.

Athletics Member NCAA. All Division II. *Intercollegiate sports:* baseball M(s), basketball M(s)/W(s), cheerleading M(c)/W(c), cross-country running M(s)/W(s), field hockey W(s), football M(s), gymnastics W(s), lacrosse W(s), rugby M(c)/W(c), soccer M(s)/W(s), softball W(s), swimming and diving M(s)/W(s), track and field M(s)/W(s), ultimate Frisbee M(c)/W(c), volleyball W(s). *Intramural sports:* badminton M/W, basketball M/W, football M/W, ice hockey M(c)/W(c), soccer M/W, softball M/W, tennis M/W, volleyball M/W.

Standardized Tests *Required:* SAT or ACT (for admission).

Costs (2012–13) *Tuition:* state resident $4285 full-time, $427 per credit hour part-time; nonresident $13,866 full-time, $441 per credit hour part-time. Full-

time tuition and fees vary according to course load and reciprocity agreements. Part-time tuition and fees vary according to course load. *Required fees:* $4285 full-time, $55 per term part-time. *Room and board:* $10,641; room only: $5859. Room and board charges vary according to board plan and housing facility. *Payment plans:* installment, deferred payment. *Waivers:* senior citizens and employees or children of employees.

Financial Aid Of all full-time matriculated undergraduates who enrolled in 2012, 6,216 applied for aid, 5,037 were judged to have need, 1,067 had their need fully met. 170 Federal Work-Study jobs (averaging $3931). In 2012, 208 non-need-based awards were made. *Average percent of need met:* 70%. *Average financial aid package:* $13,599. *Average need-based loan:* $4662. *Average need-based gift aid:* $6191. *Average non-need-based aid:* $4575. *Average indebtedness upon graduation:* $23,663. *Financial aid deadline:* 3/9.

Applying *Options:* electronic application, deferred entrance. *Application fee:* $50. *Required:* essay or personal statement, high school transcript. *Application deadlines:* 4/1 (freshmen), 8/1 (transfers). *Notification:* continuous (freshmen), continuous (transfers).

Freshman Application Contact Ms. Paula Kennedy, Associate Director of Admissions, Southern Connecticut State University, Admissions House, 131 Farnham Avenue, New Haven, CT 06515-1202. *Phone:* 203-392-5651. *Fax:* 203-392-5727.

Website: http://www.southernct.edu/.

See previous page for display ad and page 1508 for the College Close-Up.

Trinity College

Hartford, Connecticut

- **Independent** comprehensive, founded 1823
- **Urban** 100-acre campus
- **Endowment** $439.1 million
- **Coed** 2,301 undergraduate students, 95% full-time, 48% women, 52% men
- **Most difficult** entrance level, 34% of applicants were admitted

Undergraduates 2,195 full-time, 106 part-time. Students come from 48 states and territories; 53 other countries; 83% are from out of state; 6% Black or African American, non-Hispanic/Latino; 7% Hispanic/Latino; 5% Asian, non-Hispanic/Latino; 3% Two or more races, non-Hispanic/Latino; 4% Race/ethnicity unknown; 8% international; 1% transferred in; 90% live on campus. *Retention:* 88% of full-time freshmen returned.

Freshmen *Admission:* 7,720 applied, 2,605 admitted, 591 enrolled. *Test scores:* SAT critical reading scores over 500: 99%; SAT math scores over 500: 97%; SAT writing scores over 500: 97%; ACT scores over 18: 100%; SAT critical reading scores over 600: 72%; SAT math scores over 600: 75%; SAT writing scores over 600: 79%; ACT scores over 24: 93%; SAT critical reading scores over 700: 20%; SAT math scores over 700: 25%; SAT writing scores over 700: 25%; ACT scores over 30: 26%.

Faculty *Total:* 250, 70% full-time, 86% with terminal degrees. *Student/faculty ratio:* 10:1.

Academics *Calendar:* semesters. *Degrees:* bachelor's and master's. *Special study options:* accelerated degree program, adult/continuing education programs, advanced placement credit, double majors, honors programs, independent study, internships, off-campus study, student-designed majors, study abroad, summer session for credit. *ROTC:* Army (c). *Unusual degree programs:* 3-2 engineering with Rensselaer Polytechnic Institute.

Computers on Campus 249 computers/terminals and 3,000 ports are available on campus for general student use. Students can access the following: campus intranet, computer help desk, free student e-mail accounts, online (class) grades, online (class) registration, online (class) schedules, Web pages. Campuswide network is available. 100% of college-owned or -operated housing units are wired for high-speed Internet access. Wireless service is available via classrooms, computer centers, computer labs, learning centers, libraries, student centers.

Student Life *Housing:* on-campus residence required for freshman year. *Options:* coed, disabled students. Campus housing is university owned. Freshman campus housing is guaranteed. *Activities and organizations:* drama/theater group, student-run newspaper, radio station, choral group, Friends Active in Community Engagement and Service (FACES), The Mill, Student Government Association, Relay for Life, Multi-Cultural Affairs Council, national fraternities, national sororities. *Campus security:* 24-hour emergency response devices and patrols, late-night transport/escort service, controlled dormitory access. *Student services:* health clinic, personal/psychological counseling, women's center.

Athletics Member NCAA. All Division III. *Intercollegiate sports:* baseball M, basketball M/W, crew M/W, cross-country running M/W, equestrian sports M(c)/W(c), fencing M(c)/W(c), football M, golf M, ice hockey M/W, lacrosse M/W, rugby M(c)/W(c), sailing M(c)/W(c), skiing (downhill) M(c)/W(c), soccer M/W, softball W, squash M/W, swimming and diving M/W, tennis M/W, track and field M/W, ultimate Frisbee M(c)/W(c), volleyball W, water polo M(c)/W(c), wrestling M. *Intramural sports:* badminton M/W, basketball M/W, soccer M/W, softball M/W, squash M/W, tennis M/W.

Standardized Tests *Required for some:* SAT or ACT (for admission), SAT Subject Tests (for admission).

Costs (2012–13) *One-time required fee:* $25. *Comprehensive fee:* $57,530 includes full-time tuition ($43,570), mandatory fees ($2160), and room and board ($11,800). Full-time tuition and fees vary according to course load and program. Part-time tuition: $4841 per course. Part-time tuition and fees vary according to course load and program. *College room only:* $7660. Room and board charges vary according to board plan. *Payment plan:* installment. *Waivers:* adult students and employees or children of employees.

Financial Aid Of all full-time matriculated undergraduates who enrolled in 2012, 940 applied for aid, 896 were judged to have need, 896 had their need fully met. 739 Federal Work-Study jobs (averaging $1735). In 2012, 18 non-need-based awards were made. *Average percent of need met:* 100%. *Average financial aid package:* $41,862. *Average need-based loan:* $4600. *Average need-based gift aid:* $39,131. *Average non-need-based aid:* $32,371. *Average indebtedness upon graduation:* $18,868. *Financial aid deadline:* 3/1.

Applying *Options:* electronic application, early admission, early decision, deferred entrance. *Application fee:* $60. *Required:* essay or personal statement, high school transcript, 3 letters of recommendation. *Recommended:* interview. *Application deadlines:* 1/1 (freshmen), 4/1 (transfers). *Early decision deadline:* 11/15 (for plan 1), 1/1 (for plan 2). *Notification:* 4/1 (freshmen), 6/10 (transfers), 12/15 (early decision plan 1), 2/15 (early decision plan 2).

Freshman Application Contact Trinity College, 300 Summit Street, Hartford, CT 06106-3100. *Phone:* 860-297-2180.
Website: http://www.trincoll.edu/.

See previous page for display ad and page 1540 for the College Close-Up.

United States Coast Guard Academy

New London, Connecticut

- **Federally supported** 4-year, founded 1876
- **Suburban** 110-acre campus with easy access to Providence, Hartford
- **Endowment** $1.3 million
- **Coed** 1,045 undergraduate students, 100% full-time, 30% women, 70% men
- **Very difficult** entrance level, 16% of applicants were admitted

Undergraduates 1,045 full-time. Students come from 53 states and territories; 19 other countries; 94% are from out of state; 3% Black or African American, non-Hispanic/Latino; 10% Hispanic/Latino; 4% Asian, non-Hispanic/Latino; 0.9% Native Hawaiian or other Pacific Islander, non-Hispanic/Latino; 0.7% American Indian or Alaska Native, non-Hispanic/Latino; 3% Two or more races, non-Hispanic/Latino; 1% Race/ethnicity unknown; 2% international; 100% live on campus. *Retention:* 95% of full-time freshmen returned.

Freshmen *Admission:* 2,374 applied, 383 admitted, 288 enrolled. *Average high school GPA:* 3.78. *Test scores:* SAT critical reading scores over 500: 93%; SAT math scores over 500: 97%; SAT writing scores over 500: 92%; ACT scores over 18: 99%; SAT critical reading scores over 600: 49%; SAT math scores over 600: 71%; SAT writing scores over 600: 46%; ACT scores over 24: 87%; SAT critical reading scores over 700: 10%; SAT math scores over 700: 12%; SAT writing scores over 700: 6%; ACT scores over 30: 23%.

Faculty *Total:* 143, 93% full-time, 50% with terminal degrees. *Student/faculty ratio:* 8:1.

Academics *Calendar:* semesters. *Degree:* bachelor's. *Special study options:* academic remediation for entering students, double majors, English as a second language, honors programs, independent study, internships, off-campus study, summer session for credit.

Computers on Campus 325 computers/terminals are available on campus for general student use. Students can access the following: campus intranet, computer help desk, free student e-mail accounts, online (class) grades, online (class) registration, online (class) schedules. Campuswide network is available. 100% of college-owned or -operated housing units are wired for high-speed Internet access. Wireless service is available via classrooms, dorm rooms, libraries, student centers.

Student Life *Housing:* on-campus residence required through senior year. *Options:* coed. Campus housing is university owned. Freshman campus housing is guaranteed. *Activities and organizations:* drama/theater group, choral group, marching band, Companneros Club—Latino culture and traditions, Genesis Club—Multicultural awareness, Men's and Women's Lacrosse Club, Men's and Women's Rugby Club, Officers' Christian Fellowship. *Campus security:* 24-hour patrols, student patrols, late-night transport/escort service. *Student services:* health clinic, personal/psychological counseling, legal services.

Athletics Member NCAA. All Division III. *Intercollegiate sports:* baseball M, basketball M/W, bowling M(c)/W(c), cheerleading W, crew M/W, cross-country running M/W, fencing M(c)/W(c), football M, golf M(c)/W(c), ice hockey M(c), lacrosse M(c)/W(c), riflery M/W, rugby M(c)/W(c), sailing M/W, skiing (downhill) M(c)/W(c), soccer M/W, softball W, swimming and diving M/W, tennis M, track and field M/W, volleyball M(c)/W, water polo M(c), weight lifting M(c), wrestling M. *Intramural sports:* basketball M/W, football M/W, golf M/W, racquetball M/W, soccer M/W, softball M/W, swimming and diving M/W, tennis M/W.

Standardized Tests *Required:* SAT or ACT (for admission).

Costs (2012–13) *Comprehensive fee:* Tuition, room and board, and medical and dental care are provided by the US government. Each cadet receives a salary from which to pay for uniforms, supplies, and personal expenses.

Applying *Options:* electronic application, early action. *Required:* essay or personal statement, high school transcript, 3 letters of recommendation, medical examination, physical fitness examination. *Recommended:* interview. *Application deadlines:* 2/1 (freshmen), 2/1 (out-of-state freshmen), 2/1 (transfers), 11/1 (early action). *Notification:* continuous until 4/15 (freshmen), continuous until 4/15 (out-of-state freshmen), continuous until 4/15 (transfers), 1/15 (early action).

Freshman Application Contact Capt. Stephan P. Finton, Director of Admissions, United States Coast Guard Academy, 31 Mohegan Avenue, New London, CT 06320-4195. *Phone:* 860-444-8500. *Toll-free phone:* 800-883-8724. *Fax:* 860-701-6700. *E-mail:* admissions@uscga.edu.
Website: http://www.uscga.edu/.

University of Bridgeport

Bridgeport, Connecticut

- **Independent** comprehensive, founded 1927
- **Urban** 86-acre campus with easy access to New York City
- **Endowment** $24.9 million
- **Coed** 2,688 undergraduate students, 69% full-time, 68% women, 32% men
- **Moderately difficult** entrance level, 63% of applicants were admitted

Undergraduates 1,852 full-time, 836 part-time. Students come from 35 states and territories; 51 other countries; 38% are from out of state; 37% Black or African American, non-Hispanic/Latino; 18% Hispanic/Latino; 3% Asian, non-Hispanic/Latino; 0.1% Native Hawaiian or other Pacific Islander, non-Hispanic/Latino; 0.7% American Indian or Alaska Native, non-Hispanic/Latino; 3% Two or more races, non-Hispanic/Latino; 11% international; 8% transferred in; 48% live on campus. *Retention:* 62% of full-time freshmen returned.

Freshmen *Admission:* 5,736 applied, 3,641 admitted, 598 enrolled. *Average high school GPA:* 298. *Test scores:* SAT critical reading scores over 500: 25%; SAT math scores over 500: 27%; SAT writing scores over 500: 23%; ACT scores over 18: 81%; SAT critical reading scores over 600: 3%; SAT math scores over 600: 4%; SAT writing scores over 600: 4%; ACT scores over 24: 8%; SAT writing scores over 700: 1%.

Faculty *Total:* 470, 26% full-time. *Student/faculty ratio:* 15:1.

Academics *Calendar:* semesters. *Degrees:* certificates, associate, bachelor's, master's, doctoral, post-master's, and postbachelor's certificates. *Special study options:* academic remediation for entering students, accelerated degree program, adult/continuing education programs, advanced placement credit, cooperative education, distance learning, double majors, English as a second language, honors programs, independent study, internships, off-campus study, part-time degree program, services for LD students, student-designed majors, study abroad, summer session for credit. *ROTC:* Army (b).

Computers on Campus 200 computers/terminals and 200 ports are available on campus for general student use. Students can access the following: computer help desk, free student e-mail accounts, online (class) grades, online (class) registration, online (class) schedules. Campuswide network is available. 100% of college-owned or -operated housing units are wired for high-speed Internet access. Wireless service is available via classrooms, computer centers, computer labs, dorm rooms, learning centers, libraries, student centers.

Student Life *Housing:* on-campus residence required through sophomore year. *Options:* coed. Campus housing is university owned. Freshman campus housing is guaranteed. *Activities and organizations:* student-run newspaper, choral group, Student Congress, International Relations Club, Black Students Alliance, Latin America Club, Martial Arts Club, national fraternities, national sororities. *Campus security:* 24-hour emergency response devices and patrols, student patrols, late-night transport/escort service, controlled dormitory access. *Student services:* health clinic, personal/psychological counseling, women's center.

Athletics Member NCAA. All Division II. *Intercollegiate sports:* baseball M(s), basketball M(s)/W(s), cross-country running M(s)/W(s), gymnastics W(s), lacrosse W(s), soccer M(s)/W(s), softball W(s), swimming and diving M(s)/W(s), volleyball W(s). *Intramural sports:* basketball M/W, football M/W, golf M/W, racquetball M/W, soccer M/W, softball M/W, tennis M/W.

Standardized Tests *Required:* SAT or ACT (for admission).

Costs (2012–13) *Comprehensive fee:* $40,190 includes full-time tuition ($25,950), mandatory fees ($2190), and room and board ($12,050). Full-time tuition and fees vary according to course load and program. Part-time tuition: $865 per credit hour. Part-time tuition and fees vary according to course load and program. *Required fees:* $200 per term part-time. *Room and board:* Room and board charges vary according to board plan, housing facility, and student level. *Payment plans:* installment, deferred payment. *Waivers:* senior citizens and employees or children of employees.

Financial Aid Of all full-time matriculated undergraduates who enrolled in 2011, 1,420 applied for aid, 1,380 were judged to have need, 55 had their need fully met. In 2011, 243 non-need-based awards were made. *Average percent of need met:* 51%. *Average financial aid package:* $20,535. *Average need-based loan:* $4109. *Average need-based gift aid:* $7339. *Average non-need-based aid:* $9666. *Average indebtedness upon graduation:* $39,983.

Applying *Options:* electronic application, early admission, early decision, deferred entrance. *Application fee:* $25. *Required:* essay or personal statement, high school transcript, minimum 2.0 GPA. *Required for some:* 2 letters of recommendation, interview, portfolio, audition. *Recommended:* 1 letter of recommendation, interview. *Application deadlines:* rolling (freshmen), rolling (out-of-state freshmen), rolling (transfers). *Notification:* continuous (freshmen), continuous (out-of-state freshmen), continuous (transfers).

Freshman Application Contact Ms. Jessica Crowley, Director Undergraduate Admissions, University of Bridgeport, 126 Park Avenue, Bridgeport, CT 06604. *Phone:* 203-576-4812. *Toll-free phone:* 800-EXCEL-UB. *Fax:* 203-576-4941. *E-mail:* admit@bridgeport.edu. *Website:* http://www.bridgeport.edu/.

University of Connecticut

Storrs, Connecticut

- **State-supported** university, founded 1881
- **Rural** 4108-acre campus
- **Endowment** $329.0 million
- **Coed**
- **Moderately difficult** entrance level

Faculty *Student/faculty ratio:* 18:1.

Academics *Calendar:* semesters. *Degrees:* associate, bachelor's, master's, doctoral, post-master's, and postbachelor's certificates.

Student Life *Campus security:* 24-hour emergency response devices, late-night transport/escort service.

Athletics Member NCAA. All Division I except football (Division I-A).

Standardized Tests *Required:* SAT or ACT (for admission).

Costs (2012–13) *Tuition:* state resident $8712 full-time, $363 per credit part-time; nonresident $26,544 full-time, $1106 per credit part-time. Part-time tuition and fees vary according to course load. *Required fees:* $2530 full-time. *Room and board:* $11,380; room only: $6096. Room and board charges vary according to board plan and housing facility. *Payment plans:* installment, deferred payment.

Financial Aid *Of all full-time matriculated undergraduates who enrolled in 2012,* 12,118 applied for aid, 9,404 were judged to have need, 639 had their need fully met. 999 Federal Work-Study jobs (averaging $2091). 3,849 state and other part-time jobs (averaging $1845). *In 2012,* 1564 non-need-based awards were made. *Average percent of need met:* 64. *Average financial aid package:* $12,870. *Average need-based loan:* $4326. *Average need-based gift aid:* $8587. *Average non-need-based aid:* $6685. *Average indebtedness upon graduation:* $24,373.

Applying *Options:* electronic application, early action, deferred entrance. *Application fee:* $70. *Required:* essay or personal statement, high school transcript. *Recommended:* 1 letter of recommendation.

Freshman Application Contact Nathan Fuerst, Director of Undergraduate Admissions, University of Connecticut, 2131 Hillside Road, U-88, Storrs, CT 06269. *Phone:* 860-486-3137. *Fax:* 860-486-1476. *E-mail:* beahusky@uconnvm.uconn.edu. *Website:* http://www.uconn.edu/.

University of Hartford

West Hartford, Connecticut

- **Independent** comprehensive, founded 1877
- **Suburban** 320-acre campus with easy access to Hartford
- **Endowment** $114.6 million
- **Coed** 5,284 undergraduate students, 85% full-time, 51% women, 49% men
- **Moderately difficult** entrance level, 70% of applicants were admitted

Undergraduates 4,503 full-time, 781 part-time. Students come from 46 states and territories; 39 other countries; 57% are from out of state; 13% Black or African American, non-Hispanic/Latino; 8% Hispanic/Latino; 3% Asian, non-Hispanic/Latino; 0.1% Native Hawaiian or other Pacific Islander, non-Hispanic/Latino; 0.3% American Indian or Alaska Native, non-Hispanic/Latino; 1% Two or more races, non-Hispanic/Latino; 9% Race/ethnicity unknown; 4% international; 4% transferred in; 62% live on campus. *Retention:* 72% of full-time freshmen returned.

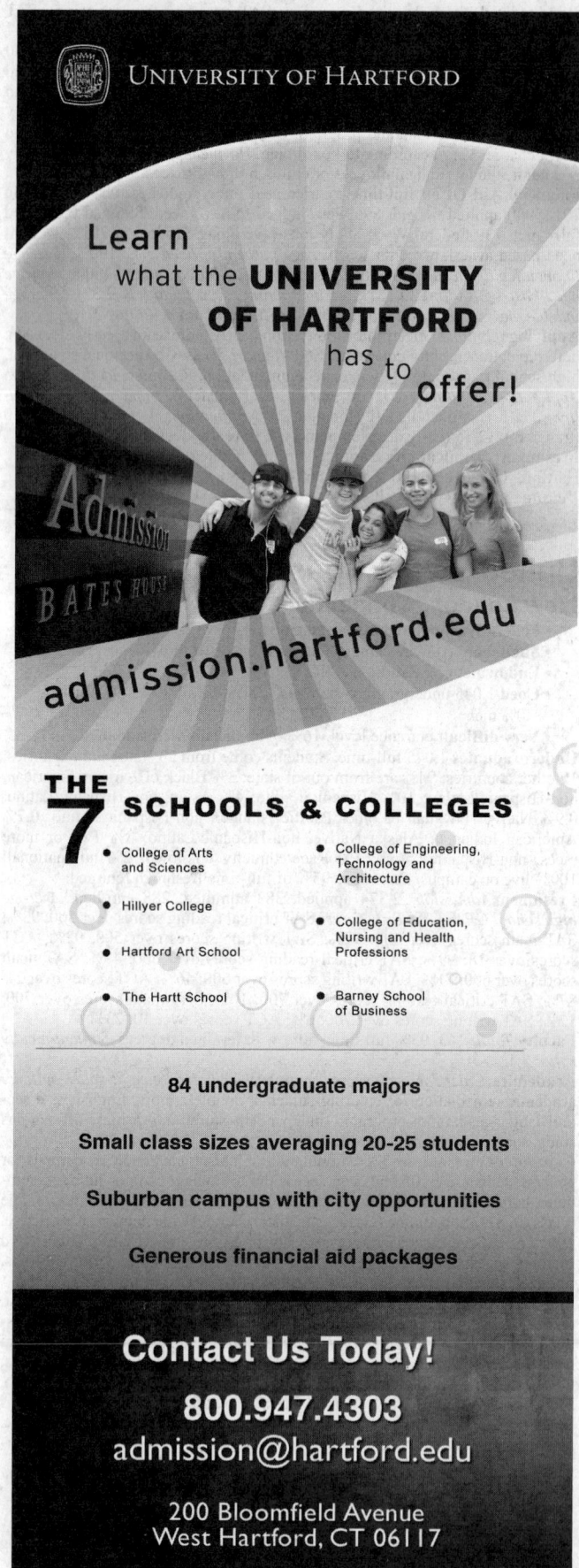

Freshmen *Admission:* 13,040 applied, 9,076 admitted, 1,289 enrolled. *Test scores:* SAT critical reading scores over 500: 54%; SAT math scores over 500: 56%; ACT scores over 18: 87%; SAT critical reading scores over 600: 15%; SAT math scores over 600: 20%; ACT scores over 24: 40%; SAT critical reading scores over 700: 2%; SAT math scores over 700: 2%; ACT scores over 30: 6%.

Faculty *Total:* 846, 41% full-time. *Student/faculty ratio:* 11:1.

Academics *Calendar:* semesters. *Degrees:* certificates, diplomas, associate, bachelor's, master's, doctoral, post-master's, and postbachelor's certificates. *Special study options:* academic remediation for entering students, adult/continuing education programs, advanced placement credit, cooperative education, distance learning, double majors, English as a second language, honors programs, independent study, internships, off-campus study, part-time degree program, services for LD students, student-designed majors, study abroad, summer session for credit. *ROTC:* Army (c), Air Force (c).

Computers on Campus 400 computers/terminals are available on campus for general student use. Students can access the following: campus intranet, computer help desk, free student e-mail accounts, online (class) grades, online (class) registration, online (class) schedules, student Web pages. Campuswide network is available. 100% of college-owned or -operated housing units are wired for high-speed Internet access. Wireless service is available via classrooms, computer centers, computer labs, libraries, student centers.

Student Life *Housing options:* coed, women-only, disabled students. Campus housing is university owned and leased by the school. Freshman campus housing is guaranteed. *Activities and organizations:* drama/theater group, student-run newspaper, radio and television station, choral group, Program Council, Brothers and Sisters United, Hillel, Student Government Association, Residence Hall Association, national fraternities, national sororities. *Campus security:* 24-hour emergency response devices and patrols, late-night transport/escort service, controlled dormitory access, bicycle patrols. *Student services:* health clinic, personal/psychological counseling, women's center, legal services.

Athletics Member NCAA. All Division I. *Intercollegiate sports:* badminton M(c)/W(c), baseball M(s), basketball M(s)/W(s), cross-country running M(s)/W(s), golf M(s)/W(s), lacrosse M(s), racquetball M(c)/W(c), rugby M(c)/W(c), soccer M(s)/W(s), softball W(s), squash M(c)/W(c), tennis M(s)/W(s), track and field M/W, volleyball M(c)/W(s). *Intramural sports:* basketball M/W, football M/W, racquetball M/W, soccer M/W, softball M/W, tennis M/W, ultimate Frisbee M/W, volleyball M/W, water polo M/W.

Standardized Tests *Required:* SAT or ACT (for admission).

Costs (2013–14) *Comprehensive fee:* $45,606 includes full-time tuition ($31,804), mandatory fees ($1554), and room and board ($12,248). Full-time tuition and fees vary according to program. Part-time tuition: $480 per credit. Part-time tuition and fees vary according to course load and program. *College room only:* $7328. Room and board charges vary according to board plan and housing facility. *Payment plans:* tuition prepayment, installment. *Waivers:* senior citizens and employees or children of employees.

Financial Aid Of all full-time matriculated undergraduates who enrolled in 2010, 4,694 applied for aid, 3,786 were judged to have need, 967 had their need fully met. 93 Federal Work-Study jobs (averaging $1212). In 2010, 908 non-need-based awards were made. *Average percent of need met:* 94%. *Average financial aid package:* $6042. *Average need-based loan:* $4325. *Average need-based gift aid:* $6042. *Average non-need-based aid:* $8823. *Average indebtedness upon graduation:* $29,598.

Applying *Options:* electronic application, early admission, deferred entrance. *Application fee:* $40. *Required:* high school transcript. *Recommended:* essay or personal statement, 2 letters of recommendation, interview. *Application deadlines:* rolling (freshmen), rolling (transfers). *Notification:* continuous (freshmen), continuous (transfers).

Freshman Application Contact Mr. Richard Zeiser, Dean of Admissions, University of Hartford, 200 Bloomfield Avenue, West Hartford, CT 06117. *Phone:* 860-768-4296. *Toll-free phone:* 800-947-4303. *Fax:* 860-768-4961. *E-mail:* admissions@hartford.edu. *Website:* http://www.hartford.edu/.

See previous page for display ad and page 1566 for the College Close-Up.

University of New Haven
West Haven, Connecticut

- **Independent** comprehensive, founded 1920
- **Suburban** 75-acre campus with easy access to Hartford, New Haven
- **Coed** 4,693 undergraduate students, 91% full-time, 50% women, 50% men
- **Moderately difficult** entrance level, 71% of applicants were admitted

Undergraduates 4,267 full-time, 426 part-time. Students come from 40 states and territories; 26 other countries; 55% are from out of state; 8% Black or African American, non-Hispanic/Latino; 3% Hispanic/Latino; 2% Asian, non-Hispanic/Latino; 0.1% Native Hawaiian or other Pacific Islander, non-Hispanic/Latino; 0.3% American Indian or Alaska Native, non-Hispanic/Latino; 2% Two or more races, non-Hispanic/Latino; 29% Race/ethnicity unknown; 6%

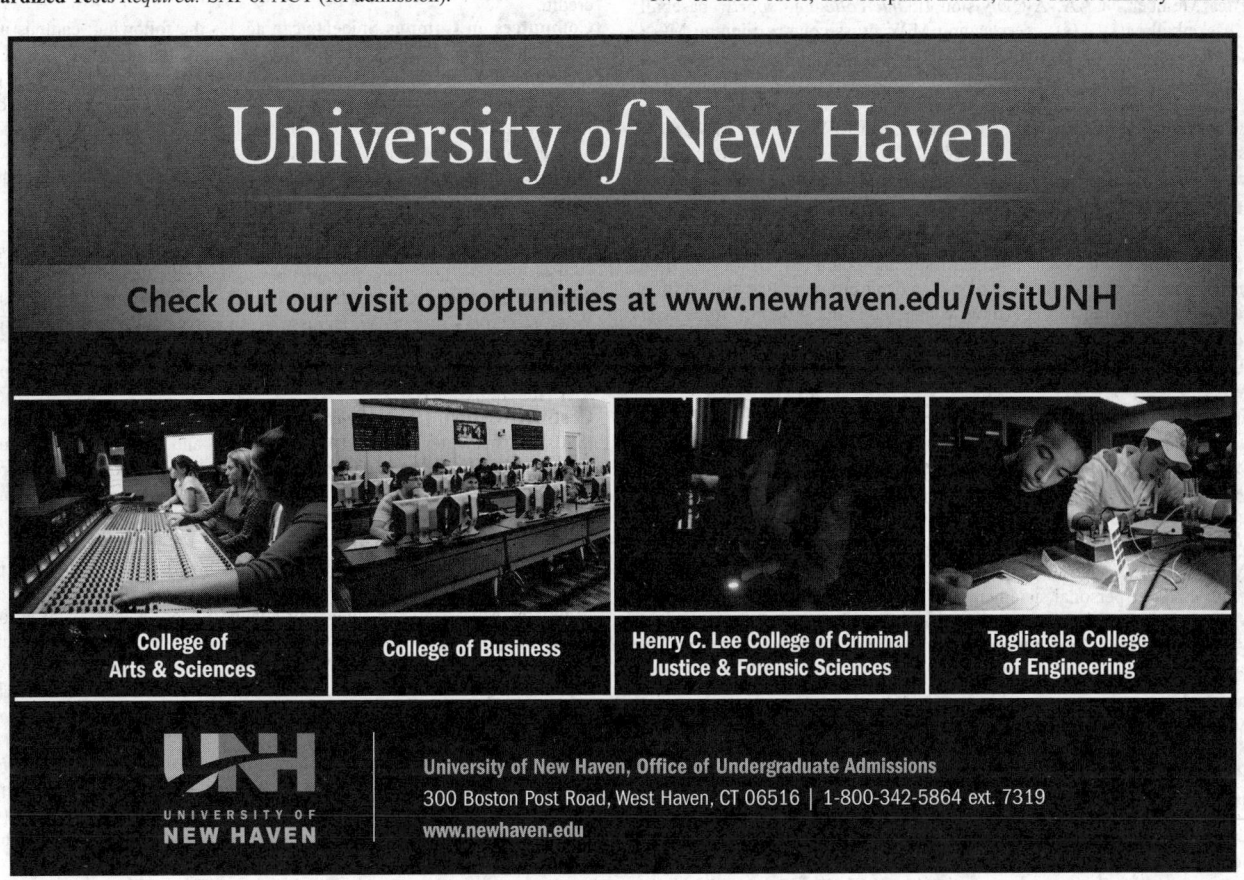

international; 5% transferred in; 56% live on campus. *Retention:* 76% of full-time freshmen returned.

Freshmen *Admission:* 10,028 applied, 7,167 admitted, 1,127 enrolled. *Average high school GPA:* 3.34. *Test scores:* SAT critical reading scores over 500: 62%; SAT math scores over 500: 68%; SAT writing scores over 500: 61%; ACT scores over 18: 93%; SAT critical reading scores over 600: 17%; SAT math scores over 600: 21%; SAT writing scores over 600: 15%; ACT scores over 24: 39%; SAT critical reading scores over 700: 1%; SAT math scores over 700: 2%; SAT writing scores over 700: 1%; ACT scores over 30: 5%.

Faculty *Total:* 572, 37% full-time, 52% with terminal degrees. *Student/faculty ratio:* 17:1.

Academics *Calendar:* 4-1-4. *Degrees:* certificates, associate, bachelor's, master's, doctoral, post-master's, and postbachelor's certificates. *Special study options:* academic remediation for entering students, accelerated degree program, adult/continuing education programs, advanced placement credit, cooperative education, distance learning, double majors, English as a second language, honors programs, independent study, internships, off-campus study, part-time degree program, services for LD students, study abroad, summer session for credit. *ROTC:* Army (b), Air Force (c).

Computers on Campus 300 computers/terminals and 250 ports are available on campus for general student use. Students can access the following: campus intranet, computer help desk, free student e-mail accounts, online (class) grades, online (class) registration, online (class) schedules, computer repair services. Campuswide network is available. 100% of college-owned or -operated housing units are wired for high-speed Internet access. Wireless service is available via entire campus.

Student Life *Housing options:* coed, disabled students. Campus housing is university owned and leased by the school. Freshman applicants given priority for college housing. *Activities and organizations:* drama/theater group, student-run newspaper, radio station, choral group, marching band, student government, Criminal Justice Club, Music Entertainment and Industry Association, Black Student Union, Fire Science Club, national fraternities, national sororities. *Campus security:* 24-hour emergency response devices and patrols, student patrols, late-night transport/escort service, controlled dormitory access, escort service, vehicle, bicycle and foot patrols, crime prevention programs. *Student services:* health clinic, personal/psychological counseling.

Athletics Member NCAA. All Division II. *Intercollegiate sports:* baseball M(s), basketball M(s)/W(s), cheerleading M/W, cross-country running M(s)/W(s), field hockey W(c), football M(s), ice hockey M(c), lacrosse M(c)/W(s), rugby M(c), soccer M(s)/W(s), softball W(s), tennis W(s), track and field M(s)/W(s), ultimate Frisbee M(c)/W(c), volleyball W(s), wrestling M(c). *Intramural sports:* basketball M/W, bowling M(c)/W(c), soccer M/W, softball M/W, table tennis M/W, tennis M/W, ultimate Frisbee M/W, volleyball M/W, weight lifting M/W.

Standardized Tests *Required:* SAT or ACT (for admission).

Costs (2012–13) *Comprehensive fee:* $46,450 includes full-time tuition ($31,500), mandatory fees ($1250), and room and board ($13,700). Full-time tuition and fees vary according to course load and program. Part-time tuition and fees vary according to class time, course load, and program. *Room and board:* Room and board charges vary according to board plan and housing facility. *Payment plan:* installment. *Waivers:* senior citizens and employees or children of employees.

Financial Aid Of all full-time matriculated undergraduates who enrolled in 2012, 3,733 applied for aid, 3,420 were judged to have need, 371 had their need fully met. In 2012, 493 non-need-based awards were made. *Average percent of need met:* 59%. *Average financial aid package:* $19,727. *Average need-based loan:* $4271. *Average need-based gift aid:* $16,067. *Average non-need-based aid:* $11,526. *Average indebtedness upon graduation:* $42,217.

Applying *Options:* electronic application, early action. *Application fee:* $75. *Required:* essay or personal statement, high school transcript. *Recommended:* interview. *Application deadlines:* rolling (freshmen), rolling (transfers), 11/15 (early action). *Notification:* continuous (freshmen), continuous (transfers), 12/17 (early action).

Freshman Application Contact Mr. Kevin Phillips, Associate Vice President for Enrollment Management, University of New Haven, Bayer Hall, 300 Boston Post Road, West Haven, CT 06516. *Phone:* 203-932-7318. *Toll-free phone:* 800-DIAL-UNH. *Fax:* 203-931-6093. *E-mail:* adminfo@newhaven.edu.

Website: http://www.newhaven.edu/.

See previous page for display ad and page 1588 for the College Close-Up.

University of Phoenix–Fairfield County Campus
Norwalk, Connecticut

Admissions Office Contact University of Phoenix–Fairfield County Campus, 535 Connecticut Avenue Suite 400, Norwalk, CT 06854-1799. *Toll-free phone:* 866-766-0766.
Website: http://www.phoenix.edu/.

University of Saint Joseph
West Hartford, Connecticut

- **Independent Roman Catholic** comprehensive, founded 1932
- **Suburban** 84-acre campus with easy access to Hartford
- **Endowment** $21.7 million
- **Undergraduate: women only; graduate: coed** 1,067 undergraduate students, 78% full-time, 99% women, 1% men
- **Moderately difficult** entrance level, 80% of applicants were admitted

Undergraduates 831 full-time, 236 part-time. 6% are from out of state; 10% Black or African American, non-Hispanic/Latino; 11% Hispanic/Latino; 3% Asian, non-Hispanic/Latino; 0.1% Native Hawaiian or other Pacific Islander, non-Hispanic/Latino; 0.2% American Indian or Alaska Native, non-Hispanic/Latino; 2% Two or more races, non-Hispanic/Latino; 20% Race/ethnicity unknown; 0.2% international; 11% transferred in; 47% live on campus. *Retention:* 75% of full-time freshmen returned.

Freshmen *Admission:* 679 applied, 540 admitted, 159 enrolled. *Average high school GPA:* 3.27. *Test scores:* SAT critical reading scores over 500: 43%; SAT math scores over 500: 46%; ACT scores over 18: 77%; SAT critical reading scores over 600: 12%; SAT math scores over 600: 5%; ACT scores over 24: 17%.

Faculty *Total:* 309, 38% full-time. *Student/faculty ratio:* 10:1.

Academics *Calendar:* semesters. *Degrees:* certificates, bachelor's, master's, doctoral, post-master's, and postbachelor's certificates. *Special study options:* accelerated degree program, adult/continuing education programs, advanced placement credit, distance learning, double majors, honors programs, independent study, internships, off-campus study, part-time degree program, services for LD students, student-designed majors, study abroad, summer session for credit.

Computers on Campus Students can access the following: campus intranet, computer help desk, free student e-mail accounts, online (class) grades, online (class) registration, online (class) schedules. Campuswide network is available. 100% of college-owned or -operated housing units are wired for high-speed Internet access. Wireless service is available via computer centers, computer labs, dorm rooms, libraries, student centers.

Student Life *Housing options:* women-only, disabled students. Campus housing is university owned. *Activities and organizations:* drama/theater group, choral group. *Campus security:* 24-hour emergency response devices and patrols, late-night transport/escort service, controlled dormitory access. *Student services:* health clinic, personal/psychological counseling.

Athletics Member NCAA. All Division III. *Intercollegiate sports:* basketball W, cross-country running W, lacrosse W, soccer W, softball W, swimming and diving W, tennis W, volleyball W.

Standardized Tests *Required:* SAT or ACT (for admission). *Recommended:* SAT (for admission).

Costs (2012–13) *Comprehensive fee:* $45,424 includes full-time tuition ($30,408), mandatory fees ($1418), and room and board ($13,598). Full-time tuition and fees vary according to course load, degree level, location, program, and student level. Part-time tuition: $688 per credit. Part-time tuition and fees vary according to course load, degree level, location, program, and student level. *Required fees:* $45 per credit part-time. *College room only:* $6274. Room and board charges vary according to board plan and housing facility. *Payment plan:* installment. *Waivers:* employees or children of employees.

Financial Aid Of all full-time matriculated undergraduates who enrolled in 2012, 800 applied for aid, 763 were judged to have need, 69 had their need fully met. In 2012, 79 non-need-based awards were made. *Average percent of need met:* 67%. *Average financial aid package:* $21,760. *Average need-based loan:* $5450. *Average need-based gift aid:* $16,990. *Average non-need-based aid:* $9620.

Applying *Options:* electronic application, deferred entrance. *Application fee:* $50. *Required:* high school transcript. *Recommended:* essay or personal statement, interview. *Application deadlines:* rolling (freshmen), rolling (out-of-state freshmen), rolling (transfers). *Notification:* continuous (freshmen), continuous (out-of-state freshmen), continuous (transfers).

Freshman Application Contact Office of Admissions, University of Saint Joseph, 1678 Asylum Avenue, West Hartford, CT 06117. *Phone:* 860-231-5216. *Toll-free phone:* 866-442-8752. *Fax:* 860-231-5744.
E-mail: admissions@usj.edu.
Website: http://www.usj.edu/.

See below for display ad and page 1600 for the College Close-Up.

Wesleyan University
Middletown, Connecticut

- **Independent** university, founded 1831
- **Small-town** 240-acre campus
- **Endowment** $616.2 million
- **Coed** 2,940 undergraduate students, 100% full-time, 52% women, 48% men
- **Most difficult** entrance level, 21% of applicants were admitted

Undergraduates 2,932 full-time, 8 part-time. 92% are from out of state; 7% Black or African American, non-Hispanic/Latino; 10% Hispanic/Latino; 9% Asian, non-Hispanic/Latino; 0.1% Native Hawaiian or other Pacific Islander, non-Hispanic/Latino; 0.1% American Indian or Alaska Native, non-Hispanic/Latino; 6% Two or more races, non-Hispanic/Latino; 9% Race/ethnicity unknown; 8% international; 2% transferred in; 98% live on campus. *Retention:* 95% of full-time freshmen returned.
Freshmen *Admission:* 10,046 applied, 2,102 admitted, 752 enrolled. *Average high school GPA:* 3.73. *Test scores:* SAT critical reading scores over 500: 99%; SAT math scores over 500: 100%; SAT writing scores over 500: 100%; ACT scores over 18: 100%; SAT critical reading scores over 600: 87%; SAT math scores over 600: 93%; SAT writing scores over 600: 89%; ACT scores over 24: 99%; SAT critical reading scores over 700: 50%; SAT math scores over 700: 55%; SAT writing scores over 700: 53%; ACT scores over 30: 68%.
Faculty *Total:* 389, 87% full-time, 91% with terminal degrees. *Student/faculty ratio:* 9:1.
Academics *Calendar:* semesters. *Degrees:* bachelor's, master's, doctoral, and post-master's certificates. *Special study options:* adult/continuing education programs, advanced placement credit, double majors, honors programs, independent study, off-campus study, services for LD students, student-designed majors, study abroad, summer session for credit. *ROTC:* Air Force (c). *Unusual degree programs:* 3-2 engineering with Columbia University, California Institute of Technology.

Computers on Campus 1,600 computers/terminals are available on campus for general student use. Students can access the following: campus intranet, computer help desk, free student e-mail accounts, online (class) grades, online (class) registration, online (class) schedules, electronic portfolio, online course drop/add, Blackboard course management system. Campuswide network is available. 100% of college-owned or -operated housing units are wired for high-speed Internet access. Wireless service is available via entire campus.
Student Life *Housing:* on-campus residence required through senior year. *Options:* coed, cooperative, disabled students. Campus housing is university owned. Freshman campus housing is guaranteed. *Activities and organizations:* drama/theater group, student-run newspaper, radio station, choral group, Environmental Organizers Network, WesDems, Ajuacampos (Latino affinity group), national fraternities, national sororities. *Campus security:* 24-hour emergency response devices and patrols, student patrols, late-night transport/escort service, controlled dormitory access. *Student services:* health clinic, personal/psychological counseling, women's center.
Athletics Member NCAA. All Division III. *Intercollegiate sports:* baseball M, basketball M/W, crew M/W, cross-country running M/W, equestrian sports M(c)/W(c), field hockey W, football M, golf M, ice hockey M/W, lacrosse M/W, rugby M(c)/W(c), sailing M(c)/W(c), skiing (cross-country) M(c)/W(c), skiing (downhill) M(c)/W(c), soccer M/W, softball W, squash M/W, swimming and diving M/W, tennis M/W, track and field M/W, volleyball M(c)/W, water polo M(c), wrestling M. *Intramural sports:* basketball M/W, ice hockey M/W, soccer M/W, softball M/W, squash M/W, ultimate Frisbee M/W, water polo M/W.
Standardized Tests *Required:* SAT and SAT Subject Tests or ACT (for admission).
Costs (2012–13) *One-time required fee:* $300. *Comprehensive fee:* $58,202 includes full-time tuition ($45,358), mandatory fees ($270), and room and board ($12,574). *Room and board:* Room and board charges vary according to board plan and housing facility. *Payment plan:* installment.
Financial Aid Of all full-time matriculated undergraduates who enrolled in 2011, 1,509 applied for aid, 1,413 were judged to have need, 1,311 had their need fully met. 1,183 Federal Work-Study jobs (averaging $2369). 100 state and other part-time jobs (averaging $2325). In 2011, 32 non-need-based awards were made. *Average percent of need met:* 100%. *Average financial aid package:* $40,364. *Average need-based loan:* $4283. *Average need-based gift aid:* $36,316. *Average non-need-based aid:* $42,362. *Average indebtedness upon graduation:* $25,864. *Financial aid deadline:* 2/15.
Applying *Options:* electronic application, early admission, early decision, deferred entrance. *Application fee:* $55. *Required:* essay or personal statement,

high school transcript, 2 letters of recommendation. *Required for some:* interview. *Recommended:* interview. *Application deadlines:* 1/1 (freshmen), 3/15 (transfers). *Early decision deadline:* 11/15 (for plan 1), 1/1 (for plan 2). *Notification:* 4/1 (freshmen), 5/15 (transfers), 12/15 (early decision plan 1), 2/15 (early decision plan 2).
Freshman Application Contact Ms. Nancy Meislahn, Dean of Admission and Financial Aid, Wesleyan University, Stewart M. Reid House, 70 Wyllys Avenue, Middletown, CT 06459-0265. *Phone:* 860-685-3000. *Fax:* 860-685-3001. *E-mail:* admissions@wesleyan.edu.
Website: http://www.wesleyan.edu/.

Western Connecticut State University
Danbury, Connecticut

- **State-supported** comprehensive, founded 1903, part of Connecticut State Colleges and Universities (ConnSCU)
- **Urban** 340-acre campus with easy access to New York City
- **Endowment** $10.5 million
- **Coed** 5,583 undergraduate students, 81% full-time, 54% women, 46% men
- **Moderately difficult** entrance level, 59% of applicants were admitted

Undergraduates 4,501 full-time, 1,082 part-time. Students come from 17 states and territories; 4 other countries; 7% are from out of state; 9% Black or African American, non-Hispanic/Latino; 13% Hispanic/Latino; 3% Asian, non-Hispanic/Latino; 0.4% Native Hawaiian or other Pacific Islander, non-Hispanic/Latino; 0.4% American Indian or Alaska Native, non-Hispanic/Latino; 2% Two or more races, non-Hispanic/Latino; 2% Race/ethnicity unknown; 0.1% international; 10% transferred in; 29% live on campus. *Retention:* 68% of full-time freshmen returned.
Freshmen *Admission:* 4,016 applied, 2,368 admitted, 836 enrolled. *Average high school GPA:* 2.97. *Test scores:* SAT critical reading scores over 500: 49%; SAT math scores over 500: 47%; SAT critical reading scores over 600: 10%; SAT math scores over 600: 11%; SAT critical reading scores over 700: 2%; SAT math scores over 700: 1%.
Faculty *Total:* 588, 39% full-time. *Student/faculty ratio:* 14:1.
Academics *Calendar:* semesters. *Degrees:* associate, bachelor's, master's, doctoral, and post-master's certificates. *Special study options:* cooperative education, distance learning, honors programs, independent study, internships, part-time degree program, services for LD students, student-designed majors, study abroad, summer session for credit. *ROTC:* Army (c), Air Force (c).
Computers on Campus 834 computers/terminals and 1,459 ports are available on campus for general student use. Students can access the following: computer help desk, free student e-mail accounts, online (class) grades, online (class) registration, online (class) schedules, 100% wireless, on-line payment. Campuswide network is available. Wireless service is available via classrooms, computer centers, computer labs, dorm rooms, libraries, student centers.
Student Life *Housing options:* coed, women-only. Campus housing is university owned. Freshman campus housing is guaranteed. *Activities and organizations:* drama/theater group, student-run newspaper, radio station, choral group, National Society of Collegiate Scholars, Criminology Club, Jazz Club, American Marketing Club, Meteorology, national fraternities, national sororities. *Campus security:* 24-hour emergency response devices and patrols, student patrols, late-night transport/escort service, controlled dormitory access. *Student services:* health clinic, personal/psychological counseling.
Athletics Member NCAA. All Division III. *Intercollegiate sports:* baseball M, basketball M/W, cheerleading W(c), field hockey W, football M, lacrosse M/W, soccer M/W, softball W, swimming and diving W, tennis M/W, volleyball W. *Intramural sports:* basketball M/W, football M, ice hockey M(c), rock climbing M(c)/W(c), softball M/W.
Standardized Tests *Required:* SAT or ACT (for admission).
Costs (2013–14) *Tuition:* state resident $4510 full-time, $188 per credit part-time; nonresident $14,594 full-time, $192 per credit part-time. Full-time tuition and fees vary according to course load, program, and reciprocity agreements. *Required fees:* $4383 full-time, $222 per credit part-time. *Room and board:* $10,907; room only: $6445. Room and board charges vary according to board plan and housing facility. *Payment plan:* installment. *Waivers:* senior citizens and employees or children of employees.
Financial Aid Of all full-time matriculated undergraduates who enrolled in 2011, 3,793 applied for aid, 3,032 were judged to have need, 71 had their need fully met. 112 Federal Work-Study jobs (averaging $2059). 23 state and other part-time jobs (averaging $1999). In 2011, 28 non-need-based awards were made. *Average percent of need met:* 63%. *Average financial aid package:* $7767. *Average need-based loan:* $4099. *Average need-based gift aid:* $4556. *Average non-need-based aid:* $7289. *Average indebtedness upon graduation:* $22,505. *Financial aid deadline:* 4/15.
Applying *Options:* electronic application, early admission, deferred entrance. *Application fee:* $50. *Required:* high school transcript, 2 letters of recommen-

dation. *Required for some:* essay or personal statement, interview. *Application deadlines:* rolling (freshmen), rolling (transfers). *Notification:* continuous (freshmen), continuous (transfers).

Freshman Application Contact Five counselors assigned by freshman's last name., Office of University Admissions, Western Connecticut State University, 181 White Street, Danbury, CT 06810. *Phone:* 203-837-9000. *Toll-free phone:* 877-837-WCSU. *Fax:* 203-837-8338. *E-mail:* admissions@wcsu.edu.
Website: http://www.wcsu.edu/.

See previous page for display ad and page 1640 for the College Close-Up.

Yale University
New Haven, Connecticut
- **Independent** university, founded 1701
- **Urban** 342-acre campus with easy access to New York City
- **Endowment** $19.3 billion
- **Coed** 5,405 undergraduate students, 100% full-time, 50% women, 50% men
- **Most difficult** entrance level, 7% of applicants were admitted

Undergraduates 5,393 full-time, 12 part-time. Students come from 50 states and territories; 86 other countries; 94% are from out of state; 7% Black or African American, non-Hispanic/Latino; 10% Hispanic/Latino; 16% Asian, non-Hispanic/Latino; 0.1% Native Hawaiian or other Pacific Islander, non-Hispanic/Latino; 0.6% American Indian or Alaska Native, non-Hispanic/Latino; 6% Two or more races, non-Hispanic/Latino; 3% Race/ethnicity unknown; 10% international; 0.4% transferred in; 88% live on campus. *Retention:* 99% of full-time freshmen returned.
Freshmen *Admission:* 28,977 applied, 2,043 admitted, 1,355 enrolled. *Test scores:* SAT critical reading scores over 500: 100%; SAT math scores over 500: 100%; SAT writing scores over 500: 100%; SAT critical reading scores over 600: 98%; SAT math scores over 600: 99%; SAT writing scores over 600: 98%; SAT critical reading scores over 700: 76%; SAT math scores over 700: 80%; SAT writing scores over 700: 81%.
Faculty *Total:* 1,666, 71% full-time, 88% with terminal degrees. *Student/faculty ratio:* 5:1.
Academics *Calendar:* semesters. *Degrees:* bachelor's, master's, doctoral, and post-master's certificates. *Special study options:* advanced placement credit, double majors, independent study, part-time degree program, services for LD students, student-designed majors, study abroad, summer session for credit. *ROTC:* Army (c), Navy (b), Air Force (b).
Computers on Campus 450 computers/terminals are available on campus for general student use. Students can access the following: campus intranet, computer help desk, free student e-mail accounts, online (class) grades, online (class) registration, online (class) schedules. Campuswide network is available. 100% of college-owned or -operated housing units are wired for high-speed Internet access. Wireless service is available via classrooms, computer centers, computer labs, learning centers, libraries, student centers.
Student Life *Housing:* on-campus residence required through sophomore year. *Options:* coed, disabled students. Campus housing is university owned. Freshman campus housing is guaranteed. *Activities and organizations:* drama/theater group, student-run newspaper, radio station, choral group, marching band, national fraternities, national sororities. *Campus security:* 24-hour emergency response devices and patrols, late-night transport/escort service, controlled dormitory access. *Student services:* health clinic, personal/psychological counseling, women's center.
Athletics Member NCAA. All Division I except football (Division I-AA). *Intercollegiate sports:* archery M(c)/W(c), badminton M(c)/W(c), baseball M, basketball M/W, cheerleading M(c)/W, crew M/W, cross-country running M/W, equestrian sports M(c)/W(c), fencing M/W, field hockey W, golf M/W, gymnastics W, ice hockey M/W, lacrosse M/W, riflery M(c)/W(c), rock climbing M(c)/W(c), rugby M(c)/W(c), sailing M/W, skiing (cross-country) M(c)/W(c), skiing (downhill) M(c)/W(c), soccer M/W, softball W, squash M/W, swimming and diving M/W, table tennis M(c)/W(c), tennis M/W, track and field M/W, ultimate Frisbee M(c)/W(c), volleyball M(c)/W, water polo M(c)/W(c), wrestling M(c)/W(c). *Intramural sports:* badminton M(c)/W(c), baseball M, basketball M/W, bowling M/W, crew M/W, cross-country running M/W, field hockey W, football M/W, golf M/W, ice hockey M/W, racquetball M/W, soccer M/W, softball M/W, squash M/W, swimming and diving M/W, table tennis M/W, tennis M/W, ultimate Frisbee M/W, volleyball M/W, water polo M/W.
Standardized Tests *Required:* SAT and SAT Subject Tests or ACT (for admission).
Costs (2013–14) *Comprehensive fee:* $57,500 includes full-time tuition ($44,000) and room and board ($13,500). *Room and board:* Room and board charges vary according to board plan.
Financial Aid Of all full-time matriculated undergraduates who enrolled in 2010, 3,145 applied for aid, 3,004 were judged to have need, 3,004 had their need fully met. *Average percent of need met:* 100%. *Average financial aid package:* $40,990. *Average need-based loan:* $2434. *Average need-based gift aid:* $38,914. *Average indebtedness upon graduation:* $9254. *Financial aid deadline:* 3/1.
Applying *Options:* electronic application, early admission, early action, deferred entrance. *Application fee:* $75. *Required:* essay or personal statement, high school transcript, 3 letters of recommendation. *Recommended:* interview. *Application deadlines:* 12/31 (freshmen), 3/1 (transfers), 11/1 (early action). *Notification:* 4/1 (freshmen), 5/15 (transfers), 12/15 (early action).
Freshman Application Contact Admissions Director, Yale University, PO Box 208234, New Haven, CT 06520. *Phone:* 203-432-9300. *E-mail:* student.questions@yale.edu.
Website: http://www.yale.edu/.

DELAWARE

Delaware State University
Dover, Delaware
- **State-supported** university, founded 1891, part of Delaware Higher Education Commission
- **Small-town** 400-acre campus
- **Coed**
- **Moderately difficult** entrance level

Faculty *Student/faculty ratio:* 15:1.
Academics *Calendar:* semesters. *Degrees:* bachelor's, master's, and doctoral.
Student Life *Campus security:* 24-hour emergency response devices and patrols, student patrols, late-night transport/escort service, controlled dormitory access.
Athletics Member NCAA. All Division I except football (Division I-AA).
Standardized Tests *Required:* SAT or ACT (for admission).
Costs (2012–13) *Tuition:* state resident $6481 full-time; nonresident $13,742 full-time. Full-time tuition and fees vary according to course load. Part-time tuition and fees vary according to course load. *Room and board:* $9386; room only: $6114. Room and board charges vary according to board plan and housing facility.
Financial Aid *Of all full-time matriculated undergraduates who enrolled in 2011,* 3,193 applied for aid, 2,954 were judged to have need, 1,023 had their need fully met. *In 2011,* 448 non-need-based awards were made. *Average percent of need met:* 48. *Average financial aid package:* $10,953. *Average need-based loan:* $3412. *Average need-based gift aid:* $6262. *Average non-need-based aid:* $7173. *Average indebtedness upon graduation:* $45,098.
Applying *Options:* electronic application, early admission. *Application fee:* $35. *Required:* high school transcript, minimum 2.0 GPA.
Freshman Application Contact Mrs. Erin Hill, Executive Director for Admissions, Delaware State University, 1200 North DuPont Highway, Dover, DE 19901-2277. *Phone:* 302-857-6351. *Toll-free phone:* 800-845-2544. *Fax:* 302-857-6352. *E-mail:* ehill@desu.edu.
Website: http://www.desu.edu/.

Goldey-Beacom College
Wilmington, Delaware
- **Independent** comprehensive, founded 1886
- **Suburban** 24-acre campus with easy access to Philadelphia
- **Endowment** $47.4 million
- **Coed** 625 undergraduate students, 74% full-time, 56% women, 44% men

Undergraduates 462 full-time, 163 part-time. Students come from 12 states and territories; 24 other countries; 33% are from out of state; 24% Black or African American, non-Hispanic/Latino; 8% Hispanic/Latino; 5% Asian, non-Hispanic/Latino; 0.2% American Indian or Alaska Native, non-Hispanic/Latino; 2% Two or more races, non-Hispanic/Latino; 3% Race/ethnicity unknown; 9% international; 9% transferred in; 32% live on campus. *Retention:* 85% of full-time freshmen returned.
Freshmen *Admission:* 96 enrolled. *Average high school GPA:* 2.9.
Faculty *Total:* 56, 32% full-time, 41% with terminal degrees. *Student/faculty ratio:* 26:1.
Academics *Calendar:* semesters. *Degrees:* associate, bachelor's, master's, and postbachelor's certificates. *Special study options:* academic remediation for entering students, accelerated degree program, advanced placement credit, cooperative education, double majors, honors programs, internships, part-time degree program, summer session for credit.
Computers on Campus 159 computers/terminals are available on campus for general student use. Students can access the following: campus intranet, computer help desk, free student e-mail accounts, online (class) grades, online

(class) schedules, campus Web. Campuswide network is available. 100% of college-owned or -operated housing units are wired for high-speed Internet access. Wireless service is available via entire campus.

Student Life *Housing options:* coed. Campus housing is university owned. *Activities and organizations:* student-run newspaper, Student Athletic Advisory Committee, Alpha Chi, Resident Student Association, Student Ambassadors, International Student Association. *Campus security:* 24-hour emergency response devices and patrols, student patrols, late-night transport/escort service.

Athletics Member NCAA. All Division II. *Intercollegiate sports:* basketball M(s)/W(s), cross-country running M(s)/W(s), golf M(s)/W, soccer M(s)/W(s), softball W(s), tennis W(s), volleyball W(s).

Standardized Tests *Required:* SAT or ACT (for admission).

Costs (2013–14) *Tuition:* $21,840 full-time, $728 per credit part-time. Full-time tuition and fees vary according to course load. Part-time tuition and fees vary according to course load. *Required fees:* $300 full-time, $10 per credit part-time. *Room only:* $5353. Room and board charges vary according to housing facility. *Payment plans:* installment, deferred payment. *Waivers:* children of alumni and employees or children of employees.

Applying *Required:* high school transcript, minimum 2.0 GPA. *Required for some:* 1 letter of recommendation, interview.

Freshman Application Contact Mr. Larry Eby, Director of Admissions, Goldey-Beacom College, 4701 Limestone Road, Wilmington, DE 19808. *Phone:* 302-225-6289. *Toll-free phone:* 800-833-4877. *Fax:* 302-996-5408. *E-mail:* admissions@gbc.edu. *Website:* http://www.gbc.edu/.

Strayer University—Christiana Campus

Newark, Delaware

Freshman Application Contact Strayer University—Christiana Campus, 240 Continental Drive, Suite 108, Newark, DE 19713. *Website:* http://www.strayer.edu/campus/christiana.

University of Delaware

Newark, Delaware

- **State-related** university, founded 1743
- **Small-town** 1000-acre campus with easy access to Philadelphia, Baltimore
- **Coed** 17,427 undergraduate students, 91% full-time, 57% women, 43% men
- **Moderately difficult** entrance level, 57% of applicants were admitted

Undergraduates 15,899 full-time, 1,528 part-time. 58% are from out of state; 5% Black or African American, non-Hispanic/Latino; 6% Hispanic/Latino; 4% Asian, non-Hispanic/Latino; 0.1% Native Hawaiian or other Pacific Islander, non-Hispanic/Latino; 0.1% American Indian or Alaska Native, non-Hispanic/Latino; 2% Two or more races, non-Hispanic/Latino; 2% Race/ethnicity unknown; 4% international; 3% transferred in; 44% live on campus. *Retention:* 92% of full-time freshmen returned.

Freshmen *Admission:* 26,225 applied, 14,829 admitted, 3,817 enrolled. *Average high school GPA:* 3.78. *Test scores:* SAT critical reading scores over 500: 92%; SAT math scores over 500: 93%; SAT writing scores over 500: 91%; ACT scores over 18: 100%; SAT critical reading scores over 600: 50%; SAT math scores over 600: 59%; SAT writing scores over 600: 50%; ACT scores over 24: 82%; SAT critical reading scores over 700: 12%; SAT math scores over 700: 13%; SAT writing scores over 700: 9%; ACT scores over 30: 17%.

Faculty *Total:* 1,484, 80% full-time, 76% with terminal degrees. *Student/faculty ratio:* 13:1.

Academics *Calendar:* 4-1-4. *Degrees:* associate, bachelor's, master's, and doctoral. *Special study options:* academic remediation for entering students, accelerated degree program, adult/continuing education programs, advanced placement credit, distance learning, double majors, English as a second language, honors programs, independent study, internships, off-campus study, part-time degree program, services for LD students, student-designed majors, study abroad, summer session for credit. *ROTC:* Army (b), Air Force (b).

Computers on Campus Students can access the following: campus intranet, computer help desk, free student e-mail accounts, online (class) grades, online (class) registration, online (class) schedules, personal Web page, Google apps. Campuswide network is available. 100% of college-owned or -operated housing units are wired for high-speed Internet access. Wireless service is available via entire campus.

Student Life *Housing:* on-campus residence required for freshman year. *Options:* coed, women-only, disabled students. Campus housing is university owned. Freshman campus housing is guaranteed. *Activities and organizations:* drama/theater group, student-run newspaper, radio station, choral group,

marching band, national fraternities, national sororities. *Campus security:* 24-hour emergency response devices and patrols, student patrols, late-night transport/escort service, controlled dormitory access. *Student services:* health clinic, personal/psychological counseling, women's center.

Athletics Member NCAA. All Division I except football (Division I-AA). *Intercollegiate sports:* baseball M(s), basketball M(s)/W(s), bowling M(c)/W(c), cheerleading M(s)/W(s), crew M(c)/W(s), cross-country running M(c)/W, equestrian sports M(c)/W(c), field hockey W(s), golf M/W, ice hockey M(c)/W(c), lacrosse M(s)/W(s), rugby M(c)/W(c), sailing M(c)/W(c), soccer M(s)/W(s), softball W(s), swimming and diving M/W(s), tennis M/W, track and field M(c)/W(s), volleyball W(s), wrestling M(c). *Intramural sports:* badminton M/W, basketball M/W, field hockey W(c), football M/W, golf M/W, lacrosse M(c)/W(c), racquetball M/W, soccer M(c)/W(c), softball M/W, squash M/W, swimming and diving M/W, table tennis M/W, tennis M/W, track and field M/W, ultimate Frisbee M/W, volleyball M(c)/W(c), water polo M/W.

Standardized Tests *Required:* SAT or ACT (for admission). *Required for some:* SAT Subject Tests (for admission). *Recommended:* SAT Subject Tests (for admission).

Costs (2013–14) *Tuition:* state resident $10,150 full-time, $423 per credit hour part-time; nonresident $27,240 full-time, $1135 per credit hour part-time. *Required fees:* $1532 full-time. *Room and board:* $10,758; room only: $6516. Room and board charges vary according to board plan, housing facility, and student level. *Payment plan:* installment. *Waivers:* senior citizens and employees or children of employees.

Financial Aid Of all full-time matriculated undergraduates who enrolled in 2012, 11,420 applied for aid, 7,979 were judged to have need, 3,687 had their need fully met. In 2012, 2984 non-need-based awards were made. *Average percent of need met:* 73%. *Average financial aid package:* $14,442. *Average need-based loan:* $7773. *Average need-based gift aid:* $7831. *Average non-need-based aid:* $6597. *Average indebtedness upon graduation:* $33,649. *Financial aid deadline:* 3/15.

Applying *Options:* electronic application, early admission, deferred entrance. *Application fee:* $75. *Required:* essay or personal statement, high school transcript, 1 letter of recommendation. *Application deadlines:* 1/15 (freshmen), 5/1 (transfers). *Notification:* 3/15 (freshmen), continuous (transfers).

Freshman Application Contact Mr. Lou Hirsh, Director of Admissions, University of Delaware, 116 Hullihen Hall, Newark, DE 19716. *Phone:* 302-831-8123. *Fax:* 302-831-6905. *E-mail:* admissions@udel.edu. *Website:* http://www.udel.edu/.

Wesley College

Dover, Delaware

- **Independent United Methodist** comprehensive, founded 1873
- **Small-town** 40-acre campus
- **Coed** 1,661 undergraduate students, 81% full-time, 49% women, 51% men
- **Moderately difficult** entrance level, 63% of applicants were admitted

Undergraduates 1,345 full-time, 316 part-time. Students come from 28 states and territories; 4 other countries; 57% are from out of state; 37% Black or African American, non-Hispanic/Latino; 6% Hispanic/Latino; 1% Asian, non-Hispanic/Latino; 1% American Indian or Alaska Native, non-Hispanic/Latino; 0.8% Two or more races, non-Hispanic/Latino; 5% Race/ethnicity unknown; 2% transferred in; 66% live on campus. *Retention:* 46% of full-time freshmen returned.

Freshmen *Admission:* 2,933 applied, 1,836 admitted, 553 enrolled. *Average high school GPA:* 2.71. *Test scores:* SAT critical reading scores over 500: 17%; SAT math scores over 500: 20%; SAT writing scores over 500: 14%; SAT critical reading scores over 600: 4%; SAT math scores over 600: 2%; SAT writing scores over 600: 2%; SAT critical reading scores over 700: 1%; SAT math scores over 700: 1%.

Faculty *Total:* 170, 41% full-time, 40% with terminal degrees. *Student/faculty ratio:* 11:1.

Academics *Calendar:* semesters. *Degrees:* certificates, associate, bachelor's, master's, post-master's, and postbachelor's certificates. *Special study options:* academic remediation for entering students, adult/continuing education programs, advanced placement credit, cooperative education, English as a second language, external degree program, freshman honors college, independent study, internships, off-campus study, part-time degree program, services for LD students, study abroad, summer session for credit. *ROTC:* Army (c).

Computers on Campus 225 computers/terminals are available on campus for general student use. Students can access the following: campus intranet, computer help desk, free student e-mail accounts, online (class) grades, online (class) registration, online (class) schedules. Campuswide network is available. 100% of college-owned or -operated housing units are wired for high-speed Internet access. Wireless service is available via entire campus.

Student Life *Housing:* on-campus residence required for freshman year. *Options:* coed, men-only, women-only. Campus housing is university owned.

Freshman campus housing is guaranteed. *Activities and organizations:* drama/ theater group, student-run newspaper, choral group, Student Activity Board, Student Government Association, National Coeducation Community Service Organization, national fraternities, national sororities. *Campus security:* 24-hour patrols, controlled dormitory access. *Student services:* health clinic, personal/psychological counseling.

Athletics Member NCAA. All Division III. *Intercollegiate sports:* baseball M, basketball M/W, field hockey W, football M, golf M/W, lacrosse M/W, soccer M/W, softball W, tennis M/W. *Intramural sports:* basketball M/W, cross-country running M/W, football M, soccer M/W, track and field M/W, volleyball M/W.

Standardized Tests *Required:* SAT (for admission). *Required for some:* special test for nursing.

Costs (2012–13) *Comprehensive fee:* $32,830 includes full-time tuition ($21,512), mandatory fees ($880), and room and board ($10,438). Full-time tuition and fees vary according to class time. *College room only:* $5096. Room and board charges vary according to board plan and housing facility. *Payment plan:* installment. *Waivers:* senior citizens and employees or children of employees.

Financial Aid Of all full-time matriculated undergraduates who enrolled in 2011, 1,265 applied for aid, 1,265 were judged to have need, 2 had their need fully met. *Average percent of need met:* 39%. *Average financial aid package:* $13,896. *Average need-based loan:* $1858. *Average need-based gift aid:* $13,896.

Applying *Options:* electronic application. *Application fee:* $25. *Required:* essay or personal statement, high school transcript, minimum 2.2 GPA, 1 letter of recommendation. *Recommended:* interview. *Application deadlines:* rolling (freshmen), rolling (transfers).

Freshman Application Contact Mr. Christopher Jester, Assistant Director of Undergraduate Admissions, Wesley College, 120 North State Street, Dover, DE 19901-3875. *Phone:* 302-736-2468. *Toll-free phone:* 800-937-5398. *E-mail:* christopher.jester@wesley.edu. *Website:* http://www.wesley.edu/.

Wilmington University

New Castle, Delaware

- **Independent** comprehensive, founded 1967
- **Suburban** 17-acre campus with easy access to Philadelphia
- **Endowment** $15.5 million
- **Coed** 8,238 undergraduate students, 63% full-time, 65% women, 35% men
- **Noncompetitive** entrance level, 97% of applicants were admitted

Undergraduates 5,205 full-time, 3,033 part-time. Students come from 41 states and territories; 25 other countries; 23% are from out of state; 22% Black or African American, non-Hispanic/Latino; 3% Hispanic/Latino; 2% Asian, non-Hispanic/Latino; 0.1% Native Hawaiian or other Pacific Islander, non-Hispanic/Latino; 0.7% American Indian or Alaska Native, non-Hispanic/Latino; 29% Race/ethnicity unknown; 19% transferred in. *Retention:* 64% of full-time freshmen returned.

Freshmen *Admission:* 1,466 applied, 1,418 admitted, 561 enrolled.

Faculty *Total:* 1,116, 8% full-time, 23% with terminal degrees. *Student/faculty ratio:* 14:1.

Academics *Calendar:* semesters. *Degrees:* certificates, associate, bachelor's, master's, doctoral, post-master's, and postbachelor's certificates. *Special study options:* academic remediation for entering students, accelerated degree program, adult/continuing education programs, cooperative education, distance learning, double majors, external degree program, independent study, internships, part-time degree program, summer session for credit. *ROTC:* Army (c), Air Force (c).

Computers on Campus 600 computers/terminals are available on campus for general student use. Students can access the following: free student e-mail accounts, online (class) grades, online (class) registration, online (class) schedules. Campuswide network is available. Wireless service is available via entire campus.

Student Life *Housing:* college housing not available. *Activities and organizations:* Student Government Association, Green Team, Photography Club, WU Student United Way, Wildcat Cheerleaders. *Campus security:* 24-hour emergency response devices and patrols, late-night transport/escort service.

Athletics Member NCAA. All Division II. *Intercollegiate sports:* baseball M(s), basketball M(s)/W(s), cross-country running M(s)/W(s), softball W(s), volleyball W(s).

Financial Aid Of all full-time matriculated undergraduates who enrolled in 2004, 1,217 applied for aid, 900 were judged to have need. 25 Federal Work-Study jobs (averaging $2000). In 2004, 74 non-need-based awards were made. *Average percent of need met:* 48%. *Average financial aid package:* $5770. *Average need-based loan:* $3889. *Average need-based gift aid:* $2464. *Aver-*

age non-need-based aid: $1100. *Average indebtedness upon graduation:* $17,486.

Applying *Options:* early admission, deferred entrance. *Application fee:* $25. *Required:* high school transcript. *Recommended:* interview. *Application deadlines:* rolling (freshmen), rolling (transfers). *Notification:* continuous (freshmen), continuous (transfers).

Freshman Application Contact Ms. Laura Morris, Director of Admissions, Wilmington University, 320 North DuPont Highway, New Castle, DE 19720-6491. *Phone:* 302-295-1179. *Toll-free phone:* 877-967-5464. *E-mail:* undergradadmissions@wilmu.edu. *Website:* http://www.wilmu.edu/.

DISTRICT OF COLUMBIA

American University

Washington, District of Columbia

- **Independent Methodist** university, founded 1893
- **Suburban** 84-acre campus with easy access to Washington, DC
- **Endowment** $466.0 million
- **Coed** 7,299 undergraduate students, 95% full-time, 59% women, 41% men
- **Very difficult** entrance level, 44% of applicants were admitted

Undergraduates 6,970 full-time, 329 part-time. Students come from 55 states and territories; 89 other countries; 86% are from out of state; 6% Black or African American, non-Hispanic/Latino; 9% Hispanic/Latino; 6% Asian, non-Hispanic/Latino; 0.1% Native Hawaiian or other Pacific Islander, non-Hispanic/Latino; 0.2% American Indian or Alaska Native, non-Hispanic/Latino; 4% Two or more races, non-Hispanic/Latino; 11% Race/ethnicity unknown; 7% international; 3% transferred in. *Retention:* 90% of full-time freshmen returned.

Freshmen *Admission:* 17,039 applied, 7,531 admitted, 1,597 enrolled. *Average high school GPA:* 3.74. *Test scores:* SAT critical reading scores over 500: 96%; SAT math scores over 500: 95%; SAT writing scores over 500: 96%; ACT scores over 18: 99%; SAT critical reading scores over 600: 74%; SAT math scores over 600: 63%; SAT writing scores over 600: 68%; ACT scores over 24: 91%; SAT critical reading scores over 700: 25%; SAT math scores over 700: 15%; SAT writing scores over 700: 18%; ACT scores over 30: 35%.

Faculty *Total:* 1,327, 55% full-time. *Student/faculty ratio:* 12:1.

Academics *Calendar:* semesters. *Degrees:* certificates, associate, bachelor's, master's, doctoral, and postbachelor's certificates. *Special study options:* accelerated degree program, advanced placement credit, cooperative education, distance learning, double majors, English as a second language, honors programs, independent study, internships, off-campus study, part-time degree program, services for LD students, student-designed majors, study abroad, summer session for credit. *ROTC:* Army (c), Air Force (c). *Unusual degree programs:* 3-2 engineering with University of Maryland College Park.

Computers on Campus 650 computers/terminals are available on campus for general student use. Students can access the following: campus intranet, computer help desk, free student e-mail accounts, online (class) grades, online (class) registration, online (class) schedules. Campuswide network is available. 100% of college-owned or -operated housing units are wired for high-speed Internet access. Wireless service is available via entire campus.

Student Life *Housing options:* coed, disabled students. Campus housing is university owned and leased by the school. Freshman campus housing is guaranteed. *Activities and organizations:* drama/theater group, student-run newspaper, radio and television station, choral group, Kennedy Political Union, Habitat for Humanity, Student Government, Amnesty International, Ethnic and religious organizations, national fraternities, national sororities. *Campus security:* 24-hour emergency response devices and patrols, late-night transport/ escort service, controlled dormitory access, E-mail and text emergency notification system. *Student services:* health clinic, personal/psychological counseling, women's center.

Athletics Member NCAA. All Division I. *Intercollegiate sports:* basketball M(s)/W(s), cross-country running M(s)/W(s), field hockey W(s), lacrosse W(s), soccer M(s)/W(s), swimming and diving M/W, track and field M(s)/ W(s), volleyball W(s), wrestling M(s). *Intramural sports:* baseball M(c)/W(c), basketball M/W, crew M(c)/W(c), equestrian sports M(c)/W(c), field hockey M(c)/W(c), football M/W, golf M(c)/W(c), gymnastics M(c)/W(c), ice hockey M(c)/W(c), lacrosse M(c)/W(c), rugby M(c)/W(c), sailing M(c)/W(c), soccer M(c)/W(c), softball M/W, table tennis M/W, tennis M/W, ultimate Frisbee M(c)/W(c), volleyball M/W, water polo M(c)/W(c), weight lifting M.

Standardized Tests *Required:* SAT or ACT (for admission).

Costs (2012–13) *Comprehensive fee:* $53,419 includes full-time tuition ($38,982), mandatory fees ($517), and room and board ($13,920). Full-time tuition and fees vary according to location. Part-time tuition: $1299 per credit hour. Part-time tuition and fees vary according to course load and location. *Required fees:* $170 per term part-time. *College room only:* $9290. Room and board charges vary according to board plan, housing facility, and location. *Payment plans:* tuition prepayment, installment. *Waivers:* employees or children of employees.

Financial Aid Of all full-time matriculated undergraduates who enrolled in 2012, 4,243 applied for aid, 3,482 were judged to have need, 799 had their need fully met. 1,407 Federal Work-Study jobs (averaging $1663). In 2012, 941 non-need-based awards were made. *Average percent of need met:* 72%. *Average financial aid package:* $27,138. *Average need-based loan:* $5052. *Average need-based gift aid:* $19,733. *Average non-need-based aid:* $17,504. *Financial aid deadline:* 2/15.

Applying *Options:* electronic application, early decision, deferred entrance. *Application fee:* $65. *Required:* essay or personal statement, high school transcript. *Required for some:* If home schooled: A description of why home-schooling was chosen for the applicant and the home-school philosophy and a detailed description of curriculum. At least two SAT Subject Tests are recommended but not required. An additional letter of recommendation is recommended but not required. *Recommended:* 2 letters of recommendation. *Application deadlines:* 1/15 (freshmen), 3/1 (transfers). *Early decision deadline:* 11/15. *Notification:* 4/1 (freshmen), continuous (transfers), 12/31 (early decision).

Freshman Application Contact Greg Grauman, Director of Admissions, American University, 4400 Massachusetts Avenue, NW, Washington, DC 20016-8001. *Phone:* 202-885-6000. *E-mail:* admissions@american.edu. *Website:* http://www.american.edu/.

The Catholic University of America
Washington, District of Columbia

- **Independent** university, founded 1887, affiliated with Roman Catholic Church
- **Urban** 184-acre campus
- **Coed** 3,694 undergraduate students, 93% full-time, 55% women, 45% men
- **Moderately difficult** entrance level, 63% of applicants were admitted

Undergraduates 3,422 full-time, 272 part-time. Students come from 48 states and territories; 41 other countries; 96% are from out of state; 5% Black or African American, non-Hispanic/Latino; 9% Hispanic/Latino; 3% Asian, non-Hispanic/Latino; 0.2% Native Hawaiian or other Pacific Islander, non-Hispanic/Latino; 0.2% American Indian or Alaska Native, non-Hispanic/Latino; 3% Two or more races, non-Hispanic/Latino; 14% Race/ethnicity unknown; 4% international; 2% transferred in; 59% live on campus. *Retention:* 84% of full-time freshmen returned.

Freshmen *Admission:* 6,361 applied, 4,017 admitted, 884 enrolled. *Average high school GPA:* 3.37. *Test scores:* SAT critical reading scores over 500: 80%; SAT math scores over 500: 79%; ACT scores over 18: 98%; SAT critical reading scores over 600: 32%; SAT math scores over 600: 34%; ACT scores over 24: 59%; SAT critical reading scores over 700: 6%; SAT math scores over 700: 5%; ACT scores over 30: 10%.

Faculty *Total:* 814, 49% full-time. *Student/faculty ratio:* 9:1.

Academics *Calendar:* semesters. *Degrees:* associate, bachelor's, master's, doctoral, post-master's, and postbachelor's certificates. *Special study options:* accelerated degree program, adult/continuing education programs, advanced placement credit, cooperative education, distance learning, double majors, English as a second language, honors programs, independent study, internships, off-campus study, part-time degree program, services for LD students, study abroad, summer session for credit. *ROTC:* Army (c), Navy (c), Air Force (c). *Unusual degree programs:* 3-2 engineering; nursing; architecture, accounting, education, psychology.

Computers on Campus 500 computers/terminals and 50 ports are available on campus for general student use. Students can access the following: campus intranet, computer help desk, free student e-mail accounts, online (class) grades, online (class) registration, online (class) schedules, Internet2, video streaming, online voting, pedagogical software. Campuswide network is available. 100% of college-owned or -operated housing units are wired for high-speed Internet access. Wireless service is available via classrooms, computer centers, computer labs, libraries, student centers.

Student Life *Housing:* on-campus residence required through sophomore year. *Options:* coed, men-only, women-only, disabled students. Campus housing is university owned. Freshman campus housing is guaranteed. *Activities and organizations:* drama/theater group, student-run newspaper, radio station, choral group, Student Nursing Association, College Republicans, CU Film Society, Alpha Phi Omega, Program Board, national fraternities, national sororities. *Campus security:* 24-hour emergency response devices and patrols, late-night transport/escort service, controlled dormitory access, controlled access of academic buildings. *Student services:* health clinic, personal/psychological counseling, legal services.

Athletics Member NCAA. All Division III. *Intercollegiate sports:* baseball M, basketball M/W, cross-country running M/W, field hockey W, football M, lacrosse M/W, soccer M/W, softball W, swimming and diving M/W, tennis M/W, track and field M/W, volleyball W. *Intramural sports:* basketball M/W, cheerleading M(c)/W(c), crew M(c)/W(c), fencing M(c)/W(c), football M/W, ice hockey M(c), rugby M(c)/W(c), sailing M(c)/W(c), soccer M/W, softball M/W, tennis M/W, ultimate Frisbee M(c)/W(c), volleyball M/W.

Standardized Tests *Required:* SAT or ACT (for admission). *Recommended:* SAT Subject Tests (for admission).

Costs (2012–13) *One-time required fee:* $425. *Comprehensive fee:* $51,094 includes full-time tuition ($36,320), mandatory fees ($500), and room and board ($14,274). Full-time tuition and fees vary according to program. Part-time tuition: $1420 per credit hour. Part-time tuition and fees vary according to course load and program. *Required fees:* $290 per year part-time. *College room only:* $8876. Room and board charges vary according to board plan and housing facility. *Payment plan:* installment. *Waivers:* employees or children of employees.

Financial Aid Of all full-time matriculated undergraduates who enrolled in 2012, 2,373 applied for aid, 2,071 were judged to have need, 866 had their need fully met. 289 Federal Work-Study jobs (averaging $1892). In 2012, 965 non-need-based awards were made. *Average percent of need met:* 77%. *Average financial aid package:* $22,879. *Average need-based loan:* $4680. *Average need-based gift aid:* $19,076. *Average non-need-based aid:* $13,666. *Financial aid deadline:* 4/10.

Applying *Options:* electronic application, early action, deferred entrance. *Application fee:* $55. *Required:* essay or personal statement, high school transcript, 1 letter of recommendation. *Required for some:* interview. *Recommended:* minimum 3.0 GPA. *Application deadlines:* 2/15 (freshmen), 7/15 (transfers), 11/15 (early action). *Notification:* 3/15 (freshmen), 12/15 (early action).

Freshman Application Contact Ms. Christine Mica, Dean, University Admissions, The Catholic University of America, 102 McMahon Hall, 620 Michigan Avenue, NE, Washington, DC 20064. *Phone:* 202-319-5305. *Toll-free phone:* 800-673-2772. *Fax:* 202-319-6533. *E-mail:* cua-admissions@cua.edu. *Website:* http://www.cua.edu/.

Corcoran College of Art and Design
Washington, District of Columbia

- **Independent** comprehensive, founded 1890
- **Urban** 7-acre campus with easy access to Washington, DC
- **Endowment** $19.2 million
- **Coed** 386 undergraduate students, 69% full-time, 68% women, 32% men
- **Moderately difficult** entrance level, 31% of applicants were admitted

Undergraduates 268 full-time, 118 part-time. Students come from 21 states and territories; 32 other countries; 79% are from out of state; 10% Black or African American, non-Hispanic/Latino; 10% Hispanic/Latino; 8% Asian, non-Hispanic/Latino; 0.5% Native Hawaiian or other Pacific Islander, non-Hispanic/Latino; 0.5% American Indian or Alaska Native, non-Hispanic/Latino; 2% Two or more races, non-Hispanic/Latino; 8% Race/ethnicity unknown; 6% international; 8% transferred in; 20% live on campus. *Retention:* 87% of full-time freshmen returned.

Freshmen *Admission:* 609 applied, 189 admitted, 49 enrolled. *Average high school GPA:* 3.1.

Faculty *Total:* 214, 12% full-time, 81% with terminal degrees. *Student/faculty ratio:* 10:1.

Academics *Calendar:* semesters. *Degrees:* certificates, associate, bachelor's, and master's. *Special study options:* academic remediation for entering students, adult/continuing education programs, advanced placement credit, independent study, internships, off-campus study, part-time degree program, services for LD students, study abroad, summer session for credit. *Unusual degree programs:* 3-2 BFA/MAT Art Education.

Computers on Campus 154 computers/terminals are available on campus for general student use. Students can access the following: campus intranet, computer help desk, free student e-mail accounts, online (class) grades, online (class) schedules. 100% of college-owned or -operated housing units are wired for high-speed Internet access. Wireless service is available via classrooms, computer centers, computer labs, dorm rooms, libraries.

Student Life *Housing options:* coed. Campus housing is leased by the school. Freshman applicants given priority for college housing. *Activities and organizations:* Student Activities Programming Board, American Society of Interior Designers, National Art Education Association, Corcoran Student Council, Society of Environmental Designers. *Campus security:* 24-hour emergency response devices and patrols, controlled dormitory access, ID check at all entrances. *Student services:* personal/psychological counseling.

Standardized Tests *Recommended:* SAT or ACT (for admission).

Costs (2013–14) *Comprehensive fee:* $44,030 includes full-time tuition ($30,930), mandatory fees ($200), and room and board ($12,900). Part-time tuition and fees vary according to course load and degree level. *College room only:* $10,400. *Payment plan:* installment. *Waivers:* employees or children of employees.

Financial Aid Of all full-time matriculated undergraduates who enrolled in 2010, 258 applied for aid, 258 were judged to have need. 58 Federal Work-Study jobs (averaging $1686). In 2010, 71 non-need-based awards were made. *Average percent of need met:* 27%. *Average financial aid package:* $19,573. *Average need-based loan:* $4042. *Average need-based gift aid:* $8974. *Average non-need-based aid:* $7324. *Average indebtedness upon graduation:* $35,562.

Applying *Options:* electronic application, early admission, early action, deferred entrance. *Application fee:* $45. *Required:* high school transcript, minimum 2.5 GPA, portfolio. *Required for some:* essay or personal statement, 1 letter of recommendation, interview. *Recommended:* essay or personal statement, minimum 3.0 GPA, 1 letter of recommendation, interview. *Application deadlines:* rolling (freshmen), rolling (transfers), 11/15 (early action). *Notification:* continuous until 3/15 (freshmen), continuous until 3/15 (transfers), 12/15 (early action).

Freshman Application Contact Corcoran College of Art and Design, 500 17th Street NW, Washington, DC 20006-4804. *Phone:* 202-639-1864. *Toll-free phone:* 888-CORCORAN.

Website: http://www.corcoran.edu/.

Gallaudet University
Washington, District of Columbia

- **Independent** university, founded 1864
- **Urban** 99-acre campus
- **Coed** 1,118 undergraduate students, 92% full-time, 54% women, 46% men
- **Moderately difficult** entrance level, 69% of applicants were admitted

Undergraduates 1,029 full-time, 89 part-time. Students come from 47 states and territories; 21 other countries; 96% are from out of state; 11% Black or African American, non-Hispanic/Latino; 8% Hispanic/Latino; 4% Asian, non-Hispanic/Latino; 0.1% Native Hawaiian or other Pacific Islander, non-Hispanic/Latino; 0.3% American Indian or Alaska Native, non-Hispanic/Latino; 6% Two or more races, non-Hispanic/Latino; 0.9% Race/ethnicity unknown; 5% international; 9% transferred in. *Retention:* 70% of full-time freshmen returned.

Freshmen *Admission:* 413 applied, 284 admitted, 201 enrolled. *Test scores:* ACT scores over 18: 42%; ACT scores over 24: 15%; ACT scores over 30: 2%.

Faculty *Total:* 185, 100% full-time, 89% with terminal degrees. *Student/faculty ratio:* 8:1.

Academics *Calendar:* semesters. *Degrees:* bachelor's, master's, doctoral, post-master's, and postbachelor's certificates (undergraduate programs are open primarily to the students with hearing-impairments). *Special study options:* academic remediation for entering students, accelerated degree program, adult/continuing education programs, advanced placement credit, distance learning, double majors, English as a second language, honors programs, independent study, internships, off-campus study, part-time degree program, services for LD students, student-designed majors, study abroad, summer session for credit.

Computers on Campus Students can access the following: campus intranet, computer help desk, free student e-mail accounts, online (class) grades, online (class) registration, online (class) schedules. Campuswide network is available.

Student Life *Housing options:* coed, disabled students. Campus housing is university owned. *Activities and organizations:* drama/theater group, student-run newspaper, Student Body Government, Delta Epsilon, Rainbow Society, Black Deaf Student Union, national fraternities, national sororities. *Campus security:* 24-hour emergency response devices and patrols, late-night transport/escort service, controlled dormitory access. *Student services:* health clinic, personal/psychological counseling.

Athletics Member NCAA. All Division III. *Intercollegiate sports:* baseball M, basketball M/W, cross-country running M/W, football M, soccer M/W, softball W, swimming and diving M/W, track and field M/W, volleyball M(c)/W. *Intramural sports:* basketball M/W, football M/W, soccer M, softball W.

Standardized Tests *Required:* SAT or ACT (for admission). *Recommended:* ACT (for admission).

Costs (2012–13) *Comprehensive fee:* $23,596 includes full-time tuition ($12,430), mandatory fees ($376), and room and board ($10,790). Full-time tuition and fees vary according to degree level. Part-time tuition: $622 per credit hour. Part-time tuition and fees vary according to degree level. *College room only:* $5960. Room and board charges vary according to board plan. *Payment plans:* installment, deferred payment. *Waivers:* employees or children of employees.

Financial Aid Of all full-time matriculated undergraduates who enrolled in 2012, 940 applied for aid, 863 were judged to have need, 227 had their need fully met. 20 Federal Work-Study jobs (averaging $1560). In 2012, 50 non-need-based awards were made. *Average percent of need met:* 76%. *Average financial aid package:* $19,287. *Average need-based loan:* $4034. *Average need-based gift aid:* $17,124. *Average non-need-based aid:* $16,569. *Average indebtedness upon graduation:* $10,347.

Applying *Options:* electronic application, deferred entrance. *Application fee:* $50. *Required:* essay or personal statement, high school transcript, 2 letters of recommendation, audiogram. *Required for some:* interview. *Application deadline:* rolling (freshmen). *Notification:* continuous (freshmen), continuous (transfers).

Freshman Application Contact Gallaudet University, 800 Florida Avenue, NE, Washington, DC 20002-3625. *Phone:* 202-651-5750. *Toll-free phone:* 800-995-0550.

Website: http://www.gallaudet.edu/.

Georgetown University
Washington, District of Columbia

- **Independent Roman Catholic (Jesuit)** university, founded 1789
- **Urban** 110-acre campus
- **Coed** 7,552 undergraduate students, 96% full-time, 56% women, 44% men
- **Most difficult** entrance level, 17% of applicants were admitted

Undergraduates 7,242 full-time, 310 part-time. Students come from 52 states and territories; 106 other countries; 97% are from out of state; 6% Black or African American, non-Hispanic/Latino; 8% Hispanic/Latino; 9% Asian, non-Hispanic/Latino; 0.1% Native Hawaiian or other Pacific Islander, non-Hispanic/Latino; 0.1% American Indian or Alaska Native, non-Hispanic/Latino; 3% Two or more races, non-Hispanic/Latino; 3% Race/ethnicity unknown; 11% international; 2% transferred in; 71% live on campus. *Retention:* 96% of full-time freshmen returned.

Freshmen *Admission:* 20,115 applied, 3,413 admitted, 1,570 enrolled. *Test scores:* SAT critical reading scores over 500: 99%; SAT math scores over 500: 99%; ACT scores over 18: 100%; SAT critical reading scores over 600: 90%; SAT math scores over 600: 92%; ACT scores over 24: 98%; SAT critical reading scores over 700: 57%; SAT math scores over 700: 56%; ACT scores over 30: 73%.

Faculty *Total:* 1,757, 55% full-time, 72% with terminal degrees. *Student/faculty ratio:* 11:1.

Academics *Calendar:* semesters. *Degrees:* certificates, bachelor's, master's, and doctoral. *Special study options:* academic remediation for entering students, adult/continuing education programs, advanced placement credit, distance learning, double majors, English as a second language, honors programs, independent study, internships, off-campus study, services for LD students, student-designed majors, study abroad, summer session for credit. *ROTC:* Army (b), Navy (c), Air Force (c). *Unusual degree programs:* 3-2 foreign service.

Computers on Campus Students can access the following: computer help desk, free student e-mail accounts, online (class) registration, online grade reports. Campuswide network is available. Wireless service is available via classrooms, computer centers, computer labs, dorm rooms, learning centers, libraries, student centers.

Student Life *Housing:* on-campus residence required through sophomore year. *Options:* coed, disabled students. Campus housing is university owned. Freshman campus housing is guaranteed. *Activities and organizations:* drama/theater group, student-run newspaper, radio and television station, choral group. *Campus security:* 24-hour emergency response devices and patrols, late-night transport/escort service, controlled dormitory access, student guards at residence halls and academic facilities. *Student services:* health clinic, personal/psychological counseling, women's center.

Athletics Member NCAA. All Division I except football (Division I-AA). *Intercollegiate sports:* baseball M(s), basketball M(s)/W(s), crew M/W, cross-country running M(s)/W(s), field hockey W, golf M(s), ice hockey M(c), lacrosse M(s)/W(s), rugby M(c)/W(c), sailing M/W, soccer M(s)/W(s), softball W(s), swimming and diving M/W, tennis M/W(s), track and field M(s)/W(s), ultimate Frisbee M(c)/W(c), volleyball M(c)/W(s), water polo M(c). *Intramural sports:* basketball M/W, cross-country running M/W, football M/W, golf M/W, racquetball M/W, soccer M/W, softball M/W, squash M/W, table tennis M/W, tennis M/W, track and field M/W, ultimate Frisbee M, volleyball M/W.

Standardized Tests *Required:* SAT or ACT (for admission). *Recommended:* SAT Subject Tests (for admission).

Costs (2012–13) *Comprehensive fee:* $56,382 includes full-time tuition ($42,360), mandatory fees ($710), and room and board ($13,312). Full-time tuition and fees vary according to course load and program. Part-time tuition and fees vary according to course load and program. *Room and board:* Room and board charges vary according to board plan and housing facility. *Payment plan:* installment.

Financial Aid Of all full-time matriculated undergraduates who enrolled in 2011, 4,150 applied for aid, 2,931 were judged to have need, 2,931 had their need fully met. 1,900 Federal Work-Study jobs (averaging $2630). *Average percent of need met:* 100%. *Average financial aid package:* $33,566. *Average need-based loan:* $4394. *Average need-based gift aid:* $31,830. *Average indebtedness upon graduation:* $28,035. *Financial aid deadline:* 2/1.

Applying *Options:* electronic application, early action, deferred entrance. *Application fee:* $70. *Required:* essay or personal statement, high school transcript, 2 letters of recommendation, interview. *Application deadlines:* 1/10 (freshmen), 3/1 (transfers), 11/1 (early action). *Notification:* 4/1 (freshmen), 6/1 (transfers), 12/15 (early action).

Freshman Application Contact Mr. Charles A. Deacon, Dean of Undergraduate Admissions, Georgetown University, 37th and O Street, NW, Washington, DC 20057. *Phone:* 202-687-3600. *Fax:* 202-687-5084. *Website:* http://www.georgetown.edu/.

The George Washington University
Washington, District of Columbia

- **Independent** university, founded 1821
- **Urban** 36-acre campus
- **Endowment** $1.6 billion
- **Coed**
- **Very difficult** entrance level

Faculty *Student/faculty ratio:* 14:1.

Academics *Calendar:* semesters. *Degrees:* certificates, associate, bachelor's, master's, doctoral, post-master's, and postbachelor's certificates.

Student Life *Campus security:* 24-hour emergency response devices and patrols, late-night transport/escort service, controlled dormitory access.

Athletics Member NCAA. All Division I.

Standardized Tests *Required:* SAT or ACT (for admission).

Costs (2012–13) *Comprehensive fee:* $56,310 includes full-time tuition ($45,735), mandatory fees ($45), and room and board ($10,530). Full-time tuition and fees vary according to student level. Part-time tuition: $1272 per credit hour. Part-time tuition and fees vary according to course load. No tuition increase for student's term of enrollment. *Required fees:* $150 per credit hour part-time. *College room only:* $7130. Room and board charges vary according to housing facility.

Financial Aid *Of all full-time matriculated undergraduates who enrolled in 2011,* 5,313 applied for aid, 4,509 were judged to have need, 3,119 had their need fully met. *In 2011,* 1310 non-need-based awards were made. *Average percent of need met:* 90. *Average financial aid package:* $39,558. *Average need-based loan:* $5725. *Average need-based gift aid:* $27,270. *Average non-need-based aid:* $15,510. *Average indebtedness upon graduation:* $32,714. *Financial aid deadline:* 2/1.

Applying *Options:* electronic application, early admission, early decision, deferred entrance. *Application fee:* $75. *Required:* essay or personal statement, high school transcript, 2 letters of recommendation. *Recommended:* interview.

Freshman Application Contact The George Washington University, 2121 I Street, NW, Washington, DC 20052. *Phone:* 202-994-6040. *Website:* http://www.gwu.edu/.

See page 1306 for the College Close-Up.

Howard University
Washington, District of Columbia

Director of Admissions Ms. Linda Sanders-Hawkins, Interim Director of Admissions, Howard University, 2400 Sixth Street, NW, Washington, DC 20059-0002. *Phone:* 202-806-2700. *Toll-free phone:* 800-822-6363. *Fax:* 202-806-4467. *E-mail:* lsanders-hawkins@howard.edu. *Website:* http://www.howard.edu/.

Potomac College
Washington, District of Columbia

- **Proprietary** 4-year, founded 1991
- **Urban** campus with easy access to Washington, DC
- **Coed** 298 undergraduate students, 85% full-time, 57% women, 43% men
- **Noncompetitive** entrance level, 100% of applicants were admitted

Undergraduates 253 full-time, 45 part-time. Students come from 29 states and territories; 60% Black or African American, non-Hispanic/Latino; 6% Hispanic/Latino; 1% Asian, non-Hispanic/Latino; 0.3% American Indian or Alaska Native, non-Hispanic/Latino; 21% Race/ethnicity unknown; 0.3% international. *Retention:* 88% of full-time freshmen returned.

Freshmen *Admission:* 81 applied, 81 admitted, 62 enrolled.

Faculty *Total:* 38, 13% full-time, 11% with terminal degrees. *Student/faculty ratio:* 10:1.

Academics *Calendar:* 6-week modules. *Degrees:* associate, bachelor's, and master's. *Special study options:* adult/continuing education programs, distance learning, external degree program, honors programs, independent study, part-time degree program, services for LD students.

Computers on Campus 28 computers/terminals are available on campus for general student use. Students can access the following: campus intranet, free student e-mail accounts, online (class) grades, online (class) schedules, Student Portal and access to Course Management System. Wireless service is available via entire campus.

Student Life *Housing:* college housing not available. *Campus security:* late-night transport/escort service.

Costs (2013–14) *Tuition:* $11,760 full-time, $490 per credit part-time. No tuition increase for student's term of enrollment. *Required fees:* $450 full-time, $450 per term part-time.

Applying *Options:* electronic application. *Required:* interview. *Application deadlines:* rolling (freshmen), rolling (transfers). *Notification:* continuous (freshmen), continuous (transfers).

Freshman Application Contact Danny Carrasco, Director of Admissions, Potomac College, 4000 Chesapeake Street, NW, Washington, DC 20016. *Phone:* 602-734-4357. *Toll-free phone:* 888-686-0876. *E-mail:* admissions@potomac.edu. *Website:* http://www.potomac.edu/.

Strayer University—Takoma Park Campus
Washington, District of Columbia

Freshman Application Contact Strayer University—Takoma Park Campus, 6830 Laurel Street, NW, Washington, DC 20012. *Website:* http://www.strayer.edu/campus/takoma-park.

Strayer University—Washington Campus
Washington, District of Columbia

Freshman Application Contact Strayer University—Washington Campus, 1133 15th Street, NW, Washington, DC 20025. *Website:* http://www.strayer.edu/campus/washington.

Trinity Washington University
Washington, District of Columbia

Director of Admissions Director of Admissions, Trinity Washington University, 125 Michigan Avenue, NE, Washington, DC 20017-1094. *Phone:* 800-492-6882. *Toll-free phone:* 800-IWANTTC. *E-mail:* admissions@trinitydc.edu. *Website:* http://www.trinitydc.edu/.

University of Phoenix–Washington D.C. Campus
Washington, District of Columbia

Freshman Application Contact Marc Booker, Sr. Director, Office of Admissions and Evaluation, University of Phoenix–Washington D.C. Campus, 4035 South Riverpoint Parkway, Mail Stop CF-L101, Phoenix, AZ 85040. *Phone:* 602-557-4609. *Toll-free phone:* 866-766-0766. *Fax:* 480-643-1156. *Website:* http://www.phoenix.edu/.

University of the District of Columbia
Washington, District of Columbia

- **District-supported** comprehensive, founded 1976
- **Urban** 28-acre campus
- **Endowment** $36.7 million
- **Coed** 4,857 undergraduate students, 43% full-time, 62% women, 38% men
- **Noncompetitive** entrance level, 50% of applicants were admitted

Undergraduates 2,087 full-time, 2,770 part-time. Students come from 39 states and territories; 95 other countries; 20% are from out of state; 37% Black or African American, non-Hispanic/Latino; 3% Hispanic/Latino; 0.4% Asian, non-Hispanic/Latino; 0.1% American Indian or Alaska Native, non-Hispanic/Latino; 52% Race/ethnicity unknown; 6% international; 9% transferred in. *Retention:* 54% of full-time freshmen returned.

Freshmen *Admission:* 7,412 applied, 3,690 admitted, 607 enrolled. *Average high school GPA:* 2.
Faculty *Total:* 218. *Student/faculty ratio:* 13:1.
Academics *Calendar:* semesters. *Degrees:* associate, bachelor's, and master's. *Special study options:* academic remediation for entering students, accelerated degree program, adult/continuing education programs, cooperative education, English as a second language, external degree program, honors programs, internships, off-campus study, part-time degree program, services for LD students, summer session for credit. *ROTC:* Army (c), Air Force (c).
Computers on Campus 1,586 computers/terminals are available on campus for general student use. Students can access the following: campus intranet, computer help desk, free student e-mail accounts, online (class) grades, online (class) registration, online (class) schedules. Campuswide network is available. Wireless service is available via classrooms, computer labs, learning centers, libraries.
Student Life *Housing options:* Campus housing is leased by the school. *Activities and organizations:* drama/theater group, student-run newspaper, choral group, marching band, Caribbean Student Association, Theater Arts Ensemble, National Association for the Advancement of Colored People, national fraternities, national sororities. *Campus security:* 24-hour emergency response devices and patrols. *Student services:* health clinic, personal/psychological counseling.
Athletics Member NCAA. All Division II. *Intercollegiate sports:* basketball M/W, golf M(s), soccer M(s), tennis M(s)/W(s), track and field M(s)/W(s), volleyball W(s).
Standardized Tests *Recommended:* SAT (for admission).
Costs (2013–14) *Tuition:* district resident $6635 full-time, $276 per credit part-time; nonresident $13,915 full-time, $580 per credit part-time. Full-time tuition and fees vary according to course load. Part-time tuition and fees vary according to course load. *Required fees:* $620 full-time, $30 per credit part-time. *Room and board:* $6600. *Payment plans:* installment, deferred payment. *Waivers:* senior citizens and employees or children of employees.
Financial Aid Of all full-time matriculated undergraduates who enrolled in 2011, 2,160 applied for aid, 1,965 were judged to have need, 789 had their need fully met. 87 Federal Work-Study jobs (averaging $2500). 92 state and other part-time jobs (averaging $2500). In 2011, 141 non-need-based awards were made. *Average percent of need met:* 98%. *Average financial aid package:* $5600. *Average need-based loan:* $2750. *Average need-based gift aid:* $3275. *Average non-need-based aid:* $2750.
Applying *Options:* electronic application, deferred entrance. *Application fee:* $35. *Required:* high school transcript. *Required for some:* GED. *Application deadlines:* 8/1 (freshmen), 8/1 (transfers). *Notification:* continuous until 8/15 (freshmen), continuous until 8/15 (transfers).
Freshman Application Contact Ms. Saundra M Carter, Acting Director, University of the District of Columbia, 4200 Connecticut Ave. NW, Washington, DC 20008. *Phone:* 202-274-6110. *Fax:* 202-274-5553. *E-mail:* scarter@udc.edu.
Website: http://www.udc.edu/.

FLORIDA

Adventist University of Health Sciences
Orlando, Florida

- **Independent** comprehensive, founded 1913
- **Urban** 9-acre campus with easy access to Orlando
- **Endowment** $6.0 million
- **Coed** 2,576 undergraduate students, 23% full-time, 80% women, 20% men
- **Minimally difficult** entrance level, 96% of applicants were admitted

Undergraduates 594 full-time, 1,982 part-time. Students come from 52 states and territories; 35% are from out of state; 15% Black or African American, non-Hispanic/Latino; 19% Hispanic/Latino; 5% Asian, non-Hispanic/Latino; 0.5% Native Hawaiian or other Pacific Islander, non-Hispanic/Latino; 0.5% American Indian or Alaska Native, non-Hispanic/Latino; 2% Two or more races, non-Hispanic/Latino; 8% Race/ethnicity unknown; 0.8% international; 24% transferred in.
Freshmen *Admission:* 358 applied, 344 admitted, 96 enrolled. *Test scores:* SAT critical reading scores over 500: 16%; ACT scores over 18: 33%; SAT critical reading scores over 600: 3%; ACT scores over 24: 1%; SAT critical reading scores over 700: 1%.
Faculty *Total:* 252, 25% full-time, 16% with terminal degrees.

Academics *Calendar:* semesters. *Degrees:* associate, bachelor's, and master's. *Special study options:* academic remediation for entering students, advanced placement credit, distance learning, independent study, services for LD students. *ROTC:* Air Force (c).
Computers on Campus 43 computers/terminals are available on campus for general student use. Students can access the following: campus intranet, computer help desk, free student e-mail accounts, online (class) grades, online (class) registration, online (class) schedules, Online registration. Campuswide network is available. Wireless service is available via entire campus.
Student Life *Housing options:* coed. Campus housing is leased by the school. *Activities and organizations:* drama/theater group, student-run newspaper. *Campus security:* 24-hour emergency response devices and patrols, late-night transport/escort service, controlled dormitory access. *Student services:* personal/psychological counseling.
Standardized Tests *Required for some:* SAT or ACT (for admission).
Financial Aid *Financial aid deadline:* 7/22.
Applying *Options:* electronic application. *Application fee:* $20. *Required:* minimum 2.7 GPA. *Required for some:* essay or personal statement, high school transcript, 3 letters of recommendation. *Application deadlines:* 7/1 (freshmen), 7/1 (out-of-state freshmen), 7/1 (transfers). *Notification:* continuous until 8/30 (freshmen), continuous until 8/30 (out-of-state freshmen), continuous until 8/30 (transfers).
Freshman Application Contact Adventist University of Health Sciences, 671 Winyah Drive, Orlando, FL 32803. *Phone:* 407-303-7742. *Toll-free phone:* 800-500-7747.
Website: http://www.adu.edu/.

American InterContinental University South Florida
Weston, Florida

Freshman Application Contact American InterContinental University South Florida, 2250 North Commerce Parkway, Suite 100, Weston, FL 33326. *Phone:* 877-564-6248. *Toll-free phone:* 888-603-4888. *Fax:* 877-564-6248. *Website:* http://www.aiuniv.edu/.

Argosy University, Sarasota
Sarasota, Florida

Freshman Application Contact Argosy University, Sarasota, 5250 17th Street, Sarasota, FL 34235. *Phone:* 941-379-0404. *Toll-free phone:* 800-331-5995.
Website: http://www.argosy.edu/sarasota/.

Argosy University, Tampa
Tampa, Florida

Freshman Application Contact Argosy University, Tampa, 1403 North Howard Avenue, Tampa, FL 33607. *Phone:* 813-393-5290. *Toll-free phone:* 800-850-6488.
Website: http://www.argosy.edu/tampa/.

The Art Institute of Fort Lauderdale
Fort Lauderdale, Florida

- **Proprietary** 4-year, founded 1968, part of Education Management Corporation
- **Urban** campus
- **Coed**

Academics *Calendar:* quarters. *Degrees:* diplomas, associate, and bachelor's.
Freshman Application Contact The Art Institute of Fort Lauderdale, 1799 Southeast 17th Street, Fort Lauderdale, FL 33316. *Phone:* 954-463-3000. *Toll-free phone:* 800-275-7603.
Website: http://www.artinstitutes.edu/fortlauderdale/.

See full-page ad on page 54 and page 1080 for the College Close-Up.

The Art Institute of Jacksonville
Jacksonville, Florida

- **Proprietary** 4-year, founded 2006, part of Education Management Corporation
- **Suburban** campus
- **Coed**

Academics *Degrees:* diplomas, associate, and bachelor's.

Freshman Application Contact The Art Institute of Jacksonville, 8775 Baypine Road, Jacksonville, FL 32256. *Phone:* 904-486-3000. *Toll-free phone:* 800-924-1589.
Website: http://www.artinstitutes.edu/jacksonville/.

See full-page ad on page 54 and page 1090 for the College Close-Up.

The Art Institute of Tampa
Tampa, Florida

- **Proprietary** 4-year, part of Education Management Corporation
- **Suburban** campus
- **Coed**

Academics *Calendar:* quarters. *Degrees:* diplomas, associate, and bachelor's.
Freshman Application Contact The Art Institute of Tampa, Parkside at Tampa Bay Park, 4401 North Himes Avenue, Suite 150, Tampa, FL 33614. *Phone:* 813-873-2112. *Toll-free phone:* 866-703-3277.
Website: http://www.artinstitutes.edu/tampa/.

See full-page ad on page 54 and page 1118 for the College Close-Up.

Ave Maria University
Ave Maria, Florida

Freshman Application Contact Ave Maria University, 5050 Ave Maria Boulevard, Ave Maria, FL 34142. *Phone:* 239-280-2487. *Toll-free phone:* 877-283-8648. *Fax:* 239-280-2559.
Website: http://www.avemaria.edu/.

The Baptist College of Florida
Graceville, Florida

- **Independent Southern Baptist** comprehensive, founded 1943
- **Small-town** 250-acre campus
- **Endowment** $5.8 million
- **Coed** 596 undergraduate students, 73% full-time, 39% women, 61% men
- **Noncompetitive** entrance level, 40% of applicants were admitted

Undergraduates 438 full-time, 158 part-time. Students come from 20 states and territories; 37% are from out of state; 6% Black or African American, non-Hispanic/Latino; 3% Hispanic/Latino; 0.2% Asian, non-Hispanic/Latino; 0.2% American Indian or Alaska Native, non-Hispanic/Latino; 1% Two or more races, non-Hispanic/Latino; 9% Race/ethnicity unknown; 12% transferred in; 44% live on campus. *Retention:* 82% of full-time freshmen returned.
Freshmen *Admission:* 162 applied, 65 admitted, 63 enrolled.
Faculty *Total:* 63, 41% full-time, 57% with terminal degrees. *Student/faculty ratio:* 13:1.
Academics *Calendar:* semesters. *Degrees:* associate, bachelor's, and master's. *Special study options:* academic remediation for entering students, advanced placement credit, distance learning, double majors, independent study, internships, part-time degree program, services for LD students, summer session for credit.
Computers on Campus 25 computers/terminals are available on campus for general student use. Students can access the following: free student e-mail accounts, online (class) grades, online (class) registration. Campuswide network is available. Wireless service is available via entire campus.
Student Life *Housing:* on-campus residence required through sophomore year. *Options:* men-only, women-only, disabled students. Campus housing is university owned. Freshman campus housing is guaranteed. *Activities and organizations:* drama/theater group, student-run radio station, choral group, Baptist Collegiate Ministry, College Choir, AACC. *Campus security:* student patrols, patrols by police officers 11 pm to 7 am. *Student services:* personal/psychological counseling.
Athletics Member NCCAA. *Intercollegiate sports:* golf M, volleyball W. *Intramural sports:* basketball M/W, football M/W, soccer M/W, softball M/W, table tennis M/W, tennis M/W, ultimate Frisbee M/W, volleyball M/W.
Standardized Tests *Required:* SAT or ACT (for admission).
Costs (2012–13) *Comprehensive fee:* $13,538 includes full-time tuition ($9000), mandatory fees ($400), and room and board ($4138). Part-time tuition: $300 per credit hour. *Room and board:* Room and board charges vary according to board plan and housing facility. *Waivers:* employees or children of employees.
Financial Aid Of all full-time matriculated undergraduates who enrolled in 2012, 738 applied for aid, 491 were judged to have need, 20 had their need fully met. 22 Federal Work-Study jobs (averaging $2306). In 2012, 12 non-need-based awards were made. *Average percent of need met:* 36%. *Average financial aid package:* $7444. *Average need-based loan:* $3488. *Average need-based gift aid:* $5177. *Average non-need-based aid:* $1750. *Average indebtedness upon graduation:* $22,803. *Financial aid deadline:* 4/15.

Applying *Options:* electronic application, deferred entrance. *Application fee:* $25. *Required:* essay or personal statement, high school transcript, 2 letters of recommendation, Christian/Church Member for 1 year minimum. *Recommended:* interview. *Application deadlines:* 8/11 (freshmen), 8/11 (transfers). *Notification:* continuous (freshmen), continuous (transfers).
Freshman Application Contact The Baptist College of Florida, 5400 College Drive, Graceville, FL 32440-1898. *Phone:* 850-263-3261 Ext. 460. *Toll-free phone:* 800-328-2660 Ext. 460.
Website: http://www.baptistcollege.edu/.

Barry University
Miami Shores, Florida

- **Independent Roman Catholic** university, founded 1940
- **Suburban** 122-acre campus with easy access to Miami
- **Endowment** $29.7 million
- **Coed** 4,619 undergraduate students, 83% full-time, 63% women, 37% men
- **Moderately difficult** entrance level, 52% of applicants were admitted

Undergraduates 3,824 full-time, 795 part-time. 19% Black or African American, non-Hispanic/Latino; 17% Hispanic/Latino; 0.9% Asian, non-Hispanic/Latino; 0.1% Native Hawaiian or other Pacific Islander, non-Hispanic/Latino; 0.3% American Indian or Alaska Native, non-Hispanic/Latino; 43% Race/ethnicity unknown; 7% international; 8% transferred in. *Retention:* 62% of full-time freshmen returned.
Freshmen *Admission:* 7,645 applied, 3,966 admitted, 625 enrolled. *Average high school GPA:* 0. *Test scores:* SAT critical reading scores over 500: 35%; SAT math scores over 500: 32%; SAT critical reading scores over 600: 7%; SAT math scores over 600: 7%.
Faculty *Total:* 838, 44% full-time. *Student/faculty ratio:* 12:1.
Academics *Calendar:* semesters. *Degrees:* certificates, bachelor's, master's, doctoral, post-master's, and postbachelor's certificates. *Special study options:* academic remediation for entering students, accelerated degree program, adult/continuing education programs, advanced placement credit, distance learning, double majors, English as a second language, honors programs, independent study, internships, off-campus study, part-time degree program, services for LD students, study abroad, summer session for credit. *ROTC:* Army (c), Air Force (c). *Unusual degree programs:* 3-2 engineering with University of Miami.
Computers on Campus 368 computers/terminals are available on campus for general student use. Students can access the following: campus intranet, computer help desk, free student e-mail accounts, online (class) grades, online (class) registration, online (class) schedules, Blackboard. Campuswide network is available. Wireless service is available via computer centers, computer labs, learning centers, student centers.
Student Life *Housing:* on-campus residence required for freshman year. *Options:* coed, men-only, women-only, disabled students. Campus housing is university owned. *Activities and organizations:* drama/theater group, student-run newspaper, radio and television station, choral group, Student Government Association, Campus Activities Board, SCUBA Society, Caribbean Students Association, Jamaican Association, national fraternities, national sororities. *Campus security:* 24-hour emergency response devices and patrols, late-night transport/escort service. *Student services:* health clinic, personal/psychological counseling.
Athletics Member NCAA. All Division II. *Intercollegiate sports:* baseball M(s), basketball M(s)/W(s), crew W(s), golf M(s)/W(s), soccer M(s)/W(s), softball W(s), tennis M(s)/W(s), volleyball W(s). *Intramural sports:* basketball M/W, football M/W, golf M/W, soccer M/W, softball M/W, volleyball M/W.
Standardized Tests *Required:* SAT or ACT (for admission).
Costs (2013–14) *Tuition:* $28,160 full-time. Part-time tuition and fees vary according to course load. *Room only:* $11,988. Room and board charges vary according to board plan.
Financial Aid Of all full-time matriculated undergraduates who enrolled in 2012, 3,352 applied for aid, 3,219 were judged to have need, 155 had their need fully met. In 2012, 65 non-need-based awards were made. *Average percent of need met:* 52%. *Average financial aid package:* $19,074. *Average need-based loan:* $4644. *Average need-based gift aid:* $7083. *Average non-need-based aid:* $10,293. *Average indebtedness upon graduation:* $38,634.
Applying *Options:* electronic application, early admission, deferred entrance. *Application fee:* $30. *Required:* high school transcript, minimum 2.0 GPA. *Required for some:* essay or personal statement. *Recommended:* interview. *Application deadlines:* rolling (freshmen), rolling (transfers). *Notification:* continuous (freshmen), continuous (transfers).
Freshman Application Contact Barry University, 11300 Northeast Second Avenue, Miami Shores, FL 33161-6695. *Phone:* 305-899-3051. *Toll-free phone:* 800-695-2279.
Website: http://www.barry.edu/.

See next page for display ad and page 1150 for the College Close-Up.

Beacon College

Leesburg, Florida

- **Independent** 4-year, founded 1989
- **Small-town** 5-acre campus with easy access to Orlando
- **Endowment** $50,000
- **Coed** 184 undergraduate students, 99% full-time, 33% women, 67% men
- **Moderately difficult** entrance level, 36% of applicants were admitted

Undergraduates 182 full-time, 2 part-time. Students come from 31 states and territories; 4 other countries; 72% are from out of state; 13% Black or African American, non-Hispanic/Latino; 6% Hispanic/Latino; 2% Asian, non-Hispanic/Latino; 0.5% Native Hawaiian or other Pacific Islander, non-Hispanic/Latino; 0.5% American Indian or Alaska Native, non-Hispanic/Latino; 0.5% Two or more races, non-Hispanic/Latino; 3% international; 11% transferred in; 86% live on campus. *Retention:* 80% of full-time freshmen returned.

Freshmen *Admission:* 138 applied, 50 admitted, 39 enrolled. *Average high school GPA:* 2.9.

Faculty *Total:* 24, 58% full-time, 50% with terminal degrees. *Student/faculty ratio:* 11:1.

Academics *Calendar:* semesters. *Degrees:* associate and bachelor's. *Special study options:* academic remediation for entering students, adult/continuing education programs, advanced placement credit, cooperative education, double majors, independent study, internships, services for LD students, summer session for credit.

Computers on Campus 72 computers/terminals and 288 ports are available on campus for general student use. Students can access the following: campus intranet, computer help desk, free student e-mail accounts, online (class) grades, online (class) schedules. Campuswide network is available. 100% of college-owned or -operated housing units are wired for high-speed Internet access. Wireless service is available via classrooms, computer centers, computer labs, dorm rooms, learning centers, libraries, student centers.

Student Life *Housing options:* coed. Campus housing is university owned and leased by the school. Freshman campus housing is guaranteed. *Activities and organizations:* drama/theater group, student-run newspaper, Florida Christian Athletes, Performance Club, Theater Goers Club, Camping Club, Beach Goers Club. *Campus security:* 24-hour emergency response devices, student patrols, late-night transport/escort service. *Student services:* health clinic, personal/psychological counseling.

Standardized Tests *Recommended:* SAT or ACT (for admission).

Costs (2013–14) *Tuition:* $30,396 full-time. *Room only:* Room and board charges vary according to board plan and housing facility. *Payment plan:* installment.

Applying *Options:* early admission, deferred entrance. *Application fee:* $50. *Required:* essay or personal statement, high school transcript, 3 letters of recommendation, Psycho-educational evaluation. *Recommended:* minimum 2.5 GPA. *Application deadlines:* rolling (freshmen), rolling (transfers). *Notification:* 8/1 (freshmen), 8/1 (transfers).

Freshman Application Contact Ms. Brenda Meli, Director of Admissions, Beacon College, 105 East Main Street, Leesburg, FL 34748. *Phone:* 352-638-9732. *Fax:* 352-787-0796. *E-mail:* bmeli@beaconcollege.edu. *Website:* http://www.beaconcollege.edu/.

Belhaven University

Orlando, Florida

Director of Admissions Jeremy Couch, Director of Admission, Belhaven University, 5200 Vineland Road, Suite 100, Orlando, FL 32811. *Phone:* 407-804-1424. *Toll-free phone:* 877-804-1424. *Fax:* 407-661-1732. *E-mail:* orlando@belhaven.edu. *Website:* http://orlando.belhaven.edu/.

Bethune-Cookman University

Daytona Beach, Florida

- **Independent Methodist** comprehensive, founded 1904
- **Urban** 60-acre campus with easy access to Orlando
- **Endowment** $41.8 million
- **Coed** 3,486 undergraduate students, 96% full-time, 59% women, 41% men
- **Minimally difficult** entrance level, 73% of applicants were admitted

Undergraduates 3,348 full-time, 138 part-time. Students come from 44 states and territories; 28 other countries; 33% are from out of state; 79% Black or African American, non-Hispanic/Latino; 2% Hispanic/Latino; 0.2% Asian, non-Hispanic/Latino; 0.5% Native Hawaiian or other Pacific Islander, non-Hispanic/Latino; 0.1% American Indian or Alaska Native, non-Hispanic/Latino; 1% Two or more races, non-Hispanic/Latino; 15% Race/ethnicity unknown; 1% international; 14% transferred in; 55% live on campus. *Retention:* 64% of full-time freshmen returned.

Freshmen *Admission:* 5,380 applied, 3,953 admitted, 899 enrolled. *Average high school GPA:* 2.86. *Test scores:* SAT critical reading scores over 500: 10%; SAT math scores over 500: 11%; SAT writing scores over 500: 8%; ACT scores over 18: 32%; SAT critical reading scores over 600: 1%; SAT math scores over 600: 1%; SAT writing scores over 600: 1%; ACT scores over 24: 1%.
Faculty *Total:* 248, 72% full-time, 38% with terminal degrees. *Student/faculty ratio:* 17:1.
Academics *Calendar:* semesters. *Degrees:* bachelor's and master's. *Special study options:* academic remediation for entering students, accelerated degree program, adult/continuing education programs, advanced placement credit, cooperative education, distance learning, double majors, honors programs, independent study, internships, part-time degree program, study abroad, summer session for credit. *ROTC:* Army (c), Air Force (c). *Unusual degree programs:* 3-2 engineering with Tuskegee University, University of Florida, Florida Atlantic University, Florida Agricultural and Mechanical University, University of Central Florida.
Computers on Campus 966 computers/terminals are available on campus for general student use. Students can access the following: campus intranet, computer help desk, free student e-mail accounts, online (class) grades, online (class) registration, online (class) schedules. Campuswide network is available. 100% of college-owned or -operated housing units are wired for high-speed Internet access. Wireless service is available via entire campus.
Student Life *Housing:* on-campus residence required for freshman year. *Options:* coed, men-only, women-only. Campus housing is university owned. Freshman campus housing is guaranteed. *Activities and organizations:* drama/theater group, student-run newspaper, radio station, choral group, marching band, Concert Chorale, marching band, Inspirational Gospel Choir, Student Government Association, national fraternities, national sororities. *Campus security:* 24-hour emergency response devices and patrols, student patrols, late-night transport/escort service. *Student services:* health clinic, personal/psychological counseling.
Athletics Member NCAA. All Division I except football (Division I-AA). *Intercollegiate sports:* baseball M(s), basketball M(s)/W(s), bowling W(s), cheerleading W, cross-country running M(s)/W(s), golf M(s)/W(s), softball W(s), tennis M(s)/W(s), track and field M(s)/W(s), volleyball W(s). *Intramural sports:* basketball M/W, bowling M/W, football M, racquetball W, soccer M/W, table tennis W.
Standardized Tests *Required:* SAT or ACT (for admission).
Costs (2013–14) *Comprehensive fee:* $22,958 includes full-time tuition ($14,410) and room and board ($8548). Full-time tuition and fees vary according to course load and degree level. Part-time tuition: $600 per credit hour. Part-time tuition and fees vary according to course load and degree level. *Room and board:* Room and board charges vary according to housing facility. *Payment plan:* installment. *Waivers:* employees or children of employees.
Financial Aid Of all full-time matriculated undergraduates who enrolled in 2012, 3,279 applied for aid, 3,206 were judged to have need, 142 had their need fully met. 295 Federal Work-Study jobs (averaging $1808). 140 state and other part-time jobs (averaging $2200). In 2012, 24 non-need-based awards were made. *Average percent of need met:* 48%. *Average financial aid package:* $13,786. *Average need-based loan:* $4331. *Average need-based gift aid:* $9893. *Average non-need-based aid:* $11,062. *Average indebtedness upon graduation:* $22,175.
Applying *Options:* electronic application, early admission, deferred entrance. *Application fee:* $25. *Required:* high school transcript, minimum 2.3 GPA, 1 letter of recommendation, medical history. *Required for some:* interview. *Recommended:* essay or personal statement. *Application deadlines:* 6/30 (freshmen), 6/30 (transfers). *Notification:* continuous (freshmen), continuous (transfers).
Freshman Application Contact Mr. Reynolda Brown, Director of Admissions, Bethune-Cookman University, 640 Dr. Mary McLeod Bethune Boulevard, Daytona Beach, FL 32114-3099. *Phone:* 386-481-2600. *Toll-free phone:* 800-448-0228. *Fax:* 386-481-2601. *E-mail:* brownr@cookman.edu. *Website:* http://www.cookman.edu/.

Broward College
Fort Lauderdale, Florida

Freshman Application Contact Willie J. Alexander, Associate Vice President for Student Affairs/College Registrar, Broward College, 225 East Las Olas Boulevard, Fort Lauderdale, FL 33301. *Phone:* 954-201-7471. *Fax:* 954-201-7466. *E-mail:* walexand@broward.edu. *Website:* http://www.broward.edu/.

Brown Mackie College–Miami
Miami, Florida

Freshman Application Contact Brown Mackie College–Miami, One Herald Plaza, Miami, FL 33132. *Phone:* 305-341-6600. *Toll-free phone:* 866-505-0335.
Website: http://www.brownmackie.edu/miami/.

See next page for display ad and page 1194 for the College Close-Up.

Carlos Albizu University, Miami Campus
Miami, Florida

- **Independent** comprehensive, founded 1980, part of Carlos Albizu University
- **Urban** 18-acre campus
- **Coed, primarily women** 322 undergraduate students, 55% full-time, 69% women, 31% men
- **Moderately difficult** entrance level, 56% of applicants were admitted

Undergraduates 178 full-time, 144 part-time. 3% Black or African American, non-Hispanic/Latino; 41% Hispanic/Latino; 53% Race/ethnicity unknown; 0.9% international; 20% transferred in. *Retention:* 63% of full-time freshmen returned.
Freshmen *Admission:* 18 applied, 10 admitted, 11 enrolled. *Average high school GPA:* 2.9.
Faculty *Total:* 48, 10% full-time, 35% with terminal degrees. *Student/faculty ratio:* 12:1.
Academics *Calendar:* trimesters. *Degrees:* certificates, diplomas, bachelor's, master's, and doctoral. *Special study options:* academic remediation for entering students, accelerated degree program, adult/continuing education programs, advanced placement credit, cooperative education, distance learning, double majors, English as a second language, independent study, internships, part-time degree program, services for LD students, summer session for credit.
Computers on Campus 187 computers/terminals are available on campus for general student use. Students can access the following: computer help desk, free student e-mail accounts, online (class) grades, online (class) registration, online (class) schedules, Campus Portal. Wireless service is available via entire campus.
Student Life *Housing:* college housing not available. *Activities and organizations:* student-run newspaper, Student Council, Psi Chi, Kappa Delta Pi, Nu Sigma Si, Future Educators of America. *Campus security:* 24-hour emergency response devices and patrols, late-night transport/escort service.
Costs (2012–13) *Tuition:* $11,304 full-time, $314 per credit part-time. Full-time tuition and fees vary according to course load, degree level, and program. Part-time tuition and fees vary according to course load, degree level, and program. *Required fees:* $744 full-time, $248 per term part-time. *Payment plan:* installment. *Waivers:* employees or children of employees.
Financial Aid Of all full-time matriculated undergraduates who enrolled in 2003, 121 applied for aid, 118 were judged to have need. 27 Federal Work-Study jobs (averaging $3059). *Average percent of need met:* 50%. *Average financial aid package:* $7925. *Average need-based loan:* $3549. *Average need-based gift aid:* $5300. *Average indebtedness upon graduation:* $23,000.
Applying *Options:* electronic application. *Application fee:* $25. *Required:* high school transcript, minimum 2.0 GPA. *Recommended:* interview. *Application deadlines:* rolling (freshmen), rolling (transfers). *Notification:* continuous (freshmen).
Freshman Application Contact Ms. Dayanes Rodriguez, Admissions Officer, Carlos Albizu University, Miami Campus, 2173 NW 99 Avenue, Miami, FL 33172. *Phone:* 305-593-1223 Ext. 218. *Toll-free phone:* 888-GO-TO-CAU (in-state); 800-GO-TO-CAU (out-of-state). *Fax:* 305-593-1854. *E-mail:* mtriana@albizu.edu.
Website: http://www.mia.albizu.edu/.

Chamberlain College of Nursing
Jacksonville, Florida

- **Proprietary** 4-year
- **Coed**

Faculty *Student/faculty ratio:* 11:1.
Academics *Calendar:* semesters. *Degree:* bachelor's.
Standardized Tests *Required:* SAT or ACT (for admission).
Costs (2013–14) *Tuition:* $16,360 full-time, $665 per credit hour part-time. Full-time tuition and fees vary according to course load. Part-time tuition and fees vary according to course load. *Required fees:* $600 full-time.

Freshman Application Contact Admissions, Chamberlain College of Nursing, 5200 Belfort Road, Jacksonville, FL 32256-6040. *Phone:* 904-251-8100. *Toll-free phone:* 888-556-8CCN.
Website: http://www.chamberlain.edu/.

Chamberlain College of Nursing
Miramar, Florida

- **Proprietary** 4-year
- **Coed** 274 undergraduate students, 44% full-time, 90% women, 10% men
- **Moderately difficult** entrance level

Undergraduates 120 full-time, 154 part-time. 7% are from out of state; 22% Black or African American, non-Hispanic/Latino; 39% Hispanic/Latino; 3% Asian, non-Hispanic/Latino; 0.4% Two or more races, non-Hispanic/Latino; 22% Race/ethnicity unknown; 3% international; 62% transferred in.
Faculty *Total:* 21, 29% full-time. *Student/faculty ratio:* 16:1.
Academics *Degree:* bachelor's.
Student Life *Housing:* college housing not available.
Standardized Tests *Required:* SAT or ACT (for admission).
Costs (2013–14) *Tuition:* $16,360 full-time, $665 per credit hour part-time. Full-time tuition and fees vary according to course load. Part-time tuition and fees vary according to course load. *Required fees:* $600 full-time. *Payment plan:* installment. *Waivers:* employees or children of employees.
Applying *Application fee:* $95. *Application deadlines:* rolling (freshmen), rolling (transfers). *Notification:* continuous (freshmen), continuous (transfers).
Freshman Application Contact Director of Recruitment, Chamberlain College of Nursing, 2300 SW 145th Avenue, Miramar, FL 33027. *Phone:* 954-885-3510.
Website: http://www.chamberlain.edu/.

Chipola College
Marianna, Florida

- **State-supported** primarily 2-year, founded 1947
- **Rural** 105-acre campus
- **Coed** 2,292 undergraduate students, 42% full-time, 63% women, 37% men
- **Noncompetitive** entrance level

Undergraduates 964 full-time, 1,328 part-time. Students come from 7 states and territories; 6 other countries; 8% are from out of state; 17% Black or African American, non-Hispanic/Latino; 3% Hispanic/Latino; 1% Asian, non-Hispanic/Latino; 0.6% American Indian or Alaska Native, non-Hispanic/Latino; 2% Two or more races, non-Hispanic/Latino; 0.1% Race/ethnicity unknown; 6% transferred in.
Freshmen *Admission:* 247 enrolled. *Average high school GPA:* 2.5. *Test scores:* SAT critical reading scores over 500: 16%; SAT math scores over 500: 36%; ACT scores over 18: 81%; SAT critical reading scores over 600: 4%; SAT math scores over 600: 12%; ACT scores over 24: 25%; ACT scores over 30: 3%.
Faculty *Total:* 127, 31% full-time, 13% with terminal degrees. *Student/faculty ratio:* 24:1.
Academics *Calendar:* semesters. *Degrees:* certificates, associate, and bachelor's. *Special study options:* academic remediation for entering students, adult/continuing education programs, advanced placement credit, distance learning, honors programs, independent study, part-time degree program, services for LD students, summer session for credit.
Computers on Campus 80 computers/terminals are available on campus for general student use. Campuswide network is available.
Student Life *Housing:* college housing not available. *Activities and organizations:* drama/theater group, student-run newspaper, choral group, Drama/Theater Group. *Campus security:* night security personnel.
Athletics Member NJCAA. *Intercollegiate sports:* baseball M(s), basketball M(s)/W(s), softball W(s).
Costs (2012–13) *Tuition:* state resident $3060 full-time, $102 per semester hour part-time; nonresident $8891 full-time, $296 per semester hour part-time. Full-time tuition and fees vary according to degree level. Part-time tuition and fees vary according to degree level. *Required fees:* $40 full-time.
Applying *Options:* early admission. *Required:* high school transcript. *Application deadlines:* rolling (freshmen), rolling (transfers). *Notification:* continuous (freshmen), continuous (transfers).
Freshman Application Contact Mrs. Kathy L. Rehberg, Registrar, Chipola College, 3094 Indian Circle, Marianna, FL 32446-3065. *Phone:* 850-718-2233. *Fax:* 850-718-2287. *E-mail:* rehbergk@chipola.edu.
Website: http://www.chipola.edu/.

City College
Almonte Springs, Florida

Director of Admissions Ms. Kimberly Bowden, Director of Admissions, City College, 177 Montgomery Road, Almonte Springs, FL 32714. *Phone:* 352-335-4000. *Fax:* 352-335-4303. *E-mail:* kbowden@citycollege.edu. *Website:* http://www.citycollege.edu/.

City College
Fort Lauderdale, Florida

Freshman Application Contact City College, 2000 West Commercial Boulevard, Suite 200, Fort Lauderdale, FL 33309. *Phone:* 954-492-5353. *Toll-free phone:* 866-314-5681. *Website:* http://www.citycollege.edu/.

City College
Gainesville, Florida

Freshman Application Contact Admissions Office, City College, 7001 Northwest 4th Boulevard, Gainesville, FL 32607. *Phone:* 352-335-4000. *Website:* http://www.citycollege.edu/.

City College
Miami, Florida

Freshman Application Contact Admissions Office, City College, 9300 South Dadeland Boulevard, Suite PH, Miami, FL 33156. *Phone:* 305-666-9242. *Fax:* 305-666-9243. *Website:* http://www.citycollege.edu/.

Clearwater Christian College
Clearwater, Florida

- **Independent nondenominational** comprehensive, founded 1966
- **Suburban** 138-acre campus with easy access to Tampa-St. Petersburg
- **Endowment** $577,109
- **Coed** 485 undergraduate students, 97% full-time, 49% women, 51% men
- **Minimally difficult** entrance level, 72% of applicants were admitted

Undergraduates 470 full-time, 15 part-time. Students come from 38 states and territories; 8 other countries; 46% are from out of state; 5% Black or African American, non-Hispanic/Latino; 10% Hispanic/Latino; 0.8% Asian, non-Hispanic/Latino; 1% Two or more races, non-Hispanic/Latino; 2% international; 7% transferred in; 75% live on campus. *Retention:* 68% of full-time freshmen returned.

Freshmen *Admission:* 353 applied, 255 admitted, 115 enrolled. *Average high school GPA:* 3.1. *Test scores:* SAT critical reading scores over 500: 66%; SAT math scores over 500: 66%; ACT scores over 18: 89%; SAT critical reading scores over 600: 19%; SAT math scores over 600: 12%; ACT scores over 24: 29%; SAT critical reading scores over 700: 3%; ACT scores over 30: 1%.

Faculty *Total:* 43, 70% full-time, 65% with terminal degrees. *Student/faculty ratio:* 14:1.

Academics *Calendar:* semesters. *Degrees:* certificates, associate, bachelor's, and master's. *Special study options:* academic remediation for entering students, advanced placement credit, distance learning, double majors, independent study, internships, off-campus study, part-time degree program, services for LD students, study abroad, summer session for credit. *ROTC:* Army (c), Navy (c), Air Force (c).

Computers on Campus 45 computers/terminals are available on campus for general student use. Students can access the following: campus intranet, computer help desk, free student e-mail accounts, online (class) grades, online (class) registration, online (class) schedules. Campuswide network is available. 100% of college-owned or -operated housing units are wired for high-speed Internet access. Wireless service is available via entire campus.

Student Life *Housing:* on-campus residence required through senior year. *Options:* men-only, women-only. Campus housing is university owned. Freshman campus housing is guaranteed. *Activities and organizations:* drama/theater group, student-run newspaper, choral group, Drama Club, Alpha Chi, College Republicans, Science Club, Student Missionary Fellowship. *Campus security:* 24-hour emergency response devices and patrols. *Student services:* personal/psychological counseling.

Athletics Member NCCAA. *Intercollegiate sports:* baseball M, basketball M/W, golf M/W, soccer M/W, softball W, volleyball W. *Intramural sports:* basketball M/W, football M, table tennis M/W, tennis M/W, volleyball M/W.

Standardized Tests *Required:* SAT or ACT (for admission).

Costs (2013–14) *Comprehensive fee:* $25,360 includes full-time tuition ($17,060) and room and board ($8300). Full-time tuition and fees vary according to student level. No tuition increase for student's term of enrollment. *College room only:* $5050. Room and board charges vary according to board plan. *Payment plan:* installment. *Waivers:* employees or children of employees.

Financial Aid Of all full-time matriculated undergraduates who enrolled in 2009, 543 applied for aid, 433 were judged to have need, 65 had their need fully met. 50 Federal Work-Study jobs (averaging $670). 20 state and other part-time jobs (averaging $612). In 2009, 132 non-need-based awards were made. *Average percent of need met:* 60%. *Average financial aid package:* $10,353. *Average need-based loan:* $4324. *Average need-based gift aid:* $7918. *Average non-need-based aid:* $2848. *Average indebtedness upon graduation:* $18,000.

Applying *Options:* electronic application, early admission, deferred entrance. *Application fee:* $35. *Required:* essay or personal statement, high school transcript, minimum 2.0 GPA, 2 letters of recommendation, Christian testimony. *Recommended:* interview. *Application deadlines:* rolling (freshmen), rolling (transfers). *Notification:* continuous (freshmen), continuous (transfers).

Freshman Application Contact Miss Colleen Gumbert, Admissions Administrative Assistant, Clearwater Christian College, 3400 Gulf-to-Bay Boulevard, Clearwater, FL 33759-4595. *Phone:* 727-726-1153 Ext. 228. *Toll-free phone:* 800-348-4463. *Fax:* 813-726-8597. *E-mail:* admissions@clearwater.edu. *Website:* http://www.clearwater.edu/.

College of Business and Technology
Miami, Florida

- **Proprietary** primarily 2-year, founded 1988
- **Coed**
- **Minimally difficult** entrance level

Faculty *Student/faculty ratio:* 15:1.

Academics *Calendar:* semesters. *Degrees:* certificates, diplomas, associate, and bachelor's.

Costs (2012–13) *Tuition:* $10,920 full-time. *Required fees:* $1400 full-time.

Applying *Options:* electronic application. *Application fee:* $25. *Required:* essay or personal statement, high school transcript, minimum 2.6 GPA, 2 letters of recommendation, interview.

Freshman Application Contact Ms. Ivis Delgado, Admissions Representative, College of Business and Technology, 8230 West Flagler Street, Miami, FL 33144. *Phone:* 305-273-4499 Ext. 2204. *Toll-free phone:* 866-626-8842. *Fax:* 305-485-4411. *E-mail:* admissions@cbt.edu. *Website:* http://www.cbt.edu/.

College of Central Florida
Ocala, Florida

- **State and locally supported** primarily 2-year, founded 1957, part of Florida Community College System
- **Small-town** 139-acre campus
- **Endowment** $40.1 million
- **Coed**
- **Noncompetitive** entrance level

Faculty *Student/faculty ratio:* 18:1.

Academics *Calendar:* semesters. *Degrees:* certificates, diplomas, associate, and bachelor's.

Student Life *Campus security:* 24-hour emergency response devices and patrols, student patrols, late-night transport/escort service.

Athletics Member NJCAA.

Standardized Tests *Recommended:* SAT (for admission), ACT (for admission), SAT or ACT (for admission), SAT and SAT Subject Tests or ACT (for admission), SAT Subject Tests (for admission).

Costs (2012–13) *Tuition:* state resident $2388 full-time, $80 per credit hour part-time; nonresident $9552 full-time, $422 per credit hour part-time. Full-time tuition and fees vary according to course level, degree level, and program. Part-time tuition and fees vary according to course level, degree level, and program. *Required fees:* $765 full-time, $26 per credit hour part-time.

Financial Aid Of all full-time matriculated undergraduates who enrolled in 2011, 85 Federal Work-Study jobs (averaging $1505).

Applying *Options:* early admission. *Application fee:* $30. *Required:* high school transcript.

Freshman Application Contact Ms. Devona Sewell, Registrar, Admission and Records, College of Central Florida, 3001 SW College Road, Ocala, FL 34474. *Phone:* 352-237-2111 Ext. 1398. *Fax:* 352-873-5882. *E-mail:* sewelld@cf.edu. *Website:* http://www.cf.edu/.

Daytona State College
Daytona Beach, Florida

- **State-supported** primarily 2-year, founded 1958, part of Florida Community College System
- **Suburban** 100-acre campus with easy access to Orlando
- **Endowment** $9.4 million
- **Coed** 15,708 undergraduate students, 41% full-time, 60% women, 40% men
- **Noncompetitive** entrance level, 99% of applicants were admitted

Undergraduates 6,429 full-time, 9,279 part-time. Students come from 51 states and territories; 130 other countries; 4% are from out of state; 13% Black or African American, non-Hispanic/Latino; 11% Hispanic/Latino; 2% Asian, non-Hispanic/Latino; 0.1% Native Hawaiian or other Pacific Islander, non-Hispanic/Latino; 0.5% American Indian or Alaska Native, non-Hispanic/Latino; 1% Two or more races, non-Hispanic/Latino; 0.9% Race/ethnicity unknown; 7% transferred in.
Freshmen *Admission:* 4,684 applied, 4,629 admitted, 1,769 enrolled.
Faculty *Total:* 931, 35% full-time, 16% with terminal degrees. *Student/faculty ratio:* 26:1.
Academics *Calendar:* semesters. *Degrees:* certificates, diplomas, associate, bachelor's, and postbachelor's certificates. *Special study options:* academic remediation for entering students, adult/continuing education programs, advanced placement credit, cooperative education, distance learning, double majors, English as a second language, external degree program, freshman honors college, honors programs, independent study, internships, off-campus study, part-time degree program, services for LD students, study abroad, summer session for credit. *ROTC:* Army (c), Air Force (c).
Computers on Campus 3,208 computers/terminals are available on campus for general student use. Students can access the following: campus intranet, computer help desk, free student e-mail accounts, online (class) grades, online (class) registration, online (class) schedules. Campuswide network is available. Wireless service is available via entire campus.
Student Life *Housing:* college housing not available. *Activities and organizations:* drama/theater group, student-run newspaper, choral group, Florida Student Nursing Association, Phi Theta Kappa, Mu Rho Chapter, Student Government Association, Campus Crusade for Christ, Student Paralegal Association, national fraternities, national sororities. *Campus security:* 24-hour emergency response devices and patrols, late-night transport/escort service. *Student services:* personal/psychological counseling, women's center.
Athletics Member NJCAA. *Intercollegiate sports:* baseball M(s), basketball M(s)/W(s), golf W(s), softball W(s), swimming and diving M(s)/W(s), volleyball W. *Intramural sports:* basketball M/W, cheerleading M/W, football M/W, golf M/W, racquetball M/W, soccer M/W, table tennis M/W, tennis M/W, volleyball M/W.
Financial Aid Of all full-time matriculated undergraduates who enrolled in 2011, 212 Federal Work-Study jobs (averaging $1479). 1 state and other part-time job (averaging $2373). In 2011, 525 non-need-based awards were made. *Average need-based loan:* $2704. *Average need-based gift aid:* $1580. *Average non-need-based aid:* $1222.
Applying *Options:* electronic application, early admission, deferred entrance. *Required:* high school transcript. *Application deadlines:* rolling (freshmen), rolling (transfers). *Notification:* continuous (freshmen), continuous (transfers).
Freshman Application Contact Dr. Karen Sanders, Director of Admissions and Recruitment, Daytona State College, 1200 International Speedway Boulevard, Daytona Beach, FL 32114. *Phone:* 386-506-3050. *E-mail:* sanderk@daytonastate.edu.
Website: http://www.daytonastate.edu/.

DeVry University
Jacksonville, Florida

Admissions Office Contact DeVry University, 5200 Belfort Road, Jacksonville, FL 32256-6040.
Website: http://www.devry.edu/locations/campuses/loc_jacksonville.jsp.

DeVry University
Miami, Florida

Admissions Office Contact DeVry University, 8700 West Flagler Street, Suite 100, Miami, FL 33174-2535. *Toll-free phone:* 866-338-7941.
Website: http://www.devry.edu/.

DeVry University
Miramar, Florida

- **Proprietary** comprehensive, founded 2002, part of DeVry University
- **Coed** 714 undergraduate students, 41% full-time, 38% women, 62% men
- **Minimally difficult** entrance level

Undergraduates 295 full-time, 419 part-time. 11% are from out of state; 22% Black or African American, non-Hispanic/Latino; 43% Hispanic/Latino; 1% Asian, non-Hispanic/Latino; 0.3% Native Hawaiian or other Pacific Islander, non-Hispanic/Latino; 0.7% Two or more races, non-Hispanic/Latino; 15% Race/ethnicity unknown; 4% international; 16% transferred in.
Freshmen *Admission:* 49 enrolled.
Faculty *Total:* 61, 30% full-time. *Student/faculty ratio:* 16:1.
Academics *Calendar:* semesters. *Degrees:* associate, bachelor's, master's, and postbachelor's certificates. *Special study options:* part-time degree program.
Student Life *Housing:* college housing not available.
Costs (2013–14) *Tuition:* $16,076 full-time, $609 per credit hour part-time. *Required fees:* $80 full-time.
Financial Aid Of all full-time matriculated undergraduates who enrolled in 2007, 204 applied for aid, 197 were judged to have need, 2 had their need fully met. In 2007, 35 non-need-based awards were made. *Average percent of need met:* 38%. *Average financial aid package:* $12,172. *Average need-based loan:* $7414. *Average need-based gift aid:* $7044. *Average non-need-based aid:* $12,256. *Average indebtedness upon graduation:* $51,131.
Applying *Application fee:* $40. *Required:* high school transcript, interview. *Application deadlines:* rolling (freshmen), rolling (transfers). *Notification:* continuous (freshmen), continuous (transfers).
Freshman Application Contact DeVry University, 2300 Southwest 145th Avenue, Miramar, FL 33027-4150. *Phone:* 954-499-9775. *Toll-free phone:* 866-338-7941.
Website: http://www.devry.edu/.

DeVry University
Orlando, Florida

- **Proprietary** comprehensive, founded 2000, part of DeVry University
- **Urban** campus
- **Coed** 1,330 undergraduate students, 41% full-time, 40% women, 60% men
- **Minimally difficult** entrance level

Undergraduates 543 full-time, 787 part-time. 15% are from out of state; 21% Black or African American, non-Hispanic/Latino; 22% Hispanic/Latino; 2% Asian, non-Hispanic/Latino; 0.3% Native Hawaiian or other Pacific Islander, non-Hispanic/Latino; 0.2% American Indian or Alaska Native, non-Hispanic/Latino; 0.8% Two or more races, non-Hispanic/Latino; 14% Race/ethnicity unknown; 2% international; 20% transferred in.
Freshmen *Admission:* 91 enrolled.
Faculty *Total:* 98, 26% full-time. *Student/faculty ratio:* 19:1.
Academics *Calendar:* semesters. *Degrees:* associate, bachelor's, master's, and postbachelor's certificates. *Special study options:* adult/continuing education programs, part-time degree program.
Computers on Campus Students can access the following: online (class) registration.
Student Life *Housing:* college housing not available.
Costs (2013–14) *Tuition:* $16,076 full-time, $609 per credit hour part-time. *Required fees:* $80 full-time.
Financial Aid Of all full-time matriculated undergraduates who enrolled in 2007, 314 applied for aid, 294 were judged to have need, 2 had their need fully met. In 2007, 35 non-need-based awards were made. *Average percent of need met:* 33%. *Average financial aid package:* $10,774. *Average need-based loan:* $7062. *Average need-based gift aid:* $5608. *Average non-need-based aid:* $18,240. *Average indebtedness upon graduation:* $23,511.
Applying *Application fee:* $40. *Required:* high school transcript, interview. *Application deadlines:* rolling (freshmen), rolling (transfers). *Notification:* continuous (freshmen), continuous (transfers).
Freshman Application Contact DeVry University, 4000 Millenia Boulevard, Orlando, FL 32839. *Phone:* 407-345-2800. *Toll-free phone:* 866-338-7941.
Website: http://www.devry.edu/.

DeVry University
Tampa, Florida

Admissions Office Contact DeVry University, 3030 North Rocky Point Drive West, Suite 100, Tampa, FL 33607-5901. *Toll-free phone:* 866-338-7941.
Website: http://www.devry.edu/.

Eckerd College
St. Petersburg, Florida

- **Independent Presbyterian** 4-year, founded 1958
- **Suburban** 188-acre campus with easy access to Tampa
- **Endowment** $45.6 million
- **Coed** 1,893 undergraduate students, 98% full-time, 59% women, 41% men
- **Moderately difficult** entrance level, 68% of applicants were admitted

Undergraduates 1,849 full-time, 44 part-time. Students come from 47 states and territories; 35 other countries; 80% are from out of state; 3% Black or African American, non-Hispanic/Latino; 8% Hispanic/Latino; 1% Asian, non-Hispanic/Latino; 0.2% Native Hawaiian or other Pacific Islander, non-Hispanic/Latino; 0.4% American Indian or Alaska Native, non-Hispanic/Latino; 3% Two or more races, non-Hispanic/Latino; 1% Race/ethnicity unknown; 4% international; 3% transferred in; 81% live on campus. *Retention:* 81% of full-time freshmen returned.

Freshmen *Admission:* 3,713 applied, 2,542 admitted, 532 enrolled. *Average high school GPA:* 3.3. *Test scores:* SAT critical reading scores over 500: 80%; SAT math scores over 500: 75%; ACT scores over 18: 98%; SAT critical reading scores over 600: 35%; SAT math scores over 600: 34%; ACT scores over 24: 70%; SAT critical reading scores over 700: 8%; SAT math scores over 700: 4%; ACT scores over 30: 13%.

Faculty *Total:* 164, 71% full-time, 80% with terminal degrees. *Student/faculty ratio:* 13:1.

Academics *Calendar:* 4-1-4. *Degree:* bachelor's. *Special study options:* accelerated degree program, adult/continuing education programs, advanced placement credit, double majors, external degree program, honors programs, independent study, internships, off-campus study, part-time degree program, services for LD students, student-designed majors, study abroad, summer session for credit. *ROTC:* Army (c), Air Force (c). *Unusual degree programs:* 3-2 engineering with Columbia University, Washington University in St. Louis.

Computers on Campus 300 computers/terminals and 2,000 ports are available on campus for general student use. Students can access the following: campus intranet, computer help desk, free student e-mail accounts, online (class) grades, online (class) registration, online (class) schedules, free computer repair shop. Campuswide network is available. 100% of college-owned or -operated housing units are wired for high-speed Internet access. Wireless service is available via entire campus.

Student Life *Housing:* on-campus residence required for freshman year. *Options:* coed, women-only. Campus housing is university owned. Freshman campus housing is guaranteed. *Activities and organizations:* drama/theater group, student-run newspaper, radio and television station, choral group, Earth Society, Water Search and Rescue Team, The Current (student newspaper), College Choir, Organization of Students. *Campus security:* 24-hour emergency response devices and patrols, student patrols, late-night transport/escort service, controlled dormitory access. *Student services:* health clinic, personal/psychological counseling, women's center.

Athletics Member NCAA. All Division II. *Intercollegiate sports:* baseball M(s), basketball M(s)/W(s), golf M(s)/W(s), sailing M/W, soccer M(s)/W(s), softball W(s), tennis M(s)/W(s), volleyball W(s). *Intramural sports:* baseball M, basketball M/W, bowling M/W, cheerleading M(c)/W(c), equestrian sports M(c)/W(c), field hockey M(c)/W(c), football M(c)/W(c), golf M(c)/W(c), lacrosse M(c)/W(c), rugby M(c)/W(c), sailing M/W, soccer M(c)/W(c), softball M/W, swimming and diving M(c)/W(c), table tennis M/W, tennis M(c)/W(c), ultimate Frisbee M(c)/W(c), volleyball M/W.

Standardized Tests *Required:* SAT or ACT (for admission). *Recommended:* SAT Subject Tests (for admission).

Costs (2013–14) *Comprehensive fee:* $47,506 includes full-time tuition ($37,046), mandatory fees ($316), and room and board ($10,144). Part-time tuition: $4361 per course. *College room only:* $5106. Room and board charges vary according to board plan and housing facility. *Payment plan:* installment. *Waivers:* employees or children of employees.

Financial Aid Of all full-time matriculated undergraduates who enrolled in 2012, 1,318 applied for aid, 1,082 were judged to have need, 195 had their need fully met. In 2012, 612 non-need-based awards were made. *Average percent of need met:* 86%. *Average financial aid package:* $26,201. *Average need-based loan:* $4672. *Average need-based gift aid:* $19,732. *Average non-need-based aid:* $12,706. *Average indebtedness upon graduation:* $33,957.

Applying *Options:* electronic application, early action, deferred entrance. *Application fee:* $40. *Required:* essay or personal statement, high school transcript, 1 letter of recommendation. *Recommended:* minimum 3.0 GPA, interview. *Application deadlines:* rolling (freshmen), rolling (transfers), 11/15 (early action). *Notification:* continuous (freshmen), continuous (transfers), 12/15 (early action).

Freshman Application Contact Ms. Donna Grosso, Eckerd College, 4200 54th Avenue South, St. Petersburg, FL 33711. *Phone:* 727-864-8331. *Toll-free phone:* 800-456-9009. *Fax:* 727-866-2304. *E-mail:* admissions@eckerd.edu. *Website:* http://www.eckerd.edu/.

Edison State College
Fort Myers, Florida

Freshman Application Contact Lauren Willison, Admissions Specialist, Edison State College, 8099 College Parkway, Fort Myers, FL 33919. *Phone:* 239-489-9257. *Toll-free phone:* 800-749-2ECC. *E-mail:* Lauren.Willison@edison.edu. *Website:* http://www.edison.edu/.

Edward Waters College
Jacksonville, Florida

- **Independent African Methodist Episcopal** 4-year, founded 1866
- **Urban** 50-acre campus
- **Coed**
- **Noncompetitive** entrance level

Faculty *Student/faculty ratio:* 9:1.

Academics *Calendar:* semesters. *Degree:* bachelor's.

Student Life *Campus security:* 24-hour emergency response devices and patrols, student patrols, late-night transport/escort service, controlled dormitory access.

Athletics Member NAIA.

Standardized Tests *Required:* SAT or ACT (for admission).

Costs (2012–13) *Comprehensive fee:* $18,028 includes full-time tuition ($11,158) and room and board ($6870). *College room only:* $3280.

Financial Aid *Of all full-time matriculated undergraduates who enrolled in 2001,* 1,242 applied for aid, 1,242 were judged to have need, 11 had their need fully met. 318 Federal Work-Study jobs (averaging $851). *In 2001,* 262 non-need-based awards were made. *Average percent of need met:* 61. *Average financial aid package:* $4835. *Average need-based loan:* $2625. *Average need-based gift aid:* $4835. *Average non-need-based aid:* $1488. *Average indebtedness upon graduation:* $9000.

Applying *Options:* electronic application. *Application fee:* $25. *Required:* high school transcript, 2 letters of recommendation, medical forms.

Freshman Application Contact Edward Waters College, 1658 Kings Road, Jacksonville, FL 32209-6199. *Phone:* 904-470-8202. *Toll-free phone:* 888-898-3191. *Website:* http://www.ewc.edu/.

Embry-Riddle Aeronautical University–Daytona
Daytona Beach, Florida

- **Independent** comprehensive, founded 1926
- **Suburban** 168-acre campus with easy access to Orlando
- **Endowment** $80.9 million
- **Coed** 4,534 undergraduate students, 93% full-time, 17% women, 83% men
- **Moderately difficult** entrance level

Undergraduates 4,225 full-time, 309 part-time. Students come from 52 states and territories; 100 other countries; 59% are from out of state; 6% Black or African American, non-Hispanic/Latino; 8% Hispanic/Latino; 5% Asian, non-Hispanic/Latino; 0.2% Native Hawaiian or other Pacific Islander, non-Hispanic/Latino; 0.6% American Indian or Alaska Native, non-Hispanic/Latino; 5% Two or more races, non-Hispanic/Latino; 8% Race/ethnicity unknown; 15% international; 6% transferred in; 40% live on campus. *Retention:* 77% of full-time freshmen returned.

Freshmen *Admission:* 941 enrolled. *Average high school GPA:* 3.56. *Test scores:* SAT critical reading scores over 500: 65%; SAT math scores over 500: 81%; ACT scores over 18: 96%; SAT critical reading scores over 600: 25%; SAT math scores over 600: 43%; ACT scores over 24: 58%; SAT critical reading scores over 700: 4%; SAT math scores over 700: 8%; ACT scores over 30: 14%.

Faculty *Total:* 392, 80% full-time, 52% with terminal degrees. *Student/faculty ratio:* 13:1.

Academics *Calendar:* semesters. *Degrees:* associate, bachelor's, master's, and doctoral. *Special study options:* academic remediation for entering students, accelerated degree program, adult/continuing education programs, advanced placement credit, cooperative education, distance learning, double majors, English as a second language, honors programs, independent study, intern-

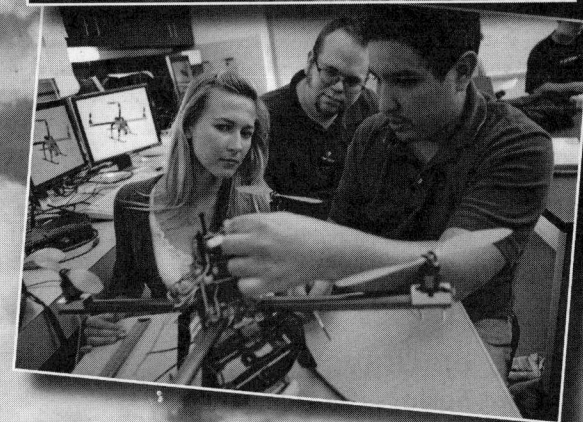

ships, part-time degree program, services for LD students, study abroad, summer session for credit. *ROTC:* Army (b), Navy (b), Air Force (b).

Computers on Campus 1,049 computers/terminals are available on campus for general student use. Students can access the following: campus intranet, computer help desk, free student e-mail accounts, online (class) grades, online (class) registration, online (class) schedules. Campuswide network is available. 100% of college-owned or -operated housing units are wired for high-speed Internet access. Wireless service is available via entire campus.

Student Life *Housing:* on-campus residence required for freshman year. *Options:* coed. Campus housing is university owned. Freshman campus housing is guaranteed. *Activities and organizations:* drama/theater group, student-run newspaper, radio station, choral group, Eagle Wing, Future Professional Pilots Association, African Student Association, Caribbean Student Association, Sigma Gamma Tau, national fraternities, national sororities. *Campus security:* 24-hour emergency response devices and patrols, student patrols, late-night transport/escort service, controlled dormitory access. *Student services:* health clinic, personal/psychological counseling, women's center.

Athletics Member NAIA. *Intercollegiate sports:* baseball M(s), basketball M(s), cheerleading M/W, cross-country running M(s)/W(s), golf M(s)/W(s), soccer M(s)/W(s), softball W(s), tennis M(s)/W(s), track and field M(s)/W(s), volleyball W(s). *Intramural sports:* basketball M/W, bowling M/W, crew M(c)/W(c), football M/W, golf M/W, ice hockey M(c), lacrosse M(c), racquetball M/W, rugby M(c), soccer M/W, softball M/W, swimming and diving M(c)/W(c), table tennis M/W, tennis M/W, ultimate Frisbee M(c)/W(c), volleyball M/W.

Standardized Tests *Required:* SAT or ACT (for admission).

Costs (2013–14) *Comprehensive fee:* $40,884 includes full-time tuition ($30,120), mandatory fees ($1214), and room and board ($9550). Part-time tuition: $1255 per credit hour. *College room only:* $5600. Room and board charges vary according to board plan and housing facility. *Payment plan:* deferred payment. *Waivers:* employees or children of employees.

Financial Aid Of all full-time matriculated undergraduates who enrolled in 2011, 3,111 applied for aid, 2,775 were judged to have need. 123 Federal Work-Study jobs (averaging $1008). 1,171 state and other part-time jobs (averaging $1700). *Average financial aid package:* $14,942. *Average need-based loan:* $4822. *Average need-based gift aid:* $9321.

Applying *Options:* electronic application, deferred entrance. *Application fee:* $50. *Required:* high school transcript, minimum 2.0 GPA, 2 letters of recommendation. *Required for some:* minimum 3.0 GPA, medical examination for flight students. *Recommended:* essay or personal statement, interview. *Application deadlines:* rolling (freshmen), rolling (out-of-state freshmen), 6/1 (transfers). *Notification:* continuous (freshmen), continuous (out-of-state freshmen), continuous (transfers).

Freshman Application Contact Embry-Riddle Aeronautical University–Daytona, 600 South Clyde Morris Boulevard, Daytona Beach, FL 32114-3900. *Phone:* 386-226-6100. *Toll-free phone:* 800-862-2416. *Fax:* 386-226-7070. *E-mail:* dbadmit@erau.edu. *Website:* http://www.embryriddle.edu/.

See display ad on this page and page 1282 for the College Close-Up.

Embry-Riddle Aeronautical University–Worldwide
Daytona Beach, Florida

- **Independent** comprehensive, founded 1970
- **Endowment** $80.9 million
- **Coed** 11,117 undergraduate students, 26% full-time, 11% women, 89% men
- **Minimally difficult** entrance level

Undergraduates 2,875 full-time, 8,242 part-time. 7% Black or African American, non-Hispanic/Latino; 9% Hispanic/Latino; 2% Asian, non-Hispanic/Latino; 0.5% Native Hawaiian or other Pacific Islander, non-Hispanic/Latino; 0.4% American Indian or Alaska Native, non-Hispanic/Latino; 7% Two or more races, non-Hispanic/Latino; 32% Race/ethnicity unknown; 1% international; 5% transferred in.

Freshmen *Admission:* 338 enrolled.

Faculty *Total:* 2,711, 5% full-time, 25% with terminal degrees.

Academics *Calendar:* 5 9-week terms. *Degrees:* certificates, associate, bachelor's, master's, and doctoral (programs offered at 100 military bases worldwide). *Special study options:* adult/continuing education programs, advanced placement credit, cooperative education, distance learning, external degree program, independent study, off-campus study, part-time degree program, services for LD students, summer session for credit.

Computers on Campus Students can access the following: free student e-mail accounts, online (class) grades, online (class) registration, online (class) schedules.

Student Life *Housing:* college housing not available.

Standardized Tests *Required for some:* SAT or ACT (for admission).

Costs (2013–14) *Tuition:* $7032 full-time, $305 per credit part-time. Full-time tuition and fees vary according to program and reciprocity agreements. Part-time tuition and fees vary according to program and reciprocity agreements. *Waivers:* employees or children of employees.

Financial Aid Of all full-time matriculated undergraduates who enrolled in 2011, 899 applied for aid, 769 were judged to have need. *Average financial aid package:* $6690. *Average need-based loan:* $4438. *Average need-based gift aid:* $4249.

Applying *Options:* electronic application, deferred entrance. *Application fee:* $50. *Required:* minimum 2.0 GPA. *Required for some:* essay or personal statement, high school transcript, 2 letters of recommendation, SAT with a minimum score of 1000 or ACT with a minimum score of 21; 300-500 word essay. *Application deadlines:* rolling (freshmen), rolling (transfers). *Notification:* continuous (freshmen), continuous (transfers).

Freshman Application Contact Embry-Riddle Aeronautical University–Worldwide, 600 South Clyde Morris Boulevard, Daytona Beach, FL 32114-3900. *Phone:* 866-509-0743. *Toll-free phone:* 800-522-6787. *Fax:* 386-226-6984. *E-mail:* ecinfo@erau.edu.
Website: http://www.embryriddle.edu/.

Everest University
Jacksonville, Florida

Director of Admissions Mr. Robin Manning, Admissions Director, Everest University, 8226 Phillips Highway, Jacksonville, FL 32256. *Phone:* 904-731-4949. *Toll-free phone:* 888-741-4270. *E-mail:* rmanning@cci.edu.
Website: http://www.everest.edu/.

Everest University
Lakeland, Florida

- **Proprietary** 4-year, founded 1890, part of Corinthian Colleges, Inc.
- **Urban** 3-acre campus with easy access to Orlando, Tampa-St. Petersburg
- **Coed**
- **Minimally difficult** entrance level

Faculty *Student/faculty ratio:* 18:1.

Academics *Calendar:* quarters. *Degrees:* certificates, diplomas, associate, and bachelor's (bachelor's degree in business administration only).

Student Life *Campus security:* 24-hour patrols.

Standardized Tests *Required:* CPAt (for admission). *Recommended:* SAT or ACT (for admission).

Costs (2012–13) *Tuition:* $452 per credit part-time. Full-time tuition and fees vary according to course load, degree level, and program. Part-time tuition and fees vary according to course load, degree level, and program.

Financial Aid *Of all full-time matriculated undergraduates who enrolled in 2002,* 679 applied for aid, 646 were judged to have need, 10 had their need fully met. 6 Federal Work-Study jobs (averaging $4863). *Average percent of need met:* 76. *Average financial aid package:* $3510. *Average need-based loan:* $3875. *Average need-based gift aid:* $1000. *Average indebtedness upon graduation:* $29,852.

Applying *Options:* early admission. *Required:* high school transcript, interview. *Recommended:* essay or personal statement, high school transcript.

Freshman Application Contact Ms. Patricia Sabol, Director of Student Services, Everest University, 995 East Memorial Boulevard, Suite 110, Lakeland, FL 33801. *Phone:* 863-686-1444 Ext. 144. *Toll-free phone:* 888-741-4270. *E-mail:* psabol@cci.edu.
Website: http://www.everest.edu/.

Everest University
Largo, Florida

Freshman Application Contact Mr. Kevin Buskirk, Director of Admissions, Everest University, 2471 McMullen Road, Clearwater, FL 33759. *Phone:* 727-725-2688. *Toll-free phone:* 888-741-4270. *Fax:* 727-796-3406. *E-mail:* kbuskirk@cci.edu.
Website: http://www.everest.edu/.

Everest University
Melbourne, Florida

Director of Admissions Mr. Timothy Alexander, Director of Admissions, Everest University, 2401 North Harbor City Boulevard, Melbourne, FL 32935-6657. *Phone:* 321-253-2929 Ext. 121.
Website: http://www.everest.edu/.

Everest University
Orange Park, Florida

Freshman Application Contact Admissions Office, Everest University, 805 Wells Road, Orange Park, FL 32073. *Phone:* 904-264-9122.
Website: http://www.everest.edu/.

Everest University
Orlando, Florida

Freshman Application Contact Joann Derosa-Weber, Director of Admissions, Everest University, 5421 Diplomat Circle, Orlando, FL 32810-5674. *Phone:* 407-628-5870. *Toll-free phone:* 800-628-5870. *Fax:* 407-628-1344.
Website: http://www.everest.edu/.

Everest University
Orlando, Florida

Director of Admissions Ms. Annette Cloin, Director of Admissions, Everest University, 9200 South Park Center Loop, Orlando, FL 32819. *Phone:* 407-851-2525 Ext. 111. *Toll-free phone:* 888-741-4270 (in-state); 888-471-4270 (out-of-state). *Fax:* 407-354-7946.
Website: http://www.everest.edu/.

Everest University
Pompano Beach, Florida

Freshman Application Contact Martin Levert, Director of Admissions, Everest University, 225 North Federal Highway, Pompano Beach, FL 33062. *Phone:* 954-783-7339. *Fax:* 954-943-2571.
Website: http://www.everest.edu/.

Everest University
Tampa, Florida

Freshman Application Contact Everest University, 3319 West Hillsborough Avenue, Tampa, FL 33614-5899. *Phone:* 813-879-6000 Ext. 129.
Website: http://www.everest.edu/.

Everest University
Tampa, Florida

Freshman Application Contact Everest University, 3924 Coconut Palm Drive, Tampa, FL 33619. *Phone:* 813-621-0041 Ext. 106. *Toll-free phone:* 888-741-4270.
Website: http://www.everest.edu/.

Everglades University
Altamonte Springs, Florida

Freshman Application Contact Everglades University, 887 East Altamonte Drive, Altamonte Springs, FL 32701. *Phone:* 407-277-0311. *Toll-free phone:* 866-289-1078.
Website: http://www.evergladesuniversity.edu/.

Everglades University
Boca Raton, Florida

Freshman Application Contact Everglades University, 5002 T-Rex Avenue, Suite 100, Boca Raton, FL 33431. *Phone:* 561-912-1211. *Toll-free phone:* 888-772-6077.
Website: http://www.evergladesuniversity.edu/.

Everglades University
Sarasota, Florida

Director of Admissions Director of Admissions, Everglades University, 6001 Lake Osprey Drive #110, Sarasota, FL 34240. *Phone:* 941-907-2262. *Toll-free phone:* 866-907-2262. *Fax:* 941-907-6634. *E-mail:* admissions-sar@evergladesuniversity.edu.
Website: http://www.evergladesuniversity.edu/.

Flagler College

St. Augustine, Florida

- **Independent** 4-year, founded 1968
- **Small-town** 32-acre campus with easy access to Jacksonville
- **Endowment** $54.9 million
- **Coed** 2,847 undergraduate students, 97% full-time, 59% women, 41% men
- **Moderately difficult** entrance level, 41% of applicants were admitted

Undergraduates 2,764 full-time, 83 part-time. Students come from 43 states and territories; 32 other countries; 36% are from out of state; 4% Black or African American, non-Hispanic/Latino; 7% Hispanic/Latino; 0.8% Asian, non-Hispanic/Latino; 0.1% Native Hawaiian or other Pacific Islander, non-Hispanic/Latino; 0.6% American Indian or Alaska Native, non-Hispanic/Latino; 2% Two or more races, non-Hispanic/Latino; 5% Race/ethnicity unknown; 3% international; 6% transferred in; 36% live on campus. *Retention:* 69% of full-time freshmen returned.

Freshmen *Admission:* 5,347 applied, 2,219 admitted, 646 enrolled. *Average high school GPA:* 3.43. *Test scores:* SAT critical reading scores over 500: 91%; SAT math scores over 500: 89%; SAT writing scores over 500: 87%; ACT scores over 18: 99%; SAT critical reading scores over 600: 25%; SAT math scores over 600: 14%; SAT writing scores over 600: 16%; ACT scores over 24: 57%; SAT critical reading scores over 700: 1%; SAT math scores over 700: 1%; SAT writing scores over 700: 1%; ACT scores over 30: 3%.

Faculty *Total:* 228, 47% full-time, 42% with terminal degrees. *Student/faculty ratio:* 18:1.

Academics *Calendar:* semesters. *Degree:* bachelor's. *Special study options:* academic remediation for entering students, advanced placement credit, double majors, independent study, internships, services for LD students, study abroad, summer session for credit.

Computers on Campus 265 computers/terminals are available on campus for general student use. Students can access the following: campus intranet, computer help desk, free student e-mail accounts, online (class) grades, online (class) registration, online (class) schedules. Campuswide network is available. 100% of college-owned or -operated housing units are wired for high-speed Internet access. Wireless service is available via entire campus.

Student Life *Housing:* on-campus residence required for freshman year. *Options:* men-only, women-only. Campus housing is university owned. Freshman campus housing is guaranteed. *Activities and organizations:* drama/theater group, student-run newspaper, radio station, choral group, Student Government Association, Inter-Varsity, Campus Crusade, Mu Epsilon Nu (men's service club), Phi Alpha Omega (women's service club). *Campus security:* 24-hour emergency response devices and patrols, late-night transport/escort service, controlled dormitory access. *Student services:* health clinic, personal/psychological counseling.

Athletics Member NCAA. All Division II. *Intercollegiate sports:* baseball M(s), basketball M(s)/W(s), cross-country running M(s)/W(s), golf M(s)/W(s), lacrosse M(c), soccer M(s)/W(s), softball W(s), tennis M(s)/W(s), volleyball M(c)/W(s). *Intramural sports:* badminton M/W, basketball M/W, bowling M/W, football M/W, soccer M/W, softball M/W, swimming and diving M/W, table tennis M/W, tennis M/W, volleyball M/W, weight lifting M/W.

Standardized Tests *Required:* SAT or ACT (for admission).

Costs (2012–13) *Comprehensive fee:* $23,690 includes full-time tuition ($15,340) and room and board ($8350). Part-time tuition: $510 per credit hour. *College room only:* $4070. Room and board charges vary according to board plan and housing facility. *Waivers:* employees or children of employees.

Financial Aid Of all full-time matriculated undergraduates who enrolled in 2012, 2,373 applied for aid, 1,779 were judged to have need, 295 had their need fully met. 285 Federal Work-Study jobs (averaging $1111). 54 state and other part-time jobs (averaging $1164). In 2012, 86 non-need-based awards were made. *Average percent of need met:* 79%. *Average financial aid package:* $11,033. *Average need-based loan:* $4122. *Average need-based gift aid:* $4650. *Average non-need-based aid:* $2990. *Average indebtedness upon graduation:* $24,519.

Applying *Options:* electronic application, early admission, early decision, deferred entrance. *Application fee:* $40. *Required:* essay or personal statement, high school transcript. *Recommended:* minimum 2.0 GPA, 1 letter of recommendation, interview, rank in upper 50% of high school class. *Application deadlines:* 3/1 (freshmen), 3/1 (transfers). *Early decision deadline:* 12/1. *Notification:* 3/30 (freshmen), 3/30 (transfers), 12/15 (early decision).

Freshman Application Contact Mr. Marc Williar, Director of Admissions, Flagler College, 74 King Street, St. Augustine, FL 32085. *Phone:* 904-819-6220. *Toll-free phone:* 800-304-4208. *Fax:* 904-819-6466. *E-mail:* admiss@flagler.edu. *Website:* http://www.flagler.edu/.

Florida Agricultural and Mechanical University

Tallahassee, Florida

- **State-supported** university, founded 1887, part of State University System of Florida
- **Urban** 419-acre campus with easy access to Jacksonville
- **Endowment** $79.9 million
- **Coed** 10,053 undergraduate students, 90% full-time, 61% women, 39% men
- **Moderately difficult** entrance level, 49% of applicants were admitted

Undergraduates 9,086 full-time, 967 part-time. Students come from 42 states and territories; 50 other countries; 16% are from out of state; 94% Black or African American, non-Hispanic/Latino; 1% Hispanic/Latino; 0.7% Asian, non-Hispanic/Latino; 0.1% American Indian or Alaska Native, non-Hispanic/Latino; 0.8% international; 5% transferred in; 27% live on campus. *Retention:* 80% of full-time freshmen returned.

Freshmen *Admission:* 5,747 applied, 2,795 admitted, 1,518 enrolled. *Average high school GPA:* 3.2. *Test scores:* SAT critical reading scores over 500: 35%; SAT math scores over 500: 34%; SAT writing scores over 500: 27%; ACT scores over 18: 84%; SAT critical reading scores over 600: 8%; SAT math scores over 600: 7%; SAT writing scores over 600: 4%; ACT scores over 24: 16%; SAT critical reading scores over 700: 1%; SAT math scores over 700: 1%; ACT scores over 30: 1%.

Faculty *Total:* 724, 76% full-time, 57% with terminal degrees. *Student/faculty ratio:* 19:1.

Academics *Calendar:* semesters. *Degrees:* associate, bachelor's, master's, doctoral, and post-master's certificates. *Special study options:* academic remediation for entering students, accelerated degree program, adult/continuing education programs, advanced placement credit, cooperative education, distance learning, double majors, honors programs, independent study, internships, off-campus study, part-time degree program, services for LD students, study abroad, summer session for credit. *ROTC:* Army (b), Navy (b), Air Force (c). *Unusual degree programs:* 3-2 business administration; occupational therapy, architecture.

Computers on Campus 4,000 computers/terminals and 8,000 ports are available on campus for general student use. Students can access the following: campus intranet, computer help desk, free student e-mail accounts, online (class) grades, online (class) registration, online (class) schedules. Campuswide network is available. 100% of college-owned or -operated housing units are wired for high-speed Internet access. Wireless service is available via classrooms, computer centers, computer labs, dorm rooms, learning centers, libraries, student centers.

Student Life *Housing:* on-campus residence required for freshman year. *Options:* coed, men-only, women-only, disabled students. Campus housing is university owned. Freshman applicants given priority for college housing. *Activities and organizations:* drama/theater group, student-run newspaper, radio and television station, choral group, marching band, National Council of Negro Women, FAMU Chapter, American Society of Mechanical Engineers, Psi Chi International Honor Society, Caribbean Student Association, Academy of Student Pharmacists/Student National Pharmaceutical Association, national fraternities, national sororities. *Campus security:* 24-hour emergency response devices and patrols, late-night transport/escort service, controlled dormitory access. *Student services:* health clinic, personal/psychological counseling.

Athletics Member NCAA. All Division I except football (Division I-AA). *Intercollegiate sports:* baseball M(s), basketball M(s)/W(s), bowling W(s), cheerleading M/W, cross-country running M(s)/W(s), golf M(s)/W(s), softball W(s), swimming and diving M(s)/W(s), tennis M(s)/W(s), track and field M(s)/W(s), volleyball W(s). *Intramural sports:* badminton M/W, basketball M/W, bowling M/W, cheerleading W, football M, golf M/W, gymnastics M/W, racquetball M/W, skiing (downhill) M/W, soccer M/W, softball M/W, swimming and diving M/W, table tennis M/W, tennis M/W, track and field M/W, ultimate Frisbee M/W, volleyball M/W, weight lifting M/W, wrestling M/W.

Standardized Tests *Required:* SAT or ACT (for admission).

Costs (2012–13) *Tuition:* state resident $4929 full-time, $164 per credit part-time; nonresident $16,869 full-time, $562 per credit part-time. *Required fees:* $258 full-time, $129 per term part-time. *Room and board:* $8754; room only: $4928. Room and board charges vary according to board plan and housing facility. *Payment plan:* tuition prepayment. *Waivers:* senior citizens and employees or children of employees.

Financial Aid Of all full-time matriculated undergraduates who enrolled in 2011, 9,766 applied for aid, 8,737 were judged to have need, 2,033 had their need fully met. 233 Federal Work-Study jobs (averaging $2300). In 2011, 89 non-need-based awards were made. *Average percent of need met:* 74%. *Average financial aid package:* $12,521. *Average need-based loan:* $3903. *Average need-based gift aid:* $5738. *Average non-need-based aid:* $3608. *Average indebtedness upon graduation:* $29,702.

Applying *Options:* electronic application, early admission. *Application fee:* $30. *Required:* essay or personal statement, high school transcript, minimum 2.5 GPA, 3 letters of recommendation. *Required for some:* interview, audition required of music major applicants. *Recommended:* minimum 3.0 GPA. *Application deadlines:* 5/15 (freshmen), 5/15 (out-of-state freshmen), 5/15 (transfers). *Notification:* continuous (freshmen), continuous (out-of-state freshmen), continuous (transfers).

Freshman Application Contact Ms. Barbara R. Cox, Director, Admissions, Florida Agricultural and Mechanical University, Office of Admissions, Florida A & M University, Tallahassee, FL 32307. *Phone:* 850-599-3796. *Toll-free phone:* 866-642-1198. *Fax:* 850-599-3069. *E-mail:* ugrdadmissions@famu.edu.

Website: http://www.famu.edu/.

Florida Atlantic University

Boca Raton, Florida

- **State-supported** university, founded 1961, part of State University System of Florida
- **Suburban** 850-acre campus with easy access to Miami, Fort Lauderdale, Palm Beach
- **Coed** 24,823 undergraduate students, 63% full-time, 56% women, 44% men
- **Moderately difficult** entrance level, 39% of applicants were admitted

Undergraduates 15,593 full-time, 9,230 part-time. Students come from 50 states and territories; 135 other countries; 5% are from out of state; 18% Black or African American, non-Hispanic/Latino; 24% Hispanic/Latino; 4% Asian, non-Hispanic/Latino; 0.1% Native Hawaiian or other Pacific Islander, non-Hispanic/Latino; 0.2% American Indian or Alaska Native, non-Hispanic/Latino; 3% Two or more races, non-Hispanic/Latino; 1% Race/ethnicity unknown; 1% international; 13% transferred in; 6% live on campus. *Retention:* 78% of full-time freshmen returned.

Freshmen *Admission:* 27,888 applied, 10,876 admitted, 3,237 enrolled. *Average high school GPA:* 3.5. *Test scores:* SAT critical reading scores over 500: 70%; SAT math scores over 500: 74%; SAT writing scores over 500: 68%; ACT scores over 18: 100%; SAT critical reading scores over 600: 17%; SAT math scores over 600: 20%; SAT writing scores over 600: 14%; ACT scores over 24: 41%; SAT critical reading scores over 700: 2%; SAT math scores over 700: 2%; SAT writing scores over 700: 1%; ACT scores over 30: 3%.

Faculty *Total:* 1,226, 60% full-time, 67% with terminal degrees. *Student/faculty ratio:* 22:1.

Academics *Calendar:* semesters. *Degrees:* certificates, associate, bachelor's, master's, doctoral, and post-master's certificates. *Special study options:* accelerated degree program, adult/continuing education programs, advanced placement credit, cooperative education, distance learning, double majors, English as a second language, freshman honors college, honors programs, independent study, internships, off-campus study, part-time degree program, services for LD students, study abroad, summer session for credit. *ROTC:* Army (b), Air Force (c).

Computers on Campus 1,000 computers/terminals are available on campus for general student use. Students can access the following: campus intranet, computer help desk, free student e-mail accounts, online (class) grades, online (class) registration, online (class) schedules. Campuswide network is available. Wireless service is available via entire campus.

Student Life *Housing:* on-campus residence required for freshman year. *Options:* coed, women-only. Campus housing is university owned. Freshman campus housing is guaranteed. *Activities and organizations:* drama/theater group, student-run newspaper, radio and television station, choral group, marching band, American Society of Civil Engineers, Dive Club, Pre-Law Society, Submarine Club, American Criminal Justice Society, national fraternities, national sororities. *Campus security:* 24-hour emergency response devices and patrols, student patrols, late-night transport/escort service, controlled dormitory access. *Student services:* health clinic, personal/psychological counseling, women's center.

Athletics Member NCAA. All Division I. *Intercollegiate sports:* baseball M(s), basketball M(s)/W(s), cheerleading M/W, cross-country running M/W, football M(s), golf M(s)/W(s), soccer M/W, softball W(s), swimming and diving M/W, tennis M/W, track and field W, volleyball W(s). *Intramural sports:* baseball M/W, bowling M/W, football M, ice hockey M(c)/W(c), lacrosse M(c), rock climbing M(c)/W(c), rugby M(c)/W(c), sailing M(c)/W(c), soccer M/W, softball W, table tennis M/W, ultimate Frisbee M/W, volleyball M/W, weight lifting M(c), wrestling M(c).

Standardized Tests *Required:* SAT or ACT (for admission).

Costs (2012–13) *Tuition:* state resident $5986 full-time, $200 per credit hour part-time; nonresident $21,543 full-time, $718 per credit hour part-time. Full-time tuition and fees vary according to course load. Part-time tuition and fees vary according to course load. *Room and board:* $11,353. Room and board charges vary according to board plan and housing facility. *Payment plans:* tuition prepayment, installment, deferred payment. *Waivers:* senior citizens and employees or children of employees.

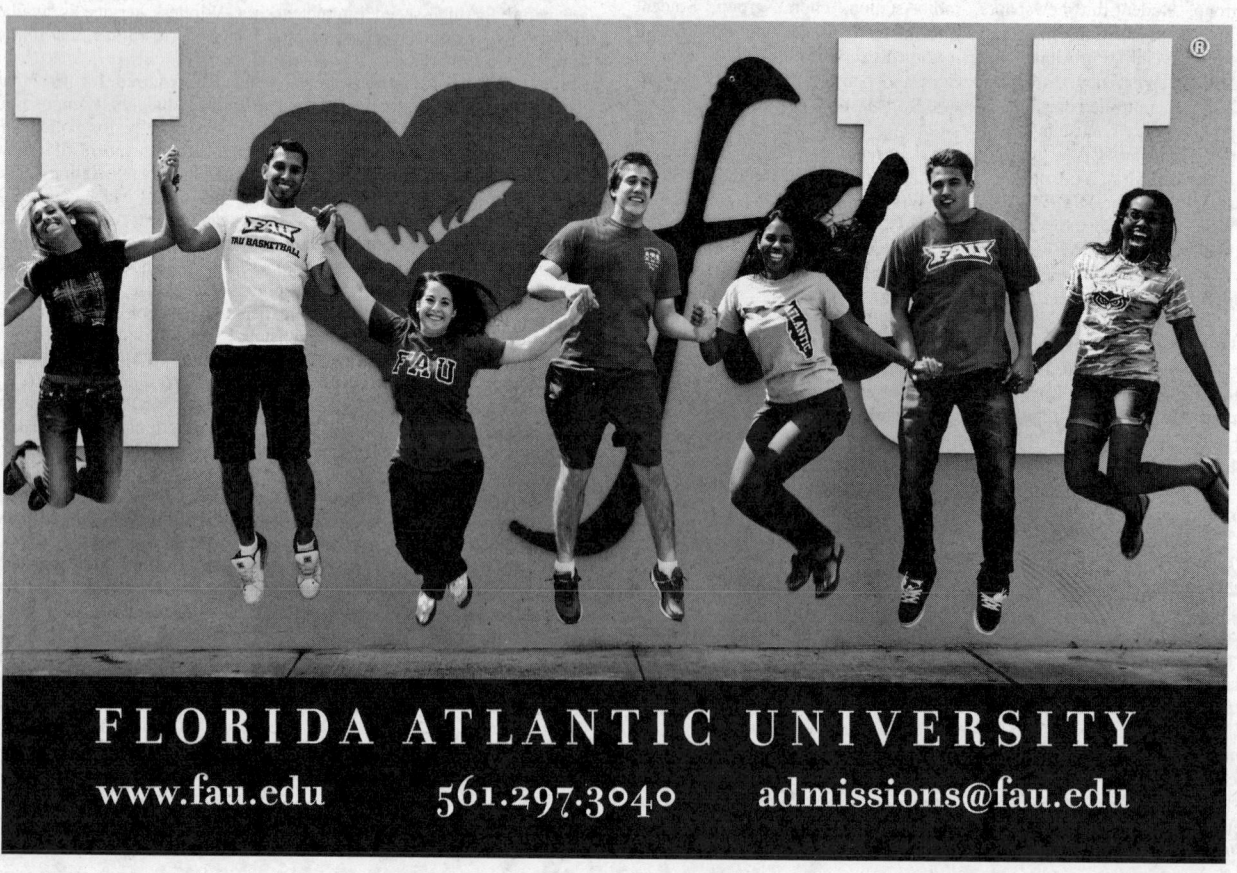

Financial Aid Of all full-time matriculated undergraduates who enrolled in 2012, 13,008 applied for aid, 10,335 were judged to have need, 1,369 had their need fully met. 187 Federal Work-Study jobs (averaging $2373). 3 state and other part-time jobs (averaging $3298). In 2012, 272 non-need-based awards were made. *Average percent of need met:* 66%. *Average financial aid package:* $10,684. *Average need-based loan:* $6777. *Average need-based gift aid:* $5871. *Average non-need-based aid:* $2502. *Average indebtedness upon graduation:* $19,281.

Applying *Options:* electronic application, early admission, deferred entrance. *Application fee:* $30. *Required:* high school transcript. *Application deadline:* 5/1 (freshmen).

Freshman Application Contact Mary Edmunds, Associate Director, Florida Atlantic University, 777 Glades Road, PO Box 3091, Boca Raton, FL 33431-0991. *Phone:* 561-297-3040. *Fax:* 561-297-2758. *Website:* http://www.fau.edu/.

See previous page for display ad and page 1296 for the College Close-Up.

Florida Christian College
Kissimmee, Florida

- **Independent** 4-year, founded 1976, affiliated with Christian Churches and Churches of Christ
- **Small-town** 40-acre campus with easy access to Orlando, Florida
- **Coed** 380 undergraduate students, 74% full-time, 44% women, 56% men
- **Minimally difficult** entrance level, 35% of applicants were admitted

Undergraduates 281 full-time, 99 part-time. Students come from 21 states and territories; 2 other countries; 12% are from out of state; 17% Black or African American, non-Hispanic/Latino; 16% Hispanic/Latino; 0.3% Two or more races, non-Hispanic/Latino; 3% Race/ethnicity unknown; 0.3% international; 11% transferred in; 62% live on campus. *Retention:* 60% of full-time freshmen returned.

Freshmen *Admission:* 526 applied, 182 admitted, 86 enrolled.

Faculty *Total:* 29, 41% full-time, 45% with terminal degrees. *Student/faculty ratio:* 18:1.

Academics *Calendar:* semesters. *Degrees:* diplomas, associate, and bachelor's. *Special study options:* academic remediation for entering students, adult/continuing education programs, advanced placement credit, distance learning, double majors, internships, part-time degree program, study abroad, summer session for credit.

Computers on Campus Students can access the following: online (class) grades, online (class) registration, online (class) schedules. Campuswide network is available. 100% of college-owned or -operated housing units are wired for high-speed Internet access. Wireless service is available via entire campus.

Student Life *Housing options:* men-only, women-only. Campus housing is university owned. *Activities and organizations:* choral group. *Campus security:* controlled dormitory access, late night trained security patrol.

Athletics Member NCCAA. *Intercollegiate sports:* baseball M, basketball M, cross-country running M/W, soccer W, volleyball W. *Intramural sports:* ultimate Frisbee M.

Standardized Tests *Required:* SAT or ACT (for admission).

Costs (2013–14) *One-time required fee:* $920. *Tuition:* $11,400 full-time. No tuition increase for student's term of enrollment. *Required fees:* $1170 full-time. *Room only:* $3200. *Payment plan:* installment. *Waivers:* employees or children of employees.

Financial Aid Of all full-time matriculated undergraduates who enrolled in 2005, 186 applied for aid, 186 were judged to have need, 5 had their need fully met. 38 Federal Work-Study jobs (averaging $1103). In 2005, 10 non-need-based awards were made. *Average percent of need met:* 46%. *Average financial aid package:* $5947. *Average need-based loan:* $3418. *Average need-based gift aid:* $2788. *Average non-need-based aid:* $2000. *Average indebtedness upon graduation:* $15,353. *Financial aid deadline:* 7/15.

Applying *Options:* early admission, deferred entrance. *Application fee:* $35. *Required:* essay or personal statement, high school transcript, 3 letters of recommendation. *Required for some:* interview. *Application deadlines:* 7/15 (freshmen), 7/15 (transfers). *Notification:* continuous until 8/25 (freshmen), continuous until 8/15 (transfers).

Freshman Application Contact Florida Christian College, 1011 Bill Beck Boulevard, Kissimmee, FL 34744-5301. *Phone:* 407-569-1172. *Toll-free phone:* 888-GO-TO-FCC. *Website:* http://www.fcc.edu/.

Florida College
Temple Terrace, Florida

- **Independent** 4-year, founded 1944
- **Small-town** 95-acre campus with easy access to Tampa
- **Endowment** $11.9 million
- **Coed** 532 undergraduate students, 95% full-time, 52% women, 48% men
- **Moderately difficult** entrance level, 73% of applicants were admitted

Undergraduates 507 full-time, 25 part-time. Students come from 34 states and territories; 5 other countries; 68% are from out of state; 5% Black or African American, non-Hispanic/Latino; 6% Hispanic/Latino; 0.6% Asian, non-Hispanic/Latino; 0.4% Native Hawaiian or other Pacific Islander, non-Hispanic/Latino; 2% American Indian or Alaska Native, non-Hispanic/Latino; 4% Two or more races, non-Hispanic/Latino; 0.2% Race/ethnicity unknown; 0.9% international; 6% transferred in; 81% live on campus.

Freshmen *Admission:* 322 applied, 234 admitted, 182 enrolled. *Test scores:* SAT critical reading scores over 500: 60%; SAT math scores over 500: 57%; SAT writing scores over 500: 51%; ACT scores over 18: 55%; SAT critical reading scores over 600: 24%; SAT math scores over 600: 21%; SAT writing scores over 600: 17%; ACT scores over 24: 20%; SAT critical reading scores over 700: 8%; SAT math scores over 700: 5%; SAT writing scores over 700: 3%; ACT scores over 30: 6%.

Faculty *Total:* 60, 65% full-time, 33% with terminal degrees. *Student/faculty ratio:* 11:1.

Academics *Calendar:* semesters. *Degrees:* associate and bachelor's. *Special study options:* academic remediation for entering students, advanced placement credit, independent study, summer session for credit. *ROTC:* Army (c), Air Force (c).

Computers on Campus 36 computers/terminals are available on campus for general student use. Students can access the following: campus intranet, computer help desk, free student e-mail accounts, online (class) grades, online (class) schedules. Campuswide network is available. 100% of college-owned or -operated housing units are wired for high-speed Internet access. Wireless service is available via classrooms, computer centers, computer labs, dorm rooms, libraries, student centers.

Student Life *Housing:* on-campus residence required through sophomore year. *Options:* men-only, women-only. Campus housing is university owned. Freshman campus housing is guaranteed. *Activities and organizations:* drama/theater group, choral group, Co-ed Societies, Circle K, NAFME, SBGA, Footlighters. *Campus security:* controlled dormitory access, evening patrols by trained security personnel. *Student services:* health clinic, personal/psychological counseling.

Athletics Member USCAA. *Intercollegiate sports:* basketball M(s)/W, cheerleading W, cross-country running M/W, soccer M(s)/W(s), volleyball W(s). *Intramural sports:* basketball M/W, football M/W, soccer M/W, softball M/W, ultimate Frisbee M/W, volleyball M/W.

Standardized Tests *Required:* SAT or ACT (for admission).

Costs (2012–13) *One-time required fee:* $150. *Comprehensive fee:* $21,390 includes full-time tuition ($13,020), mandatory fees ($800), and room and board ($7570). Part-time tuition: $520 per credit hour. Part-time tuition and fees vary according to course load. *College room only:* $3880. Room and board charges vary according to board plan and housing facility. *Payment plan:* installment. *Waivers:* employees or children of employees.

Financial Aid Of all full-time matriculated undergraduates who enrolled in 2010, 389 applied for aid, 321 were judged to have need, 29 had their need fully met. 25 Federal Work-Study jobs (averaging $831). In 2010, 65 non-need-based awards were made. *Average percent of need met:* 56%. *Average financial aid package:* $12,257. *Average need-based loan:* $3980. *Average need-based gift aid:* $6069. *Average non-need-based aid:* $2524.

Applying *Options:* electronic application. *Application fee:* $30. *Required:* high school transcript, minimum 2.0 GPA, 2 letters of recommendation. *Required for some:* essay required for international students. *Application deadlines:* 8/1 (freshmen), 8/1 (transfers). *Notification:* continuous (freshmen), continuous (transfers).

Freshman Application Contact Mrs. Colleen Engel, Assistant Director of Admissions, Florida College, 119 North Glen Arven Avenue, Temple Terrace, FL 33617. *Phone:* 813-988-5131 Ext. 152. *Fax:* 813-899-6772. *E-mail:* admissions@floridacollege.edu. *Website:* http://www.floridacollege.edu/.

Florida Gateway College
Lake City, Florida

- **State-supported** primarily 2-year, founded 1962, part of Florida Community College System
- **Small-town** 132-acre campus with easy access to Jacksonville
- **Coed** 3,073 undergraduate students, 34% full-time, 65% women, 35% men
- **Noncompetitive** entrance level

Undergraduates 1,040 full-time, 2,033 part-time. Students come from 4 states and territories; 10% Black or African American, non-Hispanic/Latino; 4% Hispanic/Latino; 0.9% Asian, non-Hispanic/Latino; 0.4% American Indian or Alaska Native, non-Hispanic/Latino; 0.4% Two or more races, non-Hispanic/Latino; 0.5% Race/ethnicity unknown; 0.1% international; 4% transferred in.
Freshmen *Admission:* 279 enrolled.
Faculty *Total:* 179, 38% full-time, 8% with terminal degrees. *Student/faculty ratio:* 16:1.
Academics *Calendar:* semesters. *Degrees:* certificates, diplomas, associate, and bachelor's. *Special study options:* academic remediation for entering students, adult/continuing education programs, advanced placement credit, cooperative education, distance learning, English as a second language, independent study, internships, off-campus study, part-time degree program, services for LD students, summer session for credit.
Computers on Campus 150 computers/terminals are available on campus for general student use. Students can access the following: free student e-mail accounts, online (class) grades, online (class) registration, online (class) schedules. Campuswide network is available. Wireless service is available via classrooms, computer centers, computer labs, learning centers, libraries.
Student Life *Housing:* college housing not available. *Activities and organizations:* drama/theater group, choral group. *Campus security:* 24-hour emergency response devices and patrols. *Student services:* personal/psychological counseling.
Costs (2012–13) *Tuition:* state resident $2480 full-time, $103 per credit hour part-time; nonresident $11,747 full-time, $392 per credit hour part-time. Full-time tuition and fees vary according to course level, course load, degree level, program, and reciprocity agreements. Part-time tuition and fees vary according to course level, course load, degree level, program, and reciprocity agreements. *Required fees:* $731 full-time, $24 per credit hour part-time. *Payment plan:* deferred payment. *Waivers:* employees or children of employees.
Applying *Required for some:* high school transcript. *Application deadlines:* rolling (freshmen), rolling (transfers). *Notification:* continuous (freshmen), continuous (transfers).
Freshman Application Contact Admissions, Florida Gateway College, 149 SE College Place, Lake City, FL 32025-8703. *Phone:* 386-755-4236. *E-mail:* admissions@fgc.edu.
Website: http://www.fgc.edu/.

Florida Gulf Coast University
Fort Myers, Florida

- **State-supported** comprehensive, founded 1991, part of State University System of Florida
- **Suburban** 760-acre campus
- **Endowment** $55.6 million
- **Coed** 12,155 undergraduate students, 80% full-time, 55% women, 45% men
- **Moderately difficult** entrance level, 68% of applicants were admitted

Undergraduates 9,704 full-time, 2,451 part-time. Students come from 44 states and territories; 87 other countries; 7% are from out of state; 7% Black or African American, non-Hispanic/Latino; 18% Hispanic/Latino; 2% Asian, non-Hispanic/Latino; 0.1% Native Hawaiian or other Pacific Islander, non-Hispanic/Latino; 0.2% American Indian or Alaska Native, non-Hispanic/Latino; 2% Two or more races, non-Hispanic/Latino; 1% Race/ethnicity unknown; 1% international; 9% transferred in; 34% live on campus. *Retention:* 76% of full-time freshmen returned.
Freshmen *Admission:* 10,073 applied, 6,811 admitted, 2,776 enrolled. *Average high school GPA:* 3.35. *Test scores:* SAT critical reading scores over 500: 56%; SAT math scores over 500: 59%; SAT writing scores over 500: 48%; ACT scores over 18: 95%; SAT critical reading scores over 600: 10%; SAT math scores over 600: 13%; SAT writing scores over 600: 8%; ACT scores over 24: 25%; SAT critical reading scores over 700: 1%; SAT math scores over 700: 1%; SAT writing scores over 700: 1%; ACT scores over 30: 2%.
Faculty *Total:* 630, 63% full-time, 47% with terminal degrees. *Student/faculty ratio:* 22:1.
Academics *Calendar:* semesters. *Degrees:* certificates, associate, bachelor's, master's, and doctoral. *Special study options:* academic remediation for entering students, accelerated degree program, advanced placement credit, cooperative education, distance learning, double majors, honors programs, independent study, internships, off-campus study, part-time degree program, services for LD students, study abroad, summer session for credit.
Computers on Campus 871 computers/terminals are available on campus for general student use. Students can access the following: online (class) registration, online admissions and advising. Campuswide network is available. 100% of college-owned or -operated housing units are wired for high-speed Internet access.
Student Life *Housing options:* coed. Campus housing is university owned. *Activities and organizations:* drama/theater group, student-run newspaper, student government, Ignite (Religious Organization), International Club, Martial Arts Club, Physical Therapy Association, national fraternities, national sororities. *Campus security:* 24-hour emergency response devices and patrols, late-night transport/escort service. *Student services:* health clinic, personal/psychological counseling.
Athletics Member NCAA. All Division I. *Intercollegiate sports:* baseball M(s), basketball M(s)/W(s), cheerleading W, cross-country running M(s)/W(s), golf M(s)/W(s), soccer M(s)/W(s), softball W(s), swimming and diving W(s), tennis M(s)/W(s), volleyball W(s). *Intramural sports:* basketball M/W, cross-country running M(c)/W(c), fencing M(c)/W(c), football M/W, ice hockey M(c), lacrosse M(c)/W(c), sailing M(c)/W(c), skiing (downhill) M(c)/W(c), soccer M/W, softball M/W, swimming and diving M(c)/W(c), table tennis M/W, tennis M(c)/W(c), ultimate Frisbee M/W, volleyball M/W, water polo M/W, weight lifting M(c)/W(c), wrestling M(c)/W(c).
Standardized Tests *Required:* SAT or ACT (for admission).
Costs (2012–13) *Tuition:* state resident $4855 full-time; nonresident $20,090 full-time. Full-time tuition and fees vary according to course load. Part-time tuition and fees vary according to course load. *Room and board:* $9424. Room and board charges vary according to board plan.
Financial Aid Of all full-time matriculated undergraduates who enrolled in 2011, 7,217 applied for aid, 4,806 were judged to have need, 419 had their need fully met. In 2011, 291 non-need-based awards were made. *Average percent of need met:* 19%. *Average financial aid package:* $9088. *Average need-based loan:* $7132. *Average need-based gift aid:* $5035. *Average non-need-based aid:* $3796. *Average indebtedness upon graduation:* $27,308. *Financial aid deadline:* 6/30.
Applying *Options:* electronic application, deferred entrance. *Application fee:* $30. *Required:* high school transcript, minimum 2.0 GPA. *Application deadlines:* 5/1 (freshmen), 7/1 (transfers). *Notification:* continuous (freshmen), continuous (transfers).
Freshman Application Contact Florida Gulf Coast University, 10501 FGCU Boulevard South, Fort Myers, FL 33965-6565. *Phone:* 239-590-7878. *Toll-free phone:* 888-889-1095.
Website: http://www.fgcu.edu/.

Florida Institute of Technology
Melbourne, Florida

- **Independent** university, founded 1958
- **Small-town** 130-acre campus with easy access to Orlando
- **Endowment** $47.1 million
- **Coed** 2,978 undergraduate students, 94% full-time, 28% women, 72% men
- **Moderately difficult** entrance level, 59% of applicants were admitted

Undergraduates 2,794 full-time, 184 part-time. Students come from 49 states and territories; 97 other countries; 47% are from out of state; 5% Black or African American, non-Hispanic/Latino; 6% Hispanic/Latino; 2% Asian, non-Hispanic/Latino; 0.1% Native Hawaiian or other Pacific Islander, non-Hispanic/Latino; 0.1% American Indian or Alaska Native, non-Hispanic/Latino; 2% Two or more races, non-Hispanic/Latino; 11% Race/ethnicity unknown; 29% international; 7% transferred in; 47% live on campus. *Retention:* 79% of full-time freshmen returned.
Freshmen *Admission:* 7,428 applied, 4,386 admitted, 756 enrolled. *Average high school GPA:* 3.6. *Test scores:* SAT critical reading scores over 500: 76%; SAT math scores over 500: 88%; ACT scores over 18: 98%; SAT critical reading scores over 600: 32%; SAT math scores over 600: 48%; ACT scores over 24: 64%; SAT critical reading scores over 700: 7%; SAT math scores over 700: 12%; ACT scores over 30: 14%.
Faculty *Total:* 467, 53% full-time, 75% with terminal degrees. *Student/faculty ratio:* 14:1.
Academics *Calendar:* semesters. *Degrees:* bachelor's, master's, doctoral, and post-master's certificates. *Special study options:* academic remediation for entering students, accelerated degree program, adult/continuing education programs, advanced placement credit, cooperative education, distance learning, double majors, English as a second language, independent study, internships, part-time degree program, services for LD students, student-designed majors, study abroad, summer session for credit. *ROTC:* Army (b).
Computers on Campus 440 computers/terminals and 75 ports are available on campus for general student use. Students can access the following: com-

puter help desk, free student e-mail accounts, online (class) grades, online (class) registration, online (class) schedules. Campuswide network is available. 100% of college-owned or -operated housing units are wired for high-speed Internet access. Wireless service is available via classrooms, computer centers, computer labs, dorm rooms, learning centers, libraries, student centers.

Student Life *Housing:* on-campus residence required through sophomore year. *Options:* coed. Campus housing is university owned. Freshman campus housing is guaranteed. *Activities and organizations:* drama/theater group, student-run newspaper, radio and television station, choral group, FITSSFF, College Players, Saudi Student House, Squamish, Phi Eta Sigma National Honor Society, national fraternities, national sororities. *Campus security:* 24-hour emergency response devices and patrols, late-night transport/escort service, controlled dormitory access. *Student services:* health clinic, personal/psychological counseling.

Athletics Member NCAA. All Division II. *Intercollegiate sports:* baseball M(s), basketball M(s)/W(s), crew M(s)/W(s), cross-country running M(s)/W(s), football M(c)/W(c), golf M(s)/W(s), lacrosse M, soccer M(s)/W(s), softball W(s), swimming and diving M(s)/W(s), tennis M(s)/W(s), track and field M(s)/W(s), ultimate Frisbee M(c)/W(c), volleyball W(s), water polo M(c)/W(c). *Intramural sports:* badminton M/W, baseball M(c)/W(c), basketball M/W, bowling M/W, cheerleading M(c)/W(c), crew M(c)/W(c), fencing M(c)/W(c), field hockey M(c)/W(c), football M/W, golf M/W, ice hockey M/W, sailing M(c)/W(c), soccer M/W, softball M/W, swimming and diving M(c)/W(c), table tennis M(c)/W(c), tennis M/W, ultimate Frisbee M/W, volleyball M/W, water polo M/W, weight lifting M/W, wrestling M(c)/W(c).

Standardized Tests *Required:* SAT or ACT (for admission).

Costs (2012–13) *Comprehensive fee:* $48,290 includes full-time tuition ($35,460), mandatory fees ($560), and room and board ($12,270). Full-time tuition and fees vary according to course load, program, and student level. Part-time tuition: $1025 per credit hour. *College room only:* $7150. Room and board charges vary according to board plan and housing facility. *Payment plan:* installment. *Waivers:* senior citizens and employees or children of employees.

Financial Aid Of all full-time matriculated undergraduates who enrolled in 2012, 1,797 applied for aid, 1,607 were judged to have need, 509 had their need fully met. 690 Federal Work-Study jobs (averaging $1930). 11 state and other part-time jobs (averaging $2661). In 2012, 661 non-need-based awards were made. *Average percent of need met:* 83%. *Average financial aid package:* $32,459. *Average need-based loan:* $4977. *Average need-based gift aid:* $21,384. *Average non-need-based aid:* $12,038. *Average indebtedness upon graduation:* $38,953.

Applying *Options:* electronic application, deferred entrance. *Required:* essay or personal statement, high school transcript, minimum 2.6 GPA, 2 letters of recommendation, SAT or ACT. *Recommended:* minimum 3.3 GPA, interview. *Application deadlines:* rolling (freshmen), rolling (transfers). *Notification:* continuous (freshmen), continuous (transfers).

Freshman Application Contact Michael J. Perry, Director of Undergraduate Admission, Florida Institute of Technology, 150 West University Boulevard, Melbourne, FL 32901-6975. *Phone:* 321-674-8030. *Toll-free phone:* 800-888-4348. *Fax:* 321-723-9468. *E-mail:* admission@fit.edu. *Website:* http://www.fit.edu/.

Florida International University
Miami, Florida

- **State-supported** university, founded 1965, part of State University System of Florida
- **Urban** 582-acre campus with easy access to Miami
- **Endowment** $132.5 million
- **Coed** 37,468 undergraduate students, 64% full-time, 55% women, 45% men
- **Moderately difficult** entrance level, 40% of applicants were admitted

Undergraduates 24,001 full-time, 13,467 part-time. Students come from 49 states and territories; 133 other countries; 3% are from out of state; 12% Black or African American, non-Hispanic/Latino; 66% Hispanic/Latino; 3% Asian, non-Hispanic/Latino; 0.1% Native Hawaiian or other Pacific Islander, non-Hispanic/Latino; 0.1% American Indian or Alaska Native, non-Hispanic/Latino; 2% Two or more races, non-Hispanic/Latino; 2% Race/ethnicity unknown; 5% international; 11% transferred in; 7% live on campus. *Retention:* 82% of full-time freshmen returned.

Freshmen *Admission:* 15,863 applied, 6,418 admitted, 4,345 enrolled. *Average high school GPA:* 3.7. *Test scores:* SAT critical reading scores over 500: 93%; SAT math scores over 500: 91%; SAT writing scores over 500: 90%; ACT scores over 18: 100%; SAT critical reading scores over 600: 30%; SAT

math scores over 600: 33%; SAT writing scores over 600: 26%; ACT scores over 24: 75%; SAT critical reading scores over 700: 3%; SAT math scores over 700: 2%; SAT writing scores over 700: 2%; ACT scores over 30: 6%.

Faculty *Total:* 2,052, 54% full-time, 65% with terminal degrees. *Student/faculty ratio:* 25:1.

Academics *Calendar:* semesters. *Degrees:* bachelor's, master's, doctoral, and postbachelor's certificates. *Special study options:* accelerated degree program, adult/continuing education programs, advanced placement credit, cooperative education, distance learning, double majors, freshman honors college, honors programs, independent study, internships, off-campus study, part-time degree program, services for LD students, study abroad, summer session for credit. *ROTC:* Army (b), Air Force (b).

Computers on Campus Students can access the following: computer help desk, free student e-mail accounts, online (class) grades, online (class) registration, online (class) schedules, online financial and cashier's information; class schedule, financial, campus maps information available on cell phones. Campuswide network is available. 100% of college-owned or -operated housing units are wired for high-speed Internet access. Wireless service is available via entire campus.

Student Life *Housing options:* coed. Campus housing is university owned. *Activities and organizations:* drama/theater group, student-run newspaper, radio station, choral group, marching band, Students for Community Service, Black Student Leadership Council, Hospitality Management Student Club, Hispanic Students Association, Haitian Students Organization, national fraternities, national sororities. *Campus security:* 24-hour emergency response devices and patrols, late-night transport/escort service, controlled dormitory access. *Student services:* health clinic, personal/psychological counseling, women's center.

Athletics Member NCAA. All Division I. *Intercollegiate sports:* baseball M(s), basketball M(s)/W(s), cross-country running M(s)/W(s), football M(s), golf W(s), soccer M(s)/W(s), softball W(s), swimming and diving W(s), tennis W(s), track and field M(s)/W(s), volleyball W(s). *Intramural sports:* badminton M(c)/W(c), baseball M(c), basketball M/W, crew M(c)/W(c), cross-country running M(c)/W(c), equestrian sports M(c)/W(c), football M/W, golf W, lacrosse M(c)/W(c), racquetball M/W, rugby M(c)/W(c), sailing M/W, soccer M/W, softball M/W, swimming and diving M(c)/W(c), table tennis M/W, tennis M(c)/W(c), ultimate Frisbee M/W, volleyball M/W, weight lifting M/W, wrestling M(c)/W(c).

Standardized Tests *Required:* SAT or ACT (for admission), TOEFL is required of all applicants whose native language is not English (for admission). *Recommended:* SAT Subject Tests (for admission).

Costs (2012–13) *Tuition:* state resident $6050 full-time, $202 per credit hour part-time; nonresident $18,449 full-time, $615 per credit hour part-time. Full-time tuition and fees vary according to course load. Part-time tuition and fees vary according to course load. *Required fees:* $367 full-time. *Room and board:* $11,330. Room and board charges vary according to board plan and housing facility. *Payment plan:* installment. *Waivers:* senior citizens and employees or children of employees.

Financial Aid Of all full-time matriculated undergraduates who enrolled in 2011, 16,384 applied for aid, 15,968 were judged to have need, 1,368 had their need fully met. 627 Federal Work-Study jobs (averaging $4424). 24 state and other part-time jobs (averaging $3678). In 2011, 2007 non-need-based awards were made. *Average percent of need met:* 17%. *Average financial aid package:* $7960. *Average need-based loan:* $9284. *Average need-based gift aid:* $5750. *Average non-need-based aid:* $455. *Average indebtedness upon graduation:* $17,706. *Financial aid deadline:* 5/15.

Applying *Options:* electronic application. *Application fee:* $30. *Required:* high school transcript, minimum 3.0 GPA. *Required for some:* portfolio, audition. *Application deadlines:* rolling (freshmen), rolling (out-of-state freshmen), rolling (transfers). *Notification:* continuous (freshmen), continuous (out-of-state freshmen), continuous (transfers).

Freshman Application Contact Mr. Barry Taylor, Director of Admissions, Florida International University, 11200 SW Eighth Street, PC 140, Miami, FL 33199. *Phone:* 305-348-2363. *Fax:* 305-348-3648. *E-mail:* admiss@fiu.edu. *Website:* http://www.fiu.edu/.

Florida Memorial University
Miami-Dade, Florida

Director of Admissions Mrs. Peggy Murray Martin, Director of Admissions and International Student Advisor, Florida Memorial University, 15800 NW 42nd Avenue, Miami-Dade, FL 33054. *Phone:* 305-626-3147. *Toll-free phone:* 800-822-1362. *Website:* http://www.fmuniv.edu/.

Florida National University

Hialeah, Florida

- **Proprietary** comprehensive, founded 1982
- **Urban** 4-acre campus with easy access to Miami
- **Coed** 2,487 undergraduate students, 73% full-time, 71% women, 29% men
- **Moderately difficult** entrance level, 83% of applicants were admitted

Undergraduates 1,825 full-time, 662 part-time. Students come from 16 states and territories; 16 other countries; 1% are from out of state; 3% Black or African American, non-Hispanic/Latino; 91% Hispanic/Latino; 0.5% Asian, non-Hispanic/Latino; 0.2% American Indian or Alaska Native, non-Hispanic/Latino; 0.4% Two or more races, non-Hispanic/Latino; 4% international; 4% transferred in. *Retention:* 78% of full-time freshmen returned.

Freshmen *Admission:* 1,394 applied, 1,161 admitted, 592 enrolled.

Faculty *Total:* 150, 61% full-time, 11% with terminal degrees. *Student/faculty ratio:* 19:1.

Academics *Calendar:* semesters. *Degrees:* certificates, diplomas, associate, bachelor's, and master's. *Special study options:* academic remediation for entering students, accelerated degree program, adult/continuing education programs, advanced placement credit, cooperative education, distance learning, English as a second language, independent study, internships, part-time degree program, services for LD students, summer session for credit.

Computers on Campus 225 computers/terminals are available on campus for general student use. Students can access the following: computer help desk, online (class) grades, online (class) registration, online (class) schedules. Campuswide network is available. Wireless service is available via entire campus.

Student Life *Housing:* college housing not available. *Activities and organizations:* student-run newspaper, Student Government Association, Bible Club, Salsa Club, W.I.C.S (Women Community Service), Criminal Justice Society, national fraternities. *Campus security:* 24-hour emergency response devices.

Standardized Tests *Required:* SAT or ACT (for admission).

Costs (2013–14) *Tuition:* $12,600 full-time, $525 per credit part-time. No tuition increase for student's term of enrollment. *Required fees:* $630 full-time. *Payment plans:* tuition prepayment, installment. *Waivers:* employees or children of employees.

Financial Aid Of all full-time matriculated undergraduates who enrolled in 2011, 1,223 applied for aid, 1,210 were judged to have need. 15 Federal Work-Study jobs (averaging $8300). *Average need-based gift aid:* $5460. *Average indebtedness upon graduation:* $8700.

Applying *Options:* electronic application, deferred entrance. *Required:* high school transcript, interview. *Application deadlines:* rolling (freshmen), rolling (transfers). *Notification:* continuous (freshmen), continuous (transfers).

Freshman Application Contact Mr. Joseph Forton, Director of Admissions, Florida National University, 4425 West Dr. Jose Regueiro Avenue (20th), Hialeah, FL 33012. *Phone:* 305-821-3333 Ext. 1071. *Fax:* 305-362-0595. *E-mail:* jforton@fnu.edu.
Website: http://www.fnu.edu/.

Florida Southern College

Lakeland, Florida

- **Independent** comprehensive, founded 1885, affiliated with United Methodist Church
- **Suburban** 113-acre campus with easy access to Tampa, Orlando
- **Endowment** $78.7 million
- **Coed** 2,040 undergraduate students, 97% full-time, 58% women, 42% men
- **Moderately difficult** entrance level, 56% of applicants were admitted

Undergraduates 1,987 full-time, 53 part-time. Students come from 45 states and territories; 40 other countries; 33% are from out of state; 6% Black or African American, non-Hispanic/Latino; 9% Hispanic/Latino; 2% Asian, non-Hispanic/Latino; 0.0% Native Hawaiian or other Pacific Islander, non-Hispanic/Latino; 0.4% American Indian or Alaska Native, non-Hispanic/Latino; 4% Two or more races, non-Hispanic/Latino; 0.1% Race/ethnicity unknown; 5% international; 5% transferred in; 70% live on campus. *Retention:* 76% of full-time freshmen returned.

Freshmen *Admission:* 4,448 applied, 2,477 admitted, 537 enrolled. *Average high school GPA:* 3.63. *Test scores:* SAT critical reading scores over 500: 79%; SAT math scores over 500: 73%; SAT writing scores over 500: 61%; ACT scores over 18: 99%; SAT critical reading scores over 600: 23%; SAT math scores over 600: 26%; SAT writing scores over 600: 17%; ACT scores over 24: 50%; SAT critical reading scores over 700: 3%; SAT math scores over 700: 3%; SAT writing scores over 700: 2%; ACT scores over 30: 9%.

Faculty *Total:* 229, 54% full-time, 55% with terminal degrees. *Student/faculty ratio:* 13:1.

Academics *Calendar:* semesters. *Degrees:* bachelor's and master's. *Special study options:* accelerated degree program, adult/continuing education programs, advanced placement credit, double majors, external degree program, honors programs, independent study, internships, off-campus study, part-time degree program, student-designed majors, study abroad, summer session for credit. *ROTC:* Army (b), Air Force (c). *Unusual degree programs:* 3-2 business administration with BA/MBA in Business Administration; engineering with Washington University in St. Louis.

Computers on Campus 500 computers/terminals and 50 ports are available on campus for general student use. Students can access the following: campus intranet, computer help desk, free student e-mail accounts, online (class) grades, online (class) registration, online (class) schedules, campus portal. Campuswide network is available. 100% of college-owned or -operated housing units are wired for high-speed Internet access. Wireless service is available via entire campus.

Student Life *Housing:* on-campus residence required through senior year. *Options:* coed, men-only, women-only, disabled students. Campus housing is university owned. Freshman campus housing is guaranteed. *Activities and organizations:* drama/theater group, student-run newspaper, television station, choral group, Student Government Association, Toastmasters, Association of Campus Entertainment, Beyond (Campus Ministry), Fellowship of Christian Athletes, national fraternities, national sororities. *Campus security:* 24-hour emergency response devices and patrols, student patrols, late-night transport/escort service, controlled dormitory access. *Student services:* health clinic, personal/psychological counseling.

Athletics Member NCAA. All Division II. *Intercollegiate sports:* baseball M(s), basketball M(s)/W(s), cheerleading W(c), cross-country running M(s)/W(s), golf M(s)/W(s), lacrosse M(s)/W(s), soccer M(s)/W(s), softball W(s), swimming and diving M(s)/W(s), tennis M(s)/W(s), track and field M(s)/W(s), volleyball M(c)/W(s). *Intramural sports:* basketball M/W, bowling M/W, cross-country running M/W, football M/W, golf M/W, soccer M/W, softball M/W, swimming and diving M/W, table tennis M/W, tennis M/W, ultimate Frisbee M/W, volleyball M/W.

Standardized Tests *Required:* SAT or ACT (for admission).

Costs (2012–13) *Comprehensive fee:* $36,300 includes full-time tuition ($26,600), mandatory fees ($600), and room and board ($9100). Full-time tuition and fees vary according to student level. Part-time tuition: $780 per semester hour. Part-time tuition and fees vary according to class time. *College room only:* $5000. Room and board charges vary according to board plan and housing facility. *Payment plan:* installment. *Waivers:* children of alumni and employees or children of employees.

Financial Aid Of all full-time matriculated undergraduates who enrolled in 2012, 1,756 applied for aid, 1,461 were judged to have need, 355 had their need fully met. 139 Federal Work-Study jobs (averaging $1500). 358 state and other part-time jobs (averaging $2142). In 2012, 478 non-need-based awards were made. *Average percent of need met:* 72%. *Average financial aid package:* $21,210. *Average need-based loan:* $4624. *Average need-based gift aid:* $15,632. *Average non-need-based aid:* $13,038. *Average indebtedness upon graduation:* $26,509. *Financial aid deadline:* 7/1.

Applying *Options:* electronic application, early admission, early decision, deferred entrance. *Application fee:* $30. *Required:* essay or personal statement, high school transcript, 1 letter of recommendation. *Recommended:* minimum 2.0 GPA, interview. *Application deadlines:* 3/1 (freshmen), rolling (transfers). *Early decision deadline:* 12/1. *Notification:* continuous (freshmen), continuous (transfers), 12/15 (early decision).

Freshman Application Contact Florida Southern College, 111 Lake Hollingsworth Drive, Lakeland, FL 33801-5698. *Phone:* 863-680-4131. *Toll-free phone:* 800-274-4131.
Website: http://www.flsouthern.edu/.

See previous page for display ad and page 1298 for the College Close-Up.

Florida State College at Jacksonville

Jacksonville, Florida

- **State-supported** primarily 2-year, founded 1963, part of Florida College System
- **Urban** 825-acre campus
- **Endowment** $28.8 million
- **Coed**
- **Noncompetitive** entrance level

Faculty *Student/faculty ratio:* 29:1.

Academics *Calendar:* semesters. *Degrees:* certificates, diplomas, associate, and bachelor's.

Student Life *Campus security:* 24-hour emergency response devices and patrols, late-night transport/escort service.

Athletics Member NJCAA.

Applying *Options:* electronic application, early admission, deferred entrance. *Application fee:* $25. *Required:* high school transcript.

Freshman Application Contact Dr. Peter Biegel, AVP, Enrollment Management, Florida State College at Jacksonville, 501 West State Street, Jacksonville, FL 32202. *Phone:* 904-632-3131. *Toll-free phone:* 888-873-1145. *Fax:* 904-632-5105. *E-mail:* pbiegel@fscj.edu.
Website: http://www.fscj.edu/.

Florida State University

Tallahassee, Florida

- **State-supported** university, founded 1851, part of State University System of Florida
- **Suburban** 451-acre campus
- **Endowment** $497.7 million
- **Coed** 32,171 undergraduate students, 89% full-time, 55% women, 45% men
- **Very difficult** entrance level, 54% of applicants were admitted

Undergraduates 28,733 full-time, 3,438 part-time. Students come from 52 states and territories; 109 other countries; 9% are from out of state; 9% Black or African American, non-Hispanic/Latino; 16% Hispanic/Latino; 3% Asian, non-Hispanic/Latino; 0.3% American Indian or Alaska Native, non-Hispanic/Latino; 2% Two or more races, non-Hispanic/Latino; 1% Race/ethnicity unknown; 0.8% international; 6% transferred in; 20% live on campus. *Retention:* 91% of full-time freshmen returned.

Freshmen *Admission:* 30,040 applied, 16,124 admitted, 5,712 enrolled. *Average high school GPA:* 3.85. *Test scores:* SAT critical reading scores over 500: 97%; SAT math scores over 500: 97%; SAT writing scores over 500: 96%; ACT scores over 18: 100%; SAT critical reading scores over 600: 51%; SAT math scores over 600: 54%; SAT writing scores over 600: 50%; ACT scores over 24: 91%; SAT critical reading scores over 700: 9%; SAT math scores over 700: 6%; SAT writing scores over 700: 7%; ACT scores over 30: 16%.

Faculty *Total:* 1,624, 77% full-time, 92% with terminal degrees. *Student/faculty ratio:* 26:1.

Academics *Calendar:* semesters. *Degrees:* certificates, associate, bachelor's, master's, doctoral, post-master's, and postbachelor's certificates. *Special study options:* accelerated degree program, advanced placement credit, cooperative education, distance learning, double majors, English as a second language, honors programs, independent study, internships, off-campus study, part-time degree program, services for LD students, study abroad, summer session for credit. *ROTC:* Army (b), Navy (c), Air Force (b).

Computers on Campus 3,821 computers/terminals are available on campus for general student use. Students can access the following: computer help desk, free student e-mail accounts, online (class) grades, online (class) registration, online (class) schedules, course home pages, course search, online fee payment. Campuswide network is available. 100% of college-owned or -operated housing units are wired for high-speed Internet access. Wireless service is available via entire campus.

Student Life *Housing options:* coed, women-only, cooperative, disabled students. Campus housing is university owned. Freshman applicants given priority for college housing. *Activities and organizations:* drama/theater group, student-run newspaper, radio and television station, choral group, marching band, student government, honors program, Golden Key Honor Society, Marching Chiefs, intramural sports, national fraternities, national sororities. *Campus security:* 24-hour emergency response devices and patrols, late-night transport/escort service, controlled dormitory access. *Student services:* health clinic, personal/psychological counseling, women's center, legal services.

Athletics Member NCAA. All Division I except football (Division I-A). *Intercollegiate sports:* baseball M(s), basketball M(s)/W(s), bowling M(c)/W(c), cheerleading M/W, cross-country running M(s)/W(s), golf M(s)/W(s), rugby M(c)/W(c), soccer M(c)/W(s), softball W(s), swimming and diving M(s)/W(s), table tennis M(c)/W(c), tennis M(s)/W(s), track and field M(s)/W(s), volleyball M(c)/W(s), wrestling M(c)/W(c). *Intramural sports:* badminton M(c)/W(c), baseball M(c), basketball M/W, bowling M/W, crew M(c)/W(c), equestrian sports M(c)/W(c), fencing M(c)/W(c), field hockey W(c), football M/W, golf M/W, gymnastics W(c), ice hockey M(c)/W(c), lacrosse M(c)/W(c), racquetball M/W, sailing M(c)/W(c), soccer M/W, softball M/W, squash M(c)/W(c), swimming and diving M/W, table tennis M/W, tennis M/W, track and field M/W, ultimate Frisbee M(c)/W(c), volleyball M/W, water polo M(c)/W(c), weight lifting M/W, wrestling M/W.

Standardized Tests *Required:* SAT or ACT (for admission).

Costs (2012–13) *Tuition:* state resident $3397 full-time, $113 per credit hour part-time; nonresident $18,564 full-time, $619 per credit hour part-time. Full-time tuition and fees vary according to course load, degree level, and location. Part-time tuition and fees vary according to course load, degree level, and location. *Required fees:* $3005 full-time, $99 per credit hour part-time, $20 per term part-time. *Room and board:* $9626; room only: $5694. Room and board charges vary according to board plan and housing facility. *Payment plans:* tuition prepayment, installment. *Waivers:* senior citizens and employees or children of employees.

Financial Aid Of all full-time matriculated undergraduates who enrolled in 2012, 24,347 applied for aid, 11,793 were judged to have need, 7,769 had their need fully met. 852 Federal Work-Study jobs (averaging $1200). 29 state and other part-time jobs (averaging $1200). In 2012, 1769 non-need-based awards were made. *Average percent of need met:* 67%. *Average financial aid package:* $9850. *Average need-based loan:* $3960. *Average need-based gift aid:* $3912. *Average non-need-based aid:* $2335. *Average indebtedness upon graduation:* $22,405.
Applying *Options:* electronic application, early admission. *Application fee:* $30. *Required:* high school transcript. *Recommended:* essay or personal statement. *Application deadlines:* 1/14 (freshmen), 1/14 (out-of-state freshmen), 7/1 (transfers). *Notification:* 3/20 (freshmen), 3/20 (out-of-state freshmen), continuous (transfers).
Freshman Application Contact Florida State University, Tallahassee, FL 32306. *Phone:* 850-644-6200.
Website: http://www.fsu.edu/.

Florida Tech University Online

Tampa, Florida

Admissions Office Contact Florida Tech University Online, 9417 Princess Palm Avenue, Tampa, FL 33619. *Toll-free phone:* 855-300-1469.
Website: http://floridatechonline.com/.

Full Sail University

Winter Park, Florida

Freshman Application Contact Ms. Mary Beth Plank, Director of Admissions, Full Sail University, 3300 University Boulevard, Winter Park, FL 32792-7437. *Phone:* 407-679-6333. *Toll-free phone:* 800-226-7625. *E-mail:* admissions@fullsail.com.
Website: http://www.fullsail.edu/.

Gulf Coast State College

Panama City, Florida

- **State-supported** primarily 2-year, founded 1957
- **Suburban** 80-acre campus
- **Endowment** $25.9 million
- **Coed**
- **Noncompetitive** entrance level

Faculty *Student/faculty ratio:* 21:1.
Academics *Calendar:* semesters. *Degrees:* certificates, associate, and bachelor's.
Student Life *Campus security:* late-night transport/escort service, patrols by trained security personnel during campus hours.
Athletics Member NJCAA.
Costs (2012–13) *One-time required fee:* $20. *Tuition:* state resident $2370 full-time, $99 per credit hour part-time; nonresident $8635 full-time, $360 per credit hour part-time. Full-time tuition and fees vary according to degree level. Part-time tuition and fees vary according to degree level.
Financial Aid *Of all full-time matriculated undergraduates who enrolled in 2011,* 145 Federal Work-Study jobs (averaging $3200). 60 state and other part-time jobs (averaging $2600).
Applying *Options:* electronic application, early admission, deferred entrance. *Application fee:* $20. *Required:* high school transcript.
Freshman Application Contact Mrs. Jackie Kuczenski, Administrative Secretary of Admissions, Gulf Coast State College, 5230 West U.S. Highway 98, Panama City, FL 32401. *Phone:* 850-769-1551 Ext. 4892. *Fax:* 850-913-3308. *E-mail:* jkuczenski@gulfcoast.edu.
Website: http://www.gulfcoast.edu/.

Herzing University

Winter Park, Florida

Director of Admissions Tessie Uranga, Director of Admissions, Herzing University, 1595 South Semoran Boulevard, Winter Park, FL 32792. *Phone:* 407-478-0500. *Toll-free phone:* 800-596-0724. *Fax:* 407-380-0269.
Website: http://www.herzing.edu/.

Hobe Sound Bible College

Hobe Sound, Florida

Freshman Application Contact Director of Admissions, Hobe Sound Bible College, PO Box 1065, Hobe Sound, FL 33475-1065. *Phone:* 772-545-1400. *E-mail:* info@hsbc.edu.
Website: http://www.hsbc.edu/.

Hodges University

Naples, Florida

- **Independent** comprehensive, founded 1990
- **Suburban** 31-acre campus with easy access to Miami
- **Endowment** $4.5 million
- **Coed** 2,067 undergraduate students, 68% full-time, 66% women, 34% men
- **Minimally difficult** entrance level, 86% of applicants were admitted

Undergraduates 1,409 full-time, 658 part-time. Students come from 7 states and territories; 6% are from out of state; 16% Black or African American, non-Hispanic/Latino; 34% Hispanic/Latino; 2% Asian, non-Hispanic/Latino; 0.3% Native Hawaiian or other Pacific Islander, non-Hispanic/Latino; 0.7% American Indian or Alaska Native, non-Hispanic/Latino; 0.6% Two or more races, non-Hispanic/Latino; 3% Race/ethnicity unknown; 15% transferred in.
Freshmen *Admission:* 240 applied, 207 admitted, 201 enrolled.
Faculty *Total:* 157, 59% full-time, 46% with terminal degrees. *Student/faculty ratio:* 14:1.
Academics *Calendar:* trimesters. *Degrees:* certificates, associate, bachelor's, and master's. *Special study options:* academic remediation for entering students, accelerated degree program, adult/continuing education programs, advanced placement credit, cooperative education, distance learning, double majors, English as a second language, external degree program, independent study, internships, part-time degree program, services for LD students, summer session for credit.
Computers on Campus 1,020 computers/terminals are available on campus for general student use. Students can access the following: Our campus intranet takes the form of a student portal that is accessible via the internet. The portal provides single sign on access to all of the above as well as our Learning Management System, online storage, library resources, a student calendar, etc. Campuswide network is available. Wireless service is available via entire campus.
Student Life *Housing:* college housing not available. *Activities and organizations:* Ambassadors, Paralegal Club, Institute of Managerial Accountants, running club, Entrepreneurial Club. *Campus security:* late-night transport/escort service, building security. *Student services:* personal/psychological counseling.
Standardized Tests *Required for some:* CPAt.
Costs (2012–13) *Tuition:* $11,760 full-time. *Required fees:* $500 full-time. *Payment plan:* installment. *Waivers:* employees or children of employees.
Financial Aid Of all full-time matriculated undergraduates who enrolled in 2010, 1,558 applied for aid, 1,402 were judged to have need, 285 had their need fully met. 50 Federal Work-Study jobs (averaging $3931). In 2010, 71 non-need-based awards were made. *Average percent of need met:* 76%. *Average financial aid package:* $9275. *Average need-based loan:* $4310. *Average need-based gift aid:* $4625. *Average non-need-based aid:* $220. *Average indebtedness upon graduation:* $18,900.
Applying *Options:* electronic application, deferred entrance. *Application fee:* $20. *Required:* essay or personal statement, high school transcript, interview. *Required for some:* 2 letters of recommendation. *Application deadlines:* rolling (freshmen), rolling (transfers). *Notification:* continuous (freshmen), continuous (transfers).
Freshman Application Contact Hodges University, 2655 Northbrooke Drive, Naples, FL 34119. *Phone:* 239-513-1122 Ext. 104. *Toll-free phone:* 800-466-8017.
Website: http://www.hodges.edu/.

Indian River State College

Fort Pierce, Florida

- **State-supported** 4-year, founded 1960, part of Florida Community College System
- **Small-town** 713-acre campus
- **Coed** 17,806 undergraduate students, 34% full-time, 60% women, 40% men
- **Noncompetitive** entrance level, 100% of applicants were admitted

Undergraduates 6,097 full-time, 11,709 part-time. Students come from 28 states and territories; 120 other countries; 15% are from out of state; 0.2% Black or African American, non-Hispanic/Latino; 15% Hispanic/Latino; 0.2% Asian, non-Hispanic/Latino; 61% Native Hawaiian or other Pacific Islander, non-Hispanic/Latino; 17% American Indian or Alaska Native, non-Hispanic/Latino; 1% Two or more races, non-Hispanic/Latino; 3% Race/ethnicity unknown; 1% international; 14% transferred in.
Freshmen *Admission:* 1,734 applied, 1,734 admitted, 1,734 enrolled.
Faculty *Total:* 874, 26% full-time, 19% with terminal degrees. *Student/faculty ratio:* 22:1.
Academics *Calendar:* semesters. *Degrees:* certificates, diplomas, associate, and bachelor's. *Special study options:* academic remediation for entering students, adult/continuing education programs, advanced placement credit, dis-

tance learning, English as a second language, independent study, part-time degree program, services for LD students, summer session for credit.

Computers on Campus 3,200 computers/terminals are available on campus for general student use. Students can access the following: computer help desk, free student e-mail accounts, online (class) grades, online (class) registration, online (class) schedules. Campuswide network is available. Wireless service is available via classrooms, computer centers, computer labs, learning centers, libraries, student centers.

Student Life *Housing:* college housing not available. *Activities and organizations:* drama/theater group, choral group. *Campus security:* 24-hour emergency response devices and patrols. *Student services:* health clinic, personal/psychological counseling, women's center.

Athletics Member NJCAA. *Intercollegiate sports:* baseball M(s), basketball M(s)/W(s), softball W(s), swimming and diving M(s)/W(s), volleyball W(s). *Intramural sports:* basketball M/W, racquetball M/W, soccer M, volleyball M/W.

Applying *Options:* early admission, deferred entrance. *Required:* high school transcript. *Application deadlines:* rolling (freshmen), rolling (transfers). *Notification:* continuous (freshmen), continuous (transfers).

Freshman Application Contact Mr. Steven Payne, Dean of Educational Services, Indian River State College, 3209 Virginia Avenue, Fort Pierce, FL 34981-5596. *Phone:* 772-462-7805. *Toll-free phone:* 866-792-4772. *E-mail:* spayne@ircc.edu.
Website: http://www.irsc.edu/.

International Academy of Design & Technology

Tampa, Florida

- **Proprietary** 4-year, founded 1984, part of Career Education Corporation
- **Urban** 1-acre campus
- **Coed**
- **Noncompetitive** entrance level

Faculty *Total:* 91. *Student/faculty ratio:* 21:1.

Academics *Calendar:* quarters. *Degrees:* associate and bachelor's. *Special study options:* academic remediation for entering students, accelerated degree program, cooperative education, distance learning, independent study, internships, part-time degree program, services for LD students, study abroad, summer session for credit.

Computers on Campus 485 computers/terminals are available on campus for general student use. Campuswide network is available.

Student Life *Housing:* college housing not available. *Activities and organizations:* Student Chapter ASID, IIDA, Emerging Professionals, United States Greenbuilding Council (USGBC), American Advertising Federation. *Campus security:* 24-hour emergency response devices, late night patrols by trained security personnel.

Standardized Tests *Required:* Wonderlic Assessment (for admission).

Costs (2012–13) *Tuition:* $14,400 full-time. *Payment plan:* installment. *Waivers:* employees or children of employees.

Financial Aid *Average percent of need met:* 48%.

Applying *Options:* electronic application, early admission, deferred entrance. *Application fee:* $50. *Required:* interview, Portfolio review for fashion design program; Wonderlic assessment. *Recommended:* high school transcript. *Application deadlines:* rolling (freshmen), rolling (out-of-state freshmen), rolling (transfers). *Notification:* continuous (freshmen), continuous (out-of-state freshmen), continuous (transfers).

Freshman Application Contact International Academy of Design & Technology, 5104 Eisenhower Boulevard, Tampa, FL 33634-7350. *Phone:* 813-881-0007. *Toll-free phone:* 888-315-6111.
Website: http://www.academy.edu/.

ITT Technical Institute

Bradenton, Florida

- **Proprietary** primarily 2-year, part of ITT Educational Services, Inc.
- **Coed**

Academics *Calendar:* quarters. *Degrees:* associate and bachelor's.

Freshman Application Contact Director of Recruitment, ITT Technical Institute, 8039 Cooper Creek Boulevard, Bradenton, FL 34201. *Phone:* 941-309-9200. *Toll-free phone:* 800-342-8684.
Website: http://www.itt-tech.edu/.

ITT Technical Institute

Deerfield Beach, Florida

- **Proprietary** 4-year
- **Coed**
- **Minimally difficult** entrance level

Academics *Degrees:* associate and bachelor's.

Freshman Application Contact Director of Recruitment, ITT Technical Institute, 700 W. Hillsboro Boulevard, Suite 100, Building 1, Deerfield Beach, FL 33441. *Phone:* 954-360-4701. *Toll-free phone:* 877-243-8548.
Website: http://www.itt-tech.edu/.

ITT Technical Institute

Fort Lauderdale, Florida

- **Proprietary** primarily 2-year, founded 1991, part of ITT Educational Services, Inc.
- **Suburban** campus
- **Coed**
- **Minimally difficult** entrance level

Academics *Calendar:* quarters. *Degrees:* associate and bachelor's.

Freshman Application Contact Director of Recruitment, ITT Technical Institute, 3401 South University Drive, Fort Lauderdale, FL 33328-2021. *Phone:* 954-476-9300. *Toll-free phone:* 800-488-7797.
Website: http://www.itt-tech.edu/.

ITT Technical Institute

Fort Myers, Florida

- **Proprietary** primarily 2-year
- **Coed**
- **Minimally difficult** entrance level

Academics *Degrees:* associate and bachelor's.

Freshman Application Contact Director of Recruitment, ITT Technical Institute, 13500 Powers Court, Suite 100, Fort Myers, FL 33912. *Phone:* 239-603-8700. *Toll-free phone:* 877-485-5313.
Website: http://www.itt-tech.edu/.

ITT Technical Institute

Jacksonville, Florida

- **Proprietary** primarily 2-year, founded 1991, part of ITT Educational Services, Inc.
- **Urban** campus
- **Coed**
- **Minimally difficult** entrance level

Academics *Calendar:* quarters. *Degrees:* associate and bachelor's.

Financial Aid *Of all full-time matriculated undergraduates who enrolled in 2011,* 5 Federal Work-Study jobs.

Freshman Application Contact Director of Recruitment, ITT Technical Institute, 7011 A.C. Skinner Parkway, Suite 140, Jacksonville, FL 32256. *Phone:* 904-573-9100. *Toll-free phone:* 800-318-1264.
Website: http://www.itt-tech.edu/.

ITT Technical Institute

Lake Mary, Florida

- **Proprietary** primarily 2-year, founded 1989, part of ITT Educational Services, Inc.
- **Suburban** campus
- **Coed**
- **Minimally difficult** entrance level

Academics *Calendar:* quarters. *Degrees:* associate and bachelor's.

Freshman Application Contact Director of Recruitment, ITT Technical Institute, 1400 South International Parkway, Lake Mary, FL 32746. *Phone:* 407-660-2900. *Toll-free phone:* 866-489-8441. *Fax:* 407-660-2566.
Website: http://www.itt-tech.edu/.

ITT Technical Institute

Miami, Florida

- **Proprietary** primarily 2-year, founded 1996, part of ITT Educational Services, Inc.
- **Coed**
- **Minimally difficult** entrance level

Academics *Calendar:* quarters. *Degrees:* associate and bachelor's.

Freshman Application Contact Director of Recruitment, ITT Technical Institute, 7955 NW 12th Street, Suite 119, Miami, FL 33126. *Phone:* 305-477-3080.
Website: http://www.itt-tech.edu/.

ITT Technical Institute
Orlando, Florida

- **Proprietary** primarily 2-year, part of ITT Educational Services, Inc.
- **Coed**

Academics *Calendar:* quarters. *Degrees:* associate and bachelor's.
Freshman Application Contact Director of Recruitment, ITT Technical Institute, 8301 Southpark Circle, Suite 100, Orlando, FL 32819. *Phone:* 407-371-6000. *Toll-free phone:* 877-201-4367.
Website: http://www.itt-tech.edu/.

ITT Technical Institute
St. Petersburg, Florida

- **Proprietary** primarily 2-year, part of ITT Educational Services, Inc.
- **Coed**
- **Minimally difficult** entrance level

Academics *Degrees:* associate and bachelor's.
Freshman Application Contact Director of Recruitment, ITT Technical Institute, 877 Executive Center Drive W., Suite 100, St. Petersburg, FL 33702. *Phone:* 727-209-4700. *Toll-free phone:* 866-488-5084.
Website: http://www.itt-tech.edu/.

ITT Technical Institute
Tallahassee, Florida

- **Proprietary** primarily 2-year
- **Coed**
- **Minimally difficult** entrance level

Academics *Degrees:* associate and bachelor's.
Freshman Application Contact Director of Recruitment, ITT Technical Institute, 2639 North Monroe Street, Building A, Suite 100, Tallahassee, FL 32303. *Phone:* 850-422-6300. *Toll-free phone:* 877-230-3559.
Website: http://www.itt-tech.edu/.

ITT Technical Institute
Tampa, Florida

- **Proprietary** primarily 2-year, founded 1981, part of ITT Educational Services, Inc.
- **Suburban** campus
- **Coed**
- **Minimally difficult** entrance level

Academics *Calendar:* quarters. *Degrees:* associate and bachelor's.
Freshman Application Contact Director of Recruitment, ITT Technical Institute, 4809 Memorial Highway, Tampa, FL 33634-7151. *Phone:* 813-885-2244. *Toll-free phone:* 800-825-2831.
Website: http://www.itt-tech.edu/.

ITT Technical Institute
West Palm Beach, Florida

- **Proprietary** 4-year
- **Coed**
- **Minimally difficult** entrance level

Academics *Degrees:* associate and bachelor's.
Freshman Application Contact Director of Recruitment, ITT Technical Institute, 1756 N. Congress Avenue, West Palm Beach, FL 33409. *Phone:* 561-233-4900. *Toll-free phone:* 877-236-8164.
Website: http://www.itt-tech.edu/.

Jacksonville University
Jacksonville, Florida

- **Independent** comprehensive, founded 1934
- **Suburban** 198-acre campus
- **Coed**
- **Moderately difficult** entrance level

Faculty *Student/faculty ratio:* 13:1.

Academics *Calendar:* semesters. *Degrees:* bachelor's, master's, and post-master's certificates.
Student Life *Campus security:* 24-hour emergency response devices and patrols, student patrols, late-night transport/escort service, controlled dormitory access, code lock doors in residence halls, trained security patrols during evening hours.
Athletics Member NCAA. All Division I except football (Division I-AA).
Standardized Tests *Required:* SAT or ACT (for admission).
Costs (2012–13) *Comprehensive fee:* $37,450 includes full-time tuition ($29,100) and room and board ($8350). *College room only:* $6010. Room and board charges vary according to board plan and housing facility.
Financial Aid *Of all full-time matriculated undergraduates who enrolled in 2011,* 1,807 applied for aid, 1,594 were judged to have need, 335 had their need fully met. *In 2011,* 409 non-need-based awards were made. *Average percent of need met:* 50. *Average financial aid package:* $18,465. *Average need-based loan:* $4549. *Average need-based gift aid:* $14,818. *Average non-need-based aid:* $10,194.
Applying *Options:* electronic application, early admission, deferred entrance. *Application fee:* $30. *Required:* high school transcript, minimum 2.0 GPA. *Required for some:* essay or personal statement. *Recommended:* interview.
Freshman Application Contact Ms. Lisa Hannasch, Director of First Year Student Admission and Enrollment, Jacksonville University, 2800 University Boulevard North, Office of Admissions, Jacksonville, FL 32211. *Phone:* 904-256-7000. *Toll-free phone:* 800-225-2027. *Fax:* 904-256-7012. *E-mail:* admissions@ju.edu.
Website: http://www.ju.edu/.

Johnson & Wales University
North Miami, Florida

Freshman Application Contact Jeff Greenip, Director of Admissions, Johnson & Wales University, 1701 Northeast 127th Street, North Miami, FL 33181. *Phone:* 305-892-7600. *Toll-free phone:* 866-598-3567. *Fax:* 305-892-7020. *E-mail:* mia@admissions.jwu.edu.
Website: http://www.jwu.edu/northmiami/.

Jones College
Jacksonville, Florida

- **Independent** 4-year, founded 1918
- **Urban** 5-acre campus
- **Coed** 496 undergraduate students, 48% full-time, 69% women, 31% men
- **Noncompetitive** entrance level

Undergraduates 240 full-time, 256 part-time. Students come from 16 states and territories; 1 other country; 8% are from out of state; 71% Black or African American, non-Hispanic/Latino; 5% Hispanic/Latino; 0.6% Asian, non-Hispanic/Latino; 0.6% American Indian or Alaska Native, non-Hispanic/Latino; 2% Two or more races, non-Hispanic/Latino; 1% Race/ethnicity unknown; 0.4% international; 11% transferred in.
Freshmen *Admission:* 27 enrolled.
Faculty *Total:* 73, 12% full-time, 25% with terminal degrees. *Student/faculty ratio:* 7:1.
Academics *Calendar:* trimesters. *Degrees:* associate and bachelor's. *Special study options:* academic remediation for entering students, accelerated degree program, adult/continuing education programs, advanced placement credit, cooperative education, distance learning, double majors, internships, part-time degree program, student-designed majors, summer session for credit.
Computers on Campus 100 computers/terminals are available on campus for general student use. Students can access the following: campus intranet, computer help desk, free student e-mail accounts, online (class) registration, online (class) schedules. Campuswide network is available. Wireless service is available via classrooms, computer centers, computer labs, student centers.
Student Life *Housing:* college housing not available. *Campus security:* late-night transport/escort service, emergency notification system through email/texting/phones.
Standardized Tests *Required for some:* CPAt.
Costs (2013–14) *Tuition:* $7320 full-time, $305 per credit hour part-time. *Required fees:* $90 full-time, $45 per term part-time. *Payment plan:* installment. *Waivers:* children of alumni and employees or children of employees.
Applying *Options:* electronic application. *Required:* interview. *Required for some:* high school transcript. *Application deadline:* rolling (freshmen). *Notification:* continuous (transfers).
Freshman Application Contact Jones College, 555 Arlington Expressway, Jacksonville, FL 32211-5588. *Phone:* 904-743-1122 Ext. 141. *Toll-free phone:* 800-631-4056.
Website: http://www.jones.edu/.

Jose Maria Vargas University

Pembroke Pines, Florida

Admissions Office Contact Jose Maria Vargas University, 8300 South Palm Drive, Pembroke Pines, FL 33025.
Website: http://www.jmvu.edu/.

Keiser University

Fort Lauderdale, Florida

Freshman Application Contact Keiser University, 1500 NW 49th Street, Fort Lauderdale, FL 33309. *Toll-free phone:* 888-534-7379.
Website: http://www.keiseruniversity.edu/.

Keiser University

Fort Myers, Florida

Admissions Office Contact Keiser University, 9100 Forum Corporate Parkway, Fort Myers, FL 33905.
Website: http://www.keiseruniversity.edu/.

Lincoln College of Technology

West Palm Beach, Florida

Director of Admissions Mr. Kevin Cassidy, Director of Admissions, Lincoln College of Technology, 2410 Metrocentre Boulevard, West Palm Beach, FL 33407. *Phone:* 561-842-8324 Ext. 117. *Fax:* 561-842-9503.
Website: http://www.lincolnedu.com/.

Lincoln Culinary Institute

West Palm Beach, Florida

- **Proprietary** 4-year
- **Urban** 14-acre campus with easy access to West Palm Beach, Fort Lauderdale, Miami
- **Coed**

Academics *Degrees:* diplomas, associate, and bachelor's (degree in science only (18 or 24 month program)).
Financial Aid *Of all full-time matriculated undergraduates who enrolled in 2011,* 28 Federal Work-Study jobs (averaging $4160).
Freshman Application Contact Lincoln Culinary Institute, 2410 Metrocentre Boulevard, West Palm Beach, FL 33407. *Phone:* 561-842-8324 Ext. 202.
Website: http://www.lincolnedu.com/campus/west-palm-beach-culinary-fl.

Lynn University

Boca Raton, Florida

- **Independent** comprehensive, founded 1962
- **Suburban** 123-acre campus with easy access to Fort Lauderdale
- **Endowment** $21.1 million
- **Coed** 1,657 undergraduate students, 90% full-time, 48% women, 52% men
- **Moderately difficult** entrance level, 95% of applicants were admitted

Undergraduates 1,499 full-time, 158 part-time. Students come from 42 states and territories; 77 other countries; 55% are from out of state; 8% Black or African American, non-Hispanic/Latino; 10% Hispanic/Latino; 0.9% Asian, non-Hispanic/Latino; 0.3% Native Hawaiian or other Pacific Islander, non-Hispanic/Latino; 0.2% American Indian or Alaska Native, non-Hispanic/Latino; 1% Two or more races, non-Hispanic/Latino; 8% Race/ethnicity unknown; 22% international; 10% transferred in; 48% live on campus. *Retention:* 69% of full-time freshmen returned.
Freshmen *Admission:* 2,162 applied, 2,047 admitted, 409 enrolled. *Average high school GPA:* 2.8. *Test scores:* SAT critical reading scores over 500: 23%; SAT math scores over 500: 32%; SAT writing scores over 500: 22%; ACT scores over 18: 72%; SAT critical reading scores over 600: 5%; SAT math scores over 600: 6%; SAT writing scores over 600: 5%; ACT scores over 24: 13%; SAT critical reading scores over 700: 1%; SAT writing scores over 700: 1%; ACT scores over 30: 1%.
Faculty *Total:* 181, 51% full-time, 46% with terminal degrees. *Student/faculty ratio:* 15:1.
Academics *Calendar:* semesters plus 3 summer sessions. *Degrees:* certificates, bachelor's, master's, doctoral, post-master's, and postbachelor's certificates. *Special study options:* academic remediation for entering students, accelerated degree program, adult/continuing education programs, advanced placement credit, cooperative education, distance learning, double majors, English as a second language, freshman honors college, honors programs,

independent study, internships, part-time degree program, services for LD students, study abroad, summer session for credit. *ROTC:* Air Force (c).
Computers on Campus Students can access the following: campus intranet, computer help desk, free student e-mail accounts, online (class) grades, online (class) registration, online (class) schedules. Campuswide network is available. Wireless service is available via classrooms, computer centers, computer labs, dorm rooms, learning centers, libraries, student centers.
Student Life *Housing:* on-campus residence required for freshman year. *Options:* coed, women-only, disabled students. Campus housing is university owned. Freshman campus housing is guaranteed. *Activities and organizations:* drama/theater group, student-run newspaper, radio and television station, Knights of the Round Table, intramural groups, student newspaper, Residence Hall Council, Activities Board, national fraternities, national sororities. *Campus security:* 24-hour emergency response devices and patrols, late-night transport/escort service, video monitor at residence entrances. *Student services:* health clinic, personal/psychological counseling, women's center.
Athletics Member NCAA. All Division II. *Intercollegiate sports:* baseball M(s), basketball M(s)/W(s), cross-country running M(s)/W(s), golf M(s)/W(s), soccer M(s)/W(s), softball W(s), swimming and diving W(s), tennis M(s)/W(s), volleyball W(s). *Intramural sports:* basketball M/W, cheerleading W(c), football M/W, golf M/W, ice hockey M(c), lacrosse M(c), rugby M(c), soccer M(c), tennis M/W, volleyball M(c).
Standardized Tests *Required:* SAT or ACT (for admission).
Costs (2013–14) *Comprehensive fee:* $44,300 includes full-time tuition ($31,900), mandatory fees ($1500), and room and board ($10,900). Full-time tuition and fees vary according to reciprocity agreements. Part-time tuition: $925 per credit. Part-time tuition and fees vary according to class time and course load. *Room and board:* Room and board charges vary according to board plan and housing facility. *Payment plans:* installment, deferred payment. *Waivers:* employees or children of employees.
Financial Aid Of all full-time matriculated undergraduates who enrolled in 2012, 1,117 applied for aid, 661 were judged to have need, 655 had their need fully met. 82 Federal Work-Study jobs (averaging $2030). 37 state and other part-time jobs (averaging $7446). In 2012, 277 non-need-based awards were made. *Average percent of need met:* 52%. *Average financial aid package:* $19,097. *Average need-based loan:* $4920. *Average need-based gift aid:* $10,250. *Average non-need-based aid:* $11,387. *Average indebtedness upon graduation:* $33,472.
Applying *Options:* electronic application, early admission, deferred entrance. *Application fee:* $45. *Required:* essay or personal statement, high school transcript, minimum 2.0 GPA. *Recommended:* minimum 3.0 GPA, interview, Interview and essay, portfolio for art and graphic design majors. *Application deadlines:* rolling (freshmen), rolling (transfers). *Notification:* continuous (freshmen), continuous (transfers).
Freshman Application Contact Stefano Papaleo, Director of Undergraduate Admission, Lynn University, Admission, 3601 North Military Trail, Boca Raton, FL 33431. *Phone:* 561-237-7831. *Toll-free phone:* 800-888-5966. *Fax:* 561-237-7100. *E-mail:* spapaleo@lynn.edu.
Website: http://www.lynn.edu/.

Miami Dade College

Miami, Florida

- **State and locally supported** primarily 2-year, founded 1960, part of Florida College System
- **Urban** campus
- **Endowment** $165.5 million
- **Coed** 66,701 undergraduate students, 39% full-time, 58% women, 42% men
- **Noncompetitive** entrance level, 100% of applicants were admitted

Undergraduates 26,211 full-time, 40,490 part-time. Students come from 43 states and territories; 185 other countries; 1% are from out of state; 17% Black or African American, non-Hispanic/Latino; 70% Hispanic/Latino; 1% Asian, non-Hispanic/Latino; 0.1% Native Hawaiian or other Pacific Islander, non-Hispanic/Latino; 0.1% American Indian or Alaska Native, non-Hispanic/Latino; 0.3% Two or more races, non-Hispanic/Latino; 3% Race/ethnicity unknown; 2% international; 3% transferred in.
Freshmen *Admission:* 10,575 applied, 10,575 admitted, 12,224 enrolled.
Faculty *Total:* 2,558, 28% full-time, 18% with terminal degrees. *Student/faculty ratio:* 30:1.
Academics *Calendar:* 16-16-6-6. *Degrees:* certificates, associate, bachelor's, and postbachelor's certificates. *Special study options:* academic remediation for entering students, accelerated degree program, adult/continuing education programs, advanced placement credit, cooperative education, distance learning, English as a second language, freshman honors college, honors programs, independent study, internships, off-campus study, part-time degree program, services for LD students, study abroad, summer session for credit. *ROTC:* Army (b), Air Force (b).

Computers on Campus 9,655 computers/terminals and 1,500 ports are available on campus for general student use. Students can access the following: campus intranet, computer help desk, free student e-mail accounts, online (class) grades, online (class) registration, online (class) schedules, admissions; student feedback of faculty; financial aid; IRS Form 1098. Campuswide network is available. Wireless service is available via classrooms, computer centers, computer labs, learning centers, libraries, student centers.

Student Life *Housing:* college housing not available. *Activities and organizations:* drama/theater group, student-run newspaper, radio and television station, choral group, Student Government Association, Phi Theta Kappa, Phi Beta Lambda (Business), Future Educators of America Professional, Kappa Delta Pi Honor Society (Education), national fraternities. *Campus security:* 24-hour emergency response devices and patrols, mass communication emergency notification systems. *Student services:* personal/psychological counseling.

Athletics Member NCAA, NJCAA. All NCAA Division I. *Intercollegiate sports:* baseball M(s), basketball M(s)/W(s), softball W(s), volleyball W(s).

Costs (2012–13) *One-time required fee:* $30. *Tuition:* state resident $2483 full-time, $83 per credit hour part-time; nonresident $9933 full-time, $331 per credit hour part-time. Full-time tuition and fees vary according to course load, degree level, and program. Part-time tuition and fees vary according to course load, degree level, and program. *Required fees:* $883 full-time, $29 per credit hour part-time. *Waivers:* employees or children of employees.

Financial Aid Of all full-time matriculated undergraduates who enrolled in 2011, 800 Federal Work-Study jobs (averaging $5000). 125 state and other part-time jobs (averaging $5000).

Applying *Options:* electronic application, early admission. *Application fee:* $30. *Required:* high school transcript. *Required for some:* Some programs such as Honors College and Medical programs have additional admissions requirements. *Application deadlines:* rolling (freshmen), rolling (out-of-state freshmen), rolling (transfers). *Notification:* continuous (freshmen), continuous (out-of-state freshmen), continuous (transfers).

Freshman Application Contact Mrs. Dulce Beltran, College Registrar, Miami Dade College, 11011 SW 104th Street, Miami, FL 33176. *Phone:* 305-237-2206. *Fax:* 305-237-2532. *E-mail:* dbeltran@mdc.edu. *Website:* http://www.mdc.edu/.

Miami International University of Art & Design
Miami, Florida

- **Proprietary** comprehensive, founded 1965, part of Education Management Corporation
- **Urban** campus
- **Coed**

Academics *Calendar:* quarters. *Degrees:* diplomas, associate, bachelor's, and master's.

Freshman Application Contact Miami International University of Art & Design, 1501 Biscayne Boulevard, Suite 100, Miami, FL 33132-1418. *Phone:* 305-428-5700. *Toll-free phone:* 800-225-9023. *Website:* http://www.artinstitutes.edu/miami/.

See full-page ad on page 54 and page 1384 for the College Close-Up.

Millennia Atlantic University
Doral, Florida

Admissions Office Contact Millennia Atlantic University, 3801 NW 97th Avenue, Doral, FL 33178. *Website:* http://www.maufl.edu/.

New College of Florida
Sarasota, Florida

- **State-supported** 4-year, founded 1960, part of State University System of Florida
- **Suburban** 119-acre campus with easy access to Tampa-St. Petersburg
- **Endowment** $28.2 million
- **Coed** 832 undergraduate students, 100% full-time, 59% women, 41% men
- **Very difficult** entrance level, 60% of applicants were admitted

Undergraduates 832 full-time. Students come from 37 states and territories; 20 other countries; 18% are from out of state; 2% Black or African American, non-Hispanic/Latino; 14% Hispanic/Latino; 2% Asian, non-Hispanic/Latino; 0.1% Native Hawaiian or other Pacific Islander, non-Hispanic/Latino; 0.2% American Indian or Alaska Native, non-Hispanic/Latino; 4% Two or more

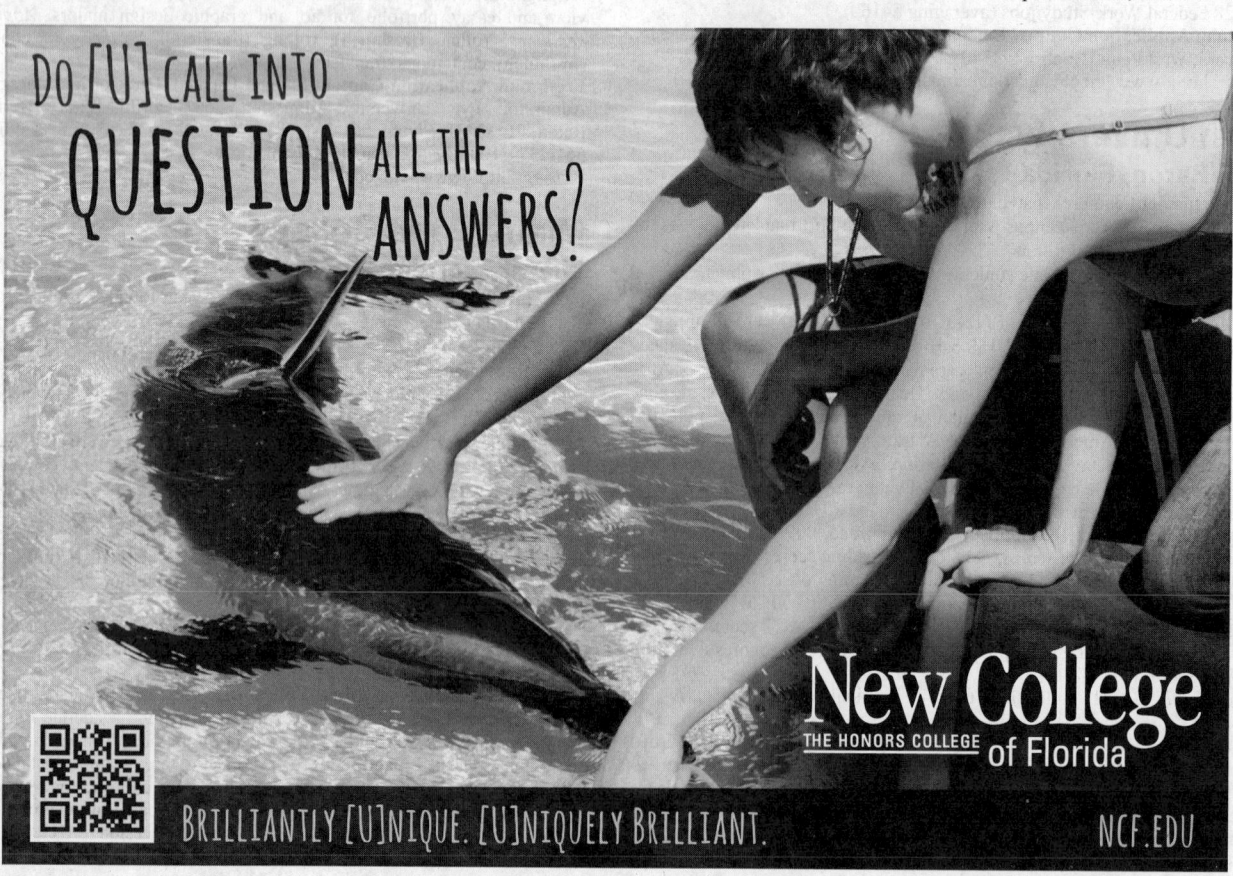

races, non-Hispanic/Latino; 3% Race/ethnicity unknown; 0.8% international; 3% transferred in; 75% live on campus. *Retention:* 83% of full-time freshmen returned.

Freshmen *Admission:* 1,348 applied, 803 admitted, 223 enrolled. *Average high school GPA:* 3.98. *Test scores:* SAT critical reading scores over 500: 100%; SAT math scores over 500: 99%; SAT writing scores over 500: 97%; ACT scores over 18: 100%; SAT critical reading scores over 600: 87%; SAT math scores over 600: 66%; SAT writing scores over 600: 72%; ACT scores over 24: 97%; SAT critical reading scores over 700: 44%; SAT math scores over 700: 16%; SAT writing scores over 700: 23%; ACT scores over 30: 40%.
Faculty *Total:* 105, 65% full-time, 91% with terminal degrees. *Student/faculty ratio:* 10:1.

Academics *Calendar:* 4-1-4. *Degree:* bachelor's. *Special study options:* cooperative education, double majors, honors programs, independent study, internships, off-campus study, services for LD students, student-designed majors, study abroad.

Computers on Campus 41 computers/terminals and 1,000 ports are available on campus for general student use. Students can access the following: campus intranet, computer help desk, free student e-mail accounts, online (class) grades, online (class) registration, online (class) schedules. Campuswide network is available. 100% of college-owned or -operated housing units are wired for high-speed Internet access. Wireless service is available via classrooms, dorm rooms, learning centers, libraries, student centers.

Student Life *Housing:* on-campus residence required through senior year. *Options:* coed, disabled students. Campus housing is university owned. Freshman campus housing is guaranteed. *Activities and organizations:* drama/theater group, student-run newspaper, radio station, choral group, PRIDE, Interfaith groups, New College Student Alliance, Feminist Majority Leadership Alliance, Sailing Club. *Campus security:* 24-hour emergency response devices and patrols, student patrols, late-night transport/escort service, controlled dormitory access, campus police are state certified police officers and available 24/7. *Student services:* health clinic, personal/psychological counseling, women's center.

Athletics *Intercollegiate sports:* sailing M/W. *Intramural sports:* archery M(c)/W(c), basketball M/W, fencing M/W, football M, racquetball M/W, sailing M(c)/W(c), soccer M(c)/W(c), softball M(c)/W(c), swimming and diving M(c)/W(c), table tennis M(c)/W(c), tennis M(c)/W(c), ultimate Frisbee M(c)/W(c), wrestling M/W.

Standardized Tests *Required:* SAT or ACT (for admission).

Costs (2013–14) *Tuition:* state resident $6783 full-time; nonresident $29,812 full-time. Full-time tuition and fees vary according to course load. *Room and board:* $8856; room only: $6078. Room and board charges vary according to board plan and housing facility. *Payment plan:* installment.

Financial Aid Of all full-time matriculated undergraduates who enrolled in 2012, 745 applied for aid, 487 were judged to have need, 137 had their need fully met. 12 Federal Work-Study jobs (averaging $2325). In 2012, 212 non-need-based awards were made. *Average percent of need met:* 80%. *Average financial aid package:* $12,186. *Average need-based loan:* $4176. *Average need-based gift aid:* $8819. *Average non-need-based aid:* $2282. *Average indebtedness upon graduation:* $16,640.

Applying *Options:* electronic application, early admission, deferred entrance. *Application fee:* $30. *Required:* essay or personal statement, high school transcript, 1 letter of recommendation. *Required for some:* interview. *Recommended:* minimum 3.0 GPA. *Application deadlines:* 4/15 (freshmen), 4/15 (out-of-state freshmen), 4/15 (transfers). *Notification:* 4/25 (freshmen), 4/25 (out-of-state freshmen), 4/25 (transfers).

Freshman Application Contact Office of Admissions, New College of Florida, 5800 Bay Shore Road, Sarasota, FL 34243-2109. *Phone:* 941-487-5000. *Fax:* 941-487-5010. *E-mail:* admissions@ncf.edu. *Website:* http://www.ncf.edu/.

See previous page for display ad and page 1410 for the College Close-Up.

New World School of the Arts
Miami, Florida
- **State-supported** 4-year, founded 1984, part of New World School of the Arts is a partnership of Miami Dade County Public Schools, Miami Dade College and the University of Florida
- **Urban** 5-acre campus with easy access to Broward, Palm Beach Counties
- **Endowment** $8.3 million
- **Coed**
- **Noncompetitive** entrance level

Faculty *Student/faculty ratio:* 5:1.
Academics *Calendar:* semesters. *Degrees:* associate and bachelor's.
Student Life *Campus security:* 24-hour patrols.
Standardized Tests *Recommended:* SAT or ACT (for admission).
Applying *Options:* early decision. *Required:* essay or personal statement, high school transcript, 2 letters of recommendation, interview, audition.

Freshman Application Contact Recruitment and Admissions Coordinator, New World School of the Arts, 300 NE Second Avenue, Miami, FL 33132. *Phone:* 305-237-7408. *Fax:* 305-237-3794. *E-mail:* nwsaadm@mdc.edu. *Website:* http://www.mdc.edu/nwsa/.

Northwest Florida State College
Niceville, Florida
- **State and locally supported** primarily 2-year, founded 1963, part of Florida College System
- **Small-town** 264-acre campus
- **Endowment** $28.6 million
- **Coed**
- **Noncompetitive** entrance level

Faculty *Student/faculty ratio:* 15:1.
Academics *Calendar:* semesters plus summer sessions. *Degrees:* certificates, associate, and bachelor's.
Athletics Member NJCAA.
Standardized Tests *Required for some:* ACT, SAT I, ACT ASSET, MAPS, or Florida College Entry Placement Test are used for placement not admission.
Costs (2012–13) *One-time required fee:* $30. *Tuition:* state resident $3234 full-time, $108 per credit part-time; nonresident $11,604 full-time, $387 per credit part-time. Full-time tuition and fees vary according to course level, course load, degree level, and reciprocity agreements. Part-time tuition and fees vary according to course level, course load, degree level, and reciprocity agreements. *Payment plans:* tuition prepayment, installment, deferred payment.
Applying *Options:* electronic application. *Required:* high school transcript.
Freshman Application Contact Ms. Christine Bishop, Dean Enrollment Services, Northwest Florida State College, 100 College Boulevard, Niceville, FL 32578. *Phone:* 850-729-5373. *Fax:* 850-729-5323. *E-mail:* registrar@nwfsc.edu.
Website: http://www.nwfsc.edu/.

Northwood University, Florida Campus
West Palm Beach, Florida
- **Private** comprehensive, founded 1982
- **Suburban** 90-acre campus
- **Endowment** $31.1 million
- **Coed** 497 undergraduate students, 97% full-time, 35% women, 65% men
- **Moderately difficult** entrance level, 54% of applicants were admitted

Undergraduates 484 full-time, 13 part-time. 38% are from out of state; 10% Black or African American, non-Hispanic/Latino; 11% Hispanic/Latino; 1% Asian, non-Hispanic/Latino; 0.6% American Indian or Alaska Native, non-Hispanic/Latino; 0.4% Two or more races, non-Hispanic/Latino; 13% Race/ethnicity unknown; 39% international; 25% transferred in; 41% live on campus. *Retention:* 56% of full-time freshmen returned.

Freshmen *Admission:* 628 applied, 339 admitted, 103 enrolled. *Average high school GPA:* 3.09. *Test scores:* SAT critical reading scores over 500: 33%; SAT math scores over 500: 58%; SAT writing scores over 500: 20%; ACT scores over 18: 81%; SAT critical reading scores over 600: 5%; SAT math scores over 600: 15%; SAT writing scores over 600: 5%; ACT scores over 24: 11%; SAT critical reading scores over 700: 1%; SAT math scores over 700: 4%; SAT writing scores over 700: 1%.
Faculty *Total:* 44, 36% full-time, 25% with terminal degrees. *Student/faculty ratio:* 20:1.
Academics *Calendar:* quarters. *Degrees:* bachelor's and master's. *Special study options:* academic remediation for entering students, accelerated degree program, adult/continuing education programs, advanced placement credit, distance learning, double majors, external degree program, honors programs, internships, off-campus study, part-time degree program, study abroad, summer session for credit.
Computers on Campus 89 computers/terminals are available on campus for general student use. Students can access the following: campus intranet, computer help desk, free student e-mail accounts, online (class) grades, online (class) registration, online (class) schedules. Campuswide network is available. 100% of college-owned or -operated housing units are wired for high-speed Internet access. Wireless service is available via entire campus.
Student Life *Housing:* on-campus residence required for freshman year. *Options:* coed, men-only. Campus housing is university owned. Freshman campus housing is guaranteed. *Activities and organizations:* drama/theater group, Student Government Association, International Club, Auto Show. *Campus security:* 24-hour emergency response devices and patrols, student patrols, late-night transport/escort service. *Student services:* health clinic, personal/psychological counseling.

Athletics Member NAIA. *Intercollegiate sports:* baseball M(s), basketball M/W, cheerleading M/W, golf M(s)/W(s), soccer M(s)/W(s), softball W(s), tennis M(s)/W(s), volleyball W(s). *Intramural sports:* basketball M/W, bowling M/W, football M, racquetball M/W, tennis M/W.

Standardized Tests *Required:* SAT or ACT (for admission). *Recommended:* SAT Subject Tests (for admission).

Costs (2013–14) *Comprehensive fee:* $32,171 includes full-time tuition ($21,000), mandatory fees ($1130), and room and board ($10,041). Part-time tuition: $811 per credit hour.

Financial Aid Of all full-time matriculated undergraduates who enrolled in 2012, 247 applied for aid, 217 were judged to have need, 38 had their need fully met. 42 Federal Work-Study jobs (averaging $2042). In 2012, 93 non-need-based awards were made. *Average percent of need met:* 62%. *Average financial aid package:* $21,509. *Average need-based loan:* $4198. *Average need-based gift aid:* $7575. *Average non-need-based aid:* $6890. *Average indebtedness upon graduation:* $27,505.

Applying *Options:* electronic application, deferred entrance. *Application fee:* $25. *Required for some:* essay or personal statement, high school transcript, interview. *Recommended:* minimum 2.0 GPA. *Application deadlines:* 8/1 (freshmen), 8/1 (out-of-state freshmen), rolling (transfers). *Notification:* continuous (freshmen), continuous (out-of-state freshmen), continuous (transfers).

Freshman Application Contact Ms. Emily Mass, Director of Admissions & Enrollment Management, Northwood University, Florida Campus, 2600 North Military Trail, West Palm Beach, FL 33409-2911. *Phone:* 800-622-9000. *Toll-free phone:* 800-622-9000. *Fax:* 561-681-7901. *E-mail:* fladmit@northwood.edu.

Website: http://www.northwood.edu/.

Nova Southeastern University

Fort Lauderdale, Florida

- **Independent** university, founded 1964
- **Suburban** 300-acre campus
- **Endowment** $69.6 million
- **Coed** 5,739 undergraduate students, 63% full-time, 70% women, 30% men
- **Moderately difficult** entrance level, 56% of applicants were admitted

Undergraduates 3,592 full-time, 2,147 part-time. Students come from 45 states and territories; 67 other countries; 16% are from out of state; 22% Black or African American, non-Hispanic/Latino; 33% Hispanic/Latino; 6% Asian, non-Hispanic/Latino; 0.2% Native Hawaiian or other Pacific Islander, non-Hispanic/Latino; 0.2% American Indian or Alaska Native, non-Hispanic/Latino; 1% Two or more races, non-Hispanic/Latino; 4% Race/ethnicity unknown; 6% international; 14% transferred in; 16% live on campus. *Retention:* 72% of full-time freshmen returned.

Freshmen *Admission:* 4,257 applied, 2,364 admitted, 724 enrolled. *Average high school GPA:* 3.6. *Test scores:* SAT critical reading scores over 500: 61%; SAT math scores over 500: 64%; ACT scores over 18: 97%; SAT critical reading scores over 600: 19%; SAT math scores over 600: 24%; ACT scores over 24: 38%; SAT critical reading scores over 700: 2%; SAT math scores over 700: 3%; ACT scores over 30: 6%.

Faculty *Total:* 1,725, 47% full-time, 81% with terminal degrees. *Student/faculty ratio:* 18:1.

Academics *Calendar:* trimesters. *Degrees:* certificates, associate, bachelor's, master's, doctoral, post-master's, and postbachelor's certificates. *Special study options:* academic remediation for entering students, adult/continuing education programs, advanced placement credit, distance learning, double majors, honors programs, independent study, internships, off-campus study, part-time degree program, services for LD students, study abroad, summer session for credit. *Unusual degree programs:* 3-2 business administration; marine biology, occupational therapy, criminal justice, psychology, mental health counseling, speech language pathology, computer science, education, physical therapy.

Computers on Campus 3,000 computers/terminals and 6,000 ports are available on campus for general student use. Students can access the following: campus intranet, computer help desk, free student e-mail accounts, online (class) grades, online (class) registration, online (class) schedules. Campus-wide network is available. 100% of college-owned or -operated housing units are wired for high-speed Internet access. Wireless service is available via entire campus.

Student Life *Housing:* on-campus residence required through sophomore year. *Options:* coed, disabled students. Campus housing is university owned. Freshman campus housing is guaranteed. *Activities and organizations:* drama/theater group, student-run newspaper, radio station, choral group, Delta Epsilon Iota, Students for Stress Resilience, International Muslim Association at NSU (IMAN), Preventative Medicine Initiative (PMI), Pre-Med Society, national fraternities, national sororities. *Campus security:* 24-hour emergency response devices and patrols, late-night transport/escort service, controlled dormitory

access, shuttle bus service. *Student services:* health clinic, personal/psychological counseling, women's center.

Athletics Member NCAA. All Division II. *Intercollegiate sports:* baseball M(s), basketball M(s)/W(s), cheerleading W, crew W(s), cross-country running M(s)/W(s), golf M(s)/W(s), soccer M(s)/W(s), softball W(s), swimming and diving M(s)/W(s), tennis W(s), track and field M(s)/W(s), volleyball W(s). *Intramural sports:* basketball M/W, golf M/W, racquetball M/W, soccer M/W, softball M/W, ultimate Frisbee M/W, volleyball M/W.

Standardized Tests *Required:* SAT or ACT (for admission).

Costs (2013–14) *Comprehensive fee:* $34,016 includes full-time tuition ($23,850), mandatory fees ($650), and room and board ($9516). Full-time tuition and fees vary according to class time and program. Part-time tuition: $795 per credit hour. Part-time tuition and fees vary according to class time, course load, and program. *College room only:* $6916. Room and board charges vary according to board plan and housing facility. *Payment plans:* installment, deferred payment. *Waivers:* employees or children of employees.

Financial Aid Of all full-time matriculated undergraduates who enrolled in 2011, 3,623 applied for aid, 3,253 were judged to have need, 333 had their need fully met. 654 Federal Work-Study jobs (averaging $3007). 1,054 state and other part-time jobs (averaging $3144). In 2011, 469 non-need-based awards were made. *Average percent of need met:* 91%. *Average financial aid package:* $19,568. *Average need-based loan:* $6782. *Average need-based gift aid:* $11,173. *Average non-need-based aid:* $5512. *Average indebtedness upon graduation:* $43,201.

Applying *Options:* electronic application, deferred entrance. *Application fee:* $50. *Recommended:* minimum 2.6 GPA, essay and transcript of high school record recommended of some. *Application deadlines:* rolling (freshmen), rolling (out-of-state freshmen), rolling (transfers). *Notification:* continuous (freshmen), continuous (out-of-state freshmen), continuous (transfers).

Freshman Application Contact Ms. Maria Dillard, Director of Enrollment Management, Nova Southeastern University, Enrollment Processing Services, 3301 College Avenue, Ft. Lauderdale, FL 33329-9905. *Phone:* 954-262-8000. *Toll-free phone:* 800-541-NOVA. *Fax:* 954-262-3811. *E-mail:* nsuinfo@nova.edu.

Website: http://www.nova.edu/.

Palm Beach Atlantic University

West Palm Beach, Florida

- **Independent nondenominational** comprehensive, founded 1968
- **Urban** 93-acre campus with easy access to Orlando, the Caribbean
- **Endowment** $70.0 million
- **Coed** 2,751 undergraduate students, 80% full-time, 63% women, 37% men
- **Moderately difficult** entrance level, 96% of applicants were admitted

Undergraduates 2,188 full-time, 563 part-time. Students come from 49 states and territories; 41 other countries; 27% are from out of state; 15% Black or African American, non-Hispanic/Latino; 14% Hispanic/Latino; 1% Asian, non-Hispanic/Latino; 0.1% Native Hawaiian or other Pacific Islander, non-Hispanic/Latino; 0.5% American Indian or Alaska Native, non-Hispanic/Latino; 1% Two or more races, non-Hispanic/Latino; 6% Race/ethnicity unknown; 4% international; 12% transferred in; 38% live on campus. *Retention:* 68% of full-time freshmen returned.

Freshmen *Admission:* 1,380 applied, 1,323 admitted, 445 enrolled. *Test scores:* SAT critical reading scores over 500: 62%; SAT math scores over 500: 56%; ACT scores over 18: 88%; SAT critical reading scores over 600: 18%; SAT math scores over 600: 16%; ACT scores over 24: 36%; SAT critical reading scores over 700: 3%; SAT math scores over 700: 1%; ACT scores over 30: 3%.

Faculty *Total:* 332, 50% full-time, 60% with terminal degrees. *Student/faculty ratio:* 13:1.

Academics *Calendar:* semesters. *Degrees:* associate, bachelor's, master's, and doctoral. *Special study options:* academic remediation for entering students, accelerated degree program, adult/continuing education programs, advanced placement credit, distance learning, double majors, honors programs, independent study, internships, part-time degree program, services for LD students, student-designed majors, study abroad, summer session for credit. *ROTC:* Army (c).

Computers on Campus 600 computers/terminals are available on campus for general student use. Students can access the following: campus intranet, computer help desk, free student e-mail accounts, online (class) grades, online (class) registration, online (class) schedules. Campuswide network is available. 100% of college-owned or -operated housing units are wired for high-speed Internet access. Wireless service is available via entire campus.

Student Life *Housing:* on-campus residence required through sophomore year. *Options:* men-only, women-only. Campus housing is university owned and leased by the school. Freshman applicants given priority for college housing. *Activities and organizations:* drama/theater group, student-run newspaper, radio station, choral group, Christian Pharmacist Fellowship International, American Latino Intercultural Coalition, N.O.W. (Night of Worship), Student Government, Club S.A.I.L. *Campus security:* 24-hour emergency response devices and patrols, late-night transport/escort service, controlled dormitory access, Security Escort Services; Lighted pathways/sidewalks; Self-defense education; Closed-circuit television system. *Student services:* health clinic, personal/psychological counseling.

Athletics Member NCAA, NCCAA. All NCAA Division II. *Intercollegiate sports:* baseball M(s), basketball M(s)/W(s), cheerleading M(c)/W(c), cross-country running W(s), fencing M(c)/W(c), lacrosse M(c)/W(c), soccer M(s)/W(s), softball W(s), tennis M(s)/W(s), volleyball W(s). *Intramural sports:* badminton M/W, basketball M/W, bowling M/W, golf M/W, racquetball M/W, soccer M/W, softball M/W, table tennis M/W, ultimate Frisbee M/W, volleyball M/W, water polo M/W.

Standardized Tests *Required:* SAT or ACT (for admission).

Costs (2013–14) *Comprehensive fee:* $33,882 includes full-time tuition ($25,232), mandatory fees ($300), and room and board ($8350). Full-time tuition and fees vary according to course load, degree level, location, and program. Part-time tuition: $590 per credit. Part-time tuition and fees vary according to course load, degree level, location, and program. *Required fees:* $99 per term part-time. *College room only:* $4700. Room and board charges vary according to board plan and housing facility. *Payment plan:* installment. *Waivers:* employees or children of employees.

Financial Aid Of all full-time matriculated undergraduates who enrolled in 2012, 1,959 applied for aid, 1,692 were judged to have need, 205 had their need fully met. 244 Federal Work-Study jobs (averaging $2460). 5 state and other part-time jobs (averaging $2009). In 2012, 425 non-need-based awards were made. *Average percent of need met:* 57%. *Average financial aid package:* $16,343. *Average need-based loan:* $4168. *Average need-based gift aid:* $12,958. *Average non-need-based aid:* $7571. *Average indebtedness upon graduation:* $24,749. *Financial aid deadline:* 8/1.

Applying *Options:* electronic application, early admission, early action, deferred entrance. *Application fee:* $50. *Required:* essay or personal statement, high school transcript. *Required for some:* interview. *Application deadlines:* rolling (freshmen), rolling (transfers). *Notification:* continuous (freshmen), continuous (transfers).

Freshman Application Contact Mr. James Zugelder, Director of Admissions, Palm Beach Atlantic University, 901 South Flagler Drive, PO Box 24708, West Palm Beach, FL 33416-4708. *Phone:* 561-803-2101. *Toll-free phone:* 888-GO-TO-PBA. *E-mail:* admissions_admissions@pba.edu. *Website:* http://www.pba.edu/.

Palm Beach State College

Lake Worth, Florida

- **State-supported** 4-year, founded 1933, part of Florida College System
- **Urban** 150-acre campus with easy access to West Palm Beach
- **Endowment** $23.0 million
- **Coed** 29,974 undergraduate students, 34% full-time, 57% women, 43% men
- **Noncompetitive** entrance level, 100% of applicants were admitted

Undergraduates 10,177 full-time, 19,797 part-time. Students come from 49 states and territories; 146 other countries; 5% are from out of state; 24% Black or African American, non-Hispanic/Latino; 24% Hispanic/Latino; 3% Asian, non-Hispanic/Latino; 0.2% Native Hawaiian or other Pacific Islander, non-Hispanic/Latino; 0.2% American Indian or Alaska Native, non-Hispanic/Latino; 2% Two or more races, non-Hispanic/Latino; 4% Race/ethnicity unknown; 2% international; 4% transferred in.

Freshmen *Admission:* 4,153 applied, 4,153 admitted, 4,153 enrolled.

Faculty *Total:* 1,473, 19% full-time, 16% with terminal degrees. *Student/faculty ratio:* 43:1.

Academics *Calendar:* semesters. *Degrees:* certificates, diplomas, associate, and bachelor's. *Special study options:* academic remediation for entering students, adult/continuing education programs, advanced placement credit, cooperative education, distance learning, double majors, English as a second language, freshman honors college, honors programs, independent study, internships, off-campus study, part-time degree program, services for LD students, student-designed majors, study abroad, summer session for credit.

Computers on Campus 2,300 computers/terminals are available on campus for general student use. Students can access the following: computer help desk, free student e-mail accounts, online (class) registration. Campuswide network is available. Wireless service is available via entire campus.

Student Life *Housing:* college housing not available. *Activities and organizations:* drama/theater group, student-run newspaper, choral group, student gov-

ernment, Phi Theta Kappa, Students for International Understanding, Black Student Union, Drama Club, national fraternities. *Campus security:* 24-hour emergency response devices and patrols. *Student services:* health clinic, women's center.

Athletics Member NJCAA. *Intercollegiate sports:* baseball M(s), basketball M(s)/W(s), softball W(s), volleyball W(s).

Standardized Tests *Recommended:* SAT and SAT Subject Tests or ACT (for admission).

Applying *Options:* electronic application, early admission, deferred entrance. *Application fee:* $20. *Application deadlines:* 8/20 (freshmen), 8/20 (transfers). *Notification:* continuous until 8/20 (freshmen), continuous until 8/20 (transfers).

Freshman Application Contact Ms. Anne Guiler, Coordinator of Distance Learning, Palm Beach State College, Lake Worth, FL 33461. *Phone:* 561-868-3032. *Fax:* 561-868-3584. *E-mail:* enrollmt@palmbeachstate.edu. *Website:* http://www.palmbeachstate.edu/.

Pensacola State College

Pensacola, Florida

- **State-supported** primarily 2-year, founded 1948, part of Florida College System
- **Urban** 130-acre campus
- **Coed** 11,862 undergraduate students, 41% full-time, 61% women, 39% men
- **Noncompetitive** entrance level

Undergraduates 4,865 full-time, 6,997 part-time. Students come from 25 states and territories; 1% are from out of state; 15% Black or African American, non-Hispanic/Latino; 5% Hispanic/Latino; 3% Asian, non-Hispanic/Latino; 0.4% Native Hawaiian or other Pacific Islander, non-Hispanic/Latino; 0.9% American Indian or Alaska Native, non-Hispanic/Latino; 4% Two or more races, non-Hispanic/Latino; 1% Race/ethnicity unknown; 0.4% international; 6% transferred in.

Freshmen *Admission:* 1,843 enrolled.

Faculty *Total:* 632, 30% full-time, 6% with terminal degrees. *Student/faculty ratio:* 25:1.

Academics *Calendar:* semesters. *Degrees:* certificates, diplomas, associate, and bachelor's. *Special study options:* academic remediation for entering students, adult/continuing education programs, advanced placement credit, cooperative education, distance learning, double majors, English as a second language, external degree program, honors programs, independent study, part-time degree program, services for LD students, summer session for credit. *ROTC:* Army (b).

Computers on Campus 500 computers/terminals are available on campus for general student use. Students can access the following: campus intranet, computer help desk, free student e-mail accounts, online (class) grades, online (class) registration, online (class) schedules. Campuswide network is available. Wireless service is available via entire campus.

Student Life *Housing:* college housing not available. *Activities and organizations:* drama/theater group, student-run newspaper, choral group. *Campus security:* 24-hour emergency response devices and patrols, late-night transport/escort service. *Student services:* health clinic, personal/psychological counseling, women's center.

Athletics Member NJCAA. *Intercollegiate sports:* baseball M(s), basketball M(s)/W(s), softball W(s), volleyball W. *Intramural sports:* archery M/W, badminton M/W, basketball M/W, bowling M/W, cross-country running M/W, gymnastics M/W, racquetball M/W, sailing M/W, swimming and diving M/W, tennis M/W, track and field M/W, volleyball M/W, weight lifting M/W, wrestling M.

Costs (2012–13) *One-time required fee:* $30. *Tuition:* state resident $2510 full-time, $105 per credit hour part-time; nonresident $10,075 full-time, $420 per credit hour part-time. Full-time tuition and fees vary according to degree level. Part-time tuition and fees vary according to degree level. *Waivers:* senior citizens and employees or children of employees.

Financial Aid Of all full-time matriculated undergraduates who enrolled in 2011, 120 Federal Work-Study jobs (averaging $3000).

Applying *Options:* electronic application, early admission. *Application fee:* $30. *Required:* high school transcript. *Application deadlines:* 8/30 (freshmen), 8/30 (transfers). *Notification:* continuous until 8/30 (freshmen), continuous until 8/30 (transfers).

Freshman Application Contact Ms. Martha Caughey, Registrar, Pensacola State College, 1000 College Boulevard, Pensacola, FL 32504-8998. *Phone:* 850-484-1600. *Fax:* 850-484-1829. *Website:* http://www.pensacolastate.edu/.

Polk State College

Winter Haven, Florida

- **State-supported** 4-year, founded 1964, part of Florida College System
- **Suburban** 98-acre campus with easy access to Orlando, Tampa
- **Endowment** $10.8 million
- **Coed** 11,862 undergraduate students, 32% full-time, 62% women, 38% men
- **Noncompetitive** entrance level

Undergraduates 3,849 full-time, 8,013 part-time. Students come from 13 states and territories; 60 other countries; 1% are from out of state; 17% Black or African American, non-Hispanic/Latino; 16% Hispanic/Latino; 2% Asian, non-Hispanic/Latino; 0.1% Native Hawaiian or other Pacific Islander, non-Hispanic/Latino; 0.2% American Indian or Alaska Native, non-Hispanic/Latino; 2% Two or more races, non-Hispanic/Latino; 3% Race/ethnicity unknown; 0.9% international; 4% transferred in. *Retention:* 55% of full-time freshmen returned.

Freshmen *Admission:* 1,849 enrolled. *Test scores:* SAT critical reading scores over 500: 44%; SAT math scores over 500: 53%; SAT writing scores over 500: 46%; ACT scores over 18: 88%; SAT critical reading scores over 600: 8%; SAT math scores over 600: 7%; SAT writing scores over 600: 10%; ACT scores over 24: 12%; SAT critical reading scores over 700: 1%; SAT math scores over 700: 1%; SAT writing scores over 700: 1%.

Faculty *Total:* 623, 30% full-time, 14% with terminal degrees. *Student/faculty ratio:* 20:1.

Academics *Calendar:* semesters 16-16-6-6. *Degrees:* certificates, associate, and bachelor's. *Special study options:* academic remediation for entering students, accelerated degree program, adult/continuing education programs, advanced placement credit, cooperative education, distance learning, double majors, English as a second language, honors programs, independent study, off-campus study, part-time degree program, services for LD students, study abroad, summer session for credit. *ROTC:* Army (c).

Computers on Campus 250 computers/terminals are available on campus for general student use. Students can access the following: computer help desk, free student e-mail accounts, online (class) grades, online (class) registration, online (class) schedules. Campuswide network is available. Wireless service is available via entire campus.

Student Life *Housing:* college housing not available. *Activities and organizations:* drama/theater group, choral group, Florida Student Nursing Association, SLAM (Student's Living a Message), Eagleteers, Student Government Association, SALO (Student Activities and Leadership Office). *Campus security:* 24-hour emergency response devices and patrols. *Student services:* personal/psychological counseling.

Athletics Member NJCAA. *Intercollegiate sports:* baseball M(s), basketball M(s), soccer W(s), softball W(s), volleyball W(s). *Intramural sports:* basketball M/W, bowling M/W, football M/W, volleyball M/W.

Costs (2012–13) *Tuition:* state resident $3307 full-time, $110 per credit hour part-time; nonresident $12,212 full-time, $407 per credit hour part-time. Full-time tuition and fees vary according to course level, course load, and degree level. Part-time tuition and fees vary according to course level, course load, and degree level. *Waivers:* employees or children of employees.

Applying *Options:* electronic application, early admission, deferred entrance. *Required:* high school transcript. *Application deadlines:* rolling (freshmen), rolling (transfers). *Notification:* continuous (freshmen), continuous (transfers).

Freshman Application Contact Polk State College, 999 Avenue H, NE, Winter Haven, FL 33881-4299. *Phone:* 863-297-1010 Ext. 5016.

Website: http://www.polk.edu/.

Polytechnic University of Puerto Rico, Miami Campus

Miami, Florida

Director of Admissions Admissions Department, Polytechnic University of Puerto Rico, Miami Campus, 8180 Northwest 36th Street, Suite 401, Miami, FL 33166. *Phone:* 305-418-4220. *Toll-free phone:* 888-729-7659. *Fax:* 305-418-4325.

Website: http://www.pupr.edu/miami/.

Polytechnic University of Puerto Rico, Orlando Campus

Winter Park, Florida

Director of Admissions Teresa Cardona, Director of Recruitment and Admission, Polytechnic University of Puerto Rico, Orlando Campus, 4800 Howell Branch Road, Winter Park, FL 32792. *Phone:* 407-677-7000. *Toll-free phone:* 888-577-POLY. *Fax:* 407-677-5082.

Website: http://www.pupr.edu/orlando/.

Rasmussen College Fort Myers

Fort Myers, Florida

- **Proprietary** primarily 2-year, part of Rasmussen College System
- **Suburban** campus
- **Coed** 798 undergraduate students
- **Minimally difficult** entrance level

Faculty *Student/faculty ratio:* 22:1.

Academics *Degrees:* certificates, diplomas, associate, and bachelor's. *Special study options:* academic remediation for entering students, accelerated degree program, adult/continuing education programs, distance learning, double majors, internships, part-time degree program, summer session for credit.

Computers on Campus 129 computers/terminals are available on campus for general student use. Students can access the following: computer help desk, free student e-mail accounts, online (class) grades, online (class) schedules. Campuswide network is available. Wireless service is available via entire campus.

Student Life *Housing:* college housing not available.

Standardized Tests *Required:* Internal Exam (for admission).

Costs (2013–14) *Tuition:* $12,600 full-time. Full-time tuition and fees vary according to course level, course load, degree level, location, and program. Part-time tuition and fees vary according to course level, course load, degree level, location, and program. *Required fees:* $1800 full-time. *Payment plans:* installment, deferred payment. *Waivers:* employees or children of employees.

Applying *Options:* electronic application, early admission, deferred entrance. *Required:* high school transcript, minimum 2.0 GPA. *Required for some:* interview. *Application deadlines:* rolling (freshmen), rolling (transfers).

Freshman Application Contact Susan Hammerstrom, Director of Admissions, Rasmussen College Fort Myers, 9160 Forum Corporate Parkway, Suite 100, Fort Myers, FL 33905. *Phone:* 239-477-2100. *Toll-free phone:* 888-549-6755. *E-mail:* susan.hammerstrom@rasmussen.edu.

Website: http://www.rasmussen.edu/.

Rasmussen College Land O' Lakes

Land O' Lakes, Florida

- **Proprietary** 4-year, part of Rasmussen College System
- **Suburban** campus
- **Coed** 182 undergraduate students
- **Minimally difficult** entrance level

Faculty *Student/faculty ratio:* 22:1.

Academics *Degrees:* certificates, diplomas, associate, and bachelor's. *Special study options:* academic remediation for entering students, accelerated degree program, adult/continuing education programs, distance learning, double majors, internships, part-time degree program, summer session for credit.

Computers on Campus 61 computers/terminals are available on campus for general student use. Students can access the following: computer help desk, free student e-mail accounts, online (class) grades, online (class) schedules. Campuswide network is available. Wireless service is available via entire campus.

Student Life *Housing:* college housing not available.

Standardized Tests *Required:* Internal Exam (for admission).

Costs (2013–14) *Tuition:* $12,600 full-time. Full-time tuition and fees vary according to course level, course load, degree level, location, and program. Part-time tuition and fees vary according to course level, course load, degree level, location, and program. *Required fees:* $1800 full-time. *Payment plans:* installment, deferred payment. *Waivers:* employees or children of employees.

Applying *Options:* electronic application, early admission, deferred entrance. *Required:* high school transcript, minimum 2.0 GPA. *Required for some:* interview. *Application deadlines:* rolling (freshmen), rolling (transfers).

Freshman Application Contact Susan Hammerstrom, Director of Admissions, Rasmussen College Land O' Lakes, 18600 Fernview Street, Land O' Lakes, FL 34638. *Phone:* 813-435-3601. *Toll-free phone:* 888-549-6755. *E-mail:* susan.hammerstrom@rasmussen.edu.

Website: http://www.rasmussen.edu/.

Rasmussen College New Port Richey

New Port Richey, Florida

- **Proprietary** primarily 2-year, part of Rasmussen College System
- **Suburban** campus
- **Coed** 893 undergraduate students
- **Minimally difficult** entrance level

Faculty *Student/faculty ratio:* 22:1.

Academics *Degrees:* certificates, diplomas, associate, and bachelor's. *Special study options:* academic remediation for entering students, accelerated degree program, adult/continuing education programs, distance learning, double majors, internships, part-time degree program, summer session for credit.

Computers on Campus 118 computers/terminals are available on campus for general student use. Students can access the following: computer help desk, free student e-mail accounts, online (class) grades, online (class) schedules. Campuswide network is available. Wireless service is available via entire campus.

Student Life *Housing:* college housing not available.

Standardized Tests *Required:* Internal Exam (for admission).

Costs (2013–14) *Tuition:* $12,600 full-time. Full-time tuition and fees vary according to course level, course load, degree level, location, and program. Part-time tuition and fees vary according to course level, course load, degree level, location, and program. *Required fees:* $1800 full-time. *Payment plans:* installment, deferred payment. *Waivers:* employees or children of employees.

Financial Aid Of all full-time matriculated undergraduates who enrolled in 2011, 6 Federal Work-Study jobs.

Applying *Options:* electronic application, early admission, deferred entrance. *Required:* high school transcript, minimum 2.0 GPA. *Required for some:* interview. *Application deadlines:* rolling (freshmen), rolling (transfers).

Freshman Application Contact Susan Hammerstrom, Director of Admissions, Rasmussen College New Port Richey, 8661 Citizens Drive, New Port Richey, FL 34654. *Phone:* 727-942-0069. *Toll-free phone:* 888-549-6755. *E-mail:* susan.hammerstrom@rasmussen.edu. *Website:* http://www.rasmussen.edu/.

Rasmussen College Ocala

Ocala, Florida

- **Proprietary** primarily 2-year, founded 1984, part of Rasmussen College System
- **Suburban** campus with easy access to Orlando
- **Coed, primarily women** 1,266 undergraduate students
- **Minimally difficult** entrance level

Faculty *Student/faculty ratio:* 22:1.

Academics *Calendar:* quarters. *Degrees:* certificates, diplomas, associate, and bachelor's. *Special study options:* academic remediation for entering students, accelerated degree program, adult/continuing education programs, distance learning, double majors, internships, part-time degree program, summer session for credit.

Computers on Campus 124 computers/terminals are available on campus for general student use. Students can access the following: computer help desk, free student e-mail accounts, online (class) grades, online (class) schedules. Campuswide network is available. Wireless service is available via entire campus.

Student Life *Housing:* college housing not available.

Standardized Tests *Required:* Internal Exam (for admission).

Costs (2013–14) *Tuition:* $12,600 full-time. Full-time tuition and fees vary according to course level, course load, degree level, location, and program. Part-time tuition and fees vary according to course level, course load, degree level, location, and program. *Required fees:* $1800 full-time. *Payment plans:* installment, deferred payment. *Waivers:* employees or children of employees.

Applying *Options:* electronic application, early admission, deferred entrance. *Required:* high school transcript, minimum 2.0 GPA. *Required for some:* interview. *Application deadlines:* rolling (freshmen), rolling (transfers).

Freshman Application Contact Susan Hammerstrom, Director of Admissions, Rasmussen College Ocala, 4755 SW 46th Court, Ocala, FL 34471. *Phone:* 352-629-1941. *Toll-free phone:* 888-549-6755. *E-mail:* susan.hammerstrom@rasmussen.edu. *Website:* http://www.rasmussen.edu/.

Rasmussen College Ocala School of Nursing

Ocala, Florida

- **Proprietary** 4-year, part of Rasmussen College System
- **Suburban** campus
- **Coed**
- **Minimally difficult** entrance level

Faculty *Student/faculty ratio:* 22:1.

Academics *Degrees:* associate and bachelor's. *Special study options:* academic remediation for entering students, accelerated degree program, adult/continuing education programs, distance learning, double majors, internships, part-time degree program, summer session for credit.

Computers on Campus Students can access the following: computer help desk, free student e-mail accounts, online (class) grades, online (class) schedules. Campuswide network is available. Wireless service is available via entire campus.

Student Life *Housing:* college housing not available.

Standardized Tests *Required:* Internal Exam (for admission).

Costs (2013–14) *Tuition:* $14,220 full-time. Full-time tuition and fees vary according to course level, course load, degree level, location, and program. Part-time tuition and fees vary according to course level, course load, degree level, location, and program. *Required fees:* $1800 full-time. *Payment plans:* installment, deferred payment. *Waivers:* employees or children of employees.

Applying *Options:* electronic application, early admission, deferred entrance. *Required:* high school transcript, minimum 2.0 GPA. *Required for some:* interview. *Application deadlines:* rolling (freshmen), rolling (transfers).

Freshman Application Contact Susan Hammerstrom, Director of Admissions, Rasmussen College Ocala School of Nursing, 2100 SW 22nd Place, Ocala, FL 34471. *Phone:* 352-291-8560. *Toll-free phone:* 888-549-6755. *E-mail:* susan.hammerstrom@rasmussen.edu. *Website:* http://www.rasmussen.edu/.

Rasmussen College Tampa/Brandon

Tampa, Florida

- **Proprietary** 4-year, part of Rasmussen College System
- **Suburban** campus
- **Coed** 300 undergraduate students
- **Minimally difficult** entrance level

Faculty *Student/faculty ratio:* 22:1.

Academics *Degrees:* certificates, diplomas, associate, and bachelor's. *Special study options:* academic remediation for entering students, accelerated degree program, adult/continuing education programs, distance learning, double majors, internships, part-time degree program, summer session for credit.

Computers on Campus 47 computers/terminals are available on campus for general student use. Students can access the following: computer help desk, free student e-mail accounts, online (class) grades, online (class) schedules. Campuswide network is available. Wireless service is available via entire campus.

Student Life *Housing:* college housing not available.

Standardized Tests *Required:* Internal Exam (for admission).

Costs (2013–14) *Tuition:* $12,600 full-time. Full-time tuition and fees vary according to course level, course load, degree level, location, and program. Part-time tuition and fees vary according to course level, course load, degree level, location, and program. *Required fees:* $1800 full-time. *Payment plans:* installment, deferred payment. *Waivers:* employees or children of employees.

Applying *Options:* electronic application, early admission, deferred entrance. *Required:* high school transcript, minimum 2.0 GPA. *Required for some:* interview. *Application deadlines:* rolling (freshmen), rolling (transfers).

Freshman Application Contact Susan Hammerstrom, Director of Admissions, Rasmussen College Tampa/Brandon, 4042 Park Oaks Boulevard, Tampa, FL 33610. *Phone:* 813-246-7600. *Toll-free phone:* 888-549-6755. *E-mail:* susan.hammerstrom@rasmussen.edu. *Website:* http://www.rasmussen.edu/.

Remington College–Tampa Campus

Tampa, Florida

Freshman Application Contact Remington College–Tampa Campus, 6302 E. Dr. Martin Luther King, Jr. Boulevard, Suite 400, Tampa, FL 33619. *Phone:* 813-932-0701. *Toll-free phone:* 800-560-6192. *Website:* http://www.remingtoncollege.edu/.

Ringling College of Art and Design

Sarasota, Florida

- **Independent** 4-year, founded 1931
- **Small-town** 49-acre campus with easy access to Tampa-St. Petersburg
- **Endowment** $26.6 million
- **Coed** 1,364 undergraduate students, 96% full-time, 61% women, 39% men
- **Moderately difficult** entrance level, 75% of applicants were admitted

Undergraduates 1,313 full-time, 51 part-time. Students come from 47 states and territories; 53 other countries; 46% are from out of state; 3% Black or African American, non-Hispanic/Latino; 14% Hispanic/Latino; 7% Asian, non-Hispanic/Latino; 0.3% Native Hawaiian or other Pacific Islander, non-Hispanic/Latino; 0.4% American Indian or Alaska Native, non-Hispanic/Latino; 3% Two or more races, non-Hispanic/Latino; 0.1% Race/ethnicity unknown;

11% international; 7% transferred in; 60% live on campus. *Retention:* 79% of full-time freshmen returned.

Freshmen *Admission:* 1,255 applied, 941 admitted, 312 enrolled. *Average high school GPA:* 3.12.

Faculty *Total:* 152, 61% full-time, 51% with terminal degrees. *Student/faculty ratio:* 12:1.

Academics *Calendar:* semesters. *Degree:* certificates and bachelor's. *Special study options:* academic remediation for entering students, advanced placement credit, independent study, internships, off-campus study, part-time degree program, services for LD students, study abroad.

Computers on Campus 879 computers/terminals are available on campus for general student use. Students can access the following: campus intranet, computer help desk, free student e-mail accounts, online (class) grades, online (class) registration, online (class) schedules, central file storage, high performance computing labs. Campuswide network is available. 100% of college-owned or -operated housing units are wired for high-speed Internet access. Wireless service is available via entire campus.

Student Life *Housing options:* coed, men-only, women-only. Campus housing is university owned. Freshman applicants given priority for college housing. *Activities and organizations:* drama/theater group, Student Government Association, Digital Painting Sketch Club, Resident Student Association, MOSAIC, Quidditch Team. *Campus security:* 24-hour emergency response devices and patrols, late-night transport/escort service, controlled dormitory access, lighted campus. *Student services:* personal/psychological counseling, legal services.

Athletics *Intramural sports:* basketball M(c)/W(c), football M(c)/W(c), soccer M(c)/W(c), table tennis M(c)/W(c), ultimate Frisbee M(c)/W(c), volleyball M(c)/W(c), weight lifting M(c)/W(c).

Costs (2012–13) *Comprehensive fee:* $47,530 includes full-time tuition ($33,960), mandatory fees ($1340), and room and board ($12,230). Full-time tuition and fees vary according to course load, program, and student level. Part-time tuition: $1583 per credit hour. Part-time tuition and fees vary according to course load, program, and student level. *College room only:* $6670. Room and board charges vary according to board plan and housing facility. *Payment plan:* installment. *Waivers:* employees or children of employees.

Financial Aid Of all full-time matriculated undergraduates who enrolled in 2012, 964 applied for aid, 870 were judged to have need, 37 had their need fully met. 168 Federal Work-Study jobs (averaging $824). In 2012, 118 non-need-based awards were made. *Average percent of need met:* 40%. *Average financial aid package:* $17,427. *Average need-based loan:* $7657. *Average need-based gift aid:* $10,881. *Average non-need-based aid:* $16,972. *Average indebtedness upon graduation:* $48,515.

Applying *Options:* electronic application, deferred entrance. *Application fee:* $70. *Required:* essay or personal statement, high school transcript, minimum 2.0 GPA, 2 letters of recommendation, portfolio, resume. *Recommended:* interview. *Application deadlines:* rolling (freshmen), rolling (transfers). *Notification:* continuous (freshmen), continuous (transfers).

Freshman Application Contact Ringling College of Art and Design, FL. *Phone:* 941-359-7523. *Toll-free phone:* 800-255-7695. *E-mail:* admissions@ringling.edu.

Website: http://www.ringling.edu/.

Rollins College
Winter Park, Florida

- **Independent** comprehensive, founded 1885
- **Suburban** 80-acre campus with easy access to Orlando
- **Endowment** $335.6 million
- **Coed** 1,884 undergraduate students, 100% full-time, 59% women, 41% men
- **Moderately difficult** entrance level, 56% of applicants were admitted

Undergraduates 1,884 full-time. Students come from 44 states and territories; 39 other countries; 45% are from out of state; 4% Black or African American, non-Hispanic/Latino; 13% Hispanic/Latino; 3% Asian, non-Hispanic/Latino; 0.2% Native Hawaiian or other Pacific Islander, non-Hispanic/Latino; 0.1% American Indian or Alaska Native, non-Hispanic/Latino; 3% Two or more races, non-Hispanic/Latino; 3% Race/ethnicity unknown; 5% international; 3% transferred in; 68% live on campus. *Retention:* 84% of full-time freshmen returned.

Freshmen *Admission:* 4,542 applied, 2,533 admitted, 518 enrolled. *Average high school GPA:* 3.3. *Test scores:* SAT critical reading scores over 500: 95%; SAT math scores over 500: 93%; SAT writing scores over 500: 91%; ACT scores over 18: 101%; SAT critical reading scores over 600: 49%; SAT math scores over 600: 53%; SAT writing scores over 600: 44%; ACT scores over 24:

86%; SAT critical reading scores over 700: 9%; SAT math scores over 700: 10%; SAT writing scores over 700: 9%; ACT scores over 30: 17%.

Faculty *Total:* 216, 100% full-time, 90% with terminal degrees. *Student/faculty ratio:* 10:1.

Academics *Calendar:* semesters. *Degrees:* bachelor's and master's. *Special study options:* academic remediation for entering students, accelerated degree program, adult/continuing education programs, advanced placement credit, double majors, honors programs, independent study, internships, off-campus study, part-time degree program, services for LD students, student-designed majors, study abroad, summer session for credit. *Unusual degree programs:* 3-2 business administration with Crummer Graduate School of Business, Rollins College; engineering with Columbia University, Washington University in St. Louis, or Auburn University; forestry with Duke University School of the Environment; Environmental Management with Duke University School of the Environment.

Computers on Campus 240 computers/terminals and 155 ports are available on campus for general student use. Students can access the following: campus intranet, computer help desk, free student e-mail accounts, online (class) grades, online (class) registration, online (class) schedules. Campuswide network is available. 100% of college-owned or -operated housing units are wired for high-speed Internet access. Wireless service is available via entire campus.

Student Life *Housing:* on-campus residence required through sophomore year. *Options:* coed, men-only, women-only, disabled students. Campus housing is university owned. Freshman campus housing is guaranteed. *Activities and organizations:* drama/theater group, student-run newspaper, radio and television station, choral group, Interfraternity Council, Panhellenic Association, Student Government Association, Rollins Entertainment Programs, National Society of Collegiate Scholars, national fraternities, national sororities. *Campus security:* 24-hour emergency response devices and patrols, late-night transport/escort service, controlled dormitory access. *Student services:* health clinic, personal/psychological counseling, women's center.

Athletics Member NCAA. All Division II. *Intercollegiate sports:* baseball M(s), basketball M(s)/W(s), crew M/W, cross-country running M/W, golf M(s)/W(s), lacrosse M/W, sailing M/W, skiing (downhill) M/W, soccer M(s)/W(s), softball W(s), swimming and diving M/W, tennis M(s)/W(s), volleyball W(s). *Intramural sports:* baseball M(c), basketball M/W, bowling M(c)/W(c), cheerleading W(c), equestrian sports W(c), football M/W, ice hockey M(c), rock climbing M(c)/W(c), soccer M(c)/W(c), softball M/W, table tennis M/W, tennis M/W, ultimate Frisbee M(c)/W(c), volleyball W(c).

Standardized Tests *Required for some:* SAT or ACT (for admission), Selection of Test Score Waived Option (TSWO) or official SAT/ACT scores (TSWO is not appropriate for applicants seeking academic merit scholarship, Honors Program, or 3/2 Accelerated Management Program consideration).

Costs (2012–13) *Comprehensive fee:* $52,370 includes full-time tuition ($39,900) and room and board ($12,470). *College room only:* $7340. Room and board charges vary according to housing facility. *Payment plan:* installment. *Waivers:* employees or children of employees.

Financial Aid Of all full-time matriculated undergraduates who enrolled in 2012, 1,289 applied for aid, 1,071 were judged to have need, 252 had their need fully met. 347 Federal Work-Study jobs (averaging $1531). In 2012, 428 non-need-based awards were made. *Average percent of need met:* 80%. *Average financial aid package:* $34,058. *Average need-based loan:* $4772. *Average need-based gift aid:* $29,722. *Average non-need-based aid:* $18,325. *Average indebtedness upon graduation:* $24,096.

Applying *Options:* electronic application, early admission, early decision, deferred entrance. *Application fee:* $40. *Required:* essay or personal statement, high school transcript, 1 letter of recommendation. *Recommended:* minimum 2.0 GPA, interview. *Application deadlines:* 2/15 (freshmen), 4/15 (transfers). *Early decision deadline:* 11/15 (for plan 1), 1/15 (for plan 2). *Notification:* 4/1 (freshmen), continuous (transfers), 12/15 (early decision plan 1), 2/1 (early decision plan 2).

Freshman Application Contact Mr. David Erdmann, Dean of Admission and Enrollment, Rollins College, 1000 Holt Avenue, Campus Box 2720, Winter Park, FL 32789. *Phone:* 407-646-2161. *Fax:* 407-646-1502. *E-mail:* admission@rollins.edu.

Website: http://www.rollins.edu/.

St. John Vianney College Seminary
Miami, Florida

Freshman Application Contact Br. Edward Van Merrienboer, Academic Dean, St. John Vianney College Seminary, 2900 Southwest 87th Avenue, Miami, FL 33165-3244. *Phone:* 305-223-4561 Ext. 13.

Website: http://www.sjvcs.edu/.

Saint Leo University

Saint Leo, Florida

- **Independent Roman Catholic** comprehensive, founded 1889
- **Rural** 259-acre campus with easy access to Tampa, Orlando
- **Endowment** $35.1 million
- **Coed** 2,167 undergraduate students, 97% full-time, 50% women, 50% men
- **Moderately difficult** entrance level, 85% of applicants were admitted

Undergraduates 2,098 full-time, 69 part-time. Students come from 44 states and territories; 56 other countries; 28% are from out of state; 11% Black or African American, non-Hispanic/Latino; 14% Hispanic/Latino; 1% Asian, non-Hispanic/Latino; 0.1% Native Hawaiian or other Pacific Islander, non-Hispanic/Latino; 0.3% American Indian or Alaska Native, non-Hispanic/Latino; 2% Two or more races, non-Hispanic/Latino; 10% Race/ethnicity unknown; 13% international; 7% transferred in; 62% live on campus. *Retention:* 73% of full-time freshmen returned.

Freshmen *Admission:* 2,648 applied, 2,239 admitted, 634 enrolled. *Average high school GPA:* 3.5. *Test scores:* SAT critical reading scores over 500: 59%; SAT math scores over 500: 61%; ACT scores over 18: 97%; SAT critical reading scores over 600: 12%; SAT math scores over 600: 10%; ACT scores over 24: 23%; SAT critical reading scores over 700: 1%; SAT math scores over 700: 1%; ACT scores over 30: 1%.

Faculty *Total:* 190, 58% full-time, 63% with terminal degrees. *Student/faculty ratio:* 15:1.

Academics *Calendar:* semesters. *Degrees:* associate, bachelor's, master's, and postbachelor's certificates. *Special study options:* academic remediation for entering students, adult/continuing education programs, advanced placement credit, distance learning, double majors, English as a second language, honors programs, independent study, internships, part-time degree program, services for LD students, study abroad, summer session for credit. *ROTC:* Army (b), Air Force (c).

Computers on Campus 150 computers/terminals are available on campus for general student use. Students can access the following: campus intranet, computer help desk, free student e-mail accounts, online (class) grades, online (class) registration, online (class) schedules, campus residents are issued a laptop for their personal use. Campuswide network is available. 100% of college-owned or -operated housing units are wired for high-speed Internet access. Wireless service is available via classrooms, computer centers, computer labs, dorm rooms, learning centers, libraries, student centers.

Student Life *Housing:* on-campus residence required through junior year. *Options:* coed, men-only, women-only, disabled students. Campus housing is university owned. Freshman applicants given priority for college housing. *Activities and organizations:* drama/theater group, student-run newspaper, radio station, choral group, Student Government Union, Campus Activities Board, Caribbean Student Association, The Quest, Intercultural Student Association, national fraternities, national sororities. *Campus security:* 24-hour emergency response devices and patrols, late-night transport/escort service, controlled dormitory access, surveillance cameras in parking lots. *Student services:* health clinic, personal/psychological counseling.

Athletics Member NCAA. All Division II. *Intercollegiate sports:* baseball M(s), basketball M(s)/W(s), cross-country running M(s)/W(s), golf M(s)/W(s), lacrosse M(s)/W(s), soccer M(s)/W(s), softball W(s), swimming and diving M(s)/W(s), tennis M(s)/W(s), volleyball W(s). *Intramural sports:* basketball M/W, field hockey M/W, football M/W, soccer M/W, tennis M/W, ultimate Frisbee M/W, water polo M/W.

Standardized Tests *Recommended:* SAT or ACT (for admission).

Costs (2013–14) *Comprehensive fee:* $24,610 includes full-time tuition ($19,240), mandatory fees ($370), and room and board ($5000). *College room only:* $4680. *Payment plans:* installment, deferred payment. *Waivers:* employees or children of employees.

Financial Aid Of all full-time matriculated undergraduates who enrolled in 2011, 1,566 applied for aid, 1,375 were judged to have need, 284 had their need fully met. 711 Federal Work-Study jobs (averaging $3220). In 2011, 92 non-need-based awards were made. *Average percent of need met:* 73%. *Average financial aid package:* $18,859. *Average need-based loan:* $4148. *Average need-based gift aid:* $13,057. *Average non-need-based aid:* $1816. *Average indebtedness upon graduation:* $30,015.

Applying *Options:* electronic application, early admission, deferred entrance. *Application fee:* $40. *Required:* high school transcript, minimum 2.7 GPA, 1 letter of recommendation. *Recommended:* minimum 3.0 GPA, interview. *Application deadlines:* 7/1 (freshmen), 8/15 (transfers). *Notification:* continuous (freshmen), continuous (transfers).

Freshman Application Contact Ms. Dana Davies, Associate Vice President of Enrollment, Saint Leo University, MC 2008, PO Box 6665, Saint Leo, FL 33574-6665. *Phone:* 352-588-8283. *Toll-free phone:* 800-334-5532. *Fax:* 352-588-8257. *E-mail:* admissions@saintleo.edu. *Website:* http://www.saintleo.edu/.

See below for display ad and page 1478 for the College Close-Up.

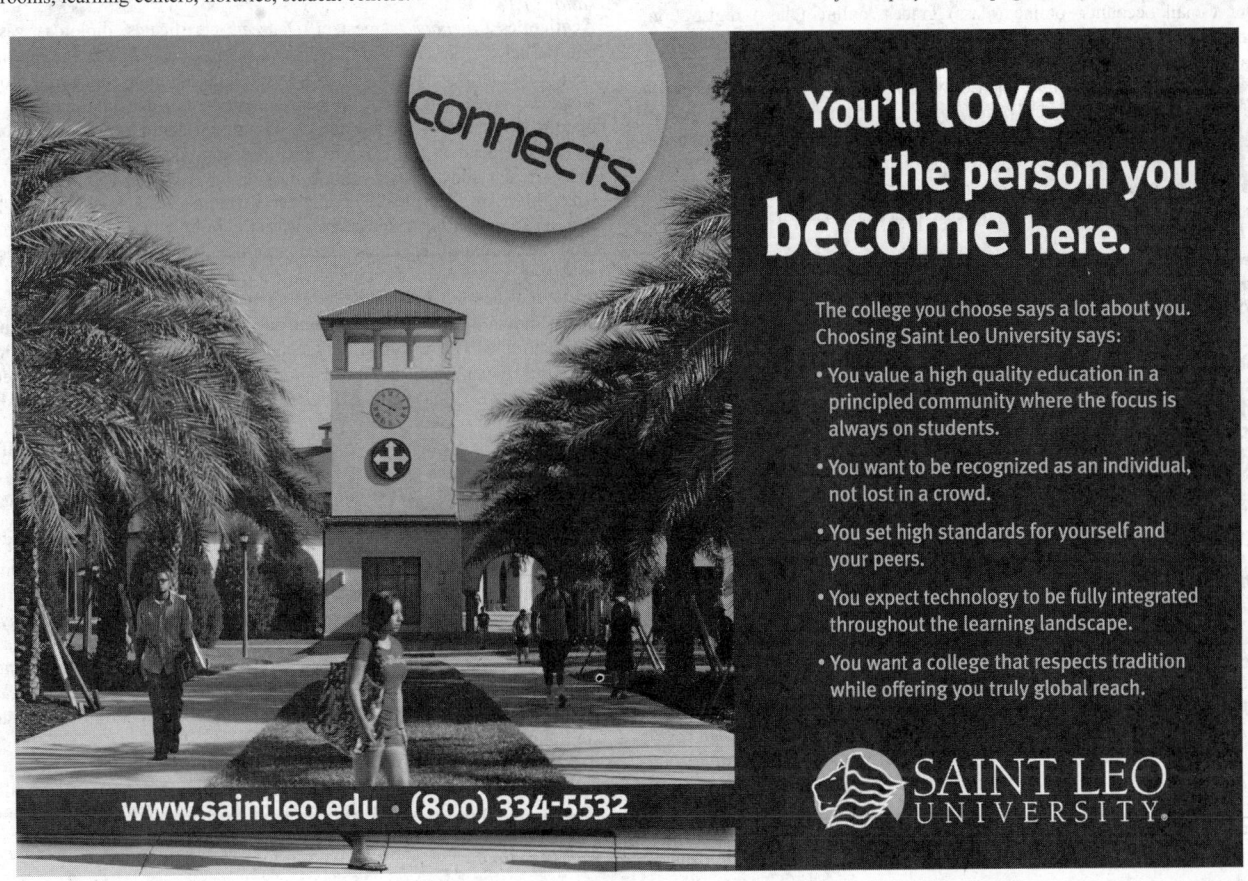

St. Petersburg College

St. Petersburg, Florida

Freshman Application Contact Ms. Susan Fell, Director of Admissions and Records, St. Petersburg College, PO Box 13489, St. Petersburg, FL 33733-3489. *Phone:* 727-341-3166. *E-mail:* information@spcollege.edu. *Website:* http://www.spcollege.edu/.

St. Thomas University

Miami Gardens, Florida

- **Independent Roman Catholic** comprehensive, founded 1961
- **Suburban** 140-acre campus
- **Coed** 1,085 undergraduate students, 93% full-time, 56% women, 44% men
- **Minimally difficult** entrance level, 39% of applicants were admitted

Undergraduates 1,013 full-time, 72 part-time. Students come from 25 states and territories; 52 other countries; 20% are from out of state; 26% Black or African American, non-Hispanic/Latino; 41% Hispanic/Latino; 0.4% Asian, non-Hispanic/Latino; 0.2% American Indian or Alaska Native, non-Hispanic/Latino; 0.9% Two or more races, non-Hispanic/Latino; 7% Race/ethnicity unknown; 13% international; 16% transferred in; 25% live on campus. *Retention:* 67% of full-time freshmen returned.

Freshmen *Admission:* 681 applied, 268 admitted, 209 enrolled. *Average high school GPA:* 2.94. *Test scores:* SAT critical reading scores over 500: 21%; SAT math scores over 500: 29%; SAT writing scores over 500: 13%; ACT scores over 18: 69%; SAT critical reading scores over 600: 2%; SAT math scores over 600: 6%; SAT writing scores over 600: 2%; ACT scores over 24: 6%.

Faculty *Total:* 238, 43% full-time, 52% with terminal degrees. *Student/faculty ratio:* 14:1.

Academics *Calendar:* semesters. *Degrees:* certificates, bachelor's, master's, doctoral, post-master's, and postbachelor's certificates. *Special study options:* academic remediation for entering students, adult/continuing education programs, advanced placement credit, distance learning, double majors, freshman honors college, honors programs, independent study, internships, part-time degree program, services for LD students, summer session for credit.

Computers on Campus 80 computers/terminals are available on campus for general student use. Students can access the following: campus intranet, free student e-mail accounts, online (class) grades, online (class) registration, online (class) schedules. Campuswide network is available. Wireless service is available via entire campus.

Student Life *Housing options:* men-only, women-only. Campus housing is university owned. *Activities and organizations:* student-run television station, choral group, Psychology Club, National Society of Leadership and Success (NSLS), Criminal Justice, Kreyol Nation, Gay Strait Alliance (GSA). *Campus security:* 24-hour emergency response devices and patrols, late-night transport/escort service, controlled dormitory access. *Student services:* health clinic, personal/psychological counseling.

Athletics Member NAIA. *Intercollegiate sports:* baseball M(s), cross-country running M(s)/W(s), golf M(s)/W(s), soccer M(s)/W(s), softball W(s), tennis M(s)/W(s), volleyball W(s). *Intramural sports:* baseball M, basketball M/W, cross-country running M/W, football M, golf M, soccer M/W, softball M/W, table tennis M/W, tennis M/W, volleyball M/W, water polo M/W, weight lifting M/W.

Standardized Tests *Required:* SAT or ACT (for admission).

Costs (2012–13) *Comprehensive fee:* $32,250 includes full-time tuition ($25,110) and room and board ($7140). Full-time tuition and fees vary according to program. Part-time tuition: $502 per credit hour. Part-time tuition and fees vary according to program. *Room and board:* Room and board charges vary according to board plan and housing facility. *Payment plan:* installment. *Waivers:* employees or children of employees.

Financial Aid Of all full-time matriculated undergraduates who enrolled in 2012, 833 applied for aid, 747 were judged to have need, 391 had their need fully met. In 2012, 189 non-need-based awards were made. *Average need-based loan:* $4295. *Average need-based gift aid:* $3604. *Average non-need-based aid:* $8365.

Applying *Options:* electronic application, deferred entrance. *Application fee:* $40. *Required:* high school transcript, minimum 2.0 GPA. *Recommended:* essay or personal statement, 1 letter of recommendation, interview. *Application deadlines:* rolling (freshmen), rolling (transfers). *Notification:* continuous (freshmen), continuous (transfers).

Freshman Application Contact Mr. Andre Lightbourne, Director of Admissions, St. Thomas University, 16401 Northwest 37th Avenue, Miami Gardens, FL 33054-6459. *Phone:* 305-628-6712. *Toll-free phone:* 800-367-9010. *Fax:* 305-628-6591. *E-mail:* signup@stu.edu. *Website:* http://www.stu.edu/.

Santa Fe College

Gainesville, Florida

Freshman Application Contact Santa Fe College, 3000 Northwest 83rd Street, Gainesville, FL 32606. *Phone:* 352-395-4177. *Website:* http://www.sfcollege.edu/.

Schiller International University

Largo, Florida

Freshman Application Contact Donald Trippe, Admissions Officer, Schiller International University, 300 East Bay Drive, Largo, FL 33770. *Phone:* 727-738-6365. *Toll-free phone:* 800-261-9571 (in-state); 800-261-9751 (out-of-state). *Fax:* 727-738-6376. *E-mail:* admissions@schiller.edu. *Website:* http://www.schiller.edu/.

Seminole State College of Florida

Sanford, Florida

- **State and locally supported** primarily 2-year, founded 1966
- **Small-town** 200-acre campus with easy access to Orlando
- **Endowment** $12.5 million
- **Coed** 19,450 undergraduate students, 39% full-time, 59% women, 41% men
- **Noncompetitive** entrance level, 100% of applicants were admitted

Undergraduates 7,559 full-time, 11,891 part-time. Students come from 88 other countries; 0.5% are from out of state; 18% Black or African American, non-Hispanic/Latino; 22% Hispanic/Latino; 3% Asian, non-Hispanic/Latino; 0.3% Native Hawaiian or other Pacific Islander, non-Hispanic/Latino; 0.3% American Indian or Alaska Native, non-Hispanic/Latino; 3% Two or more races, non-Hispanic/Latino; 0.8% Race/ethnicity unknown; 2% international; 6% transferred in.

Freshmen *Admission:* 9,901 applied, 9,901 admitted, 2,721 enrolled.

Faculty *Total:* 795, 30% full-time, 16% with terminal degrees. *Student/faculty ratio:* 27:1.

Academics *Calendar:* semesters. *Degrees:* certificates, diplomas, associate, and bachelor's. *Special study options:* academic remediation for entering students, accelerated degree program, adult/continuing education programs, advanced placement credit, cooperative education, distance learning, double majors, English as a second language, external degree program, honors programs, independent study, internships, part-time degree program, services for LD students, study abroad, summer session for credit. *ROTC:* Army (b).

Computers on Campus 250 computers/terminals are available on campus for general student use. Students can access the following: online (class) registration, online (class) schedules, Online Syallabii. Campuswide network is available. Wireless service is available via entire campus.

Student Life *Housing:* college housing not available. *Activities and organizations:* drama/theater group, student-run newspaper, choral group, Phi Beta Lambda, Phi Theta Kappa, Student Government Association, Sigma Phi Gamma, Hispanic Student Association. *Campus security:* 24-hour emergency response devices and patrols. *Student services:* personal/psychological counseling.

Athletics Member NJCAA. *Intercollegiate sports:* baseball M(s), golf W(s), softball W(s).

Standardized Tests *Required:* CPT, PERT (for admission). *Recommended:* ACT (for admission).

Costs (2013–14) *Tuition:* state resident $3131 full-time; nonresident $11,456 full-time. Full-time tuition and fees vary according to degree level and program. Part-time tuition and fees vary according to degree level and program. *Payment plan:* deferred payment. *Waivers:* senior citizens and employees or children of employees.

Applying *Options:* electronic application, early admission, deferred entrance. *Required:* high school transcript, minimum 2.0 GPA. *Application deadlines:* rolling (freshmen), rolling (transfers). *Notification:* continuous (freshmen), continuous (transfers).

Freshman Application Contact Ms. Pamela Mennechey, Associate Vice President—Student Recruitment and Enrollment, Seminole State College of Florida, Sanford, FL 32773-6199. *Phone:* 407-708-2050. *Fax:* 407-708-2395. *E-mail:* admissions@scc-fl.edu. *Website:* http://www.seminolestate.edu/.

Southeastern University

Lakeland, Florida

- **Independent** comprehensive, founded 1935, affiliated with Assemblies of God
- **Suburban** 87-acre campus with easy access to Tampa, Orlando
- **Endowment** $5.8 million
- **Coed** 2,448 undergraduate students, 86% full-time, 56% women, 44% men
- **Minimally difficult** entrance level, 70% of applicants were admitted

Undergraduates 2,106 full-time, 342 part-time. Students come from 49 states and territories; 20 other countries; 33% are from out of state; 11% Black or African American, non-Hispanic/Latino; 14% Hispanic/Latino; 1% Asian, non-Hispanic/Latino; 0.2% Native Hawaiian or other Pacific Islander, non-Hispanic/Latino; 0.4% American Indian or Alaska Native, non-Hispanic/Latino; 0.8% Two or more races, non-Hispanic/Latino; 5% Race/ethnicity unknown; 0.8% international; 6% transferred in; 54% live on campus. *Retention:* 66% of full-time freshmen returned.

Freshmen *Admission:* 1,234 applied, 859 admitted, 592 enrolled. *Average high school GPA:* 3.44. *Test scores:* SAT critical reading scores over 500: 54%; SAT math scores over 500: 45%; SAT writing scores over 500: 50%; ACT scores over 18: 81%; SAT critical reading scores over 600: 15%; SAT math scores over 600: 11%; SAT writing scores over 600: 10%; ACT scores over 24: 24%; SAT critical reading scores over 700: 2%; SAT math scores over 700: 1%; SAT writing scores over 700: 2%; ACT scores over 30: 3%.

Faculty *Total:* 169, 57% full-time, 46% with terminal degrees. *Student/faculty ratio:* 19:1.

Academics *Calendar:* semesters. *Degrees:* associate, bachelor's, and master's. *Special study options:* adult/continuing education programs, part-time degree program. *ROTC:* Army (c).

Computers on Campus Students can access the following: campus intranet, computer help desk, free student e-mail accounts, online (class) grades, online (class) registration, online (class) schedules, network programs. Campuswide network is available. 100% of college-owned or -operated housing units are wired for high-speed Internet access. Wireless service is available via entire campus.

Student Life *Housing:* on-campus residence required through senior year. *Options:* men-only, women-only. Campus housing is university owned. Freshman campus housing is guaranteed. *Activities and organizations:* drama/theater group, student-run newspaper, radio and television station, choral group. *Campus security:* 24-hour emergency response devices and patrols, late-night transport/escort service. *Student services:* health clinic, personal/psychological counseling.

Athletics Member NAIA, NCCAA. *Intercollegiate sports:* baseball M(s), basketball M(s)/W(s), cheerleading M/W, cross-country running M(s)/W(s), football M(s), golf M(s)/W(s), soccer M(s)/W(s), softball W(s), tennis M(s)/W(s), volleyball W(s). *Intramural sports:* basketball M/W, football M/W, soccer M/W, softball M/W, ultimate Frisbee M/W, volleyball M/W.

Standardized Tests *Required:* SAT or ACT (for admission).

Costs (2012–13) *Comprehensive fee:* $27,202 includes full-time tuition ($17,996), mandatory fees ($600), and room and board ($8606). Full-time tuition and fees vary according to class time, degree level, and reciprocity agreements. Part-time tuition: $750 per credit hour. Part-time tuition and fees vary according to class time, course load, degree level, and reciprocity agreements. *Required fees:* $150 per term part-time. *Room and board:* Room and board charges vary according to board plan and housing facility. *Payment plan:* installment. *Waivers:* employees or children of employees.

Financial Aid Of all full-time matriculated undergraduates who enrolled in 2011, 2,057 applied for aid, 1,814 were judged to have need, 172 had their need fully met. In 2011, 245 non-need-based awards were made. *Average percent of need met:* 2%. *Average financial aid package:* $11,535. *Average need-based loan:* $3861. *Average need-based gift aid:* $8187. *Average non-need-based aid:* $3846. *Average indebtedness upon graduation:* $24,398.

Applying *Options:* early admission, deferred entrance. *Application fee:* $40. *Required:* essay or personal statement, high school transcript, 2 letters of recommendation. *Required for some:* interview. *Application deadlines:* 5/1 (freshmen), 7/1 (transfers). *Notification:* 6/1 (freshmen), continuous (transfers).

Freshman Application Contact Southeastern University, 1000 Longfellow Boulevard, Lakeland, FL 33801-6099. *Phone:* 800-500-8760. *Toll-free phone:* 800-500-8760.

Website: http://www.seu.edu/.

South University

Royal Palm Beach, Florida

- **Proprietary** comprehensive, founded 1899, part of Education Management Corporation
- **Coed**

Academics *Calendar:* quarters. *Degrees:* associate, bachelor's, and master's.

Freshman Application Contact South University, University Centre, 9801 Belvedere Road, Royal Palm Beach, FL 33411. *Phone:* 561-273-6500. *Toll-free phone:* 866-629-2902.

Website: http://www.southuniversity.edu/west-palm-beach/.

South University

Tampa, Florida

- **Proprietary** comprehensive, part of Education Management Corporation
- **Coed**

Academics *Degrees:* associate, bachelor's, and master's.

Freshman Application Contact South University, 4401 North Himes Avenue, Suite 175, Tampa, FL 33614. *Phone:* 813-393-3800. *Toll-free phone:* 800-846-1472.

Website: http://www.southuniversity.edu/tampa/.

Southwest Florida College

Fort Myers, Florida

Freshman Application Contact Mr. Ken Reynolds, Director of Admissions, Southwest Florida College, 1685 Medical Lane, Fort Myers, FL 33907. *Phone:* 239-939-4766. *Toll-free phone:* 877-493-5147 (in-state); 877-793-5147 (out-of-state). *Fax:* 239-936-4040. *E-mail:* kreynolds@swfc.edu.

Website: http://www.swfc.edu/.

Southwest Florida College

Tampa, Florida

Director of Admissions Admissions, Southwest Florida College, 3910 Riga Boulevard, Tampa, FL 33619. *Phone:* 813-630-4401. *Toll-free phone:* 877-493-5147.

Website: http://www.swfc.edu/.

State College of Florida Manatee-Sarasota

Bradenton, Florida

- **State-supported** 4-year, founded 1957, part of Florida Community College System
- **Suburban** 100-acre campus with easy access to Tampa-St. Petersburg
- **Coed** 10,765 undergraduate students, 43% full-time, 60% women, 40% men
- **Noncompetitive** entrance level, 100% of applicants were admitted

Undergraduates 4,600 full-time, 6,165 part-time. Students come from 31 states and territories; 38 other countries; 3% are from out of state; 9% Black or African American, non-Hispanic/Latino; 13% Hispanic/Latino; 2% Asian, non-Hispanic/Latino; 0.4% American Indian or Alaska Native, non-Hispanic/Latino; 1% Two or more races, non-Hispanic/Latino; 6% Race/ethnicity unknown; 0.9% international; 4% transferred in. *Retention:* 61% of full-time freshmen returned.

Freshmen *Admission:* 2,729 applied, 2,729 admitted, 1,423 enrolled. *Test scores:* SAT critical reading scores over 500: 32%; SAT math scores over 500: 34%; SAT writing scores over 500: 37%; ACT scores over 18: 61%; SAT critical reading scores over 600: 5%; SAT math scores over 600: 6%; SAT writing scores over 600: 8%; ACT scores over 24: 19%; ACT scores over 30: 3%.

Faculty *Total:* 445, 34% full-time.

Academics *Calendar:* semesters. *Degrees:* certificates, associate, and bachelor's. *Special study options:* academic remediation for entering students, advanced placement credit, cooperative education, distance learning, English as a second language, honors programs, independent study, part-time degree program, services for LD students, summer session for credit.

Computers on Campus 1,000 computers/terminals are available on campus for general student use. Students can access the following: computer help desk, free student e-mail accounts, online (class) registration, online (class) schedules. Campuswide network is available. Wireless service is available via entire campus.

Student Life *Housing:* college housing not available. *Activities and organizations:* drama/theater group, student-run newspaper, choral group, Student Government Association, Phi Theta Kappa, American Chemical Society Student Affiliate, Campus Ministry, Medical Community Club. *Campus security:* 24-hour emergency response devices and patrols, late-night transport/escort service.

Athletics Member NJCAA. *Intercollegiate sports:* baseball M(s), basketball M(s), softball W(s), volleyball W(s). *Intramural sports:* basketball M/W, softball M/W, volleyball M/W, weight lifting M/W.

Costs (2013–14) *Tuition:* state resident $2460 full-time, $102 per credit part-time; nonresident $9276 full-time, $387 per credit part-time. *Payment plan:* deferred payment. *Waivers:* employees or children of employees.

Financial Aid Of all full-time matriculated undergraduates who enrolled in 2011, 82 Federal Work-Study jobs (averaging $2800). *Financial aid deadline:* 8/15.

Applying *Options:* early admission. *Required:* high school transcript. *Application deadlines:* 8/20 (freshmen), 8/20 (transfers). *Notification:* continuous (freshmen), continuous (transfers).

Freshman Application Contact Ms. MariLynn Lewy, AVP, Student Services, State College of Florida Manatee-Sarasota, Bradenton, FL 34206. *Phone:* 941-752-5384. *Fax:* 941-727-6380. *E-mail:* lewym@scf.edu. *Website:* http://www.scf.edu/.

Stetson University

DeLand, Florida

- **Independent** comprehensive, founded 1883
- **Small-town** 140-acre campus with easy access to Orlando
- **Endowment** $147.7 million
- **Coed** 2,516 undergraduate students, 98% full-time, 56% women, 44% men
- **Moderately difficult** entrance level, 60% of applicants were admitted

Undergraduates 2,477 full-time, 39 part-time. Students come from 42 states and territories; 47 other countries; 22% are from out of state; 7% Black or African American, non-Hispanic/Latino; 15% Hispanic/Latino; 2% Asian, non-Hispanic/Latino; 0.1% American Indian or Alaska Native, non-Hispanic/Latino; 4% Two or more races, non-Hispanic/Latino; 0.9% Race/ethnicity unknown; 4% international; 4% transferred in; 67% live on campus. *Retention:* 79% of full-time freshmen returned.

Freshmen *Admission:* 4,862 applied, 2,934 admitted, 818 enrolled. *Average high school GPA:* 3.77. *Test scores:* SAT critical reading scores over 500: 88%; SAT math scores over 500: 86%; SAT writing scores over 500: 79%; ACT scores over 18: 99%; SAT critical reading scores over 600: 44%; SAT math scores over 600: 40%; SAT writing scores over 600: 32%; ACT scores over 24: 70%; SAT critical reading scores over 700: 7%; SAT math scores over 700: 6%; SAT writing scores over 700: 4%; ACT scores over 30: 12%.

Faculty *Total:* 381, 64% full-time, 83% with terminal degrees. *Student/faculty ratio:* 12:1.

Academics *Calendar:* semesters. *Degrees:* bachelor's, master's, doctoral, and post-master's certificates. *Special study options:* accelerated degree program, adult/continuing education programs, advanced placement credit, distance learning, double majors, honors programs, independent study, internships, off-campus study, part-time degree program, services for LD students, student-designed majors, study abroad, summer session for credit. *ROTC:* Army (c). *Unusual degree programs:* 3-2 engineering; forestry with Duke University; Master of Public Administration with American University, JD with Stetson University College of Law.

Computers on Campus 500 computers/terminals are available on campus for general student use. Students can access the following: campus intranet, computer help desk, free student e-mail accounts, online (class) grades, online (class) registration, online (class) schedules. Campuswide network is available. 100% of college-owned or -operated housing units are wired for high-speed Internet access. Wireless service is available via entire campus.

Student Life *Housing:* on-campus residence required through junior year. *Options:* coed, men-only, women-only. Campus housing is university owned and leased by the school. Freshman campus housing is guaranteed. *Activities and organizations:* drama/theater group, student-run newspaper, radio station, choral group, Hatter Harvest, Wesley House, Invisible Children, Kaleidoscope, Student Government Association, national fraternities, national sororities. *Campus security:* 24-hour emergency response devices and patrols, late-night transport/escort service, controlled dormitory access. *Student services:* health clinic, personal/psychological counseling, women's center.

Athletics Member NCAA. All Division I. *Intercollegiate sports:* baseball M(s), basketball M(s)/W(s), crew M/W(s), cross-country running M(s)/W(s), football M, golf M(s)/W(s), lacrosse W(s), soccer M(s)/W(s), softball W(s), tennis M(s)/W(s), volleyball W(s). *Intramural sports:* baseball M, basketball M(c)/W, bowling M/W, equestrian sports M(c)/W(c), golf M/W, lacrosse M(c)/W(c), riflery M(c)/W(c), soccer M(c)/W, softball M/W, swimming and diving M(c)/W(c), table tennis M(c)/W(c), tennis M(c)/W(c), ultimate Frisbee M(c)/W(c), volleyball M/W.

Standardized Tests *Required for some:* SAT or ACT (for admission).

Costs (2012–13) *Comprehensive fee:* $47,332 includes full-time tuition ($36,344), mandatory fees ($300), and room and board ($10,688). Part-time tuition: $3785 per course. Part-time tuition and fees vary according to course load, location, and program. *College room only:* $6088. Room and board charges vary according to board plan and housing facility. *Payment plan:* installment. *Waivers:* employees or children of employees.

Financial Aid Of all full-time matriculated undergraduates who enrolled in 2012, 2,167 applied for aid, 1,861 were judged to have need, 406 had their need fully met. 1,061 Federal Work-Study jobs (averaging $2070). 201 state and other part-time jobs (averaging $3032). In 2012, 454 non-need-based awards were made. *Average percent of need met:* 80%. *Average financial aid package:* $32,011. *Average need-based loan:* $4824. *Average need-based gift aid:* $24,768. *Average non-need-based aid:* $18,327. *Average indebtedness upon graduation:* $32,750.

Applying *Options:* electronic application, early admission, deferred entrance. *Application fee:* $50. *Required:* essay or personal statement, high school transcript, 1 letter of recommendation. *Recommended:* interview. *Application deadlines:* rolling (freshmen), rolling (out-of-state freshmen), rolling (transfers). *Notification:* continuous (freshmen), continuous (out-of-state freshmen), continuous (transfers).

Freshman Application Contact Mr. Joel Bauman, Director of Admissions, Stetson University, Unit 8378, Griffith Hall, DeLand, FL 32723. *Phone:* 386-822-7100. *Toll-free phone:* 800-688-0101. *Fax:* 386-822-7112. *E-mail:* admissions@stetson.edu. *Website:* http://www.stetson.edu/.

Strayer University—Baymeadows Campus

Jacksonville, Florida

Freshman Application Contact Strayer University—Baymeadows Campus, 8375 Dix Ellis Trail, Suite 200, Jacksonville, FL 32256. *Website:* http://www.strayer.edu/campus/baymeadows/.

Strayer University—Brickell Campus

Miami, Florida

Freshman Application Contact Strayer University—Brickell Campus, 1201 Brickell Avenue, Suite 700, Miami, FL 33131. *Website:* http://www.strayer.edu/campus/brickell.

Strayer University—Coral Springs Campus

Coral Springs, Florida

Freshman Application Contact Strayer University—Coral Springs Campus, 5830 Coral Ridge Drive, Suite 300, Coral Springs, FL 33076. *Website:* http://www.strayer.edu/campus/coral-springs/.

Strayer University—Doral Campus

Miami, Florida

Freshman Application Contact Strayer University—Doral Campus, 11430 Northwest 20th Street, Suite 150, Miami, FL 33172. *Website:* http://www.strayer.edu/campus/doral.

Strayer University—Fort Lauderdale Campus

Fort Lauderdale, Florida

Freshman Application Contact Strayer University—Fort Lauderdale Campus, 2307 West Broward Boulevard, Suite 100, Fort Lauderdale, FL 33312. *Website:* http://www.strayer.edu/campus/fort-lauderdale/.

Strayer University—Maitland Campus

Maitland, Florida

Freshman Application Contact Strayer University—Maitland Campus, 850 Trafalgar Court, Suite 360, Maitland, FL 32751. *Website:* http://www.strayer.edu/campus/maitland/.

Strayer University—Miramar Campus

Miramar, Florida

Freshman Application Contact Strayer University—Miramar Campus, 15620 Southwest 29th Street, Miramar, FL 33027. *Website:* http://www.strayer.edu/campus/miramar.

Strayer University—Orlando East Campus

Orlando, Florida

Freshman Application Contact Strayer University—Orlando East Campus, 2200 North Alafaya Trail, Suite 500, Orlando, FL 32826.
Website: http://www.strayer.edu/campus/orlando-east/.

Strayer University—Palm Beach Gardens Campus

Palm Beach Gardens, Florida

Freshman Application Contact Strayer University—Palm Beach Gardens Campus, 11025 RCA Center Drive, Suite 200, Palm Beach Gardens, FL 33410.
Website: http://www.strayer.edu/campus/palm-beach-gardens.

Strayer University—Sand Lake Campus

Orlando, Florida

Freshman Application Contact Strayer University—Sand Lake Campus, 8541 South Park Circle, Building 900, Orlando, FL 32819.
Website: http://www.strayer.edu/campus/sand-lake/.

Strayer University—Tampa East Campus

Tampa, Florida

Freshman Application Contact Strayer University—Tampa East Campus, 6302 East Martin Luther King Boulevard, Suite 450, Tampa, FL 33619.
Website: http://www.strayer.edu/campus/tampa-east.

Strayer University—Tampa Westshore Campus

Tampa, Florida

Freshman Application Contact Strayer University—Tampa Westshore Campus, 4902 Eisenhower Boulevard, Suite 100, Tampa, FL 33634.
Website: http://www.strayer.edu/campus/tampa-westshore.

Talmudic College of Florida

Miami Beach, Florida

Freshman Application Contact Rabbi Yeshaya Greenberg, Dean of Students, Talmudic College of Florida, 1910 Alton Road, Miami Beach, FL 33139.
Phone: 305-534-7050. *Fax:* 305-534-8444. *E-mail:* yandtg@gmail.com.
Website: http://www.talmudicu.edu/.

Trinity Baptist College

Jacksonville, Florida

- **Independent Baptist** comprehensive, founded 1974
- **Urban** 148-acre campus with easy access to Jacksonville
- **Coed**
- **Moderately difficult** entrance level

Faculty *Student/faculty ratio:* 9:1.
Academics *Calendar:* semesters. *Degrees:* associate, bachelor's, and master's.
Student Life *Campus security:* 24-hour emergency response devices and patrols, controlled dormitory access.
Athletics Member NCCAA.
Standardized Tests *Required:* SAT or ACT (for admission).
Costs (2012–13) *Comprehensive fee:* $14,550 includes full-time tuition ($7990), mandatory fees ($1050), and room and board ($5510). Part-time tuition: $335 per credit hour. *College room only:* $2510. Room and board charges vary according to board plan.
Financial Aid *Of all full-time matriculated undergraduates who enrolled in 2001,* 264 applied for aid, 168 were judged to have need, 37 had their need fully met. *In 2001,* 10 non-need-based awards were made. *Average percent of need met:* 55. *Average financial aid package:* $4458. *Average need-based loan:* $2912. *Average need-based gift aid:* $2791. *Average non-need-based aid:* $1279. *Average indebtedness upon graduation:* $6425. *Financial aid deadline:* 4/15.

Applying *Options:* electronic application. *Application fee:* $30. *Required:* essay or personal statement, high school transcript, minimum 2.0 GPA, 2 letters of recommendation.
Freshman Application Contact Trinity Baptist College, FL. *Phone:* 904-596-2538. *Toll-free phone:* 800-786-2206. *E-mail:* trinity@tbc.edu.
Website: http://www.tbc.edu/.

Trinity College of Florida

New Port Richey, Florida

- **Independent nondenominational** 4-year, founded 1932
- **Small-town** 40-acre campus with easy access to Tampa
- **Endowment** $606,874
- **Coed** 219 undergraduate students, 86% full-time, 44% women, 56% men
- **Minimally difficult** entrance level, 25% of applicants were admitted

Undergraduates 189 full-time, 30 part-time. Students come from 8 states and territories; 7 other countries; 3% are from out of state; 10% Black or African American, non-Hispanic/Latino; 18% Hispanic/Latino; 0.5% Asian, non-Hispanic/Latino; 2% Two or more races, non-Hispanic/Latino; 4% Race/ethnicity unknown; 4% international; 26% transferred in; 27% live on campus. *Retention:* 45% of full-time freshmen returned.
Freshmen *Admission:* 107 applied, 27 admitted, 29 enrolled. *Average high school GPA:* 2.25. *Test scores:* SAT critical reading scores over 500: 20%; SAT writing scores over 500: 25%; ACT scores over 18: 50%.
Faculty *Total:* 23, 35% full-time, 35% with terminal degrees. *Student/faculty ratio:* 10:1.
Academics *Calendar:* semesters. *Degrees:* certificates, associate, and bachelor's. *Special study options:* academic remediation for entering students, accelerated degree program, adult/continuing education programs, advanced placement credit, cooperative education, distance learning, double majors, independent study, internships, off-campus study, part-time degree program, services for LD students, student-designed majors, summer session for credit.
Computers on Campus 17 computers/terminals and 144 ports are available on campus for general student use. Students can access the following: campus intranet, computer help desk, free student e-mail accounts, online (class) grades, online (class) registration, online (class) schedules. Campuswide network is available. 100% of college-owned or -operated housing units are wired for high-speed Internet access. Wireless service is available via entire campus.
Student Life *Housing:* on-campus residence required through senior year. *Options:* men-only, women-only, disabled students. Campus housing is university owned and leased by the school. Freshman campus housing is guaranteed. *Activities and organizations:* drama/theater group, student-run newspaper, choral group, Great Commission Missionary Fellowship, Trinity Tribune (School Newspaper), Student Government. *Campus security:* student patrols. *Student services:* personal/psychological counseling.
Athletics Member NCAA, NCCAA. All NCAA Division II. *Intercollegiate sports:* basketball M, volleyball W. *Intramural sports:* soccer M, softball M.
Standardized Tests *Required:* SAT or ACT (for admission).
Costs (2013–14) *Comprehensive fee:* $19,870 includes full-time tuition ($12,520), mandatory fees ($800), and room and board ($6550). Part-time tuition: $522 per credit hour. Part-time tuition and fees vary according to course load. *Required fees:* $400 per term part-time. *College room only:* $4450. *Payment plan:* installment. *Waivers:* senior citizens and employees or children of employees.
Financial Aid Of all full-time matriculated undergraduates who enrolled in 2012, 158 applied for aid, 150 were judged to have need, 4 had their need fully met. 28 Federal Work-Study jobs (averaging $2698). 2 state and other part-time jobs (averaging $2420). In 2012, 3 non-need-based awards were made. *Average percent of need met:* 47%. *Average financial aid package:* $10,078. *Average need-based loan:* $4015. *Average need-based gift aid:* $6254. *Average non-need-based aid:* $733. *Average indebtedness upon graduation:* $5500.
Applying *Options:* electronic application, early admission, deferred entrance. *Application fee:* $25. *Required:* essay or personal statement, high school transcript, 2 letters of recommendation, interview. *Recommended:* minimum 2.0 GPA. *Application deadlines:* 12/17 (freshmen), 12/17 (out-of-state freshmen), 12/17 (transfers). *Notification:* continuous until 12/17 (freshmen), continuous (out-of-state freshmen).
Freshman Application Contact Mr. Kevin D. O'Farrell, Admissions Committee Chairman, Trinity College of Florida, 2430 Welbilt Boulevard, Trinity, FL 34655. *Phone:* 727-376-6911 Ext. 309. *Toll-free phone:* 800-388-0869. *Fax:* 727-569-1410. *E-mail:* kofarrell@trinitycollege.edu.
Website: http://www.trinitycollege.edu/.

Universidad FLET

Miami, Florida

Director of Admissions Dalia Sosa, Admissions Director, Universidad FLET, 14540 Southwest 136th Street, Suite 108, Miami, FL 33186. *Phone:* 305-378-

8700. *Toll-free phone:* 888-376-3538. *Fax:* 305-232-5832. *E-mail:* admissiones@flet.edu. *Website:* http://www.flet.edu/.

University of Central Florida
Orlando, Florida

- **State-supported** university, founded 1963, part of State University System of Florida
- **Suburban** 1415-acre campus with easy access to Orlando
- **Endowment** $121.1 million
- **Coed** 50,968 undergraduate students, 72% full-time, 55% women, 45% men
- **Moderately difficult** entrance level, 46% of applicants were admitted

Undergraduates 36,731 full-time, 14,237 part-time. Students come from 50 states and territories; 134 other countries; 5% are from out of state; 10% Black or African American, non-Hispanic/Latino; 20% Hispanic/Latino; 5% Asian, non-Hispanic/Latino; 0.2% Native Hawaiian or other Pacific Islander, non-Hispanic/Latino; 0.3% American Indian or Alaska Native, non-Hispanic/Latino; 2% Two or more races, non-Hispanic/Latino; 1% Race/ethnicity unknown; 1% international; 12% transferred in; 17% live on campus. *Retention:* 88% of full-time freshmen returned.

Freshmen *Admission:* 33,281 applied, 15,388 admitted, 6,082 enrolled. *Average high school GPA:* 3.78. *Test scores:* SAT critical reading scores over 500: 91%; SAT math scores over 500: 94%; SAT writing scores over 500: 83%; ACT scores over 18: 100%; SAT critical reading scores over 600: 43%; SAT math scores over 600: 51%; SAT writing scores over 600: 31%; ACT scores over 24: 77%; SAT critical reading scores over 700: 7%; SAT math scores over 700: 9%; SAT writing scores over 700: 4%; ACT scores over 30: 12%.

Faculty *Total:* 1,842, 72% full-time, 66% with terminal degrees. *Student/faculty ratio:* 32:1.

Academics *Calendar:* semesters. *Degrees:* certificates, associate, bachelor's, master's, doctoral, and postbachelor's certificates. *Special study options:* accelerated degree program, adult/continuing education programs, advanced placement credit, cooperative education, distance learning, double majors, English as a second language, freshman honors college, honors programs, independent study, internships, off-campus study, part-time degree program, services for LD students, study abroad, summer session for credit. *ROTC:* Army (b), Air Force (b). *Unusual degree programs:* 3-2 engineering; nursing; history; communicative sciences and disorders; economics; computer science.

Computers on Campus 3,200 computers/terminals and 200 ports are available on campus for general student use. Students can access the following: campus intranet, computer help desk, free student e-mail accounts, online (class) grades, online (class) registration, online (class) schedules. Campuswide network is available. 100% of college-owned or -operated housing units are wired for high-speed Internet access. Wireless service is available via entire campus.

Student Life *Housing options:* coed, men-only, women-only, disabled students. Campus housing is university owned and is provided by a third party. Freshman applicants given priority for college housing. *Activities and organizations:* drama/theater group, student-run newspaper, radio and television station, choral group, marching band, Volunteer UCF, Intramural Sports, Recreation and Wellness Center Group Exercise Programs, Multicultural Student Center and Organizations, Campus Religious Organizations, national fraternities, national sororities. *Campus security:* 24-hour emergency response devices and patrols, late-night transport/escort service, controlled dormitory access. *Student services:* health clinic, personal/psychological counseling, women's center, legal services.

Athletics Member NCAA. All Division I except football (Division I-A). *Intercollegiate sports:* baseball M(s), basketball M(s)/W(s), cheerleading M(s)/W(s), crew W(s), cross-country running W(s), golf M(s)/W(s), soccer M(s)/W(s), softball W(s), tennis M(s)/W(s), track and field W(s), volleyball W(s). *Intramural sports:* badminton M/W, baseball M(c), basketball M/W, bowling M(c)/W(c), crew M(c)/W(c), equestrian sports M(c)/W(c), fencing M(c)/W(c), golf M/W, ice hockey M(c)/W(c), lacrosse M(c)/W(c), racquetball M(c)/W(c), rock climbing M(c)/W(c), rugby M(c)/W(c), soccer M(c)/W(c), softball M/W, table tennis M(c)/W(c), tennis M(c)/W(c), ultimate Frisbee M(c)/W(c), volleyball M(c)/W(c), water polo M(c)/W(c), wrestling M.

Standardized Tests *Required:* SAT or ACT (for admission).

Costs (2012–13) *Tuition:* state resident $6247 full-time, $208 per credit hour part-time; nonresident $22,345 full-time, $745 per credit hour part-time. Full-time tuition and fees vary according to course load. Part-time tuition and fees vary according to course load. *Room and board:* $9357; room only: $5400. Room and board charges vary according to board plan and housing facility. *Payment plans:* tuition prepayment, deferred payment. *Waivers:* senior citizens and employees or children of employees.

Financial Aid Of all full-time matriculated undergraduates who enrolled in 2011, 33,456 applied for aid, 29,262 were judged to have need, 3,012 had their

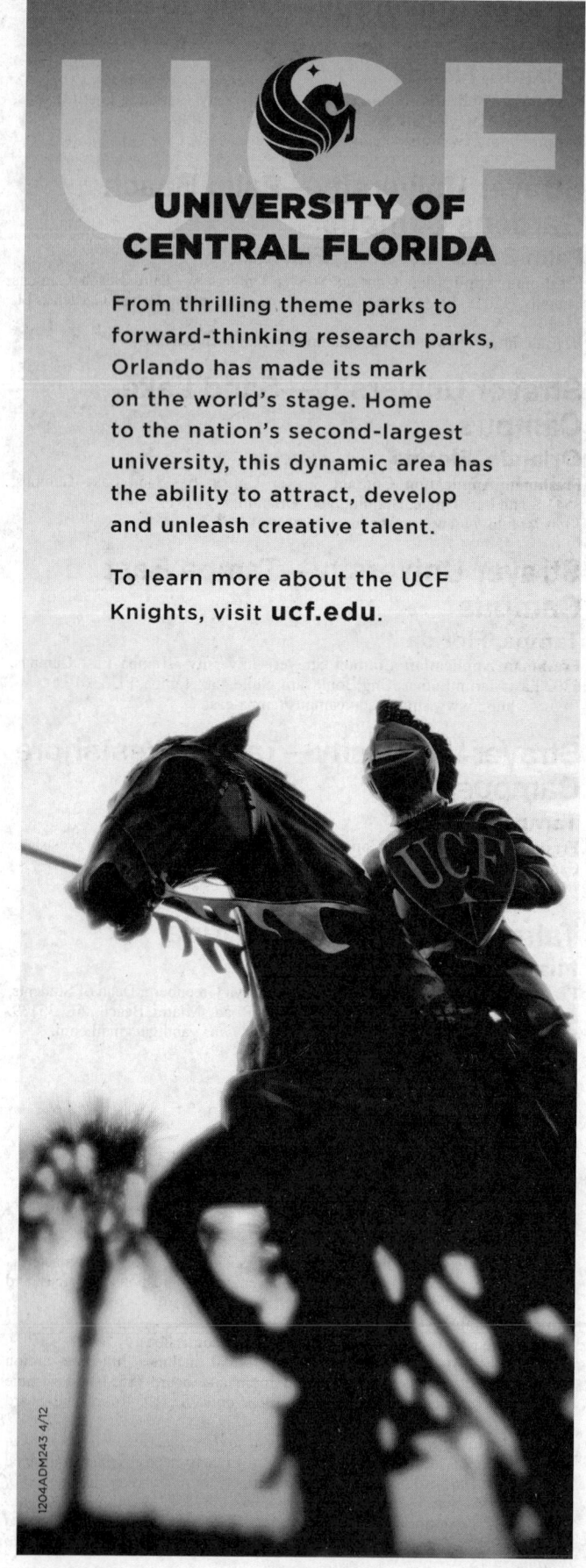

need fully met. 403 Federal Work-Study jobs (averaging $3008). In 2011, 762 non-need-based awards were made. *Average percent of need met:* 56%. *Average financial aid package:* $7028. *Average need-based loan:* $4759. *Average need-based gift aid:* $4846. *Average non-need-based aid:* $2690. *Average indebtedness upon graduation:* $20,086. *Financial aid deadline:* 6/15.
Applying *Options:* electronic application, early admission. *Application fee:* $30. *Required:* high school transcript, minimum 2.0 GPA. *Recommended:* essay or personal statement. *Application deadlines:* 3/1 (freshmen), 5/1 (transfers). *Notification:* continuous (freshmen), continuous (transfers).
Freshman Application Contact Dr. Gordon Chavis Jr., Associate Vice President, Undergraduate Admissions, Student Financial Assistance and Outreach Programs, University of Central Florida, PO Box 160111, Orlando, FL 32816-0111. *Phone:* 407-823-3000. *Fax:* 407-823-5625. *E-mail:* admission@ucf.edu.
Website: http://www.ucf.edu/.

See previous page for display ad and page 1554 for the College Close-Up.

University of Florida
Gainesville, Florida

- **State-supported** university, founded 1853, part of Board of Trustees
- **Suburban** 2000-acre campus with easy access to Jacksonville
- **Endowment** $1.3 billion
- **Coed** 32,776 undergraduate students, 92% full-time, 55% women, 45% men
- **Very difficult** entrance level, 44% of applicants were admitted

Undergraduates 30,241 full-time, 2,535 part-time. Students come from 51 states and territories; 127 other countries; 3% are from out of state; 8% Black or African American, non-Hispanic/Latino; 18% Hispanic/Latino; 8% Asian, non-Hispanic/Latino; 0.6% Native Hawaiian or other Pacific Islander, non-Hispanic/Latino; 0.3% American Indian or Alaska Native, non-Hispanic/Latino; 3% Two or more races, non-Hispanic/Latino; 3% Race/ethnicity unknown; 0.9% international; 6% transferred in; 23% live on campus. *Retention:* 96% of full-time freshmen returned.
Freshmen *Admission:* 27,419 applied, 12,092 admitted, 6,289 enrolled. *Test scores:* SAT critical reading scores over 500: 94%; SAT math scores over 500: 96%; SAT writing scores over 500: 93%; ACT scores over 18: 99%; SAT critical reading scores over 600: 66%; SAT math scores over 600: 74%; SAT writing scores over 600: 65%; ACT scores over 24: 92%; SAT critical reading scores over 700: 17%; SAT math scores over 700: 23%; SAT writing scores over 700: 17%; ACT scores over 30: 38%.
Faculty *Total:* 3,701, 93% full-time, 77% with terminal degrees. *Student/faculty ratio:* 21:1.
Academics *Calendar:* semesters. *Degrees:* bachelor's, master's, and doctoral. *Special study options:* accelerated degree program, adult/continuing education programs, advanced placement credit, cooperative education, distance learning, double majors, English as a second language, external degree program, honors programs, independent study, internships, off-campus study, part-time degree program, services for LD students, student-designed majors, study abroad, summer session for credit. *ROTC:* Army (b), Navy (b), Air Force (b). *Unusual degree programs:* 3-2 business administration.
Computers on Campus 2,200 computers/terminals and 1,000 ports are available on campus for general student use. Students can access the following: campus intranet, computer help desk, free student e-mail accounts, online (class) grades, online (class) registration, online (class) schedules, course management system. Campuswide network is available. 100% of college-owned or -operated housing units are wired for high-speed Internet access. Wireless service is available via classrooms, computer centers, computer labs, dorm rooms, learning centers, libraries, student centers.
Student Life *Housing options:* coed, disabled students. Campus housing is university owned. Freshman applicants given priority for college housing. *Activities and organizations:* drama/theater group, student-run newspaper, radio and television station, choral group, marching band, VISA—Volunteers for International Student Affairs, Fellowship of Christian Athletes, Black Student Union, Hispanic Student Association, Asian American Student Union, national fraternities, national sororities. *Campus security:* 24-hour emergency response devices and patrols, student patrols, late-night transport/escort service, controlled dormitory access, crime and rape prevention programs. *Student services:* health clinic, personal/psychological counseling, legal services.
Athletics Member NCAA. All Division I. *Intercollegiate sports:* baseball M(s), basketball M(s)/W(s), bowling M(c)/W(c), cheerleading M(s)/W(s), crew M/W, cross-country running M(s)/W(s), football M(s), golf M(s)/W(s), gymnastics W(s), lacrosse W(s), racquetball M(c)/W(c), rock climbing M/W, rugby M/W, soccer M/W(s), softball W(s), swimming and diving M/W, table tennis M(c)/W(c), tennis M(s)/W(s), track and field M(s)/W(s), ultimate Frisbee M(c)/W(c), volleyball M/W(s). *Intramural sports:* basketball M/W, bowling M/W, cheerleading W(c), cross-country running M(c)/W(c), equestrian sports M(c)/W(c), fencing M(c)/W(c), football M/W, golf M/W, gymnas-

tics W(c), ice hockey M(c), lacrosse W(c), racquetball M/W, rugby M(c)/W(c), sailing M(c)/W(c), soccer M/W, softball M/W, swimming and diving M/W, table tennis M/W, tennis M/W, track and field M/W, ultimate Frisbee M/W, volleyball M/W, water polo M(c)/W(c), wrestling M(c)/W(c).
Standardized Tests *Required:* SAT or ACT (for admission).
Costs (2012–13) *Tuition:* state resident $6143 full-time, $147 per credit hour part-time; nonresident $28,420 full-time, $855 per credit hour part-time. Full-time tuition and fees vary according to course level, location, program, and reciprocity agreements. Part-time tuition and fees vary according to course level, location, program, and reciprocity agreements. *Required fees:* $57 per credit hour part-time, $93 per credit hour part-time. *Room and board:* $9370; room only: $5240. Room and board charges vary according to board plan and housing facility. *Payment plan:* deferred payment. *Waivers:* senior citizens and employees or children of employees.
Financial Aid Of all full-time matriculated undergraduates who enrolled in 2011, 29,158 applied for aid, 19,134 were judged to have need, 4,201 had their need fully met. 964 Federal Work-Study jobs (averaging $1898). 4,506 state and other part-time jobs (averaging $2494). In 2011, 1591 non-need-based awards were made. *Average percent of need met:* 72%. *Average financial aid package:* $12,218. *Average need-based loan:* $4742. *Average need-based gift aid:* $6184. *Average non-need-based aid:* $2230. *Average indebtedness upon graduation:* $19,636.
Applying *Options:* electronic application, early admission. *Application fee:* $30. *Required:* essay or personal statement, high school transcript. *Application deadlines:* 11/1 (freshmen), rolling (transfers). *Notification:* 2/8 (freshmen), continuous (transfers).
Freshman Application Contact Office of Admissions, University of Florida, PO Box 114000, Gainesville, FL 32611-4000. *Phone:* 352-392-1365. *Website:* http://www.ufl.edu/.

University of Fort Lauderdale
Lauderhill, Florida

Admissions Office Contact University of Fort Lauderdale, 4093 NW 16th Street, Lauderhill, FL 33313.
Website: http://uftl.edu/.

University of Miami
Coral Gables, Florida

- **Independent** university, founded 1925
- **Suburban** 239-acre campus with easy access to Miami
- **Coed** 10,590 undergraduate students, 94% full-time, 51% women, 49% men
- **Very difficult** entrance level, 40% of applicants were admitted

Undergraduates 9,979 full-time, 611 part-time. Students come from 54 states and territories; 99 other countries; 52% are from out of state; 7% Black or African American, non-Hispanic/Latino; 23% Hispanic/Latino; 6% Asian, non-Hispanic/Latino; 0.1% Native Hawaiian or other Pacific Islander, non-Hispanic/Latino; 0.2% American Indian or Alaska Native, non-Hispanic/Latino; 2% Two or more races, non-Hispanic/Latino; 5% Race/ethnicity unknown; 12% international; 5% transferred in; 39% live on campus. *Retention:* 91% of full-time freshmen returned.
Freshmen *Admission:* 27,757 applied, 11,020 admitted, 2,012 enrolled. *Average high school GPA:* 4.2. *Test scores:* SAT critical reading scores over 500: 96%; SAT math scores over 500: 98%; SAT writing scores over 500: 96%; ACT scores over 18: 98%; SAT critical reading scores over 600: 76%; SAT math scores over 600: 87%; SAT writing scores over 600: 73%; ACT scores over 24: 96%; SAT critical reading scores over 700: 26%; SAT math scores over 700: 40%; SAT writing scores over 700: 23%; ACT scores over 30: 69%.
Faculty *Total:* 1,452, 72% full-time, 78% with terminal degrees. *Student/faculty ratio:* 11:1.
Academics *Calendar:* semesters. *Degrees:* certificates, bachelor's, master's, doctoral, post-master's, and postbachelor's certificates. *Special study options:* academic remediation for entering students, accelerated degree program, advanced placement credit, cooperative education, distance learning, double majors, English as a second language, honors programs, independent study, internships, off-campus study, part-time degree program, services for LD students, student-designed majors, study abroad, summer session for credit. *ROTC:* Army (b), Air Force (b).
Computers on Campus 400 computers/terminals and 600 ports are available on campus for general student use. Students can access the following: campus intranet, computer help desk, free student e-mail accounts, online (class) grades, online (class) registration, online (class) schedules, Online bill payment, online housing registration. Campuswide network is available. 100% of college-owned or -operated housing units are wired for high-speed Internet access. Wireless service is available via entire campus.

Student Life *Housing:* on-campus residence required for freshman year. *Options:* coed, disabled students. Campus housing is university owned. Freshman campus housing is guaranteed. *Activities and organizations:* drama/theater group, student-run newspaper, radio and television station, choral group, marching band, national fraternities, national sororities. *Campus security:* 24-hour emergency response devices and patrols, student patrols, late-night transport/escort service, controlled dormitory access, Programs, seminars, activities, classes and publications are available to students, faculty, staff, parents and friends. *Student services:* health clinic, personal/psychological counseling, women's center.

Athletics Member NCAA. All Division I except football (Division I-A). *Intercollegiate sports:* baseball M(s), basketball M(s)/W(s), cheerleading M/W, crew W(s), cross-country running M(s)/W(s), golf W(s), soccer W(s), swimming and diving M(s)/W(s), tennis M(s)/W(s), track and field M(s)/W(s), volleyball W(s). *Intramural sports:* badminton M(c)/W(c), baseball M(c), basketball M/W, bowling M(c)/W(c), equestrian sports M(c)/W(c), fencing M(c)/W(c), field hockey M(c)/W(c), golf M(c)/W(c), ice hockey M(c)/W(c), lacrosse M(c)/W(c), racquetball M(c)/W(c), rock climbing M(c)/W(c), rugby M(c)/W(c), sailing M(c)/W(c), soccer M(c)/W(c), softball M(c)/W(c), swimming and diving M(c)/W(c), table tennis M(c)/W(c), tennis M(c)/W(c), track and field M/W, ultimate Frisbee M(c)/W(c), volleyball M(c)/W(c), water polo M(c)/W(c), weight lifting M/W, wrestling M(c)/W(c).

Standardized Tests *Required:* SAT or ACT (for admission). *Required for some:* SAT Subject Tests (for admission).

Costs (2012–13) *Comprehensive fee:* $53,102 includes full-time tuition ($39,980), mandatory fees ($1240), and room and board ($11,882). Part-time tuition: $1660 per credit hour. Part-time tuition and fees vary according to course load. No tuition increase for student's term of enrollment. *College room only:* $6914. Room and board charges vary according to board plan and housing facility. *Payment plans:* tuition prepayment, installment. *Waivers:* employees or children of employees.

Financial Aid Of all full-time matriculated undergraduates who enrolled in 2012, 6,105 applied for aid, 4,596 were judged to have need, 1,756 had their need fully met. In 2012, 1810 non-need-based awards were made. *Average percent of need met:* 80%. *Average financial aid package:* $33,932. *Average need-based loan:* $6013. *Average need-based gift aid:* $24,812. *Average non-need-based aid:* $20,841. *Average indebtedness upon graduation:* $26,786.

Applying *Options:* electronic application, early admission, early decision, early action, deferred entrance. *Application fee:* $70. *Required:* essay or personal statement, 1 letter of recommendation, College transcript(s) and statement of good standing from prior institution(s). *Required for some:* high school transcript. *Application deadlines:* 1/1 (freshmen), 3/1 (transfers), 11/1 (early action). *Early decision deadline:* 11/1. *Notification:* 4/15 (freshmen), 3/1 (transfers), 12/15 (early decision), 2/1 (early action).

Freshman Application Contact Ms. Deanna Lynn Voss, Executive Director of Undergraduate Admission, University of Miami, PO Box 248025, Coral Gables, FL 33124. *Phone:* 305-284-4323. *Fax:* 305-284-6605. *E-mail:* admission@miami.edu.
Website: http://www.miami.edu/.

University of North Florida
Jacksonville, Florida

- **State-supported** comprehensive, founded 1965, part of State University System of Florida
- **Urban** 1300-acre campus
- **Coed** 14,398 undergraduate students, 72% full-time, 56% women, 44% men
- **Very difficult** entrance level, 52% of applicants were admitted

Undergraduates 10,308 full-time, 4,090 part-time. Students come from 41 states and territories; 53 other countries; 2% are from out of state; 10% Black or African American, non-Hispanic/Latino; 9% Hispanic/Latino; 5% Asian, non-Hispanic/Latino; 0.1% Native Hawaiian or other Pacific Islander, non-Hispanic/Latino; 0.2% American Indian or Alaska Native, non-Hispanic/Latino; 4% Two or more races, non-Hispanic/Latino; 0.5% Race/ethnicity unknown; 2% international; 9% transferred in; 20% live on campus. *Retention:* 83% of full-time freshmen returned.

Freshmen *Admission:* 10,412 applied, 5,415 admitted, 1,608 enrolled. *Average high school GPA:* 3.72. *Test scores:* SAT critical reading scores over 500: 91%; SAT math scores over 500: 91%; SAT writing scores over 500: 77%; ACT scores over 18: 100%; SAT critical reading scores over 600: 38%; SAT math scores over 600: 37%; SAT writing scores over 600: 24%; ACT scores over 24: 60%; SAT critical reading scores over 700: 6%; SAT math scores over 700: 4%; SAT writing scores over 700: 3%; ACT scores over 30: 3%.

Faculty *Total:* 827, 65% full-time, 62% with terminal degrees. *Student/faculty ratio:* 20:1.

Academics *Calendar:* semesters. *Degrees:* associate, bachelor's, master's, doctoral, post-master's, and postbachelor's certificates (doctoral degree in edu-

cation only). *Special study options:* accelerated degree program, adult/continuing education programs, advanced placement credit, cooperative education, distance learning, double majors, English as a second language, honors programs, independent study, internships, off-campus study, part-time degree program, services for LD students, student-designed majors, study abroad, summer session for credit. *ROTC:* Army (b), Navy (c).

Computers on Campus 750 computers/terminals are available on campus for general student use. Students can access the following: campus intranet, computer help desk, free student e-mail accounts, online (class) grades, online (class) registration, online (class) schedules, applications software. Campus-wide network is available. 100% of college-owned or -operated housing units are wired for high-speed Internet access. Wireless service is available via entire campus.

Student Life *Housing:* on-campus residence required for freshman year. *Options:* coed, disabled students. Campus housing is university owned. Freshman campus housing is guaranteed. *Activities and organizations:* drama/theater group, student-run newspaper, radio and television station, choral group, Student Government Association, African American Student Association, International Student Association, Filipino Student Association, National Education Association, national fraternities, national sororities. *Campus security:* 24-hour emergency response devices and patrols, late-night transport/escort service, controlled dormitory access, electronic parking lot security. *Student services:* health clinic, personal/psychological counseling, women's center.

Athletics Member NCAA. All Division I. *Intercollegiate sports:* baseball M(s), basketball M(s)/W(s), cross-country running M(s)/W(s), golf M(s)/W, soccer M(s)/W(s), softball W(s), swimming and diving W(s), tennis M(s)/W(s), track and field M(s)/W(s), volleyball W(s). *Intramural sports:* badminton M/W, basketball M/W, bowling M/W, fencing M(c)/W(c), football M/W, golf M/W, lacrosse M(c)/W(c), racquetball M(c)/W(c), rugby M(c), sailing M(c)/W(c), soccer M/W, swimming and diving M/W, table tennis M/W, track and field M/W, ultimate Frisbee M(c)/W(c), volleyball M(c)/W(c).

Standardized Tests *Required:* SAT or ACT (for admission).

Costs (2012–13) *Tuition:* state resident $4229 full-time, $208 per credit hour part-time; nonresident $17,999 full-time, $690 per credit hour part-time. Full-time tuition and fees vary according to course load. Part-time tuition and fees vary according to course load. *Required fees:* $2006 full-time. *Room and board:* $8190. Room and board charges vary according to board plan and housing facility. *Payment plan:* installment. *Waivers:* senior citizens and employees or children of employees.

Financial Aid Of all full-time matriculated undergraduates who enrolled in 2012, 8,765 applied for aid, 6,473 were judged to have need, 576 had their need fully met. 214 Federal Work-Study jobs (averaging $2814). In 2012, 1312 non-need-based awards were made. *Average percent of need met:* 90%. *Average financial aid package:* $7720. *Average need-based loan:* $4506. *Average need-based gift aid:* $5370. *Average non-need-based aid:* $2694. *Average indebtedness upon graduation:* $17,000.

Applying *Options:* electronic application, deferred entrance. *Application fee:* $30. *Required:* high school transcript, minimum 2.5 GPA, meet minimum test score requirements (460 SAT Critical Reading, 460 SAT Math, 440 SAT Writing; or 19 ACT Reading, 19 ACT Math, 18 ACT English/Writing). *Required for some:* essay or personal statement. *Recommended:* minimum 3.0 GPA. *Application deadlines:* rolling (freshmen), 5/11 (transfers). *Notification:* continuous until 1/3 (freshmen), continuous (transfers).

Freshman Application Contact Mr. John Yancey, Director of Admissions, University of North Florida, 1 UNF Drive, Jacksonville, FL 32224. *Phone:* 904-620-2624. *Fax:* 904-620-2014. *E-mail:* admissions@unf.edu.
Website: http://www.unf.edu/.

University of Phoenix–Central Florida Campus
Maitland, Florida

Freshman Application Contact Marc Booker, Sr. Director, Office of Admissions and Evaluation, University of Phoenix–Central Florida Campus, 4035 South Riverpoint Parkway, Mail Stop CF-L101, Phoenix, AZ 85040. *Phone:* 602-557-4609. *Toll-free phone:* 866-766-0766. *Fax:* 480-643-1156. *Website:* http://www.phoenix.edu/.

University of Phoenix–North Florida Campus
Jacksonville, Florida

Freshman Application Contact Marc Booker, Sr. Director, Office of Admissions and Evaluation, University of Phoenix–North Florida Campus, 4035 South Riverpoint Parkway, Mail Stop CF-L101, Phoenix, AZ 85040. *Phone:* 602-557-4609. *Toll-free phone:* 866-766-0766. *Fax:* 480-643-1156. *Website:* http://www.phoenix.edu/.

University of Phoenix–South Florida Campus

Fort Lauderdale, Florida

Freshman Application Contact Marc Booker, Sr. Director, Office of Admissions and Evaluation, University of Phoenix–South Florida Campus, 4035 South Riverpoint Parkway, Mail Stop CF-L101, Phoenix, AZ 85040. *Phone:* 602-557-4609. *Toll-free phone:* 866-766-0766. *Fax:* 480-643-1156. *Website:* http://www.phoenix.edu/.

University of Phoenix–West Florida Campus

Temple Terrace, Florida

Freshman Application Contact Marc Booker, Sr. Director, Office of Admissions and Evaluation, University of Phoenix–West Florida Campus, 4615 East Elwood Street, Mail Stop AA-K101, Phoenix, AZ 85040-1958. *Phone:* 602-557-4609. *Toll-free phone:* 866-766-0766. *Fax:* 480-643-1156. *Website:* http://www.phoenix.edu/.

University of South Florida

Tampa, Florida

- **State-supported** university, founded 1956, part of State University System of Florida
- **Urban** 1562-acre campus
- **Endowment** $334.1 million
- **Coed** 30,289 undergraduate students, 77% full-time, 56% women, 44% men
- **Moderately difficult** entrance level, 43% of applicants were admitted

Undergraduates 23,407 full-time, 6,882 part-time. Students come from 51 states and territories; 153 other countries; 7% are from out of state; 11% Black or African American, non-Hispanic/Latino; 19% Hispanic/Latino; 6% Asian, non-Hispanic/Latino; 0.2% Native Hawaiian or other Pacific Islander, non-Hispanic/Latino; 0.3% American Indian or Alaska Native, non-Hispanic/Latino; 3% Two or more races, non-Hispanic/Latino; 2% Race/ethnicity unknown; 3% international; 13% transferred in; 17% live on campus. *Retention:* 87% of full-time freshmen returned.

Freshmen *Admission:* 28,544 applied, 12,331 admitted, 3,750 enrolled. *Average high school GPA:* 3.83. *Test scores:* SAT critical reading scores over 500: 91%; SAT math scores over 500: 94%; SAT writing scores over 500: 82%; ACT scores over 18: 100%; SAT critical reading scores over 600: 40%; SAT math scores over 600: 51%; SAT writing scores over 600: 28%; ACT scores over 24: 78%; SAT critical reading scores over 700: 6%; SAT math scores over 700: 8%; SAT writing scores over 700: 4%; ACT scores over 30: 14%.

Faculty *Total:* 1,188, 93% full-time, 85% with terminal degrees. *Student/faculty ratio:* 27:1.

Academics *Calendar:* semesters. *Degrees:* associate, bachelor's, master's, and doctoral. *Special study options:* academic remediation for entering students, accelerated degree program, adult/continuing education programs, advanced placement credit, cooperative education, distance learning, double majors, English as a second language, freshman honors college, honors programs, independent study, internships, off-campus study, part-time degree program, services for LD students, student-designed majors, study abroad, summer session for credit. *ROTC:* Army (b), Navy (b), Air Force (b).

Computers on Campus 500 computers/terminals are available on campus for general student use. Students can access the following: computer help desk, free student e-mail accounts, online (class) registration, online (class) schedules. Campuswide network is available. 100% of college-owned or -operated housing units are wired for high-speed Internet access. Wireless service is available via classrooms, computer centers, computer labs, dorm rooms, libraries, student centers.

Student Life *Housing:* on-campus residence required for freshman year. *Options:* coed, men-only, women-only, cooperative, disabled students. Campus housing is university owned. Freshman campus housing is guaranteed. *Activities and organizations:* drama/theater group, student-run newspaper, radio and television station, choral group, marching band, student government, Campus Activities Board, USF Ambassadors, Student Admissions Representatives, national fraternities, national sororities. *Campus security:* 24-hour emergency response devices and patrols, student patrols, late-night transport/escort service, controlled dormitory access, residence hall lobby personnel 8 pm to 6 am. *Student services:* health clinic, personal/psychological counseling, women's center, legal services.

Athletics Member NCAA. All Division I except football (Division I-A). *Intercollegiate sports:* badminton M(c)/W(c), baseball M(s), basketball M(s)/W(s),

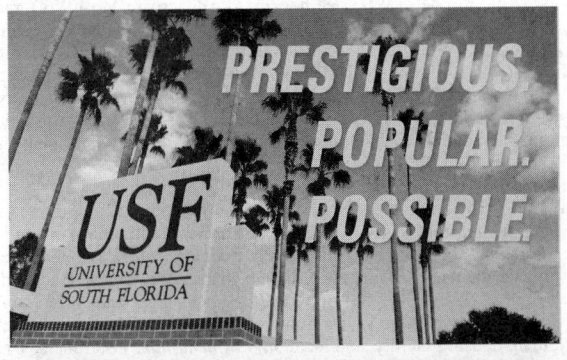

EXPERIENCE INNOVATIVE LEARNING

Imagine a university where Engineering and Arts students collaborate to develop a dancing wheelchair. At USF, it's not just possible—as one of the top-50 pubic research universities, it's what we do every day. By connecting interdisciplinary research with education in arts, sciences, health, engineering, business and beyond, students here solve real-world challenges.

DISCOVER THE VALUE OF USF

With one of the lowest tuition rates in the country , USF offers more mileage for your college budget. Plus, our location in Tampa means you'll have access to career-boosting professional, cultural, and volunteer opportunities.

VISIT USF IN TAMPA

If your plans bring you to sunny Florida, visit USF and make it a family holiday. Ride the roller coasters at Busch Gardens. Shop at International Mall and lunch in Ybor City, Tampa's Latin Quarter. Or, drive just an hour northeast of Tampa to visit a certain world-famous mouse.

APPLY FOR ADMISSION

It takes just 30 minutes to complete an online application. Apply today at usf.edu/apply!

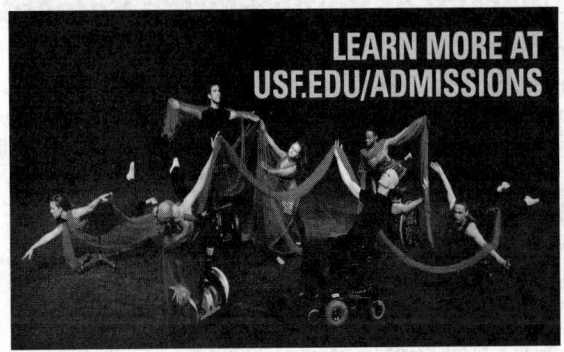

LEARN MORE AT USF.EDU/ADMISSIONS

bowling M(c)/W(c), cheerleading M(c)/W(c), crew M(c)/W(c), cross-country running M(s)/W(s), equestrian sports M(c)/W(c), fencing M(c)/W(c), field hockey W(c), golf M(s)/W(s), ice hockey M(c), lacrosse M(c)/W(c), racquetball M(c)/W(c), rugby M(c)/W(c), soccer M(s)/W(s), softball W(s), swimming and diving M(c)/W(c), tennis M(s)/W(s),.track and field M(s)/W(s), ultimate Frisbee M(c)/W(c), volleyball M(c)/W(c), water polo M(c)/W(c). *Intramural sports:* badminton M/W, basketball M/W, bowling M/W, cross-country running M/W, football M, golf M/W, racquetball M/W, soccer M/W, softball M/W, swimming and diving M/W, tennis M/W, track and field M/W, ultimate Frisbee M/W, volleyball M/W.

Standardized Tests *Required:* SAT or ACT (for admission).

Costs (2013–14) *Tuition:* state resident $4506 full-time, $209 per credit hour part-time; nonresident $14,429 full-time, $539 per credit hour part-time. Full-time tuition and fees vary according to course level, course load, and location. Part-time tuition and fees vary according to course level, course load, and location. *Required fees:* $1828 full-time, $37 per credit hour part-time. *Room and board:* $8960; room only: $5460. Room and board charges vary according to board plan, housing facility, and location. *Payment plan:* installment. *Waivers:* senior citizens.

Financial Aid Of all full-time matriculated undergraduates who enrolled in 2010, 20,144 applied for aid, 17,701 were judged to have need, 15 had their need fully met. In 2010, 4030 non-need-based awards were made. *Average percent of need met:* 47%. *Average financial aid package:* $9808. *Average need-based loan:* $4550. *Average need-based gift aid:* $6465. *Average non-need-based aid:* $2118. *Average indebtedness upon graduation:* $22,077.

Applying *Options:* electronic application, early admission. *Application fee:* $30. *Required:* minimum 2.0 GPA. *Required for some:* high school transcript, 1 letter of recommendation. *Application deadlines:* 3/1 (freshmen), 3/5 (transfers). *Notification:* continuous (freshmen), continuous (transfers).

Freshman Application Contact Ms. Amanda Dale, Associate Director of Recruitment, University of South Florida, Office of Undergraduate Admissions, 4202 East Fowler Avenue, Tampa, FL 33620-9951. *Phone:* 813-974-3350. *Fax:* 813-974-9689. *E-mail:* admissions@usf.edu. *Website:* http://www.usf.edu/.

See previous page for display ad and page 1604 for the College Close-Up.

University of South Florida–St. Petersburg Campus

St. Petersburg, Florida

- **State-supported** comprehensive, founded 1965, part of University of South Florida System
- **Urban** 50-acre campus with easy access to Tampa
- **Coed**

Faculty *Student/faculty ratio:* 13:1.

Academics *Calendar:* semesters. *Degrees:* bachelor's and master's.

Student Life *Campus security:* 24-hour emergency response devices and patrols, late-night transport/escort service, controlled dormitory access.

Standardized Tests *Required:* SAT or ACT (for admission).

Costs (2012–13) *Tuition:* state resident $5189 full-time, $173 per credit hour part-time; nonresident $14,377 full-time, $392 per credit hour part-time. *Required fees:* $10 full-time. *Room only:* $7570.

Applying *Required:* high school transcript, minimum 2.5 GPA.

Freshman Application Contact Ms. Holly Kickliter, Director, Enrollment Services, University of South Florida–St. Petersburg Campus, 140 Seventh Avenue South, St. Petersburg, FL 33701. *Phone:* 727-873-4142. *Fax:* 727-873-4525. *E-mail:* admissions@usfsp.edu. *Website:* http://www.stpt.usf.edu/.

University of South Florida Sarasota-Manatee

Sarasota, Florida

Admissions Office Contact University of South Florida Sarasota-Manatee, 8350 N Tamiami Trail, Sarasota, FL 34243. *Website:* http://www.sarasota.usf.edu/.

The University of Tampa

Tampa, Florida

- **Independent** comprehensive, founded 1931
- **Urban** 100-acre campus with easy access to Tampa-St. Petersburg, Clearwater
- **Coed** 6,143 undergraduate students, 94% full-time, 56% women, 44% men
- **Moderately difficult** entrance level, 59% of applicants were admitted

Undergraduates 5,799 full-time, 344 part-time. Students come from 50 states and territories; 122 other countries; 63% are from out of state; 6% Black or African American, non-Hispanic/Latino; 11% Hispanic/Latino; 1% Asian, non-Hispanic/Latino; 0.2% Native Hawaiian or other Pacific Islander, non-Hispanic/Latino; 0.1% American Indian or Alaska Native, non-Hispanic/Latino; 2% Two or more races, non-Hispanic/Latino; 8% Race/ethnicity unknown; 10% international; 7% transferred in; 60% live on campus. *Retention:* 74% of full-time freshmen returned.

Freshmen *Admission:* 14,704 applied, 8,668 admitted, 1,517 enrolled. *Average high school GPA:* 3.3. *Test scores:* SAT critical reading scores over 500: 67%; SAT math scores over 500: 79%; SAT writing scores over 500: 66%; SAT critical reading scores over 600: 16%; SAT math scores over 600: 23%; SAT writing scores over 600: 16%; SAT critical reading scores over 700: 1%; SAT math scores over 700: 1%; SAT writing scores over 700: 1%.

Faculty *Total:* 564, 47% full-time, 59% with terminal degrees. *Student/faculty ratio:* 16:1.

Academics *Calendar:* semesters. *Degrees:* certificates, associate, bachelor's, master's, and post-master's certificates. *Special study options:* academic remediation for entering students, adult/continuing education programs, advanced placement credit, cooperative education, double majors, English as a second language, honors programs, independent study, internships, part-time degree program, services for LD students, study abroad, summer session for credit. *ROTC:* Army (b), Navy (c), Air Force (c). *Unusual degree programs:* 3-2 chemistry/MBA joint program.

Computers on Campus 800 computers/terminals and 8,000 ports are available on campus for general student use. Students can access the following: campus intranet, computer help desk, free student e-mail accounts, online (class) grades, online (class) registration, online (class) schedules. Campus-wide network is available. 100% of college-owned or -operated housing units are wired for high-speed Internet access. Wireless service is available via entire campus.

Student Life *Housing options:* coed, disabled students. Campus housing is university owned. *Activities and organizations:* drama/theater group, student-run newspaper, radio and television station, choral group, Greek Life, student government, PEACE (volunteer organization), Student Productions, Minaret, national fraternities, national sororities. *Campus security:* 24-hour emergency response devices and patrols, student patrols, late-night transport/escort service, controlled dormitory access. *Student services:* health clinic, personal/psychological counseling, women's center.

Athletics Member NCAA. All Division II. *Intercollegiate sports:* baseball M(s), basketball M(s)/W(s), crew W(s), cross-country running M(s)/W(s), golf M(s)/W(s), lacrosse M(s), soccer M(s)/W(s), softball W(s), swimming and diving M(s)/W(s), tennis W(s), volleyball W(s). *Intramural sports:* basketball M/W, cheerleading W(c), crew M(c), field hockey W, football M/W, golf M/W, soccer M/W, softball M/W, swimming and diving M/W, table tennis W, tennis M/W, track and field M/W, ultimate Frisbee M/W, volleyball M/W.

Standardized Tests *Required:* SAT or ACT (for admission).

Costs (2012–13) *One-time required fee:* $85. *Comprehensive fee:* $34,338 includes full-time tuition ($23,520), mandatory fees ($1702), and room and board ($9116). Full-time tuition and fees vary according to class time. Part-time tuition: $500 per credit hour. Part-time tuition and fees vary according to class time. *Required fees:* $40 per term part-time. *College room only:* $4852. Room and board charges vary according to board plan and housing facility. *Payment plan:* installment. *Waivers:* employees or children of employees.

Financial Aid Of all full-time matriculated undergraduates who enrolled in 2012, 4,384 applied for aid, 3,533 were judged to have need, 666 had their need fully met. 358 Federal Work-Study jobs (averaging $2000). 2 state and other part-time jobs (averaging $2000). In 2012, 1784 non-need-based awards were made. *Average percent of need met:* 61%. *Average financial aid package:* $15,742. *Average need-based loan:* $4315. *Average need-based gift aid:* $12,880. *Average non-need-based aid:* $6487. *Average indebtedness upon graduation:* $31,032.

Applying *Options:* electronic application, early admission, early action, deferred entrance. *Application fee:* $40. *Required:* essay or personal statement, high school transcript, minimum 2.0 GPA. *Required for some:* 1 letter of recommendation. *Recommended:* interview. *Application deadlines:* rolling (freshmen), rolling (out-of-state freshmen), rolling (transfers), 5/1 (early action). *Notification:* continuous (freshmen), continuous (out-of-state freshmen), continuous (transfers), 12/15 (early action).

Freshman Application Contact Mr. Dennis Nostrand, Vice President for Enrollment, The University of Tampa, 401 West Kennedy Boulevard, Tampa, FL 33606-1480. *Phone:* 813-257-1808. *Toll-free phone:* 888-646-2738 (in-state); 888-MINARET (out-of-state). *Fax:* 813-258-7398. *E-mail:* admissions@ut.edu. *Website:* http://www.ut.edu/.

University of West Florida
Pensacola, Florida

- **State-supported** comprehensive, founded 1963, part of State University System of Florida
- **Suburban** 1600-acre campus
- **Endowment** $49.2 million
- **Coed** 10,332 undergraduate students, 73% full-time, 58% women, 42% men
- **Moderately difficult** entrance level, 61% of applicants were admitted

Undergraduates 7,559 full-time, 2,773 part-time. Students come from 50 states and territories; 92 other countries; 9% are from out of state; 12% Black or African American, non-Hispanic/Latino; 8% Hispanic/Latino; 3% Asian, non-Hispanic/Latino; 0.4% Native Hawaiian or other Pacific Islander, non-Hispanic/Latino; 0.7% American Indian or Alaska Native, non-Hispanic/Latino; 3% Two or more races, non-Hispanic/Latino; 0.2% Race/ethnicity unknown; 2% international; 12% transferred in; 20% live on campus. *Retention:* 70% of full-time freshmen returned.

Freshmen *Admission:* 13,623 applied, 8,284 admitted, 1,450 enrolled. *Average high school GPA:* 3.4. *Test scores:* SAT critical reading scores over 500: 55%; SAT math scores over 500: 51%; SAT writing scores over 500: 40%; ACT scores over 18: 96%; SAT critical reading scores over 600: 11%; SAT math scores over 600: 10%; SAT writing scores over 600: 6%; ACT scores over 24: 34%; SAT critical reading scores over 700: 1%; SAT math scores over 700: 1%; SAT writing scores over 700: 1%; ACT scores over 30: 3%.

Faculty *Total:* 603, 52% full-time. *Student/faculty ratio:* 23:1.

Academics *Calendar:* semesters. *Degrees:* associate, bachelor's, master's, doctoral, and post-master's certificates. *Special study options:* advanced placement credit, cooperative education, distance learning, English as a second language, honors programs, independent study, internships, off-campus study, part-time degree program, services for LD students, study abroad, summer session for credit. *ROTC:* Army (b), Air Force (b). *Unusual degree programs:* 3-2 business administration.

Computers on Campus 1,067 computers/terminals and 100 ports are available on campus for general student use. Students can access the following: campus intranet, computer help desk, free student e-mail accounts, online (class) grades, online (class) registration, online (class) schedules. Campus-wide network is available. 100% of college-owned or -operated housing units are wired for high-speed Internet access. Wireless service is available via entire campus.

Student Life *Housing options:* coed. Campus housing is university owned. *Activities and organizations:* drama/theater group, student-run newspaper, choral group, Marketing Association, Student Council for Exceptional Children, Inter-Varsity Christian Fellowship, Baptist Student Ministry, Golden Key Honor Society, national fraternities, national sororities. *Campus security:* 24-hour emergency response devices and patrols, student patrols, late-night transport/escort service, controlled dormitory access. *Student services:* health clinic, personal/psychological counseling.

Athletics Member NCAA. All Division II. *Intercollegiate sports:* baseball M(s), basketball M(s)/W(s), cross-country running M(s)/W(s), golf M(s)/W(s), soccer M(s)/W(s), softball W(s), tennis M(s)/W(s), volleyball W. *Intramural sports:* basketball M/W, bowling M/W, cheerleading W, fencing M/W, football M/W, sailing M/W, soccer M/W, softball W, swimming and diving M/W, tennis M/W, volleyball M/W.

Standardized Tests *Required:* SAT or ACT (for admission), SAT and SAT Subject Tests or ACT (for admission).

Costs (2012–13) *Tuition:* state resident $5072 full-time, $208 per semester hour part-time; nonresident $17,954 full-time, $637 per semester hour part-time. Full-time tuition and fees vary according to location and reciprocity agreements. Part-time tuition and fees vary according to location and reciprocity agreements. *Required fees:* $1950 full-time, $208 per semester hour part-time. *Room and board:* $9210. Room and board charges vary according to housing facility. *Payment plans:* tuition prepayment, deferred payment. *Waivers:* senior citizens and employees or children of employees.

Financial Aid Of all full-time matriculated undergraduates who enrolled in 2011, 169 Federal Work-Study jobs (averaging $1595).

Applying *Options:* electronic application, early admission, deferred entrance. *Application fee:* $30. *Required:* high school transcript, minimum 2.0 GPA. *Application deadlines:* 6/30 (freshmen), 6/30 (transfers). *Notification:* continuous (freshmen), continuous (transfers).

Freshman Application Contact Katie Condon, Director of Admissions, University of West Florida, Admissions, 11000 University Parkway, Pensacola, FL 32514. *Phone:* 850-474-2230. *Toll-free phone:* 800-263-1074. *Fax:* 850-474-3460. *E-mail:* admissions@uwf.edu. *Website:* http://www.uwf.edu/.

Valencia College
Orlando, Florida

- **State-supported** 4-year, founded 1967, part of Florida College System
- **Urban** 629-acre campus with easy access to Orlando
- **Endowment** $55.6 million
- **Coed** 42,915 undergraduate students, 40% full-time, 57% women, 43% men
- **90% of applicants were admitted**

Undergraduates 16,998 full-time, 25,917 part-time. Students come from 59 other countries; 3% are from out of state; 17% Black or African American, non-Hispanic/Latino; 31% Hispanic/Latino; 4% Asian, non-Hispanic/Latino; 0.3% Native Hawaiian or other Pacific Islander, non-Hispanic/Latino; 0.3% American Indian or Alaska Native, non-Hispanic/Latino; 2% Two or more races, non-Hispanic/Latino; 9% Race/ethnicity unknown; 1% international; 9% transferred in. *Retention:* 65% of full-time freshmen returned.

Freshmen *Admission:* 11,235 applied, 10,111 admitted, 8,055 enrolled.

Faculty *Total:* 1,602, 25% full-time, 6% with terminal degrees. *Student/faculty ratio:* 16:1.

Academics *Calendar:* semesters. *Degrees:* certificates, diplomas, associate, and bachelor's. *Special study options:* academic remediation for entering students, accelerated degree program, adult/continuing education programs, advanced placement credit, cooperative education, distance learning, double majors, English as a second language, external degree program, freshman honors college, honors programs, independent study, internships, part-time degree program, services for LD students, study abroad, summer session for credit. *ROTC:* Army (c), Navy (c), .

Computers on Campus Students can access the following: campus intranet, computer help desk, free student e-mail accounts, online (class) grades, online (class) registration, online (class) schedules, Emergency Alert System. Campuswide network is available. Wireless service is available via entire campus.

Student Life *Housing:* college housing not available. *Activities and organizations:* drama/theater group, student-run newspaper, choral group. *Campus security:* 24-hour emergency response devices and patrols, student patrols, late-night transport/escort service. *Student services:* personal/psychological counseling, legal services.

Athletics *Intramural sports:* baseball M/W, basketball M/W, racquetball M/W, rock climbing M/W, soccer M/W, softball M/W, tennis M/W, volleyball M/W, weight lifting M/W.

Costs (2013–14) *Tuition:* state resident $2377 full-time, $99 per credit part-time; nonresident $9005 full-time, $375 per credit part-time. Full-time tuition and fees vary according to course level, degree level, and program. Part-time tuition and fees vary according to course level, degree level, and program. *Payment plans:* tuition prepayment, installment. *Waivers:* senior citizens and employees or children of employees.

Financial Aid Of all full-time matriculated undergraduates who enrolled in 2010, 21,366 applied for aid, 17,532 were judged to have need, 485 had their need fully met. 242 Federal Work-Study jobs (averaging $2608). 27 state and other part-time jobs (averaging $2738). In 2010, 93 non-need-based awards were made. *Average percent of need met:* 46%. *Average financial aid package:* $7383. *Average need-based loan:* $3242. *Average need-based gift aid:* $3430. *Average non-need-based aid:* $642.

Applying *Options:* electronic application, early admission, deferred entrance. *Application fee:* $35. *Required:* $35 Application fee for lower level (1000 and 2000 level courses) students and $50 application fee for Bachelor level students. *Required for some:* high school transcript. *Application deadlines:* 8/12 (freshmen), 8/12 (out-of-state freshmen), 8/12 (transfers).

Freshman Application Contact Dr. Renee Simpson, Assistant Vice President of Admissions and Records, Valencia College, Orlando, FL 32802-3028. *Phone:* 407-582-1511. *Fax:* 407-582-1866. *E-mail:* rsimpson@valenciacollege.edu. *Website:* http://valenciacollege.edu/.

Warner University
Lake Wales, Florida

Freshman Application Contact Mr. Jason Roe, Director of Admissions, Warner University, Warner Southern Center, 13895 Highway 27, Lake Wales, FL 33859. *Phone:* 863-638-7212 Ext. 7213. *Toll-free phone:* 800-309-9563. *Fax:* 863-638-1472. *E-mail:* admissions@warner.edu. *Website:* http://www.warner.edu/.

Webber International University

Babson Park, Florida

- **Independent** comprehensive, founded 1927
- **Small-town** 110-acre campus with easy access to Orlando
- **Endowment** $4.4 million
- **Coed** 655 undergraduate students, 96% full-time, 33% women, 67% men
- **Moderately difficult** entrance level, 69% of applicants were admitted

Undergraduates 628 full-time, 27 part-time. 8% are from out of state; 24% Black or African American, non-Hispanic/Latino; 9% Hispanic/Latino; 0.9% Asian, non-Hispanic/Latino; 0.2% American Indian or Alaska Native, non-Hispanic/Latino; 2% Two or more races, non-Hispanic/Latino; 24% international; 52% live on campus. *Retention:* 52% of full-time freshmen returned.

Freshmen *Admission:* 586 applied, 404 admitted, 183 enrolled. *Average high school GPA:* 3.16. *Test scores:* SAT critical reading scores over 500: 32%; SAT math scores over 500: 37%; ACT scores over 18: 74%; SAT critical reading scores over 600: 3%; SAT math scores over 600: 5%; ACT scores over 24: 10%; SAT math scores over 700: 1%.

Faculty *Total:* 43, 47% full-time, 42% with terminal degrees. *Student/faculty ratio:* 22:1.

Academics *Calendar:* semesters. *Degrees:* associate, bachelor's, and master's. *Special study options:* academic remediation for entering students, accelerated degree program, adult/continuing education programs, advanced placement credit, cooperative education, distance learning, double majors, English as a second language, internships, part-time degree program, services for LD students, study abroad, summer session for credit.

Computers on Campus 89 computers/terminals are available on campus for general student use. Students can access the following: campus intranet, free student e-mail accounts, online (class) grades, online (class) schedules. Campuswide network is available. 100% of college-owned or -operated housing units are wired for high-speed Internet access. Wireless service is available via computer labs, libraries, student centers.

Student Life *Housing:* on-campus residence required for freshman year. *Options:* men-only, women-only. Campus housing is university owned and leased by the school. Freshman campus housing is guaranteed. *Activities and organizations:* student-run newspaper, marching band, Student Leadership Association, Phi Beta Lambda, Society of International Students, Fellowship of Christian Athletes, Marketing Club. *Campus security:* 24-hour emergency response devices and patrols, late-night transport/escort service, controlled dormitory access. *Student services:* health clinic, personal/psychological counseling.

Athletics Member NAIA. *Intercollegiate sports:* baseball M(s), basketball M(s)/W(s), bowling M(s)/W(s), cheerleading M(s)/W(s), cross-country running M(s)/W(s), football M(s), golf M(s)/W(s), soccer M(s)/W(s), softball W(s), tennis M(s)/W(s), track and field M(s)/W(s), volleyball W(s). *Intramural sports:* basketball M/W, football M/W, soccer M/W, softball W, table tennis M/W, tennis M/W, volleyball M(c)/W(c).

Standardized Tests *Required:* SAT or ACT (for admission).

Costs (2012–13) *Comprehensive fee:* $28,318 includes full-time tuition ($20,418) and room and board ($7900). Full-time tuition and fees vary according to class time and course load. Part-time tuition: $294 per credit hour. Part-time tuition and fees vary according to course load. *College room only:* $5072. Room and board charges vary according to board plan, gender, and housing facility. *Payment plan:* installment. *Waivers:* children of alumni, adult students, senior citizens, and employees or children of employees.

Financial Aid Of all full-time matriculated undergraduates who enrolled in 2012, 628 applied for aid, 382 were judged to have need, 38 had their need fully met. In 2012, 208 non-need-based awards were made. *Average percent of need met:* 58%. *Average financial aid package:* $13,062. *Average need-based loan:* $4396. *Average need-based gift aid:* $3185. *Average non-need-based aid:* $8021. *Financial aid deadline:* 8/1.

Applying *Options:* electronic application, early action. *Application fee:* $35. *Required:* high school transcript, minimum 2.0 GPA. *Required for some:* interview. *Recommended:* essay or personal statement. *Application deadlines:* 8/1 (freshmen), 8/1 (transfers), 4/1 (early action).

Freshman Application Contact Mr. Mike Mattison, Director of Admissions, Webber International University, P. O. Box 96, Babson Park, FL 33827. *Phone:* 863-638-2910. *Toll-free phone:* 800-741-1844. *Fax:* 863-638-1591. *E-mail:* admissions@webber.edu. *Website:* http://www.webber.edu/.

Yeshiva Gedolah Rabbinical College

Miami Beach, Florida

Admissions Office Contact Yeshiva Gedolah Rabbinical College, 1140 Alton Road, Miami Beach, FL 33139.

GEORGIA

Abraham Baldwin Agricultural College

Tifton, Georgia

Freshman Application Contact Mrs. Donna Webb, Director of Enrollment Services, Abraham Baldwin Agricultural College, Box 4, 2802 Moore Highway, Tifton, GA 31793-2601. *Phone:* 229-391-5004. *Toll-free phone:* 800-733-3653. *Fax:* 229-391-5002. *E-mail:* dwebb@abac.edu. *Website:* http://www.abac.edu/.

Agnes Scott College

Decatur, Georgia

- **Independent** 4-year, founded 1889, affiliated with Presbyterian Church (U.S.A.)
- **Urban** 100-acre campus with easy access to Atlanta
- **Endowment** $239.3 million
- **Undergraduate: women only; graduate: coed** 885 undergraduate students, 98% full-time, 99% women, 1% men
- **Very difficult** entrance level, 62% of applicants were admitted

Undergraduates 869 full-time, 16 part-time. Students come from 43 states and territories; 29 other countries; 37% are from out of state; 35% Black or African American, non-Hispanic/Latino; 8% Hispanic/Latino; 3% Asian, non-Hispanic/Latino; 6% Two or more races, non-Hispanic/Latino; 4% Race/ethnicity unknown; 9% international; 1% transferred in; 85% live on campus. *Retention:* 82% of full-time freshmen returned.

Freshmen *Admission:* 1,554 applied, 963 admitted, 232 enrolled. *Average high school GPA:* 3.61. *Test scores:* SAT critical reading scores over 500: 86%; SAT math scores over 500: 82%; SAT writing scores over 500: 84%; ACT scores over 18: 100%; SAT critical reading scores over 600: 50%; SAT math scores over 600: 35%; SAT writing scores over 600: 46%; ACT scores over 24: 65%; SAT critical reading scores over 700: 14%; SAT math scores over 700: 9%; SAT writing scores over 700: 9%; ACT scores over 30: 20%.

Faculty *Total:* 89, 79% full-time, 91% with terminal degrees. *Student/faculty ratio:* 11:1.

Academics *Calendar:* semesters. *Degree:* bachelor's. *Special study options:* accelerated degree program, adult/continuing education programs, advanced placement credit, double majors, independent study, internships, off-campus study, part-time degree program, services for LD students, student-designed majors, study abroad, summer session for credit. *ROTC:* Army (c), Air Force (c). *Unusual degree programs:* 3-2 engineering with Georgia Institute of Technology; nursing with Emory University; computer science with Emory University.

Computers on Campus 458 computers/terminals and 3,819 ports are available on campus for general student use. Students can access the following: campus intranet, computer help desk, free student e-mail accounts, online (class) grades, online (class) registration, online (class) schedules. Campuswide network is available. 100% of college-owned or -operated housing units are wired for high-speed Internet access. Wireless service is available via entire campus.

Student Life *Housing:* on-campus residence required through senior year. *Options:* women-only. Campus housing is university owned. Freshman campus housing is guaranteed. *Activities and organizations:* drama/theater group, student-run newspaper, television station, choral group, marching band, Programming Board, Witkaze (African-American Student organization), Student Senate, ASC-TV, International Students Association. *Campus security:* 24-hour emergency response devices and patrols, late-night transport/escort service, controlled dormitory access, security systems in apartments, public safety facility, surveillance equipment, key required for residence hall entry. *Student services:* health clinic, personal/psychological counseling.

Athletics Member NCAA. All Division III. *Intercollegiate sports:* basketball W, lacrosse W, soccer W, softball W, tennis W, volleyball W. *Intramural sports:* cross-country running W(c), swimming and diving W(c), tennis W.

Standardized Tests *Required:* SAT or ACT scores or graded writing sample, home-schooled students must submit SAT or ACT (for admission). *Required for some:* SAT and SAT Subject Tests or ACT (for admission).

Costs (2013–14) *Comprehensive fee:* $45,321 includes full-time tuition ($34,546), mandatory fees ($240), and room and board ($10,535). Full-time tuition and fees vary according to course load. Part-time tuition and fees vary according to course load. *Room and board:* Room and board charges vary according to board plan and housing facility. *Payment plan:* installment. *Waivers:* employees or children of employees.

Financial Aid Of all full-time matriculated undergraduates who enrolled in 2011, 674 applied for aid, 626 were judged to have need, 149 had their need

fully met. 292 Federal Work-Study jobs (averaging $2300). 61 state and other part-time jobs (averaging $2300). In 2011, 191 non-need-based awards were made. *Average percent of need met:* 88%. *Average financial aid package:* $30,639. *Average need-based loan:* $4340. *Average need-based gift aid:* $24,435. *Average non-need-based aid:* $18,247. *Average indebtedness upon graduation:* $26,148. *Financial aid deadline:* 5/1.

Applying *Options:* electronic application, early admission, early action, deferred entrance. *Application fee:* $35. *Required:* essay or personal statement, high school transcript, 2 letters of recommendation. *Recommended:* interview. *Application deadlines:* 3/1 (freshmen), 3/1 (transfers), 11/15 (early action). *Notification:* continuous (transfers), 12/15 (early action).

Freshman Application Contact Agnes Scott College, 141 East College Avenue, Decatur, GA 30030-3797. *Phone:* 404-471-6285. *Toll-free phone:* 800-868-8602.

Website: http://www.agnesscott.edu/.

Albany State University

Albany, Georgia

- **State-supported** comprehensive, founded 1903, part of University System of Georgia
- **Urban** 232-acre campus
- **Endowment** $1.5 million
- **Coed**
- **Minimally difficult** entrance level

Faculty *Student/faculty ratio:* 21:1.

Academics *Calendar:* semesters. *Degrees:* bachelor's, master's, and post-master's certificates.

Student Life *Campus security:* 24-hour emergency response devices and patrols, late-night transport/escort service, controlled dormitory access, Connect Ed.- Emergency E-mail, Emergency sirens, Active Shooter Team, Certified Police Officers.

Athletics Member NCAA. All Division II.

Standardized Tests *Required:* SAT or ACT (for admission).

Costs (2012–13) *Tuition:* state resident $4512 full-time; nonresident $16,416 full-time. Full-time tuition and fees vary according to course load and degree level. Part-time tuition and fees vary according to course load and degree level. *Required fees:* $1400 full-time. *Room and board:* $7388; room only: $2734. Room and board charges vary according to board plan and housing facility.

Financial Aid *Of all full-time matriculated undergraduates who enrolled in 2011, 3,608 applied for aid, 3,462 were judged to have need, 63 had their need fully met. In 2011, 2 non-need-based awards were made. Average percent of need met:* 67. *Average financial aid package:* $4910. *Average need-based loan:* $2336. *Average need-based gift aid:* $2532. *Average non-need-based aid:* $2750. *Average indebtedness upon graduation:* $32,034. *Financial aid deadline:* 6/1.

Applying *Options:* electronic application, early admission, deferred entrance. *Application fee:* $20. *Required:* high school transcript, minimum 2.2 GPA. *Required for some:* COMPASS Test.

Freshman Application Contact Mr. James Burrell, Interim Director, Enrollment Services, Albany State University, 504 College Drive, Albany, GA 31705-2717. *Phone:* 229-430-4646. *Toll-free phone:* 866-579-3498. *Fax:* 229-430-4105. *E-mail:* enrollmentservices@asurams.edu. *Website:* http://www.asurams.edu/.

American InterContinental University Atlanta

Atlanta, Georgia

Freshman Application Contact American InterContinental University Atlanta, 6600 Peachtree-Dunwoody Road, 500 Embassy Row, Atlanta, GA 30328. *Phone:* 877-564-6248. *Toll-free phone:* 800-353-1744. *Fax:* 877-564-6248.

Website: http://www.aiuniv.edu/.

Argosy University, Atlanta

Atlanta, Georgia

Freshman Application Contact Argosy University, Atlanta, 980 Hammond Drive, Suite 100, Atlanta, GA 30328. *Phone:* 770-671-1200. *Toll-free phone:* 888-671-4777.

Website: http://www.argosy.edu/atlanta/.

Armstrong Atlantic State University

Savannah, Georgia

- **State-supported** comprehensive, founded 1935, part of University System of Georgia
- **Suburban** 267-acre campus
- **Endowment** $9.0 million
- **Coed** 6,731 undergraduate students, 72% full-time, 65% women, 35% men
- **Minimally difficult** entrance level, 70% of applicants were admitted

Undergraduates 4,839 full-time, 1,892 part-time. Students come from 43 states and territories; 67 other countries; 11% are from out of state; 23% Black or African American, non-Hispanic/Latino; 6% Hispanic/Latino; 3% Asian, non-Hispanic/Latino; 0.2% Native Hawaiian or other Pacific Islander, non-Hispanic/Latino; 0.3% American Indian or Alaska Native, non-Hispanic/Latino; 4% Two or more races, non-Hispanic/Latino; 2% Race/ethnicity unknown; 2% international; 9% transferred in; 20% live on campus. *Retention:* 69% of full-time freshmen returned.

Freshmen *Admission:* 2,790 applied, 1,964 admitted, 1,065 enrolled. *Average high school GPA:* 3.16. *Test scores:* SAT critical reading scores over 500: 54%; SAT math scores over 500: 48%; ACT scores over 18: 92%; SAT critical reading scores over 600: 12%; SAT math scores over 600: 10%; ACT scores over 24: 24%; SAT critical reading scores over 700: 1%; SAT math scores over 700: 1%; ACT scores over 30: 1%.

Faculty *Total:* 424, 61% full-time. *Student/faculty ratio:* 19:1.

Academics *Calendar:* semesters. *Degrees:* certificates, associate, bachelor's, master's, doctoral, post-master's, and postbachelor's certificates. *Special study options:* academic remediation for entering students, adult/continuing education programs, advanced placement credit, cooperative education, distance learning, double majors, honors programs, independent study, internships, off-campus study, part-time degree program, services for LD students, study abroad, summer session for credit. *ROTC:* Army (b), Navy (c).

Computers on Campus 300 computers/terminals are available on campus for general student use. Students can access the following: campus intranet, computer help desk, free student e-mail accounts, online (class) grades, online (class) registration, online (class) schedules. Campuswide network is available. 100% of college-owned or -operated housing units are wired for high-speed Internet access. Wireless service is available via entire campus.

Student Life *Housing:* on-campus residence required for freshman year. *Options:* coed. Campus housing is leased by the school and is provided by a third party. Freshman applicants given priority for college housing. *Activities and organizations:* drama/theater group, student-run newspaper, choral group, Wesley Fellowship, Hispanic Outreach and Leadership at Armstrong (HOLA), Ebony Coalition, American Chemical Society, Phi Alpha Theta, national fraternities, national sororities. *Campus security:* 24-hour emergency response devices and patrols, student patrols, late-night transport/escort service, controlled dormitory access. *Student services:* health clinic, personal/psychological counseling.

Athletics Member NCAA. All Division II. *Intercollegiate sports:* baseball M(s), basketball M(s)/W(s), cheerleading M/W, cross-country running M(s), golf M(s)/W(s), softball W(s), tennis M(s)/W(s), volleyball W(s). *Intramural sports:* badminton M/W, basketball M/W, bowling M/W, football M/W, golf M/W, rugby M, soccer M/W, softball M/W, table tennis M/W, tennis M/W, ultimate Frisbee M/W, volleyball M/W.

Standardized Tests *Required:* SAT or ACT (for admission). *Required for some:* SAT Subject Tests (for admission).

Costs (2012–13) *Tuition:* state resident $4512 full-time, $150 per credit hour part-time; nonresident $16,416 full-time, $547 per credit hour part-time. Full-time tuition and fees vary according to course load, location, and program. Part-time tuition and fees vary according to course load, location, and program. *Required fees:* $1332 full-time, $666 per term part-time. *Room and board:* $9770; room only: $5908. Room and board charges vary according to board plan and housing facility. *Waivers:* senior citizens and employees or children of employees.

Financial Aid Of all full-time matriculated undergraduates who enrolled in 2011, 4,721 applied for aid, 3,777 were judged to have need, 1,963 had their need fully met. 69 Federal Work-Study jobs (averaging $3650). In 2011, 650 non-need-based awards were made. *Average percent of need met:* 82%. *Average financial aid package:* $7750. *Average need-based loan:* $4500. *Average need-based gift aid:* $4000. *Average non-need-based aid:* $3000. *Average indebtedness upon graduation:* $21,000.

Applying *Options:* electronic application, early admission, deferred entrance. *Application fee:* $25. *Required:* high school transcript, minimum 2.5 GPA, ACT/SAT Scores. *Application deadlines:* 7/15 (freshmen), 7/15 (transfers). *Notification:* continuous (freshmen), continuous (transfers).

Freshman Application Contact Armstrong Atlantic State University, 11935 Abercorn Street, Savannah, GA 31419-1997. *Phone:* 912-344-2503. *Toll-free phone:* 800-633-2349.
Website: http://www.armstrong.edu/.

The Art Institute of Atlanta
Atlanta, Georgia
- **Proprietary** 4-year, founded 1949, part of Education Management Corporation
- **Suburban** 7-acre campus
- **Coed**

Academics *Calendar:* quarters. *Degrees:* diplomas, associate, and bachelor's.
Freshman Application Contact The Art Institute of Atlanta, 6600 Peachtree Dunwoody Road, NE, 100 Embassy Row, Atlanta, GA 30328. *Phone:* 770-394-8300. *Toll-free phone:* 800-275-4242.
Website: http://www.artinstitutes.edu/atlanta/.

See full-page ad on page 54 and page 1050 for the College Close-Up.

The Art Institute of Atlanta–Decatur
Decatur, Georgia
- **Proprietary** 4-year, founded 2007, part of Education Management Corporation
- **Coed**

Academics *Calendar:* quarters. *Degrees:* diplomas, associate, and bachelor's.
Freshman Application Contact The Art Institute of Atlanta–Decatur, One West Court Square, Suite 110, Decatur, GA 30030. *Phone:* 404-942-1800. *Toll-free phone:* 866-856-6203.
Website: http://www.artinstitutes.edu/decatur/.

See full-page ad on page 54 and page 1052 for the College Close-Up.

Ashworth College
Norcross, Georgia
Freshman Application Contact Eric Ryall, Registrar, Ashworth College, 6625 The Corners Parkway, Suite 500, Norcross, GA 30092. *Phone:* 770-729-8400 Ext. 5297. *Toll-free phone:* 800-957-5412.
Website: http://www.ashworthcollege.edu/.

Bauder College
Atlanta, Georgia
- **Proprietary** 4-year, founded 1964
- **Urban** campus
- **Coed**

Academics *Calendar:* quarters. *Degrees:* certificates, associate, and bachelor's.
Freshman Application Contact Bauder College, 384 Northyards Boulevard NW, Suites 190 and 400, Atlanta, GA 30313. *Phone:* 404-237-7573. *Toll-free phone:* 800-935-1857.
Website: http://atlanta.bauder.edu/.

Berry College
Mount Berry, Georgia
- **Independent interdenominational** comprehensive, founded 1902
- **Suburban** 27,000-acre campus with easy access to Atlanta
- **Endowment** $822.0 million
- **Coed** 2,041 undergraduate students, 98% full-time, 67% women, 33% men
- **Moderately difficult** entrance level, 66% of applicants were admitted

Undergraduates 2,007 full-time, 34 part-time. Students come from 35 states and territories; 17 other countries; 27% are from out of state; 4% Black or African American, non-Hispanic/Latino; 5% Hispanic/Latino; 2% Asian, non-Hispanic/Latino; 0.1% Native Hawaiian or other Pacific Islander, non-Hispanic/Latino; 0.2% American Indian or Alaska Native, non-Hispanic/Latino; 2% Two or more races, non-Hispanic/Latino; 2% Race/ethnicity unknown; 0.9% international; 2% transferred in; 86% live on campus. *Retention:* 75% of full-time freshmen returned.
Freshmen *Admission:* 3,485 applied, 2,304 admitted, 618 enrolled. *Average high school GPA:* 3.7. *Test scores:* SAT critical reading scores over 500: 87%; SAT math scores over 500: 90%; SAT writing scores over 500: 81%; ACT scores over 18: 100%; SAT critical reading scores over 600: 39%; SAT math scores over 600: 38%; SAT writing scores over 600: 33%; ACT scores over 24:

77%; SAT critical reading scores over 700: 10%; SAT math scores over 700: 4%; SAT writing scores over 700: 6%; ACT scores over 30: 17%.
Faculty *Total:* 207, 74% full-time, 76% with terminal degrees. *Student/faculty ratio:* 13:1.
Academics *Calendar:* semesters. *Degrees:* bachelor's and master's. *Special study options:* adult/continuing education programs, advanced placement credit, double majors, honors programs, independent study, internships, part-time degree program, student-designed majors, study abroad, summer session for credit. *Unusual degree programs:* 3-2 engineering with Georgia Institute of Technology; nursing with Emory University.
Computers on Campus 200 computers/terminals and 80 ports are available on campus for general student use. Students can access the following: campus intranet, computer help desk, free student e-mail accounts, online (class) grades, online (class) registration, online (class) schedules. Campuswide network is available. 100% of college-owned or -operated housing units are wired for high-speed Internet access. Wireless service is available via classrooms, computer centers, computer labs, dorm rooms, learning centers, libraries, student centers.
Student Life *Housing:* on-campus residence required through senior year. *Options:* coed, men-only, women-only. Campus housing is university owned. Freshman campus housing is guaranteed. *Activities and organizations:* drama/theater group, student-run newspaper, choral group, Student Government Association, Campus Outreach, Block-n-Bridle, Allied Health, Athletes Bettering the Community. *Campus security:* 24-hour emergency response devices and patrols, controlled dormitory access, lighted pathways, gated campus, mobile police patrols, identification of valuables, limited access to campus, on campus police officers. *Student services:* health clinic, personal/psychological counseling.
Athletics Member NCAA. All Division III. *Intercollegiate sports:* baseball M, basketball M/W, cross-country running M/W, equestrian sports W, football M, golf M/W, lacrosse M/W, soccer M/W, softball W, swimming and diving M/W, tennis M/W, track and field M/W, volleyball W. *Intramural sports:* badminton M/W, basketball M/W, bowling M/W, cheerleading M(c)/W(c), crew M(c)/W(c), cross-country running M/W, football M/W, golf M/W, racquetball M/W, rock climbing M/W, soccer M/W, softball M/W, swimming and diving M/W, table tennis M/W, tennis M/W, ultimate Frisbee M/W, volleyball M/W, water polo M/W, weight lifting M/W.
Standardized Tests *Required:* SAT or ACT (for admission).
Costs (2012–13) *Comprehensive fee:* $37,329 includes full-time tuition ($27,450), mandatory fees ($200), and room and board ($9679). Part-time tuition: $915 per credit hour. *College room only:* $5456. Room and board charges vary according to board plan and housing facility. *Payment plan:* installment. *Waivers:* senior citizens and employees or children of employees.
Financial Aid Of all full-time matriculated undergraduates who enrolled in 2012, 1,734 applied for aid, 1,459 were judged to have need, 375 had their need fully met. 560 Federal Work-Study jobs (averaging $3508). 2,132 state and other part-time jobs (averaging $3778). In 2012, 525 non-need-based awards were made. *Average percent of need met:* 83%. *Average financial aid package:* $23,802. *Average need-based loan:* $4803. *Average need-based gift aid:* $18,578. *Average non-need-based aid:* $11,355. *Average indebtedness upon graduation:* $20,611.
Applying *Options:* electronic application, early admission. *Application fee:* $50. *Required:* essay or personal statement, high school transcript, 1 letter of recommendation. *Required for some:* 2 letters of recommendation, Home-school applicants must meet or exceed academic profile of previous freshmen class. *Recommended:* interview. *Application deadlines:* 7/26 (freshmen), 7/26 (transfers). *Notification:* continuous (freshmen), continuous (transfers).
Freshman Application Contact Mr. Timothy Tarpley, Director of Operations, Enrollment Management, Berry College, PO Box 490159, 2277 Martha Berry Highway, NW, Mount Berry, GA 30149-0159. *Phone:* 706-236-2215. *Toll-free phone:* 800-237-7942. *Fax:* 706-290-2178. *E-mail:* admissions@berry.edu. *Website:* http://www.berry.edu/.

Beulah Heights University
Atlanta, Georgia
- **Independent Pentecostal** comprehensive, founded 1918
- **Urban** 10-acre campus with easy access to Atlanta
- **Coed**
- **Noncompetitive** entrance level

Faculty *Student/faculty ratio:* 13:1.
Academics *Calendar:* semesters. *Degrees:* associate, bachelor's, and master's.
Student Life *Campus security:* 24-hour emergency response devices and patrols.
Standardized Tests *Required:* TOFEL required for international students (for admission). *Recommended:* SAT or ACT (for admission).
Costs (2012–13) *Tuition:* $5760 full-time, $240 per credit part-time. Full-time tuition and fees vary according to course load. *Room only:* $2500. Room and

board charges vary according to housing facility. *Payment plans:* installment, deferred payment.

Financial Aid *Of all full-time matriculated undergraduates who enrolled in 2009,* 113 applied for aid, 113 were judged to have need. 13 Federal Work-Study jobs (averaging $4335). *Average percent of need met:* 75. *Average financial aid package:* $5619. *Average need-based loan:* $2250. *Average need-based gift aid:* $3500. *Average indebtedness upon graduation:* $40,000.

Applying *Options:* electronic application, early admission. *Application fee:* $30. *Required:* essay or personal statement, high school transcript, minimum 2.0 GPA, 2 letters of recommendation, Statement of Faith. *Recommended:* interview.

Freshman Application Contact John Dreher, Director of Admissions, Beulah Heights University, 892 Berne Street, SE, Atlanta, GA 30316. *Phone:* 404-627-2681 Ext. 117. *Toll-free phone:* 888-777-BHBC. *E-mail:* john.dreher@beulah.org.
Website: http://www.beulah.org/.

Brenau University
Gainesville, Georgia

- **Independent** comprehensive, founded 1878
- **Small-town** 57-acre campus with easy access to Atlanta
- **Endowment** $31.7 million
- **Women only**
- **Moderately difficult** entrance level

Faculty *Student/faculty ratio:* 9:1.

Academics *Calendar:* semesters. *Degrees:* associate, bachelor's, and master's (also offers coed evening and weekend programs with significant enrollment not reflected in profile).

Student Life *Campus security:* 24-hour emergency response devices and patrols, late-night transport/escort service.

Athletics Member NAIA.

Standardized Tests *Required:* SAT or ACT (for admission).

Costs (2012–13) *Comprehensive fee:* $32,792 includes full-time tuition ($21,908) and room and board ($10,884). Full-time tuition and fees vary according to location and program. Part-time tuition and fees vary according to course load, location, and program.

Financial Aid *Of all full-time matriculated undergraduates who enrolled in 2012,* 612 applied for aid, 569 were judged to have need, 86 had their need fully met. 112 Federal Work-Study jobs (averaging $1993). *In 2012,* 40 non-need-based awards were made. *Average percent of need met:* 68. *Average financial aid package:* $19,555. *Average need-based loan:* $4667. *Average need-based gift aid:* $15,490. *Average non-need-based aid:* $12,930. *Average indebtedness upon graduation:* $23,317.

Applying *Options:* electronic application, deferred entrance. *Application fee:* $35. *Required:* high school transcript, minimum 2.5 GPA. *Required for some:* interview.

Freshman Application Contact Mr. Scott Briell, Senior Vice President, Enrollment Management and Student Services, Brenau University, Admissions, 500 Washington Street, SE, Gainesville, GA 30501. *Phone:* 770-538-4704. *Toll-free phone:* 800-252-5119. *Fax:* 770-538-4701. *E-mail:* admissions@brenau.edu.
Website: http://www.brenau.edu/.

Brewton-Parker College
Mt. Vernon, Georgia

- **Independent Southern Baptist** 4-year, founded 1904
- **Rural** 280-acre campus
- **Coed**
- **Minimally difficult** entrance level

Faculty *Student/faculty ratio:* 11:1.

Academics *Calendar:* semesters. *Degrees:* associate and bachelor's.

Student Life *Campus security:* 24-hour emergency response devices, controlled dormitory access, Campus security is provided from 6 pm to 6 am.

Athletics Member NAIA.

Standardized Tests *Required:* SAT or ACT (for admission).

Costs (2012–13) *One-time required fee:* $200. *Comprehensive fee:* $21,030 includes full-time tuition ($12,670), mandatory fees ($760), and room and board ($7600). Full-time tuition and fees vary according to course load, location, and program. Part-time tuition: $360 per credit hour. Part-time tuition and fees vary according to course load, location, and program. *Required fees:* $360 per credit hour part-time. *College room only:* $3000. Room and board charges vary according to board plan and housing facility.

Financial Aid *Of all full-time matriculated undergraduates who enrolled in 2009,* 819 applied for aid, 736 were judged to have need, 118 had their need fully met. 170 Federal Work-Study jobs (averaging $676). 114 state and other part-time jobs (averaging $466). *In 2009,* 96 non-need-based awards were

made. *Average percent of need met:* 71. *Average financial aid package:* $11,736. *Average need-based loan:* $3436. *Average need-based gift aid:* $9011. *Average non-need-based aid:* $3915. *Average indebtedness upon graduation:* $28,231. *Financial aid deadline:* 5/1.

Applying *Options:* electronic application. *Application fee:* $35. *Required:* high school transcript, minimum 2.0 GPA.

Freshman Application Contact Director of Admissions, Brewton-Parker College, PO Box 197, Mount Vernon, GA 30445. *Phone:* 912-583-3247. *Toll-free phone:* 800-342-1087. *Fax:* 912-583-3598. *E-mail:* admissions@bpc.edu.
Website: http://www.bpc.edu/.

Carver College
Atlanta, Georgia

- **Independent nondenominational** 4-year, founded 1943
- **Urban** 16-acre campus
- **Coed**
- **Noncompetitive** entrance level

Faculty *Student/faculty ratio:* 6:1.

Academics *Calendar:* semesters. *Degrees:* certificates, associate, and bachelor's.

Athletics Member NCCAA.

Costs (2012–13) *Comprehensive fee:* $11,840 includes full-time tuition ($6960) and room and board ($4880). Part-time tuition: $290 per credit hour.

Applying *Application fee:* $35. *Required:* essay or personal statement, high school transcript, minimum 2.0 GPA, 2 letters of recommendation. *Required for some:* interview. *Recommended:* interview.

Freshman Application Contact Bertha Mack, Admissions Officer, Carver College, 3870 Cascade Road SW, Atlanta, GA 30331. *Phone:* 404-527-4520. *Fax:* 404-527-4524. *E-mail:* info@carver.edu.
Website: http://www.carver.edu/.

Chamberlain College of Nursing
Atlanta, Georgia

- **Proprietary** 4-year
- **Coed** 381 undergraduate students, 43% full-time, 94% women, 6% men

Undergraduates 165 full-time, 216 part-time. 2% are from out of state; 28% Black or African American, non-Hispanic/Latino; 2% Hispanic/Latino; 4% Asian, non-Hispanic/Latino; 2% Two or more races, non-Hispanic/Latino; 35% Race/ethnicity unknown; 7% international; 82% transferred in.

Freshmen *Admission:* 4 enrolled.

Faculty *Total:* 15, 60% full-time. *Student/faculty ratio:* 22:1.

Academics *Degree:* bachelor's.

Standardized Tests *Required:* SAT or ACT (for admission).

Costs (2013–14) *Tuition:* $16,360 full-time, $665 per credit hour part-time. *Required fees:* $600 full-time.

Applying *Application fee:* $95.

Freshman Application Contact Chamberlain College of Nursing, 5775 Peachtree-Dunwoody Road, NE, Suite A100, Atlanta, GA 30342.
Website: http://www.chamberlain.edu/.

Clark Atlanta University
Atlanta, Georgia

- **Independent United Methodist** university, founded 1865
- **Urban** 126-acre campus
- **Endowment** $53.7 million
- **Coed** 2,632 undergraduate students, 94% full-time, 75% women, 25% men
- **Moderately difficult** entrance level, 69% of applicants were admitted

Undergraduates 2,484 full-time, 148 part-time. Students come from 43 states and territories; 10 other countries; 63% are from out of state; 90% Black or African American, non-Hispanic/Latino; 0.4% Hispanic/Latino; 0.2% Asian, non-Hispanic/Latino; 0.3% American Indian or Alaska Native, non-Hispanic/Latino; 8% Race/ethnicity unknown; 0.6% international; 5% transferred in; 55% live on campus. *Retention:* 61% of full-time freshmen returned.

Freshmen *Admission:* 5,801 applied, 3,975 admitted, 637 enrolled. *Average high school GPA:* 3. *Test scores:* SAT critical reading scores over 500: 19%; SAT math scores over 500: 16%; ACT scores over 18: 73%; SAT critical reading scores over 600: 3%; SAT math scores over 600: 2%; ACT scores over 24: 13%.

Faculty *Total:* 320, 53% full-time, 62% with terminal degrees. *Student/faculty ratio:* 15:1.

Academics *Calendar:* semesters. *Degrees:* bachelor's, master's, doctoral, post-master's, and postbachelor's certificates. *Special study options:* academic remediation for entering students, accelerated degree program, adult/continuing education programs, advanced placement credit, cooperative education, double majors, honors programs, independent study, internships, off-campus study, part-time degree program, services for LD students, study abroad, summer session for credit. *ROTC:* Army (c), Navy (c). *Unusual degree programs:* 3-2 engineering with Georgia Institute of Technology, Boston University, North Carolina Agricultural and Technical State University.

Computers on Campus 741 computers/terminals and 2,000 ports are available on campus for general student use. Students can access the following: computer help desk, free student e-mail accounts, online (class) grades, online (class) registration, online (class) schedules. Campuswide network is available. 100% of college-owned or -operated housing units are wired for high-speed Internet access. Wireless service is available via entire campus.

Student Life *Housing:* on-campus residence required through sophomore year. *Options:* coed, men-only, women-only. Campus housing is university owned and is provided by a third party. Freshman applicants given priority for college housing. *Activities and organizations:* drama/theater group, student-run newspaper, radio and television station, choral group, marching band, Spirit Boosters, Pre-Alumni Council, Campus Activities Board, Orientation Guides, National Association for the Advancement of Colored People, national fraternities, national sororities. *Campus security:* 24-hour emergency response devices and patrols, late-night transport/escort service, controlled dormitory access. *Student services:* health clinic, personal/psychological counseling.

Athletics Member NCAA. All Division II. *Intercollegiate sports:* baseball M(s), basketball M(s)/W(s), cross-country running M(s)/W(s), football M(s), softball W(s), tennis W(s), track and field M(s)/W(s), volleyball W(s). *Intramural sports:* basketball M/W, football M, softball W, tennis W, track and field M/W, volleyball M/W.

Standardized Tests *Required:* SAT or ACT (for admission).

Costs (2012–13) *Comprehensive fee:* $28,786 includes full-time tuition ($19,012), mandatory fees ($818), and room and board ($8956). Part-time tuition: $792 per credit hour. *Required fees:* $409 per term part-time. *Room and board:* Room and board charges vary according to board plan and housing facility. *Payment plan:* installment. *Waivers:* employees or children of employees.

Financial Aid Of all full-time matriculated undergraduates who enrolled in 2005, 3,883 applied for aid, 3,712 were judged to have need, 1,567 had their need fully met. 229 Federal Work-Study jobs (averaging $1335). *Average percent of need met:* 8%. *Average financial aid package:* $10,935. *Average need-based loan:* $4526. *Average need-based gift aid:* $3818. *Average indebtedness upon graduation:* $17,751.

Applying *Options:* electronic application, early admission, deferred entrance. *Application fee:* $35. *Required:* essay or personal statement, high school transcript, minimum 2.5 GPA, 2 letters of recommendation. *Required for some:* interview. *Application deadlines:* 6/1 (freshmen), 6/1 (out-of-state freshmen), 6/1 (transfers). *Notification:* continuous (freshmen), continuous (out-of-state freshmen), continuous (transfers).

Freshman Application Contact Mr. Dwight Sanchez, Director, Office of Admissions, Clark Atlanta University, 223 James P. Brawley Drive, SW, Atlanta, GA 30314. *Phone:* 404-880-8043. *Toll-free phone:* 800-688-3228. *Fax:* 404-880-6174. *E-mail:* cauadmissions@cau.edu. *Website:* http://www.cau.edu/.

Clayton State University
Morrow, Georgia

- **State-supported** comprehensive, founded 1969, part of University System of Georgia
- **Suburban** 163-acre campus with easy access to Atlanta
- **Endowment** $1.1 million
- **Coed** 6,808 undergraduate students, 58% full-time, 70% women, 30% men
- **Minimally difficult** entrance level, 39% of applicants were admitted

Undergraduates 3,924 full-time, 2,884 part-time. Students come from 34 states and territories; 34 other countries; 2% are from out of state; 63% Black or African American, non-Hispanic/Latino; 2% Hispanic/Latino; 0.4% Asian, non-Hispanic/Latino; 0.2% American Indian or Alaska Native, non-Hispanic/Latino; 0.2% Two or more races, non-Hispanic/Latino; 4% Race/ethnicity unknown; 1% international; 1% transferred in; 10% live on campus. *Retention:* 68% of full-time freshmen returned.

Freshmen *Admission:* 2,556 applied, 1,007 admitted, 612 enrolled. *Average high school GPA:* 3. *Test scores:* SAT critical reading scores over 500: 35%; SAT math scores over 500: 29%; ACT scores over 18: 25%; SAT critical reading scores over 600: 6%; SAT math scores over 600: 6%; ACT scores over 24: 8%; SAT critical reading scores over 700: 1%; SAT math scores over 700: 1%. **Faculty** *Total:* 367, 61% full-time, 54% with terminal degrees. *Student/faculty ratio:* 19:1.

Academics *Calendar:* semesters. *Degrees:* certificates, associate, bachelor's, and master's. *Special study options:* academic remediation for entering stu-

dents, adult/continuing education programs, advanced placement credit, cooperative education, distance learning, double majors, English as a second language, freshman honors college, honors programs, independent study, internships, off-campus study, part-time degree program, services for LD students, student-designed majors, study abroad, summer session for credit. *ROTC:* Army (b), Navy (c), Air Force (c).

Computers on Campus 3,500 computers/terminals are available on campus for general student use. Students can access the following: online (class) grades, online (class) registration, online (class) schedules. Campuswide network is available. 100% of college-owned or -operated housing units are wired for high-speed Internet access. Wireless service is available via entire campus.

Student Life *Housing:* on-campus residence required for freshman year. *Options:* coed. Campus housing is university owned. Freshman applicants given priority for college housing. *Activities and organizations:* drama/theater group, student-run newspaper, choral group, Accounting Club, International Awareness Club, Black Cultural Awareness Association, Student Government Association, music club, national fraternities, national sororities. *Campus security:* 24-hour emergency response devices and patrols, late-night transport/escort service, controlled dormitory access, lighted pathways. *Student services:* health clinic, personal/psychological counseling.

Athletics Member NCAA. All Division II. *Intercollegiate sports:* basketball M(s)/W(s), cheerleading W(s)(c), cross-country running M(s)/W(s), golf M(s), soccer M(s)/W(s), tennis W(s), track and field M(s)/W(s). *Intramural sports:* bowling M/W, softball M/W, table tennis M/W, volleyball M/W.

Standardized Tests *Required:* SAT or ACT (for admission). *Required for some:* SAT Subject Tests (for admission).

Costs (2012–13) *Tuition:* state resident $4512 full-time, $150 per credit hour part-time; nonresident $16,416 full-time, $547 per credit hour part-time. Full-time tuition and fees vary according to course load. Part-time tuition and fees vary according to course load. *Required fees:* $1404 full-time, $702 per term part-time. *Room and board:* $8862; room only: $5574. Room and board charges vary according to board plan and housing facility. *Waivers:* senior citizens and employees or children of employees.

Financial Aid Of all full-time matriculated undergraduates who enrolled in 2012, 3,574 applied for aid, 3,392 were judged to have need, 95 had their need fully met. 41 Federal Work-Study jobs (averaging $6225). In 2012, 22 non-need-based awards were made. *Average percent of need met:* 45%. *Average financial aid package:* $9145. *Average need-based loan:* $4410. *Average need-based gift aid:* $5807. *Average non-need-based aid:* $1749. *Average indebtedness upon graduation:* $28,872.

Applying *Options:* electronic application, early admission, deferred entrance. *Application fee:* $40. *Required:* high school transcript, proof of immunization. *Application deadline:* 7/17 (freshmen). *Notification:* continuous (freshmen), continuous (transfers).

Freshman Application Contact Ms. Theadora Riley, Admissions, Clayton State University, 2000 Clayton State Boulevard, Morrow, GA 30260-0285. *Phone:* 678-466-4115. *Fax:* 678-466-4149. *E-mail:* csc-info@clayton.edu. *Website:* http://www.clayton.edu/.

College of Coastal Georgia
Brunswick, Georgia

- **State-supported** 4-year, founded 1961, part of University System of Georgia
- **Small-town** 193-acre campus with easy access to Jacksonville
- **Endowment** $6.4 million
- **Coed** 3,156 undergraduate students, 57% full-time, 68% women, 32% men
- **Minimally difficult** entrance level, 88% of applicants were admitted

Undergraduates 1,792 full-time, 1,364 part-time. Students come from 38 states and territories; 8% are from out of state; 18% Black or African American, non-Hispanic/Latino; 4% Hispanic/Latino; 1% Asian, non-Hispanic/Latino; 0.2% Native Hawaiian or other Pacific Islander, non-Hispanic/Latino; 0.4% American Indian or Alaska Native, non-Hispanic/Latino; 2% Two or more races, non-Hispanic/Latino; 7% Race/ethnicity unknown; 1% international; 8% transferred in; 11% live on campus. *Retention:* 55% of full-time freshmen returned.

Freshmen *Admission:* 983 applied, 868 admitted, 619 enrolled. *Average high school GPA:* 2.98. *Test scores:* SAT critical reading scores over 500: 34%; SAT math scores over 500: 27%; ACT scores over 18: 67%; SAT critical reading scores over 600: 4%; SAT math scores over 600: 5%; ACT scores over 24: 8%. **Faculty** *Total:* 186, 46% full-time, 45% with terminal degrees. *Student/faculty ratio:* 19:1.

Academics *Calendar:* semesters. *Degrees:* associate and bachelor's. *Special study options:* academic remediation for entering students, advanced placement credit, distance learning, double majors, internships, part-time degree program, services for LD students, study abroad, summer session for credit.

Computers on Campus 395 computers/terminals and 300 ports are available on campus for general student use. Students can access the following: computer help desk, free student e-mail accounts, online (class) grades, online (class) registration, online (class) schedules. Campuswide network is available. 100% of college-owned or -operated housing units are wired for high-speed Internet access. Wireless service is available via entire campus.

Student Life *Housing options:* coed. Campus housing is university owned. Freshman campus housing is guaranteed. *Activities and organizations:* student-run newspaper, Phi Theta Kappa, Urban Gaming Club, Biology Club, Psychology Club, International Association. *Campus security:* 24-hour emergency response devices and patrols, late-night transport/escort service, controlled dormitory access. *Student services:* health clinic, personal/psychological counseling.

Athletics Member NAIA. *Intercollegiate sports:* basketball M(s)/W(s), cross-country running M(s)/W(s), golf M(s)/W(s), softball W(s), tennis M(s)/W(s), volleyball W(s). *Intramural sports:* basketball M/W, bowling M/W, cheerleading W, football M/W, golf M/W, soccer M(c)/W(c), tennis M/W, ultimate Frisbee M(c)/W(c), volleyball M/W.

Standardized Tests *Required for some:* SAT or ACT (for admission).

Costs (2012–13) *Tuition:* state resident $2277 full-time, $95 per credit hour part-time; nonresident $8411 full-time, $350 per credit hour part-time. Full-time tuition and fees vary according to course load. Part-time tuition and fees vary according to course load. *Required fees:* $1650 full-time, $830 per term part-time. *Room and board:* $8126; room only: $5126. Room and board charges vary according to board plan, housing facility, and location. *Payment plan:* installment. *Waivers:* senior citizens and employees or children of employees.

Financial Aid Of all full-time matriculated undergraduates who enrolled in 2011, 80 Federal Work-Study jobs (averaging $1500).

Applying *Options:* electronic application, early admission, deferred entrance. *Application fee:* $25. *Required:* high school transcript, minimum 2.0 GPA, Immunization records, proof of residency and SAT or ACT scores(for applicants graduating from high school within the last five years). *Application deadlines:* 7/15 (freshmen), 7/15 (transfers). *Notification:* continuous (freshmen), continuous (transfers).

Freshman Application Contact Mr. Clayton Daniels, Assistant Vice President for Enrollment Management, College of Coastal Georgia, One College Drive, Brunswick, GA 31520. *Phone:* 912-279-5730. *Toll-free phone:* 800-675-7235. *Fax:* 912-262-3072. *E-mail:* admiss@ccga.edu. *Website:* http://www.ccga.edu/.

Columbus State University
Columbus, Georgia

- **State-supported** comprehensive, founded 1958, part of University System of Georgia
- **Suburban** 132-acre campus with easy access to Atlanta
- **Endowment** $1.8 million
- **Coed** 7,025 undergraduate students, 70% full-time, 59% women, 41% men
- **Minimally difficult** entrance level, 53% of applicants were admitted

Undergraduates 4,947 full-time, 2,078 part-time. Students come from 44 states and territories; 45 other countries; 15% are from out of state; 36% Black or African American, non-Hispanic/Latino; 5% Hispanic/Latino; 2% Asian, non-Hispanic/Latino; 0.3% Native Hawaiian or other Pacific Islander, non-Hispanic/Latino; 0.5% American Indian or Alaska Native, non-Hispanic/Latino; 2% Two or more races, non-Hispanic/Latino; 1% international; 9% transferred in; 21% live on campus. *Retention:* 67% of full-time freshmen returned.

Freshmen *Admission:* 3,672 applied, 1,930 admitted, 1,159 enrolled. *Average high school GPA:* 3.09. *Test scores:* SAT critical reading scores over 500: 47%; SAT math scores over 500: 39%; SAT writing scores over 500: 38%; ACT scores over 18: 78%; SAT critical reading scores over 600: 13%; SAT math scores over 600: 12%; SAT writing scores over 600: 9%; ACT scores over 24: 18%; SAT critical reading scores over 700: 2%; SAT math scores over 700: 1%; SAT writing scores over 700: 1%; ACT scores over 30: 2%.

Faculty *Total:* 511, 55% full-time, 54% with terminal degrees. *Student/faculty ratio:* 17:1.

Academics *Calendar:* semesters. *Degrees:* certificates, associate, bachelor's, master's, doctoral, post-master's, and postbachelor's certificates. *Special study options:* academic remediation for entering students, adult/continuing education programs, advanced placement credit, cooperative education, distance learning, double majors, English as a second language, freshman honors college, honors programs, independent study, internships, off-campus study, part-time degree program, services for LD students, study abroad, summer session for credit. *ROTC:* Army (b). *Unusual degree programs:* 3-2 engineering with Georgia Institute of Technology.

Computers on Campus 1,135 computers/terminals are available on campus for general student use. Students can access the following: campus intranet, computer help desk, free student e-mail accounts, online (class) grades, online (class) registration, online (class) schedules. Campuswide network is available. 100% of college-owned or -operated housing units are wired for high-speed Internet access. Wireless service is available via entire campus.

Student Life *Housing:* on-campus residence required for freshman year. *Options:* coed, men-only, women-only, disabled students. Campus housing is university owned. Freshman applicants given priority for college housing. *Activities and organizations:* drama/theater group, student-run newspaper, choral group, Student Government Association, Student Activities Council, Campus Ministry Association, African Students Association, SABER Student Newspaper, national fraternities, national sororities. *Campus security:* 24-hour emergency response devices and patrols, late-night transport/escort service, controlled dormitory access. *Student services:* health clinic, personal/psychological counseling.

Athletics Member NCAA. All Division II except men's and women's riflery (Division I). *Intercollegiate sports:* baseball M(s), basketball M(s)/W(s), cheerleading M(s)/W(s), cross-country running M(s)/W(s), golf M(s)/W(s), riflery M(s)/W(s), soccer W(s), softball W(s), tennis M(s)/W(s), volleyball W(s). *Intramural sports:* badminton M/W, basketball M/W, bowling M/W, cross-country running M/W, football M, golf M/W, racquetball M/W, skiing (downhill) M/W, soccer M/W, softball M/W, table tennis M/W, tennis M/W, track and field M/W, volleyball M/W.

Standardized Tests *Required:* SAT or ACT (for admission).

Costs (2012–13) *Tuition:* state resident $4852 full-time, $162 per semester hour part-time; nonresident $17,128 full-time, $571 per semester hour part-time. *Required fees:* $1740 full-time, $870 per term part-time. *Room and board:* $8542. Room and board charges vary according to board plan.

Financial Aid Of all full-time matriculated undergraduates who enrolled in 2012, 4,215 applied for aid, 3,543 were judged to have need, 625 had their need fully met. In 2012, 235 non-need-based awards were made. *Average percent of need met:* 73%. *Average financial aid package:* $8997. *Average need-based loan:* $4106. *Average need-based gift aid:* $4727. *Average non-need-based aid:* $1638. *Average indebtedness upon graduation:* $25,687.

Applying *Options:* electronic application, early admission, deferred entrance. *Application fee:* $40. *Required:* high school transcript, minimum 2.4 GPA, proof of immunization. *Application deadlines:* 6/30 (freshmen), 6/30 (transfers). *Notification:* continuous (freshmen), continuous (transfers).

Freshman Application Contact Columbus State University, 4225 University Avenue, Columbus, GA 31907-5645. *Phone:* 706-507-8806. *Toll-free phone:* 866-264-2035. *Website:* http://www.columbusstate.edu/.

Covenant College
Lookout Mountain, Georgia

- **Independent** comprehensive, founded 1955, affiliated with Presbyterian Church in America
- **Suburban** 350-acre campus
- **Endowment** $25.1 million
- **Coed** 1,065 undergraduate students, 95% full-time, 57% women, 43% men
- **Moderately difficult** entrance level, 57% of applicants were admitted

Undergraduates 1,011 full-time, 54 part-time. 76% are from out of state; 3% Black or African American, non-Hispanic/Latino; 2% Hispanic/Latino; 2% Asian, non-Hispanic/Latino; 0.5% American Indian or Alaska Native, non-Hispanic/Latino; 2% Two or more races, non-Hispanic/Latino; 2% international; 3% transferred in; 83% live on campus. *Retention:* 87% of full-time freshmen returned.

Freshmen *Admission:* 1,129 applied, 644 admitted, 268 enrolled. *Average high school GPA:* 3.6. *Test scores:* SAT critical reading scores over 500: 89%; SAT math scores over 500: 85%; SAT writing scores over 500: 87%; ACT scores over 18: 100%; SAT critical reading scores over 600: 51%; SAT math scores over 600: 43%; SAT writing scores over 600: 54%; ACT scores over 24: 62%; SAT critical reading scores over 700: 19%; SAT math scores over 700: 6%; SAT writing scores over 700: 8%; ACT scores over 30: 15%.

Faculty *Total:* 101, 66% full-time, 69% with terminal degrees. *Student/faculty ratio:* 13:1.

Academics *Calendar:* semesters. *Degrees:* associate, bachelor's, and master's (master's degree in education only). *Special study options:* academic remediation for entering students, adult/continuing education programs, advanced placement credit, double majors, independent study, internships, off-campus study, part-time degree program, services for LD students, student-designed majors, study abroad, summer session for credit. *ROTC:* Army (c).

Computers on Campus Students can access the following: computer help desk, free student e-mail accounts, online (class) registration, online student information system. Campuswide network is available. 100% of college-owned or -operated housing units are wired for high-speed Internet access. Wireless service is available via classrooms, computer labs, dorm rooms, libraries.

Student Life *Housing:* on-campus residence required through junior year. *Options:* men-only, women-only. Campus housing is university owned. Freshman campus housing is guaranteed. *Activities and organizations:* drama/theater group, student-run newspaper, radio station, choral group. *Campus security:* controlled dormitory access, night security guards. *Student services:* health clinic, personal/psychological counseling, women's center.

Athletics Member NCAA, NAIA, NCCAA. All NCAA Division III. *Intercollegiate sports:* baseball M, basketball M/W, cross-country running M/W, golf M/W, soccer M/W, softball W, tennis M/W, volleyball W. *Intramural sports:* badminton M/W, basketball M/W, football M, soccer M/W, volleyball M/W.

Standardized Tests *Required:* SAT or ACT (for admission).

Costs (2013–14) *Comprehensive fee:* $36,310 includes full-time tuition ($27,500), mandatory fees ($770), and room and board ($8040). Full-time tuition and fees vary according to course load. Part-time tuition: $1150 per credit hour. Part-time tuition and fees vary according to course load. *Payment plan:* installment. *Waivers:* senior citizens and employees or children of employees.

Financial Aid Of all full-time matriculated undergraduates who enrolled in 2010, 694 applied for aid, 600 were judged to have need, 222 had their need fully met. In 2010, 228 non-need-based awards were made. *Average percent of need met:* 81%. *Average financial aid package:* $21,764. *Average need-based loan:* $6164. *Average need-based gift aid:* $15,449. *Average non-need-based aid:* $9059. *Average indebtedness upon graduation:* $21,853.

Applying *Options:* electronic application, early admission, deferred entrance. *Application fee:* $35. *Required:* essay or personal statement, high school transcript, minimum 2.5 GPA, 2 letters of recommendation, interview. *Application deadlines:* rolling (freshmen), rolling (transfers). *Notification:* continuous (freshmen).

Freshman Application Contact Mr. Philip Howlett, Assistant Director of Admissions, Covenant College, 14049 Scenic Highway, Lookout Mountain, GA 30750. *Phone:* 706-419-1145. *Toll-free phone:* 888-451-2683. *Fax:* 706-820-0893. *E-mail:* admissions@covenant.edu.

Website: http://www.covenant.edu/.

Dalton State College
Dalton, Georgia

- **State-supported** 4-year, founded 1963, part of University System of Georgia
- **Small-town** 144-acre campus
- **Endowment** $29.8 million
- **Coed** 5,047 undergraduate students, 59% full-time, 62% women, 38% men
- **Noncompetitive** entrance level, 36% of applicants were admitted

Undergraduates 2,976 full-time, 2,071 part-time. Students come from 6 states and territories; 40 other countries; 1% are from out of state; 4% Black or African American, non-Hispanic/Latino; 17% Hispanic/Latino; 1% Asian, non-Hispanic/Latino; 0.2% Native Hawaiian or other Pacific Islander, non-Hispanic/Latino; 0.5% American Indian or Alaska Native, non-Hispanic/Latino; 1% Two or more races, non-Hispanic/Latino; 6% Race/ethnicity unknown; 1% international; 5% transferred in; 4% live on campus. *Retention:* 61% of full-time freshmen returned.

Freshmen *Admission:* 3,067 applied, 1,100 admitted, 926 enrolled. *Average high school GPA:* 3.14. *Test scores:* SAT critical reading scores over 500: 39%; SAT math scores over 500: 39%; ACT scores over 18: 75%; SAT critical reading scores over 600: 9%; SAT math scores over 600: 7%; ACT scores over 24: 17%; SAT critical reading scores over 700: 1%; ACT scores over 30: 1%.

Faculty *Total:* 215, 74% full-time, 47% with terminal degrees. *Student/faculty ratio:* 21:1.

Academics *Calendar:* semesters. *Degrees:* certificates, associate, and bachelor's. *Special study options:* academic remediation for entering students, adult/continuing education programs, advanced placement credit, cooperative education, double majors, English as a second language, internships, off-campus study, part-time degree program, services for LD students, study abroad, summer session for credit.

Computers on Campus 730 computers/terminals are available on campus for general student use. Students can access the following: free student e-mail accounts, online (class) grades, online (class) registration, online (class) schedules. Campuswide network is available. Wireless service is available via computer centers, computer labs, learning centers, libraries, student centers.

Student Life *Housing options:* coed, disabled students. Campus housing is university owned. *Activities and organizations:* student-run newspaper, Kappa Delta Pi, Phi Theta Kappa, Phi Beta Lambda, Environmental Club, Radiological Technology Club. *Campus security:* 24-hour emergency response devices and patrols.

Athletics *Intercollegiate sports:* basketball M(c)/W(c), golf W(c), softball M(c)/W(c), table tennis M(c)/W(c), tennis M(c)/W(c), volleyball M(c)/W(c). *Intramural sports:* badminton M/W, basketball M/W, football M/W, softball M/W, table tennis M/W, tennis M/W, volleyball M/W.

Standardized Tests *Required:* SAT or ACT (for admission).

Costs (2013–14) *One-time required fee:* $300. *Tuition:* state resident $2276 full-time, $93 per credit hour part-time; nonresident $8411 full-time, $350 per credit hour part-time. Full-time tuition and fees vary according to course load. Part-time tuition and fees vary according to course load. *Required fees:* $886 full-time. *Room and board:* $6320; room only: $4970. Room and board charges vary according to housing facility. *Payment plan:* installment. *Waivers:* senior citizens and employees or children of employees.

Financial Aid Of all full-time matriculated undergraduates who enrolled in 2010, 2,934 applied for aid, 2,494 were judged to have need, 364 had their need fully met. In 2010, 19 non-need-based awards were made. *Average percent of need met:* 73%. *Average financial aid package:* $8334. *Average need-based loan:* $3554. *Average need-based gift aid:* $3556. *Average non-need-based aid:* $1383. *Average indebtedness upon graduation:* $6811. *Financial aid deadline:* 7/1.

Applying *Options:* electronic application, deferred entrance. *Application fee:* $30. *Required:* high school transcript. *Application deadlines:* 7/1 (freshmen), 7/1 (transfers). *Notification:* continuous (freshmen).

Freshman Application Contact Dr. Angela Harris, Assistant Vice President of Enrollment Services, Dalton State College, 650 College Drive, Dalton, GA 30720-3797. *Phone:* 706-272-4476. *Toll-free phone:* 800-829-4436. *Fax:* 706-272-2530.

Website: http://www.daltonstate.edu/.

Darton State College
Albany, Georgia

- **State-supported** primarily 2-year, founded 1965, part of University System of Georgia
- **Urban** 185-acre campus
- **Endowment** $978,169
- **Coed** 6,396 undergraduate students, 49% full-time, 70% women, 30% men
- **Minimally difficult** entrance level

Undergraduates 3,137 full-time, 3,259 part-time. Students come from 33 states and territories; 46 other countries; 7% are from out of state; 45% Black or African American, non-Hispanic/Latino; 2% Hispanic/Latino; 0.9% Asian, non-Hispanic/Latino; 0.2% Native Hawaiian or other Pacific Islander, non-Hispanic/Latino; 0.4% American Indian or Alaska Native, non-Hispanic/Latino; 0.3% Two or more races, non-Hispanic/Latino; 0.6% Race/ethnicity unknown; 1% international; 15% transferred in. *Retention:* 53% of full-time freshmen returned.

Freshmen *Admission:* 1,251 enrolled. *Average high school GPA:* 2.73. *Test scores:* SAT critical reading scores over 500: 25%; SAT math scores over 500: 23%; SAT writing scores over 500: 17%; ACT scores over 18: 42%; SAT critical reading scores over 600: 6%; SAT math scores over 600: 4%; SAT writing scores over 600: 3%; ACT scores over 24: 5%; SAT critical reading scores over 700: 1%.

Faculty *Total:* 282, 43% full-time. *Student/faculty ratio:* 21:1.

Academics *Calendar:* semesters. *Degrees:* certificates, associate, bachelor's, and postbachelor's certificates. *Special study options:* academic remediation for entering students, accelerated degree program, adult/continuing education programs, advanced placement credit, cooperative education, distance learning, double majors, English as a second language, honors programs, independent study, off-campus study, part-time degree program, services for LD students, student-designed majors, study abroad, summer session for credit. *ROTC:* Army (c).

Computers on Campus 450 computers/terminals and 4 ports are available on campus for general student use. Students can access the following: campus intranet, computer help desk, free student e-mail accounts, online (class) grades, online (class) registration, online (class) schedules. Campuswide network is available. 100% of college-owned or -operated housing units are wired for high-speed Internet access. Wireless service is available via entire campus.

Student Life *Housing options:* coed. Campus housing is university owned. *Activities and organizations:* drama/theater group, choral group, Cultural Exchange Club, Democratic, Independent, & Republican Team (D.I.R.T.), Human Services Club, Outdoor Adventure Club (OAC), Music Club. *Campus security:* 24-hour emergency response devices and patrols, student patrols, late-night transport/escort service, controlled dormitory access. *Student services:* health clinic, personal/psychological counseling.

Athletics Member NJCAA. *Intercollegiate sports:* baseball M(s), basketball W(s), cross-country running M(s)/W(s), golf M(s), soccer M(s)/W(s), softball W(s), swimming and diving M(s)/W(s), wrestling M. *Intramural sports:* badminton M/W, basketball M/W, bowling M/W, football M, racquetball M/W, table tennis M, volleyball M/W.

Standardized Tests *Required:* non-traditional students must take the COMPASS test (for admission). *Required for some:* SAT or ACT (for admission), SAT Subject Tests (for admission). *Recommended:* SAT or ACT (for admission), SAT Subject Tests (for admission).

Costs (2012–13) *Tuition:* state resident $2026 full-time, $84 per credit hour part-time; nonresident $7666 full-time, $319 per credit hour part-time. *Required fees:* $1144 full-time, $395 per course part-time. *Room and board:* $8730. Room and board charges vary according to board plan and housing facility. *Waivers:* senior citizens and employees or children of employees.

Financial Aid Of all full-time matriculated undergraduates who enrolled in 2011, 60 Federal Work-Study jobs.

Applying *Options:* electronic application, deferred entrance. *Application fee:* $20. *Required:* minimum 2.0 GPA, proof of immunization. *Required for some:* high school transcript. *Application deadlines:* 7/20 (freshmen), 7/20 (transfers). *Notification:* continuous until 7/27 (freshmen), continuous until 7/27 (transfers).

Freshman Application Contact Darton State College, 2400 Gillionville Road, Albany, GA 31707-3098. *Phone:* 229-430-6740. *Toll-free phone:* 866-775-1214.

Website: http://www.darton.edu/.

DeVry University
Alpharetta, Georgia

Freshman Application Contact DeVry University, 2555 Northwinds Parkway, Alpharetta, GA 30009. *Toll-free phone:* 866-338-7941.

Website: http://www.devry.edu/.

DeVry University
Decatur, Georgia

- **Proprietary** comprehensive, founded 1969, part of DeVry University
- **Suburban** campus
- **Coed** 2,240 undergraduate students, 31% full-time, 56% women, 44% men
- **Minimally difficult** entrance level

Undergraduates 703 full-time, 1,537 part-time. 13% are from out of state; 54% Black or African American, non-Hispanic/Latino; 3% Hispanic/Latino; 1% Asian, non-Hispanic/Latino; 0.2% Native Hawaiian or other Pacific Islander, non-Hispanic/Latino; 0.2% American Indian or Alaska Native, non-Hispanic/Latino; 0.8% Two or more races, non-Hispanic/Latino; 17% Race/ethnicity unknown; 0.6% international; 24% transferred in.

Freshmen *Admission:* 140 enrolled.

Faculty *Total:* 152, 27% full-time. *Student/faculty ratio:* 18:1.

Academics *Calendar:* semesters. *Degrees:* associate, bachelor's, master's, and postbachelor's certificates. *Special study options:* adult/continuing education programs, part-time degree program.

Student Life *Housing:* college housing not available.

Athletics *Intramural sports:* basketball M/W, football M/W, softball M/W, volleyball M/W.

Costs (2013–14) *Tuition:* $16,076 full-time, $609 per credit hour part-time. *Required fees:* $80 full-time.

Financial Aid Of all full-time matriculated undergraduates who enrolled in 2007, 488 applied for aid, 477 were judged to have need, 14 had their need fully met. In 2007, 17 non-need-based awards were made. *Average percent of need met:* 43%. *Average financial aid package:* $14,044. *Average need-based loan:* $8002. *Average need-based gift aid:* $6480. *Average non-need-based aid:* $15,251. *Average indebtedness upon graduation:* $47,994.

Applying *Application fee:* $40. *Required:* high school transcript, interview. *Application deadlines:* rolling (freshmen), rolling (transfers). *Notification:* continuous (freshmen), continuous (transfers).

Freshman Application Contact DeVry University, 1 West Court Square, Suite 100, Decatur, GA 30030-2556. *Phone:* 404-270-2700. *Toll-free phone:* 866-338-7941.

Website: http://www.devry.edu/.

DeVry University
Duluth, Georgia

Admissions Office Contact DeVry University, 3505 Koger Boulevard, Suite 170, Duluth, GA 30096-7671. *Toll-free phone:* 866-338-7941.

Website: http://www.devry.edu/.

Emmanuel College
Franklin Springs, Georgia

- **Independent** 4-year, founded 1919, affiliated with Pentecostal Holiness Church
- **Rural** 90-acre campus with easy access to Atlanta, Georgia
- **Endowment** $3.2 million
- **Coed** 806 undergraduate students, 88% full-time, 51% women, 49% men
- **Moderately difficult** entrance level, 51% of applicants were admitted

Undergraduates 711 full-time, 95 part-time. Students come from 20 states and territories; 18 other countries; 24% are from out of state; 17% Black or African American, non-Hispanic/Latino; 4% Hispanic/Latino; 0.7% Asian, non-Hispanic/Latino; 0.6% Two or more races, non-Hispanic/Latino; 4% international; 7% transferred in; 56% live on campus. *Retention:* 67% of full-time freshmen returned.

Freshmen *Admission:* 1,144 applied, 582 admitted, 188 enrolled. *Average high school GPA:* 3.18.

Faculty *Total:* 82, 61% full-time, 40% with terminal degrees. *Student/faculty ratio:* 12:1.

Academics *Calendar:* semesters. *Degrees:* associate and bachelor's. *Special study options:* academic remediation for entering students, accelerated degree program, advanced placement credit, distance learning, honors programs, independent study, internships, part-time degree program, services for LD students, study abroad, summer session for credit.

Computers on Campus 50 computers/terminals are available on campus for general student use. Students can access the following: campus intranet, computer help desk, free student e-mail accounts, online (class) grades, online (class) registration, online (class) schedules. Campuswide network is available. 100% of college-owned or -operated housing units are wired for high-speed Internet access. Wireless service is available via entire campus.

Student Life *Housing:* on-campus residence required through sophomore year. *Options:* men-only, women-only. Campus housing is university owned. Freshman campus housing is guaranteed. *Activities and organizations:* drama/theater group, choral group, Students in Free Enterprise (SIFE), Fellowship of Christian Athletes, SOS, BSU, International Students Club. *Campus security:* 24-hour patrols. *Student services:* personal/psychological counseling.

Athletics Member NAIA, NCCAA. *Intercollegiate sports:* baseball M(s), basketball M(s)/W(s), cheerleading W(s), cross-country running M(s)/W(s), golf M(s)/W(s), lacrosse M(s)/W(s), riflery M(s)/W(s), soccer M(s)/W(s), softball W(s), tennis M(s)/W(s), track and field M(s)/W(s), volleyball M(s)/W(s). *Intramural sports:* basketball M/W, football M/W, golf M/W, soccer M/W, tennis M/W, track and field M/W, volleyball M/W, weight lifting M/W.

Standardized Tests *Required:* SAT or ACT (for admission).

Costs (2012–13) *Comprehensive fee:* $22,140 includes full-time tuition ($15,700) and room and board ($6440). Part-time tuition: $630 per credit hour. *Room and board:* Room and board charges vary according to housing facility. *Payment plan:* installment. *Waivers:* senior citizens and employees or children of employees.

Financial Aid Of all full-time matriculated undergraduates who enrolled in 2011, 626 applied for aid, 573 were judged to have need, 71 had their need fully met. 335 Federal Work-Study jobs (averaging $1921). 227 state and other part-time jobs (averaging $845). In 2011, 104 non-need-based awards were made. *Average percent of need met:* 69%. *Average financial aid package:* $13,378. *Average need-based loan:* $3621. *Average need-based gift aid:* $9457. *Average non-need-based aid:* $4616. *Average indebtedness upon graduation:* $24,268. *Financial aid deadline:* 6/15.

Applying *Options:* electronic application, early admission, deferred entrance. *Application fee:* $25. *Required:* essay or personal statement, high school transcript. *Required for some:* interview. *Application deadlines:* 8/1 (freshmen), 8/1 (transfers). *Notification:* 8/1 (freshmen), continuous until 8/1 (transfers).

Freshman Application Contact Ms. Amanda Strickland, Admissions Counselor, Emmanuel College, PO Box 129, 181 Spring Street, Franklin Springs, GA 30639-0129. *Phone:* 706-245-7226 Ext. 2907. *Toll-free phone:* 800-860-8800. *E-mail:* admissions@ec.edu.

Website: http://www.ec.edu/.

Emory University
Atlanta, Georgia

- **Independent Methodist** university, founded 1836
- **Suburban** 634-acre campus with easy access to Atlanta
- **Endowment** $5.4 billion
- **Coed**
- **Most difficult** entrance level

Faculty *Student/faculty ratio:* 7:1.

Academics *Calendar:* semesters. *Degrees:* associate, bachelor's, master's, doctoral, post-master's, and postbachelor's certificates (enrollment figures include Emory University, Oxford College; application data for main campus only).

Student Life *Campus security:* 24-hour emergency response devices and patrols, student patrols, late-night transport/escort service, controlled dormitory access.

Athletics Member NCAA. All Division III.

Standardized Tests *Required:* SAT or ACT (for admission). *Recommended:* SAT Subject Tests (for admission).

Costs (2012–13) *Comprehensive fee:* $54,980 includes full-time tuition ($42,400), mandatory fees ($580), and room and board ($12,000). Full-time tuition and fees vary according to degree level and location. Part-time tuition: $1766 per credit hour. *College room only:* $7200. Room and board charges vary according to board plan, housing facility, location, and student level.

Financial Aid *Of all full-time matriculated undergraduates who enrolled in 2011,* 3,940 applied for aid, 3,591 were judged to have need, 3,591 had their need fully met. *In 2011,* 457 non-need-based awards were made. *Average percent of need met:* 100. *Average financial aid package:* $36,807. *Average need-based loan:* $4179. *Average need-based gift aid:* $33,323. *Average non-need-based aid:* $21,821. *Average indebtedness upon graduation:* $28,076. *Financial aid deadline:* 3/1.

Applying *Options:* electronic application, early admission, early decision, deferred entrance. *Application fee:* $50. *Required:* essay or personal statement, high school transcript, 1 letter of recommendation. *Recommended:* minimum 3.0 GPA.

Freshman Application Contact Mr. John Latting, Dean of Admission, Emory University, 1390 Oxford Road NE, 3rd Floor, Atlanta, GA 30322-1100. *Phone:* 404-727-6036. *Toll-free phone:* 800-727-6036. *Fax:* 404-727-4303. *E-mail:* admiss@emory.edu. *Website:* http://www.emory.edu/.

Emory University, Oxford College
Oxford, Georgia

- **Independent Methodist** primarily 2-year, founded 1836
- **Small-town** 150-acre campus with easy access to Atlanta
- **Endowment** $39.0 million
- **Coed**
- **Very difficult** entrance level

Faculty *Student/faculty ratio:* 14:1.

Academics *Calendar:* semesters. *Degrees:* associate and bachelor's.

Student Life *Campus security:* 24-hour emergency response devices and patrols, student patrols, late-night transport/escort service, controlled dormitory access.

Athletics Member NJCAA.

Standardized Tests *Required:* SAT or ACT (for admission). *Required for some:* SAT Subject Tests (for admission).

Costs (2012–13) *Comprehensive fee:* $47,054 includes full-time tuition ($36,100), mandatory fees ($478), and room and board ($10,476). Part-time tuition: $1504 per contact hour. *College room only:* $7196.

Financial Aid *Of all full-time matriculated undergraduates who enrolled in 2011,* 225 Federal Work-Study jobs (averaging $1600).

Applying *Options:* electronic application, early admission, early action, deferred entrance. *Application fee:* $50. *Required:* essay or personal statement, high school transcript, 1 letter of recommendation. *Required for some:* interview. *Recommended:* minimum 3.0 GPA, 2 letters of recommendation.

Freshman Application Contact Emory University, Oxford College, 100 Hamill Street, PO Box 1328, Oxford, GA 30054. *Phone:* 770-784-8328. *Toll-free phone:* 800-723-8328. *Website:* http://oxford.emory.edu/.

Fort Valley State University
Fort Valley, Georgia

Freshman Application Contact Mr. Donald Moore, Director of Admissions and Recruitment, Fort Valley State University, 1005 State University Drive, Fort Valley, GA 31030. *Phone:* 478-825-6307. *Toll-free phone:* 877-462-3878. *Fax:* 478-825-6169. *E-mail:* admissap@fvsu.edu. *Website:* http://www.fvsu.edu/.

Georgia College & State University
Milledgeville, Georgia

- **State-supported** comprehensive, founded 1889, part of University System of Georgia
- **Small-town** 602-acre campus
- **Endowment** $25.3 million
- **Coed** 5,568 undergraduate students, 92% full-time, 60% women, 40% men
- **Moderately difficult** entrance level, 66% of applicants were admitted

Undergraduates 5,131 full-time, 437 part-time. Students come from 24 states and territories; 40 other countries; 1% are from out of state; 5% Black or African American, non-Hispanic/Latino; 5% Hispanic/Latino; 1% Asian, non-Hispanic/Latino; 0.1% Native Hawaiian or other Pacific Islander, non-Hispanic/Latino; 0.2% American Indian or Alaska Native, non-Hispanic/Latino; 2% Two or more races, non-Hispanic/Latino; 0.5% Race/ethnicity unknown; 1% international; 6% transferred in; 37% live on campus. *Retention:* 86% of full-time freshmen returned.

Freshmen *Admission:* 3,878 applied, 2,570 admitted, 1,311 enrolled. *Average high school GPA:* 3.4. *Test scores:* SAT critical reading scores over 500: 89%; SAT math scores over 500: 89%; ACT scores over 18: 99%; SAT critical reading scores over 600: 35%; SAT math scores over 600: 39%; ACT scores over 24: 60%; SAT critical reading scores over 700: 3%; SAT math scores over 700: 3%; ACT scores over 30: 3%.

Faculty *Total:* 446, 72% full-time. *Student/faculty ratio:* 17:1.

Academics *Calendar:* semesters. *Degrees:* bachelor's, master's, doctoral, and post-master's certificates. *Special study options:* accelerated degree program, advanced placement credit, distance learning, double majors, English as a second language, external degree program, freshman honors college, honors programs, independent study, internships, part-time degree program, services for LD students, student-designed majors, study abroad, summer session for credit. *ROTC:* Army (c). *Unusual degree programs:* 3-2 engineering with Georgia Institute of Technology.

Computers on Campus 900 computers/terminals and 6,295 ports are available on campus for general student use. Students can access the following: campus intranet, computer help desk, free student e-mail accounts, online (class) grades, online (class) registration, online (class) schedules. Campus-wide network is available. 100% of college-owned or -operated housing units are wired for high-speed Internet access. Wireless service is available via entire campus.

Student Life *Housing:* on-campus residence required for freshman year. *Options:* coed, disabled students. Campus housing is university owned and leased by the school. Freshman applicants given priority for college housing. *Activities and organizations:* drama/theater group, student-run newspaper, radio station, choral group, Alpha Lambda Delta, Campus Activities Board, Alpha Delta Pi, Zeta au Alpha Sorority, Georgia College Miracle, national fraternities, national sororities. *Campus security:* 24-hour emergency response devices and patrols, student patrols, late-night transport/escort service, controlled dormitory access. *Student services:* health clinic, personal/psychological counseling, women's center.

Athletics Member NCAA. All Division II. *Intercollegiate sports:* baseball M(s), basketball M(s)/W(s), cheerleading M/W, cross-country running M(s)/W(s), golf M(s), soccer W(s), softball W(s), tennis M(s)/W(s). *Intramural sports:* basketball M/W, football M/W, rugby M(c), soccer M(c)/W(c), softball M/W, swimming and diving M(c)/W(c), ultimate Frisbee M/W, volleyball M/W, water polo M/W.

Standardized Tests *Required:* SAT or ACT (for admission). *Required for some:* SAT Subject Tests (for admission).

Costs (2012–13) *Tuition:* state resident $6634 full-time; nonresident $24,098 full-time. Full-time tuition and fees vary according to course load, location, and program. Part-time tuition and fees vary according to course load, location, and program. *Required fees:* $1984 full-time; $992 per term part-time. *Room and board:* $9268; room only: $5268. Room and board charges vary according to board plan, housing facility, and location. *Payment plan:* installment. *Waivers:* senior citizens and employees or children of employees.

Financial Aid Of all full-time matriculated undergraduates who enrolled in 2011, 4,800 applied for aid, 2,702 were judged to have need. In 2011, 52 non-need-based awards were made. *Average financial aid package:* $7418. *Average need-based loan:* $3299. *Average need-based gift aid:* $4424. *Average non-need-based aid:* $1325. *Average indebtedness upon graduation:* $18,985.

Applying *Options:* electronic application, early admission, early action, deferred entrance. *Application fee:* $40. *Required:* essay or personal statement, proof of immunization. *Required for some:* high school transcript. *Application deadlines:* 4/1 (freshmen), 4/1 (out-of-state freshmen), 7/1 (transfers), 11/1 (early action). *Notification:* continuous (freshmen), continuous (out-of-state freshmen), continuous (transfers), 12/1 (early action).

Freshman Application Contact Ms. Suzanne Pittman, Assistant Vice President for Enrollment Management, Georgia College & State University,

CPO Box 023, Milledgeville, GA 31061. *Phone:* 478-445-6283. *Toll-free phone:* 800-342-0471. *Fax:* 478-445-1336. *E-mail:* admissions@gcsu.edu. *Website:* http://www.gcsu.edu/.

Georgia Gwinnett College

Lawrenceville, Georgia

- **State-supported** 4-year, part of University System of Georgia
- **Suburban** 260-acre campus with easy access to Atlanta
- **Coed** 9,397 undergraduate students, 71% full-time, 53% women, 47% men
- **91%** of applicants were admitted

Undergraduates 6,648 full-time, 2,749 part-time. Students come from 26 states and territories; 92 other countries; 1% are from out of state; 30% Black or African American, non-Hispanic/Latino; 12% Hispanic/Latino; 8% Asian, non-Hispanic/Latino; 0.2% Native Hawaiian or other Pacific Islander, non-Hispanic/Latino; 0.2% American Indian or Alaska Native, non-Hispanic/Latino; 3% Two or more races, non-Hispanic/Latino; 2% Race/ethnicity unknown; 1% international; 9% transferred in; 8% live on campus. *Retention:* 60% of full-time freshmen returned.

Freshmen *Admission:* 4,593 applied, 4,167 admitted, 2,399 enrolled. *Average high school GPA:* 2.7. *Test scores:* SAT critical reading scores over 500: 37%; SAT math scores over 500: 38%; ACT scores over 18: 67%; SAT critical reading scores over 600: 7%; SAT math scores over 600: 9%; ACT scores over 24: 13%; SAT critical reading scores over 700: 1%; SAT math scores over 700: 1%; ACT scores over 30: 1%.

Faculty *Total:* 562, 61% full-time, 72% with terminal degrees. *Student/faculty ratio:* 20:1.

Academics *Degree:* bachelor's. *Special study options:* advanced placement credit, English as a second language, internships, services for LD students, summer session for credit. *ROTC:* Army (b).

Computers on Campus 243 computers/terminals are available on campus for general student use. Students can access the following: campus intranet, computer help desk, free student e-mail accounts, online (class) grades, online (class) registration, online (class) schedules. Campuswide network is available. 100% of college-owned or -operated housing units are wired for high-speed Internet access. Wireless service is available via entire campus.

Student Life *Housing options:* coed. Campus housing is university owned. *Campus security:* 24-hour emergency response devices and patrols. *Student services:* personal/psychological counseling.

Athletics Member NAIA. *Intercollegiate sports:* baseball M, soccer M/W, softball W, tennis M/W.

Standardized Tests *Recommended:* SAT or ACT (for admission).

Costs (2012–13) *Tuition:* state resident $3378 full-time, $113 per credit hour part-time; nonresident $12,604 full-time, $420 per credit hour part-time. No tuition increase for student's term of enrollment. *Required fees:* $1704 full-time, $1704 per year part-time. *Room and board:* $12,350; room only: $9650. Room and board charges vary according to board plan. *Payment plans:* installment, deferred payment. *Waivers:* senior citizens and employees or children of employees.

Applying *Options:* electronic application. *Application fee:* $20. *Required:* high school transcript, minimum 2.0 GPA. *Application deadlines:* 6/1 (freshmen), 6/1 (out-of-state freshmen), rolling (transfers).

Freshman Application Contact Admissions Office, Georgia Gwinnett College, 1000 University Center Lane, Lawrenceville, GA 60043. *Phone:* 678-407-5313. *Toll-free phone:* 877-704-4422. *E-mail:* ggcadmissions@ggc.edu. *Website:* http://www.ggc.edu/.

Georgia Institute of Technology

Atlanta, Georgia

- **State-supported** university, founded 1885, part of University System of Georgia
- **Urban** 400-acre campus
- **Endowment** $1.6 billion
- **Coed**
- **Very difficult** entrance level

Faculty *Student/faculty ratio:* 17:1.

Academics *Calendar:* semesters. *Degrees:* bachelor's, master's, and doctoral.

Student Life *Campus security:* 24-hour emergency response devices and patrols, late-night transport/escort service, controlled dormitory access, self defense education, lighted pathways and walks, video cameras, email and phone alerts of emergency situations.

Athletics Member NCAA. All Division I except football (Division I-A).

Standardized Tests *Required:* SAT or ACT (for admission).

Costs (2012–13) *Tuition:* state resident $7718 full-time, $2293 per term part-time; nonresident $27,022 full-time, $8017 per term part-time. Part-time tuition and fees vary according to course load. *Required fees:* $2380 full-time,

$1190 per term part-time, $1190 per term part-time. *Room and board:* $9236; room only: $5574. Room and board charges vary according to board plan and housing facility.

Financial Aid *Of all full-time matriculated undergraduates who enrolled in 2010,* 8,131 applied for aid, 5,553 were judged to have need, 1,757 had their need fully met. 369 Federal Work-Study jobs (averaging $1739). *In 2010,* 674 non-need-based awards were made. *Average percent of need met:* 58. *Average financial aid package:* $11,529. *Average need-based loan:* $5066. *Average need-based gift aid:* $10,049. *Average non-need-based aid:* $4221. *Average indebtedness upon graduation:* $23,427. *Financial aid deadline:* 3/1.

Applying *Options:* electronic application, early admission, early action. *Application fee:* $65. *Required:* essay or personal statement, high school transcript.

Freshman Application Contact Mr. Rick A. Clark Jr., Director of Undergraduate Admissions, Georgia Institute of Technology, Office of Undergraduate Admission, Atlanta, GA 30332-0320. *Phone:* 404-894-4154. *Fax:* 404-894-9511. *E-mail:* admission@gatech.edu. *Website:* http://www.gatech.edu/.

Georgia Regents University

Augusta, Georgia

- **State-supported** comprehensive, founded 1828, part of University System of Georgia
- **Urban** 650-acre campus
- **Coed**

Academics *Calendar:* semesters. *Degrees:* associate, bachelor's, master's, doctoral, post-master's, and postbachelor's certificates. *Special study options:* academic remediation for entering students, adult/continuing education programs, advanced placement credit, cooperative education, distance learning, double majors, honors programs, independent study, internships, off-campus study, services for LD students, study abroad, summer session for credit. *ROTC:* Army (b).

Computers on Campus Students can access the following: campus intranet, computer help desk, free student e-mail accounts, online (class) grades, online (class) registration, online (class) schedules. Campuswide network is available. 100% of college-owned or -operated housing units are wired for high-speed Internet access. Wireless service is available via classrooms, computer centers, computer labs, dorm rooms, learning centers, libraries, student centers.

Student Life *Housing options:* coed. Campus housing is university owned. *Activities and organizations:* drama/theater group, student-run newspaper, choral group, Student Government Association, national fraternities, national sororities. *Campus security:* 24-hour emergency response devices and patrols, late-night transport/escort service. *Student services:* health clinic, personal/psychological counseling.

Athletics Member NCAA. All Division II except men's and women's golf (Division I). *Intercollegiate sports:* baseball M(s), basketball M(s)/W(s), cross-country running M(s)/W(s), golf M(s)/W(s), softball W(s), tennis M(s)/W(s), track and field M/W. *Intramural sports:* badminton M/W, basketball M/W, football M/W, racquetball M/W, soccer M/W, softball M/W, table tennis M/W, volleyball M/W.

Costs (2012–13) *Tuition:* state resident $7434 full-time, $249 per credit hour part-time; nonresident $26,130 full-time, $871 per credit hour part-time. Full-time tuition and fees vary according to course load, location, and program. Part-time tuition and fees vary according to course load, location, and program. *Required fees:* $1646 full-time. *Room only:* $2308. *Waivers:* employees or children of employees.

Financial Aid Of all full-time matriculated undergraduates who enrolled in 2011, 300 applied for aid, 300 were judged to have need, 266 had their need fully met. In 2011, 2 non-need-based awards were made. *Average financial aid package:* $13,059. *Average need-based loan:* $4258. *Average need-based gift aid:* $3122. *Average non-need-based aid:* $1506.

Applying *Options:* electronic application. *Application fee:* $50.

Freshman Application Contact Georgia Regents University, 1120 15th Street, Augusta, GA 30912. *Phone:* 706-737-1632. *Toll-free phone:* 800-519-3388.

Website: http://www.gru.edu/.

Georgia Southern University

Statesboro, Georgia

- **State-supported** university, founded 1906, part of University System of Georgia
- **Small-town** 900-acre campus
- **Endowment** $36.0 million
- **Coed** 17,993 undergraduate students, 88% full-time, 50% women, 50% men
- **Moderately difficult** entrance level, 52% of applicants were admitted

Undergraduates 15,818 full-time, 2,175 part-time. Students come from 50 states and territories; 69 other countries; 4% are from out of state; 25% Black or African American, non-Hispanic/Latino; 4% Hispanic/Latino; 1% Asian, non-Hispanic/Latino; 0.2% Native Hawaiian or other Pacific Islander, non-Hispanic/Latino; 0.6% American Indian or Alaska Native, non-Hispanic/Latino; 2% Two or more races, non-Hispanic/Latino; 1% Race/ethnicity unknown; 1% international; 6% transferred in; 28% live on campus. *Retention:* 77% of full-time freshmen returned.

Freshmen *Admission:* 10,525 applied, 5,473 admitted, 3,604 enrolled. *Average high school GPA:* 3.21. *Test scores:* SAT critical reading scores over 500: 87%; SAT math scores over 500: 87%; SAT writing scores over 500: 70%; ACT scores over 18: 99%; SAT critical reading scores over 600: 22%; SAT math scores over 600: 27%; SAT writing scores over 600: 15%; ACT scores over 24: 39%; SAT critical reading scores over 700: 2%; SAT math scores over 700: 2%; SAT writing scores over 700: 1%; ACT scores over 30: 3%.

Faculty *Total:* 884, 86% full-time, 76% with terminal degrees. *Student/faculty ratio:* 22:1.

Academics *Calendar:* semesters. *Degrees:* bachelor's, master's, doctoral, post-master's, and postbachelor's certificates. *Special study options:* academic remediation for entering students, accelerated degree program, adult/continuing education programs, advanced placement credit, cooperative education, distance learning, double majors, English as a second language, honors programs, independent study, internships, off-campus study, part-time degree program, services for LD students, student-designed majors, study abroad, summer session for credit. *ROTC:* Army (b). *Unusual degree programs:* 3-2 engineering with Georgia Institute of Technology; Bachelor's/Graduate in Accounting and Nursing.

Computers on Campus 3,320 computers/terminals and 5,200 ports are available on campus for general student use. Students can access the following: campus intranet, computer help desk, free student e-mail accounts, online (class) grades, online (class) registration, online (class) schedules, online degree audit, online career services, and online healthcare. Campuswide network is available. 100% of college-owned or -operated housing units are wired for high-speed Internet access. Wireless service is available via entire campus.

Student Life *Housing:* on-campus residence required for freshman year. *Options:* coed, disabled students. Campus housing is university owned. Freshman applicants given priority for college housing. *Activities and organizations:* drama/theater group, student-run newspaper, radio station, choral group, marching band, Residence Hall Association, Campus Religious Ministries, Student Government Association, Club Sports and Recreation, Greek Life, national fraternities, national sororities. *Campus security:* 24-hour emergency response devices and patrols, student patrols, late-night transport/escort service, controlled dormitory access, bike police and environmental safety services. *Student services:* health clinic, personal/psychological counseling, women's center, legal services.

Athletics Member NCAA. All Division I. *Intercollegiate sports:* baseball M(s), basketball M(s)/W(s), cheerleading M/W, cross-country running W(s), football M(s), golf M(s), soccer M(s)/W(s), softball W(s), swimming and diving W(s), tennis M(s)/W(s), track and field W(s), volleyball W(s). *Intramural sports:* baseball M(c), basketball M/W, bowling M/W, cross-country running M(c)/W(c), equestrian sports M(c)/W(c), fencing M(c)/W(c), football M/W, golf M/W, racquetball M/W, rugby M(c)/W(c), soccer M/W, softball M/W, swimming and diving M/W, table tennis M/W, tennis M/W, volleyball M/W, weight lifting M/W, wrestling M(c).

Standardized Tests *Required:* SAT or ACT (for admission).

Costs (2012–13) *Tuition:* state resident $4852 full-time, $162 per credit hour part-time; nonresident $17,128 full-time, $571 per credit hour part-time. Full-time tuition and fees vary according to degree level, location, and program. Part-time tuition and fees vary according to course load, degree level, location, and program. *Required fees:* $1872 full-time, $936 per term part-time. *Room and board:* $9290; room only: $5582. Room and board charges vary according to board plan and housing facility. *Waivers:* senior citizens and employees or children of employees.

Financial Aid Of all full-time matriculated undergraduates who enrolled in 2011, 13,935 applied for aid, 10,502 were judged to have need, 778 had their need fully met. 216 Federal Work-Study jobs (averaging $1849). In 2011, 280 non-need-based awards were made. *Average percent of need met:* 49%. *Average financial aid package:* $8598. *Average need-based loan:* $4296. *Average need-based gift aid:* $5876. *Average non-need-based aid:* $1867. *Average indebtedness upon graduation:* $21,562.

Applying *Options:* electronic application, early admission, deferred entrance. *Application fee:* $30. *Required:* minimum 2.0 GPA, proof of immunization prior to enrollment. *Required for some:* high school transcript. *Application deadlines:* 5/1 (freshmen), 5/1 (out-of-state freshmen), 8/1 (transfers). *Notification:* continuous (freshmen), continuous (out-of-state freshmen), continuous (transfers).

Freshman Application Contact Mrs. Sarah Smith, Director, Georgia Southern University, PO Box 8024, Statesboro, GA 30460. *Phone:* 912-478-5391. *Fax:* 912-478-7240. *E-mail:* admissions@georgiasouthern.edu. *Website:* http://www.georgiasouthern.edu/.

Georgia Southwestern State University
Americus, Georgia

- **State-supported** comprehensive, founded 1906, part of University System of Georgia
- **Small-town** 400-acre campus
- **Endowment** $345,315
- **Coed** 2,749 undergraduate students, 72% full-time, 64% women, 36% men
- **Moderately difficult** entrance level, 66% of applicants were admitted

Undergraduates 1,982 full-time, 767 part-time. Students come from 25 states and territories; 38 other countries; 3% are from out of state; 30% Black or African American, non-Hispanic/Latino; 2% Hispanic/Latino; 1% Asian, non-Hispanic/Latino; 0.1% Native Hawaiian or other Pacific Islander, non-Hispanic/Latino; 0.2% American Indian or Alaska Native, non-Hispanic/Latino; 1% Two or more races, non-Hispanic/Latino; 0.3% Race/ethnicity unknown; 3% international; 12% transferred in; 29% live on campus. *Retention:* 63% of full-time freshmen returned.

Freshmen *Admission:* 1,308 applied, 868 admitted, 400 enrolled. *Average high school GPA:* 3.2. *Test scores:* SAT critical reading scores over 500: 40%; SAT math scores over 500: 40%; SAT writing scores over 500: 37%; ACT scores over 18: 85%; SAT critical reading scores over 600: 8%; SAT math scores over 600: 10%; SAT writing scores over 600: 5%; ACT scores over 24: 15%; SAT critical reading scores over 700: 1%.

Faculty *Total:* 169, 66% full-time, 56% with terminal degrees. *Student/faculty ratio:* 19:1.

Academics *Calendar:* semesters. *Degrees:* bachelor's, master's, post-master's, and postbachelor's certificates. *Special study options:* academic remediation for entering students, accelerated degree program, advanced placement credit, distance learning, double majors, English as a second language, honors programs, internships, off-campus study, part-time degree program, services for LD students, study abroad, summer session for credit. *Unusual degree programs:* 3-2 engineering with Georgia Institute of Technology.

Computers on Campus 250 computers/terminals are available on campus for general student use. Students can access the following: free student e-mail accounts, online (class) grades, online (class) registration, online (class) schedules. Campuswide network is available. Wireless service is available via dorm rooms.

Student Life *Housing:* on-campus residence required through sophomore year. *Options:* coed. Campus housing is university owned. Freshman campus housing is guaranteed. *Activities and organizations:* drama/theater group, student-run newspaper, choral group, SUAVE—Strong United Assertive Virtuous Educated, BOLD—Beautiful Outstanding Ladies of Distinction, Residence Hall Association, Baptist Collegiate Ministries, national fraternities, national sororities. *Campus security:* 24-hour emergency response devices and patrols, late-night transport/escort service, controlled dormitory access. *Student services:* health clinic, personal/psychological counseling.

Athletics Member NCAA. All Division II. *Intercollegiate sports:* baseball M(s), basketball M(s)/W(s), cross-country running W(s), golf M(s), soccer M(s)/W(s), softball W(s), tennis M(s)/W(s). *Intramural sports:* badminton M/W, basketball M/W, football M/W, golf M/W, racquetball M/W, softball M/W, table tennis M/W, tennis M/W, ultimate Frisbee M/W, volleyball M/W, weight lifting M/W.

Standardized Tests *Required:* SAT or ACT (for admission).

Costs (2012–13) *Tuition:* state resident $4512 full-time; nonresident $16,416 full-time. Full-time tuition and fees vary according to course load. Part-time tuition and fees vary according to course load. *Required fees:* $1268 full-time. *Room and board:* $7378; room only: $4620. Room and board charges vary according to board plan and housing facility.

Financial Aid Of all full-time matriculated undergraduates who enrolled in 2009, 1,563 applied for aid, 1,300 were judged to have need, 270 had their need fully met. 58 Federal Work-Study jobs (averaging $1493). In 2009, 114 non-need-based awards were made. *Average percent of need met:* 56%. *Average financial aid package:* $7655. *Average need-based loan:* $3914. *Average need-based gift aid:* $4475. *Average non-need-based aid:* $1886. *Average indebtedness upon graduation:* $20,505.

Applying *Options:* electronic application, early admission, early decision, deferred entrance. *Application fee:* $25. *Required:* high school transcript, minimum 2.0 GPA, proof of immunization; SAT or ACT scores. *Recommended:* interview. *Application deadlines:* 7/21 (freshmen), 7/21 (transfers). *Early deci-*

sion deadline: 12/15. *Notification:* continuous (freshmen), continuous (transfers), 1/15 (early decision).

Freshman Application Contact Mr. David Jenkins, Assistant Director of Admissions, Georgia Southwestern State University, Americus, GA 31709. *Phone:* 229-928-1273. *Toll-free phone:* 800-338-0082. *Fax:* 229-931-2983. *E-mail:* gswapps@canes.gsw.edu.
Website: http://www.gsw.edu/.

Georgia State University
Atlanta, Georgia

- **State-supported** university, founded 1913, part of University System of Georgia
- **Urban** 67-acre campus with easy access to Atlanta
- **Endowment** $112.1 million
- **Coed** 24,665 undergraduate students, 73% full-time, 59% women, 41% men
- **Moderately difficult** entrance level, 57% of applicants were admitted

Undergraduates 18,060 full-time, 6,605 part-time. Students come from 57 states and territories; 152 other countries; 3% are from out of state; 39% Black or African American, non-Hispanic/Latino; 8% Hispanic/Latino; 11% Asian, non-Hispanic/Latino; 0.1% Native Hawaiian or other Pacific Islander, non-Hispanic/Latino; 0.2% American Indian or Alaska Native, non-Hispanic/Latino; 4% Two or more races, non-Hispanic/Latino; 2% Race/ethnicity unknown; 2% international; 11% transferred in; 17% live on campus. *Retention:* 83% of full-time freshmen returned.
Freshmen *Admission:* 12,774 applied, 7,333 admitted, 3,201 enrolled. *Average high school GPA:* 3.33. *Test scores:* SAT critical reading scores over 500: 70%; SAT math scores over 500: 71%; ACT scores over 18: 97%; SAT critical reading scores over 600: 21%; SAT math scores over 600: 23%; ACT scores over 24: 38%; SAT critical reading scores over 700: 2%; SAT math scores over 700: 3%; ACT scores over 30: 4%.
Faculty *Total:* 1,658, 71% full-time, 75% with terminal degrees. *Student/faculty ratio:* 21:1.
Academics *Calendar:* semesters. *Degrees:* certificates, bachelor's, master's, doctoral, post-master's, and postbachelor's certificates. *Special study options:* advanced placement credit, cooperative education, distance learning, double majors, English as a second language, honors programs, independent study, internships, part-time degree program, services for LD students, study abroad, summer session for credit. *ROTC:* Army (b), Navy (c), Air Force (c). *Unusual degree programs:* 3-2 business administration.
Computers on Campus 685 computers/terminals and 14,095 ports are available on campus for general student use. Students can access the following: computer help desk, free student e-mail accounts, online (class) grades, online (class) registration, online (class) schedules. Campuswide network is available. 100% of college-owned or -operated housing units are wired for high-speed Internet access. Wireless service is available via entire campus.
Student Life *Housing options:* coed, disabled students. Campus housing is university owned and leased by the school. Freshman applicants given priority for college housing. *Activities and organizations:* drama/theater group, student-run newspaper, radio and television station, choral group, marching band, Spotlight Programs Board, Greek Organizations, International Student Associations Council, Academic Clubs, Sports Clubs, national fraternities, national sororities. *Campus security:* 24-hour emergency response devices and patrols, late-night transport/escort service, controlled dormitory access, Emergency Notification Center. *Student services:* health clinic, personal/psychological counseling.
Athletics Member NCAA. All Division I. *Intercollegiate sports:* baseball M(s), basketball M(s)/W(s), cheerleading M/W, crew M(c)/W(c), cross-country running M(s)/W(s), equestrian sports M(c)/W(c), football M(s), golf M(s)/W(s), ice hockey M(c), lacrosse M(c), rugby M(c)/W(c), soccer M(s)/W(s), softball W(s), squash M(c)/W(c), swimming and diving M(c)/W(c), table tennis M(c)/W(c), tennis M(s)/W(s), track and field M(s)/W(s), ultimate Frisbee M(c)/W(c), volleyball W(s). *Intramural sports:* badminton M(c)/W(c), basketball M/W, bowling M/W, football M/W, golf M/W, racquetball M/W, rock climbing M(c)/W(c), soccer M/W, softball M/W, ultimate Frisbee M/W, volleyball M/W, water polo M/W, weight lifting M/W, wrestling M(c)/W(c).
Standardized Tests *Required:* SAT or ACT (for admission).
Costs (2012–13) *Tuition:* state resident $7536 full-time, $251 per credit hour part-time; nonresident $25,746 full-time, $858 per credit hour part-time. Part-time tuition and fees vary according to course load. *Required fees:* $2128 full-time, $1064 per term part-time. *Room and board:* $11,546; room only: $7956. Room and board charges vary according to housing facility. *Waivers:* senior citizens and employees or children of employees.
Financial Aid Of all full-time matriculated undergraduates who enrolled in 2011, 15,048 applied for aid, 13,250 were judged to have need, 459 had their

need fully met. In 2011, 623 non-need-based awards were made. *Average percent of need met:* 61%. *Average financial aid package:* $9815. *Average need-based loan:* $4317. *Average need-based gift aid:* $4413. *Average non-need-based aid:* $1129. *Average indebtedness upon graduation:* $21,817. *Financial aid deadline:* 4/1.
Applying *Options:* electronic application, early admission, early action, deferred entrance. *Application fee:* $60. *Required:* high school transcript, minimum 2.8 GPA, college preparatory curriculum as specified by the University System of Georgia Board of Regents. Combined SAT of 830. Freshman Index of 2500 or higher. *Application deadlines:* 3/1 (freshmen), 6/1 (transfers), 11/1 (early action). *Notification:* 5/1 (freshmen), continuous (transfers), 1/30 (early action).
Freshman Application Contact Scott Burke, Director of Admissions, Georgia State University, PO Box 4009, Atlanta, GA 30302-4009. *Phone:* 404-413-2500. *Fax:* 404-413-2002. *E-mail:* onestopshop@gsu.edu.
Website: http://www.gsu.edu/.

Gordon State College
Barnesville, Georgia

- **State-supported** primarily 2-year, founded 1852, part of University System of Georgia
- **Small-town** 125-acre campus with easy access to Atlanta
- **Endowment** $7.5 million
- **Coed** 4,171 undergraduate students
- **Minimally difficult** entrance level, 43% of applicants were admitted

Undergraduates Students come from 9 states and territories; 1 other country; 0.1% are from out of state.
Freshmen *Admission:* 2,871 applied, 1,222 admitted.
Faculty *Total:* 207, 60% full-time, 52% with terminal degrees. *Student/faculty ratio:* 24:1.
Academics *Calendar:* semesters. *Degrees:* certificates, associate, and bachelor's. *Special study options:* academic remediation for entering students, accelerated degree program, adult/continuing education programs, advanced placement credit, cooperative education, honors programs, internships, off-campus study, part-time degree program, study abroad, summer session for credit.
Computers on Campus 466 computers/terminals and 1,000 ports are available on campus for general student use. Students can access the following: campus intranet, computer help desk, free student e-mail accounts, online (class) grades, online (class) registration, online (class) schedules. Campuswide network is available. 100% of college-owned or -operated housing units are wired for high-speed Internet access. Wireless service is available via entire campus.
Student Life *Housing:* on-campus residence required for freshman year. *Options:* coed. Campus housing is university owned. Freshman applicants given priority for college housing. *Activities and organizations:* drama/theater group, student-run newspaper, choral group, Campus Activity Board, Student Government Association, Earth wind fire (Science Club), Student African American Brotherhood (SAAB), Swazi Step Team. *Campus security:* 24-hour emergency response devices and patrols, student patrols, late-night transport/escort service, controlled dormitory access, RA's and RDs (housing) and Parking Patrol (Public Safety). *Student services:* health clinic, personal/psychological counseling.
Athletics Member NJCAA. *Intercollegiate sports:* baseball M, basketball M, soccer M/W, softball W, track and field M/W.
Financial Aid Of all full-time matriculated undergraduates who enrolled in 2011, 75 Federal Work-Study jobs (averaging $1850).
Applying *Options:* electronic application, early admission, deferred entrance. *Application fee:* $20. *Required:* high school transcript. *Application deadlines:* rolling (freshmen), rolling (transfers).
Freshman Application Contact Gordon State College, 419 College Drive, Barnesville, GA 30204-1762. *Phone:* 678-359-5021. *Toll-free phone:* 800-282-6504.
Website: http://www.gordonstate.edu/.

Herzing University
Atlanta, Georgia

Freshman Application Contact Miss Anissa Elder, Director of Admissions, Herzing University, 3393 Peachtree Road, NE, Suite 1003, Atlanta, GA 30326. *Phone:* 404-816-4533. *Toll-free phone:* 800-596-0724. *Fax:* 404-816-5576. *E-mail:* aelder@atl.herzing.edu.
Website: http://www.herzing.edu/atlanta/.

ITT Technical Institute

Atlanta, Georgia

- **Proprietary** primarily 2-year, part of ITT Educational Services, Inc.
- **Coed**
- **Minimally difficult** entrance level

Academics *Degrees:* associate and bachelor's.

Freshman Application Contact Director of Recruitment, ITT Technical Institute, 485 Oak Place, Suite 800, Atlanta, GA 30349. *Phone:* 404-765-4600. *Toll-free phone:* 877-488-6102 (in-state); 877-788-6102 (out-of-state). *Website:* http://www.itt-tech.edu/.

ITT Technical Institute

Duluth, Georgia

- **Proprietary** primarily 2-year, founded 2003, part of ITT Educational Services, Inc.
- **Coed**
- **Minimally difficult** entrance level

Academics *Calendar:* quarters. *Degrees:* associate and bachelor's.

Freshman Application Contact Director of Recruitment, ITT Technical Institute, 10700 Abbotts Bridge Road, Duluth, GA 30097. *Phone:* 678-957-8510. *Toll-free phone:* 866-489-8818. *Website:* http://www.itt-tech.edu/.

ITT Technical Institute

Kennesaw, Georgia

- **Proprietary** primarily 2-year, founded 2004, part of ITT Educational Services, Inc.
- **Coed**
- **Minimally difficult** entrance level

Academics *Calendar:* quarters. *Degrees:* associate and bachelor's.

Freshman Application Contact Director of Recruitment, ITT Technical Institute, 2065 ITT Tech Way NW, Kennesaw, GA 30144. *Phone:* 770-426-2300. *Toll-free phone:* 877-231-6415 (in-state); 800-231-6415 (out-of-state). *Website:* http://www.itt-tech.edu/.

Kennesaw State University

Kennesaw, Georgia

- **State-supported** comprehensive, founded 1963, part of University System of Georgia
- **Suburban** 384-acre campus with easy access to Atlanta
- **Endowment** $24.8 million
- **Coed** 22,684 undergraduate students, 75% full-time, 58% women, 42% men
- **Moderately difficult** entrance level, 57% of applicants were admitted

Undergraduates 16,954 full-time, 5,730 part-time. 6% are from out of state; 16% Black or African American, non-Hispanic/Latino; 7% Hispanic/Latino; 3% Asian, non-Hispanic/Latino; 0.1% Native Hawaiian or other Pacific Islander, non-Hispanic/Latino; 0.2% American Indian or Alaska Native, non-Hispanic/Latino; 3% Two or more races, non-Hispanic/Latino; 4% Race/ethnicity unknown; 2% international; 14% live on campus. *Retention:* 76% of full-time freshmen returned.

Freshmen *Admission:* 9,471 applied, 5,355 admitted, 3,088 enrolled. *Average high school GPA:* 3.2. *Test scores:* SAT critical reading scores over 500: 81%; SAT math scores over 500: 75%; SAT writing scores over 500: 62%; ACT scores over 18: 99%; SAT critical reading scores over 600: 21%; SAT math scores over 600: 20%; SAT writing scores over 600: 13%; ACT scores over 24: 33%; SAT critical reading scores over 700: 2%; SAT math scores over 700: 2%; ACT scores over 30: 2%.

Faculty *Total:* 1,356, 55% full-time, 57% with terminal degrees. *Student/faculty ratio:* 21:1.

Academics *Calendar:* semesters. *Degrees:* certificates, bachelor's, master's, doctoral, post-master's, and postbachelor's certificates. *Special study options:* adult/continuing education programs, advanced placement credit, cooperative education, distance learning, double majors, English as a second language, honors programs, internships, off-campus study, part-time degree program, services for LD students, study abroad, summer session for credit. *ROTC:* Army (c), Air Force (c).

Computers on Campus 1,650 computers/terminals and 12,000 ports are available on campus for general student use. Students can access the following: campus intranet, computer help desk, free student e-mail accounts, online (class) grades, online (class) registration, online (class) schedules. Campus-wide network is available. 100% of college-owned or -operated housing units are wired for high-speed Internet access. Wireless service is available via

classrooms, computer centers, computer labs, dorm rooms, learning centers, libraries, student centers.

Student Life *Housing options:* coed, disabled students. Campus housing is provided by a third party. Freshman applicants given priority for college housing. *Activities and organizations:* drama/theater group, student-run newspaper, radio station, choral group, Global Society, Student Government Association, Kennesaw Activities Board, African-American Student Alliance, International Student Association, national fraternities, national sororities. *Campus security:* 24-hour emergency response devices and patrols, student patrols, late-night transport/escort service, controlled dormitory access. *Student services:* health clinic, personal/psychological counseling.

Athletics Member NCAA. All Division I. *Intercollegiate sports:* baseball M(s), basketball M(s)/W(s), cheerleading W(c), cross-country running M(s)/W(s), golf M(s)/W(s), soccer W(s), softball W(s), tennis M(s)/W(s), track and field M(s)/W(s), ultimate Frisbee M(c), volleyball W(s). *Intramural sports:* archery M(c)/W(c), badminton M(c)/W(c), baseball M(c), basketball M, cross-country running M(c)/W(c), equestrian sports M(c)/W(c), fencing M(c)/W(c), football M/W, golf M/W, gymnastics M(c)/W(c), ice hockey M(c), lacrosse M(c)/W(c), rugby M(c)/W(c), soccer M(c)/W(c), softball M/W, swimming and diving M(c)/W(c), tennis M/W, ultimate Frisbee M/W, volleyball M/W, weight lifting M(c)/W(c), wrestling M(c).

Standardized Tests *Required:* SAT or ACT (for admission).

Costs (2012–13) *Tuition:* state resident $4852 full-time, $162 per credit hour part-time; nonresident $17,128 full-time, $571 per credit hour part-time. Part-time tuition and fees vary according to course load. *Required fees:* $1634 full-time, $817 per term part-time. *Room and board:* $7966. Room and board charges vary according to board plan and housing facility. *Waivers:* senior citizens and employees or children of employees.

Financial Aid Of all full-time matriculated undergraduates who enrolled in 2012, 13,937 applied for aid, 11,804 were judged to have need, 1,941 had their need fully met. 200 Federal Work-Study jobs (averaging $2557). In 2012, 80 non-need-based awards were made. *Average percent of need met:* 65%. *Average financial aid package:* $7309. *Average need-based loan:* $3293. *Average need-based gift aid:* $6121. *Average non-need-based aid:* $1295. *Average indebtedness upon graduation:* $20,666.

Applying *Options:* electronic application, early admission, deferred entrance. *Application fee:* $40. *Required:* high school transcript, minimum 2.5 GPA, proof of immunization. *Application deadlines:* 5/10 (freshmen), 6/21 (transfers). *Notification:* continuous (freshmen), continuous (transfers).

Freshman Application Contact Admissions Office, Kennesaw State University, 1000 Chastain Road, Campus Box #0115, Kennesaw, GA 30144-5591. *Phone:* 770-423-6300. *Fax:* 770-420-4435. *E-mail:* ksuadmit@kennesaw.edu. *Website:* http://www.kennesaw.edu/.

LaGrange College

LaGrange, Georgia

- **Independent United Methodist** comprehensive, founded 1831
- **Small-town** 120-acre campus with easy access to Atlanta
- **Endowment** $52.5 million
- **Coed** 834 undergraduate students, 99% full-time, 57% women, 43% men
- **Moderately difficult** entrance level, 49% of applicants were admitted

Undergraduates 823 full-time, 11 part-time. Students come from 17 states and territories; 10 other countries; 15% are from out of state; 23% Black or African American, non-Hispanic/Latino; 3% Hispanic/Latino; 1% Asian, non-Hispanic/Latino; 0.5% American Indian or Alaska Native, non-Hispanic/Latino; 2% Two or more races, non-Hispanic/Latino; 0.4% Race/ethnicity unknown; 1% international; 10% transferred in; 64% live on campus. *Retention:* 60% of full-time freshmen returned.

Freshmen *Admission:* 1,288 applied, 632 admitted, 198 enrolled. *Average high school GPA:* 3.34. *Test scores:* SAT critical reading scores over 500: 53%; SAT math scores over 500: 52%; ACT scores over 18: 95%; SAT critical reading scores over 600: 12%; SAT math scores over 600: 15%; ACT scores over 24: 32%; SAT critical reading scores over 700: 1%; SAT math scores over 700: 1%; ACT scores over 30: 1%.

Faculty *Total:* 109, 64% full-time, 55% with terminal degrees. *Student/faculty ratio:* 10:1.

Academics *Calendar:* 4-1-4. *Degrees:* certificates, bachelor's, and master's. *Special study options:* accelerated degree program, adult/continuing education programs, advanced placement credit, double majors, independent study, internships, part-time degree program, services for LD students, student-designed majors, study abroad, summer session for credit. *Unusual degree programs:* 3-2 engineering with Georgia Institute of Technology, Auburn University.

Computers on Campus 175 computers/terminals and 960 ports are available on campus for general student use. Students can access the following: campus intranet, free student e-mail accounts, online (class) grades, online (class) registration, online (class) schedules. Campuswide network is available. 100% of college-owned or -operated housing units are wired for high-speed Internet access. Wireless service is available via entire campus.

Student Life *Housing:* on-campus residence required through senior year. *Options:* coed, men-only, women-only. Campus housing is university owned. Freshman campus housing is guaranteed. *Activities and organizations:* drama/theater group, student-run newspaper, choral group, Student Government Association, Greek Life, Baptist Collegiate Ministries, Wesley Fellowship, Fellowship of Christian Athletes, national fraternities, national sororities. *Campus security:* 24-hour patrols, controlled dormitory access, A mass notification system, called e2Campus, allows the college to automatically send emergency messages to students and employees. *Student services:* health clinic, personal/psychological counseling.

Athletics Member NCAA. All Division III. *Intercollegiate sports:* baseball M, basketball M/W, cheerleading W, cross-country running M/W, football M, golf M, lacrosse W, soccer M/W, softball W, swimming and diving M/W, tennis M/W, volleyball W. *Intramural sports:* basketball M/W, softball M/W, table tennis M/W, water polo M/W.

Standardized Tests *Required:* SAT or ACT (for admission).

Costs (2012–13) *Comprehensive fee:* $34,640 includes full-time tuition ($24,302), mandatory fees ($160), and room and board ($10,178). Full-time tuition and fees vary according to class time, course load, degree level, and program. Part-time tuition: $1000 per semester hour. Part-time tuition and fees vary according to class time, course load, degree level, and program. *College room only:* $5816. Room and board charges vary according to board plan and housing facility. *Payment plan:* installment. *Waivers:* senior citizens and employees or children of employees.

Applying *Options:* electronic application, early admission, early action, deferred entrance. *Application fee:* $30. *Required:* essay or personal statement, high school transcript, SAT or ACT. *Required for some:* minimum 2.5 GPA, 1 letter of recommendation, interview. *Application deadlines:* rolling (freshmen), rolling (transfers), 12/31 (early action). *Notification:* continuous (freshmen), continuous (transfers).

Freshman Application Contact Mr. Michael Thomas, Director of Admission, LaGrange College, 601 Broad Street, LaGrange, GA 30240-2999. *Phone:* 706-880-8217. *Toll-free phone:* 800-593-2885. *Fax:* 706-880-8010. *E-mail:* mthomas@lagrange.edu.
Website: http://www.lagrange.edu/.

Life University
Marietta, Georgia
- **Independent** comprehensive, founded 1974
- **Suburban** 96-acre campus
- **Coed** 843 undergraduate students, 71% full-time, 49% women, 51% men
- **Minimally difficult** entrance level, 75% of applicants were admitted

Undergraduates 598 full-time, 245 part-time. Students come from 52 states and territories; 39 other countries; 54% are from out of state; 32% Black or African American, non-Hispanic/Latino; 8% Hispanic/Latino; 3% Asian, non-Hispanic/Latino; 1% American Indian or Alaska Native, non-Hispanic/Latino; 6% Race/ethnicity unknown; 4% international; 15% transferred in. *Retention:* 70% of full-time freshmen returned.
Freshmen *Admission:* 809 applied, 603 admitted, 39 enrolled.
Faculty *Total:* 181, 70% full-time, 73% with terminal degrees. *Student/faculty ratio:* 17:1.
Academics *Calendar:* quarters. *Degrees:* associate, bachelor's, master's, and doctoral. *Special study options:* academic remediation for entering students, accelerated degree program, advanced placement credit, double majors, English as a second language, independent study, internships, off-campus study, services for LD students, summer session for credit.
Computers on Campus Students can access the following: campus intranet, free student e-mail accounts, online (class) grades, online (class) registration. Campuswide network is available. 100% of college-owned or -operated housing units are wired for high-speed Internet access. Wireless service is available via classrooms, computer centers, computer labs, learning centers, libraries.
Student Life *Housing options:* Campus housing is university owned. *Activities and organizations:* student-run newspaper. *Campus security:* 24-hour emergency response devices and patrols, controlled dormitory access. *Student services:* health clinic.
Athletics Member NAIA. *Intramural sports:* basketball M/W, football M, rugby M, softball M/W, volleyball M/W.
Standardized Tests *Required:* SAT or ACT (for admission).
Costs (2012–13) *Comprehensive fee:* $24,832 includes full-time tuition ($11,231), mandatory fees ($747), and room and board ($12,854). Full-time tuition and fees vary according to course load. Part-time tuition: $191 per credit hour. Part-time tuition and fees vary according to course load. *Required fees:* $249 per term part-time. *Payment plan:* installment. *Waivers:* employees or children of employees.

Financial Aid Of all full-time matriculated undergraduates who enrolled in 2012, 459 applied for aid, 440 were judged to have need. 125 Federal Work-Study jobs (averaging $2000). *Average percent of need met:* 32%. *Average financial aid package:* $10,500. *Average need-based loan:* $5300. *Average need-based gift aid:* $5300. *Average indebtedness upon graduation:* $31,000.
Applying *Options:* electronic application. *Application fee:* $50. *Required:* high school transcript, minimum 2.0 GPA. *Application deadline:* 9/1 (freshmen). *Notification:* continuous (freshmen), continuous (transfers).
Freshman Application Contact Mr. Brian Gipson, Office of New Student Development, Life University, 1269 Barclay Circle, Marietta, GA 30060. *Phone:* 800-543-3202. *Toll-free phone:* 800-543-3202. *Fax:* 770-426-2895. *E-mail:* admissions@life.edu.
Website: http://www.life.edu/.

Luther Rice University
Lithonia, Georgia
- **Independent Baptist** comprehensive, founded 1962
- **Urban** 5-acre campus with easy access to Atlanta
- **Coed** 600 undergraduate students
- **Noncompetitive** entrance level, 81% of applicants were admitted

Undergraduates 31% are from out of state.
Freshmen *Admission:* 360 applied, 292 admitted.
Academics *Calendar:* semesters. *Degrees:* bachelor's and master's. *Special study options:* academic remediation for entering students, adult/continuing education programs, advanced placement credit, cooperative education, distance learning, external degree program, independent study, internships, part-time degree program, study abroad.
Student Life *Housing:* college housing not available. *Campus security:* 24-hour emergency response devices, late-night transport/escort service. *Student services:* personal/psychological counseling.
Standardized Tests *Required:* Bible examination (for admission).
Costs (2013–14) *Tuition:* $5352 full-time.
Financial Aid Of all full-time matriculated undergraduates who enrolled in 2009, 64 applied for aid, 64 were judged to have need, 50 had their need fully met. 3 Federal Work-Study jobs (averaging $6985). *Average percent of need met:* 95%. *Average financial aid package:* $6902. *Average need-based loan:* $4102. *Average need-based gift aid:* $5195. *Average indebtedness upon graduation:* $50,400.
Applying *Options:* electronic application, early admission. *Application fee:* $50. *Required:* high school transcript. *Application deadlines:* rolling (freshmen), rolling (transfers).
Freshman Application Contact Mr. Steve Pray, Admissions Counselor, Luther Rice University, 3038 Evans Mill Road, Lithonia, GA 30038-2454. *Phone:* 770-484-1204. *Toll-free phone:* 800-442-1577. *E-mail:* admissions@lru.edu.
Website: http://www.lru.edu/.

Mercer University
Macon, Georgia
- **Independent Baptist** university, founded 1833
- **Suburban** 150-acre campus with easy access to Atlanta
- **Endowment** $191.7 million
- **Coed** 2,382 undergraduate students, 97% full-time, 49% women, 51% men
- **Moderately difficult** entrance level, 63% of applicants were admitted

Undergraduates 2,318 full-time, 64 part-time. Students come from 41 states and territories; 37 other countries; 16% are from out of state; 19% Black or African American, non-Hispanic/Latino; 4% Hispanic/Latino; 7% Asian, non-Hispanic/Latino; 0.3% American Indian or Alaska Native, non-Hispanic/Latino; 2% Two or more races, non-Hispanic/Latino; 4% Race/ethnicity unknown; 4% international; 4% transferred in; 67% live on campus. *Retention:* 82% of full-time freshmen returned.
Freshmen *Admission:* 3,519 applied, 2,219 admitted, 645 enrolled. *Average high school GPA:* 3.67. *Test scores:* SAT critical reading scores over 500: 91%; SAT math scores over 500: 97%; SAT writing scores over 500: 80%; ACT scores over 18: 99%; SAT critical reading scores over 600: 41%; SAT math scores over 600: 50%; SAT writing scores over 600: 32%; ACT scores over 24: 74%; SAT critical reading scores over 700: 8%; SAT math scores over 700: 9%; SAT writing scores over 700: 6%; ACT scores over 30: 16%.
Faculty *Total:* 685, 54% full-time, 73% with terminal degrees. *Student/faculty ratio:* 13:1.
Academics *Calendar:* semesters. *Degrees:* bachelor's, master's, doctoral, and post-master's certificates. *Special study options:* accelerated degree program, adult/continuing education programs, advanced placement credit, cooperative education, distance learning, double majors, English as a second language, honors programs, independent study, internships, off-campus study, part-time

degree program, services for LD students, student-designed majors, study abroad, summer session for credit. *ROTC:* Army (b). *Unusual degree programs:* pharmacy, physical therapy, physicians assistant.

Computers on Campus Students can access the following: campus intranet, computer help desk, free student e-mail accounts, online (class) grades, online (class) registration, online (class) schedules. Campuswide network is available. 100% of college-owned or -operated housing units are wired for high-speed Internet access. Wireless service is available via entire campus.

Student Life *Housing:* on-campus residence required through sophomore year. *Options:* coed, men-only, women-only, disabled students. Campus housing is university owned. Freshman campus housing is guaranteed. *Activities and organizations:* drama/theater group, student-run newspaper, radio and television station, choral group, marching band, national fraternities, national sororities. *Campus security:* 24-hour emergency response devices and patrols, student patrols, late-night transport/escort service, controlled dormitory access, patrols by police officers. *Student services:* health clinic, personal/psychological counseling.

Athletics Member NCAA. All Division I. *Intercollegiate sports:* baseball M(s), basketball M(s)/W(s), cross-country running M(s)/W(s), football M, golf M(s)/W(s), lacrosse M(s)/W(c), soccer M(s)/W(s), softball W(s), tennis M(s)/W(s), track and field W, volleyball W(s). *Intramural sports:* basketball M/W, bowling M/W, equestrian sports W(c), football M/W, golf M/W, soccer M/W, softball M/W, tennis M/W, ultimate Frisbee W, volleyball M/W, wrestling M(c).

Standardized Tests *Required:* SAT or ACT (for admission).

Costs (2012–13) *Comprehensive fee:* $43,163 includes full-time tuition ($32,166), mandatory fees ($300), and room and board ($10,697). Full-time tuition and fees vary according to class time and location. Part-time tuition: $1072 per credit hour. Part-time tuition and fees vary according to class time, course load, and location. *Required fees:* $10 per credit hour part-time. *College room only:* $5244. Room and board charges vary according to board plan, housing facility, and location. *Payment plan:* installment. *Waivers:* employees or children of employees.

Financial Aid Of all full-time matriculated undergraduates who enrolled in 2012, 2,297 applied for aid, 1,683 were judged to have need, 435 had their need fully met. In 2012, 579 non-need-based awards were made. *Average percent of need met:* 79%. *Average financial aid package:* $29,373. *Average need-based loan:* $6074. *Average need-based gift aid:* $23,528. *Average non-need-based aid:* $18,895. *Average indebtedness upon graduation:* $31,488.

Applying *Options:* electronic application, early admission, early action, deferred entrance. *Application fee:* $50. *Required:* high school transcript, minimum 3.0 GPA. *Required for some:* 2 letters of recommendation, interview. *Recommended:* interview, counselor's evaluation. *Application deadlines:* 7/1 (freshmen), rolling (transfers), 11/1 (early action). *Notification:* continuous (freshmen), continuous (transfers), 11/15 (early action).

Freshman Application Contact Ms. Alejandra Sosa, Director of Freshman Admissions, Mercer University, 1400 Coleman Avenue, Macon, GA 31207-0003. *Phone:* 478-301-5125. *Toll-free phone:* 800-MERCER-U. *E-mail:* sosa_ac@mercer.edu.
Website: http://www.mercer.edu/.

Middle Georgia State College
Cochran, Georgia

Freshman Application Contact Ms. Jennifer Brannon, Director of Admissions, Middle Georgia State College, 1100 2nd Street, Southeast, Cochran, GA 31014. *Phone:* 478-934-3103. *Fax:* 478-934-3403. *E-mail:* admissions@mgc.edu.
Website: http://www.mgc.edu/.

Morehouse College
Atlanta, Georgia

- **Independent** 4-year, founded 1867
- **Urban** 61-acre campus
- **Endowment** $129.4 million
- **Men only** 2,377 undergraduate students, 93% full-time
- **Moderately difficult** entrance level, 66% of applicants were admitted

Undergraduates 2,221 full-time, 156 part-time. Students come from 44 states and territories; 14 other countries; 71% are from out of state; 96% Black or African American, non-Hispanic/Latino; 0.2% Hispanic/Latino; 2% Race/ethnicity unknown; 2% international; 3% transferred in; 96% live on campus. *Retention:* 80% of full-time freshmen returned.

Freshmen *Admission:* 2,576 applied, 1,711 admitted, 570 enrolled. *Average high school GPA:* 3.24. *Test scores:* SAT critical reading scores over 500: 56%; SAT math scores over 500: 60%; SAT writing scores over 500: 44%; ACT scores over 18: 83%; SAT critical reading scores over 600: 15%; SAT math scores over 600: 18%; SAT writing scores over 600: 12%; ACT scores over 24:

27%; SAT critical reading scores over 700: 2%; SAT math scores over 700: 1%; SAT writing scores over 700: 1%; ACT scores over 30: 3%.
Faculty *Total:* 223, 74% full-time, 74% with terminal degrees. *Student/faculty ratio:* 12:1.

Academics *Calendar:* semesters. *Degree:* bachelor's. *Special study options:* academic remediation for entering students, advanced placement credit, cooperative education, double majors, honors programs, internships, off-campus study, part-time degree program, services for LD students, study abroad, summer session for credit. *ROTC:* Army (b), Navy (b), Air Force (b). *Unusual degree programs:* 3-2 engineering with Georgia Tech, Boston Univ., Auburn Univ., Rensselaer Polytechnic Univ., Rochester Institute of Technology, Columbia Univ., Dartmouth College, North Carolina A&T State Univ., Univ. of Florida, Univ. of Missouri-Rolla. Univ. of Michigan.

Computers on Campus 500 computers/terminals are available on campus for general student use. Students can access the following: campus intranet, computer help desk, free student e-mail accounts, online (class) grades, online (class) registration, online (class) schedules. Campuswide network is available. 100% of college-owned or -operated housing units are wired for high-speed Internet access. Wireless service is available via entire campus.

Student Life *Housing:* on-campus residence required for freshman year. *Options:* men-only. Campus housing is university owned. Freshman campus housing is guaranteed. *Activities and organizations:* drama/theater group, student-run newspaper, choral group, marching band, Morehouse College Glee Club, Morehouse Business Association, NAACP, Morehouse Public Health Association, Pre-Law Society, national fraternities. *Campus security:* 24-hour emergency response devices and patrols, late-night transport/escort service, controlled dormitory access. *Student services:* health clinic, personal/psychological counseling.

Athletics Member NCAA. All Division II. *Intercollegiate sports:* baseball M(s), basketball M(s), cross-country running M(s), football M(s), golf M(s), tennis M(s), track and field M(s). *Intramural sports:* baseball M, basketball M, football M, golf M, soccer M, softball M, swimming and diving M, table tennis M, tennis M, weight lifting M.

Standardized Tests *Required:* SAT or ACT (for admission).

Costs (2012–13) *Comprehensive fee:* $37,416 includes full-time tuition ($22,482), mandatory fees ($2262), and room and board ($12,672). Full-time tuition and fees vary according to course load and student level. Part-time tuition and fees vary according to course load. *College room only:* $7220. Room and board charges vary according to board plan. *Waivers:* employees or children of employees.

Financial Aid Of all full-time matriculated undergraduates who enrolled in 2012, 2,359 applied for aid, 2,359 were judged to have need, 183 had their need fully met. *Average percent of need met:* 25%. *Average financial aid package:* $15,450. *Average need-based loan:* $5500. *Average need-based gift aid:* $7050. *Financial aid deadline:* 4/1.

Applying *Options:* electronic application, early admission, early decision, early action, deferred entrance. *Application fee:* $50. *Required:* essay or personal statement, high school transcript. *Recommended:* minimum 3.0 GPA, interview. *Application deadlines:* 2/15 (freshmen), 2/15 (transfers), 11/1 (early action). *Early decision deadline:* 11/1. *Notification:* 4/1 (freshmen), 4/1 (transfers), 12/15 (early decision), 12/15 (early action).

Freshman Application Contact Morehouse College, 830 Westview Drive, SW, Atlanta, GA 30314. *Phone:* 404-215-2632. *Toll-free phone:* 800-851-1254.
Website: http://www.morehouse.edu/.

Oglethorpe University
Atlanta, Georgia

- **Independent** comprehensive, founded 1835
- **Suburban** 102-acre campus with easy access to Atlanta
- **Endowment** $17.4 million
- **Coed** 1,053 undergraduate students, 92% full-time, 59% women, 41% men
- **Very difficult** entrance level, 83% of applicants were admitted

Undergraduates 971 full-time, 82 part-time. Students come from 32 states and territories; 27 other countries; 29% are from out of state; 21% Black or African American, non-Hispanic/Latino; 8% Hispanic/Latino; 3% Asian, non-Hispanic/Latino; 0.1% Native Hawaiian or other Pacific Islander, non-Hispanic/Latino; 0.2% American Indian or Alaska Native, non-Hispanic/Latino; 2% Two or more races, non-Hispanic/Latino; 25% Race/ethnicity unknown; 5% international; 4% transferred in; 57% live on campus. *Retention:* 80% of full-time freshmen returned.

Freshmen *Admission:* 2,463 applied, 2,036 admitted, 277 enrolled. *Average high school GPA:* 3.44. *Test scores:* SAT critical reading scores over 500: 93%; SAT math scores over 500: 84%; SAT writing scores over 500: 78%; ACT scores over 18: 100%; SAT critical reading scores over 600: 36%; SAT math scores over 600: 32%; SAT writing scores over 600: 27%; ACT scores over 24:

58%; SAT critical reading scores over 700: 4%; SAT math scores over 700: 4%; SAT writing scores over 700: 4%; ACT scores over 30: 6%.
Faculty *Total:* 116, 47% full-time, 65% with terminal degrees. *Student/faculty ratio:* 13:1.
Academics *Calendar:* semesters. *Degrees:* bachelor's and master's. *Special study options:* accelerated degree program, adult/continuing education programs, advanced placement credit, cooperative education, double majors, honors programs, independent study, internships, off-campus study, part-time degree program, services for LD students, student-designed majors, study abroad, summer session for credit. *ROTC:* Air Force (c). *Unusual degree programs:* 3-2 engineering with Auburn University, Georgia Institute of Technology, University of Florida, University of Southern California.
Computers on Campus Students can access the following: campus intranet, computer help desk, free student e-mail accounts, online (class) grades, online (class) registration, online (class) schedules. Campuswide network is available. 100% of college-owned or -operated housing units are wired for high-speed Internet access. Wireless service is available via classrooms, computer centers, computer labs, learning centers, libraries, student centers.
Student Life *Housing:* on-campus residence required through sophomore year. *Options:* coed. Campus housing is university owned. Freshman campus housing is guaranteed. *Activities and organizations:* drama/theater group, student-run newspaper, radio station, choral group, national fraternities, national sororities. *Campus security:* 24-hour emergency response devices and patrols, late-night transport/escort service, controlled dormitory access. *Student services:* health clinic, personal/psychological counseling.
Athletics Member NCAA. All Division III. *Intercollegiate sports:* baseball M, basketball M/W, cross-country running M/W, golf M/W, lacrosse M/W, soccer M/W, tennis M/W, track and field M/W, volleyball W. *Intramural sports:* badminton M/W, basketball M/W, football M/W, softball M/W, table tennis M/W, ultimate Frisbee M/W, volleyball M/W.
Standardized Tests *Required:* SAT or ACT (for admission).
Costs (2013–14) *Comprehensive fee:* $42,580 includes full-time tuition ($31,000), mandatory fees ($280), and room and board ($11,300). Full-time tuition and fees vary according to degree level. Part-time tuition: $1260 per credit hour. Part-time tuition and fees vary according to class time, course load, and degree level. *Room and board:* Room and board charges vary according to housing facility and location. *Payment plans:* tuition prepayment, installment. *Waivers:* employees or children of employees.
Financial Aid Of all full-time matriculated undergraduates who enrolled in 2012, 872 applied for aid, 809 were judged to have need, 90 had their need fully met. In 2012, 252 non-need-based awards were made. *Average percent of need met:* 72%. *Average financial aid package:* $27,081. *Average need-based loan:* $4146. *Average need-based gift aid:* $21,498. *Average non-need-based aid:* $15,442. *Average indebtedness upon graduation:* $22,692.
Applying *Options:* electronic application, early admission, early action, deferred entrance. *Application fee:* $40. *Required:* essay or personal statement, high school transcript, 1 letter of recommendation. *Required for some:* interview. *Recommended:* minimum 2.5 GPA, interview. *Application deadlines:* rolling (freshmen), rolling (transfers), 12/5 (early action). *Notification:* continuous (freshmen), continuous (transfers), 12/20 (early action).
Freshman Application Contact Ms. Lucy Leusch, Vice President for Enrollment and Financial Aid, Oglethorpe University, 4484 Peachtree Road, NE, Atlanta, GA 30319. *Phone:* 404-364-8307. *Toll-free phone:* 800-428-4484. *Fax:* 404-364-8491. *E-mail:* admission@oglethorpe.edu. *Website:* http://www.oglethorpe.edu/.

Paine College
Augusta, Georgia
- **Independent** Methodist 4-year, founded 1882
- **Urban** 65-acre campus with easy access to Atlanta
- **Endowment** $8.1 million
- **Coed** 837 undergraduate students, 91% full-time, 62% women, 38% men
- **Minimally difficult** entrance level, 78% of applicants were admitted

Undergraduates 765 full-time, 72 part-time. Students come from 28 states and territories; 5 other countries; 25% are from out of state; 91% Black or African American, non-Hispanic/Latino; 1% Hispanic/Latino; 0.4% Asian, non-Hispanic/Latino; 0.2% Native Hawaiian or other Pacific Islander, non-Hispanic/Latino; 0.1% American Indian or Alaska Native, non-Hispanic/Latino; 1% Two or more races, non-Hispanic/Latino; 2% Race/ethnicity unknown; 2% international; 7% transferred in; 48% live on campus. *Retention:* 52% of full-time freshmen returned.
Freshmen *Admission:* 2,142 applied, 1,666 admitted, 176 enrolled. *Average high school GPA:* 2.6. *Test scores:* SAT critical reading scores over 500: 10%; SAT math scores over 500: 5%; SAT writing scores over 500: 7%; ACT scores over 18: 33%; SAT critical reading scores over 600: 2%; SAT writing scores over 600: 2%.

Faculty *Total:* 79, 67% full-time, 59% with terminal degrees. *Student/faculty ratio:* 13:1.
Academics *Calendar:* semesters. *Degree:* bachelor's. *Special study options:* academic remediation for entering students, accelerated degree program, advanced placement credit, distance learning, double majors, honors programs, independent study, internships, off-campus study, part-time degree program, services for LD students, study abroad, summer session for credit. *ROTC:* Army (c). *Unusual degree programs:* 3-2 engineering with Tuskegee University.
Computers on Campus 130 computers/terminals and 696 ports are available on campus for general student use. Students can access the following: campus intranet, computer help desk, free student e-mail accounts, online (class) grades, online (class) registration, online (class) schedules. Campuswide network is available. 100% of college-owned or -operated housing units are wired for high-speed Internet access. Wireless service is available via entire campus.
Student Life *Housing options:* men-only, women-only. Campus housing is university owned. Freshman applicants given priority for college housing. *Activities and organizations:* drama/theater group, student-run newspaper, choral group, Wesley Fellowship, Alpha Kappa Mu National Honor Society, Pre-Alumni Council, Honda All-Stars, Creme de la Creme Models, national fraternities, national sororities. *Campus security:* 24-hour emergency response devices and patrols, late-night transport/escort service. *Student services:* health clinic, personal/psychological counseling.
Athletics Member NCAA. All Division II. *Intercollegiate sports:* baseball M(s), basketball M(s)/W(s), cross-country running M(s)/W(s), golf M(s), softball W(s), track and field M(s)/W(s), volleyball W(s). *Intramural sports:* baseball M, basketball M/W, cheerleading M/W, football M, soccer M/W, softball M/W, table tennis M/W, tennis M/W, track and field M/W, volleyball M/W, weight lifting M/W.
Standardized Tests *Required:* SAT or ACT (for admission).
Costs (2012–13) *Comprehensive fee:* $18,594 includes full-time tuition ($11,550), mandatory fees ($952), and room and board ($6092). Full-time tuition and fees vary according to course load, location, and reciprocity agreements. Part-time tuition: $481 per semester hour. Part-time tuition and fees vary according to course load, location, and reciprocity agreements. *Room and board:* Room and board charges vary according to housing facility. *Payment plans:* installment, deferred payment. *Waivers:* children of alumni and employees or children of employees.
Financial Aid *Average indebtedness upon graduation:* $2304.
Applying *Options:* electronic application, early admission, deferred entrance. *Application fee:* $35. *Required:* essay or personal statement, high school transcript, minimum 2.0 GPA, 3 letters of recommendation. *Required for some:* score of 500 on each Georgia high school exit exam. *Application deadlines:* 7/1 (freshmen), 7/1 (out-of-state freshmen), 7/1 (transfers). *Notification:* continuous (freshmen), continuous (out-of-state freshmen), continuous (transfers).
Freshman Application Contact Mr. Marshall Rainey, Director of Admissions, Paine College, 1235 15th Street, Augusta, GA 30901-3182. *Phone:* 706-821-8320. *Toll-free phone:* 800-476-7703. *Fax:* 706-821-8691. *E-mail:* mrainey@paine.edu. *Website:* http://www.paine.edu/.

Piedmont College
Demorest, Georgia
- **Independent** comprehensive, founded 1897, affiliated with United Church of Christ
- **Rural** 186-acre campus with easy access to Atlanta
- **Endowment** $49.7 million
- **Coed** 1,294 undergraduate students, 87% full-time, 68% women, 32% men
- **Moderately difficult** entrance level, 56% of applicants were admitted

Undergraduates 1,127 full-time, 167 part-time. Students come from 21 states and territories; 7 other countries; 6% are from out of state; 10% Black or African American, non-Hispanic/Latino; 3% Hispanic/Latino; 1% Asian, non-Hispanic/Latino; 0.1% Native Hawaiian or other Pacific Islander, non-Hispanic/Latino; 0.5% American Indian or Alaska Native, non-Hispanic/Latino; 0.6% Two or more races, non-Hispanic/Latino; 3% Race/ethnicity unknown; 0.2% international; 9% transferred in; 45% live on campus. *Retention:* 75% of full-time freshmen returned.
Freshmen *Admission:* 901 applied, 509 admitted, 210 enrolled. *Average high school GPA:* 3.49. *Test scores:* SAT critical reading scores over 500: 57%; SAT math scores over 500: 58%; ACT scores over 18: 96%; SAT critical reading scores over 600: 18%; SAT math scores over 600: 22%; ACT scores over 24: 38%; SAT critical reading scores over 700: 3%; SAT math scores over 700: 3%; ACT scores over 30: 9%.
Faculty *Total:* 245, 46% full-time, 70% with terminal degrees. *Student/faculty ratio:* 16:1.

Academics *Calendar:* semesters. *Degrees:* bachelor's, master's, doctoral, and post-master's certificates. *Special study options:* accelerated degree program, adult/continuing education programs, advanced placement credit, cooperative education, distance learning, double majors, honors programs, independent study, internships, off-campus study, part-time degree program, services for LD students, student-designed majors, study abroad, summer session for credit. *Unusual degree programs:* 3-2 engineering with Georgia Institute of Technology; Engineering Physics (Primarily for Mechanical Engineering).
Computers on Campus 150 computers/terminals are available on campus for general student use. Students can access the following: free student e-mail accounts, online (class) grades, online (class) schedules. Campuswide network is available. Wireless service is available via classrooms, computer centers, computer labs, dorm rooms, learning centers, libraries, student centers.
Student Life *Housing:* on-campus residence required through sophomore year. *Options:* coed, men-only, women-only, disabled students. Campus housing is university owned. Freshman campus housing is guaranteed. *Activities and organizations:* drama/theater group, student-run newspaper, radio and television station, choral group, Campus Activity Board, Residence Hall Council, Outdoor Club, Team Piedmont, Alpha PSI Omega. *Campus security:* 24-hour emergency response devices and patrols, late-night transport/escort service. *Student services:* personal/psychological counseling.
Athletics Member NCAA. All Division III. *Intercollegiate sports:* baseball M, basketball M/W, cross-country running M/W, golf M/W, lacrosse M/W, soccer M/W, softball W, tennis M/W, volleyball W. *Intramural sports:* cheerleading W.
Standardized Tests *Required:* SAT or ACT (for admission).
Costs (2013–14) *Comprehensive fee:* $29,260 includes full-time tuition ($20,730) and room and board ($8530). Full-time tuition and fees vary according to course load, degree level, location, and program. Part-time tuition: $864 per credit. Part-time tuition and fees vary according to course load, degree level, location, and program. *College room only:* $4744. *Payment plan:* installment. *Waivers:* employees or children of employees.
Financial Aid Of all full-time matriculated undergraduates who enrolled in 2012, 1,026 applied for aid, 946 were judged to have need, 140 had their need fully met. 82 Federal Work-Study jobs (averaging $1966). 316 state and other part-time jobs (averaging $1910). In 2012, 127 non-need-based awards were made. *Average percent of need met:* 70%. *Average financial aid package:* $17,250. *Average need-based loan:* $4486. *Average need-based gift aid:* $12,208. *Average non-need-based aid:* $10,628. *Average indebtedness upon graduation:* $18,129.
Applying *Options:* electronic application, early admission, deferred entrance. *Required:* high school transcript, minimum 2.0 GPA. *Required for some:* interview. *Recommended:* essay or personal statement. *Application deadlines:* 7/1 (freshmen), 7/1 (transfers).
Freshman Application Contact Ms. Brenda Boonstra, Director of Undergraduate Admissions, Piedmont College, PO Box 10, 165 Central Avenue, Demorest, GA 30535. *Phone:* 706-776-0103 Ext. 1188. *Toll-free phone:* 800-277-7020. *Fax:* 706-776-6635. *E-mail:* bboonstra@piedmont.edu. *Website:* http://www.piedmont.edu/.

Point University

East Point, Georgia

- **Independent Christian** 4-year, founded 1937
- **Small-town** 52-acre campus with easy access to Atlanta, Georgia
- **Coed** 1,483 undergraduate students, 88% full-time, 58% women, 42% men
- **Moderately difficult** entrance level, 56% of applicants were admitted

Undergraduates 1,306 full-time, 177 part-time. 16% are from out of state; 59% Black or African American, non-Hispanic/Latino; 3% Hispanic/Latino; 0.5% Asian, non-Hispanic/Latino; 0.2% Native Hawaiian or other Pacific Islander, non-Hispanic/Latino; 0.1% American Indian or Alaska Native, non-Hispanic/Latino; 0.4% Two or more races, non-Hispanic/Latino; 3% Race/ethnicity unknown; 13% transferred in; 75% live on campus. *Retention:* 50% of full-time freshmen returned.
Freshmen *Admission:* 721 applied, 405 admitted, 254 enrolled. *Average high school GPA:* 3.15. *Test scores:* SAT critical reading scores over 500: 32%; SAT math scores over 500: 25%; ACT scores over 18: 73%; SAT critical reading scores over 600: 10%; SAT math scores over 600: 6%; ACT scores over 24: 11%; SAT critical reading scores over 700: 2%; ACT scores over 30: 1%.
Faculty *Total:* 129, 24% full-time, 28% with terminal degrees. *Student/faculty ratio:* 22:1.
Academics *Calendar:* semesters. *Degrees:* associate and bachelor's. *Special study options:* academic remediation for entering students, accelerated degree program, adult/continuing education programs, advanced placement credit, cooperative education, distance learning, double majors, independent study, internships, part-time degree program, services for LD students, study abroad, summer session for credit.

Computers on Campus 115 computers/terminals are available on campus for general student use. Students can access the following: campus intranet, computer help desk, free student e-mail accounts, online (class) grades, online (class) registration, online (class) schedules. Campuswide network is available. 100% of college-owned and -operated housing units are wired for high-speed Internet access. Wireless service is available via entire campus.
Student Life *Housing:* on-campus residence required through sophomore year. *Options:* men-only, women-only. Campus housing is leased by the school. Freshman applicants given priority for college housing. *Activities and organizations:* drama/theater group, student-run newspaper, choral group, Student Government Association, Global Mission Conference, Campus Life Ministers, Student Transition Team, Sunday Night Live. *Campus security:* 24-hour patrols, student patrols. *Student services:* health clinic, personal/psychological counseling.
Athletics Member NAIA, NCCAA. *Intercollegiate sports:* baseball M(s), basketball M(s)/W(s), cheerleading W(s), cross-country running M(s)/W(s), football M(s)(c), golf M(s)/W(s), lacrosse M(s), soccer M(s)/W(s), softball W(s), tennis M(s)/W(s), volleyball W(s). *Intramural sports:* basketball W, table tennis M/W, ultimate Frisbee M/W, volleyball M/W, weight lifting M/W.
Standardized Tests *Required:* SAT or ACT (for admission).
Applying *Options:* electronic application, early admission, deferred entrance. *Application fee:* $25. *Required:* high school transcript, minimum 2.0 GPA, 1 letter of recommendation, SAT or ACT for some, COMPASS for some, college transcript if applicable. *Required for some:* essay or personal statement, interview. *Application deadlines:* 8/5 (freshmen), 8/5 (out-of-state freshmen), 8/5 (transfers). *Notification:* continuous (freshmen), continuous (out-of-state freshmen), continuous (transfers).
Freshman Application Contact Ms. Tiffany Wood, Director of Admission, Point University, 507 West 10th Street, West Point, GA 31833. *Phone:* 706-385-1019. *Toll-free phone:* 855-37-POINT. *Fax:* 706-645-9473. *E-mail:* admissions@point.edu.
Website: http://point.edu/.

Reinhardt University

Waleska, Georgia

- **Independent** comprehensive, founded 1883, affiliated with United Methodist Church
- **Rural** 600-acre campus with easy access to Atlanta
- **Endowment** $41.5 million
- **Coed**
- **Moderately difficult** entrance level

Faculty *Student/faculty ratio:* 12:1.
Academics *Calendar:* semesters. *Degrees:* associate, bachelor's, and master's.
Student Life *Campus security:* 24-hour emergency response devices and patrols, late-night transport/escort service, controlled dormitory access.
Athletics Member NAIA.
Standardized Tests *Required:* SAT or ACT (for admission).
Costs (2012–13) *Comprehensive fee:* $25,248 includes full-time tuition ($17,950), mandatory fees ($340), and room and board ($6958). Full-time tuition and fees vary according to location and program. Part-time tuition: $598 per credit hour. Part-time tuition and fees vary according to course load, location, and program. *Required fees:* $85 per term part-time. *Room and board:* Room and board charges vary according to board plan and housing facility.
Financial Aid Of all full-time matriculated undergraduates who enrolled in 2009, 1,601 applied for aid, 1,382 were judged to have need, 56 had their need fully met. In 2009, 235 non-need-based awards were made. *Average percent of need met:* 27. *Average financial aid package:* $9523. *Average need-based loan:* $3631. *Average need-based gift aid:* $7417. *Average non-need-based aid:* $4221. *Average indebtedness upon graduation:* $21,096.
Applying *Options:* electronic application, early admission, deferred entrance. *Application fee:* $25. *Required:* high school transcript, minimum 2.0 GPA.
Freshman Application Contact Ms. Julie Fleming, Director of Admissions, Reinhardt University, 7300 Reinhardt College Circle, Waleska, GA 30183-0128. *Phone:* 770-720-5526. *Fax:* 770-720-5602. *E-mail:* admissions@mail.reinhardt.edu.
Website: http://www.reinhardt.edu/.

Savannah College of Art and Design

Savannah, Georgia

- **Independent** comprehensive, founded 1978
- **Urban** campus
- **Coed** 9,182 undergraduate students, 84% full-time, 64% women, 36% men
- **Moderately difficult** entrance level, 62% of applicants were admitted

Undergraduates 7,754 full-time, 1,428 part-time. Students come from 54 states and territories; 101 other countries; 77% are from out of state; 9% Black or African American, non-Hispanic/Latino; 6% Hispanic/Latino; 5% Asian, non-Hispanic/Latino; 0.2% Native Hawaiian or other Pacific Islander, non-Hispanic/Latino; 0.5% American Indian or Alaska Native, non-Hispanic/Latino; 0.2% Two or more races, non-Hispanic/Latino; 17% Race/ethnicity unknown; 11% international; 7% transferred in; 41% live on campus. *Retention:* 81% of full-time freshmen returned.

Freshmen *Admission:* 8,977 applied, 5,535 admitted, 1,794 enrolled. *Average high school GPA:* 3.46. *Test scores:* SAT critical reading scores over 500: 63%; SAT math scores over 500: 58%; SAT writing scores over 500: 57%; ACT scores over 18: 90%; SAT critical reading scores over 600: 24%; SAT math scores over 600: 18%; SAT writing scores over 600: 19%; ACT scores over 24: 45%; SAT critical reading scores over 700: 4%; SAT math scores over 700: 2%; SAT writing scores over 700: 2%; ACT scores over 30: 7%.

Faculty *Total:* 657, 79% full-time, 72% with terminal degrees. *Student/faculty ratio:* 18:1.

Academics *Calendar:* quarters. *Degrees:* certificates, bachelor's, master's, and postbachelor's certificates. *Special study options:* advanced placement credit, distance learning, double majors, English as a second language, independent study, internships, off-campus study, part-time degree program, services for LD students, study abroad, summer session for credit. *ROTC:* Army (c).

Computers on Campus 3,400 computers/terminals are available on campus for general student use. Students can access the following: campus intranet, computer help desk, free student e-mail accounts, online (class) grades, online (class) registration, online (class) schedules. Campuswide network is available. 100% of college-owned or -operated housing units are wired for high-speed Internet access. Wireless service is available via entire campus.

Student Life *Housing options:* coed, women-only, disabled students. Campus housing is university owned and leased by the school. Freshman applicants given priority for college housing. *Activities and organizations:* drama/theater group, student-run newspaper, radio station, choral group, Gamers' Guild, Contemporary Animation Society, Circus Club, Expressions Dance Club, Queers and Allies. *Campus security:* 24-hour emergency response devices and patrols, student patrols, late-night transport/escort service, controlled dormitory access, Video camera surveillance. *Student services:* health clinic, personal/psychological counseling.

Athletics Member NAIA. *Intercollegiate sports:* cross-country running M(s)/W(s), equestrian sports M(s)/W(s), golf M(s)/W(s), lacrosse M(s)/W(s), soccer M(s)/W(s), swimming and diving M(s)/W(s), tennis M(s)/W(s), track and field M(s)/W(s). *Intramural sports:* basketball M/W, soccer M/W, tennis M/W, volleyball M/W.

Standardized Tests *Required:* SAT or ACT (for admission).

Costs (2012–13) *Comprehensive fee:* $45,395 includes full-time tuition ($31,905), mandatory fees ($500), and room and board ($12,990). Full-time tuition and fees vary according to course load and degree level. Part-time tuition: $709 per quarter hour. Part-time tuition and fees vary according to course load and degree level. *College room only:* $8220. Room and board charges vary according to board plan, housing facility, and location. *Payment plan:* installment. *Waivers:* employees or children of employees.

Financial Aid Of all full-time matriculated undergraduates who enrolled in 2012, 5,059 applied for aid, 4,478 were judged to have need, 375 had their need fully met. In 2012, 2435 non-need-based awards were made. *Average percent of need met:* 20%. *Average financial aid package:* $25,296. *Average need-based loan:* $3975. *Average need-based gift aid:* $6465. *Average non-need-based aid:* $9612. *Average indebtedness upon graduation:* $37,776.

Applying *Options:* electronic application, early admission, deferred entrance. *Application fee:* $35. *Required:* high school transcript. *Required for some:* essay or personal statement, high school transcript, College transcripts required for transfer students; Portfolio/audition recommended for all performing arts, riding, writing, or visual arts applicants. *Recommended:* essay or personal statement, minimum 3.0 GPA, 3 letters of recommendation, interview. *Application deadlines:* rolling (freshmen), rolling (transfers). *Notification:* continuous (freshmen), continuous (transfers).

Freshman Application Contact Margaret Kross, Savannah College of Art and Design, 342 Bull Street, PO Box 3146, Savannah, GA 31402-3146. *Phone:* 912-525-5100. *Toll-free phone:* 800-869-7223. *Fax:* 912-525-5983. *E-mail:* admission@scad.edu. *Website:* http://www.scad.edu/.

Savannah State University

Savannah, Georgia

Freshman Application Contact Mrs. Carol Dolan, Assistant Director of Admissions for Operations, Savannah State University, PO Box 20209, Savannah, GA 31404. *Phone:* 912-358-4014. *Toll-free phone:* 800-788-0478. *Fax:* 912-358-4517. *E-mail:* dolanc@savannahstate.edu. *Website:* http://www.savannahstate.edu/.

Shorter University

Rome, Georgia

- **Independent Baptist** comprehensive, founded 1873
- **Small-town** 155-acre campus with easy access to Atlanta
- **Endowment** $20.1 million
- **Coed**
- **Moderately difficult** entrance level

Faculty *Student/faculty ratio:* 13:1.

Academics *Calendar:* semesters. *Degrees:* associate, bachelor's, and master's.

Student Life *Campus security:* 24-hour emergency response devices and patrols.

Athletics Member NAIA.

Standardized Tests *Required:* SAT or ACT (for admission).

Financial Aid *Of all full-time matriculated undergraduates who enrolled in 2011,* 1,312 applied for aid, 1,176 were judged to have need, 235 had their need fully met. 133 Federal Work-Study jobs (averaging $2417). 82 state and other part-time jobs (averaging $2335). *In 2011,* 159 non-need-based awards were made. *Average percent of need met:* 65. *Average financial aid package:* $16,072. *Average need-based loan:* $4054. *Average need-based gift aid:* $12,875. *Average non-need-based aid:* $5738. *Average indebtedness upon graduation:* $25,441.

Applying *Options:* electronic application, early admission, deferred entrance. *Application fee:* $25. *Required:* essay or personal statement, high school transcript. *Required for some:* interview, audition for music and theater programs. *Recommended:* minimum 2.0 GPA, 1 letter of recommendation, interview.

Freshman Application Contact Shorter University, 315 Shorter Avenue, Rome, GA 30165. *Phone:* 706-233-7342. *Toll-free phone:* 800-868-6980. *Website:* http://www.shorter.edu/.

See next page for display ad and page 1498 for the College Close-Up.

Southern Polytechnic State University

Marietta, Georgia

- **State-supported** comprehensive, founded 1948, part of University System of Georgia
- **Suburban** 198-acre campus with easy access to Atlanta
- **Endowment** $3.1 million
- **Coed** 5,402 undergraduate students, 72% full-time, 18% women, 82% men
- **Moderately difficult** entrance level, 79% of applicants were admitted

Undergraduates 3,863 full-time, 1,539 part-time. Students come from 41 states and territories; 51 other countries; 2% are from out of state; 22% Black or African American, non-Hispanic/Latino; 8% Hispanic/Latino; 6% Asian, non-Hispanic/Latino; 0.1% Native Hawaiian or other Pacific Islander, non-Hispanic/Latino; 0.2% American Indian or Alaska Native, non-Hispanic/Latino; 3% Two or more races, non-Hispanic/Latino; 1% Race/ethnicity unknown; 4% international; 13% transferred in; 25% live on campus. *Retention:* 76% of full-time freshmen returned.

Freshmen *Admission:* 1,535 applied, 1,212 admitted, 790 enrolled. *Average high school GPA:* 3.28. *Test scores:* SAT critical reading scores over 500: 80%; SAT math scores over 500: 91%; SAT writing scores over 500: 62%; ACT scores over 18: 99%; SAT critical reading scores over 600: 29%; SAT math scores over 600: 46%; SAT writing scores over 600: 15%; ACT scores over 24: 53%; SAT critical reading scores over 700: 4%; SAT math scores over 700: 7%; SAT writing scores over 700: 1%; ACT scores over 30: 7%.

Faculty *Total:* 309, 71% full-time, 61% with terminal degrees. *Student/faculty ratio:* 19:1.

Academics *Calendar:* semesters. *Degrees:* certificates, associate, bachelor's, master's, and postbachelor's certificates. *Special study options:* advanced placement credit, cooperative education, distance learning, double majors, honors programs, independent study, internships, off-campus study, part-time degree program, services for LD students, student-designed majors, study abroad, summer session for credit. *ROTC:* Army (c), Navy (c), Air Force (c).

Computers on Campus 1,400 computers/terminals and 250 ports are available on campus for general student use. Students can access the following: campus intranet, computer help desk, free student e-mail accounts, online (class) grades, online (class) registration, online (class) schedules. Campuswide network is available. 100% of college-owned or -operated housing units are wired for high-speed Internet access. Wireless service is available via classrooms, computer centers, computer labs, dorm rooms, learning centers, libraries, student centers.

Student Life *Housing:* on-campus residence required for freshman year. *Options:* coed, men-only, women-only, cooperative, disabled students. Campus housing is university owned. Freshman applicants given priority for college housing. *Activities and organizations:* drama/theater group, student-run newspaper, radio station, International Student Association, Campus Activities Board, National Society of Black Engineers, Baptist Collegiate Ministries, American Society of Civil Engineers, national fraternities, national sororities. *Campus security:* 24-hour emergency response devices and patrols, late-night transport/escort service, controlled dormitory access. *Student services:* health clinic, personal/psychological counseling.

Athletics Member NAIA. *Intercollegiate sports:* baseball M(s), basketball M(s)/W(s), soccer M(s). *Intramural sports:* badminton M/W, basketball M/W, bowling M/W, football M/W, golf M/W, racquetball M/W, soccer M/W, softball M/W, swimming and diving M(c)/W(c), table tennis M/W, ultimate Frisbee M/W, volleyball M/W, weight lifting M/W.

Standardized Tests *Required:* SAT or ACT (for admission).

Costs (2012–13) *Tuition:* state resident $5256 full-time, $175 per semester hour part-time; nonresident $18,704 full-time, $623 per semester hour part-time. Full-time tuition and fees vary according to course load. Part-time tuition and fees vary according to course load. *Required fees:* $1422 full-time, $711 per term part-time. *Room and board:* $7280; room only: $4020. Room and board charges vary according to board plan and housing facility. *Waivers:* senior citizens and employees or children of employees.

Financial Aid Of all full-time matriculated undergraduates who enrolled in 2011, 3,871 applied for aid, 3,871 were judged to have need, 548 had their need fully met. 254 Federal Work-Study jobs (averaging $4000). *Average percent of need met:* 61%. *Average financial aid package:* $2851. *Average need-based loan:* $2100. *Average need-based gift aid:* $2117. *Average non-need-based aid:* $4482. *Average indebtedness upon graduation:* $22,250.

Applying *Options:* electronic application, deferred entrance. *Application fee:* $40. *Required:* high school transcript, minimum 2.5 GPA, proof of immunization, international students have additional requirements, 19 academic CPC units. *Application deadlines:* 7/1 (freshmen), 7/1 (out-of-state freshmen), 7/1 (transfers). *Notification:* continuous (freshmen), continuous (out-of-state freshmen), continuous (transfers).

Freshman Application Contact Mr. Gary Bush, Director of Admissions, Southern Polytechnic State University, 1100 South Marietta Parkway, Marietta, GA 30060. *Phone:* 678-915-7468. *Toll-free phone:* 800-635-3204. *Fax:* 678-915-7496. *E-mail:* gbush@spsu.edu. *Website:* http://www.spsu.edu/.

South University

Savannah, Georgia

- **Proprietary** comprehensive, founded 1899, part of Education Management Corporation
- **Coed**

Academics *Calendar:* quarters. *Degrees:* associate, bachelor's, master's, and doctoral.

Freshman Application Contact South University, 709 Mall Boulevard, Savannah, GA 31406. *Phone:* 912-201-8000. *Toll-free phone:* 866-629-2901. *Website:* http://www.southuniversity.edu/savannah/.

Spelman College

Atlanta, Georgia

- **Independent** 4-year, founded 1881
- **Urban** 39-acre campus with easy access to Atlanta
- **Women only** 2,145 undergraduate students, 97% full-time
- **Very difficult** entrance level, 38% of applicants were admitted

Undergraduates 2,074 full-time, 71 part-time. Students come from 9 states and territories; 45 other countries; 73% are from out of state; 82% Black or African American, non-Hispanic/Latino; 0.4% Hispanic/Latino; 0.1% Asian, non-Hispanic/Latino; 2% Two or more races, non-Hispanic/Latino; 14% Race/ethnicity unknown; 0.7% international; 1% transferred in; 65% live on campus. *Retention:* 90% of full-time freshmen returned.

Freshmen *Admission:* 6,081 applied, 2,312 admitted, 523 enrolled. *Average high school GPA:* 3.56. *Test scores:* SAT critical reading scores over 500: 60%; SAT math scores over 500: 56%; ACT scores over 18: 93%; SAT critical reading scores over 600: 18%; SAT math scores over 600: 9%; ACT scores over 24: 34%; SAT critical reading scores over 700: 2%; SAT math scores over 700: 1%; ACT scores over 30: 4%.

Faculty *Total:* 247, 70% full-time, 73% with terminal degrees. *Student/faculty ratio:* 11:1.

Academics *Calendar:* semesters. *Degree:* bachelor's. *Special study options:* adult/continuing education programs, double majors, honors programs, independent study, internships, part-time degree program, services for LD students, student-designed majors, study abroad. *ROTC:* Army (c), Navy (c), Air Force (c). *Unusual degree programs:* 3-2 engineering with North Carolina Agricultural and Technical State University, Rensselaer Polytechnic Institute, Georgia Institute of Technology, Boston University, The University of Alabama in Huntsville, Auburn University.

Computers on Campus 770 computers/terminals and 115 ports are available on campus for general student use. Students can access the following: computer help desk, free student e-mail accounts, online (class) grades, online (class) registration, online (class) schedules. Campuswide network is available. 85% of college-owned or -operated housing units are wired for high-speed Internet access.

Student Life *Housing:* on-campus residence required for freshman year. *Options:* women-only. Campus housing is university owned and leased by the school. Freshman applicants given priority for college housing. *Activities and organizations:* drama/theater group, student-run newspaper, choral group, marching band, national sororities. *Campus security:* 24-hour emergency response devices and patrols, late-night transport/escort service, controlled dormitory access, Lighted pathways/sidewalks. *Student services:* health clinic, women's center.

Athletics Member NCAA. *Intercollegiate sports:* basketball W, cross-country running W, golf W, soccer W, tennis W, track and field W, volleyball W. *Intramural sports:* softball W, swimming and diving W.

Standardized Tests *Required:* SAT or ACT (for admission).

Costs (2012–13) *One-time required fee:* $250. *Comprehensive fee:* $35,335 includes full-time tuition ($20,569), mandatory fees ($3225), and room and board ($11,541). Full-time tuition and fees vary according to course load. Part-time tuition: $860 per credit hour. Part-time tuition and fees vary according to course load. $1,612.50 per term fees are optional if a student registers for less than six semester hours. *Required fees:* $1613 per term part-time. *Room and board:* Room and board charges vary according to board plan and housing facility. *Payment plans:* installment, deferred payment. *Waivers:* employees or children of employees.

Financial Aid Of all full-time matriculated undergraduates who enrolled in 2012, 1,834 applied for aid, 1,732 were judged to have need, 227 had their need fully met. 148 Federal Work-Study jobs (averaging $1470). In 2012, 7 non-need-based awards were made. *Average percent of need met:* 39%. *Average financial aid package:* $14,391. *Average need-based loan:* $4330. *Average need-based gift aid:* $12,190. *Average non-need-based aid:* $3429. *Average indebtedness upon graduation:* $33,898.

Applying *Options:* electronic application, early admission, early decision, early action, deferred entrance. *Application fee:* $35. *Required:* essay or personal statement, high school transcript, minimum 2.0 GPA, 2 letters of recommendation. *Required for some:* interview. *Application deadlines:* 2/1 (freshmen), 4/1 (transfers), 11/15 (early action). *Early decision deadline:* 11/1. *Notification:* 4/1 (freshmen), 5/1 (transfers), 12/15 (early decision), 12/31 (early action).

Freshman Application Contact Ms. Arlene Cash, Vice President for Admissions and Orientation, Spelman College, 350 Spelman Lane, SW, Atlanta, GA 30314-4399. *Phone:* 404-681-3643. *Toll-free phone:* 800-982-2411. *Fax:* 404-270-5201. *E-mail:* admiss@spelman.edu. *Website:* http://www.spelman.edu/.

Strayer University—Augusta Campus

Augusta, Georgia

Freshman Application Contact Strayer University—Augusta Campus, 1330 Augusta West Parkway, Augusta, GA 30909. *Website:* http://www.strayer.edu/campus/augusta/.

Strayer University—Chamblee Campus

Atlanta, Georgia

Freshman Application Contact Strayer University—Chamblee Campus, 3355 Northeast Expressway, Suite 100, Atlanta, GA 30341. *Website:* http://www.strayer.edu/campus/chamblee/.

Strayer University—Cobb County Campus

Atlanta, Georgia

Freshman Application Contact Strayer University—Cobb County Campus, 3101 Towercreek Parkway, SE, Suite 700, Atlanta, GA 30339-3256. *Website:* http://www.strayer.edu/campus/cobb-county/.

Strayer University—Columbus Campus

Columbus, Georgia

Freshman Application Contact Strayer University—Columbus Campus, 6003 Veterans Parkway, Suite 100, Columbus, GA 31909. *Website:* http://www.strayer.edu/campus/columbus_ga.

Strayer University—Douglasville Campus

Douglasville, Georgia

Freshman Application Contact Strayer University—Douglasville Campus, 4655 Timber Ridge Drive, Douglasville, GA 30135. *Website:* http://www.strayer.edu/campus/douglasville/.

Strayer University—Lithonia Campus

Lithonia, Georgia

Freshman Application Contact Strayer University—Lithonia Campus, 3120 Stonecrest Boulevard, Suite 200, Lithonia, GA 30038. *Website:* http://www.strayer.edu/campus/lithonia/.

Strayer University—Morrow Campus

Morrow, Georgia

Freshman Application Contact Strayer University—Morrow Campus, 3000 Corporate Center Drive, Suite 100, Morrow, GA 30260. *Website:* http://www.strayer.edu/campus/morrow.

Strayer University—Roswell Campus

Roswell, Georgia

Freshman Application Contact Strayer University—Roswell Campus, 100 Mansell Court East, Suite 100, Roswell, GA 30076. *Website:* http://www.strayer.edu/campus/roswell.

Strayer University—Savannah Campus

Savannah, Georgia

Freshman Application Contact Strayer University—Savannah Campus, 20 Martin Court, Savannah, GA 31419. *Website:* http://www.strayer.edu/campus/savannah/.

Thomas University

Thomasville, Georgia

- **Independent** comprehensive, founded 1950
- **Small-town** 24-acre campus
- **Endowment** $4.2 million
- **Coed** 882 undergraduate students, 59% full-time, 56% women, 44% men
- **Minimally difficult** entrance level

Undergraduates 519 full-time, 363 part-time. Students come from 14 states and territories; 10 other countries; 26% are from out of state; 27% Black or African American, non-Hispanic/Latino; 4% Hispanic/Latino; 0.9% Asian, non-Hispanic/Latino; 0.1% Native Hawaiian or other Pacific Islander, non-Hispanic/Latino; 0.6% American Indian or Alaska Native, non-Hispanic/Latino; 11% Race/ethnicity unknown; 2% international; 22% transferred in; 9% live on campus.

Freshmen *Admission:* 71 applied, 142 enrolled.

Faculty *Total:* 53, 96% full-time, 70% with terminal degrees. *Student/faculty ratio:* 6:1.

Academics *Calendar:* semesters. *Degrees:* associate, bachelor's, master's, and postbachelor's certificates. *Special study options:* academic remediation for entering students, accelerated degree program, adult/continuing education programs, advanced placement credit, cooperative education, distance learning, double majors, independent study, internships, part-time degree program, services for LD students, study abroad, summer session for credit.

Computers on Campus 80 computers/terminals are available on campus for general student use. Students can access the following: free student e-mail accounts, online (class) schedules. Campuswide network is available.

Student Life *Housing options:* coed. Campus housing is university owned. Freshman applicants given priority for college housing. *Activities and organi-*

zations: drama/theater group, student-run newspaper, choral group, Student Government Association, Professional Management Association, National Society for Leadership and Success. *Campus security:* late-night transport/escort service, controlled dormitory access, evening security guards. *Student services:* personal/psychological counseling.

Athletics Member NAIA. *Intercollegiate sports:* baseball M(s), golf M(s)/W, soccer M(s)/W(s), softball W(s). *Intramural sports:* football M/W, table tennis M/W, tennis M/W, volleyball M/W.

Standardized Tests *Recommended:* SAT (for admission), SAT and SAT Subject Tests or ACT (for admission).

Applying *Options:* electronic application, early admission, deferred entrance. *Application fee:* $25. *Required:* high school transcript. *Application deadlines:* rolling (freshmen), rolling (transfers). *Notification:* continuous (freshmen), continuous (transfers).

Freshman Application Contact Mrs. Kerri Knight, Thomas University Office of Admission, Thomas University, 1501 Millpond Road, Thomasville, GA 31792. *Phone:* 229-227-6942 Ext. 1074. *Toll-free phone:* 800-538-9784. *Fax:* 229-227-6919. *E-mail:* kknight@thomasu.edu.
Website: http://www.thomasu.edu/.

Toccoa Falls College

Toccoa Falls, Georgia

Freshman Application Contact Toccoa Falls College, 107 North Chapel Drive, Toccoa Falls, GA 30598. *Phone:* 888-785-5624.
Website: http://www.tfc.edu/.

Truett-McConnell College

Cleveland, Georgia

- **Independent Baptist** 4-year, founded 1946
- **Rural** 310-acre campus with easy access to Atlanta
- **Coed**
- **Minimally difficult** entrance level

Faculty *Student/faculty ratio:* 13:1.

Academics *Calendar:* semesters. *Degrees:* associate and bachelor's.

Student Life *Campus security:* 24-hour weekday patrols, 10-hour weekend patrols by trained security personnel.

Athletics Member NAIA, NCCAA.

Standardized Tests *Required:* SAT or ACT (for admission).

Financial Aid *Of all full-time matriculated undergraduates who enrolled in 2011,* 509 applied for aid, 330 were judged to have need, 37 had their need fully met. 24 Federal Work-Study jobs (averaging $1205). *In 2011,* 40 non-need-based awards were made. *Average percent of need met:* 67. *Average financial aid package:* $13,759. *Average need-based loan:* $3581. *Average need-based gift aid:* $11,135. *Average non-need-based aid:* $6872. *Average indebtedness upon graduation:* $19,921.

Applying *Options:* electronic application, early admission, deferred entrance. *Application fee:* $25. *Required:* essay or personal statement, high school transcript, minimum 2.0 GPA. *Required for some:* 1 letter of recommendation, interview.

Freshman Application Contact Truett-McConnell College, 100 Alumni Drive, Cleveland, GA 30528. *Phone:* 706-865-2134 Ext. 210. *Toll-free phone:* 800-226-8621.
Website: http://www.truett.edu/.

University of Atlanta

Atlanta, Georgia

Freshman Application Contact Bill Kay, Vice President for Enrollment Management, University of Atlanta, 6685 Peachtree Industrial Boulevard, Atlanta, GA 30360. *Phone:* 404-424-8410 Ext. 5555. *Toll-free phone:* 800-533-3378. *Fax:* 678-736-8042. *E-mail:* bkay@uofa.edu.
Website: http://www.uofa.edu/.

University of Georgia

Athens, Georgia

- **State-supported** comprehensive, founded 1785, part of University System of Georgia
- **Suburban** 759-acre campus with easy access to Atlanta
- **Endowment** $744.3 million
- **Coed** 26,259 undergraduate students, 93% full-time, 57% women, 43% men
- **Moderately difficult** entrance level, 56% of applicants were admitted

Undergraduates 24,514 full-time, 1,745 part-time. Students come from 55 states and territories; 121 other countries; 9% are from out of state; 7% Black or African American, non-Hispanic/Latino; 5% Hispanic/Latino; 8% Asian, non-Hispanic/Latino; 0.1% Native Hawaiian or other Pacific Islander, non-Hispanic/Latino; 0.1% American Indian or Alaska Native, non-Hispanic/Latino; 2% Two or more races, non-Hispanic/Latino; 2% Race/ethnicity unknown; 1% international; 5% transferred in; 28% live on campus. *Retention:* 94% of full-time freshmen returned.

Freshmen *Admission:* 18,458 applied, 10,352 admitted, 4,936 enrolled. *Average high school GPA:* 3.83. *Test scores:* SAT critical reading scores over 500: 94%; SAT math scores over 500: 96%; SAT writing scores over 500: 94%; ACT scores over 18: 100%; SAT critical reading scores over 600: 59%; SAT math scores over 600: 68%; SAT writing scores over 600: 60%; ACT scores over 24: 90%; SAT critical reading scores over 700: 14%; SAT math scores over 700: 16%; SAT writing scores over 700: 14%; ACT scores over 30: 28%.

Faculty *Total:* 2,205, 83% full-time, 89% with terminal degrees. *Student/faculty ratio:* 18:1.

Academics *Calendar:* semesters. *Degrees:* certificates, bachelor's, master's, doctoral, post-master's, and postbachelor's certificates. *Special study options:* academic remediation for entering students, accelerated degree program, adult/continuing education programs, advanced placement credit, cooperative education, distance learning, double majors, honors programs, independent study, internships, off-campus study, part-time degree program, services for LD students, student-designed majors, study abroad, summer session for credit. *ROTC:* Army (b), Air Force (b).

Computers on Campus 3,046 computers/terminals are available on campus for general student use. Students can access the following: campus intranet, computer help desk, free student e-mail accounts, online (class) grades, online (class) registration, online (class) schedules. Campuswide network is available. 100% of college-owned or -operated housing units are wired for high-speed Internet access. Wireless service is available via classrooms, computer centers, computer labs, dorm rooms, learning centers, libraries, student centers.

Student Life *Housing:* on-campus residence required for freshman year. *Options:* coed, women-only, disabled students. Campus housing is university owned. Freshman campus housing is guaranteed. *Activities and organizations:* drama/theater group, student-run newspaper, radio and television station, choral group, marching band, intramurals, Recreational sports program, Communiversity, University Union, Red Coat Band, national fraternities, national sororities. *Campus security:* 24-hour emergency response devices and patrols, late-night transport/escort service, controlled dormitory access. *Student services:* health clinic, personal/psychological counseling, women's center, legal services.

Athletics Member NCAA. All Division I except football (Division I-A). *Intercollegiate sports:* badminton M(c)/W(c), baseball M(s), basketball M(s)/W(s), cheerleading M(c)/W(c), crew M(c)/W(c), cross-country running M(s)/W(s), equestrian sports W(s), fencing M(c)/W(c), golf M(s)/W(s), gymnastics W(s), ice hockey M(c), lacrosse M(c)/W(c), racquetball M(c)/W(c), rugby M(c)/W(c), sailing M(c)/W(c), soccer W(s), softball W(s), swimming and diving M(s)/W(s), tennis M(s)/W(s), track and field M(s)/W(s), ultimate Frisbee M(c)/W(c), volleyball W(s), water polo M(c)/W(c), wrestling M(c). *Intramural sports:* badminton M/W, basketball M/W, football M/W, golf M/W, racquetball M/W, soccer M/W, softball M/W, tennis M/W, ultimate Frisbee M/W, volleyball M/W.

Standardized Tests *Required:* SAT or ACT (for admission). *Recommended:* SAT Subject Tests (for admission).

Costs (2012–13) *Tuition:* state resident $9842 full-time; nonresident $28,052 full-time. Full-time tuition and fees vary according to course load, location, and program. Part-time tuition and fees vary according to course load, location, and program. *Room and board:* $8970; room only: $5088. Room and board charges vary according to board plan and housing facility. *Waivers:* senior citizens.

Financial Aid Of all full-time matriculated undergraduates who enrolled in 2012, 16,376 applied for aid, 9,680 were judged to have need, 1,858 had their need fully met. 407 Federal Work-Study jobs (averaging $2764). In 2012, 1481 non-need-based awards were made. *Average percent of need met:* 66%. *Average financial aid package:* $10,797. *Average need-based loan:* $4206. *Average need-based gift aid:* $8433. *Average non-need-based aid:* $1924. *Average indebtedness upon graduation:* $19,621.

Applying *Options:* electronic application, early admission, early action, deferred entrance. *Application fee:* $60. *Required:* high school transcript, counselor evaluation. *Recommended:* essay or personal statement, minimum 2.0 GPA. *Application deadlines:* 1/15 (freshmen), 4/1 (transfers), 10/15 (early action). *Notification:* 4/1 (freshmen), continuous (transfers), 12/1 (early action).

Freshman Application Contact Mr. Charles Carabello, Associate Director for Enrollment Management, University of Georgia, Terrell Hall, Athens, GA 30602. *Phone:* 706-542-8776. *Fax:* 706-542-1466. *E-mail:* admproc@uga.edu.
Website: http://www.uga.edu/.

University of North Georgia

Dahlonega, Georgia

- **State-supported** comprehensive, founded 1873, part of University System of Georgia
- **Small-town** 140-acre campus with easy access to Atlanta
- **Endowment** $21.8 million
- **Coed** 5,851 undergraduate students, 84% full-time, 57% women, 43% men
- **Moderately difficult** entrance level, 56% of applicants were admitted

Undergraduates 4,889 full-time, 962 part-time. Students come from 39 states and territories; 47 other countries; 6% are from out of state; 3% Black or African American, non-Hispanic/Latino; 4% Hispanic/Latino; 2% Asian, non-Hispanic/Latino; 0.1% Native Hawaiian or other Pacific Islander, non-Hispanic/Latino; 0.2% American Indian or Alaska Native, non-Hispanic/Latino; 2% Two or more races, non-Hispanic/Latino; 2% Race/ethnicity unknown; 0.9% international; 8% transferred in; 37% live on campus. *Retention:* 78% of full-time freshmen returned.

Freshmen *Admission:* 4,226 applied, 2,377 admitted, 1,125 enrolled. *Average high school GPA:* 3.51. *Test scores:* SAT critical reading scores over 500: 84%; SAT math scores over 500: 77%; ACT scores over 18: 98%; SAT critical reading scores over 600: 28%; SAT math scores over 600: 27%; ACT scores over 24: 49%; SAT critical reading scores over 700: 3%; SAT math scores over 700: 2%; ACT scores over 30: 3%.

Faculty *Total:* 353, 70% full-time. *Student/faculty ratio:* 20:1.

Academics *Calendar:* semesters. *Degrees:* certificates, associate, bachelor's, master's, doctoral, and post-master's certificates. *Special study options:* academic remediation for entering students, accelerated degree program, advanced placement credit, cooperative education, distance learning, double majors, English as a second language, external degree program, freshman honors college, honors programs, independent study, internships, part-time degree program, services for LD students, study abroad, summer session for credit. *ROTC:* Army (b). *Unusual degree programs:* 3-2 engineering with Georgia Institute of Technology, Clemson University; industrial management, computer science with Georgia Institute of Technology.

Computers on Campus 707 computers/terminals are available on campus for general student use. Students can access the following: computer help desk, free student e-mail accounts, online (class) grades, online (class) registration, online (class) schedules. Campuswide network is available. 100% of college-owned or -operated housing units are wired for high-speed Internet access. Wireless service is available via classrooms, computer centers, computer labs, dorm rooms, learning centers, libraries.

Student Life *Housing:* on-campus residence required through sophomore year. *Options:* coed, men-only, women-only. Campus housing is university owned. Freshman campus housing is guaranteed. *Activities and organizations:* drama/theater group, student-run newspaper, choral group, Student Government Association, Commuter Council, Graduate Student Senate, Student Activities Board, Greek organizations, national fraternities, national sororities. *Campus security:* 24-hour emergency response devices and patrols, late-night transport/escort service, controlled dormitory access. *Student services:* health clinic, personal/psychological counseling.

Athletics Member NCAA. All Division II. *Intercollegiate sports:* baseball M(s), basketball M(s)/W(s), cheerleading M/W, cross-country running M(c)/W(s), equestrian sports W(c), golf M(s)/W(s), lacrosse M(c)/W(c), riflery M(s)/W(s), soccer M(s)/W(s), softball W(s), tennis M(s)/W(s), wrestling M(c). *Intramural sports:* basketball M/W, football M/W, golf M(c)/W(c), rugby M/W, soccer M/W, softball M/W, table tennis M/W, ultimate Frisbee M/W, volleyball M/W, water polo M/W.

Standardized Tests *Required:* SAT or ACT (for admission). *Required for some:* SAT and SAT Subject Tests or ACT (for admission).

Costs (2013–14) *Tuition:* state resident $4852 full-time, $162 per credit hour part-time; nonresident $17,128 full-time, $571 per credit hour part-time. Part-time tuition and fees vary according to course load. *Required fees:* $1718 full-time. *Room and board:* $8430; room only: $4760. Room and board charges vary according to board plan and housing facility. *Waivers:* senior citizens and employees or children of employees.

Financial Aid Of all full-time matriculated undergraduates who enrolled in 2012, 4,087 applied for aid, 3,066 were judged to have need, 792 had their need fully met. 95 Federal Work-Study jobs (averaging $2000). 115 state and other part-time jobs (averaging $1500). In 2012, 110 non-need-based awards were made. *Average percent of need met:* 62%. *Average financial aid package:* $12,650. *Average need-based loan:* $5352. *Average need-based gift aid:* $4900. *Average non-need-based aid:* $1109. *Average indebtedness upon graduation:* $12,166.

Applying *Options:* electronic application, early admission. *Application fee:* $30. *Required:* high school transcript, minimum 2.0 GPA, proof of immunization. *Application deadlines:* 7/1 (freshmen), rolling (transfers). *Notification:* continuous (freshmen), continuous (transfers).

Freshman Application Contact Jennifer Chadwick, Director of Admissions, University of North Georgia, Admissions Center, Dahlonega, GA 30533. *Phone:* 706-864-1800. *Toll-free phone:* 800-498-9581. *Fax:* 706-864-1478. *E-mail:* admissions@northgeorgia.edu. *Website:* http://www.ung.edu/.

University of Phoenix–Atlanta Campus

Sandy Springs, Georgia

Freshman Application Contact Marc Booker, Sr. Director, Office of Admissions and Evaluation, University of Phoenix–Atlanta Campus, 4035 South Riverpoint Parkway, Mail Stop CF-L101, Phoenix, AZ 85040. *Phone:* 602-557-4609. *Toll-free phone:* 866-766-0766. *Fax:* 480-643-1156. *Website:* http://www.phoenix.edu/.

University of Phoenix–Augusta Campus

Augusta, Georgia

Admissions Office Contact University of Phoenix–Augusta Campus, 3150 Perimeter Parkway, Augusta, GA 30909-4583. *Toll-free phone:* 866-766-0766. *Website:* http://www.phoenix.edu/.

University of Phoenix–Columbus Georgia Campus

Columbus, Georgia

Freshman Application Contact Marc Booker, Sr. Director, Office of Admissions and Evaluation, University of Phoenix–Columbus Georgia Campus, 4035 South Riverpoint Parkway, Mail Stop CF-L101, Phoenix, AZ 85040. *Phone:* 602-557-4609. *Toll-free phone:* 866-766-0766. *Fax:* 480-643-1156. *Website:* http://www.phoenix.edu/.

University of Phoenix–Savannah Campus

Savannah, Georgia

Admissions Office Contact University of Phoenix–Savannah Campus, 8001 Chatham Center Drive, Suite 200, Savannah, GA 31405-7400. *Toll-free phone:* 866-766-0766. *Website:* http://www.phoenix.edu/.

University of West Georgia

Carrollton, Georgia

- **State-supported** comprehensive, founded 1933, part of University System of Georgia
- **Small-town** 645-acre campus with easy access to Atlanta
- **Endowment** $19.7 million
- **Coed** 9,963 undergraduate students, 82% full-time, 61% women, 39% men
- **Minimally difficult** entrance level, 56% of applicants were admitted

Undergraduates 8,178 full-time, 1,785 part-time. Students come from 41 states and territories; 56 other countries; 3% are from out of state; 31% Black or African American, non-Hispanic/Latino; 4% Hispanic/Latino; 1% Asian, non-Hispanic/Latino; 0.1% Native Hawaiian or other Pacific Islander, non-Hispanic/Latino; 0.2% American Indian or Alaska Native, non-Hispanic/Latino; 3% Two or more races, non-Hispanic/Latino; 4% Race/ethnicity unknown; 1% international; 6% transferred in; 27% live on campus. *Retention:* 70% of full-time freshmen returned.

Freshmen *Admission:* 6,435 applied, 3,589 admitted, 2,070 enrolled. *Average high school GPA:* 3.08. *Test scores:* SAT critical reading scores over 500: 37%; SAT math scores over 500: 35%; SAT writing scores over 500: 30%; ACT scores over 18: 82%; SAT critical reading scores over 600: 8%; SAT math scores over 600: 5%; SAT writing scores over 600: 3%; ACT scores over 24: 12%; SAT critical reading scores over 700: 1%; ACT scores over 30: 1%.

Faculty *Total:* 644, 70% full-time, 61% with terminal degrees. *Student/faculty ratio:* 19:1.

Academics *Calendar:* semesters. *Degrees:* bachelor's, master's, doctoral, post-master's, and postbachelor's certificates. *Special study options:* academic remediation for entering students, accelerated degree program, adult/continuing education programs, advanced placement credit, cooperative education, distance learning, double majors, English as a second language, external degree program, honors programs, independent study, internships, off-campus study, part-time degree program, services for LD students, study abroad, summer session for credit. *ROTC:* Air Force (c). *Unusual degree programs:* 3-2 engineering with Georgia Institute of Technology, Auburn University, Mercer University, University of Georgia.

Computers on Campus 1,200 computers/terminals are available on campus for general student use. Students can access the following: campus intranet, computer help desk, free student e-mail accounts, online (class) grades, online (class) registration, online (class) schedules. Campuswide network is available. 100% of college-owned or -operated housing units are wired for high-speed Internet access. Wireless service is available via entire campus.

Student Life *Housing:* on-campus residence required for freshman year. *Options:* coed, women-only, disabled students. Campus housing is university owned and leased by the school. Freshman campus housing is guaranteed. *Activities and organizations:* drama/theater group, student-run newspaper, radio and television station, choral group, marching band, Black Student Alliance, Student Activities Council, Baptist Student Union, Campus Outreach, United Voices Gospel Choir, national fraternities, national sororities. *Campus security:* 24-hour emergency response devices and patrols, late-night transport/escort service, controlled dormitory access. *Student services:* health clinic, personal/psychological counseling.

Athletics Member NCAA. All Division II. *Intercollegiate sports:* baseball M(s), basketball M(s)/W(s), cheerleading M(s)/W(s), cross-country running M(s)/W(s), football M(s)/W(s), golf M(s)/W(s), soccer W(s), softball W(s), tennis W(s), track and field W(s), volleyball W(s). *Intramural sports:* basketball M/W, football M/W, soccer M/W, softball M/W, tennis M/W, ultimate Frisbee M/W, volleyball M/W.

Standardized Tests *Required:* SAT or ACT (for admission).

Costs (2012–13) *Tuition:* state resident $4852 full-time, $162 per semester hour part-time; nonresident $17,128 full-time, $571 per semester hour part-time. Full-time tuition and fees vary according to course load and location. Part-time tuition and fees vary according to course load and location. *Required fees:* $1858 full-time, $46 per semester hour part-time, $512 per term part-time. *Room and board:* $7482; room only: $4100. Room and board charges vary according to board plan and housing facility. *Waivers:* senior citizens and employees or children of employees.

Financial Aid Of all full-time matriculated undergraduates who enrolled in 2012, 7,056 applied for aid, 6,083 were judged to have need, 1,793 had their need fully met. 223 Federal Work-Study jobs (averaging $1455). 1,059 state and other part-time jobs (averaging $1230). In 2012, 321 non-need-based awards were made. *Average percent of need met:* 51%. *Average financial aid package:* $8957. *Average need-based loan:* $4078. *Average need-based gift aid:* $5700. *Average non-need-based aid:* $1584. *Average indebtedness upon graduation:* $18,603.

Applying *Options:* electronic application, early admission, deferred entrance. *Application fee:* $40. *Required:* high school transcript, minimum 2.4 GPA, proof of immunization. *Application deadlines:* 6/1 (freshmen), 6/1 (out-of-state freshmen), 6/1 (transfers). *Notification:* continuous (freshmen), continuous (out-of-state freshmen), continuous (transfers).

Freshman Application Contact Ms. Ketty Ballard, Associate Director (Recruiting), University of West Georgia, 1601 Maple Street, Carrollton, GA 30118. *Phone:* 678-839-5600. *Fax:* 678-839-4747. *E-mail:* admiss@westga.edu.
Website: http://www.westga.edu/.

Valdosta State University

Valdosta, Georgia

- **State-supported** university, founded 1906, part of University System of Georgia
- **Small-town** 180-acre campus
- **Endowment** $23.3 million
- **Coed** 10,290 undergraduate students, 86% full-time, 59% women, 41% men
- **Moderately difficult** entrance level, 59% of applicants were admitted

Undergraduates 8,859 full-time, 1,431 part-time. Students come from 47 states and territories; 68 other countries; 5% are from out of state; 35% Black or African American, non-Hispanic/Latino; 4% Hispanic/Latino; 1% Asian, non-Hispanic/Latino; 0.2% Native Hawaiian or other Pacific Islander, non-Hispanic/Latino; 0.2% American Indian or Alaska Native, non-Hispanic/Latino; 2% Two or more races, non-Hispanic/Latino; 3% Race/ethnicity unknown; 2% international; 6% transferred in; 28% live on campus. *Retention:* 67% of full-time freshmen returned.

Freshmen *Admission:* 6,268 applied, 3,713 admitted, 1,918 enrolled. *Average high school GPA:* 3.12. *Test scores:* SAT critical reading scores over 500: 55%; SAT math scores over 500: 48%; SAT writing scores over 500: 42%; ACT scores over 18: 92%; SAT critical reading scores over 600: 11%; SAT math

scores over 600: 8%; SAT writing scores over 600: 6%; ACT scores over 24: 16%; SAT critical reading scores over 700: 1%; ACT scores over 30: 2%.
Faculty *Total:* 644, 75% full-time, 66% with terminal degrees. *Student/faculty ratio:* 21:1.

Academics *Calendar:* semesters. *Degrees:* certificates, associate, bachelor's, master's, doctoral, post-master's, and postbachelor's certificates. *Special study options:* accelerated degree program, adult/continuing education programs, advanced placement credit, cooperative education, distance learning, double majors, English as a second language, external degree program, honors programs, independent study, internships, off-campus study, part-time degree program, services for LD students, study abroad, summer session for credit. *ROTC:* Air Force (b). *Unusual degree programs:* 3-2 engineering with Georgia Institute of Technology, Atlanta, GA.

Computers on Campus 1,225 computers/terminals are available on campus for general student use. Students can access the following: campus intranet, computer help desk, free student e-mail accounts, online (class) grades, online (class) registration, online (class) schedules. Campuswide network is available. 100% of college-owned or -operated housing units are wired for high-speed Internet access. Wireless service is available via classrooms, computer centers, computer labs, dorm rooms, learning centers, libraries, student centers.

Student Life *Housing:* on-campus residence required for freshman year. *Options:* coed, disabled students. Campus housing is university owned. Freshman applicants given priority for college housing. *Activities and organizations:* drama/theater group, student-run newspaper, radio station, choral group, marching band, Interfraternity Council, College Panhellenic Council, Black Student League, Residence Hall Association, Alpha Lambda Delta Freshmen Honor Society, national fraternities, national sororities. *Campus security:* 24-hour emergency response devices and patrols, late-night transport/escort service, controlled dormitory access, bicycle patrols, security cameras. *Student services:* health clinic, personal/psychological counseling.

Athletics Member NCAA. All Division II. *Intercollegiate sports:* baseball M(s), basketball M(s)/W(s), cheerleading M(c)/W(c), cross-country running M(s)/W(s), fencing M(c)/W(c), football M(s), golf M(s), lacrosse M(c)/W(c), rugby M(c), soccer M(c)/W(s), softball W(s), table tennis M(c)/W(c), tennis M(s)/W(s), ultimate Frisbee M(c)/W(c), volleyball W(s), wrestling M(c). *Intramural sports:* badminton M/W, basketball M/W, bowling M/W, field hockey M/W, football M/W, golf M/W, racquetball M/W, soccer M/W, softball M/W, swimming and diving M/W, table tennis M/W, tennis M/W, volleyball M/W.

Standardized Tests *Required:* SAT or ACT (for admission).

Costs (2012–13) *Tuition:* state resident $3882 full-time, $162 per credit hour part-time; nonresident $13,703 full-time, $571 per credit hour part-time. Full-time tuition and fees vary according to course load, location, program, and reciprocity agreements. Part-time tuition and fees vary according to course load, location, program, and reciprocity agreements. *Required fees:* $1910 full-time, $955 per term part-time. *Room and board:* $7070; room only: $3560. Room and board charges vary according to board plan and housing facility. *Waivers:* senior citizens and employees or children of employees.

Financial Aid Of all full-time matriculated undergraduates who enrolled in 2012, 8,487 applied for aid, 7,353 were judged to have need, 1,819 had their need fully met. 157 Federal Work-Study jobs (averaging $3067). In 2012, 91 non-need-based awards were made. *Average percent of need met:* 83%. *Average financial aid package:* $14,321. *Average need-based loan:* $4352. *Average need-based gift aid:* $5975. *Average non-need-based aid:* $1933. *Average indebtedness upon graduation:* $23,826.

Applying *Options:* electronic application, early admission, deferred entrance. *Application fee:* $40. *Required:* high school transcript. *Application deadlines:* 6/15 (freshmen), 6/15 (out-of-state freshmen), 6/15 (transfers). *Notification:* continuous until 8/1 (freshmen), continuous until 8/1 (out-of-state freshmen), continuous until 8/1 (transfers).

Freshman Application Contact Mr. Ryan M. Hogan, Associate Director of Admissions, Valdosta State University, Office of Admissions, 1500 North Patterson Street, Valdosta, GA 31698. *Phone:* 229-333-5791. *Toll-free phone:* 800-618-1878. *Fax:* 229-333-5482. *E-mail:* admissions@valdosta.edu.
Website: http://www.valdosta.edu/.

Wesleyan College

Macon, Georgia

- **Independent United Methodist** comprehensive, founded 1836
- **Suburban** 200-acre campus with easy access to Atlanta
- **Endowment** $55.0 million
- **Undergraduate: women only; graduate: coed** 648 undergraduate students, 68% full-time, 100% women
- **Moderately difficult** entrance level, 51% of applicants were admitted

Undergraduates 439 full-time, 209 part-time. Students come from 21 states and territories; 27 other countries; 14% are from out of state; 31% Black or African American, non-Hispanic/Latino; 4% Hispanic/Latino; 1% Asian, non-

Hispanic/Latino; 0.2% Native Hawaiian or other Pacific Islander, non-Hispanic/Latino; 3% Two or more races, non-Hispanic/Latino; 2% Race/ethnicity unknown; 18% international; 3% transferred in; 82% live on campus. *Retention:* 83% of full-time freshmen returned.

Freshmen *Admission:* 690 applied, 351 admitted, 121 enrolled. *Average high school GPA:* 3.3. *Test scores:* SAT critical reading scores over 500: 60%; SAT math scores over 500: 44%; SAT writing scores over 500: 53%; ACT scores over 18: 75%; SAT critical reading scores over 600: 18%; SAT math scores over 600: 16%; SAT writing scores over 600: 18%; ACT scores over 24: 19%; SAT critical reading scores over 700: 1%; SAT math scores over 700: 7%; SAT writing scores over 700: 1%.

Faculty *Total:* 114, 45% full-time, 45% with terminal degrees. *Student/faculty ratio:* 8:1.

Academics *Calendar:* semesters. *Degrees:* bachelor's and master's. *Special study options:* adult/continuing education programs, advanced placement credit, cooperative education, double majors, honors programs, independent study, internships, off-campus study, part-time degree program, services for LD students, student-designed majors, study abroad, summer session for credit. *ROTC:* Army (c). *Unusual degree programs:* 3-2 engineering with Georgia Tech, Auburn University and Mercer University.

Computers on Campus 40 computers/terminals are available on campus for general student use. Students can access the following: campus intranet, computer help desk, free student e-mail accounts, online (class) grades, online (class) registration, online (class) schedules, online payment. Campuswide network is available. 85% of college-owned or -operated housing units are wired for high-speed Internet access. Wireless service is available via classrooms, computer centers, computer labs, learning centers, libraries, student centers.

Student Life *Housing:* on-campus residence required through senior year. *Options:* women-only, disabled students. Campus housing is university owned. Freshman campus housing is guaranteed. *Activities and organizations:* drama/theater group, student-run newspaper, choral group, Student Recreation Council, Campus Activities Board, Student Government Association, Council on Religious Concerns, Christian Fellowship. *Campus security:* 24-hour emergency response devices and patrols, late-night transport/escort service, controlled dormitory access. *Student services:* health clinic, women's center.

Athletics Member NCAA. All Division III. *Intercollegiate sports:* basketball W, cross-country running W, equestrian sports W, soccer W, softball W, tennis W, volleyball W. *Intramural sports:* basketball W, cross-country running W, equestrian sports W, soccer W, softball W, tennis W, volleyball W.

Standardized Tests *Required:* SAT or ACT (for admission).

Costs (2012–13) *Comprehensive fee:* $27,400 includes full-time tuition ($19,000) and room and board ($8400). Full-time tuition and fees vary according to degree level, program, and reciprocity agreements. Part-time tuition and fees vary according to degree level, program, and reciprocity agreements. *Room and board:* Room and board charges vary according to board plan and housing facility. *Payment plans:* installment, deferred payment. *Waivers:* senior citizens and employees or children of employees.

Financial Aid Of all full-time matriculated undergraduates who enrolled in 2012, 340 applied for aid, 316 were judged to have need, 42 had their need fully met. In 2012, 129 non-need-based awards were made. *Average percent of need met:* 73%. *Average financial aid package:* $17,573. *Average need-based loan:* $4438. *Average need-based gift aid:* $13,911. *Average non-need-based aid:* $12,088. *Average indebtedness upon graduation:* $34,368.

Applying *Options:* electronic application, early admission, early decision, early action, deferred entrance. *Application fee:* $30. *Required:* high school transcript, minimum 2.0 GPA, 1 letter of recommendation. *Required for some:* interview. *Recommended:* essay or personal statement, 2 letters of recommendation. *Application deadlines:* 2/15 (freshmen), rolling (transfers), 1/15 (early action). *Early decision deadline:* 11/15. *Notification:* continuous (freshmen), continuous (transfers), 12/15 (early decision).

Freshman Application Contact Mr. Stephen Farr, Vice President for Enrollment Services, Wesleyan College, 4760 Forsyth Road, Macon, GA 31210-4462. *Phone:* 478-757-3700. *Toll-free phone:* 800-447-6610. *Fax:* 478-757-4030. *E-mail:* admissions@wesleyancollege.edu. *Website:* http://www.wesleyancollege.edu/.

Westwood College–Atlanta Midtown
Atlanta, Georgia

Freshman Application Contact Westwood College–Atlanta Midtown, 1100 Spring Street, Suite 102, Atlanta, GA 30309. *Phone:* 404-745-9862. *Toll-free phone:* 800-613-4595.
Website: http://www.westwood.edu/.

Westwood College–Atlanta Northlake
Atlanta, Georgia

Freshman Application Contact Westwood College–Atlanta Northlake, 2309 Parklake Drive, NE, Building 10, Atlanta, GA 30345. *Phone:* 404-962-2998. *Toll-free phone:* 866-821-6145.
Website: http://www.westwood.edu/.

Young Harris College
Young Harris, Georgia

- **Independent United Methodist** 4-year, founded 1886
- **Small-town** 800-acre campus
- **Endowment** $93.7 million
- **Coed** 1,034 undergraduate students, 97% full-time, 54% women, 46% men
- **Moderately difficult** entrance level, 48% of applicants were admitted

Undergraduates 999 full-time, 35 part-time. Students come from 24 states and territories; 26 other countries; 14% are from out of state; 6% Black or African American, non-Hispanic/Latino; 6% Hispanic/Latino; 0.8% Asian, non-Hispanic/Latino; 0.4% Native Hawaiian or other Pacific Islander, non-Hispanic/Latino; 0.2% American Indian or Alaska Native, non-Hispanic/Latino; 0.5% Two or more races, non-Hispanic/Latino; 3% Race/ethnicity unknown; 3% transferred in; 87% live on campus. *Retention:* 65% of full-time freshmen returned.

Freshmen *Admission:* 2,061 applied, 993 admitted, 388 enrolled. *Average high school GPA:* 3.15. *Test scores:* SAT critical reading scores over 500: 51%; SAT math scores over 500: 46%; SAT writing scores over 500: 42%; ACT scores over 18: 82%; SAT critical reading scores over 600: 11%; SAT math scores over 600: 9%; SAT writing scores over 600: 9%; ACT scores over 24: 22%; SAT critical reading scores over 700: 1%; SAT writing scores over 700: 1%; ACT scores over 30: 2%.

Faculty *Total:* 105, 73% full-time, 58% with terminal degrees. *Student/faculty ratio:* 12:1.

Academics *Calendar:* semesters. *Degree:* bachelor's. *Special study options:* adult/continuing education programs, advanced placement credit, cooperative education, double majors, honors programs, internships, part-time degree program, services for LD students, study abroad, summer session for credit.

Computers on Campus 99 computers/terminals are available on campus for general student use. Students can access the following: campus intranet, computer help desk, free student e-mail accounts, online (class) grades, online (class) registration, online (class) schedules. Campuswide network is available. 100% of college-owned or -operated housing units are wired for high-speed Internet access. Wireless service is available via entire campus.

Student Life *Housing:* on-campus residence required through senior year. *Options:* coed, men-only, women-only, disabled students. Campus housing is university owned. Freshman campus housing is guaranteed. *Activities and organizations:* drama/theater group, student-run newspaper, choral group, Greek life, religious organizations/Bible study, intramural sports, Student Government Association, Campus Activities Board, national fraternities, national sororities. *Campus security:* 24-hour emergency response devices and patrols, student patrols, late-night transport/escort service, controlled dormitory access. *Student services:* health clinic, personal/psychological counseling.

Athletics Member NCAA. All Division II. *Intercollegiate sports:* baseball M(s), basketball M(s)/W(s), cheerleading M(s)/W(s), cross-country running M(s)/W(s), golf M(s)/W(s), lacrosse M(s)/W(s), soccer M(s)/W(s), softball W(s), tennis M(s)/W(s). *Intramural sports:* basketball M/W, football M/W, soccer M/W, softball M/W, ultimate Frisbee M/W, volleyball M/W, weight lifting M/W.

Standardized Tests *Required:* SAT or ACT (for admission).

Costs (2013–14) *Comprehensive fee:* $34,940 includes full-time tuition ($24,500), mandatory fees ($780), and room and board ($9660). Full-time tuition and fees vary according to course load. Part-time tuition: $675 per credit hour. Part-time tuition and fees vary according to course load. *Room and board:* Room and board charges vary according to housing facility. *Payment plan:* installment. *Waivers:* employees or children of employees.

Financial Aid Of all full-time matriculated undergraduates who enrolled in 2010, 677 applied for aid, 613 were judged to have need, 146 had their need fully met. In 2010, 212 non-need-based awards were made. *Average percent of need met:* 81%. *Average financial aid package:* $17,157. *Average need-based loan:* $3190. *Average need-based gift aid:* $14,754. *Average non-need-based aid:* $12,162. *Average indebtedness upon graduation:* $23,728.

Applying *Options:* electronic application. *Required:* high school transcript. *Application deadlines:* rolling (freshmen), rolling (out-of-state freshmen), rolling (transfers). *Notification:* continuous (freshmen), continuous (out-of-state freshmen), continuous (transfers).

Freshman Application Contact Mr. Clinton G. Hobbs, Vice President for Enrollment Management, Young Harris College, PO Box 116, Young Harris,

GA 30582-0098. *Phone:* 706-379-3111. *Toll-free phone:* 800-241-3754. *Fax:* 706-379-3108. *E-mail:* admissions@yhc.edu.
Website: http://www.yhc.edu/.

HAWAII

Argosy University, Hawai`i
Honolulu, Hawaii

Freshman Application Contact Argosy University, Hawai`i, 400 ASB Tower, 1001 Bishop Street, Honolulu, HI 96813. *Phone:* 808-536-5555. *Toll-free phone:* 888-323-2777.
Website: http://www.argosy.edu/hawaii/.

Brigham Young University–Hawaii
Laie, Hawaii

Freshman Application Contact Mr. Arapata P. Meha, Brigham Young University–Hawaii, 55-220 Kulanui Street, Laie, HI 96762-1294. *Phone:* 808-675-3731. *Fax:* 808-675-3741. *E-mail:* admissions@byuh.edu.
Website: http://www.byuh.edu/.

Chaminade University of Honolulu
Honolulu, Hawaii

- **Independent Roman Catholic** comprehensive, founded 1955
- **Urban** 62-acre campus with easy access to Honolulu
- **Endowment** $9.3 million
- **Coed**
- **Moderately difficult** entrance level

Faculty *Student/faculty ratio:* 13:1.
Academics *Calendar:* semesters. *Degrees:* associate, bachelor's, master's, and postbachelor's certificates.
Student Life *Campus security:* 24-hour emergency response devices and patrols, late-night transport/escort service, controlled dormitory access.
Athletics Member NCAA. All Division II.

Standardized Tests *Required:* SAT or ACT (for admission), TOEFL for international students (for admission).
Costs (2012–13) *Comprehensive fee:* $30,620 includes full-time tuition ($19,200), mandatory fees ($130), and room and board ($11,290). Full-time tuition and fees vary according to course load. Part-time tuition: $640 per credit hour. Part-time tuition and fees vary according to course load. *Room and board:* Room and board charges vary according to board plan and housing facility.
Applying *Options:* electronic application, deferred entrance. *Application fee:* $50. *Required:* essay or personal statement, high school transcript, minimum 2.5 GPA. *Required for some:* minimum 2.8 GPA, 2 letters of recommendation, interview. *Recommended:* minimum 3.0 GPA, 2 letters of recommendation.
Freshman Application Contact Office of Admissions, Chaminade University of Honolulu, 3140 Waialae Avenue, Honolulu, HI 96816-1578. *Phone:* 808-739-8340. *Toll-free phone:* 800-735-3733. *Fax:* 808-739-4647. *E-mail:* admissions@chaminade.edu.
Website: http://www.chaminade.edu/.

Hawai`i Pacific University
Honolulu, Hawaii

- **Independent** comprehensive, founded 1965
- **Urban** 140-acre campus
- **Endowment** $61.0 million
- **Coed** 6,168 undergraduate students, 64% full-time, 55% women, 45% men
- **Moderately difficult** entrance level, 72% of applicants were admitted

Undergraduates 3,944 full-time, 2,224 part-time. Students come from 51 states and territories; 65 other countries; 30% are from out of state; 6% Black or African American, non-Hispanic/Latino; 14% Hispanic/Latino; 21% Asian, non-Hispanic/Latino; 3% Native Hawaiian or other Pacific Islander, non-Hispanic/Latino; 0.6% American Indian or Alaska Native, non-Hispanic/Latino; 12% Two or more races, non-Hispanic/Latino; 5% Race/ethnicity unknown; 10% international; 12% transferred in; 10% live on campus. *Retention:* 69% of full-time freshmen returned.
Freshmen *Admission:* 4,129 applied, 2,980 admitted, 475 enrolled. *Average high school GPA:* 3.39. *Test scores:* SAT critical reading scores over 500: 43%; SAT math scores over 500: 48%; SAT writing scores over 500: 38%; ACT scores over 18: 81%; SAT critical reading scores over 600: 9%; SAT math scores over 600: 10%; SAT writing scores over 600: 6%; ACT scores over 24:

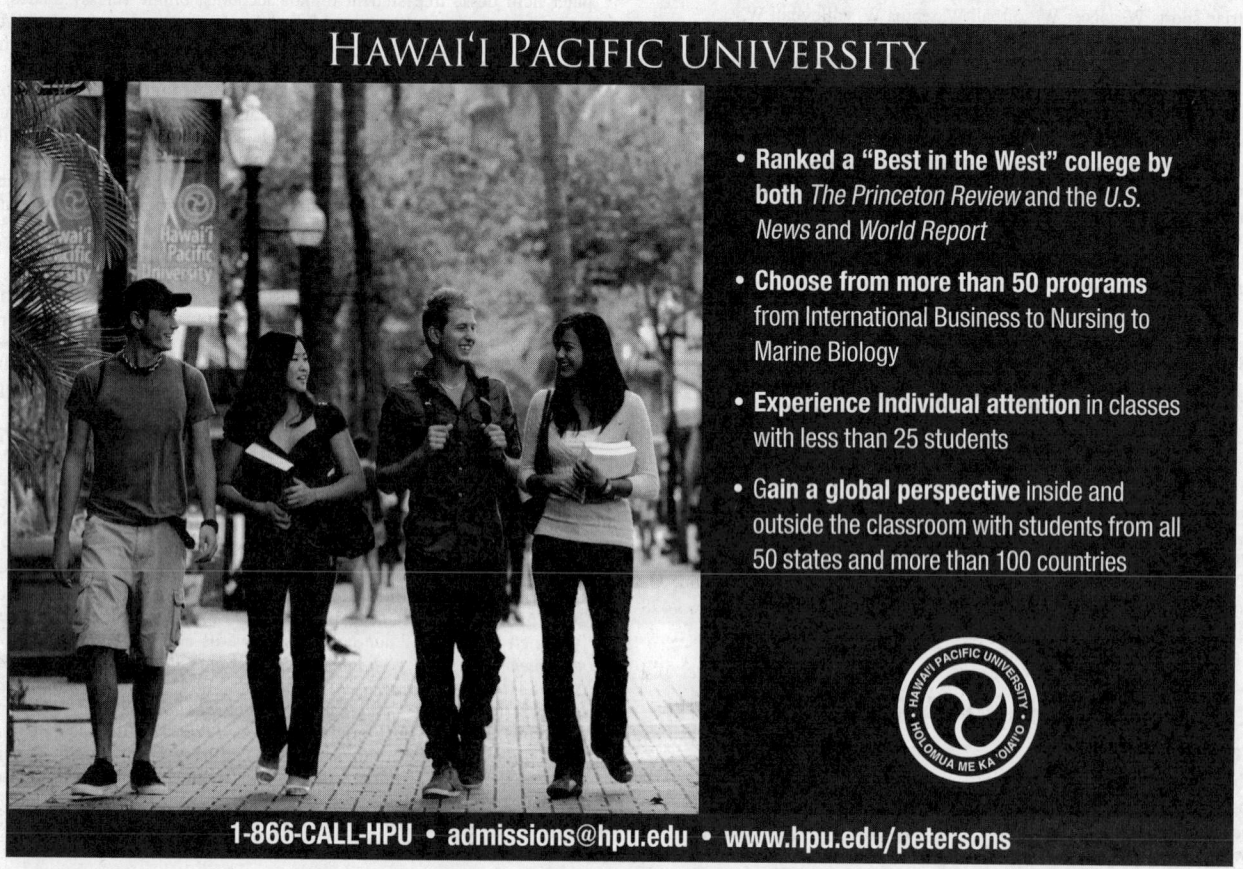

23%; SAT critical reading scores over 700: 1%; SAT math scores over 700: 1%; ACT scores over 30: 4%.

Faculty *Total:* 696, 38% full-time, 48% with terminal degrees. *Student/faculty ratio:* 14:1.

Academics *Calendar:* semesters. *Degrees:* certificates, associate, bachelor's, master's, post-master's, and postbachelor's certificates. *Special study options:* academic remediation for entering students, accelerated degree program, adult/continuing education programs, advanced placement credit, cooperative education, distance learning, double majors, English as a second language, freshman honors college, honors programs, independent study, internships, off-campus study, part-time degree program, services for LD students, student-designed majors, study abroad, summer session for credit. *ROTC:* Army (c), Air Force (c). *Unusual degree programs:* 3-2 engineering with Washington University in St. Louis, University of Southern California.

Computers on Campus 590 computers/terminals are available on campus for general student use. Students can access the following: campus intranet, computer help desk, free student e-mail accounts, online (class) grades, online (class) registration, online (class) schedules. Campuswide network is available. Wireless service is available via entire campus.

Student Life *Housing options:* coed. Campus housing is university owned and is provided by a third party. Freshman applicants given priority for college housing. *Activities and organizations:* drama/theater group, student-run newspaper, choral group, Student Government Association, Circle K International, Psychology Club, Student Nurses Association, Outspoken LGBT Cooperative. *Campus security:* 24-hour emergency response devices and patrols, student patrols, late-night transport/escort service, controlled dormitory access, Rave Alert System. *Student services:* personal/psychological counseling.

Athletics Member NCAA. All Division II. *Intercollegiate sports:* baseball M(s), basketball M(s)/W(s), cheerleading M(s)/W(s), cross-country running M(s)/W(s), golf M(s), soccer M(s)/W(s), softball W(s), tennis M(s)/W(s), volleyball W(s). *Intramural sports:* basketball M/W, football M/W, soccer M/W, softball M/W, table tennis M/W, tennis M/W, ultimate Frisbee M/W, volleyball M/W.

Standardized Tests *Required:* SAT or ACT (for admission).

Costs (2013–14) *Comprehensive fee:* $32,630 includes full-time tuition ($19,980), mandatory fees ($100), and room and board ($12,550). Full-time tuition and fees vary according to course level, course load, degree level, location, program, and student level. Part-time tuition and fees vary according to course level, course load, degree level, location, program, and student level. *Room and board:* Room and board charges vary according to housing facility. *Payment plan:* installment. *Waivers:* employees or children of employees.

Financial Aid Of all full-time matriculated undergraduates who enrolled in 2010, 3,031 applied for aid, 1,933 were judged to have need, 470 had their need fully met. 157 Federal Work-Study jobs (averaging $3000). In 2010, 182 non-need-based awards were made. *Average percent of need met:* 78%. *Average financial aid package:* $17,448. *Average need-based loan:* $6159. *Average need-based gift aid:* $2031. *Average non-need-based aid:* $2153. *Average indebtedness upon graduation:* $32,172.

Applying *Options:* electronic application, early admission, deferred entrance. *Application fee:* $50. *Required:* high school transcript, minimum 2.5 GPA. *Required for some:* interview. *Recommended:* essay or personal statement, 2 letters of recommendation. *Application deadlines:* rolling (freshmen), rolling (transfers). *Notification:* continuous (transfers).

Freshman Application Contact Ms. Sara Sato, Assistant Vice President, Enrollment Management, Hawai`i Pacific University, 1164 Bishop Street, Honolulu, HI 96813-2785. *Phone:* 808-543-8095. *Toll-free phone:* 866-225-5478. *Fax:* 808-543-8065. *E-mail:* admissions@hpu.edu. *Website:* http://www.hpu.edu/.

See previous page for display ad and page 1318 for the College Close-Up.

Remington College–Honolulu Campus

Honolulu, Hawaii

Director of Admissions Louis LaMair, Director of Recruitment, Remington College–Honolulu Campus, 1111 Bishop Street, Suite 400, Honolulu, HI 96813. *Phone:* 808-942-1000. *Fax:* 808-533-3064. *E-mail:* louis.lamair@remingtoncollege.edu. *Website:* http://www.remingtoncollege.edu/.

University of Hawaii at Hilo

Hilo, Hawaii

- **State-supported** comprehensive, founded 1970, part of University of Hawaii System
- **Small-town** 115-acre campus
- **Endowment** $2.8 million
- **Coed** 3,568 undergraduate students, 79% full-time, 59% women, 41% men
- **Moderately difficult** entrance level, 28% of applicants were admitted

Undergraduates 2,818 full-time, 750 part-time. Students come from 50 states and territories; 26 other countries; 23% are from out of state; 1% Black or African American, non-Hispanic/Latino; 10% Hispanic/Latino; 19% Asian, non-Hispanic/Latino; 12% Native Hawaiian or other Pacific Islander, non-Hispanic/Latino; 0.4% American Indian or Alaska Native, non-Hispanic/Latino; 30% Two or more races, non-Hispanic/Latino; 0.4% Race/ethnicity unknown; 5% international; 18% transferred in; 22% live on campus. *Retention:* 70% of full-time freshmen returned.

Freshmen *Admission:* 1,639 applied, 453 admitted, 453 enrolled. *Test scores:* SAT critical reading scores over 500: 40%; SAT math scores over 500: 43%; SAT writing scores over 500: 30%; ACT scores over 18: 81%; SAT critical reading scores over 600: 9%; SAT math scores over 600: 12%; SAT writing scores over 600: 7%; ACT scores over 24: 27%; SAT critical reading scores over 700: 1%; SAT math scores over 700: 1%; ACT scores over 30: 1%.

Faculty *Total:* 300, 76% full-time. *Student/faculty ratio:* 14:1.

Academics *Calendar:* semesters. *Degrees:* certificates, bachelor's, master's, doctoral, and postbachelor's certificates. *Special study options:* advanced placement credit, distance learning, double majors, English as a second language, honors programs, independent study, internships, off-campus study, part-time degree program, services for LD students, student-designed majors, study abroad, summer session for credit.

Computers on Campus 600 computers/terminals are available on campus for general student use. Students can access the following: online (class) registration. Campuswide network is available.

Student Life *Housing options:* coed. Campus housing is university owned. *Activities and organizations:* drama/theater group, student-run newspaper, choral group, International Student Association, Hawaiian Leadership and Development, Delta Sigma Pi Business Fraternity, University Canoe Club, Samoan Club. *Campus security:* 24-hour emergency response devices and patrols, controlled dormitory access. *Student services:* health clinic, personal/psychological counseling, women's center.

Athletics Member NCAA. All Division II except baseball (Division I). *Intercollegiate sports:* baseball M(s), basketball M(s), cross-country running M(s)/W(s), golf M(s), softball W(s), tennis M(s)/W(s), volleyball W(s). *Intramural sports:* archery M/W, badminton M/W, basketball M/W, bowling M/W, golf M/W, soccer M/W, softball M/W, table tennis M/W, tennis M/W, volleyball M/W, weight lifting M/W.

Standardized Tests *Required:* SAT or ACT (for admission).

Costs (2013–14) *Tuition:* state resident $6192 full-time, $258 per credit part-time; nonresident $17,952 full-time, $748 per credit part-time. Full-time tuition and fees vary according to reciprocity agreements. Part-time tuition and fees vary according to course load. *Required fees:* $304 full-time. *Room and board:* Room and board charges vary according to board plan and housing facility.

Financial Aid Of all full-time matriculated undergraduates who enrolled in 2012, 2,278 applied for aid, 1,768 were judged to have need, 347 had their need fully met. 160 Federal Work-Study jobs (averaging $1631). 526 state and other part-time jobs (averaging $2172). In 2012, 27 non-need-based awards were made. *Average percent of need met:* 70%. *Average financial aid package:* $11,389. *Average need-based loan:* $4273. *Average need-based gift aid:* $4963. *Average non-need-based aid:* $1870. *Average indebtedness upon graduation:* $13,035.

Applying *Options:* electronic application, deferred entrance. *Application fee:* $50. *Required:* high school transcript. *Recommended:* minimum 3.0 GPA. *Application deadlines:* 7/1 (freshmen), 7/1 (transfers). *Notification:* 7/31 (freshmen), 7/31 (transfers).

Freshman Application Contact Mr. Curtis Nishioka, Student Services Specialist/Director of Admissions, University of Hawaii at Hilo, 200 West Kawili Street, Hilo, HI 96720-4091. *Phone:* 808-974-7414. *Toll-free phone:* 800-897-4456. *Fax:* 808-933-0861. *E-mail:* uhhao@hawaii.edu. *Website:* http://www.uhh.hawaii.edu/.

University of Hawaii at Manoa
Honolulu, Hawaii

- **State-supported** university, founded 1907, part of University of Hawaii System
- **Urban** 320,300-acre campus with easy access to Honolulu
- **Endowment** $201.5 million
- **Coed** 14,655 undergraduate students, 82% full-time, 54% women, 46% men
- **Moderately difficult** entrance level, 81% of applicants were admitted

Undergraduates 11,975 full-time, 2,680 part-time. Students come from 63 states and territories; 50 other countries; 23% are from out of state; 2% Black or African American, non-Hispanic/Latino; 2% Hispanic/Latino; 40% Asian, non-Hispanic/Latino; 17% Native Hawaiian or other Pacific Islander, non-Hispanic/Latino; 0.3% American Indian or Alaska Native, non-Hispanic/Latino; 14% Two or more races, non-Hispanic/Latino; 0.2% Race/ethnicity unknown; 3% international; 13% transferred in; 23% live on campus. *Retention:* 79% of full-time freshmen returned.

Freshmen *Admission:* 6,810 applied, 5,528 admitted, 1,964 enrolled. *Average high school GPA:* 3.46. *Test scores:* SAT critical reading scores over 500: 66%; SAT math scores over 500: 78%; SAT writing scores over 500: 63%; ACT scores over 18: 98%; SAT critical reading scores over 600: 19%; SAT math scores over 600: 33%; SAT writing scores over 600: 18%; ACT scores over 24: 50%; SAT critical reading scores over 700: 3%; SAT math scores over 700: 5%; SAT writing scores over 700: 2%; ACT scores over 30: 3%.

Faculty *Total:* 1,265, 95% full-time, 85% with terminal degrees. *Student/faculty ratio:* 14:1.

Academics *Calendar:* semesters. *Degrees:* certificates, bachelor's, master's, doctoral, and postbachelor's certificates. *Special study options:* accelerated degree program, advanced placement credit, cooperative education, distance learning, double majors, English as a second language, honors programs, independent study, internships, off-campus study, part-time degree program, services for LD students, student-designed majors, study abroad, summer session for credit. *ROTC:* Army (b), Air Force (b).

Computers on Campus 400 computers/terminals are available on campus for general student use. Students can access the following: campus intranet, computer help desk, free student e-mail accounts, online (class) grades, online (class) registration, online (class) schedules. Campuswide network is available. 99% of college-owned or -operated housing units are wired for high-speed Internet access. Wireless service is available via entire campus.

Student Life *Housing options:* coed, disabled students. Campus housing is university owned. Freshman applicants given priority for college housing. *Activities and organizations:* drama/theater group, student-run newspaper, radio station, choral group, marching band, Associated Students of University of Hawaii (ASUH), Campus Center Board, Broadcast Communication Authority, Board of Publications, Student Activities and Program Fee Board, national fraternities, national sororities. *Campus security:* 24-hour emergency response devices and patrols, student patrols, late-night transport/escort service, controlled dormitory access. *Student services:* health clinic, personal/psychological counseling, women's center.

Athletics Member NCAA. All Division I except football (Division I-A). *Intercollegiate sports:* archery M, baseball M(s), basketball M(s)/W(s), cheerleading M(s)/W(s), cross-country running W(s), golf M(s)/W(s), sailing M/W, soccer W(s), softball W(s), swimming and diving M(s)/W(s), tennis M(s)/W(s), track and field W(s), volleyball M(s)/W(s), water polo W(s). *Intramural sports:* badminton M/W, basketball M/W, crew M/W, cross-country running M/W, golf M/W, rugby M, sailing M/W, soccer M, softball M, swimming and diving M/W, table tennis M/W, tennis M/W, track and field M/W, ultimate Frisbee M/W, volleyball M/W, weight lifting M/W, wrestling M/W.

Standardized Tests *Required:* SAT or ACT (for admission).

Costs (2013–14) *Tuition:* area resident $9144 full-time; state resident $9144 full-time, $381 per credit part-time; nonresident $26,712 full-time, $1113 per credit part-time. Full-time tuition and fees vary according to class time, course level, course load, degree level, program, reciprocity agreements, and student level. Part-time tuition and fees vary according to class time, course level, course load, degree level, program, reciprocity agreements, and student level. *Required fees:* $740 full-time. *Room and board:* $10,029; room only: $6820. Room and board charges vary according to board plan and housing facility. *Payment plan:* installment. *Waivers:* minority students, adult students, senior citizens, and employees or children of employees.

Financial Aid Of all full-time matriculated undergraduates who enrolled in 2011, 9,105 applied for aid, 6,540 were judged to have need, 1,578 had their need fully met. 419 Federal Work-Study jobs (averaging $2161). In 2011, 2216 non-need-based awards were made. *Average percent of need met:* 70%. *Average financial aid package:* $11,498. *Average need-based loan:* $4467. *Average need-based gift aid:* $7836. *Average non-need-based aid:* $8592. *Average indebtedness upon graduation:* $21,405.

Applying *Options:* electronic application. *Application fee:* $70. *Required:* high school transcript, minimum 2.8 GPA. *Application deadlines:* 5/1 (freshmen), 5/1 (transfers). *Notification:* continuous (freshmen), continuous (transfers).

Freshman Application Contact Ms. Lisa Buto, Student Services Specialist, University of Hawaii at Manoa, 2600 Campus Road, Room 001, Honolulu, HI 96822. *Phone:* 808-956-8975. *Toll-free phone:* 800-823-9771. *Fax:* 808-956-4148. *E-mail:* ar-info@hawaii.edu.
Website: http://manoa.hawaii.edu/.

University of Hawaii Maui College
Kahului, Hawaii

Freshman Application Contact Mr. Stephen Kameda, Director of Admissions and Records, University of Hawaii Maui College, 310 Kaahumanu Avenue, Kahului, HI 96732. *Phone:* 808-984-3267. *Toll-free phone:* 800-479-6692. *Fax:* 808-242-9618. *E-mail:* kameda@hawaii.edu.
Website: http://maui.hawaii.edu/.

University of Hawaii–West Oahu
Pearl City, Hawaii

- **State-supported** 4-year, founded 1976, part of University of Hawaii System
- **Small-town** campus with easy access to Honolulu
- **Coed** 1,997 undergraduate students, 42% full-time, 66% women, 34% men
- **Moderately difficult** entrance level, 51% of applicants were admitted

Undergraduates 830 full-time, 1,167 part-time. 20% are from out of state; 2% Black or African American, non-Hispanic/Latino; 1% Hispanic/Latino; 41% Asian, non-Hispanic/Latino; 28% Native Hawaiian or other Pacific Islander, non-Hispanic/Latino; 0.3% American Indian or Alaska Native, non-Hispanic/Latino; 14% Two or more races, non-Hispanic/Latino; 0.1% Race/ethnicity unknown; 0.4% international; 25% transferred in. *Retention:* 67% of full-time freshmen returned.

Freshmen *Admission:* 908 applied, 467 admitted, 301 enrolled. *Average high school GPA:* 3.3.

Faculty *Total:* 101, 50% full-time, 55% with terminal degrees. *Student/faculty ratio:* 18:1.

Academics *Calendar:* semesters. *Degree:* certificates and bachelor's. *Special study options:* part-time degree program. *ROTC:* Army (c), Air Force (c).

Computers on Campus Students can access the following: computer help desk, free student e-mail accounts, online (class) grades, online (class) registration, online (class) schedules. Campuswide network is available. Wireless service is available via classrooms.

Student Life *Housing:* college housing not available. *Campus security:* 24-hour emergency response devices and patrols, late-night transport/escort service. *Student services:* personal/psychological counseling.

Standardized Tests *Required for some:* SAT (for admission), ACT (for admission), SAT or ACT (for admission).

Costs (2013–14) *Tuition:* state resident $5592 full-time, $254 per credit hour part-time; nonresident $16,656 full-time, $734 per credit hour part-time. *Payment plan:* installment. *Waivers:* employees or children of employees.

Financial Aid Of all full-time matriculated undergraduates who enrolled in 2011, 240 applied for aid, 240 were judged to have need. In 2011, 6 non-need-based awards were made. *Average percent of need met:* 50%. *Average financial aid package:* $8380. *Average need-based loan:* $4346. *Average need-based gift aid:* $5326. *Average non-need-based aid:* $917.

Applying *Options:* deferred entrance. *Application fee:* $50. *Required:* minimum 2.7 GPA. *Required for some:* high school transcript, 2 letters of recommendation, college transcripts. *Application deadlines:* 3/1 (freshmen), 3/1 (transfers). *Notification:* continuous (freshmen), continuous (transfers).

Freshman Application Contact Robyn Oshiro, University of Hawaii–West Oahu, 96-129 Ala Ike Street, Pearl City, HI 96782. *Phone:* 808-454-4700. *Toll-free phone:* 866-299-8656. *Fax:* 808-453-6075. *E-mail:* admissions@hawaii.edu.
Website: http://www.uhwo.hawaii.edu/.

University of Phoenix–Hawaii Campus
Honolulu, Hawaii

Freshman Application Contact Marc Booker, Sr. Director, Office of Admissions and Evaluation, University of Phoenix–Hawaii Campus, 4035 South Riverpoint Parkway, Mail Stop CF-L101, Phoenix, AZ 85040. *Phone:* 602-557-4609. *Toll-free phone:* 866-766-0766. *Fax:* 480-643-1156.
Website: http://www.phoenix.edu/.

IDAHO

Boise Bible College

Boise, Idaho

Freshman Application Contact Russell Grove, Director of Admissions, Boise Bible College, 8695 West Marigold Street, Boise, ID 83714-1220. *Phone:* 208-376-7731. *Toll-free phone:* 800-893-7755. *Fax:* 208-376-7743. *E-mail:* rgrove@boisebible.edu.
Website: http://www.boisebible.edu/.

Boise State University

Boise, Idaho

- **State-supported** university, founded 1932, part of Idaho System of Higher Education
- **Urban** 216-acre campus
- **Endowment** $75.3 million
- **Coed** 19,653 undergraduate students, 65% full-time, 53% women, 47% men
- **Moderately difficult** entrance level, 85% of applicants were admitted

Undergraduates 12,783 full-time, 6,870 part-time. Students come from 50 states and territories; 68 other countries; 12% are from out of state; 2% Black or African American, non-Hispanic/Latino; 8% Hispanic/Latino; 2% Asian, non-Hispanic/Latino; 0.5% Native Hawaiian or other Pacific Islander, non-Hispanic/Latino; 0.8% American Indian or Alaska Native, non-Hispanic/Latino; 2% Two or more races, non-Hispanic/Latino; 5% Race/ethnicity unknown; 3% international; 15% transferred in; 12% live on campus. *Retention:* 71% of full-time freshmen returned.
Freshmen *Admission:* 5,184 applied, 4,426 admitted, 2,373 enrolled. *Average high school GPA:* 3.43. *Test scores:* SAT critical reading scores over 500: 65%; SAT math scores over 500: 69%; SAT writing scores over 500: 55%; ACT scores over 18: 91%; SAT critical reading scores over 600: 20%; SAT math scores over 600: 27%; SAT writing scores over 600: 15%; ACT scores over 24: 40%; SAT critical reading scores over 700: 3%; SAT math scores over 700: 2%; SAT writing scores over 700: 1%; ACT scores over 30: 5%.
Faculty *Total:* 1,272, 48% full-time, 32% with terminal degrees. *Student/faculty ratio:* 20:1.
Academics *Calendar:* semesters. *Degrees:* associate, bachelor's, master's, doctoral, and postbachelor's certificates. *Special study options:* academic remediation for entering students, adult/continuing education programs, advanced placement credit, cooperative education, distance learning, double majors, English as a second language, freshman honors college, honors program, independent study, internships, off-campus study, part-time degree program, services for LD students, student-designed majors, study abroad, summer session for credit. *ROTC:* Army (b).
Computers on Campus 900 computers/terminals are available on campus for general student use. Students can access the following: computer help desk, free student e-mail accounts, online (class) grades, online (class) registration, online (class) schedules. Campuswide network is available. 100% of college-owned or -operated housing units are wired for high-speed Internet access. Wireless service is available via classrooms, computer labs, dorm rooms, learning centers, libraries, student centers.
Student Life *Housing options:* coed, men-only, women-only. Campus housing is university owned. Freshman applicants given priority for college housing. *Activities and organizations:* drama/theater group, student-run newspaper, radio station, choral group, marching band, Latter-Day Saints Student Association, Residence Hall Association, Organization of Student Social Workers, Marching Band Association, Teacher Education Association, national fraternities, national sororities. *Campus security:* 24-hour emergency response devices and patrols, late-night transport/escort service. *Student services:* health clinic, personal/psychological counseling, women's center, legal services.
Athletics Member NCAA. All Division I except football (Division I-A). *Intercollegiate sports:* basketball M(s)/W(s), cross-country running M(s)/W(s), golf M(s)/W(s), gymnastics W(s), soccer W(s), softball W(s), swimming and diving W(s), tennis M(s)/W(s), track and field M(s)/W(s), volleyball W(s), wrestling M(s). *Intramural sports:* baseball M, basketball M/W, bowling M/W, lacrosse W(c), racquetball M/W, rock climbing M/W, skiing (downhill) M(c)/W(c), soccer M/W, softball M/W, tennis M/W, volleyball M/W, weight lifting M/W.
Standardized Tests *Required:* SAT or ACT (for admission).
Costs (2013–14) *Tuition:* state resident $3990 full-time, $239 per credit hour part-time; nonresident $15,430 full-time, $331 per credit hour part-time. Full-time tuition and fees vary according to reciprocity agreements. *Required fees:* $1894 full-time, $92 per credit hour part-time, $92 per credit hour part-time. *Room and board:* $7174; room only: $3674. Room and board charges vary according to board plan and housing facility. *Payment plan:* installment. *Waivers:* senior citizens and employees or children of employees.
Financial Aid Of all full-time matriculated undergraduates who enrolled in 2011, 9,175 applied for aid, 8,877 were judged to have need, 2,536 had their need fully met. 819 Federal Work-Study jobs (averaging $3815). 880 state and other part-time jobs (averaging $3796). In 2011, 1124 non-need-based awards were made. *Average percent of need met:* 22%. *Average financial aid package:* $9464. *Average need-based loan:* $7321. *Average need-based gift aid:* $4641. *Average non-need-based aid:* $1392. *Average indebtedness upon graduation:* $24,905. *Financial aid deadline:* 6/30.
Applying *Options:* electronic application. *Application fee:* $50. *Required for some:* high school transcript. *Application deadlines:* 5/15 (freshmen), 5/15 (transfers). *Notification:* continuous (freshmen), continuous (transfers).
Freshman Application Contact Ms. Niki Callison, Associate Director/Admissions, Boise State University, Boise State University, 1910 University Drive, Boise, ID 83725. *Phone:* 208-426-2715. *Toll-free phone:* 800-824-7017. *E-mail:* bsuinfo@boisestate.edu.
Website: http://www.boisestate.edu/.

Brigham Young University–Idaho

Rexburg, Idaho

Freshman Application Contact Brigham Young University–Idaho, Rexburg, ID 83460. *Phone:* 208-496-1310.
Website: http://www.byui.edu/.

Broadview University–Boise

Meridian, Idaho

- **Proprietary** 4-year, part of Globe Education Network (GEN) which is composed of Globe University, Minnesota School of Business, Broadview University, The Institute of Production and Recording and Minnesota School of Cosmetology
- **Small-town** 4-acre campus
- **Coed**

Faculty *Student/faculty ratio:* 5:1.
Academics *Degrees:* diplomas, associate, and bachelor's.
Student Life *Campus security:* 24-hour emergency response devices, late-night transport/escort service.
Standardized Tests *Required:* ACCUPLACER is required of all applicants unless documentation of a minimum ACT composite score of 21 or documentation of a minimum composite score of 1485 on the SAT is presented (for admission).
Costs (2012–13) *Tuition:* $14,400 full-time, $435 per credit part-time. Full-time tuition and fees vary according to course level, course load, degree level, location, and program. Part-time tuition and fees vary according to course level, course load, degree level, location, and program. *Required fees:* $1548 full-time, $43 per credit part-time.
Applying *Options:* electronic application. *Application fee:* $50. *Required:* high school transcript, interview. *Required for some:* essay or personal statement, 2 letters of recommendation, GED certificate in lieu of high school transcript.
Freshman Application Contact Broadview University–Boise, 2750 East Gala Court, Meridian, ID 83642. *Phone:* 208-577-2900. *Toll-free phone:* 877-572-5757.
Website: http://www.broadviewuniversity.edu/.

Brown Mackie College–Boise

Boise, Idaho

Freshman Application Contact Brown Mackie College–Boise, 9050 West Overland Road, Suite 100, Boise, ID 83709. *Phone:* 208-321-8800.
Website: http://www.brownmackie.edu/boise/.

See next page for display ad and page 1174 for the College Close-Up.

The College of Idaho

Caldwell, Idaho

- **Independent** comprehensive, founded 1891
- **Suburban** 50-acre campus
- **Endowment** $91.7 million
- **Coed** 1,042 undergraduate students, 96% full-time, 58% women, 42% men
- **Moderately difficult** entrance level, 65% of applicants were admitted

Undergraduates 1,003 full-time, 39 part-time. Students come from 29 states and territories; 53 other countries; 17% are from out of state; 1% Black or African American, non-Hispanic/Latino; 14% Hispanic/Latino; 3% Asian, non-

Hispanic/Latino; 0.8% Native Hawaiian or other Pacific Islander, non-Hispanic/Latino; 0.8% American Indian or Alaska Native, non-Hispanic/Latino; 15% Race/ethnicity unknown; 10% international; 3% transferred in; 62% live on campus. *Retention:* 83% of full-time freshmen returned.

Freshmen *Admission:* 1,388 applied, 901 admitted, 292 enrolled. *Average high school GPA:* 3.64. *Test scores:* SAT critical reading scores over 500: 67%; SAT math scores over 500: 68%; SAT writing scores over 500: 61%; ACT scores over 18: 96%; SAT critical reading scores over 600: 37%; SAT math scores over 600: 30%; SAT writing scores over 600: 26%; ACT scores over 24: 57%; SAT critical reading scores over 700: 13%; SAT math scores over 700: 3%; SAT writing scores over 700: 2%; ACT scores over 30: 14%.

Faculty *Total:* 113, 66% full-time, 68% with terminal degrees. *Student/faculty ratio:* 12:1.

Academics *Calendar:* 12-6-12 week calendar. *Degrees:* bachelor's and master's. *Special study options:* advanced placement credit, cooperative education, double majors, English as a second language, honors programs, independent study, internships, off-campus study, part-time degree program, services for LD students, study abroad. *ROTC:* Army (c). *Unusual degree programs:* 3-2 nursing with Idaho State University; law, speech language pathology, pharmacy, medical laboratory science.

Computers on Campus 475 computers/terminals are available on campus for general student use. Students can access the following: campus intranet, computer help desk, free student e-mail accounts, online (class) grades, online (class) registration, online (class) schedules, online course syllabi, course assignments, course discussion, College of Idaho catalog. Campuswide network is available. 100% of college-owned or -operated housing units are wired for high-speed Internet access. Wireless service is available via entire campus.

Student Life *Housing:* on-campus residence required through junior year. *Options:* coed, disabled students. Campus housing is university owned. Freshman campus housing is guaranteed. *Activities and organizations:* drama/theater group, student-run newspaper, choral group, ISO- International Student Organization, ALAS- Association of Latino American Students, Potter's Clay, GSCA- Gay-Straight Campus Alliance, AFRO- Africans Friends Relatives and Others, national fraternities, national sororities. *Campus security:* 24-hour emergency response devices and patrols, student patrols, late-night transport/escort service, controlled dormitory access. *Student services:* health clinic, personal/psychological counseling, women's center.

Athletics Member NAIA. *Intercollegiate sports:* baseball M(s), basketball M(s)/W(s), cross-country running M(s)/W(s), golf M(s)/W(s), skiing (downhill) M(s)/W(s), soccer M(s)/W(s), softball W(s), swimming and diving M(s)/W(s), tennis W(s), track and field M(s)/W(s), volleyball W(s). *Intramural sports:* badminton M/W, basketball M/W, football M/W, soccer M/W, softball M/W, ultimate Frisbee M/W, volleyball M/W.

Standardized Tests *Required:* SAT or ACT (for admission).

Costs (2013–14) *One-time required fee:* $355. *Comprehensive fee:* $31,646 includes full-time tuition ($22,600), mandatory fees ($400), and room and board ($8646). Part-time tuition: $940 per credit. Part-time tuition and fees vary according to course load. *Room and board:* Room and board charges vary according to board plan and housing facility. *Payment plans:* installment, deferred payment. *Waivers:* employees or children of employees.

Financial Aid Of all full-time matriculated undergraduates who enrolled in 2012, 707 applied for aid, 707 were judged to have need, 123 had their need fully met. 151 Federal Work-Study jobs (averaging $800). 46 state and other part-time jobs (averaging $800). In 2012, 215 non-need-based awards were made. *Average percent of need met:* 93%. *Average financial aid package:* $23,706. *Average need-based loan:* $4561. *Average need-based gift aid:* $7240. *Average non-need-based aid:* $12,358. *Average indebtedness upon graduation:* $27,008.

Applying *Options:* electronic application, early admission, early action, deferred entrance. *Required:* essay or personal statement, high school transcript, 1 letter of recommendation. *Recommended:* interview, class rank, extracurricular resume. *Application deadlines:* 8/1 (freshmen), 8/1 (transfers), 11/15 (early action). *Notification:* continuous (freshmen), continuous (transfers), 11/15 (early action).

Freshman Application Contact Brian Bava, Dean of Enrollment Management, The College of Idaho, 2112 Cleveland Boulevard, Caldwell, ID 83605-4432. *Phone:* 208-459-5319. *Toll-free phone:* 800-244-3246. *Fax:* 208-459-. *E-mail:* admission@collegeofidaho.edu. *Website:* http://www.collegeofidaho.edu/.

Idaho State University
Pocatello, Idaho

- **State-supported** university, founded 1901
- **Urban** 1100-acre campus
- **Coed**
- **Minimally difficult** entrance level

Faculty *Student/faculty ratio:* 15:1.

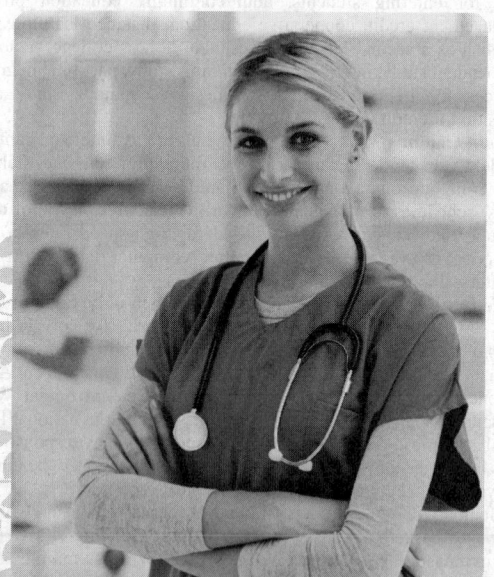

Academics *Calendar:* semesters. *Degrees:* certificates, associate, bachelor's, master's, doctoral, post-master's, and postbachelor's certificates.

Student Life *Campus security:* 24-hour emergency response devices and patrols, late-night transport/escort service, controlled dormitory access.

Athletics Member NCAA. All Division I except football (Division I-AA).

Standardized Tests *Required:* SAT or ACT (for admission). *Recommended:* ACT (for admission).

Costs (2012–13) *One-time required fee:* $40. *Tuition:* state resident $4418 full-time, $304 per credit hour part-time; nonresident $16,218 full-time, $494 per credit hour part-time. Full-time tuition and fees vary according to course load, program, and reciprocity agreements. Part-time tuition and fees vary according to course load and reciprocity agreements. *Required fees:* $1652 full-time. *Room and board:* $5838; room only: $2520. Room and board charges vary according to board plan and housing facility.

Financial Aid *Of all full-time matriculated undergraduates who enrolled in 2010,* 6,664 applied for aid, 6,040 were judged to have need, 157 had their need fully met. *In 2010,* 353 non-need-based awards were made. *Average percent of need met:* 53. *Average financial aid package:* $9376. *Average need-based loan:* $3869. *Average need-based gift aid:* $4792. *Average non-need-based aid:* $1810. *Average indebtedness upon graduation:* $21,939. *Financial aid deadline:* 3/1.

Applying *Options:* electronic application, early admission, deferred entrance. *Application fee:* $40. *Required:* high school transcript, minimum 2.0 GPA.

Freshman Application Contact Admissions and Registration Office, Idaho State University, 921 South 7th, Stop 8270, Pocatello, ID 83209-8270. *Phone:* 208-282-2475. *Fax:* 208-282-4511. *E-mail:* info@isu.edu. *Website:* http://www.isu.edu/.

ITT Technical Institute

Boise, Idaho

- **Proprietary** primarily 2-year, founded 1906, part of ITT Educational Services, Inc.
- **Urban** campus
- **Coed**
- **Minimally difficult** entrance level

Academics *Calendar:* quarters. *Degrees:* associate and bachelor's.

Financial Aid *Of all full-time matriculated undergraduates who enrolled in 2011,* 9 Federal Work-Study jobs (averaging $5500).

Freshman Application Contact Director of Recruitment, ITT Technical Institute, 12302 West Explorer Drive, Boise, ID 83713. *Phone:* 208-322-8844. *Toll-free phone:* 800-666-4888. *Fax:* 208-322-0173. *Website:* http://www.itt-tech.edu/.

Lewis-Clark State College

Lewiston, Idaho

- **State-supported** 4-year, founded 1893
- **Small-town** 44-acre campus
- **Coed** 4,525 undergraduate students, 56% full-time, 60% women, 40% men
- **Minimally difficult** entrance level, 99% of applicants were admitted

Undergraduates 2,549 full-time, 1,976 part-time. 20% are from out of state; 0.7% Black or African American, non-Hispanic/Latino; 5% Hispanic/Latino; 1% Asian, non-Hispanic/Latino; 0.2% Native Hawaiian or other Pacific Islander, non-Hispanic/Latino; 2% American Indian or Alaska Native, non-Hispanic/Latino; 3% Two or more races, non-Hispanic/Latino; 2% Race/ethnicity unknown; 2% international; 9% transferred in. *Retention:* 50% of full-time freshmen returned.

Freshmen *Admission:* 1,006 applied, 997 admitted, 515 enrolled. *Average high school GPA:* 3.02. *Test scores:* SAT math scores over 500: 42%; ACT scores over 18: 76%; SAT math scores over 600: 10%; ACT scores over 24: 21%; SAT math scores over 700: 1%; ACT scores over 30: 1%.

Faculty *Total:* 260, 65% full-time. *Student/faculty ratio:* 16:1.

Academics *Calendar:* semesters. *Degrees:* certificates, associate, and bachelor's. *Special study options:* adult/continuing education programs, part-time degree program, study abroad. *ROTC:* Army (c), Navy (c), Air Force (c).

Computers on Campus Students can access the following: online (class) registration. Campuswide network is available.

Student Life *Housing options:* coed. Campus housing is university owned, leased by the school and is provided by a third party. *Campus security:* 24-hour emergency response devices and patrols, student patrols, late-night transport/escort service.

Athletics Member NAIA. *Intercollegiate sports:* baseball M(s), basketball M(s)/W(s), cross-country running M(s)/W(s), golf M(s)/W(s), tennis M(s)/W(s), volleyball W(s). *Intramural sports:* badminton M/W, baseball M/W, bas-ketball M/W, bowling M/W, field hockey M/W, football M/W, golf M/W, lacrosse M/W, rock climbing M/W, rugby M/W, skiing (cross-country) M/W, skiing (downhill) M/W, soccer M/W, softball M/W, table tennis M/W, tennis M/W, track and field M/W, volleyball M/W, weight lifting M/W.

Standardized Tests *Required for some:* SAT or ACT (for admission).

Costs (2012–13) *Tuition:* state resident $5562 full-time; nonresident $15,476 full-time. Full-time tuition and fees vary according to course load and reciprocity agreements. *Room and board:* Room and board charges vary according to board plan and housing facility. *Payment plan:* deferred payment. *Waivers:* senior citizens and employees or children of employees.

Financial Aid Of all full-time matriculated undergraduates who enrolled in 2011, 2,348 applied for aid, 2,082 were judged to have need, 351 had their need fully met. 91 Federal Work-Study jobs (averaging $1380). 89 state and other part-time jobs (averaging $1412). In 2011, 159 non-need-based awards were made. *Average percent of need met:* 17%. *Average financial aid package:* $8172. *Average need-based loan:* $3783. *Average need-based gift aid:* $4328. *Average non-need-based aid:* $2130.

Applying *Options:* electronic application, deferred entrance. *Application fee:* $35. *Required:* high school transcript, minimum 2.0 GPA. *Required for some:* interview. *Application deadlines:* rolling (freshmen), rolling (transfers). *Notification:* continuous (freshmen), continuous (transfers).

Freshman Application Contact Soo Lee Bruce-Smith, Coordinator of New Student Recruitment, Lewis-Clark State College, 500 Eighth Avenue, Lewiston, ID 83501-2698. *Phone:* 208-792-2210. *Toll-free phone:* 800-933-5272. *Fax:* 208-792-2876. *E-mail:* admissions@lcsc.edu. *Website:* http://www.lcsc.edu/.

New Saint Andrews College

Moscow, Idaho

- **Independent Christian** comprehensive, founded 1993
- **Small-town** campus
- **Coed** 149 undergraduate students, 87% full-time, 64% women, 36% men
- **Moderately difficult** entrance level, 78% of applicants were admitted

Undergraduates 130 full-time, 19 part-time. Students come from 29 states and territories; 5 other countries; 75% are from out of state; 0.7% Black or African American, non-Hispanic/Latino; 1% Hispanic/Latino; 1% Asian, non-Hispanic/Latino; 2% American Indian or Alaska Native, non-Hispanic/Latino; 31% Race/ethnicity unknown; 4% international; 3% transferred in. *Retention:* 87% of full-time freshmen returned.

Freshmen *Admission:* 89 applied, 69 admitted, 46 enrolled. *Test scores:* SAT critical reading scores over 500: 97%; SAT math scores over 500: 73%; ACT scores over 18: 100%; SAT critical reading scores over 600: 76%; SAT math scores over 600: 46%; ACT scores over 24: 80%; SAT critical reading scores over 700: 31%; SAT math scores over 700: 10%; ACT scores over 30: 25%.

Faculty *Total:* 16, 38% full-time, 50% with terminal degrees. *Student/faculty ratio:* 15:1.

Academics *Calendar:* 4 8-week terms. *Degrees:* associate, bachelor's, master's, and postbachelor's certificates. *Special study options:* advanced placement credit, independent study, part-time degree program, summer session for credit.

Computers on Campus 6 computers/terminals and 6 ports are available on campus for general student use. Students can access the following: campus intranet, free student e-mail accounts, online (class) grades, online (class) registration, online (class) schedules. Campuswide network is available. Wireless service is available via entire campus.

Student Life *Housing:* college housing not available. *Activities and organizations:* drama/theater group, choral group, Students for the Relief of the Oppressed, Nursing Home Visits and Elderly Assistance (snow and leaf removal), Blood Drives, Fall Carnival, St. Andrews Day Food Bank Drive. *Campus security:* 24-hour emergency response devices. *Student services:* personal/psychological counseling.

Standardized Tests *Required:* SAT or ACT (for admission).

Costs (2013–14) *Tuition:* $11,200 full-time, $950 per course part-time. Full-time tuition and fees vary according to program. Part-time tuition and fees vary according to program. No tuition increase for student's term of enrollment. *Payment plan:* installment. *Waivers:* employees or children of employees.

Applying *Options:* electronic application, deferred entrance. *Application fee:* $40. *Required:* essay or personal statement, high school transcript, 2 letters of recommendation. *Required for some:* interview. *Application deadlines:* 2/15 (freshmen), 2/15 (transfers). *Notification:* 3/15 (freshmen), 3/15 (transfers).

Freshman Application Contact Mr. John Sawyer, Director of Student Recruitment, New Saint Andrews College, PO Box 9025, Moscow, ID 83843. *Phone:* 208-882-1566 Ext. 100. *Fax:* 208-882-4293. *E-mail:* info@nsa.edu. *Website:* http://www.nsa.edu/.

Northwest Nazarene University
Nampa, Idaho

- **Independent** comprehensive, founded 1913, affiliated with Church of the Nazarene
- **Small-town** 85-acre campus with easy access to Boise
- **Endowment** $25.9 million
- **Coed** 1,477 undergraduate students, 78% full-time, 55% women, 45% men
- **Moderately difficult** entrance level, 67% of applicants were admitted

Undergraduates 1,154 full-time, 323 part-time. 51% are from out of state; 1% Black or African American, non-Hispanic/Latino; 6% Hispanic/Latino; 2% Asian, non-Hispanic/Latino; 0.4% Native Hawaiian or other Pacific Islander, non-Hispanic/Latino; 0.5% American Indian or Alaska Native, non-Hispanic/Latino; 1% Two or more races, non-Hispanic/Latino; 12% Race/ethnicity unknown; 3% international; 5% transferred in; 67% live on campus. *Retention:* 80% of full-time freshmen returned.
Freshmen *Admission:* 993 applied, 667 admitted, 243 enrolled. *Average high school GPA:* 3.54. *Test scores:* SAT critical reading scores over 500: 66%; SAT math scores over 500: 66%; SAT writing scores over 500: 63%; ACT scores over 18: 93%; SAT critical reading scores over 600: 26%; SAT math scores over 600: 30%; SAT writing scores over 600: 19%; ACT scores over 24: 50%; SAT critical reading scores over 700: 3%; SAT math scores over 700: 9%; SAT writing scores over 700: 2%; ACT scores over 30: 13%.
Faculty *Total:* 107, 96% full-time, 73% with terminal degrees. *Student/faculty ratio:* 14:1.
Academics *Calendar:* semesters. *Degrees:* bachelor's, master's, doctoral, and post-master's certificates. *Special study options:* academic remediation for entering students, accelerated degree program, adult/continuing education programs, advanced placement credit, cooperative education, distance learning, double majors, English as a second language, freshman honors college, honors programs, independent study, internships, off-campus study, part-time degree program, services for LD students, student-designed majors, study abroad, summer session for credit. *ROTC:* Army (b).
Computers on Campus 213 computers/terminals and 1,200 ports are available on campus for general student use. Students can access the following: campus intranet, computer help desk, free student e-mail accounts, online (class) grades, online (class) registration, online (class) schedules. Campuswide network is available. 99% of college-owned or -operated housing units are wired for high-speed Internet access. Wireless service is available via entire campus.
Student Life *Housing:* on-campus residence required through sophomore year. *Options:* men-only, women-only, disabled students. Campus housing is university owned. Freshman campus housing is guaranteed. *Activities and organizations:* drama/theater group, student-run newspaper, choral group, Students in Free Enterprise (SIFE), Student Government Association, Fellowship of Christian Athletes, The Crusader newspaper, The Oasis yearbook. *Campus security:* 24-hour emergency response devices and patrols, student patrols, late-night transport/escort service, controlled dormitory access, residence hall check-in system, on-campus police hub. *Student services:* health clinic, personal/psychological counseling.
Athletics Member NCAA. All Division II. *Intercollegiate sports:* baseball M(s), basketball M(s)/W(s), cheerleading W(c), cross-country running M(s)/W(s), golf M(s)/W(s), soccer M/W(s), softball W(s), track and field M(s)/W(s), volleyball W(s). *Intramural sports:* basketball M/W, cross-country running M/W, football M/W, lacrosse M/W, softball M/W, table tennis M/W, tennis M/W, ultimate Frisbee M/W, volleyball M/W.
Standardized Tests *Required:* SAT or ACT (for admission).
Costs (2013–14) *Comprehensive fee:* $32,950 includes full-time tuition ($26,150), mandatory fees ($400), and room and board ($6400). Full-time tuition and fees vary according to course load, degree level, program, and reciprocity agreements. Part-time tuition: $1130 per semester hour. *Room and board:* Room and board charges vary according to board plan. *Payment plans:* tuition prepayment, installment. *Waivers:* minority students, children of alumni, and employees or children of employees.
Financial Aid Of all full-time matriculated undergraduates who enrolled in 2011, 1,044 applied for aid, 960 were judged to have need, 149 had their need fully met. 151 Federal Work-Study jobs (averaging $769). In 2011, 206 non-need-based awards were made. *Average percent of need met:* 68%. *Average financial aid package:* $17,811. *Average need-based loan:* $4759. *Average need-based gift aid:* $11,653. *Average non-need-based aid:* $8263. *Average indebtedness upon graduation:* $28,872.
Applying *Options:* electronic application, early action, deferred entrance. *Application fee:* $25. *Required:* essay or personal statement, high school transcript, minimum 2.5 GPA, 2 letters of recommendation. *Required for some:* interview. *Application deadlines:* 8/15 (freshmen), 8/15 (transfers), 12/15 (early action). *Notification:* continuous (freshmen), continuous (transfers), 1/15 (early action).

Freshman Application Contact Northwest Nazarene University, 623 S. University Blvd., Nampa, ID 83686-5897. *Phone:* 208-467-8950. *Toll-free phone:* 877-668-4968.
Website: http://www.nnu.edu/.

Stevens-Henager College–Boise
Boise, Idaho

Director of Admissions David Breck, Director of Admission, Stevens-Henager College–Boise, 1444 South Entertainment Avenue, Boise, ID 83709. *Phone:* 208-383-4540. *Toll-free phone:* 800-622-2670 (in-state); 800-622-2640 (out-of-state). *Fax:* 208-345-6999.
Website: http://www.stevenshenager.edu/.

University of Idaho
Moscow, Idaho

- **State-supported** university, founded 1889
- **Small-town** 1450-acre campus
- **Endowment** $187.6 million
- **Coed** 9,928 undergraduate students, 82% full-time, 47% women, 53% men
- **Moderately difficult** entrance level, 66% of applicants were admitted

Undergraduates 8,138 full-time, 1,790 part-time. Students come from 45 states and territories; 46 other countries; 26% are from out of state; 1% Black or African American, non-Hispanic/Latino; 8% Hispanic/Latino; 2% Asian, non-Hispanic/Latino; 0.3% Native Hawaiian or other Pacific Islander, non-Hispanic/Latino; 0.9% American Indian or Alaska Native, non-Hispanic/Latino; 3% Two or more races, non-Hispanic/Latino; 2% Race/ethnicity unknown; 3% international; 7% transferred in; 39% live on campus. *Retention:* 77% of full-time freshmen returned.
Freshmen *Admission:* 7,467 applied, 4,903 admitted, 1,617 enrolled. *Average high school GPA:* 3.38. *Test scores:* SAT critical reading scores over 500: 69%; SAT math scores over 500: 72%; SAT writing scores over 500: 59%; ACT scores over 18: 93%; SAT critical reading scores over 600: 24%; SAT math scores over 600: 29%; SAT writing scores over 600: 17%; ACT scores over 24: 47%; SAT critical reading scores over 700: 4%; SAT math scores over 700: 4%; SAT writing scores over 700: 3%; ACT scores over 30: 7%.
Faculty *Total:* 687, 79% full-time, 71% with terminal degrees. *Student/faculty ratio:* 18:1.
Academics *Calendar:* semesters. *Degrees:* certificates, bachelor's, master's, doctoral, post-master's, and postbachelor's certificates. *Special study options:* academic remediation for entering students, accelerated degree program, adult/continuing education programs, advanced placement credit, cooperative education, distance learning, double majors, English as a second language, honors programs, independent study, internships, off-campus study, part-time degree program, services for LD students, study abroad, summer session for credit. *ROTC:* Army (b), Navy (b), Air Force (c).
Computers on Campus 530 computers/terminals are available on campus for general student use. Students can access the following: campus intranet, computer help desk, free student e-mail accounts, online (class) grades, online (class) registration, online (class) schedules. Campuswide network is available. 100% of college-owned or -operated housing units are wired for high-speed Internet access. Wireless service is available via entire campus.
Student Life *Housing:* on-campus residence required for freshman year. *Options:* coed, men-only, women-only, cooperative, disabled students. Campus housing is university owned. Freshman campus housing is guaranteed. *Activities and organizations:* drama/theater group, student-run newspaper, radio and television station, choral group, marching band, Pre-Med club, Student Alumni Relations Board, Vandal Volunteers Club, National Society of Collegiate Scholars, University of Idaho Polo, national fraternities, national sororities. *Campus security:* 24-hour emergency response devices and patrols, late-night transport/escort service, controlled dormitory access, contracted services with the city of Moscow police department. *Student services:* health clinic, personal/psychological counseling, women's center.
Athletics Member NCAA. All Division I except football (Division I-A). *Intercollegiate sports:* basketball M(s)/W(s), cross-country running M(s)/W(s), golf M(s)/W(s), soccer W(s), swimming and diving W(s), tennis M(s)/W(s), track and field M(s)/W(s), volleyball W(s). *Intramural sports:* badminton M/W, basketball M/W, bowling M/W, equestrian sports M(c)/W(c), football M, golf M/W, ice hockey M(c)/W(c), lacrosse M(c)/W(c), racquetball M/W, rock climbing M(c)/W(c), rugby M(c)/W(c), skiing (cross-country) M/W, skiing (downhill) M(c)/W(c), soccer M/W, softball M/W, swimming and diving M/W, table tennis M/W, tennis M/W, track and field M/W, ultimate Frisbee M/W, volleyball M/W, water polo M(c)/W(c), weight lifting M/W, wrestling M.
Standardized Tests *Required:* SAT or ACT (for admission).
Costs (2012–13) *Tuition:* state resident $4230 full-time, $253 per credit hour part-time; nonresident $17,018 full-time, $892 per credit hour part-time. Full-

time tuition and fees vary according to course load, degree level, program, and reciprocity agreements. Part-time tuition and fees vary according to course load, degree level, and program. *Required fees:* $1982 full-time, $59 per credit hour part-time. *Room and board:* $7682. Room and board charges vary according to board plan and housing facility. *Payment plans:* installment, deferred payment. *Waivers:* senior citizens and employees or children of employees.

Financial Aid Of all full-time matriculated undergraduates who enrolled in 2011, 6,857 applied for aid, 5,798 were judged to have need, 1,512 had their need fully met. 383 Federal Work-Study jobs (averaging $1786). 163 state and other part-time jobs (averaging $1852). In 2011, 1517 non-need-based awards were made. *Average percent of need met:* 75%. *Average financial aid package:* $13,347. *Average need-based loan:* $7441. *Average need-based gift aid:* $4671. *Average non-need-based aid:* $4996. *Average indebtedness upon graduation:* $26,809.

Applying *Options:* electronic application, deferred entrance. *Application fee:* $50. *Required:* high school transcript, minimum 2.2 GPA. *Required for some:* essay or personal statement. *Application deadlines:* 8/1 (freshmen), rolling (transfers). *Notification:* continuous (freshmen), continuous (transfers).

Freshman Application Contact Ms. Melissa Goodwin, Associate Director, Admissions, University of Idaho, 875 Perimeter Drive MS 4264, Moscow, ID 83844-4264. *Phone:* 208-885-6326. *Toll-free phone:* 888-884-3246. *Fax:* 208-885-9119. *E-mail:* admissions@uidaho.edu.
Website: http://www.uidaho.edu/.

University of Phoenix–Idaho Campus
Meridian, Idaho

Freshman Application Contact Marc Booker, Sr. Director, Office of Admissions and Evaluation, University of Phoenix–Idaho Campus, 4305 South Riverpoint Parkway, Mail Stop CF-L101, Phoenix, AZ 85040. *Phone:* 602-557-4609. *Toll-free phone:* 866-766-0766. *Fax:* 480-643-1156.
Website: http://www.phoenix.edu/.

ILLINOIS

American Academy of Art
Chicago, Illinois

- **Proprietary** 4-year, founded 1923
- **Urban** campus with easy access to Chicago
- **Coed** 432 undergraduate students
- **Moderately difficult** entrance level

Undergraduates 20% are from out of state. *Retention:* 78% of full-time freshmen returned.

Faculty *Student/faculty ratio:* 15:1.

Academics *Calendar:* trimesters. *Degree:* bachelor's. *Special study options:* academic remediation for entering students, accelerated degree program, adult/continuing education programs, independent study, internships, part-time degree program, study abroad, summer session for credit.

Student Life *Housing:* college housing not available. *Options:* Campus housing is provided by a third party. *Campus security:* 24-hour emergency response devices.

Financial Aid *Average percent of need met:* 70%.

Applying *Options:* electronic application. *Application fee:* $25. *Required:* high school transcript, interview. *Application deadlines:* rolling (freshmen), rolling (transfers).

Freshman Application Contact Mr. Stuart Rosenbloom, Director of Admissions, American Academy of Art, 332 South Michigan Avenue, Suite 300, Chicago, IL 60604-4302. *Phone:* 312-461-0600 Ext. 159. *Toll-free phone:* 888-461-0600. *E-mail:* srosenbloom@aaart.edu.
Website: http://www.aaart.edu/.

American InterContinental University Online
Hoffman Estates, Illinois

Director of Admissions Jennifer Ziegenmier, Senior Vice President of Admissions and Marketing, American InterContinental University Online, 5550 Prairie Stone Parkway, Suite 400, Hoffman Estates, IL 60192. *Phone:* 877-564-6248. *Toll-free phone:* 877-701-3800. *E-mail:* jziegenmier@aiuonline.edu.
Website: http://www.aiuniv.edu/.

Argosy University, Chicago
Chicago, Illinois

Freshman Application Contact Argosy University, Chicago, 225 North Michigan Avenue, Suite 1300, Chicago, IL 60601. *Phone:* 312-777-7600. *Toll-free phone:* 800-626-4123.
Website: http://www.argosy.edu/chicago/.

Argosy University, Schaumburg
Schaumburg, Illinois

Freshman Application Contact Argosy University, Schaumburg, 999 North Plaza Drive, Suite 111, Schaumburg, IL 60173-5403. *Phone:* 847-969-4900. *Toll-free phone:* 866-290-2777.
Website: http://www.argosy.edu/schaumburg/.

Augustana College
Rock Island, Illinois

- **Independent** 4-year, founded 1860, affiliated with Evangelical Lutheran Church in America
- **Suburban** 115-acre campus
- **Endowment** $115.9 million
- **Coed** 2,551 undergraduate students, 99% full-time, 57% women, 43% men
- **Moderately difficult** entrance level, 69% of applicants were admitted

Undergraduates 2,532 full-time, 19 part-time. Students come from 34 states and territories; 25 other countries; 15% are from out of state; 4% Black or African American, non-Hispanic/Latino; 7% Hispanic/Latino; 2% Asian, non-Hispanic/Latino; 0.1% Native Hawaiian or other Pacific Islander, non-Hispanic/Latino; 0.4% American Indian or Alaska Native, non-Hispanic/Latino; 2% Two or more races, non-Hispanic/Latino; 3% Race/ethnicity unknown; 2% international; 2% transferred in; 73% live on campus. *Retention:* 84% of full-time freshmen returned.

Freshmen *Admission:* 4,230 applied, 2,912 admitted, 656 enrolled. *Average high school GPA:* 3.25. *Test scores:* SAT critical reading scores over 500: 78%; SAT math scores over 500: 89%; ACT scores over 18: 99%; SAT critical reading scores over 600: 45%; SAT math scores over 600: 56%; ACT scores over 24: 69%; SAT critical reading scores over 700: 11%; SAT math scores over 700: 34%; SAT writing scores over 700: 14%; ACT scores over 30: 14%.

Faculty *Total:* 286, 62% full-time, 69% with terminal degrees. *Student/faculty ratio:* 12:1.

Academics *Calendar:* quarters. *Degree:* bachelor's. *Special study options:* advanced placement credit, double majors, honors programs, independent study, internships, part-time degree program, services for LD students, student-designed majors, study abroad, summer session for credit. *Unusual degree programs:* 3-2 engineering with Washington University in St. Louis, University of Illinois, Iowa State University of Science and Technology, Northern Illinois University; forestry with Duke University; occupational therapy with Washington University in St. Louis, landscape architecture with University of Illinois, environmental studies with Duke University.

Computers on Campus 600 computers/terminals and 1,800 ports are available on campus for general student use. Students can access the following: campus intranet, computer help desk, free student e-mail accounts, online (class) grades, online (class) registration, online (class) schedules. Campus-wide network is available. 100% of college-owned or -operated housing units are wired for high-speed Internet access. Wireless service is available via classrooms, computer centers, computer labs, libraries, student centers.

Student Life *Housing:* on-campus residence required through junior year. *Options:* coed, men-only, women-only. Campus housing is university owned. Freshman campus housing is guaranteed. *Activities and organizations:* drama/theater group, student-run newspaper, radio station, choral group, College Union Board of Managers, Student Government Association, student newspaper, student radio station, service organizations (APO, Dance Marathon committee). *Campus security:* 24-hour emergency response devices and patrols, late-night transport/escort service, controlled dormitory access. *Student services:* health clinic, personal/psychological counseling, women's center.

Athletics Member NCAA. All Division III. *Intercollegiate sports:* baseball M, basketball M/W, cheerleading M(c)/W(c), crew M(c)/W(c), cross-country running M/W, equestrian sports M(c)/W(c), fencing M(c)/W(c), football M, golf M/W, ice hockey M(c), lacrosse M/W, soccer M/W, softball W, swimming and diving M/W, tennis M/W, track and field M/W, ultimate Frisbee M(c)/W(c), volleyball M/W, wrestling M. *Intramural sports:* badminton M/W, basketball M/W, bowling M/W, cross-country running M/W, football M/W, golf M/W, racquetball M/W, rugby M, skiing (cross-country) M/W, skiing (downhill) M/W, soccer M/W, softball M/W, swimming and diving M/W, table tennis M/W, tennis M/W, track and field M/W, ultimate Frisbee M/W, volleyball M/W, wrestling M.

Standardized Tests *Required for some:* SAT or ACT (for admission). *Recommended:* SAT or ACT (for admission).

Costs (2013–14) *Comprehensive fee:* $43,398 includes full-time tuition ($34,614) and room and board ($8784). Full-time tuition and fees vary according to student level. Part-time tuition and fees vary according to course load. *Room and board:* Room and board charges vary according to board plan and housing facility. *Payment plans:* tuition prepayment, installment. *Waivers:* employees or children of employees.

Financial Aid Of all full-time matriculated undergraduates who enrolled in 2011, 2,201 applied for aid, 1,890 were judged to have need, 409 had their need fully met. 1,293 Federal Work-Study jobs (averaging $2319). In 2011, 575 non-need-based awards were made. *Average percent of need met:* 85%. *Average financial aid package:* $24,211. *Average need-based loan:* $4705. *Average need-based gift aid:* $18,374. *Average non-need-based aid:* $14,382. *Average indebtedness upon graduation:* $34,120.

Applying *Options:* electronic application, deferred entrance. *Application fee:* $30. *Required:* high school transcript. *Required for some:* essay or personal statement, interview. *Recommended:* essay or personal statement, 1 letter of recommendation, interview. *Application deadlines:* rolling (freshmen), rolling (transfers). *Notification:* continuous (freshmen), continuous (transfers).

Freshman Application Contact Dane Rowley, Director of Admissions, Augustana College, 639 38th Street, Rock Island, IL 61201-2296. *Phone:* 309-794-7142. *Toll-free phone:* 800-798-8100. *Fax:* 309-794-8797. *E-mail:* admissions@augustana.edu.
Website: http://www.augustana.edu/.

Aurora University
Aurora, Illinois

- **Independent** comprehensive, founded 1893
- **Suburban** 32-acre campus with easy access to Chicago
- **Endowment** $38.5 million
- **Coed** 3,015 undergraduate students, 87% full-time, 64% women, 36% men
- **Moderately difficult** entrance level, 75% of applicants were admitted

Undergraduates 2,629 full-time, 386 part-time. Students come from 25 states and territories; 5 other countries; 9% are from out of state; 8% Black or African American, non-Hispanic/Latino; 17% Hispanic/Latino; 2% Asian, non-Hispanic/Latino; 0.1% Native Hawaiian or other Pacific Islander, non-Hispanic/Latino; 0.2% American Indian or Alaska Native, non-Hispanic/Latino; 2% Two or more races, non-Hispanic/Latino; 3% Race/ethnicity unknown; 0.2% international; 16% transferred in; 23% live on campus. *Retention:* 70% of full-time freshmen returned.

Freshmen *Admission:* 2,219 applied, 1,655 admitted, 525 enrolled. *Average high school GPA:* 3.22. *Test scores:* SAT critical reading scores over 500: 39%; SAT math scores over 500: 45%; ACT scores over 18: 98%; SAT critical reading scores over 600: 6%; SAT math scores over 600: 6%; ACT scores over 24: 29%; ACT scores over 30: 2%.

Faculty *Total:* 382, 32% full-time, 44% with terminal degrees. *Student/faculty ratio:* 17:1.

Academics *Calendar:* semesters. *Degrees:* bachelor's, master's, doctoral, post-master's, and postbachelor's certificates. *Special study options:* academic remediation for entering students, accelerated degree program, adult/continuing education programs, advanced placement credit, distance learning, double majors, honors programs, independent study, internships, off-campus study, part-time degree program, services for LD students, student-designed majors, study abroad, summer session for credit. *ROTC:* Army (c).

Computers on Campus 167 computers/terminals are available on campus for general student use. Students can access the following: campus intranet, computer help desk, free student e-mail accounts, online (class) grades, online (class) registration, online (class) schedules, Moodle Learning Management System. Campuswide network is available. 100% of college-owned or -operated housing units are wired for high-speed Internet access. Wireless service is available via classrooms, computer labs, dorm rooms, learning centers, libraries, student centers.

Student Life *Housing options:* coed. Campus housing is university owned. Freshman applicants given priority for college housing. *Activities and organizations:* drama/theater group, student-run newspaper, radio station, choral group, Aurora University Student Association, Latin American Student Organization, Student Nursing Association, Social Work Association, Future Educators Association, national fraternities, national sororities. *Campus security:* 24-hour emergency response devices and patrols, late-night transport/escort service, controlled dormitory access. *Student services:* health clinic, personal/psychological counseling.

Athletics Member NCAA. All Division III. *Intercollegiate sports:* baseball M, basketball M/W, cross-country running M/W, football M, golf M/W, ice hockey M(c), lacrosse M/W, soccer M/W, softball W, tennis M/W, track and

field M/W, volleyball W. *Intramural sports:* basketball M/W, football M/W, soccer M/W, softball M/W, volleyball M/W.

Standardized Tests *Required:* SAT or ACT (for admission).

Costs (2013–14) *Comprehensive fee:* $30,262 includes full-time tuition ($20,500), mandatory fees ($220), and room and board ($9542). Full-time tuition and fees vary according to location. Part-time tuition: $590 per semester hour. Part-time tuition and fees vary according to course load, location, and program. *Room and board:* Room and board charges vary according to board plan, housing facility, and location. *Payment plans:* installment, deferred payment. *Waivers:* senior citizens and employees or children of employees.

Financial Aid Of all full-time matriculated undergraduates who enrolled in 2012, 2,345 applied for aid, 2,108 were judged to have need, 432 had their need fully met. 1,266 Federal Work-Study jobs (averaging $1572). 28 state and other part-time jobs (averaging $8759). In 2012, 458 non-need-based awards were made. *Average percent of need met:* 83%. *Average financial aid package:* $17,248. *Average need-based loan:* $4418. *Average need-based gift aid:* $6537. *Average non-need-based aid:* $7766. *Average indebtedness upon graduation:* $25,484.

Applying *Options:* electronic application, deferred entrance. *Application fee:* $25. *Required:* high school transcript, minimum 2.0 GPA. *Required for some:* 2 letters of recommendation, interview. *Recommended:* essay or personal statement, interview. *Application deadlines:* 5/1 (freshmen), 5/1 (out-of-state freshmen), rolling (transfers). *Notification:* continuous (transfers).

Freshman Application Contact Mr. James Lancaster, Director, Freshman Admission, Aurora University, 347 South Gladstone Avenue, Aurora, IL 60506-4892. *Phone:* 630-844-5533. *Toll-free phone:* 800-742-5281. *Fax:* 630-844-5535. *E-mail:* admission@aurora.edu.
Website: http://www.aurora.edu/.

Benedictine University
Lisle, Illinois

- **Independent Roman Catholic** comprehensive, founded 1887
- **Suburban** 108-acre campus with easy access to Chicago
- **Endowment** $28.5 million
- **Coed** 3,724 undergraduate students, 78% full-time, 61% women, 39% men
- **Moderately difficult** entrance level, 39% of applicants were admitted

Undergraduates 2,916 full-time, 808 part-time. Students come from 50 states and territories; 17 other countries; 8% are from out of state; 10% Black or African American, non-Hispanic/Latino; 7% Hispanic/Latino; 14% Asian, non-Hispanic/Latino; 0.4% Native Hawaiian or other Pacific Islander, non-Hispanic/Latino; 0.3% American Indian or Alaska Native, non-Hispanic/Latino; 24% Race/ethnicity unknown; 2% international; 8% transferred in; 18% live on campus. *Retention:* 73% of full-time freshmen returned.

Freshmen *Admission:* 1,586 applied, 612 admitted, 612 enrolled. *Average high school GPA:* 3.32. *Test scores:* ACT scores over 18: 89%; ACT scores over 24: 35%; ACT scores over 30: 4%.

Faculty *Total:* 702, 21% full-time, 31% with terminal degrees. *Student/faculty ratio:* 18:1.

Academics *Calendar:* semesters. *Degrees:* certificates, associate, bachelor's, master's, doctoral, and postbachelor's certificates. *Special study options:* academic remediation for entering students, accelerated degree program, adult/continuing education programs, advanced placement credit, distance learning, double majors, English as a second language, honors programs, independent study, internships, off-campus study, part-time degree program, services for LD students, study abroad, summer session for credit. *ROTC:* Army (c). *Unusual degree programs:* 3-2 engineering with University of Illinois at Urbana–Champaign, Illinois Institute of Technology, Purdue University; nursing with Rush University-Clinical Life Science. Respiratory Care and Perfusion Technology.

Computers on Campus 200 computers/terminals are available on campus for general student use. Students can access the following: computer help desk, free student e-mail accounts, online (class) grades, online (class) registration, online (class) schedules. Campuswide network is available. 100% of college-owned or -operated housing units are wired for high-speed Internet access. Wireless service is available via computer centers, dorm rooms, libraries, student centers.

Student Life *Housing options:* coed, men-only, women-only. Campus housing is university owned and is provided by a third party. Freshman campus housing is guaranteed. *Activities and organizations:* student-run newspaper, television station, choral group, Student Senate, MSA-Muslim Student Association, AMSA-American Medical Student Association, The Candor-Student Newspaper, Programming Board. *Campus security:* 24-hour emergency response devices and patrols, late-night transport/escort service, controlled dormitory access. *Student services:* health clinic, personal/psychological counseling.

Athletics Member NCAA. All Division III. *Intercollegiate sports:* baseball M, basketball M/W, cross-country running M/W, football M, golf M/W, soccer M/

W, softball W, tennis W, track and field M/W, volleyball W. *Intramural sports:* basketball M/W, bowling M/W, cheerleading W(c), football M/W, lacrosse M(c), softball M/W, table tennis M/W, volleyball M/W.
Standardized Tests *Required:* SAT or ACT (for admission).
Costs (2012–13) *Comprehensive fee:* $34,230 includes full-time tuition ($24,850), mandatory fees ($1000), and room and board ($8380). Full-time tuition and fees vary according to class time, degree level, and location. Part-time tuition: $830 per credit hour. Part-time tuition and fees vary according to class time and degree level. *Required fees:* $15 per credit hour part-time. *College room only:* $5860. Room and board charges vary according to board plan, housing facility, and location. *Payment plans:* installment, deferred payment. *Waivers:* employees or children of employees.
Financial Aid Of all full-time matriculated undergraduates who enrolled in 2012, 2,408 applied for aid, 2,241 were judged to have need. 215 Federal Work-Study jobs (averaging $1264). In 2012, 312 non-need-based awards were made. *Average financial aid package:* $16,870. *Average need-based loan:* $4478. *Average need-based gift aid:* $7229. *Average non-need-based aid:* $9799. *Average indebtedness upon graduation:* $19,560.
Applying *Options:* electronic application, deferred entrance. *Application fee:* $40. *Required:* essay or personal statement, high school transcript. *Required for some:* interview. *Recommended:* rank in upper 50% of high school class. *Application deadlines:* rolling (freshmen), rolling (transfers). *Notification:* continuous (freshmen), continuous (transfers).
Freshman Application Contact Ms. Kari Gibbons, Dean of Enrollment, Benedictine University, 5700 College Road, Lisle, IL 60532-0900. *Phone:* 630-829-6300. *Toll-free phone:* 888-829-6363. *Fax:* 630-829-6301. *E-mail:* admissions@ben.edu.
Website: http://www.ben.edu/.

Blackburn College
Carlinville, Illinois
- **Independent Presbyterian** 4-year, founded 1837
- **Small-town** 80-acre campus with easy access to St. Louis
- **Endowment** $11.1 million
- **Coed** 546 undergraduate students, 97% full-time, 58% women, 42% men
- **Moderately difficult** entrance level, 70% of applicants were admitted

Undergraduates 531 full-time, 15 part-time. Students come from 18 states and territories; 2 other countries; 9% are from out of state; 9% Black or African American, non-Hispanic/Latino; 1% Hispanic/Latino; 0.7% Asian, non-Hispanic/Latino; 0.6% Native Hawaiian or other Pacific Islander, non-Hispanic/Latino; 1% American Indian or Alaska Native, non-Hispanic/Latino; 0.6% Two or more races, non-Hispanic/Latino; 2% Race/ethnicity unknown; 0.4% international; 11% transferred in; 67% live on campus. *Retention:* 71% of full-time freshmen returned.
Freshmen *Admission:* 423 applied, 296 admitted, 138 enrolled. *Average high school GPA:* 3.29. *Test scores:* ACT scores over 18: 83%; ACT scores over 24: 38%; ACT scores over 30: 5%.
Faculty *Total:* 73, 52% full-time, 52% with terminal degrees. *Student/faculty ratio:* 12:1.
Academics *Calendar:* semesters. *Degree:* bachelor's. *Special study options:* advanced placement credit, cooperative education, double majors, honors programs, independent study, internships, off-campus study, services for LD students, student-designed majors, study abroad, summer session for credit. *Unusual degree programs:* 3-2 engineering with Washington University in St. Louis or University of Missouri, Kansas City.
Computers on Campus 202 computers/terminals are available on campus for general student use. Students can access the following: computer help desk, free student e-mail accounts, online (class) grades, online (class) registration, online (class) schedules. Campuswide network is available. 100% of college-owned or -operated housing units are wired for high-speed Internet access. Wireless service is available via libraries, student centers.
Student Life *Housing:* on-campus residence required through junior year. *Options:* coed, men-only, women-only. Campus housing is university owned. Freshman campus housing is guaranteed. *Activities and organizations:* drama/theater group, student-run newspaper, radio station, choral group, Habitat for Humanity, Residence Hall Association, Newman Club, Blackburn Common Ground. *Campus security:* student patrols, late-night transport/escort service. *Student services:* personal/psychological counseling.
Athletics Member NCAA. All Division III. *Intercollegiate sports:* baseball M, basketball M/W, cross-country running M/W, golf M, soccer M/W, softball W, tennis W, volleyball W. *Intramural sports:* badminton M/W, basketball M/W, football M/W, golf M/W, racquetball M/W, soccer M/W, softball M/W, table tennis M/W, tennis M/W, ultimate Frisbee M/W, volleyball M/W.
Standardized Tests *Required:* SAT or ACT (for admission).
Costs (2013–14) *Comprehensive fee:* $24,906 includes full-time tuition ($18,146), mandatory fees ($300), and room and board ($6460). Full-time tuition and fees vary according to student level. Part-time tuition: $605 per credit hour. Part-time tuition and fees vary according to student level. *College room only:* $3748. Room and board charges vary according to board plan and housing facility. *Payment plan:* installment. *Waivers:* employees or children of employees.
Financial Aid Of all full-time matriculated undergraduates who enrolled in 2009, 581 applied for aid, 502 were judged to have need, 194 had their need fully met. 388 Federal Work-Study jobs (averaging $2653). 113 state and other part-time jobs (averaging $2337). In 2009, 62 non-need-based awards were made. *Average percent of need met:* 80%. *Average financial aid package:* $13,873. *Average need-based loan:* $4107. *Average need-based gift aid:* $11,209. *Average non-need-based aid:* $5163. *Average indebtedness upon graduation:* $20,077.
Applying *Options:* electronic application, deferred entrance. *Application fee:* $20. *Required:* high school transcript, minimum 2.0 GPA. *Required for some:* essay or personal statement, 3 letters of recommendation, interview. *Recommended:* minimum 2.5 GPA. *Application deadlines:* rolling (freshmen), rolling (out-of-state freshmen), rolling (transfers). *Notification:* continuous (freshmen), continuous (out-of-state freshmen), continuous (transfers).
Freshman Application Contact Mrs. Alisha Kapp, Director of Admission, Blackburn College, 700 College Avenue, Carlinville, IL 62626. *Phone:* 217-854-3231 Ext. 4252. *Toll-free phone:* 800-233-3550. *E-mail:* admit@mail.blackburn.edu.
Website: http://www.blackburn.edu/.

Blessing-Rieman College of Nursing
Quincy, Illinois
- **Independent** comprehensive, founded 1985
- **Small-town** 1-acre campus
- **Endowment** $6.7 million
- **Coed, primarily women**
- **Moderately difficult** entrance level

Faculty *Student/faculty ratio:* 12:1.
Academics *Calendar:* semesters. *Degrees:* bachelor's and master's.
Student Life *Campus security:* 24-hour patrols, late-night transport/escort service, controlled dormitory access.
Standardized Tests *Required:* SAT or ACT (for admission).
Financial Aid Of all full-time matriculated undergraduates who enrolled in 2009, 186 applied for aid, 186 were judged to have need, 186 had their need fully met. *Average percent of need met:* 100. *Average need-based loan:* $2394. *Average need-based gift aid:* $7902. *Average indebtedness upon graduation:* $20,000.
Applying *Options:* electronic application, deferred entrance. *Required:* high school transcript, minimum 3.0 GPA. *Recommended:* essay or personal statement, interview.
Freshman Application Contact Ms. Heather Mutter, Admissions Counselor, Blessing-Rieman College of Nursing, Broadway at 11th Street, POB 7005, Quincy, IL 62305-7005. *Phone:* 217-228-5520 Ext. 6979. *Toll-free phone:* 800-877-9140 Ext. 6964. *Fax:* 217-223-4661. *E-mail:* admissions@brcn.edu.
Website: http://www.brcn.edu/.

Bradley University
Peoria, Illinois
- **Independent** comprehensive, founded 1897
- **Suburban** 85-acre campus
- **Endowment** $243.0 million
- **Coed** 4,872 undergraduate students, 95% full-time, 53% women, 47% men
- **Moderately difficult** entrance level, 63% of applicants were admitted

Undergraduates 4,631 full-time, 241 part-time. Students come from 41 states and territories; 38 other countries; 12% are from out of state; 7% Black or African American, non-Hispanic/Latino; 6% Hispanic/Latino; 4% Asian, non-Hispanic/Latino; 0.1% Native Hawaiian or other Pacific Islander, non-Hispanic/Latino; 0.3% American Indian or Alaska Native, non-Hispanic/Latino; 1% Two or more races, non-Hispanic/Latino; 0.5% Race/ethnicity unknown; 0.7% international; 6% transferred in; 66% live on campus. *Retention:* 86% of full-time freshmen returned.
Freshmen *Admission:* 7,562 applied, 4,787 admitted, 1,016 enrolled. *Average high school GPA:* 3.7. *Test scores:* SAT critical reading scores over 500: 80%; SAT math scores over 500: 79%; SAT writing scores over 500: 59%; ACT scores over 18: 100%; SAT critical reading scores over 600: 34%; SAT math scores over 600: 48%; SAT writing scores over 600: 23%; ACT scores over 24: 71%; SAT critical reading scores over 700: 7%; SAT math scores over 700: 14%; SAT writing scores over 700: 4%; ACT scores over 30: 16%.
Faculty *Total:* 579, 61% full-time, 51% with terminal degrees. *Student/faculty ratio:* 12:1.

Academics *Calendar:* semesters. *Degrees:* certificates, bachelor's, master's, and doctoral. *Special study options:* advanced placement credit, cooperative education, distance learning, double majors, honors programs, independent study, internships, off-campus study, part-time degree program, services for LD students, student-designed majors, study abroad, summer session for credit. *ROTC:* Army (b).

Computers on Campus 2,500 computers/terminals are available on campus for general student use. Students can access the following: computer help desk, free student e-mail accounts, online (class) grades, online (class) registration, online (class) schedules. Campuswide network is available. 100% of college-owned or -operated housing units are wired for high-speed Internet access. Wireless service is available via classrooms, computer centers, computer labs, dorm rooms, learning centers, libraries, student centers.

Student Life *Housing:* on-campus residence required through sophomore year. *Options:* coed. Campus housing is university owned, leased by the school and is provided by a third party. Freshman campus housing is guaranteed. *Activities and organizations:* drama/theater group, student-run newspaper, radio station, choral group, Habitat for Humanity, Alpha Phi Omega Co-Ed Service Fraternity, Activities Council of Bradley University, CRU (Campus Christian group), Dance Marathon, national fraternities, national sororities. *Campus security:* 24-hour emergency response devices and patrols, late-night transport/escort service, controlled dormitory access, emergency text messaging, mass notification/emergency communication system in 20 academic buildings. *Student services:* health clinic, personal/psychological counseling.

Athletics Member NCAA. All Division I. *Intercollegiate sports:* baseball M(s), basketball M(s)/W(s), cheerleading M/W, cross-country running M(s)/W(s), golf M(s)/W(s), ice hockey M(c), soccer M(s), softball W(s), tennis M(s)/W(s), track and field M(s)/W(s), volleyball M(c)/W(s). *Intramural sports:* badminton M/W, basketball M/W, bowling M/W, football M, racquetball M/W, rock climbing M/W, soccer M/W, swimming and diving M/W, table tennis M/W, tennis M/W, ultimate Frisbee M/W, volleyball M/W, water polo M/W, wrestling M.

Standardized Tests *Required:* SAT or ACT (for admission).

Costs (2013–14) *One-time required fee:* $200. *Comprehensive fee:* $38,714 includes full-time tuition ($29,320), mandatory fees ($344), and room and board ($9050). Full-time tuition and fees vary according to course load and program. Part-time tuition: $740 per credit. Part-time tuition and fees vary according to course load and program. *College room only:* $5250. Room and board charges vary according to board plan. *Payment plans:* installment, deferred payment. *Waivers:* senior citizens and employees or children of employees.

Financial Aid Of all full-time matriculated undergraduates who enrolled in 2012, 3,849 applied for aid, 3,324 were judged to have need, 515 had their need fully met. In 2012, 927 non-need-based awards were made. *Average percent of need met:* 68%. *Average financial aid package:* $18,951. *Average need-based loan:* $5874. *Average need-based gift aid:* $14,351. *Average non-need-based aid:* $7744. *Average indebtedness upon graduation:* $26,109.

Applying *Options:* electronic application, early admission, deferred entrance. *Application fee:* $35. *Required:* essay or personal statement, high school transcript, 1 letter of recommendation. *Recommended:* interview. *Application deadlines:* rolling (freshmen), rolling (out-of-state freshmen), rolling (transfers).

Freshman Application Contact Mr. Justin Ball, Director of Admissions, Bradley University, 1501 West Bradley Avenue, Peoria, IL 61625-0002. *Phone:* 309-677-1000. *Toll-free phone:* 800-447-6460. *Fax:* 309-677-2797. *E-mail:* admissions@bradley.edu. *Website:* http://www.bradley.edu/.

Chamberlain College of Nursing
Addison, Illinois

- **Proprietary** 4-year
- **Coed**

Faculty *Student/faculty ratio:* 30:1.
Academics *Calendar:* semesters. *Degrees:* bachelor's and master's.
Standardized Tests *Required:* SAT or ACT (for admission).
Costs (2013–14) *Tuition:* $16,360 full-time, $665 per credit hour part-time. Full-time tuition and fees vary according to course load. Part-time tuition and fees vary according to course load. *Required fees:* $600 full-time.
Freshman Application Contact Admissions, Chamberlain College of Nursing, 1221 N. Swift Road, Addison, IL 60101-6106. *Phone:* 630-953-3680. *Toll-free phone:* 888-556-8CCN.
Website: http://www.chamberlain.edu/.

Chamberlain College of Nursing
Chicago, Illinois

- **Proprietary** 4-year
- **Coed**

Faculty *Student/faculty ratio:* 16:1.
Academics *Calendar:* semesters. *Degree:* bachelor's.
Standardized Tests *Required:* SAT or ACT (for admission).
Costs (2013–14) *Tuition:* $16,360 full-time, $665 per credit hour part-time. Full-time tuition and fees vary according to course load. Part-time tuition and fees vary according to course load. *Required fees:* $600 full-time.
Freshman Application Contact Admissions, Chamberlain College of Nursing, 3300 N. Campbell Avenue, Chicago, IL 60618. *Phone:* 773-961-3000. *Toll-free phone:* 888-556-8CCN.
Website: http://www.chamberlain.edu/.

Chicago State University
Chicago, Illinois

- **State-supported** comprehensive, founded 1867
- **Urban** 161-acre campus
- **Endowment** $2.0 million
- **Coed** 4,618 undergraduate students, 65% full-time, 72% women, 28% men
- **Minimally difficult** entrance level, 32% of applicants were admitted

Undergraduates 3,012 full-time, 1,606 part-time. Students come from 29 states and territories; 2 other countries; 2% are from out of state; 83% Black or African American, non-Hispanic/Latino; 7% Hispanic/Latino; 0.7% Asian, non-Hispanic/Latino; 0.2% American Indian or Alaska Native, non-Hispanic/Latino; 6% Race/ethnicity unknown; 12% transferred in. *Retention:* 54% of full-time freshmen returned.

Freshmen *Admission:* 3,702 applied, 1,179 admitted, 323 enrolled. *Average high school GPA:* 3.09. *Test scores:* ACT scores over 18: 45%; ACT scores over 24: 7%.

Faculty *Total:* 291, 97% full-time, 41% with terminal degrees. *Student/faculty ratio:* 11:1.

Academics *Calendar:* semesters. *Degrees:* bachelor's, master's, doctoral, and postbachelor's certificates. *Special study options:* academic remediation for entering students, accelerated degree program, adult/continuing education programs, advanced placement credit, cooperative education, distance learning, double majors, external degree program, freshman honors college, honors programs, independent study, internships, off-campus study, part-time degree program, services for LD students, student-designed majors, study abroad, summer session for credit. *ROTC:* Army (b), Navy (c), Air Force (c).

Computers on Campus 75 computers/terminals and 250 ports are available on campus for general student use. Students can access the following: free student e-mail accounts, online (class) grades, online (class) registration, online (class) schedules. Campuswide network is available. 100% of college-owned or -operated housing units are wired for high-speed Internet access. Wireless service is available via libraries.

Student Life *Housing options:* coed. Campus housing is university owned. *Activities and organizations:* drama/theater group, student-run newspaper, radio station, choral group, Math/Computer Science Club, Geographic Society Club, Gospel Choir, Movie Club, national fraternities, national sororities. *Campus security:* 24-hour emergency response devices and patrols, student patrols, late-night transport/escort service, controlled dormitory access. *Student services:* health clinic, personal/psychological counseling, women's center.

Athletics Member NCAA. All Division I. *Intercollegiate sports:* baseball M(s), basketball M(s)/W(s), cross-country running M(s)/W(s), golf M(s)/W(s), tennis M(s)/W(s), track and field M(s)/W(s), volleyball W(s).

Standardized Tests *Required:* SAT or ACT (for admission).

Costs (2012–13) *Tuition:* state resident $6840 full-time; nonresident $13,606 full-time. No tuition increase for student's term of enrollment. *Required fees:* $2414 full-time. *Room and board:* $8221. *Payment plan:* tuition prepayment.

Financial Aid Of all full-time matriculated undergraduates who enrolled in 2011, 3,286 applied for aid, 3,286 were judged to have need, 3 had their need fully met. In 2011, 33 non-need-based awards were made. *Average percent of need met:* 35%. *Average financial aid package:* $9559. *Average need-based loan:* $4192. *Average need-based gift aid:* $7543. *Average non-need-based aid:* $5020. *Average indebtedness upon graduation:* $30,237. *Financial aid deadline:* 6/30.

Applying *Options:* electronic application. *Application fee:* $25. *Required:* high school transcript, minimum 2.5 GPA. *Required for some:* essay or personal statement, interview. *Notification:* continuous (freshmen), continuous (transfers).

Freshman Application Contact Mr. John Martinez, Associate Director of Admissions, Chicago State University, 95th Street at King Drive, ADM 200,

Chicago, IL 60628. *Phone:* 773-995-3578. *Fax:* 773-995-3820. *E-mail:* jmarti21@csu.edu.
Website: http://www.csu.edu/.

Christian Life College
Mount Prospect, Illinois

Freshman Application Contact Christian Life College, 400 East Gregory Street, Mount Prospect, IL 60056. *Phone:* 847-259-1840 Ext. 100.
Website: http://www.christianlifecollege.edu/.

Columbia College Chicago
Chicago, Illinois

- **Independent** comprehensive, founded 1890
- **Urban** campus with easy access to Chicago
- **Endowment** $109.2 million
- **Coed** 10,310 undergraduate students, 89% full-time, 53% women, 47% men
- **Moderately difficult** entrance level, 85% of applicants were admitted

Undergraduates 9,224 full-time, 1,086 part-time. Students come from 52 states and territories; 46 other countries; 37% are from out of state; 17% Black or African American, non-Hispanic/Latino; 13% Hispanic/Latino; 3% Asian, non-Hispanic/Latino; 0.1% Native Hawaiian or other Pacific Islander, non-Hispanic/Latino; 0.3% American Indian or Alaska Native, non-Hispanic/Latino; 3% Two or more races, non-Hispanic/Latino; 5% Race/ethnicity unknown; 2% international; 9% transferred in; 18% live on campus. *Retention:* 64% of full-time freshmen returned.

Freshmen *Admission:* 7,416 applied, 6,304 admitted, 2,091 enrolled. *Average high school GPA:* 3.07. *Test scores:* SAT critical reading scores over 500: 60%; SAT math scores over 500: 49%; SAT writing scores over 500: 57%; ACT scores over 18: 82%; SAT critical reading scores over 600: 22%; SAT math scores over 600: 14%; SAT writing scores over 600: 18%; ACT scores over 24: 34%; SAT critical reading scores over 700: 3%; SAT math scores over 700: 2%; SAT writing scores over 700: 1%; ACT scores over 30: 4%.

Faculty *Total:* 1,675, 23% full-time. *Student/faculty ratio:* 11:1.

Academics *Calendar:* semesters. *Degrees:* certificates, diplomas, bachelor's, master's, and postbachelor's certificates. *Special study options:* academic remediation for entering students, adult/continuing education programs, advanced placement credit, cooperative education, distance learning, English as a second language, honors programs, independent study, internships, off-campus study, part-time degree program, services for LD students, student-designed majors, study abroad, summer session for credit.

Computers on Campus 851 computers/terminals are available on campus for general student use. Students can access the following: campus intranet, computer help desk, free student e-mail accounts, online (class) grades, online (class) registration, online (class) schedules. Campuswide network is available. 100% of college-owned or -operated housing units are wired for high-speed Internet access. Wireless service is available via entire campus.

Student Life *Housing options:* coed. Campus housing is university owned and leased by the school. Freshman applicants given priority for college housing. *Activities and organizations:* drama/theater group, student-run newspaper, radio and television station, choral group, Columbia Urban Music Association, International Student Organization, Acianza Latina, Marketing Club. *Campus security:* 24-hour emergency response devices and patrols, late-night transport/escort service, controlled dormitory access, escort upon request. *Student services:* health clinic, personal/psychological counseling.

Athletics *Intercollegiate sports:* baseball M(c), basketball M(c), lacrosse M(c). *Intramural sports:* cheerleading M/W, cross-country running M/W, fencing M/W, football M/W, rugby M/W, soccer M/W, softball W, swimming and diving M/W, tennis M/W, ultimate Frisbee M/W, volleyball M/W.

Standardized Tests *Recommended:* SAT or ACT (for admission).

Costs (2012–13) *Comprehensive fee:* $33,670 includes full-time tuition ($21,200), mandatory fees ($550), and room and board ($11,920). Full-time tuition and fees vary according to course load. Part-time tuition: $732 per credit hour. Part-time tuition and fees vary according to course load. *Room and board:* Room and board charges vary according to housing facility.

Financial Aid Of all full-time matriculated undergraduates who enrolled in 2009, 7,243 applied for aid, 6,428 were judged to have need, 5,780 had their need fully met. *Average percent of need met:* 29%. *Average financial aid package:* $8922. *Average need-based loan:* $4337. *Average need-based gift aid:* $2347.

Applying *Options:* electronic application, deferred entrance. *Application fee:* $35. *Required:* essay or personal statement, high school transcript, 1 letter of recommendation. *Recommended:* minimum 2.0 GPA, interview. *Application deadlines:* rolling (freshmen), rolling (out-of-state freshmen), rolling (transfers). *Notification:* continuous (freshmen), continuous (out-of-state freshmen), continuous (transfers).

Freshman Application Contact Mr. Murphy Monroe, Executive Director of Admissions, Columbia College Chicago, 600 South Michigan Avenue, Chicago, IL 60605-1996. *Phone:* 312-369-7133. *Fax:* 312-344-8024. *E-mail:* admissions@colum.edu.
Website: http://www.colum.edu/.

See previous page for display ad and page 1252 for the College Close-Up.

Concordia University Chicago
River Forest, Illinois

- **Independent** comprehensive, founded 1864, affiliated with Lutheran Church–Missouri Synod, part of Concordia University System
- **Suburban** 40-acre campus with easy access to Chicago
- **Coed** 1,515 undergraduate students, 93% full-time, 62% women, 38% men
- **Moderately difficult** entrance level, 55% of applicants were admitted

Undergraduates 1,407 full-time, 108 part-time. 28% are from out of state; 13% Black or African American, non-Hispanic/Latino; 21% Hispanic/Latino; 2% Asian, non-Hispanic/Latino; 0.1% Native Hawaiian or other Pacific Islander, non-Hispanic/Latino; 3% Two or more races, non-Hispanic/Latino; 1% Race/ethnicity unknown; 0.4% international; 8% transferred in; 55% live on campus.
Freshmen *Admission:* 3,524 applied, 1,952 admitted, 318 enrolled. *Average high school GPA:* 3.05. *Test scores:* SAT critical reading scores over 500: 56%; SAT math scores over 500: 59%; ACT scores over 18: 90%; SAT critical reading scores over 600: 22%; SAT math scores over 600: 11%; ACT scores over 24: 24%; SAT math scores over 700: 7%; ACT scores over 30: 4%.
Faculty *Total:* 507, 25% full-time, 34% with terminal degrees. *Student/faculty ratio:* 19:1.
Academics *Calendar:* semesters. *Degrees:* certificates, bachelor's, master's, doctoral, and post-master's certificates. *Special study options:* adult/continuing education programs, part-time degree program.
Computers on Campus Students can access the following: campus intranet, computer help desk, free student e-mail accounts, online (class) grades, online (class) registration, online (class) schedules. Campuswide network is available. 100% of college-owned or -operated housing units are wired for high-speed Internet access. Wireless service is available via libraries, student centers.
Student Life *Housing options:* coed, disabled students. Campus housing is university owned. *Campus security:* 24-hour emergency response devices and patrols, student patrols, late-night transport/escort service, controlled dormitory access, emergency call boxes.
Athletics Member NCAA. All Division III. *Intercollegiate sports:* baseball M, basketball M/W, cheerleading M/W, cross-country running M/W, football M, golf M, soccer M/W, softball W, tennis M/W, track and field M/W, volleyball W. *Intramural sports:* badminton M/W, basketball M/W, bowling M/W, football W, swimming and diving M/W, table tennis M/W, tennis M/W, volleyball M/W.
Standardized Tests *Required:* SAT or ACT (for admission).
Costs (2013–14) *Comprehensive fee:* $36,452 includes full-time tuition ($27,044), mandatory fees ($744), and room and board ($8664). Full-time tuition and fees vary according to program. Part-time tuition: $845 per credit hour. Part-time tuition and fees vary according to program. *College room only:* $4264. *Payment plan:* installment. *Waivers:* minority students, children of alumni, senior citizens, and employees or children of employees.
Financial Aid Of all full-time matriculated undergraduates who enrolled in 2010, 1,217 applied for aid, 1,105 were judged to have need, 215 had their need fully met. In 2010, 159 non-need-based awards were made. *Average percent of need met:* 77%. *Average financial aid package:* $18,748. *Average need-based loan:* $4141. *Average need-based gift aid:* $13,938. *Average non-need-based aid:* $9594. *Average indebtedness upon graduation:* $31,856. *Financial aid deadline:* 8/15.
Applying *Options:* electronic application, deferred entrance. *Required:* high school transcript, minimum 2.0 GPA, 1 letter of recommendation. *Required for some:* essay or personal statement, interview. *Application deadlines:* rolling (freshmen), rolling (transfers).
Freshman Application Contact Ms. Gwen Kanelos, Director of Admission, Concordia University Chicago, 7400 Augusta Street, River Forest, IL 60305. *Phone:* 708-209-3101. *Toll-free phone:* 800-285-2668. *Fax:* 708-209-3473. *E-mail:* gwen.kanelos@cuchicago.edu.
Website: http://www.cuchicago.edu/.

DePaul University
Chicago, Illinois

- **Independent Roman Catholic** university, founded 1898
- **Urban** 36-acre campus with easy access to Chicago
- **Endowment** $349.2 million
- **Coed** 16,498 undergraduate students, 83% full-time, 54% women, 46% men
- **Moderately difficult** entrance level, 62% of applicants were admitted

Undergraduates 13,657 full-time, 2,841 part-time. Students come from 51 states and territories; 75 other countries; 19% are from out of state; 8% Black or African American, non-Hispanic/Latino; 17% Hispanic/Latino; 7% Asian, non-Hispanic/Latino; 0.3% Native Hawaiian or other Pacific Islander, non-Hispanic/Latino; 0.1% American Indian or Alaska Native, non-Hispanic/Latino; 3% Two or more races, non-Hispanic/Latino; 6% Race/ethnicity unknown; 2% international; 11% transferred in; 17% live on campus. *Retention:* 85% of full-time freshmen returned.
Freshmen *Admission:* 18,160 applied, 11,318 admitted, 2,593 enrolled. *Average high school GPA:* 3.58. *Test scores:* SAT critical reading scores over 500: 84%; SAT math scores over 500: 82%; ACT scores over 18: 99%; SAT critical reading scores over 600: 43%; SAT math scores over 600: 39%; ACT scores over 24: 67%; SAT critical reading scores over 700: 7%; SAT math scores over 700: 5%; ACT scores over 30: 13%.
Faculty *Total:* 1,987, 49% full-time, 51% with terminal degrees. *Student/faculty ratio:* 16:1.
Academics *Calendar:* quarters; semesters for law school. *Degrees:* certificates, bachelor's, master's, doctoral, post-master's, and postbachelor's certificates. *Special study options:* academic remediation for entering students, accelerated degree program, adult/continuing education programs, advanced placement credit, cooperative education, distance learning, double majors, English as a second language, freshman honors college, honors programs, independent study, internships, off-campus study, part-time degree program, services for LD students, student-designed majors, study abroad, summer session for credit. *ROTC:* Army (b). *Unusual degree programs:* 3-2 business administration; engineering with Illinois Institute of Technology.
Computers on Campus 1,800 computers/terminals and 400 ports are available on campus for general student use. Students can access the following: campus intranet, computer help desk, free student e-mail accounts, online (class) grades, online (class) registration, online (class) schedules, tuition payments, degree progress, financial aid, transcript requests, housing services, student employment information. Campuswide network is available. 100% of college-owned or -operated housing units are wired for high-speed Internet access. Wireless service is available via entire campus.
Student Life *Housing options:* coed, disabled students. Campus housing is university owned, leased by the school and is provided by a third party. Freshman applicants given priority for college housing. *Activities and organizations:* drama/theater group, student-run newspaper, radio station, choral group, Panhellenic Association, DePaul Activities Board, Student Government Association, Community Service Organizations, Catholic Campus Ministry, national fraternities, national sororities. *Campus security:* 24-hour emergency response devices and patrols, late-night transport/escort service, controlled dormitory access, security lighting, prevention/awareness programs, on-campus police officers, video cameras, smoke detectors in residence halls, etc. *Student services:* health clinic, personal/psychological counseling, women's center, legal services.
Athletics Member NCAA. All Division I. *Intercollegiate sports:* basketball M(s)/W(s), cross-country running M(s)/W(s), golf M(s), soccer M(s)/W(s), softball W(s), tennis M(s)/W(s), track and field M(s)/W(s), volleyball W(s). *Intramural sports:* badminton M/W, baseball M(c), basketball M/W, football M/W, golf M(c)/W(c), ice hockey M(c)/W(c), lacrosse M(c)/W(c), racquetball M/W, rugby M(c)/W(c), skiing (downhill) M(c)/W(c), soccer M/W, softball M/W, table tennis M/W, tennis M/W, ultimate Frisbee M(c)/W(c), volleyball M/W, water polo M/W.
Standardized Tests *Recommended:* SAT and SAT Subject Tests or ACT (for admission).
Costs (2012–13) *Comprehensive fee:* $44,012 includes full-time tuition ($31,650), mandatory fees ($645), and room and board ($11,717). Full-time tuition and fees vary according to course load and program. Part-time tuition: $530 per credit hour. Part-time tuition and fees vary according to course load and program. *College room only:* $8486. Room and board charges vary according to board plan, housing facility, and location. *Payment plans:* installment, deferred payment. *Waivers:* employees or children of employees.
Financial Aid Of all full-time matriculated undergraduates who enrolled in 2011, 10,211 applied for aid, 9,991 were judged to have need, 653 had their need fully met. In 2011, 697 non-need-based awards were made. *Average percent of need met:* 61%. *Average financial aid package:* $19,411. *Average need-based loan:* $4621. *Average need-based gift aid:* $14,031. *Average non-need-based aid:* $8882. *Average indebtedness upon graduation:* $27,486.

Applying *Options:* electronic application, early action, deferred entrance. *Application fee:* $40. *Required:* essay or personal statement, high school transcript, minimum 2.0 GPA. *Required for some:* minimum 3.0 GPA, interview, audition/interviews required for the School of Music and Theatre School applicants. *Recommended:* minimum 2.8 GPA. *Application deadlines:* 2/1 (freshmen), rolling (transfers), 11/15 (early action). *Notification:* 3/15 (freshmen), continuous (transfers), 1/15 (early action).

Freshman Application Contact Carlene Klaas-Kennelly, Dean of Undergraduate Admission, DePaul University, 1 East Jackson Boulevard, Suite 9000, Chicago, IL 60604. *Phone:* 312-362-8300. *Toll-free phone:* 800-4DE-PAUL. *E-mail:* admission@depaul.edu. *Website:* http://www.depaul.edu/.

DeVry University
Addison, Illinois

Freshman Application Contact DeVry University, 1221 North Swift Road, Addison, IL 60101-6106. *Toll-free phone:* 866-338-7941. *Website:* http://www.devry.edu/.

DeVry University
Chicago, Illinois

- **Proprietary** comprehensive, founded 1931, part of DeVry University
- **Urban** campus
- **Coed** 1,634 undergraduate students, 56% full-time, 40% women, 60% men
- **Minimally difficult** entrance level

Undergraduates 915 full-time, 719 part-time. 9% are from out of state; 31% Black or African American, non-Hispanic/Latino; 34% Hispanic/Latino; 6% Asian, non-Hispanic/Latino; 0.4% Native Hawaiian or other Pacific Islander, non-Hispanic/Latino; 0.2% American Indian or Alaska Native, non-Hispanic/Latino; 0.7% Two or more races, non-Hispanic/Latino; 11% Race/ethnicity unknown; 2% international; 13% transferred in.

Freshmen *Admission:* 135 enrolled.

Faculty *Total:* 130, 28% full-time. *Student/faculty ratio:* 18:1.

Academics *Calendar:* semesters. *Degrees:* associate, bachelor's, master's, and postbachelor's certificates. *Special study options:* adult/continuing education programs, part-time degree program.

Student Life *Housing:* college housing not available.

Costs (2013–14) *Tuition:* $16,076 full-time, $609 per credit hour part-time. *Required fees:* $80 full-time.

Financial Aid Of all full-time matriculated undergraduates who enrolled in 2007, 479 applied for aid, 467 were judged to have need, 5 had their need fully met. In 2007, 14 non-need-based awards were made. *Average percent of need met:* 48%. *Average financial aid package:* $16,145. *Average need-based loan:* $8033. *Average need-based gift aid:* $8371. *Average non-need-based aid:* $11,220. *Average indebtedness upon graduation:* $49,157.

Applying *Application fee:* $40. *Required:* high school transcript, interview. *Application deadlines:* rolling (freshmen), rolling (transfers). *Notification:* continuous (freshmen), continuous (transfers).

Freshman Application Contact DeVry University, 3300 North Campbell Avenue, Chicago, IL 60618-5994. *Phone:* 773-929-8500. *Toll-free phone:* 866-338-7941. *Website:* http://www.devry.edu/.

DeVry University
Downers Grove, Illinois

Admissions Office Contact DeVry University, 3005 Highland Parkway, Downers Grove, IL 60515. *Toll-free phone:* 866-338-7941. *Website:* http://www.devry.edu/.

DeVry University
Elgin, Illinois

Admissions Office Contact DeVry University, Randall Point, 2250 Point Boulevard, Suite 250, Elgin, IL 60123. *Toll-free phone:* 866-338-7941. *Website:* http://www.devry.edu/.

DeVry University
Gurnee, Illinois

Admissions Office Contact DeVry University, 1075 Tri-State Parkway, Suite 800, Gurnee, IL 60031-9126. *Toll-free phone:* 866-338-7941. *Website:* http://www.devry.edu/.

DeVry University
Naperville, Illinois

Director of Admissions Admissions Office, DeVry University, 2056 Westings Avenue, Suite 40, Naperville, IL 60563-2361. *Toll-free phone:* 866-338-7941. *Website:* http://www.devry.edu/.

DeVry University
Tinley Park, Illinois

Freshman Application Contact DeVry University, 18624 West Creek Drive, Tinley Park, IL 60477. *Toll-free phone:* 866-338-7941. *Website:* http://www.devry.edu/.

DeVry University Online
Addison, Illinois

- **Proprietary** comprehensive, founded 2000
- **Coed** 19,104 undergraduate students, 21% full-time, 54% women, 46% men
- **Minimally difficult** entrance level

Undergraduates 3,938 full-time, 15,166 part-time. 89% are from out of state; 18% Black or African American, non-Hispanic/Latino; 8% Hispanic/Latino; 2% Asian, non-Hispanic/Latino; 0.4% Native Hawaiian or other Pacific Islander, non-Hispanic/Latino; 0.7% American Indian or Alaska Native, non-Hispanic/Latino; 1% Two or more races, non-Hispanic/Latino; 17% Race/ethnicity unknown; 0.8% international; 26% transferred in.

Freshmen *Admission:* 1,267 enrolled.

Faculty *Total:* 2,809, 1.0% full-time. *Student/faculty ratio:* 12:1.

Academics *Calendar:* semesters. *Degrees:* associate, bachelor's, master's, and postbachelor's certificates.

Costs (2013–14) *Tuition:* $16,076 full-time, $609 per credit hour part-time. *Required fees:* $80 full-time.

Financial Aid Of all full-time matriculated undergraduates who enrolled in 2006, 810 applied for aid, 785 were judged to have need, 9 had their need fully met. In 2006, 146 non-need-based awards were made. *Average percent of need met:* 36%. *Average financial aid package:* $10,560. *Average need-based loan:* $6201. *Average need-based gift aid:* $7114. *Average non-need-based aid:* $10,591. *Average indebtedness upon graduation:* $35,423.

Applying *Application fee:* $40. *Required:* high school transcript, interview. *Application deadlines:* rolling (freshmen), rolling (transfers). *Notification:* continuous (freshmen), continuous (transfers).

Freshman Application Contact DeVry University Online, 1221 North Swift Road, Addison, IL 60101-6106. *Phone:* 877-496-9050. *Toll-free phone:* 866-338-7941. *Website:* http://www.devry.edu/.

Dominican University
River Forest, Illinois

- **Independent Roman Catholic** comprehensive, founded 1901
- **Suburban** 30-acre campus with easy access to Chicago
- **Endowment** $23.3 million
- **Coed** 1,995 undergraduate students, 90% full-time, 68% women, 32% men
- **Moderately difficult** entrance level, 57% of applicants were admitted

Undergraduates 1,794 full-time, 201 part-time. Students come from 31 states and territories; 23 other countries; 8% are from out of state; 8% Black or African American, non-Hispanic/Latino; 34% Hispanic/Latino; 4% Asian, non-Hispanic/Latino; 0.3% Native Hawaiian or other Pacific Islander, non-Hispanic/Latino; 0.2% American Indian or Alaska Native, non-Hispanic/Latino; 1% Two or more races, non-Hispanic/Latino; 2% Race/ethnicity unknown; 2% international; 5% transferred in; 29% live on campus. *Retention:* 80% of full-time freshmen returned.

Freshmen *Admission:* 3,056 applied, 1,745 admitted, 406 enrolled. *Average high school GPA:* 3.44. *Test scores:* SAT math scores over 500: 68%; SAT writing scores over 500: 82%; ACT scores over 18: 98%; SAT math scores over 600: 27%; SAT writing scores over 600: 41%; ACT scores over 24: 33%; SAT writing scores over 700: 5%; ACT scores over 30: 5%.

Faculty *Total:* 404, 38% full-time, 58% with terminal degrees. *Student/faculty ratio:* 11:1.

Academics *Calendar:* semesters. *Degrees:* certificates, bachelor's, master's, doctoral, post-master's, and postbachelor's certificates. *Special study options:* accelerated degree program, adult/continuing education programs, advanced placement credit, distance learning, double majors, English as a second language, honors programs, independent study, internships, off-campus study, part-time degree program, services for LD students, study abroad, summer session for credit. *Unusual degree programs:* 3-2 business administration; engineering with Illinois Institute of Technology; nursing with Rush University; Library Science, Occupational Therapy (Rush University), Pharmacy (Midwestern).

Computers on Campus 550 computers/terminals are available on campus for general student use. Students can access the following: campus intranet, computer help desk, free student e-mail accounts, online (class) grades, online (class) registration, online (class) schedules. Campuswide network is available. 100% of college-owned or -operated housing units are wired for high-speed Internet access. Wireless service is available via entire campus.

Student Life *Housing options:* coed. Campus housing is university owned and leased by the school. Freshman campus housing is guaranteed. *Activities and organizations:* drama/theater group, student-run newspaper, choral group, Polish Club, Commuter Student Association, Nutrition Club, Organization of Latin American Students, Fashion Club. *Campus security:* 24-hour emergency response devices and patrols, student patrols, late-night transport/escort service, controlled dormitory access, Door alarms. *Student services:* health clinic, personal/psychological counseling.

Athletics Member NCAA. All Division III. *Intercollegiate sports:* baseball M, basketball M/W, cross-country running M/W, golf M, soccer M/W, softball W, tennis M/W, volleyball M/W. *Intramural sports:* basketball M/W, bowling M/W, football M/W, racquetball M/W, soccer M, ultimate Frisbee M/W, volleyball W.

Standardized Tests *Required:* SAT or ACT (for admission).

Costs (2013–14) *One-time required fee:* $250. *Comprehensive fee:* $37,508 includes full-time tuition ($28,440), mandatory fees ($250), and room and board ($8818). Full-time tuition and fees vary according to course load. Part-time tuition: $948 per credit hour. Part-time tuition and fees vary according to course load. *Required fees:* $40 part-time. *Room and board:* Room and board charges vary according to board plan and housing facility. *Payment plan:* deferred payment. *Waivers:* employees or children of employees.

Financial Aid Of all full-time matriculated undergraduates who enrolled in 2012, 1,632 applied for aid, 1,538 were judged to have need, 176 had their need fully met. 365 Federal Work-Study jobs (averaging $2500). 157 state and other part-time jobs (averaging $2500). In 2012, 124 non-need-based awards were made. *Average percent of need met:* 70%. *Average financial aid package:* $20,810. *Average need-based loan:* $4224. *Average need-based gift aid:* $17,633. *Average non-need-based aid:* $8317. *Average indebtedness upon graduation:* $28,281.

Applying *Options:* electronic application, deferred entrance. *Application fee:* $25. *Required:* high school transcript. *Required for some:* interview. *Recommended:* essay or personal statement. *Application deadlines:* rolling (freshmen), rolling (transfers). *Notification:* continuous (freshmen), continuous (transfers).

Freshman Application Contact Mr. Glenn Hamilton, Assistant Vice President, Enrollment Management, Dominican University, 7900 West Division Street, River Forest, IL 60305. *Phone:* 708-524-6800. *Toll-free phone:* 800-828-8475. *Fax:* 708-524-6864. *E-mail:* domadmis@dom.edu. *Website:* http://www.dom.edu/.

Eastern Illinois University

Charleston, Illinois

- **State-supported** comprehensive, founded 1895
- **Small-town** 320-acre campus
- **Endowment** $51.6 million
- **Coed** 8,975 undergraduate students, 88% full-time, 59% women, 41% men
- **Moderately difficult** entrance level, 65% of applicants were admitted

Undergraduates 7,906 full-time, 1,069 part-time. Students come from 35 states and territories; 30 other countries; 2% are from out of state; 17% Black or African American, non-Hispanic/Latino; 4% Hispanic/Latino; 0.8% Asian, non-Hispanic/Latino; 0.1% Native Hawaiian or other Pacific Islander, non-Hispanic/Latino; 0.2% American Indian or Alaska Native, non-Hispanic/Latino; 2% Two or more races, non-Hispanic/Latino; 3% Race/ethnicity unknown; 0.7% international; 11% transferred in; 36% live on campus. *Retention:* 79% of full-time freshmen returned.

Freshmen *Admission:* 6,710 applied, 4,337 admitted, 1,295 enrolled. *Average high school GPA:* 3.09. *Test scores:* ACT scores over 18: 89%; ACT scores over 24: 28%; ACT scores over 30: 3%.

Faculty *Total:* 720, 81% full-time, 61% with terminal degrees. *Student/faculty ratio:* 15:1.

Academics *Calendar:* semesters. *Degrees:* bachelor's, master's, post-master's, and postbachelor's certificates. *Special study options:* academic remediation for entering students, accelerated degree program, adult/continuing education programs, advanced placement credit, cooperative education, distance learning, double majors, freshman honors college, honors programs, independent study, internships, off-campus study, part-time degree program, services for

LD students, study abroad, summer session for credit. *ROTC:* Army (b). *Unusual degree programs:* 3-2 engineering with University of Illinois at Urbana-Champaign and Southern Illinois University at Carbondale.

Computers on Campus 582 computers/terminals and 10,000 ports are available on campus for general student use. Students can access the following: computer help desk, free student e-mail accounts, online (class) grades, online (class) registration, online (class) schedules. Campuswide network is available. 100% of college-owned or -operated housing units are wired for high-speed Internet access. Wireless service is available via classrooms, computer centers, computer labs, dorm rooms, learning centers, libraries, student centers.

Student Life *Housing:* on-campus residence required for freshman year. *Options:* coed, men-only, women-only. Campus housing is university owned. Freshman campus housing is guaranteed. *Activities and organizations:* drama/theater group, student-run newspaper, radio and television station, choral group, marching band, Illinois Student Education Association, Math Energy at Eastern Illinois University, Black Student Union, Alpha Gamma, Alpha Phi, national fraternities, national sororities. *Campus security:* 24-hour emergency response devices and patrols, student patrols, late-night transport/escort service, AlertEIU and warning sirens. *Student services:* health clinic, personal/psychological counseling, women's center, legal services.

Athletics Member NCAA. All Division I except football (Division I-AA). *Intercollegiate sports:* badminton M(c)/W(c), baseball M(s), basketball M(s)/W(s), cross-country running M(s)/W(s), equestrian sports M(c)/W(c), golf M(s)/W(s), ice hockey M(c), lacrosse W(c), racquetball M(c)/W(c), rugby W(s), soccer M(s)/W(s), softball W(s), swimming and diving M(s)/W(s), tennis M(s)/W(s), track and field M(s)/W(s), ultimate Frisbee M(c)/W(c), volleyball M(c)/W(s), water polo M(c)/W(c). *Intramural sports:* badminton M/W, basketball M/W, bowling M/W, racquetball M/W, soccer M/W, softball M/W, table tennis M/W, tennis M/W, volleyball M/W, weight lifting M/W.

Standardized Tests *Required:* SAT or ACT (for admission).

Costs (2012–13) *Tuition:* state resident $8370 full-time, $279 per credit hour part-time; nonresident $25,110 full-time, $837 per credit hour part-time. Full-time tuition and fees vary according to course load and student level. Part-time tuition and fees vary according to course load and student level. No tuition increase for student's term of enrollment. *Required fees:* $2560 full-time, $92 per credit hour part-time. *Room and board:* $9174. Room and board charges vary according to board plan and housing facility. *Payment plan:* installment. *Waivers:* senior citizens and employees or children of employees.

Financial Aid Of all full-time matriculated undergraduates who enrolled in 2012, 6,895 applied for aid, 5,284 were judged to have need, 444 had their need fully met. 294 Federal Work-Study jobs (averaging $991). 2,680 state and other part-time jobs (averaging $1440). In 2012, 354 non-need-based awards were made. *Average percent of need met:* 60%. *Average financial aid package:* $10,231. *Average need-based loan:* $4194. *Average need-based gift aid:* $3594. *Average non-need-based aid:* $4002. *Average indebtedness upon graduation:* $28,575.

Applying *Options:* electronic application, deferred entrance. *Application fee:* $30. *Required:* high school transcript, minimum 2.3 GPA, standardized test scores, audition for music program. *Required for some:* essay or personal statement, 2 letters of recommendation, standardized test scores, audition for music program. *Application deadlines:* rolling (freshmen), rolling (out-of-state freshmen), rolling (transfers). *Notification:* continuous (freshmen), continuous (out-of-state freshmen), continuous (transfers).

Freshman Application Contact Brenda Major, Director of Admissions, Eastern Illinois University, 600 Lincoln Avenue, Charleston, IL 61920. *Phone:* 217-581-2223. *Toll-free phone:* 877-581-2348 (in-state); 800-252-5711 (out-of-state). *Fax:* 217-581-7060. *E-mail:* admissions@eiu.edu. *Website:* http://www.eiu.edu/.

East-West University

Chicago, Illinois

- **Independent** 4-year, founded 1978
- **Urban** 1-acre campus with easy access to Chicago
- **Endowment** $56.1 million
- **Coed** 755 undergraduate students, 98% full-time, 54% women, 46% men
- **Minimally difficult** entrance level, 89% of applicants were admitted

Undergraduates 737 full-time, 18 part-time. Students come from 7 states and territories; 14 other countries; 7% are from out of state; 65% Black or African American, non-Hispanic/Latino; 15% Hispanic/Latino; 12% Asian, non-Hispanic/Latino; 0.7% Native Hawaiian or other Pacific Islander, non-Hispanic/Latino; 0.5% American Indian or Alaska Native, non-Hispanic/Latino; 3% Two or more races, non-Hispanic/Latino; 0.7% Race/ethnicity unknown; 12% transferred in. *Retention:* 71% of full-time freshmen returned.

Freshmen *Admission:* 1,008 applied, 896 admitted, 260 enrolled. *Average high school GPA:* 2.67. *Test scores:* ACT scores over 18: 39%; ACT scores over 24: 4%.

Faculty *Total:* 67, 27% full-time. *Student/faculty ratio:* 15:1.

Academics *Calendar:* quarters. *Degrees:* certificates, associate, and bachelor's. *Special study options:* academic remediation for entering students, advanced placement credit, cooperative education, double majors, English as a second language, external degree program, honors programs, internships, part-time degree program, summer session for credit.

Computers on Campus 144 computers/terminals are available on campus for general student use. Students can access the following: computer help desk, free student e-mail accounts, online (class) grades, online (class) registration, online (class) schedules. Campuswide network is available.

Student Life *Activities and organizations:* drama/theater group, student-run newspaper, choral group, student government, performing arts, Black Student Union, Latino Student Association, Multicultural Student Association. *Student services:* personal/psychological counseling.

Athletics *Intercollegiate sports:* basketball M.

Standardized Tests *Required:* ACT (for admission).

Costs (2013–14) *Tuition:* $17,550 full-time. *Required fees:* $1470 full-time. *Room only:* $7641.

Financial Aid Of all full-time matriculated undergraduates who enrolled in 2010, 53 Federal Work-Study jobs (averaging $4500). *Average indebtedness upon graduation:* $3500.

Applying *Options:* electronic application, early decision. *Application fee:* $40. *Required:* essay or personal statement, high school transcript, minimum 2.0 GPA, interview. *Required for some:* 1 letter of recommendation. *Application deadlines:* rolling (freshmen), rolling (transfers). *Early decision deadline:* 7/1. **Freshman Application Contact** Bryan Lambert, Director of Enrollment, East-West University, 816 South Michigan Avenue, Chicago, IL 60605-2103. *Phone:* 312-939-0112 Ext. 1701. *Website:* http://www.eastwest.edu/.

Ellis University

Chicago, Illinois

Freshman Application Contact Office of Admissions, Ellis University, 111 North Canal Street, Suite 380, Chicago, IL 60606-7204. *Phone:* 312-669-5000. *Toll-free phone:* 877-355-4762. *E-mail:* admissions@ellis.edu. *Website:* http://www.ellis.edu/.

Elmhurst College

Elmhurst, Illinois

- **Independent** comprehensive, founded 1871, affiliated with United Church of Christ
- **Suburban** 38-acre campus with easy access to Chicago
- **Endowment** $92.0 million
- **Coed**
- **Moderately difficult** entrance level

Faculty *Student/faculty ratio:* 14:1.

Academics *Calendar:* 4-1-4. *Degrees:* bachelor's and master's.

Student Life *Campus security:* 24-hour emergency response devices and patrols, late-night transport/escort service, controlled dormitory access.

Athletics Member NCAA. All Division III.

Standardized Tests *Required:* SAT or ACT (for admission).

Costs (2012–13) *Comprehensive fee:* $40,588 includes full-time tuition ($31,450), mandatory fees ($200), and room and board ($8938). Part-time tuition: $896 per semester hour. Part-time tuition and fees vary according to course load. *College room only:* $5460. Room and board charges vary according to board plan and housing facility.

Financial Aid *Of all full-time matriculated undergraduates who enrolled in 2012,* 2,761 applied for aid, 2,244 were judged to have need, 899 had their need fully met. 396 Federal Work-Study jobs (averaging $877). 361 state and other part-time jobs (averaging $1610). *In 2012,* 472 non-need-based awards were made. *Average percent of need met:* 73. *Average financial aid package:* $21,775. *Average need-based loan:* $4394. *Average need-based gift aid:* $19,165. *Average non-need-based aid:* $13,219. *Average indebtedness upon graduation:* $29,787.

Applying *Options:* electronic application, deferred entrance. *Required:* high school transcript. *Required for some:* essay or personal statement, interview. *Recommended:* essay or personal statement, interview.

Freshman Application Contact Mrs. Stephanie Levenson, Director of Admission, Elmhurst College, Elmhurst College, Admission Office, 190 South Prospect Avenue, Elmhurst, IL 60126-3296. *Phone:* 630-617-3400. *Toll-free phone:* 800-697-1871. *Fax:* 630-617-5501. *E-mail:* admit@elmhurst.edu. *Website:* http://www.elmhurst.edu/.

Eureka College

Eureka, Illinois

Freshman Application Contact Dr. Brian Sajko, Dean of Admissions and Financial Aid, Eureka College, 300 East College Avenue, Eureka, IL 61530. *Phone:* 309-467-6350. *Toll-free phone:* 888-4-EUREKA. *Fax:* 309-467-6576. *E-mail:* admissions@eureka.edu. *Website:* http://www.eureka.edu/.

Governors State University

University Park, Illinois

- **State-supported** upper-level, founded 1969
- **Suburban** 750-acre campus with easy access to Chicago
- **Coed** 3,178 undergraduate students, 40% full-time, 68% women, 32% men

Undergraduates 1,269 full-time, 1,909 part-time. 3% are from out of state; 37% Black or African American, non-Hispanic/Latino; 9% Hispanic/Latino; 1% Asian, non-Hispanic/Latino; 0.1% Native Hawaiian or other Pacific Islander, non-Hispanic/Latino; 0.4% American Indian or Alaska Native, non-Hispanic/Latino; 0.9% Two or more races, non-Hispanic/Latino; 7% Race/ethnicity unknown; 0.5% international; 29% transferred in.

Faculty *Total:* 413, 50% full-time, 35% with terminal degrees. *Student/faculty ratio:* 11:1.

Academics *Calendar:* trimesters. *Degrees:* certificates, bachelor's, master's, doctoral, post-master's, and postbachelor's certificates. *Special study options:* adult/continuing education programs, advanced placement credit, distance learning, double majors, honors programs, independent study, internships, off-campus study, part-time degree program, services for LD students, student-designed majors, summer session for credit.

Computers on Campus Students can access the following: computer help desk, free student e-mail accounts, online (class) grades, online (class) registration, online (class) schedules, student portal. Campuswide network is available.

Student Life *Housing:* college housing not available. *Activities and organizations:* student-run newspaper, choral group. *Campus security:* 24-hour emergency response devices and patrols, late-night transport/escort service. *Student services:* personal/psychological counseling.

Athletics *Intramural sports:* badminton M/W, basketball M/W, racquetball M/W, skiing (cross-country) M/W, softball M/W, table tennis M/W, volleyball M/W.

Costs (2012–13) *Tuition:* state resident $7470 full-time, $249 per credit hour part-time; nonresident $14,940 full-time, $498 per credit hour part-time. Full-time tuition and fees vary according to course load, reciprocity agreements, and student level. Part-time tuition and fees vary according to course load, reciprocity agreements, and student level. No tuition increase for student's term of enrollment. *Required fees:* $1646 full-time, $46 per credit hour part-time, $133 per term part-time. *Payment plans:* installment, deferred payment. *Waivers:* senior citizens and employees or children of employees.

Financial Aid Of all full-time matriculated undergraduates who enrolled in 2010, 859 applied for aid, 807 were judged to have need, 120 had their need fully met. In 2010, 40 non-need-based awards were made. *Average percent of need met:* 65%. *Average financial aid package:* $4795. *Average need-based loan:* $2227. *Average need-based gift aid:* $3087. *Average non-need-based aid:* $2055.

Applying *Options:* electronic application, deferred entrance. *Application deadline:* rolling (transfers).

Application Contact Ms. Yakeea Daniels, Director of Admissions, Governors State University, One University Parkway, University Park, IL 60466. *Phone:* 708-534-4490. *Toll-free phone:* 800-GSU-8GSU. *Fax:* 708-235-7455. *E-mail:* ydaniels@govst.edu. *Website:* http://www.govst.edu/.

Greenville College

Greenville, Illinois

- **Independent Free Methodist** comprehensive, founded 1892
- **Small-town** 12-acre campus with easy access to St. Louis
- **Endowment** $13.8 million
- **Coed** 1,224 undergraduate students, 94% full-time, 49% women, 51% men
- **Moderately difficult** entrance level, 74% of applicants were admitted

Undergraduates 1,155 full-time, 69 part-time. Students come from 40 states and territories; 8 other countries; 32% are from out of state; 8% Black or African American, non-Hispanic/Latino; 4% Hispanic/Latino; 0.8% Asian, non-Hispanic/Latino; 0.5% American Indian or Alaska Native, non-Hispanic/Latino; 2% Two or more races, non-Hispanic/Latino; 6% Race/ethnicity

unknown; 2% international; 10% transferred in; 76% live on campus. *Retention:* 62% of full-time freshmen returned.

Freshmen *Admission:* 1,101 applied, 810 admitted, 262 enrolled. *Average high school GPA:* 3.16. *Test scores:* SAT critical reading scores over 500: 53%; SAT math scores over 500: 67%; ACT scores over 18: 82%; SAT critical reading scores over 600: 28%; SAT math scores over 600: 20%; ACT scores over 24: 35%; SAT critical reading scores over 700: 3%; SAT math scores over 700: 6%; ACT scores over 30: 6%.

Faculty *Total:* 185, 34% full-time, 34% with terminal degrees. *Student/faculty ratio:* 14:1.

Academics *Calendar:* 4-1-4. *Degrees:* bachelor's and master's. *Special study options:* academic remediation for entering students, accelerated degree program, adult/continuing education programs, advanced placement credit, cooperative education, distance learning, double majors, external degree program, honors programs, independent study, internships, off-campus study, part-time degree program, student-designed majors, study abroad, summer session for credit. *Unusual degree programs:* 3-2 engineering with University of Illinois at Urbana-Champaign; Washington University in St. Louis; nursing with St. John's College of Nursing; chiropractic at Logan College of Chiropractic.

Computers on Campus 65 computers/terminals are available on campus for general student use. Students can access the following: campus intranet, computer help desk, free student e-mail accounts, online (class) grades, online (class) registration, online (class) schedules. Campuswide network is available. 100% of college-owned or -operated housing units are wired for high-speed Internet access. Wireless service is available via entire campus.

Student Life *Housing:* on-campus residence required through senior year. *Options:* men-only, women-only. Campus housing is university owned. Freshman campus housing is guaranteed. *Activities and organizations:* drama/theater group, student-run newspaper, radio station, choral group, marching band, Campus Activity Board, Greenville Student Outreach, Greenville College Student Association, Circle K, Music and Entertainment Industry Student Association. *Campus security:* 24-hour emergency response devices and patrols, late-night transport/escort service, controlled dormitory access. *Student services:* personal/psychological counseling.

Athletics Member NCAA, NCCAA. All NCAA Division III. *Intercollegiate sports:* baseball M, basketball M/W, cross-country running M/W, football M, soccer M/W, softball W, tennis M/W, track and field M/W, volleyball W. *Intramural sports:* basketball M/W, cheerleading W, football M/W, softball M/W, ultimate Frisbee M/W, volleyball M/W.

Standardized Tests *Required:* SAT or ACT (for admission).

Costs (2012–13) *Comprehensive fee:* $30,496 includes full-time tuition ($22,750), mandatory fees ($170), and room and board ($7576). Full-time tuition and fees vary according to degree level. Part-time tuition: $482 per credit hour. Part-time tuition and fees vary according to course load and degree level. *College room only:* $3664. Room and board charges vary according to housing facility. *Waivers:* senior citizens and employees or children of employees.

Financial Aid Of all full-time matriculated undergraduates who enrolled in 2011, 1,136 applied for aid, 1,052 were judged to have need, 89 had their need fully met. In 2011, 149 non-need-based awards were made. *Average percent of need met:* 68%. *Average financial aid package:* $16,597. *Average need-based loan:* $4288. *Average need-based gift aid:* $12,880. *Average non-need-based aid:* $6970. *Average indebtedness upon graduation:* $23,976.

Applying *Options:* electronic application, early admission, deferred entrance. *Required:* essay or personal statement, high school transcript, minimum 2.3 GPA, agreement to code of conduct. *Required for some:* interview. *Application deadlines:* rolling (freshmen), rolling (transfers). *Notification:* continuous (freshmen), continuous (transfers).

Freshman Application Contact Mr. John R. Massena, Director of Undergraduate Admissions, Greenville College, 315 East College Avenue, Greenville, IL 62246. *Phone:* 618-664-7100. *Toll-free phone:* 800-345-4440. *Fax:* 618-664-9841. *E-mail:* admissions@greenville.edu. *Website:* http://www.greenville.edu/.

Harrington College of Design
Chicago, Illinois

- **Proprietary** comprehensive, founded 1931, part of Career Education Corporation
- **Urban** campus with easy access to Chicago
- **Coed, primarily women**
- **Noncompetitive** entrance level

Faculty *Student/faculty ratio:* 14:1.

Academics *Calendar:* semesters. *Degrees:* associate, bachelor's, and master's.

Student Life *Campus security:* 24-hour emergency response devices and patrols.

Standardized Tests *Recommended:* SAT or ACT (for admission).

Costs (2012–13) *Tuition:* $18,250 full-time, $4750 per term part-time. Full-time tuition and fees vary according to course load, degree level, and program. Part-time tuition and fees vary according to course load, degree level, and program. *Required fees:* $1050 full-time, $410 per term part-time.

Financial Aid *Average percent of need met:* 30. *Average financial aid package:* $3500.

Applying *Options:* electronic application. *Application fee:* $50. *Required:* high school transcript, interview. *Recommended:* essay or personal statement, 1 letter of recommendation.

Freshman Application Contact Harrington College of Design, 200 West Madison Street, Chicago, IL 60605-1496. *Phone:* 312-697-8051. *Toll-free phone:* 866-590-4423 (in-state); 877-939-4975 (out-of-state). *Website:* http://www.harrington.edu/.

Hebrew Theological College
Skokie, Illinois

Freshman Application Contact Rabbi Berish Cardash, Hebrew Theological College, 7135 North Carpenter Road, Skokie, IL 60077-3263. *Phone:* 847-982-2500. *Website:* http://www.htc.edu/.

Illinois College
Jacksonville, Illinois

- **Independent interdenominational** comprehensive, founded 1829
- **Small-town** 62-acre campus with easy access to St. Louis
- **Coed** 970 undergraduate students, 99% full-time, 49% women, 51% men
- **Moderately difficult** entrance level, 58% of applicants were admitted

Undergraduates 961 full-time, 9 part-time. 13% are from out of state; 8% Black or African American, non-Hispanic/Latino; 5% Hispanic/Latino; 0.4% Asian, non-Hispanic/Latino; 0.1% Native Hawaiian or other Pacific Islander, non-Hispanic/Latino; 3% Two or more races, non-Hispanic/Latino; 2% Race/ethnicity unknown; 3% international; 5% transferred in; 84% live on campus. *Retention:* 72% of full-time freshmen returned.

Freshmen *Admission:* 2,357 applied, 1,370 admitted, 285 enrolled. *Average high school GPA:* 3.56. *Test scores:* ACT scores over 18: 90%; ACT scores over 24: 47%; ACT scores over 30: 5%.

Faculty *Total:* 104, 77% full-time, 67% with terminal degrees. *Student/faculty ratio:* 11:1.

Academics *Calendar:* semesters. *Degrees:* bachelor's and master's.

Computers on Campus Students can access the following: computer help desk, free student e-mail accounts, online (class) grades, online (class) registration, online (class) schedules. Campuswide network is available. Wireless service is available via entire campus.

Student Life *Housing:* on-campus residence required through sophomore year. *Options:* coed, men-only, women-only. Campus housing is university owned. Freshman campus housing is guaranteed. *Campus security:* 24-hour emergency response devices and patrols, late-night transport/escort service, controlled dormitory access.

Athletics Member NCAA. All Division III. *Intercollegiate sports:* baseball M, cheerleading W, cross-country running M/W, football M, golf M/W, soccer M/W, softball W, swimming and diving M/W, tennis M/W, track and field M/W, volleyball W. *Intramural sports:* badminton M/W, basketball M/W, fencing M/W, football M, racquetball M/W, softball M/W, swimming and diving M/W, volleyball M/W, water polo M/W, weight lifting M/W.

Costs (2012–13) *Comprehensive fee:* $35,000 includes full-time tuition ($26,000), mandatory fees ($500), and room and board ($8500). Part-time tuition: $800 per semester hour. *Required fees:* $125 per term part-time. *College room only:* $4600. Room and board charges vary according to board plan and housing facility. *Payment plans:* installment, deferred payment. *Waivers:* employees or children of employees.

Financial Aid Of all full-time matriculated undergraduates who enrolled in 2012, 863 applied for aid, 783 were judged to have need, 176 had their need fully met. 556 Federal Work-Study jobs (averaging $1911). In 2012, 167 non-need-based awards were made. *Average percent of need met:* 87%. *Average financial aid package:* $23,156. *Average need-based loan:* $4904. *Average need-based gift aid:* $17,895. *Average non-need-based aid:* $13,684. *Average indebtedness upon graduation:* $29,762.

Applying *Options:* electronic application, early admission, early action, deferred entrance. *Required:* high school transcript, 1 letter of recommendation. *Required for some:* essay or personal statement. *Recommended:* essay or personal statement, minimum 2.5 GPA, interview. *Application deadlines:* rolling (freshmen), 12/15 (early action). *Notification:* continuous (freshmen).

Freshman Application Contact Mr. Rick Bystry, Associate Director of Admission, Illinois College, 1101 West College, Jacksonville, IL 62650.

Phone: 217-245-3030. *Toll-free phone:* 866-464-5265. *Fax:* 217-245-3034. *E-mail:* admissions@ic.edu. *Website:* http://www.ic.edu/.

The Illinois Institute of Art–Chicago
Chicago, Illinois
- **Proprietary** 4-year, founded 1916, part of Education Management Corporation
- **Urban** campus
- **Coed**

Academics *Calendar:* quarters. *Degrees:* diplomas, associate, and bachelor's. **Freshman Application Contact** The Illinois Institute of Art–Chicago, 350 North Orleans Street, Chicago, IL 60654. *Phone:* 312-280-3500. *Toll-free phone:* 800-351-3450. *Website:* http://www.artinstitutes.edu/chicago/.

See full-page ad on page 54 and page 1332 for the College Close-Up.

The Illinois Institute of Art–Schaumburg
Schaumburg, Illinois
- **Proprietary** 4-year, part of Education Management Corporation
- **Suburban** campus
- **Coed**

Academics *Calendar:* quarters. *Degrees:* diplomas, associate, and bachelor's. **Freshman Application Contact** The Illinois Institute of Art–Schaumburg, 1000 North Plaza Drive, Suite 100, Schaumburg, IL 60173. *Phone:* 847-619-3450. *Toll-free phone:* 800-314-3450. *Website:* http://www.artinstitutes.edu/schaumburg/.

See full-page ad on page 54 and page 1334 for the College Close-Up.

The Illinois Institute of Art–Tinley Park
Tinley Park, Illinois
- **Proprietary** 4-year, part of Education Management Corporation
- **Coed**

Academics *Degrees:* diplomas, associate, and bachelor's. **Freshman Application Contact** The Illinois Institute of Art–Tinley Park, 18670 Graphic Drive, Tinley Park, IL 60477. *Phone:* 708-781-4200. *Toll-free phone:* 877-342-3298. *Website:* http://www.artinstitutes.edu/tinleypark.

See full-page ad on page 54 and page 1336 for the College Close-Up.

Illinois Institute of Technology
Chicago, Illinois
- **Independent** comprehensive, founded 1890
- **Urban** 120-acre campus with easy access to Chicago
- **Endowment** $180.2 million
- **Coed** 2,801 undergraduate students, 93% full-time, 31% women, 69% men
- **Moderately difficult** entrance level, 55% of applicants were admitted

Undergraduates 2,610 full-time, 191 part-time. Students come from 51 states and territories; 72 other countries; 23% are from out of state; 7% Black or African American, non-Hispanic/Latino; 13% Hispanic/Latino; 10% Asian, non-Hispanic/Latino; 0.7% Native Hawaiian or other Pacific Islander, non-Hispanic/Latino; 0.4% American Indian or Alaska Native, non-Hispanic/Latino; 0.5% Two or more races, non-Hispanic/Latino; 6% Race/ethnicity unknown; 23% international; 10% transferred in; 60% live on campus. *Retention:* 92% of full-time freshmen returned. **Freshmen** *Admission:* 2,597 applied, 1,427 admitted, 408 enrolled. *Average high school GPA:* 3.92. *Test scores:* SAT critical reading scores over 500: 83%; SAT math scores over 500: 98%; SAT writing scores over 500: 85%; ACT scores over 18: 100%; SAT critical reading scores over 600: 39%; SAT math scores over 600: 83%; SAT writing scores over 600: 38%; ACT scores over 24: 81%; SAT critical reading scores over 700: 7%; SAT math scores over 700: 29%; SAT writing scores over 700: 4%; ACT scores over 30: 25%. **Faculty** *Total:* 742, 55% full-time. *Student/faculty ratio:* 12:1. **Academics** *Calendar:* semesters. *Degrees:* bachelor's, master's, and doctoral. *Special study options:* advanced placement credit, cooperative education, distance learning, double majors, English as a second language, independent study, internships, off-campus study, part-time degree program, services for

LD students, study abroad, summer session for credit. *ROTC:* Army (b), Navy (b), Air Force (b). *Unusual degree programs:* 3-2 engineering; BS in Political Science/Master of Public Administration; BS in Psychology/MS in Personnel and Human Resources Development; BS in Psychology/MS.in Rehabilitation Counseling Dual Degree Program. **Computers on Campus** 500 computers/terminals are available on campus for general student use. Students can access the following: campus intranet, computer help desk, free student e-mail accounts, online (class) grades, online (class) registration, online (class) schedules. Campuswide network is available. 100% of college-owned or -operated housing units are wired for high-speed Internet access. Wireless service is available via classrooms, computer centers, computer labs, dorm rooms, learning centers, libraries, student centers. **Student Life** *Housing:* on-campus residence required for freshman year. *Options:* coed. Campus housing is university owned and is provided by a third party. Freshman applicants given priority for college housing. *Activities and organizations:* drama/theater group, student-run newspaper, radio station, choral group, Union Board, International Students Association, Student Government Association, Greek Council, Commuter Student Associate, national fraternities, national sororities. *Campus security:* 24-hour emergency response devices and patrols, late-night transport/escort service, controlled dormitory access. *Student services:* health clinic, personal/psychological counseling, women's center, legal services. **Athletics** Member NAIA. *Intercollegiate sports:* badminton M(c)/W(c), baseball M(s), basketball M/W, bowling M(c)/W(c), cross-country running M(s)/W(s), lacrosse M(c)/W, rugby M(c)/W(c), soccer M(s)/W(s), swimming and diving M(s)/W(s), track and field M/W, ultimate Frisbee M(c)/W(c), volleyball M(c)/W(s). *Intramural sports:* badminton M/W, basketball M/W, bowling M/W, field hockey M/W, football M/W, racquetball M/W, soccer M/W, softball M/W, squash M/W, table tennis M/W, tennis M(c)/W(c), track and field M(c)/W(c), ultimate Frisbee M/W, volleyball M/W. **Standardized Tests** *Required:* SAT or ACT (for admission). **Costs (2013–14)** *Tuition:* $38,512 full-time, $1204 per credit part-time. Full-time tuition and fees vary according to student level. Part-time tuition and fees vary according to course load and student level. *Room only:* Room and board charges vary according to board plan and housing facility. *Payment plan:* installment. *Waivers:* employees or children of employees. **Financial Aid** Of all full-time matriculated undergraduates who enrolled in 2011, 1,631 applied for aid, 1,552 were judged to have need, 209 had their need fully met. In 2011, 883 non-need-based awards were made. *Average percent of need met:* 76%. *Average financial aid package:* $29,712. *Average need-based loan:* $4831. *Average need-based gift aid:* $24,381. *Average non-need-based aid:* $16,867. *Average indebtedness upon graduation:* $29,581. **Applying** *Options:* electronic application, early admission, early action, deferred entrance. *Required:* essay or personal statement, high school transcript, 1 letter of recommendation. *Recommended:* interview. *Application deadlines:* 8/1 (freshmen), 6/1 (transfers), 12/1 (early action). *Notification:* continuous (freshmen), continuous (transfers), 11/15 (early action). **Freshman Application Contact** Mr. Alfred Nunez, Director, Undergraduate Admissions Office, Illinois Institute of Technology, Office of Undergraduate Admission, Perlstein 101, 10 West 33rd Street, Chicago, IL 60616. *Phone:* 312-567-3025. *Toll-free phone:* 866-472-3448. *Fax:* 312-567-6939. *E-mail:* admission@iit.edu. *Website:* http://www.iit.edu/.

Illinois State University
Normal, Illinois
- **State-supported** university, founded 1857
- **Urban** 490-acre campus
- **Endowment** $67.3 million
- **Coed** 18,257 undergraduate students, 94% full-time, 55% women, 45% men
- **Moderately difficult** entrance level, 74% of applicants were admitted

Undergraduates 17,140 full-time, 1,117 part-time. Students come from 43 states and territories; 39 other countries; 3% are from out of state; 6% Black or African American, non-Hispanic/Latino; 7% Hispanic/Latino; 2% Asian, non-Hispanic/Latino; 0.1% Native Hawaiian or other Pacific Islander, non-Hispanic/Latino; 0.2% American Indian or Alaska Native, non-Hispanic/Latino; 2% Two or more races, non-Hispanic/Latino; 1% Race/ethnicity unknown; 0.5% international; 10% transferred in; 34% live on campus. *Retention:* 82% of full-time freshmen returned. **Freshmen** *Admission:* 12,407 applied, 9,177 admitted, 3,088 enrolled. *Average high school GPA:* 3.36. *Test scores:* ACT scores over 18: 99%; ACT scores over 24: 50%; ACT scores over 30: 4%. **Faculty** *Total:* 1,212, 71% full-time, 66% with terminal degrees. *Student/faculty ratio:* 19:1. **Academics** *Calendar:* semesters. *Degrees:* bachelor's, master's, doctoral, post-master's, and postbachelor's certificates. *Special study options:* academic remediation for entering students, accelerated degree program, adult/continuing education programs, advanced placement credit, cooperative education, distance learning, double majors, English as a second language, honors programs, independent study, internships, off-campus study, part-time degree program, services for LD students, student-designed majors, study abroad, summer session for credit. *ROTC:* Army (b). *Unusual degree programs:* 3-2 engineering with University of Illinois or Bradley University.

Computers on Campus 2,445 computers/terminals and 2,445 ports are available on campus for general student use. Students can access the following: campus intranet, computer help desk, free student e-mail accounts, online (class) grades, online (class) registration, online (class) schedules. Campuswide network is available. 100% of college-owned or -operated housing units are wired for high-speed Internet access. Wireless service is available via classrooms, computer centers, computer labs, libraries, student centers.

Student Life *Housing:* on-campus residence required through sophomore year. *Options:* coed, women-only, disabled students. Campus housing is university owned. Freshman campus housing is guaranteed. *Activities and organizations:* drama/theater group, student-run newspaper, radio and television station, choral group, marching band, national fraternities, national sororities. *Campus security:* 24-hour emergency response devices and patrols, late-night transport/escort service, controlled dormitory access. *Student services:* health clinic, personal/psychological counseling, women's center, legal services.

Athletics Member NCAA. All Division I except football (Division I-AA). *Intercollegiate sports:* baseball M(s), basketball M(s)/W(s), cross-country running M(s)/W(s), golf M(s)/W(s), gymnastics W(s), soccer W(s), softball W(s), swimming and diving W(s), tennis M(s)/W(s), track and field M(s)/W(s), volleyball W(s). *Intramural sports:* baseball M, basketball M/W(c), bowling M(c)/W(c), cheerleading W(c), cross-country running M(c)/W(c), equestrian sports M(c)/W(c), fencing M(c)/W(c), field hockey W, golf W, ice hockey M(c), lacrosse M(c)/W(c), racquetball M/W, rugby M(c)/W(c), soccer M(c)/W(c), softball W(c), tennis M(c)/W(c), ultimate Frisbee M(c)/W(c), volleyball M(c)/W(c), water polo M(c)/W(c), wrestling M(c).

Standardized Tests *Required:* SAT or ACT (for admission).

Costs (2012–13) *Tuition:* state resident $12,726 full-time; nonresident $20,887 full-time. Full-time tuition and fees vary according to course load and degree level. Part-time tuition and fees vary according to course load and degree level. No tuition increase for student's term of enrollment. *Room and board:* $9364. Room and board charges vary according to board plan, housing facility, and location. *Payment plan:* installment. *Waivers:* minority students, senior citizens, and employees or children of employees.

Financial Aid Of all full-time matriculated undergraduates who enrolled in 2011, 13,511 applied for aid, 10,479 were judged to have need, 619 had their need fully met. 372 Federal Work-Study jobs (averaging $1980). 56 state and other part-time jobs (averaging $1529). In 2011, 328 non-need-based awards were made. *Average percent of need met:* 51%. *Average financial aid package:* $7364. *Average need-based loan:* $3854. *Average need-based gift aid:* $3222. *Average non-need-based aid:* $2221. *Average indebtedness upon graduation:* $27,910.

Applying *Options:* electronic application, deferred entrance. *Application fee:* $40. *Required:* essay or personal statement, high school transcript. *Application deadlines:* 3/1 (freshmen), 4/1 (transfers). *Notification:* continuous (freshmen), continuous (transfers).

Freshman Application Contact Mrs. Stacy Ramsey, Acting Director of Admissions, Illinois State University, Campus Box 2200, Normal, IL 61790-2200. *Phone:* 309-438-2181. *Toll-free phone:* 800-366-2478. *Fax:* 309-438-3932. *E-mail:* admissions@ilstu.edu.
Website: http://www.illinoisstate.edu/.

Illinois Wesleyan University
Bloomington, Illinois

- **Independent** 4-year, founded 1850
- **Suburban** 79-acre campus
- **Coed** 2,013 undergraduate students, 100% full-time, 58% women, 42% men
- **Very difficult** entrance level, 60% of applicants were admitted

Undergraduates 2,008 full-time, 5 part-time. 12% are from out of state; 5% Black or African American, non-Hispanic/Latino; 5% Hispanic/Latino; 5% Asian, non-Hispanic/Latino; 0.0% Native Hawaiian or other Pacific Islander, non-Hispanic/Latino; 0.4% American Indian or Alaska Native, non-Hispanic/Latino; 0.3% Two or more races, non-Hispanic/Latino; 7% Race/ethnicity unknown; 4% international; 2% transferred in; 71% live on campus. *Retention:* 89% of full-time freshmen returned.

Freshmen *Admission:* 3,297 applied, 1,963 admitted, 490 enrolled. *Average high school GPA:* 3.5. *Test scores:* SAT critical reading scores over 500: 93%; SAT math scores over 500: 97%; ACT scores over 18: 100%; SAT critical reading scores over 600: 44%; SAT math scores over 600: 64%; ACT scores over 24: 89%; SAT critical reading scores over 700: 10%; SAT math scores over 700: 26%; ACT scores over 30: 26%.

Faculty *Total:* 226, 72% full-time, 77% with terminal degrees. *Student/faculty ratio:* 11:1.

Academics *Calendar:* 4-4-1. *Degree:* bachelor's. *ROTC:* Army (c). *Unusual degree programs:* 3-2 engineering with Case Western Reserve University, Northwestern University, Washington University in St. Louis, Dartmouth College, University of Illinois; forestry with Duke University; occupational therapy.

Computers on Campus Students can access the following: campus intranet, computer help desk, free student e-mail accounts, online (class) grades, online (class) registration, online (class) schedules. Campuswide network is available. Wireless service is available via entire campus.

Student Life *Housing:* on-campus residence required through sophomore year. *Options:* coed, disabled students. Campus housing is university owned. Freshman campus housing is guaranteed. *Campus security:* 24-hour emergency response devices and patrols, late-night transport/escort service, controlled dormitory access, emergency response team.

Athletics Member NCAA. All Division III. *Intercollegiate sports:* baseball M, basketball M/W, cheerleading M(c)/W(c), cross-country running M/W, football M, golf M/W, lacrosse M(c), soccer M/W, softball W, swimming and diving M/W, tennis M/W, track and field M/W, ultimate Frisbee M(c)/W(c), volleyball M(c)/W, water polo M(c). *Intramural sports:* badminton M/W, basketball M/W, football M/W, golf M/W, racquetball M/W, soccer M/W, softball M/W, tennis M/W, volleyball M/W.

Standardized Tests *Required:* SAT or ACT (for admission).

Costs (2012–13) *Comprehensive fee:* $46,792 includes full-time tuition ($37,774), mandatory fees ($180), and room and board ($8838). Part-time tuition: $1180 per credit hour. *College room only:* $5584. *Payment plan:* installment.

Financial Aid Of all full-time matriculated undergraduates who enrolled in 2012, 1,580 applied for aid, 1,293 were judged to have need, 499 had their need fully met. In 2012, 608 non-need-based awards were made. *Average percent of need met:* 87%. *Average financial aid package:* $26,643. *Average need-based loan:* $5346. *Average need-based gift aid:* $20,554. *Average non-need-based aid:* $13,661. *Average indebtedness upon graduation:* $32,964.

Applying *Options:* electronic application, early admission, early action, deferred entrance. *Required:* essay or personal statement, high school transcript, minimum 2.0 GPA, 1 letter of recommendation. *Recommended:* minimum 3.0 GPA, 2 letters of recommendation, interview. *Application deadlines:* rolling (freshmen), 8/15 (transfers), 11/15 (early action). *Notification:* continuous (freshmen), continuous (transfers), 1/15 (early action).

Freshman Application Contact Mr. Tony Bankston, Dean of Admissions, Illinois Wesleyan University, PO Box 2900, Bloomington, IL 61702-2900. *Phone:* 309-556-3031. *Toll-free phone:* 800-332-2498. *Fax:* 309-556-3820. *E-mail:* iwuadmit@iwu.edu.
Website: http://www.iwu.edu/.

International Academy of Design & Technology
Chicago, Illinois

Freshman Application Contact Ms. Suzanne Reichart, Director of Student Management, International Academy of Design & Technology, One North State Street, Suite 500, Chicago, IL 60602. *Phone:* 312-980-9200. *Toll-free phone:* 877-458-6111. *Fax:* 312-541-3929. *E-mail:* sreichart@iadtchicago.edu.
Website: http://www.iadtchicago.edu/.

ITT Technical Institute
Mount Prospect, Illinois

- **Proprietary** primarily 2-year, founded 1986, part of ITT Educational Services, Inc.
- **Suburban** campus
- **Coed**
- **Minimally difficult** entrance level

Academics *Calendar:* quarters. *Degrees:* associate and bachelor's.
Freshman Application Contact Director of Recruitment, ITT Technical Institute, 1401 Feehanville Drive, Mount Prospect, IL 60056. *Phone:* 847-375-8800.
Website: http://www.itt-tech.edu/.

ITT Technical Institute

Oak Brook, Illinois

- **Proprietary** primarily 2-year, founded 1998, part of ITT Educational Services, Inc.
- **Coed**
- **Minimally difficult** entrance level

Academics *Calendar:* quarters. *Degrees:* associate and bachelor's.
Freshman Application Contact Director of Recruitment, ITT Technical Institute, 800 Jorie Boulevard, Suite 100, Oak Brook, IL 60523. *Phone:* 630-472-7000. *Toll-free phone:* 877-488-0001.
Website: http://www.itt-tech.edu/.

ITT Technical Institute

Orland Park, Illinois

- **Proprietary** primarily 2-year, founded 1993, part of ITT Educational Services, Inc.
- **Suburban** campus
- **Coed**
- **Minimally difficult** entrance level

Academics *Calendar:* quarters. *Degrees:* associate and bachelor's.
Financial Aid *Of all full-time matriculated undergraduates who enrolled in 2011*, 6 Federal Work-Study jobs (averaging $4000).
Freshman Application Contact Director of Recruitment, ITT Technical Institute, 11551 184th Place, Orland Park, IL 60467. *Phone:* 708-326-3200.
Website: http://www.itt-tech.edu/.

ITT Technical Institute

Springfield, Illinois

- **Proprietary** 4-year
- **Coed**
- **Minimally difficult** entrance level

Academics *Degrees:* associate and bachelor's.
Freshman Application Contact Director of Recruitment, ITT Technical Institute, 2501 Wabash Avenue, Springfield, IL 62704. *Phone:* 217-547-5700.
Toll-free phone: 877-263-2374.
Website: http://www.itt-tech.edu/.

Judson University

Elgin, Illinois

- **Independent Baptist** comprehensive, founded 1963
- **Suburban** 90-acre campus with easy access to Chicago
- **Endowment** $11.4 million
- **Coed** 1,018 undergraduate students, 73% full-time, 55% women, 45% men
- **Moderately difficult** entrance level, 65% of applicants were admitted

Undergraduates 747 full-time, 271 part-time. Students come from 35 states and territories; 24 other countries; 18% are from out of state; 6% Black or African American, non-Hispanic/Latino; 9% Hispanic/Latino; 1% Asian, non-Hispanic/Latino; 0.2% Native Hawaiian or other Pacific Islander, non-Hispanic/Latino; 1% Two or more races, non-Hispanic/Latino; 15% Race/ethnicity unknown; 3% international; 16% transferred in; 65% live on campus. *Retention:* 73% of full-time freshmen returned.
Freshmen *Admission:* 711 applied, 464 admitted, 163 enrolled. *Average high school GPA:* 3.3. *Test scores:* SAT critical reading scores over 500: 53%; SAT math scores over 500: 79%; ACT scores over 18: 96%; SAT critical reading scores over 600: 18%; SAT math scores over 600: 29%; ACT scores over 24: 49%; SAT critical reading scores over 700: 4%; SAT math scores over 700: 4%; ACT scores over 30: 6%.
Faculty *Total:* 218, 28% full-time, 44% with terminal degrees. *Student/faculty ratio:* 8:1.
Academics *Calendar:* semesters. *Degrees:* bachelor's, master's, and postbachelor's certificates. *Special study options:* academic remediation for entering students, accelerated degree program, adult/continuing education programs, advanced placement credit, distance learning, double majors, honors programs, independent study, internships, off-campus study, part-time degree program, services for LD students, student-designed majors, study abroad, summer session for credit. *ROTC:* Army (c).
Computers on Campus 90 computers/terminals are available on campus for general student use. Students can access the following: campus intranet, computer help desk, free student e-mail accounts, online (class) grades, online (class) registration, online (class) schedules. Campuswide network is available. 100% of college-owned or -operated housing units are wired for high-speed Internet access. Wireless service is available via entire campus.

Student Life *Housing:* on-campus residence required through senior year. *Options:* coed, men-only, women-only, disabled students. Campus housing is university owned. Freshman campus housing is guaranteed. *Activities and organizations:* drama/theater group, choral group, Judson Student Organization, University Ministries, Judson Choir, Fellowship of Christian Athletes, Judson Business Network. *Campus security:* 24-hour emergency response devices and patrols, controlled dormitory access. *Student services:* health clinic, personal/psychological counseling.
Athletics Member NAIA, NCCAA. *Intercollegiate sports:* baseball M(s), basketball M(s)/W(s), cheerleading W(s), cross-country running M(s)/W(s), golf M(s), lacrosse M(s), soccer M(s)/W(s), softball W(s), tennis M(s)/W(s), track and field M(s)/W(s), volleyball W(s). *Intramural sports:* basketball M/W, football M, racquetball M/W, soccer M/W, ultimate Frisbee M/W, volleyball M/W.
Standardized Tests *Required:* SAT or ACT (for admission).
Costs (2013–14) *Comprehensive fee:* $36,520 includes full-time tuition ($26,750), mandatory fees ($780), and room and board ($8990). Full-time tuition and fees vary according to course load and program. Part-time tuition: $1100 per credit. Part-time tuition and fees vary according to course load and program. *Room and board:* Room and board charges vary according to board plan. *Payment plan:* installment. *Waivers:* adult students, senior citizens, and employees or children of employees.
Applying *Options:* electronic application. *Application fee:* $50. *Required:* high school transcript, minimum 2.5 GPA, Minimum 21 ACT; lifestyle statement; portfolios for some majors. *Required for some:* essay or personal statement, 1 letter of recommendation. *Application deadlines:* rolling (freshmen), rolling (out-of-state freshmen), rolling (transfers). *Notification:* continuous (freshmen), continuous (out-of-state freshmen), continuous (transfers).
Freshman Application Contact Mrs. Nancy Binger, Executive Director of Enrollment Services, Judson University, Judson University, 1151 North State Street, Elgin, IL 60123. *Phone:* 847-628-2512. *Toll-free phone:* 800-879-5376. *Fax:* 847-628-2526. *E-mail:* nbinger@judsonu.edu.
Website: http://www.judsonu.edu/.

Kendall College

Chicago, Illinois

Freshman Application Contact Mr. Thomas Marigliano, Director of Enrollment, Kendall College, 900 North North Branch Street, Chicago, IL 60642. *Toll-free phone:* 888-90-KENDALL. *E-mail:* admissions@kendall.edu.
Website: http://www.kendall.edu/.

Knox College

Galesburg, Illinois

- **Independent** 4-year, founded 1837
- **Small-town** 82-acre campus with easy access to Peoria; Quad Cities
- **Endowment** $84.4 million
- **Coed** 1,430 undergraduate students, 97% full-time, 57% women, 43% men
- **Very difficult** entrance level, 78% of applicants were admitted

Undergraduates 1,392 full-time, 38 part-time. Students come from 45 states and territories; 36 other countries; 55% are from out of state; 6% Black or African American, non-Hispanic/Latino; 9% Hispanic/Latino; 5% Asian, non-Hispanic/Latino; 0.3% American Indian or Alaska Native, non-Hispanic/Latino; 3% Two or more races, non-Hispanic/Latino; 2% Race/ethnicity unknown; 11% international; 3% transferred in; 85% live on campus. *Retention:* 88% of full-time freshmen returned.
Freshmen *Admission:* 2,208 applied, 1,713 admitted, 377 enrolled. *Average high school GPA:* 3.3. *Test scores:* SAT critical reading scores over 500: 94%; SAT math scores over 500: 92%; SAT writing scores over 500: 96%; ACT scores over 18: 100%; SAT critical reading scores over 600: 63%; SAT math scores over 600: 66%; SAT writing scores over 600: 58%; ACT scores over 24: 86%; SAT critical reading scores over 700: 30%; SAT math scores over 700: 24%; SAT writing scores over 700: 21%; ACT scores over 30: 38%.
Faculty *Total:* 140, 79% full-time, 85% with terminal degrees. *Student/faculty ratio:* 12:1.
Academics *Calendar:* trimesters. *Degree:* bachelor's. *Special study options:* advanced placement credit, double majors, honors programs, independent study, internships, off-campus study, part-time degree program, services for LD students, student-designed majors, study abroad. *Unusual degree programs:* 3-2 engineering with University of Illinois at Urbana, Washington University, Columbia University, Rensselaer Polytechnic Institute; forestry with Duke University; nursing with Rush University's College of Nursing.
Computers on Campus 200 computers/terminals and 100 ports are available on campus for general student use. Students can access the following: campus intranet, computer help desk, free student e-mail accounts, online (class) grades, online (class) registration, online (class) schedules, Transcripts, EDR, Moodle. Campuswide network is available. 100% of college-owned or -oper-

ated housing units are wired for high-speed Internet access. Wireless service is available via entire campus.

Student Life *Housing:* on-campus residence required through sophomore year. *Options:* coed, men-only, women-only, disabled students. Campus housing is university owned. Freshman campus housing is guaranteed. *Activities and organizations:* drama/theater group, student-run newspaper, radio station, choral group, Student-Run Radio Station (WVKC), International Club, Student Newspaper (The Knox Student), Common Ground, Terpsichore (Dance Collective), national fraternities, national sororities. *Campus security:* 24-hour emergency response devices and patrols, late-night transport/escort service. *Student services:* health clinic, personal/psychological counseling.

Athletics Member NCAA. All Division III. *Intercollegiate sports:* baseball M, basketball M/W, cross-country running M/W, football M, golf M/W, soccer M/W, softball W, swimming and diving M/W, tennis M/W, track and field M/W, volleyball W, wrestling M. *Intramural sports:* badminton M(c)/W(c), basketball M/W, fencing M(c)/W(c), lacrosse M(c)/W(c), soccer M/W, softball M/W, ultimate Frisbee M(c)/W(c), volleyball M/W, water polo M(c)/W(c).

Standardized Tests *Required for some:* SAT or ACT (for admission).

Costs (2013–14) *Comprehensive fee:* $47,352 includes full-time tuition ($38,286), mandatory fees ($666), and room and board ($8400). Full-time tuition and fees vary according to course load. Part-time tuition and fees vary according to course load. *College room only:* $4206. Room and board charges vary according to housing facility. *Payment plan:* installment. *Waivers:* employees or children of employees.

Financial Aid Of all full-time matriculated undergraduates who enrolled in 2012, 1,199 applied for aid, 1,090 were judged to have need, 303 had their need fully met. In 2012, 304 non-need-based awards were made. *Average percent of need met:* 87%. *Average financial aid package:* $28,374. *Average need-based loan:* $5252. *Average need-based gift aid:* $22,949. *Average non-need-based aid:* $12,870. *Average indebtedness upon graduation:* $27,542.

Applying *Options:* electronic application, early admission, early action, deferred entrance. *Application fee:* $40. *Required:* essay or personal statement, high school transcript, 2 letters of recommendation. *Recommended:* interview. *Application deadlines:* 2/1 (freshmen), 4/1 (transfers), 12/1 (early action). *Notification:* 3/31 (freshmen), 5/15 (transfers), 12/31 (early action).

Freshman Application Contact Mr. Paul Steenis, Dean of Admission, Knox College, 2 East South Street, Campus Box148, Galesburg, IL 61401. *Phone:* 309-341-7100. *Toll-free phone:* 800-678-KNOX. *Fax:* 309-341-7070. *E-mail:* admission@knox.edu.

Website: http://www.knox.edu/.

Lake Forest College
Lake Forest, Illinois

- **Independent** comprehensive, founded 1857
- **Suburban** 107-acre campus with easy access to Chicago
- **Endowment** $70.9 million
- **Coed**
- **Moderately difficult** entrance level

Faculty *Student/faculty ratio:* 13:1.

Academics *Calendar:* semesters. *Degrees:* bachelor's, master's, and postbachelor's certificates.

Student Life *Campus security:* 24-hour emergency response devices and patrols, student patrols, late-night transport/escort service, controlled dormitory access.

Athletics Member NCAA. All Division III.

Standardized Tests *Required for some:* SAT or ACT (for admission).

Costs (2012–13) *Comprehensive fee:* $47,350 includes full-time tuition ($37,660), mandatory fees ($640), and room and board ($9050). *College room only:* $4440.

Financial Aid *Of all full-time matriculated undergraduates who enrolled in 2011,* 1,270 applied for aid, 1,189 were judged to have need, 396 had their need fully met. *In 2011,* 218 non-need-based awards were made. *Average percent of need met:* 86. *Average financial aid package:* $26,740. *Average need-based loan:* $4900. *Average need-based gift aid:* $26,740. *Average non-need-based aid:* $14,500. *Average indebtedness upon graduation:* $30,200. *Financial aid deadline:* 5/1.

Applying *Options:* electronic application, early decision, early action, deferred entrance. *Required:* essay or personal statement, high school transcript, 1 letter of recommendation. *Recommended:* interview.

Freshman Application Contact Mr. William Motzer Jr., Vice President for Admissions and Career Services, Lake Forest College, 555 North Sheridan Road, Lake Forest, IL 60045-2338. *Phone:* 847-735-5000. *Toll-free phone:* 800-828-4751. *Fax:* 847-735-6271. *E-mail:* admissions@lakeforest.edu.

Website: http://www.lakeforest.edu/.

Lakeview College of Nursing
Danville, Illinois

Application Contact Admissions Office, Lakeview College of Nursing, 903 North Logan Avenue, Danville, IL 61832. *Phone:* 217-443-5238. *Fax:* 217-442-2279. *E-mail:* admission@lakeviewcol.edu.

Website: http://www.lakeviewcol.edu/.

Lewis University
Romeoville, Illinois

- **Independent** comprehensive, founded 1932, affiliated with Roman Catholic Church
- **Suburban** 410-acre campus with easy access to Chicago
- **Endowment** $40.8 million
- **Coed** 4,579 undergraduate students, 79% full-time, 56% women, 44% men
- **Moderately difficult** entrance level, 56% of applicants were admitted

Undergraduates 3,611 full-time, 968 part-time. Students come from 37 states and territories; 21 other countries; 6% are from out of state; 8% Black or African American, non-Hispanic/Latino; 16% Hispanic/Latino; 3% Asian, non-Hispanic/Latino; 0.2% Native Hawaiian or other Pacific Islander, non-Hispanic/Latino; 0.4% American Indian or Alaska Native, non-Hispanic/Latino; 1% Two or more races, non-Hispanic/Latino; 6% Race/ethnicity unknown; 0.9% international; 9% transferred in; 28% live on campus. *Retention:* 82% of full-time freshmen returned.

Freshmen *Admission:* 5,568 applied, 3,115 admitted, 673 enrolled. *Average high school GPA:* 3.31. *Test scores:* SAT critical reading scores over 500: 66%; SAT math scores over 500: 78%; SAT writing scores over 500: 89%; ACT scores over 18: 96%; SAT critical reading scores over 600: 33%; SAT math scores over 600: 33%; SAT writing scores over 600: 11%; ACT scores over 24: 39%; SAT math scores over 700: 11%; ACT scores over 30: 4%.

Faculty *Total:* 662, 32% full-time, 33% with terminal degrees. *Student/faculty ratio:* 13:1.

Academics *Calendar:* semesters. *Degrees:* certificates, associate, bachelor's, master's, doctoral, and post-master's certificates. *Special study options:* academic remediation for entering students, accelerated degree program, adult/continuing education programs, advanced placement credit, distance learning, double majors, English as a second language, honors programs, independent study, internships, off-campus study, part-time degree program, services for LD students, student-designed majors, study abroad, summer session for credit. *ROTC:* Army (c), Air Force (c).

Computers on Campus 350 computers/terminals are available on campus for general student use. Students can access the following: campus intranet, computer help desk, free student e-mail accounts, online (class) grades, online (class) registration, online (class) schedules, online help, online billing, online financial aid, online payments, online application for admission, online housing application, online application for graduation, Blackboard course management system. Campuswide network is available. 100% of college-owned or -operated housing units are wired for high-speed Internet access. Wireless service is available via entire campus.

Student Life *Housing options:* coed. Campus housing is university owned. Freshman campus housing is guaranteed. *Activities and organizations:* drama/theater group, student-run newspaper, radio and television station, choral group, Student Governing Board, Student Nurses Association, Latin American Student Organization, Theta Kappa Pi Sorority, Delta Sigma Pi (business fraternity), national fraternities, national sororities. *Campus security:* 24-hour emergency response devices and patrols, student patrols, late-night transport/escort service, controlled dormitory access. *Student services:* health clinic, personal/psychological counseling.

Athletics Member NCAA. All Division II. *Intercollegiate sports:* baseball M(s), basketball M(s)/W(s), cheerleading W(s)(c), cross-country running M(s)/W(s), golf M(s)/W(s), ice hockey M(c), rugby M(c), soccer M(s)/W(s), softball W(s), swimming and diving M(s)/W(s), tennis M(s)/W(s), track and field M(s)/W(s), volleyball M(s)/W(s). *Intramural sports:* badminton M/W, basketball M/W, bowling M/W, football M/W, soccer M/W, softball M/W, table tennis M/W, volleyball M(c)/W.

Standardized Tests *Required:* SAT or ACT (for admission).

Costs (2013–14) *Comprehensive fee:* $36,310 includes full-time tuition ($26,780) and room and board ($9530). Full-time tuition and fees vary according to course load and program. Part-time tuition: $780 per credit. Part-time tuition and fees vary according to course load and program. *Required fees:* $780 per credit part-time. *College room only:* $6160. Room and board charges vary according to board plan and housing facility. *Payment plan:* installment. *Waivers:* children of alumni, adult students, and employees or children of employees.

Financial Aid Of all full-time matriculated undergraduates who enrolled in 2012, 3,128 applied for aid, 2,813 were judged to have need, 519 had their

need fully met. 1,833 Federal Work-Study jobs (averaging $3261). 205 state and other part-time jobs (averaging $3156). In 2012, 556 non-need-based awards were made. *Average percent of need met:* 73%. *Average financial aid package:* $18,333. *Average need-based loan:* $4432. *Average need-based gift aid:* $12,713. *Average non-need-based aid:* $8735. *Average indebtedness upon graduation:* $31,400. *Financial aid deadline:* 5/1.

Applying *Options:* electronic application, deferred entrance. *Application fee:* $40. *Required:* high school transcript, minimum 2.0 GPA. *Required for some:* interview. *Application deadlines:* 8/1 (freshmen), 8/1 (out-of-state freshmen), rolling (transfers). *Notification:* continuous (freshmen), continuous (out-of-state freshmen), continuous (transfers).

Freshman Application Contact Mr. Ryan Cockerill, Director of Admission, Lewis University, Box 297, One University Parkway, Romeoville, IL 60446. *Phone:* 815-836-5237. *Toll-free phone:* 800-897-9000. *Fax:* 815-836-5002. *E-mail:* admissions@lewisu.edu.
Website: http://www.lewisu.edu/.

Lexington College

Chicago, Illinois

Freshman Application Contact Mrs. Carmen Larios, Admissions Director, Lexington College, 310 South Peoria Street, Suite 512, Chicago, IL 60607-3534. *Phone:* 312-226-6294 Ext. 226. *Fax:* 312-226-6405. *E-mail:* admissions@lexingtoncollege.edu.
Website: http://www.lexingtoncollege.edu/.

Lincoln Christian University

Lincoln, Illinois

- **Independent** 4-year, founded 1944, affiliated with Christian Churches and Churches of Christ
- **Small-town** 227-acre campus
- **Endowment** $4.2 million
- **Coed** 679 undergraduate students, 85% full-time, 53% women, 47% men
- **Moderately difficult** entrance level, 67% of applicants were admitted

Undergraduates 580 full-time, 99 part-time. Students come from 33 states and territories; 3 other countries; 31% are from out of state; 6% Black or African American, non-Hispanic/Latino; 3% Hispanic/Latino; 0.7% Asian, non-Hispanic/Latino; 1% American Indian or Alaska Native, non-Hispanic/Latino; 1% Two or more races, non-Hispanic/Latino; 3% Race/ethnicity unknown; 2% international; 12% transferred in; 51% live on campus. *Retention:* 75% of full-time freshmen returned.

Freshmen *Admission:* 335 applied, 224 admitted, 100 enrolled. *Average high school GPA:* 3.34. *Test scores:* SAT math scores over 500: 40%; ACT scores over 18: 81%; SAT math scores over 600: 27%; ACT scores over 24: 41%; SAT math scores over 700: 7%; ACT scores over 30: 6%.

Faculty *Total:* 118, 31% full-time, 37% with terminal degrees. *Student/faculty ratio:* 14:1.

Academics *Calendar:* semesters. *Degrees:* certificates, associate, bachelor's, master's, and doctoral. *Special study options:* academic remediation for entering students, adult/continuing education programs, advanced placement credit, distance learning, double majors, external degree program, honors programs, independent study, internships, off-campus study, part-time degree program, services for LD students, study abroad, summer session for credit. *Unusual degree programs:* 3-2 teacher education.

Computers on Campus 51 computers/terminals are available on campus for general student use. Students can access the following: campus intranet, computer help desk, free student e-mail accounts, online (class) grades, online (class) registration, online (class) schedules. Campuswide network is available. 100% of college-owned or -operated housing units are wired for high-speed Internet access. Wireless service is available via entire campus.

Student Life *Housing:* on-campus residence required through senior year. *Options:* men-only, women-only. Campus housing is university owned. Freshman campus housing is guaranteed. *Activities and organizations:* drama/theater group, choral group, Chorale, Student Cabinet, American Association of Christian Counselors (AACC)—Student Chapter, Cheerleading. *Campus security:* 24-hour emergency response devices, student patrols, controlled dormitory access. *Student services:* personal/psychological counseling.

Athletics Member NCCAA. *Intercollegiate sports:* baseball M, basketball M/W, soccer M/W, volleyball W. *Intramural sports:* badminton M/W, basketball M/W, soccer M/W, ultimate Frisbee M/W, volleyball M/W.

Standardized Tests *Required:* SAT or ACT (for admission).

Costs (2012–13) *One-time required fee:* $240. *Comprehensive fee:* $22,140 includes full-time tuition ($15,060) and room and board ($7080). Full-time tuition and fees vary according to location. Part-time tuition: $502 per credit hour. Part-time tuition and fees vary according to location. *Required fees:* $8 per credit hour part-time. *College room only:* $3398. *Payment plans:* install-

ment, deferred payment. *Waivers:* senior citizens and employees or children of employees.

Financial Aid Of all full-time matriculated undergraduates who enrolled in 2010, 631 applied for aid, 559 were judged to have need, 50 had their need fully met. 97 Federal Work-Study jobs (averaging $1107). 156 state and other part-time jobs (averaging $1345). In 2010, 49 non-need-based awards were made. *Average percent of need met:* 53%. *Average financial aid package:* $10,423. *Average need-based loan:* $3991. *Average need-based gift aid:* $3897. *Average non-need-based aid:* $5210. *Average indebtedness upon graduation:* $16,165.

Applying *Options:* electronic application, deferred entrance. *Application fee:* $25. *Required:* essay or personal statement, high school transcript, 3 letters of recommendation. *Required for some:* interview. *Application deadlines:* rolling (freshmen), rolling (out-of-state freshmen), rolling (transfers). *Notification:* continuous (freshmen), continuous (out-of-state freshmen), continuous (transfers).

Freshman Application Contact Mrs. Mary K. Davis, Admissions Office Manager, Lincoln Christian University, 100 Campus View Drive, Lincoln, IL 62656. *Phone:* 217-732-3168 Ext. 2251. *Toll-free phone:* 888-522-5228. *Fax:* 217-732-4199. *E-mail:* admissions@lincolnchristian.edu.
Website: http://www.lincolnchristian.edu/.

Lincoln College–Normal

Normal, Illinois

Freshman Application Contact Mr. Steve Puck, Director of Admissions, Lincoln College–Normal, 715 West Raab Road, Normal, IL 61761. *Phone:* 309-268-4314. *Toll-free phone:* 800-569-0558. *Fax:* 309-862-3352. *E-mail:* spuck@lincolncollege.edu.
Website: http://www.lincolncollege.edu/normal/.

Lindenwood University–Belleville

Belleville, Illinois

Admissions Office Contact Lindenwood University–Belleville, 2600 West Main Street, Belleville, IL 62226.
Website: http://belleville.lindenwood.edu/.

Loyola University Chicago

Chicago, Illinois

- **Independent Roman Catholic (Jesuit)** university, founded 1870
- **Urban** 105-acre campus
- **Endowment** $406.0 million
- **Coed** 9,723 undergraduate students, 92% full-time, 63% women, 37% men
- **Moderately difficult** entrance level, 58% of applicants were admitted

Undergraduates 8,952 full-time, 771 part-time. Students come from 50 states and territories; 77 other countries; 34% are from out of state; 4% Black or African American, non-Hispanic/Latino; 12% Hispanic/Latino; 10% Asian, non-Hispanic/Latino; 0.1% Native Hawaiian or other Pacific Islander, non-Hispanic/Latino; 0.1% American Indian or Alaska Native, non-Hispanic/Latino; 5% Two or more races, non-Hispanic/Latino; 3% Race/ethnicity unknown; 2% international; 7% transferred in; 41% live on campus. *Retention:* 87% of full-time freshmen returned.

Freshmen *Admission:* 19,657 applied, 11,395 admitted, 2,003 enrolled. *Average high school GPA:* 3.76. *Test scores:* SAT critical reading scores over 500: 92%; SAT math scores over 500: 90%; SAT writing scores over 500: 89%; ACT scores over 18: 100%; SAT critical reading scores over 600: 48%; SAT math scores over 600: 50%; SAT writing scores over 600: 44%; ACT scores over 24: 89%; SAT critical reading scores over 700: 12%; SAT math scores over 700: 10%; SAT writing scores over 700: 7%; ACT scores over 30: 24%.

Faculty *Total:* 1,463, 49% full-time. *Student/faculty ratio:* 14:1.

Academics *Calendar:* semesters. *Degrees:* certificates, bachelor's, master's, doctoral, post-master's, and postbachelor's certificates (also offers adult part-time program with significant enrollment not reflected in profile). *Special study options:* academic remediation for entering students, accelerated degree program, adult/continuing education programs, advanced placement credit, cooperative education, distance learning, double majors, English as a second language, freshman honors college, honors programs, independent study, internships, off-campus study, part-time degree program, services for LD students, study abroad, summer session for credit. *ROTC:* Army (c), Navy (c), Air Force (c). *Unusual degree programs:* 3-2 business administration; engineering with BS Physics and Engineering, Columbia University in NYC; BS Physics and Engineering, Washington University, St. Louis; social work; political science, sociology, psychology, computer science, biology, education, accounting, information technology, criminal justice, environmental studies, women's studies, applied human perception.

Computers on Campus 1,464 computers/terminals are available on campus for general student use. Students can access the following: campus intranet, computer help desk, free student e-mail accounts, online (class) grades, online (class) registration, online (class) schedules. Campuswide network is available. 100% of college-owned or -operated housing units are wired for high-speed Internet access. Wireless service is available via entire campus.

Student Life *Housing:* on-campus residence required through sophomore year. *Options:* coed, disabled students. Campus housing is university owned. Freshman campus housing is guaranteed. *Activities and organizations:* drama/theater group, student-run newspaper, radio station, Department of Programming, Panhellenic Sororities, American Medical Association, Habitat for Humanity, Globe Med, national fraternities, national sororities. *Campus security:* 24-hour emergency response devices and patrols, late-night transport/escort service, controlled dormitory access, Loyola Alert, a special service to provide personalized, time-sensitive alerts to students, faculty, staff & other personnel at Loyola. *Student services:* health clinic, personal/psychological counseling, women's center.

Athletics Member NCAA. All Division I. *Intercollegiate sports:* basketball M(s)/W(s), cheerleading M/W, cross-country running M(s)/W(s), golf M(s)/W(s), soccer M(s)/W(s), softball W(s), track and field M(s)/W(s), volleyball M(s)/W(s). *Intramural sports:* badminton M/W, baseball M(c), basketball M/W, cross-country running M(c)/W(c), fencing M(c)/W(c), football M(c), ice hockey M(c)/W(c), lacrosse M(c)/W(c), racquetball M/W, rugby M(c)/W(c), soccer M(c)/W(c), softball W(c), swimming and diving M(c)/W(c), table tennis M(c)/W(c), tennis M(c)/W(c), ultimate Frisbee M(c)/W(c), volleyball M(c)/W(c), water polo M(c)/W(c).

Standardized Tests *Required:* SAT or ACT (for admission).

Costs (2013–14) *Comprehensive fee:* $48,403 includes full-time tuition ($34,343), mandatory fees ($1160), and room and board ($12,900). Full-time tuition and fees vary according to location, program, and student level. Part-time tuition: $690 per credit. Part-time tuition and fees vary according to course load. *Required fees:* $158 per term part-time. *College room only:* $8114. Room and board charges vary according to board plan, housing facility, and location. *Payment plans:* installment, deferred payment. *Waivers:* senior citizens and employees or children of employees.

Financial Aid Of all full-time matriculated undergraduates who enrolled in 2012, 7,190 applied for aid, 6,452 were judged to have need, 655 had their need fully met. 5,148 Federal Work-Study jobs (averaging $2131). In 2012, 1600 non-need-based awards were made. *Average percent of need met:* 79%. *Average financial aid package:* $29,572. *Average need-based loan:* $4736. *Average need-based gift aid:* $18,304. *Average non-need-based aid:* $10,775. *Average indebtedness upon graduation:* $36,328.

Applying *Options:* electronic application. *Required:* essay or personal statement, high school transcript, minimum 2.0 GPA. *Recommended:* interview. *Notification:* continuous (freshmen), continuous (out-of-state freshmen), continuous (transfers).

Freshman Application Contact Ms. Lori Greene, Director of Undergraduate Admissions, Loyola University Chicago, 1032 West Sheridan Road, Chicago, IL 60660. *Phone:* 773-508-3075. *Toll-free phone:* 800-262-2373. *E-mail:* admission@luc.edu.
Website: http://www.luc.edu/.

MacMurray College
Jacksonville, Illinois

Freshman Application Contact Ms. Alicia Zeone, Assistant Director of Admission, MacMurray College, MacMurray College, 447 East College Avenue, Jacksonville, IL 62650. *Phone:* 217-479-7059. *Toll-free phone:* 800-252-7485. *Fax:* 217-291-0702. *E-mail:* alicia.zeone@mac.edu.
Website: http://www.mac.edu/.

McKendree University
Lebanon, Illinois

- **Independent** comprehensive, founded 1828, affiliated with United Methodist Church
- **Suburban** 234-acre campus with easy access to St. Louis, MO; Belleville, IL
- **Endowment** $28.6 million
- **Coed** 2,356 undergraduate students, 71% full-time, 56% women, 44% men
- **Moderately difficult** entrance level, 68% of applicants were admitted

Undergraduates 1,667 full-time, 689 part-time. Students come from 24 states and territories; 9 other countries; 32% are from out of state; 9% Black or African American, non-Hispanic/Latino; 2% Hispanic/Latino; 1% Asian, non-Hispanic/Latino; 0.2% American Indian or Alaska Native, non-Hispanic/Latino; 4% Two or more races, non-Hispanic/Latino; 1% international; 5% transferred in; 60% live on campus. *Retention:* 81% of full-time freshmen returned.

Freshmen *Admission:* 1,359 applied, 925 admitted, 290 enrolled. *Average high school GPA:* 3.4. *Test scores:* SAT critical reading scores over 500: 62%; SAT math scores over 500: 63%; SAT writing scores over 500: 13%; ACT scores over 18: 93%; SAT math scores over 600: 13%; ACT scores over 24: 37%; ACT scores over 30: 4%.

Faculty *Total:* 313, 31% full-time, 44% with terminal degrees. *Student/faculty ratio:* 13:1.

Academics *Calendar:* semesters. *Degrees:* associate, bachelor's, master's, doctoral, and post-master's certificates. *Special study options:* academic remediation for entering students, accelerated degree program, adult/continuing education programs, advanced placement credit, cooperative education, distance learning, double majors, honors programs, independent study, internships, off-campus study, part-time degree program, services for LD students, student-designed majors, study abroad, summer session for credit. *ROTC:* Army (c), Air Force (c). *Unusual degree programs:* 3-2 engineering with Engineering program with Missouri Science and Technology or University of Illinois-Champaign; occupational therapy with Washington University in St. Louis.

Computers on Campus 168 computers/terminals and 1,061 ports are available on campus for general student use. Students can access the following: campus intranet, computer help desk, free student e-mail accounts, online (class) grades, online (class) registration, online (class) schedules. Campuswide network is available. 100% of college-owned or -operated housing units are wired for high-speed Internet access. Wireless service is available via entire campus.

Student Life *Housing:* on-campus residence required through junior year. *Options:* coed, disabled students. Campus housing is university owned and leased by the school. Freshman campus housing is guaranteed. *Activities and organizations:* drama/theater group, student-run newspaper, radio station, choral group, marching band, Wonders of Wellness, Center for Public Service, Campus Ministries, APO, Debate, national fraternities, national sororities. *Campus security:* 24-hour emergency response devices and patrols, student patrols, late-night transport/escort service, controlled dormitory access. *Student services:* health clinic, personal/psychological counseling.

Athletics Member NCAA. All Division II. *Intercollegiate sports:* baseball M(s), basketball M(s)/W(s), bowling M(c)/W(s), cheerleading W(s)(c), cross-country running M(s)/W(s), football M(s), golf M(s)/W(s), ice hockey M(c), lacrosse W(s), soccer M(s)/W(s), softball W(s), tennis M(s)/W(s), track and field M(s)/W(s), volleyball M(s)(c)/W(s), wrestling M(s). *Intramural sports:* basketball M/W, football M/W, softball M/W, table tennis M/W, ultimate Frisbee M/W, volleyball M/W.

Standardized Tests *Required:* SAT or ACT (for admission).

Costs (2013–14) *Comprehensive fee:* $34,740 includes full-time tuition ($25,050), mandatory fees ($1000), and room and board ($8690). Full-time tuition and fees vary according to course load, degree level, and location. Part-time tuition: $830 per credit hour. Part-time tuition and fees vary according to course load, degree level, and location. *College room only:* $4620. Room and board charges vary according to board plan and housing facility. *Payment plans:* installment, deferred payment. *Waivers:* children of alumni and employees or children of employees.

Financial Aid Of all full-time matriculated undergraduates who enrolled in 2012, 1,366 applied for aid, 1,243 were judged to have need, 219 had their need fully met. 767 Federal Work-Study jobs (averaging $1784). 99 state and other part-time jobs (averaging $1148). In 2012, 212 non-need-based awards were made. *Average percent of need met:* 71%. *Average financial aid package:* $17,998. *Average need-based loan:* $4147. *Average need-based gift aid:* $14,459. *Average non-need-based aid:* $9033. *Average indebtedness upon graduation:* $23,005.

Applying *Options:* electronic application, deferred entrance. *Required:* essay or personal statement, high school transcript, minimum 2.5 GPA, 1 letter of recommendation, rank in upper 50% of high school class, ACT score of 20 or higher. *Required for some:* interview. *Application deadlines:* rolling (freshmen), rolling (transfers). *Notification:* continuous (freshmen), continuous (transfers).

Freshman Application Contact Mrs. Josie Blasdel, Director of Undergraduate Admission, McKendree University, 701 College Road, Lebanon, IL 62254. *Phone:* 618-537-6836. *Toll-free phone:* 800-232-7228. *Fax:* 618-537-6496. *E-mail:* jlblasdel@mckendree.edu.
Website: http://www.mckendree.edu/.

Midstate College
Peoria, Illinois

Freshman Application Contact Ms. Jessica Hancock, Director of Admissions, Midstate College, 411 West Northmoor Road, Peoria, IL 61614. *Phone:* 309-692-4092. *Toll-free phone:* 800-251-4299. *Fax:* 309-692-3893. *E-mail:* jhancock2@midstate.edu.
Website: http://www.midstate.edu/.

Millikin University
Decatur, Illinois

- **Independent** comprehensive, founded 1901, affiliated with Presbyterian Church (U.S.A.)
- **Suburban** 75-acre campus
- **Endowment** $105.5 million
- **Coed** 2,264 undergraduate students, 95% full-time, 59% women, 41% men
- **Moderately difficult** entrance level, 55% of applicants were admitted

Undergraduates 2,161 full-time, 103 part-time. Students come from 32 states and territories; 13 other countries; 11% are from out of state; 12% Black or African American, non-Hispanic/Latino; 5% Hispanic/Latino; 0.9% Asian, non-Hispanic/Latino; 0.2% Native Hawaiian or other Pacific Islander, non-Hispanic/Latino; 0.3% American Indian or Alaska Native, non-Hispanic/Latino; 3% Two or more races, non-Hispanic/Latino; 0.2% Race/ethnicity unknown; 1% international; 6% transferred in; 61% live on campus. *Retention:* 78% of full-time freshmen returned.

Freshmen *Admission:* 3,998 applied, 2,217 admitted, 532 enrolled. *Average high school GPA:* 3.36. *Test scores:* SAT critical reading scores over 500: 60%; SAT math scores over 500: 51%; SAT writing scores over 500: 54%; ACT scores over 18: 94%; SAT critical reading scores over 600: 29%; SAT math scores over 600: 18%; SAT writing scores over 600: 23%; ACT scores over 24: 45%; SAT critical reading scores over 700: 3%; SAT math scores over 700: 5%; SAT writing scores over 700: 5%; ACT scores over 30: 7%.

Faculty *Total:* 305, 50% full-time, 53% with terminal degrees. *Student/faculty ratio:* 11:1.

Academics *Calendar:* semesters. *Degrees:* bachelor's and master's. *Special study options:* accelerated degree program, adult/continuing education programs, advanced placement credit, double majors, English as a second language, honors programs, independent study, internships, off-campus study, part-time degree program, services for LD students, student-designed majors, study abroad, summer session for credit. *Unusual degree programs:* 3-2 engineering with Washington University in St. Louis; occupational therapy with Washington University; pharmacy with Midwestern University.

Computers on Campus 282 computers/terminals and 318 ports are available on campus for general student use. Students can access the following: computer help desk, free student e-mail accounts, online (class) grades, online (class) registration, online (class) schedules, online degree audit; online financials (view and pay bills; view financial aid). Campuswide network is available. 100% of college-owned or -operated housing units are wired for high-speed Internet access. Wireless service is available via classrooms, computer centers, computer labs, dorm rooms, learning centers, libraries, student centers.

Student Life *Housing:* on-campus residence required through junior year. *Options:* coed, women-only, disabled students. Campus housing is university owned, leased by the school and is provided by a third party. Freshman campus housing is guaranteed. *Activities and organizations:* drama/theater group, student-run newspaper, radio station, choral group, University Center Board, Multicultural Student Council, Student Housing Council, Panhellenic Council, Interfraternity Council, national fraternities, national sororities. *Campus security:* 24-hour emergency response devices and patrols, late-night transport/escort service, controlled dormitory access. *Student services:* health clinic, personal/psychological counseling.

Athletics Member NCAA. All Division III. *Intercollegiate sports:* baseball M, basketball M/W, cheerleading M/W, cross-country running M/W, football M, golf M/W, soccer M/W, softball W, swimming and diving M/W, tennis W, track and field M/W, volleyball W. *Intramural sports:* basketball M/W, bowling M/W, football M, soccer M/W, softball M/W, volleyball M/W.

Standardized Tests *Required:* SAT or ACT (for admission).

Costs (2012–13) *Comprehensive fee:* $37,614 includes full-time tuition ($27,852), mandatory fees ($792), and room and board ($8970). Part-time tuition: $931 per credit hour. *Required fees:* $22 per credit hour part-time. *College room only:* $5000. Room and board charges vary according to board plan and housing facility. *Payment plan:* installment. *Waivers:* employees or children of employees.

Financial Aid Of all full-time matriculated undergraduates who enrolled in 2011, 1,932 applied for aid, 1,724 were judged to have need, 914 had their need fully met. 598 Federal Work-Study jobs (averaging $989). 300 state and other part-time jobs (averaging $781). In 2011, 180 non-need-based awards were made. *Average percent of need met:* 92%. *Average financial aid package:* $22,924. *Average need-based loan:* $4520. *Average need-based gift aid:* $9940. *Average non-need-based aid:* $11,192. *Average indebtedness upon graduation:* $29,871.

Applying *Options:* electronic application, deferred entrance. *Required:* high school transcript, minimum 2.0 GPA, 2 letters of recommendation. *Required for some:* audition for music/theatre, art portfolio review. *Recommended:* interview. *Application deadlines:* rolling (freshmen), rolling (out-of-state freshmen), rolling (transfers). *Notification:* continuous (freshmen), continuous (out-of-state freshmen), continuous (transfers).

Freshman Application Contact Mr. Joe Havis, Director, Office of Admission, Millikin University, 1184 West Main Street, Decatur, IL 62522-2084. *Phone:* 217-424-6210. *Toll-free phone:* 800-373-7733. *Fax:* 217-425-4669. *E-mail:* admis@millikin.edu. *Website:* http://www.millikin.edu/.

Monmouth College
Monmouth, Illinois

- **Independent** 4-year, founded 1853, affiliated with Presbyterian Church
- **Small-town** 106-acre campus
- **Endowment** $77.7 million
- **Coed** 1,247 undergraduate students, 99% full-time, 54% women, 46% men
- **Moderately difficult** entrance level, 62% of applicants were admitted

Undergraduates 1,234 full-time, 13 part-time. Students come from 19 states and territories; 9 other countries; 7% are from out of state; 13% Black or African American, non-Hispanic/Latino; 9% Hispanic/Latino; 0.6% Asian, non-Hispanic/Latino; 0.3% Native Hawaiian or other Pacific Islander, non-Hispanic/Latino; 1% American Indian or Alaska Native, non-Hispanic/Latino; 0.6% Two or more races, non-Hispanic/Latino; 5% Race/ethnicity unknown; 0.8% international; 4% transferred in; 92% live on campus. *Retention:* 75% of full-time freshmen returned.

Freshmen *Admission:* 1,930 applied, 1,187 admitted, 343 enrolled. *Average high school GPA:* 3.2. *Test scores:* ACT scores over 18: 88%; ACT scores over 24: 26%; ACT scores over 30: 4%.

Faculty *Total:* 118, 73% full-time, 65% with terminal degrees. *Student/faculty ratio:* 13:1.

Academics *Calendar:* semesters. *Degree:* bachelor's. *Special study options:* academic remediation for entering students, advanced placement credit, double majors, English as a second language, honors programs, independent study, internships, off-campus study, part-time degree program, services for LD students, student-designed majors, study abroad. *ROTC:* Army (c). *Unusual degree programs:* engineering with Case Western Reserve University; University of Southern California (joint five-year and six-year coordinated programs); nursing with Rush University College of Nursing; Joint five-year and six-year occupational therapy and medical technology Masters programs with Rush University; atmospheric science with Creighton University.

Computers on Campus 140 computers/terminals are available on campus for general student use. Students can access the following: campus intranet, computer help desk, free student e-mail accounts, online (class) grades, online (class) registration, online (class) schedules, 11 PC labs and 3 specialized Mac labs. Campuswide network is available. 100% of college-owned or -operated housing units are wired for high-speed Internet access. Wireless service is available via entire campus.

Student Life *Housing:* on-campus residence required through senior year. *Options:* coed, men-only, women-only, disabled students. Campus housing is university owned. Freshman campus housing is guaranteed. *Activities and organizations:* drama/theater group, student-run newspaper, radio and television station, choral group, marching band, Fighting Scots Marching Band and Jazz Band, Associated Students of Monmouth College, Crimson Masque (theatre), Alternative Spring Break, Coalition for Ethnic Awareness, national fraternities, national sororities. *Campus security:* 24-hour emergency response devices, late-night transport/escort service, controlled dormitory access, night security. *Student services:* personal/psychological counseling.

Athletics Member NCAA. All Division III. *Intercollegiate sports:* baseball M, basketball M/W, cross-country running M/W, football M, golf M/W, soccer M/W, softball W, swimming and diving M/W, tennis M/W, track and field M/W, volleyball W, water polo M/W. *Intramural sports:* archery M/W, badminton M/W, baseball M, cheerleading W(c), lacrosse W(c), soccer M/W, swimming and diving M/W, table tennis M/W, tennis M/W, ultimate Frisbee M/W, volleyball M/W, water polo M(c)/W(c), wrestling M.

Standardized Tests *Required:* SAT or ACT (for admission).

Costs (2013–14) *One-time required fee:* $190. *Comprehensive fee:* $39,100 includes full-time tuition ($31,500) and room and board ($7600). Full-time tuition and fees vary according to course load. *Room and board:* Room and board charges vary according to board plan and housing facility. *Payment plan:* installment. *Waivers:* employees or children of employees.

Financial Aid Of all full-time matriculated undergraduates who enrolled in 2012, 1,169 applied for aid, 1,078 were judged to have need, 191 had their need fully met. In 2012, 153 non-need-based awards were made. *Average percent of need met:* 85%. *Average financial aid package:* $27,194. *Average need-based loan:* $4524. *Average need-based gift aid:* $21,934. *Average non-need-based aid:* $13,824. *Average indebtedness upon graduation:* $31,578.

Applying *Options:* electronic application, deferred entrance. *Required:* high school transcript. *Required for some:* interview. *Recommended:* essay or personal statement, minimum 2.7 GPA, interview. *Application deadlines:* rolling (freshmen), rolling (transfers). *Notification:* continuous (freshmen), continuous (transfers).

Freshman Application Contact Mr. Phil Betz, Director of Admissions, Monmouth College, Monmouth College, 700 East Broadway, Monmouth, IL 61462-1988. *Phone:* 309-457-2132. *Toll-free phone:* 800-747-2687. *Fax:* 309-457-2141. *E-mail:* admissions@monmouthcollege.edu. *Website:* http://www.monm.edu/.

Moody Bible Institute
Chicago, Illinois

- **Independent nondenominational** comprehensive, founded 1886
- **Urban** 25-acre campus with easy access to Chicago
- **Endowment** $27.8 million
- **Coed**
- **Moderately difficult** entrance level

Faculty *Student/faculty ratio:* 20:1.
Academics *Calendar:* semesters. *Degrees:* associate, bachelor's, master's, and postbachelor's certificates.
Student Life *Campus security:* 24-hour emergency response devices and patrols, student patrols, late-night transport/escort service, controlled dormitory access.
Athletics Member NCCAA.
Standardized Tests *Required:* SAT and SAT Subject Tests or ACT (for admission).
Applying *Options:* electronic application, early admission, early decision. *Required:* essay or personal statement, high school transcript, minimum 2.0 GPA, 4 letters of recommendation, Christian testimony. *Required for some:* interview.
Freshman Application Contact Ms. Jacqueline Holman, Admissions Office, Moody Bible Institute, 820 North LaSalle Boulevard, Chicago, IL 60610. *Phone:* 312-329-4307. *Toll-free phone:* 800-967-4MBI. *Fax:* 312-329-8987. *E-mail:* admissions@moody.edu. *Website:* http://www.moody.edu/.

National Louis University
Chicago, Illinois

- **Independent** university, founded 1886
- **Urban** 12-acre campus
- **Endowment** $29.0 million
- **Coed**
- **Minimally difficult** entrance level

Faculty *Student/faculty ratio:* 8:1.
Academics *Calendar:* quarters. *Degrees:* bachelor's, master's, doctoral, postmaster's, and postbachelor's certificates.
Student Life *Campus security:* 24-hour emergency response devices and patrols.
Standardized Tests *Required for some:* SAT or ACT (for admission).
Financial Aid *Of all full-time matriculated undergraduates who enrolled in 2011,* 772 applied for aid, 736 were judged to have need, 10 had their need fully met. 66 Federal Work-Study jobs (averaging $3890). *In 2011,* 52 non-need-based awards were made. *Average percent of need met:* 43. *Average financial aid package:* $12,225. *Average need-based loan:* $4426. *Average need-based gift aid:* $8302. *Average non-need-based aid:* $5605. *Average indebtedness upon graduation:* $29,900.
Applying *Options:* electronic application, deferred entrance. *Application fee:* $40. *Required:* high school transcript, minimum 2.0 GPA. *Required for some:* 2 letters of recommendation. *Recommended:* interview.
Freshman Application Contact National Louis University, 1000 Capitol Drive, Wheeling, IL 60090. *Phone:* 888-NLU-TODAY. *Toll-free phone:* 888-658-8632. *Website:* http://www.nl.edu/.

North Central College
Naperville, Illinois

- **Independent United Methodist** comprehensive, founded 1861
- **Suburban** 63-acre campus with easy access to Chicago
- **Endowment** $91.3 million
- **Coed** 2,755 undergraduate students, 93% full-time, 57% women, 43% men
- **Moderately difficult** entrance level, 60% of applicants were admitted

Undergraduates 2,560 full-time, 195 part-time. Students come from 30 states and territories; 22 other countries; 7% are from out of state; 4% Black or African American, non-Hispanic/Latino; 8% Hispanic/Latino; 2% Asian, non-His-

panic/Latino; 0.1% Native Hawaiian or other Pacific Islander, non-Hispanic/Latino; 0.2% American Indian or Alaska Native, non-Hispanic/Latino; 2% Two or more races, non-Hispanic/Latino; 4% Race/ethnicity unknown; 0.9% international; 10% transferred in; 54% live on campus. *Retention:* 78% of full-time freshmen returned.
Freshmen *Admission:* 3,987 applied, 2,401 admitted, 552 enrolled. *Average high school GPA:* 3.6. *Test scores:* ACT scores over 18: 99%; ACT scores over 24: 59%; ACT scores over 30: 9%.
Faculty *Total:* 256, 51% full-time, 62% with terminal degrees. *Student/faculty ratio:* 16:1.
Academics *Calendar:* quarters. *Degrees:* bachelor's, master's, and postbachelor's certificates. *Special study options:* academic remediation for entering students, accelerated degree program, advanced placement credit, double majors, English as a second language, honors programs, independent study, internships, off-campus study, part-time degree program, services for LD students, student-designed majors, study abroad, summer session for credit. *ROTC:* Army (c), Air Force (c). *Unusual degree programs:* 3-2 engineering with Washington University in St. Louis; University of Illinois at Urbana-Champaign; Marquette University; University of Minnesota, Twin Cities Campus.
Computers on Campus 254 computers/terminals are available on campus for general student use. Students can access the following: campus intranet, computer help desk, free student e-mail accounts, online (class) grades, online (class) registration, online (class) schedules, software packages. Campuswide network is available. 100% of college-owned or -operated housing units are wired for high-speed Internet access. Wireless service is available via computer centers, computer labs, dorm rooms, learning centers, libraries, student centers.
Student Life *Housing options:* coed, men-only, women-only, disabled students. Campus housing is university owned. Freshman applicants given priority for college housing. *Activities and organizations:* drama/theater group, student-run newspaper, radio station, choral group, College Union Activities Board, WONC (student radio station), Cardinals in Action (service group), Students in Free Enterprise (SIFE), Residence Hall Association. *Campus security:* 24-hour emergency response devices and patrols, late-night transport/escort service, controlled dormitory access. *Student services:* health clinic, personal/psychological counseling.
Athletics Member NCAA. All Division III. *Intercollegiate sports:* baseball M, basketball M/W, cheerleading W, cross-country running M/W, football M, golf M/W, lacrosse W, soccer M/W, softball W, swimming and diving M/W, tennis M/W, track and field M/W, volleyball W, wrestling M. *Intramural sports:* badminton M/W, basketball M/W, football M/W, golf M/W, racquetball M/W, soccer M/W, softball M/W, ultimate Frisbee M/W, volleyball M/W.
Standardized Tests *Required:* SAT or ACT (for admission). *Recommended:* ACT (for admission).
Costs (2012–13) *Comprehensive fee:* $39,954 includes full-time tuition ($30,891), mandatory fees ($180), and room and board ($8883). Part-time tuition: $750 per credit hour. Part-time tuition and fees vary according to course load. *Required fees:* $20 per term part-time. *Room and board:* Room and board charges vary according to housing facility. *Payment plan:* installment. *Waivers:* senior citizens and employees or children of employees.
Financial Aid Of all full-time matriculated undergraduates who enrolled in 2012, 2,179 applied for aid, 1,955 were judged to have need, 391 had their need fully met. 1,297 Federal Work-Study jobs (averaging $163). In 2012, 530 non-need-based awards were made. *Average percent of need met:* 73%. *Average financial aid package:* $22,061. *Average need-based loan:* $4737. *Average need-based gift aid:* $16,944. *Average non-need-based aid:* $12,632. *Average indebtedness upon graduation:* $33,304.
Applying *Options:* electronic application, deferred entrance. *Application fee:* $25. *Required:* high school transcript, minimum 2.5 GPA. *Required for some:* interview. *Recommended:* essay or personal statement, 1 letter of recommendation. *Application deadlines:* rolling (freshmen), rolling (out-of-state freshmen), rolling (transfers). *Notification:* continuous (freshmen), continuous (out-of-state freshmen), continuous (transfers).
Freshman Application Contact Ms. Martha Stolze, Director of Freshman Admission, North Central College, 30 North Brainard Street, PO Box 3063, Naperville, IL 60566-7063. *Phone:* 630-637-5800. *Toll-free phone:* 800-411-1861. *Fax:* 630-637-5819. *E-mail:* admissions@noctrl.edu. *Website:* http://www.northcentralcollege.edu/.

Northeastern Illinois University
Chicago, Illinois

- **State-supported** comprehensive, founded 1961
- **Urban** 67-acre campus with easy access to Chicago
- **Endowment** $2.9 million
- **Coed** 9,140 undergraduate students, 60% full-time, 56% women, 44% men
- **Minimally difficult** entrance level, 63% of applicants were admitted

Undergraduates 5,464 full-time, 3,676 part-time. Students come from 15 states and territories; 104 other countries; 1% are from out of state; 10% Black or African American, non-Hispanic/Latino; 34% Hispanic/Latino; 9% Asian, non-Hispanic/Latino; 0.3% Native Hawaiian or other Pacific Islander, non-Hispanic/Latino; 0.2% American Indian or Alaska Native, non-Hispanic/Latino; 2% Two or more races, non-Hispanic/Latino; 2% Race/ethnicity unknown; 4% international; 15% transferred in. *Retention:* 62% of full-time freshmen returned.
Freshmen *Admission:* 5,295 applied, 3,331 admitted, 1,040 enrolled. *Average high school GPA:* 2.87. *Test scores:* ACT scores over 18: 59%; ACT scores over 24: 9%.
Faculty *Total:* 669, 61% full-time, 54% with terminal degrees. *Student/faculty ratio:* 16:1.
Academics *Calendar:* semesters. *Degrees:* bachelor's and master's. *Special study options:* academic remediation for entering students, adult/continuing education programs, advanced placement credit, cooperative education, distance learning, double majors, English as a second language, external degree program, honors programs, independent study, internships, off-campus study, part-time degree program, services for LD students, study abroad, summer session for credit. *ROTC:* Army (c), Air Force (c).
Computers on Campus 520 computers/terminals are available on campus for general student use. Students can access the following: computer help desk, free student e-mail accounts, online (class) grades, online (class) registration, online (class) schedules, productivity software. Campuswide network is available. Wireless service is available via classrooms, computer centers, computer labs, learning centers, libraries, student centers.
Student Life *Housing:* college housing not available. *Activities and organizations:* drama/theater group, student-run newspaper, radio station, choral group, Student Government Association, United Greek Council, Anime Club, Honors Society, Latinas in Power, national fraternities, national sororities. *Campus security:* 24-hour emergency response devices and patrols, late-night transport/escort service. *Student services:* health clinic, personal/psychological counseling, women's center.
Athletics *Intramural sports:* badminton M/W, baseball M(c), basketball M/W, cross-country running M/W, football M/W, ice hockey M(c), racquetball M/W, soccer M(c)/W(c), softball M/W, table tennis M/W, tennis M/W, volleyball M(c)/W(c), weight lifting M/W.
Standardized Tests *Required:* SAT or ACT (for admission).
Costs (2013–14) *Tuition:* state resident $8610 full-time, $287 per credit hour part-time; nonresident $14,700 full-time, $550 per credit hour part-time. Full-time tuition and fees vary according to student level. Part-time tuition and fees vary according to student level. No tuition increase for student's term of enrollment. *Required fees:* $1316 full-time. *Payment plan:* deferred payment. *Waivers:* senior citizens and employees or children of employees.
Financial Aid Of all full-time matriculated undergraduates who enrolled in 2011, 4,410 applied for aid, 3,912 were judged to have need, 80 had their need fully met. 65 Federal Work-Study jobs (averaging $3073). 221 state and other part-time jobs (averaging $3757). In 2011, 141 non-need-based awards were made. *Average percent of need met:* 31%. *Average financial aid package:* $8196. *Average need-based loan:* $4610. *Average need-based gift aid:* $6735. *Average non-need-based aid:* $3240. *Average indebtedness upon graduation:* $12,100.
Applying *Options:* electronic application, deferred entrance. *Application fee:* $30. *Required:* high school transcript. *Application deadlines:* 7/1 (freshmen), 7/1 (transfers). *Notification:* 9/1 (freshmen), continuous (transfers).
Freshman Application Contact Ms. Zarrin Kerwell, Admissions Counselor, Northeastern Illinois University, 5500 North St. Louis Avenue, Chicago, IL 60625. *Phone:* 773-442-4026. *Fax:* 773-794-6243. *E-mail:* admrec@neiu.edu. *Website:* http://www.neiu.edu/.

Northern Illinois University

De Kalb, Illinois

- **State-supported** university, founded 1895
- **Small-town** 650-acre campus with easy access to Chicago
- **Endowment** $3.0 million
- **Coed** 16,552 undergraduate students, 88% full-time, 50% women, 50% men
- **Moderately difficult** entrance level, 52% of applicants were admitted

Undergraduates 14,494 full-time, 2,058 part-time. Students come from 28 states and territories; 91 other countries; 2% are from out of state; 16% Black or African American, non-Hispanic/Latino; 12% Hispanic/Latino; 5% Asian, non-Hispanic/Latino; 0.1% Native Hawaiian or other Pacific Islander, non-Hispanic/Latino; 0.2% American Indian or Alaska Native, non-Hispanic/Latino; 2% Two or more races, non-Hispanic/Latino; 2% Race/ethnicity unknown; 1% international; 12% transferred in; 28% live on campus. *Retention:* 70% of full-time freshmen returned.

Freshmen *Admission:* 17,842 applied, 9,242 admitted, 2,664 enrolled. *Average high school GPA:* 3.13. *Test scores:* ACT scores over 18: 85%; ACT scores over 24: 33%; ACT scores over 30: 5%.
Faculty *Total:* 1,148, 78% full-time, 74% with terminal degrees. *Student/faculty ratio:* 17:1.
Academics *Calendar:* semesters. *Degrees:* bachelor's, master's, and doctoral. *Special study options:* accelerated degree program, adult/continuing education programs, advanced placement credit, cooperative education, double majors, honors programs, independent study, internships, off-campus study, part-time degree program, services for LD students, student-designed majors, study abroad, summer session for credit. *ROTC:* Army (b), Air Force (c).
Computers on Campus 1,500 computers/terminals are available on campus for general student use. Students can access the following: computer help desk, free student e-mail accounts, online (class) grades, online (class) registration, online (class) schedules. Campuswide network is available. 90% of college-owned or -operated housing units are wired for high-speed Internet access. Wireless service is available via entire campus.
Student Life *Housing:* on-campus residence required for freshman year. *Options:* coed. Campus housing is university owned. Freshman applicants given priority for college housing. *Activities and organizations:* drama/theater group, student-run newspaper, radio station, choral group, marching band, American Marketing Association, Delta Sigma Pi, Pi Sigma Epsilon, Black Choir, Student Volunteer Choir, national fraternities, national sororities. *Campus security:* 24-hour emergency response devices and patrols, student patrols, late-night transport/escort service, controlled dormitory access. *Student services:* health clinic, personal/psychological counseling, women's center, legal services.
Athletics Member NCAA. All Division I except football (Division I-A). *Intercollegiate sports:* baseball M(s), basketball M(s)/W(s), cross-country running W, golf M(s)/W(s), gymnastics W(s), soccer M(s)/W(s), softball W(s), swimming and diving M(s)/W(s), tennis M(s)/W(s), volleyball W(s), wrestling M(s). *Intramural sports:* archery M(c)/W(c), badminton M/W, basketball M/W, bowling M(c)/W(c), cross-country running W, football M/W, golf M/W, ice hockey M(c)/W(c), lacrosse M(c)/W(c), racquetball M/W, rugby M(c)/W(c), skiing (downhill) M(c)/W(c), soccer M/W, softball M/W, table tennis M/W, tennis M/W, track and field M(c)/W(c), volleyball M/W, water polo M(c)/W(c), weight lifting M(c)/W(c).
Standardized Tests *Required:* SAT or ACT (for admission).
Costs (2012–13) *Tuition:* state resident $11,484 full-time; nonresident $20,377 full-time. Full-time tuition and fees vary according to course load, location, and student level. Part-time tuition and fees vary according to course load, location, and student level. No tuition increase for student's term of enrollment. *Required fees:* $1577 full-time. *Room and board:* $10,648. Room and board charges vary according to board plan and housing facility.
Financial Aid Of all full-time matriculated undergraduates who enrolled in 2011, 13,091 applied for aid, 11,578 were judged to have need, 933 had their need fully met. 6,400 Federal Work-Study jobs (averaging $3042). *Average percent of need met:* 60%. *Average financial aid package:* $11,698. *Average need-based loan:* $4388. *Average need-based gift aid:* $7511. *Average indebtedness upon graduation:* $30,521.
Applying *Options:* electronic application. *Application fee:* $40. *Required:* high school transcript, high school rank. *Application deadlines:* 8/1 (freshmen), 8/1 (transfers). *Notification:* continuous (freshmen), continuous (transfers).
Freshman Application Contact Dr. Kimberley Buster-Williams, Director of Admissions, Northern Illinois University, Office of Admissions, DeKalb, IL 60115-2857. *Phone:* 815-753-0446. *Toll-free phone:* 800-892-3050. *E-mail:* admission-info@niu.edu.
Website: http://www.niu.edu/.

North Park University

Chicago, Illinois

Freshman Application Contact Office of Admissions, North Park University, 3225 West Foster Avenue, Chicago, IL 60625-4895. *Phone:* 773-244-5500. *Toll-free phone:* 800-888-NPC8. *Fax:* 773-583-0858. *E-mail:* afao@northpark.edu.
Website: http://www.northpark.edu/.

Northwestern University

Evanston, Illinois

Freshman Application Contact Mr. Christopher Watson, Dean of Undergraduate Admission, Northwestern University, PO Box 3060, Evanston, IL 60204-3060. *Phone:* 847-491-7271. *E-mail:* ug-admission@northwestern.edu.
Website: http://www.northwestern.edu/.

Olivet Nazarene University

Bourbonnais, Illinois

Freshman Application Contact Olivet Nazarene University, One University Avenue, Bourbonnais, IL 60914. *Phone:* 815-939-5203. *Toll-free phone:* 800-648-1463.
Website: http://www.olivet.edu/.

See below for display ad and page 1430 for the College Close-Up.

Principia College

Elsah, Illinois

- **Independent Christian Science** 4-year, founded 1910
- **Rural** 2600-acre campus with easy access to St. Louis
- **Endowment** $458.7 million
- **Coed** 489 undergraduate students, 97% full-time, 55% women, 45% men
- **Moderately difficult** entrance level, 59% of applicants were admitted

Undergraduates 476 full-time, 13 part-time. Students come from 36 states and territories; 22 other countries; 91% are from out of state; 1% Black or African American, non-Hispanic/Latino; 0.4% Asian, non-Hispanic/Latino; 3% Two or more races, non-Hispanic/Latino; 12% Race/ethnicity unknown; 15% international; 5% transferred in; 100% live on campus. *Retention:* 79% of full-time freshmen returned.

Freshmen *Admission:* 195 applied, 115 admitted, 114 enrolled. *Average high school GPA:* 3.3. *Test scores:* SAT critical reading scores over 500: 69%; SAT math scores over 500: 60%; SAT writing scores over 500: 60%; ACT scores over 18: 98%; SAT critical reading scores over 600: 32%; SAT math scores over 600: 25%; SAT writing scores over 600: 24%; ACT scores over 24: 42%; SAT critical reading scores over 700: 10%; SAT math scores over 700: 7%; SAT writing scores over 700: 10%; ACT scores over 30: 10%.

Faculty *Total:* 85, 89% full-time, 40% with terminal degrees. *Student/faculty ratio:* 7:1.

Academics *Calendar:* quarters. *Degree:* bachelor's. *Special study options:* accelerated degree program, advanced placement credit, double majors, honors programs, independent study, internships, off-campus study, student-designed majors, study abroad. *Unusual degree programs:* 3-2 engineering with Washington University in St. Louis, Southern Illinois University at Edwardsville, University of Southern California.

Computers on Campus 200 computers/terminals are available on campus for general student use. Students can access the following: online (class) registration. Campuswide network is available. Wireless service is available via classrooms, computer centers, computer labs, dorm rooms, libraries, student centers.

Student Life *Housing:* on-campus residence required through senior year. *Options:* men-only, women-only. Campus housing is university owned. Freshman campus housing is guaranteed. *Activities and organizations:* drama/theater group, student-run newspaper, radio and television station, choral group, Christian Science Organization, student newspaper, International Students Association, student radio station, student government. *Campus security:* 24-hour patrols. *Student services:* health clinic.

Athletics Member NCAA. All Division III. *Intercollegiate sports:* baseball M, basketball M/W, cross-country running M/W, soccer M/W, softball W, swimming and diving M/W, tennis M/W, track and field M/W, volleyball W. *Intramural sports:* basketball M/W, rugby M(c), soccer M/W, softball M/W.

Standardized Tests *Required:* SAT or ACT (for admission). *Recommended:* SAT Subject Tests (for admission).

Costs (2013–14) *Comprehensive fee:* $36,480 includes full-time tuition ($25,500), mandatory fees ($480), and room and board ($10,500). Full-time tuition and fees vary according to course load. Part-time tuition and fees vary according to course load. *College room only:* $5000. *Payment plan:* installment.

Financial Aid Of all full-time matriculated undergraduates who enrolled in 2012, 385 applied for aid, 372 were judged to have need, 172 had their need fully met. In 2012, 109 non-need-based awards were made. *Average percent of need met:* 83%. *Average financial aid package:* $26,856. *Average need-based loan:* $4566. *Average need-based gift aid:* $22,681. *Average non-need-based aid:* $18,408.

Applying *Options:* electronic application, deferred entrance. *Required:* essay or personal statement, high school transcript, minimum 2.3 GPA, 3 letters of recommendation, Christian Science commitment. *Required for some:* interview. *Recommended:* interview. *Application deadlines:* rolling (freshmen), rolling (transfers). *Notification:* continuous (freshmen), continuous (transfers).

Freshman Application Contact Mr. Brian McCauley, Dean of Enrollment Management, Principia College, One Maybeck Place, Elsah, IL 62028-9799. *Phone:* 618-374-5180. *Toll-free phone:* 800-277-4648 Ext. 2804. *Website:* http://www.principiacollege.edu/.

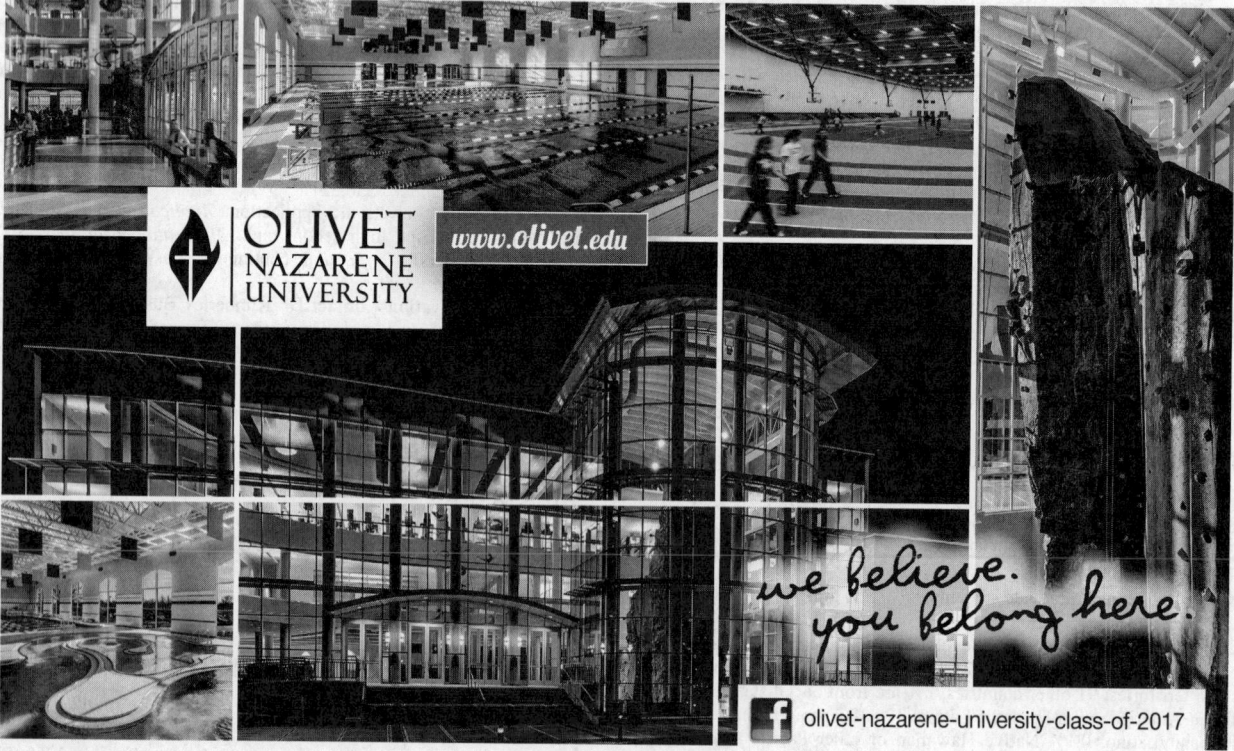

OLIVET NAZARENE UNIVERSITY
www.olivet.edu
we believe. you belong here.
olivet-nazarene-university-class-of-2017

NOW OPEN! To take a tour of our new 168,000-square-foot Student Life and Recreation Center, schedule your campus visit at *www.olivet.edu* or call the Office of Admissions at 800-648-1463.

Quincy University

Quincy, Illinois

- **Independent Roman Catholic** comprehensive, founded 1860
- **Small-town** 70-acre campus
- **Endowment** $15.9 million
- **Coed** 1,226 undergraduate students, 90% full-time, 58% women, 42% men
- **Moderately difficult** entrance level, 91% of applicants were admitted

Undergraduates 1,102 full-time, 124 part-time. Students come from 23 states and territories; 3 other countries; 25% are from out of state; 10% Black or African American, non-Hispanic/Latino; 1% Hispanic/Latino; 0.7% Asian, non-Hispanic/Latino; 0.3% Native Hawaiian or other Pacific Islander, non-Hispanic/Latino; 1% American Indian or Alaska Native, non-Hispanic/Latino; 1% Two or more races, non-Hispanic/Latino; 20% Race/ethnicity unknown; 1% international; 7% transferred in; 63% live on campus. *Retention:* 70% of full-time freshmen returned.

Freshmen *Admission:* 1,034 applied, 945 admitted, 262 enrolled. *Average high school GPA:* 3.34. *Test scores:* SAT critical reading scores over 500: 36%; SAT math scores over 500: 45%; ACT scores over 18: 90%; SAT critical reading scores over 600: 9%; ACT scores over 24: 32%; ACT scores over 30: 2%.

Faculty *Total:* 165, 33% full-time, 37% with terminal degrees. *Student/faculty ratio:* 14:1.

Academics *Calendar:* semesters. *Degrees:* associate, bachelor's, and master's. *Special study options:* academic remediation for entering students, accelerated degree program, adult/continuing education programs, advanced placement credit, distance learning, double majors, honors programs, independent study, internships, off-campus study, part-time degree program, student-designed majors, study abroad, summer session for credit.

Computers on Campus 131 computers/terminals are available on campus for general student use. Students can access the following: campus intranet, computer help desk, free student e-mail accounts, online (class) grades, online (class) registration, online (class) schedules. Campuswide network is available. 100% of college-owned or -operated housing units are wired for high-speed Internet access. Wireless service is available via classrooms, computer centers, computer labs, dorm rooms, learning centers, libraries, student centers.

Student Life *Housing:* on-campus residence required through junior year. *Options:* coed, disabled students. Campus housing is university owned. Freshman campus housing is guaranteed. *Activities and organizations:* drama/theater group, student-run newspaper, choral group, marching band, Student Senate, Kappa Kappa Psi, Student Programming Board, Minority Student Association, Students in Free Enterprise (SIFE), national fraternities, national sororities. *Campus security:* 24-hour emergency response devices and patrols, student patrols, late-night transport/escort service, controlled dormitory access, self-defense education, shuttle buses, lighted pathways/sidewalks. *Student services:* health clinic, personal/psychological counseling.

Athletics Member NCAA. All Division II except volleyball (Division I). *Intercollegiate sports:* baseball M(s), basketball M(s)/W(s), cheerleading M(c)/W(c), cross-country running M(s)/W(s), football M(s), golf M(s)/W(s), soccer M(s)/W(s), softball W(s), tennis M(s)/W(s), volleyball M(s)/W(s). *Intramural sports:* basketball M/W, bowling M/W, football M/W, racquetball M/W, soccer M/W, softball M/W, table tennis M/W, volleyball M/W.

Standardized Tests *Required:* SAT or ACT (for admission).

Costs (2013–14) *Comprehensive fee:* $35,714 includes full-time tuition ($24,974), mandatory fees ($860), and room and board ($9880). Part-time tuition: $585 per semester hour. Part-time tuition and fees vary according to course load. *Required fees:* $30 per semester hour part-time. *College room only:* $5500. Room and board charges vary according to board plan, housing facility, and student level. *Payment plan:* installment. *Waivers:* senior citizens and employees or children of employees.

Financial Aid Of all full-time matriculated undergraduates who enrolled in 2012, 1,027 applied for aid, 966 were judged to have need, 188 had their need fully met. 410 Federal Work-Study jobs (averaging $2000). 35 state and other part-time jobs (averaging $2000). In 2012, 38 non-need-based awards were made. *Average percent of need met:* 72%. *Average financial aid package:* $23,101. *Average need-based loan:* $4312. *Average need-based gift aid:* $19,152. *Average non-need-based aid:* $11,836. *Average indebtedness upon graduation:* $26,080.

Applying *Options:* electronic application, deferred entrance. *Application fee:* $25. *Required:* essay or personal statement, high school transcript, minimum 2.5 GPA. *Required for some:* 1 letter of recommendation, audition required of music majors, portfolio recommended for art majors. *Recommended:* interview. *Application deadlines:* rolling (freshmen), rolling (out-of-state freshmen), rolling (transfers). *Notification:* continuous (freshmen), continuous (out-of-state freshmen), continuous (transfers).

Freshman Application Contact Mrs. Syndi Peck, Vice President of Enrollment Management, Quincy University, Admissions Office, 1800 College Avenue, Quincy, IL 62301-2699. *Phone:* 217-228-5210. *Toll-free phone:* 800-688-4295. *E-mail:* admissions@quincy.edu. *Website:* http://www.quincy.edu/.

Rasmussen College Aurora

Aurora, Illinois

- **Proprietary** primarily 2-year, part of Rasmussen College System
- **Suburban** campus
- **Coed** 366 undergraduate students
- **Minimally difficult** entrance level

Faculty *Student/faculty ratio:* 22:1.

Academics *Degrees:* certificates, diplomas, associate, and bachelor's. *Special study options:* academic remediation for entering students, accelerated degree program, adult/continuing education programs, distance learning, double majors, internships, part-time degree program, summer session for credit.

Computers on Campus 87 computers/terminals are available on campus for general student use. Students can access the following: computer help desk, free student e-mail accounts, online (class) grades, online (class) schedules. Campuswide network is available. Wireless service is available via entire campus.

Student Life *Housing:* college housing not available.

Standardized Tests *Required:* Internal Exam (for admission).

Costs (2013–14) *Tuition:* $12,600 full-time. Full-time tuition and fees vary according to course level, course load, degree level, location, and program. Part-time tuition and fees vary according to course level, course load, degree level, location, and program. *Required fees:* $1800 full-time. *Payment plans:* installment, deferred payment. *Waivers:* employees or children of employees.

Applying *Options:* electronic application, early admission, deferred entrance. *Required:* high school transcript, minimum 2.0 GPA. *Required for some:* interview. *Application deadlines:* rolling (freshmen), rolling (transfers).

Freshman Application Contact Susan Hammerstrom, Director of Admissions, Rasmussen College Aurora, 2363 Sequoia Drive, Aurora, IL 60506. *Phone:* 630-888-3500. *Toll-free phone:* 888-549-6755. *E-mail:* susan.hammerstrom@rasmussen.edu. *Website:* http://www.rasmussen.edu/.

Rasmussen College Mokena/Tinley Park

Mokena, Illinois

- **Proprietary** 4-year, part of Rasmussen College System
- **Suburban** campus
- **Coed** 249 undergraduate students
- **Minimally difficult** entrance level

Faculty *Student/faculty ratio:* 22:1.

Academics *Degrees:* certificates, diplomas, associate, and bachelor's. *Special study options:* academic remediation for entering students, accelerated degree program, adult/continuing education programs, distance learning, double majors, internships, part-time degree program, summer session for credit.

Computers on Campus 73 computers/terminals are available on campus for general student use. Students can access the following: computer help desk, free student e-mail accounts, online (class) grades, online (class) schedules. Campuswide network is available. Wireless service is available via entire campus.

Student Life *Housing:* college housing not available.

Standardized Tests *Required:* Internal Exam (for admission).

Costs (2013–14) *Tuition:* $12,600 full-time. Full-time tuition and fees vary according to course level, course load, degree level, location, and program. Part-time tuition and fees vary according to course level, course load, degree level, location, and program. *Required fees:* $1800 full-time. *Payment plans:* installment, deferred payment. *Waivers:* employees or children of employees.

Applying *Options:* electronic application, early admission, deferred entrance. *Required:* high school transcript, minimum 2.0 GPA. *Required for some:* interview. *Application deadlines:* rolling (freshmen), rolling (transfers).

Freshman Application Contact Susan Hammerstrom, Director of Admissions, Rasmussen College Mokena/Tinley Park, 8650 West Spring Lake Road, Mokena, IL 60448. *Phone:* 815-534-3300. *Toll-free phone:* 888-549-6755. *Website:* http://www.rasmussen.edu/.

Rasmussen College Rockford
Rockford, Illinois

- **Proprietary** primarily 2-year, part of Rasmussen College System
- **Suburban** campus
- **Coed** 713 undergraduate students
- **Minimally difficult** entrance level

Faculty *Student/faculty ratio:* 22:1.

Academics *Degrees:* certificates, diplomas, associate, and bachelor's. *Special study options:* academic remediation for entering students, accelerated degree program, adult/continuing education programs, distance learning, double majors, internships, part-time degree program, summer session for credit.

Computers on Campus 103 computers/terminals are available on campus for general student use. Students can access the following: computer help desk, free student e-mail accounts, online (class) grades, online (class) schedules. Campuswide network is available. Wireless service is available via entire campus.

Student Life *Housing:* college housing not available.

Standardized Tests *Required:* Internal Exam (for admission).

Costs (2013–14) *Tuition:* $12,600 full-time. Full-time tuition and fees vary according to course level, course load, degree level, location, and program. Part-time tuition and fees vary according to course level, course load, degree level, location, and program. *Required fees:* $1800 full-time. *Payment plans:* installment, deferred payment. *Waivers:* employees or children of employees.

Applying *Options:* electronic application, early admission, deferred entrance. *Required:* high school transcript, minimum 2.0 GPA. *Required for some:* interview. *Application deadlines:* rolling (freshmen), rolling (transfers).

Freshman Application Contact Susan Hammerstrom, Director of Admissions, Rasmussen College Rockford, 6000 East State Street, Fourth Floor, Rockford, IL 61108-2513. *Phone:* 815-316-4800. *Toll-free phone:* 888-549-6755. *E-mail:* susan.hammerstrom@rasmussen.edu. *Website:* http://www.rasmussen.edu/.

Rasmussen College Romeoville/Joliet
Romeoville, Illinois

- **Proprietary** 4-year, part of Rasmussen College System
- **Suburban** campus
- **Coed** 475 undergraduate students
- **Minimally difficult** entrance level

Faculty *Student/faculty ratio:* 22:1.

Academics *Degrees:* certificates, diplomas, associate, and bachelor's. *Special study options:* academic remediation for entering students, accelerated degree program, adult/continuing education programs, distance learning, double majors, internships, part-time degree program, summer session for credit.

Computers on Campus 87 computers/terminals are available on campus for general student use. Students can access the following: computer help desk, free student e-mail accounts, online (class) grades, online (class) schedules. Campuswide network is available. Wireless service is available via entire campus.

Student Life *Housing:* college housing not available.

Standardized Tests *Required:* Internal Exam (for admission).

Costs (2013–14) *Tuition:* $12,600 full-time. Full-time tuition and fees vary according to course level, course load, degree level, location, and program. Part-time tuition and fees vary according to course level, course load, degree level, location, and program. *Required fees:* $1800 full-time. *Payment plans:* installment, deferred payment. *Waivers:* employees or children of employees.

Applying *Options:* electronic application, early admission, deferred entrance. *Required:* high school transcript, minimum 2.0 GPA. *Required for some:* interview. *Application deadlines:* rolling (freshmen), rolling (transfers).

Freshman Application Contact Susan Hammerstrom, Director of Admissions, Rasmussen College Romeoville/Joliet, 1400 W. Normantown Road, Romeoville, IL 60446. *Phone:* 815-306-2600. *Toll-free phone:* 888-549-6755. *E-mail:* susan.hammerstrom@rasmussen.edu. *Website:* http://www.rasmussen.edu/.

Resurrection University
Chicago, Illinois

- **Independent** upper-level, founded 1982
- **Urban** 10-acre campus with easy access to Chicago
- **Endowment** $1.5 million
- **Coed, primarily women** 392 undergraduate students, 82% full-time, 83% women, 17% men
- **Moderately difficult** entrance level, 94% of applicants were admitted

Undergraduates 323 full-time, 69 part-time. Students come from 2 states and territories; 1 other country; 13% Black or African American, non-Hispanic/Latino; 19% Hispanic/Latino; 18% Asian, non-Hispanic/Latino; 0.8% Native Hawaiian or other Pacific Islander, non-Hispanic/Latino; 3% Two or more races, non-Hispanic/Latino; 12% Race/ethnicity unknown; 0.3% international; 99% transferred in.

Freshmen *Admission:* 252 applied, 237 admitted.

Faculty *Total:* 56, 43% full-time, 11% with terminal degrees. *Student/faculty ratio:* 13:1.

Academics *Calendar:* semesters. *Degrees:* certificates, bachelor's, and master's. *Special study options:* academic remediation for entering students, accelerated degree program, advanced placement credit, independent study, part-time degree program, summer session for credit.

Computers on Campus 36 computers/terminals are available on campus for general student use. Students can access the following: campus intranet, computer help desk, free student e-mail accounts, online (class) grades, online (class) registration, online (class) schedules. Campuswide network is available. Wireless service is available via entire campus.

Student Life *Housing:* college housing not available. *Campus security:* 24-hour emergency response devices and patrols, late-night transport/escort service. *Student services:* personal/psychological counseling.

Costs (2013–14) *Tuition:* $11,349 full-time, $769 per credit hour part-time. *Required fees:* $290 full-time, $140 per term part-time. *Payment plans:* installment, deferred payment. *Waivers:* employees or children of employees.

Financial Aid Of all full-time matriculated undergraduates who enrolled in 2011, 304 applied for aid, 304 were judged to have need, 76 had their need fully met. 17 Federal Work-Study jobs (averaging $1700). In 2011, 16 non-need-based awards were made. *Average percent of need met:* 85%. *Average financial aid package:* $15,500. *Average need-based loan:* $5500. *Average need-based gift aid:* $3000. *Average non-need-based aid:* $3000.

Applying *Options:* electronic application, deferred entrance. *Application fee:* $50. *Application deadline:* 4/1 (transfers). *Notification:* 5/15 (transfers).

Application Contact Resurrection University, 1431 N. Claremont Avenue, Chicago, IL 60622. *Website:* http://www.resu.edu/.

Robert Morris University Illinois
Chicago, Illinois

- **Independent** comprehensive, founded 1913
- **Urban** campus with easy access to Chicago
- **Endowment** $51.1 million
- **Coed** 3,230 undergraduate students, 95% full-time, 54% women, 46% men
- **Minimally difficult** entrance level, 28% of applicants were admitted

Undergraduates 3,065 full-time, 165 part-time. Students come from 31 states and territories; 20 other countries; 8% are from out of state; 33% Black or African American, non-Hispanic/Latino; 23% Hispanic/Latino; 3% Asian, non-Hispanic/Latino; 0.3% Native Hawaiian or other Pacific Islander, non-Hispanic/Latino; 0.4% American Indian or Alaska Native, non-Hispanic/Latino; 1% Two or more races, non-Hispanic/Latino; 1% Race/ethnicity unknown; 1% international; 15% transferred in; 10% live on campus. *Retention:* 49% of full-time freshmen returned.

Freshmen *Admission:* 3,386 applied, 946 admitted, 756 enrolled. *Average high school GPA:* 2.7. *Test scores:* ACT scores over 18: 63%; ACT scores over 24: 19%; ACT scores over 30: 1%.

Faculty *Total:* 261, 48% full-time, 20% with terminal degrees. *Student/faculty ratio:* 20:1.

Academics *Calendar:* 5 ten-week academic sessions per year. *Degrees:* associate, bachelor's, and master's. *Special study options:* accelerated degree program, adult/continuing education programs, advanced placement credit, double majors, honors programs, internships, part-time degree program, services for LD students, study abroad, summer session for credit. *ROTC:* Army (c).

Computers on Campus 1,740 computers/terminals are available on campus for general student use. Students can access the following: computer help desk, free student e-mail accounts, online (class) grades, online (class) registration, online (class) schedules, online credentials, online payments, online student accounts, online degree audit. Campuswide network is available. Wireless service is available via entire campus.

Student Life *Housing options:* coed. *Activities and organizations:* student-run newspaper, choral group, marching band, UNA-USA, Architectural Technology Club, Sigma Beta Delta, LEX, Film Club. *Campus security:* controlled dormitory access, Roaming security visits our metropolitan campuses on an intermittent schedule and are sent to other campuses as needed. *Student services:* personal/psychological counseling.

Athletics Member NAIA, USCAA. *Intercollegiate sports:* baseball M(s), basketball M(s)/W(s), bowling M(s)/W(s), cheerleading M(s)/W(s), cross-country running M(s)/W(s), field hockey W(s)(c), football M(s), golf M(s)/W(s), ice hockey M/W, lacrosse M(s)/W(s), soccer M(s)/W(s), softball W(s), swimming and diving W(s), tennis W(s), track and field W(s), volleyball M(s)/W(s).

Intramural sports: bowling M/W, cross-country running M/W, golf M/W, softball M/W, tennis M/W, volleyball M/W.

Standardized Tests *Required for some:* SAT or ACT (for admission).

Costs (2013–14) *Comprehensive fee:* $34,554 includes full-time tuition ($22,800) and room and board ($11,754). Part-time tuition: $633 per credit hour. Part-time tuition and fees vary according to course load. *College room only:* $10,500. Room and board charges vary according to housing facility. *Payment plan:* installment. *Waivers:* employees or children of employees.

Financial Aid Of all full-time matriculated undergraduates who enrolled in 2012, 3,907 applied for aid, 3,615 were judged to have need, 155 had their need fully met. 148 Federal Work-Study jobs (averaging $1907). In 2012, 93 non-need-based awards were made. *Average percent of need met:* 47%. *Average financial aid package:* $14,319. *Average need-based loan:* $4151. *Average need-based gift aid:* $11,372. *Average non-need-based aid:* $9229. *Average indebtedness upon graduation:* $30,133.

Applying *Options:* electronic application, deferred entrance. *Application fee:* $20. *Required:* ACT scores (Nursing and Surgical Tech applicants). *Required for some:* high school transcript. *Recommended:* interview. *Application deadlines:* rolling (freshmen), rolling (out-of-state freshmen), rolling (transfers). *Notification:* continuous (freshmen), continuous (out-of-state freshmen), continuous (transfers).

Freshman Application Contact Ms. Connie Esparza, Vice President for Marketing, Robert Morris University Illinois, 401 South State Street, Chicago, IL 60605. *Phone:* 312-935-4541. *Toll-free phone:* 800-RMC-5960. *Fax:* 312-935-4140. *E-mail:* enroll@robertmorris.edu.
Website: http://www.robertmorris.edu/.

Rockford College
Rockford, Illinois

- **Independent** comprehensive, founded 1847
- **Suburban** 150-acre campus with easy access to Chicago
- **Endowment** $10.5 million
- **Coed** 1,022 undergraduate students, 86% full-time, 62% women, 38% men
- **Moderately difficult** entrance level, 40% of applicants were admitted

Undergraduates 881 full-time, 141 part-time. Students come from 25 states and territories; 5 other countries; 9% are from out of state; 7% Black or African American, non-Hispanic/Latino; 6% Hispanic/Latino; 2% Asian, non-Hispanic/Latino; 0.4% Native Hawaiian or other Pacific Islander, non-Hispanic/Latino; 0.2% American Indian or Alaska Native, non-Hispanic/Latino; 6% Two or more races, non-Hispanic/Latino; 9% Race/ethnicity unknown; 2% international; 17% transferred in; 41% live on campus. *Retention:* 61% of full-time freshmen returned.

Freshmen *Admission:* 1,455 applied, 584 admitted, 105 enrolled. *Average high school GPA:* 3.1. *Test scores:* SAT critical reading scores over 500: 56%; SAT math scores over 500: 75%; SAT writing scores over 500: 44%; ACT scores over 18: 90%; SAT critical reading scores over 600: 13%; SAT math scores over 600: 38%; SAT writing scores over 600: 13%; ACT scores over 24: 26%; SAT critical reading scores over 700: 6%; SAT math scores over 700: 6%; ACT scores over 30: 3%.

Faculty *Total:* 162, 44% full-time, 40% with terminal degrees. *Student/faculty ratio:* 9:1.

Academics *Calendar:* semesters. *Degrees:* bachelor's and master's. *Special study options:* academic remediation for entering students, accelerated degree program, adult/continuing education programs, advanced placement credit, double majors, English as a second language, honors programs, independent study, internships, off-campus study, part-time degree program, services for LD students, study abroad, summer session for credit. *ROTC:* Army (c).

Computers on Campus 131 computers/terminals are available on campus for general student use. Students can access the following: campus intranet, computer help desk, free student e-mail accounts, online (class) grades, online (class) registration, online (class) schedules, online bill payment. Campuswide network is available. 100% of college-owned or -operated housing units are wired for high-speed Internet access. Wireless service is available via entire campus.

Student Life *Housing options:* coed, disabled students. Campus housing is university owned. *Activities and organizations:* drama/theater group, student-run newspaper, radio station, choral group, Student Government Association, Multicultural Club, RAGE (Regent Athletics Getting Excited), Psychology Society, Nursing Student Organization. *Campus security:* 24-hour emergency response devices and patrols, late-night transport/escort service, controlled dormitory access. *Student services:* health clinic, personal/psychological counseling.

Athletics Member NCAA. All Division III. *Intercollegiate sports:* baseball M, basketball M/W, cross-country running M/W, football M, golf M, soccer M/W, softball W, tennis M/W, track and field M/W, volleyball W. *Intramural sports:* basketball M/W, bowling M/W, football M/W, softball M/W, volleyball M/W.

Standardized Tests *Required:* SAT or ACT (for admission).

Costs (2012–13) *Comprehensive fee:* $33,630 includes full-time tuition ($26,210), mandatory fees ($100), and room and board ($7320). Full-time tuition and fees vary according to course load. Part-time tuition: $715 per credit. Part-time tuition and fees vary according to course load. *Required fees:* $40 per term part-time. *College room only:* $4070. Room and board charges vary according to board plan and housing facility. *Payment plan:* installment. *Waivers:* employees or children of employees.

Financial Aid Of all full-time matriculated undergraduates who enrolled in 2011, 917 applied for aid, 867 were judged to have need, 78 had their need fully met. 141 Federal Work-Study jobs (averaging $696). 206 state and other part-time jobs (averaging $745). In 2011, 76 non-need-based awards were made. *Average percent of need met:* 64%. *Average financial aid package:* $16,725. *Average need-based loan:* $4828. *Average need-based gift aid:* $12,342. *Average non-need-based aid:* $7404. *Average indebtedness upon graduation:* $22,245.

Applying *Options:* electronic application, early admission, deferred entrance. *Required:* high school transcript, SAT/ACT score. *Required for some:* essay or personal statement, minimum 2.7 GPA, 2 letters of recommendation. *Recommended:* minimum 2.7 GPA. *Application deadlines:* rolling (freshmen), rolling (out-of-state freshmen), rolling (transfers). *Notification:* continuous (freshmen), continuous (out-of-state freshmen), continuous (transfers).

Freshman Application Contact Ms. Rebecca Miziniak, Assistant Director of Admission, Rockford College, 5050 East State Street, Rockford, IL 61108-2393. *Phone:* 815-226-4050. *Toll-free phone:* 800-892-2984. *Fax:* 815-226-2822. *E-mail:* rcadmissions@rockford.edu.
Website: http://www.rockford.edu/.

Roosevelt University
Chicago, Illinois

- **Independent** comprehensive, founded 1945
- **Urban** campus with easy access to Chicago
- **Endowment** $74.4 million
- **Coed** 3,795 undergraduate students, 73% full-time, 64% women, 36% men
- **Moderately difficult** entrance level, 75% of applicants were admitted

Undergraduates 2,779 full-time, 1,016 part-time. Students come from 30 states and territories; 41 other countries; 16% are from out of state; 21% Black or African American, non-Hispanic/Latino; 17% Hispanic/Latino; 5% Asian, non-Hispanic/Latino; 0.2% Native Hawaiian or other Pacific Islander, non-Hispanic/Latino; 0.2% American Indian or Alaska Native, non-Hispanic/Latino; 4% Two or more races, non-Hispanic/Latino; 2% Race/ethnicity unknown; 3% international; 19% transferred in; 23% live on campus. *Retention:* 58% of full-time freshmen returned.

Freshmen *Admission:* 3,862 applied, 2,904 admitted, 553 enrolled. *Average high school GPA:* 3.17. *Test scores:* SAT critical reading scores over 500: 72%; SAT math scores over 500: 65%; SAT writing scores over 500: 60%; ACT scores over 18: 99%; SAT critical reading scores over 600: 28%; SAT math scores over 600: 22%; SAT writing scores over 600: 13%; ACT scores over 24: 35%; SAT critical reading scores over 700: 6%; ACT scores over 30: 4%.

Faculty *Total:* 722, 34% full-time. *Student/faculty ratio:* 12:1.

Academics *Calendar:* semesters. *Degrees:* bachelor's, master's, doctoral, and postbachelor's certificates. *Special study options:* academic remediation for entering students, accelerated degree program, adult/continuing education programs, advanced placement credit, distance learning, double majors, English as a second language, honors programs, independent study, internships, off-campus study, part-time degree program, services for LD students, student-designed majors, study abroad, summer session for credit.

Computers on Campus 646 computers/terminals are available on campus for general student use. Students can access the following: campus intranet, computer help desk, free student e-mail accounts, online (class) grades, online (class) registration, online (class) schedules. Campuswide network is available. 100% of college-owned or -operated housing units are wired for high-speed Internet access. Wireless service is available via classrooms, computer centers, computer labs, dorm rooms, libraries, student centers.

Student Life *Housing:* on-campus residence required through sophomore year. *Options:* coed. Campus housing is university owned, leased by the school and is provided by a third party. Freshman campus housing is guaranteed. *Activities and organizations:* student-run newspaper, radio station, International Student Union, RU Proud, Association of Latin Americans (ALAS), student government, Residence Hall Council, national fraternities, national sororities. *Campus security:* 24-hour emergency response devices and patrols, late-night transport/escort service, controlled dormitory access. *Student services:* personal/psychological counseling.

Athletics Member NAIA. *Intercollegiate sports:* baseball M, basketball M/W, cross-country running M/W, golf M, soccer M/W, softball W, tennis M/W, volleyball W.

Standardized Tests *Required:* SAT or ACT (for admission).

Costs (2012–13) *Comprehensive fee:* $38,050 includes full-time tuition ($25,950) and room and board ($12,100). Full-time tuition and fees vary according to course load, program, and reciprocity agreements. Part-time tuition: $699 per credit. Part-time tuition and fees vary according to course load, program, and reciprocity agreements. *Room and board:* Room and board charges vary according to board plan and housing facility. *Payment plan:* installment. *Waivers:* employees or children of employees.

Financial Aid Of all full-time matriculated undergraduates who enrolled in 2011, 2,675 applied for aid, 2,281 were judged to have need, 177 had their need fully met. In 2011, 529 non-need-based awards were made. *Average percent of need met:* 75%. *Average financial aid package:* $20,970. *Average need-based loan:* $8827. *Average need-based gift aid:* $8927. *Average non-need-based aid:* $6718.

Applying *Options:* electronic application, deferred entrance. *Application fee:* $25. *Required:* high school transcript, minimum 2.5 GPA, audition for music and theater programs. *Required for some:* essay or personal statement, interview. *Recommended:* essay or personal statement. *Application deadlines:* 8/15 (freshmen), rolling (transfers). *Notification:* continuous (freshmen), continuous (transfers).

Freshman Application Contact Ms. Asia Mitchell, Director of Admission, Roosevelt University, 430 South Michigan Avenue, Chicago, IL 60605-1394. *Phone:* 312-341-2107. *Toll-free phone:* 877-APPLYRU. *Fax:* 312-341-3253. *E-mail:* amitchell@roosevelt.edu. *Website:* http://www.roosevelt.edu/.

Rush University
Chicago, Illinois

Application Contact Rush University, 600 South Paulina, Chicago, IL 60612-3832. *Phone:* 312-942-7100. *Website:* http://www.rushu.rush.edu/.

Saint Anthony College of Nursing
Rockford, Illinois

Application Contact Ms. Nancy Sanders, Assistant Dean for Admissions and Student Affairs, Saint Anthony College of Nursing, 5658 East State Street, Rockford, IL 61108-2468. *Phone:* 815-395-5100. *Fax:* 815-395-2275. *E-mail:* info@sacn.edu. *Website:* http://www.sacn.edu/.

St. Augustine College
Chicago, Illinois

Freshman Application Contact Ms. Gloria Quiroz, Director of Admissions, St. Augustine College, 1333-1345 West Argyle, Chicago, IL 60640-3501. *Phone:* 773-878-3256. *Fax:* 773-878-0937. *E-mail:* info@staugustine.edu. *Website:* http://www.staugustine.edu/.

Saint Francis Medical Center College of Nursing
Peoria, Illinois

- **Independent Roman Catholic** upper-level, founded 1986
- **Urban** campus
- **Coed, primarily women** 402 undergraduate students, 73% full-time, 89% women, 11% men
- **49% of applicants were admitted**

Undergraduates 294 full-time, 108 part-time. Students come from 4 states and territories; 2 other countries; 1% are from out of state; 5% Black or African American, non-Hispanic/Latino; 4% Hispanic/Latino; 2% Asian, non-Hispanic/Latino; 0.5% Native Hawaiian or other Pacific Islander, non-Hispanic/Latino; 0.2% American Indian or Alaska Native, non-Hispanic/Latino; 0.2% international; 23% transferred in; 3% live on campus.

Freshmen *Admission:* 190 applied, 93 admitted.

Faculty *Total:* 62, 56% full-time, 26% with terminal degrees. *Student/faculty ratio:* 8:1.

Academics *Calendar:* semesters. *Degrees:* bachelor's, master's, doctoral, and post-master's certificates. *Special study options:* accelerated degree program, advanced placement credit, distance learning, independent study, summer session for credit.

Computers on Campus 49 computers/terminals and 53 ports are available on campus for general student use. Students can access the following: campus intranet, computer help desk, free student e-mail accounts, online (class) grades, online (class) registration, online (class) schedules. Campuswide net-

work is available. 100% of college-owned or -operated housing units are wired for high-speed Internet access. Wireless service is available via entire campus.

Student Life *Housing options:* coed. Campus housing is university owned. *Activities and organizations:* Student Senate, SNAI, Minority Student Association, Tau Omicron. *Campus security:* 24-hour emergency response devices and patrols, controlled dormitory access. *Student services:* health clinic, personal/psychological counseling.

Costs (2013–14) *Tuition:* $16,368 full-time, $528 per hour part-time. Full-time tuition and fees vary according to course load. Part-time tuition and fees vary according to course load. *Required fees:* $596 full-time. *Room only:* $3200. *Payment plan:* installment. *Waivers:* employees or children of employees.

Financial Aid Of all full-time matriculated undergraduates who enrolled in 2012, 253 applied for aid, 211 were judged to have need, 16 had their need fully met. In 2012, 14 non-need-based awards were made. *Average percent of need met:* 61%. *Average financial aid package:* $11,259. *Average need-based loan:* $5429. *Average need-based gift aid:* $7558. *Average non-need-based aid:* $1737.

Applying *Options:* deferred entrance. *Application fee:* $50.

Application Contact Saint Francis Medical Center College of Nursing, 511 Northeast Greenleaf Street, Peoria, IL 61603-3783. *Phone:* 309-624-8980. *Website:* http://www.sfmccon.edu/.

St. John's College
Springfield, Illinois

Application Contact St. John's College, 729 East Carpenter Street, Springfield, IL 62702. *Phone:* 217-525-5628. *Website:* http://www.stjohnscollegespringfield.edu/.

Saint Xavier University
Chicago, Illinois

- **Independent Roman Catholic** comprehensive, founded 1847
- **Urban** 70-acre campus
- **Endowment** $7.1 million
- **Coed**
- **Moderately difficult** entrance level

Faculty *Student/faculty ratio:* 14:1.

Academics *Calendar:* semesters. *Degrees:* certificates, bachelor's, master's, post-master's, and postbachelor's certificates.

Student Life *Campus security:* 24-hour emergency response devices and patrols, late-night transport/escort service.

Athletics Member NAIA.

Standardized Tests *Required:* SAT or ACT (for admission).

Costs (2012–13) *Comprehensive fee:* $37,600 includes full-time tuition ($27,330), mandatory fees ($780), and room and board ($9490). *Room and board:* Room and board charges vary according to board plan and housing facility.

Financial Aid Of all full-time matriculated undergraduates who enrolled in 2011, 2,362 applied for aid, 2,233 were judged to have need, 395 had their need fully met. 1,757 Federal Work-Study jobs (averaging $2377). In 2011, 206 non-need-based awards were made. *Average percent of need met:* 79. *Average financial aid package:* $21,941. *Average need-based loan:* $4584. *Average need-based gift aid:* $15,477. *Average non-need-based aid:* $8470. *Average indebtedness upon graduation:* $32,095.

Applying *Options:* electronic application, deferred entrance. *Application fee:* $25. *Required:* high school transcript. *Recommended:* essay or personal statement, minimum 2.5 GPA, interview.

Freshman Application Contact Dr. Kathleen Carlson, Vice President, Saint Xavier University, 3700 West 103rd Street, Chicago, IL 60655-3105. *Phone:* 773-298-3305. *Toll-free phone:* 800-462-9288. *E-mail:* carlson@sxu.edu. *Website:* http://www.sxu.edu/.

School of the Art Institute of Chicago
Chicago, Illinois

- **Independent** comprehensive, founded 1866
- **Urban** 1-acre campus with easy access to Chicago
- **Endowment** $186.3 million
- **Coed** 2,627 undergraduate students, 91% full-time, 70% women, 30% men
- **Very difficult** entrance level, 78% of applicants were admitted

Undergraduates 2,387 full-time, 240 part-time. Students come from 50 states and territories; 68 other countries; 62% are from out of state; 4% Black or African American, non-Hispanic/Latino; 5% Hispanic/Latino; 12% Asian, non-Hispanic/Latino; 0.2% Native Hawaiian or other Pacific Islander, non-Hispanic/Latino; 0.7% American Indian or Alaska Native, non-Hispanic/Latino;

3% Two or more races, non-Hispanic/Latino; 2% Race/ethnicity unknown; 22% international; 10% transferred in; 25% live on campus. *Retention:* 79% of full-time freshmen returned.

Freshmen *Admission:* 3,004 applied, 2,352 admitted, 563 enrolled. *Average high school GPA:* 3.4. *Test scores:* SAT critical reading scores over 500: 85%; SAT math scores over 500: 77%; ACT scores over 18: 98%; SAT critical reading scores over 600: 45%; SAT math scores over 600: 31%; ACT scores over 24: 54%; SAT critical reading scores over 700: 11%; SAT math scores over 700: 1%; ACT scores over 30: 6%.

Faculty *Total:* 744, 22% full-time. *Student/faculty ratio:* 9:1.

Academics *Calendar:* semesters. *Degrees:* certificates, bachelor's, master's, and postbachelor's certificates. *Special study options:* academic remediation for entering students, advanced placement credit, cooperative education, double majors, English as a second language, independent study, internships, off-campus study, part-time degree program, services for LD students, student-designed majors, study abroad, summer session for credit.

Computers on Campus 300 computers/terminals and 945 ports are available on campus for general student use. Students can access the following: campus intranet, computer help desk, free student e-mail accounts, online (class) grades, online (class) registration, online (class) schedules. Campuswide network is available. 100% of college-owned or -operated housing units are wired for high-speed Internet access. Wireless service is available via entire campus.

Student Life *Housing options:* coed, disabled students. Campus housing is university owned. *Activities and organizations:* drama/theater group, student-run newspaper, radio and television station, Student Association/Student Union Galleries, Korean Student Association, InterVarsity, Curatorial Community, Good 'Ol Futbol. *Campus security:* 24-hour emergency response devices and patrols, late-night transport/escort service, controlled dormitory access. *Student services:* health clinic, personal/psychological counseling.

Standardized Tests *Required:* SAT or ACT (for admission).

Costs (2012–13) *One-time required fee:* $150. *Comprehensive fee:* $52,830 includes full-time tuition ($38,340), mandatory fees ($680), and room and board ($13,810). Full-time tuition and fees vary according to course load, degree level, and program. Part-time tuition: $1278 per credit hour. Part-time tuition and fees vary according to course load, degree level, and program. *Required fees:* $235 per term part-time. *College room only:* $10,400. Room and board charges vary according to board plan. *Payment plan:* installment. *Waivers:* employees or children of employees.

Financial Aid Of all full-time matriculated undergraduates who enrolled in 2011, 1,418 applied for aid, 1,287 were judged to have need, 69 had their need fully met. In 2011, 873 non-need-based awards were made. *Average percent of need met:* 77%. *Average financial aid package:* $33,404. *Average need-based loan:* $4835. *Average need-based gift aid:* $15,671. *Average non-need-based aid:* $6469. *Average indebtedness upon graduation:* $39,914.

Applying *Options:* electronic application, early action, deferred entrance. *Application fee:* $65. *Required:* essay or personal statement, high school transcript, 1 letter of recommendation, portfolio. *Recommended:* interview. *Application deadlines:* 6/1 (freshmen), 8/15 (transfers), 1/3 (early action). *Notification:* continuous (freshmen), continuous (transfers), 2/15 (early action).

Freshman Application Contact Mr. Larry Lee, Interim Director, Undergraduate Admissions, School of the Art Institute of Chicago, 36 South Wabash, Chicago, IL 60603. *Phone:* 312-629-6100. *Toll-free phone:* 800-232-SAIC. *Fax:* 312-629-6101. *E-mail:* ugadmiss@saic.edu. *Website:* http://www.saic.edu/.

See below for display ad and page 1492 for the College Close-Up.

Shimer College
Chicago, Illinois

- **Independent** 4-year, founded 1853
- **Urban** 3-acre campus with easy access to Chicago, Milwaukee
- **Coed** 127 undergraduate students, 83% full-time, 49% women, 51% men
- **Moderately difficult** entrance level, 74% of applicants were admitted

Undergraduates 105 full-time, 22 part-time. 52% are from out of state; 2% Black or African American, non-Hispanic/Latino; 4% Hispanic/Latino; 4% Asian, non-Hispanic/Latino; 7% Two or more races, non-Hispanic/Latino; 6% Race/ethnicity unknown; 12% transferred in; 5% live on campus. *Retention:* 84% of full-time freshmen returned.

Freshmen *Admission:* 31 applied, 23 admitted, 16 enrolled. *Average high school GPA:* 3.13. *Test scores:* SAT critical reading scores over 500: 100%; SAT math scores over 500: 67%; SAT writing scores over 500: 100%; ACT scores over 18: 100%; SAT critical reading scores over 600: 100%; SAT writing scores over 600: 67%; ACT scores over 24: 100%; SAT critical reading scores over 700: 34%.

Faculty *Total:* 15, 73% full-time, 87% with terminal degrees. *Student/faculty ratio:* 9:1.

Academics *Calendar:* semesters. *Degree:* bachelor's. *Special study options:* adult/continuing education programs, cooperative education, double majors, independent study, internships, off-campus study, part-time degree program, student-designed majors, study abroad, summer session for credit.

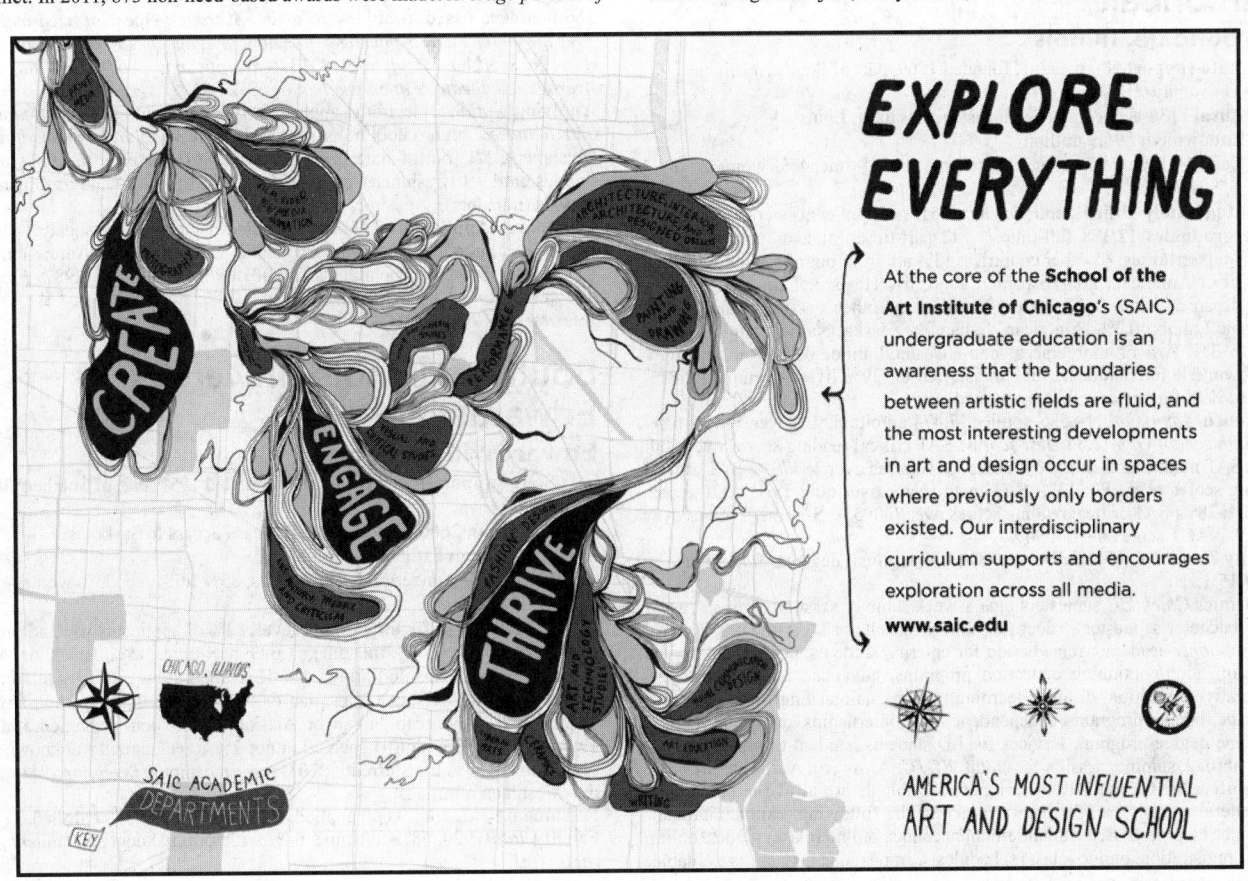

Computers on Campus Students can access the following: campus intranet, computer help desk, free student e-mail accounts, online (class) schedules. Campuswide network is available. 100% of college-owned or -operated housing units are wired for high-speed Internet access. Wireless service is available via entire campus.

Student Life *Housing options:* coed, disabled students. Campus housing is university owned and leased by the school. Freshman campus housing is guaranteed. *Activities and organizations:* drama/theater group, student-run newspaper, radio station, choral group. *Campus security:* 24-hour emergency response devices, late-night transport/escort service. *Student services:* personal/psychological counseling.

Athletics *Intramural sports:* baseball M, basketball M/W, cross-country running M/W, soccer M/W, softball W, track and field M/W, volleyball M/W.

Standardized Tests *Required for some:* SAT and SAT Subject Tests or ACT (for admission).

Costs (2013–14) *Comprehensive fee:* $41,856 includes full-time tuition ($26,510), mandatory fees ($4720), and room and board ($10,626). Full-time tuition and fees vary according to class time, course load, and program. Part-time tuition and fees vary according to class time, course load, and program. *Room and board:* Room and board charges vary according to housing facility. *Payment plan:* installment. *Waivers:* adult students, senior citizens, and employees or children of employees.

Financial Aid Of all full-time matriculated undergraduates who enrolled in 2010, 95 applied for aid, 84 were judged to have need, 4 had their need fully met. In 2010, 14 non-need-based awards were made. *Average percent of need met:* 59%. *Average financial aid package:* $20,388. *Average need-based loan:* $5630. *Average need-based gift aid:* $13,889. *Average non-need-based aid:* $6525. *Average indebtedness upon graduation:* $33,500.

Applying *Options:* electronic application. *Application fee:* $25. *Required:* essay or personal statement, high school transcript, 1 letter of recommendation, interview. *Application deadlines:* rolling (freshmen), rolling (transfers). *Notification:* continuous (freshmen), continuous (transfers).

Freshman Application Contact Ms. Amy Pritts, Director of Admission, Shimer College, 3424 South State Street, Chicago, IL 60616. *Phone:* 312-235-3504. *Toll-free phone:* 800-215-7173. *Fax:* 888-808-3133. *E-mail:* admission@shimer.edu.
Website: http://www.shimer.edu/.

Southern Illinois University Carbondale

Carbondale, Illinois

- **State-supported** university, founded 1869, part of Southern Illinois University
- **Rural** 1136-acre campus with easy access to St. Louis
- **Endowment** $95.9 million
- **Coed** 14,130 undergraduate students, 88% full-time, 45% women, 55% men
- **Moderately difficult** entrance level, 51% of applicants were admitted

Undergraduates 12,388 full-time, 1,742 part-time. Students come from 47 states and territories; 45 other countries; 13% are from out of state; 22% Black or African American, non-Hispanic/Latino; 6% Hispanic/Latino; 2% Asian, non-Hispanic/Latino; 0.2% Native Hawaiian or other Pacific Islander, non-Hispanic/Latino; 0.3% American Indian or Alaska Native, non-Hispanic/Latino; 3% Two or more races, non-Hispanic/Latino; 0.2% Race/ethnicity unknown; 3% international; 13% transferred in; 29% live on campus. *Retention:* 61% of full-time freshmen returned.

Freshmen *Admission:* 14,535 applied, 7,474 admitted, 2,321 enrolled. *Average high school GPA:* 2.82. *Test scores:* SAT critical reading scores over 500: 46%; SAT math scores over 500: 60%; ACT scores over 18: 79%; SAT critical reading scores over 600: 13%; SAT math scores over 600: 18%; ACT scores over 24: 28%; SAT critical reading scores over 700: 3%; SAT math scores over 700: 3%; ACT scores over 30: 4%.

Faculty *Total:* 996, 87% full-time, 78% with terminal degrees. *Student/faculty ratio:* 15:1.

Academics *Calendar:* semesters plus 8-week summer session. *Degrees:* associate, bachelor's, master's, doctoral, and postbachelor's certificates. *Special study options:* academic remediation for entering students, accelerated degree program, adult/continuing education programs, advanced placement credit, cooperative education, distance learning, double majors, English as a second language, honors programs, independent study, internships, off-campus study, part-time degree program, services for LD students, student-designed majors, study abroad, summer session for credit. *ROTC:* Army (b), Air Force (b).

Computers on Campus 1,856 computers/terminals are available on campus for general student use. Students can access the following: campus intranet, computer help desk, free student e-mail accounts, online (class) grades, online (class) registration, online (class) schedules. Campuswide network is available.

100% of college-owned or -operated housing units are wired for high-speed Internet access. Wireless service is available via classrooms, computer centers, computer labs, dorm rooms, learning centers, libraries, student centers.

Student Life *Housing:* on-campus residence required for freshman year. *Options:* coed, women-only, disabled students. Campus housing is university owned. Freshman campus housing is guaranteed. *Activities and organizations:* drama/theater group, student-run newspaper, radio and television station, choral group, marching band, Undergraduate Student Government, Graduate Professional Student Government, Interfraternity Council, Student Programming Council, International Student Council, national fraternities, national sororities. *Campus security:* 24-hour emergency response devices and patrols, student patrols, late-night transport/escort service, controlled dormitory access, well-lit pathways, night safety vans, student transit system. *Student services:* health clinic, personal/psychological counseling, women's center, legal services.

Athletics Member NCAA. All Division I except football (Division I-AA). *Intercollegiate sports:* baseball M(s), basketball M(s)/W(s), cheerleading M/W, cross-country running M(s)/W(s), golf M(s)/W(s), softball W(s), swimming and diving M(s)/W(s), tennis M(s)/W(s), track and field M(s)/W(s), volleyball W(s). *Intramural sports:* archery M(c)/W(c), badminton M(c)/W(c), baseball M(c), basketball M/W, bowling M(c)/W(c), equestrian sports M(c)/W(c), fencing M(c)/W(c), football M, gymnastics M(c)/W(c), lacrosse M(c)/W(c), racquetball M/W, rock climbing M(c)/W(c), rugby M(c)/W(c), sailing M(c)/W(c), skiing (downhill) M(c)/W(c), soccer M(c)/W(c), softball M/W(c), swimming and diving M/W, table tennis M(c)/W(c), tennis M(c)/W(c), track and field M/W, ultimate Frisbee M(c)/W(c), volleyball M(c)/W(c), water polo M(c)/W(c), weight lifting M(c)/W(c).

Standardized Tests *Required:* SAT or ACT (for admission).

Costs (2012–13) *Tuition:* state resident $8169 full-time, $272 per credit hour part-time; nonresident $20,422 full-time, $681 per credit hour part-time. Full-time tuition and fees vary according to course load, program, and student level. Part-time tuition and fees vary according to course load, program, and student level. No tuition increase for student's term of enrollment. *Required fees:* $3359 full-time, $156 per credit hour part-time. *Room and board:* $9126. Room and board charges vary according to board plan and housing facility. *Payment plan:* installment. *Waivers:* children of alumni, senior citizens, and employees or children of employees.

Financial Aid Of all full-time matriculated undergraduates who enrolled in 2012, 9,944 applied for aid, 8,742 were judged to have need, 283 had their need fully met. 1,672 Federal Work-Study jobs (averaging $1301). In 2012, 156 non-need-based awards were made. *Average percent of need met:* 39%. *Average financial aid package:* $12,466. *Average need-based loan:* $4469. *Average need-based gift aid:* $2137. *Average non-need-based aid:* $4931. *Average indebtedness upon graduation:* $32,652.

Applying *Options:* electronic application, deferred entrance. *Application fee:* $30. *Required:* high school transcript, SAT or ACT. *Application deadlines:* 5/1 (freshmen), 5/1 (out-of-state freshmen), rolling (transfers). *Notification:* continuous until 9/1 (freshmen), continuous until 9/1 (out-of-state freshmen), continuous (transfers).

Freshman Application Contact Katharine Suski, Associate Director, Southern Illinois University Carbondale, Undergraduate Admissions, 425 Clocktower Drive, Carbondale, IL 62901. *Phone:* 618-453-2987. *Fax:* 618-453-4609. *E-mail:* ksuski@siu.edu.
Website: http://www.siuc.edu/.

Southern Illinois University Edwardsville

Edwardsville, Illinois

- **State-supported** comprehensive, founded 1957, part of Southern Illinois University
- **Suburban** 2660-acre campus with easy access to St. Louis
- **Endowment** $16.5 million
- **Coed** 11,341 undergraduate students, 85% full-time, 53% women, 47% men
- **Moderately difficult** entrance level, 82% of applicants were admitted

Undergraduates 9,648 full-time, 1,693 part-time. 15% Black or African American, non-Hispanic/Latino; 4% Hispanic/Latino; 1% Asian, non-Hispanic/Latino; 0.1% Native Hawaiian or other Pacific Islander, non-Hispanic/Latino; 0.3% American Indian or Alaska Native, non-Hispanic/Latino; 3% Two or more races, non-Hispanic/Latino; 2% Race/ethnicity unknown; 0.9% international; 11% transferred in; 30% live on campus. *Retention:* 71% of full-time freshmen returned.

Freshmen *Admission:* 7,660 applied, 6,272 admitted, 2,075 enrolled.

Faculty *Total:* 920, 68% full-time, 66% with terminal degrees. *Student/faculty ratio:* 18:1.

Academics *Calendar:* semesters. *Degrees:* bachelor's, master's, doctoral, post-master's, and postbachelor's certificates. *Special study options:* academic remediation for entering students, accelerated degree program, advanced placement credit, cooperative education, distance learning, double majors, English as a second language, honors programs, independent study, internships, off-campus study, part-time degree program, services for LD students, student-designed majors, study abroad, summer session for credit. *ROTC:* Army (b), Air Force (c). *Unusual degree programs:* 3-2 engineering.

Computers on Campus 600 computers/terminals are available on campus for general student use. Students can access the following: campus intranet, computer help desk, free student e-mail accounts, online (class) grades, online (class) registration, online (class) schedules, online job finder. Campuswide network is available. 100% of college-owned or -operated housing units are wired for high-speed Internet access. Wireless service is available via entire campus.

Student Life *Housing options:* coed, disabled students. Campus housing is university owned. Freshman applicants given priority for college housing. *Activities and organizations:* drama/theater group, student-run newspaper, radio and television station, choral group, national fraternities, national sororities. *Campus security:* 24-hour emergency response devices and patrols, student patrols, late-night transport/escort service, controlled dormitory access, 24-hour ID check at residence hall entrances, emergency call boxes located throughout campus. *Student services:* health clinic, personal/psychological counseling, legal services.

Athletics Member NCAA. All Division I. *Intercollegiate sports:* baseball M(s), basketball M(s)/W(s), cross-country running M(s)/W(s), golf M(s)/W(s), soccer M(s)/W(s), softball W(s), tennis M(s)/W(s), track and field M(s)/W(s), volleyball W(s), wrestling M(s). *Intramural sports:* badminton M/W, basketball M/W, bowling M/W, cheerleading M/W, fencing M/W, football M, ice hockey M, racquetball M/W, rock climbing M/W, rugby M, soccer M/W, softball M/W, table tennis M/W, tennis M/W, ultimate Frisbee M/W, volleyball M/W, water polo M/W, weight lifting M/W.

Standardized Tests *Required:* SAT or ACT (for admission).

Costs (2012–13) *Tuition:* state resident $6948 full-time, $232 per credit hour part-time; nonresident $17,370 full-time. Full-time tuition and fees vary according to course load. Part-time tuition and fees vary according to course load. No tuition increase for student's term of enrollment. *Required fees:* $2303 full-time, $273 per credit hour part-time. *Room and board:* $8281. Room and board charges vary according to board plan and housing facility. *Payment plan:* installment. *Waivers:* senior citizens and employees or children of employees.

Financial Aid Of all full-time matriculated undergraduates who enrolled in 2011, 7,785 applied for aid, 6,715 were judged to have need, 1,649 had their need fully met. In 2011, 209 non-need-based awards were made. *Average percent of need met:* 54%. *Average financial aid package:* $11,214. *Average need-based loan:* $4499. *Average need-based gift aid:* $8930. *Average non-need-based aid:* $7620. *Average indebtedness upon graduation:* $25,998.

Applying *Options:* electronic application, deferred entrance. *Application fee:* $30. *Required:* high school transcript. *Recommended:* minimum 2.5 GPA. *Application deadline:* 5/1 (freshmen). *Notification:* continuous (freshmen), continuous (transfers).

Freshman Application Contact Mr. Todd Burrell, Director of Admissions, Southern Illinois University Edwardsville, Campus Box 1600, Rendleman Hall, Edwardsville, IL 62026-1600. *Phone:* 618-650-3705. *Toll-free phone:* 800-447-SIUE. *Fax:* 618-650-5013. *E-mail:* admissions@siue.edu. *Website:* http://www.siue.edu/.

Telshe Yeshiva–Chicago
Chicago, Illinois

Freshman Application Contact Rosh Hayeshiva, Telshe Yeshiva–Chicago, 3535 West Foster Avenue, Chicago, IL 60625-5598. *Phone:* 773-463-7738.

Trinity Christian College
Palos Heights, Illinois

- **Independent Christian Reformed** comprehensive, founded 1959
- **Suburban** 53-acre campus with easy access to Chicago
- **Endowment** $7.9 million
- **Coed** 1,346 undergraduate students, 80% full-time, 65% women, 35% men
- **Moderately difficult** entrance level, 82% of applicants were admitted

Undergraduates 1,075 full-time, 271 part-time. 28% are from out of state; 9% Black or African American, non-Hispanic/Latino; 9% Hispanic/Latino; 2% Asian, non-Hispanic/Latino; 0.2% Native Hawaiian or other Pacific Islander, non-Hispanic/Latino; 0.6% American Indian or Alaska Native, non-Hispanic/Latino; 0.9% Two or more races, non-Hispanic/Latino; 2% Race/ethnicity

unknown; 2% international; 7% transferred in; 45% live on campus. *Retention:* 80% of full-time freshmen returned.

Freshmen *Admission:* 691 applied, 569 admitted, 187 enrolled. *Average high school GPA:* 3.32. *Test scores:* SAT critical reading scores over 500: 72%; SAT math scores over 500: 57%; ACT scores over 18: 86%; SAT critical reading scores over 600: 51%; SAT math scores over 600: 14%; ACT scores over 24: 34%; SAT critical reading scores over 700: 22%; SAT math scores over 700: 7%; ACT scores over 30: 9%.

Faculty *Total:* 157, 53% full-time, 43% with terminal degrees. *Student/faculty ratio:* 11:1.

Academics *Calendar:* semesters plus 2 week interim term. *Degrees:* bachelor's and master's. *Special study options:* academic remediation for entering students, adult/continuing education programs, advanced placement credit, cooperative education, double majors, English as a second language, honors programs, independent study, internships, off-campus study, part-time degree program, services for LD students, study abroad, summer session for credit.

Computers on Campus 170 computers/terminals are available on campus for general student use. Students can access the following: campus intranet, computer help desk, free student e-mail accounts, online (class) grades, online (class) registration, online (class) schedules. Campuswide network is available. 100% of college-owned or -operated housing units are wired for high-speed Internet access. Wireless service is available via entire campus.

Student Life *Housing options:* coed. Campus housing is university owned. Freshman campus housing is guaranteed. *Activities and organizations:* drama/theater group, student-run newspaper, choral group, Student Association, student ministries, campus newspaper, Pro-Life Task Force, PACE (prison tutoring program). *Campus security:* 24-hour emergency response devices and patrols, student patrols, late-night transport/escort service, security cameras, Code Blue Emergency Phones. *Student services:* health clinic, personal/psychological counseling.

Athletics Member NAIA, NCCAA. *Intercollegiate sports:* baseball M(s), basketball M(s)/W(s), cross-country running M(s)/W(s), golf M(s), soccer M(s)/W(s), softball W(s), track and field M(s)/W(s), volleyball W(s). *Intramural sports:* badminton M/W, basketball M/W, football M/W, soccer M/W, volleyball M/W.

Standardized Tests *Required:* SAT or ACT (for admission). *Required for some:* SAT (for admission), SAT and SAT Subject Tests or ACT (for admission), SAT Subject Tests (for admission). *Recommended:* ACT (for admission).

Costs (2013–14) *Comprehensive fee:* $31,955 includes full-time tuition ($23,098), mandatory fees ($415), and room and board ($8442). Part-time tuition: $772 per credit hour. *Room and board:* Room and board charges vary according to board plan. *Payment plan:* installment. *Waivers:* employees or children of employees.

Financial Aid Of all full-time matriculated undergraduates who enrolled in 2012, 923 applied for aid, 837 were judged to have need, 117 had their need fully met. 98 Federal Work-Study jobs (averaging $1500). 352 state and other part-time jobs (averaging $1895). In 2012, 167 non-need-based awards were made. *Average percent of need met:* 66%. *Average financial aid package:* $15,289. *Average need-based loan:* $4560. *Average need-based gift aid:* $11,690. *Average non-need-based aid:* $6200. *Average indebtedness upon graduation:* $28,124.

Applying *Options:* electronic application, deferred entrance. *Application fee:* $20. *Required:* essay or personal statement, high school transcript, minimum 2.3 GPA, interview. *Required for some:* 1 letter of recommendation. *Application deadline:* rolling (freshmen). *Notification:* continuous (freshmen), continuous (transfers).

Freshman Application Contact Jeremy Klyn, Director of Admissions, Trinity Christian College, 6601 West College Drive, Palos Heights, IL 60463. *Phone:* 708-239-4708. *Fax:* 708-239-4826. *E-mail:* admissions@trnty.edu. *Website:* http://www.trnty.edu/.

Trinity College of Nursing and Health Sciences
Rock Island, Illinois

- **Independent** 4-year, founded 1994
- **Urban** 2-acre campus
- **Endowment** $1.3 million
- **Coed** 232 undergraduate students, 51% full-time, 92% women, 8% men
- **Moderately difficult** entrance level, 50% of applicants were admitted

Undergraduates 119 full-time, 113 part-time. 46% are from out of state; 4% Black or African American, non-Hispanic/Latino; 5% Hispanic/Latino; 2% Asian, non-Hispanic/Latino; 0.4% Native Hawaiian or other Pacific Islander, non-Hispanic/Latino; 1% Two or more races, non-Hispanic/Latino; 3% Race/ethnicity unknown; 17% transferred in. *Retention:* 100% of full-time freshmen returned.

Freshmen *Admission:* 4 applied, 2 admitted. *Average high school GPA:* 3.42. *Test scores:* ACT scores over 18: 82%; ACT scores over 24: 24%; ACT scores over 30: 1%.

Faculty *Total:* 26, 62% full-time, 12% with terminal degrees. *Student/faculty ratio:* 9:1.

Academics *Calendar:* semesters. *Degrees:* associate and bachelor's (general education requirements are taken off campus, usually at Black Hawk College, Eastern Iowa Community College District and Western Illinois University). *Special study options:* accelerated degree program, adult/continuing education programs, advanced placement credit, distance learning, independent study, internships, off-campus study, part-time degree program, services for LD students, study abroad, summer session for credit.

Computers on Campus 20 computers/terminals are available on campus for general student use. Students can access the following: computer help desk, free student e-mail accounts, online (class) grades, online (class) schedules. Campuswide network is available. Wireless service is available via entire campus.

Student Life *Housing:* college housing not available. *Activities and organizations:* Student Government Association, Phi Theta Kappa, BSN Honor Society. *Campus security:* 24-hour emergency response devices. *Student services:* personal/psychological counseling.

Standardized Tests *Required for some:* ACT (for admission).

Costs (2013–14) *Tuition:* $22,680 full-time, $648 per credit hour part-time. Full-time tuition and fees vary according to degree level, program, and student level. Part-time tuition and fees vary according to degree level, program, and student level. *Required fees:* $2302 full-time. *Payment plan:* installment.

Financial Aid Of all full-time matriculated undergraduates who enrolled in 2012, 106 applied for aid, 106 were judged to have need. *Average indebtedness upon graduation:* $9500.

Applying *Options:* electronic application, early admission, early decision. *Application fee:* $50. *Required:* minimum 2.5 GPA. *Required for some:* essay or personal statement, high school transcript, minimum 3.0 GPA, interview. *Application deadlines:* rolling (freshmen), rolling (out-of-state freshmen), rolling (transfers). *Early decision deadline:* 12/1. *Notification:* continuous until 2/1 (freshmen), continuous until 2/1 (out-of-state freshmen), continuous until 2/1 (transfers), 12/15 (early decision).

Freshman Application Contact Ms. Lori Perez, Admissions Representative, Trinity College of Nursing and Health Sciences, 2122—25th Avenue, Rock Island, IL 61201. *Phone:* 309-779-7700. *Fax:* 309-779-7748. *E-mail:* PerezLJ@ihs.org.

Website: http://www.trinitycollegeqc.edu/.

Trinity International University
Deerfield, Illinois

Freshman Application Contact Mr. Aaron Mahl, Director of Undergraduate Admissions, Trinity International University, 2065 Half Day Road, Deerfield, IL 60015-1284. *Phone:* 847-317-7000. *Toll-free phone:* 800-822-3225. *Fax:* 847-317-8097. *E-mail:* tcadmissions@tiu.edu.

Website: http://www.tiu.edu/.

University of Chicago
Chicago, Illinois

- **Independent** university, founded 1891
- **Urban** 215-acre campus
- **Endowment** $6.6 million
- **Coed** 5,590 undergraduate students, 99% full-time, 47% women, 53% men
- **Most difficult** entrance level, 13% of applicants were admitted

Undergraduates 5,531 full-time, 59 part-time. 81% are from out of state; 5% Black or African American, non-Hispanic/Latino; 8% Hispanic/Latino; 18% Asian, non-Hispanic/Latino; 0.2% American Indian or Alaska Native, non-Hispanic/Latino; 3% Two or more races, non-Hispanic/Latino; 10% Race/ethnicity unknown; 9% international; 0.3% transferred in; 55% live on campus. *Retention:* 99% of full-time freshmen returned.

Freshmen *Admission:* 25,273 applied, 3,345 admitted, 1,527 enrolled. *Average high school GPA:* 4.28. *Test scores:* SAT critical reading scores over 500: 100%; SAT math scores over 500: 100%; SAT writing scores over 500: 100%; ACT scores over 18: 100%; SAT critical reading scores over 600: 100%; SAT math scores over 600: 99%; SAT writing scores over 600: 99%; ACT scores over 24: 100%; SAT critical reading scores over 700: 83%; SAT math scores over 700: 81%; SAT writing scores over 700: 78%; ACT scores over 30: 88%.

Faculty *Total:* 1,723, 73% full-time, 89% with terminal degrees. *Student/faculty ratio:* 6:1.

Academics *Calendar:* quarters. *Degrees:* bachelor's, master's, and doctoral. *Special study options:* accelerated degree program, adult/continuing education programs, advanced placement credit, double majors, independent study,

internships, off-campus study, student-designed majors, study abroad, summer session for credit. *ROTC:* Army (c), Air Force (c). *Unusual degree programs:* 3-2 business administration; social work; public policy, social sciences (MAPSS), international relations.

Computers on Campus 300 computers/terminals are available on campus for general student use. Students can access the following: campus intranet, computer help desk, free student e-mail accounts, online (class) grades, online (class) registration, online (class) schedules. Campuswide network is available. 100% of college-owned or -operated housing units are wired for high-speed Internet access. Wireless service is available via entire campus.

Student Life *Housing:* on-campus residence required for freshman year. *Options:* coed, men-only, women-only, disabled students. Campus housing is university owned. Freshman campus housing is guaranteed. *Activities and organizations:* drama/theater group, student-run newspaper, radio and television station, choral group, University Theatre, Model United Nations, Council on University Programming, Documentary Films, South Asian Students Association, national fraternities, national sororities. *Campus security:* 24-hour emergency response devices and patrols, student patrols, late-night transport/escort service, controlled dormitory access. *Student services:* health clinic, personal/psychological counseling, women's center.

Athletics Member NCAA. All Division III. *Intercollegiate sports:* baseball M, basketball M/W, cross-country running M/W, football M, soccer M/W, softball W, swimming and diving M/W, tennis M/W, track and field M/W, volleyball W, wrestling M. *Intramural sports:* archery M/W, badminton M/W, basketball M/W, bowling M/W, football M/W, racquetball M/W, soccer M/W, softball M/W, squash M/W, swimming and diving M/W, table tennis M/W, tennis M/W, track and field M/W, ultimate Frisbee M/W, volleyball M/W, water polo M/W.

Standardized Tests *Required:* SAT or ACT (for admission).

Costs (2012–13) *One-time required fee:* $1035. *Comprehensive fee:* $57,711 includes full-time tuition ($43,581), mandatory fees ($993), and room and board ($13,137). Part-time tuition and fees vary according to course load. *Room and board:* Room and board charges vary according to board plan and housing facility. *Payment plans:* tuition prepayment, installment. *Waivers:* employees or children of employees.

Financial Aid Of all full-time matriculated undergraduates who enrolled in 2012, 2,866 applied for aid, 2,483 were judged to have need, 2,483 had their need fully met. In 2012, 635 non-need-based awards were made. *Average percent of need met:* 100%. *Average financial aid package:* $40,089. *Average need-based loan:* $4697. *Average need-based gift aid:* $36,600. *Average non-need-based aid:* $11,955. *Average indebtedness upon graduation:* $22,663. *Financial aid deadline:* 2/1.

Applying *Options:* electronic application, early admission, early action, deferred entrance. *Application fee:* $75. *Required:* essay or personal statement, high school transcript, 2 letters of recommendation, 2 teacher recommendations required. *Recommended:* interview. *Application deadlines:* 1/2 (freshmen), 3/1 (transfers), 11/1 (early action). *Notification:* 4/1 (freshmen), 5/9 (transfers), 12/17 (early action).

Freshman Application Contact Mr. James G. Nondorf, Vice President for Enrollment and Student Advancement and Dean of Admissions and Financial Aid, University of Chicago, Rosenwald Hall, 1101 East 58th Street, Suite 105, Chicago, IL 60637. *Phone:* 773-702-8650. *Fax:* 773-702-4199. *E-mail:* collegeadmissions@uchicago.edu.

Website: http://www.uchicago.edu/.

University of Illinois at Chicago
Chicago, Illinois

- **State-supported** university, founded 1946, part of University of Illinois System
- **Urban** 240-acre campus with easy access to Chicago
- **Endowment** $217.2 million
- **Coed** 16,678 undergraduate students, 92% full-time, 51% women, 49% men
- **Moderately difficult** entrance level, 64% of applicants were admitted

Undergraduates 15,381 full-time, 1,297 part-time. Students come from 42 states and territories; 40 other countries; 2% are from out of state; 8% Black or African American, non-Hispanic/Latino; 24% Hispanic/Latino; 22% Asian, non-Hispanic/Latino; 0.5% Native Hawaiian or other Pacific Islander, non-Hispanic/Latino; 0.1% American Indian or Alaska Native, non-Hispanic/Latino; 2% Two or more races, non-Hispanic/Latino; 2% Race/ethnicity unknown; 2% international; 9% transferred in; 19% live on campus. *Retention:* 78% of full-time freshmen returned.

Freshmen *Admission:* 14,380 applied, 9,193 admitted, 3,123 enrolled. *Average high school GPA:* 3.26. *Test scores:* SAT critical reading scores over 500: 70%; SAT math scores over 500: 82%; SAT writing scores over 500: 72%; ACT scores over 18: 100%; SAT critical reading scores over 600: 31%; SAT math scores over 600: 48%; SAT writing scores over 600: 29%; ACT scores over 24: 52%; SAT critical reading scores over 700: 9%; SAT math scores over 700: 14%; SAT writing scores over 700: 10%; ACT scores over 30: 8%.

Faculty *Total:* 1,672, 72% full-time, 67% with terminal degrees. *Student/faculty ratio:* 18:1.

Academics *Calendar:* semesters. *Degrees:* bachelor's, master's, doctoral, post-master's, and postbachelor's certificates. *Special study options:* academic remediation for entering students, accelerated degree program, advanced placement credit, cooperative education, distance learning, double majors, honors programs, independent study, internships, off-campus study, part-time degree program, services for LD students, student-designed majors, study abroad, summer session for credit. *ROTC:* Army (b), Navy (c), Air Force (c).

Computers on Campus 910 computers/terminals are available on campus for general student use. Students can access the following: campus intranet, computer help desk, free student e-mail accounts, online (class) grades, online (class) registration, online (class) schedules. Campuswide network is available. 100% of college-owned or -operated housing units are wired for high-speed Internet access. Wireless service is available via classrooms, computer centers, computer labs, dorm rooms, libraries, student centers.

Student Life *Housing options:* coed. Campus housing is university owned. *Activities and organizations:* drama/theater group, student-run newspaper, radio station, choral group, MBA Association, StudentsMuslim Student Association, Society of Automotive Engineers, Pakistani Student Organization, Society of Future Physicians, national fraternities, national sororities. *Campus security:* 24-hour emergency response devices and patrols, student patrols, late-night transport/escort service, controlled dormitory access, housing ID stickers, guest escort policy, 24-hour closed circuit videos for exits and entrances, security screen for first floor. *Student services:* health clinic, personal/psychological counseling, women's center, legal services.

Athletics Member NCAA. All Division I. *Intercollegiate sports:* baseball M(s), basketball M(s)/W(s), cross-country running M(s)/W(s), gymnastics M(s)/W(s), soccer M(s), softball W(s), swimming and diving M(s)/W(s), tennis M(s)/W(s), track and field M(s)/W(s), volleyball W(s). *Intramural sports:* badminton M/W, basketball M/W, bowling M/W, fencing M(c)/W(c), field hockey W, football M/W, golf M/W, racquetball M/W, rugby M(c)/W(c), soccer M/W, softball M/W, squash M/W, table tennis M/W, tennis M/W, volleyball M(c)/W(c), water polo M(c)/W(c), wrestling M.

Standardized Tests *Required:* SAT or ACT (for admission).

Costs (2013–14) *Tuition:* state resident $10,406 full-time; nonresident $22,796 full-time. Full-time tuition and fees vary according to degree level and program. Part-time tuition and fees vary according to course load, degree level, and program. No tuition increase for student's term of enrollment. *Required fees:* $2948 full-time, $1193 per term part-time. *Room and board:* $10,882; room only: $7462. Room and board charges vary according to board plan and housing facility. *Payment plan:* installment. *Waivers:* senior citizens and employees or children of employees.

Financial Aid Of all full-time matriculated undergraduates who enrolled in 2011, 12,832 applied for aid, 11,725 were judged to have need, 1,071 had their need fully met. 939 Federal Work-Study jobs (averaging $2000). 2,808 state and other part-time jobs (averaging $2700). In 2011, 433 non-need-based awards were made. *Average percent of need met:* 63%. *Average financial aid package:* $14,016. *Average need-based loan:* $4568. *Average need-based gift aid:* $12,474. *Average non-need-based aid:* $3800. *Average indebtedness upon graduation:* $22,256.

Applying *Options:* electronic application. *Application fee:* $50. *Required:* essay or personal statement, high school transcript, auditions required of music and theater majors; portfolios required of art majors. *Application deadlines:* 1/15 (freshmen), 3/31 (transfers). *Notification:* continuous until 11/30 (freshmen), continuous (transfers).

Freshman Application Contact Ms. Maureen Woods SAC, Associate Director, Admissions Undergraduate, University of Illinois at Chicago, 1100 SSB, m/c 018, Chicago, IL 60607-7128. *Phone:* 312-996-4111. *Fax:* 312-413-7628. *E-mail:* uic.admit@uic.edu.

Website: http://www.uic.edu/.

University of Illinois at Springfield
Springfield, Illinois

- **State-supported** comprehensive, founded 1969, part of University of Illinois System
- **Suburban** 746-acre campus
- **Endowment** $11.2 million
- **Coed** 3,054 undergraduate students, 64% full-time, 51% women, 49% men
- **Moderately difficult** entrance level, 56% of applicants were admitted

Undergraduates 1,948 full-time, 1,106 part-time. Students come from 50 states and territories; 15 other countries; 11% are from out of state; 12% Black or African American, non-Hispanic/Latino; 6% Hispanic/Latino; 3% Asian, non-Hispanic/Latino; 0.2% Native Hawaiian or other Pacific Islander, non-

Hispanic/Latino; 0.3% American Indian or Alaska Native, non-Hispanic/Latino; 2% Two or more races, non-Hispanic/Latino; 4% Race/ethnicity unknown; 3% international; 21% transferred in; 28% live on campus. *Retention:* 72% of full-time freshmen returned.

Freshmen *Admission:* 1,506 applied, 849 admitted, 270 enrolled. *Average high school GPA:* 3.35. *Test scores:* ACT scores over 18: 94%; ACT scores over 24: 39%; ACT scores over 30: 7%.

Faculty *Total:* 374, 57% full-time, 59% with terminal degrees. *Student/faculty ratio:* 12:1.

Academics *Calendar:* semesters. *Degrees:* bachelor's, master's, doctoral, post-master's, and postbachelor's certificates. *Special study options:* academic remediation for entering students, advanced placement credit, cooperative education, distance learning, English as a second language, honors programs, independent study, internships, off-campus study, part-time degree program, services for LD students, study abroad, summer session for credit.

Computers on Campus 390 computers/terminals and 27 ports are available on campus for general student use. Students can access the following: campus intranet, computer help desk, free student e-mail accounts, online (class) grades, online (class) registration, online (class) schedules. Campuswide network is available. 100% of college-owned or -operated housing units are wired for high-speed Internet access. Wireless service is available via entire campus.

Student Life *Housing:* on-campus residence required for freshman year. *Options:* coed, disabled students. Campus housing is university owned. Freshman campus housing is guaranteed. *Activities and organizations:* drama/theater group, student-run newspaper, radio station, choral group, Student Activities Committee, Christian Student Fellowship, DODGE—Dodge Ball Club, Black Student Union, Black Male Collegiate Society. *Campus security:* 24-hour emergency response devices and patrols, late-night transport/escort service, controlled dormitory access. *Student services:* health clinic, personal/psychological counseling, women's center.

Athletics Member NCAA. All Division II. *Intercollegiate sports:* baseball M(s), basketball M(s)/W(s), golf M(s)/W(s), soccer M(s)/W(s), softball W(s), tennis M(s)/W(s), volleyball W(s). *Intramural sports:* badminton M/W, baseball M(c), basketball M/W, football M/W, racquetball M/W, soccer M/W, softball M/W, squash M(c)/W, table tennis M/W, ultimate Frisbee M/W, volleyball M/W.

Standardized Tests *Required:* SAT or ACT (for admission).

Costs (2013–14) *Tuition:* state resident $9248 full-time, $308 per credit hour part-time; nonresident $18,398 full-time, $613 per credit hour part-time. Full-time tuition and fees vary according to course load. Part-time tuition and fees vary according to course load. No tuition increase for student's term of enrollment. *Required fees:* $1884 full-time. *Room and board:* $10,350; room only: $7000. Room and board charges vary according to board plan and housing facility. *Payment plan:* installment. *Waivers:* senior citizens and employees or children of employees.

Financial Aid Of all full-time matriculated undergraduates who enrolled in 2011, 1,703 applied for aid, 1,421 were judged to have need, 90 had their need fully met. In 2011, 278 non-need-based awards were made. *Average percent of need met:* 66%. *Average financial aid package:* $11,392. *Average need-based loan:* $4362. *Average need-based gift aid:* $8473. *Average non-need-based aid:* $5003. *Average indebtedness upon graduation:* $21,057. *Financial aid deadline:* 11/15.

Applying *Options:* electronic application, deferred entrance. *Application fee:* $50. *Required:* high school transcript. *Application deadlines:* rolling (freshmen), rolling (transfers). *Notification:* continuous (transfers).

Freshman Application Contact Dr. Lori Giordano, Interim Director of Student Services/ Admissions, University of Illinois at Springfield, Springfield, IL 62703. *Phone:* 217-206-4847. *Toll-free phone:* 888-977-4847. *E-mail:* admissions@uis.edu.

Website: http://www.uis.edu/.

University of Illinois at Urbana–Champaign
Champaign, Illinois

- **State-supported** university, founded 1867, part of University of Illinois System
- **Urban** 1783-acre campus
- **Endowment** $24.0 billion
- **Coed** 32,281 undergraduate students, 96% full-time, 44% women, 56% men
- **Very difficult** entrance level, 63% of applicants were admitted

Undergraduates 31,118 full-time, 1,163 part-time. Students come from 52 states and territories; 119 other countries; 8% are from out of state; 5% Black or African American, non-Hispanic/Latino; 7% Hispanic/Latino; 14% Asian, non-Hispanic/Latino; 0.2% Native Hawaiian or other Pacific Islander, non-Hispanic/Latino; 0.1% American Indian or Alaska Native, non-Hispanic/

Latino; 2% Two or more races, non-Hispanic/Latino; 0.7% Race/ethnicity unknown; 14% international; 4% transferred in; 50% live on campus. *Retention:* 94% of full-time freshmen returned.

Freshmen *Admission:* 31,454 applied, 19,924 admitted, 6,921 enrolled. *Test scores:* SAT critical reading scores over 500: 93%; SAT math scores over 500: 99%; SAT writing scores over 500: 95%; ACT scores over 18: 100%; SAT critical reading scores over 600: 56%; SAT math scores over 600: 93%; SAT writing scores over 600: 66%; ACT scores over 24: 90%; SAT critical reading scores over 700: 19%; SAT math scores over 700: 71%; SAT writing scores over 700: 17%; ACT scores over 30: 41%.

Faculty *Total:* 1,854, 100% full-time, 93% with terminal degrees. *Student/faculty ratio:* 19:1.

Academics *Calendar:* semesters. *Degrees:* certificates, bachelor's, master's, doctoral, post-master's, and postbachelor's certificates. *Special study options:* academic remediation for entering students, accelerated degree program, advanced placement credit, cooperative education, distance learning, double majors, English as a second language, honors programs, independent study, internships, off-campus study, services for LD students, student-designed majors, study abroad, summer session for credit. *ROTC:* Army (b), Navy (b), Air Force (b). *Unusual degree programs:* 3-2 business administration; engineering; accounting.

Computers on Campus Students can access the following: computer help desk, free student e-mail accounts, online (class) grades, online (class) registration, online (class) schedules. Campuswide network is available. 100% of college-owned or -operated housing units are wired for high-speed Internet access. Wireless service is available via entire campus.

Student Life *Housing:* on-campus residence required for freshman year. *Options:* coed, men-only, women-only, cooperative, disabled students. Campus housing is university owned and is provided by a third party. Freshman campus housing is guaranteed. *Activities and organizations:* drama/theater group, student-run newspaper, radio and television station, choral group, marching band, Volunteer Illini Project, October Lovers, Illini Pride Student Board, National Society of Collegiate Scholars, Phi Eta Sigma Freshman Honor Society, national fraternities, national sororities. *Campus security:* 24-hour emergency response devices and patrols, student patrols, late-night transport/escort service, controlled dormitory access, safety training classes, ID cards with safety numbers. *Student services:* health clinic, personal/psychological counseling, women's center, legal services.

Athletics Member NCAA. All Division I except football (Division I-A). *Intercollegiate sports:* baseball M(s), basketball M(s)/W(s), cheerleading M/W, cross-country running M(s)/W(s), golf M(s)/W(s), gymnastics M(s)/W(s), soccer W(s), softball W(s), swimming and diving W(s), tennis M(s)/W(s), track and field M(s)/W(s), volleyball W(s), wrestling M(s). *Intramural sports:* archery M(c)/W(c), badminton M/W, baseball M(c), basketball M/W, bowling M(c)/W(c), cheerleading M(c)/W(c), crew M(c)/W(c), cross-country running M/W, equestrian sports M(c)/W(c), fencing M(c)/W(c), field hockey M(c)/W(c), football M/W(c), golf M/W, gymnastics M(c)/W(c), ice hockey M(c)/W(c), lacrosse M(c)/W(c), racquetball M/W, riflery M(c)/W(c), rock climbing M(c)/W(c), rugby M(c)/W(c), sailing M(c)/W(c), skiing (cross-country) M(c)/W(c), skiing (downhill) M(c)/W(c), soccer M/W, softball M/W, squash M(c)/W(c), swimming and diving W(c), table tennis M(c)/W(c), tennis M/W, ultimate Frisbee M(c)/W(c), volleyball M/W, water polo M(c)/W(c), weight lifting M(c)/W(c), wrestling M.

Standardized Tests *Required:* SAT or ACT (for admission).

Costs (2013–14) *Tuition:* state resident $11,834 full-time; nonresident $26,216 full-time. Full-time tuition and fees vary according to program and student level. No tuition increase for student's term of enrollment. *Required fees:* $3504 full-time. *Room and board:* $10,636. Room and board charges vary according to board plan, housing facility, and location. *Payment plan:* installment. *Waivers:* senior citizens and employees or children of employees.

Financial Aid Of all full-time matriculated undergraduates who enrolled in 2010, 18,196 applied for aid, 14,487 were judged to have need, 3,087 had their need fully met. In 2010, 3299 non-need-based awards were made. *Average percent of need met:* 65%. *Average financial aid package:* $13,501. *Average need-based loan:* $4605. *Average need-based gift aid:* $11,504. *Average non-need-based aid:* $3742. *Average indebtedness upon graduation:* $22,975.

Applying *Options:* electronic application, early admission, deferred entrance. *Application fee:* $50. *Required:* essay or personal statement, high school transcript. *Required for some:* An application essay is required for all potential students. Auditions or portfolios may be required of some applicants depending on their field of study. *Application deadlines:* 1/2 (freshmen), 3/1 (transfers). *Notification:* 2/17 (freshmen), 4/15 (transfers).

Freshman Application Contact Stacey Kostell, Director of Admissions, University of Illinois at Urbana–Champaign, 901 West Illinois, Urbana, IL 61801. *Phone:* 217-333-0302. *Fax:* 217-244-4614. *E-mail:* ugradadmissions@uiuc.edu.

Website: http://www.illinois.edu/.

University of Phoenix–Chicago Campus
Schaumburg, Illinois

Freshman Application Contact Marc Booker, Sr. Director, Office of Admissions and Evaluation, University of Phoenix–Chicago Campus, 4035 South Riverpoint Parkway, Mail Stop CF-L101, Phoenix, AZ 85040-1958. *Phone:* 602-557-4609. *Toll-free phone:* 866-766-0766. *Fax:* 480-643-1156. *Website:* http://www.phoenix.edu/.

University of St. Francis
Joliet, Illinois

- **Independent Roman Catholic** comprehensive, founded 1920
- **Suburban** 24-acre campus with easy access to Chicago
- **Endowment** $10.2 million
- **Coed** 1,423 undergraduate students, 96% full-time, 68% women, 32% men
- **Moderately difficult** entrance level, 51% of applicants were admitted

Undergraduates 1,361 full-time, 62 part-time. Students come from 17 states and territories; 6% are from out of state; 8% Black or African American, non-Hispanic/Latino; 14% Hispanic/Latino; 2% Asian, non-Hispanic/Latino; 0.4% Native Hawaiian or other Pacific Islander, non-Hispanic/Latino; 0.5% American Indian or Alaska Native, non-Hispanic/Latino; 2% Two or more races, non-Hispanic/Latino; 0.1% Race/ethnicity unknown; 1% international; 14% transferred in; 26% live on campus. *Retention:* 79% of full-time freshmen returned.

Freshmen *Admission:* 1,718 applied, 884 admitted, 220 enrolled. *Average high school GPA:* 3.43. *Test scores:* SAT critical reading scores over 500: 29%; SAT math scores over 500: 43%; SAT writing scores over 500: 29%; ACT scores over 18: 97%; SAT math scores over 600: 14%; ACT scores over 24: 37%; ACT scores over 30: 5%.

Faculty *Total:* 254, 36% full-time, 38% with terminal degrees. *Student/faculty ratio:* 12:1.

Academics *Calendar:* semesters. *Degrees:* bachelor's, master's, doctoral, and post-master's certificates. *Special study options:* academic remediation for entering students, accelerated degree program, adult/continuing education programs, advanced placement credit, distance learning, double majors, English as a second language, honors programs, independent study, internships, off-campus study, part-time degree program, services for LD students, student-designed majors, study abroad, summer session for credit. *ROTC:* Army (c).

Computers on Campus 476 computers/terminals and 1,500 ports are available on campus for general student use. Students can access the following: campus intranet, computer help desk, free student e-mail accounts, online (class) grades, online (class) registration, online (class) schedules, billing/payment. Campuswide network is available. 100% of college-owned or -operated housing units are wired for high-speed Internet access. Wireless service is available via entire campus.

Student Life *Housing options:* coed. Campus housing is university owned. Freshman campus housing is guaranteed. *Activities and organizations:* drama/theater group, student-run newspaper, radio and television station, choral group, Justice League, Student Business Association, International Club, Student Nurses Association, Student Activities Board. *Campus security:* 24-hour emergency response devices and patrols, student patrols, late-night transport/escort service, controlled dormitory access, First Response trained security personnel. *Student services:* health clinic, personal/psychological counseling.

Athletics Member NAIA. *Intercollegiate sports:* baseball M(s), basketball M(s)/W(s), cheerleading W(s), cross-country running M(s)/W(s), football M(s), golf M(s)/W(s), soccer M(s)/W(s), softball W(s), tennis M(s)/W(s), track and field M(s)/W(s), volleyball W(s). *Intramural sports:* basketball M/W, bowling M/W, volleyball M/W.

Standardized Tests *Required:* SAT or ACT (for admission).

Costs (2012–13) *Comprehensive fee:* $35,092 includes full-time tuition ($26,374), mandatory fees ($450), and room and board ($8268). Full-time tuition and fees vary according to degree level and location. Part-time tuition: $795 per credit hour. Part-time tuition and fees vary according to degree level. *Room and board:* Room and board charges vary according to board plan and housing facility. *Payment plans:* installment, deferred payment. *Waivers:* children of alumni and employees or children of employees.

Financial Aid Of all full-time matriculated undergraduates who enrolled in 2011, 1,225 applied for aid, 1,129 were judged to have need, 786 had their need fully met. 160 Federal Work-Study jobs (averaging $1249). 309 state and other part-time jobs (averaging $1283). In 2011, 196 non-need-based awards were made. *Average percent of need met:* 63%. *Average financial aid package:* $20,987. *Average need-based loan:* $4749. *Average need-based gift aid:* $8251. *Average non-need-based aid:* $9093. *Average indebtedness upon graduation:* $26,393.

Applying *Options:* electronic application, deferred entrance. *Application fee:* $30. *Required:* high school transcript, minimum 2.5 GPA. *Required for some:* essay or personal statement, 2 letters of recommendation, interview. *Application deadline:* 8/1 (freshmen). *Notification:* continuous (freshmen), continuous (transfers).

Freshman Application Contact Ms. Cynthia Cruz, Director of Undergraduate Admissions, University of St. Francis, 500 North Wilcox Street, Joliet, IL 60435-6188. *Phone:* 800-735-7500. *Toll-free phone:* 800-735-7500. *Fax:* 815-740-5032. *E-mail:* ccruz@stfrancis.edu.
Website: http://www.stfrancis.edu/.

VanderCook College of Music

Chicago, Illinois

- **Independent** 4-year, founded 1909
- **Urban** 1-acre campus with easy access to Downtown Chicago
- **Coed** 139 undergraduate students, 78% full-time, 50% women, 50% men

Undergraduates 108 full-time, 31 part-time. Students come from 13 states and territories; 3 other countries; 25% are from out of state; 2% transferred in; 15% live on campus. *Retention:* 90% of full-time freshmen returned.
Freshmen *Admission:* 27 enrolled. *Average high school GPA:* 3.27. *Test scores:* ACT scores over 18: 100%; ACT scores over 24: 52%; ACT scores over 30: 8%.
Faculty *Total:* 33, 27% full-time, 30% with terminal degrees. *Student/faculty ratio:* 9:1.
Academics *Calendar:* semesters. *Degrees:* bachelor's, master's, and postbachelor's certificates. *Special study options:* advanced placement credit, distance learning, independent study, internships, part-time degree program.
Computers on Campus 21 computers/terminals are available on campus for general student use. Students can access the following: campus intranet, free student e-mail accounts. Campuswide network is available. Wireless service is available via entire campus.
Student Life *Housing options:* coed, disabled students. Campus housing is provided by a third party. *Activities and organizations:* choral group, NAME (National Association for Music Education), ACDA (American Choral Directors Association), NBA (National Band Association), ASTA (American String Teachers Association), national fraternities, national sororities. *Campus security:* 24-hour emergency response devices and patrols, late-night transport/escort service.
Standardized Tests *Required for some:* SAT or ACT (for admission).
Costs (2012–13) *Comprehensive fee:* $34,742 includes full-time tuition ($22,776), mandatory fees ($1340), and room and board ($10,626). Full-time tuition and fees vary according to course level, course load, degree level, and program. Part-time tuition: $950 per semester hour. Part-time tuition and fees vary according to course level, course load, degree level, and program. *Required fees:* $1040 per year part-time. *College room only:* $5546. Room and board charges vary according to board plan and housing facility. *Payment plan:* installment. *Waivers:* employees or children of employees.
Financial Aid Of all full-time matriculated undergraduates who enrolled in 2006, 7 Federal Work-Study jobs (averaging $500). 37 state and other part-time jobs (averaging $959).
Applying *Required:* essay or personal statement, high school transcript, 3 letters of recommendation, interview, audition. *Required for some:* minimum 3.0 GPA. *Recommended:* minimum 3.0 GPA.
Freshman Application Contact Ms. Amy Lenting, Director of Admissions, VanderCook College of Music, 3140 South Federal Street, Chicago, IL 60616. *Phone:* 312-788-1120 Ext. 230. *Fax:* 312-225-5211. *E-mail:* admissions@vandercook.edu.
Website: http://www.vandercook.edu/.

Western Illinois University

Macomb, Illinois

- **State-supported** comprehensive, founded 1899
- **Small-town** 1050-acre campus
- **Endowment** $28.4 million
- **Coed** 10,263 undergraduate students, 89% full-time, 48% women, 52% men
- **Moderately difficult** entrance level, 63% of applicants were admitted

Undergraduates 9,161 full-time, 1,102 part-time. Students come from 36 states and territories; 55 other countries; 6% are from out of state; 16% Black or African American, non-Hispanic/Latino; 7% Hispanic/Latino; 0.8% Asian, non-Hispanic/Latino; 0.1% Native Hawaiian or other Pacific Islander, non-Hispanic/Latino; 0.2% American Indian or Alaska Native, non-Hispanic/Latino; 2% Two or more races, non-Hispanic/Latino; 4% Race/ethnicity unknown; 1% international; 13% transferred in; 42% live on campus. *Retention:* 68% of full-time freshmen returned.

Freshmen *Admission:* 10,326 applied, 6,481 admitted, 1,754 enrolled. *Average high school GPA:* 3.04.
Faculty *Total:* 737, 90% full-time, 68% with terminal degrees. *Student/faculty ratio:* 15:1.
Academics *Calendar:* semesters. *Degrees:* bachelor's, master's, doctoral, and postbachelor's certificates. *Special study options:* academic remediation for entering students, adult/continuing education programs, advanced placement credit, distance learning, double majors, English as a second language, external degree program, freshman honors college, honors programs, independent study, internships, off-campus study, part-time degree program, services for LD students, student-designed majors, study abroad, summer session for credit. *ROTC:* Army (b).
Computers on Campus 1,000 computers/terminals are available on campus for general student use. Students can access the following: online (class) registration. Campuswide network is available. 100% of college-owned or -operated housing units are wired for high-speed Internet access. Wireless service is available via classrooms, computer labs, dorm rooms, libraries, student centers.
Student Life *Housing:* on-campus residence required through sophomore year. *Options:* coed, men-only, women-only. Campus housing is university owned. Freshman campus housing is guaranteed. *Activities and organizations:* drama/theater group, student-run newspaper, radio and television station, choral group, marching band, Student Government Association, Black Student Association, University Union Board, International Friendship Club, Bureau of Cultural Affairs, national fraternities, national sororities. *Campus security:* 24-hour emergency response devices and patrols, student patrols, late-night transport/escort service, controlled dormitory access. *Student services:* health clinic, personal/psychological counseling, women's center, legal services.
Athletics Member NCAA. All Division I except football (Division I-AA). *Intercollegiate sports:* baseball M(s), basketball M(s)/W(s), cross-country running M(s)/W(s), golf M(s)/W, soccer M(s)/W(s), softball W(s), swimming and diving M(s)/W(s), tennis M(s)/W(s), track and field M(s)/W(s), volleyball W(s). *Intramural sports:* badminton M/W, basketball M/W, bowling M/W, cheerleading M/W, cross-country running M/W, football M/W, golf M/W, lacrosse M, racquetball M/W, rugby M/W, soccer M/W, softball M/W, swimming and diving M/W, table tennis M/W, tennis M/W, ultimate Frisbee M/W, volleyball M/W, water polo M/W.
Standardized Tests *Required:* SAT or ACT (for admission).
Costs (2012–13) *Tuition:* state resident $8010 full-time; nonresident $12,018 full-time. Full-time tuition and fees vary according to course load and student level. Part-time tuition and fees vary according to course load and student level. No tuition increase for student's term of enrollment. *Required fees:* $1945 full-time. *Room and board:* $8820; room only: $5370. Room and board charges vary according to board plan, housing facility, and student level. *Waivers:* senior citizens and employees or children of employees.
Financial Aid Of all full-time matriculated undergraduates who enrolled in 2012, 7,694 applied for aid, 6,685 were judged to have need, 1,917 had their need fully met. 140 Federal Work-Study jobs (averaging $2736). 1,523 state and other part-time jobs (averaging $1117). In 2012, 247 non-need-based awards were made. *Average percent of need met:* 55%. *Average financial aid package:* $9985. *Average need-based loan:* $4327. *Average need-based gift aid:* $7737. *Average non-need-based aid:* $3205. *Average indebtedness upon graduation:* $24,993.
Applying *Options:* electronic application, deferred entrance. *Application fee:* $30. *Required:* high school transcript, minimum 2.5 GPA. *Application deadlines:* 5/15 (freshmen), rolling (transfers). *Notification:* continuous (freshmen), continuous (transfers).
Freshman Application Contact Western Illinois University, 1 University Circle, Macomb, IL 61455-1390. *Phone:* 309-298-3157. *Toll-free phone:* 877-742-5948.
Website: http://www.wiu.edu/.

Westwood College–Chicago Du Page

Woodridge, Illinois

Freshman Application Contact Westwood College–Chicago Du Page, 7155 Janes Avenue, Woodridge, IL 60517. *Phone:* 630-434-8250. *Toll-free phone:* 866-721-7647.
Website: http://www.westwood.edu/.

Westwood College–Chicago Loop Campus

Chicago, Illinois

Freshman Application Contact Westwood College–Chicago Loop Campus, 1 North State Street, Suite 1000, Chicago, IL 60602. *Phone:* 312-739-0890. *Toll-free phone:* 800-693-5411.
Website: http://www.westwood.edu/.

Westwood College–Chicago O'Hare Airport
Chicago, Illinois

Freshman Application Contact Westwood College–Chicago O'Hare Airport, 8501 West Higgins Road, Suite 100, Chicago, IL 60631. *Phone:* 773-380-6801. *Toll-free phone:* 866-235-2457.
Website: http://www.westwood.edu/.

Westwood College–Chicago River Oaks
Calumet City, Illinois

Freshman Application Contact Westwood College–Chicago River Oaks, 80 River Oaks Drive, Suite 111, Calumet City, IL 60409. *Phone:* 708-832-9760. *Toll-free phone:* 888-549-4960.
Website: http://www.westwood.edu/.

Wheaton College
Wheaton, Illinois

- **Independent nondenominational** comprehensive, founded 1860
- **Suburban** 80-acre campus with easy access to Chicago
- **Endowment** $312.9 million
- **Coed** 2,508 undergraduate students, 97% full-time, 51% women, 49% men
- **Very difficult** entrance level, 69% of applicants were admitted

Undergraduates 2,435 full-time, 73 part-time. Students come from 51 states and territories; 37 other countries; 74% are from out of state; 2% Black or African American, non-Hispanic/Latino; 4% Hispanic/Latino; 7% Asian, non-Hispanic/Latino; 0.1% Native Hawaiian or other Pacific Islander, non-Hispanic/Latino; 0.2% American Indian or Alaska Native, non-Hispanic/Latino; 3% Two or more races, non-Hispanic/Latino; 1% Race/ethnicity unknown; 2% international; 3% transferred in; 90% live on campus. *Retention:* 95% of full-time freshmen returned.

Freshmen *Admission:* 1,959 applied, 1,346 admitted, 598 enrolled. *Average high school GPA:* 3.71. *Test scores:* SAT critical reading scores over 500: 99%; SAT math scores over 500: 98%; SAT writing scores over 500: 98%; ACT scores over 18: 100%; SAT critical reading scores over 600: 78%; SAT math scores over 600: 80%; SAT writing scores over 600: 77%; ACT scores over 24: 93%; SAT critical reading scores over 700: 39%; SAT math scores over 700: 26%; SAT writing scores over 700: 28%; ACT scores over 30: 47%.

Faculty *Total:* 283, 70% full-time, 84% with terminal degrees. *Student/faculty ratio:* 12:1.

Academics *Calendar:* semesters. *Degrees:* bachelor's, master's, doctoral, and postbachelor's certificates. *Special study options:* advanced placement credit, double majors, independent study, internships, off-campus study, services for LD students, student-designed majors, study abroad, summer session for credit. *ROTC:* Army (b), Air Force (c). *Unusual degree programs:* 3-2 engineering with University of Illinois, Washington University in St. Louis, Illinois Institute of Technology, University of Minnesota; nursing with Emory University, Johns Hopkins University, Rush University, Vanderbilt University, Case Western Reserve University.

Computers on Campus 125 computers/terminals and 3,500 ports are available on campus for general student use. Students can access the following: campus intranet, computer help desk, free student e-mail accounts, online (class) grades, online (class) registration, online (class) schedules, financial information, degree requirements evaluation. Campuswide network is available. 100% of college-owned or -operated housing units are wired for high-speed Internet access. Wireless service is available via entire campus.

Student Life *Housing:* on-campus residence required through senior year. *Options:* coed, men-only, women-only, cooperative, disabled students. Campus housing is university owned. Freshman campus housing is guaranteed. *Activities and organizations:* drama/theater group, student-run newspaper, choral group, Discipleship small groups, Intramurals, Club Sports, Christian Service Council, Student Government. *Campus security:* 24-hour emergency response devices and patrols, student patrols, late-night transport/escort service, controlled dormitory access. *Student services:* health clinic, personal/psychological counseling.

Athletics Member NCAA. All Division III. *Intercollegiate sports:* baseball M, basketball M/W, cheerleading W(c), crew M(c)/W(c), cross-country running M/W, football M, golf M/W, ice hockey M(c), lacrosse M(c)/W(c), soccer M/W, softball W, swimming and diving M/W, tennis M/W, track and field M/W, volleyball M(c)/W, water polo M(c), wrestling M. *Intramural sports:* basketball M/W, golf M/W, soccer M/W, softball M, ultimate Frisbee M/W, volleyball M/W.

Standardized Tests *Required:* SAT or ACT (for admission).

Costs (2012–13) *Comprehensive fee:* $38,680 includes full-time tuition ($30,120) and room and board ($8560). Part-time tuition: $1255 per credit

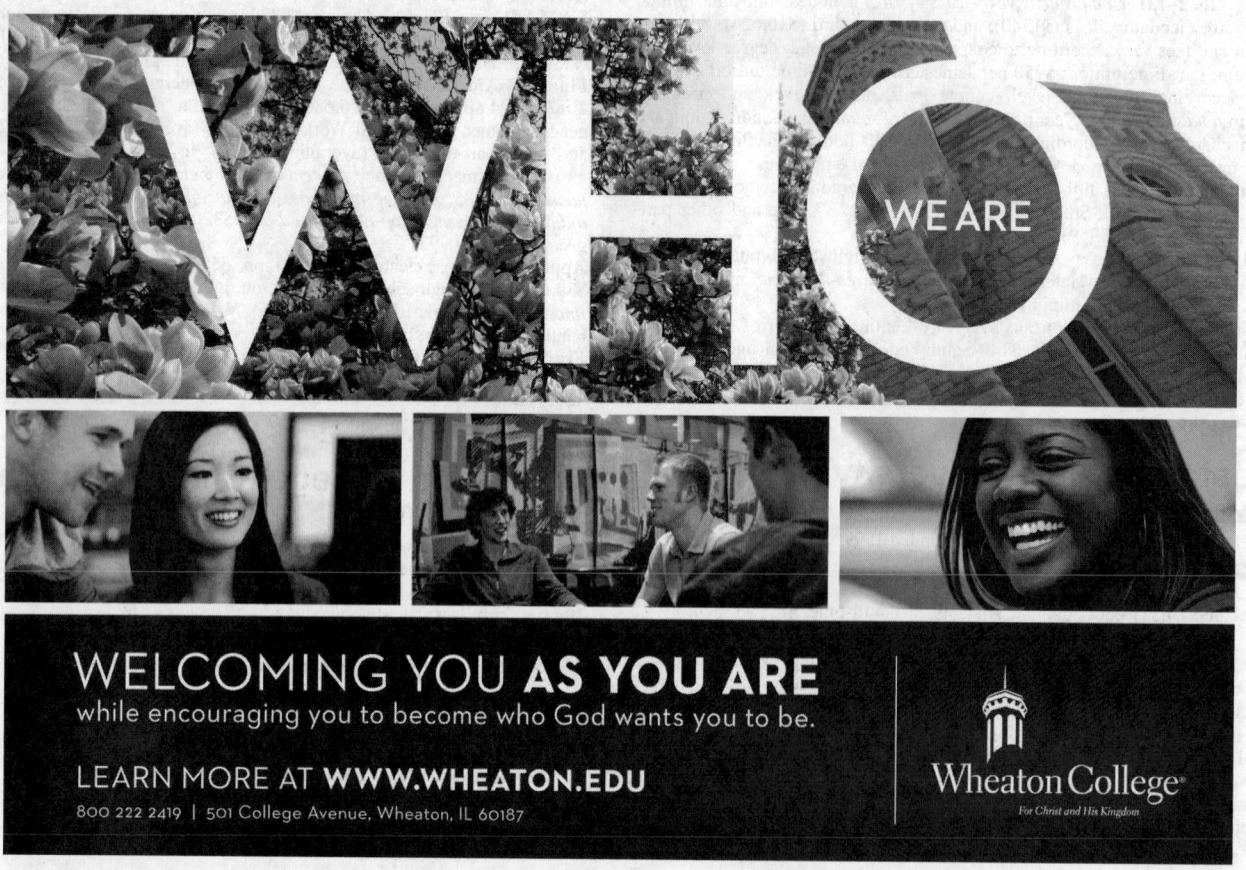

hour. Part-time tuition and fees vary according to course load. *College room only:* $5050. Room and board charges vary according to board plan and housing facility. *Payment plans:* installment, deferred payment.

Financial Aid Of all full-time matriculated undergraduates who enrolled in 2011, 1,638 applied for aid, 1,312 were judged to have need, 304 had their need fully met. 172 Federal Work-Study jobs (averaging $1331). In 2011, 329 non-need-based awards were made. *Average percent of need met:* 88%. *Average financial aid package:* $22,384. *Average need-based loan:* $4848. *Average need-based gift aid:* $18,382. *Average non-need-based aid:* $5068. *Average indebtedness upon graduation:* $24,067.

Applying *Options:* electronic application, early action, deferred entrance. *Application fee:* $50. *Required:* essay or personal statement, high school transcript, 2 letters of recommendation. *Recommended:* interview. *Application deadlines:* 1/10 (freshmen), 3/1 (transfers), 11/1 (early action). *Notification:* 4/1 (freshmen), 4/1 (transfers), 12/31 (early action).

Freshman Application Contact Ms. Shawn Leftwich, Director of Admissions, Wheaton College, 501 College Avenue, Wheaton, IL 60187-5593. *Phone:* 630-752-5011. *Toll-free phone:* 800-222-2419. *Fax:* 630-752-5285. *E-mail:* admissions@wheaton.edu. *Website:* http://www.wheaton.edu/.

See previous page for display ad and page 1646 for the College Close-Up.

INDIANA

Anderson University

Anderson, Indiana

- **Independent** comprehensive, founded 1917, affiliated with Church of God
- **Suburban** 163-acre campus with easy access to Indianapolis
- **Endowment** $21.7 million
- **Coed** 2,034 undergraduate students, 92% full-time, 59% women, 41% men
- **Moderately difficult** entrance level, 54% of applicants were admitted

Undergraduates 1,868 full-time, 166 part-time. Students come from 42 states and territories; 21 other countries; 25% are from out of state; 6% Black or African American, non-Hispanic/Latino; 3% Hispanic/Latino; 0.4% Asian, non-Hispanic/Latino; 0.1% Native Hawaiian or other Pacific Islander, non-Hispanic/Latino; 0.2% American Indian or Alaska Native, non-Hispanic/Latino; 0.6% Two or more races, non-Hispanic/Latino; 6% Race/ethnicity unknown; 3% international; 4% transferred in; 62% live on campus. *Retention:* 75% of full-time freshmen returned.

Freshmen *Admission:* 2,894 applied, 1,563 admitted, 519 enrolled. *Average high school GPA:* 3.4. *Test scores:* SAT critical reading scores over 500: 62%; SAT math scores over 500: 64%; ACT scores over 18: 95%; SAT critical reading scores over 600: 15%; SAT math scores over 600: 18%; ACT scores over 24: 50%; SAT critical reading scores over 700: 1%; SAT math scores over 700: 1%; ACT scores over 30: 3%.

Faculty *Total:* 274, 49% full-time, 34% with terminal degrees. *Student/faculty ratio:* 11:1.

Academics *Calendar:* semesters. *Degrees:* associate, bachelor's, master's, and doctoral. *Special study options:* academic remediation for entering students, accelerated degree program, adult/continuing education programs, advanced placement credit, distance learning, double majors, honors programs, independent study, internships, off-campus study, part-time degree program, services for LD students, student-designed majors, study abroad, summer session for credit. *Unusual degree programs:* 3-2 engineering with Purdue University.

Computers on Campus 338 computers/terminals are available on campus for general student use. Students can access the following: campus intranet, computer help desk, free student e-mail accounts, online (class) grades, online (class) registration, online (class) schedules, microcomputer software. Campuswide network is available. 100% of college-owned or -operated housing units are wired for high-speed Internet access. Wireless service is available via entire campus.

Student Life *Housing:* on-campus residence required through junior year. *Options:* men-only, women-only. Campus housing is university owned. Freshman campus housing is guaranteed. *Activities and organizations:* drama/theater group, student-run newspaper, radio station, choral group, Adult and Continuing Education Students Association, Multicultural Student Union, Campus Ministries. *Campus security:* 24-hour emergency response devices and patrols, student patrols, late-night transport/escort service, controlled dormitory access, 24-hour crime line. *Student services:* health clinic, personal/psychological counseling.

Athletics Member NCAA. All Division III. *Intercollegiate sports:* baseball M, basketball M/W, cross-country running M/W, football M, golf M/W, soccer M/ W, softball W, tennis M/W, track and field M/W, volleyball W. *Intramural sports:* badminton M/W, basketball M/W, bowling M/W, cheerleading M(c)/ W(c), rugby M(c), soccer M/W, softball M/W, tennis M/W, volleyball M/W.

Standardized Tests *Required:* SAT or ACT (for admission).

Costs (2013–14) *Comprehensive fee:* $35,310 includes full-time tuition ($26,120), mandatory fees ($80), and room and board ($9110). Part-time tuition: $1089 per semester hour. Part-time tuition and fees vary according to course load. *College room only:* $5830. Room and board charges vary according to board plan and housing facility. *Payment plan:* installment. *Waivers:* employees or children of employees.

Financial Aid Of all full-time matriculated undergraduates who enrolled in 2011, 1,752 applied for aid, 1,596 were judged to have need, 663 had their need fully met. 1,011 Federal Work-Study jobs (averaging $2611). In 2011, 306 non-need-based awards were made. *Average percent of need met:* 82%. *Average financial aid package:* $20,419. *Average need-based loan:* $4382. *Average need-based gift aid:* $14,057. *Average non-need-based aid:* $11,396. *Average indebtedness upon graduation:* $32,363.

Applying *Options:* electronic application, deferred entrance. *Application fee:* $25. *Required:* high school transcript, minimum 2.0 GPA, 2 letters of recommendation, lifestyle statement. *Required for some:* interview. *Recommended:* essay or personal statement. *Application deadlines:* 7/1 (freshmen), rolling (transfers). *Notification:* 9/1 (freshmen), continuous until 9/1 (transfers).

Freshman Application Contact Mr. Joe Davis, Director of Admissions, Anderson University, 1100 East 5th Street, Anderson, IN 46012-3495. *Phone:* 765-641-4076. *Toll-free phone:* 800-428-6414. *Fax:* 765-641-3851. *E-mail:* info@anderson.edu. *Website:* http://www.anderson.edu/.

The Art Institute of Indianapolis

Indianapolis, Indiana

- **Proprietary** 4-year, part of Education Management Corporation
- **Suburban** campus
- **Coed**

Academics *Degrees:* certificates, associate, and bachelor's.

Freshman Application Contact The Art Institute of Indianapolis, 3500 Depauw Boulevard, Suite 1010, Indianapolis, IN 46268. *Phone:* 317-613-4800. *Toll-free phone:* 866-441-9031. *Website:* http://www.artinstitutes.edu/indianapolis/.

See full-page ad on page 54 and page 1088 for the College Close-Up.

Ball State University

Muncie, Indiana

- **State-supported** university, founded 1918
- **Suburban** 1140-acre campus with easy access to Indianapolis
- **Endowment** $165.5 million
- **Coed** 16,652 undergraduate students, 94% full-time, 57% women, 43% men
- **Moderately difficult** entrance level, 61% of applicants were admitted

Undergraduates 15,597 full-time, 1,055 part-time. Students come from 50 states and territories; 44 other countries; 10% are from out of state; 6% Black or African American, non-Hispanic/Latino; 3% Hispanic/Latino; 0.8% Asian, non-Hispanic/Latino; 0.1% Native Hawaiian or other Pacific Islander, non-Hispanic/Latino; 0.1% American Indian or Alaska Native, non-Hispanic/Latino; 2% Two or more races, non-Hispanic/Latino; 2% Race/ethnicity unknown; 2% international; 4% transferred in; 42% live on campus. *Retention:* 77% of full-time freshmen returned.

Freshmen *Admission:* 16,896 applied, 10,333 admitted, 3,556 enrolled. *Average high school GPA:* 3.35. *Test scores:* SAT critical reading scores over 500: 67%; SAT math scores over 500: 68%; SAT writing scores over 500: 59%; ACT scores over 18: 98%; SAT critical reading scores over 600: 19%; SAT math scores over 600: 21%; SAT writing scores over 600: 15%; ACT scores over 24: 25%; SAT critical reading scores over 700: 2%; SAT math scores over 700: 2%; SAT writing scores over 700: 1%; ACT scores over 30: 3%.

Faculty *Total:* 1,140, 83% full-time, 67% with terminal degrees. *Student/faculty ratio:* 16:1.

Academics *Calendar:* semesters. *Degrees:* associate, bachelor's, master's, doctoral, post-master's, and postbachelor's certificates. *Special study options:* accelerated degree program, adult/continuing education programs, advanced placement credit, cooperative education, distance learning, double majors, English as a second language, external degree program, freshman honors college, honors programs, independent study, internships, part-time degree program, services for LD students, student-designed majors, study abroad, summer session for credit. *ROTC:* Army (b). *Unusual degree programs:* 3-2 engineering with Purdue University, Tri-State University.

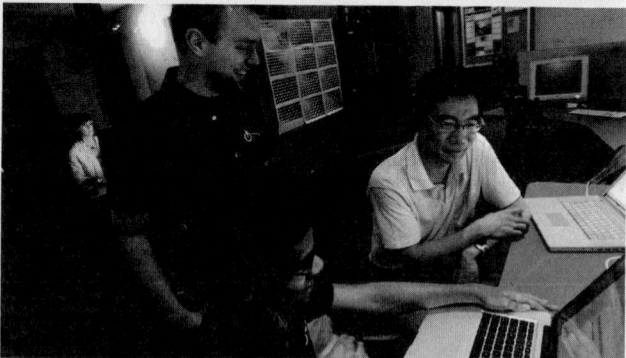

Ball State welcomes students from around the world.

Collaborate with peers and expert faculty in a welcoming, immersive environment at **Ball State University**, one of the top schools in the Midwest region of the United States.

About 700 international students from 60 countries enroll each year in our more than 180 undergraduate and 120 graduate programs.

Our Rinker Center for International Programs provides:

- **personal attention** in advising and mentoring
- lasting bonds through our **friendship family program**
- active **student organizations** that connect you with peers
- **knowledgeable staff** to help you navigate decisions about transportation and documentation.

BALL STATE
UNIVERSITY
EDUCATION REDEFINED®
www.bsu.edu/international

Computers on Campus 888 computers/terminals and 21,135 ports are available on campus for general student use. Students can access the following: campus intranet, computer help desk, free student e-mail accounts, online (class) grades, online (class) registration, online (class) schedules, room reservations, testing and test results, manage and pay tuition, order/buy textbooks, request room repairs, order transcripts, manage meal plan, manage and prepay long distance service, undergraduate degree progress report. Campuswide network is available. 100% of college-owned or -operated housing units are wired for high-speed Internet access. Wireless service is available via entire campus.

Student Life *Housing:* on-campus residence required for freshman year. *Options:* coed, men-only, women-only, disabled students. Campus housing is university owned. Freshman campus housing is guaranteed. *Activities and organizations:* drama/theater group, student-run newspaper, radio and television station, choral group, marching band, Epsilon Sigma Alpha International, WCRD- Student Radio Station, Golden Key Honor Society, Excellence in Leadership (EIL), Student Voluntary Services, national fraternities, national sororities. *Campus security:* 24-hour emergency response devices and patrols, late-night transport/escort service, controlled dormitory access. *Student services:* health clinic, personal/psychological counseling, women's center, legal services.

Athletics Member NCAA. All Division I except football (Division I-A). *Intercollegiate sports:* baseball M(s)/W(c), basketball M(s)/W(s), bowling M(c)/W(c), cheerleading M/W, cross-country running W(s), equestrian sports M(c)/W(c), fencing M(c)/W(c), field hockey W(s), golf M(s)/W(s), gymnastics W(s), lacrosse M(c)/W(c), racquetball M(c)/W(c), rock climbing M(c)/W(c), rugby M(c)/W(c), soccer M(c)/W(s), softball W(s), swimming and diving M(s)/W(s), tennis M(s)/W(s), track and field W(s), ultimate Frisbee M(c)/W(c), volleyball M(s)/W(s), water polo M(c)/W(c), wrestling M(c). *Intramural sports:* badminton M/W, basketball M/W, bowling M/W, golf M/W, racquetball M/W, soccer M/W, softball M/W, swimming and diving M/W, table tennis M/W, tennis M/W, track and field M/W, ultimate Frisbee M/W, volleyball M/W.

Standardized Tests *Required for some:* SAT or ACT (for admission).

Costs (2013–14) *Tuition:* state resident $8318 full-time, $270 per credit hour part-time; nonresident $22,988 full-time, $906 per credit hour part-time. Full-time tuition and fees vary according to course load, program, and reciprocity agreements. Part-time tuition and fees vary according to course load and reciprocity agreements. *Required fees:* $662 full-time. *Room and board:* $8870. Room and board charges vary according to board plan and housing facility. *Payment plan:* installment. *Waivers:* senior citizens and employees or children of employees.

Financial Aid Of all full-time matriculated undergraduates who enrolled in 2012, 13,112 applied for aid, 10,327 were judged to have need, 3,185 had their need fully met. 512 Federal Work-Study jobs (averaging $2253). In 2012, 1329 non-need-based awards were made. *Average percent of need met:* 65%. *Average financial aid package:* $10,255. *Average need-based loan:* $4300. *Average need-based gift aid:* $6027. *Average non-need-based aid:* $7166. *Average indebtedness upon graduation:* $27,373.

Applying *Options:* electronic application, deferred entrance. *Application fee:* $55. *Required:* high school transcript. *Required for some:* essay or personal statement. *Application deadlines:* 8/15 (freshmen), rolling (transfers). *Notification:* continuous (freshmen), continuous (transfers).

Freshman Application Contact Ball State University, 2000 West University Avenue, Muncie, IN 47306-1099. *Phone:* 765-285-8300. *Toll-free phone:* 800-482-4BSU.

Website: http://www.bsu.edu/.

See this page for display ad and page 1144 for the College Close-Up.

Bethel College
Mishawaka, Indiana

- **Independent** comprehensive, founded 1947, affiliated with Missionary Church
- **Suburban** 80-acre campus
- **Endowment** $8.2 million
- **Coed** 1,801 undergraduate students, 79% full-time, 67% women, 33% men
- **Minimally difficult** entrance level, 73% of applicants were admitted

Undergraduates 1,416 full-time, 385 part-time. Students come from 31 states and territories; 15 other countries; 24% are from out of state; 12% Black or African American, non-Hispanic/Latino; 5% Hispanic/Latino; 0.5% Asian, non-Hispanic/Latino; 0.1% Native Hawaiian or other Pacific Islander, non-Hispanic/Latino; 0.3% American Indian or Alaska Native, non-Hispanic/Latino; 2% Two or more races, non-Hispanic/Latino; 2% international; 13% transferred in; 45% live on campus. *Retention:* 75% of full-time freshmen returned.

Freshmen *Admission:* 956 applied, 702 admitted, 233 enrolled. *Average high school GPA:* 3.42. *Test scores:* SAT critical reading scores over 500: 59%; SAT math scores over 500: 60%; SAT writing scores over 500: 48%; ACT scores over 18: 89%; SAT critical reading scores over 600: 20%; SAT math scores over 600: 24%; SAT writing scores over 600: 13%; ACT scores over 24: 49%; SAT critical reading scores over 700: 2%; SAT math scores over 700: 2%; SAT writing scores over 700: 1%; ACT scores over 30: 8%.

Faculty *Total:* 221, 37% full-time, 32% with terminal degrees. *Student/faculty ratio:* 13:1.

Academics *Calendar:* semesters. *Degrees:* associate, bachelor's, and master's. *Special study options:* academic remediation for entering students, accelerated degree program, adult/continuing education programs, advanced placement credit, distance learning, double majors, honors programs, independent study, internships, off-campus study, part-time degree program, services for LD students, student-designed majors, study abroad, summer session for credit. *ROTC:* Army (c), Air Force (c). *Unusual degree programs:* 3-2 engineering with University of Notre Dame, Trine University.

Computers on Campus 160 computers/terminals are available on campus for general student use. Students can access the following: computer help desk, free student e-mail accounts, online (class) grades, online (class) registration, online (class) schedules. Campuswide network is available. 100% of college-owned or -operated housing units are wired for high-speed Internet access. Wireless service is available via entire campus.

Student Life *Housing:* on-campus residence required through sophomore year. *Options:* men-only, women-only. Campus housing is university owned. *Activities and organizations:* drama/theater group, student-run newspaper, radio station, choral group, International Student Fellowship, Students for Life, Student Council, Spiritual Life Team. *Campus security:* 24-hour emergency response devices and patrols, late-night transport/escort service, controlled dormitory access. *Student services:* health clinic, personal/psychological counseling.

Athletics Member NAIA, NCCAA. *Intercollegiate sports:* baseball M(s), basketball M(s)/W(s), cheerleading M(s)/W(s), cross-country running M(s)/W(s), golf M(s)/W(s), soccer M(s)/W(s), softball W(s), tennis M(s)/W(s), track and field M(s)/W(s), volleyball W(s). *Intramural sports:* badminton M/W, basketball M/W, football M/W, soccer M/W, softball M/W, table tennis M/W, tennis M/W, ultimate Frisbee M/W, volleyball M/W.

Standardized Tests *Required:* SAT or ACT (for admission).

Costs (2013–14) *Comprehensive fee:* $32,430 includes full-time tuition ($24,620), mandatory fees ($350), and room and board ($7460). Full-time tuition and fees vary according to program. Part-time tuition: $782 per credit. Part-time tuition and fees vary according to program. *College room only:*

$3560. Room and board charges vary according to board plan and housing facility. *Payment plan:* installment. *Waivers:* employees or children of employees.

Financial Aid Of all full-time matriculated undergraduates who enrolled in 2012, 1,332 applied for aid, 1,239 were judged to have need, 179 had their need fully met. 53 Federal Work-Study jobs (averaging $2536). In 2012, 131 non-need-based awards were made. *Average percent of need met:* 66%. *Average financial aid package:* $16,405. *Average need-based loan:* $4473. *Average need-based gift aid:* $7754. *Average non-need-based aid:* $8067. *Average indebtedness upon graduation:* $24,207. *Financial aid deadline:* 3/10.

Applying *Options:* electronic application, early admission, deferred entrance. *Application fee:* $25. *Required:* high school transcript, minimum 2.0 GPA, 1 letter of recommendation. *Recommended:* essay or personal statement, minimum 2.5 GPA, interview. *Application deadlines:* 8/15 (freshmen), 8/15 (transfers). *Notification:* continuous (freshmen), continuous (transfers).

Freshman Application Contact Ms. Stephanie Hochstetler, Associate Director of Admission, Bethel College, 1001 Bethel Circle, Mishawaka, IN 46545. *Phone:* 574-807-7600. *Toll-free phone:* 800-422-4101. *Fax:* 574-807-7650. *E-mail:* admissions@bethelcollege.edu. *Website:* http://www.bethelcollege.edu/.

Brown Mackie College–Fort Wayne
Fort Wayne, Indiana

Freshman Application Contact Brown Mackie College–Fort Wayne, 3000 East Coliseum Boulevard, Fort Wayne, IN 46805. *Phone:* 260-484-4400. *Toll-free phone:* 866-433-2289.
Website: http://www.brownmackie.edu/fortwayne/.

See below for display ad and page 1182 for the College Close-Up.

Brown Mackie College–Indianapolis
Indianapolis, Indiana

Freshman Application Contact Brown Mackie College–Indianapolis, 1200 North Meridian Street, Suite 100, Indianapolis, IN 46204. *Phone:* 317-554-8301. *Toll-free phone:* 866-255-0279.
Website: http://www.brownmackie.edu/indianapolis/.

See below for display ad and page 1186 for the College Close-Up.

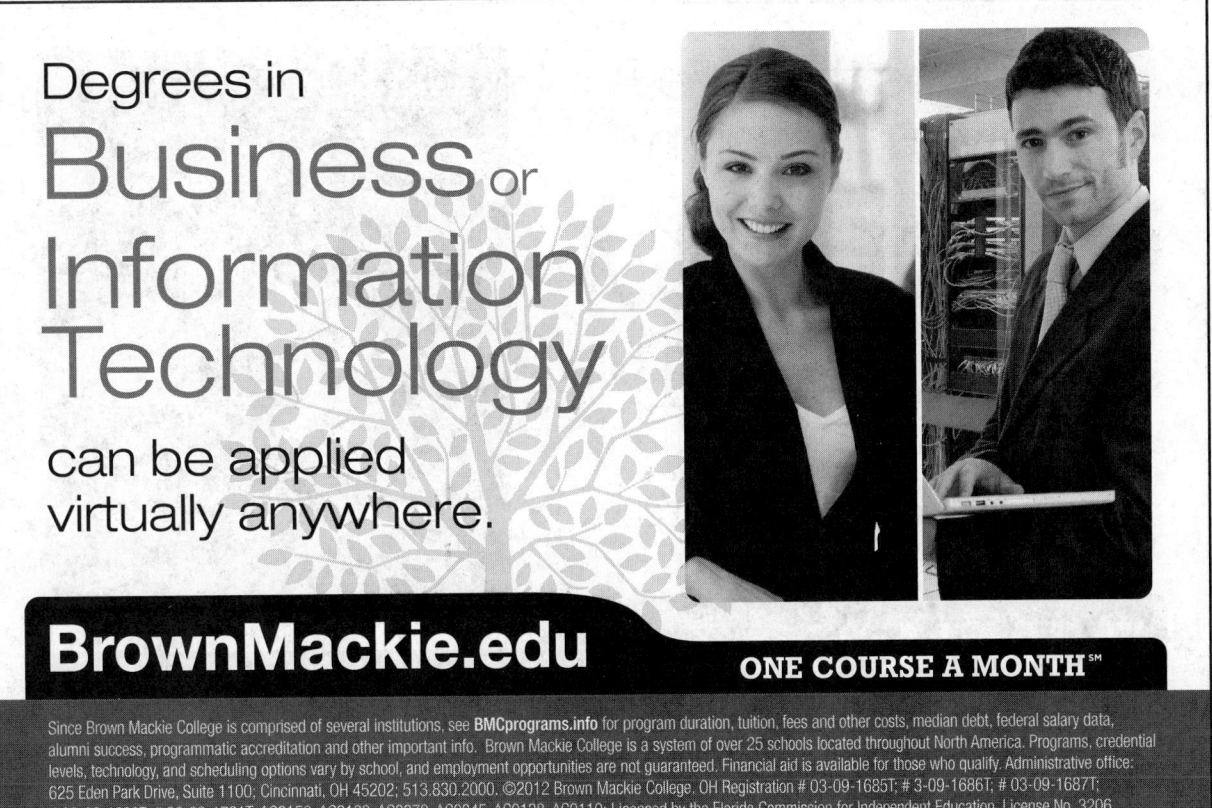

Brown Mackie College–Merrillville

Merrillville, Indiana

Freshman Application Contact Brown Mackie College–Merrillville, 1000 East 80th Place, Suite 205S, Merrillville, IN 46410. *Phone:* 219-769-3321. *Toll-free phone:* 800-258-3321.
Website: http://www.brownmackie.edu/merrillville/.

See below for display ad and page 1192 for the College Close-Up.

Brown Mackie College–Michigan City

Michigan City, Indiana

Freshman Application Contact Brown Mackie College–Michigan City, 325 East US Highway 20, Michigan City, IN 46360. *Phone:* 219-877-3100. *Toll-free phone:* 800-519-2416.
Website: http://www.brownmackie.edu/michigancity/.

See below for display ad and page 1196 for the College Close-Up.

Brown Mackie College–South Bend

South Bend, Indiana

Freshman Application Contact Brown Mackie College–South Bend, 3454 Douglas Road, South Bend, IN 46635. *Phone:* 574-237-0774. *Toll-free phone:* 800-743-2447.
Website: http://www.brownmackie.edu/southbend/.

See below for display ad and page 1210 for the College Close-Up.

Butler University

Indianapolis, Indiana

- **Independent** comprehensive, founded 1855
- **Urban** 290-acre campus with easy access to Indianapolis
- **Endowment** $146.0 million
- **Coed** 4,020 undergraduate students, 98% full-time, 60% women, 40% men
- **Very difficult** entrance level, 66% of applicants were admitted

Undergraduates 3,943 full-time, 77 part-time. Students come from 45 states and territories; 49 other countries; 48% are from out of state; 3% Black or Afri-can American, non-Hispanic/Latino; 3% Hispanic/Latino; 3% Asian, non-Hispanic/Latino; 0.4% American Indian or Alaska Native, non-Hispanic/Latino; 0.7% Two or more races, non-Hispanic/Latino; 4% Race/ethnicity unknown; 2% international; 3% transferred in; 69% live on campus. *Retention:* 91% of full-time freshmen returned.

Freshmen *Admission:* 9,682 applied, 6,379 admitted, 1,101 enrolled. *Average high school GPA:* 3.79. *Test scores:* SAT critical reading scores over 500: 86%; SAT math scores over 500: 91%; SAT writing scores over 500: 82%; ACT scores over 18: 101%; SAT critical reading scores over 600: 40%; SAT math scores over 600: 52%; SAT writing scores over 600: 38%; ACT scores over 24: 88%; SAT critical reading scores over 700: 7%; SAT math scores over 700: 7%; SAT writing scores over 700: 4%; ACT scores over 30: 29%.

Faculty *Total:* 480, 71% full-time. *Student/faculty ratio:* 11:1.

Academics *Calendar:* semesters. *Degrees:* associate, bachelor's, master's, and doctoral. *Special study options:* adult/continuing education programs, advanced placement credit, cooperative education, double majors, honors programs, independent study, internships, off-campus study, part-time degree program, services for LD students, student-designed majors, study abroad, summer session for credit. *ROTC:* Army (b), Air Force (c). *Unusual degree programs:* 3-2 engineering with Indiana University-Purdue University Indianapolis.

Computers on Campus 450 computers/terminals are available on campus for general student use. Students can access the following: campus intranet, computer help desk, free student e-mail accounts, online (class) grades, online (class) registration, online (class) schedules. Campuswide network is available. 100% of college-owned or -operated housing units are wired for high-speed Internet access. Wireless service is available via entire campus.

Student Life *Housing:* on-campus residence required through junior year. *Options:* coed, women-only. Campus housing is university owned. Freshman campus housing is guaranteed. *Activities and organizations:* drama/theater group, student-run newspaper, television station, choral group, marching band, Dawg Pound, Student Government Association, Academic Service Honoraries, Alpha Phi Omega, Mortar Board, national fraternities, national sororities. *Campus security:* 24-hour emergency response devices and patrols, late-night transport/escort service, controlled dormitory access. *Student services:* health clinic, personal/psychological counseling.

Athletics Member NCAA. All Division I except football (Division III). *Intercollegiate sports:* baseball M(s), basketball M(s)/W(s), crew M(c)/W(c), cross-country running M(s)/W(s), football M, golf M(s)/W(s), ice hockey M(c), rugby M(c), soccer M(s)/W(s), softball W(s), swimming and diving W, tennis M(s)/W(s), track and field M/W, volleyball W(s). *Intramural sports:* badminton M/W, baseball M, basketball M/W, bowling M/W, football M, soccer M/W, softball M/W, swimming and diving M/W, table tennis M/W, tennis M/W, track and field M/W, volleyball M/W, weight lifting M/W.

Standardized Tests *Required:* SAT or ACT (for admission).

Costs (2013–14) *One-time required fee:* $288. *Comprehensive fee:* $44,248 includes full-time tuition ($32,280), mandatory fees ($858), and room and board ($11,110). Full-time tuition and fees vary according to course load, degree level, and program. Part-time tuition and fees vary according to course load, degree level, and program. *College room only:* $5370. Room and board charges vary according to housing facility. *Payment plan:* installment. *Waivers:* employees or children of employees.

Financial Aid Of all full-time matriculated undergraduates who enrolled in 2012, 3,793 applied for aid, 2,782 were judged to have need, 439 had their need fully met. 287 Federal Work-Study jobs (averaging $975). In 2012, 924 non-need-based awards were made. *Average percent of need met:* 72%. *Average financial aid package:* $22,467. *Average need-based loan:* $4861. *Average need-based gift aid:* $18,179. *Average non-need-based aid:* $11,459. *Average indebtedness upon graduation:* $35,210.

Applying *Options:* electronic application, early action, deferred entrance. *Application fee:* $35. *Required:* essay or personal statement, high school transcript, 1 letter of recommendation. *Required for some:* Audition/interview/portfolio required for applicants to JCFA. Four years of math and science STRONGLY recommended for students interested in COPHS majors and natural sciences. *Recommended:* 1 letter of recommendation. *Application deadlines:* rolling (freshmen), rolling (out-of-state freshmen), 8/15 (transfers), 11/1 (early action). *Notification:* continuous (freshmen), continuous (out-of-state freshmen), continuous (transfers), 12/15 (early action).

Freshman Application Contact Mr. Scott Ham, Director of Admissions, Butler University, 4600 Sunset Avenue, Indianapolis, IN 46208-3485. *Phone:* 317-940-8100. *Toll-free phone:* 888-940-8100. *Fax:* 317-940-8150. *E-mail:* admission@butler.edu.

Website: http://www.butler.edu/.

Calumet College of Saint Joseph

Whiting, Indiana

- **Independent Roman Catholic** comprehensive, founded 1951
- **Urban** 25-acre campus with easy access to Chicago
- **Endowment** $3.6 million
- **Coed** 867 undergraduate students, 51% full-time, 46% women, 54% men
- **Noncompetitive** entrance level, 33% of applicants were admitted

Undergraduates 438 full-time, 429 part-time. Students come from 2 states and territories; 1% are from out of state; 26% Black or African American, non-Hispanic/Latino; 31% Hispanic/Latino; 1% Asian, non-Hispanic/Latino; 0.6% American Indian or Alaska Native, non-Hispanic/Latino; 0.1% Two or more races, non-Hispanic/Latino; 0.7% international; 14% transferred in. *Retention:* 56% of full-time freshmen returned.

Freshmen *Admission:* 553 applied, 181 admitted, 134 enrolled. *Average high school GPA:* 2.55. *Test scores:* SAT critical reading scores over 500: 9%; SAT math scores over 500: 16%; SAT writing scores over 500: 3%; ACT scores over 18: 39%; SAT critical reading scores over 600: 2%; SAT math scores over 600: 2%; ACT scores over 24: 2%.

Faculty *Total:* 130, 25% full-time, 38% with terminal degrees. *Student/faculty ratio:* 10:1.

Academics *Calendar:* semesters. *Degrees:* certificates, associate, bachelor's, and master's. *Special study options:* academic remediation for entering students, accelerated degree program, adult/continuing education programs, advanced placement credit, cooperative education, distance learning, double majors, external degree program, honors programs, independent study, internships, part-time degree program, services for LD students, summer session for credit.

Computers on Campus 161 computers/terminals are available on campus for general student use. Students can access the following: computer help desk, free student e-mail accounts, online (class) grades, online (class) registration, online (class) schedules. Campuswide network is available. Wireless service is available via classrooms, libraries, student centers.

Student Life *Housing:* college housing not available. *Activities and organizations:* drama/theater group, student-run newspaper, Student Government, Los Amigos Hispanic Club, Criminal Justice Club, Drama Club, GIVE. *Campus security:* day and night security, emergency alert system. *Student services:* personal/psychological counseling.

Athletics Member NAIA. *Intercollegiate sports:* baseball M(s), basketball M(s)/W(s), bowling M(s)/W(s), cross-country running M(s)/W(s), golf M(s), soccer M(s)/W(s), softball W(s), tennis M(s)/W(s), track and field M(s)/W(s), volleyball W(s), wrestling M(s).

Standardized Tests *Required for some:* ACT COMPASS. *Recommended:* SAT or ACT (for admission).

Costs (2013–14) *Tuition:* $15,420 full-time, $490 per credit part-time. Full-time tuition and fees vary according to course load and program. Part-time tuition and fees vary according to course load and program. *Required fees:* $200 full-time, $100 per term part-time. *Payment plan:* deferred payment. *Waivers:* children of alumni, senior citizens, and employees or children of employees.

Financial Aid Of all full-time matriculated undergraduates who enrolled in 2011, 444 applied for aid, 408 were judged to have need, 53 had their need fully met. 29 Federal Work-Study jobs (averaging $2207). In 2011, 15 non-need-based awards were made. *Average percent of need met:* 67%. *Average financial aid package:* $12,760. *Average need-based loan:* $2094. *Average need-based gift aid:* $8071. *Average non-need-based aid:* $2962. *Average indebtedness upon graduation:* $23,000.

Applying *Options:* electronic application, deferred entrance. *Required:* high school transcript. *Required for some:* essay or personal statement, interview. *Recommended:* minimum 2.0 GPA. *Application deadlines:* rolling (freshmen), rolling (out-of-state freshmen), rolling (transfers). *Notification:* continuous (transfers).

Freshman Application Contact Miss Rebecca Leevey, Assistant Director of Recruitment and Enrollment, Calumet College of Saint Joseph, 2400 New York Avenue, Whiting, IN 46394. *Phone:* 219-473-4218. *Toll-free phone:* 877-700-9100. *Fax:* 219-473-4336. *E-mail:* admissions@ccsj.edu.

Website: http://www.ccsj.edu/.

Chamberlain College of Nursing

Indianapolis, Indiana

- **Proprietary** 4-year
- **Coed** 124 undergraduate students, 53% full-time, 83% women, 17% men

Undergraduates 66 full-time, 58 part-time. 30% Black or African American, non-Hispanic/Latino; 3% Hispanic/Latino; 2% Asian, non-Hispanic/Latino; 0.8% American Indian or Alaska Native, non-Hispanic/Latino; 12% Race/ethnicity unknown; 2% international; 93% transferred in.

Freshmen *Admission:* 2 enrolled.

Faculty *Total:* 3, 100% full-time. *Student/faculty ratio:* 28:1.

Academics *Degree:* bachelor's.

Standardized Tests *Required:* SAT or ACT (for admission).

Costs (2013–14) *Tuition:* $16,360 full-time, $665 per credit hour part-time. *Required fees:* $600 full-time.

Applying *Application fee:* $95.

Freshman Application Contact Chamberlain College of Nursing, 9100 Keystone Crossing, Suite 600, Indianapolis, IN 46240.

Website: http://www.chamberlain.edu/.

Crossroads Bible College

Indianapolis, Indiana

- **Independent Baptist** 4-year, founded 1980
- **Urban** 6-acre campus with easy access to Indianapolis
- **Coed**
- **Noncompetitive** entrance level

Faculty *Student/faculty ratio:* 7:1.

Academics *Calendar:* semesters. *Degrees:* certificates, associate, and bachelor's.

Student Life *Campus security:* 24-hour emergency response devices, student patrols, late-night transport/escort service.

Costs (2012–13) *Tuition:* $9480 full-time, $395 per credit hour part-time. *Required fees:* $500 full-time, $250 per term part-time. *Room only:* $3400.

Financial Aid Of all full-time matriculated undergraduates who enrolled in 2010, 133 applied for aid, 133 were judged to have need, 130 had their need fully met. 14 Federal Work-Study jobs (averaging $1509). *Average percent of need met:* 98. *Average financial aid package:* $7945. *Average need-based loan:* $5500. *Average need-based gift aid:* $5662. *Average indebtedness upon graduation:* $9618. *Financial aid deadline:* 6/30.

Applying *Options:* electronic application, deferred entrance. *Application fee:* $10. *Required:* essay or personal statement, high school transcript. *Required for some:* interview.

Freshman Application Contact Michael Garrison, Admissions Counselor, Crossroads Bible College, 601 North Shortridge Road, Indianapolis, IN 46219. *Phone:* 317-789-8266. *Toll-free phone:* 800-822-3119. *E-mail:* admissions@crossroads.edu.

Website: http://www.crossroads.edu/.

DePauw University

Greencastle, Indiana

- **Independent** 4-year, founded 1837, affiliated with United Methodist Church
- **Small-town** 655-acre campus with easy access to Indianapolis
- **Coed** 2,336 undergraduate students, 99% full-time, 55% women, 45% men
- **Moderately difficult** entrance level, 63% of applicants were admitted

Undergraduates 2,307 full-time, 29 part-time. 58% are from out of state; 6% Black or African American, non-Hispanic/Latino; 4% Hispanic/Latino; 3% Asian, non-Hispanic/Latino; 0.3% American Indian or Alaska Native, non-Hispanic/Latino; 4% Two or more races, non-Hispanic/Latino; 3% Race/ethnicity unknown; 11% international; 0.9% transferred in; 95% live on campus. *Retention:* 89% of full-time freshmen returned.

Freshmen *Admission:* 4,835 applied, 3,023 admitted, 578 enrolled. *Average high school GPA:* 3.51. *Test scores:* SAT critical reading scores over 500: 87%; SAT math scores over 500: 91%; SAT writing scores over 500: 86%; ACT scores over 18: 100%; SAT critical reading scores over 600: 49%; SAT math scores over 600: 60%; SAT writing scores over 600: 49%; ACT scores over 24: 83%; SAT critical reading scores over 700: 10%; SAT math scores over 700: 21%; SAT writing scores over 700: 9%; ACT scores over 30: 25%.

Faculty *Total:* 267, 85% full-time, 92% with terminal degrees. *Student/faculty ratio:* 10:1.

Academics *Calendar:* 4-1-4. *Degree:* bachelor's. *Special study options:* part-time degree program. *ROTC:* Army (c), Air Force (c). *Unusual degree programs:* 3-2 engineering with Columbia University, Washington University in St. Louis.

Computers on Campus Students can access the following: online (class) registration. Campuswide network is available.

Student Life *Housing:* on-campus residence required through senior year. *Options:* coed, disabled students. Campus housing is university owned. Freshman campus housing is guaranteed. *Activities and organizations:* drama/theater group, student-run newspaper, radio and television station, choral group, national fraternities, national sororities. *Campus security:* 24-hour emergency response devices and patrols, student patrols, late-night transport/escort service, controlled dormitory access. *Student services:* health clinic, personal/psychological counseling, women's center.

Athletics Member NCAA. All Division III. *Intercollegiate sports:* baseball M, basketball M/W, cheerleading M(c)/W(c), crew M(c)/W(c), cross-country running M/W, field hockey W, football M, golf M/W, rugby M(c), soccer M/W, softball W, swimming and diving M/W, tennis M/W, track and field M/W, volleyball W. *Intramural sports:* badminton M/W, basketball M/W, bowling M/W, football M/W, golf M, racquetball M/W, soccer M/W, softball M/W, table tennis M/W, tennis M/W, ultimate Frisbee M/W, volleyball M/W.

Standardized Tests *Required:* SAT or ACT (for admission).

Costs (2013–14) *Comprehensive fee:* $48,950 includes full-time tuition ($38,280), mandatory fees ($470), and room and board ($10,200). Part-time tuition: $1196 per credit hour. *Room and board:* Room and board charges vary according to board plan. *Payment plan:* installment. *Waivers:* employees or children of employees.

Financial Aid Of all full-time matriculated undergraduates who enrolled in 2011, 1,509 applied for aid, 1,318 were judged to have need, 377 had their need fully met. 518 Federal Work-Study jobs (averaging $1658). 260 state and other part-time jobs (averaging $2800). In 2011, 948 non-need-based awards were made. *Average percent of need met:* 87%. *Average financial aid package:* $29,804. *Average need-based loan:* $4284. *Average need-based gift aid:* $25,718. *Average non-need-based aid:* $16,638. *Average indebtedness upon graduation:* $22,755. *Financial aid deadline:* 3/1.

Applying *Options:* electronic application, early admission, early decision, early action, deferred entrance. *Application fee:* $40. *Required:* essay or personal statement, high school transcript, 1 letter of recommendation. *Recommended:* interview. *Application deadlines:* 2/1 (freshmen), 3/1 (transfers), 12/1 (early action). *Early decision deadline:* 11/1. *Notification:* 4/1 (transfers), 1/1 (early decision), 1/31 (early action).

Freshman Application Contact Earl Macam, Director of Admission, DePauw University, 313 South Locust Street, Greencastle, IN 46135. *Phone:* 765-658-4006. *Toll-free phone:* 800-447-2495. *Fax:* 765-658-4007. *E-mail:* emacam@depauw.edu.

Website: http://www.depauw.edu/.

DeVry University

Indianapolis, Indiana

Freshman Application Contact DeVry University, 9100 Keystone Crossing, Suite 350, Indianapolis, IN 46240-2158. *Toll-free phone:* 866-338-7941.

Website: http://www.devry.edu/.

DeVry University

Merrillville, Indiana

Admissions Office Contact DeVry University, Twin Towers, 1000 East 80th Place, Suite 222 Mall, Merrillville, IN 46410-5673. *Toll-free phone:* 866-338-7941.

Website: http://www.devry.edu/.

Earlham College

Richmond, Indiana

- **Independent** comprehensive, founded 1847, affiliated with Society of Friends
- **Small-town** 800-acre campus with easy access to Cincinnati, Indianapolis, Dayton
- **Endowment** $289.4 million
- **Coed** 1,087 undergraduate students, 98% full-time, 56% women, 44% men
- **Very difficult** entrance level, 75% of applicants were admitted

Undergraduates 1,065 full-time, 22 part-time. Students come from 43 states and territories; 76 other countries; 81% are from out of state; 10% Black or African American, non-Hispanic/Latino; 6% Hispanic/Latino; 2% Asian, non-Hispanic/Latino; 0.3% Native Hawaiian or other Pacific Islander, non-Hispanic/Latino; 0.7% American Indian or Alaska Native, non-Hispanic/Latino; 2% Two or more races, non-Hispanic/Latino; 18% Race/ethnicity unknown; 18% international; 1% transferred in; 96% live on campus. *Retention:* 83% of full-time freshmen returned.

Freshmen *Admission:* 1,408 applied, 1,055 admitted, 286 enrolled. *Average high school GPA:* 3.4. *Test scores:* SAT critical reading scores over 500: 81%; SAT math scores over 500: 84%; SAT writing scores over 500: 81%; ACT scores over 18: 96%; SAT critical reading scores over 600: 52%; SAT math scores over 600: 45%; SAT writing scores over 600: 46%; ACT scores over 24: 65%; SAT critical reading scores over 700: 23%; SAT math scores over 700: 11%; SAT writing scores over 700: 7%; ACT scores over 30: 25%.

Faculty *Total:* 120, 87% full-time, 91% with terminal degrees. *Student/faculty ratio:* 10:1.

Academics *Calendar:* semesters. *Degrees:* bachelor's and master's. *Special study options:* accelerated degree program, advanced placement credit, double majors, English as a second language, independent study, internships, off-campus study, services for LD students, student-designed majors, study abroad. *Unusual degree programs:* 3-2 engineering with Columbia University, University of Michigan, Rensselaer Polytechnic Institute.

Computers on Campus Students can access the following: campus intranet, computer help desk, free student e-mail accounts, online (class) grades, online (class) registration, online (class) schedules. Campuswide network is available. 100% of college-owned or -operated housing units are wired for high-speed Internet access. Wireless service is available via entire campus.

Student Life *Housing:* on-campus residence required through senior year. *Options:* coed, men-only, women-only, disabled students. Campus housing is university owned. Freshman campus housing is guaranteed. *Activities and organizations:* drama/theater group, student-run newspaper, radio station, choral group, Gospel Revelations Chorus, Dance Alloy, club sports, student government, Black Student Union. *Campus security:* 24-hour emergency response devices and patrols, student patrols, late-night transport/escort service, controlled dormitory access. *Student services:* health clinic, personal/psychological counseling, women's center.

Athletics Member NCAA. All Division III. *Intercollegiate sports:* baseball M, basketball M/W, cheerleading W(c), cross-country running M/W, equestrian sports W(c), field hockey W, football M, lacrosse M(c)/W(c), rugby M(c)/W(c), soccer M/W, tennis M/W, track and field M/W, ultimate Frisbee M(c)/W(c), volleyball M(c)/W. *Intramural sports:* basketball M/W, bowling M/W, football M, racquetball M/W, soccer M/W.

Standardized Tests *Recommended:* SAT or ACT (for admission).

Costs (2013–14) *Comprehensive fee:* $49,710 includes full-time tuition ($40,600), mandatory fees ($850), and room and board ($8260). Part-time tuition: $1353 per credit. *College room only:* $4190. Room and board charges vary according to board plan. *Payment plans:* tuition prepayment, installment, deferred payment. *Waivers:* employees or children of employees.

Financial Aid Of all full-time matriculated undergraduates who enrolled in 2011, 719 applied for aid, 660 were judged to have need, 296 had their need fully met. In 2011, 170 non-need-based awards were made. *Average percent of need met:* 96%. *Average financial aid package:* $36,001. *Average need-based loan:* $5043. *Average need-based gift aid:* $21,544. *Average non-need-based aid:* $8204. *Average indebtedness upon graduation:* $26,089. *Financial aid deadline:* 3/1.

Applying *Options:* electronic application, early admission, early decision, early action, deferred entrance. *Required:* essay or personal statement, high school transcript, minimum 2.8 GPA, 2 letters of recommendation. *Recom-*

mended: interview. *Application deadlines:* 2/1 (freshmen), 4/1 (transfers), 12/1 (early action). *Early decision deadline:* 11/1. *Notification:* 3/1 (freshmen), 4/15 (transfers), 12/1 (early decision), 2/1 (early action).
Freshman Application Contact Ms. Nancy Sinex, Director of Admissions, Earlham College, 801 National Road West, Richmond, IN 47374. *Phone:* 765-983-1600. *Toll-free phone:* 800-327-5426. *Fax:* 765-983-1560. *E-mail:* admission@earlham.edu.
Website: http://www.earlham.edu/.

Franklin College

Franklin, Indiana

- **Independent** 4-year, founded 1834, affiliated with American Baptist Churches in the U.S.A.
- **Small-town** 187-acre campus with easy access to Indianapolis
- **Endowment** $80.1 million
- **Coed** 1,053 undergraduate students, 96% full-time, 51% women, 49% men
- **Moderately difficult** entrance level, 60% of applicants were admitted

Undergraduates 1,006 full-time, 47 part-time. Students come from 20 states and territories; 8 other countries; 7% are from out of state; 5% Black or African American, non-Hispanic/Latino; 0.7% Hispanic/Latino; 0.6% Asian, non-Hispanic/Latino; 0.5% American Indian or Alaska Native, non-Hispanic/Latino; 3% Two or more races, non-Hispanic/Latino; 6% Race/ethnicity unknown; 3% transferred in; 76% live on campus. *Retention:* 77% of full-time freshmen returned.
Freshmen *Admission:* 1,926 applied, 1,147 admitted, 286 enrolled. *Average high school GPA:* 3.4. *Test scores:* SAT critical reading scores over 500: 44%; SAT math scores over 500: 56%; SAT writing scores over 500: 38%; ACT scores over 18: 96%; SAT critical reading scores over 600: 9%; SAT math scores over 600: 14%; SAT writing scores over 600: 7%; ACT scores over 24: 33%; ACT scores over 30: 3%.
Faculty *Total:* 103, 72% full-time, 69% with terminal degrees. *Student/faculty ratio:* 11:1.
Academics *Calendar:* 4-1-4. *Degree:* bachelor's. *Special study options:* academic remediation for entering students, advanced placement credit, cooperative education, double majors, independent study, internships, off-campus study, part-time degree program, services for LD students, study abroad, summer session for credit. *ROTC:* Army (c). *Unusual degree programs:* 3-2 engineering with Indiana University—Purdue University Indianapolis.

Computers on Campus 150 computers/terminals are available on campus for general student use. Students can access the following: online (class) registration. Campuswide network is available. Wireless service is available via classrooms, computer centers, computer labs, learning centers, libraries, student centers.
Student Life *Housing:* on-campus residence required through junior year. *Options:* coed. Campus housing is university owned. Freshman campus housing is guaranteed. *Activities and organizations:* drama/theater group, student-run newspaper, radio and television station, choral group, FLOW, FC Volunteers, Student Entertainment Board, Student Congress, national fraternities, national sororities. *Campus security:* 24-hour emergency response devices and patrols, late-night transport/escort service. *Student services:* health clinic, personal/psychological counseling.
Athletics Member NCAA. All Division III. *Intercollegiate sports:* baseball M, basketball M/W, cross-country running M/W, football M, golf M/W, soccer M/W, softball W, tennis M/W, track and field M/W, volleyball W. *Intramural sports:* basketball M/W, softball M, volleyball W.
Standardized Tests *Required:* SAT or ACT (for admission).
Costs (2013–14) *One-time required fee:* $380. *Comprehensive fee:* $34,845 includes full-time tuition ($26,710), mandatory fees ($185), and room and board ($7950). Part-time tuition: $380 per credit. *College room only:* $4720. Room and board charges vary according to board plan. *Payment plan:* installment. *Waivers:* senior citizens and employees or children of employees.
Financial Aid Of all full-time matriculated undergraduates who enrolled in 2011, 971 applied for aid, 885 were judged to have need, 106 had their need fully met. In 2011, 131 non-need-based awards were made. *Average percent of need met:* 74%. *Average financial aid package:* $20,017. *Average need-based loan:* $4562. *Average need-based gift aid:* $15,833. *Average non-need-based aid:* $10,037. *Average indebtedness upon graduation:* $34,160.
Applying *Options:* electronic application, deferred entrance. *Application fee:* $30. *Required:* essay or personal statement, high school transcript. *Required for some:* interview. *Application deadline:* rolling (freshmen). *Notification:* continuous (freshmen), continuous (transfers).
Freshman Application Contact Ms. Jennifer Bostrom, Director of Admissions, Franklin College, 101 Branigin Boulevard, Franklin, IN 46131-2623. *Phone:* 317-738-8062. *Toll-free phone:* 800-852-0232. *Fax:* 317-738-8274.
Website: http://www.franklincollege.edu/.

See below for display ad and page 1300 for the College Close-Up.

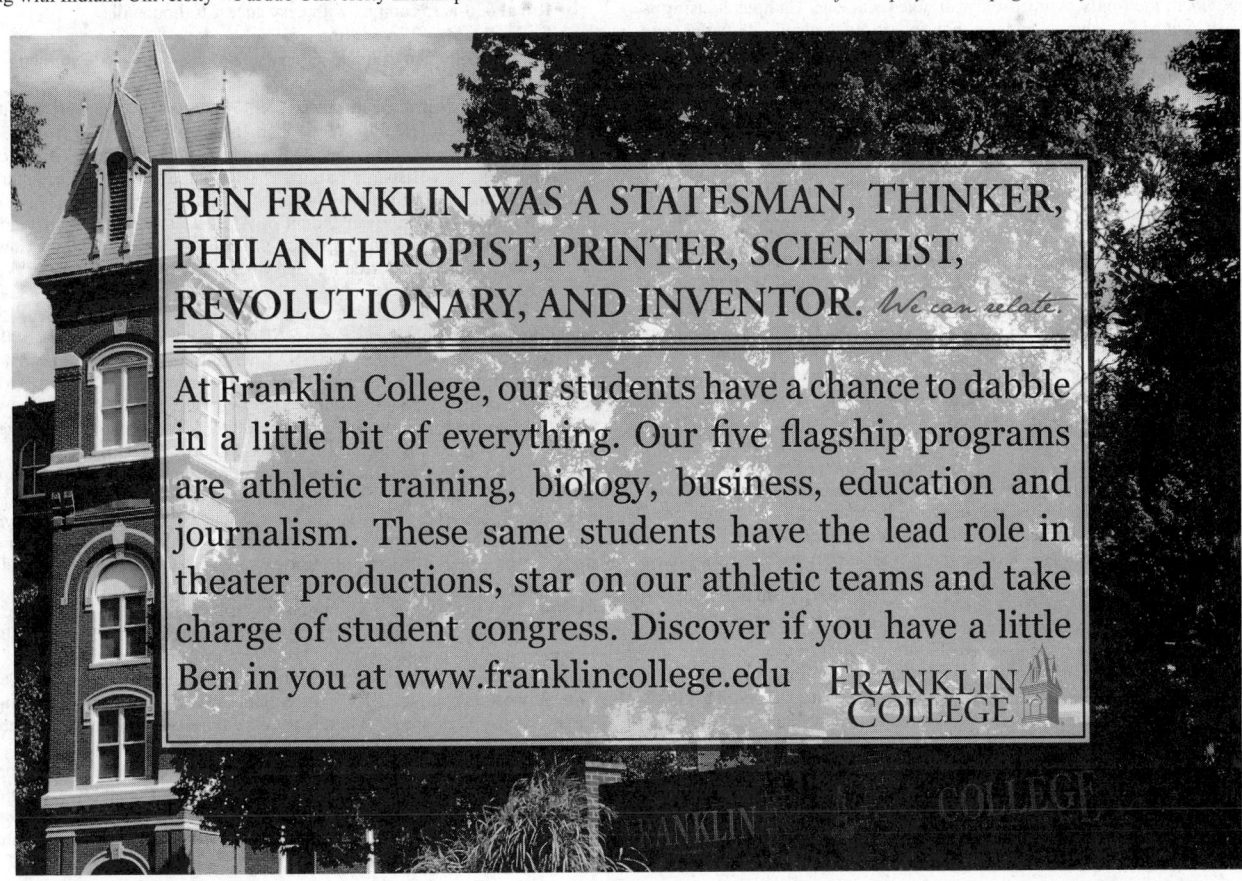

Goshen College

Goshen, Indiana

- **Independent Mennonite** comprehensive, founded 1894
- **Small-town** 135-acre campus
- **Endowment** $94.0 million
- **Coed** 884 undergraduate students, 91% full-time, 60% women, 40% men
- **Moderately difficult** entrance level, 60% of applicants were admitted

Undergraduates 807 full-time, 77 part-time. Students come from 37 states and territories; 37 other countries; 49% are from out of state; 3% Black or African American, non-Hispanic/Latino; 10% Hispanic/Latino; 1% Asian, non-Hispanic/Latino; 2% Two or more races, non-Hispanic/Latino; 0.9% Race/ethnicity unknown; 9% international; 7% transferred in; 70% live on campus. *Retention:* 83% of full-time freshmen returned.

Freshmen *Admission:* 608 applied, 365 admitted, 168 enrolled. *Average high school GPA:* 3.44. *Test scores:* SAT critical reading scores over 500: 61%; SAT math scores over 500: 77%; SAT writing scores over 500: 56%; ACT scores over 18: 94%; SAT critical reading scores over 600: 30%; SAT math scores over 600: 41%; SAT writing scores over 600: 28%; ACT scores over 24: 53%; SAT critical reading scores over 700: 11%; SAT math scores over 700: 11%; SAT writing scores over 700: 4%; ACT scores over 30: 12%.

Faculty *Total:* 94, 76% full-time, 51% with terminal degrees. *Student/faculty ratio:* 10:1.

Academics *Calendar:* semesters. *Degrees:* certificates, bachelor's, and master's. *Special study options:* academic remediation for entering students, accelerated degree program, adult/continuing education programs, advanced placement credit, distance learning, double majors, independent study, internships, off-campus study, part-time degree program, services for LD students, student-designed majors, study abroad, summer session for credit. *Unusual degree programs:* 3-2 engineering with Case Western Reserve University, University of Illinois at Urbana-Champaign, University of Notre Dame, Washington University in St. Louis.

Computers on Campus 160 computers/terminals and 2,000 ports are available on campus for general student use. Students can access the following: campus intranet, computer help desk, free student e-mail accounts, online (class) grades, online (class) registration, online (class) schedules. Campuswide network is available. 100% of college-owned or -operated housing units are wired for high-speed Internet access. Wireless service is available via entire campus.

Student Life *Housing:* on-campus residence required through junior year. *Options:* coed, men-only, women-only, disabled students. Campus housing is university owned. Freshman campus housing is guaranteed. *Activities and organizations:* drama/theater group, student-run newspaper, radio and television station, choral group, International Student Club, Latino Student Union, PAX—Peace Club, Goshen Student Women's Organization, Business Club. *Campus security:* 24-hour emergency response devices and patrols, late-night transport/escort service. *Student services:* health clinic, personal/psychological counseling.

Athletics Member NAIA. *Intercollegiate sports:* baseball M(s), basketball M(s)/W(s), cross-country running M(s)/W(s), golf M(s)/W(s), soccer M(s)/W(s), softball W(s), tennis M(s)/W(s), track and field M(s)/W(s), volleyball W(s). *Intramural sports:* badminton M/W, baseball M, basketball M/W, cross-country running M/W, racquetball M/W, soccer M/W, softball W, table tennis M/W, tennis M/W, ultimate Frisbee M/W, volleyball M/W, weight lifting M/W.

Standardized Tests *Required:* SAT or ACT (for admission).

Costs (2013–14) *Comprehensive fee:* $37,960 includes full-time tuition ($28,500) and room and board ($9460). Full-time tuition and fees vary according to degree level and program. Part-time tuition: $1190 per credit hour. Part-time tuition and fees vary according to course load, degree level, and program. *College room only:* $5060. Room and board charges vary according to board plan and housing facility. *Waivers:* employees or children of employees.

Financial Aid Of all full-time matriculated undergraduates who enrolled in 2011, 731 applied for aid, 663 were judged to have need, 81 had their need fully met. In 2011, 200 non-need-based awards were made. *Average percent of need met:* 80%. *Average financial aid package:* $19,900. *Average need-based loan:* $4875. *Average need-based gift aid:* $16,306. *Average non-need-based aid:* $11,206. *Average indebtedness upon graduation:* $21,953.

Applying *Options:* electronic application, deferred entrance. *Application fee:* $25. *Required:* essay or personal statement, high school transcript, minimum 2.0 GPA, 1 letter of recommendation. *Recommended:* minimum 2.8 GPA, interview, rank in upper 50% of high school class. *Application deadlines:* 8/15 (freshmen), 8/15 (transfers). *Notification:* continuous (freshmen), continuous (transfers).

Freshman Application Contact Dr. Dan Koop Liechty, Director of Admission, Goshen College, 1700 South Main Street, Goshen, IN 46526-4794. *Phone:* 574-535-7535. *Toll-free phone:* 800-348-7422. *Fax:* 574-535-7609. *E-mail:* dankl@goshen.edu. *Website:* http://www.goshen.edu/.

Grace College

Winona Lake, Indiana

- **Independent** comprehensive, founded 1948, affiliated with Fellowship of Grace Brethren Churches
- **Small-town** 160-acre campus
- **Endowment** $8.3 million
- **Coed**
- **Moderately difficult** entrance level

Faculty *Student/faculty ratio:* 27:1.

Academics *Calendar:* semesters. *Degrees:* certificates, diplomas, associate, bachelor's, master's, and doctoral.

Student Life *Campus security:* student patrols, late-night transport/escort service, controlled dormitory access, evening patrols by trained security personnel.

Athletics Member NAIA, NCCAA.

Standardized Tests *Required:* SAT or ACT (for admission).

Costs (2012–13) *Comprehensive fee:* $30,744 includes full-time tuition ($23,290) and room and board ($7454). Full-time tuition and fees vary according to course load, degree level, location, and program. Part-time tuition: $775 per credit hour. Part-time tuition and fees vary according to course load, degree level, location, and program. *College room only:* $3900. Room and board charges vary according to board plan and housing facility.

Financial Aid Of all full-time matriculated undergraduates who enrolled in 2009, 1,276 applied for aid, 1,273 were judged to have need. *Average financial aid package:* $11,338.

Applying *Options:* electronic application, early admission, early action, deferred entrance. *Application fee:* $30. *Required:* essay or personal statement, high school transcript, minimum 2.3 GPA, 2 letters of recommendation, personal statement of faith. *Required for some:* interview.

Freshman Application Contact Mrs. Jessica Hauck, Admissions Office, Grace College, 200 Seminary Drive, Winona Lake, IN 46590. *Phone:* 574-372-5100 Ext. 6008. *Toll-free phone:* 800-54-GRACE. *Fax:* 574-372-5120. *E-mail:* enroll@grace.edu. *Website:* http://www.grace.edu/.

Hanover College

Hanover, Indiana

- **Independent Presbyterian** 4-year, founded 1827
- **Rural** 630-acre campus with easy access to Louisville
- **Endowment** $127.9 million
- **Coed** 1,123 undergraduate students, 99% full-time, 56% women, 44% men
- **Moderately difficult** entrance level, 64% of applicants were admitted

Undergraduates 1,116 full-time, 7 part-time. Students come from 23 states and territories; 11 other countries; 31% are from out of state; 4% Black or African American, non-Hispanic/Latino; 2% Hispanic/Latino; 0.7% Asian, non-Hispanic/Latino; 0.1% Native Hawaiian or other Pacific Islander, non-Hispanic/Latino; 0.4% American Indian or Alaska Native, non-Hispanic/Latino; 2% Two or more races, non-Hispanic/Latino; 3% Race/ethnicity unknown; 3% international; 0.9% transferred in; 95% live on campus. *Retention:* 83% of full-time freshmen returned.

Freshmen *Admission:* 3,633 applied, 2,322 admitted, 372 enrolled. *Average high school GPA:* 3.66. *Test scores:* SAT critical reading scores over 500: 76%; SAT math scores over 500: 75%; SAT writing scores over 500: 65%; ACT scores over 18: 100%; SAT critical reading scores over 600: 32%; SAT math scores over 600: 30%; SAT writing scores over 600: 23%; ACT scores over 24: 63%; SAT critical reading scores over 700: 5%; SAT math scores over 700: 3%; SAT writing scores over 700: 3%; ACT scores over 30: 15%.

Faculty *Total:* 101, 95% full-time, 97% with terminal degrees. *Student/faculty ratio:* 12:1.

Academics *Calendar:* 4-4-1. *Degree:* bachelor's. *Special study options:* advanced placement credit, cooperative education, double majors, independent study, internships, off-campus study, services for LD students, student-designed majors, study abroad.

Computers on Campus 120 computers/terminals and 1,550 ports are available on campus for general student use. Students can access the following: campus intranet, computer help desk, free student e-mail accounts, online (class) grades, online (class) registration, online (class) schedules. Campuswide network is available. 100% of college-owned or -operated housing units are wired for high-speed Internet access. Wireless service is available via entire campus.

Student Life *Housing:* on-campus residence required through senior year. *Options:* coed, men-only, women-only. Campus housing is university owned and leased by the school. Freshman campus housing is guaranteed. *Activities and organizations:* drama/theater group, student-run newspaper, radio and television station, choral group, marching band, Student Senate, Campus Crusade for Christ, Campus Activities Board, People for Peace, Love Out Loud, national fraternities, national sororities. *Campus security:* 24-hour emergency response devices and patrols, late-night transport/escort service, controlled dormitory access. *Student services:* health clinic, personal/psychological counseling.

Athletics Member NCAA. All Division III. *Intercollegiate sports:* baseball M, basketball M/W, cross-country running M/W, football M, golf M/W, lacrosse M, soccer M/W, softball W, tennis M/W, track and field M/W, volleyball W. *Intramural sports:* basketball M/W, football M/W, rugby M(c)/W(c), soccer M/W, softball M/W, ultimate Frisbee M(c), volleyball M/W.

Standardized Tests *Required:* SAT or ACT (for admission).

Costs (2012–13) *One-time required fee:* $250. *Comprehensive fee:* $39,498 includes full-time tuition ($29,668), mandatory fees ($600), and room and board ($9230). Full-time tuition and fees vary according to reciprocity agreements. Part-time tuition: $3296 per unit. Part-time tuition and fees vary according to course load and reciprocity agreements. *College room only:* $4588. Room and board charges vary according to housing facility and location. *Payment plan:* installment. *Waivers:* senior citizens and employees or children of employees.

Financial Aid Of all full-time matriculated undergraduates who enrolled in 2011, 1,007 applied for aid, 912 were judged to have need, 195 had their need fully met. 356 Federal Work-Study jobs (averaging $1675). In 2011, 199 non-need-based awards were made. *Average percent of need met:* 81%. *Average financial aid package:* $25,527. *Average need-based loan:* $4601. *Average need-based gift aid:* $20,938. *Average non-need-based aid:* $15,202. *Average indebtedness upon graduation:* $27,626.

Applying *Options:* electronic application, early admission, early action, deferred entrance. *Application fee:* $40. *Required:* essay or personal statement, high school transcript, 1 letter of recommendation. *Recommended:* interview. *Application deadlines:* 3/1 (freshmen), rolling (transfers), 12/1 (early action). *Notification:* continuous (freshmen), continuous (transfers), 12/20 (early action).

Freshman Application Contact Mr. Christopher Gage, Dean of Admission, Hanover College, PO Box 108, Hanover, IN 47243-0108. *Phone:* 812-866-7021. *Toll-free phone:* 800-213-2178. *Fax:* 812-866-7098. *E-mail:* admission@hanover.edu. *Website:* http://www.hanover.edu/.

Harrison College
Elkhart, Indiana
Freshman Application Contact Matt Brady, Director of Admissions, Harrison College, 56075 Parkway Avenue, Elkhart, IN 46516. *Phone:* 574-522-0397. *Toll-free phone:* 888-544-4422. *E-mail:* matt.brady@harrison.edu. *Website:* http://www.harrison.edu/.

Harrison College
Evansville, Indiana
Freshman Application Contact Mr. Bryan Barber, Harrison College, 4601 Theater Drive, Evansville, IN 47715. *Phone:* 812-476-6000. *Toll-free phone:* 888-544-4422 (in-state); 888-554-4422 (out-of-state). *Fax:* 812-471-8576. *E-mail:* bryan.barber@harrison.edu. *Website:* http://www.harrison.edu/.

Harrison College
Fort Wayne, Indiana
Freshman Application Contact Mr. Matt Wallace, Associate Director of Admissions, Harrison College, 6413 North Clinton Street, Fort Wayne, IN 46825. *Phone:* 260-471-7667. *Toll-free phone:* 888-544-4422. *Fax:* 260-471-6918. *E-mail:* matt.wallace@harrison.edu. *Website:* http://www.harrison.edu/.

Harrison College
Indianapolis, Indiana
Freshman Application Contact Mr. Ted Lukomski, Director of Admissions, Harrison College, 550 East Washington Street, Indianapolis, IN 46204. *Phone:* 317-264-5656. *Toll-free phone:* 888-544-4422. *Fax:* 317-264-5650. *E-mail:* ted.lukomski@ibcschools.edu. *Website:* http://www.harrison.edu/.

Harrison College
Lafayette, Indiana
Freshman Application Contact Ms. Stacy Golleher, Associate Director of Admissions, Harrison College, 4705 Meijer Court, Lafayette, IN 47905. *Phone:* 765-447-9550. *Toll-free phone:* 888-544-4422. *Fax:* 765-447-0868. *E-mail:* stacy.golleher@harrison.edu. *Website:* http://www.harrison.edu/.

Harrison College
Muncie, Indiana
Freshman Application Contact Mr. Jeremy Linder, Associate Director of Admissions, Harrison College, Muncie, IN 47303. *Phone:* 765-288-8681. *Toll-free phone:* 888-544-4422. *Fax:* 765-288-8797. *E-mail:* Jeremy.linder@harrison.edu. *Website:* http://www.harrison.edu/.

Harrison College
Terre Haute, Indiana
Freshman Application Contact Sarah Stultz, Associate Director of Admissions, Harrison College, 1378 South State Road 46, Terre Haute, IN 47803. *Phone:* 812-877-2100. *Toll-free phone:* 888-544-4422. *Fax:* 812-877-4440. *E-mail:* sarah.stultz@harrison.edu. *Website:* http://www.harrison.edu/.

Holy Cross College
Notre Dame, Indiana
- **Independent Roman Catholic** 4-year, founded 1966
- **Suburban** 150-acre campus with easy access to Chicago, Indianapolis
- **Endowment** $1.4 million
- **Coed** 450 undergraduate students, 93% full-time, 40% women, 60% men
- **Moderately difficult** entrance level, 81% of applicants were admitted

Undergraduates 420 full-time, 30 part-time. Students come from 29 states and territories; 6 other countries; 47% are from out of state; 7% Black or African American, non-Hispanic/Latino; 10% Hispanic/Latino; 1% Asian, non-Hispanic/Latino; 0.2% American Indian or Alaska Native, non-Hispanic/Latino; 1% Two or more races, non-Hispanic/Latino; 11% international; 7% transferred in; 52% live on campus. *Retention:* 64% of full-time freshmen returned.

Freshmen *Admission:* 493 applied, 401 admitted, 116 enrolled. *Average high school GPA:* 3.05. *Test scores:* SAT critical reading scores over 500: 52%; SAT math scores over 500: 51%; SAT writing scores over 500: 30%; ACT scores over 18: 86%; SAT critical reading scores over 600: 5%; SAT math scores over 600: 10%; SAT writing scores over 600: 5%; ACT scores over 24: 27%; ACT scores over 30: 3%.

Faculty *Total:* 48, 46% full-time, 27% with terminal degrees. *Student/faculty ratio:* 14:1.

Academics *Calendar:* semesters. *Degrees:* associate and bachelor's. *Special study options:* academic remediation for entering students, advanced placement credit, double majors, freshman honors college, honors programs, independent study, internships, off-campus study, student-designed majors, study abroad, summer session for credit. *ROTC:* Army (c), Air Force (c).

Computers on Campus 91 computers/terminals are available on campus for general student use. Students can access the following: campus intranet, free student e-mail accounts, online (class) registration, online (class) schedules. Campuswide network is available. 100% of college-owned or -operated housing units are wired for high-speed Internet access. Wireless service is available via entire campus.

Student Life *Housing:* on-campus residence required for freshman year. *Options:* men-only, women-only, disabled students. Campus housing is university owned. Freshman applicants given priority for college housing. *Activities and organizations:* drama/theater group, student-run newspaper, choral group, marching band, Student Government Association, Campus Ministry, Intramural athletics, Commuter Student Organization, Circle K. *Campus security:* 24-hour emergency response devices and patrols, late-night transport/escort service, controlled dormitory access. *Student services:* personal/psychological counseling.

Athletics Member NAIA. *Intercollegiate sports:* baseball M(s), basketball M(s), crew M, golf W(s), ice hockey M(c), lacrosse M, soccer M(s)/W(s), track and field M/W, water polo M/W. *Intramural sports:* basketball M/W, cheerleading M/W, football M/W, rugby M, skiing (downhill) M(c)/W(c), softball M/W, table tennis M/W, tennis M/W, ultimate Frisbee M/W, volleyball M/W, weight lifting M/W.

Standardized Tests *Required:* SAT or ACT (for admission).

Costs (2013–14) *Comprehensive fee:* $34,345 includes full-time tuition ($24,500), mandatory fees ($950), and room and board ($8895). Full-time tuition and fees vary according to course load. Part-time tuition: $825 per semester hour. Part-time tuition and fees vary according to course load. No tuition increase for student's term of enrollment. *Room and board:* Room and board charges vary according to board plan and housing facility. *Payment plan:* installment. *Waivers:* employees or children of employees.

Applying *Options:* electronic application, deferred entrance. *Required:* high school transcript, Freshmen applicants and Transfer applicants with fewer than 24 transferable credits are required to submit ACT or SAT scores. *Required for some:* essay or personal statement. *Recommended:* minimum 2.5 GPA, interview. *Application deadlines:* rolling (freshmen), rolling (out-of-state freshmen), rolling (transfers). *Notification:* continuous (freshmen), continuous (out-of-state freshmen), continuous (transfers).

Freshman Application Contact Mr. Adam DeBeck, Office of Admissions, Holy Cross College, 54515 SR 933 N, PO Box 308, Notre Dame, IN 46556. *Phone:* 574-239-8400. *Fax:* 574-239-8323. *E-mail:* admissions@hcc-nd.edu. *Website:* http://www.hcc-nd.edu/.

Huntington University
Huntington, Indiana

- **Independent** comprehensive, founded 1897, affiliated with Church of the United Brethren in Christ
- **Small-town** 170-acre campus with easy access to Fort Wayne
- **Endowment** $20.6 million
- **Coed** 1,134 undergraduate students, 92% full-time, 58% women, 42% men
- **Moderately difficult** entrance level, 97% of applicants were admitted

Undergraduates 1,041 full-time, 93 part-time. Students come from 36 states and territories; 19 other countries; 38% are from out of state; 2% Black or African American, non-Hispanic/Latino; 3% Hispanic/Latino; 0.4% Asian, non-Hispanic/Latino; 0.1% Native Hawaiian or other Pacific Islander, non-Hispanic/Latino; 0.4% American Indian or Alaska Native, non-Hispanic/Latino; 0.6% Two or more races, non-Hispanic/Latino; 3% international; 5% transferred in; 74% live on campus. *Retention:* 73% of full-time freshmen returned.

Freshmen *Admission:* 824 applied, 802 admitted, 239 enrolled. *Average high school GPA:* 3.46. *Test scores:* SAT critical reading scores over 500: 56%; SAT math scores over 500: 53%; SAT writing scores over 500: 42%; ACT scores over 18: 95%; SAT critical reading scores over 600: 18%; SAT math scores over 600: 16%; SAT writing scores over 600: 13%; ACT scores over 24: 44%; SAT critical reading scores over 700: 5%; SAT math scores over 700: 1%; ACT scores over 30: 4%.

Faculty *Total:* 109, 53% full-time, 55% with terminal degrees. *Student/faculty ratio:* 13:1.

Academics *Calendar:* 4-1-4. *Degrees:* associate, bachelor's, and master's. *Special study options:* academic remediation for entering students, accelerated degree program, adult/continuing education programs, advanced placement credit, distance learning, double majors, English as a second language, independent study, internships, off-campus study, part-time degree program, services for LD students, study abroad, summer session for credit. *Unusual degree programs:* 3-2 Athletic Training (three-year program at Huntington/two-year graduate program at Manchester University).

Computers on Campus 209 computers/terminals and 3,167 ports are available on campus for general student use. Students can access the following: campus intranet, computer help desk, free student e-mail accounts, online (class) grades, online (class) registration, online (class) schedules. Campus-wide network is available. 100% of college-owned or -operated housing units are wired for high-speed Internet access. Wireless service is available via classrooms, computer centers, computer labs, dorm rooms, learning centers, libraries, student centers.

Student Life *Housing:* on-campus residence required through junior year. *Options:* men-only, women-only, disabled students. Campus housing is university owned. Freshman campus housing is guaranteed. *Activities and organizations:* drama/theater group, student-run newspaper, radio and television station, choral group, Film Club, Ultimate Frisbee Club, Mu Kappa, Social Work Student Council, Investment Club. *Campus security:* 24-hour emergency response devices, late-night transport/escort service, campus police on duty from 6 pm to 6 am.

Athletics Member NAIA, NCCAA. *Intercollegiate sports:* baseball M(s), basketball M(s)/W(s), bowling M(s)/W(s), cheerleading M/W, cross-country running M(s)/W(s), golf M(s), soccer M(s)/W(s), softball W(s), tennis M(s)/W(s), track and field M(s)/W(s), ultimate Frisbee M(c), volleyball W(s). *Intramural sports:* basketball M/W, football M/W, racquetball M/W, soccer M/W, table tennis M/W, volleyball M/W.

Standardized Tests *Required:* SAT or ACT (for admission).

Costs (2013–14) *Comprehensive fee:* $32,220 includes full-time tuition ($23,300), mandatory fees ($740), and room and board ($8180). Full-time

tuition and fees vary according to course load, degree level, and program. Part-time tuition: $700 per credit. Part-time tuition and fees vary according to course load, degree level, and program. *Room and board:* Room and board charges vary according to board plan. *Payment plan:* installment. *Waivers:* minority students, children of alumni, and employees or children of employees.

Financial Aid Of all full-time matriculated undergraduates who enrolled in 2012, 907 applied for aid, 834 were judged to have need, 73 had their need fully met. 86 Federal Work-Study jobs (averaging $1875). In 2012, 140 non-need-based awards were made. *Average percent of need met:* 68%. *Average financial aid package:* $16,801. *Average need-based loan:* $4728. *Average need-based gift aid:* $13,973. *Average non-need-based aid:* $10,201. *Average indebtedness upon graduation:* $31,149.

Applying *Options:* electronic application, deferred entrance. *Application fee:* $20. *Required:* essay or personal statement, high school transcript, minimum 2.3 GPA. *Recommended:* interview. *Application deadlines:* 8/1 (freshmen), rolling (transfers). *Notification:* 10/1 (freshmen), continuous (transfers).

Freshman Application Contact Huntington University, 2303 College Avenue, Huntington, IN 46750-1299. *Phone:* 260-356-6000 Ext. 4016. *Toll-free phone:* 800-642-6493. *Website:* http://www.huntington.edu/.

Indiana State University
Terre Haute, Indiana

- **State-supported** university, founded 1865
- **Small-town** 91-acre campus with easy access to Indianapolis
- **Endowment** $47.6 million
- **Coed** 10,076 undergraduate students, 86% full-time, 54% women, 46% men
- **Moderately difficult** entrance level, 86% of applicants were admitted

Undergraduates 8,675 full-time, 1,401 part-time. Students come from 53 states and territories; 43 other countries; 17% are from out of state; 17% Black or African American, non-Hispanic/Latino; 3% Hispanic/Latino; 1% Asian, non-Hispanic/Latino; 0.1% Native Hawaiian or other Pacific Islander, non-Hispanic/Latino; 0.2% American Indian or Alaska Native, non-Hispanic/Latino; 3% Two or more races, non-Hispanic/Latino; 1% Race/ethnicity unknown; 4% international; 7% transferred in; 36% live on campus. *Retention:* 61% of full-time freshmen returned.

Freshmen *Admission:* 10,709 applied, 9,245 admitted, 2,664 enrolled. *Average high school GPA:* 3.06. *Test scores:* SAT critical reading scores over 500: 31%; SAT math scores over 500: 34%; SAT writing scores over 500: 23%; ACT scores over 18: 62%; SAT critical reading scores over 600: 6%; SAT math scores over 600: 6%; SAT writing scores over 600: 3%; ACT scores over 24: 15%; SAT critical reading scores over 700: 1%; ACT scores over 30: 1%.

Faculty *Total:* 689, 70% full-time, 57% with terminal degrees. *Student/faculty ratio:* 19:1.

Academics *Calendar:* semesters. *Degrees:* certificates, associate, bachelor's, master's, doctoral, post-master's, and postbachelor's certificates. *Special study options:* academic remediation for entering students, accelerated degree program, adult/continuing education programs, advanced placement credit, cooperative education, distance learning, double majors, English as a second language, freshman honors college, honors programs, independent study, internships, off-campus study, part-time degree program, services for LD students, study abroad, summer session for credit. *ROTC:* Army (b), Air Force (b).

Computers on Campus 395 computers/terminals are available on campus for general student use. Students can access the following: campus intranet, computer help desk, free student e-mail accounts, online (class) grades, online (class) registration, online (class) schedules. Campuswide network is available. 100% of college-owned or -operated housing units are wired for high-speed Internet access. Wireless service is available via entire campus.

Student Life *Housing:* on-campus residence required for freshman year. *Options:* coed, men-only, women-only, disabled students. Campus housing is university owned. Freshman campus housing is guaranteed. *Activities and organizations:* drama/theater group, student-run newspaper, radio station, choral group, marching band, Union Board, Student Government Association, Panhellenic Council (sororities), Interfraternity Council (fraternities), Residence Hall Association, national fraternities, national sororities. *Campus security:* 24-hour emergency response devices and patrols, student patrols, late-night transport/escort service. *Student services:* health clinic, personal/psychological counseling, women's center.

Athletics Member NCAA. All Division I except football (Division I-AA). *Intercollegiate sports:* baseball M(s), basketball M(s)/W(s), cross-country running M(s)/W(s), golf W(s), soccer W(s), softball W(s), track and field M(s)/W(s), volleyball W(s). *Intramural sports:* badminton M/W, basketball M/W, racquetball M/W, soccer M/W, softball M/W, swimming and diving M/W, track and field M/W, ultimate Frisbee M/W, volleyball M/W.

Standardized Tests *Required:* SAT or ACT (for admission).
Costs (2012–13) *Tuition:* state resident $7898 full-time, $286 per credit hour part-time; nonresident $17,444 full-time, $617 per credit hour part-time. Part-time tuition and fees vary according to course load. *Required fees:* $200 full-time, $100 per term part-time. *Room and board:* $8262. Room and board charges vary according to board plan, housing facility, and student level. *Payment plans:* installment, deferred payment. *Waivers:* senior citizens and employees or children of employees.
Financial Aid Of all full-time matriculated undergraduates who enrolled in 2011, 7,198 applied for aid, 6,075 were judged to have need, 657 had their need fully met. 1,092 Federal Work-Study jobs (averaging $2207). In 2011, 799 non-need-based awards were made. *Average percent of need met:* 81%. *Average financial aid package:* $9735. *Average need-based loan:* $3842. *Average need-based gift aid:* $6095. *Average non-need-based aid:* $3694. *Average indebtedness upon graduation:* $24,484.
Applying *Options:* electronic application, deferred entrance. *Application fee:* $25. *Required:* high school transcript. *Required for some:* interview. *Application deadline:* 8/15 (freshmen). *Notification:* continuous (freshmen), continuous (transfers).
Freshman Application Contact Mr. Richard Toomey, Assistant Vice President Enrollment Management, Indiana State University, 218 North Sixth Street, Erickson Hall, Terre Haute, IN 47809-9989. *Phone:* 812-237-2121. *Toll-free phone:* 800-468-6478. *Fax:* 812-237-8023. *E-mail:* admisu@isugw.indstate.edu.
Website: http://www.indstate.edu/.

Indiana Tech

Fort Wayne, Indiana

- **Independent** comprehensive, founded 1930
- **Urban** 42-acre campus
- **Endowment** $47.1 million
- **Coed** 4,470 undergraduate students, 66% full-time, 58% women, 42% men
- **Moderately difficult** entrance level, 65% of applicants were admitted

Undergraduates 2,969 full-time, 1,501 part-time. Students come from 41 states and territories; 10 other countries; 16% are from out of state; 25% Black or African American, non-Hispanic/Latino; 3% Hispanic/Latino; 0.4% Asian, non-Hispanic/Latino; 0.2% Native Hawaiian or other Pacific Islander, non-Hispanic/Latino; 0.3% American Indian or Alaska Native, non-Hispanic/Latino; 2% Two or more races, non-Hispanic/Latino; 21% Race/ethnicity unknown; 0.4% international; 2% transferred in; 48% live on campus. *Retention:* 73% of full-time freshmen returned.
Freshmen *Admission:* 3,172 applied, 2,054 admitted, 593 enrolled. *Average high school GPA:* 2.82. *Test scores:* SAT critical reading scores over 500: 33%; SAT math scores over 500: 43%; SAT writing scores over 500: 22%; ACT scores over 18: 74%; SAT critical reading scores over 600: 4%; SAT math scores over 600: 11%; SAT writing scores over 600: 2%; ACT scores over 24: 17%; SAT math scores over 700: 1%.
Faculty *Total:* 306, 13% full-time. *Student/faculty ratio:* 19:1.
Academics *Calendar:* semesters. *Degrees:* associate, bachelor's, master's, and doctoral. *Special study options:* academic remediation for entering students, accelerated degree program, adult/continuing education programs, advanced placement credit, cooperative education, distance learning, double majors, external degree program, honors programs, independent study, internships, part-time degree program, services for LD students, student-designed majors, summer session for credit. *ROTC:* Army (c).
Computers on Campus 398 computers/terminals and 398 ports are available on campus for general student use. Students can access the following: computer help desk, free student e-mail accounts, online (class) grades, online (class) registration, online (class) schedules. Campuswide network is available. 100% of college-owned or -operated housing units are wired for high-speed Internet access. Wireless service is available via entire campus.
Student Life *Housing:* on-campus residence required through sophomore year. *Options:* coed. Campus housing is university owned. Freshman campus housing is guaranteed. *Activities and organizations:* student-run newspaper, Student Board, Student Ambassadors, NSBE, SHRM, Sport Recreation and Leisure Society, national fraternities. *Campus security:* 24-hour emergency response devices and patrols, student patrols, late-night transport/escort service, controlled dormitory access.
Athletics Member NAIA. *Intercollegiate sports:* baseball M(s), basketball M(s)/W(s), bowling M(s)/W(s), cheerleading M(s)/W(s), cross-country running M(s)/W(s), golf M(s)/W(s), lacrosse M(s)/W(s), soccer M(s)/W(s), softball M(s)/W(s), tennis M(s)/W(s), track and field M(s)/W(s), volleyball W(s), wrestling M(s). *Intramural sports:* basketball M/W, bowling M/W, football M, table tennis M/W, ultimate Frisbee M/W.
Standardized Tests *Required:* SAT or ACT (for admission).

Costs (2013–14) *Comprehensive fee:* $34,240 includes full-time tuition ($24,450), mandatory fees ($410), and room and board ($9380). Full-time tuition and fees vary according to class time, course load, and program. Part-time tuition: $480 per credit hour. Part-time tuition and fees vary according to class time, course load, and program. *Room and board:* Room and board charges vary according to housing facility. *Payment plan:* installment. *Waivers:* employees or children of employees.
Financial Aid Of all full-time matriculated undergraduates who enrolled in 2011, 2,433 applied for aid, 2,325 were judged to have need, 841 had their need fully met. 103 Federal Work-Study jobs (averaging $1488). In 2011, 11 non-need-based awards were made. *Average financial aid package:* $17,433. *Average need-based loan:* $640. *Average need-based gift aid:* $7179. *Average non-need-based aid:* $8722.
Applying *Options:* electronic application. *Application fee:* $50. *Required:* minimum 2.0 GPA. *Required for some:* high school transcript, minimum 3.0 GPA, 2 letters of recommendation, Interview with the Director of Software Engineering and college-level math courses for the Software Engineering program, Interview with the Director for the Pre-Law program. *Recommended:* Interview with the Director of Software Engineering and college-level math courses for the Software Engineering program, Interview with the Director for the Pre-Law program. *Application deadlines:* 8/15 (freshmen), 8/15 (transfers). *Notification:* continuous until 8/15 (freshmen), continuous until 8/15 (transfers).
Freshman Application Contact Ms. Monica Chamberlain, Associate Vice President of Enrollment Management, Indiana Tech, 1600 East Washington Boulevard, Fort Wayne, IN 46803. *Phone:* 260-422-5561 Ext. 2348. *Toll-free phone:* 800-937-2448. *Fax:* 260-422-7696. *E-mail:* admissions@indianatech.edu.
Website: http://www.indianatech.edu/.

Indiana University Bloomington

Bloomington, Indiana

- **State-supported** university, founded 1820, part of Indiana University System
- **Small-town** 1937-acre campus with easy access to Indianapolis
- **Endowment** $692.1 million
- **Coed** 32,371 undergraduate students, 96% full-time, 51% women, 49% men
- **Moderately difficult** entrance level, 74% of applicants were admitted

Undergraduates 30,949 full-time, 1,422 part-time. Students come from 51 states and territories; 135 other countries; 28% are from out of state; 4% Black or African American, non-Hispanic/Latino; 4% Hispanic/Latino; 4% Asian, non-Hispanic/Latino; 0.1% Native Hawaiian or other Pacific Islander, non-Hispanic/Latino; 0.1% American Indian or Alaska Native, non-Hispanic/Latino; 3% Two or more races, non-Hispanic/Latino; 0.6% Race/ethnicity unknown; 11% international; 3% transferred in; 38% live on campus. *Retention:* 88% of full-time freshmen returned.
Freshmen *Admission:* 35,247 applied, 26,228 admitted, 7,192 enrolled. *Average high school GPA:* 3.6. *Test scores:* SAT critical reading scores over 500: 82%; SAT math scores over 500: 90%; SAT writing scores over 500: 80%; ACT scores over 18: 99%; SAT critical reading scores over 600: 36%; SAT math scores over 600: 52%; SAT writing scores over 600: 33%; ACT scores over 24: 80%; SAT critical reading scores over 700: 8%; SAT math scores over 700: 14%; SAT writing scores over 700: 6%; ACT scores over 30: 24%.
Faculty *Total:* 2,284, 85% full-time, 72% with terminal degrees. *Student/faculty ratio:* 18:1.
Academics *Calendar:* semesters plus 2 summer sessions. *Degrees:* certificates, bachelor's, master's, doctoral, post-master's, and postbachelor's certificates. *Special study options:* academic remediation for entering students, accelerated degree program, adult/continuing education programs, advanced placement credit, cooperative education, distance learning, double majors, English as a second language, external degree program, freshman honors college, honors programs, independent study, internships, off-campus study, part-time degree program, services for LD students, student-designed majors, study abroad, summer session for credit. *ROTC:* Army (b), Air Force (b). *Unusual degree programs:* 3-2 accounting.
Computers on Campus Students can access the following: campus intranet, computer help desk, free student e-mail accounts, online (class) grades, online (class) registration, online (class) schedules. Campuswide network is available. 100% of college-owned or -operated housing units are wired for high-speed Internet access. Wireless service is available via entire campus.
Student Life *Housing:* on-campus residence required for freshman year. *Options:* coed, men-only, women-only, cooperative, disabled students. Campus housing is university owned. Freshman applicants given priority for college housing. *Activities and organizations:* drama/theater group, student-run newspaper, radio and television station, choral group, marching band, Union Board, Student Association, Student Foundation, Habitat for Humanity, Stu-

dent Athletic Board, national fraternities, national sororities. *Campus security:* 24-hour emergency response devices and patrols, late-night transport/escort service, safety seminars, lighted pathways, escort service, shuttle bus service, emergency telephones. *Student services:* health clinic, personal/psychological counseling, women's center, legal services.

Athletics Member NCAA. All Division I except football (Division I-A). *Intercollegiate sports:* baseball M(s), basketball M(s)/W(s), crew W(s), cross-country running M(s)/W(s), field hockey W, golf M(s)/W(s), soccer M(s)/W(s), softball W(s), swimming and diving M(s)/W(s), tennis M(s)/W(s), track and field M(s)/W(s), volleyball W(s), water polo W(s), wrestling M(s). *Intramural sports:* archery M/W, badminton M(c)/W(c), baseball M/W, basketball M/W, bowling M(c)/W(c), crew M(c)/W(c), cross-country running M/W, equestrian sports M(c)/W(c), fencing M(c)/W(c), field hockey W(c), golf M/W, gymnastics M/W, ice hockey M/W, lacrosse M(c)/W, racquetball M(c)/W(c), riflery M(c)/W(c), rugby M(c)/W(c), sailing M(c)/W(c), skiing (downhill) M(c)/W(c), soccer M/W(c), softball M/W, squash M/W, swimming and diving M/W, table tennis M/W, tennis M(c)/W, track and field M/W, ultimate Frisbee M(c)/W(c), volleyball M/W, water polo M(c)/W, weight lifting M(c)/W(c), wrestling M(c).

Standardized Tests *Required:* SAT or ACT (for admission). *Recommended:* SAT Subject Tests (for admission).

Costs (2012–13) *Tuition:* state resident $8750 full-time, $273 per credit hour part-time; nonresident $30,200 full-time, $944 per credit hour part-time. Full-time tuition and fees vary according to location and program. Part-time tuition and fees vary according to course load, location, and program. *Required fees:* $1283 full-time. *Room and board:* $8853; room only: $5853. Room and board charges vary according to board plan and housing facility. *Payment plan:* deferred payment. *Waivers:* employees or children of employees.

Financial Aid Of all full-time matriculated undergraduates who enrolled in 2011, 19,119 applied for aid, 14,268 were judged to have need, 1,617 had their need fully met. In 2011, 5558 non-need-based awards were made. *Average percent of need met:* 88%. *Average financial aid package:* $11,366. *Average need-based loan:* $4449. *Average need-based gift aid:* $9866. *Average non-need-based aid:* $7351. *Average indebtedness upon graduation:* $28,769.

Applying *Options:* electronic application, deferred entrance. *Application fee:* $55. *Required:* high school transcript. *Recommended:* interview. *Application deadlines:* rolling (freshmen), rolling (transfers). *Notification:* continuous (freshmen), continuous (transfers).

Freshman Application Contact Ms. Mary Ellen Anderson, Director of Admissions, Indiana University Bloomington, 300 North Jordan Avenue, Bloomington, IN 47405-1106. *Phone:* 812-855-0661. *Fax:* 812-855-5102. *E-mail:* iuadmit@indiana.edu.
Website: http://www.iub.edu/.

Indiana University East

Richmond, Indiana

- **State-supported** comprehensive, founded 1971, part of Indiana University System
- **Small-town** 182-acre campus with easy access to Indianapolis
- **Endowment** $4.1 million
- **Coed** 4,052 undergraduate students, 49% full-time, 65% women, 35% men
- **Moderately difficult** entrance level, 60% of applicants were admitted

Undergraduates 1,988 full-time, 2,064 part-time. Students come from 33 states and territories; 25 other countries; 20% are from out of state; 3% Black or African American, non-Hispanic/Latino; 2% Hispanic/Latino; 0.7% Asian, non-Hispanic/Latino; 0.0% Native Hawaiian or other Pacific Islander, non-Hispanic/Latino; 0.2% American Indian or Alaska Native, non-Hispanic/Latino; 2% Two or more races, non-Hispanic/Latino; 2% Race/ethnicity unknown; 0.4% international; 10% transferred in. *Retention:* 67% of full-time freshmen returned.

Freshmen *Admission:* 1,266 applied, 756 admitted, 383 enrolled. *Average high school GPA:* 3.15. *Test scores:* SAT critical reading scores over 500: 33%; SAT math scores over 500: 38%; ACT scores over 18: 80%; SAT critical reading scores over 600: 4%; SAT math scores over 600: 6%; ACT scores over 24: 28%; ACT scores over 30: 2%.

Faculty *Total:* 271, 38% full-time, 34% with terminal degrees. *Student/faculty ratio:* 16:1.

Academics *Calendar:* semesters. *Degrees:* certificates, bachelor's, master's, and postbachelor's certificates. *Special study options:* academic remediation for entering students, adult/continuing education programs, advanced placement credit, cooperative education, distance learning, double majors, external degree program, honors programs, independent study, internships, off-campus study, part-time degree program, services for LD students, study abroad, summer session for credit.

Computers on Campus Students can access the following: campus intranet, computer help desk, free student e-mail accounts, online (class) grades, online

(class) registration, online (class) schedules. Campuswide network is available. Wireless service is available via entire campus.

Student Life *Housing:* college housing not available. *Activities and organizations:* drama/theater group, student-run newspaper, television station, Student Government Association, Cultural Inclusive Awareness, Psychology Club, Sociology Club, Humanities Club. *Campus security:* 24-hour emergency response devices, late-night transport/escort service, safety awareness, lighted pathways, 14-hour foot and vehicle patrol. *Student services:* personal/psychological counseling.

Athletics Member NAIA. *Intercollegiate sports:* basketball M/W, cheerleading W, cross-country running M/W, golf M/W, tennis M/W, track and field M/W, volleyball W. *Intramural sports:* basketball M(c)/W(c), softball M/W, volleyball M/W.

Standardized Tests *Required:* SAT or ACT (for admission).

Costs (2012–13) *Tuition:* state resident $5964 full-time, $199 per credit hour part-time; nonresident $16,894 full-time, $563 per credit hour part-time. Full-time tuition and fees vary according to course load, location, program, and reciprocity agreements. Part-time tuition and fees vary according to course load, location, program, and reciprocity agreements. *Required fees:* $532 full-time. *Payment plan:* deferred payment. *Waivers:* employees or children of employees.

Financial Aid Of all full-time matriculated undergraduates who enrolled in 2011, 1,774 applied for aid, 1,579 were judged to have need, 101 had their need fully met. In 2011, 66 non-need-based awards were made. *Average percent of need met:* 95%. *Average financial aid package:* $8506. *Average need-based loan:* $3800. *Average need-based gift aid:* $6273. *Average non-need-based aid:* $1968. *Average indebtedness upon graduation:* $30,632.

Applying *Options:* electronic application, early admission, deferred entrance. *Application fee:* $35. *Required:* high school transcript. *Recommended:* minimum 2.0 GPA. *Application deadlines:* rolling (freshmen), rolling (transfers). *Notification:* continuous (freshmen), continuous (transfers).

Freshman Application Contact Ms. Molly Vanderpool, Director of Admissions, Indiana University East, 2325 Chester Boulevard, Whitewater Hall 151, Richmond, IN 47374-1289. *Phone:* 765-973-8208. *Toll-free phone:* 800-959-EAST. *Fax:* 765-973-8209. *E-mail:* applynow@iue.edu. *Website:* http://www.iue.edu/.

Indiana University Kokomo

Kokomo, Indiana

- **State-supported** comprehensive, founded 1945, part of Indiana University System
- **Small-town** 51-acre campus with easy access to Indianapolis
- **Endowment** $4.1 million
- **Coed** 3,581 undergraduate students, 52% full-time, 64% women, 36% men
- **Minimally difficult** entrance level, 70% of applicants were admitted

Undergraduates 1,869 full-time, 1,712 part-time. Students come from 13 states and territories; 19 other countries; 1% are from out of state; 4% Black or African American, non-Hispanic/Latino; 3% Hispanic/Latino; 1% Asian, non-Hispanic/Latino; 0.1% Native Hawaiian or other Pacific Islander, non-Hispanic/Latino; 0.2% American Indian or Alaska Native, non-Hispanic/Latino; 2% Two or more races, non-Hispanic/Latino; 12% Race/ethnicity unknown; 0.1% international; 8% transferred in. *Retention:* 63% of full-time freshmen returned.

Freshmen *Admission:* 1,023 applied, 720 admitted, 450 enrolled. *Average high school GPA:* 3. *Test scores:* SAT critical reading scores over 500: 33%; SAT math scores over 500: 43%; ACT scores over 18: 77%; SAT critical reading scores over 600: 6%; SAT math scores over 600: 6%; ACT scores over 24: 22%.

Faculty *Total:* 194, 51% full-time, 37% with terminal degrees. *Student/faculty ratio:* 18:1.

Academics *Calendar:* semesters. *Degrees:* certificates, associate, bachelor's, master's, and postbachelor's certificates. *Special study options:* academic remediation for entering students, accelerated degree program, adult/continuing education programs, advanced placement credit, distance learning, double majors, English as a second language, external degree program, freshman honors college, honors programs, independent study, internships, part-time degree program, services for LD students, study abroad, summer session for credit. *ROTC:* Army (b).

Computers on Campus Students can access the following: campus intranet, computer help desk, free student e-mail accounts, online (class) grades, online (class) registration, online (class) schedules. Campuswide network is available. Wireless service is available via entire campus.

Student Life *Housing:* college housing not available. *Activities and organizations:* drama/theater group, student-run newspaper, radio station, choral group. *Campus security:* 24-hour patrols, late-night transport/escort service, campus police, lighted pathways. *Student services:* personal/psychological counseling.

Athletics Member NAIA. *Intercollegiate sports:* basketball M, cross-country running M/W, volleyball W. *Intramural sports:* basketball M, soccer M/W, softball M/W, volleyball M/W.

Standardized Tests *Required:* SAT or ACT (for admission).

Costs (2012–13) *Tuition:* state resident $5949 full-time, $198 per credit hour part-time; nonresident $16,894 full-time, $563 per credit hour part-time. Full-time tuition and fees vary according to course load, location, and program. Part-time tuition and fees vary according to course load, location, and program. *Required fees:* $592 full-time. *Payment plan:* deferred payment. *Waivers:* employees or children of employees.

Financial Aid Of all full-time matriculated undergraduates who enrolled in 2011, 1,589 applied for aid, 1,354 were judged to have need, 35 had their need fully met. In 2011, 68 non-need-based awards were made. *Average percent of need met:* 92%. *Average financial aid package:* $7708. *Average need-based loan:* $3650. *Average need-based gift aid:* $5970. *Average non-need-based aid:* $1531. *Average indebtedness upon graduation:* $26,217.

Applying *Options:* electronic application, deferred entrance. *Application fee:* $35. *Required:* high school transcript. *Application deadline:* rolling (freshmen). *Notification:* continuous (freshmen), continuous (transfers).

Freshman Application Contact Ms. Angie Siders, Director of Admissions, Indiana University Kokomo, Kelley Student Center, Room 230, 2300 South Washington Street, Kokomo, IN 46904-9003. *Phone:* 765-455-9217. *Toll-free phone:* 888-875-4485. *Fax:* 765-455-9537. *E-mail:* iuadmis@iuk.edu. *Website:* http://www.iuk.edu/.

Indiana University Northwest

Gary, Indiana

- **State-supported** comprehensive, founded 1959, part of Indiana University System
- **Urban** 38-acre campus with easy access to Chicago
- **Endowment** $6.8 million
- **Coed** 5,636 undergraduate students, 58% full-time, 67% women, 33% men
- **Minimally difficult** entrance level, 69% of applicants were admitted

Undergraduates 3,260 full-time, 2,376 part-time. Students come from 14 states and territories; 33 other countries; 2% are from out of state; 20% Black or African American, non-Hispanic/Latino; 15% Hispanic/Latino; 2% Asian, non-Hispanic/Latino; 0.2% Native Hawaiian or other Pacific Islander, non-Hispanic/Latino; 0.2% American Indian or Alaska Native, non-Hispanic/Latino; 1% Two or more races, non-Hispanic/Latino; 7% Race/ethnicity unknown; 0.1% international; 6% transferred in. *Retention:* 67% of full-time freshmen returned.

Freshmen *Admission:* 1,704 applied, 1,173 admitted, 743 enrolled. *Average high school GPA:* 2.73. *Test scores:* SAT critical reading scores over 500: 33%; SAT math scores over 500: 33%; SAT writing scores over 500: 25%; ACT scores over 18: 70%; SAT critical reading scores over 600: 7%; SAT math scores over 600: 7%; SAT writing scores over 600: 4%; ACT scores over 24: 28%; ACT scores over 30: 1%.

Faculty *Total:* 424, 44% full-time, 41% with terminal degrees. *Student/faculty ratio:* 15:1.

Academics *Calendar:* semesters. *Degrees:* certificates, associate, bachelor's, master's, and postbachelor's certificates. *Special study options:* academic remediation for entering students, accelerated degree program, adult/continuing education programs, advanced placement credit, cooperative education, distance learning, double majors, external degree program, honors programs, independent study, internships, off-campus study, part-time degree program, services for LD students, student-designed majors, study abroad, summer session for credit. *ROTC:* Army (b).

Computers on Campus Students can access the following: campus intranet, computer help desk, free student e-mail accounts, online (class) grades, online (class) registration, online (class) schedules. Campuswide network is available. Wireless service is available via entire campus.

Student Life *Housing:* college housing not available. *Activities and organizations:* drama/theater group, student-run newspaper, radio station, choral group, Student Government Association, Student Ambassadors, Student Nurses Association, Dental Education, International Affairs Club, national fraternities, national sororities. *Campus security:* 24-hour emergency response devices and patrols, late-night transport/escort service, lighted pathways. *Student services:* health clinic, personal/psychological counseling.

Athletics Member NAIA. *Intercollegiate sports:* baseball M, basketball M/W, golf M/W, volleyball W. *Intramural sports:* basketball M(c)/W(c), bowling M(c)/W(c), fencing M(c)/W(c), golf M(c)/W(c), ice hockey M(c), soccer M(c)/W(c), softball M(c)/W(c), table tennis M(c)/W(c), tennis M(c)/W(c), volleyball M(c)/W(c).

Standardized Tests *Required:* SAT or ACT (for admission).

Costs (2012–13) *Tuition:* state resident $6043 full-time, $201 per credit hour part-time; nonresident $16,894 full-time, $563 per credit hour part-time. Full-

time tuition and fees vary according to course load, location, and program. Part-time tuition and fees vary according to course load, location, and program. *Required fees:* $583 full-time. *Payment plans:* installment, deferred payment. *Waivers:* employees or children of employees.

Financial Aid Of all full-time matriculated undergraduates who enrolled in 2011, 2,843 applied for aid, 2,599 were judged to have need, 41 had their need fully met. In 2011, 113 non-need-based awards were made. *Average percent of need met:* 90%. *Average financial aid package:* $8382. *Average need-based loan:* $3904. *Average need-based gift aid:* $6361. *Average non-need-based aid:* $4097. *Average indebtedness upon graduation:* $30,369.

Applying *Options:* electronic application, deferred entrance. *Application fee:* $35. *Required:* high school transcript, minimum 2.0 GPA. *Application deadlines:* rolling (freshmen), rolling (transfers). *Notification:* continuous (freshmen), continuous (transfers).

Freshman Application Contact Dr. Linda B. Templeton, Director of Admissions, Indiana University Northwest, Hawthorn Hall 101, 3400 Broadway, Gary, IN 46408-1197. *Phone:* 219-980-6991. *Toll-free phone:* 800-968-7486. *Fax:* 219-981-4219. *E-mail:* admit@iun.edu. *Website:* http://www.iun.edu/.

Indiana University–Purdue University Fort Wayne

Fort Wayne, Indiana

- **State-supported** comprehensive, founded 1917, part of Indiana University System and Purdue University System
- **Urban** 683-acre campus
- **Endowment** $41.6 million
- **Coed** 13,117 undergraduate students, 60% full-time, 55% women, 45% men
- **Minimally difficult** entrance level, 82% of applicants were admitted

Undergraduates 7,870 full-time, 5,247 part-time. Students come from 43 states and territories; 53 other countries; 3% are from out of state; 6% Black or African American, non-Hispanic/Latino; 5% Hispanic/Latino; 2% Asian, non-Hispanic/Latino; 0.3% American Indian or Alaska Native, non-Hispanic/Latino; 3% Two or more races, non-Hispanic/Latino; 0.7% Race/ethnicity unknown; 2% international; 5% transferred in; 6% live on campus. *Retention:* 60% of full-time freshmen returned.

Freshmen *Admission:* 3,270 applied, 2,686 admitted, 1,629 enrolled. *Average high school GPA:* 3.2. *Test scores:* SAT critical reading scores over 500: 48%; SAT math scores over 500: 54%; SAT writing scores over 500: 37%; ACT scores over 18: 87%; SAT critical reading scores over 600: 11%; SAT math scores over 600: 16%; SAT writing scores over 600: 7%; ACT scores over 24: 29%; SAT critical reading scores over 700: 1%; SAT math scores over 700: 2%; SAT writing scores over 700: 1%; ACT scores over 30: 5%.

Faculty *Total:* 860, 50% full-time, 47% with terminal degrees. *Student/faculty ratio:* 17:1.

Academics *Calendar:* semesters. *Degrees:* certificates, associate, bachelor's, master's, and postbachelor's certificates. *Special study options:* academic remediation for entering students, accelerated degree program, adult/continuing education programs, advanced placement credit, cooperative education, distance learning, double majors, English as a second language, honors programs, independent study, internships, off-campus study, part-time degree program, services for LD students, student-designed majors, study abroad, summer session for credit. *ROTC:* Army (b).

Computers on Campus 642 computers/terminals are available on campus for general student use. Students can access the following: computer help desk, free student e-mail accounts, online (class) grades, online (class) registration, online (class) schedules, student academic records. Campuswide network is available. 100% of college-owned or -operated housing units are wired for high-speed Internet access. Wireless service is available via entire campus.

Student Life *Housing options:* coed. Campus housing is provided by a third party. *Activities and organizations:* drama/theater group, student-run newspaper, television station, choral group, Campus Ministry, Delta Sigma Pi, Chi Alpha Christian Fellowship, IPFW OUTspoken (previously named United Sexualities), Live Action Combat Club. *Campus security:* 24-hour emergency response devices and patrols, late-night transport/escort service, controlled dormitory access. *Student services:* health clinic, personal/psychological counseling, women's center.

Athletics Member NCAA. All Division I. *Intercollegiate sports:* baseball M(s), basketball M(s)/W(s), cross-country running M(s)/W(s), golf M(s)/W(s), soccer M(s)/W(s), softball W(s), tennis M(s)/W(s), track and field W(s), volleyball M(s)/W(s). *Intramural sports:* basketball M/W, golf M/W, racquetball M/W, softball W, tennis M/W, ultimate Frisbee M/W, volleyball M/W.

Standardized Tests *Required:* SAT or ACT (for admission).

Costs (2012–13) *Tuition:* state resident $6001 full-time, $222 per credit hour part-time; nonresident $15,640 full-time, $579 per credit hour part-time. Full-

time tuition and fees vary according to course load. Part-time tuition and fees vary according to course load. *Required fees:* $875 full-time, $32 per credit hour part-time. *Room only:* $7210. Room and board charges vary according to housing facility. *Payment plans:* installment, deferred payment. *Waivers:* senior citizens and employees or children of employees.

Financial Aid Of all full-time matriculated undergraduates who enrolled in 2011, 7,574 applied for aid, 6,716 were judged to have need, 226 had their need fully met. 969 Federal Work-Study jobs (averaging $3000). In 2011, 73 non-need-based awards were made. *Average percent of need met:* 46%. *Average financial aid package:* $9283. *Average need-based loan:* $3784. *Average need-based gift aid:* $5831. *Average non-need-based aid:* $2892. *Average indebtedness upon graduation:* $26,498.

Applying *Options:* electronic application, deferred entrance. *Application fee:* $50. *Required:* high school transcript, minimum 2.8 GPA. *Recommended:* rank in upper 50% of high school class. *Application deadlines:* 8/1 (freshmen), 8/1 (out-of-state freshmen), 8/1 (transfers). *Notification:* continuous (freshmen), continuous (out-of-state freshmen), continuous (transfers).

Freshman Application Contact Angela Morren, Undergraduate Applications Coordinator, Indiana University–Purdue University Fort Wayne, 2101 East Coliseum Boulevard, Fort Wayne, IN 46805-1499. *Phone:* 260-481-6142. *Toll-free phone:* 800-324-4739. *Fax:* 260-481-6880. *E-mail:* morrena@ipfw.edu.
Website: http://www.ipfw.edu/.

Indiana University–Purdue University Indianapolis
Indianapolis, Indiana

- **State-supported** university, founded 1969, part of Indiana University System
- **Urban** 509-acre campus
- **Endowment** $512.1 million
- **Coed** 22,271 undergraduate students, 72% full-time, 57% women, 43% men
- **Moderately difficult** entrance level, 67% of applicants were admitted

Undergraduates 16,127 full-time, 6,144 part-time. Students come from 51 states and territories; 141 other countries; 3% are from out of state; 11% Black or African American, non-Hispanic/Latino; 5% Hispanic/Latino; 3% Asian, non-Hispanic/Latino; 0.1% American Indian or Alaska Native, non-Hispanic/Latino; 3% Two or more races, non-Hispanic/Latino; 2% Race/ethnicity unknown; 3% international; 8% transferred in; 6% live on campus. *Retention:* 72% of full-time freshmen returned.

Freshmen *Admission:* 11,350 applied, 7,612 admitted, 3,279 enrolled. *Average high school GPA:* 3.3. *Test scores:* SAT critical reading scores over 500: 48%; SAT math scores over 500: 53%; SAT writing scores over 500: 39%; ACT scores over 18: 86%; SAT critical reading scores over 600: 13%; SAT math scores over 600: 17%; SAT writing scores over 600: 9%; ACT scores over 24: 35%; SAT critical reading scores over 700: 2%; SAT math scores over 700: 2%; SAT writing scores over 700: 1%; ACT scores over 30: 7%.

Faculty *Total:* 3,256, 69% full-time, 66% with terminal degrees. *Student/faculty ratio:* 17:1.

Academics *Calendar:* semesters. *Degrees:* certificates, associate, bachelor's, master's, doctoral, and postbachelor's certificates. *Special study options:* academic remediation for entering students, accelerated degree program, adult/continuing education programs, advanced placement credit, cooperative education, distance learning, double majors, English as a second language, external degree program, freshman honors college, honors programs, independent study, internships, off-campus study, part-time degree program, services for LD students, student-designed majors, study abroad, summer session for credit. *ROTC:* Army (b), Air Force (c).

Computers on Campus Students can access the following: campus intranet, computer help desk, free student e-mail accounts, online (class) grades, online (class) registration, online (class) schedules. Campuswide network is available. Wireless service is available via entire campus.

Student Life *Housing options:* coed. Campus housing is university owned. *Activities and organizations:* drama/theater group, student-run newspaper, choral group, national fraternities, national sororities. *Campus security:* 24-hour emergency response devices and patrols, late-night transport/escort service, controlled dormitory access, lighted pathways, self-defense education. *Student services:* health clinic, personal/psychological counseling, women's center.

Athletics Member NCAA. All Division I. *Intercollegiate sports:* basketball M(s)/W(s), cross-country running M(s)/W(s), golf M(s)/W(s), soccer M(s)/W(s), softball W(s), swimming and diving M(s)/W(s), tennis M(s)/W(s), track and field M/W, volleyball W(s). *Intramural sports:* badminton M/W, baseball M, basketball M/W, cross-country running M/W, football M/W, golf M/W, racquetball M/W, soccer M/W, softball M/W, swimming and diving M/W, table

tennis M/W, tennis M/W, track and field M/W, ultimate Frisbee M/W, volleyball M/W, water polo M/W.

Standardized Tests *Required:* SAT or ACT (for admission).

Costs (2012–13) *Tuition:* state resident $7623 full-time, $254 per credit hour part-time; nonresident $28,080 full-time, $936 per credit hour part-time. Full-time tuition and fees vary according to course load, location, and program. Part-time tuition and fees vary according to course load, location, and program. *Required fees:* $982 full-time. *Room and board:* $7944. Room and board charges vary according to housing facility. *Payment plans:* installment, deferred payment. *Waivers:* employees or children of employees.

Financial Aid Of all full-time matriculated undergraduates who enrolled in 2011, 13,390 applied for aid, 11,613 were judged to have need, 430 had their need fully met. In 2011, 873 non-need-based awards were made. *Average percent of need met:* 90%. *Average financial aid package:* $9465. *Average need-based loan:* $4220. *Average need-based gift aid:* $7361. *Average non-need-based aid:* $5022. *Average indebtedness upon graduation:* $30,752.

Applying *Options:* electronic application, deferred entrance. *Application fee:* $50. *Required:* high school transcript. *Required for some:* interview. *Recommended:* portfolio for art program. *Application deadlines:* 5/1 (freshmen), rolling (transfers). *Notification:* continuous (freshmen), continuous (transfers).

Freshman Application Contact Mr. Chris J. Foley, Director of Admissions, Indiana University–Purdue University Indianapolis, 420 University Boulevard, Campus Center 255, Indianapolis, IN 46202-5143. *Phone:* 317-274-4591. *Fax:* 317-278-1862. *E-mail:* apply@iupui.edu.
Website: http://www.iupui.edu/.

Indiana University South Bend
South Bend, Indiana

- **State-supported** comprehensive, founded 1922, part of Indiana University System
- **Suburban** 103-acre campus with easy access to Chicago
- **Endowment** $8.6 million
- **Coed** 7,860 undergraduate students, 53% full-time, 62% women, 38% men
- **Moderately difficult** entrance level, 72% of applicants were admitted

Undergraduates 4,134 full-time, 3,726 part-time. Students come from 26 states and territories; 76 other countries; 3% are from out of state; 7% Black or African American, non-Hispanic/Latino; 6% Hispanic/Latino; 1% Asian, non-Hispanic/Latino; 0.1% Native Hawaiian or other Pacific Islander, non-Hispanic/Latino; 0.2% American Indian or Alaska Native, non-Hispanic/Latino; 2% Two or more races, non-Hispanic/Latino; 3% Race/ethnicity unknown; 1% international; 5% transferred in; 6% live on campus. *Retention:* 63% of full-time freshmen returned.

Freshmen *Admission:* 2,354 applied, 1,693 admitted, 950 enrolled. *Average high school GPA:* 3.03. *Test scores:* SAT critical reading scores over 500: 37%; SAT math scores over 500: 38%; SAT writing scores over 500: 26%; ACT scores over 18: 81%; SAT critical reading scores over 600: 8%; SAT math scores over 600: 8%; SAT writing scores over 600: 5%; ACT scores over 24: 22%; SAT critical reading scores over 700: 1%; SAT math scores over 700: 1%; ACT scores over 30: 1%.

Faculty *Total:* 535, 53% full-time, 43% with terminal degrees. *Student/faculty ratio:* 14:1.

Academics *Calendar:* semesters. *Degrees:* certificates, diplomas, associate, bachelor's, master's, and postbachelor's certificates. *Special study options:* accelerated degree program, adult/continuing education programs, advanced placement credit, distance learning, double majors, English as a second language, external degree program, freshman honors college, honors programs, independent study, internships, off-campus study, part-time degree program, services for LD students, study abroad, summer session for credit. *ROTC:* Army (c), Navy (c), Air Force (c).

Computers on Campus Students can access the following: campus intranet, computer help desk, free student e-mail accounts, online (class) grades, online (class) registration, online (class) schedules. Campuswide network is available. Wireless service is available via entire campus.

Student Life *Housing options:* coed. Campus housing is university owned. *Activities and organizations:* drama/theater group, student-run newspaper, choral group, national fraternities, national sororities. *Campus security:* 24-hour emergency response devices and patrols, late-night transport/escort service, safety seminars, lighted pathways. *Student services:* health clinic, personal/psychological counseling, women's center.

Athletics Member NAIA. *Intercollegiate sports:* basketball M(s)/W(s), volleyball W. *Intramural sports:* badminton M/W, baseball M, basketball M/W, bowling M(c)/W(c), cheerleading M(c)/W(c), cross-country running M/W, football M/W, golf M(c)/W(c), racquetball M/W, soccer M(c)/W(c), softball M/W(c), table tennis M/W, tennis M/W, ultimate Frisbee M/W, volleyball M(c)/W(c).

Standardized Tests *Required:* SAT or ACT (for admission).

Costs (2012–13) *Tuition:* state resident $6138 full-time, $205 per credit hour part-time; nonresident $16,894 full-time, $563 per credit hour part-time. Full-time tuition and fees vary according to course load, location, and program. Part-time tuition and fees vary according to course load, location, and program. *Required fees:* $590 full-time. *Room only:* $6838. Room and board charges vary according to housing facility. *Payment plan:* deferred payment. *Waivers:* employees or children of employees.

Financial Aid Of all full-time matriculated undergraduates who enrolled in 2011, 3,775 applied for aid, 3,363 were judged to have need, 69 had their need fully met. In 2011, 81 non-need-based awards were made. *Average percent of need met:* 92%. *Average financial aid package:* $8536. *Average need-based loan:* $3891. *Average need-based gift aid:* $6572. *Average non-need-based aid:* $5516. *Average indebtedness upon graduation:* $27,417.

Applying *Options:* electronic application, deferred entrance. *Application fee:* $35. *Required:* high school transcript, minimum 2.0 GPA. *Required for some:* interview. *Application deadlines:* rolling (freshmen), rolling (transfers). *Notification:* continuous (freshmen), continuous (transfers).

Freshman Application Contact Ms. Connie Peterson-Miller, Director of Admissions, Indiana University South Bend, 1700 Mishawaka Avenue, PO Box 7111, South Bend, IN 46634-7111. *Phone:* 574-520-4839. *Toll-free phone:* 877-GO-2-IUSB. *Fax:* 574-520-4834. *E-mail:* admissions@iusb.edu. *Website:* http://www.iusb.edu/.

Indiana University Southeast

New Albany, Indiana

- **State-supported** comprehensive, founded 1941, part of Indiana University System
- **Suburban** 178-acre campus with easy access to Louisville
- **Endowment** $10.5 million
- **Coed** 6,203 undergraduate students, 60% full-time, 58% women, 42% men
- **Minimally difficult** entrance level, 78% of applicants were admitted

Undergraduates 3,751 full-time, 2,452 part-time. Students come from 18 states and territories; 36 other countries; 28% are from out of state; 6% Black or African American, non-Hispanic/Latino; 3% Hispanic/Latino; 1% Asian, non-Hispanic/Latino; 0.1% Native Hawaiian or other Pacific Islander, non-Hispanic/Latino; 0.2% American Indian or Alaska Native, non-Hispanic/Latino; 2% Two or more races, non-Hispanic/Latino; 1% Race/ethnicity unknown; 0.3% international; 8% transferred in; 6% live on campus. *Retention:* 59% of full-time freshmen returned.

Freshmen *Admission:* 2,147 applied, 1,673 admitted, 917 enrolled. *Average high school GPA:* 3.05. *Test scores:* SAT critical reading scores over 500: 41%; SAT math scores over 500: 36%; SAT writing scores over 500: 26%; ACT scores over 18: 77%; SAT critical reading scores over 600: 8%; SAT math scores over 600: 6%; SAT writing scores over 600: 5%; ACT scores over 24: 20%; SAT critical reading scores over 700: 1%; ACT scores over 30: 2%.

Faculty *Total:* 498, 42% full-time, 41% with terminal degrees. *Student/faculty ratio:* 15:1.

Academics *Calendar:* semesters. *Degrees:* certificates, associate, bachelor's, master's, and postbachelor's certificates. *Special study options:* academic remediation for entering students, accelerated degree program, adult/continuing education programs, advanced placement credit, distance learning, double majors, external degree program, honors programs, independent study, internships, off-campus study, part-time degree program, services for LD students, student-designed majors, study abroad, summer session for credit. *ROTC:* Army (c), Air Force (c).

Computers on Campus Students can access the following: campus intranet, computer help desk, free student e-mail accounts, online (class) grades, online (class) registration, online (class) schedules. Campuswide network is available. Wireless service is available via entire campus.

Student Life *Housing options:* coed. Campus housing is university owned. *Activities and organizations:* drama/theater group, student-run newspaper, choral group, national fraternities, national sororities. *Campus security:* 24-hour emergency response devices and patrols, self-defense education, lighted pathways, police department on campus. *Student services:* personal/psychological counseling.

Athletics Member NAIA. *Intercollegiate sports:* baseball M, basketball M(s)/W(s), cheerleading W, softball W, tennis M/W, volleyball W(s). *Intramural sports:* basketball M/W, bowling M/W, cross-country running M/W, golf M/W, soccer M/W, softball M/W, tennis M/W, ultimate Frisbee M/W, volleyball M/W.

Standardized Tests *Required:* SAT or ACT (for admission).

Costs (2012–13) *Tuition:* state resident $5960 full-time, $199 per credit hour part-time; nonresident $16,894 full-time, $563 per credit hour part-time. Full-time tuition and fees vary according to course load, location, program, and reciprocity agreements. Part-time tuition and fees vary according to course load, location, program, and reciprocity agreements. *Required fees:* $616 full-time.

Room only: $6570. Room and board charges vary according to board plan and housing facility. *Payment plan:* deferred payment. *Waivers:* employees or children of employees.

Financial Aid Of all full-time matriculated undergraduates who enrolled in 2011, 3,426 applied for aid, 2,830 were judged to have need, 81 had their need fully met. In 2011, 166 non-need-based awards were made. *Average percent of need met:* 93%. *Average financial aid package:* $7802. *Average need-based loan:* $3813. *Average need-based gift aid:* $6007. *Average non-need-based aid:* $1968. *Average indebtedness upon graduation:* $24,609.

Applying *Options:* electronic application, early admission, deferred entrance. *Application fee:* $35. *Required:* high school transcript. *Required for some:* interview. *Application deadlines:* rolling (freshmen), rolling (transfers). *Notification:* continuous (freshmen), continuous (transfers).

Freshman Application Contact Ms. Chris Crews, Acting Director of Admission, Indiana University Southeast, University Center South Room 102, 4201 Grant Line Road, New Albany, IN 47150. *Phone:* 812-941-2212. *Toll-free phone:* 800-852-8835. *Fax:* 812-941-2595. *E-mail:* admissions@ius.edu. *Website:* http://www.ius.edu/.

Indiana Wesleyan University

Marion, Indiana

- **Independent Wesleyan** comprehensive, founded 1920
- **Small-town** 300-acre campus with easy access to Indianapolis
- **Coed** 2,999 undergraduate students, 93% full-time, 64% women, 36% men
- **Moderately difficult** entrance level, 66% of applicants were admitted

Undergraduates 2,798 full-time, 201 part-time. 2% Black or African American, non-Hispanic/Latino; 3% Hispanic/Latino; 0.6% Asian, non-Hispanic/Latino; 0.2% Native Hawaiian or other Pacific Islander, non-Hispanic/Latino; 0.2% American Indian or Alaska Native, non-Hispanic/Latino; 2% Two or more races, non-Hispanic/Latino; 0.2% Race/ethnicity unknown; 0.3% international; 80% live on campus. *Retention:* 74% of full-time freshmen returned.

Freshmen *Admission:* 3,429 applied, 2,272 admitted, 725 enrolled. *Average high school GPA:* 3.65. *Test scores:* SAT critical reading scores over 500: 67%; SAT math scores over 500: 70%; SAT writing scores over 500: 61%; ACT scores over 18: 94%; SAT critical reading scores over 600: 25%; SAT math scores over 600: 24%; SAT writing scores over 600: 20%; ACT scores over 24: 57%; SAT critical reading scores over 700: 4%; SAT math scores over 700: 3%; SAT writing scores over 700: 3%; ACT scores over 30: 5%.

Faculty *Total:* 300, 55% full-time, 38% with terminal degrees. *Student/faculty ratio:* 14:1.

Academics *Calendar:* semesters. *Degrees:* certificates, associate, bachelor's, master's, doctoral, post-master's, and postbachelor's certificates (also offers adult program with significant enrollment not reflected in profile). *Special study options:* academic remediation for entering students, advanced placement credit, distance learning, double majors, freshman honors college, honors programs, independent study, internships, off-campus study, part-time degree program, services for LD students, study abroad, summer session for credit. *ROTC:* Army (b).

Computers on Campus 691 computers/terminals are available on campus for general student use. Students can access the following: campus intranet, computer help desk, free student e-mail accounts, online (class) grades, online (class) registration, online (class) schedules. Campuswide network is available. 100% of college-owned or -operated housing units are wired for high-speed Internet access. Wireless service is available via entire campus.

Student Life *Housing:* on-campus residence required through junior year. *Options:* men-only, women-only. Campus housing is university owned. Freshman campus housing is guaranteed. *Activities and organizations:* drama/theater group, student-run newspaper, radio and television station, choral group, Student Government Organization, Student Activities Council, University Players, World Christian Fellowship, Sixth Man Club. *Campus security:* 24-hour emergency response devices and patrols, late-night transport/escort service, controlled dormitory access. *Student services:* health clinic, personal/psychological counseling.

Athletics Member NAIA, NCCAA. *Intercollegiate sports:* baseball M(s), basketball M(s)/W(s), cheerleading M(s)/W(s), cross-country running M(s)/W(s), golf M(s)/W(s), soccer M(s)/W(s), softball W(s), tennis M(s)/W(s), track and field M(s)/W(s), volleyball W(s). *Intramural sports:* badminton M/W, basketball M/W, bowling M/W, football M/W, golf M/W, racquetball M/W, soccer M/W, softball M/W, swimming and diving M/W, table tennis M/W, tennis M/W, ultimate Frisbee M/W, volleyball M/W, weight lifting M/W.

Standardized Tests *Required:* SAT or ACT (for admission), TOEFL for non-English speaking, and some non-resident alien students (for admission).

Costs (2013–14) *Comprehensive fee:* $31,188 includes full-time tuition ($23,628) and room and board ($7560). Full-time tuition and fees vary according to course load and degree level. Part-time tuition: $662 per credit hour. Part-time tuition and fees vary according to course load and degree level.

Room and board: Room and board charges vary according to board plan. *Payment plan:* installment. *Waivers:* employees or children of employees.

Financial Aid Of all full-time matriculated undergraduates who enrolled in 2011, 2,832 applied for aid, 2,351 were judged to have need, 846 had their need fully met. In 2011, 386 non-need-based awards were made. *Average percent of need met:* 80%. *Average financial aid package:* $21,404. *Average need-based loan:* $6479. *Average need-based gift aid:* $12,739. *Average non-need-based aid:* $4459. *Average indebtedness upon graduation:* $22,940.

Applying *Options:* electronic application, deferred entrance. *Application fee:* $25. *Required:* essay or personal statement, high school transcript, minimum 2.5 GPA, 2 letters of recommendation. *Application deadlines:* rolling (freshmen), rolling (out-of-state freshmen), rolling (transfers). *Notification:* continuous (freshmen), continuous (out-of-state freshmen), continuous (transfers).

Freshman Application Contact Mr. Daniel Solms, Director of Admissions, Indiana Wesleyan University, 4201 South Washington Street, Marion, IN 46953. *Phone:* 866-468-6498 Ext. 2138. *Toll-free phone:* 866-468-6498. *Fax:* 765-677-2333. *E-mail:* admissions@indwes.edu.
Website: http://www.indwes.edu/.

International Business College
Fort Wayne, Indiana

- **Private** 4-year, founded 1889
- **Suburban** campus
- **Coed** 559 undergraduate students
- **72%** of applicants were admitted

Freshmen *Admission:* 860 applied, 615 admitted.
Academics *Calendar:* semesters. *Degrees:* diplomas, associate, and bachelor's. *Special study options:* accelerated degree program, internships.
Freshman Application Contact Admissions Office, International Business College, 5699 Coventry Lane, Fort Wayne, IN 46804. *Phone:* 260-459-4500. *Toll-free phone:* 800-589-6363.
Website: http://www.ibcfortwayne.edu/.

ITT Technical Institute
Fort Wayne, Indiana

- **Proprietary** primarily 2-year, founded 1967, part of ITT Educational Services, Inc.
- **Coed**
- **Minimally difficult** entrance level

Academics *Calendar:* quarters. *Degrees:* associate and bachelor's.
Freshman Application Contact Director of Recruitment, ITT Technical Institute, 2810 Dupont Commerce Court, Fort Wayne, IN 46825. *Phone:* 260-497-6200. *Toll-free phone:* 800-866-4488. *Fax:* 260-497-6299.
Website: http://www.itt-tech.edu/.

ITT Technical Institute
Indianapolis, Indiana

- **Proprietary** 4-year
- **Coed**
- **Minimally difficult** entrance level

Academics *Degrees:* associate and bachelor's.
Freshman Application Contact Director of Recruitment, ITT Technical Institute, 2525 N. Shadeland Avenue, Suite 103, Indianapolis, IN 46219. *Phone:* 317-351-3800. *Toll-free phone:* 877-264-1057.
Website: http://www.itt-tech.edu/.

ITT Technical Institute
Indianapolis, Indiana

- **Proprietary** comprehensive, founded 1966, part of ITT Educational Services, Inc.
- **Suburban** campus
- **Coed**
- **Minimally difficult** entrance level

Academics *Calendar:* quarters. *Degrees:* associate, bachelor's, and master's.
Freshman Application Contact Director of Recruitment, ITT Technical Institute, 9511 Angola Court, Indianapolis, IN 46268-1119. *Phone:* 317-875-8640. *Toll-free phone:* 800-937-4488.
Website: http://www.itt-tech.edu/.

ITT Technical Institute
Merrillville, Indiana

- **Proprietary** primarily 2-year
- **Coed**
- **Minimally difficult** entrance level

Academics *Degrees:* associate and bachelor's.
Freshman Application Contact Director of Recruitment, ITT Technical Institute, 8488 Georgia Street, Merrillville, IN 46410. *Phone:* 219-738-6100. *Toll-free phone:* 877-418-8134.
Website: http://www.itt-tech.edu/.

ITT Technical Institute
Newburgh, Indiana

- **Proprietary** primarily 2-year, founded 1966, part of ITT Educational Services, Inc.
- **Coed**
- **Minimally difficult** entrance level

Academics *Calendar:* quarters. *Degrees:* associate and bachelor's.
Freshman Application Contact Director of Recruitment, ITT Technical Institute, 10999 Stahl Road, Newburgh, IN 47630-7430. *Phone:* 812-858-1600. *Toll-free phone:* 800-832-4488.
Website: http://www.itt-tech.edu/.

ITT Technical Institute
South Bend, Indiana

- **Proprietary** 4-year, part of ITT Educational Services, Inc.
- **Coed**
- **Minimally difficult** entrance level

Academics *Calendar:* quarters. *Degrees:* associate and bachelor's.
Freshman Application Contact Director of Recruitment, ITT Technical Institute, 17390 Dugdale Drive, Suite 100, South Bend, IN 46635. *Phone:* 574-247-8300. *Toll-free phone:* 877-474-1926.
Website: http://www.itt-tech.edu/.

Manchester University
North Manchester, Indiana

- **Independent** comprehensive, founded 1889, affiliated with Church of the Brethren
- **Small-town** 125-acre campus
- **Endowment** $42.9 million
- **Coed** 1,257 undergraduate students, 98% full-time, 52% women, 48% men
- **Moderately difficult** entrance level, 64% of applicants were admitted

Undergraduates 1,232 full-time, 25 part-time. Students come from 21 states and territories; 23 other countries; 8% are from out of state; 3% Black or African American, non-Hispanic/Latino; 4% Hispanic/Latino; 0.6% Asian, non-Hispanic/Latino; 0.1% Native Hawaiian or other Pacific Islander, non-Hispanic/Latino; 0.2% American Indian or Alaska Native, non-Hispanic/Latino; 3% Two or more races, non-Hispanic/Latino; 0.3% Race/ethnicity unknown; 2% international; 2% transferred in; 75% live on campus. *Retention:* 68% of full-time freshmen returned.

Freshmen *Admission:* 3,861 applied, 2,473 admitted, 372 enrolled. *Average high school GPA:* 3.36. *Test scores:* SAT critical reading scores over 500: 53%; SAT math scores over 500: 67%; SAT writing scores over 500: 47%; ACT scores over 18: 89%; SAT critical reading scores over 600: 12%; SAT math scores over 600: 22%; SAT writing scores over 600: 8%; ACT scores over 24: 44%; SAT critical reading scores over 700: 2%; SAT math scores over 700: 1%; SAT writing scores over 700: 1%; ACT scores over 30: 4%.

Faculty *Total:* 102, 73% full-time, 73% with terminal degrees. *Student/faculty ratio:* 15:1.

Academics *Calendar:* 4-1-4. *Degrees:* certificates, associate, bachelor's, master's, and doctoral. *Special study options:* accelerated degree program, advanced placement credit, distance learning, double majors, honors programs, independent study, internships, off-campus study, part-time degree program, services for LD students, student-designed majors, study abroad, summer session for credit. *Unusual degree programs:* 3-2 engineering with institutions such as Washington University in St. Louis, Purdue University, Ohio State University.

Computers on Campus 222 computers/terminals are available on campus for general student use. Students can access the following: campus intranet, computer help desk, free student e-mail accounts, online (class) grades, online (class) registration, online (class) schedules. Campuswide network is available. 100% of college-owned or -operated housing units are wired for high-speed

Internet access. Wireless service is available via computer centers, computer labs, dorm rooms, learning centers, libraries, student centers.

Student Life *Housing:* on-campus residence required through junior year. *Options:* coed, disabled students. Campus housing is university owned. Freshman campus housing is guaranteed. *Activities and organizations:* drama/theater group, student-run newspaper, radio station, choral group, A Cappella Choir, American Chemical Society, Accounting and Business Club, Circle K, Student Education Association. *Campus security:* 24-hour emergency response devices and patrols, student patrols, late-night transport/escort service, alarm system, locked residence hall entrances. *Student services:* health clinic, personal/psychological counseling.

Athletics Member NCAA. All Division III. *Intercollegiate sports:* baseball M, basketball M/W, cheerleading W, cross-country running M/W, equestrian sports W, football M, golf M/W, soccer M/W, softball W, tennis M/W, track and field M/W, volleyball W, wrestling M. *Intramural sports:* basketball M/W, football M/W, soccer M/W, softball M/W, volleyball M/W.

Standardized Tests *Required:* SAT or ACT (for admission).

Costs (2013–14) *One-time required fee:* $250. *Comprehensive fee:* $37,170 includes full-time tuition ($27,000), mandatory fees ($920), and room and board ($9250). Part-time tuition: $700 per credit hour. Part-time tuition and fees vary according to course load. *Required fees:* $25 part-time. *College room only:* $5500. Room and board charges vary according to board plan and housing facility. *Payment plan:* installment. *Waivers:* employees or children of employees.

Financial Aid Of all full-time matriculated undergraduates who enrolled in 2012, 1,139 applied for aid, 1,070 were judged to have need, 253 had their need fully met. In 2012, 79 non-need-based awards were made. *Average financial aid package:* $24,423. *Average need-based loan:* $4218. *Average need-based gift aid:* $19,591. *Average non-need-based aid:* $14,241. *Average indebtedness upon graduation:* $29,039.

Applying *Options:* electronic application. *Application fee:* $25. *Required:* high school transcript, 1 letter of recommendation, rank in upper 50% of high school class. *Required for some:* essay or personal statement, minimum 3.0 GPA. *Recommended:* minimum 2.3 GPA. *Application deadlines:* rolling (freshmen), rolling (transfers). *Notification:* continuous (freshmen), continuous (transfers).

Freshman Application Contact Mr. Adam Hohman, Associate Director of Admissions, Manchester University, 604 East College Avenue, North Manchester, IN 46962-1225. *Phone:* 260-982-5235. *Toll-free phone:* 800-852-3648. *Fax:* 260-982-5239. *E-mail:* arhohman@manchester.edu. *Website:* http://www.manchester.edu/.

Marian University

Indianapolis, Indiana

Freshman Application Contact Marian University, 3200 Cold Spring Road, Indianapolis, IN 46222-1997. *Phone:* 317-955-6300. *Toll-free phone:* 800-772-7264. *Fax:* 317-955-6401. *E-mail:* admissions@marian.edu. *Website:* http://www.marian.edu/.

Martin University

Indianapolis, Indiana

Freshman Application Contact Ms. Brenda Shaheed, Director of Enrollment Management, Martin University, 2171 Avondale Place, PO Box 18567, Indianapolis, IN 46218-3867. *Phone:* 317-543-3237. *Fax:* 317-543-4790. *Website:* http://www.martin.edu/.

Mid-America College of Funeral Service

Jeffersonville, Indiana

Freshman Application Contact Mr. Richard Nelson, Dean of Students, Mid-America College of Funeral Service, 3111 Hamburg Pike, Jeffersonville, IN 47130-9630. *Phone:* 812-288-8878. *Toll-free phone:* 800-221-6158. *Fax:* 812-288-5942. *E-mail:* macfs@mindspring.com. *Website:* http://www.mid-america.edu/.

Oakland City University

Oakland City, Indiana

- **Independent General Baptist** comprehensive, founded 1885
- **Rural** 20-acre campus
- **Coed** 2,301 undergraduate students, 21% full-time, 61% women, 39% men
- **Minimally difficult** entrance level, 48% of applicants were admitted

Undergraduates 480 full-time, 1,821 part-time. 15% are from out of state; 5% Black or African American, non-Hispanic/Latino; 4% Hispanic/Latino; 0.9% Asian, non-Hispanic/Latino; 0.2% Native Hawaiian or other Pacific Islander, non-Hispanic/Latino; 0.4% American Indian or Alaska Native, non-Hispanic/Latino; 0.7% Two or more races, non-Hispanic/Latino; 2% Race/ethnicity unknown; 0.6% transferred in; 33% live on campus. *Retention:* 75% of full-time freshmen returned.

Freshmen *Admission:* 514 applied, 246 admitted, 111 enrolled. *Average high school GPA:* 3.09. *Test scores:* SAT critical reading scores over 500: 29%; SAT math scores over 500: 36%; SAT writing scores over 500: 25%; ACT scores over 18: 70%; SAT critical reading scores over 600: 3%; SAT math scores over 600: 7%; SAT writing scores over 600: 5%; ACT scores over 24: 24%; ACT scores over 30: 2%.

Faculty *Total:* 202, 18% full-time, 63% with terminal degrees. *Student/faculty ratio:* 15:1.

Academics *Calendar:* semesters. *Degrees:* certificates, associate, bachelor's, master's, and doctoral. *Special study options:* academic remediation for entering students, accelerated degree program, adult/continuing education programs, advanced placement credit, external degree program, part-time degree program, services for LD students, summer session for credit.

Computers on Campus 92 computers/terminals are available on campus for general student use. Students can access the following: campus intranet, free student e-mail accounts, online (class) grades, online (class) schedules. Campuswide network is available. 100% of college-owned or -operated housing units are wired for high-speed Internet access. Wireless service is available via entire campus.

Student Life *Housing:* on-campus residence required for freshman year. *Options:* men-only, women-only. Campus housing is university owned. Freshman campus housing is guaranteed. *Activities and organizations:* drama/theater group, student-run newspaper, choral group, Student Government Association, Good News Players, Art Guild, FOCUS, intramural sports. *Campus security:* 24-hour patrols, student patrols. *Student services:* personal/psychological counseling.

Athletics Member NCAA, NCCAA. All NCAA Division II. *Intercollegiate sports:* baseball M(s), basketball M(s)/W(s), cheerleading W(s), cross-country running M(s)/W(s), golf M(s)/W(s), soccer M(s)/W(s), softball W(s), tennis M(s)/W(s), volleyball W(s). *Intramural sports:* archery M/W, badminton M/W, basketball M/W, bowling M/W, football M, golf M/W, soccer M/W, softball M/W, table tennis M/W, tennis M/W, volleyball M/W.

Standardized Tests *Required:* SAT or ACT (for admission). *Required for some:* SAT or ACT (for admission).

Costs (2013–14) *Comprehensive fee:* $26,700 includes full-time tuition ($18,600) and room and board ($8100). Full-time tuition and fees vary according to degree level. Part-time tuition: $620 per credit hour. *College room only:* $2800. Room and board charges vary according to board plan and housing facility. *Payment plan:* deferred payment.

Financial Aid Of all full-time matriculated undergraduates who enrolled in 2007, 150 Federal Work-Study jobs (averaging $1600). 4 state and other part-time jobs (averaging $1500). *Average percent of need met:* 90%.

Applying *Options:* electronic application, early admission, deferred entrance. *Application fee:* $35. *Required:* essay or personal statement, high school transcript, minimum 2.0 GPA. *Recommended:* interview. *Application deadlines:* rolling (freshmen), rolling (transfers). *Notification:* continuous (freshmen), continuous (transfers).

Freshman Application Contact Ms. Kim Heldt, Director of Admissions, Oakland City University, 138 North Lucretia Street, Oakland City, IN 47660. *Phone:* 812-749-1222. *Toll-free phone:* 800-737-5125. *Website:* http://www.oak.edu/.

Purdue University

West Lafayette, Indiana

- **State-supported** university, founded 1869, part of Purdue University System
- **Suburban** 2602-acre campus with easy access to Indianapolis
- **Endowment** $1.9 billion
- **Coed** 30,147 undergraduate students, 95% full-time, 43% women, 57% men
- **Moderately difficult** entrance level, 61% of applicants were admitted

Undergraduates 28,739 full-time, 1,408 part-time. Students come from 52 states and territories; 90 other countries; 31% are from out of state; 3% Black or African American, non-Hispanic/Latino; 4% Hispanic/Latino; 5% Asian, non-Hispanic/Latino; 0.1% Native Hawaiian or other Pacific Islander, non-Hispanic/Latino; 0.2% American Indian or Alaska Native, non-Hispanic/Latino; 2% Two or more races, non-Hispanic/Latino; 2% Race/ethnicity unknown; 16% international; 2% transferred in; 35% live on campus. *Retention:* 91% of full-time freshmen returned.

Freshmen *Admission:* 30,903 applied, 18,951 admitted, 6,349 enrolled. *Average high school GPA:* 3.7. *Test scores:* SAT critical reading scores over 500: 81%; SAT math scores over 500: 92%; SAT writing scores over 500: 80%; ACT scores over 18: 100%; SAT critical reading scores over 600: 35%; SAT math scores over 600: 60%; SAT writing scores over 600: 33%; ACT scores over 24: 79%; SAT critical reading scores over 700: 7%; SAT math scores over 700: 21%; SAT writing scores over 700: 5%; ACT scores over 30: 27%.

Faculty *Total:* 2,314, 88% full-time. *Student/faculty ratio:* 14:1.

Academics *Calendar:* semesters. *Degrees:* certificates, associate, bachelor's, master's, doctoral, post-master's, and postbachelor's certificates. *Special study options:* accelerated degree program, adult/continuing education programs, advanced placement credit, cooperative education, distance learning, double majors, freshman honors college, honors programs, independent study, internships, part-time degree program, services for LD students, study abroad, summer session for credit. *ROTC:* Army (b), Navy (b), Air Force (b). *Unusual degree programs:* 3-2 business administration; engineering; forestry; nursing; social work; pharmacy.

Computers on Campus 5,217 computers/terminals and 17,822 ports are available on campus for general student use. Students can access the following: campus intranet, computer help desk, free student e-mail accounts, online (class) grades, online (class) registration, online (class) schedules. Campus-wide network is available. 100% of college-owned or -operated housing units are wired for high-speed Internet access. Wireless service is available via classrooms, computer centers, computer labs, learning centers, libraries, student centers.

Student Life *Housing options:* coed, men-only, women-only, cooperative, disabled students. Campus housing is university owned. Freshman applicants given priority for college housing. *Activities and organizations:* drama/theater group, student-run newspaper, radio and television station, choral group, marching band, student government, Golden Key National Honor Society, Society of Women Engineers, Purdue student union board, Krannert Graduate Student Association, national fraternities, national sororities. *Campus security:* 24-hour emergency response devices and patrols, student patrols, late-night transport/escort service, controlled dormitory access. *Student services:* health clinic, personal/psychological counseling, women's center.

Athletics Member NCAA. All Division I except football (Division I-A). *Intercollegiate sports:* baseball M(s), basketball M(s)/W(s), cross-country running M(s)/W(s), golf M(s)/W(s), soccer W(s), softball W(s), swimming and diving M(s)/W(s), tennis M(s)/W(s), track and field M(s)/W(s), volleyball W(s), wrestling M(s). *Intramural sports:* archery M(c)/W(c), badminton M(c)/W(c), baseball M(c), bowling M(c)/W(c), crew M(c)/W(c), cross-country running M(c)/W(c), equestrian sports M(c)/W(c), fencing M(c)/W(c), gymnastics M(c)/W(c), ice hockey M(c), lacrosse M(c)/W(c), racquetball M(c)/W(c), riflery M(c)/W(c), rock climbing M(c)/W(c), rugby M(c)/W(c), sailing M(c)/W(c), soccer M(c)/W(c), squash M(c)/W(c), swimming and diving M(c)/W(c), table tennis M(c)/W(c), tennis M(c)/W(c), track and field M(c)/W(c), ultimate Frisbee M(c)/W(c), volleyball M(c)/W(c), water polo M(c)/W(c).

Standardized Tests *Required:* SAT or ACT (for admission).

Costs (2012–13) *Tuition:* state resident $9900 full-time; nonresident $28,702 full-time. Full-time tuition and fees vary according to course load and program. Part-time tuition and fees vary according to course load. *Required fees:* $566 full-time. *Room and board:* $9990; room only: $5196. Room and board charges vary according to board plan and housing facility. *Payment plan:* installment. *Waivers:* senior citizens and employees or children of employees.

Financial Aid Of all full-time matriculated undergraduates who enrolled in 2012, 18,211 applied for aid, 14,269 were judged to have need, 5,007 had their need fully met. 1,935 Federal Work-Study jobs (averaging $2373). In 2012, 2478 non-need-based awards were made. *Average percent of need met:* 85%. *Average financial aid package:* $12,300. *Average need-based loan:* $4776. *Average need-based gift aid:* $10,702. *Average non-need-based aid:* $6321. *Average indebtedness upon graduation:* $27,798.

Applying *Options:* electronic application, early admission, deferred entrance. *Application fee:* $50. *Required:* high school transcript. *Application deadlines:* 3/1 (freshmen), rolling (transfers). *Notification:* continuous (freshmen).

Freshman Application Contact Ms. Pamela T. Horne, Assistant Vice President for Enrollment Management and Dean of Admissions, Purdue University, 475 Stadium Mall Drive, Schleman Hall, West Lafayette, IN 47907-2050. *Phone:* 765-494-1776. *Fax:* 765-494-0544. *E-mail:* admissions@purdue.edu.

Website: http://www.purdue.edu/.

Purdue University Calumet
Hammond, Indiana

- **State-supported** comprehensive, founded 1951, part of Purdue University System
- **Urban** 202-acre campus with easy access to Chicago
- **Endowment** $12.9 million
- **Coed** 8,912 undergraduate students, 58% full-time, 58% women, 42% men
- **Moderately difficult** entrance level, 51% of applicants were admitted

Undergraduates 5,140 full-time, 3,772 part-time. 20% are from out of state; 14% Black or African American, non-Hispanic/Latino; 15% Hispanic/Latino; 2% Asian, non-Hispanic/Latino; 0.1% Native Hawaiian or other Pacific Islander, non-Hispanic/Latino; 0.3% American Indian or Alaska Native, non-Hispanic/Latino; 1% Two or more races, non-Hispanic/Latino; 8% Race/ethnicity unknown; 6% international; 6% transferred in; 6% live on campus. *Retention:* 69% of full-time freshmen returned.

Freshmen *Admission:* 3,759 applied, 1,918 admitted, 994 enrolled. *Average high school GPA:* 3.03. *Test scores:* SAT critical reading scores over 500: 41%; SAT writing scores over 500: 32%; SAT critical reading scores over 600: 8%; SAT writing scores over 600: 6%; SAT critical reading scores over 700: 2%; SAT writing scores over 700: 1%.

Faculty *Total:* 606, 51% full-time, 42% with terminal degrees. *Student/faculty ratio:* 17:1.

Academics *Calendar:* semesters. *Degrees:* certificates, associate, bachelor's, master's, post-master's, and postbachelor's certificates. *Special study options:* academic remediation for entering students, accelerated degree program, adult/continuing education programs, advanced placement credit, cooperative education, distance learning, double majors, English as a second language, freshman honors college, honors programs, independent study, internships, part-time degree program, services for LD students, study abroad, summer session for credit. *ROTC:* Army (b).

Computers on Campus 1,500 computers/terminals and 100 ports are available on campus for general student use. Students can access the following: campus intranet, computer help desk, free student e-mail accounts, online (class) grades, online (class) registration, online (class) schedules. Campus-wide network is available. 100% of college-owned or -operated housing units are wired for high-speed Internet access. Wireless service is available via learning centers, libraries, student centers.

Student Life *Housing options:* coed. Campus housing is university owned. *Activities and organizations:* drama/theater group, student-run newspaper, choral group, Purdue University Gamers Guild, Biology Club, American Society of Civil Engineers, Purdue Calumet Ambassadors, Society for Human Resources Management, national fraternities, national sororities. *Campus security:* 24-hour emergency response devices and patrols, student patrols, late-night transport/escort service. *Student services:* health clinic, personal/psychological counseling.

Athletics Member NAIA. *Intercollegiate sports:* baseball M, basketball M(s)/W(s), cross-country running M/W, golf M, soccer M/W, softball W, tennis M/W, volleyball W. *Intramural sports:* badminton M/W, bowling M/W, football M/W, golf M/W, racquetball M/W, soccer M/W, softball M/W, swimming and diving M/W, table tennis M/W, ultimate Frisbee M/W, volleyball M/W.

Standardized Tests *Required:* SAT or ACT (for admission).

Costs (2012–13) *Tuition:* state resident $6991 full-time, $232 per credit hour part-time; nonresident $15,169 full-time, $524 per credit hour part-time. Full-time tuition and fees vary according to course load and program. Part-time tuition and fees vary according to course load and program. *Room and board:* $7717; room only: $5170. Room and board charges vary according to housing facility. *Payment plan:* deferred payment. *Waivers:* senior citizens and employees or children of employees.

Financial Aid Of all full-time matriculated undergraduates who enrolled in 2011, 4,882 applied for aid, 4,373 were judged to have need, 345 had their need fully met. 68 Federal Work-Study jobs (averaging $2478). In 2011, 186 non-need-based awards were made. *Average percent of need met:* 18%. *Average financial aid package:* $7306. *Average need-based loan:* $3469. *Average need-based gift aid:* $5330. *Average non-need-based aid:* $4348. *Average indebtedness upon graduation:* $26,273.

Applying *Options:* electronic application. *Application fee:* $25. *Required:* high school transcript, minimum 2.0 GPA. *Application deadlines:* 8/9 (freshmen), 8/9 (out-of-state freshmen), 8/9 (transfers). *Notification:* continuous (freshmen), continuous (out-of-state freshmen), continuous (transfers).

Freshman Application Contact Purdue University Calumet, 2200 169th Street, Hammond, IN 46323-2094. *Phone:* 219-989-2287. *Toll-free phone:* 800-447-8738.

Website: http://www.purduecal.edu/.

Purdue University North Central
Westville, Indiana

- **State-supported** comprehensive, founded 1967, part of Purdue University System
- **Rural** 305-acre campus with easy access to Chicago
- **Endowment** $3.5 million
- **Coed** 5,982 undergraduate students, 45% full-time, 59% women, 41% men
- **Minimally difficult** entrance level, 72% of applicants were admitted

Undergraduates 2,701 full-time, 3,281 part-time. Students come from 7 states and territories; 12 other countries; 2% are from out of state; 5% Black or African American, non-Hispanic/Latino; 10% Hispanic/Latino; 1% Asian, non-Hispanic/Latino; 0.1% Native Hawaiian or other Pacific Islander, non-Hispanic/Latino; 0.5% American Indian or Alaska Native, non-Hispanic/Latino; 2% Two or more races, non-Hispanic/Latino; 0.2% Race/ethnicity unknown; 0.3% international; 5% transferred in. *Retention:* 62% of full-time freshmen returned.
Freshmen *Admission:* 1,582 applied, 1,141 admitted, 655 enrolled. *Average high school GPA:* 2.93. *Test scores:* SAT critical reading scores over 500: 35%; SAT math scores over 500: 42%; SAT writing scores over 500: 29%; ACT scores over 18: 82%; SAT critical reading scores over 600: 8%; SAT math scores over 600: 9%; SAT writing scores over 600: 3%; ACT scores over 24: 20%; SAT critical reading scores over 700: 1%; SAT math scores over 700: 1%; ACT scores over 30: 1%.
Faculty *Total:* 277, 43% full-time, 35% with terminal degrees. *Student/faculty ratio:* 17:1.
Academics *Calendar:* semesters. *Degrees:* certificates, associate, bachelor's, master's, and postbachelor's certificates. *Special study options:* academic remediation for entering students, advanced placement credit, distance learning, double majors, honors programs, independent study, internships, off-campus study, services for LD students, study abroad, summer session for credit.
Computers on Campus 450 computers/terminals and 65 ports are available on campus for general student use. Students can access the following: campus intranet, computer help desk, free student e-mail accounts, online (class) grades, online (class) registration, online (class) schedules. Campuswide network is available. Wireless service is available via entire campus.
Student Life *Housing:* college housing not available. *Activities and organizations:* drama/theater group, student-run newspaper, choral group, Dean's Leadership Group, Society of Human Resource Management, PLAYCE (Early Childhood Education), Astronomy Club, PNC Veteran's. *Campus security:* 24-hour emergency response devices and patrols, late-night transport/escort service. *Student services:* personal/psychological counseling.
Athletics Member NAIA. *Intercollegiate sports:* cheerleading M/W.
Standardized Tests *Recommended:* SAT or ACT (for admission).
Costs (2012–13) *Tuition:* state resident $6440 full-time, $215 per credit hour part-time; nonresident $16,164 full-time, $539 per credit hour part-time. Full-time tuition and fees vary according to reciprocity agreements. Part-time tuition and fees vary according to reciprocity agreements. *Required fees:* $605 full-time, $20 per credit hour part-time. *Payment plans:* installment, deferred payment. *Waivers:* senior citizens and employees or children of employees.
Financial Aid Of all full-time matriculated undergraduates who enrolled in 2010, 2,809 applied for aid, 2,150 were judged to have need, 438 had their need fully met. 62 Federal Work-Study jobs (averaging $1607). In 2010, 25 non-need-based awards were made. *Average percent of need met:* 50%. *Average financial aid package:* $7339. *Average need-based loan:* $3702. *Average need-based gift aid:* $5930. *Average non-need-based aid:* $1473. *Average indebtedness upon graduation:* $20,153. *Financial aid deadline:* 6/30.
Applying *Options:* electronic application, deferred entrance. *Required:* high school transcript. *Required for some:* minimum 2.0 GPA. *Application deadlines:* 8/15 (freshmen), 8/15 (transfers). *Notification:* continuous (freshmen), continuous (transfers).
Freshman Application Contact Ms. Janice Whisler, Director Enrollment/Outreach Recruitment, Purdue University North Central, 1401 South U.S. Highway 421, Westville, IN 46391. *Phone:* 219-785-5415. *Toll-free phone:* 800-872-1231. *Fax:* 219-785-5538. *E-mail:* jwhisler@pnc.edu. *Website:* http://www.pnc.edu/.

Rose-Hulman Institute of Technology
Terre Haute, Indiana

- **Independent** comprehensive, founded 1874
- **Suburban** 200-acre campus with easy access to Indianapolis
- **Endowment** $181.9 million
- **Coed, primarily men**
- **Very difficult** entrance level

Faculty *Student/faculty ratio:* 12:1.
Academics *Calendar:* quarters. *Degrees:* bachelor's and master's.

Student Life *Campus security:* 24-hour emergency response devices and patrols, late-night transport/escort service, controlled dormitory access.
Athletics Member NCAA. All Division III.
Standardized Tests *Required:* SAT or ACT (for admission).
Costs (2012–13) *One-time required fee:* $2400. *Comprehensive fee:* $50,013 includes full-time tuition ($38,313), mandatory fees ($765), and room and board ($10,935). Full-time tuition and fees vary according to course load. Part-time tuition: $1118 per credit hour. Part-time tuition and fees vary according to course load. *College room only:* $6705. Room and board charges vary according to board plan. *Payment plans:* tuition prepayment, installment.
Financial Aid *Of all full-time matriculated undergraduates who enrolled in 2012,* 1,619 applied for aid, 1,445 were judged to have need, 206 had their need fully met. 419 Federal Work-Study jobs (averaging $1297). 560 state and other part-time jobs (averaging $1300). *In 2012,* 611 non-need-based awards were made. *Average percent of need met:* 72. *Average financial aid package:* $26,703. *Average need-based loan:* $5147. *Average need-based gift aid:* $21,881. *Average non-need-based aid:* $11,441. *Average indebtedness upon graduation:* $44,965.
Applying *Options:* electronic application, deferred entrance. *Application fee:* $40. *Required:* high school transcript, 1 letter of recommendation, curricular. *Recommended:* essay or personal statement, interview.
Freshman Application Contact Mrs. Lisa Norton, Director of Admissions, Rose-Hulman Institute of Technology, 5500 Wabash Avenue, CM 1, Terre Haute, IN 47803-3920. *Phone:* 812-877-8213. *Toll-free phone:* 800-248-7448. *Fax:* 812-877-8941. *E-mail:* admissions@rose-hulman.edu. *Website:* http://www.rose-hulman.edu/.

Saint Joseph's College
Rensselaer, Indiana

- **Independent Roman Catholic** comprehensive, founded 1889
- **Small-town** 180-acre campus
- **Endowment** $24.2 million
- **Coed** 1,074 undergraduate students, 92% full-time, 61% women, 39% men
- **Moderately difficult** entrance level, 62% of applicants were admitted

Undergraduates 986 full-time, 88 part-time. Students come from 22 states and territories; 9 other countries; 23% are from out of state; 10% Black or African American, non-Hispanic/Latino; 4% Hispanic/Latino; 0.7% Asian, non-Hispanic/Latino; 0.1% Native Hawaiian or other Pacific Islander, non-Hispanic/Latino; 0.8% American Indian or Alaska Native, non-Hispanic/Latino; 2% Two or more races, non-Hispanic/Latino; 3% Race/ethnicity unknown; 0.5% international; 4% transferred in; 67% live on campus. *Retention:* 67% of full-time freshmen returned.
Freshmen *Admission:* 1,718 applied, 1,061 admitted, 235 enrolled. *Average high school GPA:* 3.14. *Test scores:* SAT critical reading scores over 500: 35%; SAT math scores over 500: 43%; ACT scores over 18: 89%; SAT critical reading scores over 600: 6%; SAT math scores over 600: 10%; ACT scores over 24: 36%; ACT scores over 30: 5%.
Faculty *Total:* 119, 50% full-time, 41% with terminal degrees. *Student/faculty ratio:* 13:1.
Academics *Calendar:* semesters. *Degrees:* diplomas, associate, bachelor's, and master's. *Special study options:* academic remediation for entering students, accelerated degree program, advanced placement credit, double majors, honors programs, independent study, internships, part-time degree program, services for LD students, student-designed majors, study abroad, summer session for credit.
Computers on Campus 69 computers/terminals and 114 ports are available on campus for general student use. Students can access the following: campus intranet, computer help desk, free student e-mail accounts, online (class) grades, online (class) registration, online (class) schedules. Campuswide network is available. 100% of college-owned or -operated housing units are wired for high-speed Internet access. Wireless service is available via entire campus.
Student Life *Housing:* on-campus residence required through senior year. *Options:* coed, men-only, women-only, disabled students. Campus housing is university owned. Freshman campus housing is guaranteed. *Activities and organizations:* drama/theater group, student-run newspaper, radio and television station, choral group, marching band, Gallagher Charitable Society, Cup O' Joe, Habitat for Humanity, Science Club, Alpha Lambda Delta. *Campus security:* 24-hour emergency response devices and patrols, student patrols, late-night transport/escort service. *Student services:* health clinic, personal/psychological counseling.
Athletics Member NCAA. All Division II. *Intercollegiate sports:* baseball M(s), basketball M(s)/W(s), cheerleading M(s)(c)/W(s)(c), cross-country running M(s)/W(s), football M(s), golf M(s)/W(s), soccer M(s)/W(s), softball W(s), tennis M(s)/W(s), track and field M(s)/W(s), volleyball W(s). *Intramural sports:* basketball M/W, lacrosse M(c)/W(c), rugby M(c)/W(c), soccer M/W, softball M/W, ultimate Frisbee M/W, volleyball M/W.

Standardized Tests *Required:* SAT or ACT (for admission).
Costs (2012–13) *Comprehensive fee:* $35,600 includes full-time tuition ($27,160), mandatory fees ($190), and room and board ($8250). Full-time tuition and fees vary according to reciprocity agreements. *Part-time tuition:* $910 per credit. Part-time tuition and fees vary according to course load and reciprocity agreements. *College room only:* $4010. Room and board charges vary according to housing facility. *Payment plan:* installment. *Waivers:* minority students, children of alumni, and employees or children of employees.
Financial Aid Of all full-time matriculated undergraduates who enrolled in 2011, 800 applied for aid, 713 were judged to have need, 200 had their need fully met. 107 Federal Work-Study jobs (averaging $935). In 2011, 82 non-need-based awards were made. *Average percent of need met:* 81%. *Average financial aid package:* $24,940. *Average need-based loan:* $4362. *Average need-based gift aid:* $17,827. *Average non-need-based aid:* $14,628. *Average indebtedness upon graduation:* $30,963.
Applying *Options:* electronic application, deferred entrance. *Application fee:* $25. *Required:* high school transcript, minimum 2.0 GPA. *Required for some:* essay or personal statement. *Recommended:* interview. *Application deadlines:* rolling (freshmen), rolling (transfers). *Notification:* continuous (freshmen), continuous (transfers).
Freshman Application Contact Vacant, Vice President for Enrollment Management, Saint Joseph's College, PO Box 815, Rensselaer, IN 47978-0850. *Phone:* 219-866-6170. *Toll-free phone:* 800-447-8781. *Fax:* 219-866-6122. *E-mail:* admissions@saintjoe.edu.
Website: http://www.saintjoe.edu/.

Saint Mary-of-the-Woods College
Saint Mary of the Woods, Indiana

- **Independent Roman Catholic** comprehensive, founded 1840
- **Rural** 67-acre campus with easy access to Indianapolis
- **Endowment** $10.6 million
- **Coed, primarily women** 795 undergraduate students, 54% full-time, 96% women, 4% men
- **Moderately difficult** entrance level, 64% of applicants were admitted

Undergraduates 431 full-time, 364 part-time. Students come from 36 states and territories; 7 other countries; 24% are from out of state; 4% Black or African American, non-Hispanic/Latino; 2% Hispanic/Latino; 0.3% Asian, non-Hispanic/Latino; 0.8% American Indian or Alaska Native, non-Hispanic/Latino; 9% Race/ethnicity unknown; 0.8% international; 10% transferred in. *Retention:* 74% of full-time freshmen returned.
Freshmen *Admission:* 424 applied, 270 admitted, 72 enrolled. *Average high school GPA:* 3.16. *Test scores:* SAT critical reading scores over 500: 52%; SAT math scores over 500: 26%; SAT writing scores over 500: 29%; ACT scores over 18: 82%; SAT critical reading scores over 600: 10%; SAT math scores over 600: 2%; SAT writing scores over 600: 2%; ACT scores over 24: 21%.
Faculty *Total:* 64, 98% full-time, 94% with terminal degrees. *Student/faculty ratio:* 8:1.
Academics *Calendar:* semesters. *Degrees:* certificates, associate, bachelor's, master's, and postbachelor's certificates (also offers external degree program with significant enrollment not reflected in profile). *Special study options:* academic remediation for entering students, accelerated degree program, adult/continuing education programs, advanced placement credit, distance learning, double majors, external degree program, honors programs, independent study, internships, off-campus study, part-time degree program, student-designed majors, study abroad, summer session for credit. *ROTC:* Army (c), Air Force (c).
Computers on Campus 85 computers/terminals are available on campus for general student use. Students can access the following: campus intranet, computer help desk, free student e-mail accounts, online (class) grades, online (class) schedules. Campuswide network is available. 100% of college-owned or -operated housing units are wired for high-speed Internet access. Wireless service is available via entire campus.
Student Life *Housing:* on-campus residence required through senior year. *Options:* women-only. Campus housing is university owned. Freshman campus housing is guaranteed. *Activities and organizations:* drama/theater group, student-run newspaper, choral group, Student Activities Committee, Chorale, Student Senate, Woods Newspaper. *Campus security:* 24-hour emergency response devices and patrols, late-night transport/escort service. *Student services:* health clinic, personal/psychological counseling.
Athletics Member USCAA. *Intercollegiate sports:* basketball W(s), cross-country running W(s), equestrian sports W(s), golf W(s), soccer W(s), softball W(s).
Standardized Tests *Required:* SAT or ACT (for admission).
Costs (2012–13) *One-time required fee:* $225. *Comprehensive fee:* $37,472 includes full-time tuition ($26,872), mandatory fees ($800), and room and board ($9800). Full-time tuition and fees vary according to program and student level. *Part-time tuition:* $482 per credit hour. Part-time tuition and fees

vary according to course load. No tuition increase for student's term of enrollment. *Required fees:* $150 per term part-time. *College room only:* $3826. Room and board charges vary according to housing facility. *Payment plan:* installment. *Waivers:* employees or children of employees.
Financial Aid Of all full-time matriculated undergraduates who enrolled in 2012, 431 applied for aid, 394 were judged to have need, 218 had their need fully met. 80 Federal Work-Study jobs (averaging $827). In 2012, 14 non-need-based awards were made. *Average percent of need met:* 27%. *Average financial aid package:* $15,450. *Average need-based loan:* $4503. *Average need-based gift aid:* $8563. *Average non-need-based aid:* $7512. *Average indebtedness upon graduation:* $18,742.
Applying *Options:* electronic application, early admission, deferred entrance. *Application fee:* $30. *Required:* essay or personal statement, high school transcript, minimum 2.5 GPA, 1 letter of recommendation. *Required for some:* interview.
Freshman Application Contact Ms. Beth Terrell, Vice President for Enrollment Management, Saint Mary-of-the-Woods College, Rooney Library, SMWC, Saint Mary of the Woods, IN 47876. *Phone:* 812-535-5106. *Toll-free phone:* 800-926-SMWC. *Fax:* 812-535-5010. *E-mail:* smwcadms@smwc.edu. *Website:* http://www.smwc.edu/.

Saint Mary's College
Notre Dame, Indiana

- **Independent Roman Catholic** 4-year, founded 1844
- **Suburban** 100-acre campus with easy access to Chicago
- **Endowment** $123.3 million
- **Women only** 1,469 undergraduate students, 99% full-time
- **Moderately difficult** entrance level, 85% of applicants were admitted

Undergraduates 1,456 full-time, 13 part-time. Students come from 42 states and territories; 14 other countries; 73% are from out of state; 1% Black or African American, non-Hispanic/Latino; 10% Hispanic/Latino; 1% Asian, non-Hispanic/Latino; 0.1% American Indian or Alaska Native, non-Hispanic/Latino; 2% Two or more races, non-Hispanic/Latino; 4% Race/ethnicity unknown; 2% international; 2% transferred in; 87% live on campus. *Retention:* 88% of full-time freshmen returned.
Freshmen *Admission:* 1,482 applied, 1,256 admitted, 417 enrolled. *Average high school GPA:* 3.75. *Test scores:* SAT critical reading scores over 500: 81%; SAT math scores over 500: 76%; SAT writing scores over 500: 80%; ACT scores over 18: 99%; SAT critical reading scores over 600: 38%; SAT math scores over 600: 34%; SAT writing scores over 600: 34%; ACT scores over 24: 74%; SAT critical reading scores over 700: 7%; SAT math scores over 700: 5%; SAT writing scores over 700: 7%; ACT scores over 30: 14%.
Faculty *Total:* 196, 63% full-time, 68% with terminal degrees. *Student/faculty ratio:* 10:1.
Academics *Calendar:* semesters. *Degree:* bachelor's. *Special study options:* academic remediation for entering students, accelerated degree program, advanced placement credit, cooperative education, distance learning, double majors, English as a second language, independent study, internships, off-campus study, part-time degree program, services for LD students, student-designed majors, study abroad, summer session for credit. *ROTC:* Army (c), Navy (c), Air Force (c). *Unusual degree programs:* 3-2 engineering with University of Notre Dame.
Computers on Campus 303 computers/terminals and 1,456 ports are available on campus for general student use. Students can access the following: campus intranet, computer help desk, free student e-mail accounts, online (class) grades, online (class) registration, online (class) schedules. Campuswide network is available. 100% of college-owned or -operated housing units are wired for high-speed Internet access. Wireless service is available via classrooms, computer centers, computer labs, dorm rooms, learning centers, libraries, student centers.
Student Life *Housing:* on-campus residence required through junior year. *Options:* women-only. Campus housing is university owned. Freshman campus housing is guaranteed. *Activities and organizations:* drama/theater group, student-run newspaper, radio and television station, choral group, marching band, Student Government Association, Dance Marathon, Class Boards, Residence Hall Association, Student Diversity Board. *Campus security:* 24-hour emergency response devices and patrols, late-night transport/escort service, controlled dormitory access. *Student services:* health clinic, personal/psychological counseling, women's center.
Athletics Member NCAA. All Division III. *Intercollegiate sports:* basketball W, cross-country running W, field hockey W(c), golf W, soccer W, softball W, swimming and diving W, tennis W, volleyball W. *Intramural sports:* cheerleading W(c), lacrosse W(c), volleyball W(c).
Standardized Tests *Required:* SAT or ACT (for admission).
Costs (2012–13) *Comprehensive fee:* $43,420 includes full-time tuition ($32,560), mandatory fees ($720), and room and board ($10,140). Part-time tuition: $1290 per credit hour. *Required fees:* $360 per term part-time. *College*

room only: $6250. Room and board charges vary according to board plan and housing facility. *Payment plan:* installment. *Waivers:* employees or children of employees.

Financial Aid Of all full-time matriculated undergraduates who enrolled in 2012, 1,118 applied for aid, 815 were judged to have need, 198 had their need fully met. In 2012, 508 non-need-based awards were made. *Average percent of need met:* 84%. *Average financial aid package:* $27,360. *Average need-based loan:* $4753. *Average need-based gift aid:* $22,653. *Average non-need-based aid:* $12,125. *Average indebtedness upon graduation:* $31,891. *Financial aid deadline:* 3/1.

Applying *Options:* electronic application, early admission, early decision, deferred entrance. *Required:* essay or personal statement, high school transcript, 1 letter of recommendation, 16 high school academic units; at least two years of study of the same foreign language. *Recommended:* interview. *Application deadlines:* 2/15 (freshmen), 4/15 (transfers). *Early decision deadline:* 11/15. *Notification:* continuous (freshmen), continuous (transfers), 12/15 (early decision).

Freshman Application Contact Ms. Kristin McAndrew, Director of Admission, Saint Mary's College, Notre Dame, IN 46556. *Phone:* 574-284-4587. *Toll-free phone:* 800-551-7621. *Fax:* 574-284-4841. *E-mail:* admission@saintmarys.edu.
Website: http://www.saintmarys.edu/.

See this page for display ad and page 1482 for the College Close-Up.

Strayer University—North Indianapolis Campus

Indianapolis, Indiana

Freshman Application Contact Strayer University—North Indianapolis Campus, 9025 N. River Road, Suite 400, Indianapolis, IN 46240.
Website: http://www.strayer.edu/campus/north-indianapolis.

Taylor University

Upland, Indiana

- **Independent interdenominational** comprehensive, founded 1846
- **Rural** 950-acre campus with easy access to Indianapolis
- **Endowment** $67.5 million
- **Coed** 2,237 undergraduate students, 83% full-time, 56% women, 44% men
- **Moderately difficult** entrance level, 84% of applicants were admitted

Undergraduates 1,846 full-time, 391 part-time. Students come from 42 states and territories; 27 other countries; 63% are from out of state; 2% Black or African American, non-Hispanic/Latino; 2% Hispanic/Latino; 2% Asian, non-Hispanic/Latino; 0.2% Native Hawaiian or other Pacific Islander, non-Hispanic/Latino; 0.4% American Indian or Alaska Native, non-Hispanic/Latino; 0.8% Two or more races, non-Hispanic/Latino; 4% international; 2% transferred in; 86% live on campus. *Retention:* 88% of full-time freshmen returned.

Freshmen *Admission:* 1,787 applied, 1,493 admitted, 498 enrolled. *Average high school GPA:* 3.71. *Test scores:* SAT critical reading scores over 500: 80%; SAT math scores over 500: 81%; SAT writing scores over 500: 73%; ACT scores over 18: 99%; SAT critical reading scores over 600: 47%; SAT math scores over 600: 44%; SAT writing scores over 600: 36%; ACT scores over 24: 84%; SAT critical reading scores over 700: 14%; SAT math scores over 700: 13%; SAT writing scores over 700: 8%; ACT scores over 30: 25%.

Faculty *Total:* 253, 53% full-time, 59% with terminal degrees. *Student/faculty ratio:* 12:1.

Academics *Calendar:* 4-1-4. *Degrees:* certificates, diplomas, associate, bachelor's, and master's. *Special study options:* academic remediation for entering students, advanced placement credit, cooperative education, distance learning, double majors, English as a second language, honors programs, independent study, internships, off-campus study, part-time degree program, services for LD students, student-designed majors, study abroad, summer session for credit.

Computers on Campus 437 computers/terminals are available on campus for general student use. Students can access the following: campus intranet, computer help desk, free student e-mail accounts, online (class) grades, online (class) registration, online (class) schedules. Campuswide network is available. 100% of college-owned or -operated housing units are wired for high-speed Internet access. Wireless service is available via entire campus.

Student Life *Housing:* on-campus residence required through junior year. *Options:* men-only, women-only. Campus housing is university owned and is provided by a third party. Freshman campus housing is guaranteed. *Activities and organizations:* drama/theater group, student-run newspaper, radio and television station, choral group, TWO (Taylor World Outreach), IFC (Integration of Faith and Culture), Spring Break Mission Trips, Community Outreach, TSO (Taylor Student Organization). *Campus security:* 24-hour patrols, student patrols, late-night transport/escort service. *Student services:* health clinic, personal/psychological counseling.

Athletics Member NAIA. *Intercollegiate sports:* baseball M(s), basketball M(s)/W(s), cross-country running M(s)/W(s), football M(s), golf M(s)/W(s), soccer M(s)/W(s), softball W(s), tennis M(s)/W(s), track and field M(s)/W(s), volleyball W(s). *Intramural sports:* badminton M/W, basketball M/W, equestrian sports W(c), lacrosse M(c)/W(c), racquetball M/W, soccer M/W, softball M/W, tennis M/W, ultimate Frisbee M/W, volleyball M/W.

Standardized Tests *Required:* SAT or ACT (for admission).

Costs (2012–13) *Comprehensive fee:* $35,845 includes full-time tuition ($27,850), mandatory fees ($238), and room and board ($7757). Full-time tuition and fees vary according to course load. Part-time tuition: $981 per credit hour. Part-time tuition and fees vary according to course load. *Required fees:* $37 per term part-time. *College room only:* $4041. Room and board charges vary according to board plan and housing facility. *Payment plan:* installment. *Waivers:* senior citizens and employees or children of employees.

Financial Aid Of all full-time matriculated undergraduates who enrolled in 2012, 1,335 applied for aid, 1,147 were judged to have need, 253 had their need fully met. 831 Federal Work-Study jobs (averaging $564). In 2012, 473 non-need-based awards were made. *Average percent of need met:* 71%. *Average financial aid package:* $18,428. *Average need-based loan:* $4735. *Average need-based gift aid:* $14,266. *Average non-need-based aid:* $8147. *Average indebtedness upon graduation:* $26,003. *Financial aid deadline:* 3/10.

Applying *Options:* electronic application, early action, deferred entrance. *Application fee:* $25. *Required:* essay or personal statement, high school transcript, 2 letters of recommendation, interview. *Recommended:* minimum 2.8 GPA. *Application deadlines:* rolling (freshmen), rolling (transfers), 12/1 (early action). *Notification:* continuous (freshmen), continuous (transfers), 12/20 (early action).

Freshman Application Contact Ms. Lisa Wallace, Visit Coordinator, Taylor University, 236 West Reade Avenue, Upland, IN 46989-1001. *Phone:* 765-998-5134. *Toll-free phone:* 800-882-3456. *Fax:* 765-998-4925. *E-mail:* admissions@taylor.edu.
Website: http://www.taylor.edu/.

Trine University

Angola, Indiana

- **Independent** comprehensive, founded 1884
- **Small-town** 400-acre campus
- **Endowment** $22.7 million
- **Coed** 1,943 undergraduate students, 77% full-time, 37% women, 63% men
- **Moderately difficult** entrance level, 72% of applicants were admitted

Undergraduates 1,498 full-time, 445 part-time. Students come from 29 states and territories; 14 other countries; 36% are from out of state; 2% Black or African American, non-Hispanic/Latino; 2% Hispanic/Latino; 0.4% Asian, non-Hispanic/Latino; 0.3% Native Hawaiian or other Pacific Islander, non-Hispanic/Latino; 0.3% American Indian or Alaska Native, non-Hispanic/Latino; 1% Two or more races, non-Hispanic/Latino; 4% Race/ethnicity unknown; 4% international; 2% transferred in; 56% live on campus. *Retention:* 69% of full-time freshmen returned.

Freshmen *Admission:* 2,867 applied, 2,052 admitted, 421 enrolled. *Average high school GPA:* 3.46. *Test scores:* SAT critical reading scores over 500: 58%; SAT math scores over 500: 78%; ACT scores over 18: 100%; SAT critical reading scores over 600: 18%; SAT math scores over 600: 40%; ACT scores over 24: 59%; SAT critical reading scores over 700: 4%; SAT math scores over 700: 5%; ACT scores over 30: 16%.

Faculty *Total:* 137, 58% full-time, 39% with terminal degrees. *Student/faculty ratio:* 15:1.

Academics *Calendar:* semesters. *Degrees:* associate, bachelor's, and master's. *Special study options:* academic remediation for entering students, adult/continuing education programs, advanced placement credit, cooperative education, distance learning, double majors, English as a second language, honors programs, internships, part-time degree program, student-designed majors, study abroad, summer session for credit. *ROTC:* Air Force (c). *Unusual degree programs:* 3-2 engineering.

Computers on Campus 700 computers/terminals and 1,170 ports are available on campus for general student use. Students can access the following: computer help desk, free student e-mail accounts, online (class) grades, online (class) registration, online (class) schedules, online campus billing accounts. Campuswide network is available. 100% of college-owned or -operated housing units are wired for high-speed Internet access. Wireless service is available via entire campus.

Student Life *Housing:* on-campus residence required through senior year. *Options:* coed, men-only, women-only. Campus housing is university owned and is provided by a third party. Freshman campus housing is guaranteed. *Activities and organizations:* drama/theater group, student-run newspaper,

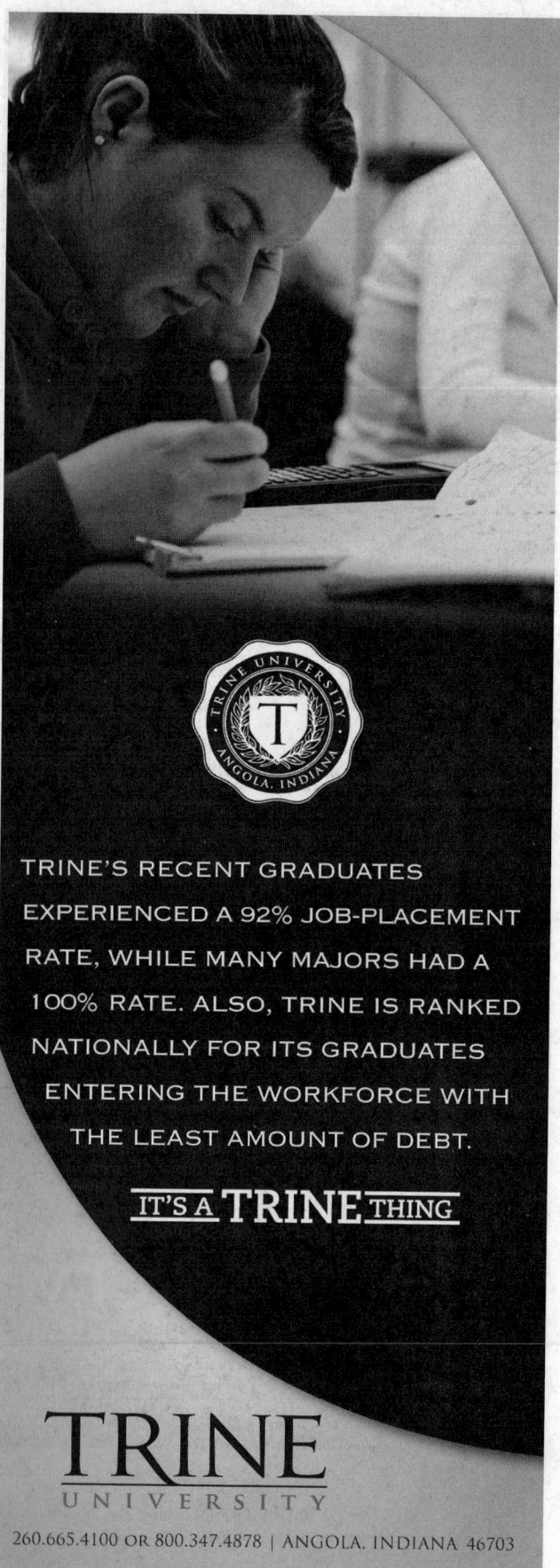

radio station, choral group, marching band, Campus Christian House, Fellowship of Christian Athletes, Multicultural Student Organization, Math Club, Trine Disc Golf Collective, national fraternities, national sororities. *Campus security:* 24-hour emergency response devices and patrols, late-night transport/escort service, controlled dormitory access. *Student services:* health clinic, personal/psychological counseling.

Athletics Member NCAA. All Division III. *Intercollegiate sports:* baseball M, basketball M/W, cross-country running M/W, field hockey W, football M, golf M/W, lacrosse M/W, soccer M/W, softball W, tennis M/W, track and field M/W, volleyball W, wrestling M. *Intramural sports:* badminton M/W, basketball M/W, football M, golf M/W, racquetball M/W, softball M/W, table tennis M/W, volleyball M/W.

Standardized Tests *Required:* SAT or ACT (for admission).

Costs (2013–14) *Comprehensive fee:* $38,350 includes full-time tuition ($28,700), mandatory fees ($150), and room and board ($9500). Full-time tuition and fees vary according to degree level, location, and program. Part-time tuition: $890 per credit hour. Part-time tuition and fees vary according to degree level, location, and program. *Room and board:* Room and board charges vary according to board plan and housing facility. *Payment plan:* installment. *Waivers:* employees or children of employees.

Financial Aid Of all full-time matriculated undergraduates who enrolled in 2012, 1,449 applied for aid, 1,181 were judged to have need, 370 had their need fully met. In 2012, 77 non-need-based awards were made. *Average percent of need met:* 79%. *Average financial aid package:* $21,543. *Average need-based loan:* $4174. *Average need-based gift aid:* $4306. *Average non-need-based aid:* $11,251. *Average indebtedness upon graduation:* $32,662.

Applying *Options:* electronic application, deferred entrance. *Required:* high school transcript, minimum 2.5 GPA. *Recommended:* essay or personal statement, 2 letters of recommendation, interview. *Application deadlines:* 8/1 (freshmen), 8/1 (transfers). *Notification:* 8/15 (freshmen), continuous until 8/15 (transfers).

Freshman Application Contact Mr. Scott Goplin, Dean of Admission, Trine University, 1 University Avenue, Angola, IN 46703. *Phone:* 260-665-4365. *Toll-free phone:* 800-347-4TSU. *Fax:* 260-665-4578. *E-mail:* admit@trine.edu.

Website: http://www.trine.edu/.

See previous page for display ad and page 1538 for the College Close-Up.

University of Evansville

Evansville, Indiana

- **Independent** comprehensive, founded 1854, affiliated with United Methodist Church
- **Urban** 75-acre campus
- **Endowment** $74.4 million
- **Coed** 2,612 undergraduate students, 93% full-time, 60% women, 40% men
- **Moderately difficult** entrance level, 80% of applicants were admitted

Undergraduates 2,418 full-time, 194 part-time. Students come from 42 states and territories; 45 other countries; 43% are from out of state; 3% Black or African American, non-Hispanic/Latino; 3% Hispanic/Latino; 1% Asian, non-Hispanic/Latino; 0.1% Native Hawaiian or other Pacific Islander, non-Hispanic/Latino; 0.1% American Indian or Alaska Native, non-Hispanic/Latino; 2% Two or more races, non-Hispanic/Latino; 5% Race/ethnicity unknown; 7% international; 3% transferred in; 66% live on campus. *Retention:* 85% of full-time freshmen returned.

Freshmen *Admission:* 2,879 applied, 2,305 admitted, 518 enrolled. *Average high school GPA:* 3.81. *Test scores:* SAT critical reading scores over 500: 78%; SAT math scores over 500: 80%; SAT writing scores over 500: 74%; ACT scores over 18: 99%; SAT critical reading scores over 600: 38%; SAT math scores over 600: 41%; SAT writing scores over 600: 29%; ACT scores over 24: 74%; SAT critical reading scores over 700: 9%; SAT math scores over 700: 4%; SAT writing scores over 700: 5%; ACT scores over 30: 19%.

Faculty *Total:* 238, 75% full-time. *Student/faculty ratio:* 13:1.

Academics *Calendar:* semesters. *Degrees:* associate, bachelor's, master's, and doctoral. *Special study options:* accelerated degree program, adult/continuing education programs, advanced placement credit, cooperative education, distance learning, double majors, English as a second language, external degree program, honors programs, independent study, internships, part-time degree program, services for LD students, student-designed majors, study abroad, summer session for credit. *ROTC:* Army (c).

Computers on Campus 385 computers/terminals and 3,000 ports are available on campus for general student use. Students can access the following: campus intranet, computer help desk, free student e-mail accounts, online (class) grades, online (class) registration, online (class) schedules. Campus-wide network is available. 100% of college-owned or -operated housing units

are wired for high-speed Internet access. Wireless service is available via entire campus.

Student Life *Housing:* on-campus residence required for freshman year. *Options:* coed, men-only, women-only. Campus housing is university owned. Freshman campus housing is guaranteed. *Activities and organizations:* drama/theater group, student-run newspaper, radio station, choral group, Phi Eta Sigma, International Club, PT Club, Student Christian Fellowship, Alpha Omicron Pi, national fraternities, national sororities. *Campus security:* 24-hour emergency response devices and patrols, student patrols, late-night transport/escort service, controlled dormitory access. *Student services:* health clinic, personal/psychological counseling.

Athletics Member NCAA. All Division I. *Intercollegiate sports:* baseball M(s), basketball M(s)/W(s), cross-country running M(s)/W(s), golf M(s)/W(s), soccer M(s)/W(s), softball W(s), swimming and diving M(s)/W(s), tennis W(s), volleyball W(s). *Intramural sports:* badminton M/W, basketball M/W, racquetball M/W, soccer M/W, tennis M/W, ultimate Frisbee M/W, volleyball M/W.

Standardized Tests *Required:* SAT or ACT (for admission).

Costs (2012–13) *Comprehensive fee:* $40,566 includes full-time tuition ($29,740), mandatory fees ($816), and room and board ($10,010). Part-time tuition: $830 per credit hour. Part-time tuition and fees vary according to course load. *Required fees:* $50 per term part-time. *College room only:* $5230. Room and board charges vary according to board plan and housing facility. *Payment plan:* installment. *Waivers:* minority students, children of alumni, adult students, senior citizens, and employees or children of employees.

Financial Aid Of all full-time matriculated undergraduates who enrolled in 2012, 1,964 applied for aid, 1,724 were judged to have need, 463 had their need fully met. 389 Federal Work-Study jobs (averaging $1408). 32 state and other part-time jobs (averaging $1365). In 2012, 485 non-need-based awards were made. *Average percent of need met:* 82%. *Average financial aid package:* $25,232. *Average need-based loan:* $5036. *Average need-based gift aid:* $21,872. *Average non-need-based aid:* $16,302. *Average indebtedness upon graduation:* $27,679.

Applying *Options:* electronic application, early action, deferred entrance. *Application fee:* $35. *Required:* essay or personal statement, high school transcript, 1 letter of recommendation. *Required for some:* interview. *Recommended:* minimum 3.0 GPA, interview. *Application deadlines:* 2/1 (freshmen), rolling (transfers), 12/1 (early action). *Notification:* 2/15 (freshmen), continuous (transfers), 12/15 (early action).

Freshman Application Contact Don Vos, Dean of Admission, University of Evansville, 1800 Lincoln Avenue, Evansville, IN 47722. *Phone:* 812-488-2468. *Toll-free phone:* 800-423-8633 Ext. 2468. *Fax:* 812-488-4076. *E-mail:* admission@evansville.edu.

Website: http://www.evansville.edu/.

University of Indianapolis

Indianapolis, Indiana

- **Independent** comprehensive, founded 1902, affiliated with United Methodist Church
- **Urban** 65-acre campus with easy access to Indianapolis
- **Endowment** $72.7 million
- **Coed**
- **Moderately difficult** entrance level

Faculty *Student/faculty ratio:* 15:1.

Academics *Calendar:* semesters. *Degrees:* associate, bachelor's, master's, and doctoral.

Student Life *Campus security:* 24-hour emergency response devices and patrols, student patrols, late-night transport/escort service, emergency call boxes.

Athletics Member NCAA. All Division II.

Standardized Tests *Required:* SAT or ACT (for admission).

Costs (2012–13) *Comprehensive fee:* $32,920 includes full-time tuition ($23,590), mandatory fees ($240), and room and board ($9090). Part-time tuition: $982 per credit hour. Part-time tuition and fees vary according to course load. *College room only:* $4300. Room and board charges vary according to board plan and housing facility.

Financial Aid Of all full-time matriculated undergraduates who enrolled in 2011, 3,493 applied for aid, 3,121 were judged to have need, 301 had their need fully met. *In 2011,* 513 non-need-based awards were made. *Average percent of need met:* 60. *Average financial aid package:* $15,228. *Average need-based loan:* $4499. *Average need-based gift aid:* $7322. *Average non-need-based aid:* $7746. *Average indebtedness upon graduation:* $32,495.

Applying *Options:* electronic application, deferred entrance. *Application fee:* $25. *Required:* high school transcript, minimum 2.0 GPA. *Required for some:* interview.

Freshman Application Contact Mr. Ronald Wilks, Director of Admissions, University of Indianapolis, 1400 East Hanna Avenue, Indianapolis, IN 46227-

3697. *Phone:* 317-788-3216. *Toll-free phone:* 800-232-8634 Ext. 3216. *Fax:* 317-788-3300. *E-mail:* admissions@uindy.edu. *Website:* http://www.uindy.edu/.

See below for display ad and page 1568 for the College Close-Up.

University of Notre Dame
Notre Dame, Indiana

- **Independent Roman Catholic** university, founded 1842
- **Suburban** 1250-acre campus
- **Endowment** $7.6 billion
- **Coed** 8,475 undergraduate students, 100% full-time, 47% women, 53% men
- **Most difficult** entrance level, 23% of applicants were admitted

Undergraduates 8,462 full-time, 13 part-time. Students come from 51 states and territories; 40 other countries; 92% are from out of state; 3% Black or African American, non-Hispanic/Latino; 10% Hispanic/Latino; 7% Asian, non-Hispanic/Latino; 0.4% American Indian or Alaska Native, non-Hispanic/Latino; 3% Two or more races, non-Hispanic/Latino; 0.7% Race/ethnicity unknown; 4% international; 80% live on campus. *Retention:* 97% of full-time freshmen returned.

Freshmen *Admission:* 16,957 applied, 3,947 admitted, 2,014 enrolled. *Test scores:* SAT critical reading scores over 500: 99%; SAT math scores over 500: 99%; SAT writing scores over 500: 98%; SAT critical reading scores over 600: 93%; SAT math scores over 600: 96%; SAT writing scores over 600: 91%; ACT scores over 24: 100%; SAT critical reading scores over 700: 57%; SAT math scores over 700: 66%; SAT writing scores over 700: 53%; ACT scores over 30: 90%.

Faculty *Total:* 1,221, 89% full-time, 86% with terminal degrees. *Student/faculty ratio:* 11:1.

Academics *Calendar:* semesters. *Degrees:* bachelor's, master's, and doctoral. *Special study options:* advanced placement credit, double majors, honors programs, independent study, internships, off-campus study, services for LD students, student-designed majors, study abroad, summer session for credit. *ROTC:* Army (b), Navy (b), Air Force (b).

Computers on Campus 200 computers/terminals are available on campus for general student use. Students can access the following: computer help desk, free student e-mail accounts, online (class) grades, online (class) registration, online (class) schedules. Campuswide network is available. Wireless service is available via entire campus.

Student Life *Housing:* on-campus residence required for freshman year. *Options:* men-only, women-only. Campus housing is university owned. Freshman campus housing is guaranteed. *Activities and organizations:* drama/theater group, student-run newspaper, radio station, choral group, marching band, marching band, Circle K, Finance Club, Notre Dame/St. Mary's Right to Life. *Campus security:* 24-hour emergency response devices and patrols, student patrols, late-night transport/escort service, controlled dormitory access, crime prevention and personal safety workshops, full-time trained police investigators, fire sprinklers in all residence halls. *Student services:* health clinic, personal/psychological counseling, women's center.

Athletics Member NCAA. All Division I except football (Division I-A). *Intercollegiate sports:* baseball M(s), basketball M(s)/W(s), crew W(s), cross-country running M(s)/W(s), fencing M(s)/W(s), golf M(s)/W(s), ice hockey M(s), lacrosse M(s)/W(s), soccer M(s)/W(s), softball W(s), swimming and diving M(s)/W(s), tennis M(s)/W(s), track and field M(s)/W(s), volleyball W(s). *Intramural sports:* badminton M/W, baseball M, basketball M/W, bowling M(c)/W(c), crew M(c), cross-country running M/W, equestrian sports M(c)/W(c), field hockey M(c)/W(c), football M/W, golf M/W, gymnastics M(c)/W(c), ice hockey M/W(c), lacrosse M/W, racquetball M/W, rock climbing M(c)/W(c), rugby M(c)/W(c), sailing M(c)/W(c), skiing (cross-country) M(c)/W(c), skiing (downhill) M(c)/W(c), soccer M/W, softball M/W, squash M(c)/W(c), tennis M/W, ultimate Frisbee M/W, volleyball M(c)/W(c), water polo M(c)/W(c).

Standardized Tests *Required:* SAT or ACT (for admission). *Required for some:* SAT Subject Tests (for admission).

Costs (2012–13) *Comprehensive fee:* $54,905 includes full-time tuition ($42,464), mandatory fees ($507), and room and board ($11,934). Part-time tuition: $1769 per credit hour. *Payment plan:* installment. *Waivers:* employees or children of employees.

Financial Aid Of all full-time matriculated undergraduates who enrolled in 2012, 5,150 applied for aid, 4,252 were judged to have need, 4,242 had their need fully met. 1,677 Federal Work-Study jobs (averaging $2402). 3,291 state and other part-time jobs (averaging $2993). In 2012, 389 non-need-based awards were made. *Average percent of need met:* 100%. *Average financial aid package:* $38,818. *Average need-based loan:* $5358. *Average need-based gift aid:* $29,440. *Average non-need-based aid:* $10,182. *Average indebtedness upon graduation:* $29,480.

Applying *Options:* electronic application, early action, deferred entrance. *Application fee:* $75. *Required:* essay or personal statement, high school transcript, 1 letter of recommendation. *Application deadlines:* 12/31 (freshmen), 4/

15 (transfers), 11/1 (early action). *Notification:* 4/10 (freshmen), 12/21 (early action).

Freshman Application Contact Office of Undergraduate Admissions, University of Notre Dame, 220 Main Building, Notre Dame, IN 46556-5612. *Phone:* 574-631-7505. *Fax:* 574-631-8865. *E-mail:* admissions@nd.edu. *Website:* http://www.nd.edu/.

University of Phoenix–Indianapolis Campus

Indianapolis, Indiana

Freshman Application Contact Marc Booker, Sr. Director, Office of Admissions and Evaluation, University of Phoenix–Indianapolis Campus, 4035 South Riverpoint Parkway, Mail Stop CF-L101, Phoenix, AZ 85040. *Phone:* 602-557-4609. *Toll-free phone:* 866-766-0766. *Fax:* 480-643-1156. *Website:* http://www.phoenix.edu/.

University of Phoenix–Northwest Indiana Campus

Merrillville, Indiana

Admissions Office Contact University of Phoenix–Northwest Indiana Campus, 359 East 81st Avenue, Merrillville, IN 46410. *Toll-free phone:* 866-766-0766. *Website:* http://www.phoenix.edu/.

University of Saint Francis

Fort Wayne, Indiana

- **Independent Roman Catholic** comprehensive, founded 1890
- **Suburban** 74-acre campus
- **Endowment** $14.8 million
- **Coed**
- **Moderately difficult** entrance level

Faculty *Student/faculty ratio:* 15:1.

Academics *Calendar:* semesters. *Degrees:* certificates, associate, bachelor's, master's, and postbachelor's certificates.

Student Life *Campus security:* 24-hour emergency response devices and patrols, late-night transport/escort service, controlled dormitory access.

Athletics Member NAIA.

Standardized Tests *Required:* SAT or ACT (for admission).

Costs (2012–13) *Comprehensive fee:* $32,730 includes full-time tuition ($23,560), mandatory fees ($1000), and room and board ($8170). Full-time tuition and fees vary according to course load. Part-time tuition: $730 per credit hour. Part-time tuition and fees vary according to course load. *Required fees:* $20 per credit hour part-time. *Room and board:* Room and board charges vary according to board plan and housing facility.

Financial Aid *Of all full-time matriculated undergraduates who enrolled in 2009,* 1,477 applied for aid, 1,316 were judged to have need, 258 had their need fully met. 629 Federal Work-Study jobs (averaging $1411). *In 2009,* 146 non-need-based awards were made. *Average percent of need met:* 72. *Average financial aid package:* $16,158. *Average need-based loan:* $4028. *Average need-based gift aid:* $12,247. *Average non-need-based aid:* $5446. *Average indebtedness upon graduation:* $28,428. *Financial aid deadline:* 6/30.

Applying *Options:* electronic application, deferred entrance. *Application fee:* $20. *Required:* high school transcript, minimum 2.3 GPA. *Required for some:* interview. *Recommended:* essay or personal statement.

Freshman Application Contact Mr. JP Spagnolo, Director of Admissions, University of Saint Francis, 2701 Spring Street, Fort Wayne, IN 46808. *Phone:* 260-399-8000. *Toll-free phone:* 800-729-4732. *E-mail:* admis@sf.edu. *Website:* http://www.sf.edu/.

University of Southern Indiana

Evansville, Indiana

- **State-supported** comprehensive, founded 1965, part of Indiana Commission for Higher Education
- **Suburban** 330-acre campus
- **Coed** 9,502 undergraduate students, 83% full-time, 60% women, 40% men
- **Moderately difficult** entrance level, 72% of applicants were admitted

Undergraduates 7,902 full-time, 1,600 part-time. Students come from 44 states and territories; 37 other countries; 8% are from out of state; 5% Black or African American, non-Hispanic/Latino; 0.9% Hispanic/Latino; 0.7% Asian, non-Hispanic/Latino; 0.1% Native Hawaiian or other Pacific Islander, non-Hispanic/Latino; 0.3% American Indian or Alaska Native, non-Hispanic/Latino; 2% Two or more races, non-Hispanic/Latino; 3% Race/ethnicity unknown; 3% international; 7% transferred in; 27% live on campus. *Retention:* 67% of full-time freshmen returned.

Freshmen *Admission:* 6,279 applied, 4,505 admitted, 1,880 enrolled. *Average high school GPA:* 3.2. *Test scores:* SAT critical reading scores over 500: 49%; SAT math scores over 500: 55%; SAT writing scores over 500: 38%; ACT scores over 18: 89%; SAT critical reading scores over 600: 10%; SAT math scores over 600: 14%; SAT writing scores over 600: 8%; ACT scores over 24: 31%; SAT critical reading scores over 700: 1%; SAT math scores over 700: 1%; SAT writing scores over 700: 1%; ACT scores over 30: 2%.

Faculty *Total:* 681, 49% full-time, 45% with terminal degrees. *Student/faculty ratio:* 17:1.

Academics *Calendar:* semesters. *Degrees:* certificates, associate, bachelor's, master's, doctoral, and postbachelor's certificates. *Special study options:* academic remediation for entering students, adult/continuing education programs, advanced placement credit, cooperative education, distance learning, double majors, English as a second language, honors programs, independent study, internships, part-time degree program, services for LD students, study abroad, summer session for credit. *ROTC:* Army (b).

Computers on Campus 306 computers/terminals are available on campus for general student use. Students can access the following: computer help desk, free student e-mail accounts, online (class) grades, online (class) registration, online (class) schedules. Campuswide network is available. 100% of college-owned or -operated housing units are wired for high-speed Internet access. Wireless service is available via entire campus.

Student Life *Housing options:* coed. Campus housing is university owned. *Activities and organizations:* drama/theater group, student-run newspaper, radio station, choral group, Activities Programming Board, Interfraternity Council, Panhellenic Council, International Student Organization, Habitat for Humanity, national fraternities, national sororities. *Campus security:* 24-hour emergency response devices and patrols, student patrols, late-night transport/escort service, controlled dormitory access. *Student services:* health clinic, personal/psychological counseling.

Athletics Member NCAA. All Division II. *Intercollegiate sports:* baseball M(s), basketball M(s)/W(s), bowling M(c)/W(c), cheerleading M/W, cross-country running M(s)/W(s), golf M(s)/W(s), lacrosse M(c), rugby M(c)/W(c), soccer M(s)/W(s), softball W(s), tennis M(s)/W(s), ultimate Frisbee M(c)/W(c), volleyball W(s), wrestling M(c). *Intramural sports:* badminton M/W, basketball M/W, bowling M/W, football M/W, golf M/W, rock climbing M/W, skiing (downhill) M/W, soccer M/W, softball M/W, swimming and diving M/W, table tennis M/W, tennis M/W, volleyball M/W.

Standardized Tests *Required:* SAT or ACT (for admission).

Costs (2013–14) *One-time required fee:* $100. *Tuition:* state resident $6085 full-time, $203 per credit hour part-time; nonresident $14,485 full-time, $483 per credit hour part-time. Full-time tuition and fees vary according to course load, program, and reciprocity agreements. Part-time tuition and fees vary according to course load, program, and reciprocity agreements. *Required fees:* $240 full-time. *Room and board:* $7502; room only: $4032. Room and board charges vary according to board plan and housing facility. *Payment plan:* installment. *Waivers:* employees or children of employees.

Financial Aid Of all full-time matriculated undergraduates who enrolled in 2012, 7,718 applied for aid, 5,022 were judged to have need, 280 had their need fully met. 78 Federal Work-Study jobs (averaging $2177). In 2012, 707 non-need-based awards were made. *Average percent of need met:* 59%. *Average financial aid package:* $8289. *Average need-based loan:* $4071. *Average need-based gift aid:* $5073. *Average non-need-based aid:* $3008. *Average indebtedness upon graduation:* $19,429. *Financial aid deadline:* 3/1.

Applying *Options:* electronic application. *Application fee:* $40. *Required:* high school transcript. *Required for some:* interview. *Recommended:* essay or personal statement, minimum 2.0 GPA. *Application deadline:* 8/10 (freshmen). *Notification:* continuous (freshmen), continuous (transfers).

Freshman Application Contact Mr. Eric Otto, Director of Admission, University of Southern Indiana, 8600 University Boulevard, Evansville, IN 47712-3590. *Phone:* 812-464-1765. *Toll-free phone:* 800-467-1965. *Fax:* 812-465-7154. *E-mail:* enroll@usi.edu. *Website:* http://www.usi.edu/.

Valparaiso University

Valparaiso, Indiana

- **Independent** university, founded 1859, affiliated with Lutheran Church
- **Small-town** 320-acre campus with easy access to Chicago
- **Endowment** $163.5 million
- **Coed** 2,980 undergraduate students, 96% full-time, 53% women, 47% men
- **Moderately difficult** entrance level, 80% of applicants were admitted

Undergraduates 2,855 full-time, 125 part-time. Students come from 46 states and territories; 47 other countries; 59% are from out of state; 5% Black or African American, non-Hispanic/Latino; 7% Hispanic/Latino; 2% Asian, non-Hispanic/Latino; 0.1% Native Hawaiian or other Pacific Islander, non-Hispanic/Latino; 0.2% American Indian or Alaska Native, non-Hispanic/Latino; 2% Two or more races, non-Hispanic/Latino; 1% Race/ethnicity unknown; 7% international; 6% transferred in; 65% live on campus. *Retention:* 87% of full-time freshmen returned.
Freshmen *Admission:* 5,555 applied, 4,423 admitted, 772 enrolled. *Average high school GPA:* 3.6. *Test scores:* SAT critical reading scores over 500: 77%; SAT math scores over 500: 82%; SAT writing scores over 500: 69%; ACT scores over 18: 98%; SAT critical reading scores over 600: 27%; SAT math scores over 600: 36%; SAT writing scores over 600: 21%; ACT scores over 24: 69%; SAT critical reading scores over 700: 6%; SAT math scores over 700: 6%; SAT writing scores over 700: 2%; ACT scores over 30: 21%.
Faculty *Total:* 380, 70% full-time, 71% with terminal degrees. *Student/faculty ratio:* 13:1.
Academics *Calendar:* semesters. *Degrees:* certificates, associate, bachelor's, master's, doctoral, post-master's, and postbachelor's certificates. *Special study options:* accelerated degree program, adult/continuing education programs, advanced placement credit, cooperative education, distance learning, double majors, English as a second language, freshman honors college, honors programs, independent study, internships, off-campus study, part-time degree program, services for LD students, student-designed majors, study abroad, summer session for credit. *ROTC:* Army (c), Air Force (c).
Computers on Campus 500 computers/terminals are available on campus for general student use. Students can access the following: campus intranet, computer help desk, free student e-mail accounts, online (class) grades, online (class) registration, online (class) schedules, Web academic information, degree audit. Campuswide network is available. 100% of college-owned or -operated housing units are wired for high-speed Internet access. Wireless service is available via classrooms, computer centers, computer labs, dorm rooms, learning centers, libraries, student centers.
Student Life *Housing:* on-campus residence required through junior year. *Options:* coed, women-only. Campus housing is university owned and leased by the school. Freshman campus housing is guaranteed. *Activities and organizations:* drama/theater group, student-run newspaper, radio station, choral group, Union Board, student government, student volunteer organization, chapel programs, national fraternities. *Campus security:* 24-hour emergency response devices and patrols, late-night transport/escort service, controlled dormitory access. *Student services:* health clinic, personal/psychological counseling, legal services.
Athletics Member NCAA. All Division I. *Intercollegiate sports:* baseball M(s), basketball M(s)/W(s), bowling W(s), cross-country running M(s)/W(s), football M, golf M(s)/W(s), soccer M(s)/W(s), softball W(s), swimming and diving M(s)/W(s), tennis M(s)/W(s), track and field M(s)/W(s), volleyball W(s). *Intramural sports:* badminton M/W, basketball M/W, bowling M/W, football M/W, golf M/W, racquetball M/W, soccer M(c)/W(c), softball M/W, table tennis M/W, tennis M(c)/W(c), ultimate Frisbee M(c)/W(c), volleyball M/W.
Standardized Tests *Required:* SAT or ACT (for admission).
Costs (2012–13) *Comprehensive fee:* $41,414 includes full-time tuition ($31,170), mandatory fees ($1080), and room and board ($9164). Full-time tuition and fees vary according to course load and program. Part-time tuition: $1400 per credit hour. Part-time tuition and fees vary according to course load and program. *Required fees:* $96 per term part-time. *College room only:* $5564. Room and board charges vary according to housing facility and student level. *Payment plans:* tuition prepayment, installment. *Waivers:* employees or children of employees.
Financial Aid Of all full-time matriculated undergraduates who enrolled in 2011, 2,245 applied for aid, 2,054 were judged to have need, 499 had their need fully met. In 2011, 529 non-need-based awards were made. *Average percent of need met:* 77%. *Average financial aid package:* $22,150. *Average need-based loan:* $5133. *Average need-based gift aid:* $19,174. *Average non-need-based aid:* $13,880. *Average indebtedness upon graduation:* $31,957.
Applying *Options:* electronic application, deferred entrance. *Required:* essay or personal statement, high school transcript. *Required for some:* interview. *Recommended:* 2 letters of recommendation, interview. *Application deadlines:* rolling (freshmen), rolling (out-of-state freshmen), rolling (transfers). *Notification:* continuous (freshmen), continuous (out-of-state freshmen), continuous (transfers).
Freshman Application Contact Mr. T. Scott Henne, Director of Freshman Recruitment, Valparaiso University, Kretzmann Hall, 1700 Chapel Drive, Valparaiso, IN 46383-6493. *Phone:* 219-464-5011. *Toll-free phone:* 888-GO-VALPO. *Fax:* 219-464-6898. *E-mail:* undergrad.admission@valpo.edu. *Website:* http://www.valpo.edu/.

Vincennes University
Vincennes, Indiana
- **State-supported** primarily 2-year, founded 1801
- **Small-town** 100-acre campus
- **Coed** 17,530 undergraduate students, 35% full-time, 45% women, 55% men
- **Noncompetitive** entrance level

Undergraduates 6,199 full-time, 11,331 part-time. 11% Black or African American, non-Hispanic/Latino; 2% Hispanic/Latino; 0.4% Asian, non-Hispanic/Latino; 0.2% Native Hawaiian or other Pacific Islander, non-Hispanic/Latino; 0.3% American Indian or Alaska Native, non-Hispanic/Latino; 1% Two or more races, non-Hispanic/Latino; 11% Race/ethnicity unknown; 0.6% international. *Retention:* 69% of full-time freshmen returned.
Freshmen *Admission:* 2,644 enrolled.
Faculty *Total:* 1,614, 15% full-time. *Student/faculty ratio:* 14:1.
Academics *Calendar:* semesters. *Degrees:* certificates, associate, and bachelor's. *Special study options:* academic remediation for entering students, adult/continuing education programs, advanced placement credit, distance learning, double majors, English as a second language, external degree program, honors programs, off-campus study, part-time degree program, services for LD students, summer session for credit. *ROTC:* Army (c), Air Force (c).
Computers on Campus Campuswide network is available.
Student Life *Housing:* on-campus residence required for freshman year. *Options:* coed, men-only, women-only, disabled students. Campus housing is university owned. Freshman campus housing is guaranteed. *Activities and organizations:* drama/theater group, student-run newspaper, radio and television station, choral group, national fraternities, national sororities. *Campus security:* 24-hour emergency response devices and patrols, student patrols, late-night transport/escort service, controlled dormitory access, surveillance cameras. *Student services:* health clinic, personal/psychological counseling.
Athletics Member NJCAA. *Intercollegiate sports:* baseball M, basketball M/W, bowling M, cross-country running M/W, golf M, tennis M, track and field M/W, volleyball W.
Costs (2012–13) *Tuition:* state resident $4882 full-time, $2013 per year part-time; nonresident $11,542 full-time, $4580 per year part-time. Full-time tuition and fees vary according to course level, course load, location, and program. Part-time tuition and fees vary according to course level, course load, location, and program. *Room and board:* $8152. Room and board charges vary according to board plan, gender, and housing facility.
Financial Aid Of all full-time matriculated undergraduates who enrolled in 2011, 220 Federal Work-Study jobs (averaging $1072).
Applying *Options:* electronic application, early admission, deferred entrance. *Application fee:* $20. *Required:* high school transcript. *Required for some:* interview. *Application deadlines:* rolling (freshmen), rolling (transfers). *Notification:* continuous until 8/1 (freshmen), continuous (transfers).
Freshman Application Contact Vincennes University, 1002 North First Street, Vincennes, IN 47591-5202. *Phone:* 812-888-4313. *Toll-free phone:* 800-742-9198.
Website: http://www.vinu.edu/.

Vincennes University Jasper Campus
Jasper, Indiana
Freshman Application Contact Ms. Louann Gilbert, Admissions Director, Vincennes University Jasper Campus, 850 College Avenue, Jasper, IN 47546-9393. *Phone:* 812-482-3030. *Toll-free phone:* 800-809-VUJC. *Fax:* 812-481-5960. *E-mail:* lagilbert@vinu.edu.
Website: http://vujc.vinu.edu/.

Wabash College
Crawfordsville, Indiana
- **Independent** 4-year, founded 1832
- **Small-town** 60-acre campus with easy access to Indianapolis
- **Endowment** $322.9 million
- **Men only** 906 undergraduate students, 100% full-time
- **Moderately difficult** entrance level, 67% of applicants were admitted

Undergraduates 904 full-time, 2 part-time. Students come from 35 states and territories; 11 other countries; 26% are from out of state; 6% Black or African American, non-Hispanic/Latino; 5% Hispanic/Latino; 1% Asian, non-Hispanic/Latino; 0.4% Native Hawaiian or other Pacific Islander, non-Hispanic/Latino; 0.6% American Indian or Alaska Native, non-Hispanic/Latino; 3% Two or more races, non-Hispanic/Latino; 1% Race/ethnicity unknown; 7% international; 0.6% transferred in; 87% live on campus. *Retention:* 86% of full-time freshmen returned.
Freshmen *Admission:* 1,331 applied, 892 admitted, 252 enrolled. *Average high school GPA:* 3.62. *Test scores:* SAT critical reading scores over 500: 80%;

SAT math scores over 500: 88%; SAT writing scores over 500: 69%; ACT scores over 18: 99%; SAT critical reading scores over 600: 36%; SAT math scores over 600: 48%; SAT writing scores over 600: 25%; ACT scores over 24: 59%; SAT critical reading scores over 700: 11%; SAT math scores over 700: 11%; SAT writing scores over 700: 6%; ACT scores over 30: 14%. **Faculty** *Total:* 97, 94% full-time, 95% with terminal degrees. *Student/faculty ratio:* 10:1.

Academics *Calendar:* semesters. *Degree:* bachelor's. *Special study options:* advanced placement credit, double majors, independent study, internships, off-campus study, services for LD students, study abroad. *Unusual degree programs:* 3-2 engineering with Purdue University, Columbia University, Washington University in St. Louis; accounting with Indiana University.

Computers on Campus 350 computers/terminals are available on campus for general student use. Students can access the following: campus intranet, computer help desk, free student e-mail accounts, online (class) grades, online (class) schedules, online course management, degree audit, expenses. Campuswide network is available. 100% of college-owned or -operated housing units are wired for high-speed Internet access. Wireless service is available via entire campus.

Student Life *Housing:* on-campus residence required through sophomore year. *Options:* men-only. Campus housing is university owned. Freshman campus housing is guaranteed. *Activities and organizations:* drama/theater group, student-run newspaper, radio station, choral group, Sphinx Club, Alpha Phi Omega, The Bachelor, Malcolm X Institute of Black Studies, Wabash Christian Fellowship, national fraternities. *Campus security:* 24-hour emergency response devices and patrols, late-night transport/escort service. *Student services:* health clinic, personal/psychological counseling.

Athletics Member NCAA. All Division III. *Intercollegiate sports:* baseball M, basketball M, crew M(c), cross-country running M, football M, golf M, lacrosse M(c), rugby M(c), soccer M, swimming and diving M, tennis M, track and field M, volleyball M(c), water polo M(c), wrestling M. *Intramural sports:* badminton M, basketball M, bowling M, cross-country running M, football M, golf M, racquetball M, soccer M, softball M, swimming and diving M, table tennis M, tennis M, track and field M, volleyball M, weight lifting M, wrestling M.

Standardized Tests *Required:* SAT or ACT (for admission).

Costs (2013–14) *Comprehensive fee:* $44,160 includes full-time tuition ($35,000), mandatory fees ($650), and room and board ($8510). Part-time tuition: $5833 per course. *College room only:* $4310. Room and board charges vary according to board plan and housing facility. *Payment plans:* tuition prepayment, installment. *Waivers:* employees or children of employees.

Financial Aid Of all full-time matriculated undergraduates who enrolled in 2012, 805 applied for aid, 732 were judged to have need, 597 had their need fully met. 784 state and other part-time jobs (averaging $3227). In 2012, 131 non-need-based awards were made. *Average percent of need met:* 97%. *Average financial aid package:* $29,423. *Average need-based loan:* $5426. *Average need-based gift aid:* $17,749. *Average non-need-based aid:* $16,274. *Average indebtedness upon graduation:* $28,919. *Financial aid deadline:* 3/1.

Applying *Options:* electronic application, early admission, early decision, early action, deferred entrance. *Application fee:* $40. *Required:* high school transcript. *Recommended:* essay or personal statement, 1 letter of recommendation, interview. *Application deadlines:* rolling (freshmen), 3/15 (transfers), 12/1 (early action). *Early decision deadline:* 11/15. *Notification:* continuous (freshmen), continuous until 4/1 (transfers), 12/1 (early decision), 12/22 (early action).

Freshman Application Contact Mr. Steven J. Klein, Dean of Admissions, Wabash College, PO Box 362, Crawfordsville, IN 47933-0352. *Phone:* 765-361-6225. *Toll-free phone:* 800-345-5385. *Fax:* 765-361-6437. *E-mail:* admissions@wabash.edu. *Website:* http://www.wabash.edu/.

IOWA

AIB College of Business
Des Moines, Iowa

- **Independent** 4-year, founded 1921
- **Urban** 20-acre campus
- **Endowment** $7.0 million
- **Coed** 905 undergraduate students, 67% full-time, 60% women, 40% men
- **Minimally difficult** entrance level, 94% of applicants were admitted

Undergraduates 610 full-time, 295 part-time. Students come from 26 states and territories; 7 other countries; 8% are from out of state; 4% Black or African American, non-Hispanic/Latino; 4% Hispanic/Latino; 3% Asian, non-Hispanic/Latino; 0.1% Native Hawaiian or other Pacific Islander, non-Hispanic/Latino; 0.8% American Indian or Alaska Native, non-Hispanic/Latino; 3%

Two or more races, non-Hispanic/Latino; 11% Race/ethnicity unknown; 3% international; 13% transferred in; 36% live on campus. *Retention:* 73% of full-time freshmen returned.

Freshmen *Admission:* 229 applied, 216 admitted, 165 enrolled. *Average high school GPA:* 3. *Test scores:* ACT scores over 18: 79%; ACT scores over 24: 4%.

Faculty *Total:* 59, 34% full-time, 14% with terminal degrees. *Student/faculty ratio:* 21:1.

Academics *Calendar:* quarters. *Degrees:* associate and bachelor's. *Special study options:* academic remediation for entering students, advanced placement credit, cooperative education, distance learning, double majors, independent study, internships, part-time degree program, services for LD students, summer session for credit.

Computers on Campus 346 computers/terminals and 1,256 ports are available on campus for general student use. Students can access the following: campus intranet, computer help desk, free student e-mail accounts, online (class) grades, online (class) schedules. Campuswide network is available. 100% of college-owned or -operated housing units are wired for high-speed Internet access.

Student Life *Housing options:* coed, disabled students. Campus housing is university owned. *Activities and organizations:* Student Government Association, Business Management Association, Enactus (formerly Students in Free Enterprise), Hospitality and Travel Management Association, Institute of Management Accountants, national sororities. *Campus security:* 24-hour emergency response devices and patrols, late-night transport/escort service, controlled dormitory access, video security. *Student services:* personal/psychological counseling.

Athletics Member NAIA. *Intercollegiate sports:* baseball M(s), basketball M(s)/W(s), bowling M(s)/W(s), cheerleading M(s)/W(s), golf M(s)/W(s), soccer M(s)/W(s), softball W(s), volleyball W(s). *Intramural sports:* badminton M/W, basketball M/W, bowling M/W, football M/W, softball M/W, table tennis M/W, tennis M/W, ultimate Frisbee M/W, volleyball M/W.

Standardized Tests *Required for some:* Nelson-Denny if no ACT score. *Recommended:* ACT (for admission).

Costs (2013–14) *Tuition:* $14,550 full-time, $1275 per course part-time. Full-time tuition and fees vary according to course load. Part-time tuition and fees vary according to course load. No tuition increase for student's term of enrollment. *Required fees:* $300 full-time, $100 per term part-time. *Room only:* $3984. Room and board charges vary according to housing facility. *Payment plans:* installment, deferred payment. *Waivers:* employees or children of employees.

Financial Aid Of all full-time matriculated undergraduates who enrolled in 2011, 104 Federal Work-Study jobs (averaging $1135). 1 state and other part-time job (averaging $457).

Applying *Options:* electronic application. *Required:* high school transcript, minimum 2.0 GPA. *Recommended:* interview. *Application deadlines:* rolling (freshmen), rolling (out-of-state freshmen), rolling (transfers). *Notification:* continuous (freshmen), continuous (out-of-state freshmen), continuous (transfers).

Freshman Application Contact AIB College of Business, 2500 Fleur Drive, Des Moines, IA 50321-1799. *Phone:* 515-246-5336. *Toll-free phone:* 800-444-1921. *Website:* http://www.aib.edu/.

Allen College
Waterloo, Iowa

- **Independent** comprehensive, founded 1989
- **Suburban** 20-acre campus
- **Endowment** $1.9 million
- **Coed, primarily women** 385 undergraduate students, 64% full-time, 93% women, 7% men
- **Moderately difficult** entrance level, 11% of applicants were admitted

Undergraduates 247 full-time, 138 part-time. Students come from 10 states and territories; 1 other country; 5% are from out of state; 2% Black or African American, non-Hispanic/Latino; 0.3% Hispanic/Latino; 1% Asian, non-Hispanic/Latino; 1% Two or more races, non-Hispanic/Latino; 0.5% international; 38% transferred in; 5% live on campus.

Freshmen *Admission:* 9 applied, 1 admitted, 1 enrolled.

Faculty *Total:* 42, 67% full-time, 29% with terminal degrees. *Student/faculty ratio:* 12:1.

Academics *Calendar:* semesters. *Degrees:* certificates, associate, bachelor's, master's, doctoral, and post-master's certificates (liberal arts and general education courses offered at either University of North Iowa or Wartburg College). *Special study options:* accelerated degree program, advanced placement credit, cooperative education, distance learning, honors programs, independent study, internships, off-campus study, part-time degree program. *ROTC:* Army (c).

Unusual degree programs: 3-2 nursing with Wartburg College, Loras College, Central College, Simpson College.

Computers on Campus 32 computers/terminals are available on campus for general student use. Students can access the following: campus intranet, computer help desk, free student e-mail accounts, online (class) grades, online (class) schedules. Campuswide network is available. 100% of college-owned or -operated housing units are wired for high-speed Internet access. Wireless service is available via entire campus.

Student Life *Housing options:* coed. Campus housing is university owned. *Activities and organizations:* choral group, Allen Student Nurses' Association, Nurses' Christian Fellowship. *Campus security:* 24-hour patrols, controlled dormitory access. *Student services:* health clinic, personal/psychological counseling.

Standardized Tests *Required for some:* SAT or ACT (for admission).

Costs (2013–14) *Comprehensive fee:* $26,110 includes full-time tuition ($16,771), mandatory fees ($2058), and room and board ($7281). Full-time tuition and fees vary according to course load and program. Part-time tuition: $541 per credit. Part-time tuition and fees vary according to course load and program. *Required fees:* $73 per credit part-time. *College room only:* $3641. *Payment plan:* deferred payment. *Waivers:* employees or children of employees.

Financial Aid Of all full-time matriculated undergraduates who enrolled in 2010, 288 applied for aid, 252 were judged to have need, 6 had their need fully met. 15 Federal Work-Study jobs (averaging $2380). In 2010, 14 non-need-based awards were made. *Average percent of need met:* 33%. *Average financial aid package:* $10,231. *Average need-based loan:* $10,088. *Average need-based gift aid:* $6524. *Average non-need-based aid:* $3928. *Average indebtedness upon graduation:* $20,231.

Applying *Options:* electronic application. *Application fee:* $50. *Required:* minimum 3.0 GPA. *Required for some:* essay or personal statement, high school transcript, 1 letter of recommendation, interview. *Recommended:* GPA requirements are based on grades in specific general education courses, not on a cumulative GPA. *Application deadlines:* 2/1 (freshmen), 2/1 (transfers). *Notification:* continuous until 3/1 (freshmen), continuous until 3/1 (transfers). **Freshman Application Contact** Ashlee Gilstrap, Education Secretary, Student Services, Allen College, Barrett Forum, 1825 Logan Avenue, Waterloo, IA 50703. *Phone:* 319-226-2014. *Fax:* 319-226-2010. *E-mail:* allencollegeadmissions@ihs.org.
Website: http://www.allencollege.edu/.

Ashford University
Clinton, Iowa

Director of Admissions Ms. Waunita M. Sullivan, Director of Enrollment, Ashford University, 400 North Bluff Boulevard, PO Box 2967, Clinton, IA 52733-2967. *Phone:* 563-242-4023 Ext. 3401. *Toll-free phone:* 866-711-1700. *E-mail:* admissns@tfu.edu.
Website: http://www.ashford.edu/.

Briar Cliff University
Sioux City, Iowa

- **Independent Roman Catholic** comprehensive, founded 1930
- **Suburban** 75-acre campus
- **Endowment** $9.5 million
- **Coed**
- **Moderately difficult** entrance level

Faculty *Student/faculty ratio:* 12:1.

Academics *Calendar:* (3 10-week terms plus 2 5-week summer sessions). *Degrees:* associate, bachelor's, master's, post-master's, and postbachelor's certificates.

Student Life *Campus security:* 24-hour emergency response devices and patrols, student patrols, late-night transport/escort service, controlled dormitory access.

Athletics Member NAIA.

Standardized Tests *Required:* SAT or ACT (for admission).

Costs (2012–13) *Comprehensive fee:* $33,184 includes full-time tuition ($24,520), mandatory fees ($1122), and room and board ($7542). Part-time tuition: $810 per hour. *Room and board:* Room and board charges vary according to board plan and housing facility. *Payment plans:* installment, deferred payment.

Financial Aid *Of all full-time matriculated undergraduates who enrolled in 2011,* 833 applied for aid, 724 were judged to have need, 571 had their need fully met. 237 Federal Work-Study jobs (averaging $1500). 183 state and other part-time jobs (averaging $1500). *In 2011,* 144 non-need-based awards were made. *Average percent of need met:* 79. *Average financial aid package:* $19,220. *Average need-based loan:* $4825. *Average need-based gift aid:* $7155. *Average non-need-based aid:* $6752. *Average indebtedness upon graduation:* $29,487. *Financial aid deadline:* 3/15.

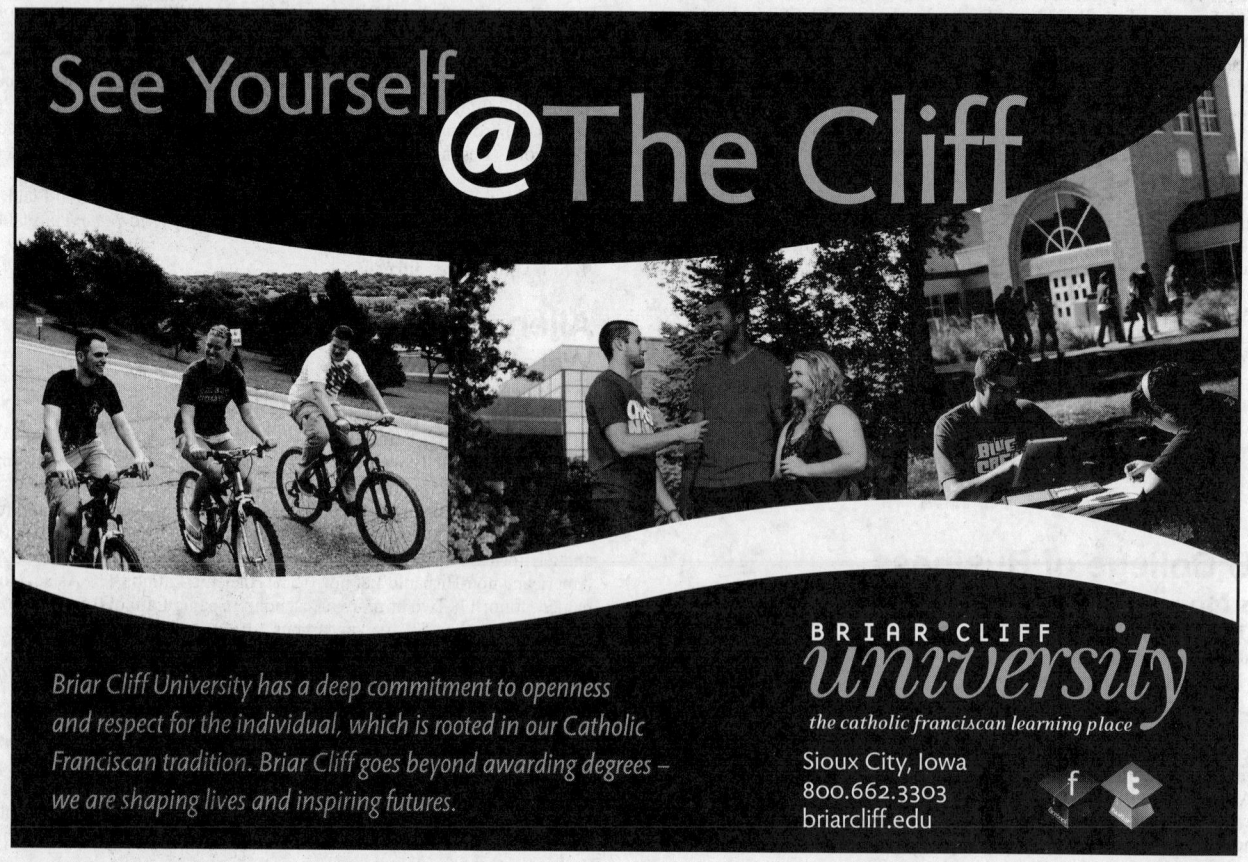

Applying *Options:* electronic application, early admission, deferred entrance. *Application fee:* $20. *Required:* high school transcript, minimum 2.0 GPA. *Required for some:* essay or personal statement, 3 letters of recommendation, interview.

Freshman Application Contact Mr. Brian Eben, Assistant Vice President for Enrollment Management, Briar Cliff University, 3303 Rebecca Street, Sioux City, IA 51104. *Phone:* 712-279-5200. *Toll-free phone:* 800-662-3303. *Fax:* 712-279-1632. *E-mail:* admissions@briarcliff.edu. *Website:* http://www.briarcliff.edu/.

See previous page for display ad and page 1166 for the College Close-Up.

Buena Vista University

Storm Lake, Iowa

- **Independent** comprehensive, founded 1891, affiliated with Presbyterian Church (U.S.A.)
- **Small-town** 60-acre campus
- **Endowment** $114.2 million
- **Coed** 913 undergraduate students, 98% full-time, 51% women, 49% men
- **Moderately difficult** entrance level, 71% of applicants were admitted

Undergraduates 896 full-time, 17 part-time. Students come from 27 states and territories; 9 other countries; 21% are from out of state; 3% Black or African American, non-Hispanic/Latino; 7% Hispanic/Latino; 1% Asian, non-Hispanic/Latino; 0.2% American Indian or Alaska Native, non-Hispanic/Latino; 2% Two or more races, non-Hispanic/Latino; 4% Race/ethnicity unknown; 4% international; 6% transferred in; 87% live on campus. *Retention:* 77% of full-time freshmen returned.

Freshmen *Admission:* 1,223 applied, 871 admitted, 228 enrolled. *Average high school GPA:* 3.4. *Test scores:* ACT scores over 18: 95%; ACT scores over 24: 40%; ACT scores over 30: 7%.

Faculty *Total:* 119, 74% full-time, 54% with terminal degrees. *Student/faculty ratio:* 9:1.

Academics *Calendar:* 4-1-4. *Degrees:* bachelor's and master's. *Special study options:* academic remediation for entering students, adult/continuing education programs, advanced placement credit, distance learning, double majors, English as a second language, external degree program, honors programs, independent study, internships, off-campus study, part-time degree program, services for LD students, student-designed majors, study abroad, summer session for credit. *ROTC:* Army (b). *Unusual degree programs:* 3-2 engineering with Washington University in St. Louis.

Computers on Campus 400 computers/terminals are available on campus for general student use. Students can access the following: computer help desk, free student e-mail accounts, online (class) grades, online (class) registration, online (class) schedules. Campuswide network is available. 100% of college-owned or -operated housing units are wired for high-speed Internet access. Wireless service is available via entire campus.

Student Life *Housing:* on-campus residence required through senior year. *Options:* coed, men-only, women-only. Campus housing is university owned. Freshman campus housing is guaranteed. *Activities and organizations:* drama/theater group, student-run newspaper, radio and television station, choral group, Student Activities Board, Student orientation staff, Esprit De Corps, Student Senate, Marketing Association. *Campus security:* 24-hour emergency response devices, late-night transport/escort service, controlled dormitory access, night security patrols. *Student services:* health clinic, personal/psychological counseling.

Athletics Member NCAA. All Division III. *Intercollegiate sports:* baseball M, basketball M/W, cross-country running M/W, football M, golf M/W, soccer M/W, softball W, tennis M/W, track and field M/W, volleyball W, wrestling M. *Intramural sports:* basketball M/W, football M, racquetball M/W, softball M/W, volleyball M/W.

Standardized Tests *Required:* SAT or ACT (for admission).

Costs (2012–13) *Comprehensive fee:* $36,494 includes full-time tuition ($28,314) and room and board ($8180). Full-time tuition and fees vary according to location. Part-time tuition and fees vary according to location. No tuition increase for student's term of enrollment. *Room and board:* Room and board charges vary according to board plan. *Payment plan:* installment. *Waivers:* employees or children of employees.

Financial Aid Of all full-time matriculated undergraduates who enrolled in 2012, 810 applied for aid, 743 were judged to have need, 349 had their need fully met. 365 Federal Work-Study jobs (averaging $1145). 252 state and other part-time jobs (averaging $1655). In 2012, 27 non-need-based awards were made. *Average percent of need met:* 83%. *Average financial aid package:* $30,793. *Average need-based loan:* $5223. *Average need-based gift aid:* $18,894. *Average non-need-based aid:* $11,269.

Applying *Options:* electronic application, deferred entrance. *Required:* high school transcript. *Required for some:* essay or personal statement, interview. *Recommended:* minimum 3.0 GPA. *Notification:* continuous (freshmen), continuous (transfers).

Freshman Application Contact Bridget Kurkowski, Director of Admissions, Buena Vista University, 610 West Fourth Street, Storm Lake, IA 50588. *Phone:* 712-749-2078. *Toll-free phone:* 800-383-9600. *E-mail:* admissions@bvu.edu. *Website:* http://www.bvu.edu/.

Central College

Pella, Iowa

- **Independent** 4-year, founded 1853, affiliated with Reformed Church in America
- **Small-town** 169-acre campus with easy access to Des Moines
- **Endowment** $68.1 million
- **Coed** 1,486 undergraduate students, 98% full-time, 54% women, 46% men
- **Moderately difficult** entrance level, 65% of applicants were admitted

Undergraduates 1,461 full-time, 25 part-time. Students come from 32 states and territories; 12 other countries; 19% are from out of state; 2% Black or African American, non-Hispanic/Latino; 3% Hispanic/Latino; 1% Asian, non-Hispanic/Latino; 0.2% Native Hawaiian or other Pacific Islander, non-Hispanic/Latino; 0.3% American Indian or Alaska Native, non-Hispanic/Latino; 1% Two or more races, non-Hispanic/Latino; 2% Race/ethnicity unknown; 0.4% international; 3% transferred in; 94% live on campus. *Retention:* 83% of full-time freshmen returned.

Freshmen *Admission:* 2,471 applied, 1,616 admitted, 320 enrolled. *Average high school GPA:* 3.61. *Test scores:* SAT critical reading scores over 500: 54%; SAT math scores over 500: 71%; ACT scores over 18: 98%; SAT critical reading scores over 600: 16%; SAT math scores over 600: 21%; ACT scores over 24: 55%; SAT critical reading scores over 700: 4%; SAT math scores over 700: 8%; ACT scores over 30: 8%.

Faculty *Total:* 120, 82% full-time, 72% with terminal degrees. *Student/faculty ratio:* 13:1.

Academics *Calendar:* semesters. *Degree:* bachelor's. *Special study options:* cooperative education, double majors, honors programs, independent study, internships, off-campus study, part-time degree program, services for LD students, student-designed majors, study abroad, summer session for credit. *Unusual degree programs:* 3-2 engineering with Washington University in St. Louis, University of Iowa, and Iowa State University; nursing with Allen College; Palmer College of Chiropractic.

Computers on Campus 322 computers/terminals and 1,500 ports are available on campus for general student use. Students can access the following: campus intranet, computer help desk, free student e-mail accounts, online (class) grades, online (class) registration, online (class) schedules. Campuswide network is available. 100% of college-owned or -operated housing units are wired for high-speed Internet access. Wireless service is available via entire campus.

Student Life *Housing:* on-campus residence required through senior year. *Options:* coed, men-only, women-only, disabled students. Campus housing is university owned. Freshman campus housing is guaranteed. *Activities and organizations:* drama/theater group, student-run newspaper, choral group, Campus Activities Board, Fellowship of Christian Athletes, Central Volunteer Center, Health Professions, Economics, Accounting, Management (EAM) Club. *Campus security:* 24-hour emergency response devices and patrols, late-night transport/escort service, controlled dormitory access. *Student services:* health clinic, personal/psychological counseling.

Athletics Member NCAA. All Division III. *Intercollegiate sports:* baseball M, basketball M/W, cross-country running M/W, football M, golf M/W, soccer M/W, softball W, tennis M/W, track and field M/W, volleyball W, wrestling M. *Intramural sports:* basketball M/W, football M, racquetball M/W, rugby M, soccer M/W, softball M/W, volleyball M/W.

Standardized Tests *Required:* SAT or ACT (for admission).

Costs (2013–14) *Comprehensive fee:* $40,680 includes full-time tuition ($30,700) and room and board ($9980). Part-time tuition: $1279 per credit. Part-time tuition and fees vary according to course load. *College room only:* $4892. Room and board charges vary according to board plan. *Payment plan:* installment. *Waivers:* employees or children of employees.

Financial Aid Of all full-time matriculated undergraduates who enrolled in 2012, 1,274 applied for aid, 1,183 were judged to have need, 217 had their need fully met. In 2012, 219 non-need-based awards were made. *Average percent of need met:* 77%. *Average financial aid package:* $24,093. *Average need-based loan:* $4413. *Average need-based gift aid:* $18,374. *Average non-need-based aid:* $14,260. *Average indebtedness upon graduation:* $27,790.

Applying *Options:* electronic application, deferred entrance. *Application fee:* $25. *Required:* high school transcript. *Required for some:* essay or personal statement, 3 letters of recommendation, interview. *Recommended:* minimum 2.7 GPA. *Application deadlines:* 8/15 (freshmen), rolling (transfers). *Notification:* continuous (freshmen), continuous (transfers).

Freshman Application Contact Chevy Freiburger, Director of Admissions, Central College, 812 University, Pella, IA 50112. *Phone:* 641-628-7637. *Toll-free phone:* 877-462-3687. *Fax:* 641-628-5983. *E-mail:* freiburgerc@central.edu.
Website: http://www.central.edu/.

Clarke University
Dubuque, Iowa

- **Independent Roman Catholic** comprehensive, founded 1843
- **Urban** 55-acre campus
- **Endowment** $28.9 million
- **Coed** 967 undergraduate students, 86% full-time, 66% women, 34% men
- **Moderately difficult** entrance level, 74% of applicants were admitted

Undergraduates 829 full-time, 138 part-time. Students come from 28 states and territories; 8 other countries; 39% are from out of state; 3% Black or African American, non-Hispanic/Latino; 2% Hispanic/Latino; 0.8% Asian, non-Hispanic/Latino; 0.2% Native Hawaiian or other Pacific Islander, non-Hispanic/Latino; 0.1% American Indian or Alaska Native, non-Hispanic/Latino; 0.5% Two or more races, non-Hispanic/Latino; 1% international; 9% transferred in; 42% live on campus. *Retention:* 81% of full-time freshmen returned.
Freshmen *Admission:* 1,034 applied, 763 admitted, 155 enrolled. *Average high school GPA:* 3.47. *Test scores:* SAT critical reading scores over 500: 25%; SAT math scores over 500: 63%; ACT scores over 18: 98%; ACT scores over 24: 51%; ACT scores over 30: 5%.
Faculty *Total:* 160, 53% full-time, 37% with terminal degrees. *Student/faculty ratio:* 10:1.
Academics *Calendar:* semesters. *Degrees:* associate, bachelor's, master's, and doctoral. *Special study options:* accelerated degree program, adult/continuing education programs, advanced placement credit, cooperative education, distance learning, double majors, English as a second language, honors programs, independent study, internships, off-campus study, part-time degree program, student-designed majors, study abroad, summer session for credit. *ROTC:* Army (c).
Computers on Campus 237 computers/terminals are available on campus for general student use. Students can access the following: campus intranet, computer help desk, free student e-mail accounts, online (class) grades, online (class) registration, online (class) schedules. Campuswide network is available. Wireless service is available via classrooms, computer centers, computer labs, dorm rooms, learning centers, libraries, student centers.
Student Life *Housing:* on-campus residence required through sophomore year. *Options:* coed, men-only, women-only. Campus housing is university owned. Freshman campus housing is guaranteed. *Activities and organizations:* drama/theater group, student-run newspaper, radio station, choral group, Admissions Student Team, Student Multicultural Organization, concert choir, campus ministry, student government. *Campus security:* 24-hour emergency response devices and patrols, late-night transport/escort service, controlled dormitory access. *Student services:* health clinic, personal/psychological counseling.
Athletics Member NAIA. *Intercollegiate sports:* baseball M(s), basketball M(s)/W(s), bowling M(s)/W(s), cheerleading W, cross-country running M(s)/W(s), golf M(s)/W(s), soccer M(s)/W(s), softball W(s), tennis W(s), track and field M(s)/W(s), volleyball M(s)/W(s). *Intramural sports:* badminton M/W, basketball M/W, bowling M/W, football M/W, golf M/W, racquetball M/W, skiing (cross-country) M/W, skiing (downhill) M/W, softball M/W, table tennis M/W, tennis M/W, track and field M/W, volleyball M/W, water polo M/W, weight lifting M/W.
Standardized Tests *Required:* SAT or ACT (for admission).
Costs (2013–14) *Comprehensive fee:* $36,400 includes full-time tuition ($27,100), mandatory fees ($900), and room and board ($8400). Part-time tuition: $690 per credit. *College room only:* $4100. Room and board charges vary according to housing facility. *Payment plans:* installment, deferred payment. *Waivers:* children of alumni, adult students, senior citizens, and employees or children of employees.
Financial Aid Of all full-time matriculated undergraduates who enrolled in 2012, 749 applied for aid, 702 were judged to have need, 132 had their need fully met. 311 Federal Work-Study jobs (averaging $1316). In 2012, 86 non-need-based awards were made. *Average percent of need met:* 68%. *Average financial aid package:* $21,509. *Average need-based loan:* $4494. *Average need-based gift aid:* $17,141. *Average non-need-based aid:* $15,913. *Average indebtedness upon graduation:* $26,865.
Applying *Options:* electronic application, deferred entrance. *Application fee:* $25. *Required:* high school transcript, minimum 2.0 GPA. *Application deadlines:* rolling (freshmen), rolling (transfers). *Notification:* 7/15 (freshmen), continuous until 8/15 (transfers).
Freshman Application Contact Ms. Emily Kruse, Assistant Director of Admissions, Clarke University, 1550 Clarke Drive, Dubuque, IA 52001-3198.

Phone: 563-588-6436. *Toll-free phone:* 800-383-2345. *E-mail:* admissions@clarke.edu.
Website: http://www.clarke.edu/.

Coe College
Cedar Rapids, Iowa

- **Independent** comprehensive, founded 1851, affiliated with Presbyterian Church
- **Urban** 53-acre campus
- **Endowment** $87.5 million
- **Coed** 1,364 undergraduate students, 96% full-time, 53% women, 47% men
- **Moderately difficult** entrance level, 67% of applicants were admitted

Undergraduates 1,304 full-time, 60 part-time. Students come from 40 states and territories; 15 other countries; 43% are from out of state; 4% Black or African American, non-Hispanic/Latino; 4% Hispanic/Latino; 3% Asian, non-Hispanic/Latino; 0.4% Native Hawaiian or other Pacific Islander, non-Hispanic/Latino; 0.1% American Indian or Alaska Native, non-Hispanic/Latino; 3% Two or more races, non-Hispanic/Latino; 6% Race/ethnicity unknown; 2% international; 2% transferred in; 84% live on campus. *Retention:* 81% of full-time freshmen returned.
Freshmen *Admission:* 2,509 applied, 1,674 admitted, 364 enrolled. *Average high school GPA:* 3.58. *Test scores:* SAT critical reading scores over 500: 76%; SAT math scores over 500: 78%; SAT writing scores over 500: 67%; ACT scores over 18: 100%; SAT critical reading scores over 600: 32%; SAT math scores over 600: 38%; SAT writing scores over 600: 30%; ACT scores over 24: 72%; SAT critical reading scores over 700: 3%; SAT math scores over 700: 8%; ACT scores over 30: 13%.
Faculty *Total:* 169, 54% full-time, 66% with terminal degrees. *Student/faculty ratio:* 11:1.
Academics *Calendar:* 4-4-1. *Degrees:* bachelor's and master's. *Special study options:* accelerated degree program, advanced placement credit, double majors, English as a second language, honors programs, independent study, internships, off-campus study, part-time degree program, services for LD students, student-designed majors, study abroad, summer session for credit. *ROTC:* Army (b), Air Force (c).
Computers on Campus 300 computers/terminals are available on campus for general student use. Students can access the following: campus intranet, computer help desk, free student e-mail accounts, online (class) grades, online (class) registration, online (class) schedules. Campuswide network is available. 100% of college-owned or -operated housing units are wired for high-speed Internet access. Wireless service is available via entire campus.
Student Life *Housing:* on-campus residence required through senior year. *Options:* coed, men-only, women-only, disabled students. Campus housing is university owned. Freshman campus housing is guaranteed. *Activities and organizations:* drama/theater group, student-run newspaper, radio station, choral group, Student Activities Committee, Student Senate, Up 'til Dawn, Cedar Rapids Dance Marathon, Alpha Sigma Alpha Sorority, national fraternities, national sororities. *Campus security:* 24-hour emergency response devices and patrols, late-night transport/escort service, controlled dormitory access. *Student services:* health clinic, personal/psychological counseling.
Athletics Member NCAA. All Division III. *Intercollegiate sports:* baseball M, basketball M/W, cheerleading W, cross-country running M/W, football M, golf M/W, soccer M/W, softball W, swimming and diving M/W, tennis M/W, track and field M/W, volleyball W, wrestling M. *Intramural sports:* badminton M/W, basketball M/W, cross-country running M(c)/W(c), football M/W, racquetball M/W, rock climbing M/W, rugby M(c)/W(c), soccer M/W, softball M/W, squash M/W, swimming and diving M(c)/W(c), table tennis M/W, tennis M/W, ultimate Frisbee M(c)/W(c), volleyball M/W.
Standardized Tests *Required:* SAT or ACT (for admission).
Costs (2013–14) *Comprehensive fee:* $43,480 includes full-time tuition ($35,400), mandatory fees ($330), and room and board ($7750). Part-time tuition: $4035 per course. Part-time tuition and fees vary according to course load. *College room only:* $3450. Room and board charges vary according to housing facility. *Payment plan:* installment. *Waivers:* adult students, senior citizens, and employees or children of employees.
Financial Aid Of all full-time matriculated undergraduates who enrolled in 2011, 1,149 applied for aid, 1,048 were judged to have need, 194 had their need fully met. 523 Federal Work-Study jobs (averaging $1656). 228 state and other part-time jobs (averaging $1421). In 2011, 240 non-need-based awards were made. *Average percent of need met:* 80%. *Average financial aid package:* $27,104. *Average need-based loan:* $5061. *Average need-based gift aid:* $22,297. *Average non-need-based aid:* $18,489. *Average indebtedness upon graduation:* $29,500.
Applying *Options:* electronic application, early admission, early action, deferred entrance. *Application fee:* $30. *Required:* essay or personal statement, high school transcript, 1 letter of recommendation. *Recommended:* minimum

3.0 GPA, interview. *Application deadlines:* 3/1 (freshmen), rolling (transfers), 12/10 (early action). *Notification:* 3/15 (freshmen), continuous (transfers).
Freshman Application Contact Ms. Julie Staker, Dean of Admission, Coe College, 1220 1st Avenue, NE, Cedar Rapids, IA 52402-5070. *Phone:* 319-399-8500. *Toll-free phone:* 877-225-5263. *Fax:* 319-399-8816. *E-mail:* admission@coe.edu.
Website: http://www.coe.edu/.

Cornell College
Mount Vernon, Iowa

- **Independent Methodist** 4-year, founded 1853
- **Small-town** 129-acre campus
- **Endowment** $65.0 million
- **Coed** 1,180 undergraduate students, 99% full-time, 55% women, 45% men
- **Moderately difficult** entrance level, 53% of applicants were admitted

Undergraduates 1,171 full-time, 9 part-time. Students come from 49 states and territories; 19 other countries; 83% are from out of state; 5% Black or African American, non-Hispanic/Latino; 11% Hispanic/Latino; 4% Asian, non-Hispanic/Latino; 0.3% Native Hawaiian or other Pacific Islander, non-Hispanic/Latino; 0.9% American Indian or Alaska Native, non-Hispanic/Latino; 2% Two or more races, non-Hispanic/Latino; 5% Race/ethnicity unknown; 6% international; 3% transferred in; 92% live on campus. *Retention:* 84% of full-time freshmen returned.
Freshmen *Admission:* 2,716 applied, 1,436 admitted, 302 enrolled. *Average high school GPA:* 3.53. *Test scores:* SAT critical reading scores over 500: 89%; SAT math scores over 500: 88%; SAT writing scores over 500: 85%; ACT scores over 18: 99%; SAT critical reading scores over 600: 50%; SAT math scores over 600: 59%; SAT writing scores over 600: 50%; ACT scores over 24: 81%; SAT critical reading scores over 700: 22%; SAT math scores over 700: 23%; SAT writing scores over 700: 10%; ACT scores over 30: 25%.
Faculty *Total:* 116, 77% full-time, 89% with terminal degrees. *Student/faculty ratio:* 12:1.
Academics *Calendar:* 9 3&S1/&I2-week terms. *Degree:* bachelor's. *Special study options:* advanced placement credit, double majors, English as a second language, honors programs, independent study, internships, off-campus study, services for LD students, student-designed majors, study abroad. *Unusual degree programs:* 3-2 engineering with University of Minnesota; forestry with Duke University; environmental management with Duke University; Architecture with Washington University–St. Louis.
Computers on Campus 190 computers/terminals and 1,200 ports are available on campus for general student use. Students can access the following: campus intranet, computer help desk, free student e-mail accounts, online (class) grades, online (class) registration, online (class) schedules. Campuswide network is available. 100% of college-owned or -operated housing units are wired for high-speed Internet access. Wireless service is available via entire campus.
Student Life *Housing:* on-campus residence required through senior year. *Options:* coed, women-only. Campus housing is university owned. Freshman campus housing is guaranteed. *Activities and organizations:* drama/theater group, student-run newspaper, radio station, choral group, Student-initiated Living-learning Community, Lunch Buddies/Youth Mentoring, Chess and Games Club, PAAC (Performing Arts and Activities Council), Fellowship of Christian Athletes (FCA). *Campus security:* 24-hour emergency response devices and patrols, late-night transport/escort service, controlled dormitory access. *Student services:* health clinic, personal/psychological counseling, women's center.
Athletics Member NCAA. All Division III. *Intercollegiate sports:* baseball M, basketball M/W, cheerleading M/W, cross-country running M/W, fencing M(c)/W(c), football M, lacrosse M(c)/W(c), soccer M/W, softball W, tennis M/W, track and field M/W, ultimate Frisbee M(c)/W(c), volleyball M(c)/W, wrestling M. *Intramural sports:* badminton M/W, basketball M/W, bowling M/W, cross-country running M/W, football M/W, golf M/W, ice hockey M/W, racquetball M/W, soccer M/W, softball M/W, table tennis M/W, tennis M/W, track and field M/W, ultimate Frisbee M/W, volleyball M/W, weight lifting M/W, wrestling M/W.
Standardized Tests *Required:* SAT or ACT (for admission). *Recommended:* SAT Subject Tests (for admission).
Costs (2012–13) *Comprehensive fee:* $42,605 includes full-time tuition ($34,480), mandatory fees ($225), and room and board ($7900). Part-time tuition: $2586 per course. Part-time tuition and fees vary according to course load and reciprocity agreements. *Required fees:* $113 per year part-time. *College room only:* $3700. Room and board charges vary according to board plan and housing facility. *Payment plan:* installment. *Waivers:* employees or children of employees.
Financial Aid Of all full-time matriculated undergraduates who enrolled in 2012, 964 applied for aid, 877 were judged to have need, 152 had their need fully met. 585 Federal Work-Study jobs (averaging $1165). In 2012, 219 non-need-based awards were made. *Average percent of need met:* 84%. *Average financial aid package:* $30,087. *Average need-based loan:* $4775. *Average need-based gift aid:* $20,435. *Average non-need-based aid:* $11,535. *Average indebtedness upon graduation:* $27,227. *Financial aid deadline:* 3/1.
Applying *Options:* electronic application, early admission, early decision, early action, deferred entrance. *Application fee:* $30. *Required:* essay or personal statement, high school transcript, 1 letter of recommendation. *Recommended:* interview. *Application deadlines:* 2/1 (freshmen), 3/1 (transfers), 12/1 (early action). *Early decision deadline:* 11/1 (for plan 1), 2/1 (for plan 2). *Notification:* 3/20 (freshmen), continuous (transfers), 12/15 (early decision plan 1), 3/15 (early decision plan 2), 2/1 (early action).
Freshman Application Contact Ms. Marie Schofer, Director of Admissions, Cornell College, 600 First Street SW, Mount Vernon, IA 52314-1098. *Phone:* 319-895-4477. *Toll-free phone:* 800-747-1112. *Fax:* 319-895-4451. *E-mail:* admissions@cornellcollege.edu.
Website: http://www.cornellcollege.edu/.

Divine Word College
Epworth, Iowa

Freshman Application Contact Divine Word College, 102 Jacoby Drive SW, Epworth, IA 52045-0380. *Phone:* 563-876-3353. *Toll-free phone:* 800-553-3321.
Website: http://www.dwci.edu/.

Dordt College
Sioux Center, Iowa

- **Independent Christian Reformed** comprehensive, founded 1955
- **Small-town** 110-acre campus
- **Endowment** $29.0 million
- **Coed** 1,379 undergraduate students, 97% full-time, 48% women, 52% men
- **Moderately difficult** entrance level, 79% of applicants were admitted

Undergraduates 1,344 full-time, 35 part-time. Students come from 37 states and territories; 18 other countries; 62% are from out of state; 2% Black or African American, non-Hispanic/Latino; 2% Hispanic/Latino; 0.7% Asian, non-Hispanic/Latino; 0.2% American Indian or Alaska Native, non-Hispanic/Latino; 2% Race/ethnicity unknown; 9% international; 4% transferred in; 90% live on campus. *Retention:* 80% of full-time freshmen returned.
Freshmen *Admission:* 1,102 applied, 872 admitted, 342 enrolled. *Average high school GPA:* 3.5. *Test scores:* SAT critical reading scores over 500: 64%; SAT math scores over 500: 71%; SAT writing scores over 500: 56%; ACT scores over 18: 97%; SAT critical reading scores over 600: 26%; SAT math scores over 600: 38%; SAT writing scores over 600: 21%; ACT scores over 24: 61%; SAT critical reading scores over 700: 9%; SAT math scores over 700: 11%; SAT writing scores over 700: 3%; ACT scores over 30: 16%.
Faculty *Total:* 102, 74% full-time, 70% with terminal degrees. *Student/faculty ratio:* 14:1.
Academics *Calendar:* semesters. *Degrees:* associate, bachelor's, and master's. *Special study options:* academic remediation for entering students, advanced placement credit, distance learning, double majors, English as a second language, freshman honors college, honors programs, independent study, internships, off-campus study, part-time degree program, services for LD students, student-designed majors, study abroad.
Computers on Campus 200 computers/terminals are available on campus for general student use. Students can access the following: campus intranet, computer help desk, free student e-mail accounts, online (class) grades, online (class) registration, online (class) schedules. Campuswide network is available. 100% of college-owned or -operated housing units are wired for high-speed Internet access. Wireless service is available via entire campus.
Student Life *Housing:* on-campus residence required through senior year. *Options:* men-only, women-only, disabled students. Campus housing is university owned. Freshman campus housing is guaranteed. *Activities and organizations:* drama/theater group, student-run newspaper, radio station, choral group, PLIA, Future Teachers, Ag Club, Lacrosse Club, Defenders of Life. *Campus security:* 24-hour emergency response devices, student patrols, late-night transport/escort service, controlled dormitory access. *Student services:* health clinic, personal/psychological counseling.
Athletics Member NAIA. *Intercollegiate sports:* baseball M(s), basketball M(s)/W(s), cross-country running M(s)/W(s), football M(s), golf M(s)/W(s), ice hockey M(s), lacrosse M, soccer M(s)/W(s), softball W(s), track and field M(s)/W(s), volleyball W(s). *Intramural sports:* basketball M/W, bowling M/W, field hockey M/W, gymnastics M/W, ice hockey M, lacrosse M, racquetball M/W, skiing (cross-country) M/W, soccer M/W, softball M/W, swimming and diving M/W, table tennis M/W, tennis M/W, track and field M/W, ultimate Frisbee M/W, volleyball M/W, weight lifting M/W.

Standardized Tests *Required:* SAT or ACT (for admission).

Costs (2012–13) *Comprehensive fee:* $32,750 includes full-time tuition ($25,100), mandatory fees ($420), and room and board ($7230). Full-time tuition and fees vary according to course load. Part-time tuition: $960 per quarter hour. *College room only:* $3700. Room and board charges vary according to board plan and housing facility. *Payment plan:* installment. *Waivers:* senior citizens and employees or children of employees.

Financial Aid Of all full-time matriculated undergraduates who enrolled in 2012, 980 applied for aid, 866 were judged to have need, 244 had their need fully met. 446 Federal Work-Study jobs (averaging $1500). 497 state and other part-time jobs (averaging $1500). In 2012, 227 non-need-based awards were made. *Average percent of need met:* 78%. *Average financial aid package:* $20,194. *Average need-based loan:* $5297. *Average need-based gift aid:* $13,426. *Average non-need-based aid:* $17,166. *Average indebtedness upon graduation:* $21,859.

Applying *Options:* electronic application, deferred entrance. *Required:* high school transcript, minimum 2.3 GPA. *Required for some:* essay or personal statement, interview. *Application deadlines:* 8/1 (freshmen), 8/1 (transfers). *Notification:* 8/1 (freshmen), continuous until 9/1 (transfers).

Freshman Application Contact Mr. Quentin Van Essen, Executive Director of Admissions, Dordt College, 498 4th Avenue, NE, Sioux Center, IA 51250-1697. *Phone:* 712-722-6080. *Toll-free phone:* 800-343-6738. *Fax:* 712-722-6035. *E-mail:* admissions@dordt.edu. *Website:* http://www.dordt.edu/.

Drake University
Des Moines, Iowa

- **Independent** university, founded 1881
- **Urban** 120-acre campus
- **Endowment** $149.3 million
- **Coed** 3,365 undergraduate students, 95% full-time, 57% women, 43% men
- **Moderately difficult** entrance level, 66% of applicants were admitted

Undergraduates 3,189 full-time, 176 part-time. Students come from 46 states and territories; 39 other countries; 62% are from out of state; 3% Black or African American, non-Hispanic/Latino; 3% Hispanic/Latino; 3% Asian, non-Hispanic/Latino; 0.1% Native Hawaiian or other Pacific Islander, non-Hispanic/Latino; 0.2% American Indian or Alaska Native, non-Hispanic/Latino; 2% Two or more races, non-Hispanic/Latino; 2% Race/ethnicity unknown; 8% international; 4% transferred in; 71% live on campus. *Retention:* 88% of full-time freshmen returned.

Freshmen *Admission:* 6,357 applied, 4,188 admitted, 848 enrolled. *Average high school GPA:* 3.7. *Test scores:* SAT critical reading scores over 500: 78%; SAT math scores over 500: 93%; ACT scores over 18: 99%; SAT critical reading scores over 600: 45%; SAT math scores over 600: 60%; ACT scores over 24: 82%; SAT critical reading scores over 700: 7%; SAT math scores over 700: 12%; ACT scores over 30: 24%.

Faculty *Total:* 450, 64% full-time, 61% with terminal degrees. *Student/faculty ratio:* 12:1.

Academics *Calendar:* semesters. *Degrees:* bachelor's, master's, doctoral, post-master's, and postbachelor's certificates. *Special study options:* accelerated degree program, advanced placement credit, cooperative education, distance learning, double majors, English as a second language, honors programs, independent study, internships, off-campus study, part-time degree program, services for LD students, student-designed majors, study abroad, summer session for credit. *ROTC:* Army (b), Air Force (c). *Unusual degree programs:* 3-2 journalism and law, arts and sciences and law, accounting.

Computers on Campus 1,000 computers/terminals are available on campus for general student use. Students can access the following: campus intranet, computer help desk, free student e-mail accounts, online (class) grades, online (class) registration, online (class) schedules. Campuswide network is available. 100% of college-owned or -operated housing units are wired for high-speed Internet access. Wireless service is available via classrooms, computer centers, computer labs, dorm rooms, libraries, student centers.

Student Life *Housing:* on-campus residence required through sophomore year. *Options:* coed, disabled students. Campus housing is university owned and is provided by a third party. Freshman campus housing is guaranteed. *Activities and organizations:* drama/theater group, student-run newspaper, radio and television station, choral group, marching band, Student Activities Board, Drake Magazine, Dog Pound Pep Squad, Alpha Phi Omega, Residence Hall Association, national fraternities, national sororities. *Campus security:* 24-hour emergency response devices and patrols, late-night transport/escort service, 24-hour desk attendants in residence halls. *Student services:* health clinic, personal/psychological counseling, legal services.

Athletics Member NCAA. All Division I except football (Division I-AA). *Intercollegiate sports:* basketball M(s)/W(s), cheerleading M(s)/W(s), crew W, cross-country running M(s)/W(s), golf M(s)/W, soccer M(s)/W(s), softball

W(s), tennis M(s)/W(s), track and field M(s)/W(s), volleyball W(s). *Intramural sports:* badminton M/W, basketball M/W, football M/W, golf M/W, racquetball M/W, soccer M(c)/W, softball M/W, swimming and diving M/W, tennis M/W, volleyball M/W(c).

Standardized Tests *Required:* SAT or ACT (for admission).

Costs (2013–14) *Comprehensive fee:* $39,580 includes full-time tuition ($30,734), mandatory fees ($146), and room and board ($8700). Full-time tuition and fees vary according to course load, program, and student level. Part-time tuition: $610 per hour. Part-time tuition and fees vary according to class time and program. *College room only:* $4470. Room and board charges vary according to board plan. *Payment plan:* installment. *Waivers:* children of alumni, senior citizens, and employees or children of employees.

Financial Aid Of all full-time matriculated undergraduates who enrolled in 2012, 2,341 applied for aid, 1,940 were judged to have need, 513 had their need fully met. 1,616 Federal Work-Study jobs (averaging $1871). In 2012, 1029 non-need-based awards were made. *Average percent of need met:* 75%. *Average financial aid package:* $21,650. *Average need-based loan:* $4554. *Average need-based gift aid:* $14,719. *Average non-need-based aid:* $11,607. *Average indebtedness upon graduation:* $32,114.

Applying *Options:* electronic application, early admission, deferred entrance. *Application fee:* $25. *Required:* essay or personal statement, high school transcript. *Recommended:* interview. *Application deadlines:* 3/1 (freshmen), rolling (transfers). *Notification:* continuous (freshmen), continuous (transfers).

Freshman Application Contact Ms. Laura Linn, Director of Admission, Drake University, 2507 University Avenue, Des Moines, IA 50311. *Phone:* 515-271-3181 Ext. 3182. *Toll-free phone:* 800-44-DRAKE Ext. 3181. *Fax:* 515-271-2831. *E-mail:* admission@drake.edu. *Website:* http://www.drake.edu/.

Emmaus Bible College
Dubuque, Iowa

- **Independent nondenominational** 4-year, founded 1941
- **Small-town** 22-acre campus
- **Coed**
- **Noncompetitive** entrance level

Academics *Calendar:* semesters. *Degrees:* certificates, associate, and bachelor's.

Student Life *Campus security:* 24-hour emergency response devices, student patrols, controlled dormitory access.

Athletics Member NCCAA.

Standardized Tests *Required:* SAT or ACT (for admission).

Costs (2012–13) *Comprehensive fee:* $20,700 includes full-time tuition ($13,750), mandatory fees ($750), and room and board ($6200). Full-time tuition and fees vary according to course load and program. Part-time tuition and fees vary according to course load and program.

Financial Aid *Of all full-time matriculated undergraduates who enrolled in 2005,* 212 applied for aid, 145 were judged to have need. *Average percent of need met:* 74. *Average financial aid package:* $5216. *Average need-based loan:* $3652. *Average need-based gift aid:* $2852.

Applying *Options:* electronic application, deferred entrance. *Application fee:* $25. *Required:* essay or personal statement, high school transcript, 2 letters of recommendation.

Freshman Application Contact Emmaus Bible College, 2570 Asbury Road, Dubuque, IA 52001-3097. *Phone:* 563-588-8000 Ext. 1310. *Toll-free phone:* 800-397-2425. *Website:* http://www.emmaus.edu/.

Faith Baptist Bible College and Theological Seminary
Ankeny, Iowa

- **Independent** comprehensive, founded 1921, affiliated with General Association of Regular Baptist Churches
- **Suburban** 52-acre campus
- **Endowment** $4.0 million
- **Coed** 261 undergraduate students, 90% full-time, 52% women, 48% men
- **Minimally difficult** entrance level, 65% of applicants were admitted

Undergraduates 234 full-time, 27 part-time. Students come from 26 states and territories; 7 other countries; 44% are from out of state; 2% Black or African American, non-Hispanic/Latino; 0.8% Hispanic/Latino; 1% Asian, non-Hispanic/Latino; 0.8% Native Hawaiian or other Pacific Islander, non-Hispanic/Latino; 1% American Indian or Alaska Native, non-Hispanic/Latino; 5% transferred in; 75% live on campus. *Retention:* 72% of full-time freshmen returned.

Freshmen *Admission:* 191 applied, 125 admitted, 70 enrolled. *Average high school GPA:* 3.41. *Test scores:* SAT critical reading scores over 500: 100%;

SAT math scores over 500: 75%; SAT writing scores over 500: 75%; ACT scores over 18: 83%; SAT critical reading scores over 600: 75%; SAT math scores over 600: 25%; SAT writing scores over 600: 75%; ACT scores over 24: 42%; SAT critical reading scores over 700: 50%; ACT scores over 30: 3%.

Faculty *Total:* 29, 62% full-time, 52% with terminal degrees. *Student/faculty ratio:* 11:1.

Academics *Calendar:* semesters. *Degrees:* associate, bachelor's, and master's. *Special study options:* academic remediation for entering students, adult/continuing education programs, advanced placement credit, double majors, independent study, internships, part-time degree program, summer session for credit.

Computers on Campus 45 computers/terminals and 250 ports are available on campus for general student use. Students can access the following: free student e-mail accounts, online (class) registration. Campuswide network is available. 100% of college-owned or -operated housing units are wired for high-speed Internet access. Wireless service is available via entire campus.

Student Life *Housing:* on-campus residence required through senior year. *Options:* men-only, women-only, disabled students. Campus housing is university owned. Freshman campus housing is guaranteed. *Activities and organizations:* drama/theater group, choral group, Student Association, Student Missionary Fellowship, Intramural Sports, Photo Club, Chapel Orchestra. *Campus security:* 24-hour emergency response devices and patrols, late-night transport/escort service. *Student services:* personal/psychological counseling.

Athletics Member NCCAA. *Intercollegiate sports:* basketball M/W, cross-country running M/W, soccer M/W, track and field M/W, volleyball W. *Intramural sports:* basketball M/W, football M, ultimate Frisbee M/W, volleyball M/W.

Standardized Tests *Required:* SAT or ACT (for admission).

Costs (2012–13) *One-time required fee:* $230. *Comprehensive fee:* $21,008 includes full-time tuition ($14,560), mandatory fees ($460), and room and board ($5988). Full-time tuition and fees vary according to course load and degree level. Part-time tuition: $532 per credit hour. Part-time tuition and fees vary according to course load and degree level. *Required fees:* $230 per term part-time. *College room only:* $2812. *Payment plan:* installment. *Waivers:* employees or children of employees.

Financial Aid Of all full-time matriculated undergraduates who enrolled in 2004, 311 applied for aid, 290 were judged to have need, 5 had their need fully met. In 2004, 21 non-need-based awards were made. *Average percent of need met:* 48%. *Average financial aid package:* $7124. *Average need-based loan:* $3142. *Average need-based gift aid:* $6299. *Average non-need-based aid:* $2465. *Average indebtedness upon graduation:* $15,006.

Applying *Options:* electronic application, deferred entrance. *Required:* essay or personal statement, high school transcript, 2 letters of recommendation. *Required for some:* interview. *Recommended:* minimum 2.0 GPA. *Application deadlines:* 8/1 (freshmen), 8/1 (transfers). *Notification:* 9/1 (freshmen), continuous until 9/1 (transfers).

Freshman Application Contact Mrs. Krisanna Sternquist, Admissions Secretary, Faith Baptist Bible College and Theological Seminary, 1900 NW 4th Street, Ankeny, IA 50023. *Phone:* 515-964-0601. *Toll-free phone:* 888-FAITH 4U. *Fax:* 515-964-1638. *E-mail:* admissions@faith.edu. *Website:* http://www.faith.edu/.

Graceland University

Lamoni, Iowa

- **Independent Community of Christ** comprehensive, founded 1895
- **Rural** 170-acre campus with easy access to Des Moines
- **Endowment** $35.3 million
- **Coed** 1,515 undergraduate students, 79% full-time, 57% women, 43% men
- **Moderately difficult** entrance level, 48% of applicants were admitted

Undergraduates 1,203 full-time, 312 part-time. Students come from 44 states and territories; 40 other countries; 69% are from out of state; 9% Black or African American, non-Hispanic/Latino; 2% Hispanic/Latino; 0.3% Asian, non-Hispanic/Latino; 1% Native Hawaiian or other Pacific Islander, non-Hispanic/Latino; 0.5% American Indian or Alaska Native, non-Hispanic/Latino; 3% Two or more races, non-Hispanic/Latino; 8% Race/ethnicity unknown; 8% international; 6% transferred in; 72% live on campus. *Retention:* 68% of full-time freshmen returned.

Freshmen *Admission:* 1,676 applied, 802 admitted, 260 enrolled. *Average high school GPA:* 3.2. *Test scores:* SAT critical reading scores over 500: 32%; SAT math scores over 500: 48%; ACT scores over 18: 84%; SAT critical reading scores over 600: 10%; SAT math scores over 600: 16%; ACT scores over 24: 35%; SAT critical reading scores over 700: 2%; ACT scores over 30: 4%.

Faculty *Total:* 97, 57% full-time, 62% with terminal degrees. *Student/faculty ratio:* 13:1.

Academics *Calendar:* 4-1-4. *Degrees:* bachelor's, master's, doctoral, and post-master's certificates. *Special study options:* academic remediation for

entering students, accelerated degree program, adult/continuing education programs, advanced placement credit, cooperative education, distance learning, double majors, English as a second language, freshman honors college, honors programs, independent study, internships, off-campus study, part-time degree program, services for LD students, student-designed majors, study abroad, summer session for credit.

Computers on Campus 249 computers/terminals and 1,046 ports are available on campus for general student use. Students can access the following: campus intranet, computer help desk, free student e-mail accounts, online (class) grades, online (class) registration, online (class) schedules. Campuswide network is available. 100% of college-owned or -operated housing units are wired for high-speed Internet access. Wireless service is available via classrooms, computer centers, computer labs, dorm rooms, learning centers, libraries, student centers.

Student Life *Housing:* on-campus residence required through sophomore year. *Options:* men-only, women-only. Campus housing is university owned. Freshman campus housing is guaranteed. *Activities and organizations:* drama/theater group, student-run newspaper, radio station, choral group, International Club, Student Athletic Trainers, Outreach International, Art Student Society, Students in Free Enterprise (SIFE). *Campus security:* 24-hour emergency response devices and patrols, late-night transport/escort service, controlled dormitory access. *Student services:* health clinic, personal/psychological counseling.

Athletics Member NAIA. *Intercollegiate sports:* baseball M(s), basketball M(s)/W(s), cheerleading M(s)/W(s), cross-country running M(s)/W(s), football M(s), golf M(s)/W(s), soccer M(s)/W(s), softball W(s), tennis M(s)/W(s), track and field M(s)/W(s), ultimate Frisbee M(c)/W(c), volleyball M(s)/W(s). *Intramural sports:* basketball M/W, football M/W, golf M/W, racquetball M/W, soccer M/W, softball M/W, swimming and diving M/W, table tennis M/W, ultimate Frisbee M/W, volleyball M/W.

Standardized Tests *Required:* SAT or ACT (for admission), TOEFL for all students whose first language is not English (for admission).

Costs (2013–14) *Comprehensive fee:* $31,420 includes full-time tuition ($23,180), mandatory fees ($350), and room and board ($7890). Full-time tuition and fees vary according to course load. Part-time tuition: $725 per credit. Part-time tuition and fees vary according to course load. *Room and board:* Room and board charges vary according to board plan, housing facility, and location. *Payment plan:* installment. *Waivers:* senior citizens and employees or children of employees.

Financial Aid Of all full-time matriculated undergraduates who enrolled in 2012, 1,053 applied for aid, 795 were judged to have need, 112 had their need fully met. 186 Federal Work-Study jobs (averaging $1522). 375 state and other part-time jobs (averaging $1490). In 2012, 338 non-need-based awards were made. *Average percent of need met:* 72%. *Average financial aid package:* $18,973. *Average need-based loan:* $4963. *Average need-based gift aid:* $14,979. *Average non-need-based aid:* $11,028. *Average indebtedness upon graduation:* $39,022.

Applying *Options:* electronic application, deferred entrance. *Required:* high school transcript, minimum 2.5 GPA, Students must meet 2 out of the following 3 requirements to be considered for admission: rank in top half of class; score a minimum of 21 on ACT or 960 on the SAT; have a 2.5 high school GPA (on a 4.0 scale). *Required for some:* essay or personal statement, 2 letters of recommendation, interview. *Application deadlines:* rolling (freshmen), rolling (out-of-state freshmen), rolling (transfers). *Notification:* continuous (freshmen), continuous (out-of-state freshmen), continuous (transfers).

Freshman Application Contact Mr. Kevin Brown, Director of Admissions, Graceland University, 1 University Place, Lamoni, IA 50140. *Phone:* 641-784-5149. *Toll-free phone:* 866-GRACELAND. *Fax:* 641-784-5480. *E-mail:* admissions@graceland.edu. *Website:* http://www.graceland.edu/.

Grand View University

Des Moines, Iowa

- **Independent** comprehensive, founded 1896, affiliated with Evangelical Lutheran Church in America
- **Urban** 25-acre campus
- **Endowment** $16.4 million
- **Coed** 2,195 undergraduate students, 81% full-time, 59% women, 41% men
- **Minimally difficult** entrance level, 92% of applicants were admitted

Undergraduates 1,785 full-time, 410 part-time. Students come from 34 states and territories; 16 other countries; 14% are from out of state; 7% Black or African American, non-Hispanic/Latino; 3% Hispanic/Latino; 3% Asian, non-Hispanic/Latino; 0.2% Native Hawaiian or other Pacific Islander, non-Hispanic/Latino; 0.5% American Indian or Alaska Native, non-Hispanic/Latino; 3% Two or more races, non-Hispanic/Latino; 8% Race/ethnicity unknown; 2%

international; 18% transferred in; 35% live on campus. *Retention:* 73% of full-time freshmen returned.

Freshmen *Admission:* 821 applied, 758 admitted, 292 enrolled. *Average high school GPA:* 3.13. *Test scores:* SAT critical reading scores over 500: 27%; SAT math scores over 500: 43%; SAT writing scores over 500: 100%; ACT scores over 18: 88%; SAT math scores over 600: 12%; ACT scores over 24: 19%; ACT scores over 30: 1%.

Faculty *Total:* 269, 35% full-time, 43% with terminal degrees. *Student/faculty ratio:* 14:1.

Academics *Calendar:* semesters. *Degrees:* bachelor's, master's, and postbachelor's certificates. *Special study options:* academic remediation for entering students, accelerated degree program, adult/continuing education programs, advanced placement credit, cooperative education, distance learning, double majors, freshman honors college, honors programs, independent study, internships, off-campus study, part-time degree program, services for LD students, student-designed majors, study abroad, summer session for credit. *ROTC:* Army (c), Air Force (c). *Unusual degree programs:* 3-2 engineering with Iowa State University; hospital administration with The University of Iowa.

Computers on Campus 313 computers/terminals are available on campus for general student use. Students can access the following: campus intranet, computer help desk, free student e-mail accounts, online (class) grades, online (class) registration, online (class) schedules. Campuswide network is available. 100% of college-owned or -operated housing units are wired for high-speed Internet access. Wireless service is available via classrooms, computer labs, libraries, student centers.

Student Life *Housing:* on-campus residence required through sophomore year. *Options:* coed. Campus housing is university owned. Freshman applicants given priority for college housing. *Activities and organizations:* drama/theater group, student-run newspaper, radio and television station, choral group, Nursing Student Association, Art Club, Science Club, Education Club, Business Club. *Campus security:* 24-hour emergency response devices and patrols, late-night transport/escort service, controlled dormitory access, night security patrols. *Student services:* health clinic, personal/psychological counseling.

Athletics Member NAIA. *Intercollegiate sports:* baseball M(s), basketball M(s)/W(s), bowling M(s)/W(s), cheerleading W(s), cross-country running M(s)/W(s), football M(s), golf M(s)/W(s), soccer M(s)/W(s), softball W(s), tennis M(s)/W(s), track and field M(s)/W(s), volleyball M(s)/W(s), wrestling M(s). *Intramural sports:* basketball M/W, football M/W, soccer M/W, table tennis M/W, ultimate Frisbee M/W, volleyball M/W.

Standardized Tests *Required:* SAT or ACT (for admission).

Costs (2013–14) *Comprehensive fee:* $29,972 includes full-time tuition ($22,208), mandatory fees ($500), and room and board ($7264). Full-time tuition and fees vary according to class time and course load. Part-time tuition: $553 per credit hour. Part-time tuition and fees vary according to class time and course load. *Room and board:* Room and board charges vary according to board plan and housing facility. *Payment plan:* installment. *Waivers:* children of alumni, senior citizens, and employees or children of employees.

Financial Aid Of all full-time matriculated undergraduates who enrolled in 2012, 1,632 applied for aid, 1,486 were judged to have need, 377 had their need fully met. 396 Federal Work-Study jobs (averaging $1353). 1 state and other part-time job (averaging $2250). In 2012, 235 non-need-based awards were made. *Average percent of need met:* 78%. *Average financial aid package:* $17,334. *Average need-based loan:* $4052. *Average need-based gift aid:* $12,983. *Average non-need-based aid:* $6810. *Average indebtedness upon graduation:* $33,464.

Applying *Options:* electronic application. *Required:* high school transcript. *Recommended:* minimum 2.0 GPA. *Application deadlines:* 8/15 (freshmen), 8/15 (transfers). *Notification:* 9/15 (freshmen), continuous until 9/15 (transfers).

Freshman Application Contact Ms. Diane Schaefer, Director of Admissions, Grand View University, 1200 Grandview Avenue, Des Moines, IA 50316-1599. *Phone:* 515-263-2810. *Toll-free phone:* 800-444-6083. *Fax:* 515-263-2974. *E-mail:* admissions@grandview.edu. *Website:* http://www.grandview.edu/.

See below for display ad and page 1308 for the College Close-Up.

Grinnell College
Grinnell, Iowa

- **Independent** 4-year, founded 1846
- **Small-town** 120-acre campus
- **Endowment** $1.4 billion
- **Coed** 1,674 undergraduate students, 96% full-time, 54% women, 46% men
- **Very difficult** entrance level, 36% of applicants were admitted

Undergraduates 1,615 full-time, 59 part-time. Students come from 50 states and territories; 54 other countries; 88% are from out of state; 5% Black or African American, non-Hispanic/Latino; 7% Hispanic/Latino; 7% Asian, non-Hispanic/Latino; 0.2% Native Hawaiian or other Pacific Islander, non-Hispanic/Latino; 4% Two or more races, non-Hispanic/Latino; 6% Race/ethnicity

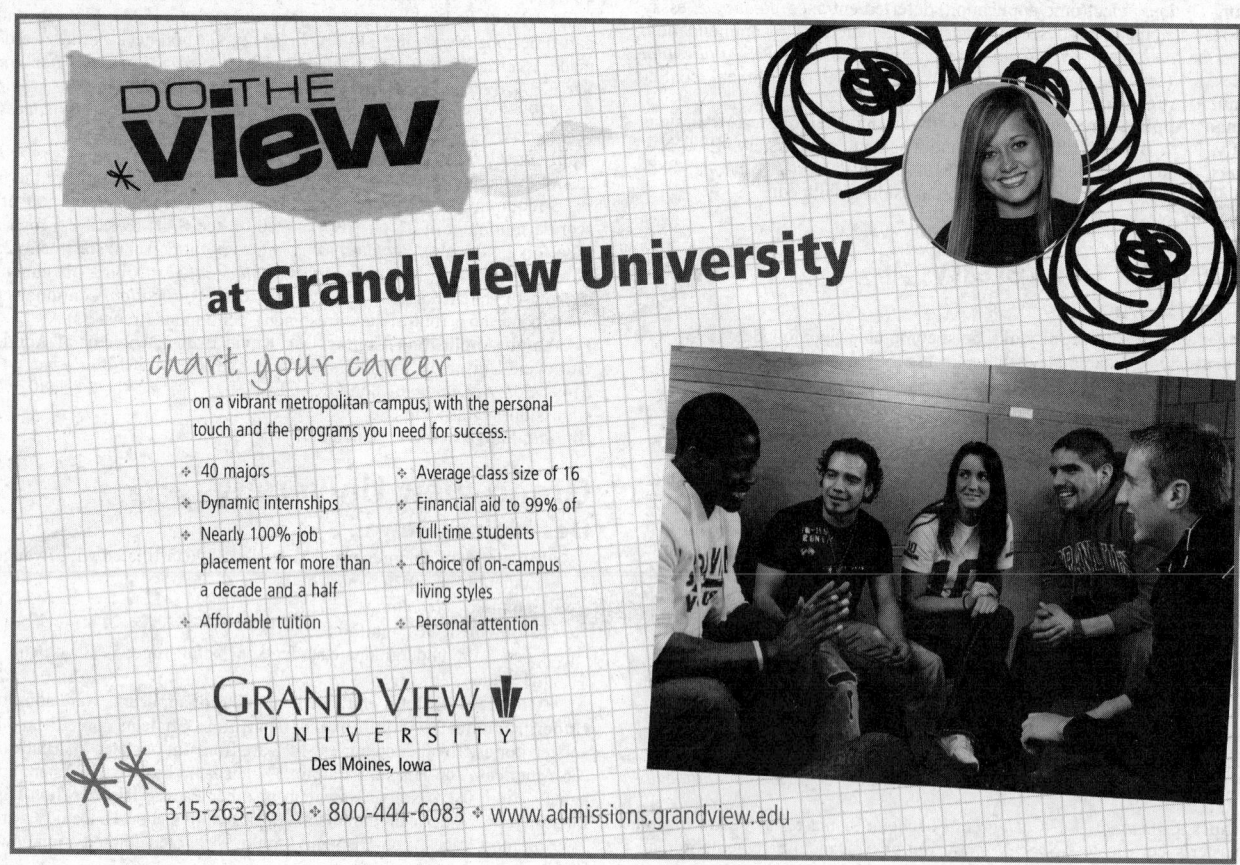

unknown; 12% international; 0.8% transferred in; 82% live on campus. *Retention:* 95% of full-time freshmen returned.

Freshmen *Admission:* 4,021 applied, 1,458 admitted, 444 enrolled. *Test scores:* SAT critical reading scores over 500: 97%; SAT math scores over 500: 97%; ACT scores over 18: 100%; SAT critical reading scores over 600: 85%; SAT math scores over 600: 90%; ACT scores over 24: 98%; SAT critical reading scores over 700: 48%; SAT math scores over 700: 47%; ACT scores over 30: 70%.

Faculty *Total:* 211, 76% full-time, 88% with terminal degrees. *Student/faculty ratio:* 9:1.

Academics *Calendar:* semesters. *Degree:* bachelor's. *Special study options:* accelerated degree program, advanced placement credit, double majors, independent study, internships, off-campus study, services for LD students, student-designed majors, study abroad. *Unusual degree programs:* 3-2 engineering with Columbia University, California Institute of Technology, Rensselaer Polytechnic Institute, Washington University in St, Louis; architecture with Washington University in St. Louis, law at Columbia University.

Computers on Campus Students can access the following: campus intranet, computer help desk, free student e-mail accounts, online (class) grades, online (class) schedules. Campuswide network is available. 100% of college-owned or -operated housing units are wired for high-speed Internet access. Wireless service is available via entire campus.

Student Life *Housing:* on-campus residence required through sophomore year. *Options:* coed, cooperative, disabled students. Campus housing is university owned. Freshman campus housing is guaranteed. *Activities and organizations:* drama/theater group, student-run newspaper, radio station, choral group, Concerned Black Students, International Student Organization, Student Organization of Latinas/Latinos, Campus Democrats, Ultimate Frisbee. *Campus security:* 24-hour emergency response devices and patrols, student patrols, late-night transport/escort service, controlled dormitory access. *Student services:* health clinic, personal/psychological counseling.

Athletics Member NCAA. All Division III. *Intercollegiate sports:* baseball M, basketball M/W, cross-country running M/W, football M, golf M/W, soccer M/W, softball W, swimming and diving M/W, tennis M/W, track and field M/W, volleyball W. *Intramural sports:* archery M(c)/W(c), badminton M/W, baseball M(c)/W(c), basketball M/W, equestrian sports M(c)/W(c), fencing M(c)/W(c), rugby M(c)/W(c), sailing M(c)/W(c), soccer M/W, softball M/W, tennis M/W, ultimate Frisbee M(c)/W, volleyball M/W, water polo M/W.

Standardized Tests *Required:* SAT or ACT (for admission).

Costs (2012–13) *Comprehensive fee:* $50,618 includes full-time tuition ($40,628), mandatory fees ($376), and room and board ($9614). Part-time tuition: $1270 per credit hour. *College room only:* $4504. Room and board charges vary according to board plan and housing facility. *Payment plan:* installment. *Waivers:* employees or children of employees.

Financial Aid Of all full-time matriculated undergraduates who enrolled in 2012, 1,250 applied for aid, 1,162 were judged to have need, 1,162 had their need fully met. 591 Federal Work-Study jobs (averaging $1200). 334 state and other part-time jobs (averaging $1364). In 2012, 223 non-need-based awards were made. *Average percent of need met:* 100%. *Average financial aid package:* $38,306. *Average need-based loan:* $3484. *Average need-based gift aid:* $32,984. *Average non-need-based aid:* $13,626. *Average indebtedness upon graduation:* $16,226. *Financial aid deadline:* 2/1.

Applying *Options:* electronic application, early admission, early decision, deferred entrance. *Application fee:* $30. *Required:* essay or personal statement, high school transcript, 3 letters of recommendation. *Recommended:* interview. *Application deadlines:* 1/15 (freshmen), 4/1 (transfers). *Early decision deadline:* 11/15 (for plan 1), 1/1 (for plan 2). *Notification:* 4/1 (freshmen), 5/20 (transfers), 12/15 (early decision plan 1), 2/1 (early decision plan 2).

Freshman Application Contact Mr. Joseph Bagnoli, Vice President for Enrollment, Grinnell College, 1103 Park Street, Grinnell, IA 50112. *Phone:* 641-269-3600. *Toll-free phone:* 800-247-0113. *Fax:* 641-269-4800. *E-mail:* askgrin@grinnell.edu.
Website: http://www.grinnell.edu/.

Hamilton Technical College

Davenport, Iowa

Freshman Application Contact Hamilton Technical College, 1011 East 53rd Street, Davenport, IA 52807-2653. *Phone:* 563-386-3570. *Toll-free phone:* 866-966-4825.
Website: http://www.hamiltontechcollege.edu/.

INSTE Bible College

Ankeny, Iowa

Director of Admissions Admissions, INSTE Bible College, 2302 SW 3rd Street, Ankeny, IA 50023. *Phone:* 515-289-9200. *Fax:* 515-289-9201. *E-mail:* inste@inste.edu.
Website: http://www.inste.edu/.

Iowa State University of Science and Technology

Ames, Iowa

- **State-supported** university, founded 1858
- **Suburban** 1795-acre campus with easy access to Des Moines
- **Endowment** $604.9 million
- **Coed** 25,555 undergraduate students, 95% full-time, 44% women, 56% men
- **Moderately difficult** entrance level, 83% of applicants were admitted

Undergraduates 24,206 full-time, 1,349 part-time. Students come from 54 states and territories; 101 other countries; 28% are from out of state; 3% Black or African American, non-Hispanic/Latino; 4% Hispanic/Latino; 3% Asian, non-Hispanic/Latino; 0.1% Native Hawaiian or other Pacific Islander, non-Hispanic/Latino; 0.2% American Indian or Alaska Native, non-Hispanic/Latino; 2% Two or more races, non-Hispanic/Latino; 3% Race/ethnicity unknown; 8% international; 7% transferred in; 34% live on campus. *Retention:* 86% of full-time freshmen returned.

Freshmen *Admission:* 16,539 applied, 13,648 admitted, 5,366 enrolled. *Average high school GPA:* 3.55. *Test scores:* SAT critical reading scores over 500: 67%; SAT math scores over 500: 84%; ACT scores over 18: 98%; SAT critical reading scores over 600: 30%; SAT math scores over 600: 55%; ACT scores over 24: 62%; SAT critical reading scores over 700: 8%; SAT math scores over 700: 18%; ACT scores over 30: 14%.

Faculty *Total:* 1,745, 83% full-time, 88% with terminal degrees. *Student/faculty ratio:* 18:1.

Academics *Calendar:* semesters. *Degrees:* bachelor's, master's, doctoral, post-master's, and postbachelor's certificates. *Special study options:* academic remediation for entering students, accelerated degree program, adult/continuing education programs, advanced placement credit, cooperative education, distance learning, double majors, English as a second language, external degree program, freshman honors college, honors programs, independent study, internships, off-campus study, part-time degree program, services for LD students, student-designed majors, study abroad, summer session for credit. *ROTC:* Army (b), Navy (b), Air Force (b). *Unusual degree programs:* 3-2 engineering with William Penn College.

Computers on Campus 2,400 computers/terminals are available on campus for general student use. Students can access the following: campus intranet, computer help desk, free student e-mail accounts, online (class) grades, online (class) registration, online (class) schedules, network services. Campuswide network is available. 100% of college-owned or -operated housing units are wired for high-speed Internet access. Wireless service is available via entire campus.

Student Life *Housing options:* coed, men-only, women-only, disabled students. Campus housing is university owned. Freshman applicants given priority for college housing. *Activities and organizations:* drama/theater group, student-run newspaper, radio and television station, choral group, marching band, Student Government, Student Alumni Association, Residence Hall Associations, national fraternities, national sororities. *Campus security:* 24-hour emergency response devices and patrols, student patrols, late-night transport/escort service, controlled dormitory access, crime prevention programs, threat assessment team, motor vehicle help van. *Student services:* health clinic, personal/psychological counseling, women's center, legal services.

Athletics Member NCAA. All Division I except football (Division I-A). *Intercollegiate sports:* basketball M(s)/W(s), cross-country running M(s)/W(s), golf M(s)/W(s), gymnastics W(s), soccer W(s), softball W(s), swimming and diving M(s)/W(s), tennis W(s), track and field M(s)/W(s), volleyball W(s), wrestling M(s). *Intramural sports:* archery M(c)/W(c), badminton M(c)/W(c), basketball M/W, bowling M(c)/W(c), cross-country running M/W, equestrian sports M(c)/W(c), fencing M(c)/W(c), football M/W, golf M/W, ice hockey M(c)/W(c), lacrosse M(c)/W(c), racquetball M(c)/W(c), riflery M(c)/W(c), rugby M(c)/W(c), sailing M(c)/W(c), skiing (cross-country) M(c)/W(c), skiing (downhill) M(c)/W(c), soccer M(c)/W(c), softball M/W, squash M/W, swimming and diving M/W, table tennis M(c)/W(c), tennis M/W, volleyball M(c)/W(c), water polo M(c)/W(c), weight lifting M(c)/W(c), wrestling M/W.

Standardized Tests *Required:* SAT or ACT (for admission).

Costs (2012–13) *Tuition:* state resident $6648 full-time, $277 per semester hour part-time; nonresident $18,760 full-time, $782 per semester hour part-time. Full-time tuition and fees vary according to class time, degree level, and

program. Part-time tuition and fees vary according to class time, course load, degree level, and program. *Required fees:* $1078 full-time. *Room and board:* $7721; room only: $4093. Room and board charges vary according to board plan and housing facility. *Payment plans:* installment, deferred payment.
Financial Aid Of all full-time matriculated undergraduates who enrolled in 2010, 16,487 applied for aid, 12,210 were judged to have need, 4,916 had their need fully met. In 2010, 6060 non-need-based awards were made. *Average percent of need met:* 81%. *Average financial aid package:* $11,954. *Average need-based loan:* $4453. *Average need-based gift aid:* $6720. *Average non-need-based aid:* $2613. *Average indebtedness upon graduation:* $29,455.
Applying *Options:* electronic application, early admission, deferred entrance. *Application fee:* $40. *Required:* high school transcript, Regent Admission Index (RAI) of at least 245 and meet minimum HS course requirements. *Application deadlines:* 7/1 (freshmen), 7/1 (transfers). *Notification:* continuous (freshmen), continuous (transfers).
Freshman Application Contact Mr. Phil Caffrey, Associate Director for Freshman Admissions, Iowa State University of Science and Technology, 100 Enrollment Services Center, Ames, IA 50011-2010. *Phone:* 515-294-5836. *Toll-free phone:* 800-262-3810. *Fax:* 515-294-2592. *E-mail:* admissions@iastate.edu.
Website: http://www.iastate.edu/.

Iowa Wesleyan College
Mount Pleasant, Iowa

- **Independent United Methodist** 4-year, founded 1842
- **Small-town** 60-acre campus
- **Endowment** $13.1 million
- **Coed** 650 undergraduate students, 76% full-time, 59% women, 41% men
- **Moderately difficult** entrance level, 56% of applicants were admitted

Undergraduates 497 full-time, 153 part-time. Students come from 30 states and territories; 11 other countries; 36% are from out of state; 9% Black or African American, non-Hispanic/Latino; 6% Hispanic/Latino; 0.3% Asian, non-Hispanic/Latino; 0.3% Native Hawaiian or other Pacific Islander, non-Hispanic/Latino; 0.3% American Indian or Alaska Native, non-Hispanic/Latino; 1% Two or more races, non-Hispanic/Latino; 13% Race/ethnicity unknown; 7% international; 15% transferred in; 68% live on campus. *Retention:* 43% of full-time freshmen returned.
Freshmen *Admission:* 1,274 applied, 716 admitted, 111 enrolled. *Average high school GPA:* 2.99. *Test scores:* SAT math scores over 500: 67%.
Faculty *Total:* 105, 46% full-time, 35% with terminal degrees. *Student/faculty ratio:* 12:1.
Academics *Calendar:* semesters. *Degree:* bachelor's. *Special study options:* academic remediation for entering students, adult/continuing education programs, advanced placement credit, cooperative education, distance learning, double majors, honors programs, independent study, internships, off-campus study, part-time degree program, services for LD students, student-designed majors, study abroad, summer session for credit. *Unusual degree programs:* 3-2 forestry with Iowa State University of Science and Technology, Duke University; pre-physical therapy program with St. Ambrose University; medical technology program with St. Luke's Hospital in Cedar Rapids, IA.
Computers on Campus 97 computers/terminals are available on campus for general student use. Students can access the following: campus intranet, computer help desk, free student e-mail accounts, online (class) grades, online (class) schedules. Campuswide network is available. 100% of college-owned or -operated housing units are wired for high-speed Internet access. Wireless service is available via entire campus.
Student Life *Housing:* on-campus residence required through senior year. *Options:* coed, men-only, women-only. Campus housing is university owned. Freshman campus housing is guaranteed. *Activities and organizations:* student-run radio station, choral group, Student Union Board, Student Senate, Commuter Club, Choir, Student Ambassadors, national sororities. *Campus security:* late-night transport/escort service, controlled dormitory access, evening patrols by trained security personnel. *Student services:* health clinic, personal/psychological counseling.
Athletics Member NCAA. All Division III except track and field (Division II). *Intercollegiate sports:* baseball M, basketball M/W, cross-country running M/W, football M, golf M/W, soccer M/W, softball W, track and field M/W, volleyball W. *Intramural sports:* badminton M/W, basketball M/W, cheerleading M/W, football M/W, soccer M/W, softball M/W, table tennis M/W, tennis M/W, track and field M/W, volleyball M/W, weight lifting M/W.
Standardized Tests *Required:* SAT or ACT (for admission).
Costs (2012–13) *Comprehensive fee:* $32,280 includes full-time tuition ($24,300) and room and board ($7980). Part-time tuition: $610 per credit hour. Part-time tuition and fees vary according to class time, course load, and location. *College room only:* $3140. Room and board charges vary according to

board plan and housing facility. *Payment plans:* installment, deferred payment. *Waivers:* employees or children of employees.
Financial Aid Of all full-time matriculated undergraduates who enrolled in 2011, 529 applied for aid, 462 were judged to have need, 36 had their need fully met. 115 Federal Work-Study jobs (averaging $2000). In 2011, 66 non-need-based awards were made. *Average percent of need met:* 73%. *Average financial aid package:* $20,538. *Average need-based loan:* $4380. *Average need-based gift aid:* $14,975. *Average non-need-based aid:* $8311. *Average indebtedness upon graduation:* $32,666.
Applying *Options:* electronic application, early admission, deferred entrance. *Application fee:* $20. *Required:* high school transcript, minimum 2.5 GPA, minimum ACT score of 19 or SAT of 890. *Required for some:* essay or personal statement, 1 letter of recommendation, interview. *Application deadlines:* 8/15 (freshmen), 8/15 (transfers).
Freshman Application Contact Dean Mark T. Petty, Associate Vice President and Dean for Admissions, Iowa Wesleyan College, 601 N Main Street, Mount Pleasant, IA 52641. *Phone:* 319-385-6231. *Toll-free phone:* 800-582-2383. *Fax:* 319-385-6240. *E-mail:* mpetty@iwc.edu.
Website: http://www.iwc.edu/.

ITT Technical Institute
Cedar Rapids, Iowa

- **Proprietary** primarily 2-year
- **Coed**
- **Minimally difficult** entrance level

Academics *Degrees:* associate and bachelor's.
Freshman Application Contact Director of Recruitment, ITT Technical Institute, 3735 Queen Court SW, Cedar Rapids, IA 52404. *Phone:* 319-297-3400. *Toll-free phone:* 877-320-4625.
Website: http://www.itt-tech.edu/.

ITT Technical Institute
Clive, Iowa

- **Proprietary** primarily 2-year, part of ITT Educational Services, Inc.
- **Coed**
- **Minimally difficult** entrance level

Academics *Degrees:* associate and bachelor's.
Freshman Application Contact Director of Recruitment, ITT Technical Institute, 1860 Northwest 118th Street, Suite 110, Clive, IA 50325. *Phone:* 515-327-5500. *Toll-free phone:* 877-526-7312.
Website: http://www.itt-tech.edu/.

Kaplan University, Cedar Falls
Cedar Falls, Iowa

Freshman Application Contact Kaplan University, Cedar Falls, 7009 Nordic Drive, Cedar Falls, IA 50613. *Phone:* 319-277-0220. *Toll-free phone:* 866-527-5268 (in-state); 800-527-5268 (out-of-state).
Website: http://www.cedarfalls.kaplanuniversity.edu/.

Kaplan University, Cedar Rapids
Cedar Rapids, Iowa

Freshman Application Contact Kaplan University, Cedar Rapids, 3165 Edgewood Parkway, SW, Cedar Rapids, IA 52404. *Phone:* 319-363-0481. *Toll-free phone:* 866-527-5268 (in-state); 800-527-5268 (out-of-state).
Website: http://www.cedarrapids.kaplanuniversity.edu/.

Kaplan University, Council Bluffs
Council Bluffs, Iowa

Freshman Application Contact Kaplan University, Council Bluffs, 1751 Madison Avenue, Council Bluffs, IA 51503. *Phone:* 712-328-4212. *Toll-free phone:* 866-527-5268 (in-state); 800-527-5268 (out-of-state).
Website: http://www.councilbluffs.kaplanuniversity.edu/.

Kaplan University, Davenport Campus
Davenport, Iowa

Freshman Application Contact Kaplan University, Davenport Campus, 1801 East Kimberly Road, Suite 1, Davenport, IA 52807-2095. *Phone:* 563-355-3500. *Toll-free phone:* 866-527-5268 (in-state); 800-527-5268 (out-of-state).
Website: http://www.davenport.kaplanuniversity.edu/.

Kaplan University, Des Moines

Urbandale, Iowa

Freshman Application Contact Kaplan University, Des Moines, 4655 121st Street, Urbandale, IA 50323. *Phone:* 515-727-2100. *Toll-free phone:* 866-527-5268 (in-state); 800-527-5268 (out-of-state).
Website: http://www.desmoines.kaplanuniversity.edu/.

Kaplan University, Mason City Campus

Mason City, Iowa

Freshman Application Contact Kaplan University, Mason City Campus, 2570 4th Street, SW, Mason City, IA 50401. *Phone:* 641-423-2530. *Toll-free phone:* 866-527-5268 (in-state); 800-527-5268 (out-of-state).
Website: http://masoncity.kaplanuniversity.edu/.

Loras College

Dubuque, Iowa

- **Independent Roman Catholic** comprehensive, founded 1839
- **Suburban** 60-acre campus
- **Endowment** $22.0 million
- **Coed**
- **Moderately difficult** entrance level

Faculty *Student/faculty ratio:* 12:1.
Academics *Calendar:* semesters. *Degrees:* associate, bachelor's, and master's.
Student Life *Campus security:* 24-hour emergency response devices and patrols, late-night transport/escort service, controlled dormitory access.
Athletics Member NCAA. All Division III.
Standardized Tests *Required for some:* SAT (for admission). *Recommended:* ACT (for admission).
Costs (2012–13) *Comprehensive fee:* $35,815 includes full-time tuition ($26,813), mandatory fees ($1352), and room and board ($7650). Full-time tuition and fees vary according to course load and degree level. Part-time tuition: $559 per credit hour. *College room only:* $3875. Room and board charges vary according to board plan and housing facility.
Financial Aid *Of all full-time matriculated undergraduates who enrolled in 2011,* 1,222 applied for aid, 1,064 were judged to have need, 585 had their need fully met. *In 2011,* 378 non-need-based awards were made. *Average percent of need met:* 76. *Average financial aid package:* $20,663. *Average need-based loan:* $4772. *Average need-based gift aid:* $16,144. *Average non-need-based aid:* $13,567. *Average indebtedness upon graduation:* $32,704.
Applying *Options:* electronic application, deferred entrance. *Application fee:* $25. *Required:* high school transcript, minimum 2.5 GPA. *Required for some:* interview. *Recommended:* essay or personal statement, 1 letter of recommendation.
Freshman Application Contact Ms. Sharon Lyons, Director of Admissions, Loras College, 1450 Alta Vista, Dubuque, IA 52004-0178. *Phone:* 563-588-7829. *Toll-free phone:* 800-245-6727. *Fax:* 563-588-7119. *E-mail:* adms@loras.edu.
Website: http://www.loras.edu/.

Luther College

Decorah, Iowa

- **Independent** 4-year, founded 1861, affiliated with Evangelical Lutheran Church in America
- **Small-town** 200-acre campus
- **Endowment** $118.1 million
- **Coed** 2,473 undergraduate students, 98% full-time, 56% women, 44% men
- **Moderately difficult** entrance level, 70% of applicants were admitted

Undergraduates 2,421 full-time, 52 part-time. Students come from 38 states and territories; 46 other countries; 68% are from out of state; 1% Black or African American, non-Hispanic/Latino; 3% Hispanic/Latino; 2% Asian, non-Hispanic/Latino; 2% Two or more races, non-Hispanic/Latino; 0.6% Race/ethnicity unknown; 5% international; 1% transferred in; 85% live on campus. *Retention:* 88% of full-time freshmen returned.
Freshmen *Admission:* 3,556 applied, 2,495 admitted, 645 enrolled. *Average high school GPA:* 3.63. *Test scores:* SAT critical reading scores over 500: 66%; SAT math scores over 500: 78%; SAT writing scores over 500: 60%; ACT scores over 18: 99%; SAT critical reading scores over 600: 28%; SAT math scores over 600: 36%; SAT writing scores over 600: 25%; ACT scores over 24: 75%; SAT critical reading scores over 700: 8%; SAT math scores over 700: 8%; SAT writing scores over 700: 4%; ACT scores over 30: 17%.
Faculty *Total:* 255, 70% full-time, 76% with terminal degrees. *Student/faculty ratio:* 12:1.

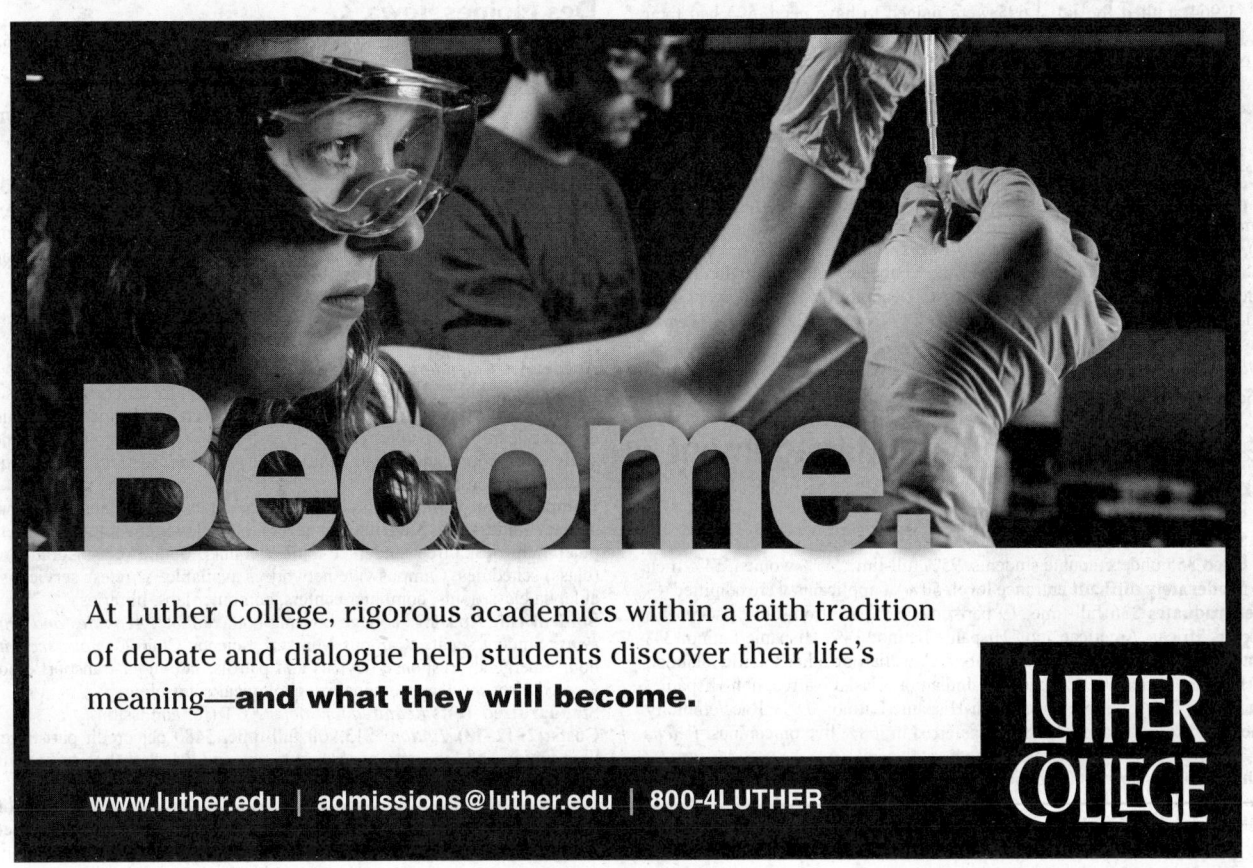

Academics *Calendar:* 4-1-4. *Degree:* bachelor's. *Special study options:* academic remediation for entering students, advanced placement credit, double majors, honors programs, independent study, internships, off-campus study, part-time degree program, services for LD students, student-designed majors, study abroad, summer session for credit. *Unusual degree programs:* 3-2 engineering with Washington University in St. Louis; University of Minnesota, Twin Cities Campus; environmental management, resource management with Duke University.

Computers on Campus 546 computers/terminals are available on campus for general student use. Students can access the following: campus intranet, computer help desk, free student e-mail accounts, online (class) grades, online (class) registration, online (class) schedules. Campuswide network is available. 64% of college-owned or -operated housing units are wired for high-speed Internet access. Wireless service is available via entire campus.

Student Life *Housing:* on-campus residence required through senior year. *Options:* coed, disabled students. Campus housing is university owned. Freshman campus housing is guaranteed. *Activities and organizations:* drama/theater group, student-run newspaper, radio station, choral group, Alpha Phi Omega, college ministries, recreational sports, Student Activities Council, Diversity groups. *Campus security:* 24-hour emergency response devices and patrols, late-night transport/escort service, controlled dormitory access. *Student services:* health clinic, personal/psychological counseling, women's center.

Athletics Member NCAA. All Division III. *Intercollegiate sports:* baseball M, basketball M/W, cross-country running M/W, football M, golf M/W, soccer M/W, softball W, swimming and diving M/W, tennis M/W, track and field M/W, ultimate Frisbee M(c)/W(c), volleyball W, wrestling M. *Intramural sports:* archery M/W, badminton M/W, basketball M/W, bowling M/W, football M/W, golf M/W, lacrosse W(c), racquetball M/W, rugby M(c)/W(c), soccer M/W, softball M/W, table tennis M/W, tennis M/W, track and field M/W, ultimate Frisbee M(c)/W(c), volleyball M/W.

Standardized Tests *Required:* SAT or ACT (for admission).

Costs (2013–14) *Comprehensive fee:* $44,330 includes full-time tuition ($37,330), mandatory fees ($150), and room and board ($6850). Full-time tuition and fees vary according to course load. Part-time tuition: $1334 per credit hour. Part-time tuition and fees vary according to course load. *College room only:* $3240. Room and board charges vary according to board plan and housing facility. *Payment plan:* installment. *Waivers:* employees or children of employees.

Financial Aid Of all full-time matriculated undergraduates who enrolled in 2012, 1,964 applied for aid, 1,695 were judged to have need, 504 had their need fully met. 1,066 Federal Work-Study jobs (averaging $1988). 1,110 state and other part-time jobs (averaging $1678). In 2012, 256 non-need-based awards were made. *Average percent of need met:* 86%. *Average financial aid package:* $27,771. *Average need-based loan:* $4840. *Average need-based gift aid:* $20,503. *Average non-need-based aid:* $14,833. *Average indebtedness upon graduation:* $35,619.

Applying *Options:* electronic application, deferred entrance. *Application fee:* $25. *Required:* essay or personal statement, high school transcript, 1 letter of recommendation. *Recommended:* interview. *Notification:* continuous (freshmen), continuous (transfers).

Freshman Application Contact Mr. Kirk Neubauer, Director of Recruiting Services, Luther College, 700 College Drive, Decorah, IA 52101. *Phone:* 563-387-1287. *Toll-free phone:* 800-458-8437. *Fax:* 563-387-2159. *E-mail:* admissions@luther.edu. *Website:* http://www.luther.edu/.

See previous page for display ad and page 1368 for the College Close-Up.

Maharishi University of Management
Fairfield, Iowa

- **Independent** university, founded 1971
- **Small-town** campus
- **Coed** 355 undergraduate students, 95% full-time, 46% women, 54% men
- **Moderately difficult** entrance level, 50% of applicants were admitted

Undergraduates 336 full-time, 19 part-time. 83% are from out of state; 9% Black or African American, non-Hispanic/Latino; 14% Hispanic/Latino; 3% Asian, non-Hispanic/Latino; 0.3% Native Hawaiian or other Pacific Islander, non-Hispanic/Latino; 0.9% American Indian or Alaska Native, non-Hispanic/Latino; 4% Two or more races, non-Hispanic/Latino; 0.9% Race/ethnicity unknown; 13% international; 48% transferred in; 68% live on campus. *Retention:* 77% of full-time freshmen returned.

Freshmen *Admission:* 100 applied, 50 admitted, 35 enrolled. *Average high school GPA:* 2.8.

Faculty *Total:* 94, 72% full-time, 40% with terminal degrees. *Student/faculty ratio:* 12:1.

Academics *Calendar:* semesters. *Degrees:* certificates, diplomas, bachelor's, master's, doctoral, post-master's, and postbachelor's certificates. *Special study options:* adult/continuing education programs.

Computers on Campus Students can access the following: campus intranet, computer help desk, free student e-mail accounts, online (class) grades, online (class) schedules. Campuswide network is available. 100% of college-owned or -operated housing units are wired for high-speed Internet access.

Student Life *Housing:* on-campus residence required through senior year. *Options:* men-only, women-only. Campus housing is university owned. Freshman campus housing is guaranteed. *Campus security:* 24-hour emergency response devices and patrols, late-night transport/escort service, controlled dormitory access.

Athletics *Intercollegiate sports:* soccer M(c)/W(c), ultimate Frisbee M(c)/W(c), volleyball M(c)/W(c). *Intramural sports:* archery M/W, badminton M/W, basketball M/W, football M/W, gymnastics M/W, rock climbing M/W, sailing M/W, soccer M/W, table tennis M/W, tennis M/W, ultimate Frisbee M/W, volleyball M/W.

Costs (2013–14) *Comprehensive fee:* $33,830 includes full-time tuition ($26,000), mandatory fees ($430), and room and board ($7400). Part-time tuition: $350 per credit hour. Part-time tuition and fees vary according to course load. *Payment plan:* installment.

Financial Aid Of all full-time matriculated undergraduates who enrolled in 2006, 150 applied for aid, 148 were judged to have need, 32 had their need fully met. 120 Federal Work-Study jobs (averaging $1422). 7 state and other part-time jobs (averaging $2729). In 2006, 5 non-need-based awards were made. *Average percent of need met:* 89%. *Average financial aid package:* $23,963. *Average need-based loan:* $8281. *Average need-based gift aid:* $14,082. *Average non-need-based aid:* $9300. *Average indebtedness upon graduation:* $22,691.

Applying *Options:* electronic application, early admission, deferred entrance. *Application fee:* $25. *Required:* essay or personal statement, high school transcript, minimum 2.5 GPA, 2 letters of recommendation. *Recommended:* interview. *Application deadline:* 8/1 (freshmen). *Notification:* continuous until 8/15 (freshmen).

Freshman Application Contact Maharishi University of Management, Office of Admissions, Fairfield, IA 52557. *Phone:* 641-472-1110. *Toll-free phone:* 800-369-6480. *Fax:* 641-472-1179. *E-mail:* admissions@mum.edu. *Website:* http://www.mum.edu/.

Mercy College of Health Sciences
Des Moines, Iowa

- **Independent** 4-year, founded 1995, affiliated with Roman Catholic Church
- **Urban** 5-acre campus
- **Coed, primarily women** 846 undergraduate students, 46% full-time, 88% women, 12% men
- **84%** of applicants were admitted

Undergraduates 390 full-time, 456 part-time. Students come from 13 states and territories; 2% are from out of state; 3% Black or African American, non-Hispanic/Latino; 3% Hispanic/Latino; 4% Asian, non-Hispanic/Latino; 0.7% American Indian or Alaska Native, non-Hispanic/Latino; 0.1% Two or more races, non-Hispanic/Latino; 4% Race/ethnicity unknown.

Freshmen *Admission:* 111 applied, 93 admitted, 43 enrolled.

Faculty *Total:* 117, 44% full-time, 14% with terminal degrees. *Student/faculty ratio:* 7:1.

Academics *Calendar:* semesters. *Degrees:* certificates, associate, and bachelor's. *Special study options:* academic remediation for entering students, accelerated degree program, advanced placement credit, cooperative education, distance learning, double majors, English as a second language, independent study, off-campus study, part-time degree program, services for LD students, summer session for credit.

Computers on Campus 46 computers/terminals are available on campus for general student use. Students can access the following: campus intranet, computer help desk, free student e-mail accounts, online (class) grades, online (class) schedules. Campuswide network is available. Wireless service is available via classrooms, computer centers, computer labs, libraries.

Student Life *Housing:* college housing not available. *Activities and organizations:* Student senate, Campus Ministry, Science Club. *Campus security:* 24-hour emergency response devices and patrols, late-night transport/escort service. *Student services:* personal/psychological counseling.

Standardized Tests *Required for some:* ACT (for admission).

Costs (2012–13) *Tuition:* $13,900 full-time, $480 per credit part-time. Full-time tuition and fees vary according to course load. Part-time tuition and fees vary according to course load.

Financial Aid Of all full-time matriculated undergraduates who enrolled in 2003, 331 applied for aid, 322 were judged to have need, 3 had their need fully met. 11 Federal Work-Study jobs (averaging $1964). In 2003, 9 non-need-based awards were made. *Average percent of need met:* 29%. *Average financial aid package:* $7670. *Average need-based loan:* $2492. *Average need-based gift aid:* $5132. *Average non-need-based aid:* $6697. *Average indebtedness upon graduation:* $17,567. *Financial aid deadline:* 7/1.

Applying *Options:* electronic application. *Required:* high school transcript, minimum 2.3 GPA. *Required for some:* interview.

Freshman Application Contact Kara Donovan, Director of Admissions, Mercy College of Health Sciences, 928 Sixth Avenue, Des Moines, IA 50309-1239. *Phone:* 515-643-6604. *Toll-free phone:* 800-637-2994. *Fax:* 515-643-6698. *E-mail:* kdonovan@mercydesmoines.org. *Website:* http://www.mchs.edu/.

Morningside College

Sioux City, Iowa

- **Independent** comprehensive, founded 1894, affiliated with United Methodist Church
- **Suburban** 69-acre campus
- **Endowment** $38.1 million
- **Coed** 1,242 undergraduate students, 97% full-time, 51% women, 49% men
- **Moderately difficult** entrance level, 63% of applicants were admitted

Undergraduates 1,199 full-time, 43 part-time. Students come from 21 states and territories; 9 other countries; 35% are from out of state; 1% Black or African American, non-Hispanic/Latino; 6% Hispanic/Latino; 0.5% Asian, non-Hispanic/Latino; 0.2% Native Hawaiian or other Pacific Islander, non-Hispanic/Latino; 0.5% American Indian or Alaska Native, non-Hispanic/Latino; 2% Two or more races, non-Hispanic/Latino; 5% Race/ethnicity unknown; 2% international; 6% transferred in; 60% live on campus. *Retention:* 68% of full-time freshmen returned.

Freshmen *Admission:* 2,048 applied, 1,281 admitted, 273 enrolled. *Average high school GPA:* 3.4.

Faculty *Total:* 180, 43% full-time, 29% with terminal degrees. *Student/faculty ratio:* 14:1.

Academics *Calendar:* semesters. *Degrees:* bachelor's and master's. *Special study options:* academic remediation for entering students, adult/continuing education programs, advanced placement credit, distance learning, double majors, English as a second language, honors programs, independent study, internships, off-campus study, part-time degree program, services for LD students, student-designed majors, study abroad, summer session for credit. *ROTC:* Army (c).

Computers on Campus 150 computers/terminals are available on campus for general student use. Students can access the following: campus intranet, computer help desk, free student e-mail accounts, online (class) grades, online (class) registration, online (class) schedules, academic and financial records. Campuswide network is available. 100% of college-owned or -operated housing units are wired for high-speed Internet access. Wireless service is available via entire campus.

Student Life *Housing:* on-campus residence required through junior year. *Options:* coed. Campus housing is university owned. Freshman campus housing is guaranteed. *Activities and organizations:* drama/theater group, student-run newspaper, radio and television station, choral group, Student Government/Activities Council, Student Ambassadors, Homecoming Committee, national fraternities, national sororities. *Campus security:* 24-hour emergency response devices, student patrols, late-night transport/escort service, controlled dormitory access, 20-hour patrols by trained security personnel. *Student services:* health clinic, personal/psychological counseling, women's center.

Athletics Member NCAA, NAIA. All NCAA Division II. *Intercollegiate sports:* baseball M(s), basketball M(s)/W(s), cross-country running M(s)/W(s), football M(s), golf M(s)/W(s), soccer M(s)/W(s), softball W(s), swimming and diving M(s)/W(s), tennis M(s)/W(s), track and field M(s)/W(s), volleyball W(s), wrestling M(s). *Intramural sports:* basketball M/W, bowling M/W, ultimate Frisbee M/W, volleyball M/W.

Standardized Tests *Required:* SAT or ACT (for admission).

Costs (2012–13) *Comprehensive fee:* $32,620 includes full-time tuition ($23,780), mandatory fees ($1220), and room and board ($7620). Part-time tuition and fees vary according to course load. *College room only:* $3900. Room and board charges vary according to housing facility. *Payment plan:* installment. *Waivers:* children of alumni, senior citizens, and employees or children of employees.

Financial Aid Of all full-time matriculated undergraduates who enrolled in 2012, 1,102 applied for aid, 1,013 were judged to have need, 351 had their need fully met. 530 Federal Work-Study jobs (averaging $1020). 341 state and other part-time jobs (averaging $1843). In 2012, 1149 non-need-based awards were made. *Average percent of need met:* 82%. *Average financial aid package:* $24,394. *Average need-based loan:* $4766. *Average need-based gift aid:* $7138. *Average non-need-based aid:* $8200. *Average indebtedness upon graduation:* $36,140.

Applying *Options:* electronic application, deferred entrance. *Required:* high school transcript, 20 ACT/1410 SAT and either rank in top half of class or 2.5

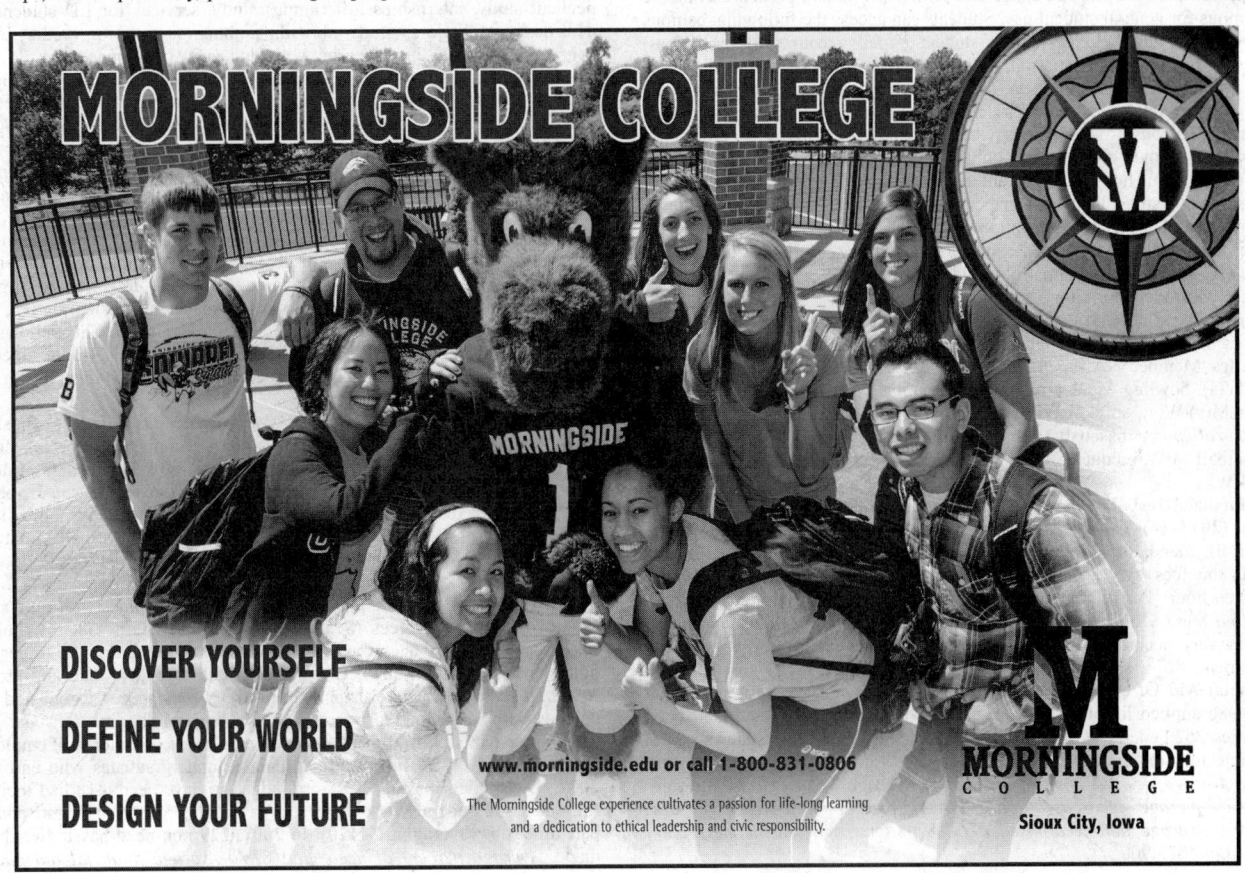

GPA required. *Recommended:* minimum 2.5 GPA, interview. *Application deadlines:* rolling (freshmen), rolling (out-of-state freshmen), rolling (transfers). *Notification:* continuous (freshmen), continuous (out-of-state freshmen), continuous (transfers).

Freshman Application Contact Mrs. Stephanie Peters, Director of Admissions, Morningside College, 1501 Morningside Avenue, Sioux City, IA 51106. *Phone:* 712-274-5111. *Toll-free phone:* 800-831-0806 Ext. 5111. *Fax:* 712-274-5101. *E-mail:* mscadm@morningside.edu. *Website:* http://www.morningside.edu/.

See previous page for display ad and page 1402 for the College Close-Up.

Mount Mercy University
Cedar Rapids, Iowa

- **Independent Roman Catholic** comprehensive, founded 1928
- **Suburban** 40-acre campus with easy access to Iowa City
- **Endowment** $23.1 million
- **Coed** 1,513 undergraduate students, 60% full-time, 69% women, 31% men
- **Moderately difficult** entrance level, 70% of applicants were admitted

Undergraduates 915 full-time, 598 part-time. Students come from 6 states and territories; 10 other countries; 4% are from out of state; 3% Black or African American, non-Hispanic/Latino; 3% Hispanic/Latino; 1% Asian, non-Hispanic/Latino; 0.1% Native Hawaiian or other Pacific Islander, non-Hispanic/Latino; 0.2% American Indian or Alaska Native, non-Hispanic/Latino; 0.3% Two or more races, non-Hispanic/Latino; 5% Race/ethnicity unknown; 4% international; 19% transferred in; 38% live on campus. *Retention:* 75% of full-time freshmen returned.

Freshmen *Admission:* 532 applied, 371 admitted, 158 enrolled. *Average high school GPA:* 3.4. *Test scores:* ACT scores over 18: 96%; ACT scores over 24: 30%.

Faculty *Total:* 152, 57% full-time, 51% with terminal degrees. *Student/faculty ratio:* 13:1.

Academics *Calendar:* 4-1-4. *Degrees:* bachelor's and master's. *Special study options:* academic remediation for entering students, accelerated degree program, adult/continuing education programs, advanced placement credit, double majors, honors programs, independent study, internships, off-campus study, part-time degree program, services for LD students, study abroad, summer session for credit.

Computers on Campus 120 computers/terminals and 200 ports are available on campus for general student use. Students can access the following: campus intranet, computer help desk, free student e-mail accounts, online (class) grades, online (class) registration, online (class) schedules. Campuswide network is available. 100% of college-owned or -operated housing units are wired for high-speed Internet access. Wireless service is available via entire campus.

Student Life *Housing:* on-campus residence required through sophomore year. *Options:* coed, men-only, women-only. Campus housing is university owned. Freshman campus housing is guaranteed. *Activities and organizations:* drama/theater group, student-run newspaper, choral group, Student Ambassadors, Mount Mercy University Association of Nursing Students, Cheerleaders, Best Buddies, Student Government Association. *Campus security:* 24-hour emergency response devices and patrols, student patrols, late-night transport/escort service, controlled dormitory access, The Mount Mercy University Department of Public Safety is operational 24 hours a day, seven days a week. *Student services:* health clinic, personal/psychological counseling.

Athletics Member NAIA. *Intercollegiate sports:* baseball M(s), basketball M(s)/W(s), bowling M/W, cross-country running M(s)/W(s), golf M(s)/W(s), soccer M(s)/W(s), softball W(s), track and field M(s)/W(s), volleyball W(s). *Intramural sports:* baseball M, basketball M/W, bowling M/W, cheerleading W, football M/W, racquetball M/W, tennis M/W, volleyball M/W, weight lifting M/W.

Standardized Tests *Required:* SAT or ACT (for admission).

Costs (2013–14) *Comprehensive fee:* $34,385 includes full-time tuition ($26,160), mandatory fees ($150), and room and board ($8075). Full-time tuition and fees vary according to course load. Part-time tuition: $710 per semester hour. Part-time tuition and fees vary according to course load. *Required fees:* $150 per year part-time. *Room and board:* Room and board charges vary according to board plan and housing facility. *Payment plan:* installment. *Waivers:* employees or children of employees.

Financial Aid Of all full-time matriculated undergraduates who enrolled in 2011, 986 applied for aid, 907 were judged to have need, 127 had their need fully met. 262 Federal Work-Study jobs (averaging $1398). 225 state and other part-time jobs (averaging $998). In 2011, 139 non-need-based awards were made. *Average percent of need met:* 67%. *Average financial aid package:* $16,281. *Average need-based loan:* $4451. *Average need-based gift aid:* $12,207. *Average non-need-based aid:* $8708. *Average indebtedness upon graduation:* $28,900.

Applying *Options:* electronic application, deferred entrance. *Required:* high school transcript, minimum 2.5 GPA. *Required for some:* 1 letter of recommendation. *Application deadlines:* 8/15 (freshmen), 8/15 (transfers). *Notification:* continuous (freshmen), continuous (transfers).

Freshman Application Contact Ms. Lauren Garcia, Assistant Director of Admissions, Mount Mercy University, 1330 Elmhurst Drive, NE, Cedar Rapids, IA 52402. *Phone:* 319-368-6460. *Toll-free phone:* 800-248-4504. *Fax:* 319-363-5270. *E-mail:* lgarcia@mtmercy.edu. *Website:* http://www.mtmercy.edu/.

Northwestern College
Orange City, Iowa

- **Independent** 4-year, founded 1882, affiliated with Reformed Church in America
- **Small-town** 100-acre campus
- **Endowment** $41.3 million
- **Coed** 1,241 undergraduate students, 94% full-time, 57% women, 43% men
- **Moderately difficult** entrance level, 74% of applicants were admitted

Undergraduates 1,169 full-time, 72 part-time. Students come from 33 states and territories; 23 other countries; 46% are from out of state; 2% Black or African American, non-Hispanic/Latino; 5% Hispanic/Latino; 0.9% Asian, non-Hispanic/Latino; 0.6% American Indian or Alaska Native, non-Hispanic/Latino; 0.9% Two or more races, non-Hispanic/Latino; 1% Race/ethnicity unknown; 3% international; 4% transferred in; 89% live on campus. *Retention:* 77% of full-time freshmen returned.

Freshmen *Admission:* 1,193 applied, 878 admitted, 302 enrolled. *Average high school GPA:* 3.53. *Test scores:* SAT critical reading scores over 500: 56%; SAT math scores over 500: 56%; SAT writing scores over 500: 51%; ACT scores over 18: 95%; SAT critical reading scores over 600: 29%; SAT math scores over 600: 36%; SAT writing scores over 600: 14%; ACT scores over 24: 56%; SAT critical reading scores over 700: 7%; SAT math scores over 700: 7%; SAT writing scores over 700: 2%; ACT scores over 30: 13%.

Faculty *Total:* 126, 67% full-time, 54% with terminal degrees. *Student/faculty ratio:* 12:1.

Academics *Calendar:* semesters. *Degrees:* certificates, bachelor's, and post-bachelor's certificates. *Special study options:* academic remediation for entering students, advanced placement credit, cooperative education, distance learning, double majors, English as a second language, honors programs, independent study, internships, off-campus study, services for LD students, student-designed majors, study abroad, summer session for credit. *Unusual degree programs:* 3-2 engineering with University of Minnesota.

Computers on Campus 250 computers/terminals are available on campus for general student use. Students can access the following: campus intranet, computer help desk, free student e-mail accounts, online (class) grades, online (class) registration, online (class) schedules, online degree audits. Campuswide network is available. 100% of college-owned or -operated housing units are wired for high-speed Internet access. Wireless service is available via entire campus.

Student Life *Housing:* on-campus residence required through senior year. *Options:* men-only, women-only, disabled students. Campus housing is university owned. Freshman campus housing is guaranteed. *Activities and organizations:* drama/theater group, student-run newspaper, television station, choral group, Drama Ministries Ensemble, Acappella Choir, Psi Chi, Fellowship of Christian Athletes, International Club. *Campus security:* 24-hour emergency response devices, controlled dormitory access. *Student services:* health clinic, personal/psychological counseling.

Athletics Member NAIA. *Intercollegiate sports:* baseball M(s), basketball M(s)/W(s), cheerleading M/W, cross-country running M(s)/W(s), football M(s), golf M(s)/W(s), soccer M(s)/W(s), softball W(s), tennis W(s), track and field M(s)/W(s), volleyball W(s), wrestling M(s). *Intramural sports:* badminton M/W, basketball M/W, bowling M/W, cheerleading M/W, football M/W, golf M/W, lacrosse M/W, racquetball M/W, soccer M/W, softball M, table tennis M/W, tennis M/W, ultimate Frisbee M/W, volleyball M/W.

Standardized Tests *Required:* SAT or ACT (for admission).

Costs (2013–14) *Comprehensive fee:* $34,848 includes full-time tuition ($26,614), mandatory fees ($150), and room and board ($8084). Full-time tuition and fees vary according to program. Part-time tuition: $570 per credit hour. Part-time tuition and fees vary according to course load and program. *Required fees:* $50 per term part-time. *Room and board:* Room and board charges vary according to board plan and housing facility. *Payment plans:* tuition prepayment, installment. *Waivers:* employees or children of employees.

Financial Aid Of all full-time matriculated undergraduates who enrolled in 2007, 997 applied for aid, 997 were judged to have need, 418 had their need fully met. 354 Federal Work-Study jobs (averaging $1120). 412 state and other part-time jobs (averaging $1120). In 2007, 229 non-need-based awards were made. *Average percent of need met:* 87%. *Average financial aid package:*

$16,330. *Average need-based loan:* $4453. *Average need-based gift aid:* $6289. *Average non-need-based aid:* $5562. *Average indebtedness upon graduation:* $23,817.

Applying *Options:* electronic application, early admission, deferred entrance. *Application fee:* $25. *Required:* essay or personal statement, high school transcript, minimum 2.0 GPA, 1 letter of recommendation. *Recommended:* minimum 2.5 GPA, interview. *Application deadlines:* rolling (freshmen), rolling (transfers). *Notification:* continuous (freshmen), continuous (transfers).

Freshman Application Contact Mr. Kenton Pauls, Dean of Enrollment Management, Northwestern College, 101 7th Street SW, Orange City, IA 51041-1996. *Phone:* 712-737-7130. *Toll-free phone:* 800-747-4757. *Fax:* 712-707-7164. *E-mail:* admissions@nwciowa.edu. *Website:* http://www.nwciowa.edu/.

Palmer College of Chiropractic

Davenport, Iowa

Freshman Application Contact Ms. Lisa Gisel, Undergraduate Admissions Representative, Palmer College of Chiropractic, 1000 Brady Street, Davenport, IA 52803-5287. *Phone:* 563-884-5743. *Toll-free phone:* 800-722-3648. *Fax:* 563-884-5226. *E-mail:* lisa.gisel@palmer.edu. *Website:* http://www.palmer.edu/.

St. Ambrose University

Davenport, Iowa

- **Independent Roman Catholic** comprehensive, founded 1882
- **Urban** 118-acre campus
- **Endowment** $105.2 million
- **Coed** 2,794 undergraduate students, 87% full-time, 58% women, 42% men
- **Moderately difficult** entrance level, 73% of applicants were admitted

Undergraduates 2,419 full-time, 375 part-time. Students come from 25 states and territories; 14 other countries; 57% are from out of state; 3% Black or African American, non-Hispanic/Latino; 1% Hispanic/Latino; 1% Asian, non-Hispanic/Latino; 0.1% Native Hawaiian or other Pacific Islander, non-Hispanic/Latino; 0.1% American Indian or Alaska Native, non-Hispanic/Latino; 1% Two or more races, non-Hispanic/Latino; 4% Race/ethnicity unknown; 1% international; 9% transferred in; 60% live on campus. *Retention:* 78% of full-time freshmen returned.

Freshmen *Admission:* 3,309 applied, 2,422 admitted, 582 enrolled. *Average high school GPA:* 3.28. *Test scores:* ACT scores over 18: 96%; ACT scores over 24: 41%; ACT scores over 30: 9%.

Faculty *Total:* 425, 50% full-time, 41% with terminal degrees. *Student/faculty ratio:* 11:1.

Academics *Calendar:* 4-1-4. *Degrees:* certificates, bachelor's, master's, doctoral, and post-master's certificates. *Special study options:* academic remediation for entering students, accelerated degree program, adult/continuing education programs, advanced placement credit, cooperative education, distance learning, double majors, external degree program, independent study, internships, off-campus study, part-time degree program, services for LD students, student-designed majors, study abroad, summer session for credit. *Unusual degree programs:* 3-2 physical therapy, occupational therapy, special education.

Computers on Campus 276 computers/terminals and 517 ports are available on campus for general student use. Students can access the following: campus intranet, computer help desk, free student e-mail accounts, online (class) grades, online (class) registration, online (class) schedules, online course syllabi, online class listings, and online payments. Campuswide network is available. 100% of college-owned or -operated housing units are wired for high-speed Internet access. Wireless service is available via classrooms, libraries, student centers.

Student Life *Housing:* on-campus residence required through sophomore year. *Options:* coed, men-only, women-only, disabled students. Campus housing is university owned. Freshman campus housing is guaranteed. *Activities and organizations:* drama/theater group, student-run newspaper, radio and television station, choral group, Up 'til Dawn, SOTA, Ambrosinas for Obama, Amnesty International, SPTO. *Campus security:* 24-hour emergency response devices and patrols, late-night transport/escort service, controlled dormitory access, police officer on campus 10 pm to 6 am. *Student services:* health clinic, personal/psychological counseling, women's center.

Athletics Member NAIA. *Intercollegiate sports:* baseball M(s), basketball M(s)/W(s), bowling M(s)/W(s), cheerleading M(s)/W(s), cross-country running M(s)/W(s), football M(s), golf M(s)/W(s), lacrosse M(s), soccer M(s)/W(s), softball W(s), tennis M(s)/W(s), track and field M(s)/W(s), volleyball M(s)/W(s). *Intramural sports:* badminton M/W, baseball M/W, basketball M/W, bowling M/W, football M/W, golf M/W, racquetball M/W, skiing (down-hill) M/W, soccer M/W, softball M/W, table tennis M/W, tennis M/W, volleyball M/W.

Standardized Tests *Required:* SAT or ACT (for admission). *Recommended:* ACT (for admission).

Costs (2013–14) *Comprehensive fee:* $35,756 includes full-time tuition ($26,500), mandatory fees ($240), and room and board ($9016). Full-time tuition and fees vary according to course load, location, program, and reciprocity agreements. Part-time tuition: $820 per credit hour. Part-time tuition and fees vary according to course load and location. *College room only:* $5500. Room and board charges vary according to board plan and housing facility. *Payment plan:* installment. *Waivers:* senior citizens and employees or children of employees.

Financial Aid Of all full-time matriculated undergraduates who enrolled in 2012, 2,111 applied for aid, 1,871 were judged to have need, 430 had their need fully met. 567 Federal Work-Study jobs (averaging $1850). 279 state and other part-time jobs (averaging $1850). In 2012, 479 non-need-based awards were made. *Average percent of need met:* 70%. *Average financial aid package:* $18,133. *Average need-based loan:* $4284. *Average need-based gift aid:* $12,076. *Average non-need-based aid:* $10,538. *Average indebtedness upon graduation:* $37,236.

Applying *Options:* electronic application, deferred entrance. *Application fee:* $25. *Required:* high school transcript, minimum 2.5 GPA, rank in upper 50% of high school class. *Required for some:* interview. *Recommended:* interview. *Application deadlines:* rolling (freshmen), rolling (transfers). *Notification:* 10/1 (freshmen), continuous (transfers).

Freshman Application Contact St. Ambrose University, 518 West Locust Street, Davenport, IA 52803-2898. *Phone:* 563-333-6300 Ext. 6311. *Toll-free phone:* 800-383-2627. *Website:* http://www.sau.edu/.

Simpson College

Indianola, Iowa

- **Independent United Methodist** comprehensive, founded 1860
- **Suburban** 80-acre campus with easy access to Des Moines
- **Endowment** $69.2 million
- **Coed** 1,844 undergraduate students, 77% full-time, 54% women, 46% men
- **Moderately difficult** entrance level, 89% of applicants were admitted

Undergraduates 1,423 full-time, 421 part-time. Students come from 29 states and territories; 5 other countries; 11% are from out of state; 2% Black or African American, non-Hispanic/Latino; 2% Hispanic/Latino; 1% Asian, non-Hispanic/Latino; 0.3% American Indian or Alaska Native, non-Hispanic/Latino; 2% Two or more races, non-Hispanic/Latino; 4% Race/ethnicity unknown; 1% international; 4% transferred in; 87% live on campus. *Retention:* 82% of full-time freshmen returned.

Freshmen *Admission:* 1,385 applied, 1,228 admitted, 415 enrolled. *Test scores:* ACT scores over 18: 99%; ACT scores over 24: 53%; ACT scores over 30: 11%.

Faculty *Total:* 202, 49% full-time, 53% with terminal degrees. *Student/faculty ratio:* 12:1.

Academics *Calendar:* 4-4-1. *Degrees:* bachelor's, master's, and postbachelor's certificates. *Special study options:* accelerated degree program, adult/continuing education programs, advanced placement credit, cooperative education, double majors, independent study, internships, off-campus study, part-time degree program, services for LD students, student-designed majors, study abroad, summer session for credit. *Unusual degree programs:* 3-2 engineering with Washington University in St. Louis, MO; Iowa State University in Ames, IA; Institute of Technology (University of Minnesota) in Minneapolis, MN; nursing with Allen College (Waterloo, IA).

Computers on Campus 374 computers/terminals are available on campus for general student use. Students can access the following: campus intranet, computer help desk, free student e-mail accounts, online (class) grades, online (class) registration, online (class) schedules, wireless campus. Campuswide network is available. 100% of college-owned or -operated housing units are wired for high-speed Internet access. Wireless service is available via entire campus.

Student Life *Housing:* on-campus residence required through junior year. *Options:* coed. Campus housing is university owned. Freshman campus housing is guaranteed. *Activities and organizations:* drama/theater group, student-run newspaper, radio station, choral group, Religious Life Community, Campus Activities Board, Student Government Association, Residence Hall Association, Intramurals, national fraternities, national sororities. *Campus security:* 24-hour emergency response devices and patrols, student patrols, late-night transport/escort service, controlled dormitory access, Safe (Simpson Alert for Emergencies) Students and staff/faculty will receive phone calls in case of campus emergency, including weather. *Student services:* health clinic, personal/psychological counseling, women's center.

Athletics Member NCAA. All Division III. *Intercollegiate sports:* baseball M, basketball M/W, cheerleading M/W, cross-country running M/W, football M, golf M/W, soccer M/W, softball W, swimming and diving M/W, tennis M/W, track and field M/W, volleyball W, wrestling M. *Intramural sports:* badminton M/W, basketball M/W, bowling M/W, football M/W, golf M/W, racquetball M/W, rugby M, soccer M/W, softball M/W, swimming and diving M/W, table tennis M/W, tennis M/W, ultimate Frisbee M/W, volleyball M/W.

Standardized Tests *Required:* SAT or ACT (for admission).

Costs (2013–14) *One-time required fee:* $200. *Comprehensive fee:* $38,962 includes full-time tuition ($30,423), mandatory fees ($576), and room and board ($7963). Full-time tuition and fees vary according to class time, course load, degree level, and program. Part-time tuition: $355 per credit hour. Part-time tuition and fees vary according to class time, course load, degree level, and program. *College room only:* $3860. Room and board charges vary according to board plan and housing facility. *Payment plan:* installment. *Waivers:* children of alumni, senior citizens, and employees or children of employees.

Financial Aid Of all full-time matriculated undergraduates who enrolled in 2012, 1,419 applied for aid, 1,211 were judged to have need, 320 had their need fully met. 343 Federal Work-Study jobs (averaging $1079). 449 state and other part-time jobs (averaging $1372). In 2012, 205 non-need-based awards were made. *Average percent of need met:* 88%. *Average financial aid package:* $27,785. *Average need-based loan:* $3785. *Average need-based gift aid:* $18,784. *Average non-need-based aid:* $16,534. *Average indebtedness upon graduation:* $35,228.

Applying *Options:* electronic application, deferred entrance. *Required:* high school transcript, online or paper application, guidance counselor recommendation form. *Recommended:* minimum 3.0 GPA, interview. *Application deadlines:* 8/15 (freshmen), 8/15 (transfers). *Notification:* continuous (freshmen), continuous (transfers).

Freshman Application Contact Deborah Tierney, Vice President for Enrollment, Simpson College, 701 North C Street, Indianola, IA 50125. *Phone:* 515-961-1624. *Toll-free phone:* 800-362-2454. *Fax:* 515-961-1870. *E-mail:* admiss@simpson.edu.
Website: http://www.simpson.edu/.

See next page for display ad and page 1502 for the College Close-Up.

University of Dubuque
Dubuque, Iowa

- **Independent Presbyterian** comprehensive, founded 1852
- **Suburban** 77-acre campus
- **Endowment** $87.1 million
- **Coed**
- **Moderately difficult** entrance level

Faculty *Student/faculty ratio:* 15:1.

Academics *Calendar:* semesters. *Degrees:* associate, bachelor's, master's, and doctoral.

Student Life *Campus security:* 24-hour patrols, late-night transport/escort service, controlled dormitory access.

Athletics Member NCAA. All Division III.

Standardized Tests *Required:* SAT or ACT (for admission).

Costs (2012–13) *Comprehensive fee:* $32,410 includes full-time tuition ($23,540), mandatory fees ($990), and room and board ($7880). *College room only:* $3920. Room and board charges vary according to board plan, housing facility, and location.

Financial Aid *Of all full-time matriculated undergraduates who enrolled in 2011,* 1,487 applied for aid, 1,364 were judged to have need, 230 had their need fully met. 185 Federal Work-Study jobs (averaging $1500). 194 state and other part-time jobs (averaging $1500). *In 2011,* 164 non-need-based awards were made. *Average percent of need met:* 71. *Average financial aid package:* $19,029. *Average need-based loan:* $6655. *Average need-based gift aid:* $13,102. *Average non-need-based aid:* $7912. *Average indebtedness upon graduation:* $31,906.

Applying *Options:* electronic application. *Application fee:* $25. *Required:* essay or personal statement, high school transcript, minimum 2.5 GPA, 2 letters of recommendation. *Recommended:* interview.

Freshman Application Contact Mr. Jesse James, Director of Admissions, University of Dubuque, 2000 University Avenue, Dubuque, IA 52001-5099. *Phone:* 563-589-3214. *Toll-free phone:* 800-722-5583. *Fax:* 563-589-3690. *E-mail:* admissns@dbq.edu.
Website: http://www.dbq.edu/.

See below for display ad and page 1560 for the College Close-Up.

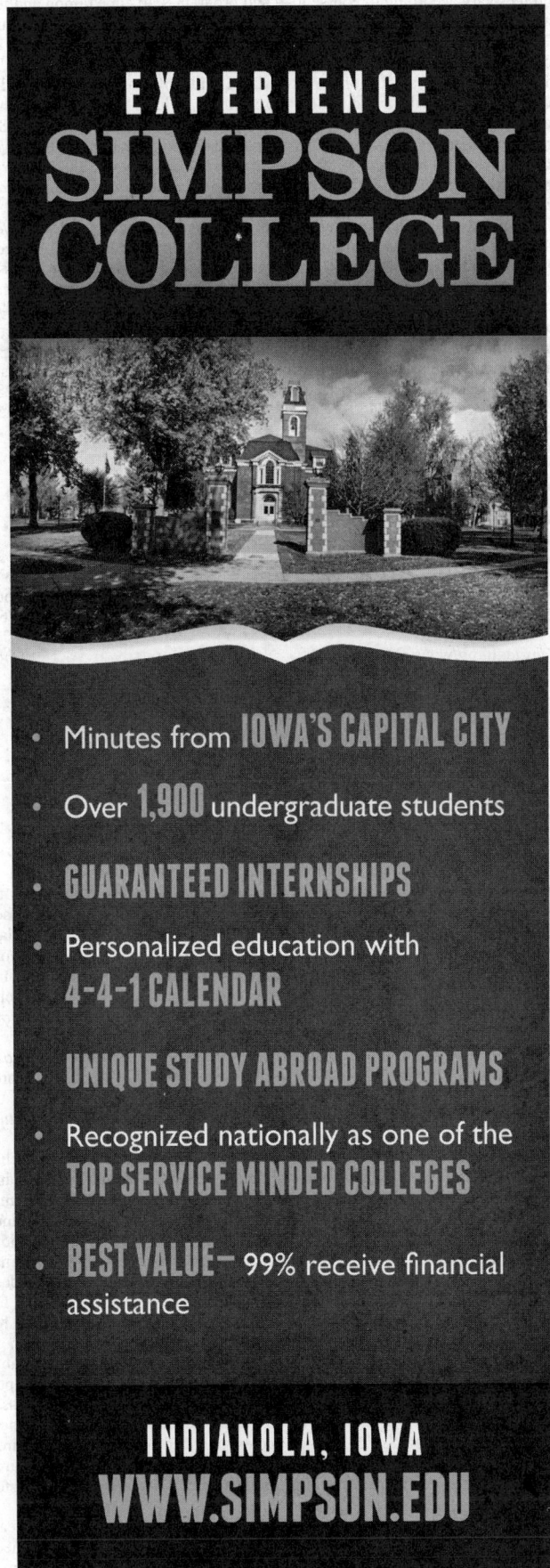
The University of Iowa

Iowa City, Iowa

- **State-supported** university, founded 1847
- **Small-town** 1900-acre campus
- **Endowment** $981.1 million
- **Coed** 21,999 undergraduate students, 89% full-time, 52% women, 48% men
- **Moderately difficult** entrance level, 78% of applicants were admitted

Undergraduates 19,639 full-time, 2,360 part-time. Students come from 53 states and territories; 58 other countries; 39% are from out of state; 3% Black or African American, non-Hispanic/Latino; 5% Hispanic/Latino; 3% Asian, non-Hispanic/Latino; 0.1% Native Hawaiian or other Pacific Islander, non-Hispanic/Latino; 0.2% American Indian or Alaska Native, non-Hispanic/Latino; 2% Two or more races, non-Hispanic/Latino; 4% Race/ethnicity unknown; 9% international; 5% transferred in; 31% live on campus. *Retention:* 86% of full-time freshmen returned.

Freshmen *Admission:* 19,430 applied, 15,240 admitted, 4,470 enrolled. *Average high school GPA:* 3.62. *Test scores:* SAT critical reading scores over 500: 68%; SAT math scores over 500: 89%; SAT writing scores over 500: 74%; ACT scores over 18: 98%; SAT critical reading scores over 600: 37%; SAT math scores over 600: 65%; SAT writing scores over 600: 31%; ACT scores over 24: 65%; SAT critical reading scores over 700: 13%; SAT math scores over 700: 24%; SAT writing scores over 700: 7%; ACT scores over 30: 12%.

Faculty *Total:* 1,635, 95% full-time, 97% with terminal degrees. *Student/faculty ratio:* 16:1.

Academics *Calendar:* semesters. *Degrees:* bachelor's, master's, doctoral, post-master's, and postbachelor's certificates. *Special study options:* accelerated degree program, adult/continuing education programs, advanced placement credit, cooperative education, distance learning, double majors, English as a second language, external degree program, honors programs, independent study, internships, off-campus study, part-time degree program, services for LD students, student-designed majors, study abroad, summer session for credit. *ROTC:* Army (b), Air Force (b).

Computers on Campus 1,386 computers/terminals are available on campus for general student use. Students can access the following: computer help desk, free student e-mail accounts, online (class) grades, online (class) registration, online (class) schedules, online degree process, financial aid summary, university bill. Campuswide network is available. 100% of college-owned or -operated housing units are wired for high-speed Internet access. Wireless service is available via classrooms, computer centers, computer labs, dorm rooms, learning centers, libraries, student centers.

Student Life *Housing options:* coed, disabled students. Campus housing is university owned and leased by the school. *Activities and organizations:* drama/theater group, student-run newspaper, radio and television station, choral group, marching band, Association of Residence Halls, Graduate Student Senate, National Society of Collegiate Scholars, Organization for the Active Support of International Students (OASIS), Dance Marathon, national fraternities, national sororities. *Campus security:* 24-hour emergency response devices and patrols, late-night transport/escort service, controlled dormitory access. *Student services:* health clinic, personal/psychological counseling, women's center, legal services.

Athletics Member NCAA. All Division I except football (Division I-A). *Intercollegiate sports:* baseball M(s), basketball M(s)/W(s), crew M(c)/W(s), cross-country running M(s)/W(s), field hockey W(s), golf M(s)/W(s), gymnastics M(s)/W(s), ice hockey M(c), lacrosse M(c)/W(c), rugby M(c)/W(c), sailing M(c)/W(c), soccer M(c)/W(s), softball W(s), swimming and diving M(s)/W(s), table tennis M(c)/W(c), tennis M(s)/W(s), track and field M(s)/W(s), ultimate Frisbee M(c)/W(c), volleyball M(c)/W(s), wrestling M(s). *Intramural sports:* badminton M/W, basketball M/W, bowling M/W, fencing M(c)/W(c), football M/W, golf M/W, racquetball M/W, rugby M(c)/W(c), sailing M(c)/W(c), skiing (cross-country) M(c)/W(c), skiing (downhill) M(c)/W(c), soccer M/W, softball M/W, table tennis M/W, tennis M/W, track and field M/W, ultimate Frisbee M/W, volleyball M/W, water polo M(c)/W(c), wrestling M.

Standardized Tests *Required:* SAT or ACT (for admission).

Costs (2013–14) *Tuition:* state resident $6678 full-time, $279 per semester hour part-time; nonresident $25,548 full-time, $1065 per semester hour part-time. Full-time tuition and fees vary according to course load, program, and student level. Part-time tuition and fees vary according to course load, program, and student level. *Required fees:* $1383 full-time, $72 per semester hour part-time. *Room and board:* $9420. Room and board charges vary according to board plan and housing facility. *Payment plan:* installment.

Financial Aid Of all full-time matriculated undergraduates who enrolled in 2010, 12,721 applied for aid, 8,983 were judged to have need, 2,622 had their need fully met. In 2010, 6564 non-need-based awards were made. *Average percent of need met:* 65%. *Average financial aid package:* $11,504. *Average need-based loan:* $5315. *Average need-based gift aid:* $6603. *Average non-need-based aid:* $4543. *Average indebtedness upon graduation:* $27,480.

Applying *Options:* electronic application, early admission, deferred entrance. *Application fee:* $40. *Required:* high school transcript, Must submit ACT or SAT score; must meet Regent Admission Index (RAI) requirement: residents 245 or above; nonresidents 255 or above. *Application deadlines:* 4/1 (freshmen), 4/1 (transfers). *Notification:* continuous (freshmen), continuous (transfers).

Freshman Application Contact Mr. Michael Barron, Assistant Provost for Enrollment Management and Executive Director of Admissions, The University of Iowa, 107 Calvin Hall, Iowa City, IA 52242. *Phone:* 319-335-3847. *Toll-free phone:* 800-553-4692. *Fax:* 319-335-1535. *E-mail:* admissions@uiowa.edu.
Website: http://www.uiowa.edu/.

University of Northern Iowa
Cedar Falls, Iowa

- **State-supported** comprehensive, founded 1876, part of Board of Regents, State of Iowa
- **Small-town** 916-acre campus
- **Endowment** $75.5 million
- **Coed** 10,655 undergraduate students, 91% full-time, 57% women, 43% men
- **Moderately difficult** entrance level, 78% of applicants were admitted

Undergraduates 9,679 full-time, 976 part-time. Students come from 38 states and territories; 45 other countries; 5% are from out of state; 3% Black or African American, non-Hispanic/Latino; 3% Hispanic/Latino; 1% Asian, non-Hispanic/Latino; 0.2% American Indian or Alaska Native, non-Hispanic/Latino; 1% Two or more races, non-Hispanic/Latino; 2% Race/ethnicity unknown; 3% international; 9% transferred in; 34% live on campus. *Retention:* 81% of full-time freshmen returned.

Freshmen *Admission:* 4,322 applied, 3,350 admitted, 1,704 enrolled. *Average high school GPA:* 3.21. *Test scores:* ACT scores over 18: 96%; ACT scores over 24: 42%; ACT scores over 30: 5%.

Faculty *Total:* 788, 76% full-time, 66% with terminal degrees. *Student/faculty ratio:* 16:1.

Academics *Calendar:* semesters. *Degrees:* bachelor's, master's, and doctoral. *Special study options:* academic remediation for entering students, accelerated degree program, adult/continuing education programs, advanced placement credit, cooperative education, distance learning, double majors, English as a second language, external degree program, honors programs, independent study, internships, off-campus study, part-time degree program, services for LD students, student-designed majors, study abroad, summer session for credit. *ROTC:* Army (b). *Unusual degree programs:* 3-2 nursing with University of Iowa; medical technology with St. Luke's Hospital/University of Iowa Medical School, cytotechnology with Mayo School of Health-Related Sciences, Wisconsin State Laboratory of Hygiene and Mercy School of Cytotechnology, chiropractic with Logan College of Chiropractic.

Computers on Campus 1,900 computers/terminals are available on campus for general student use. Students can access the following: campus intranet, computer help desk, free student e-mail accounts, online (class) grades, online (class) registration, online (class) schedules, course registration, student account, degree audit, program of study. Campuswide network is available. 100% of college-owned or -operated housing units are wired for high-speed Internet access. Wireless service is available via entire campus.

Student Life *Housing options:* coed, women-only, disabled students. Campus housing is university owned. Freshman campus housing is guaranteed. *Activities and organizations:* drama/theater group, student-run newspaper, radio and television station, choral group, marching band, Catholic Student Association, National Society of Collegiate Scholars, Accounting Club, Phi Eta Sigma, Students Today Alumni Tomorrow, national fraternities, national sororities. *Campus security:* 24-hour emergency response devices and patrols, student patrols, late-night transport/escort service, controlled dormitory access. *Student services:* health clinic, personal/psychological counseling.

Athletics Member NCAA. All Division I except football (Division I-AA). *Intercollegiate sports:* basketball M(s)/W(s), cross-country running M(s)/W(s), golf M(s)/W(s), soccer W(s), softball W(s), swimming and diving W(s), tennis W(s), track and field M(s)/W(s), volleyball W(s), wrestling M(s). *Intramural sports:* badminton M/W, baseball M(c), basketball M/W, bowling M(c)/W(c), cheerleading M/W, crew M(c)/W(c), cross-country running M(c)/W(c), football M(c), golf M(c)/W(c), ice hockey M(c), racquetball M(c)/W(c), rugby M(c)/W(c), skiing (cross-country) M(c)/W(c), skiing (downhill) M(c)/W(c), soccer M(c)/W(c), softball M(c)/W(c), swimming and diving M(c)/W(c), table tennis M/W, tennis M(c)/W(c), track and field M(c)/W(c), ultimate Frisbee M(c)/W(c), volleyball M/W(c), weight lifting M/W, wrestling M.

Standardized Tests *Required:* SAT or ACT (for admission). *Recommended:* ACT (for admission).

Costs (2012–13) *Tuition:* state resident $6648 full-time, $277 per hour part-time; nonresident $15,734 full-time, $656 per hour part-time. Full-time tuition

and fees vary according to course load and program. Part-time tuition and fees vary according to course load and program. *Required fees:* $987 full-time. *Room and board:* $7597; room only: $3703. Room and board charges vary according to board plan and housing facility. *Payment plan:* installment.

Financial Aid Of all full-time matriculated undergraduates who enrolled in 2011, 8,007 applied for aid, 6,468 were judged to have need, 994 had their need fully met. 433 Federal Work-Study jobs (averaging $1417). In 2011, 823 non-need-based awards were made. *Average percent of need met:* 68%. *Average financial aid package:* $7828. *Average need-based loan:* $3832. *Average need-based gift aid:* $4227. *Average non-need-based aid:* $3473. *Average indebtedness upon graduation:* $23,575.

Applying *Options:* electronic application, deferred entrance. *Application fee:* $40. *Required:* high school transcript, A Regent Admission Index (RAI) score of 245 guarantees admission. High school requirements include 4 years of English; 3 years each of math, science and social studies, and 2 or more years of electives, which may include foreign language and fine arts. *Required for some:* interview. *Application deadlines:* 8/15 (freshmen), 8/15 (transfers). *Notification:* 9/1 (freshmen), 9/1 (transfers).

Freshman Application Contact Amy Schipper, Assistant Director, University of Northern Iowa, 002 Gilchrist, Cedar Falls, IA 50614. *Phone:* 319-273-2281. *Toll-free phone:* 800-772-2037. *Fax:* 319-273-2885. *E-mail:* admissions@uni.edu.
Website: http://www.uni.edu/.

University of Phoenix–Des Moines Campus
Des Moines, Iowa

Admissions Office Contact University of Phoenix–Des Moines Campus, 6600 Westown Parkway, Des Moines, IA 50266. *Toll-free phone:* 866-766-0766.
Website: http://www.phoenix.edu/.

Upper Iowa University
Fayette, Iowa

- **Independent** comprehensive, founded 1857
- **Rural** 80-acre campus with easy access to Minneapolis, Chicago
- **Endowment** $9.0 million
- **Coed** 4,645 undergraduate students, 65% full-time, 60% women, 40% men
- **Moderately difficult** entrance level, 62% of applicants were admitted

Undergraduates 3,008 full-time, 1,637 part-time. Students come from 50 states and territories; 35 other countries; 60% are from out of state; 16% Black or African American, non-Hispanic/Latino; 4% Hispanic/Latino; 1% Asian, non-Hispanic/Latino; 0.1% Native Hawaiian or other Pacific Islander, non-Hispanic/Latino; 0.5% American Indian or Alaska Native, non-Hispanic/Latino; 0.6% Two or more races, non-Hispanic/Latino; 7% Race/ethnicity unknown; 3% international; 2% transferred in; 50% live on campus. *Retention:* 68% of full-time freshmen returned.

Freshmen *Admission:* 1,160 applied, 714 admitted, 230 enrolled. *Average high school GPA:* 3.21. *Test scores:* ACT scores over 18: 91%; ACT scores over 24: 38%; ACT scores over 30: 2%.

Faculty *Total:* 586, 14% full-time, 32% with terminal degrees. *Student/faculty ratio:* 19:1.

Academics *Calendar:* 4 8-week terms. *Degrees:* certificates, associate, bachelor's, and master's (enrollment figures include extended learning centers and online and distance education programs). *Special study options:* academic remediation for entering students, accelerated degree program, adult/continuing education programs, advanced placement credit, cooperative education, distance learning, double majors, English as a second language, external degree program, freshman honors college, honors programs, independent study, internships, off-campus study, part-time degree program, services for LD students, student-designed majors, study abroad, summer session for credit.

Computers on Campus 600 computers/terminals and 444 ports are available on campus for general student use. Students can access the following: campus intranet, computer help desk, free student e-mail accounts, online (class) grades, online (class) registration, online (class) schedules. Campuswide network is available. 100% of college-owned or -operated housing units are wired for high-speed Internet access. Wireless service is available via classrooms, computer centers, computer labs, dorm rooms, learning centers, libraries, student centers.

Student Life *Housing:* on-campus residence required through sophomore year. *Options:* coed, men-only, women-only. Campus housing is university owned. Freshman campus housing is guaranteed. *Activities and organizations:* drama/theater group, student-run newspaper, choral group, Beta Phi Omega, Peacock

Entertainment Crew, Greek Council, Student Government Association, International Student Association. *Campus security:* late-night transport/escort service, controlled dormitory access. *Student services:* health clinic, personal/psychological counseling.

Athletics Member NCAA. All Division II. *Intercollegiate sports:* baseball M(s), basketball M(s)/W(s), football M(s), golf M(s)/W(s), soccer M(s)/W(s), softball W(s), tennis M/W, volleyball W(s), wrestling M. *Intramural sports:* badminton M/W, basketball M/W, bowling M/W, cheerleading M(c)/W(c), football M, golf M/W, soccer M/W, softball M/W, table tennis M/W, ultimate Frisbee M/W, volleyball M/W.

Standardized Tests *Required:* SAT or ACT (for admission).

Costs (2013–14) *Comprehensive fee:* $31,910 includes full-time tuition ($24,400) and room and board ($7510). Full-time tuition and fees vary according to degree level, location, and program. *College room only:* $3028. Room and board charges vary according to board plan, housing facility, and location. *Payment plan:* installment. *Waivers:* employees or children of employees.

Financial Aid Of all full-time matriculated undergraduates who enrolled in 2012, 742 applied for aid, 742 were judged to have need. 228 Federal Work-Study jobs (averaging $1860). In 2012, 200 non-need-based awards were made. *Average percent of need met:* 33%. *Average financial aid package:* $8015. *Average need-based loan:* $3800. *Average need-based gift aid:* $6819. *Average non-need-based aid:* $6100. *Average indebtedness upon graduation:* $27,361.

Applying *Options:* electronic application. *Required:* high school transcript, minimum 2.0 GPA. *Required for some:* essay or personal statement, interview. *Application deadlines:* rolling (freshmen), rolling (out-of-state freshmen), rolling (transfers).

Freshman Application Contact Mr. Storm M Schmitt, Executive Director of Admissions, Upper Iowa University, 605 Washington Street, Parker Fox Hall, Fayette, IA 52142. *Phone:* 563-425-5857. *Toll-free phone:* 800-553-4150. *Fax:* 563-4255323. *E-mail:* schmitts@uiu.edu. *Website:* http://www.uiu.edu/.

Vatterott College

Des Moines, Iowa

Freshman Application Contact Mr. Henry Franken, Co-Director, Vatterott College, 7000 Fleur Drive, Suite 290, Des Moines, IA 50321. *Phone:* 515-309-9000. *Toll-free phone:* 888-553-6627. *Fax:* 515-309-0366. *Website:* http://www.vatterott.edu/.

Waldorf College

Forest City, Iowa

- **Independent Lutheran** 4-year, founded 1903, part of Columbia Southern Education Group
- **Rural** 51-acre campus
- **Coed** 1,105 undergraduate students, 84% full-time, 34% women, 66% men
- **Moderately difficult** entrance level, 51% of applicants were admitted

Undergraduates 925 full-time, 180 part-time. Students come from 46 states and territories; 2 other countries; 82% are from out of state; 15% Black or African American, non-Hispanic/Latino; 6% Hispanic/Latino; 2% Asian, non-Hispanic/Latino; 0.6% American Indian or Alaska Native, non-Hispanic/Latino; 0.9% Two or more races, non-Hispanic/Latino; 8% Race/ethnicity unknown; 6% transferred in; 70% live on campus. *Retention:* 47% of full-time freshmen returned.

Freshmen *Admission:* 1,039 applied, 526 admitted, 155 enrolled. *Average high school GPA:* 3. *Test scores:* ACT scores over 18: 83%; ACT scores over 24: 23%.

Faculty *Total:* 41, 93% full-time, 56% with terminal degrees. *Student/faculty ratio:* 15:1.

Academics *Calendar:* semesters. *Degrees:* associate and bachelor's. *Special study options:* academic remediation for entering students, adult/continuing education programs, advanced placement credit, cooperative education, distance learning, double majors, freshman honors college, honors programs, independent study, internships, part-time degree program, services for LD students, summer session for credit.

Computers on Campus 500 computers/terminals are available on campus for general student use. Students can access the following: campus intranet, computer help desk, free student e-mail accounts, online (class) grades, all students receive laptops. Campuswide network is available. 100% of college-owned or -operated housing units are wired for high-speed Internet access. Wireless service is available via computer centers, computer labs, learning centers, libraries, student centers.

Student Life *Housing:* on-campus residence required through junior year. *Options:* coed, men-only, women-only, cooperative, disabled students. Campus housing is university owned and leased by the school. Freshman campus housing is guaranteed. *Activities and organizations:* drama/theater group, student-run newspaper, radio and television station, choral group, Student Activities Team, Education Club, Campus Ministry groups, Intramurals, Radio/TV/Newspaper. *Campus security:* 24-hour emergency response devices, student patrols, late-night transport/escort service, controlled dormitory access, evening and night patrols by trained security personnel, camera surveillance system. *Student services:* health clinic, personal/psychological counseling.

Athletics Member NAIA. *Intercollegiate sports:* baseball M(s), basketball M(s)/W(s), cheerleading W(s), cross-country running M(s)/W(s), football M(s), golf M(s)/W(s), ice hockey M(s)(c), soccer M(s)/W(s), softball W(s), track and field M(c)/W(c), volleyball W(s), wrestling M(s)/W(s). *Intramural sports:* basketball M/W, bowling M/W, football M, racquetball M/W, skiing (cross-country) M/W, skiing (downhill) M/W, soccer M/W, softball M/W, table tennis M/W, tennis M/W, ultimate Frisbee M/W, volleyball M/W.

Standardized Tests *Required:* SAT or ACT (for admission).

Costs (2013–14) *Comprehensive fee:* $27,172 includes full-time tuition ($19,266), mandatory fees ($1050), and room and board ($6856). Full-time tuition and fees vary according to class time, course load, and program. *Room and board:* Room and board charges vary according to board plan and housing facility. *Payment plans:* installment, deferred payment. *Waivers:* employees or children of employees.

Financial Aid Of all full-time matriculated undergraduates who enrolled in 2011, 958 applied for aid, 745 were judged to have need, 84 had their need fully met. In 2011, 51 non-need-based awards were made. *Average percent of need met:* 64%. *Average financial aid package:* $12,615. *Average need-based loan:* $3966. *Average need-based gift aid:* $9483. *Average non-need-based aid:* $4661. *Average indebtedness upon graduation:* $19,744.

Applying *Options:* electronic application, early admission. *Required:* high school transcript, ACT or SAT scores. *Required for some:* interview. *Recommended:* minimum 2.0 GPA. *Application deadlines:* rolling (freshmen), rolling (out-of-state freshmen), rolling (transfers). *Notification:* continuous (freshmen), continuous (out-of-state freshmen), continuous (transfers).

Freshman Application Contact Scott Pitcher, Director for Admissions, Waldorf College, 106 South 6th Street, Forest City, IA 50436. *Phone:* 641-585-8112. *Toll-free phone:* 800-292-1903. *Fax:* 641-585-8125. *E-mail:* admissions@waldorf.edu. *Website:* http://www.waldorf.edu/.

Wartburg College

Waverly, Iowa

- **Independent Lutheran** 4-year, founded 1852
- **Small-town** 118-acre campus
- **Endowment** $45.7 million
- **Coed** 1,747 undergraduate students, 96% full-time, 53% women, 47% men
- **Moderately difficult** entrance level, 70% of applicants were admitted

Undergraduates 1,673 full-time, 74 part-time. Students come from 29 states and territories; 52 other countries; 26% are from out of state; 6% Black or African American, non-Hispanic/Latino; 2% Hispanic/Latino; 0.9% Asian, non-Hispanic/Latino; 0.1% Native Hawaiian or other Pacific Islander, non-Hispanic/Latino; 0.1% American Indian or Alaska Native, non-Hispanic/Latino; 2% Two or more races, non-Hispanic/Latino; 1% Race/ethnicity unknown; 8% international; 1% transferred in; 86% live on campus. *Retention:* 76% of full-time freshmen returned.

Freshmen *Admission:* 2,389 applied, 1,682 admitted, 484 enrolled. *Average high school GPA:* 3.47. *Test scores:* SAT critical reading scores over 500: 67%; SAT math scores over 500: 78%; SAT writing scores over 500: 66%; ACT scores over 18: 95%; SAT critical reading scores over 600: 17%; SAT math scores over 600: 23%; SAT writing scores over 600: 12%; ACT scores over 24: 52%; SAT critical reading scores over 700: 6%; SAT math scores over 700: 3%; SAT writing scores over 700: 3%; ACT scores over 30: 10%.

Faculty *Total:* 160, 68% full-time, 66% with terminal degrees. *Student/faculty ratio:* 11:1.

Academics *Calendar:* 4-4-1. *Degree:* bachelor's. *Special study options:* academic remediation for entering students, accelerated degree program, advanced placement credit, double majors, honors programs, independent study, internships, off-campus study, part-time degree program, services for LD students, student-designed majors, study abroad, summer session for credit. *Unusual degree programs:* 3-2 nursing with Allen College.

Computers on Campus 250 computers/terminals are available on campus for general student use. Students can access the following: campus intranet, computer help desk, free student e-mail accounts, online (class) grades, online (class) registration, online (class) schedules. Campuswide network is available. 100% of college-owned or -operated housing units are wired for high-speed Internet access. Wireless service is available via entire campus.

Student Life *Housing:* on-campus residence required through senior year. *Options:* coed, men-only, women-only, disabled students. Campus housing is university owned. Freshman campus housing is guaranteed. *Activities and organizations:* drama/theater group, student-run newspaper, radio and television station, choral group, Entertainment To Knight, Student Senate, Campus Ministry, Symphonic Band, Wartburg Choir. *Campus security:* 24-hour emergency response devices and patrols, late-night transport/escort service, controlled dormitory access. *Student services:* health clinic, personal/psychological counseling.

Athletics Member NCAA. All Division III. *Intercollegiate sports:* baseball M, basketball M/W, cheerleading W, cross-country running M/W, football M, golf M/W, soccer M/W, softball W, tennis M/W, track and field M/W, volleyball W, wrestling M. *Intramural sports:* badminton M/W, basketball M/W, bowling M/W, golf M/W, racquetball M/W, rugby W(c), softball M/W, tennis M/W, ultimate Frisbee M/W, volleyball M/W.

Standardized Tests *Required:* SAT or ACT (for admission).

Costs (2013–14) *Tuition:* $33,400 full-time. *Required fees:* $850 full-time. *Room only:* $4150. Room and board charges vary according to board plan. *Payment plan:* installment. *Waivers:* minority students, children of alumni, and employees or children of employees.

Financial Aid Of all full-time matriculated undergraduates who enrolled in 2012, 1,509 applied for aid, 1,336 were judged to have need, 309 had their need fully met. 408 Federal Work-Study jobs (averaging $1246). 905 state and other part-time jobs (averaging $1549). In 2012, 384 non-need-based awards were made. *Average percent of need met:* 80%. *Average financial aid package:* $23,882. *Average need-based loan:* $4986. *Average need-based gift aid:* $18,984. *Average non-need-based aid:* $15,836. *Average indebtedness upon graduation:* $36,567.

Applying *Options:* electronic application, early action, deferred entrance. *Required:* high school transcript, minimum 2.0 GPA. *Required for some:* interview. *Recommended:* secondary school report. *Application deadlines:* rolling (freshmen), rolling (transfers), 12/1 (early action). *Notification:* continuous (freshmen), continuous (transfers).

Freshman Application Contact Mr. Todd Coleman, Assistant Vice President for Admissions, Wartburg College, 100 Wartburg Boulevard, PO Box 1003, Waverly, IA 50677-0903. *Phone:* 319-352-8264. *Toll-free phone:* 800-772-2085. *Fax:* 319-352-8579. *E-mail:* admissions@wartburg.edu. *Website:* http://www.wartburg.edu/.

William Penn University
Oskaloosa, Iowa

- **Independent** comprehensive, founded 1873, affiliated with Society of Friends
- **Rural** 60-acre campus with easy access to Des Moines
- **Endowment** $6.6 million
- **Coed** 1,697 undergraduate students, 97% full-time, 49% women, 51% men
- **Moderately difficult** entrance level, 54% of applicants were admitted

Undergraduates 1,648 full-time, 49 part-time. Students come from 48 states and territories; 15 other countries; 29% are from out of state; 1% Black or African American, non-Hispanic/Latino; 7% Hispanic/Latino; 1% Asian, non-Hispanic/Latino; 0.8% Native Hawaiian or other Pacific Islander, non-Hispanic/Latino; 0.6% American Indian or Alaska Native, non-Hispanic/Latino; 1% Two or more races, non-Hispanic/Latino; 5% Race/ethnicity unknown; 2% international; 42% transferred in; 40% live on campus. *Retention:* 61% of full-time freshmen returned.

Freshmen *Admission:* 841 applied, 450 admitted, 256 enrolled. *Average high school GPA:* 2.88. *Test scores:* ACT scores over 18: 69%; ACT scores over 24: 11%; ACT scores over 30: 1%.

Faculty *Total:* 50, 98% full-time, 30% with terminal degrees. *Student/faculty ratio:* 15:1.

Academics *Calendar:* semesters. *Degrees:* associate, bachelor's, and master's. *Special study options:* academic remediation for entering students, adult/continuing education programs, advanced placement credit, cooperative education, distance learning, double majors, honors programs, independent study, internships, part-time degree program, services for LD students, study abroad, summer session for credit. *Unusual degree programs:* 3-2 engineering with Iowa State University College of Engineering.

Computers on Campus 85 computers/terminals are available on campus for general student use. Students can access the following: computer help desk, free student e-mail accounts, online (class) grades, online (class) schedules. Campuswide network is available. 100% of college-owned or -operated housing units are wired for high-speed Internet access. Wireless service is available via classrooms, computer labs, libraries.

Student Life *Housing:* on-campus residence required through sophomore year. *Options:* coed, men-only, women-only. Campus housing is university owned. Freshman campus housing is guaranteed. *Activities and organizations:* drama/theater group, student-run newspaper, radio and television station, choral group, marching band, Student Government Association, Computer Club, InterVarsity/Campus Ministries, College Republicans, Education Club. *Campus security:* 24-hour emergency response devices and patrols, late-night transport/escort service, controlled dormitory access. *Student services:* health clinic, personal/psychological counseling.

Athletics Member NAIA. *Intercollegiate sports:* baseball M(s), basketball M(s)/W(s), bowling M(s)/W(s), cheerleading M(s)/W(s), cross-country running M(s)/W(s), football M(s), golf M(s)/W(s), soccer M(s)/W(s), softball W(s), track and field M(s)/W(s), volleyball W(s), wrestling M(s). *Intramural sports:* basketball M/W, football M, table tennis M/W, volleyball M/W, weight lifting M/W.

Standardized Tests *Required:* SAT or ACT (for admission).

Costs (2012–13) *Comprehensive fee:* $28,682 includes full-time tuition ($22,750), mandatory fees ($460), and room and board ($5472). Part-time tuition: $450 per credit hour. *College room only:* $2002. Room and board charges vary according to board plan and housing facility. *Payment plan:* installment. *Waivers:* senior citizens and employees or children of employees.

Financial Aid Of all full-time matriculated undergraduates who enrolled in 2005, 808 applied for aid, 768 were judged to have need, 238 had their need fully met. 511 Federal Work-Study jobs (averaging $1287). 1 state and other part-time job (averaging $1103). In 2005, 2 non-need-based awards were made. *Average percent of need met:* 82%. *Average financial aid package:* $17,782. *Average need-based loan:* $4600. *Average need-based gift aid:* $11,300. *Average non-need-based aid:* $4500. *Average indebtedness upon graduation:* $22,169.

Applying *Options:* electronic application, deferred entrance. *Application fee:* $20. *Required:* high school transcript, minimum 2.0 GPA. *Required for some:* essay or personal statement, interview. *Notification:* continuous (freshmen), continuous (out-of-state freshmen), continuous (transfers).

Freshman Application Contact Kerra Strong, Director of Admissions, William Penn University, 201 Trueblood Avenue, Oskaloosa, IA 52577-1799. *Phone:* 641-673-1012. *Toll-free phone:* 800-779-7366. *Fax:* 641-673-2113. *E-mail:* admissions@wmpenn.edu. *Website:* http://www.wmpenn.edu/.

KANSAS

The Art Institutes International–Kansas City
Lenexa, Kansas

- **Proprietary** 4-year, founded 2008, part of Education Management Corporation
- **Coed**

Academics *Degrees:* diplomas, associate, and bachelor's.

Freshman Application Contact The Art Institutes International–Kansas City, 8208 Melrose Drive, Lenexa, KS 66214. *Phone:* 913-217-4600. *Toll-free phone:* 866-530-8508. *Website:* http://www.artinstitutes.edu/kansascity/.

See full-page ad on page 54 and page 1134 for the College Close-Up.

Baker University
Baldwin City, Kansas

- **Independent United Methodist** comprehensive, founded 1858
- **Small-town** 26-acre campus with easy access to Kansas City
- **Endowment** $33.8 million
- **Coed** 936 undergraduate students, 87% full-time, 47% women, 53% men
- **Moderately difficult** entrance level, 85% of applicants were admitted

Undergraduates 818 full-time, 118 part-time. Students come from 22 states and territories; 9 other countries; 25% are from out of state; 10% Black or African American, non-Hispanic/Latino; 4% Hispanic/Latino; 1% Asian, non-Hispanic/Latino; 0.5% Native Hawaiian or other Pacific Islander, non-Hispanic/Latino; 3% American Indian or Alaska Native, non-Hispanic/Latino; 0.6% Two or more races, non-Hispanic/Latino; 5% Race/ethnicity unknown; 2% international; 6% transferred in; 74% live on campus. *Retention:* 75% of full-time freshmen returned.

Freshmen *Admission:* 775 applied, 657 admitted, 202 enrolled. *Average high school GPA:* 3.47. *Test scores:* ACT scores over 18: 95%; ACT scores over 24: 45%; ACT scores over 30: 6%.

Faculty *Total:* 98, 58% full-time, 56% with terminal degrees. *Student/faculty ratio:* 13:1.

Academics *Calendar:* 4-1-4, semesters for nursing program. *Degrees:* bachelor's, master's, and doctoral (profile includes information primarily for undergraduate residential campus in Baldwin City, KS). *Special study options:* advanced placement credit, double majors, honors programs, independent study, internships, services for LD students, student-designed majors, study abroad, summer session for credit. *ROTC:* Army (c), Air Force (c). *Unusual degree programs:* 3-2 engineering with Washington University in St. Louis, University of Kansas, University of Missouri Kansas City; forestry with Duke University.

Computers on Campus 140 computers/terminals are available on campus for general student use. Students can access the following: computer help desk, free student e-mail accounts, online (class) grades, online (class) registration, online (class) schedules. Campuswide network is available. 100% of college-owned or -operated housing units are wired for high-speed Internet access. Wireless service is available via classrooms, computer labs, libraries, student centers.

Student Life *Housing:* on-campus residence required through senior year. *Options:* coed, men-only, women-only, disabled students. Campus housing is university owned. Freshman campus housing is guaranteed. *Activities and organizations:* drama/theater group, student-run newspaper, radio and television station, choral group, Cardinal Key, Earth We Are, Mungano, Fellowship of Christian Athletes, Student Activities Council, national fraternities, national sororities. *Campus security:* 24-hour emergency response devices and patrols, student patrols, controlled dormitory access. *Student services:* health clinic, personal/psychological counseling.

Athletics Member NAIA. *Intercollegiate sports:* baseball M(s), basketball M(s)/W(s), bowling W(s), cheerleading M(s)/W(s), cross-country running M(s)/W(s), football M(s), golf M(s)/W(s), soccer M(s)/W(s), softball W(s), tennis M(s)/W(s), track and field M(s)/W(s), volleyball W(s), wrestling M(s). *Intramural sports:* basketball M/W, football M/W, softball M/W, table tennis M/W, volleyball M/W.

Standardized Tests *Required:* SAT or ACT (for admission).

Costs (2012–13) *One-time required fee:* $80. *Comprehensive fee:* $32,070 includes full-time tuition ($24,470) and room and board ($7600). Full-time tuition and fees vary according to course load, degree level, location, and program. Part-time tuition: $740 per credit hour. Part-time tuition and fees vary according to course load, degree level, location, and program. *Room and board:* Room and board charges vary according to board plan and housing facility. *Payment plan:* installment. *Waivers:* senior citizens and employees or children of employees.

Financial Aid Of all full-time matriculated undergraduates who enrolled in 2008, 839 applied for aid, 713 were judged to have need, 268 had their need fully met. In 2008, 180 non-need-based awards were made. *Average percent of need met:* 84%. *Average financial aid package:* $13,600. *Average need-based loan:* $5622. *Average need-based gift aid:* $6787. *Average non-need-based aid:* $9006. *Average indebtedness upon graduation:* $26,869.

Applying *Options:* electronic application, deferred entrance. *Required:* high school transcript, 1 letter of recommendation. *Required for some:* essay or personal statement, interview. *Application deadlines:* rolling (freshmen), rolling (transfers).

Freshman Application Contact Mr. Kevin Kropf, Director of Enrollment Management, Baker University, PO Box 65, Baldwin City, KS 66006-0065. *Phone:* 785-594-8327. *Toll-free phone:* 800-873-4282. *Fax:* 785-594-8353. *E-mail:* admissions@bakeru.edu. *Website:* http://www.bakeru.edu/.

Barclay College

Haviland, Kansas

- **Independent** comprehensive, founded 1917, affiliated with Society of Friends
- **Rural** 17-acre campus
- **Endowment** $700,000
- **Coed** 239 undergraduate students, 90% full-time, 51% women, 49% men
- **Minimally difficult** entrance level, 72% of applicants were admitted

Undergraduates 216 full-time, 23 part-time. Students come from 30 states and territories; 3 other countries; 67% are from out of state; 4% Black or African American, non-Hispanic/Latino; 6% Hispanic/Latino; 0.8% Asian, non-Hispanic/Latino; 0.4% American Indian or Alaska Native, non-Hispanic/Latino; 0.8% Two or more races, non-Hispanic/Latino; 2% international; 12% transferred in; 78% live on campus. *Retention:* 71% of full-time freshmen returned.

Freshmen *Admission:* 79 applied, 57 admitted, 40 enrolled. *Test scores:* SAT critical reading scores over 500: 20%; SAT math scores over 500: 40%; SAT writing scores over 500: 20%; ACT scores over 18: 68%; SAT critical reading scores over 600: 20%; ACT scores over 24: 9%.

Faculty *Total:* 33, 30% full-time, 33% with terminal degrees. *Student/faculty ratio:* 13:1.

Academics *Calendar:* semesters. *Degrees:* certificates, associate, bachelor's, and master's. *Special study options:* academic remediation for entering students, adult/continuing education programs, advanced placement credit, distance learning, double majors, external degree program, independent study, internships, off-campus study, part-time degree program. *Unusual degree programs:* 3-2 nursing with Pratt Community College.

Computers on Campus 28 computers/terminals are available on campus for general student use. Students can access the following: campus intranet, computer help desk, free student e-mail accounts, online (class) grades, online (class) registration, online (class) schedules. Campuswide network is available. 100% of college-owned or -operated housing units are wired for high-speed Internet access. Wireless service is available via entire campus.

Student Life *Housing:* on-campus residence required through senior year. *Options:* men-only, women-only. Campus housing is university owned. Freshman campus housing is guaranteed. *Activities and organizations:* drama/theater group, choral group, Pep Club, Drama Club, Missions Club. *Campus security:* student patrols. *Student services:* personal/psychological counseling.

Athletics *Intercollegiate sports:* basketball M/W, cheerleading M/W, soccer M, tennis M/W, volleyball W. *Intramural sports:* basketball M/W, volleyball M/W.

Standardized Tests *Required:* SAT or ACT (for admission).

Costs (2012–13) *Comprehensive fee:* $21,590 includes full-time tuition ($11,000), mandatory fees ($3590), and room and board ($7000). Part-time tuition and fees vary according to course load. *College room only:* $2800. Room and board charges vary according to board plan and housing facility. *Payment plan:* installment. *Waivers:* employees or children of employees.

Financial Aid Of all full-time matriculated undergraduates who enrolled in 2003, 163 applied for aid, 163 were judged to have need, 145 had their need fully met. 33 Federal Work-Study jobs (averaging $1200). 67 state and other part-time jobs (averaging $600). In 2003, 4 non-need-based awards were made. *Average percent of need met:* 85%. *Average financial aid package:* $6700. *Average need-based loan:* $3750. *Average need-based gift aid:* $1500. *Average non-need-based aid:* $1500. *Average indebtedness upon graduation:* $10,000.

Applying *Options:* electronic application, early admission, deferred entrance. *Application fee:* $15. *Required:* essay or personal statement, high school transcript, minimum 2.3 GPA, 2 letters of recommendation, interview. *Application deadlines:* 9/1 (freshmen), 9/1 (transfers). *Notification:* continuous (freshmen), continuous (transfers).

Freshman Application Contact Mr. Justin Kendall, Admissions Recruiter, Barclay College, 607 North Kingman, Haviland, KS 67059. *Phone:* 620-862-5252 Ext. 21. *Toll-free phone:* 800-862-0226. *Fax:* 620-862-5242. *E-mail:* jkendall@barclaycollege.edu. *Website:* http://www.barclaycollege.edu/.

Benedictine College

Atchison, Kansas

- **Independent Roman Catholic** comprehensive, founded 1859
- **Small-town** 225-acre campus with easy access to Kansas City
- **Endowment** $16.6 million
- **Coed** 2,086 undergraduate students, 83% full-time, 53% women, 47% men
- **Moderately difficult** entrance level, 61% of applicants were admitted

Undergraduates 1,735 full-time, 351 part-time. Students come from 42 states and territories; 14 other countries; 71% are from out of state; 4% Black or African American, non-Hispanic/Latino; 7% Hispanic/Latino; 0.8% Asian, non-Hispanic/Latino; 0.5% Native Hawaiian or other Pacific Islander, non-Hispanic/Latino; 0.4% American Indian or Alaska Native, non-Hispanic/Latino; 3% Two or more races, non-Hispanic/Latino; 4% Race/ethnicity unknown; 2% international; 3% transferred in; 82% live on campus. *Retention:* 78% of full-time freshmen returned.

Freshmen *Admission:* 3,347 applied, 2,042 admitted, 488 enrolled. *Average high school GPA:* 3.48. *Test scores:* ACT scores over 18: 96%; ACT scores over 24: 51%; ACT scores over 30: 11%.

Faculty *Total:* 158, 65% full-time. *Student/faculty ratio:* 16:1.

Academics *Calendar:* semesters. *Degrees:* bachelor's and master's. *Special study options:* academic remediation for entering students, advanced placement credit, cooperative education, distance learning, double majors, English as a second language, independent study, internships, off-campus study, part-time degree program, services for LD students, student-designed majors, study abroad, summer session for credit. *ROTC:* Army (c). *Unusual degree pro-*

grams: 3-2 engineering with Kansas State University, University of Missouri-Columbia, South Dakota School of Mines and Technology; occupational therapy with Washington University in St. Louis.

Computers on Campus 100 computers/terminals are available on campus for general student use. Students can access the following: computer help desk, free student e-mail accounts, online (class) grades, online (class) registration, online (class) schedules. Campuswide network is available. 100% of college-owned or -operated housing units are wired for high-speed Internet access. Wireless service is available via entire campus.

Student Life *Housing:* on-campus residence required through senior year. *Options:* men-only, women-only. Campus housing is university owned. Freshman campus housing is guaranteed. *Activities and organizations:* drama/theater group, student-run newspaper, choral group, marching band, student government, Students in Free Enterprise (SIFE), Knights of Columbus, Concert Chorale/Chamber Singers, Ravens Respect Life. *Campus security:* 24-hour emergency response devices and patrols, late-night transport/escort service, controlled dormitory access. *Student services:* health clinic, personal/psychological counseling.

Athletics Member NAIA. *Intercollegiate sports:* baseball M(s), basketball M(s)/W(s), cheerleading M(s)/W(s), cross-country running M(s)/W(s), football M(s), soccer M(s)/W(s), softball W(s), track and field M(s)/W(s), volleyball W(s), wrestling M(s). *Intramural sports:* basketball M/W, football M/W, golf M/W, lacrosse M/W, racquetball M/W, rugby M/W, soccer M/W, softball M/W, table tennis M/W, ultimate Frisbee M/W, volleyball M/W.

Standardized Tests *Required:* SAT or ACT (for admission).

Costs (2012–13) *Comprehensive fee:* $31,365 includes full-time tuition ($22,550), mandatory fees ($625), and room and board ($8190). Full-time tuition and fees vary according to course load and degree level. Part-time tuition and fees vary according to course load and degree level. *College room only:* $4540. Room and board charges vary according to board plan and housing facility. *Payment plan:* installment. *Waivers:* senior citizens and employees or children of employees.

Financial Aid Of all full-time matriculated undergraduates who enrolled in 2012, 1,436 applied for aid, 1,247 were judged to have need, 261 had their need fully met. 347 Federal Work-Study jobs (averaging $1314). In 2012, 327 non-need-based awards were made. *Average percent of need met:* 76%. *Average financial aid package:* $18,831. *Average need-based loan:* $4646. *Average need-based gift aid:* $14,222. *Average non-need-based aid:* $9688. *Average indebtedness upon graduation:* $26,980.

Applying *Options:* electronic application, deferred entrance. *Application fee:* $50. *Required:* high school transcript, minimum 2.0 GPA, 1 letter of recommendation. *Required for some:* interview. *Application deadlines:* rolling (freshmen), rolling (out-of-state freshmen), rolling (transfers). *Notification:* continuous (freshmen), continuous (transfers).

Freshman Application Contact Benedictine College, 1020 North 2nd Street, Atchison, KS 66002-1499. *Phone:* 913-367-5340 Ext. 2476. *Toll-free phone:* 800-467-5340.

Website: http://www.benedictine.edu/.

Bethany College

Lindsborg, Kansas

- **Independent Lutheran** 4-year, founded 1881
- **Small-town** 80-acre campus
- **Endowment** $23.0 million
- **Coed**
- **Moderately difficult** entrance level

Faculty *Student/faculty ratio:* 13:1.

Academics *Calendar:* 4-1-4. *Degree:* bachelor's.

Student Life *Campus security:* 24-hour emergency response devices, late-night transport/escort service, controlled dormitory access, night patrols by security personnel.

Athletics Member NAIA.

Standardized Tests *Required:* SAT or ACT (for admission).

Costs (2012–13) *Comprehensive fee:* $29,510 includes full-time tuition ($22,024), mandatory fees ($600), and room and board ($6886). Part-time tuition: $460 per credit hour. Part-time tuition and fees vary according to course load. *College room only:* $3550. Room and board charges vary according to board plan and housing facility.

Financial Aid *Of all full-time matriculated undergraduates who enrolled in 2011,* 541 applied for aid, 466 were judged to have need, 188 had their need fully met. 381 Federal Work-Study jobs (averaging $1342). *In 2011,* 1 non-need-based awards were made. *Average percent of need met:* 91. *Average*

financial aid package: $22,887. *Average need-based loan:* $7529. *Average need-based gift aid:* $6935. *Average non-need-based aid:* $4800. *Average indebtedness upon graduation:* $22,015.

Applying *Options:* electronic application, deferred entrance. *Required:* high school transcript, minimum 2.5 GPA. *Required for some:* essay or personal statement, 1 letter of recommendation, interview.

Freshman Application Contact Vicki Cornett, Assistant director of Recruitment, Bethany College, 335 East Swensson Avenue, Lindsborg, KS 67456-1895. *Phone:* 785-227-3311 Ext. 8388. *Toll-free phone:* 800-826-2281. *Fax:* 785-227-8993. *E-mail:* cornettv@bethanylb.edu.

Website: http://www.bethanylb.edu/.

Bethel College

North Newton, Kansas

- **Independent** 4-year, founded 1887, affiliated with Mennonite Church USA
- **Small-town** 60-acre campus with easy access to Wichita
- **Coed** 472 undergraduate students, 96% full-time, 55% women, 45% men
- **Moderately difficult** entrance level, 65% of applicants were admitted

Undergraduates 451 full-time, 21 part-time. 28% are from out of state; 9% Black or African American, non-Hispanic/Latino; 9% Hispanic/Latino; 1% Asian, non-Hispanic/Latino; 0.4% American Indian or Alaska Native, non-Hispanic/Latino; 2% Two or more races, non-Hispanic/Latino; 2% international; 13% transferred in; 72% live on campus. *Retention:* 62% of full-time freshmen returned.

Freshmen *Admission:* 521 applied, 338 admitted, 101 enrolled. *Average high school GPA:* 3.44. *Test scores:* SAT critical reading scores over 500: 53%; SAT math scores over 500: 53%; SAT writing scores over 500: 54%; ACT scores over 18: 92%; SAT critical reading scores over 600: 26%; SAT math scores over 600: 33%; SAT writing scores over 600: 14%; ACT scores over 24: 47%; SAT critical reading scores over 700: 13%; SAT math scores over 700: 13%; SAT writing scores over 700: 7%; ACT scores over 30: 9%.

Faculty *Total:* 58, 64% full-time, 50% with terminal degrees. *Student/faculty ratio:* 9:1.

Academics *Calendar:* 4-1-4. *Degree:* certificates and bachelor's. *Special study options:* part-time degree program. *Unusual degree programs:* 3-2 engineering with Kansas State University, University of Kansas, Wichita State University.

Computers on Campus Students can access the following: campus intranet, computer help desk, free student e-mail accounts, online (class) grades, online (class) registration, online (class) schedules. Campuswide network is available. Wireless service is available via entire campus.

Student Life *Housing:* on-campus residence required through senior year. *Options:* Campus housing is university owned. Freshman campus housing is guaranteed. *Activities and organizations:* drama/theater group, student-run newspaper, radio and television station, choral group. *Student services:* health clinic, personal/psychological counseling.

Athletics Member NAIA. *Intercollegiate sports:* basketball M(s)/W(s), cross-country running M(s)/W(s), football M(s), golf M(s)/W(s), soccer M(s)/W(s), tennis M(s)/W(s), track and field M(s)/W(s), volleyball W(s). *Intramural sports:* badminton M/W, baseball M, basketball M/W, bowling M/W, cross-country running M/W, golf M/W, soccer M/W, softball M/W, table tennis M/W, tennis M/W, ultimate Frisbee M/W, volleyball M/W.

Standardized Tests *Required:* SAT or ACT (for admission).

Costs (2013–14) *One-time required fee:* $200. *Comprehensive fee:* $31,480 includes full-time tuition ($23,500) and room and board ($7980). *College room only:* $4310.

Financial Aid Of all full-time matriculated undergraduates who enrolled in 2011, 442 applied for aid, 419 were judged to have need, 172 had their need fully met. In 2011, 69 non-need-based awards were made. *Average percent of need met:* 92%. *Average financial aid package:* $22,638. *Average need-based loan:* $8088. *Average need-based gift aid:* $5065. *Average non-need-based aid:* $8984. *Average indebtedness upon graduation:* $20,356.

Applying *Options:* deferred entrance. *Application fee:* $20. *Required:* high school transcript, minimum 2.5 GPA. *Required for some:* essay or personal statement, 2 letters of recommendation. *Recommended:* interview. *Application deadlines:* rolling (freshmen), rolling (transfers). *Notification:* continuous (freshmen), continuous (transfers).

Freshman Application Contact Mr. Todd H. Moore, Vice President for Admissions, Bethel College, 300 East 27th Street, North Newton, KS 67117-0531. *Phone:* 316-284-5230. *Toll-free phone:* 800-522-1887 Ext. 230. *Fax:* 316-284-5870. *E-mail:* admissions@bethelks.edu.

Website: http://www.bethelks.edu/.

Brown Mackie College–Kansas City

Lenexa, Kansas

Freshman Application Contact Brown Mackie College–Kansas City, 9705 Lenexa Drive, Lenexa, KS 66215. *Phone:* 913-768-1900. *Toll-free phone:* 800-635-9101.
Website: http://www.brownmackie.edu/kansascity/.

See below for display ad and page 1188 for the College Close-Up.

Brown Mackie College–Salina

Salina, Kansas

Freshman Application Contact Brown Mackie College–Salina, 2106 South 9th Street, Salina, KS 67401-2810. *Phone:* 785-825-5422. *Toll-free phone:* 800-365-0433.
Website: http://www.brownmackie.edu/salina/.

See below for display ad and page 1206 for the College Close-Up.

Central Christian College of Kansas

McPherson, Kansas

Freshman Application Contact Central Christian College of Kansas, 1200 South Main, PO Box 1403, McPherson, KS 67460-5799. *Phone:* 620-241-0723 Ext. 380. *Toll-free phone:* 800-835-0078.
Website: http://www.centralchristian.edu/.

Cleveland Chiropractic College–Kansas City Campus

Overland Park, Kansas

- **Independent** comprehensive, founded 1922
- **Suburban** 34-acre campus with easy access to Kansas City
- **Coed** 79 undergraduate students, 94% full-time, 34% women, 66% men
- **Noncompetitive** entrance level, 100% of applicants were admitted

Undergraduates 74 full-time, 5 part-time. Students come from 10 states and territories; 1 other country; 47% are from out of state; 5% Hispanic/Latino; 3% Asian, non-Hispanic/Latino; 3% American Indian or Alaska Native, non-Hispanic/Latino; 1% Two or more races, non-Hispanic/Latino; 15% Race/ethnicity unknown; 1% international; 41% transferred in. *Retention:* 50% of full-time freshmen returned.
Freshmen *Admission:* 1 applied, 1 admitted, 1 enrolled. *Test scores:* ACT scores over 18: 100%; ACT scores over 24: 100%.
Faculty *Total:* 53, 81% full-time, 89% with terminal degrees. *Student/faculty ratio:* 11:1.
Academics *Calendar:* trimesters. *Degrees:* associate, bachelor's, and doctoral. *Special study options:* academic remediation for entering students, accelerated degree program, advanced placement credit, cooperative education, internships, services for LD students, summer session for credit.
Computers on Campus 30 computers/terminals are available on campus for general student use. Students can access the following: computer help desk, free student e-mail accounts, online (class) grades, online (class) schedules, educational software. Campuswide network is available. Wireless service is available via entire campus.
Student Life *Housing:* college housing not available. *Campus security:* 24-hour patrols. *Student services:* health clinic, personal/psychological counseling.
Standardized Tests *Required for some:* SAT or ACT (for admission).
Costs (2013–14) *Tuition:* $7000 full-time. Full-time tuition and fees vary according to course load and program. Part-time tuition and fees vary according to course load and program. *Required fees:* $440 full-time. *Payment plan:* installment.
Applying *Options:* electronic application, deferred entrance. *Application fee:* $50. *Required:* high school transcript, minimum 2.5 GPA. *Required for some:*

interview. *Application deadlines:* rolling (freshmen), rolling (out-of-state freshmen), rolling (transfers). *Notification:* continuous (freshmen), continuous (out-of-state freshmen), continuous (transfers).
Freshman Application Contact Ms. Melissa Denton, Director of Admissions, Cleveland Chiropractic College–Kansas City Campus, 10850 Lowell Avenue, Overland Park, KS 66210. *Phone:* 913-234-0750. *Toll-free phone:* 800-467-2252. *Fax:* 913-234-0906. *E-mail:* kc.admissions@cleveland.edu. *Website:* http://www.cleveland.edu/.

Donnelly College

Kansas City, Kansas

Freshman Application Contact Mr. Edward Marquez, Director of Admissions, Donnelly College, 608 North 18th Street, Kansas City, KS 66102. *Phone:* 913-621-8713. *Fax:* 913-621-8719. *E-mail:* admissions@donnelly.edu.
Website: http://www.donnelly.edu/.

Emporia State University

Emporia, Kansas

- **State-supported** comprehensive, founded 1863, part of Kansas State Board of Regents
- **Small-town** 207-acre campus with easy access to Wichita
- **Endowment** $59.6 million
- **Coed** 3,773 undergraduate students, 89% full-time, 60% women, 40% men
- **Noncompetitive** entrance level, 72% of applicants were admitted

Undergraduates 3,343 full-time, 430 part-time. Students come from 31 states and territories; 19 other countries; 9% are from out of state; 6% Black or African American, non-Hispanic/Latino; 6% Hispanic/Latino; 0.9% Asian, non-Hispanic/Latino; 0.2% Native Hawaiian or other Pacific Islander, non-Hispanic/Latino; 0.4% American Indian or Alaska Native, non-Hispanic/Latino; 5% Two or more races, non-Hispanic/Latino; 2% Race/ethnicity unknown; 7% international; 12% transferred in; 6% live on campus. *Retention:* 70% of full-time freshmen returned.
Freshmen *Admission:* 1,753 applied, 1,268 admitted, 621 enrolled. *Average high school GPA:* 3.33. *Test scores:* SAT critical reading scores over 500: 57%; SAT math scores over 500: 64%; ACT scores over 18: 90%; SAT critical reading scores over 600: 43%; SAT math scores over 600: 28%; ACT scores over 24: 55%; SAT critical reading scores over 700: 14%; SAT math scores over 700: 7%; ACT scores over 30: 4%.
Faculty *Total:* 296, 88% full-time, 73% with terminal degrees. *Student/faculty ratio:* 16:1.
Academics *Calendar:* semesters. *Degrees:* bachelor's, master's, doctoral, post-master's, and postbachelor's certificates. *Special study options:* academic remediation for entering students, accelerated degree program, adult/continuing education programs, advanced placement credit, cooperative education, distance learning, double majors, English as a second language, honors programs, independent study, internships, off-campus study, part-time degree program, services for LD students, study abroad, summer session for credit. *Unusual degree programs:* 3-2 engineering with Kansas State University, University of Kansas, Wichita State University.
Computers on Campus 410 computers/terminals are available on campus for general student use. Students can access the following: campus intranet, computer help desk, free student e-mail accounts, online (class) grades, online (class) registration, online (class) schedules. Campuswide network is available. 100% of college-owned or -operated housing units are wired for high-speed Internet access. Wireless service is available via classrooms, computer centers, computer labs, libraries.
Student Life *Housing:* on-campus residence required for freshman year. *Options:* coed, men-only, women-only, disabled students. Campus housing is university owned. Freshman campus housing is guaranteed. *Activities and organizations:* drama/theater group, student-run newspaper, radio station, choral group, marching band, Union Activities Council, Associated Student Government, Black Student Union, national fraternities, national sororities. *Campus security:* 24-hour emergency response devices and patrols, student patrols, late-night transport/escort service, controlled dormitory access, 24-hour residence hall monitoring, safety and self-awareness programs. *Student services:* health clinic, personal/psychological counseling, women's center, legal services.
Athletics Member NCAA. All Division II. *Intercollegiate sports:* baseball M(s), basketball M(s)/W(s), cheerleading M(s)/W(s), cross-country running M(s)/W(s), football M(s), soccer W(s), softball W(s), tennis M(s)/W(s), track

and field M(s)/W(s), volleyball W(s). *Intramural sports:* badminton M/W, basketball M/W, fencing M(c)/W(c), football M/W, rugby M(c), soccer M(c)/W(c), softball M/W, table tennis M/W, tennis M/W, volleyball M/W.
Standardized Tests *Required:* SAT or ACT (for admission).
Costs (2012–13) *Tuition:* state resident $4102 full-time, $137 per credit hour part-time; nonresident $15,156 full-time, $505 per credit hour part-time. Full-time tuition and fees vary according to course load, degree level, and location. Part-time tuition and fees vary according to course load, degree level, and location. *Required fees:* $1170 full-time, $70 per credit hour part-time, $70 per credit hour part-time. *Room and board:* $6629; room only: $3438. Room and board charges vary according to board plan, housing facility, and location. *Payment plans:* installment, deferred payment. *Waivers:* senior citizens and employees or children of employees.
Financial Aid Of all full-time matriculated undergraduates who enrolled in 2012, 2,603 applied for aid, 2,127 were judged to have need, 296 had their need fully met. 241 Federal Work-Study jobs (averaging $1933). 11 state and other part-time jobs (averaging $1682). In 2012, 416 non-need-based awards were made. *Average percent of need met:* 65%. *Average financial aid package:* $6600. *Average need-based loan:* $6481. *Average need-based gift aid:* $5215. *Average non-need-based aid:* $1647. *Average indebtedness upon graduation:* $23,538.
Applying *Options:* electronic application, early admission, deferred entrance. *Application fee:* $30. *Required:* high school transcript. *Recommended:* minimum 2.0 GPA. *Application deadlines:* rolling (freshmen), rolling (out-of-state freshmen), rolling (transfers). *Notification:* continuous (freshmen), continuous (out-of-state freshmen), continuous (transfers).
Freshman Application Contact Ms. Laura Eddy, Director of Admissions, Emporia State University, 1200 Commercial Street, Campus Box 4034, Emporia, KS 66801-5087. *Phone:* 620-341-5465. *Toll-free phone:* 877-GOTOESU (in-state); 877-468-6378 (out-of-state). *Fax:* 620-341-5599. *E-mail:* go2esu@emporia.edu.
Website: http://www.emporia.edu/.

Fort Hays State University

Hays, Kansas

- **State-supported** comprehensive, founded 1902
- **Small-town** 200-acre campus
- **Coed**
- **Noncompetitive** entrance level

Faculty *Student/faculty ratio:* 18:1.
Academics *Calendar:* semesters. *Degrees:* certificates, associate, bachelor's, master's, and post-master's certificates.
Student Life *Campus security:* 24-hour emergency response devices and patrols.
Standardized Tests *Required:* SAT or ACT (for admission).
Financial Aid *Of all full-time matriculated undergraduates who enrolled in 2007, 3,244 applied for aid, 2,653 were judged to have need, 483 had their need fully met. In 2007, 1162 non-need-based awards were made. Average percent of need met: 62. Average financial aid package: $5955. Average need-based loan: $3634. Average need-based gift aid: $3390. Average non-need-based aid: $3358. Average indebtedness upon graduation: $15,601.*
Applying *Application fee:* $35. *Required:* high school transcript.
Freshman Application Contact Tricia Cline, Director, Admissions, Fort Hays State University, 600 Park Street, Hays, KS 67601-4099. *Phone:* 785-628-4091. *Toll-free phone:* 800-628-FHSU. *E-mail:* tcline@fhsu.edu.
Website: http://www.fhsu.edu/.

Friends University

Wichita, Kansas

- **Independent** comprehensive, founded 1898, affiliated with Christian non-denominational
- **Urban** 55-acre campus
- **Endowment** $40.1 million
- **Coed** 1,769 undergraduate students, 81% full-time, 56% women, 44% men
- **Moderately difficult** entrance level, 58% of applicants were admitted

Undergraduates 1,428 full-time, 341 part-time. Students come from 18 states and territories; 11 other countries; 19% are from out of state; 11% Black or African American, non-Hispanic/Latino; 4% Hispanic/Latino; 3% Asian, non-Hispanic/Latino; 0.3% Native Hawaiian or other Pacific Islander, non-Hispanic/Latino; 2% American Indian or Alaska Native, non-Hispanic/Latino; 5% Two or more races, non-Hispanic/Latino; 4% Race/ethnicity unknown; 6%

transferred in; 46% live on campus. *Retention:* 60% of full-time freshmen returned.

Freshmen *Admission:* 786 applied, 456 admitted, 196 enrolled. *Average high school GPA:* 3.38. *Test scores:* SAT critical reading scores over 500: 33%; SAT math scores over 500: 38%; ACT scores over 18: 81%; SAT critical reading scores over 600: 13%; SAT math scores over 600: 13%; ACT scores over 24: 37%; ACT scores over 30: 4%.

Faculty *Total:* 206, 36% full-time. *Student/faculty ratio:* 11:1.

Academics *Calendar:* semesters. *Degrees:* associate, bachelor's, master's, and postbachelor's certificates. *Special study options:* academic remediation for entering students, accelerated degree program, adult/continuing education programs, advanced placement credit, cooperative education, distance learning, double majors, honors programs, independent study, internships, off-campus study, part-time degree program, services for LD students, student-designed majors, study abroad, summer session for credit.

Computers on Campus 360 computers/terminals are available on campus for general student use. Students can access the following: campus intranet, computer help desk, free student e-mail accounts, online (class) grades, online (class) registration, online (class) schedules. Campuswide network is available. 90% of college-owned or -operated housing units are wired for high-speed Internet access. Wireless service is available via entire campus.

Student Life *Housing options:* coed. Campus housing is university owned. *Activities and organizations:* drama/theater group, student-run newspaper, choral group, Concert Choir, Singing Quakers, Zoo Science Club, Psychology Club, Spanish Club. *Campus security:* 24-hour patrols, late-night transport/escort service, controlled dormitory access. *Student services:* health clinic, personal/psychological counseling.

Athletics Member NAIA. *Intercollegiate sports:* baseball M(s), basketball M(s)/W(s), cheerleading M(s)/W(s), cross-country running M(s)/W(s), football M(s), golf M(s), soccer M(s)/W(s), softball W(s), tennis M(s)/W(s), track and field M(s)/W(s), volleyball W(s). *Intramural sports:* basketball M/W, football M/W, racquetball M/W, soccer M/W, table tennis M/W, tennis M/W, ultimate Frisbee M/W, volleyball M/W.

Standardized Tests *Required for some:* SAT or ACT (for admission). *Recommended:* ACT (for admission), SAT and SAT Subject Tests or ACT (for admission).

Costs (2012–13) *Comprehensive fee:* $29,100 includes full-time tuition ($22,320), mandatory fees ($180), and room and board ($6600). Full-time tuition and fees vary according to course load and degree level. Part-time tuition: $738 per credit hour. Part-time tuition and fees vary according to course load and degree level. *Required fees:* $6 per credit hour part-time. *College room only:* $3200. Room and board charges vary according to board plan and housing facility. *Payment plan:* installment. *Waivers:* senior citizens and employees or children of employees.

Financial Aid Of all full-time matriculated undergraduates who enrolled in 2006, 1,290 applied for aid, 1,160 were judged to have need, 279 had their need fully met. 239 Federal Work-Study jobs (averaging $1221). 185 state and other part-time jobs (averaging $1608). In 2006, 227 non-need-based awards were made. *Average percent of need met:* 66%. *Average financial aid package:* $11,219. *Average need-based loan:* $4098. *Average need-based gift aid:* $7092. *Average non-need-based aid:* $7792. *Average indebtedness upon graduation:* $17,750.

Applying *Options:* electronic application. *Application fee:* $35. *Required:* High school transcripts are not required for adult students enrolling in degree completion programs. Auditions are required for music, dance and theater programs. Portfolios are required for art program. Admission for traditional undergraduate students is based on student's hs GPA x ACT score. *Required for some:* high school transcript, interview. *Application deadlines:* rolling (freshmen), rolling (out-of-state freshmen), rolling (transfers). *Notification:* continuous (freshmen), continuous (out-of-state freshmen), continuous (transfers).

Freshman Application Contact Mr. Jim Allen, Director of CBASE Admissions, Friends University, 2100 West University Avenue, Wichita, KS 67213. *Phone:* 316-295-5100. *Toll-free phone:* 800-794-6945. *Fax:* 316-295-5101. *E-mail:* learn@friends.edu. *Website:* http://www.friends.edu/.

Haskell Indian Nations University

Lawrence, Kansas

Freshman Application Contact Ms. Patty Grant, Recruitment Officer, Haskell Indian Nations University, 155 Indian Avenue, #5031, Lawrence, KS 66046-4800. *Phone:* 785-749-8437 Ext. 437. *Website:* http://www.haskell.edu/.

ITT Technical Institute

Overland Park, Kansas

- **Proprietary** 4-year
- **Coed**
- **Minimally difficult** entrance level

Academics *Degrees:* associate and bachelor's.

Freshman Application Contact Director of Recruitment, ITT Technical Institute, 7600 West 119th Street, Suite 100, Overland Park, KS 66213. *Phone:* 913-253-1300. *Toll-free phone:* 877-327-9026. *Website:* http://www.itt-tech.edu/.

ITT Technical Institute

Wichita, Kansas

- **Proprietary** 4-year, part of ITT Educational Services, Inc.
- **Coed**
- **Minimally difficult** entrance level

Academics *Calendar:* quarters. *Degrees:* associate and bachelor's.

Freshman Application Contact Director of Recruitment, ITT Technical Institute, 8111 E. 32nd Street North, Suite 103, Wichita, KS 67226. *Phone:* 316-609-4100. *Toll-free phone:* 877-207-1047. *Website:* http://www.itt-tech.edu/.

Kansas State University

Manhattan, Kansas

- **State-supported** university, founded 1863, part of Kansas Board of Regents
- **Suburban** 668-acre campus
- **Endowment** $329.2 million
- **Coed** 19,853 undergraduate students, 90% full-time, 48% women, 52% men
- **Noncompetitive** entrance level, 99% of applicants were admitted

Undergraduates 17,798 full-time, 2,055 part-time. Students come from 52 states and territories; 79 other countries; 16% are from out of state; 4% Black or African American, non-Hispanic/Latino; 6% Hispanic/Latino; 1% Asian, non-Hispanic/Latino; 0.1% Native Hawaiian or other Pacific Islander, non-Hispanic/Latino; 0.4% American Indian or Alaska Native, non-Hispanic/Latino; 3% Two or more races, non-Hispanic/Latino; 2% Race/ethnicity unknown; 6% international; 8% transferred in. *Retention:* 80% of full-time freshmen returned.

Freshmen *Admission:* 9,273 applied, 9,180 admitted, 3,874 enrolled. *Average high school GPA:* 3.45. *Test scores:* ACT scores over 18: 95%; ACT scores over 24: 57%; ACT scores over 30: 13%.

Faculty *Total:* 1,203, 83% full-time, 79% with terminal degrees. *Student/faculty ratio:* 20:1.

Academics *Calendar:* semesters. *Degrees:* certificates, associate, bachelor's, master's, doctoral, and postbachelor's certificates. *Special study options:* academic remediation for entering students, accelerated degree program, adult/continuing education programs, advanced placement credit, cooperative education, distance learning, double majors, English as a second language, freshman honors college, honors programs, independent study, internships, off-campus study, part-time degree program, services for LD students, study abroad, summer session for credit. *ROTC:* Army (b), Air Force (b). *Unusual degree programs:* 3-2 engineering; biology, kinesiology, horticulture, master of public health, biochemistry.

Computers on Campus Students can access the following: computer help desk, free student e-mail accounts, online (class) grades, online (class) registration, online (class) schedules. Campuswide network is available. Wireless service is available via entire campus.

Student Life *Housing options:* coed, men-only, women-only, cooperative. Campus housing is university owned. *Activities and organizations:* drama/theater group, student-run newspaper, radio and television station, choral group, marching band, athletic department groups, marching band, Union Governing Board, theater productions, debate team, national fraternities, national sororities. *Campus security:* 24-hour emergency response devices and patrols, late-night transport/escort service, controlled dormitory access. *Student services:* health clinic, personal/psychological counseling, women's center, legal services.

Athletics Member NCAA. All Division I except football (Division I-A). *Intercollegiate sports:* baseball M(s), basketball M(s)/W(s), crew W(s), cross-country running M(s)/W(s), golf M(s)/W(s), tennis W(s), track and field M(s)/W(s), volleyball W(s). *Intramural sports:* badminton M/W, basketball M/W, bowling M/W, crew M/W, cross-country running M/W, football M/W, golf M/W, ice hockey M, lacrosse M, racquetball M/W, soccer M/W, softball M/W, table tennis M/W, tennis M/W, track and field M/W, volleyball M/W, water polo M/W, weight lifting M/W, wrestling M.

Standardized Tests *Required for some:* SAT or ACT (for admission). *Recommended:* SAT or ACT (for admission).

Costs (2012–13) *Tuition:* state resident $7317 full-time; nonresident $19,416 full-time. Full-time tuition and fees vary according to course load, degree level, location, program, and reciprocity agreements. Part-time tuition and fees vary according to course load, degree level, location, program, and reciprocity agreements. *Required fees:* $730 full-time. *Room and board:* $7450. Room and board charges vary according to board plan, housing facility, and location. *Payment plans:* installment, deferred payment. *Waivers:* employees or children of employees.

Financial Aid Of all full-time matriculated undergraduates who enrolled in 2011, 11,815 applied for aid, 9,128 were judged to have need, 1,603 had their need fully met. In 2011, 1091 non-need-based awards were made. *Average percent of need met:* 81%. *Average financial aid package:* $11,182. *Average need-based loan:* $4188. *Average need-based gift aid:* $4143. *Average non-need-based aid:* $3497. *Average indebtedness upon graduation:* $25,147.

Applying *Options:* electronic application, early admission. *Application fee:* $30. *Required:* high school transcript, minimum 2.0 GPA. *Application deadlines:* rolling (freshmen), rolling (out-of-state freshmen), rolling (transfers). *Notification:* continuous (freshmen), continuous (out-of-state freshmen), continuous (transfers).

Freshman Application Contact Ms. Molly McGaughey, Associate Director of Admissions, Kansas State University, 119 Anderson Hall, Manhattan, KS 66506. *Phone:* 785-532-6250. *Toll-free phone:* 800-432-8270. *Fax:* 785-532-6393. *E-mail:* k-state@k-state.edu.
Website: http://www.k-state.edu/.

Kansas Wesleyan University

Salina, Kansas

- **Independent United Methodist** comprehensive, founded 1886
- **Urban** 28-acre campus
- **Endowment** $19.8 million
- **Coed** 711 undergraduate students, 90% full-time, 58% women, 42% men
- **Moderately difficult** entrance level, 48% of applicants were admitted

Undergraduates 637 full-time, 74 part-time. Students come from 19 states and territories; 15 other countries; 37% are from out of state; 7% Black or African American, non-Hispanic/Latino; 10% Hispanic/Latino; 0.7% Asian, non-Hispanic/Latino; 0.6% Native Hawaiian or other Pacific Islander, non-Hispanic/Latino; 1% American Indian or Alaska Native, non-Hispanic/Latino; 0.6% Two or more races, non-Hispanic/Latino; 3% international; 12% transferred in; 57% live on campus. *Retention:* 48% of full-time freshmen returned.

Freshmen *Admission:* 728 applied, 349 admitted, 139 enrolled. *Average high school GPA:* 3.46. *Test scores:* ACT scores over 18: 97%; ACT scores over 24: 31%; ACT scores over 30: 1%.

Faculty *Total:* 80, 54% full-time, 34% with terminal degrees. *Student/faculty ratio:* 13:1.

Academics *Calendar:* 2 semesters with a summer term. *Degrees:* associate, bachelor's, and master's. *Special study options:* academic remediation for entering students, adult/continuing education programs, advanced placement credit, distance learning, double majors, English as a second language, honors programs, independent study, internships, off-campus study, part-time degree program, student-designed majors, study abroad, summer session for credit.

Computers on Campus 130 computers/terminals are available on campus for general student use. Students can access the following: campus intranet, free student e-mail accounts, online (class) grades, online (class) schedules. Campuswide network is available. 100% of college-owned or -operated housing units are wired for high-speed Internet access. Wireless service is available via classrooms, dorm rooms, learning centers, libraries, student centers.

Student Life *Housing:* on-campus residence required through sophomore year. *Options:* coed, men-only, women-only. Campus housing is university owned. Freshman campus housing is guaranteed. *Activities and organizations:* drama/theater group, student-run newspaper, choral group, Fellowship of Christian Athletes, Student government, Wesleyan Chorale, Multicultural Student Association, Business Club. *Campus security:* 24-hour emergency response devices, student patrols, late-night transport/escort service, controlled dormi-

tory access, evening patrols by security. *Student services:* personal/psychological counseling.

Athletics Member NAIA. *Intercollegiate sports:* baseball M(s), basketball M(s)/W(s), cheerleading M(s)/W(s), cross-country running M(s)/W(s), football M(s), golf M(s)/W(s), soccer M(s)/W(s), softball W(s), tennis M(s)/W(s), track and field M(s)/W(s), volleyball W(s). *Intramural sports:* basketball M/W, bowling M/W, fencing M/W, football W, golf M/W, racquetball M/W, softball M/W, table tennis M/W, volleyball M/W, weight lifting M/W.

Standardized Tests *Required:* SAT or ACT (for admission).

Costs (2013–14) *One-time required fee:* $100. *Comprehensive fee:* $31,400 includes full-time tuition ($23,800) and room and board ($7600). Part-time tuition and fees vary according to course load. *College room only:* $2600. Room and board charges vary according to housing facility. *Payment plan:* installment. *Waivers:* children of alumni, senior citizens, and employees or children of employees.

Financial Aid Of all full-time matriculated undergraduates who enrolled in 2001, 497 applied for aid, 452 were judged to have need, 429 had their need fully met. 100 Federal Work-Study jobs (averaging $790). 62 state and other part-time jobs (averaging $790). In 2001, 45 non-need-based awards were made. *Average percent of need met:* 95%. *Average financial aid package:* $15,495. *Average need-based loan:* $3739. *Average need-based gift aid:* $4346. *Average non-need-based aid:* $6553.

Applying *Options:* electronic application, deferred entrance. *Application fee:* $20. *Required:* high school transcript, minimum 2.5 GPA. *Application deadlines:* rolling (freshmen), rolling (transfers). *Notification:* continuous (freshmen), continuous (transfers).

Freshman Application Contact Kansas Wesleyan University, 100 East Claflin Avenue, Salina, KS 67401-6196. *Phone:* 785-827-5541 Ext. 1285. *Toll-free phone:* 800-874-1154 Ext. 1285.
Website: http://www.kwu.edu/.

Manhattan Christian College

Manhattan, Kansas

Director of Admissions Eric Ingmire, Director of Admissions, Manhattan Christian College, 1415 Anderson Avenue, Manhattan, KS 66502-4081. *Phone:* 785-539-3571 Ext. 324. *Toll-free phone:* 877-246-4622. *E-mail:* admit@mccks.edu.
Website: http://www.mccks.edu/.

McPherson College

McPherson, Kansas

- **Independent** 4-year, founded 1887, affiliated with Church of the Brethren
- **Small-town** 26-acre campus
- **Coed**
- **Moderately difficult** entrance level

Faculty *Student/faculty ratio:* 13:1.

Academics *Calendar:* 4-1-4. *Degree:* bachelor's.

Student Life *Campus security:* student patrols, controlled dormitory access.

Athletics Member NAIA.

Standardized Tests *Required:* SAT or ACT (for admission).

Costs (2012–13) *Comprehensive fee:* $29,565 includes full-time tuition ($21,801) and room and board ($7764). Full-time tuition and fees vary according to course load and program. *College room only:* $3206.

Financial Aid Of all full-time matriculated undergraduates who enrolled in 2011, 547 applied for aid, 495 were judged to have need, 114 had their need fully met. 300 Federal Work-Study jobs (averaging $978). In 2011, 85 non-need-based awards were made. *Average percent of need met:* 83. *Average financial aid package:* $21,302. *Average need-based loan:* $8194. *Average need-based gift aid:* $6328. *Average non-need-based aid:* $8097. *Average indebtedness upon graduation:* $27,529.

Applying *Options:* electronic application, deferred entrance. *Application fee:* $25. *Required:* high school transcript, minimum 2.0 GPA.

Freshman Application Contact Mr. Matt Pfannenstiel, Director of Admissions, McPherson College, 1600 East Euclid, McPherson, KS 67460. *Phone:* 800-365-7402. *Toll-free phone:* 800-365-7402. *E-mail:* admiss@mcpherson.edu.
Website: http://www.mcpherson.edu/.

MidAmerica Nazarene University

Olathe, Kansas

- **Independent** comprehensive, founded 1966, affiliated with Church of the Nazarene
- **Suburban** 105-acre campus with easy access to Kansas City
- **Coed**
- **Moderately difficult** entrance level

Faculty *Student/faculty ratio:* 10:1.

Academics *Calendar:* semesters. *Degrees:* associate, bachelor's, master's, post-master's, and postbachelor's certificates.

Student Life *Campus security:* 24-hour emergency response devices and patrols, student patrols, late-night transport/escort service, controlled dormitory access.

Athletics Member NAIA.

Standardized Tests *Required:* SAT or ACT (for admission).

Costs (2012–13) *Comprehensive fee:* $28,500 includes full-time tuition ($20,500), mandatory fees ($1000), and room and board ($7000). Full-time tuition and fees vary according to course load. Part-time tuition: $700 per credit hour. Part-time tuition and fees vary according to course load. *Required fees:* $250 per term part-time. *Room and board:* Room and board charges vary according to board plan and housing facility.

Financial Aid *Of all full-time matriculated undergraduates who enrolled in 2008,* 796 applied for aid, 692 were judged to have need, 97 had their need fully met. *In 2008,* 187 non-need-based awards were made. *Average percent of need met:* 65. *Average financial aid package:* $13,686. *Average need-based loan:* $5638. *Average need-based gift aid:* $8989. *Average non-need-based aid:* $4891. *Average indebtedness upon graduation:* $28,859.

Applying *Options:* electronic application, deferred entrance. *Application fee:* $25. *Required:* high school transcript, minimum 2.0 GPA. *Recommended:* TOEFL recommended.

Freshman Application Contact Mr. Dennis Miller, Associate Director of Admissions, MidAmerica Nazarene University, 2030 East College Way, Olathe, KS 66062-1899. *Phone:* 913-971-3380. *Toll-free phone:* 800-800-8887. *Fax:* 913-971-3481. *E-mail:* admissions@mnu.edu. *Website:* http://www.mnu.edu/.

See below for display ad and page 1388 for the College Close-Up.

Newman University

Wichita, Kansas

- **Independent Roman Catholic** comprehensive, founded 1933
- **Urban** 61-acre campus
- **Endowment** $19.5 million
- **Coed** 2,384 undergraduate students, 48% full-time, 63% women, 37% men
- **Minimally difficult** entrance level, 44% of applicants were admitted

Undergraduates 1,149 full-time, 1,235 part-time. Students come from 22 states and territories; 25 other countries; 12% are from out of state; 6% Black or African American, non-Hispanic/Latino; 11% Hispanic/Latino; 4% Asian, non-Hispanic/Latino; 0.1% Native Hawaiian or other Pacific Islander, non-Hispanic/Latino; 1% American Indian or Alaska Native, non-Hispanic/Latino; 3% Two or more races, non-Hispanic/Latino; 0.4% Race/ethnicity unknown; 5% international; 11% transferred in; 14% live on campus. *Retention:* 69% of full-time freshmen returned.

Freshmen *Admission:* 2,454 applied, 1,088 admitted, 192 enrolled. *Average high school GPA:* 3.64. *Test scores:* SAT critical reading scores over 500: 67%; SAT math scores over 500: 88%; SAT writing scores over 500: 50%; ACT scores over 18: 99%; SAT critical reading scores over 600: 25%; SAT math scores over 600: 75%; SAT writing scores over 600: 17%; ACT scores over 24: 55%; SAT critical reading scores over 700: 17%; SAT math scores over 700: 13%; ACT scores over 30: 20%.

Faculty *Total:* 233, 38% full-time, 31% with terminal degrees. *Student/faculty ratio:* 13:1.

Academics *Calendar:* semesters. *Degrees:* associate, bachelor's, and master's. *Special study options:* academic remediation for entering students, accelerated degree program, adult/continuing education programs, advanced placement credit, cooperative education, distance learning, double majors, honors programs, independent study, internships, off-campus study, part-time degree program, services for LD students, student-designed majors, study abroad, summer session for credit. *Unusual degree programs:* 3-2 Occupational therapy with Washington University in St. Louis.

Computers on Campus 90 computers/terminals and 300 ports are available on campus for general student use. Students can access the following: computer help desk, free student e-mail accounts, online (class) grades, online (class) registration, online (class) schedules. Campuswide network is available.

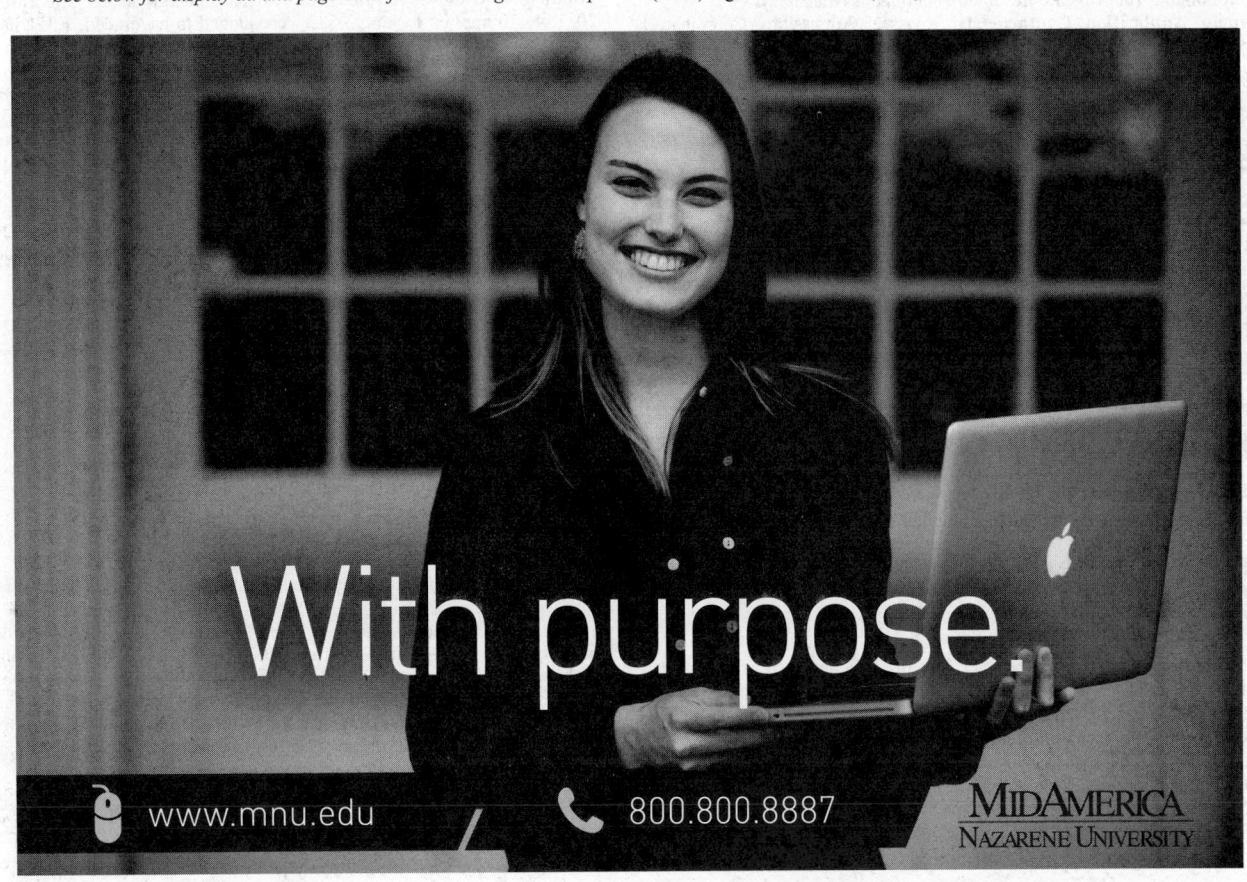

100% of college-owned or -operated housing units are wired for high-speed Internet access. Wireless service is available via classrooms, computer centers, computer labs, dorm rooms, learning centers, libraries, student centers. **Student Life** *Housing:* on-campus residence required through sophomore year. *Options:* coed, men-only, women-only, cooperative, disabled students. Campus housing is university owned. Freshman campus housing is guaranteed. *Activities and organizations:* drama/theater group, student-run newspaper, choral group, Newman University Medical Professionals Club (NUMPC), Hispanic American Leadership Organization (HALO), Chemistry Club, Math Club, Art Club. *Campus security:* 24-hour emergency response devices and patrols, student patrols, late-night transport/escort service, controlled dormitory access. *Student services:* personal/psychological counseling.
Athletics Member NCAA. All Division II. *Intercollegiate sports:* baseball M(s)/W, basketball M(s)/W(s), bowling M(s)(c)/W(s)(c), cross-country running M(s)/W(s), golf M(s)/W(s), soccer M(s)/W(s), softball W(s), tennis M(s)/W(s), volleyball W(s), wrestling M(s). *Intramural sports:* baseball M, basketball M/W, bowling M/W, football M/W, golf M/W, soccer M/W, softball M/W, table tennis M/W, volleyball M/W, weight lifting M/W.
Standardized Tests *Required for some:* SAT or ACT (for admission).
Costs (2012–13) *Comprehensive fee:* $28,688 includes full-time tuition ($21,388), mandatory fees ($910), and room and board ($6390). Full-time tuition and fees vary according to class time, course load, location, and program. Part-time tuition: $713 per credit hour. Part-time tuition and fees vary according to class time, course load, location, and program. *Required fees:* $15 per credit hour part-time. *College room only:* $3200. Room and board charges vary according to board plan and housing facility. *Payment plan:* installment. *Waivers:* employees or children of employees.
Financial Aid Of all full-time matriculated undergraduates who enrolled in 2009, 1,074 applied for aid, 919 were judged to have need, 146 had their need fully met. 66 Federal Work-Study jobs (averaging $1037). 80 state and other part-time jobs (averaging $994). In 2009, 43 non-need-based awards were made. *Average percent of need met:* 62%. *Average financial aid package:* $14,370. *Average need-based loan:* $4065. *Average need-based gift aid:* $4869. *Average non-need-based aid:* $5673. *Average indebtedness upon graduation:* $23,996.
Applying *Options:* electronic application, early admission, deferred entrance. *Application fee:* $20. *Required:* high school transcript, minimum 2.0 GPA. *Recommended:* interview. *Application deadlines:* rolling (freshmen), rolling (out-of-state freshmen), rolling (transfers). *Notification:* continuous (freshmen), continuous (out-of-state freshmen), continuous (transfers).
Freshman Application Contact Jann Reusser, Admissions Coordinator, Newman University, 3100 McCormick Avenue, Wichita, KS 67213. *Phone:* 316-942-4291 Ext. 2144. *Toll-free phone:* 877-NEWMANU. *Fax:* 316-942-4483. *E-mail:* reusserj@newmanu.edu.
Website: http://www.newmanu.edu/.

Ottawa University
Ottawa, Kansas

Freshman Application Contact Ottawa University, 1001 South Cedar, Ottawa, KS 66067-3399. *Phone:* 785-229-1051. *Toll-free phone:* 800-755-5200.
Website: http://www.ottawa.edu/.

Pittsburg State University
Pittsburg, Kansas

- **State-supported** comprehensive, founded 1903, part of Kansas State Board of Regents
- **Small-town** 630-acre campus
- **Endowment** $57.2 million
- **Coed** 5,984 undergraduate students, 88% full-time, 48% women, 52% men
- **Minimally difficult** entrance level, 79% of applicants were admitted

Undergraduates 5,256 full-time, 728 part-time. Students come from 39 states and territories; 41 other countries; 26% are from out of state; 3% Black or African American, non-Hispanic/Latino; 4% Hispanic/Latino; 0.5% Asian, non-Hispanic/Latino; 0.2% Native Hawaiian or other Pacific Islander, non-Hispanic/Latino; 2% American Indian or Alaska Native, non-Hispanic/Latino; 3% Two or more races, non-Hispanic/Latino; 0.1% Race/ethnicity unknown; 5% international; 9% transferred in; 18% live on campus. *Retention:* 69% of full-time freshmen returned.

Freshmen *Admission:* 2,771 applied, 2,197 admitted, 1,102 enrolled. *Average high school GPA:* 3.3. *Test scores:* ACT scores over 18: 88%; ACT scores over 24: 33%; ACT scores over 30: 4%.
Faculty *Total:* 411, 76% full-time, 68% with terminal degrees.
Academics *Calendar:* semesters. *Degrees:* certificates, associate, bachelor's, master's, and post-master's certificates. *Special study options:* academic remediation for entering students, adult/continuing education programs, advanced placement credit, cooperative education, distance learning, double majors, English as a second language, freshman honors college, honors programs, independent study, internships, off-campus study, part-time degree program, services for LD students, student-designed majors, study abroad, summer session for credit. *ROTC:* Army (b).
Computers on Campus 425 computers/terminals are available on campus for general student use. Students can access the following: campus intranet, computer help desk, free student e-mail accounts, online (class) grades, online (class) registration, online (class) schedules. Campuswide network is available. 100% of college-owned or -operated housing units are wired for high-speed Internet access. Wireless service is available via entire campus.
Student Life *Housing:* on-campus residence required for freshman year. *Options:* coed, disabled students. Campus housing is university owned. Freshman applicants given priority for college housing. *Activities and organizations:* drama/theater group, student-run newspaper, radio and television station, choral group, marching band, Student Government Association, student yearbook, student newspaper, Student Activities Council, Students in Free Enterprise (SIFE), national fraternities, national sororities. *Campus security:* 24-hour emergency response devices and patrols, controlled dormitory access. *Student services:* health clinic, personal/psychological counseling, legal services.
Athletics Member NCAA. All Division II. *Intercollegiate sports:* baseball M(s), basketball M(s)/W(s), cheerleading M(s)/W(s), cross-country running M(s)/W(s), football M(s), golf M(s), softball W(s), track and field M(s)/W(s), volleyball W(s). *Intramural sports:* badminton M/W, basketball M/W, football M/W, lacrosse M(c), racquetball M/W, rugby M(c), soccer M(c)/W(c), softball M/W, table tennis M/W, tennis M/W, ultimate Frisbee M/W, volleyball M/W.
Standardized Tests *Required:* ACT (for admission).
Costs (2012–13) *Tuition:* state resident $5494 full-time; nonresident $15,050 full-time. Part-time tuition and fees vary according to course load. *Room and board:* $6758. Room and board charges vary according to board plan and housing facility. *Payment plan:* installment. *Waivers:* employees or children of employees.
Financial Aid Of all full-time matriculated undergraduates who enrolled in 2011, 4,410 applied for aid, 3,522 were judged to have need, 1,372 had their need fully met. In 2011, 429 non-need-based awards were made. *Average percent of need met:* 81%. *Average financial aid package:* $8274. *Average need-based loan:* $4287. *Average need-based gift aid:* $4361. *Average non-need-based aid:* $2441. *Average indebtedness upon graduation:* $21,377.
Applying *Options:* electronic application, deferred entrance. *Application fee:* $30. *Required:* high school transcript. *Required for some:* minimum 2.0 GPA. *Application deadlines:* rolling (freshmen), rolling (transfers).
Freshman Application Contact Director of Admission, Pittsburg State University, 1701 South Broadway, Pittsburg, KS 66762. *Phone:* 620-235-4251. *Toll-free phone:* 800-854-7488. *Fax:* 620-235-6003. *E-mail:* psuadmit@pittstate.edu.
Website: http://www.pittstate.edu/.

Southwestern College
Winfield, Kansas

- **Independent United Methodist** comprehensive, founded 1885
- **Small-town** 70-acre campus with easy access to Wichita
- **Endowment** $19.9 million
- **Coed** 1,304 undergraduate students, 40% full-time, 45% women, 55% men
- **Minimally difficult** entrance level, 88% of applicants were admitted

Undergraduates 523 full-time, 781 part-time. Students come from 47 states and territories; 9 other countries; 37% are from out of state; 10% Black or African American, non-Hispanic/Latino; 7% Hispanic/Latino; 0.6% Asian, non-Hispanic/Latino; 0.1% Native Hawaiian or other Pacific Islander, non-Hispanic/Latino; 2% American Indian or Alaska Native, non-Hispanic/Latino; 4% Two or more races, non-Hispanic/Latino; 12% Race/ethnicity unknown; 2% international; 4% transferred in; 72% live on campus. *Retention:* 60% of full-time freshmen returned.
Freshmen *Admission:* 339 applied, 298 admitted, 148 enrolled. *Average high school GPA:* 3.44. *Test scores:* SAT critical reading scores over 500: 31%; SAT math scores over 500: 39%; SAT writing scores over 500: 25%; ACT scores over 18: 89%; SAT critical reading scores over 600: 6%; SAT math scores over

600: 10%; SAT writing scores over 600: 3%; ACT scores over 24: 40%; SAT critical reading scores over 700: 3%; SAT math scores over 700: 3%; ACT scores over 30: 3%.

Faculty *Total:* 119, 38% full-time, 29% with terminal degrees. *Student/faculty ratio:* 12:1.

Academics *Calendar:* semesters. *Degrees:* certificates, bachelor's, master's, post-master's, and postbachelor's certificates. *Special study options:* accelerated degree program, adult/continuing education programs, advanced placement credit, distance learning, double majors, honors programs, independent study, internships, off-campus study, part-time degree program, student-designed majors, study abroad, summer session for credit.

Computers on Campus 15 computers/terminals are available on campus for general student use. Students can access the following: campus intranet, computer help desk, free student e-mail accounts, online (class) grades, online (class) registration, online (class) schedules. Campuswide network is available. 100% of college-owned or -operated housing units are wired for high-speed Internet access. Wireless service is available via entire campus.

Student Life *Housing:* on-campus residence required through sophomore year. *Options:* coed, men-only, women-only. Campus housing is university owned. Freshman campus housing is guaranteed. *Activities and organizations:* drama/theater group, student-run newspaper, radio and television station, choral group, Discipleship SC, Leadership SC, Acappella Choir, Concert Band, Southwestern Singers, national fraternities, national sororities. *Campus security:* 24-hour emergency response devices and patrols, late-night transport/escort service, controlled dormitory access. *Student services:* health clinic, personal/psychological counseling.

Athletics Member NAIA. *Intercollegiate sports:* basketball M(s)/W(s), cross-country running M(s)/W(s), football M(s), golf M(s)/W(s), soccer M(s)/W(s), softball W(s), tennis M(s)/W(s), track and field M(s)/W(s), volleyball W(s). *Intramural sports:* basketball M/W, softball M/W, tennis M/W, ultimate Frisbee M(c)/W(c), volleyball M/W.

Standardized Tests *Required:* SAT or ACT (for admission).

Costs (2013–14) *Comprehensive fee:* $30,522 includes full-time tuition ($23,736), mandatory fees ($150), and room and board ($6636). Full-time tuition and fees vary according to class time, course load, degree level, location, and program. Part-time tuition: $989 per credit hour. Part-time tuition and fees vary according to class time, course load, degree level, location, and program. *College room only:* $3000. Room and board charges vary according to board plan and housing facility. *Payment plan:* installment. *Waivers:* senior citizens and employees or children of employees.

Financial Aid Of all full-time matriculated undergraduates who enrolled in 2011, 507 applied for aid, 465 were judged to have need, 56 had their need fully met. 177 Federal Work-Study jobs (averaging $1204). 140 state and other part-time jobs (averaging $1143). In 2011, 99 non-need-based awards were made. *Average percent of need met:* 69%. *Average financial aid package:* $18,444. *Average need-based loan:* $5110. *Average need-based gift aid:* $13,106. *Average non-need-based aid:* $8119. *Average indebtedness upon graduation:* $34,056. *Financial aid deadline:* 8/15.

Applying *Options:* electronic application. *Application fee:* $25. *Required:* high school transcript, minimum 2.5 GPA. *Required for some:* 2 letters of recommendation, interview. *Recommended:* essay or personal statement. *Application deadlines:* 8/1 (freshmen), 8/1 (out-of-state freshmen), 8/1 (transfers). *Notification:* continuous (freshmen), continuous (out-of-state freshmen), continuous (transfers).

Freshman Application Contact Southwestern College, 100 College Street, Winfield, KS 67156-2499. *Phone:* 620-229-6364. *Toll-free phone:* 800-846-1543.
Website: http://www.sckans.edu/.

Sterling College

Sterling, Kansas

- **Independent Presbyterian** 4-year, founded 1887
- **Rural** 46-acre campus
- **Endowment** $13.3 million
- **Coed** 653 undergraduate students, 88% full-time, 45% women, 55% men
- **Minimally difficult** entrance level, 51% of applicants were admitted

Undergraduates 577 full-time, 76 part-time. Students come from 36 states and territories; 2 other countries; 47% are from out of state; 9% Black or African American, non-Hispanic/Latino; 6% Hispanic/Latino; 2% Native Hawaiian or other Pacific Islander, non-Hispanic/Latino; 2% American Indian or Alaska Native, non-Hispanic/Latino; 4% Race/ethnicity unknown; 0.5% international; 9% transferred in; 76% live on campus. *Retention:* 55% of full-time freshmen returned.

Freshmen *Admission:* 806 applied, 415 admitted, 139 enrolled. *Average high school GPA:* 3.3. *Test scores:* SAT critical reading scores over 500: 38%; SAT

math scores over 500: 33%; SAT writing scores over 500: 14%; ACT scores over 18: 93%; SAT math scores over 600: 5%; ACT scores over 24: 36%; ACT scores over 30: 7%.

Faculty *Total:* 63, 63% full-time, 40% with terminal degrees. *Student/faculty ratio:* 12:1.

Academics *Calendar:* 4-1-4. *Degree:* bachelor's. *Special study options:* advanced placement credit, distance learning, double majors, honors programs, independent study, internships, off-campus study, services for LD students, student-designed majors, study abroad, summer session for credit. *Unusual degree programs:* 3-2 biology/medical technology with Wichita State University.

Computers on Campus 50 computers/terminals are available on campus for general student use. Students can access the following: campus intranet, computer help desk, free student e-mail accounts, online (class) grades, online (class) registration, online (class) schedules. Campuswide network is available. 100% of college-owned or -operated housing units are wired for high-speed Internet access. Wireless service is available via entire campus.

Student Life *Housing:* on-campus residence required through senior year. *Options:* men-only, women-only. Campus housing is university owned. Freshman campus housing is guaranteed. *Activities and organizations:* drama/theater group, student-run newspaper, radio and television station, choral group, Fellowship of Christian Athletes, Student Activities Council, Bible study groups, theatre, Mission teams. *Campus security:* controlled dormitory access, late night security patrol. *Student services:* health clinic, personal/psychological counseling.

Athletics Member NAIA. *Intercollegiate sports:* baseball M(s), basketball M(s)/W(s), cross-country running M(s)/W(s), football M(s), golf M(s)/W(s), soccer M(s)/W(s), softball W(s), track and field M(s)/W(s), volleyball W(s). *Intramural sports:* basketball M/W, softball M/W, ultimate Frisbee M/W, volleyball M/W.

Standardized Tests *Required:* SAT or ACT (for admission).

Costs (2013–14) *Comprehensive fee:* $28,722 includes full-time tuition ($20,950), mandatory fees ($250), and room and board ($7522). Part-time tuition: $392 per credit hour. *Room and board:* Room and board charges vary according to board plan and housing facility. *Payment plan:* installment. *Waivers:* senior citizens and employees or children of employees.

Financial Aid Of all full-time matriculated undergraduates who enrolled in 2004, 449 applied for aid, 363 were judged to have need, 176 had their need fully met. 169 Federal Work-Study jobs (averaging $501). 196 state and other part-time jobs (averaging $808). In 2004, 77 non-need-based awards were made. *Average percent of need met:* 100%. *Average financial aid package:* $15,375. *Average need-based loan:* $4214. *Average need-based gift aid:* $7863. *Average non-need-based aid:* $6817. *Average indebtedness upon graduation:* $9647.

Applying *Options:* electronic application, deferred entrance. *Application fee:* $25. *Required:* high school transcript, minimum 2.2 GPA. *Required for some:* 2 letters of recommendation. *Recommended:* essay or personal statement, interview. *Application deadlines:* rolling (freshmen), rolling (transfers). *Notification:* continuous (freshmen), continuous (transfers).

Freshman Application Contact Marge Jones, Admissions Office Manager, Sterling College, 125 West Cooper, Sterling, KS 67579. *Phone:* 620-278-4275. *Toll-free phone:* 800-346-1017. *Fax:* 620-278-4416. *E-mail:* admissions@sterling.edu.
Website: http://www.sterling.edu/.

Tabor College

Hillsboro, Kansas

- **Independent Mennonite Brethren** comprehensive, founded 1908
- **Small-town** 87-acre campus with easy access to Wichita
- **Endowment** $6.1 million
- **Coed** 760 undergraduate students, 76% full-time, 48% women, 52% men
- **Moderately difficult** entrance level, 85% of applicants were admitted

Undergraduates 580 full-time, 180 part-time. Students come from 31 states and territories; 7 other countries; 52% are from out of state; 7% Black or African American, non-Hispanic/Latino; 9% Hispanic/Latino; 0.7% Asian, non-Hispanic/Latino; 0.5% Native Hawaiian or other Pacific Islander, non-Hispanic/Latino; 0.5% American Indian or Alaska Native, non-Hispanic/Latino; 2% Two or more races, non-Hispanic/Latino; 11% Race/ethnicity unknown; 1% international; 9% transferred in; 86% live on campus. *Retention:* 56% of full-time freshmen returned.

Freshmen *Admission:* 367 applied, 312 admitted, 142 enrolled. *Average high school GPA:* 3.31. *Test scores:* SAT critical reading scores over 500: 30%; SAT math scores over 500: 50%; ACT scores over 18: 90%; SAT critical reading scores over 600: 13%; SAT math scores over 600: 15%; ACT scores over 24: 38%; SAT math scores over 700: 4%; ACT scores over 30: 4%.

Faculty *Total:* 75, 48% full-time, 41% with terminal degrees. *Student/faculty ratio:* 16:1.

Academics *Calendar:* 4-1-4. *Degrees:* associate, bachelor's, and master's. *Special study options:* academic remediation for entering students, accelerated degree program, adult/continuing education programs, advanced placement credit, cooperative education, distance learning, double majors, honors programs, independent study, internships, off-campus study, part-time degree program, services for LD students, student-designed majors, study abroad.

Computers on Campus 40 computers/terminals are available on campus for general student use. Students can access the following: campus intranet, computer help desk, free student e-mail accounts, online (class) grades, online (class) registration, online (class) schedules. Campuswide network is available. 100% of college-owned or -operated housing units are wired for high-speed Internet access. Wireless service is available via entire campus.

Student Life *Housing:* on-campus residence required through senior year. *Options:* men-only, women-only, disabled students. Campus housing is university owned. Freshman campus housing is guaranteed. *Activities and organizations:* drama/theater group, student-run newspaper, choral group, Student Activities Board, Campus Ministries Council, Multi-Cultural Student Union, Business Club, Science Club. *Campus security:* Emergency Alert System. *Student services:* personal/psychological counseling.

Athletics Member NAIA. *Intercollegiate sports:* baseball M(s), basketball M(s)/W(s), bowling M(s)/W(s), cheerleading M(s)/W(s), cross-country running M(s)/W(s), football M(s), soccer M(s)/W(s), softball W(s), tennis M(s)/W(s), track and field M(s)/W(s), volleyball W(s). *Intramural sports:* basketball M/W, football M/W, soccer M/W, volleyball M/W.

Standardized Tests *Required:* SAT or ACT (for admission).

Costs (2012–13) *One-time required fee:* $175. *Comprehensive fee:* $29,860 includes full-time tuition ($21,160), mandatory fees ($580), and room and board ($8120). Full-time tuition and fees vary according to course load. Part-time tuition: $440 per credit hour. Part-time tuition and fees vary according to course load. *Required fees:* $15 per credit hour part-time, $140 per term part-time. *College room only:* $3220. Room and board charges vary according to board plan, housing facility, and location. *Payment plan:* installment. *Waivers:* employees or children of employees.

Financial Aid Of all full-time matriculated undergraduates who enrolled in 2010, 590 applied for aid, 490 were judged to have need, 87 had their need fully met. 213 Federal Work-Study jobs (averaging $593). In 2010, 86 non-need-based awards were made. *Average percent of need met:* 79%. *Average financial aid package:* $20,301. *Average need-based loan:* $7704. *Average need-based gift aid:* $4702. *Average non-need-based aid:* $7559. *Average indebtedness upon graduation:* $27,380. *Financial aid deadline:* 8/15.

Applying *Options:* electronic application, early admission, deferred entrance. *Application fee:* $30. *Required:* essay or personal statement, high school transcript, minimum 2.0 GPA. *Required for some:* 1 letter of recommendation. *Recommended:* interview. *Application deadlines:* rolling (freshmen), rolling (out-of-state freshmen), rolling (transfers).

Freshman Application Contact Mr. Lee Waldron, Director of Admissions, Tabor College, Tabor College, 400 South Jefferson, Hillsboro, KS 67063. *Phone:* 620-947-3121 Ext. 1723. *Toll-free phone:* 800-822-6799. *Fax:* 620-947-6276. *E-mail:* leew@tabor.edu. *Website:* http://www.tabor.edu/.

The University of Kansas

Lawrence, Kansas

- **State-supported** university, founded 1866, part of Kansas Board of Regents System
- **Suburban** 1000-acre campus with easy access to Kansas City
- **Endowment** $1.6 billion
- **Coed** 19,169 undergraduate students, 89% full-time, 50% women, 50% men
- **Moderately difficult** entrance level, 92% of applicants were admitted

Undergraduates 17,130 full-time, 2,039 part-time. Students come from 52 states and territories; 76 other countries; 22% are from out of state; 4% Black or African American, non-Hispanic/Latino; 6% Hispanic/Latino; 4% Asian, non-Hispanic/Latino; 0.1% Native Hawaiian or other Pacific Islander, non-Hispanic/Latino; 0.6% American Indian or Alaska Native, non-Hispanic/Latino; 4% Two or more races, non-Hispanic/Latino; 0.6% Race/ethnicity unknown; 5% international; 7% transferred in; 24% live on campus. *Retention:* 79% of full-time freshmen returned.

Freshmen *Admission:* 12,389 applied, 11,433 admitted, 3,771 enrolled. *Average high school GPA:* 3.5. *Test scores:* ACT scores over 18: 97%; ACT scores over 24: 63%; ACT scores over 30: 16%.

Faculty *Total:* 1,722, 77% full-time, 79% with terminal degrees. *Student/faculty ratio:* 19:1.

Academics *Calendar:* semesters. *Degrees:* certificates, bachelor's, master's, doctoral, and postbachelor's certificates (University of Kansas is a single institution with academic programs and facilities at two primary locations: Lawrence and Kansas City). *Special study options:* academic remediation for entering students, accelerated degree program, advanced placement credit, cooperative education, distance learning, double majors, English as a second language, honors programs, independent study, internships, part-time degree program, services for LD students, study abroad, summer session for credit. *ROTC:* Army (b), Navy (b), Air Force (b).

Computers on Campus 1,500 computers/terminals are available on campus for general student use. Students can access the following: campus intranet, computer help desk, free student e-mail accounts, online (class) grades, online (class) registration, online (class) schedules. Campuswide network is available. 100% of college-owned or -operated housing units are wired for high-speed Internet access. Wireless service is available via entire campus.

Student Life *Housing options:* coed, women-only, cooperative. Campus housing is university owned. *Activities and organizations:* drama/theater group, student-run newspaper, radio and television station, choral group, marching band, Hillel, National Society of Collegiate Scholars, International Student Association, Panhellenic Association, Chinese Students & Scholars Friendship Association, national fraternities, national sororities. *Campus security:* 24-hour emergency response devices and patrols, late-night transport/escort service, controlled dormitory access, University police department. *Student services:* health clinic, personal/psychological counseling, women's center, legal services.

Athletics Member NCAA. All Division I except football (Division I-A). *Intercollegiate sports:* baseball M(s), basketball M(s)/W(s), crew W(s), cross-country running M(s)/W(s), golf M(s)/W(s), ice hockey M(c), rugby M(c), soccer W(s), softball W(s), swimming and diving W(s), tennis W(s), track and field M(s)/W(s), volleyball W(s). *Intramural sports:* baseball M(c), basketball M/W, bowling M(c)/W(c), crew M(c)/W(c), fencing M(c)/W(c), football M/W, golf M(c)/W(c), lacrosse M(c)/W(c), racquetball M(c)/W(c), rock climbing M(c)/W(c), rugby M(c), sailing M(c)/W(c), soccer M(c)/W(c), softball M(c)/W(c), swimming and diving M(c)/W(c), table tennis M(c)/W(c), tennis M(c)/W(c), ultimate Frisbee M(c)/W(c), volleyball W(c), water polo M(c).

Standardized Tests *Required:* SAT or ACT (for admission).

Costs (2012–13) *Tuition:* state resident $8790 full-time, $293 per credit hour part-time; nonresident $22,860 full-time, $762 per credit hour part-time. Full-time tuition and fees vary according to program, reciprocity agreements, and student level. Part-time tuition and fees vary according to program, reciprocity agreements, and student level. No tuition increase for student's term of enrollment. *Required fees:* $888 full-time, $74 per credit hour part-time, $74 per credit hour part-time. *Room and board:* $7258; room only: $3804. Room and board charges vary according to board plan and housing facility. *Payment plan:* installment. *Waivers:* employees or children of employees.

Financial Aid Of all full-time matriculated undergraduates who enrolled in 2011, 11,283 applied for aid, 8,343 were judged to have need, 969 had their need fully met. 404 Federal Work-Study jobs (averaging $2416). 40 state and other part-time jobs (averaging $3695). In 2011, 1643 non-need-based awards were made. *Average percent of need met:* 55%. *Average financial aid package:* $8844. *Average need-based loan:* $4380. *Average need-based gift aid:* $5013. *Average non-need-based aid:* $3731. *Average indebtedness upon graduation:* $23,468.

Applying *Options:* electronic application. *Application fee:* $30. *Required:* high school transcript, minimum 2.0 GPA, Kansas Board of Regents admissions criteria. *Required for some:* minimum 2.5 GPA. *Application deadlines:* 4/1 (freshmen), 4/1 (out-of-state freshmen), 5/1 (transfers). *Notification:* continuous (freshmen), continuous (out-of-state freshmen), continuous (transfers).

Freshman Application Contact Ms. Lisa Pinamonti Kress, Director of Admissions, The University of Kansas, KU Visitor Center, 1502 Iowa Street, Lawrence, KS 66045-7576. *Phone:* 785-864-3911. *Toll-free phone:* 888-686-7323. *Fax:* 785-864-5006. *E-mail:* adm@ku.edu. *Website:* http://www.ku.edu/.

University of Phoenix–Wichita Campus

Wichita, Kansas

Freshman Application Contact Marc Booker, Sr. Director, Office of Admissions and Evaluation, University of Phoenix–Wichita Campus, 4035 South Riverpoint Parkway, Mail Stop CF-L101, Phoenix, AZ 85040. *Phone:* 602-557-4609. *Toll-free phone:* 866-766-0766. *Fax:* 480-643-1156. *Website:* http://www.phoenix.edu/.

University of Saint Mary

Leavenworth, Kansas

- **Independent Roman Catholic** comprehensive, founded 1923
- **Small-town** 240-acre campus with easy access to Kansas City
- **Endowment** $15.6 million
- **Coed** 816 undergraduate students, 67% full-time, 64% women, 36% men
- **Moderately difficult** entrance level, 47% of applicants were admitted

Undergraduates 544 full-time, 272 part-time. Students come from 25 states and territories; 4 other countries; 40% are from out of state; 14% Black or African American, non-Hispanic/Latino; 6% Hispanic/Latino; 2% Asian, non-Hispanic/Latino; 0.3% Native Hawaiian or other Pacific Islander, non-Hispanic/Latino; 0.7% American Indian or Alaska Native, non-Hispanic/Latino; 11% Race/ethnicity unknown; 0.7% international; 10% transferred in; 40% live on campus. *Retention:* 64% of full-time freshmen returned.
Freshmen *Admission:* 733 applied, 342 admitted, 103 enrolled. *Average high school GPA:* 3.23. *Test scores:* SAT critical reading scores over 500: 33%; SAT math scores over 500: 46%; ACT scores over 18: 94%; SAT critical reading scores over 600: 4%; SAT math scores over 600: 13%; ACT scores over 24: 29%; ACT scores over 30: 4%.
Faculty *Total:* 148, 34% full-time, 30% with terminal degrees. *Student/faculty ratio:* 10:1.
Academics *Calendar:* semesters. *Degrees:* associate, bachelor's, master's, and doctoral. *Special study options:* academic remediation for entering students, adult/continuing education programs, advanced placement credit, cooperative education, distance learning, double majors, honors programs, independent study, internships, off-campus study, part-time degree program, services for LD students, student-designed majors, study abroad, summer session for credit. *ROTC:* Army (c), Air Force (c).
Computers on Campus 45 computers/terminals are available on campus for general student use. Students can access the following: campus intranet, computer help desk, free student e-mail accounts, online (class) grades, online (class) registration, online (class) schedules. Campuswide network is available. 100% of college-owned or -operated housing units are wired for high-speed Internet access. Wireless service is available via entire campus.
Student Life *Housing:* on-campus residence required through sophomore year. *Options:* coed. Campus housing is university owned. Freshman campus housing is guaranteed. *Activities and organizations:* drama/theater group, choral group, Student Government Association, BACCHUS, Theatrical Union, campus ministry, Amnesty International. *Campus security:* 24-hour patrols, late-night transport/escort service, controlled dormitory access. *Student services:* personal/psychological counseling.
Athletics Member NAIA. *Intercollegiate sports:* baseball M(s), basketball M(s)/W(s), cheerleading M(s)/W(s), cross-country running M(s)/W(s), football M(s), soccer M(s)/W(s), softball W(s), track and field M(s)/W(s), volleyball W(s). *Intramural sports:* badminton M/W, basketball M/W, bowling M/W, football M, racquetball M/W, soccer M/W, softball W, table tennis M/W, ultimate Frisbee M/W, volleyball M/W, weight lifting M/W.
Standardized Tests *Required:* SAT or ACT (for admission).
Costs (2012–13) *Comprehensive fee:* $29,230 includes full-time tuition ($21,500), mandatory fees ($480), and room and board ($7250). Full-time tuition and fees vary according to class time, course load, location, and program. Part-time tuition: $410 per credit. Part-time tuition and fees vary according to class time, course load, location, and program. *Required fees:* $115 per term part-time. *Room and board:* Room and board charges vary according to board plan and housing facility. *Payment plan:* installment. *Waivers:* senior citizens and employees or children of employees.
Financial Aid *Average percent of need met:* 82%.
Applying *Options:* electronic application. *Application fee:* $25. *Required:* high school transcript, minimum 2.5 GPA. *Recommended:* 1 letter of recommendation, interview. *Application deadlines:* rolling (freshmen), rolling (transfers). *Notification:* continuous (freshmen), continuous (transfers).
Freshman Application Contact Mr. Ken Wuertzberger, Director of Admissions, University of Saint Mary, 4100 South Fourth Street, Leavenworth, KS 66048. *Phone:* 913-758-6118. *Toll-free phone:* 800-752-7043. *Fax:* 913-758-6140. *E-mail:* admiss@stmary.edu.
Website: http://www.stmary.edu/.

Washburn University

Topeka, Kansas

- **City-supported** comprehensive, founded 1865
- **Urban** 160-acre campus with easy access to Kansas City
- **Endowment** $120.0 million
- **Coed** 6,389 undergraduate students, 66% full-time, 59% women, 41% men
- **Noncompetitive** entrance level, 96% of applicants were admitted

Undergraduates 4,213 full-time, 2,176 part-time. Students come from 43 states and territories; 37 other countries; 7% are from out of state; 9% transferred in; 14% live on campus. *Retention:* 67% of full-time freshmen returned.
Freshmen *Admission:* 1,916 applied, 1,830 admitted, 876 enrolled. *Average high school GPA:* 3.3. *Test scores:* ACT scores over 18: 89%; ACT scores over 24: 35%; ACT scores over 30: 4%.
Faculty *Total:* 555, 49% full-time, 59% with terminal degrees. *Student/faculty ratio:* 15:1.
Academics *Calendar:* semesters. *Degrees:* certificates, associate, bachelor's, master's, doctoral, and postbachelor's certificates. *Special study options:* academic remediation for entering students, adult/continuing education programs, advanced placement credit, cooperative education, distance learning, double majors, English as a second language, honors programs, independent study, internships, off-campus study, part-time degree program, services for LD students, student-designed majors, study abroad, summer session for credit. *ROTC:* Army (b), Navy (c), Air Force (c). *Unusual degree programs:* 3-2 engineering with University of Kansas, Kansas State University.
Computers on Campus 560 computers/terminals are available on campus for general student use. Students can access the following: campus intranet, computer help desk, free student e-mail accounts, online (class) grades, online (class) registration, online (class) schedules. Campuswide network is available. 100% of college-owned or -operated housing units are wired for high-speed Internet access. Wireless service is available via entire campus.
Student Life *Housing options:* coed. Campus housing is university owned. *Activities and organizations:* drama/theater group, student-run newspaper, television station, choral group, marching band, national fraternities, national sororities. *Campus security:* 24-hour emergency response devices and patrols, student patrols, late-night transport/escort service. *Student services:* health clinic, personal/psychological counseling, legal services.
Athletics Member NCAA. All Division II. *Intercollegiate sports:* baseball M(s), basketball M(s)/W(s), cheerleading M(s)/W(s), football M(s), golf M(s), soccer W(s), softball W(s), tennis M(s)/W(s), volleyball W(s). *Intramural sports:* badminton M/W, basketball M/W, crew M(c)/W(c), football M/W, golf M/W, rugby M(c), soccer M/W, softball M/W, table tennis M/W, tennis M/W, volleyball M/W.
Standardized Tests *Required:* ACT (for admission).
Costs (2012–13) *Tuition:* state resident $5400 full-time, $225 per credit hour part-time; nonresident $12,216 full-time, $509 per credit hour part-time. Full-time tuition and fees vary according to program. Part-time tuition and fees vary according to program. *Required fees:* $86 full-time, $21 per term part-time. *Room and board:* $6216; room only: $3501. Room and board charges vary according to board plan and housing facility. *Payment plan:* installment. *Waivers:* senior citizens and employees or children of employees.
Financial Aid Of all full-time matriculated undergraduates who enrolled in 2012, 3,732 applied for aid, 2,620 were judged to have need, 381 had their need fully met. 348 Federal Work-Study jobs (averaging $2417). 13 state and other part-time jobs (averaging $2623). In 2012, 574 non-need-based awards were made. *Average percent of need met:* 43%. *Average financial aid package:* $9315. *Average need-based loan:* $4354. *Average need-based gift aid:* $4884. *Average non-need-based aid:* $2371. *Average indebtedness upon graduation:* $17,955.
Applying *Options:* electronic application. *Application fee:* $20. *Required:* high school transcript. *Application deadlines:* 8/1 (freshmen), 8/1 (transfers). *Notification:* continuous (freshmen), continuous (transfers).
Freshman Application Contact Ms. Kris Klima, Director of Admissions, Washburn University, 1700 SW College, MO 114, Topeka, KS 66621. *Phone:* 785-670-1030. *Toll-free phone:* 800-332-0291. *Fax:* 785-670-1113. *E-mail:* admissions@washburn.edu.
Website: http://www.washburn.edu/.

Wichita State University

Wichita, Kansas

- **State-supported** university, founded 1895, part of Kansas State Board of Education
- **Urban** 335-acre campus
- **Endowment** $220.1 million
- **Coed** 12,192 undergraduate students, 71% full-time, 54% women, 46% men
- **Noncompetitive** entrance level, 95% of applicants were admitted

Undergraduates 8,670 full-time, 3,522 part-time. Students come from 47 states and territories; 82 other countries; 4% are from out of state; 6% Black or African American, non-Hispanic/Latino; 8% Hispanic/Latino; 7% Asian, non-Hispanic/Latino; 0.1% Native Hawaiian or other Pacific Islander, non-Hispanic/Latino; 1% American Indian or Alaska Native, non-Hispanic/Latino; 2% Two or more races, non-Hispanic/Latino; 4% Race/ethnicity unknown; 7% international; 11% transferred in; 8% live on campus. *Retention:* 70% of full-time freshmen returned.
Freshmen *Admission:* 3,515 applied, 3,347 admitted, 1,359 enrolled. *Average high school GPA:* 3.38. *Test scores:* SAT critical reading scores over 500: 56%; SAT math scores over 500: 70%; ACT scores over 18: 86%; SAT critical reading scores over 600: 28%; SAT math scores over 600: 36%; ACT scores over 24: 46%; SAT critical reading scores over 700: 7%; SAT math scores over 700: 13%; ACT scores over 30: 6%.
Faculty *Total:* 814, 56% full-time, 56% with terminal degrees. *Student/faculty ratio:* 20:1.
Academics *Calendar:* semesters. *Degrees:* certificates, associate, bachelor's, master's, doctoral, post-master's, and postbachelor's certificates. *Special study options:* academic remediation for entering students, accelerated degree program, advanced placement credit, cooperative education, distance learning, double majors, English as a second language, freshman honors college, honors programs, independent study, internships, off-campus study, part-time degree program, services for LD students, study abroad, summer session for credit. *Unusual degree programs:* 3-2 nursing; accounting.
Computers on Campus 1,500 computers/terminals are available on campus for general student use. Students can access the following: computer help desk, free student e-mail accounts, online (class) grades, online (class) registration, online (class) schedules, online Blackboard. Campuswide network is available. 100% of college-owned or -operated housing units are wired for high-speed Internet access. Wireless service is available via entire campus.
Student Life *Housing:* on-campus residence required for freshman year. *Options:* coed, disabled students. Campus housing is university owned. *Activities and organizations:* drama/theater group, student-run newspaper, radio and television station, choral group, Golden Key Honor Society, WSU Green Group, Criminal Justice Society, Future Health Care Professionals, Students in Free Enterprise (SIFE), national fraternities, national sororities. *Campus security:* 24-hour emergency response devices and patrols, student patrols, late-night transport/escort service, controlled dormitory access, bicycle patrols by campus security. *Student services:* health clinic, personal/psychological counseling, women's center, legal services.
Athletics Member NCAA. All Division I. *Intercollegiate sports:* baseball M(s), basketball M(s)/W(s), bowling M(s)/W(s), cheerleading M/W, cross-country running M(s)/W(s), golf M(s)/W(s), ice hockey M(c), rock climbing M(c)/W(c), soccer M(c), softball W(s), table tennis M(c)/W(c), tennis M(s)/W(s), track and field M(s)/W(s), volleyball M(c)/W(s), wrestling M(c)/W(c). *Intramural sports:* badminton M/W, basketball M/W, bowling M/W, crew M/W, football M/W, golf M/W, racquetball M/W, soccer M/W, softball M/W, swimming and diving M/W, table tennis M/W, tennis M/W, track and field M/W, volleyball M/W.
Standardized Tests *Required for some:* SAT or ACT (for admission). *Recommended:* SAT or ACT (for admission).
Costs (2012–13) *Tuition:* state resident $5205 full-time, $174 per credit hour part-time; nonresident $13,239 full-time, $441 per credit hour part-time. Full-time tuition and fees vary according to course load, degree level, and student level. Part-time tuition and fees vary according to course load, degree level, and student level. *Required fees:* $1237 full-time. *Room and board:* $6460. Room and board charges vary according to board plan and housing facility. *Payment plan:* installment. *Waivers:* senior citizens and employees or children of employees.
Financial Aid Of all full-time matriculated undergraduates who enrolled in 2011, 7,040 applied for aid, 4,176 were judged to have need, 2,671 had their need fully met. 112 Federal Work-Study jobs (averaging $3144). In 2011, 1281 non-need-based awards were made. *Average percent of need met:* 63%. *Average financial aid package:* $7926. *Average need-based loan:* $4690. *Average need-based gift aid:* $4136. *Average non-need-based aid:* $2014. *Average indebtedness upon graduation:* $21,068.

Applying *Options:* electronic application, deferred entrance. *Application fee:* $30. *Required for some:* minimum 2.5 GPA, rank in upper one-third of high school class or complete the pre-college curriculum with a minimum 2.0 GPA (2.5 GPA for nonresidents). *Recommended:* high school transcript. *Application deadlines:* rolling (freshmen), rolling (transfers). *Notification:* continuous (freshmen), continuous (transfers).
Freshman Application Contact Wichita State University, 1845 North Fairmount, Wichita, KS 67260. *Phone:* 316-978-3085. *Toll-free phone:* 800-362-2594.
Website: http://www.wichita.edu/.

KENTUCKY

Alice Lloyd College

Pippa Passes, Kentucky

- **Independent** 4-year, founded 1923
- **Rural** 175-acre campus
- **Endowment** $29.0 million
- **Coed** 608 undergraduate students, 96% full-time, 53% women, 47% men
- **Moderately difficult** entrance level, 6% of applicants were admitted

Undergraduates 581 full-time, 27 part-time. Students come from 10 states and territories; 2 other countries; 17% are from out of state; 1% Black or African American, non-Hispanic/Latino; 0.7% Hispanic/Latino; 0.2% Native Hawaiian or other Pacific Islander, non-Hispanic/Latino; 0.2% American Indian or Alaska Native, non-Hispanic/Latino; 1% Race/ethnicity unknown; 0.3% international; 6% transferred in; 80% live on campus. *Retention:* 54% of full-time freshmen returned.
Freshmen *Admission:* 3,081 applied, 200 admitted, 200 enrolled. *Average high school GPA:* 3.3. *Test scores:* SAT critical reading scores over 500: 50%; SAT math scores over 500: 33%; SAT writing scores over 500: 20%; ACT scores over 18: 85%; SAT critical reading scores over 600: 8%; SAT math scores over 600: 8%; ACT scores over 24: 19%.
Faculty *Total:* 38, 76% full-time, 47% with terminal degrees. *Student/faculty ratio:* 18:1.
Academics *Calendar:* semesters. *Degree:* bachelor's. *Special study options:* academic remediation for entering students, advanced placement credit, double majors, independent study, internships, part-time degree program, student-designed majors.
Computers on Campus 85 computers/terminals and 550 ports are available on campus for general student use. Students can access the following: campus intranet, computer help desk, free student e-mail accounts. Campuswide network is available. Wireless service is available via computer centers, computer labs, dorm rooms, learning centers, libraries.
Student Life *Housing:* on-campus residence required through senior year. *Options:* men-only, women-only. Campus housing is university owned. *Activities and organizations:* drama/theater group, student-run newspaper, radio and television station, choral group, Phi Beta Lambda, ALC Scholastic Society, Math/Science Club, Allied Health Sciences Club, Alpha Chi National Honor Society. *Campus security:* 24-hour patrols, late-night transport/escort service. *Student services:* health clinic, personal/psychological counseling.
Athletics Member NAIA. *Intercollegiate sports:* baseball M(s), basketball M(s)/W(s), cheerleading W, golf M/W, softball W. *Intramural sports:* badminton M/W, basketball M/W, cross-country running M/W, football M, racquetball M/W, soccer M/W, softball M/W, swimming and diving M/W, table tennis M/W, tennis M/W, volleyball M/W, weight lifting M/W.
Standardized Tests *Required:* SAT or ACT (for admission).
Costs (2012–13) *Comprehensive fee:* $15,240 includes full-time tuition ($8500), mandatory fees ($1600), and room and board ($5140). Full-time tuition and fees vary according to course load, location, and program. Part-time tuition: $212 per credit hour. Part-time tuition and fees vary according to course load and program. *College room only:* $2470. Room and board charges vary according to location. *Waivers:* employees or children of employees.
Financial Aid Of all full-time matriculated undergraduates who enrolled in 2011, 602 applied for aid, 529 were judged to have need, 91 had their need fully met. 342 Federal Work-Study jobs (averaging $2320). 262 state and other part-time jobs (averaging $2320). In 2011, 92 non-need-based awards were made. *Average percent of need met:* 69%. *Average financial aid package:* $10,309. *Average need-based loan:* $1851. *Average need-based gift aid:* $7303. *Average non-need-based aid:* $4486. *Average indebtedness upon graduation:* $9065.
Applying *Options:* deferred entrance. *Required:* high school transcript, minimum 2.3 GPA, interview. *Required for some:* essay or personal statement, 2

letters of recommendation. *Application deadlines:* rolling (freshmen), rolling (transfers). *Notification:* continuous (freshmen), continuous (transfers).
Freshman Application Contact Mr. Ronnie Collins, Director of Admissions, Alice Lloyd College, 100 Purpose Road, Pippa Passes, KY 41844. *Phone:* 606-368-6036. *Toll-free phone:* 888-280-4252. *Fax:* 606-368-6215. *E-mail:* ronniecollins@alc.edu.
Website: http://www.alc.edu/.

Asbury University

Wilmore, Kentucky

- **Independent nondenominational** comprehensive, founded 1890
- **Small-town** 400-acre campus with easy access to Lexington
- **Endowment** $38.0 million
- **Coed** 1,529 undergraduate students, 89% full-time, 61% women, 39% men
- **Moderately difficult** entrance level, 63% of applicants were admitted

Undergraduates 1,363 full-time, 166 part-time. Students come from 44 states and territories; 25 other countries; 49% are from out of state; 3% Black or African American, non-Hispanic/Latino; 3% Hispanic/Latino; 0.4% Asian, non-Hispanic/Latino; 0.1% Native Hawaiian or other Pacific Islander, non-Hispanic/Latino; 0.4% American Indian or Alaska Native, non-Hispanic/Latino; 4% Two or more races, non-Hispanic/Latino; 3% Race/ethnicity unknown; 1% international; 3% transferred in; 86% live on campus. *Retention:* 84% of full-time freshmen returned.
Freshmen *Admission:* 1,260 applied, 798 admitted, 322 enrolled. *Average high school GPA:* 3.62. *Test scores:* SAT critical reading scores over 500: 78%; SAT math scores over 500: 73%; ACT scores over 18: 98%; SAT critical reading scores over 600: 37%; SAT math scores over 600: 30%; ACT scores over 24: 56%; SAT critical reading scores over 700: 12%; SAT math scores over 700: 2%; ACT scores over 30: 12%.
Faculty *Total:* 187, 46% full-time, 51% with terminal degrees. *Student/faculty ratio:* 13:1.
Academics *Calendar:* semesters. *Degrees:* associate, bachelor's, and master's. *Special study options:* adult/continuing education programs, advanced placement credit, distance learning, double majors, off-campus study, study abroad, summer session for credit. *ROTC:* Army (c), Air Force (c). *Unusual degree programs:* 3-2 engineering with University of Kentucky.
Computers on Campus 250 computers/terminals and 950 ports are available on campus for general student use. Students can access the following: campus intranet, computer help desk, free student e-mail accounts, online (class) grades, online (class) registration, online (class) schedules. Campuswide network is available. 100% of college-owned or -operated housing units are wired for high-speed Internet access. Wireless service is available via classrooms, computer centers, computer labs, dorm rooms, learning centers, libraries, student centers.
Student Life *Housing:* on-campus residence required through senior year. *Options:* men-only, women-only. Campus housing is university owned. Freshman campus housing is guaranteed. *Activities and organizations:* drama/theater group, student-run newspaper, radio and television station, choral group, Fellowship of Christian Athletes, Impact (community service), Christian Service Association, ministry teams, Student-Faculty Council. *Campus security:* 24-hour emergency response devices, late-night transport/escort service, controlled dormitory access, late night security personnel. *Student services:* health clinic, personal/psychological counseling.
Athletics Member NAIA, NCCAA. *Intercollegiate sports:* baseball M(s), basketball M(s)/W(s), cross-country running M(s)/W(s), golf M(s)/W(s), soccer M(s)/W(s), softball W(s), swimming and diving M(s)/W(s), tennis M(s)/W(s), volleyball W(s). *Intramural sports:* basketball M/W, football M/W, golf M/W, racquetball M/W, soccer M/W, softball M/W, ultimate Frisbee M/W, volleyball M/W.
Standardized Tests *Required:* SAT or ACT (for admission). *Required for some:* ACT (for admission).
Costs (2013–14) *Comprehensive fee:* $32,038 includes full-time tuition ($25,894), mandatory fees ($182), and room and board ($5962). Full-time tuition and fees vary according to course load, location, and program. Part-time tuition: $996 per credit. Part-time tuition and fees vary according to course load, location, and program. *Room and board:* Room and board charges vary according to board plan, housing facility, and location. *Payment plan:* installment. *Waivers:* senior citizens and employees or children of employees.
Financial Aid Of all full-time matriculated undergraduates who enrolled in 2012, 1,019 applied for aid, 891 were judged to have need, 204 had their need fully met. In 2012, 125 non-need-based awards were made. *Average percent of need met:* 81%. *Average financial aid package:* $19,597. *Average need-based loan:* $4038. *Average need-based gift aid:* $12,669. *Average non-need-based aid:* $11,431. *Average indebtedness upon graduation:* $26,854.

Applying *Options:* electronic application, early admission, deferred entrance. *Required:* essay or personal statement, high school transcript, minimum 2.5 GPA, 1 letter of recommendation. *Required for some:* interview. *Application deadlines:* rolling (freshmen), rolling (transfers). *Notification:* continuous (freshmen), continuous (transfers).
Freshman Application Contact Mrs. Lisa D. Harper, Director of Admissions, Asbury University, One Macklem Drive, Wilmore, KY 40390. *Phone:* 800-888-1818. *Toll-free phone:* 800-888-1818. *E-mail:* admissions@asbury.edu. *Website:* http://www.asbury.edu/.

Beckfield College

Florence, Kentucky

Freshman Application Contact Mrs. Leah Boerger, Director of Admissions, Beckfield College, 16 Spiral Drive, Florence, KY 41042. *Phone:* 859-371-9393. *E-mail:* lboerger@beckfield.edu.
Website: http://www.beckfield.edu/.

Bellarmine University

Louisville, Kentucky

- **Independent Roman Catholic** comprehensive, founded 1950
- **Suburban** 144-acre campus with easy access to Louisville
- **Coed** 2,730 undergraduate students, 86% full-time, 65% women, 35% men
- **Moderately difficult** entrance level, 86% of applicants were admitted

Undergraduates 2,344 full-time, 386 part-time. 33% are from out of state; 0.2% Black or African American, non-Hispanic/Latino; 4% Hispanic/Latino; 4% Asian, non-Hispanic/Latino; 2% Native Hawaiian or other Pacific Islander, non-Hispanic/Latino; 0.2% American Indian or Alaska Native, non-Hispanic/Latino; 83% Two or more races, non-Hispanic/Latino; 3% Race/ethnicity unknown; 1% international; 3% transferred in; 44% live on campus. *Retention:* 81% of full-time freshmen returned.
Freshmen *Admission:* 4,317 applied, 3,716 admitted, 607 enrolled. *Average high school GPA:* 3.51. *Test scores:* SAT critical reading scores over 500: 75%; SAT math scores over 500: 71%; ACT scores over 18: 100%; SAT critical reading scores over 600: 26%; SAT math scores over 600: 26%; ACT scores over 24: 59%; SAT critical reading scores over 700: 3%; SAT math scores over 700: 3%; ACT scores over 30: 8%.
Faculty *Total:* 376, 41% full-time, 49% with terminal degrees. *Student/faculty ratio:* 12:1.
Academics *Calendar:* semesters. *Degrees:* bachelor's, master's, doctoral, and postbachelor's certificates. *Special study options:* adult/continuing education programs, part-time degree program. *ROTC:* Army (c), Air Force (c).
Computers on Campus 434 computers/terminals and 434 ports are available on campus for general student use. Students can access the following: campus intranet, computer help desk, free student e-mail accounts, online (class) grades, online (class) registration, online (class) schedules. Campuswide network is available. 100% of college-owned or -operated housing units are wired for high-speed Internet access. Wireless service is available via classrooms, computer centers, computer labs, dorm rooms, learning centers, libraries, student centers.
Student Life *Housing:* on-campus residence required through junior year. *Options:* coed, men-only, women-only, disabled students. Campus housing is university owned. Freshman campus housing is guaranteed. *Activities and organizations:* student government, Bellarmine Activities Council, Knights Nation, Fellowship of Christian Athletes, Delta Sigma Pi. *Campus security:* 24-hour emergency response devices and patrols, student patrols, late-night transport/escort service, controlled dormitory access, 24-hour locked residence hall entrances, security cameras.
Athletics Member NCAA. All Division II except lacrosse (Division I). *Intercollegiate sports:* baseball M(s), basketball M(s)/W(s), bowling M/W(s), cross-country running M(s)/W(s), field hockey W(s), golf M(s)/W(s), lacrosse M(s), soccer M(s)/W(s), softball W(s), swimming and diving M(c)/W(c), tennis M(s)/W(s), track and field M(s)/W(s), volleyball W(s). *Intramural sports:* basketball M/W, bowling M/W, football M/W, golf M/W, soccer M/W, softball M/W, table tennis M/W, tennis M/W, ultimate Frisbee M/W, volleyball M/W, weight lifting M/W.
Standardized Tests *Required:* SAT or ACT (for admission).
Costs (2013–14) *Comprehensive fee:* $42,950 includes full-time tuition ($31,900), mandatory fees ($1280), and room and board ($9770). Part-time tuition: $755 per credit hour. *College room only:* $5990. Room and board charges vary according to board plan and housing facility. *Payment plan:* installment. *Waivers:* senior citizens and employees or children of employees.

Financial Aid Of all full-time matriculated undergraduates who enrolled in 2012, 1,962 applied for aid, 1,796 were judged to have need, 330 had their need fully met. 251 Federal Work-Study jobs (averaging $1688). In 2012, 477 non-need-based awards were made. *Average percent of need met:* 73%. *Average financial aid package:* $26,374. *Average need-based loan:* $4329. *Average need-based gift aid:* $19,713. *Average non-need-based aid:* $18,457. *Average indebtedness upon graduation:* $28,722.

Applying *Options:* electronic application, early action. *Application fee:* $25. *Required:* high school transcript, minimum 2.5 GPA, 1 letter of recommendation. *Required for some:* essay or personal statement. *Recommended:* interview. *Application deadlines:* 8/15 (freshmen), rolling (transfers), 11/1 (early action). *Notification:* continuous (freshmen), continuous (transfers), 11/15 (early action).

Freshman Application Contact Mr. Timothy A. Sturgeon, Dean of Admission, Bellarmine University, 2001 Newburg Road, Louisville, KY 40205-0671. *Phone:* 502-272-8131. *Toll-free phone:* 800-274-4723 Ext. 8131. *E-mail:* admissions@bellarmine.edu. *Website:* http://www.bellarmine.edu/.

Berea College

Berea, Kentucky

- **Independent** 4-year, founded 1855
- **Small-town** 140-acre campus
- **Endowment** $978.7 million
- **Coed** 1,658 undergraduate students, 97% full-time, 57% women, 43% men
- **Moderately difficult** entrance level, 32% of applicants were admitted

Undergraduates 1,601 full-time, 57 part-time. 56% are from out of state; 14% Black or African American, non-Hispanic/Latino; 4% Hispanic/Latino; 1% Asian, non-Hispanic/Latino; 0.3% American Indian or Alaska Native, non-Hispanic/Latino; 6% Two or more races, non-Hispanic/Latino; 2% Race/ethnicity unknown; 7% international; 3% transferred in; 84% live on campus. *Retention:* 82% of full-time freshmen returned.

Freshmen *Admission:* 1,694 applied, 539 admitted, 391 enrolled. *Average high school GPA:* 3.42. *Test scores:* SAT critical reading scores over 500: 85%; SAT math scores over 500: 87%; SAT writing scores over 500: 79%; ACT scores over 18: 99%; SAT critical reading scores over 600: 42%; SAT math scores over 600: 43%; SAT writing scores over 600: 30%; ACT scores over 24: 64%; SAT critical reading scores over 700: 12%; SAT math scores over 700: 5%; SAT writing scores over 700: 8%; ACT scores over 30: 7%.

Faculty *Total:* 171, 75% full-time, 77% with terminal degrees. *Student/faculty ratio:* 11:1.

Academics *Calendar:* 4-1-4. *Degree:* bachelor's. *Special study options:* academic remediation for entering students, advanced placement credit, double majors, English as a second language, honors programs, independent study, internships, off-campus study, services for LD students, student-designed majors, study abroad, summer session for credit. *Unusual degree programs:* 3-2 engineering with Washington University in St. Louis, University of Kentucky.

Computers on Campus 7,000 ports are available on campus for general student use. Students can access the following: campus intranet, computer help desk, free student e-mail accounts, online (class) grades, online (class) registration, online (class) schedules. Campuswide network is available. 100% of college-owned or -operated housing units are wired for high-speed Internet access. Wireless service is available via classrooms, learning centers, libraries, student centers.

Student Life *Housing:* on-campus residence required through senior year. *Options:* men-only, women-only. Campus housing is university owned. Freshman campus housing is guaranteed. *Activities and organizations:* drama/theater group, student-run newspaper, choral group, Campus Activities Board, Cosmopolitan Club, CELTS (Center for Excellence in Learning through Service), Black Cultural Center, African Student Association. *Campus security:* 24-hour emergency response devices and patrols, late-night transport/escort service, controlled dormitory access, crime prevention programs. *Student services:* health clinic, personal/psychological counseling, women's center.

Athletics Member NAIA. *Intercollegiate sports:* baseball M, basketball M/W, cross-country running M/W, golf M, soccer M/W, softball W, swimming and diving M/W, tennis M/W, track and field M/W, volleyball W. *Intramural sports:* basketball M/W, football M/W, racquetball M/W, soccer M/W, softball M/W, ultimate Frisbee M/W, volleyball M/W.

Standardized Tests *Required:* SAT or ACT (for admission).

Financial Aid Of all full-time matriculated undergraduates who enrolled in 2012, 1,604 applied for aid, 1,604 were judged to have need. *Average percent of need met:* 100%. *Average financial aid package:* $27,666. *Average need-based loan:* $1289. *Average need-based gift aid:* $25,569. *Average indebtedness upon graduation:* $7224.

Applying *Options:* electronic application. *Required:* essay or personal statement, high school transcript, interview, financial aid application. *Recommended:* 2 letters of recommendation. *Application deadlines:* 4/30 (freshmen), rolling (transfers). *Notification:* continuous (freshmen), continuous (transfers).

Freshman Application Contact Mr. Luke Hodson, Director of Admissions/Operations, Berea College, CPO 2220, Berea, KY 40404. *Phone:* 859-985-3500. *Toll-free phone:* 800-326-5948. *Fax:* 859-985-3512. *E-mail:* admissions@berea.edu. *Website:* http://www.berea.edu/.

Brescia University

Owensboro, Kentucky

- **Independent Roman Catholic** comprehensive, founded 1950
- **Urban** 9-acre campus
- **Endowment** $10.3 million
- **Coed**
- **Moderately difficult** entrance level

Faculty *Student/faculty ratio:* 13:1.

Academics *Calendar:* semesters. *Degrees:* certificates, associate, bachelor's, master's, and postbachelor's certificates.

Student Life *Campus security:* 24-hour emergency response devices, late-night transport/escort service, controlled dormitory access.

Athletics Member NAIA.

Standardized Tests *Required:* SAT or ACT (for admission).

Costs (2012–13) *One-time required fee:* $200. *Comprehensive fee:* $26,940 includes full-time tuition ($18,500), mandatory fees ($440), and room and board ($8000). Full-time tuition and fees vary according to course load and degree level. Part-time tuition: $540 per credit hour. Part-time tuition and fees vary according to course load and degree level. *Room and board:* Room and board charges vary according to board plan and housing facility.

Financial Aid *Of all full-time matriculated undergraduates who enrolled in 2009,* 609 applied for aid, 581 were judged to have need. 64 Federal Work-Study jobs (averaging $1200). 15 state and other part-time jobs (averaging $2500). *Average indebtedness upon graduation:* $18,638.

Applying *Options:* electronic application, deferred entrance. *Application fee:* $25. *Required:* high school transcript, GPA coincides with test scores. *Required for some:* essay or personal statement, 1 letter of recommendation, interview.

Freshman Application Contact Brescia University, 717 Frederica Street, Owensboro, KY 42301-3023. *Phone:* 270-686-4241 Ext. 241. *Toll-free phone:* 877-273-7242. *Website:* http://www.brescia.edu/.

Brown Mackie College–Louisville

Louisville, Kentucky

Freshman Application Contact Brown Mackie College–Louisville, 3605 Fern Valley Road, Louisville, KY 40219. *Phone:* 502-968-7191. *Toll-free phone:* 800-999-7387. *Website:* http://www.brownmackie.edu/louisville/.

See next page for display ad and page 1190 for the College Close-Up.

Brown Mackie College–Northern Kentucky

Fort Mitchell, Kentucky

Freshman Application Contact Brown Mackie College–Northern Kentucky, 309 Buttermilk Pike, Fort Mitchell, KY 41017-2191. *Phone:* 859-341-5627. *Toll-free phone:* 800-888-1445. *Website:* http://www.brownmackie.edu/northernkentucky/.

See next page for display ad and page 1200 for the College Close-Up.

Campbellsville University

Campbellsville, Kentucky

- **Independent** comprehensive, founded 1906, affiliated with Kentucky Baptist Convention
- **Small-town** 90-acre campus
- **Endowment** $910.2 million
- **Coed** 3,132 undergraduate students, 63% full-time, 59% women, 41% men
- **Moderately difficult** entrance level, 67% of applicants were admitted

Undergraduates 1,967 full-time, 1,165 part-time. Students come from 35 states and territories; 37 other countries; 12% are from out of state; 11% Black or African American, non-Hispanic/Latino; 1% Hispanic/Latino; 0.4% Asian, non-Hispanic/Latino; 0.1% Native Hawaiian or other Pacific Islander, non-Hispanic/Latino; 0.2% American Indian or Alaska Native, non-Hispanic/Latino; 0.5% Two or more races, non-Hispanic/Latino; 3% Race/ethnicity unknown; 5% international; 8% transferred in; 57% live on campus. *Retention:* 63% of full-time freshmen returned.

Freshmen *Admission:* 2,477 applied, 1,651 admitted, 579 enrolled. *Average high school GPA:* 3.18. *Test scores:* SAT critical reading scores over 500: 39%; SAT math scores over 500: 53%; SAT writing scores over 500: 38%; SAT critical reading scores over 600: 19%; SAT math scores over 600: 23%; SAT writing scores over 600: 13%; SAT critical reading scores over 700: 7%; SAT math scores over 700: 3%.

Faculty *Total:* 311, 47% full-time, 29% with terminal degrees. *Student/faculty ratio:* 13:1.

Academics *Calendar:* semesters. *Degrees:* certificates, associate, bachelor's, master's, and postbachelor's certificates. *Special study options:* academic remediation for entering students, accelerated degree program, adult/continuing education programs, advanced placement credit, distance learning, double majors, English as a second language, honors programs, independent study, internships, off-campus study, part-time degree program, study abroad, summer session for credit. *ROTC:* Army (c). *Unusual degree programs:* 3-2 engineering with University of Kentucky.

Computers on Campus 220 computers/terminals are available on campus for general student use. Students can access the following: campus intranet, computer help desk, free student e-mail accounts, online (class) grades, online (class) registration, online (class) schedules. Campuswide network is available.

Student Life *Housing:* on-campus residence required through sophomore year. *Options:* men-only, women-only. Campus housing is university owned. Freshman campus housing is guaranteed. *Activities and organizations:* drama/theater group, student-run newspaper, radio and television station, choral group, marching band, Student Government Association, Baptist Student Union, Phi Beta Lambda, African-American Leadership League, Fellowship of Christian Athletes. *Campus security:* 24-hour emergency response devices and patrols, student patrols, late-night transport/escort service, controlled dormitory access. *Student services:* health clinic, personal/psychological counseling.

Athletics Member NAIA. *Intercollegiate sports:* baseball M(s), basketball M(s)/W(s), bowling M(s)/W(s), cheerleading M(s)/W(s), cross-country running M(s)/W(s), football M(s), golf M(s)/W(s), soccer M(s)/W(s), softball W(s), swimming and diving M(s)/W(s), tennis M(s)/W(s), track and field M(s)/W(s), volleyball W(s), wrestling M(s)/W(s). *Intramural sports:* basketball M/W, bowling M/W, football M/W, racquetball M/W, soccer M/W, swimming and diving M/W, table tennis M/W, tennis M/W, volleyball M/W, weight lifting M/W.

Standardized Tests *Required:* SAT or ACT (for admission).

Costs (2013–14) *Comprehensive fee:* $30,396 includes full-time tuition ($21,696), mandatory fees ($500), and room and board ($8200). Part-time tuition: $904 per credit hour. *Room and board:* Room and board charges vary according to housing facility. *Payment plan:* installment. *Waivers:* adult students, senior citizens, and employees or children of employees.

Financial Aid Of all full-time matriculated undergraduates who enrolled in 2011, 1,655 applied for aid, 1,575 were judged to have need, 193 had their need fully met. 375 Federal Work-Study jobs (averaging $1675). 32 state and other part-time jobs (averaging $1650). In 2011, 102 non-need-based awards were made. *Average percent of need met:* 70%. *Average financial aid package:* $15,848. *Average need-based loan:* $3649. *Average need-based gift aid:* $12,914. *Average non-need-based aid:* $7147. *Average indebtedness upon graduation:* $10,183.

Applying *Options:* electronic application, deferred entrance. *Application fee:* $20. *Required:* high school transcript, minimum 2.0 GPA. *Recommended:* essay or personal statement, minimum 3.0 GPA, interview. *Application deadlines:* rolling (freshmen), rolling (transfers). *Notification:* continuous (freshmen), continuous (transfers).

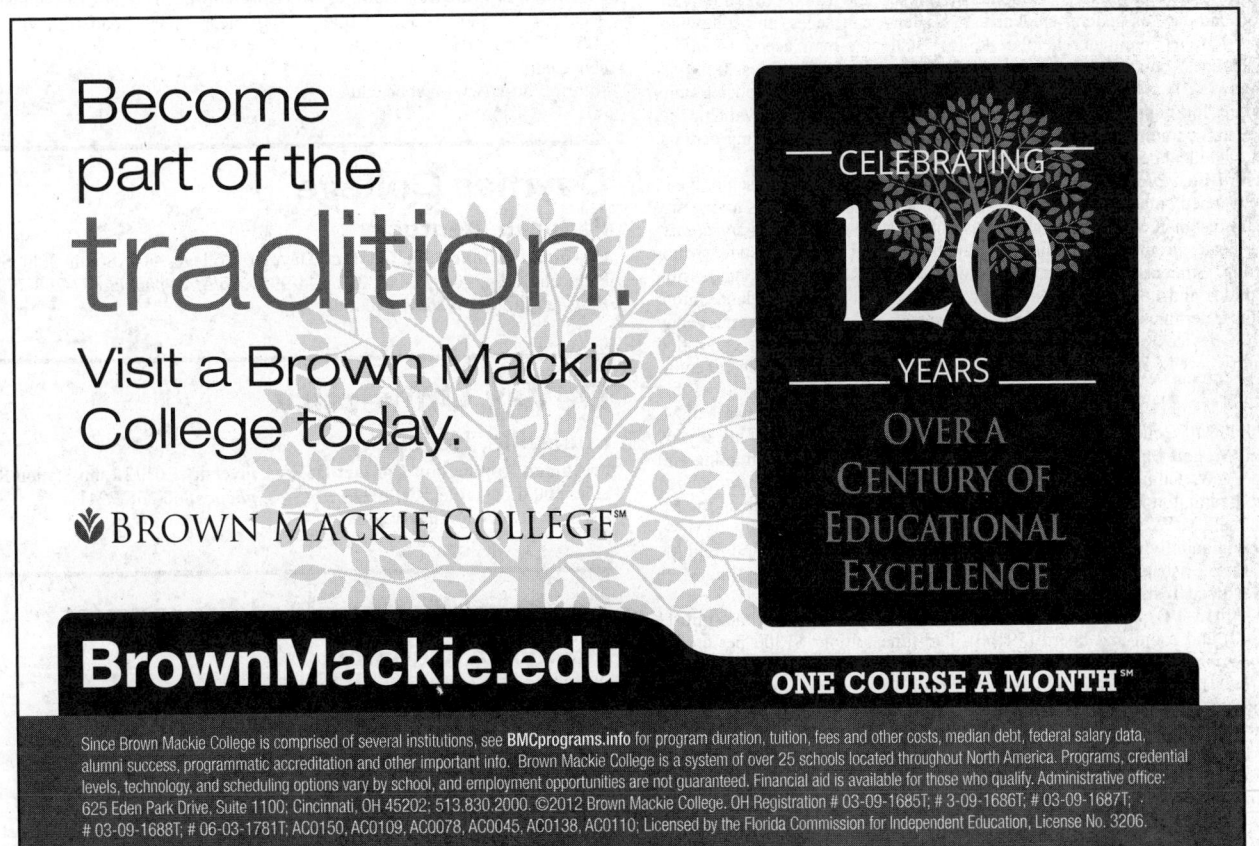

Freshman Application Contact Mr. David Walters, Vice President for Admissions and Student Services, Campbellsville University, 1 University Drive, Campbellsville, KY 42718-2799. *Phone:* 270-789-5220 Ext. 5007. *Toll-free phone:* 800-264-6014. *Fax:* 270-789-5071. *E-mail:* admissions@campbellsville.edu.
Website: http://www.campbellsville.edu/.

Centre College
Danville, Kentucky

- **Independent** 4-year, founded 1819, affiliated with Presbyterian Church (U.S.A.)
- **Small-town** 152-acre campus
- **Endowment** $182.2 million
- **Coed** 1,344 undergraduate students, 100% full-time, 53% women, 47% men
- **Very difficult** entrance level, 70% of applicants were admitted

Undergraduates 1,343 full-time, 1 part-time. Students come from 44 states and territories; 10 other countries; 40% are from out of state; 5% Black or African American, non-Hispanic/Latino; 2% Hispanic/Latino; 3% Asian, non-Hispanic/Latino; 3% Two or more races, non-Hispanic/Latino; 0.1% Race/ethnicity unknown; 3% international; 0.7% transferred in; 99% live on campus. *Retention:* 91% of full-time freshmen returned.
Freshmen *Admission:* 2,539 applied, 1,768 admitted, 351 enrolled. *Average high school GPA:* 3.68. *Test scores:* SAT critical reading scores over 500: 92%; SAT math scores over 500: 95%; SAT writing scores over 500: 90%; ACT scores over 18: 100%; SAT critical reading scores over 600: 62%; SAT math scores over 600: 69%; SAT writing scores over 600: 63%; ACT scores over 24: 91%; SAT critical reading scores over 700: 24%; SAT math scores over 700: 26%; SAT writing scores over 700: 16%; ACT scores over 30: 38%.
Faculty *Total:* 142, 82% full-time, 89% with terminal degrees. *Student/faculty ratio:* 11:1.
Academics *Calendar:* 4-1-4. *Degree:* bachelor's. *Special study options:* advanced placement credit, cooperative education, double majors, honors programs, independent study, internships, off-campus study, services for LD students, student-designed majors, study abroad. *ROTC:* Army (c), Air Force (c). *Unusual degree programs:* 3-2 engineering with Washington University in St. Louis, Columbia University, Vanderbilt University, University of Kentucky.
Computers on Campus 425 computers/terminals and 1,500 ports are available on campus for general student use. Students can access the following: campus intranet, computer help desk, free student e-mail accounts, online (class) grades, online (class) registration, online (class) schedules. Campus-wide network is available. 100% of college-owned or -operated housing units are wired for high-speed Internet access. Wireless service is available via classrooms, computer centers, computer labs, dorm rooms, learning centers, libraries, student centers.
Student Life *Housing:* on-campus residence required through senior year. *Options:* coed, men-only, disabled students. Campus housing is university owned. Freshman campus housing is guaranteed. *Activities and organizations:* drama/theater group, student-run newspaper, radio and television station, choral group, Student Government Association, campus newspaper, admission tour guides and hosts, Christian fellowship group, Diversity Student Union, national fraternities, national sororities. *Campus security:* 24-hour emergency response devices and patrols, late-night transport/escort service, controlled dormitory access. *Student services:* health clinic, personal/psychological counseling.
Athletics Member NCAA. All Division III. *Intercollegiate sports:* baseball M, basketball M/W, cheerleading W, cross-country running M/W, field hockey W, football M, golf M/W, lacrosse M/W, soccer M/W, softball W, swimming and diving M/W, tennis M/W, track and field M/W, volleyball W. *Intramural sports:* badminton M/W, basketball M/W, bowling M/W, equestrian sports M/W, football M/W, golf M/W, racquetball M/W, soccer M/W, softball M/W, swimming and diving M/W, table tennis M/W, tennis M/W, track and field M/W, ultimate Frisbee M/W, volleyball M/W, weight lifting M/W, wrestling M.
Standardized Tests *Required:* SAT or ACT (for admission).
Costs (2013–14) *Comprehensive fee:* $45,100 includes full-time tuition ($36,000) and room and board ($9100). Part-time tuition: $1300 per credit. *College room only:* $4550. Room and board charges vary according to board plan. *Payment plan:* installment. *Waivers:* adult students, senior citizens, and employees or children of employees.
Financial Aid Of all full-time matriculated undergraduates who enrolled in 2012, 1,000 applied for aid, 841 were judged to have need, 238 had their need fully met. 369 Federal Work-Study jobs (averaging $1535). 2 state and other part-time jobs (averaging $2790). In 2012, 445 non-need-based awards were made. *Average percent of need met:* 84%. *Average financial aid package:* $26,961. *Average need-based loan:* $4600. *Average need-based gift aid:*

$23,643. *Average non-need-based aid:* $17,231. *Average indebtedness upon graduation:* $25,500. *Financial aid deadline:* 1/31.
Applying *Options:* electronic application, early admission, early action, deferred entrance. *Application fee:* $40. *Required:* essay or personal statement, high school transcript, 1 letter of recommendation. *Recommended:* interview. *Application deadlines:* 2/1 (freshmen), rolling (transfers), 12/1 (early action). *Notification:* 3/15 (freshmen), 1/15 (early action).
Freshman Application Contact Mr. Bob Nesmith, Director of Admissions, Centre College, 600 West Walnut Street, Danville, KY 40422-1394. *Phone:* 859-238-5350. *Toll-free phone:* 800-423-6236. *Fax:* 859-238-5373. *E-mail:* admission@centre.edu.
Website: http://www.centre.edu/.

Clear Creek Baptist Bible College
Pineville, Kentucky

- **Independent Southern Baptist** 4-year, founded 1926
- **Rural** 700-acre campus
- **Coed, primarily men**
- **Noncompetitive** entrance level

Faculty *Student/faculty ratio:* 13:1.
Academics *Calendar:* semesters. *Degrees:* certificates, diplomas, associate, and bachelor's.
Student Life *Campus security:* 24-hour emergency response devices, student patrols.
Costs (2012–13) *Comprehensive fee:* $8840 includes full-time tuition ($5220), mandatory fees ($150), and room and board ($3470). *College room only:* $1870.
Financial Aid Of all full-time matriculated undergraduates who enrolled in 2012, 111 applied for aid, 107 were judged to have need, 2 had their need fully met. 35 Federal Work-Study jobs (averaging $1088). In 2012, 17 non-need-based awards were made. *Average percent of need met:* 68. *Average financial aid package:* $6823. *Average need-based gift aid:* $6823. *Average non-need-based aid:* $3042.
Applying *Options:* electronic application, deferred entrance. *Application fee:* $50. *Required:* essay or personal statement, 4 letters of recommendation. *Recommended:* high school transcript, interview.
Freshman Application Contact Mr. Billy Howell, Director of Admissions, Clear Creek Baptist Bible College, 300 Clear Creek Road, Pineville, KY 40977. *Phone:* 606-337-3196 Ext. 103. *Fax:* 606-337-1631. *E-mail:* bhowell@ccbbc.edu.
Website: http://www.ccbbc.edu/.

Daymar College
Paducah, Kentucky

Freshman Application Contact Daymar College, 509 South 30th Street, Paducah, KY 42001. *Phone:* 270-444-9950. *Toll-free phone:* 877-258-7796.
Website: http://www.daymarcollege.edu/.

DeVry University
Louisville, Kentucky

Freshman Application Contact DeVry University, 10172 Linn Station Road, Suite 300, Louisville, KY 40223. *Toll-free phone:* 866-338-7941.
Website: http://www.devry.edu/.

Eastern Kentucky University
Richmond, Kentucky

- **State-supported** comprehensive, founded 1906
- **Small-town** 500-acre campus with easy access to Lexington
- **Endowment** $55.6 million
- **Coed**
- **Noncompetitive** entrance level

Faculty *Student/faculty ratio:* 15:1.
Academics *Calendar:* semesters. *Degrees:* associate, bachelor's, master's, doctoral, post-master's, and postbachelor's certificates.

Student Life *Campus security:* 24-hour emergency response devices and patrols, student patrols, late-night transport/escort service, controlled dormitory access.

Athletics Member NCAA. All Division I.

Standardized Tests *Required:* SAT or ACT (for admission).

Costs (2012–13) *Tuition:* state resident $7320 full-time, $305 per credit hour part-time; nonresident $16,464 full-time, $686 per credit hour part-time. Part-time tuition and fees vary according to course load. *Room and board:* $7316. Room and board charges vary according to board plan and housing facility.

Financial Aid *Of all full-time matriculated undergraduates who enrolled in 2012,* 9,368 applied for aid, 7,962 were judged to have need, 3,061 had their need fully met. 1,200 Federal Work-Study jobs (averaging $1800). 1,200 state and other part-time jobs (averaging $1800). *In 2012,* 1196 non-need-based awards were made. *Average percent of need met:* 85. *Average financial aid package:* $9932. *Average need-based loan:* $3806. *Average need-based gift aid:* $5736. *Average non-need-based aid:* $5743. *Average indebtedness upon graduation:* $26,150.

Applying *Options:* electronic application, deferred entrance. *Application fee:* $30. *Required:* high school transcript, minimum 2.0 GPA.

Freshman Application Contact Mr. Stephen Byrn, Director of Admissions, Eastern Kentucky University, SSB CPO 54, 521 Lancaster Avenue, Richmond, KY 40475-3102. *Phone:* 859-622-2106. *Toll-free phone:* 800-465-9191. *Fax:* 859-622-8024. *E-mail:* admissions@eku.edu. *Website:* http://www.eku.edu/.

Georgetown College

Georgetown, Kentucky

- **Independent** comprehensive, founded 1829, affiliated with Baptist Church
- **Suburban** 104-acre campus with easy access to Cincinnati
- **Endowment** $41.1 million
- **Coed** 1,116 undergraduate students, 97% full-time, 54% women, 46% men
- **Moderately difficult** entrance level, 82% of applicants were admitted

Undergraduates 1,087 full-time, 29 part-time. Students come from 25 states and territories; 12 other countries; 22% are from out of state; 10% Black or African American, non-Hispanic/Latino; 3% Hispanic/Latino; 0.6% Asian, non-Hispanic/Latino; 0.1% American Indian or Alaska Native, non-Hispanic/Latino; 1% Two or more races, non-Hispanic/Latino; 2% international; 3% transferred in; 91% live on campus. *Retention:* 75% of full-time freshmen returned.

Freshmen *Admission:* 1,735 applied, 1,426 admitted, 237 enrolled. *Average high school GPA:* 3.41. *Test scores:* SAT critical reading scores over 500: 61%; SAT math scores over 500: 56%; ACT scores over 18: 96%; SAT critical reading scores over 600: 34%; SAT math scores over 600: 12%; ACT scores over 24: 45%; SAT critical reading scores over 700: 6%; SAT math scores over 700: 6%; ACT scores over 30: 6%.

Faculty *Total:* 148, 78% full-time, 79% with terminal degrees. *Student/faculty ratio:* 9:1.

Academics *Calendar:* semesters. *Degrees:* bachelor's and master's. *Special study options:* advanced placement credit, cooperative education, distance learning, double majors, English as a second language, honors programs, independent study, internships, off-campus study, part-time degree program, student-designed majors, study abroad, summer session for credit. *ROTC:* Army (c), Air Force (c). *Unusual degree programs:* 3-2 engineering with University of Kentucky; nursing with University of Kentucky; University of Kentucky, Patterson School of Diplomacy.

Computers on Campus 175 computers/terminals are available on campus for general student use. Students can access the following: campus intranet, computer help desk, free student e-mail accounts, online (class) grades, online (class) registration, online (class) schedules. Campuswide network is available. 100% of college-owned or -operated housing units are wired for high-speed Internet access. Wireless service is available via classrooms, computer centers, computer labs, dorm rooms, learning centers, libraries, student centers.

Student Life *Housing:* on-campus residence required through senior year. *Options:* men-only, women-only. Campus housing is university owned. Freshman campus housing is guaranteed. *Activities and organizations:* drama/theater group, student-run newspaper, radio station, choral group, Campus Ministries, Association of Georgetown Students, Harper-Gatton Leadership Center, President's Ambassadors, Phi Beta Lambda, national fraternities, national sororities. *Campus security:* 24-hour patrols, late-night transport/escort service. *Student services:* health clinic, personal/psychological counseling.

Athletics Member NAIA. *Intercollegiate sports:* baseball M(s), basketball M(s)/W(s), cheerleading W(s), cross-country running M(s)/W(s), football M(s), golf M(s)/W(s), lacrosse W(s), soccer M(s)/W(s), softball W(s), tennis M(s)/W(s), track and field M(s)/W(s), volleyball W(s). *Intramural sports:* basketball M/W, football M/W, golf M/W, racquetball M/W, soccer M/W, softball M/W, table tennis M/W, tennis M/W, ultimate Frisbee M/W, volleyball M/W.

Standardized Tests *Required:* SAT or ACT (for admission). *Recommended:* ACT (for admission).

Costs (2012–13) *Comprehensive fee:* $38,690 includes full-time tuition ($30,770) and room and board ($7920). Full-time tuition and fees vary according to course load and degree level. Part-time tuition: $1270 per credit hour. Part-time tuition and fees vary according to degree level. *College room only:* $3820. Room and board charges vary according to board plan and housing facility. *Payment plan:* installment. *Waivers:* employees or children of employees.

Financial Aid Of all full-time matriculated undergraduates who enrolled in 2012, 951 applied for aid, 889 were judged to have need, 438 had their need fully met. 561 Federal Work-Study jobs (averaging $936). In 2012, 187 non-need-based awards were made. *Average percent of need met:* 84%. *Average financial aid package:* $26,633. *Average need-based loan:* $4724. *Average need-based gift aid:* $18,640. *Average non-need-based aid:* $14,958. *Average indebtedness upon graduation:* $26,730. *Financial aid deadline:* 3/15.

Applying *Options:* electronic application, early decision, early action, deferred entrance. *Application fee:* $30. *Required:* high school transcript, minimum 2.5 GPA. *Required for some:* essay or personal statement, interview. *Application deadlines:* 8/1 (freshmen), rolling (transfers). *Notification:* 10/1 (freshmen), continuous (out-of-state freshmen), continuous (transfers).

Freshman Application Contact Ms. Julie Sams, Assistant Director of Admissions, Georgetown College, 400 East College Street, Georgetown, KY 40324. *Phone:* 502-863-8013. *Toll-free phone:* 800-788-9985. *Fax:* 502-868-7733. *E-mail:* admissions@georgetowncollege.edu. *Website:* http://www.georgetowncollege.edu/.

ITT Technical Institute

Lexington, Kentucky

- **Proprietary** 4-year, founded 2006, part of ITT Educational Services, Inc.
- **Coed**
- **Minimally difficult** entrance level

Academics *Degrees:* associate and bachelor's.

Freshman Application Contact Director of Recruitment, ITT Technical Institute, 2473 Fortune Drive, Suite 180, Lexington, KY 40509. *Phone:* 859-246-3300. *Toll-free phone:* 800-519-8151. *Website:* http://www.itt-tech.edu/.

ITT Technical Institute

Louisville, Kentucky

- **Proprietary** primarily 2-year, founded 1993, part of ITT Educational Services, Inc.
- **Suburban** campus
- **Coed**
- **Minimally difficult** entrance level

Academics *Calendar:* quarters. *Degrees:* associate and bachelor's.

Freshman Application Contact Director of Recruitment, ITT Technical Institute, 9500 Ormsby Station Road, Suite 100, Louisville, KY 40223. *Phone:* 502-327-7424. *Toll-free phone:* 888-790-7427. *Website:* http://www.itt-tech.edu/.

Kentucky Christian University

Grayson, Kentucky

- **Independent** comprehensive, founded 1919, affiliated with Christian Churches and Churches of Christ
- **Small-town** 121-acre campus
- **Endowment** $6.1 million
- **Coed** 574 undergraduate students, 95% full-time, 45% women, 55% men
- **Moderately difficult** entrance level, 58% of applicants were admitted

Undergraduates 546 full-time, 28 part-time. Students come from 30 states and territories; 4 other countries; 47% are from out of state; 12% Black or African American, non-Hispanic/Latino; 1% Hispanic/Latino; 0.3% Asian, non-Hispanic/Latino; 5% American Indian or Alaska Native, non-Hispanic/Latino; 0.5% Two or more races, non-Hispanic/Latino; 9% Race/ethnicity unknown;

0.8% international; 11% transferred in; 82% live on campus. *Retention:* 57% of full-time freshmen returned.

Freshmen *Admission:* 806 applied, 469 admitted, 199 enrolled. *Average high school GPA:* 3.02. *Test scores:* SAT critical reading scores over 500: 35%; SAT math scores over 500: 47%; SAT writing scores over 500: 29%; ACT scores over 18: 83%; SAT critical reading scores over 600: 12%; SAT writing scores over 600: 6%; ACT scores over 24: 24%; ACT scores over 30: 3%.

Faculty *Total:* 55, 67% full-time, 36% with terminal degrees. *Student/faculty ratio:* 13:1.

Academics *Calendar:* semesters. *Degrees:* bachelor's and master's. *Special study options:* academic remediation for entering students, accelerated degree program, adult/continuing education programs, advanced placement credit, cooperative education, double majors, external degree program, independent study, internships, off-campus study, part-time degree program, summer session for credit.

Computers on Campus 55 computers/terminals and 48 ports are available on campus for general student use. Students can access the following: computer help desk, free student e-mail accounts, online (class) grades, online (class) registration, online (class) schedules. Campuswide network is available. 100% of college-owned or -operated housing units are wired for high-speed Internet access. Wireless service is available via classrooms, dorm rooms, learning centers, libraries, student centers.

Student Life *Housing:* on-campus residence required through sophomore year. *Options:* men-only, women-only, disabled students. Campus housing is university owned. Freshman campus housing is guaranteed. *Activities and organizations:* drama/theater group, choral group, marching band. *Campus security:* 24-hour emergency response devices, late-night transport/escort service, controlled dormitory access. *Student services:* health clinic, personal/psychological counseling.

Athletics Member NCAA, NAIA, NCCAA. All NCAA Division II. *Intercollegiate sports:* basketball M/W, cheerleading M(c)/W(c), cross-country running M/W, football M/W, soccer M/W, volleyball W.

Standardized Tests *Required:* SAT or ACT (for admission).

Costs (2013–14) *One-time required fee:* $100. *Comprehensive fee:* $24,318 includes full-time tuition ($17,088), mandatory fees ($330), and room and board ($6900). Part-time tuition: $534 per credit hour. Part-time tuition and fees vary according to class time, program, and reciprocity agreements. *Required fees:* $534 per credit hour part-time. *Room and board:* Room and board charges vary according to housing facility. *Payment plan:* installment. *Waivers:* employees or children of employees.

Financial Aid Of all full-time matriculated undergraduates who enrolled in 2007, 507 applied for aid, 458 were judged to have need, 57 had their need fully met. 241 Federal Work-Study jobs (averaging $1219). 56 state and other part-time jobs (averaging $1403). In 2007, 55 non-need-based awards were made. *Average percent of need met:* 67%. *Average financial aid package:* $9798. *Average need-based loan:* $3792. *Average need-based gift aid:* $4474. *Average non-need-based aid:* $4320. *Average indebtedness upon graduation:* $24,703.

Applying *Options:* electronic application. *Application fee:* $35. *Required:* essay or personal statement, high school transcript, 2 letters of recommendation. *Required for some:* 3 letters of recommendation, interview. *Application deadlines:* rolling (freshmen), rolling (transfers). *Notification:* continuous (freshmen), continuous (transfers).

Freshman Application Contact Ms. Sheree Greer, Director of Admissions, Kentucky Christian University, 100 Academic Parkway, Grayson, KY 41143. *Phone:* 606-474-3186. *Toll-free phone:* 800-522-3181. *Fax:* 606-474-3155. *E-mail:* sgreer@kcu.edu. *Website:* http://www.kcu.edu/.

Kentucky Mountain Bible College

Vancleve, Kentucky

- **Independent interdenominational** 4-year, founded 1931
- **Rural** 400-acre campus with easy access to Lexington
- **Coed**
- **Minimally difficult** entrance level

Faculty *Student/faculty ratio:* 5:1.

Academics *Calendar:* semesters. *Degrees:* associate and bachelor's.

Student Life *Campus security:* student patrols.

Standardized Tests *Required:* ACT (for admission).

Costs (2012–13) *Comprehensive fee:* $10,790 includes full-time tuition ($6000), mandatory fees ($690), and room and board ($4100). Full-time tuition and fees vary according to program. Part-time tuition: $200 per credit. Part-time tuition and fees vary according to program. *Required fees:* $585 per year part-time. *College room only:* $1400. Room and board charges vary according to board plan and housing facility.

Applying *Application fee:* $25. *Required:* essay or personal statement, high school transcript, minimum 2.0 GPA, testimony of religious life. *Recommended:* interview.

Freshman Application Contact Mr. David Lorimer, Director of Recruiting, Kentucky Mountain Bible College, PO Box 10, Vancleve, KY 41385. *Phone:* 606-693-5000 Ext. 138. *Toll-free phone:* 800-879-KMBC. *Fax:* 606-693-4884. *E-mail:* kmbc@kmbc.edu. *Website:* http://www.kmbc.edu/.

Kentucky State University

Frankfort, Kentucky

- **State-related** comprehensive, founded 1886
- **Small-town** 915-acre campus with easy access to Louisville
- **Endowment** $28.6 million
- **Coed** 2,296 undergraduate students, 78% full-time, 59% women, 41% men
- **Minimally difficult** entrance level, 45% of applicants were admitted

Undergraduates 1,782 full-time, 514 part-time. Students come from 30 states and territories; 10 other countries; 43% are from out of state; 57% Black or African American, non-Hispanic/Latino; 0.8% Hispanic/Latino; 0.3% Asian, non-Hispanic/Latino; 0.2% Native Hawaiian or other Pacific Islander, non-Hispanic/Latino; 1% Two or more races, non-Hispanic/Latino; 22% Race/ethnicity unknown; 0.5% international; 8% transferred in; 37% live on campus. *Retention:* 46% of full-time freshmen returned.

Freshmen *Admission:* 4,193 applied, 1,866 admitted, 323 enrolled. *Average high school GPA:* 2.44. *Test scores:* SAT critical reading scores over 500: 13%; SAT math scores over 500: 11%; SAT writing scores over 500: 9%; ACT scores over 18: 37%; ACT scores over 24: 5%; ACT scores over 30: 2%.

Faculty *Total:* 162, 83% full-time, 53% with terminal degrees. *Student/faculty ratio:* 14:1.

Academics *Calendar:* semesters. *Degrees:* associate, bachelor's, and master's. *Special study options:* academic remediation for entering students, adult/continuing education programs, advanced placement credit, cooperative education, distance learning, double majors, English as a second language, external degree program, honors programs, independent study, internships, off-campus study, part-time degree program, services for LD students, student-designed majors, study abroad, summer session for credit. *ROTC:* Army (c), Air Force (c). *Unusual degree programs:* 3-2 engineering with University of Kentucky, University of Maryland at College Park, Vanderbilt University, Florida A&M University.

Computers on Campus 450 computers/terminals and 200 ports are available on campus for general student use. Students can access the following: campus intranet, computer help desk, free student e-mail accounts, online (class) grades, online (class) registration, online (class) schedules, accept financial aid awards. Campuswide network is available. 100% of college-owned or -operated housing units are wired for high-speed Internet access. Wireless service is available via entire campus.

Student Life *Housing:* on-campus residence required through sophomore year. *Options:* coed, men-only, women-only. Campus housing is university owned. Freshman applicants given priority for college housing. *Activities and organizations:* drama/theater group, student-run newspaper, television station, choral group, marching band, Student Government Association, NAACP, Apostolic Lighthouse Organization, Whitney Young Council, Kentucky Education Association, national fraternities, national sororities. *Campus security:* 24-hour emergency response devices and patrols, controlled dormitory access. *Student services:* health clinic, personal/psychological counseling.

Athletics Member NCAA. All Division II. *Intercollegiate sports:* baseball M(s), basketball M(s)/W(s), cross-country running M(s)/W(s), football M(s), golf M(s), softball W(s), track and field M(s)/W(s), volleyball W(s).

Standardized Tests *Required:* SAT or ACT (for admission).

Costs (2012–13) *Tuition:* state resident $6108 full-time, $229 per credit hour part-time; nonresident $15,708 full-time, $585 per credit hour part-time. Full-time tuition and fees vary according to course load. Part-time tuition and fees vary according to course load. *Required fees:* $750 full-time, $25 per credit hour part-time. *Room and board:* $6580; room only: $3340. Room and board charges vary according to board plan and housing facility. *Payment plan:* deferred payment. *Waivers:* children of alumni, senior citizens, and employees or children of employees.

Financial Aid Of all full-time matriculated undergraduates who enrolled in 2012, 1,621 applied for aid, 1,621 were judged to have need, 31 had their need fully met. 205 Federal Work-Study jobs (averaging $1730). In 2012, 2 non-need-based awards were made. *Average percent of need met:* 45%. *Average financial aid package:* $10,279. *Average need-based loan:* $4019. *Average need-based gift aid:* $6898. *Average non-need-based aid:* $2013. *Average indebtedness upon graduation:* $39,623.

Applying *Options:* electronic application, early admission. *Application fee:* $30. *Required:* high school transcript. *Required for some:* essay or personal statement, 2 letters of recommendation, interview. *Recommended:* minimum 2.0 GPA. *Application deadlines:* rolling (freshmen), rolling (transfers).
Freshman Application Contact Mr. Juan Alexander, Director of Admission, Kentucky State University, 400 East Main Street, Academic Suite Building 312, Frankfort, KY 40601. *Phone:* 502- 597-6322. *Fax:* 502-597-5814. *E-mail:* juan.alexander@kysu.edu.
Website: http://www.kysu.edu/.

Kentucky Wesleyan College
Owensboro, Kentucky
- **Independent Methodist** 4-year, founded 1858
- **Suburban** 52-acre campus
- **Endowment** $27.9 million
- **Coed** 678 undergraduate students, 95% full-time, 49% women, 51% men
- **Moderately difficult** entrance level, 21% of applicants were admitted

Undergraduates 641 full-time, 37 part-time. Students come from 25 states and territories; 8 other countries; 28% are from out of state; 10% Black or African American, non-Hispanic/Latino; 2% Hispanic/Latino; 0.3% Asian, non-Hispanic/Latino; 0.6% American Indian or Alaska Native, non-Hispanic/Latino; 12% Race/ethnicity unknown; 1% international; 8% transferred in; 45% live on campus. *Retention:* 54% of full-time freshmen returned.
Freshmen *Admission:* 910 applied, 193 admitted, 158 enrolled. *Average high school GPA:* 3.24. *Test scores:* SAT critical reading scores over 500: 40%; SAT math scores over 500: 54%; SAT writing scores over 500: 28%; ACT scores over 18: 85%; SAT critical reading scores over 600: 15%; SAT math scores over 600: 25%; SAT writing scores over 600: 14%; ACT scores over 24: 29%; SAT critical reading scores over 700: 4%; SAT math scores over 700: 4%; ACT scores over 30: 3%.
Faculty *Total:* 75, 64% full-time, 56% with terminal degrees. *Student/faculty ratio:* 12:1.
Academics *Calendar:* semesters. *Degree:* bachelor's. *Special study options:* academic remediation for entering students, accelerated degree program, adult/continuing education programs, advanced placement credit, cooperative education, distance learning, double majors, honors programs, independent study, internships, off-campus study, part-time degree program, services for LD students, student-designed majors, study abroad, summer session for credit. *ROTC:* Army (c). *Unusual degree programs:* 3-2 engineering with Auburn University, University of Kentucky; nursing with University of Louisville.
Computers on Campus 125 computers/terminals are available on campus for general student use. Students can access the following: campus intranet, computer help desk, free student e-mail accounts, online (class) grades, online (class) registration, online (class) schedules. Campuswide network is available. 100% of college-owned or -operated housing units are wired for high-speed Internet access. Wireless service is available via entire campus.
Student Life *Housing:* on-campus residence required through senior year. *Options:* coed, men-only, women-only, disabled students. Campus housing is university owned. Freshman campus housing is guaranteed. *Activities and organizations:* drama/theater group, student-run newspaper, radio station, choral group, marching band, Student Government Association, Student Activities Programming Board, Campus Ministries, Pre Professional, St Jude Up 'Til Dawn Executive Board, national fraternities, national sororities. *Campus security:* 24-hour emergency response devices, late-night transport/escort service, controlled dormitory access, 12-hour patrols by trained security personnel. *Student services:* health clinic, personal/psychological counseling, women's center.
Athletics Member NCAA. All Division II. *Intercollegiate sports:* baseball M(s), basketball M(s)/W(s), cheerleading M/W, cross-country running M(s)/W(s), football M(s)/W(s), golf M(s)/W(s), soccer M(s)/W(s), softball W(s), tennis W(s), track and field M(s)/W(s), volleyball W(s). *Intramural sports:* basketball M/W, soccer M/W, softball M, volleyball M/W.
Standardized Tests *Required:* SAT or ACT (for admission).
Costs (2013–14) *Comprehensive fee:* $28,700 includes full-time tuition ($20,600), mandatory fees ($600), and room and board ($7500). Full-time tuition and fees vary according to course load. Part-time tuition: $585 per credit. Part-time tuition and fees vary according to course load. *Room and board:* Room and board charges vary according to board plan and housing facility. *Payment plans:* installment, deferred payment. *Waivers:* children of alumni, senior citizens, and employees or children of employees.
Financial Aid Of all full-time matriculated undergraduates who enrolled in 2011, 702 applied for aid, 653 were judged to have need, 107 had their need fully met. 117 Federal Work-Study jobs (averaging $1427). In 2011, 89 non-need-based awards were made. *Average percent of need met:* 69%. *Average financial aid package:* $15,970. *Average need-based loan:* $3930. *Average*

need-based gift aid: $12,886. *Average non-need-based aid:* $9561. *Financial aid deadline:* 3/15.
Applying *Options:* electronic application, early admission, deferred entrance. *Required:* high school transcript. *Notification:* continuous (freshmen), continuous (transfers).
Freshman Application Contact Kentucky Wesleyan College, 3000 Frederica Street, Owensboro, KY 42301. *Phone:* 270-852-3120. *Toll-free phone:* 800-999-0592 (in-state); 800-990-0592 (out-of-state).
Website: http://www.kwc.edu/.

Lindsey Wilson College
Columbia, Kentucky
- **Independent United Methodist** comprehensive, founded 1903
- **Rural** 225-acre campus
- **Endowment** $14.3 million
- **Coed** 2,217 undergraduate students, 95% full-time, 60% women, 40% men
- **Minimally difficult** entrance level, 65% of applicants were admitted

Undergraduates 2,107 full-time, 110 part-time. Students come from 30 states and territories; 27 other countries; 18% are from out of state; 9% Black or African American, non-Hispanic/Latino; 0.6% Hispanic/Latino; 0.7% Asian, non-Hispanic/Latino; 0.5% American Indian or Alaska Native, non-Hispanic/Latino; 2% Two or more races, non-Hispanic/Latino; 12% Race/ethnicity unknown; 0.3% international; 15% transferred in; 52% live on campus. *Retention:* 58% of full-time freshmen returned.
Freshmen *Admission:* 2,928 applied, 1,915 admitted, 526 enrolled. *Average high school GPA:* 3.22. *Test scores:* ACT scores over 18: 87%; ACT scores over 24: 28%; ACT scores over 30: 2%.
Faculty *Total:* 256, 43% full-time. *Student/faculty ratio:* 14:1.
Academics *Calendar:* semesters. *Degrees:* associate, bachelor's, and master's. *Special study options:* academic remediation for entering students, accelerated degree program, adult/continuing education programs, advanced placement credit, cooperative education, double majors, English as a second language, independent study, internships, off-campus study, part-time degree program, services for LD students, student-designed majors, study abroad, summer session for credit.
Computers on Campus 120 computers/terminals are available on campus for general student use. Students can access the following: campus intranet, computer help desk, free student e-mail accounts, online (class) grades, online (class) registration, online (class) schedules. Campuswide network is available. 100% of college-owned or -operated housing units are wired for high-speed Internet access. Wireless service is available via entire campus.
Student Life *Housing:* on-campus residence required through senior year. *Options:* men-only, women-only. Campus housing is university owned. Freshman campus housing is guaranteed. *Activities and organizations:* drama/theater group, student-run newspaper, choral group, marching band. *Campus security:* 24-hour emergency response devices and patrols. *Student services:* health clinic, personal/psychological counseling, women's center.
Athletics Member NAIA. *Intercollegiate sports:* baseball M(s), basketball M(s)/W(s), bowling M(s)/W(s), cheerleading M(s)/W(s), cross-country running M(s)/W(s), football M(s)/W(s), golf M(s)/W(s), soccer M(s)/W(s), softball W(s), swimming and diving M(s)/W(s), tennis M(s)/W(s), track and field M(s)/W(s), volleyball W(s), wrestling M(s). *Intramural sports:* basketball M/W, football M/W, softball M/W, table tennis M/W, tennis M/W, volleyball M/W, weight lifting M/W.
Standardized Tests *Required for some:* SAT or ACT (for admission).
Costs (2013–14) *Comprehensive fee:* $30,470 includes full-time tuition ($21,840), mandatory fees ($230), and room and board ($8400). Full-time tuition and fees vary according to location. Part-time tuition: $910 per credit hour. Part-time tuition and fees vary according to location. *College room only:* $3100. *Payment plan:* installment. *Waivers:* senior citizens and employees or children of employees.
Financial Aid Of all full-time matriculated undergraduates who enrolled in 2012, 2,092 applied for aid, 1,994 were judged to have need, 429 had their need fully met. 290 Federal Work-Study jobs (averaging $2140). 20 state and other part-time jobs (averaging $2063). *Average indebtedness upon graduation:* $27,542.
Applying *Options:* electronic application. *Required:* high school transcript. *Recommended:* interview. *Application deadlines:* rolling (freshmen), rolling (transfers). *Notification:* continuous (freshmen), continuous (transfers).
Freshman Application Contact Mrs. Charity Ferguson, Assistant Director of Admissions, Lindsey Wilson College, 210 Lindsey Wilson Street, Columbia, KY 42728-1298. *Phone:* 270-384-8100. *Toll-free phone:* 800-264-0138. *Fax:* 270-384-8591.
Website: http://www.lindsey.edu/.

Mid-Continent University
Mayfield, Kentucky

- **Independent Southern Baptist** comprehensive, founded 1949
- **Small-town** 60-acre campus
- **Endowment** $3.4 million
- **Coed** 2,174 undergraduate students, 80% full-time, 62% women, 38% men
- **Minimally difficult** entrance level, 87% of applicants were admitted

Undergraduates 1,731 full-time, 443 part-time. Students come from 21 states and territories; 10 other countries; 18% are from out of state; 14% Black or African American, non-Hispanic/Latino; 2% Hispanic/Latino; 0.2% Asian, non-Hispanic/Latino; 0.1% Native Hawaiian or other Pacific Islander, non-Hispanic/Latino; 0.3% American Indian or Alaska Native, non-Hispanic/Latino; 1% Two or more races, non-Hispanic/Latino; 2% Race/ethnicity unknown; 0.6% international; 18% transferred in; 5% live on campus. *Retention:* 60% of full-time freshmen returned.

Freshmen *Admission:* 419 applied, 365 admitted, 261 enrolled. *Average high school GPA:* 2.87.

Faculty *Total:* 199, 23% full-time, 18% with terminal degrees. *Student/faculty ratio:* 20:1.

Academics *Calendar:* semesters. *Degrees:* certificates, associate, bachelor's, and master's. *Special study options:* academic remediation for entering students, accelerated degree program, adult/continuing education programs, advanced placement credit, distance learning, double majors, English as a second language, independent study, off-campus study, part-time degree program, student-designed majors, summer session for credit.

Computers on Campus 43 computers/terminals are available on campus for general student use. Students can access the following: free student e-mail accounts, online (class) grades, online (class) schedules. Campuswide network is available. 100% of college-owned or -operated housing units are wired for high-speed Internet access. Wireless service is available via entire campus.

Student Life *Housing:* on-campus residence required through sophomore year. *Options:* men-only, women-only. Campus housing is university owned. *Activities and organizations:* drama/theater group, student-run newspaper, choral group, Student Government Association, Baptist Student Union, Psychology Club, International Club, Ministry Association. *Campus security:* 24-hour emergency response devices, late-night transport/escort service, controlled dormitory access, night patrols by trained security personnel. *Student services:* personal/psychological counseling.

Athletics Member NAIA, NCCAA. *Intercollegiate sports:* baseball M(s), basketball M(s)/W(s), soccer M(s), softball W(s), volleyball W(s). *Intramural sports:* cheerleading M/W.

Standardized Tests *Required:* SAT or ACT (for admission).

Financial Aid Of all full-time matriculated undergraduates who enrolled in 2009, 2,161 applied for aid, 2,117 were judged to have need, 58 had their need fully met. 72 Federal Work-Study jobs (averaging $2126). In 2009, 52 non-need-based awards were made. *Average percent of need met:* 35%. *Average financial aid package:* $8454. *Average need-based loan:* $3523. *Average need-based gift aid:* $6356. *Average non-need-based aid:* $8564. *Average indebtedness upon graduation:* $11,005.

Applying *Options:* electronic application, early admission, deferred entrance. *Application fee:* $50. *Required:* high school transcript. *Required for some:* essay or personal statement, minimum 2.0 GPA, 1 letter of recommendation, interview. *Application deadlines:* rolling (freshmen), rolling (out-of-state freshmen), rolling (transfers). *Notification:* continuous (freshmen), continuous (out-of-state freshmen), continuous (transfers).

Freshman Application Contact Mr. Karl Hatton, Acting Dean of Students/Enrollment, Mid-Continent University, 99 Powell Road East, Mayfield, KY 42066. *Phone:* 270-247-8521 Ext. 312. *Toll-free phone:* 866-894-8878. *Fax:* 270-247-9475. *E-mail:* advantage@midcontinent.edu. *Website:* http://www.midcontinent.edu/.

Midway College
Midway, Kentucky

Freshman Application Contact Midway College, 512 East Stephens Street, Midway, KY 40347-1120. *Phone:* 859-846-5799. *Toll-free phone:* 800-755-0031. *Website:* http://www.midway.edu/.

Morehead State University
Morehead, Kentucky

- **State-supported** comprehensive, founded 1922
- **Small-town** 1016-acre campus
- **Coed** 9,725 undergraduate students, 61% full-time, 61% women, 39% men
- **Minimally difficult** entrance level, 84% of applicants were admitted

Undergraduates 5,897 full-time, 3,828 part-time. 14% are from out of state; 3% Black or African American, non-Hispanic/Latino; 1% Hispanic/Latino; 0.3% Asian, non-Hispanic/Latino; 0.1% Native Hawaiian or other Pacific Islander, non-Hispanic/Latino; 0.2% American Indian or Alaska Native, non-Hispanic/Latino; 1% Two or more races, non-Hispanic/Latino; 2% Race/ethnicity unknown; 0.9% international; 5% transferred in; 35% live on campus. *Retention:* 66% of full-time freshmen returned.

Freshmen *Admission:* 5,230 applied, 4,419 admitted, 1,649 enrolled. *Average high school GPA:* 3.32. *Test scores:* SAT critical reading scores over 500: 39%; SAT math scores over 500: 58%; SAT writing scores over 500: 30%; ACT scores over 18: 90%; SAT critical reading scores over 600: 13%; SAT math scores over 600: 14%; SAT writing scores over 600: 3%; ACT scores over 24: 35%; SAT critical reading scores over 700: 4%; SAT math scores over 700: 1%; SAT writing scores over 700: 1%; ACT scores over 30: 3%.

Faculty *Total:* 479, 80% full-time. *Student/faculty ratio:* 17:1.

Academics *Calendar:* semesters. *Degrees:* associate, bachelor's, master's, doctoral, post-master's, and postbachelor's certificates. *Special study options:* academic remediation for entering students, accelerated degree program, adult/continuing education programs, advanced placement credit, cooperative education, distance learning, double majors, honors programs, independent study, internships, off-campus study, part-time degree program, services for LD students, student-designed majors, study abroad, summer session for credit. *ROTC:* Army (b). *Unusual degree programs:* 3-2 engineering with Chemical Engineering : 3 years (96 hours) at Morehead State University, transfer to University of Kentucky to an approved engineering program.

Computers on Campus 1,000 computers/terminals and 1,820 ports are available on campus for general student use. Students can access the following: campus intranet, computer help desk, free student e-mail accounts, online (class) grades, online (class) registration, online (class) schedules. Campuswide network is available. 100% of college-owned or -operated housing units are wired for high-speed Internet access. Wireless service is available via entire campus.

Student Life *Housing:* on-campus residence required through sophomore year. *Options:* coed, disabled students. Campus housing is university owned. Freshman applicants given priority for college housing. *Activities and organizations:* drama/theater group, student-run newspaper, radio and television station, choral group, marching band, national fraternities, national sororities. *Campus security:* 24-hour emergency response devices and patrols, student patrols, late-night transport/escort service, controlled dormitory access. *Student services:* health clinic, personal/psychological counseling.

Athletics Member NCAA. All Division I except football (Division I-AA). *Intercollegiate sports:* baseball M(s), basketball M(s)/W(s), bowling M(c)/W(c), cheerleading M/W, cross-country running M(s)/W(s), equestrian sports M(c)/W(c), golf M(s), riflery M(s)/W(s), soccer W(s), softball W(s), tennis M(s)/W(s), track and field M(s)/W(s), volleyball W(s). *Intramural sports:* archery M/W, badminton M/W, basketball M/W, bowling M/W, football M/W, golf M/W, racquetball M/W, soccer M(c)/W(c), softball M/W, swimming and diving M/W, table tennis M/W, tennis M/W, track and field M/W, volleyball M/W.

Standardized Tests *Required:* SAT or ACT (for admission).

Costs (2013–14) *Tuition:* $276 per credit hour part-time; nonresident $690 per credit hour part-time. Full-time tuition and fees vary according to course load, degree level, location, reciprocity agreements, and student level. Part-time tuition and fees vary according to course load, degree level, location, reciprocity agreements, and student level. *Room and board:* Room and board charges vary according to board plan and housing facility. *Payment plan:* installment. *Waivers:* children of alumni, senior citizens, and employees or children of employees.

Financial Aid Of all full-time matriculated undergraduates who enrolled in 2012, 5,152 applied for aid, 4,577 were judged to have need, 986 had their need fully met. 438 Federal Work-Study jobs (averaging $2048). 731 state and other part-time jobs (averaging $2371). In 2012, 732 non-need-based awards were made. *Average percent of need met:* 63%. *Average financial aid package:* $10,305. *Average need-based loan:* $3646. *Average need-based gift aid:* $4960. *Average non-need-based aid:* $6602. *Average indebtedness upon graduation:* $28,768.

Applying *Options:* electronic application, early admission, deferred entrance. *Application fee:* $30. *Required:* high school transcript. *Required for some:* essay or personal statement, 1 letter of recommendation, interview. *Application*

deadlines: rolling (freshmen), rolling (transfers). *Notification:* continuous (freshmen), continuous (transfers).
Freshman Application Contact Mr. Jeffrey Liles, Assistant Vice President for Enrollment Services, Morehead State University, 100 Admissions Center, Morehead, KY 40351. *Phone:* 606-783-2000. *Toll-free phone:* 800-585-6781. *Fax:* 606-783-5038. *E-mail:* admissions@moreheadstate.edu. *Website:* http://www.moreheadstate.edu/.

Murray State University
Murray, Kentucky

- **State-supported** comprehensive, founded 1922, part of Kentucky Council on Post Secondary Education
- **Small-town** 238-acre campus
- **Endowment** $59.0 million
- **Coed** 8,891 undergraduate students, 80% full-time, 59% women, 41% men
- **Moderately difficult** entrance level, 82% of applicants were admitted

Undergraduates 7,090 full-time, 1,801 part-time. Students come from 44 states and territories; 51 other countries; 29% are from out of state; 7% Black or African American, non-Hispanic/Latino; 2% Hispanic/Latino; 0.8% Asian, non-Hispanic/Latino; 0.1% Native Hawaiian or other Pacific Islander, non-Hispanic/Latino; 0.2% American Indian or Alaska Native, non-Hispanic/Latino; 1% Two or more races, non-Hispanic/Latino; 2% Race/ethnicity unknown; 5% international; 8% transferred in; 36% live on campus. *Retention:* 70% of full-time freshmen returned.
Freshmen *Admission:* 4,573 applied, 3,760 admitted, 1,626 enrolled. *Average high school GPA:* 3.35. *Test scores:* ACT scores over 18: 98%; ACT scores over 24: 45%; ACT scores over 30: 5%.
Faculty *Total:* 611, 69% full-time, 66% with terminal degrees. *Student/faculty ratio:* 16:1.
Academics *Calendar:* semesters. *Degrees:* certificates, associate, bachelor's, master's, doctoral, and post-master's certificates. *Special study options:* academic remediation for entering students, adult/continuing education programs, advanced placement credit, cooperative education, distance learning, double majors, English as a second language, external degree program, freshman honors college, honors programs, independent study, internships, off-campus study, part-time degree program, services for LD students, study abroad, summer session for credit. *ROTC:* Army (b). *Unusual degree programs:* 3-2 Biology, Chemistry with the University of Louisville Medical School.
Computers on Campus 1,800 computers/terminals are available on campus for general student use. Students can access the following: campus intranet, computer help desk, free student e-mail accounts, online (class) grades, online (class) registration, online (class) schedules, billing accounts. Campuswide network is available. 100% of college-owned or -operated housing units are wired for high-speed Internet access. Wireless service is available via entire campus.
Student Life *Housing:* on-campus residence required through sophomore year. *Options:* coed, women-only, disabled students. Campus housing is university owned. *Activities and organizations:* drama/theater group, student-run newspaper, radio and television station, choral group, marching band, student government, Baptist Student Union, Christ Ambassadors, Residential Colleges, Greek Organizations, national fraternities, national sororities. *Campus security:* 24-hour emergency response devices and patrols, student patrols, late-night transport/escort service, controlled dormitory access. *Student services:* health clinic, personal/psychological counseling, women's center, legal services.
Athletics Member NCAA. All Division I except football (Division I-AA). *Intercollegiate sports:* baseball M(s), basketball M(s)/W(s), cheerleading W, crew M(c)/W(c), cross-country running W(s), equestrian sports M(c)/W(c), golf M(s)/W(s), riflery M(s)/W(s), soccer W(s), softball W(s), tennis M(s)/W(s), track and field W(s), volleyball W(s). *Intramural sports:* basketball M/W, bowling M/W, fencing M/W, field hockey M/W, football M/W, golf M/W, racquetball M/W, rugby M, sailing M/W, soccer M/W, softball M/W, swimming and diving M/W, track and field M/W, volleyball M/W, weight lifting M/W.
Standardized Tests *Required:* SAT or ACT (for admission). *Recommended:* ACT (for admission).
Costs (2012–13) *Tuition:* state resident $5880 full-time, $285 per credit hour part-time; nonresident $7942 full-time, $369 per credit hour part-time. Full-time tuition and fees vary according to reciprocity agreements. Part-time tuition and fees vary according to reciprocity agreements. *Required fees:* $960 full-time. *Room and board:* $7638; room only: $4430. Room and board charges vary according to board plan and housing facility. *Payment plan:* installment. *Waivers:* children of alumni, senior citizens, and employees or children of employees.

Financial Aid Of all full-time matriculated undergraduates who enrolled in 2012, 5,318 applied for aid, 4,460 were judged to have need, 813 had their need fully met. 264 Federal Work-Study jobs (averaging $2088). 1,332 state and other part-time jobs (averaging $2913). In 2012, 227 non-need-based awards were made. *Average percent of need met:* 29%. *Average financial aid package:* $10,810. *Average need-based loan:* $6671. *Average need-based gift aid:* $5611. *Average non-need-based aid:* $3224. *Average indebtedness upon graduation:* $20,644.
Applying *Options:* electronic application. *Application fee:* $30. *Required:* high school transcript, minimum 3.0 GPA, Pre-College Curricula. *Notification:* continuous until 8/1 (freshmen), continuous until 1/8 (out-of-state freshmen), continuous until 8/1 (transfers).
Freshman Application Contact Ms. Lesa Harris, Director of Undergraduate Admissions, Murray State University, 102 Curris Center, Murray, KY 42701-0009. *Phone:* 270-809-3750. *Toll-free phone:* 800-272-4678. *Fax:* 270-809-3780. *E-mail:* admissions@murraystate.edu. *Website:* http://www.murraystate.edu/.

National College
Lexington, Kentucky

Director of Admissions Kim Thomasson, Campus Director, National College, 2376 Sir Barton Way, Lexington, KY 40509. *Phone:* 859-253-0621. *Toll-free phone:* 888-9-JOBREADY. *Website:* http://www.national-college.edu/.

National College
Louisville, Kentucky

Director of Admissions Vincent C. Tinebra, Campus Director, National College, 4205 Dixie Highway, Louisville, KY 40216. *Phone:* 502-447-7634. *Toll-free phone:* 888-9-JOBREADY. *Website:* http://www.national-college.edu/.

Northern Kentucky University
Highland Heights, Kentucky

- **State-supported** comprehensive, founded 1968
- **Suburban** 398-acre campus with easy access to Cincinnati
- **Endowment** $68.9 million
- **Coed**
- **Moderately difficult** entrance level

Faculty *Student/faculty ratio:* 17:1.
Academics *Calendar:* semesters. *Degrees:* certificates, associate, bachelor's, master's, doctoral, post-master's, and postbachelor's certificates.
Student Life *Campus security:* 24-hour emergency response devices and patrols, late-night transport/escort service, controlled dormitory access.
Athletics Member NCAA. All Division II.
Standardized Tests *Required:* SAT or ACT (for admission).
Costs (2012–13) *Tuition:* state resident $7872 full-time, $328 per credit hour part-time; nonresident $15,744 full-time, $656 per credit hour part-time. Full-time tuition and fees vary according to course load and reciprocity agreements. Part-time tuition and fees vary according to course load and reciprocity agreements. *Required fees:* $192 full-time. *Room and board:* $7430. Room and board charges vary according to board plan and housing facility.
Financial Aid Of all full-time matriculated undergraduates who enrolled in 2012, 7,913 applied for aid, 6,566 were judged to have need, 919 had their need fully met. In 2012, 755 non-need-based awards were made. *Average percent of need met:* 53. *Average financial aid package:* $8506. *Average need-based loan:* $3656. *Average need-based gift aid:* $5107. *Average non-need-based aid:* $4405. *Average indebtedness upon graduation:* $13,432.
Applying *Options:* electronic application, early admission, deferred entrance. *Application fee:* $40. *Required:* high school transcript. *Required for some:* some programs require separate applications.
Freshman Application Contact Office of Admissions, Northern Kentucky University, Lucas Administrative Center, 400 Nunn Drive, Highland Heights, KY 41099. *Phone:* 859-572-5220. *Toll-free phone:* 800-637-9948. *Fax:* 859-572-6665. *E-mail:* admitnku@nku.edu. *Website:* http://www.nku.edu/.

See next page for display ad and page 1420 for the College Close-Up.

St. Catharine College

St. Catharine, Kentucky

Director of Admissions Ms. Amy C. Carrico, Director of Admissions, St. Catharine College, 2735 Bardstown Road, St. Catharine, KY 40061-9499. *Phone:* 859-336-5082. *Toll-free phone:* 800-599-2000. *Website:* http://www.sccky.edu/.

Southern Baptist Theological Seminary

Louisville, Kentucky

Freshman Application Contact Dr. Daniel DeWitt, Southern Baptist Theological Seminary, 2825 Lexington Road, Louisville, KY 40280-0004. *Phone:* 502-897-4011 Ext. 4617. *Website:* http://www.sbts.edu/.

Spalding University

Louisville, Kentucky

- **Independent** comprehensive, founded 1814, affiliated with Roman Catholic Church
- **Urban** 5-acre campus with easy access to Louisville
- **Endowment** $11.5 million
- **Coed** 1,371 undergraduate students, 72% full-time, 74% women, 26% men
- **Moderately difficult** entrance level, 43% of applicants were admitted

Undergraduates 983 full-time, 388 part-time. Students come from 13 states and territories; 7 other countries; 10% are from out of state; 29% Black or African American, non-Hispanic/Latino; 3% Hispanic/Latino; 1% Asian, non-Hispanic/Latino; 0.1% Native Hawaiian or other Pacific Islander, non-Hispanic/Latino; 0.4% American Indian or Alaska Native, non-Hispanic/Latino; 3% Two or more races, non-Hispanic/Latino; 4% Race/ethnicity unknown; 0.4%

international; 14% transferred in; 8% live on campus. *Retention:* 73% of full-time freshmen returned.

Freshmen *Admission:* 790 applied, 338 admitted, 171 enrolled. *Average high school GPA:* 3.04. *Test scores:* SAT critical reading scores over 500: 22%; SAT math scores over 500: 17%; ACT scores over 18: 66%; ACT scores over 24: 8%.

Faculty *Total:* 169, 53% full-time, 51% with terminal degrees. *Student/faculty ratio:* 11:1.

Academics *Calendar:* other. *Degrees:* certificates, associate, bachelor's, master's, doctoral, post-master's, and postbachelor's certificates. *Special study options:* academic remediation for entering students, accelerated degree program, adult/continuing education programs, advanced placement credit, cooperative education, distance learning, double majors, independent study, internships, off-campus study, part-time degree program, services for LD students, study abroad, summer session for credit. *ROTC:* Army (c), Air Force (c). *Unusual degree programs:* 3-2 occupational therapy.

Computers on Campus 250 computers/terminals are available on campus for general student use. Students can access the following: computer help desk, free student e-mail accounts, online (class) grades, online (class) registration, online (class) schedules. Campuswide network is available. 100% of college-owned or -operated housing units are wired for high-speed Internet access. Wireless service is available via entire campus.

Student Life *Housing options:* coed, disabled students. Campus housing is university owned. *Activities and organizations:* Egan Service Learning Program, Student Government Association, Student Occupational Therapy Association, Residence Hall Advisory Council, Best Buddies. *Campus security:* 24-hour emergency response devices and patrols, late-night transport/escort service, controlled dormitory access, outdoor emergency call stations located in various locations around campus. *Student services:* personal/psychological counseling.

Athletics Member NCAA, USCAA. All Division III. *Intercollegiate sports:* baseball M, basketball M/W, bowling W, cross-country running M/W, golf M/W, soccer M/W, softball W, track and field M/W, volleyball W.

Standardized Tests *Required:* SAT or ACT (for admission).

Costs (2012–13) *Comprehensive fee:* $28,950 includes full-time tuition ($20,550) and room and board ($8400). Full-time tuition and fees vary according to course load and program. Part-time tuition and fees vary according to course load and program. *College room only:* $5600. Room and board charges vary according to board plan. *Payment plans:* installment, deferred payment. *Waivers:* employees or children of employees.

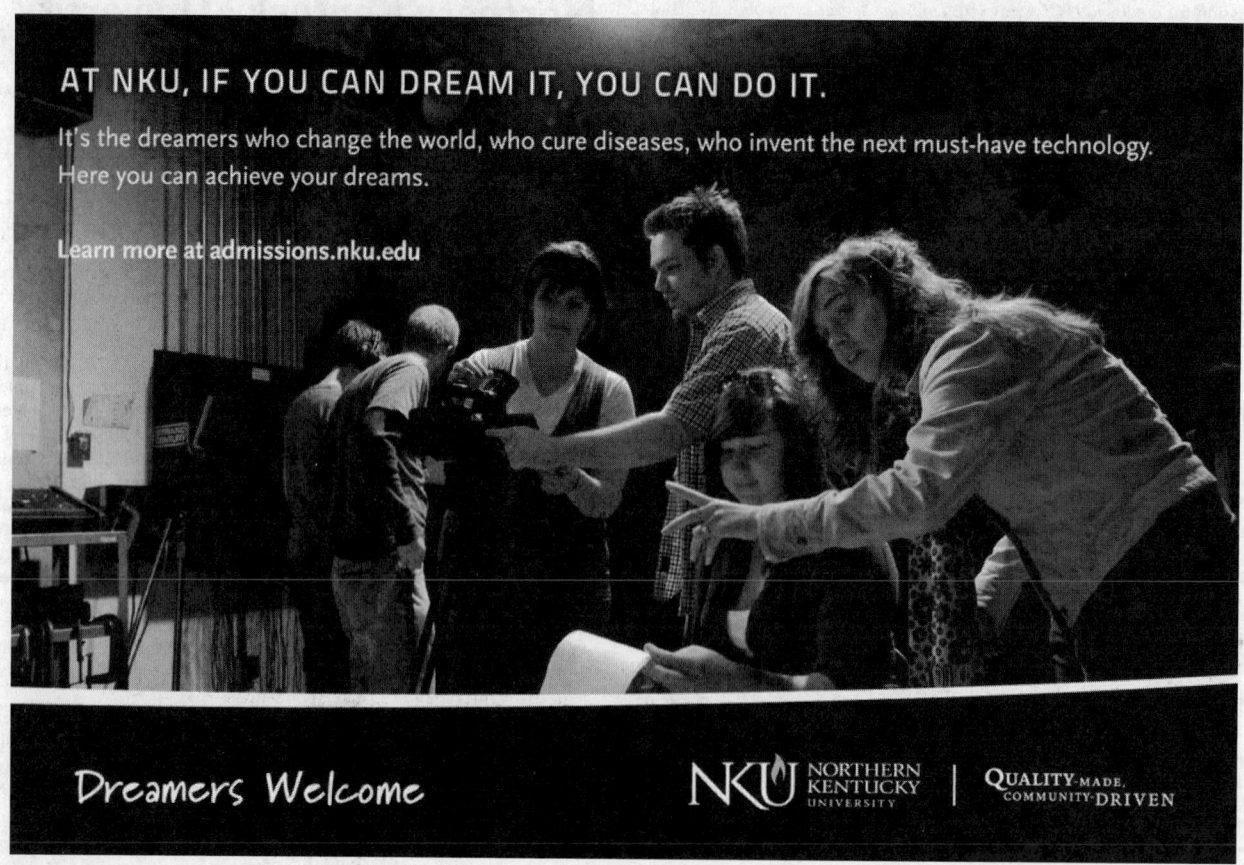

Financial Aid *Average percent of need met:* 75%. *Average financial aid package:* $11,500.
Applying *Options:* electronic application, early admission, deferred entrance. *Application fee:* $20. *Required:* high school transcript, minimum 2.5 GPA. *Required for some:* essay or personal statement. *Recommended:* interview. *Application deadlines:* rolling (freshmen), rolling (out-of-state freshmen), rolling (transfers). *Notification:* continuous (freshmen), continuous (out-of-state freshmen), continuous (transfers).
Freshman Application Contact Mr. Matt Elder, Associate Director of Admissions, Spalding University, 845 South Third Street, Louisville, KY 40203. *Phone:* 502-873-4177. *Toll-free phone:* 800-896-8941. *E-mail:* admissions@spalding.edu.
Website: http://www.spalding.edu/.

Strayer University—Florence Campus

Florence, Kentucky

Freshman Application Contact Strayer University—Florence Campus, 7300 Turfway Road, Suite 250, Florence, KY 41042.
Website: http://www.strayer.edu/campus/florence.

Strayer University—Lexington Campus

Lexington, Kentucky

Freshman Application Contact Strayer University—Lexington Campus, 220 Lexington Green Circle, Suite 550, Lexington, KY 40503.
Website: http://www.strayer.edu/campus/lexington/.

Strayer University—Louisville Campus

Louisville, Kentucky

Freshman Application Contact Strayer University—Louisville Campus, 2650 Eastpoint Parkway, Suite 100, Louisville, KY 40223.
Website: http://www.strayer.edu/campus/louisville/.

Sullivan College of Technology and Design

Louisville, Kentucky

- **Proprietary** primarily 2-year, founded 1961, part of The Sullivan University System, Inc.
- **Suburban** 10-acre campus with easy access to Louisville
- **Coed** 457 undergraduate students, 69% full-time, 32% women, 68% men
- **Moderately difficult** entrance level

Undergraduates 316 full-time, 141 part-time. Students come from 5 states and territories; 1 other country; 11% are from out of state; 18% Black or African American, non-Hispanic/Latino; 5% Hispanic/Latino; 1% Asian, non-Hispanic/Latino; 0.2% American Indian or Alaska Native, non-Hispanic/Latino; 8% Two or more races, non-Hispanic/Latino; 18% transferred in; 7% live on campus.
Freshmen *Admission:* 83 enrolled.
Faculty *Total:* 65, 46% full-time. *Student/faculty ratio:* 12:1.
Academics *Calendar:* quarters. *Degrees:* associate and bachelor's. *Special study options:* academic remediation for entering students, accelerated degree program, adult/continuing education programs, advanced placement credit, double majors, independent study, internships, part-time degree program, services for LD students, summer session for credit.
Computers on Campus 232 computers/terminals and 16 ports are available on campus for general student use. Students can access the following: campus intranet, computer help desk, free student e-mail accounts, online (class) grades, online (class) schedules, wireless Internet. Campuswide network is available. 50% of college-owned or -operated housing units are wired for high-

speed Internet access. Wireless service is available via classrooms, computer centers, computer labs, dorm rooms, learning centers, libraries, student centers.
Student Life *Housing options:* coed. Campus housing is university owned and leased by the school. Freshman applicants given priority for college housing. *Activities and organizations:* ASID, IIDA, ADDA, ADFED, Skills USA. *Campus security:* late-night transport/escort service, controlled dormitory access, telephone alarm device during hours school is open; patrols by trained security personnel while classes are in session.
Standardized Tests *Required:* Career Performance Assessment Test (CPAt) or ACT or SAT Language and Math scores in place of CPAt results (for admission). *Recommended:* SAT or ACT (for admission).
Costs (2013–14) *One-time required fee:* $100. *Comprehensive fee:* $27,560 includes full-time tuition ($17,340), mandatory fees ($1400), and room and board ($8820). Full-time tuition and fees vary according to course load, degree level, and program. Part-time tuition: $425 per quarter hour. Part-time tuition and fees vary according to course load, degree level, and program. No tuition increase for student's term of enrollment. *Room and board:* Room and board charges vary according to board plan. *Payment plan:* installment. *Waivers:* employees or children of employees.
Applying *Options:* electronic application, deferred entrance. *Application fee:* $100. *Required:* high school transcript, interview, CPAT Exam or ACT/SAT Scores. *Application deadlines:* rolling (freshmen), rolling (out-of-state freshmen), rolling (transfers). *Notification:* continuous (freshmen), continuous (out-of-state freshmen), continuous (transfers).
Freshman Application Contact Mr. Aamer Z. Chauhdri, Director of Admissions, Sullivan College of Technology and Design, 3901 Atkinson Square Drive, Louisville, KY 40218. *Phone:* 502-456-6509 Ext. 8220. *Toll-free phone:* 800-884-6528. *Fax:* 502-456-2341. *E-mail:* achauhdri@sctd.edu. *Website:* http://www.sctd.edu/.

Sullivan University

Louisville, Kentucky

- **Proprietary** comprehensive, founded 1864
- **Urban** 15-acre campus
- **Coed** 3,999 undergraduate students, 55% full-time, 60% women, 40% men
- **Minimally difficult** entrance level, 63% of applicants were admitted

Undergraduates 2,182 full-time, 1,817 part-time. Students come from 44 states and territories; 63 other countries; 15% are from out of state; 21% Black or African American, non-Hispanic/Latino; 0.2% Hispanic/Latino; 1% Asian, non-Hispanic/Latino; 0.1% Native Hawaiian or other Pacific Islander, non-Hispanic/Latino; 0.5% American Indian or Alaska Native, non-Hispanic/Latino; 10% Two or more races, non-Hispanic/Latino; 10% Race/ethnicity unknown; 0.2% international; 6% live on campus.
Freshmen *Admission:* 1,151 applied, 724 admitted, 308 enrolled.
Faculty *Total:* 340, 45% full-time, 35% with terminal degrees. *Student/faculty ratio:* 18:1.
Academics *Calendar:* quarters. *Degrees:* certificates, diplomas, associate, bachelor's, master's, doctoral, post-master's, and postbachelor's certificates. *Special study options:* academic remediation for entering students, accelerated degree program, adult/continuing education programs, cooperative education, distance learning, double majors, independent study, internships, part-time degree program, services for LD students, student-designed majors, summer session for credit.
Computers on Campus 92 computers/terminals are available on campus for general student use. Students can access the following: campus intranet, computer help desk, free student e-mail accounts, online (class) grades, online (class) schedules. Campuswide network is available. Wireless service is available via entire campus.
Student Life *Housing options:* coed, men-only, women-only, disabled students. Campus housing is university owned. Freshman campus housing is guaranteed. *Activities and organizations:* choral group, Student Activities Committee, Student Veterans Association, Sullivan Christian Fellowship, People 2 People Club, Glee Club. *Campus security:* 24-hour patrols, late-night transport/escort service, controlled dormitory access. *Student services:* personal/psychological counseling.
Athletics *Intramural sports:* basketball M/W, bowling M/W, soccer M/W, softball M/W, volleyball M/W.
Standardized Tests *Required:* Acceptable SAT, ACT, Sullivan Admissions Placement Assessment Scores Required (for admission).
Financial Aid Of all full-time matriculated undergraduates who enrolled in 2002, 6,028 applied for aid, 5,247 were judged to have need. 31 Federal Work-Study jobs (averaging $2065). In 2002, 374 non-need-based awards were made. *Average non-need-based aid:* $2000. *Average indebtedness upon graduation:* $15,000.

Applying *Options:* electronic application, deferred entrance. *Application fee:* $50. *Required:* high school transcript, interview. *Required for some:* essay or personal statement, 2 letters of recommendation, Certain programs require criminal background checks and no felony convictions. Some drug and abuse related misdemeanors will exclude applicants from being accepted into several programs. *Application deadlines:* rolling (freshmen), rolling (transfers). *Notification:* continuous (freshmen), continuous (transfers).
Freshman Application Contact Mr. Brian Willett, Director of Admissions, Sullivan University, 3101 Bardstown Road, Louisville, KY 40205. *Phone:* 502-456-6505. *Toll-free phone:* 800-844-1354. *Fax:* 502-456-0040. *E-mail:* admissions@sullivan.edu.
Website: http://www.sullivan.edu/.

Thomas More College

Crestview Hills, Kentucky

- **Independent Roman Catholic** comprehensive, founded 1921
- **Suburban** 100-acre campus with easy access to Cincinnati
- **Endowment** $14.0 million
- **Coed** 1,652 undergraduate students, 76% full-time, 52% women, 48% men
- **Moderately difficult** entrance level, 88% of applicants were admitted

Undergraduates 1,258 full-time, 394 part-time. Students come from 16 states and territories; 3 other countries; 49% are from out of state; 8% Black or African American, non-Hispanic/Latino; 2% Hispanic/Latino; 0.6% Asian, non-Hispanic/Latino; 0.3% American Indian or Alaska Native, non-Hispanic/Latino; 1% Two or more races, non-Hispanic/Latino; 11% Race/ethnicity unknown; 0.4% international; 4% transferred in; 27% live on campus. *Retention:* 66% of full-time freshmen returned.
Freshmen *Admission:* 1,093 applied, 965 admitted, 266 enrolled. *Average high school GPA:* 3.3. *Test scores:* SAT critical reading scores over 500: 48%; SAT math scores over 500: 64%; ACT scores over 18: 97%; SAT critical reading scores over 600: 16%; SAT math scores over 600: 18%; ACT scores over 24: 38%; SAT critical reading scores over 700: 6%; SAT math scores over 700: 8%; ACT scores over 30: 7%.
Faculty *Total:* 159, 48% full-time, 48% with terminal degrees. *Student/faculty ratio:* 14:1.

Academics *Calendar:* semesters. *Degrees:* certificates, associate, bachelor's, and master's. *Special study options:* academic remediation for entering students, accelerated degree program, adult/continuing education programs, advanced placement credit, cooperative education, distance learning, double majors, honors programs, independent study, internships, off-campus study, part-time degree program, services for LD students, student-designed majors, study abroad, summer session for credit. *ROTC:* Army (c), Air Force (c). *Unusual degree programs:* 3-2 engineering with Choice of locations.
Computers on Campus 100 computers/terminals are available on campus for general student use. Students can access the following: campus intranet, computer help desk, free student e-mail accounts, online (class) grades, online (class) registration, online (class) schedules. Campuswide network is available. 100% of college-owned or -operated housing units are wired for high-speed Internet access. Wireless service is available via entire campus.
Student Life *Housing options:* coed, men-only, women-only, disabled students. Campus housing is university owned. *Activities and organizations:* drama/theater group, choral group, Student Government Association, Student Activities Board, More Ministry, Outdoors Adventure Club, International Student Society, national fraternities, national sororities. *Campus security:* 24-hour emergency response devices and patrols, late-night transport/escort service, controlled dormitory access. *Student services:* health clinic, personal/psychological counseling.
Athletics Member NCAA. All Division III. *Intercollegiate sports:* baseball M, basketball M/W, cross-country running M/W, football M, golf M/W, soccer M/W, softball W, tennis M/W, volleyball W. *Intramural sports:* basketball M/W, football M, soccer M/W, softball M/W, volleyball M/W.
Standardized Tests *Required:* SAT or ACT (for admission).
Costs (2013–14) *Comprehensive fee:* $34,720 includes full-time tuition ($26,500), mandatory fees ($720), and room and board ($7500). Full-time tuition and fees vary according to student level. Part-time tuition: $590 per credit. Part-time tuition and fees vary according to student level. *Required fees:* $30 per hour part-time, $15 per term part-time. *College room only:* $3500. Room and board charges vary according to board plan and housing facility. *Payment plans:* installment, deferred payment. *Waivers:* senior citizens and employees or children of employees.
Financial Aid Of all full-time matriculated undergraduates who enrolled in 2012, 1,028 applied for aid, 700 were judged to have need, 156 had their need fully met. 125 Federal Work-Study jobs (averaging $1530). 169 state and other part-time jobs (averaging $195). In 2012, 170 non-need-based awards were made. *Average percent of need met:* 71%. *Average financial aid package:* $19,944. *Average need-based loan:* $4185. *Average need-based gift aid:*

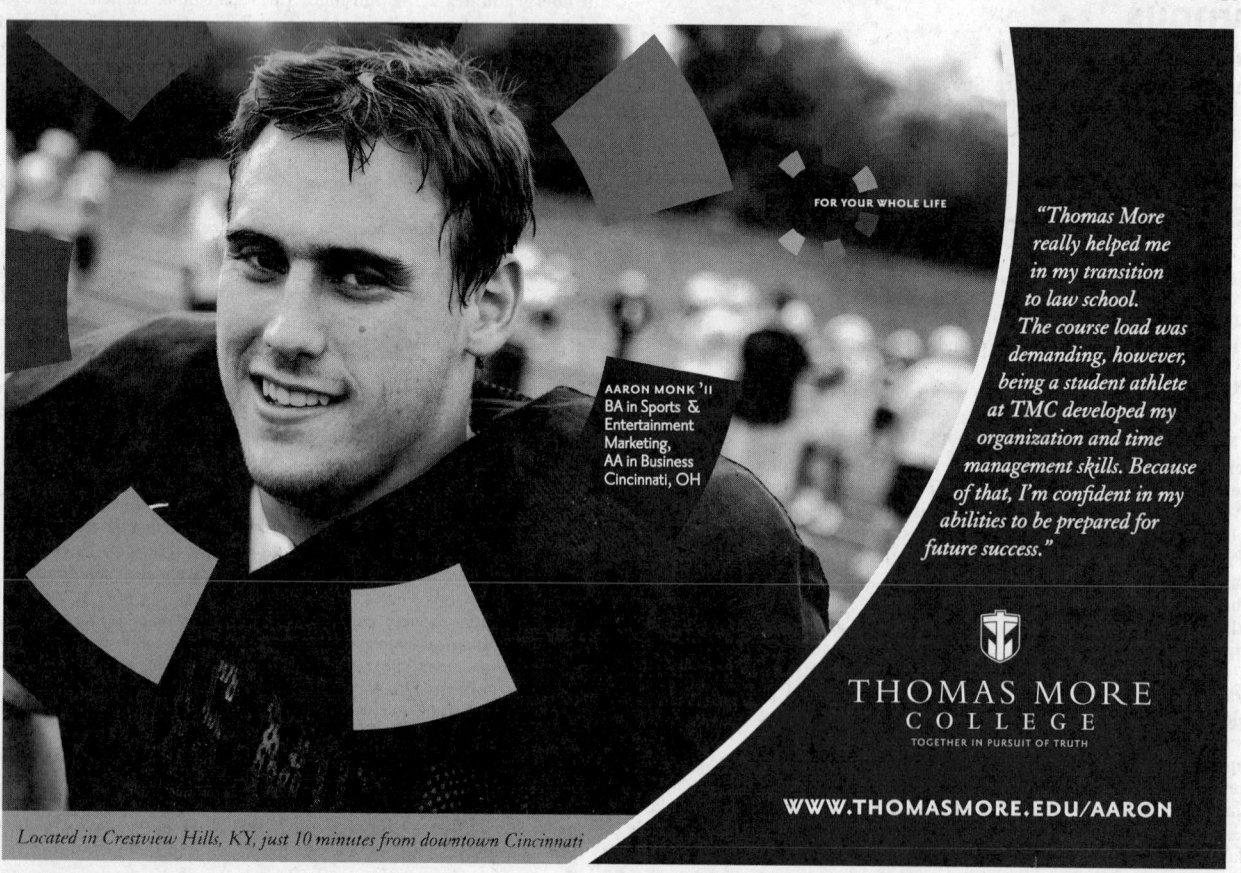

FOR YOUR WHOLE LIFE

AARON MONK '11
BA in Sports & Entertainment Marketing, AA in Business
Cincinnati, OH

"Thomas More really helped me in my transition to law school. The course load was demanding, however, being a student athlete at TMC developed my organization and time management skills. Because of that, I'm confident in my abilities to be prepared for future success."

THOMAS MORE
COLLEGE
TOGETHER IN PURSUIT OF TRUTH

WWW.THOMASMORE.EDU/AARON

Located in Crestview Hills, KY, just 10 minutes from downtown Cincinnati

$15,461. *Average non-need-based aid:* $13,433. *Average indebtedness upon graduation:* $32,650.

Applying *Options:* electronic application, deferred entrance. *Application fee:* $25. *Required:* high school transcript, minimum 2.5 GPA. *Required for some:* 2 letters of recommendation. *Application deadlines:* 8/1 (freshmen), 8/1 (transfers). *Notification:* continuous (freshmen), continuous (transfers).

Freshman Application Contact Mr. Billy Sarge, Associate Director of Admissions, Thomas More College, 333 Thomas More Parkway, Crestview Hills, KY 41017-3495. *Phone:* 859-344-3332. *Toll-free phone:* 800-825-4557. *Fax:* 859-344-3444. *E-mail:* admissions@thomasmore.edu. *Website:* http://www.thomasmore.edu/.

See previous page for display ad and page 1536 for the College Close-Up.

Transylvania University

Lexington, Kentucky

- **Independent** 4-year, founded 1780, affiliated with Christian Church (Disciples of Christ)
- **Urban** 40-acre campus with easy access to Cincinnati, Louisville
- **Coed** 1,074 undergraduate students, 99% full-time, 58% women, 42% men
- **Very difficult** entrance level, 85% of applicants were admitted

Undergraduates 1,060 full-time, 14 part-time. Students come from 28 states and territories; 6 other countries; 18% are from out of state; 3% Black or African American, non-Hispanic/Latino; 2% Hispanic/Latino; 2% Asian, non-Hispanic/Latino; 0.1% American Indian or Alaska Native, non-Hispanic/Latino; 2% Two or more races, non-Hispanic/Latino; 4% Race/ethnicity unknown; 1% international; 2% transferred in; 76% live on campus. *Retention:* 88% of full-time freshmen returned.

Freshmen *Admission:* 1,569 applied, 1,332 admitted, 333 enrolled. *Average high school GPA:* 3.72. *Test scores:* SAT critical reading scores over 500: 80%; SAT math scores over 500: 81%; ACT scores over 18: 100%; SAT critical reading scores over 600: 40%; SAT math scores over 600: 42%; ACT scores over 24: 82%; SAT critical reading scores over 700: 10%; SAT math scores over 700: 6%; ACT scores over 30: 26%.

Faculty *Total:* 108, 83% full-time, 86% with terminal degrees. *Student/faculty ratio:* 11:1.

Academics *Calendar:* 4-4-1. *Degree:* bachelor's. *Special study options:* advanced placement credit, double majors, independent study, internships, off-campus study, part-time degree program, services for LD students, student-designed majors, study abroad, summer session for credit. *ROTC:* Army (c), Air Force (c). *Unusual degree programs:* 3-2 engineering with University of Kentucky, Vanderbilt University.

Computers on Campus 200 computers/terminals and 200 ports are available on campus for general student use. Students can access the following: campus intranet, computer help desk, free student e-mail accounts, online (class) grades, online (class) registration, online (class) schedules. Campuswide network is available. 100% of college-owned or -operated housing units are wired for high-speed Internet access. Wireless service is available via classrooms, computer centers, computer labs, dorm rooms, learning centers, libraries, student centers.

Student Life *Housing:* on-campus residence required through junior year. *Options:* coed, men-only, women-only, disabled students. Campus housing is university owned. Freshman campus housing is guaranteed. *Activities and organizations:* drama/theater group, student-run newspaper, radio station, choral group, Student Government Association, Delta Sigma Phi, Phi Mu, Delta Delta Delta, Chi Omega, national fraternities, national sororities. *Campus security:* 24-hour emergency response devices and patrols, late-night transport/escort service, controlled dormitory access. *Student services:* health clinic, personal/psychological counseling.

Athletics Member NCAA. All Division III. *Intercollegiate sports:* baseball M, basketball M/W, cheerleading M/W, cross-country running M/W, equestrian sports M/W, field hockey W, golf M/W, lacrosse M/W, soccer M/W, softball W, swimming and diving M/W, tennis M/W, track and field M/W, volleyball W. *Intramural sports:* badminton M/W, basketball M/W, cross-country running M/W, equestrian sports M/W, golf M/W, lacrosse M/W, racquetball M/W, soccer M/W, softball M/W, swimming and diving M/W, table tennis M/W, tennis M/W, track and field M/W, ultimate Frisbee M/W, volleyball M/W, weight lifting M/W.

Standardized Tests *Required:* SAT or ACT (for admission).

Costs (2012–13) *Comprehensive fee:* $38,615 includes full-time tuition ($28,645), mandatory fees ($1220), and room and board ($8750). Part-time tuition: $3175 per course. Part-time tuition and fees vary according to course load. *Room and board:* Room and board charges vary according to board plan, housing facility, and location. *Payment plan:* installment. *Waivers:* employees or children of employees.

Financial Aid Of all full-time matriculated undergraduates who enrolled in 2012, 816 applied for aid, 727 were judged to have need, 155 had their need fully met. 430 Federal Work-Study jobs (averaging $1713). 48 state and other part-time jobs (averaging $7107). In 2012, 320 non-need-based awards were made. *Average percent of need met:* 81%. *Average financial aid package:* $24,373. *Average need-based loan:* $4295. *Average need-based gift aid:* $20,083. *Average non-need-based aid:* $13,690. *Average indebtedness upon graduation:* $26,604.

Applying *Options:* electronic application, early admission, early action, deferred entrance. *Required:* essay or personal statement, high school transcript, minimum 2.8 GPA, 2 letters of recommendation. *Required for some:* interview. *Recommended:* interview. *Application deadlines:* 2/1 (freshmen), rolling (transfers), 12/1 (early action). *Notification:* 3/1 (freshmen), 1/15 (early action).

Freshman Application Contact Mr. Bradley Goan, Vice President for Enrollment and Dean of Admissions, Transylvania University, 300 North Broadway, Lexington, KY 40508-1797. *Phone:* 859-233-4242. *Toll-free phone:* 800-872-6798. *Fax:* 859-281-3649. *E-mail:* admissions@transy.edu. *Website:* http://www.transy.edu/.

Union College

Barbourville, Kentucky

- **Independent United Methodist** comprehensive, founded 1879
- **Small-town** 100-acre campus
- **Coed** 781 undergraduate students, 92% full-time, 45% women, 55% men
- **Moderately difficult** entrance level, 77% of applicants were admitted

Undergraduates 720 full-time, 61 part-time. Students come from 28 states and territories; 9 other countries; 29% are from out of state; 12% Black or African American, non-Hispanic/Latino; 3% Hispanic/Latino; 0.1% Asian, non-Hispanic/Latino; 0.1% Native Hawaiian or other Pacific Islander, non-Hispanic/Latino; 0.4% American Indian or Alaska Native, non-Hispanic/Latino; 1% Two or more races, non-Hispanic/Latino; 0.6% Race/ethnicity unknown; 4% international; 9% transferred in; 39% live on campus. *Retention:* 53% of full-time freshmen returned.

Freshmen *Admission:* 1,127 applied, 863 admitted, 214 enrolled. *Average high school GPA:* 2.87. *Test scores:* ACT scores over 18: 83%; ACT scores over 24: 19%; ACT scores over 30: 3%.

Faculty *Total:* 110, 60% full-time, 64% with terminal degrees. *Student/faculty ratio:* 12:1.

Academics *Calendar:* semesters. *Degrees:* bachelor's, master's, post-master's, and postbachelor's certificates. *Special study options:* academic remediation for entering students, accelerated degree program, advanced placement credit, double majors, English as a second language, honors programs, independent study, off-campus study, part-time degree program, services for LD students, student-designed majors, study abroad, summer session for credit.

Computers on Campus 230 computers/terminals and 450 ports are available on campus for general student use. Students can access the following: campus intranet, computer help desk, free student e-mail accounts, online (class) grades, online (class) registration, online (class) schedules. Campuswide network is available. 100% of college-owned or -operated housing units are wired for high-speed Internet access. Wireless service is available via classrooms, computer centers, computer labs, dorm rooms, learning centers, libraries, student centers.

Student Life *Housing:* on-campus residence required through sophomore year. *Options:* men-only, women-only. Campus housing is university owned. Freshman campus housing is guaranteed. *Activities and organizations:* drama/theater group, choral group, Special Performers, Off-campus Trips, Open Mic Night, Bingo Night, Movie Fest. *Campus security:* 24-hour emergency response devices and patrols, late-night transport/escort service, controlled dormitory access. *Student services:* health clinic, personal/psychological counseling.

Athletics Member NAIA. *Intercollegiate sports:* baseball M(s), basketball M(s)/W(s), bowling M(s)/W(s), cheerleading M(s)/W(s), cross-country running M(s)/W(s), football M(s), golf M(s)/W(s), soccer M(s)/W(s), softball W(s), swimming and diving M(s)/W(s), track and field W(s), volleyball W(s). *Intramural sports:* basketball M/W, football M, soccer M/W, softball M/W, table tennis M/W, ultimate Frisbee M/W, volleyball M/W, water polo W.

Standardized Tests *Required:* SAT or ACT (for admission).

Costs (2012–13) *Comprehensive fee:* $27,450 includes full-time tuition ($19,900), mandatory fees ($900), and room and board ($6650). Full-time tuition and fees vary according to course load. Part-time tuition: $325 per credit hour. Part-time tuition and fees vary according to course load. *College room only:* $3000. Room and board charges vary according to board plan and housing facility. *Payment plan:* installment. *Waivers:* senior citizens and employees or children of employees.

Financial Aid Of all full-time matriculated undergraduates who enrolled in 2012, 725 applied for aid, 676 were judged to have need, 74 had their need fully met. 111 Federal Work-Study jobs (averaging $1500). 78 state and other part-time jobs (averaging $1500). In 2012, 67 non-need-based awards were made. *Average percent of need met:* 66%. *Average financial aid package:* $18,963. *Average need-based loan:* $4258. *Average need-based gift aid:* $14,835. *Average non-need-based aid:* $11,626. *Average indebtedness upon graduation:* $18,843.

Applying *Options:* electronic application, deferred entrance. *Application fee:* $10. *Required:* high school transcript, minimum 2.0 GPA. *Required for some:* interview. *Application deadlines:* rolling (freshmen), rolling (out-of-state freshmen), rolling (transfers). *Notification:* continuous (freshmen), continuous (out-of-state freshmen), continuous (transfers).

Freshman Application Contact Dr. Jerry Jackson EdD, Vice President for Enrollment Management, Union College, 310 College Street, Barbourville, KY 40906. *Phone:* 606-546-1222. *Toll-free phone:* 800-489-8646. *Fax:* 606-546-1667. *E-mail:* jjackson@unionky.edu.
Website: http://www.unionky.edu/.

University of Kentucky
Lexington, Kentucky

- **State-supported** university, founded 1865
- **Urban** 685-acre campus with easy access to Cincinnati, Louisville
- **Coed** 20,827 undergraduate students, 92% full-time, 50% women, 50% men
- **Moderately difficult** entrance level, 67% of applicants were admitted

Undergraduates 19,178 full-time, 1,649 part-time. Students come from 53 states and territories; 71 other countries; 21% are from out of state; 8% Black or African American, non-Hispanic/Latino; 3% Hispanic/Latino; 2% Asian, non-Hispanic/Latino; 0.1% Native Hawaiian or other Pacific Islander, non-Hispanic/Latino; 0.2% American Indian or Alaska Native, non-Hispanic/Latino; 2% Two or more races, non-Hispanic/Latino; 3% Race/ethnicity unknown; 2% international; 6% transferred in; 26% live on campus. *Retention:* 81% of full-time freshmen returned.

Freshmen *Admission:* 18,802 applied, 12,655 admitted, 4,647 enrolled. *Average high school GPA:* 3.46. *Test scores:* SAT critical reading scores over 500: 77%; SAT math scores over 500: 80%; SAT writing scores over 500: 76%; ACT scores over 18: 99%; SAT critical reading scores over 600: 31%; SAT math scores over 600: 39%; SAT writing scores over 600: 29%; ACT scores over 24: 66%; SAT critical reading scores over 700: 9%; SAT math scores over 700: 10%; SAT writing scores over 700: 6%; ACT scores over 30: 17%.

Faculty *Total:* 1,683, 81% full-time, 86% with terminal degrees. *Student/faculty ratio:* 18:1.

Academics *Calendar:* semesters. *Degrees:* bachelor's, master's, doctoral, and postbachelor's certificates. *Special study options:* academic remediation for entering students, accelerated degree program, adult/continuing education programs, advanced placement credit, cooperative education, distance learning, double majors, English as a second language, honors programs, independent study, internships, off-campus study, part-time degree program, services for LD students, study abroad, summer session for credit. *ROTC:* Army (b), Air Force (b). *Unusual degree programs:* 3-2 business administration.

Computers on Campus Students can access the following: computer help desk, free student e-mail accounts, online (class) grades, online (class) registration, online (class) schedules. Campuswide network is available. Wireless service is available via entire campus.

Student Life *Housing options:* coed, men-only, women-only, disabled students. Campus housing is university owned and leased by the school. *Activities and organizations:* drama/theater group, student-run newspaper, radio station, choral group, marching band, Student Activities Board, Student Government Association, Campus Progressive Coalition, Ski and Snowboard Club, Society of Women Engineers, national fraternities, national sororities. *Campus security:* 24-hour emergency response devices and patrols, late-night transport/escort service, controlled dormitory access. *Student services:* health clinic, personal/psychological counseling, women's center, legal services.

Athletics Member NCAA. All Division I except football (Division I-A). *Intercollegiate sports:* baseball M(s), basketball M(s)/W(s), cross-country running M(s)/W(s), golf M(s)/W(s), gymnastics W(s), riflery M(s)/W(s), soccer M(s)/W(s), softball W(s), swimming and diving M(s)/W(s), tennis M(s)/W(s), track and field M(s)/W(s), volleyball W(s). *Intramural sports:* archery M/W, badminton M/W, basketball M/W, fencing M/W, football M/W, golf M/W, ice hockey M, lacrosse M, rugby M, soccer M/W, softball M/W, swimming and diving M/W, table tennis M/W, tennis M/W, track and field M/W, volleyball M/W.

Standardized Tests *Required:* SAT or ACT (for admission).

Costs (2012–13) *Tuition:* state resident $8610 full-time, $359 per credit hour part-time; nonresident $18,798 full-time, $783 per credit hour part-time. Full-time tuition and fees vary according to degree level, program, reciprocity agreements, and student level. Part-time tuition and fees vary according to degree level, program, reciprocity agreements, and student level. *Required fees:* $1066 full-time, $30 per credit hour part-time. *Room and board:* $10,192; room only: $4510. Room and board charges vary according to board plan and housing facility. *Payment plan:* installment. *Waivers:* senior citizens and employees or children of employees.

Financial Aid Of all full-time matriculated undergraduates who enrolled in 2010, 11,548 applied for aid, 9,092 were judged to have need, 1,659 had their need fully met. In 2010, 6780 non-need-based awards were made. *Average percent of need met:* 63%. *Average financial aid package:* $9963. *Average need-based loan:* $4123. *Average need-based gift aid:* $5306. *Average non-need-based aid:* $7297. *Average indebtedness upon graduation:* $21,774.

Applying *Options:* electronic application, deferred entrance. *Application fee:* $50. *Required:* high school transcript, minimum 2.0 GPA. *Application deadlines:* 2/15 (freshmen), 8/1 (transfers). *Notification:* continuous (freshmen).

Freshman Application Contact Ms. Michelle Nordin, Associate Director of Admissions, University of Kentucky, 100 W.D. Funkhouser Building, Lexington, KY 40506-0054. *Phone:* 859-257-2000. *Toll-free phone:* 866-900-GO-UK. *E-mail:* admissio@uky.edu.
Website: http://www.uky.edu/.

University of Louisville
Louisville, Kentucky

- **State-supported** university, founded 1798
- **Urban** 345-acre campus with easy access to Louisville
- **Endowment** $755.1 million
- **Coed** 15,727 undergraduate students, 78% full-time, 52% women, 48% men
- **Moderately difficult** entrance level, 73% of applicants were admitted

Undergraduates 12,192 full-time, 3,535 part-time. Students come from 47 states and territories; 58 other countries; 15% are from out of state; 12% Black or African American, non-Hispanic/Latino; 3% Hispanic/Latino; 3% Asian, non-Hispanic/Latino; 0.1% Native Hawaiian or other Pacific Islander, non-Hispanic/Latino; 0.1% American Indian or Alaska Native, non-Hispanic/Latino; 3% Two or more races, non-Hispanic/Latino; 0.2% Race/ethnicity unknown; 2% international; 7% transferred in; 27% live on campus. *Retention:* 77% of full-time freshmen returned.

Freshmen *Admission:* 7,892 applied, 5,738 admitted, 2,705 enrolled. *Average high school GPA:* 3.49. *Test scores:* SAT critical reading scores over 500: 77%; SAT math scores over 500: 80%; ACT scores over 18: 99%; SAT critical reading scores over 600: 31%; SAT math scores over 600: 43%; ACT scores over 24: 59%; SAT critical reading scores over 700: 9%; SAT math scores over 700: 11%; ACT scores over 30: 17%.

Faculty *Total:* 2,299, 73% full-time, 80% with terminal degrees. *Student/faculty ratio:* 17:1.

Academics *Calendar:* semesters. *Degrees:* certificates, associate, bachelor's, master's, doctoral, post-master's, and postbachelor's certificates. *Special study options:* academic remediation for entering students, accelerated degree program, adult/continuing education programs, advanced placement credit, cooperative education, distance learning, double majors, English as a second language, honors programs, independent study, internships, off-campus study, part-time degree program, services for LD students, student-designed majors, study abroad, summer session for credit. *ROTC:* Army (b), Air Force (b). *Unusual degree programs:* 3-2 engineering; Bachelor of Arts/Science and Master of Public Health.

Computers on Campus 400 computers/terminals are available on campus for general student use. Students can access the following: campus intranet, computer help desk, free student e-mail accounts, online (class) grades, online (class) registration, online (class) schedules. Campuswide network is available. 100% of college-owned or -operated housing units are wired for high-speed Internet access. Wireless service is available via entire campus.

Student Life *Housing:* on-campus residence required for freshman year. *Options:* coed, cooperative, disabled students. Campus housing is university owned and is provided by a third party. Freshman applicants given priority for college housing. *Activities and organizations:* drama/theater group, student-run newspaper, radio station, choral group, marching band, Baptist Campus Ministry, Society of Porter Scholars, Association of Black Students, common-Ground, Phi Eta Sigma, national fraternities, national sororities. *Campus security:* 24-hour emergency response devices and patrols, late-night transport/escort service, controlled dormitory access, The University of Louisville Alert notification system. *Student services:* health clinic, personal/psychological counseling, women's center.

Athletics Member NCAA. All Division I except football (Division I-A). *Intercollegiate sports:* baseball M(s), basketball M(s)/W(s), crew W(s), cross-country running M(s)/W(s), field hockey W(s), golf M(s)/W(s), lacrosse W(s), soccer M(s)/W(s), softball W(s), swimming and diving M(s)/W(s), tennis M(s)/W(s), track and field M(s)/W(s), ultimate Frisbee M(c)/W(c), volleyball W(s). *Intramural sports:* badminton M/W, basketball M/W, bowling M/W, cross-country running M/W, equestrian sports W(c), fencing M/W, football M/W, golf M/W, gymnastics W(c), ice hockey M, lacrosse M(c)/W(c), racquetball M/W, rugby M(c), soccer M/W, softball W, swimming and diving M/W, table tennis M/W, tennis M/W, track and field M/W, ultimate Frisbee M/W, volleyball M/W.

Standardized Tests *Required:* SAT or ACT (for admission). *Required for some:* TOEFL for students whose primary language is not English.

Costs (2012–13) *Tuition:* state resident $9466 full-time, $395 per credit hour part-time; nonresident $22,950 full-time, $957 per credit hour part-time. Full-time tuition and fees vary according to reciprocity agreements. Part-time tuition and fees vary according to course load and reciprocity agreements. *Room and board:* $7570; room only: $4650. Room and board charges vary according to board plan and housing facility. *Payment plan:* installment. *Waivers:* senior citizens and employees or children of employees.

Financial Aid Of all full-time matriculated undergraduates who enrolled in 2010, 10,402 applied for aid, 8,833 were judged to have need, 1,571 had their need fully met. 395 Federal Work-Study jobs (averaging $3280). In 2010, 1573 non-need-based awards were made. *Average percent of need met:* 59%. *Average financial aid package:* $9987. *Average need-based loan:* $4070. *Average need-based gift aid:* $7561. *Average non-need-based aid:* $7368. *Average indebtedness upon graduation:* $19,812.

Applying *Options:* electronic application, deferred entrance. *Application fee:* $40. *Required:* high school transcript, minimum 2.5 GPA. *Application deadlines:* 2/15 (freshmen), 7/1 (transfers). *Notification:* continuous (freshmen), continuous (transfers).

Freshman Application Contact Ms. Jenny L. Sawyer, Executive Director of Admissions, University of Louisville, 2301 South Third Street, Houchens Room 150, Louisville, KY 40292-0001. *Phone:* 502-852-6531. *Toll-free phone:* 800-334-8635. *Fax:* 502-852-4776. *E-mail:* admitme@louisville.edu. *Website:* http://www.louisville.edu/.

University of Phoenix–Louisville Campus
Louisville, Kentucky

Admissions Office Contact University of Phoenix–Louisville Campus, 10400 Linn Station Road, Louisville, KY 40223-3839. *Toll-free phone:* 866-766-0766.
Website: http://www.phoenix.edu/.

University of Pikeville
Pikeville, Kentucky

- **Independent** comprehensive, founded 1889, affiliated with Presbyterian Church (U.S.A.)
- **Small-town** 25-acre campus
- **Endowment** $10.7 million
- **Coed** 1,620 undergraduate students, 75% full-time, 52% women, 48% men
- **Noncompetitive** entrance level, 100% of applicants were admitted

Undergraduates 1,219 full-time, 401 part-time. Students come from 25 states and territories; 10 other countries; 20% are from out of state; 8% Black or African American, non-Hispanic/Latino; 1% Hispanic/Latino; 0.8% Asian, non-Hispanic/Latino; 0.1% American Indian or Alaska Native, non-Hispanic/Latino; 0.4% Race/ethnicity unknown; 1% international; 9% transferred in; 60% live on campus. *Retention:* 52% of full-time freshmen returned.

Freshmen *Admission:* 1,858 applied, 1,858 admitted, 368 enrolled. *Average high school GPA:* 3.13. *Test scores:* SAT math scores over 500: 32%; SAT writing scores over 500: 16%; ACT scores over 18: 72%; SAT math scores over 600: 8%; ACT scores over 24: 18%; ACT scores over 30: 1%.

Faculty *Total:* 109, 62% full-time, 43% with terminal degrees. *Student/faculty ratio:* 16:1.

Academics *Calendar:* semesters. *Degrees:* associate, bachelor's, master's, and doctoral. *Special study options:* academic remediation for entering students, advanced placement credit, double majors, English as a second language, independent study, internships, part-time degree program, services for LD students,

student-designed majors, study abroad, summer session for credit. *ROTC:* Army (b).

Computers on Campus 166 computers/terminals are available on campus for general student use. Students can access the following: computer help desk, free student e-mail accounts, online (class) grades, online (class) schedules. Campuswide network is available. 90% of college-owned or -operated housing units are wired for high-speed Internet access. Wireless service is available via entire campus.

Student Life *Housing options:* coed, men-only, women-only. Campus housing is university owned. *Activities and organizations:* drama/theater group, student-run newspaper, choral group, student government, Phi Beta Lambda, Lambda Sigma, Concert Choir, Student Nurses at PC. *Campus security:* 24-hour emergency response devices and patrols, controlled dormitory access. *Student services:* personal/psychological counseling.

Athletics Member NAIA. *Intercollegiate sports:* baseball M(s), basketball M(s)/W(s), bowling M(s)/W(s), cheerleading M(s)/W(s), cross-country running M(s)/W(s), football M(s), golf M(s)/W(s), lacrosse W(s)(c), soccer M(s)/W(s), softball W(s), tennis M(s)/W(s), track and field M(s)/W(s), volleyball W(s).

Costs (2012–13) *Comprehensive fee:* $23,750 includes full-time tuition ($17,050) and room and board ($6700). Full-time tuition and fees vary according to course load. Part-time tuition: $710 per credit hour. Part-time tuition and fees vary according to course load. *Room and board:* Room and board charges vary according to housing facility. *Payment plan:* installment. *Waivers:* senior citizens and employees or children of employees.

Financial Aid Of all full-time matriculated undergraduates who enrolled in 2012, 1,191 applied for aid, 1,183 were judged to have need, 508 had their need fully met. 190 Federal Work-Study jobs (averaging $1736). *Average percent of need met:* 83%. *Average financial aid package:* $19,231. *Average need-based loan:* $4062. *Average need-based gift aid:* $13,831. *Average indebtedness upon graduation:* $24,954.

Applying *Options:* electronic application, deferred entrance. *Required:* high school transcript. *Application deadlines:* 8/15 (freshmen), 8/15 (out-of-state freshmen), 8/15 (transfers). *Notification:* continuous (freshmen), continuous (out-of-state freshmen), continuous (transfers).

Freshman Application Contact Mr. Gary Justice, Director of Admissions, University of Pikeville, 147 Sycamore Street, Pikeville, KY 41501. *Phone:* 606-218-5251. *Toll-free phone:* 866-232-7700. *Fax:* 606-218-5255. *E-mail:* wewantyou@pc.edu. *Website:* http://www.upike.edu/.

University of the Cumberlands
Williamsburg, Kentucky

- **Independent Kentucky Baptist** comprehensive, founded 1889
- **Rural** 100-acre campus with easy access to Knoxville
- **Endowment** $70.5 million
- **Coed** 1,864 undergraduate students, 79% full-time, 49% women, 51% men
- **Moderately difficult** entrance level, 69% of applicants were admitted

Undergraduates 1,481 full-time, 383 part-time. Students come from 45 states and territories; 31 other countries; 36% are from out of state; 6% Black or African American, non-Hispanic/Latino; 2% Hispanic/Latino; 0.4% Asian, non-Hispanic/Latino; 0.1% Native Hawaiian or other Pacific Islander, non-Hispanic/Latino; 0.4% American Indian or Alaska Native, non-Hispanic/Latino; 0.2% Two or more races, non-Hispanic/Latino; 7% Race/ethnicity unknown; 6% international; 4% transferred in; 77% live on campus. *Retention:* 63% of full-time freshmen returned.

Freshmen *Admission:* 2,460 applied, 1,698 admitted, 459 enrolled. *Average high school GPA:* 3.3. *Test scores:* SAT critical reading scores over 500: 28%; SAT math scores over 500: 52%; ACT scores over 18: 89%; SAT critical reading scores over 600: 4%; SAT math scores over 600: 8%; ACT scores over 24: 24%; ACT scores over 30: 1%.

Faculty *Total:* 194, 58% full-time, 69% with terminal degrees. *Student/faculty ratio:* 13:1.

Academics *Calendar:* semesters. *Degrees:* bachelor's, master's, doctoral, post-master's, and postbachelor's certificates. *Special study options:* academic remediation for entering students, accelerated degree program, adult/continuing education programs, advanced placement credit, cooperative education, distance learning, double majors, honors programs, independent study, internships, part-time degree program, student-designed majors, study abroad, summer session for credit. *ROTC:* Army (b). *Unusual degree programs:* 3-2 engineering with University of Kentucky; Physician Assistant.

Computers on Campus 225 computers/terminals are available on campus for general student use. Students can access the following: campus intranet, computer help desk, free student e-mail accounts, online (class) grades, online

(class) registration, online (class) schedules. Campuswide network is available. 100% of college-owned or -operated housing units are wired for high-speed Internet access. Wireless service is available via entire campus.

Student Life *Housing:* on-campus residence required through senior year. *Options:* men-only, women-only. Campus housing is university owned. Freshman campus housing is guaranteed. *Activities and organizations:* drama/theater group, student-run newspaper, radio and television station, choral group, marching band, Baptist Campus Ministries, Student Government Association, Campus Activity Board, Mountain Outreach, Fellowship of Christian Athletes. *Campus security:* 24-hour emergency response devices and patrols, student patrols, late-night transport/escort service. *Student services:* health clinic.

Athletics Member NAIA. *Intercollegiate sports:* archery M(s)/W(s), baseball M(s), basketball M(s)/W(s), bowling M(s)/W(s), cheerleading M(s)/W(s), cross-country running M(s)/W(s), football M(s), golf M(s)/W(s), soccer M(s)/W(s), softball W(s), swimming and diving M(s)/W(s), tennis M(s)/W(s), track and field M(s)/W(s), volleyball W(s), wrestling M(s)/W(s). *Intramural sports:* badminton M/W, basketball M/W, bowling M/W, football M/W, golf M/W, soccer M/W, softball M/W, table tennis M/W, tennis M/W, volleyball M/W.

Standardized Tests *Required:* SAT or ACT (for admission).

Costs (2013–14) *Comprehensive fee:* $27,140 includes full-time tuition ($19,640) and room and board ($7500). Part-time tuition: $590 per credit. Part-time tuition and fees vary according to course load. *Required fees:* $90 per term part-time. *Payment plan:* installment. *Waivers:* senior citizens and employees or children of employees.

Financial Aid Of all full-time matriculated undergraduates who enrolled in 2012, 1,371 applied for aid, 1,295 were judged to have need, 207 had their need fully met. 763 Federal Work-Study jobs (averaging $2029). 15 state and other part-time jobs (averaging $2462). In 2012, 186 non-need-based awards were made. *Average percent of need met:* 76%. *Average financial aid package:* $18,582. *Average need-based loan:* $3780. *Average need-based gift aid:* $14,482. *Average non-need-based aid:* $8489. *Average indebtedness upon graduation:* $20,090.

Applying *Options:* electronic application, deferred entrance. *Application fee:* $30. *Required:* high school transcript, minimum 2.0 GPA. *Required for some:* essay or personal statement, interview. *Application deadlines:* rolling (freshmen), rolling (transfers). *Notification:* continuous (freshmen), continuous (transfers).

Freshman Application Contact Mrs. Erica Harris, Director of Admissions, University of the Cumberlands, 6178 College Station Drive, Williamsburg, KY

40769. *Phone:* 606-539-4241. *Toll-free phone:* 800-343-1609. *Fax:* 606-539-4303. *E-mail:* admiss@ucumberlands.edu.
Website: http://www.ucumberlands.edu/.

See below for display ad and page 1608 for the College Close-Up.

Western Kentucky University

Bowling Green, Kentucky

- **State-supported** comprehensive, founded 1906
- **Suburban** 235-acre campus with easy access to Nashville
- **Endowment** $110,043
- **Coed** 18,101 undergraduate students, 77% full-time, 58% women, 42% men
- **Minimally difficult** entrance level, 92% of applicants were admitted

Undergraduates 13,868 full-time, 4,233 part-time. Students come from 47 states and territories; 60 other countries; 16% are from out of state; 11% Black or African American, non-Hispanic/Latino; 2% Hispanic/Latino; 0.9% Asian, non-Hispanic/Latino; 0.1% Native Hawaiian or other Pacific Islander, non-Hispanic/Latino; 0.3% American Indian or Alaska Native, non-Hispanic/Latino; 2% Two or more races, non-Hispanic/Latino; 2% Race/ethnicity unknown; 3% international; 6% transferred in; 29% live on campus. *Retention:* 71% of full-time freshmen returned.

Freshmen *Admission:* 8,526 applied, 7,871 admitted, 3,375 enrolled. *Average high school GPA:* 3.14. *Test scores:* SAT critical reading scores over 500: 47%; SAT math scores over 500: 48%; ACT scores over 18: 80%; SAT critical reading scores over 600: 18%; SAT math scores over 600: 21%; ACT scores over 24: 32%; SAT critical reading scores over 700: 5%; SAT math scores over 700: 4%; ACT scores over 30: 6%.

Faculty *Total:* 1,131, 69% full-time, 54% with terminal degrees. *Student/faculty ratio:* 19:1.

Academics *Calendar:* semesters. *Degrees:* certificates, associate, bachelor's, master's, doctoral, post-master's, and postbachelor's certificates. *Special study options:* academic remediation for entering students, accelerated degree program, adult/continuing education programs, advanced placement credit, cooperative education, distance learning, double majors, English as a second language, external degree program, freshman honors college, honors programs, independent study, internships, off-campus study, part-time degree program, services for LD students, student-designed majors, study abroad,

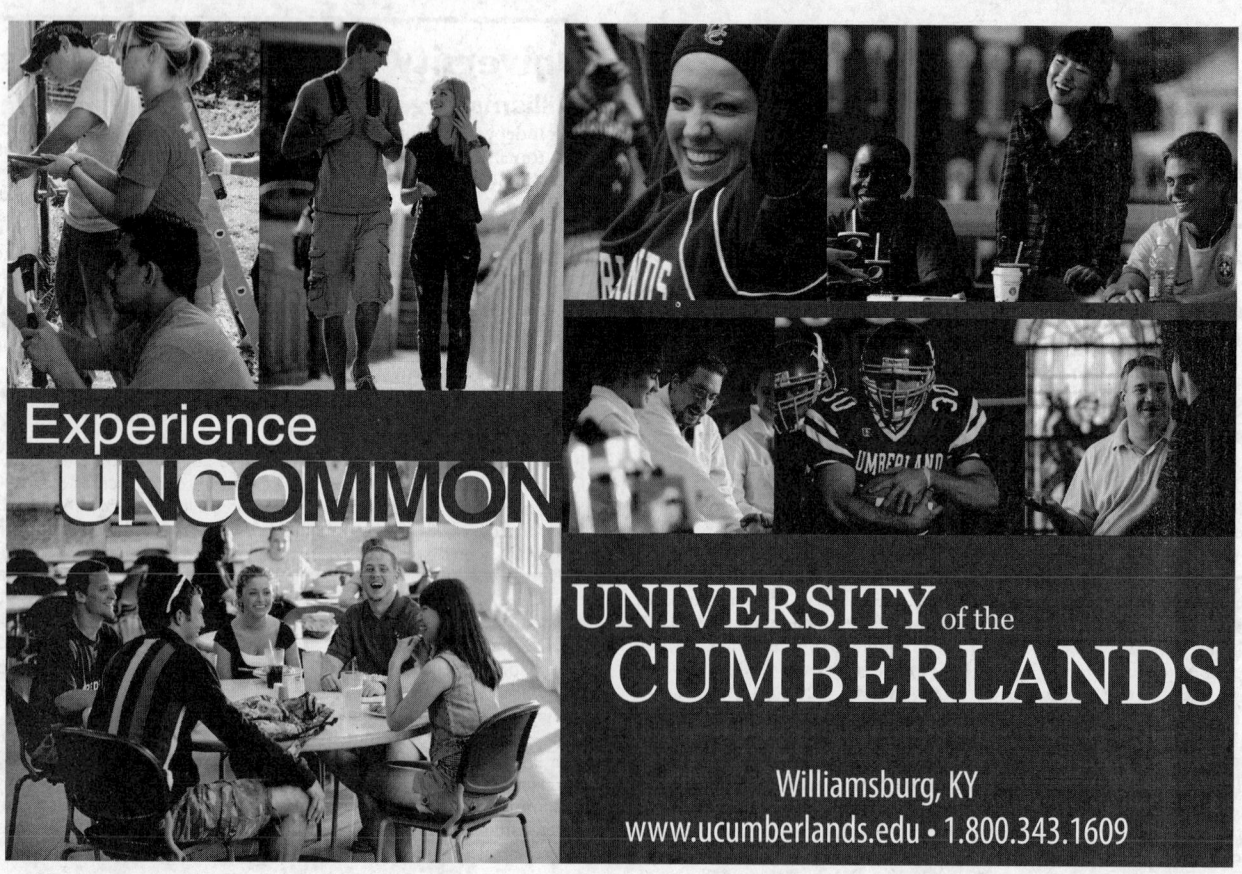

summer session for credit. *ROTC:* Army (b), Air Force (c). *Unusual degree programs:* 3-2 engineering with Western Kentucky University has cooperative agreements with a number of engineering schools.

Computers on Campus 542 computers/terminals are available on campus for general student use. Students can access the following: campus intranet, computer help desk, free student e-mail accounts, online (class) grades, online (class) registration, online (class) schedules. Campuswide network is available. 100% of college-owned or -operated housing units are wired for high-speed Internet access. Wireless service is available via entire campus.

Student Life *Housing:* on-campus residence required through sophomore year. *Options:* coed, men-only, women-only. Campus housing is university owned. Freshman applicants given priority for college housing. *Activities and organizations:* drama/theater group, student-run newspaper, radio and television station, choral group, marching band, Student Government Association, Campus Activities Board, Campus Crusade for Christ, Campus Ministries, Residence Hall Association, national fraternities, national sororities. *Campus security:* 24-hour emergency response devices and patrols, student patrols, late-night transport/escort service, controlled dormitory access. *Student services:* health clinic, personal/psychological counseling, women's center.

Athletics Member NCAA. All Division I except football (Division I-A). *Intercollegiate sports:* baseball M(s), basketball M(s)/W(s), cross-country running M(s)/W(s), golf M(s)/W(s), soccer W, softball W(s), swimming and diving M(s)/W(s), tennis M(s)/W(s), track and field M(s)/W(s), volleyball W(s). *Intramural sports:* badminton M/W, basketball M/W, bowling M(c)/W(c), fencing M(c)/W(c), field hockey M(c)/W(c), football M/W, golf M/W, lacrosse M(c)/W(c), racquetball M/W, rugby M(c)/W(c), soccer M/W, softball M/W, table tennis M/W, tennis M(c)/W(c), ultimate Frisbee M(c)/W(c), volleyball M/W.

Standardized Tests *Required:* SAT or ACT (for admission).

Costs (2012–13) *Tuition:* state resident $8472 full-time, $353 per credit hour part-time; nonresident $21,000 full-time, $875 per credit hour part-time. Full-time tuition and fees vary according to course load, location, program, and reciprocity agreements. Part-time tuition and fees vary according to course load, location, program, and reciprocity agreements. *Room and board:* $7320; room only: $4170. Room and board charges vary according to board plan and housing facility. *Payment plan:* installment. *Waivers:* children of alumni, senior citizens, and employees or children of employees.

Financial Aid Of all full-time matriculated undergraduates who enrolled in 2011, 11,413 applied for aid, 9,400 were judged to have need, 2,758 had their need fully met. 820 Federal Work-Study jobs (averaging $2408). 1,649 state and other part-time jobs (averaging $2677). In 2011, 1303 non-need-based awards were made. *Average percent of need met:* 30%. *Average financial aid package:* $13,194. *Average need-based loan:* $3822. *Average need-based gift aid:* $4856. *Average non-need-based aid:* $4927. *Average indebtedness upon graduation:* $26,110.

Applying *Options:* electronic application. *Application fee:* $40. *Required:* high school transcript, minimum 2.5 GPA. *Required for some:* minimum 2.0 GPA. *Recommended:* minimum 2.5 GPA. *Application deadlines:* 8/1 (freshmen), 8/1 (transfers). *Notification:* continuous (freshmen), continuous (transfers).

Freshman Application Contact Western Kentucky University, 1906 College Heights Boulevard, Bowling Green, KY 42101. *Phone:* 270-745-2551. *Toll-free phone:* 800-495-8463.
Website: http://www.wku.edu/.

LOUISIANA

Centenary College of Louisiana

Shreveport, Louisiana

- **Independent United Methodist** comprehensive, founded 1825
- **Suburban** 65-acre campus with easy access to Shreveport
- **Coed** 698 undergraduate students, 96% full-time, 56% women, 44% men
- **Moderately difficult** entrance level, 64% of applicants were admitted

Undergraduates 673 full-time, 25 part-time. 13% Black or African American, non-Hispanic/Latino; 5% Hispanic/Latino; 3% Asian, non-Hispanic/Latino; 0.3% Native Hawaiian or other Pacific Islander, non-Hispanic/Latino; 0.6% American Indian or Alaska Native, non-Hispanic/Latino; 4% Two or more races, non-Hispanic/Latino; 0.3% Race/ethnicity unknown; 3% international; 56% live on campus. *Retention:* 69% of full-time freshmen returned.

Freshmen *Admission:* 933 applied, 598 admitted, 158 enrolled. *Average high school GPA:* 3.53. *Test scores:* SAT critical reading scores over 500: 74%; SAT math scores over 500: 80%; ACT scores over 18: 99%; SAT critical reading scores over 600: 39%; SAT math scores over 600: 39%; ACT scores over 24:

65%; SAT critical reading scores over 700: 2%; SAT math scores over 700: 7%; ACT scores over 30: 9%.

Faculty *Total:* 124, 47% full-time, 54% with terminal degrees. *Student/faculty ratio:* 9:1.

Academics *Calendar:* 4-4-1. *Degrees:* bachelor's and master's. *Special study options:* adult/continuing education programs, advanced placement credit, double majors, honors programs, independent study, internships, off-campus study, part-time degree program, services for LD students, student-designed majors, study abroad, summer session for credit. *Unusual degree programs:* 3-2 engineering with Columbia University, University of Southern California, Case Western Reserve University, Texas A&M University, Louisiana, Washington University in St. Louis; communication disorders with Louisiana State University Medical Center School of Medicine in Shreveport.

Computers on Campus Students can access the following: free student e-mail accounts, online (class) grades, online (class) registration, online (class) schedules. Campuswide network is available. Wireless service is available via classrooms, dorm rooms, libraries, student centers.

Student Life *Housing:* on-campus residence required through senior year. *Options:* coed, women-only. Campus housing is university owned. Freshman campus housing is guaranteed. *Activities and organizations:* drama/theater group, student-run newspaper, radio station, choral group, intramural sports, Residence Life, FCA, Church Career/Campus Ministries, student media, national fraternities, national sororities. *Campus security:* 24-hour emergency response devices and patrols, late-night transport/escort service, controlled dormitory access. *Student services:* health clinic, personal/psychological counseling.

Athletics Member NCAA. All Division III. *Intercollegiate sports:* baseball M, basketball M/W, cheerleading M(c)/W(c), cross-country running M/W, golf M/W, gymnastics W, lacrosse M(c), soccer M/W, softball W, swimming and diving M/W, tennis M/W, volleyball W. *Intramural sports:* basketball M/W, cheerleading W, football M/W, golf M, lacrosse M, soccer M/W, softball M/W, table tennis M/W, tennis M/W, volleyball M/W.

Standardized Tests *Required:* SAT or ACT (for admission).

Costs (2012–13) *Comprehensive fee:* $38,836 includes full-time tuition ($29,500) and room and board ($9336). Full-time tuition and fees vary according to degree level. Part-time tuition: $880 per credit hour. Part-time tuition and fees vary according to course load, degree level, and program. *College room only:* $4816. Room and board charges vary according to board plan and housing facility. *Payment plans:* installment, deferred payment. *Waivers:* employees or children of employees.

Financial Aid Of all full-time matriculated undergraduates who enrolled in 2012, 481 applied for aid, 386 were judged to have need, 79 had their need fully met. 170 Federal Work-Study jobs (averaging $1933). 33 state and other part-time jobs (averaging $1217). In 2012, 155 non-need-based awards were made. *Average percent of need met:* 74%. *Average financial aid package:* $29,507. *Average need-based loan:* $5423. *Average need-based gift aid:* $25,230. *Average non-need-based aid:* $13,568. *Average indebtedness upon graduation:* $21,820.

Applying *Options:* electronic application, early admission, early action, deferred entrance. *Application fee:* $30. *Required:* essay or personal statement, high school transcript, minimum 2.0 GPA, 1 letter of recommendation. *Recommended:* interview, class rank. *Application deadlines:* 8/1 (freshmen), 8/1 (out-of-state freshmen), 8/15 (transfers), 12/15 (early action). *Notification:* continuous (freshmen), continuous (out-of-state freshmen), continuous (transfers).

Freshman Application Contact Mrs. Gail Roberson, Director of Admission, Centenary College of Louisiana, Office of Admission, 2911 Centenary Boulevard, Shreveport, LA 71134-1188. *Phone:* 318-869-5701. *Toll-free phone:* 800-234-4448. *Fax:* 318-869-5005.
Website: http://www.centenary.edu/.

Dillard University

New Orleans, Louisiana

- **Independent interdenominational** 4-year, founded 1869
- **Urban** 55-acre campus
- **Endowment** $54.8 million
- **Coed** 1,307 undergraduate students, 93% full-time, 72% women, 28% men
- **Moderately difficult** entrance level, 33% of applicants were admitted

Undergraduates 1,222 full-time, 85 part-time. Students come from 30 states and territories; 14 other countries; 35% are from out of state; 93% Black or African American, non-Hispanic/Latino; 0.5% Hispanic/Latino; 0.2% Asian, non-Hispanic/Latino; 0.5% Two or more races, non-Hispanic/Latino; 3% Race/ethnicity unknown; 2% international; 7% transferred in; 43% live on campus. *Retention:* 68% of full-time freshmen returned.

Freshmen *Admission:* 7,496 applied, 2,505 admitted, 351 enrolled. *Average high school GPA:* 2.88. *Test scores:* SAT critical reading scores over 500: 19%; SAT math scores over 500: 15%; SAT writing scores over 500: 18%; ACT scores over 18: 57%; SAT critical reading scores over 600: 2%; SAT math scores over 600: 3%; SAT writing scores over 600: 1%; ACT scores over 24: 6%.

Faculty *Student/faculty ratio:* 14:1.

Academics *Calendar:* semesters. *Degree:* bachelor's. *Special study options:* academic remediation for entering students, advanced placement credit, cooperative education, double majors, English as a second language, external degree program, honors programs, independent study, internships, part-time degree program, services for LD students, study abroad, summer session for credit. *ROTC:* Army (c), Air Force (c). *Unusual degree programs:* 3-2 engineering with Columbia University, Tulane University, University of New Orleans, Georgia Institute of Technology; biology with Boston University School of Medicine, Meharry Medical College School of Medicine, New York College of Podiatric Medicine and Ohio College of Medicine; public health with LSU Health Sciences Center School of Public Health and Tulane School of Public Health and Tropical Medicine.

Computers on Campus 75 computers/terminals and 300 ports are available on campus for general student use. Students can access the following: free student e-mail accounts, online (class) grades, online (class) registration, online (class) schedules. Campuswide network is available. 100% of college-owned or -operated housing units are wired for high-speed Internet access. Wireless service is available via dorm rooms, student centers.

Student Life *Housing:* on-campus residence required for freshman year. *Options:* coed, men-only, women-only, disabled students. Campus housing is university owned and leased by the school. Freshman campus housing is guaranteed. *Activities and organizations:* drama/theater group, student-run newspaper, radio and television station, choral group, Student Government Association, Student Activities Board, National Pan-Hellenic Council, Collegiate 100, Class Councils, national fraternities, national sororities. *Campus security:* 24-hour emergency response devices and patrols, late-night transport/escort service, controlled dormitory access. *Student services:* health clinic, personal/psychological counseling, legal services.

Athletics Member NAIA. *Intercollegiate sports:* basketball M(s)/W(s), cross-country running M(s)/W(s), track and field M(s)/W(s), volleyball W(s). *Intramural sports:* basketball M/W, football M/W, tennis M/W, volleyball M/W, weight lifting M/W.

Standardized Tests *Required:* SAT or ACT (for admission), minimum SAT score of 870 (math and verbal) or minimum ACT composite score of 18 (for admission).

Costs (2013–14) *Comprehensive fee:* $23,536 includes full-time tuition ($13,650), mandatory fees ($1200), and room and board ($8686). Part-time tuition and fees vary according to course load. *College room only:* $5690. Room and board charges vary according to housing facility and student level. *Payment plan:* installment. *Waivers:* employees or children of employees.

Financial Aid Of all full-time matriculated undergraduates who enrolled in 2011, 1,157 applied for aid, 1,118 were judged to have need, 73 had their need fully met. 237 Federal Work-Study jobs (averaging $1366). In 2011, 24 non-need-based awards were made. *Average percent of need met:* 58%. *Average financial aid package:* $13,641. *Average need-based loan:* $4262. *Average need-based gift aid:* $9650. *Average non-need-based aid:* $7655. *Average indebtedness upon graduation:* $36,241.

Applying *Options:* electronic application, early admission. *Application fee:* $30. *Required:* high school transcript, minimum 2.5 GPA, 2 letters of recommendation. *Required for some:* essay or personal statement. *Application deadlines:* rolling (freshmen), rolling (out-of-state freshmen), rolling (transfers). *Notification:* continuous (freshmen), continuous (out-of-state freshmen), continuous (transfers).

Freshman Application Contact Dr. Alecia Cyprian, Assistant Vice President of Enrollment Management, Dillard University, 2601 Gentilly Boulevard, New Orleans, LA 70122-3097. *Phone:* 504-816-4670. *Toll-free phone:* 800-216-8094. *Fax:* 504-816-4895. *E-mail:* acyprian@dillard.edu. *Website:* http://www.dillard.edu/.

Grambling State University

Grambling, Louisiana

- **State-supported** university, founded 1901, part of University of Louisiana System
- **Small-town** 433-acre campus with easy access to Shreveport
- **Endowment** $10.7 million
- **Coed** 4,435 undergraduate students, 92% full-time, 60% women, 40% men
- **Noncompetitive** entrance level, 42% of applicants were admitted

Undergraduates 4,087 full-time, 348 part-time. Students come from 40 states and territories; 26 other countries; 35% are from out of state; 88% Black or African American, non-Hispanic/Latino; 1% Hispanic/Latino; 0.3% Asian, non-Hispanic/Latino; 0.2% American Indian or Alaska Native, non-Hispanic/Latino; 1% Two or more races, non-Hispanic/Latino; 0.9% Race/ethnicity unknown; 6% international; 7% transferred in; 87% live on campus. *Retention:* 69% of full-time freshmen returned.

Freshmen *Admission:* 5,154 applied, 2,170 admitted, 756 enrolled. *Average high school GPA:* 2.8. *Test scores:* SAT math scores over 500: 18%; ACT scores over 18: 45%; SAT math scores over 600: 2%; ACT scores over 24: 1%; SAT math scores over 700: 1%.

Faculty *Total:* 239, 92% full-time, 55% with terminal degrees. *Student/faculty ratio:* 21:1.

Academics *Calendar:* semesters. *Degrees:* associate, bachelor's, master's, doctoral, and post-master's certificates. *Special study options:* academic remediation for entering students, adult/continuing education programs, advanced placement credit, cooperative education, distance learning, double majors, honors programs, internships, off-campus study, part-time degree program, services for LD students, summer session for credit. *ROTC:* Army (b), Air Force (c).

Computers on Campus Students can access the following: campus intranet, computer help desk, free student e-mail accounts, online (class) grades, online (class) registration, online (class) schedules. Campuswide network is available. Wireless service is available via classrooms, computer centers, computer labs, dorm rooms, learning centers, libraries, student centers.

Student Life *Housing:* college housing not available. *Options:* coed, men-only, women-only, disabled students. Campus housing is provided by a third party. Freshman applicants given priority for college housing. *Activities and organizations:* drama/theater group, student-run newspaper, radio and television station, choral group, marching band, Tiger Marching Band, Black Dynasty Modeling Troupe, Academic and Professional Clubs, sororities, fraternities, national fraternities, national sororities. *Campus security:* 24-hour patrols, student patrols, controlled dormitory access. *Student services:* health clinic, personal/psychological counseling.

Athletics Member NCAA. All Division I except football (Division I-AA). *Intercollegiate sports:* baseball M(s), basketball M(s)/W(s), bowling W(s), cross-country running M/W, soccer W, softball W(s), tennis W(s), track and field M(s)/W(s), volleyball W(s). *Intramural sports:* badminton M/W, basketball M/W, bowling M(c)/W(c), racquetball M(c)/W(c), soccer M(c)/W(c), softball M/W, table tennis M/W, tennis M(c)/W(c), volleyball M(c)/W(c), weight lifting M(c)/W(c).

Standardized Tests *Required:* SAT or ACT (for admission).

Costs (2012–13) *Tuition:* state resident $3932 full-time, $164 per credit hour part-time; nonresident $12,302 full-time, $164 per credit hour part-time. Full-time tuition and fees vary according to course load, degree level, and student level. Part-time tuition and fees vary according to course load, degree level, and student level. *Required fees:* $1308 full-time, $164 per credit hour part-time, $349 per term part-time. *Room and board:* $9674; room only: $5880. Room and board charges vary according to housing facility. *Payment plans:* installment, deferred payment. *Waivers:* children of alumni, senior citizens, and employees or children of employees.

Financial Aid Of all full-time matriculated undergraduates who enrolled in 2007, 4,191 applied for aid, 3,931 were judged to have need, 309 had their need fully met. 1,141 Federal Work-Study jobs (averaging $1310). 431 state and other part-time jobs (averaging $1487). In 2007, 200 non-need-based awards were made. *Average percent of need met:* 80%. *Average financial aid package:* $6800. *Average need-based loan:* $3813. *Average need-based gift aid:* $2928. *Average non-need-based aid:* $2328. *Average indebtedness upon graduation:* $29,416. *Financial aid deadline:* 4/1.

Applying *Options:* electronic application, early admission. *Application fee:* $20. *Required:* high school transcript, minimum 2.0 GPA. *Application deadlines:* 6/30 (freshmen), 6/30 (transfers). *Notification:* 8/1 (freshmen), continuous until 8/1 (transfers).

Freshman Application Contact Ms. Annie L. Moss, Director of Admissions and Recruitment, Grambling State University, GSU Box 4200, Grambling, LA 71245. *Phone:* 318-274-6423. *Toll-free phone:* 800-569-4714. *Fax:* 318-274-3292. *E-mail:* mossa@gram.edu. *Website:* http://www.gram.edu/.

Herzing University

Kenner, Louisiana

Director of Admissions Genny Bordelon, Director of Admissions, Herzing University, 2500 Williams Boulevard, Kenner, LA 70062. *Phone:* 504-733-0074. *Toll-free phone:* 800-596-0724. *Fax:* 504-733-0020. *Website:* http://www.herzing.edu/.

ITT Technical Institute

Baton Rouge, Louisiana

- **Proprietary** primarily 2-year
- **Coed**

Academics *Degrees:* associate and bachelor's.
Freshman Application Contact Director of Recruitment, ITT Technical Institute, 14111 Airline Highway, Suite 101, Baton Rouge, LA 70817. *Phone:* 225-754-5800. *Toll-free phone:* 800-295-8485.
Website: http://www.itt-tech.edu/.

ITT Technical Institute

St. Rose, Louisiana

- **Proprietary** primarily 2-year, founded 1998, part of ITT Educational Services, Inc.
- **Coed**
- **Minimally difficult** entrance level

Academics *Calendar:* quarters. *Degrees:* associate and bachelor's.
Freshman Application Contact Director of Recruitment, ITT Technical Institute, 140 James Drive East, St. Rose, LA 70087. *Phone:* 504-463-0338.
Toll-free phone: 866-463-0338.
Website: http://www.itt-tech.edu/.

Louisiana College

Pineville, Louisiana

- **Independent Southern Baptist** comprehensive, founded 1906
- **Small-town** 81-acre campus
- **Endowment** $29.3 million
- **Coed** 1,153 undergraduate students, 93% full-time, 50% women, 50% men
- **Moderately difficult** entrance level, 74% of applicants were admitted

Undergraduates 1,068 full-time, 85 part-time. 18% Black or African American, non-Hispanic/Latino; 3% Hispanic/Latino; 1% Asian, non-Hispanic/Latino; 0.1% Native Hawaiian or other Pacific Islander, non-Hispanic/Latino; 1% American Indian or Alaska Native, non-Hispanic/Latino; 0.9% Two or more races, non-Hispanic/Latino; 2% Race/ethnicity unknown; 1% international; 60% live on campus. *Retention:* 56% of full-time freshmen returned.
Freshmen *Admission:* 820 applied, 606 admitted, 461 enrolled. *Average high school GPA:* 3.17. *Test scores:* ACT scores over 18: 86%; ACT scores over 24: 31%; ACT scores over 30: 5%.
Faculty *Total:* 115, 70% full-time, 48% with terminal degrees. *Student/faculty ratio:* 13:1.
Academics *Calendar:* semesters. *Degrees:* associate, bachelor's, and master's. *Special study options:* academic remediation for entering students, accelerated degree program, adult/continuing education programs, advanced placement credit, cooperative education, distance learning, double majors, honors programs, independent study, internships, part-time degree program, services for LD students, student-designed majors, study abroad, summer session for credit. *ROTC:* Army (b).
Computers on Campus 233 computers/terminals are available on campus for general student use. Students can access the following: campus intranet, free student e-mail accounts, online (class) grades, online (class) registration, online (class) schedules. Campuswide network is available. 100% of college-owned or -operated housing units are wired for high-speed Internet access.
Student Life *Housing:* on-campus residence required through junior year. *Options:* men-only, women-only. Campus housing is university owned. Freshman campus housing is guaranteed. *Activities and organizations:* drama/theater group, student-run newspaper, radio station, choral group, marching band, Baptist Student Union, Delta Xi Omega, Student Government Association, Union Board, Lambda Chi Beta. *Campus security:* 24-hour emergency response devices and patrols, student patrols, late-night transport/escort service, controlled dormitory access. *Student services:* health clinic, personal/psychological counseling.
Athletics Member NCAA. All Division III. *Intercollegiate sports:* baseball M, basketball M/W, cheerleading M/W, cross-country running M/W, football M, golf M, soccer M/W, softball W, tennis M/W. *Intramural sports:* badminton M/W, basketball M/W, football M/W, racquetball M/W, soccer M/W, softball M/W, table tennis M/W, tennis M/W, ultimate Frisbee M/W, volleyball M/W, water polo M/W.
Standardized Tests *Required:* SAT or ACT (for admission).

Costs (2013–14) *Comprehensive fee:* $18,228 includes full-time tuition ($12,150), mandatory fees ($1630), and room and board ($4448). Full-time tuition and fees vary according to course load. Part-time tuition: $405 per credit hour. Part-time tuition and fees vary according to course load. *Room and board:* Room and board charges vary according to board plan and housing facility. *Payment plan:* installment.
Financial Aid Of all full-time matriculated undergraduates who enrolled in 2012, 1,186 applied for aid, 901 were judged to have need, 181 had their need fully met. In 2012, 270 non-need-based awards were made. *Average percent of need met:* 64%. *Average financial aid package:* $11,049. *Average need-based loan:* $3168. *Average need-based gift aid:* $8842. *Average non-need-based aid:* $5032.
Applying *Options:* electronic application, early admission. *Application fee:* $25. *Required:* high school transcript, minimum 2.0 GPA, class rank. *Required for some:* 3 letters of recommendation. *Recommended:* interview. *Application deadline:* 8/15 (freshmen). *Notification:* continuous (freshmen), continuous (transfers).
Freshman Application Contact Mr. Byron McGee, Director of Enrollment Management, Louisiana College, LC Box 566, Pineville, LA 71359. *Phone:* 318-487-7439. *Toll-free phone:* 800-487-1906. *Fax:* 318-487-7550. *E-mail:* admissions@lacollege.edu.
Website: http://www.lacollege.edu/.

Louisiana State University and Agricultural and Mechanical College

Baton Rouge, Louisiana

- **State-supported** university, founded 1860, part of Louisiana State University System
- **Urban** 2000-acre campus with easy access to New Orleans
- **Endowment** $348.8 million
- **Coed** 24,626 undergraduate students, 92% full-time, 51% women, 49% men
- **Moderately difficult** entrance level, 76% of applicants were admitted

Undergraduates 22,681 full-time, 1,945 part-time. Students come from 51 states and territories; 80 other countries; 20% are from out of state; 11% Black or African American, non-Hispanic/Latino; 5% Hispanic/Latino; 3% Asian, non-Hispanic/Latino; 0.1% Native Hawaiian or other Pacific Islander, non-Hispanic/Latino; 0.3% American Indian or Alaska Native, non-Hispanic/Latino; 2% Two or more races, non-Hispanic/Latino; 0.8% Race/ethnicity unknown; 2% international; 3% transferred in; 27% live on campus. *Retention:* 83% of full-time freshmen returned.
Freshmen *Admission:* 16,169 applied, 12,326 admitted, 5,725 enrolled. *Average high school GPA:* 3.4. *Test scores:* SAT critical reading scores over 500: 79%; SAT math scores over 500: 85%; ACT scores over 18: 100%; SAT critical reading scores over 600: 31%; SAT math scores over 600: 42%; ACT scores over 24: 66%; SAT critical reading scores over 700: 7%; SAT math scores over 700: 8%; ACT scores over 30: 13%.
Faculty *Total:* 1,399, 88% full-time, 87% with terminal degrees. *Student/faculty ratio:* 23:1.
Academics *Calendar:* semesters. *Degrees:* bachelor's, master's, doctoral, and post-master's certificates. *Special study options:* accelerated degree program, adult/continuing education programs, advanced placement credit, cooperative education, distance learning, double majors, English as a second language, freshman honors college, honors programs, independent study, internships, off-campus study, part-time degree program, services for LD students, student-designed majors, study abroad, summer session for credit. *ROTC:* Army (b), Navy (c), Air Force (b).
Computers on Campus 1,400 computers/terminals and 8,500 ports are available on campus for general student use. Students can access the following: computer help desk, free student e-mail accounts, online (class) grades, online (class) registration, online (class) schedules, free software for download, personal Web sites, storage, discounts on hardware, virtual computer lab. Campuswide network is available. 100% of college-owned or -operated housing units are wired for high-speed Internet access. Wireless service is available via entire campus.
Student Life *Housing options:* coed, men-only, women-only, disabled students. Campus housing is university owned. *Activities and organizations:* drama/theater group, student-run newspaper, radio and television station, choral group, marching band, intramural athletics, student political organizations, student professional organizations, religious organizations, cultural organizations, national fraternities, national sororities. *Campus security:* 24-hour emergency response devices and patrols, late-night transport/escort service,

controlled dormitory access, self-defense education, crime prevention programs. *Student services:* health clinic, personal/psychological counseling, women's center, legal services.

Athletics Member NCAA. All Division I except football (Division I-A). *Intercollegiate sports:* baseball M(s), basketball M(s)/W(s), cheerleading M/W, cross-country running M(s)/W(s), golf M(s)/W(s), gymnastics W(s), soccer W(s), softball W(s), swimming and diving M(s)/W(s), tennis M(s)/W(s), track and field M(s)/W(s), volleyball W(s). *Intramural sports:* badminton M/W, basketball M/W, bowling M(c)/W(c), crew M(c)/W(c), equestrian sports W(c), football M/W, lacrosse M(c)/W(c), racquetball M/W, rugby M(c), soccer M(c)/W(c), softball M/W, table tennis M/W, tennis M(c)/W(c), ultimate Frisbee M(c)/W(c), volleyball M(c)/W(c), water polo M(c)/W(c), weight lifting M(c)/W(c).

Standardized Tests *Required:* SAT or ACT (for admission).

Costs (2013–14) *Tuition:* state resident $5193 full-time; nonresident $20,469 full-time. Part-time tuition and fees vary according to course load. *Required fees:* $1796 full-time. *Room and board:* $10,218; room only: $6600. Room and board charges vary according to board plan and housing facility. *Payment plan:* deferred payment. *Waivers:* employees or children of employees.

Financial Aid Of all full-time matriculated undergraduates who enrolled in 2011, 11,945 applied for aid, 8,751 were judged to have need, 2,122 had their need fully met. 550 Federal Work-Study jobs (averaging $1400). 4,597 state and other part-time jobs (averaging $2600). In 2011, 3395 non-need-based awards were made. *Average percent of need met:* 70%. *Average financial aid package:* $13,772. *Average need-based loan:* $6130. *Average need-based gift aid:* $9036. *Average non-need-based aid:* $6101. *Average indebtedness upon graduation:* $20,125.

Applying *Options:* electronic application, early admission, deferred entrance. *Application fee:* $40. *Required:* high school transcript, minimum 3.0 GPA, 22 ACT (1030 SAT) with a minimum critical reading score of 18 ACT (450 SAT), and a math score of 19 ACT (460 SAT). *Required for some:* essay or personal statement. *Application deadlines:* 4/15 (freshmen), 4/15 (transfers). *Notification:* continuous (freshmen), continuous (transfers).

Freshman Application Contact Ms. Guadalupe Lamadrid, Associate Director, Undergraduate Admissions, Louisiana State University and Agricultural and Mechanical College, 1146 Pleasant Hall, Baton Rouge, LA 70803. *Phone:* 225-578-1175. *Fax:* 225-578-4433. *E-mail:* glamadrid@lsu.edu.
Website: http://www.lsu.edu/.

Louisiana State University at Alexandria

Alexandria, Louisiana

- **State-supported** 4-year, founded 1960, part of Louisiana State University System
- **Rural** 3114-acre campus
- **Endowment** $13.8 million
- **Coed** 2,407 undergraduate students, 50% full-time, 70% women, 30% men
- **Moderately difficult** entrance level, 61% of applicants were admitted

Undergraduates 1,196 full-time, 1,211 part-time. Students come from 16 states and territories; 7 other countries; 2% are from out of state; 18% Black or African American, non-Hispanic/Latino; 3% Hispanic/Latino; 1% Asian, non-Hispanic/Latino; 1% American Indian or Alaska Native, non-Hispanic/Latino; 2% Two or more races, non-Hispanic/Latino; 0.5% Race/ethnicity unknown; 0.1% international; 7% transferred in; 8% live on campus. *Retention:* 49% of full-time freshmen returned.

Freshmen *Admission:* 991 applied, 606 admitted, 371 enrolled. *Average high school GPA:* 3.12.

Faculty *Total:* 139, 62% full-time, 47% with terminal degrees. *Student/faculty ratio:* 15:1.

Academics *Calendar:* semesters. *Degrees:* certificates, associate, bachelor's, and postbachelor's certificates. *Special study options:* academic remediation for entering students, accelerated degree program, adult/continuing education programs, advanced placement credit, cooperative education, distance learning, double majors, independent study, internships, part-time degree program, services for LD students, summer session for credit.

Computers on Campus 325 computers/terminals are available on campus for general student use. Students can access the following: campus intranet, computer help desk, free student e-mail accounts, online (class) grades, online (class) registration, online (class) schedules. Campuswide network is available. 100% of college-owned or -operated housing units are wired for high-speed Internet access. Wireless service is available via entire campus.

Student Life *Housing:* on-campus residence required for freshman year. *Options:* coed, disabled students. Campus housing is university owned. Freshman applicants given priority for college housing. *Activities and organizations:* drama/theater group, student-run newspaper, choral group, Student Government Association. *Campus security:* 24-hour emergency response devices and patrols. *Student services:* personal/psychological counseling.

Athletics Member NAIA. *Intramural sports:* baseball M, softball W.

Standardized Tests *Required:* SAT or ACT (for admission).

Financial Aid Of all full-time matriculated undergraduates who enrolled in 2011, 53 Federal Work-Study jobs (averaging $1226). 76 state and other part-time jobs (averaging $1261).

Applying *Options:* electronic application, early admission. *Application fee:* $20. *Required:* high school transcript. *Required for some:* minimum 2.0 GPA. *Application deadlines:* rolling (freshmen), rolling (transfers). *Notification:* continuous (freshmen), continuous (transfers).

Freshman Application Contact Ms. Shelly Kieffer, Director of Admissions and Recruiting, Louisiana State University at Alexandria, 8100 Highway 71 South, Alexandria, LA 71302-9121. *Phone:* 318-473-6424. *Toll-free phone:* 888-473-6417. *Fax:* 318-473-6418. *E-mail:* admissions@lsua.edu.
Website: http://www.lsua.edu/.

Louisiana State University Health Sciences Center

New Orleans, Louisiana

Freshman Application Contact Louisiana State University Health Sciences Center, 433 Bolivar Street, New Orleans, LA 70112-2223. *Phone:* 504-568-4829.
Website: http://www.lsuhsc.edu/.

Louisiana State University in Shreveport

Shreveport, Louisiana

- **State-supported** comprehensive, founded 1965, part of Louisiana State University System
- **Urban** 200-acre campus
- **Endowment** $16.3 million
- **Coed** 4,124 undergraduate students, 56% full-time, 59% women, 41% men
- **Moderately difficult** entrance level, 68% of applicants were admitted

Undergraduates 2,306 full-time, 1,818 part-time. Students come from 43 states and territories; 12 other countries; 6% are from out of state; 23% Black or African American, non-Hispanic/Latino; 4% Hispanic/Latino; 2% Asian, non-Hispanic/Latino; 0.1% Native Hawaiian or other Pacific Islander, non-Hispanic/Latino; 1% American Indian or Alaska Native, non-Hispanic/Latino; 6% Race/ethnicity unknown; 2% international; 9% transferred in. *Retention:* 65% of full-time freshmen returned.

Freshmen *Admission:* 543 applied, 370 admitted, 370 enrolled. *Average high school GPA:* 3.25. *Test scores:* ACT scores over 18: 95%; ACT scores over 24: 38%; ACT scores over 30: 3%.

Faculty *Total:* 188, 68% full-time, 58% with terminal degrees. *Student/faculty ratio:* 21:1.

Academics *Calendar:* semesters plus 8-week and two 4-week summer terms. *Degrees:* certificates, bachelor's, master's, and post-master's certificates. *Special study options:* academic remediation for entering students, accelerated degree program, adult/continuing education programs, advanced placement credit, cooperative education, distance learning, double majors, English as a second language, honors programs, independent study, internships, off-campus study, part-time degree program, services for LD students, student-designed majors, summer session for credit. *ROTC:* Army (b).

Computers on Campus Students can access the following: computer help desk, free student e-mail accounts, online (class) grades, online (class) registration, online (class) schedules. Campuswide network is available. Wireless service is available via entire campus.

Student Life *Housing:* college housing not available. *Options:* Campus housing is provided by a third party. *Activities and organizations:* drama/theater group, student-run newspaper, choral group, national fraternities, national sororities. *Campus security:* 24-hour emergency response devices and patrols, student patrols, controlled dormitory access. *Student services:* personal/psychological counseling.

Athletics Member NAIA. *Intercollegiate sports:* baseball M(s), basketball M(s)/W(s), soccer M(s)/W(s), tennis W(s). *Intramural sports:* archery M, basketball M/W, lacrosse M, racquetball M/W, softball M/W, table tennis M/W, volleyball M/W.

Standardized Tests *Required:* SAT or ACT (for admission).

Costs (2012–13) *Tuition:* state resident $3882 full-time, $162 per credit hour part-time; nonresident $10,617 full-time, $442 per credit hour part-time. *Required fees:* $1060 full-time, $44 per credit hour part-time. *Waivers:* employees or children of employees.

Applying *Options:* electronic application, early admission, early decision. *Application fee:* $10. *Required for some:* high school transcript, minimum 2.0 GPA. *Application deadline:* rolling (freshmen).

Freshman Application Contact Louisiana State University in Shreveport, 1 University Place, Shreveport, LA 71115-2399. *Phone:* 318-797-5063. *Toll-free phone:* 800-229-5957.

Website: http://www.lsus.edu/.

Louisiana Tech University

Ruston, Louisiana

Freshman Application Contact Mrs. Jan B. Albritton, Director of Admissions, Louisiana Tech University, PO Box 3168, Ruston, LA 71272. *Phone:* 318-257-3036. *Toll-free phone:* 800-528-3241. *Fax:* 318-257-2499. *E-mail:* bulldog@latech.edu.

Website: http://www.latech.edu/.

Loyola University New Orleans

New Orleans, Louisiana

- **Independent Roman Catholic (Jesuit)** comprehensive, founded 1912
- **Suburban** 26-acre campus with easy access to New Orleans
- **Endowment** $249.0 million
- **Coed** 3,200 undergraduate students, 93% full-time, 58% women, 42% men
- **Moderately difficult** entrance level, 66% of applicants were admitted

Undergraduates 2,986 full-time, 214 part-time. Students come from 53 states and territories; 48 other countries; 58% are from out of state; 15% Black or African American, non-Hispanic/Latino; 15% Hispanic/Latino; 4% Asian, non-Hispanic/Latino; 0.9% American Indian or Alaska Native, non-Hispanic/Latino; 2% Two or more races, non-Hispanic/Latino; 7% Race/ethnicity unknown; 4% international; 4% transferred in; 65% live on campus. *Retention:* 74% of full-time freshmen returned.

Freshmen *Admission:* 6,486 applied, 4,257 admitted, 870 enrolled. *Average high school GPA:* 3.66. *Test scores:* SAT critical reading scores over 500: 96%; SAT math scores over 500: 93%; SAT writing scores over 500: 93%; ACT scores over 18: 100%; SAT critical reading scores over 600: 53%; SAT math scores over 600: 43%; SAT writing scores over 600: 49%; ACT scores over 24: 73%; SAT critical reading scores over 700: 10%; SAT math scores over 700: 4%; SAT writing scores over 700: 7%; ACT scores over 30: 12%.

Faculty *Total:* 492, 64% full-time, 75% with terminal degrees. *Student/faculty ratio:* 10:1.

Academics *Calendar:* semesters. *Degrees:* bachelor's, master's, doctoral, post-master's, and postbachelor's certificates. *Special study options:* accelerated degree program, adult/continuing education programs, advanced placement credit, cooperative education, distance learning, double majors, English as a second language, external degree program, honors programs, independent study, internships, off-campus study, part-time degree program, services for LD students, student-designed majors, study abroad, summer session for credit. *ROTC:* Army (c), Navy (c), Air Force (c). *Unusual degree programs:* 3-2 engineering with Tulane University.

Computers on Campus 525 computers/terminals and 2,500 ports are available on campus for general student use. Students can access the following: campus intranet, computer help desk, free student e-mail accounts, online (class) grades, online (class) registration, online (class) schedules. Campuswide network is available. 100% of college-owned or -operated housing units are wired for high-speed Internet access. Wireless service is available via entire campus.

Student Life *Housing:* on-campus residence required through sophomore year. *Options:* coed, disabled students. Campus housing is university owned. Freshman campus housing is guaranteed. *Activities and organizations:* drama/theater group, student-run newspaper, radio station, choral group, University Programming Board, Student Government Association, Black Student Union, Loyola University Community Action Program (LUCAP), Panhellenic Council, national fraternities, national sororities. *Campus security:* 24-hour emer-

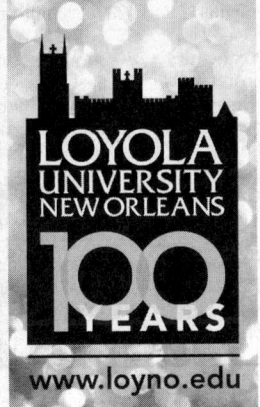

gency response devices and patrols, student patrols, late-night transport/escort service, controlled dormitory access, self-defense education, bicycle patrols, closed circuit TV monitors, door alarms, crime prevention programs, card access control. *Student services:* health clinic, personal/psychological counseling, women's center.

Athletics Member NAIA. *Intercollegiate sports:* baseball M, basketball M(s)/W(s), cheerleading M(c)/W(c), cross-country running M/W, golf M(c)/W(c), racquetball M/W, rugby M(c), sailing M(c)/W(c), soccer M(c)/W(c), swimming and diving M/W, tennis M/W, track and field M/W, ultimate Frisbee M(c)/W(c), volleyball W. *Intramural sports:* basketball M/W, soccer M/W, softball M/W, swimming and diving M/W, volleyball M/W, weight lifting M/W.

Standardized Tests *Required:* SAT or ACT (for admission).

Costs (2013–14) *Comprehensive fee:* $48,795 includes full-time tuition ($35,504), mandatory fees ($1106), and room and board ($12,185). Part-time tuition: $1012 per credit. *College room only:* $7250. Room and board charges vary according to board plan and housing facility. *Payment plan:* installment. *Waivers:* senior citizens and employees or children of employees.

Financial Aid Of all full-time matriculated undergraduates who enrolled in 2012, 2,257 applied for aid, 1,989 were judged to have need, 316 had their need fully met. In 2012, 837 non-need-based awards were made. *Average percent of need met:* 72%. *Average financial aid package:* $26,626. *Average need-based loan:* $4208. *Average need-based gift aid:* $22,391. *Average non-need-based aid:* $15,158. *Average indebtedness upon graduation:* $23,178. *Financial aid deadline:* 6/1.

Applying *Options:* electronic application, early admission. *Application fee:* $20. *Required:* essay or personal statement, high school transcript, 1 letter of recommendation. *Required for some:* interview. *Recommended:* interview. *Application deadlines:* rolling (freshmen), rolling (transfers). *Notification:* continuous (freshmen).

Freshman Application Contact Mr. Keith E. Gramling, Director, Admissions, Loyola University New Orleans, 6363 St. Charles Avenue, Campus Box 18, New Orleans, LA 70118. *Phone:* 504-865-3240. *Toll-free phone:* 800-4-LOYOLA. *Fax:* 504-865-3383. *E-mail:* admit@loyno.edu. *Website:* http://www.loyno.edu/.

See previous page for display ad and page 1366 for the College Close-Up.

McNeese State University

Lake Charles, Louisiana

- **State-supported** comprehensive, founded 1939, part of University of Louisiana System
- **Suburban** 766-acre campus
- **Coed** 7,711 undergraduate students, 79% full-time, 62% women, 38% men
- **Moderately difficult** entrance level, 61% of applicants were admitted

Undergraduates 6,082 full-time, 1,629 part-time. Students come from 38 states and territories; 47 other countries; 8% are from out of state; 18% Black or African American, non-Hispanic/Latino; 1% Hispanic/Latino; 1% Asian, non-Hispanic/Latino; 0.1% Native Hawaiian or other Pacific Islander, non-Hispanic/Latino; 0.8% American Indian or Alaska Native, non-Hispanic/Latino; 1% Two or more races, non-Hispanic/Latino; 0.3% Race/ethnicity unknown; 4% international; 4% transferred in; 9% live on campus. *Retention:* 68% of full-time freshmen returned.

Freshmen *Admission:* 3,547 applied, 2,152 admitted, 1,315 enrolled. *Average high school GPA:* 3.35. *Test scores:* ACT scores over 18: 95%; ACT scores over 24: 29%; ACT scores over 30: 2%.

Faculty *Total:* 428, 68% full-time, 50% with terminal degrees. *Student/faculty ratio:* 21:1.

Academics *Calendar:* semesters. *Degrees:* associate, bachelor's, master's, post-master's, and postbachelor's certificates. *Special study options:* academic remediation for entering students, accelerated degree program, advanced placement credit, cooperative education, distance learning, double majors, English as a second language, freshman honors college, honors programs, independent study, internships, off-campus study, part-time degree program, services for LD students, study abroad, summer session for credit.

Computers on Campus 700 computers/terminals are available on campus for general student use. Students can access the following: computer help desk, free student e-mail accounts, online (class) grades, online (class) registration, online (class) schedules. Campuswide network is available. Wireless service is available via entire campus.

Student Life *Housing options:* coed. Campus housing is university owned and is provided by a third party. *Activities and organizations:* drama/theater group, student-run newspaper, choral group, marching band, Student Government Association, International Students Association, Resident Student Association, national fraternities, national sororities. *Campus security:* 24-hour emergency

response devices and patrols, late-night transport/escort service, controlled dormitory access. *Student services:* health clinic, personal/psychological counseling, women's center.

Athletics Member NCAA. All Division I except football (Division I-AA). *Intercollegiate sports:* baseball M(s), basketball M(s)/W(s), cross-country running M(s)/W(s), golf M(s)/W(s), soccer W(s), softball W(s), tennis W(s), track and field M(s)/W(s), volleyball W(s). *Intramural sports:* badminton M/W, baseball M, basketball M/W, football M/W, golf M/W, racquetball M/W, soccer M/W, softball W, swimming and diving M/W, table tennis M/W, tennis M/W, volleyball M/W, water polo M/W, weight lifting M/W.

Standardized Tests *Required:* SAT or ACT (for admission).

Costs (2012–13) *Tuition:* state resident $5120 full-time; nonresident $11,454 full-time. Full-time tuition and fees vary according to course load. Part-time tuition and fees vary according to course load. *Room and board:* $7468. Room and board charges vary according to board plan and housing facility. *Waivers:* senior citizens and employees or children of employees.

Financial Aid Of all full-time matriculated undergraduates who enrolled in 2007, 3,331 were judged to have need, 556 had their need fully met. In 2007, 1527 non-need-based awards were made. *Average percent of need met:* 64%. *Average financial aid package:* $6705. *Average need-based loan:* $3899. *Average need-based gift aid:* $4085. *Average non-need-based aid:* $2847.

Applying *Options:* electronic application, early admission, deferred entrance. *Application fee:* $20. *Required:* high school transcript, minimum 2.0 GPA. *Application deadlines:* rolling (freshmen), rolling (transfers). *Notification:* continuous (freshmen), continuous (transfers).

Freshman Application Contact Ms. Kara Smith, Director of Admissions and Recruiting, McNeese State University, Box 91740, Lake Charles, LA 70609. *Phone:* 337-475-5504. *Toll-free phone:* 800-622-3352. *Fax:* 337-475-5978. *E-mail:* ksmith2@mcneese.edu. *Website:* http://www.mcneese.edu/.

New Orleans Baptist Theological Seminary

New Orleans, Louisiana

Director of Admissions Dr. Paul E. Gregoire Jr., Registrar/Director of Admissions, New Orleans Baptist Theological Seminary, 3939 Gentilly Boulevard, New Orleans, LA 70126-4858. *Phone:* 504-282-4455 Ext. 3337. *Toll-free phone:* 800-662-8701. *Website:* http://www.nobts.edu/.

Nicholls State University

Thibodaux, Louisiana

- **State-supported** comprehensive, founded 1948, part of University of Louisiana System
- **Small-town** 210-acre campus with easy access to New Orleans
- **Endowment** $15.2 million
- **Coed** 6,012 undergraduate students, 80% full-time, 62% women, 38% men
- **Noncompetitive** entrance level, 92% of applicants were admitted

Undergraduates 4,782 full-time, 1,230 part-time. Students come from 18 states and territories; 42 other countries; 4% are from out of state; 20% Black or African American, non-Hispanic/Latino; 3% Hispanic/Latino; 1% Asian, non-Hispanic/Latino; 0.1% Native Hawaiian or other Pacific Islander, non-Hispanic/Latino; 2% American Indian or Alaska Native, non-Hispanic/Latino; 2% Two or more races, non-Hispanic/Latino; 2% Race/ethnicity unknown; 2% international; 4% transferred in; 26% live on campus. *Retention:* 69% of full-time freshmen returned.

Freshmen *Admission:* 2,336 applied, 2,144 admitted, 1,253 enrolled. *Average high school GPA:* 3.17. *Test scores:* ACT scores over 18: 88%; ACT scores over 24: 25%; ACT scores over 30: 1%.

Faculty *Total:* 298, 88% full-time, 51% with terminal degrees. *Student/faculty ratio:* 20:1.

Academics *Calendar:* semesters. *Degrees:* associate, bachelor's, master's, and post-master's certificates. *Special study options:* academic remediation for entering students, accelerated degree program, adult/continuing education programs, advanced placement credit, cooperative education, distance learning, double majors, English as a second language, honors programs, independent study, internships, off-campus study, part-time degree program, services for LD students, study abroad, summer session for credit.

Computers on Campus 1,500 computers/terminals and 1,500 ports are available on campus for general student use. Students can access the following:

campus intranet, free student e-mail accounts, online (class) grades, online (class) registration, online (class) schedules, course management system—Moodle. Campuswide network is available. 100% of college-owned or -operated housing units are wired for high-speed Internet access. Wireless service is available via entire campus.

Student Life *Housing:* on-campus residence required for freshman year. *Options:* coed, men-only, women-only, disabled students. Campus housing is university owned. Freshman campus housing is guaranteed. *Activities and organizations:* drama/theater group, student-run newspaper, radio and television station, choral group, marching band, Student Government Association, Student Programming Association, Residence Hall Association, Food Advisory Association, national fraternities, national sororities. *Campus security:* 24-hour emergency response devices and patrols, student patrols, late-night transport/escort service. *Student services:* health clinic, personal/psychological counseling, women's center, legal services.

Athletics Member NCAA. All Division I except football (Division I-AA). *Intercollegiate sports:* baseball M(s), basketball M(s)/W(s), cross-country running M(s)/W(s), golf M(s)/W(s), soccer W(s), softball W(s), tennis M/W(s), track and field M(s)/W(s), volleyball W(s). *Intramural sports:* basketball M/W, football M/W, softball M/W, volleyball M/W.

Standardized Tests *Required:* SAT or ACT (for admission).

Costs (2013–14) *Tuition:* state resident $3924 full-time; nonresident $12,774 full-time. Part-time tuition and fees vary according to course load. *Required fees:* $1755 full-time. *Room and board:* $8560; room only: $5670. Room and board charges vary according to board plan, housing facility, and location. *Payment plans:* installment, deferred payment. *Waivers:* employees or children of employees.

Financial Aid Of all full-time matriculated undergraduates who enrolled in 2010, 4,109 applied for aid, 2,833 were judged to have need, 471 had their need fully met. In 2010, 437 non-need-based awards were made. *Average percent of need met:* 66%. *Average financial aid package:* $8358. *Average need-based loan:* $3153. *Average need-based gift aid:* $6401. *Average non-need-based aid:* $3731. *Average indebtedness upon graduation:* $25,036. *Financial aid deadline:* 6/30.

Applying *Options:* electronic application, early admission, deferred entrance. *Application fee:* $20. *Required:* high school transcript. *Application deadlines:* rolling (freshmen), rolling (transfers). *Notification:* 9/1 (freshmen), continuous until 8/28 (transfers).

Freshman Application Contact Mrs. Becky L. Durocher, Director of Admissions, Nicholls State University, PO Box 2004-NSU, Thibodaux, LA 70310. *Phone:* 985-448-4507. *Toll-free phone:* 877-NICHOLLS. *Fax:* 985-448-4929. *E-mail:* nicholls@nicholls.edu.
Website: http://www.nicholls.edu/.

Northwestern State University of Louisiana

Natchitoches, Louisiana

- **State-supported** comprehensive, founded 1884, part of University of Louisiana System
- **Small-town** 916-acre campus
- **Endowment** $10.9 million
- **Coed** 8,312 undergraduate students, 64% full-time, 68% women, 32% men
- **Moderately difficult** entrance level, 85% of applicants were admitted

Undergraduates 5,294 full-time, 3,018 part-time. Students come from 48 states and territories; 21 other countries; 9% are from out of state; 30% Black or African American, non-Hispanic/Latino; 4% Hispanic/Latino; 0.6% Asian, non-Hispanic/Latino; 0.1% Native Hawaiian or other Pacific Islander, non-Hispanic/Latino; 1% American Indian or Alaska Native, non-Hispanic/Latino; 3% Two or more races, non-Hispanic/Latino; 5% Race/ethnicity unknown; 0.6% international; 7% transferred in; 19% live on campus. *Retention:* 68% of full-time freshmen returned.

Freshmen *Admission:* 3,238 applied, 2,750 admitted, 1,369 enrolled. *Average high school GPA:* 3.24. *Test scores:* SAT critical reading scores over 500: 47%; SAT math scores over 500: 51%; ACT scores over 18: 90%; SAT critical reading scores over 600: 11%; SAT math scores over 600: 14%; ACT scores over 24: 27%; SAT critical reading scores over 700: 1%; SAT math scores over 700: 1%; ACT scores over 30: 2%.

Faculty *Total:* 498, 54% full-time, 45% with terminal degrees. *Student/faculty ratio:* 20:1.

Academics *Calendar:* semesters. *Degrees:* associate, bachelor's, master's, post-master's, and postbachelor's certificates. *Special study options:* academic remediation for entering students, adult/continuing education programs, advanced placement credit, cooperative education, distance learning, double

majors, freshman honors college, honors programs, independent study, internships, part-time degree program, services for LD students, study abroad, summer session for credit. *ROTC:* Army (b), Air Force (c).

Computers on Campus 1,500 computers/terminals and 1,500 ports are available on campus for general student use. Students can access the following: computer help desk, free student e-mail accounts, online (class) grades, online (class) registration, online (class) schedules. Campuswide network is available. 100% of college-owned or -operated housing units are wired for high-speed Internet access. Wireless service is available via classrooms, computer centers, computer labs, dorm rooms, learning centers, libraries, student centers.

Student Life *Housing:* on-campus residence required through junior year. *Options:* coed, disabled students. Campus housing is university owned and is provided by a third party. Freshman applicants given priority for college housing. *Activities and organizations:* drama/theater group, student-run newspaper, radio and television station, choral group, marching band, national fraternities, national sororities. *Campus security:* 24-hour emergency response devices and patrols, student patrols, late-night transport/escort service, controlled dormitory access. *Student services:* health clinic, personal/psychological counseling.

Athletics Member NCAA. All Division I except football (Division I-AA). *Intercollegiate sports:* baseball M(s), basketball M(s)/W(s), cross-country running M(s)/W(s), soccer W(s), softball W(s), tennis W(s), track and field M(s)/W(s), volleyball W(s). *Intramural sports:* archery M(c)/W(c), badminton M/W, basketball M/W, bowling M/W, crew M(c)/W(c), fencing M(c)/W(c), football M/W, golf M/W, racquetball M/W, soccer M(c)/W(c), softball M/W, swimming and diving M/W, table tennis M/W, tennis M/W, volleyball M/W.

Standardized Tests *Required:* SAT or ACT (for admission).

Costs (2012–13) *Tuition:* state resident $3938 full-time; nonresident $13,304 full-time. Full-time tuition and fees vary according to course load and location. Part-time tuition and fees vary according to course load and location. *Required fees:* $1542 full-time. *Room and board:* $7826; room only: $4896. Room and board charges vary according to board plan, housing facility, and location. *Payment plan:* installment. *Waivers:* senior citizens and employees or children of employees.

Financial Aid Of all full-time matriculated undergraduates who enrolled in 2010, 3,016 applied for aid, 2,673 were judged to have need, 983 had their need fully met. 211 Federal Work-Study jobs (averaging $1455). 114 state and other part-time jobs. In 2010, 2596 non-need-based awards were made. *Average percent of need met:* 48%. *Average financial aid package:* $7433. *Average need-based loan:* $7419. *Average need-based gift aid:* $5236. *Average non-need-based aid:* $5057. *Average indebtedness upon graduation:* $15,176.

Applying *Options:* electronic application, deferred entrance. *Application fee:* $20. *Required:* high school transcript, minimum 2.0 GPA, college preparatory curriculum. *Application deadlines:* 7/6 (freshmen), 7/6 (out-of-state freshmen), 7/6 (transfers). *Notification:* continuous (freshmen), continuous (out-of-state freshmen), continuous (transfers).

Freshman Application Contact Ms. Jana Lucky, Director of University Recruiting, Northwestern State University of Louisiana, 175 Sam Sibley Drive, Recruiting Office, Student Services Center, 1st Floor, Natchitoches, LA 71497. *Phone:* 318-357-4503. *Toll-free phone:* 800-327-1903. *Fax:* 318-357-5567. *E-mail:* recruiting@nsula.edu.
Website: http://www.nsula.edu/.

Our Lady of Holy Cross College

New Orleans, Louisiana

Director of Admissions Donna Kennedy, Director of Admissions and Financial Aid, Our Lady of Holy Cross College, 4123 Woodland Drive, New Orleans, LA 70131-7399. *Phone:* 504-398-2175. *Toll-free phone:* 800-259-7744. *E-mail:* dkennedy@olhcc.edu.
Website: http://www.olhcc.edu/.

Our Lady of the Lake College

Baton Rouge, Louisiana

- **Independent Roman Catholic** comprehensive, founded 1990
- **Suburban** 5-acre campus with easy access to New Orleans
- **Endowment** $8.6 million
- **Coed, primarily women**
- **Minimally difficult** entrance level

Faculty *Student/faculty ratio:* 18:1.

Academics *Calendar:* semesters. *Degrees:* certificates, diplomas, associate, bachelor's, master's, and postbachelor's certificates.

Student Life *Campus security:* 24-hour patrols.

COLLEGES AT-A-GLANCE

Standardized Tests *Required:* SAT or ACT (for admission), ACT ASSET (for admission).

Financial Aid *Of all full-time matriculated undergraduates who enrolled in 2008,* 684 applied for aid, 546 were judged to have need, 10 had their need fully met. *Average financial aid package:* $5175. *Average need-based loan:* $3664. *Average need-based gift aid:* $2486. *Average indebtedness upon graduation:* $12,019.

Applying *Options:* electronic application, early admission, deferred entrance. *Application fee:* $35. *Required:* high school transcript, minimum 2.0 GPA.

Freshman Application Contact Mrs. Rebecca Cannon, Director of Admissions, Our Lady of the Lake College, 7434 Perkins Road, Baton Rouge, LA 70808. *Phone:* 225-768-1718. *E-mail:* admissions@ololcollege.edu. *Website:* http://www.ololcollege.edu/.

Saint Joseph Seminary College

Saint Benedict, Louisiana

- **Independent Roman Catholic** 4-year, founded 1891
- **Rural** 1800-acre campus with easy access to New Orleans
- **Endowment** $1.1 million
- **Coed, primarily men** 107 undergraduate students, 97% full-time, 100% men
- **Minimally difficult** entrance level

Undergraduates 104 full-time, 3 part-time. Students come from 8 states and territories; 5 other countries; 45% are from out of state; 19% Hispanic/Latino; 5% Asian, non-Hispanic/Latino; 37% transferred in; 100% live on campus. *Retention:* 50% of full-time freshmen returned.

Freshmen *Admission:* 10 admitted, 11 enrolled. *Average high school GPA:* 3.25. *Test scores:* ACT scores over 18: 55%; ACT scores over 24: 22%.

Faculty *Total:* 22, 45% full-time, 32% with terminal degrees. *Student/faculty ratio:* 3:1.

Academics *Calendar:* semesters. *Degrees:* bachelor's (Religious Studies Institute is coed). *Special study options:* academic remediation for entering students, adult/continuing education programs, advanced placement credit, English as a second language, services for LD students.

Computers on Campus 14 computers/terminals and 90 ports are available on campus for general student use. Students can access the following: campus intranet, computer help desk, free student e-mail accounts. Campuswide network is available. 100% of college-owned or -operated housing units are wired for high-speed Internet access. Wireless service is available via entire campus.

Student Life *Housing:* on-campus residence required through senior year. *Options:* men-only. Campus housing is university owned. Freshman campus housing is guaranteed. *Activities and organizations:* drama/theater group, student-run newspaper, choral group, student government, yearbook. *Campus security:* 24-hour emergency response devices, controlled dormitory access, entrance gate. *Student services:* health clinic, personal/psychological counseling.

Athletics *Intramural sports:* football M, golf M.

Standardized Tests *Required:* ACT (for admission).

Costs (2012–13) *One-time required fee:* $150. *Comprehensive fee:* $28,180 includes full-time tuition ($13,500), mandatory fees ($1640), and room and board ($13,040). Part-time tuition: $175 per credit hour. *College room only:* $6850.

Financial Aid Of all full-time matriculated undergraduates who enrolled in 2009, 33 applied for aid, 33 were judged to have need, 33 had their need fully met. *Average percent of need met:* 100%. *Average financial aid package:* $4105. *Average need-based gift aid:* $4105. *Average indebtedness upon graduation:* $5000.

Applying *Options:* early admission, deferred entrance. *Required:* high school transcript, minimum 2.0 GPA. *Application deadlines:* rolling (freshmen), rolling (transfers). *Notification:* continuous (freshmen), continuous (transfers).

Freshman Application Contact Saint Joseph Seminary College, 75376 River Road, St. Benedict, LA 70457. *Phone:* 985-867-2273. *Fax:* 985-327-1085. *E-mail:* registrar@sjasc.edu. *Website:* http://www.sjasc.edu/.

Southeastern Louisiana University

Hammond, Louisiana

- **State-supported** comprehensive, founded 1925, part of University of Louisiana System
- **Small-town** 375-acre campus with easy access to New Orleans
- **Endowment** $28.4 million
- **Coed** 14,240 undergraduate students, 74% full-time, 61% women, 39% men
- **Moderately difficult** entrance level, 80% of applicants were admitted

Undergraduates 10,474 full-time, 3,766 part-time. Students come from 46 states and territories; 43 other countries; 3% are from out of state; 15% Black or African American, non-Hispanic/Latino; 3% Hispanic/Latino; 0.8% Asian, non-Hispanic/Latino; 0.1% Native Hawaiian or other Pacific Islander, non-Hispanic/Latino; 0.4% American Indian or Alaska Native, non-Hispanic/Latino; 2% Two or more races, non-Hispanic/Latino; 2% Race/ethnicity unknown; 2% international; 5% transferred in; 18% live on campus. *Retention:* 69% of full-time freshmen returned.

Freshmen *Admission:* 3,811 applied, 3,034 admitted, 2,471 enrolled. *Average high school GPA:* 3.18. *Test scores:* ACT scores over 18: 95%; ACT scores over 24: 31%; ACT scores over 30: 2%.

Faculty *Total:* 610, 80% full-time, 59% with terminal degrees. *Student/faculty ratio:* 23:1.

Academics *Calendar:* semesters. *Degrees:* associate, bachelor's, master's, and doctoral. *Special study options:* adult/continuing education programs, advanced placement credit, distance learning, double majors, English as a second language, honors programs, independent study, internships, off-campus study, part-time degree program, services for LD students, study abroad, summer session for credit. *ROTC:* Army (c).

Computers on Campus 1,622 computers/terminals and 600 ports are available on campus for general student use. Students can access the following: campus intranet, computer help desk, free student e-mail accounts, online (class) grades, online (class) registration, online (class) schedules, campus Webmail, student newspaper, transcripts, bookstore. Campuswide network is available. 100% of college-owned or -operated housing units are wired for high-speed Internet access. Wireless service is available via classrooms, computer centers, computer labs, dorm rooms, learning centers, libraries, student centers.

Student Life *Housing:* on-campus residence required through sophomore year. *Options:* coed, women-only, disabled students. Campus housing is university owned. *Activities and organizations:* drama/theater group, student-run newspaper, radio and television station, choral group, marching band, Catholic Student Association, Gamma Beta Phi, National Society of Collegiate Scholars, Sigma Alpha Lambda, Student Nurses' Association, national fraternities, national sororities. *Campus security:* 24-hour emergency response devices and patrols, student patrols, late-night transport/escort service, controlled dormitory access, video cameras, motorist assistance. *Student services:* health clinic, personal/psychological counseling.

Athletics Member NCAA. All Division I except football (Division I-AA). *Intercollegiate sports:* baseball M(s), basketball M(s)/W(s), cross-country running M(s)/W(s), golf M(s), soccer W(s), softball W(s), tennis W(s), track and field M(s)/W(s), volleyball W(s). *Intramural sports:* baseball M/W, basketball M/W, football M/W, racquetball M/W, rugby M(c), soccer M/W, softball M/W, tennis M/W, volleyball M/W, weight lifting M/W.

Standardized Tests *Required:* SAT or ACT (for admission).

Costs (2012–13) *Tuition:* state resident $5427 full-time; nonresident $16,285 full-time. Full-time tuition and fees vary according to course load. Part-time tuition and fees vary according to course load. *Room and board:* $6510; room only: $4260. Room and board charges vary according to board plan and housing facility. *Waivers:* employees or children of employees.

Financial Aid Of all full-time matriculated undergraduates who enrolled in 2011, 8,373 applied for aid, 6,164 were judged to have need, 2,272 had their need fully met. In 2011, 1061 non-need-based awards were made. *Average financial aid package:* $8238. *Average need-based loan:* $3791. *Average need-based gift aid:* $4823. *Average non-need-based aid:* $2787. *Average indebtedness upon graduation:* $19,661.

Applying *Options:* electronic application, early admission, deferred entrance. *Application fee:* $20. *Required:* proof of immunization required for all, college transcripts and statement of good standing required for some. *Required for some:* high school transcript, minimum 2.5 GPA. *Application deadlines:* 8/1 (freshmen), 8/1 (out-of-state freshmen), 8/1 (transfers). *Notification:* continuous (freshmen), continuous (out-of-state freshmen), continuous (transfers).

Freshman Application Contact Ms. Lori Fairburn, Director, Enrollment Services, Southeastern Louisiana University, SLU 10752, Hammond, LA

70402. *Phone:* 985-549-5637. *Toll-free phone:* 800-222-7358. *Fax:* 985-549-5882. *E-mail:* admissions@selu.edu. *Website:* http://www.selu.edu/.

Southern University and Agricultural and Mechanical College

Baton Rouge, Louisiana

Freshman Application Contact Ms. Velva Thomas, Director of Admissions, Southern University and Agricultural and Mechanical College, PO Box 9901, Baton Rouge, LA 70813. *Phone:* 225-771-2430. *Fax:* 225-771-2500. *E-mail:* velva_thomas@subr.edu. *Website:* http://www.subr.edu/.

Southern University at New Orleans

New Orleans, Louisiana

Freshman Application Contact Southern University at New Orleans, 6400 Press Drive, New Orleans, LA 70126-1009. *Phone:* 504-286-5033. *Website:* http://www.suno.edu/.

Southwest University

Kenner, Louisiana

Freshman Application Contact Admissions Office, Southwest University, 2200 Veterans Memorial Blvd., Kenner, LA 70062. *Phone:* 504-468-2900. *Toll-free phone:* 800-433-5923. *Fax:* 504-468-3213. *E-mail:* admissions@southwest.edu. *Website:* http://www.southwest.edu/.

Strayer University—Metairie Campus

Metairie, Louisiana

Freshman Application Contact Strayer University—Metairie Campus, 111 Veterans Memorial Boulevard, Suite 420, Metairie, LA 70005. *Website:* http://www.strayer.edu/campus/metairie.

Tulane University

New Orleans, Louisiana

- **Independent** university, founded 1834
- **Urban** 110-acre campus
- **Endowment** $121.1 million
- **Coed** 8,423 undergraduate students, 76% full-time, 58% women, 42% men
- **Very difficult** entrance level, 27% of applicants were admitted

Undergraduates 6,443 full-time, 1,980 part-time. Students come from 53 states and territories; 79 other countries; 71% are from out of state; 10% Black or African American, non-Hispanic/Latino; 6% Hispanic/Latino; 4% Asian, non-Hispanic/Latino; 0.4% American Indian or Alaska Native, non-Hispanic/Latino; 3% Two or more races, non-Hispanic/Latino; 4% Race/ethnicity unknown; 3% international; 0.9% transferred in; 44% live on campus. *Retention:* 89% of full-time freshmen returned.

Freshmen *Admission:* 30,080 applied, 8,203 admitted, 1,641 enrolled. *Average high school GPA:* 3.51. *Test scores:* SAT critical reading scores over 500: 99%; SAT math scores over 500: 98%; SAT writing scores over 500: 99%; ACT scores over 18: 100%; SAT critical reading scores over 600: 87%; SAT math scores over 600: 88%; SAT writing scores over 600: 89%; ACT scores over 24: 98%; SAT critical reading scores over 700: 35%; SAT math scores over 700: 32%; SAT writing scores over 700: 39%; ACT scores over 30: 62%.

Faculty *Total:* 1,179, 55% full-time, 72% with terminal degrees. *Student/faculty ratio:* 9:1.

Academics *Calendar:* semesters plus 3 summer sessions. *Degrees:* certificates, associate, bachelor's, master's, doctoral, and postbachelor's certificates. *Special study options:* accelerated degree program, adult/continuing education programs, advanced placement credit, cooperative education, distance learning, double majors, English as a second language, freshman honors college, honors programs, independent study, internships, off-campus study, part-time degree program, services for LD students, student-designed majors, study abroad, summer session for credit. *ROTC:* Army (b), Navy (b), Air Force (b). *Unusual degree programs:* 3-2 business administration; public health tropical medicine, science and engineering.

Computers on Campus 556 computers/terminals are available on campus for general student use. Students can access the following: campus intranet, computer help desk, free student e-mail accounts, online (class) grades, online (class) registration, online (class) schedules. Campuswide network is available. 100% of college-owned or -operated housing units are wired for high-speed Internet access. Wireless service is available via entire campus.

Student Life *Housing:* on-campus residence required through sophomore year. *Options:* coed, women-only, disabled students. Campus housing is university owned. Freshman campus housing is guaranteed. *Activities and organizations:* drama/theater group, student-run newspaper, radio and television station, choral group, marching band, Community Action Council of Tulane Students (CACTUS), Associated Student Body, Tulane University Campus Programming (TUCP), Association of Club Sports (ACS), National Pan-Hellenic Council, national fraternities, national sororities. *Campus security:* 24-hour emergency response devices and patrols, student patrols, late-night transport/escort service, controlled dormitory access, on and off-campus shuttle service, crime prevention programs, lighted pathways. *Student services:* health clinic, personal/psychological counseling, women's center, legal services.

Athletics Member NCAA. All Division I except football (Division I-A). *Intercollegiate sports:* baseball M(s), basketball M(s)/W(s), crew M(c)/W(c), cross-country running M(s)/W(s), golf W(s), gymnastics M(c)/W(c), ice hockey M(c)/W(c), lacrosse M(c)/W(c), rugby M(c), sailing M(c)/W(c), soccer M(c)/W(s), swimming and diving M(c)/W(s), tennis M(s)/W(s), track and field M(c)/W(s), volleyball M(c)/W(s), water polo M(c)/W(c). *Intramural sports:* baseball M(c), cheerleading M(c)/W(c), crew M(c)/W(c), cross-country running M(c), fencing M(c)/W(c), field hockey M(c)/W(c), gymnastics M(c)/W(c), ice hockey M(c), lacrosse M(c)/W(c), racquetball M(c)/W(c), rock climbing M(c)/W(c), rugby M(c), sailing M(c)/W(c), soccer M(c)/W(c), swimming and diving M(c)/W(c), tennis M(c)/W(c), track and field M(c)/W, ultimate Frisbee M(c)/W(c), volleyball M(c)/W(c), water polo M(c)/W(c).

Standardized Tests *Required:* SAT or ACT (for admission).

Costs (2012–13) *Comprehensive fee:* $56,787 includes full-time tuition ($41,500), mandatory fees ($3740), and room and board ($11,547). *College room only:* $6597. Room and board charges vary according to board plan and housing facility. *Payment plans:* tuition prepayment, installment. *Waivers:* employees or children of employees.

Financial Aid Of all full-time matriculated undergraduates who enrolled in 2011, 3,432 applied for aid, 2,627 were judged to have need, 1,773 had their need fully met. 1,372 Federal Work-Study jobs (averaging $2843). 138 state and other part-time jobs (averaging $7328). In 2011, 2276 non-need-based awards were made. *Average percent of need met:* 91%. *Average financial aid package:* $32,387. *Average need-based loan:* $7237. *Average need-based gift aid:* $27,164. *Average non-need-based aid:* $21,157. *Average indebtedness upon graduation:* $35,100.

Applying *Options:* electronic application, early action, deferred entrance. *Required:* essay or personal statement, high school transcript, 1 letter of recommendation. *Application deadlines:* 1/15 (freshmen), 6/1 (transfers). *Notification:* 4/1 (freshmen), continuous (transfers).

Freshman Application Contact Earl Retif, Vice President for Enrollment Management and University Registrar, Tulane University, Office of Admissions, 210 Gibson Hall, New Orleans, LA 70118. *Phone:* 504-865-5731. *Toll-free phone:* 800-873-9283. *Fax:* 504-862-8715. *E-mail:* undergrad.admission@tulane.edu. *Website:* http://www.tulane.edu/.

University of Louisiana at Lafayette

Lafayette, Louisiana

- **State-supported** university, founded 1898, part of University of Louisiana System
- **Urban** 1375-acre campus
- **Endowment** $112.3 million
- **Coed** 15,143 undergraduate students, 83% full-time, 57% women, 43% men
- **Moderately difficult** entrance level, 60% of applicants were admitted

Undergraduates 12,542 full-time, 2,601 part-time. Students come from 49 states and territories; 74 other countries; 5% are from out of state; 21% Black or African American, non-Hispanic/Latino; 3% Hispanic/Latino; 2% Asian, non-Hispanic/Latino; 0.5% American Indian or Alaska Native, non-Hispanic/Latino; 1% Two or more races, non-Hispanic/Latino; 1% Race/ethnicity unknown; 2% international; 4% transferred in; 17% live on campus. *Retention:* 74% of full-time freshmen returned.

Freshmen *Admission:* 9,262 applied, 5,591 admitted, 2,728 enrolled. *Average high school GPA:* 3.28. *Test scores:* SAT math scores over 500: 63%; ACT scores over 18: 98%; SAT math scores over 600: 24%; ACT scores over 24: 39%; SAT math scores over 700: 2%; ACT scores over 30: 3%.

Faculty *Total:* 754, 79% full-time, 56% with terminal degrees. *Student/faculty ratio:* 22:1.

Academics *Calendar:* semesters. *Degrees:* bachelor's, master's, doctoral, post-master's, and postbachelor's certificates. *Special study options:* academic remediation for entering students, accelerated degree program, adult/continuing education programs, advanced placement credit, cooperative education, distance learning, double majors, honors programs, independent study, internships, part-time degree program, services for LD students, student-designed majors, study abroad, summer session for credit. *ROTC:* Army (b).

Computers on Campus 413 computers/terminals and 800 ports are available on campus for general student use. Students can access the following: campus intranet, computer help desk, free student e-mail accounts, online (class) grades, online (class) registration, online (class) schedules. Campuswide network is available. 98% of college-owned or -operated housing units are wired for high-speed Internet access. Wireless service is available via libraries.

Student Life *Housing:* on-campus residence required for freshman year. *Options:* coed, men-only, women-only. Campus housing is university owned. Freshman campus housing is guaranteed. *Activities and organizations:* drama/theater group, student-run newspaper, radio station, choral group, marching band, Union Program Council, Chi Alpha, Student Government Association, Greek Council, Newman Club, national fraternities, national sororities. *Campus security:* 24-hour emergency response devices and patrols, late-night transport/escort service, controlled dormitory access. *Student services:* health clinic, personal/psychological counseling, women's center, legal services.

Athletics Member NCAA. All Division I except football (Division I-A). *Intercollegiate sports:* baseball M(s), basketball M(s)/W(s), cross-country running M(s)/W(s), golf M(s), soccer W, softball W(s), tennis M(s)/W(s), track and field M(s)/W(s), volleyball W(s). *Intramural sports:* badminton M/W, baseball M, basketball M/W, bowling M/W, cross-country running M/W, football M/W, golf M/W, ice hockey M, lacrosse M, racquetball M/W, rugby M/W, sailing M/W, soccer M/W, softball M/W, swimming and diving M/W, table tennis M/W, tennis M/W, track and field M/W, volleyball M/W, water polo M/W, weight lifting M/W.

Standardized Tests *Required:* SAT or ACT (for admission).

Costs (2012–13) *Tuition:* state resident $3926 full-time, $164 per credit hour part-time; nonresident $12,896 full-time, $537 per credit hour part-time. Full-time tuition and fees vary according to course load. Part-time tuition and fees vary according to course load. *Required fees:* $1448 full-time. *Room and board:* $8102. Room and board charges vary according to board plan and housing facility.

Financial Aid Of all full-time matriculated undergraduates who enrolled in 2011, 10,446 applied for aid, 7,142 were judged to have need, 630 had their need fully met. In 2011, 905 non-need-based awards were made. *Average percent of need met:* 55%. *Average financial aid package:* $7636. *Average need-based loan:* $3596. *Average need-based gift aid:* $5931. *Average non-need-based aid:* $1851.

Applying *Options:* electronic application, early admission, deferred entrance. *Application fee:* $25. *Required:* high school transcript, minimum 2.0 GPA, core requirements, no remedial courses. *Application deadlines:* rolling (freshmen), rolling (transfers).

Freshman Application Contact Mr. Andy Benoit Jr., Director of Enrollment Services and Recruitment, University of Louisiana at Lafayette, PO Drawer 41210, Lafayette, LA 70504. *Phone:* 337-482-6473. *Toll-free phone:* 800-752-6553. *Fax:* 337-482-1317. *E-mail:* admissions@louisiana.edu. *Website:* http://www.louisiana.edu/.

University of Louisiana at Monroe

Monroe, Louisiana

- **State-supported** university, founded 1931, part of University of Louisiana System
- **Urban** 238-acre campus
- **Coed** 7,298 undergraduate students, 71% full-time, 63% women, 37% men
- **Moderately difficult** entrance level, 49% of applicants were admitted

Undergraduates 5,184 full-time, 2,114 part-time. Students come from 46 states and territories; 58 other countries; 10% are from out of state; 27% Black or African American, non-Hispanic/Latino; 2% Hispanic/Latino; 1% Asian, non-Hispanic/Latino; 0.1% Native Hawaiian or other Pacific Islander, non-Hispanic/Latino; 0.4% American Indian or Alaska Native, non-Hispanic/Latino; 2% Two or more races, non-Hispanic/Latino; 2% Race/ethnicity unknown; 3% international; 5% transferred in; 22% live on campus. *Retention:* 68% of full-time freshmen returned.

Freshmen *Admission:* 2,641 applied, 1,302 admitted, 1,166 enrolled. *Average high school GPA:* 3.35. *Test scores:* SAT critical reading scores over 500: 37%; SAT math scores over 500: 49%; ACT scores over 18: 94%; SAT critical reading scores over 600: 10%; SAT math scores over 600: 18%; ACT scores over 24: 44%; SAT math scores over 700: 1%; ACT scores over 30: 9%.

Faculty *Total:* 407, 45% full-time. *Student/faculty ratio:* 18:1.

Academics *Calendar:* semesters. *Degrees:* associate, bachelor's, master's, doctoral, post-master's, and postbachelor's certificates. *Special study options:* academic remediation for entering students, accelerated degree program, advanced placement credit, cooperative education, distance learning, double majors, English as a second language, external degree program, honors programs, independent study, internships, off-campus study, study abroad, summer session for credit. *ROTC:* Army (c), Air Force (c).

Computers on Campus Students can access the following: campus intranet, computer help desk, free student e-mail accounts, online (class) grades, online (class) registration, online (class) schedules. Campuswide network is available. 100% of college-owned or -operated housing units are wired for high-speed Internet access. Wireless service is available via entire campus.

Student Life *Housing:* on-campus residence required through sophomore year. *Options:* coed, men-only, women-only. Campus housing is university owned and leased by the school. Freshman applicants given priority for college housing. *Activities and organizations:* drama/theater group, student-run newspaper, radio station, marching band, Maroon Platoon, Alpha Lambda Delta, Louisiana Pharmacist Alliance, Association for Students in Kinesiology, Pre-Pharmacy Organization/Sound of Today, national fraternities, national sororities. *Campus security:* 24-hour emergency response devices and patrols, student patrols, late-night transport/escort service. *Student services:* health clinic, personal/psychological counseling.

Athletics Member NCAA. All Division I except football (Division I-A). *Intercollegiate sports:* baseball M(s), basketball M(s)/W(s), cheerleading M(s)/W(s), cross-country running M(s)/W(s), golf M(s)/W, racquetball M/W, soccer M/W(s), softball W(s), swimming and diving M(s)/W(s), tennis M/W, track and field M(s)/W(s), volleyball M/W(s), weight lifting M/W. *Intramural sports:* archery M/W, badminton M/W, basketball M/W, bowling M/W, cross-country running M/W, football M/W, golf M/W, soccer M/W, softball M/W, swimming and diving M/W, table tennis M/W, tennis W, track and field M/W, volleyball W.

Standardized Tests *Required:* SAT or ACT (for admission).

Costs (2012–13) *Tuition:* state resident $5443 full-time; nonresident $14,263 full-time. Full-time tuition and fees vary according to course load. Part-time tuition and fees vary according to course load. *Room and board:* $6486; room only: $3830. Room and board charges vary according to board plan and housing facility. *Payment plan:* deferred payment. *Waivers:* children of alumni, senior citizens, and employees or children of employees.

Applying *Options:* electronic application, early admission, deferred entrance. *Application fee:* $20. *Required:* high school transcript. *Application deadlines:* rolling (freshmen), rolling (out-of-state freshmen), rolling (transfers). *Notification:* continuous (freshmen), continuous (out-of-state freshmen), continuous (transfers).

Freshman Application Contact Ms. Frances Self, Assistant Director of Admissions, University of Louisiana at Monroe, Office of Recruitment and Admissions, Sandel Hall, 4020 Northeast Drive, Monroe, LA 71209. *Phone:* 318-342-5430. *Toll-free phone:* 800-372-5127. *Fax:* 318-342-1915. *E-mail:* admissions@ulm.edu. *Website:* http://www.ulm.edu/.

University of New Orleans

New Orleans, Louisiana

- **State-supported** university, founded 1958, part of University of Louisiana System
- **Urban** 345-acre campus
- **Endowment** $17.6 million
- **Coed** 7,689 undergraduate students, 76% full-time, 50% women, 50% men
- **Moderately difficult** entrance level, 49% of applicants were admitted

Undergraduates 5,828 full-time, 1,861 part-time. Students come from 48 states and territories; 59 other countries; 4% are from out of state; 15% Black or African American, non-Hispanic/Latino; 9% Hispanic/Latino; 7% Asian, non-Hispanic/Latino; 0.1% Native Hawaiian or other Pacific Islander, non-Hispanic/Latino; 0.4% American Indian or Alaska Native, non-Hispanic/Latino; 2% Two or more races, non-Hispanic/Latino; 6% Race/ethnicity unknown; 4% international; 10% transferred in; 8% live on campus. *Retention:* 65% of full-time freshmen returned.
Freshmen *Admission:* 3,237 applied, 1,592 admitted, 882 enrolled. *Average high school GPA:* 3.1. *Test scores:* SAT critical reading scores over 500: 67%; SAT math scores over 500: 71%; ACT scores over 18: 97%; SAT critical reading scores over 600: 36%; SAT math scores over 600: 34%; ACT scores over 24: 36%; SAT critical reading scores over 700: 5%; SAT math scores over 700: 6%; ACT scores over 30: 3%.
Faculty *Total:* 519, 62% full-time, 65% with terminal degrees. *Student/faculty ratio:* 21:1.
Academics *Calendar:* semesters. *Degrees:* bachelor's, master's, and doctoral. *Special study options:* adult/continuing education programs, advanced placement credit, cooperative education, distance learning, double majors, English as a second language, honors programs, independent study, internships, off-campus study, part-time degree program, services for LD students, study abroad, summer session for credit. *ROTC:* Army (b), Navy (c), Air Force (c). *Unusual degree programs:* 3-2 engineering with Xavier University of Louisiana; Southern University at New Orleans; Loyola University, New Orleans; Dillard University.
Computers on Campus 1,208 computers/terminals and 1,191 ports are available on campus for general student use. Students can access the following: campus intranet, computer help desk, free student e-mail accounts, online (class) grades, online (class) registration, online (class) schedules, classes in Moodle. Campuswide network is available. 100% of college-owned or -operated housing units are wired for high-speed Internet access. Wireless service is available via entire campus.
Student Life *Housing options:* coed, disabled students. Campus housing is university owned, leased by the school and is provided by a third party. *Activities and organizations:* drama/theater group, student-run newspaper, choral group, Student Activities Council, Student Government, International Student Organization, VASA, Greek Life, national fraternities, national sororities. *Campus security:* 24-hour emergency response devices and patrols, late-night transport/escort service, controlled dormitory access. *Student services:* health clinic, personal/psychological counseling, women's center, legal services.
Athletics Member NCAA. All Division I. *Intercollegiate sports:* baseball M(s), basketball M(s)/W(s), cross-country running M(s)/W(s), golf M(s)/W(s), tennis M(s)/W(s), track and field M(s)/W(s), volleyball W(s). *Intramural sports:* basketball M/W, football M/W, racquetball M/W, soccer M/W, softball M/W, volleyball M/W.
Standardized Tests *Required:* SAT or ACT (for admission).
Costs (2012–13) *Tuition:* state resident $5164 full-time; nonresident $17,176 full-time. Full-time tuition and fees vary according to course load, location, and program. Part-time tuition and fees vary according to course load, location, and program. *Required fees:* $758 full-time. *Room and board:* $8310. Room and board charges vary according to board plan and housing facility. *Payment plan:* installment. *Waivers:* senior citizens and employees or children of employees.
Financial Aid Of all full-time matriculated undergraduates who enrolled in 2012, 4,702 applied for aid, 4,135 were judged to have need, 241 had their need fully met. 150 Federal Work-Study jobs (averaging $2361). 366 state and other part-time jobs (averaging $1660). In 2012, 42 non-need-based awards were made. *Average percent of need met:* 48%. *Average financial aid package:* $8174. *Average need-based loan:* $4120. *Average need-based gift aid:* $5702. *Average non-need-based aid:* $1458. *Average indebtedness upon graduation:* $18,271.
Applying *Options:* electronic application, early admission, deferred entrance. *Application fee:* $20. *Required:* high school transcript, Core Requirements (19 units). *Required for some:* minimum 2.5 GPA. *Application deadlines:* 7/25 (freshmen), 6/1 (out-of-state freshmen), 7/25 (transfers).

Freshman Application Contact University of New Orleans, 2000 Lakeshore Drive, New Orleans, LA 70148. *Phone:* 504-280-6595. *Toll-free phone:* 800-256-5866.
Website: http://www.uno.edu/.

University of Phoenix–Louisiana Campus

Metairie, Louisiana

Freshman Application Contact Marc Booker, Sr. Director, Office of Admissions and Evaluation, University of Phoenix–Louisiana Campus, 4035 South Riverpoint Parkway, Mail Stop CF-L101, Phoenix, AZ 85040. *Phone:* 602-557-4609. *Toll-free phone:* 866-766-0766. *Fax:* 480-643-1156.
Website: http://www.phoenix.edu/.

Xavier University of Louisiana

New Orleans, Louisiana

- **Independent Roman Catholic** comprehensive, founded 1925
- **Urban** 23-acre campus
- **Coed** 2,525 undergraduate students, 95% full-time, 71% women, 29% men
- **Moderately difficult** entrance level, 64% of applicants were admitted

Undergraduates 2,399 full-time, 126 part-time. 48% are from out of state; 78% Black or African American, non-Hispanic/Latino; 2% Hispanic/Latino; 10% Asian, non-Hispanic/Latino; 0.2% American Indian or Alaska Native, non-Hispanic/Latino; 3% Two or more races, non-Hispanic/Latino; 1% Race/ethnicity unknown; 2% international; 5% transferred in; 47% live on campus. *Retention:* 65% of full-time freshmen returned.
Freshmen *Admission:* 3,987 applied, 2,532 admitted, 661 enrolled. *Average high school GPA:* 3.33. *Test scores:* SAT critical reading scores over 500: 46%; SAT math scores over 500: 42%; SAT writing scores over 500: 34%; ACT scores over 18: 89%; SAT critical reading scores over 600: 12%; SAT math scores over 600: 13%; SAT writing scores over 600: 8%; ACT scores over 24: 38%; SAT critical reading scores over 700: 1%; SAT math scores over 700: 1%; SAT writing scores over 700: 1%; ACT scores over 30: 2%.
Faculty *Total:* 261, 90% full-time, 89% with terminal degrees. *Student/faculty ratio:* 13:1.
Academics *Calendar:* semesters. *Degrees:* bachelor's, master's, and doctoral. *Special study options:* academic remediation for entering students, accelerated degree program, adult/continuing education programs, advanced placement credit, cooperative education, double majors, freshman honors college, honors programs, independent study, internships, off-campus study, part-time degree program, services for LD students, study abroad, summer session for credit. *ROTC:* Army (c), Navy (c), Air Force (c). *Unusual degree programs:* 3-2 business administration with Tulane University; engineering with Tulane University, University of Maryland, University of New Orleans, Georgia Institute of Technology, University of Wisconsin-Madison, Morgan State University, Southern University and Agricultural and Mechanical College; biostatistics with Louisiana State University Medical Center.
Computers on Campus Students can access the following: computer help desk, free student e-mail accounts, online (class) grades, online (class) registration, online (class) schedules. Campuswide network is available. 100% of college-owned or -operated housing units are wired for high-speed Internet access. Wireless service is available via entire campus.
Student Life *Housing options:* coed, men-only, women-only, disabled students. Campus housing is university owned. Freshman applicants given priority for college housing. *Activities and organizations:* drama/theater group, student-run newspaper, television station, choral group, Mobilization at Xavier, AWARE, NAACP, California Club, Beta Beta Beta (Biology Club), national fraternities, national sororities. *Campus security:* 24-hour emergency response devices and patrols, student patrols, bicycle patrols. *Student services:* health clinic, personal/psychological counseling.
Athletics Member NAIA. *Intercollegiate sports:* basketball M(s)/W(s), cross-country running M/W, tennis M(s)/W(s). *Intramural sports:* badminton M/W, basketball M/W, football M/W, golf M/W, softball M/W, swimming and diving M/W, table tennis M/W, tennis M/W, track and field M/W, volleyball M/W.
Standardized Tests *Required:* SAT or ACT (for admission).
Costs (2013–14) *Comprehensive fee:* $26,300 includes full-time tuition ($17,700), mandatory fees ($1000), and room and board ($7600). Part-time tuition: $775 per credit hour. Part-time tuition and fees vary according to course load. *Room and board:* Room and board charges vary according to

housing facility. *Payment plan:* installment. *Waivers:* employees or children of employees.

Financial Aid Of all full-time matriculated undergraduates who enrolled in 2010, 2,455 applied for aid, 2,271 were judged to have need, 17 had their need fully met. 319 Federal Work-Study jobs (averaging $1082). In 2010, 73 non-need-based awards were made. *Average percent of need met:* 13%. *Average financial aid package:* $17,465. *Average need-based loan:* $4729. *Average need-based gift aid:* $6179. *Average non-need-based aid:* $9257. *Average indebtedness upon graduation:* $46,474.

Applying *Options:* electronic application, early action. *Application fee:* $25. *Required:* high school transcript, minimum 2.0 GPA, 1 letter of recommendation. *Required for some:* interview. *Application deadlines:* 7/1 (freshmen), 6/1 (transfers), 1/15 (early action). *Notification:* continuous (freshmen), continuous (transfers), 2/15 (early action).

Freshman Application Contact Mr. Winston Brown, Dean of Admissions, Xavier University of Louisiana, 7325 Palmetto Street, New Orleans, LA 70125. *Phone:* 504-520-7388. *Toll-free phone:* 877-XAVIERU. *Fax:* 504-520-7941. *E-mail:* apply@xula.edu.
Website: http://www.xula.edu/.

MAINE

Bates College
Lewiston, Maine

- **Independent** 4-year, founded 1855
- **Small-town** 109-acre campus
- **Endowment** $216.2 million
- **Coed** 1,753 undergraduate students, 100% full-time, 53% women, 47% men
- **Most difficult** entrance level, 27% of applicants were admitted

Undergraduates 1,753 full-time. Students come from 44 states and territories; 71 other countries; 89% are from out of state; 4% Black or African American, non-Hispanic/Latino; 5% Hispanic/Latino; 4% Asian, non-Hispanic/Latino; 0.4% American Indian or Alaska Native, non-Hispanic/Latino; 4% Two or more races, non-Hispanic/Latino; 2% Race/ethnicity unknown; 6% international; 0.9% transferred in; 92% live on campus. *Retention:* 95% of full-time freshmen returned.

Freshmen *Admission:* 4,906 applied, 1,304 admitted, 503 enrolled. *Test scores:* SAT critical reading scores over 500: 100%; SAT math scores over 500: 100%; SAT writing scores over 500: 100%; ACT scores over 18: 100%; SAT critical reading scores over 600: 91%; SAT math scores over 600: 93%; SAT writing scores over 600: 93%; ACT scores over 24: 100%; SAT critical reading scores over 700: 37%; SAT math scores over 700: 36%; SAT writing scores over 700: 45%; ACT scores over 30: 75%.

Faculty *Total:* 195, 86% full-time, 88% with terminal degrees. *Student/faculty ratio:* 10:1.

Academics *Calendar:* 4-4-1. *Degree:* bachelor's. *Special study options:* accelerated degree program, advanced placement credit, double majors, honors programs, independent study, internships, off-campus study, services for LD students, student-designed majors, study abroad. *Unusual degree programs:* 3-2 engineering with Columbia University, Rensselaer Polytechnic Institute, Case Western Reserve University, Washington University in St. Louis, Dartmouth College.

Computers on Campus 175 computers/terminals and 2,075 ports are available on campus for general student use. Students can access the following: computer help desk, free student e-mail accounts, online (class) grades, online (class) registration, online (class) schedules, course web pages, course evaluation, financial records. Campuswide network is available. 100% of college-owned or -operated housing units are wired for high-speed Internet access. Wireless service is available via classrooms, computer labs, dorm rooms, learning centers, libraries, student centers.

Student Life *Housing:* on-campus residence required through senior year. *Options:* coed, men-only, women-only. Campus housing is university owned. Freshman campus housing is guaranteed. *Activities and organizations:* drama/theater group, student-run newspaper, radio station, choral group, Outing Club (outdoor recreation), International Club, Chase Hall Committee (student activities planning), Representative Assembly, WRBC (student radio station). *Campus security:* 24-hour emergency response devices and patrols, student patrols, late-night transport/escort service, controlled dormitory access. *Student services:* health clinic, personal/psychological counseling, women's center.

Athletics Member NCAA. All Division III. *Intercollegiate sports:* baseball M, basketball M/W, crew M/W, cross-country running M/W, equestrian sports M(c)/W(c), fencing M(c)/W(c), field hockey W, football M, golf M/W, ice

hockey M(c)/W(c), lacrosse M/W, rugby M(c)/W(c), sailing M(c)/W(c), skiing (cross-country) M/W, skiing (downhill) M/W, soccer M/W, softball W, squash M/W, swimming and diving M/W, tennis M/W, track and field M/W, ultimate Frisbee M(c)/W(c), volleyball M(c)/W(c), water polo M(c)/W(c). *Intramural sports:* basketball M/W, bowling M/W, ice hockey M/W, racquetball M/W, soccer M/W, softball M/W, squash M/W, tennis M/W, volleyball M/W.

Costs (2012–13) *Comprehensive fee:* $57,235 includes full-time tuition ($44,040), mandatory fees ($260), and room and board ($12,935). *Payment plans:* tuition prepayment, installment. *Waivers:* employees or children of employees.

Financial Aid Of all full-time matriculated undergraduates who enrolled in 2012, 872 applied for aid, 800 were judged to have need, 720 had their need fully met. 438 Federal Work-Study jobs (averaging $1826). 251 state and other part-time jobs (averaging $1764). *Average percent of need met:* 100%. *Average financial aid package:* $38,887. *Average need-based loan:* $3523. *Average need-based gift aid:* $36,058. *Average indebtedness upon graduation:* $24,515. *Financial aid deadline:* 2/15.

Applying *Options:* electronic application, early admission, early decision, deferred entrance. *Application fee:* $60. *Required:* essay or personal statement, high school transcript, 3 letters of recommendation. *Recommended:* interview. *Application deadlines:* 1/1 (freshmen), 3/1 (transfers). *Early decision deadline:* 11/15 (for plan 1), 1/1 (for plan 2). *Notification:* 4/1 (freshmen), 6/1 (transfers), 12/20 (early decision plan 1), 2/15 (early decision plan 2).

Freshman Application Contact Leigh Weisenburger, Dean of Admission and Financial Aid, Bates College, 23 Campus Ave, Lindholm House, Bates College, Lewiston, ME 04240-6028. *Phone:* 855-228-3755. *Fax:* 207-786-6025. *E-mail:* admission@bates.edu.
Website: http://www.bates.edu/.

Bowdoin College
Brunswick, Maine

- **Independent** 4-year, founded 1794
- **Small-town** 205-acre campus with easy access to Portland
- **Endowment** $902.4 million
- **Coed** 1,839 undergraduate students, 100% full-time, 50% women, 50% men
- **Most difficult** entrance level, 16% of applicants were admitted

Undergraduates 1,831 full-time, 8 part-time. Students come from 49 states and territories; 27 other countries; 87% are from out of state; 5% Black or African American, non-Hispanic/Latino; 13% Hispanic/Latino; 7% Asian, non-Hispanic/Latino; 0.1% Native Hawaiian or other Pacific Islander, non-Hispanic/Latino; 0.1% American Indian or Alaska Native, non-Hispanic/Latino; 6% Two or more races, non-Hispanic/Latino; 0.6% Race/ethnicity unknown; 4% international; 0.1% transferred in; 92% live on campus. *Retention:* 97% of full-time freshmen returned.

Freshmen *Admission:* 6,716 applied, 1,060 admitted, 492 enrolled. *Test scores:* SAT critical reading scores over 500: 99%; SAT math scores over 500: 99%; SAT writing scores over 500: 100%; ACT scores over 18: 100%; SAT critical reading scores over 600: 95%; SAT math scores over 600: 96%; SAT writing scores over 600: 96%; ACT scores over 24: 100%; SAT critical reading scores over 700: 64%; SAT math scores over 700: 62%; SAT writing scores over 700: 62%; ACT scores over 30: 85%.

Faculty *Total:* 228, 82% full-time, 98% with terminal degrees. *Student/faculty ratio:* 9:1.

Academics *Calendar:* semesters. *Degrees:* bachelor's (SAT or ACT considered if submitted. Test scores are required for home-schooled applicants). *Special study options:* accelerated degree program, advanced placement credit, double majors, independent study, off-campus study, services for LD students, student-designed majors, study abroad. *Unusual degree programs:* 3-2 engineering with California Institute of Technology, Columbia University, Dartmouth College, University of Maine Orono; Law with Columbia University.

Computers on Campus 600 computers/terminals and 650 ports are available on campus for general student use. Students can access the following: campus intranet, computer help desk, free student e-mail accounts, online (class) grades, online (class) schedules, training classes on variety of desktop and academic software, 24/7 software support, free equipment loaner pool: laptops, video and digital cameras, sound and lighting systems, iPads, iPods. Campuswide network is available. 100% of college-owned or -operated housing units are wired for high-speed Internet access. Wireless service is available via entire campus.

Student Life *Housing:* on-campus residence required through sophomore year. *Options:* coed, disabled students. Campus housing is university owned. Freshman campus housing is guaranteed. *Activities and organizations:* drama/theater group, student-run newspaper, radio and television station, choral group, Outing Club, Intramural Sports, Community Service Volunteer Programs,

WBOR 91.1 FM, Bowdoin Orient. *Campus security:* 24-hour emergency response devices and patrols, late-night transport/escort service, controlled dormitory access, self-defense education, whistle program, safe ride service. *Student services:* health clinic, personal/psychological counseling, women's center.

Athletics Member NCAA. All Division III except men's and women's sailing (Division I), men's and women's skiing (cross-country) (Division I), men's and women's squash (Division I). *Intercollegiate sports:* baseball M, basketball M/W, crew M(c)/W(c), cross-country running M/W, equestrian sports M(c)/W(c), fencing M(c)/W(c), field hockey W, football M, golf M/W, ice hockey M/W, lacrosse M/W, rugby M(c)/W, sailing M/W, skiing (cross-country) M/W, soccer M/W, softball W, squash M/W, swimming and diving M/W, tennis M/W, track and field M/W, ultimate Frisbee M(c)/W(c), volleyball M(c)/W, water polo M(c)/W(c). *Intramural sports:* badminton M/W, basketball M/W, cheerleading M(c)/W(c), football M/W, ice hockey M/W, lacrosse M(c)/W(c), rock climbing M(c)/W(c), skiing (cross-country) M(c)/W(c), skiing (downhill) M(c)/W(c), soccer M/W, softball M/W, table tennis M(c)/W(c), tennis M/W.

Costs (2012–13) *Comprehensive fee:* $56,128 includes full-time tuition ($43,676), mandatory fees ($442), and room and board ($12,010). *College room only:* $5620. Room and board charges vary according to board plan. *Payment plans:* installment, deferred payment. *Waivers:* employees or children of employees.

Financial Aid Of all full-time matriculated undergraduates who enrolled in 2011, 974 applied for aid, 813 were judged to have need, 813 had their need fully met. 412 Federal Work-Study jobs (averaging $1338). 322 state and other part-time jobs (averaging $2236). In 2011, 89 non-need-based awards were made. *Average percent of need met:* 100%. *Average financial aid package:* $40,196. *Average need-based gift aid:* $35,975. *Average non-need-based aid:* $1000. *Average indebtedness upon graduation:* $17,569. *Financial aid deadline:* 2/15.

Applying *Options:* electronic application, early admission, early decision, deferred entrance. *Application fee:* $60. *Required:* essay or personal statement, high school transcript, 3 letters of recommendation. *Recommended:* interview. *Application deadlines:* 1/1 (freshmen), 1/1 (out-of-state freshmen), 3/1 (transfers). *Early decision deadline:* 11/15 (for plan 1), 1/1 (for plan 2). *Notification:* 4/5 (freshmen), 4/5 (out-of-state freshmen), 5/1 (transfers), 12/15 (early decision plan 1), 2/15 (early decision plan 2).

Freshman Application Contact Jacob Daly, Assistant Dean of Admissions, Bowdoin College, 5000 College Station, Brunswick, ME 04011-8411. *Phone:* 207-725-3730. *Fax:* 207-725-3101. *E-mail:* admissions@bowdoin.edu. *Website:* http://www.bowdoin.edu/.

Colby College
Waterville, Maine

- **Independent** 4-year, founded 1813
- **Small-town** 714-acre campus
- **Endowment** $599.6 million
- **Coed** 1,863 undergraduate students, 100% full-time, 55% women, 45% men
- **Most difficult** entrance level, 29% of applicants were admitted

Undergraduates 1,863 full-time. Students come from 48 states and territories; 76 other countries; 87% are from out of state; 3% Black or African American, non-Hispanic/Latino; 5% Hispanic/Latino; 6% Asian, non-Hispanic/Latino; 0.1% Native Hawaiian or other Pacific Islander, non-Hispanic/Latino; 0.1% American Indian or Alaska Native, non-Hispanic/Latino; 4% Two or more races, non-Hispanic/Latino; 15% Race/ethnicity unknown; 6% international; 0.3% transferred in; 93% live on campus. *Retention:* 95% of full-time freshmen returned.

Freshmen *Admission:* 5,241 applied, 1,518 admitted, 493 enrolled. *Test scores:* SAT critical reading scores over 500: 97%; SAT math scores over 500: 98%; SAT writing scores over 500: 98%; ACT scores over 18: 100%; SAT critical reading scores over 600: 79%; SAT math scores over 600: 87%; SAT writing scores over 600: 81%; ACT scores over 24: 99%; SAT critical reading scores over 700: 30%; SAT math scores over 700: 37%; SAT writing scores over 700: 32%; ACT scores over 30: 62%.

Faculty *Total:* 216, 77% full-time, 88% with terminal degrees. *Student/faculty ratio:* 10:1.

Academics *Calendar:* 4-1-4. *Degree:* bachelor's. *Special study options:* advanced placement credit, double majors, honors programs, independent study, internships, off-campus study, services for LD students, student-designed majors, study abroad. *ROTC:* Army (c). *Unusual degree programs:* 3-2 engineering with Dartmouth College and Columbia University.

Computers on Campus 350 computers/terminals are available on campus for general student use. Students can access the following: campus intranet, computer help desk, free student e-mail accounts, online (class) grades, online (class) registration, online (class) schedules, portal. Campuswide network is available. 100% of college-owned or -operated housing units are wired for high-speed Internet access. Wireless service is available via classrooms, computer centers, computer labs, dorm rooms, learning centers, libraries, student centers.

Student Life *Housing:* on-campus residence required through senior year. *Options:* coed. Campus housing is university owned. Freshman campus housing is guaranteed. *Activities and organizations:* drama/theater group, student-run newspaper, radio station, choral group, Outing Club, volunteer center, WMHB-FM (College Radio Station), student government, Powder and Wig (theater). *Campus security:* 24-hour emergency response devices and patrols, late-night transport/escort service, controlled dormitory access, campus lighting, student emergency response team, self-defense class, property id program, party monitors. *Student services:* health clinic, personal/psychological counseling, women's center.

Athletics Member NCAA. All Division III except men's and women's skiing (downhill) (Division I). *Intercollegiate sports:* baseball M, basketball M/W, crew M/W, cross-country running M/W, equestrian sports M(c)/W(c), fencing M(c)/W(c), field hockey W, football M, golf M/W, ice hockey M/W, lacrosse M/W, rugby M(c)/W(c), skiing (downhill) M/W, soccer M/W, softball W, squash M/W, swimming and diving M/W, tennis M/W, track and field M/W, ultimate Frisbee M(c)/W(c), volleyball M(c)/W(c), water polo M(c)/W(c). *Intramural sports:* basketball M/W, field hockey M/W, football M, soccer M/W, softball M/W.

Standardized Tests *Required:* Students must submit either (a) SAT, (b) ACT, or (c) three SAT Subject Tests of their choice (for admission).

Costs (2012–13) *Comprehensive fee:* $55,700. Part-time tuition and fees vary according to course load. *Room and board:* Room and board charges vary according to housing facility. *Payment plan:* installment. *Waivers:* employees or children of employees.

Financial Aid Of all full-time matriculated undergraduates who enrolled in 2012, 886 applied for aid, 698 were judged to have need, 694 had their need fully met. 409 Federal Work-Study jobs (averaging $1697). 147 state and other part-time jobs (averaging $1768). In 2012, 36 non-need-based awards were made. *Average percent of need met:* 100%. *Average financial aid package:* $38,613. *Average need-based loan:* $811. *Average need-based gift aid:* $36,924. *Average non-need-based aid:* $3754. *Average indebtedness upon graduation:* $24,453. *Financial aid deadline:* 2/1.

Applying *Options:* electronic application, early admission, early decision, deferred entrance. *Required:* essay or personal statement, high school transcript, 2 letters of recommendation. *Recommended:* interview. *Application deadlines:* 1/1 (freshmen), 1/1 (out-of-state freshmen), 3/1 (transfers). *Early decision deadline:* 11/15 (for plan 1), 1/1 (for plan 2). *Notification:* 4/1 (freshmen), 4/1 (out-of-state freshmen), 5/15 (transfers), 12/15 (early decision plan 1), 2/10 (early decision plan 2).

Freshman Application Contact Mr. Steve Thomas, Director of Admissions, Colby College, Mayflower Hill, Waterville, ME 04901-8840. *Phone:* 207-859-4800. *Toll-free phone:* 800-723-3032. *Fax:* 207-859-4828. *E-mail:* admissions@colby.edu.
Website: http://www.colby.edu/.

See previous page for display ad and page 1244 for the College Close-Up.

College of the Atlantic

Bar Harbor, Maine

- **Independent** comprehensive, founded 1969
- **Small-town** 35-acre campus
- **Endowment** $29.3 million
- **Coed** 330 undergraduate students, 94% full-time, 72% women, 28% men
- **Very difficult** entrance level, 71% of applicants were admitted

Undergraduates 309 full-time, 21 part-time. Students come from 38 states and territories; 34 other countries; 82% are from out of state; 1% Black or African American, non-Hispanic/Latino; 3% Hispanic/Latino; 1% Asian, non-Hispanic/Latino; 0.3% American Indian or Alaska Native, non-Hispanic/Latino; 3% Two or more races, non-Hispanic/Latino; 4% Race/ethnicity unknown; 17% international; 9% transferred in; 44% live on campus. *Retention:* 83% of full-time freshmen returned.

Freshmen *Admission:* 378 applied, 267 admitted, 73 enrolled. *Average high school GPA:* 3.62. *Test scores:* SAT critical reading scores over 500: 98%; SAT math scores over 500: 93%; SAT writing scores over 500: 95%; ACT scores over 18: 100%; SAT critical reading scores over 600: 83%; SAT math scores over 600: 66%; SAT writing scores over 600: 73%; ACT scores over 24: 91%; SAT critical reading scores over 700: 23%; SAT math scores over 700: 18%; SAT writing scores over 700: 18%; ACT scores over 30: 36%.

Faculty *Total:* 44, 68% full-time, 82% with terminal degrees. *Student/faculty ratio:* 9:1.

Academics *Calendar:* trimesters. *Degrees:* bachelor's and master's. *Special study options:* academic remediation for entering students, accelerated degree program, advanced placement credit, cooperative education, independent

study, internships, off-campus study, part-time degree program, services for LD students, student-designed majors, study abroad, summer session for credit.

Computers on Campus 45 computers/terminals and 85 ports are available on campus for general student use. Students can access the following: computer help desk, free student e-mail accounts, online (class) grades, online (class) registration, online (class) schedules, online billing, grades, transcript, financial aid and course management system. Campuswide network is available. 100% of college-owned or -operated housing units are wired for high-speed Internet access. Wireless service is available via entire campus.

Student Life *Housing:* on-campus residence required for freshman year. *Options:* coed. Campus housing is university owned. Freshman campus housing is guaranteed. *Activities and organizations:* drama/theater group, student-run newspaper, choral group, All College Meeting, Open Mic, Outdoor Program, Campus Committee on Sustainability, Theater Club. *Campus security:* 24-hour emergency response devices and patrols, late-night transport/escort service. *Student services:* health clinic, personal/psychological counseling.

Athletics *Intramural sports:* badminton M/W, basketball M/W, bowling M/W, fencing M/W(c), ice hockey M/W, rock climbing M/W, sailing M/W, skiing (cross-country) M/W, soccer M/W, softball M/W, table tennis M/W, ultimate Frisbee M/W, volleyball M/W, water polo M/W.

Standardized Tests *Recommended:* SAT or ACT (for admission).

Costs (2013–14) *Comprehensive fee:* $48,210 includes full-time tuition ($38,403), mandatory fees ($549), and room and board ($9258). Full-time tuition and fees vary according to course load. Part-time tuition: $4267 per credit. Part-time tuition and fees vary according to course load. *Required fees:* $183 per term part-time. *College room only:* $5952. Room and board charges vary according to board plan. *Payment plan:* installment. *Waivers:* employees or children of employees.

Financial Aid Of all full-time matriculated undergraduates who enrolled in 2012, 272 applied for aid, 265 were judged to have need, 135 had their need fully met. 210 Federal Work-Study jobs (averaging $2511). 53 state and other part-time jobs (averaging $2336). In 2012, 22 non-need-based awards were made. *Average percent of need met:* 95%. *Average financial aid package:* $35,359. *Average need-based loan:* $4620. *Average need-based gift aid:* $30,483. *Average non-need-based aid:* $5996. *Average indebtedness upon graduation:* $22,473.

Applying *Options:* electronic application, early admission, early decision, deferred entrance. *Application fee:* $50. *Required:* essay or personal statement, high school transcript, 3 letters of recommendation. *Required for some:* interview. *Recommended:* minimum 3.0 GPA, interview. *Application deadlines:* 2/15 (freshmen), 4/1 (transfers). *Early decision deadline:* 12/1 (for plan 1), 1/10 (for plan 2). *Notification:* 4/1 (freshmen), 4/25 (transfers), 12/15 (early decision plan 1), 1/25 (early decision plan 2).

Freshman Application Contact Ms. Sarah Baker, Dean of Admission, College of the Atlantic, 105 Eden Street, Bar Harbor, ME 04609-1198. *Phone:* 207-801-5640. *Toll-free phone:* 800-528-0025. *Fax:* 207-288-4126. *E-mail:* inquiry@coa.edu.
Website: http://www.coa.edu/.

Husson University

Bangor, Maine

- **Independent** comprehensive, founded 1898
- **Suburban** 208-acre campus
- **Endowment** $9.2 million
- **Coed** 2,409 undergraduate students, 82% full-time, 58% women, 42% men
- **Moderately difficult** entrance level, 77% of applicants were admitted

Undergraduates 1,969 full-time, 440 part-time. Students come from 35 states and territories; 11 other countries; 12% are from out of state; 4% Black or African American, non-Hispanic/Latino; 1% Hispanic/Latino; 1% Asian, non-Hispanic/Latino; 0.2% Native Hawaiian or other Pacific Islander, non-Hispanic/Latino; 0.5% American Indian or Alaska Native, non-Hispanic/Latino; 1% Two or more races, non-Hispanic/Latino; 2% Race/ethnicity unknown; 2% international; 5% transferred in; 36% live on campus. *Retention:* 72% of full-time freshmen returned.

Freshmen *Admission:* 1,509 applied, 1,155 admitted, 368 enrolled. *Average high school GPA:* 3.3. *Test scores:* SAT critical reading scores over 500: 36%; SAT math scores over 500: 38%; SAT writing scores over 500: 36%; ACT scores over 18: 87%; SAT critical reading scores over 600: 5%; SAT math scores over 600: 8%; SAT writing scores over 600: 5%; ACT scores over 24: 16%; SAT critical reading scores over 700: 1%; SAT math scores over 700: 1%.

Faculty *Total:* 320, 37% full-time, 45% with terminal degrees. *Student/faculty ratio:* 16:1.

Academics *Calendar:* semesters. *Degrees:* certificates, associate, bachelor's, master's, doctoral, post-master's, and postbachelor's certificates. *Special study options:* academic remediation for entering students, adult/continuing education programs, advanced placement credit, cooperative education, distance learning, double majors, independent study, internships, part-time degree program, services for LD students, student-designed majors, summer session for credit. *ROTC:* Army (b), Navy (c). *Unusual degree programs:* 3-2 business administration; occupational therapy.

Computers on Campus 116 computers/terminals and 116 ports are available on campus for general student use. Students can access the following: campus intranet, computer help desk, free student e-mail accounts, online (class) grades, online (class) registration, online (class) schedules. Campuswide network is available. 100% of college-owned or -operated housing units are wired for high-speed Internet access. Wireless service is available via entire campus.

Student Life *Housing:* on-campus residence required through sophomore year. *Options:* coed. Campus housing is university owned and leased by the school. Freshman campus housing is guaranteed. *Activities and organizations:* drama/theater group, student-run newspaper, radio station, student government, Organization of Student Nurses, Organization of Physical Therapy Students, Accounting Society, Criminal Justice Club, national fraternities. *Campus security:* 24-hour emergency response devices and patrols, late-night transport/escort service, controlled dormitory access. *Student services:* health clinic, personal/psychological counseling.

Athletics Member NCAA. All Division III. *Intercollegiate sports:* baseball M, basketball M/W, cross-country running M/W, field hockey W, football M, golf M, lacrosse M/W, soccer M/W, softball W, swimming and diving W, track and field W, volleyball W. *Intramural sports:* baseball M, basketball M/W, cheerleading M/W, football M, ice hockey M/W, lacrosse M, soccer M/W, softball M/W, swimming and diving M/W, tennis M/W, volleyball M/W, water polo M/W.

Standardized Tests *Required:* SAT or ACT (for admission).

Costs (2013–14) *Comprehensive fee:* $23,386 includes full-time tuition ($14,760), mandatory fees ($370), and room and board ($8256). Full-time tuition and fees vary according to class time. Part-time tuition: $492 per credit. Part-time tuition and fees vary according to class time and course load. *Required fees:* $370 per year part-time. *College room only:* $4102. Room and board charges vary according to board plan and housing facility. *Payment plans:* tuition prepayment, installment. *Waivers:* senior citizens and employees or children of employees.

Financial Aid Of all full-time matriculated undergraduates who enrolled in 2012, 1,827 applied for aid, 1,649 were judged to have need, 93 had their need fully met. 1,000 Federal Work-Study jobs (averaging $1300). In 2012, 125 non-need-based awards were made. *Average percent of need met:* 59%. *Average financial aid package:* $12,322. *Average need-based loan:* $4085. *Average need-based gift aid:* $8130. *Average non-need-based aid:* $2691. *Average indebtedness upon graduation:* $33,385.

Applying *Options:* electronic application, deferred entrance. *Application fee:* $40. *Required:* essay or personal statement, high school transcript, 1 letter of recommendation. *Recommended:* interview. *Application deadlines:* 8/15 (freshmen), 8/15 (transfers). *Notification:* continuous (freshmen), continuous (transfers).

Freshman Application Contact Ms. Carlena Bean, Director of Admissions, Husson University, 1 College Circle, Bangor, ME 04401-2999. *Phone:* 207-941-7067. *Toll-free phone:* 800-4-HUSSON. *Fax:* 207-941-7935. *E-mail:* beanc@husson.edu. *Website:* http://www.husson.edu/.

Maine College of Art

Portland, Maine

Freshman Application Contact Stacy Howe, Admissions Operations Coordinator, Maine College of Art, 522 Congress Street, Portland, ME 04101-3987. *Phone:* 207-699-5026. *Toll-free phone:* 800-699-1509. *Fax:* 207-699-5080. *E-mail:* admissions@meca.edu. *Website:* http://www.meca.edu/.

Maine Maritime Academy

Castine, Maine

- **State-supported** comprehensive, founded 1941
- **Small-town** 35-acre campus
- **Endowment** $20.0 million
- **Coed, primarily men** 993 undergraduate students, 100% full-time, 19% women, 81% men
- **Moderately difficult** entrance level, 29% of applicants were admitted

Undergraduates 993 full-time. Students come from 35 states and territories; 6 other countries; 30% are from out of state; 0.7% Black or African American, non-Hispanic/Latino; 0.7% Hispanic/Latino; 0.5% Asian, non-Hispanic/Latino; 0.1% American Indian or Alaska Native, non-Hispanic/Latino; 1% international; 4% transferred in; 78% live on campus. *Retention:* 85% of full-time freshmen returned.

Freshmen *Admission:* 1,000 applied, 287 admitted, 320 enrolled. *Average high school GPA:* 2.9.

Faculty *Total:* 90, 77% full-time, 22% with terminal degrees. *Student/faculty ratio:* 15:1.

Academics *Calendar:* semesters. *Degrees:* associate, bachelor's, and master's. *Special study options:* academic remediation for entering students, adult/continuing education programs, advanced placement credit, cooperative education, double majors, honors programs, independent study, internships, student-designed majors, study abroad. *ROTC:* Army (c), Navy (b).

Computers on Campus 40 computers/terminals are available on campus for general student use. Students can access the following: computer help desk, free student e-mail accounts, online (class) registration, online (class) schedules. Campuswide network is available. 100% of college-owned or -operated housing units are wired for high-speed Internet access. Wireless service is available via classrooms, dorm rooms, learning centers, libraries, student centers.

Student Life *Housing:* on-campus residence required through junior year. *Options:* coed. Campus housing is university owned. Freshman campus housing is guaranteed. *Activities and organizations:* drama/theater group, choral group, marching band, Rugby Club, yacht club, Alpha Phi Omega (community service), Chess Club, Drill Team. *Campus security:* 24-hour emergency response devices and patrols, late-night transport/escort service, controlled dormitory access. *Student services:* health clinic, personal/psychological counseling, women's center.

Athletics Member NCAA. All Division III. *Intercollegiate sports:* basketball M/W, cross-country running M/W, football M, lacrosse M, sailing M/W, soccer M/W, softball W, volleyball W. *Intramural sports:* basketball M/W, golf M/W, ice hockey M, racquetball M/W, riflery M/W, rock climbing M, rugby M/W, sailing M/W, skiing (downhill) M/W, softball M/W, squash M/W, swimming and diving M/W, tennis M/W, volleyball M, weight lifting M/W.

Standardized Tests *Required:* SAT or ACT (for admission).

Costs (2012–13) *Tuition:* state resident $8800 full-time, $334 per credit part-time; nonresident $18,800 full-time, $645 per credit part-time. Full-time tuition and fees vary according to course load and program. Part-time tuition and fees vary according to course load and program. *Required fees:* $2725 full-time. *Room and board:* $9548; room only: $3628. Room and board charges vary according to board plan. *Payment plan:* installment.

Financial Aid Of all full-time matriculated undergraduates who enrolled in 2012, 849 applied for aid, 750 were judged to have need, 82 had their need fully met. 342 Federal Work-Study jobs (averaging $788). In 2012, 34 non-need-based awards were made. *Average percent of need met:* 47%. *Average financial aid package:* $9455. *Average need-based loan:* $4770. *Average need-based gift aid:* $6296. *Average non-need-based aid:* $4001. *Average indebtedness upon graduation:* $41,672.

Applying *Options:* electronic application, early admission, early decision, deferred entrance. *Required:* high school transcript, 1 letter of recommendation, physical examination. *Recommended:* interview. *Application deadlines:* 7/1 (freshmen), 7/1 (transfers), 12/31 (early action). *Early decision deadline:* 12/31. *Notification:* 2/15 (early decision), 2/15 (early action).

Freshman Application Contact Maine Maritime Academy, Castine, ME 04420. *Phone:* 207-326-2215. *Toll-free phone:* 800-464-6565 (in-state); 800-227-8465 (out-of-state). *Website:* http://www.mainemaritime.edu/.

New England School of Communications

Bangor, Maine

- **Independent** 4-year, founded 1981
- **Small-town** 200-acre campus
- **Coed, primarily men** 499 undergraduate students, 93% full-time, 21% women, 79% men
- **Minimally difficult** entrance level, 61% of applicants were admitted

Undergraduates 462 full-time, 37 part-time. Students come from 18 states and territories; 1 other country; 33% are from out of state; 2% Black or African American, non-Hispanic/Latino; 1% Hispanic/Latino; 0.6% Asian, non-Hispanic/Latino; 0.4% American Indian or Alaska Native, non-Hispanic/Latino; 0.2% international; 6% transferred in; 50% live on campus. *Retention:* 64% of full-time freshmen returned.

Freshmen *Admission:* 325 applied, 199 admitted, 108 enrolled. *Average high school GPA:* 2.91.

Faculty *Total:* 73, 33% full-time, 18% with terminal degrees. *Student/faculty ratio:* 12:1.

Academics *Calendar:* semesters. *Degree:* bachelor's. *Special study options:* adult/continuing education programs, advanced placement credit, cooperative education, internships, off-campus study, part-time degree program, services for LD students, summer session for credit. *ROTC:* Army (c).

Computers on Campus 195 computers/terminals are available on campus for general student use. Students can access the following: campus intranet, computer help desk, free student e-mail accounts, online (class) grades, online (class) schedules. Campuswide network is available. 100% of college-owned or -operated housing units are wired for high-speed Internet access. Wireless service is available via classrooms, computer centers, computer labs, dorm rooms, learning centers, libraries, student centers.

Student Life *Housing:* on-campus residence required through sophomore year. *Options:* coed, disabled students. Campus housing is university owned and leased by the school. Freshman applicants given priority for college housing. *Activities and organizations:* drama/theater group, student-run newspaper, radio and television station, choral group, marching band, Audio Engineering Society (AES), Society of Professional Journalists (SPJ), Public Relations Student Society of America (PRSSA), GAMERS club, Husson University Theatre, national fraternities, national sororities. *Campus security:* 24-hour emergency response devices and patrols, late-night transport/escort service. *Student services:* health clinic, personal/psychological counseling.

Athletics *Intramural sports:* baseball M, basketball M/W, cheerleading M/W, field hockey W, football M, lacrosse M/W, skiing (downhill) M/W, soccer M/W, softball M/W, swimming and diving M/W, table tennis M/W, tennis M/W, ultimate Frisbee M/W, volleyball M/W, water polo M/W.

Standardized Tests *Required:* Wonderlic aptitude test (for admission). *Recommended:* SAT or ACT (for admission).

Costs (2013–14) *One-time required fee:* $100. *Comprehensive fee:* $22,410 includes full-time tuition ($13,034); mandatory fees ($1070), and room and board ($8306). *College room only:* $4102.

Financial Aid Of all full-time matriculated undergraduates who enrolled in 2012, 430 applied for aid, 369 were judged to have need. In 2012, 24 non-need-based awards were made. *Average need-based loan:* $4193. *Average need-based gift aid:* $4691. *Average non-need-based aid:* $815. *Average indebtedness upon graduation:* $34,426.

Applying *Options:* electronic application, deferred entrance. *Application fee:* $25. *Required:* essay or personal statement, high school transcript, minimum 2.0 GPA, 2 letters of recommendation, interview. *Required for some:* placement test. *Application deadlines:* rolling (freshmen), rolling (out-of-state freshmen), rolling (transfers). *Notification:* continuous (freshmen), continuous (out-of-state freshmen), continuous (transfers).

Freshman Application Contact Ms. Louise Grant, Director of Admissions, New England School of Communications, 1 College Circle, Bangor, ME 04401. *Phone:* 207-941-7176 Ext. 1093. *Toll-free phone:* 888-877-1876. *Fax:* 207-947-3987. *E-mail:* info@nescom.edu.
Website: http://www.nescom.edu/.

Saint Joseph's College of Maine

Standish, Maine

- **Independent** comprehensive, founded 1912, affiliated with Roman Catholic Church
- **Small-town** 350-acre campus
- **Endowment** $9.2 million
- **Coed**
- **Moderately difficult** entrance level

Faculty *Student/faculty ratio:* 14:1.

Academics *Calendar:* semesters. *Degrees:* certificates, bachelor's, master's, and post-master's certificates (profile does not include enrollment in distance learning master's program).

Student Life *Campus security:* 24-hour emergency response devices and patrols, late-night transport/escort service, controlled dormitory access.

Athletics Member NCAA. All Division III.

Standardized Tests *Required:* SAT or ACT (for admission).

Costs (2012–13) *Comprehensive fee:* $40,400 includes full-time tuition ($29,000) and room and board ($11,400). Part-time tuition and fees vary according to course load. *Room and board:* Room and board charges vary according to board plan.

Financial Aid *Of all full-time matriculated undergraduates who enrolled in 2009,* 946 applied for aid, 864 were judged to have need, 99 had their need fully met. 408 Federal Work-Study jobs (averaging $1382). *In 2009,* 172 non-need-based awards were made. *Average percent of need met:* 78. *Average financial aid package:* $20,192. *Average need-based loan:* $6858. *Average need-based gift aid:* $13,447. *Average non-need-based aid:* $8155. *Average indebtedness upon graduation:* $36,071.

Applying *Options:* electronic application, early action, deferred entrance. *Required:* essay or personal statement, high school transcript, minimum 2.0 GPA, 2 letters of recommendation, SAT or ACT Scores. *Recommended:* interview.

Freshman Application Contact Kathleen Davis, Vice President for Enrollment Management, Saint Joseph's College of Maine, 278 Whites Bridge Road, Standish, ME 04084-5263. *Phone:* 207-893-7746. *Toll-free phone:* 800-338-7057. *Fax:* 207-893-7862. *E-mail:* admission@sjcme.edu.
Website: http://www.sjcme.edu/.

Thomas College

Waterville, Maine

Freshman Application Contact Mr. James Love, Dean of Admissions, Thomas College, 180 West River Road, Waterville, ME 04901. *Phone:* 207-859-1101. *Toll-free phone:* 800-339-7001. *Fax:* 207-859-1114. *E-mail:* admiss@thomas.edu.
Website: http://www.thomas.edu/.

Unity College

Unity, Maine

- **Independent** 4-year, founded 1965
- **Rural** 265-acre campus
- **Endowment** $13.2 million
- **Coed** 537 undergraduate students, 99% full-time, 53% women, 47% men
- **Moderately difficult** entrance level, 87% of applicants were admitted

Undergraduates 533 full-time, 4 part-time. Students come from 35 states and territories; 77% are from out of state; 1% Black or African American, non-Hispanic/Latino; 2% Hispanic/Latino; 1% Asian, non-Hispanic/Latino; 0.4% Native Hawaiian or other Pacific Islander, non-Hispanic/Latino; 1% American Indian or Alaska Native, non-Hispanic/Latino; 2% Two or more races, non-Hispanic/Latino; 6% transferred in; 65% live on campus. *Retention:* 75% of full-time freshmen returned.

Freshmen *Admission:* 402 applied, 350 admitted, 120 enrolled. *Average high school GPA:* 3.25.

Faculty *Total:* 65, 58% full-time, 55% with terminal degrees. *Student/faculty ratio:* 11:1.

Academics *Calendar:* semesters. *Degrees:* associate and bachelor's. *Special study options:* academic remediation for entering students, accelerated degree program, advanced placement credit, cooperative education, double majors, honors programs, independent study, internships, off-campus study, part-time degree program, services for LD students, study abroad. *ROTC:* Army (c). *Unusual degree programs:* 3-2 business administration with Husson University Bangor, Maine; MS in Criminal Justice with Husson University Bangor Maine.

Computers on Campus 100 computers/terminals and 150 ports are available on campus for general student use. Students can access the following: campus intranet, computer help desk, free student e-mail accounts, online (class) grades, online (class) registration, online (class) schedules. Campuswide network is available. 100% of college-owned or -operated housing units are wired for high-speed Internet access. Wireless service is available via entire campus.

Student Life *Housing:* on-campus residence required through sophomore year. *Options:* coed, cooperative. Campus housing is university owned. Freshman campus housing is guaranteed. *Activities and organizations:* drama/theater group, Woodsmen Team, Ultimate Frisbee, Outing Club. *Campus security:* 24-hour emergency response devices and patrols. *Student services:* health clinic, personal/psychological counseling.

Athletics *Intercollegiate sports:* basketball M/W, cross-country running M/W, soccer M/W, volleyball W. *Intramural sports:* baseball M, basketball M/W, cross-country running M/W, golf M/W, ice hockey M/W, soccer W, softball M/W, table tennis M/W, tennis M/W, ultimate Frisbee M/W, volleyball M/W, weight lifting M/W.

Standardized Tests *Required for some:* SAT or ACT (for admission). *Recommended:* SAT or ACT (for admission).

Costs (2012–13) *Comprehensive fee:* $32,814 includes full-time tuition ($23,000), mandatory fees ($1100), and room and board ($8714). Part-time tuition: $860 per credit hour. Part-time tuition and fees vary according to course load. *Room and board:* Room and board charges vary according to board plan and housing facility. *Payment plan:* installment. *Waivers:* employees or children of employees.

Financial Aid Of all full-time matriculated undergraduates who enrolled in 2010, 506 applied for aid, 459 were judged to have need, 31 had their need fully met. 375 Federal Work-Study jobs (averaging $1573). 4 state and other part-time jobs (averaging $1200). In 2010, 74 non-need-based awards were made. *Average percent of need met:* 75%. *Average financial aid package:* $17,369. *Average need-based loan:* $5677. *Average need-based gift aid:* $11,156. *Average non-need-based aid:* $3166.

Applying *Options:* electronic application, early admission, early action, deferred entrance. *Application fee:* $25. *Required:* essay or personal statement, high school transcript, 2 letters of recommendation. *Required for some:* interview. *Recommended:* minimum 2.0 GPA, interview. *Application deadlines:* rolling (freshmen), rolling (transfers).

Freshman Application Contact Mr. Joe Saltalamachia, Senior Associate Director of Admissions, Unity College, 90 Quaker Hill Road, Unity, ME 04988. *Phone:* 207-948-9205. *E-mail:* jsalty@unity.edu. *Website:* http://www.unity.edu/.

University of Maine

Orono, Maine

- **State-supported** university, founded 1865, part of University of Maine System
- **Small-town** 3300-acre campus
- **Endowment** $159.6 million
- **Coed**
- **Moderately difficult** entrance level

Faculty *Student/faculty ratio:* 15:1.

Academics *Calendar:* semesters. *Degrees:* bachelor's, master's, doctoral, and post-master's certificates.

Student Life *Campus security:* 24-hour emergency response devices and patrols, late-night transport/escort service, controlled dormitory access, area emergency text and email message system.

Athletics Member NCAA. All Division I except football (Division I-AA).

Standardized Tests *Required:* SAT or ACT (for admission).

Costs (2012–13) *Tuition:* state resident $8370 full-time, $279 per credit part-time; nonresident $24,090 full-time, $803 per credit part-time. Full-time tuition and fees vary according to course load and program. Part-time tuition and fees vary according to course load and program. *Required fees:* $2218 full-time. *Room and board:* $8644. Room and board charges vary according to board plan and housing facility.

Financial Aid *Of all full-time matriculated undergraduates who enrolled in 2012,* 6,258 applied for aid, 5,298 were judged to have need, 723 had their need fully met. 1,162 Federal Work-Study jobs (averaging $2612). *In 2012,* 358 non-need-based awards were made. *Average percent of need met:* 80. *Average financial aid package:* $14,973. *Average need-based loan:* $4407. *Average need-based gift aid:* $7353. *Average non-need-based aid:* $4254. *Average indebtedness upon graduation:* $32,438.

Applying *Options:* electronic application, early admission, early action, deferred entrance. *Application fee:* $40. *Required:* essay or personal statement,

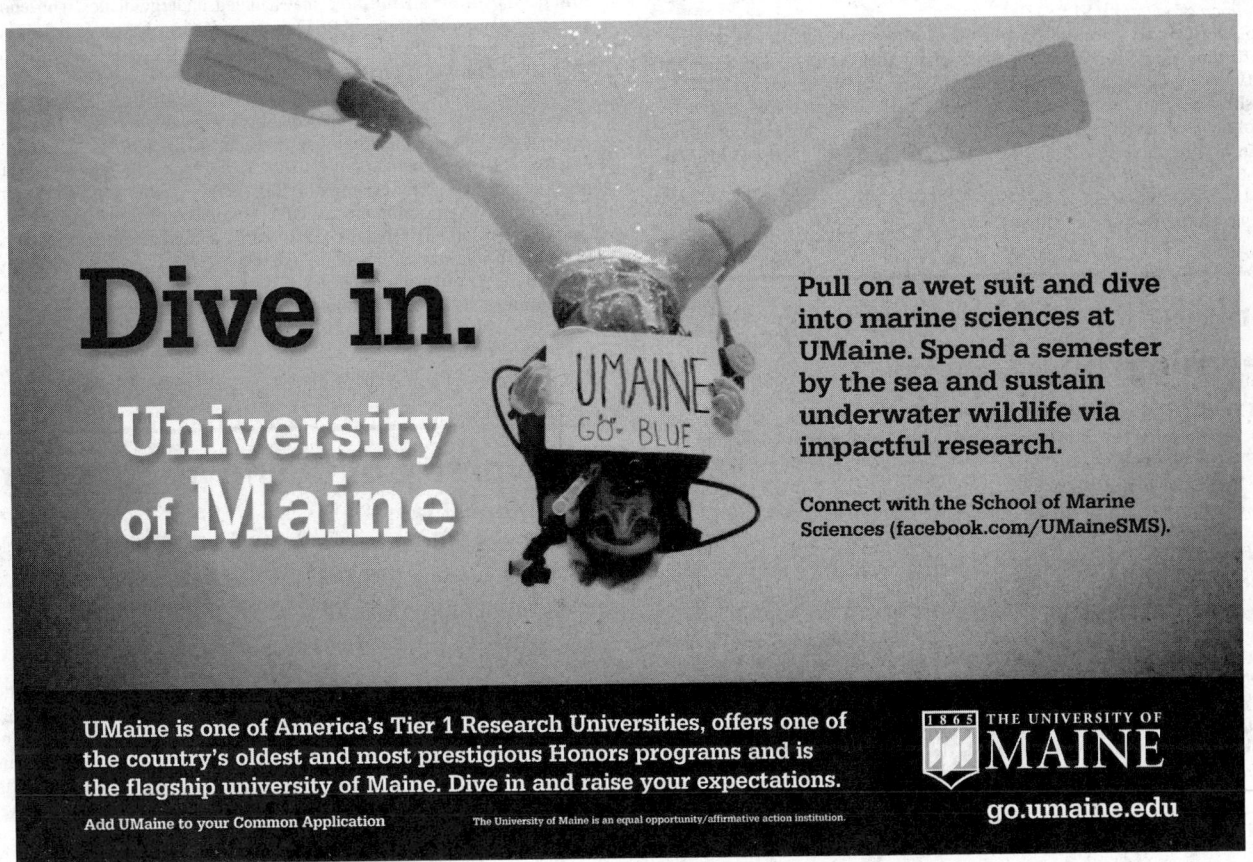

high school transcript, 1 letter of recommendation. *Required for some:* audition for music majors.

Freshman Application Contact Ms. Sharon Oliver, Director of Admissions, University of Maine, 5713 Chadbourne Hall, Orono, ME 04469-5713. *Phone:* 207-581-1561. *Toll-free phone:* 877-486-2364. *Fax:* 207-581-1213. *E-mail:* um-admit@maine.edu.
Website: http://www.umaine.edu/.

See previous page for display ad and page 1570 for the College Close-Up.

University of Maine at Augusta

Augusta, Maine

- **State-supported** 4-year, founded 1965, part of University of Maine System
- **Small-town** 159-acre campus
- **Endowment** $5.0 million
- **Coed**
- **Noncompetitive** entrance level

Faculty *Student/faculty ratio:* 17:1.
Academics *Calendar:* semesters. *Degrees:* certificates, associate, bachelor's, and postbachelor's certificates (also offers some graduate courses and continuing education programs with significant enrollment not reflected in profile).
Student Life *Campus security:* 24-hour emergency response devices, late-night transport/escort service.
Athletics Member USCAA.
Standardized Tests *Recommended:* SAT or ACT (for admission).
Costs (2012–13) *Tuition:* state resident $6510 full-time, $217 per credit hour part-time; nonresident $15,750 full-time, $525 per credit hour part-time. Full-time tuition and fees vary according to course load, location, program, and reciprocity agreements. Part-time tuition and fees vary according to course load, location, program, and reciprocity agreements. *Required fees:* $938 full-time, $31 per credit hour part-time.
Financial Aid *Of all full-time matriculated undergraduates who enrolled in 2008,* 1,604 applied for aid, 1,435 were judged to have need, 258 had their need fully met. 220 Federal Work-Study jobs (averaging $1500). *In 2008,* 135 non-need-based awards were made. *Average percent of need met:* 70. *Average financial aid package:* $8467. *Average need-based loan:* $4063. *Average need-based gift aid:* $4828. *Average non-need-based aid:* $4862. *Average indebtedness upon graduation:* $15,842.
Applying *Options:* electronic application, early admission, deferred entrance. *Application fee:* $40. *Required:* high school transcript. *Required for some:* interview, music audition. *Recommended:* essay or personal statement.
Freshman Application Contact Jonathan H. Henry, Vice President of Enrollment Management and Director of Admissions, University of Maine at Augusta, 46 University Drive, Robinson Hall, Augusta, ME 04330. *Phone:* 207-621-3136. *Toll-free phone:* 877-862-1234 Ext. 3185 (in-state); 877-862-1234 (out-of-state). *Fax:* 207-621-3333. *E-mail:* umaadm@maine.edu.
Website: http://www.uma.maine.edu/.

University of Maine at Farmington

Farmington, Maine

- **State-supported** comprehensive, founded 1863, part of University of Maine System
- **Small-town** 50-acre campus
- **Coed** 2,029 undergraduate students, 93% full-time, 64% women, 36% men
- **Moderately difficult** entrance level, 86% of applicants were admitted

Undergraduates 1,886 full-time, 143 part-time. 16% are from out of state; 0.4% Black or African American, non-Hispanic/Latino; 1% Hispanic/Latino; 2% Asian, non-Hispanic/Latino; 0.7% Native Hawaiian or other Pacific Islander, non-Hispanic/Latino; 0.1% American Indian or Alaska Native, non-Hispanic/Latino; 2% Two or more races, non-Hispanic/Latino; 9% Race/ethnicity unknown; 0.3% international; 6% transferred in; 50% live on campus. *Retention:* 71% of full-time freshmen returned.
Freshmen *Admission:* 1,488 applied, 1,279 admitted, 424 enrolled. *Test scores:* SAT critical reading scores over 500: 49%; SAT math scores over 500: 44%; SAT critical reading scores over 600: 15%; SAT math scores over 600: 10%; SAT critical reading scores over 700: 2%; SAT math scores over 700: 1%.

Faculty *Total:* 171, 71% full-time, 70% with terminal degrees. *Student/faculty ratio:* 14:1.
Academics *Calendar:* semesters plus May term and 2 5-week summer terms. *Degrees:* certificates, bachelor's, and master's. *Special study options:* academic remediation for entering students, accelerated degree program, advanced placement credit, distance learning, double majors, honors programs, independent study, internships, off-campus study, part-time degree program, services for LD students, student-designed majors, study abroad, summer session for credit.
Computers on Campus Students can access the following: campus intranet, computer help desk, free student e-mail accounts, online (class) grades, online (class) registration, online (class) schedules, laptop initiative. Campuswide network is available. 100% of college-owned or -operated housing units are wired for high-speed Internet access. Wireless service is available via entire campus.
Student Life *Housing options:* coed, women-only. Campus housing is university owned and is provided by a third party. Freshman campus housing is guaranteed. *Activities and organizations:* drama/theater group, student-run newspaper, radio station, choral group, Program Board, Intramural Board, Campus Residence Council, campus radio station, Commuter Council. *Campus security:* 24-hour emergency response devices and patrols, late-night transport/escort service, controlled dormitory access, safety whistles. *Student services:* health clinic, personal/psychological counseling.
Athletics Member NCAA, NAIA. All NCAA Division III. *Intercollegiate sports:* baseball M, basketball M/W, cross-country running M/W, field hockey W, golf M, ice hockey M(c), lacrosse M(c)/W(c), soccer M/W, softball W, tennis M(c)/W(c), ultimate Frisbee M(c)/W(c), volleyball W. *Intramural sports:* basketball M/W, cheerleading M(c)/W(c), football M/W, ice hockey M(c)/W(c), rugby M(c)/W(c), skiing (cross-country) M(c)/W(c), skiing (downhill) M(c)/W(c), soccer M/W, softball M/W, swimming and diving M/W, tennis M/W, ultimate Frisbee M/W, volleyball M/W.
Standardized Tests *Required:* SAT or ACT (for admission).
Costs (2013–14) *Tuition:* state resident $8352 full-time, $261 per credit hour part-time; nonresident $17,440 full-time, $545 per credit hour part-time. Full-time tuition and fees vary according to course load, reciprocity agreements, and student level. Part-time tuition and fees vary according to course load, reciprocity agreements, and student level. *Required fees:* $785 full-time. *Room and board:* $8454; room only: $4500. Room and board charges vary according to board plan and housing facility. *Payment plan:* installment. *Waivers:* minority students, senior citizens, and employees or children of employees.
Financial Aid *Of all full-time matriculated undergraduates who enrolled in 2011,* 1,751 applied for aid, 1,557 were judged to have need, 142 had their need fully met. In 2011, 59 non-need-based awards were made. *Average percent of need met:* 65%. *Average financial aid package:* $10,348. *Average need-based loan:* $7275. *Average need-based gift aid:* $6383. *Average non-need-based aid:* $2431. *Average indebtedness upon graduation:* $26,319.
Applying *Options:* electronic application, early admission, early action, deferred entrance. *Application fee:* $40. *Required:* essay or personal statement, high school transcript, minimum 2.0 GPA, 1 letter of recommendation. *Required for some:* minimum 2.5 GPA. *Recommended:* interview. *Application deadlines:* rolling (freshmen), 12/1 (early action). *Notification:* continuous (freshmen), continuous (transfers), 1/8 (early action).
Freshman Application Contact Ms. Lisa Elrich, Associate Director of Admissions, University of Maine at Farmington, 246 Main Street, Farmington, ME 04938-1994. *Phone:* 207-778-7050. *Fax:* 207-778-8182. *E-mail:* umfadmit@maine.edu.
Website: http://www.umf.maine.edu/.

University of Maine at Fort Kent

Fort Kent, Maine

- **State-supported** 4-year, founded 1878, part of University of Maine System
- **Rural** 52-acre campus
- **Endowment** $2.0 million
- **Coed** 1,169 undergraduate students, 52% full-time, 63% women, 37% men
- **Minimally difficult** entrance level, 57% of applicants were admitted

Undergraduates 610 full-time, 559 part-time. Students come from 22 states and territories; 11 other countries; 6% are from out of state; 2% Black or African American, non-Hispanic/Latino; 1% Hispanic/Latino; 0.3% Asian, non-Hispanic/Latino; 1% Native Hawaiian or other Pacific Islander, non-Hispanic/Latino; 1% American Indian or Alaska Native, non-Hispanic/Latino; 12% Race/ethnicity unknown; 7% international; 11% transferred in; 25% live on campus. *Retention:* 64% of full-time freshmen returned.

Freshmen *Admission:* 561 applied, 318 admitted, 181 enrolled. *Average high school GPA:* 2.98. *Test scores:* SAT critical reading scores over 500: 27%; SAT math scores over 500: 25%; SAT writing scores over 500: 22%; SAT critical reading scores over 600: 2%; SAT math scores over 600: 2%; SAT writing scores over 600: 3%.

Faculty *Total:* 74, 41% full-time, 41% with terminal degrees. *Student/faculty ratio:* 18:1.

Academics *Calendar:* semesters. *Degrees:* certificates, associate, and bachelor's. *Special study options:* academic remediation for entering students, accelerated degree program, advanced placement credit, cooperative education, distance learning, double majors, English as a second language, external degree program, honors programs, independent study, internships, part-time degree program, services for LD students, student-designed majors, summer session for credit.

Computers on Campus 100 computers/terminals are available on campus for general student use. Students can access the following: campus intranet, computer help desk, free student e-mail accounts, online (class) grades, online (class) registration, online (class) schedules. Campuswide network is available. Wireless service is available via entire campus.

Student Life *Housing:* on-campus residence required for freshman year. *Options:* Campus housing is university owned. Freshman applicants given priority for college housing. *Activities and organizations:* drama/theater group, choral group, Student Nurses Organization, Student Teachers Educational Professional Society, Student Senate, Performing Arts Club, Dorm Council, national fraternities, national sororities. *Campus security:* controlled dormitory access, 8-hour night patrols by security personnel 11pm-7am. *Student services:* health clinic, personal/psychological counseling.

Athletics Member USCAA. *Intercollegiate sports:* basketball M/W, soccer M/W, volleyball W. *Intramural sports:* basketball M/W, racquetball M/W, soccer M/W, softball M/W, volleyball M/W.

Standardized Tests *Required for some:* SAT (for admission), SAT and SAT Subject Tests or ACT (for admission). *Recommended:* SAT and SAT Subject Tests or ACT (for admission).

Costs (2013–14) *Tuition:* state resident $6600 full-time, $220 per credit hour part-time; nonresident $16,560 full-time, $552 per credit hour part-time. Full-time tuition and fees vary according to course load and reciprocity agreements. Part-time tuition and fees vary according to reciprocity agreements. *Required fees:* $975 full-time, $33 per credit hour part-time. *Room and board:* $7400; room only: $4000. Room and board charges vary according to board plan and housing facility. *Payment plan:* installment.

Financial Aid Of all full-time matriculated undergraduates who enrolled in 2010, 444 applied for aid, 402 were judged to have need, 87 had their need fully met. In 2010, 1 non-need-based awards were made. *Average percent of need met:* 70%. *Average financial aid package:* $10,121. *Average need-based loan:* $5696. *Average need-based gift aid:* $5991. *Average non-need-based aid:* $3000. *Average indebtedness upon graduation:* $9506.

Applying *Options:* electronic application, deferred entrance. *Application fee:* $40. *Required:* essay or personal statement, high school transcript. *Required for some:* interview. *Application deadlines:* rolling (freshmen), rolling (out-of-state freshmen), rolling (transfers). *Notification:* continuous (freshmen), continuous (out-of-state freshmen), continuous (transfers).

Freshman Application Contact University of Maine at Fort Kent, 23 University Drive, Fort Kent, ME 04743-1292. *Phone:* 207-834-7600. *Toll-free phone:* 888-TRY-UMFK.

Website: http://www.umfk.maine.edu/.

University of Maine at Machias

Machias, Maine

- **State-supported** 4-year, founded 1909, part of University of Maine System
- **Rural** 42-acre campus
- **Coed** 925 undergraduate students, 51% full-time, 71% women, 29% men
- **Moderately difficult** entrance level, 83% of applicants were admitted

Undergraduates 473 full-time, 452 part-time. 21% are from out of state; 3% Black or African American, non-Hispanic/Latino; 2% Hispanic/Latino; 0.1% Asian, non-Hispanic/Latino; 3% American Indian or Alaska Native, non-Hispanic/Latino; 2% Two or more races, non-Hispanic/Latino; 15% Race/ethnicity unknown; 1% international; 6% transferred in; 41% live on campus. *Retention:* 67% of full-time freshmen returned.

Freshmen *Admission:* 442 applied, 365 admitted, 135 enrolled. *Test scores:* SAT math scores over 500: 31%; SAT math scores over 600: 7%; SAT math scores over 700: 2%.

Faculty *Total:* 89, 35% full-time, 46% with terminal degrees. *Student/faculty ratio:* 13:1.

Academics *Calendar:* semesters. *Degrees:* certificates, associate, and bachelor's. *Special study options:* academic remediation for entering students, advanced placement credit, cooperative education, distance learning, double

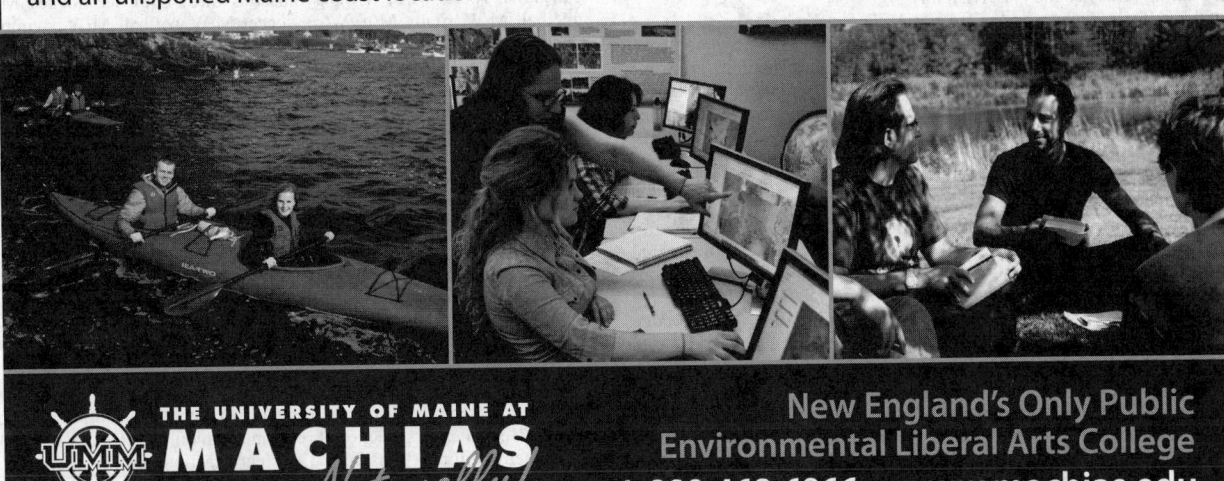

majors, independent study, internships, off-campus study, part-time degree program, services for LD students, student-designed majors, study abroad, summer session for credit.

Student Life *Housing:* on-campus residence required through sophomore year. *Options:* coed, disabled students. Campus housing is university owned.

Athletics Member NAIA. *Intercollegiate sports:* basketball M/W, cross-country running M/W, lacrosse M(c)/W(c), soccer M/W, volleyball W. *Intramural sports:* basketball M/W, cheerleading W, fencing M/W, football M/W, soccer M/W, softball W, water polo M/W.

Standardized Tests *Required:* SAT or ACT (for admission).

Costs (2013–14) *Tuition:* state resident $6600 full-time, $222 per credit hour part-time; nonresident $18,480 full-time, $616 per credit hour part-time. *Required fees:* $820 full-time. *Room and board:* $7900; room only: $4000.

Financial Aid Of all full-time matriculated undergraduates who enrolled in 2002, 512 applied for aid, 419 were judged to have need, 108 had their need fully met. 140 Federal Work-Study jobs (averaging $1621). 83 state and other part-time jobs (averaging $1660). In 2002, 44 non-need-based awards were made. *Average percent of need met:* 83%. *Average financial aid package:* $8182. *Average need-based loan:* $3356. *Average need-based gift aid:* $4847. *Average non-need-based aid:* $5051. *Average indebtedness upon graduation:* $14,873.

Applying *Options:* electronic application, early admission, early action, deferred entrance. *Application fee:* $40. *Required:* essay or personal statement, high school transcript, 1 letter of recommendation. *Required for some:* minimum 2.0 GPA, interview. *Recommended:* minimum 2.5 GPA, 2 letters of recommendation, interview. *Application deadlines:* 8/15 (freshmen), rolling (transfers), 12/15 (early action). *Notification:* continuous (freshmen), continuous (transfers).

Freshman Application Contact Director of Admissions, University of Maine at Machias, 9 O'Brien Avenue, Machias, ME 04654. *Phone:* 207-255-1318. *Toll-free phone:* 888-GOTOUMM (in-state); 888-468-6866 (out-of-state). *Fax:* 207-255-1363. *E-mail:* ummadmissions@maine.edu. *Website:* http://umm.maine.edu/.

See previous page for display ad and page 1572 for the College Close-Up.

University of Maine at Presque Isle

Presque Isle, Maine

- **State-supported** 4-year, founded 1903, part of University of Maine System
- **Small-town** 150-acre campus
- **Endowment** $6.1 million
- **Coed**
- **Minimally difficult** entrance level

Faculty *Student/faculty ratio:* 22:1.

Academics *Calendar:* semesters. *Degrees:* certificates, associate, and bachelor's.

Student Life *Campus security:* student patrols, controlled dormitory access, crime prevention programs, lighted pathways, security cameras.

Athletics Member NCAA, USCAA. All Division III except men's and women's skiing (cross-country) (Division I).

Standardized Tests *Recommended:* SAT or ACT (for admission).

Costs (2012–13) *Tuition:* state resident $6600 full-time, $220 per credit part-time; nonresident $16,560 full-time, $552 per credit part-time. Full-time tuition and fees vary according to course load, location, and reciprocity agreements. Part-time tuition and fees vary according to course load, location, and reciprocity agreements. *Required fees:* $835 full-time, $18 per credit part-time, $51 per term part-time. *Room and board:* $7422; room only: $4240. Room and board charges vary according to board plan and housing facility. *Payment plans:* installment, deferred payment.

Financial Aid *Of all full-time matriculated undergraduates who enrolled in 2012,* 645 applied for aid, 592 were judged to have need, 172 had their need fully met. 265 Federal Work-Study jobs (averaging $2406). *In 2012,* 26 non-need-based awards were made. *Average percent of need met:* 80. *Average financial aid package:* $10,832. *Average need-based loan:* $5461. *Average need-based gift aid:* $6428. *Average non-need-based aid:* $2740. *Average indebtedness upon graduation:* $18,052.

Applying *Options:* electronic application, early admission, early action, deferred entrance. *Application fee:* $40. *Required:* essay or personal statement, high school transcript, minimum 2.0 GPA. *Required for some:* 1 letter of recommendation, interview.

Freshman Application Contact University of Maine at Presque Isle, 181 Main Street, Presque Isle, ME 04769-2888. *Phone:* 207-768-9453. *Website:* http://www.umpi.edu/.

University of New England

Biddeford, Maine

- **Independent** comprehensive, founded 1831
- **Small-town** 540-acre campus
- **Endowment** $27.1 million
- **Coed** 2,637 undergraduate students, 81% full-time, 69% women, 31% men
- **Moderately difficult** entrance level, 86% of applicants were admitted

Undergraduates 2,148 full-time, 489 part-time. Students come from 49 states and territories; 8 other countries; 64% are from out of state; 1% Black or African American, non-Hispanic/Latino; 0.2% Hispanic/Latino; 2% Asian, non-Hispanic/Latino; 0.2% Native Hawaiian or other Pacific Islander, non-Hispanic/Latino; 0.5% American Indian or Alaska Native, non-Hispanic/Latino; 0.9% Two or more races, non-Hispanic/Latino; 19% Race/ethnicity unknown; 0.6% international; 3% transferred in; 63% live on campus. *Retention:* 75% of full-time freshmen returned.

Freshmen *Admission:* 3,885 applied, 3,346 admitted, 633 enrolled. *Average high school GPA:* 3.2. *Test scores:* SAT critical reading scores over 500: 63%; SAT math scores over 500: 73%; ACT scores over 18: 93%; SAT critical reading scores over 600: 15%; SAT math scores over 600: 22%; ACT scores over 24: 51%; SAT critical reading scores over 700: 2%; SAT math scores over 700: 1%; ACT scores over 30: 4%.

Faculty *Total:* 437, 57% full-time, 67% with terminal degrees. *Student/faculty ratio:* 13:1.

Academics *Calendar:* semesters. *Degrees:* associate, bachelor's, master's, doctoral, post-master's, and postbachelor's certificates. *Special study options:* academic remediation for entering students, accelerated degree program, adult/continuing education programs, advanced placement credit, cooperative education, distance learning, double majors, honors programs, independent study, internships, off-campus study, part-time degree program, services for LD students, study abroad, summer session for credit. *ROTC:* Army (c). *Unusual degree programs:* 3-2 Physician Assistant.

Computers on Campus 91 computers/terminals are available on campus for general student use. Students can access the following: campus intranet, computer help desk, free student e-mail accounts, online (class) grades, online (class) registration, online (class) schedules. Campuswide network is available. 100% of college-owned or -operated housing units are wired for high-speed Internet access. Wireless service is available via classrooms, computer centers, computer labs, dorm rooms, learning centers, libraries, student centers.

Student Life *Housing:* on-campus residence required through junior year. *Options:* coed, women-only, disabled students. Campus housing is university owned. *Activities and organizations:* drama/theater group, student-run newspaper, choral group, student government, Outing Club, Campus Programming Board, Earth's Eco, Dance Team. *Campus security:* 24-hour emergency response devices and patrols, late-night transport/escort service, controlled dormitory access. *Student services:* health clinic, personal/psychological counseling.

Athletics Member NCAA. All Division III. *Intercollegiate sports:* basketball M/W, cross-country running M/W, field hockey W, golf M, ice hockey M/W, lacrosse M/W, soccer M/W, softball W, swimming and diving W, volleyball W. *Intramural sports:* baseball M(c), basketball M/W, cheerleading M(c)/W(c), equestrian sports M(c)/W(c), gymnastics M(c)/W(c), ice hockey M/W, racquetball M/W, rugby M(c)/W(c), soccer M/W, softball M/W, swimming and diving M(c), table tennis M/W, tennis M/W, ultimate Frisbee M/W, volleyball M(c)/W, water polo M/W.

Standardized Tests *Required:* SAT or ACT (for admission).

Costs (2012–13) *Comprehensive fee:* $44,370 includes full-time tuition ($30,750), mandatory fees ($1120), and room and board ($12,500). Part-time tuition: $1090 per credit hour. *Room and board:* Room and board charges vary according to board plan, housing facility, and location. *Payment plan:* installment. *Waivers:* children of alumni and employees or children of employees.

Financial Aid Of all full-time matriculated undergraduates who enrolled in 2008, 1,777 applied for aid, 1,648 were judged to have need, 306 had their need fully met. 850 Federal Work-Study jobs (averaging $1946). In 2008, 332 non-need-based awards were made. *Average percent of need met:* 83%. *Average financial aid package:* $23,956. *Average need-based loan:* $10,836. *Average need-based gift aid:* $12,857. *Average non-need-based aid:* $8424. *Average indebtedness upon graduation:* $44,325.

Applying *Options:* electronic application, early admission, deferred entrance. *Application fee:* $40. *Required:* essay or personal statement, high school transcript. *Recommended:* 1 letter of recommendation. *Application deadlines:* 2/15 (freshmen), rolling (transfers), 12/1 (early action). *Notification:* continuous (freshmen), continuous (transfers).

Freshman Application Contact Stacy Gato, Executive Director of University Admissions, University of New England, 111 Hills Beach Road, Biddeford,

ME 04005-9526. *Phone:* 207-477-4863. *Toll-free phone:* 800-477-4UNE. *Fax:* 207-602-5900. *E-mail:* admissions@une.edu. *Website:* http://www.une.edu/.

See below for display ad and page 1584 for the College Close-Up.

University of Southern Maine

Portland, Maine

- **State-supported** comprehensive, founded 1878, part of University of Maine System
- **Urban** 144-acre campus
- **Endowment** $121.0 million
- **Coed** 7,407 undergraduate students, 61% full-time, 56% women, 44% men
- **Moderately difficult** entrance level, 83% of applicants were admitted

Undergraduates 4,551 full-time, 2,856 part-time. Students come from 34 states and territories; 19 other countries; 19% are from out of state; 3% Black or African American, non-Hispanic/Latino; 2% Hispanic/Latino; 2% Asian, non-Hispanic/Latino; 0.1% Native Hawaiian or other Pacific Islander, non-Hispanic/Latino; 0.9% American Indian or Alaska Native, non-Hispanic/Latino; 2% Two or more races, non-Hispanic/Latino; 9% Race/ethnicity unknown; 1% international; 13% transferred in; 14% live on campus. *Retention:* 64% of full-time freshmen returned.

Freshmen *Admission:* 3,900 applied, 3,231 admitted, 865 enrolled. *Average high school GPA:* 3.01. *Test scores:* SAT critical reading scores over 500: 51%; SAT math scores over 500: 51%; SAT writing scores over 500: 47%; ACT scores over 18: 92%; SAT critical reading scores over 600: 11%; SAT math scores over 600: 13%; SAT writing scores over 600: 10%; ACT scores over 24: 41%; SAT critical reading scores over 700: 2%; SAT math scores over 700: 1%; SAT writing scores over 700: 1%; ACT scores over 30: 3%.

Faculty *Total:* 680, 53% full-time, 55% with terminal degrees. *Student/faculty ratio:* 15:1.

Academics *Calendar:* semesters. *Degrees:* certificates, bachelor's, master's, doctoral, post-master's, and postbachelor's certificates. *Special study options:* academic remediation for entering students, accelerated degree program, adult/continuing education programs, advanced placement credit, cooperative education, distance learning, double majors, English as a second language, honors programs, independent study, internships, off-campus study, part-time degree program, services for LD students, student-designed majors, study abroad, summer session for credit. *ROTC:* Army (c), Air Force (c). *Unusual degree programs:* 3-2 business administration.

Computers on Campus 219 computers/terminals are available on campus for general student use. Students can access the following: campus intranet, computer help desk, free student e-mail accounts, online (class) grades, online (class) registration, online (class) schedules. Campuswide network is available. 100% of college-owned or -operated housing units are wired for high-speed Internet access. Wireless service is available via entire campus.

Student Life *Housing options:* coed, disabled students. Campus housing is university owned. Freshman applicants given priority for college housing. *Activities and organizations:* drama/theater group, student-run newspaper, radio station, choral group, Outing and Ski Clubs, Gorham Events Board, Commuter Student Group, Circle K, national fraternities, national sororities. *Campus security:* 24-hour emergency response devices and patrols, late-night transport/escort service, controlled dormitory access, security lighting, preventive programs within residence halls. *Student services:* health clinic, personal/psychological counseling, women's center, legal services.

Athletics Member NCAA. All Division III. *Intercollegiate sports:* baseball M, basketball M/W, cross-country running M/W, fencing M/W(c), field hockey W, golf M/W, ice hockey M/W, lacrosse M/W, sailing M/W, soccer M/W, softball W, tennis M/W, track and field M/W, volleyball W, wrestling M. *Intramural sports:* baseball M, basketball M/W, cheerleading M(c)/W(c), football M/W, ice hockey M/W, lacrosse M(c)/W(c), racquetball M/W, rugby M(c)/W(c), skiing (downhill) M(c)/W(c), soccer M/W, softball M/W, squash M/W, table tennis M/W, tennis M/W, ultimate Frisbee M/W, volleyball M/W, weight lifting M/W.

Standardized Tests *Required:* SAT or ACT (for admission).

Costs (2012–13) *Tuition:* state resident $7590 full-time, $253 per credit hour part-time; nonresident $19,950 full-time, $665 per credit hour part-time. Full-time tuition and fees vary according to course load, degree level, and reciprocity agreements. Part-time tuition and fees vary according to course load, degree level, and reciprocity agreements. *Required fees:* $1330 full-time. *Room and board:* $9130; room only: $4978. Room and board charges vary according to board plan, housing facility, and location. *Payment plan:* installment.

Financial Aid Of all full-time matriculated undergraduates who enrolled in 2011, 3,899 applied for aid, 3,535 were judged to have need, 193 had their need fully met. In 2011, 139 non-need-based awards were made. *Average percent of need met:* 51%. *Average financial aid package:* $1080. *Average need-based loan:* $8331. *Average need-based gift aid:* $5008. *Average non-need-based aid:* $4070.

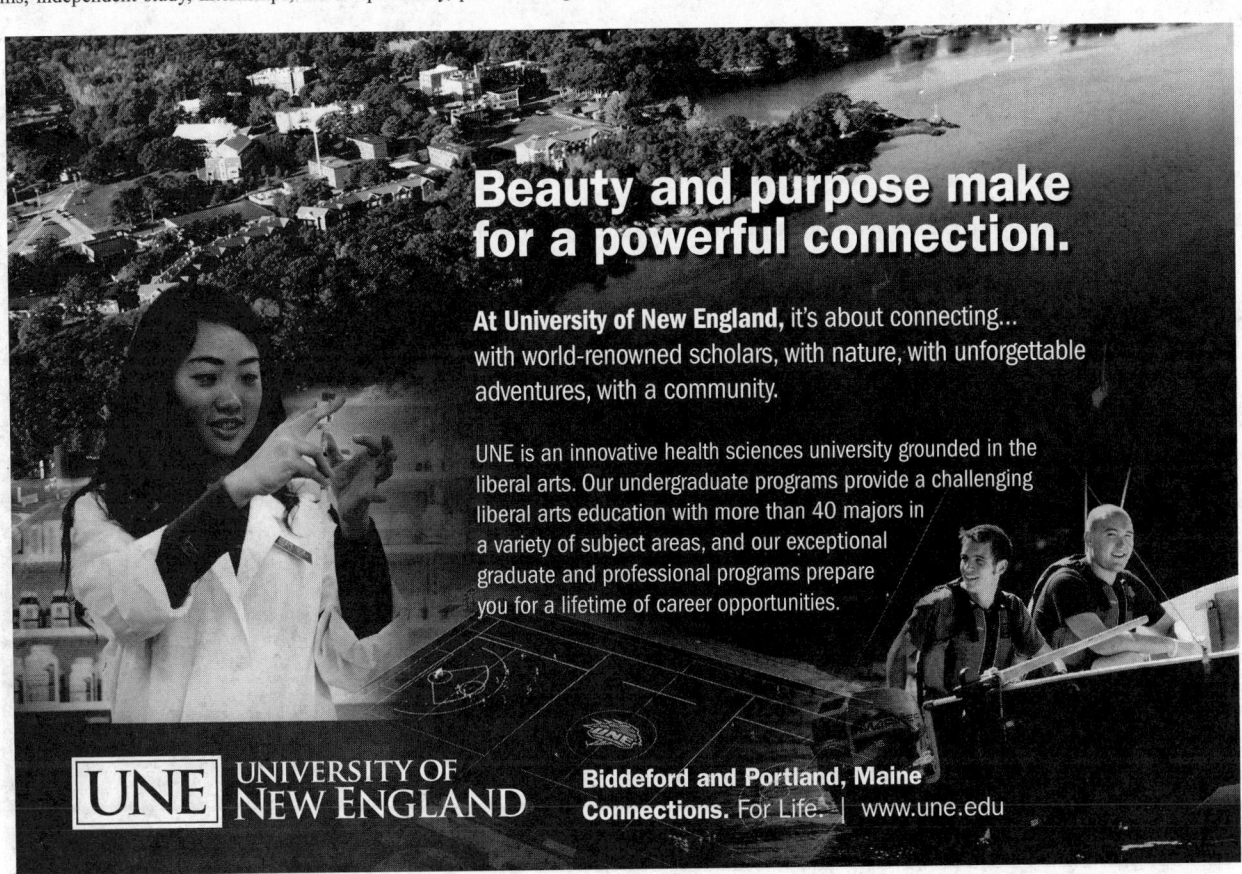

Applying *Options:* electronic application, early admission, deferred entrance. *Application fee:* $40. *Required:* essay or personal statement, high school transcript. *Required for some:* interview, auditions for music majors. *Recommended:* 1 letter of recommendation, interview. *Application deadlines:* 2/15 (freshmen), 2/15 (transfers). *Notification:* continuous (freshmen), continuous (out-of-state freshmen), continuous (transfers).

Freshman Application Contact Mr. John Barker, Director of Technology for Graduate and Undergraduate Admission, University of Southern Maine, Portland, ME 04104-9300. *Phone:* 207-780-5724. *Toll-free phone:* 800-800-4USM Ext. 5670. *E-mail:* usmadm@usm.maine.edu.
Website: http://www.usm.maine.edu/.

MARYLAND

Bowie State University

Bowie, Maryland

- **State-supported** comprehensive, founded 1865, part of University System of Maryland
- **Small-town** 295-acre campus with easy access to Baltimore and Washington, DC
- **Endowment** $5.4 million
- **Coed** 4,283 undergraduate students, 82% full-time, 62% women, 38% men
- **Minimally difficult** entrance level, 48% of applicants were admitted

Undergraduates 3,493 full-time, 790 part-time. Students come from 31 states and territories; 9% are from out of state; 89% Black or African American, non-Hispanic/Latino; 3% Hispanic/Latino; 2% Asian, non-Hispanic/Latino; 0.1% Native Hawaiian or other Pacific Islander, non-Hispanic/Latino; 0.1% American Indian or Alaska Native, non-Hispanic/Latino; 2% Two or more races, non-Hispanic/Latino; 1% Race/ethnicity unknown; 0.8% international; 11% transferred in; 34% live on campus. *Retention:* 67% of full-time freshmen returned.

Freshmen *Admission:* 2,632 applied, 1,267 admitted, 484 enrolled. *Average high school GPA:* 2.53. *Test scores:* SAT critical reading scores over 500: 23%; SAT math scores over 500: 18%; SAT critical reading scores over 600: 3%; SAT math scores over 600: 3%.

Faculty *Total:* 408, 53% full-time, 88% with terminal degrees. *Student/faculty ratio:* 16:1.

Academics *Calendar:* semesters. *Degrees:* certificates, bachelor's, master's, doctoral, and postbachelor's certificates. *Special study options:* academic remediation for entering students, adult/continuing education programs, advanced placement credit, cooperative education, distance learning, double majors, external degree program, honors programs, independent study, internships, off-campus study, part-time degree program, services for LD students, study abroad, summer session for credit. *ROTC:* Army (b). *Unusual degree programs:* 3-2 engineering with George Washington University, University of Maryland College Park, Howard University.

Computers on Campus 3,144 computers/terminals are available on campus for general student use. Students can access the following: computer help desk, free student e-mail accounts, online (class) grades, online (class) registration. Campuswide network is available. Wireless service is available via entire campus.

Student Life *Housing options:* coed, men-only, women-only. Campus housing is university owned and is provided by a third party. Freshman applicants given priority for college housing. *Activities and organizations:* drama/theater group, student-run newspaper, radio and television station, choral group, marching band, NSAP Student Leadership Institute, Honda Campus All-Star Challenge, national fraternities, national sororities. *Campus security:* 24-hour emergency response devices and patrols, student patrols, late-night transport/escort service, controlled dormitory access. *Student services:* health clinic, personal/psychological counseling.

Athletics Member NCAA. All Division II. *Intercollegiate sports:* basketball M(s)/W(s), bowling W, cross-country running M(s)/W(s), football M(s), softball W(s), tennis W(s), track and field M(s)/W(s), volleyball W(s).

Standardized Tests *Required:* SAT or ACT (for admission).

Costs (2012–13) *Tuition:* state resident $4683 full-time, $207 per credit hour part-time; nonresident $15,239 full-time, $641 per credit hour part-time. Part-time tuition and fees vary according to course load. *Required fees:* $1956 full-time, $87 per credit hour part-time. *Room and board:* $9597. Room and board charges vary according to board plan and housing facility. *Payment plans:* installment, deferred payment. *Waivers:* senior citizens and employees or children of employees.

Financial Aid Of all full-time matriculated undergraduates who enrolled in 2011, 2,664 applied for aid, 2,658 were judged to have need, 1,071 had their need fully met. 68 Federal Work-Study jobs (averaging $2627). In 2011, 40

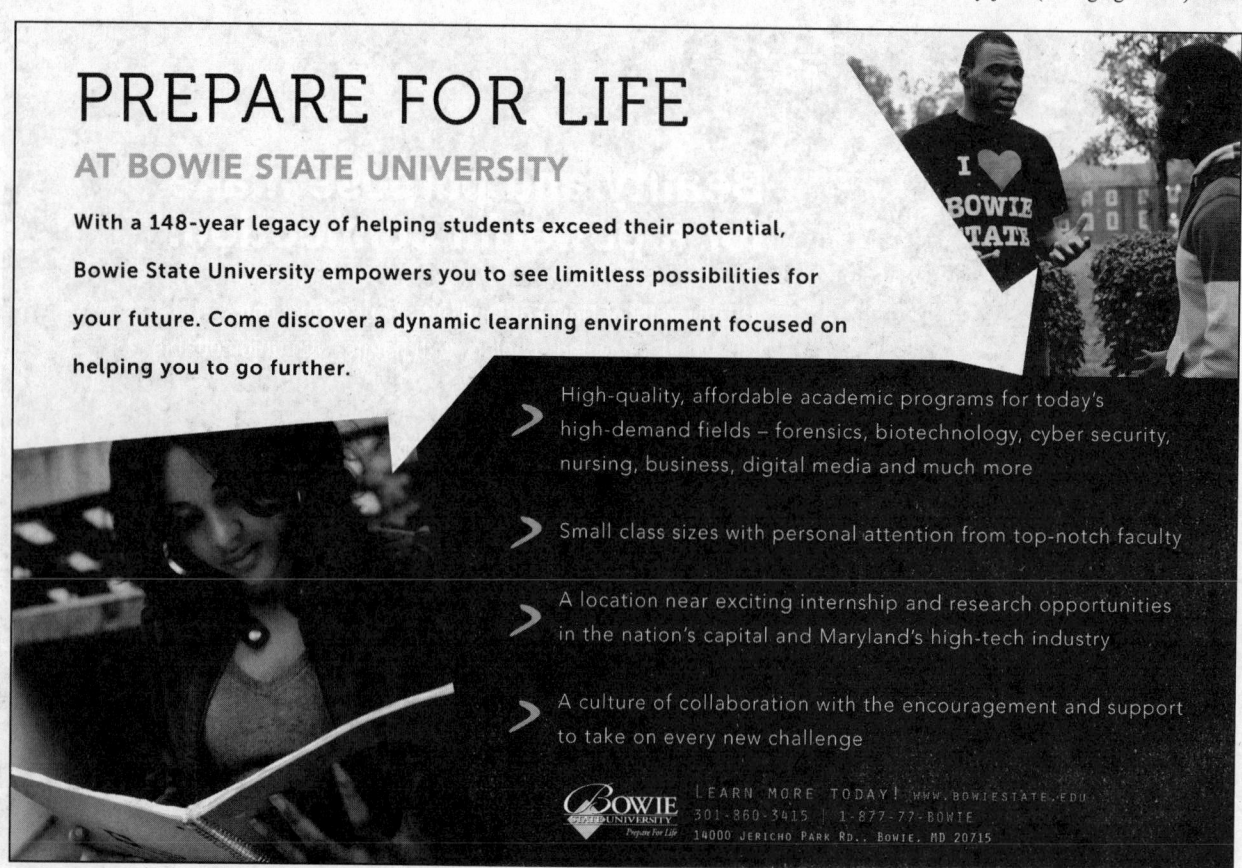

non-need-based awards were made. *Average percent of need met: 46%. Average financial aid package:* $8287. *Average need-based loan:* $4161. *Average need-based gift aid:* $6335. *Average indebtedness upon graduation:* $24,291.
Applying *Options:* electronic application. *Application fee:* $40. *Required:* high school transcript, minimum 2.0 GPA. *Application deadlines:* 4/1 (freshmen), 4/1 (transfers). *Notification:* continuous (freshmen), continuous (transfers).
Freshman Application Contact Mr. Lonnie Morris, Director of Admissions, Bowie State University, Administration Building, 1st Floor. *Phone:* 301-860-3415. *Toll-free phone:* 877-772-6943. *Fax:* 301-860-3438. *E-mail:* sholt@bowiestate.edu.
Website: http://www.bowiestate.edu/.

See previous page for display ad and page 1164 for the College Close-Up.

Capitol College

Laurel, Maryland

Director of Admissions Mr. George Walls, Director of Recruiting and Admissions, Capitol College, 11301 Springfield Road, Laurel, MD 20708-9759. *Phone:* 301-953-3200 Ext. 3033. *Toll-free phone:* 800-950-1992. *E-mail:* ghwalls@capitol-college.edu.
Website: http://www.capitol-college.edu/.

Coppin State University

Baltimore, Maryland

Freshman Application Contact Ms. Michelle Gross, Director of Admissions, Coppin State University, 2500 West North Avenue, Baltimore, MD 21216-3698. *Phone:* 410-951-3600. *Toll-free phone:* 800-635-3674. *Fax:* 410-523-7351. *E-mail:* mgross@coppin.edu.
Website: http://www.coppin.edu/.

DeVry University

Bethesda, Maryland

Freshman Application Contact DeVry University, 4550 Montgomery Avenue, Suite 100 North, Bethesda, MD 20814-3304. *Toll-free phone:* 866-338-7941.
Website: http://www.devry.edu/.

Faith Theological Seminary

Baltimore, Maryland

- **Independent** comprehensive, affiliated with Christian non-denominational
- **Urban** campus
- **Coed**

Academics *Degrees:* bachelor's, master's, and doctoral.
Costs (2012–13) *Tuition:* $4800 full-time, $200 per hour part-time. *Required fees:* $280 full-time. *Payment plans:* tuition prepayment, installment.
Applying *Application fee:* $50. *Required:* essay or personal statement, high school transcript, 2 letters of recommendation, photos. *Required for some:* interview. *Recommended:* interview.
Freshman Application Contact Faith Theological Seminary, 529 Walker Avenue, Baltimore, MD 21212. *Phone:* 410-323-6211.
Website: http://www.faiththeological.org/.

Frostburg State University

Frostburg, Maryland

- **State-supported** comprehensive, founded 1898, part of University System of Maryland
- **Small-town** 260-acre campus with easy access to Baltimore and Washington, DC
- **Endowment** $14.7 million
- **Coed** 4,631 undergraduate students, 92% full-time, 49% women, 51% men
- **Moderately difficult** entrance level, 59% of applicants were admitted

Undergraduates 4,253 full-time, 378 part-time. Students come from 31 states and territories; 41 other countries; 8% are from out of state; 25% Black or African American, non-Hispanic/Latino; 3% Hispanic/Latino; 1% Asian, non-Hispanic/Latino; 0.3% Native Hawaiian or other Pacific Islander, non-Hispanic/Latino; 0.1% American Indian or Alaska Native, non-Hispanic/Latino; 4% Two or more races, non-Hispanic/Latino; 1% Race/ethnicity unknown; 1% international; 10% transferred in; 32% live on campus. *Retention:* 72% of full-time freshmen returned.
Freshmen *Admission:* 3,951 applied, 2,340 admitted, 814 enrolled. *Average high school GPA:* 3.2. *Test scores:* SAT critical reading scores over 500: 42%; SAT math scores over 500: 45%; SAT writing scores over 500: 35%; ACT scores over 18: 81%; SAT critical reading scores over 600: 8%; SAT math scores over 600: 11%; SAT writing scores over 600: 6%; ACT scores over 24: 15%; SAT critical reading scores over 700: 1%; SAT math scores over 700: 1%; SAT writing scores over 700: 1%.
Faculty *Total:* 378, 65% full-time, 61% with terminal degrees. *Student/faculty ratio:* 17:1.
Academics *Calendar:* semesters. *Degrees:* certificates, bachelor's, master's, doctoral, post-master's, and postbachelor's certificates. *Special study options:* adult/continuing education programs, advanced placement credit, cooperative education, distance learning, double majors, freshman honors college, honors programs, independent study, internships, off-campus study, part-time degree program, services for LD students, study abroad, summer session for credit. *Unusual degree programs:* business administration with Management/Accounting; engineering with University of Maryland.
Computers on Campus 577 computers/terminals are available on campus for general student use. Students can access the following: campus intranet, computer help desk, free student e-mail accounts, online (class) grades, online (class) registration, online (class) schedules. Campuswide network is available. 100% of college-owned or -operated housing units are wired for high-speed Internet access. Wireless service is available via entire campus.
Student Life *Housing options:* coed, men-only, women-only. Campus housing is university owned and is provided by a third party. *Activities and organizations:* drama/theater group, student-run newspaper, radio and television station, choral group, marching band, Student Government Association, Black Student Association, Campus Activities Board, Residence Hall Association, University Programming Council, national fraternities, national sororities. *Campus security:* 24-hour emergency response devices and patrols, student patrols, late-night transport/escort service, controlled dormitory access, bicycle patrols. *Student services:* health clinic, personal/psychological counseling, women's center.
Athletics Member NCAA. All Division III. *Intercollegiate sports:* baseball M, basketball M/W, cross-country running M/W, field hockey W, football M, lacrosse M/W, soccer M/W, softball W, swimming and diving M/W, tennis M/W, track and field M/W, volleyball W. *Intramural sports:* basketball M/W, football M/W, lacrosse M(c), racquetball M/W, rugby M(c), soccer M/W, softball M/W, tennis M/W, volleyball M(c)/W, wrestling M.
Standardized Tests *Required:* SAT or ACT (for admission).
Costs (2013–14) *Tuition:* state resident $5630 full-time, $233 per credit part-time; nonresident $16,278 full-time, $457 per credit part-time. Full-time tuition and fees vary according to location. Part-time tuition and fees vary according to course load and location. *Required fees:* $2098 full-time, $96 per credit part-time, $25 per term part-time. *Room and board:* $7990; room only: $3762. Room and board charges vary according to board plan and housing facility. *Payment plans:* installment, deferred payment. *Waivers:* senior citizens and employees or children of employees.
Financial Aid Of all full-time matriculated undergraduates who enrolled in 2012, 3,616 applied for aid, 2,684 were judged to have need, 410 had their need fully met. 147 Federal Work-Study jobs (averaging $635). In 2012, 755 non-need-based awards were made. *Average percent of need met: 62%. Average financial aid package:* $8855. *Average need-based loan:* $4010. *Average need-based gift aid:* $6388. *Average non-need-based aid:* $3100. *Average indebtedness upon graduation:* $20,736.
Applying *Options:* electronic application, early admission. *Application fee:* $30. *Required:* high school transcript, minimum 2.0 GPA. *Required for some:*

essay or personal statement. *Recommended:* interview. *Application deadlines:* 2/15 (freshmen), 2/30 (out-of-state freshmen), 6/1 (transfers).
Freshman Application Contact Frostburg State University, 101 Braddock Road, Frostburg, MD 21532-1099. *Phone:* 301-687-4201.
Website: http://www.frostburg.edu/.

Goucher College
Baltimore, Maryland

- **Independent** comprehensive, founded 1885
- **Suburban** 287-acre campus with easy access to Baltimore and Washington, DC
- **Endowment** $183.7 million
- **Coed** 1,484 undergraduate students, 97% full-time, 66% women, 34% men
- **Moderately difficult** entrance level, 72% of applicants were admitted

Undergraduates 1,446 full-time, 38 part-time. Students come from 46 states and territories; 49 other countries; 73% are from out of state; 9% Black or African American, non-Hispanic/Latino; 7% Hispanic/Latino; 3% Asian, non-Hispanic/Latino; 0.2% Native Hawaiian or other Pacific Islander, non-Hispanic/Latino; 0.3% American Indian or Alaska Native, non-Hispanic/Latino; 5% Two or more races, non-Hispanic/Latino; 9% Race/ethnicity unknown; 3% international; 3% transferred in; 86% live on campus. *Retention:* 84% of full-time freshmen returned.
Freshmen *Admission:* 3,615 applied, 2,593 admitted, 410 enrolled. *Average high school GPA:* 3.16. *Test scores:* SAT critical reading scores over 500: 80%; SAT math scores over 500: 72%; SAT writing scores over 500: 77%; ACT scores over 18: 96%; SAT critical reading scores over 600: 40%; SAT math scores over 600: 35%; SAT writing scores over 600: 38%; ACT scores over 24: 63%; SAT critical reading scores over 700: 11%; SAT math scores over 700: 5%; SAT writing scores over 700: 6%; ACT scores over 30: 13%.
Faculty *Total:* 218, 62% full-time, 72% with terminal degrees. *Student/faculty ratio:* 9:1.
Academics *Calendar:* semesters. *Degrees:* bachelor's, master's, and postbachelor's certificates. *Special study options:* adult/continuing education programs, advanced placement credit, distance learning, double majors, independent study, internships, off-campus study, part-time degree program, services for LD students, student-designed majors, study abroad, summer session for credit. *ROTC:* Army (c), Air Force (c). *Unusual degree programs:* 3-2 engineering with Johns Hopkins University, Columbia University FU Foundation School of Engineering and Applied Science.
Computers on Campus 200 computers/terminals are available on campus for general student use. Students can access the following: campus intranet, computer help desk, free student e-mail accounts, online (class) grades, online (class) registration, online (class) schedules, transcripts, financial aid information, billing, ePortfolios, academic progress reports, study abroad plan. Campuswide network is available. 100% of college-owned or -operated housing units are wired for high-speed Internet access. Wireless service is available via entire campus.
Student Life *Housing:* on-campus residence required through sophomore year. *Options:* coed, men-only, women-only, disabled students. Campus housing is university owned. Freshman campus housing is guaranteed. *Activities and organizations:* drama/theater group, student-run newspaper, radio station, choral group, Student Government Association, The Quindecim, Earthworks / Ag Co-op / Gear (Environmental action clubs), Hillel, Umoja: The Black Student Union. *Campus security:* 24-hour emergency response devices and patrols, late-night transport/escort service, controlled dormitory access, e2 campus alerts. *Student services:* health clinic, personal/psychological counseling.
Athletics Member NCAA. All Division III. *Intercollegiate sports:* basketball M/W, cross-country running M/W, equestrian sports M/W, field hockey W, lacrosse M/W, soccer M/W, swimming and diving M/W, tennis M/W, track and field M/W, volleyball W. *Intramural sports:* basketball M/W, fencing M(c)/W(c), soccer M/W, ultimate Frisbee M/W.
Costs (2013–14) *Comprehensive fee:* $50,252 includes full-time tuition ($38,462), mandatory fees ($622), and room and board ($11,168). Part-time tuition: $1282 per credit hour. *College room only:* $6664. Room and board charges vary according to board plan and housing facility. *Payment plans:* tuition prepayment, installment. *Waivers:* employees or children of employees.
Financial Aid Of all full-time matriculated undergraduates who enrolled in 2012, 1,039 applied for aid, 914 were judged to have need, 99 had their need fully met. 436 Federal Work-Study jobs (averaging $1041). In 2012, 277 non-need-based awards were made. *Average percent of need met:* 76%. *Average financial aid package:* $28,225. *Average need-based loan:* $4102. *Average need-based gift aid:* $24,804. *Average non-need-based aid:* $14,301. *Average indebtedness upon graduation:* $29,135.

Applying *Options:* electronic application, early admission, early decision, early action, deferred entrance. *Application fee:* $55. *Required:* essay or personal statement, high school transcript. *Recommended:* 3 letters of recommendation, interview. *Application deadlines:* 2/1 (freshmen), 4/1 (transfers), 12/1 (early action). *Early decision deadline:* 11/15 (for plan 1), 1/15 (for plan 2). *Notification:* 4/1 (freshmen), 6/1 (transfers), 12/15 (early decision plan 1), 2/15 (early decision plan 2), 2/1 (early action).
Freshman Application Contact Mr. Carlton E. Surbeck, Director of Admissions, Goucher College, 1021 Dulaney Valley Road, Baltimore, MD 21204. *Phone:* 410-337-6100. *Toll-free phone:* 800-468-2437. *Fax:* 410-337-6354. *E-mail:* admissions@goucher.edu.
Website: http://www.goucher.edu/.

Hood College
Frederick, Maryland

- **Independent** comprehensive, founded 1893
- **Suburban** 50-acre campus with easy access to Baltimore and Washington, DC
- **Endowment** $62.1 million
- **Coed** 1,434 undergraduate students, 89% full-time, 66% women, 34% men
- **Moderately difficult** entrance level, 77% of applicants were admitted

Undergraduates 1,281 full-time, 153 part-time. Students come from 32 states and territories; 23 other countries; 23% are from out of state; 12% Black or African American, non-Hispanic/Latino; 7% Hispanic/Latino; 3% Asian, non-Hispanic/Latino; 0.1% Native Hawaiian or other Pacific Islander, non-Hispanic/Latino; 0.1% American Indian or Alaska Native, non-Hispanic/Latino; 4% Two or more races, non-Hispanic/Latino; 3% Race/ethnicity unknown; 3% international; 9% transferred in; 54% live on campus. *Retention:* 77% of full-time freshmen returned.
Freshmen *Admission:* 1,788 applied, 1,379 admitted, 271 enrolled. *Average high school GPA:* 3.53. *Test scores:* SAT critical reading scores over 500: 67%; SAT math scores over 500: 67%; SAT writing scores over 500: 61%; ACT scores over 18: 93%; SAT critical reading scores over 600: 31%; SAT math scores over 600: 23%; SAT writing scores over 600: 22%; ACT scores over 24: 50%; SAT critical reading scores over 700: 4%; SAT math scores over 700: 5%; SAT writing scores over 700: 2%; ACT scores over 30: 5%.
Faculty *Total:* 262, 34% full-time, 63% with terminal degrees. *Student/faculty ratio:* 12:1.
Academics *Calendar:* semesters. *Degrees:* certificates, bachelor's, master's, and postbachelor's certificates (also offers adult program with significant enrollment not reflected in profile). *Special study options:* academic remediation for entering students, advanced placement credit, double majors, English as a second language, honors programs, independent study, internships, off-campus study, part-time degree program, services for LD students, student-designed majors, study abroad, summer session for credit. *ROTC:* Army (b). *Unusual degree programs:* 3-2 engineering with George Washington University.
Computers on Campus 283 computers/terminals are available on campus for general student use. Students can access the following: campus intranet, computer help desk, free student e-mail accounts, online (class) grades, online (class) registration, online (class) schedules. Campuswide network is available. 100% of college-owned or -operated housing units are wired for high-speed Internet access. Wireless service is available via entire campus.
Student Life *Housing:* on-campus residence required through sophomore year. *Options:* coed, women-only. Campus housing is university owned and leased by the school. Freshman campus housing is guaranteed. *Activities and organizations:* drama/theater group, student-run newspaper, radio station, choral group, Education Club, Black Student Union, Campus Activities Board, International Club, Hood Today (newspaper). *Campus security:* 24-hour emergency response devices and patrols, late-night transport/escort service, controlled dormitory access. *Student services:* health clinic, personal/psychological counseling.
Athletics Member NCAA. All Division III. *Intercollegiate sports:* basketball M/W, cross-country running M/W, equestrian sports M(c)/W(c), field hockey W, golf M, lacrosse M/W, soccer M/W, softball W, swimming and diving M/W, tennis M/W, track and field M/W, volleyball W.
Standardized Tests *Required:* SAT or ACT (for admission).
Costs (2012–13) *Comprehensive fee:* $43,210 includes full-time tuition ($31,840), mandatory fees ($460), and room and board ($10,910). Part-time tuition: $920 per credit hour. *Required fees:* $150 per term part-time. *College room only:* $5700. Room and board charges vary according to board plan and housing facility. *Payment plan:* installment. *Waivers:* employees or children of employees.

Financial Aid Of all full-time matriculated undergraduates who enrolled in 2012, 1,141 applied for aid, 1,066 were judged to have need, 168 had their need fully met. 372 Federal Work-Study jobs (averaging $2000). 49 state and other part-time jobs (averaging $2000). In 2012, 181 non-need-based awards were made. *Average percent of need met:* 76%. *Average financial aid package:* $25,598. *Average need-based loan:* $4320. *Average need-based gift aid:* $21,551. *Average non-need-based aid:* $14,658. *Average indebtedness upon graduation:* $18,250.

Applying *Options:* electronic application, early decision, early action, deferred entrance. *Application fee:* $35. *Required:* essay or personal statement, high school transcript, minimum 2.0 GPA, 2 letters of recommendation. *Recommended:* interview. *Application deadlines:* 8/15 (freshmen), 8/15 (out-of-state freshmen), rolling (transfers), 12/1 (early action). *Early decision deadline:* 11/15 (for plan 1), 12/15 (for plan 2). *Notification:* continuous (freshmen), continuous (out-of-state freshmen), continuous (transfers), 12/1 (early decision plan 1), 1/1 (early decision plan 2), 12/15 (early action).

Freshman Application Contact Mr. David Adams, Director of Admissions, Hood College, 401 Rosemont Avenue, Frederick, MD 21701. *Phone:* 301-696-3400. *Toll-free phone:* 800-922-1599. *Fax:* 301-696-3819. *E-mail:* admissions@hood.edu.
Website: http://www.hood.edu/.

ITT Technical Institute

Hanover, Maryland

- **Proprietary** 4-year
- **Coed**
- **Minimally difficult** entrance level

Academics *Degrees:* associate and bachelor's.

Freshman Application Contact Director of Recruitment, ITT Technical Institute, 7030 Dorsey Road, Suite 100, Hanover, MD 21076. *Phone:* 410-694-4700. *Toll-free phone:* 877-243-6993.
Website: http://www.itt-tech.edu/.

ITT Technical Institute

Owings Mills, Maryland

- **Proprietary** primarily 2-year, founded 2005
- **Coed**
- **Minimally difficult** entrance level

Academics *Calendar:* quarters. *Degrees:* associate and bachelor's.

Freshman Application Contact Director of Recruitment, ITT Technical Institute, 11301 Red Run Boulevard, Owings Mills, MD 21117. *Phone:* 443-394-7115. *Toll-free phone:* 877-411-6782.
Website: http://www.itt-tech.edu/.

The Johns Hopkins University

Baltimore, Maryland

- **Independent** university, founded 1876
- **Urban** 140-acre campus with easy access to Baltimore and Washington, DC
- **Endowment** $2.7 billion
- **Coed** 5,192 undergraduate students, 99% full-time, 48% women, 52% men
- **Most difficult** entrance level, 18% of applicants were admitted

Undergraduates 5,164 full-time, 28 part-time. Students come from 53 states and territories; 71 other countries; 88% are from out of state; 5% Black or African American, non-Hispanic/Latino; 10% Hispanic/Latino; 19% Asian, non-Hispanic/Latino; 0.1% Native Hawaiian or other Pacific Islander, non-Hispanic/Latino; 0.1% American Indian or Alaska Native, non-Hispanic/Latino; 4% Two or more races, non-Hispanic/Latino; 2% Race/ethnicity unknown; 9% international; 0.9% transferred in; 54% live on campus. *Retention:* 97% of full-time freshmen returned.

Freshmen *Admission:* 20,502 applied, 3,626 admitted, 1,330 enrolled. *Average high school GPA:* 3.72. *Test scores:* SAT critical reading scores over 500: 99%; SAT math scores over 500: 100%; SAT writing scores over 500: 99%; ACT scores over 18: 100%; SAT critical reading scores over 600: 91%; SAT math scores over 600: 95%; SAT writing scores over 600: 91%; ACT scores

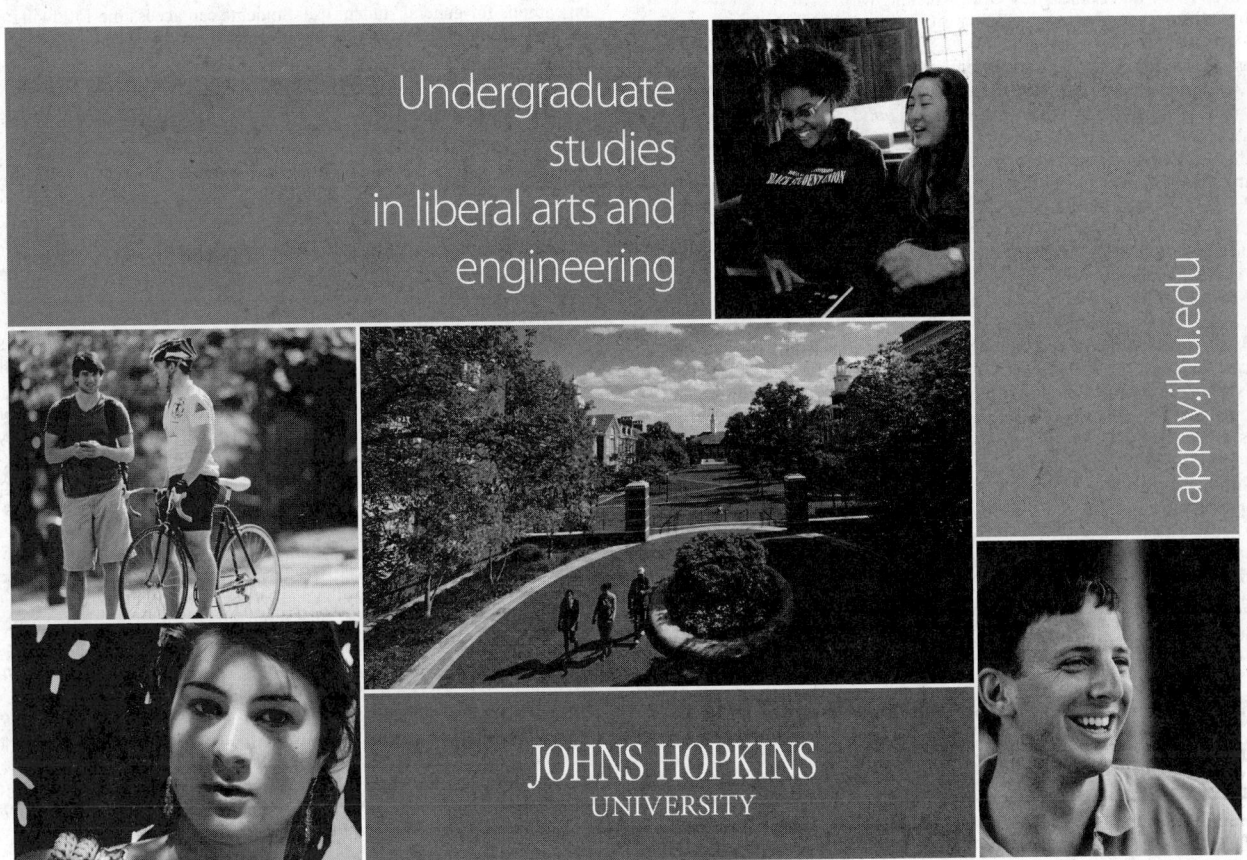

Undergraduate studies in liberal arts and engineering

apply.jhu.edu

JOHNS HOPKINS
UNIVERSITY

over 24: 100%; SAT critical reading scores over 700: 47%; SAT math scores over 700: 65%; SAT writing scores over 700: 55%; ACT scores over 30: 82%.
Faculty *Total:* 609, 83% full-time, 91% with terminal degrees. *Student/faculty ratio:* 13:1.
Academics *Calendar:* 4-1-4. *Degrees:* certificates, diplomas, bachelor's, master's, doctoral, post-master's, and postbachelor's certificates. *Special study options:* adult/continuing education programs, advanced placement credit, double majors, honors programs, independent study, internships, off-campus study, part-time degree program, services for LD students, student-designed majors, study abroad, summer session for credit. *ROTC:* Army (b), Air Force (c). *Unusual degree programs:* 3-2 engineering; international studies with Johns Hopkins University, School of Advanced International Studies (Washington, DC); biology; classics; German; history; neuroscience; public policy; mathematics; education.
Computers on Campus 200 computers/terminals and 4,000 ports are available on campus for general student use. Students can access the following: campus intranet, computer help desk, free student e-mail accounts, online (class) grades, online (class) registration, online (class) schedules. Campuswide network is available. 100% of college-owned or -operated housing units are wired for high-speed Internet access. Wireless service is available via classrooms, computer centers, computer labs, dorm rooms, libraries.
Student Life *Housing:* on-campus residence required through sophomore year. *Options:* coed, disabled students. Campus housing is university owned. Freshman campus housing is guaranteed. *Activities and organizations:* drama/theater group, student-run newspaper, radio station, choral group, The Outdoors Club, JHU Tutorial Project, The Barn Stormers (theater group), Inter-Asian Council, News-letter (student paper), national fraternities, national sororities. *Campus security:* 24-hour emergency response devices and patrols, student patrols, late-night transport/escort service, controlled dormitory access, CCTV monitoring of public areas. *Student services:* health clinic, personal/psychological counseling.
Athletics Member NCAA. All Division III except men's and women's lacrosse (Division I). *Intercollegiate sports:* baseball M, basketball M/W, cross-country running M/W, fencing M/W, field hockey W, football M, lacrosse M(s)/W(s), soccer M/W, swimming and diving M/W, tennis M/W, track and field M/W, volleyball W, water polo M, wrestling M. *Intramural sports:* badminton M(c)/W(c), basketball M/W, equestrian sports M(c)/W(c), field hockey W(c), football M/W, golf M(c)/W(c), ice hockey M(c), lacrosse M(c)/W(c), rock climbing M/W, rugby M(c)/W(c), soccer M/W, softball W(c), squash M(c)/W(c), table tennis M(c)/W(c), tennis M(c)/W(c), ultimate Frisbee M(c)/W(c), volleyball M(c)/W(c), water polo M(c)/W(c), wrestling M(c).
Standardized Tests *Required:* SAT or ACT (for admission). *Recommended:* SAT Subject Tests (for admission).
Costs (2013–14) *Comprehensive fee:* $59,802 includes full-time tuition ($45,470), mandatory fees ($500), and room and board ($13,832). Part-time tuition: $1515 per credit hour. *College room only:* $7920. Room and board charges vary according to board plan and housing facility. *Payment plan:* installment. *Waivers:* employees or children of employees.
Financial Aid Of all full-time matriculated undergraduates who enrolled in 2012, 2,532 applied for aid, 2,297 were judged to have need, 2,279 had their need fully met. 1,839 Federal Work-Study jobs (averaging $2296). In 2012, 56 non-need-based awards were made. *Average percent of need met:* 99%. *Average financial aid package:* $36,312. *Average need-based loan:* $4242. *Average need-based gift aid:* $33,476. *Average non-need-based aid:* $30,898. *Average indebtedness upon graduation:* $23,092. *Financial aid deadline:* 3/1.
Applying *Options:* electronic application, early admission, early decision, deferred entrance. *Application fee:* $70. *Required:* essay or personal statement, high school transcript, 2 letters of recommendation. *Recommended:* 3 letters of recommendation, interview. *Application deadlines:* 1/1 (freshmen), 3/15 (transfers). *Early decision deadline:* 11/1. *Notification:* 4/1 (freshmen), 5/31 (transfers), 12/15 (early decision).
Freshman Application Contact Mr. John Birney, Senior Associate Director of Undergraduate Admissions, The Johns Hopkins University, Mason Hall, 3400 North Charles Street, Baltimore, MD 21218-2699. *Phone:* 410-516-8171. *Fax:* 410-516-6025. *E-mail:* gotojhu@jhu.edu.
Website: http://www.jhu.edu/.

See previous page for display ad and page 1338 for the College Close-Up.

Kaplan University, Hagerstown Campus

Hagerstown, Maryland

Freshman Application Contact Kaplan University, Hagerstown Campus, 18618 Crestwood Drive, Hagerstown, MD 21742-2797. *Phone:* 301-739-2680

Ext. 217. *Toll-free phone:* 866-527-5268 (in-state); 800-527-5268 (out-of-state).
Website: http://www.ku-hagerstown.com/.

Loyola University Maryland

Baltimore, Maryland

- **Independent Roman Catholic (Jesuit)** university, founded 1852
- **Urban** 89-acre campus with easy access to Washington, DC
- **Endowment** $159.3 million
- **Coed** 3,917 undergraduate students, 99% full-time, 61% women, 39% men
- **Moderately difficult** entrance level, 65% of applicants were admitted

Undergraduates 3,875 full-time, 42 part-time. Students come from 38 states and territories; 61 other countries; 82% are from out of state; 5% Black or African American, non-Hispanic/Latino; 8% Hispanic/Latino; 3% Asian, non-Hispanic/Latino; 0.2% American Indian or Alaska Native, non-Hispanic/Latino; 2% Two or more races, non-Hispanic/Latino; 0.8% Race/ethnicity unknown; 0.6% international; 2% transferred in; 82% live on campus. *Retention:* 88% of full-time freshmen returned.
Freshmen *Admission:* 12,664 applied, 8,187 admitted, 1,072 enrolled. *Average high school GPA:* 3.39. *Test scores:* SAT critical reading scores over 500: 92%; SAT math scores over 500: 90%; ACT scores over 18: 100%; SAT critical reading scores over 600: 43%; SAT math scores over 600: 51%; ACT scores over 24: 84%; SAT critical reading scores over 700: 7%; SAT math scores over 700: 7%; ACT scores over 30: 15%.
Faculty *Total:* 556, 63% full-time, 56% with terminal degrees. *Student/faculty ratio:* 12:1.
Academics *Calendar:* semesters. *Degrees:* bachelor's, master's, doctoral, post-master's, and postbachelor's certificates. *Special study options:* accelerated degree program, advanced placement credit, cooperative education, double majors, honors programs, independent study, internships, off-campus study, part-time degree program, services for LD students, study abroad, summer session for credit. *ROTC:* Army (b), Air Force (c). *Unusual degree programs:* nursing with Johns Hopkins University School of Nursing (The Loyola-Hopkins dual-degree program allows students to earn two degrees in five years).
Computers on Campus 690 computers/terminals and 50 ports are available on campus for general student use. Students can access the following: campus intranet, computer help desk, free student e-mail accounts, online (class) grades, online (class) registration, online (class) schedules, entire campus has unlimited wireless access. Campuswide network is available. 100% of college-owned or -operated housing units are wired for high-speed Internet access. Wireless service is available via entire campus.
Student Life *Housing options:* coed, cooperative. Campus housing is university owned. Freshman campus housing is guaranteed. *Activities and organizations:* drama/theater group, student-run newspaper, radio and television station, choral group, Student Government Association, Resident Affairs Council (RAC), Relay for Life, Resident Assistants (RA), The Evergreens. *Campus security:* 24-hour emergency response devices and patrols, late-night transport/escort service, controlled dormitory access. *Student services:* health clinic, personal/psychological counseling, women's center.
Athletics Member NCAA. All Division I. *Intercollegiate sports:* basketball M(s)/W(s), crew M(s)/W(s), cross-country running M(s)/W(s), golf M(s), lacrosse M(s)/W(s), soccer M(s)/W(s), swimming and diving M(s)/W(s), tennis M(s)/W(s), track and field W(s), volleyball W(s). *Intramural sports:* badminton M(c)/W(c), baseball M(c), basketball M(c)/W(c), field hockey W(c), ice hockey M(c), lacrosse M(c)/W(c), riflery M(c)/W(c), rugby M(c), sailing M(c)/W(c), soccer M(c)/W(c), softball W(c), swimming and diving M(c)/W(c), tennis M(c)/W(c), ultimate Frisbee M(c)/W(c), volleyball M(c)/W(c), water polo M(c)/W(c).
Costs (2012–13) *One-time required fee:* $165. *Comprehensive fee:* $54,550 includes full-time tuition ($41,030), mandatory fees ($1400), and room and board ($12,120). Full-time tuition and fees vary according to course load. Part-time tuition: $665 per credit. Part-time tuition and fees vary according to course load. *Required fees:* $25 per term part-time. *College room only:* $9120. Room and board charges vary according to housing facility. *Payment plan:* installment. *Waivers:* employees or children of employees.
Financial Aid Of all full-time matriculated undergraduates who enrolled in 2011, 2,645 applied for aid, 2,230 were judged to have need, 2,218 had their need fully met. In 2011, 350 non-need-based awards were made. *Average percent of need met:* 98%. *Average financial aid package:* $26,915. *Average need-based loan:* $5105. *Average need-based gift aid:* $20,270. *Average non-need-based aid:* $15,140. *Average indebtedness upon graduation:* $32,392. *Financial aid deadline:* 2/15.

Applying *Options:* electronic application, early admission, early action, deferred entrance. *Application fee:* $50. *Required:* essay or personal statement, high school transcript. *Application deadlines:* 1/15 (freshmen), 1/15 (out-of-state freshmen), 7/15 (transfers), 11/1 (early action). *Notification:* 4/1 (freshmen), 4/1 (out-of-state freshmen), continuous (transfers), 1/15 (early action). **Freshman Application Contact** Loyola University Maryland, 4501 North Charles Street, Baltimore, MD 21210-2699. *Phone:* 410-617-2000. *Toll-free phone:* 800-221-9107. *Website:* http://www.loyola.edu/.

See below for display ad and page 1364 for the College Close-Up.

Maple Springs Baptist Bible College and Seminary
Capitol Heights, Maryland

- **Independent Baptist** comprehensive, founded 1986
- **Suburban** 1-acre campus with easy access to Washington, DC
- **Coed** 74 undergraduate students, 4% full-time, 55% women, 45% men
- **Minimally difficult** entrance level, 100% of applicants were admitted

Undergraduates 3 full-time, 71 part-time. Students come from 3 states and territories; 32% are from out of state; 96% Black or African American, non-Hispanic/Latino; 4% Hispanic/Latino. *Retention:* 75% of full-time freshmen returned.
Freshmen *Admission:* 2 applied, 2 admitted, 1 enrolled.
Faculty *Total:* 23, 13% full-time, 100% with terminal degrees.
Academics *Calendar:* semesters. *Degrees:* certificates, diplomas, associate, bachelor's, master's, and doctoral. *Special study options:* academic remediation for entering students, accelerated degree program, adult/continuing education programs, external degree program, independent study, internships, part-time degree program.
Student Life *Housing:* college housing not available. *Activities and organizations:* student-run newspaper. *Campus security:* 24-hour emergency response devices, part-time security personnel.
Standardized Tests *Required:* math and English placement examination for all new students who do not have college English and math grades of C or above (for admission).

Costs (2012–13) *Tuition:* $4470 full-time, $2230 per term part-time. Full-time tuition and fees vary according to degree level. Part-time tuition and fees vary according to degree level. *Required fees:* $120 full-time, $165 per credit part-time, $60 per term part-time. *Payment plan:* installment.
Financial Aid *Financial aid deadline:* 4/30.
Applying *Options:* deferred entrance. *Application fee:* $50. *Required:* essay or personal statement, high school transcript, 2 letters of recommendation, interview. *Application deadlines:* rolling (freshmen), rolling (transfers). *Notification:* continuous (freshmen), continuous (transfers).
Freshman Application Contact Ms. Jeannie Bowman, Assistant Director of Admissions and Records, Maple Springs Baptist Bible College and Seminary, 4130 Belt Road, Capitol Heights, MD 20743. *Phone:* 301-736-3631. *Fax:* 301-735-6507.
Website: http://www.msbbcs.edu/.

Maryland Institute College of Art
Baltimore, Maryland

- **Independent** comprehensive, founded 1826
- **Urban** 16-acre campus with easy access to Washington, DC
- **Endowment** $62.9 million
- **Coed** 1,827 undergraduate students, 99% full-time, 71% women, 29% men
- **Very difficult** entrance level, 52% of applicants were admitted

Undergraduates 1,809 full-time, 18 part-time. Students come from 49 states and territories; 49 other countries; 77% are from out of state; 5% Black or African American, non-Hispanic/Latino; 4% Hispanic/Latino; 12% Asian, non-Hispanic/Latino; 0.1% Native Hawaiian or other Pacific Islander, non-Hispanic/Latino; 0.3% American Indian or Alaska Native, non-Hispanic/Latino; 8% Two or more races, non-Hispanic/Latino; 9% Race/ethnicity unknown; 7% international; 5% transferred in; 42% live on campus. *Retention:* 85% of full-time freshmen returned.
Freshmen *Admission:* 3,139 applied, 1,627 admitted, 414 enrolled. *Average high school GPA:* 3.45. *Test scores:* SAT critical reading scores over 500: 87%; SAT math scores over 500: 78%; SAT writing scores over 500: 86%; SAT critical reading scores over 600: 53%; SAT math scores over 600: 35%; SAT writing scores over 600: 44%; SAT critical reading scores over 700: 17%; SAT math scores over 700: 5%; SAT writing scores over 700: 10%.

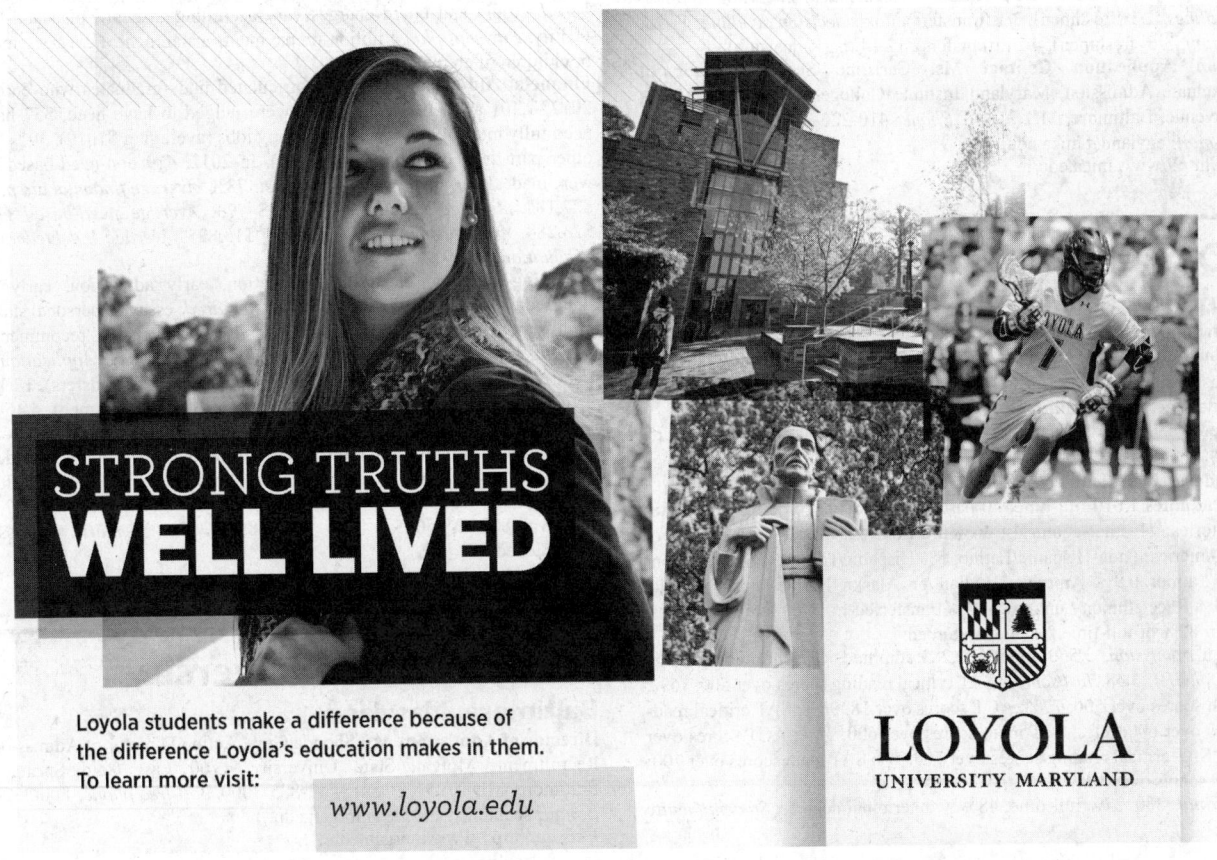

Faculty *Total:* 363, 40% full-time, 79% with terminal degrees. *Student/faculty ratio:* 9:1.

Academics *Calendar:* semesters. *Degrees:* bachelor's, master's, and postbachelor's certificates. *Special study options:* accelerated degree program, adult/continuing education programs, advanced placement credit, distance learning, double majors, English as a second language, independent study, internships, off-campus study, services for LD students, student-designed majors, study abroad, summer session for credit. *ROTC:* Army (c).

Computers on Campus 650 computers/terminals and 750 ports are available on campus for general student use. Students can access the following: campus intranet, computer help desk, free student e-mail accounts, online (class) grades, online (class) registration, online (class) schedules, campus Portal, online gallery space, network storage space, personal Web sites, online software training tutorials (Lynda.com), and Learning management system (Moodle). Campuswide network is available. 100% of college-owned or -operated housing units are wired for high-speed Internet access. Wireless service is available via classrooms, computer centers, computer labs, dorm rooms, learning centers, libraries, student centers.

Student Life *Housing options:* coed, disabled students. Campus housing is university owned. Freshman campus housing is guaranteed. *Activities and organizations:* drama/theater group, student-run radio station, choral group, Soccer Club, Urban Gaming Club, Black Student Union, Students of Sustainability, National Art Educators Association. *Campus security:* 24-hour emergency response devices and patrols, student patrols, late-night transport/escort service, controlled dormitory access, self-defense education, 24-hour building security, safety awareness programs, campus patrols by city police. *Student services:* health clinic, personal/psychological counseling.

Athletics *Intramural sports:* soccer M(c)/W(c), volleyball M(c)/W(c).

Standardized Tests *Required:* SAT or ACT (for admission).

Costs (2012–13) *One-time required fee:* $160. *Comprehensive fee:* $50,220 includes full-time tuition ($37,900), mandatory fees ($1440), and room and board ($10,880). *Part-time tuition:* $1580 per credit. *Required fees:* $720 per term part-time. *College room only:* $8200. Room and board charges vary according to board plan and housing facility. *Payment plan:* installment. *Waivers:* employees or children of employees.

Financial Aid *Average indebtedness upon graduation:* $17,472.

Applying *Options:* early admission, early decision, deferred entrance. *Application fee:* $60. *Required:* essay or personal statement, high school transcript, 3 letters of recommendation, art portfolio. *Recommended:* interview. *Application deadlines:* 2/1 (freshmen), 3/1 (transfers). *Early decision deadline:* 11/29. *Notification:* 3/6 (freshmen), 4/24 (transfers), 12/14 (early decision).

Freshman Application Contact Ms. Christine Seese, Director of Undergraduate Admission, Maryland Institute College of Art, 1300 Mount Royal Avenue, Baltimore, MD 21217. *Phone:* 410-225-2222. *Fax:* 410-225-2337. *E-mail:* cgyland@mica.edu.

Website: http://www.mica.edu/.

McDaniel College

Westminster, Maryland

- **Independent** comprehensive, founded 1867
- **Suburban** 160-acre campus with easy access to Baltimore and Washington, D.C.
- **Endowment** $88.4 million
- **Coed** 1,650 undergraduate students, 98% full-time, 54% women, 46% men
- **Moderately difficult** entrance level, 64% of applicants were admitted

Undergraduates 1,610 full-time, 40 part-time. Students come from 33 states and territories; 21 other countries; 36% are from out of state; 12% Black or African American, non-Hispanic/Latino; 5% Hispanic/Latino; 4% Asian, non-Hispanic/Latino; 0.9% American Indian or Alaska Native, non-Hispanic/Latino; 3% Race/ethnicity unknown; 3% transferred in; 84% live on campus. *Retention:* 82% of full-time freshmen returned.

Freshmen *Admission:* 3,560 applied, 2,283 admitted, 437 enrolled. *Average high school GPA:* 3.48. *Test scores:* SAT critical reading scores over 500: 75%; SAT math scores over 500: 77%; ACT scores over 18: 96%; SAT critical reading scores over 600: 30%; SAT math scores over 600: 33%; ACT scores over 24: 55%; SAT critical reading scores over 700: 7%; SAT math scores over 700: 4%; ACT scores over 30: 9%.

Faculty *Total:* 380, 27% full-time, 48% with terminal degrees. *Student/faculty ratio:* 11:1.

Academics *Calendar:* 4-1-4. *Degrees:* bachelor's, master's, and postbachelor's certificates. *Special study options:* academic remediation for entering students, adult/continuing education programs, advanced placement credit, distance learning, double majors, honors programs, independent study, internships, off-campus study, part-time degree program, services for LD students, student-designed majors, study abroad, summer session for credit. *ROTC:* Army (b). *Unusual degree programs:* 3-2 engineering with University of Maryland; environmental policy science with Duke University.

Computers on Campus 320 computers/terminals and 1,228 ports are available on campus for general student use. Students can access the following: campus intranet, computer help desk, free student e-mail accounts, online (class) grades, online (class) registration, online (class) schedules, online billing summaries, financial aid letter, tax information. Campuswide network is available. 100% of college-owned or -operated housing units are wired for high-speed Internet access. Wireless service is available via entire campus.

Student Life *Housing:* on-campus residence required through junior year. *Options:* coed, men-only, women-only, disabled students. Campus housing is university owned. Freshman campus housing is guaranteed. *Activities and organizations:* drama/theater group, student-run newspaper, radio and television station, choral group, Student Government Association, Black Student Union, International Club, Maryland State Legislature, Up 'til Dawn, national fraternities, national sororities. *Campus security:* 24-hour emergency response devices and patrols, late-night transport/escort service, About half patrol force sworn as campus police. All are certified to US DOT First Responder standards. *Student services:* health clinic, personal/psychological counseling.

Athletics Member NCAA. All Division III. *Intercollegiate sports:* baseball M, basketball M/W, cross-country running M/W, field hockey W, football M, golf M/W, lacrosse M/W, soccer M/W, softball W, swimming and diving M/W, tennis M/W, track and field M/W, volleyball W, wrestling M. *Intramural sports:* badminton M/W, basketball M/W, cheerleading M(c)/W(c), football M, golf M/W, soccer M/W, softball M/W, ultimate Frisbee M(c)/W(c), volleyball M/W.

Standardized Tests *Required:* SAT or ACT (for admission), SAT Optional Plan for students who are in the top 10% of their class if their HS ranks; otherwise, a cumulative GPA of a 3.5 or higher. SAT Subject Tests considered if submitted (for admission).

Costs (2013–14) *Comprehensive fee:* $45,600 includes full-time tuition ($36,960) and room and board ($8640). Full-time tuition and fees vary according to course load. *Part-time tuition:* $1155 per credit hour. Part-time tuition and fees vary according to course load and reciprocity agreements. *Room and board:* Room and board charges vary according to board plan and housing facility. *Payment plans:* tuition prepayment, installment. *Waivers:* employees or children of employees.

Financial Aid Of all full-time matriculated undergraduates who enrolled in 2012, 1,301 applied for aid, 1,195 were judged to have need, 357 had their need fully met. 349 Federal Work-Study jobs (averaging $1019). 301 state and other part-time jobs (averaging $732). In 2012, 419 non-need-based awards were made. *Average percent of need met:* 78%. *Average financial aid package:* $27,184. *Average need-based loan:* $4773. *Average need-based gift aid:* $23,284. *Average non-need-based aid:* $15,825. *Average indebtedness upon graduation:* $31,919.

Applying *Options:* electronic application, early admission, early action, deferred entrance. *Application fee:* $50. *Required:* essay or personal statement, high school transcript, minimum 2.5 GPA, 2 letters of recommendation. *Required for some:* interview. *Recommended:* interview. *Application deadlines:* 2/15 (freshmen), 2/5 (out-of-state freshmen), 4/1 (transfers), 12/1 (early action). *Notification:* 3/9 (freshmen), 3/9 (out-of-state freshmen), 4/15 (transfers), 12/21 (early action).

Freshman Application Contact Ms. Florence Hines, Vice President for Enrollment Management and Dean of Admissions, McDaniel College, 2 College Hill, Westminster, MD 21157-4390. *Phone:* 410-857-2230. *Toll-free phone:* 800-638-5005. *Fax:* 410-857-2757. *E-mail:* admissions@mcdaniel.edu.

Website: http://www.mcdaniel.edu/.

Morgan State University

Baltimore, Maryland

Director of Admissions Ms. Shonda Gray, Acting Director of Admissions and Recruitment, Morgan State University, 1700 East Cold Spring Lane, Baltimore, MD 21251. *Phone:* 443-885-3000. *Toll-free phone:* 800-332-6674. *E-mail:* shantell.saunders@morgan.edu.

Website: http://www.morgan.edu/.

Mount St. Mary's University

Emmitsburg, Maryland

- **Independent Roman Catholic** comprehensive, founded 1808
- **Rural** 1400-acre campus with easy access to Baltimore and Washington, DC
- **Endowment** $41.5 million
- **Coed** 1,842 undergraduate students, 95% full-time, 54% women, 46% men
- **Moderately difficult** entrance level, 55% of applicants were admitted

Undergraduates 1,755 full-time, 87 part-time. Students come from 36 states and territories; 16 other countries; 48% are from out of state; 10% Black or African American, non-Hispanic/Latino; 9% Hispanic/Latino; 2% Asian, non-Hispanic/Latino; 0.2% Native Hawaiian or other Pacific Islander, non-Hispanic/Latino; 0.3% American Indian or Alaska Native, non-Hispanic/Latino; 3% Two or more races, non-Hispanic/Latino; 2% Race/ethnicity unknown; 1% international; 2% transferred in; 82% live on campus. *Retention:* 80% of full-time freshmen returned.

Freshmen *Admission:* 5,283 applied, 2,930 admitted, 447 enrolled. *Average high school GPA:* 3.37. *Test scores:* SAT critical reading scores over 500: 83%; SAT math scores over 500: 79%; SAT writing scores over 500: 71%; ACT scores over 18: 88%; SAT critical reading scores over 600: 26%; SAT math scores over 600: 28%; SAT writing scores over 600: 26%; ACT scores over 24: 22%; SAT critical reading scores over 700: 2%; SAT math scores over 700: 3%; SAT writing scores over 700: 2%; ACT scores over 30: 2%.

Faculty *Total:* 193, 59% full-time, 65% with terminal degrees. *Student/faculty ratio:* 14:1.

Academics *Calendar:* semesters. *Degrees:* bachelor's, master's, post-master's, and postbachelor's certificates. *Special study options:* academic remediation for entering students, accelerated degree program, adult/continuing education programs, advanced placement credit, double majors, honors programs, independent study, internships, off-campus study, part-time degree program, services for LD students, student-designed majors, study abroad, summer session for credit. *ROTC:* Army (c). *Unusual degree programs:* 3-2 nursing with Johns Hopkins University, Shenandoah University.

Computers on Campus 80 computers/terminals are available on campus for general student use. Students can access the following: campus intranet, computer help desk, free student e-mail accounts, online (class) grades, online (class) registration, online (class) schedules, tuition payment, course management system. Campuswide network is available. 100% of college-owned or -operated housing units are wired for high-speed Internet access. Wireless service is available via entire campus.

Student Life *Housing:* on-campus residence required for freshman year. *Options:* coed, disabled students. Campus housing is university owned. Freshman campus housing is guaranteed. *Activities and organizations:* drama/theater group, student-run newspaper, radio and television station, choral group, Mount Students for Life, CRUX—Outdoor Adventures, Campus Ministry Student Organization, Circle K, Mount Chorale. *Campus security:* 24-hour emergency response devices and patrols, late-night transport/escort service, controlled dormitory access. *Student services:* health clinic, personal/psychological counseling.

Athletics Member NCAA. All Division I. *Intercollegiate sports:* baseball M(s), basketball M(s)/W(s), cheerleading W(c), cross-country running M(s)/W(s), equestrian sports M(c)/W(c), ice hockey M(c)/W(c), lacrosse M(s)/W(s), rugby M(c)/W(c), soccer W(s), softball W(s), swimming and diving W(s), tennis M(s)/W(s), track and field M(s)/W(s). *Intramural sports:* basketball M, field hockey M/W, skiing (downhill) M/W, soccer M/W, softball M/W, tennis M/W, ultimate Frisbee M/W, volleyball W.

Standardized Tests *Required:* SAT or ACT (for admission).

Costs (2012–13) *Comprehensive fee:* $43,972 includes full-time tuition ($32,224), mandatory fees ($730), and room and board ($11,018). Full-time tuition and fees vary according to location and program. Part-time tuition: $1076 per credit hour. Part-time tuition and fees vary according to location and program. *College room only:* $5392. Room and board charges vary according to board plan. *Payment plan:* installment. *Waivers:* employees or children of employees.

Financial Aid Of all full-time matriculated undergraduates who enrolled in 2012, 1,406 applied for aid, 1,249 were judged to have need, 277 had their need fully met. 121 Federal Work-Study jobs (averaging $1559). 528 state and other part-time jobs (averaging $1181). In 2012, 439 non-need-based awards were made. *Average percent of need met:* 72%. *Average financial aid package:* $22,587. *Average need-based loan:* $4571. *Average need-based gift aid:*

$18,245. *Average non-need-based aid:* $13,462. *Average indebtedness upon graduation:* $32,311. *Financial aid deadline:* 3/1.

Applying *Options:* electronic application, early action, deferred entrance. *Application fee:* $45. *Required:* high school transcript, minimum 2.0 GPA, 1 letter of recommendation. *Recommended:* essay or personal statement, minimum 3.0 GPA, interview. *Application deadlines:* 3/1 (freshmen), 6/1 (transfers), 12/1 (early action). *Notification:* continuous (freshmen), continuous (transfers), 12/25 (early action).

Freshman Application Contact Mr. Michael Post, Dean of Admissions and Enrollment Management, Mount St. Mary's University, 16300 Old Emmitsburg Road, Emmitsburg, MD 21727. *Phone:* 301-447-5214. *Toll-free phone:* 800-448-4347. *Fax:* 301-447-5860. *E-mail:* admissions@msmary.edu. *Website:* http://www.msmary.edu/.

National Labor College

Silver Spring, Maryland

Director of Admissions Carol Rodgers, Associate Provost for External Relations and Director of Admissions, National Labor College, 10000 New Hampshire Avenue, Silver Spring, MD 20903. *Phone:* 301-431-5440. *Toll-free phone:* 888-427-8100. *E-mail:* crodgers@nlc.edu. *Website:* http://www.nlc.edu/.

Ner Israel Rabbinical College

Baltimore, Maryland

Freshman Application Contact Ner Israel Rabbinical College, 400 Mount Wilson Lane, Baltimore, MD 21208. *Phone:* 410-484-7200.

Notre Dame of Maryland University

Baltimore, Maryland

- **Independent Roman Catholic** comprehensive, founded 1873
- **Urban** 58-acre campus with easy access to Baltimore and Washington, DC
- **Endowment** $26.3 million
- **Coed, primarily women**
- **Moderately difficult** entrance level

Faculty *Student/faculty ratio:* 12:1.

Academics *Calendar:* 4-1-4. *Degrees:* bachelor's, master's, doctoral, post-master's, and postbachelor's certificates (offers coed undergraduate program for adult students).

Student Life *Campus security:* 24-hour emergency response devices and patrols, late-night transport/escort service, controlled dormitory access, emergency call boxes.

Athletics Member NCAA. All Division III.

Standardized Tests *Required:* SAT or ACT (for admission).

Costs (2012–13) *Comprehensive fee:* $41,000 includes full-time tuition ($29,850), mandatory fees ($1000), and room and board ($10,150). *Room and board:* Room and board charges vary according to board plan.

Financial Aid *Of all full-time matriculated undergraduates who enrolled in 2011,* 503 applied for aid, 445 were judged to have need, 71 had their need fully met. 92 Federal Work-Study jobs (averaging $902). *In 2011,* 43 non-need-based awards were made. *Average percent of need met:* 66. *Average financial aid package:* $21,479. *Average need-based loan:* $4104. *Average need-based gift aid:* $17,446. *Average non-need-based aid:* $13,689. *Average indebtedness upon graduation:* $27,265.

Applying *Options:* electronic application, early admission, early action, deferred entrance. *Application fee:* $45. *Required:* essay or personal statement, high school transcript, minimum 2.0 GPA, 2 letters of recommendation. *Recommended:* minimum 3.0 GPA, interview, resume.

Freshman Application Contact Notre Dame of Maryland University, 4701 North Charles Street, Baltimore, MD 21210-2476. *Phone:* 410-532-5332. *Toll-free phone:* 800-435-0200. *Website:* http://www.ndm.edu/.

Peabody Conservatory of The Johns Hopkins University

Baltimore, Maryland

- **Independent** comprehensive, founded 1857
- **Urban** 1-acre campus with easy access to Washington, DC
- **Endowment** $84.2 million
- **Coed** 312 undergraduate students, 96% full-time, 47% women, 53% men
- **Very difficult** entrance level, 40% of applicants were admitted

Undergraduates 300 full-time, 12 part-time. Students come from 35 states and territories; 15 other countries; 73% are from out of state; 6% Black or African American, non-Hispanic/Latino; 4% Hispanic/Latino; 15% Asian, non-Hispanic/Latino; 1% Native Hawaiian or other Pacific Islander, non-Hispanic/Latino; 5% Two or more races, non-Hispanic/Latino; 3% Race/ethnicity unknown; 24% international; 4% transferred in; 40% live on campus. *Retention:* 99% of full-time freshmen returned.

Freshmen *Admission:* 750 applied, 298 admitted, 61 enrolled.

Faculty *Total:* 177, 46% full-time, 21% with terminal degrees. *Student/faculty ratio:* 6:1.

Academics *Calendar:* semesters. *Degrees:* certificates, diplomas, bachelor's, master's, doctoral, post-master's, and postbachelor's certificates. *Special study options:* academic remediation for entering students, accelerated degree program, advanced placement credit, double majors, English as a second language, honors programs, independent study, internships, off-campus study, services for LD students.

Computers on Campus 40 computers/terminals are available on campus for general student use. Students can access the following: campus intranet, computer help desk, free student e-mail accounts, online (class) grades, online (class) registration, online (class) schedules, word processing, music processing. Campuswide network is available. 100% of college-owned or -operated housing units are wired for high-speed Internet access. Wireless service is available via entire campus.

Student Life *Housing:* on-campus residence required through sophomore year. *Options:* coed. Campus housing is university owned. Freshman campus housing is guaranteed. *Activities and organizations:* choral group. *Campus security:* 24-hour emergency response devices and patrols, late-night transport/escort service, controlled dormitory access. *Student services:* health clinic, personal/psychological counseling.

Standardized Tests *Required for some:* SAT or ACT (for admission).

Costs (2012–13) *One-time required fee:* $700. *Comprehensive fee:* $51,595 includes full-time tuition ($38,450), mandatory fees ($465), and room and board ($12,680). Full-time tuition and fees vary according to program. Part-time tuition: $1097 per semester hour. Part-time tuition and fees vary according to course load. *Room and board:* Room and board charges vary according to board plan. *Payment plan:* installment.

Financial Aid Of all full-time matriculated undergraduates who enrolled in 2012, 199 applied for aid, 172 were judged to have need, 42 had their need fully met. 103 Federal Work-Study jobs (averaging $1892). In 2012, 80 non-need-based awards were made. *Average percent of need met:* 74%. *Average financial aid package:* $16,339. *Average need-based loan:* $5478. *Average need-based gift aid:* $12,778. *Average non-need-based aid:* $18,524. *Average indebtedness upon graduation:* $33,961.

Applying *Application fee:* $100. *Required:* essay or personal statement, high school transcript, 3 letters of recommendation, interview, audition. *Recommended:* minimum 3.0 GPA. *Application deadlines:* 12/1 (freshmen), 12/1 (transfers). *Notification:* 4/1 (freshmen), 4/1 (transfers).

Freshman Application Contact Mr. David Lane, Director of Admissions, Peabody Conservatory of The Johns Hopkins University, Peabody Conservatory Admissions Office, One East Mount Vernon Place, Baltimore, MD 21202-2397. *Phone:* 410-234-4848. *Toll-free phone:* 800-368-2521. *Website:* http://www.peabody.jhu.edu/.

St. John's College

Annapolis, Maryland

- **Independent** comprehensive, founded 1784
- **Small-town** 36-acre campus with easy access to Baltimore and Washington, DC
- **Endowment** $86.3 million
- **Coed** 449 undergraduate students, 100% full-time, 45% women, 55% men
- **Moderately difficult** entrance level, 82% of applicants were admitted

Undergraduates 447 full-time, 2 part-time. Students come from 42 states and territories; 15 other countries; 85% are from out of state; 2% Black or African

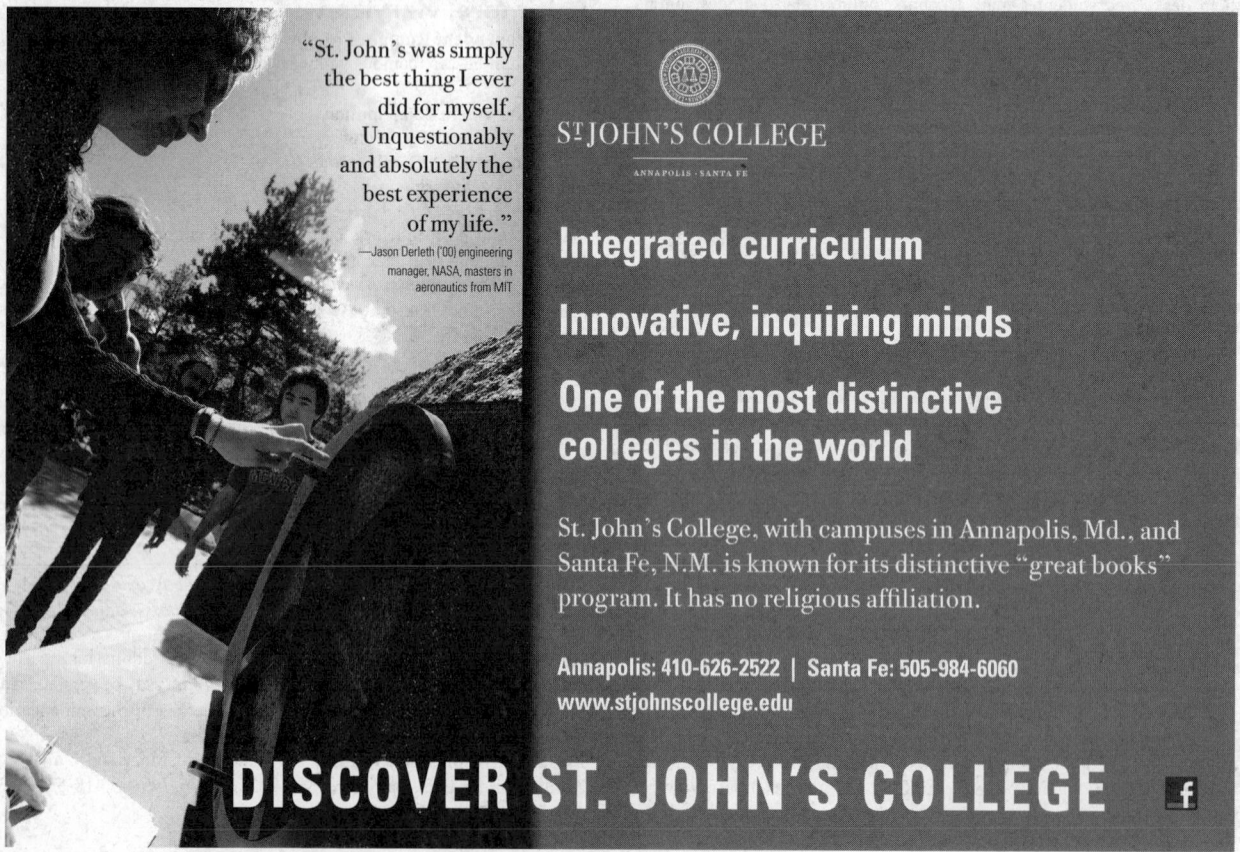

American, non-Hispanic/Latino; 7% Hispanic/Latino; 2% Asian, non-Hispanic/Latino; 0.4% American Indian or Alaska Native, non-Hispanic/Latino; 3% Two or more races, non-Hispanic/Latino; 2% Race/ethnicity unknown; 9% international; 74% live on campus. *Retention:* 81% of full-time freshmen returned.

Freshmen *Admission:* 378 applied, 311 admitted, 118 enrolled. *Test scores:* SAT critical reading scores over 500: 99%; SAT math scores over 500: 93%; SAT writing scores over 500: 99%; SAT critical reading scores over 600: 83%; SAT math scores over 600: 69%; SAT writing scores over 600: 64%; SAT critical reading scores over 700: 38%; SAT math scores over 700: 23%; SAT writing scores over 700: 21%.

Faculty *Total:* 63, 92% full-time, 73% with terminal degrees. *Student/faculty ratio:* 8:1.

Academics *Calendar:* semesters. *Degrees:* bachelor's and master's.

Computers on Campus 24 computers/terminals and 12 ports are available on campus for general student use. Students can access the following: computer help desk, free student e-mail accounts. Campuswide network is available. 100% of college-owned or -operated housing units are wired for high-speed Internet access. Wireless service is available via computer labs, dorm rooms, libraries.

Student Life *Housing:* on-campus residence required for freshman year. *Options:* coed. Campus housing is university owned. Freshman campus housing is guaranteed. *Activities and organizations:* drama/theater group, student-run newspaper, choral group, King William's Players (drama), Reality (social), Delegate Council (student government), Waltz (social), Student Committee on Instruction (advisory). *Campus security:* 24-hour emergency response devices and patrols, late-night transport/escort service, controlled dormitory access. *Student services:* health clinic, personal/psychological counseling.

Athletics *Intercollegiate sports:* crew M(c)/W(c), fencing M(c)/W(c). *Intramural sports:* badminton M/W, basketball M/W, fencing M/W, football W, racquetball M/W, sailing M/W, soccer M/W, softball M/W, squash M/W, table tennis M/W, tennis M/W, track and field M/W, volleyball M/W, weight lifting M/W.

Standardized Tests *Required for some:* SAT or ACT (for admission). *Recommended:* SAT or ACT (for admission).

Costs (2012–13) *Comprehensive fee:* $55,648 includes full-time tuition ($44,554), mandatory fees ($450), and room and board ($10,644). *Room and board:* Room and board charges vary according to board plan. *Payment plan:* installment. *Waivers:* employees or children of employees.

Financial Aid Of all full-time matriculated undergraduates who enrolled in 2012, 356 applied for aid, 322 were judged to have need, 32 had their need fully met. 99 Federal Work-Study jobs (averaging $1894). 88 state and other part-time jobs (averaging $2075). In 2012, 19 non-need-based awards were made. *Average percent of need met:* 98%. *Average financial aid package:* $33,665. *Average need-based loan:* $4842. *Average need-based gift aid:* $28,695. *Average non-need-based aid:* $16,340. *Average indebtedness upon graduation:* $29,265.

Applying *Options:* electronic application, early admission, deferred entrance. *Required:* essay or personal statement, high school transcript, 2 letters of recommendation. *Recommended:* interview. *Application deadline:* rolling (freshmen). *Notification:* continuous (freshmen).

Freshman Application Contact Ms. Sarah Morse, Director of Admissions, St. John's College, PO Box 2800, 60 College Avenue, Annapolis, MD 21404. *Phone:* 410-626-2522. *Toll-free phone:* 800-727-9238. *Fax:* 410-269-7916. *E-mail:* admissions@sjca.edu.
Website: http://www.stjohnscollege.edu/.

See previous page for display ad and page 1470 for the College Close-Up.

St. Mary's College of Maryland
St. Mary's City, Maryland

- **State-supported** comprehensive, founded 1840
- **Rural** 361-acre campus
- **Endowment** $25.9 million
- **Coed** 1,901 undergraduate students, 97% full-time, 59% women, 41% men
- **Very difficult** entrance level, 72% of applicants were admitted

Undergraduates 1,837 full-time, 64 part-time. Students come from 31 states and territories; 35 other countries; 11% are from out of state; 7% Black or African American, non-Hispanic/Latino; 5% Hispanic/Latino; 2% Asian, non-Hispanic/Latino; 0.1% Native Hawaiian or other Pacific Islander, non-Hispanic/Latino; 4% Two or more races, non-Hispanic/Latino; 2% Race/ethnicity unknown; 2% international; 4% transferred in; 86% live on campus. *Retention:* 87% of full-time freshmen returned.

Freshmen *Admission:* 1,985 applied, 1,430 admitted, 419 enrolled. *Average high school GPA:* 3.34. *Test scores:* SAT critical reading scores over 500: 93%;

SAT math scores over 500: 89%; SAT writing scores over 500: 89%; ACT scores over 18: 100%; SAT critical reading scores over 600: 62%; SAT math scores over 600: 53%; SAT writing scores over 600: 52%; ACT scores over 24: 84%; SAT critical reading scores over 700: 17%; SAT math scores over 700: 10%; SAT writing scores over 700: 12%; ACT scores over 30: 27%.

Faculty *Total:* 225, 63% full-time, 76% with terminal degrees. *Student/faculty ratio:* 12:1.

Academics *Calendar:* semesters. *Degrees:* bachelor's and master's. *Special study options:* advanced placement credit, cooperative education, double majors, freshman honors college, honors programs, independent study, internships, off-campus study, part-time degree program, services for LD students, student-designed majors, study abroad, summer session for credit. *Unusual degree programs:* 3-2 engineering with University of Maryland, College Park.

Computers on Campus 390 computers/terminals and 500 ports are available on campus for general student use. Students can access the following: campus intranet, computer help desk, free student e-mail accounts, online (class) grades, online (class) registration, online (class) schedules, Blackboard. Campuswide network is available. 100% of college-owned or -operated housing units are wired for high-speed Internet access. Wireless service is available via classrooms, computer centers, computer labs, learning centers, libraries, student centers.

Student Life *Housing options:* coed, men-only, women-only, cooperative, disabled students. Campus housing is university owned. Freshman campus housing is guaranteed. *Activities and organizations:* drama/theater group, student-run newspaper, radio station, choral group, Crew, Acappella groups, SEAC (Student Environmental Action Coalition), Dance Club, Outdoors Club. *Campus security:* 24-hour emergency response devices and patrols, late-night transport/escort service, controlled dormitory access. *Student services:* health clinic, personal/psychological counseling.

Athletics Member NCAA. All Division III. *Intercollegiate sports:* badminton M/W, baseball M, basketball M/W, cheerleading M/W, crew M(c)/W(c), cross-country running M/W, equestrian sports M(c)/W(c), fencing M(c)/W(c), field hockey W, lacrosse M/W, rock climbing M(c)/W(c), rugby M(c)/W(c), sailing M/W, soccer M/W, swimming and diving M/W, tennis M/W, ultimate Frisbee M(c)/W(c), volleyball W. *Intramural sports:* badminton M/W, basketball M/W, football M/W, lacrosse M/W, soccer M/W, softball M/W, volleyball M/W.

Standardized Tests *Required:* SAT or ACT (for admission).

Costs (2012–13) *Tuition:* state resident $12,245 full-time, $195 per credit hour part-time; nonresident $25,045 full-time, $195 per credit hour part-time. Full-time tuition and fees vary according to course load and degree level. Part-time tuition and fees vary according to course load and degree level. *Required fees:* $2528 full-time. *Room and board:* $11,305; room only: $6385. Room and board charges vary according to board plan and housing facility. *Payment plan:* installment. *Waivers:* senior citizens and employees or children of employees.

Financial Aid Of all full-time matriculated undergraduates who enrolled in 2011, 1,250 applied for aid, 833 were judged to have need, 48 had their need fully met. 114 Federal Work-Study jobs (averaging $561). In 2011, 401 non-need-based awards were made. *Average percent of need met:* 64%. *Average financial aid package:* $12,652. *Average need-based loan:* $4363. *Average need-based gift aid:* $9345. *Average non-need-based aid:* $3849. *Average indebtedness upon graduation:* $23,834.

Applying *Options:* electronic application, early admission, early decision, deferred entrance. *Application fee:* $50. *Required:* essay or personal statement, high school transcript, 2 letters of recommendation, Prospective students should apply online through the Common Application. *Recommended:* interview. *Application deadlines:* 1/1 (freshmen), 4/1 (transfers). *Early decision deadline:* 11/1 (for plan 1), 1/1 (for plan 2). *Notification:* 4/1 (freshmen), 5/15 (transfers), 12/15 (early decision plan 1), 2/15 (early decision plan 2).

Freshman Application Contact Mr. Richard J. Edgar, Director of Admissions, St. Mary's College of Maryland, 18952 East Fisher Road, St. Mary's City, MD 20686-3001. *Phone:* 240-895-5000. *Toll-free phone:* 800-492-7181. *Fax:* 240-895-5001. *E-mail:* admissions@smcm.edu.
Website: http://www.smcm.edu/.

Salisbury University
Salisbury, Maryland

- **State-supported** comprehensive, founded 1925, part of University System of Maryland
- **Small-town** 161-acre campus
- **Endowment** $56.1 million
- **Coed** 7,969 undergraduate students, 92% full-time, 57% women, 43% men
- **Moderately difficult** entrance level, 53% of applicants were admitted

Undergraduates 7,323 full-time, 646 part-time. Students come from 29 states and territories; 63 other countries; 135% are from out of state; 11% Black or African American, non-Hispanic/Latino; 5% Hispanic/Latino; 2% Asian, non-Hispanic/Latino; 0.1% Native Hawaiian or other Pacific Islander, non-Hispanic/Latino; 0.2% American Indian or Alaska Native, non-Hispanic/Latino; 3% Two or more races, non-Hispanic/Latino; 2% Race/ethnicity unknown; 0.8% international; 12% transferred in; 38% live on campus. *Retention:* 84% of full-time freshmen returned.

Freshmen *Admission:* 8,866 applied, 4,676 admitted, 1,232 enrolled. *Average high school GPA:* 3.71. *Test scores:* SAT critical reading scores over 500: 94%; SAT math scores over 500: 95%; SAT writing scores over 500: 91%; ACT scores over 18: 100%; SAT critical reading scores over 600: 31%; SAT math scores over 600: 42%; SAT writing scores over 600: 29%; ACT scores over 24: 57%; SAT critical reading scores over 700: 3%; SAT math scores over 700: 4%; SAT writing scores over 700: 2%; ACT scores over 30: 5%.

Faculty *Total:* 661, 61% full-time, 56% with terminal degrees. *Student/faculty ratio:* 16:1.

Academics *Calendar:* 4-1-4. *Degrees:* bachelor's, master's, doctoral, and postbachelor's certificates. *Special study options:* accelerated degree program, adult/continuing education programs, advanced placement credit, cooperative education, distance learning, double majors, English as a second language, honors programs, independent study, internships, off-campus study, part-time degree program, services for LD students, student-designed majors, study abroad, summer session for credit. *ROTC:* Army (b), Air Force (c). *Unusual degree programs:* 3-2 engineering with Pre-Engineering Program with University of Maryland College Park, Old Dominion University, and Widener University; social work with Social Work and Sociology Dual Degree Program with University of Maryland Eastern Shore; Biology and Environmental Marine Science with University of Maryland Eastern Shore.

Computers on Campus 531 computers/terminals and 3,552 ports are available on campus for general student use. Students can access the following: campus intranet, computer help desk, free student e-mail accounts, online (class) grades, online (class) registration, online (class) schedules, University accounts. Campuswide network is available. 100% of college-owned or -operated housing units are wired for high-speed Internet access. Wireless service is available via entire campus.

Student Life *Housing options:* coed, disabled students. Campus housing is university owned. Freshman applicants given priority for college housing. *Activities and organizations:* drama/theater group, student-run newspaper, radio and television station, choral group, Student Government Association, Radio (WXSU), Student Organization for Activity Planning (SOAP), Campus Crusade for Christ, Greek Council, national fraternities, national sororities. *Campus security:* 24-hour emergency response devices and patrols, student patrols, late-night transport/escort service, controlled dormitory access, Lighted pathways, Sidewalks, 24-hour University Police protection. *Student services:* health clinic, personal/psychological counseling.

Athletics Member NCAA. All Division III. *Intercollegiate sports:* baseball M, basketball M/W, cross-country running M/W, field hockey W, football M, lacrosse M/W, soccer M/W, softball W, swimming and diving M/W, tennis M/W, track and field M/W, volleyball W. *Intramural sports:* basketball M(c)/W(c), equestrian sports W(c), fencing M(c)/W(c), field hockey W(c), football M/W, golf M(c)/W(c), ice hockey M(c), lacrosse M(c)/W(c), racquetball M/W, rock climbing M/W, rugby M(c)/W(c), sailing M(c)/W(c), soccer M(c)/W(c), softball M/W, ultimate Frisbee M(c)/W(c), volleyball M/W, water polo M/W.

Standardized Tests *Required for some:* SAT or ACT (for admission).

Costs (2012–13) *Tuition:* state resident $5576 full-time, $231 per credit hour part-time; nonresident $13,922 full-time, $578 per credit hour part-time. Full-time tuition and fees vary according to degree level. Part-time tuition and fees vary according to course load and degree level. *Required fees:* $2124 full-time, $77 per credit hour part-time. *Room and board:* $9120; room only: $5250. Room and board charges vary according to board plan and housing facility. *Payment plan:* installment. *Waivers:* senior citizens and employees or children of employees.

Financial Aid Of all full-time matriculated undergraduates who enrolled in 2010, 5,031 applied for aid, 3,523 were judged to have need, 435 had their need fully met. 76 Federal Work-Study jobs (averaging $1970). In 2010, 690 non-need-based awards were made. *Average percent of need met:* 53%. *Average financial aid package:* $7488. *Average need-based loan:* $4023. *Average need-based gift aid:* $4933. *Average non-need-based aid:* $2067. *Average indebtedness upon graduation:* $20,693.

Applying *Options:* electronic application, early admission, early action. *Application fee:* $50. *Required:* essay or personal statement, high school transcript, minimum 2.0 GPA. *Application deadlines:* 1/15 (freshmen), rolling (transfers), 12/1 (early action). *Notification:* 3/15 (freshmen), continuous (transfers), 1/15 (early action).

Freshman Application Contact Mrs. Elizabeth Skoglund, Director of Admissions, Salisbury University, Admissions House, 1101 Camden Avenue, Salisbury, MD 21801. *Phone:* 410-543-6161. *Toll-free phone:* 888-543-0148. *Fax:* 410-546-6016. *E-mail:* admissions@salisbury.edu. *Website:* http://www.salisbury.edu/.

See below for display ad and page 1490 for the College Close-Up.

Sojourner-Douglass College

Baltimore, Maryland

- **Independent** comprehensive, founded 1980
- **Urban** 15-acre campus with easy access to Baltimore
- **Coed, primarily women**
- **Noncompetitive** entrance level

Faculty *Student/faculty ratio:* 5:1.

Academics *Calendar:* trimesters. *Degrees:* bachelor's and master's (offers only evening and weekend programs).

Costs (2012–13) *Tuition:* $8650 full-time. *Required fees:* $200 full-time.

Financial Aid *Of all full-time matriculated undergraduates who enrolled in 2008,* 1,412 applied for aid, 1,412 were judged to have need. 16 Federal Work-Study jobs (averaging $7462). *Average percent of need met:* 35. *Average financial aid package:* $4080. *Average need-based loan:* $6722. *Average need-based gift aid:* $4800. *Average indebtedness upon graduation:* $34,750.

Applying *Options:* deferred entrance. *Application fee:* $25. *Required:* essay or personal statement, high school transcript, 2 letters of recommendation, interview, resume.

Freshman Application Contact Sojourner-Douglass College, 500 North Caroline Street, Baltimore, MD 21205-1814. *Phone:* 410-276-0306 Ext. 251. *Website:* http://sdc.edu/.

Stevenson University

Stevenson, Maryland

- **Independent** comprehensive, founded 1952
- **Suburban** 168-acre campus with easy access to Baltimore
- **Endowment** $44.8 million
- **Coed** 3,904 undergraduate students, 83% full-time, 65% women, 35% men
- **Moderately difficult** entrance level, 59% of applicants were admitted

Undergraduates 3,227 full-time, 677 part-time. 15% are from out of state; 27% Black or African American, non-Hispanic/Latino; 4% Hispanic/Latino; 3% Asian, non-Hispanic/Latino; 0.2% Native Hawaiian or other Pacific Islander, non-Hispanic/Latino; 0.3% American Indian or Alaska Native, non-Hispanic/Latino; 2% Two or more races, non-Hispanic/Latino; 5% Race/ethnicity unknown; 0.4% international; 10% transferred in; 47% live on campus. *Retention:* 69% of full-time freshmen returned.

Freshmen *Admission:* 5,735 applied, 3,369 admitted, 861 enrolled. *Average high school GPA:* 3.38. *Test scores:* SAT critical reading scores over 500: 47%; SAT math scores over 500: 52%; SAT writing scores over 500: 44%; ACT scores over 18: 72%; SAT critical reading scores over 600: 9%; SAT math scores over 600: 12%; SAT writing scores over 600: 9%; ACT scores over 24: 26%; SAT math scores over 700: 1%; ACT scores over 30: 1%.

Faculty *Total:* 502, 24% full-time. *Student/faculty ratio:* 15:1.

Academics *Calendar:* semesters. *Degrees:* bachelor's and master's. *Special study options:* academic remediation for entering students, accelerated degree program, adult/continuing education programs, advanced placement credit, cooperative education, distance learning, double majors, honors programs, independent study, internships, off-campus study, part-time degree program, services for LD students, student-designed majors, study abroad, summer session for credit. *ROTC:* Army (c), Air Force (c).

Computers on Campus 300 computers/terminals and 1,000 ports are available on campus for general student use. Students can access the following: campus intranet, computer help desk, free student e-mail accounts, online (class) grades, online (class) registration, online (class) schedules. Campus-wide network is available. 100% of college-owned or -operated housing units are wired for high-speed Internet access. Wireless service is available via entire campus.

Student Life *Housing options:* Campus housing is university owned. Freshman applicants given priority for college housing. *Activities and organizations:* drama/theater group, student-run newspaper, radio station, choral group, marching band, Student Government Association, MAP, Black Student Union, National Student Nurses Association, Phi Sigma, national sororities. *Campus security:* 24-hour emergency response devices and patrols, late-night transport/escort service, controlled dormitory access, patrols by trained security personnel during campus hours. *Student services:* health clinic, personal/psychological counseling.

Athletics Member NCAA. All Division III. *Intercollegiate sports:* baseball M, basketball M/W, cheerleading M/W, cross-country running M/W, field hockey W, football M, golf M/W, ice hockey W, lacrosse M/W, soccer M/W, softball W, tennis M/W, track and field M/W, volleyball M/W. *Intramural sports:* bad-

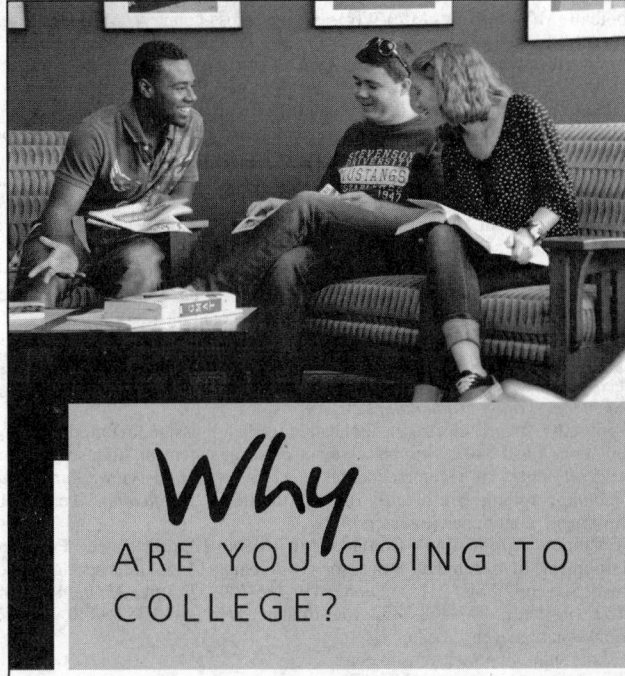

Why

ARE YOU GOING TO COLLEGE?

IF YOU ARE LIKE THE STUDENTS AT STEVENSON, YOU ARE GOING TO COLLEGE BECAUSE AT THE END OF FOUR YEARS, YOU WANT TO BE READY TO TAKE ON THE WORLD.

»» Career-focused academic programs prepare you for the real world. Typical placement rate? **92 PERCENT**.

»» Small classes allow professors to become mentors. Average class size? **17 STUDENTS**.

»» From smart classrooms to new residence halls, Stevenson's campus resources go beyond your expectations. Capacity of SU's new stadium? **3,500 SEATS**.

IMAGINE YOUR FUTURE. DESIGN YOUR CAREER. IT ALL STARTS TODAY.

PLAN YOUR VISIT AND APPLY ONLINE AT **STEVENSON.EDU**

STEVENSON
U N I V E R S I T Y
Imagine your future. Design your career.®

minton M/W, baseball M, basketball M/W, fencing M(c)/W(c), field hockey W, football M/W, sailing M(c)/W(c), skiing (cross-country) M/W(c), skiing (downhill) M/W, softball W, table tennis M/W, tennis M/W, volleyball M. **Standardized Tests** *Required:* SAT or ACT (for admission).

Costs (2012–13) *Comprehensive fee:* $37,204 includes full-time tuition ($23,562), mandatory fees ($1748), and room and board ($11,894). Full-time tuition and fees vary according to degree level. Part-time tuition: $596 per credit hour. Part-time tuition and fees vary according to course load and degree level. *Required fees:* $75 per term part-time. *College room only:* $7888. Room and board charges vary according to board plan and housing facility. *Payment plans:* installment, deferred payment. *Waivers:* employees or children of employees.

Financial Aid Of all full-time matriculated undergraduates who enrolled in 2009, 2,097 applied for aid, 1,806 were judged to have need, 530 had their need fully met. 225 Federal Work-Study jobs (averaging $2000). In 2009, 555 non-need-based awards were made. *Average percent of need met:* 63%. *Average financial aid package:* $14,124. *Average need-based loan:* $4095. *Average need-based gift aid:* $10,967. *Average non-need-based aid:* $6920. *Average indebtedness upon graduation:* $20,779.

Applying *Options:* electronic application, early admission, deferred entrance. *Application fee:* $40. *Required:* essay or personal statement, high school transcript, 2 letters of recommendation. *Recommended:* interview. *Application deadlines:* rolling (freshmen), rolling (transfers). *Notification:* continuous (freshmen), continuous (transfers).

Freshman Application Contact Mr. Mark Hergan, Vice President, Enrollment Management, Stevenson University, 1525 Greenspring Valley Road, Stevenson, MD 21153. *Phone:* 410-486-7001. *Toll-free phone:* 877-468-6852 (in-state); 877-468-3852 (out-of-state). *Fax:* 410-352-4440. *E-mail:* admissions@stevenson.edu.
Website: http://www.stevenson.edu/.

See previous page for display ad and page 1522 for the College Close-Up.

Stratford University

Baltimore, Maryland

- **Proprietary** comprehensive, founded 1972
- **Urban** 6-acre campus with easy access to Baltimore and Washington, DC
- **Coed** 347 undergraduate students, 21% full-time, 54% women, 46% men
- **Minimally difficult** entrance level, 71% of applicants were admitted

Undergraduates 72 full-time, 275 part-time. 12% are from out of state; 70% Black or African American, non-Hispanic/Latino; 2% Hispanic/Latino; 1% Asian, non-Hispanic/Latino; 0.9% Two or more races, non-Hispanic/Latino; 2% Race/ethnicity unknown; 14% transferred in. *Retention:* 87% of full-time freshmen returned.

Freshmen *Admission:* 162 applied, 115 admitted. *Average high school GPA:* 2. **Faculty** *Total:* 31, 42% full-time, 23% with terminal degrees. *Student/faculty ratio:* 20:1.

Academics *Calendar:* semesters. *Degrees:* certificates, associate, bachelor's, and master's. *Special study options:* academic remediation for entering students, accelerated degree program, adult/continuing education programs, advanced placement credit, cooperative education, internships, off-campus study, part-time degree program, services for LD students, summer session for credit.

Computers on Campus 40 computers/terminals are available on campus for general student use. Students can access the following: campus intranet, computer help desk, free student e-mail accounts, online (class) grades, online (class) schedules. Campuswide network is available. Wireless service is available via entire campus.

Student Life *Housing:* college housing not available. *Options:* Campus housing is provided by a third party. *Activities and organizations:* student-run newspaper, Chai Eta Psi / Eta Psi Xi, Gardening Club, Epicurean Club, Enactus, Event Planning Club. *Campus security:* late-night transport/escort service, controlled dormitory access. *Student services:* personal/psychological counseling.

Costs (2013–14) *One-time required fee:* $850. *Tuition:* $14,986 full-time, $370 per quarter hour part-time. Full-time tuition and fees vary according to course load and program. Part-time tuition and fees vary according to course load and program. *Required fees:* $2376 full-time, $176 per quarter hour part-time. *Payment plan:* installment. *Waivers:* employees or children of employees.

Financial Aid Of all full-time matriculated undergraduates who enrolled in 2011, 136 Federal Work-Study jobs (averaging $533).

Applying *Options:* electronic application, early action, deferred entrance. *Application fee:* $50. *Required:* essay or personal statement, high school transcript, minimum 2.0 GPA, interview. *Required for some:* letters of recommendation. *Application deadlines:* rolling (freshmen), rolling (out-of-state

freshmen), rolling (transfers). *Notification:* continuous (freshmen), continuous (out-of-state freshmen), continuous (transfers).

Freshman Application Contact Stratford University, Baltimore, MD. *Phone:* 410-752-4710 Ext. 5390. *Toll-free phone:* 800-624-9926 (in-state); 800-624-9926 Ext. 120 (out-of-state).
Website: http://www.stratford.edu/.

Strayer University—Anne Arundel Campus

Millersville, Maryland

Freshman Application Contact Strayer University—Anne Arundel Campus, 1520 Jabez Run, Millersville, MD 21108.
Website: http://www.strayer.edu/campus/anne-arundel.

Strayer University—Owings Mills Campus

Owings Mills, Maryland

Freshman Application Contact Strayer University—Owings Mills Campus, 500 Redland Court, Suite 100, Owings Mills, MD 21117.
Website: http://www.strayer.edu/campus/owings-mills.

Strayer University—Prince George's Campus

Suitland, Maryland

Freshman Application Contact Strayer University—Prince George's Campus, 4710 Auth Place, First Floor, Suitland, MD 20746.
Website: http://www.strayer.edu/campus/prince-georges.

Strayer University—Rockville Campus

Rockville, Maryland

Freshman Application Contact Strayer University—Rockville Campus, 4 Research Place, Suite 100, Rockville, MD 20850.
Website: http://www.strayer.edu/campus/rockville.

Strayer University—White Marsh Campus

Baltimore, Maryland

Freshman Application Contact Strayer University—White Marsh Campus, 9920 Franklin Square Drive, Suite 200, Baltimore, MD 21236.
Website: http://www.strayer.edu/campus/white-marsh.

Towson University

Towson, Maryland

- **State-supported** university, founded 1866, part of University System of Maryland
- **Suburban** 321-acre campus with easy access to Baltimore and Washington, DC
- **Endowment** $4.4 million
- **Coed**
- **Moderately difficult** entrance level

Faculty *Student/faculty ratio:* 17:1.

Academics *Calendar:* semesters. *Degrees:* bachelor's, master's, doctoral, post-master's, and postbachelor's certificates.

Student Life *Campus security:* 24-hour emergency response devices and patrols, late-night transport/escort service, controlled dormitory access.

Athletics Member NCAA. All Division I except football (Division I-AA).

Standardized Tests *Required:* SAT or ACT (for admission).

Costs (2012–13) *Tuition:* state resident $5660 full-time, $246 per credit hour part-time; nonresident $17,282 full-time, $723 per credit hour part-time. Full-time tuition and fees vary according to course load. Part-time tuition and fees vary according to course load. *Required fees:* $2472 full-time, $103 per credit hour part-time. *Room and board:* $10,338; room only: $5910. Room and board charges vary according to board plan and housing facility.

Financial Aid *Of all full-time matriculated undergraduates who enrolled in 2012,* 11,207 applied for aid, 8,488 were judged to have need, 996 had their need fully met. 365 Federal Work-Study jobs (averaging $1729). *In 2012,* 967 non-need-based awards were made. *Average percent of need met:* 60. *Average financial aid package:* $9169. *Average need-based loan:* $4051. *Average need-based gift aid:* $7816. *Average non-need-based aid:* $4441. *Average indebtedness upon graduation:* $23,812.

Applying *Options:* electronic application, early admission, deferred entrance. *Application fee:* $45. *Required:* high school transcript. *Required for some:* essay or personal statement, interview. *Recommended:* minimum 3.0 GPA, 2 letters of recommendation.

Freshman Application Contact Mr. Brian Hazlett, Director of Admissions, Towson University, 8000 York Road, Towson, MD 21252. *Phone:* 410-704-2113. *Fax:* 410-704-3030. *E-mail:* admissions@towson.edu. *Website:* http://www.towson.edu/.

United States Naval Academy

Annapolis, Maryland

- **Federally supported** 4-year, founded 1845
- **Small-town** 338-acre campus with easy access to Baltimore and Washington, DC
- **Coed, primarily men** 4,536 undergraduate students, 100% full-time, 21% women, 79% men
- **Very difficult** entrance level, 6% of applicants were admitted

Undergraduates 4,536 full-time. Students come from 54 states and territories; 31 other countries; 93% are from out of state; 7% Black or African American, non-Hispanic/Latino; 12% Hispanic/Latino; 5% Asian, non-Hispanic/Latino; 0.7% Native Hawaiian or other Pacific Islander, non-Hispanic/Latino; 0.4% American Indian or Alaska Native, non-Hispanic/Latino; 8% Two or more races, non-Hispanic/Latino; 1% Race/ethnicity unknown; 1% international; 100% live on campus. *Retention:* 97% of full-time freshmen returned.

Freshmen *Admission:* 20,601 applied, 1,211 admitted, 1,186 enrolled. *Test scores:* SAT critical reading scores over 500: 92%; SAT math scores over 500: 99%; SAT critical reading scores over 600: 60%; SAT math scores over 600: 79%; SAT critical reading scores over 700: 17%; SAT math scores over 700: 27%.

Faculty *Total:* 528, 91% full-time, 68% with terminal degrees. *Student/faculty ratio:* 9:1.

Academics *Calendar:* semesters. *Degree:* bachelor's. *Special study options:* academic remediation for entering students, advanced placement credit, double majors, honors programs, independent study, off-campus study, study abroad, summer session for credit.

Computers on Campus 6,100 computers/terminals and 8,000 ports are available on campus for general student use. Students can access the following: campus intranet, computer help desk, free student e-mail accounts, online (class) grades, online (class) registration, online (class) schedules. Campus-wide network is available. 100% of college-owned or -operated housing units are wired for high-speed Internet access. Wireless service is available via classrooms, computer labs, libraries.

Student Life *Housing:* on-campus residence required through senior year. *Options:* coed. Campus housing is university owned. Freshman campus housing is guaranteed. *Activities and organizations:* drama/theater group, student-run radio station, choral group, marching band, Mountaineering Club, Semper Fi, Black Studies Club, Midshipmen Action Club, Martial Arts Club. *Campus security:* 24-hour emergency response devices and patrols, campus gate security. *Student services:* health clinic, personal/psychological counseling, legal services.

Athletics Member NCAA. All Division I except football (Division I-A). *Intercollegiate sports:* baseball M, basketball M/W, cheerleading M(c)/W(c), crew M/W, cross-country running M/W, fencing M(c)/W(c), field hockey W(c), golf M/W, gymnastics M/W(c), ice hockey M(c)/W(c), lacrosse M/W, riflery M/W, rugby M(c)/W(c), sailing M/W, skiing (downhill) M(c)/W(c), soccer M/W, softball W(c), squash M, swimming and diving M/W, tennis M/W, track and

field M/W, volleyball M(c)/W, water polo M, weight lifting M(c)/W(c), wrestling M. *Intramural sports:* basketball M/W, cross-country running M/W, football M/W, lacrosse M(c)/W(c), racquetball M/W, sailing M/W, soccer M/W, softball M/W, volleyball M/W, weight lifting M/W.

Standardized Tests *Required:* SAT or ACT (for admission).

Costs (2013–14) *Comprehensive fee:* No tuition increase for student's term of enrollment. The Navy pays for the tuition, room and board, medical and dental care of Naval Academy midshipmen.

Applying *Options:* electronic application, early action. *Required:* essay or personal statement, high school transcript, 2 letters of recommendation, interview, age 17-22, medical exam, authorized nomination, candidate fitness test. *Application deadline:* 1/31 (freshmen). *Notification:* continuous until 4/15 (freshmen).

Freshman Application Contact Capt. Ann Kubera, Director of Admissions, United States Naval Academy, 52 King George Street, United States Naval Academy, Annapolis, MD 21402. *Phone:* 410-293-4361. *Fax:* 410-293-4348. *E-mail:* webmail@usna.edu. *Website:* http://www.usna.edu/.

University of Baltimore

Baltimore, Maryland

Freshman Application Contact Ms. Brigid H. Lawler, Director, Freshman Admission, University of Baltimore, 1420 North Charles Street, Baltimore, MD 21201. *Phone:* 410-837-4777. *Fax:* 410-837-4793. *E-mail:* admissions@ubalt.edu. *Website:* http://www.ubalt.edu/.

University of Maryland, Baltimore County

Baltimore, Maryland

- **State-supported** university, founded 1963, part of University System of Maryland
- **Suburban** 530-acre campus with easy access to Washington, DC
- **Endowment** $59.7 million
- **Coed** 10,953 undergraduate students, 86% full-time, 45% women, 55% men
- **Moderately difficult** entrance level, 60% of applicants were admitted

Undergraduates 9,371 full-time, 1,582 part-time. Students come from 40 states and territories; 85 other countries; 6% are from out of state; 16% Black or African American, non-Hispanic/Latino; 5% Hispanic/Latino; 20% Asian, non-Hispanic/Latino; 0.2% Native Hawaiian or other Pacific Islander, non-Hispanic/Latino; 0.2% American Indian or Alaska Native, non-Hispanic/Latino; 3% Two or more races, non-Hispanic/Latino; 4% Race/ethnicity unknown; 4% international; 12% transferred in; 34% live on campus. *Retention:* 85% of full-time freshmen returned.

Freshmen *Admission:* 8,514 applied, 5,138 admitted, 1,560 enrolled. *Average high school GPA:* 3.71. *Test scores:* SAT critical reading scores over 500: 92%; SAT math scores over 500: 97%; SAT writing scores over 500: 89%; ACT scores over 18: 98%; SAT critical reading scores over 600: 48%; SAT math scores over 600: 69%; SAT writing scores over 600: 47%; ACT scores over 24: 82%; SAT critical reading scores over 700: 11%; SAT math scores over 700: 19%; SAT writing scores over 700: 9%; ACT scores over 30: 24%.

Faculty *Total:* 776, 64% full-time, 67% with terminal degrees. *Student/faculty ratio:* 20:1.

Academics *Calendar:* 4-1-4. *Degrees:* bachelor's, master's, doctoral, and postbachelor's certificates. *Special study options:* academic remediation for entering students, adult/continuing education programs, advanced placement credit, cooperative education, distance learning, double majors, English as a second language, external degree program, freshman honors college, honors programs, independent study, internships, off-campus study, part-time degree program, services for LD students, student-designed majors, study abroad, summer session for credit. *ROTC:* Army (c), Air Force (c).

Computers on Campus 965 computers/terminals are available on campus for general student use. Students can access the following: campus intranet, computer help desk, free student e-mail accounts, online (class) grades, online (class) registration, online (class) schedules, student account information. Campuswide network is available. 100% of college-owned or -operated housing units are wired for high-speed Internet access. Wireless service is available via classrooms, computer centers, computer labs, libraries, student centers.

Student Life *Housing options:* coed, disabled students. Campus housing is university owned and is provided by a third party. Freshman campus housing is guaranteed. *Activities and organizations:* drama/theater group, student-run newspaper, radio station, choral group, Student Government Association, Student Events Board, Retriever Weekly, Resident Student Association, Freedom Alliance, national fraternities, national sororities. *Campus security:* 24-hour emergency response devices and patrols, late-night transport/escort service. *Student services:* health clinic, personal/psychological counseling, women's center, legal services.

Athletics Member NCAA. All Division I. *Intercollegiate sports:* badminton M(c)/W(c), baseball M(s), basketball M(s)/W(s), bowling M(c)/W(c), crew M(c)/W(c), cross-country running M(s)/W(s), fencing M(c)/W(c), field hockey W(c), ice hockey M(c), lacrosse M(s)/W(s), rugby M(c)/W(c), sailing M(c)/W(c), skiing (downhill) M(c)/W(c), soccer M(s)/W(s), softball W(s), swimming and diving M(s)/W(s), tennis M(s)/W(s), track and field M(s)/W(s), ultimate Frisbee M(c)/W(c), volleyball M(c)/W(c), wrestling M(c). *Intramural sports:* basketball M/W, football M/W, lacrosse M(c)/W(c), soccer M(c)/W(c), softball M/W, tennis M(c)/W(c), volleyball M/W/W(c).

Standardized Tests *Required:* SAT or ACT (for admission).

Costs (2012–13) *One-time required fee:* $125. *Tuition:* state resident $7085 full-time, $295 per credit hour part-time; nonresident $18,146 full-time, $754 per credit hour part-time. Full-time tuition and fees vary according to location and program. Part-time tuition and fees vary according to location and program. *Required fees:* $2679 full-time, $115 per credit hour part-time. *Room and board:* $10,142; room only: $6126. Room and board charges vary according to board plan and housing facility. *Payment plan:* installment. *Waivers:* senior citizens and employees or children of employees.

Financial Aid Of all full-time matriculated undergraduates who enrolled in 2012, 6,100 applied for aid, 4,894 were judged to have need, 471 had their need fully met. 94 Federal Work-Study jobs (averaging $2089). In 2012, 1064 non-need-based awards were made. *Average percent of need met:* 56%. *Average financial aid package:* $10,436. *Average need-based loan:* $4228. *Average need-based gift aid:* $7396. *Average non-need-based aid:* $8443. *Average indebtedness upon graduation:* $22,601.

Applying *Options:* electronic application, early admission, early action, deferred entrance. *Application fee:* $50. *Required:* essay or personal statement, high school transcript. *Recommended:* minimum 3.0 GPA, 2 letters of recommendation. *Application deadlines:* 2/1 (freshmen), 5/31 (transfers), 11/1 (early action). *Notification:* continuous (freshmen), continuous (transfers), 12/15 (early action).

Freshman Application Contact Mr. Dale Bittinger, Director of Admissions, University of Maryland, Baltimore County, 1000 Hilltop Circle, Baltimore, MD 21250. *Phone:* 410-455-2291. *Toll-free phone:* 800-UMBC-4U2 (in-state); 800-862-2402 (out-of-state). *Fax:* 410-455-1094. *E-mail:* admissions@umbc.edu.
Website: http://www.umbc.edu/.

University of Maryland, College Park

College Park, Maryland

- **State-supported** university, founded 1856, part of University System of Maryland
- **Suburban** 1500-acre campus with easy access to Baltimore and Washington, DC
- **Endowment** $377.1 million
- **Coed** 26,487 undergraduate students, 92% full-time, 47% women, 53% men
- **Moderately difficult** entrance level, 47% of applicants were admitted

Undergraduates 24,448 full-time, 2,039 part-time. Students come from 48 states and territories; 103 other countries; 23% are from out of state; 12% Black or African American, non-Hispanic/Latino; 8% Hispanic/Latino; 15% Asian, non-Hispanic/Latino; 0.1% Native Hawaiian or other Pacific Islander, non-Hispanic/Latino; 0.1% American Indian or Alaska Native, non-Hispanic/Latino; 3% Two or more races, non-Hispanic/Latino; 3% Race/ethnicity unknown; 3% international; 7% transferred in; 47% live on campus. *Retention:* 94% of full-time freshmen returned.

Freshmen *Admission:* 25,255 applied, 11,825 admitted, 3,903 enrolled. *Average high school GPA:* 4.07. *Test scores:* SAT critical reading scores over 500: 94%; SAT math scores over 500: 96%; SAT critical reading scores over 600: 68%; SAT math scores over 600: 80%; SAT critical reading scores over 700: 21%; SAT math scores over 700: 37%.

Faculty *Total:* 2,375, 71% full-time, 80% with terminal degrees. *Student/faculty ratio:* 18:1.

Academics *Calendar:* semesters. *Degrees:* certificates, bachelor's, master's, doctoral, post-master's, and postbachelor's certificates. *Special study options:* academic remediation for entering students, accelerated degree program, adult/

continuing education programs, advanced placement credit, cooperative education, distance learning, double majors, English as a second language, external degree program, honors programs, independent study, internships, off-campus study, part-time degree program, services for LD students, student-designed majors, study abroad, summer session for credit. *ROTC:* Army (b), Navy (c), Air Force (b).

Computers on Campus 3,890 computers/terminals are available on campus for general student use. Students can access the following: campus intranet, computer help desk, free student e-mail accounts, online (class) grades, online (class) registration, online (class) schedules, student account information, financial aid summary. Campuswide network is available. 100% of college-owned or -operated housing units are wired for high-speed Internet access. Wireless service is available via entire campus.

Student Life *Housing options:* coed, women-only, cooperative, disabled students. Campus housing is university owned and is provided by a third party. Freshman campus housing is guaranteed. *Activities and organizations:* drama/theater group, student-run newspaper, radio and television station, choral group, marching band, Student Government Association, Residence Hall Association, Black Student Union, Asian-American Student Union/Jewish Student Union, Commuter Students Association, national fraternities, national sororities. *Campus security:* 24-hour emergency response devices and patrols, student patrols, late-night transport/escort service, controlled dormitory access, campus police, video camera surveillance. *Student services:* health clinic, personal/psychological counseling, women's center, legal services.

Athletics Member NCAA. All Division I except football (Division I-A). *Intercollegiate sports:* baseball M(s), basketball M(s)/W(s), cheerleading W(s), cross-country running M/W(s), field hockey W(s), golf M(s)/W(s), gymnastics W, lacrosse M(s)/W(s), soccer M(s)/W(s), softball W(s), swimming and diving M/W, tennis M/W, track and field M/W(s), volleyball W(s), water polo W(s), wrestling M(s). *Intramural sports:* badminton M(c)/W(c), baseball M(c), basketball M/W, crew M(c)/W(c), cross-country running M/W, equestrian sports M(c)/W(c), fencing M(c)/W(c), field hockey W(c), football M/W, golf M/W, ice hockey M(c)/W(c), lacrosse M(c)/W(c), racquetball M(c)/W(c), rock climbing M(c)/W(c), rugby M(c)/W(c), sailing M(c)/W(c), soccer M(c)/W(c), softball W, squash M(c)/W(c), swimming and diving M(c)/W(c), table tennis M/W, tennis M/W, track and field M/W, ultimate Frisbee M/W, volleyball M(c)/W(c), water polo M(c)/W(c), weight lifting M/W, wrestling M.

Standardized Tests *Required:* SAT or ACT (for admission).

Costs (2012–13) *Tuition:* state resident $7175 full-time, $299 per credit hour part-time; nonresident $25,554 full-time, $1065 per credit hour part-time. Part-time tuition and fees vary according to course load. *Required fees:* $1734 full-time, $400 per term part-time. *Room and board:* $9893; room only: $5918. Room and board charges vary according to board plan and housing facility. *Payment plans:* installment, deferred payment. *Waivers:* employees or children of employees.

Financial Aid Of all full-time matriculated undergraduates who enrolled in 2011, 14,885 applied for aid, 11,002 were judged to have need, 1,619 had their need fully met. 2,130 Federal Work-Study jobs (averaging $2154). In 2011, 2985 non-need-based awards were made. *Average percent of need met:* 63%. *Average financial aid package:* $11,026. *Average need-based loan:* $4691. *Average need-based gift aid:* $6840. *Average non-need-based aid:* $6482. *Average indebtedness upon graduation:* $25,276.

Applying *Options:* electronic application, early admission, early action, deferred entrance. *Application fee:* $65. *Required:* essay or personal statement, high school transcript. *Required for some:* Resume of activities; audition for music applicants; drawing requirement for architecture applicants. *Recommended:* 2 letters of recommendation. *Application deadlines:* 1/20 (freshmen), 6/1 (transfers), 11/1 (early action). *Notification:* 4/1 (freshmen), continuous (transfers), 1/31 (early action).

Freshman Application Contact Ms. Barbara Gill, Director of Undergraduate Admissions, University of Maryland, College Park, College Park, MD 20742. *Phone:* 301-314-8385. *Toll-free phone:* 800-422-5867. *Fax:* 301-314-9693. *Website:* http://www.maryland.edu/.

University of Maryland Eastern Shore

Princess Anne, Maryland

- **State-supported** university, founded 1886, part of University System of Maryland
- **Rural** 744-acre campus
- **Coed** 3,758 undergraduate students, 92% full-time, 57% women, 43% men
- **Moderately difficult** entrance level, 57% of applicants were admitted

Undergraduates 3,449 full-time, 309 part-time. 19% are from out of state; 77% Black or African American, non-Hispanic/Latino; 2% Hispanic/Latino; 1% Asian, non-Hispanic/Latino; 0.1% Native Hawaiian or other Pacific Islander, non-Hispanic/Latino; 0.1% American Indian or Alaska Native, non-Hispanic/Latino; 4% Two or more races, non-Hispanic/Latino; 2% Race/ethnicity unknown; 3% international; 6% transferred in; 60% live on campus.
Freshmen *Admission:* 4,409 applied, 2,535 admitted, 886 enrolled. *Average high school GPA:* 2.8. *Test scores:* SAT critical reading scores over 500: 20%; SAT math scores over 500: 20%; ACT scores over 18: 40%; SAT critical reading scores over 600: 4%; SAT math scores over 600: 3%; ACT scores over 24: 5%.
Faculty *Total:* 345, 63% full-time, 58% with terminal degrees. *Student/faculty ratio:* 16:1.
Academics *Calendar:* semesters. *Degrees:* certificates, bachelor's, master's, and doctoral. *Special study options:* part-time degree program. *ROTC:* Army (c).
Computers on Campus Students can access the following: computer help desk, free student e-mail accounts, online (class) grades, online (class) registration, online (class) schedules. Campuswide network is available. Wireless service is available via classrooms, computer centers, computer labs, learning centers, libraries, student centers.
Student Life *Housing options:* coed, men-only, women-only. Campus housing is university owned. *Campus security:* 24-hour emergency response devices and patrols, student patrols, late-night transport/escort service, controlled dormitory access.
Athletics Member NCAA. All Division I. *Intercollegiate sports:* baseball M(s), basketball M(s)/W(s), cheerleading M/W, cross-country running M/W, softball W, tennis M(s)/W, track and field M/W, volleyball W, wrestling M. *Intramural sports:* basketball M/W, bowling W, cheerleading M/W, cross-country running M/W, soccer M/W, softball W, swimming and diving M/W, table tennis M/W, tennis M/W, track and field M/W, volleyball M/W, wrestling M.
Standardized Tests *Required:* SAT or ACT (for admission).
Costs (2013–14) *Tuition:* state resident $4628 full-time, $193 per credit hour part-time; nonresident $13,134 full-time, $484 per credit hour part-time. Full-time tuition and fees vary according to course load. Part-time tuition and fees vary according to course load. *Required fees:* $2370 full-time. *Room and board:* $8374; room only: $4324. Room and board charges vary according to board plan and housing facility. *Payment plans:* installment, deferred payment. *Waivers:* senior citizens and employees or children of employees.
Financial Aid Of all full-time matriculated undergraduates who enrolled in 2011, 3,352 applied for aid, 2,909 were judged to have need. 80 Federal Work-Study jobs (averaging $2647). In 2011, 150 non-need-based awards were made. *Average percent of need met:* 51%. *Average financial aid package:* $9034. *Average need-based loan:* $4031. *Average need-based gift aid:* $7174. *Average non-need-based aid:* $12,202. *Average indebtedness upon graduation:* $27,215.
Applying *Options:* electronic application, deferred entrance. *Application fee:* $25. *Required:* essay or personal statement, high school transcript, minimum 2.5 GPA, 3 letters of recommendation. *Required for some:* essay or personal statement, interview. *Application deadlines:* 7/15 (freshmen), 5/1 (transfers).
Freshman Application Contact University of Maryland Eastern Shore, Princess Anne, MD 21853-1299. *Phone:* 410-651-6410.
Website: http://www.umes.edu/.

University of Maryland University College
Adelphi, Maryland

- **State-supported** comprehensive, founded 1947, part of University System of Maryland
- **Suburban** campus with easy access to Washington, DC
- **Coed** 28,273 undergraduate students, 22% full-time, 51% women, 49% men
- **Noncompetitive** entrance level, 100% of applicants were admitted

Undergraduates 6,144 full-time, 22,129 part-time. Students come from 54 states and territories; 26 other countries; 44% are from out of state; 31% Black or African American, non-Hispanic/Latino; 8% Hispanic/Latino; 4% Asian, non-Hispanic/Latino; 0.4% Native Hawaiian or other Pacific Islander, non-Hispanic/Latino; 0.5% American Indian or Alaska Native, non-Hispanic/Latino; 3% Two or more races, non-Hispanic/Latino; 10% Race/ethnicity unknown; 1% international; 13% transferred in.
Freshmen *Admission:* 3,308 applied, 3,307 admitted, 1,406 enrolled.
Faculty *Total:* 2,712, 8% full-time, 66% with terminal degrees. *Student/faculty ratio:* 18:1.

Academics *Calendar:* semesters. *Degrees:* certificates, associate, bachelor's, master's, doctoral, post-master's, and postbachelor's certificates (offers primarily part-time evening and weekend degree programs at more than 30 off-campus locations in Maryland and the Washington, DC area, and more than 180 military communities in Europe and Asia with military enrollment not reflected in this profile; associate of arts program available to military students only). *Special study options:* accelerated degree program, advanced placement credit, cooperative education, distance learning, double majors, external degree program, independent study, off-campus study, part-time degree program, services for LD students, summer session for credit.
Computers on Campus 363 computers/terminals are available on campus for general student use. Students can access the following: computer help desk, online (class) grades, online (class) registration, online (class) schedules. Campuswide network is available. Wireless service is available via entire campus.
Student Life *Housing:* college housing not available. *Campus security:* 24-hour emergency response devices and patrols, late-night transport/escort service.
Costs (2012–13) *Tuition:* state resident $6024 full-time, $251 per credit hour part-time; nonresident $11,976 full-time, $499 per credit hour part-time. *Required fees:* $360 full-time, $15 per credit hour part-time. *Payment plan:* installment. *Waivers:* senior citizens and employees or children of employees.
Financial Aid Of all full-time matriculated undergraduates who enrolled in 2011, 3,608 applied for aid, 3,427 were judged to have need, 32 had their need fully met. *Average percent of need met:* 31%. *Average financial aid package:* $7382. *Average need-based loan:* $4213. *Average need-based gift aid:* $4586.
Applying *Options:* electronic application, deferred entrance. *Application fee:* $50. *Required:* high school transcript. *Application deadlines:* rolling (freshmen), rolling (transfers). *Notification:* continuous (freshmen), continuous (transfers).
Freshman Application Contact University of Maryland University College, 3501 University Boulevard East, Adelphi, MD 20783. *Phone:* 800-888-UMUC (8682). *Toll-free phone:* 800-888-8682. *E-mail:* enroll@umuc.edu. *Website:* http://www.umuc.edu/.

University of Phoenix–Maryland Campus
Columbia, Maryland

Freshman Application Contact Marc Booker, Sr. Director, Office of Admissions and Evaluation, University of Phoenix–Maryland Campus, 4035 South Riverpoint Parkway, Mail Stop CF-L101, Phoenix, AZ 85040. *Phone:* 602-557-4609. *Toll-free phone:* 866-766-0766. *Fax:* 480-643-1156. *Website:* http://www.phoenix.edu/.

Washington Adventist University
Takoma Park, Maryland

- **Independent Seventh-day Adventist** comprehensive, founded 1904
- **Suburban** campus
- **Coed**
- **Moderately difficult** entrance level

Faculty *Student/faculty ratio:* 14:1.
Academics *Calendar:* semesters. *Degrees:* certificates, associate, bachelor's, and master's.
Student Life *Campus security:* 24-hour emergency response devices and patrols, late-night transport/escort service.
Athletics Member NCAA. All Division II.
Standardized Tests *Required:* SAT or ACT (for admission).
Costs (2012–13) *Comprehensive fee:* $27,820 includes full-time tuition ($18,900), mandatory fees ($1320), and room and board ($7600). Part-time tuition: $760 per credit hour. Part-time tuition and fees vary according to class time and course load. *Required fees:* $433 per term part-time. *Room and board:* Room and board charges vary according to housing facility.
Financial Aid *Of all full-time matriculated undergraduates who enrolled in 2009,* 883 applied for aid, 702 were judged to have need.
Applying *Options:* electronic application, early admission, deferred entrance. *Application fee:* $25. *Required:* essay or personal statement, high school transcript, minimum 2.5 GPA, 2 letters of recommendation. *Required for some:* interview.
Freshman Application Contact Elaine Oliver, Associate Vice President, Enrollment Services, Washington Adventist University, 7600 Flower Avenue,

Takoma Park, MD 20912. *Phone:* 301-891-4502. *Toll-free phone:* 800-835-4212. *Fax:* 301-971-4230. *E-mail:* enroll@cuc.edu. *Website:* http://www.wau.edu/.

Washington Bible College

Lanham, Maryland

Freshman Application Contact Mr. Mark D. Johnson, Director of Admissions, Washington Bible College, 6511 Princess Garden Parkway, Lanham, MD 20706-3599. *Phone:* 877-793-7227. *Toll-free phone:* 877-793-7227 Ext. 1212. *Fax:* 301-552-2775. *E-mail:* admissions@bible.edu. *Website:* http://www.bible.edu/.

Washington College

Chestertown, Maryland

- **Independent** comprehensive, founded 1782
- **Small-town** 140-acre campus with easy access to Baltimore and Washington, DC
- **Endowment** $173.0 million
- **Coed** 1,562 undergraduate students, 97% full-time, 60% women, 40% men
- **Moderately difficult** entrance level, 66% of applicants were admitted

Undergraduates 1,519 full-time, 43 part-time. 49% are from out of state; 3% Black or African American, non-Hispanic/Latino; 4% Hispanic/Latino; 2% Asian, non-Hispanic/Latino; 0.1% American Indian or Alaska Native, non-Hispanic/Latino; 2% Two or more races, non-Hispanic/Latino; 5% Race/ethnicity unknown; 5% international; 2% transferred in; 85% live on campus. *Retention:* 85% of full-time freshmen returned.
Freshmen *Admission:* 4,484 applied, 2,976 admitted, 447 enrolled. *Average high school GPA:* 3.48. *Test scores:* SAT critical reading scores over 500: 91%; SAT math scores over 500: 88%; ACT scores over 18: 100%; SAT critical reading scores over 600: 43%; SAT math scores over 600: 41%; ACT scores over 24: 68%; SAT critical reading scores over 700: 5%; SAT math scores over 700: 4%; ACT scores over 30: 9%.
Faculty *Total:* 172, 53% full-time, 72% with terminal degrees. *Student/faculty ratio:* 12:1.
Academics *Calendar:* semesters. *Degrees:* bachelor's and master's. *Special study options:* advanced placement credit, double majors, English as a second language, honors programs, independent study, internships, off-campus study, part-time degree program, services for LD students, student-designed majors, study abroad. *Unusual degree programs:* 3-2 engineering with University of Maryland, College Park; nursing with Johns Hopkins University.
Computers on Campus 100 computers/terminals and 225 ports are available on campus for general student use. Students can access the following: campus intranet, computer help desk, free student e-mail accounts, online (class) grades, online (class) registration, online (class) schedules, thousands of wireless addresses available for students. Campuswide network is available. 100% of college-owned or -operated housing units are wired for high-speed Internet access. Wireless service is available via entire campus.
Student Life *Housing:* on-campus residence required through sophomore year. *Options:* coed, men-only, women-only, disabled students. Campus housing is university owned. Freshman campus housing is guaranteed. *Activities and organizations:* drama/theater group, student-run newspaper, radio station, choral group, Writers Union, Student Government Association, Hands Out, Omicron Delta Kappa, Dale Adams Society, national fraternities, national sororities. *Campus security:* 24-hour emergency response devices and patrols, student patrols, late-night transport/escort service, controlled dormitory access. *Student services:* health clinic, personal/psychological counseling.
Athletics Member NCAA. All Division III. *Intercollegiate sports:* baseball M, basketball M/W, cheerleading W(c), crew M/W, equestrian sports M(c)/W(c), field hockey W, ice hockey M(c), lacrosse M/W, rugby M(c)/W(c), sailing M/W, soccer M/W, softball W, swimming and diving M/W, tennis M/W, volleyball W, water polo M(c)/W(c). *Intramural sports:* basketball M/W, football M/W, lacrosse M(c), racquetball M/W, rugby M/W, sailing M/W, soccer M/W, squash M/W, table tennis M/W, tennis M/W, ultimate Frisbee M/W.
Standardized Tests *Required:* SAT or ACT (for admission).
Costs (2013–14) *Comprehensive fee:* $48,768 includes full-time tuition ($39,208), mandatory fees ($736), and room and board ($8824). Part-time tuition: $1578 per credit hour. Part-time tuition and fees vary according to course load. *College room only:* $4482. Room and board charges vary according to board plan, housing facility, and location. *Payment plans:* tuition prepayment, installment. *Waivers:* employees or children of employees.

Financial Aid Of all full-time matriculated undergraduates who enrolled in 2011, 1,040 applied for aid, 914 were judged to have need, 265 had their need fully met. In 2011, 358 non-need-based awards were made. *Average percent of need met:* 75%. *Average financial aid package:* $24,814. *Average need-based loan:* $3812. *Average need-based gift aid:* $21,015. *Average non-need-based aid:* $14,063. *Average indebtedness upon graduation:* $37,303.
Applying *Options:* electronic application, early admission, early decision, early action, deferred entrance. *Application fee:* $50. *Required:* essay or personal statement, high school transcript, 1 letter of recommendation. *Required for some:* interview. *Recommended:* interview. *Application deadlines:* rolling (freshmen), 12/1 (early action). *Early decision deadline:* 11/1. *Notification:* continuous (freshmen), 12/1 (early decision), 1/15 (early action).
Freshman Application Contact Mr. Kevin Coveney, Vice President for Admissions and Enrollment Management, Washington College, 300 Washington Avenue, Chesterton, MD 21620. *Phone:* 410-778-7700. *Toll-free phone:* 800-422-1782. *Fax:* 410-778-7287. *E-mail:* admissions_office@washcoll.edu. *Website:* http://www.washcoll.edu/.

Yeshiva College of the Nation's Capital

Silver Spring, Maryland

Admissions Office Contact Yeshiva College of the Nation's Capital, 1216 Arcola Avenue, Silver Spring, MD 20902. *Website:* http://www.yeshiva.edu/.

MASSACHUSETTS

American International College

Springfield, Massachusetts

Freshman Application Contact Miss Kim LaBlanc, Director of Freshman Admissions, American International College, 1000 State Street, Springfield, MA 01109-3189. *Phone:* 413-205-3275. *Toll-free phone:* 800-242-3142. *Fax:* 413-205-3051. *E-mail:* kim.lablanc@aic.edu. *Website:* http://www.aic.edu/.

Amherst College

Amherst, Massachusetts

- **Independent** 4-year, founded 1821
- **Small-town** 1020-acre campus
- **Endowment** $1.6 billion
- **Coed** 1,817 undergraduate students, 100% full-time, 49% women, 51% men
- **Most difficult** entrance level, 13% of applicants were admitted

Undergraduates 1,817 full-time. Students come from 50 states and territories; 50 other countries; 86% are from out of state; 11% Black or African American, non-Hispanic/Latino; 12% Hispanic/Latino; 12% Asian, non-Hispanic/Latino; 0.1% American Indian or Alaska Native, non-Hispanic/Latino; 6% Two or more races, non-Hispanic/Latino; 9% Race/ethnicity unknown; 10% international; 0.7% transferred in; 99% live on campus. *Retention:* 98% of full-time freshmen returned.
Freshmen *Admission:* 8,565 applied, 1,110 admitted, 463 enrolled. *Test scores:* SAT critical reading scores over 500: 100%; SAT math scores over 500: 100%; SAT writing scores over 500: 100%; ACT scores over 18: 100%; SAT critical reading scores over 600: 98%; SAT math scores over 600: 98%; SAT writing scores over 600: 96%; ACT scores over 24: 99%; SAT critical reading scores over 700: 65%; SAT math scores over 700: 64%; SAT writing scores over 700: 61%; ACT scores over 30: 80%.
Faculty *Total:* 253, 83% full-time, 97% with terminal degrees. *Student/faculty ratio:* 8:1.
Academics *Calendar:* semesters. *Degree:* bachelor's. *Special study options:* double majors, honors programs, independent study, off-campus study, student-designed majors, study abroad. *ROTC:* Army (c), Air Force (c).
Computers on Campus 182 computers/terminals are available on campus for general student use. Students can access the following: campus intranet, com-

puter help desk, free student e-mail accounts, online (class) grades, online (class) schedules. Campuswide network is available. 100% of college-owned or -operated housing units are wired for high-speed Internet access. Wireless service is available via entire campus.

Student Life *Housing:* on-campus residence required through senior year. *Options:* coed, cooperative, disabled students. Campus housing is university owned. Freshman campus housing is guaranteed. *Activities and organizations:* drama/theater group, student-run newspaper, radio station, choral group, choral groups, WAMH (campus radio station), OUTREACH (community service), literary magazines, The Amherst Student (school newspaper). *Campus security:* 24-hour emergency response devices and patrols, student patrols, late-night transport/escort service, controlled dormitory access. *Student services:* health clinic, personal/psychological counseling, women's center.

Athletics Member NCAA. All Division III. *Intercollegiate sports:* baseball M, basketball M/W, crew M(c)/W(c), cross-country running M/W, equestrian sports M(c)/W(c), fencing M(c)/W(c), field hockey W, football M, golf M/W, ice hockey M/W, lacrosse M/W, rugby M(c)/W(c), sailing M(c)/W(c), skiing (downhill) M(c)/W(c), soccer M/W, softball W, squash M/W, swimming and diving M/W, tennis M/W, track and field M/W, ultimate Frisbee M(c)/W(c), volleyball M(c)/W, water polo M(c)/W(c), wrestling M(c)/W(c). *Intramural sports:* badminton M/W, basketball M/W, golf M/W, ice hockey M/W, soccer M/W, softball M/W, squash M/W, table tennis M/W, tennis M/W, track and field M/W, volleyball M/W.

Standardized Tests *Required:* SAT and SAT Subject Tests or ACT (for admission).

Costs (2012–13) *Comprehensive fee:* $56,260 includes full-time tuition ($43,860), mandatory fees ($750), and room and board ($11,650). *College room only:* $6310. *Payment plans:* installment, deferred payment.

Financial Aid Of all full-time matriculated undergraduates who enrolled in 2012, 1,197 applied for aid, 1,067 were judged to have need, 1,067 had their need fully met. 616 Federal Work-Study jobs (averaging $1672). 245 state and other part-time jobs (averaging $1680). *Average percent of need met:* 100%. *Average financial aid package:* $44,888. *Average need-based loan:* $2898. *Average need-based gift aid:* $43,424. *Average indebtedness upon graduation:* $14,566.

Applying *Options:* electronic application, early admission, early decision, deferred entrance. *Application fee:* $60. *Required:* essay or personal statement, high school transcript, 3 letters of recommendation. *Application deadlines:* 1/1 (freshmen), 3/1 (transfers). *Early decision deadline:* 11/15. *Notification:* 4/1 (freshmen), 6/1 (transfers), 12/15 (early decision).

Freshman Application Contact Mr. Thomas H. Parker, Dean of Admission and Financial Aid, Amherst College, PO Box 5000, Amherst, MA 01002-5000. *Phone:* 413-542-2328. *Fax:* 413-542-2040. *E-mail:* admission@amherst.edu. *Website:* http://www.amherst.edu/.

Anna Maria College

Paxton, Massachusetts

- **Independent Roman Catholic** comprehensive, founded 1946
- **Rural** 192-acre campus with easy access to Boston
- **Endowment** $4.7 million
- **Coed**
- **Minimally difficult** entrance level

Faculty *Student/faculty ratio:* 12:1.

Academics *Calendar:* semesters. *Degrees:* certificates, associate, bachelor's, master's, post-master's, and postbachelor's certificates.

Student Life *Campus security:* 24-hour emergency response devices and patrols, late-night transport/escort service, controlled dormitory access.

Athletics Member NCAA. All Division III.

Standardized Tests *Required:* SAT or ACT (for admission).

Costs (2012–13) *Comprehensive fee:* $41,906 includes full-time tuition ($28,752), mandatory fees ($1704), and room and board ($11,450). Full-time tuition and fees vary according to course load and program. Part-time tuition and fees vary according to class time, course load, and program. *Room and board:* Room and board charges vary according to board plan and housing facility.

Financial Aid *Of all full-time matriculated undergraduates who enrolled in 2011,* 771 applied for aid, 717 were judged to have need, 152 had their need fully met. 123 Federal Work-Study jobs (averaging $1816). *In 2011,* 18 non-need-based awards were made. *Average financial aid package:* $22,424. *Average need-based loan:* $2248. *Average need-based gift aid:* $9483. *Average non-need-based aid:* $3542. *Average indebtedness upon graduation:* $38,436.

Applying *Options:* electronic application, deferred entrance. *Application fee:* $40. *Required:* high school transcript, minimum 2.0 GPA. *Required for some:* essay or personal statement, audition for music programs, portfolio for art programs. *Recommended:* 1 letter of recommendation, interview.

Freshman Application Contact Ms. Meghan McDonough, Director of Admissions, Anna Maria College, Box O, Sunset Lane, Paxton, MA 01612. *Phone:* 508-849-3586. *Fax:* 508-849-3362. *E-mail:* admissions@annamaria.edu.
Website: http://www.annamaria.edu/.

See previous page for display ad and page 1044 for the College Close-Up.

Assumption College

Worcester, Massachusetts

- **Independent Roman Catholic** comprehensive, founded 1904
- **Suburban** 180-acre campus with easy access to Boston
- **Endowment** $79.2 million
- **Coed** 2,056 undergraduate students, 99% full-time, 60% women, 40% men
- **Moderately difficult** entrance level, 75% of applicants were admitted

Undergraduates 2,031 full-time, 25 part-time. Students come from 25 states and territories; 28 other countries; 37% are from out of state; 4% Black or African American, non-Hispanic/Latino; 6% Hispanic/Latino; 2% Asian, non-Hispanic/Latino; 0.1% American Indian or Alaska Native, non-Hispanic/Latino; 2% Two or more races, non-Hispanic/Latino; 11% Race/ethnicity unknown; 0.7% international; 2% transferred in; 92% live on campus. *Retention:* 81% of full-time freshmen returned.

Freshmen *Admission:* 4,440 applied, 3,345 admitted, 559 enrolled. *Average high school GPA:* 3.29. *Test scores:* SAT critical reading scores over 500: 81%; SAT math scores over 500: 87%; ACT scores over 18: 100%; SAT critical reading scores over 600: 25%; SAT math scores over 600: 29%; ACT scores over 24: 63%; SAT math scores over 700: 2%; ACT scores over 30: 12%.

Faculty *Total:* 228, 64% full-time, 79% with terminal degrees. *Student/faculty ratio:* 12:1.

Academics *Calendar:* semesters. *Degrees:* bachelor's, master's, post-master's, and postbachelor's certificates. *Special study options:* advanced placement credit, double majors, honors programs, independent study, internships, off-campus study, part-time degree program, services for LD students, student-designed majors, study abroad, summer session for credit. *ROTC:* Army (c), Air Force (c). *Unusual degree programs:* 3-2 business administration; engineering with University of Notre Dame; forestry with Duke University; nursing with Massachusetts College of Pharmacy and Health Sciences; special education, rehabilitation counseling, school counseling; law (JD) with Duquesne U Sch of Law, Western NE Col Sch of Law, Vermont Law Sch; optometry with New England Col of Optometry; osteopathic medicine with Des Moines U; environmental science management with Duke U; see catalog for others.

Computers on Campus 361 computers/terminals and 1,900 ports are available on campus for general student use. Students can access the following: campus intranet, computer help desk, free student e-mail accounts, online (class) grades, online (class) registration, online (class) schedules. Campus-wide network is available. 100% of college-owned or -operated housing units are wired for high-speed Internet access. Wireless service is available via entire campus.

Student Life *Housing options:* coed, women-only, disabled students. Campus housing is university owned. Freshman campus housing is guaranteed. *Activities and organizations:* drama/theater group, student-run newspaper, television station, choral group, Volunteer center, Campus Activities Board, Student government, Campus Ministry, Intramural sports. *Campus security:* 24-hour emergency response devices and patrols, student patrols, late-night transport/escort service, controlled dormitory access, front gate security, well-lit pathways. *Student services:* health clinic, personal/psychological counseling.

Athletics Member NCAA. All Division II. *Intercollegiate sports:* baseball M, basketball M(s)/W(s), crew W, cross-country running M/W, field hockey W, football M, golf M, ice hockey M, lacrosse M/W, soccer M/W, softball W, swimming and diving W, tennis M/W, track and field M/W, volleyball W. *Intramural sports:* badminton M/W, basketball M/W(c), cheerleading M(c)/W(c), equestrian sports M(c)/W(c), football M, golf M/W, ice hockey M/W, racquetball M/W, soccer M/W, softball M/W, table tennis M/W, tennis M/W, ultimate Frisbee M/W, volleyball M(c)/W(c).

Costs (2012–13) *Comprehensive fee:* $44,395 includes full-time tuition ($33,390), mandatory fees ($415), and room and board ($10,590). Full-time tuition and fees vary according to course load and reciprocity agreements. Part-time tuition: $1113 per credit hour. Part-time tuition and fees vary according to course load. *College room only:* $6660. Room and board charges vary according to housing facility. *Waivers:* employees or children of employees.

Financial Aid Of all full-time matriculated undergraduates who enrolled in 2012, 1,744 applied for aid, 1,589 were judged to have need, 300 had their need fully met. 464 Federal Work-Study jobs (averaging $1456). In 2012, 338 non-need-based awards were made. *Average percent of need met:* 75%. *Aver-*

age financial aid package: $24,802. *Average need-based loan:* $4887. *Average need-based gift aid:* $19,344. *Average non-need-based aid:* $10,808. *Average indebtedness upon graduation:* $34,579. *Financial aid deadline:* 2/15.

Applying *Options:* electronic application, early action, deferred entrance. *Application fee:* $50. *Required:* essay or personal statement, high school transcript, 1 letter of recommendation. *Recommended:* interview. *Application deadlines:* 2/15 (freshmen), 7/1 (transfers), 11/1 (early action). *Notification:* continuous (freshmen), continuous (transfers), 12/15 (early action).

Freshman Application Contact Ms. Kathleen Murphy, Dean of Enrollment, Assumption College, 500 Salisbury Street, Worcester, MA 01609-1296. *Phone:* 508-767-7110. *Toll-free phone:* 866-477-7776. *Fax:* 508-799-4412. *E-mail:* admiss@assumption.edu.

Website: http://www.assumption.edu/.

See previous page for display ad and page 1138 for the College Close-Up.

Babson College

Wellesley, Massachusetts

- **Independent** comprehensive, founded 1919
- **Suburban** 370-acre campus with easy access to Boston
- **Coed** 2,015 undergraduate students, 100% full-time, 44% women, 56% men
- **Very difficult** entrance level, 30% of applicants were admitted

Undergraduates 2,015 full-time. Students come from 41 states and territories; 70% are from out of state; 4% Black or African American, non-Hispanic/Latino; 10% Hispanic/Latino; 12% Asian, non-Hispanic/Latino; 0.2% American Indian or Alaska Native, non-Hispanic/Latino; 2% Two or more races, non-Hispanic/Latino; 8% Race/ethnicity unknown; 27% international; 2% transferred in; 85% live on campus. *Retention:* 94% of full-time freshmen returned.

Freshmen *Admission:* 5,512 applied, 1,648 admitted, 470 enrolled. *Average high school GPA:* 3.6. *Test scores:* SAT critical reading scores over 500: 94%; SAT math scores over 500: 99%; SAT writing scores over 500: 97%; ACT scores over 18: 99%; SAT critical reading scores over 600: 52%; SAT math scores over 600: 82%; SAT writing scores over 600: 65%; ACT scores over 24: 92%; SAT critical reading scores over 700: 8%; SAT math scores over 700: 31%; SAT writing scores over 700: 13%; ACT scores over 30: 22%.

Faculty *Total:* 261, 62% full-time, 67% with terminal degrees. *Student/faculty ratio:* 15:1.

Academics *Calendar:* semesters. *Degrees:* bachelor's, master's, and post-master's certificates. *Special study options:* advanced placement credit, freshman honors college, honors programs, independent study, internships, off-campus study, services for LD students, student-designed majors, study abroad, summer session for credit. *ROTC:* Army (c), Navy (c), Air Force (c).

Computers on Campus Students can access the following: campus intranet, computer help desk, free student e-mail accounts, online (class) grades, online (class) registration, online (class) schedules, network drives and folders; students are also issued an IBM Thinkpad. Campuswide network is available. Wireless service is available via entire campus.

Student Life *Housing:* on-campus residence required for freshman year. *Options:* coed, men-only, disabled students. Campus housing is university owned. Freshman campus housing is guaranteed. *Activities and organizations:* drama/theater group, student-run newspaper, radio station, choral group, Student Government Association, Free Press, Dance Ensemble, Asian Pacific Student Association, College Radio, national fraternities, national sororities. *Campus security:* 24-hour emergency response devices and patrols, late-night transport/escort service, controlled dormitory access. *Student services:* health clinic, personal/psychological counseling, women's center.

Athletics Member NCAA. All Division III. *Intercollegiate sports:* baseball M, basketball M/W, cheerleading W(c), cross-country running M/W, field hockey W, golf M, ice hockey M/W(c), lacrosse M/W, rugby M(c)/W(c), skiing (downhill) M/W, soccer M/W, softball W, swimming and diving M/W, tennis M/W, track and field M/W, volleyball W. *Intramural sports:* basketball M/W, football M, ice hockey M/W, racquetball M/W, soccer M/W, softball M/W, squash M/W, tennis M/W, ultimate Frisbee M/W, volleyball M/W, wrestling M(c).

Standardized Tests *Required:* SAT or ACT (for admission). *Recommended:* TOEFL or IELTS for non-native English speakers.

Costs (2013–14) *Comprehensive fee:* $57,662 includes full-time tuition ($43,520) and room and board ($14,142). *College room only:* $9126. Room and board charges vary according to board plan and housing facility. *Waivers:* employees or children of employees.

Financial Aid Of all full-time matriculated undergraduates who enrolled in 2012, 960 applied for aid, 884 were judged to have need, 327 had their need fully met. In 2012, 137 non-need-based awards were made. *Average percent of need met:* 95%. *Average financial aid package:* $34,782. *Average need-based loan:* $4072. *Average need-based gift aid:* $29,177. *Average non-need-based*

aid: $24,000. *Average indebtedness upon graduation:* $31,918. *Financial aid deadline:* 2/15.

Applying *Options:* electronic application, early decision, early action, deferred entrance. *Application fee:* $75. *Required:* essay or personal statement, high school transcript, 2 letters of recommendation. *Recommended:* interview. *Application deadlines:* 1/1 (freshmen), 4/1 (transfers), 11/1 (early action). *Early decision deadline:* 11/1. *Notification:* 4/1 (freshmen), 5/15 (transfers), 12/15 (early decision), 1/1 (early action).

Freshman Application Contact Mrs. Adrienne Ramsey, Associate Director of Undergraduate Admission, Babson College, Lunder Undergraduate Admission Center, Babson Park, MA 02457-0310. *Phone:* 781-239-5522. *Toll-free phone:* 800-488-3696. *Fax:* 781-239-4135. *E-mail:* ugradadmission@babson.edu.

Website: http://www.babson.edu/.

See previous page for display ad and page 1140 for the College Close-Up.

Bard College at Simon's Rock

Great Barrington, Massachusetts

- **Independent** 4-year, founded 1964
- **Small-town** 210-acre campus with easy access to Boston, New York City
- **Coed**
- **Moderately difficult** entrance level

Faculty *Student/faculty ratio:* 7:1.

Academics *Calendar:* semesters. *Degrees:* associate and bachelor's.

Student Life *Campus security:* 24-hour patrols, controlled dormitory access.

Financial Aid *Of all full-time matriculated undergraduates who enrolled in 2011,* 271 applied for aid, 245 were judged to have need, 38 had their need fully met. 156 Federal Work-Study jobs (averaging $1000). *In 2011,* 73 non-need-based awards were made. *Average percent of need met:* 77. *Average financial aid package:* $34,687. *Average need-based loan:* $4721. *Average need-based gift aid:* $17,845. *Average non-need-based aid:* $16,504. *Average indebtedness upon graduation:* $30,000.

Applying *Application fee:* $50. *Required:* essay or personal statement, high school transcript, 3 letters of recommendation, interview, school report, parent supplement.

Freshman Application Contact Steven Coleman, Director of Admissions, Bard College at Simon's Rock, 84 Alford Road, Great Barrington, MA 01230-9702. *Phone:* 413-528-7228. *Toll-free phone:* 800-235-7186. *Fax:* 413-541-0081. *E-mail:* admit@simons-rock.edu.

Website: http://www.simons-rock.edu/.

See this page for display ad and page 1146 for the College Close-Up.

Bay Path College

Longmeadow, Massachusetts

- **Independent** comprehensive, founded 1897
- **Suburban** 48-acre campus with easy access to Hartford, CT and Boston, MA
- **Endowment** $31.7 million
- **Undergraduate: women only; graduate: coed** 1,558 undergraduate students, 81% full-time, 100% women
- **Moderately difficult** entrance level, 61% of applicants were admitted

Undergraduates 1,259 full-time, 299 part-time. Students come from 18 states and territories; 3 other countries; 37% are from out of state; 12% Black or African American, non-Hispanic/Latino; 14% Hispanic/Latino; 1% Asian, non-Hispanic/Latino; 0.2% Native Hawaiian or other Pacific Islander, non-Hispanic/Latino; 0.4% American Indian or Alaska Native, non-Hispanic/Latino; 2% Two or more races, non-Hispanic/Latino; 14% Race/ethnicity unknown; 0.4% international; 19% transferred in; 63% live on campus. *Retention:* 74% of full-time freshmen returned.

Freshmen *Admission:* 978 applied, 600 admitted, 155 enrolled. *Average high school GPA:* 3.19. *Test scores:* SAT critical reading scores over 500: 44%; SAT math scores over 500: 44%; SAT writing scores over 500: 45%; ACT scores over 18: 64%; SAT critical reading scores over 600: 7%; SAT math scores over 600: 11%; SAT writing scores over 600: 8%; ACT scores over 24: 20%; SAT critical reading scores over 700: 1%; SAT math scores over 700: 10%; ACT scores over 30: 1%.

Faculty *Total:* 230, 24% full-time, 43% with terminal degrees. *Student/faculty ratio:* 12:1.

Academics *Calendar:* semesters. *Degrees:* certificates, associate, bachelor's, master's, post-master's, and postbachelor's certificates. *Special study options:* academic remediation for entering students, accelerated degree program, adult/

continuing education programs, advanced placement credit, cooperative education, distance learning, double majors, English as a second language, honors programs, independent study, internships, off-campus study, part-time degree program, services for LD students, student-designed majors, study abroad, summer session for credit. *ROTC:* Army (c), Air Force (c).

Computers on Campus 350 computers/terminals are available on campus for general student use. Students can access the following: campus intranet, computer help desk, free student e-mail accounts, online (class) grades, online (class) registration, online (class) schedules. Campuswide network is available. 100% of college-owned or -operated housing units are wired for high-speed Internet access. Wireless service is available via entire campus.

Student Life *Housing options:* women-only. Campus housing is university owned. Freshman campus housing is guaranteed. *Activities and organizations:* drama/theater group, choral group, student government, Black Student Association, Golden Z Service Club, Alliance, Women of Culture. *Campus security:* 24-hour emergency response devices and patrols, late-night transport/escort service, controlled dormitory access. *Student services:* health clinic, personal/psychological counseling.

Athletics Member NCAA. All Division III. *Intercollegiate sports:* basketball W, cross-country running W, field hockey W, lacrosse W, soccer W, softball W, tennis W, volleyball W. *Intramural sports:* ice hockey W(c).

Standardized Tests *Required:* SAT or ACT (for admission).

Costs (2012–13) *Comprehensive fee:* $39,972 includes full-time tuition ($28,532) and room and board ($11,440). Part-time tuition: $480 per credit. Part-time tuition and fees vary according to course load. *Room and board:* Room and board charges vary according to board plan. *Payment plan:* installment. *Waivers:* employees or children of employees.

Financial Aid Of all full-time matriculated undergraduates who enrolled in 2012, 619 applied for aid, 579 were judged to have need, 45 had their need fully met. In 2012, 55 non-need-based awards were made. *Average percent of need met:* 66%. *Average financial aid package:* $22,819. *Average need-based loan:* $5267. *Average need-based gift aid:* $17,432. *Average non-need-based aid:* $12,028. *Average indebtedness upon graduation:* $31,456.

Applying *Options:* electronic application, early admission, early action, deferred entrance. *Application fee:* $25. *Required:* high school transcript. *Required for some:* interview. *Recommended:* essay or personal statement, minimum 2.0 GPA, interview. *Application deadlines:* rolling (freshmen), rolling (transfers), 12/15 (early action). *Notification:* continuous (freshmen), continuous (transfers), 1/2 (early action).

Freshman Application Contact Stefanie Sanchez, Bay Path College, 588 Longmeadow Street, Longmeadow, MA 01106-2292. *Phone:* 413-565-1000. *Toll-free phone:* 800-782-7284 Ext. 1331. *Website:* http://www.baypath.edu/.

Bay State College
Boston, Massachusetts

- **Independent** primarily 2-year, founded 1946
- **Urban** campus
- **Coed** 1,153 undergraduate students
- **Minimally difficult** entrance level, 59% of applicants were admitted

Undergraduates 14% are from out of state. *Retention:* 76% of full-time freshmen returned.

Freshmen *Admission:* 1,761 applied, 1,045 admitted.

Faculty *Student/faculty ratio:* 16:1.

Academics *Calendar:* semesters. *Degrees:* diplomas, associate, and bachelor's. *Special study options:* academic remediation for entering students, adult/continuing education programs, advanced placement credit, cooperative education, English as a second language, independent study, internships, part-time degree program.

Computers on Campus Campuswide network is available.

Student Life *Housing options:* coed, women-only. Campus housing is provided by a third party. *Campus security:* late-night transport/escort service, controlled dormitory access, 14-hour patrols by trained security personnel. *Student services:* personal/psychological counseling.

Standardized Tests *Recommended:* SAT or ACT (for admission).

Financial Aid Of all full-time matriculated undergraduates who enrolled in 2011, 20 Federal Work-Study jobs (averaging $2600).

Applying *Options:* early admission. *Application fee:* $40. *Required:* high school transcript, minimum 2.3 GPA. *Recommended:* interview. *Application deadlines:* rolling (freshmen), rolling (transfers).

Freshman Application Contact Julia Croft, Director of Admissions, Bay State College, 122 Commonwealth Avenue, Boston, MA 02116. *Phone:* 617-217-9115. *Toll-free phone:* 800-81-LEARN. *Fax:* 617-536-1735. *E-mail:* admissions@baystate.edu. *Website:* http://www.baystate.edu/.

See below for display ad and page 1152 for the College Close-Up.

Becker College

Worcester, Massachusetts

- **Independent** 4-year, founded 1784
- **Urban** 100-acre campus with easy access to Boston
- **Coed** 1,826 undergraduate students, 77% full-time, 58% women, 42% men
- **Moderately difficult** entrance level, 62% of applicants were admitted

Undergraduates 1,403 full-time, 423 part-time. Students come from 33 states and territories; 19 other countries; 31% are from out of state; 7% Black or African American, non-Hispanic/Latino; 8% Hispanic/Latino; 1% Asian, non-Hispanic/Latino; 0.1% Native Hawaiian or other Pacific Islander, non-Hispanic/Latino; 0.3% American Indian or Alaska Native, non-Hispanic/Latino; 2% Two or more races, non-Hispanic/Latino; 23% Race/ethnicity unknown; 0.6% international; 10% transferred in; 39% live on campus. *Retention:* 65% of full-time freshmen returned.

Freshmen *Admission:* 3,350 applied, 2,088 admitted, 381 enrolled. *Average high school GPA:* 2.97. *Test scores:* SAT critical reading scores over 500: 46%; SAT math scores over 500: 48%; SAT writing scores over 500: 37%; ACT scores over 18: 85%; SAT critical reading scores over 600: 16%; SAT math scores over 600: 16%; SAT writing scores over 600: 10%; ACT scores over 24: 28%; SAT critical reading scores over 700: 2%; SAT math scores over 700: 3%; SAT writing scores over 700: 1%; ACT scores over 30: 5%.

Faculty *Total:* 193, 23% full-time, 26% with terminal degrees. *Student/faculty ratio:* 16:1.

Academics *Calendar:* semesters. *Degrees:* associate and bachelor's (also includes Leicester, MA small town campus). *Special study options:* academic remediation for entering students, accelerated degree program, adult/continuing education programs, advanced placement credit, cooperative education, distance learning, honors programs, independent study, internships, off-campus study, part-time degree program, services for LD students, study abroad. *ROTC:* Army (c).

Computers on Campus 155 computers/terminals are available on campus for general student use. Students can access the following: campus intranet, computer help desk, free student e-mail accounts, online (class) grades, online (class) registration, online (class) schedules. Campuswide network is available. 100% of college-owned or -operated housing units are wired for high-speed Internet access. Wireless service is available via entire campus.

Student Life *Housing options:* coed, men-only, women-only. Campus housing is university owned and leased by the school. Freshman applicants given priority for college housing. *Activities and organizations:* drama/theater group, student-run newspaper, television station, choral group, Student government, Student Activities Committee, Black Student Union, Animal Health Club, Drama Club. *Campus security:* 24-hour emergency response devices and patrols, late-night transport/escort service, controlled dormitory access. *Student services:* health clinic, personal/psychological counseling.

Athletics Member NCAA. *Intercollegiate sports:* baseball M, basketball M/W, cheerleading M/W, equestrian sports M/W, field hockey W, football M, golf M, ice hockey M, lacrosse M/W, soccer M/W, softball W, tennis M/W, volleyball W. *Intramural sports:* basketball M/W, bowling M/W, skiing (downhill) M(c)/W(c), soccer M/W, table tennis M/W, volleyball M/W.

Standardized Tests *Required:* SAT or ACT (for admission).

Costs (2012–13) *Comprehensive fee:* $41,390 includes full-time tuition ($28,900), mandatory fees ($1440), and room and board ($11,050). Full-time tuition and fees vary according to class time, course load, and program. Part-time tuition: $1200 per credit hour. Part-time tuition and fees vary according to class time, course load, and program. *Room and board:* Room and board charges vary according to board plan and housing facility. *Payment plan:* installment. *Waivers:* senior citizens and employees or children of employees.

Financial Aid Of all full-time matriculated undergraduates who enrolled in 2009, 1,679 applied for aid, 1,524 were judged to have need, 27 had their need fully met. 338 Federal Work-Study jobs (averaging $1404). In 2009, 504 non-need-based awards were made. *Average percent of need met:* 74%. *Average financial aid package:* $14,056. *Average need-based loan:* $4031. *Average need-based gift aid:* $12,854. *Average non-need-based aid:* $14,032. *Average indebtedness upon graduation:* $31,800.

Applying *Options:* electronic application, early admission, early action, deferred entrance. *Required:* high school transcript, minimum 2.0 GPA, 1 letter of recommendation. *Required for some:* interview. *Recommended:* essay or personal statement. *Application deadlines:* rolling (freshmen), rolling (transfers), 11/15 (early action). *Notification:* continuous (freshmen), continuous (transfers), 12/15 (early action).

Freshman Application Contact Office of Admissions, Becker College, 61 Sever Street, Worcester, MA 01609. *Phone:* 508-373-9400. *Toll-free phone:* 877-5BECKER. *Fax:* 508-890-1500. *E-mail:* admissions@becker.edu. *Website:* http://www.becker.edu/.

Benjamin Franklin Institute of Technology

Boston, Massachusetts

Freshman Application Contact Ms. Brittainy Johnson, Associate Director of Admissions, Benjamin Franklin Institute of Technology, Boston, MA 02116. *Phone:* 617-423-4630 Ext. 122. *Toll-free phone:* 877-400-BFIT. *Fax:* 617-482-3706. *E-mail:* bjohnson@bfit.edu. *Website:* http://www.bfit.edu/.

Bentley University

Waltham, Massachusetts

- **Independent** comprehensive, founded 1917
- **Suburban** 163-acre campus with easy access to Boston
- **Endowment** $207.8 million
- **Coed** 4,228 undergraduate students, 96% full-time, 41% women, 59% men
- **Very difficult** entrance level, 43% of applicants were admitted

Undergraduates 4,066 full-time, 162 part-time. Students come from 40 states and territories; 83 other countries; 52% are from out of state; 3% Black or African American, non-Hispanic/Latino; 7% Hispanic/Latino; 7% Asian, non-Hispanic/Latino; 0.1% American Indian or Alaska Native, non-Hispanic/Latino; 1% Two or more races, non-Hispanic/Latino; 8% Race/ethnicity unknown; 13% international; 3% transferred in; 79% live on campus. *Retention:* 94% of full-time freshmen returned.

Freshmen *Admission:* 6,695 applied, 2,902 admitted, 911 enrolled. *Test scores:* SAT critical reading scores over 500: 92%; SAT math scores over 500: 99%; SAT writing scores over 500: 93%; ACT scores over 18: 100%; SAT critical reading scores over 600: 48%; SAT math scores over 600: 78%; SAT writing scores over 600: 50%; ACT scores over 24: 91%; SAT critical reading scores over 700: 7%; SAT math scores over 700: 19%; SAT writing scores over 700: 10%; ACT scores over 30: 20%.

Faculty *Total:* 448, 63% full-time, 67% with terminal degrees. *Student/faculty ratio:* 14:1.

Academics *Calendar:* semesters. *Degrees:* associate, bachelor's, master's, doctoral, post-master's, and postbachelor's certificates. *Special study options:* accelerated degree program, adult/continuing education programs, advanced placement credit, double majors, honors programs, independent study, internships, off-campus study, services for LD students, student-designed majors, study abroad, summer session for credit. *ROTC:* Army (c), Air Force (c).

Computers on Campus 4,489 computers/terminals and 10,752 ports are available on campus for general student use. Students can access the following: campus intranet, computer help desk, free student e-mail accounts, online (class) grades, online (class) registration, online (class) schedules, Grade checking, online admission, Blackboard, resume review, student employment, interlibrary loan, free software. Campuswide network is available. 100% of college-owned or -operated housing units are wired for high-speed Internet access. Wireless service is available via entire campus.

Student Life *Housing options:* coed, disabled students. Campus housing is university owned and leased by the school. Freshman campus housing is guaranteed. *Activities and organizations:* drama/theater group, student-run newspaper, radio and television station, choral group, Bentley Entrepreneurship Society, Campus Activities Board, Delta Sigma Pi, Bentley Investment Group, National Association of Black Accountants, national fraternities, national sororities. *Campus security:* 24-hour emergency response devices and patrols, late-night transport/escort service, controlled dormitory access, security cameras, Community Policing Team, self-defense classes, CPR and first-aid training. *Student services:* health clinic, personal/psychological counseling, women's center.

Athletics Member NCAA. All Division II except ice hockey (Division I). *Intercollegiate sports:* baseball M, basketball M(s)/W(s), cross-country running M/W, field hockey W, football M, golf M, ice hockey M(s), lacrosse M/W, soccer M/W, softball W, swimming and diving M/W, tennis M/W, track and field M/W. *Intramural sports:* basketball M/W, cheerleading W(c), football M, golf M(c)/W(c), racquetball M(c)/W(c), rugby M(c)/W(c), sailing M(c)/W(c), skiing (cross-country) M(c)/W(c), skiing (downhill) M(c)/W(c), soccer M/W, softball M/W, volleyball M/W, water polo M(c), wrestling M(c).

Standardized Tests *Required:* SAT or ACT (for admission). *Required for some:* TOEFL (or IELTS) is required form non-native English speakers unless the student receives at least 577 (paper-based) or 90 (Internet-based) on the writing section of the SAT.

Costs (2012–13) *Comprehensive fee:* $52,588 includes full-time tuition ($38,130), mandatory fees ($1498), and room and board ($12,960). Part-time tuition: $1932 per course. Part-time tuition and fees vary according to class time and course load. *Required fees:* $45 per term part-time. *College room only:* $7790. Room and board charges vary according to board plan and housing facility. *Payment plan:* installment. *Waivers:* employees or children of employees.

Financial Aid Of all full-time matriculated undergraduates who enrolled in 2012, 2,496 applied for aid, 1,943 were judged to have need, 859 had their need fully met. 950 Federal Work-Study jobs (averaging $1494). 644 state and other part-time jobs (averaging $1458). In 2012, 668 non-need-based awards were made. *Average percent of need met:* 95%. *Average financial aid package:* $31,152. *Average need-based loan:* $5055. *Average need-based gift aid:* $23,737. *Average non-need-based aid:* $15,803. *Average indebtedness upon graduation:* $30,375. *Financial aid deadline:* 2/1.

Applying *Options:* electronic application, early admission, early action, deferred entrance. *Application fee:* $50. *Required:* essay or personal statement, high school transcript, 2 letters of recommendation. *Required for some:* interview. *Application deadlines:* 1/15 (freshmen), 1/15 (out-of-state freshmen), 11/15 (early action). *Notification:* 4/1 (freshmen), 4/1 (out-of-state freshmen), 1/15 (early action).

Freshman Application Contact Office of Undergraduate Admissions, Bentley University, 175 Forest Street, Waltham, MA 02452. *Phone:* 781-891-2244. *Toll-free phone:* 800-523-2354. *Fax:* 781-891-3414. *E-mail:* ugadmission@bentley.edu.
Website: http://www.bentley.edu/.

See this page for display ad and page 1156 for the College Close-Up.

Berklee College of Music
Boston, Massachusetts

- **Independent** comprehensive, founded 1945
- **Urban** campus
- **Coed** 4,447 undergraduate students, 91% full-time, 30% women, 70% men
- **Moderately difficult** entrance level, 19% of applicants were admitted

Undergraduates 4,049 full-time, 398 part-time. 84% are from out of state; 6% Black or African American, non-Hispanic/Latino; 9% Hispanic/Latino; 3% Asian, non-Hispanic/Latino; 0.2% Native Hawaiian or other Pacific Islander, non-Hispanic/Latino; 0.1% American Indian or Alaska Native, non-Hispanic/Latino; 3% Two or more races, non-Hispanic/Latino; 8% Race/ethnicity unknown; 29% international; 3% transferred in; 17% live on campus. *Retention:* 82% of full-time freshmen returned.

Freshmen *Admission:* 5,538 applied, 1,061 admitted, 778 enrolled.

Faculty *Total:* 569, 42% full-time, 13% with terminal degrees. *Student/faculty ratio:* 13:1.

Academics *Calendar:* semesters. *Degrees:* diplomas, bachelor's, and master's.

Computers on Campus Students can access the following: free student e-mail accounts, online (class) grades, online (class) registration, online (class) schedules. Campuswide network is available. Wireless service is available via entire campus.

Student Life *Housing options:* coed. Campus housing is university owned. Freshman applicants given priority for college housing. *Campus security:* 24-hour patrols.

Athletics *Intramural sports:* ice hockey M/W, rock climbing M/W, soccer M/W, table tennis M/W.

Costs (2012–13) *Comprehensive fee:* $53,440 includes full-time tuition ($35,450), mandatory fees ($1040), and room and board ($16,950). Part-time tuition: $1255 per credit hour. *Payment plans:* tuition prepayment, deferred payment. *Waivers:* employees or children of employees.

Financial Aid Of all full-time matriculated undergraduates who enrolled in 2011, 1,851 applied for aid, 1,708 were judged to have need, 70 had their need fully met. In 2011, 701 non-need-based awards were made. *Average percent of need met:* 35%. *Average financial aid package:* $16,897. *Average need-based loan:* $5325. *Average need-based gift aid:* $13,432. *Average non-need-based aid:* $14,394. *Financial aid deadline:* 5/1.

Applying *Options:* electronic application, early action, deferred entrance. *Application fee:* $150. *Required:* essay or personal statement, high school transcript, 2 letters of recommendation, interview, 2 years of formal music study and audition. *Application deadlines:* 1/15 (freshmen), 1/15 (transfers), 11/1 (early action). *Notification:* 3/31 (freshmen), 3/31 (transfers), 1/31 (early action).

Freshman Application Contact Mr. Damien Bracken, Director of Admissions, Berklee College of Music, 1140 Boylston Street, Boston, MA

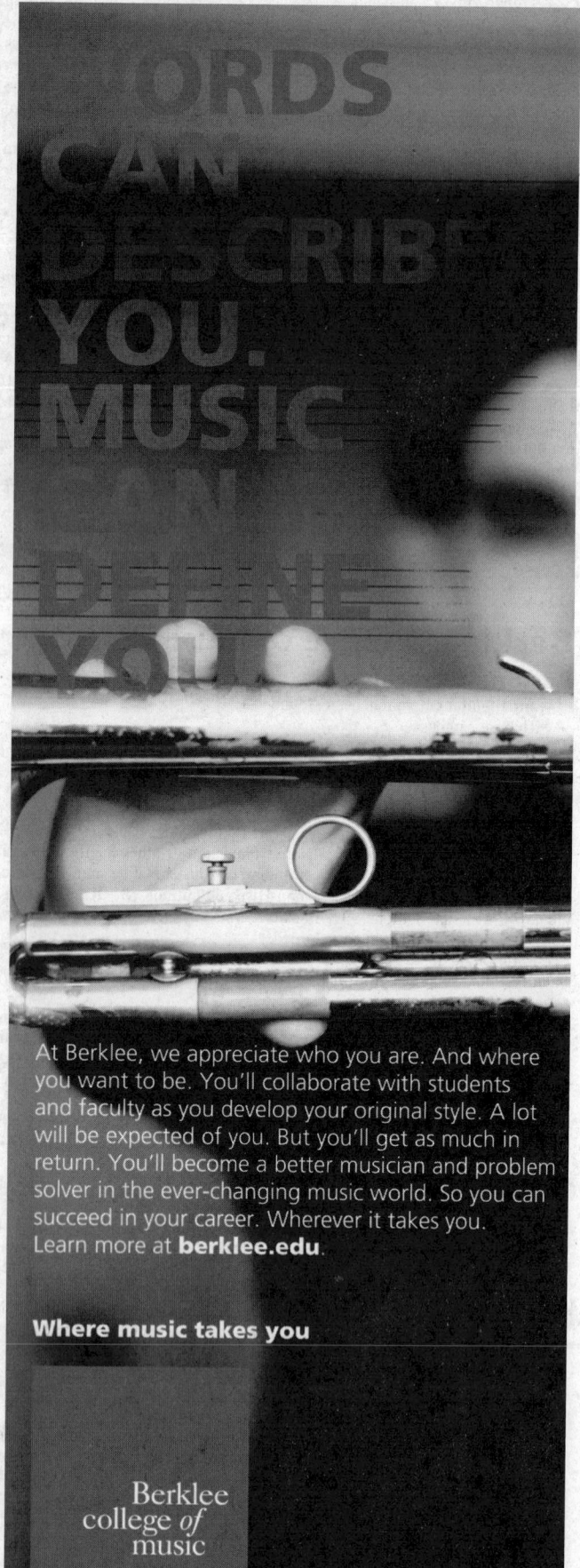

At Berklee, we appreciate who you are. And where you want to be. You'll collaborate with students and faculty as you develop your original style. A lot will be expected of you. But you'll get as much in return. You'll become a better musician and problem solver in the ever-changing music world. So you can succeed in your career. Wherever it takes you. Learn more at **berklee.edu**.

Where music takes you

Berklee
college *of*
music

02215-3693. *Phone:* 617-747-2222. *Toll-free phone:* 800-BERKLEE. *Fax:* 617-747-2047. *E-mail:* admissions@berklee.edu.
Website: http://www.berklee.edu/.

See this page for display ad and page 1158 for the College Close-Up.

Boston Architectural College

Boston, Massachusetts

- **Independent** comprehensive, founded 1889
- **Urban** 1-acre campus
- **Endowment** $8.7 million
- **Coed** 466 undergraduate students, 98% full-time, 33% women, 67% men
- **Noncompetitive** entrance level, 100% of applicants were admitted

Undergraduates 455 full-time, 11 part-time. Students come from 35 states and territories; 4 other countries; 51% are from out of state; 6% Black or African American, non-Hispanic/Latino; 14% Hispanic/Latino; 8% Asian, non-Hispanic/Latino; 0.6% American Indian or Alaska Native, non-Hispanic/Latino; 2% Two or more races, non-Hispanic/Latino; 8% Race/ethnicity unknown; 9% transferred in. *Retention:* 62% of full-time freshmen returned.
Freshmen *Admission:* 100 applied, 100 admitted, 20 enrolled. *Average high school GPA:* 2.9.
Faculty *Total:* 229, 5% full-time, 26% with terminal degrees. *Student/faculty ratio:* 4:1.
Academics *Calendar:* semesters. *Degrees:* certificates, bachelor's, and master's. *Special study options:* adult/continuing education programs, advanced placement credit, distance learning, independent study, internships, off-campus study, summer session for credit.
Computers on Campus 78 computers/terminals are available on campus for general student use. Students can access the following: campus intranet, computer help desk, free student e-mail accounts, online (class) grades, online (class) registration, online (class) schedules. Campuswide network is available. Wireless service is available via entire campus.
Student Life *Housing:* college housing not available. *Activities and organizations:* Atelier, Student Government, American Institute of Architectural Students, BAC Interior Design Society (IIDA and ASID), National Organization of Minority Architecture Students (NOMAS), Student American Society of Landscape Architects (SASLA). *Campus security:* 24-hour emergency response devices and patrols, late-night transport/escort service, electronically operated building access and CCTV systems. *Student services:* personal/psychological counseling.
Financial Aid Of all full-time matriculated undergraduates who enrolled in 2010, 505 applied for aid, 486 were judged to have need, 12 had their need fully met. 57 Federal Work-Study jobs (averaging $2680). In 2010, 73 non-need-based awards were made. *Average percent of need met:* 34%. *Average financial aid package:* $9472. *Average need-based loan:* $4951. *Average need-based gift aid:* $5359. *Average non-need-based aid:* $3634. *Average indebtedness upon graduation:* $34,874.
Applying *Options:* electronic application. *Application fee:* $50. *Required:* essay or personal statement, high school transcript, resumes, creative exercise. *Recommended:* interview. *Application deadlines:* rolling (freshmen), rolling (out-of-state freshmen), rolling (transfers). *Notification:* continuous (freshmen), continuous (out-of-state freshmen), continuous (transfers).
Freshman Application Contact Richard Moyer, Director of Admission, Boston Architectural College, 320 Newbury Street, Boston, MA 02115-2795. *Phone:* 617-585-0256. *Toll-free phone:* 877-585-0100. *Fax:* 617-585-0121. *E-mail:* admissions@the-bac.edu.
Website: http://www.the-bac.edu/.

Boston Baptist College

Boston, Massachusetts

- **Independent Baptist** 4-year, founded 1976
- **Suburban** 8-acre campus with easy access to Boston, Providence
- **Coed**
- **Moderately difficult** entrance level

Faculty *Student/faculty ratio:* 9:1.
Academics *Calendar:* semesters. *Degrees:* certificates, diplomas, associate, and bachelor's.
Student Life *Campus security:* 24-hour emergency response devices, student patrols, late-night transport/escort service, controlled dormitory access.
Standardized Tests *Required for some:* SAT or ACT (for admission).
Costs (2012–13) *Comprehensive fee:* $22,750 includes full-time tuition ($13,500), mandatory fees ($1500), and room and board ($7750). Part-time

tuition: $391 per credit. *College room only:* $4600. Room and board charges vary according to board plan.

Applying *Options:* deferred entrance. *Application fee:* $50. *Required:* essay or personal statement, high school transcript, 1 letter of recommendation. *Recommended:* 1 letter of recommendation.

Freshman Application Contact Mrs. Karen Fox, Director of Admissions, Boston Baptist College, 950 Metropolitan Avenue, Boston, MA 02136. *Phone:* 617-364-3510 Ext. 217. *Toll-free phone:* 888-235-2014. *Fax:* 617-399-8220. *E-mail:* kfox@boston.edu.

Website: http://www.boston.edu/.

Boston College

Chestnut Hill, Massachusetts

- **Independent Roman Catholic (Jesuit)** university, founded 1863
- **Suburban** 338-acre campus with easy access to Boston
- **Endowment** $1.8 billion
- **Coed** 9,110 undergraduate students, 100% full-time, 53% women, 47% men
- **Very difficult** entrance level, 29% of applicants were admitted

Undergraduates 9,110 full-time. Students come from 53 states and territories; 59 other countries; 73% are from out of state; 4% Black or African American, non-Hispanic/Latino; 11% Hispanic/Latino; 10% Asian, non-Hispanic/Latino; 0.1% American Indian or Alaska Native, non-Hispanic/Latino; 3% Two or more races, non-Hispanic/Latino; 8% Race/ethnicity unknown; 4% international; 1% transferred in; 85% live on campus. *Retention:* 95% of full-time freshmen returned.

Freshmen *Admission:* 34,061 applied, 9,813 admitted, 2,405 enrolled. *Test scores:* SAT critical reading scores over 500: 98%; SAT math scores over 500: 98%; SAT writing scores over 500: 98%; ACT scores over 18: 100%; SAT critical reading scores over 600: 84%; SAT math scores over 600: 89%; SAT writing scores over 600: 89%; ACT scores over 24: 97%; SAT critical reading scores over 700: 33%; SAT math scores over 700: 46%; SAT writing scores over 700: 43%; ACT scores over 30: 72%.

Faculty *Total:* 1,363, 55% full-time, 95% with terminal degrees. *Student/faculty ratio:* 14:1.

Academics *Calendar:* semesters. *Degrees:* bachelor's, master's, doctoral, and post-master's certificates (also offers continuing education program with significant enrollment not reflected in profile). *Special study options:* accelerated degree program, advanced placement credit, double majors, honors programs, independent study, internships, off-campus study, part-time degree program, services for LD students, student-designed majors, study abroad, summer session for credit. *ROTC:* Army (c), Navy (c), Air Force (c).

Computers on Campus 1,000 computers/terminals are available on campus for general student use. Students can access the following: campus intranet, computer help desk, free student e-mail accounts, online (class) grades, online (class) registration, online (class) schedules. Campuswide network is available. 100% of college-owned or -operated housing units are wired for high-speed Internet access. Wireless service is available via entire campus.

Student Life *Housing options:* coed, women-only. Campus housing is university owned. Freshman campus housing is guaranteed. *Activities and organizations:* drama/theater group, student-run newspaper, radio and television station, choral group, marching band, UGBC and individual School Senates, Asian Caucus, Appalachia Volunteers, Dance Marathon, 4Boston. *Campus security:* 24-hour emergency response devices and patrols, late-night transport/escort service, controlled dormitory access. *Student services:* health clinic, personal/psychological counseling, women's center.

Athletics Member NCAA. All Division I except football (Division I-A). *Intercollegiate sports:* baseball M(s), basketball M(s)/W(s), cheerleading M(c)/W(c), crew W(s), cross-country running M(s)/W(s), fencing M/W, field hockey W(s), golf M(s)/W(s), ice hockey M(s)/W(s), lacrosse W(s), sailing M/W, skiing (downhill) M/W, soccer M(s)/W(s), softball W(s), swimming and diving M(s)/W(s), tennis M(s)/W(s), track and field M(s)/W(s), volleyball W(s). *Intramural sports:* badminton M/W, basketball M(c)/W(c), crew M(c), cross-country running M(c)/W(c), equestrian sports M(c)/W(c), field hockey W(c), golf M(c)/W(c), ice hockey M/W, lacrosse M(c)/W(c), racquetball M/W, rugby M(c)/W(c), soccer M(c)/W(c), softball M/W, squash M/W, tennis M/W, track and field M(c)/W(c), ultimate Frisbee M(c)/W(c), volleyball M(c)/W(c), water polo M(c)/W(c).

Standardized Tests *Required:* SAT and SAT Subject Tests or ACT (for admission).

Costs (2012–13) *One-time required fee:* $458. *Comprehensive fee:* $56,486 includes full-time tuition ($43,140), mandatory fees ($738), and room and board ($12,608). *College room only:* $7790. Room and board charges vary according to housing facility. *Payment plan:* installment. *Waivers:* employees or children of employees.

Financial Aid Of all full-time matriculated undergraduates who enrolled in 2011, 4,435 applied for aid, 3,865 were judged to have need, 3,865 had their need fully met. 3,156 Federal Work-Study jobs (averaging $2143). In 2011, 176 non-need-based awards were made. *Average percent of need met:* 100%. *Average financial aid package:* $34,578. *Average need-based loan:* $5403. *Average need-based gift aid:* $28,586. *Average non-need-based aid:* $15,634. *Average indebtedness upon graduation:* $20,975.

Applying *Options:* electronic application, early admission, early action, deferred entrance. *Application fee:* $70. *Required:* essay or personal statement, high school transcript, 2 letters of recommendation. *Application deadlines:* 1/1 (freshmen), 3/15 (transfers), 11/1 (early action). *Notification:* 4/15 (freshmen), 6/1 (transfers), 12/25 (early action).

Freshman Application Contact Office of Undergraduate Admissions, Boston College, 140 Commonwealth Avenue, Devlin 208, Chestnut Hill, MA 02467-3809. *Phone:* 617-552-3100. *Toll-free phone:* 800-360-2522. *Fax:* 617-552-0798.

Website: http://www.bc.edu/.

See page 1160 for the College Close-Up.

The Boston Conservatory

Boston, Massachusetts

- **Independent** comprehensive, founded 1867
- **Urban** campus with easy access to Boston
- **Coed** 544 undergraduate students, 98% full-time, 61% women, 39% men
- **Moderately difficult** entrance level, 46% of applicants were admitted

Undergraduates 533 full-time, 11 part-time. Students come from 40 states and territories; 28 other countries; 88% are from out of state; 4% transferred in; 30% live on campus. *Retention:* 76% of full-time freshmen returned.

Freshmen *Admission:* 1,080 applied, 502 admitted, 182 enrolled. *Average high school GPA:* 3.49. *Test scores:* SAT critical reading scores over 500: 72%; SAT math scores over 500: 73%; ACT scores over 18: 94%; SAT critical reading scores over 600: 32%; SAT math scores over 600: 27%; ACT scores over 24: 63%; SAT critical reading scores over 700: 10%; SAT math scores over 700: 4%; ACT scores over 30: 14%.

Faculty *Total:* 202, 44% full-time, 18% with terminal degrees. *Student/faculty ratio:* 4:1.

Academics *Calendar:* semesters. *Degrees:* diplomas, bachelor's, master's, post-master's, and postbachelor's certificates. *Special study options:* advanced placement credit, cooperative education, double majors, English as a second language, independent study, internships, off-campus study, summer session for credit.

Computers on Campus 20 computers/terminals are available on campus for general student use. Students can access the following: campus intranet, computer help desk, free student e-mail accounts. Campuswide network is available. 100% of college-owned or -operated housing units are wired for high-speed Internet access. Wireless service is available via entire campus.

Student Life *Housing options:* coed. Campus housing is university owned. Freshman campus housing is guaranteed. *Activities and organizations:* drama/theater group, choral group, Student Government Association, BoCo Cares, The Tent, Sigma Alpha Iota, Phi Mu Alpha, national fraternities, national sororities. *Campus security:* 24-hour emergency response devices and patrols, controlled dormitory access. *Student services:* personal/psychological counseling.

Standardized Tests *Required:* SAT or ACT (for admission).

Costs (2012–13) *Comprehensive fee:* $56,380 includes full-time tuition ($37,300), mandatory fees ($2000), and room and board ($17,080). Full-time tuition and fees vary according to course load, degree level, and program. Part-time tuition: $1750 per credit hour. Part-time tuition and fees vary according to course load, degree level, and program. *College room only:* $10,700. Room and board charges vary according to board plan and housing facility. *Payment plan:* installment. *Waivers:* employees or children of employees.

Financial Aid Of all full-time matriculated undergraduates who enrolled in 2008, 335 applied for aid, 293 were judged to have need, 23 had their need fully met. In 2008, 20 non-need-based awards were made. *Average percent of need met:* 0%. *Average financial aid package:* $13,967. *Average need-based loan:* $4257. *Average need-based gift aid:* $12,772. *Average non-need-based aid:* $9235. *Average indebtedness upon graduation:* $34,931.

Applying *Options:* electronic application, deferred entrance. *Application fee:* $110. *Required:* essay or personal statement, high school transcript, minimum 2.7 GPA, 2 letters of recommendation, audition. *Required for some:* interview. *Application deadlines:* 12/1 (freshmen), 12/1 (transfers). *Notification:* 4/1 (freshmen), 4/1 (transfers).

Freshman Application Contact The Boston Conservatory, 8 The Fenway, Boston, MA 02215. *Phone:* 617-912-9153.

Website: http://www.bostonconservatory.edu/.

Boston University

Boston, Massachusetts

- **Independent** university, founded 1839
- **Urban** 132-acre campus
- **Endowment** $1.2 billion
- **Coed** 18,306 undergraduate students, 91% full-time, 60% women, 40% men
- **Very difficult** entrance level, 46% of applicants were admitted

Undergraduates 16,634 full-time, 1,672 part-time. Students come from 52 states and territories; 101 other countries; 77% are from out of state; 3% Black or African American, non-Hispanic/Latino; 9% Hispanic/Latino; 14% Asian, non-Hispanic/Latino; 0.1% Native Hawaiian or other Pacific Islander, non-Hispanic/Latino; 0.1% American Indian or Alaska Native, non-Hispanic/Latino; 3% Two or more races, non-Hispanic/Latino; 8% Race/ethnicity unknown; 13% international; 2% transferred in; 77% live on campus. *Retention:* 92% of full-time freshmen returned.

Freshmen *Admission:* 44,005 applied, 20,071 admitted, 3,877 enrolled. *Average high school GPA:* 3.57. *Test scores:* SAT critical reading scores over 500: 93%; SAT math scores over 500: 99%; SAT writing scores over 500: 97%; ACT scores over 18: 100%; SAT critical reading scores over 600: 63%; SAT math scores over 600: 82%; SAT writing scores over 600: 75%; ACT scores over 24: 95%; SAT critical reading scores over 700: 17%; SAT math scores over 700: 33%; SAT writing scores over 700: 21%; ACT scores over 30: 34%.

Faculty *Total:* 2,630, 62% full-time. *Student/faculty ratio:* 13:1.

Academics *Calendar:* semesters. *Degrees:* bachelor's, master's, doctoral, post-master's, and postbachelor's certificates. *Special study options:* accelerated degree program, adult/continuing education programs, advanced placement credit, cooperative education, distance learning, double majors, English as a second language, honors programs, independent study, internships, off-campus study, part-time degree program, services for LD students, student-designed majors, study abroad, summer session for credit. *ROTC:* Army (b), Navy (b), Air Force (b).

Computers on Campus 250 computers/terminals and 1,650 ports are available on campus for general student use. Students can access the following: campus intranet, computer help desk, free student e-mail accounts, online (class) grades, online (class) registration, online (class) schedules, research and educational networks. Campuswide network is available. 77% of college-owned or -operated housing units are wired for high-speed Internet access. Wireless service is available via classrooms, computer labs, dorm rooms, libraries, student centers.

Student Life *Housing:* on-campus residence required for freshman year. *Options:* coed, women-only, cooperative, disabled students. Campus housing is university owned. Freshman campus housing is guaranteed. *Activities and organizations:* drama/theater group, student-run newspaper, radio and television station, choral group, marching band, performing and acappella groups, cultural organizations, service organizations, student government, residence hall associations, national fraternities, national sororities. *Campus security:* 24-hour emergency response devices and patrols, late-night transport/escort service, controlled dormitory access, security personnel at residence hall entrances, self-defense education, well-lit sidewalks. *Student services:* health clinic, personal/psychological counseling, women's center.

Athletics Member NCAA. All Division I. *Intercollegiate sports:* archery M(c)/W(c), badminton M(c)/W(c), baseball M(c), basketball M(s)/W(s), cheerleading M(c)/W(c), crew M(s)/W(s), cross-country running M(s)/W(s), equestrian sports M(c)/W(c), fencing M(c)/W(c), field hockey W(s), golf M(c)/W, gymnastics M(c)/W(c), ice hockey M(s)/W(s), lacrosse M/W(s), rugby M(c)/W(c), sailing M(c)/W(c), skiing (downhill) M(c)/W(c), soccer M(s)/W(s), softball W(s), squash M(c), swimming and diving M(s)/W(s), table tennis M(c)/W(c), tennis M/W(s), track and field M(s)/W(s), ultimate Frisbee M(c)/W(c), volleyball M(c)/W(c), water polo M(c)/W(c), wrestling M(s). *Intramural sports:* basketball M/W, football M/W, ice hockey M, soccer M/W, softball M/W, swimming and diving M/W, tennis M/W, volleyball M/W.

Standardized Tests *Required:* SAT or ACT (for admission). *Required for some:* SAT Subject Tests (for admission).

Costs (2012–13) *Comprehensive fee:* $56,184 includes full-time tuition ($42,400), mandatory fees ($594), and room and board ($13,190). Full-time tuition and fees vary according to class time. Part-time tuition: $1325 per credit hour. Part-time tuition and fees vary according to class time and course load. *Required fees:* $40 per term part-time. *College room only:* $8600. Room and board charges vary according to board plan and housing facility. *Payment plans:* tuition prepayment, installment. *Waivers:* employees or children of employees.

Financial Aid Of all full-time matriculated undergraduates who enrolled in 2012, 7,741 applied for aid, 7,110 were judged to have need, 3,286 had their

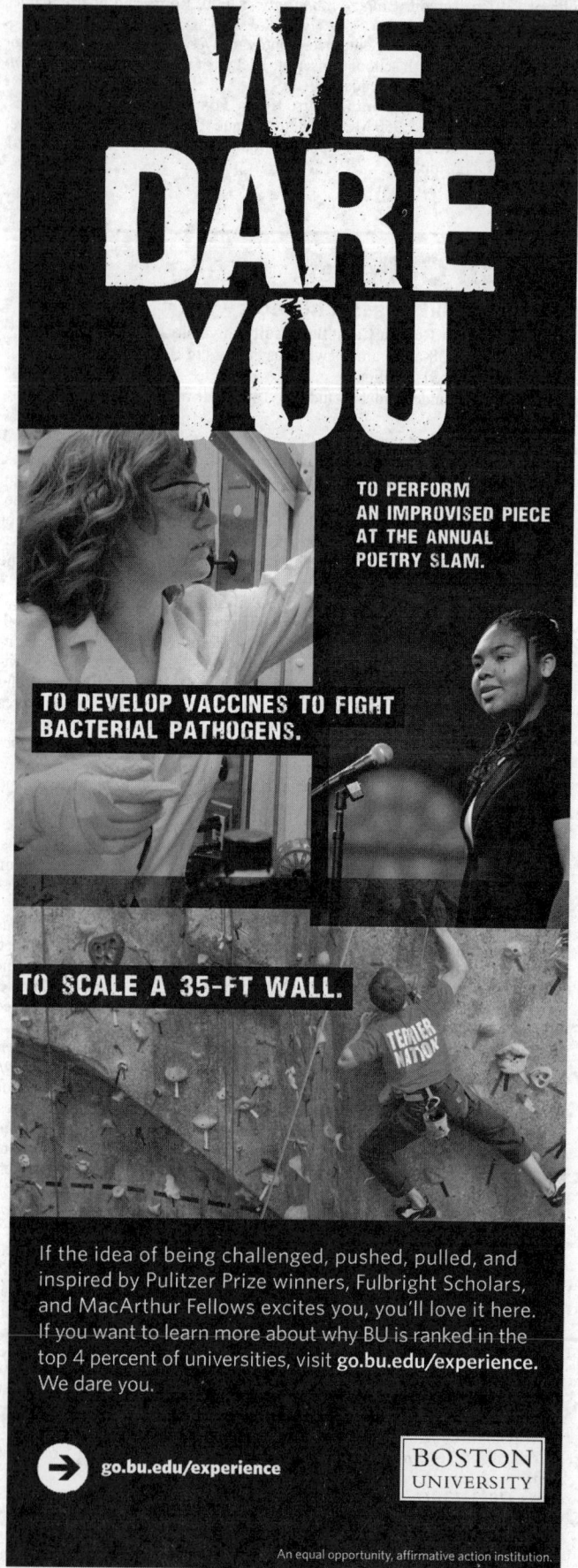

WE DARE YOU

TO PERFORM AN IMPROVISED PIECE AT THE ANNUAL POETRY SLAM.

TO DEVELOP VACCINES TO FIGHT BACTERIAL PATHOGENS.

TO SCALE A 35-FT WALL.

If the idea of being challenged, pushed, pulled, and inspired by Pulitzer Prize winners, Fulbright Scholars, and MacArthur Fellows excites you, you'll love it here. If you want to learn more about why BU is ranked in the top 4 percent of universities, visit **go.bu.edu/experience**. We dare you.

→ **go.bu.edu/experience**

BOSTON UNIVERSITY

An equal opportunity, affirmative action institution.

need fully met. 3,238 Federal Work-Study jobs (averaging $1930). 129 state and other part-time jobs (averaging $13,114). In 2012, 1148 non-need-based awards were made. *Average percent of need met:* 89%. *Average financial aid package:* $37,038. *Average need-based loan:* $7631. *Average need-based gift aid:* $25,047. *Average non-need-based aid:* $22,631. *Average indebtedness upon graduation:* $36,150. *Financial aid deadline:* 2/15.

Applying *Options:* electronic application, early admission, early decision, deferred entrance. *Application fee:* $80. *Required:* essay or personal statement, high school transcript, 2 letters of recommendation. *Required for some:* interview, audition, portfolio. *Application deadlines:* 1/1 (freshmen), 3/1 (transfers). *Early decision deadline:* 11/1. *Notification:* 4/1 (freshmen), continuous until 6/1 (transfers), 12/15 (early decision).

Freshman Application Contact Ms. Kelly Walter, Associate Vice-president and Executive Director of Admissions, Boston University, 121 Bay State Road, Boston, MA 02215. *Phone:* 617-353-2300. *Fax:* 617-353-9695. *E-mail:* admissions@bu.edu.

Website: http://www.bu.edu/.

See previous page for display ad and page 1162 for the College Close-Up.

Brandeis University

Waltham, Massachusetts

- **Independent** university, founded 1948
- **Suburban** 235-acre campus with easy access to Boston
- **Endowment** $703.7 million
- **Coed**
- **Most difficult** entrance level

Faculty *Student/faculty ratio:* 10:1.

Academics *Calendar:* semesters. *Degrees:* bachelor's, master's, doctoral, and postbachelor's certificates.

Student Life *Campus security:* 24-hour emergency response devices and patrols, late-night transport/escort service, controlled dormitory access.

Athletics Member NCAA. All Division III.

Standardized Tests *Required:* SAT or ACT (for admission).

Costs (2012–13) *Comprehensive fee:* $56,550 includes full-time tuition ($42,682), mandatory fees ($1612), and room and board ($12,256). Full-time tuition and fees vary according to student level. Part-time tuition and fees vary according to course load. *College room only:* $6812. Room and board charges vary according to board plan and housing facility. *Payment plans:* tuition prepayment, installment.

Financial Aid *Of all full-time matriculated undergraduates who enrolled in 2011,* 2,115 applied for aid, 1,822 were judged to have need, 844 had their need fully met. *In 2011,* 240 non-need-based awards were made. *Average percent of need met:* 90. *Average financial aid package:* $33,633. *Average need-based loan:* $4156. *Average need-based gift aid:* $30,179. *Average non-need-based aid:* $21,351. *Average indebtedness upon graduation:* $27,906. *Financial aid deadline:* 2/1.

Applying *Options:* electronic application, early decision, deferred entrance. *Application fee:* $55. *Required:* essay or personal statement, high school transcript, 2 letters of recommendation. *Recommended:* interview.

Freshman Application Contact Mr. Mark D. Spencer, Dean of Admissions, Brandeis University, 415 South Street, PO Box 549110, Waltham, MA 02454-9110. *Phone:* 781-736-3500. *Toll-free phone:* 800-622-0622. *Fax:* 781-736-3536. *E-mail:* admissions@brandeis.edu.

Website: http://www.brandeis.edu/.

Bridgewater State University

Bridgewater, Massachusetts

- **State-supported** comprehensive, founded 1840, part of Massachusetts Department of Higher Education
- **Suburban** 278-acre campus with easy access to Boston
- **Endowment** $26.7 million
- **Coed** 9,684 undergraduate students, 83% full-time, 58% women, 42% men
- **Moderately difficult** entrance level, 73% of applicants were admitted

Undergraduates 8,032 full-time, 1,652 part-time. Students come from 27 states and territories; 22 other countries; 4% are from out of state; 7% Black or African American, non-Hispanic/Latino; 5% Hispanic/Latino; 2% Asian, non-Hispanic/Latino; 0.1% Native Hawaiian or other Pacific Islander, non-Hispanic/Latino; 0.3% American Indian or Alaska Native, non-Hispanic/Latino; 2% Two or more races, non-Hispanic/Latino; 1% Race/ethnicity unknown;

0.6% international; 11% transferred in; 35% live on campus. *Retention:* 81% of full-time freshmen returned.

Freshmen *Admission:* 6,170 applied, 4,525 admitted, 1,454 enrolled. *Average high school GPA:* 3.2. *Test scores:* SAT critical reading scores over 500: 52%; SAT math scores over 500: 60%; ACT scores over 18: 96%; SAT critical reading scores over 600: 11%; SAT math scores over 600: 13%; ACT scores over 24: 11%; SAT critical reading scores over 700: 1%; SAT math scores over 700: 1%; ACT scores over 30: 2%.

Faculty *Total:* 775, 41% full-time. *Student/faculty ratio:* 20:1.

Academics *Calendar:* semesters. *Degrees:* bachelor's, master's, post-master's, and postbachelor's certificates. *Special study options:* academic remediation for entering students, accelerated degree program, adult/continuing education programs, advanced placement credit, distance learning, double majors, English as a second language, honors programs, independent study, internships, off-campus study, part-time degree program, services for LD students, study abroad, summer session for credit. *ROTC:* Army (c), Air Force (c).

Computers on Campus 675 computers/terminals and 12 ports are available on campus for general student use. Students can access the following: campus intranet, computer help desk, free student e-mail accounts, online (class) grades, online (class) registration, online (class) schedules, student account information, application software. Campuswide network is available. 100% of college-owned or -operated housing units are wired for high-speed Internet access. Wireless service is available via entire campus.

Student Life *Housing options:* coed, disabled students. Campus housing is university owned. Freshman applicants given priority for college housing. *Activities and organizations:* drama/theater group, student-run newspaper, radio station, choral group, Dance Company, African American Society (Afro-Am), Program Committee, Panhellenic Association, Inter-Fraternity Council, national fraternities, national sororities. *Campus security:* 24-hour emergency response devices and patrols, late-night transport/escort service, controlled dormitory access, 24-Hour patrols by BSU Police. *Student services:* health clinic, personal/psychological counseling.

Athletics Member NCAA. All Division III. *Intercollegiate sports:* baseball M, basketball M/W, cross-country running M/W, field hockey W, football M, lacrosse W, soccer M/W, softball W, swimming and diving M/W, tennis M/W, track and field M/W, volleyball W, wrestling M. *Intramural sports:* badminton M/W, basketball M/W, equestrian sports M(c)/W(c), field hockey W, football M/W, golf M(c)/W(c), ice hockey M(c), lacrosse M(c), rugby W(c), soccer M/W, softball M/W, ultimate Frisbee M(c)/W(c), volleyball M/W.

Standardized Tests *Required:* SAT or ACT (for admission).

Costs (2013–14) *Tuition:* state resident $910 full-time, $38 per credit hour part-time; nonresident $7050 full-time, $294 per credit hour part-time. Full-time tuition and fees vary according to class time. *Required fees:* $7142 full-time, $292 per credit hour part-time. *Room and board:* $10,700; room only: $7000. Room and board charges vary according to board plan and housing facility. *Payment plan:* installment. *Waivers:* senior citizens and employees or children of employees.

Financial Aid Of all full-time matriculated undergraduates who enrolled in 2011, 7,601 applied for aid, 5,041 were judged to have need, 351 had their need fully met. 526 Federal Work-Study jobs (averaging $1710). In 2011, 31 non-need-based awards were made. *Average financial aid package:* $10,368. *Average need-based loan:* $3997. *Average need-based gift aid:* $4146. *Average non-need-based aid:* $5278. *Average indebtedness upon graduation:* $30,189.

Applying *Options:* electronic application, early action, deferred entrance. *Application fee:* $40. *Required:* high school transcript, minimum 2.0 GPA, SAT or ACT Scores. *Recommended:* essay or personal statement, . *Application deadlines:* 2/15 (freshmen), 2/15 (out-of-state freshmen), 2/15 (transfers), 11/15 (early action). *Notification:* continuous until 4/15 (freshmen), continuous until 4/15 (out-of-state freshmen), continuous until 4/15 (transfers), 12/15 (early action).

Freshman Application Contact Mr. Gregg Meyer, Dean of University Admissions, Bridgewater State University, Gates House, 40 Cedar Street, Bridgewater, MA 02325. *Phone:* 508-531-1237. *Fax:* 508-531-1746. *E-mail:* admission@bridgew.edu.

Website: http://www.bridgew.edu/.

Cambridge College

Cambridge, Massachusetts

- **Independent** comprehensive, founded 1971
- **Urban** campus with easy access to Boston
- **Endowment** $11.4 million
- **Coed** 1,090 undergraduate students, 25% full-time, 67% women, 33% men
- **Noncompetitive** entrance level, 64% of applicants were admitted

Undergraduates 270 full-time, 820 part-time. Students come from 7 states and territories; 13% are from out of state; 32% Black or African American, non-Hispanic/Latino; 24% Hispanic/Latino; 3% Asian, non-Hispanic/Latino; 0.3% Native Hawaiian or other Pacific Islander, non-Hispanic/Latino; 0.3% American Indian or Alaska Native, non-Hispanic/Latino; 1% Two or more races, non-Hispanic/Latino; 17% Race/ethnicity unknown; 5% international; 7% transferred in. *Retention:* 41% of full-time freshmen returned.

Freshmen *Admission:* 107 applied, 68 admitted, 68 enrolled.

Faculty *Total:* 453, 4% full-time, 59% with terminal degrees. *Student/faculty ratio:* 13:1.

Academics *Calendar:* trimesters. *Degrees:* certificates, bachelor's, master's, doctoral, and post-master's certificates. *Special study options:* accelerated degree program, adult/continuing education programs, advanced placement credit, distance learning, independent study, internships, part-time degree program, services for LD students, summer session for credit.

Computers on Campus Students can access the following: computer help desk, free student e-mail accounts, online (class) grades, online (class) registration, online (class) schedules. Campuswide network is available. Wireless service is available via entire campus.

Student Life *Housing:* college housing not available.

Financial Aid Of all full-time matriculated undergraduates who enrolled in 2011, 219 applied for aid, 208 were judged to have need. *Average financial aid package:* $8094. *Average need-based loan:* $4302. *Average need-based gift aid:* $4912.

Applying *Options:* electronic application, deferred entrance. *Application fee:* $30. *Required:* essay or personal statement, high school transcript, 1 letter of recommendation, resume, health insurance, immunizations form, application form. *Recommended:* interview. *Application deadlines:* rolling (freshmen), rolling (out-of-state freshmen), rolling (transfers). *Notification:* continuous (freshmen), continuous (out-of-state freshmen), continuous (transfers).

Freshman Application Contact Denise Haile, Director of Admissions, Cambridge College, 1000 Massachusetts Avenue, Cambridge, MA 02138-5304. *Phone:* 800-877-4725. *Toll-free phone:* 800-877-4723. *Fax:* 617-349-3561. *E-mail:* denise.haile@cambridgecollege.edu. *Website:* http://www.cambridgecollege.edu/.

Clark University

Worcester, Massachusetts

- **Independent** university, founded 1887
- **Urban** 50-acre campus with easy access to Boston
- **Endowment** $320.5 million
- **Coed** 2,352 undergraduate students, 96% full-time, 58% women, 42% men
- **Moderately difficult** entrance level, 70% of applicants were admitted

Undergraduates 2,253 full-time, 99 part-time. Students come from 42 states and territories; 70 other countries; 60% are from out of state; 4% Black or African American, non-Hispanic/Latino; 6% Hispanic/Latino; 5% Asian, non-Hispanic/Latino; 0.1% American Indian or Alaska Native, non-Hispanic/Latino; 2% Two or more races, non-Hispanic/Latino; 7% Race/ethnicity unknown; 11% international; 2% transferred in; 71% live on campus. *Retention:* 92% of full-time freshmen returned.

Freshmen *Admission:* 4,297 applied, 3,010 admitted, 594 enrolled. *Average high school GPA:* 3.49. *Test scores:* SAT critical reading scores over 500: 86%; SAT math scores over 500: 87%; SAT writing scores over 500: 86%; ACT scores over 18: 99%; SAT critical reading scores over 600: 44%; SAT math scores over 600: 48%; SAT writing scores over 600: 45%; ACT scores over 24: 80%; SAT critical reading scores over 700: 12%; SAT math scores over 700: 12%; SAT writing scores over 700: 7%; ACT scores over 30: 21%.

Faculty *Total:* 291, 68% full-time. *Student/faculty ratio:* 10:1.

Academics *Calendar:* semesters. *Degrees:* bachelor's, master's, doctoral, and post-master's certificates. *Special study options:* academic remediation for entering students, accelerated degree program, adult/continuing education programs, advanced placement credit, double majors, English as a second language, honors programs, independent study, internships, off-campus study, part-time degree program, services for LD students, student-designed majors, study abroad, summer session for credit. *ROTC:* Army (c), Navy (c), Air Force (c). *Unusual degree programs:* 3-2 business administration; engineering with Columbia University, Washington University in St. Louis, Worcester Polytechnic Institute; environmental studies, international development, community planning, biology, biochemistry, chemistry, physics, economics, history, communications, public administration, geographic information systems.

Computers on Campus 149 computers/terminals and 4,000 ports are available on campus for general student use. Students can access the following: campus intranet, computer help desk, free student e-mail accounts, online (class) grades, online (class) registration, online (class) schedules, online

course support. Campuswide network is available. 100% of college-owned or-operated housing units are wired for high-speed Internet access. Wireless service is available via entire campus.

Student Life *Housing:* on-campus residence required through sophomore year. *Options:* coed, women-only, disabled students. Campus housing is university owned. Freshman campus housing is guaranteed. *Activities and organizations:* drama/theater group, student-run newspaper, radio and television station, choral group, marching band, International Students Association, Outing Club, Science Fiction People of Clark, Ballroom Dance Team and Club, Hillel. *Campus security:* 24-hour emergency response devices and patrols, student patrols, late-night transport/escort service, controlled dormitory access. *Student services:* health clinic, personal/psychological counseling, women's center.

Athletics Member NCAA, NAIA. All NCAA Division III. *Intercollegiate sports:* baseball M, basketball M/W, crew M/W, cross-country running M/W, field hockey W, lacrosse M, soccer M/W, softball W, swimming and diving M/W, tennis M/W, volleyball W. *Intramural sports:* basketball M/W, equestrian sports M(c)/W(c), football M/W, ice hockey M(c)/W(c), lacrosse W(c), racquetball M/W, soccer M/W, softball M/W, track and field M(c)/W(c), ultimate Frisbee M(c)/W(c), volleyball M(c)/W(c), water polo M/W.

Costs (2013–14) *Comprehensive fee:* $47,020 includes full-time tuition ($39,200), mandatory fees ($350), and room and board ($7470). Part-time tuition: $1225 per credit hour. *Required fees:* $1225 per credit hour part-time. *College room only:* $4170. Room and board charges vary according to board plan and housing facility. *Payment plans:* tuition prepayment, installment. *Waivers:* employees or children of employees.

Financial Aid Of all full-time matriculated undergraduates who enrolled in 2012, 1,613 applied for aid, 1,290 were judged to have need, 871 had their need fully met. 1,000 Federal Work-Study jobs (averaging $2000). In 2012, 666 non-need-based awards were made. *Average percent of need met:* 95%. *Average financial aid package:* $32,364. *Average need-based loan:* $3778. *Average need-based gift aid:* $25,010. *Average non-need-based aid:* $15,601. *Average indebtedness upon graduation:* $25,175. *Financial aid deadline:* 2/1.

Applying *Options:* electronic application, early admission, early action, deferred entrance. *Application fee:* $55. *Required:* essay or personal statement, high school transcript, 2 letters of recommendation. *Recommended:* interview. *Application deadlines:* 1/15 (freshmen), 4/15 (transfers), 11/15 (early action). *Notification:* 4/1 (freshmen), 6/1 (transfers), 12/23 (early action).

Freshman Application Contact Mr. Donald Honeman, Dean of Admissions, Clark University, Admissions House, 950 Main Street, Worcester, MA 01610. *Phone:* 508-793-7431. *Toll-free phone:* 800-GO-CLARK. *Fax:* 508-793-8821. *E-mail:* admissions@clarku.edu. *Website:* http://www.clarku.edu/.

College of the Holy Cross

Worcester, Massachusetts

- **Independent Roman Catholic (Jesuit)** 4-year, founded 1843
- **Suburban** 174-acre campus with easy access to Boston
- **Endowment** $589.8 million
- **Coed** 2,926 undergraduate students, 99% full-time, 51% women, 49% men
- **Very difficult** entrance level, 34% of applicants were admitted

Undergraduates 2,891 full-time, 35 part-time. Students come from 48 states and territories; 21 other countries; 63% are from out of state; 5% Black or African American, non-Hispanic/Latino; 10% Hispanic/Latino; 5% Asian, non-Hispanic/Latino; 0.2% American Indian or Alaska Native, non-Hispanic/Latino; 2% Two or more races, non-Hispanic/Latino; 8% Race/ethnicity unknown; 1% international; 0.5% transferred in; 91% live on campus. *Retention:* 95% of full-time freshmen returned.

Freshmen *Admission:* 7,228 applied, 2,424 admitted, 763 enrolled. *Average high school GPA:* 3.88. *Test scores:* SAT critical reading scores over 500: 99%; SAT math scores over 500: 99%; SAT writing scores over 500: 99%; ACT scores over 18: 100%; SAT critical reading scores over 600: 78%; SAT math scores over 600: 85%; SAT writing scores over 600: 82%; ACT scores over 24: 98%; SAT critical reading scores over 700: 26%; SAT math scores over 700: 21%; SAT writing scores over 700: 28%; ACT scores over 30: 39%.

Faculty *Total:* 316, 86% full-time, 91% with terminal degrees. *Student/faculty ratio:* 10:1.

Academics *Calendar:* semesters. *Degrees:* bachelor's (standardized tests are optional for admission to the College of Holy Cross). *Special study options:* accelerated degree program, advanced placement credit, double majors, honors programs, independent study, internships, off-campus study, services for LD students, student-designed majors, study abroad. *ROTC:* Army (c), Navy (b), Air Force (c). *Unusual degree programs:* 3-2 engineering with Columbia University.

Computers on Campus 485 computers/terminals are available on campus for general student use. Students can access the following: computer help desk, free student e-mail accounts, online (class) registration. Campuswide network is available. 100% of college-owned or -operated housing units are wired for high-speed Internet access. Wireless service is available via classrooms, computer centers, computer labs, dorm rooms, libraries, student centers.

Student Life *Housing:* on-campus residence required through sophomore year. *Options:* coed, disabled students. Campus housing is university owned. Freshman campus housing is guaranteed. *Activities and organizations:* drama/theater group, student-run newspaper, radio station, choral group, marching band, SPUD (community service organization), choral and music groups, Campus Activities Board, Student Government Association, Purple Key Society. *Campus security:* 24-hour emergency response devices and patrols, late-night transport/escort service, controlled dormitory access. *Student services:* health clinic, personal/psychological counseling.

Athletics Member NCAA. All Division I except football (Division I-AA). *Intercollegiate sports:* baseball M, basketball M(s)/W(s), crew M/W, cross-country running M/W, field hockey W(s), golf M/W, ice hockey M(s)/W, lacrosse M/W, soccer M(s)/W(s), softball W, swimming and diving M/W, tennis M/W, track and field M/W, volleyball W. *Intramural sports:* baseball M(c), basketball M(c)/W, equestrian sports M(c)/W(c), field hockey W(c), football M/W, golf M(c)/W(c), ice hockey M(c), lacrosse M(c)/W(c), rugby M(c)/W(c), sailing M(c)/W(c), skiing (downhill) M(c)/W(c), soccer M(c)/W(c), softball M/W, swimming and diving M(c)/W(c), tennis M(c)/W(c), ultimate Frisbee M(c)/W(c), volleyball M(c)/W(c), water polo M(c)/W(c).

Costs (2013–14) *Comprehensive fee:* $56,232 includes full-time tuition ($43,660), mandatory fees ($612), and room and board ($11,960). *College room only:* $6450. Room and board charges vary according to housing facility. *Payment plan:* installment. *Waivers:* employees or children of employees.

Financial Aid Of all full-time matriculated undergraduates who enrolled in 2012, 1,892 applied for aid, 1,761 were judged to have need, 1,682 had their need fully met. 1,108 Federal Work-Study jobs (averaging $1638). In 2012, 36 non-need-based awards were made. *Average percent of need met:* 100%. *Average financial aid package:* $33,123. *Average need-based loan:* $5492. *Average need-based gift aid:* $30,191. *Average non-need-based aid:* $28,625. *Average indebtedness upon graduation:* $26,567. *Financial aid deadline:* 2/1.

Applying *Options:* electronic application, early admission, early decision, deferred entrance. *Application fee:* $60. *Required:* essay or personal statement, high school transcript, 2 letters of recommendation. *Recommended:* interview. *Application deadlines:* 1/15 (freshmen), 4/1 (transfers). *Early decision deadline:* 12/15. *Notification:* 4/1 (freshmen), continuous (transfers), 1/15 (early decision).

Freshman Application Contact College of the Holy Cross, 1 College Street, Worcester, MA 01610-2395. *Phone:* 508-793-2443. *Toll-free phone:* 800-442-2421.

Website: http://www.holycross.edu/.

Curry College
Milton, Massachusetts

- **Independent** comprehensive, founded 1879
- **Suburban** 135-acre campus with easy access to Boston
- **Coed** 2,769 undergraduate students, 72% full-time, 62% women, 38% men
- **Moderately difficult** entrance level, 84% of applicants were admitted

Undergraduates 1,995 full-time, 774 part-time. Students come from 32 states and territories; 7 other countries; 21% are from out of state; 8% Black or African American, non-Hispanic/Latino; 5% Hispanic/Latino; 2% Asian, non-Hispanic/Latino; 0.1% Native Hawaiian or other Pacific Islander, non-Hispanic/Latino; 0.4% American Indian or Alaska Native, non-Hispanic/Latino; 1% Two or more races, non-Hispanic/Latino; 17% Race/ethnicity unknown; 0.9% international; 3% transferred in; 50% live on campus. *Retention:* 69% of full-time freshmen returned.

Freshmen *Admission:* 5,494 applied, 4,621 admitted, 584 enrolled. *Average high school GPA:* 2.72. *Test scores:* SAT critical reading scores over 500: 27%; SAT math scores over 500: 30%; SAT writing scores over 500: 29%; ACT scores over 18: 75%; SAT critical reading scores over 600: 3%; SAT math scores over 600: 3%; SAT writing scores over 600: 4%; ACT scores over 24: 8%.

Faculty *Total:* 292, 43% full-time. *Student/faculty ratio:* 12:1.

Academics *Calendar:* semesters. *Degrees:* certificates, bachelor's, and master's. *Special study options:* academic remediation for entering students, accelerated degree program, adult/continuing education programs, advanced placement credit, double majors, external degree program, honors programs, independent study, internships, off-campus study, part-time degree program, services for LD students, student-designed majors, study abroad, summer session for credit. *ROTC:* Army (c).

Computers on Campus 245 computers/terminals and 2,500 ports are available on campus for general student use. Students can access the following: campus intranet, computer help desk, free student e-mail accounts, online (class) grades, online (class) registration, online (class) schedules, library online catalog and research databases. Campuswide network is available. 100% of college-owned or -operated housing units are wired for high-speed Internet access. Wireless service is available via entire campus.

Student Life *Housing options:* coed, men-only, women-only. Campus housing is university owned. *Activities and organizations:* drama/theater group, student-run newspaper, radio and television station, choral group, student radio station, student government, Campus Activities Board, student newspaper, Drama Club. *Campus security:* 24-hour emergency response devices and patrols, late-night transport/escort service, controlled dormitory access. *Student services:* health clinic, personal/psychological counseling.

Athletics Member NCAA. All Division III. *Intercollegiate sports:* baseball M, basketball M/W, cross-country running W, football M, ice hockey M, lacrosse M/W, soccer M/W, softball W, tennis M/W. *Intramural sports:* basketball M/W, cheerleading M/W, equestrian sports W, rugby M/W, skiing (downhill) M/W, softball M/W, tennis M/W, ultimate Frisbee M/W, volleyball M/W.

Standardized Tests *Required for some:* SAT or ACT (for admission), TOEFL for international applicants. The College's Program for the Advancement of Learning does not require nor does it consider SAT or ACT scores during the admissions process.

Costs (2012–13) *One-time required fee:* $290. *Comprehensive fee:* $46,225 includes full-time tuition ($31,900), mandatory fees ($1565), and room and board ($12,760). Full-time tuition and fees vary according to class time and location. Part-time tuition: $1063 per credit hour. Part-time tuition and fees vary according to class time, course load, and location. *College room only:* $7160. Room and board charges vary according to board plan and housing facility. *Payment plan:* installment. *Waivers:* children of alumni and employees or children of employees.

Financial Aid Of all full-time matriculated undergraduates who enrolled in 2012, 1,483 applied for aid, 1,483 were judged to have need, 85 had their need fully met. 832 Federal Work-Study jobs (averaging $1851). In 2012, 203 non-need-based awards were made. *Average percent of need met:* 67%. *Average financial aid package:* $21,860. *Average need-based loan:* $4435. *Average need-based gift aid:* $13,856. *Average non-need-based aid:* $5607. *Average indebtedness upon graduation:* $41,876.

Applying *Options:* electronic application, early admission, early action, deferred entrance. *Application fee:* $50. *Required:* essay or personal statement, high school transcript, minimum 2.0 GPA, 1 letter of recommendation, supplemental form for Common Application subscribers and Program for Advancement of Learning. *Required for some:* interview. *Recommended:* interview. *Application deadlines:* 4/1 (freshmen), 7/1 (transfers), 12/1 (early action). *Notification:* continuous (freshmen), continuous (transfers), 12/15 (early action).

Freshman Application Contact Ms. Jane P. Fidler, Dean of Admission, Curry College, 1071 Blue Hill Avenue, Milton, MA 02186. *Phone:* 617-333-2210. *Toll-free phone:* 800-669-0686. *Fax:* 617-333-2114. *E-mail:* curryadm@curry.edu.
Website: http://www.curry.edu/.

See previous page for display ad and page 1260 for the College Close-Up.

Dean College

Franklin, Massachusetts

Freshman Application Contact Mr. James Fowler, Dean College, 99 Main Street, Franklin, MA 02038. *Phone:* 508-541-1547. *Toll-free phone:* 877-TRY-DEAN. *Fax:* 508-541-8726. *E-mail:* jfowler@dean.edu.
Website: http://www.dean.edu/.

See page 1264 for the College Close-Up.

Eastern Nazarene College

Quincy, Massachusetts

- **Independent** comprehensive, founded 1918, affiliated with Church of the Nazarene
- **Urban** 17-acre campus with easy access to Boston
- **Endowment** $12.9 million
- **Coed**
- **Moderately difficult** entrance level

Faculty *Student/faculty ratio:* 17:1.

Academics *Calendar:* semesters. *Degrees:* certificates, associate, bachelor's, and master's.

Student Life *Campus security:* 24-hour emergency response devices and patrols, student patrols, late-night transport/escort service, controlled dormitory access.

Athletics Member NCAA. All Division III.

Standardized Tests *Required:* SAT or ACT (for admission). *Recommended:* SAT and SAT Subject Tests or ACT (for admission), SAT Subject Tests (for admission).

Costs (2012–13) *Comprehensive fee:* $35,184 includes full-time tuition ($25,944), mandatory fees ($940), and room and board ($8300). Full-time tuition and fees vary according to class time, course load, degree level, location, program, and reciprocity agreements. Part-time tuition: $1081 per credit. Part-time tuition and fees vary according to class time, degree level, location, program, and reciprocity agreements. *Required fees:* $350 per term part-time. *Room and board:* Room and board charges vary according to board plan and housing facility.

Financial Aid *Of all full-time matriculated undergraduates who enrolled in 2011,* 526 applied for aid, 447 were judged to have need, 119 had their need fully met. *In 2011,* 65 non-need-based awards were made. *Average percent of need met:* 72. *Average financial aid package:* $23,272. *Average need-based loan:* $8724. *Average need-based gift aid:* $11,487. *Average non-need-based aid:* $11,001.

Applying *Options:* electronic application, early admission, deferred entrance. *Required:* high school transcript, minimum 2.0 GPA, 1 letter of recommendation. *Recommended:* essay or personal statement, minimum 3.0 GPA, 2 letters of recommendation, interview.

Freshman Application Contact Mr. Andrew R. Wright, Director of Admissions, Eastern Nazarene College, 23 East Elm Avenue, Quincy, MA 02170. *Phone:* 617-745-3864. *Toll-free phone:* 800-88-ENC88. *Fax:* 617-745-3992. *E-mail:* andrew.wright@enc.edu.
Website: http://www.enc.edu/.

Elms College

Chicopee, Massachusetts

Freshman Application Contact Mr. Joseph Wagner, Director of Admissions, Elms College, Chicopee, MA 01013-2839. *Phone:* 413-592-3189 Ext. 350. *Toll-free phone:* 800-255-ELMS. *Fax:* 413-594-2781. *E-mail:* admissions@elms.edu.
Website: http://www.elms.edu/.

Emerson College

Boston, Massachusetts

- **Independent** comprehensive, founded 1880
- **Urban** campus
- **Endowment** $117.1 million
- **Coed** 3,675 undergraduate students, 98% full-time, 62% women, 38% men
- **Very difficult** entrance level, 48% of applicants were admitted

Undergraduates 3,586 full-time, 89 part-time. Students come from 44 states and territories; 43 other countries; 77% are from out of state; 3% Black or African American, non-Hispanic/Latino; 10% Hispanic/Latino; 4% Asian, non-Hispanic/Latino; 0.1% Native Hawaiian or other Pacific Islander, non-Hispanic/Latino; 0.1% American Indian or Alaska Native, non-Hispanic/Latino; 4% Two or more races, non-Hispanic/Latino; 14% Race/ethnicity unknown; 4% international; 5% transferred in; 57% live on campus. *Retention:* 88% of full-time freshmen returned.

Freshmen *Admission:* 7,465 applied, 3,615 admitted, 866 enrolled. *Average high school GPA:* 3.6. *Test scores:* SAT critical reading scores over 500: 98%; SAT math scores over 500: 94%; SAT writing scores over 500: 98%; ACT scores over 18: 100%; SAT critical reading scores over 600: 70%; SAT math scores over 600: 56%; SAT writing scores over 600: 71%; ACT scores over 24: 93%; SAT critical reading scores over 700: 18%; SAT math scores over 700: 8%; SAT writing scores over 700: 17%; ACT scores over 30: 22%.

Faculty *Total:* 444, 42% full-time, 52% with terminal degrees. *Student/faculty ratio:* 13:1.

Academics *Calendar:* semesters. *Degrees:* certificates, bachelor's, master's, and doctoral. *Special study options:* adult/continuing education programs, advanced placement credit, double majors, honors programs, independent study, internships, off-campus study, part-time degree program, services for LD students, student-designed majors, study abroad, summer session for credit.

Computers on Campus 480 computers/terminals and 1,900 ports are available on campus for general student use. Students can access the following: computer help desk, free student e-mail accounts, online (class) registration, online (class) schedules. Campuswide network is available. 100% of college-owned or -operated housing units are wired for high-speed Internet access. Wireless service is available via entire campus.

Student Life *Housing:* on-campus residence required through sophomore year. *Options:* coed. Campus housing is university owned. Freshman campus housing is guaranteed. *Activities and organizations:* drama/theater group, student-run newspaper, radio and television station, choral group, EIV (Emerson Independent Video), National Broadcasting Society (student chapter), EmComm (student marketing agency), Emerson Channel (campus television), Berkeley Beacon (student newspaper), national fraternities, national sororities. *Campus security:* 24-hour emergency response devices and patrols, late-night transport/escort service, controlled dormitory access. *Student services:* health clinic, personal/psychological counseling.

Athletics Member NCAA. All Division III. *Intercollegiate sports:* baseball M, basketball M/W, cross-country running M/W, golf M(c)/W(c), ice hockey M(c), lacrosse M/W, soccer M/W, softball W, tennis M/W, track and field W, volleyball M/W. *Intramural sports:* weight lifting M/W.

Standardized Tests *Required:* SAT or ACT (for admission).

Costs (2013–14) *Comprehensive fee:* $50,246 includes full-time tuition ($35,072), mandatory fees ($658), and room and board ($14,516). *Room and board:* Room and board charges vary according to board plan. *Payment plan:* installment. *Waivers:* employees or children of employees.

Financial Aid Of all full-time matriculated undergraduates who enrolled in 2011, 2,329 applied for aid, 2,031 were judged to have need, 885 had their need fully met. 462 Federal Work-Study jobs (averaging $2000). 56 state and other part-time jobs (averaging $11,683). In 2011, 204 non-need-based awards were made. *Average percent of need met:* 72%. *Average financial aid package:* $18,643. *Average need-based loan:* $4407. *Average need-based gift aid:* $16,237. *Average non-need-based aid:* $13,825. *Average indebtedness upon graduation:* $22,844.

Applying *Options:* electronic application, early admission, early action, deferred entrance. *Application fee:* $65. *Required:* essay or personal statement, high school transcript, 1 letter of recommendation. *Required for some:* interview. *Application deadlines:* 1/5 (freshmen), 3/1 (transfers), 11/1 (early action). *Notification:* 4/1 (freshmen), 5/1 (transfers), 12/15 (early action).

Freshman Application Contact Emerson College, 120 Boylston Street, Boston, MA 02116-4624. *Phone:* 617-824-8600.
Website: http://www.emerson.edu/.
See below for display ad and page 1284 for the College Close-Up.

Emmanuel College

Boston, Massachusetts

- **Independent Roman Catholic** comprehensive, founded 1919
- **Urban** 17-acre campus
- **Endowment** $64.7 million
- **Coed** 2,198 undergraduate students, 83% full-time, 72% women, 28% men
- **Moderately difficult** entrance level, 50% of applicants were admitted

Undergraduates 1,828 full-time, 370 part-time. Students come from 33 states and territories; 35 other countries; 39% are from out of state; 6% Black or African American, non-Hispanic/Latino; 6% Hispanic/Latino; 3% Asian, non-Hispanic/Latino; 0.3% American Indian or Alaska Native, non-Hispanic/Latino; 2% Two or more races, non-Hispanic/Latino; 12% Race/ethnicity unknown; 1% international; 2% transferred in; 74% live on campus. *Retention:* 81% of full-time freshmen returned.

Freshmen *Admission:* 7,851 applied, 3,926 admitted, 553 enrolled. *Average high school GPA:* 3.58. *Test scores:* SAT critical reading scores over 500: 83%; SAT math scores over 500: 81%; SAT writing scores over 500: 82%; ACT scores over 18: 99%; SAT critical reading scores over 600: 29%; SAT math scores over 600: 28%; SAT writing scores over 600: 28%; ACT scores over 24: 57%; SAT critical reading scores over 700: 3%; SAT math scores over 700: 2%; SAT writing scores over 700: 2%; ACT scores over 30: 3%.

Faculty *Total:* 242, 42% full-time, 61% with terminal degrees. *Student/faculty ratio:* 14:1.

Academics *Calendar:* semesters. *Degrees:* bachelor's, master's, post-master's, and postbachelor's certificates. *Special study options:* academic remediation for entering students, accelerated degree program, adult/continuing education programs, advanced placement credit, distance learning, double majors, honors programs, independent study, internships, off-campus study, part-time degree program, services for LD students, student-designed majors, study abroad, summer session for credit. *ROTC:* Army (c), Air Force (c).

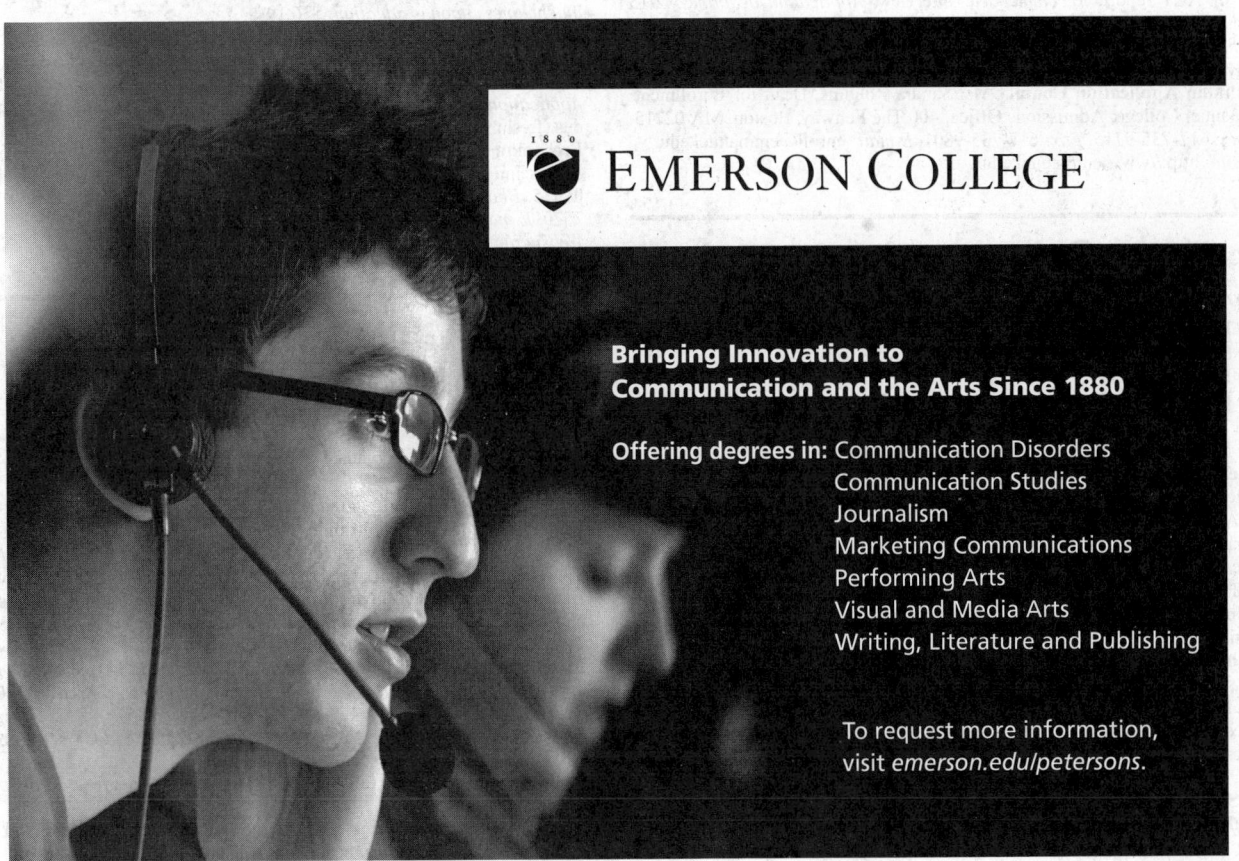

Computers on Campus 117 computers/terminals are available on campus for general student use. Students can access the following: campus intranet, computer help desk, free student e-mail accounts, online (class) grades, online (class) registration, online (class) schedules, software applications. Campuswide network is available. 100% of college-owned or -operated housing units are wired for high-speed Internet access. Wireless service is available via entire campus.

Student Life *Housing options:* coed, disabled students. Campus housing is university owned and leased by the school. Freshman campus housing is guaranteed. *Activities and organizations:* drama/theater group, student-run newspaper, radio station, choral group, EC Superfans, Black Student Union, OUTSpoken (LGBTQ Club), Psychology Club, Campus Activities and Student Events. *Campus security:* 24-hour emergency response devices and patrols, late-night transport/escort service, controlled dormitory access, 24-hour staffed residence hall desks and security office, closed-circuit surveillance in public areas, off-campus escorts, bike patrol. *Student services:* health clinic, personal/psychological counseling.

Athletics Member NCAA. All Division III. *Intercollegiate sports:* basketball M/W, cross-country running M/W, golf M, lacrosse M/W, soccer M/W, softball W, tennis W, track and field M/W, volleyball M/W. *Intramural sports:* badminton M/W, baseball M(c), basketball M/W, bowling M/W, cheerleading M(c)/W(c), field hockey W(c), racquetball M/W, soccer M/W, softball M/W, tennis M/W, volleyball M/W.

Standardized Tests *Required:* SAT or ACT (for admission).

Costs (2012–13) *One-time required fee:* $225. *Comprehensive fee:* $46,640 includes full-time tuition ($33,450), mandatory fees ($200), and room and board ($12,990). Full-time tuition and fees vary according to course load, degree level, and program. Part-time tuition and fees vary according to program. *Room and board:* Room and board charges vary according to housing facility. *Payment plan:* installment. *Waivers:* employees or children of employees.

Financial Aid Of all full-time matriculated undergraduates who enrolled in 2012, 1,631 applied for aid, 1,505 were judged to have need, 864 had their need fully met. In 2012, 265 non-need-based awards were made. *Average percent of need met:* 74%. *Average financial aid package:* $26,204. *Average need-based loan:* $4747. *Average need-based gift aid:* $18,336. *Average non-need-based aid:* $10,978.

Applying *Options:* electronic application, early admission, early decision, early action, deferred entrance. *Application fee:* $60. *Required:* essay or personal statement, high school transcript, 2 letters of recommendation, Official SAT or ACT report. *Recommended:* interview. *Application deadlines:* 2/15 (freshmen), 4/1 (transfers), 11/15 (early action). *Early decision deadline:* 11/1. *Notification:* 12/1 (freshmen), 12/1 (transfers), 12/1 (early decision), 12/15 (early action).

Freshman Application Contact Ms. Sandra Robbins, Dean for Enrollment, Emmanuel College, Admissions Office, 400 The Fenway, Boston, MA 02115. *Phone:* 617-735-9715. *Fax:* 617-735-9801. *E-mail:* enroll@emmanuel.edu. *Website:* http://www.emmanuel.edu/.

Endicott College

Beverly, Massachusetts

- **Independent** comprehensive, founded 1939
- **Suburban** 235-acre campus with easy access to Boston
- **Endowment** $44.9 million
- **Coed** 2,762 undergraduate students, 90% full-time, 58% women, 42% men
- **Moderately difficult** entrance level, 63% of applicants were admitted

Undergraduates 2,498 full-time, 264 part-time. Students come from 28 states and territories; 24 other countries; 51% are from out of state; 2% Black or African American, non-Hispanic/Latino; 3% Hispanic/Latino; 0.7% Asian, non-Hispanic/Latino; 0.1% Native Hawaiian or other Pacific Islander, non-Hispanic/Latino; 0.3% American Indian or Alaska Native, non-Hispanic/Latino; 2% Two or more races, non-Hispanic/Latino; 10% Race/ethnicity unknown; 2% international; 2% transferred in; 83% live on campus. *Retention:* 83% of full-time freshmen returned.

Freshmen *Admission:* 3,661 applied, 2,321 admitted, 645 enrolled. *Average high school GPA:* 3.25. *Test scores:* SAT critical reading scores over 500: 72%; SAT math scores over 500: 74%; SAT writing scores over 500: 71%; ACT scores over 18: 96%; SAT critical reading scores over 600: 16%; SAT math scores over 600: 20%; SAT writing scores over 600: 17%; ACT scores over 24: 45%; SAT critical reading scores over 700: 1%; SAT math scores over 700: 1%; SAT writing scores over 700: 1%.

Faculty *Total:* 386, 24% full-time, 40% with terminal degrees. *Student/faculty ratio:* 14:1.

Academics *Calendar:* semesters. *Degrees:* certificates, associate, bachelor's, master's, doctoral, and postbachelor's certificates. *Special study options:* accelerated degree program, adult/continuing education programs, advanced placement credit, cooperative education, distance learning, honors programs, independent study, internships, off-campus study, part-time degree program, services for LD students, student-designed majors, study abroad, summer session for credit. *ROTC:* Army (c).

Computers on Campus 237 computers/terminals are available on campus for general student use. Students can access the following: campus intranet, computer help desk, free student e-mail accounts, online (class) grades, online (class) registration, online (class) schedules. Campuswide network is available. 100% of college-owned or -operated housing units are wired for high-speed Internet access. Wireless service is available via entire campus.

Student Life *Housing options:* coed, women-only, disabled students. Campus housing is university owned. Freshman campus housing is guaranteed. *Activities and organizations:* drama/theater group, student-run newspaper, radio and television station, choral group, Campus Activities Board, Student Senate, Intramurals, Sailing Club, Shipmates. *Campus security:* 24-hour emergency response devices and patrols, student patrols, late-night transport/escort service, controlled dormitory access, license plate recognition, crime prevention programs, rape awareness defense, property identification, security cameras, front gate. *Student services:* health clinic, personal/psychological counseling.

Athletics Member NCAA. All Division III. *Intercollegiate sports:* baseball M, basketball M/W, cheerleading W(c), crew M(c)/W(c), cross-country running M/W, equestrian sports M/W, field hockey W, football M, golf M/W(c), ice hockey M(c)/W(c), lacrosse M/W, rugby M(c)/W(c), sailing M(c)/W(c), soccer M/W, softball W, tennis M/W, volleyball M/W. *Intramural sports:* basketball M/W, football M/W, racquetball M/W, soccer M/W, softball M/W, tennis M/W, volleyball M/W.

Standardized Tests *Required:* SAT or ACT (for admission).

Costs (2012–13) *Comprehensive fee:* $41,366 includes full-time tuition ($27,666), mandatory fees ($500), and room and board ($13,200). *College room only:* $9100. Room and board charges vary according to board plan and housing facility. *Payment plans:* tuition prepayment, installment. *Waivers:* employees or children of employees.

Financial Aid Of all full-time matriculated undergraduates who enrolled in 2012, 2,114 applied for aid, 1,583 were judged to have need, 172 had their need fully met. 619 Federal Work-Study jobs (averaging $2000). In 2012, 411 non-need-based awards were made. *Average percent of need met:* 63%. *Average financial aid package:* $19,525. *Average need-based loan:* $4556. *Average need-based gift aid:* $10,563. *Average non-need-based aid:* $7749. *Average indebtedness upon graduation:* $36,198.

Applying *Options:* electronic application. *Application fee:* $50. *Required:* essay or personal statement, high school transcript, minimum 2.5 GPA, 1 letter of recommendation. *Required for some:* interview. *Recommended:* interview. *Application deadlines:* 2/15 (freshmen), 3/15 (transfers). *Notification:* continuous (freshmen), continuous (transfers).

Freshman Application Contact Mr. Thomas J. Redman, Vice President of Admission and Financial Aid, Endicott College, 376 Hale Street, Beverly, MA 01915. *Phone:* 978-921-1000. *Toll-free phone:* 800-325-1114. *Fax:* 978-232-2520. *E-mail:* admissio@endicott.edu. *Website:* http://www.endicott.edu/.

Fisher College

Boston, Massachusetts

- **Independent** 4-year, founded 1903
- **Urban** campus with easy access to Boston
- **Coed** 1,751 undergraduate students, 60% full-time, 75% women, 25% men
- **Minimally difficult** entrance level, 64% of applicants were admitted

Undergraduates 1,056 full-time, 695 part-time. 34% are from out of state; 12% Black or African American, non-Hispanic/Latino; 8% Hispanic/Latino; 2% Asian, non-Hispanic/Latino; 0.4% American Indian or Alaska Native, non-Hispanic/Latino; 3% Two or more races, non-Hispanic/Latino; 19% Race/ethnicity unknown; 8% international; 2% transferred in; 47% live on campus. *Retention:* 65% of full-time freshmen returned.

Freshmen *Admission:* 2,460 applied, 1,572 admitted, 349 enrolled. *Average high school GPA:* 2.31. *Test scores:* SAT critical reading scores over 500: 15%; SAT math scores over 500: 15%; ACT scores over 18: 57%; SAT critical reading scores over 600: 3%; SAT math scores over 600: 3%; ACT scores over 24: 7%; SAT critical reading scores over 700: 1%.

Faculty *Total:* 155, 19% full-time, 23% with terminal degrees. *Student/faculty ratio:* 18:1.

Academics *Calendar:* semesters. *Degrees:* certificates, associate, and bachelor's. *Special study options:* academic remediation for entering students, adult/

continuing education programs, advanced placement credit, distance learning, English as a second language, honors programs, independent study, internships, off-campus study, part-time degree program, services for LD students, study abroad, summer session for credit. *ROTC:* Army (c).

Computers on Campus 137 computers/terminals are available on campus for general student use. Students can access the following: campus intranet, computer help desk, free student e-mail accounts, online (class) grades, online (class) registration, online (class) schedules. Campuswide network is available. 100% of college-owned or -operated housing units are wired for high-speed Internet access. Wireless service is available via entire campus.

Student Life *Housing options:* coed, women-only. Campus housing is university owned and leased by the school. *Activities and organizations:* drama/theater group, choral group. *Campus security:* 24-hour emergency response devices and patrols, controlled dormitory access. *Student services:* health clinic, personal/psychological counseling, women's center.

Athletics Member NAIA. *Intercollegiate sports:* baseball M, basketball M/W, soccer M/W, softball W.

Standardized Tests *Required for some:* SAT or ACT (for admission).

Costs (2013–14) *Comprehensive fee:* $40,699 includes full-time tuition ($25,780), mandatory fees ($995), and room and board ($13,924). Part-time tuition: $300 per credit. *Room and board:* Room and board charges vary according to housing facility. *Payment plan:* installment.

Financial Aid Of all full-time matriculated undergraduates who enrolled in 2012, 1,047 applied for aid, 879 were judged to have need.

Applying *Options:* electronic application, deferred entrance. *Application fee:* $50. *Required:* high school transcript. *Required for some:* essay or personal statement, interview. *Recommended:* minimum 2.0 GPA. *Application deadlines:* rolling (freshmen), rolling (transfers). *Notification:* continuous (freshmen), continuous (transfers).

Freshman Application Contact Mr. Robert Melaragni, Dean of Admissions, Fisher College, Boston, MA 02116. *Phone:* 617-236-8818. *Fax:* 617-236-5473. *E-mail:* admissions@fisher.edu. *Website:* http://www.fisher.edu/.

Fitchburg State University

Fitchburg, Massachusetts

- **State-supported** comprehensive, founded 1894, part of Massachusetts Public Higher Education System
- **Suburban** 78-acre campus with easy access to Boston
- **Endowment** $15.0 million
- **Coed**
- **Moderately difficult** entrance level

Faculty *Student/faculty ratio:* 16:1.

Academics *Calendar:* semesters. *Degrees:* certificates, bachelor's, master's, post-master's, and postbachelor's certificates.

Student Life *Campus security:* 24-hour emergency response devices and patrols, student patrols, late-night transport/escort service, controlled dormitory access.

Athletics Member NCAA. All Division III.

Standardized Tests *Required:* SAT or ACT (for admission).

Costs (2012–13) *Tuition:* state resident $970 full-time; nonresident $7050 full-time. Full-time tuition and fees vary according to class time and reciprocity agreements. Part-time tuition and fees vary according to class time and reciprocity agreements. *Required fees:* $7740 full-time. *Room and board:* $8602; room only: $5652. Room and board charges vary according to board plan and housing facility.

Financial Aid *Of all full-time matriculated undergraduates who enrolled in 2009,* 3,132 applied for aid, 1,934 were judged to have need, 1,742 had their need fully met. 248 Federal Work-Study jobs (averaging $1076). *In 2009,* 76 non-need-based awards were made. *Average percent of need met:* 93. *Average financial aid package:* $8645. *Average need-based loan:* $3679. *Average need-based gift aid:* $4336. *Average non-need-based aid:* $1292. *Average indebtedness upon graduation:* $19,902.

Applying *Options:* electronic application, deferred entrance. *Application fee:* $25. *Required:* essay or personal statement, high school transcript, minimum 2.0 GPA, 16 core courses.

Freshman Application Contact Kay Reynolds, Director of Admissions, Fitchburg State University, 160 Pearl Street, Fitchburg, MA 01420-2697.

Phone: 978-665-3144. *Toll-free phone:* 800-705-9692. *Fax:* 978-665-4540. *E-mail:* admissions@fitchburgstate.edu. *Website:* http://www.fitchburgstate.edu/.

See previous page for display ad and page 1292 for the College Close-Up.

Framingham State University

Framingham, Massachusetts

- **State-supported** 4-year, founded 1839, part of Massachusetts Public Higher Education System
- **Suburban** 73-acre campus with easy access to Boston
- **Endowment** $21.8 million
- **Coed** 4,490 undergraduate students, 85% full-time, 63% women, 37% men
- **Moderately difficult** entrance level, 52% of applicants were admitted

Undergraduates 3,804 full-time, 686 part-time. 4% are from out of state; 7% Black or African American, non-Hispanic/Latino; 8% Hispanic/Latino; 3% Asian, non-Hispanic/Latino; 0.1% American Indian or Alaska Native, non-Hispanic/Latino; 2% Two or more races, non-Hispanic/Latino; 4% Race/ethnicity unknown; 0.1% international; 11% transferred in; 52% live on campus. *Retention:* 74% of full-time freshmen returned.

Freshmen *Admission:* 5,433 applied, 2,807 admitted, 826 enrolled. *Average high school GPA:* 3.16. *Test scores:* SAT critical reading scores over 500: 40%; SAT math scores over 500: 33%; SAT writing scores over 500: 41%; ACT scores over 18: 7%; SAT critical reading scores over 600: 1%; SAT math scores over 600: 1%; SAT writing scores over 600: 3%.

Faculty *Total:* 313, 56% full-time, 49% with terminal degrees. *Student/faculty ratio:* 16:1.

Academics *Calendar:* semesters. *Degrees:* bachelor's, master's, and postbachelor's certificates. *Special study options:* advanced placement credit, cooperative education, distance learning, double majors, English as a second language, honors programs, independent study, internships, off-campus study, part-time degree program, services for LD students, student-designed majors, study abroad, summer session for credit.

Computers on Campus 216 computers/terminals and 3,500 ports are available on campus for general student use. Students can access the following: computer help desk, free student e-mail accounts, online (class) grades, online (class) registration, online (class) schedules. Campuswide network is available. 100% of college-owned or -operated housing units are wired for high-speed Internet access. Wireless service is available via entire campus.

Student Life *Housing options:* coed, women-only. Campus housing is university owned. Freshman applicants given priority for college housing. *Activities and organizations:* drama/theater group, student-run newspaper, radio station, choral group, Dance Club, Student Union Activities Board, Gatepost (student newspaper), Student Government Association, Hilltop Players (theater group). *Campus security:* 24-hour emergency response devices and patrols, student patrols, late-night transport/escort service, controlled dormitory access. *Student services:* health clinic, personal/psychological counseling.

Athletics Member NCAA. All Division III. *Intercollegiate sports:* baseball M, basketball M/W, cross-country running M/W, field hockey W, football M, ice hockey M, lacrosse W, soccer M/W, softball W, volleyball W. *Intramural sports:* badminton M/W, basketball M/W, cheerleading M(c)/W(c), football M/W, golf M/W, rugby M(c)/W(c), soccer M/W, tennis M/W, ultimate Frisbee M/W, volleyball M/W, weight lifting M/W.

Standardized Tests *Required:* SAT or ACT (for admission).

Costs (2012–13) *Tuition:* state resident $970 full-time, $162 per course part-time; nonresident $7050 full-time, $1175 per course part-time. Full-time tuition and fees vary according to class time. Part-time tuition and fees vary according to class time and course load. *Required fees:* $7110 full-time, $1250 per course part-time. *Room and board:* $9540; room only: $6380. Room and board charges vary according to board plan and housing facility. *Payment plans:* tuition prepayment, installment. *Waivers:* senior citizens and employees or children of employees.

Financial Aid Of all full-time matriculated undergraduates who enrolled in 2009, 2,362 applied for aid, 1,624 were judged to have need, 895 had their need fully met. In 2009, 74 non-need-based awards were made. *Average percent of need met:* 76%. *Average financial aid package:* $6880. *Average need-based loan:* $4950. *Average need-based gift aid:* $4090. *Average non-need-based aid:* $2208. *Average indebtedness upon graduation:* $19,300.

Applying *Options:* electronic application, early action, deferred entrance. *Application fee:* $45. *Required:* high school transcript, minimum 2.0 GPA, Minimum of 16 college preparatory courses in specified areas. *Recommended:* minimum 3.0 GPA. *Application deadlines:* 2/15 (freshmen), 11/15 (early

action). *Notification:* continuous (freshmen), continuous (transfers), 12/15 (early action).

Freshman Application Contact Ms. Shayna Eddy, Associate Dean of Admissions, Framingham State University, 100 State Street, PO Box 9101, Framingham, MA 01701-9101. *Phone:* 508-626-4500. *Fax:* 508-626-4017. *E-mail:* admissions@framingham.edu. *Website:* http://www.framingham.edu/.

Franklin W. Olin College of Engineering

Needham, Massachusetts

- **Independent** 4-year, founded 2002
- **Suburban** 75-acre campus with easy access to Boston
- **Coed** 355 undergraduate students, 100% full-time, 47% women, 53% men
- **Most difficult** entrance level, 16% of applicants were admitted

Undergraduates 355 full-time. Students come from 38 states and territories; 10 other countries; 87% are from out of state; 0.9% Black or African American, non-Hispanic/Latino; 0.6% Hispanic/Latino; 17% Asian, non-Hispanic/Latino; 6% Two or more races, non-Hispanic/Latino; 11% Race/ethnicity unknown; 7% international; 0.6% transferred in; 100% live on campus. *Retention:* 96% of full-time freshmen returned.

Freshmen *Admission:* 768 applied, 126 admitted, 81 enrolled. *Average high school GPA:* 3.9. *Test scores:* SAT critical reading scores over 500: 100%; SAT math scores over 500: 100%; SAT writing scores over 500: 100%; ACT scores over 18: 100%; SAT critical reading scores over 600: 100%; SAT math scores over 600: 99%; SAT writing scores over 600: 100%; ACT scores over 24: 100%; SAT critical reading scores over 700: 76%; SAT math scores over 700: 89%; SAT writing scores over 700: 64%; ACT scores over 30: 97%.

Faculty *Total:* 48, 73% full-time, 88% with terminal degrees. *Student/faculty ratio:* 9:1.

Academics *Degree:* bachelor's. *Special study options:* independent study, internships, off-campus study, services for LD students, student-designed majors, study abroad.

Computers on Campus 410 computers/terminals and 2,364 ports are available on campus for general student use. Students can access the following: campus intranet, computer help desk, free student e-mail accounts, online (class) grades, online (class) registration, online (class) schedules. Campuswide network is available. 100% of college-owned or -operated housing units are wired for high-speed Internet access. Wireless service is available via entire campus.

Student Life *Housing:* on-campus residence required through senior year. *Options:* coed, disabled students. Campus housing is university owned. Freshman campus housing is guaranteed. *Activities and organizations:* drama/theater group, student-run newspaper, choral group, Greening Olin, Olin Fire Arts Club, Support, Encourage and Recognize Volunteerism (SERV), Olin Entrepreneurial Group, Open. *Campus security:* 24-hour emergency response devices and patrols, controlled dormitory access. *Student services:* health clinic, personal/psychological counseling.

Athletics *Intercollegiate sports:* soccer M(c)/W(c), ultimate Frisbee M(c)/W(c). *Intramural sports:* basketball M/W, softball M/W, volleyball M/W.

Standardized Tests *Required:* SAT or ACT (for admission), SAT Subject Tests (for admission).

Costs (2013–14) *One-time required fee:* $2656. *Comprehensive fee:* $57,500 includes full-time tuition ($42,000), mandatory fees ($500), and room and board ($15,000). Part-time tuition: $1400 per credit. *College room only:* $9000. *Payment plan:* installment.

Financial Aid Of all full-time matriculated undergraduates who enrolled in 2012, 177 applied for aid, 135 were judged to have need, 135 had their need fully met. In 2012, 207 non-need-based awards were made. *Average percent of need met:* 100%. *Average financial aid package:* $33,543. *Average need-based loan:* $3178. *Average need-based gift aid:* $17,058. *Average non-need-based aid:* $25,390. *Average indebtedness upon graduation:* $12,541. *Financial aid deadline:* 2/15.

Applying *Options:* electronic application, deferred entrance. *Application fee:* $80. *Required:* essay or personal statement, high school transcript, 3 letters of recommendation, interview. *Application deadline:* 1/1 (freshmen). *Notification:* 3/21 (freshmen).

Freshman Application Contact Franklin W. Olin College of Engineering, Olin Way, Needham, MA 02492-1200. *Phone:* 781-292-2250. *Fax:* 781-292-2310. *E-mail:* info@olin.edu. *Website:* http://www.olin.edu/.

Gordon College

Wenham, Massachusetts

- **Independent nondenominational** comprehensive, founded 1889
- **Suburban** 450-acre campus with easy access to Boston
- **Endowment** $29.0 million
- **Coed** 1,580 undergraduate students, 98% full-time, 62% women, 38% men
- **Moderately difficult** entrance level, 40% of applicants were admitted

Undergraduates 1,548 full-time, 32 part-time. Students come from 41 states and territories; 69 other countries; 68% are from out of state; 3% Black or African American, non-Hispanic/Latino; 7% Hispanic/Latino; 3% Asian, non-Hispanic/Latino; 0.4% Native Hawaiian or other Pacific Islander, non-Hispanic/Latino; 3% Two or more races, non-Hispanic/Latino; 0.1% Race/ethnicity unknown; 4% international; 4% transferred in; 90% live on campus. *Retention:* 80% of full-time freshmen returned.

Freshmen *Admission:* 4,008 applied, 1,615 admitted, 465 enrolled. *Average high school GPA:* 3.56. *Test scores:* SAT critical reading scores over 500: 81%; SAT math scores over 500: 81%; SAT writing scores over 500: 85%; ACT scores over 18: 100%; SAT critical reading scores over 600: 41%; SAT math scores over 600: 41%; SAT writing scores over 600: 45%; ACT scores over 24: 67%; SAT critical reading scores over 700: 9%; SAT math scores over 700: 6%; SAT writing scores over 700: 9%; ACT scores over 30: 17%.

Faculty *Total:* 177, 52% full-time, 45% with terminal degrees. *Student/faculty ratio:* 13:1.

Academics *Calendar:* semesters. *Degrees:* bachelor's and master's. *Special study options:* academic remediation for entering students, advanced placement credit, cooperative education, double majors, honors programs, independent study, internships, off-campus study, part-time degree program, services for LD students, student-designed majors, study abroad, summer session for credit. *ROTC:* Army (c). *Unusual degree programs:* 3-2 engineering with University of Southern California.

Computers on Campus 100 computers/terminals are available on campus for general student use. Students can access the following: campus intranet, computer help desk, free student e-mail accounts, online (class) grades, online (class) registration, online (class) schedules. Campuswide network is available. 100% of college-owned or -operated housing units are wired for high-speed Internet access. Wireless service is available via entire campus.

Student Life *Housing:* on-campus residence required through senior year. *Options:* coed, men-only, women-only, disabled students. Campus housing is university owned. Freshman campus housing is guaranteed. *Activities and organizations:* drama/theater group, student-run newspaper, radio station, choral group, Student government association, Student ministries and volunteer programs, Diverse music ensembles, Intramural sports, Short-term missions. *Campus security:* 24-hour emergency response devices and patrols, late-night transport/escort service, controlled dormitory access, video cameras. *Student services:* health clinic, personal/psychological counseling.

Athletics Member NCAA. All Division III. *Intercollegiate sports:* baseball M, basketball M/W, cross-country running M/W, field hockey W, lacrosse M/W, soccer M/W, softball W, swimming and diving M/W, tennis M/W, track and field M/W, volleyball W. *Intramural sports:* badminton M/W, basketball M/W, cheerleading W(c), football M/W, ice hockey M(c)/W(c), soccer M/W, table tennis M/W, ultimate Frisbee M/W, volleyball M/W, water polo M/W.

Standardized Tests *Required:* SAT or ACT (for admission). *Recommended:* SAT Subject Tests (for admission).

Costs (2013–14) *Comprehensive fee:* $42,660 includes full-time tuition ($31,820), mandatory fees ($1410), and room and board ($9430). Full-time tuition and fees vary according to course load and program. Part-time tuition: $1125 per credit. Part-time tuition and fees vary according to course load and program. *College room only:* $6250. Room and board charges vary according to board plan and housing facility. *Payment plan:* installment. *Waivers:* employees or children of employees.

Financial Aid Of all full-time matriculated undergraduates who enrolled in 2012, 1,309 applied for aid, 1,151 were judged to have need, 179 had their need fully met. 766 Federal Work-Study jobs (averaging $1536). In 2012, 377 non-need-based awards were made. *Average percent of need met:* 68%. *Average financial aid package:* $19,992. *Average need-based loan:* $4586. *Average need-based gift aid:* $15,295. *Average non-need-based aid:* $11,629. *Average indebtedness upon graduation:* $37,662.

Applying *Options:* electronic application, early admission, early decision, early action, deferred entrance. *Application fee:* $50. *Required:* high school transcript, 2 letters of recommendation, interview, Pastoral recommendation and statement of Christian faith. *Recommended:* essay or personal statement, minimum 3.0 GPA. *Application deadlines:* rolling (freshmen), rolling (transfers), 11/15 (early action). *Early decision deadline:* 11/1. *Notification:* continuous until 9/15 (freshmen), continuous (transfers), 12/1 (early decision), 12/15 (early action).

Freshman Application Contact Ms. June Bodoni, Executive Director of Admissions and Advancement Operations, Gordon College, 255 Grapevine Road, Wenham, MA 01984. *Phone:* 978-867-4218. *Toll-free phone:* 866-464-6736. *Fax:* 978-867-4682. *E-mail:* admissions@gordon.edu. *Website:* http://www.gordon.edu/.

Hampshire College

Amherst, Massachusetts

- **Independent** 4-year, founded 1965
- **Small-town** 800-acre campus
- **Endowment** $28.9 million
- **Coed** 1,484 undergraduate students, 100% full-time, 58% women, 42% men
- **Moderately difficult** entrance level, 64% of applicants were admitted

Undergraduates 1,484 full-time. Students come from 47 states and territories; 19 other countries; 82% are from out of state; 3% Black or African American, non-Hispanic/Latino; 9% Hispanic/Latino; 2% Asian, non-Hispanic/Latino; 0.1% American Indian or Alaska Native, non-Hispanic/Latino; 5% Two or more races, non-Hispanic/Latino; 10% Race/ethnicity unknown; 5% international; 3% transferred in; 80% live on campus. *Retention:* 82% of full-time freshmen returned.

Freshmen *Admission:* 2,856 applied, 1,819 admitted, 366 enrolled. *Average high school GPA:* 3.45. *Test scores:* SAT critical reading scores over 500: 97%; SAT math scores over 500: 87%; SAT writing scores over 500: 94%; ACT scores over 18: 100%; SAT critical reading scores over 600: 78%; SAT math scores over 600: 56%; SAT writing scores over 600: 68%; ACT scores over 24: 92%; SAT critical reading scores over 700: 30%; SAT math scores over 700: 12%; SAT writing scores over 700: 19%; ACT scores over 30: 27%.

Faculty *Total:* 145, 72% full-time. *Student/faculty ratio:* 12:1.

Academics *Calendar:* 4-1-4. *Degree:* bachelor's. *Special study options:* independent study, internships, off-campus study, services for LD students, student-designed majors, study abroad. *ROTC:* Army (c).

Computers on Campus 215 computers/terminals are available on campus for general student use. Students can access the following: campus intranet, computer help desk, free student e-mail accounts, online (class) grades, online (class) registration, online (class) schedules. Campuswide network is available. 100% of college-owned or -operated housing units are wired for high-speed Internet access. Wireless service is available via entire campus.

Student Life *Housing:* on-campus residence required through senior year. *Options:* coed, men-only, women-only, cooperative, disabled students. Campus housing is university owned. Freshman campus housing is guaranteed. *Activities and organizations:* drama/theater group, student-run newspaper, radio station, choral group, Red Scare Frisbee, Queer Community Alliance, Excalibur (fantasy/role playing), Sports Coop, Circus Folks Unite. *Campus security:* 24-hour emergency response devices and patrols. *Student services:* health clinic, personal/psychological counseling, women's center.

Athletics Member USCAA. *Intercollegiate sports:* basketball M(c)/W(c), cross-country running M/W, equestrian sports M(c)/W(c), fencing M/W, soccer M/W, ultimate Frisbee M/W. *Intramural sports:* basketball M/W, equestrian sports M(c)/W(c), rock climbing M(c)/W(c), soccer M/W, table tennis M(c)/W(c), ultimate Frisbee M/W.

Standardized Tests *Recommended:* SAT and SAT Subject Tests or ACT (for admission).

Costs (2013–14) *Comprehensive fee:* $58,655 includes full-time tuition ($45,100), mandatory fees ($1525), and room and board ($12,030). *College room only:* $7680. Room and board charges vary according to board plan. *Payment plan:* installment. *Waivers:* employees or children of employees.

Financial Aid Of all full-time matriculated undergraduates who enrolled in 2012, 1,035 applied for aid, 870 were judged to have need, 596 had their need fully met. 800 Federal Work-Study jobs (averaging $2264). 137 state and other part-time jobs (averaging $2217). In 2012, 282 non-need-based awards were made. *Average percent of need met:* 91%. *Average financial aid package:* $35,849. *Average need-based loan:* $3536. *Average need-based gift aid:* $29,910. *Average non-need-based aid:* $8913. *Average indebtedness upon graduation:* $22,550.

Applying *Options:* electronic application, early admission, early decision, early action, deferred entrance. *Application fee:* $60. *Required:* essay or personal statement, high school transcript, 1 letter of recommendation. *Recommended:* interview. *Application deadlines:* 1/1 (freshmen), 3/1 (transfers), 12/1 (early action). *Early decision deadline:* 11/15 (for plan 1), 1/1 (for plan 2). *Notification:* 4/1 (freshmen), 4/15 (transfers), 12/15 (early decision plan 1), 2/1 (early decision plan 2), 2/1 (early action).

Freshman Application Contact Ms. Julie Richardson, Director of Admissions, Hampshire College, Hampshire College, 893 West Street,

Amherst, MA 01002. *Phone:* 413-559-5471. *Toll-free phone:* 877-937-4267. *Fax:* 413-559-5631. *E-mail:* admissions@hampshire.edu. *Website:* http://www.hampshire.edu/.

Harvard University

Cambridge, Massachusetts

- **Independent** university, founded 1636
- **Urban** 380-acre campus with easy access to Boston
- **Endowment** $32.0 billion
- **Coed**
- **Most difficult** entrance level

Faculty *Student/faculty ratio:* 7:1.

Academics *Calendar:* semesters. *Degrees:* bachelor's, master's, and doctoral.

Student Life *Campus security:* 24-hour emergency response devices and patrols, late-night transport/escort service, controlled dormitory access, required and optional safety courses.

Athletics Member NCAA. All Division I except football (Division I-AA).

Standardized Tests *Required:* SAT or ACT (for admission), SAT Subject Tests (for admission).

Costs (2012–13) *Comprehensive fee:* $54,496 includes full-time tuition ($37,576), mandatory fees ($3290), and room and board ($13,630). *College room only:* $8366. *Payment plans:* tuition prepayment, installment.

Financial Aid *Of all full-time matriculated undergraduates who enrolled in 2012,* 4,327 applied for aid, 4,026 were judged to have need, 4,026 had their need fully met. 1,042 Federal Work-Study jobs (averaging $2832). 2,185 state and other part-time jobs (averaging $2859). *Average percent of need met:* 100. *Average financial aid package:* $45,561. *Average need-based loan:* $5656. *Average need-based gift aid:* $42,464. *Average indebtedness upon graduation:* $13,098.

Applying *Options:* electronic application, early action, deferred entrance. *Application fee:* $75. *Required:* essay or personal statement, high school transcript. *Recommended:* 2 letters of recommendation, interview.

Freshman Application Contact Harvard University, Cambridge, MA 02138. *Phone:* 617-495-1551. *Website:* http://www.harvard.edu/.

Hellenic College

Brookline, Massachusetts

- **Independent Greek Orthodox** comprehensive, founded 1937
- **Suburban** 52-acre campus with easy access to Boston
- **Endowment** $25.9 million
- **Coed**
- **Minimally difficult** entrance level

Faculty *Student/faculty ratio:* 9:1.

Academics *Calendar:* semesters. *Degrees:* bachelor's and master's (also offers graduate degree programs through Holy Cross Greek Orthodox School of Theology).

Student Life *Campus security:* controlled dormitory access.

Standardized Tests *Required:* SAT or ACT (for admission). *Required for some:* SAT Subject Tests (for admission).

Financial Aid *Of all full-time matriculated undergraduates who enrolled in 2008,* 59 applied for aid, 57 were judged to have need. *In 2008,* 1 non-need-based awards were made. *Average percent of need met:* 80. *Average financial aid package:* $9500. *Average need-based loan:* $5500. *Average non-need-based aid:* $5000. *Average indebtedness upon graduation:* $15,000.

Applying *Options:* electronic application, early action, deferred entrance. *Application fee:* $50. *Required:* essay or personal statement, high school transcript, minimum 2.0 GPA, interview, health certificate, SAT or ACT Scores.

Freshman Application Contact Mr. Gregory Floor, Director of Admissions, Hellenic College, 50 Goddard Avenue, Brookline, MA 02445-7496. *Phone:* 617-850-1285. *Toll-free phone:* 866-424-2338. *Fax:* 617-850-1460. *E-mail:* admissions@hchc.edu. *Website:* http://www.hchc.edu/.

Hult International Business School

Cambridge, Massachusetts

Admissions Office Contact Hult International Business School, One Education Street, Cambridge, MA 02141. *Website:* http://www.hult.edu/.

ITT Technical Institute

Norwood, Massachusetts

- **Proprietary** primarily 2-year, founded 1990, part of ITT Educational Services, Inc.
- **Suburban** campus
- **Coed**
- **Minimally difficult** entrance level

Academics *Calendar:* quarters. *Degrees:* associate and bachelor's.

Freshman Application Contact Director of Recruitment, ITT Technical Institute, 333 Providence Highway, Norwood, MA 02062. *Phone:* 781-278-7200. *Toll-free phone:* 800-879-8324. *Website:* http://www.itt-tech.edu/.

ITT Technical Institute

Wilmington, Massachusetts

- **Proprietary** primarily 2-year, founded 2000, part of ITT Educational Services, Inc.
- **Coed**
- **Minimally difficult** entrance level

Academics *Calendar:* quarters. *Degrees:* associate and bachelor's.

Freshman Application Contact Director of Recruitment, ITT Technical Institute, 200 Ballardvale Street, Suite 200, Wilmington, MA 01887. *Phone:* 978-658-2636. *Toll-free phone:* 800-430-5097. *Website:* http://www.itt-tech.edu/.

Lasell College

Newton, Massachusetts

- **Independent** comprehensive, founded 1851
- **Suburban** 50-acre campus with easy access to Boston
- **Endowment** $30.0 million
- **Coed** 1,655 undergraduate students, 99% full-time, 64% women, 36% men
- **Moderately difficult** entrance level, 70% of applicants were admitted

Undergraduates 1,632 full-time, 23 part-time. Students come from 36 states and territories; 21 other countries; 44% are from out of state; 8% Black or African American, non-Hispanic/Latino; 7% Hispanic/Latino; 2% Asian, non-Hispanic/Latino; 0.4% Native Hawaiian or other Pacific Islander, non-Hispanic/Latino; 0.5% American Indian or Alaska Native, non-Hispanic/Latino; 3% Two or more races, non-Hispanic/Latino; 1% Race/ethnicity unknown; 3% international; 4% transferred in; 78% live on campus. *Retention:* 72% of full-time freshmen returned.

Freshmen *Admission:* 3,998 applied, 2,798 admitted, 558 enrolled. *Average high school GPA:* 2.84. *Test scores:* SAT critical reading scores over 500: 46%; SAT math scores over 500: 44%; SAT writing scores over 500: 42%; ACT scores over 18: 90%; SAT critical reading scores over 600: 9%; SAT math scores over 600: 7%; SAT writing scores over 600: 6%; ACT scores over 24: 21%.

Faculty *Total:* 229, 34% full-time, 59% with terminal degrees. *Student/faculty ratio:* 15:1.

Academics *Calendar:* semesters. *Degrees:* bachelor's and master's. *Special study options:* advanced placement credit, cooperative education, double majors, English as a second language, honors programs, independent study, internships, part-time degree program, student-designed majors, study abroad, summer session for credit.

Computers on Campus 200 computers/terminals are available on campus for general student use. Students can access the following: campus intranet, computer help desk, free student e-mail accounts, online (class) grades, online

(class) registration, online (class) schedules, Online tutoring in various subjects. Campuswide network is available. 100% of college-owned or -operated housing units are wired for high-speed Internet access. Wireless service is available via entire campus.

Student Life *Housing options:* coed, women-only, cooperative. Campus housing is university owned. Freshman campus housing is guaranteed. *Activities and organizations:* drama/theater group, student-run newspaper, radio station, choral group, Campus Activities Board, Tennis Club, Lasell College Radio Station, Students Advocating for Equality, Lasell Environmental Action Force. *Campus security:* 24-hour emergency response devices and patrols, late-night transport/escort service, controlled dormitory access. *Student services:* health clinic, personal/psychological counseling.

Athletics Member NCAA. All Division III. *Intercollegiate sports:* baseball M, basketball M/W, cross-country running M/W, field hockey W, lacrosse M/W, soccer M/W, softball W, track and field M/W, volleyball M/W. *Intramural sports:* basketball M/W, cheerleading M(c)/W(c), crew M(c)/W(c), rugby M(c), skiing (downhill) M(c)/W(c), tennis M(c)/W(c).

Standardized Tests *Required:* SAT or ACT (for admission).

Costs (2012–13) *Comprehensive fee:* $41,300 includes full-time tuition ($27,800), mandatory fees ($1200), and room and board ($12,300). Full-time tuition and fees vary according to program. Part-time tuition: $940 per credit hour. Part-time tuition and fees vary according to course load and program. *Required fees:* $300 per term part-time. *Room and board:* Room and board charges vary according to board plan. *Payment plan:* installment. *Waivers:* children of alumni and employees or children of employees.

Financial Aid Of all full-time matriculated undergraduates who enrolled in 2011, 1,345 applied for aid, 1,222 were judged to have need, 294 had their need fully met. In 2011, 252 non-need-based awards were made. *Average percent of need met:* 66%. *Average financial aid package:* $20,448. *Average need-based loan:* $4400. *Average need-based gift aid:* $16,616. *Average non-need-based aid:* $8607. *Average indebtedness upon graduation:* $39,559.

Applying *Options:* electronic application, deferred entrance. *Application fee:* $40. *Required:* essay or personal statement, high school transcript, 2 letters of recommendation, college preparatory program. *Recommended:* interview. *Application deadlines:* rolling (freshmen), rolling (transfers). *Notification:* continuous (freshmen), continuous (transfers).

Freshman Application Contact Lasell College, 1844 Commonwealth Avenue, Newton, MA 02466-2709. *Phone:* 617-243-2225. *Toll-free phone:* 888-LASELL-4.

Website: http://www.lasell.edu/.

Lesley University
Cambridge, Massachusetts
- **Independent** comprehensive, founded 1909
- **Urban** campus with easy access to Boston
- **Coed** 1,568 undergraduate students, 93% full-time, 76% women, 24% men
- **64%** of applicants were admitted

Undergraduates 1,451 full-time, 117 part-time. 56% are from out of state; 3% Black or African American, non-Hispanic/Latino; 6% Hispanic/Latino; 4% Asian, non-Hispanic/Latino; 0.1% Native Hawaiian or other Pacific Islander, non-Hispanic/Latino; 0.7% American Indian or Alaska Native, non-Hispanic/Latino; 4% Two or more races, non-Hispanic/Latino; 8% Race/ethnicity unknown; 2% international; 7% transferred in; 54% live on campus. *Retention:* 79% of full-time freshmen returned.

Freshmen *Admission:* 2,718 applied, 1,737 admitted, 335 enrolled. *Average high school GPA:* 3.02. *Test scores:* SAT critical reading scores over 500: 77%; SAT math scores over 500: 60%; SAT writing scores over 500: 72%; SAT critical reading scores over 600: 29%; SAT math scores over 600: 20%; SAT writing scores over 600: 22%; SAT critical reading scores over 700: 5%; SAT math scores over 700: 1%; SAT writing scores over 700: 1%.

Faculty *Total:* 270, 26% full-time, 45% with terminal degrees. *Student/faculty ratio:* 28:1.

Academics *Calendar:* semesters. *Degrees:* associate, bachelor's, master's, doctoral, post-master's, and postbachelor's certificates. *Special study options:* academic remediation for entering students, accelerated degree program, adult/continuing education programs, advanced placement credit, distance learning, double majors, external degree program, freshman honors college, honors programs, independent study, internships, off-campus study, part-time degree program, services for LD students, student-designed majors, study abroad, summer session for credit.

Computers on Campus Students can access the following: free student e-mail accounts, online (class) registration. Campuswide network is available. Wireless service is available via classrooms, student centers.

Student Life *Housing options:* coed, women-only. Campus housing is university owned and leased by the school. Freshman applicants given priority for college housing. *Activities and organizations:* drama/theater group, choral group. *Campus security:* 24-hour emergency response devices and patrols, late-night transport/escort service, controlled dormitory access. *Student services:* health clinic, personal/psychological counseling.

Athletics Member NCAA. All Division III except baseball (Division II). *Intercollegiate sports:* baseball M, basketball M/W, cross-country running M/W, soccer M/W, softball W, volleyball M/W. *Intramural sports:* swimming and diving M/W, tennis M.

Standardized Tests *Required:* SAT or ACT (for admission).

Costs (2013–14) *Comprehensive fee:* $46,250 includes full-time tuition ($32,000), mandatory fees ($250), and room and board ($14,000). Full-time tuition and fees vary according to class time, course level, course load, degree level, location, program, reciprocity agreements, and student level. Part-time tuition: $1310 per credit hour. *College room only:* $8550. Room and board charges vary according to housing facility. *Payment plan:* installment. *Waivers:* employees or children of employees.

Financial Aid Of all full-time matriculated undergraduates who enrolled in 2010, 1,337 applied for aid, 1,034 were judged to have need, 155 had their need fully met. In 2010, 224 non-need-based awards were made. *Average percent of need met:* 70%. *Average financial aid package:* $16,579. *Average need-based loan:* $4534. *Average need-based gift aid:* $14,563. *Average non-need-based aid:* $10,358. *Average indebtedness upon graduation:* $18,000.

Applying *Options:* electronic application, early action, deferred entrance. *Application fee:* $50. *Required:* essay or personal statement, high school transcript. *Recommended:* interview. *Application deadlines:* rolling (freshmen), rolling (transfers). *Notification:* continuous (freshmen), continuous (transfers).

Freshman Application Contact Lesley University, 29 Everett Street, Cambridge, MA 02138-2790. *Phone:* 617-349-8800. *Toll-free phone:* 800-999-1959 Ext. 8800.

Website: http://www.lesley.edu/.

Massachusetts College of Art and Design
Boston, Massachusetts
- **State-supported** comprehensive, founded 1873, part of Massachusetts Public Higher Education System
- **Urban** 5-acre campus
- **Endowment** $13.6 million
- **Coed** 2,172 undergraduate students, 75% full-time, 68% women, 32% men
- **Very difficult** entrance level, 70% of applicants were admitted

Undergraduates 1,637 full-time, 535 part-time. Students come from 26 states and territories; 49 other countries; 29% are from out of state; 3% Black or African American, non-Hispanic/Latino; 5% Hispanic/Latino; 6% Asian, non-Hispanic/Latino; 0.1% Native Hawaiian or other Pacific Islander, non-Hispanic/Latino; 0.3% American Indian or Alaska Native, non-Hispanic/Latino; 2% Two or more races, non-Hispanic/Latino; 11% Race/ethnicity unknown; 2% international; 6% transferred in; 38% live on campus. *Retention:* 88% of full-time freshmen returned.

Freshmen *Admission:* 1,381 applied, 967 admitted, 353 enrolled. *Average high school GPA:* 3.39. *Test scores:* SAT critical reading scores over 500: 79%; SAT math scores over 500: 74%; SAT writing scores over 500: 74%; SAT critical reading scores over 600: 38%; SAT math scores over 600: 25%; SAT writing scores over 600: 31%; SAT critical reading scores over 700: 7%; SAT math scores over 700: 3%; SAT writing scores over 700: 2%.

Faculty *Total:* 277, 38% full-time. *Student/faculty ratio:* 10:1.

Academics *Calendar:* semesters. *Degrees:* certificates, bachelor's, master's, and postbachelor's certificates. *Special study options:* double majors, independent study, internships, off-campus study, part-time degree program, student-designed majors, study abroad, summer session for credit.

Computers on Campus 370 computers/terminals are available on campus for general student use. Students can access the following: campus intranet, computer help desk, free student e-mail accounts, online (class) grades, online (class) registration, online (class) schedules. Campuswide network is available. 100% of college-owned or -operated housing units are wired for high-speed Internet access. Wireless service is available via entire campus.

Student Life *Housing options:* coed. Campus housing is university owned. Freshman campus housing is guaranteed. *Activities and organizations:* drama/theater group, student-run newspaper, radio station, International Students' Club, Design Research Unit, Spectrum, film society, Event Works. *Campus security:* 24-hour emergency response devices and patrols, late-night transport/

escort service, security lighting, self-defense workshops. *Student services:* health clinic, personal/psychological counseling, women's center.

Athletics *Intramural sports:* basketball M/W, ice hockey M, sailing M/W, softball M/W, table tennis M/W, volleyball M/W.

Standardized Tests *Required:* SAT or ACT (for admission).

Costs (2012–13) *Tuition:* state resident $10,400 full-time; nonresident $27,500 full-time. Part-time tuition and fees vary according to course load. *Room and board:* $12,150. Room and board charges vary according to board plan and housing facility. *Payment plan:* installment. *Waivers:* senior citizens and employees or children of employees.

Financial Aid Of all full-time matriculated undergraduates who enrolled in 2011, 1,326 applied for aid, 1,112 were judged to have need. 171 Federal Work-Study jobs (averaging $1217). In 2011, 43 non-need-based awards were made. *Average financial aid package:* $9074. *Average need-based loan:* $4251. *Average need-based gift aid:* $6670. *Average non-need-based aid:* $4551.

Applying *Options:* electronic application, early action, deferred entrance. *Application fee:* $50. *Required:* essay or personal statement, high school transcript, 2 letters of recommendation, portfolio required; for GPA between 2.0 and 2.9, SAT/ACT scores considered with GPA on sliding scale. *Recommended:* minimum 3.0 GPA. *Application deadlines:* 2/1 (freshmen), 2/1 (transfers), 12/1 (early action). *Notification:* 1/5 (early action).

Freshman Application Contact Massachusetts College of Art and Design, 621 Huntington Avenue, Boston, MA 02115. *Phone:* 617-879-7230. *Fax:* 617-879-7250. *E-mail:* admissions@massart.edu. *Website:* http://www.massart.edu/.

Massachusetts College of Liberal Arts

North Adams, Massachusetts

- **State-supported** comprehensive, founded 1894, part of Massachusetts State University System
- **Small-town** 105-acre campus with easy access to Albany-Schenectady-Troy New York Metro Area
- **Coed** 1,600 undergraduate students, 88% full-time, 59% women, 41% men
- **Moderately difficult** entrance level, 67% of applicants were admitted

Undergraduates 1,408 full-time, 192 part-time. Students come from 15 states and territories; 1 other country; 23% are from out of state; 9% Black or African American, non-Hispanic/Latino; 6% Hispanic/Latino; 0.9% Asian, non-Hispanic/Latino; 0.1% Native Hawaiian or other Pacific Islander, non-Hispanic/Latino; 0.2% American Indian or Alaska Native, non-Hispanic/Latino; 2% Two or more races, non-Hispanic/Latino; 4% Race/ethnicity unknown; 9% transferred in; 63% live on campus. *Retention:* 75% of full-time freshmen returned.

Freshmen *Admission:* 1,689 applied, 1,135 admitted, 313 enrolled. *Average high school GPA:* 3.06. *Test scores:* SAT critical reading scores over 500: 65%; SAT math scores over 500: 56%; ACT scores over 18: 91%; SAT critical reading scores over 600: 20%; SAT math scores over 600: 12%; ACT scores over 24: 39%; SAT critical reading scores over 700: 4%; SAT math scores over 700: 1%; ACT scores over 30: 9%.

Faculty *Total:* 174, 49% full-time, 50% with terminal degrees. *Student/faculty ratio:* 13:1.

Academics *Calendar:* semesters. *Degrees:* certificates, bachelor's, master's, and post-master's certificates. *Special study options:* academic remediation for entering students, accelerated degree program, adult/continuing education programs, advanced placement credit, cooperative education, distance learning, double majors, honors programs, independent study, internships, off-campus study, part-time degree program, services for LD students, student-designed majors, study abroad, summer session for credit. *Unusual degree programs:* 3-2 engineering with University of Massachusetts at Amherst; podiatric medicine with the New York School of Podiatric Medicine.

Computers on Campus 140 computers/terminals are available on campus for general student use. Students can access the following: campus intranet, computer help desk, free student e-mail accounts, online (class) grades, online (class) registration, online (class) schedules. Campuswide network is available. 100% of college-owned or -operated housing units are wired for high-speed Internet access. Wireless service is available via entire campus.

Student Life *Housing:* on-campus residence required through junior year. *Options:* coed, disabled students. Campus housing is university owned. Freshman campus housing is guaranteed. *Activities and organizations:* drama/theater group, student-run newspaper, radio and television station, choral group, Student Activities Council, Student Government Association, The Beacon (Student Newspaper), Harlequin-Musical Theatre Company, Dance Company,

national fraternities, national sororities. *Campus security:* 24-hour emergency response devices and patrols, late-night transport/escort service, controlled dormitory access, escort service. *Student services:* health clinic, personal/psychological counseling, women's center.

Athletics Member NCAA. All Division III. *Intercollegiate sports:* baseball M, basketball M/W, cross-country running M/W, golf M, soccer M/W, softball W, tennis M/W. *Intramural sports:* basketball M/W, cross-country running M/W, equestrian sports M(c)/W(c), football M, golf M/W, lacrosse M(c)/W(c), racquetball M/W, rugby M(c)/W(c), skiing (cross-country) M(c)/W(c), skiing (downhill) M(c)/W(c), soccer M/W, softball M/W, squash M/W, swimming and diving M/W, tennis M/W, volleyball M/W, weight lifting M(c)/W(c), wrestling M(c)/W(c).

Standardized Tests *Required:* SAT or ACT (for admission).

Costs (2012–13) *Tuition:* state resident $1030 full-time, $43 per credit part-time; nonresident $9975 full-time, $416 per credit part-time. Part-time tuition and fees vary according to course load. *Required fees:* $7495 full-time, $253 per credit part-time. *Room and board:* $9102. Room and board charges vary according to board plan and housing facility. *Payment plan:* installment. *Waivers:* senior citizens and employees or children of employees.

Financial Aid Of all full-time matriculated undergraduates who enrolled in 2012, 1,263 applied for aid, 1,042 were judged to have need, 758 had their need fully met. In 2012, 64 non-need-based awards were made. *Average percent of need met:* 84%. *Average financial aid package:* $14,131. *Average need-based loan:* $4147. *Average need-based gift aid:* $6297. *Average non-need-based aid:* $3390. *Average indebtedness upon graduation:* $29,534.

Applying *Options:* electronic application, early admission, early action, deferred entrance. *Application fee:* $40. *Required:* essay or personal statement, high school transcript, minimum 3.0 GPA, 1 letter of recommendation. *Required for some:* interview, sliding scale applies (GPA and SAT) if below 3.0. *Application deadlines:* rolling (freshmen), rolling (transfers), 12/1 (early action). *Notification:* continuous (freshmen), continuous (transfers), 12/15 (early action).

Freshman Application Contact Massachusetts College of Liberal Arts, 375 Church Street, North Adams, MA 01247-4100. *Phone:* 413-662-5416. *Toll-free phone:* 800-989-MCLA. *Website:* http://www.mcla.edu/.

Massachusetts College of Pharmacy and Health Sciences

Boston, Massachusetts

- **Independent** university, founded 1823
- **Urban** 3-acre campus
- **Endowment** $258.0 million
- **Coed** 3,627 undergraduate students, 95% full-time, 67% women, 33% men
- **90%** of applicants were admitted

Undergraduates 3,439 full-time, 188 part-time. Students come from 48 states and territories; 35 other countries; 37% are from out of state; 4% Black or African American, non-Hispanic/Latino; 2% Hispanic/Latino; 25% Asian, non-Hispanic/Latino; 0.1% Native Hawaiian or other Pacific Islander, non-Hispanic/Latino; 0.1% American Indian or Alaska Native, non-Hispanic/Latino; 0.6% Two or more races, non-Hispanic/Latino; 20% Race/ethnicity unknown; 9% international; 13% transferred in; 20% live on campus. *Retention:* 85% of full-time freshmen returned.

Freshmen *Admission:* 4,939 applied, 4,444 admitted, 911 enrolled. *Average high school GPA:* 3.49. *Test scores:* SAT critical reading scores over 500: 63%; SAT math scores over 500: 79%; SAT writing scores over 500: 70%; ACT scores over 18: 97%; SAT critical reading scores over 600: 16%; SAT math scores over 600: 38%; SAT writing scores over 600: 22%; ACT scores over 24: 52%; SAT critical reading scores over 700: 1%; SAT math scores over 700: 7%; SAT writing scores over 700: 2%; ACT scores over 30: 4%.

Faculty *Total:* 259, 100% full-time, 77% with terminal degrees. *Student/faculty ratio:* 23:1.

Academics *Calendar:* semesters. *Degrees:* certificates, bachelor's, master's, doctoral, post-master's, and postbachelor's certificates. *Special study options:* accelerated degree program, adult/continuing education programs, advanced placement credit, distance learning, double majors, independent study, internships, off-campus study, part-time degree program, services for LD students, study abroad, summer session for credit.

Computers on Campus 507 computers/terminals are available on campus for general student use. Students can access the following: computer help desk, free student e-mail accounts, online (class) grades, online (class) registration, online (class) schedules. Campuswide network is available. 100% of college-

owned or -operated housing units are wired for high-speed Internet access. Wireless service is available via entire campus.

Student Life *Housing options:* coed. Campus housing is university owned, leased by the school and is provided by a third party. Freshman campus housing is guaranteed. *Activities and organizations:* drama/theater group, student-run newspaper, choral group, Residence Hall Council, Vietnamese Student Association, Student Government Association, Campus Activities Board, Student Indian Organization, national fraternities. *Campus security:* 24-hour emergency response devices and patrols, late-night transport/escort service, controlled dormitory access, electronically operated academic area entrances, security guards at entrance. *Student services:* health clinic, personal/psychological counseling.

Athletics *Intramural sports:* basketball M/W, bowling M/W, cross-country running M/W, field hockey M/W, football M/W, racquetball M/W, soccer M/W, softball M/W, tennis M/W, ultimate Frisbee M/W, volleyball M/W.

Standardized Tests *Required:* SAT or ACT (for admission).

Costs (2012–13) *Comprehensive fee:* $40,888 includes full-time tuition ($26,600), mandatory fees ($840), and room and board ($13,448). Full-time tuition and fees vary according to course load, degree level, location, program, and student level. Part-time tuition: $980 per credit. *Required fees:* $220 per term part-time. *College room only:* $10,400. Room and board charges vary according to board plan, housing facility, and location. *Payment plan:* installment. *Waivers:* employees or children of employees.

Financial Aid Of all full-time matriculated undergraduates who enrolled in 2009, 2,146 applied for aid, 1,953 were judged to have need, 953 had their need fully met. In 2009, 371 non-need-based awards were made. *Average percent of need met:* 41%. *Average financial aid package:* $12,035. *Average need-based loan:* $5305. *Average need-based gift aid:* $8612. *Average non-need-based aid:* $11,269.

Applying *Options:* electronic application, early action, deferred entrance. *Required:* essay or personal statement, 2 letters of recommendation. *Required for some:* high school transcript, interview. *Application deadlines:* rolling (freshmen), 2/1 (transfers), 11/15 (early action). *Notification:* continuous until 2/15 (freshmen), continuous (transfers), 12/19 (early action).

Freshman Application Contact Sandra Hernandez, Visit Concierge, Massachusetts College of Pharmacy and Health Sciences, 179 Longwood Avenue, Boston, MA 02115. *Phone:* 617-732-2850. *Fax:* 617-732-2118. *E-mail:* admissions@mcphs.edu.
Website: http://www.mcphs.edu/.

Massachusetts Institute of Technology

Cambridge, Massachusetts

- **Independent** university, founded 1861
- **Urban** 168-acre campus with easy access to Boston
- **Endowment** $10.1 billion
- **Coed** 4,503 undergraduate students, 99% full-time, 45% women, 55% men
- **Most difficult** entrance level, 9% of applicants were admitted

Undergraduates 4,480 full-time, 23 part-time. Students come from 54 states and territories; 92 other countries; 91% are from out of state; 6% Black or African American, non-Hispanic/Latino; 15% Hispanic/Latino; 24% Asian, non-Hispanic/Latino; 0.3% American Indian or Alaska Native, non-Hispanic/Latino; 4% Two or more races, non-Hispanic/Latino; 3% Race/ethnicity unknown; 10% international; 0.5% transferred in; 90% live on campus. *Retention:* 97% of full-time freshmen returned.

Freshman *Admission:* 18,109 applied, 1,620 admitted, 1,135 enrolled. *Test scores:* SAT critical reading scores over 500: 100%; SAT math scores over 500: 100%; SAT writing scores over 500: 100%; ACT scores over 18: 100%; SAT critical reading scores over 600: 94%; SAT math scores over 600: 100%; SAT writing scores over 600: 96%; ACT scores over 24: 100%; SAT critical reading scores over 700: 67%; SAT math scores over 700: 94%; SAT writing scores over 700: 70%; ACT scores over 30: 95%.

Faculty *Total:* 1,447, 82% full-time, 88% with terminal degrees. *Student/faculty ratio:* 8:1.

Academics *Calendar:* 4-1-4. *Degrees:* bachelor's, master's, and doctoral. *Special study options:* advanced placement credit, cooperative education, double majors, English as a second language, independent study, internships, off-campus study, services for LD students, study abroad. *ROTC:* Army (b), Navy (b), Air Force (b).

Computers on Campus 1,100 computers/terminals and 50,000 ports are available on campus for general student use. Students can access the following: campus intranet, computer help desk, free student e-mail accounts, online (class) grades, online (class) registration, online (class) schedules. Campus-

wide network is available. 100% of college-owned or -operated housing units are wired for high-speed Internet access. Wireless service is available via entire campus.

Student Life *Housing:* on-campus residence required for freshman year. *Options:* coed, women-only, cooperative, disabled students. Campus housing is university owned. Freshman campus housing is guaranteed. *Activities and organizations:* drama/theater group, student-run newspaper, radio and television station, choral group, marching band, Educational Studies Program, Dance Troupe, Science Fiction Society, The Tech (student newspaper), Anime Club, national fraternities, national sororities. *Campus security:* 24-hour emergency response devices and patrols, late-night transport/escort service, controlled dormitory access. *Student services:* health clinic, personal/psychological counseling.

Athletics Member NCAA. All Division III except men's and women's crew (Division I). *Intercollegiate sports:* baseball M, basketball M/W, crew M/W, cross-country running M/W, fencing M/W, field hockey W, football M, lacrosse M/W, riflery M/W, sailing M/W, soccer M/W, softball W, squash M, swimming and diving M/W, tennis M/W, track and field M/W, volleyball M/W, water polo M. *Intramural sports:* archery M(c)/W(c), badminton M/W, basketball M/W, bowling M/W, cheerleading M(c)/W(c), crew M(c)/W(c), golf M(c)/W(c), gymnastics M(c)/W(c), ice hockey M/W, rugby M(c)/W(c), soccer M/W, softball M/W, table tennis M/W, tennis M/W, ultimate Frisbee M/W, volleyball M/W, water polo M/W, wrestling M(c).

Standardized Tests *Required:* SAT or ACT (for admission), SAT Subject Tests (for admission).

Costs (2012–13) *Comprehensive fee:* $54,238 includes full-time tuition ($41,770), mandatory fees ($280), and room and board ($12,188). Part-time tuition: $650 per unit. Part-time tuition and fees vary according to course load. *College room only:* $7554. Room and board charges vary according to board plan and housing facility. *Payment plan:* installment. *Waivers:* employees or children of employees.

Financial Aid Of all full-time matriculated undergraduates who enrolled in 2011, 3,222 applied for aid, 2,803 were judged to have need, 2,803 had their need fully met. 849 Federal Work-Study jobs (averaging $2585). 1,091 state and other part-time jobs (averaging $2964). *Average percent of need met:* 100%. *Average financial aid package:* $38,604. *Average need-based loan:* $3511. *Average need-based gift aid:* $35,993. *Average indebtedness upon graduation:* $20,794. *Financial aid deadline:* 2/15.

Applying *Options:* electronic application, early action, deferred entrance. *Application fee:* $75. *Required:* essay or personal statement, high school transcript, 2 letters of recommendation, SAT, ACT or TOEFL. Two SAT II Subject tests: one in math and one in science. *Recommended:* interview. *Application deadlines:* 1/1 (freshmen), 2/15 (transfers), 11/1 (early action). *Notification:* 3/20 (freshmen), 5/1 (transfers), 12/20 (early action).

Freshman Application Contact Admissions Counselors, Massachusetts Institute of Technology, 77 Massachusetts Avenue, Building 3-108, Cambridge, MA 02139-4307. *Phone:* 617-253-3400. *Fax:* 617-258-8304. *E-mail:* admissions@mit.edu.
Website: http://web.mit.edu/.

Massachusetts Maritime Academy

Buzzards Bay, Massachusetts

- **State-supported** comprehensive, founded 1891, part of Massachusetts State University System
- **Small-town** 55-acre campus with easy access to Boston, Providence
- **Endowment** $7.4 million
- **Coed, primarily men** 1,312 undergraduate students, 97% full-time, 10% women, 90% men
- **Moderately difficult** entrance level, 77% of applicants were admitted

Undergraduates 1,269 full-time, 43 part-time. Students come from 29 states and territories; 4 other countries; 23% are from out of state; 2% Black or African American, non-Hispanic/Latino; 2% Hispanic/Latino; 2% Asian, non-Hispanic/Latino; 0.6% American Indian or Alaska Native, non-Hispanic/Latino; 0.3% Two or more races, non-Hispanic/Latino; 1% Race/ethnicity unknown; 0.8% international; 3% transferred in; 95% live on campus. *Retention:* 89% of full-time freshmen returned.

Freshmen *Admission:* 787 applied, 608 admitted, 305 enrolled. *Average high school GPA:* 3. *Test scores:* SAT critical reading scores over 500: 58%; SAT math scores over 500: 75%; SAT writing scores over 500: 43%; ACT scores over 18: 95%; SAT critical reading scores over 600: 12%; SAT math scores over 600: 25%; SAT writing scores over 600: 6%; ACT scores over 24: 45%; SAT math scores over 700: 1%.

Faculty *Total:* 137, 52% full-time, 31% with terminal degrees. *Student/faculty ratio:* 13:1.

Academics *Calendar:* semesters plus sea term. *Degrees:* bachelor's and master's. *Special study options:* academic remediation for entering students, advanced placement credit, cooperative education, distance learning, double majors, internships, off-campus study, part-time degree program, services for LD students, study abroad, summer session for credit. *ROTC:* Army (c), Navy (b).

Computers on Campus 150 computers/terminals and 1,000 ports are available on campus for general student use. Students can access the following: campus intranet, computer help desk, free student e-mail accounts, online (class) grades, online (class) registration, online (class) schedules, course-supported e-learning, wireless available campus wide. Campuswide network is available. 100% of college-owned or -operated housing units are wired for high-speed Internet access. Wireless service is available via entire campus.

Student Life *Housing:* on-campus residence required for freshman year. *Options:* coed, disabled students. Campus housing is university owned. Freshman campus housing is guaranteed. *Activities and organizations:* drama/theater group, student-run newspaper, choral group, marching band, club hockey, water sports, sailing/crew, rugby club, scuba club. *Campus security:* 24-hour emergency response devices and patrols, student patrols, late-night transport/escort service, controlled dormitory access. *Student services:* health clinic, personal/psychological counseling, women's center.

Athletics Member NCAA. All Division III. *Intercollegiate sports:* baseball M, crew M/W, cross-country running M/W, football M, lacrosse M/W, riflery M/W, sailing M/W, soccer M/W, softball W, track and field M/W, volleyball W. *Intramural sports:* basketball M/W, golf M(c)/W(c), ice hockey M(c), racquetball M/W, rugby M(c), skiing (cross-country) M(c)/W(c), skiing (downhill) M(c)/W(c), soccer M, softball M/W, squash M/W, swimming and diving M/W, table tennis M/W, tennis M/W, ultimate Frisbee M/W, volleyball M/W, water polo M/W, weight lifting M(c)/W(c).

Standardized Tests *Required:* SAT and SAT Subject Tests or ACT (for admission).

Financial Aid Of all full-time matriculated undergraduates who enrolled in 2011, 911 applied for aid, 645 were judged to have need, 152 had their need fully met. 115 Federal Work-Study jobs (averaging $1000). In 2011, 87 non-need-based awards were made. *Average percent of need met:* 70%. *Average financial aid package:* $9510. *Average need-based loan:* $3938. *Average need-based gift aid:* $5192. *Average non-need-based aid:* $3296. *Average indebtedness upon graduation:* $32,400.

Applying *Options:* electronic application, early action, deferred entrance. *Application fee:* $50. *Required:* essay or personal statement, high school transcript, minimum 2.0 GPA, 2 letters of recommendation, for students transferring between 12 and 23 credits minimum college GPA 2.5; for less than 23 transferable credits minimum college GPA 2.0 and meet admission standards for freshman applicants; for more than 24 transferable credits minimum college GPA 2.0. *Recommended:* interview. *Application deadlines:* rolling (freshmen), rolling (out-of-state freshmen), rolling (transfers), 11/1 (early action). *Notification:* continuous (freshmen), continuous (out-of-state freshmen), continuous (transfers).

Freshman Application Contact Cmdr. Sam White, Director of Admissions, Massachusetts Maritime Academy, 101 Academy Drive, Blinn Hall, Buzzards Bay, MA 02532. *Phone:* 508-830-5031. *Toll-free phone:* 800-544-3411. *Fax:* 508-830-5077. *E-mail:* jmclaughlin@maritime.edu. *Website:* http://www.maritime.edu/.

Merrimack College

North Andover, Massachusetts

- **Independent Roman Catholic** comprehensive, founded 1947
- **Suburban** 220-acre campus with easy access to Boston
- **Endowment** $35.1 million
- **Coed** 2,429 undergraduate students, 95% full-time, 48% women, 52% men
- **Moderately difficult** entrance level, 77% of applicants were admitted

Undergraduates 2,309 full-time, 120 part-time. Students come from 20 states and territories; 18 other countries; 27% are from out of state; 3% Black or African American, non-Hispanic/Latino; 7% Hispanic/Latino; 2% Asian, non-Hispanic/Latino; 0.1% American Indian or Alaska Native, non-Hispanic/Latino; 1% Two or more races, non-Hispanic/Latino; 12% Race/ethnicity unknown; 6% international; 3% transferred in; 71% live on campus. *Retention:* 80% of full-time freshmen returned.

Freshmen *Admission:* 5,661 applied, 4,358 admitted, 699 enrolled. *Test scores:* SAT critical reading scores over 500: 56%; SAT math scores over 500: 66%; SAT writing scores over 500: 55%; ACT scores over 18: 95%; SAT critical reading scores over 600: 12%; SAT math scores over 600: 22%; SAT writ-

ing scores over 600: 13%; ACT scores over 24: 33%; SAT critical reading scores over 700: 1%; SAT math scores over 700: 1%; SAT writing scores over 700: 1%.

Faculty *Total:* 315, 44% full-time. *Student/faculty ratio:* 12:1.

Academics *Calendar:* semesters. *Degrees:* bachelor's, master's, post-master's, and postbachelor's certificates. *Special study options:* academic remediation for entering students, adult/continuing education programs, advanced placement credit, cooperative education, double majors, English as a second language, honors programs, independent study, internships, off-campus study, part-time degree program, services for LD students, student-designed majors, study abroad, summer session for credit. *ROTC:* Air Force (c).

Computers on Campus Students can access the following: campus intranet, computer help desk, free student e-mail accounts, online (class) grades, online (class) registration, online (class) schedules. Campuswide network is available. 100% of college-owned or -operated housing units are wired for high-speed Internet access. Wireless service is available via entire campus.

Student Life *Housing options:* coed, disabled students. Campus housing is university owned. Freshman applicants given priority for college housing. *Activities and organizations:* drama/theater group, student-run newspaper, television station, choral group, Programming Board, Student Government; Class Councils, Greek Life, A.L.A.N.A, national fraternities, national sororities. *Campus security:* 24-hour emergency response devices and patrols, student patrols, late-night transport/escort service, controlled dormitory access, staffed dorm entrances. *Student services:* health clinic, personal/psychological counseling.

Athletics Member NCAA. All Division II except men's and women's ice hockey (Division I). *Intercollegiate sports:* baseball M(s), basketball M(s)/W(s), crew W(s), cross-country running M(s)/W(s), field hockey W(s), football M(s), golf M(s), ice hockey M(s)/W(s), lacrosse M(s)/W(s), soccer M(s)/W(s), softball W(s), swimming and diving W(s), tennis M(s)/W(s), track and field M(s)/W(s), volleyball W(s). *Intramural sports:* baseball M(c), cheerleading W(c), ice hockey M(c), lacrosse M(c)/W(c), rugby M(c)/W(c), ultimate Frisbee M(c)/W(c).

Costs (2012–13) *Comprehensive fee:* $45,610 includes full-time tuition ($32,720), mandatory fees ($1200), and room and board ($11,690). Part-time tuition and fees vary according to class time, course level, course load, and degree level. *Room and board:* Room and board charges vary according to board plan and housing facility. *Payment plan:* installment. *Waivers:* senior citizens and employees or children of employees.

Financial Aid Of all full-time matriculated undergraduates who enrolled in 2012, 1,804 applied for aid, 1,628 were judged to have need, 254 had their need fully met. 129 Federal Work-Study jobs (averaging $1239). 488 state and other part-time jobs (averaging $915). In 2012, 481 non-need-based awards were made. *Average percent of need met:* 64%. *Average financial aid package:* $20,669. *Average need-based loan:* $4522. *Average need-based gift aid:* $17,029. *Average non-need-based aid:* $9757. *Financial aid deadline:* 2/15.

Applying *Options:* electronic application, early admission, early decision, early action, deferred entrance. *Required:* essay or personal statement, high school transcript, 1 letter of recommendation, first quarter senior grades. *Required for some:* interview. *Recommended:* interview. *Application deadlines:* 2/15 (freshmen), 8/1 (transfers), 11/15 (early action). *Early decision deadline:* 11/15. *Notification:* continuous until 3/15 (freshmen), continuous (transfers), 12/15 (early decision), 12/25 (early action).

Freshman Application Contact Admissions Office, Merrimack College, Austin Hall, A22, North Andover, MA 01845. *Phone:* 978-837-5100. *Fax:* 978-837-5133. *E-mail:* admission@merrimack.edu. *Website:* http://www.merrimack.edu/.

Montserrat College of Art

Beverly, Massachusetts

- **Independent** 4-year, founded 1970
- **Suburban** 10-acre campus with easy access to Boston
- **Endowment** $670,985
- **Coed**
- **Moderately difficult** entrance level

Faculty *Student/faculty ratio:* 12:1.

Academics *Calendar:* semesters. *Degrees:* diplomas, bachelor's, and post-bachelor's certificates.

Student Life *Campus security:* 24-hour emergency response devices and patrols, student patrols, late-night transport/escort service, controlled dormitory access.

Standardized Tests *Required for some:* SAT or ACT (for admission).

Costs (2012–13) *Tuition:* $25,500 full-time, $1065 per credit part-time. *Required fees:* $1100 full-time, $50 per credit part-time. *Room only:* $7300.

Financial Aid *Of all full-time matriculated undergraduates who enrolled in 2005,* 281 applied for aid, 227 were judged to have need. 65 Federal Work-Study jobs (averaging $847). *Average financial aid package:* $9947. *Average need-based loan:* $4196. *Average need-based gift aid:* $4548.

Applying *Options:* electronic application, early action, deferred entrance. *Application fee:* $50. *Required:* essay or personal statement, high school transcript, minimum 2.0 GPA, 2 letters of recommendation, portfolio. *Recommended:* minimum 2.0 GPA, interview.

Freshman Application Contact Mr. Jeffrey Newell, Director of Admissions, Montserrat College of Art, 23 Essex Street, Beverly, MA 01915. *Phone:* 978-921-4242 Ext. 1152. *Toll-free phone:* 800-836-0487. *Fax:* 978-921-4241. *E-mail:* jeffrey.newell@montserrat.edu.
Website: http://www.montserrat.edu/.

Mount Holyoke College

South Hadley, Massachusetts

- **Independent** comprehensive, founded 1837
- **Small-town** 800-acre campus with easy access to Springfield
- **Endowment** $594.0 million
- **Women only** 2,322 undergraduate students, 98% full-time
- **Very difficult** entrance level, 42% of applicants were admitted

Undergraduates 2,287 full-time, 35 part-time. Students come from 45 states and territories; 78 other countries; 77% are from out of state; 6% Black or African American, non-Hispanic/Latino; 8% Hispanic/Latino; 7% Asian, non-Hispanic/Latino; 4% Two or more races, non-Hispanic/Latino; 3% Race/ethnicity unknown; 23% international; 2% transferred in; 95% live on campus. *Retention:* 92% of full-time freshmen returned.

Freshmen *Admission:* 3,876 applied, 1,631 admitted, 496 enrolled. *Average high school GPA:* 3.74. *Test scores:* SAT critical reading scores over 500: 99%; SAT math scores over 500: 99%; SAT writing scores over 500: 100%; ACT scores over 18: 100%; SAT critical reading scores over 600: 82%; SAT math scores over 600: 80%; SAT writing scores over 600: 86%; ACT scores over 24: 96%; SAT critical reading scores over 700: 37%; SAT math scores over 700: 31%; SAT writing scores over 700: 38%; ACT scores over 30: 53%.

Faculty *Total:* 268, 84% full-time, 93% with terminal degrees. *Student/faculty ratio:* 10:1.

Academics *Calendar:* semesters. *Degrees:* bachelor's, master's, and postbachelor's certificates. *Special study options:* adult/continuing education programs, advanced placement credit, cooperative education, double majors, English as a second language, independent study, internships, off-campus study, part-time degree program, services for LD students, student-designed majors, study abroad. *ROTC:* Army (c), Air Force (c). *Unusual degree programs:* 3-2 engineering with Dartmouth College, University of Massachusetts, California Institute of Technology.

Computers on Campus 447 computers/terminals and 800 ports are available on campus for general student use. Students can access the following: campus intranet, computer help desk, free student e-mail accounts, online (class) grades, online (class) registration, online (class) schedules, personal Web pages. Campuswide network is available. 100% of college-owned or -operated housing units are wired for high-speed Internet access. Wireless service is available via classrooms, computer centers, computer labs, dorm rooms, learning centers, libraries, student centers.

Student Life *Housing:* on-campus residence required through senior year. *Options:* women-only, disabled students. Campus housing is university owned. Freshman campus housing is guaranteed. *Activities and organizations:* drama/theater group, student-run newspaper, radio station, choral group, Student Government Association, Model UN, Mount Holyoke African and Caribbean Student Association (MHCASA), Ice Hockey, Rugby. *Campus security:* 24-hour emergency response devices and patrols, student patrols, late-night transport/escort service, controlled dormitory access, police officers on-campus. *Student services:* health clinic, personal/psychological counseling.

Athletics Member NCAA. All Division III. *Intercollegiate sports:* basketball W, crew W, cross-country running W, equestrian sports W, field hockey W, golf W, lacrosse W, soccer W, squash W, swimming and diving W, tennis W, track and field W, volleyball W. *Intramural sports:* cheerleading W(c), equestrian sports W(c), fencing W(c), ice hockey W(c), rugby W(c), sailing W(c), ultimate Frisbee W(c).

Standardized Tests *Required for some:* SAT Subject Tests (for admission).

Costs (2013–14) *Comprehensive fee:* $53,596 includes full-time tuition ($41,270), mandatory fees ($186), and room and board ($12,140). Part-time tuition: $1290 per credit hour. *College room only:* $5940. *Payment plans:* tuition prepayment, installment. *Waivers:* employees or children of employees.

Financial Aid *Of all full-time matriculated undergraduates who enrolled in 2012,* 1,774 applied for aid, 1,644 were judged to have need, 1,644 had their need fully met. 912 Federal Work-Study jobs (averaging $1806). 432 state and other part-time jobs (averaging $1851). In 2012, 296 non-need-based awards were made. *Average percent of need met:* 100%. *Average financial aid package:* $35,643. *Average need-based loan:* $5042. *Average need-based gift aid:* $30,163. *Average non-need-based aid:* $16,222. *Average indebtedness upon graduation:* $22,691. *Financial aid deadline:* 3/1.

Applying *Options:* electronic application, early admission, early decision, deferred entrance. *Application fee:* $60. *Required:* essay or personal statement, high school transcript, 2 letters of recommendation. *Recommended:* interview. *Application deadlines:* 1/15 (freshmen), 5/15 (transfers). *Early decision deadline:* 11/15 (for plan 1), 1/1 (for plan 2). *Notification:* 4/1 (freshmen), continuous (transfers), 1/1 (early decision plan 1), 2/1 (early decision plan 2).

Freshman Application Contact Ms. Diane Anci, Vice President of Enrollment and Dean of Admission, Mount Holyoke College, Office of Admission, Mount Holyoke College, South Hadley, MA 01075. *Phone:* 413-538-2023. *Fax:* 413-538-2409. *E-mail:* admission@mtholyoke.edu. *Website:* http://www.mtholyoke.edu/.

Mount Ida College

Newton, Massachusetts

- **Independent** comprehensive, founded 1899
- **Suburban** 72-acre campus with easy access to Boston
- **Coed**
- **Moderately difficult** entrance level

Faculty *Student/faculty ratio:* 14:1.

Academics *Calendar:* semesters. *Degrees:* certificates, associate, bachelor's, and master's.

Student Life *Campus security:* 24-hour emergency response devices and patrols, student patrols, late-night transport/escort service, controlled dormitory access, secured campus entrance.

Athletics Member NCAA. All Division III.

Standardized Tests *Required:* SAT or ACT (for admission).

Costs (2012–13) *Comprehensive fee:* $39,429 includes full-time tuition ($26,664), mandatory fees ($265), and room and board ($12,500). Part-time tuition: $705 per credit. Part-time tuition and fees vary according to course load.

Financial Aid *Of all full-time matriculated undergraduates who enrolled in 2009,* 1,231 applied for aid, 1,111 were judged to have need, 77 had their need fully met. In 2009, 234 non-need-based awards were made. *Average percent of need met:* 58. *Average financial aid package:* $15,105. *Average need-based loan:* $4063. *Average need-based gift aid:* $11,328. *Average indebtedness upon graduation:* $34,911.

Applying *Options:* electronic application, deferred entrance. *Application fee:* $45. *Required:* high school transcript, 1 letter of recommendation, SAT or ACT scores. *Required for some:* interview. *Recommended:* essay or personal statement, minimum 2.0 GPA.

Freshman Application Contact Calvin Conyers, Assistant Dean of Admissions, Mount Ida College, 777 Dedham Street, Newton, MA 02459-3310. *Phone:* 617-928-4553. *Fax:* 617-928-4507. *E-mail:* admissions@mountida.edu.
Website: http://www.mountida.edu/.

Newbury College

Brookline, Massachusetts

- **Independent** 4-year, founded 1962
- **Suburban** 10-acre campus with easy access to Boston
- **Endowment** $1.6 million
- **Coed** 1,003 undergraduate students, 88% full-time, 58% women, 42% men
- **Minimally difficult** entrance level, 62% of applicants were admitted

Undergraduates 883 full-time, 120 part-time. Students come from 28 states and territories; 13 other countries; 29% are from out of state; 32% Black or African American, non-Hispanic/Latino; 16% Hispanic/Latino; 7% Asian, non-Hispanic/Latino; 3% international; 4% transferred in; 35% live on campus. *Retention:* 61% of full-time freshmen returned.

Freshmen *Admission:* 5,543 applied, 3,443 admitted, 286 enrolled. *Average high school GPA:* 2.65. *Test scores:* SAT critical reading scores over 500: 20%; SAT math scores over 500: 24%; SAT writing scores over 500: 15%; ACT scores over 18: 50%; SAT critical reading scores over 600: 2%; SAT math scores over 600: 2%; SAT writing scores over 600: 3%; ACT scores over 24: 8%.

Faculty *Total:* 107, 33% full-time, 30% with terminal degrees. *Student/faculty ratio:* 16:1.

Academics *Calendar:* semesters. *Degrees:* certificates, associate, and bachelor's. *Special study options:* academic remediation for entering students, accelerated degree program, adult/continuing education programs, advanced placement credit, cooperative education, distance learning, double majors, honors programs, independent study, internships, off-campus study, part-time degree program, services for LD students, student-designed majors, study abroad, summer session for credit.

Computers on Campus 122 computers/terminals are available on campus for general student use. Students can access the following: campus intranet, computer help desk, free student e-mail accounts, online (class) grades, online (class) registration, online (class) schedules, Online software and document storage. Campuswide network is available. 100% of college-owned or -operated housing units are wired for high-speed Internet access. Wireless service is available via entire campus.

Student Life *Housing options:* coed. Campus housing is university owned and leased by the school. Freshman applicants given priority for college housing. *Activities and organizations:* drama/theater group, student-run radio and television station, choral group, Innkeeper's Club, Campus Activities Board, Step Team, Fashion Forward Club, Commuter Council/Residence Hall Council. *Campus security:* 24-hour emergency response devices and patrols, late-night transport/escort service. *Student services:* personal/psychological counseling.

Athletics Member NCAA. All Division III. *Intercollegiate sports:* baseball M, basketball M/W, cross-country running M/W, golf M, soccer M/W, softball W, tennis M/W, volleyball M/W.

Costs (2013–14) *One-time required fee:* $175. *Comprehensive fee:* $41,850 includes full-time tuition ($27,850), mandatory fees ($1100), and room and board ($12,900). Full-time tuition and fees vary according to program and reciprocity agreements. Part-time tuition and fees vary according to class time, course load, program, and reciprocity agreements. *Room and board:* Room and board charges vary according to housing facility. *Payment plan:* installment. *Waivers:* employees or children of employees.

Financial Aid Of all full-time matriculated undergraduates who enrolled in 2012, 826 applied for aid, 783 were judged to have need, 1 had their need fully met. 197 Federal Work-Study jobs (averaging $1592). In 2012, 36 non-need-based awards were made. *Average percent of need met:* 47%. *Average financial aid package:* $12,974. *Average need-based loan:* $4500. *Average need-based gift aid:* $11,712. *Average non-need-based aid:* $10,313. *Average indebtedness upon graduation:* $29,530.

Applying *Options:* electronic application. *Application fee:* $25. *Required:* essay or personal statement, high school transcript, 2 letters of recommendation. *Required for some:* interview. *Recommended:* minimum 2.0 GPA. *Application deadlines:* 9/1 (freshmen), 9/1 (transfers). *Notification:* continuous (freshmen), continuous (transfers).

Freshman Application Contact Jonathan DiNuzzo, Application Coordinator, Newbury College, 129 Fisher Avenue, Brookline, MA 02445-5796. *Phone:* 617-730-7003. *Toll-free phone:* 800-NEWBURY. *Fax:* 617-731-9618. *E-mail:* admissions@newbury.edu. *Website:* http://www.newbury.edu/.

New England College of Business and Finance

Boston, Massachusetts

Freshman Application Contact New England College of Business and Finance, 10 High Street, Suite 204, Boston, MA 02111-2645. *Phone:* 617-951-2350 Ext. 6912. *Toll-free phone:* 800-997-1673. *Website:* http://necb.edu/.

New England Conservatory of Music

Boston, Massachusetts

- **Independent** comprehensive, founded 1867
- **Urban** 2-acre campus
- **Endowment** $112.1 million
- **Coed** 436 undergraduate students, 93% full-time, 44% women, 56% men
- **Very difficult** entrance level, 33% of applicants were admitted

Undergraduates 406 full-time, 30 part-time. Students come from 37 states and territories; 25 other countries; 86% are from out of state; 2% Black or African American, non-Hispanic/Latino; 5% Hispanic/Latino; 10% Asian, non-Hispanic/Latino; 3% Two or more races, non-Hispanic/Latino; 4% Race/eth-

nicity unknown; 32% international; 5% transferred in; 30% live on campus. *Retention:* 93% of full-time freshmen returned.

Freshmen *Admission:* 1,098 applied, 363 admitted, 102 enrolled.

Faculty *Total:* 234, 40% full-time, 12% with terminal degrees. *Student/faculty ratio:* 6:1.

Academics *Calendar:* semesters. *Degrees:* certificates, diplomas, bachelor's, master's, doctoral, post-master's, and postbachelor's certificates. *Special study options:* advanced placement credit, double majors, English as a second language, independent study, internships, off-campus study, services for LD students, study abroad, summer session for credit.

Computers on Campus 70 computers/terminals and 200 ports are available on campus for general student use. Students can access the following: campus intranet, computer help desk, free student e-mail accounts, online (class) grades, online (class) registration, online (class) schedules, online activity effective Fall 2010. Campuswide network is available. 100% of college-owned or -operated housing units are wired for high-speed Internet access. Wireless service is available via entire campus.

Student Life *Housing:* on-campus residence required for freshman year. *Options:* coed. Campus housing is university owned. Freshman campus housing is guaranteed. *Activities and organizations:* drama/theater group, student-run newspaper, choral group, Fellowship with Christ, Hillel, The Penguin (newspaper), Rockin' Rangers Theatre Improv. *Campus security:* 24-hour patrols, late-night transport/escort service. *Student services:* health clinic, personal/psychological counseling.

Costs (2012–13) *Comprehensive fee:* $50,805 includes full-time tuition ($38,000), mandatory fees ($455), and room and board ($12,350). Part-time tuition: $1210 per credit. *Room and board:* Room and board charges vary according to board plan. *Waivers:* employees or children of employees.

Financial Aid Of all full-time matriculated undergraduates who enrolled in 2011, 261 applied for aid, 216 were judged to have need, 34 had their need fully met. 103 Federal Work-Study jobs (averaging $1608). In 2011, 182 non-need-based awards were made. *Average percent of need met:* 61%. *Average financial aid package:* $23,951. *Average need-based loan:* $6102. *Average need-based gift aid:* $17,843. *Average non-need-based aid:* $15,922. *Average indebtedness upon graduation:* $25,189.

Applying *Options:* electronic application, deferred entrance. *Application fee:* $115. *Required:* essay or personal statement, high school transcript, minimum 2.8 GPA, 2 letters of recommendation, audition recording, repertoire list. *Application deadlines:* 12/1 (freshmen), 12/1 (transfers). *Notification:* 4/1 (freshmen), 4/1 (transfers).

Freshman Application Contact New England Conservatory of Music, 290 Huntington Avenue, Boston, MA 02115-5000. *Phone:* 617-585-1103. *Website:* http://necmusic.edu/.

The New England Institute of Art

Brookline, Massachusetts

- **Proprietary** 4-year, part of Education Management Corporation
- **Urban** campus
- **Coed**

Academics *Calendar:* semesters. *Degrees:* certificates, associate, and bachelor's.

Freshman Application Contact The New England Institute of Art, 10 Brookline Place West, Brookline, MA 02445. *Phone:* 617-739-1700. *Toll-free phone:* 800-903-4425. *Website:* http://www.artinstitutes.edu/boston/.

See full-page ad on page 54 and page 1412 for the College Close-Up.

Nichols College

Dudley, Massachusetts

- **Independent** comprehensive, founded 1815
- **Suburban** 210-acre campus with easy access to Boston
- **Endowment** $11.9 million
- **Coed**
- **Moderately difficult** entrance level

Faculty *Student/faculty ratio:* 18:1.

Academics *Calendar:* semesters. *Degrees:* certificates, associate, bachelor's, and master's.

Student Life *Campus security:* 24-hour emergency response devices and patrols, student patrols, late-night transport/escort service.

Athletics Member NCAA. All Division III.

Standardized Tests *Required:* SAT or ACT (for admission).

Costs (2012–13) *Comprehensive fee:* $42,440 includes full-time tuition ($31,440), mandatory fees ($300), and room and board ($10,700). *College room only:* $5800. Room and board charges vary according to housing facility.

Financial Aid *Of all full-time matriculated undergraduates who enrolled in 2012,* 961 applied for aid, 949 were judged to have need, 32 had their need fully met. 387 Federal Work-Study jobs (averaging $1470). *In 2012,* 54 non-need-based awards were made. *Average percent of need met:* 78. *Average financial aid package:* $21,795. *Average need-based loan:* $3940. *Average need-based gift aid:* $17,830. *Average non-need-based aid:* $9984. *Average indebtedness upon graduation:* $30,890.

Applying *Options:* electronic application, deferred entrance. *Application fee:* $25. *Required:* essay or personal statement, high school transcript, 1 letter of recommendation. *Required for some:* interview.

Freshman Application Contact Ms. Marie Keegan, Admissions Assistant, Nichols College, 124 Center Road, Dudley, MA 01571. *Phone:* 508-213-2203. *Toll-free phone:* 800-470-3379. *Fax:* 508-943-9885. *E-mail:* admissions@nichols.edu.

Website: http://www.nichols.edu/.

Northeastern University

Boston, Massachusetts

- **Independent** university, founded 1898
- **Urban** 73-acre campus
- **Endowment** $578.3 million
- **Coed** 16,685 undergraduate students, 100% full-time, 50% women, 50% men
- **Very difficult** entrance level, 32% of applicants were admitted

Undergraduates 16,685 full-time. Students come from 52 states and territories; 122 other countries; 71% are from out of state; 3% Black or African American, non-Hispanic/Latino; 6% Hispanic/Latino; 9% Asian, non-Hispanic/Latino; 0.1% American Indian or Alaska Native, non-Hispanic/Latino; 3% Two or more races, non-Hispanic/Latino; 12% Race/ethnicity unknown; 15% international; 4% transferred in; 54% live on campus. *Retention:* 96% of full-time freshmen returned.

Freshmen *Admission:* 44,208 applied, 14,084 admitted, 2,664 enrolled. *Test scores:* SAT critical reading scores over 500: 98%; SAT math scores over 500: 99%; SAT writing scores over 500: 98%; SAT critical reading scores over 600: 86%; SAT math scores over 600: 92%; SAT writing scores over 600: 82%; SAT critical reading scores over 700: 35%; SAT math scores over 700: 51%; SAT writing scores over 700: 31%.

Faculty *Total:* 1,536, 72% full-time. *Student/faculty ratio:* 14:1.

Academics *Calendar:* semesters. *Degrees:* bachelor's, master's, doctoral, and post-master's certificates. *Special study options:* academic remediation for entering students, accelerated degree program, adult/continuing education programs, advanced placement credit, cooperative education, distance learning, double majors, English as a second language, honors programs, independent study, internships, off-campus study, part-time degree program, services for LD students, student-designed majors, study abroad, summer session for credit. *ROTC:* Army (b), Navy (c), Air Force (c). *Unusual degree programs:* 3-2 engineering; nursing; biochemistry/biotechnology, biology/biotechnology, chemistry, communication studies/communication, media & cultural studies, computer science, criminal justice, economics, English, health sciences/public health, history, math, physics, pol. science, sociology, speech-language pathology/audiology.

Computers on Campus 1,993 computers/terminals and 1,382 ports are available on campus for general student use. Students can access the following: campus intranet, computer help desk, free student e-mail accounts, online (class) grades, online (class) registration, online (class) schedules. Campus-wide network is available. 100% of college-owned or -operated housing units are wired for high-speed Internet access. Wireless service is available via entire campus.

Student Life *Housing:* on-campus residence required through sophomore year. *Options:* coed. Campus housing is university owned and leased by the school. Freshman campus housing is guaranteed. *Activities and organizations:* drama/theater group, student-run newspaper, radio and television station, choral group, Student Government Association, Council for University Programs, Resident Student Association, Society of Collegiate Scholars, No Limits Dance Crew, national fraternities, national sororities. *Campus security:* 24-hour emergency response devices and patrols, student patrols, late-night transport/escort service, controlled dormitory access, Public Safety website. *Student services:* health clinic, personal/psychological counseling.

Athletics Member NCAA. All Division I. *Intercollegiate sports:* baseball M(s), basketball M(s)/W(s), cheerleading M(c)/W(c), crew M(s)/W(s), cross-country running M(s)/W(s), field hockey W(s), golf M(c)/W(c), ice hockey M(s)/W(s), lacrosse M(c)/W(c), racquetball M(c)/W(c), rugby M(c)/W(c), sailing M(c)/W(c), soccer M(s)/W(s), softball M(c)/W, swimming and diving W(s), table tennis M(c)/W(c), tennis M(c)/W, track and field M(s)/W(s), ultimate Frisbee M(c)/W, volleyball W(s), water polo M(c)/W(c), wrestling M(c).

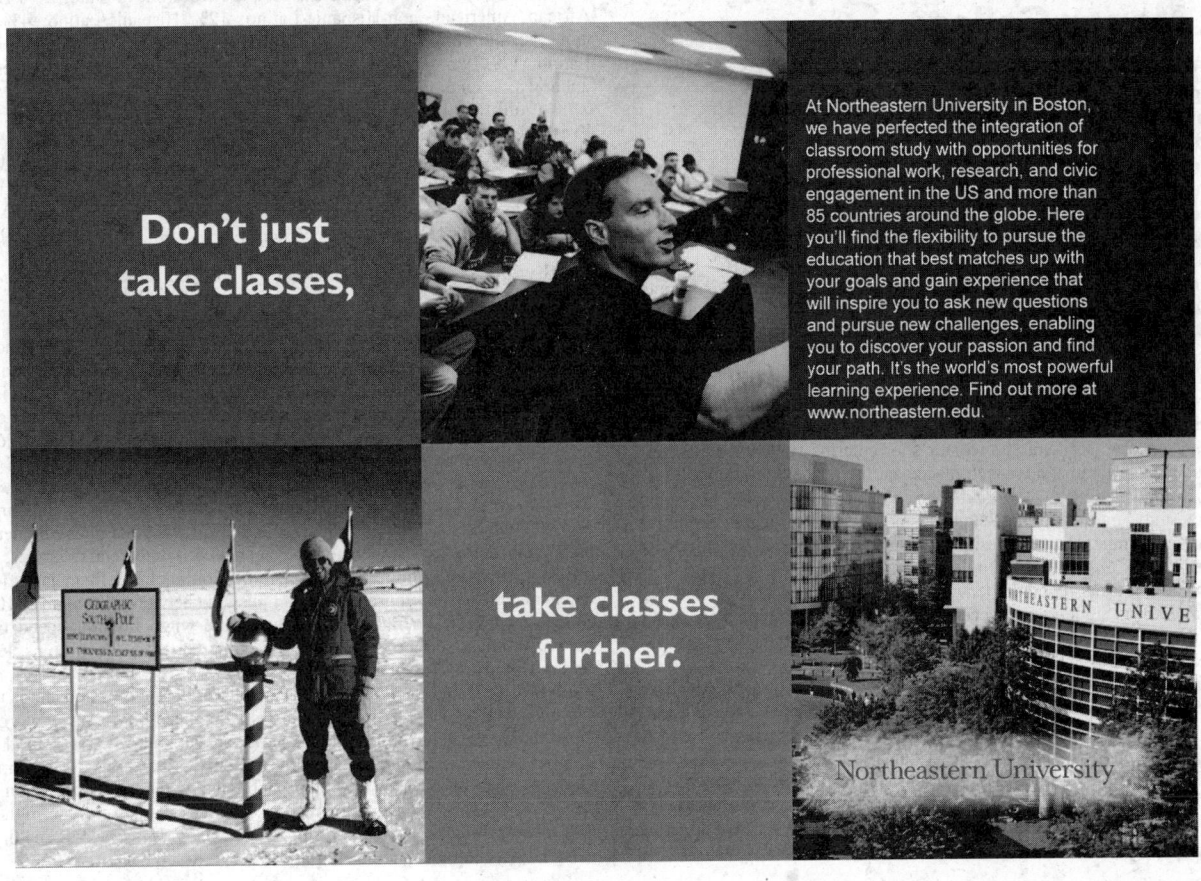

Don't just take classes, take classes further.

At Northeastern University in Boston, we have perfected the integration of classroom study with opportunities for professional work, research, and civic engagement in the US and more than 85 countries around the globe. Here you'll find the flexibility to pursue the education that best matches up with your goals and gain experience that will inspire you to ask new questions and pursue new challenges, enabling you to discover your passion and find your path. It's the world's most powerful learning experience. Find out more at www.northeastern.edu.

Northeastern University

Intramural sports: basketball M/W, cheerleading M(c)/W(c), field hockey W(c), golf M(c)/W(c), racquetball M/W, skiing (cross-country) M(c)/W(c), skiing (downhill) M(c)/W(c), soccer M/W, squash M(c)/W(c), swimming and diving M(c)/W(c), volleyball M(c)/W(c), weight lifting M(c).

Standardized Tests *Required:* SAT or ACT (for admission).

Costs (2012–13) *Comprehensive fee:* $53,356 includes full-time tuition ($39,320), mandatory fees ($416), and room and board ($13,620). *College room only:* $7240. Room and board charges vary according to board plan and housing facility. *Payment plan:* installment. *Waivers:* employees or children of employees.

Financial Aid Of all full-time matriculated undergraduates who enrolled in 2012, 9,646 applied for aid, 7,470 were judged to have need, 2,001 had their need fully met. In 2012, 4081 non-need-based awards were made. *Average percent of need met:* 70%. *Average financial aid package:* $22,787. *Average need-based loan:* $4700. *Average need-based gift aid:* $18,575. *Average non-need-based aid:* $11,629.

Applying *Options:* electronic application, early admission, early action, deferred entrance. *Application fee:* $75. *Required:* essay or personal statement, high school transcript, 2 letters of recommendation. *Application deadlines:* 1/15 (freshmen), 5/1 (transfers), 11/1 (early action). *Notification:* continuous until 4/1 (freshmen), continuous (transfers), 12/31 (early action).

Freshman Application Contact Jimmie Foster Jr., Dean of Undergraduate Admissions and Orientation, Northeastern University, 360 Huntington Avenue, 260 West Village F, Boston, MA 02115. *Phone:* 617-373-2200. *Fax:* 617-373-8780. *E-mail:* admissions@neu.edu.
Website: http://www.northeastern.edu/.

See previous page for display ad and page 1418 for the College Close-Up.

Northpoint Bible College

Haverhill, Massachusetts

Director of Admissions Helen Brouillette, Admissions Director, Northpoint Bible College, 320 South Main Street, Haverhill, MA 01835. *Phone:* 800-356-4014. *Toll-free phone:* 800-356-4014. *E-mail:* admissions@zbc.edu. *Website:* http://northpoint.edu/.

Pine Manor College

Chestnut Hill, Massachusetts

- **Independent** 4-year, founded 1911
- **Suburban** 55-acre campus
- **Endowment** $8.6 million
- **Women only** 317 undergraduate students, 97% full-time
- **Moderately difficult** entrance level, 64% of applicants were admitted

Undergraduates 306 full-time, 11 part-time. Students come from 18 states and territories; 15 other countries; 28% are from out of state; 27% Black or African American, non-Hispanic/Latino; 17% Hispanic/Latino; 6% Asian, non-Hispanic/Latino; 0.3% American Indian or Alaska Native, non-Hispanic/Latino; 19% Two or more races, non-Hispanic/Latino; 11% Race/ethnicity unknown; 11% international; 5% transferred in. *Retention:* 50% of full-time freshmen returned.

Freshmen *Admission:* 392 applied, 250 admitted, 122 enrolled.

Faculty *Total:* 70, 61% with terminal degrees. *Student/faculty ratio:* 10:1.

Academics *Calendar:* semesters. *Degrees:* associate, bachelor's, and master's. *Special study options:* academic remediation for entering students, adult/continuing education programs, advanced placement credit, double majors, English as a second language, external degree program, honors programs, independent study, internships, off-campus study, part-time degree program, services for LD students, student-designed majors, study abroad, summer session for credit.

Computers on Campus 85 computers/terminals are available on campus for general student use. Students can access the following: computer help desk, free student e-mail accounts, online (class) grades, online (class) schedules. Campuswide network is available.

Student Life *Housing options:* Campus housing is university owned. *Activities and organizations:* drama/theater group, student-run newspaper, radio station, choral group, African American, Latina, Asian, Native American and All (ALANA), Community Service Committee, International Student Club, The Model UN, Student Government Association (SGA). *Campus security:* 24-hour emergency response devices and patrols, student patrols, late-night transport/escort service, controlled dormitory access. *Student services:* health clinic, personal/psychological counseling, women's center.

Athletics Member NCAA. All Division III. *Intercollegiate sports:* basketball W, cross-country running W, field hockey W, lacrosse W, soccer W, softball W, tennis W, volleyball W.

Standardized Tests *Required:* SAT or ACT (for admission).

Costs (2013–14) *Comprehensive fee:* $37,051 includes full-time tuition ($24,301) and room and board ($12,750). Full-time tuition and fees vary according to course load. Part-time tuition: $725 per credit. Part-time tuition and fees vary according to course load. *Room and board:* Room and board charges vary according to housing facility. *Payment plan:* installment. *Waivers:* children of alumni and employees or children of employees.

Financial Aid Of all full-time matriculated undergraduates who enrolled in 2011, 263 applied for aid, 262 were judged to have need, 2 had their need fully met. 140 Federal Work-Study jobs (averaging $950). In 2011, 28 non-need-based awards were made. *Average percent of need met:* 70%. *Average financial aid package:* $23,000. *Average need-based loan:* $5200. *Average need-based gift aid:* $17,200. *Average non-need-based aid:* $10,700. *Average indebtedness upon graduation:* $30,660.

Applying *Options:* electronic application, deferred entrance. *Application fee:* $25. *Required:* essay or personal statement, high school transcript, SAT or ACT Scores. *Recommended:* minimum 2.0 GPA, interview. *Application deadlines:* rolling (freshmen), rolling (transfers). *Notification:* continuous (freshmen), continuous (transfers).

Freshman Application Contact Pine Manor College, 400 Heath Street, Chestnut Hill, MA 02467. *Phone:* 617-731-7107. *Toll-free phone:* 800-762-1357.
Website: http://www.pmc.edu/.

Regis College

Weston, Massachusetts

- **Independent Roman Catholic** comprehensive, founded 1927
- **Small-town** 131-acre campus with easy access to Boston
- **Endowment** $15.4 million
- **Coed** 1,149 undergraduate students, 79% full-time, 78% women, 22% men
- **Moderately difficult** entrance level, 73% of applicants were admitted

Undergraduates 902 full-time, 247 part-time. Students come from 21 states and territories; 11 other countries; 13% are from out of state; 21% Black or African American, non-Hispanic/Latino; 12% Hispanic/Latino; 4% Asian, non-Hispanic/Latino; 0.3% American Indian or Alaska Native, non-Hispanic/Latino; 1% Two or more races, non-Hispanic/Latino; 13% Race/ethnicity unknown; 1% international; 2% transferred in; 57% live on campus. *Retention:* 77% of full-time freshmen returned.

Freshmen *Admission:* 2,041 applied, 1,484 admitted, 278 enrolled. *Average high school GPA:* 2.97. *Test scores:* SAT critical reading scores over 500: 39%; SAT math scores over 500: 34%; SAT writing scores over 500: 36%; ACT scores over 18: 80%; SAT critical reading scores over 600: 5%; SAT math scores over 600: 4%; SAT writing scores over 600: 7%; ACT scores over 24: 29%; ACT scores over 30: 3%.

Faculty *Total:* 177, 41% full-time, 53% with terminal degrees. *Student/faculty ratio:* 13:1.

Academics *Calendar:* semesters. *Degrees:* associate, bachelor's, master's, doctoral, and post-master's certificates. *Special study options:* academic remediation for entering students, accelerated degree program, adult/continuing education programs, advanced placement credit, double majors, English as a second language, honors programs, independent study, internships, off-campus study, part-time degree program, services for LD students, student-designed majors, study abroad, summer session for credit. *ROTC:* Army (c). *Unusual degree programs:* 3-2 business administration; communication.

Computers on Campus 196 computers/terminals are available on campus for general student use. Students can access the following: campus intranet, computer help desk, free student e-mail accounts, online (class) grades, online (class) registration, online (class) schedules, online bills, financial aid award letters and check-in requirements. Campuswide network is available. 100% of college-owned or -operated housing units are wired for high-speed Internet access. Wireless service is available via computer labs, dorm rooms, learning centers, libraries, student centers.

Student Life *Housing options:* coed, women-only. Campus housing is university owned. Freshman campus housing is guaranteed. *Activities and organizations:* drama/theater group, student-run newspaper, radio station, choral group, Campus Ministry, SGA-Student Government Association, Asian American Student Organization, Dynasty Step Club, Black Student Organization. *Campus security:* 24-hour emergency response devices and patrols, late-night transport/escort service, controlled dormitory access. *Student services:* health clinic, personal/psychological counseling.

Athletics Member NCAA. All Division III. *Intercollegiate sports:* basketball M/W, field hockey W, lacrosse M/W, soccer M/W, softball W, swimming and diving M/W, tennis M/W, track and field M/W, volleyball M/W.

Standardized Tests *Required:* SAT or ACT (for admission).

Costs (2012–13) *One-time required fee:* $200. *Comprehensive fee:* $45,860 includes full-time tuition ($33,060) and room and board ($12,800). Full-time tuition and fees vary according to course load. Part-time tuition and fees vary according to class time. *Payment plan:* installment. *Waivers:* employees or children of employees.

Financial Aid Of all full-time matriculated undergraduates who enrolled in 2008, 695 applied for aid, 644 were judged to have need, 93 had their need fully met. 436 Federal Work-Study jobs (averaging $2000). 40 state and other part-time jobs (averaging $1500). In 2008, 66 non-need-based awards were made. *Average percent of need met:* 59%. *Average financial aid package:* $22,111. *Average need-based loan:* $4849. *Average need-based gift aid:* $12,529. *Average non-need-based aid:* $8231. *Average indebtedness upon graduation:* $24,178.

Applying *Options:* electronic application, early admission, early action, deferred entrance. *Application fee:* $50. *Required:* essay or personal statement, high school transcript, minimum 2.0 GPA, 2 letters of recommendation. *Required for some:* interview. *Recommended:* minimum 3.0 GPA, interview, rank in upper 50% of high school class. *Application deadlines:* rolling (freshmen), rolling (transfers), 12/1 (early action). *Notification:* 12/23 (early action).

Freshman Application Contact Ms. Wanda Suriel, Director of Admission, Regis College, 235 Wellesley Street, Weston, MA 02493. *Phone:* 781-768-7100. *Toll-free phone:* 866-438-7344. *Fax:* 781-768-7071. *E-mail:* admission@regiscollege.edu.
Website: http://www.regiscollege.edu/.

Salem State University

Salem, Massachusetts

- **State-supported** comprehensive, founded 1854, part of Massachusetts Public Higher Education System
- **Urban** 62-acre campus with easy access to Boston
- **Coed** 7,741 undergraduate students, 76% full-time, 61% women, 39% men
- **Minimally difficult** entrance level, 69% of applicants were admitted

Undergraduates 5,862 full-time, 1,879 part-time. Students come from 50 other countries; 3% are from out of state; 11% transferred in; 28% live on campus. *Retention:* 74% of full-time freshmen returned.

Freshmen *Admission:* 4,855 applied, 3,364 admitted, 1,095 enrolled. *Average high school GPA:* 3.09. *Test scores:* SAT critical reading scores over 500: 49%; SAT math scores over 500: 49%; SAT writing scores over 500: 43%; SAT critical reading scores over 600: 10%; SAT math scores over 600: 9%; SAT writing scores over 600: 7%; SAT critical reading scores over 700: 1%.

Faculty *Total:* 783, 44% full-time.

Academics *Calendar:* semesters. *Degrees:* certificates, bachelor's, master's, and post-master's certificates. *Special study options:* academic remediation for entering students, accelerated degree program, adult/continuing education programs, advanced placement credit, distance learning, double majors, English as a second language, honors programs, independent study, internships, off-campus study, part-time degree program, services for LD students, student-designed majors, study abroad, summer session for credit. *ROTC:* Army (c), Air Force (c).

Computers on Campus 255 computers/terminals are available on campus for general student use. Students can access the following: campus intranet, computer help desk, free student e-mail accounts, online (class) grades, online (class) registration, online (class) schedules. Campuswide network is available. 100% of college-owned or -operated housing units are wired for high-speed Internet access. Wireless service is available via entire campus.

Student Life *Housing options:* coed. Campus housing is university owned. Freshman applicants given priority for college housing. *Activities and organizations:* drama/theater group, student-run newspaper, radio and television station, choral group, Student Government Association, Program Council, Residence Hall Association, Multicultural Student Association, Hispanic-American Society, national fraternities, national sororities. *Campus security:* 24-hour emergency response devices and patrols, late-night transport/escort service, controlled dormitory access. *Student services:* health clinic, personal/psychological counseling, women's center, legal services.

Athletics Member NCAA. All Division III. *Intercollegiate sports:* baseball M, basketball M/W, cross-country running M/W, field hockey W, golf M, ice hockey M/W(c), lacrosse M/W, soccer M/W, softball W, tennis M/W, volleyball W. *Intramural sports:* basketball M/W, cheerleading M/W, football M/W, ice hockey M/W, rugby M/W, ultimate Frisbee M/W, volleyball M/W.

Standardized Tests *Required:* SAT or ACT (for admission).

Costs (2012–13) *Tuition:* state resident $910 full-time, $38 per credit hour part-time; nonresident $7050 full-time, $294 per credit hour part-time. Full-time tuition and fees vary according to class time and course load. Part-time tuition and fees vary according to class time and course load. *Required fees:* $7140 full-time, $298 per credit hour part-time. *Room only:* $8292. Room and board charges vary according to board plan and housing facility. *Payment plan:* installment. *Waivers:* senior citizens and employees or children of employees.

Financial Aid Of all full-time matriculated undergraduates who enrolled in 2009, 286 Federal Work-Study jobs (averaging $3000).

Applying *Options:* electronic application, early action, deferred entrance. *Application fee:* $40. *Required:* high school transcript, minimum 2.0 GPA. *Required for some:* interview. *Application deadlines:* 5/1 (freshmen), rolling (transfers). *Notification:* continuous (freshmen), continuous (transfers).

Freshman Application Contact Dr. Mary Dunn, Assistant Dean for Undergraduate Admissions, Salem State University, 352 Lafayette Street, Salem, MA 01970. *Phone:* 978-542-6202. *Fax:* 978-542-6893. *E-mail:* admissions@salemstate.edu.
Website: http://www.salemstate.edu/.

School of the Museum of Fine Arts, Boston

Boston, Massachusetts

- **Independent** comprehensive, founded 1876
- **Urban** 14-acre campus with easy access to Boston
- **Endowment** $22.7 million
- **Coed** 594 undergraduate students, 71% full-time, 70% women, 30% men
- **Moderately difficult** entrance level, 82% of applicants were admitted

Undergraduates 422 full-time, 172 part-time. Students come from 36 states and territories; 37 other countries; 65% are from out of state; 3% Black or African American, non-Hispanic/Latino; 8% Hispanic/Latino; 4% Asian, non-Hispanic/Latino; 0.5% American Indian or Alaska Native, non-Hispanic/Latino; 4% Two or more races, non-Hispanic/Latino; 23% Race/ethnicity unknown; 8% international; 7% transferred in; 10% live on campus. *Retention:* 68% of full-time freshmen returned.

Freshmen *Admission:* 701 applied, 572 admitted, 94 enrolled.

Faculty *Total:* 147, 33% full-time, 71% with terminal degrees. *Student/faculty ratio:* 9:1.

Academics *Calendar:* semesters. *Degrees:* certificates, diplomas, bachelor's, master's, and postbachelor's certificates. *Special study options:* adult/continuing education programs, double majors, independent study, internships, off-campus study, part-time degree program, services for LD students, student-designed majors, study abroad, summer session for credit.

Computers on Campus 100 computers/terminals are available on campus for general student use. Students can access the following: campus intranet, computer help desk, free student e-mail accounts, online (class) grades, online (class) registration, online (class) schedules. Campuswide network is available. 100% of college-owned or -operated housing units are wired for high-speed Internet access. Wireless service is available via entire campus.

Student Life *Housing options:* coed. Campus housing is leased by the school. Freshman applicants given priority for college housing. *Activities and organizations:* GLBT Group, Student Body, Inc and Student Voice, Library Sounds, SMFARM (garden group—smfa farm), CRU @ SMFA. *Campus security:* 24-hour emergency response devices and patrols, late night taxis service between buildings. *Student services:* health clinic, personal/psychological counseling.

Standardized Tests *Recommended:* Test scores are considered if submitted.

Costs (2012–13) *Comprehensive fee:* $50,018 includes full-time tuition ($36,828), mandatory fees ($1200), and room and board ($11,990). Full-time tuition and fees vary according to course load, degree level, program, and student level. *Part-time tuition:* $1370 per unit. Part-time tuition and fees vary according to class time, course load, program, and student level. *Room and board:* Room and board charges vary according to board plan and housing facility. *Payment plan:* installment. *Waivers:* employees or children of employees.

Financial Aid Of all full-time matriculated undergraduates who enrolled in 2011, 322 applied for aid, 287 were judged to have need, 52 had their need fully met. In 2011, 30 non-need-based awards were made. *Average percent of need met:* 52%. *Average financial aid package:* $21,284. *Average need-based loan:* $4462. *Average need-based gift aid:* $13,373. *Average non-need-based aid:* $8782.

Applying *Options:* electronic application, deferred entrance. *Application fee:* $65. *Required:* essay or personal statement, high school transcript, 2 letters of recommendation, portfolio. *Recommended:* interview. *Application deadlines:* rolling (freshmen), rolling (out-of-state freshmen), rolling (transfers). *Notifica-*

tion: continuous (freshmen), continuous (out-of-state freshmen), continuous (transfers).

Freshman Application Contact Ms. Robyn Reed, Associate Dean of Admissions, School of the Museum of Fine Arts, Boston, 230 The Fenway, Boston, MA 02115. *Phone:* 617-369-3626. *Toll-free phone:* 800-643-6078. *Fax:* 617-369-4264. *E-mail:* admissions@smfa.edu. *Website:* http://www.smfa.edu/.

Simmons College

Boston, Massachusetts

- **Independent** university, founded 1899
- **Urban** 12-acre campus with easy access to Boston
- **Undergraduate: women only; graduate: coed** 1,792 undergraduate students, 92% full-time, 100% women
- **Moderately difficult** entrance level, 48% of applicants were admitted

Undergraduates 1,647 full-time, 145 part-time. 37% are from out of state; 7% Black or African American, non-Hispanic/Latino; 6% Hispanic/Latino; 8% Asian, non-Hispanic/Latino; 0.1% Native Hawaiian or other Pacific Islander, non-Hispanic/Latino; 0.2% American Indian or Alaska Native, non-Hispanic/Latino; 3% Two or more races, non-Hispanic/Latino; 4% Race/ethnicity unknown; 3% international; 3% transferred in; 55% live on campus. *Retention:* 85% of full-time freshmen returned.

Freshmen *Admission:* 4,440 applied, 2,145 admitted, 401 enrolled. *Average high school GPA:* 3.15. *Test scores:* SAT critical reading scores over 500: 82%; SAT math scores over 500: 87%; SAT writing scores over 500: 88%; ACT scores over 18: 99%; SAT critical reading scores over 600: 35%; SAT math scores over 600: 34%; SAT writing scores over 600: 42%; ACT scores over 24: 64%; SAT critical reading scores over 700: 6%; SAT math scores over 700: 5%; SAT writing scores over 700: 7%; ACT scores over 30: 11%.

Faculty *Total:* 623, 35% full-time, 43% with terminal degrees. *Student/faculty ratio:* 11:1.

Academics *Calendar:* semesters. *Degrees:* certificates, bachelor's, master's, doctoral, post-master's, and postbachelor's certificates. *Special study options:* academic remediation for entering students, accelerated degree program, adult/continuing education programs, advanced placement credit, cooperative education, distance learning, double majors, honors programs, independent study, internships, off-campus study, part-time degree program, services for LD stu-

dents, student-designed majors, study abroad, summer session for credit. *ROTC:* Army (c), Navy (c). *Unusual degree programs:* 3-2 business administration; nursing; social work; teaching, physician assistant, pharmacy with Massachusetts College of Pharmacy & Health Sciences.

Computers on Campus 350 computers/terminals and 1,000 ports are available on campus for general student use. Students can access the following: campus intranet, computer help desk, free student e-mail accounts, online (class) grades, online (class) registration, online (class) schedules. Campus-wide network is available. 100% of college-owned or -operated housing units are wired for high-speed Internet access. Wireless service is available via entire campus.

Student Life *Housing:* on-campus residence required for freshman year. *Options:* coed, women-only. Campus housing is university owned. Freshman applicants given priority for college housing. *Activities and organizations:* drama/theater group, student-run newspaper, radio station, choral group, Student Government Association, Black Students Organization, Campus Activities Board, Asian Students Association, Simmons Voice. *Campus security:* 24-hour emergency response devices and patrols, late-night transport/escort service, controlled dormitory access. *Student services:* health clinic, personal/psychological counseling, women's center.

Athletics Member NCAA. All Division III. *Intercollegiate sports:* basketball W, crew W, cross-country running W, field hockey W, lacrosse W, soccer W, softball W, swimming and diving W, tennis W, volleyball W. *Intramural sports:* basketball M/W, rugby W(c), soccer M/W, volleyball M/W.

Standardized Tests *Required:* SAT or ACT (for admission).

Costs (2013–14) *Comprehensive fee:* $48,770 includes full-time tuition ($34,350), mandatory fees ($1020), and room and board ($13,400). Full-time tuition and fees vary according to course load and program. Part-time tuition: $1178 per credit hour. Part-time tuition and fees vary according to course load and program. *Room and board:* Room and board charges vary according to board plan. *Payment plan:* installment. *Waivers:* employees or children of employees.

Financial Aid Of all full-time matriculated undergraduates who enrolled in 2010, 1,363 applied for aid, 1,252 were judged to have need, 100 had their need fully met. 1,040 Federal Work-Study jobs (averaging $2333). In 2010, 289 non-need-based awards were made. *Average percent of need met:* 64%. *Average financial aid package:* $22,495. *Average need-based loan:* $4800. *Average need-based gift aid:* $16,075. *Average non-need-based aid:* $8815.

Applying *Options:* electronic application, early action, deferred entrance. *Application fee:* $55. *Required:* essay or personal statement, high school transcript, 2 letters of recommendation, Test scores. *Recommended:* minimum 3.0

GPA, interview. *Application deadlines:* 2/1 (freshmen), 2/1 (out-of-state freshmen), 4/1 (transfers), 12/1 (early action). *Notification:* 3/15 (freshmen), 3/15 (out-of-state freshmen), 1/15 (early action).
Freshman Application Contact Simmons College, 300 The Fenway, Boston, MA 02115. *Phone:* 617-521-2051. *Toll-free phone:* 800-345-8468. *Website:* http://www.simmons.edu/.

See previous page for display ad and page 1500 for the College Close-Up.

Smith College

Northampton, Massachusetts

- **Independent** comprehensive, founded 1871
- **Small-town** 147-acre campus with easy access to Hartford
- **Undergraduate: women only; graduate: coed** 2,664 undergraduate students, 99% full-time, 100% women
- **Very difficult** entrance level, 42% of applicants were admitted

Undergraduates 2,643 full-time, 21 part-time. 78% are from out of state; 5% Black or African American, non-Hispanic/Latino; 9% Hispanic/Latino; 12% Asian, non-Hispanic/Latino; 0.1% Native Hawaiian or other Pacific Islander, non-Hispanic/Latino; 0.2% American Indian or Alaska Native, non-Hispanic/Latino; 4% Two or more races, non-Hispanic/Latino; 11% Race/ethnicity unknown; 12% international; 2% transferred in; 95% live on campus. *Retention:* 93% of full-time freshmen returned.
Freshmen *Admission:* 4,341 applied, 1,842 admitted, 651 enrolled. *Average high school GPA:* 3.92. *Test scores:* SAT critical reading scores over 500: 99%; SAT math scores over 500: 97%; SAT writing scores over 500: 99%; ACT scores over 18: 100%; SAT critical reading scores over 600: 82%; SAT math scores over 600: 76%; SAT writing scores over 600: 85%; ACT scores over 24: 94%; SAT critical reading scores over 700: 37%; SAT math scores over 700: 29%; SAT writing scores over 700: 34%; ACT scores over 30: 35%.
Faculty *Total:* 299, 92% full-time, 98% with terminal degrees. *Student/faculty ratio:* 9:1.
Academics *Calendar:* semesters. *Degrees:* bachelor's, master's, doctoral, post-master's, and postbachelor's certificates. *Special study options:* adult/continuing education programs, part-time degree program. *ROTC:* Army (c), Air Force (c).
Computers on Campus Students can access the following: campus intranet, computer help desk, free student e-mail accounts, online (class) grades, online (class) registration, online (class) schedules. Campuswide network is available. 100% of college-owned or -operated housing units are wired for high-speed Internet access. Wireless service is available via classrooms, computer centers, computer labs, dorm rooms, learning centers, libraries, student centers.
Student Life *Housing:* on-campus residence required through senior year. *Options:* women-only, cooperative. Campus housing is university owned. Freshman campus housing is guaranteed. *Campus security:* 24-hour emergency response devices and patrols, late-night transport/escort service, self-defense workshops, emergency telephones, programs in crime and sexual assault prevention.
Athletics Member NCAA. All Division III. *Intercollegiate sports:* basketball W, crew W, cross-country running W, equestrian sports W, field hockey W, lacrosse W, skiing (downhill) W, soccer W, softball W, squash W, swimming and diving W, tennis W, track and field W, volleyball W. *Intramural sports:* badminton W(c), cheerleading W(c), crew W, equestrian sports W(c), fencing W(c), golf W(c), ice hockey W(c), rock climbing W, rugby W(c), soccer W, squash W, ultimate Frisbee W(c).
Costs (2012–13) *Comprehensive fee:* $55,320 includes full-time tuition ($41,190), mandatory fees ($270), and room and board ($13,860). Part-time tuition: $1290 per credit hour. *College room only:* $6940. *Payment plans:* tuition prepayment, installment. *Waivers:* employees or children of employees.
Financial Aid Of all full-time matriculated undergraduates who enrolled in 2012, 1,915 applied for aid, 1,658 were judged to have need, 1,658 had their need fully met. In 2012, 102 non-need-based awards were made. *Average percent of need met:* 100%. *Average financial aid package:* $39,120. *Average need-based loan:* $4513. *Average need-based gift aid:* $34,654. *Average non-need-based aid:* $17,691. *Average indebtedness upon graduation:* $23,071. *Financial aid deadline:* 2/15.
Applying *Options:* electronic application, early admission, early decision, deferred entrance. *Application fee:* $60. *Required:* essay or personal statement, high school transcript, 3 letters of recommendation. *Recommended:* interview. *Application deadlines:* 1/15 (freshmen), 5/15 (transfers). *Early decision deadline:* 11/15 (for plan 1), 1/2 (for plan 2). *Notification:* 4/1 (freshmen), 6/1 (transfers), 12/15 (early decision plan 1), 2/2 (early decision plan 2).
Freshman Application Contact Ms. Debra Shaver, Director of Admissions, Smith College, 7 College Lane, Northampton, MA 01063. *Phone:* 413-585-

2500. *Toll-free phone:* 800-383-3232. *Fax:* 413-585-2527. *E-mail:* admission@smith.edu.
Website: http://www.smith.edu/.

See previous page for display ad and page 1506 for the College Close-Up.

Springfield College

Springfield, Massachusetts

Freshman Application Contact Richard K. Veres, Director of Undergraduate Admissions, Springfield College, 263 Alden Street, Springfield, MA 01109. *Phone:* 413-748-3136. *Toll-free phone:* 800-343-1257. *Fax:* 413-748-3694. *E-mail:* admissions@spfldcol.edu.
Website: http://www.spfldcol.edu/.

See below for display ad and page 1512 for the College Close-Up.

Stonehill College

Easton, Massachusetts

- **Independent Roman Catholic** 4-year, founded 1948
- **Suburban** 384-acre campus with easy access to Boston
- **Endowment** $146.7 million
- **Coed** 2,599 undergraduate students, 100% full-time, 61% women, 39% men
- **Very difficult** entrance level, 80% of applicants were admitted

Undergraduates 2,590 full-time, 9 part-time. Students come from 31 states and territories; 8 other countries; 55% are from out of state; 3% Black or African American, non-Hispanic/Latino; 4% Hispanic/Latino; 2% Asian, non-Hispanic/Latino; 2% Two or more races, non-Hispanic/Latino; 3% Race/ethnicity unknown; 0.5% international; 0.7% transferred in; 93% live on campus. *Retention:* 86% of full-time freshmen returned.

Freshmen *Admission:* 6,117 applied, 4,890 admitted, 814 enrolled. *Average high school GPA:* 3.28. *Test scores:* SAT critical reading scores over 500: 84%; SAT math scores over 500: 87%; SAT writing scores over 500: 88%; ACT scores over 18: 99%; SAT critical reading scores over 600: 35%; SAT math scores over 600: 43%; SAT writing scores over 600: 42%; ACT scores over 24:

77%; SAT critical reading scores over 700: 5%; SAT math scores over 700: 5%; SAT writing scores over 700: 7%; ACT scores over 30: 5%.
Faculty *Total:* 278, 60% full-time, 67% with terminal degrees. *Student/faculty ratio:* 13:1.

Academics *Calendar:* semesters. *Degree:* bachelor's. *Special study options:* advanced placement credit, double majors, honors programs, independent study, internships, off-campus study, part-time degree program, services for LD students, student-designed majors, study abroad, summer session for credit. *ROTC:* Army (b). *Unusual degree programs:* 3-2 engineering with University of Notre Dame.

Computers on Campus 403 computers/terminals and 300 ports are available on campus for general student use. Students can access the following: campus intranet, computer help desk, free student e-mail accounts, online (class) grades, online (class) registration, online (class) schedules, Learning Management System; online degree evaluation and planning; add funds to ID online and use at off campus locations; online housing contracts and room lottery; online financial aid awards; online time sheets and payments for campus jobs; and ebill. Campuswide network is available. 100% of college-owned or -operated housing units are wired for high-speed Internet access. Wireless service is available via entire campus.

Student Life *Housing options:* coed, women-only, disabled students. Campus housing is university owned. *Activities and organizations:* drama/theater group, student-run newspaper, radio station, choral group, Into the Streets, Recreation/Intramural Sports Teams, Dance Club, Student Government Association, Education Society. *Campus security:* 24-hour emergency response devices and patrols, late-night transport/escort service, controlled dormitory access. *Student services:* health clinic, personal/psychological counseling, women's center.

Athletics Member NCAA. All Division II. *Intercollegiate sports:* baseball M(s), basketball M(s)/W(s), bowling M(c)/W(c), cheerleading M(c)/W(c), cross-country running M(s)/W(s), equestrian sports W, field hockey W(s), football M(s), golf M(c)/W(c), ice hockey M, lacrosse M(c)/W(s), rugby M(c)/W(c), soccer M(s)/W(s), softball W(s), tennis M(s)/W(s), track and field M(s)/W(s), ultimate Frisbee M(c)/W(c), volleyball M(c)/W(s), wrestling M(c). *Intramural sports:* basketball M/W, field hockey M/W, soccer M/W, softball M/W, tennis M/W, volleyball M/W.

Costs (2013–14) *Comprehensive fee:* $49,970 includes full-time tuition ($36,160) and room and board ($13,810). Part-time tuition: $1205 per credit. Part-time tuition and fees vary according to course load. *Room and board:* Room and board charges vary according to board plan. *Payment plans:* tuition prepayment, installment. *Waivers:* employees or children of employees.

Financial Aid Of all full-time matriculated undergraduates who enrolled in 2012, 2,090 applied for aid, 1,506 were judged to have need, 722 had their need fully met. In 2012, 743 non-need-based awards were made. *Average percent of need met:* 90%. *Average financial aid package:* $26,199. *Average need-based loan:* $5002. *Average need-based gift aid:* $20,657. *Average non-need-based aid:* $10,836. *Average indebtedness upon graduation:* $27,794.

Applying *Options:* electronic application, early decision, early action, deferred entrance. *Application fee:* $60. *Required:* essay or personal statement, high school transcript, 2 letters of recommendation. *Required for some:* interview. *Recommended:* campus visit. *Application deadlines:* 1/15 (freshmen), 4/1 (transfers), 11/1 (early action). *Early decision deadline:* 11/1. *Notification:* 3/15 (freshmen), continuous until 5/31 (transfers), 12/25 (early decision), 1/15 (early action).

Freshman Application Contact Stonehill College, 320 Washington Street, Easton, MA 02357-5610. *Phone:* 508-565-1373. *Fax:* 508-565-1545. *E-mail:* admission@stonehill.edu.
Website: http://www.stonehill.edu/.

See below for display ad and page 1524 for the College Close-Up.

Suffolk University

Boston, Massachusetts

- **Independent** comprehensive, founded 1906
- **Urban** 2-acre campus
- **Endowment** $130.0 million
- **Coed** 5,770 undergraduate students, 93% full-time, 56% women, 44% men
- **Moderately difficult** entrance level, 78% of applicants were admitted

Undergraduates 5,364 full-time, 406 part-time. Students come from 43 states and territories; 105 other countries; 33% are from out of state; 5% Black or African American, non-Hispanic/Latino; 10% Hispanic/Latino; 7% Asian, non-Hispanic/Latino; 0.2% American Indian or Alaska Native, non-Hispanic/Latino; 1% Two or more races, non-Hispanic/Latino; 17% Race/ethnicity unknown; 17% international; 8% transferred in; 22% live on campus. *Retention:* 76% of full-time freshmen returned.

Freshmen *Admission:* 9,418 applied, 7,380 admitted, 1,240 enrolled. *Average high school GPA:* 3.15. *Test scores:* SAT critical reading scores over 500: 54%; SAT math scores over 500: 57%; SAT writing scores over 500: 55%; ACT scores over 18: 87%; SAT critical reading scores over 600: 15%; SAT math scores over 600: 17%; SAT writing scores over 600: 15%; ACT scores over 24: 35%; SAT critical reading scores over 700: 1%; SAT math scores over 700: 1%; SAT writing scores over 700: 1%; ACT scores over 30: 4%.

Faculty *Total:* 863, 45% full-time, 57% with terminal degrees. *Student/faculty ratio:* 12:1.

Academics *Calendar:* semesters. *Degrees:* certificates, diplomas, associate, bachelor's, master's, doctoral, post-master's, and postbachelor's certificates (doctoral degree in law). *Special study options:* academic remediation for entering students, accelerated degree program, adult/continuing education programs, advanced placement credit, cooperative education, distance learning, double majors, English as a second language, freshman honors college, honors programs, independent study, internships, off-campus study, part-time degree program, services for LD students, study abroad, summer session for credit. *ROTC:* Army (c).

Computers on Campus 539 computers/terminals are available on campus for general student use. Students can access the following: campus intranet, computer help desk, free student e-mail accounts, online (class) grades, online (class) registration, online (class) schedules. Campuswide network is available. 100% of college-owned or -operated housing units are wired for high-speed Internet access. Wireless service is available via entire campus.

Student Life *Housing options:* coed. Campus housing is university owned. Freshman applicants given priority for college housing. *Activities and organizations:* drama/theater group, student-run newspaper, radio and television station, choral group, Student Government Association, Program Committee, Suffolk Free Radio, Black Student Union, Journey Leadership Program, national fraternities. *Campus security:* 24-hour emergency response devices, late-night transport/escort service, controlled dormitory access. *Student services:* health clinic, personal/psychological counseling, women's center.

Athletics Member NCAA. All Division III. *Intercollegiate sports:* baseball M, basketball M/W, cross-country running M/W, golf M, ice hockey M, soccer M, softball W, tennis M/W, volleyball W. *Intramural sports:* basketball M/W, soccer M/W, softball M/W, volleyball M/W.

Standardized Tests *Required:* SAT or ACT (for admission).

Costs (2012–13) *One-time required fee:* $200. *Comprehensive fee:* $45,522 includes full-time tuition ($30,672), mandatory fees ($120), and room and board ($14,730). Part-time tuition and fees vary according to course load. *College room only:* $12,124. Room and board charges vary according to board plan and housing facility. *Payment plans:* installment, deferred payment. *Waivers:* children of alumni, senior citizens, and employees or children of employees.

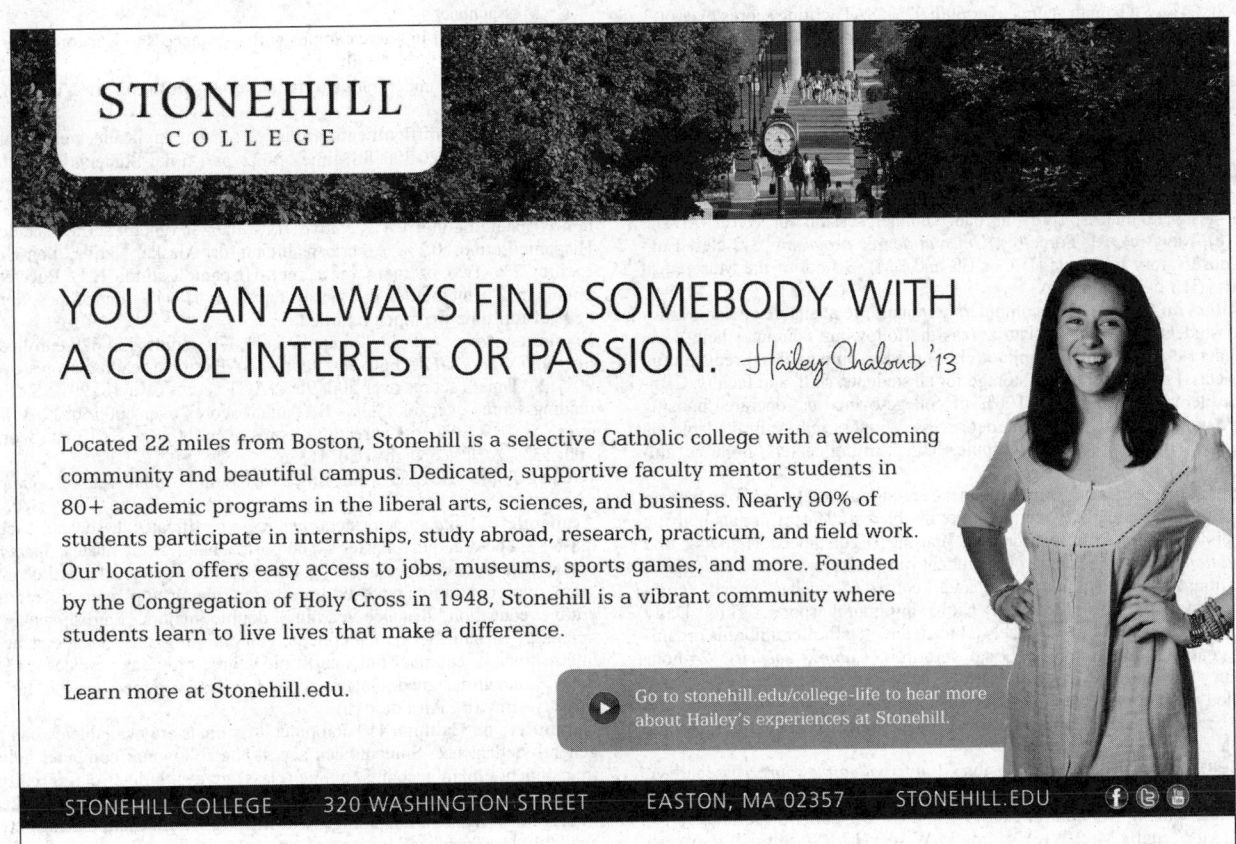

Financial Aid Of all full-time matriculated undergraduates who enrolled in 2012, 3,738 applied for aid, 3,461 were judged to have need, 294 had their need fully met. 1,104 Federal Work-Study jobs (averaging $2394). 428 state and other part-time jobs (averaging $3125). In 2012, 391 non-need-based awards were made. *Average percent of need met:* 65%. *Average financial aid package:* $22,115. *Average need-based loan:* $4677. *Average need-based gift aid:* $14,463. *Average non-need-based aid:* $8872. *Average indebtedness upon graduation:* $33,823. *Financial aid deadline:* 2/15.

Applying *Options:* electronic application, early action, deferred entrance. *Application fee:* $50. *Required:* essay or personal statement, high school transcript, 2 letters of recommendation. *Required for some:* interview. *Recommended:* minimum 2.5 GPA. *Application deadlines:* 2/15 (freshmen), 6/30 (transfers), 11/15 (early action). *Notification:* 3/20 (freshmen), continuous (transfers), 12/20 (early action).

Freshman Application Contact Mr. John Hamel, Associate Vice President/Director Undergraduate Admissions, Suffolk University, 8 Ashburton Place, Boston, MA 02108. *Phone:* 617-573-8460. *Toll-free phone:* 800-6-SUFFOLK. *Fax:* 617-742-4291. *E-mail:* admission@suffolk.edu. *Website:* http://www.suffolk.edu/.

Tufts University
Medford, Massachusetts

- **Independent** university, founded 1852
- **Suburban** 150-acre campus with easy access to Boston
- **Endowment** $1.4 billion
- **Coed** 5,255 undergraduate students, 98% full-time, 51% women, 49% men
- **Most difficult** entrance level, 21% of applicants were admitted

Undergraduates 5,167 full-time, 88 part-time. Students come from 52 states and territories; 60 other countries; 77% are from out of state; 4% Black or African American, non-Hispanic/Latino; 7% Hispanic/Latino; 10% Asian, non-Hispanic/Latino; 0.1% American Indian or Alaska Native, non-Hispanic/Latino; 4% Two or more races, non-Hispanic/Latino; 11% Race/ethnicity unknown; 7% international; 2% transferred in; 64% live on campus. *Retention:* 97% of full-time freshmen returned.

Freshmen *Admission:* 16,369 applied, 3,503 admitted, 1,307 enrolled. *Test scores:* SAT critical reading scores over 500: 100%; SAT math scores over 500: 100%; SAT writing scores over 500: 100%; SAT critical reading scores over 600: 94%; SAT math scores over 600: 97%; SAT writing scores over 600: 96%; SAT critical reading scores over 700: 64%; SAT math scores over 700: 69%; SAT writing scores over 700: 64%.

Faculty *Total:* 1,045, 67% full-time, 82% with terminal degrees. *Student/faculty ratio:* 9:1.

Academics *Calendar:* semesters. *Degrees:* bachelor's, master's, doctoral, post-master's, and postbachelor's certificates. *Special study options:* adult/continuing education programs, advanced placement credit, double majors, independent study, internships, off-campus study, services for LD students, student-designed majors, study abroad, summer session for credit. *ROTC:* Army (c), Navy (c), Air Force (c). *Unusual degree programs:* 3-2 New England Conservatory of Music (BA or BS and BM), School of the Museum of Fine Arts (BA or BS and BFA).

Computers on Campus 300 computers/terminals are available on campus for general student use. Students can access the following: computer help desk, free student e-mail accounts, online (class) grades, online (class) registration, online (class) schedules, Cloud storage for all students, staff, and faculty. Campuswide network is available. 100% of college-owned or -operated housing units are wired for high-speed Internet access. Wireless service is available via classrooms, computer centers, computer labs, learning centers, libraries, student centers.

Student Life *Housing:* on-campus residence required through sophomore year. *Options:* coed, women-only, cooperative, disabled students. Campus housing is university owned. Freshman campus housing is guaranteed. *Activities and organizations:* drama/theater group, student-run newspaper, radio and television station, choral group, marching band, Leonard Carmichael Society (community service), Tufts Mountain Club, intramural sports, Tufts Daily (newspaper), Pen, Paint, and Pretzels (student directed theater umbrella organization), national fraternities, national sororities. *Campus security:* 24-hour emergency response devices and patrols, late-night transport/escort service, controlled dormitory access, security lighting, call boxes to campus police. *Student services:* health clinic, personal/psychological counseling, women's center, legal services.

Athletics Member NCAA. All Division III. *Intercollegiate sports:* baseball M, basketball M/W, crew M/W, cross-country running M/W, equestrian sports M(c)/W(c), fencing W, field hockey W, football M, golf M, ice hockey M, lacrosse M/W, rugby M(c)/W(c), sailing M/W, soccer M/W, softball W, squash M/W, swimming and diving M/W, tennis M/W, track and field M/W, ultimate Frisbee M(c)/W(c), volleyball M(c)/W, water polo M(c)/W(c). *Intramural sports:* badminton M/W, baseball M(c), basketball M/W, cheerleading W, fencing M(c), field hockey W(c), football M(c)/W(c), ice hockey M(c), lacrosse M(c)/W(c), racquetball M/W, skiing (downhill) M/W, soccer M/W, softball M/W(c), table tennis M(c)/W(c), tennis M/W, volleyball M/W.

Standardized Tests *Required:* SAT and SAT Subject Tests or ACT (for admission).

Costs (2013–14) *Comprehensive fee:* $58,780 includes full-time tuition ($45,590), mandatory fees ($1008), and room and board ($12,182). *College room only:* $6630. Room and board charges vary according to board plan. *Payment plans:* tuition prepayment, installment. *Waivers:* employees or children of employees.

Financial Aid Of all full-time matriculated undergraduates who enrolled in 2012, 2,396 applied for aid, 2,077 were judged to have need, 2,049 had their need fully met. 1,605 Federal Work-Study jobs (averaging $1803). 93 state and other part-time jobs (averaging $1891). In 2012, 89 non-need-based awards were made. *Average percent of need met:* 100%. *Average financial aid package:* $34,802. *Average need-based loan:* $4016. *Average need-based gift aid:* $31,716. *Average non-need-based aid:* $500. *Average indebtedness upon graduation:* $23,068. *Financial aid deadline:* 2/15.

Applying *Options:* electronic application, early decision, deferred entrance. *Application fee:* $70. *Required:* essay or personal statement, high school transcript, 2 letters of recommendation, Common Application, the Tufts Supplement, and standardized testing. *Recommended:* interview. *Application deadlines:* 1/1 (freshmen), 3/15 (transfers). *Early decision deadline:* 11/1 (for plan 1), 1/1 (for plan 2). *Notification:* 4/1 (freshmen), 5/15 (transfers), 12/15 (early decision plan 1), 2/1 (early decision plan 2).

Freshman Application Contact Mr. Lee Coffin, Office of Undergraduate Admissions, Tufts University, Bendetson Hall, Medford, MA 02155. *Phone:* 617-627-3170. *Fax:* 617-627-3860. *E-mail:* admissions.inquiry@ase.tufts.edu. *Website:* http://www.tufts.edu/.

University of Massachusetts Amherst
Amherst, Massachusetts

- **State-supported** university, founded 1863, part of University of Massachusetts
- **Small-town** 1463-acre campus with easy access to Hartford
- **Endowment** $230.6 million
- **Coed** 21,928 undergraduate students, 93% full-time, 49% women, 51% men
- **Moderately difficult** entrance level, 63% of applicants were admitted

Undergraduates 20,306 full-time, 1,622 part-time. Students come from 51 states and territories; 69 other countries; 21% are from out of state; 4% Black or African American, non-Hispanic/Latino; 5% Hispanic/Latino; 7% Asian, non-Hispanic/Latino; 0.1% Native Hawaiian or other Pacific Islander, non-Hispanic/Latino; 0.1% American Indian or Alaska Native, non-Hispanic/Latino; 2% Two or more races, non-Hispanic/Latino; 12% Race/ethnicity unknown; 2% international; 5% transferred in; 61% live on campus. *Retention:* 88% of full-time freshmen returned.

Freshmen *Admission:* 34,326 applied, 21,470 admitted, 4,679 enrolled. *Average high school GPA:* 3.66. *Test scores:* SAT critical reading scores over 500: 90%; SAT math scores over 500: 96%; ACT scores over 18: 99%; SAT critical reading scores over 600: 43%; SAT math scores over 600: 60%; ACT scores over 24: 80%; SAT critical reading scores over 700: 8%; SAT math scores over 700: 13%; ACT scores over 30: 16%.

Faculty *Total:* 1,361, 89% full-time, 90% with terminal degrees. *Student/faculty ratio:* 18:1.

Academics *Calendar:* semesters. *Degrees:* certificates, associate, bachelor's, master's, doctoral, post-master's, and postbachelor's certificates. *Special study options:* academic remediation for entering students, accelerated degree program, adult/continuing education programs, advanced placement credit, cooperative education, distance learning, double majors, English as a second language, freshman honors college, honors programs, independent study, internships, off-campus study, part-time degree program, services for LD students, student-designed majors, study abroad, summer session for credit. *ROTC:* Army (b), Air Force (b).

Computers on Campus 419 computers/terminals are available on campus for general student use. Students can access the following: computer help desk, free student e-mail accounts, online (class) grades, online (class) registration, online (class) schedules, online housing assignments, bill payment, Learning Management System, file storage, web hosting, blogs. Campuswide network is available. 100% of college-owned or -operated housing units are wired for high-speed Internet access. Wireless service is available via classrooms, computer centers, computer labs, dorm rooms, learning centers, libraries, student centers. **Student Life** *Housing:* on-campus residence required for freshman year. *Options:* coed, men-only, women-only, disabled students. Campus housing is university owned. Freshman campus housing is guaranteed. *Activities and organizations:* drama/theater group, student-run newspaper, radio and television station, choral group, marching band, Minutemen Marching Band, Theater Guild, Ski Club, Outing Club, student newspaper, national fraternities, national sororities. *Campus security:* 24-hour emergency response devices and patrols, student patrols, late-night transport/escort service, controlled dormitory access. *Student services:* health clinic, personal/psychological counseling, women's center, legal services.

Athletics Member NCAA. All Division I except football (Division I-A). *Intercollegiate sports:* baseball M(s), basketball M(s)/W(s), crew W(s), cross-country running M(s)/W(s), field hockey W(s), ice hockey M(s), lacrosse M(s)/W(s), soccer M(s)/W(s), softball W(s), swimming and diving M(s)/W(s), tennis W(s), track and field M(s)/W(s). *Intramural sports:* archery M(c)/W(c), badminton M/W, baseball M(c), basketball M/W, cheerleading M/W, equestrian sports M(c)/W(c), fencing M(c)/W(c), field hockey W, football M/W, ice hockey M(c)/W(c), lacrosse M(c)/W(c), racquetball M/W, rugby M(c)/W(c), sailing M(c)/W(c), skiing (downhill) M(c)/W(c), soccer M/W, softball M/W, swimming and diving M(c)/W(c), table tennis M/W, tennis M/W, ultimate Frisbee M(c)/W(c), volleyball M/W, water polo M(c), wrestling M(c)/W(c).

Standardized Tests *Required:* SAT or ACT (for admission).

Costs (2012–13) *One-time required fee:* $185. *Tuition:* state resident $1714 full-time, $72 per credit part-time; nonresident $9937 full-time, $414 per credit part-time. Full-time tuition and fees vary according to class time, course load, location, program, reciprocity agreements, and student level. Part-time tuition and fees vary according to class time, course load, location, program, reciprocity agreements, and student level. *Required fees:* $11,701 full-time, $672 per credit part-time. *Room and board:* $10,767; room only: $5563. Room and board charges vary according to board plan and housing facility. *Payment plan:* installment. *Waivers:* senior citizens and employees or children of employees.

Financial Aid Of all full-time matriculated undergraduates who enrolled in 2011, 16,780 applied for aid, 12,475 were judged to have need, 2,049 had their need fully met. 3,517 Federal Work-Study jobs (averaging $1733). In 2011, 1391 non-need-based awards were made. *Average percent of need met:* 85%. *Average financial aid package:* $15,039. *Average need-based loan:* $4636.

Average need-based gift aid: $9408. *Average non-need-based aid:* $3531. *Average indebtedness upon graduation:* $27,945.

Applying *Options:* electronic application, early action, deferred entrance. *Application fee:* $75. *Required:* essay or personal statement, high school transcript, SAT or ACT. *Recommended:* minimum 3.0 GPA. *Application deadlines:* 1/15 (freshmen), 1/15 (out-of-state freshmen), 4/15 (transfers), 11/1 (early action). *Notification:* continuous (freshmen), continuous (out-of-state freshmen), continuous (transfers), 12/15 (early action).

Freshman Application Contact Mr. Kevin Kelly, Director, Undergraduate Admissions, University of Massachusetts Amherst, 37 Mather Drive, Amherst, MA 01003. *Phone:* 413-545-0222. *Fax:* 413-545-4312. *E-mail:* mail@admissions.umass.edu.

Website: http://www.umass.edu/.

University of Massachusetts Boston

Boston, Massachusetts

- **State-supported** university, founded 1964, part of University of Massachusetts
- **Urban** 187-acre campus
- **Endowment** $51.9 million
- **Coed** 12,124 undergraduate students, 69% full-time, 56% women, 44% men
- **Moderately difficult** entrance level, 61% of applicants were admitted

Undergraduates 8,426 full-time, 3,698 part-time. Students come from 39 states and territories; 143 other countries; 5% are from out of state; 15% Black or African American, non-Hispanic/Latino; 11% Hispanic/Latino; 11% Asian, non-Hispanic/Latino; 0.0% Native Hawaiian or other Pacific Islander, non-Hispanic/Latino; 0.2% American Indian or Alaska Native, non-Hispanic/Latino; 2% Two or more races, non-Hispanic/Latino; 8% Race/ethnicity unknown; 8% international; 15% transferred in. *Retention:* 79% of full-time freshmen returned.

Freshmen *Admission:* 7,876 applied, 4,835 admitted, 1,267 enrolled. *Average high school GPA:* 3.18. *Test scores:* SAT critical reading scores over 500: 64%; SAT math scores over 500: 74%; SAT critical reading scores over 600: 19%;

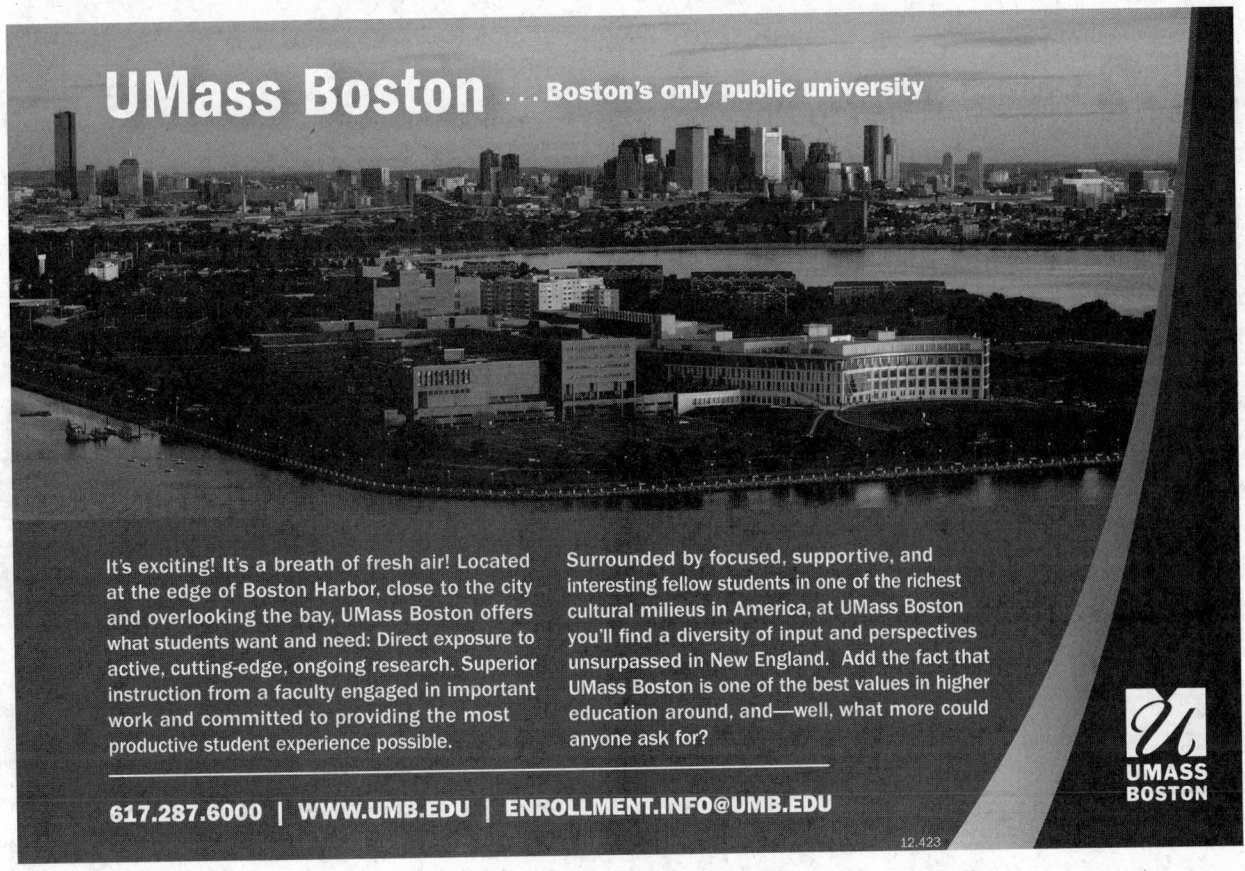

SAT math scores over 600: 27%; SAT critical reading scores over 700: 3%; SAT math scores over 700: 4%.

Faculty *Total:* 1,193, 49% full-time, 65% with terminal degrees. *Student/faculty ratio:* 15:1.

Academics *Calendar:* semesters. *Degrees:* certificates, bachelor's, master's, doctoral, post-master's, and postbachelor's certificates. *Special study options:* academic remediation for entering students, accelerated degree program, adult/continuing education programs, advanced placement credit, cooperative education, distance learning, double majors, English as a second language, freshman honors college, honors programs, independent study, internships, off-campus study, part-time degree program, services for LD students, student-designed majors, study abroad, summer session for credit. *ROTC:* Army (c), Navy (c), Air Force (c).

Computers on Campus 350 computers/terminals are available on campus for general student use. Students can access the following: computer help desk, free student e-mail accounts, online (class) grades, online (class) registration, online (class) schedules. Campuswide network is available. Wireless service is available via entire campus.

Student Life *Housing:* college housing not available. *Activities and organizations:* drama/theater group, student-run newspaper, radio station, choral group, Student Arts & Events Council, Haitian Student Association, Golden Key Honor Society, Campus Kitchens, Mass Media. *Campus security:* 24-hour emergency response devices and patrols, late-night transport/escort service, crime prevention program, bicycle patrols. *Student services:* health clinic, personal/psychological counseling, women's center, legal services.

Athletics Member NCAA. All Division III. *Intercollegiate sports:* baseball M, basketball M/W, cross-country running M/W, ice hockey M, lacrosse M, soccer M/W, softball W, tennis M/W, track and field M/W, volleyball W. *Intramural sports:* badminton M/W, basketball M/W, racquetball M/W, sailing M/W, soccer M/W, softball M/W, squash M/W, volleyball M/W.

Standardized Tests *Required:* SAT (for admission), ACT (for admission), SAT or ACT (for admission). *Recommended:* SAT and SAT Subject Tests or ACT (for admission), SAT Subject Tests (for admission).

Costs (2012–13) *Tuition:* state resident $11,320 full-time; nonresident $25,504 full-time. Full-time tuition and fees vary according to program. Part-time tuition and fees vary according to program. *Required fees:* $646 full-time.

Financial Aid Of all full-time matriculated undergraduates who enrolled in 2011, 6,227 applied for aid, 5,491 were judged to have need, 2,735 had their need fully met. 547 Federal Work-Study jobs (averaging $3701). In 2011, 208 non-need-based awards were made. *Average percent of need met:* 91%. *Average financial aid package:* $14,889. *Average need-based loan:* $6988. *Average*

need-based gift aid: $8882. *Average non-need-based aid:* $4501. *Average indebtedness upon graduation:* $25,499.

Applying *Options:* electronic application, deferred entrance. *Application fee:* $40. *Required:* high school transcript, minimum 2.5 GPA. *Required for some:* essay or personal statement, minimum 2.8 GPA, interview. *Recommended:* essay or personal statement. *Application deadlines:* 4/1 (freshmen), 6/15 (transfers). *Notification:* continuous (freshmen), continuous (transfers).

Freshman Application Contact Mr. John Drew, Director of Undergraduate Admissions, University of Massachusetts Boston, 100 Morrissey Boulevard, Boston, MA 02125-3393. *Phone:* 617-287-6000. *Fax:* 617-287-5999. *E-mail:* enrollment.info@umb.edu.

Website: http://www.umb.edu/.

See previous page for display ad and page 1574 for the College Close-Up.

University of Massachusetts Dartmouth

North Dartmouth, Massachusetts

- **State-supported** university, founded 1895, part of University of Massachusetts
- **Suburban** 710-acre campus with easy access to Boston, Providence
- **Endowment** $39.0 million
- **Coed** 7,562 undergraduate students, 87% full-time, 48% women, 52% men
- **Moderately difficult** entrance level, 72% of applicants were admitted

Undergraduates 6,580 full-time, 982 part-time. Students come from 32 states and territories; 38 other countries; 4% are from out of state; 11% Black or African American, non-Hispanic/Latino; 6% Hispanic/Latino; 3% Asian, non-Hispanic/Latino; 0.2% American Indian or Alaska Native, non-Hispanic/Latino; 3% Two or more races, non-Hispanic/Latino; 6% Race/ethnicity unknown; 2% international; 6% transferred in; 55% live on campus. *Retention:* 74% of full-time freshmen returned.

Freshmen *Admission:* 8,063 applied, 5,816 admitted, 1,577 enrolled. *Average high school GPA:* 3.2. *Test scores:* SAT critical reading scores over 500: 41%; SAT math scores over 500: 74%; SAT writing scores over 500: 56%; ACT scores over 18: 96%; SAT critical reading scores over 600: 6%; SAT math scores over 600: 24%; SAT writing scores over 600: 14%; ACT scores over 24:

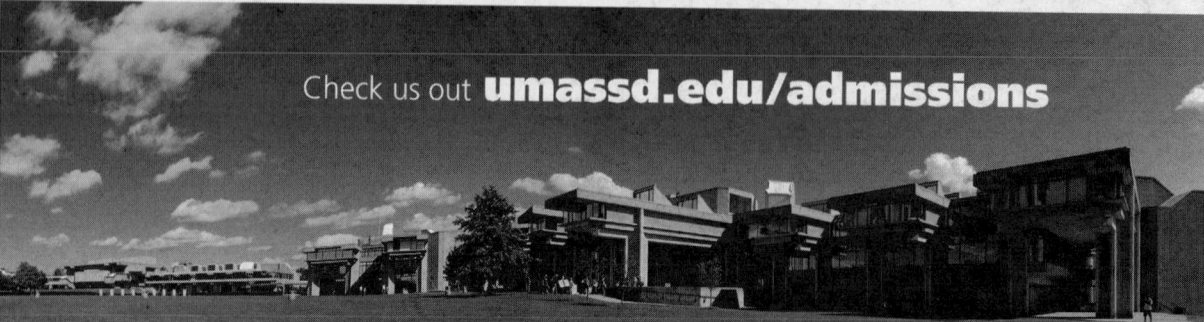

43%; SAT critical reading scores over 700: 1%; SAT math scores over 700: 2%; SAT writing scores over 700: 2%; ACT scores over 30: 6%.

Faculty *Total:* 660, 57% full-time, 58% with terminal degrees. *Student/faculty ratio:* 18:1.

Academics *Calendar:* semesters. *Degrees:* certificates, bachelor's, master's, doctoral, post-master's, and postbachelor's certificates. *Special study options:* academic remediation for entering students, advanced placement credit, cooperative education, distance learning, double majors, honors programs, independent study, internships, off-campus study, part-time degree program, services for LD students, student-designed majors, study abroad, summer session for credit. *ROTC:* Army (c).

Computers on Campus 368 computers/terminals are available on campus for general student use. Students can access the following: campus intranet, computer help desk, free student e-mail accounts, online (class) grades, online (class) registration, online (class) schedules. Campuswide network is available. 100% of college-owned or -operated housing units are wired for high-speed Internet access. Wireless service is available via entire campus.

Student Life *Housing options:* coed, disabled students. Campus housing is university owned. *Activities and organizations:* drama/theater group, student-run newspaper, radio station, choral group, Student Activities Board, Ski & Snowboard Club, Phi Sigma Sigma, American Red Cross Club, Pride Alliance, national fraternities, national sororities. *Campus security:* 24-hour emergency response devices and patrols, student patrols, late-night transport/escort service, controlled dormitory access. *Student services:* health clinic, personal/psychological counseling, women's center, legal services.

Athletics Member NCAA. All Division III. *Intercollegiate sports:* baseball M, basketball M/W, cheerleading W, cross-country running M/W, equestrian sports W(c), field hockey W, football M, golf M, ice hockey M, lacrosse M/W, soccer M/W, softball W, swimming and diving M/W, tennis M/W, track and field M/W, volleyball W. *Intramural sports:* badminton M/W, basketball M/W, rugby M(c)/W(c), sailing W, skiing (downhill) M(c)/W(c), soccer M/W, softball M/W, table tennis M/W, tennis M/W, ultimate Frisbee M/W, volleyball M/W.

Standardized Tests *Required:* SAT or ACT (for admission).

Costs (2012–13) *Tuition:* state resident $1417 full-time; nonresident $8099 full-time. Full-time tuition and fees vary according to class time, program, and reciprocity agreements. Part-time tuition and fees vary according to class time, course load, program, and reciprocity agreements. *Required fees:* $10,264 full-time. *Room and board:* Room and board charges vary according to board plan and housing facility. *Payment plan:* installment. *Waivers:* senior citizens and employees or children of employees.

Financial Aid Of all full-time matriculated undergraduates who enrolled in 2012, 5,458 applied for aid, 4,650 were judged to have need, 1,874 had their need fully met. In 2012, 337 non-need-based awards were made. *Average percent of need met:* 86%. *Average financial aid package:* $15,281. *Average need-based loan:* $7872. *Average need-based gift aid:* $8637. *Average non-need-based aid:* $4377. *Average indebtedness upon graduation:* $32,349.

Applying *Options:* electronic application, early admission, early action, deferred entrance. *Application fee:* $40. *Required:* essay or personal statement, high school transcript, minimum 3.0 GPA. *Recommended:* essay or personal statement, 1 letter of recommendation. *Application deadlines:* rolling (freshmen), rolling (transfers), 11/15 (early action). *Notification:* continuous (freshmen), continuous (transfers), 12/15 (early action).

Freshman Application Contact University of Massachusetts Dartmouth, 285 Old Westport Road, North Dartmouth, MA 02747-2300. *Phone:* 508-999-8605. *Fax:* 508-999-8755. *E-mail:* admissions@umassd.edu. *Website:* http://www.umassd.edu/.

See previous page for display ad and page 1576 for the College Close-Up.

University of Massachusetts Lowell

Lowell, Massachusetts

- **State-supported** university, founded 1894, part of University of Massachusetts
- **Urban** 100-acre campus with easy access to Boston
- **Endowment** $49.5 million
- **Coed**
- **Moderately difficult** entrance level

Faculty *Student/faculty ratio:* 14:1.

Academics *Calendar:* semesters. *Degrees:* associate, bachelor's, master's, doctoral, post-master's, and postbachelor's certificates.

Student Life *Campus security:* 24-hour emergency response devices and patrols, late-night transport/escort service, controlled dormitory access.

Athletics Member NCAA. All Division II except ice hockey (Division I).

Standardized Tests *Required:* SAT or ACT (for admission).

Costs (2012–13) *One-time required fee:* $200. *Tuition:* state resident $1454 full-time, $61 per credit part-time; nonresident $8567 full-time, $357 per credit part-time. Part-time tuition and fees vary according to course load. *Required fees:* $10,398 full-time, $433 per credit part-time. *Room and board:* $10,282; room only: $6854. Room and board charges vary according to board plan and housing facility.

Financial Aid *Of all full-time matriculated undergraduates who enrolled in 2011,* 6,703 applied for aid, 5,327 were judged to have need, 2,999 had their need fully met. 175 Federal Work-Study jobs (averaging $2450). 663 state and other part-time jobs (averaging $3026). *In 2011,* 568 non-need-based awards were made. *Average percent of need met:* 92. *Average financial aid package:* $13,549. *Average need-based loan:* $7028. *Average need-based gift aid:* $7398. *Average non-need-based aid:* $3830. *Average indebtedness upon graduation:* $29,212.

Applying *Options:* electronic application, early action, deferred entrance. *Application fee:* $60. *Required:* essay or personal statement, high school transcript, minimum 3.0 GPA, 1 letter of recommendation, Audition for music students.

Freshman Application Contact Admissions Office, University of Massachusetts Lowell, 883 Broadway Street, Room 110, Lowell, MA 01854-5104. *Phone:* 978-934-3931. *Fax:* 978-934-3086. *E-mail:* admissions@umi.edu.

Website: http://www.uml.edu/.

See previous page for display ad and page 1578 for the College Close-Up.

University of Phoenix–Boston Campus

Braintree, Massachusetts

Freshman Application Contact Marc Booker, Sr. Director, Office of Admissions and Evaluation, University of Phoenix–Boston Campus, 4035 South Riverpoint Parkway, Mail Stop CF-L101, Phoenix, AZ 85040. *Phone:* 602-557-4609. *Toll-free phone:* 866-766-0766. *Fax:* 480-643-1156.
Website: http://www.phoenix.edu/.

University of Phoenix–Central Massachusetts Campus

Westborough, Massachusetts

Freshman Application Contact Marc Booker, Sr. Director, Office of Admissions and Evaluation, University of Phoenix–Central Massachusetts Campus, 4035 South Riverpoint Parkway, Mail Stop CF-L101, Phoenix, AZ 85040. *Phone:* 602-557-4609. *Toll-free phone:* 866-766-0766. *Fax:* 480-643-1156.
Website: http://www.phoenix.edu/.

Wellesley College

Wellesley, Massachusetts

- **Independent** 4-year, founded 1870
- **Suburban** 500-acre campus with easy access to Boston
- **Endowment** $1.5 billion
- **Women only** 2,483 undergraduate students, 95% full-time
- **Most difficult** entrance level, 30% of applicants were admitted

Undergraduates 2,366 full-time, 117 part-time. Students come from 49 states and territories; 80 other countries; 84% are from out of state; 6% Black or African American, non-Hispanic/Latino; 10% Hispanic/Latino; 21% Asian, non-Hispanic/Latino; 5% Two or more races, non-Hispanic/Latino; 3% Race/ethnicity unknown; 12% international; 0.6% transferred in; 93% live on campus. *Retention:* 97% of full-time freshmen returned.

Freshmen *Admission:* 4,478 applied, 1,349 admitted, 585 enrolled. *Test scores:* SAT critical reading scores over 500: 100%; SAT math scores over 500: 100%; SAT writing scores over 500: 100%; ACT scores over 18: 100%; SAT critical reading scores over 600: 90%; SAT math scores over 600: 87%; SAT writing scores over 600: 92%; ACT scores over 24: 97%; SAT critical reading scores over 700: 53%; SAT math scores over 700: 48%; SAT writing scores over 700: 56%; ACT scores over 30: 64%.

Faculty *Total:* 346, 83% full-time, 94% with terminal degrees. *Student/faculty ratio:* 7:1.

Academics *Calendar:* semesters. *Degrees:* bachelor's (double bachelor's degree with Massachusetts Institute of Technology). *Special study options:* adult/continuing education programs, advanced placement credit, double majors, honors programs, independent study, internships, off-campus study, part-time degree program, services for LD students, student-designed majors, study abroad, summer session for credit. *ROTC:* Army (c), Air Force (c).

Unusual degree programs: 3-2 engineering with Massachusetts Institute of Technology, Dartmouth College, Columbia University; architecture; aeronautics and astronautics; urban studies and planning with Massachusetts Institute of Technology; international economics and finance with Brandeis University.

Computers on Campus 200 computers/terminals and 200 ports are available on campus for general student use. Students can access the following: campus intranet, computer help desk, free student e-mail accounts, online (class) grades, online (class) registration, online (class) schedules. Campuswide network is available. 100% of college-owned or -operated housing units are wired for high-speed Internet access. Wireless service is available via entire campus.

Student Life *Housing options:* women-only, cooperative. Campus housing is university owned. Freshman campus housing is guaranteed. *Activities and organizations:* drama/theater group, student-run newspaper, radio and television station, choral group, student government, radio station, cultural clubs, rugby club, theater groups. *Campus security:* 24-hour emergency response devices and patrols, late-night transport/escort service, controlled dormitory access. *Student services:* health clinic, personal/psychological counseling, women's center.

Athletics Member NCAA. All Division III. *Intercollegiate sports:* basketball W, crew W, cross-country running W, fencing W, field hockey W, golf W, lacrosse W, rugby W(c), sailing W(c), skiing (downhill) W(c), soccer W, softball W, squash W, swimming and diving W, tennis W, track and field W, ultimate Frisbee W(c), volleyball W. *Intramural sports:* archery W, badminton W(c), basketball W, cheerleading W(c), crew W, equestrian sports W(c), ice hockey W(c), racquetball W(c), sailing W(c), skiing (cross-country) W, skiing (downhill) W, soccer W, softball W, squash W(c), swimming and diving W, table tennis W(c), tennis W, volleyball W, water polo W, weight lifting W.

Standardized Tests *Required:* SAT and SAT Subject Tests or ACT (for admission).

Costs (2013–14) *Comprehensive fee:* $57,042 includes full-time tuition ($43,288), mandatory fees ($266), and room and board ($13,488). Part-time tuition: $1352 per credit hour. Part-time tuition and fees vary according to course load. *College room only:* $6846. *Payment plans:* tuition prepayment, installment. *Waivers:* employees or children of employees.

Financial Aid Of all full-time matriculated undergraduates who enrolled in 2011, 1,596 applied for aid, 1,395 were judged to have need, 1,395 had their need fully met. *Average percent of need met:* 100%. *Average financial aid package:* $38,903. *Average need-based loan:* $3145. *Average need-based gift aid:* $36,971. *Average indebtedness upon graduation:* $13,579.

Applying *Options:* electronic application, early admission, early decision, deferred entrance. *Application fee:* $50. *Required:* essay or personal statement, high school transcript, 3 letters of recommendation, first senior marking period grades and mid-year report. *Required for some:* interview. *Recommended:* interview. *Application deadlines:* 1/15 (freshmen), 1/15 (out-of-state freshmen), 3/1 (transfers). *Early decision deadline:* 11/1. *Notification:* 4/1 (freshmen), 4/1 (out-of-state freshmen), 5/15 (transfers), 12/15 (early decision).

Freshman Application Contact Director of Admission, Wellesley College, 106 Central Street, Wellesley, MA 02481. *Phone:* 781-283-2270. *Fax:* 781-283-3678. *E-mail:* admission@wellesley.edu.
Website: http://www.wellesley.edu/.

Wentworth Institute of Technology

Boston, Massachusetts

- **Independent** comprehensive, founded 1904
- **Urban** 31-acre campus
- **Endowment** $74.4 million
- **Coed** 4,003 undergraduate students, 90% full-time, 18% women, 82% men
- **Moderately difficult** entrance level, 61% of applicants were admitted

Undergraduates 3,592 full-time, 411 part-time. Students come from 36 states and territories; 49 other countries; 36% are from out of state; 5% Black or African American, non-Hispanic/Latino; 4% Hispanic/Latino; 6% Asian, non-Hispanic/Latino; 0.2% American Indian or Alaska Native, non-Hispanic/Latino; 3% Two or more races, non-Hispanic/Latino; 18% Race/ethnicity unknown; 4% international; 3% transferred in; 49% live on campus. *Retention:* 82% of full-time freshmen returned.

Freshmen *Admission:* 5,650 applied, 3,442 admitted, 1,068 enrolled. *Average high school GPA:* 2.99. *Test scores:* SAT critical reading scores over 500: 60%; SAT writing scores over 500: 55%; SAT critical reading scores over 600: 14%;

SAT writing scores over 600: 12%; SAT critical reading scores over 700: 1%; SAT writing scores over 700: 1%.

Faculty *Total:* 310, 47% full-time, 32% with terminal degrees. *Student/faculty ratio:* 16:1.

Academics *Calendar:* semesters for freshmen and sophomores, trimesters for juniors and seniors. *Degrees:* associate, bachelor's, and master's. *Special study options:* academic remediation for entering students, advanced placement credit, cooperative education, internships, off-campus study, part-time degree program, services for LD students, study abroad, summer session for credit. *ROTC:* Army (c), Air Force (c).

Computers on Campus 320 computers/terminals and 200 ports are available on campus for general student use. Students can access the following: campus intranet, computer help desk, free student e-mail accounts, online (class) grades, online (class) registration, online (class) schedules. Campuswide network is available. 100% of college-owned or -operated housing units are wired for high-speed Internet access. Wireless service is available via entire campus.

Student Life *Housing:* on-campus residence required through sophomore year. *Options:* coed. Campus housing is university owned. Freshman campus housing is guaranteed. *Activities and organizations:* student-run radio station, Intramural Sports, Wentworth Events Board, Multicultural Student Association, Phi Sigma Pi, Major Particular Professional Student Associations. *Campus security:* 24-hour emergency response devices and patrols, student patrols, late-night transport/escort service, controlled dormitory access. *Student services:* health clinic, personal/psychological counseling, women's center.

Athletics Member NCAA. All Division III. *Intercollegiate sports:* baseball M, basketball M/W, crew M(c)/W(c), golf M, ice hockey M, lacrosse M/W(c), riflery M/W, rugby M(c)/W(c), soccer M/W, softball W, tennis M/W, ultimate Frisbee M(c)/W(c), volleyball M/W.

Standardized Tests *Required:* SAT or ACT (for admission).

Costs (2013–14) *Comprehensive fee:* $40,476 includes full-time tuition ($27,950) and room and board ($12,526). Part-time tuition: $875 per credit hour. Part-time tuition and fees vary according to course load and degree level. *Required fees:* $440 per credit hour part-time. *College room only:* $11,384. Room and board charges vary according to board plan and housing facility. *Payment plan:* installment. *Waivers:* employees or children of employees.

Financial Aid Of all full-time matriculated undergraduates who enrolled in 2011, 2,253 applied for aid, 2,129 were judged to have need, 420 had their need fully met. 571 Federal Work-Study jobs (averaging $1300). In 2011, 120 non-need-based awards were made. *Average financial aid package:* $14,957. *Average need-based loan:* $4342. *Average need-based gift aid:* $6277. *Aver-*

age non-need-based aid: $6079. *Average indebtedness upon graduation:* $20,371.

Applying *Options:* electronic application, deferred entrance. *Application fee:* $50. *Required:* essay or personal statement, high school transcript, 1 letter of recommendation. *Recommended:* minimum 2.0 GPA, interview. *Application deadlines:* 5/1 (freshmen), 5/1 (out-of-state freshmen), 5/1 (transfers). *Notification:* continuous (freshmen), continuous (transfers).

Freshman Application Contact Ms. Amy Dufour, Associate Director of Admissions, Wentworth Institute of Technology, 550 Huntington Avenue, Boston, MA 02115. *Phone:* 617-989-4116. *Toll-free phone:* 800-556-0610. *Fax:* 617-989-4010. *E-mail:* dufoura@wit.edu. *Website:* http://www.wit.edu/.

See below for display ad and page 1636 for the College Close-Up.

Western New England University

Springfield, Massachusetts

- **Independent** comprehensive, founded 1919
- **Suburban** 215-acre campus
- **Endowment** $34.1 million
- **Coed**
- **Moderately difficult** entrance level

Faculty *Student/faculty ratio:* 14:1.

Academics *Calendar:* semesters. *Degrees:* associate, bachelor's, master's, and doctoral.

Student Life *Campus security:* 24-hour emergency response devices and patrols, student patrols, late-night transport/escort service, controlled dormitory access, security cameras.

Athletics Member NCAA. All Division III.

Standardized Tests *Required:* SAT or ACT (for admission).

Costs (2012–13) *Comprehensive fee:* $44,056 includes full-time tuition ($29,738), mandatory fees ($2174), and room and board ($12,144). Full-time tuition and fees vary according to program. Part-time tuition: $560 per credit hour. Part-time tuition and fees vary according to location and program. *Room and board:* Room and board charges vary according to board plan and housing facility. *Payment plans:* tuition prepayment, installment.

Financial Aid Of all full-time matriculated undergraduates who enrolled in 2012, 2,256 applied for aid, 1,991 were judged to have need, 218 had their

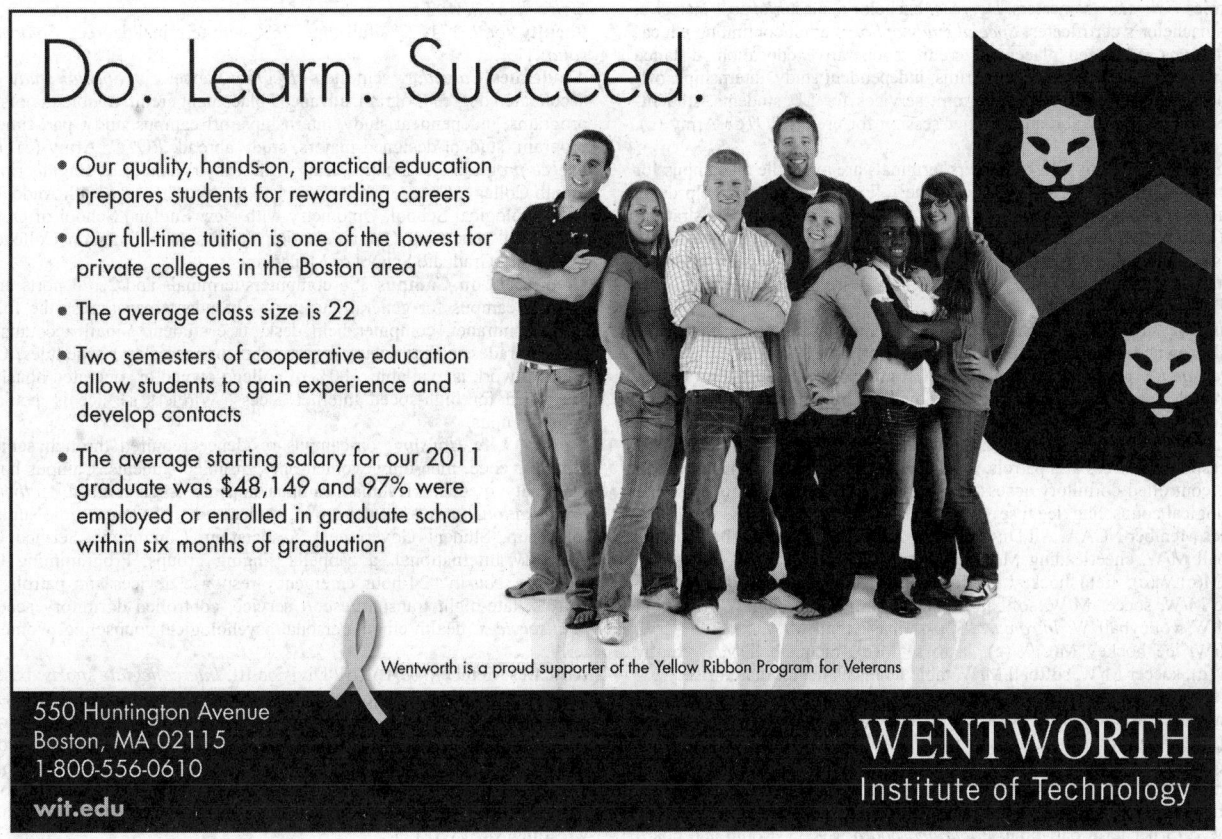

need fully met. *In 2012,* 371 non-need-based awards were made. *Average percent of need met:* 69. *Average financial aid package:* $21,920. *Average need-based loan:* $4159. *Average need-based gift aid:* $16,656. *Average non-need-based aid:* $11,226. *Financial aid deadline:* 4/15.

Applying *Options:* electronic application. *Application fee:* $40. *Required:* high school transcript, 1 letter of recommendation. *Recommended:* essay or personal statement, interview.

Freshman Application Contact Dr. Charles R. Pollock, Vice President of Enrollment Management, Western New England University, Springfield, MA 01119. *Phone:* 413-782-1321. *Toll-free phone:* 800-325-1122 Ext. 1321. *Fax:* 413-782-1777. *E-mail:* learn@wne.edu.
Website: http://www.wne.edu/.

Westfield State University

Westfield, Massachusetts

- **State-supported** comprehensive, founded 1838, part of Massachusetts Public Higher Education System
- **Suburban** 256-acre campus
- **Coed** 5,368 undergraduate students, 88% full-time, 53% women, 47% men
- **Moderately difficult** entrance level, 64% of applicants were admitted

Undergraduates 4,712 full-time, 656 part-time. Students come from 17 states and territories; 14 other countries; 7% are from out of state; 4% Black or African American, non-Hispanic/Latino; 6% Hispanic/Latino; 0.8% Asian, non-Hispanic/Latino; 0.1% Native Hawaiian or other Pacific Islander, non-Hispanic/Latino; 0.2% American Indian or Alaska Native, non-Hispanic/Latino; 3% Two or more races, non-Hispanic/Latino; 4% Race/ethnicity unknown; 0.6% international; 7% transferred in; 54% live on campus. *Retention:* 81% of full-time freshmen returned.

Freshmen *Admission:* 4,941 applied, 3,174 admitted, 997 enrolled. *Average high school GPA:* 3.08. *Test scores:* SAT critical reading scores over 500: 53%; SAT math scores over 500: 62%; SAT writing scores over 500: 50%; ACT scores over 18: 87%; SAT critical reading scores over 600: 9%; SAT math scores over 600: 13%; SAT writing scores over 600: 8%; ACT scores over 24: 30%; SAT critical reading scores over 700: 1%; SAT math scores over 700: 1%.

Faculty *Total:* 469, 48% full-time, 56% with terminal degrees. *Student/faculty ratio:* 17:1.

Academics *Calendar:* semesters. *Degrees:* bachelor's, master's, post-master's, and postbachelor's certificates. *Special study options:* adult/continuing education programs, advanced placement credit, cooperative education, distance learning, double majors, honors programs, independent study, internships, off-campus study, part-time degree program, services for LD students, student-designed majors, study abroad, summer session for credit. *ROTC:* Army (c), Air Force (c).

Computers on Campus 640 computers/terminals are available on campus for general student use. Students can access the following: computer help desk, free student e-mail accounts, online (class) grades, online (class) registration, online (class) schedules, online transcripts and billing information, web portal. Campuswide network is available. 100% of college-owned or -operated housing units are wired for high-speed Internet access. Wireless service is available via entire campus.

Student Life *Housing options:* coed, disabled students. Campus housing is university owned. Freshman applicants given priority for college housing. *Activities and organizations:* drama/theater group, student-run newspaper, radio and television station, choral group, Student National Education Association, Student Government Association, Campus Activities Board, The Dance Company, Multicultural Student Association. *Campus security:* 24-hour emergency response devices and patrols, student patrols, late-night transport/escort service, controlled dormitory access. *Student services:* health clinic, personal/psychological counseling, legal services.

Athletics Member NCAA. All Division III. *Intercollegiate sports:* baseball M, basketball M/W, cheerleading M/W, cross-country running M/W, equestrian sports M(c)/W(c), field hockey W, football M, golf M/W, ice hockey M, lacrosse M/W, soccer M/W, softball W, swimming and diving W, track and field M/W, volleyball W. *Intramural sports:* basketball M/W, football M/W, golf M/W, ice hockey M(c)/W(c), lacrosse M(c), racquetball M/W, rugby M(c)/W(c), soccer M/W, softball M/W, table tennis M/W, ultimate Frisbee M/W, volleyball M/W, water polo M/W.

Standardized Tests *Required:* SAT or ACT (for admission).

Costs (2012–13) *Tuition:* state resident $970 full-time, $260 per credit hour part-time; nonresident $7050 full-time, $260 per credit hour part-time. Full-time tuition and fees vary according to program and reciprocity agreements. Part-time tuition and fees vary according to course load. *Required fees:* $7327 full-time, $75 per term part-time. *Room and board:* $9233. Room and board

charges vary according to board plan and housing facility. *Payment plan:* installment. *Waivers:* senior citizens and employees or children of employees.

Financial Aid Of all full-time matriculated undergraduates who enrolled in 2011, 4,144 applied for aid, 2,998 were judged to have need, 407 had their need fully met. 307 Federal Work-Study jobs (averaging $1558). In 2011, 53 non-need-based awards were made. *Average percent of need met:* 68%. *Average financial aid package:* $7666. *Average need-based loan:* $4062. *Average need-based gift aid:* $5279. *Average non-need-based aid:* $4289. *Average indebtedness upon graduation:* $24,825.

Applying *Options:* electronic application, deferred entrance. *Application fee:* $50. *Required:* high school transcript, minimum 3.0 GPA. *Required for some:* interview, audition for music major, portfolio for art major, also sliding scale minimum high school GPA using SAT/ACT scores for GPAs between 2.0 and 3.0. *Application deadlines:* 3/1 (freshmen), 3/1 (out-of-state freshmen), 3/1 (transfers). *Notification:* continuous until 3/15 (freshmen), continuous until 3/15 (out-of-state freshmen), continuous until 3/15 (transfers).

Freshman Application Contact Dr. Kelly Hart, Director of Admissions, Westfield State University, 333 Western Avenue, Westfield, MA 01002. *Phone:* 413-572-5218. *Fax:* 413-572-0520. *E-mail:* admission@westfield.ma.edu.
Website: http://www.wsc.ma.edu/.

Wheaton College

Norton, Massachusetts

- **Independent** 4-year, founded 1834
- **Suburban** 400-acre campus with easy access to Boston
- **Endowment** $159.5 million
- **Coed** 1,619 undergraduate students, 100% full-time, 64% women, 36% men
- **Very difficult** entrance level, 64% of applicants were admitted

Undergraduates 1,613 full-time, 6 part-time. Students come from 42 states and territories; 38 other countries; 64% are from out of state; 5% Black or African American, non-Hispanic/Latino; 7% Hispanic/Latino; 3% Asian, non-Hispanic/Latino; 0.1% American Indian or Alaska Native, non-Hispanic/Latino; 3% Two or more races, non-Hispanic/Latino; 1% Race/ethnicity unknown; 8% international; 0.7% transferred in; 95% live on campus. *Retention:* 86% of full-time freshmen returned.

Freshmen *Admission:* 4,046 applied, 2,603 admitted, 466 enrolled. *Average high school GPA:* 3.5.

Faculty *Total:* 171, 77% full-time, 76% with terminal degrees. *Student/faculty ratio:* 11:1.

Academics *Calendar:* semesters. *Degree:* bachelor's. *Special study options:* accelerated degree program, advanced placement credit, double majors, honors programs, independent study, internships, off-campus study, part-time degree program, student-designed majors, study abroad. *ROTC:* Army (c). *Unusual degree programs:* 3-2 engineering with Thayer School of Engineering, Dartmouth College; George Washington University; Theology with Andover Newton Theological School, Optometry with New England School of Optometry, Integrated Marketing Communication Studies with Emerson College, Clark University Graduate School of Management.

Computers on Campus 356 computers/terminals and 2,175 ports are available on campus for general student use. Students can access the following: campus intranet, computer help desk, free student e-mail accounts, online (class) grades, online (class) registration, online (class) schedules. Campuswide network is available. 100% of college-owned or -operated housing units are wired for high-speed Internet access. Wireless service is available via entire campus.

Student Life *Housing:* on-campus residence required through senior year. *Options:* coed, men-only, women-only, disabled students. Campus housing is university owned. Freshman campus housing is guaranteed. *Activities and organizations:* drama/theater group, student-run newspaper, radio station, choral group, Student Government Association, Community Service Council, Amnesty International, a cappella singing groups, Programming Council. *Campus security:* 24-hour emergency response devices and patrols, student patrols, late-night transport/escort service, controlled dormitory access. *Student services:* health clinic, personal/psychological counseling, women's center.

Athletics Member NCAA. All Division III. *Intercollegiate sports:* baseball M, basketball M/W, cross-country running M/W, field hockey W, lacrosse M/W, soccer M/W, softball W, swimming and diving M/W, tennis M/W, track and field M/W, volleyball W. *Intramural sports:* archery M(c)/W, badminton M/W, basketball M/W, equestrian sports M(c)/W(c), field hockey W(c), golf M(c)/W(c), ice hockey M(c)/W(c), rugby M(c)/W(c), sailing M(c)/W(c), soccer M/W, softball M/W, tennis M/W, ultimate Frisbee M(c)/W(c), volleyball M/W, wrestling M(c)/W(c).

Costs (2013–14) *One-time required fee:* $50. *Comprehensive fee:* $56,574 includes full-time tuition ($44,780), mandatory fees ($294), and room and board ($11,500). *College room only:* $6140. *Payment plans:* tuition prepayment, installment. *Waivers:* employees or children of employees.

Financial Aid Of all full-time matriculated undergraduates who enrolled in 2011, 1,132 applied for aid, 1,007 were judged to have need, 501 had their need fully met. 807 Federal Work-Study jobs (averaging $1672). 295 state and other part-time jobs (averaging $1590). In 2011, 231 non-need-based awards were made. *Average percent of need met:* 96%. *Average financial aid package:* $33,908. *Average need-based loan:* $4431. *Average need-based gift aid:* $27,876. *Average non-need-based aid:* $12,374. *Average indebtedness upon graduation:* $25,778. *Financial aid deadline:* 2/1.

Applying *Options:* electronic application, early admission, early decision, early action, deferred entrance. *Application fee:* $50. *Required:* essay or personal statement, high school transcript, 2 letters of recommendation. *Recommended:* interview. *Application deadlines:* 1/15 (freshmen), 3/1 (transfers), 11/15 (early action). *Early decision deadline:* 11/15. *Notification:* 4/1 (freshmen), continuous (transfers), 12/15 (early decision), 1/15 (early action).

Freshman Application Contact Gail Berson, Vice President for Enrollment and Dean of Admission and Student Aid, Wheaton College, 26 East Main Street, Norton, MA 02766. *Phone:* 508-286-8251. *Toll-free phone:* 800-394-6003. *Fax:* 508-286-8271. *E-mail:* admission@wheatoncollege.edu. *Website:* http://www.wheatoncollege.edu/.

Wheelock College

Boston, Massachusetts

- **Independent** comprehensive, founded 1888
- **Urban** 6-acre campus
- **Endowment** $43.7 million
- **Coed, primarily women**
- **Minimally difficult** entrance level

Faculty *Student/faculty ratio:* 9:1.

Academics *Calendar:* semesters. *Degrees:* bachelor's, master's, post-master's, and postbachelor's certificates.

Student Life *Campus security:* 24-hour patrols, late-night transport/escort service, controlled dormitory access.

Athletics Member NCAA. All Division III.

Standardized Tests *Required:* SAT or ACT (for admission).

Costs (2012–13) *Comprehensive fee:* $43,755 includes full-time tuition ($29,860), mandatory fees ($1095), and room and board ($12,800). Full-time tuition and fees vary according to course load. Part-time tuition: $935 per credit hour. Part-time tuition and fees vary according to course load. *Required fees:* $62 per credit part-time.

Financial Aid Of all full-time matriculated undergraduates who enrolled in 2012, 752 applied for aid, 704 were judged to have need, 86 had their need fully met. 160 Federal Work-Study jobs (averaging $1800). In 2012, 108 non-need-based awards were made. *Average percent of need met:* 62. *Average financial aid package:* $20,934. *Average need-based loan:* $4683. *Average need-based gift aid:* $16,565. *Average non-need-based aid:* $12,901. *Average indebtedness upon graduation:* $49,439.

Applying *Options:* electronic application, early admission, early action, deferred entrance. *Application fee:* $15. *Required:* essay or personal statement, high school transcript, minimum 2.0 GPA, 1 letter of recommendation. *Recommended:* interview.

Freshman Application Contact Ms. Kristen Harrington, Director of Undergraduate Admissions, Wheelock College, 200 The Riverway, Boston, MA 02215. *Phone:* 617-879-2206. *Toll-free phone:* 800-734-5212. *Fax:* 617-879-2449. *E-mail:* kharrington@wheelock.edu. *Website:* http://www.wheelock.edu/.

Williams College

Williamstown, Massachusetts

- **Independent** 4-year, founded 1793
- **Small-town** 450-acre campus with easy access to Albany, NY
- **Endowment** $1.8 billion
- **Coed** 2,052 undergraduate students, 98% full-time, 52% women, 48% men
- **Most difficult** entrance level, 17% of applicants were admitted

Undergraduates 2,013 full-time, 39 part-time. Students come from 50 states and territories; 63 other countries; 86% are from out of state; 8% Black or African American, non-Hispanic/Latino; 12% Hispanic/Latino; 11% Asian, non-Hispanic/Latino; 0.3% American Indian or Alaska Native, non-Hispanic/

Latino; 5% Two or more races, non-Hispanic/Latino; 6% international; 0.3% transferred in; 94% live on campus. *Retention:* 96% of full-time freshmen returned.

Freshmen *Admission:* 7,069 applied, 1,203 admitted, 547 enrolled. *Test scores:* SAT critical reading scores over 500: 100%; SAT math scores over 500: 100%; SAT writing scores over 500: 100%; ACT scores over 18: 100%; SAT critical reading scores over 600: 95%; SAT math scores over 600: 93%; SAT writing scores over 600: 96%; ACT scores over 24: 99%; SAT critical reading scores over 700: 66%; SAT math scores over 700: 62%; SAT writing scores over 700: 69%; ACT scores over 30: 77%.

Faculty *Total:* 334, 82% full-time, 92% with terminal degrees. *Student/faculty ratio:* 7:1.

Academics *Calendar:* 4-1-4. *Degrees:* bachelor's and master's. *Special study options:* double majors, independent study, internships, off-campus study, student-designed majors, study abroad. *ROTC:* Air Force (c). *Unusual degree programs:* 3-2 engineering with Columbia University, Washington University in St. Louis, Oxford-Style tutorials, Dartmouth College.

Computers on Campus 252 computers/terminals are available on campus for general student use. Students can access the following: computer help desk, free student e-mail accounts, online (class) grades, online (class) registration. Campuswide network is available. 100% of college-owned or -operated housing units are wired for high-speed Internet access. Wireless service is available via entire campus.

Student Life *Housing:* on-campus residence required for freshman year. *Options:* coed, cooperative. Campus housing is university owned. *Activities and organizations:* drama/theater group, student-run newspaper, radio station, choral group, marching band. *Student services:* health clinic, personal/psychological counseling.

Athletics Member NCAA. All Division III except men's and women's skiing (cross-country) (Division I), men's and women's skiing (downhill) (Division I). *Intercollegiate sports:* baseball M, basketball M/W, crew M/W, cross-country running M/W, equestrian sports M(c)/W(c), field hockey W, football M, golf M/W(c), ice hockey M/W, lacrosse M/W, rugby M(c)/W(c), sailing M(c)/W(c), skiing (cross-country) M/W, skiing (downhill) M/W, soccer M/W, softball W, squash M/W, swimming and diving M/W, tennis M/W, track and field M/W, volleyball M(c)/W, water polo M(c)/W(c), wrestling M. *Intramural sports:* badminton M/W, baseball M(c), basketball M/W, fencing M(c)/W(c), gymnastics M(c)/W(c), ice hockey M/W, skiing (cross-country) M/W, skiing (downhill) M/W, soccer M/W, softball M/W, ultimate Frisbee M(c)/W(c), volleyball M/W, water polo M/W.

Standardized Tests *Required:* SAT and SAT Subject Tests or ACT (for admission).

Costs (2012–13) *Comprehensive fee:* $54,560 includes full-time tuition ($42,938), mandatory fees ($252), and room and board ($11,370). *College room only:* $5780. Room and board charges vary according to board plan. *Payment plan:* installment.

Financial Aid Of all full-time matriculated undergraduates who enrolled in 2010, 1,280 applied for aid, 1,169 were judged to have need, 1,169 had their need fully met. 465 Federal Work-Study jobs (averaging $1844). 464 state and other part-time jobs (averaging $1915). *Average percent of need met:* 100%. *Average financial aid package:* $40,185. *Average need-based gift aid:* $37,836. *Average indebtedness upon graduation:* $8801. *Financial aid deadline:* 2/1.

Applying *Options:* electronic application, early admission, early decision, deferred entrance. *Application fee:* $65. *Required:* essay or personal statement, high school transcript, 2 letters of recommendation. *Application deadlines:* 1/1 (freshmen), 1/1 (out-of-state freshmen), 3/15 (transfers). *Early decision deadline:* 11/10. *Notification:* 4/7 (freshmen), 4/7 (out-of-state freshmen), 5/1 (transfers), 12/15 (early decision).

Freshman Application Contact Mr. Richard L. Nesbitt, Director of Admission, Williams College, 33 Stetson Court, Williamstown, MA 01267. *Phone:* 413-597-2211. *Fax:* 413-597-4052. *E-mail:* admission@williams.edu. *Website:* http://www.williams.edu/.

Worcester Polytechnic Institute

Worcester, Massachusetts

- **Independent** university, founded 1865
- **Suburban** 80-acre campus with easy access to Boston
- **Endowment** $358.6 million
- **Coed** 3,952 undergraduate students, 96% full-time, 32% women, 68% men
- **Very difficult** entrance level, 53% of applicants were admitted

Undergraduates 3,787 full-time, 165 part-time. Students come from 49 states and territories; 70 other countries; 53% are from out of state; 3% Black or African American, non-Hispanic/Latino; 7% Hispanic/Latino; 5% Asian, non-His-

panic/Latino; 0.2% American Indian or Alaska Native, non-Hispanic/Latino; 3% Two or more races, non-Hispanic/Latino; 2% Race/ethnicity unknown; 12% international; 1% transferred in; 45% live on campus. *Retention:* 96% of full-time freshmen returned.

Freshmen *Admission:* 7,585 applied, 3,986 admitted, 951 enrolled. *Average high school GPA:* 3.8. *Test scores:* SAT critical reading scores over 500: 93%; SAT math scores over 500: 100%; SAT writing scores over 500: 95%; ACT scores over 18: 100%; SAT critical reading scores over 600: 61%; SAT math scores over 600: 93%; SAT writing scores over 600: 61%; ACT scores over 24: 96%; SAT critical reading scores over 700: 16%; SAT math scores over 700: 42%; SAT writing scores over 700: 14%; ACT scores over 30: 46%.

Faculty *Total:* 460, 66% full-time, 76% with terminal degrees. *Student/faculty ratio:* 14:1.

Academics *Calendar:* 4 7-week terms. *Degrees:* bachelor's, master's, and doctoral. *Special study options:* accelerated degree program, advanced placement credit, cooperative education, distance learning, double majors, English as a second language, independent study, internships, off-campus study, part-time degree program, services for LD students, student-designed majors, study abroad, summer session for credit. *ROTC:* Army (b), Navy (c), Air Force (b). *Unusual degree programs:* business administration; engineering.

Computers on Campus 500 computers/terminals and 775 ports are available on campus for general student use. Students can access the following: campus intranet, computer help desk, free student e-mail accounts, online (class) grades, online (class) registration, online (class) schedules, online course content. Campuswide network is available. 100% of college-owned or -operated housing units are wired for high-speed Internet access. Wireless service is available via entire campus.

Student Life *Housing options:* coed, men-only, women-only, disabled students. Campus housing is university owned. Freshman campus housing is guaranteed. *Activities and organizations:* drama/theater group, student-run newspaper, radio station, choral group, marching band, Student Government Association, Social Committee (Student Events Programming Board), Music Association (all music-performing groups), intramural and club sports, International Student Council, national fraternities, national sororities. *Campus security:* 24-hour emergency response devices and patrols, student patrols, late-night transport/escort service, controlled dormitory access. *Student services:* health clinic, personal/psychological counseling.

Athletics Member NCAA. All Division III. *Intercollegiate sports:* baseball M, basketball M/W, crew M/W, cross-country running M/W, field hockey W, football M, soccer M/W, softball W, swimming and diving M/W, track and field M/W, volleyball W, water polo M(c)/W(c), wrestling M. *Intramural sports:* baseball M/W, basketball M/W, cheerleading M(c)/W(c), cross-country running M(c)/W(c), fencing M(c)/W(c), golf M(c)/W(c), ice hockey M(c)/W(c), lacrosse M(c)/W(c), racquetball M/W, rugby M(c)/W(c), sailing M(c)/W(c), skiing (cross-country) M(c)/W(c), skiing (downhill) M(c)/W(c), soccer M/W, softball M/W, squash M/W, swimming and diving M/W, table tennis M/W, tennis M(c)/W(c), track and field M/W, ultimate Frisbee M(c)/W(c), volleyball M(c)/W, water polo M(c)/W(c), wrestling M(c).

Standardized Tests *Required for some:* SAT or ACT (for admission), IELTS or TOEFL.

Costs (2013–14) *One-time required fee:* $200. *Comprehensive fee:* $55,860 includes full-time tuition ($42,178), mandatory fees ($600), and room and board ($13,082). Part-time tuition: $1172 per credit hour. Part-time tuition and fees vary according to course load. *College room only:* $7466. Room and board charges vary according to board plan and housing facility. *Payment plans:* tuition prepayment, installment, deferred payment. *Waivers:* employees or children of employees.

Financial Aid Of all full-time matriculated undergraduates who enrolled in 2011, 2,862 applied for aid, 2,569 were judged to have need, 935 had their need fully met. 749 Federal Work-Study jobs (averaging $956). In 2011, 1033 non-need-based awards were made. *Average percent of need met:* 72%. *Average financial aid package:* $30,954. *Average need-based loan:* $2746. *Average need-based gift aid:* $19,699. *Average non-need-based aid:* $15,854.

Applying *Options:* electronic application, early admission, early action, deferred entrance. *Application fee:* $60. *Required:* essay or personal statement, high school transcript, 2 letters of recommendation. *Required for some:* interview. *Application deadlines:* 2/1 (freshmen), 4/15 (transfers), 11/10 (early action). *Notification:* 4/1 (freshmen), continuous (transfers), 12/20 (early action).

Freshman Application Contact Mr. Edward J. Connor, Dean of Admissions, Worcester Polytechnic Institute, 100 Institute Road, Worcester, MA 01609-2280. *Phone:* 508-831-5286. *Fax:* 508-831-5875. *E-mail:* admissions@wpi.edu.

Website: http://www.wpi.edu/.

See below for display ad and page 1656 for the College Close-Up.

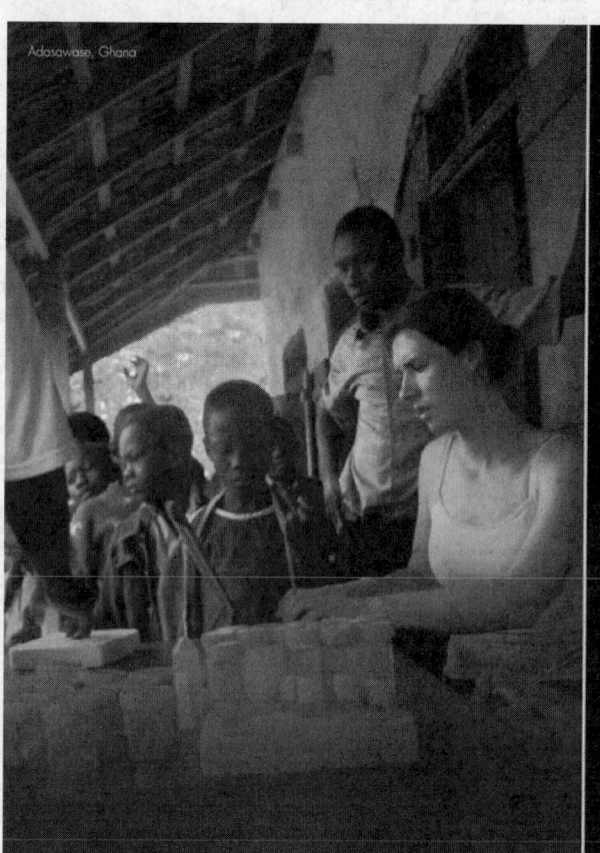

Worcester State University

Worcester, Massachusetts

- **State-supported** comprehensive, founded 1874, part of Massachusetts Public Higher Education System
- **Urban** 58-acre campus with easy access to Boston
- **Endowment** $10.6 million
- **Coed** 5,307 undergraduate students, 75% full-time, 60% women, 40% men
- **Moderately difficult** entrance level, 68% of applicants were admitted

Undergraduates 3,973 full-time, 1,334 part-time. Students come from 21 states and territories; 13 other countries; 3% are from out of state; 6% Black or African American, non-Hispanic/Latino; 7% Hispanic/Latino; 3% Asian, non-Hispanic/Latino; 0.1% Native Hawaiian or other Pacific Islander, non-Hispanic/Latino; 0.4% American Indian or Alaska Native, non-Hispanic/Latino; 2% Two or more races, non-Hispanic/Latino; 6% Race/ethnicity unknown; 0.8% international; 10% transferred in; 31% live on campus. *Retention:* 78% of full-time freshmen returned.

Freshmen *Admission:* 3,434 applied, 2,340 admitted, 784 enrolled. *Average high school GPA:* 3.14. *Test scores:* SAT critical reading scores over 500: 47%; SAT math scores over 500: 58%; SAT writing scores over 500: 46%; ACT scores over 18: 85%; SAT critical reading scores over 600: 9%; SAT math scores over 600: 11%; SAT writing scores over 600: 7%; ACT scores over 24: 21%; SAT critical reading scores over 700: 1%; ACT scores over 30: 1%.

Faculty *Total:* 422, 46% full-time, 48% with terminal degrees. *Student/faculty ratio:* 18:1.

Academics *Calendar:* semesters. *Degrees:* bachelor's, master's, post-master's, and postbachelor's certificates. *Special study options:* academic remediation for entering students, accelerated degree program, adult/continuing education programs, advanced placement credit, distance learning, double majors, English as a second language, honors programs, independent study, internships, off-campus study, part-time degree program, services for LD students, study abroad, summer session for credit. *ROTC:* Army (c), Navy (c), Air Force (c).

Computers on Campus 500 computers/terminals and 1,700 ports are available on campus for general student use. Students can access the following: campus intranet, computer help desk, free student e-mail accounts, online (class) grades, online (class) registration, online (class) schedules. Campus-wide network is available. 100% of college-owned or -operated housing units are wired for high-speed Internet access. Wireless service is available via entire campus.

Student Life *Housing options:* coed, men-only, women-only, disabled students. Campus housing is university owned. *Activities and organizations:* drama/theater group, student-run newspaper, radio and television station, choral group, Senate, SEC (Student Events Committee), TWA (Third World Alliance), WSCW (radio station), Dance Company/Club. *Campus security:* 24-hour emergency response devices and patrols, late-night transport/escort service, controlled dormitory access, well-lit campus and limited access to campus at night. *Student services:* health clinic, personal/psychological counseling.

Athletics Member NCAA. All Division III. *Intercollegiate sports:* baseball M, basketball M/W, cross-country running M/W, field hockey W, football M, golf M, ice hockey M, lacrosse W, soccer M/W, softball W, tennis W, track and field M/W, volleyball W. *Intramural sports:* basketball M/W, cheerleading M/W, equestrian sports M/W, football M, soccer M/W, softball M/W, ultimate Frisbee M/W.

Standardized Tests *Required:* SAT or ACT (for admission).

Costs (2012–13) *Tuition:* state resident $970 full-time, $40 per credit part-time; nonresident $7050 full-time, $294 per credit part-time. Full-time tuition and fees vary according to class time, course load, degree level, and reciprocity agreements. Part-time tuition and fees vary according to class time, course load, degree level, and reciprocity agreements. *Required fees:* $7187 full-time, $278 per credit part-time. *Room and board:* $10,500; room only: $7380. Room and board charges vary according to board plan and housing facility. *Payment plan:* installment. *Waivers:* senior citizens and employees or children of employees.

Financial Aid Of all full-time matriculated undergraduates who enrolled in 2011, 3,213 applied for aid, 2,217 were judged to have need, 1,004 had their need fully met. 200 Federal Work-Study jobs (averaging $1500). In 2011, 50 non-need-based awards were made. *Average percent of need met:* 83%. *Average financial aid package:* $11,002. *Average need-based loan:* $3077. *Average need-based gift aid:* $4596. *Average non-need-based aid:* $2268. *Average indebtedness upon graduation:* $20,449. *Financial aid deadline:* 5/1.

Applying *Options:* electronic application, deferred entrance. *Application fee:* $40. *Required:* high school transcript, minimum 2.0 GPA. *Required for some:* essay or personal statement. *Application deadlines:* 5/1 (freshmen), 6/1 (transfers). *Notification:* continuous (freshmen), continuous (transfers).

Freshman Application Contact Ms. Sarah Whitney, Clerk of Admissions, Worcester State University, 486 Chandler Street, Administration Building, Worcester, MA 01602-2597. *Phone:* 508-929-8040. *Toll-free phone:* 866-WSC-CALL. *Fax:* 508-929-8183. *E-mail:* admissions@worcester.edu. *Website:* http://www.worcester.edu/.

MICHIGAN

Adrian College

Adrian, Michigan

- **Independent** comprehensive, founded 1859, affiliated with United Methodist Church
- **Small-town** 100-acre campus with easy access to Detroit, Toledo
- **Coed**
- **Moderately difficult** entrance level

Faculty *Student/faculty ratio:* 14:1.

Academics *Calendar:* semesters. *Degrees:* associate, bachelor's, and master's.

Student Life *Campus security:* 24-hour patrols, student patrols, late-night transport/escort service.

Athletics Member NCAA. All Division III.

Standardized Tests *Required:* SAT or ACT (for admission). *Recommended:* ACT (for admission).

Costs (2012–13) *Comprehensive fee:* $37,952 includes full-time tuition ($28,606), mandatory fees ($550), and room and board ($8796). *College room only:* $4226. Room and board charges vary according to board plan and housing facility.

Financial Aid *Of all full-time matriculated undergraduates who enrolled in 2012,* 1,581 applied for aid, 1,498 were judged to have need, 127 had their need fully met. 1,155 Federal Work-Study jobs (averaging $1800). 72 state and other part-time jobs (averaging $1800). *In 2012,* 200 non-need-based awards were made. *Average percent of need met:* 74. *Average financial aid package:* $24,428. *Average need-based loan:* $4104. *Average need-based gift aid:* $19,428. *Average non-need-based aid:* $12,964. *Average indebtedness upon graduation:* $30,645.

Applying *Options:* electronic application, deferred entrance. *Required:* high school transcript. *Required for some:* essay or personal statement. *Recommended:* interview.

Freshman Application Contact Mr. Frank Hribar, Vice President for Enrollment, Adrian College, 110 S. Madison St., Adrian, MI 49221. *Phone:* 800-877-2246. *Toll-free phone:* 800-877-2246. *Fax:* 517-264-3331. *E-mail:* admissions@adrian.edu. *Website:* http://www.adrian.edu/.

Albion College

Albion, Michigan

- **Independent Methodist** 4-year, founded 1835
- **Small-town** 565-acre campus with easy access to Detroit
- **Endowment** $161.2 million
- **Coed** 1,382 undergraduate students, 98% full-time, 49% women, 51% men
- **Moderately difficult** entrance level, 70% of applicants were admitted

Undergraduates 1,353 full-time, 29 part-time. Students come from 20 states and territories; 23 other countries; 9% are from out of state; 4% Black or African American, non-Hispanic/Latino; 3% Hispanic/Latino; 1% Asian, non-Hispanic/Latino; 0.2% American Indian or Alaska Native, non-Hispanic/Latino; 4% Two or more races, non-Hispanic/Latino; 3% Race/ethnicity unknown; 4% international; 3% transferred in; 90% live on campus. *Retention:* 73% of full-time freshmen returned.

Freshmen *Admission:* 2,383 applied, 1,673 admitted, 360 enrolled. *Average high school GPA:* 3.4. *Test scores:* SAT critical reading scores over 500: 61%; SAT math scores over 500: 71%; ACT scores over 18: 96%; SAT critical reading scores over 600: 32%; SAT math scores over 600: 39%; ACT scores over 24: 59%; SAT critical reading scores over 700: 6%; SAT math scores over 700: 16%; ACT scores over 30: 11%.

Faculty *Total:* 151, 70% full-time, 79% with terminal degrees. *Student/faculty ratio:* 11:1.

Academics *Calendar:* semesters. *Degree:* bachelor's. *Special study options:* advanced placement credit, double majors, honors programs, independent study, internships, off-campus study, part-time degree program, services for LD students, student-designed majors, study abroad, summer session for credit. *Unusual degree programs:* 3-2 engineering with Columbia University,

University of Michigan, Case Western Reserve University, Michigan Technological University, Washington University in St. Louis; forestry with Duke University, Washington University in St. Louis; nursing with Case Western Reserve University; public policy studies with University of Michigan, fine arts with Bank Street College of Education.

Computers on Campus 120 computers/terminals and 2,000 ports are available on campus for general student use. Students can access the following: computer help desk, free student e-mail accounts, online (class) grades, online (class) registration, online (class) schedules, online student account and financial aid. Campuswide network is available. 100% of college-owned or -operated housing units are wired for high-speed Internet access. Wireless service is available via classrooms, computer centers, computer labs, dorm rooms, learning centers, libraries, student centers.

Student Life *Housing options:* coed, men-only, women-only, cooperative. Campus housing is university owned. Freshman campus housing is guaranteed. *Activities and organizations:* drama/theater group, student-run newspaper, radio station, choral group, marching band, Greek Life (Fraternities and Sororities), Student Senate (Student Government), Umbrella (Diversity Groups), Union Board (Programming Board), Spiritual Life (Religious Centered groups), national fraternities, national sororities. *Campus security:* 24-hour emergency response devices and patrols, student patrols, late-night transport/escort service, controlled dormitory access. *Student services:* health clinic, personal/psychological counseling, women's center.

Athletics Member NCAA. All Division III. *Intercollegiate sports:* baseball M, basketball M/W, cross-country running M/W, equestrian sports M/W, football M, golf M/W, lacrosse M/W, soccer M/W, softball W, swimming and diving M/W, tennis M/W, track and field M/W, volleyball M(c)/W. *Intramural sports:* basketball M/W, cheerleading M(c)/W(c), equestrian sports M(c)/W(c), football M/W, ice hockey M(c)/W(c), racquetball M/W, rugby M/W, sailing M(c)/W(c), soccer M/W, softball M/W, swimming and diving M/W, tennis M/W, ultimate Frisbee M/W, volleyball M/W, water polo M(c)/W(c).

Standardized Tests *Required:* SAT or ACT (for admission).

Costs (2012–13) *One-time required fee:* $185. *Comprehensive fee:* $43,884 includes full-time tuition ($33,600), mandatory fees ($594), and room and board ($9690). Full-time tuition and fees vary according to course load. Part-time tuition: $1430 per credit hour. Part-time tuition and fees vary according to course load. *Required fees:* $297 per term part-time. *College room only:* $4740. Room and board charges vary according to board plan and housing facility. *Payment plans:* installment, deferred payment. *Waivers:* employees or children of employees.

Financial Aid Of all full-time matriculated undergraduates who enrolled in 2012, 1,063 applied for aid, 949 were judged to have need, 185 had their need fully met. 401 Federal Work-Study jobs (averaging $1094). In 2012, 387 non-need-based awards were made. *Average percent of need met:* 80%. *Average financial aid package:* $26,466. *Average need-based loan:* $5296. *Average need-based gift aid:* $21,488. *Average non-need-based aid:* $15,585. *Average indebtedness upon graduation:* $36,029.

Applying *Options:* electronic application, early action, deferred entrance. *Required:* essay or personal statement, high school transcript, minimum 3.0 GPA, 1 letter of recommendation. *Recommended:* interview. *Application deadlines:* rolling (freshmen), rolling (transfers), 12/1 (early action). *Notification:* continuous (freshmen), continuous (transfers), 11/1 (early action).

Freshman Application Contact Albion College, 611 East Porter Street, Albion, MI 49224-1831. *Phone:* 517-629-0757. *Toll-free phone:* 800-858-6770.
Website: http://www.albion.edu/.

Alma College

Alma, Michigan

- **Independent Presbyterian** 4-year, founded 1886
- **Small-town** 125-acre campus
- **Endowment** $96.5 million
- **Coed** 1,464 undergraduate students, 97% full-time, 55% women, 45% men
- **Moderately difficult** entrance level, 72% of applicants were admitted

Undergraduates 1,414 full-time, 50 part-time. Students come from 28 states and territories; 14 other countries; 8% are from out of state; 3% Black or African American, non-Hispanic/Latino; 2% Hispanic/Latino; 1% Asian, non-Hispanic/Latino; 1% American Indian or Alaska Native, non-Hispanic/Latino; 2% Two or more races, non-Hispanic/Latino; 4% Race/ethnicity unknown; 0.8% international; 4% transferred in; 90% live on campus. *Retention:* 80% of full-time freshmen returned.

Freshmen *Admission:* 2,232 applied, 1,604 admitted, 427 enrolled. *Average high school GPA:* 3.5. *Test scores:* SAT critical reading scores over 500: 64%; SAT math scores over 500: 58%; SAT writing scores over 500: 53%; ACT

scores over 18: 94%; SAT critical reading scores over 600: 28%; SAT math scores over 600: 39%; SAT writing scores over 600: 24%; ACT scores over 24: 47%; SAT critical reading scores over 700: 18%; SAT math scores over 700: 10%; SAT writing scores over 700: 10%; ACT scores over 30: 5%.

Faculty *Total:* 174, 55% full-time, 63% with terminal degrees. *Student/faculty ratio:* 12:1.

Academics *Calendar:* 4-4-1. *Degree:* bachelor's. *Special study options:* academic remediation for entering students, advanced placement credit, double majors, honors programs, independent study, internships, off-campus study, services for LD students, student-designed majors, study abroad, summer session for credit. *ROTC:* Army (c). *Unusual degree programs:* 3-2 engineering with University of Michigan, Michigan Technological University; occupational therapy with Washington University in St. Louis.

Computers on Campus 298 computers/terminals are available on campus for general student use. Students can access the following: campus intranet, computer help desk, free student e-mail accounts, online (class) grades, online (class) registration, online (class) schedules. Campuswide network is available. 100% of college-owned or -operated housing units are wired for high-speed Internet access. Wireless service is available via entire campus.

Student Life *Housing:* on-campus residence required through senior year. *Options:* coed, disabled students. Campus housing is university owned. Freshman campus housing is guaranteed. *Activities and organizations:* drama/theater group, student-run newspaper, radio station, choral group, marching band, Ambassadors, Alma College Union Board, New Life Campus Ministries, Student Congress, Alpha Phi Omega, national fraternities, national sororities. *Campus security:* 24-hour emergency response devices and patrols, controlled dormitory access. *Student services:* health clinic, personal/psychological counseling.

Athletics Member NCAA. All Division III. *Intercollegiate sports:* baseball M, basketball M/W, bowling W, cheerleading M/W, cross-country running M/W, football M, golf M/W, lacrosse M/W, soccer M/W, softball W, swimming and diving M/W, tennis M/W, track and field M/W, volleyball W, wrestling M. *Intramural sports:* basketball M/W, equestrian sports W(c), football M, softball M/W, ultimate Frisbee M/W, volleyball M/W.

Standardized Tests *Required:* SAT or ACT (for admission).

Costs (2012–13) *Comprehensive fee:* $40,050 includes full-time tuition ($30,700), mandatory fees ($360), and room and board ($8990). Part-time tuition: $1000 per credit hour. Part-time tuition and fees vary according to course load. *College room only:* $4495. Room and board charges vary according to board plan and housing facility. *Payment plans:* installment, deferred payment. *Waivers:* employees or children of employees.

Financial Aid Of all full-time matriculated undergraduates who enrolled in 2012, 1,323 applied for aid, 1,182 were judged to have need, 148 had their need fully met. 514 Federal Work-Study jobs (averaging $1227). In 2012, 218 non-need-based awards were made. *Average percent of need met:* 87%. *Average financial aid package:* $26,245. *Average need-based loan:* $3980. *Average need-based gift aid:* $19,594. *Average non-need-based aid:* $14,480. *Average indebtedness upon graduation:* $31,297.

Applying *Options:* electronic application, deferred entrance. *Application fee:* $25. *Required:* essay or personal statement, high school transcript, minimum 3.0 GPA. *Required for some:* 3 letters of recommendation. *Recommended:* interview. *Application deadlines:* rolling (freshmen), rolling (out-of-state freshmen), rolling (transfers). *Notification:* continuous (freshmen), continuous (out-of-state freshmen), continuous (transfers).

Freshman Application Contact Amanda Slenski, Director of Admissions, Alma College, Admissions Office, Alma, MI 48801-1599. *Phone:* 800-321-2562. *Toll-free phone:* 800-321-ALMA. *Fax:* 989-463-7057. *E-mail:* admissions@alma.edu.
Website: http://www.alma.edu/.

Andrews University

Berrien Springs, Michigan

- **Independent Seventh-day Adventist** university, founded 1874
- **Small-town** 1650-acre campus
- **Endowment** $37.7 million
- **Coed** 1,917 undergraduate students, 89% full-time, 56% women, 44% men
- **Moderately difficult** entrance level, 38% of applicants were admitted

Undergraduates 1,704 full-time, 213 part-time. Students come from 50 states and territories; 55 other countries; 72% are from out of state; 24% Black or African American, non-Hispanic/Latino; 15% Hispanic/Latino; 11% Asian, non-Hispanic/Latino; 0.7% Native Hawaiian or other Pacific Islander, non-Hispanic/Latino; 0.2% American Indian or Alaska Native, non-Hispanic/Latino; 3% Two or more races, non-Hispanic/Latino; 1% Race/ethnicity

unknown; 14% international; 7% transferred in; 69% live on campus. *Retention:* 79% of full-time freshmen returned.

Freshmen *Admission:* 2,551 applied, 958 admitted, 388 enrolled. *Average high school GPA:* 3.44. *Test scores:* SAT critical reading scores over 500: 65%; SAT math scores over 500: 56%; SAT writing scores over 500: 60%; ACT scores over 18: 93%; SAT critical reading scores over 600: 30%; SAT math scores over 600: 26%; SAT writing scores over 600: 24%; ACT scores over 24: 53%; SAT critical reading scores over 700: 6%; SAT math scores over 700: 9%; SAT writing scores over 700: 4%; ACT scores over 30: 12%.

Faculty *Total:* 292, 78% full-time, 62% with terminal degrees. *Student/faculty ratio:* 10:1.

Academics *Calendar:* semesters. *Degrees:* associate, bachelor's, master's, doctoral, post-master's, and postbachelor's certificates. *Special study options:* academic remediation for entering students, accelerated degree program, adult/continuing education programs, advanced placement credit, cooperative education, distance learning, double majors, English as a second language, freshman honors college, honors programs, internships, off-campus study, part-time degree program, student-designed majors, study abroad, summer session for credit. *Unusual degree programs:* 3-2 physical therapy and architecture.

Computers on Campus 130 computers/terminals are available on campus for general student use. Students can access the following: campus intranet, computer help desk, free student e-mail accounts, online (class) grades, online (class) registration, online (class) schedules, degree audit. Campuswide network is available. 99% of college-owned or -operated housing units are wired for high-speed Internet access. Wireless service is available via classrooms, computer centers, computer labs, learning centers, libraries, student centers.

Student Life *Housing:* on-campus residence required through senior year. *Options:* men-only, women-only. Campus housing is university owned. Freshman campus housing is guaranteed. *Activities and organizations:* drama/theater group, student-run newspaper, radio station, choral group. *Campus security:* 24-hour emergency response devices and patrols, controlled dormitory access. *Student services:* health clinic, personal/psychological counseling. **Athletics** *Intramural sports:* basketball M/W, football M/W, golf M/W, gymnastics M/W, racquetball M/W, soccer M/W, softball M/W, volleyball M/W, water polo M/W.

Standardized Tests *Required:* SAT or ACT (for admission).

Costs (2012–13) *Comprehensive fee:* $32,006 includes full-time tuition ($23,700), mandatory fees ($778), and room and board ($7528). Full-time tuition and fees vary according to course load. Part-time tuition: $988 per credit hour. Part-time tuition and fees vary according to course load. *College room only:* $4008. Room and board charges vary according to board plan. *Payment plan:* installment. *Waivers:* senior citizens and employees or children of employees.

Financial Aid Of all full-time matriculated undergraduates who enrolled in 2012, 1,237 applied for aid, 1,143 were judged to have need, 155 had their need fully met. 868 Federal Work-Study jobs (averaging $956). 1 state and other part-time job (averaging $1500). In 2012, 566 non-need-based awards were made. *Average percent of need met:* 85%. *Average financial aid package:* $25,910. *Average need-based loan:* $4553. *Average need-based gift aid:* $5598. *Average non-need-based aid:* $8152. *Average indebtedness upon graduation:* $33,249.

Applying *Options:* electronic application, deferred entrance. *Application fee:* $30. *Required:* high school transcript, minimum 2.3 GPA, 2 letters of recommendation. *Application deadlines:* rolling (freshmen), rolling (transfers). *Notification:* continuous (freshmen), continuous (transfers).

Freshman Application Contact Shanna Leak, Undergraduate Admissions Coordinator, Andrews University, Berrien Springs, MI 49104. *Phone:* 800-253-2874. *Toll-free phone:* 800-253-2874. *Fax:* 269-471-3228. *E-mail:* enroll@andrews.edu.
Website: http://www.andrews.edu/.

Aquinas College

Grand Rapids, Michigan

- **Independent Roman Catholic** comprehensive, founded 1886
- **Suburban** 107-acre campus with easy access to Detroit, Chicago, Grand Rapids
- **Endowment** $32.2 million
- **Coed**
- **Moderately difficult** entrance level

Faculty *Student/faculty ratio:* 13:1.

Academics *Calendar:* semesters. *Degrees:* associate, bachelor's, and master's.

Student Life *Campus security:* 24-hour emergency response devices and patrols, student patrols, late-night transport/escort service, controlled dormitory access.

Athletics Member NAIA.

Standardized Tests *Required:* SAT or ACT (for admission).

Costs (2012–13) *Comprehensive fee:* $33,060 includes full-time tuition ($25,070), mandatory fees ($180), and room and board ($7810). Full-time

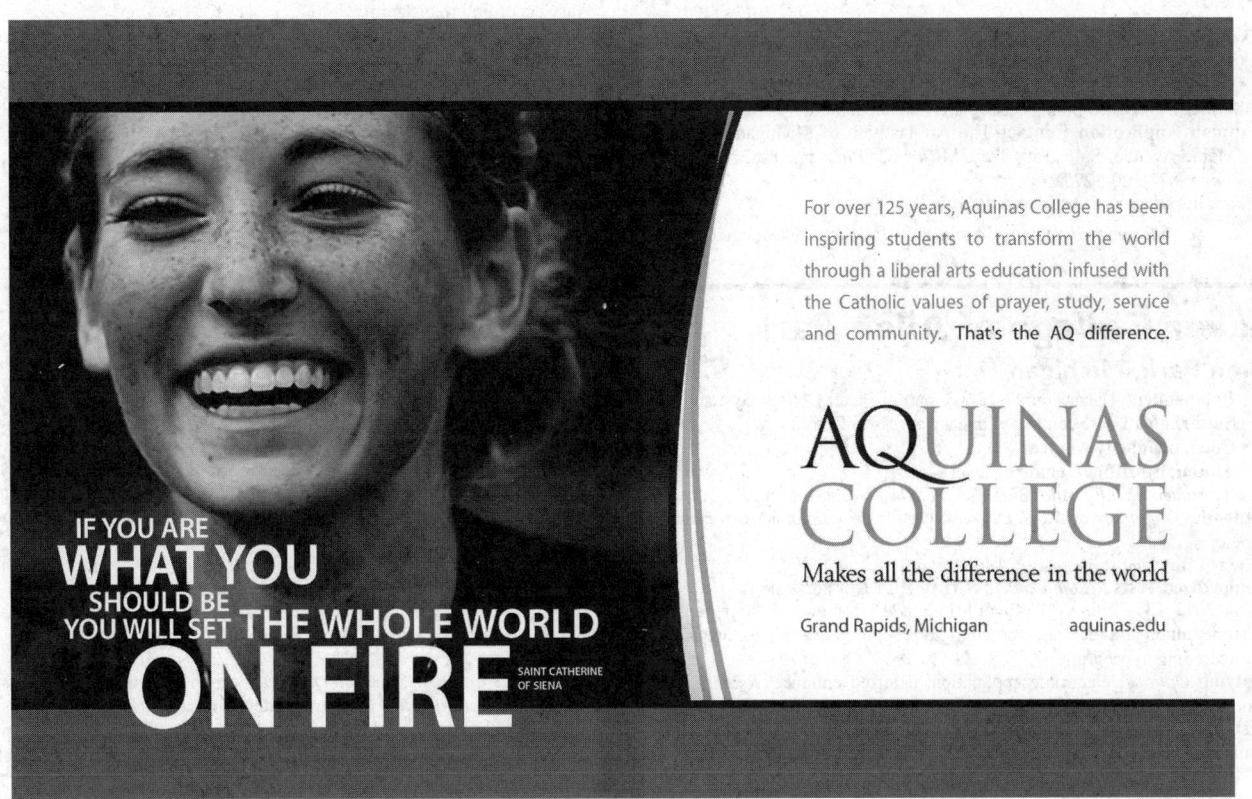

tuition and fees vary according to course load. Part-time tuition: $498 per credit hour. Part-time tuition and fees vary according to course load. *College room only:* $3644. Room and board charges vary according to board plan and housing facility. *Payment plans:* installment, deferred payment.

Financial Aid *Of all full-time matriculated undergraduates who enrolled in 2011,* 1,375 applied for aid, 1,244 were judged to have need, 540 had their need fully met. *In 2011,* 218 non-need-based awards were made. *Average percent of need met:* 85. *Average financial aid package:* $21,214. *Average need-based loan:* $4108. *Average need-based gift aid:* $17,106. *Average non-need-based aid:* $15,827. *Average indebtedness upon graduation:* $20,694. *Financial aid deadline:* 8/15.

Applying *Options:* electronic application, early admission, deferred entrance. *Required:* high school transcript, minimum 2.5 GPA. *Required for some:* essay or personal statement, interview.

Freshman Application Contact Ms. Rebecca Roberts, Admissions Office Applications Specialist, Aquinas College, 1607 Robinson Road, SE, Grand Rapids, MI 49506-1799. *Phone:* 616-632-2900. *Toll-free phone:* 800-678-9593. *Fax:* 616-732-4469. *E-mail:* admissions@aquinas.edu. *Website:* http://www.aquinas.edu/.

See previous page for display ad and page 1046 for the College Close-Up.

The Art Institute of Michigan

Novi, Michigan

- **Proprietary** 4-year, part of Education Management Corporation
- **Coed**

Academics *Degrees:* diplomas, associate, and bachelor's.

Freshman Application Contact The Art Institute of Michigan, 28125 Cabot Drive, Suite 120, Novi, MI 48377. *Phone:* 248-675-3800. *Toll-free phone:* 800-479-0087. *Website:* http://www.artinstitutes.edu/detroit/.

See full-page ad on page 54 and page 1094 for the College Close-Up.

The Art Institute of Michigan– Troy

Troy, Michigan

- **Proprietary** 4-year
- **Coed**

Academics *Degrees:* diplomas, associate, and bachelor's.

Freshman Application Contact The Art Institute of Michigan–Troy, 1414 East Maple Avenue, Suite 150, Troy, MI 48083. *Phone:* 248-837-3200. *Toll-free phone:* 877-320-3275. *Website:* http://www.artinstitutes.edu/troy.

See full-page ad on page 54 and page 1096 for the College Close-Up.

Baker College of Allen Park

Allen Park, Michigan

- **Independent** 4-year, founded 2003, part of Baker College System
- **Suburban** 13-acre campus with easy access to Detroit
- **Coed, primarily women**
- **Minimally difficult** entrance level

Faculty *Student/faculty ratio:* 34:1.

Academics *Calendar:* quarters. *Degrees:* certificates, diplomas, associate, and bachelor's.

Student Life *Campus security:* 24-hour patrols.

Standardized Tests *Recommended:* SAT or ACT (for admission).

Costs (2012–13) *Tuition:* $7740 full-time, $215 per quarter hour part-time. Full-time tuition and fees vary according to program. Part-time tuition and fees vary according to program.

Applying *Options:* electronic application, deferred entrance. *Required:* high school transcript, interview.

Freshman Application Contact Mr. Steve Peterson, Vice President of Admissions, Baker College of Allen Park, 4500 Enterprise Drive, Allen Park, MI 48101. *Phone:* 313-425-3700. *Toll-free phone:* 800-767-4120. *E-mail:* steve.peterson@baker.edu. *Website:* http://www.baker.edu/.

Baker College of Auburn Hills

Auburn Hills, Michigan

- **Independent** 4-year, founded 1911, part of Baker College System
- **Urban** 10-acre campus with easy access to Detroit
- **Coed**
- **Minimally difficult** entrance level

Faculty *Student/faculty ratio:* 41:1.

Academics *Calendar:* quarters. *Degrees:* certificates, diplomas, associate, bachelor's, and postbachelor's certificates.

Student Life *Campus security:* 24-hour emergency response devices.

Standardized Tests *Recommended:* SAT or ACT (for admission).

Costs (2012–13) *Tuition:* $7740 full-time, $215 per quarter hour part-time. Full-time tuition and fees vary according to program. Part-time tuition and fees vary according to program.

Applying *Options:* early admission, deferred entrance. *Application fee:* $20. *Required:* high school transcript.

Freshman Application Contact Ms. Nicole Chirco, Director of Admissions, Baker College of Auburn Hills, 1500 University Drive, Auburn Hills, MI 48326-1586. *Phone:* 248-340-0600. *Toll-free phone:* 888-429-0410. *Fax:* 248-340-0608. *Website:* http://www.baker.edu/.

Baker College of Cadillac

Cadillac, Michigan

- **Independent** 4-year, founded 1986, part of Baker College System
- **Small-town** 40-acre campus
- **Coed**
- **Minimally difficult** entrance level

Faculty *Student/faculty ratio:* 42:1.

Academics *Calendar:* quarters. *Degrees:* certificates, diplomas, associate, and bachelor's.

Student Life *Campus security:* 24-hour emergency response devices.

Standardized Tests *Recommended:* SAT or ACT (for admission).

Costs (2012–13) *Tuition:* $7740 full-time, $215 per quarter hour part-time. Full-time tuition and fees vary according to program. Part-time tuition and fees vary according to program.

Applying *Options:* early admission, deferred entrance. *Application fee:* $20. *Required:* high school transcript. *Recommended:* interview.

Freshman Application Contact Ms. Audrey Charmoli, Director of Admissions, Baker College of Cadillac, 9600 East 13th Street, Cadillac, MI 49601. *Phone:* 231-876-3100. *Toll-free phone:* 888-313-3463. *Fax:* 231-775-8505. *E-mail:* audrey.charmoli@baker.edu. *Website:* http://www.baker.edu/.

Baker College of Clinton Township

Clinton Township, Michigan

- **Independent** 4-year, founded 1990, part of Baker College System
- **Urban** 30-acre campus with easy access to Detroit
- **Coed** 5,138 undergraduate students, 58% full-time, 69% women, 31% men
- **Minimally difficult** entrance level, 100% of applicants were admitted

Undergraduates 2,980 full-time, 2,158 part-time. Students come from 2 states and territories; 27% Black or African American, non-Hispanic/Latino; 2% Hispanic/Latino; 1% Asian, non-Hispanic/Latino; 0.6% American Indian or Alaska Native, non-Hispanic/Latino; 1% Race/ethnicity unknown.

Freshmen *Admission:* 2,010 applied, 2,010 admitted.

Faculty *Total:* 208, 8% full-time, 12% with terminal degrees. *Student/faculty ratio:* 45:1.

Academics *Calendar:* quarters. *Degrees:* certificates, diplomas, associate, and bachelor's. *Special study options:* academic remediation for entering students, advanced placement credit, cooperative education, external degree program, internships, part-time degree program, services for LD students, summer session for credit.

Computers on Campus 127 computers/terminals are available on campus for general student use. Campuswide network is available.

Student Life *Housing:* college housing not available. *Campus security:* 24-hour emergency response devices and patrols, evening security guard. *Student services:* personal/psychological counseling.

Standardized Tests *Required for some:* SAT or ACT (for admission).

Costs (2013–14) *Tuition:* $7920 full-time, $220 per quarter hour part-time. Full-time tuition and fees vary according to program. Part-time tuition and fees vary according to program. *Waivers:* employees or children of employees.

Applying *Options:* electronic application, early admission, deferred entrance. *Application fee:* $20. *Required:* high school transcript. *Application deadlines:* rolling (freshmen), rolling (transfers).

Freshman Application Contact Ms. Annette Looser, Vice President for Admissions, Baker College of Clinton Township, 34401 South Gratiot Avenue, Clinton Township, MI 48035. *Phone:* 586-791-3000. *Toll-free phone:* 888-272-2842. *Fax:* 586-791-6811. *E-mail:* annette.looser@baker.edu. *Website:* http://www.baker.edu/.

Baker College of Flint

Flint, Michigan

- **Independent** 4-year, founded 1911, part of Baker College System
- **Urban** 53-acre campus with easy access to Detroit
- **Coed**
- **Minimally difficult** entrance level

Faculty *Student/faculty ratio:* 31:1.

Academics *Calendar:* quarters. *Degrees:* certificates, diplomas, associate, and bachelor's.

Student Life *Campus security:* 24-hour patrols, late-night transport/escort service, controlled dormitory access, video monitoring of high traffic areas.

Standardized Tests *Recommended:* SAT or ACT (for admission).

Costs (2012–13) *Tuition:* $7740 full-time, $215 per quarter hour part-time. Full-time tuition and fees vary according to program. Part-time tuition and fees vary according to program. *Room only:* $3000. Room and board charges vary according to housing facility.

Applying *Options:* early admission, deferred entrance. *Application fee:* $20. *Required:* high school transcript.

Freshman Application Contact Ms. Jodi Cunez, Vice President for Admissions, Baker College of Flint, 1050 West Bristol Road, Flint, MI 48507-5508. *Phone:* 810-766-4008. *Toll-free phone:* 800-964-4299. *Fax:* 810-766-4049.

Website: http://www.baker.edu/.

Baker College of Jackson

Jackson, Michigan

- **Independent** 4-year, founded 1994, part of Baker College System
- **Suburban** 42-acre campus with easy access to Lansing
- **Coed**
- **Minimally difficult** entrance level

Faculty *Student/faculty ratio:* 36:1.

Academics *Calendar:* quarters. *Degrees:* certificates, diplomas, associate, and bachelor's.

Student Life *Campus security:* 24-hour emergency response devices.

Standardized Tests *Recommended:* SAT or ACT (for admission).

Costs (2012–13) *Tuition:* $7740 full-time, $215 per quarter hour part-time. Full-time tuition and fees vary according to program. Part-time tuition and fees vary according to program.

Applying *Options:* electronic application, early admission, deferred entrance. *Application fee:* $20. *Required:* high school transcript.

Freshman Application Contact Mr. Kevin Pnacek, Vice President for Admissions, Baker College of Jackson, 2800 Springport Road, Jackson, MI 49202. *Phone:* 517-788-7800. *Toll-free phone:* 888-343-3683. *Fax:* 517-789-7331. *E-mail:* kevin.pnacek@baker.edu. *Website:* http://www.baker.edu/.

Baker College of Muskegon

Muskegon, Michigan

- **Independent** 4-year, founded 1888, part of Baker College System
- **Suburban** 45-acre campus with easy access to Grand Rapids
- **Coed**
- **Minimally difficult** entrance level

Faculty *Student/faculty ratio:* 55:1.

Academics *Calendar:* quarters. *Degrees:* certificates, diplomas, associate, and bachelor's.

Student Life *Campus security:* 24-hour emergency response devices and patrols, late-night transport/escort service, controlled dormitory access, 24-hour security camera surveillance.

Standardized Tests *Recommended:* SAT or ACT (for admission).

Costs (2012–13) *Tuition:* $7740 full-time, $215 per quarter hour part-time. Full-time tuition and fees vary according to program. Part-time tuition and fees vary according to program.

Applying *Options:* electronic application, early admission, deferred entrance. *Application fee:* $20. *Required:* high school transcript.

Freshman Application Contact Ms. Kathy Jacobson, Vice President of Admissions, Baker College of Muskegon, 1903 Marquette Avenue, Muskegon, MI 49442-3497. *Phone:* 231-777-5207. *Toll-free phone:* 800-937-0337. *Fax:* 231-777-5201. *E-mail:* kathy.jacobson@baker.edu. *Website:* http://www.baker.edu/.

Baker College of Owosso

Owosso, Michigan

- **Independent** 4-year, founded 1984, part of Baker College System
- **Small-town** 52-acre campus
- **Coed**
- **Minimally difficult** entrance level

Faculty *Student/faculty ratio:* 40:1.

Academics *Calendar:* quarters. *Degrees:* certificates, diplomas, associate, and bachelor's.

Student Life *Campus security:* 24-hour emergency response devices and patrols, late-night transport/escort service, controlled dormitory access.

Standardized Tests *Recommended:* SAT or ACT (for admission).

Costs (2012–13) *Tuition:* $7740 full-time, $215 per quarter hour part-time. Full-time tuition and fees vary according to program. Part-time tuition and fees vary according to program. *Room only:* $3000. Room and board charges vary according to housing facility.

Applying *Options:* early admission, deferred entrance. *Application fee:* $20. *Required:* high school transcript.

Freshman Application Contact Mr. Michael Konopacke, Vice President for Admissions, Baker College of Owosso, 1020 South Washington Street, Owosso, MI 48867-4400. *Phone:* 989-729-3350. *Toll-free phone:* 800-879-3797. *Fax:* 989-729-3441. *E-mail:* mike.konopacke@baker.edu. *Website:* http://www.baker.edu/.

Baker College of Port Huron

Port Huron, Michigan

- **Independent** 4-year, founded 1990, part of Baker College System
- **Urban** 10-acre campus with easy access to Detroit
- **Coed** 1,177 undergraduate students, 65% full-time, 73% women, 27% men
- **Minimally difficult** entrance level, 100% of applicants were admitted

Undergraduates 765 full-time, 412 part-time. Students come from 1 other state; 3% Black or African American, non-Hispanic/Latino; 2% Hispanic/Latino; 0.2% Asian, non-Hispanic/Latino; 0.1% American Indian or Alaska Native, non-Hispanic/Latino; 0.1% Race/ethnicity unknown.

Freshmen *Admission:* 334 applied, 334 admitted.

Faculty *Total:* 126, 10% full-time, 7% with terminal degrees. *Student/faculty ratio:* 28:1.

Academics *Calendar:* quarters. *Degrees:* diplomas, associate, and bachelor's. *Special study options:* academic remediation for entering students, accelerated degree program, advanced placement credit, cooperative education, distance learning, double majors, external degree program, independent study, internships, part-time degree program, services for LD students, summer session for credit.

Computers on Campus 165 computers/terminals are available on campus for general student use. Students can access the following: online (class) registration, software. Campuswide network is available.

Student Life *Housing:* college housing not available. *Activities and organizations:* Travel Club, Student Association Dental Hygienists of America. *Campus security:* 24-hour emergency response devices, late-night transport/escort service. *Student services:* personal/psychological counseling.

Standardized Tests *Recommended:* SAT or ACT (for admission).

Costs (2013–14) *Tuition:* $7920 full-time, $220 per quarter hour part-time. Full-time tuition and fees vary according to program. Part-time tuition and fees vary according to program. *Waivers:* employees or children of employees.
Applying *Options:* early admission, deferred entrance. *Application fee:* $20. *Required:* high school transcript, interview. *Application deadlines:* 9/24 (freshmen), rolling (transfers). *Notification:* continuous (freshmen), continuous (transfers).
Freshman Application Contact Mr. Daniel Kenny, Vice President for Admissions, Baker College of Port Huron, 3403 Lapeer Road, Port Huron, MI 48060-2597. *Phone:* 810-985-7000. *Toll-free phone:* 888-262-2442. *Fax:* 810-985-7066. *E-mail:* kenny_d@porthuron.baker.edu.
Website: http://www.baker.edu/.

Calvin College
Grand Rapids, Michigan

- **Independent Christian Reformed** comprehensive, founded 1876
- **Suburban** 400-acre campus with easy access to Grand Rapids
- **Endowment** $107.8 million
- **Coed** 3,930 undergraduate students, 96% full-time, 53% women, 47% men
- **Moderately difficult** entrance level, 75% of applicants were admitted

Undergraduates 3,763 full-time, 167 part-time. Students come from 48 states and territories; 56 other countries; 45% are from out of state; 3% Black or African American, non-Hispanic/Latino; 3% Hispanic/Latino; 4% Asian, non-Hispanic/Latino; 0.3% American Indian or Alaska Native, non-Hispanic/Latino; 2% Two or more races, non-Hispanic/Latino; 2% Race/ethnicity unknown; 10% international; 3% transferred in; 61% live on campus. *Retention:* 86% of full-time freshmen returned.
Freshmen *Admission:* 3,284 applied, 2,478 admitted, 977 enrolled. *Average high school GPA:* 3.67. *Test scores:* SAT critical reading scores over 500: 79%; SAT math scores over 500: 85%; ACT scores over 18: 99%; SAT critical reading scores over 600: 46%; SAT math scores over 600: 55%; ACT scores over 24: 76%; SAT critical reading scores over 700: 14%; SAT math scores over 700: 15%; ACT scores over 30: 25%.
Faculty *Total:* 394, 77% full-time, 69% with terminal degrees. *Student/faculty ratio:* 12:1.

Academics *Calendar:* 4-1-4. *Degrees:* bachelor's and master's. *Special study options:* academic remediation for entering students, accelerated degree program, advanced placement credit, distance learning, double majors, honors programs, independent study, internships, off-campus study, part-time degree program, services for LD students, student-designed majors, study abroad, summer session for credit. *ROTC:* Army (c). *Unusual degree programs:* 3-2 occupational therapy with Washington University in St. Louis.
Computers on Campus 1,025 computers/terminals and 2,656 ports are available on campus for general student use. Students can access the following: campus intranet, computer help desk, free student e-mail accounts, online (class) grades, online (class) registration, online (class) schedules. Campus-wide network is available. 100% of college-owned or -operated housing units are wired for high-speed Internet access. Wireless service is available via classrooms, computer centers, computer labs, dorm rooms, learning centers, libraries, student centers.
Student Life *Housing:* on-campus residence required through sophomore year. *Options:* men-only, women-only. Campus housing is university owned. Freshman campus housing is guaranteed. *Activities and organizations:* drama/theater group, student-run newspaper, choral group, Dance Guild, Airband (Lip-syncing contest), Chimes (Student Newspaper), International Reconciliation Organization, Knight Investment Management Organization. *Campus security:* 24-hour emergency response devices and patrols, student patrols, late-night transport/escort service, controlled dormitory access, crime prevention programs, crime alert bulletins. *Student services:* health clinic, personal/psychological counseling.
Athletics Member NCAA. All Division III. *Intercollegiate sports:* baseball M, basketball M/W, cross-country running M/W, equestrian sports M(c)/W(c), golf M/W, ice hockey M(c), lacrosse M/W, rugby M(c)/W(c), soccer M/W, softball W, swimming and diving M/W, tennis M/W, track and field M/W, ultimate Frisbee M(c)/W(c), volleyball M(c)/W. *Intramural sports:* badminton M/W, basketball M/W, cross-country running M/W, football M/W, golf M/W, racquetball M/W, rock climbing M/W, soccer M/W, softball M/W, swimming and diving M/W, tennis M/W, track and field M/W, volleyball M/W, water polo M/W.
Standardized Tests *Required for some:* SAT or ACT (for admission).
Costs (2013–14) *Comprehensive fee:* $37,585 includes full-time tuition ($28,025), mandatory fees ($225), and room and board ($9335). Full-time tuition and fees vary according to degree level and program. Part-time tuition: $670 per credit hour. Part-time tuition and fees vary according to course load and degree level. *Room and board:* Room and board charges vary according to

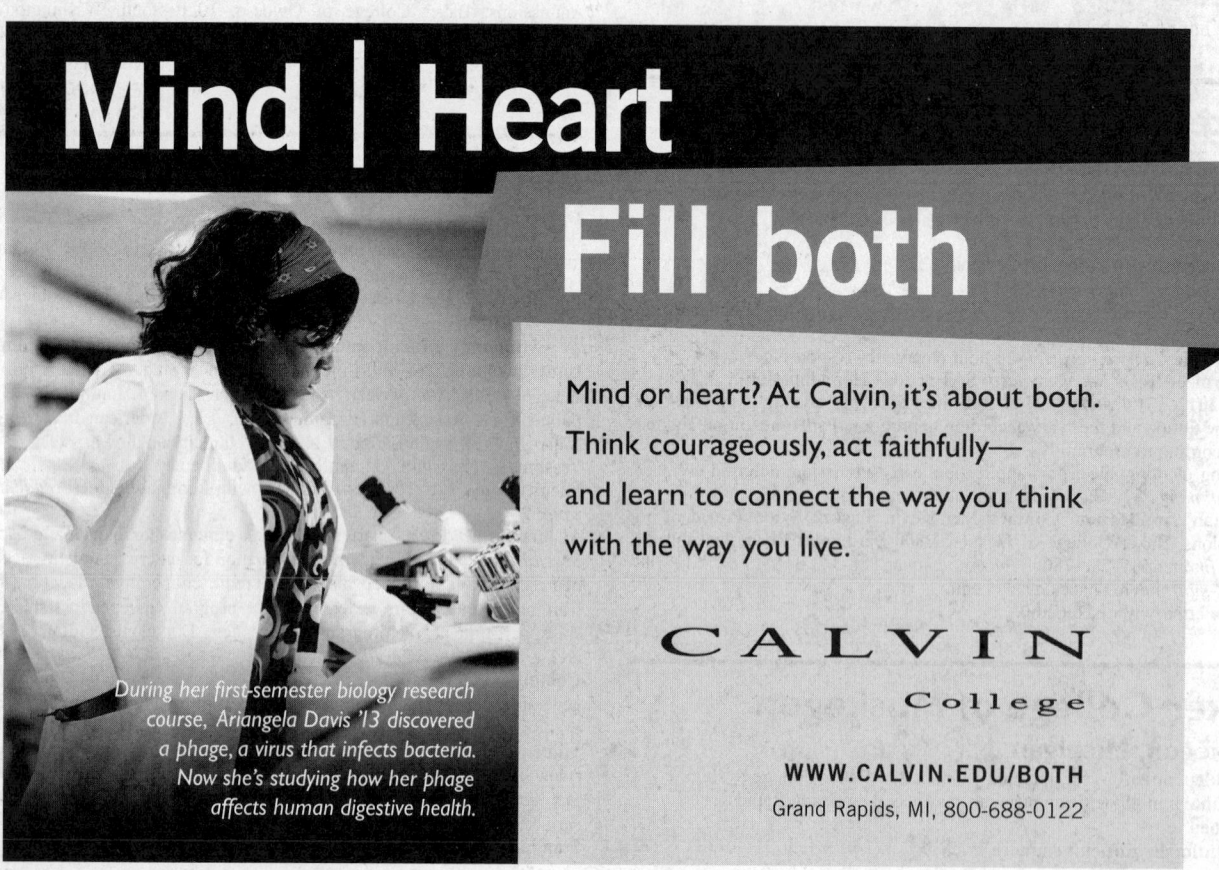

board plan and housing facility. *Payment plans:* tuition prepayment, installment. *Waivers:* employees or children of employees.

Financial Aid Of all full-time matriculated undergraduates who enrolled in 2012, 3,114 applied for aid, 2,436 were judged to have need, 394 had their need fully met. 1,241 Federal Work-Study jobs (averaging $1544). 977 state and other part-time jobs (averaging $1518). In 2012, 1129 non-need-based awards were made. *Average percent of need met:* 70%. *Average financial aid package:* $19,642. *Average need-based loan:* $6740. *Average need-based gift aid:* $12,967. *Average non-need-based aid:* $6573. *Average indebtedness upon graduation:* $32,957.

Applying *Options:* electronic application, deferred entrance. *Application fee:* $35. *Required:* essay or personal statement, high school transcript, minimum 2.5 GPA, 1 letter of recommendation. *Recommended:* interview. *Application deadlines:* 8/15 (freshmen), rolling (transfers). *Notification:* continuous (freshmen).

Freshman Application Contact Mr. Ben Arendt, Director of Admissions, Calvin College, 3201 Burton Street, SE, Grand Rapids, MI 49546. *Phone:* 616-526-6106. *Toll-free phone:* 800-688-0122. *Fax:* 616-526-6777. *E-mail:* admissions@calvin.edu.
Website: http://www.calvin.edu/.

See previous page for display ad and page 1222 for the College Close-Up.

Central Michigan University

Mount Pleasant, Michigan

- **State-supported** university, founded 1892
- **Small-town** 854-acre campus
- **Endowment** $81.2 million
- **Coed** 21,332 undergraduate students, 87% full-time, 56% women, 44% men
- **Moderately difficult** entrance level, 64% of applicants were admitted

Undergraduates 18,564 full-time, 2,768 part-time. Students come from 50 states and territories; 55 other countries; 3% are from out of state; 7% Black or African American, non-Hispanic/Latino; 3% Hispanic/Latino; 0.9% Asian, non-Hispanic/Latino; 0.6% American Indian or Alaska Native, non-Hispanic/Latino; 1% Two or more races, non-Hispanic/Latino; 6% Race/ethnicity unknown; 2% international; 6% transferred in; 31% live on campus. *Retention:* 75% of full-time freshmen returned.

Freshmen *Admission:* 17,769 applied, 11,333 admitted, 3,417 enrolled. *Average high school GPA:* 3.33. *Test scores:* SAT critical reading scores over 500: 49%; SAT math scores over 500: 57%; ACT scores over 18: 94%; SAT critical reading scores over 600: 18%; SAT math scores over 600: 20%; ACT scores over 24: 35%; SAT critical reading scores over 700: 1%; SAT math scores over 700: 4%; ACT scores over 30: 4%.

Faculty *Total:* 1,113, 69% full-time, 65% with terminal degrees. *Student/faculty ratio:* 22:1.

Academics *Calendar:* semesters. *Degrees:* bachelor's, master's, doctoral, post-master's, and postbachelor's certificates. *Special study options:* academic remediation for entering students, accelerated degree program, adult/continuing education programs, advanced placement credit, distance learning, double majors, English as a second language, freshman honors college, honors programs, independent study, internships, off-campus study, part-time degree program, services for LD students, student-designed majors, study abroad, summer session for credit. *ROTC:* Army (b), Air Force (c). *Unusual degree programs:* 3-2 apparel product development and merchandising technology; computer science; economics; experimental psychology; geographic information science; human development and family studies; mathematics; political science.

Computers on Campus 3,000 computers/terminals and 10,000 ports are available on campus for general student use. Students can access the following: campus intranet, computer help desk, free student e-mail accounts, online (class) grades, online (class) registration, online (class) schedules, Blackboard. Campuswide network is available. 100% of college-owned or -operated housing units are wired for high-speed Internet access. Wireless service is available via entire campus.

Student Life *Housing:* on-campus residence required for freshman year. *Options:* coed, men-only, women-only, disabled students. Campus housing is university owned. Freshman campus housing is guaranteed. *Activities and organizations:* drama/theater group, student-run newspaper, radio and television station, choral group, marching band, Residence Hall Assembly, Student Government Association, High Adventure Club, Fellowship of Christian Athletes, College Republicans, national fraternities, national sororities. *Campus security:* 24-hour emergency response devices and patrols, student patrols, late-night transport/escort service, controlled dormitory access. *Student services:* health clinic, personal/psychological counseling, women's center, legal services.

Athletics Member NCAA. All Division I except football (Division I-A). *Intercollegiate sports:* baseball M(s), basketball M(s)/W(s), cross-country running M(s)/W(s), field hockey W(s), gymnastics W(s), soccer W(s), softball W(s), track and field M(s)/W(s), volleyball W(s), wrestling M(s). *Intramural sports:* archery M/W, baseball M(c), basketball M/W, bowling M/W, cheerleading W(c), cross-country running M/W, equestrian sports M(c)/W(c), football M/W, golf M(c)/W(c), ice hockey M(c)/W(c), lacrosse M(c)/W(c), racquetball M/W, rugby M(c)/W(c), skiing (downhill) M(c)/W(c), soccer M(c)/W(c), softball M/W, swimming and diving M(c)/W(c), table tennis M(c)/W(c), tennis M(c)/W(c), ultimate Frisbee M(c)/W(c), volleyball M(c)/W(c), water polo M(c)/W(c), weight lifting M(c)/W(c), wrestling M.

Standardized Tests *Required:* SAT or ACT (for admission). *Recommended:* ACT (for admission).

Costs (2012–13) *Tuition:* state resident $10,950 full-time, $365 per credit hour part-time; nonresident $23,670 full-time, $789 per credit hour part-time. Full-time tuition and fees vary according to location. Part-time tuition and fees vary according to location. *Room and board:* $8368; room only: $4184. Room and board charges vary according to board plan, housing facility, location, and student level. *Payment plan:* installment. *Waivers:* children of alumni, senior citizens, and employees or children of employees.

Financial Aid Of all full-time matriculated undergraduates who enrolled in 2012, 14,712 applied for aid, 11,539 were judged to have need, 6,661 had their need fully met. 902 Federal Work-Study jobs (averaging $1382). 4,302 state and other part-time jobs (averaging $2477). In 2012, 1509 non-need-based awards were made. *Average percent of need met:* 85%. *Average financial aid package:* $11,867. *Average need-based loan:* $6791. *Average need-based gift aid:* $5869. *Average non-need-based aid:* $4045. *Average indebtedness upon graduation:* $31,520.

Applying *Options:* electronic application, early admission, early action, deferred entrance. *Application fee:* $35. *Required:* high school transcript. *Required for some:* essay or personal statement, interview. *Application deadlines:* rolling (freshmen), rolling (transfers). *Notification:* continuous (freshmen), continuous (transfers).

Freshman Application Contact Central Michigan University, Mount Pleasant, MI 48859. *Phone:* 989-774-1169. *Toll-free phone:* 888-292-5366. *Website:* http://www.cmich.edu/.

Cleary University

Ann Arbor, Michigan

- **Independent** comprehensive, founded 1883
- **Suburban** 32-acre campus with easy access to Detroit, Ann Arbor
- **Endowment** $998,704
- **Coed** 618 undergraduate students, 43% full-time, 57% women, 43% men
- **Moderately difficult** entrance level, 48% of applicants were admitted

Undergraduates 268 full-time, 350 part-time. Students come from 11 states and territories; 2% are from out of state; 7% Black or African American, non-Hispanic/Latino; 1% Hispanic/Latino; 1% Asian, non-Hispanic/Latino; 0.2% American Indian or Alaska Native, non-Hispanic/Latino; 11% Race/ethnicity unknown; 14% transferred in. *Retention:* 75% of full-time freshmen returned.

Freshmen *Admission:* 81 applied, 39 admitted, 30 enrolled. *Test scores:* ACT scores over 18: 77%; ACT scores over 24: 27%.

Faculty *Total:* 78, 15% with terminal degrees. *Student/faculty ratio:* 15:1.

Academics *Calendar:* quarters. *Degrees:* certificates, associate, bachelor's, and master's. *Special study options:* accelerated degree program, adult/continuing education programs, advanced placement credit, cooperative education, distance learning, double majors, honors programs, independent study, internships, off-campus study, part-time degree program, summer session for credit.

Computers on Campus 26 computers/terminals are available on campus for general student use. Students can access the following: free student e-mail accounts, online (class) grades, online (class) schedules. Campuswide network is available. Wireless service is available via entire campus.

Student Life *Housing:* college housing not available. *Activities and organizations:* Cleary Professional Accounting Associates, Human Resources & Organizational Leadership Association, Event and Meeting Planning Student Association, Veterans Club, Accounting/Fraud Examiners Club. *Campus security:* 24-hour emergency response devices, access to facilities limited to authorized persons. *Student services:* personal/psychological counseling.

Athletics Member USCAA. *Intercollegiate sports:* cross-country running M(s)/W(s), golf M(s)/W(s).

Standardized Tests *Required:* SAT or ACT (for admission). *Required for some:* SAT Subject Tests (for admission).

Financial Aid Of all full-time matriculated undergraduates who enrolled in 2009, 391 applied for aid, 391 were judged to have need, 13 had their need fully met. In 2009, 60 non-need-based awards were made. *Average percent of* *need met:* 42%. *Average financial aid package:* $12,759. *Average need-based loan:* $1193. *Average need-based gift aid:* $1265. *Average non-need-based aid:* $2258. *Average indebtedness upon graduation:* $20,830. *Financial aid deadline:* 7/1.

Applying *Options:* electronic application, early admission, deferred entrance. *Application fee:* $25. *Required:* high school transcript, minimum 2.5 GPA. *Required for some:* essay or personal statement, First-Time/First Year Students: minimum ACT score of 19. Minimum high school GPA of 2.0 required for non-traditional and transfer students. *Recommended:* interview. *Application deadlines:* 7/15 (freshmen), 7/15 (out-of-state freshmen), 7/15 (transfers).

Freshman Application Contact Carrie Bonofiglio, Director of Admissions, Cleary University, 3750 Cleary Drive, Howell, MI 48843. *Phone:* 800-686-1883. *Toll-free phone:* 800-686-1883. *Fax:* 517-338-3336. *E-mail:* admissions@cleary.edu.
Website: http://www.cleary.edu/.

College for Creative Studies

Detroit, Michigan

- **Independent** comprehensive, founded 1926
- **Urban** 11-acre campus
- **Coed** 1,386 undergraduate students, 80% full-time, 51% women, 49% men
- **Moderately difficult** entrance level, 45% of applicants were admitted

Undergraduates 1,109 full-time, 277 part-time. 17% are from out of state; 8% Black or African American, non-Hispanic/Latino; 5% Hispanic/Latino; 5% Asian, non-Hispanic/Latino; 0.1% Native Hawaiian or other Pacific Islander, non-Hispanic/Latino; 0.4% American Indian or Alaska Native, non-Hispanic/Latino; 3% Two or more races, non-Hispanic/Latino; 14% Race/ethnicity unknown; 6% international; 11% transferred in; 29% live on campus. *Retention:* 76% of full-time freshmen returned.

Freshmen *Admission:* 1,615 applied, 720 admitted, 305 enrolled. *Average high school GPA:* 3.18.

Faculty *Total:* 252, 19% full-time. *Student/faculty ratio:* 11:1.

Academics *Calendar:* semesters. *Degrees:* bachelor's, master's, and postbachelor's certificates. *Special study options:* part-time degree program.

Computers on Campus Campuswide network is available.

Student Life *Housing options:* coed. Campus housing is university owned. *Campus security:* 24-hour patrols, late-night transport/escort service, controlled dormitory access.

Standardized Tests *Required:* SAT or ACT (for admission).

Costs (2013–14) *Comprehensive fee:* $43,760 includes full-time tuition ($34,320), mandatory fees ($1390), and room and board ($8050). Part-time tuition: $1144 per credit hour. *College room only:* $5150.

Applying *Options:* electronic application, deferred entrance. *Application fee:* $35. *Required:* essay or personal statement, high school transcript, portfolio. *Required for some:* interview. *Recommended:* minimum 2.5 GPA. *Application deadlines:* 7/1 (freshmen), rolling (transfers). *Notification:* continuous (freshmen).

Freshman Application Contact Office of Admissions, College for Creative Studies, 201 East Kirby, Detroit, MI 48202-4034. *Phone:* 800-952-2787. *Toll-free phone:* 800-952-ARTS. *Fax:* 313-872-2739. *E-mail:* admissions@collegeforcreativestudies.edu.
Website: http://www.collegeforcreativestudies.edu/.

Concordia University Ann Arbor

Ann Arbor, Michigan

- **Independent** comprehensive, founded 1963, affiliated with Lutheran Church–Missouri Synod, part of Concordia University System
- **Suburban** 187-acre campus with easy access to Detroit
- **Endowment** $7.6 million
- **Coed**
- **Moderately difficult** entrance level

Faculty *Student/faculty ratio:* 11:1.

Academics *Calendar:* semesters. *Degrees:* associate, bachelor's, master's, and postbachelor's certificates.

Student Life *Campus security:* 24-hour emergency response devices and patrols, late-night transport/escort service, controlled dormitory access.

Athletics Member NAIA.

Standardized Tests *Required:* SAT or ACT (for admission). *Recommended:* ACT (for admission).

Costs (2012–13) *Comprehensive fee:* $30,762 includes full-time tuition ($22,464) and room and board ($8298). Full-time tuition and fees vary according to location and program. Part-time tuition: $936 per credit hour. Part-time tuition and fees vary according to course load, location, and program. *Room and board:* Room and board charges vary according to housing facility.

Financial Aid *Of all full-time matriculated undergraduates who enrolled in 2010,* 392 applied for aid, 336 were judged to have need, 79 had their need fully met. 112 Federal Work-Study jobs (averaging $803). 68 state and other part-time jobs (averaging $1169). *In 2010,* 76 non-need-based awards were made. *Average percent of need met:* 74. *Average financial aid package:* $16,032. *Average need-based loan:* $4636. *Average need-based gift aid:* $12,065. *Average non-need-based aid:* $6821. *Average indebtedness upon graduation:* $17,032.

Applying *Options:* electronic application, deferred entrance. *Application fee:* $25. *Required:* high school transcript. *Required for some:* essay or personal statement, 1 letter of recommendation, interview. *Recommended:* minimum 2.5 GPA.

Freshman Application Contact Mr. Ben Limback, Director of Admissions, Concordia University Ann Arbor, 4090 Geddes Road, Ann Arbor, MI 48105-2797. *Phone:* 734-995-7311. *Toll-free phone:* 877-995-7520 (in-state); 877-955-7520 (out-of-state). *Fax:* 734-995-4610. *E-mail:* admissions@cuaa.edu.
Website: http://www.cuaa.edu/.

Cornerstone University

Grand Rapids, Michigan

- **Independent nondenominational** comprehensive, founded 1941
- **Suburban** 132-acre campus
- **Endowment** $6.6 million
- **Coed** 2,125 undergraduate students, 80% full-time, 62% women, 38% men
- **Minimally difficult** entrance level, 63% of applicants were admitted

Undergraduates 1,693 full-time, 432 part-time. Students come from 34 states and territories; 12 other countries; 22% are from out of state; 10% Black or African American, non-Hispanic/Latino; 4% Hispanic/Latino; 0.3% Asian, non-Hispanic/Latino; 0.6% American Indian or Alaska Native, non-Hispanic/Latino; 1% Two or more races, non-Hispanic/Latino; 1% international; 3% transferred in; 62% live on campus. *Retention:* 74% of full-time freshmen returned.

Freshmen *Admission:* 2,062 applied, 1,293 admitted, 343 enrolled. *Average high school GPA:* 3.5. *Test scores:* SAT critical reading scores over 500: 79%; SAT math scores over 500: 70%; SAT writing scores over 500: 83%; ACT scores over 18: 96%; SAT critical reading scores over 600: 37%; SAT math scores over 600: 45%; SAT writing scores over 600: 28%; ACT scores over 24: 50%; SAT critical reading scores over 700: 9%; SAT math scores over 700: 6%; SAT writing scores over 700: 3%; ACT scores over 30: 10%.

Faculty *Total:* 114, 46% full-time, 32% with terminal degrees. *Student/faculty ratio:* 24:1.

Academics *Calendar:* semesters. *Degrees:* diplomas, associate, bachelor's, and master's. *Special study options:* academic remediation for entering students, accelerated degree program, adult/continuing education programs, advanced placement credit, distance learning, double majors, English as a second language, honors programs, independent study, internships, off-campus study, part-time degree program, services for LD students, study abroad, summer session for credit. *ROTC:* Army (c).

Computers on Campus 1,300 computers/terminals are available on campus for general student use. Students can access the following: campus intranet, computer help desk, free student e-mail accounts, online (class) grades, online (class) registration, online (class) schedules. Campuswide network is available. 100% of college-owned or -operated housing units are wired for high-speed Internet access. Wireless service is available via entire campus.

Student Life *Housing:* on-campus residence required through sophomore year. *Options:* men-only, women-only, disabled students. Campus housing is university owned. Freshman campus housing is guaranteed. *Activities and organizations:* drama/theater group, student-run newspaper, choral group, student government, Student Education Association, Breakpoint, Student Activities Council, International Justice Mission. *Campus security:* 24-hour emergency response devices and patrols, student patrols, late-night transport/escort service, controlled dormitory access. *Student services:* health clinic, personal/psychological counseling.

Athletics Member NAIA. *Intercollegiate sports:* baseball M(s), basketball M(s)/W(s), cheerleading W(s), cross-country running M(s)/W(s), golf M(s)/W, soccer M(s)/W(s), softball W(s), track and field M(s)/W(s), volleyball W(s). *Intramural sports:* basketball M/W, football M, soccer M/W, softball M/W, volleyball M/W.

Standardized Tests *Required:* SAT or ACT (for admission).

Costs (2013–14) *Comprehensive fee:* $32,078 includes full-time tuition ($23,598), mandatory fees ($570), and room and board ($7910). Full-time tuition and fees vary according to course load and reciprocity agreements. Part-time tuition: $905 per credit. Part-time tuition and fees vary according to course load. *Required fees:* $185 per term part-time. *Room and board:* Room and board charges vary according to board plan and housing facility. *Payment plan:* installment. *Waivers:* employees or children of employees.

Financial Aid Of all full-time matriculated undergraduates who enrolled in 2012, 1,118 applied for aid, 1,031 were judged to have need, 156 had their need fully met. 242 Federal Work-Study jobs (averaging $1213). In 2012, 133 non-need-based awards were made. *Average percent of need met:* 69%. *Average financial aid package:* $18,938. *Average need-based loan:* $4652. *Average need-based gift aid:* $14,649. *Average non-need-based aid:* $8441. *Average indebtedness upon graduation:* $32,071.

Applying *Options:* electronic application, deferred entrance. *Application fee:* $25. *Required:* essay or personal statement, high school transcript, minimum 2.5 GPA, 1 letter of recommendation, pastoral letter. *Recommended:* interview. *Application deadlines:* rolling (freshmen), rolling (transfers). *Notification:* continuous (freshmen), continuous (transfers).

Freshman Application Contact Mrs. Lisa Link, Office of Admissions, Cornerstone University, 1001 East Beltline Avenue, NE, Grand Rapids, MI 49525. *Phone:* 616-222-1426. *Toll-free phone:* 800-787-9778. *Fax:* 616-222-1400. *E-mail:* admissions@cornerstone.edu. *Website:* http://www.cornerstone.edu/.

Davenport University

Grand Rapids, Michigan

- **Independent** comprehensive, founded 1866
- **Suburban** campus
- **Endowment** $16.2 million
- **Coed** 8,882 undergraduate students, 27% full-time, 63% women, 37% men
- **Minimally difficult** entrance level, 95% of applicants were admitted

Undergraduates 2,425 full-time, 6,457 part-time. Students come from 53 states and territories; 32 other countries; 2% are from out of state; 19% Black or African American, non-Hispanic/Latino; 2% Hispanic/Latino; 2% Asian, non-Hispanic/Latino; 0.1% Native Hawaiian or other Pacific Islander, non-Hispanic/Latino; 0.4% American Indian or Alaska Native, non-Hispanic/Latino; 2% Two or more races, non-Hispanic/Latino; 19% Race/ethnicity unknown; 2% international; 11% transferred in; 4% live on campus. *Retention:* 69% of full-time freshmen returned.

Freshmen *Admission:* 1,324 applied, 1,255 admitted, 728 enrolled.

Faculty *Total:* 982, 16% full-time, 23% with terminal degrees. *Student/faculty ratio:* 14:1.

Academics *Calendar:* semesters. *Degrees:* diplomas, associate, bachelor's, master's, post-master's, and postbachelor's certificates. *Special study options:* academic remediation for entering students, accelerated degree program, adult/continuing education programs, advanced placement credit, cooperative education, distance learning, English as a second language, independent study, internships, part-time degree program, services for LD students, study abroad, summer session for credit.

Computers on Campus 3,098 computers/terminals are available on campus for general student use. Students can access the following: campus intranet, computer help desk, free student e-mail accounts, online (class) grades, online (class) registration, online (class) schedules. Campuswide network is available. 100% of college-owned or -operated housing units are wired for high-speed Internet access. Wireless service is available via entire campus.

Student Life *Housing options:* coed. Campus housing is university owned. Freshman applicants given priority for college housing. *Activities and organizations:* student-run newspaper, Business Professionals of America, Delta Epsilon Chi, Student government, Health Occupations Students of America, Connect. *Campus security:* 24-hour emergency response devices and patrols, late-night transport/escort service, controlled dormitory access. *Student services:* personal/psychological counseling.

Athletics Member NAIA. *Intercollegiate sports:* baseball M(s), basketball M(s)/W(s), bowling M(s)/W(s), cheerleading W(s), cross-country running M(s)/W(s), golf M(s)/W(s), ice hockey M(s)/W(s), lacrosse M(s)/W(s), rugby M(s)/W(s), soccer M(s)/W(s), softball M(s)/W(s), tennis M(s)/W(s), track and field M(s)/W(s), volleyball W(s).

Standardized Tests *Recommended:* SAT or ACT (for admission).

Costs (2012–13) *Comprehensive fee:* $21,456 includes full-time tuition ($12,672), mandatory fees ($350), and room and board ($8434). Full-time tuition and fees vary according to location and program. Part-time tuition: $528 per credit hour. Part-time tuition and fees vary according to location and program. *Room and board:* Room and board charges vary according to board plan and housing facility. *Payment plan:* installment. *Waivers:* employees or children of employees.

Applying *Options:* electronic application, deferred entrance. *Application fee:* $25. *Required:* high school transcript. *Recommended:* interview. *Application deadlines:* rolling (freshmen), rolling (out-of-state freshmen), rolling (transfers). *Notification:* continuous (freshmen), continuous (out-of-state freshmen), continuous (transfers).

Freshman Application Contact Mr. Daryl Kingrey, Executive Director of Admissions, Davenport University, 6191 Kraft Avenue SE, Grand Rapids, MI 49512. *Phone:* 616-451-3511. *Toll-free phone:* 800-925-3884 (in-state); 866-925-3884 (out-of-state). *E-mail:* daryl.kingrey@davenport.edu. *Website:* http://www.davenport.edu/.

DeVry University

Southfield, Michigan

Freshman Application Contact DeVry University, 26999 Central Park Boulevard, Suite 125, Southfield, MI 48076. *Toll-free phone:* 866-338-7941. *Website:* http://www.devry.edu/.

Eastern Michigan University

Ypsilanti, Michigan

- **State-supported** comprehensive, founded 1849
- **Suburban** 460-acre campus with easy access to Detroit
- **Endowment** $51.4 million
- **Coed** 18,914 undergraduate students, 70% full-time, 58% women, 42% men
- **Moderately difficult** entrance level, 65% of applicants were admitted

Undergraduates 13,178 full-time, 5,736 part-time. Students come from 45 states and territories; 26 other countries; 8% are from out of state; 22% Black or African American, non-Hispanic/Latino; 3% Hispanic/Latino; 2% Asian, non-Hispanic/Latino; 0.1% Native Hawaiian or other Pacific Islander, non-Hispanic/Latino; 0.4% American Indian or Alaska Native, non-Hispanic/Latino; 2% Two or more races, non-Hispanic/Latino; 5% Race/ethnicity unknown; 2% international; 11% transferred in; 22% live on campus. *Retention:* 75% of full-time freshmen returned.

Freshmen *Admission:* 11,538 applied, 7,513 admitted, 2,646 enrolled. *Average high school GPA:* 3.18. *Test scores:* SAT critical reading scores over 500: 56%; SAT math scores over 500: 61%; SAT writing scores over 500: 45%; ACT scores over 18: 84%; SAT critical reading scores over 600: 16%; SAT math scores over 600: 19%; SAT writing scores over 600: 13%; ACT scores over 24: 29%; SAT critical reading scores over 700: 2%; SAT math scores over 700: 4%; SAT writing scores over 700: 1%; ACT scores over 30: 3%.

Faculty *Total:* 1,226, 62% full-time, 57% with terminal degrees. *Student/faculty ratio:* 19:1.

Academics *Calendar:* semesters. *Degrees:* bachelor's, master's, doctoral, post-master's, and postbachelor's certificates. *Special study options:* academic remediation for entering students, accelerated degree program, advanced placement credit, cooperative education, distance learning, double majors, English as a second language, external degree program, honors programs, independent study, internships, part-time degree program, services for LD students, student-designed majors, study abroad, summer session for credit. *ROTC:* Army (b), Navy (c), Air Force (c). *Unusual degree programs:* accounting, occupational therapy.

Computers on Campus 1,600 computers/terminals and 200 ports are available on campus for general student use. Students can access the following: campus intranet, computer help desk, free student e-mail accounts, online (class) grades, online (class) registration, online (class) schedules, Wireless internet connections are available for all students. Campuswide network is available. 100% of college-owned or -operated housing units are wired for high-speed Internet access. Wireless service is available via entire campus.

Student Life *Housing:* on-campus residence required through sophomore year. *Options:* coed, disabled students. Campus housing is university owned. *Activities and organizations:* drama/theater group, student-run newspaper, radio and television station, choral group, marching band, International Student Association, Golden Key International Honor Society, Psychology Club, Indian Student Association, GREEN (Gathering Resources to Educate about our Environment and Nature), national fraternities, national sororities. *Campus security:* 24-hour emergency response devices and patrols, student patrols, late-night transport/escort service, controlled dormitory access, bicycle patrols, local police in dormitories, self-defense education, lighted pathways, bike lock lease program. *Student services:* health clinic, personal/psychological counseling, women's center, legal services.

Athletics Member NCAA. All Division I except football (Division I-A). *Intercollegiate sports:* baseball M(s), basketball M(s)/W(s), crew W(s), cross-country running M(s)/W(s), golf M(s)/W(s), gymnastics W(s), soccer W(s), softball W(s), swimming and diving M(s)/W(s), tennis W(s), track and field M(s)/W(s), volleyball W(s), wrestling M(s). *Intramural sports:* badminton M/W, basketball M/W, bowling M/W, cross-country running M/W, golf M/W, ice hockey M(c), racquetball M/W, soccer M/W, softball M/W, swimming and diving M/W, table tennis M/W, track and field M/W, ultimate Frisbee M(c)/W(c), volleyball M/W, weight lifting M(c)/W(c).

Standardized Tests *Required:* SAT or ACT (for admission).

Costs (2012–13) *One-time required fee:* $300. *Tuition:* state resident $7701 full-time, $257 per credit hour part-time; nonresident $22,683 full-time, $756 per credit hour part-time. Full-time tuition and fees vary according to course level and reciprocity agreements. Part-time tuition and fees vary according to course level and reciprocity agreements. *Required fees:* $1325 full-time, $41 per credit hour part-time, $48 per term part-time. *Room and board:* $8286; room only: $3952. Room and board charges vary according to board plan, housing facility, and location. *Payment plan:* installment. *Waivers:* employees or children of employees.

Financial Aid Of all full-time matriculated undergraduates who enrolled in 2011, 10,505 applied for aid, 9,294 were judged to have need, 126 had their need fully met. 808 Federal Work-Study jobs (averaging $1474). In 2011, 1368 non-need-based awards were made. *Average percent of need met:* 64%. *Average financial aid package:* $8751. *Average need-based loan:* $4116. *Average need-based gift aid:* $4348. *Average non-need-based aid:* $4559. *Average indebtedness upon graduation:* $25,133.

Applying *Options:* electronic application, deferred entrance. *Application fee:* $30. *Required:* high school transcript, minimum 2.0 GPA. *Required for some:* 1 letter of recommendation, interview. *Application deadlines:* rolling (freshmen), rolling (out-of-state freshmen), rolling (transfers). *Notification:* continuous (freshmen), continuous (out-of-state freshmen), continuous (transfers).

Freshman Application Contact Eastern Michigan University, Ypsilanti, MI 48197. *Phone:* 734-487-3060. *Toll-free phone:* 800-GO TO EMU. *Website:* http://www.emich.edu/.

Ferris State University

Big Rapids, Michigan

- **State-supported** comprehensive, founded 1884
- **Small-town** 941-acre campus with easy access to Grand Rapids
- **Endowment** $35.2 million
- **Coed** 13,261 undergraduate students, 71% full-time, 51% women, 49% men
- **Minimally difficult** entrance level, 71% of applicants were admitted

Undergraduates 9,366 full-time, 3,895 part-time. Students come from 48 states and territories; 30 other countries; 5% are from out of state; 7% Black or African American, non-Hispanic/Latino; 3% Hispanic/Latino; 2% Asian, non-Hispanic/Latino; 0.1% Native Hawaiian or other Pacific Islander, non-Hispanic/Latino; 0.5% American Indian or Alaska Native, non-Hispanic/Latino; 2% Two or more races, non-Hispanic/Latino; 4% Race/ethnicity unknown; 2% international; 10% transferred in; 28% live on campus. *Retention:* 70% of full-time freshmen returned.

Freshmen *Admission:* 9,457 applied, 6,709 admitted, 2,139 enrolled. *Average high school GPA:* 3.2. *Test scores:* ACT scores over 18: 84%; ACT scores over 24: 32%; ACT scores over 30: 5%.

Faculty *Total:* 969, 59% full-time, 31% with terminal degrees. *Student/faculty ratio:* 16:1.

Academics *Calendar:* semesters. *Degrees:* certificates, associate, bachelor's, master's, doctoral, and postbachelor's certificates (associate degree). *Special study options:* academic remediation for entering students, accelerated degree program, adult/continuing education programs, advanced placement credit, cooperative education, distance learning, double majors, English as a second language, external degree program, freshman honors college, honors programs, independent study, internships, off-campus study, part-time degree program, services for LD students, student-designed majors, study abroad, summer session for credit. *ROTC:* Army (c).

Computers on Campus 1,930 computers/terminals are available on campus for general student use. Students can access the following: campus intranet, computer help desk, free student e-mail accounts, online (class) grades, online (class) registration, online (class) schedules. Campuswide network is available. 100% of college-owned or -operated housing units are wired for high-speed Internet access. Wireless service is available via entire campus.

Student Life *Housing:* on-campus residence required through sophomore year. *Options:* coed, disabled students. Campus housing is university owned. Freshman campus housing is guaranteed. *Activities and organizations:* drama/theater group, student-run newspaper, radio and television station, choral group, Panhellenic Council, Interfraternal Council, Music Industry Management Association, Pre-Pharmacy Organization, Crafter's Anonymous, national fra-

ternities, national sororities. *Campus security:* 24-hour emergency response devices, student patrols, late-night transport/escort service, controlled dormitory access. *Student services:* health clinic, personal/psychological counseling.

Athletics Member NCAA. All Division II. *Intercollegiate sports:* basketball M(s)/W(s), cheerleading M/W, cross-country running M(s)/W(s), football M(s), golf M(s)/W(s), ice hockey M(s), soccer W(s), softball W(s), tennis M(s)/W(s), track and field M(s)/W(s), volleyball W(s). *Intramural sports:* basketball M/W, bowling M(c)/W(c), cheerleading M(c)/W(c), cross-country running M(c)/W(c), equestrian sports M(c)/W(c), football M/W, golf M(c)/W(c), ice hockey M/W, lacrosse M(c)/W(c), rugby M(c)/W(c), soccer M/W, softball M/W, table tennis M(c)/W(c), tennis M(c)/W(c), ultimate Frisbee M(c)/W(c), volleyball M(c)/W(c).

Standardized Tests *Required:* SAT or ACT (for admission).

Costs (2012–13) *One-time required fee:* $162. *Tuition:* state resident $10,710 full-time, $357 per credit hour part-time; nonresident $16,080 full-time, $536 per credit hour part-time. Full-time tuition and fees vary according to location and program. Part-time tuition and fees vary according to location. *Room and board:* $8744. Room and board charges vary according to board plan and housing facility. *Payment plan:* deferred payment. *Waivers:* employees or children of employees.

Financial Aid Of all full-time matriculated undergraduates who enrolled in 2012, 8,526 applied for aid, 7,009 were judged to have need, 896 had their need fully met. 481 Federal Work-Study jobs (averaging $2293). 270 state and other part-time jobs (averaging $1610). In 2012, 957 non-need-based awards were made. *Average percent of need met:* 61%. *Average financial aid package:* $10,495. *Average need-based loan:* $4560. *Average need-based gift aid:* $4645. *Average non-need-based aid:* $4465. *Average indebtedness upon graduation:* $36,930.

Applying *Options:* electronic application. *Application fee:* $30. *Required:* high school transcript, minimum 2.5 GPA, SAT or ACT. *Application deadlines:* 8/1 (freshmen), 7/1 (transfers). *Notification:* continuous (freshmen), continuous (transfers).

Freshman Application Contact Mr. Jason Daday, Associate Director of Admissions, Ferris State University, 1201 South Street, CSS201, Big Rapids, MI 49307-2742. *Phone:* 231-591-3106. *Toll-free phone:* 800-433-7747. *Fax:* 231-591-2242. *E-mail:* dadayja@ferris.edu. *Website:* http://www.ferris.edu/.

Finlandia University

Hancock, Michigan

Freshman Application Contact Martin Kinard, Finlandia University, 601 Quincy Street, Hancock, MI 49930. *Phone:* 906-487-7352. *Toll-free phone:* 877-202-5491. *Fax:* 906-487-7383. *E-mail:* admissions@finlandia.edu. *Website:* http://www.finlandia.edu/.

Grace Bible College

Grand Rapids, Michigan

Freshman Application Contact Mr. Kevin Gilliam, Director of Enrollment, Grace Bible College, 1101 Aldon Street, SW, PO Box 910, Grand Rapids, MI 49509. *Phone:* 616-538-2330 Ext. 239. *Toll-free phone:* 800-968-1887. *Fax:* 616-538-0599. *E-mail:* gbc@gbcol.edu. *Website:* http://www.gbcol.edu/.

Grand Valley State University

Allendale, Michigan

- **State-supported** comprehensive, founded 1960
- **Small-town** 1337-acre campus with easy access to Grand Rapids
- **Endowment** $75.3 million
- **Coed** 21,317 undergraduate students, 88% full-time, 58% women, 42% men
- **Moderately difficult** entrance level, 82% of applicants were admitted

Undergraduates 18,663 full-time, 2,654 part-time. Students come from 39 states and territories; 73 other countries; 5% are from out of state; 5% Black or African American, non-Hispanic/Latino; 4% Hispanic/Latino; 2% Asian, non-Hispanic/Latino; 0.1% Native Hawaiian or other Pacific Islander, non-Hispanic/Latino; 0.4% American Indian or Alaska Native, non-Hispanic/Latino; 2% Two or more races, non-Hispanic/Latino; 0.7% Race/ethnicity unknown; 1% international; 8% transferred in; 27% live on campus. *Retention:* 82% of full-time freshmen returned.

Freshmen *Admission:* 17,880 applied, 14,596 admitted, 3,966 enrolled. *Average high school GPA:* 3.5. *Test scores:* ACT scores over 18: 96%; ACT scores over 24: 50%; ACT scores over 30: 6%.

Faculty *Total:* 1,678, 65% full-time, 53% with terminal degrees. *Student/faculty ratio:* 17:1.

Academics *Calendar:* semesters. *Degrees:* certificates, bachelor's, master's, doctoral, post-master's, and postbachelor's certificates. *Special study options:* academic remediation for entering students, accelerated degree program, adult/continuing education programs, advanced placement credit, cooperative education, distance learning, double majors, English as a second language, freshman honors college, honors programs, independent study, internships, part-time degree program, services for LD students, study abroad, summer session for credit.

Computers on Campus 2,600 computers/terminals are available on campus for general student use. Students can access the following: campus intranet, computer help desk, free student e-mail accounts, online (class) grades, online (class) registration, online (class) schedules, transcript, degree audit, credit card payments. Campuswide network is available. 100% of college-owned or -operated housing units are wired for high-speed Internet access. Wireless service is available via entire campus.

Student Life *Housing options:* coed. Campus housing is university owned. Freshman campus housing is guaranteed. *Activities and organizations:* drama/theater group, student-run newspaper, radio and television station, choral group, marching band, Habitat for Humanity, Alternative Breaks, Hospitality and tourism Management Club, Dance Troupe, Colleges Against Cancer, national fraternities, national sororities. *Campus security:* 24-hour emergency response devices and patrols, student patrols, late-night transport/escort service, controlled dormitory access. *Student services:* health clinic, personal/psychological counseling, women's center.

Athletics Member NCAA. All Division II. *Intercollegiate sports:* baseball M(s), basketball M(s)/W(s), cheerleading M(c)/W(c), crew M(c)/W(c), cross-country running M(s)/W(s), football M(s), golf M(s)/W(s), ice hockey M(c), lacrosse M(c)/W, rugby M(c)/W(c), sailing M(c)/W(c), skiing (downhill) M(c)/W(c), soccer M(c)/W(s), softball W(s), swimming and diving M(s)/W(s), tennis M(s)/W(s), track and field M(s)/W(s), volleyball M(c)/W(s), water polo M(c)/W(c), wrestling M(c). *Intramural sports:* archery M/W, badminton M/W, basketball M/W, bowling M/W, cheerleading M/W, crew M/W, cross-country running M/W, fencing M/W, field hockey M/W, football M/W, golf M/W, gymnastics M/W, lacrosse M/W, racquetball M/W, skiing (cross-country) M/W, skiing (downhill) M/W, soccer M/W, softball M/W, squash M/W, swimming and diving M/W, tennis M/W, volleyball M/W, water polo M/W, weight lifting M/W, wrestling M.

Standardized Tests *Required:* SAT or ACT (for admission).

Costs (2012–13) *Tuition:* state resident $10,078 full-time, $420 per credit hour part-time; nonresident $14,568 full-time, $607 per credit hour part-time. Full-time tuition and fees vary according to course level, degree level, program, and student level. Part-time tuition and fees vary according to course level, course load, degree level, program, and student level. *Room and board:* $7920; room only: $5400. Room and board charges vary according to board plan, housing facility, and location. *Payment plans:* installment, deferred payment. *Waivers:* employees or children of employees.

Financial Aid Of all full-time matriculated undergraduates who enrolled in 2012, 15,412 applied for aid, 12,340 were judged to have need, 1,365 had their need fully met. 2,041 Federal Work-Study jobs (averaging $2905). In 2012, 2270 non-need-based awards were made. *Average percent of need met:* 60%. *Average financial aid package:* $9226. *Average need-based loan:* $4486. *Average need-based gift aid:* $6133. *Average non-need-based aid:* $2440. *Average indebtedness upon graduation:* $28,728.

Applying *Options:* electronic application. *Application fee:* $30. *Required:* high school transcript. *Required for some:* essay or personal statement, interview. *Application deadlines:* 5/1 (freshmen), 7/24 (transfers). *Notification:* 5/1 (freshmen), continuous (transfers).

Freshman Application Contact Ms. Jodi Chycinski, Director of Admissions, Grand Valley State University, 1 Campus Drive, Allendale, MI 49401. *Phone:* 616-331-2025. *Toll-free phone:* 800-748-0246. *Fax:* 616-331-2000. *E-mail:* go2gvsu@gvsu.edu.

Website: http://www.gvsu.edu/.

Great Lakes Christian College
Lansing, Michigan

- **Independent** 4-year, founded 1949, affiliated with Christian Churches and Churches of Christ
- **Suburban** 47-acre campus
- **Endowment** $442,503
- **Coed**
- **Moderately difficult** entrance level

Faculty *Student/faculty ratio:* 14:1.

Academics *Calendar:* semesters. *Degrees:* associate and bachelor's.

Student Life *Campus security:* controlled dormitory access, evening security patrols.

Athletics Member NCCAA.

Standardized Tests *Required:* SAT or ACT (for admission).

Costs (2012–13) *One-time required fee:* $200. *Comprehensive fee:* $22,642 includes full-time tuition ($13,312), mandatory fees ($1330), and room and board ($8000). Part-time tuition: $416 per credit hour. *Room and board:* Room and board charges vary according to board plan and housing facility.

Applying *Options:* electronic application. *Application fee:* $30. *Required:* essay or personal statement, high school transcript, minimum 2.3 GPA, 3 letters of recommendation.

Freshman Application Contact Mrs. Judy Carter, Admissions Office Manager, Great Lakes Christian College, 6211 West Willow Highway, Lansing, MI 48917-1299. *Phone:* 517-321-0242 Ext. 221. *Toll-free phone:* 800-YES-GLCC. *Fax:* 517-321-5902. *E-mail:* jcarter@glcc.edu.
Website: http://www.glcc.edu/.

Griggs University
Berrien Springs, Michigan

Freshman Application Contact Ms. Linda Lundberg, Enrollment Officer, Griggs University, PO Box 4437, Silver Spring, MD 20914-4437. *Phone:* 301-680-6590. *Toll-free phone:* 800-782-4769. *Fax:* 301-680-6577. *E-mail:* LLundberg@griggs.edu.
Website: http://www.griggs.edu/college.html.

Hillsdale College
Hillsdale, Michigan

- **Independent** comprehensive, founded 1844
- **Small-town** 250-acre campus
- **Endowment** $350.0 million
- **Coed** 1,434 undergraduate students, 98% full-time, 53% women, 47% men
- **Very difficult** entrance level, 49% of applicants were admitted

Undergraduates 1,399 full-time, 35 part-time. Students come from 47 states and territories; 8 other countries; 64% are from out of state; 2% transferred in; 75% live on campus. *Retention:* 98% of full-time freshmen returned.

Freshmen *Admission:* 2,018 applied, 989 admitted, 388 enrolled. *Average high school GPA:* 3.75. *Test scores:* SAT critical reading scores over 500: 100%; SAT math scores over 500: 98%; SAT writing scores over 500: 100%; ACT scores over 18: 100%; SAT critical reading scores over 600: 90%; SAT math scores over 600: 73%; SAT writing scores over 600: 84%; ACT scores over 24: 96%; SAT critical reading scores over 700: 43%; SAT math scores over 700: 25%; SAT writing scores over 700: 40%; ACT scores over 30: 44%.

Faculty *Total:* 163, 72% full-time, 88% with terminal degrees. *Student/faculty ratio:* 10:1.

Academics *Calendar:* semesters. *Degrees:* bachelor's, master's, and doctoral. *Special study options:* accelerated degree program, advanced placement credit, double majors, honors programs, independent study, internships, off-campus study, part-time degree program, study abroad, summer session for credit. *Unusual degree programs:* 3-2 engineering with Northwestern University, Trine University.

Computers on Campus 220 computers/terminals are available on campus for general student use. Students can access the following: computer help desk, free student e-mail accounts, online (class) grades, online (class) registration, online (class) schedules. Campuswide network is available. 100% of college-owned or -operated housing units are wired for high-speed Internet access. Wireless service is available via entire campus.

Student Life *Housing:* on-campus residence required through sophomore year. *Options:* men-only, women-only. Campus housing is university owned. Freshman campus housing is guaranteed. *Activities and organizations:* drama/theater group, student-run newspaper, choral group, Inter-Varsity Christian Fellowship, Varsity H-Club, Student Federation, Young Life, College Republicans, national fraternities, national sororities. *Campus security:* 24-hour emergency response devices and patrols, late-night transport/escort service, controlled dormitory access. *Student services:* health clinic, personal/psychological counseling.

Athletics Member NCAA. All Division II. *Intercollegiate sports:* baseball M(s), basketball M(s)/W(s), cheerleading M/W, cross-country running M(s)/W(s), equestrian sports W, football M(s), riflery M(s)/W(s), rugby M(c), soccer M/W, softball W(s), swimming and diving W(s), tennis W(s), track and field M(s)/W(s), volleyball W(s). *Intramural sports:* basketball M/W, bowling M/W, equestrian sports W(c), football M/W, ice hockey M(c), racquetball M/W, riflery M(c)/W(c), skiing (downhill) M(c)/W(c), soccer M(c)/W(c), softball M/W, swimming and diving W, table tennis M/W, tennis M/W, track and field M/W, ultimate Frisbee M/W, volleyball M/W.

Standardized Tests *Required:* SAT or ACT (for admission). *Recommended:* SAT Subject Tests (for admission).

Costs (2013–14) *Comprehensive fee:* $31,890 includes full-time tuition ($22,250), mandatory fees ($640), and room and board ($9000). Part-time tuition: $880 per credit. College room only: $4460. Room and board charges vary according to board plan. *Payment plans:* tuition prepayment, installment. *Waivers:* children of alumni and employees or children of employees.

Financial Aid Of all full-time matriculated undergraduates who enrolled in 2010, 689 applied for aid, 617 were judged to have need, 248 had their need fully met. In 2010, 672 non-need-based awards were made. *Average percent of need met:* 70%. *Average financial aid package:* $17,800. *Average need-based loan:* $5950. *Average need-based gift aid:* $7860. *Average non-need-based aid:* $10,100. *Average indebtedness upon graduation:* $16,600. *Financial aid deadline:* 4/1.

Applying *Options:* electronic application, early admission, early decision, early action. *Required:* essay or personal statement, high school transcript, 2 letters of recommendation. *Required for some:* minimum 3.5 GPA, interview. *Recommended:* minimum 3.5 GPA, interview. *Application deadlines:* 2/15 (freshmen), 2/15 (out-of-state freshmen), 2/15 (transfers), 12/15 (early action). *Early decision deadline:* 11/15. *Notification:* 4/1 (freshmen), 4/1 (out-of-state freshmen), 4/1 (transfers), 12/1 (early decision), 2/15 (early action).

Freshman Application Contact Mr. Jeffrey S. Lantis, Director of Admissions, Hillsdale College, 33 East College Street, Hillsdale, MI 49242-1298. *Phone:* 517-607-2327. *Fax:* 517-607-2223. *E-mail:* admissions@hillsdale.edu.
Website: http://www.hillsdale.edu/.

See below for display ad and page 1322 for the College Close-Up.

Hope College
Holland, Michigan

- **Independent** 4-year, founded 1866, affiliated with Reformed Church in America
- **Suburban** 45-acre campus with easy access to Grand Rapids
- **Endowment** $150.9 million
- **Coed** 3,343 undergraduate students, 96% full-time, 60% women, 40% men
- **Moderately difficult** entrance level, 85% of applicants were admitted

Undergraduates 3,205 full-time, 138 part-time. Students come from 44 states and territories; 35 other countries; 31% are from out of state; 2% Black or African American, non-Hispanic/Latino; 6% Hispanic/Latino; 2% Asian, non-Hispanic/Latino; 0.1% American Indian or Alaska Native, non-Hispanic/Latino; 2% Two or more races, non-Hispanic/Latino; 2% international; 2% transferred in; 81% live on campus. *Retention:* 90% of full-time freshmen returned.

Freshmen *Admission:* 3,491 applied, 2,970 admitted, 889 enrolled. *Average high school GPA:* 3.77. *Test scores:* SAT critical reading scores over 500: 81%; SAT math scores over 500: 85%; ACT scores over 18: 99%; SAT critical reading scores over 600: 47%; SAT math scores over 600: 50%; ACT scores over 24: 74%; SAT critical reading scores over 700: 16%; SAT math scores over 700: 16%; ACT scores over 30: 22%.

Faculty *Total:* 329, 69% full-time. *Student/faculty ratio:* 12:1.

Academics *Calendar:* semesters. *Degree:* bachelor's. *Special study options:* advanced placement credit, double majors, English as a second language, independent study, internships, off-campus study, part-time degree program, services for LD students, student-designed majors, study abroad, summer session for credit. *ROTC:* Army (c).

Computers on Campus 300 computers/terminals and 5,000 ports are available on campus for general student use. Students can access the following: campus intranet, computer help desk, free student e-mail accounts, online (class) grades, online (class) registration, online (class) schedules. Campus-wide network is available. 100% of college-owned or -operated housing units

are wired for high-speed Internet access. Wireless service is available via entire campus.

Student Life *Housing:* on-campus residence required through junior year. *Options:* coed, men-only, women-only, disabled students. Campus housing is university owned and leased by the school. Freshman campus housing is guaranteed. *Activities and organizations:* drama/theater group, student-run newspaper, radio station, choral group, Social Activities Committee, Greek Life, Dance Marathon, Hockey Club, Relay for Life, national fraternities, national sororities. *Campus security:* 24-hour emergency response devices and patrols, late-night transport/escort service, controlled dormitory access. *Student services:* health clinic, personal/psychological counseling.

Athletics Member NCAA. All Division III. *Intercollegiate sports:* baseball M, basketball M/W, cheerleading M/W, cross-country running M/W, football M, golf M/W, ice hockey M(c), lacrosse M/W, sailing M(c)/W(c), soccer M/W, softball W, swimming and diving M/W, tennis M/W, track and field M/W, volleyball W. *Intramural sports:* basketball M/W, bowling M/W, football M/W, racquetball M/W, soccer M/W, softball M/W, tennis M/W, ultimate Frisbee M/W, volleyball M/W, water polo M/W.

Standardized Tests *Required:* SAT or ACT (for admission).

Costs (2013–14) *Comprehensive fee:* $37,530 includes full-time tuition ($28,550), mandatory fees ($170), and room and board ($8810). *College room only:* $4040. Room and board charges vary according to board plan. *Payment plan:* installment. *Waivers:* employees or children of employees.

Financial Aid Of all full-time matriculated undergraduates who enrolled in 2012, 2,385 applied for aid, 1,981 were judged to have need, 529 had their need fully met. 240 Federal Work-Study jobs (averaging $1425). 516 state and other part-time jobs (averaging $793). In 2012, 793 non-need-based awards were made. *Average percent of need met:* 78%. *Average financial aid package:* $22,197. *Average need-based loan:* $4706. *Average need-based gift aid:* $16,796. *Average non-need-based aid:* $7919. *Average indebtedness upon graduation:* $37,010.

Applying *Options:* electronic application, early admission, deferred entrance. *Application fee:* $50. *Required:* essay or personal statement, high school transcript. *Required for some:* 1 letter of recommendation. *Recommended:* interview. *Application deadlines:* rolling (freshmen), rolling (transfers). *Notification:* continuous (freshmen), continuous (transfers).

Freshman Application Contact Admissions Office, Hope College, 69 East 10th Street, PO Box 9000, Holland, MI 49422-9000. *Phone:* 616-395-7850. *Toll-free phone:* 800-968-7850. *E-mail:* admissions@hope.edu. *Website:* http://www.hope.edu/.

ITT Technical Institute

Canton, Michigan

- **Proprietary** primarily 2-year, founded 2002, part of ITT Educational Services, Inc.
- **Coed**
- **Minimally difficult** entrance level

Academics *Calendar:* quarters. *Degrees:* associate and bachelor's.
Freshman Application Contact Director of Recruitment, ITT Technical Institute, 1905 South Haggerty Road, Canton, MI 48188-2025. *Phone:* 784-397-7800. *Toll-free phone:* 800-247-4477. *Website:* http://www.itt-tech.edu/.

ITT Technical Institute

Dearborn, Michigan

- **Proprietary** primarily 2-year, part of ITT Educational Services, Inc.
- **Coed**

Academics *Calendar:* quarters. *Degrees:* associate and bachelor's.
Freshman Application Contact Director of Recruitment, ITT Technical Institute, 19855 W. Outer Drive, Suite L10W, Dearborn, MI 48124. *Phone:* 313-278-5208. *Toll-free phone:* 800-605-0801. *Website:* http://www.itt-tech.edu/.

ITT Technical Institute

Grand Rapids, Michigan

- **Proprietary** 4-year
- **Coed**
- **Minimally difficult** entrance level

Academics *Degrees:* associate and bachelor's.
Freshman Application Contact Director of Recruitment, ITT Technical Institute, 3518 Plainfield Avenue NE, Grand Rapids, MI 49525. *Phone:* 616-365-4800. *Toll-free phone:* 877-264-1715. *Website:* http://www.itt-tech.edu/.

ITT Technical Institute

Southfield, Michigan

- **Proprietary** 4-year
- **Coed**
- **Minimally difficult** entrance level

Academics *Degrees:* associate and bachelor's.
Freshman Application Contact Director of Recruitment, ITT Technical Institute, 26700 Lahser Road, Suite 100, Southfield, MI 48033. *Phone:* 248-603-6100. *Toll-free phone:* 877-363-3221. *Website:* http://www.itt-tech.edu/.

ITT Technical Institute

Swartz Creek, Michigan

- **Proprietary** primarily 2-year, founded 2005, part of ITT Educational Services, Inc.
- **Coed**
- **Minimally difficult** entrance level

Academics *Calendar:* quarters. *Degrees:* associate and bachelor's.
Freshman Application Contact Director of Recruitment, ITT Technical Institute, 6359 Miller Road, Swartz Creek, MI 48473. *Phone:* 810-628-2500. *Toll-free phone:* 800-514-6564. *Website:* http://www.itt-tech.edu/.

ITT Technical Institute

Troy, Michigan

- **Proprietary** primarily 2-year, founded 1987, part of ITT Educational Services, Inc.
- **Coed**
- **Minimally difficult** entrance level

Academics *Calendar:* quarters. *Degrees:* associate and bachelor's.
Freshman Application Contact Director of Recruitment, ITT Technical Institute, 1522 East Big Beaver Road, Troy, MI 48083-1905. *Phone:* 248-524-1800. *Toll-free phone:* 800-832-6817. *Fax:* 248-524-1965. *Website:* http://www.itt-tech.edu/.

ITT Technical Institute

Wyoming, Michigan

- **Proprietary** primarily 2-year, part of ITT Educational Services, Inc.
- **Coed**
- **Minimally difficult** entrance level

Academics *Calendar:* quarters. *Degrees:* associate and bachelor's.
Freshman Application Contact Director of Recruitment, ITT Technical Institute, 1980 Metro Court SW, Wyoming, MI 49519. *Phone:* 616-406-1200. *Toll-free phone:* 800-632-4676. *Website:* http://www.itt-tech.edu/.

Kalamazoo College

Kalamazoo, Michigan

- **Independent** 4-year, founded 1833, affiliated with American Baptist Churches in the U.S.A.
- **Suburban** 60-acre campus with easy access to Grand Rapids
- **Endowment** $169.5 million
- **Coed** 1,379 undergraduate students, 99% full-time, 58% women, 42% men
- **Very difficult** entrance level, 69% of applicants were admitted

Undergraduates 1,366 full-time, 13 part-time. Students come from 38 states and territories; 32 other countries; 38% are from out of state; 4% Black or African American, non-Hispanic/Latino; 9% Hispanic/Latino; 5% Asian, non-Hispanic/Latino; 0.1% Native Hawaiian or other Pacific Islander, non-Hispanic/Latino; 0.4% American Indian or Alaska Native, non-Hispanic/Latino; 3% Two or more races, non-Hispanic/Latino; 6% Race/ethnicity unknown; 7% international; 0.7% transferred in; 70% live on campus. *Retention:* 94% of full-time freshmen returned.

Freshmen *Admission:* 2,294 applied, 1,583 admitted, 334 enrolled. *Average high school GPA:* 3.61. *Test scores:* SAT critical reading scores over 500: 84%; SAT math scores over 500: 84%; SAT writing scores over 500: 87%; ACT scores over 18: 100%; SAT critical reading scores over 600: 57%; SAT math scores over 600: 59%; SAT writing scores over 600: 55%; ACT scores over 24: 90%; SAT critical reading scores over 700: 14%; SAT math scores over 700: 15%; SAT writing scores over 700: 12%; ACT scores over 30: 33%.

Faculty *Total:* 114, 84% full-time, 85% with terminal degrees. *Student/faculty ratio:* 12:1.

Academics *Calendar:* quarters. *Degree:* bachelor's. *Special study options:* advanced placement credit, double majors, independent study, internships, off-campus study, services for LD students, student-designed majors, study abroad. *ROTC:* Army (c). *Unusual degree programs:* 3-2 engineering with The University of Michigan and Washington University in St. Louis, Missouri, but any ABET accredited program is acceptable for the 3/2 engineering program.

Computers on Campus 250 computers/terminals are available on campus for general student use. Students can access the following: campus intranet, computer help desk, free student e-mail accounts, online (class) grades, online (class) registration, online (class) schedules, RCC—Residential computer consultant. Campuswide network is available. 100% of college-owned or -operated housing units are wired for high-speed Internet access. Wireless service is available via entire campus.

Student Life *Housing:* on-campus residence required through junior year. *Options:* coed, disabled students. Campus housing is university owned. Freshman campus housing is guaranteed. *Activities and organizations:* drama/theater group, student-run newspaper, radio station, choral group, Frelon Dance Company, Acappella Groups, Environmental Student Organization, Kaleidoscope, Student Commission. *Campus security:* 24-hour emergency response devices and patrols, late-night transport/escort service, controlled dormitory access. *Student services:* health clinic, personal/psychological counseling.

Athletics Member NCAA. All Division III. *Intercollegiate sports:* baseball M, basketball M/W, cross-country running M/W, football M, golf M/W, lacrosse W, soccer M/W, softball W, swimming and diving M/W, tennis M/W, volley-ball W. *Intramural sports:* badminton M/W, basketball M/W, cheerleading W, lacrosse W(c), racquetball M/W, soccer M/W, softball M/W, table tennis M/W, tennis M/W, ultimate Frisbee M(c)/W(c), volleyball M/W.

Standardized Tests *Required:* SAT or ACT (for admission).

Costs (2012–13) *Comprehensive fee:* $45,984 includes full-time tuition ($37,392), mandatory fees ($318), and room and board ($8274). *College room only:* $4035. Room and board charges vary according to board plan. *Payment plan:* installment. *Waivers:* employees or children of employees.

Financial Aid Of all full-time matriculated undergraduates who enrolled in 2012, 901 applied for aid, 796 were judged to have need, 294 had their need fully met. 550 Federal Work-Study jobs (averaging $2440). In 2012, 442 non-need-based awards were made. *Average percent of need met:* 86%. *Average financial aid package:* $31,025. *Average need-based loan:* $4954. *Average need-based gift aid:* $23,909. *Average non-need-based aid:* $13,467. *Average indebtedness upon graduation:* $27,845.

Applying *Options:* electronic application, early decision, early action, deferred entrance. *Application fee:* $40. *Required:* essay or personal statement, high school transcript, 2 letters of recommendation, Common Application Supplement. *Recommended:* minimum 3.0 GPA, interview. *Application deadlines:* 2/1 (freshmen), 5/1 (transfers), 11/20 (early action). *Early decision deadline:* 11/10. *Notification:* 4/1 (freshmen), 5/15 (transfers), 11/20 (early decision), 12/20 (early action).

Freshman Application Contact Records Processing Team, Kalamazoo College, Mandelle Hall, 1200 Academy Street, Kalamazoo, MI 49006-3295. *Phone:* 269-337-5759. *Toll-free phone:* 800-253-3602. *Fax:* 269-337-7390. *E-mail:* admission.records@kzoo.edu. *Website:* http://www.kzoo.edu/.

Kettering University

Flint, Michigan

- **Independent** comprehensive, founded 1919
- **Urban** 85-acre campus with easy access to Detroit
- **Endowment** $65.9 million
- **Coed, primarily men**
- **Very difficult** entrance level

Faculty *Student/faculty ratio:* 13:1.

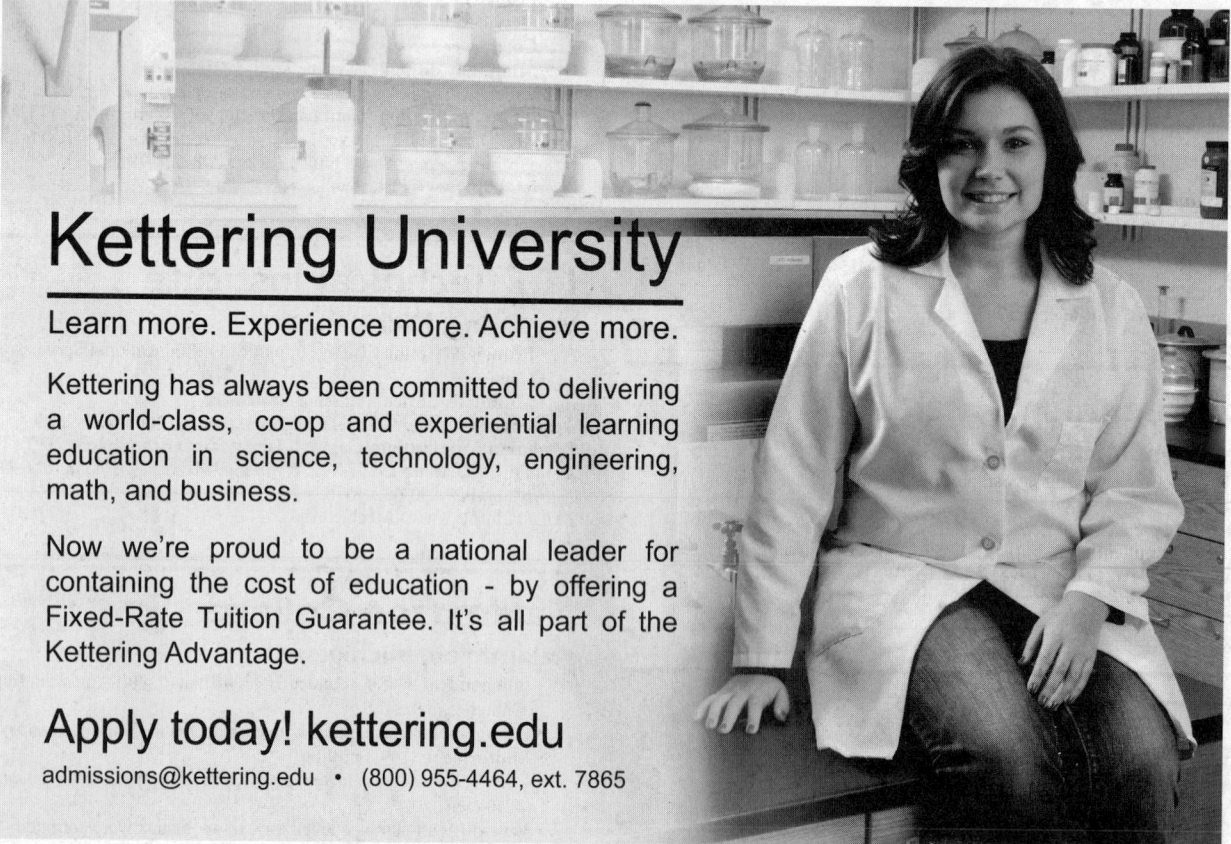

Academics *Calendar:* semesters (11 weeks of full-time study plus 12 weeks of paid co-op experience per semester). *Degrees:* bachelor's and master's.

Student Life *Campus security:* 24-hour emergency response devices and patrols, late-night transport/escort service, controlled dormitory access, security card access to all campus buildings 24/7 except the campus center main entrance which is secure 11pm-7am.

Standardized Tests *Required:* SAT or ACT (for admission).

Costs (2012–13) *Comprehensive fee:* $40,606 includes full-time tuition ($33,946) and room and board ($6660). Part-time tuition: $1132 per credit. No tuition increase for student's term of enrollment. *College room only:* $4150.

Financial Aid *Of all full-time matriculated undergraduates who enrolled in 2012,* 1,300 applied for aid, 1,232 were judged to have need, 170 had their need fully met. *In 2012,* 375 non-need-based awards were made. *Average percent of need met:* 63. *Average financial aid package:* $20,987. *Average need-based loan:* $4388. *Average need-based gift aid:* $15,267. *Average non-need-based aid:* $12,325.

Applying *Options:* electronic application, deferred entrance. *Application fee:* $35. *Required:* high school transcript. *Required for some:* essay or personal statement. *Recommended:* minimum 3.0 GPA, interview.

Freshman Application Contact Ms. Karen Full, Director, International and Undergraduate Admissions, Kettering University, 1700 University Avenue, Flint, MI 48504-6214. *Phone:* 810-762-7496. *Toll-free phone:* 800-955-4464 Ext. 7865 (in-state); 800-955-4464 (out-of-state). *Fax:* 810-762-9837. *E-mail:* admissions@kettering.edu.

Website: http://www.kettering.edu/.

See previous page for display ad and page 1342 for the College Close-Up.

Kuyper College

Grand Rapids, Michigan

- **Independent Christian** 4-year, founded 1939
- **Suburban** 34-acre campus with easy access to Grand Rapids
- **Endowment** $7.4 million
- **Coed** 312 undergraduate students, 88% full-time, 54% women, 46% men
- **Moderately difficult** entrance level

Undergraduates 276 full-time, 36 part-time. 12% are from out of state; 3% Black or African American, non-Hispanic/Latino; 0.6% Hispanic/Latino; 2% Asian, non-Hispanic/Latino; 0.6% American Indian or Alaska Native, non-Hispanic/Latino; 2% Two or more races, non-Hispanic/Latino; 9% Race/ethnicity unknown; 4% international; 51% live on campus. *Retention:* 69% of full-time freshmen returned.

Freshmen *Admission:* 46 enrolled. *Average high school GPA:* 3.18.

Faculty *Total:* 37, 35% full-time, 30% with terminal degrees. *Student/faculty ratio:* 15:1.

Academics *Calendar:* semesters. *Degrees:* certificates, associate, bachelor's, and postbachelor's certificates. *Special study options:* academic remediation for entering students, advanced placement credit, cooperative education, distance learning, double majors, independent study, internships, off-campus study, part-time degree program, services for LD students, study abroad, summer session for credit. *ROTC:* Army (c).

Computers on Campus 70 computers/terminals and 70 ports are available on campus for general student use. Students can access the following: campus intranet, computer help desk, free student e-mail accounts, online (class) grades, online (class) registration, online (class) schedules. Campuswide network is available. 100% of college-owned or -operated housing units are wired for high-speed Internet access. Wireless service is available via entire campus.

Student Life *Housing:* on-campus residence required through sophomore year. *Options:* coed. Campus housing is university owned. Freshman campus housing is guaranteed. *Activities and organizations:* drama/theater group, choral group, intramurals, Student Activities Club, Helping and Nurturing During Service, yearbook, Roots. *Campus security:* 24-hour emergency response devices, student patrols, late-night transport/escort service, controlled dormitory access. *Student services:* health clinic, personal/psychological counseling.

Athletics Member NCCAA. *Intercollegiate sports:* basketball M/W, soccer M, volleyball W. *Intramural sports:* basketball M/W, football M/W, soccer M/W, softball M/W, table tennis M/W, ultimate Frisbee M/W, volleyball M/W.

Financial Aid *Of all full-time matriculated undergraduates who enrolled in 2012,* 266 applied for aid, 253 were judged to have need, 24 had their need fully met. 12 Federal Work-Study jobs (averaging $2487). 110 state and other part-time jobs (averaging $2636). In 2012, 18 non-need-based awards were made. *Average percent of need met:* 70%. *Average financial aid package:* $13,714. *Average need-based loan:* $3395. *Average need-based gift aid:* $11,755. *Average non-need-based aid:* $5773. *Average indebtedness upon graduation:* $13,615.

Applying *Options:* electronic application, deferred entrance. *Required:* essay or personal statement, high school transcript, minimum 2.5 GPA. *Recom-*

mended: interview. *Application deadlines:* rolling (freshmen), rolling (transfers). *Notification:* continuous (freshmen), continuous (transfers).

Freshman Application Contact Admissions Office, Kuyper College, 3333 East Beltline Avenue, NE, Grand Rapids, MI 49525. *Phone:* 616-222-3000 Ext. 632. *Fax:* 616-222-3045. *E-mail:* admissions@kuyper.edu.

Website: http://www.kuyper.edu/.

Lake Superior State University

Sault Sainte Marie, Michigan

- **State-supported** comprehensive, founded 1946
- **Small-town** 115-acre campus
- **Endowment** $8.2 million
- **Coed** 2,523 undergraduate students, 83% full-time, 50% women, 50% men
- **Moderately difficult** entrance level, 90% of applicants were admitted

Undergraduates 2,105 full-time, 418 part-time. Students come from 36 states and territories; 15 other countries; 8% are from out of state; 2% Black or African American, non-Hispanic/Latino; 2% Hispanic/Latino; 0.6% Asian, non-Hispanic/Latino; 8% American Indian or Alaska Native, non-Hispanic/Latino; 0.1% Two or more races, non-Hispanic/Latino; 2% Race/ethnicity unknown; 7% international; 7% transferred in; 34% live on campus. *Retention:* 70% of full-time freshmen returned.

Freshmen *Admission:* 1,425 applied, 1,278 admitted, 442 enrolled. *Average high school GPA:* 3.22. *Test scores:* ACT scores over 18: 91%; ACT scores over 24: 34%; ACT scores over 30: 4%.

Faculty *Total:* 184, 63% full-time, 38% with terminal degrees. *Student/faculty ratio:* 17:1.

Academics *Calendar:* semesters. *Degrees:* certificates, associate, bachelor's, master's, and postbachelor's certificates. *Special study options:* advanced placement credit, cooperative education, distance learning, double majors, freshman honors college, honors programs, independent study, internships, off-campus study, part-time degree program, services for LD students, student-designed majors, study abroad, summer session for credit.

Computers on Campus 350 computers/terminals are available on campus for general student use. Students can access the following: campus intranet, computer help desk, free student e-mail accounts, online (class) grades, online (class) registration, online (class) schedules. Campuswide network is available. 100% of college-owned or -operated housing units are wired for high-speed Internet access. Wireless service is available via entire campus.

Student Life *Housing:* on-campus residence required through sophomore year. *Options:* coed, men-only, women-only. Campus housing is university owned. Freshman campus housing is guaranteed. *Activities and organizations:* drama/theater group, student-run newspaper, radio station, choral group, Enactus (Formally known as SIFE), SAILS—Student Alumni Involved in Lake State, Fisheries and Wildlife, Harry Potter Club, Dance Company, national fraternities, national sororities. *Campus security:* 24-hour emergency response devices and patrols, student patrols, late-night transport/escort service. *Student services:* health clinic, personal/psychological counseling.

Athletics Member NCAA. All Division II except ice hockey (Division I). *Intercollegiate sports:* basketball M(s)/W(s), cross-country running M(s)/W(s), golf M(s)/W(s), ice hockey M(s), softball W(s), tennis M(s)/W(s), track and field M(s)/W(s), volleyball W(s). *Intramural sports:* basketball M/W, football M/W, ice hockey M/W(c), racquetball M/W, riflery M/W, soccer M/W, swimming and diving M/W, tennis M/W, volleyball M/W, water polo M/W, wrestling M(c).

Standardized Tests *Required:* SAT or ACT (for admission).

Costs (2012–13) *One-time required fee:* $125. *Tuition:* state resident $9540 full-time, $398 per credit hour part-time; nonresident $14,310 full-time, $596 per credit hour part-time. Full-time tuition and fees vary according to program and reciprocity agreements. Part-time tuition and fees vary according to course load, location, program, and reciprocity agreements. *Required fees:* $175 full-time. *Room and board:* $8481. Room and board charges vary according to board plan and housing facility. *Payment plans:* installment, deferred payment. *Waivers:* minority students, children of alumni, senior citizens, and employees or children of employees.

Financial Aid *Of all full-time matriculated undergraduates who enrolled in 2011,* 1,762 applied for aid, 1,533 were judged to have need, 385 had their need fully met. In 2011, 285 non-need-based awards were made. *Average percent of need met:* 61%. *Average financial aid package:* $9347. *Average need-based loan:* $4171. *Average need-based gift aid:* $5548. *Average non-need-based aid:* $3515. *Average indebtedness upon graduation:* $28,500.

Applying *Options:* electronic application, deferred entrance. *Application fee:* $25. *Required:* high school transcript. *Required for some:* SAT or ACT for students out of high school for less than 26 months or have less than 19 transferable credits. *Application deadlines:* rolling (freshmen), rolling (transfers). *Notification:* continuous (freshmen), continuous (transfers).

Freshman Application Contact Lake Superior State University, 650 West Easterday Avenue, Sault Sainte Marie, MI 49783. *Phone:* 906-635-2231. *Toll-free phone:* 888-800-LSSU Ext. 2231.
Website: http://www.lssu.edu/.

Lawrence Technological University

Southfield, Michigan

- **Independent** university, founded 1932
- **Suburban** 102-acre campus with easy access to Detroit
- **Endowment** $50.0 million
- **Coed** 3,065 undergraduate students, 45% full-time, 25% women, 75% men
- **Moderately difficult** entrance level, 44% of applicants were admitted

Undergraduates 1,382 full-time, 1,683 part-time. Students come from 21 states and territories; 29 other countries; 3% are from out of state; 9% Black or African American, non-Hispanic/Latino; 2% Hispanic/Latino; 30% Asian, non-Hispanic/Latino; 0.4% American Indian or Alaska Native, non-Hispanic/Latino; 10% Race/ethnicity unknown; 5% international; 6% transferred in; 18% live on campus. *Retention:* 74% of full-time freshmen returned.

Freshmen *Admission:* 1,819 applied, 794 admitted, 341 enrolled. *Average high school GPA:* 3.38. *Test scores:* SAT critical reading scores over 500: 65%; SAT math scores over 500: 92%; ACT scores over 18: 90%; SAT critical reading scores over 600: 35%; SAT math scores over 600: 56%; ACT scores over 24: 58%; SAT critical reading scores over 700: 5%; SAT math scores over 700: 6%; ACT scores over 30: 16%.

Faculty *Total:* 398, 29% full-time, 68% with terminal degrees. *Student/faculty ratio:* 11:1.

Academics *Calendar:* semesters. *Degrees:* certificates, associate, bachelor's, master's, doctoral, and postbachelor's certificates. *Special study options:* academic remediation for entering students, accelerated degree program, adult/continuing education programs, advanced placement credit, cooperative education, distance learning, double majors, English as a second language, honors programs, independent study, internships, off-campus study, part-time degree program, services for LD students, study abroad, summer session for credit. *ROTC:* Air Force (c).

Computers on Campus 126 computers/terminals and 3,170 ports are available on campus for general student use. Students can access the following: campus intranet, computer help desk, free student e-mail accounts, online (class) grades, online (class) registration, online (class) schedules, degree audit, Blackboard, SCT Banner (student information), Personal websites, Document collection. Campuswide network is available. 50% of college-owned or -operated housing units are wired for high-speed Internet access. Wireless service is available via entire campus.

Student Life *Housing options:* coed, disabled students. Campus housing is university owned. Freshman applicants given priority for college housing. *Activities and organizations:* drama/theater group, student-run newspaper, American Institute of Architecture Students, American Society of Mechanical Engineers, Institute of Electric and Electronic Engineers, American Society of Civil Engineers, student government, national fraternities, national sororities. *Campus security:* 24-hour emergency response devices and patrols, late-night transport/escort service, controlled dormitory access. *Student services:* personal/psychological counseling.

Athletics Member NAIA. *Intercollegiate sports:* basketball M(s)/W(s), bowling M(s), cross-country running M/W, ice hockey M, lacrosse M(s), soccer M(s)/W(s), volleyball W(s). *Intramural sports:* badminton M/W, basketball M/W, football M, golf M/W, racquetball M/W, skiing (downhill) M/W, soccer M(c)/W, softball M/W, table tennis M/W, tennis M/W, ultimate Frisbee M, volleyball M.

Standardized Tests *Required:* ACT (preferred) (for admission). *Required for some:* SAT or ACT (for admission).

Costs (2012–13) *Comprehensive fee:* $36,857 includes full-time tuition ($27,300), mandatory fees ($570), and room and board ($8987). Full-time tuition and fees vary according to course level, degree level, location, program, and student level. Part-time tuition: $910 per credit hour. Part-time tuition and fees vary according to course level, degree level, location, program, and student level. *Required fees:* $285 per term part-time. *College room only:* $4959. Room and board charges vary according to board plan and housing facility. *Payment plan:* installment. *Waivers:* employees or children of employees.

Financial Aid Of all full-time matriculated undergraduates who enrolled in 2011, 1,243 applied for aid, 988 were judged to have need, 150 had their need fully met. 61 Federal Work-Study jobs (averaging $2380). In 2011, 195 non-need-based awards were made. *Average percent of need met:* 66%. *Average financial aid package:* $21,796. *Average need-based loan:* $8292. *Average*

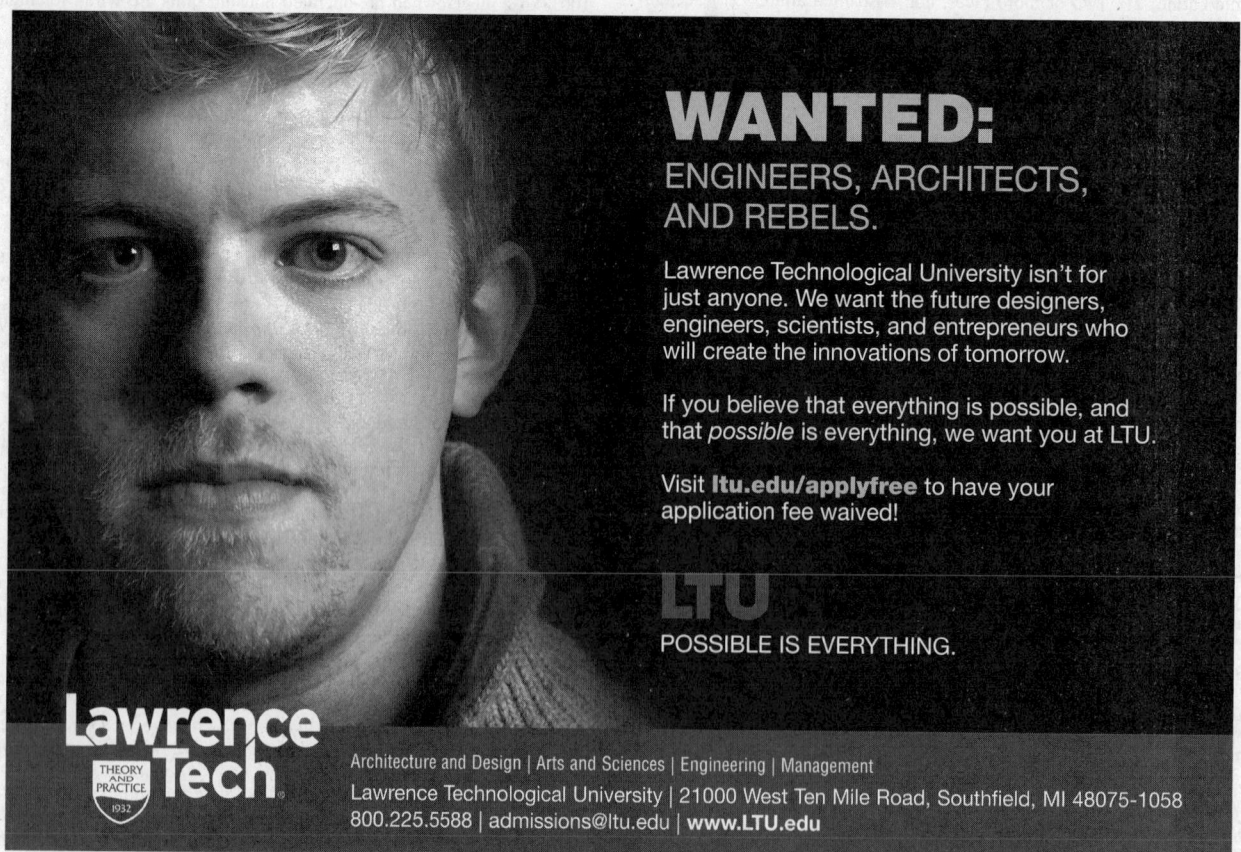

need-based gift aid: $12,631. *Average non-need-based aid:* $10,381. *Average indebtedness upon graduation:* $41,529.

Applying *Options:* electronic application, early admission, deferred entrance. *Application fee:* $30. *Required:* high school transcript, minimum 2.5 GPA. *Required for some:* essay or personal statement, minimum 2.8 GPA, 1 letter of recommendation, interview. *Application deadlines:* 8/15 (freshmen), 8/15 (transfers). *Notification:* continuous until 8/26 (freshmen), 8/26 (transfers).

Freshman Application Contact Jane Rohrback, Director of Admissions, Lawrence Technological University, 21000 West Ten Mile Road, Southfield, MI 48075. *Phone:* 248-204-3160. *Toll-free phone:* 800-225-5588. *Fax:* 248-204-2228. *E-mail:* admissions@ltu.edu.
Website: http://www.ltu.edu/.

See previous page for display ad and page 1346 for the College Close-Up.

Madonna University

Livonia, Michigan

- **Independent Roman Catholic** comprehensive, founded 1947
- **Suburban** 49-acre campus with easy access to Detroit
- **Endowment** $29.0 million
- **Coed** 3,205 undergraduate students, 51% full-time, 71% women, 29% men
- **Moderately difficult** entrance level, 70% of applicants were admitted

Undergraduates 1,625 full-time, 1,580 part-time. Students come from 7 states and territories; 26 other countries; 1% are from out of state; 14% Black or African American, non-Hispanic/Latino; 4% Hispanic/Latino; 1% Asian, non-Hispanic/Latino; 0.1% Native Hawaiian or other Pacific Islander, non-Hispanic/Latino; 0.5% American Indian or Alaska Native, non-Hispanic/Latino; 2% Two or more races, non-Hispanic/Latino; 0.6% Race/ethnicity unknown; 9% international; 16% transferred in; 7% live on campus. *Retention:* 83% of full-time freshmen returned.

Freshmen *Admission:* 537 applied, 376 admitted, 160 enrolled. *Average high school GPA:* 3.3. *Test scores:* SAT critical reading scores over 500: 60%; SAT math scores over 500: 50%; SAT writing scores over 500: 60%; ACT scores over 18: 91%; SAT critical reading scores over 600: 30%; SAT math scores over 600: 10%; SAT writing scores over 600: 20%; ACT scores over 24: 36%; SAT writing scores over 700: 10%; ACT scores over 30: 1%.

Faculty *Total:* 415, 31% full-time, 30% with terminal degrees. *Student/faculty ratio:* 10:1.

Academics *Calendar:* semesters. *Degrees:* certificates, diplomas, associate, bachelor's, master's, doctoral, post-master's, and postbachelor's certificates. *Special study options:* academic remediation for entering students, accelerated degree program, adult/continuing education programs, advanced placement credit, cooperative education, distance learning, double majors, English as a second language, independent study, internships, off-campus study, part-time degree program, services for LD students, student-designed majors, study abroad, summer session for credit. *ROTC:* Army (c).

Computers on Campus 243 computers/terminals and 243 ports are available on campus for general student use. Students can access the following: campus intranet, computer help desk, free student e-mail accounts, online (class) grades, online (class) registration, online (class) schedules, online payments, online statements, online Unofficial Transcripts. Campuswide network is available. 100% of college-owned or -operated housing units are wired for high-speed Internet access. Wireless service is available via classrooms, computer labs, dorm rooms, learning centers, libraries, student centers.

Student Life *Housing options:* men-only, women-only. Campus housing is university owned. Freshman campus housing is guaranteed. *Activities and organizations:* drama/theater group, student-run newspaper, radio station, choral group, Campus Ministry, Red Cross Club, Madonna University Nursing Student Association, Broadcast & Film Club, Society of Future Teachers. *Campus security:* 24-hour emergency response devices and patrols, late-night transport/escort service, controlled dormitory access. *Student services:* personal/psychological counseling.

Athletics Member NAIA. *Intercollegiate sports:* baseball M(s), basketball M(s)/W(s), cross-country running M(s)/W(s), golf M(s)/W(s), soccer M(s)/W(s), softball W(s), volleyball W(s). *Intramural sports:* basketball M/W, volleyball M/W.

Standardized Tests *Required:* SAT or ACT (for admission).

Costs (2012–13) *Comprehensive fee:* $22,994 includes full-time tuition ($15,180), mandatory fees ($120), and room and board ($7694). Full-time tuition and fees vary according to course load. Part-time tuition: $506 per credit hour. Part-time tuition and fees vary according to course load. *Required fees:* $60 per term part-time. *College room only:* $4178. Room and board charges vary according to board plan. *Payment plan:* deferred payment. *Waivers:* senior citizens and employees or children of employees.

Financial Aid Of all full-time matriculated undergraduates who enrolled in 2007, 862 applied for aid, 698 were judged to have need, 122 had their need fully met. In 2007, 172 non-need-based awards were made. *Average percent of need met:* 56%. *Average financial aid package:* $7396. *Average need-based loan:* $3862. *Average need-based gift aid:* $4508. *Average non-need-based aid:* $2427.

Applying *Options:* electronic application, deferred entrance. *Application fee:* $25. *Required:* essay or personal statement, high school transcript, minimum 2.8 GPA. *Required for some:* 2 letters of recommendation. *Recommended:* interview. *Application deadlines:* rolling (freshmen), rolling (transfers). *Notification:* continuous (freshmen), continuous (transfers).

Freshman Application Contact Mr. Mike Quattro, Director of Enrollment Management, Madonna University, 36600 Schoolcraft Road, Livonia, MI 48150-1173. *Phone:* 734-432-5341. *Toll-free phone:* 800-852-4951. *Fax:* 734-432-5424. *E-mail:* admissions@madonna.edu.
Website: http://www.madonna.edu/.

Marygrove College

Detroit, Michigan

Freshman Application Contact Mr. John Ambrose, Director of Undergraduate Admissions, Marygrove College, Admissions Office, Detroit, MI 48221-2599. *Phone:* 313-927-1236. *Toll-free phone:* 866-313-1297. *Fax:* 313-927-1345. *E-mail:* info@marygrove.edu.
Website: http://www.marygrove.edu/.

Michigan Jewish Institute

West Bloomfield, Michigan

Freshman Application Contact Mr. Dov Stein, Michigan Jewish Institute, 6890 Maple Road, West Bloomfield, MI 48322. *Phone:* 248-414-6900 Ext. 103. *Toll-free phone:* 888-INFO-MJI. *Fax:* 248-414-6907. *E-mail:* dstein@mji.edu.
Website: http://www.mji.edu/.

Michigan State University

East Lansing, Michigan

- **State-supported** university, founded 1855
- **Suburban** 5192-acre campus with easy access to Detroit
- **Endowment** $1.4 billion
- **Coed** 37,454 undergraduate students, 92% full-time, 50% women, 50% men
- **Moderately difficult** entrance level, 71% of applicants were admitted

Undergraduates 34,296 full-time, 3,158 part-time. Students come from 55 states and territories; 96 other countries; 9% are from out of state; 7% Black or African American, non-Hispanic/Latino; 4% Hispanic/Latino; 4% Asian, non-Hispanic/Latino; 0.1% Native Hawaiian or other Pacific Islander, non-Hispanic/Latino; 0.3% American Indian or Alaska Native, non-Hispanic/Latino; 2% Two or more races, non-Hispanic/Latino; 1% Race/ethnicity unknown; 11% international; 4% transferred in; 42% live on campus. *Retention:* 91% of full-time freshmen returned.

Freshmen *Admission:* 30,224 applied, 21,327 admitted, 8,354 enrolled. *Average high school GPA:* 3.61. *Test scores:* SAT critical reading scores over 500: 55%; SAT math scores over 500: 85%; SAT writing scores over 500: 60%; ACT scores over 18: 98%; SAT critical reading scores over 600: 23%; SAT math scores over 600: 57%; SAT writing scores over 600: 21%; ACT scores over 24: 73%; SAT critical reading scores over 700: 6%; SAT math scores over 700: 22%; SAT writing scores over 700: 4%; ACT scores over 30: 14%.

Faculty *Total:* 2,789, 85% full-time, 82% with terminal degrees. *Student/faculty ratio:* 16:1.

Academics *Calendar:* semesters. *Degrees:* certificates, bachelor's, master's, doctoral, and post-master's certificates. *Special study options:* academic remediation for entering students, accelerated degree program, adult/continuing education programs, advanced placement credit, cooperative education, distance learning, double majors, English as a second language, freshman honors college, honors programs, independent study, internships, off-campus study, part-time degree program, services for LD students, student-designed majors, study abroad, summer session for credit. *ROTC:* Army (b), Air Force (b). *Unusual degree programs:* 3-2 engineering.

Computers on Campus Students can access the following: campus intranet, computer help desk, free student e-mail accounts, online (class) grades, online (class) registration, online (class) schedules. Campuswide network is available. 100% of college-owned or -operated housing units are wired for high-speed Internet access. Wireless service is available via classrooms, computer centers, computer labs, dorm rooms, learning centers, libraries, student centers.

Student Life *Housing:* on-campus residence required for freshman year. *Options:* coed, women-only, cooperative, disabled students. Campus housing is university owned. Freshman campus housing is guaranteed. *Activities and organizations:* drama/theater group, student-run newspaper, radio and television station, choral group, marching band, national fraternities, national sororities. *Campus security:* 24-hour emergency response devices and patrols, late-night transport/escort service, controlled dormitory access, self-defense workshops. *Student services:* health clinic, personal/psychological counseling, women's center, legal services.

Athletics Member NCAA. All Division I except football (Division I-A). *Intercollegiate sports:* archery M(c)/W(c), baseball M(s), basketball M(s)/W(s), cheerleading M/W, crew M(c)/W(s), cross-country running M(s)/W(s), equestrian sports M(c)/W(c), fencing M(c)/W(c), field hockey W(s), golf M(s)/W(s), gymnastics W(s), ice hockey M(s)/W(c), lacrosse M(c)/W(c), riflery M(c)/W(c), rugby M(c)/W(c), sailing M(c)/W(c), skiing (cross-country) M(c)/W(c), skiing (downhill) M(c)/W(c), soccer M(s)/W(s), softball W(s), swimming and diving M(s)/W(s), table tennis M/W, tennis M(s)/W(s), track and field M(s)/W(s), volleyball M(c)/W(s), water polo M(c)/W(c), wrestling M(s). *Intramural sports:* archery M/W, badminton M/W, baseball M, basketball M/W, bowling M/W, cheerleading W(c), cross-country running M/W, fencing M/W, field hockey W, football M/W, golf M/W, ice hockey M/W, lacrosse M/W, racquetball M/W, riflery M/W, rugby M/W, sailing M/W, skiing (cross-country) M/W, skiing (downhill) M/W, soccer M/W, softball M/W, squash M/W, swimming and diving M/W, table tennis M(c)/W(c), tennis M/W, track and field M/W, ultimate Frisbee M(c)/W(c), volleyball M/W, water polo M/W, weight lifting M/W, wrestling M.

Standardized Tests *Required:* SAT or ACT (for admission).

Costs (2013–14) *Tuition:* state resident $13,800 full-time, $421 per credit hour part-time; nonresident $33,608 full-time, $1086 per credit hour part-time. Full-time tuition and fees vary according to course load, program, and student level. Part-time tuition and fees vary according to course load, program, and student level. *Room and board:* $8476; room only: $3500. Room and board charges vary according to board plan and housing facility. *Payment plan:* deferred payment. *Waivers:* employees or children of employees.

Financial Aid Of all full-time matriculated undergraduates who enrolled in 2012, 21,827 applied for aid, 17,044 were judged to have need, 2,293 had their need fully met. In 2012, 1054 non-need-based awards were made. *Average*

percent of need met: 61%. *Average financial aid package:* $11,509. *Average need-based loan:* $4167. *Average need-based gift aid:* $8949. *Average non-need-based aid:* $10,362. *Average indebtedness upon graduation:* $24,987.

Applying *Options:* electronic application, early action. *Application fee:* $50. *Required:* essay or personal statement, high school transcript. *Application deadlines:* rolling (freshmen), rolling (out-of-state freshmen), rolling (transfers). *Notification:* continuous (freshmen), continuous (out-of-state freshmen), continuous (transfers).

Freshman Application Contact James Cotter, Director of Admissions, Michigan State University, 250 Administration Building, East Lansing, MI 48824. *Phone:* 517-355-8332. *Fax:* 517-353-1647. *E-mail:* admis@msu.edu. *Website:* http://www.msu.edu/.

Michigan Technological University

Houghton, Michigan

- **State-supported** university, founded 1885
- **Small-town** 925-acre campus
- **Coed**
- **Moderately difficult** entrance level

Faculty *Student/faculty ratio:* 13:1.

Academics *Calendar:* semesters. *Degrees:* certificates, associate, bachelor's, master's, doctoral, and postbachelor's certificates.

Student Life *Campus security:* 24-hour emergency response devices and patrols, late-night transport/escort service, controlled dormitory access.

Athletics Member NCAA. All Division II except ice hockey (Division I).

Standardized Tests *Required:* SAT or ACT (for admission).

Costs (2012–13) *Tuition:* state resident $13,095 full-time, $437 per credit hour part-time; nonresident $27,000 full-time, $900 per credit hour part-time. Full-time tuition and fees vary according to course load and program. Part-time tuition and fees vary according to course load and program. *Required fees:* $258 full-time, $129 per term part-time. *Room and board:* $8865; room only: $4742. Room and board charges vary according to board plan and housing facility. *Payment plans:* installment, deferred payment.

Financial Aid *Of all full-time matriculated undergraduates who enrolled in 2011,* 4,121 applied for aid, 3,447 were judged to have need, 537 had their need fully met. *In 2011,* 1138 non-need-based awards were made. *Average percent of need met:* 70. *Average financial aid package:* $11,903. *Average need-based loan:* $4554. *Average need-based gift aid:* $5675. *Average non-need-based aid:* $4931. *Average indebtedness upon graduation:* $33,141.

Applying *Options:* electronic application, deferred entrance. *Required:* high school transcript. *Recommended:* minimum 2.8 GPA, interview.

Freshman Application Contact Ms. Allison Carter, Director of Admissions, Michigan Technological University, 1400 Townsend Drive, Houghton, MI 49931-1295. *Phone:* 906-487-1888. *Toll-free phone:* 888-MTU-1885. *Fax:* 906-487-2125. *E-mail:* mtu4u@mtu.edu.
Website: http://www.mtu.edu/.

See previous page for display ad and page 1386 for the College Close-Up.

Northern Michigan University

Marquette, Michigan

- **State-supported** comprehensive, founded 1899
- **Small-town** 300-acre campus
- **Coed** 8,451 undergraduate students, 90% full-time, 53% women, 47% men
- **Minimally difficult** entrance level, 68% of applicants were admitted

Undergraduates 7,587 full-time, 864 part-time. 19% are from out of state; 3% Black or African American, non-Hispanic/Latino; 2% Hispanic/Latino; 0.4% Asian, non-Hispanic/Latino; 1% American Indian or Alaska Native, non-Hispanic/Latino; 2% Two or more races, non-Hispanic/Latino; 22% Race/ethnicity unknown; 0.9% international; 7% transferred in; 38% live on campus. *Retention:* 72% of full-time freshmen returned.

Freshmen *Admission:* 6,841 applied, 4,636 admitted, 1,659 enrolled. *Average high school GPA:* 3.13. *Test scores:* ACT scores over 18: 86%; ACT scores over 24: 30%; ACT scores over 30: 4%.

Faculty *Student/faculty ratio:* 22:1.

Academics *Calendar:* semesters. *Degrees:* certificates, diplomas, associate, bachelor's, master's, post-master's, and postbachelor's certificates. *Special study options:* adult/continuing education programs, part-time degree program. *ROTC:* Army (b).

Computers on Campus Students can access the following: campus intranet, computer help desk, free student e-mail accounts, online (class) grades, online (class) registration, online (class) schedules. Campuswide network is available. 100% of college-owned or -operated housing units are wired for high-speed Internet access. Wireless service is available via entire campus.

Student Life *Housing:* on-campus residence required through sophomore year. *Options:* coed, disabled students. Campus housing is university owned. Freshman campus housing is guaranteed. *Campus security:* 24-hour emergency response devices and patrols, student patrols, late-night transport/escort service.

Athletics Member NCAA. All Division II except ice hockey (Division I). *Intercollegiate sports:* crew M(c)/W(c), cross-country running W(s), football M(s), golf M(s), ice hockey M(s)/W(c), lacrosse M(c), rugby M(c)/W(c), skiing (cross-country) M(s)/W(s), skiing (downhill) M(c)/W(c), soccer M(c)/W(s), track and field M(c)/W(s), ultimate Frisbee M/W, volleyball W(s). *Intramural sports:* badminton M/W, basketball M/W, cheerleading M/W, football M/W, ice hockey M/W, racquetball M/W, soccer M/W, softball M/W, table tennis M/W, ultimate Frisbee M/W, volleyball M/W, water polo M/W.

Standardized Tests *Required:* SAT or ACT (for admission).

Costs (2013–14) *One-time required fee:* $225. *Tuition:* state resident $8646 full-time, $324 per credit hour part-time; nonresident $13,542 full-time, $521 per credit hour part-time. Full-time tuition and fees vary according to program. Part-time tuition and fees vary according to program. *Required fees:* $64 full-time. *Room and board:* $8404; room only: $4208. Room and board charges vary according to board plan and housing facility. *Payment plans:* installment, deferred payment. *Waivers:* senior citizens and employees or children of employees.

Financial Aid Of all full-time matriculated undergraduates who enrolled in 2011, 7,336 applied for aid, 5,369 were judged to have need, 588 had their need fully met. In 2011, 397 non-need-based awards were made. *Average percent of need met:* 61%. *Average financial aid package:* $9094. *Average need-based loan:* $4145. *Average need-based gift aid:* $5365. *Average non-need-based aid:* $2868. *Average indebtedness upon graduation:* $29,371.

Applying *Options:* electronic application, deferred entrance. *Application fee:* $30. *Required:* high school transcript. *Required for some:* minimum 2.3 GPA. *Application deadlines:* rolling (freshmen), rolling (transfers). *Notification:* continuous (freshmen), continuous (transfers).

Freshman Application Contact Ms. Gerri Daniels, Director of Admissions, Northern Michigan University, 1401 Presque Isle Avenue, Marquette, MI 49855. *Phone:* 906-227-2650. *Toll-free phone:* 800-682-9797. *Fax:* 906-227-1747. *E-mail:* admiss@nmu.edu.
Website: http://www.nmu.edu/.

Northwood University, Michigan Campus

Midland, Michigan

- **Independent** comprehensive, founded 1959
- **Small-town** 434-acre campus
- **Endowment** $31.1 million
- **Coed** 1,536 undergraduate students, 95% full-time, 38% women, 62% men
- **Moderately difficult** entrance level, 68% of applicants were admitted

Undergraduates 1,456 full-time, 80 part-time. Students come from 21 states and territories; 24 other countries; 11% are from out of state; 8% Black or African American, non-Hispanic/Latino; 3% Hispanic/Latino; 0.5% Asian, non-Hispanic/Latino; 0.4% American Indian or Alaska Native, non-Hispanic/Latino; 0.7% Two or more races, non-Hispanic/Latino; 7% Race/ethnicity unknown; 9% international; 13% transferred in; 41% live on campus. *Retention:* 77% of full-time freshmen returned.

Freshmen *Admission:* 1,258 applied, 851 admitted, 323 enrolled. *Average high school GPA:* 3.26. *Test scores:* ACT scores over 18: 94%; ACT scores over 24: 35%; ACT scores over 30: 3%.

Faculty *Total:* 130, 41% full-time, 25% with terminal degrees. *Student/faculty ratio:* 21:1.

Academics *Calendar:* quarters. *Degrees:* associate, bachelor's, and master's. *Special study options:* academic remediation for entering students, accelerated degree program, adult/continuing education programs, advanced placement credit, cooperative education, distance learning, double majors, external degree program, honors programs, internships, off-campus study, part-time degree program, services for LD students, study abroad, summer session for credit.

Computers on Campus 215 computers/terminals are available on campus for general student use. Students can access the following: campus intranet, computer help desk, free student e-mail accounts, online (class) grades, online (class) registration, online (class) schedules. Campuswide network is available. 100% of college-owned or -operated housing units are wired for high-speed Internet access. Wireless service is available via entire campus.

Student Life *Housing:* on-campus residence required for freshman year. *Options:* men-only, women-only. Campus housing is university owned. Freshman campus housing is guaranteed. *Activities and organizations:* drama/theater group, student-run newspaper, Student Senate, intramural sports/club sports, campus art, Northwood University International Auto Show (NUTAS), national fraternities, national sororities. *Campus security:* 24-hour emergency response devices and patrols, late-night transport/escort service, controlled dormitory access. *Student services:* health clinic, personal/psychological counseling.

Athletics Member NCAA. All Division II. *Intercollegiate sports:* baseball M(s), basketball M(s)/W(s), cheerleading M(s)/W(s), cross-country running M(s)/W(s), football M(s), golf M(s)/W(s), soccer M(s)/W(s), softball W(s), tennis M(s)/W(s), track and field M(s)/W(s), volleyball W(s). *Intramural sports:* badminton M/W, baseball M(c), basketball M/W, football M, ice hockey M(c), lacrosse M(c), soccer M(c)/W, softball M/W, table tennis M/W, tennis M/W, ultimate Frisbee M/W, volleyball M/W.

Standardized Tests *Required:* SAT or ACT (for admission).

Costs (2012–13) *Comprehensive fee:* $29,766 includes full-time tuition ($20,040), mandatory fees ($956), and room and board ($8770). Part-time tuition: $776 per credit hour. *College room only:* $4570. Room and board charges vary according to board plan. *Payment plan:* installment. *Waivers:* employees or children of employees.

Financial Aid Of all full-time matriculated undergraduates who enrolled in 2012, 1,127 applied for aid, 998 were judged to have need, 242 had their need fully met. 101 Federal Work-Study jobs (averaging $1612). In 2012, 288 non-need-based awards were made. *Average percent of need met:* 62%. *Average financial aid package:* $18,858. *Average need-based loan:* $4243. *Average need-based gift aid:* $5480. *Average non-need-based aid:* $7197. *Average indebtedness upon graduation:* $32,457.

Applying *Options:* electronic application, early admission, deferred entrance. *Application fee:* $25. *Required:* essay or personal statement, high school transcript. *Recommended:* 1 letter of recommendation, interview. *Application deadlines:* 8/1 (freshmen), 8/1 (out-of-state freshmen), rolling (transfers). *Notification:* continuous (freshmen), continuous (out-of-state freshmen), continuous (transfers).

Freshman Application Contact Mr. Greg Stiffler, Director of Admission, Northwood University, Michigan Campus, 4000 Whiting Drive, Midland, MI 48640. *Phone:* 989-837-4273. *Toll-free phone:* 800-457-7878. *Fax:* 989-837-4490. *E-mail:* miadmit@northwood.edu.
Website: http://www.northwood.edu/.

Oakland University
Rochester, Michigan

- **State-supported** university, founded 1957
- **Suburban** 1444-acre campus with easy access to Detroit
- **Endowment** $50.9 million
- **Coed** 16,190 undergraduate students, 73% full-time, 60% women, 40% men
- **Moderately difficult** entrance level, 62% of applicants were admitted

Undergraduates 11,880 full-time, 4,310 part-time. 19% are from out of state; 8% Black or African American, non-Hispanic/Latino; 2% Hispanic/Latino; 4% Asian, non-Hispanic/Latino; 0.1% Native Hawaiian or other Pacific Islander, non-Hispanic/Latino; 0.3% American Indian or Alaska Native, non-Hispanic/Latino; 2% Two or more races, non-Hispanic/Latino; 5% Race/ethnicity unknown; 1% international; 12% transferred in; 14% live on campus. *Retention:* 70% of full-time freshmen returned.
Freshmen *Admission:* 12,152 applied, 7,551 admitted, 2,464 enrolled. *Average high school GPA:* 3.37. *Test scores:* ACT scores over 18: 95%; ACT scores over 24: 44%; ACT scores over 30: 8%.
Faculty *Total:* 560. *Student/faculty ratio:* 21:1.
Academics *Calendar:* semesters. *Degrees:* bachelor's, master's, doctoral, post-master's, and postbachelor's certificates. *Special study options:* academic remediation for entering students, accelerated degree program, advanced placement credit, cooperative education, distance learning, double majors, English as a second language, honors programs, independent study, internships, off-campus study, part-time degree program, services for LD students, student-designed majors, study abroad, summer session for credit. *ROTC:* Air Force (c).
Computers on Campus Students can access the following: computer help desk, free student e-mail accounts, online (class) grades, online (class) registration, online (class) schedules. Campuswide network is available. 100% of college-owned or -operated housing units are wired for high-speed Internet access. Wireless service is available via entire campus.
Student Life *Housing options:* coed, cooperative, disabled students. Campus housing is university owned. Freshman applicants given priority for college housing. *Activities and organizations:* drama/theater group, student-run newspaper, radio and television station, choral group, American Marketing Association (AMA), International Allies Organization, Psi Chi—Psychology Student Association, Student Michigan Education Association (SMEA), Student Nurses Association of Oakland University (SNAOU), national fraternities, national sororities. *Campus security:* 24-hour emergency response devices and patrols, student patrols, late-night transport/escort service, controlled dormitory access, state certified police officers, security lighting, extensive camera system, self-defense/alcohol abuse classes. *Student services:* health clinic, personal/psychological counseling.
Athletics Member NCAA. All Division I except ice hockey (Division III). *Intercollegiate sports:* baseball M(s), basketball M(s)/W(s), cross-country running M(s)/W(s), golf M(s)/W(s), ice hockey M, soccer M(s)/W(s), softball W(s), swimming and diving M(s)/W(s), tennis W(s), track and field M/W, volleyball W(s). *Intramural sports:* basketball M/W, bowling M/W, equestrian sports M(c)/W(c), fencing M(c)/W(c), ice hockey M(c), lacrosse M(c)/W(c), rugby M(c), soccer M/W, tennis M(c)/W(c), volleyball M/W, water polo M(c)/W(c), wrestling M(c).
Standardized Tests *Required for some:* ACT (for admission). *Recommended:* SAT or ACT (for admission).
Costs (2013–14) *Tuition:* state resident $11,183 full-time, $341 per credit hour part-time; nonresident $25,598 full-time, $796 per credit hour part-time. Full-time tuition and fees vary according to program and student level. Part-time tuition and fees vary according to program and student level. *Room and board:* $8208. Room and board charges vary according to housing facility. *Payment plans:* installment, deferred payment. *Waivers:* senior citizens and employees or children of employees.
Financial Aid Of all full-time matriculated undergraduates who enrolled in 2012, 9,192 applied for aid, 7,843 were judged to have need, 513 had their need fully met. In 2012, 1238 non-need-based awards were made. *Average percent of need met:* 70%. *Average financial aid package:* $12,511. *Average*

need-based loan: $4127. *Average need-based gift aid:* $4552. *Average non-need-based aid:* $3091. *Average indebtedness upon graduation:* $19,697.
Applying *Options:* electronic application, deferred entrance. *Required:* high school transcript, minimum 2.5 GPA. *Required for some:* minimum 3.0 GPA, interview, audition. *Application deadlines:* rolling (freshmen), rolling (transfers). *Notification:* continuous (freshmen), continuous (transfers).
Freshman Application Contact Ms. Eleanor L Reynolds, Interim Assistant Vice President, Student Affairs, Oakland University, Rochester, MI 48309-4401. *Phone:* 248-370-3364. *Toll-free phone:* 800-OAK-UNIV. *Fax:* 248-370-4462. *E-mail:* ouinfo@oakland.edu.
Website: http://www.oakland.edu/.

Olivet College
Olivet, Michigan

- **Independent** 4-year, founded 1844, affiliated with Congregational Christian Church
- **Small-town** 92-acre campus with easy access to Lansing, Battle Creek
- **Coed** 1,164 undergraduate students, 91% full-time, 45% women, 55% men
- **Minimally difficult** entrance level, 53% of applicants were admitted

Undergraduates 1,057 full-time, 107 part-time. Students come from 10 states and territories; 2 other countries; 8% Black or African American, non-Hispanic/Latino; 3% Hispanic/Latino; 0.3% Asian, non-Hispanic/Latino; 0.3% Native Hawaiian or other Pacific Islander, non-Hispanic/Latino; 0.3% American Indian or Alaska Native, non-Hispanic/Latino; 2% Two or more races, non-Hispanic/Latino; 5% Race/ethnicity unknown; 49% live on campus. *Retention:* 71% of full-time freshmen returned.
Freshmen *Admission:* 2,379 applied, 1,252 admitted, 305 enrolled.
Faculty *Total:* 90, 51% full-time. *Student/faculty ratio:* 17:1.
Academics *Calendar:* 4-4-1. *Degrees:* bachelor's and master's. *Special study options:* advanced placement credit, cooperative education, double majors, honors programs, independent study, internships, part-time degree program, student-designed majors, summer session for credit. *ROTC:* Air Force (c). *Unusual degree programs:* 3-2 engineering with Michigan Technological University.
Computers on Campus 118 computers/terminals are available on campus for general student use. Students can access the following: campus intranet, computer help desk, free student e-mail accounts, online (class) grades, online (class) registration, online (class) schedules. Campuswide network is available. Wireless service is available via entire campus.
Student Life *Housing:* on-campus residence required through junior year. *Options:* coed, men-only, women-only. Campus housing is university owned. Freshman campus housing is guaranteed. *Activities and organizations:* drama/theater group, student-run newspaper, radio station, choral group, marching band, Mathletes math club, Common Ground service club, Student Athletes club, Psych Club, Olivet College Vets. *Campus security:* 24-hour emergency response devices and patrols, student patrols, late-night transport/escort service, Security cameras in all dorms and campus surveillance. *Student services:* health clinic, personal/psychological counseling, women's center.
Athletics Member NCAA. All Division III. *Intercollegiate sports:* baseball M, basketball M/W, cross-country running M/W, football M, golf M/W, lacrosse M/W, soccer M/W, softball W, swimming and diving M/W, tennis W, track and field M/W, volleyball W, wrestling M. *Intramural sports:* basketball M/W, bowling M/W, cheerleading M/W, football M/W, softball M/W, volleyball M/W.
Standardized Tests *Required:* SAT or ACT (for admission).
Financial Aid Of all full-time matriculated undergraduates who enrolled in 2011, 1,089 applied for aid, 1,032 were judged to have need, 165 had their need fully met. 201 Federal Work-Study jobs (averaging $886). In 2011, 99 non-need-based awards were made. *Average percent of need met:* 81%. *Average financial aid package:* $17,446. *Average need-based loan:* $4631. *Average need-based gift aid:* $11,382. *Average non-need-based aid:* $10,950. *Average indebtedness upon graduation:* $24,890.
Applying *Options:* electronic application, deferred entrance. *Application fee:* $25. *Required:* high school transcript. *Required for some:* essay or personal statement, interview. *Recommended:* minimum 2.6 GPA. *Application deadlines:* rolling (freshmen), rolling (transfers). *Notification:* continuous (freshmen), continuous (transfers).
Freshman Application Contact Olivet College, 320 South Main Street, Olivet, MI 49076-9701. *Phone:* 269-749-7635. *Toll-free phone:* 800-456-7189.
Website: http://www.olivetcollege.edu/.

The Robert B. Miller College

Battle Creek, Michigan

Admissions Office Contact The Robert B. Miller College, 450 North Avenue, Battle Creek, MI 49017.
Website: http://www.millercollege.edu/.

Rochester College

Rochester Hills, Michigan

Freshman Application Contact Mr. Larry Norman, Dean of Admissions, Rochester College, 800 West Avon Road, Rochester Hills, MI 48307-2764. *Phone:* 248-218-2190. *Toll-free phone:* 800-521-6010. *Fax:* 248-218-2035. *E-mail:* admissions@rc.edu.
Website: http://www.rc.edu/.

Sacred Heart Major Seminary

Detroit, Michigan

- **Independent Roman Catholic** comprehensive, founded 1919
- **Urban** 24-acre campus
- **Coed**
- **Moderately difficult** entrance level

Faculty *Student/faculty ratio:* 6:1.
Academics *Calendar:* semesters. *Degrees:* diplomas, associate, bachelor's, master's, and postbachelor's certificates.
Standardized Tests *Required:* SAT or ACT (for admission).
Costs (2012–13) *Comprehensive fee:* $25,445 includes full-time tuition ($16,405), mandatory fees ($100), and room and board ($8940). Part-time tuition: $385 per credit hour. *Required fees:* $50 per term part-time. *Payment plans:* installment, deferred payment.
Financial Aid *Of all full-time matriculated undergraduates who enrolled in 2010,* 24 applied for aid, 24 were judged to have need, 4 had their need fully met. *In 2010,* 23 non-need-based awards were made. *Average percent of need met:* 67. *Average financial aid package:* $17,584. *Average need-based loan:* $4492. *Average need-based gift aid:* $16,052. *Average non-need-based aid:* $3830.
Applying *Options:* early admission, deferred entrance. *Application fee:* $30. *Required:* essay or personal statement, high school transcript, minimum 2.0 GPA, 1 letter of recommendation, interview.
Freshman Application Contact Fr. Michael Byrnes, Vice Rector, Sacred Heart Major Seminary, 2701 Chicago Boulevard, Detroit, MI 48206. *Phone:* 313-883-8552. *Fax:* 313-868-6400.
Website: http://www.shms.edu/.

Saginaw Valley State University

University Center, Michigan

- **State-supported** comprehensive, founded 1963
- **Small-town** 782-acre campus
- **Endowment** $44.2 million
- **Coed** 9,052 undergraduate students, 86% full-time, 56% women, 44% men
- **Moderately difficult** entrance level, 85% of applicants were admitted

Undergraduates 7,784 full-time, 1,268 part-time. Students come from 17 states and territories; 26 other countries; 1% are from out of state; 11% Black or African American, non-Hispanic/Latino; 3% Hispanic/Latino; 0.8% Asian, non-Hispanic/Latino; 0.1% Native Hawaiian or other Pacific Islander, non-Hispanic/Latino; 0.3% American Indian or Alaska Native, non-Hispanic/Latino; 1% Two or more races, non-Hispanic/Latino; 5% Race/ethnicity unknown; 6% international; 6% transferred in; 30% live on campus. *Retention:* 70% of full-time freshmen returned.
Freshmen *Admission:* 6,262 applied, 5,340 admitted, 1,653 enrolled. *Average high school GPA:* 3.19. *Test scores:* ACT scores over 18: 87%; ACT scores over 24: 28%; ACT scores over 30: 3%.
Faculty *Total:* 767, 39% full-time. *Student/faculty ratio:* 20:1.
Academics *Calendar:* semesters plus summer session. *Degrees:* bachelor's, master's, and post-master's certificates. *Special study options:* academic remediation for entering students, accelerated degree program, adult/continuing

education programs, advanced placement credit, cooperative education, distance learning, double majors, English as a second language, honors programs, independent study, internships, part-time degree program, services for LD students, student-designed majors, study abroad, summer session for credit.
Computers on Campus 1,033 computers/terminals are available on campus for general student use. Students can access the following: computer help desk, free student e-mail accounts, online (class) grades, online (class) registration, online (class) schedules. Campuswide network is available. Wireless service is available via dorm rooms, libraries, student centers.
Student Life *Housing options:* men-only, women-only, disabled students. Campus housing is university owned. Freshman campus housing is guaranteed. *Activities and organizations:* drama/theater group, student-run newspaper, choral group, marching band, His House Christian Fellowship, Criminal Justice Society, Delta Sigma Pi, Alpha Phi Omega, International Students Club, national fraternities, national sororities. *Campus security:* 24-hour emergency response devices and patrols, student patrols, late-night transport/escort service, controlled dormitory access, rape prevention program. *Student services:* health clinic, personal/psychological counseling.
Athletics Member NCAA. All Division II. *Intercollegiate sports:* baseball M(s), basketball M(s)/W(s), bowling M(s), cheerleading M/W, cross-country running M(s)/W(s), equestrian sports M(c)/W(c), football M(s), golf M(s), gymnastics M(c)/W, ice hockey M(c), lacrosse M(c)/W(c), rugby M(c)/W(c), soccer M(s)/W(s), softball W(s), tennis M(c)/W(s), track and field M(s)/W(s), ultimate Frisbee M(c)/W(c), volleyball W(s), wrestling M(c). *Intramural sports:* badminton M/W, basketball M/W, football M/W, golf M/W, soccer M/W, softball M/W, tennis M/W, volleyball M/W.
Standardized Tests *Required:* ACT (for admission).
Costs (2013–14) *Tuition:* state resident $7682 full-time, $256 per credit hour part-time; nonresident $18,626 full-time, $621 per credit hour part-time. Full-time tuition and fees vary according to course level, course load, location, and program. Part-time tuition and fees vary according to course level, course load, location, and program. *Required fees:* $438 full-time, $15 per credit hour part-time. *Room and board:* $8190; room only: $5560. Room and board charges vary according to board plan, housing facility, and student level. *Payment plan:* installment. *Waivers:* employees or children of employees.
Financial Aid Of all full-time matriculated undergraduates who enrolled in 2010, 6,168 applied for aid, 4,295 were judged to have need, 728 had their need fully met. In 2010, 705 non-need-based awards were made. *Average percent of need met:* 63%. *Average financial aid package:* $7086. *Average need-based loan:* $3816. *Average need-based gift aid:* $3432. *Average non-need-based aid:* $3745. *Average indebtedness upon graduation:* $24,000.
Applying *Options:* electronic application, deferred entrance. *Application fee:* $30. *Required:* high school transcript. *Recommended:* minimum 2.5 GPA. *Application deadlines:* rolling (freshmen), rolling (transfers). *Notification:* continuous (freshmen), continuous (transfers).
Freshman Application Contact Jennifer Pahl, Director of Admissions, Saginaw Valley State University, 7400 Bay Road, University Center, MI 48710-0001. *Phone:* 989-964-4200. *Toll-free phone:* 800-968-9500. *Fax:* 989-790-0180. *E-mail:* admissions@svsu.edu.
Website: http://www.svsu.edu/.

Siena Heights University

Adrian, Michigan

- **Independent Roman Catholic** comprehensive, founded 1919
- **Small-town** 140-acre campus with easy access to Detroit, Toledo
- **Coed** 2,322 undergraduate students, 51% full-time, 56% women, 44% men
- **Moderately difficult** entrance level, 60% of applicants were admitted

Undergraduates 1,173 full-time, 1,149 part-time. Students come from 5 other countries; 13% Black or African American, non-Hispanic/Latino; 4% Hispanic/Latino; 1% Asian, non-Hispanic/Latino; 0.1% Native Hawaiian or other Pacific Islander, non-Hispanic/Latino; 0.7% American Indian or Alaska Native, non-Hispanic/Latino; 3% Two or more races, non-Hispanic/Latino; 5% Race/ethnicity unknown; 0.3% international; 21% transferred in. *Retention:* 63% of full-time freshmen returned.
Freshmen *Admission:* 1,815 applied, 1,089 admitted, 277 enrolled.
Faculty *Student/faculty ratio:* 17:1.
Academics *Calendar:* semesters. *Degrees:* associate, bachelor's, and master's. *Special study options:* academic remediation for entering students, accelerated degree program, adult/continuing education programs, advanced placement credit, cooperative education, distance learning, double majors, English as a second language, independent study, internships, off-campus study, part-time degree program, services for LD students, student-designed majors, study abroad, summer session for credit.

Computers on Campus Students can access the following: campus intranet, computer help desk, free student e-mail accounts, online (class) grades, online (class) registration, online (class) schedules. Campuswide network is available. 100% of college-owned or -operated housing units are wired for high-speed Internet access. Wireless service is available via entire campus.

Student Life *Housing:* on-campus residence required through junior year. *Options:* coed, disabled students. Campus housing is university owned and is provided by a third party. Freshman campus housing is guaranteed. *Activities and organizations:* drama/theater group, student-run newspaper, choral group, marching band, national fraternities, national sororities. *Campus security:* 24-hour emergency response devices and patrols, student patrols, late-night transport/escort service. *Student services:* health clinic, personal/psychological counseling.

Athletics Member NAIA. *Intercollegiate sports:* baseball M(s), basketball M(s)/W(s), bowling M(s)/W(s), cheerleading M/W, cross-country running M(s)/W(s), football M(s), golf M(s)/W(s), lacrosse M(s)/W(s), soccer M(s)/W(s), softball W(s), track and field M(s)/W(s), volleyball M(s)/W(s). *Intramural sports:* basketball M/W, softball M/W, volleyball M/W.

Standardized Tests *Required:* SAT or ACT (for admission).

Costs (2013–14) *Comprehensive fee:* $30,280 includes full-time tuition ($21,250), mandatory fees ($320), and room and board ($8710). Full-time tuition and fees vary according to course load, location, and program. Part-time tuition and fees vary according to course load, location, and program. *Room and board:* Room and board charges vary according to board plan, housing facility, and location. *Payment plans:* installment, deferred payment. *Waivers:* senior citizens and employees or children of employees.

Financial Aid In 2002, 166 non-need-based awards were made. *Average percent of need met:* 66%. *Average financial aid package:* $12,200. *Average indebtedness upon graduation:* $13,500.

Applying *Options:* electronic application, deferred entrance. *Required:* high school transcript. *Required for some:* essay or personal statement, interview. *Application deadlines:* rolling (freshmen), rolling (out-of-state freshmen), rolling (transfers).

Freshman Application Contact Ms. Sarah Johnson, Director of Admissions, Siena Heights University, 1247 East Siena Heights Drive, Adrian, MI 49221. *Phone:* 517-264-7185. *Toll-free phone:* 800-521-0009. *Fax:* 517-264-7745. *E-mail:* sjohnson@sienaheights.edu.
Website: http://www.sienaheights.edu/.

South University

Novi, Michigan

- **Proprietary** comprehensive, part of Education Management Corporation
- **Coed**

Academics *Degrees:* associate, bachelor's, and master's.

Freshman Application Contact South University, 41555 Twelve Mile Road, Novi, MI 48377. *Phone:* 248-675-0200. *Toll-free phone:* 877-693-2085. *Website:* http://www.southuniversity.edu/novi.aspx.

Spring Arbor University

Spring Arbor, Michigan

- **Independent Free Methodist** comprehensive, founded 1873
- **Rural** 100-acre campus
- **Endowment** $9.8 million
- **Coed** 3,058 undergraduate students, 70% full-time, 69% women, 31% men
- **Moderately difficult** entrance level, 70% of applicants were admitted

Undergraduates 2,137 full-time, 921 part-time. Students come from 24 states and territories; 11 other countries; 12% are from out of state; 13% Black or African American, non-Hispanic/Latino; 3% Hispanic/Latino; 0.9% Asian, non-Hispanic/Latino; 0.5% American Indian or Alaska Native, non-Hispanic/Latino; 1% Two or more races, non-Hispanic/Latino; 5% Race/ethnicity unknown; 1% international; 3% transferred in; 73% live on campus. *Retention:* 77% of full-time freshmen returned.

Freshmen *Admission:* 2,674 applied, 1,885 admitted, 314 enrolled. *Average high school GPA:* 3.39. *Test scores:* SAT critical reading scores over 500: 52%; SAT math scores over 500: 57%; SAT writing scores over 500: 57%; ACT scores over 18: 91%; SAT critical reading scores over 600: 33%; SAT math scores over 600: 24%; SAT writing scores over 600: 33%; ACT scores over 24:

46%; SAT critical reading scores over 700: 9%; SAT math scores over 700: 10%; SAT writing scores over 700: 5%; ACT scores over 30: 5%.

Faculty *Total:* 143, 57% full-time, 44% with terminal degrees. *Student/faculty ratio:* 15:1.

Academics *Calendar:* 4-1-4. *Degrees:* associate, bachelor's, master's, and postbachelor's certificates. *Special study options:* academic remediation for entering students, accelerated degree program, adult/continuing education programs, advanced placement credit, distance learning, double majors, English as a second language, honors programs, independent study, internships, off-campus study, part-time degree program, services for LD students, student-designed majors, study abroad, summer session for credit. *ROTC:* Army (b), Air Force (c). *Unusual degree programs:* 3-2 engineering with University of Michigan.

Computers on Campus 251 computers/terminals and 1,193 ports are available on campus for general student use. Students can access the following: campus intranet, computer help desk, free student e-mail accounts, online (class) grades, online (class) registration, online (class) schedules. Campuswide network is available. 100% of college-owned or -operated housing units are wired for high-speed Internet access. Wireless service is available via entire campus.

Student Life *Housing:* on-campus residence required through senior year. *Options:* men-only, women-only, disabled students. Campus housing is university owned. Freshman campus housing is guaranteed. *Activities and organizations:* drama/theater group, student-run newspaper, radio and television station, choral group, Inter-faith Shelter Ministries, Band of Brothers, Action Jackson, Circle of Sisters, Heartside Homeless. *Campus security:* 24-hour emergency response devices and patrols, student patrols, late-night transport/escort service, controlled dormitory access. *Student services:* health clinic, personal/psychological counseling.

Athletics Member NAIA, NCCAA. *Intercollegiate sports:* baseball M(s), basketball M(s)/W(s), cross-country running M(s)/W(s), golf M(s)/W(s), soccer M(s)/W(s), softball W(s), tennis M(s)/W(s), track and field M(s)/W(s), volleyball W(s). *Intramural sports:* basketball M/W, field hockey M, football M/W, soccer M/W, softball M/W, table tennis M/W, tennis M/W, ultimate Frisbee M/W, volleyball M/W.

Standardized Tests *Required:* SAT or ACT (for admission). *Recommended:* ACT (for admission).

Costs (2012–13) *Comprehensive fee:* $30,438 includes full-time tuition ($21,998), mandatory fees ($540), and room and board ($7900). Full-time tuition and fees vary according to course load, degree level, and program. Part-time tuition: $535 per credit hour. Part-time tuition and fees vary according to course load, degree level, program, and reciprocity agreements. *Required fees:* $255 per term part-time. *College room only:* $3710. Room and board charges vary according to board plan and housing facility. *Payment plan:* installment. *Waivers:* employees or children of employees.

Financial Aid Of all full-time matriculated undergraduates who enrolled in 2010, 1,577 applied for aid, 1,374 were judged to have need, 287 had their need fully met. In 2010, 4 non-need-based awards were made. *Average percent of need met:* 83%. *Average financial aid package:* $19,186. *Average need-based loan:* $4730. *Average need-based gift aid:* $12,161. *Average non-need-based aid:* $3073. *Average indebtedness upon graduation:* $28,212.

Applying *Options:* electronic application, early admission, deferred entrance. *Application fee:* $30. *Required:* high school transcript. *Required for some:* essay or personal statement, interview. *Recommended:* minimum 2.6 GPA, Guidance counselor's form and ACT score of 20 or SAT score of 930 recommended. *Application deadlines:* 8/1 (freshmen), 8/1 (out-of-state freshmen), rolling (transfers). *Notification:* continuous (freshmen), continuous (out-of-state freshmen), continuous (transfers).

Freshman Application Contact Mr. Randy Comfort, Executive Director of Admissions, Spring Arbor University, 106 East Main Street, Spring Arbor, MI 49283-9799. *Phone:* 517-750-1200 Ext. 1468. *Toll-free phone:* 800-968-0011. *Fax:* 517-750-6620. *E-mail:* admissions@arbor.edu.
Website: http://www.arbor.edu/.

University of Detroit Mercy

Detroit, Michigan

Freshman Application Contact Office of Admissions, University of Detroit Mercy, 4001 West McNichols Road, Detroit, MI 48221-3038. *Phone:* 313-993-1245. *Toll-free phone:* 800-635-5020. *Fax:* 313-993-3326. *E-mail:* admissions@udmercy.edu.
Website: http://www.udmercy.edu/.

University of Michigan

Ann Arbor, Michigan

- **State-supported** university, founded 1817
- **Small-town** 3177-acre campus
- **Endowment** $7.7 billion
- **Coed** 27,407 undergraduate students, 97% full-time, 49% women, 51% men
- **Very difficult** entrance level, 41% of applicants were admitted

Undergraduates 26,538 full-time, 869 part-time. Students come from 56 states and territories; 93 other countries; 36% are from out of state; 4% Black or African American, non-Hispanic/Latino; 4% Hispanic/Latino; 12% Asian, non-Hispanic/Latino; 0.2% American Indian or Alaska Native, non-Hispanic/Latino; 3% Two or more races, non-Hispanic/Latino; 4% Race/ethnicity unknown; 6% international; 3% transferred in; 37% live on campus. *Retention:* 96% of full-time freshmen returned.

Freshmen *Admission:* 39,584 applied, 16,073 admitted, 6,236 enrolled. *Average high school GPA:* 3.79. *Test scores:* SAT critical reading scores over 500: 97%; SAT math scores over 500: 99%; SAT writing scores over 500: 98%; ACT scores over 18: 100%; SAT critical reading scores over 600: 78%; SAT math scores over 600: 92%; SAT writing scores over 600: 84%; ACT scores over 24: 95%; SAT critical reading scores over 700: 27%; SAT math scores over 700: 52%; SAT writing scores over 700: 38%; ACT scores over 30: 54%.

Faculty *Total:* 3,139, 81% full-time, 88% with terminal degrees. *Student/faculty ratio:* 16:1.

Academics *Calendar:* trimesters. *Degrees:* bachelor's, master's, doctoral, post-master's, and postbachelor's certificates. *Special study options:* accelerated degree program, adult/continuing education programs, advanced placement credit, cooperative education, distance learning, double majors, English as a second language, external degree program, honors programs, independent study, internships, off-campus study, part-time degree program, services for LD students, student-designed majors, study abroad, summer session for credit. *ROTC:* Army (b), Navy (b), Air Force (b). *Unusual degree programs:* 3-2 business administration; engineering; music; art and design.

Computers on Campus 2,529 computers/terminals are available on campus for general student use. Students can access the following: campus intranet, computer help desk, free student e-mail accounts, online (class) grades, online (class) registration, online (class) schedules, file storage. Campuswide network is available. 97% of college-owned or -operated housing units are wired for high-speed Internet access. Wireless service is available via entire campus.

Student Life *Housing options:* coed, women-only, cooperative. Campus housing is university owned. Freshman campus housing is guaranteed. *Activities and organizations:* drama/theater group, student-run newspaper, radio and television station, choral group, marching band, Hillel Society, K-Grams (Kids' Program), M-Powered Entrepreneurial Club, Dance Marathon, Alternative Spring Break, national fraternities, national sororities. *Campus security:* 24-hour emergency response devices and patrols, student patrols, late-night transport/escort service, controlled dormitory access, Safewalk, Night Owl ride service. *Student services:* health clinic, personal/psychological counseling, women's center, legal services.

Athletics Member NCAA. All Division I except football (Division I-AA). *Intercollegiate sports:* baseball M(s), basketball M(s)/W(s), crew M(c), cross-country running M(s)/W(s), field hockey W(s), golf M(s)/W(s), gymnastics M(s)/W(s), ice hockey M(s), soccer M(s)/W(s), softball W(s), swimming and diving M(s)/W(s), tennis M(s)/W(s), track and field M(s)/W(s), volleyball W(s), water polo W(s), wrestling M(s). *Intramural sports:* badminton M/W, baseball M(c)/W(c), basketball M/W, crew M(c)/W(c), fencing M(c)/W(c), field hockey M(c)/W(c), golf M/W, gymnastics W(c), ice hockey M(c)/W(c), lacrosse M(c)/W(c), racquetball M/W, riflery M(c)/W(c), rugby M(c)/W(c), sailing M(c)/W(c), soccer M(c)/W(c), softball M(c)/W(c), swimming and diving M(c)/W(c), table tennis M/W, tennis M(c)/W(c), track and field M/W, ultimate Frisbee M(c)/W(c), volleyball M/W, water polo M(c)/W(c), wrestling M(c).

Standardized Tests *Required:* SAT or ACT (for admission). *Required for some:* SAT Subject Tests (for admission).

Costs (2012–13) *Tuition:* state resident $13,625 full-time, $504 per credit hour part-time; nonresident $40,302 full-time, $1592 per credit hour part-time. Full-time tuition and fees vary according to course load, program, and student level. Part-time tuition and fees vary according to course load, program, and student level. *Required fees:* $194 full-time, $97 per term part-time. *Room and board:* $9752. Room and board charges vary according to board plan and housing facility. *Payment plan:* installment.

Financial Aid Of all full-time matriculated undergraduates who enrolled in 2011, 14,089 applied for aid, 10,748 were judged to have need, 8,472 had their need fully met. 2,982 Federal Work-Study jobs (averaging $1607). In 2011, 4455 non-need-based awards were made. *Average percent of need met:* 85%. *Average financial aid package:* $19,334. *Average need-based loan:* $5231. *Average need-based gift aid:* $13,256. *Average non-need-based aid:* $9756. *Average indebtedness upon graduation:* $27,815. *Financial aid deadline:* 5/31.

Applying *Options:* electronic application, early action, deferred entrance. *Application fee:* $65. *Required:* essay or personal statement, high school transcript. *Required for some:* interview, audition for School of Music, Theatre and Dance; portfolio for School of Art and Design. *Application deadlines:* 2/1 (freshmen), 2/1 (out-of-state freshmen), 2/1 (transfers), 10/31 (early action). *Notification:* continuous (freshmen), continuous (out-of-state freshmen), continuous (transfers), 12/22 (early action).

Freshman Application Contact University of Michigan, Ann Arbor, MI 48109. *Phone:* 734-764-7433.

Website: http://www.umich.edu/.

University of Michigan–Dearborn

Dearborn, Michigan

- **State-supported** comprehensive, founded 1959, part of University of Michigan System
- **Suburban** 210-acre campus with easy access to Detroit
- **Coed** 7,328 undergraduate students, 66% full-time, 51% women, 49% men
- **Moderately difficult** entrance level, 60% of applicants were admitted

Undergraduates 4,869 full-time, 2,459 part-time. 12% Black or African American, non-Hispanic/Latino; 5% Hispanic/Latino; 6% Asian, non-Hispanic/Latino; 0.5% American Indian or Alaska Native, non-Hispanic/Latino; 3% Two or more races, non-Hispanic/Latino; 4% Race/ethnicity unknown; 3% international; 12% transferred in.

Freshmen *Admission:* 4,807 applied, 2,908 admitted, 871 enrolled.

Faculty *Total:* 571, 55% full-time, 64% with terminal degrees.

Academics *Calendar:* semesters. *Degrees:* bachelor's, master's, and doctoral. *Special study options:* adult/continuing education programs, part-time degree program. *ROTC:* Army (b).

Computers on Campus Students can access the following: computer help desk, free student e-mail accounts, online (class) grades, online (class) registration, online (class) schedules, tuition and application payments accepted online. Campuswide network is available. Wireless service is available via entire campus.

Student Life *Housing:* college housing not available. *Campus security:* 24-hour emergency response devices and patrols, late-night transport/escort service.

Athletics Member NAIA. *Intercollegiate sports:* basketball M(s)/W(s), bowling M(c)/W(c), cheerleading M(c)/W(c), cross-country running M(c)/W(c), ice hockey M(c), rugby M(c), soccer M(c)/W(c), softball W(s), ultimate Frisbee M(c), volleyball W(s). *Intramural sports:* basketball M/W, cross-country running M(c)/W(c), fencing M(c)/W(c), volleyball M/W.

Standardized Tests *Required:* SAT or ACT (for admission).

Costs (2012–13) *Tuition:* state resident $9876 full-time, $391 per credit hour part-time; nonresident $22,290 full-time, $887 per credit hour part-time. Full-time tuition and fees vary according to course level, course load, degree level, program, and student level. Part-time tuition and fees vary according to course level, course load, degree level, program, and student level. *Required fees:* $606 full-time, $245 part-time. *Payment plan:* installment. *Waivers:* senior citizens and employees or children of employees.

Financial Aid Of all full-time matriculated undergraduates who enrolled in 2011, 3,805 applied for aid, 3,168 were judged to have need, 51 had their need fully met. 146 Federal Work-Study jobs (averaging $1565). In 2011, 538 non-need-based awards were made. *Average percent of need met:* 72%. *Average financial aid package:* $10,439. *Average need-based loan:* $4457. *Average need-based gift aid:* $5297. *Average non-need-based aid:* $4563. *Average indebtedness upon graduation:* $23,437.

Applying *Options:* electronic application, deferred entrance. *Application fee:* $30. *Required:* high school transcript, minimum 3.0 GPA. *Required for some:* interview. *Application deadlines:* rolling (freshmen), rolling (transfers). *Notification:* continuous (freshmen), continuous (transfers).

Freshman Application Contact Ms. Deb Peffer, Interim Director of Admissions, University of Michigan–Dearborn, 4901 Evergreen Road, Room 1145 UC, Dearborn, MI 48128-1491. *Phone:* 313-593-5100. *Fax:* 313-436-9167. *E-mail:* admissions@umd.umich.edu.

Website: http://www.umd.umich.edu/.

University of Michigan–Flint

Flint, Michigan

- **State-supported** comprehensive, founded 1956, part of University of Michigan System
- **Urban** 72-acre campus with easy access to Detroit, Lansing
- **Endowment** $77.4 million
- **Coed** 6,984 undergraduate students, 63% full-time, 61% women, 39% men
- **Moderately difficult** entrance level, 74% of applicants were admitted

Undergraduates 4,379 full-time, 2,605 part-time. Students come from 42 states and territories; 35 other countries; 1% are from out of state; 12% Black or African American, non-Hispanic/Latino; 4% Hispanic/Latino; 2% Asian, non-Hispanic/Latino; 0.1% Native Hawaiian or other Pacific Islander, non-Hispanic/Latino; 0.8% American Indian or Alaska Native, non-Hispanic/Latino; 3% Two or more races, non-Hispanic/Latino; 4% Race/ethnicity unknown; 4% international; 12% transferred in; 4% live on campus. *Retention:* 74% of full-time freshmen returned.

Freshmen *Admission:* 2,638 applied, 1,947 admitted, 626 enrolled. *Average high school GPA:* 3.31. *Test scores:* SAT critical reading scores over 500: 67%; SAT writing scores over 500: 70%; ACT scores over 18: 89%; SAT critical reading scores over 600: 33%; SAT writing scores over 600: 10%; ACT scores over 24: 36%; SAT critical reading scores over 700: 22%; ACT scores over 30: 5%.

Faculty *Total:* 549, 52% full-time, 47% with terminal degrees. *Student/faculty ratio:* 16:1.

Academics *Calendar:* semesters. *Degrees:* bachelor's, master's, doctoral, post-master's, and postbachelor's certificates. *Special study options:* academic remediation for entering students, accelerated degree program, adult/continuing education programs, advanced placement credit, cooperative education, distance learning, double majors, English as a second language, honors programs, independent study, internships, off-campus study, part-time degree program, services for LD students, student-designed majors, study abroad, summer session for credit. *ROTC:* Army (c), Navy (c), Air Force (c).

Computers on Campus 507 computers/terminals are available on campus for general student use. Students can access the following: campus intranet, computer help desk, free student e-mail accounts, online (class) grades, online (class) registration, online (class) schedules. Campuswide network is available. 100% of college-owned or -operated housing units are wired for high-speed Internet access. Wireless service is available via entire campus.

Student Life *Housing options:* coed. Campus housing is university owned. *Activities and organizations:* drama/theater group, student-run newspaper, choral group, International Student Organization, Muslim Student Association, Kappa Sigma Fraternity, Inter-Varsity Christian Fellowship, national fraternities, national sororities. *Campus security:* 24-hour emergency response devices and patrols, student patrols, late-night transport/escort service, controlled dormitory access. *Student services:* health clinic, personal/psychological counseling, women's center.

Athletics *Intramural sports:* basketball M(c)/W(c), bowling M(c)/W(c), cheerleading M(c)/W(c), football M(c), golf M(c)/W(c), ice hockey M(c)/W(c), lacrosse M(c)/W(c), soccer M(c)/W(c), ultimate Frisbee M(c)/W(c), volleyball M(c)/W(c), wrestling M(c)/W(c).

Standardized Tests *Required:* SAT or ACT (for admission).

Costs (2013–14) *Tuition:* state resident $9102 full-time, $359 per credit hour part-time; nonresident $17,754 full-time, $717 per credit hour part-time. Full-time tuition and fees vary according to course level, course load, degree level, program, and student level. Part-time tuition and fees vary according to course level, course load, degree level, program, and student level. *Required fees:* $412 full-time, $157 per term part-time. *Room and board:* $7506; room only: $4692. Room and board charges vary according to housing facility. *Payment plan:* installment. *Waivers:* senior citizens.

Financial Aid Of all full-time matriculated undergraduates who enrolled in 2011, 3,852 applied for aid, 3,431 were judged to have need, 159 had their need fully met. 292 Federal Work-Study jobs (averaging $1999). In 2011, 93 non-need-based awards were made. *Average percent of need met:* 73%. *Average financial aid package:* $11,775. *Average need-based loan:* $4230. *Average need-based gift aid:* $4380. *Average non-need-based aid:* $3268. *Average indebtedness upon graduation:* $26,899.

Applying *Options:* electronic application, deferred entrance. *Application fee:* $30. *Required:* high school transcript. *Application deadlines:* 8/20 (freshmen), rolling (out-of-state freshmen), 8/20 (transfers). *Notification:* continuous (freshmen), continuous (out-of-state freshmen), continuous (transfers).

Freshman Application Contact University of Michigan–Flint, 303 East Kearsley Street, Flint, MI 48502-1950. *Phone:* 810-762-3300. *Toll-free phone:* 800-942-5636.

Website: http://www.umflint.edu/.

University of Phoenix–Detroit Campus

Southfield, Michigan

Admissions Office Contact University of Phoenix–Detroit Campus, 26999 Central Park Boulevard, Suite 100, Southfield, MI 48076. *Toll-free phone:* 866-766-0766.

Website: http://www.phoenix.edu/.

University of Phoenix–Metro Detroit Campus

Troy, Michigan

Freshman Application Contact Marc Booker, Sr. Director, Office of Admissions and Evaluation, University of Phoenix–Metro Detroit Campus, 4035 South Riverpoint Parkway, Mail Stop CF-L101, Phoenix, AZ 85040. *Phone:* 602-557-4609. *Toll-free phone:* 866-766-0766. *Fax:* 480-643-1156. *Website:* http://www.phoenix.edu/.

University of Phoenix–West Michigan Campus

Walker, Michigan

Freshman Application Contact Marc Booker, Sr. Director, Office of Admissions and Evaluation, University of Phoenix–West Michigan Campus, 4035 South Riverpoint Parkway, Mail Stop CF-L101, Phoenix, AZ 85040. *Phone:* 602-557-4609. *Toll-free phone:* 866-766-0766. *Fax:* 480-643-1156. *Website:* http://www.phoenix.edu/.

Walsh College of Accountancy and Business Administration

Troy, Michigan

Application Contact Walsh College of Accountancy and Business Administration, 3838 Livernois Road, PO Box 7006, Troy, MI 48007-7006. *Phone:* 248-823-1344. *Toll-free phone:* 800-925-7401. *Website:* http://www.walshcollege.edu/.

Wayne State University

Detroit, Michigan

- **State-supported** university, founded 1868
- **Urban** 200-acre campus with easy access to Detroit
- **Endowment** $260.8 million
- **Coed** 19,342 undergraduate students, 64% full-time, 57% women, 43% men
- **Minimally difficult** entrance level, 81% of applicants were admitted

Undergraduates 12,471 full-time, 6,871 part-time. Students come from 43 states and territories; 50 other countries; 2% are from out of state; 23% Black or African American, non-Hispanic/Latino; 3% Hispanic/Latino; 8% Asian, non-Hispanic/Latino; 0.4% American Indian or Alaska Native, non-Hispanic/Latino; 1% Two or more races, non-Hispanic/Latino; 12% Race/ethnicity unknown; 2% international; 11% transferred in; 11% live on campus. *Retention:* 75% of full-time freshmen returned.

Freshmen *Admission:* 10,249 applied, 8,255 admitted, 2,338 enrolled. *Average high school GPA:* 3.27. *Test scores:* ACT scores over 18: 81%; ACT scores over 24: 39%; ACT scores over 30: 7%.

Faculty *Total:* 1,873, 56% full-time. *Student/faculty ratio:* 16:1.

Academics *Calendar:* semesters. *Degrees:* certificates, bachelor's, master's, doctoral, post-master's, and postbachelor's certificates. *Special study options:* academic remediation for entering students, accelerated degree program, adult/continuing education programs, advanced placement credit, cooperative education, distance learning, double majors, English as a second language, freshman honors college, honors programs, independent study, internships, off-campus study, part-time degree program, services for LD students, study abroad, summer session for credit. *ROTC:* Army (b), Navy (c), Air Force (c).

Computers on Campus 2,877 computers/terminals are available on campus for general student use. Students can access the following: computer help desk, free student e-mail accounts, online (class) grades, online (class) registration, online (class) schedules. Campuswide network is available. 100% of college-owned or -operated housing units are wired for high-speed Internet access. Wireless service is available via entire campus.

Student Life *Housing options:* coed, women-only, disabled students. Campus housing is university owned. Freshman applicants given priority for college housing. *Activities and organizations:* student-run newspaper, choral group, marching band, Muslim Students Association, Honors Students Association, Indian Students Association, American Medical Students Association-Pre-Med Chapter, national fraternities, national sororities. *Campus security:* 24-hour emergency response devices and patrols, late-night transport/escort service, controlled dormitory access. *Student services:* health clinic, personal/psychological counseling, legal services.

Athletics Member NCAA. All Division II except men's and women's fencing (Division I). *Intercollegiate sports:* baseball M(s), basketball M(s)/W(s), cross-country running M(s)/W(s), fencing M(s)/W(s), football M(s), golf M(s), softball W(s), swimming and diving M(s)/W(s), tennis M(s)/W(s), volleyball W(s). *Intramural sports:* badminton M/W, basketball M/W, field hockey M/W, football M/W, ice hockey M(c), lacrosse M(c)/W(c), racquetball M/W, rock climbing M/W, rugby M(c)/W(c), soccer M/W, softball M/W, table tennis M/W, tennis M/W, ultimate Frisbee M/W, volleyball M/W, weight lifting M/W.

Standardized Tests *Required:* SAT or ACT (for admission).

Costs (2013–14) *Tuition:* state resident $325 per credit hour part-time; nonresident $746 per credit hour part-time. Full-time tuition and fees vary according to course load, program, reciprocity agreements, and student level. Part-time tuition and fees vary according to course load, program, reciprocity agreements, and student level. *Room and board:* $8504; room only: $5384. Room and board charges vary according to board plan and housing facility. *Payment plan:* installment. *Waivers:* senior citizens and employees or children of employees.

Financial Aid Of all full-time matriculated undergraduates who enrolled in 2010, 10,933 applied for aid, 9,967 were judged to have need, 9,748 had their need fully met. 283 Federal Work-Study jobs (averaging $2650). In 2010, 1559 non-need-based awards were made. *Average percent of need met:* 69%. *Average financial aid package:* $16,101. *Average need-based loan:* $4460. *Average need-based gift aid:* $6653. *Average non-need-based aid:* $4330. *Average indebtedness upon graduation:* $22,420. *Financial aid deadline:* 4/30.

Applying *Options:* electronic application, deferred entrance. *Required:* minimum 2.0 GPA. *Required for some:* ACT. *Application deadlines:* 8/26 (freshmen), 8/26 (out-of-state freshmen), 8/26 (transfers). *Notification:* continuous until 8/26 (freshmen), continuous until 8/26 (out-of-state freshmen), continuous until 8/26 (transfers).

Freshman Application Contact Ms. La Joyce Brown, Associate Director, Recruitment and Outreach, Wayne State University, 42 West Warren, Undergraduate Admissions, Student Development and Campus Life, Detroit 48202. *Phone:* 313-577-4906. *Toll-free phone:* 877-WSU-INFO. *E-mail:* admissions@wayne.edu.
Website: http://www.wayne.edu/.

Western Michigan University

Kalamazoo, Michigan

- **State-supported** university, founded 1903
- **Urban** 1200-acre campus
- **Endowment** $204.1 million
- **Coed** 19,478 undergraduate students, 84% full-time, 50% women, 50% men
- **Moderately difficult** entrance level, 83% of applicants were admitted

Undergraduates 16,303 full-time, 3,175 part-time. Students come from 40 states and territories; 65 other countries; 7% are from out of state; 11% Black or African American, non-Hispanic/Latino; 4% Hispanic/Latino; 1% Asian, non-Hispanic/Latino; 0.2% Native Hawaiian or other Pacific Islander, non-Hispanic/Latino; 0.4% American Indian or Alaska Native, non-Hispanic/Latino; 3% Two or more races, non-Hispanic/Latino; 1% Race/ethnicity

unknown; 3% international; 9% transferred in; 27% live on campus. *Retention:* 73% of full-time freshmen returned.

Freshmen *Admission:* 13,985 applied, 11,654 admitted, 3,026 enrolled. *Average high school GPA:* 3.28. *Test scores:* ACT scores over 18: 87%; ACT scores over 24: 32%; ACT scores over 30: 3%.

Faculty *Total:* 1,456, 63% full-time. *Student/faculty ratio:* 18:1.

Academics *Calendar:* semesters. *Degrees:* bachelor's, master's, doctoral, post-master's, and postbachelor's certificates. *Special study options:* academic remediation for entering students, accelerated degree program, adult/continuing education programs, advanced placement credit, cooperative education, distance learning, double majors, English as a second language, freshman honors college, honors programs, independent study, internships, off-campus study, part-time degree program, services for LD students, student-designed majors, study abroad, summer session for credit. *ROTC:* Army (b).

Computers on Campus 2,309 computers/terminals are available on campus for general student use. Students can access the following: computer help desk, free student e-mail accounts, online (class) grades, online (class) registration, online (class) schedules. Campuswide network is available. 100% of college-owned or -operated housing units are wired for high-speed Internet access. Wireless service is available via entire campus.

Student Life *Housing options:* coed, men-only, women-only, disabled students. Campus housing is university owned. Freshman campus housing is guaranteed. *Activities and organizations:* drama/theater group, student-run newspaper, radio station, choral group, marching band, Campus Activities Board, Western Student Association, Young Black Male Support Network, Drive Safe Kalamazoo, Alternative Spring Break, national fraternities, national sororities. *Campus security:* 24-hour emergency response devices and patrols, student patrols, late-night transport/escort service, controlled dormitory access. *Student services:* health clinic, personal/psychological counseling, women's center, legal services.

Athletics Member NCAA. All Division I except football (Division I-A). *Intercollegiate sports:* baseball M(s), basketball M(s)/W(s), cross-country running W(s), golf W(s), gymnastics W(s), ice hockey M(s), soccer M(s)/W(s), softball W(s), tennis M(s)/W(s), track and field W(s), volleyball W(s). *Intramural sports:* baseball M(c)/W(c), basketball M/W, bowling M(c)/W(c), cheerleading W(c), equestrian sports M(c)/W(c), football M/W(c), golf M/W, ice hockey M/W(c), lacrosse M(c)/W(c), racquetball M/W, rugby M(c)/W(c), sailing M(c)/W(c), skiing (downhill) M(c)/W(c), soccer M/W, softball M/W, swimming and diving M(c)/W(c), tennis M/W, ultimate Frisbee M/W, volleyball M/W, wrestling M(c).

Standardized Tests *Required:* SAT or ACT (for admission).

Costs (2012–13) *One-time required fee:* $300. *Tuition:* state resident $9138 full-time, $316 per credit hour part-time; nonresident $22,418 full-time, $775 per credit hour part-time. Full-time tuition and fees vary according to course load, location, program, and student level. Part-time tuition and fees vary according to course load, location, program, and student level. *Required fees:* $844 full-time, $228 per term part-time. *Room and board:* $8414; room only: $4340. Room and board charges vary according to board plan. *Payment plan:* installment. *Waivers:* senior citizens and employees or children of employees.

Financial Aid Of all full-time matriculated undergraduates who enrolled in 2011, 14,698 applied for aid, 12,466 were judged to have need, 2,424 had their need fully met. In 2011, 1711 non-need-based awards were made. *Average percent of need met:* 77%. *Average financial aid package:* $14,685. *Average need-based loan:* $3855. *Average need-based gift aid:* $5256. *Average non-need-based aid:* $3817. *Average indebtedness upon graduation:* $30,867.

Applying *Options:* electronic application. *Application fee:* $35. *Required:* high school transcript. *Required for some:* interview. *Application deadlines:* rolling (freshmen), 9/1 (transfers). *Notification:* continuous (freshmen), continuous (transfers).

Freshman Application Contact Western Michigan University, 1903 West Michigan Avenue, Kalamazoo, MI 49008. *Phone:* 269-387-2000. *E-mail:* askwmu@wmich.edu.
Website: http://www.wmich.edu/.

Yeshiva Gedolah of Greater Detroit

Oak Park, Michigan

Director of Admissions Rabbi P. Rushnawitz, Director, Yeshiva Gedolah of Greater Detroit, 24600 Greenfield, Oak Park, MI 48237-1544.

MINNESOTA

Academy College

Bloomington, Minnesota

Freshman Application Contact Ms. Tracey Schantz, Director, Academy College, Bloomington, MN 55420. *Phone:* 952-851-0066. *Toll-free phone:* 800-292-9149. *Fax:* 952-851-0094. *E-mail:* admissions@academycollege.edu. *Website:* http://www.academycollege.edu/.

Argosy University, Twin Cities

Eagan, Minnesota

Freshman Application Contact Argosy University, Twin Cities, 1515 Central Parkway, Eagan, MN 55121. *Phone:* 651-846-2882. *Toll-free phone:* 888-844-2004.
Website: http://www.argosy.edu/twincities/.

The Art Institutes International Minnesota

Minneapolis, Minnesota

- **Proprietary** 4-year, founded 1964, part of Education Management Corporation
- **Urban** campus
- **Coed**

Academics *Calendar:* quarters. *Degrees:* diplomas, associate, and bachelor's.
Freshman Application Contact The Art Institutes International Minnesota, 15 South 9th Street, Minneapolis, MN 55402. *Phone:* 612-332-3361. *Toll-free phone:* 800-777-3643.
Website: http://www.artinstitutes.edu/minneapolis/.

See full-page ad on page 54 and page 1136 for the College Close-Up.

Augsburg College

Minneapolis, Minnesota

- **Independent Lutheran** comprehensive, founded 1869
- **Urban** 23-acre campus with easy access to Minneapolis-St. Paul
- **Endowment** $29.8 million
- **Coed** 2,998 undergraduate students, 79% full-time, 57% women, 43% men
- **Moderately difficult** entrance level, 69% of applicants were admitted

Undergraduates 2,357 full-time, 641 part-time. Students come from 35 states and territories; 30 other countries; 9% are from out of state; 10% Black or African American, non-Hispanic/Latino; 5% Hispanic/Latino; 8% Asian, non-Hispanic/Latino; 0.3% Native Hawaiian or other Pacific Islander, non-Hispanic/Latino; 2% American Indian or Alaska Native, non-Hispanic/Latino; 3% Two or more races, non-Hispanic/Latino; 7% Race/ethnicity unknown; 2% international; 10% transferred in; 51% live on campus. *Retention:* 79% of full-time freshmen returned.
Freshmen *Admission:* 1,853 applied, 1,271 admitted, 381 enrolled. *Average high school GPA:* 3.08. *Test scores:* SAT critical reading scores over 500: 83%; SAT math scores over 500: 80%; ACT scores over 18: 89%; SAT critical reading scores over 600: 37%; SAT math scores over 600: 43%; ACT scores over 24: 40%; SAT critical reading scores over 700: 14%; SAT math scores over 700: 3%; ACT scores over 30: 3%.
Faculty *Total:* 400, 48% full-time, 69% with terminal degrees. *Student/faculty ratio:* 14:1.
Academics *Calendar:* semesters for undergraduate programs; trimesters for graduate programs and weekend college. *Degrees:* certificates, bachelor's, master's, doctoral, post-master's, and postbachelor's certificates. *Special study options:* academic remediation for entering students, adult/continuing education programs, advanced placement credit, cooperative education, double majors, English as a second language, freshman honors college, honors programs, independent study, internships, off-campus study, part-time degree program, services for LD students, student-designed majors, study abroad, summer session for credit. *ROTC:* Army (c), Navy (c), Air Force (c). *Unusual*

degree programs: 3-2 engineering with Michigan Technological University, University of Minnesota, Twin Cities Campus.
Computers on Campus 260 computers/terminals are available on campus for general student use. Students can access the following: campus intranet, computer help desk, free student e-mail accounts, online (class) grades, online (class) registration, online (class) schedules. Campuswide network is available. 100% of college-owned or -operated housing units are wired for high-speed Internet access. Wireless service is available via entire campus.
Student Life *Housing options:* coed, men-only, women-only, disabled students. Campus housing is university owned. Freshman applicants given priority for college housing. *Activities and organizations:* drama/theater group, student-run newspaper, radio station, choral group, Student Activities Council, student government, newspaper/yearbook, campus ministry, intramurals. *Campus security:* 24-hour emergency response devices and patrols, student patrols, late-night transport/escort service, controlled dormitory access. *Student services:* health clinic, personal/psychological counseling, women's center.
Athletics Member NCAA. All Division III. *Intercollegiate sports:* baseball M, basketball M/W, cross-country running M/W, football M, golf M/W, ice hockey M/W, lacrosse W, soccer M/W, softball W, swimming and diving W, track and field M/W, volleyball W, wrestling M. *Intramural sports:* basketball M/W, football M, skiing (cross-country) M(c)/W(c), skiing (downhill) M(c)/W(c), softball M/W, volleyball M/W, wrestling M.
Standardized Tests *Recommended:* SAT or ACT (for admission).
Financial Aid Of all full-time matriculated undergraduates who enrolled in 2010, 2,338 applied for aid, 2,033 were judged to have need, 233 had their need fully met. 363 Federal Work-Study jobs (averaging $2850). 818 state and other part-time jobs (averaging $2843). In 2010, 292 non-need-based awards were made. *Average percent of need met:* 67%. *Average financial aid package:* $20,143. *Average need-based loan:* $4902. *Average need-based gift aid:* $16,115. *Average non-need-based aid:* $8739. *Average indebtedness upon graduation:* $24,311. *Financial aid deadline:* 8/15.
Applying *Options:* electronic application, deferred entrance. *Application fee:* $25. *Required:* essay or personal statement, high school transcript, minimum 2.5 GPA, interview. *Required for some:* 2 letters of recommendation. *Application deadlines:* 8/15 (freshmen), 8/15 (transfers). *Notification:* continuous (freshmen), continuous (transfers).
Freshman Application Contact Ms. Marissa Machado, Senior Associate Director of Admissions, Augsburg College, 2211 Riverside Avenue, Minneapolis, MN 55454-1351. *Phone:* 612-330-1586. *Toll-free phone:* 800-788-5678. *Fax:* 612-330-1590. *E-mail:* admissions@augsburg.edu. *Website:* http://www.augsburg.edu/.

Bemidji State University

Bemidji, Minnesota

- **State-supported** comprehensive, founded 1919, part of Minnesota State Colleges and Universities System
- **Small-town** 89-acre campus
- **Coed** 4,744 undergraduate students, 74% full-time, 55% women, 45% men
- **Moderately difficult** entrance level, 42% of applicants were admitted

Undergraduates 3,524 full-time, 1,220 part-time. 12% are from out of state; 1% Black or African American, non-Hispanic/Latino; 1% Hispanic/Latino; 0.6% Asian, non-Hispanic/Latino; 3% American Indian or Alaska Native, non-Hispanic/Latino; 2% Two or more races, non-Hispanic/Latino; 6% Race/ethnicity unknown; 3% international; 7% transferred in; 30% live on campus. *Retention:* 69% of full-time freshmen returned.
Freshmen *Admission:* 3,121 applied, 1,317 admitted, 772 enrolled. *Average high school GPA:* 3.14. *Test scores:* ACT scores over 18: 91%; ACT scores over 24: 23%; ACT scores over 30: 1%.
Faculty *Total:* 260, 59% full-time, 46% with terminal degrees. *Student/faculty ratio:* 21:1.
Academics *Calendar:* semesters. *Degrees:* certificates, associate, bachelor's, master's, and postbachelor's certificates. *Special study options:* adult/continuing education programs, part-time degree program.
Computers on Campus Students can access the following: computer help desk, free student e-mail accounts, online (class) grades, online (class) registration, online (class) schedules. Wireless service is available via entire campus.
Student Life *Housing options:* coed, disabled students. Campus housing is university owned. Freshman applicants given priority for college housing. *Campus security:* 24-hour emergency response devices and patrols, late-night transport/escort service, controlled dormitory access.
Athletics Member NCAA. All Division II except men's and women's ice hockey (Division I). *Intercollegiate sports:* baseball M(s), basketball M(s)/W(s), cross-country running W(s), football M(s), golf M(s)/W(s), ice hockey M(s)/W(s), soccer W(s), softball W(s), tennis W(s), track and field W(s), vol-

leyball W(s). *Intramural sports:* basketball M/W, football M, ice hockey M/W, soccer M/W, softball M/W, volleyball M/W.

Standardized Tests *Required:* SAT or ACT (for admission).

Costs (2012–13) *Tuition:* state resident $7146 full-time; nonresident $7146 full-time. Full-time tuition and fees vary according to course load, location, program, and reciprocity agreements. Part-time tuition and fees vary according to course load, location, program, and reciprocity agreements. *Required fees:* $960 full-time. *Room and board:* $6970. Room and board charges vary according to board plan and housing facility. *Payment plan:* installment. *Waivers:* senior citizens and employees or children of employees.

Financial Aid Of all full-time matriculated undergraduates who enrolled in 2012, 2,847 applied for aid, 2,265 were judged to have need, 398 had their need fully met. 234 Federal Work-Study jobs (averaging $1245). 185 state and other part-time jobs (averaging $1583). In 2012, 560 non-need-based awards were made. *Average percent of need met:* 66%. *Average financial aid package:* $9240. *Average need-based loan:* $4033. *Average need-based gift aid:* $5472. *Average non-need-based aid:* $10,304.

Applying *Options:* electronic application, deferred entrance. *Application fee:* $20. *Required:* high school transcript. *Required for some:* essay or personal statement, interview. *Application deadlines:* rolling (freshmen), rolling (transfers). *Notification:* continuous (freshmen), continuous (transfers).

Freshman Application Contact Bemidji State University, 1500 Birchmont Drive, NE, Bemidji, MN 56601-2699. *Phone:* 218-755-2602. *Toll-free phone:* 800-475-2001.

Website: http://www.bemidjistate.edu/.

Bethany Lutheran College

Mankato, Minnesota

- **Independent Lutheran** 4-year, founded 1927
- **Small-town** 50-acre campus with easy access to Minneapolis-St. Paul
- **Endowment** $37.4 million
- **Coed** 600 undergraduate students, 95% full-time, 52% women, 48% men
- **Moderately difficult** entrance level, 78% of applicants were admitted

Undergraduates 570 full-time, 30 part-time. Students come from 24 states and territories; 9 other countries; 26% are from out of state; 2% Black or African American, non-Hispanic/Latino; 3% Hispanic/Latino; 0.5% Asian, non-Hispanic/Latino; 2% Two or more races, non-Hispanic/Latino; 12% Race/ethnicity unknown; 1% international; 6% transferred in; 65% live on campus. *Retention:* 72% of full-time freshmen returned.

Freshmen *Admission:* 441 applied, 344 admitted, 137 enrolled. *Average high school GPA:* 3.35. *Test scores:* ACT scores over 18: 92%; ACT scores over 24: 52%; ACT scores over 30: 11%.

Faculty *Total:* 79, 52% full-time, 28% with terminal degrees. *Student/faculty ratio:* 10:1.

Academics *Calendar:* semesters. *Degree:* bachelor's. *Special study options:* academic remediation for entering students, advanced placement credit, cooperative education, double majors, independent study, internships, services for LD students, student-designed majors, study abroad. *ROTC:* Army (c). *Unusual degree programs:* 3-2 engineering with University of Minnesota-Twin Cities.

Computers on Campus 100 computers/terminals are available on campus for general student use. Students can access the following: computer help desk, free student e-mail accounts, online (class) grades, online (class) registration, online (class) schedules. Campuswide network is available. 100% of college-owned or -operated housing units are wired for high-speed Internet access. Wireless service is available via entire campus.

Student Life *Housing:* on-campus residence required through sophomore year. *Options:* men-only, women-only. Campus housing is university owned. Freshman campus housing is guaranteed. *Activities and organizations:* drama/theater group, student-run newspaper, choral group, Bethany Activities Committee, Student Senate, Scholastic Leadership Society, PAMA (Promoting Awareness, spurring Motivation, and encouraging Action), Bethany Society of Royal Scientists. *Campus security:* 24-hour emergency response devices and patrols, late-night transport/escort service, controlled dormitory access. *Student services:* personal/psychological counseling.

Athletics Member NCAA. All Division III. *Intercollegiate sports:* baseball M, basketball M/W, cross-country running M/W, equestrian sports M(c)/W(c), golf M/W, soccer M/W, softball W, tennis M/W, track and field M/W, volleyball W. *Intramural sports:* basketball M/W, football M/W, racquetball M/W, table tennis M/W, tennis M/W, ultimate Frisbee M/W, volleyball M/W.

Standardized Tests *Required:* SAT or ACT (for admission).

Costs (2012–13) *One-time required fee:* $130. *Comprehensive fee:* $30,250 includes full-time tuition ($22,810), mandatory fees ($330), and room and board ($7110). Part-time tuition: $960 per credit. Part-time tuition and fees vary according to course load. *Required fees:* $165 per term part-time. *College*

room only: $3310. Room and board charges vary according to board plan and housing facility. *Payment plan:* installment. *Waivers:* senior citizens and employees or children of employees.

Financial Aid Of all full-time matriculated undergraduates who enrolled in 2011, 559 applied for aid, 505 were judged to have need, 72 had their need fully met. 25 Federal Work-Study jobs (averaging $1637). 267 state and other part-time jobs (averaging $821). In 2011, 80 non-need-based awards were made. *Average percent of need met:* 81%. *Average financial aid package:* $18,694. *Average need-based loan:* $5621. *Average need-based gift aid:* $13,352. *Average non-need-based aid:* $6292. *Average indebtedness upon graduation:* $31,884.

Applying *Options:* electronic application. *Required:* essay or personal statement, high school transcript, minimum 2.4 GPA. *Required for some:* interview. *Recommended:* minimum 3.2 GPA, interview. *Application deadline:* 7/1 (freshmen). *Notification:* continuous (transfers).

Freshman Application Contact Mr. Don Westphal, Dean of Admissions, Bethany Lutheran College, 700 Luther Drive, Mankato, MN 56001. *Phone:* 507-344-7320. *Toll-free phone:* 800-944-3066. *Fax:* 507-344-7376. *E-mail:* dwestpha@blc.edu.

Website: http://www.blc.edu/.

Bethel University

St. Paul, Minnesota

- **Independent** comprehensive, founded 1871, affiliated with Baptist General Conference
- **Suburban** 247-acre campus with easy access to Minneapolis-St. Paul
- **Endowment** $25.9 million
- **Coed** 3,467 undergraduate students, 79% full-time, 63% women, 37% men
- **Moderately difficult** entrance level, 71% of applicants were admitted

Undergraduates 2,743 full-time, 724 part-time. Students come from 40 states and territories; 8 other countries; 22% are from out of state; 5% Black or African American, non-Hispanic/Latino; 2% Hispanic/Latino; 3% Asian, non-Hispanic/Latino; 0.1% Native Hawaiian or other Pacific Islander, non-Hispanic/Latino; 0.1% American Indian or Alaska Native, non-Hispanic/Latino; 2% Two or more races, non-Hispanic/Latino; 3% Race/ethnicity unknown; 0.1% international; 4% transferred in; 60% live on campus. *Retention:* 83% of full-time freshmen returned.

Freshmen *Admission:* 2,684 applied, 1,908 admitted, 659 enrolled. *Average high school GPA:* 3.51. *Test scores:* ACT scores over 18: 97%; ACT scores over 24: 64%; ACT scores over 30: 16%.

Faculty *Total:* 306, 59% full-time, 59% with terminal degrees. *Student/faculty ratio:* 12:1.

Academics *Calendar:* 4-1-4. *Degrees:* associate, bachelor's, master's, doctoral, post-master's, and postbachelor's certificates. *Special study options:* academic remediation for entering students, accelerated degree program, adult/continuing education programs, advanced placement credit, double majors, honors programs, independent study, internships, off-campus study, part-time degree program, services for LD students, student-designed majors, study abroad, summer session for credit. *ROTC:* Army (c), Air Force (c). *Unusual degree programs:* 3-2 engineering with University of Minnesota; other institutions by arrangement.

Computers on Campus 420 computers/terminals are available on campus for general student use. Students can access the following: campus intranet, computer help desk, free student e-mail accounts, online (class) grades, online (class) registration, online (class) schedules. Campuswide network is available. 100% of college-owned or -operated housing units are wired for high-speed Internet access. Wireless service is available via classrooms, computer centers, computer labs, dorm rooms, learning centers, libraries, student centers.

Student Life *Housing:* on-campus residence required through sophomore year. *Options:* coed, disabled students. Campus housing is university owned. Freshman campus housing is guaranteed. *Activities and organizations:* drama/theater group, student-run newspaper, radio station, choral group. *Campus security:* 24-hour emergency response devices and patrols, student patrols, late-night transport/escort service, controlled dormitory access, video surveillance for residence halls, academic buildings, and parking lots. *Student services:* health clinic, personal/psychological counseling.

Athletics Member NCAA. All Division III. *Intercollegiate sports:* baseball M, basketball M/W, cross-country running M/W, football M, golf M/W, ice hockey M/W, soccer M/W, softball W, tennis M/W, track and field M/W, volleyball M(c)/W. *Intramural sports:* badminton M/W, basketball M/W, football M, ice hockey M(c), lacrosse M(c)/W(c), rugby M(c), softball M/W, volleyball W.

Standardized Tests *Required:* SAT or ACT (for admission).

Costs (2012–13) *Comprehensive fee:* $39,740 includes full-time tuition ($30,700), mandatory fees ($140), and room and board ($8900). Part-time tuition: $1280 per credit. Part-time tuition and fees vary according to course load. *College room only:* $5100. Room and board charges vary according to board plan. *Payment plans:* tuition prepayment, installment. *Waivers:* employees or children of employees.

Financial Aid Of all full-time matriculated undergraduates who enrolled in 2011, 2,342 applied for aid, 2,042 were judged to have need, 356 had their need fully met. 350 Federal Work-Study jobs (averaging $2500). 1,500 state and other part-time jobs (averaging $2500). In 2011, 561 non-need-based awards were made. *Average percent of need met:* 74%. *Average financial aid package:* $21,159. *Average need-based loan:* $4364. *Average need-based gift aid:* $15,466. *Average non-need-based aid:* $8352. *Average indebtedness upon graduation:* $32,483.

Applying *Options:* electronic application, early admission, deferred entrance. *Required:* essay or personal statement, high school transcript, rank in upper 50% of high school class. *Required for some:* 2 letters of recommendation. *Recommended:* minimum 2.5 GPA, interview. *Application deadlines:* rolling (freshmen), rolling (out-of-state freshmen), rolling (transfers). *Notification:* continuous (freshmen), continuous (out-of-state freshmen), continuous (transfers).

Freshman Application Contact Office of Admissions, Bethel University, 3900 Bethel Drive, St. Paul, MN 55112. *Phone:* 651-638-6242. *Toll-free phone:* 800-255-8706 Ext. 6242. *Fax:* 651-635-1490. *E-mail:* buadmissions-cas@bethel.edu.
Website: http://www.bethel.edu/.

Brown College
Mendota Heights, Minnesota

Freshman Application Contact Mr. Mark Fredrichs, Registrar, Brown College, 1440 Northland Drive, Mendota Heights, MN 55120. *Phone:* 651-905-3400. *Toll-free phone:* 866-551-0049. *Fax:* 651-905-3550.
Website: http://www.browncollege.edu/.

Capella University
Minneapolis, Minnesota

- **Proprietary** upper-level, founded 1993
- **Urban** campus
- **Coed**
- **Minimally difficult** entrance level

Academics *Calendar:* quarters. *Degrees:* certificates, bachelor's, master's, doctoral, post-master's, and postbachelor's certificates (offers only distance learning degree programs).

Financial Aid *Average percent of need met:* 90. *Average financial aid package:* $10,500. *Average indebtedness upon graduation:* $8000.

Applying *Options:* electronic application. *Application fee:* $50.

Application Contact Enrollment Services, Capella University, 225 South Sixth Street, Capella Tower, 9th Floor, Minneapolis, MN 55402. *Phone:* 866-2837921. *Toll-free phone:* 866-283-7921. *Fax:* 612-977-5060. *E-mail:* info@capella.edu.
Website: http://www.capella.edu/.

Carleton College
Northfield, Minnesota

- **Independent** 4-year, founded 1866
- **Small-town** 955-acre campus with easy access to Minneapolis-St. Paul
- **Endowment** $653.5 million
- **Coed** 2,055 undergraduate students, 99% full-time, 53% women, 47% men
- **Very difficult** entrance level, 26% of applicants were admitted

Undergraduates 2,037 full-time, 18 part-time. Students come from 52 states and territories; 38 other countries; 78% are from out of state; 3% Black or African American, non-Hispanic/Latino; 6% Hispanic/Latino; 8% Asian, non-Hispanic/Latino; 0.0% Native Hawaiian or other Pacific Islander, non-Hispanic/Latino; 0.0% American Indian or Alaska Native, non-Hispanic/Latino; 5% Two or more races, non-Hispanic/Latino; 2% Race/ethnicity unknown; 8% international; 0.3% transferred in; 94% live on campus. *Retention:* 98% of full-time freshmen returned.

Freshmen *Admission:* 5,856 applied, 1,496 admitted, 528 enrolled. *Test scores:* SAT critical reading scores over 500: 100%; SAT math scores over 500: 100%; SAT writing scores over 500: 99%; ACT scores over 18: 100%; SAT critical reading scores over 600: 94%; SAT math scores over 600: 96%; SAT writing scores over 600: 93%; ACT scores over 24: 99%; SAT critical reading scores over 700: 61%; SAT math scores over 700: 61%; SAT writing scores over 700: 54%; ACT scores over 30: 73%.

Faculty *Total:* 243, 87% full-time, 93% with terminal degrees. *Student/faculty ratio:* 9:1.

Academics *Calendar:* three courses for each of three terms. *Degree:* bachelor's. *Special study options:* accelerated degree program, advanced placement credit, double majors, independent study, internships, off-campus study, services for LD students, student-designed majors, study abroad. *Unusual degree programs:* 3-2 engineering with Columbia University (3-2 program) and Washington University in St. Louis (4-2 program).

Computers on Campus 388 computers/terminals and 220 ports are available on campus for general student use. Students can access the following: campus intranet, computer help desk, free student e-mail accounts, online (class) grades, online (class) registration, online (class) schedules. Campuswide network is available. 100% of college-owned or -operated housing units are wired for high-speed Internet access. Wireless service is available via classrooms, computer centers, computer labs, dorm rooms, learning centers, libraries, student centers.

Student Life *Housing:* on-campus residence required through senior year. *Options:* coed, disabled students. Campus housing is university owned. Freshman campus housing is guaranteed. *Activities and organizations:* drama/theater group, student-run newspaper, radio station, choral group, CANOE (Carleton Association of Nature and Outdoor Enthusiasts), Farm Club, Ebony II, WHIMS (Women in Math and Science), Amnesty International. *Campus security:* 24-hour emergency response devices and patrols, student patrols, late-night transport/escort service, controlled dormitory access, Emergency Notification Service (cell phone text and email alerts). *Student services:* health clinic, personal/psychological counseling, women's center.

Athletics Member NCAA. All Division III. *Intercollegiate sports:* badminton M(c)/W(c), baseball M, basketball M/W, crew M(c)/W(c), cross-country running M/W, equestrian sports M(c)/W(c), fencing M(c)/W(c), field hockey W(c), football M, golf M/W, gymnastics W(c), ice hockey M(c)/W(c), lacrosse M(c)/W(c), rugby M(c)/W(c), sailing M(c)/W(c), skiing (cross-country) M(c)/W(c), skiing (downhill) M(c)/W(c), soccer M/W, softball W, swimming and diving M/W, tennis M/W, track and field M/W, ultimate Frisbee M(c)/W(c), volleyball M(c)/W, water polo M(c)/W(c). *Intramural sports:* badminton M/W, basketball M/W, soccer M/W, softball M/W, table tennis M/W, tennis M/W, ultimate Frisbee M/W, volleyball M/W.

Standardized Tests *Required:* SAT or ACT (for admission). *Recommended:* SAT Subject Tests (for admission).

Costs (2012–13) *Comprehensive fee:* $55,998 includes full-time tuition ($44,184), mandatory fees ($261), and room and board ($11,553). *College room only:* $6069. Room and board charges vary according to board plan. *Payment plans:* tuition prepayment, installment. *Waivers:* employees or children of employees.

Financial Aid Of all full-time matriculated undergraduates who enrolled in 2011, 1,716 applied for aid, 1,134 were judged to have need, 1,134 had their need fully met. 357 Federal Work-Study jobs (averaging $2555). 1,326 state and other part-time jobs (averaging $2503). In 2011, 131 non-need-based awards were made. *Average percent of need met:* 100%. *Average financial aid package:* $37,454. *Average need-based loan:* $4690. *Average need-based gift aid:* $31,320. *Average non-need-based aid:* $2622. *Average indebtedness upon graduation:* $17,289. *Financial aid deadline:* 2/15.

Applying *Options:* electronic application, early admission, early decision, deferred entrance. *Application fee:* $30. *Required:* essay or personal statement, high school transcript, 2 letters of recommendation, common application supplement. *Recommended:* interview. *Application deadlines:* 1/15 (freshmen), 3/31 (transfers). *Early decision deadline:* 11/15 (for plan 1), 1/15 (for plan 2). *Notification:* 4/15 (freshmen), 5/15 (transfers), 12/15 (early decision plan 1), 2/15 (early decision plan 2).

Freshman Application Contact Carleton College, One North College Street, Northfield, MN 55057-4001. *Phone:* 507-222-4190. *Toll-free phone:* 800-995-2275.
Website: http://www.carleton.edu/.

College of Saint Benedict

Saint Joseph, Minnesota

- **Independent Roman Catholic** 4-year, founded 1887
- **Small-town** 3500-acre campus with easy access to Minneapolis-St. Paul
- **Endowment** $43.2 million
- **Women only** 2,070 undergraduate students, 98% full-time
- **Moderately difficult** entrance level, 77% of applicants were admitted

Undergraduates 2,037 full-time, 33 part-time. Students come from 30 states and territories; 22 other countries; 17% are from out of state; 2% Black or African American, non-Hispanic/Latino; 4% Hispanic/Latino; 6% Asian, non-Hispanic/Latino; 0.7% American Indian or Alaska Native, non-Hispanic/Latino; 0.1% Two or more races, non-Hispanic/Latino; 6% international; 1% transferred in; 85% live on campus. *Retention:* 89% of full-time freshmen returned.
Freshmen *Admission:* 1,938 applied, 1,487 admitted, 490 enrolled. *Average high school GPA:* 3.68. *Test scores:* SAT critical reading scores over 500: 69%; SAT math scores over 500: 71%; SAT writing scores over 500: 75%; ACT scores over 18: 99%; SAT critical reading scores over 600: 28%; SAT math scores over 600: 30%; SAT writing scores over 600: 36%; ACT scores over 24: 67%; SAT critical reading scores over 700: 12%; SAT math scores over 700: 8%; SAT writing scores over 700: 10%; ACT scores over 30: 14%.
Faculty *Total:* 189, 80% full-time, 75% with terminal degrees. *Student/faculty ratio:* 12:1.
Academics *Calendar:* semesters. *Degrees:* bachelor's (coordinate with Saint John's University for men). *Special study options:* advanced placement credit, double majors, English as a second language, honors programs, independent study, internships, off-campus study, services for LD students, student-designed majors, study abroad. *ROTC:* Army (c). *Unusual degree programs:* 3-2 engineering with University of Minnesota.
Computers on Campus 980 computers/terminals and 3,000 ports are available on campus for general student use. Students can access the following: campus intranet, computer help desk, free student e-mail accounts, online (class) grades, online (class) registration, online (class) schedules, online student accounts. Campuswide network is available. 100% of college-owned or -operated housing units are wired for high-speed Internet access. Wireless service is available via entire campus.
Student Life *Housing:* on-campus residence required through senior year. *Options:* women-only, disabled students. Campus housing is university owned. Freshman campus housing is guaranteed. *Activities and organizations:* drama/theater group, student-run newspaper, radio station, choral group, China Cross Cultural Communications Club, Outskirts Snow Crew, Buddhist Meditation Club, Dance Team, AKS Sorority. *Campus security:* 24-hour emergency response devices and patrols, student patrols, late-night transport/escort service, controlled dormitory access, well-lit pathways, closed circuit TV monitors. *Student services:* health clinic, personal/psychological counseling, women's center.
Athletics Member NCAA. All Division III. *Intercollegiate sports:* basketball W, crew W(c), cross-country running W, golf W, ice hockey W, lacrosse W(c), riflery W(c), rugby W(c), skiing (cross-country) W(c), soccer W, softball W, swimming and diving W, tennis W, track and field W, ultimate Frisbee W(c), volleyball W, water polo W(c). *Intramural sports:* badminton W, basketball W, football W, golf W(c), racquetball W, rock climbing W(c), skiing (downhill) W(c), soccer W, softball W, table tennis W, tennis W, volleyball W.
Standardized Tests *Required:* SAT or ACT (for admission).
Costs (2012–13) *Comprehensive fee:* $45,489 includes full-time tuition ($35,298), mandatory fees ($920), and room and board ($9271). Part-time tuition: $1471 per semester hour. Part-time tuition and fees vary according to course load. *College room only:* $4463. Room and board charges vary according to board plan and housing facility. *Payment plan:* installment. *Waivers:* employees or children of employees.
Financial Aid Of all full-time matriculated undergraduates who enrolled in 2012, 1,590 applied for aid, 1,409 were judged to have need, 496 had their need fully met. 632 Federal Work-Study jobs (averaging $2507). 884 state and other part-time jobs (averaging $2503). In 2012, 513 non-need-based awards were made. *Average percent of need met:* 86%. *Average financial aid package:* $28,920. *Average need-based loan:* $5097. *Average need-based gift aid:* $22,145. *Average non-need-based aid:* $13,827. *Average indebtedness upon graduation:* $40,030.
Applying *Options:* electronic application, early action, deferred entrance. *Required:* essay or personal statement, high school transcript, 1 letter of recommendation. *Recommended:* minimum 3.0 GPA, interview. *Application deadlines:* rolling (freshmen), rolling (transfers), 11/15 (early action). *Notification:* continuous (freshmen), continuous (transfers), 12/15 (early action).
Freshman Application Contact Ms. Karen Backes, Dean of Admissions, College of Saint Benedict, College of Saint Benedict, 37 South College Avenue, St. Joseph, MN 56374. *Phone:* 320-363-5055. *Toll-free phone:* 800-544-1489. *Fax:* 320-363-5650. *E-mail:* admissions@csbsju.edu. *Website:* http://www.csbsju.edu/.

The College of St. Scholastica

Duluth, Minnesota

- **Independent** comprehensive, founded 1912, affiliated with Roman Catholic Church
- **Suburban** 186-acre campus
- **Endowment** $48.8 million
- **Coed** 2,877 undergraduate students, 86% full-time, 68% women, 32% men
- **Moderately difficult** entrance level, 78% of applicants were admitted

Undergraduates 2,464 full-time, 413 part-time. Students come from 35 states and territories; 36 other countries; 14% are from out of state; 2% Black or African American, non-Hispanic/Latino; 2% Hispanic/Latino; 1% Asian, non-Hispanic/Latino; 0.1% Native Hawaiian or other Pacific Islander, non-Hispanic/Latino; 2% American Indian or Alaska Native, non-Hispanic/Latino; 2% Two or more races, non-Hispanic/Latino; 8% Race/ethnicity unknown; 3% international; 15% transferred in; 52% live on campus. *Retention:* 81% of full-time freshmen returned.
Freshmen *Admission:* 1,833 applied, 1,435 admitted, 475 enrolled. *Average high school GPA:* 3.49. *Test scores:* SAT critical reading scores over 500: 55%; SAT math scores over 500: 80%; SAT writing scores over 500: 60%; ACT scores over 18: 97%; SAT critical reading scores over 600: 35%; SAT math scores over 600: 35%; SAT writing scores over 600: 30%; ACT scores over 24: 47%; SAT critical reading scores over 700: 20%; SAT math scores over 700: 10%; SAT writing scores over 700: 5%; ACT scores over 30: 6%.
Faculty *Total:* 383, 45% full-time, 36% with terminal degrees. *Student/faculty ratio:* 13:1.
Academics *Calendar:* semesters. *Degrees:* certificates, bachelor's, master's, doctoral, post-master's, and postbachelor's certificates. *Special study options:* accelerated degree program, adult/continuing education programs, advanced placement credit, distance learning, double majors, external degree program, honors programs, independent study, internships, off-campus study, part-time degree program, services for LD students, student-designed majors, study abroad, summer session for credit. *ROTC:* Air Force (c). *Unusual degree programs:* 3-2 occupational therapy.
Computers on Campus 488 computers/terminals are available on campus for general student use. Students can access the following: campus intranet, computer help desk, free student e-mail accounts, online (class) grades, online (class) registration, online (class) schedules, student account information and transcripts online. Campuswide network is available. 100% of college-owned or -operated housing units are wired for high-speed Internet access. Wireless service is available via classrooms, computer centers, computer labs, dorm rooms, learning centers, libraries, student centers.
Student Life *Housing:* on-campus residence required through sophomore year. *Options:* coed, disabled students. Campus housing is university owned. Freshman campus housing is guaranteed. *Activities and organizations:* drama/theater group, student-run newspaper, television station, choral group, Campus Activity Board, Inter-Varsity, Habitat for Humanity, SHIMA, Volunteers Involved Through Action. *Campus security:* 24-hour emergency response devices and patrols, late-night transport/escort service, controlled dormitory access, student door monitor at night. *Student services:* health clinic, personal/psychological counseling.
Athletics Member NCAA. All Division III. *Intercollegiate sports:* baseball M, basketball M/W, cross-country running M/W, football M, ice hockey M/W, skiing (cross-country) M/W, soccer M/W, softball W, tennis M/W, track and field M/W, volleyball W. *Intramural sports:* basketball M/W, football M/W, soccer M/W, tennis M/W, volleyball M/W.
Standardized Tests *Required:* SAT or ACT (for admission).
Costs (2013–14) *Comprehensive fee:* $39,960 includes full-time tuition ($31,416), mandatory fees ($196), and room and board ($8348). Full-time tuition and fees vary according to class time and program. Part-time tuition: $981 per credit. Part-time tuition and fees vary according to class time, course load, and program. *College room only:* $4644. Room and board charges vary according to board plan and housing facility. *Payment plan:* installment. *Waivers:* senior citizens and employees or children of employees.
Financial Aid Of all full-time matriculated undergraduates who enrolled in 2012, 2,142 applied for aid, 1,973 were judged to have need, 413 had their need fully met. In 2012, 143 non-need-based awards were made. *Average percent of need met:* 69%. *Average financial aid package:* $20,491. *Average need-based loan:* $4569. *Average need-based gift aid:* $6830. *Average non-need-based aid:* $11,928. *Average indebtedness upon graduation:* $39,918.

Applying *Options:* electronic application, deferred entrance. *Required:* high school transcript. *Required for some:* minimum 2.0 GPA, interview. *Recommended:* interview. *Application deadlines:* rolling (freshmen), rolling (transfers). *Notification:* continuous (freshmen), continuous (transfers).
Freshman Application Contact Mr. Eric Berg, Vice President for Enrollment Management, The College of St. Scholastica, 1200 Kenwood Avenue, Duluth, MN 55811-4199. *Phone:* 218-723-6053. *Toll-free phone:* 800-249-6412. *E-mail:* admissions@css.edu.
Website: http://www.css.edu/.

Concordia College
Moorhead, Minnesota

- **Independent** comprehensive, founded 1891, affiliated with Evangelical Lutheran Church in America
- **Suburban** 113-acre campus
- **Endowment** $78.7 million
- **Coed** 2,603 undergraduate students, 98% full-time, 62% women, 38% men
- **Moderately difficult** entrance level, 78% of applicants were admitted

Undergraduates 2,554 full-time, 49 part-time. Students come from 34 states and territories; 35 other countries; 32% are from out of state; 1% Black or African American, non-Hispanic/Latino; 1% Hispanic/Latino; 2% Asian, non-Hispanic/Latino; 0.4% American Indian or Alaska Native, non-Hispanic/Latino; 2% Two or more races, non-Hispanic/Latino; 5% Race/ethnicity unknown; 4% international; 3% transferred in; 63% live on campus. *Retention:* 80% of full-time freshmen returned.
Freshmen *Admission:* 2,350 applied, 1,825 admitted, 633 enrolled. *Average high school GPA:* 3.6. *Test scores:* SAT critical reading scores over 500: 72%; SAT math scores over 500: 75%; SAT writing scores over 500: 64%; ACT scores over 18: 99%; SAT critical reading scores over 600: 34%; SAT math scores over 600: 44%; SAT writing scores over 600: 31%; ACT scores over 24: 61%; SAT critical reading scores over 700: 13%; SAT math scores over 700: 13%; SAT writing scores over 700: 5%; ACT scores over 30: 12%.
Faculty *Total:* 252, 71% full-time, 65% with terminal degrees. *Student/faculty ratio:* 13:1.
Academics *Calendar:* semesters. *Degrees:* bachelor's and master's. *Special study options:* advanced placement credit, cooperative education, double majors, honors programs, independent study, internships, off-campus study, part-time degree program, services for LD students, student-designed majors, study abroad, summer session for credit. *ROTC:* Army (c), Air Force (c). *Unusual degree programs:* 3-2 engineering with Institute of Technology (IT) at the University of Minnesota.
Computers on Campus 570 computers/terminals and 87 ports are available on campus for general student use. Students can access the following: campus intranet, computer help desk, free student e-mail accounts, online (class) grades, online (class) registration, online (class) schedules, online degree audit. Campuswide network is available. 100% of college-owned or -operated housing units are wired for high-speed Internet access. Wireless service is available via entire campus.
Student Life *Housing:* on-campus residence required through sophomore year. *Options:* coed, women-only. Campus housing is university owned. Freshman applicants given priority for college housing. *Activities and organizations:* drama/theater group, student-run newspaper, radio and television station, choral group, Campus Service Commission, Habitat for Humanity, Lead Now, Colleges Against Cancer (Relay for Life), Campus Ministry Commission. *Campus security:* 24-hour emergency response devices and patrols, late-night transport/escort service, controlled dormitory access, well-lighted campus. *Student services:* health clinic, personal/psychological counseling, women's center.
Athletics Member NCAA. All Division III. *Intercollegiate sports:* baseball M, basketball M/W, cheerleading W(c), cross-country running M/W, football M, golf M/W, ice hockey M/W, soccer M/W, softball W, swimming and diving W, tennis M/W, track and field M/W, volleyball M(c)/W, wrestling M. *Intramural sports:* basketball M/W, bowling M/W, football M, ice hockey M(c), lacrosse M(c)/W(c), rugby W(c), skiing (cross-country) M(c)/W(c), skiing (downhill) M(c)/W(c), swimming and diving M/W, tennis M(c)/W(c), ultimate Frisbee M(c)/W(c), volleyball M/W.
Standardized Tests *Required:* SAT or ACT (for admission).
Costs (2013–14) *Comprehensive fee:* $39,974 includes full-time tuition ($32,600), mandatory fees ($214), and room and board ($7160). Full-time tuition and fees vary according to course load and degree level. Part-time tuition: $1280 per contact hour. Part-time tuition and fees vary according to course load and degree level. *College room only:* $3090. Room and board charges vary according to board plan and housing facility. *Payment plan:* installment. *Waivers:* employees or children of employees.

Financial Aid Of all full-time matriculated undergraduates who enrolled in 2011, 2,266 applied for aid, 2,005 were judged to have need, 321 had their need fully met. 1,549 Federal Work-Study jobs (averaging $1775). 1,011 state and other part-time jobs (averaging $2719). In 2011, 607 non-need-based awards were made. *Average percent of need met:* 88%. *Average financial aid package:* $24,124. *Average need-based loan:* $8026. *Average need-based gift aid:* $16,144. *Average non-need-based aid:* $10,920. *Average indebtedness upon graduation:* $38,075.
Applying *Options:* electronic application, early admission, deferred entrance. *Application fee:* $20. *Required:* high school transcript, 2 letters of recommendation. *Application deadlines:* rolling (freshmen), rolling (transfers). *Notification:* continuous (freshmen), continuous (transfers).
Freshman Application Contact Mr. Scott D. Ellingson, Dean of Admissions, Concordia College, 901 8th Street South, Moorhead, MN 56562. *Phone:* 218-299-3004. *Toll-free phone:* 800-699-9897. *Fax:* 218-299-4720. *E-mail:* sellings@cord.edu.
Website: http://www.concordiacollege.edu/.

Concordia University, St. Paul
St. Paul, Minnesota

- **Independent** comprehensive, founded 1893, affiliated with Lutheran Church–Missouri Synod
- **Urban** 37-acre campus with easy access to Minneapolis/St. Paul
- **Endowment** $26.9 million
- **Coed** 1,824 undergraduate students, 54% full-time, 60% women, 40% men
- **Minimally difficult** entrance level, 65% of applicants were admitted

Undergraduates 988 full-time, 836 part-time. Students come from 43 states and territories; 4 other countries; 16% are from out of state; 11% Black or African American, non-Hispanic/Latino; 5% Hispanic/Latino; 6% Asian, non-Hispanic/Latino; 0.5% Native Hawaiian or other Pacific Islander, non-Hispanic/Latino; 0.7% American Indian or Alaska Native, non-Hispanic/Latino; 4% Two or more races, non-Hispanic/Latino; 4% Race/ethnicity unknown; 0.5% international; 16% transferred in; 26% live on campus. *Retention:* 71% of full-time freshmen returned.
Freshmen *Admission:* 935 applied, 611 admitted, 181 enrolled. *Average high school GPA:* 3.19. *Test scores:* ACT scores over 18: 84%; ACT scores over 24: 33%; ACT scores over 30: 3%.
Faculty *Total:* 325, 25% full-time, 41% with terminal degrees. *Student/faculty ratio:* 15:1.
Academics *Calendar:* semesters. *Degrees:* certificates, associate, bachelor's, master's, post-master's, and postbachelor's certificates. *Special study options:* academic remediation for entering students, accelerated degree program, adult/continuing education programs, advanced placement credit, distance learning, double majors, honors programs, independent study, internships, off-campus study, part-time degree program, services for LD students, student-designed majors, study abroad, summer session for credit. *ROTC:* Army (c), Air Force (c). *Unusual degree programs:* 3-2 engineering with University of Minnesota.
Computers on Campus Students can access the following: campus intranet, computer help desk, free student e-mail accounts, online (class) grades, online (class) registration, online (class) schedules, undergraduate students in traditional programs are issued wireless laptops that can be used anywhere on campus. Campuswide network is available. 100% of college-owned or -operated housing units are wired for high-speed Internet access. Wireless service is available via entire campus.
Student Life *Housing:* on-campus residence required for freshman year. *Options:* coed, men-only, women-only, disabled students. Campus housing is university owned. Freshman campus housing is guaranteed. *Activities and organizations:* drama/theater group, student-run newspaper, television station, choral group. *Campus security:* 24-hour emergency response devices and patrols, student patrols, late-night transport/escort service, controlled dormitory access. *Student services:* health clinic, personal/psychological counseling.
Athletics Member NCAA. All Division II. *Intercollegiate sports:* baseball M(s), basketball M(s)/W(s), cross-country running M(s)/W(s), football M(s), golf M(s)/W(s), soccer W(s), softball W(s), track and field M(s)/W(s), volleyball W(s). *Intramural sports:* basketball M/W, football M/W, lacrosse W, racquetball M/W, softball M/W, volleyball M/W.
Standardized Tests *Required:* ACT (for admission).
Costs (2013–14) *Comprehensive fee:* $27,450 includes full-time tuition ($19,700) and room and board ($7750). Full-time tuition and fees vary according to program. Part-time tuition: $635 per credit. Part-time tuition and fees vary according to course load and program. *Room and board:* Room and board charges vary according to board plan and housing facility. *Payment plan:* installment. *Waivers:* employees or children of employees.

Financial Aid Of all full-time matriculated undergraduates who enrolled in 2012, 858 applied for aid, 793 were judged to have need, 131 had their need fully met. In 2012, 69 non-need-based awards were made. *Average percent of need met:* 72%. *Average financial aid package:* $22,531. *Average need-based loan:* $4773. *Average need-based gift aid:* $17,791. *Average non-need-based aid:* $9737. *Average indebtedness upon graduation:* $42,020.

Applying *Options:* electronic application, early admission, deferred entrance. *Application fee:* $30. *Required:* high school transcript, 2 letters of recommendation. *Required for some:* essay or personal statement. *Recommended:* minimum 2.0 GPA. *Application deadlines:* 8/1 (freshmen), 8/1 (transfers). *Notification:* continuous (freshmen), continuous (transfers).

Freshman Application Contact Ms. Kristin Vogel, Director of Undergraduate Admission, Concordia University, St. Paul, 1282 Concordia Ave, St. Paul, MN 55104-5494. *Phone:* 651-641-8230. *Toll-free phone:* 800-333-4705. *Fax:* 651-603-6320. *E-mail:* admission@csp.edu. *Website:* http://www.csp.edu/.

Crossroads College

Rochester, Minnesota

- **Independent** 4-year, founded 1913, affiliated with Christian Churches and Churches of Christ
- **Urban** 40-acre campus with easy access to Minneapolis-St. Paul
- **Endowment** $934,902
- **Coed** 154 undergraduate students, 87% full-time, 58% women, 42% men
- **Noncompetitive** entrance level, 29% of applicants were admitted

Undergraduates 134 full-time, 20 part-time. Students come from 7 states and territories; 1 other country; 27% are from out of state; 6% Black or African American, non-Hispanic/Latino; 3% Hispanic/Latino; 3% Asian, non-Hispanic/Latino; 0.6% Native Hawaiian or other Pacific Islander, non-Hispanic/Latino; 0.6% American Indian or Alaska Native, non-Hispanic/Latino; 1% Two or more races, non-Hispanic/Latino; 1% Race/ethnicity unknown; 0.6% international; 16% transferred in. *Retention:* 67% of full-time freshmen returned.

Freshmen *Admission:* 85 applied, 25 admitted, 27 enrolled. *Average high school GPA:* 2.87. *Test scores:* SAT critical reading scores over 500: 50%.

Faculty *Total:* 28, 25% full-time. *Student/faculty ratio:* 10:1.

Academics *Calendar:* semesters. *Degrees:* associate and bachelor's. *Special study options:* academic remediation for entering students, adult/continuing education programs, advanced placement credit, cooperative education, distance learning, double majors, external degree program, independent study, internships, student-designed majors, summer session for credit.

Computers on Campus 15 computers/terminals are available on campus for general student use. Students can access the following: campus intranet, computer help desk, free student e-mail accounts, online (class) grades, online (class) registration, online (class) schedules. Campuswide network is available. 80% of college-owned or -operated housing units are wired for high-speed Internet access. Wireless service is available via entire campus.

Student Life *Housing:* on-campus residence required through sophomore year. *Options:* men-only, women-only, disabled students. Campus housing is university owned. Freshman campus housing is guaranteed. *Activities and organizations:* drama/theater group, choral group, Musical Outreach Concert Choir, Adoration, Ambassadors Mission Group, Staged Reactions (drama group). *Campus security:* student patrols, late-night transport/escort service. *Student services:* personal/psychological counseling.

Athletics *Intercollegiate sports:* basketball M/W, golf M/W, racquetball M/W, tennis M/W, volleyball W, weight lifting M/W. *Intramural sports:* basketball M/W, soccer M(c)/W(c).

Standardized Tests *Required:* SAT or ACT (for admission).

Applying *Options:* electronic application, deferred entrance. *Required:* essay or personal statement, high school transcript, minimum 2.0 GPA, 3 letters of recommendation. *Recommended:* interview. *Application deadlines:* 8/15 (freshmen), 8/15 (transfers). *Notification:* continuous until 9/1 (freshmen), continuous until 9/1 (transfers).

Freshman Application Contact Mr. Christopher Williams, Director of Admissions, Crossroads College, 920 Mayowood Road, SW, Rochester, MN 55902-2382. *Phone:* 507-288-4563 Ext. 304. *Toll-free phone:* 800-456-7651. *Fax:* 507-288-9046. *E-mail:* admissions@crossroadscollege.edu. *Website:* http://www.crossroadscollege.edu/.

Crown College

St. Bonifacius, Minnesota

- **Independent** comprehensive, founded 1916, affiliated with The Christian and Missionary Alliance
- **Small-town** 215-acre campus with easy access to Minneapolis-St. Paul
- **Endowment** $6.5 million
- **Coed** 1,088 undergraduate students, 81% full-time, 57% women, 43% men
- **Minimally difficult** entrance level, 56% of applicants were admitted

Undergraduates 885 full-time, 203 part-time. Students come from 34 states and territories; 11 other countries; 39% are from out of state; 3% Black or African American, non-Hispanic/Latino; 4% Hispanic/Latino; 7% Asian, non-Hispanic/Latino; 0.6% American Indian or Alaska Native, non-Hispanic/Latino; 0.3% Two or more races, non-Hispanic/Latino; 3% Race/ethnicity unknown; 3% international; 5% transferred in; 79% live on campus. *Retention:* 79% of full-time freshmen returned.

Freshmen *Admission:* 838 applied, 471 admitted, 185 enrolled. *Average high school GPA:* 3.22. *Test scores:* SAT critical reading scores over 500: 78%; SAT math scores over 500: 63%; ACT scores over 18: 95%; SAT critical reading scores over 600: 32%; SAT math scores over 600: 27%; ACT scores over 24: 44%; SAT critical reading scores over 700: 5%; SAT math scores over 700: 9%; ACT scores over 30: 4%.

Faculty *Total:* 160, 21% full-time, 14% with terminal degrees. *Student/faculty ratio:* 15:1.

Academics *Calendar:* semesters. *Degrees:* certificates, associate, bachelor's, master's, and postbachelor's certificates. *Special study options:* academic remediation for entering students, accelerated degree program, adult/continuing education programs, advanced placement credit, distance learning, double majors, English as a second language, external degree program, honors programs, independent study, internships, part-time degree program, services for LD students, study abroad, summer session for credit. *ROTC:* Army (c).

Computers on Campus 95 computers/terminals are available on campus for general student use. Students can access the following: campus intranet, computer help desk, free student e-mail accounts, online (class) registration. Campuswide network is available. 95% of college-owned or -operated housing units are wired for high-speed Internet access. Wireless service is available via classrooms, computer labs, dorm rooms, libraries, student centers.

Student Life *Housing:* on-campus residence required through senior year. *Options:* men-only, women-only. Campus housing is university owned. Freshman campus housing is guaranteed. *Activities and organizations:* drama/theater group, student-run newspaper, radio station, choral group, Hmong Student Fellowship, Global Impact Team, Student Activities Board, Student Senate, Storm Chaser Newspaper. *Campus security:* 24-hour emergency response devices, student patrols, late-night transport/escort service, controlled dormitory access. *Student services:* health clinic, personal/psychological counseling.

Athletics Member NCAA. All Division III. *Intercollegiate sports:* baseball M, basketball M/W, cross-country running M/W, football M, golf M, soccer M/W, softball W, volleyball W. *Intramural sports:* basketball M/W, track and field M(c)/W(c), volleyball M/W.

Standardized Tests *Required:* SAT or ACT (for admission).

Costs (2013–14) *Comprehensive fee:* $29,910 includes full-time tuition ($22,430) and room and board ($7480). Full-time tuition and fees vary according to course load and program. *Part-time tuition:* $950 per credit. Part-time tuition and fees vary according to course load and program. *College room only:* $3890. Room and board charges vary according to board plan and housing facility. *Payment plan:* installment. *Waivers:* employees or children of employees.

Financial Aid *Financial aid deadline:* 8/1.

Applying *Options:* electronic application, early admission, deferred entrance. *Application fee:* $20. *Required:* essay or personal statement, high school transcript, minimum 2.0 GPA. *Required for some:* interview. *Application deadlines:* rolling (freshmen), rolling (out-of-state freshmen), rolling (transfers). *Notification:* continuous (freshmen), continuous (out-of-state freshmen), continuous (transfers).

Freshman Application Contact Mr. Bret Hyder, Assistant Director of Admissions, Crown College, 8700 College View Drive, St. Bonifacius, MN 55375-9001. *Phone:* 952-446-4142. *Toll-free phone:* 800-68-CROWN. *Fax:* 952-446-4149. *E-mail:* admissions@crown.edu. *Website:* http://www.crown.edu/.

DeVry University

Edina, Minnesota

Freshman Application Contact DeVry University, 7700 France Avenue South, Suite 575, Edina, MN 55435. *Toll-free phone:* 866-338-7941. *Website:* http://www.devry.edu/.

Dunwoody College of Technology

Minneapolis, Minnesota

- **Independent** primarily 2-year, founded 1914
- **Urban** 12-acre campus with easy access to Minneapolis, Minnesota
- **Coed, primarily men** 1,131 undergraduate students, 78% full-time, 13% women, 87% men
- **Minimally difficult** entrance level, 58% of applicants were admitted

Undergraduates 881 full-time, 250 part-time. 3% are from out of state; 6% Black or African American, non-Hispanic/Latino; 2% Hispanic/Latino; 5% Asian, non-Hispanic/Latino; 0.2% Native Hawaiian or other Pacific Islander, non-Hispanic/Latino; 0.7% American Indian or Alaska Native, non-Hispanic/Latino; 5% Two or more races, non-Hispanic/Latino; 15% Race/ethnicity unknown. *Retention:* 67% of full-time freshmen returned.

Freshmen *Admission:* 494 applied, 286 admitted, 202 enrolled. *Average high school GPA:* 2.42.

Faculty *Total:* 130, 60% full-time, 5% with terminal degrees. *Student/faculty ratio:* 10:1.

Academics *Calendar:* quarters. *Degrees:* diplomas, associate, and bachelor's. *Special study options:* academic remediation for entering students, distance learning, independent study, internships, study abroad, summer session for credit.

Computers on Campus 300 computers/terminals are available on campus for general student use. Students can access the following: campus intranet, computer help desk, free student e-mail accounts, online (class) grades, online (class) schedules. Campuswide network is available. Wireless service is available via entire campus.

Student Life *Housing:* college housing not available. *Activities and organizations:* Student Government, Historic Green. *Campus security:* 24-hour emergency response devices, late-night transport/escort service. *Student services:* personal/psychological counseling, women's center.

Standardized Tests *Recommended:* SAT or ACT (for admission).

Costs (2013–14) *Tuition:* $17,077 full-time. *Required fees:* $1437 full-time. *Payment plans:* installment, deferred payment.

Financial Aid Of all full-time matriculated undergraduates who enrolled in 2011, 1,068 applied for aid, 959 were judged to have need, 41 had their need fully met. 24 Federal Work-Study jobs (averaging $4601). 17 state and other part-time jobs (averaging $3206). In 2011, 45 non-need-based awards were made. *Average percent of need met:* 41%. *Average financial aid package:* $11,546. *Average need-based loan:* $4532. *Average need-based gift aid:* $8624. *Average non-need-based aid:* $2518. *Average indebtedness upon graduation:* $9937.

Applying *Options:* electronic application. *Application fee:* $50. *Required:* essay or personal statement, high school transcript, minimum 2.5 GPA, interview. *Required for some:* minimum 3.0 GPA, . *Application deadline:* rolling (freshmen). *Notification:* continuous (freshmen).

Freshman Application Contact Bonney Bielen, Director of Admissions and Student Services, Dunwoody College of Technology, 818 Dunwoody Boulevard, Minneapolis, MN 55403. *Phone:* 612-374-5800. *Toll-free phone:* 800-292-4625.

Website: http://www.dunwoody.edu/.

Globe University–Minneapolis

Minneapolis, Minnesota

- **Proprietary** comprehensive, part of Globe Education Network (GEN) which is composed of Globe University, Minnesota School of Business, Broadview University, The Institute of Production and Recording and Minnesota School of Cosmetology
- **Urban** campus
- **Coed**

Faculty *Student/faculty ratio:* 14:1.

Academics *Degrees:* diplomas, associate, bachelor's, master's, and doctoral.

Student Life *Campus security:* 24-hour emergency response devices, late-night transport/escort service.

Standardized Tests *Required:* ACCUPLACER is required of all applicants unless documentation of a minimum ACT composite score of 21 or documentation of a minimum composite score of 1485 on the SAT is presented (for admission).

Costs (2012–13) *Tuition:* $15,300 full-time, $460 per credit part-time. Full-time tuition and fees vary according to course load, degree level, location, and program. Part-time tuition and fees vary according to course load, degree level, location, and program. *Required fees:* $1548 full-time, $43 per credit part-time.

Applying *Options:* electronic application. *Application fee:* $50. *Required:* high school transcript, interview. *Required for some:* essay or personal statement, 2 letters of recommendation, GED certificate in lieu of high school transcript.

Freshman Application Contact Globe University–Minneapolis, 80 South 8th Street, Suite 51, Minneapolis, MN 55402. *Phone:* 612-455-3000. *Website:* http://www.globeuniversity.edu/.

Globe University–Woodbury

Woodbury, Minnesota

- **Proprietary** comprehensive, founded 1885, part of Globe Education Network (GEN) which is composed of Globe University, Minnesota School of Business, Broadview University, The Institute of Production and Recording and Minnesota School of Cosmetology
- **Suburban** 5-acre campus with easy access to Minneapolis-St. Paul
- **Coed**

Faculty *Student/faculty ratio:* 15:1.

Academics *Calendar:* quarters. *Degrees:* diplomas, associate, bachelor's, master's, and doctoral.

Student Life *Campus security:* 24-hour emergency response devices, late-night transport/escort service.

Standardized Tests *Required:* ACCUPLACER is required of all applicants unless documentation of a minimum ACT composite score of 21 or documentation of a minimum composite score of 1485 on the SAT is presented (for admission).

Costs (2012–13) *Tuition:* $15,300 full-time, $460 per credit part-time. Full-time tuition and fees vary according to course level, course load, degree level, location, and program. Part-time tuition and fees vary according to course level, course load, degree level, location, and program. *Required fees:* $1548 full-time, $43 per credit part-time.

Applying *Options:* electronic application. *Application fee:* $50. *Required:* high school transcript, interview. *Required for some:* essay or personal statement, 2 letters of recommendation, GED certificate in lieu of high school transcript.

Freshman Application Contact Globe University–Woodbury, 8089 Globe Drive, Woodbury, MN 55125. *Phone:* 651-730-5100. *Toll-free phone:* 800-231-0660.

Website: http://www.globeuniversity.edu/.

Gustavus Adolphus College

St. Peter, Minnesota

- **Independent** 4-year, founded 1862, affiliated with Evangelical Lutheran Church in America
- **Small-town** 340-acre campus with easy access to Minneapolis-St. Paul
- **Endowment** $108.3 million
- **Coed** 2,524 undergraduate students, 98% full-time, 56% women, 44% men
- **Very difficult** entrance level, 63% of applicants were admitted

Undergraduates 2,482 full-time, 42 part-time. Students come from 41 states and territories; 20 other countries; 18% are from out of state; 3% Black or African American, non-Hispanic/Latino; 3% Hispanic/Latino; 4% Asian, non-Hispanic/Latino; 0.5% American Indian or Alaska Native, non-Hispanic/Latino; 2% Two or more races, non-Hispanic/Latino; 1% Race/ethnicity unknown; 2% international; 2% transferred in; 95% live on campus. *Retention:* 90% of full-time freshmen returned.

Freshmen *Admission:* 4,881 applied, 3,096 admitted, 678 enrolled. *Average high school GPA:* 3.66. *Test scores:* ACT scores over 18: 100%; ACT scores over 24: 88%; ACT scores over 30: 27%.

Faculty *Total:* 230, 83% full-time, 77% with terminal degrees. *Student/faculty ratio:* 12:1.

Academics *Calendar:* 4-1-4. *Degree:* bachelor's. *Special study options:* accelerated degree program, advanced placement credit, cooperative education, double majors, honors programs, independent study, internships, off-campus study, services for LD students, student-designed majors, study abroad, summer session for credit. *ROTC:* Army (c). *Unusual degree programs:* 3-2 engineering with Minnesota State University, Mankato; University of Minnesota; social work; occupational therapy with Washington University in St. Louis.

Computers on Campus 440 computers/terminals and 5,000 ports are available on campus for general student use. Students can access the following: computer help desk, free student e-mail accounts, online (class) grades, online (class) registration, online (class) schedules. Campuswide network is available. 100% of college-owned or -operated housing units are wired for high-speed Internet access. Wireless service is available via entire campus.

Student Life *Housing:* on-campus residence required through senior year. *Options:* coed. Campus housing is university owned. Freshman campus housing is guaranteed. *Activities and organizations:* drama/theater group, student-run newspaper, radio and television station, choral group, Proclaim, Big Partner/Little Partner, Study Buddies, I am...We are, Pound Pals, national fraternities, national sororities. *Campus security:* 24-hour emergency response devices and patrols, late-night transport/escort service, controlled dormitory access. *Student services:* health clinic, personal/psychological counseling, women's center.

Athletics Member NCAA. All Division III. *Intercollegiate sports:* baseball M, basketball M/W, cross-country running M/W, football M, golf M/W, gymnastics W, ice hockey M/W, lacrosse M(c), rugby M(c)/W(c), skiing (cross-country) M/W, soccer M/W, softball W, swimming and diving M/W, tennis M/W, track and field M/W, ultimate Frisbee M(c)/W(c), volleyball M(c)/W. *Intramural sports:* badminton M/W, basketball M/W, football M, golf M/W, ice hockey M/W, racquetball M/W, rugby M/W, skiing (cross-country) M/W, skiing (downhill) M/W, soccer M/W, softball M/W, swimming and diving M/W, tennis M/W, track and field M/W, ultimate Frisbee M/W, volleyball M/W, water polo M/W, weight lifting M/W.

Standardized Tests *Recommended:* SAT or ACT (for admission).

Costs (2012–13) *One-time required fee:* $450. *Comprehensive fee:* $46,486 includes full-time tuition ($37,210), mandatory fees ($396), and room and board ($8880). *Part-time tuition:* $5080 per course. *College room only:* $5710. Room and board charges vary according to board plan and housing facility. *Payment plans:* tuition prepayment, installment.

Financial Aid Of all full-time matriculated undergraduates who enrolled in 2011, 1,948 applied for aid, 1,752 were judged to have need, 423 had their need fully met. In 2011, 667 non-need-based awards were made. *Average percent of need met:* 88%. *Average financial aid package:* $28,080. *Average need-based loan:* $4648. *Average need-based gift aid:* $23,250. *Average non-need-based aid:* $12,657. *Average indebtedness upon graduation:* $28,401. *Financial aid deadline:* 4/15.

Applying *Options:* electronic application, early admission, early action, deferred entrance. *Required:* essay or personal statement, high school transcript, 1 letter of recommendation. *Recommended:* interview. *Application deadlines:* 4/1 (freshmen), rolling (transfers), 11/1 (early action). *Notification:* continuous (freshmen), continuous (transfers), 11/20 (early action).

Freshman Application Contact Dr. Tom M. Crady, Vice President for Enrollment Management, Gustavus Adolphus College, 800 West College Avenue, St. Peter, MN 56082-1498. *Phone:* 507-933-7676. *Toll-free phone:* 800-GUSTAVU(S). *Fax:* 507-933-7474. *E-mail:* admission@gac.edu. *Website:* http://www.gustavus.edu/.

Hamline University

St. Paul, Minnesota

- **Independent** comprehensive, founded 1854, affiliated with United Methodist Church
- **Urban** 60-acre campus with easy access to Minneapolis-St. Paul
- **Coed** 2,140 undergraduate students, 93% full-time, 59% women, 41% men
- **Moderately difficult** entrance level, 70% of applicants were admitted

Undergraduates 1,998 full-time, 142 part-time. Students come from 40 states and territories; 39 other countries; 18% are from out of state; 6% Black or African American, non-Hispanic/Latino; 5% Hispanic/Latino; 6% Asian, non-Hispanic/Latino; 0.1% Native Hawaiian or other Pacific Islander, non-Hispanic/Latino; 0.5% American Indian or Alaska Native, non-Hispanic/Latino; 4% Two or more races, non-Hispanic/Latino; 6% Race/ethnicity unknown; 2% international; 7% transferred in; 41% live on campus. *Retention:* 81% of full-time freshmen returned.

Freshmen *Admission:* 3,282 applied, 2,297 admitted, 541 enrolled. *Average high school GPA:* 3.42. *Test scores:* SAT critical reading scores over 500: 78%;

SAT math scores over 500: 80%; SAT writing scores over 500: 73%; ACT scores over 18: 96%; SAT critical reading scores over 600: 38%; SAT math scores over 600: 41%; SAT writing scores over 600: 31%; ACT scores over 24: 57%; SAT critical reading scores over 700: 15%; SAT math scores over 700: 15%; SAT writing scores over 700: 3%; ACT scores over 30: 11%.

Faculty *Total:* 448, 44% full-time, 63% with terminal degrees. *Student/faculty ratio:* 12:1.

Academics *Calendar:* 4-1-4. *Degrees:* bachelor's, master's, doctoral, post-master's, and postbachelor's certificates. *Special study options:* academic remediation for entering students, advanced placement credit, distance learning, double majors, English as a second language, honors programs, independent study, internships, off-campus study, part-time degree program, services for LD students, student-designed majors, study abroad, summer session for credit. *ROTC:* Army (c), Air Force (c). *Unusual degree programs:* 3-2 engineering with University of Minnesota, Washington University in St. Louis.

Computers on Campus 300 computers/terminals and 500 ports are available on campus for general student use. Students can access the following: campus intranet, computer help desk, free student e-mail accounts, online (class) grades, online (class) registration, online (class) schedules. Campuswide network is available. 99% of college-owned or -operated housing units are wired for high-speed Internet access. Wireless service is available via entire campus.

Student Life *Housing options:* coed. Campus housing is university owned. Freshman campus housing is guaranteed. *Activities and organizations:* drama/theater group, student-run newspaper, radio and television station, choral group, Student Congress (HUSC), Hand in Hand (elementary school mentoring program), Residence Hall Association, PRIDE, Hamline Oracle (student newspaper), national fraternities. *Campus security:* 24-hour emergency response devices and patrols, late-night transport/escort service, controlled dormitory access, Security cameras on campus and in residence halls. Security officers are trained as first responders. *Student services:* health clinic, personal/psychological counseling, women's center.

Athletics Member NCAA. All Division III. *Intercollegiate sports:* baseball M, basketball M/W, cheerleading W(c), cross-country running M/W, football M, gymnastics W, ice hockey M/W, lacrosse M(c)/W(c), soccer M/W, softball W, swimming and diving M/W, tennis M/W, track and field M/W, ultimate Frisbee M(c)/W(c), volleyball W. *Intramural sports:* basketball M/W, football M/W, racquetball M/W, rock climbing M(c)/W(c), soccer M/W, volleyball M/W.

Standardized Tests *Required:* SAT or ACT (for admission).

Costs (2012–13) *Comprehensive fee:* $42,452 includes full-time tuition ($33,236), mandatory fees ($516), and room and board ($8700). *Part-time tuition:* $1040 per credit. Part-time tuition and fees vary according to course load. *Required fees:* $444 per year part-time. *College room only:* $4500. Room and board charges vary according to board plan and housing facility. *Payment plan:* installment. *Waivers:* employees or children of employees.

Financial Aid Of all full-time matriculated undergraduates who enrolled in 2012, 1,783 applied for aid, 1,676 were judged to have need, 243 had their need fully met. 472 Federal Work-Study jobs (averaging $2356). 885 state and other part-time jobs (averaging $2362). In 2012, 202 non-need-based awards were made. *Average percent of need met:* 78%. *Average financial aid package:* $22,368. *Average need-based loan:* $4664. *Average need-based gift aid:* $19,659. *Average non-need-based aid:* $11,840. *Average indebtedness upon graduation:* $40,472.

Applying *Options:* electronic application, early admission, early action, deferred entrance. *Required:* essay or personal statement, high school transcript, 1 letter of recommendation, ACT or SAT. *Recommended:* interview. *Application deadlines:* rolling (freshmen), rolling (out-of-state freshmen), rolling (transfers), 12/1 (early action). *Notification:* continuous (freshmen), continuous (out-of-state freshmen), continuous (transfers), 12/20 (early action).

Freshman Application Contact Mr. Milyon Trulove, Director of Admission, Hamline University, 1536 Hewitt Avenue, MS-C1930, St. Paul, MN 55104. *Phone:* 651-523-2207. *Toll-free phone:* 800-753-9753. *Fax:* 651-523-2458. *E-mail:* admission@hamline.edu. *Website:* http://www.hamline.edu/.

Herzing University

Minneapolis, Minnesota

Freshman Application Contact Ms. Shelly Larson, Director of Admissions, Herzing University, 5700 West Broadway, Minneapolis, MN 55428. *Phone:* 763-231-3155. *Toll-free phone:* 800-596-0724. *Fax:* 763-535-9205. *E-mail:* info@mpls.herzing.edu. *Website:* http://www.herzing.edu/minneapolis.

ITT Technical Institute

Brooklyn Center, Minnesota

- **Proprietary** primarily 2-year, part of ITT Educational Services, Inc.
- **Coed**

Academics *Calendar:* quarters. *Degrees:* associate and bachelor's.
Freshman Application Contact Director of Recruitment, ITT Technical Institute, 6120 Earle Brown Drive, Suite 100, Brooklyn Center, MN 55430. *Phone:* 763-549-5900. *Toll-free phone:* 800-216-8883.
Website: http://www.itt-tech.edu/.

ITT Technical Institute

Eden Prairie, Minnesota

- **Proprietary** primarily 2-year, founded 2003, part of ITT Educational Services, Inc.
- **Coed**
- **Minimally difficult** entrance level

Academics *Calendar:* quarters. *Degrees:* associate and bachelor's.
Freshman Application Contact Director of Recruitment, ITT Technical Institute, 8911 Columbine Road, Eden Prairie, MN 55347. *Phone:* 952-914-5300. *Toll-free phone:* 888-488-9646.
Website: http://www.itt-tech.edu/.

Macalester College

St. Paul, Minnesota

- **Independent Presbyterian** 4-year, founded 1874
- **Urban** 53-acre campus
- **Endowment** $654.2 million
- **Coed** 2,070 undergraduate students, 98% full-time, 60% women, 40% men
- **Very difficult** entrance level, 37% of applicants were admitted

Undergraduates 2,035 full-time, 35 part-time. Students come from 94 other countries; 81% are from out of state; 3% Black or African American, non-Hispanic/Latino; 6% Hispanic/Latino; 7% Asian, non-Hispanic/Latino; 0.2% American Indian or Alaska Native, non-Hispanic/Latino; 5% Two or more races, non-Hispanic/Latino; 13% international; 0.6% transferred in; 62% live on campus. *Retention:* 94% of full-time freshmen returned.
Freshmen *Admission:* 6,030 applied, 2,214 admitted, 534 enrolled. *Test scores:* SAT critical reading scores over 500: 97%; SAT math scores over 500: 99%; SAT writing scores over 500: 98%; ACT scores over 18: 100%; SAT critical reading scores over 600: 85%; SAT math scores over 600: 91%; SAT writing scores over 600: 85%; ACT scores over 24: 99%; SAT critical reading scores over 700: 45%; SAT math scores over 700: 41%; SAT writing scores over 700: 35%; ACT scores over 30: 63%.
Faculty *Total:* 237, 73% full-time, 84% with terminal degrees. *Student/faculty ratio:* 10:1.
Academics *Calendar:* semesters. *Degree:* bachelor's. *Special study options:* advanced placement credit, double majors, honors programs, independent study, internships, off-campus study, part-time degree program, services for LD students, student-designed majors, study abroad, summer session for credit. *ROTC:* Army (c), Navy (c), Air Force (c). *Unusual degree programs:* 3-2 engineering with Washington University in St. Louis, University of Minnesota; architecture with Washington University in St. Louis.
Computers on Campus 500 computers/terminals and 2,500 ports are available on campus for general student use. Students can access the following: campus intranet, computer help desk, free student e-mail accounts, online (class) grades, online (class) registration, online (class) schedules, Web space, online course management (LMS), shared calendars, Room and Board transactions. Campuswide network is available. 100% of college-owned or -operated housing units are wired for high-speed Internet access. Wireless service is available via entire campus.
Student Life *Housing:* on-campus residence required through sophomore year. *Options:* coed, men-only, women-only, cooperative. Campus housing is university owned. Freshman campus housing is guaranteed. *Activities and organizations:* drama/theater group, student-run newspaper, radio station, choral group, Community Service Organization, Outing Club (outdoor recreation), Multicultural Organization, International Organization, campus publications. *Campus security:* 24-hour emergency response devices and patrols, late-night transport/escort service. *Student services:* health clinic, personal/psychological counseling.

Athletics Member NCAA. All Division III. *Intercollegiate sports:* baseball M, basketball M/W, crew M(c)/W(c), cross-country running M/W, football M, golf M/W, ice hockey M(c)/W(c), lacrosse W(c), rugby M(c)/W(c), skiing (cross-country) M(c)/W(c), soccer M/W, softball W, swimming and diving M/W, tennis M/W, track and field M/W, ultimate Frisbee M(c)/W(c), volleyball M(c)/W, water polo M(c)/W. *Intramural sports:* basketball M/W, racquetball M/W, soccer M/W, softball M/W, table tennis M/W, ultimate Frisbee M/W.
Standardized Tests *Required:* SAT or ACT (for admission).
Costs (2013–14) *Comprehensive fee:* $55,456 includes full-time tuition ($45,167), mandatory fees ($221), and room and board ($10,068). Full-time tuition and fees vary according to course load. Part-time tuition: $1411 per credit. Part-time tuition and fees vary according to course load. *College room only:* $5412. Room and board charges vary according to board plan and housing facility. *Payment plan:* installment. *Waivers:* employees or children of employees.
Financial Aid Of all full-time matriculated undergraduates who enrolled in 2012, 1,619 applied for aid, 1,465 were judged to have need, 1,465 had their need fully met. In 2012, 95 non-need-based awards were made. *Average percent of need met:* 100%. *Average financial aid package:* $37,519. *Average need-based loan:* $4197. *Average need-based gift aid:* $31,864. *Average non-need-based aid:* $9729. *Average indebtedness upon graduation:* $23,285. *Financial aid deadline:* 3/1.
Applying *Options:* electronic application, early admission, early decision, deferred entrance. *Application fee:* $40. *Required:* essay or personal statement, high school transcript, 2 letters of recommendation. *Recommended:* interview. *Application deadlines:* 1/15 (freshmen), 4/15 (transfers). *Early decision deadline:* 11/15 (for plan 1), 1/2 (for plan 2). *Notification:* 3/30 (freshmen), 5/15 (transfers), 12/15 (early decision plan 1), 2/7 (early decision plan 2).
Freshman Application Contact Mr. Lorne T. Robinson, Dean of Admissions and Financial Aid, Macalester College, 1600 Grand Avenue, St. Paul, MN 55105-1899. *Phone:* 651-696-6357. *Toll-free phone:* 800-231-7974. *Fax:* 651-696-6724. *E-mail:* admissions@macalester.edu.
Website: http://www.macalester.edu/.

Martin Luther College

New Ulm, Minnesota

- **Independent** comprehensive, founded 1995, affiliated with Wisconsin Evangelical Lutheran Synod
- **Small-town** 50-acre campus
- **Coed** 742 undergraduate students, 94% full-time, 49% women, 51% men
- **Moderately difficult** entrance level, 97% of applicants were admitted

Undergraduates 694 full-time, 48 part-time. 83% are from out of state; 0.4% Black or African American, non-Hispanic/Latino; 0.4% Hispanic/Latino; 0.5% Asian, non-Hispanic/Latino; 0.3% American Indian or Alaska Native, non-Hispanic/Latino; 1% Two or more races, non-Hispanic/Latino; 0.1% Race/ethnicity unknown; 2% international; 4% transferred in; 89% live on campus. *Retention:* 84% of full-time freshmen returned.
Freshmen *Admission:* 223 applied, 217 admitted, 179 enrolled. *Average high school GPA:* 3.5. *Test scores:* ACT scores over 18: 99%; ACT scores over 24: 63%; ACT scores over 30: 13%.
Faculty *Total:* 73, 63% full-time, 44% with terminal degrees. *Student/faculty ratio:* 13:1.
Academics *Calendar:* semesters. *Degrees:* certificates, diplomas, bachelor's, and master's.
Computers on Campus Campuswide network is available.
Student Life *Housing:* on-campus residence required through junior year. *Options:* men-only, women-only. Campus housing is university owned. *Activities and organizations:* drama/theater group, choral group. *Student services:* health clinic, personal/psychological counseling.
Athletics Member NCAA, NAIA. All NCAA Division III. *Intercollegiate sports:* baseball M, basketball M/W, cross-country running M/W, football M, golf M, soccer M/W, softball W, tennis M/W, track and field M/W, volleyball W. *Intramural sports:* badminton M/W, basketball M/W, bowling M/W, football M, soccer M/W, softball M/W, tennis M/W, volleyball M/W.
Standardized Tests *Required:* ACT (for admission).
Costs (2013–14) *Comprehensive fee:* $17,160 includes full-time tuition ($12,300) and room and board ($4860). *Payment plan:* installment.
Financial Aid Of all full-time matriculated undergraduates who enrolled in 2010, 611 applied for aid, 543 were judged to have need, 76 had their need fully met. In 2010, 99 non-need-based awards were made. *Average percent of need met:* 69%. *Average financial aid package:* $8935. *Average need-based loan:* $4068. *Average need-based gift aid:* $5996. *Average non-need-based aid:* $2090. *Average indebtedness upon graduation:* $22,176. *Financial aid deadline:* 4/15.

Applying *Options:* deferred entrance. *Required:* high school transcript, minimum 2.0 GPA. *Application deadlines:* 5/1 (freshmen), 5/1 (transfers). *Notification:* continuous (freshmen), continuous (transfers).
Freshman Application Contact Prof. Ronald Brutlag, Director of Admissions, Martin Luther College, 1995 Luther Court, New Ulm, MN 56073. *Phone:* 507-354-8221 Ext. 280. *Toll-free phone:* 877-MLC-1995. *E-mail:* brutlaro@mlc-wels.edu.
Website: http://www.mlc-wels.edu/.

McNally Smith College of Music

Saint Paul, Minnesota

- **Proprietary** comprehensive, founded 1985
- **Urban** 1-acre campus with easy access to Minneapolis-St. Paul
- **Coed** 629 undergraduate students, 79% full-time, 24% women, 76% men
- **Moderately difficult** entrance level, 65% of applicants were admitted

Undergraduates 498 full-time, 131 part-time. Students come from 36 states and territories; 12 other countries; 42% are from out of state; 11% Black or African American, non-Hispanic/Latino; 4% Hispanic/Latino; 3% Asian, non-Hispanic/Latino; 0.3% American Indian or Alaska Native, non-Hispanic/Latino; 3% international; 7% transferred in; 15% live on campus. *Retention:* 80% of full-time freshmen returned.
Freshmen *Admission:* 521 applied, 338 admitted, 120 enrolled. *Average high school GPA:* 2.91. *Test scores:* SAT critical reading scores over 500: 36%; SAT math scores over 500: 54%; SAT critical reading scores over 600: 13%; SAT math scores over 600: 22%.
Faculty *Total:* 126, 47% full-time. *Student/faculty ratio:* 8:1.
Academics *Calendar:* semesters. *Degrees:* diplomas, associate, bachelor's, and master's. *Special study options:* academic remediation for entering students, advanced placement credit, cooperative education, distance learning, double majors, independent study, internships, off-campus study, part-time degree program, services for LD students, study abroad, summer session for credit.
Computers on Campus 40 computers/terminals are available on campus for general student use. Students can access the following: campus intranet, computer help desk, free student e-mail accounts, online (class) grades, online (class) registration, online (class) schedules. Campuswide network is available. Wireless service is available via entire campus.
Student Life *Housing options:* coed. Campus housing is leased by the school. Freshman applicants given priority for college housing. *Activities and organizations:* student-run newspaper, choral group, Student Advisory Board, Audio Engineering Society, Minnesota Songwriters Association, Jazz Club, intramural sports. *Campus security:* 24-hour emergency response devices and patrols, late-night transport/escort service. *Student services:* personal/psychological counseling.
Standardized Tests *Required for some:* ACT (for admission), SAT or ACT (for admission). *Recommended:* ACT (for admission), SAT or ACT (for admission).
Costs (2012–13) *Comprehensive fee:* $31,090 includes full-time tuition ($23,790), mandatory fees ($2200), and room and board ($5100). Full-time tuition and fees vary according to course load and degree level. Part-time tuition: $915 per credit hour. Part-time tuition and fees vary according to course load and degree level. No tuition increase for student's term of enrollment. *Required fees:* $450 per term part-time. *Room and board:* Room and board charges vary according to board plan and housing facility. *Payment plans:* tuition prepayment, installment, deferred payment. *Waivers:* employees or children of employees.
Financial Aid Of all full-time matriculated undergraduates who enrolled in 2011, 514 applied for aid, 469 were judged to have need. 38 Federal Work-Study jobs (averaging $1983). 23 state and other part-time jobs (averaging $1292). *Average percent of need met:* 32%. *Average financial aid package:* $7419. *Average need-based loan:* $4114. *Average need-based gift aid:* $6096. *Financial aid deadline:* 8/1.
Applying *Options:* electronic application. *Application fee:* $75. *Required:* essay or personal statement, high school transcript, minimum 2.0 GPA, interview. *Required for some:* audition or demo recording. *Recommended:* minimum 2.5 GPA. *Application deadline:* 8/1 (freshmen). *Notification:* continuous until 8/1 (freshmen).
Freshman Application Contact Mrs. Katie Marshall, Admissions Representative, McNally Smith College of Music, 19 Exchange Street East, St. Paul, MN 55101. *Phone:* 651-361-3451. *Toll-free phone:* 800-594-9500. *Fax:* 651-291-0366. *E-mail:* katie.marshall@mcnallysmith.edu.
Website: http://www.mcnallysmith.edu/.

Metropolitan State University

St. Paul, Minnesota

- **State-supported** comprehensive, founded 1971, part of Minnesota State Colleges and Universities System
- **Urban** campus with easy access to Minneapolis-St. Paul
- **Endowment** $2.4 million
- **Coed**
- **Minimally difficult** entrance level

Faculty *Student/faculty ratio:* 17:1.
Academics *Calendar:* semesters. *Degrees:* certificates, bachelor's, master's, doctoral, and postbachelor's certificates (offers primarily part-time evening degree programs).
Student Life *Campus security:* 24-hour emergency response devices, late-night transport/escort service.
Standardized Tests *Recommended:* SAT or ACT (for admission).
Costs (2012–13) *Tuition:* state resident $6329 full-time, $211 per credit hour part-time; nonresident $12,914 full-time, $430 per credit hour part-time. Full-time tuition and fees vary according to degree level, program, and reciprocity agreements. Part-time tuition and fees vary according to degree level, program, and reciprocity agreements. *Required fees:* $313 full-time, $10 per credit hour part-time.
Applying *Options:* electronic application, deferred entrance. *Application fee:* $20. *Required:* high school transcript, minimum 2.0 GPA.
Freshman Application Contact Mr. Daryl Johnson, Director, Metropolitan State University, 700 East 7th Street, St. Paul, MN 55106. *Phone:* 651-793-1227. *Fax:* 651-793-1546. *E-mail:* daryl.johnson@metrostate.edu.
Website: http://www.metrostate.edu/.

Minneapolis College of Art and Design

Minneapolis, Minnesota

Freshman Application Contact Minneapolis College of Art and Design, 2501 Stevens Avenue, Minneapolis, MN 55404-4347. *Phone:* 612-874-3762. *Toll-free phone:* 800-874-6223.
Website: http://www.mcad.edu/.

Minnesota School of Business–Blaine

Blaine, Minnesota

- **Proprietary** 4-year, part of Globe Education Network (GEN) which is composed of Globe University, Minnesota School of Business, Broadview University, The Institute of Production and Recording and Minnesota School of Cosmetology
- **Suburban** 7-acre campus with easy access to Minneapolis-St. Paul
- **Coed, primarily women**

Faculty *Student/faculty ratio:* 11:1.
Academics *Degrees:* diplomas, associate, and bachelor's.
Student Life *Campus security:* 24-hour emergency response devices, late-night transport/escort service.
Costs (2012–13) *Tuition:* $15,300 full-time, $460 per credit part-time. Full-time tuition and fees vary according to course load, degree level, location, and program. Part-time tuition and fees vary according to course load, degree level, location, and program. *Required fees:* $1548 full-time, $43 per credit part-time.
Applying *Options:* electronic application. *Application fee:* $50. *Required:* high school transcript, interview. *Required for some:* essay or personal statement, 2 letters of recommendation, GED certificate in lieu of high school transcript.
Freshman Application Contact Minnesota School of Business–Blaine, 3680 Pheasant Ridge Drive NE, Blaine, MN 55449. *Phone:* 763-225-8000.
Website: http://www.msbcollege.edu/.

Minnesota School of Business–Brooklyn Center

Brooklyn Center, Minnesota

- **Proprietary** primarily 2-year, founded 1989, part of Globe Education Network (GEN) which is composed of Globe University, Minnesota School of Business, Broadview University, The Institute of Production and Recording and Minnesota School of Cosmetology
- **Suburban** 4-acre campus with easy access to Minneapolis-St. Paul
- **Coed**
- 68% of applicants were admitted

Faculty *Student/faculty ratio:* 10:1.

Academics *Calendar:* quarters. *Degrees:* diplomas, associate, and bachelor's.

Student Life *Campus security:* 24-hour emergency response devices, late-night transport/escort service.

Standardized Tests *Required:* ACCUPLACER is required of all applicants unless documentation of a minimum ACT composite score of 21 or documentation of a minimum composite score of 1485 on the SAT is presented (for admission).

Costs (2012–13) *Tuition:* $15,300 full-time, $460 per credit part-time. Full-time tuition and fees vary according to course load, degree level, location, and program. Part-time tuition and fees vary according to course load, degree level, location, and program. *Required fees:* $1548 full-time, $43 per credit part-time.

Applying *Options:* electronic application. *Application fee:* $50. *Required:* high school transcript, interview, High school transcript or GED. *Required for some:* essay or personal statement, 2 letters of recommendation.

Freshman Application Contact Minnesota School of Business–Brooklyn Center, 5910 Shingle Creek Parkway, Brooklyn Center, MN 55430. *Phone:* 763-566-7777.

Website: http://www.msbcollege.edu/.

Minnesota School of Business–Elk River

Elk River, Minnesota

- **Proprietary** 4-year, part of Globe Education Network (GEN) which is composed of Globe University, Minnesota School of Business, Broadview University, The Institute of Production and Recording and Minnesota School of Cosmetology
- **Suburban** 4-acre campus with easy access to Minneapolis-St. Paul
- **Coed**

Faculty *Student/faculty ratio:* 16:1.

Academics *Degrees:* diplomas, associate, and bachelor's.

Student Life *Campus security:* 24-hour emergency response devices, late-night transport/escort service.

Standardized Tests *Required:* ACCUPLACER is required of all applicants unless documentation of a minimum ACT composite score of 21 or documentation of a minimum composite score of 1485 on the SAT is presented (for admission).

Costs (2012–13) *Tuition:* $15,300 full-time, $460 per credit part-time. Full-time tuition and fees vary according to course load, degree level, location, and program. Part-time tuition and fees vary according to course load, degree level, location, and program. *Required fees:* $1548 full-time, $43 per credit part-time.

Applying *Options:* electronic application. *Application fee:* $50. *Required:* high school transcript, interview, High school transcript or GED required of all applicants. *Required for some:* essay or personal statement, 2 letters of recommendation.

Freshman Application Contact Minnesota School of Business–Elk River, 11500 193rd Avenue NW, Elk River, MN 55330. *Phone:* 763-367-7000.

Website: http://www.msbcollege.edu/.

Minnesota School of Business–Lakeville

Lakeville, Minnesota

- **Proprietary** 4-year, part of Globe Education Network (GEN) which is composed of Globe University, Minnesota School of Business, Broadview University, The Institute of Production and Recording and Minnesota School of Cosmetology
- **Small-town** 3-acre campus with easy access to Minneapolis-St. Paul
- **Coed**

Faculty *Student/faculty ratio:* 11:1.

Academics *Degrees:* diplomas, associate, and bachelor's.

Student Life *Campus security:* 24-hour emergency response devices, late-night transport/escort service.

Standardized Tests *Required:* ACCUPLACER is required of all applicants unless documentation of a minimum ACT composite score of 21 or documentation of a minimum composite score of 1485 on the SAT is presented (for admission).

Costs (2012–13) *Tuition:* $15,300 full-time, $460 per credit part-time. Full-time tuition and fees vary according to course load, degree level, location, and program. Part-time tuition and fees vary according to course load, degree level, location, and program. *Required fees:* $1548 full-time, $43 per credit part-time.

Applying *Options:* electronic application. *Application fee:* $50. *Required:* high school transcript, interview. *Required for some:* essay or personal statement, 2 letters of recommendation, GED certificate in lieu of high school transcript.

Freshman Application Contact Minnesota School of Business–Lakeville, 17685 Juniper Path, Lakeville, MN 55044. *Phone:* 952-892-9000.

Website: http://www.msbcollege.edu/.

Minnesota School of Business–Moorhead

Moorhead, Minnesota

- **Proprietary** 4-year, part of Globe Education Network (GEN) which is composed of Globe University, Minnesota School of Business, Broadview University, The Institute of Production and Recording and Minnesota School of Cosmetology
- **Small-town** 5-acre campus
- **Coed**

Faculty *Student/faculty ratio:* 12:1.

Academics *Degrees:* diplomas, associate, and bachelor's.

Student Life *Campus security:* 24-hour emergency response devices, late-night transport/escort service.

Standardized Tests *Required:* ACCUPLACER is required of all applicants unless documentation of a minimum ACT composite score of 21 or documentation of a minimum composite score of 1485 on the SAT is presented (for admission).

Applying *Options:* electronic application. *Application fee:* $50. *Required:* high school transcript, interview, High school transcript or GED required of all applicants. *Required for some:* essay or personal statement, 2 letters of recommendation.

Freshman Application Contact Minnesota School of Business–Moorhead, 2777 34th Street South, Moorhead, MN 56560. *Phone:* 218-422-1000.

Website: http://www.msbcollege.edu/.

Minnesota School of Business–Plymouth

Minneapolis, Minnesota

- **Proprietary** primarily 2-year, founded 2002, part of Globe Education Network (GEN) which is composed of Globe University, Minnesota School of Business, Broadview University, The Institute of Production and Recording and Minnesota School of Cosmetology
- **Suburban** 7-acre campus with easy access to Minneapolis-St. Paul
- **Coed**

Faculty *Student/faculty ratio:* 21:1.

Academics *Calendar:* quarters. *Degrees:* diplomas, associate, and bachelor's.
Student Life *Campus security:* 24-hour emergency response devices, late-night transport/escort service.
Standardized Tests *Required:* ACCUPLACER is required of all applicants unless documentation of a minimum ACT composite score of 21 or documentation of a minimum composite score of 1485 on the SAT is presented (for admission).
Costs (2012–13) *Tuition:* $15,300 full-time, $460 per credit part-time. Full-time tuition and fees vary according to course load, degree level, location, and program. Part-time tuition and fees vary according to course load, degree level, location, and program. *Required fees:* $1548 full-time, $43 per credit part-time.
Applying *Options:* electronic application. *Application fee:* $50. *Required:* high school transcript, interview, High school transcript or GED required of all applicants. *Required for some:* essay or personal statement, 2 letters of recommendation.
Freshman Application Contact Minnesota School of Business–Plymouth, Plymouth, MN 55447. *Phone:* 763-476-2000. *Fax:* 763-476-1000.
Website: http://www.msbcollege.edu/.

Minnesota School of Business–Richfield

Richfield, Minnesota

- **Proprietary** primarily 2-year, founded 1877, part of Globe Education Network (GEN) which is composed of Globe University, Minnesota School of Business, Broadview University, The Institute of Production and Recording and Minnesota School of Cosmetology
- **Urban** 3-acre campus with easy access to Minneapolis-St. Paul
- **Coed**

Faculty *Student/faculty ratio:* 16:1.
Academics *Calendar:* quarters. *Degrees:* diplomas, associate, and bachelor's.
Student Life *Campus security:* 24-hour emergency response devices, late-night transport/escort service.
Standardized Tests *Required:* ACCUPLACER is required of all applicants unless documentation of a minimum ACT composite score of 21 or documentation of a minimum composite score of 1485 on the SAT is presented (for admission).
Costs (2012–13) *Tuition:* $15,300 full-time, $460 per credit part-time. Full-time tuition and fees vary according to course load, degree level, location, and program. Part-time tuition and fees vary according to course load, degree level, location, and program. *Required fees:* $1548 full-time, $43 per credit part-time.
Applying *Options:* electronic application. *Application fee:* $50. *Required:* high school transcript, interview, High school transcript or GED required of all applicants. Application fee for Nursing Program is $100. *Required for some:* essay or personal statement, 2 letters of recommendation.
Freshman Application Contact Minnesota School of Business–Richfield, 1401 West 76th Street, Suite 500, Richfield, MN 55423. *Phone:* 612-861-2000. *Toll-free phone:* 800-752-4223.
Website: http://www.msbcollege.edu/.

Minnesota School of Business–Rochester

Rochester, Minnesota

- **Proprietary** comprehensive, part of Globe Education Network (GEN) which is composed of Globe University, Minnesota School of Business, Broadview University, The Institute of Production and Recording and Minnesota School of Cosmetology
- **Small-town** 5-acre campus
- **Coed**

Faculty *Student/faculty ratio:* 23:1.
Academics *Calendar:* quarters. *Degrees:* diplomas, associate, bachelor's, and master's.
Student Life *Campus security:* 24-hour emergency response devices, late-night transport/escort service.
Standardized Tests *Required:* ACCUPLACER is required of all applicants unless documentation of a minimum ACT composite score of 21 or documen-

tation of a minimum composite score of 1485 on the SAT is presented (for admission).
Costs (2012–13) *Tuition:* $15,300 full-time, $460 per credit part-time. Full-time tuition and fees vary according to course level, course load, degree level, location, and program. Part-time tuition and fees vary according to course level, course load, degree level, location, and program. *Required fees:* $1548 full-time, $43 per credit part-time.
Applying *Options:* electronic application. *Application fee:* $50. *Required:* high school transcript, interview, High school transcript or GED required of all applicants. *Required for some:* essay or personal statement, 2 letters of recommendation.
Freshman Application Contact Minnesota School of Business–Rochester, 2521 Pennington Drive, NW, Rochester, MN 55901. *Phone:* 507-586-9500. *Toll-free phone:* 888-662-8772.
Website: http://www.msbcollege.edu/.

Minnesota School of Business–St. Cloud

Waite Park, Minnesota

- **Proprietary** primarily 2-year, founded 2004, part of Globe Education Network (GEN) which is composed of Globe University, Minnesota School of Business, Broadview University, The Institute of Production and Recording and Minnesota School of Cosmetology
- **Small-town** 2-acre campus
- **Coed**

Faculty *Student/faculty ratio:* 22:1.
Academics *Calendar:* quarters. *Degrees:* diplomas, associate, and bachelor's.
Student Life *Campus security:* 24-hour emergency response devices, late-night transport/escort service.
Standardized Tests *Required:* ACCUPLACER is required of all applicants unless documentation of a minimum ACT composite score of 21 or documentation of a minimum composite score of 1485 on the SAT is presented (for admission).
Costs (2012–13) *Tuition:* $15,300 full-time, $460 per credit part-time. Full-time tuition and fees vary according to course level, course load, degree level, location, and program. Part-time tuition and fees vary according to course level, course load, degree level, location, and program. *Required fees:* $1548 full-time, $43 per credit part-time.
Applying *Options:* electronic application. *Application fee:* $50. *Required:* high school transcript, interview, High school transcript or GED required of all applicants. *Required for some:* essay or personal statement, 2 letters of recommendation.
Freshman Application Contact Minnesota School of Business–St. Cloud, 1201 2nd Street South, Waite Park, MN 56387. *Phone:* 320-257-2000. *Toll-free phone:* 866-403-3333.
Website: http://www.msbcollege.edu/.

Minnesota School of Business–Shakopee

Shakopee, Minnesota

- **Proprietary** primarily 2-year, founded 2004, part of Globe Education Network (GEN) which is composed of Globe University, Minnesota School of Business, Broadview University, The Institute of Production and Recording and Minnesota School of Cosmetology
- **Suburban** 1-acre campus
- **Coed**

Faculty *Student/faculty ratio:* 15:1.
Academics *Calendar:* quarters. *Degrees:* diplomas, associate, and bachelor's.
Student Life *Campus security:* 24-hour emergency response devices, late-night transport/escort service.
Standardized Tests *Required:* ACCUPLACER is required of all applicants unless documentation of a minimum ACT composite score of 21 or documentation of a minimum composite score of 1485 on the SAT is presented (for admission).
Applying *Options:* electronic application. *Application fee:* $50. *Required:* high school transcript, interview, High school transcript or GED required of all applicants. *Required for some:* essay or personal statement, 2 letters of recommendation.

Freshman Application Contact Minnesota School of Business–Shakopee, 1200 Shakopee Town Square, Shakopee, MN 55379. *Phone:* 952-345-1200. *Toll-free phone:* 866-766-1200.
Website: http://www.msbcollege.edu/.

Minnesota State University Mankato

Mankato, Minnesota

- **State-supported** university, founded 1868, part of Minnesota State Colleges and Universities System
- **Small-town** 303-acre campus with easy access to Minneapolis-St. Paul
- **Coed** 13,285 undergraduate students, 86% full-time, 51% women, 49% men
- **Moderately difficult** entrance level, 61% of applicants were admitted

Undergraduates 11,468 full-time, 1,817 part-time. Students come from 45 states and territories; 76 other countries; 17% are from out of state; 4% Black or African American, non-Hispanic/Latino; 3% Hispanic/Latino; 3% Asian, non-Hispanic/Latino; 0.1% Native Hawaiian or other Pacific Islander, non-Hispanic/Latino; 0.2% American Indian or Alaska Native, non-Hispanic/Latino; 2% Two or more races, non-Hispanic/Latino; 3% Race/ethnicity unknown; 5% international; 8% transferred in; 25% live on campus. *Retention:* 70% of full-time freshmen returned.
Freshmen *Admission:* 7,787 applied, 4,762 admitted, 2,311 enrolled. *Test scores:* ACT scores over 18: 89%; ACT scores over 24: 29%; ACT scores over 30: 2%.
Faculty *Total:* 762, 62% full-time, 58% with terminal degrees. *Student/faculty ratio:* 27:1.
Academics *Calendar:* semesters. *Degrees:* certificates, associate, bachelor's, master's, doctoral, and post-master's certificates. *Special study options:* academic remediation for entering students, accelerated degree program, adult/continuing education programs, advanced placement credit, cooperative education, distance learning, double majors, English as a second language, external degree program, honors programs, independent study, internships, off-campus study, part-time degree program, services for LD students, student-designed majors, study abroad, summer session for credit. *ROTC:* Army (b).
Computers on Campus 900 computers/terminals are available on campus for general student use. Students can access the following: campus intranet, computer help desk, free student e-mail accounts, online (class) grades, online (class) registration, online (class) schedules. Campuswide network is available. Wireless service is available via entire campus.
Student Life *Housing options:* coed. Campus housing is university owned and leased by the school. Freshman applicants given priority for college housing. *Activities and organizations:* drama/theater group, student-run newspaper, radio station, choral group, national fraternities, national sororities. *Campus security:* 24-hour emergency response devices and patrols, student patrols, late-night transport/escort service, Night Owl security program in residence halls, closed circuit cameras in parking lots. *Student services:* health clinic, personal/psychological counseling, women's center, legal services.
Athletics Member NCAA. All Division II except men's and women's ice hockey (Division I). *Intercollegiate sports:* baseball M(s), basketball M(s)/W(s), cheerleading M/W, cross-country running M(s)/W(s), football M(s), golf M(s)/W(s), ice hockey M(s)/W(s), soccer W(s), softball W(s), swimming and diving W(s), tennis M(s)/W(s), track and field M(s)/W(s), volleyball W(s), wrestling M(s). *Intramural sports:* archery M/W, basketball M/W, fencing M/W, football M, golf M/W, ice hockey M/W, lacrosse M/W, racquetball M/W, rock climbing M/W, rugby M/W, sailing M/W, skiing (downhill) M/W, soccer M/W, softball M/W, swimming and diving W, table tennis W, tennis M/W, track and field M/W, volleyball M/W, wrestling M.
Standardized Tests *Required:* SAT or ACT (for admission). *Required for some:* SAT or ACT (for admission).
Costs (2013–14) *Tuition:* state resident $7532 full-time, $262 per credit hour part-time; nonresident $15,010 full-time, $564 per credit hour part-time. Full-time tuition and fees vary according to course load, location, and reciprocity agreements. Part-time tuition and fees vary according to course load, location, and reciprocity agreements. *Required fees:* $864 full-time, $36 per credit hour part-time. *Room and board:* $7053. Room and board charges vary according to board plan and housing facility. *Payment plan:* installment. *Waivers:* employees or children of employees.
Financial Aid Of all full-time matriculated undergraduates who enrolled in 2011, 9,360 applied for aid, 6,896 were judged to have need, 2,087 had their need fully met. 493 Federal Work-Study jobs (averaging $3571). 526 state and other part-time jobs (averaging $3390). In 2011, 458 non-need-based awards were made. *Average percent of need met:* 79%. *Average financial aid package:* $8396. *Average need-based loan:* $4200. *Average need-based gift aid:* $4756.

Average non-need-based aid: $3097. *Average indebtedness upon graduation:* $29,415.
Applying *Options:* electronic application, early admission, deferred entrance. *Application fee:* $20. *Required:* high school transcript. *Required for some:* essay or personal statement, 3 letters of recommendation, personal statement required for some. *Application deadlines:* rolling (freshmen), rolling (transfers). *Notification:* continuous (freshmen), continuous (transfers).
Freshman Application Contact Office of Admissions, Minnesota State University Mankato, 122 Taylor Center, Mankato, MN 56001. *Phone:* 507-389-1822. *Toll-free phone:* 800-722-0544. *Fax:* 507-389-1511. *E-mail:* admissions@mnsu.edu.
Website: http://www.mnsu.edu/.

Minnesota State University Moorhead

Moorhead, Minnesota

- **State-supported** comprehensive, founded 1885, part of Minnesota State Colleges and Universities System
- **Urban** 119-acre campus
- **Endowment** $7.8 million
- **Coed** 6,426 undergraduate students, 82% full-time, 59% women, 41% men
- **Moderately difficult** entrance level, 84% of applicants were admitted

Undergraduates 5,276 full-time, 1,150 part-time. Students come from 39 states and territories; 57 other countries; 36% are from out of state; 2% Black or African American, non-Hispanic/Latino; 1% Hispanic/Latino; 1% Asian, non-Hispanic/Latino; 0.7% American Indian or Alaska Native, non-Hispanic/Latino; 3% Two or more races, non-Hispanic/Latino; 5% Race/ethnicity unknown; 7% international; 11% transferred in; 26% live on campus. *Retention:* 68% of full-time freshmen returned.
Freshmen *Admission:* 3,748 applied, 3,135 admitted, 1,098 enrolled. *Test scores:* SAT critical reading scores over 500: 43%; SAT math scores over 500: 63%; ACT scores over 18: 95%; SAT critical reading scores over 600: 8%; SAT math scores over 600: 21%; ACT scores over 24: 37%; SAT math scores over 700: 3%; ACT scores over 30: 3%.
Faculty *Total:* 469, 42% full-time, 56% with terminal degrees. *Student/faculty ratio:* 21:1.
Academics *Calendar:* semesters. *Degrees:* certificates, associate, bachelor's, master's, doctoral, post-master's, and postbachelor's certificates. *Special study options:* academic remediation for entering students, adult/continuing education programs, advanced placement credit, distance learning, double majors, English as a second language, honors programs, independent study, internships, off-campus study, part-time degree program, services for LD students, student-designed majors, study abroad, summer session for credit. *ROTC:* Army (c), Air Force (c).
Computers on Campus 2,200 computers/terminals are available on campus for general student use. Students can access the following: computer help desk, free student e-mail accounts, online (class) grades, online (class) registration, online (class) schedules. Campuswide network is available. 100% of college-owned or -operated housing units are wired for high-speed Internet access. Wireless service is available via entire campus.
Student Life *Housing options:* coed, men-only, women-only, disabled students. Campus housing is university owned. *Activities and organizations:* drama/theater group, student-run newspaper, radio and television station, choral group, Chi Alpha, International Student Organization, Student Orientation Counselor & Friends, Education Minnesota Student Program, Student Senate, national fraternities, national sororities. *Campus security:* 24-hour emergency response devices and patrols, student patrols, late-night transport/escort service, controlled dormitory access. *Student services:* health clinic, personal/psychological counseling, women's center.
Athletics Member NCAA. All Division II. *Intercollegiate sports:* basketball M/W, cross-country running M/W, football M, golf W, soccer W, softball W, swimming and diving W, tennis W, track and field M/W, volleyball W, wrestling M. *Intramural sports:* badminton M/W, baseball M(c)/W(c), basketball M/W, fencing M(c)/W(c), football M/W, ice hockey M/W, lacrosse M(c)/W(c), racquetball M/W, rugby M(c)/W(c), soccer M(c)/W(c), tennis M/W, ultimate Frisbee M/W, volleyball M/W.
Standardized Tests *Required:* SAT or ACT (for admission).
Costs (2012–13) *Tuition:* state resident $6898 full-time, $222 per credit hour part-time; nonresident $13,796 full-time, $445 per credit hour part-time. Full-time tuition and fees vary according to course load, degree level, program, and reciprocity agreements. Part-time tuition and fees vary according to course load, degree level, program, and reciprocity agreements. *Required fees:* $936 full-time, $42 per credit hour part-time. *Room and board:* $6984; room only:

$4310. Room and board charges vary according to board plan and housing facility. *Payment plan:* installment. *Waivers:* senior citizens and employees or children of employees.

Financial Aid Of all full-time matriculated undergraduates who enrolled in 2011, 4,448 applied for aid, 3,498 were judged to have need. 428 Federal Work-Study jobs (averaging $1357). 215 state and other part-time jobs (averaging $1471). *Average need-based loan:* $4285.

Applying *Options:* electronic application, early admission, deferred entrance. *Application fee:* $20. *Required:* high school transcript. *Application deadlines:* 8/1 (freshmen), 8/1 (out-of-state freshmen), 8/1 (transfers).

Freshman Application Contact Mr. Adam Jenkins, Interim Director of Admissions, Minnesota State University Moorhead, Owens Hall, Moorhead, MN 56563-0002. *Phone:* 218-477-2549. *Toll-free phone:* 800-593-7246. *Fax:* 218-477-4374. *E-mail:* dragon@mnstate.edu.
Website: http://www.mnstate.edu/.

National American University

Roseville, Minnesota

Director of Admissions Mr. Steve Grunlan, Director of Admissions, National American University, 1500 West Highway 36, Roseville, MN 55113. *Phone:* 651-644-1265.
Website: http://www.national.edu/.

North Central University

Minneapolis, Minnesota

Freshman Application Contact Ms. Sigi Shawa, Assistant Director, North Central University, 910 Elliot Avenue, Minneapolis, MN 55404-1322. *Phone:* 612-343-4460. *Toll-free phone:* 800-289-6222. *Fax:* 612-343-4146. *E-mail:* admissions@northcentral.edu.
Website: http://www.northcentral.edu/.

Northwestern College

St. Paul, Minnesota

- **Independent nondenominational** comprehensive, founded 1902
- **Suburban** 107-acre campus with easy access to Minneapolis-St. Paul
- **Coed** 3,086 undergraduate students, 65% full-time, 59% women, 41% men
- **Moderately difficult** entrance level, 59% of applicants were admitted

Undergraduates 2,012 full-time, 1,074 part-time. Students come from 34 states and territories; 12 other countries; 27% are from out of state; 3% Black or African American, non-Hispanic/Latino; 1% Hispanic/Latino; 4% Asian, non-Hispanic/Latino; 0.5% American Indian or Alaska Native, non-Hispanic/Latino; 2% Two or more races, non-Hispanic/Latino; 3% Race/ethnicity unknown; 0.6% international; 5% transferred in; 67% live on campus. *Retention:* 80% of full-time freshmen returned.

Freshmen *Admission:* 2,253 applied, 1,322 admitted, 398 enrolled. *Average high school GPA:* 3.51. *Test scores:* SAT critical reading scores over 500: 88%; SAT math scores over 500: 67%; ACT scores over 18: 97%; SAT critical reading scores over 600: 45%; SAT math scores over 600: 62%; ACT scores over 24: 56%; SAT critical reading scores over 700: 16%; SAT math scores over 700: 36%; ACT scores over 30: 12%.

Faculty *Total:* 159, 61% full-time, 61% with terminal degrees. *Student/faculty ratio:* 17:1.

Academics *Calendar:* semesters. *Degrees:* certificates, associate, bachelor's, master's, and postbachelor's certificates. *Special study options:* academic remediation for entering students, adult/continuing education programs, advanced placement credit, distance learning, double majors, honors programs, independent study, internships, off-campus study, part-time degree program, services for LD students, student-designed majors, study abroad, summer session for credit. *ROTC:* Army (c), Air Force (c). *Unusual degree programs:* 3-2 engineering with University of Minnesota-Twin Cities; Dual B.A./M.Div. in Pastoral Studies.

Computers on Campus 200 computers/terminals and 1,350 ports are available on campus for general student use. Students can access the following: campus intranet, computer help desk, free student e-mail accounts, online (class) grades, online (class) registration, online (class) schedules, network file space, personal web site, integrated student portal, b/w and color printing, virtual labs. Campuswide network is available. 100% of college-owned or -operated housing units are wired for high-speed Internet access. Wireless service is

available via classrooms, computer centers, computer labs, dorm rooms, learning centers, libraries, student centers.

Student Life *Housing:* on-campus residence required through junior year. *Options:* men-only, women-only, disabled students. Campus housing is university owned. Freshman campus housing is guaranteed. *Activities and organizations:* drama/theater group, student-run newspaper, radio and television station, choral group, Northwestern Student Association (student government), The Gathering (religious group), Student Missions Fellowship, Guardian Angels, Outreach Ministries. *Campus security:* 24-hour emergency response devices and patrols, late-night transport/escort service, controlled dormitory access, gated access to main campus, emergency notification system. *Student services:* health clinic, personal/psychological counseling.

Athletics Member NCAA, NCCAA. All NCAA Division III. *Intercollegiate sports:* baseball M, basketball M/W, cross-country running M/W, football M, golf M/W, ice hockey M(c), soccer M/W, softball W, tennis M/W, track and field M/W, volleyball M(c)/W. *Intramural sports:* basketball M/W, football M/W, softball M/W, table tennis M/W, tennis M/W, volleyball M/W.

Standardized Tests *Required:* SAT or ACT (for admission).

Costs (2013–14) *Comprehensive fee:* $35,170 includes full-time tuition ($26,740), mandatory fees ($220), and room and board ($8210). Full-time tuition and fees vary according to course load. Part-time tuition: $1140 per semester hour. Part-time tuition and fees vary according to course load. *Required fees:* $65 per term part-time. *College room only:* $4820. Room and board charges vary according to board plan and student level. *Payment plan:* installment. *Waivers:* children of alumni and employees or children of employees.

Financial Aid Of all full-time matriculated undergraduates who enrolled in 2012, 1,661 applied for aid, 1,529 were judged to have need, 166 had their need fully met. 187 Federal Work-Study jobs (averaging $4151). 281 state and other part-time jobs (averaging $4267). In 2012, 272 non-need-based awards were made. *Average percent of need met:* 67%. *Average financial aid package:* $18,390. *Average need-based loan:* $4468. *Average need-based gift aid:* $13,504. *Average non-need-based aid:* $8213. *Average indebtedness upon graduation:* $24,299.

Applying *Options:* electronic application, early admission, deferred entrance. *Application fee:* $25. *Required:* essay or personal statement, high school transcript, minimum 2.0 GPA, 2 letters of recommendation, lifestyle agreement, statement of Christian faith. *Required for some:* interview. *Recommended:* minimum 3.0 GPA. *Application deadlines:* 8/1 (freshmen), 8/1 (out-of-state freshmen), 8/1 (transfers). *Notification:* continuous (freshmen), continuous (out-of-state freshmen), continuous (transfers).

Freshman Application Contact Mr. Kenneth K. Faffler, Director of Admissions, Northwestern College, Officer of Admissions, 3003 Snelling Avenue North, 212 Nazareth Hall, St. Paul, MN 55113-1598. *Phone:* 651-631-5111. *Toll-free phone:* 800-827-6827. *Fax:* 651-631-5680. *E-mail:* admissions@nwc.edu.
Website: http://www.nwc.edu/.

Oak Hills Christian College

Bemidji, Minnesota

Freshman Application Contact Shelly Fast, Assistant Director of Admissions, Oak Hills Christian College, 1600 Oak Hills Road SW, Bemidji, MN 56601. *Phone:* 218-751-8670 Ext. 1285. *Toll-free phone:* 888-751-8670 Ext. 1285. *Fax:* 218-751-8825. *E-mail:* admissions@oakhills.edu.
Website: http://www.oakhills.edu/.

Rasmussen College Blaine

Blaine, Minnesota

- **Proprietary** 4-year, part of Rasmussen College System
- **Suburban** campus
- **Coed** 500 undergraduate students
- **Minimally difficult** entrance level

Faculty *Student/faculty ratio:* 22:1.

Academics *Degrees:* certificates, diplomas, associate, and bachelor's. *Special study options:* academic remediation for entering students, accelerated degree program, adult/continuing education programs, distance learning, double majors, internships, part-time degree program, summer session for credit.

Computers on Campus 81 computers/terminals are available on campus for general student use. Students can access the following: computer help desk, free student e-mail accounts, online (class) grades, online (class) schedules. Campuswide network is available. Wireless service is available via entire campus.

Student Life *Housing:* college housing not available.
Standardized Tests *Required:* Internal Exam (for admission).
Costs (2013–14) *Tuition:* $14,220 full-time. Full-time tuition and fees vary according to course level, course load, degree level, location, and program. Part-time tuition and fees vary according to course level, course load, degree level, location, and program. *Required fees:* $1800 full-time. *Payment plans:* installment, deferred payment. *Waivers:* employees or children of employees.
Applying *Options:* electronic application, early admission, deferred entrance. *Required:* high school transcript, minimum 2.0 GPA. *Required for some:* interview. *Application deadlines:* rolling (freshmen), rolling (transfers).
Freshman Application Contact Susan Hammerstrom, Director of Admissions, Rasmussen College Blaine, 3629 95th Avenue NE, Blaine, MN 55014. *Phone:* 763-795-4720. *Toll-free phone:* 888-549-6755. *E-mail:* susan.hammerstrom@rasmussen.edu.
Website: http://www.rasmussen.edu/.

Rasmussen College Bloomington

Bloomington, Minnesota

- **Proprietary** primarily 2-year, founded 1904, part of Rasmussen College System
- **Suburban** campus with easy access to Minneapolis/St. Paul
- **Coed** 546 undergraduate students
- **Minimally difficult** entrance level

Faculty *Student/faculty ratio:* 22:1.
Academics *Calendar:* quarters. *Degrees:* certificates, diplomas, associate, and bachelor's. *Special study options:* academic remediation for entering students, accelerated degree program, adult/continuing education programs, distance learning, double majors, internships, part-time degree program, summer session for credit.
Computers on Campus 68 computers/terminals are available on campus for general student use. Students can access the following: computer help desk, free student e-mail accounts, online (class) grades, online (class) schedules. Campuswide network is available. Wireless service is available via entire campus.
Student Life *Housing:* college housing not available.
Standardized Tests *Required:* Internal Exam (for admission).
Costs (2013–14) *Tuition:* $14,220 full-time. Full-time tuition and fees vary according to course level, course load, degree level, location, and program. Part-time tuition and fees vary according to course level, course load, degree level, location, and program. *Required fees:* $1800 full-time. *Payment plans:* installment, deferred payment. *Waivers:* employees or children of employees.
Financial Aid Of all full-time matriculated undergraduates who enrolled in 2011, 3 state and other part-time jobs (averaging $4338).
Applying *Options:* electronic application, early admission, deferred entrance. *Required:* high school transcript, minimum 2.0 GPA. *Required for some:* interview. *Application deadlines:* rolling (freshmen), rolling (transfers).
Freshman Application Contact Susan Hammerstrom, Director of Admissions, Rasmussen College Bloomington, 4400 West 78th Street, Bloomington, MN 55305. *Phone:* 952-545-2000. *Toll-free phone:* 888-549-6755.
Website: http://www.rasmussen.edu/.

Rasmussen College Brooklyn Park

Brooklyn Park, Minnesota

- **Proprietary** primarily 2-year, part of Rasmussen College System
- **Suburban** campus
- **Coed** 892 undergraduate students
- **Minimally difficult** entrance level

Faculty *Student/faculty ratio:* 22:1.
Academics *Degrees:* certificates, diplomas, associate, and bachelor's. *Special study options:* academic remediation for entering students, accelerated degree program, adult/continuing education programs, distance learning, double majors, internships, part-time degree program, summer session for credit.
Computers on Campus 80 computers/terminals are available on campus for general student use. Students can access the following: computer help desk, free student e-mail accounts, online (class) grades, online (class) schedules. Campuswide network is available. Wireless service is available via entire campus.
Student Life *Housing:* college housing not available.
Standardized Tests *Required:* Internal Exam (for admission).

Costs (2013–14) *Tuition:* $14,220 full-time. Full-time tuition and fees vary according to course level, course load, degree level, location, and program. Part-time tuition and fees vary according to course level, course load, degree level, location, and program. *Required fees:* $1800 full-time. *Payment plans:* installment, deferred payment. *Waivers:* employees or children of employees.
Applying *Options:* electronic application, early admission, deferred entrance. *Required:* high school transcript, minimum 2.0 GPA. *Required for some:* interview. *Application deadlines:* rolling (freshmen), rolling (transfers).
Freshman Application Contact Susan Hammerstrom, Director of Admissions, Rasmussen College Brooklyn Park, 8301 93rd Avenue North, Brooklyn Park, MN 55445-1512. *Phone:* 763-493-4500. *Toll-free phone:* 888-549-6755. *E-mail:* susan.hammerstrom@rasmussen.edu.
Website: http://www.rasmussen.edu/.

Rasmussen College Eagan

Eagan, Minnesota

- **Proprietary** primarily 2-year, founded 1904, part of Rasmussen College System
- **Suburban** campus with easy access to Minneapolis/St. Paul
- **Coed, primarily women** 883 undergraduate students
- **Minimally difficult** entrance level

Faculty *Student/faculty ratio:* 22:1.
Academics *Calendar:* quarters. *Degrees:* certificates, diplomas, associate, and bachelor's. *Special study options:* academic remediation for entering students, accelerated degree program, adult/continuing education programs, distance learning, double majors, internships, part-time degree program, summer session for credit.
Computers on Campus 93 computers/terminals are available on campus for general student use. Students can access the following: computer help desk, free student e-mail accounts, online (class) grades, online (class) schedules. Campuswide network is available. Wireless service is available via entire campus.
Student Life *Housing:* college housing not available.
Standardized Tests *Required:* Internal Exam (for admission).
Costs (2013–14) *Tuition:* $14,220 full-time. Full-time tuition and fees vary according to course level, course load, degree level, location, and program. Part-time tuition and fees vary according to course level, course load, degree level, location, and program. *Required fees:* $1800 full-time. *Payment plans:* installment, deferred payment. *Waivers:* employees or children of employees.
Applying *Options:* electronic application, early admission, deferred entrance. *Required:* high school transcript, minimum 2.0 GPA. *Required for some:* interview. *Application deadlines:* rolling (freshmen), rolling (transfers).
Freshman Application Contact Susan Hammerstrom, Director of Admissions, Rasmussen College Eagan, 3500 Federal Drive, Eagan, MN 55122-1346. *Phone:* 651-687-9000. *Toll-free phone:* 888-549-6755. *E-mail:* susan.hammerstrom@rasmussen.edu.
Website: http://www.rasmussen.edu/.

Rasmussen College Lake Elmo/ Woodbury

Lake Elmo, Minnesota

- **Proprietary** primarily 2-year, part of Rasmussen College System
- **Suburban** campus
- **Coed** 682 undergraduate students
- **Minimally difficult** entrance level

Faculty *Student/faculty ratio:* 22:1.
Academics *Degrees:* certificates, diplomas, associate, and bachelor's. *Special study options:* academic remediation for entering students, accelerated degree program, adult/continuing education programs, distance learning, double majors, internships, part-time degree program, summer session for credit.
Computers on Campus 85 computers/terminals are available on campus for general student use. Students can access the following: computer help desk, free student e-mail accounts, online (class) grades, online (class) schedules. Campuswide network is available. Wireless service is available via entire campus.
Student Life *Housing:* college housing not available.
Standardized Tests *Required:* Internal Exam (for admission).
Costs (2013–14) *Tuition:* $14,220 full-time. Full-time tuition and fees vary according to course level, course load, degree level, location, and program. Part-time tuition and fees vary according to course level, course load, degree

level, location, and program. *Required fees:* $1800 full-time. *Payment plans:* installment, deferred payment. *Waivers:* employees or children of employees.
Applying *Options:* electronic application, early admission, deferred entrance. *Required:* high school transcript, minimum 2.0 GPA. *Required for some:* interview. *Application deadlines:* rolling (freshmen), rolling (transfers).
Freshman Application Contact Susan Hammerstrom, Director of Admissions, Rasmussen College Lake Elmo/Woodbury, 8565 Eagle Point Circle, Lake Elmo, MN 55042. *Phone:* 651-259-6600. *Toll-free phone:* 888-549-6755. *E-mail:* susan.hammerstrom@rasmussen.edu. *Website:* http://www.rasmussen.edu/.

Rasmussen College Mankato

Mankato, Minnesota

- **Proprietary** primarily 2-year, founded 1904, part of Rasmussen College System
- **Suburban** campus
- **Coed, primarily women** 745 undergraduate students
- **Minimally difficult** entrance level

Faculty *Student/faculty ratio:* 22:1.
Academics *Calendar:* quarters. *Degrees:* certificates, diplomas, associate, and bachelor's. *Special study options:* academic remediation for entering students, accelerated degree program, adult/continuing education programs, distance learning, double majors, internships, part-time degree program, summer session for credit.
Computers on Campus 116 computers/terminals are available on campus for general student use. Students can access the following: computer help desk, free student e-mail accounts, online (class) grades, online (class) schedules. Campuswide network is available. Wireless service is available via entire campus.
Student Life *Housing:* college housing not available.
Standardized Tests *Required:* Internal Exam (for admission).
Costs (2013–14) *Tuition:* $14,220 full-time. Full-time tuition and fees vary according to course level, course load, degree level, location, and program. Part-time tuition and fees vary according to course level, course load, degree level, location, and program. *Required fees:* $1800 full-time. *Payment plans:* installment, deferred payment. *Waivers:* employees or children of employees.
Financial Aid Of all full-time matriculated undergraduates who enrolled in 2011, 15 Federal Work-Study jobs (averaging $4000). 13 state and other part-time jobs (averaging $4000).
Applying *Options:* electronic application, early admission, deferred entrance. *Required:* high school transcript, minimum 2.0 GPA. *Required for some:* interview. *Application deadlines:* rolling (freshmen), rolling (transfers).
Freshman Application Contact Susan Hammerstrom, Director of Admissions, Rasmussen College Mankato, 130 Saint Andrews Drive, Mankato, MN 56001. *Phone:* 507-625-6556. *Toll-free phone:* 888-549-6755. *E-mail:* susan.hammerstrom@rasmussen.edu. *Website:* http://www.rasmussen.edu/.

Rasmussen College Moorhead

Moorhead, Minnesota

- **Proprietary** primarily 2-year, part of Rasmussen College System
- **Suburban** campus
- **Coed** 420 undergraduate students
- **Minimally difficult** entrance level

Faculty *Student/faculty ratio:* 22:1.
Academics *Degrees:* certificates, diplomas, associate, and bachelor's. *Special study options:* academic remediation for entering students, accelerated degree program, adult/continuing education programs, distance learning, double majors, internships, part-time degree program, summer session for credit.
Computers on Campus 31 computers/terminals are available on campus for general student use. Students can access the following: computer help desk, free student e-mail accounts, online (class) grades, online (class) schedules. Campuswide network is available. Wireless service is available via entire campus.
Student Life *Housing:* college housing not available.
Standardized Tests *Required:* Internal Exam (for admission).
Costs (2013–14) *Tuition:* $14,220 full-time. Full-time tuition and fees vary according to course level, course load, degree level, location, and program. Part-time tuition and fees vary according to course level, course load, degree level, location, and program. *Required fees:* $1800 full-time. *Payment plans:* installment, deferred payment. *Waivers:* employees or children of employees.

Applying *Options:* electronic application, early admission, deferred entrance. *Required:* high school transcript, minimum 2.0 GPA. *Required for some:* interview. *Application deadlines:* rolling (freshmen), rolling (transfers).
Freshman Application Contact Susan Hammerstrom, Director of Admissions, Rasmussen College Moorhead, 1250 29th Avenue South, Moorhead, MN 56560. *Phone:* 218-304-6200. *Toll-free phone:* 888-549-6755. *E-mail:* susan.hammerstrom@rasmussen.edu. *Website:* http://www.rasmussen.edu/.

Rasmussen College St. Cloud

St. Cloud, Minnesota

- **Proprietary** primarily 2-year, founded 1904, part of Rasmussen College System
- **Suburban** campus
- **Coed, primarily women** 845 undergraduate students
- **Minimally difficult** entrance level

Faculty *Student/faculty ratio:* 22:1.
Academics *Calendar:* quarters. *Degrees:* certificates, diplomas, associate, and bachelor's. *Special study options:* academic remediation for entering students, accelerated degree program, adult/continuing education programs, distance learning, double majors, internships, part-time degree program, summer session for credit.
Computers on Campus 91 computers/terminals are available on campus for general student use. Students can access the following: computer help desk, free student e-mail accounts, online (class) grades, online (class) schedules. Campuswide network is available. Wireless service is available via entire campus.
Student Life *Housing:* college housing not available.
Standardized Tests *Required:* Internal Exam (for admission).
Costs (2013–14) *Tuition:* $14,220 full-time. Full-time tuition and fees vary according to course level, course load, degree level, location, and program. Part-time tuition and fees vary according to course level, course load, degree level, location, and program. *Required fees:* $1800 full-time. *Payment plans:* installment, deferred payment. *Waivers:* employees or children of employees.
Financial Aid Of all full-time matriculated undergraduates who enrolled in 2011, 34 Federal Work-Study jobs (averaging $866). 51 state and other part-time jobs (averaging $700).
Applying *Options:* electronic application, early admission, deferred entrance. *Required:* high school transcript, minimum 2.0 GPA. *Required for some:* interview. *Application deadlines:* rolling (freshmen), rolling (transfers).
Freshman Application Contact Susan Hammerstrom, Director of Admissions, Rasmussen College St. Cloud, 226 Park Avenue South, St. Cloud, MN 56301-3713. *Phone:* 320-251-5600. *Toll-free phone:* 888-549-6755. *E-mail:* susan.hammerstrom@rasmussen.edu. *Website:* http://www.rasmussen.edu/.

Rochester Community and Technical College

Rochester, Minnesota

Director of Admissions Mr. Troy Tynsky, Director of Admissions, Rochester Community and Technical College, 851 30th Avenue, SE, Rochester, MN 55904-4999. *Phone:* 507-280-3509. *Website:* http://www.rctc.edu/.

St. Catherine University

St. Paul, Minnesota

- **Independent Roman Catholic** comprehensive, founded 1905
- **Urban** 110-acre campus with easy access to Minneapolis
- **Undergraduate: women only; graduate: coed**
- **Moderately difficult** entrance level

Faculty *Student/faculty ratio:* 12:1.
Academics *Calendar:* 4-1-4. *Degrees:* certificates, associate, bachelor's, master's, doctoral, post-master's, and postbachelor's certificates.
Student Life *Campus security:* 24-hour emergency response devices and patrols, student patrols, late-night transport/escort service, controlled dormitory access.
Athletics Member NCAA. All Division III.

Standardized Tests *Required:* SAT or ACT (for admission).

Costs (2012–13) *Comprehensive fee:* $41,564 includes full-time tuition ($32,896), mandatory fees ($380), and room and board ($8288). Full-time tuition and fees vary according to class time and degree level. Part-time tuition and fees vary according to class time and degree level. *College room only:* $4670. Room and board charges vary according to board plan and housing facility.

Financial Aid *Of all full-time matriculated undergraduates who enrolled in 2011,* 1,759 applied for aid, 1,654 were judged to have need, 218 had their need fully met. *In 2011,* 91 non-need-based awards were made. *Average percent of need met:* 85. *Average financial aid package:* $26,200. *Average need-based loan:* $4800. *Average need-based gift aid:* $10,200. *Average non-need-based aid:* $9500. *Average indebtedness upon graduation:* $35,237.

Applying *Options:* deferred entrance. *Required:* high school transcript, 1 letter of recommendation. *Required for some:* essay or personal statement, interview. *Recommended:* interview.

Freshman Application Contact Ms. Cory Piper-Hauswirth, Associate Director of Admission and Financial Aid, St. Catherine University, 2004 Randolph Avenue, St. Paul, MN 55105. *Phone:* 651-690-6047. *Toll-free phone:* 800-945-4599. *E-mail:* stkate@stkate.edu. *Website:* http://www.stkate.edu/.

St. Cloud State University

St. Cloud, Minnesota

- **State-supported** comprehensive, founded 1869, part of Minnesota State Colleges and Universities System
- **Suburban** 922-acre campus with easy access to Minneapolis-St. Paul
- **Endowment** $15.6 million
- **Coed**
- **Moderately difficult** entrance level

Faculty *Student/faculty ratio:* 21:1.

Academics *Calendar:* semesters. *Degrees:* certificates, diplomas, associate, bachelor's, master's, doctoral, post-master's, and postbachelor's certificates.

Student Life *Campus security:* 24-hour emergency response devices and patrols, student patrols, late-night transport/escort service.

Athletics Member NCAA. All Division II except men's and women's ice hockey (Division I).

Standardized Tests *Required:* SAT or ACT (for admission).

Costs (2012–13) *Tuition:* state resident $6584 full-time; nonresident $14,226 full-time. Full-time tuition and fees vary according to course load and reciprocity agreements. Part-time tuition and fees vary according to course load and reciprocity agreements. *Required fees:* $855 full-time. *Room and board:* $6994. Room and board charges vary according to board plan and housing facility.

Financial Aid *Of all full-time matriculated undergraduates who enrolled in 2010,* 9,249 applied for aid, 7,281 were judged to have need, 1,295 had their need fully met. *In 2010,* 1961 non-need-based awards were made. *Average percent of need met:* 65. *Average financial aid package:* $8400. *Average need-based loan:* $4200. *Average need-based gift aid:* $5000. *Average non-need-based aid:* $9000. *Average indebtedness upon graduation:* $28,819.

Applying *Options:* electronic application, deferred entrance. *Application fee:* $20. *Required:* high school transcript. *Required for some:* ACT/SAT score.

Freshman Application Contact Mr. Richard Shearer, Director of Admissions, St. Cloud State University, 720 4th Avenue South, AS 115, St. Cloud, MN 56301-4498. *Phone:* 320-308-2244. *Toll-free phone:* 877-654-7278. *Fax:* 320-308-2243. *E-mail:* scsu4u@stcloudstate.edu. *Website:* http://www.stcloudstate.edu/.

Saint John's University

Collegeville, Minnesota

- **Independent Roman Catholic** comprehensive, founded 1857
- **Rural** 3500-acre campus with easy access to Minneapolis-St. Paul
- **Endowment** $141.5 million
- **Men only** 1,854 undergraduate students, 98% full-time
- **Moderately difficult** entrance level, 75% of applicants were admitted

Undergraduates 1,823 full-time, 31 part-time. Students come from 36 states and territories; 26 other countries; 18% are from out of state; 3% Black or African American, non-Hispanic/Latino; 4% Hispanic/Latino; 3% Asian, non-Hispanic/Latino; 0.3% Native Hawaiian or other Pacific Islander, non-Hispanic/Latino; 1% American Indian or Alaska Native, non-Hispanic/Latino; 0.1% Two or more races, non-Hispanic/Latino; 6% international; 1% transferred in; 84% live on campus. *Retention:* 89% of full-time freshmen returned.

Freshmen *Admission:* 1,595 applied, 1,193 admitted, 449 enrolled. *Average high school GPA:* 3.49. *Test scores:* SAT critical reading scores over 500: 67%; SAT math scores over 500: 68%; SAT writing scores over 500: 63%; ACT scores over 18: 99%; SAT critical reading scores over 600: 22%; SAT math scores over 600: 27%; SAT writing scores over 600: 15%; ACT scores over 24: 61%; SAT math scores over 700: 6%; SAT writing scores over 700: 2%; ACT scores over 30: 15%.

Faculty *Total:* 167, 80% full-time, 75% with terminal degrees. *Student/faculty ratio:* 12:1.

Academics *Calendar:* semesters. *Degrees:* bachelor's and master's (coordinate with College of Saint Benedict for women). *Special study options:* advanced placement credit, double majors, English as a second language, honors programs, independent study, internships, off-campus study, services for LD students, student-designed majors, study abroad. *ROTC:* Army (b). *Unusual degree programs:* 3-2 engineering with University of Minnesota.

Computers on Campus 980 computers/terminals and 3,000 ports are available on campus for general student use. Students can access the following: campus intranet, computer help desk, free student e-mail accounts, online (class) grades, online (class) registration, online (class) schedules, online student accounts. Campuswide network is available. 100% of college-owned or -operated housing units are wired for high-speed Internet access. Wireless service is available via entire campus.

Student Life *Housing:* on-campus residence required through senior year. *Options:* men-only, disabled students. Campus housing is university owned. Freshman campus housing is guaranteed. *Activities and organizations:* drama/theater group, student-run newspaper, radio station, choral group, China Cross Cultural Communications Club, Outskirts Snow Crew, Buddhist Meditation Club, Magis, Johnball club. *Campus security:* 24-hour emergency response devices and patrols, student patrols, late-night transport/escort service, controlled dormitory access, well-lit pathways, 911 center on campus, closed circuit TV monitors. *Student services:* health clinic, personal/psychological counseling.

Athletics Member NCAA. All Division III. *Intercollegiate sports:* baseball M, basketball M, crew M(c), cross-country running M, football M, golf M, ice hockey M, lacrosse M(c), riflery M(c), rugby M(c), skiing (cross-country) M(c), soccer M, swimming and diving M, tennis M, track and field M, ultimate Frisbee M(c), volleyball M(c), water polo M(c), wrestling M. *Intramural sports:* basketball M, football M, racquetball M, rock climbing M(c), skiing (downhill) M(c), soccer M, softball M, table tennis M, ultimate Frisbee M, volleyball M.

Standardized Tests *Required:* SAT or ACT (for admission).

Costs (2012–13) *Comprehensive fee:* $44,125 includes full-time tuition ($34,838), mandatory fees ($648), and room and board ($8639). Part-time tuition: $1452 per credit hour. Part-time tuition and fees vary according to course load. *College room only:* $4350. Room and board charges vary according to board plan and housing facility. *Payment plan:* installment. *Waivers:* employees or children of employees.

Financial Aid *Of all full-time matriculated undergraduates who enrolled in 2012,* 1,340 applied for aid, 1,184 were judged to have need, 452 had their need fully met. 465 Federal Work-Study jobs (averaging $2727). 690 state and other part-time jobs (averaging $2752). In 2012, 508 non-need-based awards were made. *Average percent of need met:* 87%. *Average financial aid package:* $26,628. *Average need-based loan:* $4099. *Average need-based gift aid:* $21,605. *Average non-need-based aid:* $13,277. *Average indebtedness upon graduation:* $34,889.

Applying *Options:* electronic application, early action, deferred entrance. *Required:* essay or personal statement, high school transcript, 1 letter of recommendation. *Recommended:* minimum 3.0 GPA, interview. *Application deadlines:* rolling (freshmen), rolling (transfers), 11/15 (early action). *Notification:* continuous (freshmen), continuous (transfers), 12/15 (early action).

Freshman Application Contact Mr. Matt Beirne, Director of Admission, Saint John's University, Saint John's University, 2850 Abbey Plaza, Collegeville, MN 56321-7155. *Phone:* 320-363-5055. *Toll-free phone:* 800-544-1489. *Fax:* 320-363-5650. *E-mail:* admissions@csbsju.edu. *Website:* http://www.csbsju.edu/.

Saint Mary's University of Minnesota

Winona, Minnesota

- **Independent Roman Catholic** comprehensive, founded 1912
- **Small-town** 350-acre campus
- **Endowment** $44.0 million
- **Coed** 1,985 undergraduate students, 67% full-time, 53% women, 47% men
- **Moderately difficult** entrance level, 79% of applicants were admitted

Undergraduates 1,332 full-time, 653 part-time. Students come from 30 states and territories; 18 other countries; 42% are from out of state; 5% Black or African American, non-Hispanic/Latino; 5% Hispanic/Latino; 2% Asian, non-Hispanic/Latino; 0.1% Native Hawaiian or other Pacific Islander, non-Hispanic/Latino; 0.1% American Indian or Alaska Native, non-Hispanic/Latino; 0.3% Two or more races, non-Hispanic/Latino; 30% Race/ethnicity unknown; 2% international; 8% transferred in; 88% live on campus. *Retention:* 75% of full-time freshmen returned.

Freshmen *Admission:* 1,704 applied, 1,346 admitted, 328 enrolled. *Average high school GPA:* 3.21. *Test scores:* SAT critical reading scores over 500: 44%; SAT math scores over 500: 67%; SAT writing scores over 500: 50%; ACT scores over 18: 89%; SAT math scores over 600: 23%; SAT writing scores over 600: 17%; ACT scores over 24: 33%; SAT math scores over 700: 6%; ACT scores over 30: 5%.

Faculty *Total:* 555, 19% full-time, 50% with terminal degrees. *Student/faculty ratio:* 16:1.

Academics *Calendar:* semesters. *Degrees:* certificates, diplomas, bachelor's, master's, doctoral, post-master's, and postbachelor's certificates. *Special study options:* academic remediation for entering students, accelerated degree program, adult/continuing education programs, advanced placement credit, cooperative education, distance learning, double majors, English as a second language, honors programs, independent study, internships, off-campus study, part-time degree program, services for LD students, student-designed majors, study abroad, summer session for credit. *ROTC:* Army (c).

Computers on Campus 200 computers/terminals and 50 ports are available on campus for general student use. Students can access the following: campus intranet, computer help desk, free student e-mail accounts, online (class) grades, online (class) registration, online (class) schedules. Campuswide network is available. 100% of college-owned or -operated housing units are wired for high-speed Internet access. Wireless service is available via computer centers, computer labs, dorm rooms, libraries, student centers.

Student Life *Housing:* on-campus residence required through sophomore year. *Options:* coed, men-only, women-only, disabled students. Campus housing is university owned. Freshman campus housing is guaranteed. *Activities and organizations:* drama/theater group, student-run newspaper, radio station, choral group, Student Activity Committee, PR Business Club, Serving Others United in Love (Soul)—Mission Trips, Colleges Against Cancer, Club Hockey, national fraternities, national sororities. *Campus security:* 24-hour emergency response devices and patrols, late-night transport/escort service, controlled dormitory access. *Student services:* health clinic, personal/psychological counseling.

Athletics Member NCAA. All Division III. *Intercollegiate sports:* baseball M, basketball M/W, cross-country running M/W, golf M/W, ice hockey M/W, soccer M/W, softball W, swimming and diving M/W, tennis M/W, track and field M/W, volleyball W. *Intramural sports:* basketball M/W, cheerleading W(c), fencing M(c)/W(c), field hockey M/W, football M/W, ice hockey M, lacrosse M(c)/W(c), rugby M(c), skiing (downhill) M(c)/W(c), soccer M/W, softball M/W, tennis M/W, ultimate Frisbee M/W, volleyball M/W, water polo M(c)/W(c).

Standardized Tests *Required:* SAT or ACT (for admission).

Costs (2013–14) *Comprehensive fee:* $37,015 includes full-time tuition ($28,790), mandatory fees ($525), and room and board ($7700). Full-time tuition and fees vary according to course load. Part-time tuition: $960 per credit. Part-time tuition and fees vary according to course load. *Required fees:* $525 per year part-time. *College room only:* $4310. Room and board charges vary according to board plan and housing facility. *Payment plan:* installment. *Waivers:* employees or children of employees.

Financial Aid Of all full-time matriculated undergraduates who enrolled in 2012, 1,122 applied for aid, 1,034 were judged to have need, 195 had their need fully met. 172 Federal Work-Study jobs (averaging $1630). 288 state and other part-time jobs (averaging $1731). In 2012, 236 non-need-based awards were made. *Average percent of need met:* 70%. *Average financial aid package:* $20,127. *Average need-based loan:* $4820. *Average need-based gift aid:* $16,251. *Average non-need-based aid:* $10,611. *Average indebtedness upon graduation:* $35,134.

Applying *Options:* electronic application, early admission, deferred entrance. *Application fee:* $25. *Required:* essay or personal statement, high school transcript, minimum 2.5 GPA. *Required for some:* interview. *Recommended:* 2 letters of recommendation. *Application deadlines:* 5/1 (freshmen), rolling (transfers). *Notification:* continuous (freshmen), continuous (transfers).

Freshman Application Contact Ms. Brandi DeFries, Vice President for Enrollment Management, Saint Mary's University of Minnesota, 700 Terrace Heights, Winona, MN 55987-1399. *Phone:* 507-457-1700. *Toll-free phone:* 800-635-5987. *Fax:* 507-457-1722. *E-mail:* admission@smumn.edu. *Website:* http://www.smumn.edu/.

St. Olaf College

Northfield, Minnesota

- **Independent Lutheran** 4-year, founded 1874
- **Small-town** 300-acre campus with easy access to Minneapolis-St. Paul
- **Endowment** $333.5 million
- **Coed** 3,176 undergraduate students, 98% full-time, 56% women, 44% men
- **Very difficult** entrance level, 60% of applicants were admitted

Undergraduates 3,128 full-time, 48 part-time. Students come from 50 states and territories; 63 other countries; 49% are from out of state; 2% Black or African American, non-Hispanic/Latino; 4% Hispanic/Latino; 5% Asian, non-Hispanic/Latino; 0.1% Native Hawaiian or other Pacific Islander, non-Hispanic/Latino; 0.2% American Indian or Alaska Native, non-Hispanic/Latino; 3% Two or more races, non-Hispanic/Latino; 0.3% Race/ethnicity unknown; 5% international; 0.6% transferred in; 91% live on campus. *Retention:* 93% of full-time freshmen returned.

Freshmen *Admission:* 3,937 applied, 2,377 admitted, 864 enrolled. *Average high school GPA:* 3.62. *Test scores:* SAT critical reading scores over 500: 90%; SAT math scores over 500: 96%; SAT writing scores over 500: 91%; ACT scores over 18: 100%; SAT critical reading scores over 600: 70%; SAT math scores over 600: 70%; SAT writing scores over 600: 67%; ACT scores over 24: 91%; SAT critical reading scores over 700: 29%; SAT math scores over 700: 27%; SAT writing scores over 700: 23%; ACT scores over 30: 44%.

Faculty *Total:* 340, 66% full-time, 79% with terminal degrees. *Student/faculty ratio:* 12:1.

Academics *Calendar:* 4-1-4. *Degree:* bachelor's. *Special study options:* advanced placement credit, double majors, English as a second language, independent study, internships, off-campus study, part-time degree program, services for LD students, student-designed majors, study abroad, summer session for credit. *Unusual degree programs:* 3-2 engineering with Washington University in St. Louis and University of Minnesota in Minneapolis.

Computers on Campus 1,154 computers/terminals and 3,300 ports are available on campus for general student use. Students can access the following: campus intranet, computer help desk, free student e-mail accounts, online (class) grades, online (class) registration, online (class) schedules. Campuswide network is available. 100% of college-owned or -operated housing units are wired for high-speed Internet access. Wireless service is available via entire campus.

Student Life *Housing:* on-campus residence required through senior year. *Options:* coed, disabled students. Campus housing is university owned. Freshman campus housing is guaranteed. *Activities and organizations:* drama/theater group, student-run newspaper, radio and television station, choral group, Student Government Association, Ultimate Frisbee Teams, Ole Spring Relief, Taiko Drumming, SELAH. *Campus security:* 24-hour emergency response devices and patrols, late-night transport/escort service, controlled dormitory access, lighted pathways and sidewalks, first-year only dorms, quiet halls. *Student services:* health clinic, personal/psychological counseling.

Athletics Member NCAA. All Division III. *Intercollegiate sports:* baseball M, basketball M/W, cross-country running M/W, football M, golf M/W, ice hockey M/W, skiing (cross-country) M/W, skiing (downhill) M/W, soccer M/W, softball W, swimming and diving M/W, tennis M/W, track and field M/W, volleyball W, wrestling M. *Intramural sports:* badminton M(c)/W(c), basketball M/W, bowling M/W, crew M(c)/W(c), equestrian sports M(c)/W(c), fencing M(c)/W(c), field hockey M, football M/W, golf M/W, ice hockey M(c), lacrosse M(c)/W(c), rugby M(c)/W(c), skiing (cross-country) M/W, skiing (downhill) M(c)/W(c), soccer M/W, softball M/W, swimming and diving M/W, table tennis M/W, tennis M/W, ultimate Frisbee M/W, volleyball M(c)/W.

Standardized Tests *Required:* SAT or ACT (for admission).

Costs (2012–13) *Comprehensive fee:* $48,650 includes full-time tuition ($39,560) and room and board ($9090). Full-time tuition and fees vary according to course load. Part-time tuition: $4945 per course. Part-time tuition and fees vary according to course load. *College room only:* $4260. Room and board charges vary according to board plan and housing facility. *Payment plan:* installment. *Waivers:* senior citizens and employees or children of employees.

Financial Aid Of all full-time matriculated undergraduates who enrolled in 2012, 2,359 applied for aid, 2,116 were judged to have need, 2,116 had their need fully met. 851 Federal Work-Study jobs (averaging $1973). 1,277 state and other part-time jobs (averaging $1828). In 2012, 681 non-need-based awards were made. *Average percent of need met:* 100%. *Average financial aid package:* $33,967. *Average need-based loan:* $4694. *Average need-based gift aid:* $26,194. *Average non-need-based aid:* $11,438. *Average indebtedness upon graduation:* $27,637. *Financial aid deadline:* 3/1.

Applying *Options:* electronic application, early decision, deferred entrance. *Application fee:* $40. *Required:* essay or personal statement, high school transcript, 1 letter of recommendation. *Recommended:* interview. *Application deadlines:* 1/15 (freshmen), 2/1 (transfers). *Early decision deadline:* 11/15 (for plan 1), 1/15 (for plan 2). *Notification:* 3/15 (freshmen), 3/15 (transfers), 12/15 (early decision plan 1), 2/15 (early decision plan 2).

Freshman Application Contact Brad Lindberg, Director of Admissions, St. Olaf College, 1520 St. Olaf Avenue, Northfield, MN 55057. *Phone:* 507-786-3025. *Toll-free phone:* 800-800-3025. *Fax:* 507-786-3832. *E-mail:* admissions@stolaf.edu. *Website:* http://www.stolaf.edu/.

Southwest Minnesota State University

Marshall, Minnesota

- **State-supported** comprehensive, founded 1963, part of Minnesota State Colleges and Universities System
- **Small-town** 216-acre campus
- **Coed**
- **Minimally difficult** entrance level

Faculty *Student/faculty ratio:* 18:1.

Academics *Calendar:* semesters. *Degrees:* associate, bachelor's, master's, and postbachelor's certificates.

Student Life *Campus security:* 24-hour emergency response devices and patrols, student patrols, late-night transport/escort service, controlled dormitory access.

Athletics Member NCAA. All Division II.

Standardized Tests *Required:* SAT or ACT (for admission). *Recommended:* ACT (for admission).

Financial Aid Of all full-time matriculated undergraduates who enrolled in 2011, 1,809 applied for aid, 1,503 were judged to have need, 209 had their need fully met. 101 Federal Work-Study jobs (averaging $2271). 139 state and other part-time jobs (averaging $2136). In 2011, 268 non-need-based awards were made. *Average percent of need met:* 53. *Average financial aid package:* $8151. *Average need-based loan:* $4039. *Average need-based gift aid:* $4917. *Average non-need-based aid:* $2676. *Average indebtedness upon graduation:* $26,394.

Applying *Options:* electronic application, early admission, deferred entrance. *Application fee:* $20. *Required:* high school transcript, minimum 3.0 GPA, top half of graduating class or 21 ACT. *Required for some:* interview.

Freshman Application Contact Mr. Andrew Hlubeck, Director of Admissions, Southwest Minnesota State University, Southwest Minnesota State University, 1501 State Street, Marshall, MN 56258. *Phone:* 507-537-6286. *Toll-free phone:* 800-642-0684. *Fax:* 507-537-7145. *E-mail:* andrew.hlubek@smsu.edu. *Website:* http://www.smsu.edu/.

University of Minnesota, Crookston

Crookston, Minnesota

- **State-supported** 4-year, founded 1966, part of University of Minnesota System
- **Rural** 237-acre campus
- **Endowment** $11.4 million
- **Coed** 2,764 undergraduate students, 50% full-time, 52% women, 48% men
- **Moderately difficult** entrance level, 73% of applicants were admitted

Undergraduates 1,393 full-time, 1,371 part-time. Students come from 40 states and territories; 17 other countries; 27% are from out of state; 7% Black or African American, non-Hispanic/Latino; 2% Hispanic/Latino; 2% Asian, non-Hispanic/Latino; 0.2% Native Hawaiian or other Pacific Islander, non-Hispanic/Latino; 0.6% American Indian or Alaska Native, non-Hispanic/Latino; 2% Two or more races, non-Hispanic/Latino; 2% Race/ethnicity unknown; 7% international; 9% transferred in; 39% live on campus. *Retention:* 73% of full-time freshmen returned.

Freshmen *Admission:* 650 applied, 472 admitted, 241 enrolled. *Average high school GPA:* 3.21. *Test scores:* SAT critical reading scores over 500: 40%; SAT math scores over 500: 67%; SAT writing scores over 500: 29%; ACT scores over 18: 93%; SAT critical reading scores over 600: 13%; SAT math scores over 600: 13%; ACT scores over 24: 38%; SAT math scores over 700: 7%; ACT scores over 30: 3%.

Faculty *Total:* 90, 81% full-time, 40% with terminal degrees. *Student/faculty ratio:* 19:1.

Academics *Calendar:* semesters. *Degree:* bachelor's. *Special study options:* academic remediation for entering students, advanced placement credit, distance learning, double majors, English as a second language, external degree program, honors programs, independent study, internships, off-campus study, part-time degree program, services for LD students, student-designed majors, study abroad, summer session for credit. *ROTC:* Air Force (c).

Computers on Campus 25 computers/terminals are available on campus for general student use. Students can access the following: campus intranet, computer help desk, free student e-mail accounts, online (class) grades, online (class) registration, online (class) schedules, personal Web pages. Campuswide network is available. 100% of college-owned or -operated housing units are wired for high-speed Internet access. Wireless service is available via entire campus.

Student Life *Housing options:* coed, disabled students. Campus housing is university owned. Freshman applicants given priority for college housing. *Activities and organizations:* drama/theater group, choral group, Students in Free Enterprise (SIFE), Natural Resources Club, Horseman's Association, Multicultural and International Club, Ag-Arama Planning Club, national fraternities. *Campus security:* 24-hour emergency response devices, student patrols, controlled dormitory access. *Student services:* health clinic, personal/psychological counseling, women's center.

Athletics Member NCAA. All Division II. *Intercollegiate sports:* baseball M(s), basketball M(s)/W(s), equestrian sports W(s), football M(s), golf M(s)/W(s), soccer W(s), softball W(s), tennis W(s), volleyball W(s). *Intramural sports:* basketball M/W, football M/W, golf M/W, ice hockey M(c), racquetball M/W, soccer M(c)/W, softball M/W, table tennis M/W, tennis M/W, volleyball M/W.

Standardized Tests *Required:* SAT or ACT (for admission). *Recommended:* ACT (for admission).

Costs (2012–13) *Tuition:* state resident $10,030 full-time, $386 per semester hour part-time; nonresident $10,030 full-time, $386 per semester hour part-time. Full-time tuition and fees vary according to course load and reciprocity agreements. Part-time tuition and fees vary according to course load and reciprocity agreements. *Required fees:* $1425 full-time. *Room and board:* $7018; room only: $3170. Room and board charges vary according to board plan and housing facility. *Payment plan:* installment. *Waivers:* senior citizens.

Financial Aid Of all full-time matriculated undergraduates who enrolled in 2012, 1,092 applied for aid, 937 were judged to have need, 212 had their need fully met. 138 Federal Work-Study jobs (averaging $490). 77 state and other part-time jobs (averaging $644). In 2012, 98 non-need-based awards were made. *Average percent of need met:* 73%. *Average financial aid package:* $11,905. *Average need-based loan:* $4873. *Average need-based gift aid:* $8019. *Average non-need-based aid:* $2441. *Average indebtedness upon graduation:* $27,608.

Applying *Options:* electronic application, deferred entrance. *Application fee:* $30. *Required:* high school transcript, minimum 2.0 GPA, ACT composite 21 or SAT 980. *Application deadlines:* rolling (freshmen), rolling (out-of-state freshmen), rolling (transfers). *Notification:* continuous (freshmen), continuous (out-of-state freshmen), continuous (transfers).

Freshman Application Contact Dr. Peter Phaiah PhD, Associate Vice Chancellor for Student Affairs, University of Minnesota, Crookston, 2900 University Avenue, Crookston, MN 56716-5001. *Phone:* 218-281-8505. *Toll-free phone:* 800-862-6466. *Fax:* 218-281-8588. *E-mail:* phaiah@umn.edu. *Website:* http://www.umcrookston.edu/.

University of Minnesota, Duluth

Duluth, Minnesota

- **State-supported** comprehensive, founded 1947, part of University of Minnesota System
- **Suburban** 250-acre campus
- **Endowment** $66.5 million
- **Coed** 10,346 undergraduate students, 89% full-time, 47% women, 53% men
- **Moderately difficult** entrance level, 78% of applicants were admitted

Undergraduates 9,176 full-time, 1,170 part-time. Students come from 34 states and territories; 29 other countries; 11% are from out of state; 2% Black or African American, non-Hispanic/Latino; 2% Hispanic/Latino; 4% Asian, non-Hispanic/Latino; 0.2% Native Hawaiian or other Pacific Islander, non-Hispanic/Latino; 1% American Indian or Alaska Native, non-Hispanic/Latino; 0.9% Race/ethnicity unknown; 2% international; 5% transferred in; 26% live on campus. *Retention:* 79% of full-time freshmen returned.
Freshmen *Admission:* 6,763 applied, 5,254 admitted, 1,881 enrolled. *Average high school GPA:* 3.41. *Test scores:* SAT critical reading scores over 500: 63%; SAT math scores over 500: 74%; SAT writing scores over 500: 61%; ACT scores over 18: 98%; SAT critical reading scores over 600: 20%; SAT math scores over 600: 26%; SAT writing scores over 600: 11%; ACT scores over 24: 50%; SAT critical reading scores over 700: 4%; SAT math scores over 700: 11%; ACT scores over 30: 4%.
Faculty *Total:* 596, 80% full-time, 64% with terminal degrees. *Student/faculty ratio:* 20:1.
Academics *Calendar:* semesters. *Degrees:* bachelor's, master's, doctoral, and postbachelor's certificates. *Special study options:* academic remediation for entering students, adult/continuing education programs, advanced placement credit, cooperative education, distance learning, double majors, English as a second language, external degree program, honors programs, independent study, internships, off-campus study, part-time degree program, services for LD students, student-designed majors, study abroad, summer session for credit. *ROTC:* Air Force (b).
Computers on Campus 590 computers/terminals are available on campus for general student use. Students can access the following: campus intranet, computer help desk, free student e-mail accounts, online (class) grades, online (class) registration, online (class) schedules. Campuswide network is available. 100% of college-owned or -operated housing units are wired for high-speed Internet access. Wireless service is available via entire campus.
Student Life *Housing options:* coed, men-only, women-only, disabled students. Campus housing is university owned. Freshman applicants given priority for college housing. *Activities and organizations:* drama/theater group, student-run newspaper, radio station, choral group, marching band, national fraternities, national sororities. *Campus security:* 24-hour emergency response devices and patrols, late-night transport/escort service. *Student services:* health clinic, personal/psychological counseling, women's center.
Athletics Member NCAA. All Division II except men's and women's ice hockey (Division I). *Intercollegiate sports:* baseball M(s), basketball M(s)/W(s), cheerleading W(c), crew M(c)/W(c), cross-country running M(s)/W(s), football M(s), ice hockey M(s)/W(s), lacrosse M(s)(c)/W(c), rock climbing M(c)/W(c), rugby M(c)/W(c), skiing (cross-country) M(c)/W(c), skiing (downhill) M(c)/W(c), soccer M(c)/W(s), softball W(s), swimming and diving M(c)/W(c), tennis W(s), track and field M(s)/W(s), ultimate Frisbee M(c)/W(c), volleyball M(c)/W(s). *Intramural sports:* badminton M/W, basketball M/W, bowling M/W, football M/W, golf M/W, ice hockey M/W, sailing M/W, skiing (cross-country) M/W, skiing (downhill) M/W, soccer M/W, softball M/W, table tennis M/W, tennis M/W, ultimate Frisbee M/W, volleyball M/W, water polo M/W.
Standardized Tests *Required:* SAT or ACT (for admission).
Costs (2012–13) *Tuition:* state resident $11,720 full-time, $451 per credit part-time; nonresident $14,385 full-time, $553 per credit part-time. Full-time tuition and fees vary according to course load, program, and reciprocity agreements. Part-time tuition and fees vary according to course load, program, and reciprocity agreements. *Required fees:* $1028 full-time, $109 per term part-time. *Room and board:* $6732. Room and board charges vary according to board plan and housing facility. *Payment plan:* installment. *Waivers:* employees or children of employees.
Financial Aid Of all full-time matriculated undergraduates who enrolled in 2011, 7,729 applied for aid, 5,901 were judged to have need, 1,311 had their need fully met. 205 Federal Work-Study jobs (averaging $2115). 347 state and other part-time jobs (averaging $2281). In 2011, 1016 non-need-based awards were made. *Average percent of need met:* 69%. *Average financial aid package:* $10,738. *Average need-based loan:* $4863. *Average need-based gift aid:* $7304. *Average non-need-based aid:* $3222. *Average indebtedness upon graduation:* $31,711.

Applying *Options:* electronic application. *Application fee:* $35. *Required:* high school transcript. *Application deadlines:* 12/15 (freshmen), 8/1 (transfers). *Notification:* continuous (freshmen), continuous (transfers).
Freshman Application Contact Office of Admissions, University of Minnesota, Duluth, 25 Solon Campus Center, 1117 University Drive, Duluth, MN 55812-3000. *Phone:* 218-726-7171. *Toll-free phone:* 800-232-1339. *Fax:* 218-726-6394. *E-mail:* umdadmis@d.umn.edu.
Website: http://www.d.umn.edu/.

University of Minnesota, Morris

Morris, Minnesota

Freshman Application Contact University of Minnesota, Morris, 600 East 4th Street, Morris, MN 56267-2134. *Phone:* 320-539-6035. *Toll-free phone:* 800-992-8863. *Fax:* 320-589-1673. *E-mail:* admissions@morris.umn.edu. *Website:* http://www.mrs.umn.edu/.

University of Minnesota, Twin Cities Campus

Minneapolis, Minnesota

- **State-supported** comprehensive, founded 1851, part of University of Minnesota System
- **Urban** 2000-acre campus
- **Coed** 34,469 undergraduate students, 84% full-time, 51% women, 49% men
- **Moderately difficult** entrance level, 50% of applicants were admitted

Undergraduates 29,125 full-time, 5,344 part-time. Students come from 51 states and territories; 88 other countries; 26% are from out of state; 4% Black or African American, non-Hispanic/Latino; 3% Hispanic/Latino; 8% Asian, non-Hispanic/Latino; 0.1% Native Hawaiian or other Pacific Islander, non-Hispanic/Latino; 0.3% American Indian or Alaska Native, non-Hispanic/Latino; 3% Two or more races, non-Hispanic/Latino; 0.9% Race/ethnicity unknown; 8% international; 6% transferred in; 21% live on campus. *Retention:* 91% of full-time freshmen returned.
Freshmen *Admission:* 38,174 applied, 18,900 admitted, 5,514 enrolled. *Test scores:* SAT critical reading scores over 500: 87%; SAT math scores over 500: 97%; SAT writing scores over 500: 91%; ACT scores over 18: 99%; SAT critical reading scores over 600: 57%; SAT math scores over 600: 82%; SAT writing scores over 600: 58%; ACT scores over 24: 91%; SAT critical reading scores over 700: 23%; SAT math scores over 700: 46%; SAT writing scores over 700: 15%; ACT scores over 30: 30%.
Faculty *Total:* 2,837, 67% full-time, 68% with terminal degrees. *Student/faculty ratio:* 21:1.
Academics *Calendar:* semesters. *Degrees:* certificates, diplomas, bachelor's, master's, doctoral, post-master's, and postbachelor's certificates. *Special study options:* academic remediation for entering students, accelerated degree program, adult/continuing education programs, advanced placement credit, cooperative education, distance learning, double majors, English as a second language, external degree program, freshman honors college, honors programs, independent study, internships, off-campus study, part-time degree program, services for LD students, student-designed majors, study abroad, summer session for credit. *ROTC:* Army (b), Navy (b), Air Force (b).
Computers on Campus Students can access the following: computer help desk, free student e-mail accounts, online (class) grades, online (class) registration, online (class) schedules. Campuswide network is available.
Student Life *Housing options:* coed, cooperative, disabled students. Campus housing is university owned. Freshman campus housing is guaranteed. *Activities and organizations:* drama/theater group, student-run newspaper, radio and television station, choral group, marching band, student government, national fraternities, national sororities. *Campus security:* 24-hour emergency response devices and patrols, student patrols, late-night transport/escort service, controlled dormitory access, safety/security orientation, security lighting. *Student services:* health clinic, personal/psychological counseling, women's center, legal services.
Athletics Member NCAA. All Division I except football (Division I-A). *Intercollegiate sports:* baseball M(s), basketball M(s)/W(s), cross-country running M(s)/W(s), golf M(s)/W(s), gymnastics M(s)/W(s), ice hockey M(s)/W(s), soccer W(s), softball W(s), swimming and diving M(s)/W(s), tennis M(s)/W(s), track and field M(s)/W(s), volleyball W(s), wrestling M(s). *Intramural sports:* baseball M/W, basketball M/W, bowling M/W, crew M/W, football M/W, golf M/W, ice hockey M/W, rugby M/W, skiing (cross-country) M/W, ski-

ing (downhill) M/W, soccer M/W, softball M/W, tennis M/W, volleyball M/W, water polo M/W, wrestling M/W.

Standardized Tests *Required:* SAT or ACT (for admission).

Costs (2012–13) *Tuition:* state resident $12,060 full-time, $464 per credit part-time; nonresident $17,310 full-time, $666 per credit part-time. Full-time tuition and fees vary according to program and reciprocity agreements. Part-time tuition and fees vary according to course load, program, and reciprocity agreements. *Required fees:* $1399 full-time. *Room and board:* $8000; room only: $4548. Room and board charges vary according to board plan, housing facility, and location. *Payment plan:* installment. *Waivers:* senior citizens.

Financial Aid Of all full-time matriculated undergraduates who enrolled in 2012, 19,887 applied for aid, 15,094 were judged to have need, 3,897 had their need fully met. In 2012, 3472 non-need-based awards were made. *Average percent of need met:* 70%. *Average financial aid package:* $12,756. *Average need-based loan:* $5890. *Average need-based gift aid:* $8154. *Average non-need-based aid:* $6276. *Average indebtedness upon graduation:* $29,702.

Applying *Options:* electronic application, early admission, deferred entrance. *Application fee:* $45. *Required:* high school transcript. *Recommended:* minimum 2.0 GPA. *Application deadlines:* rolling (freshmen), rolling (transfers). *Notification:* continuous (freshmen), continuous (transfers).

Freshman Application Contact Rachelle Hernandez, Interim Director of Admissions, University of Minnesota, Twin Cities Campus, 240 Williamson, Minneapolis, MN 55455-0213. *Phone:* 612-625-2008. *Toll-free phone:* 800-752-1000. *Fax:* 612-626-1693. *E-mail:* admissions@tc.umn.edu. *Website:* http://www.umn.edu/tc/.

University of Phoenix–Minneapolis/St. Louis Park Campus

St. Louis Park, Minnesota

Admissions Office Contact University of Phoenix–Minneapolis/St. Louis Park Campus, 435 Ford Road Suite #1000, St. Louis Park, MN 55426. *Toll-free phone:* 866-766-0766.
Website: http://www.phoenix.edu/.

University of St. Thomas

St. Paul, Minnesota

- **Independent Roman Catholic** university, founded 1885
- **Urban** 78-acre campus with easy access to Minneapolis
- **Coed** 6,336 undergraduate students, 96% full-time, 47% women, 53% men
- **Moderately difficult** entrance level, 27% of applicants were admitted

Undergraduates 6,073 full-time, 263 part-time. Students come from 43 states and territories; 60 other countries; 19% are from out of state; 3% Black or African American, non-Hispanic/Latino; 4% Hispanic/Latino; 4% Asian, non-Hispanic/Latino; 0.1% American Indian or Alaska Native, non-Hispanic/Latino; 3% Two or more races, non-Hispanic/Latino; 2% Race/ethnicity unknown; 3% international; 4% transferred in; 42% live on campus. *Retention:* 88% of full-time freshmen returned.

Freshmen *Admission:* 5,362 applied, 1,447 admitted, 1,447 enrolled. *Average high school GPA:* 3.56. *Test scores:* SAT critical reading scores over 500: 92%; SAT math scores over 500: 92%; ACT scores over 18: 100%; SAT critical reading scores over 600: 40%; SAT math scores over 600: 55%; ACT scores over 24: 70%; SAT critical reading scores over 700: 16%; SAT math scores over 700: 8%; ACT scores over 30: 15%.

Faculty *Student/faculty ratio:* 14:1.

Academics *Calendar:* 4-1-4. *Degrees:* certificates, bachelor's, master's, doctoral, post-master's, and postbachelor's certificates. *Special study options:* advanced placement credit, double majors, English as a second language, honors programs, independent study, internships, off-campus study, part-time degree program, services for LD students, student-designed majors, study abroad, summer session for credit. *ROTC:* Army (c), Navy (c), Air Force (b). *Unusual degree programs:* 3-2 engineering with University of Notre Dame, Washington University in St. Louis, University of Minnesota-Twin Cities, Kettering University.

Computers on Campus Students can access the following: online (class) registration. Campuswide network is available. Wireless service is available via entire campus.

Student Life *Housing options:* men-only, women-only. Campus housing is university owned. Freshman applicants given priority for college housing.

Activities and organizations: drama/theater group, student-run newspaper, radio and television station, choral group. *Campus security:* 24-hour emergency response devices and patrols, late-night transport/escort service, controlled dormitory access. *Student services:* health clinic, personal/psychological counseling, women's center, legal services.

Athletics Member NCAA. All Division III. *Intercollegiate sports:* baseball M, basketball M/W, cross-country running M/W, football M, golf M/W, ice hockey M/W, lacrosse M(c)/W(c), soccer M/W, softball W, swimming and diving M/W, tennis M/W, volleyball W. *Intramural sports:* badminton M/W, basketball M/W, crew M(c)/W(c), golf M/W, racquetball M/W, sailing M(c)/W, skiing (downhill) M(c)/W(c), soccer M/W, table tennis M/W, tennis M/W, track and field M(c)/W(c), volleyball M/W.

Standardized Tests *Required:* SAT or ACT (for admission).

Costs (2012–13) *Comprehensive fee:* $42,565 includes full-time tuition ($33,040), mandatory fees ($747), and room and board ($8778). Full-time tuition and fees vary according to course load, degree level, and program. Part-time tuition: $1032 per credit hour. Part-time tuition and fees vary according to course load, degree level, and program. *College room only:* $5546. Room and board charges vary according to board plan and housing facility. *Waivers:* senior citizens and employees or children of employees.

Financial Aid Of all full-time matriculated undergraduates who enrolled in 2012, 4,358 applied for aid, 3,586 were judged to have need, 560 had their need fully met. 1,430 Federal Work-Study jobs (averaging $2850). 1,003 state and other part-time jobs (averaging $2808). In 2012, 630 non-need-based awards were made. *Average percent of need met:* 82%. *Average financial aid package:* $23,164. *Average need-based loan:* $7909. *Average need-based gift aid:* $16,990. *Average non-need-based aid:* $13,822. *Average indebtedness upon graduation:* $36,077.

Applying *Options:* electronic application, deferred entrance. *Required:* essay or personal statement, high school transcript. *Recommended:* interview. *Application deadlines:* rolling (freshmen), rolling (transfers). *Notification:* continuous (freshmen), continuous (transfers).

Freshman Application Contact University of St. Thomas, 2115 Summit Avenue, St. Paul, MN 55105-1096. *Phone:* 651-962-6150. *Toll-free phone:* 800-328-6819.
Website: http://www.stthomas.edu/.

Walden University

Minneapolis, Minnesota

- **Proprietary** upper-level, founded 1970, part of Laureate
- **Coed** 8,695 undergraduate students, 10% full-time, 75% women, 25% men
- **96% of applicants were admitted**

Undergraduates 886 full-time, 7,809 part-time. Students come from 55 states and territories; 48 other countries; 98% are from out of state; 37% Black or African American, non-Hispanic/Latino; 6% Hispanic/Latino; 1% Asian, non-Hispanic/Latino; 0.2% Native Hawaiian or other Pacific Islander, non-Hispanic/Latino; 0.5% American Indian or Alaska Native, non-Hispanic/Latino; 2% Two or more races, non-Hispanic/Latino; 12% Race/ethnicity unknown; 0.7% international; 24% transferred in.

Freshmen *Admission:* 520 applied, 501 admitted.

Faculty *Total:* 2,705, 10% full-time, 85% with terminal degrees.

Academics *Calendar:* quarter/semester depending on program. *Degrees:* bachelor's, master's, doctoral, post-master's, and postbachelor's certificates. *Special study options:* academic remediation for entering students, accelerated degree program, distance learning, internships, off-campus study, part-time degree program, services for LD students, student-designed majors, study abroad, summer session for credit.

Computers on Campus Students can access the following: free student e-mail accounts, online (class) grades, online (class) registration, online (class) schedules.

Student Life *Student services:* personal/psychological counseling, legal services.

Costs (2012–13) *Tuition:* $13,050 full-time, $290 per credit hour part-time. Full-time tuition and fees vary according to course level, course load, and program. Part-time tuition and fees vary according to course level, course load, and program. *Required fees:* $285 full-time, $95 per term part-time. *Payment plan:* installment. *Waivers:* employees or children of employees.

Financial Aid Of all full-time matriculated undergraduates who enrolled in 2009, 908 applied for aid, 878 were judged to have need, 7 had their need fully met. In 2009, 17 non-need-based awards were made. *Average percent of need met:* 26%. *Average financial aid package:* $6301. *Average need-based loan:* $3755. *Average need-based gift aid:* $3222. *Average non-need-based aid:* $1225.

Applying *Options:* electronic application, deferred entrance. *Application fee:* $50. *Application deadline:* rolling (transfers). *Notification:* continuous (transfers).

Application Contact Walden University, 100 Washington South, Minneapolis, MN 55401. *Phone:* 800-925-3368. *Toll-free phone:* 866-492-5336. *Website:* http://www.waldenu.edu/.

Winona State University
Winona, Minnesota

- **State-supported** comprehensive, founded 1858, part of Minnesota State Colleges and Universities System
- **Small-town** 40-acre campus
- **Endowment** $15.0 million
- **Coed**
- **Moderately difficult** entrance level

Faculty *Student/faculty ratio:* 22:1.

Academics *Calendar:* semesters. *Degrees:* associate, bachelor's, master's, doctoral, post-master's, and postbachelor's certificates.

Student Life *Campus security:* 24-hour emergency response devices and patrols, student patrols, late-night transport/escort service, controlled dormitory access, security cameras.

Athletics Member NCAA. All Division II.

Standardized Tests *Required:* SAT or ACT (for admission).

Costs (2012–13) *Tuition:* state resident $6860 full-time, $229 per credit part-time; nonresident $12,460 full-time, $415 per credit hour part-time. Full-time tuition and fees vary according to location and reciprocity agreements. Part-time tuition and fees vary according to course load, location, and reciprocity agreements. *Required fees:* $1850 full-time. *Room and board:* $7690. Room and board charges vary according to board plan, housing facility, and location.

Financial Aid *Of all full-time matriculated undergraduates who enrolled in 2011,* 6,019 applied for aid, 4,540 were judged to have need, 490 had their need fully met. 183 Federal Work-Study jobs (averaging $1926). 308 state and other part-time jobs (averaging $2027). *In 2011,* 808 non-need-based awards were made. *Average percent of need met:* 50. *Average financial aid package:* $7280. *Average need-based loan:* $4076. *Average need-based gift aid:* $4593. *Average non-need-based aid:* $2748. *Average indebtedness upon graduation:* $32,576.

Applying *Options:* electronic application, early admission, early action, deferred entrance. *Application fee:* $20. *Required:* high school transcript, class rank. *Required for some:* essay or personal statement, minimum 3.0 GPA, interview.

Freshman Application Contact Carl Stange, Director of Admissions, Winona State University, 170 West Sanborn, Winona, MN 55987. *Phone:* 507-457-5100. *Toll-free phone:* 800-DIAL WSU. *Fax:* 507-457-5620. *E-mail:* admissions@winona.edu. *Website:* http://www.winona.edu/.

MISSISSIPPI

Alcorn State University
Alcorn State, Mississippi

- **State-supported** comprehensive, founded 1871, part of Mississippi Institutions of Higher Learning
- **Rural** 1756-acre campus
- **Endowment** $10.2 million
- **Coed** 3,208 undergraduate students, 88% full-time, 65% women, 35% men
- **Moderately difficult** entrance level, 47% of applicants were admitted

Undergraduates 2,831 full-time, 377 part-time. Students come from 38 states and territories; 16 other countries; 13% are from out of state; 93% Black or African American, non-Hispanic/Latino; 0.8% Hispanic/Latino; 0.4% Asian, non-Hispanic/Latino; 0.1% American Indian or Alaska Native, non-Hispanic/Latino; 0.5% Two or more races, non-Hispanic/Latino; 1% international; 5% transferred in; 52% live on campus. *Retention:* 69% of full-time freshmen returned.

Freshmen *Admission:* 3,663 applied, 1,726 admitted, 581 enrolled. *Average high school GPA:* 2.92. *Test scores:* SAT critical reading scores over 500: 14%; SAT math scores over 500: 31%; ACT scores over 18: 48%; SAT critical read-

ing scores over 600: 3%; SAT math scores over 600: 3%; ACT scores over 24: 8%.

Faculty *Total:* 214, 79% full-time, 64% with terminal degrees. *Student/faculty ratio:* 18:1.

Academics *Calendar:* semesters. *Degrees:* associate, bachelor's, master's, and post-master's certificates. *Special study options:* academic remediation for entering students, accelerated degree program, adult/continuing education programs, advanced placement credit, cooperative education, distance learning, double majors, honors programs, independent study, internships, off-campus study, part-time degree program, study abroad, summer session for credit. *ROTC:* Army (b).

Computers on Campus 500 computers/terminals and 2,500 ports are available on campus for general student use. Students can access the following: campus intranet, computer help desk, free student e-mail accounts, online (class) grades, online (class) registration, online (class) schedules. Campus-wide network is available. 100% of college-owned or -operated housing units are wired for high-speed Internet access. Wireless service is available via classrooms, computer centers, computer labs, dorm rooms, learning centers, libraries, student centers.

Student Life *Housing options:* men-only, women-only. Campus housing is university owned. Freshman campus housing is guaranteed. *Activities and organizations:* drama/theater group, student-run newspaper, radio and television station, choral group, marching band, marching band, Gospel Choir, interfaith choir, national fraternities, national sororities. *Campus security:* 24-hour emergency response devices and patrols, late-night transport/escort service. *Student services:* health clinic, personal/psychological counseling.

Athletics Member NCAA. All Division I. *Intercollegiate sports:* baseball M(s), basketball M(s)/W(s), cross-country running M(s)/W(s), football M(s), golf M(s)/W(s), soccer W(s), softball W(s), tennis M(s)/W(s), track and field M(s)/W(s), volleyball W(s). *Intramural sports:* basketball M/W, football M.

Standardized Tests *Required:* SAT or ACT (for admission).

Costs (2012–13) *Tuition:* state resident $5724 full-time, $238 per credit hour part-time; nonresident $14,162 full-time, $586 per credit hour part-time. Full-time tuition and fees vary according to course load. Part-time tuition and fees vary according to course load. *Room and board:* $7999. Room and board charges vary according to housing facility. *Payment plan:* installment. *Waivers:* employees or children of employees.

Financial Aid Of all full-time matriculated undergraduates who enrolled in 2012, 1,332 applied for aid, 1,299 were judged to have need, 101 had their need fully met. 368 Federal Work-Study jobs (averaging $1497). In 2012, 545 non-need-based awards were made. *Average percent of need met:* 49%. *Average financial aid package:* $14,832. *Average need-based loan:* $3791. *Average need-based gift aid:* $5405. *Average non-need-based aid:* $6930. *Average indebtedness upon graduation:* $29,001.

Applying *Options:* electronic application, deferred entrance. *Required:* high school transcript, minimum 2.0 GPA. *Application deadlines:* rolling (freshmen), rolling (transfers). *Notification:* continuous (freshmen), continuous (transfers).

Freshman Application Contact Mr. Emanuel Barnes, Director of Admissions, Alcorn State University, 1000 ASU Drive, #300, Alcorn State, MS 39096-7500. *Phone:* 601-877-6147. *Toll-free phone:* 800-222-6790. *Fax:* 601-877-6347. *E-mail:* ebarnes@alcorn.edu. *Website:* http://www.alcorn.edu/.

Belhaven University
Jackson, Mississippi

- **Independent Presbyterian** comprehensive, founded 1883
- **Urban** 42-acre campus
- **Endowment** $5.0 million
- **Coed** 2,545 undergraduate students, 47% full-time, 64% women, 36% men
- **Moderately difficult** entrance level, 66% of applicants were admitted

Undergraduates 1,206 full-time, 1,339 part-time. Students come from 42 states and territories; 27 other countries; 51% are from out of state; 46% Black or African American, non-Hispanic/Latino; 6% Hispanic/Latino; 1% Asian, non-Hispanic/Latino; 1% Native Hawaiian or other Pacific Islander, non-Hispanic/Latino; 0.6% American Indian or Alaska Native, non-Hispanic/Latino; 2% Two or more races, non-Hispanic/Latino; 2% Race/ethnicity unknown; 3% international; 51% transferred in; 20% live on campus. *Retention:* 72% of full-time freshmen returned.

Freshmen *Admission:* 1,301 applied, 857 admitted, 296 enrolled. *Average high school GPA:* 3.15. *Test scores:* SAT critical reading scores over 500: 67%; SAT math scores over 500: 68%; ACT scores over 18: 76%; SAT critical reading scores over 600: 35%; SAT math scores over 600: 29%; ACT scores over

24: 21%; SAT critical reading scores over 700: 6%; SAT math scores over 700: 6%; ACT scores over 30: 2%.

Faculty *Total:* 335, 30% full-time, 21% with terminal degrees. *Student/faculty ratio:* 11:1.

Academics *Calendar:* semesters. *Degrees:* certificates, associate, bachelor's, and master's. *Special study options:* academic remediation for entering students, accelerated degree program, adult/continuing education programs, advanced placement credit, distance learning, double majors, English as a second language, honors programs, independent study, internships, off-campus study, part-time degree program, student-designed majors, study abroad, summer session for credit. *ROTC:* Army (c), Air Force (c). *Unusual degree programs:* 3-2 engineering with Mississippi State University.

Computers on Campus 36 computers/terminals are available on campus for general student use. Students can access the following: campus intranet, computer help desk, free student e-mail accounts, online (class) grades, online (class) registration, online (class) schedules. Campuswide network is available. 100% of college-owned or -operated housing units are wired for high-speed Internet access. Wireless service is available via classrooms, computer labs, dorm rooms, libraries, student centers.

Student Life *Housing:* on-campus residence required through sophomore year. *Options:* men-only, women-only. Campus housing is university owned. Freshman campus housing is guaranteed. *Activities and organizations:* drama/theater group, student-run newspaper, choral group, marching band, Belhaven Activities Team, intramurals, Reformed University Fellowship, Quartertone, Sports Medicine: Exercise Science Club. *Campus security:* 24-hour emergency response devices and patrols, late-night transport/escort service, controlled dormitory access. *Student services:* health clinic, personal/psychological counseling.

Athletics Member NAIA. *Intercollegiate sports:* baseball M(s), basketball M(s)/W(s), cross-country running M(s)/W(s), football M(s), golf M(s)/W(s), soccer M(s)/W(s), softball W(s), tennis M(s)/W(s), volleyball W(s). *Intramural sports:* basketball M/W, football M/W, soccer M/W, softball M/W, volleyball M/W.

Standardized Tests *Required:* SAT or ACT (for admission).

Costs (2013–14) *Comprehensive fee:* $26,090 includes full-time tuition ($19,200) and room and board ($6890). Part-time tuition: $375 per credit. Part-time tuition and fees vary according to course load. *Room and board:* Room and board charges vary according to housing facility. *Payment plan:* installment. *Waivers:* employees or children of employees.

Applying *Options:* electronic application, early admission, deferred entrance. *Application fee:* $25. *Required:* high school transcript, minimum 2.0 GPA, 1 letter of recommendation. *Required for some:* essay or personal statement, interview. *Application deadlines:* rolling (freshmen), rolling (out-of-state freshmen), rolling (transfers). *Notification:* continuous (freshmen), continuous (out-of-state freshmen), continuous (transfers).

Freshman Application Contact Ms. Suzanne T. Sullivan, Assistant VP for Traditional and Online Admissions, Belhaven University, 1500 Peachtree Street, Jackson, MS 39202. *Phone:* 601-968-5940. *Toll-free phone:* 800-960-5940. *Fax:* 601-968-8946. *E-mail:* admission@belhaven.edu. *Website:* http://www.belhaven.edu/.

Blue Mountain College

Blue Mountain, Mississippi

- **Independent Southern Baptist** comprehensive, founded 1873
- **Rural** 44-acre campus with easy access to Memphis
- **Endowment** $11.2 million
- **Coed** 502 undergraduate students, 91% full-time, 60% women, 40% men
- **Moderately difficult** entrance level, 31% of applicants were admitted

Undergraduates 459 full-time, 43 part-time. Students come from 18 states and territories; 4 other countries; 21% are from out of state; 11% Black or African American, non-Hispanic/Latino; 1% Hispanic/Latino; 0.2% American Indian or Alaska Native, non-Hispanic/Latino; 1% international; 14% transferred in; 52% live on campus. *Retention:* 85% of full-time freshmen returned.

Freshmen *Admission:* 416 applied, 131 admitted, 69 enrolled. *Average high school GPA:* 3.5. *Test scores:* SAT critical reading scores over 500: 100%; SAT math scores over 500: 50%; SAT writing scores over 500: 75%; ACT scores over 18: 81%; SAT math scores over 600: 25%; ACT scores over 24: 27%; ACT scores over 30: 5%.

Faculty *Total:* 44, 73% full-time, 66% with terminal degrees. *Student/faculty ratio:* 13:1.

Academics *Calendar:* semesters. *Degrees:* bachelor's and master's. *Special study options:* academic remediation for entering students, accelerated degree program, advanced placement credit, distance learning, double majors, honors programs, internships, part-time degree program, summer session for credit. *Unusual degree programs:* 3-2 nursing with Union University.

Computers on Campus 41 computers/terminals are available on campus for general student use. Students can access the following: computer help desk, free student e-mail accounts, online (class) grades, online (class) registration, online (class) schedules. Campuswide network is available. 100% of college-owned or -operated housing units are wired for high-speed Internet access. Wireless service is available via classrooms, computer centers, computer labs, dorm rooms, learning centers, libraries, student centers.

Student Life *Housing:* on-campus residence required through junior year. *Options:* men-only, women-only. Campus housing is university owned. *Activities and organizations:* drama/theater group, choral group, Baptist Student Union, Student Body Association, Intramural Association, Ministerial Association, Mississippi Association of Educators/Student Program. *Campus security:* 24-hour emergency response devices and patrols.

Athletics Member NAIA. *Intercollegiate sports:* baseball M(s), basketball M(s)/W(s), cross-country running M(s)/W(s), golf M(s)/W(s), softball W(s). *Intramural sports:* basketball M/W, football M, soccer M, softball M/W, swimming and diving M/W, table tennis W, tennis W, track and field M/W, ultimate Frisbee M, volleyball M/W.

Standardized Tests *Required:* SAT or ACT (for admission).

Costs (2012–13) *Comprehensive fee:* $13,230 includes full-time tuition ($8250), mandatory fees ($980), and room and board ($4000). Full-time tuition and fees vary according to course load and degree level. Part-time tuition: $275 per semester hour. Part-time tuition and fees vary according to course load and degree level. *Required fees:* $365 per term part-time. *Room and board:* Room and board charges vary according to board plan. *Payment plans:* installment, deferred payment. *Waivers:* employees or children of employees.

Financial Aid Of all full-time matriculated undergraduates who enrolled in 2012, 484 applied for aid, 458 were judged to have need, 375 had their need fully met. 56 Federal Work-Study jobs (averaging $507). 55 state and other part-time jobs (averaging $406). In 2012, 251 non-need-based awards were made. *Average percent of need met:* 45%. *Average financial aid package:* $9636. *Average need-based loan:* $4490. *Average need-based gift aid:* $4173. *Average indebtedness upon graduation:* $3839.

Applying *Options:* electronic application, deferred entrance. *Application fee:* $10. *Required for some:* high school transcript. *Recommended:* minimum 2.0 GPA. *Application deadlines:* rolling (freshmen), rolling (out-of-state freshmen), rolling (transfers). *Notification:* continuous (freshmen), continuous (out-of-state freshmen), continuous (transfers).

Freshman Application Contact Miss Maria Teel, Director of Admissions, Blue Mountain College, PO Box 160, Blue Mountain, MS 38610-0160. *Phone:* 662-685-4771 Ext. 176. *Toll-free phone:* 800-235-0136. *Fax:* 662-685-4776. *E-mail:* mteel@bmc.edu. *Website:* http://www.bmc.edu/.

Delta State University

Cleveland, Mississippi

- **State-supported** comprehensive, founded 1924, part of Mississippi Institutions of Higher Learning
- **Small-town** 274-acre campus
- **Coed** 2,756 undergraduate students, 82% full-time, 60% women, 40% men
- **Noncompetitive** entrance level, 89% of applicants were admitted

Undergraduates 2,253 full-time, 503 part-time. Students come from 30 states and territories; 19 other countries; 9% are from out of state; 36% Black or African American, non-Hispanic/Latino; 1% Hispanic/Latino; 0.7% Asian, non-Hispanic/Latino; 0.2% American Indian or Alaska Native, non-Hispanic/Latino; 0.5% Two or more races, non-Hispanic/Latino; 0.4% Race/ethnicity unknown; 2% international; 15% transferred in; 24% live on campus. *Retention:* 61% of full-time freshmen returned.

Freshmen *Admission:* 510 applied, 456 admitted, 384 enrolled. *Average high school GPA:* 3.2. *Test scores:* SAT critical reading scores over 500: 36%; SAT math scores over 500: 55%; ACT scores over 18: 80%; SAT critical reading scores over 600: 9%; SAT math scores over 600: 9%; ACT scores over 24: 21%; ACT scores over 30: 1%.

Faculty *Total:* 257, 72% full-time, 58% with terminal degrees. *Student/faculty ratio:* 20:1.

Academics *Calendar:* semesters. *Degrees:* bachelor's, master's, doctoral, and post-master's certificates. *Special study options:* academic remediation for entering students, adult/continuing education programs, advanced placement credit, cooperative education, distance learning, double majors, freshman honors college, honors programs, independent study, internships, part-time degree program, services for LD students, summer session for credit. *ROTC:* Army (b).

Computers on Campus 533 computers/terminals are available on campus for general student use. Students can access the following: campus intranet, com-

puter help desk, free student e-mail accounts, online (class) grades, online (class) registration, online (class) schedules. Campuswide network is available. 100% of college-owned or -operated housing units are wired for high-speed Internet access. Wireless service is available via classrooms, computer centers, dorm rooms, libraries, student centers.

Student Life *Housing:* on-campus residence required for freshman year. *Options:* men-only, women-only, disabled students. Campus housing is university owned. Freshman campus housing is guaranteed. *Activities and organizations:* drama/theater group, student-run newspaper, choral group, marching band, Student Government Association, Student Alumni Association, Baptist Student Union, Union Program Council, Delta Volunteers, national fraternities, national sororities. *Campus security:* 24-hour emergency response devices and patrols, late-night transport/escort service, controlled dormitory access. *Student services:* health clinic, personal/psychological counseling.

Athletics Member NCAA. All Division II. *Intercollegiate sports:* baseball M(s), basketball M(s)/W(s), cheerleading M(s)/W(s), cross-country running W(s), football M(s), golf M(s), soccer M(s)/W(s), softball W(s), swimming and diving M(s)/W(s), tennis M(s)/W(s). *Intramural sports:* archery M/W, badminton M/W, basketball M/W, bowling M/W, cross-country running M/W, football M/W, golf M/W, racquetball M/W, soccer M/W, softball M/W, swimming and diving M/W, table tennis M/W, tennis M/W, ultimate Frisbee M/W, volleyball M/W.

Standardized Tests *Required:* ACT (for admission). *Recommended:* SAT or ACT (for admission).

Costs (2013–14) *Tuition:* state resident $5724 full-time; nonresident $5724 full-time. Part-time tuition and fees vary according to course load. *Room and board:* $7100; room only: $4508. Room and board charges vary according to housing facility. *Payment plan:* installment. *Waivers:* children of alumni, senior citizens, and employees or children of employees.

Financial Aid Of all full-time matriculated undergraduates who enrolled in 2010, 1,937 applied for aid, 1,713 were judged to have need. 279 Federal Work-Study jobs (averaging $1850). 265 state and other part-time jobs (averaging $1168). *Average financial aid package:* $9518. *Average need-based gift aid:* $4852. *Average indebtedness upon graduation:* $19,717.

Applying *Options:* electronic application, deferred entrance. *Application fee:* $25. *Required:* high school transcript, minimum 2.0 GPA. *Required for some:* interview for art, music majors. *Application deadlines:* rolling (freshmen), rolling (out-of-state freshmen), rolling (transfers). *Notification:* continuous (freshmen), continuous (out-of-state freshmen), continuous (transfers).

Freshman Application Contact Delta State University, Highway 8 West, Cleveland, MS 38733-0001. *Phone:* 662-846-4655. *Toll-free phone:* 800-468-6378.

Website: http://www.deltastate.edu/.

ITT Technical Institute

Madison, Mississippi

- **Proprietary** 4-year, part of ITT Educational Services, Inc.
- **Coed**
- **Minimally difficult** entrance level

Academics *Calendar:* quarters. *Degrees:* associate and bachelor's.

Freshman Application Contact Director of Recruitment, ITT Technical Institute, 382 Galleria Parkway, Suite 100, Madison, MS 39110. *Phone:* 601-607-4500. *Toll-free phone:* 800-209-2521.

Website: http://www.itt-tech.edu/.

Jackson State University

Jackson, Mississippi

Freshman Application Contact Mrs. Linda Rush, Director, Marketing and Recruitment, Jackson State University, PO Box 17330, 1400 John R. Lynch Street, Jackson, MS 39217. *Phone:* 601-979-2911. *Toll-free phone:* 800-848-6817. *E-mail:* schatman@ccaix.jsums.edu.

Website: http://www.jsums.edu/.

Millsaps College

Jackson, Mississippi

- **Independent United Methodist** comprehensive, founded 1890
- **Urban** 100-acre campus
- **Endowment** $92.1 million
- **Coed** 849 undergraduate students, 98% full-time, 50% women, 50% men
- **Moderately difficult** entrance level, 55% of applicants were admitted

Undergraduates 833 full-time, 16 part-time. Students come from 25 states and territories; 18 other countries; 56% are from out of state; 11% Black or African American, non-Hispanic/Latino; 2% Hispanic/Latino; 5% Asian, non-Hispanic/Latino; 0.1% Native Hawaiian or other Pacific Islander, non-Hispanic/Latino; 0.7% American Indian or Alaska Native, non-Hispanic/Latino; 0.4% Two or more races, non-Hispanic/Latino; 3% Race/ethnicity unknown; 2% international; 4% transferred in; 84% live on campus. *Retention:* 78% of full-time freshmen returned.

Freshmen *Admission:* 2,255 applied, 1,235 admitted, 211 enrolled. *Average high school GPA:* 3.57. *Test scores:* SAT critical reading scores over 500: 74%; SAT math scores over 500: 88%; SAT writing scores over 500: 71%; ACT scores over 18: 100%; SAT critical reading scores over 600: 33%; SAT math scores over 600: 30%; SAT writing scores over 600: 16%; ACT scores over 24: 73%; SAT critical reading scores over 700: 7%; SAT math scores over 700: 10%; SAT writing scores over 700: 3%; ACT scores over 30: 19%.

Faculty *Total:* 120, 78% full-time, 86% with terminal degrees. *Student/faculty ratio:* 8:1.

Academics *Calendar:* semesters. *Degrees:* bachelor's and master's. *Special study options:* accelerated degree program, advanced placement credit, double majors, honors programs, independent study, internships, off-campus study, part-time degree program, services for LD students, student-designed majors, study abroad, summer session for credit. *ROTC:* Army (c), Air Force (c). *Unusual degree programs:* 3-2 engineering with Auburn University, Columbia University, Vanderbilt University; nursing with University of Mississippi Medical Center School of Nursing, Vanderbilt University.

Computers on Campus 150 computers/terminals are available on campus for general student use. Students can access the following: campus intranet, computer help desk, free student e-mail accounts, online (class) grades, online (class) registration, online (class) schedules, online transcripts. Campuswide network is available. 100% of college-owned or -operated housing units are wired for high-speed Internet access. Wireless service is available via entire campus.

Student Life *Housing:* on-campus residence required through sophomore year. *Options:* coed, men-only, women-only, disabled students. Campus housing is university owned. Freshman campus housing is guaranteed. *Activities and organizations:* drama/theater group, student-run newspaper, choral group, Campus Ministry Team, Student Body Association, SAPS (Campus Programming Board), Inter-fraternity/Panhellenic Councils, intramural sports, national fraternities, national sororities. *Campus security:* 24-hour emergency response devices and patrols, student patrols, late-night transport/escort service, controlled dormitory access, self-defense education, lighted pathways. *Student services:* health clinic, personal/psychological counseling.

Athletics Member NCAA. All Division III. *Intercollegiate sports:* baseball M, basketball M/W, cross-country running M/W, football M, golf M/W, lacrosse M/W, soccer M/W, softball W, tennis M/W, track and field M/W, volleyball W. *Intramural sports:* basketball M/W, bowling M/W, cheerleading W(c), fencing M(c)/W(c), football M/W, golf M/W, lacrosse W(c), racquetball M/W, soccer M/W, softball M/W, table tennis M/W, tennis M/W, ultimate Frisbee M(c)/W(c), volleyball M/W.

Standardized Tests *Required:* SAT or ACT (for admission).

Costs (2012–13) *Comprehensive fee:* $41,800 includes full-time tuition ($29,052), mandatory fees ($1922), and room and board ($10,826). Part-time tuition and fees vary according to course load. *College room only:* $6110. Room and board charges vary according to housing facility. *Payment plan:* installment. *Waivers:* employees or children of employees.

Financial Aid Of all full-time matriculated undergraduates who enrolled in 2012, 601 applied for aid, 498 were judged to have need, 124 had their need fully met. In 2012, 285 non-need-based awards were made. *Average percent of need met:* 81%. *Average financial aid package:* $27,049. *Average need-based loan:* $4840. *Average need-based gift aid:* $21,545. *Average non-need-based aid:* $18,124. *Average indebtedness upon graduation:* $28,965.

Applying *Options:* electronic application, early admission, early action, deferred entrance. *Required:* essay or personal statement, high school transcript, minimum 2.5 GPA, 1 letter of recommendation, secondary school report. *Required for some:* interview. *Application deadlines:* 2/1 (freshmen), 2/1 (out-of-state freshmen), 7/1 (transfers), 12/1 (early action). *Notification:* continuous until 3/15 (freshmen), continuous until 3/15 (out-of-state freshmen), continuous until 3/15 (transfers), 1/15 (early action).

Freshman Application Contact Dr. Robert Alexander, Millsaps College, 1701 North State Street, Jackson, MS 39210-0001. *Phone:* 601-974-1050. *Toll-free phone:* 800-352-1050. *Fax:* 601-974-1059. *E-mail:* admissions@millsaps.edu.
Website: http://www.millsaps.edu/.

Mississippi College
Clinton, Mississippi

- **Independent Southern Baptist** comprehensive, founded 1826, part of Mississippi Baptist Convention
- **Suburban** 474-acre campus with easy access to Jackson
- **Endowment** $61.1 million
- **Coed** 3,042 undergraduate students, 86% full-time, 61% women, 39% men
- **Moderately difficult** entrance level, 58% of applicants were admitted

Undergraduates 2,623 full-time, 419 part-time. Students come from 36 states and territories; 10 other countries; 24% are from out of state; 24% Black or African American, non-Hispanic/Latino; 2% Hispanic/Latino; 1% Asian, non-Hispanic/Latino; 0.6% American Indian or Alaska Native, non-Hispanic/Latino; 0.6% Two or more races, non-Hispanic/Latino; 2% Race/ethnicity unknown; 3% international; 10% transferred in; 49% live on campus. *Retention:* 73% of full-time freshmen returned.
Freshmen *Admission:* 2,178 applied, 1,266 admitted, 482 enrolled. *Average high school GPA:* 3.43. *Test scores:* SAT critical reading scores over 500: 61%; SAT math scores over 500: 67%; ACT scores over 18: 97%; SAT critical reading scores over 600: 32%; SAT math scores over 600: 21%; ACT scores over 24: 47%; SAT critical reading scores over 700: 7%; SAT math scores over 700: 8%; ACT scores over 30: 10%.
Faculty *Total:* 461, 44% full-time, 62% with terminal degrees. *Student/faculty ratio:* 15:1.
Academics *Calendar:* semesters. *Degrees:* bachelor's, master's, doctoral, post-master's, and postbachelor's certificates. *Special study options:* academic remediation for entering students, accelerated degree program, adult/continuing education programs, advanced placement credit, cooperative education, distance learning, double majors, English as a second language, honors programs, independent study, internships, part-time degree program, services for LD students, study abroad, summer session for credit. *ROTC:* Army (b), Air Force (b). *Unusual degree programs:* 3-2 engineering with Auburn University, University of Mississippi; law, medicine with University of Mississippi.
Computers on Campus 492 computers/terminals and 1,200 ports are available on campus for general student use. Students can access the following: campus intranet, computer help desk, free student e-mail accounts, online (class) grades, online (class) registration, online (class) schedules. Campuswide network is available. 100% of college-owned or -operated housing units are wired for high-speed Internet access. Wireless service is available via classrooms, computer centers, computer labs, dorm rooms, learning centers, libraries, student centers.
Student Life *Housing:* on-campus residence required through junior year. *Options:* men-only, women-only, disabled students. Campus housing is university owned. Freshman applicants given priority for college housing. *Activities and organizations:* drama/theater group, student-run newspaper, radio station, choral group, marching band, Baptist Student Union, Nenamoosha Social Tribe, Laguna Social Tribe, Civitan Service Club, Shawreth Service Club. *Campus security:* 24-hour emergency response devices and patrols, late-night transport/escort service, controlled dormitory access. *Student services:* health clinic, personal/psychological counseling.
Athletics Member NCAA. All Division III. *Intercollegiate sports:* baseball M, basketball M/W, cross-country running M/W, football M, golf M, soccer M/W, softball W, tennis M/W, track and field M/W, volleyball W. *Intramural sports:* badminton M/W, basketball M/W, cheerleading M/W, equestrian sports W, field hockey M/W, football M/W, soccer M/W, softball M/W, table tennis M/W, tennis M/W, volleyball M/W.
Standardized Tests *Required:* SAT or ACT (for admission).
Costs (2013–14) *Comprehensive fee:* $22,018 includes full-time tuition ($14,120), mandatory fees ($748), and room and board ($7150). Full-time tuition and fees vary according to course load. Part-time tuition: $442 per credit hour. Part-time tuition and fees vary according to course load. *Required fees:* $188 per term part-time. *Room and board:* Room and board charges vary according to housing facility. *Payment plan:* installment. *Waivers:* employees or children of employees.
Financial Aid Of all full-time matriculated undergraduates who enrolled in 2011, 2,617 applied for aid, 1,707 were judged to have need, 406 had their need fully met. 285 Federal Work-Study jobs (averaging $929). In 2011, 896 non-need-based awards were made. *Average percent of need met:* 71%. *Average financial aid package:* $16,315. *Average need-based loan:* $7823. *Average*

need-based gift aid: $9161. *Average non-need-based aid:* $10,133. *Average indebtedness upon graduation:* $26,677.
Applying *Options:* electronic application, early admission, early decision, deferred entrance. *Application fee:* $25. *Required:* high school transcript. *Required for some:* 2 letters of recommendation. *Recommended:* minimum 2.0 GPA, interview. *Application deadlines:* rolling (freshmen), rolling (out-of-state freshmen), rolling (transfers). *Early decision deadline:* 12/1. *Notification:* continuous (freshmen), continuous (out-of-state freshmen), continuous (transfers), 12/15 (early decision).
Freshman Application Contact Mr. William Kyle Brantley, Director of Admissions, Mississippi College, Box 4026, 200 South Capitol Street, Clinton, MS 39058-0001. *Phone:* 601-925-3800. *Toll-free phone:* 800-738-1236. *Fax:* 601-925-3804. *E-mail:* enrollment-services@mc.edu.
Website: http://www.mc.edu/.

Mississippi State University
Mississippi State, Mississippi

- **State-supported** university, founded 1878, part of Mississippi Institutions of Higher Learning
- **Small-town** 4200-acre campus
- **Endowment** $320.5 million
- **Coed** 16,390 undergraduate students, 92% full-time, 48% women, 52% men
- **Moderately difficult** entrance level, 69% of applicants were admitted

Undergraduates 15,004 full-time, 1,386 part-time. Students come from 52 states and territories; 58 other countries; 22% are from out of state; 22% Black or African American, non-Hispanic/Latino; 2% Hispanic/Latino; 1% Asian, non-Hispanic/Latino; 0.1% Native Hawaiian or other Pacific Islander, non-Hispanic/Latino; 0.5% American Indian or Alaska Native, non-Hispanic/Latino; 1% Two or more races, non-Hispanic/Latino; 1% Race/ethnicity unknown; 2% international; 10% transferred in; 27% live on campus. *Retention:* 81% of full-time freshmen returned.
Freshmen *Admission:* 10,449 applied, 7,245 admitted, 2,894 enrolled. *Average high school GPA:* 3.29. *Test scores:* SAT critical reading scores over 500: 68%; SAT math scores over 500: 73%; ACT scores over 18: 90%; SAT critical reading scores over 600: 30%; SAT math scores over 600: 37%; ACT scores over 24: 47%; SAT critical reading scores over 700: 5%; SAT math scores over 700: 7%; ACT scores over 30: 10%.
Faculty *Total:* 1,005, 88% full-time, 76% with terminal degrees. *Student/faculty ratio:* 19:1.
Academics *Calendar:* semesters. *Degrees:* associate, bachelor's, master's, doctoral, and post-master's certificates. *Special study options:* academic remediation for entering students, accelerated degree program, adult/continuing education programs, advanced placement credit, cooperative education, distance learning, double majors, English as a second language, freshman honors college, honors programs, independent study, internships, off-campus study, part-time degree program, services for LD students, student-designed majors, study abroad, summer session for credit. *ROTC:* Army (b), Air Force (b).
Computers on Campus 1,000 computers/terminals and 1,000 ports are available on campus for general student use. Students can access the following: campus intranet, computer help desk, free student e-mail accounts, online (class) grades, online (class) registration, online (class) schedules, campuswide wireless Internet access. Campuswide network is available. 100% of college-owned or -operated housing units are wired for high-speed Internet access. Wireless service is available via entire campus.
Student Life *Housing:* on-campus residence required for freshman year. *Options:* coed, men-only, women-only, disabled students. Campus housing is university owned. *Activities and organizations:* drama/theater group, student-run newspaper, radio and television station, choral group, marching band, Student Association, Black Student Alliance, Residence Hall Association, Fashion Board, Campus Activities Board, national fraternities, national sororities. *Campus security:* 24-hour emergency response devices and patrols, late-night transport/escort service, controlled dormitory access, bicycle patrols, crime prevention program, RAD program, general law enforcement services. *Student services:* health clinic, personal/psychological counseling.
Athletics Member NCAA. All Division I except football (Division I-A). *Intercollegiate sports:* baseball M(s), basketball M(s)/W(s), cheerleading M(s)/W(s), cross-country running M(s)/W(s), golf M(s)/W(s), soccer W(s), softball W(s), tennis M(s)/W(s), track and field M(s)/W(s), volleyball W(s). *Intramural sports:* badminton M(c)/W(c), basketball M/W, bowling M/W, cross-country running M(c)/W(c), fencing M(c)/W(c), football M/W, golf M/W, ice hockey M(c), lacrosse M(c), racquetball M/W, riflery M/W, rugby M(c)/W(c), soccer M(c)/W(c), softball M(c)/W(c), swimming and diving M(c)/W(c), table tennis M(c)/W(c), tennis M(c)/W(c), ultimate Frisbee M/W, volleyball M(c)/W(c), water polo M/W.

Standardized Tests *Required:* SAT or ACT (for admission).
Costs (2013–14) *Tuition:* state resident $6264 full-time, $261 per credit hour part-time; nonresident $15,828 full-time, $660 per credit hour part-time. Part-time tuition and fees vary according to course load. *Room and board:* $8486; room only: $4936. Room and board charges vary according to board plan, housing facility, and student level. *Payment plans:* tuition prepayment, installment. *Waivers:* children of alumni, senior citizens, and employees or children of employees.
Financial Aid Of all full-time matriculated undergraduates who enrolled in 2011, 10,844 applied for aid, 9,344 were judged to have need, 2,150 had their need fully met. 682 Federal Work-Study jobs (averaging $3424). In 2011, 2575 non-need-based awards were made. *Average percent of need met:* 62%. *Average financial aid package:* $12,310. *Average need-based loan:* $3944. *Average need-based gift aid:* $5180. *Average non-need-based aid:* $3208. *Average indebtedness upon graduation:* $26,139.
Applying *Options:* electronic application. *Application fee:* $40. *Required:* high school transcript, minimum 2.0 GPA. *Application deadlines:* 8/1 (freshmen), 8/1 (transfers). *Notification:* continuous (freshmen), continuous (transfers).
Freshman Application Contact Ms. Lori Ball, Interim Director of Admissions and Scholarships, Mississippi State University, PO Box 6334, Mississippi State, MS 39762. *Phone:* 662-325-2224. *Fax:* 662-325-1MSU. *E-mail:* admit@msstate.edu.
Website: http://www.msstate.edu/.

Mississippi University for Women
Columbus, Mississippi

- **State-supported** comprehensive, founded 1884, part of Mississippi Institutions of Higher Learning
- **Small-town** 110-acre campus
- **Endowment** $39.8 million
- **Coed, primarily women** 2,503 undergraduate students, 80% full-time, 83% women, 17% men
- **Moderately difficult** entrance level, 44% of applicants were admitted

Undergraduates 2,009 full-time, 494 part-time. Students come from 26 states and territories; 10 other countries; 9% are from out of state; 38% Black or African American, non-Hispanic/Latino; 0.7% Hispanic/Latino; 2% Asian, non-Hispanic/Latino; 0.1% American Indian or Alaska Native, non-Hispanic/Latino; 0.2% Two or more races, non-Hispanic/Latino; 1% international; 22% transferred in; 28% live on campus. *Retention:* 74% of full-time freshmen returned.
Freshmen *Admission:* 1,542 applied, 679 admitted, 193 enrolled. *Average high school GPA:* 3.32. *Test scores:* SAT critical reading scores over 500: 20%; SAT math scores over 500: 80%; ACT scores over 18: 88%; SAT critical reading scores over 600: 20%; SAT math scores over 600: 60%; ACT scores over 24: 43%; SAT critical reading scores over 700: 20%; SAT math scores over 700: 20%; ACT scores over 30: 5%.
Faculty *Total:* 214, 61% full-time, 49% with terminal degrees. *Student/faculty ratio:* 15:1.
Academics *Calendar:* semesters. *Degrees:* associate, bachelor's, master's, doctoral, and post-master's certificates. *Special study options:* academic remediation for entering students, adult/continuing education programs, advanced placement credit, distance learning, double majors, freshman honors college, honors programs, independent study, internships, off-campus study, part-time degree program, services for LD students, study abroad, summer session for credit. *ROTC:* Army (c), Air Force (c). *Unusual degree programs:* 3-2 engineering with Auburn University, Mississippi State University.
Computers on Campus 352 computers/terminals and 1,220 ports are available on campus for general student use. Students can access the following: campus intranet, computer help desk, free student e-mail accounts, online (class) grades, online (class) registration, online (class) schedules. Campuswide network is available. 100% of college-owned or -operated housing units are wired for high-speed Internet access. Wireless service is available via entire campus.
Student Life *Housing options:* men-only, women-only, disabled students. Campus housing is university owned. Freshman campus housing is guaranteed. *Activities and organizations:* drama/theater group, student-run newspaper, radio station, choral group, Student Government Association, Toastmasters, Wesley Foundation, Modeling Squad, national fraternities, national sororities. *Campus security:* 24-hour emergency response devices and patrols, controlled dormitory access. *Student services:* health clinic, personal/psychological counseling, women's center.
Athletics *Intramural sports:* basketball M/W, bowling M/W, football M/W, golf M/W, racquetball M/W, soccer M/W, softball M/W, table tennis M/W, tennis M/W, track and field M/W, ultimate Frisbee M/W, volleyball M/W.

Standardized Tests *Required for some:* SAT or ACT (for admission). *Recommended:* SAT or ACT (for admission).
Costs (2013–14) *Tuition:* state resident $5316 full-time, $222 per credit hour part-time; nonresident $14,484 full-time, $604 per credit hour part-time. Part-time tuition and fees vary according to course load. *Room and board:* $5991; room only: $3454. Room and board charges vary according to housing facility. *Payment plan:* installment. *Waivers:* employees or children of employees.
Financial Aid Of all full-time matriculated undergraduates who enrolled in 2011, 1,664 applied for aid, 1,512 were judged to have need, 1,025 had their need fully met. 60 Federal Work-Study jobs (averaging $1958). 185 state and other part-time jobs (averaging $1719). In 2011, 223 non-need-based awards were made. *Average percent of need met:* 69%. *Average financial aid package:* $8810. *Average need-based loan:* $4826. *Average need-based gift aid:* $5399. *Average non-need-based aid:* $5628. *Average indebtedness upon graduation:* $22,398.
Applying *Options:* electronic application, early admission. *Required:* high school transcript. *Required for some:* minimum 2.0 GPA, interview, rank in upper 50% of high school class. *Application deadlines:* rolling (freshmen), rolling (out-of-state freshmen), rolling (transfers). *Notification:* continuous (freshmen), continuous (out-of-state freshmen), continuous (transfers).
Freshman Application Contact Mississippi University for Women, 1100 College Street, MUW-1600, Columbus, MS 39701-9998. *Phone:* 662-329-7106. *Toll-free phone:* 877-GO 2 THE W.
Website: http://www.muw.edu/.

Mississippi Valley State University
Itta Bena, Mississippi

- **State-supported** comprehensive, founded 1946, part of Mississippi Institutions of Higher Learning
- **Small-town** 450-acre campus
- **Endowment** $1.7 million
- **Coed** 2,168 undergraduate students, 84% full-time, 61% women, 39% men
- **Minimally difficult** entrance level, 24% of applicants were admitted

Undergraduates 1,826 full-time, 342 part-time. Students come from 28 states and territories; 6 other countries; 13% are from out of state; 90% Black or African American, non-Hispanic/Latino; 0.8% Hispanic/Latino; 6% Race/ethnicity unknown; 10% transferred in; 38% live on campus. *Retention:* 61% of full-time freshmen returned.
Freshmen *Admission:* 4,740 applied, 1,128 admitted, 392 enrolled. *Average high school GPA:* 2.77. *Test scores:* ACT scores over 18: 36%; ACT scores over 24: 4%.
Faculty *Total:* 165, 81% full-time, 54% with terminal degrees. *Student/faculty ratio:* 15:1.
Academics *Calendar:* semesters. *Degrees:* bachelor's and master's. *Special study options:* academic remediation for entering students, cooperative education, distance learning, double majors, freshman honors college, honors programs, internships, part-time degree program, summer session for credit. *ROTC:* Army (b).
Computers on Campus 285 computers/terminals are available on campus for general student use. Students can access the following: computer help desk, free student e-mail accounts, online (class) registration. Campuswide network is available.
Student Life *Housing options:* men-only, women-only. Campus housing is university owned. *Activities and organizations:* drama/theater group, student-run newspaper, radio and television station, choral group, marching band, Student Government Association, Baptist Student Union, Black Student Fellowship, National Education Association, national fraternities, national sororities. *Campus security:* 24-hour emergency response devices and patrols, controlled dormitory access. *Student services:* health clinic, personal/psychological counseling.
Athletics Member NCAA. All Division I except football (Division I-AA). *Intercollegiate sports:* baseball M(s), basketball M(s)/W(s), bowling W, cross-country running M(s)/W(s), golf M(s)/W(s), softball W(s), tennis M(s)/W(s), track and field M(s)/W(s). *Intramural sports:* baseball M, basketball M/W, cross-country running M/W, football M, golf M/W, softball M/W, tennis M/W, track and field M/W.
Standardized Tests *Required:* SAT or ACT (for admission).
Costs (2013–14) *Tuition:* state resident $5628 full-time, $235 per hour part-time; nonresident $14,076 full-time, $352 per hour part-time. *Required fees:* $150 full-time. *Room and board:* $6510. *Payment plan:* installment. *Waivers:* employees or children of employees.
Applying *Options:* deferred entrance. *Required:* high school transcript. *Required for some:* 2.5 letters of recommendation. *Recommended:* interview.

Application deadlines: rolling (freshmen), rolling (transfers). *Notification:* continuous (freshmen), continuous (transfers).
Freshman Application Contact Mississippi Valley State University, 14000 Highway 82 West, Itta Bena, MS 38941-1400. *Phone:* 662-254-3345. *Toll-free phone:* 800-844-6885.
Website: http://www.mvsu.edu/.

Rust College

Holly Springs, Mississippi

- **Independent United Methodist** 4-year, founded 1866
- **Rural** 126-acre campus with easy access to Memphis
- **Endowment** $21.4 million
- **Coed**
- **Minimally difficult** entrance level

Faculty *Student/faculty ratio:* 17:1.
Academics *Calendar:* semesters. *Degrees:* associate and bachelor's.
Student Life *Campus security:* 24-hour emergency response devices and patrols, late-night transport/escort service, controlled dormitory access.
Athletics Member NCAA. All Division III.
Standardized Tests *Required:* ACT (for admission).
Costs (2012–13) *Comprehensive fee:* $12,150 includes full-time tuition ($8300) and room and board ($3850). Full-time tuition and fees vary according to course load. Part-time tuition and fees vary according to course load.
Financial Aid *Of all full-time matriculated undergraduates who enrolled in 2004,* 806 applied for aid, 806 were judged to have need, 481 had their need fully met. 492 Federal Work-Study jobs (averaging $714). 189 state and other part-time jobs (averaging $546). *In 2004,* 112 non-need-based awards were made. *Average percent of need met:* 60. *Average financial aid package:* $5067. *Average need-based loan:* $2158. *Average need-based gift aid:* $4281. *Average non-need-based aid:* $2795. *Average indebtedness upon graduation:* $9314.
Applying *Application fee:* $10. *Required:* high school transcript, minimum 2.2 GPA, 2 letters of recommendation.
Freshman Application Contact Mr. Johnny B. McDonald, Director of Enrollment Services, Rust College, 150 Rust Avenue, Holly Springs, MS 38635-2328. *Phone:* 601-252-8000 Ext. 4065. *Toll-free phone:* 888-886-8492 Ext. 4065. *Fax:* 662-252-8895. *E-mail:* admissions@rustcollege.edu.
Website: http://www.rustcollege.edu/.

Southeastern Baptist College

Laurel, Mississippi

Freshman Application Contact Mrs. Emma Bond, Director of Admissions, Southeastern Baptist College, 4229 Highway 15 North, Laurel, MS 39440-1096. *Phone:* 601-426-6346.
Website: http://www.southeasternbaptist.edu/.

Strayer University—Jackson Campus

Jackson, Mississippi

Freshman Application Contact Strayer University—Jackson Campus, 460 Briarwood Drive, Suite 200, Jackson, MS 39206.
Website: http://www.strayer.edu/campus/jackson.

Tougaloo College

Tougaloo, Mississippi

Freshman Application Contact Ms. Juno Jacobs, Director of Admissions, Tougaloo College, 500 West County Line Road, Tougaloo, MS 39174. *Phone:* 601-977-7765. *Toll-free phone:* 888-42GALOO. *Fax:* 601-977-4501. *E-mail:* jjacobs@tougaloo.edu.
Website: http://www.tougaloo.edu/.

University of Mississippi

Oxford, Mississippi

- **State-supported** university, founded 1844, part of Mississippi Institutions of Higher Learning
- **Small-town** 3350-acre campus with easy access to Memphis
- **Endowment** $461.9 million
- **Coed** 16,060 undergraduate students, 93% full-time, 55% women, 45% men
- **Moderately difficult** entrance level, 61% of applicants were admitted

Undergraduates 14,933 full-time, 1,127 part-time. Students come from 50 states and territories; 70 other countries; 37% are from out of state; 17% Black or African American, non-Hispanic/Latino; 3% Hispanic/Latino; 2% Asian, non-Hispanic/Latino; 0.1% Native Hawaiian or other Pacific Islander, non-Hispanic/Latino; 0.3% American Indian or Alaska Native, non-Hispanic/Latino; 2% Two or more races, non-Hispanic/Latino; 0.1% Race/ethnicity unknown; 1% international; 10% transferred in. *Retention:* 81% of full-time freshmen returned.
Freshmen *Admission:* 13,934 applied, 8,507 admitted, 3,373 enrolled. *Test scores:* SAT critical reading scores over 500: 69%; SAT math scores over 500: 71%; ACT scores over 18: 95%; SAT critical reading scores over 600: 25%; SAT math scores over 600: 28%; ACT scores over 24: 51%; SAT critical reading scores over 700: 5%; SAT math scores over 700: 4%; ACT scores over 30: 12%.
Faculty *Total:* 875, 91% full-time, 80% with terminal degrees. *Student/faculty ratio:* 19:1.
Academics *Calendar:* semesters. *Degrees:* bachelor's, master's, doctoral, and post-master's certificates. *Special study options:* academic remediation for entering students, accelerated degree program, adult/continuing education programs, advanced placement credit, cooperative education, distance learning, double majors, English as a second language, freshman honors college, honors programs, independent study, internships, part-time degree program, services for LD students, student-designed majors, study abroad, summer session for credit. *ROTC:* Army (b), Navy (b), Air Force (b).
Computers on Campus 50 computers/terminals and 20 ports are available on campus for general student use. Students can access the following: campus intranet, computer help desk, free student e-mail accounts, online (class) grades, online (class) registration, online (class) schedules, application for admission, registration for orientation. Campuswide network is available. 100% of college-owned or -operated housing units are wired for high-speed Internet access. Wireless service is available via classrooms, computer centers, computer labs, learning centers, libraries, student centers.
Student Life *Housing:* on-campus residence required for freshman year. *Options:* men-only, women-only. Campus housing is university owned, leased by the school and is provided by a third party. Freshman campus housing is guaranteed. *Activities and organizations:* drama/theater group, student-run newspaper, radio and television station, choral group, marching band, Associated Student Body, Gospel Choir, sport clubs, Black Student Union, Student Programming Board, national fraternities, national sororities. *Campus security:* 24-hour emergency response devices and patrols, late-night transport/escort service, controlled dormitory access, crime prevention programs. *Student services:* health clinic, personal/psychological counseling, women's center.
Athletics Member NCAA. All Division I except football (Division I-A). *Intercollegiate sports:* baseball M(s), basketball M(s)/W(s), cheerleading M(s)/W(s), cross-country running M(s)/W(s), fencing M(c)/W(c), golf M(s)/W(s), ice hockey M, lacrosse M/W, riflery W(s), rugby M(c), soccer M(c)/W(s), softball W(s), tennis M(s)/W(s), track and field M(s)/W(s), volleyball M(c)/W(s). *Intramural sports:* badminton M/W, basketball M/W, bowling M/W, crew M(c)/W(c), football M/W, golf M/W, racquetball M/W, riflery M(c), soccer M/W, softball M/W, swimming and diving M/W, table tennis M(c)/W(c), tennis M/W, track and field M/W, ultimate Frisbee M/W, volleyball M/W, water polo M/W.
Standardized Tests *Required:* SAT or ACT (for admission).
Costs (2012–13) *Tuition:* state resident $6282 full-time, $262 per credit hour part-time; nonresident $16,266 full-time, $678 per credit hour part-time. Full-time tuition and fees vary according to course load and program. Part-time tuition and fees vary according to course load and program. *Room and board:* $9200. Room and board charges vary according to board plan and housing facility. *Payment plan:* tuition prepayment. *Waivers:* children of alumni, senior citizens, and employees or children of employees.
Financial Aid *Of all full-time matriculated undergraduates who enrolled in 2011,* 9,799 applied for aid, 7,671 were judged to have need, 825 had their need fully met. 422 Federal Work-Study jobs (averaging $1325). In 2011, 1812 non-need-based awards were made. *Average percent of need met:* 74%. *Average financial aid package:* $7583. *Average need-based loan:* $4389. *Average*

need-based gift aid: $6857. *Average non-need-based aid:* $5747. *Average indebtedness upon graduation:* $23,986.

Applying *Options:* electronic application. *Application fee:* $35. *Required:* high school transcript, minimum 2.0 GPA. *Application deadlines:* rolling (freshmen), rolling (out-of-state freshmen), rolling (transfers). *Notification:* continuous (freshmen), continuous (out-of-state freshmen), continuous (transfers).

Freshman Application Contact Mr. Jody Lowe, Associate Director of Enrollment Services, University of Mississippi, 145 Martindale Student Services Center, University, MS 38677. *Phone:* 662-915-7226. *Toll-free phone:* 800-653-6477. *Fax:* 662-915-5869. *E-mail:* admissions@olemiss.edu. *Website:* http://www.olemiss.edu/.

University of Mississippi Medical Center

Jackson, Mississippi

Application Contact Ms. Barbara Westerfield, Director of Student Records and Registrar, University of Mississippi Medical Center, 2500 North State Street, Jackson, MS 39216-4505. *Phone:* 601-984-1080. *Fax:* 601-984-1079. *Website:* http://www.umc.edu/.

University of Southern Mississippi

Hattiesburg, Mississippi

- **State-supported** university, founded 1910, part of Mississippi Institutions of Higher Learning
- **Suburban** 1090-acre campus
- **Endowment** $64.7 million
- **Coed** 13,658 undergraduate students, 83% full-time, 62% women, 38% men
- **Moderately difficult** entrance level, 65% of applicants were admitted

Undergraduates 11,393 full-time, 2,265 part-time. Students come from 47 states and territories; 33 other countries; 12% are from out of state; 31% Black or African American, non-Hispanic/Latino; 3% Hispanic/Latino; 1% Asian, non-Hispanic/Latino; 0.1% Native Hawaiian or other Pacific Islander, non-Hispanic/Latino; 0.3% American Indian or Alaska Native, non-Hispanic/Latino; 1% Two or more races, non-Hispanic/Latino; 3% Race/ethnicity unknown; 0.6% international; 13% transferred in; 45% live on campus. *Retention:* 75% of full-time freshmen returned.

Freshmen *Admission:* 7,076 applied, 4,581 admitted, 1,945 enrolled. *Average high school GPA:* 3.18. *Test scores:* SAT critical reading scores over 500: 65%; SAT math scores over 500: 59%; ACT scores over 18: 88%; SAT critical reading scores over 600: 22%; SAT math scores over 600: 18%; ACT scores over 24: 34%; SAT critical reading scores over 700: 4%; ACT scores over 30: 6%.

Faculty *Total:* 903, 76% full-time, 66% with terminal degrees. *Student/faculty ratio:* 18:1.

Academics *Calendar:* semesters. *Degrees:* certificates, bachelor's, master's, doctoral, post-master's, and postbachelor's certificates. *Special study options:* academic remediation for entering students, accelerated degree program, advanced placement credit, cooperative education, distance learning, double majors, English as a second language, honors programs, independent study, internships, off-campus study, part-time degree program, services for LD students, study abroad, summer session for credit. *ROTC:* Army (c), Air Force (b).

Computers on Campus 500 computers/terminals and 1,439 ports are available on campus for general student use. Students can access the following: campus intranet, computer help desk, free student e-mail accounts, online (class) grades, online (class) registration, online (class) schedules. Campus-wide network is available. 100% of college-owned or -operated housing units are wired for high-speed Internet access. Wireless service is available via entire campus.

Student Life *Housing options:* men-only, women-only, disabled students. Campus housing is university owned. Freshman applicants given priority for college housing. *Activities and organizations:* drama/theater group, student-run newspaper, radio station, choral group, marching band, Southern Miss Activities Council, Residence Halls Associations, Student Government Association, Baptist Student Union, African American Student Organization, national fraternities, national sororities. *Campus security:* 24-hour emergency response devices and patrols, late-night transport/escort service, controlled dormitory access. *Student services:* health clinic, personal/psychological counseling, women's center, legal services.

Athletics Member NCAA. All Division I. *Intercollegiate sports:* baseball M(s), basketball M(s)/W(s), cheerleading M/W, cross-country running W(s), football M(s)/W(s), golf M(s)/W(s), soccer W(s), softball W(s), tennis M(s)/W(s), track and field M(s)/W(s), volleyball W(s). *Intramural sports:* badminton M/W, basketball M/W, bowling M/W, fencing M/W, racquetball M/W, riflery M/W, rugby M, soccer M/W, softball M/W, table tennis M/W, tennis M/W, track and field M/W, ultimate Frisbee M/W, volleyball M/W.

Standardized Tests *Required:* SAT or ACT (for admission).

Costs (2013–14) *Tuition:* state resident $6336 full-time, $264 per credit hour part-time; nonresident $14,448 full-time, $602 per credit hour part-time. Part-time tuition and fees vary according to course load and degree level. *Room and board:* $6907. Room and board charges vary according to board plan and housing facility. *Payment plan:* installment. *Waivers:* children of alumni, senior citizens, and employees or children of employees.

Financial Aid Of all full-time matriculated undergraduates who enrolled in 2010, 9,128 applied for aid, 8,130 were judged to have need, 1,707 had their need fully met. In 2010, 552 non-need-based awards were made. *Average percent of need met:* 75%. *Average financial aid package:* $12,199. *Average need-based loan:* $4391. *Average need-based gift aid:* $406. *Average non-need-based aid:* $3905. *Average indebtedness upon graduation:* $23,975.

Applying *Options:* electronic application, early admission. *Application fee:* $35. *Required:* high school transcript, minimum 2.0 GPA. *Application deadlines:* 7/1 (freshmen), 7/1 (transfers).

Freshman Application Contact Mr. Jason Beverly, Senior Admissions Counselor, University of Southern Mississippi, 118 College Drive, #5166, Hattiesburg, MS 39406-1000. *Phone:* 601-266-5000. *Fax:* 601-266-5148. *E-mail:* admissions@usm.edu. *Website:* http://www.usm.edu/.

William Carey University

Hattiesburg, Mississippi

Freshman Application Contact Mr. William N. Curry, Dean of Enrollment Management, William Carey University, 498 Tuscan Avenue, Hattiesburg, MS 39401-5499. *Phone:* 601-318-6051. *Toll-free phone:* 800-962-5991. *Fax:* 601-318-6154. *E-mail:* admissions@wmcarey.edu. *Website:* http://www.wmcarey.edu/.

MISSOURI

The Art Institute of St. Louis

St. Charles, Missouri

Admissions Office Contact The Art Institute of St. Louis, 1520 South Fifth Street, St. Charles, MO 63303. *Website:* http://www.artinstitutes.edu/st-louis/.

See full-page ad on page 54 and page 1110 for the College Close-Up.

Avila University

Kansas City, Missouri

- **Independent Roman Catholic** comprehensive, founded 1916
- **Suburban** 50-acre campus
- **Coed** 1,219 undergraduate students, 81% full-time, 63% women, 37% men
- **Minimally difficult** entrance level, 53% of applicants were admitted

Undergraduates 988 full-time, 231 part-time. Students come from 23 states and territories; 16 other countries; 32% are from out of state; 18% Black or African American, non-Hispanic/Latino; 6% Hispanic/Latino; 1% Asian, non-Hispanic/Latino; 0.4% Native Hawaiian or other Pacific Islander, non-Hispanic/Latino; 1% American Indian or Alaska Native, non-Hispanic/Latino; 2% Two or more races, non-Hispanic/Latino; 4% international; 13% transferred in; 28% live on campus. *Retention:* 65% of full-time freshmen returned.

Freshmen *Admission:* 1,170 applied, 619 admitted, 138 enrolled. *Average high school GPA:* 3.26. *Test scores:* SAT critical reading scores over 500: 40%; SAT math scores over 500: 40%; ACT scores over 18: 93%; SAT critical reading scores over 600: 30%; SAT math scores over 600: 20%; ACT scores over 24: 35%; SAT math scores over 700: 10%; ACT scores over 30: 2%.

Faculty *Total:* 209, 31% full-time, 43% with terminal degrees. *Student/faculty ratio:* 14:1.

Academics *Calendar:* semesters. *Degrees:* bachelor's, master's, and postbachelor's certificates. *Special study options:* academic remediation for entering students, accelerated degree program, adult/continuing education programs, advanced placement credit, cooperative education, distance learning, double majors, English as a second language, independent study, internships, off-campus study, part-time degree program, services for LD students, study abroad, summer session for credit. *ROTC:* Army (c). *Unusual degree programs:* 3-2 occupational therapy, physical therapy, law with Rockhurst University, University of Missouri-Kansas City.

Computers on Campus 180 computers/terminals and 225 ports are available on campus for general student use. Students can access the following: campus intranet, computer help desk, free student e-mail accounts, online (class) grades, online (class) registration, online (class) schedules. Campuswide network is available. 100% of college-owned or -operated housing units are wired for high-speed Internet access. Wireless service is available via entire campus.

Student Life *Housing:* on-campus residence required through sophomore year. *Options:* coed, men-only, women-only. Campus housing is university owned. Freshman campus housing is guaranteed. *Activities and organizations:* drama/theater group, student-run newspaper, choral group, Avila Ambassadors, Avila Student Nurses Association, Campus Ministries, Saudi Arabian Student Association, Avila University Theatre Company. *Campus security:* 24-hour emergency response devices, student patrols, late-night transport/escort service, controlled dormitory access. *Student services:* health clinic, personal/psychological counseling.

Athletics Member NAIA. *Intercollegiate sports:* baseball M(s), basketball M(s)/W(s), cheerleading W(s), cross-country running M(s)/W(s), football M(s), golf M(s)/W(s), soccer M(s)/W(s), softball W(s), volleyball W(s). *Intramural sports:* bowling M/W, table tennis M/W.

Standardized Tests *Required:* SAT or ACT (for admission).

Costs (2013–14) *Comprehensive fee:* $31,650 includes full-time tuition ($24,000), mandatory fees ($850), and room and board ($6800). Full-time tuition and fees vary according to course load and program. Part-time tuition: $600 per credit hour. Part-time tuition and fees vary according to course load and program. No tuition increase for student's term of enrollment. *Required fees:* $30 per credit hour part-time. *College room only:* $3400. Room and board charges vary according to board plan and housing facility. *Payment plans:* installment, deferred payment. *Waivers:* children of alumni, senior citizens, and employees or children of employees.

Financial Aid Of all full-time matriculated undergraduates who enrolled in 2008, 1,927 applied for aid, 1,852 were judged to have need, 1,846 had their need fully met. 161 Federal Work-Study jobs (averaging $903). 55 state and other part-time jobs (averaging $885). In 2008, 60 non-need-based awards were made. *Average percent of need met:* 35%. *Average financial aid package:* $12,976. *Average need-based loan:* $5465. *Average need-based gift aid:* $7854. *Average non-need-based aid:* $9152. *Average indebtedness upon graduation:* $16,508.

Applying *Options:* electronic application, early admission. *Required:* high school transcript, minimum 2.5 GPA, secondary school report. *Required for some:* essay or personal statement. *Recommended:* interview. *Application deadlines:* 8/15 (freshmen), 8/15 (transfers). *Notification:* 8/15 (freshmen), 8/15 (transfers).

Freshman Application Contact Ms. Bethany Bauer, Associate Director of Admissions, Avila University, 11901 Wornall Road, Kansas City, MO 64145. *Phone:* 816-501-2400. *Toll-free phone:* 800-GO-AVILA. *Fax:* 816-501-2453. *E-mail:* bethany.bauer@avila.edu. *Website:* http://www.avila.edu/.

Baptist Bible College
Springfield, Missouri

Freshman Application Contact Mr. Terry Allcorn, Director of Admissions, Baptist Bible College, 628 East Kearney Street, Springfield, MO 65803-3498. *Phone:* 417-268-6000. *Toll-free phone:* 800-228-5754. *Fax:* 417-268-6694. *Website:* http://www.gobbc.edu/.

Brown Mackie College–St. Louis
Fenton, Missouri

Freshman Application Contact Brown Mackie College–St. Louis, #2 Soccer Park Road, Fenton, MO 63026. *Phone:* 636-651-3290. *Website:* http://www.brownmackie.edu/st-louis/.

See below for display ad and page 1204 for the College Close-Up.

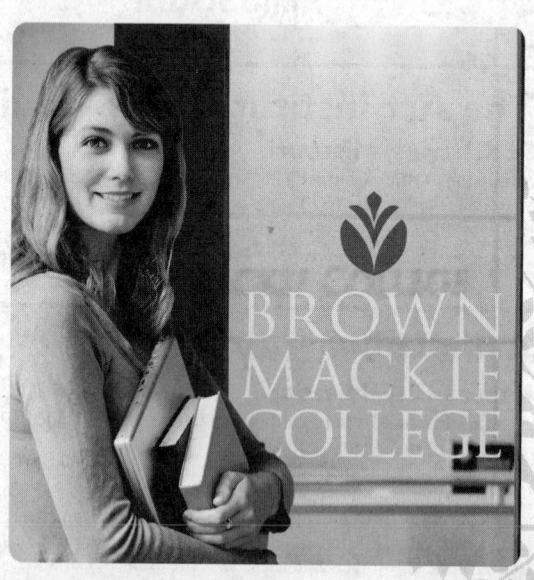

Calvary Bible College and Theological Seminary

Kansas City, Missouri

- **Independent nondenominational** comprehensive, founded 1932
- **Suburban** 55-acre campus
- **Coed**
- **Minimally difficult** entrance level

Academics *Calendar:* semesters. *Degrees:* certificates, diplomas, associate, bachelor's, and master's.

Student Life *Campus security:* late-night transport/escort service, night patrols by trained security personnel.

Athletics Member NCCAA.

Standardized Tests *Required:* SAT or ACT (for admission).

Costs (2012–13) *Comprehensive fee:* $15,116 includes full-time tuition ($9300), mandatory fees ($816), and room and board ($5000). Part-time tuition: $310 per credit. No tuition increase for student's term of enrollment. *Required fees:* $29 per credit part-time, $120 per term part-time. *Room and board:* Room and board charges vary according to housing facility.

Financial Aid *Financial aid deadline:* 4/1.

Applying *Options:* electronic application. *Application fee:* $25. *Required:* essay or personal statement, high school transcript, 2 letters of recommendation, statement of faith.

Freshman Application Contact Bob Crank, Director of Admissions, Calvary Bible College and Theological Seminary, 15800 Calvary Road, Kansas City, MO 64147-1341. *Phone:* 816-322-0110 Ext. 1321. *Toll-free phone:* 800-326-3960. *Fax:* 816-331-4474. *E-mail:* admissions@calvary.edu. *Website:* http://www.calvary.edu/.

Central Bible College

Springfield, Missouri

Director of Admissions James Bell, Executive Director for Enrollment Services, Central Bible College, 3000 North Grant Avenue, Springfield, MO 65803-1096. *Phone:* 417-833-2551 Ext. 1290. *Toll-free phone:* 800-831-4222. *E-mail:* jbell@cbcag.edu. *Website:* http://www.cbcag.edu/.

Central Christian College of the Bible

Moberly, Missouri

Freshman Application Contact Mr. Aaron Merritt, Director of Admissions, Central Christian College of the Bible, 911 Urbandale Drive East, Moberly, MO 65270-1997. *Phone:* 660-263-3900. *Toll-free phone:* 888-263-3900. *Fax:* 660-263-3936. *E-mail:* admissions@cccb.edu. *Website:* http://www.cccb.edu/.

Central Methodist University

Fayette, Missouri

- **Independent Methodist** comprehensive, founded 1854
- **Small-town** 80-acre campus
- **Coed** 1,173 undergraduate students, 99% full-time, 51% women, 49% men
- **Moderately difficult** entrance level, 67% of applicants were admitted

Undergraduates 1,158 full-time, 15 part-time. 10% are from out of state; 6% Black or African American, non-Hispanic/Latino; 2% Hispanic/Latino; 0.6% Asian, non-Hispanic/Latino; 0.5% Native Hawaiian or other Pacific Islander, non-Hispanic/Latino; 0.8% American Indian or Alaska Native, non-Hispanic/Latino; 2% Two or more races, non-Hispanic/Latino; 4% Race/ethnicity unknown; 3% international; 9% transferred in; 85% live on campus. *Retention:* 72% of full-time freshmen returned.

Freshmen *Admission:* 1,344 applied, 897 admitted, 302 enrolled. *Average high school GPA:* 3.42. *Test scores:* ACT scores over 18: 95%; ACT scores over 24: 27%; ACT scores over 30: 3%.

Faculty *Total:* 123, 51% full-time, 31% with terminal degrees. *Student/faculty ratio:* 14:1.

Academics *Calendar:* semesters. *Degrees:* associate and bachelor's. *Special study options:* accelerated degree program, adult/continuing education programs, distance learning, double majors, honors programs, independent study, internships, off-campus study, part-time degree program, services for LD students, study abroad, summer session for credit. *ROTC:* Army (c), Air Force (c). *Unusual degree programs:* 3-2 engineering with University of Missouri-Rolla.

Computers on Campus 72 computers/terminals are available on campus for general student use. Students can access the following: campus intranet, computer help desk, free student e-mail accounts, online (class) grades, online (class) schedules. Campuswide network is available. 100% of college-owned or -operated housing units are wired for high-speed Internet access. Wireless service is available via classrooms, computer centers, computer labs, learning centers, libraries, student centers.

Student Life *Housing:* on-campus residence required through senior year. *Options:* coed, men-only, women-only. Campus housing is university owned. Freshman applicants given priority for college housing. *Activities and organizations:* drama/theater group, student-run newspaper, radio and television station, choral group, marching band, Student Government Association, Students in Free Enterprise (SIFE), Alpha Phi Omega, Beta Beta Beta, Campus Ministries, national fraternities. *Campus security:* 24-hour emergency response devices, late-night transport/escort service, controlled dormitory access. *Student services:* health clinic, personal/psychological counseling.

Athletics Member NAIA. *Intercollegiate sports:* baseball M(s), basketball M(s)/W(s), cross-country running M(s)/W(s), football M(s), soccer M(s)/W(s), softball W(s), track and field M(s)/W(s), volleyball W(s). *Intramural sports:* basketball M/W, football M/W, racquetball M/W, soccer M/W, softball M/W, tennis M/W, track and field M/W, volleyball M/W, water polo M/W.

Standardized Tests *Required:* SAT or ACT (for admission).

Costs (2013–14) *Tuition:* $20,590 full-time, $190 per credit hour part-time. Full-time tuition and fees vary according to location. Part-time tuition and fees vary according to course load and location. *Room only:* Room and board charges vary according to board plan and housing facility. *Payment plan:* installment. *Waivers:* children of alumni and employees or children of employees.

Financial Aid Of all full-time matriculated undergraduates who enrolled in 2011, 999 applied for aid, 939 were judged to have need, 155 had their need fully met. In 2011, 199 non-need-based awards were made. *Average percent of need met:* 29%. *Average financial aid package:* $17,098. *Average need-based loan:* $4185. *Average need-based gift aid:* $4990. *Average non-need-based aid:* $11,267. *Average indebtedness upon graduation:* $22,086.

Applying *Options:* electronic application, deferred entrance. *Application fee:* $20. *Required:* high school transcript, minimum 2.5 GPA. *Required for some:* 2 letters of recommendation. *Application deadlines:* rolling (freshmen), rolling (transfers). *Notification:* continuous (freshmen), continuous (transfers).

Freshman Application Contact Mr. Larry Anderson, Director of Admissions, Central Methodist University, 411 Central Methodist Square, Fayette, MO 65248-1198. *Phone:* 660-248-6247. *Toll-free phone:* 888-CMU-1854 (in-state); 877-CMU-1854 (out-of-state). *Fax:* 660-248-1872. *E-mail:* admissions@centralmethodist.edu. *Website:* http://www.centralmethodist.edu/.

Chamberlain College of Nursing

St. Louis, Missouri

- **Proprietary** 4-year, founded 1889, part of DeVry University
- **Urban** campus
- **Coed** 540 undergraduate students, 68% full-time, 92% women, 8% men
- **Moderately difficult** entrance level

Undergraduates 368 full-time, 172 part-time. 22% are from out of state; 12% Black or African American, non-Hispanic/Latino; 1% Hispanic/Latino; 2% Asian, non-Hispanic/Latino; 0.2% Native Hawaiian or other Pacific Islander, non-Hispanic/Latino; 0.2% American Indian or Alaska Native, non-Hispanic/Latino; 2% Two or more races, non-Hispanic/Latino; 2% Race/ethnicity unknown; 0.2% international; 37% transferred in.

Freshmen *Admission:* 9 enrolled.

Faculty *Total:* 246, 19% full-time. *Student/faculty ratio:* 31:1.

Academics *Calendar:* semesters. *Degree:* bachelor's. *Special study options:* part-time degree program.

Student Life *Campus security:* 24-hour patrols, late-night transport/escort service, controlled dormitory access.

Standardized Tests *Required:* SAT or ACT (for admission).

Costs (2013–14) *Tuition:* $16,360 full-time, $665 per credit hour part-time. *Required fees:* $600 full-time.

Applying *Application fee:* $95. *Required:* essay or personal statement, high school transcript. *Required for some:* interview. *Application deadlines:* rolling (freshmen), rolling (transfers). *Notification:* continuous (freshmen), continuous (transfers).
Freshman Application Contact Admissions, Chamberlain College of Nursing, 11830 Westline Industrial Drive, Suite 106, St. Louis, MO 63146. *Phone:* 314-991-6200. *Toll-free phone:* 888-556-8CCN.
Website: http://www.chamberlain.edu/.

City Vision College

Kansas City, Missouri

- **Independent Christian** upper-level
- **Coed** 63 undergraduate students, 57% full-time, 56% women, 44% men

Undergraduates 36 full-time, 27 part-time. Students come from 23 states and territories; 1 other country; 93% are from out of state; 32% Black or African American, non-Hispanic/Latino; 3% Hispanic/Latino; 2% American Indian or Alaska Native, non-Hispanic/Latino; 5% Two or more races, non-Hispanic/Latino; 2% Race/ethnicity unknown; 46% transferred in.
Faculty *Total:* 19, 11% with terminal degrees. *Student/faculty ratio:* 3:1.
Academics *Degree:* certificates and bachelor's. *Special study options:* adult/continuing education programs, distance learning, double majors, internships, part-time degree program, summer session for credit.
Computers on Campus Students can access the following: computer help desk, online (class) grades, online (class) registration, online (class) schedules, All the course materials, weekly outlines, lectures and assignments. All the courses are online based.
Costs (2013–14) *One-time required fee:* $25. *Tuition:* $6000 full-time, $3000 per year part-time. Full-time tuition and fees vary according to course load. Part-time tuition and fees vary according to course load. *Waivers:* employees or children of employees.
Financial Aid Of all full-time matriculated undergraduates who enrolled in 2011, 22 applied for aid, 22 were judged to have need. *Average percent of need met:* 100%. *Average financial aid package:* $2770. *Average need-based gift aid:* $2770.
Applying *Options:* electronic application. *Application fee:* $25. *Application deadline:* rolling (transfers). *Notification:* continuous (transfers).
Application Contact City Vision College, PO Box 413188, Kansas City, MO 64141-3188. *Phone:* 816-960-2008.
Website: http://www.cityvision.edu/.

College of the Ozarks

Point Lookout, Missouri

- **Independent Presbyterian** 4-year, founded 1906
- **Small-town** 1000-acre campus
- **Endowment** $298.2 million
- **Coed** 1,379 undergraduate students, 99% full-time, 57% women, 43% men
- **Moderately difficult** entrance level, 9% of applicants were admitted

Undergraduates 1,361 full-time, 18 part-time. Students come from 25 states and territories; 22 other countries; 21% are from out of state; 0.7% Black or African American, non-Hispanic/Latino; 2% Hispanic/Latino; 0.3% Asian, non-Hispanic/Latino; 0.1% Native Hawaiian or other Pacific Islander, non-Hispanic/Latino; 0.4% American Indian or Alaska Native, non-Hispanic/Latino; 2% Two or more races, non-Hispanic/Latino; 2% international; 3% transferred in; 80% live on campus. *Retention:* 87% of full-time freshmen returned.
Freshmen *Admission:* 3,048 applied, 289 admitted, 245 enrolled. *Average high school GPA:* 3.58. *Test scores:* ACT scores over 18: 96%; ACT scores over 24: 37%; ACT scores over 30: 3%.
Faculty *Total:* 129, 64% full-time, 41% with terminal degrees. *Student/faculty ratio:* 14:1.
Academics *Calendar:* semesters. *Degree:* bachelor's. *Special study options:* academic remediation for entering students, advanced placement credit, double majors, independent study, internships, off-campus study, services for LD students, student-designed majors. *ROTC:* Army (b). *Unusual degree programs:* 3-2 engineering with Missouri University Science and Technology; JD with University of Missouri, Medical Technology with Cox Medical Center.
Computers on Campus 164 computers/terminals and 1,150 ports are available on campus for general student use. Students can access the following: campus intranet, computer help desk, free student e-mail accounts, online (class) grades, online (class) registration, online (class) schedules. Campus-wide network is available. 100% of college-owned or -operated housing units

are wired for high-speed Internet access. Wireless service is available via classrooms, dorm rooms, libraries, student centers.
Student Life *Housing:* on-campus residence required through senior year. *Options:* men-only, women-only. Campus housing is university owned. *Activities and organizations:* drama/theater group, student-run newspaper, radio station, choral group, Students in Free Enterprise (SIFE), Student Senate, Baptist Student Union, Aggie Club, Business Undergraduate Society. *Campus security:* 24-hour emergency response devices and patrols, controlled dormitory access, front gate closed 6 p.m. to 5 a.m., Security checks cars for proper credentials for entry. *Student services:* health clinic, personal/psychological counseling.
Athletics Member NAIA. *Intercollegiate sports:* baseball M(s), basketball M(s)/W(s), cheerleading M/W, volleyball W(s). *Intramural sports:* basketball M/W, football M, racquetball M/W, softball M/W, tennis M/W, volleyball M/W.
Standardized Tests *Required:* SAT or ACT (for admission).
Costs (2013–14) *Comprehensive fee:* includes mandatory fees ($430) and room and board ($5900). *Part-time tuition:* $295 per credit. Part-time tuition and fees vary according to course load. Each student participates in the on-campus work program for 15 hours per week and two forty-hour work weeks. Earnings from participation in the work program, plus any federal and/or state aid for which students qualify, plus a College of the Ozarks Cost of Education Scholarship combine to meet each student?s full tuition charge. *College room only:* $2900. *Payment plan:* installment.
Financial Aid Of all full-time matriculated undergraduates who enrolled in 2011, 1,337 applied for aid, 1,289 were judged to have need, 375 had their need fully met. 777 Federal Work-Study jobs (averaging $4638). 580 state and other part-time jobs (averaging $1957). In 2011, 82 non-need-based awards were made. *Average percent of need met:* 85%. *Average financial aid package:* $18,686. *Average need-based gift aid:* $14,692. *Average non-need-based aid:* $14,077. *Average indebtedness upon graduation:* $7062.
Applying *Options:* electronic application. *Required:* high school transcript, 2 letters of recommendation, interview, medical history, financial statement. *Recommended:* minimum 3.0 GPA. *Application deadlines:* 2/15 (freshmen), 2/15 (transfers). *Notification:* continuous (freshmen), continuous (transfers).
Freshman Application Contact Mrs. Gayle Groves, Admissions Secretary, College of the Ozarks, PO Box 17, Point Lookout, MO 65726. *Phone:* 417-690-2636. *Toll-free phone:* 800-222-0525. *Fax:* 417-335-2618. *E-mail:* admiss4@cofo.edu.
Website: http://www.cofo.edu/.

Colorado Technical University North Kansas City

North Kansas City, Missouri

Director of Admissions Angela Vietti, Director of Admissions, Colorado Technical University North Kansas City, 520 East 19th Avenue, North Kansas City, MO 64116. *Phone:* 888-404-7555. *E-mail:* avietti@kc.coloradotech.edu. *Website:* http://kc.coloradotech.edu/.

Columbia College

Columbia, Missouri

- **Independent** comprehensive, founded 1851, affiliated with Christian Church (Disciples of Christ)
- **Urban** 33-acre campus
- **Endowment** $93.5 million
- **Coed** 953 undergraduate students, 83% full-time, 58% women, 42% men
- **Moderately difficult** entrance level, 69% of applicants were admitted

Undergraduates 793 full-time, 160 part-time. Students come from 19 states and territories; 30 other countries; 11% are from out of state; 5% Black or African American, non-Hispanic/Latino; 3% Hispanic/Latino; 1% Asian, non-Hispanic/Latino; 0.1% Native Hawaiian or other Pacific Islander, non-Hispanic/Latino; 1% American Indian or Alaska Native, non-Hispanic/Latino; 2% Two or more races, non-Hispanic/Latino; 5% Race/ethnicity unknown; 9% international; 14% transferred in; 34% live on campus. *Retention:* 67% of full-time freshmen returned.
Freshmen *Admission:* 571 applied, 393 admitted, 148 enrolled. *Average high school GPA:* 3.42. *Test scores:* SAT critical reading scores over 500: 29%; SAT math scores over 500: 71%; ACT scores over 18: 95%; SAT critical reading scores over 600: 14%; SAT math scores over 600: 29%; ACT scores over 24: 50%; ACT scores over 30: 5%.

Faculty *Total:* 118, 58% full-time, 53% with terminal degrees. *Student/faculty ratio:* 11:1.

Academics *Calendar:* semesters. *Degrees:* associate, bachelor's, and master's (offers continuing education program with significant enrollment not reflected in profile). *Special study options:* adult/continuing education programs, advanced placement credit, cooperative education, distance learning, double majors, English as a second language, honors programs, independent study, internships, off-campus study, part-time degree program, services for LD students, student-designed majors, study abroad, summer session for credit. *ROTC:* Army (c), Navy (c), Air Force (c).

Computers on Campus 121 computers/terminals are available on campus for general student use. Students can access the following: campus intranet, computer help desk, free student e-mail accounts, online (class) grades, online (class) registration, online (class) schedules. Campuswide network is available. 100% of college-owned or -operated housing units are wired for high-speed Internet access. Wireless service is available via entire campus.

Student Life *Housing:* on-campus residence required through sophomore year. *Options:* coed, women-only, disabled students. Campus housing is university owned. Freshman campus housing is guaranteed. *Activities and organizations:* drama/theater group, choral group, Elysium Players, Student Government Association, International Club, Chi Alpha Christian Fellowship, The Pride. *Campus security:* 24-hour emergency response devices and patrols, late-night transport/escort service, controlled dormitory access. *Student services:* health clinic, personal/psychological counseling.

Athletics Member NAIA. *Intercollegiate sports:* basketball M(s)/W(s), cross-country running M(s)/W(s), golf M(s)/W(s), soccer M(s)/W(s), softball W(s), volleyball W(s). *Intramural sports:* basketball M/W, football M/W, soccer M/W, softball M/W, volleyball M/W.

Standardized Tests *Required:* SAT or ACT (for admission).

Costs (2013–14) *Tuition:* $19,386 full-time, $417 per credit hour part-time. Full-time tuition and fees vary according to class time, course load, degree level, and program. Part-time tuition and fees vary according to class time, course load, degree level, and location. No tuition increase for student's term of enrollment. *Room only:* Room and board charges vary according to board plan and housing facility. *Payment plans:* installment, deferred payment. *Waivers:* children of alumni, senior citizens, and employees or children of employees.

Financial Aid Of all full-time matriculated undergraduates who enrolled in 2011, 552 applied for aid, 504 were judged to have need, 60 had their need fully met. 139 Federal Work-Study jobs (averaging $2336). 171 state and other part-time jobs (averaging $1960). In 2011, 35 non-need-based awards were made. *Average percent of need met:* 56%. *Average financial aid package:* $11,081. *Average need-based loan:* $4297. *Average need-based gift aid:* $4026. *Average non-need-based aid:* $9034. *Average indebtedness upon graduation:* $11,726.

Applying *Options:* electronic application, deferred entrance. *Application fee:* $35. *Required:* high school transcript, minimum 2.5 GPA. *Required for some:* essay or personal statement, interview. *Application deadlines:* 8/13 (freshmen), 8/13 (transfers). *Notification:* continuous (freshmen), continuous (transfers).

Freshman Application Contact Daniel Kruse, Senior Admissions Counselor, Columbia College, 1001 Rogers Street, Columbia, MO 65216. *Phone:* 573-875-7358. *Toll-free phone:* 800-231-2391. *Fax:* 573-875-7506. *E-mail:* admissions@ccis.edu.
Website: http://www.ccis.edu/.

Conception Seminary College

Conception, Missouri

Freshman Application Contact Br. Etienne Huard OSB, Director of Recruitment and Admissions, Conception Seminary College, PO Box 502, Conception, MO 64433-0502. *Phone:* 660-944-2886. *Fax:* 660-944-2829. *E-mail:* vocations@conception.edu.
Website: http://www.conception.edu/.

Cox College

Springfield, Missouri

Freshman Application Contact Cox College, 1423 North Jefferson, Springfield, MO 65802. *Phone:* 417-269-3083. *Toll-free phone:* 866-898-5355.
Website: http://www.coxcollege.edu/.

Culver-Stockton College

Canton, Missouri

- **Independent** 4-year, founded 1853, affiliated with Christian Church (Disciples of Christ)
- **Rural** 143-acre campus
- **Endowment** $20.1 million
- **Coed** 769 undergraduate students, 92% full-time, 47% women, 53% men
- **Moderately difficult** entrance level, 62% of applicants were admitted

Undergraduates 710 full-time, 59 part-time. Students come from 27 states and territories; 13 other countries; 47% are from out of state; 12% Black or African American, non-Hispanic/Latino; 4% Hispanic/Latino; 0.3% Asian, non-Hispanic/Latino; 0.3% Native Hawaiian or other Pacific Islander, non-Hispanic/Latino; 0.5% American Indian or Alaska Native, non-Hispanic/Latino; 2% Two or more races, non-Hispanic/Latino; 0.5% Race/ethnicity unknown; 2% international; 10% transferred in; 83% live on campus. *Retention:* 68% of full-time freshmen returned.

Freshmen *Admission:* 1,162 applied, 715 admitted, 217 enrolled. *Average high school GPA:* 3.18. *Test scores:* ACT scores over 18: 83%; ACT scores over 24: 20%; ACT scores over 30: 2%.

Faculty *Total:* 89, 55% full-time, 42% with terminal degrees. *Student/faculty ratio:* 12:1.

Academics *Calendar:* semesters. *Degree:* bachelor's. *Special study options:* academic remediation for entering students, adult/continuing education programs, advanced placement credit, distance learning, double majors, honors programs, independent study, internships, off-campus study, part-time degree program, services for LD students, student-designed majors, study abroad, summer session for credit. *Unusual degree programs:* 3-2 occupational therapy with Washington University in St. Louis.

Computers on Campus 100 computers/terminals and 50 ports are available on campus for general student use. Students can access the following: campus intranet, computer help desk, free student e-mail accounts, online (class) grades, online (class) registration, online (class) schedules. Campuswide network is available. 100% of college-owned or -operated housing units are wired for high-speed Internet access. Wireless service is available via entire campus.

Student Life *Housing:* on-campus residence required through senior year. *Options:* coed. Campus housing is university owned. Freshman campus housing is guaranteed. *Activities and organizations:* drama/theater group, student-run newspaper, radio and television station, choral group, Up 'til Dawn (benefiting St. Jude's Hospital), Interfraternity Council/Panhellenic Council, Student Government Association, Students in Free Enterprise (SIFE), Campus Programming Council, national fraternities, national sororities. *Campus security:* 24-hour emergency response devices and patrols, late-night transport/escort service, controlled dormitory access, lighted pathways/sidewalks; self defense education is currently offered on campus. *Student services:* personal/psychological counseling.

Athletics Member NAIA. *Intercollegiate sports:* baseball M(s), basketball M(s)/W(s), cheerleading M(s)/W(s), cross-country running M(s)/W(s), football M(s), golf M(s)/W(s), soccer M(s)/W(s), softball W(s), track and field M(s)/W(s), volleyball W(s). *Intramural sports:* basketball M/W, bowling M/W, football M/W, golf M/W, racquetball M/W, softball M/W, volleyball M/W.

Standardized Tests *Required:* SAT or ACT (for admission).

Costs (2013–14) *One-time required fee:* $200. *Comprehensive fee:* $30,900 includes full-time tuition ($23,000), mandatory fees ($300), and room and board ($7600). *Part-time tuition:* $540 per credit hour. *Required fees:* $13 per credit hour part-time. *College room only:* $3400. Room and board charges vary according to board plan and housing facility. *Payment plan:* installment. *Waivers:* senior citizens and employees or children of employees.

Financial Aid Of all full-time matriculated undergraduates who enrolled in 2012, 654 applied for aid, 616 were judged to have need, 117 had their need fully met. 81 Federal Work-Study jobs (averaging $1015). 276 state and other part-time jobs (averaging $1115). In 2012, 70 non-need-based awards were made. *Average percent of need met:* 77%. *Average financial aid package:* $20,614. *Average need-based loan:* $4150. *Average need-based gift aid:* $16,903. *Average non-need-based aid:* $10,282. *Average indebtedness upon graduation:* $24,859. *Financial aid deadline:* 6/1.

Applying *Options:* electronic application, deferred entrance. *Required:* high school transcript, minimum 2.0 GPA. *Recommended:* essay or personal statement, 1 letter of recommendation, interview. *Application deadlines:* rolling (freshmen), rolling (transfers). *Notification:* continuous (freshmen), continuous (transfers).

Freshman Application Contact Misty McBee, Director of Admission, Culver-Stockton College, One College Hill, Canton, MO 63435-1299. *Phone:* 573-288-6507. *Toll-free phone:* 800-537-1883. *Fax:* 573-288-6618. *E-mail:* admissions@culver.edu.
Website: http://www.culver.edu/.

DeVry University

Kansas City, Missouri

- **Proprietary** comprehensive, founded 1931, part of DeVry University
- **Urban** campus
- **Coed** 695 undergraduate students, 44% full-time, 33% women, 67% men
- **Minimally difficult** entrance level

Undergraduates 306 full-time, 389 part-time. 40% are from out of state; 16% Black or African American, non-Hispanic/Latino; 4% Hispanic/Latino; 2% Asian, non-Hispanic/Latino; 0.4% Native Hawaiian or other Pacific Islander, non-Hispanic/Latino; 0.7% American Indian or Alaska Native, non-Hispanic/Latino; 1% Two or more races, non-Hispanic/Latino; 12% Race/ethnicity unknown; 0.3% international; 18% transferred in.
Freshmen *Admission:* 51 enrolled.
Faculty *Total:* 76, 32% full-time. *Student/faculty ratio:* 13:1.
Academics *Calendar:* semesters. *Degrees:* associate, bachelor's, master's, and postbachelor's certificates. *Special study options:* adult/continuing education programs, part-time degree program.
Computers on Campus Students can access the following: online (class) registration.
Student Life *Housing:* college housing not available.
Costs (2013–14) *Tuition:* $16,076 full-time, $609 per credit hour part-time. *Required fees:* $80 full-time.
Financial Aid Of all full-time matriculated undergraduates who enrolled in 2007, 294 applied for aid, 281 were judged to have need, 12 had their need fully met. In 2007, 30 non-need-based awards were made. *Average percent of need met:* 40%. *Average financial aid package:* $11,948. *Average need-based loan:* $8396. *Average need-based gift aid:* $5419. *Average non-need-based aid:* $13,609. *Average indebtedness upon graduation:* $8969.
Applying *Application fee:* $40. *Required:* high school transcript, interview. *Application deadlines:* rolling (freshmen), rolling (transfers). *Notification:* continuous (freshmen), continuous (transfers).
Freshman Application Contact DeVry University, 11224 Holmes Road, Kansas City, MO 64131. *Phone:* 816-943-7300. *Toll-free phone:* 866-338-7941.
Website: http://www.devry.edu/.

DeVry University

Kansas City, Missouri

Admissions Office Contact DeVry University, City Center Square, 1100 Main Street, Suite 118, Kansas City, MO 64105-2112. *Toll-free phone:* 866-338-7941.
Website: http://www.devry.edu/.

DeVry University

St. Louis, Missouri

Admissions Office Contact DeVry University, 1801 Park 270 Drive, Suite 260, St. Louis, MO 63146-4020. *Toll-free phone:* 866-338-7941.
Website: http://www.devry.edu/.

Drury University

Springfield, Missouri

- **Independent** comprehensive, founded 1873
- **Urban** 80-acre campus
- **Endowment** $56.2 million
- **Coed** 1,607 undergraduate students, 98% full-time, 54% women, 46% men
- **Moderately difficult** entrance level, 82% of applicants were admitted

Undergraduates 1,575 full-time, 32 part-time. Students come from 30 states and territories; 38 other countries; 19% are from out of state; 3% Black or African American, non-Hispanic/Latino; 3% Hispanic/Latino; 2% Asian, non-Hispanic/Latino; 0.5% American Indian or Alaska Native, non-Hispanic/Latino; 0.4% Race/ethnicity unknown; 9% international; 6% transferred in; 54% live on campus. *Retention:* 83% of full-time freshmen returned.

Freshmen *Admission:* 1,043 applied, 860 admitted, 364 enrolled. *Average high school GPA:* 3.62. *Test scores:* ACT scores over 18: 100%; ACT scores over 24: 65%; ACT scores over 30: 14%.
Faculty *Total:* 169, 80% full-time, 82% with terminal degrees. *Student/faculty ratio:* 12:1.
Academics *Calendar:* semesters. *Degrees:* bachelor's and master's (also offers evening program with significant enrollment not reflected in profile). *Special study options:* academic remediation for entering students, accelerated degree program, adult/continuing education programs, advanced placement credit, cooperative education, distance learning, double majors, English as a second language, honors programs, independent study, internships, off-campus study, part-time degree program, services for LD students, student-designed majors, study abroad, summer session for credit. *ROTC:* Army (c). *Unusual degree programs:* 3-2 engineering with Washington University in St. Louis; international management with American Graduate School of International Management, occupational therapy with Washington University in St. Louis.
Computers on Campus 389 computers/terminals are available on campus for general student use. Students can access the following: campus intranet, computer help desk, free student e-mail accounts, online (class) grades, online (class) registration, online (class) schedules, digital imaging lab, online bill payment/student information. Campuswide network is available. 100% of college-owned or -operated housing units are wired for high-speed Internet access. Wireless service is available via entire campus.
Student Life *Housing:* on-campus residence required through junior year. *Options:* coed, men-only, women-only. Campus housing is university owned and leased by the school. Freshman campus housing is guaranteed. *Activities and organizations:* drama/theater group, student-run newspaper, radio and television station, choral group, Drury Volunteer Corps (DVC), International Student Association, Lambda Chi Alpha, Zeta Tau Alpha, Kappa Delta, national fraternities, national sororities. *Campus security:* 24-hour emergency response devices and patrols, student patrols, late-night transport/escort service, controlled dormitory access, security cameras in parking areas, police substation on campus, well-lit campus. *Student services:* health clinic, personal/psychological counseling.
Athletics Member NCAA. All Division II. *Intercollegiate sports:* baseball M(s), basketball M(s)/W(s), cheerleading M(s)/W(s), cross-country running M(s)/W(s), golf M(s)/W(s), soccer M(s)/W(s), softball W(s), swimming and diving M(s)/W(s), tennis M(s)/W(s), track and field M(s)/W(s), volleyball W(s). *Intramural sports:* basketball M/W, cross-country running M(c)/W(c), football M/W, ice hockey M(c), soccer M/W, softball M/W, tennis M/W, ultimate Frisbee M/W, volleyball M/W.
Standardized Tests *Required:* SAT or ACT (for admission).
Costs (2013–14) *One-time required fee:* $150. *Comprehensive fee:* $30,615 includes full-time tuition ($21,700), mandatory fees ($715), and room and board ($8200). Full-time tuition and fees vary according to class time. Part-time tuition and fees vary according to class time. *Room and board:* Room and board charges vary according to board plan and housing facility. *Payment plans:* tuition prepayment, installment, deferred payment. *Waivers:* minority students, children of alumni, and employees or children of employees.
Financial Aid Of all full-time matriculated undergraduates who enrolled in 2012, 1,562 applied for aid, 1,531 were judged to have need, 1,432 had their need fully met. 332 Federal Work-Study jobs (averaging $2500). In 2012, 63 non-need-based awards were made. *Average percent of need met:* 83%. *Average financial aid package:* $8465. *Average need-based loan:* $6500. *Average need-based gift aid:* $7075. *Average non-need-based aid:* $4684. *Average indebtedness upon graduation:* $21,550.
Applying *Options:* electronic application, deferred entrance. *Application fee:* $25. *Required:* essay or personal statement, high school transcript, minimum 2.7 GPA, 1 letter of recommendation. *Recommended:* interview. *Application deadlines:* 8/1 (freshmen), rolling (transfers). *Notification:* continuous (freshmen), continuous (transfers).
Freshman Application Contact Ms. Dawn Hiles, Dean of Enrollment Management, Drury University, 900 North Benton Ave., Springfield, MO 65802. *Phone:* 417-873-7614. *Toll-free phone:* 800-922-2274. *Fax:* 417-866-3873. *E-mail:* druryad@drury.edu.
Website: http://www.drury.edu/.

Evangel University

Springfield, Missouri

- **Independent** comprehensive, founded 1955, affiliated with Assemblies of God
- **Urban** 80-acre campus
- **Coed** 1,879 undergraduate students, 91% full-time, 57% women, 43% men
- **Moderately difficult** entrance level, 67% of applicants were admitted

Undergraduates 1,704 full-time, 175 part-time. 47% are from out of state; 5% Black or African American, non-Hispanic/Latino; 5% Hispanic/Latino; 1% Asian, non-Hispanic/Latino; 1% American Indian or Alaska Native, non-Hispanic/Latino; 3% Two or more races, non-Hispanic/Latino; 7% Race/ethnicity unknown; 0.6% international; 7% transferred in; 68% live on campus.
Freshmen *Admission:* 1,260 applied, 839 admitted, 384 enrolled.
Faculty *Total:* 154, 70% full-time, 42% with terminal degrees.
Academics *Calendar:* semesters. *Degrees:* associate, bachelor's, and master's. ROTC: Army (c).
Computers on Campus Students can access the following: computer help desk, free student e-mail accounts, online (class) grades, online (class) registration, online (class) schedules, online payment. Campuswide network is available. Wireless service is available via classrooms, computer labs, learning centers, libraries, student centers.
Student Life *Housing:* on-campus residence required through senior year. *Options:* coed, men-only, women-only. Campus housing is university owned. *Campus security:* 24-hour emergency response devices and patrols, student patrols, late-night transport/escort service, controlled dormitory access.
Athletics Member NAIA. *Intercollegiate sports:* baseball M(s), basketball M(s)/W(s), cross-country running M(s)/W(s), football M(s), golf M(s)/W(s), softball W(s), tennis M(s)/W(s), track and field M(s)/W(s), volleyball W(s). *Intramural sports:* baseball M, basketball M/W, football M, golf M/W, soccer M/W, softball W, tennis M/W, volleyball W.
Standardized Tests *Required:* SAT or ACT (for admission).
Costs (2012–13) *Comprehensive fee:* $25,690 includes full-time tuition ($17,930), mandatory fees ($1120), and room and board ($6640). Full-time tuition and fees vary according to course load. Part-time tuition: $747 per credit hour. Part-time tuition and fees vary according to course load. *College room only:* $3430. Room and board charges vary according to board plan. *Payment plan:* installment. *Waivers:* employees or children of employees.
Financial Aid Of all full-time matriculated undergraduates who enrolled in 2011, 1,642 applied for aid, 1,476 were judged to have need, 127 had their need fully met. 1,135 Federal Work-Study jobs (averaging $1825). 88 state and other part-time jobs (averaging $1244). In 2011, 145 non-need-based awards were made. *Average percent of need met:* 60%. *Average financial aid package:* $14,057. *Average need-based loan:* $4640. *Average need-based gift aid:* $8980. *Average non-need-based aid:* $3938. *Average indebtedness upon graduation:* $34,434.
Applying *Options:* electronic application, deferred entrance. *Application fee:* $25. *Required:* essay or personal statement, high school transcript, interview.

Recommended: minimum 2.0 GPA. *Application deadline:* rolling (freshmen). *Notification:* continuous (freshmen).
Freshman Application Contact Evangel University, 1111 North Glenstone, Springfield, MO 65802. *Phone:* 417-865-2811 Ext. 7205. *Toll-free phone:* 800-382-6435. *Fax:* 417-865-9599. *E-mail:* admissions@evangel.edu. *Website:* http://www.evangel.edu/.

See below for display ad and page 1286 for the College Close-Up.

Everest College
Springfield, Missouri

Freshman Application Contact Admissions Office, Everest College, 1010 West Sunshine, Springfield, MO 65807-2488. *Phone:* 417-864-7220. *Toll-free phone:* 888-741-4270. *Fax:* 417-864-5697. *Website:* http://www.everest.edu/.

Fontbonne University
St. Louis, Missouri

- **Independent Roman Catholic** comprehensive, founded 1917
- **Suburban** 13-acre campus with easy access to St. Louis
- **Endowment** $20.3 million
- **Coed**
- **Moderately difficult** entrance level

Faculty *Student/faculty ratio:* 11:1.
Academics *Calendar:* semesters. *Degrees:* certificates, bachelor's, master's, and postbachelor's certificates.
Student Life *Campus security:* 24-hour patrols, late-night transport/escort service, controlled dormitory access.
Athletics Member NCAA, NAIA. All NCAA Division III.
Standardized Tests *Required:* SAT or ACT (for admission).
Costs (2012–13) *Comprehensive fee:* $30,654 includes full-time tuition ($22,054) and room and board ($8600). Full-time tuition and fees vary according to program. Part-time tuition and fees vary according to program. *Room*

and board: Room and board charges vary according to board plan and housing facility.

Financial Aid *In 2003,* 502 non-need-based awards were made. *Average percent of need met:* 86. *Average financial aid package:* $15,600.

Applying *Options:* electronic application, early admission, deferred entrance. *Application fee:* $25. *Required:* high school transcript, minimum 2.5 GPA. *Required for some:* essay or personal statement. *Recommended:* 2 letters of recommendation, interview.

Freshman Application Contact Dr. Greg Taylor, Executive Vice President, Fontbonne University, 6800 Wydown Boulevard, St. Louis, MO 63105. *Phone:* 314-889-1400. *Toll-free phone:* 800-205-5862. *Fax:* 314-889-1451. *E-mail:* gtaylor@fontbonne.edu.

Website: http://www.fontbonne.edu/.

Global University

Springfield, Missouri

- **Independent** comprehensive, founded 1948, affiliated with Assemblies of God
- **Small-town** campus
- **Coed** 4,176 undergraduate students, 9% full-time, 34% women, 66% men
- **Noncompetitive** entrance level

Undergraduates 381 full-time, 3,795 part-time. Students come from 50 states and territories; 127 other countries; 98% are from out of state.

Faculty *Total:* 633, 13% full-time, 46% with terminal degrees. *Student/faculty ratio:* 11:1.

Academics *Calendar:* continuous. *Degrees:* certificates, diplomas, associate, bachelor's, master's, doctoral, and postbachelor's certificates (offers only external degree programs). *Special study options:* adult/continuing education programs, distance learning, double majors, external degree program, independent study, off-campus study, part-time degree program.

Computers on Campus Students can access the following: free student e-mail accounts.

Student Life *Campus security:* 24-hour emergency response devices.

Costs (2013–14) *Tuition:* $3870 full-time, $129 per credit part-time.

Applying *Application fee:* $40. *Required:* high school transcript. *Required for some:* 1 letter of recommendation. *Recommended:* essay or personal statement. *Application deadlines:* rolling (freshmen), rolling (transfers).

Freshman Application Contact Rev. Todd Waggoner, Enrollment and International Student Services Director, Global University, 1211 South Glenstone Avenue, Springfield, MO 65804. *Phone:* 417-862-9533 Ext. 2335. *Toll-free phone:* 800-443-1083. *Fax:* 417-863-9621. *E-mail:* twaggoner@globaluniversity.edu.

Website: http://www.globaluniversity.edu/.

Goldfarb School of Nursing at Barnes-Jewish College

St. Louis, Missouri

- **Independent** comprehensive, founded 1902
- **Urban** campus
- **Endowment** $20.0 million
- **Coed, primarily women** 637 undergraduate students, 99% full-time, 89% women, 11% men
- **Moderately difficult** entrance level

Undergraduates 631 full-time, 6 part-time. Students come from 15 states and territories; 10 other countries; 25% are from out of state; 6% Black or African American, non-Hispanic/Latino; 2% Hispanic/Latino; 3% Asian, non-Hispanic/Latino; 0.3% Native Hawaiian or other Pacific Islander, non-Hispanic/Latino; 0.2% American Indian or Alaska Native, non-Hispanic/Latino; 1% Two or more races, non-Hispanic/Latino; 5% Race/ethnicity unknown; 100% transferred in.

Faculty *Total:* 50, 86% full-time, 60% with terminal degrees. *Student/faculty ratio:* 8:1.

Academics *Calendar:* trimesters. *Degrees:* bachelor's, master's, doctoral, and post-master's certificates. *Special study options:* accelerated degree program, advanced placement credit, independent study, off-campus study, services for LD students, summer session for credit.

Computers on Campus 160 computers/terminals are available on campus for general student use. Students can access the following: campus intranet, computer help desk, free student e-mail accounts, software, research databases. Campuswide network is available. Wireless service is available via entire campus.

Student Life *Housing:* college housing not available. *Activities and organizations:* student-run newspaper, Student Nurses Association. *Campus security:* 24-hour patrols, late-night transport/escort service. *Student services:* health clinic, personal/psychological counseling.

Costs (2013–14) *Tuition:* $25,768 full-time. Full-time tuition and fees vary according to course load and degree level. Part-time tuition and fees vary according to course load and degree level. *Required fees:* $1565 full-time. *Payment plan:* installment.

Applying *Options:* deferred entrance. *Application fee:* $50. *Application deadline:* rolling (transfers). *Notification:* continuous (transfers).

Freshman Application Contact Goldfarb School of Nursing at Barnes-Jewish College, 4483 Duncan Avenue, St. Louis, MO 63110. *Phone:* 314-362-9155. *Toll-free phone:* 800-832-9009.

Website: http://www.barnesjewishcollege.edu/.

Graceland University

Independence, Missouri

Freshman Application Contact Admissions, Graceland University, 1401 West Truman Road, Independence, MO 64050-3434. *Phone:* 816-833-0524. *Toll-free phone:* 866-GRACELAND. *E-mail:* gic@graceland.edu. *Website:* http://www.graceland.edu/.

Grantham University

Kansas City, Missouri

- **Proprietary** comprehensive, founded 1951
- **Urban** campus with easy access to Kansas City
- **Coed** 7,898 undergraduate students, 54% full-time, 32% women, 68% men
- **Noncompetitive** entrance level

Undergraduates 4,267 full-time, 3,631 part-time.

Faculty *Total:* 10, 100% full-time. *Student/faculty ratio:* 17:1.

Academics *Calendar:* continuous. *Degrees:* associate, bachelor's, and master's (offers only external degree programs). *Special study options:* academic remediation for entering students, accelerated degree program, adult/continuing education programs, advanced placement credit, distance learning, external degree program, independent study, part-time degree program, student-designed majors.

Computers on Campus Students can access the following: free student e-mail accounts, online (class) grades, online (class) registration, online (class) schedules.

Student Life *Housing:* college housing not available.

Costs (2012–13) *One-time required fee:* $30. *Tuition:* $6360 full-time, $265 per credit hour part-time. *Required fees:* $120 full-time, $30 per term part-time. *Payment plans:* installment, deferred payment. *Waivers:* employees or children of employees.

Applying *Options:* electronic application. *Application fee:* $30. *Application deadlines:* rolling (freshmen), rolling (out-of-state freshmen), rolling (transfers). *Notification:* continuous (freshmen), continuous (out-of-state freshmen), continuous (transfers).

Freshman Application Contact Mr. Les Hyde, Vice President Admissions, Grantham University, 7200 NW 86th Street, Kansas City, MO 64153. *Phone:* 800-955-2527. *Toll-free phone:* 800-955-2527. *Fax:* 816-595-5757. *E-mail:* admissions@grantham.edu.

Website: http://www.grantham.edu/.

Hannibal-LaGrange University

Hannibal, Missouri

- **Independent Southern Baptist** comprehensive, founded 1858
- **Small-town** 110-acre campus
- **Coed**
- **Minimally difficult** entrance level

Faculty *Student/faculty ratio:* 13:1.

Academics *Calendar:* semesters. *Degrees:* certificates, associate, bachelor's, and master's.

Student Life *Campus security:* 24-hour emergency response devices and patrols, controlled dormitory access.

Athletics Member NAIA.

Standardized Tests *Required:* SAT or ACT (for admission).

Costs (2012–13) *Comprehensive fee:* $24,370 includes full-time tuition ($17,150), mandatory fees ($650), and room and board ($6570). Full-time tuition and fees vary according to course load, degree level, program, and reciprocity agreements. Part-time tuition: $571 per credit. Part-time tuition and fees vary according to course load, degree level, program, and reciprocity agreements. *Room and board:* Room and board charges vary according to housing facility.
Financial Aid *Of all full-time matriculated undergraduates who enrolled in 2011,* 80 Federal Work-Study jobs (averaging $750).
Applying *Options:* electronic application, early admission, deferred entrance. *Application fee:* $25. *Required:* high school transcript, minimum 2.0 GPA. *Required for some:* GED.
Freshman Application Contact Dr. Raymond Carty, Vice President for Enrollment Management, Hannibal-LaGrange University, 2800 Palmyra Road, Hannibal, MO 63401-1999. *Phone:* 573-629-2278. *Toll-free phone:* 800-HLG-1119. *E-mail:* admissio@hlg.edu.
Website: http://www.hlg.edu/.

Harris-Stowe State University

St. Louis, Missouri

- **State-supported** 4-year, founded 1857, part of Missouri Coordinating Board for Higher Education
- **Urban** 22-acre campus
- **Coed** 1,484 undergraduate students, 74% full-time, 65% women, 35% men
- **Noncompetitive** entrance level, 100% of applicants were admitted

Undergraduates 1,096 full-time, 388 part-time. Students come from 15 states and territories; 5 other countries; 11% are from out of state; 84% Black or African American, non-Hispanic/Latino; 2% Hispanic/Latino; 0.3% Asian, non-Hispanic/Latino; 0.1% American Indian or Alaska Native, non-Hispanic/Latino; 3% Two or more races, non-Hispanic/Latino; 2% Race/ethnicity unknown; 0.2% international; 11% transferred in; 15% live on campus. *Retention:* 44% of full-time freshmen returned.
Freshmen *Admission:* 884 applied, 884 admitted, 320 enrolled. *Average high school GPA:* 2.4. *Test scores:* ACT scores over 18: 26%; ACT scores over 24: 2%.
Faculty *Total:* 203, 27% full-time, 37% with terminal degrees. *Student/faculty ratio:* 12:1.
Academics *Calendar:* semesters. *Degree:* bachelor's. *Special study options:* academic remediation for entering students, advanced placement credit, cooperative education, internships, off-campus study, part-time degree program, services for LD students, student-designed majors, summer session for credit. *ROTC:* Army (c), Air Force (c). *Unusual degree programs:* 3-2 engineering with Saint Louis University.
Computers on Campus 333 computers/terminals are available on campus for general student use. Students can access the following: computer help desk, free student e-mail accounts, online (class) grades, online (class) registration, online (class) schedules. Campuswide network is available. 100% of college-owned or -operated housing units are wired for high-speed Internet access. Wireless service is available via entire campus.
Student Life *Housing options:* coed. Campus housing is university owned. Freshman applicants given priority for college housing. *Activities and organizations:* drama/theater group, choral group, Drama Club, Concert chorale, Student Government Association, Multicultural Council, Student Ambassadors, national fraternities, national sororities. *Campus security:* 24-hour emergency response devices and patrols, late-night transport/escort service, controlled dormitory access. *Student services:* health clinic, personal/psychological counseling.
Athletics Member NAIA. *Intercollegiate sports:* baseball M(s), basketball M(s)/W(s), cheerleading M(s)/W(s), soccer M(s)/W(s), softball W(s), volleyball W(s).
Standardized Tests *Required for some:* institutional placement test. *Recommended:* SAT or ACT (for admission).
Financial Aid Of all full-time matriculated undergraduates who enrolled in 2008, 990 applied for aid, 890 were judged to have need, 200 had their need fully met. 86 Federal Work-Study jobs (averaging $2000). 80 state and other part-time jobs (averaging $2000). *Average percent of need met:* 90%. *Average financial aid package:* $9500. *Average need-based loan:* $5000. *Average need-based gift aid:* $4500. *Average non-need-based aid:* $3000. *Average indebtedness upon graduation:* $16,000.
Applying *Options:* electronic application, early admission, deferred entrance. *Application fee:* $15. *Required:* high school transcript. *Application deadlines:* rolling (freshmen), rolling (transfers). *Notification:* continuous (freshmen), continuous (transfers).
Freshman Application Contact Meghan Sprung, Assistant Director of Admissions, Harris-Stowe State University, 3026 Laclede Avenue, St. Louis, MO 63103. *Phone:* 314-340-3300. *Fax:* 314-340-3555. *E-mail:* admissions@hssu.edu.
Website: http://www.hssu.edu/.

Hickey College

St. Louis, Missouri

- **Private** 4-year, founded 1933
- **Suburban** campus with easy access to St. Louis
- **Coed** 500 undergraduate students
- 71% of applicants were admitted

Freshmen *Admission:* 916 applied, 651 admitted.
Academics *Calendar:* semesters. *Degrees:* diplomas, associate, and bachelor's. *Special study options:* accelerated degree program, internships.
Freshman Application Contact Admissions Office, Hickey College, 940 West Port Plaza, Suite 101, St. Louis, MO 63146. *Phone:* 314-434-2212. *Toll-free phone:* 800-777-1544.
Website: http://www.hickeycollege.edu/.

See next page for display ad and page 1320 for the College Close-Up.

ITT Technical Institute

Arnold, Missouri

- **Proprietary** primarily 2-year, founded 1997, part of ITT Educational Services, Inc.
- **Coed**
- **Minimally difficult** entrance level

Academics *Calendar:* quarters. *Degrees:* associate and bachelor's.
Freshman Application Contact Director of Recruitment, ITT Technical Institute, 1930 Meyer Drury Drive, Arnold, MO 63010. *Phone:* 636-464-6600. *Toll-free phone:* 888-488-1082.
Website: http://www.itt-tech.edu/.

ITT Technical Institute

Earth City, Missouri

- **Proprietary** primarily 2-year, founded 1936, part of ITT Educational Services, Inc.
- **Suburban** campus
- **Coed**
- **Minimally difficult** entrance level

Academics *Calendar:* quarters. *Degrees:* associate and bachelor's.
Freshman Application Contact Director of Recruitment, ITT Technical Institute, 3640 Corporate Trail Drive, Earth City, MO 63045. *Phone:* 314-298-7800. *Toll-free phone:* 800-235-5488.
Website: http://www.itt-tech.edu/.

ITT Technical Institute

Kansas City, Missouri

- **Proprietary** primarily 2-year, founded 2004, part of ITT Educational Services, Inc.
- **Coed**
- **Minimally difficult** entrance level

Academics *Calendar:* quarters. *Degrees:* associate and bachelor's.
Freshman Application Contact Director of Recruitment, ITT Technical Institute, 9150 East 41st Terrace, Kansas City, MO 64133. *Phone:* 816-276-1400. *Toll-free phone:* 877-488-1442.
Website: http://www.itt-tech.edu/.

ITT Technical Institute

Springfield, Missouri

- **Proprietary** 4-year, part of ITT Educational Services, Inc.
- **Coed**
- **Minimally difficult** entrance level

Academics *Calendar:* quarters. *Degrees:* associate and bachelor's.

Freshman Application Contact Director of Recruitment, ITT Technical Institute, 3216 South National Avenue, Springfield, MO 65807. *Phone:* 417-877-4800. *Toll-free phone:* 877-219-4387.

Website: http://www.itt-tech.edu/.

Kansas City Art Institute

Kansas City, Missouri

- **Independent** 4-year, founded 1885
- **Urban** 18-acre campus
- **Endowment** $43.7 million
- **Coed**
- **Moderately difficult** entrance level

Academics *Calendar:* semesters. *Degree:* bachelor's.

Student Life *Campus security:* 24-hour emergency response devices and patrols, late-night transport/escort service, controlled dormitory access.

Standardized Tests *Required:* SAT or ACT (for admission).

Costs (2012–13) *Comprehensive fee:* $41,364 includes full-time tuition ($31,992) and room and board ($9372).

Financial Aid *Of all full-time matriculated undergraduates who enrolled in 2012,* 780 applied for aid, 745 were judged to have need, 80 had their need fully met. 140 Federal Work-Study jobs (averaging $1205). 200 state and other part-time jobs (averaging $1000). *In 2012,* 120 non-need-based awards were made. *Average percent of need met:* 64. *Average financial aid package:* $22,050. *Average need-based loan:* $4579. *Average need-based gift aid:* $17,504. *Average non-need-based aid:* $13,052. *Average indebtedness upon graduation:* $26,660.

Applying *Options:* electronic application, deferred entrance. *Application fee:* $35. *Required:* essay or personal statement, high school transcript, minimum 2.5 GPA, 2 letters of recommendation, portfolio, statement of purpose. *Recommended:* interview.

Freshman Application Contact Mr. Gerald Valet, Director of Admission Technology, Kansas City Art Institute, 4415 Warwick Boulevard, Kansas City, MO 64111-1874. *Phone:* 816-474-5224. *Toll-free phone:* 800-522-5224. *Fax:* 816-802-3309. *E-mail:* admiss@kcai.edu.

Website: http://www.kcai.edu/.

Lincoln University

Jefferson City, Missouri

- **State-supported** comprehensive, founded 1866, part of Missouri Coordinating Board for Higher Education
- **Small-town** 171-acre campus
- **Endowment** $1.5 million
- **Coed** 3,013 undergraduate students, 64% full-time, 58% women, 42% men
- **Noncompetitive** entrance level, 43% of applicants were admitted

Undergraduates 1,927 full-time, 1,086 part-time. Students come from 36 states and territories; 16 other countries; 16% are from out of state; 44% Black or African American, non-Hispanic/Latino; 2% Hispanic/Latino; 0.3% Asian, non-Hispanic/Latino; 0.4% American Indian or Alaska Native, non-Hispanic/Latino; 0.6% Two or more races, non-Hispanic/Latino; 2% Race/ethnicity unknown; 2% international; 7% transferred in; 22% live on campus. *Retention:* 36% of full-time freshmen returned.

Freshmen *Admission:* 2,487 applied, 1,059 admitted, 449 enrolled. *Average high school GPA:* 2.7. *Test scores:* SAT critical reading scores over 500: 30%; SAT math scores over 500: 20%; ACT scores over 18: 49%; SAT critical reading scores over 600: 20%; ACT scores over 24: 7%.

Faculty *Total:* 214, 62% full-time. *Student/faculty ratio:* 15:1.

Academics *Calendar:* semesters. *Degrees:* associate, bachelor's, master's, and post-master's certificates. *Special study options:* academic remediation for entering students, accelerated degree program, adult/continuing education programs, advanced placement credit, distance learning, double majors, honors programs, independent study, internships, off-campus study, part-time degree program, services for LD students, study abroad, summer session for credit. *ROTC:* Army (b), Navy (c), Air Force (c).

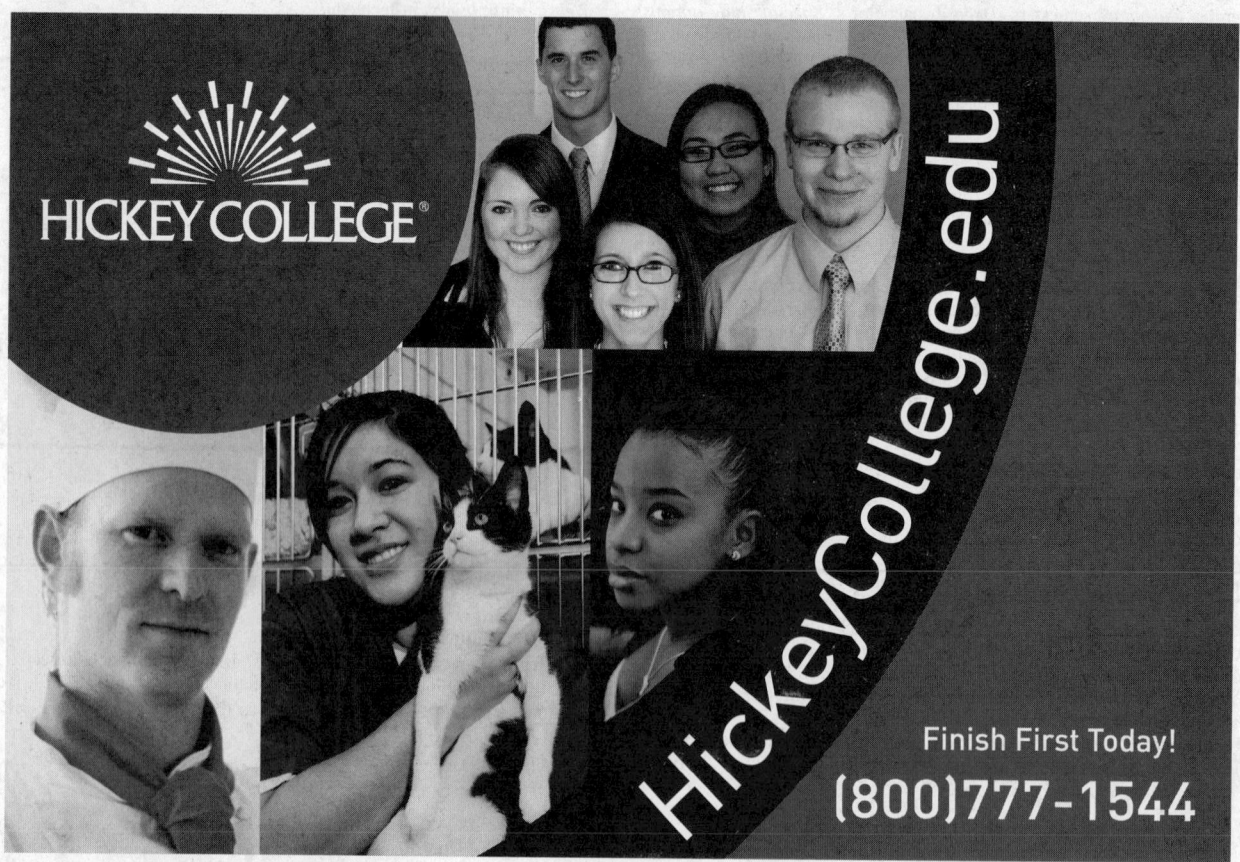

Computers on Campus 250 computers/terminals and 1,100 ports are available on campus for general student use. Students can access the following: campus intranet, computer help desk, free student e-mail accounts, online (class) grades, online (class) registration, online (class) schedules. Campus-wide network is available. 100% of college-owned or -operated housing units are wired for high-speed Internet access. Wireless service is available via entire campus.

Student Life *Housing:* on-campus residence required through sophomore year. *Options:* coed, men-only, women-only. Campus housing is university owned. *Activities and organizations:* drama/theater group, student-run newspaper, radio and television station, choral group, marching band, Student Government Association (SGA), Lincoln University Band, Alpha Kappa Mu, Army ROTC, International Students Association, national fraternities, national sororities. *Campus security:* 24-hour emergency response devices and patrols, student patrols, late-night transport/escort service, controlled dormitory access, security-related training upon request, Operation ID-ent, Timely Warnings, text message safety alerts, webpage with helpful tips. *Student services:* health clinic, personal/psychological counseling.

Athletics Member NCAA. All Division II. *Intercollegiate sports:* baseball M(s), basketball M(s)/W(s), cheerleading W(s), cross-country running W(s), football M(s), golf M(s)/W(s), softball W(s), tennis W(s), track and field M(s)/W(s). *Intramural sports:* basketball M/W, bowling M/W, volleyball M/W, weight lifting M/W.

Standardized Tests *Required:* SAT or ACT (for admission).

Costs (2012–13) *Tuition:* state resident $6150 full-time, $205 per credit hour part-time; nonresident $12,150 full-time, $405 per credit hour part-time. Full-time tuition and fees vary according to location and reciprocity agreements. Part-time tuition and fees vary according to location and reciprocity agreements. *Required fees:* $474 full-time, $17 per credit hour part-time, $36 part-time. *Room and board:* $4750; room only: $2626. Room and board charges vary according to board plan and housing facility. *Payment plans:* installment, deferred payment. *Waivers:* employees or children of employees.

Financial Aid Of all full-time matriculated undergraduates who enrolled in 2012, 1,719 applied for aid, 1,551 were judged to have need, 57 had their need fully met. 125 Federal Work-Study jobs (averaging $1490). 188 state and other part-time jobs (averaging $3078). In 2012, 1 non-need-based awards were made. *Average percent of need met:* 58%. *Average financial aid package:* $9876. *Average need-based loan:* $4128. *Average need-based gift aid:* $5467. *Average non-need-based aid:* $2000. *Average indebtedness upon graduation:* $27,910.

Applying *Options:* electronic application, deferred entrance. *Application fee:* $20. *Required:* high school transcript. *Required for some:* minimum 2.0 GPA, audition for sacred music and music education. *Application deadlines:* 7/15 (freshmen), 7/15 (out-of-state freshmen), 7/15 (transfers). *Notification:* continuous (freshmen), continuous (out-of-state freshmen), continuous (transfers).
Freshman Application Contact Annette Crowder, Director of Admissions, Lincoln University, Office of Admissions, 820 Chestnut Street, B-7 Young Hall, Jefferson City, MO 65102-0029. *Phone:* 573-681-5599. *Toll-free phone:* 800-521-5052. *Fax:* 573-681-5889. *E-mail:* enroll@lincolnu.edu. *Website:* http://www.lincolnu.edu/.

Lindenwood University

St. Charles, Missouri

- **Independent Presbyterian** comprehensive, founded 1827
- **Suburban** 500-acre campus with easy access to St. Louis
- **Endowment** $108.9 million
- **Coed** 8,296 undergraduate students, 89% full-time, 54% women, 46% men
- **Moderately difficult** entrance level, 66% of applicants were admitted

Undergraduates 7,399 full-time, 897 part-time. Students come from 47 states and territories; 88 other countries; 27% are from out of state; 14% Black or African American, non-Hispanic/Latino; 4% Hispanic/Latino; 0.6% Asian, non-Hispanic/Latino; 0.2% Native Hawaiian or other Pacific Islander, non-Hispanic/Latino; 0.4% American Indian or Alaska Native, non-Hispanic/Latino; 2% Two or more races, non-Hispanic/Latino; 10% Race/ethnicity unknown; 10% international; 7% transferred in; 52% live on campus. *Retention:* 72% of full-time freshmen returned.
Freshmen *Admission:* 2,807 applied, 1,846 admitted, 1,351 enrolled. *Average high school GPA:* 3.25. *Test scores:* SAT critical reading scores over 500: 49%; SAT math scores over 500: 62%; SAT writing scores over 500: 30%; ACT scores over 18: 97%; SAT critical reading scores over 600: 14%; SAT math scores over 600: 14%; SAT writing scores over 600: 10%; ACT scores over 24: 33%; SAT critical reading scores over 700: 3%; SAT math scores over 700: 2%; ACT scores over 30: 6%.
Faculty *Total:* 920, 25% full-time, 33% with terminal degrees. *Student/faculty ratio:* 17:1.

Academics *Calendar:* 4-1-4 for daytime programs; quarters and trimesters for evening programs. *Degrees:* bachelor's, master's, doctoral, post-master's, and postbachelor's certificates. *Special study options:* academic remediation for entering students, accelerated degree program, adult/continuing education programs, advanced placement credit, distance learning, double majors, English as a second language, external degree program, freshman honors college, honors programs, independent study, internships, off-campus study, part-time degree program, services for LD students, student-designed majors, study abroad, summer session for credit. *ROTC:* Army (b). *Unusual degree programs:* 3-2 engineering with University of Missouri-Columbia.

Computers on Campus 240 computers/terminals are available on campus for general student use. Students can access the following: campus intranet, computer help desk, free student e-mail accounts, online (class) grades, online (class) registration, online (class) schedules, Blackboard. Campuswide network is available. 100% of college-owned or -operated housing units are wired for high-speed Internet access. Wireless service is available via classrooms, computer centers, computer labs, dorm rooms, learning centers, libraries, student centers.

Student Life *Housing options:* men-only, women-only. Campus housing is university owned. Freshman applicants given priority for college housing. *Activities and organizations:* drama/theater group, student-run newspaper, radio and television station, choral group, marching band, Social Work Student Association, Kappa Delta Pi, International Student Fellowship, Cru, Delta Zeta, national fraternities, national sororities. *Campus security:* 24-hour emergency response devices and patrols, late-night transport/escort service, controlled dormitory access. *Student services:* health clinic, personal/psychological counseling.

Athletics Member NCAA, NAIA, USCAA. All NCAA Division II. *Intercollegiate sports:* baseball M(s), basketball M(s)/W(s), bowling M(s)/W(s), cheerleading M(s)/W(s), cross-country running M(s)/W(s), field hockey W(s), football M(s), golf M(s)/W(s), gymnastics W(s), ice hockey M(s)/W(s), lacrosse M(s)/W(s), riflery M(s)/W(s), rugby M(s)/W(s), soccer M(s)/W(s), softball W(s), swimming and diving M(s)/W(s), table tennis M(s)/W(s), tennis M(s)/W(s), track and field M(s)/W(s), volleyball M(s)/W(s), water polo M(s)/W(s), weight lifting M(s)/W(s), wrestling M(s)/W(s).

Standardized Tests *Required:* SAT or ACT (for admission).

Costs (2012–13) *Comprehensive fee:* $22,180 includes full-time tuition ($14,250), mandatory fees ($350), and room and board ($7580). Full-time tuition and fees vary according to program. Part-time tuition: $412 per credit hour. Part-time tuition and fees vary according to course load. *College room only:* $4180. *Payment plans:* installment, deferred payment. *Waivers:* senior citizens and employees or children of employees.

Financial Aid Of all full-time matriculated undergraduates who enrolled in 2012, 5,148 applied for aid, 3,984 were judged to have need, 2,984 had their need fully met. In 2012, 2219 non-need-based awards were made. *Average percent of need met:* 90%. *Average financial aid package:* $9093. *Average need-based loan:* $4579. *Average need-based gift aid:* $4819. *Average non-need-based aid:* $3319.

Applying *Options:* electronic application, deferred entrance. *Application fee:* $30. *Required:* high school transcript, minimum 2.5 GPA, Personal resume indicating community service, youth leadership, clubs, organizations, and non-academic experience. *Recommended:* essay or personal statement, 3 letters of recommendation, interview. *Application deadlines:* rolling (freshmen), rolling (transfers). *Notification:* continuous (freshmen), continuous (transfers). **Freshman Application Contact** Lindenwood University, 209 South Kingshighway, St. Charles, MO 63301-1695. *Phone:* 636-949-4949. *Website:* http://www.lindenwood.edu/.

See previous page for display ad and page 1358 for the College Close-Up.

Logan University–College of Chiropractic

Chesterfield, Missouri

- **Independent** upper-level, founded 1935
- **Suburban** 111-acre campus with easy access to St. Louis
- **Endowment** $13.9 million
- **Coed** 96 undergraduate students, 48% full-time, 45% women, 55% men
- **Moderately difficult** entrance level, 72% of applicants were admitted

Undergraduates 46 full-time, 50 part-time. 2% Black or African American, non-Hispanic/Latino; 1% Asian, non-Hispanic/Latino; 2% Two or more races, non-Hispanic/Latino; 24% Race/ethnicity unknown; 1% international.

Freshmen *Admission:* 108 applied, 78 admitted.

Faculty *Total:* 102, 48% full-time. *Student/faculty ratio:* 12:1.

Academics *Calendar:* trimesters. *Degrees:* bachelor's, master's, and doctoral. *Special study options:* adult/continuing education programs, advanced place-

ment credit, distance learning, independent study, internships, part-time degree program, services for LD students.

Computers on Campus 95 computers/terminals and 1,000 ports are available on campus for general student use. Students can access the following: computer help desk, free student e-mail accounts, online (class) grades, online (class) registration, online (class) schedules, on-line classes, course homepages, wireless technologies, Academic Software Solutions for teaching and learning, library resources, academic records access. Campuswide network is available. Wireless service is available via entire campus.

Student Life *Housing:* college housing not available. *Activities and organizations:* Pi Kappa Chi, Lambda Kappa Chi, Chiro Sigma, Student American Chiropractic Association, Omega Sigma Pi, national fraternities, national sororities. *Campus security:* 24-hour patrols, late-night transport/escort service. *Student services:* health clinic, personal/psychological counseling.

Athletics *Intercollegiate sports:* basketball M(c)/W(c), golf M(c), soccer M(c), tennis M(c). *Intramural sports:* basketball M/W, football M, ice hockey M, softball M/W, volleyball M/W.

Costs (2013–14) *Tuition:* $4800 full-time, $200 per credit hour part-time. *Required fees:* $420 full-time, $140 per term part-time. *Waivers:* employees or children of employees.

Financial Aid Of all full-time matriculated undergraduates who enrolled in 1999, 160 applied for aid, 160 were judged to have need, 130 had their need fully met. 130 Federal Work-Study jobs (averaging $2693). *Average percent of need met:* 100%. *Average need-based loan:* $3500. *Average need-based gift aid:* $3000.

Applying *Options:* electronic application, deferred entrance. *Application fee:* $50. *Application deadline:* rolling (transfers). *Notification:* continuous (transfers).

Application Contact Logan University–College of Chiropractic, 1851 Schoettler Road, Chesterfield, MO 63006-1065. *Phone:* 636-227-2100. *Toll-free phone:* 800-533-9210. *Fax:* 636-207-2425. *E-mail:* loganadm@logan.edu. *Website:* http://www.logan.edu/.

Maryville University of Saint Louis

St. Louis, Missouri

- **Independent** comprehensive, founded 1872
- **Suburban** 130-acre campus with easy access to St. Louis
- **Endowment** $34.1 million
- **Coed** 2,980 undergraduate students, 58% full-time, 73% women, 27% men
- **Moderately difficult** entrance level, 71% of applicants were admitted

Undergraduates 1,725 full-time, 1,255 part-time. Students come from 34 states and territories; 30 other countries; 17% are from out of state; 9% Black or African American, non-Hispanic/Latino; 2% Hispanic/Latino; 1% Asian, non-Hispanic/Latino; 0.2% Native Hawaiian or other Pacific Islander, non-Hispanic/Latino; 0.3% American Indian or Alaska Native, non-Hispanic/Latino; 2% Two or more races, non-Hispanic/Latino; 8% Race/ethnicity unknown; 2% international; 13% transferred in; 22% live on campus. *Retention:* 87% of full-time freshmen returned.

Freshmen *Admission:* 1,281 applied, 913 admitted, 368 enrolled. *Average high school GPA:* 3.6. *Test scores:* ACT scores over 18: 99%; ACT scores over 24: 71%; ACT scores over 30: 9%.

Faculty *Total:* 433, 26% full-time, 50% with terminal degrees. *Student/faculty ratio:* 12:1.

Academics *Calendar:* semesters. *Degrees:* bachelor's, master's, doctoral, and postbachelor's certificates. *Special study options:* accelerated degree program, adult/continuing education programs, advanced placement credit, cooperative education, distance learning, double majors, English as a second language, honors programs, independent study, internships, off-campus study, part-time degree program, services for LD students, study abroad, summer session for credit. *ROTC:* Army (c). *Unusual degree programs:* 3-2 business administration; engineering with Washington University in St. Louis; social work with Saint Louis University; education.

Computers on Campus 530 computers/terminals are available on campus for general student use. Students can access the following: campus intranet, computer help desk, free student e-mail accounts, online (class) grades, online (class) registration, online (class) schedules, specialized software, university catalog. Campuswide network is available. 100% of college-owned or -operated housing units are wired for high-speed Internet access. Wireless service is available via entire campus.

Student Life *Housing options:* coed. Campus housing is university owned. *Activities and organizations:* drama/theater group, student-run newspaper, choral group, Campus Activities Board, Physical Therapy Club, Student Nurses

Association, Community Service Club. *Campus security:* 24-hour emergency response devices and patrols, late-night transport/escort service, controlled dormitory access, video security system in residence halls, self-defense and education programs. *Student services:* health clinic, personal/psychological counseling.

Athletics Member NCAA. All Division II. *Intercollegiate sports:* baseball M(s), basketball M(s)/W(s), cross-country running M(s)/W(s), golf M(s)/W(s), soccer M(s)/W(s), softball W(s), tennis M(s)/W(s), track and field M(s)/W(s), volleyball W(s), wrestling M(s). *Intramural sports:* basketball M/W, cheerleading M/W, football M/W, soccer M/W, softball W, volleyball M/W.

Standardized Tests *Required:* SAT or ACT (for admission).

Costs (2012–13) *Comprehensive fee:* $32,988 includes full-time tuition ($22,786), mandatory fees ($960), and room and board ($9242). Full-time tuition and fees vary according to course load. Part-time tuition: $683 per credit hour. Part-time tuition and fees vary according to class time. *Required fees:* $240 per term part-time. *Room and board:* Room and board charges vary according to board plan and housing facility. *Payment plans:* installment, deferred payment. *Waivers:* senior citizens and employees or children of employees.

Financial Aid Of all full-time matriculated undergraduates who enrolled in 2012, 1,380 applied for aid, 1,258 were judged to have need, 206 had their need fully met. 273 Federal Work-Study jobs (averaging $658). 133 state and other part-time jobs (averaging $2435). In 2012, 332 non-need-based awards were made. *Average percent of need met:* 56%. *Average financial aid package:* $16,507. *Average need-based loan:* $4794. *Average need-based gift aid:* $10,871. *Average non-need-based aid:* $7317. *Average indebtedness upon graduation:* $21,835.

Applying *Options:* electronic application, deferred entrance. *Application fee:* $30. *Required:* high school transcript, minimum 2.5 GPA. *Required for some:* essay or personal statement, interview, audition, portfolio. *Application deadlines:* 8/15 (freshmen), rolling (transfers). *Notification:* continuous (freshmen), continuous (transfers).

Freshman Application Contact Ms. Shani Lenore-Jenkins, Assistant Vice President of Enrollment, Maryville University of Saint Louis, 650 Maryville University Drive, St. Louis, MO 63141-7299. *Phone:* 314-529-9350. *Toll-free phone:* 800-627-9855. *Fax:* 314-529-9927. *E-mail:* admissions@maryville.edu.
Website: http://www.maryville.edu/.

Metro Business College

Cape Girardeau, Missouri

Director of Admissions Ms. Kyla Evans, Admissions Director, Metro Business College, 1732 North Kingshighway, Cape Girardeau, MO 63701. *Phone:* 573-334-9181. *Toll-free phone:* 888-206-4545. *Fax:* 573-334-0617. *Website:* http://www.metrobusinesscollege.edu/.

Missouri Baptist University

St. Louis, Missouri

- **Independent Southern Baptist** comprehensive, founded 1964
- **Suburban** 65-acre campus with easy access to Saint Louis
- **Endowment** $3.6 million
- **Coed** 3,850 undergraduate students, 37% full-time, 59% women, 41% men
- **Moderately difficult** entrance level, 58% of applicants were admitted

Undergraduates 1,429 full-time, 2,421 part-time. Students come from 34 states and territories; 13 other countries; 19% are from out of state; 11% Black or African American, non-Hispanic/Latino; 3% Hispanic/Latino; 0.8% Asian, non-Hispanic/Latino; 0.4% American Indian or Alaska Native, non-Hispanic/Latino; 1% Two or more races, non-Hispanic/Latino; 2% Race/ethnicity unknown; 2% international; 9% transferred in; 14% live on campus. *Retention:* 60% of full-time freshmen returned.

Freshmen *Admission:* 900 applied, 520 admitted, 242 enrolled. *Average high school GPA:* 3.06.

Faculty *Total:* 309, 24% full-time, 27% with terminal degrees. *Student/faculty ratio:* 12:1.

Academics *Calendar:* semesters. *Degrees:* certificates, associate, bachelor's, master's, doctoral, post-master's, and postbachelor's certificates. *Special study options:* academic remediation for entering students, accelerated degree program, adult/continuing education programs, advanced placement credit, distance learning, double majors, honors programs, independent study, internships, off-campus study, part-time degree program, services for LD students, student-designed majors, study abroad, summer session for credit. *ROTC:* Army (c).

Computers on Campus 100 computers/terminals are available on campus for general student use. Students can access the following: campus intranet, computer help desk, free student e-mail accounts, online (class) grades, online (class) registration, online (class) schedules. Campuswide network is available. 100% of college-owned or -operated housing units are wired for high-speed Internet access. Wireless service is available via entire campus.

Student Life *Housing options:* men-only, women-only. Campus housing is university owned. *Activities and organizations:* drama/theater group, student-run radio station, choral group, Baptist Collegiate Ministry, Students in Free Enterprise (SIFE), Missouri State Teacher's Association, Fellowship of Christian Athletes, Ministerial Alliance. *Campus security:* 24-hour emergency response devices and patrols, late-night transport/escort service, controlled dormitory access, self-defense classes. *Student services:* personal/psychological counseling.

Athletics Member NAIA. *Intercollegiate sports:* baseball M(s), basketball M(s)/W(s), bowling M(s)(c)/W(s)(c), cheerleading M(s)/W(s), cross-country running M(s)/W(s), golf M(s)/W(s), lacrosse M(s)(c)/W(s)(c), soccer M(s)/W(s), softball W(s), tennis M(s)/W(s), track and field M(s)/W(s), volleyball M(s)/W(s), wrestling M(s)/W(s). *Intramural sports:* basketball M/W, football M/W, soccer M/W, softball M/W, volleyball M/W.

Standardized Tests *Required for some:* SAT or ACT (for admission).

Costs (2012–13) *Comprehensive fee:* $28,884 includes full-time tuition ($19,730), mandatory fees ($924), and room and board ($8230). Full-time tuition and fees vary according to course load and location. Part-time tuition: $680 per credit. Part-time tuition and fees vary according to course load and location. *Required fees:* $22 per credit part-time, $30 per term part-time. *Room and board:* Room and board charges vary according to board plan and housing facility. *Payment plan:* installment. *Waivers:* children of alumni, senior citizens, and employees or children of employees.

Financial Aid Of all full-time matriculated undergraduates who enrolled in 2012, 1,266 applied for aid, 598 were judged to have need, 69 had their need fully met. 527 Federal Work-Study jobs (averaging $1797). 25 state and other part-time jobs (averaging $1359). In 2012, 541 non-need-based awards were made. *Average financial aid package:* $14,435. *Average need-based loan:* $3890. *Average need-based gift aid:* $5389. *Average non-need-based aid:* $10,456. *Average indebtedness upon graduation:* $21,479.

Applying *Options:* electronic application. *Application fee:* $30. *Required:* high school transcript, minimum 2.0 GPA, 1 letter of recommendation. *Application deadlines:* rolling (freshmen), rolling (out-of-state freshmen), rolling (transfers). *Notification:* continuous (freshmen), continuous (out-of-state freshmen), continuous (transfers).

Freshman Application Contact Mr. Aaron Black, Director of Admissions, Missouri Baptist University, One College Park Drive, St. Louis, MO 63141-8660. *Phone:* 877-434-1115. *Toll-free phone:* 877-434-1115 Ext. 2290. *Fax:* 314-434-7596. *E-mail:* admissions@mobap.edu.
Website: http://www.mobap.edu/.

Missouri College

Brentwood, Missouri

Director of Admissions Mr. Doug Brinker, Admissions Director, Missouri College, 1405 South Hanley Road, Brentwood, MO 63117. *Phone:* 314-821-7700. *Toll-free phone:* 800-216-6732. *Fax:* 314-821-0891.
Website: http://www.missouricollege.edu/.

Missouri Southern State University

Joplin, Missouri

- **State-supported** comprehensive, founded 1937
- **Small-town** 350-acre campus
- **Coed**
- **Moderately difficult** entrance level

Faculty *Student/faculty ratio:* 18:1.

Academics *Calendar:* semesters. *Degrees:* certificates, associate, bachelor's, and master's.

Student Life *Campus security:* 24-hour emergency response devices and patrols, late-night transport/escort service, controlled dormitory access, security at campus events, emergency vehicle assistance, safety awareness information to students.

Athletics Member NCAA. All Division II.

Standardized Tests *Required:* SAT or ACT (for admission), SAT and SAT Subject Tests or ACT (for admission). *Required for some:* Michigan Test of English Language Proficiency. *Recommended:* ACT (for admission).
Costs (2012–13) *Tuition:* state resident $4564 full-time, $143 per credit hour part-time; nonresident $9128 full-time, $297 per credit hour part-time. Full-time tuition and fees vary according to course load. *Required fees:* $526 full-time. *Room and board:* $5976. Room and board charges vary according to board plan and housing facility.
Financial Aid *Of all full-time matriculated undergraduates who enrolled in 2012,* 2,596 applied for aid, 2,213 were judged to have need, 186 had their need fully met. *In 2012,* 272 non-need-based awards were made. *Average percent of need met:* 45. *Average financial aid package:* $10,790. *Average need-based loan:* $4353. *Average need-based gift aid:* $4588. *Average non-need-based aid:* $3035. *Average indebtedness upon graduation:* $20,005.
Applying *Options:* electronic application, deferred entrance. *Application fee:* $25. *Required:* high school transcript, class rank. *Required for some:* 2 letters of recommendation.
Freshman Application Contact Mr. Derek Skaggs, Director of Enrollment Services, Missouri Southern State University, 3950 East Newman Road, Joplin, MO 64801-1595. *Phone:* 417-625-9537. *Toll-free phone:* 866-818-MSSU. *Fax:* 417-659-4429. *E-mail:* admissions@mssu.edu.
Website: http://www.mssu.edu/.

Missouri State University
Springfield, Missouri

- **State-supported** comprehensive, founded 1905
- **Suburban** 225-acre campus
- **Endowment** $63.0 million
- **Coed** 17,434 undergraduate students, 77% full-time, 56% women, 44% men
- **Moderately difficult** entrance level, 83% of applicants were admitted

Undergraduates 13,465 full-time, 3,969 part-time. Students come from 50 states and territories; 83 other countries; 8% are from out of state; 4% Black or African American, non-Hispanic/Latino; 3% Hispanic/Latino; 1% Asian, non-Hispanic/Latino; 0.2% Native Hawaiian or other Pacific Islander, non-Hispanic/Latino; 0.6% American Indian or Alaska Native, non-Hispanic/Latino; 3% Two or more races, non-Hispanic/Latino; 2% Race/ethnicity unknown; 4% international; 9% transferred in; 23% live on campus. *Retention:* 75% of full-time freshmen returned.
Freshmen *Admission:* 7,342 applied, 6,113 admitted, 2,566 enrolled. *Average high school GPA:* 3.57. *Test scores:* SAT critical reading scores over 500: 71%; SAT math scores over 500: 70%; ACT scores over 18: 97%; SAT critical reading scores over 600: 24%; SAT math scores over 600: 30%; ACT scores over 24: 49%; SAT critical reading scores over 700: 5%; SAT math scores over 700: 2%; ACT scores over 30: 8%.
Faculty *Total:* 1,056, 66% full-time, 61% with terminal degrees. *Student/faculty ratio:* 20:1.
Academics *Calendar:* semesters. *Degrees:* certificates, bachelor's, master's, doctoral, post-master's, and postbachelor's certificates. *Special study options:* accelerated degree program, advanced placement credit, cooperative education, distance learning, double majors, English as a second language, freshman honors college, honors programs, independent study, internships, off-campus study, part-time degree program, services for LD students, student-designed majors, study abroad, summer session for credit. *ROTC:* Army (b).
Computers on Campus 1,940 computers/terminals and 1,190 ports are available on campus for general student use. Students can access the following: campus intranet, computer help desk, free student e-mail accounts, online (class) grades, online (class) registration, online (class) schedules. Campus-wide network is available. 100% of college-owned or -operated housing units are wired for high-speed Internet access. Wireless service is available via classrooms, computer centers, computer labs, learning centers, libraries, student centers.
Student Life *Housing:* on-campus residence required for freshman year. *Options:* coed, disabled students. Campus housing is university owned. Freshman campus housing is guaranteed. *Activities and organizations:* drama/theater group, student-run newspaper, radio and television station, choral group, marching band, Residence Hall Association, Campus Ministries, Fraternity and Sorority Life, Student Government Association, Student Activities Council, national fraternities, national sororities. *Campus security:* 24-hour emergency response devices and patrols, late-night transport/escort service, controlled dormitory access, on-campus police substation. *Student services:* health clinic, personal/psychological counseling, legal services.
Athletics Member NCAA. All Division I except football (Division I-AA). *Intercollegiate sports:* baseball M(s), basketball M(s)/W(s), bowling M(c)/W(c), cross-country running W(s), equestrian sports M(c)/W(c), field hockey

W(s), golf M(s)/W(s), ice hockey M(c), lacrosse M(c), racquetball M(c)/W(c), soccer M(s)/W(s), softball W(s), swimming and diving M(s)/W(s), track and field W(s), ultimate Frisbee M(c)/W(c), volleyball M(c)/W(c), wrestling M(c). *Intramural sports:* basketball M/W, bowling M/W, football M/W, golf M/W, racquetball M/W, soccer M/W, softball M/W, table tennis M/W, tennis M/W, track and field W, ultimate Frisbee M/W, volleyball M/W, weight lifting M/W.
Standardized Tests *Required:* SAT or ACT (for admission).
Costs (2012–13) *Tuition:* state resident $6014 full-time, $200 per credit hour part-time; nonresident $12,360 full-time, $412 per credit hour part-time. Full-time tuition and fees vary according to course level, course load, and program. Part-time tuition and fees vary according to course level, course load, and program. *Required fees:* $778 full-time. *Room and board:* $6844. Room and board charges vary according to board plan, housing facility, and location. *Payment plan:* deferred payment. *Waivers:* children of alumni, senior citizens, and employees or children of employees.
Financial Aid Of all full-time matriculated undergraduates who enrolled in 2012, 9,868 applied for aid, 7,997 were judged to have need, 934 had their need fully met. In 2012, 642 non-need-based awards were made. *Average percent of need met:* 88%. *Average financial aid package:* $7987. *Average need-based loan:* $4246. *Average need-based gift aid:* $5201. *Average non-need-based aid:* $4200. *Average indebtedness upon graduation:* $20,545.
Applying *Options:* electronic application. *Application fee:* $35. *Required:* high school transcript. *Required for some:* essay or personal statement, interview. *Application deadlines:* 7/20 (freshmen), 7/20 (transfers). *Notification:* continuous (freshmen), continuous (transfers).
Freshman Application Contact Mr. Andrew Wright, Director of Admissions, Missouri State University, 901 South National Avenue, Springfield, MO 65897. *Phone:* 417-836-5517. *Toll-free phone:* 800-492-7900. *Fax:* 417-836-5137. *E-mail:* info@missouristate.edu.
Website: http://www.missouristate.edu/.

Missouri Tech
St. Charles, Missouri

Freshman Application Contact Mr. Bob Honaker, Director of Admissions, Missouri Tech, 1167 Corporate Lake Drive, St. Louis, MO 63132. *Phone:* 314-569-3600. *Toll-free phone:* 800-960-TECH. *Fax:* 314-569-1167.
Website: http://www.motech.edu/.

Missouri University of Science and Technology
Rolla, Missouri

- **State-supported** university, founded 1870, part of University of Missouri System
- **Small-town** 284-acre campus
- **Endowment** $138.0 million
- **Coed, primarily men** 5,843 undergraduate students, 90% full-time, 23% women, 77% men
- **Very difficult** entrance level, 90% of applicants were admitted

Undergraduates 5,260 full-time, 583 part-time. 16% are from out of state; 4% Black or African American, non-Hispanic/Latino; 2% Hispanic/Latino; 2% Asian, non-Hispanic/Latino; 0.2% Native Hawaiian or other Pacific Islander, non-Hispanic/Latino; 0.4% American Indian or Alaska Native, non-Hispanic/Latino; 1% Two or more races, non-Hispanic/Latino; 4% Race/ethnicity unknown; 5% international; 6% transferred in; 51% live on campus. *Retention:* 85% of full-time freshmen returned.
Freshmen *Admission:* 2,842 applied, 2,545 admitted, 1,124 enrolled. *Average high school GPA:* 3.53. *Test scores:* SAT critical reading scores over 500: 84%; SAT math scores over 500: 96%; ACT scores over 18: 100%; SAT critical reading scores over 600: 46%; SAT math scores over 600: 81%; ACT scores over 24: 90%; SAT critical reading scores over 700: 20%; SAT math scores over 700: 29%; ACT scores over 30: 35%.
Faculty *Total:* 493, 70% full-time, 80% with terminal degrees. *Student/faculty ratio:* 17:1.
Academics *Calendar:* semesters. *Degrees:* certificates, bachelor's, master's, doctoral, and postbachelor's certificates. *Special study options:* academic remediation for entering students, accelerated degree program, adult/continuing education programs, advanced placement credit, cooperative education, distance learning, double majors, English as a second language, freshman honors college, honors programs, independent study, internships, off-campus study, part-time degree program, services for LD students, study abroad, summer session for credit. *ROTC:* Army (b), Navy (c), Air Force (b).

Computers on Campus 980 computers/terminals and 4,500 ports are available on campus for general student use. Students can access the following: campus intranet, computer help desk, free student e-mail accounts, online (class) grades, online (class) registration, online (class) schedules. Campus-wide network is available. 100% of college-owned or -operated housing units are wired for high-speed Internet access. Wireless service is available via entire campus.

Student Life *Housing:* on-campus residence required through sophomore year. *Options:* coed, men-only, women-only, cooperative, disabled students. Campus housing is university owned, leased by the school and is provided by a third party. Freshman campus housing is guaranteed. *Activities and organizations:* drama/theater group, student-run newspaper, radio station, choral group, marching band, student government, Student Union Board, Residence Hall Association, academic organizations, service organizations, national fraternities, national sororities. *Campus security:* 24-hour emergency response devices and patrols, student patrols, late-night transport/escort service, controlled dormitory access, crime prevention programs. *Student services:* health clinic, personal/psychological counseling.

Athletics Member NCAA. All Division II. *Intercollegiate sports:* baseball M(s), basketball M(s)/W(s), cross-country running M(s)/W(s), football M(s), soccer M(s)/W(s), softball W(s), swimming and diving M(s), track and field M(s)/W(s), volleyball W(s). *Intramural sports:* badminton M/W, basketball M/W, bowling M/W, cross-country running M/W, football M/W, golf M/W, racquetball M/W, soccer M/W, softball M/W, swimming and diving M/W, table tennis M/W, tennis M/W, track and field M/W, ultimate Frisbee M/W, volleyball M/W, weight lifting M/W.

Standardized Tests *Required:* SAT or ACT (for admission). *Recommended:* ACT (for admission).

Costs (2012–13) *Tuition:* state resident $8082 full-time, $269 per credit hour part-time; nonresident $22,398 full-time, $747 per credit hour part-time. Full-time tuition and fees vary according to course load, degree level, and program. Part-time tuition and fees vary according to course load, degree level, and program. *Required fees:* $1268 full-time, $269 per credit hour part-time. *Room and board:* $8900; room only: $5610. Room and board charges vary according to board plan, housing facility, and location. *Payment plan:* installment. *Waivers:* employees or children of employees.

Financial Aid Of all full-time matriculated undergraduates who enrolled in 2012, 4,068 applied for aid, 3,232 were judged to have need, 558 had their need fully met. 125 Federal Work-Study jobs (averaging $2414). In 2012, 576 non-need-based awards were made. *Average percent of need met:* 64%. *Average financial aid package:* $10,235. *Average need-based loan:* $4533. *Average need-based gift aid:* $6963. *Average non-need-based aid:* $5249. *Average indebtedness upon graduation:* $21,659.

Applying *Options:* electronic application, early admission, deferred entrance. *Application fee:* $50. *Required:* high school transcript. *Recommended:* essay or personal statement. *Application deadlines:* 7/1 (freshmen), 7/1 (transfers). *Notification:* continuous (freshmen), continuous (transfers).

Freshman Application Contact Ms. Lynn Stichnote, Admissions Office, Missouri University of Science and Technology, 300 West 13th Street, 106 Parker Hall, Rolla, MO 65401. *Phone:* 573-341-4165. *Toll-free phone:* 800-522-0938. *Fax:* 573-341-4082. *E-mail:* admissions@mst.edu. *Website:* http://www.mst.edu/.

Missouri Valley College

Marshall, Missouri

Freshman Application Contact Ms. Debi Bultmann, Admissions Office Manager, Missouri Valley College, 500 East College, Marshall, MO 65340-3197. *Phone:* 660-831-4125. *Fax:* 660-831-4233. *E-mail:* admissions@moval.edu. *Website:* http://www.moval.edu/.

Missouri Western State University

St. Joseph, Missouri

- **State-supported** comprehensive, founded 1915
- **Suburban** 744-acre campus with easy access to Kansas City
- **Coed** 5,885 undergraduate students, 69% full-time, 56% women, 44% men
- **Noncompetitive** entrance level, 100% of applicants were admitted

Undergraduates 4,077 full-time, 1,808 part-time. Students come from 32 states and territories; 21 other countries; 8% are from out of state; 11% Black or African American, non-Hispanic/Latino; 1% Hispanic/Latino; 0.9% Asian, non-Hispanic/Latino; 0.3% Native Hawaiian or other Pacific Islander, non-Hispanic/Latino; 1% American Indian or Alaska Native, non-Hispanic/Latino; 3% Two or more races, non-Hispanic/Latino; 4% Race/ethnicity unknown; 0.7% international; 6% transferred in; 21% live on campus. *Retention:* 58% of full-time freshmen returned.

Freshmen *Admission:* 3,472 applied, 3,472 admitted, 1,074 enrolled. *Average high school GPA:* 3.1. *Test scores:* ACT scores over 18: 73%; ACT scores over 24: 21%; ACT scores over 30: 2%.

Faculty *Total:* 393, 47% full-time, 45% with terminal degrees. *Student/faculty ratio:* 19:1.

Academics *Calendar:* semesters. *Degrees:* certificates, associate, bachelor's, master's, and postbachelor's certificates. *Special study options:* academic remediation for entering students, accelerated degree program, adult/continuing education programs, advanced placement credit, distance learning, double majors, English as a second language, freshman honors college, honors programs, independent study, internships, off-campus study, part-time degree program, services for LD students, student-designed majors, study abroad, summer session for credit. *ROTC:* Army (b).

Computers on Campus 618 computers/terminals are available on campus for general student use. Students can access the following: campus intranet, computer help desk, free student e-mail accounts, online (class) grades, online (class) registration, online (class) schedules, Personal online storage. Campus-wide network is available. 100% of college-owned or -operated housing units are wired for high-speed Internet access. Wireless service is available via entire campus.

Student Life *Housing:* on-campus residence required for freshman year. *Options:* coed, disabled students. Campus housing is university owned. *Activities and organizations:* drama/theater group, student-run newspaper, choral group, marching band, national fraternities, national sororities. *Campus security:* 24-hour emergency response devices and patrols, student patrols, late-night transport/escort service, controlled dormitory access. *Student services:* health clinic, personal/psychological counseling, women's center.

Athletics Member NCAA. All Division II. *Intercollegiate sports:* baseball M(s), basketball M(s)/W(s), football M(s), golf M(s)/W(s), soccer W(s), softball W(s), tennis W(s), volleyball W(s). *Intramural sports:* badminton M/W, basketball M/W, football M/W, racquetball M/W, soccer M/W, table tennis M/W, ultimate Frisbee M/W, volleyball M/W.

Standardized Tests *Required:* SAT or ACT (for admission).

Costs (2012–13) *Tuition:* state resident $5667 full-time, $189 per credit hour part-time; nonresident $11,171 full-time, $372 per credit hour part-time. Full-time tuition and fees vary according to location and program. Part-time tuition and fees vary according to location and program. *Required fees:* $718 full-time. *Room and board:* $6918. Room and board charges vary according to board plan and housing facility. *Payment plan:* installment. *Waivers:* senior citizens and employees or children of employees.

Financial Aid Of all full-time matriculated undergraduates who enrolled in 2012, 3,816 applied for aid, 3,120 were judged to have need, 269 had their need fully met. 356 Federal Work-Study jobs (averaging $1262). 809 state and other part-time jobs (averaging $1612). In 2012, 383 non-need-based awards were made. *Average percent of need met:* 62%. *Average financial aid package:* $7948. *Average need-based loan:* $3733. *Average need-based gift aid:* $5415. *Average non-need-based aid:* $3308. *Average indebtedness upon graduation:* $22,287.

Applying *Options:* electronic application, early admission. *Application fee:* $15. *Required:* high school transcript. *Application deadlines:* 5/1 (freshmen), 6/1 (transfers). *Notification:* continuous (freshmen), continuous (transfers).

Freshman Application Contact Mr. Howard McCauley, Dean of Enrollment Management, Missouri Western State University, 4525 Downs Drive, St. Joseph, MO 64507-2294. *Phone:* 816-271-4266. *Toll-free phone:* 800-662-7041. *Fax:* 816-271-5833. *E-mail:* admission@missouriwestern.edu. *Website:* http://www.missouriwestern.edu/.

National American University

Kansas City, Missouri

Director of Admissions Admissions Office, National American University, 7490 Northwest 87th Street, Kansas City, MO 64153. *Phone:* 816-412-5500. *E-mail:* zradmissions@national.edu. *Website:* http://www.national.edu/.

Northwest Missouri State University

Maryville, Missouri

- **State-supported** comprehensive, founded 1905, part of Missouri Coordinating Board for Higher Education
- **Small-town** 370-acre campus with easy access to Kansas City
- **Coed** 6,014 undergraduate students, 89% full-time, 56% women, 44% men
- **Moderately difficult** entrance level, 88% of applicants were admitted

Undergraduates 5,335 full-time, 679 part-time. Students come from 48 states and territories; 27 other countries; 26% are from out of state; 6% Black or African American, non-Hispanic/Latino; 3% Hispanic/Latino; 0.7% Asian, non-Hispanic/Latino; 0.2% Native Hawaiian or other Pacific Islander, non-Hispanic/Latino; 0.2% American Indian or Alaska Native, non-Hispanic/Latino; 2% Two or more races, non-Hispanic/Latino; 2% Race/ethnicity unknown; 2% international; 5% transferred in; 38% live on campus. *Retention:* 67% of full-time freshmen returned.

Freshmen *Admission:* 4,412 applied, 3,889 admitted, 1,357 enrolled. *Average high school GPA:* 3.32. *Test scores:* SAT critical reading scores over 500: 53%; SAT math scores over 500: 65%; ACT scores over 18: 93%; SAT math scores over 600: 18%; ACT scores over 24: 35%; SAT math scores over 700: 6%; ACT scores over 30: 3%.

Faculty *Total:* 300, 82% full-time, 57% with terminal degrees. *Student/faculty ratio:* 23:1.

Academics *Calendar:* trimesters. *Degrees:* certificates, bachelor's, master's, post-master's, and postbachelor's certificates. *Special study options:* academic remediation for entering students, advanced placement credit, distance learning, double majors, English as a second language, honors programs, independent study, internships, off-campus study, part-time degree program, services for LD students, study abroad, summer session for credit. *ROTC:* Army (b).

Computers on Campus 7,000 computers/terminals and 6,000 ports are available on campus for general student use. Students can access the following: campus intranet, computer help desk, free student e-mail accounts, online (class) grades, online (class) registration, online (class) schedules, online courses with library and databases. Campuswide network is available. 100% of college-owned or -operated housing units are wired for high-speed Internet access. Wireless service is available via classrooms, computer centers, computer labs, dorm rooms, learning centers, libraries, student centers.

Student Life *Housing:* on-campus residence required for freshman year. *Options:* coed, disabled students. Campus housing is university owned. Freshman campus housing is guaranteed. *Activities and organizations:* drama/theater group, student-run newspaper, radio and television station, choral group, marching band, student government, Residence Hall Association, Greek Life, national fraternities, national sororities. *Campus security:* 24-hour emergency response devices and patrols, student patrols, late-night transport/escort service, controlled dormitory access, security personnel are all police officers. *Student services:* health clinic, personal/psychological counseling, women's center.

Athletics Member NCAA. All Division II. *Intercollegiate sports:* baseball M(s), basketball M(s)/W(s), cheerleading M(s)/W(s), cross-country running M(s)/W(s), football M(s), golf W(s), soccer W(s), softball W(s), tennis M(s)/W(s), track and field M(s)/W(s), volleyball W(s). *Intramural sports:* badminton M/W, basketball M/W, cross-country running M/W, football M/W, golf M/W, racquetball M/W, skiing (cross-country) M/W, soccer W(c), softball W, swimming and diving M/W, table tennis M/W, tennis M/W, track and field M/W, volleyball M/W, wrestling M(c).

Standardized Tests *Required:* SAT or ACT (for admission).

Costs (2012–13) *One-time required fee:* $140. *Tuition:* state resident $5237 full-time, $175 per credit hour part-time; nonresident $11,345 full-time, $378 per credit hour part-time. Full-time tuition and fees vary according to course load, location, and reciprocity agreements. Part-time tuition and fees vary according to course load and location. *Required fees:* $2483 full-time, $83 per credit hour part-time. *Room and board:* $8614; room only: $5538. Room and board charges vary according to board plan and housing facility. *Payment plans:* installment, deferred payment. *Waivers:* senior citizens and employees or children of employees.

Financial Aid Of all full-time matriculated undergraduates who enrolled in 2011, 4,786 applied for aid, 3,821 were judged to have need, 1,496 had their need fully met. 413 Federal Work-Study jobs (averaging $1183). 1,055 state and other part-time jobs (averaging $1538). In 2011, 498 non-need-based awards were made. *Average percent of need met:* 67%. *Average financial aid package:* $8597. *Average need-based loan:* $3889. *Average need-based gift aid:* $5590. *Average non-need-based aid:* $2307. *Average indebtedness upon graduation:* $23,400.

Applying *Options:* electronic application, deferred entrance. *Application fee:* $25. *Required:* high school transcript, minimum 2.0 GPA. *Required for some:* interview. *Application deadlines:* rolling (freshmen), rolling (out-of-state freshmen), rolling (transfers). *Notification:* continuous (freshmen), continuous (out-of-state freshmen), continuous (transfers).

Freshman Application Contact Ms. Tammi Grow, Associate Director of Admission, Northwest Missouri State University, 800 University Drive, Maryville, MO 64468-6001. *Phone:* 660-562-1146. *Toll-free phone:* 800-633-1175. *Fax:* 660-562-1146. *E-mail:* admissions@nwmissouri.edu. *Website:* http://www.nwmissouri.edu/.

Ozark Christian College

Joplin, Missouri

Freshman Application Contact Mr. Troy B. Nelson, Executive Director of Admissions, Ozark Christian College, 1111 North Main Street, Joplin, MO 64801-4804. *Phone:* 417-624-2518. *Toll-free phone:* 800-299-4622. *Fax:* 417-624-0090. *E-mail:* occadmin@occ.edu. *Website:* http://www.occ.edu/.

Park University

Parkville, Missouri

- **Independent** comprehensive, founded 1875
- **Suburban** 800-acre campus with easy access to Kansas City
- **Endowment** $42.5 million
- **Coed** 1,674 undergraduate students, 72% full-time, 56% women, 44% men
- **Moderately difficult** entrance level, 69% of applicants were admitted

Undergraduates 1,204 full-time, 470 part-time. Students come from 49 states and territories; 96 other countries; 20% are from out of state; 10% Black or African American, non-Hispanic/Latino; 5% Hispanic/Latino; 0.4% Asian, non-Hispanic/Latino; 0.1% Native Hawaiian or other Pacific Islander, non-Hispanic/Latino; 0.8% American Indian or Alaska Native, non-Hispanic/Latino; 3% Two or more races, non-Hispanic/Latino; 19% international; 16% transferred in; 20% live on campus. *Retention:* 61% of full-time freshmen returned.

Freshmen *Admission:* 778 applied, 539 admitted, 212 enrolled. *Average high school GPA:* 3.3. *Test scores:* ACT scores over 18: 79%; ACT scores over 24: 24%; ACT scores over 30: 5%.

Faculty *Total:* 174, 54% full-time. *Student/faculty ratio:* 11:1.

Academics *Calendar:* semesters. *Degrees:* associate, bachelor's, master's, and postbachelor's certificates. *Special study options:* academic remediation for entering students, adult/continuing education programs, advanced placement credit, distance learning, double majors, English as a second language, external degree program, honors programs, independent study, internships, off-campus study, part-time degree program, services for LD students, student-designed majors, summer session for credit. *ROTC:* Army (b).

Computers on Campus 143 computers/terminals are available on campus for general student use. Students can access the following: online (class) registration. Campuswide network is available.

Student Life *Housing:* on-campus residence required through junior year. *Options:* coed. Campus housing is university owned. Freshman campus housing is guaranteed. *Activities and organizations:* drama/theater group, student-run newspaper, radio station, choral group, World Student Union, Student Senate, Radio Club, Latin American Student Organization, marketing club. *Campus security:* 24-hour patrols, student patrols, late-night transport/escort service. *Student services:* health clinic, personal/psychological counseling.

Athletics Member NAIA. *Intercollegiate sports:* baseball M(s), basketball M(s)/W(s), cross-country running M(s)/W(s), golf W(s), soccer M(s)/W(s), softball W(s), track and field M(s)/W(s), volleyball M(s)/W(s). *Intramural sports:* basketball M/W, softball M/W, volleyball M/W.

Standardized Tests *Required:* SAT or ACT (for admission).

Costs (2013–14) *Comprehensive fee:* $17,051 includes full-time tuition ($9800), mandatory fees ($100), and room and board ($7151). Full-time tuition and fees vary according to course load. Part-time tuition: $350 per credit. Part-time tuition and fees vary according to course load. *College room only:* $3525. Room and board charges vary according to housing facility. *Waivers:* senior citizens and employees or children of employees.

Financial Aid Of all full-time matriculated undergraduates who enrolled in 2011, 756 applied for aid, 594 were judged to have need, 96 had their need fully met. 104 Federal Work-Study jobs (averaging $2496). 127 state and other part-time jobs (averaging $3306). In 2011, 152 non-need-based awards were made. *Average percent of need met:* 67%. *Average financial aid package:*

$10,512. *Average need-based loan:* $4519. *Average need-based gift aid:* $4659. *Average non-need-based aid:* $8862. *Average indebtedness upon graduation:* $21,558.

Applying *Options:* electronic application, early admission, deferred entrance. *Application fee:* $25. *Required:* high school transcript, minimum 2.0 GPA. *Required for some:* 2 letters of recommendation, interview. *Recommended:* essay or personal statement. *Application deadlines:* 8/1 (freshmen), 8/1 (transfers). *Notification:* continuous (freshmen), continuous (transfers).

Freshman Application Contact Eric Blair, Director of Undergraduate Admissions, Park University, 8700 NW River Park Drive, Campus Box 1, Parkville, MO 64152. *Phone:* 816-584-6858. *Toll-free phone:* 800-745-7275. *Fax:* 816-741-4462. *E-mail:* admissions@mail.park.edu. *Website:* http://www.park.edu/.

Ranken Technical College

St. Louis, Missouri

Director of Admissions Ms. Elizabeth Keserauskis, Director of Admissions, Ranken Technical College, 4431 Finney Avenue, St. Louis, MO 63113. *Phone:* 314-371-0233 Ext. 4811. *Toll-free phone:* 866-4-RANKEN. *Website:* http://www.ranken.edu/.

Research College of Nursing

Kansas City, Missouri

- **Independent** comprehensive, founded 1980, part of Rockhurst University
- **Urban** 66-acre campus with easy access to Kansas City
- **Coed, primarily women** 306 undergraduate students, 98% full-time, 93% women, 7% men
- **Moderately difficult** entrance level, 73% of applicants were admitted

Undergraduates 300 full-time, 6 part-time. Students come from 7 states and territories; 6% Black or African American, non-Hispanic/Latino; 3% Hispanic/Latino; 1% Asian, non-Hispanic/Latino; 0.3% Native Hawaiian or other Pacific Islander, non-Hispanic/Latino; 0.3% American Indian or Alaska Native, non-Hispanic/Latino; 0.3% Two or more races, non-Hispanic/Latino; 13% Race/ethnicity unknown; 2% transferred in.

Freshmen *Admission:* 339 applied, 249 admitted, 83 enrolled. *Average high school GPA:* 3.53. *Test scores:* ACT scores over 18: 100%; ACT scores over 24: 56%; ACT scores over 30: 4%.

Faculty *Total:* 29, 90% full-time, 14% with terminal degrees. *Student/faculty ratio:* 7:1.

Academics *Calendar:* semesters. *Degrees:* bachelor's and master's (bachelor's degree offered jointly with Rockhurst College). *Special study options:* accelerated degree program, advanced placement credit, double majors, honors programs, independent study, services for LD students, study abroad, summer session for credit. *ROTC:* Army (c).

Computers on Campus 125 computers/terminals are available on campus for general student use. Students can access the following: online (class) registration. Campuswide network is available.

Student Life *Housing options:* coed, men-only, women-only. Campus housing is university owned. Freshman campus housing is guaranteed. *Activities and organizations:* drama/theater group, student-run newspaper, radio station, choral group, national fraternities, national sororities. *Campus security:* 24-hour emergency response devices and patrols, late-night transport/escort service, controlled dormitory access. *Student services:* health clinic, personal/psychological counseling.

Athletics Member NCAA. All Division II. *Intercollegiate sports:* baseball M(s), basketball M(s)/W(s), golf M(s)/W(s), soccer M(s)/W(s), softball W(s), tennis M(s)/W(s), volleyball W(s). *Intramural sports:* badminton M/W, basketball M/W, cross-country running M/W, field hockey M/W, golf M/W, lacrosse M/W, racquetball M/W, rugby M/W, soccer M/W, softball M/W, table tennis M/W, tennis M/W, volleyball M/W, weight lifting M.

Standardized Tests *Required:* SAT or ACT (for admission).

Costs (2012–13) *Comprehensive fee:* $38,300 includes full-time tuition ($29,100), mandatory fees ($740), and room and board ($8460). Part-time tuition: $970 per credit hour. Part-time tuition and fees vary according to class time. *College room only:* $5060. Room and board charges vary according to board plan, housing facility, and location. *Payment plans:* installment, deferred payment. *Waivers:* senior citizens and employees or children of employees.

Applying *Options:* electronic application, deferred entrance. *Required:* high school transcript, 1 letter of recommendation, ACT or SAT. *Recommended:* minimum 2.8 GPA, interview. *Application deadlines:* 6/30 (freshmen), 2/15

(transfers). *Notification:* 8/15 (freshmen), 6/20 (out-of-state freshmen), 3/15 (transfers).

Freshman Application Contact Mr. Lane Ramey, Vice-President for Enrollment Services, Research College of Nursing, 1100 Rockhurst Road, Kansas dCity, MO 64110. *Phone:* 816-501-2012. *E-mail:* lane.ramey@rockhurst.edu. *Website:* http://www.researchcollege.edu/.

Rockhurst University

Kansas City, Missouri

- **Independent Roman Catholic (Jesuit)** comprehensive, founded 1910
- **Urban** 35-acre campus
- **Endowment** $32.7 million
- **Coed** 2,160 undergraduate students, 69% full-time, 60% women, 40% men
- **Moderately difficult** entrance level, 78% of applicants were admitted

Undergraduates 1,486 full-time, 674 part-time. Students come from 26 states and territories; 18 other countries; 29% are from out of state; 6% Black or African American, non-Hispanic/Latino; 5% Hispanic/Latino; 3% Asian, non-Hispanic/Latino; 0.2% Native Hawaiian or other Pacific Islander, non-Hispanic/Latino; 0.5% American Indian or Alaska Native, non-Hispanic/Latino; 1% Two or more races, non-Hispanic/Latino; 6% Race/ethnicity unknown; 0.8% international; 3% transferred in; 52% live on campus. *Retention:* 86% of full-time freshmen returned.

Freshmen *Admission:* 2,184 applied, 1,714 admitted, 447 enrolled. *Average high school GPA:* 3.57. *Test scores:* SAT critical reading scores over 500: 71%; SAT math scores over 500: 78%; ACT scores over 18: 99%; SAT critical reading scores over 600: 25%; SAT math scores over 600: 43%; ACT scores over 24: 69%; SAT critical reading scores over 700: 4%; SAT math scores over 700: 4%; ACT scores over 30: 14%.

Faculty *Total:* 253, 49% full-time, 60% with terminal degrees. *Student/faculty ratio:* 13:1.

Academics *Calendar:* semesters. *Degrees:* certificates, bachelor's, master's, doctoral, and postbachelor's certificates. *Special study options:* academic remediation for entering students, accelerated degree program, advanced placement credit, cooperative education, distance learning, double majors, freshman honors college, honors programs, independent study, internships, off-campus study, part-time degree program, services for LD students, study abroad, summer session for credit. *ROTC:* Army (c).

Computers on Campus 240 computers/terminals are available on campus for general student use. Students can access the following: campus intranet, computer help desk, free student e-mail accounts, online (class) grades, online (class) registration, online (class) schedules. Campuswide network is available. 100% of college-owned or -operated housing units are wired for high-speed Internet access. Wireless service is available via entire campus.

Student Life *Housing:* on-campus residence required through sophomore year. *Options:* coed, men-only, women-only, disabled students. Campus housing is university owned. Freshman campus housing is guaranteed. *Activities and organizations:* drama/theater group, student-run newspaper, choral group, Student Activities Board, Student Senate, Delta Sigma Pi Business Fraternity, Student Organization of Latinos, Rockhurst University Players (theatre troupe), national fraternities, national sororities. *Campus security:* 24-hour emergency response devices and patrols, late-night transport/escort service, controlled dormitory access, closed-circuit TV monitors. *Student services:* health clinic, personal/psychological counseling.

Athletics Member NCAA. All Division II. *Intercollegiate sports:* baseball M(s), basketball M(s)/W(s), golf M(s)/W(s), soccer M(s)/W(s), softball W(s), tennis M(s)/W(s), volleyball W(s). *Intramural sports:* basketball M/W, bowling M/W, cheerleading M/W, field hockey W, football M/W, ice hockey M, lacrosse M, soccer M/W, softball M/W, tennis M/W, ultimate Frisbee M/W, volleyball M/W.

Standardized Tests *Required:* SAT or ACT (for admission).

Costs (2012–13) *Comprehensive fee:* $37,900 includes full-time tuition ($29,100), mandatory fees ($740), and room and board ($8060). Full-time tuition and fees vary according to class time and course load. Part-time tuition and fees vary according to class time and course load. *College room only:* $5060. Room and board charges vary according to board plan and housing facility. *Payment plans:* installment, deferred payment. *Waivers:* senior citizens and employees or children of employees.

Financial Aid Of all full-time matriculated undergraduates who enrolled in 2012, 1,297 applied for aid, 1,297 were judged to have need, 72 had their need fully met. In 2012, 165 non-need-based awards were made. *Average percent of need met:* 85%. *Average financial aid package:* $28,936. *Average need-based loan:* $3819. *Average need-based gift aid:* $7077. *Average non-need-based aid:* $15,146. *Average indebtedness upon graduation:* $20,003.

Applying *Options:* electronic application, deferred entrance. *Application fee:* $25. *Required:* high school transcript, minimum 2.0 GPA, 1 letter of recommendation. *Required for some:* essay or personal statement, interview. *Application deadlines:* 6/30 (freshmen), rolling (transfers). *Notification:* continuous (freshmen), continuous (transfers).

Freshman Application Contact Kyle Johnson, Director of Freshman Admissions, Rockhurst University, 1100 Rockhurst Road, Kansas City, MO 64110-2561. *Phone:* 816-501-4100. *Toll-free phone:* 800-842-6776. *Fax:* 816-501-4142. *E-mail:* admission@rockhurst.edu.
Website: http://www.rockhurst.edu/.

Saint Louis Christian College

Florissant, Missouri

- **Independent Christian** 4-year, founded 1956
- **Suburban** 20-acre campus with easy access to St. Louis
- **Endowment** $1.0 million
- **Coed** 246 undergraduate students, 78% full-time, 39% women, 61% men
- **Minimally difficult** entrance level, 27% of applicants were admitted

Undergraduates 192 full-time, 54 part-time. Students come from 15 states and territories; 1 other country; 37% are from out of state; 35% Black or African American, non-Hispanic/Latino; 3% Hispanic/Latino; 1% Asian, non-Hispanic/Latino; 0.4% American Indian or Alaska Native, non-Hispanic/Latino; 2% Two or more races, non-Hispanic/Latino; 2% international; 53% live on campus. *Retention:* 48% of full-time freshmen returned.

Freshmen *Admission:* 124 applied, 34 admitted, 23 enrolled. *Average high school GPA:* 3.21.

Faculty *Total:* 27, 41% full-time, 22% with terminal degrees. *Student/faculty ratio:* 13:1.

Academics *Calendar:* semesters. *Degrees:* associate and bachelor's. *Special study options:* academic remediation for entering students, accelerated degree program, adult/continuing education programs, advanced placement credit, double majors, English as a second language, internships, part-time degree program, services for LD students, study abroad, summer session for credit.

Computers on Campus 11 computers/terminals are available on campus for general student use. Students can access the following: free student e-mail accounts, online (class) schedules. Campuswide network is available. Wireless service is available via classrooms, computer labs, libraries, student centers.

Student Life *Housing:* on-campus residence required through senior year. *Options:* men-only, women-only. Campus housing is university owned. *Activities and organizations:* drama/theater group, choral group, World Christians Unlimited, Drama Club, pep band. *Campus security:* 24-hour emergency response devices and patrols, controlled dormitory access, night security. *Student services:* personal/psychological counseling.

Athletics Member NCCAA. *Intercollegiate sports:* baseball M, basketball M/W, cross-country running W, volleyball W. *Intramural sports:* basketball M/W, ultimate Frisbee M/W, volleyball M/W.

Standardized Tests *Required:* SAT or ACT (for admission).

Costs (2013–14) *Comprehensive fee:* $12,215 includes full-time tuition ($8215) and room and board ($4000). *Room and board:* Room and board charges vary according to housing facility. *Waivers:* employees or children of employees.

Financial Aid Of all full-time matriculated undergraduates who enrolled in 2012, 176 applied for aid, 161 were judged to have need, 13 had their need fully met. In 2012, 34 non-need-based awards were made. *Average percent of need met:* 74%. *Average financial aid package:* $18,610. *Average need-based loan:* $3542. *Average need-based gift aid:* $15,064. *Average non-need-based aid:* $9127. *Average indebtedness upon graduation:* $22,586.

Applying *Options:* electronic application, early admission. *Required:* essay or personal statement, high school transcript, 2 letters of recommendation, 18+ on ACT. *Required for some:* interview. *Recommended:* minimum 2.0 GPA. *Application deadlines:* 8/7 (freshmen), 8/7 (transfers). *Notification:* continuous (freshmen), continuous (transfers).

Freshman Application Contact Larry Osborn, Admissions Director, Saint Louis Christian College, 1360 Grandview Drive, Florissant, MO 63033. *Phone:* 314-837-6777 Ext. 1303. *Toll-free phone:* 800-887-SLCC. *E-mail:* losborn@slcconline.edu.
Website: http://www.slcconline.edu/.

St. Louis College of Pharmacy

St. Louis, Missouri

- **Independent** comprehensive, founded 1864
- **Urban** 5-acre campus with easy access to St. Louis
- **Endowment** $113.6 million
- **Coed** 714 undergraduate students, 99% full-time, 58% women, 42% men
- **Moderately difficult** entrance level, 70% of applicants were admitted

Undergraduates 707 full-time, 7 part-time. Students come from 29 states and territories; 2 other countries; 51% are from out of state; 5% Black or African American, non-Hispanic/Latino; 1% Hispanic/Latino; 22% Asian, non-Hispanic/Latino; 0.3% Native Hawaiian or other Pacific Islander, non-Hispanic/Latino; 0.6% American Indian or Alaska Native, non-Hispanic/Latino; 1% Two or more races, non-Hispanic/Latino; 4% Race/ethnicity unknown; 0.7% international; 6% transferred in; 40% live on campus. *Retention:* 92% of full-time freshmen returned.

Freshmen *Admission:* 528 applied, 370 admitted, 247 enrolled. *Average high school GPA:* 3.65. *Test scores:* ACT scores over 18: 100%; SAT math scores over 600: 100%; ACT scores over 24: 91%; SAT math scores over 700: 60%; ACT scores over 30: 21%.

Faculty *Total:* 134, 62% full-time, 83% with terminal degrees. *Student/faculty ratio:* 18:1.

Academics *Calendar:* semesters. *Degree:* doctoral. *Special study options:* academic remediation for entering students, advanced placement credit, internships, summer session for credit. *ROTC:* Army (c), Navy (c), Air Force (c).

Computers on Campus 6 computers/terminals and 2,200 ports are available on campus for general student use. Students can access the following: campus intranet, computer help desk, free student e-mail accounts, online (class) grades, online (class) registration, online (class) schedules. Campuswide network is available. 100% of college-owned or -operated housing units are wired for high-speed Internet access. Wireless service is available via entire campus.

Student Life *Housing options:* coed. Campus housing is university owned. Freshman applicants given priority for college housing. *Activities and organizations:* drama/theater group, student-run newspaper, choral group, Outdoor Club, Student Body Union, International Student Organization, Student ambassadors, Student Organization for Drug and Alcohol Awareness, national fraternities, national sororities. *Campus security:* 24-hour emergency response devices and patrols, late-night transport/escort service, controlled dormitory access. *Student services:* personal/psychological counseling.

Athletics Member NAIA. *Intercollegiate sports:* basketball M/W, cross-country running M/W, softball W, tennis M/W, track and field M/W, volleyball W. *Intramural sports:* basketball M/W, cheerleading W, cross-country running M/W, football M/W, golf M/W, soccer M/W, softball M/W, table tennis M/W, tennis M/W, volleyball M/W, weight lifting M/W.

Standardized Tests *Required:* SAT or ACT (for admission).

Costs (2013–14) *Comprehensive fee:* $35,405 includes full-time tuition ($25,800), mandatory fees ($325), and room and board ($9280). Full-time tuition and fees vary according to student level. Part-time tuition: $845 per credit. *College room only:* $5475. Room and board charges vary according to housing facility. *Payment plan:* installment. *Waivers:* employees or children of employees.

Financial Aid Of all full-time matriculated undergraduates who enrolled in 2012, 626 applied for aid, 561 were judged to have need, 45 had their need fully met. 366 Federal Work-Study jobs (averaging $767). In 2012, 128 non-need-based awards were made. *Average percent of need met:* 46%. *Average financial aid package:* $14,171. *Average need-based loan:* $5875. *Average need-based gift aid:* $9054. *Average non-need-based aid:* $6366. *Average indebtedness upon graduation:* $119,711.

Applying *Options:* electronic application, early decision. *Application fee:* $50. *Required:* essay or personal statement, high school transcript, minimum 3.0 GPA, 2 letters of recommendation, letter of reference from science teacher. *Required for some:* interview. *Application deadlines:* 2/1 (freshmen), 2/1 (transfers). *Early decision deadline:* 12/15. *Notification:* 3/1 (freshmen), 5/1 (transfers), 1/15 (early decision).

Freshman Application Contact Connie Horrall, Administrative Assistant, St. Louis College of Pharmacy, 4588 Parkview Place, St. Louis, MO 63110-1088. *Phone:* 314-446-8328. *Toll-free phone:* 800-278-5267 (in-state); 800-278-267 (out-of-state). *Fax:* 314-446-8310. *E-mail:* chorrall@stlcop.edu.
Website: http://www.stlcop.edu/.

See next page for display ad and page 1480 for the College Close-Up.

Are you inquisitive, interested in health and wellness, love math and science, and enjoy helping people?

Earn a degree that allows you to benefit individuals and the community. Become an integral part of a close-knit campus with nearly 50 student organizations. Take advantage of the surrounding world class medical community, the expertise of faculty, and all St. Louis has to offer.

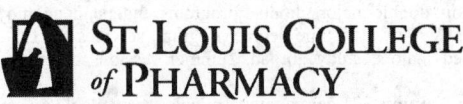

ST. LOUIS COLLEGE of PHARMACY

EST. 1864

4588 PARKVIEW PLACE
ST. LOUIS, MO 63110-1088
314.367.8700 1.800.2STLCOP
WWW.STLCOP.EDU

Saint Louis University

St. Louis, Missouri

- **Independent Roman Catholic (Jesuit)** university, founded 1818
- **Urban** 269-acre campus
- **Endowment** $852.8 million
- **Coed** 8,806 undergraduate students, 90% full-time, 59% women, 41% men
- **Moderately difficult** entrance level, 64% of applicants were admitted

Undergraduates 7,914 full-time, 892 part-time. Students come from 48 states and territories; 49 other countries; 61% are from out of state; 7% Black or African American, non-Hispanic/Latino; 4% Hispanic/Latino; 8% Asian, non-Hispanic/Latino; 0.2% American Indian or Alaska Native, non-Hispanic/Latino; 4% Two or more races, non-Hispanic/Latino; 4% Race/ethnicity unknown; 8% international; 5% transferred in; 52% live on campus. *Retention:* 88% of full-time freshmen returned.

Freshmen *Admission:* 13,060 applied, 8,314 admitted, 1,687 enrolled. *Average high school GPA:* 3.77. *Test scores:* SAT critical reading scores over 500: 88%; SAT math scores over 500: 93%; ACT scores over 18: 100%; SAT critical reading scores over 600: 54%; SAT math scores over 600: 57%; ACT scores over 24: 85%; SAT critical reading scores over 700: 13%; SAT math scores over 700: 16%; ACT scores over 30: 31%.

Faculty *Total:* 1,340, 55% full-time, 57% with terminal degrees. *Student/faculty ratio:* 12:1.

Academics *Calendar:* semesters. *Degrees:* certificates, bachelor's, master's, doctoral, post-master's, and postbachelor's certificates. *Special study options:* academic remediation for entering students, accelerated degree program, adult/continuing education programs, advanced placement credit, cooperative education, distance learning, double majors, English as a second language, honors programs, independent study, internships, off-campus study, part-time degree program, services for LD students, student-designed majors, study abroad, summer session for credit. *ROTC:* Army (c), Air Force (b). *Unusual degree programs:* 3-2 engineering with Washington University in St. Louis.

Computers on Campus 581 computers/terminals and 5,050 ports are available on campus for general student use. Students can access the following: campus intranet, computer help desk, free student e-mail accounts, online (class) grades, online (class) registration, online (class) schedules. Campus-wide network is available. 100% of college-owned or -operated housing units are wired for high-speed Internet access. Wireless service is available via entire campus.

Student Life *Housing:* on-campus residence required through sophomore year. *Options:* coed, men-only, women-only, disabled students. Campus housing is university owned and leased by the school. Freshman campus housing is guaranteed. *Activities and organizations:* drama/theater group, student-run newspaper, radio and television station, choral group, Alpha Phi Omega, Oriflamme, Student Activities Board, Interfraternity Council, Panhellenic Council, national fraternities, national sororities. *Campus security:* 24-hour emergency response devices and patrols, late-night transport/escort service, controlled dormitory access, crime prevention program, bicycle patrols, pamphlets, posters, films, identification of valuables, video cameras. *Student services:* health clinic, personal/psychological counseling, women's center.

Athletics Member NCAA. All Division I. *Intercollegiate sports:* badminton M(c)/W(c), baseball M(s), basketball M(s)/W(s), bowling M(c)/W(c), crew M(c)/W(c), cross-country running M(s)/W(s), fencing M(c)/W(c), field hockey W(s), golf M(c)/W(c), ice hockey M(c), lacrosse M(c)/W(c), racquetball M(c)/W(c), rugby M(c)/W(c), soccer M(s)/W(s), softball W(s), swimming and diving M(s)/W(s), table tennis M(c)/W(c), tennis M(s)/W(s), track and field M(s)/W(s), ultimate Frisbee M(c)/W(c), volleyball M(c)/W(c), water polo M(c). *Intramural sports:* badminton M/W, basketball M/W, bowling M/W, football M/W, golf M/W, racquetball M/W, soccer M/W, softball M/W, squash M/W, swimming and diving M/W, table tennis M/W, tennis M/W, ultimate Frisbee M/W, volleyball M/W.

Standardized Tests *Required:* SAT or ACT (for admission).

Costs (2012–13) *Comprehensive fee:* $44,878 includes full-time tuition ($34,740), mandatory fees ($526), and room and board ($9612). Full-time tuition and fees vary according to location and program. Part-time tuition: $1215 per credit hour. Part-time tuition and fees vary according to location and program. *Required fees:* $153 per term part-time. *College room only:* $5444. Room and board charges vary according to board plan, housing facility, and location. *Payment plan:* installment. *Waivers:* children of alumni and employees or children of employees.

Financial Aid Of all full-time matriculated undergraduates who enrolled in 2011, 5,069 applied for aid, 4,511 were judged to have need, 638 had their need fully met. 846 Federal Work-Study jobs (averaging $1737). 45 state and other part-time jobs (averaging $2122). In 2011, 1911 non-need-based awards were made. *Average percent of need met:* 65%. *Average financial aid package:* $25,925. *Average need-based loan:* $4743. *Average need-based gift aid:*

$19,167. *Average non-need-based aid:* $12,403. *Average indebtedness upon graduation:* $36,797.

Applying *Options:* electronic application, deferred entrance. *Required:* essay or personal statement, high school transcript, minimum 2.5 GPA. *Recommended:* 2 letters of recommendation, interview, secondary school report form and health examination. *Application deadlines:* 8/20 (freshmen), 8/20 (out-of-state freshmen), 8/20 (transfers). *Notification:* 9/15 (freshmen), 9/15 (out-of-state freshmen), continuous until 2/1 (transfers).

Freshman Application Contact Jean M. Gilman, Dean of Undergraduate Admission, Saint Louis University, 221 North Grand Boulevard, DuBourg Hall, Room 100, St. Louis, MO 63103-2097. *Phone:* 314-977-2500. *Toll-free phone:* 800-758-3678. *Fax:* 314-977-7136. *E-mail:* admitme@slu.edu. *Website:* http://www.slu.edu/.

Saint Luke's College of Health Sciences

Kansas City, Missouri

Application Contact Mrs. Jennifer Wright, Student Services Associate, Saint Luke's College of Health Sciences, 8320 Ward Parkway, Suite 300, Kansas City, MO 64114. *Phone:* 816-932-8629. *Fax:* 816-932-9064. *Website:* http://www.saintlukescollege.edu/.

Southeast Missouri State University

Cape Girardeau, Missouri

- **State-supported** comprehensive, founded 1873, part of Missouri Coordinating Board for Higher Education
- **Small-town** 400-acre campus
- **Endowment** $57.2 million
- **Coed** 10,541 undergraduate students, 78% full-time, 57% women, 43% men
- **Moderately difficult** entrance level, 97% of applicants were admitted

Undergraduates 8,206 full-time, 2,335 part-time. Students come from 39 states and territories; 46 other countries; 15% are from out of state; 9% Black or African American, non-Hispanic/Latino; 1% Hispanic/Latino; 0.9% Asian, non-Hispanic/Latino; 0.4% American Indian or Alaska Native, non-Hispanic/Latino; 0.2% Two or more races, non-Hispanic/Latino; 4% Race/ethnicity unknown; 6% international; 6% transferred in; 30% live on campus. *Retention:* 74% of full-time freshmen returned.

Freshmen *Admission:* 4,161 applied, 4,046 admitted, 1,888 enrolled. *Average high school GPA:* 3.3. *Test scores:* SAT critical reading scores over 500: 49%; SAT math scores over 500: 56%; ACT scores over 18: 95%; SAT critical reading scores over 600: 14%; SAT math scores over 600: 30%; ACT scores over 24: 38%; SAT critical reading scores over 700: 5%; SAT math scores over 700: 5%; ACT scores over 30: 5%.

Faculty *Total:* 598, 66% full-time, 56% with terminal degrees. *Student/faculty ratio:* 22:1.

Academics *Calendar:* semesters. *Degrees:* certificates, associate, bachelor's, master's, post-master's, and postbachelor's certificates. *Special study options:* academic remediation for entering students, accelerated degree program, adult/continuing education programs, advanced placement credit, distance learning, double majors, English as a second language, honors programs, independent study, internships, part-time degree program, services for LD students, student-designed majors, study abroad, summer session for credit. *ROTC:* Air Force (b).

Computers on Campus 1,550 computers/terminals and 2,000 ports are available on campus for general student use. Students can access the following: campus intranet, computer help desk, free student e-mail accounts, online (class) grades, online (class) registration, online (class) schedules. Campuswide network is available. 100% of college-owned or -operated housing units are wired for high-speed Internet access. Wireless service is available via classrooms, computer centers, computer labs, dorm rooms, learning centers, libraries, student centers.

Student Life *Housing:* on-campus residence required through sophomore year. *Options:* coed, men-only, women-only, disabled students. Campus housing is university owned. *Activities and organizations:* drama/theater group, student-run newspaper, radio and television station, choral group, marching band, Student Government, Panhellenic Council, Interfraternity Council, Residence Hall Association, Student Activities Council, national fraternities, national sororities. *Campus security:* 24-hour emergency response devices and patrols, late-

night transport/escort service, controlled dormitory access. *Student services:* health clinic, personal/psychological counseling.

Athletics Member NCAA. All Division I. *Intercollegiate sports:* baseball M(s), basketball M(s)/W(s), cheerleading M(s)/W(s), cross-country running M(s)/W(s), football M(s), gymnastics W(s), soccer W(s), softball W(s), tennis W(s), track and field M(s)/W(s), volleyball W(s). *Intramural sports:* baseball M(c)/W(c), basketball M(c)/W, bowling M/W, equestrian sports M(c)/W(c), fencing M(c)/W(c), football M/W, golf M(c)/W(c), racquetball M/W, riflery M(c)/W(c), rock climbing M(c)/W(c), rugby M(c)/W(c), soccer M/W, softball M/W, swimming and diving M(c)/W(c), table tennis M/W, tennis M/W, ultimate Frisbee M/W, volleyball M(c)/W(c).

Standardized Tests *Required:* SAT or ACT (for admission).

Costs (2012–13) *Tuition:* state resident $5814 full-time, $194 per credit hour part-time; nonresident $11,049 full-time, $368 per credit hour part-time. Full-time tuition and fees vary according to course load and location. Part-time tuition and fees vary according to course load and location. *Required fees:* $936 full-time, $31 per credit hour part-time. *Room and board:* $8110; room only: $5420. Room and board charges vary according to board plan and housing facility. *Payment plans:* installment, deferred payment. *Waivers:* senior citizens and employees or children of employees.

Financial Aid Of all full-time matriculated undergraduates who enrolled in 2011, 6,288 applied for aid, 5,026 were judged to have need, 683 had their need fully met. 207 Federal Work-Study jobs (averaging $1473). 1,512 state and other part-time jobs (averaging $1883). In 2011, 1207 non-need-based awards were made. *Average percent of need met:* 58%. *Average financial aid package:* $8191. *Average need-based loan:* $4017. *Average need-based gift aid:* $5213. *Average non-need-based aid:* $4051. *Average indebtedness upon graduation:* $24,398.

Applying *Options:* electronic application, deferred entrance. *Application fee:* $30. *Required:* high school transcript, minimum 2.0 GPA. *Application deadlines:* 7/1 (freshmen), 7/1 (out-of-state freshmen), 7/1 (transfers). *Notification:* 9/1 (freshmen), 9/1 (out-of-state freshmen), continuous (transfers).

Freshman Application Contact Southeast Missouri State University, One University Plaza, Cape Girardeau, MO 63701-4799. *Phone:* 573-651-2590. *Website:* http://www.semo.edu/.

Southwest Baptist University

Bolivar, Missouri

- **Independent Southern Baptist** comprehensive, founded 1878
- **Small-town** 152-acre campus
- **Endowment** $20.7 million
- **Coed** 3,009 undergraduate students, 69% full-time, 64% women, 36% men
- **Moderately difficult** entrance level, 59% of applicants were admitted

Undergraduates 2,065 full-time, 944 part-time. Students come from 40 states and territories; 19 other countries; 29% are from out of state; 4% Black or African American, non-Hispanic/Latino; 1% Hispanic/Latino; 0.8% Asian, non-Hispanic/Latino; 0.8% American Indian or Alaska Native, non-Hispanic/Latino; 27% Race/ethnicity unknown; 1% international; 3% transferred in; 63% live on campus. *Retention:* 67% of full-time freshmen returned.

Freshmen *Admission:* 1,912 applied, 1,125 admitted, 521 enrolled. *Average high school GPA:* 3. *Test scores:* SAT critical reading scores over 500: 44%; SAT math scores over 500: 44%; ACT scores over 18: 89%; SAT critical reading scores over 600: 19%; SAT math scores over 600: 12%; ACT scores over 24: 47%; SAT critical reading scores over 700: 2%; ACT scores over 30: 6%.

Faculty *Total:* 304, 42% full-time. *Student/faculty ratio:* 14:1.

Academics *Calendar:* 4-1-4. *Degrees:* associate, bachelor's, master's, doctoral, and post-master's certificates. *Special study options:* academic remediation for entering students, advanced placement credit, cooperative education, distance learning, double majors, honors programs, independent study, internships, off-campus study, part-time degree program, services for LD students, student-designed majors, study abroad, summer session for credit. *ROTC:* Army (c).

Computers on Campus 321 computers/terminals are available on campus for general student use. Students can access the following: computer help desk, free student e-mail accounts, online (class) grades, online (class) registration, online (class) schedules. Campuswide network is available. 90% of college-owned or -operated housing units are wired for high-speed Internet access. Wireless service is available via entire campus.

Student Life *Housing:* on-campus residence required through junior year. *Options:* men-only, women-only, disabled students. Campus housing is university owned. Freshman campus housing is guaranteed. *Activities and organizations:* drama/theater group, student-run newspaper, choral group, Enactus, Student Government Association, Fellowship of Christian Athletes, Student Missouri State Teachers Association, PSY CHI. *Campus security:* 24-hour emergency response devices and patrols, controlled dormitory access. *Student services:* health clinic, personal/psychological counseling.

Athletics Member NCAA. All Division II. *Intercollegiate sports:* baseball M(s), basketball M(s)/W(s), cheerleading M/W, cross-country running M(s)/W(s), football M(s), golf M(s), soccer M/W(s), softball W(s), tennis M(s)/W(s), track and field M(s)/W(s), volleyball W(s). *Intramural sports:* basketball M/W, football M/W, soccer M/W, softball M/W, table tennis M/W, volleyball M/W.

Standardized Tests *Required:* SAT or ACT (for admission).

Costs (2012–13) *Comprehensive fee:* $25,500 includes full-time tuition ($18,360), mandatory fees ($790), and room and board ($6350). Full-time tuition and fees vary according to course load and location. Part-time tuition and fees vary according to course load and location. *College room only:* $3150. Room and board charges vary according to board plan and housing facility. *Payment plan:* installment. *Waivers:* employees or children of employees.

Financial Aid Of all full-time matriculated undergraduates who enrolled in 2012, 2,001 applied for aid, 1,613 were judged to have need, 257 had their need fully met. 351 Federal Work-Study jobs (averaging $1800). In 2012, 325 non-need-based awards were made. *Average percent of need met: 68%. Average financial aid package: $15,142. Average need-based loan: $4171. Average need-based gift aid: $4942. Average non-need-based aid: $8960.*

Applying *Options:* electronic application. *Application fee:* $30. *Required:* high school transcript, minimum 2.5 GPA. *Required for some:* 3 letters of recommendation. *Recommended:* essay or personal statement, interview. *Application deadlines:* rolling (freshmen), rolling (transfers). *Notification:* continuous (freshmen), continuous (transfers).

Freshman Application Contact Mr. Darren Crowder, Director of Admissions, Southwest Baptist University, 1600 University Avenue, Bolivar, MO 65613-2597. *Phone:* 417-328-1817. *Toll-free phone:* 800-526-5859. *Fax:* 417-328-1808. *E-mail:* dcrowder@sbuniv.edu.
Website: http://www.sbuniv.edu/.

Stephens College

Columbia, Missouri

- **Independent** comprehensive, founded 1833
- **Urban** 86-acre campus
- **Endowment** $34.7 million
- **Coed, primarily women** 673 undergraduate students, 82% full-time, 98% women, 2% men
- **Moderately difficult** entrance level, 63% of applicants were admitted

Undergraduates 553 full-time, 120 part-time. Students come from 44 states and territories; 1 other country; 47% are from out of state; 15% Black or African American, non-Hispanic/Latino; 2% Hispanic/Latino; 0.6% Asian, non-Hispanic/Latino; 0.3% Native Hawaiian or other Pacific Islander, non-Hispanic/Latino; 1% American Indian or Alaska Native, non-Hispanic/Latino; 5% Two or more races, non-Hispanic/Latino; 3% Race/ethnicity unknown; 9% transferred in; 67% live on campus. *Retention:* 74% of full-time freshmen returned.

Freshmen *Admission:* 683 applied, 430 admitted, 140 enrolled. *Average high school GPA:* 3.35. *Test scores:* SAT critical reading scores over 500: 74%; SAT math scores over 500: 56%; SAT writing scores over 500: 57%; ACT scores over 18: 88%; SAT critical reading scores over 600: 22%; SAT math scores over 600: 17%; SAT writing scores over 600: 13%; ACT scores over 24: 48%; SAT critical reading scores over 700: 9%; ACT scores over 30: 3%.

Faculty *Total:* 104, 50% full-time, 33% with terminal degrees. *Student/faculty ratio:* 11:1.

Academics *Calendar:* semesters. *Degrees:* certificates, associate, bachelor's, master's, post-master's, and postbachelor's certificates. *Special study options:* academic remediation for entering students, accelerated degree program, adult/continuing education programs, advanced placement credit, cooperative education, distance learning, double majors, external degree program, freshman honors college, honors programs, independent study, internships, off-campus study, part-time degree program, services for LD students, student-designed majors, study abroad, summer session for credit. *ROTC:* Army (c), Navy (c), Air Force (c). *Unusual degree programs:* 3-2 occupational therapy with Washington University in St. Louis.

Computers on Campus 107 computers/terminals and 1 port are available on campus for general student use. Students can access the following: computer help desk, free student e-mail accounts, online (class) grades, online (class) schedules. Campuswide network is available. 100% of college-owned or -operated housing units are wired for high-speed Internet access. Wireless service is available via entire campus.

Student Life *Housing:* on-campus residence required through senior year. *Options:* women-only. Campus housing is university owned and is provided by a third party. Freshman campus housing is guaranteed. *Activities and organiza-*tions: drama/theater group, student-run newspaper, radio and television station, choral group, IFA, Warehouse Theatre, Student government, American Marketing Association (AMA), national sororities. *Campus security:* 24-hour emergency response devices and patrols, student patrols, late-night transport/escort service, controlled dormitory access. *Student services:* health clinic, personal/psychological counseling.

Athletics Member NAIA. *Intercollegiate sports:* basketball W(s), cross-country running W(s), golf W(s), soccer W(s), softball W(s), tennis W(s), volleyball W(s). *Intramural sports:* equestrian sports W(c).

Standardized Tests *Required:* SAT or ACT (for admission).

Costs (2012–13) *One-time required fee:* $200. *Comprehensive fee:* $37,510 includes full-time tuition ($27,210) and room and board ($10,300). Full-time tuition and fees vary according to course load, degree level, program, and reciprocity agreements. *Part-time tuition:* $700 per credit hour. Part-time tuition and fees vary according to course load, degree level, and program. *College room only:* $6900. Room and board charges vary according to board plan and housing facility. *Payment plan:* installment. *Waivers:* employees or children of employees.

Financial Aid Of all full-time matriculated undergraduates who enrolled in 2011, 545 applied for aid, 514 were judged to have need. 106 Federal Work-Study jobs (averaging $1525). 92 state and other part-time jobs (averaging $1516). In 2011, 46 non-need-based awards were made. *Average percent of need met: 73%. Average financial aid package: $20,846. Average need-based loan: $3842. Average need-based gift aid: $15,787. Average non-need-based aid: $8384. Average indebtedness upon graduation: $22,293.*

Applying *Options:* electronic application, deferred entrance. *Application fee:* $25. *Required:* essay or personal statement, high school transcript, minimum 2.0 GPA. *Required for some:* 1 letter of recommendation, audition mandatory for dance, recommended for theater. *Recommended:* minimum 2.5 GPA, interview. *Notification:* continuous until 9/15 (freshmen), continuous until 9/15 (transfers).

Freshman Application Contact Ms. Casey Pletz, Admissions Manager, Stephens College, 1200 East Broadway, Box 2121, Columbia, MO 65215-0002. *Phone:* 573-876-7207. *Toll-free phone:* 800-876-7207. *Fax:* 573-876-7237. *E-mail:* apply@stephens.edu.
Website: http://www.stephens.edu/.

Stevens Institute of Business & Arts

St. Louis, Missouri

- **Proprietary** 4-year, founded 1947
- **Urban** campus
- **Coed, primarily women**
- **Moderately difficult** entrance level

Faculty *Student/faculty ratio:* 10:1.

Academics *Calendar:* quarters. *Degrees:* diplomas, associate, and bachelor's.

Student Life *Campus security:* 24-hour emergency response devices, late-night transport/escort service.

Standardized Tests *Required for some:* SAT or ACT (for admission).

Costs (2012–13) *Tuition:* $225 per quarter hour part-time. No tuition increase for student's term of enrollment.

Applying *Application fee:* $15. *Required:* essay or personal statement, high school transcript, interview. *Required for some:* minimum 2.8 GPA.

Freshman Application Contact Mr. John Willmon, Director of Admissions, Stevens Institute of Business & Arts, 1521 Washington Avenue, St. Louis, MO 63102. *Phone:* 314-421-0949 Ext. 1119. *Toll-free phone:* 800-871-0949. *Fax:* 314-421-0304. *E-mail:* admission@siba.edu.
Website: http://www.siba.edu/.

Truman State University

Kirksville, Missouri

- **State-supported** comprehensive, founded 1867
- **Small-town** 140-acre campus
- **Endowment** $29.3 million
- **Coed** 5,872 undergraduate students, 91% full-time, 59% women, 41% men
- **Moderately difficult** entrance level, 74% of applicants were admitted

Undergraduates 5,357 full-time, 515 part-time. Students come from 39 states and territories; 54 other countries; 17% are from out of state; 4% Black or African American, non-Hispanic/Latino; 3% Hispanic/Latino; 2% Asian, non-Hispanic/Latino; 0.1% Native Hawaiian or other Pacific Islander, non-Hispanic/

COLLEGES AT-A-GLANCE

Latino; 0.3% American Indian or Alaska Native, non-Hispanic/Latino; 2% Two or more races, non-Hispanic/Latino; 2% Race/ethnicity unknown; 6% international; 3% transferred in; 45% live on campus. *Retention:* 89% of full-time freshmen returned.

Freshmen *Admission:* 4,445 applied, 3,275 admitted, 1,271 enrolled. *Average high school GPA:* 3.76. *Test scores:* SAT critical reading scores over 500: 89%; SAT math scores over 500: 92%; ACT scores over 18: 100%; SAT critical reading scores over 600: 66%; SAT math scores over 600: 56%; ACT scores over 24: 83%; SAT critical reading scores over 700: 32%; SAT math scores over 700: 14%; ACT scores over 30: 25%.

Faculty *Total:* 373, 85% full-time, 80% with terminal degrees. *Student/faculty ratio:* 17:1.

Academics *Calendar:* semesters. *Degrees:* bachelor's and master's. *Special study options:* accelerated degree program, advanced placement credit, cooperative education, double majors, honors programs, independent study, internships, off-campus study, part-time degree program, services for LD students, student-designed majors, study abroad, summer session for credit. *ROTC:* Army (b). *Unusual degree programs:* 3-2 engineering with Missouri University of Science and Technology, University of Missouri–Columbia.

Computers on Campus 738 computers/terminals and 3,690 ports are available on campus for general student use. Students can access the following: campus intranet, computer help desk, free student e-mail accounts, online (class) grades, online (class) registration, online (class) schedules. Campus-wide network is available. 100% of college-owned or -operated housing units are wired for high-speed Internet access. Wireless service is available via entire campus.

Student Life *Housing:* on-campus residence required for freshman year. *Options:* coed, disabled students. Campus housing is university owned. Freshman campus housing is guaranteed. *Activities and organizations:* drama/theater group, student-run newspaper, radio and television station, choral group, marching band, Nursing Students' Association (NSA), Beta Beta Beta (Biology Honors), Alpha Phi Omega (co-ed service fraternity), Communication Disorders Association, American Medical Student Association (AMSA), national fraternities, national sororities. *Campus security:* 24-hour emergency response devices and patrols, student patrols, late-night transport/escort service, controlled dormitory access, patrols by commissioned officers, perimeter access system, dual 911 call center for campus & community, emergency text messaging system. *Student services:* health clinic, personal/psychological counseling, women's center.

Athletics Member NCAA. All Division II. *Intercollegiate sports:* baseball M(s), basketball M(s)/W(s), bowling M(c)/W(c), cheerleading M(c)/W(c), cross-country running M(s)/W(s), equestrian sports M(c)/W(c), football M(s), golf W(s), lacrosse W(c), riflery M(c)/W(c), rock climbing M(c)/W(c), rugby M(c)/W(c), soccer M(s)/W(s), softball W(s), swimming and diving M/W(s), tennis M(s)/W(s), track and field M(s)/W(s), ultimate Frisbee M(c)/W(c), volleyball M(c)/W(s), weight lifting M(c)/W(c), wrestling M(s). *Intramural sports:* badminton M/W, basketball M/W, cross-country running M/W, football M/W, skiing (cross-country) M(c)/W(c), skiing (downhill) M(c)/W(c), soccer M/W, softball M/W, swimming and diving M/W, table tennis M/W, tennis M/W, track and field M/W, ultimate Frisbee M/W, volleyball M/W.

Standardized Tests *Required:* SAT or ACT (for admission).

Costs (2012–13) *One-time required fee:* $315. *Tuition:* state resident $6978 full-time, $291 per credit hour part-time; nonresident $12,714 full-time, $530 per credit hour part-time. Full-time tuition and fees vary according to course load and program. Part-time tuition and fees vary according to course load and program. *Required fees:* $238 full-time. *Room and board:* $7504. Room and board charges vary according to housing facility. *Payment plan:* installment. *Waivers:* children of alumni, senior citizens, and employees or children of employees.

Financial Aid Of all full-time matriculated undergraduates who enrolled in 2011, 3,950 applied for aid, 2,863 were judged to have need, 978 had their need fully met. 489 Federal Work-Study jobs (averaging $1742). 1,493 state and other part-time jobs (averaging $1226). In 2011, 1929 non-need-based awards were made. *Average percent of need met:* 82%. *Average financial aid package:* $10,707. *Average need-based loan:* $4182. *Average need-based gift aid:* $6520. *Average non-need-based aid:* $5334. *Average indebtedness upon graduation:* $22,922.

Applying *Options:* electronic application, deferred entrance. *Required:* essay or personal statement, high school transcript, official college entrance exam scores required, activities list/resume recommended. *Recommended:* minimum 3.0 GPA, interview. *Application deadlines:* rolling (freshmen), rolling (out-of-state freshmen), rolling (transfers). *Notification:* continuous until 9/15 (freshmen), continuous until 9/15 (out-of-state freshmen), continuous (transfers).

Freshman Application Contact Melody Chambers, Director of Admissions, Truman State University, Ruth Towne Museum and Visitors Center, 100 East Normal Avenue, Kirksville, MO 63501-4221. *Phone:* 660-785-4114. *Toll-free phone:* 800-892-7792. *Fax:* 660-785-7456. *E-mail:* mchamber@truman.edu. *Website:* http://www.truman.edu/.

See below for display ad and page 1542 for the College Close-Up.

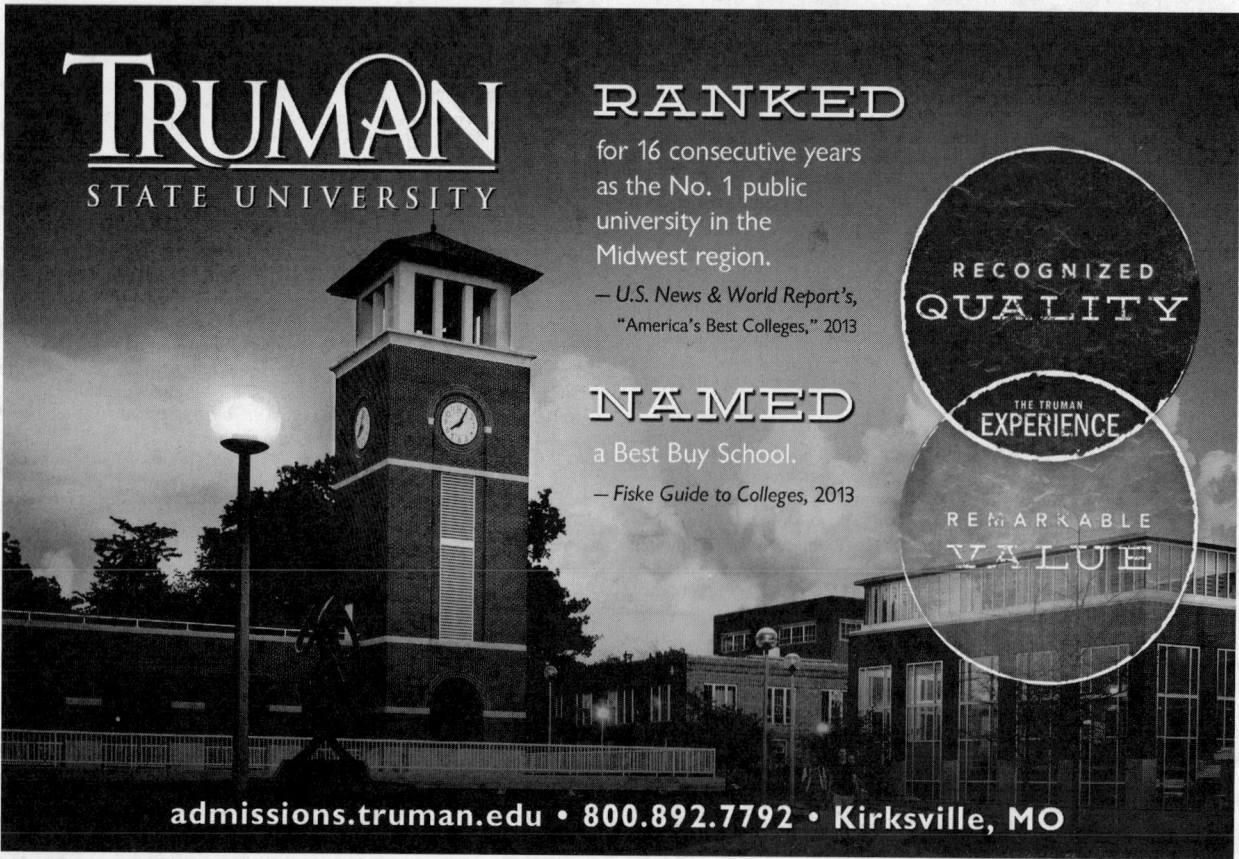

University of Central Missouri

Warrensburg, Missouri

- **State-supported** comprehensive, founded 1871
- **Small-town** 1561-acre campus with easy access to Kansas City
- **Endowment** $27.8 million
- **Coed**
- **Moderately difficult** entrance level

Faculty *Student/faculty ratio:* 17:1.

Academics *Calendar:* semesters. *Degrees:* associate, bachelor's, master's, post-master's, and postbachelor's certificates.

Student Life *Campus security:* 24-hour emergency response devices and patrols, student patrols, late-night transport/escort service, controlled dormitory access, canine patrol.

Athletics Member NCAA. All Division II.

Standardized Tests *Required:* SAT or ACT (for admission).

Financial Aid *Of all full-time matriculated undergraduates who enrolled in 2010,* 4,917 applied for aid, 3,106 were judged to have need, 346 had their need fully met. 330 Federal Work-Study jobs (averaging $1576). 1,165 state and other part-time jobs (averaging $1913). *In 2010,* 966 non-need-based awards were made. *Average percent of need met:* 84. *Average financial aid package:* $10,020. *Average need-based loan:* $4224. *Average need-based gift aid:* $4195. *Average non-need-based aid:* $8975. *Average indebtedness upon graduation:* $23,323.

Applying *Options:* electronic application, deferred entrance. *Application fee:* $30. *Required:* high school transcript, rank in upper two-thirds of high school class.

Freshman Application Contact Ms. Ann Nordyke, Director of Admissions, University of Central Missouri, 1400 Ward Edwards, Warrensburg, MO 64093. *Phone:* 660-543-4170. *Toll-free phone:* 800-729-8266. *Fax:* 660-543-8517. *E-mail:* admit@ucmo.edu.
Website: http://www.ucmo.edu/.

University of Missouri

Columbia, Missouri

- **State-supported** university, founded 1839, part of University of Missouri System
- **Suburban** 1262-acre campus
- **Endowment** $620.0 million
- **Coed** 26,996 undergraduate students, 93% full-time, 52% women, 48% men
- **Moderately difficult** entrance level, 81% of applicants were admitted

Undergraduates 25,178 full-time, 1,818 part-time. Students come from 53 states and territories; 84 other countries; 21% are from out of state; 8% Black or African American, non-Hispanic/Latino; 3% Hispanic/Latino; 2% Asian, non-Hispanic/Latino; 0.3% American Indian or Alaska Native, non-Hispanic/Latino; 2% Two or more races, non-Hispanic/Latino; 1% Race/ethnicity unknown; 3% international; 5% transferred in; 27% live on campus. *Retention:* 84% of full-time freshmen returned.

Freshmen *Admission:* 20,564 applied, 16,752 admitted, 6,501 enrolled. *Test scores:* SAT critical reading scores over 500: 81%; SAT math scores over 500: 87%; ACT scores over 18: 99%; SAT critical reading scores over 600: 42%; SAT math scores over 600: 46%; ACT scores over 24: 71%; SAT critical reading scores over 700: 11%; SAT math scores over 700: 10%; ACT scores over 30: 16%.

Faculty *Total:* 1,489, 92% full-time, 92% with terminal degrees. *Student/faculty ratio:* 20:1.

Academics *Calendar:* semesters. *Degrees:* bachelor's, master's, doctoral, and post-master's certificates. *Special study options:* accelerated degree program, adult/continuing education programs, advanced placement credit, cooperative education, distance learning, double majors, English as a second language, external degree program, freshman honors college, honors programs, independent study, internships, off-campus study, part-time degree program, services for LD students, student-designed majors, study abroad, summer session for credit. *ROTC:* Army (b), Navy (b), Air Force (b). *Unusual degree programs:* 3-2 accountancy, physical therapy, occupational therapy.

Computers on Campus 1,242 computers/terminals are available on campus for general student use. Students can access the following: computer help desk, free student e-mail accounts, online (class) grades, online (class) registration, online (class) schedules. Campuswide network is available. 90% of college-owned or -operated housing units are wired for high-speed Internet access. Wireless service is available via classrooms, computer centers, computer labs, dorm rooms, learning centers, libraries, student centers.

Student Life *Housing:* on-campus residence required for freshman year. *Options:* coed, men-only, women-only, disabled students. Campus housing is university owned. Freshman campus housing is guaranteed. *Activities and organizations:* drama/theater group, student-run newspaper, radio and television station, choral group, marching band, Academic organizations, Greek organizations, religious organizations, sports clubs, Student Governance, national fraternities, national sororities. *Campus security:* 24-hour emergency response devices and patrols, late-night transport/escort service, controlled dormitory access. *Student services:* health clinic, personal/psychological counseling, women's center, legal services.

Athletics Member NCAA. All Division I except football (Division I-A). *Intercollegiate sports:* baseball M(s), basketball M(s)/W(s), cross-country running M(s)/W(s), golf M(s)/W(s), gymnastics W(s), soccer W(s), softball W(s), swimming and diving M(s)/W(s), tennis W(s), track and field M(s)/W(s), volleyball W(s), wrestling M(s). *Intramural sports:* archery M(c)/W(c), badminton M(c), baseball M(c), basketball M(c)/W(c), bowling M(c)/W(c), fencing M(c)/W(c), field hockey W(c), ice hockey M(c), lacrosse M(c)/W(c), racquetball M(c)/W(c), rugby M(c)/W(c), soccer M(c)/W(c), softball W(c), swimming and diving M(c)/W(c), table tennis M(c)/W(c), tennis M(c)/W(c), ultimate Frisbee M(c)/W(c), volleyball M(c)/W(c), water polo M(c)/W(c), weight lifting M(c)/W(c).

Standardized Tests *Required:* SAT or ACT (for admission). *Recommended:* ACT (for admission).

Costs (2012–13) *Tuition:* state resident $8082 full-time; nonresident $22,191 full-time. Full-time tuition and fees vary according to course load, program, and reciprocity agreements. Part-time tuition and fees vary according to course load, program, and reciprocity agreements. *Required fees:* $1175 full-time. *Room and board:* $8944; room only: $5564. Room and board charges vary according to board plan and housing facility. *Payment plan:* installment. *Waivers:* senior citizens and employees or children of employees.

Financial Aid Of all full-time matriculated undergraduates who enrolled in 2011, 16,967 applied for aid, 12,452 were judged to have need, 1,772 had their need fully met. In 2011, 4067 non-need-based awards were made. *Average percent of need met:* 80%. *Average financial aid package:* $13,342. *Average need-based loan:* $4459. *Average need-based gift aid:* $7438. *Average non-need-based aid:* $3541. *Average indebtedness upon graduation:* $23,588.

Applying *Options:* electronic application, deferred entrance. *Application fee:* $50. *Required:* high school transcript, specific high school curriculum. *Application deadlines:* rolling (freshmen), rolling (transfers). *Notification:* continuous (freshmen), continuous (transfers).

Freshman Application Contact Ms. Barbara Rupp, Director of Admissions, University of Missouri, 230 Jesse Hall, Columbia, MO 65211. *Phone:* 573-882-7786. *Toll-free phone:* 800-225-6075. *Fax:* 573-882-7887. *E-mail:* mu4u@missouri.edu.
Website: http://www.missouri.edu/.

University of Missouri–Kansas City

Kansas City, Missouri

- **State-supported** university, founded 1929, part of University of Missouri System
- **Urban** 191-acre campus with easy access to Kansas City
- **Endowment** $235.5 million
- **Coed** 10,626 undergraduate students, 65% full-time, 58% women, 42% men
- **Moderately difficult** entrance level, 68% of applicants were admitted

Undergraduates 6,894 full-time, 3,732 part-time. Students come from 43 states and territories; 38 other countries; 22% are from out of state; 14% Black or African American, non-Hispanic/Latino; 6% Hispanic/Latino; 5% Asian, non-Hispanic/Latino; 0.2% Native Hawaiian or other Pacific Islander, non-Hispanic/Latino; 0.4% American Indian or Alaska Native, non-Hispanic/Latino; 3% Two or more races, non-Hispanic/Latino; 6% Race/ethnicity unknown; 4% international; 14% transferred in; 8% live on campus. *Retention:* 69% of full-time freshmen returned.

Freshmen *Admission:* 4,452 applied, 3,009 admitted, 1,125 enrolled. *Average high school GPA:* 3.27. *Test scores:* SAT critical reading scores over 500: 82%; SAT math scores over 500: 86%; ACT scores over 18: 88%; SAT critical reading scores over 600: 51%; SAT math scores over 600: 51%; ACT scores over 24: 51%; SAT critical reading scores over 700: 21%; SAT math scores over 700: 28%; ACT scores over 30: 14%.

Faculty *Total:* 1,187, 64% full-time, 71% with terminal degrees. *Student/faculty ratio:* 13:1.

Academics *Calendar:* semesters. *Degrees:* bachelor's, master's, doctoral, and post-master's certificates. *Special study options:* accelerated degree program, adult/continuing education programs, advanced placement credit, cooperative education, distance learning, double majors, English as a second language, honors programs, independent study, internships, off-campus study, part-time degree program, services for LD students, student-designed majors, study abroad, summer session for credit. *ROTC:* Army (b), Air Force (c).

Computers on Campus 400 computers/terminals are available on campus for general student use. Students can access the following: campus intranet, computer help desk, free student e-mail accounts, online (class) grades, online (class) registration, online (class) schedules. Campuswide network is available. 100% of college-owned or -operated housing units are wired for high-speed Internet access. Wireless service is available via classrooms, computer labs, dorm rooms, libraries, student centers.

Student Life *Housing options:* coed, disabled students. Campus housing is university owned. *Activities and organizations:* drama/theater group, student-run newspaper, radio station, choral group, Activities and Programs Council, International Student Council, Alpha Phi Omega, Omicron Delta Kappa, Greek Organizations, national fraternities, national sororities. *Campus security:* 24-hour emergency response devices and patrols, late-night transport/escort service, controlled dormitory access. *Student services:* health clinic, personal/psychological counseling, women's center, legal services.

Athletics Member NCAA. All Division I. *Intercollegiate sports:* basketball M(s)/W(s), cross-country running M(s)/W(s), golf M(s)/W(s), soccer M(s)/W(s), softball W(s), tennis M(s)/W(s), track and field M(s)/W(s), volleyball W(s). *Intramural sports:* badminton M/W, basketball M/W, football M/W, racquetball M/W, soccer M/W, softball M/W, swimming and diving M/W, table tennis M/W, volleyball M/W.

Standardized Tests *Required:* SAT or ACT (for admission).

Costs (2012–13) *Tuition:* state resident $7968 full-time, $266 per credit hour part-time; nonresident $20,502 full-time, $683 per credit hour part-time. Full-time tuition and fees vary according to course load and program. Part-time tuition and fees vary according to course load and program. *Required fees:* $1252 full-time, $64 per credit hour part-time. *Room and board:* $11,428. Room and board charges vary according to board plan and housing facility. *Payment plan:* installment. *Waivers:* employees or children of employees.

Financial Aid Of all full-time matriculated undergraduates who enrolled in 2012, 5,338 applied for aid, 4,754 were judged to have need, 282 had their need fully met. 472 Federal Work-Study jobs (averaging $3975). In 2012, 960 non-need-based awards were made. *Average percent of need met:* 49%. *Average financial aid package:* $9513. *Average need-based loan:* $8272. *Average need-based gift aid:* $6346. *Average non-need-based aid:* $4493. *Average indebtedness upon graduation:* $24,326.

Applying *Options:* electronic application, deferred entrance. *Application fee:* $45. *Required:* high school transcript. *Required for some:* essay or personal statement, interview. *Application deadlines:* rolling (freshmen), rolling (transfers). *Notification:* continuous (freshmen), continuous (transfers).

Freshman Application Contact Ms. Sara Gillham, Associate Director of Recruitment, University of Missouri–Kansas City, Office of Admissions, 5100 Rockhill Road, Kansas City, MO 64110-2499. *Phone:* 816-235-1111. *Toll-free phone:* 800-775-8652. *Fax:* 816-235-5544. *E-mail:* admit@umkc.edu. *Website:* http://www.umkc.edu/.

University of Missouri–St. Louis

St. Louis, Missouri

- **State-supported** university, founded 1963, part of University of Missouri System
- **Suburban** 350-acre campus
- **Endowment** $55.3 million
- **Coed** 13,349 undergraduate students, 45% full-time, 58% women, 42% men
- **Moderately difficult** entrance level, 69% of applicants were admitted

Undergraduates 6,069 full-time, 7,280 part-time. Students come from 36 states and territories; 48 other countries; 10% are from out of state; 20% Black or African American, non-Hispanic/Latino; 2% Hispanic/Latino; 4% Asian, non-Hispanic/Latino; 0.1% Native Hawaiian or other Pacific Islander, non-Hispanic/Latino; 0.3% American Indian or Alaska Native, non-Hispanic/Latino; 1% Two or more races, non-Hispanic/Latino; 7% Race/ethnicity unknown; 4% international; 14% transferred in; 8% live on campus. *Retention:* 78% of full-time freshmen returned.

Freshmen *Admission:* 1,936 applied, 1,329 admitted, 546 enrolled. *Average high school GPA:* 3408. *Test scores:* SAT math scores over 500: 68%; ACT scores over 18: 98%; SAT math scores over 600: 39%; ACT scores over 24: 53%; SAT math scores over 700: 7%; ACT scores over 30: 7%.

Faculty *Total:* 1,005, 48% full-time, 47% with terminal degrees. *Student/faculty ratio:* 16:1.

Academics *Calendar:* semesters. *Degrees:* bachelor's, master's, doctoral, post-master's, and postbachelor's certificates. *Special study options:* accelerated degree program, adult/continuing education programs, advanced placement credit, cooperative education, distance learning, double majors, English as a second language, freshman honors college, honors programs, independent study, internships, off-campus study, part-time degree program, services for LD students, student-designed majors, study abroad, summer session for credit. *ROTC:* Army (c), Air Force (c). *Unusual degree programs:* 3-2 engineering with Washington University; economics, history, philosophy, political science and sociology.

Computers on Campus 1,280 computers/terminals and 1,280 ports are available on campus for general student use. Students can access the following: campus intranet, computer help desk, free student e-mail accounts, online (class) grades, online (class) registration, online (class) schedules. Campuswide network is available. 90% of college-owned or -operated housing units are wired for high-speed Internet access. Wireless service is available via classrooms, computer centers, computer labs, dorm rooms, learning centers, libraries, student centers.

Student Life *Housing options:* coed, men-only, women-only, disabled students. Campus housing is university owned and is provided by a third party. *Activities and organizations:* drama/theater group, student-run newspaper, radio station, choral group, Student Government Association, Associated Black Collegians, Pierre laclede Honors College Student Association, Residence Hall Association, UMSL Radio Station, national fraternities, national sororities. *Campus security:* 24-hour emergency response devices and patrols, late-night transport/escort service, controlled dormitory access. *Student services:* health clinic, personal/psychological counseling, women's center.

Athletics Member NCAA. All Division II. *Intercollegiate sports:* baseball M(s), basketball M(s)/W(s), cheerleading W, golf M(s)/W(s), ice hockey M(c), soccer M(s)/W(s), softball W(s), table tennis M(c)/W(c), tennis M(s)/W(s), volleyball W(s). *Intramural sports:* badminton M/W, basketball M/W, bowling M/W, football M/W, golf M/W, racquetball M/W, rock climbing M/W, skiing (downhill) M/W, soccer M/W, softball M/W, table tennis M/W, tennis M/W, volleyball M/W, weight lifting M/W.

Standardized Tests *Required:* SAT or ACT (for admission).

Costs (2013–14) *Tuition:* state resident $9474 full-time, $316 per credit hour part-time; nonresident $24,429 full-time, $814 per credit hour part-time. Full-time tuition and fees vary according to course load, program, and reciprocity agreements. Part-time tuition and fees vary according to course load, program, and reciprocity agreements. *Room and board:* $8830; room only: $5200. Room and board charges vary according to board plan and housing facility. *Payment plan:* installment. *Waivers:* senior citizens and employees or children of employees.

Financial Aid Of all full-time matriculated undergraduates who enrolled in 2012, 4,725 applied for aid, 4,207 were judged to have need, 725 had their need fully met. 66 Federal Work-Study jobs (averaging $3365). In 2012, 198 non-need-based awards were made. *Average percent of need met:* 63%. *Average financial aid package:* $11,828. *Average need-based loan:* $4533. *Average need-based gift aid:* $6760. *Average non-need-based aid:* $4341. *Average indebtedness upon graduation:* $24,377.

Applying *Options:* electronic application. *Application fee:* $35. *Required:* high school transcript, minimum 2.0 GPA, CBHE core requirements. *Required for some:* essay or personal statement, 2 letters of recommendation, interview. *Application deadlines:* 8/23 (freshmen), 8/23 (out-of-state freshmen), rolling (transfers). *Notification:* continuous until 10/1 (freshmen), continuous until 10/1 (out-of-state freshmen), continuous (transfers).

Freshman Application Contact Mr. Andrew L. Griffin, Associate Director of Admissions, University of Missouri–St. Louis, 351 Millennium Student Center, One University Boulevard, St. Louis, MO 63121-4400. *Phone:* 314-516-6941. *Toll-free phone:* 888-GO2-UMSL (in-state); 888-GO2-USML (out-of-state). *Fax:* 314-516-5310. *E-mail:* askdrew@umsl.edu. *Website:* http://www.umsl.edu/.

University of Phoenix–Kansas City Campus

Kansas City, Missouri

Freshman Application Contact Marc Booker, Sr. Director, Office of Admissions and Evaluation, University of Phoenix–Kansas City Campus, 4035 South Riverpoint Parkway, Mail Stop CF-L101, Phoenix, AZ 85040. *Phone:* 602-557-4609. *Toll-free phone:* 866-766-0766. *Fax:* 480-643-1156. *Website:* http://www.phoenix.edu/.

University of Phoenix–St. Louis Campus

St. Louis, Missouri

Freshman Application Contact Marc Booker, Sr. Director, Office of Admissions and Evaluation, University of Phoenix–St. Louis Campus, 4035 South Riverpoint Parkway, Mail Stop CF-L101, Phoenix, AZ 85040. *Phone:* 602-557-4609. *Toll-free phone:* 866-766-0766. *Fax:* 480-643-1156. *Website:* http://www.phoenix.edu/.

University of Phoenix–Springfield Campus

Springfield, Missouri

Freshman Application Contact Marc Booker, Sr. Director, Office of Admissions and Evaluation, University of Phoenix–Springfield Campus, 4035 South Riverpoint Parkway, Mail Stop CF-L101, Phoenix, AZ 85040. *Phone:* 602-557-4609. *Toll-free phone:* 866-766-0766. *Fax:* 480-643-1156. *Website:* http://www.phoenix.edu/.

Vatterott College

Berkeley, Missouri

Director of Admissions Ann Farajallah, Director of Admissions, Vatterott College, 8580 Evans Avenue, Berkeley, MO 63134. *Phone:* 314-264-1020. *Toll-free phone:* 888-553-6627. *Website:* http://www.vatterott.edu/.

Vatterott College

Sunset Hills, Missouri

Director of Admissions Director of Admission, Vatterott College, 12900 Maurer Industrial Drive, Sunset Hills, MO 63127. *Phone:* 314-843-4200. *Toll-free phone:* 888-553-6627. *Fax:* 314-843-1709. *Website:* http://www.vatterott.edu/.

Washington University in St. Louis

St. Louis, Missouri

- **Independent** university, founded 1853
- **Suburban** 169-acre campus
- **Endowment** $5.3 billion
- **Coed** 7,259 undergraduate students, 89% full-time, 52% women, 48% men
- **Most difficult** entrance level, 18% of applicants were admitted

Undergraduates 6,455 full-time, 804 part-time. Students come from 54 states and territories; 55 other countries; 93% are from out of state; 6% Black or African American, non-Hispanic/Latino; 5% Hispanic/Latino; 17% Asian, non-Hispanic/Latino; 0.1% American Indian or Alaska Native, non-Hispanic/Latino; 4% Two or more races, non-Hispanic/Latino; 1% Race/ethnicity unknown; 8% international; 0.5% transferred in; 79% live on campus. *Retention:* 96% of full-time freshmen returned.
Freshmen *Admission:* 27,265 applied, 4,876 admitted, 1,637 enrolled. *Test scores:* SAT critical reading scores over 500: 100%; SAT math scores over 500: 100%; SAT writing scores over 500: 100%; ACT scores over 18: 100%; SAT critical reading scores over 600: 99%; SAT math scores over 600: 99%; SAT writing scores over 600: 99%; ACT scores over 24: 100%; SAT critical reading scores over 700: 75%; SAT math scores over 700: 86%; SAT writing scores over 700: 73%; ACT scores over 30: 96%.
Faculty *Total:* 1,102, 86% full-time, 84% with terminal degrees. *Student/faculty ratio:* 7:1.
Academics *Calendar:* semesters. *Degrees:* certificates, bachelor's, master's, doctoral, post-master's, and postbachelor's certificates. *Special study options:* accelerated degree program, adult/continuing education programs, advanced placement credit, cooperative education, distance learning, double majors, English as a second language, independent study, internships, off-campus study, part-time degree program, services for LD students, student-designed majors, study abroad, summer session for credit. *ROTC:* Army (b), Air Force (c). *Unusual degree programs:* 3-2 business administration; engineering; social work; art, occupational therapy, physical therapy.
Computers on Campus 2,500 computers/terminals are available on campus for general student use. Students can access the following: campus intranet, computer help desk, free student e-mail accounts, online (class) grades, online (class) registration, online (class) schedules. Campuswide network is available. 90% of college-owned or -operated housing units are wired for high-speed Internet access. Wireless service is available via classrooms, computer centers, computer labs, dorm rooms, learning centers, libraries, student centers.
Student Life *Housing:* on-campus residence required for freshman year. *Options:* coed, men-only, women-only, cooperative. Campus housing is university owned. Freshman campus housing is guaranteed. *Activities and organizations:* drama/theater group, student-run newspaper, radio and television station, choral group, national fraternities, national sororities. *Campus security:* 24-hour emergency response devices and patrols, student patrols, late-night transport/escort service, controlled dormitory access. *Student services:* health clinic, personal/psychological counseling, women's center.
Athletics Member NCAA. All Division III. *Intercollegiate sports:* baseball M, basketball M/W, crew M(c)/W(c), cross-country running M/W, equestrian sports M(c)/W(c), fencing M(c)/W(c), field hockey W(c), football M, golf M(c)/W, gymnastics M(c)/W(c), ice hockey M(c), lacrosse M(c)/W(c), rugby M(c)/W(c), sailing M(c)/W(c), soccer M/W, softball W, swimming and diving M/W, table tennis M(c)/W(c), tennis M/W, track and field M/W, ultimate Frisbee M(c)/W(c), volleyball M(c)/W, water polo M(c)/W(c). *Intramural sports:* badminton M/W, basketball M/W, bowling M/W, cross-country running M/W, football M/W, golf M/W, racquetball M/W, soccer M(c)/W(c), softball M/W, swimming and diving M/W, table tennis M/W, tennis M/W, track and field M/W, ultimate Frisbee M/W, volleyball M/W, water polo M/W.
Standardized Tests *Required:* SAT or ACT (for admission).
Costs (2013–14) *Comprehensive fee:* $58,818 includes full-time tuition ($44,100), mandatory fees ($741), and room and board ($13,977). *College room only:* $9437. Room and board charges vary according to board plan and housing facility. *Payment plans:* tuition prepayment, installment. *Waivers:* employees or children of employees.
Financial Aid Of all full-time matriculated undergraduates who enrolled in 2012, 4,285 applied for aid, 2,586 were judged to have need, 2,456 had their need fully met. 1,121 Federal Work-Study jobs (averaging $2040). In 2012, 822 non-need-based awards were made. *Average percent of need met:* 100%. *Average financial aid package:* $34,558. *Average need-based loan:* $6229. *Average need-based gift aid:* $31,295. *Average non-need-based aid:* $6072. *Financial aid deadline:* 2/1.
Applying *Options:* electronic application, early admission, early decision, deferred entrance. *Application fee:* $75. *Required:* essay or personal statement, high school transcript, 2 letters of recommendation. *Recommended:* minimum 3.0 GPA, Portfolios are required for students applying to the College of Art. Portfolios are strongly encouraged for students applying to the College of Architecture. *Application deadlines:* 1/15 (freshmen), 4/15 (transfers). *Early decision deadline:* 11/15. *Notification:* 4/1 (freshmen), continuous (transfers), 12/15 (early decision).
Freshman Application Contact Ms. Julie Shimabukuro, Director of Admissions, Washington University in St. Louis, Campus Box 1089, One Brookings Drive, St. Louis, MO 63130-4899. *Phone:* 314-935-6000. *Toll-free phone:* 800-638-0700. *Fax:* 314-935-4290. *E-mail:* admissions@wustl.edu. *Website:* http://www.wustl.edu/.

Webster University

St. Louis, Missouri

- **Independent** comprehensive, founded 1915
- **Suburban** 47-acre campus with easy access to St. Louis
- **Endowment** $86.5 million
- **Coed** 2,995 undergraduate students, 82% full-time, 56% women, 44% men
- **Moderately difficult** entrance level, 59% of applicants were admitted

Undergraduates 2,449 full-time, 546 part-time. Students come from 40 states and territories; 37 other countries; 23% are from out of state; 11% Black or African American, non-Hispanic/Latino; 3% Hispanic/Latino; 2% Asian, non-Hispanic/Latino; 0.3% American Indian or Alaska Native, non-Hispanic/Latino; 2% Two or more races, non-Hispanic/Latino; 7% Race/ethnicity unknown; 2% international; 11% transferred in; 25% live on campus. *Retention:* 79% of full-time freshmen returned.

Freshmen *Admission:* 1,706 applied, 1,008 admitted, 415 enrolled. *Average high school GPA:* 3.46. *Test scores:* ACT scores over 18: 91%; ACT scores over 24: 51%; ACT scores over 30: 7%.

Faculty *Total:* 641, 30% full-time, 31% with terminal degrees. *Student/faculty ratio:* 11:1.

Academics *Calendar:* semesters. *Degrees:* certificates, bachelor's, master's, doctoral, post-master's, and postbachelor's certificates. *Special study options:* academic remediation for entering students, accelerated degree program, adult/continuing education programs, advanced placement credit, cooperative education, distance learning, double majors, English as a second language, independent study, internships, off-campus study, part-time degree program, services for LD students, student-designed majors, study abroad, summer session for credit. *ROTC:* Army (c), Air Force (c). *Unusual degree programs:* 3-2 engineering with University of Missouri-Columbia, Washington University in St. Louis; Architecture with Washington University in St. Louis, Athletic Training with Saint Louis University, Chiropractic with Logan College of Chiropractic, Occupational Therapy with Washington University School of Medicine.

Computers on Campus 661 computers/terminals and 250 ports are available on campus for general student use. Students can access the following: campus intranet, computer help desk, free student e-mail accounts, online (class) grades, online (class) registration, online (class) schedules. Campuswide network is available. 100% of college-owned or -operated housing units are wired for high-speed Internet access. Wireless service is available via entire campus.

Student Life *Housing:* on-campus residence required for freshman year. *Options:* coed. Campus housing is university owned. Freshman applicants given priority for college housing. *Activities and organizations:* drama/theater group, student-run newspaper, radio and television station, choral group, Student Government Association, Association for African American Collegians, International Student Association, Commuter Council, Residential Housing Association, national sororities. *Campus security:* 24-hour emergency response devices and patrols, student patrols, late-night transport/escort service, controlled dormitory access. *Student services:* health clinic, personal/psychological counseling, women's center.

Athletics Member NCAA. All Division III. *Intercollegiate sports:* baseball M, basketball M/W, cross-country running M/W, golf M, soccer M/W, softball W, tennis M/W, track and field M/W, volleyball W. *Intramural sports:* basketball M/W, bowling M/W, cheerleading M(c)/W(c), football M/W, soccer M(c)/W(c), swimming and diving M(c)/W(c), volleyball M/W.

Standardized Tests *Required:* SAT or ACT (for admission).

Costs (2012–13) *Comprehensive fee:* $32,960 includes full-time tuition ($23,010) and room and board ($9950). Full-time tuition and fees vary according to program. Part-time tuition: $590 per credit hour. Part-time tuition and fees vary according to location. *College room only:* $5520. Room and board charges vary according to board plan, housing facility, and location. *Payment plan:* installment. *Waivers:* employees or children of employees.

Financial Aid Of all full-time matriculated undergraduates who enrolled in 2012, 2,111 applied for aid, 1,716 were judged to have need, 2 had their need fully met. 966 Federal Work-Study jobs (averaging $2216). 838 state and other part-time jobs (averaging $1086). In 2012, 97 non-need-based awards were made. *Average percent of need met:* 32%. *Average financial aid package:* $11,677. *Average need-based loan:* $4136. *Average need-based gift aid:* $6462. *Average non-need-based aid:* $5474. *Average indebtedness upon graduation:* $29,723.

Applying *Options:* electronic application, early admission, deferred entrance. *Application fee:* $35. *Required:* essay or personal statement, high school transcript, minimum 2.5 GPA, 1 letter of recommendation. *Required for some:* minimum 3.0 GPA, audition required for dance, music, theatre, and musical theatre students; portfolio required for art and film students. *Recommended:* minimum 3.0 GPA, interview. *Application deadlines:* 8/1 (freshmen), 8/1 (out-of-state freshmen), 8/1 (transfers). *Notification:* continuous (freshmen), continuous (out-of-state freshmen), continuous (transfers).

Freshman Application Contact Mr. Andrew Laue, Associate Director of Undergraduate Admission, Webster University, 470 East Lockwood Avenue, St. Louis, MO 63119-3194. *Phone:* 314-246-7712. *Toll-free phone:* 800-75-ENROL. *Fax:* 314-246-7122. *E-mail:* lauear@webster.edu. *Website:* http://www.webster.edu/.

Westminster College
Fulton, Missouri

- **Independent** 4-year, founded 1851, affiliated with Presbyterian Church
- **Small-town** 80-acre campus
- **Endowment** $46.2 million
- **Coed** 1,084 undergraduate students, 99% full-time, 44% women, 56% men
- **Moderately difficult** entrance level, 72% of applicants were admitted

Undergraduates 1,074 full-time, 10 part-time. Students come from 32 states and territories; 66 other countries; 20% are from out of state; 6% Black or African American, non-Hispanic/Latino; 4% Hispanic/Latino; 1% Asian, non-Hispanic/Latino; 0.1% Native Hawaiian or other Pacific Islander, non-Hispanic/Latino; 2% American Indian or Alaska Native, non-Hispanic/Latino; 1% Two or more races, non-Hispanic/Latino; 2% Race/ethnicity unknown; 15% international; 5% transferred in; 85% live on campus. *Retention:* 83% of full-time freshmen returned.

Freshmen *Admission:* 1,420 applied, 1,021 admitted, 260 enrolled. *Average high school GPA:* 3.43. *Test scores:* SAT critical reading scores over 500: 44%; SAT math scores over 500: 54%; SAT writing scores over 500: 41%; SAT critical reading scores over 600: 6%; SAT math scores over 600: 27%; SAT writing scores over 600: 3%; SAT critical reading scores over 700: 3%; SAT math scores over 700: 5%.

Faculty *Total:* 97, 66% full-time, 67% with terminal degrees. *Student/faculty ratio:* 14:1.

Academics *Calendar:* semesters. *Degree:* bachelor's. *Special study options:* academic remediation for entering students, advanced placement credit, cooperative education, double majors, English as a second language, honors programs, independent study, internships, off-campus study, part-time degree program, services for LD students, student-designed majors, study abroad, summer session for credit. *ROTC:* Army (c), Air Force (c). *Unusual degree programs:* 3-2 engineering with Washington University in St. Louis, University of Missouri-Columbia; nursing with Golfarb School of Nursing at Barnes-Jewish College in St. Louis.

Computers on Campus 188 computers/terminals are available on campus for general student use. Students can access the following: campus intranet, computer help desk, free student e-mail accounts, online (class) grades, online (class) registration, online (class) schedules. Campuswide network is available. 100% of college-owned or -operated housing units are wired for high-speed Internet access. Wireless service is available via entire campus.

Student Life *Housing:* on-campus residence required through junior year. *Options:* coed, men-only, women-only. Campus housing is university owned. Freshman campus housing is guaranteed. *Activities and organizations:* drama/theater group, student-run newspaper, choral group, Student Government Association, Environmentally Concerned Students, International Student Club, Habitat for Humanity, Little Brother/Little Sister, national fraternities, national sororities. *Campus security:* 24-hour emergency response devices and patrols, late-night transport/escort service, controlled dormitory access, well-lit campus. *Student services:* health clinic, personal/psychological counseling, women's center.

Athletics Member NCAA. All Division III. *Intercollegiate sports:* baseball M, basketball M/W, cross-country running M/W, football M, golf M/W, soccer M/W, softball M/W, tennis M/W, track and field M/W, volleyball W. *Intramural sports:* basketball M/W, football M, table tennis M/W, volleyball M/W.

Standardized Tests *Required:* SAT or ACT (for admission).

Costs (2012–13) *Comprehensive fee:* $29,300 includes full-time tuition ($19,750), mandatory fees ($1100), and room and board ($8450). Part-time tuition: $800 per credit hour. *College room only:* $4500. Room and board charges vary according to board plan and housing facility. *Payment plan:* installment. *Waivers:* children of alumni and employees or children of employees.

Financial Aid Of all full-time matriculated undergraduates who enrolled in 2012, 824 applied for aid, 656 were judged to have need, 293 had their need fully met. 658 Federal Work-Study jobs (averaging $1408). 259 state and other part-time jobs (averaging $2042). In 2012, 418 non-need-based awards were made. *Average percent of need met:* 80%. *Average financial aid package:* $18,710. *Average need-based loan:* $4061. *Average need-based gift aid:* $13,812. *Average non-need-based aid:* $10,431. *Average indebtedness upon graduation:* $26,723.

Applying *Options:* electronic application, early admission, deferred entrance. *Required:* high school transcript, 1 letter of recommendation. *Required for some:* interview. *Recommended:* essay or personal statement, minimum 2.5 GPA. *Notification:* 8/1 (freshmen), continuous (transfers).

Freshman Application Contact Mr. George Wolf, Vice President and Dean of Enrollment Services, Westminster College, 501 Westminster Avenue, Fulton,

MO 65251-1299. *Phone:* 573-592-5251. *Toll-free phone:* 800-475-3361. *Fax:* 573-592-5255. *E-mail:* admissions@westminster-mo.edu. *Website:* http://www.westminster-mo.edu/.

William Jewell College

Liberty, Missouri

- **Independent** 4-year, founded 1849
- **Suburban** 200-acre campus with easy access to Kansas City
- **Endowment** $62.5 million
- **Coed** 1,052 undergraduate students, 96% full-time, 58% women, 42% men
- **Moderately difficult** entrance level, 61% of applicants were admitted

Undergraduates 1,011 full-time, 41 part-time. Students come from 31 states and territories; 17 other countries; 37% are from out of state; 5% Black or African American, non-Hispanic/Latino; 3% Hispanic/Latino; 0.6% Asian, non-Hispanic/Latino; 0.1% Native Hawaiian or other Pacific Islander, non-Hispanic/Latino; 1% American Indian or Alaska Native, non-Hispanic/Latino; 4% Two or more races, non-Hispanic/Latino; 1% Race/ethnicity unknown; 3% international; 3% transferred in; 85% live on campus. *Retention:* 73% of full-time freshmen returned.

Freshmen *Admission:* 3,006 applied, 1,831 admitted, 305 enrolled. *Average high school GPA:* 3.69. *Test scores:* SAT critical reading scores over 500: 83%; SAT math scores over 500: 83%; ACT scores over 18: 99%; SAT critical reading scores over 600: 34%; SAT math scores over 600: 34%; ACT scores over 24: 64%; SAT critical reading scores over 700: 11%; SAT math scores over 700: 8%; ACT scores over 30: 15%.

Faculty *Total:* 141, 52% full-time, 47% with terminal degrees. *Student/faculty ratio:* 11:1.

Academics *Calendar:* semesters. *Degrees:* bachelor's (also offers evening program with significant enrollment not reflected in profile). *Special study options:* accelerated degree program, advanced placement credit, cooperative education, distance learning, double majors, honors programs, independent study, internships, off-campus study, services for LD students, student-designed majors, study abroad, summer session for credit. *ROTC:* Army (c). *Unusual degree programs:* 3-2 engineering with Washington University in St. Louis, University of Kansas, Vanderbilt University, Columbia University, Missouri University of Science and Technology; forestry with Duke University; occupational therapy with Washington University in St. Louis.

Computers on Campus 220 computers/terminals are available on campus for general student use. Students can access the following: campus intranet, computer help desk, free student e-mail accounts, online (class) grades, online (class) registration, online (class) schedules. Campuswide network is available. 100% of college-owned or -operated housing units are wired for high-speed Internet access. Wireless service is available via classrooms, dorm rooms, learning centers, libraries, student centers.

Student Life *Housing:* on-campus residence required through senior year. *Options:* coed, men-only, women-only, disabled students. Campus housing is university owned. Freshman campus housing is guaranteed. *Activities and organizations:* drama/theater group, student-run newspaper, radio station, choral group, College Union Activities, Intramurals, Mosaic, Student Senate, Black Student Association, national fraternities, national sororities. *Campus security:* 24-hour emergency response devices and patrols, late-night transport/escort service, controlled dormitory access. *Student services:* health clinic, personal/psychological counseling.

Athletics Member NCAA. All Division II. *Intercollegiate sports:* baseball M(s), basketball M(s)/W(s), cheerleading M(s)/W(s), cross-country running M(s)/W(s), football M(s), golf M(s)/W(s), soccer M(s)/W(s), softball W(s), swimming and diving M(s)/W(s), tennis M(s)/W(s), track and field M(s)/W(s), volleyball W(s). *Intramural sports:* racquetball M/W, soccer M/W, softball M/W, tennis M/W, ultimate Frisbee M/W, volleyball M/W.

Standardized Tests *Recommended:* SAT or ACT (for admission).

Costs (2013–14) *Comprehensive fee:* $39,120 includes full-time tuition ($30,800), mandatory fees ($300), and room and board ($8020). Full-time tuition and fees vary according to class time, course load, program, and student level. Part-time tuition: $890 per credit. *Room and board:* Room and board charges vary according to board plan and housing facility. *Payment plan:* installment. *Waivers:* employees or children of employees.

Financial Aid Of all full-time matriculated undergraduates who enrolled in 2012, 784 applied for aid, 783 were judged to have need, 157 had their need fully met. 541 Federal Work-Study jobs (averaging $1565). In 2012, 216 non-need-based awards were made. *Average percent of need met:* 71%. *Average financial aid package:* $22,308. *Average need-based loan:* $4955. *Average need-based gift aid:* $20,311. *Average non-need-based aid:* $13,634. *Average indebtedness upon graduation:* $31,324.

Applying *Options:* electronic application, deferred entrance. *Application fee:* $25. *Required:* essay or personal statement, high school transcript. *Required for some:* interview. *Recommended:* interview. *Application deadlines:* 8/15 (freshmen), rolling (transfers). *Notification:* continuous (transfers).

Freshman Application Contact Mr. Clint Chapman, Dean of Admission, William Jewell College, 500 College Hill, Liberty, MO 64068-1843. *Phone:* 816-415-7872. *Toll-free phone:* 888-2JEWELL. *Fax:* 816-415-5040. *E-mail:* chapmanc@william.jewell.edu. *Website:* http://www.jewell.edu/.

William Woods University

Fulton, Missouri

- **Independent** comprehensive, founded 1870, affiliated with Christian Church (Disciples of Christ)
- **Rural** campus with easy access to St. Louis
- **Coed**
- **Moderately difficult** entrance level

Faculty *Student/faculty ratio:* 12:1.

Academics *Calendar:* semesters. *Degrees:* associate, bachelor's, master's, and post-master's certificates.

Student Life *Campus security:* 24-hour emergency response devices and patrols, late-night transport/escort service, controlled dormitory access.

Athletics Member NAIA.

Standardized Tests *Required:* SAT or ACT (for admission).

Costs (2012–13) *Comprehensive fee:* $27,100 includes full-time tuition ($19,200) and room and board ($7900). Full-time tuition and fees vary according to degree level and program. Part-time tuition and fees vary according to course load, degree level, and program. *College room only:* $4000. Room and board charges vary according to board plan and housing facility.

Financial Aid Of all full-time matriculated undergraduates who enrolled in 2011, 800 applied for aid, 711 were judged to have need, 147 had their need fully met. In 2011, 236 non-need-based awards were made. *Average percent of need met:* 55. *Average financial aid package:* $14,416. *Average need-based loan:* $4193. *Average need-based gift aid:* $10,713. *Average non-need-based aid:* $7170. *Average indebtedness upon graduation:* $22,032.

Applying *Options:* deferred entrance. *Application fee:* $25. *Required:* high school transcript, minimum 2.5 GPA, 16 hours college preparatory units. *Required for some:* essay or personal statement, 2 letters of recommendation. *Recommended:* interview.

Freshman Application Contact Ms. Sharon Horn, Admissions Data Analyst, William Woods University, One University Avenue, Fulton, MO 65251. *Phone:* 573-592-4221. *Toll-free phone:* 800-995-3159 Ext. 4221. *Fax:* 573-592-1146. *E-mail:* admissions@williamwoods.edu. *Website:* http://www.williamwoods.edu/.

MONTANA

Carroll College

Helena, Montana

- **Independent Roman Catholic** 4-year, founded 1909
- **Small-town** 61-acre campus
- **Endowment** $27.3 million
- **Coed** 1,464 undergraduate students, 93% full-time, 58% women, 42% men
- **Moderately difficult** entrance level, 62% of applicants were admitted

Undergraduates 1,364 full-time, 100 part-time. Students come from 33 states and territories; 7 other countries; 50% are from out of state; 0.5% Black or African American, non-Hispanic/Latino; 3% Hispanic/Latino; 1% Asian, non-Hispanic/Latino; 0.3% Native Hawaiian or other Pacific Islander, non-Hispanic/Latino; 1% American Indian or Alaska Native, non-Hispanic/Latino; 0.8% Two or more races, non-Hispanic/Latino; 11% Race/ethnicity unknown; 1% international; 3% transferred in. *Retention:* 86% of full-time freshmen returned.

Freshmen *Admission:* 2,529 applied, 1,574 admitted, 383 enrolled. *Average high school GPA:* 3.54. *Test scores:* SAT critical reading scores over 500: 77%; SAT math scores over 500: 78%; SAT writing scores over 500: 72%; ACT scores over 18: 96%; SAT critical reading scores over 600: 29%; SAT math scores over 600: 35%; SAT writing scores over 600: 24%; ACT scores over 24:

58%; SAT critical reading scores over 700: 4%; SAT math scores over 700: 5%; SAT writing scores over 700: 4%; ACT scores over 30: 6%.

Faculty *Total:* 170, 54% full-time. *Student/faculty ratio:* 12:1.

Academics *Calendar:* semesters. *Degrees:* associate and bachelor's. *Special study options:* accelerated degree program, adult/continuing education programs, advanced placement credit, cooperative education, double majors, English as a second language, freshman honors college, honors programs, independent study, internships, part-time degree program, student-designed majors, study abroad, summer session for credit. *ROTC:* Army (b). *Unusual degree programs:* 3-2 engineering with Columbia University, University of Southern California, University of Notre Dame, Montana State University, Gonzaga University, Montana College of Mineral Science and Technology, University of Minnesota.

Computers on Campus Students can access the following: campus intranet, computer help desk, free student e-mail accounts, online (class) grades, online (class) registration, online (class) schedules, online book order. Campuswide network is available. 100% of college-owned or -operated housing units are wired for high-speed Internet access. Wireless service is available via entire campus.

Student Life *Housing:* on-campus residence required through sophomore year. *Options:* coed. Campus housing is university owned. Freshman campus housing is guaranteed. *Activities and organizations:* drama/theater group, student-run newspaper, radio station, choral group, student government, Carroll Outreach Team, Carroll Adventure and Mountaineering Program, Up 'Til Dawn, Engineers Without Borders. *Campus security:* 24-hour emergency response devices, late-night transport/escort service, controlled dormitory access. *Student services:* health clinic, personal/psychological counseling.

Athletics Member NAIA. *Intercollegiate sports:* basketball M(s)/W(s), cheerleading M(s)/W(s), cross-country running M(s)/W(s), football M(s), golf M(s)/W(s), soccer W(s), track and field M(s)/W(s), volleyball W(s).

Standardized Tests *Required:* SAT or ACT (for admission). *Required for some:* SAT Subject Tests (for admission).

Costs (2012–13) *Comprehensive fee:* $34,616 includes full-time tuition ($26,004), mandatory fees ($550), and room and board ($8062). Full-time tuition and fees vary according to course load. Part-time tuition: $1094 per credit hour. Part-time tuition and fees vary according to course load. *Required fees:* $138 per term part-time. *College room only:* $4292. Room and board charges vary according to board plan and housing facility. *Payment plan:* installment. *Waivers:* senior citizens and employees or children of employees.

Financial Aid Of all full-time matriculated undergraduates who enrolled in 2011, 1,012 applied for aid, 880 were judged to have need, 114 had their need fully met. 226 Federal Work-Study jobs (averaging $2087). In 2011, 409 non-need-based awards were made. *Average percent of need met:* 69%. *Average financial aid package:* $18,415. *Average need-based loan:* $1470. *Average need-based gift aid:* $13,760. *Average non-need-based aid:* $10,304. *Average indebtedness upon graduation:* $28,005.

Applying *Options:* electronic application, deferred entrance. *Application fee:* $35. *Required:* essay or personal statement, high school transcript. *Required for some:* interview. *Recommended:* interview. *Application deadlines:* 2/15 (freshmen), 2/15 (out-of-state freshmen), 6/15 (transfers), 11/1 (early action). *Notification:* continuous (freshmen), continuous (out-of-state freshmen), continuous (transfers), rolling (early action).

Freshman Application Contact Director of Admission, Carroll College, 1601 North Benton Avenue, Helena, MT 59625-0002. *Phone:* 406-447-4384. *Toll-free phone:* 800-992-3648. *E-mail:* admission@carroll.edu. *Website:* http://www.carroll.edu/.

Montana State University

Bozeman, Montana

- **State-supported** university, founded 1893, part of Montana University System
- **Small-town** 1781-acre campus
- **Endowment** $92.9 million
- **Coed** 12,772 undergraduate students, 83% full-time, 46% women, 54% men
- **Moderately difficult** entrance level, 58% of applicants were admitted

Undergraduates 10,598 full-time, 2,174 part-time. Students come from 50 states and territories; 66 other countries; 34% are from out of state; 0.6% Black or African American, non-Hispanic/Latino; 3% Hispanic/Latino; 0.8% Asian, non-Hispanic/Latino; 2% American Indian or Alaska Native, non-Hispanic/Latino; 3% Two or more races, non-Hispanic/Latino; 1% Race/ethnicity unknown; 3% international; 7% transferred in; 25% live on campus. *Retention:* 74% of full-time freshmen returned.

Freshmen *Admission:* 12,081 applied, 6,955 admitted, 2,710 enrolled. *Average high school GPA:* 3.29. *Test scores:* SAT critical reading scores over 500: 76%; SAT math scores over 500: 78%; SAT writing scores over 500: 67%; ACT scores over 18: 94%; SAT critical reading scores over 600: 35%; SAT math scores over 600: 40%; SAT writing scores over 600: 27%; ACT scores over 24: 57%; SAT critical reading scores over 700: 9%; SAT math scores over 700: 9%; SAT writing scores over 700: 4%; ACT scores over 30: 12%.

Faculty *Total:* 917, 63% full-time, 56% with terminal degrees. *Student/faculty ratio:* 18:1.

Academics *Calendar:* semesters. *Degrees:* certificates, associate, bachelor's, master's, doctoral, post-master's, and postbachelor's certificates. *Special study options:* academic remediation for entering students, adult/continuing education programs, advanced placement credit, distance learning, double majors, English as a second language, honors programs, independent study, internships, off-campus study, part-time degree program, services for LD students, student-designed majors, study abroad, summer session for credit. *ROTC:* Army (b), Air Force (b).

Computers on Campus 850 computers/terminals are available on campus for general student use. Students can access the following: computer help desk, free student e-mail accounts, online (class) registration, online (class) schedules. Campuswide network is available. 100% of college-owned or -operated housing units are wired for high-speed Internet access. Wireless service is available via entire campus.

Student Life *Housing:* on-campus residence required for freshman year. *Options:* coed, men-only, women-only. Campus housing is university owned. Freshman campus housing is guaranteed. *Activities and organizations:* drama/theater group, student-run newspaper, radio and television station, choral group, marching band, Spurs, Inter-Varsity Christian Fellowship, Campus Crusade for Christ, Fangs, Mortar Board, national fraternities, national sororities. *Campus security:* 24-hour emergency response devices and patrols, student patrols, late-night transport/escort service, 24-hour residence hall monitoring. *Student services:* health clinic, personal/psychological counseling, women's center, legal services.

Athletics Member NCAA. All Division I except football (Division I-AA). *Intercollegiate sports:* basketball M(s)/W(s), cheerleading M(s)/W(s), cross-country running M(s)/W(s), golf W(s), skiing (cross-country) M(s)/W(s), skiing (downhill) M(s)/W(s), tennis M(s)/W(s), track and field M(s)/W(s), volleyball W(s). *Intramural sports:* archery W, badminton M/W, baseball M, basketball M/W, bowling M/W, cross-country running M/W, fencing M/W, football M, golf M/W, gymnastics M/W, racquetball M/W, rugby M/W, skiing (cross-country) M/W, skiing (downhill) M/W, soccer M/W, softball M/W, swimming and diving M/W, table tennis M/W, tennis M/W, track and field M/W, ultimate Frisbee M/W, volleyball M/W, water polo M/W, weight lifting M/W, wrestling M.

Standardized Tests *Required:* SAT or ACT (for admission).

Costs (2012–13) *Tuition:* state resident $5330 full-time, $222 per credit part-time; nonresident $18,599 full-time, $779 per credit part-time. Full-time tuition and fees vary according to course load, degree level, and program. Part-time tuition and fees vary according to course load, degree level, and program. *Required fees:* $1419 full-time, $106 per credit part-time. *Room and board:* $8070. Room and board charges vary according to board plan and housing facility. *Payment plans:* installment, deferred payment. *Waivers:* minority students, senior citizens, and employees or children of employees.

Financial Aid Of all full-time matriculated undergraduates who enrolled in 2010, 6,411 applied for aid, 5,169 were judged to have need, 195 had their need fully met. In 2010, 279 non-need-based awards were made. *Average percent of need met:* 74%. *Average financial aid package:* $12,062. *Average need-based loan:* $4413. *Average need-based gift aid:* $5504. *Average non-need-based aid:* $1674. *Average indebtedness upon graduation:* $25,682.

Applying *Options:* electronic application, early admission, deferred entrance. *Application fee:* $30. *Required:* high school transcript, minimum 2.5 GPA. *Application deadlines:* rolling (freshmen), rolling (out-of-state freshmen), rolling (transfers). *Notification:* continuous (freshmen), continuous (out-of-state freshmen), continuous (transfers).

Freshman Application Contact Ms. Ronda Russell, Director of New Student Services, Montana State University, PO Box 172190, Bozeman, MT 59717-2190. *Phone:* 406-994-2452. *Toll-free phone:* 888-MSU-CATS. *Fax:* 406-994-1923. *E-mail:* admissions@montana.edu. *Website:* http://www.montana.edu/.

Montana State University Billings

Billings, Montana

- **State-supported** comprehensive, founded 1927, part of Montana University System
- **Urban** 92-acre campus
- **Endowment** $15.6 million
- **Coed**
- **Moderately difficult** entrance level

Faculty *Student/faculty ratio:* 19:1.

Academics *Calendar:* semesters. *Degrees:* certificates, associate, bachelor's, master's, and postbachelor's certificates.

Student Life *Campus security:* 24-hour emergency response devices and patrols, late-night transport/escort service, controlled dormitory access.

Athletics Member NCAA. All Division II.

Standardized Tests *Required:* SAT or ACT (for admission).

Costs (2012–13) *Tuition:* state resident $4397 full-time, $158 per credit hour part-time; nonresident $16,726 full-time, $522 per credit hour part-time. Full-time tuition and fees vary according to course load, degree level, and location. Part-time tuition and fees vary according to course load, degree level, and location. *Required fees:* $1314 full-time. *Room and board:* $6320. Room and board charges vary according to board plan and housing facility.

Financial Aid *Of all full-time matriculated undergraduates who enrolled in 2011,* 2,698 applied for aid, 2,261 were judged to have need, 79 had their need fully met. 265 Federal Work-Study jobs (averaging $1275). 86 state and other part-time jobs (averaging $1679). *In 2011,* 80 non-need-based awards were made. *Average percent of need met:* 71. *Average financial aid package:* $9806. *Average need-based loan:* $3445. *Average need-based gift aid:* $5034. *Average non-need-based aid:* $2337. *Average indebtedness upon graduation:* $27,178.

Applying *Options:* electronic application, early admission, deferred entrance. *Application fee:* $30. *Required:* high school transcript, minimum 2.5 GPA.

Freshman Application Contact Ms. Shelly Andersen, Associate Director of Admissions, Montana State University Billings, 1500 University Drive, Billings, MT 59101. *Phone:* 406-657-2158. *Toll-free phone:* 800-565-6782. *Fax:* 406-657-2302. *E-mail:* sandersen@msubillings.edu. *Website:* http://www.msubillings.edu/.

Montana State University–Northern

Havre, Montana

- **State-supported** comprehensive, founded 1929, part of Montana University System
- **Small-town** campus
- **Coed**
- **Moderately difficult** entrance level

Faculty *Student/faculty ratio:* 15:1.

Academics *Calendar:* semesters. *Degrees:* certificates, diplomas, associate, bachelor's, and master's.

Athletics Member NAIA.

Standardized Tests *Required:* SAT or ACT (for admission).

Costs (2012–13) *Tuition:* state resident $3765 full-time, $232 per credit hour part-time; nonresident $14,943 full-time, $635 per credit hour part-time. Full-time tuition and fees vary according to course level, course load, degree level, location, reciprocity agreements, and student level. Part-time tuition and fees vary according to course level, course load, degree level, location, reciprocity agreements, and student level. *Required fees:* $1305 full-time. *Room and board:* $6275; room only: $2147. Room and board charges vary according to board plan.

Financial Aid *Of all full-time matriculated undergraduates who enrolled in 2012,* 772 applied for aid, 686 were judged to have need, 21 had their need fully met. 61 Federal Work-Study jobs, 25 state and other part-time jobs. *In 2012,* 7 non-need-based awards were made. *Average percent of need met:* 60. *Average financial aid package:* $10,291. *Average need-based loan:* $3522. *Average need-based gift aid:* $4826. *Average non-need-based aid:* $715. *Average indebtedness upon graduation:* $21,365.

Applying *Options:* early admission, deferred entrance. *Application fee:* $30. *Required:* high school transcript. *Required for some:* minimum 2.0 GPA.

Freshman Application Contact Montana State University–Northern, PO Box 7751, Havre, MT 59501-7751. *Phone:* 406-265-3704. *Toll-free phone:* 800-662-6132. *Website:* http://www.msun.edu/.

Montana Tech of The University of Montana

Butte, Montana

- **State-supported** comprehensive, founded 1895, part of Montana University System
- **Small-town** 56-acre campus
- **Endowment** $26.3 million
- **Coed** 2,646 undergraduate students, 83% full-time, 41% women, 59% men
- **Moderately difficult** entrance level, 90% of applicants were admitted

Undergraduates 2,186 full-time, 460 part-time. Students come from 31 states and territories; 9 other countries; 13% are from out of state; 0.5% Black or African American, non-Hispanic/Latino; 2% Hispanic/Latino; 0.8% Asian, non-Hispanic/Latino; 2% American Indian or Alaska Native, non-Hispanic/Latino; 0.1% Two or more races, non-Hispanic/Latino; 6% Race/ethnicity unknown; 6% international; 8% transferred in; 12% live on campus. *Retention:* 66% of full-time freshmen returned.

Freshmen *Admission:* 822 applied, 737 admitted, 426 enrolled. *Average high school GPA:* 3.39. *Test scores:* SAT critical reading scores over 500: 75%; SAT math scores over 500: 87%; SAT writing scores over 500: 55%; ACT scores over 18: 94%; SAT critical reading scores over 600: 33%; SAT math scores over 600: 41%; SAT writing scores over 600: 15%; ACT scores over 24: 53%; SAT critical reading scores over 700: 4%; SAT math scores over 700: 9%; SAT writing scores over 700: 1%; ACT scores over 30: 8%.

Faculty *Total:* 213, 63% full-time. *Student/faculty ratio:* 15:1.

Academics *Calendar:* semesters. *Degrees:* certificates, diplomas, associate, bachelor's, master's, and postbachelor's certificates. *Special study options:* academic remediation for entering students, adult/continuing education programs, advanced placement credit, cooperative education, distance learning, double majors, external degree program, honors programs, independent study, internships, part-time degree program, services for LD students, student-designed majors, summer session for credit. *Unusual degree programs:* engineering.

Computers on Campus 585 computers/terminals are available on campus for general student use. Students can access the following: campus intranet, computer help desk, free student e-mail accounts, online (class) grades, online (class) registration, online (class) schedules. Campuswide network is available. 100% of college-owned or -operated housing units are wired for high-speed Internet access. Wireless service is available via entire campus.

Student Life *Housing:* on-campus residence required for freshman year. *Options:* coed, disabled students. Campus housing is university owned. Freshman campus housing is guaranteed. *Activities and organizations:* student-run newspaper, radio station, choral group, Circle K, Ski/Snowboard Club, BSU, Hockey Club, Dance Club. *Campus security:* 24-hour patrols, controlled dormitory access. *Student services:* health clinic, personal/psychological counseling.

Athletics Member NAIA. *Intercollegiate sports:* basketball M(s)/W(s), football M(s), golf M(s)/W(s), volleyball W(s). *Intramural sports:* basketball M/W, cheerleading M(c)/W(c), football M/W, ice hockey M(c)/W(c), racquetball M/W, rugby M(c)/W(c), skiing (cross-country) M(c)/W(c), skiing (downhill) M(c)/W(c), softball M/W, volleyball M/W.

Standardized Tests *Required:* SAT or ACT (for admission).

Costs (2012–13) *Tuition:* state resident $5177 full-time, $215 per credit part-time; nonresident $17,432 full-time, $726 per credit part-time. Full-time tuition and fees vary according to course load, degree level, location, program, and student level. Part-time tuition and fees vary according to course load, degree level, location, program, and student level. *Required fees:* $1516 full-time, $69 per credit hour part-time. *Room and board:* $7626; room only: $3392. Room and board charges vary according to board plan. *Payment plan:* installment. *Waivers:* minority students, senior citizens, and employees or children of employees.

Financial Aid Of all full-time matriculated undergraduates who enrolled in 2011, 1,625 applied for aid, 1,301 were judged to have need, 448 had their need fully met. In 2011, 257 non-need-based awards were made. *Average percent of need met:* 84%. *Average financial aid package:* $10,505. *Average need-based loan:* $3825. *Average need-based gift aid:* $5285. *Average non-need-based aid:* $3213. *Average indebtedness upon graduation:* $25,360.

Applying *Options:* electronic application, deferred entrance. *Application fee:* $30. *Required:* high school transcript, proof of immunization. *Required for some:* minimum 2.5 GPA. *Application deadlines:* rolling (freshmen), rolling (transfers). *Notification:* continuous (freshmen), continuous (transfers).

Freshman Application Contact Montana Tech of The University of Montana, 1300 West Park Street, Butte, MT 59701-8997. *Phone:* 406-496-4568. *Toll-free phone:* 800-445-TECH. *Website:* http://www.mtech.edu/.

Rocky Mountain College

Billings, Montana

- **Independent interdenominational** comprehensive, founded 1878
- **Urban** 60-acre campus
- **Endowment** $22.2 million
- **Coed** 1,007 undergraduate students, 96% full-time, 49% women, 51% men
- **Moderately difficult** entrance level, 64% of applicants were admitted

Undergraduates 969 full-time, 38 part-time. Students come from 48 states and territories; 20 other countries; 44% are from out of state; 3% Black or African American, non-Hispanic/Latino; 4% Hispanic/Latino; 0.6% Asian, non-Hispanic/Latino; 0.5% Native Hawaiian or other Pacific Islander, non-Hispanic/Latino; 2% American Indian or Alaska Native, non-Hispanic/Latino; 2% Two or more races, non-Hispanic/Latino; 2% Race/ethnicity unknown; 4% international; 8% transferred in; 49% live on campus. *Retention:* 67% of full-time freshmen returned.

Freshmen *Admission:* 1,347 applied, 856 admitted, 262 enrolled. *Average high school GPA:* 3.36. *Test scores:* SAT critical reading scores over 500: 53%; SAT math scores over 500: 56%; SAT writing scores over 500: 29%; ACT scores over 18: 91%; SAT critical reading scores over 600: 6%; SAT math scores over 600: 12%; SAT writing scores over 600: 4%; ACT scores over 24: 36%; SAT math scores over 700: 1%; ACT scores over 30: 1%.

Faculty *Total:* 127, 51% full-time, 46% with terminal degrees. *Student/faculty ratio:* 12:1.

Academics *Calendar:* semesters. *Degrees:* associate, bachelor's, and master's. *Special study options:* academic remediation for entering students, accelerated degree program, adult/continuing education programs, advanced placement credit, distance learning, double majors, English as a second language, honors programs, independent study, internships, off-campus study, part-time degree program, services for LD students, student-designed majors, study abroad, summer session for credit. *ROTC:* Army (b). *Unusual degree programs:* 3-2 athletic training with Montana State University Billings.

Computers on Campus 129 computers/terminals are available on campus for general student use. Students can access the following: campus intranet, computer help desk, free student e-mail accounts, online (class) grades, online (class) registration, online (class) schedules. Campuswide network is available. 100% of college-owned or -operated housing units are wired for high-speed Internet access. Wireless service is available via entire campus.

Student Life *Housing:* on-campus residence required through sophomore year. *Options:* coed, disabled students. Campus housing is university owned. Freshman campus housing is guaranteed. *Activities and organizations:* drama/theater group, student-run newspaper, choral group, Outdoor Recreation/Climbing Club, Students in Free Enterprise (SIFE), Flight Team/Club, Residence Hall Association, OISTERS, Organization of Interested Students Toward Environmentally Responsible Solutions. *Campus security:* 24-hour emergency response devices, student patrols, late-night transport/escort service, controlled dormitory access, security cameras. *Student services:* health clinic, personal/psychological counseling.

Athletics Member NAIA. *Intercollegiate sports:* basketball M(s)/W(s), cheerleading W(s), cross-country running M(s)/W(s), equestrian sports M(c)/W(c), football M(s), golf M(s)/W(s), skiing (downhill) M(s)/W(s), soccer M(s)/W(s), volleyball W(s). *Intramural sports:* basketball M/W, football M, golf M/W, racquetball M/W, skiing (downhill) M/W, soccer M/W, softball M/W, tennis M/W, volleyball M/W.

Standardized Tests *Required:* SAT or ACT (for admission).

Costs (2013–14) *Comprehensive fee:* $31,148 includes full-time tuition ($23,228), mandatory fees ($490), and room and board ($7430). Full-time tuition and fees vary according to course load, degree level, and program. Part-time tuition: $968 per credit. Part-time tuition and fees vary according to course load, degree level, and program. *College room only:* $3462. Room and board charges vary according to board plan and housing facility. *Payment plan:* installment. *Waivers:* employees or children of employees.

Financial Aid Of all full-time matriculated undergraduates who enrolled in 2012, 817 applied for aid, 746 were judged to have need, 132 had their need fully met. 166 Federal Work-Study jobs (averaging $824). 81 state and other part-time jobs (averaging $920). In 2012, 65 non-need-based awards were made. *Average percent of need met:* 71%. *Average financial aid package:* $18,988. *Average need-based loan:* $4590. *Average need-based gift aid:* $14,404. *Average non-need-based aid:* $9860. *Average indebtedness upon graduation:* $30,948.

Applying *Options:* electronic application, early admission, early action, deferred entrance. *Application fee:* $35. *Required:* high school transcript, minimum 2.5 GPA. *Required for some:* essay or personal statement, 2 letters of recommendation, interview. *Application deadlines:* rolling (freshmen), rolling (transfers). *Notification:* continuous (freshmen), continuous (transfers).

Freshman Application Contact Kelly Edwards, Rocky Mountain College, 1511 Poly Drive, Vice President for Enrollment Services, Billings, MT 59102. *Phone:* 406-657-1026. *Toll-free phone:* 800-877-6259. *Fax:* 406-259-9751. *E-mail:* admissions@rocky.edu. *Website:* http://www.rocky.edu/.

Salish Kootenai College

Pablo, Montana

Freshman Application Contact Ms. Jackie Moran, Admissions Officer, Salish Kootenai College, PO Box 70, Pablo, MT 59855-0117. *Phone:* 406-275-4866. *Fax:* 406-275-4810. *E-mail:* jackie_moran@skc.edu. *Website:* http://www.skc.edu/.

University of Great Falls

Great Falls, Montana

- **Independent Roman Catholic** comprehensive, founded 1932
- **Urban** 40-acre campus
- **Coed** 974 undergraduate students, 68% full-time, 65% women, 35% men
- **Noncompetitive** entrance level, 84% of applicants were admitted

Undergraduates 667 full-time, 307 part-time. 47% are from out of state; 3% Black or African American, non-Hispanic/Latino; 5% Hispanic/Latino; 0.9% Asian, non-Hispanic/Latino; 2% Native Hawaiian or other Pacific Islander, non-Hispanic/Latino; 4% American Indian or Alaska Native, non-Hispanic/Latino; 2% Two or more races, non-Hispanic/Latino; 4% Race/ethnicity unknown; 1% international; 13% transferred in; 34% live on campus. *Retention:* 66% of full-time freshmen returned.

Freshmen *Admission:* 828 applied, 693 admitted, 142 enrolled. *Average high school GPA:* 3.2. *Test scores:* SAT critical reading scores over 500: 40%; SAT math scores over 500: 48%; SAT writing scores over 500: 36%; ACT scores over 18: 85%; SAT critical reading scores over 600: 20%; SAT math scores over 600: 14%; SAT writing scores over 600: 14%; ACT scores over 24: 32%; SAT critical reading scores over 700: 5%; SAT writing scores over 700: 1%; ACT scores over 30: 1%.

Faculty *Total:* 116, 38% full-time, 41% with terminal degrees. *Student/faculty ratio:* 13:1.

Academics *Calendar:* semesters. *Degrees:* certificates, associate, bachelor's, and master's. *Special study options:* adult/continuing education programs, part-time degree program.

Computers on Campus Students can access the following: campus intranet, computer help desk, free student e-mail accounts, online (class) grades, online (class) registration, online (class) schedules. Campuswide network is available. Wireless service is available via classrooms, computer centers, computer labs, dorm rooms, learning centers, libraries, student centers.

Student Life *Housing:* on-campus residence required through sophomore year. *Options:* coed. Campus housing is university owned and leased by the school. Freshman campus housing is guaranteed. *Campus security:* 24-hour emergency response devices and patrols, late-night transport/escort service, controlled dormitory access.

Athletics Member NAIA. *Intercollegiate sports:* basketball M(s)/W(s), cheerleading M(s)/W(s), cross-country running M/W, equestrian sports M(s)/W(s), golf M(s)/W(s), soccer M(s)/W(s), softball W, track and field M(s)/W(s), volleyball W(s), wrestling M(s). *Intramural sports:* basketball M/W, equestrian sports M/W(c), football M/W, golf M/W, skiing (downhill) M/W, soccer M/W, softball W, table tennis M/W, track and field M/W, ultimate Frisbee M/W, volleyball M/W, wrestling M.

Standardized Tests *Required:* SAT or ACT (for admission). *Recommended:* SAT and SAT Subject Tests or ACT (for admission), SAT Subject Tests (for admission).

Costs (2013–14) *Comprehensive fee:* $27,760 includes full-time tuition ($19,860), mandatory fees ($1100), and room and board ($6800). Full-time tuition and fees vary according to course load. Part-time tuition: $607 per credit hour. Part-time tuition and fees vary according to course load, location, and program. *College room only:* $3900. Room and board charges vary according to housing facility. *Payment plan:* installment. *Waivers:* employees or children of employees.

Financial Aid Of all full-time matriculated undergraduates who enrolled in 2012, 595 applied for aid, 547 were judged to have need, 14 had their need fully met. In 2012, 60 non-need-based awards were made. *Average percent of need met:* 65%. *Average financial aid package:* $16,581. *Average need-based loan:* $4193. *Average need-based gift aid:* $9473. *Average non-need-based aid:* $7517. *Average indebtedness upon graduation:* $25,690.

Applying *Options:* electronic application, early admission, deferred entrance. *Application fee:* $35. *Required:* high school transcript. *Recommended:* essay or personal statement, interview. *Application deadlines:* 9/1 (freshmen), rolling (transfers). *Notification:* continuous (freshmen), continuous (transfers).
Freshman Application Contact Kelly Braun, Assistant Director of Admissions, University of Great Falls, 1301 20th Street South, Great Falls, MT 59405. *Phone:* 406-791-5202 Ext. 5211. *Toll-free phone:* 800-856-9544. *Fax:* 406-791-5209. *E-mail:* enroll@ugf.edu.
Website: http://www.ugf.edu/.

The University of Montana

Missoula, Montana

Freshman Application Contact Ms. Juana Alcala, Manager, Enrollment Services, The University of Montana, Missoula, MT 59812-0002. *Phone:* 406-243-6266. *Toll-free phone:* 800-462-8636. *Fax:* 406-243-5711. *E-mail:* admiss@umontana.edu.
Website: http://www.umt.edu/.

The University of Montana Western

Dillon, Montana

- **State-supported** 4-year, founded 1893, part of Montana University System
- **Small-town** 30-acre campus
- **Endowment** $3.4 million
- **Coed** 1,483 undergraduate students, 83% full-time, 57% women, 43% men
- **Minimally difficult** entrance level, 75% of applicants were admitted

Undergraduates 1,233 full-time, 250 part-time. Students come from 40 states and territories; 3 other countries; 22% are from out of state; 1% Black or African American, non-Hispanic/Latino; 2% Hispanic/Latino; 0.7% Asian, non-Hispanic/Latino; 2% Native Hawaiian or other Pacific Islander, non-Hispanic/Latino; 2% American Indian or Alaska Native, non-Hispanic/Latino; 0.9% Two or more races, non-Hispanic/Latino; 4% Race/ethnicity unknown; 0.2% international; 11% transferred in; 25% live on campus. *Retention:* 77% of full-time freshmen returned.
Freshmen *Admission:* 602 applied, 454 admitted, 290 enrolled. *Average high school GPA:* 3. *Test scores:* SAT critical reading scores over 500: 38%; SAT math scores over 500: 45%; ACT scores over 18: 70%; SAT critical reading scores over 600: 13%; SAT math scores over 600: 11%; ACT scores over 24: 16%; SAT critical reading scores over 700: 1%; SAT math scores over 700: 1%; ACT scores over 30: 1%.
Faculty *Total:* 108, 59% full-time, 59% with terminal degrees. *Student/faculty ratio:* 17:1.
Academics *Calendar:* semesters. *Degrees:* certificates, associate, bachelor's, and postbachelor's certificates. *Special study options:* academic remediation for entering students, advanced placement credit, cooperative education, distance learning, double majors, honors programs, independent study, internships, off-campus study, part-time degree program, services for LD students, study abroad, summer session for credit.
Computers on Campus 140 computers/terminals and 140 ports are available on campus for general student use. Students can access the following: campus intranet, computer help desk, free student e-mail accounts, online (class) grades, online (class) registration, online (class) schedules. Campuswide network is available. Wireless service is available via entire campus.
Student Life *Housing:* on-campus residence required for freshman year. *Options:* coed, men-only, women-only, disabled students. Campus housing is university owned. Freshman campus housing is guaranteed. *Activities and organizations:* drama/theater group, student-run radio station, choral group, Chi Alpha, Drama Club, Humans in Performance, Western Gaming Alliance, Rodeo Club. *Campus security:* 24-hour emergency response devices and patrols, student patrols, late-night transport/escort service. *Student services:* health clinic, personal/psychological counseling.
Athletics Member NAIA. *Intercollegiate sports:* basketball M(s)/W(s), equestrian sports M(s)/W(s), football M(s), volleyball W(s). *Intramural sports:* basketball M/W, cheerleading M(c)/W(c), equestrian sports M(c)/W(c), football M/W, racquetball M/W, rock climbing M(c)/W(c), rugby M(c)/W(c), skiing (downhill) M(c)/W(c), softball M/W, ultimate Frisbee M/W, volleyball M/W, wrestling M(c).

Standardized Tests *Required:* SAT or ACT (for admission).
Costs (2013–14) *Tuition:* state resident $3699 full-time, $153 per credit part-time; nonresident $13,532 full-time, $562 per credit part-time. Full-time tuition and fees vary according to course load, location, program, reciprocity agreements, and student level. Part-time tuition and fees vary according to course load, location, program, reciprocity agreements, and student level. *Required fees:* $1020 full-time, $134 per credit part-time. *Room and board:* $6180; room only: $2310. Room and board charges vary according to housing facility. *Payment plans:* installment, deferred payment. *Waivers:* minority students, senior citizens, and employees or children of employees.
Financial Aid Of all full-time matriculated undergraduates who enrolled in 2010, 951 applied for aid, 886 were judged to have need, 82 had their need fully met. 107 Federal Work-Study jobs (averaging $2610). 131 state and other part-time jobs (averaging $2406). In 2010, 6 non-need-based awards were made. *Average percent of need met:* 17%. *Average financial aid package:* $3317. *Average need-based loan:* $4044. *Average need-based gift aid:* $3045. *Average non-need-based aid:* $1860. *Average indebtedness upon graduation:* $23,629.
Applying *Options:* electronic application, early admission, deferred entrance. *Application fee:* $30. *Required:* high school transcript, MMR, ACT or SAT, high school self report form. *Application deadlines:* rolling (freshmen), rolling (transfers). *Notification:* continuous (freshmen), continuous (transfers).
Freshman Application Contact Mrs. Janet Jones, Admissions Evaluator, The University of Montana Western, 710 South Atlantic, Dillon, MT 59725. *Phone:* 406-683-7331. *Toll-free phone:* 877-683-7331. *E-mail:* j_jones@umwestern.edu.
Website: http://www.umwestern.edu/.

NEBRASKA

Bellevue University

Bellevue, Nebraska

- **Independent** comprehensive, founded 1965
- **Suburban** 50-acre campus with easy access to Omaha
- **Endowment** $43.6 million
- **Coed**
- **Noncompetitive** entrance level

Faculty *Student/faculty ratio:* 40:1.
Academics *Calendar:* semesters for day division, trimesters for evening division. *Degrees:* bachelor's, master's, and doctoral.
Student Life *Campus security:* 24-hour emergency response devices.
Athletics Member NAIA.
Costs (2012–13) *Tuition:* $7500 full-time, $250 per credit hour part-time. Full-time tuition and fees vary according to course load. Part-time tuition and fees vary according to course load. *Required fees:* $200 full-time, $100 per term part-time.
Financial Aid *Of all full-time matriculated undergraduates who enrolled in 2003, 2,477 applied for aid, 2,477 were judged to have need. 44 Federal Work-Study jobs (averaging $1793). In 2003, 912 non-need-based awards were made. Average financial aid package: $4107. Average need-based loan: $3326. Average need-based gift aid: $2325. Average non-need-based aid: $1134.*
Applying *Options:* electronic application, deferred entrance. *Application fee:* $50. *Required:* high school transcript.
Freshman Application Contact Nick Baker, Director of Undergraduate Enrollment, Bellevue University, 1000 Galvin Road South, Bellevue, NE 68005-3098. *Phone:* 402-557-7250. *Toll-free phone:* 800-756-7920. *E-mail:* nick.baker@bellevue.edu.
Website: http://www.bellevue.edu/.

Chadron State College

Chadron, Nebraska

Freshman Application Contact Ms. Tena Cook, Director of Admissions, Chadron State College, 1000 Main Street, Chadron, NE 69337-2690. *Phone:* 308-432-6263. *Toll-free phone:* 800-242-3766. *Fax:* 308-432-6229. *E-mail:* inquire@csc.edu.
Website: http://www.csc.edu/.

Clarkson College

Omaha, Nebraska

- **Independent** comprehensive, founded 1888
- **Urban** 3-acre campus
- **Endowment** $937,115
- **Coed, primarily women**
- **Moderately difficult** entrance level

Faculty *Student/faculty ratio:* 8:1.

Academics *Calendar:* semesters. *Degrees:* certificates, associate, bachelor's, master's, and post-master's certificates.

Student Life *Campus security:* 24-hour emergency response devices and patrols, student patrols, late-night transport/escort service, controlled dormitory access.

Standardized Tests *Required for some:* SAT or ACT (for admission).

Financial Aid *Of all full-time matriculated undergraduates who enrolled in 2001,* 109 applied for aid, 94 were judged to have need, 22 had their need fully met. 40 Federal Work-Study jobs (averaging $2500). *In 2001,* 15 non-need-based awards were made. *Average percent of need met:* 71. *Average financial aid package:* $8291. *Average need-based loan:* $3365. *Average need-based gift aid:* $5434. *Average non-need-based aid:* $4374. *Average indebtedness upon graduation:* $13,931.

Applying *Options:* electronic application, deferred entrance. *Application fee:* $35. *Required:* essay or personal statement, high school transcript, minimum 2.5 GPA. *Required for some:* minimum 3.0 GPA, 2 letters of recommendation. *Recommended:* minimum 3.0 GPA.

Freshman Application Contact Clarkson College, 101 South 42nd Street, Omaha, NE 68131-2739. *Phone:* 402-552-3100. *Toll-free phone:* 800-647-5500.

Website: http://www.clarksoncollege.edu/.

College of Saint Mary

Omaha, Nebraska

- **Independent Roman Catholic** comprehensive, founded 1923
- **Urban** 25-acre campus
- **Endowment** $7.9 million
- **Women only** 782 undergraduate students, 81% full-time
- **Minimally difficult** entrance level, 52% of applicants were admitted

Undergraduates 632 full-time, 150 part-time. Students come from 18 states and territories; 7 other countries; 15% are from out of state; 7% Black or African American, non-Hispanic/Latino; 11% Hispanic/Latino; 1% Asian, non-Hispanic/Latino; 0.3% Native Hawaiian or other Pacific Islander, non-Hispanic/Latino; 0.4% American Indian or Alaska Native, non-Hispanic/Latino; 2% Two or more races, non-Hispanic/Latino; 1% Race/ethnicity unknown; 0.1% international; 14% transferred in; 34% live on campus. *Retention:* 69% of full-time freshmen returned.

Freshmen *Admission:* 402 applied, 208 admitted, 91 enrolled. *Average high school GPA:* 3.44. *Test scores:* ACT scores over 18: 94%; ACT scores over 24: 25%; ACT scores over 30: 1%.

Faculty *Total:* 158, 37% full-time, 38% with terminal degrees. *Student/faculty ratio:* 9:1.

Academics *Calendar:* semesters. *Degrees:* certificates, associate, bachelor's, master's, doctoral, and postbachelor's certificates. *Special study options:* academic remediation for entering students, accelerated degree program, advanced placement credit, distance learning, double majors, honors programs, independent study, internships, part-time degree program, services for LD students, study abroad, summer session for credit. *ROTC:* Army (c), Air Force (c).

Computers on Campus 170 computers/terminals and 300 ports are available on campus for general student use. Students can access the following: campus intranet, computer help desk, free student e-mail accounts, online (class) grades, online (class) registration, online (class) schedules. Campuswide network is available. 100% of college-owned or -operated housing units are wired for high-speed Internet access. Wireless service is available via entire campus.

Student Life *Housing:* on-campus residence required through sophomore year. *Options:* women-only. Campus housing is university owned. Freshman campus housing is guaranteed. *Activities and organizations:* drama/theater group, choral group, Students Against Violence (SAV), Campus Activities Board, Student Education Association of Nebraska, Student Occupational Therapy Club, Student Nurses Association. *Campus security:* 24-hour emergency response devices and patrols, late-night transport/escort service, controlled dormitory access, surveillance cameras at residence hall entrances; CSM Alert Text Message System. *Student services:* health clinic, personal/psychological counseling.

Athletics Member NAIA. *Intercollegiate sports:* basketball W(s), cross-country running W(s), golf W(s), soccer W(s), softball W(s), swimming and diving W(s), volleyball W(s). *Intramural sports:* basketball W, bowling W, volleyball W, water polo W.

Standardized Tests *Required:* Students graduating high school within the past five years with less than 12 transfer credits are required to submit ACT scores. The minimum ACT score for admission is 18 (for admission).

Costs (2012–13) *Comprehensive fee:* $32,110 includes full-time tuition ($24,830), mandatory fees ($480), and room and board ($6800). Full-time tuition and fees vary according to location and program. Part-time tuition: $825 per credit. Part-time tuition and fees vary according to class time, course load, location, and program. *Required fees:* $16 per credit part-time. *Payment plans:* installment, deferred payment. *Waivers:* senior citizens and employees or children of employees.

Financial Aid Of all full-time matriculated undergraduates who enrolled in 2012, 631 applied for aid, 592 were judged to have need, 49 had their need fully met. 161 Federal Work-Study jobs (averaging $1739). 10 state and other part-time jobs (averaging $7160). In 2012, 36 non-need-based awards were made. *Average percent of need met:* 61%. *Average financial aid package:* $17,850. *Average need-based loan:* $6047. *Average need-based gift aid:* $12,160. *Average non-need-based aid:* $7904. *Average indebtedness upon graduation:* $31,522.

Applying *Options:* electronic application. *Application fee:* $30. *Required:* high school transcript, minimum 2.0 GPA. *Required for some:* essay or personal statement, 3 letters of recommendation, interview. *Application deadlines:* rolling (freshmen), rolling (transfers). *Notification:* continuous (freshmen), continuous (transfers).

Freshman Application Contact CSM Enrollment Services, College of Saint Mary, 7000 Mercy Road, Omaha, NE 68106. *Phone:* 402-399-2355. *Toll-free phone:* 800-926-5534. *Fax:* 402-399-2412. *E-mail:* enroll@csm.edu. *Website:* http://www.csm.edu/.

Concordia University, Nebraska

Seward, Nebraska

- **Independent** comprehensive, founded 1894, affiliated with Lutheran Church–Missouri Synod
- **Small-town** 120-acre campus with easy access to Omaha
- **Endowment** $36.8 million
- **Coed** 1,481 undergraduate students, 78% full-time, 53% women, 47% men
- **Moderately difficult** entrance level, 76% of applicants were admitted

Undergraduates 1,159 full-time, 322 part-time. Students come from 40 states and territories; 10 other countries; 52% are from out of state; 3% Black or African American, non-Hispanic/Latino; 3% Hispanic/Latino; 0.4% Asian, non-Hispanic/Latino; 0.2% Native Hawaiian or other Pacific Islander, non-Hispanic/Latino; 0.1% American Indian or Alaska Native, non-Hispanic/Latino; 8% Race/ethnicity unknown; 1% international; 4% transferred in; 73% live on campus. *Retention:* 79% of full-time freshmen returned.

Freshmen *Admission:* 1,288 applied, 980 admitted, 296 enrolled. *Average high school GPA:* 3.5. *Test scores:* SAT critical reading scores over 500: 49%; SAT math scores over 500: 72%; ACT scores over 18: 97%; SAT critical reading scores over 600: 18%; SAT math scores over 600: 33%; ACT scores over 24: 45%; SAT math scores over 700: 5%; ACT scores over 30: 5%.

Faculty *Total:* 161, 37% full-time, 47% with terminal degrees. *Student/faculty ratio:* 14:1.

Academics *Calendar:* 4-4-1. *Degrees:* bachelor's, master's, and postbachelor's certificates. *Special study options:* academic remediation for entering students, accelerated degree program, adult/continuing education programs, advanced placement credit, distance learning, double majors, English as a second language, independent study, internships, off-campus study, part-time degree program, services for LD students, study abroad, summer session for credit. *ROTC:* Army (c), Air Force (c).

Computers on Campus 220 computers/terminals and 1,508 ports are available on campus for general student use. Students can access the following: campus intranet, computer help desk, free student e-mail accounts, online (class) grades, online (class) registration, online (class) schedules, academic plans, human resource data. Campuswide network is available. 100% of college-owned or -operated housing units are wired for high-speed Internet access. Wireless service is available via entire campus.

Student Life *Housing:* on-campus residence required through junior year. *Options:* men-only, women-only, disabled students. Campus housing is university owned. Freshman campus housing is guaranteed. *Activities and organizations:* drama/theater group, student-run newspaper, choral group, Student

Activities Council, Musical Groups, Curtain/Drama Club, Student Senate, Concordia Youth Ministry. *Campus security:* 24-hour emergency response devices and patrols, controlled dormitory access. *Student services:* health clinic, personal/psychological counseling.

Athletics Member NAIA. *Intercollegiate sports:* baseball M(s), basketball M(s)/W(s), cross-country running M(s)/W(s), football M(s), golf M(s)/W(s), soccer M(s)/W(s), softball W(s), tennis M(s)/W(s), track and field M(s)/W(s), volleyball W(s), wrestling M(s). *Intramural sports:* badminton M/W, basketball M/W, bowling M/W, cross-country running M/W, soccer M/W, softball M/W, table tennis M/W, tennis M/W, volleyball M/W.

Standardized Tests *Required:* SAT or ACT (for admission).

Costs (2013–14) *Comprehensive fee:* $31,450 includes full-time tuition ($24,500), mandatory fees ($250), and room and board ($6700). Part-time tuition: $765 per credit hour. *College room only:* $2750. Room and board charges vary according to board plan and housing facility. *Payment plan:* installment. *Waivers:* employees or children of employees.

Financial Aid Of all full-time matriculated undergraduates who enrolled in 2012, 1,011 applied for aid, 884 were judged to have need, 224 had their need fully met. 70 Federal Work-Study jobs (averaging $1454). In 2012, 119 non-need-based awards were made. *Average percent of need met:* 77%. *Average financial aid package:* $18,594. *Average need-based loan:* $4555. *Average need-based gift aid:* $14,340. *Average non-need-based aid:* $11,370. *Average indebtedness upon graduation:* $27,222.

Applying *Options:* deferred entrance. *Required:* high school transcript. *Recommended:* interview. *Application deadlines:* 8/1 (freshmen), 8/1 (transfers). *Notification:* continuous (freshmen), continuous (transfers).

Freshman Application Contact Mr. Aaron W. Roberts, Director of Undergraduate Recruitment, Concordia University, Nebraska, 800 North Columbia Avenue, Seward, NE 68434-1556. *Phone:* 800-535-5494 Ext. 7233. *Toll-free phone:* 800-535-5494. *Fax:* 402-643-4073. *E-mail:* admiss@cune.edu.
Website: http://www.cune.edu/.

Creative Center

Omaha, Nebraska

- **Proprietary** 4-year, founded 1993
- **Urban** 2-acre campus with easy access to Omaha
- **Coed** 102 undergraduate students, 98% full-time, 66% women, 34% men

Undergraduates 100 full-time, 2 part-time. *Retention:* 82% of full-time freshmen returned.

Faculty *Total:* 16, 31% full-time. *Student/faculty ratio:* 13:1.

Academics *Calendar:* semesters. *Degrees:* associate and bachelor's. *Special study options:* accelerated degree program, part-time degree program, services for LD students.

Computers on Campus 8 computers/terminals are available on campus for general student use. Students can access the following: campus intranet, computer help desk, All students receive a laptop computer and software- included in tuition and fees. Campuswide network is available. Wireless service is available via entire campus.

Student Life *Housing:* college housing not available.

Costs (2013–14) *Tuition:* $27,600 full-time. Part-time tuition and fees vary according to program. *Required fees:* $3555 full-time.

Applying *Required:* essay or personal statement, high school transcript, 1 letter of recommendation, interview, portfolio. *Recommended:* minimum 2.0 GPA.

Freshman Application Contact Mr. Richard Caldwell, Director of Admissions, Creative Center, 10850 Emmet Street, Omaha, NE 68164. *Phone:* 402-898-1000 Ext. 216. *Toll-free phone:* 888-898-1789. *Fax:* 402-898-1301. *E-mail:* rich_c@creativecenter.edu.
Website: http://www.creativecenter.edu/.

Creighton University

Omaha, Nebraska

- **Independent Roman Catholic (Jesuit)** university, founded 1878
- **Urban** 130-acre campus with easy access to Omaha
- **Endowment** $299.9 million
- **Coed** 4,032 undergraduate students, 95% full-time, 59% women, 41% men
- **Moderately difficult** entrance level, 78% of applicants were admitted

Undergraduates 3,813 full-time, 219 part-time. Students come from 51 states and territories; 42 other countries; 68% are from out of state; 3% Black or African American, non-Hispanic/Latino; 6% Hispanic/Latino; 10% Asian, non-Hispanic/Latino; 0.3% Native Hawaiian or other Pacific Islander, non-Hispanic/Latino; 0.5% American Indian or Alaska Native, non-Hispanic/Latino; 4% Two or more races, non-Hispanic/Latino; 1% Race/ethnicity unknown; 2% international; 1% transferred in; 49% live on campus. *Retention:* 90% of full-time freshmen returned.

Freshmen *Admission:* 5,361 applied, 4,192 admitted, 945 enrolled. *Average high school GPA:* 3.76. *Test scores:* SAT critical reading scores over 500: 89%; SAT math scores over 500: 92%; SAT writing scores over 500: 82%; ACT scores over 18: 100%; SAT critical reading scores over 600: 44%; SAT math scores over 600: 55%; SAT writing scores over 600: 41%; ACT scores over 24: 78%; SAT critical reading scores over 700: 10%; SAT math scores over 700: 14%; SAT writing scores over 700: 9%; ACT scores over 30: 21%.

Faculty *Total:* 764, 70% full-time, 77% with terminal degrees. *Student/faculty ratio:* 12:1.

Academics *Calendar:* semesters. *Degrees:* certificates, diplomas, associate, bachelor's, master's, doctoral, post-master's, and postbachelor's certificates. *Special study options:* academic remediation for entering students, accelerated degree program, adult/continuing education programs, advanced placement credit, distance learning, double majors, English as a second language, external degree program, freshman honors college, honors programs, independent study, internships, off-campus study, part-time degree program, services for LD students, study abroad, summer session for credit. *ROTC:* Army (b), Air Force (c). *Unusual degree programs:* 3-2 engineering with University of Detroit Mercy.

Computers on Campus 550 computers/terminals are available on campus for general student use. Students can access the following: campus intranet, computer help desk, free student e-mail accounts, online (class) grades, online (class) registration, online (class) schedules, financial aid information. Campuswide network is available. 100% of college-owned or -operated housing units are wired for high-speed Internet access. Wireless service is available via entire campus.

Student Life *Housing:* on-campus residence required through sophomore year. *Options:* coed, women-only, disabled students. Campus housing is university owned. Freshman campus housing is guaranteed. *Activities and organizations:* drama/theater group, student-run newspaper, choral group, Birdcage (Athletic Boosters), Pre-Medical Society, Student Nurses Association, Alpha Kappa Psi (business majors), Omicron Delta Kappa (Greek Leadership), national fraternities, national sororities. *Campus security:* 24-hour emergency response devices and patrols, student patrols, late-night transport/escort service, controlled dormitory access. *Student services:* health clinic, personal/psychological counseling, women's center.

Athletics Member NCAA. All Division I. *Intercollegiate sports:* baseball M(s), basketball M(s)/W(s), crew W(s), cross-country running M(s)/W(s), golf M(s)/W(s), soccer M(s)/W(s), softball W(s), tennis M(s)/W(s), volleyball W(s). *Intramural sports:* basketball M/W, crew M(c), football M/W, golf M/W, lacrosse M(c), racquetball M/W, rugby M(c), soccer M/W, tennis M/W, ultimate Frisbee M/W, volleyball M/W, weight lifting M(c)/W(c).

Standardized Tests *Required:* SAT or ACT (for admission).

Costs (2012–13) *Comprehensive fee:* $42,776 includes full-time tuition ($31,856), mandatory fees ($1474), and room and board ($9446). Full-time tuition and fees vary according to course load and degree level. Part-time tuition: $996 per credit hour. Part-time tuition and fees vary according to course load and degree level. *Required fees:* $184 per degree program part-time. *College room only:* $5350. Room and board charges vary according to board plan and housing facility. *Payment plan:* installment. *Waivers:* adult students and employees or children of employees.

Financial Aid Of all full-time matriculated undergraduates who enrolled in 2012, 2,679 applied for aid, 2,256 were judged to have need, 565 had their need fully met. In 2012, 1269 non-need-based awards were made. *Average percent of need met:* 83%. *Average financial aid package:* $27,505. *Average need-based loan:* $5683. *Average need-based gift aid:* $21,524. *Average non-need-based aid:* $15,118. *Average indebtedness upon graduation:* $36,333.

Applying *Options:* electronic application, deferred entrance. *Application fee:* $40. *Required:* essay or personal statement, high school transcript, minimum 2.8 GPA, 1 letter of recommendation. *Application deadlines:* 2/15 (freshmen), 8/1 (transfers). *Notification:* continuous (freshmen), continuous (transfers).

Freshman Application Contact Ms. Sarah Richardson, Director of Admissions and Scholarships, Creighton University, 2500 California Plaza, Omaha, NE 68178-0001. *Phone:* 402-280-2703. *Toll-free phone:* 800-282-5835. *Fax:* 402-280-2685. *E-mail:* williampierce@creighton.edu.
Website: http://www.creighton.edu/.

Doane College

Crete, Nebraska

- **Independent** comprehensive, founded 1872, affiliated with United Church of Christ
- **Small-town** 300-acre campus with easy access to Omaha
- **Endowment** $77.8 million
- **Coed** 1,149 undergraduate students, 99% full-time, 51% women, 49% men
- **Moderately difficult** entrance level, 76% of applicants were admitted

Undergraduates 1,138 full-time, 11 part-time. Students come from 29 states and territories; 7 other countries; 17% are from out of state; 3% Black or African American, non-Hispanic/Latino; 5% Hispanic/Latino; 1% Asian, non-Hispanic/Latino; 0.2% Native Hawaiian or other Pacific Islander, non-Hispanic/Latino; 0.3% American Indian or Alaska Native, non-Hispanic/Latino; 1% Two or more races, non-Hispanic/Latino; 1% Race/ethnicity unknown; 1% international; 5% transferred in; 82% live on campus. *Retention:* 76% of full-time freshmen returned.

Freshmen *Admission:* 1,733 applied, 1,325 admitted, 337 enrolled. *Average high school GPA:* 3.49. *Test scores:* ACT scores over 18: 96%; ACT scores over 24: 47%; ACT scores over 30: 6%.

Faculty *Total:* 123, 63% full-time, 67% with terminal degrees. *Student/faculty ratio:* 12:1.

Academics *Calendar:* 4-1-4. *Degrees:* bachelor's, master's, and post-master's certificates (non-traditional undergraduate programs and graduate programs offered at Lincoln campus). *Special study options:* advanced placement credit, cooperative education, double majors, English as a second language, honors programs, independent study, internships, off-campus study, student-designed majors, study abroad, summer session for credit. *ROTC:* Army (c), Air Force (c). *Unusual degree programs:* 3-2 engineering with Columbia University, Washington University in St. Louis; forestry with Duke University; environmental studies with Duke University.

Computers on Campus 250 computers/terminals and 1,000 ports are available on campus for general student use. Students can access the following: campus intranet, computer help desk, free student e-mail accounts, online (class) grades, online (class) registration, online (class) schedules. Campuswide network is available. 100% of college-owned or -operated housing units are wired for high-speed Internet access. Wireless service is available via entire campus.

Student Life *Housing:* on-campus residence required through senior year. *Options:* coed, women-only. Campus housing is university owned. Freshman campus housing is guaranteed. *Activities and organizations:* drama/theater group, student-run newspaper, radio and television station, choral group, marching band, Student Activities Council, Hansen Leadership Program, band/choir, Doane Ambassadors, Doane Art League. *Campus security:* 24-hour emergency response devices and patrols, student patrols, late-night transport/escort service, controlled dormitory access, evening patrols by trained security personnel. *Student services:* health clinic, personal/psychological counseling.

Athletics Member NAIA. *Intercollegiate sports:* baseball M(s), basketball M(s)/W(s), cross-country running M(s)/W(s), football M(s), golf M(s)/W(s), soccer M(s)/W(s), softball W(s), tennis M/W, track and field M(s)/W(s), volleyball W(s). *Intramural sports:* baseball M(c)/W(c), basketball M/W, bowling M/W, football M/W, golf M/W, ice hockey M, racquetball M(c)/W(c), softball M/W, swimming and diving M/W, table tennis M(c)/W(c), tennis M/W, volleyball M/W, water polo M/W.

Standardized Tests *Required:* SAT or ACT (for admission).

Costs (2012–13) *Comprehensive fee:* $32,220 includes full-time tuition ($24,460), mandatory fees ($620), and room and board ($7140). Full-time tuition and fees vary according to location. Part-time tuition: $815 per credit hour. Part-time tuition and fees vary according to course load and location. *Room and board:* Room and board charges vary according to board plan, housing facility, and location. *Payment plan:* installment. *Waivers:* senior citizens and employees or children of employees.

Financial Aid Of all full-time matriculated undergraduates who enrolled in 2012, 1,014 applied for aid, 1,010 were judged to have need, 264 had their need fully met. In 2012, 80 non-need-based awards were made. *Average percent of need met:* 83%. *Average financial aid package:* $19,073. *Average need-based loan:* $4379. *Average need-based gift aid:* $14,569. *Average non-need-based aid:* $11,128. *Average indebtedness upon graduation:* $26,803.

Applying *Options:* electronic application, early admission, deferred entrance. *Required:* high school transcript, 2 letters of recommendation. *Required for some:* interview. *Recommended:* minimum 2.0 GPA. *Application deadlines:* rolling (freshmen), rolling (transfers). *Notification:* continuous (freshmen), continuous (transfers).

Freshman Application Contact Doane College, 1014 Boswell Avenue, Crete, NE 68333-2430. *Phone:* 800-333-6263. *Toll-free phone:* 800-333-6263. *Website:* http://www.doane.edu/.

Grace University

Omaha, Nebraska

- **Independent interdenominational** comprehensive, founded 1943
- **Urban** 15-acre campus with easy access to Omaha
- **Endowment** $890,668
- **Coed** 366 undergraduate students, 78% full-time, 57% women, 43% men
- **Moderately difficult** entrance level, 64% of applicants were admitted

Undergraduates 287 full-time, 79 part-time. Students come from 26 states and territories; 6 other countries; 39% are from out of state; 7% Black or African American, non-Hispanic/Latino; 8% Hispanic/Latino; 2% Asian, non-Hispanic/Latino; 1% Native Hawaiian or other Pacific Islander, non-Hispanic/Latino; 0.3% American Indian or Alaska Native, non-Hispanic/Latino; 0.5% Two or more races, non-Hispanic/Latino; 0.8% Race/ethnicity unknown; 0.3% international; 10% transferred in; 60% live on campus. *Retention:* 70% of full-time freshmen returned.

Freshmen *Admission:* 228 applied, 146 admitted, 97 enrolled. *Average high school GPA:* 3.26.

Faculty *Total:* 50, 50% full-time, 90% with terminal degrees. *Student/faculty ratio:* 18:1.

Academics *Calendar:* semesters. *Degrees:* certificates, associate, bachelor's, and master's. *Special study options:* academic remediation for entering students, accelerated degree program, adult/continuing education programs, advanced placement credit, cooperative education, distance learning, double majors, external degree program, independent study, internships, off-campus study, part-time degree program, services for LD students, student-designed majors, study abroad, summer session for credit. *ROTC:* Army (c), Air Force (c). *Unusual degree programs:* 3-2 nursing with Clarkson College.

Computers on Campus 45 computers/terminals are available on campus for general student use. Students can access the following: campus intranet, computer help desk, free student e-mail accounts, online (class) grades, online (class) registration, online (class) schedules. Campuswide network is available. 100% of college-owned or -operated housing units are wired for high-speed Internet access. Wireless service is available via entire campus.

Student Life *Housing:* on-campus residence required through junior year. *Options:* men-only, women-only. Campus housing is university owned. Freshman applicants given priority for college housing. *Activities and organizations:* drama/theater group, student-run radio station, choral group, band, yearbook. *Campus security:* student patrols, late-night transport/escort service, controlled dormitory access. *Student services:* health clinic, personal/psychological counseling.

Athletics Member NCCAA. *Intercollegiate sports:* basketball M/W, soccer M, volleyball W. *Intramural sports:* basketball M/W, volleyball M/W.

Standardized Tests *Required:* SAT or ACT (for admission).

Costs (2012–13) *Comprehensive fee:* $23,320 includes full-time tuition ($16,816), mandatory fees ($550), and room and board ($5954). Part-time tuition: $473 per credit hour. Part-time tuition and fees vary according to course load. *College room only:* $2800. Room and board charges vary according to board plan and student level. *Payment plan:* installment. *Waivers:* children of alumni, senior citizens, and employees or children of employees.

Financial Aid Of all full-time matriculated undergraduates who enrolled in 2009, 247 applied for aid, 211 were judged to have need, 34 had their need fully met. 37 Federal Work-Study jobs (averaging $1103). 45 state and other part-time jobs (averaging $1101). In 2009, 57 non-need-based awards were made. *Average percent of need met:* 72%. *Average financial aid package:* $12,607. *Average need-based loan:* $4089. *Average need-based gift aid:* $8841. *Average non-need-based aid:* $5924. *Average indebtedness upon graduation:* $21,586.

Applying *Options:* electronic application, early admission, deferred entrance. *Application fee:* $20. *Required:* essay or personal statement, high school transcript, minimum 2.8 GPA. *Required for some:* interview. *Application deadlines:* rolling (freshmen), rolling (transfers).

Freshman Application Contact Angela Wayman, Director of Admissions, Grace University, 1311 South Ninth Street, Omaha, NE 68108. *Phone:* 402-449-2831. *Toll-free phone:* 800-383-1422. *Fax:* 402-341-9587. *E-mail:* admissions@graceuniversity.com. *Website:* http://www.graceuniversity.edu/.

Hastings College

Hastings, Nebraska

Freshman Application Contact Ms. Mary Molliconi, Director of Admissions, Hastings College, 710 North Turner Avenue, Hastings, NE

68901-7621. *Phone:* 402-461-7320. *Toll-free phone:* 800-532-7642. *Fax:* 402-461-7490. *E-mail:* mmolliconi@hastings.edu. *Website:* http://www.hastings.edu/.

ITT Technical Institute

Omaha, Nebraska

- **Proprietary** primarily 2-year, founded 1991, part of ITT Educational Services, Inc.
- **Urban** campus
- **Coed**
- **Minimally difficult** entrance level

Academics *Calendar:* quarters. *Degrees:* associate and bachelor's.
Freshman Application Contact Director of Recruitment, ITT Technical Institute, 1120 North 103rd Plaza, Suite 200, Omaha, NE 68114. *Phone:* 402-331-2900. *Toll-free phone:* 800-677-9260.
Website: http://www.itt-tech.edu/.

Kaplan University, Lincoln

Lincoln, Nebraska

Freshman Application Contact Kaplan University, Lincoln, 1821 K Street, Lincoln, NE 68501-2826. *Phone:* 402-474-5315. *Toll-free phone:* 866-527-5268 (in-state); 800-527-5268 (out-of-state).
Website: http://www.lincoln.kaplanuniversity.edu/.

Kaplan University, Omaha

Omaha, Nebraska

Freshman Application Contact Kaplan University, Omaha, 5425 North 103rd Street, Omaha, NE 68134. *Phone:* 402-572-8500. *Toll-free phone:* 866-527-5268 (in-state); 800-527-5268 (out-of-state).
Website: http://www.omaha.kaplanuniversity.edu/.

Midland University

Fremont, Nebraska

Freshman Application Contact Mr. Todd Hansen, Associate Director of Admissions, Midland University, Fremont, NE 68025-4200. *Phone:* 402-941-6504. *Toll-free phone:* 800-642-8382 Ext. 6501. *Fax:* 402-941-6513. *E-mail:* admissions@mlc.edu.
Website: http://www.midlandu.edu/.

Nebraska Christian College

Papillion, Nebraska

Freshman Application Contact Ms. Alisha Livengood, Associate Director of Admissions, Nebraska Christian College, 12550 South 114th Steet, Papillion, NE 68046. *Phone:* 402-935-9407.
Website: http://www.nechristian.edu/.

Nebraska Methodist College

Omaha, Nebraska

- **Independent** comprehensive, founded 1891, affiliated with United Methodist Church
- **Urban** 7-acre campus
- **Coed, primarily women** 738 undergraduate students, 62% full-time, 90% women, 10% men
- **Moderately difficult** entrance level, 51% of applicants were admitted

Undergraduates 454 full-time, 284 part-time. Students come from 10 states and territories; 15% are from out of state; 3% Black or African American, non-Hispanic/Latino; 3% Hispanic/Latino; 2% Asian, non-Hispanic/Latino; 0.3% Native Hawaiian or other Pacific Islander, non-Hispanic/Latino; 0.5% Ameri-

can Indian or Alaska Native, non-Hispanic/Latino; 0.8% Two or more races, non-Hispanic/Latino; 4% Race/ethnicity unknown; 0.4% international; 9% transferred in; 11% live on campus. *Retention:* 72% of full-time freshmen returned.
Freshmen *Admission:* 109 applied, 56 admitted, 29 enrolled. *Average high school GPA:* 3.51. *Test scores:* ACT scores over 18: 100%; ACT scores over 24: 28%; ACT scores over 30: 3%.
Faculty *Total:* 61, 82% full-time, 30% with terminal degrees. *Student/faculty ratio:* 12:1.
Academics *Calendar:* semesters. *Degrees:* certificates, associate, bachelor's, master's, and post-master's certificates. *Special study options:* academic remediation for entering students, accelerated degree program, adult/continuing education programs, advanced placement credit, distance learning, external degree program, independent study, internships, services for LD students, summer session for credit. *ROTC:* Army (c), Air Force (c).
Computers on Campus 47 computers/terminals are available on campus for general student use. Students can access the following: campus intranet, computer help desk, free student e-mail accounts, online (class) grades, online (class) registration, online (class) schedules. Campuswide network is available. 100% of college-owned or -operated housing units are wired for high-speed Internet access. Wireless service is available via entire campus.
Student Life *Housing options:* coed. Campus housing is university owned. Freshman applicants given priority for college housing. *Activities and organizations:* Student Senate, Student Nurses Association, Methodist Allied Health Student Association, Student Ambassadors, Residence Hall Council. *Campus security:* 24-hour emergency response devices and patrols, late-night transport/escort service, controlled dormitory access. *Student services:* health clinic, personal/psychological counseling.
Standardized Tests *Required:* SAT or ACT (for admission).
Costs (2013–14) *Tuition:* $15,840 full-time, $528 per credit hour part-time. Full-time tuition and fees vary according to degree level and program. Part-time tuition and fees vary according to degree level and program. *Required fees:* $1227 full-time. *Room only:* $6160. Room and board charges vary according to housing facility. *Payment plan:* installment. *Waivers:* employees or children of employees.
Financial Aid Of all full-time matriculated undergraduates who enrolled in 2012, 413 applied for aid, 358 were judged to have need, 30 had their need fully met. 25 Federal Work-Study jobs (averaging $1605). In 2012, 50 non-need-based awards were made. *Average percent of need met:* 43%. *Average financial aid package:* $8564. *Average need-based loan:* $4244. *Average need-based gift aid:* $5717. *Average non-need-based aid:* $3819. *Average indebtedness upon graduation:* $39,753.
Applying *Options:* electronic application, deferred entrance. *Application fee:* $25. *Required:* essay or personal statement, high school transcript, minimum 2.5 GPA. *Application deadlines:* rolling (freshmen), rolling (out-of-state freshmen), rolling (transfers).
Freshman Application Contact Ms. Sara Hanson, Director of Enrollment Services, Nebraska Methodist College, 720 North 87th Street, Omaha, NE 68114. *Phone:* 402-354-7111. *Toll-free phone:* 800-335-5510. *Fax:* 402-354-7020. *E-mail:* sara.hanson@methodistcollege.edu.
Website: http://www.methodistcollege.edu/.

Nebraska Wesleyan University

Lincoln, Nebraska

- **Independent United Methodist** comprehensive, founded 1887
- **Suburban** 50-acre campus with easy access to Omaha
- **Endowment** $48.1 million
- **Coed**
- **Moderately difficult** entrance level

Faculty *Student/faculty ratio:* 14:1.
Academics *Calendar:* semesters. *Degrees:* certificates, bachelor's, master's, post-master's, and postbachelor's certificates.
Student Life *Campus security:* 24-hour emergency response devices, late-night transport/escort service, controlled dormitory access.
Athletics Member NCAA, NAIA. All NCAA Division III.
Standardized Tests *Required:* SAT or ACT (for admission).
Costs (2012–13) *One-time required fee:* $120. *Comprehensive fee:* $33,042 includes full-time tuition ($25,468), mandatory fees ($450), and room and board ($7124). Part-time tuition: $958 per credit hour. Part-time tuition and fees vary according to class time and location. *Room and board:* Room and board charges vary according to board plan and housing facility.
Financial Aid *Of all full-time matriculated undergraduates who enrolled in 2011,* 1,215 applied for aid, 1,071 were judged to have need, 217 had their need fully met. 129 Federal Work-Study jobs (averaging $868). 431 state and other part-time jobs (averaging $1551). *In 2011,* 344 non-need-based awards

were made. *Average percent of need met:* 69. *Average financial aid package:* $17,243. *Average need-based loan:* $4630. *Average need-based gift aid:* $12,523. *Average non-need-based aid:* $9199. *Average indebtedness upon graduation:* $25,490.

Applying *Options:* electronic application, deferred entrance. *Application fee:* $20. *Required:* high school transcript. *Required for some:* essay or personal statement. *Recommended:* interview.

Freshman Application Contact Mr. David Duzik, Director of Admissions, Nebraska Wesleyan University, 5000 Saint Paul Avenue, Lincoln, NE 68504. *Phone:* 402-465-2144. *Toll-free phone:* 800-541-3818. *Fax:* 402-465-2177. *E-mail:* admissions@nebrwesleyan.edu.
Website: http://www.nebrwesleyan.edu/.

Peru State College

Peru, Nebraska

- **State-supported** comprehensive, founded 1867, part of Nebraska State College System
- **Rural** 104-acre campus
- **Coed**
- **Noncompetitive** entrance level

Faculty *Student/faculty ratio:* 24:1.
Academics *Calendar:* semesters. *Degrees:* bachelor's and master's.
Student Life *Campus security:* 24-hour emergency response devices and patrols, late-night transport/escort service.
Athletics Member NAIA.
Standardized Tests *Required for some:* SAT or ACT (for admission).
Costs (2012–13) *Tuition:* state resident $4200 full-time; nonresident $4200 full-time. Full-time tuition and fees vary according to course level, course load, and location. Part-time tuition and fees vary according to course level, course load, and location. *Room and board:* $5970; room only: $3162. Room and board charges vary according to board plan and housing facility.
Applying *Options:* electronic application. *Required:* high school transcript.
Freshman Application Contact Ms. Micki Willis, Vice President for Enrollment Management and Student Affairs, Peru State College, PO Box 10, Peru, NE 68421. *Phone:* 402-872-2221. *Toll-free phone:* 800-742-4412 (in-state); 800-741-4412 (out-of-state). *Fax:* 402-872-2296. *E-mail:* mwillis@peru.edu.
Website: http://www.peru.edu/.

St. Gregory the Great Seminary

Seward, Nebraska

Freshman Application Contact Rev. Peter M. Mitchell, Dean of Men, St. Gregory the Great Seminary, 800 Fletcher Road, Seward, NE 68434. *Phone:* 402-643-4052. *Fax:* 402-643-6964. *E-mail:* sggs@stgregoryseminary.edu.
Website: http://www.stgregoryseminary.edu/.

Union College

Lincoln, Nebraska

- **Independent Seventh-day Adventist** comprehensive, founded 1891
- **Suburban** 26-acre campus with easy access to Omaha
- **Endowment** $14.0 million
- **Coed** 795 undergraduate students, 85% full-time, 59% women, 41% men
- **Moderately difficult** entrance level, 45% of applicants were admitted

Undergraduates 673 full-time, 122 part-time. Students come from 48 states and territories; 32 other countries; 76% are from out of state; 4% Black or African American, non-Hispanic/Latino; 13% Hispanic/Latino; 4% Asian, non-Hispanic/Latino; 1% Native Hawaiian or other Pacific Islander, non-Hispanic/Latino; 0.8% American Indian or Alaska Native, non-Hispanic/Latino; 3% Two or more races, non-Hispanic/Latino; 2% Race/ethnicity unknown; 7% international; 9% transferred in; 62% live on campus. *Retention:* 72% of full-time freshmen returned.
Freshmen *Admission:* 1,251 applied, 563 admitted, 148 enrolled. *Average high school GPA:* 3.3. *Test scores:* SAT math scores over 500: 38%; SAT writing scores over 500: 44%; ACT scores over 18: 81%; SAT math scores over 600: 24%; SAT writing scores over 600: 14%; ACT scores over 24: 33%; SAT math scores over 700: 5%; SAT writing scores over 700: 3%; ACT scores over 30: 3%.

Faculty *Total:* 118, 47% full-time, 29% with terminal degrees. *Student/faculty ratio:* 10:1.
Academics *Calendar:* semesters. *Degrees:* associate, bachelor's, and master's. *Special study options:* accelerated degree program, adult/continuing education programs, advanced placement credit, cooperative education, double majors, English as a second language, honors programs, independent study, internships, off-campus study, part-time degree program, services for LD students, student-designed majors, study abroad, summer session for credit.
Computers on Campus 85 computers/terminals are available on campus for general student use. Students can access the following: free student e-mail accounts, online (class) grades, online (class) registration, online (class) schedules. Campuswide network is available. 100% of college-owned or -operated housing units are wired for high-speed Internet access. Wireless service is available via entire campus.
Student Life *Housing:* on-campus residence required through junior year. *Options:* men-only, women-only. Campus housing is university owned. Freshman campus housing is guaranteed. *Activities and organizations:* drama/theater group, student-run newspaper, choral group. *Campus security:* 24-hour emergency response devices, student patrols, late-night transport/escort service. *Student services:* health clinic, personal/psychological counseling.
Athletics *Intercollegiate sports:* basketball M/W, golf M, volleyball W. *Intramural sports:* basketball M/W, football M/W, gymnastics M(c)/W(c), softball M/W, ultimate Frisbee M/W, volleyball M/W.
Standardized Tests *Required:* SAT or ACT (for admission).
Costs (2013–14) *Comprehensive fee:* $26,840 includes full-time tuition ($19,550), mandatory fees ($920), and room and board ($6370). Full-time tuition and fees vary according to course load, degree level, and program. Part-time tuition: $815 per credit hour. Part-time tuition and fees vary according to program. *College room only:* $3620. Room and board charges vary according to housing facility. *Payment plan:* installment. *Waivers:* employees or children of employees.
Financial Aid *Financial aid deadline:* 7/31.
Applying *Options:* electronic application. *Required:* high school transcript, minimum 2.5 GPA, 3 letters of recommendation. *Required for some:* essay or personal statement, interview. *Application deadlines:* rolling (freshmen), rolling (transfers). *Notification:* continuous (freshmen), continuous (transfers).
Freshman Application Contact Jennifer Enos, Admissions Assistant Director, Union College, 3800 South 48th Street, Lincoln, NE 68506. *Phone:* 402-486-2600 Ext. 2052. *Toll-free phone:* 800-228-4600. *Fax:* 402-486-2895. *E-mail:* ucenroll@ucollege.edu.
Website: http://www.ucollege.edu/.

University of Nebraska at Kearney

Kearney, Nebraska

- **State-supported** comprehensive, founded 1903, part of University of Nebraska System
- **Small-town** 235-acre campus
- **Coed** 5,648 undergraduate students, 88% full-time, 56% women, 44% men
- **Moderately difficult** entrance level, 77% of applicants were admitted

Undergraduates 4,964 full-time, 684 part-time. 9% are from out of state; 1% Black or African American, non-Hispanic/Latino; 8% Hispanic/Latino; 0.8% Asian, non-Hispanic/Latino; 0.2% American Indian or Alaska Native, non-Hispanic/Latino; 1% Two or more races, non-Hispanic/Latino; 0.2% Race/ethnicity unknown; 9% international; 6% transferred in; 50% live on campus. *Retention:* 79% of full-time freshmen returned.
Freshmen *Admission:* 2,895 applied, 2,215 admitted, 1,136 enrolled. *Average high school GPA:* 3.39. *Test scores:* ACT scores over 18: 93%; ACT scores over 24: 40%; ACT scores over 30: 5%.
Faculty *Total:* 406, 75% full-time, 64% with terminal degrees. *Student/faculty ratio:* 16:1.
Academics *Calendar:* semesters. *Degrees:* bachelor's, master's, and post-master's certificates. *Special study options:* part-time degree program. *ROTC:* Army (b).
Computers on Campus 600 computers/terminals and 8,500 ports are available on campus for general student use. Students can access the following: computer help desk, free student e-mail accounts, online (class) grades, online (class) registration, online (class) schedules, online degree audit, online personal information update, online bill viewing and payment, online financial aid awards and acceptance. Campuswide network is available. Wireless service is available via entire campus.
Student Life *Housing:* on-campus residence required for freshman year. *Options:* coed. Campus housing is university owned. Freshman campus hous-

ing is guaranteed. *Activities and organizations:* drama/theater group, student-run newspaper, radio and television station, marching band, national fraternities, national sororities. *Campus security:* 24-hour emergency response devices and patrols, late-night transport/escort service. *Student services:* health clinic.

Athletics Member NCAA. All Division II. *Intercollegiate sports:* baseball M(s), basketball M(s)/W(s), cross-country running M(s)/W(s), football M(s), golf M(s)/W(s), soccer W, softball W(s), swimming and diving W(s), tennis M(s)/W(s), track and field M(s)/W(s), volleyball W(s), wrestling M(s). *Intramural sports:* badminton M/W, basketball M/W, cross-country running M/W, football M/W, golf M/W, racquetball M/W, soccer M/W, softball M/W, tennis M/W, volleyball M/W, water polo M/W, wrestling M/W.

Standardized Tests *Required:* SAT and SAT Subject Tests or ACT (for admission).

Costs (2012–13) *Tuition:* state resident $5235 full-time, $175 per credit hour part-time; nonresident $10,740 full-time, $358 per credit hour part-time. Full-time tuition and fees vary according to course level, course load, degree level, and location. Part-time tuition and fees vary according to course level, course load, degree level, and location. *Required fees:* $1271 full-time, $25 per credit hour part-time, $264 per term part-time. *Room and board:* $8038; room only: $4114. Room and board charges vary according to board plan and housing facility. *Payment plan:* installment. *Waivers:* employees or children of employees.

Financial Aid Of all full-time matriculated undergraduates who enrolled in 2011, 3,369 applied for aid, 2,836 were judged to have need, 943 had their need fully met. In 2011, 179 non-need-based awards were made. *Average percent of need met:* 74%. *Average financial aid package:* $9889. *Average need-based loan:* $3945. *Average need-based gift aid:* $6024. *Average non-need-based aid:* $2209.

Applying *Options:* electronic application. *Application fee:* $45. *Required:* high school transcript, rank in upper 50% of high school class. *Application deadlines:* 9/1 (freshmen), rolling (transfers). *Notification:* continuous (freshmen), continuous (transfers).

Freshman Application Contact Mr. Dusty Newton, Director of Admissions, University of Nebraska at Kearney, 905 West 25th Street, Kearney, NE 68849-0001. *Phone:* 308-865-8702. *Toll-free phone:* 800-532-7639. *Fax:* 308-865-8987. *E-mail:* admissionsug@unk.edu.
Website: http://www.unk.edu/.

University of Nebraska at Omaha

Omaha, Nebraska

- **State-supported** university, founded 1908, part of University of Nebraska System
- **Urban** 503-acre campus
- **Coed** 12,136 undergraduate students, 75% full-time, 52% women, 48% men
- **Minimally difficult** entrance level, 80% of applicants were admitted

Undergraduates 9,147 full-time, 2,989 part-time. Students come from 47 states and territories; 79 other countries; 7% are from out of state; 7% Black or African American, non-Hispanic/Latino; 7% Hispanic/Latino; 3% Asian, non-Hispanic/Latino; 0.1% Native Hawaiian or other Pacific Islander, non-Hispanic/Latino; 0.4% American Indian or Alaska Native, non-Hispanic/Latino; 2% Two or more races, non-Hispanic/Latino; 3% Race/ethnicity unknown; 3% international; 10% transferred in; 11% live on campus. *Retention:* 72% of full-time freshmen returned.

Freshmen *Admission:* 4,536 applied, 3,630 admitted, 1,761 enrolled. *Average high school GPA:* 3.4. *Test scores:* ACT scores over 18: 89%; ACT scores over 24: 41%; ACT scores over 30: 11%.

Faculty *Total:* 984, 51% full-time, 54% with terminal degrees. *Student/faculty ratio:* 17:1.

Academics *Calendar:* semesters. *Degrees:* bachelor's, master's, doctoral, post-master's, and postbachelor's certificates. *Special study options:* adult/continuing education programs, advanced placement credit, cooperative education, distance learning, double majors, English as a second language, honors programs, independent study, internships, off-campus study, part-time degree program, services for LD students, student-designed majors, study abroad, summer session for credit. *ROTC:* Army (c), Air Force (b).

Computers on Campus 2,450 computers/terminals are available on campus for general student use. Students can access the following: computer help desk, free student e-mail accounts, online (class) grades, online (class) registration, online (class) schedules. Campuswide network is available. 100% of college-owned or -operated housing units are wired for high-speed Internet access. Wireless service is available via classrooms, computer centers, computer labs, dorm rooms, learning centers, libraries, student centers.

Student Life *Housing options:* coed. Campus housing is university owned and leased by the school. *Activities and organizations:* drama/theater group, stu-

dent-run newspaper, radio and television station, choral group, marching band, Student Programming Board-Maverick Productions, student government, Greek Life, Emerging Leaders, PRSSA—Public Relations student society of America, national fraternities, national sororities. *Campus security:* 24-hour emergency response devices and patrols, late-night transport/escort service, controlled dormitory access. *Student services:* health clinic, personal/psychological counseling, women's center, legal services.

Athletics Member NCAA. All Division I. *Intercollegiate sports:* baseball M(s), basketball M(s)/W(s), golf M(s)/W(s), ice hockey M(s), soccer M(s)/W(s), softball W(s), swimming and diving W(s), tennis M(s)/W(s), volleyball W(s). *Intramural sports:* bowling M/W, fencing M/W, field hockey M/W, golf M/W, lacrosse M/W, racquetball M/W, riflery M/W, rugby M/W, soccer M/W, softball M/W, track and field M/W, ultimate Frisbee M/W, volleyball M/W.

Standardized Tests *Required:* SAT or ACT (for admission).

Costs (2013–14) *Tuition:* state resident $5180 full-time, $197 per credit part-time; nonresident $15,520 full-time, $598 per credit part-time. *Required fees:* $1370 full-time. *Room and board:* $8090.

Financial Aid Of all full-time matriculated undergraduates who enrolled in 2011, 6,501 applied for aid, 5,557 were judged to have need, 1,540 had their need fully met. In 2011, 323 non-need-based awards were made. *Average percent of need met:* 68%. *Average financial aid package:* $8931. *Average need-based loan:* $3939. *Average need-based gift aid:* $5266. *Average non-need-based aid:* $1642. *Average indebtedness upon graduation:* $25,145.

Applying *Options:* electronic application, deferred entrance. *Application fee:* $45. *Required:* high school transcript. *Application deadlines:* 8/1 (freshmen), 8/1 (transfers). *Notification:* continuous (freshmen), continuous (transfers).

Freshman Application Contact University of Nebraska at Omaha, 6001 Dodge Street, Omaha, NE 68182. *Phone:* 402-554-2416. *Toll-free phone:* 800-858-8648.
Website: http://www.unomaha.edu/.

University of Nebraska–Lincoln

Lincoln, Nebraska

- **State-supported** university, founded 1869, part of University of Nebraska System
- **Urban** 622-acre campus with easy access to Omaha
- **Endowment** $1.2 billion
- **Coed** 19,103 undergraduate students, 93% full-time, 46% women, 54% men
- **Moderately difficult** entrance level, 64% of applicants were admitted

Undergraduates 17,766 full-time, 1,337 part-time. Students come from 51 states and territories; 89 other countries; 16% are from out of state; 2% Black or African American, non-Hispanic/Latino; 4% Hispanic/Latino; 2% Asian, non-Hispanic/Latino; 0.1% Native Hawaiian or other Pacific Islander, non-Hispanic/Latino; 0.3% American Indian or Alaska Native, non-Hispanic/Latino; 2% Two or more races, non-Hispanic/Latino; 2% Race/ethnicity unknown; 5% international; 5% transferred in; 41% live on campus. *Retention:* 84% of full-time freshmen returned.

Freshmen *Admission:* 10,350 applied, 6,662 admitted, 3,937 enrolled. *Test scores:* SAT critical reading scores over 500: 79%; SAT math scores over 500: 87%; ACT scores over 18: 99%; SAT critical reading scores over 600: 45%; SAT math scores over 600: 59%; ACT scores over 24: 63%; SAT critical reading scores over 700: 17%; SAT math scores over 700: 21%; ACT scores over 30: 20%.

Faculty *Total:* 1,089, 98% full-time, 96% with terminal degrees. *Student/faculty ratio:* 20:1.

Academics *Calendar:* semesters. *Degrees:* associate, bachelor's, master's, doctoral, post-master's, and postbachelor's certificates. *Special study options:* accelerated degree program, adult/continuing education programs, advanced placement credit, cooperative education, distance learning, double majors, English as a second language, honors programs, independent study, internships, off-campus study, part-time degree program, services for LD students, student-designed majors, study abroad, summer session for credit. *ROTC:* Army (b), Navy (b), Air Force (b).

Computers on Campus 600 computers/terminals are available on campus for general student use. Students can access the following: campus intranet, computer help desk, free student e-mail accounts, online (class) grades, online (class) registration, online (class) schedules. Campuswide network is available. 100% of college-owned or -operated housing units are wired for high-speed Internet access. Wireless service is available via entire campus.

Student Life *Housing:* on-campus residence required for freshman year. *Options:* coed, women-only, cooperative, disabled students. Campus housing is university owned. Freshman campus housing is guaranteed. *Activities and organizations:* drama/theater group, student-run newspaper, radio station, choral group, marching band, Student Alumni Association, University Ambassadors, University Program Council, Golden Key Honor Society, ASUN (Association of Students of the University of Nebraska, student body government), national fraternities, national sororities. *Campus security:* 24-hour emergency response devices and patrols, late-night transport/escort service, controlled dormitory access. *Student services:* health clinic, personal/psychological counseling, women's center, legal services.

Athletics Member NCAA. All Division I except football (Division I-A). *Intercollegiate sports:* baseball M(s), basketball M(s)/W(s), bowling W(s), cross-country running M(s)/W(s), golf M(s)/W(s), gymnastics M(s)/W(s), riflery W(s), soccer W(s), softball W(s), swimming and diving W(s), tennis M(s)/W(s), track and field M(s)/W(s), volleyball W(s), wrestling M(s). *Intramural sports:* badminton M/W, baseball M(c)/W(c), basketball M/W, bowling M(c)/W, crew M(c)/W(c), cross-country running M(c)/W(c), golf M/W, ice hockey M(c)/W(c), lacrosse M(c)/W(c), racquetball M(c)/W(c), riflery M(c)/W(c), rock climbing M(c)/W(c), rugby M(c)/W(c), soccer M(c)/W(c), softball M(c)/W(c), swimming and diving M(c)/W(c), table tennis M(c)/W(c), tennis M(c)/W(c), ultimate Frisbee M(c)/W(c), volleyball M(c)/W(c), water polo M(c)/W(c), weight lifting M/W, wrestling M/W.

Standardized Tests *Required:* SAT or ACT (for admission). *Recommended:* ACT (for admission).

Costs (2012–13) *Tuition:* state resident $6480 full-time, $216 per credit hour part-time; nonresident $19,230 full-time, $641 per credit hour part-time. Full-time tuition and fees vary according to course load, program, and reciprocity agreements. Part-time tuition and fees vary according to course load, program, and reciprocity agreements. *Required fees:* $1417 full-time, $11 per credit hour part-time, $299 per term part-time. *Room and board:* $9122. Room and board charges vary according to board plan and housing facility. *Payment plan:* installment. *Waivers:* employees or children of employees.

Financial Aid Of all full-time matriculated undergraduates who enrolled in 2011, 11,021 applied for aid, 8,480 were judged to have need, 1,377 had their need fully met. 1,142 Federal Work-Study jobs (averaging $2115). In 2011, 998 non-need-based awards were made. *Average percent of need met:* 78%. *Average financial aid package:* $12,087. *Average need-based loan:* $4171. *Average need-based gift aid:* $6731. *Average non-need-based aid:* $5059. *Average indebtedness upon graduation:* $23,280.

Applying *Options:* electronic application. *Application fee:* $45. *Required:* high school transcript. *Required for some:* rank in upper 50% of high school class. *Application deadlines:* 5/1 (freshmen), 5/1 (transfers). *Notification:* continuous (freshmen), continuous (transfers).

Freshman Application Contact Ms. Amber Hunter, Associate Dean—Enrollment Management, University of Nebraska–Lincoln, 1410 Q Street, Lincoln, NE 68588-0417. *Phone:* 402-472-2023. *Toll-free phone:* 800-742-8800. *Fax:* 402-472-0670. *E-mail:* admissions@unl.edu. *Website:* http://www.unl.edu/.

University of Nebraska Medical Center
Omaha, Nebraska

- **State-supported** upper-level, founded 1869, part of University of Nebraska System
- **Urban** 16-acre campus
- **Endowment** $11.9 million
- **Coed**

Faculty *Student/faculty ratio:* 3:1.

Academics *Calendar:* semesters. *Degrees:* bachelor's, master's, doctoral, post-master's, and postbachelor's certificates.

Student Life *Campus security:* 24-hour emergency response devices and patrols, late-night transport/escort service.

Financial Aid *Of all full-time matriculated undergraduates who enrolled in 2008,* 863 applied for aid, 729 were judged to have need, 103 had their need fully met. 53 Federal Work-Study jobs (averaging $663). *In 2008,* 181 non-need-based awards were made. *Average percent of need met:* 56. *Average financial aid package:* $8239. *Average need-based loan:* $4871. *Average need-based gift aid:* $4760. *Average non-need-based aid:* $8607. *Average indebtedness upon graduation:* $29,188.

Applying *Options:* electronic application, deferred entrance. *Application fee:* $45.

Application Contact University of Nebraska Medical Center, Nebraska Medical Center, Omaha, NE 68198. *Toll-free phone:* 800-626-8431 Ext. 6468. *Website:* http://www.unmc.edu/.

University of Phoenix–Omaha Campus
Omaha, Nebraska

Admissions Office Contact University of Phoenix–Omaha Campus, 13321 California Street, Suite 200, Omaha, NE 68154-5240. *Toll-free phone:* 866-766-0766.
Website: http://www.phoenix.edu/.

Wayne State College
Wayne, Nebraska

- **State-supported** comprehensive, founded 1910, part of Nebraska State College System
- **Small-town** 128-acre campus
- **Endowment** $12.2 million
- **Coed** 3,020 undergraduate students, 92% full-time, 57% women, 43% men
- **Noncompetitive** entrance level, 100% of applicants were admitted

Undergraduates 2,779 full-time, 241 part-time. Students come from 29 states and territories; 18 other countries; 14% are from out of state; 3% Black or African American, non-Hispanic/Latino; 6% Hispanic/Latino; 0.4% Asian, non-Hispanic/Latino; 0.1% Native Hawaiian or other Pacific Islander, non-Hispanic/Latino; 0.7% American Indian or Alaska Native, non-Hispanic/Latino; 1% Two or more races, non-Hispanic/Latino; 8% Race/ethnicity unknown; 0.5% international; 7% transferred in; 47% live on campus. *Retention:* 70% of full-time freshmen returned.

Freshmen *Admission:* 2,278 applied, 2,278 admitted, 695 enrolled. *Average high school GPA:* 3.21. *Test scores:* ACT scores over 18: 79%; ACT scores over 24: 29%; ACT scores over 30: 3%.

Faculty *Total:* 216, 57% full-time, 54% with terminal degrees. *Student/faculty ratio:* 20:1.

Academics *Calendar:* semesters. *Degrees:* bachelor's, master's, and post-master's certificates. *Special study options:* adult/continuing education programs, advanced placement credit, cooperative education, distance learning, double majors, honors programs, independent study, internships, off-campus study, part-time degree program, services for LD students, student-designed majors, study abroad, summer session for credit. *ROTC:* Army (b).

Computers on Campus 365 computers/terminals are available on campus for general student use. Students can access the following: campus intranet, computer help desk, free student e-mail accounts, online (class) grades, online (class) registration, online (class) schedules. Campuswide network is available. 100% of college-owned or -operated housing units are wired for high-speed Internet access. Wireless service is available via classrooms, computer centers, computer labs, learning centers, libraries, student centers.

Student Life *Housing:* on-campus residence required for freshman year. *Options:* coed. Campus housing is university owned. Freshman campus housing is guaranteed. *Activities and organizations:* drama/theater group, student-run newspaper, radio and television station, choral group, marching band, national fraternities, national sororities. *Campus security:* 24-hour emergency response devices and patrols, student patrols, late-night transport/escort service, controlled dormitory access. *Student services:* health clinic, personal/psychological counseling.

Athletics Member NCAA. All Division II. *Intercollegiate sports:* baseball M(s), basketball M(s)/W(s), cheerleading M(c)/W(c), cross-country running M(s)/W(s), football M(s), golf M(s)/W(s), rugby M(c)/W(c), soccer M(c)/W(s), softball W(s), track and field M(s)/W(s), volleyball W(s), wrestling M(c). *Intramural sports:* archery M/W, badminton M/W, basketball M/W, bowling M/W, football M/W, golf M/W, racquetball M/W, softball M/W, swimming and diving M/W, table tennis M/W, tennis M/W, track and field M/W, volleyball M/W, weight lifting M/W, wrestling M.

Standardized Tests *Recommended:* SAT or ACT (for admission).

Costs (2012–13) *Tuition:* state resident $4200 full-time, $140 per credit hour part-time; nonresident $8400 full-time, $280 per credit hour part-time. Full-time tuition and fees vary according to course level and course load. Part-time tuition and fees vary according to course level and course load. *Required fees:* $1320 full-time, $52 per credit hour part-time. *Room and board:* $5960; room only: $2880. Room and board charges vary according to board plan and housing facility. *Payment plan:* installment. *Waivers:* employees or children of employees.

Financial Aid Of all full-time matriculated undergraduates who enrolled in 2012, 2,448 applied for aid, 1,965 were judged to have need, 848 had their need fully met. In 2012, 225 non-need-based awards were made. *Average per-*

cent of need met: 61%. *Average financial aid package:* $8179. *Average need-based loan:* $3895. *Average need-based gift aid:* $4049. *Average non-need-based aid:* $3508.

Applying *Options:* electronic application, deferred entrance. *Required:* high school transcript. *Application deadlines:* rolling (freshmen), rolling (out-of-state freshmen), rolling (transfers). *Notification:* continuous (freshmen), continuous (out-of-state freshmen), continuous (transfers).

Freshman Application Contact Mr. Kevin Halle, Director of Admissions, Wayne State College, 1111 Main Street, Wayne, NE 68787. *Phone:* 402-375-7234. *Toll-free phone:* 866-WSC-CATS. *Fax:* 402-375-7204. *E-mail:* admit1@wsc.edu.
Website: http://www.wsc.edu/.

York College
York, Nebraska

Freshman Application Contact Ms. Janae Parsons, York College, 1125 East 8th Street, York, NE 68467-2699. *Phone:* 402-363-5627. *Toll-free phone:* 800-950-9675. *Fax:* 402-363-5623. *E-mail:* enroll@york.edu.
Website: http://www.york.edu/.

NEVADA

The Art Institute of Las Vegas
Henderson, Nevada

- **Proprietary** 4-year, founded 2002, part of Education Management Corporation
- **Suburban** campus
- **Coed**

Academics *Calendar:* quarters. *Degrees:* diplomas, associate, and bachelor's.
Freshman Application Contact The Art Institute of Las Vegas, 2350 Corporate Circle Drive, Henderson, NV 89074. *Phone:* 702-369-9944. *Toll-free phone:* 800-833-2678.
Website: http://www.artinstitutes.edu/lasvegas/.

See full-page ad on page 54 and page 1092 for the College Close-Up.

College of Southern Nevada
North Las Vegas, Nevada

Freshman Application Contact Admissions and Records, College of Southern Nevada, 3200 East Cheyenne Avenue, North Las Vegas, NV 89030-4296. *Phone:* 702-651-4060.
Website: http://www.csn.edu/.

DeVry University
Henderson, Nevada

Freshman Application Contact DeVry University, 2490 Paseo Verde Parkway, Henderson, NV 89074-7120. *Toll-free phone:* 866-338-7941.
Website: http://www.devry.edu/.

Great Basin College
Elko, Nevada

Freshman Application Contact Ms. Janice King, Director of Admissions and Registrar, Great Basin College, 1500 College Parkway, Elko, NV 89801-3348. *Phone:* 775-753-2361. *Fax:* 775-753-2311. *E-mail:* janicek@gwmail.gbcnv.edu.
Website: http://www.gbcnv.edu/.

ITT Technical Institute
Henderson, Nevada

- **Proprietary** primarily 2-year, founded 1997, part of ITT Educational Services, Inc.
- **Coed**
- **Minimally difficult** entrance level

Academics *Degrees:* associate and bachelor's.
Financial Aid *Of all full-time matriculated undergraduates who enrolled in 2011,* 6 Federal Work-Study jobs (averaging $5000).
Freshman Application Contact Director of Recruitment, ITT Technical Institute, 168 North Gibson Road, Henderson, NV 89014. *Phone:* 702-558-5404. *Toll-free phone:* 800-488-8459.
Website: http://www.itt-tech.edu/.

ITT Technical Institute
North Las Vegas, Nevada

- **Proprietary** primarily 2-year, part of ITT Educational Services, Inc.
- **Coed**

Academics *Calendar:* quarters. *Degrees:* associate and bachelor's.
Freshman Application Contact Director of Recruitment, ITT Technical Institute, 3825 W. Cheyenne Avenue, Suite 600, North Las Vegas, NV 89032. *Phone:* 702-240-0967. *Toll-free phone:* 877-832-8442.
Website: http://www.itt-tech.edu/.

Morrison University
Reno, Nevada

Freshman Application Contact Mr. Charles Timinsky, Director of Enrollment, Morrison University, 10315 Professional Circle, Suite 201, Reno, NV 89521. *Phone:* 775-850-0700 Ext. 101. *Toll-free phone:* 866-381-6050. *Fax:* 775-850-0711. *E-mail:* ctiminsky@morrison.neumont.edu.
Website: http://anthem.edu/morrison/.

Nevada State College at Henderson
Henderson, Nevada

Freshman Application Contact Ms. Patricia Ring, Registrar, Nevada State College at Henderson, Office of Admissions and Records, 1125 Nevada State Drive, Henderson, NV 89002. *Phone:* 702-992-2114. *Fax:* 702-992-2111. *E-mail:* admissions@nsc.nevada.edu.
Website: http://www.nsc.nevada.edu/.

Pima Medical Institute
Las Vegas, Nevada

Freshman Application Contact Admissions Office, Pima Medical Institute, 3333 East Flamingo Road, Las Vegas, NV 89121. *Phone:* 702-458-9650 Ext. 202. *Toll-free phone:* 800-477-PIMA.
Website: http://www.pmi.edu/.

Sierra Nevada College
Incline Village, Nevada

- **Independent** comprehensive, founded 1969
- **Small-town** 20-acre campus with easy access to Reno
- **Endowment** $4.1 million
- **Coed** 536 undergraduate students, 96% full-time, 41% women, 59% men
- **Moderately difficult** entrance level, 69% of applicants were admitted

Undergraduates 515 full-time, 21 part-time. Students come from 34 states and territories; 12 other countries; 84% are from out of state; 2% Black or African American, non-Hispanic/Latino; 2% Hispanic/Latino; 2% Asian, non-Hispanic/Latino; 0.4% Native Hawaiian or other Pacific Islander, non-Hispanic/Latino; 2% American Indian or Alaska Native, non-Hispanic/Latino; 5% Race/ethnicity unknown; 9% international; 14% transferred in; 52% live on campus. *Retention:* 79% of full-time freshmen returned.

Freshmen *Admission:* 709 applied, 491 admitted, 70 enrolled. *Average high school GPA:* 2.93. *Test scores:* SAT critical reading scores over 500: 47%; SAT math scores over 500: 47%; SAT writing scores over 500: 42%; ACT scores over 18: 86%; SAT critical reading scores over 600: 14%; SAT math scores over 600: 12%; SAT writing scores over 600: 13%; ACT scores over 24: 41%; SAT critical reading scores over 700: 4%; SAT math scores over 700: 2%.

Faculty *Total:* 127, 27% full-time, 26% with terminal degrees. *Student/faculty ratio:* 11:1.

Academics *Calendar:* semesters. *Degrees:* bachelor's and master's. *Special study options:* academic remediation for entering students, accelerated degree program, adult/continuing education programs, advanced placement credit, cooperative education, double majors, English as a second language, external degree program, honors programs, independent study, internships, part-time degree program, services for LD students, student-designed majors, study abroad, summer session for credit. *Unusual degree programs:* 3-2 Master of Teaching, elementary or secondary education.

Computers on Campus 50 computers/terminals are available on campus for general student use. Students can access the following: computer help desk, free student e-mail accounts, online (class) grades, online (class) schedules. Campuswide network is available. 100% of college-owned or -operated housing units are wired for high-speed Internet access. Wireless service is available via entire campus.

Student Life *Housing:* on-campus residence required through sophomore year. *Options:* coed. Campus housing is university owned. Freshman campus housing is guaranteed. *Activities and organizations:* student-run newspaper, choral group, Film Club, International Club, Sustainability Club, Rock Climbing Club, First Generation Club. *Campus security:* 24-hour emergency response devices and patrols, controlled dormitory access.

Athletics *Intercollegiate sports:* rock climbing M/W, skiing (downhill) M(s)/W(s). *Intramural sports:* rock climbing M/W, skiing (downhill) M/W, soccer M/W, softball M/W, volleyball M/W.

Standardized Tests *Required:* SAT or ACT (for admission).

Costs (2013–14) *Comprehensive fee:* $40,255 includes full-time tuition ($27,753), mandatory fees ($730), and room and board ($11,772). Full-time tuition and fees vary according to degree level and location. Part-time tuition: $1180 per credit. Part-time tuition and fees vary according to degree level and location. *College room only:* $5900. Room and board charges vary according

to board plan. *Payment plan:* installment. *Waivers:* employees or children of employees.

Financial Aid Of all full-time matriculated undergraduates who enrolled in 2012, 363 applied for aid, 339 were judged to have need, 18 had their need fully met. 248 Federal Work-Study jobs (averaging $410). In 2012, 189 non-need-based awards were made. *Average percent of need met:* 55%. *Average financial aid package:* $20,100. *Average need-based loan:* $4750. *Average need-based gift aid:* $14,169. *Average non-need-based aid:* $6500. *Average indebtedness upon graduation:* $27,000.

Applying *Options:* electronic application, deferred entrance. *Required:* essay or personal statement, high school transcript, minimum 2.6 GPA. *Required for some:* 1 letter of recommendation. *Recommended:* interview. *Application deadlines:* rolling (freshmen), rolling (transfers). *Notification:* continuous (freshmen), continuous (transfers).

Freshman Application Contact Ms. Julie Hernandez, Sierra Nevada College, 999 Tahoe Boulevard, Incline Village, NV 89451. *Phone:* 866-412-4636. *Fax:* 775-831-6223. *E-mail:* admissions@sierranevada.edu. *Website:* http://www.sierranevada.edu/.

University of Nevada, Las Vegas

Las Vegas, Nevada

- **State-supported** university, founded 1957, part of Nevada System of Higher Education
- **Urban** campus
- **Coed** 22,432 undergraduate students, 71% full-time, 55% women, 45% men
- **Moderately difficult** entrance level, 81% of applicants were admitted

Undergraduates 15,885 full-time, 6,547 part-time. 14% are from out of state; 8% Black or African American, non-Hispanic/Latino; 21% Hispanic/Latino; 16% Asian, non-Hispanic/Latino; 2% Native Hawaiian or other Pacific Islander, non-Hispanic/Latino; 0.4% American Indian or Alaska Native, non-Hispanic/Latino; 6% Two or more races, non-Hispanic/Latino; 2% Race/ethnicity unknown; 4% international; 10% transferred in; 5% live on campus. *Retention:* 76% of full-time freshmen returned.

Freshmen *Admission:* 6,366 applied, 5,133 admitted, 3,294 enrolled. *Average high school GPA:* 3.24. *Test scores:* SAT critical reading scores over 500: 49%; SAT math scores over 500: 52%; SAT writing scores over 500: 37%; ACT

scores over 18: 83%; SAT critical reading scores over 600: 11%; SAT math scores over 600: 16%; SAT writing scores over 600: 6%; ACT scores over 24: 28%; SAT critical reading scores over 700: 1%; SAT math scores over 700: 1%; ACT scores over 30: 2%.
Faculty *Student/faculty ratio:* 21:1.
Academics *Calendar:* semesters. *Degrees:* certificates, bachelor's, master's, doctoral, post-master's, and postbachelor's certificates. *Special study options:* academic remediation for entering students, adult/continuing education programs, advanced placement credit, cooperative education, distance learning, double majors, English as a second language, honors programs, independent study, internships, part-time degree program, services for LD students, study abroad, summer session for credit. *ROTC:* Army (b), Air Force (b).
Computers on Campus Students can access the following: computer help desk, free student e-mail accounts, online (class) grades, online (class) registration, online (class) schedules. Campuswide network is available. 100% of college-owned or -operated housing units are wired for high-speed Internet access. Wireless service is available via entire campus.
Student Life *Housing options:* coed, disabled students. Campus housing is university owned. Freshman applicants given priority for college housing. *Activities and organizations:* drama/theater group, student-run newspaper, radio and television station, choral group, marching band, national fraternities, national sororities. *Campus security:* 24-hour emergency response devices and patrols, late-night transport/escort service, controlled dormitory access. *Student services:* health clinic, personal/psychological counseling, women's center, legal services.
Athletics Member NCAA. All Division I except football (Division I-A). *Intercollegiate sports:* baseball M(s), basketball M(s)/W(s), cheerleading M(s)/W(s), cross-country running W(s), golf M(s), soccer M(s)/W(s), softball W(s), swimming and diving M(s)/W(s), tennis M(s)/W(s), track and field W(s), volleyball W(s). *Intramural sports:* badminton M/W, basketball M/W, bowling M/W, football M/W, golf M/W, racquetball M/W, soccer M/W, softball M/W, swimming and diving M/W, tennis M/W, volleyball M/W.
Standardized Tests *Required:* SAT or ACT (for admission).
Costs (2013–14) *Tuition:* state resident $6089 full-time, $192 per credit hour part-time; nonresident $19,999 full-time, $402 per credit hour part-time. Full-time tuition and fees vary according to course level, program, and reciprocity agreements. Part-time tuition and fees vary according to course level, program, and reciprocity agreements. *Required fees:* $496 full-time. *Room and board:* $10,524; room only: $5880. Room and board charges vary according to board plan. *Payment plan:* deferred payment. *Waivers:* employees or children of employees.
Financial Aid Of all full-time matriculated undergraduates who enrolled in 2011, 10,548 applied for aid, 9,267 were judged to have need, 1,109 had their need fully met. In 2011, 760 non-need-based awards were made. *Average percent of need met:* 55%. *Average financial aid package:* $8164. *Average need-based loan:* $4145. *Average need-based gift aid:* $5046. *Average non-need-based aid:* $2879. *Average indebtedness upon graduation:* $20,896.
Applying *Options:* electronic application, early admission, deferred entrance. *Application fee:* $60. *Required:* high school transcript, minimum 3.0 GPA. *Required for some:* 2 letters of recommendation. *Application deadlines:* 7/1 (freshmen), 7/1 (transfers). *Notification:* continuous (freshmen), continuous (transfers).
Freshman Application Contact Director of Admissions, University of Nevada, Las Vegas, 4505 Maryland Parkway, Box 451021, Las Vegas, NV 89154-1021. *Phone:* 702-774-8658. *Fax:* 702-774-8008. *E-mail:* admissions@unlv.edu.
Website: http://www.unlv.edu/.

See previous page for display ad and page 1582 for the College Close-Up.

University of Nevada, Reno

Reno, Nevada

- **State-supported** university, founded 1874, part of Nevada System of Higher Education
- **Urban** 200-acre campus
- **Coed** 15,082 undergraduate students, 82% full-time, 53% women, 47% men
- **Moderately difficult** entrance level, 83% of applicants were admitted

Undergraduates 12,415 full-time, 2,667 part-time. Students come from 46 states and territories; 39 other countries; 21% are from out of state; 4% Black or African American, non-Hispanic/Latino; 15% Hispanic/Latino; 6% Asian, non-Hispanic/Latino; 0.4% Native Hawaiian or other Pacific Islander, non-Hispanic/Latino; 0.9% American Indian or Alaska Native, non-Hispanic/Latino; 6% Two or more races, non-Hispanic/Latino; 0.8% Race/ethnicity unknown; 2% international; 7% transferred in; 14% live on campus. *Retention:* 79% of full-time freshmen returned.

Freshmen *Admission:* 7,753 applied, 6,434 admitted, 2,885 enrolled. *Average high school GPA:* 3.35. *Test scores:* SAT critical reading scores over 500: 67%; SAT math scores over 500: 69%; SAT writing scores over 500: 56%; ACT scores over 18: 92%; SAT critical reading scores over 600: 21%; SAT math scores over 600: 26%; SAT writing scores over 600: 15%; ACT scores over 24: 46%; SAT critical reading scores over 700: 3%; SAT math scores over 700: 3%; SAT writing scores over 700: 2%; ACT scores over 30: 6%.
Faculty *Total:* 566, 96% full-time, 89% with terminal degrees. *Student/faculty ratio:* 29:1.
Academics *Calendar:* semesters. *Degrees:* associate, bachelor's, master's, doctoral, post-master's, and postbachelor's certificates. *Special study options:* academic remediation for entering students, adult/continuing education programs, advanced placement credit, distance learning, double majors, English as a second language, honors programs, independent study, internships, off-campus study, part-time degree program, services for LD students, study abroad, summer session for credit. *ROTC:* Army (b). *Unusual degree programs:* 3-2 biotechnology.
Computers on Campus 725 computers/terminals are available on campus for general student use. Students can access the following: computer help desk, free student e-mail accounts, online (class) grades, online (class) registration, online (class) schedules. Campuswide network is available. 100% of college-owned or -operated housing units are wired for high-speed Internet access. Wireless service is available via entire campus.
Student Life *Housing options:* coed, men-only, women-only, disabled students. Campus housing is university owned. Freshman applicants given priority for college housing. *Activities and organizations:* drama/theater group, student-run newspaper, radio station, choral group, marching band, Intervarsity Christian Fellowship, Student Ambassadors, Young Democrats, Asian American Association, Blue Crew, national fraternities, national sororities. *Campus security:* 24-hour emergency response devices and patrols, late-night transport/escort service, controlled dormitory access. *Student services:* health clinic, personal/psychological counseling, women's center, legal services.
Athletics Member NCAA. All Division I except football (Division I-A). *Intercollegiate sports:* baseball M(s), basketball M(s)/W(s), cheerleading M(c)/W(c), cross-country running W(s), golf M(s)/W(s), riflery M(s)/W(s), soccer W(s), softball W(s), swimming and diving W(s), tennis M(s)/W(s), track and field W(s), volleyball W(s). *Intramural sports:* basketball M/W, bowling M/W, cross-country running M/W, equestrian sports M/W, football M, golf M/W, racquetball M/W, rock climbing M/W, rugby M/W, skiing (cross-country) M/W, skiing (downhill) M/W, soccer M/W, softball M/W, swimming and diving M/W, table tennis M/W, tennis M/W, track and field M/W, ultimate Frisbee M/W, volleyball M/W, water polo M/W.
Standardized Tests *Required:* SAT or ACT (for admission).
Costs (2013–14) *Tuition:* state resident $5745 full-time, $192 per credit hour part-time; nonresident $19,655 full-time, $403 per credit hour part-time. Full-time tuition and fees vary according to course level, course load, degree level, and program. Part-time tuition and fees vary according to course level, course load, degree level, and program. *Required fees:* $620 full-time. *Room and board:* $9518. Room and board charges vary according to board plan and housing facility. *Waivers:* employees or children of employees.
Financial Aid Of all full-time matriculated undergraduates who enrolled in 2011, 8,623 applied for aid, 7,364 were judged to have need, 622 had their need fully met. In 2011, 1730 non-need-based awards were made. *Average percent of need met:* 62%. *Average financial aid package:* $8367. *Average need-based loan:* $4290. *Average need-based gift aid:* $5490. *Average non-need-based aid:* $1843. *Average indebtedness upon graduation:* $19,500.
Applying *Options:* electronic application, early admission, deferred entrance. *Application fee:* $60. *Required:* high school transcript, minimum 3.0 GPA. *Application deadlines:* 5/31 (freshmen), rolling (transfers). *Notification:* continuous (freshmen), continuous (transfers).
Freshman Application Contact Dr. Steve Maples, Director of Undergraduate Admissions, University of Nevada, Reno, Mail Stop 120, Reno, NV 89557. *Phone:* 775-784-4700. *Toll-free phone:* 866-263-8232. *Fax:* 775-784-4283. *E-mail:* asknevada@unr.edu.
Website: http://www.unr.edu/.

University of Phoenix–Las Vegas Campus

Las Vegas, Nevada

Freshman Application Contact Marc Booker, Sr. Director, Office of Admissions and Evaluation, University of Phoenix–Las Vegas Campus, 4305 South Riverpoint Parkway, Mail Stop CF-L101, Phoenix, AZ 85040. *Phone:* 602-557-4609. *Toll-free phone:* 866-766-0766. *Fax:* 480-643-1156.
Website: http://www.phoenix.edu/.

University of Phoenix–Northern Nevada Campus

Reno, Nevada

Freshman Application Contact Marc Booker, Sr. Director, Office of Admissions and Evaluation, University of Phoenix–Northern Nevada Campus, 4035 South Riverpoint Parkway, Mail Stop CF-L101, Phoenix, AZ 85040. *Phone:* 602-557-4609. *Toll-free phone:* 866-766-0766. *Fax:* 480-643-1156. *Website:* http://www.phoenix.edu/.

Western Nevada College

Carson City, Nevada

Freshman Application Contact Admissions and Records, Western Nevada College, 2201 West College Parkway, Carson City, NV 89703. *Phone:* 775-445-2377. *Fax:* 775-445-3147. *E-mail:* wncc_aro@wncc.edu. *Website:* http://www.wnc.edu/.

NEW HAMPSHIRE

Colby-Sawyer College

New London, New Hampshire

Freshman Application Contact Director of Admissions and Financial Aid, Colby-Sawyer College, 541 Main Street, New London, NH 03257-4648. *Phone:* 603-526-3700. *Toll-free phone:* 800-272-1015. *Fax:* 603-526-3452. *E-mail:* admissions@colby-sawyer.edu. *Website:* http://www.colby-sawyer.edu/.

College of Saint Mary Magdalen

Warner, New Hampshire

Freshman Application Contact Admissions Director, College of Saint Mary Magdalen, 511 Kearsarge Mountain Road, Warner, NH 03278. *Phone:* 603-456-2656. *Toll-free phone:* 877-498-1723. *Fax:* 603-456-2660. *E-mail:* admissions@magdalen.edu. *Website:* http://www.magdalen.edu/.

Daniel Webster College

Nashua, New Hampshire

- **Independent** comprehensive, founded 1965
- **Suburban** 59-acre campus with easy access to Boston
- **Coed** 603 undergraduate students, 90% full-time, 20% women, 80% men
- **Moderately difficult** entrance level, 64% of applicants were admitted

Undergraduates 544 full-time, 59 part-time. Students come from 19 states and territories; 15 other countries; 54% are from out of state; 3% Black or African American, non-Hispanic/Latino; 2% Hispanic/Latino; 1% Asian, non-Hispanic/Latino; 0.2% Native Hawaiian or other Pacific Islander, non-Hispanic/Latino; 0.2% American Indian or Alaska Native, non-Hispanic/Latino; 0.5% Two or more races, non-Hispanic/Latino; 54% Race/ethnicity unknown; 10% transferred in; 51% live on campus. *Retention:* 58% of full-time freshmen returned.
Freshmen *Admission:* 656 applied, 419 admitted, 145 enrolled. *Average high school GPA:* 2.96. *Test scores:* SAT math scores over 500: 51%; SAT writing scores over 500: 28%; ACT scores over 18: 73%; SAT math scores over 600: 17%; SAT writing scores over 600: 3%; ACT scores over 24: 13%; SAT math scores over 700: 3%.
Faculty *Total:* 85, 27% full-time, 22% with terminal degrees. *Student/faculty ratio:* 13:1.
Academics *Calendar:* semesters. *Degrees:* bachelor's and master's. *Special study options:* academic remediation for entering students, accelerated degree program, advanced placement credit, distance learning, double majors, inde-

pendent study, internships, off-campus study, part-time degree program, summer session for credit. *ROTC:* Army (c), Air Force (c).
Computers on Campus 50 computers/terminals and 535 ports are available on campus for general student use. Students can access the following: campus intranet, computer help desk, free student e-mail accounts, online (class) grades, online (class) registration, online (class) schedules. Campuswide network is available. 100% of college-owned or -operated housing units are wired for high-speed Internet access. Wireless service is available via entire campus.
Student Life *Housing:* on-campus residence required through sophomore year. *Options:* coed, men-only, disabled students. Campus housing is university owned. Freshman campus housing is guaranteed. *Activities and organizations:* drama/theater group, Student Activity Board, Gaming Guild, SATCA (Student Air Traffic Controllers Association), AIAA (American Institute of Aeronautics and Astronautics), Culinary Club. *Campus security:* 24-hour emergency response devices and patrols, controlled dormitory access. *Student services:* health clinic, personal/psychological counseling.
Athletics Member NCAA. All Division III. *Intercollegiate sports:* baseball M, basketball M/W, cross-country running M/W, field hockey W, golf M, ice hockey M(c), lacrosse M/W, soccer M/W, softball W, volleyball M/W. *Intramural sports:* basketball M/W, football M/W, ultimate Frisbee M/W, volleyball M/W.
Standardized Tests *Required:* SAT or ACT (for admission).
Costs (2012–13) *Comprehensive fee:* $25,380 includes full-time tuition ($15,090) and room and board ($10,290). Full-time tuition and fees vary according to course load. Part-time tuition: $503 per credit. Part-time tuition and fees vary according to course load. *College room only:* $5050. Room and board charges vary according to board plan and housing facility. *Payment plan:* installment. *Waivers:* employees or children of employees.
Financial Aid Of all full-time matriculated undergraduates who enrolled in 2011, 400 applied for aid, 339 were judged to have need. 247 Federal Work-Study jobs (averaging $1889). In 2011, 5 non-need-based awards were made. *Average percent of need met:* 58%. *Average financial aid package:* $12,190. *Average need-based loan:* $4865. *Average need-based gift aid:* $4886. *Average non-need-based aid:* $4650. *Average indebtedness upon graduation:* $51,063.
Applying *Options:* electronic application, early admission, deferred entrance. *Required:* high school transcript. *Recommended:* interview. *Application deadlines:* rolling (freshmen), rolling (out-of-state freshmen), rolling (transfers). *Notification:* continuous (freshmen), continuous (out-of-state freshmen), continuous (transfers).
Freshman Application Contact Mrs. Jennifer O'Neal, Manager of Admissions, Daniel Webster College, 20 University Drive, Nashua, NH 03063-1300. *Phone:* 800-794-6188. *Toll-free phone:* 800-325-6876. *E-mail:* nilsson@dwc.edu. *Website:* http://www.dwc.edu/.

Dartmouth College

Hanover, New Hampshire

- **Independent** university, founded 1769
- **Small-town** 269-acre campus
- **Endowment** $3.5 billion
- **Coed** 4,193 undergraduate students, 99% full-time, 50% women, 50% men
- **Most difficult** entrance level, 10% of applicants were admitted

Undergraduates 4,139 full-time, 54 part-time. Students come from 54 states and territories; 69 other countries; 96% are from out of state; 7% Black or African American, non-Hispanic/Latino; 8% Hispanic/Latino; 14% Asian, non-Hispanic/Latino; 0.1% Native Hawaiian or other Pacific Islander, non-Hispanic/Latino; 2% American Indian or Alaska Native, non-Hispanic/Latino; 4% Two or more races, non-Hispanic/Latino; 9% Race/ethnicity unknown; 8% international; 0.4% transferred in; 85% live on campus. *Retention:* 97% of full-time freshmen returned.
Freshmen *Admission:* 23,110 applied, 2,260 admitted, 1,095 enrolled. *Test scores:* SAT critical reading scores over 500: 100%; SAT math scores over 500: 100%; SAT writing scores over 500: 99%; SAT critical reading scores over 600: 94%; SAT math scores over 600: 97%; SAT writing scores over 600: 93%; SAT critical reading scores over 700: 68%; SAT math scores over 700: 73%; SAT writing scores over 700: 69%.
Faculty *Total:* 702, 79% full-time, 91% with terminal degrees. *Student/faculty ratio:* 8:1.
Academics *Calendar:* quarters. *Degrees:* bachelor's, master's, and doctoral. *Special study options:* advanced placement credit, double majors, honors programs, independent study, internships, off-campus study, services for LD students, student-designed majors, study abroad, summer session for credit. *ROTC:* Army (c). *Unusual degree programs:* 3-2 engineering.

Computers on Campus 200 computers/terminals are available on campus for general student use. Students can access the following: campus intranet, computer help desk, free student e-mail accounts, online (class) grades, online (class) registration, online (class) schedules. Campuswide network is available. 100% of college-owned or -operated housing units are wired for high-speed Internet access. Wireless service is available via entire campus.

Student Life *Housing:* on-campus residence required for freshman year. *Options:* coed, cooperative. Campus housing is university owned. Freshman campus housing is guaranteed. *Activities and organizations:* drama/theater group, student-run newspaper, radio and television station, choral group, marching band, Dartmouth Student Assembly, Dartmouth Outing Club, national fraternities, national sororities. *Campus security:* 24-hour emergency response devices and patrols, student patrols, late-night transport/escort service, controlled dormitory access. *Student services:* health clinic, personal/psychological counseling, women's center.

Athletics Member NCAA. All Division I except football (Division I-AA). *Intercollegiate sports:* badminton M(c)/W(c), baseball M, basketball M/W, cheerleading M(c)/W(c), crew M/W, cross-country running M/W, equestrian sports M/W, fencing M(c)/W(c), field hockey W, golf M/W, gymnastics M(c)/W(c), ice hockey M/W, lacrosse M/W, rugby M(c)/W(c), sailing M/W, skiing (cross-country) M/W, skiing (downhill) M/W, soccer M/W, softball W, squash M/W, swimming and diving M/W, table tennis M(c)/W(c), tennis M/W, track and field M/W, ultimate Frisbee M(c)/W(c), volleyball M(c)/W, water polo M(c)/W(c), wrestling M(c). *Intramural sports:* baseball M, basketball M/W, cross-country running M/W, football M/W, golf M/W, ice hockey M/W, lacrosse M/W, rugby M/W, skiing (cross-country) M/W, skiing (downhill) M/W, soccer M/W, softball M/W, squash M/W, swimming and diving M/W, table tennis M/W, tennis M/W, track and field M/W, volleyball M/W, water polo M/W, weight lifting M/W, wrestling M.

Standardized Tests *Required:* SAT or ACT (for admission), SAT Subject Tests (for admission).

Costs (2012–13) *Comprehensive fee:* $58,166 includes full-time tuition ($43,782), mandatory fees ($1430), and room and board ($12,954). Full-time tuition and fees vary according to student level. *College room only:* $7755. Room and board charges vary according to board plan. *Payment plans:* tuition prepayment, installment.

Financial Aid Of all full-time matriculated undergraduates who enrolled in 2011, 2,429 applied for aid, 2,127 were judged to have need, 2,127 had their need fully met. *Average percent of need met:* 100%. *Average financial aid package:* $41,339. *Average need-based loan:* $3586. *Average need-based gift aid:* $38,188. *Average indebtedness upon graduation:* $16,615. *Financial aid deadline:* 2/1.

Applying *Options:* electronic application, early admission, early decision, deferred entrance. *Application fee:* $80. *Required:* essay or personal statement, high school transcript, 2 letters of recommendation, peer evaluation. *Recommended:* interview. *Application deadlines:* 1/1 (freshmen), 3/1 (transfers). *Early decision deadline:* 11/1. *Notification:* 4/1 (freshmen), 5/15 (transfers), 12/15 (early decision).

Freshman Application Contact Maria Laskaris, Dean of Admissions and Financial Aid, Dartmouth College, 6016 McNutt Hall, Hanover, NH 03755. *Phone:* 603-646-2875. *E-mail:* admissions.reply@dartmouth.edu. *Website:* http://www.dartmouth.edu/.

Franklin Pierce University

Rindge, New Hampshire

- **Independent** university, founded 1962
- **Rural** 1000-acre campus
- **Endowment** $7.7 million
- **Coed** 1,737 undergraduate students, 86% full-time, 54% women, 46% men
- **Minimally difficult** entrance level, 85% of applicants were admitted

Undergraduates 1,497 full-time, 240 part-time. 79% are from out of state; 3% Black or African American, non-Hispanic/Latino; 5% Hispanic/Latino; 0.4% Asian, non-Hispanic/Latino; 0.1% Native Hawaiian or other Pacific Islander, non-Hispanic/Latino; 0.4% American Indian or Alaska Native, non-Hispanic/Latino; 1% Two or more races, non-Hispanic/Latino; 13% Race/ethnicity unknown; 2% international; 3% transferred in; 86% live on campus. *Retention:* 63% of full-time freshmen returned.

Freshmen *Admission:* 3,544 applied, 3,004 admitted, 538 enrolled. *Average high school GPA:* 2.71. *Test scores:* SAT critical reading scores over 500: 38%; SAT math scores over 500: 44%; SAT writing scores over 500: 34%; ACT scores over 18: 73%; SAT critical reading scores over 600: 6%; SAT math scores over 600: 8%; SAT writing scores over 600: 5%; ACT scores over 24: 16%; SAT critical reading scores over 700: 1%; ACT scores over 30: 2%.

Faculty *Total:* 315, 30% full-time, 44% with terminal degrees. *Student/faculty ratio:* 14:1.

Academics *Calendar:* differs by branch and program. *Degrees:* certificates, associate, bachelor's, master's, doctoral, post-master's, and postbachelor's certificates (profile does not reflect significant enrollment at 6 continuing education sites; master's degree is only offered at these sites). *Special study options:* academic remediation for entering students, accelerated degree program, adult/continuing education programs, advanced placement credit, distance learning, double majors, English as a second language, external degree program, freshman honors college, honors programs, independent study, internships, off-campus study, part-time degree program, services for LD students, student-designed majors, study abroad, summer session for credit. *ROTC:* Army (c), Air Force (c). *Unusual degree programs:* business administration.

Computers on Campus 60 computers/terminals and 200 ports are available on campus for general student use. Students can access the following: campus intranet, computer help desk, free student e-mail accounts, online (class) grades, online (class) registration, online (class) schedules. Campuswide network is available. 100% of college-owned or -operated housing units are wired for high-speed Internet access. Wireless service is available via classrooms, computer labs, libraries, student centers.

Student Life *Housing:* on-campus residence required through senior year. *Options:* coed. Campus housing is university owned. Freshman campus housing is guaranteed. *Activities and organizations:* drama/theater group, student-run newspaper, radio and television station, choral group, Outing Club, WFPR Radio, Student Senate, Law Club, Business Club. *Campus security:* 24-hour emergency response devices and patrols, student patrols, late-night transport/escort service, controlled dormitory access. *Student services:* health clinic, personal/psychological counseling.

Athletics Member NCAA. All Division II. *Intercollegiate sports:* baseball M(s), basketball M(s)/W(s), crew M/W, cross-country running M/W, field hockey W(s), golf M, ice hockey M, lacrosse M/W, soccer M(s)/W(s), softball W(s), tennis M(s)/W(s), volleyball W(s). *Intramural sports:* baseball M, basketball M/W, cheerleading W(c), cross-country running M/W, fencing M(c)/W(c), field hockey W, football M, golf M, ice hockey M, lacrosse M/W, rugby M/W, soccer M/W, softball W, tennis M/W, volleyball M/W.

Standardized Tests *Required:* SAT or ACT (for admission).

Costs (2013–14) *Comprehensive fee:* $41,210 includes full-time tuition ($28,250), mandatory fees ($1700), and room and board ($11,260). Full-time tuition and fees vary according to course load, degree level, location, and program. Part-time tuition: $945 per credit hour. Part-time tuition and fees vary according to course load, degree level, location, and program. *College room only:* $6634. Room and board charges vary according to board plan, housing facility, and student level. *Payment plan:* installment. *Waivers:* senior citizens and employees or children of employees.

Financial Aid Of all full-time matriculated undergraduates who enrolled in 2012, 1,234 applied for aid, 1,124 were judged to have need, 224 had their need fully met. 804 Federal Work-Study jobs (averaging $1429). In 2012, 212 non-need-based awards were made. *Average percent of need met:* 75%. *Average financial aid package:* $24,077. *Average need-based loan:* $4800. *Average need-based gift aid:* $19,218. *Average non-need-based aid:* $12,604. *Average indebtedness upon graduation:* $35,551.

Applying *Options:* electronic application, early admission, deferred entrance. *Application fee:* $40. *Required:* essay or personal statement, high school transcript, 1 letter of recommendation. *Required for some:* minimum 2.0 GPA. *Recommended:* minimum 2.2 GPA, interview. *Application deadlines:* rolling (freshmen), rolling (out-of-state freshmen), rolling (transfers). *Notification:* continuous (freshmen), continuous (out-of-state freshmen), continuous (transfers).

Freshman Application Contact Office of Admissions, Franklin Pierce University, 40 University Drive, Rindge, NH 03461. *Phone:* 603-899-4050. *Toll-free phone:* 800-437-0048. *Fax:* 603-899-4394. *E-mail:* admissions@franklinpierce.edu. *Website:* http://www.franklinpierce.edu/.

Granite State College

Concord, New Hampshire

- **State and locally supported** comprehensive, founded 1972, part of University System of New Hampshire
- **Suburban** campus
- **Endowment** $2.0 million
- **Coed** 1,737 undergraduate students, 51% full-time, 71% women, 29% men
- **Noncompetitive** entrance level, 100% of applicants were admitted

Undergraduates 879 full-time, 858 part-time. Students come from 24 states and territories; 11% are from out of state; 1% Black or African American, non-

COLLEGES AT-A-GLANCE

Hispanic/Latino; 2% Hispanic/Latino; 0.4% Asian, non-Hispanic/Latino; 0.6% American Indian or Alaska Native, non-Hispanic/Latino; 2% Two or more races, non-Hispanic/Latino; 9% Race/ethnicity unknown; 0.1% international; 16% transferred in. *Retention:* 75% of full-time freshmen returned.
Freshmen *Admission:* 354 applied, 354 admitted, 124 enrolled.
Faculty *Total:* 189, 3% full-time, 38% with terminal degrees. *Student/faculty ratio:* 11:1.
Academics *Calendar:* trimesters. *Degrees:* associate, bachelor's, master's, and postbachelor's certificates (offers primarily part-time degree programs; courses offered at 50 locations in New Hampshire). *Special study options:* academic remediation for entering students, accelerated degree program, adult/continuing education programs, advanced placement credit, cooperative education, distance learning, double majors, independent study, internships, off-campus study, part-time degree program, services for LD students, student-designed majors, summer session for credit. *ROTC:* Army (c), Air Force (c).
Computers on Campus 139 computers/terminals are available on campus for general student use. Students can access the following: campus intranet, computer help desk, free student e-mail accounts, online (class) grades, online (class) registration, online (class) schedules. Campuswide network is available. Wireless service is available via entire campus.
Student Life *Housing:* college housing not available. *Activities and organizations:* Alumni Learner Association, Green Team. *Campus security:* UNH Alert, a system that provides emergency notifications via text and voice messages.
Costs (2012–13) *Tuition:* state resident $6840 full-time, $285 per credit part-time; nonresident $7080 full-time, $295 per credit part-time. *Required fees:* $75 per term part-time. *Payment plan:* deferred payment. *Waivers:* senior citizens and employees or children of employees.
Applying *Options:* electronic application. *Required for some:* high school transcript, self-certify high school graduate or GED. *Application deadlines:* rolling (freshmen), rolling (out-of-state freshmen), rolling (transfers). *Notification:* continuous (freshmen), continuous (out-of-state freshmen), continuous (transfers).
Freshman Application Contact Ms. Cortney Vachon, Associate Registrar, Granite State College, 25 Hall Street, Concord, NH 03301. *Phone:* 603-228-3000. *Toll-free phone:* 888-228-3000. *Fax:* 603-513-1386. *E-mail:* gsc.admissions@granite.edu.
Website: http://www.granite.edu/.

Hesser College, Concord

Concord, New Hampshire

- **Proprietary** primarily 2-year
- **Coed**

Academics *Degrees:* diplomas, associate, and bachelor's.
Freshman Application Contact Hesser College, Concord, 16 Foundry Street, Concord, NH 03301. *Phone:* 603-225-9200. *Toll-free phone:* 800-935-1824.
Website: http://www.hesser.edu/.

Hesser College, Manchester

Manchester, New Hampshire

- **Proprietary** primarily 2-year, founded 1900
- **Urban** campus
- **Coed**

Academics *Calendar:* semesters. *Degrees:* diplomas, associate, and bachelor's.
Financial Aid *Of all full-time matriculated undergraduates who enrolled in 2011,* 700 Federal Work-Study jobs (averaging $1000).
Freshman Application Contact Hesser College, Manchester, 3 Sundial Avenue, Manchester, NH 03103. *Phone:* 603-668-6660. *Toll-free phone:* 800-935-1824.
Website: http://www.hesser.edu/.

Hesser College, Nashua

Nashua, New Hampshire

- **Proprietary** primarily 2-year
- **Coed**

Academics *Degrees:* diplomas, associate, and bachelor's.

Freshman Application Contact Hesser College, Nashua, 410 Amherst Street, Nashua, NH 03063. *Phone:* 603-883-0404. *Toll-free phone:* 800-935-1824.
Website: http://www.hesser.edu/.

Hesser College, Portsmouth

Portsmouth, New Hampshire

- **Proprietary** primarily 2-year
- **Coed**

Academics *Degrees:* diplomas, associate, and bachelor's.
Freshman Application Contact Hesser College, Portsmouth, 170 Commerce Way, Portsmouth, NH 03801. *Phone:* 603-436-5300. *Toll-free phone:* 800-935-1824.
Website: http://www.hesser.edu/.

Hesser College, Salem

Salem, New Hampshire

- **Proprietary** primarily 2-year
- **Coed**

Academics *Degrees:* diplomas, associate, and bachelor's.
Freshman Application Contact Hesser College, Salem, 11 Manor Parkway, Salem, NH 03079. *Phone:* 603-898-3480. *Toll-free phone:* 800-935-1824.
Website: http://www.hesser.edu/.

Keene State College

Keene, New Hampshire

- **State-supported** comprehensive, founded 1909, part of University System of New Hampshire
- **Small-town** 160-acre campus
- **Coed** 4,933 undergraduate students, 94% full-time, 57% women, 43% men
- **Moderately difficult** entrance level, 78% of applicants were admitted

Undergraduates 4,657 full-time, 276 part-time. Students come from 29 states and territories; 4 other countries; 50% are from out of state; 0.8% Black or African American, non-Hispanic/Latino; 3% Hispanic/Latino; 0.9% Asian, non-Hispanic/Latino; 0.2% American Indian or Alaska Native, non-Hispanic/Latino; 1% Two or more races, non-Hispanic/Latino; 11% Race/ethnicity unknown; 4% transferred in; 54% live on campus. *Retention:* 76% of full-time freshmen returned.
Freshmen *Admission:* 6,315 applied, 4,956 admitted, 1,186 enrolled. *Average high school GPA:* 2.98. *Test scores:* SAT critical reading scores over 500: 45%; SAT math scores over 500: 48%; SAT writing scores over 500: 45%; ACT scores over 18: 86%; SAT critical reading scores over 600: 8%; SAT math scores over 600: 8%; SAT writing scores over 600: 7%; ACT scores over 24: 19%; SAT critical reading scores over 700: 1%; SAT math scores over 700: 1%; ACT scores over 30: 2%.
Faculty *Total:* 464, 44% full-time, 39% with terminal degrees. *Student/faculty ratio:* 17:1.
Academics *Calendar:* semesters. *Degrees:* certificates, bachelor's, master's, post-master's, and postbachelor's certificates. *Special study options:* advanced placement credit, cooperative education, double majors, English as a second language, freshman honors college, honors programs, independent study, internships, off-campus study, part-time degree program, services for LD students, student-designed majors, study abroad, summer session for credit. *ROTC:* Army (c), Air Force (c). *Unusual degree programs:* 3-2 engineering with Clarkson University, University of New Hampshire.
Computers on Campus 600 computers/terminals are available on campus for general student use. Students can access the following: campus intranet, computer help desk, free student e-mail accounts, online (class) grades, online (class) registration, online (class) schedules, Student web pages. Campuswide network is available. 100% of college-owned or -operated housing units are wired for high-speed Internet access. Wireless service is available via classrooms, computer centers, computer labs, dorm rooms, learning centers, libraries, student centers.
Student Life *Housing:* on-campus residence required through sophomore year. *Options:* coed, women-only. Campus housing is university owned. Freshman campus housing is guaranteed. *Activities and organizations:* drama/theater group, student-run newspaper, radio and television station, choral group, Social Activities Council, Humans vs. Zobies, Student Government, Phi Sigma

Sigma Sorority, Delta Phi Epsilon Sorority, national fraternities, national sororities. *Campus security:* 24-hour emergency response devices and patrols, late-night transport/escort service, controlled dormitory access. *Student services:* health clinic, personal/psychological counseling, women's center.

Athletics Member NCAA. All Division III. *Intercollegiate sports:* baseball M, basketball M/W, cheerleading W, cross-country running M/W, field hockey W, lacrosse M/W, rugby M(c)/W(c), soccer M/W, softball W, swimming and diving M/W, track and field M/W, ultimate Frisbee M(c)/W(c), volleyball W. *Intramural sports:* badminton M/W, basketball M/W, bowling M/W, fencing M(c)/W(c), football M/W, ice hockey M(c)/W(c), racquetball M/W, skiing (downhill) M(c)/W(c), soccer M/W, softball M/W, table tennis M/W, tennis M/W, ultimate Frisbee M/W, volleyball M/W, water polo M/W.

Standardized Tests *Required:* SAT or ACT (for admission).

Costs (2012–13) *Tuition:* state resident $10,410 full-time, $440 per credit hour part-time; nonresident $17,310 full-time, $720 per credit hour part-time. Part-time tuition and fees vary according to course load. *Required fees:* $2366 full-time, $94 per credit hour part-time. *Room and board:* $8762. Room and board charges vary according to board plan and housing facility. *Payment plan:* installment. *Waivers:* senior citizens and employees or children of employees.

Financial Aid Of all full-time matriculated undergraduates who enrolled in 2011, 4,015 applied for aid, 3,135 were judged to have need, 365 had their need fully met. 1,492 Federal Work-Study jobs (averaging $2207). 688 state and other part-time jobs (averaging $1171). In 2011, 333 non-need-based awards were made. *Average percent of need met:* 65%. *Average financial aid package:* $10,272. *Average need-based loan:* $4392. *Average need-based gift aid:* $5926. *Average non-need-based aid:* $2654. *Average indebtedness upon graduation:* $33,248. *Financial aid deadline:* 3/1.

Applying *Options:* electronic application, deferred entrance. *Application fee:* $50. *Required:* essay or personal statement, high school transcript, 1 letter of recommendation. *Application deadlines:* 4/1 (freshmen), rolling (transfers). *Notification:* continuous (freshmen), continuous (transfers).

Freshman Application Contact Ms. Margaret Richmond, Director of Admissions, Keene State College, 229 Main Street, Keene, NH 03435-2604. *Phone:* 603-358-2273. *Toll-free phone:* 800-KSC-1909. *Fax:* 603-358-2767. *E-mail:* mrichmon@keene.edu. *Website:* http://www.keene.edu/.

New England College

Henniker, New Hampshire

- **Independent** comprehensive, founded 1946
- **Small-town** 225-acre campus with easy access to Boston
- **Endowment** $8.1 million
- **Coed** 1,127 undergraduate students, 92% full-time, 49% women, 51% men
- **Minimally difficult** entrance level, 65% of applicants were admitted

Undergraduates 1,041 full-time, 85 part-time. Students come from 51 states and territories; 17 other countries; 67% are from out of state; 12% Black or African American, non-Hispanic/Latino; 4% Hispanic/Latino; 2% Asian, non-Hispanic/Latino; 0.2% Native Hawaiian or other Pacific Islander, non-Hispanic/Latino; 0.8% American Indian or Alaska Native, non-Hispanic/Latino; 0.1% Two or more races, non-Hispanic/Latino; 17% Race/ethnicity unknown; 4% international; 13% transferred in; 47% live on campus. *Retention:* 63% of full-time freshmen returned.

Freshmen *Admission:* 3,723 applied, 2,404 admitted, 335 enrolled. *Average high school GPA:* 2.66. *Test scores:* SAT critical reading scores over 500: 24%; SAT math scores over 500: 35%; SAT writing scores over 500: 22%; ACT scores over 18: 61%; SAT critical reading scores over 600: 5%; SAT math scores over 600: 5%; SAT writing scores over 600: 6%; ACT scores over 24: 28%; SAT math scores over 700: 1%; SAT writing scores over 700: 1%.

Faculty *Total:* 180, 38% full-time, 41% with terminal degrees. *Student/faculty ratio:* 11:1.

Academics *Calendar:* semesters. *Degrees:* associate, bachelor's, master's, and doctoral. *Special study options:* academic remediation for entering students, accelerated degree program, adult/continuing education programs, advanced placement credit, distance learning, double majors, English as a second language, honors programs, independent study, internships, off-campus study, part-time degree program, services for LD students, student-designed majors, study abroad, summer session for credit. *ROTC:* Army (c), Air Force (c). *Unusual degree programs:* 3-2 business administration; engineering with Clarkson University; nursing with Massachusetts College of Pharmacy and Health Sciences; Education BA/MED; Political Science BA/MA.

Computers on Campus 191 computers/terminals and 350 ports are available on campus for general student use. Students can access the following: campus intranet, computer help desk, free student e-mail accounts, online (class) grades, online (class) registration, online (class) schedules. Campuswide net-

work is available. 100% of college-owned or -operated housing units are wired for high-speed Internet access. Wireless service is available via entire campus.

Student Life *Housing:* on-campus residence required through sophomore year. *Options:* coed. Campus housing is university owned. Freshman campus housing is guaranteed. *Activities and organizations:* drama/theater group, student-run newspaper, radio station, Student Senate, Campus Activities Board, Role Playing Association, International Student Association, Political Science Club, national fraternities, national sororities. *Campus security:* 24-hour emergency response devices and patrols, student patrols, late-night transport/escort service, controlled dormitory access, Emergency Text System. *Student services:* health clinic, personal/psychological counseling, women's center.

Athletics Member NCAA. All Division III. *Intercollegiate sports:* baseball M, basketball M/W, cross-country running M/W, field hockey W, ice hockey M/W, lacrosse M/W, soccer M/W, softball W. *Intramural sports:* basketball M/W, cheerleading W, golf M/W, ice hockey M/W, lacrosse M/W, rugby M/W, soccer M/W, softball W, table tennis M/W, tennis M/W, ultimate Frisbee M/W, volleyball M/W.

Costs (2013–14) *Comprehensive fee:* $44,178 includes full-time tuition ($31,394), mandatory fees ($350), and room and board ($12,434). Full-time tuition and fees vary according to class time, course load, degree level, location, program, and reciprocity agreements. Part-time tuition: $385 per credit. Part-time tuition and fees vary according to class time, course load, degree level, location, and program. *College room only:* $5750. Room and board charges vary according to board plan and housing facility. *Payment plan:* installment. *Waivers:* children of alumni, adult students, senior citizens, and employees or children of employees.

Financial Aid Of all full-time matriculated undergraduates who enrolled in 2012, 833 applied for aid, 792 were judged to have need, 153 had their need fully met. 247 Federal Work-Study jobs (averaging $17,556). In 2012, 170 non-need-based awards were made. *Average percent of need met:* 74%. *Average financial aid package:* $25,290. *Average need-based loan:* $4865. *Average need-based gift aid:* $16,485. *Average non-need-based aid:* $12,686. *Average indebtedness upon graduation:* $33,797.

Applying *Options:* electronic application, deferred entrance. *Application fee:* $35. *Required:* essay or personal statement, high school transcript, 3 letters of recommendation. *Recommended:* interview. *Application deadlines:* 9/7 (freshmen), 9/7 (out-of-state freshmen), 9/7 (transfers). *Notification:* continuous (freshmen), continuous (out-of-state freshmen), continuous (transfers).

Freshman Application Contact Sean Kelley, Associate Director of Undergraduate Admissions, New England College, 102 Bridge Street, Henniker, NH 03242. *Phone:* 603-428 2341. *Toll-free phone:* 800-521-7642. *Fax:* 603-428 3155. *E-mail:* vsalyer@nec.edu. *Website:* http://www.nec.edu/.

New Hampshire Institute of Art

Manchester, New Hampshire

Freshman Application Contact Ms. Amanda Abbott, Assistant Director of Enrollment, New Hampshire Institute of Art, 148 Concord Street, Manchester, NH 03104-4158. *Phone:* 866-241-4918 Ext. 576. *Toll-free phone:* 866-241-4918. *Fax:* 603-647-0658. *E-mail:* aabbott@nhia.edu. *Website:* http://www.nhia.edu/.

Plymouth State University

Plymouth, New Hampshire

- **State-supported** comprehensive, founded 1871, part of University System of New Hampshire
- **Small-town** 170-acre campus with easy access to Manchester, NH
- **Endowment** $9.1 million
- **Coed** 4,238 undergraduate students, 93% full-time, 48% women, 52% men
- **Moderately difficult** entrance level, 76% of applicants were admitted

Undergraduates 3,926 full-time, 312 part-time. Students come from 29 states and territories; 23 other countries; 41% are from out of state; 1% Black or African American, non-Hispanic/Latino; 2% Hispanic/Latino; 1% Asian, non-Hispanic/Latino; 0.2% American Indian or Alaska Native, non-Hispanic/Latino; 1% Two or more races, non-Hispanic/Latino; 1% Race/ethnicity unknown; 1% international; 5% transferred in; 53% live on campus. *Retention:* 74% of full-time freshmen returned.

Freshmen *Admission:* 4,940 applied, 3,778 admitted, 933 enrolled. *Average high school GPA:* 2.89. *Test scores:* SAT critical reading scores over 500: 38%; SAT math scores over 500: 45%; SAT writing scores over 500: 35%; ACT scores over 18: 77%; SAT critical reading scores over 600: 5%; SAT math scores over 600: 10%; SAT writing scores over 600: 4%; ACT scores over 24: 11%; SAT critical reading scores over 700: 1%; SAT math scores over 700: 1%.

Faculty *Total:* 418, 45% full-time, 51% with terminal degrees. *Student/faculty ratio:* 17:1.

Academics *Calendar:* semesters. *Degrees:* certificates, bachelor's, master's, doctoral, post-master's, and postbachelor's certificates. *Special study options:* adult/continuing education programs, advanced placement credit, distance learning, double majors, English as a second language, honors programs, independent study, internships, off-campus study, part-time degree program, services for LD students, student-designed majors, study abroad, summer session for credit. *ROTC:* Army (c), Air Force (c).

Computers on Campus 900 computers/terminals are available on campus for general student use. Students can access the following: campus intranet, computer help desk, free student e-mail accounts, online (class) grades, online (class) registration, online (class) schedules, degree audit, academic history, account status. Campuswide network is available. 100% of college-owned or -operated housing units are wired for high-speed Internet access. Wireless service is available via entire campus.

Student Life *Housing:* on-campus residence required for freshman year. *Options:* coed. Campus housing is university owned. Freshman applicants given priority for college housing. *Activities and organizations:* drama/theater group, student-run newspaper, radio station, choral group, Programming Activities in College Environment, Student Senate, Marketing Association of Plymouth State, CommonGround—Environmental and Social Justice Organization, PSU Pep Band, national sororities. *Campus security:* 24-hour emergency response devices and patrols, student patrols, late-night transport/escort service, controlled dormitory access, shuttle bus service, crime prevention programs, self-defense education. *Student services:* health clinic, personal/psychological counseling, women's center.

Athletics Member NCAA. All Division III. *Intercollegiate sports:* baseball M, basketball M/W, cheerleading W, field hockey W, football M, ice hockey M/W, lacrosse M/W, skiing (cross-country) M/W, skiing (downhill) M/W, soccer M/W, softball W, swimming and diving W, tennis W, volleyball W, wrestling M. *Intramural sports:* basketball M/W, cross-country running M(c)/W(c), rugby M(c)/W(c), sailing M(c)/W(c), soccer M/W, softball M/W, table tennis M/W, ultimate Frisbee M/W, volleyball M/W.

Standardized Tests *Required:* SAT or ACT (for admission).

Costs (2012–13) *One-time required fee:* $198. *Tuition:* state resident $10,410 full-time, $435 per credit hour part-time; nonresident $17,310 full-time, $720 per credit hour part-time. Full-time tuition and fees vary according to reciprocity agreements. Part-time tuition and fees vary according to reciprocity agreements. *Required fees:* $2150 full-time, $92 per credit hour part-time. *Room and board:* $9440; room only: $6370. Room and board charges vary according to board plan and housing facility. *Payment plan:* installment. *Waivers:* senior citizens and employees or children of employees.

Financial Aid Of all full-time matriculated undergraduates who enrolled in 2011, 3,595 applied for aid, 2,867 were judged to have need, 264 had their need fully met. 1,880 Federal Work-Study jobs (averaging $2239). In 2011, 259 non-need-based awards were made. *Average percent of need met:* 55%. *Average financial aid package:* $9202. *Average need-based loan:* $4189. *Average need-based gift aid:* $5794. *Average non-need-based aid:* $3503. *Average indebtedness upon graduation:* $31,214.

Applying *Options:* electronic application, deferred entrance. *Application fee:* $50. *Required:* essay or personal statement, high school transcript, 1 letter of recommendation. *Required for some:* interview. *Application deadlines:* 4/1 (freshmen), 4/1 (transfers). *Notification:* continuous until 11/1 (freshmen), continuous until 11/1 (transfers).

Freshman Application Contact Mr. Andrew B Palumbo, AVP of Enrollment Management/Director of Admissions, Plymouth State University, 17 High Street, MSC #52, Plymouth, NH 03264-1595. *Phone:* 603-535-2237. *Toll-free phone:* 800-842-6900. *Fax:* 603-535-2714. *E-mail:* plymouthadmit@plymouth.edu. *Website:* http://www.plymouth.edu/.

Rivier University

Nashua, New Hampshire

- **Independent Roman Catholic** comprehensive, founded 1933
- **Suburban** 68-acre campus with easy access to Boston
- **Endowment** $39.3 million
- **Coed** 1,559 undergraduate students, 58% full-time, 81% women, 19% men
- **Moderately difficult** entrance level, 83% of applicants were admitted

Undergraduates 912 full-time, 647 part-time. Students come from 15 states and territories; 1 other country; 39% are from out of state; 2% Black or African

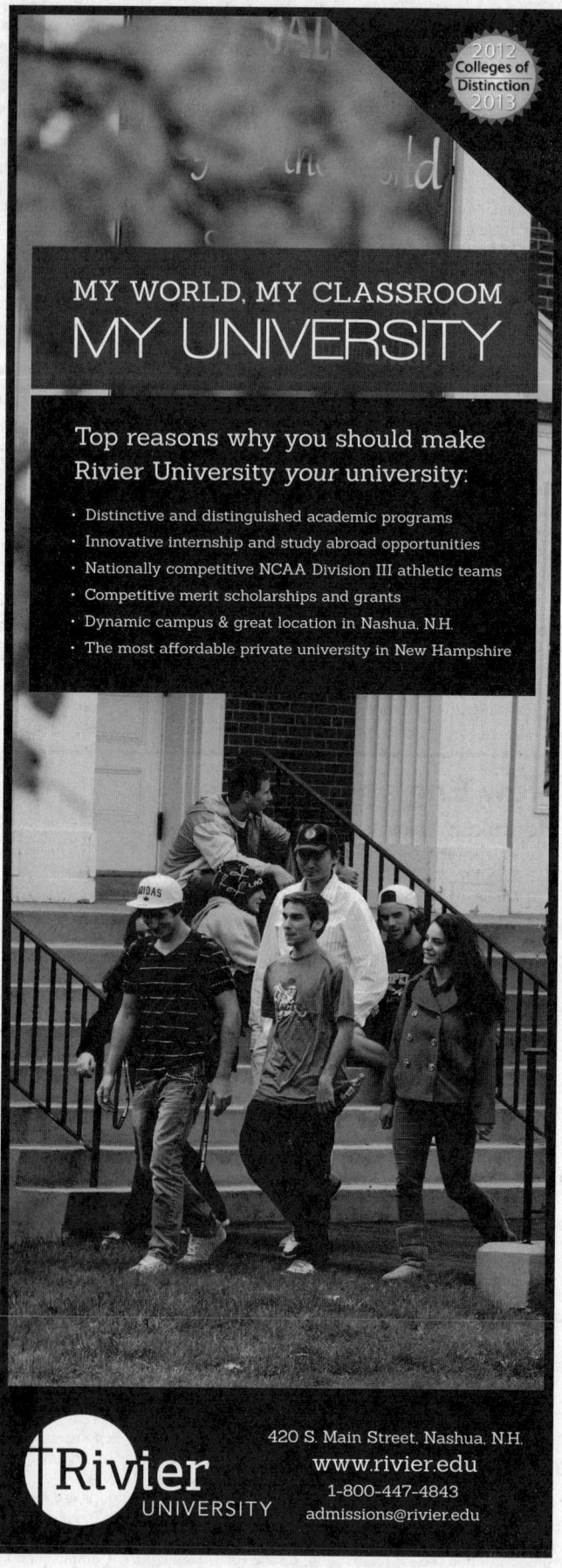

American, non-Hispanic/Latino; 4% Hispanic/Latino; 3% Asian, non-Hispanic/Latino; 0.1% Native Hawaiian or other Pacific Islander, non-Hispanic/Latino; 0.1% American Indian or Alaska Native, non-Hispanic/Latino; 0.8% Two or more races, non-Hispanic/Latino; 14% Race/ethnicity unknown; 10% transferred in; 49% live on campus. *Retention:* 78% of full-time freshmen returned.

Freshmen *Admission:* 776 applied, 643 admitted, 225 enrolled. *Average high school GPA:* 3. *Test scores:* SAT critical reading scores over 500: 31%; SAT math scores over 500: 34%; SAT writing scores over 500: 33%; ACT scores over 18: 61%; SAT critical reading scores over 600: 7%; SAT math scores over 600: 6%; SAT writing scores over 600: 4%; ACT scores over 24: 13%; SAT critical reading scores over 700: 1%; SAT math scores over 700: 1%.

Faculty *Total:* 200, 36% full-time, 38% with terminal degrees. *Student/faculty ratio:* 17:1.

Academics *Calendar:* semesters. *Degrees:* certificates, associate, bachelor's, master's, doctoral, post-master's, and postbachelor's certificates. *Special study options:* advanced placement credit, distance learning, double majors, independent study, internships, off-campus study, part-time degree program, services for LD students, study abroad, summer session for credit. *ROTC:* Air Force (c).

Computers on Campus 175 computers/terminals and 200 ports are available on campus for general student use. Students can access the following: campus intranet, computer help desk, free student e-mail accounts, online (class) grades, online (class) registration, online (class) schedules. Campuswide network is available. 100% of college-owned or -operated housing units are wired for high-speed Internet access. Wireless service is available via entire campus.

Student Life *Housing options:* coed. Campus housing is university owned. Freshman campus housing is guaranteed. *Activities and organizations:* drama/theater group, choral group, Student Government Association, Student Program Board, Outdoor Club, Student Nurses Association, Habitat for Humanity. *Campus security:* 24-hour emergency response devices and patrols, late-night transport/escort service, controlled dormitory access. *Student services:* health clinic, personal/psychological counseling.

Athletics Member NCAA. All Division III. *Intercollegiate sports:* baseball M, basketball M/W, cross-country running M/W, field hockey W, lacrosse M/W, soccer M/W, softball W, volleyball M/W. *Intramural sports:* basketball M/W, volleyball M/W.

Standardized Tests *Required:* SAT or ACT (for admission). *Required for some:* nursing exam.

Costs (2012–13) *One-time required fee:* $275. *Comprehensive fee:* $36,873 includes full-time tuition ($26,430), mandatory fees ($325), and room and board ($10,118). Full-time tuition and fees vary according to program and reciprocity agreements. Part-time tuition: $881 per credit. Part-time tuition and fees vary according to class time, course load, program, and reciprocity agreements. *Required fees:* $25 per year part-time. *College room only:* $5500. Room and board charges vary according to board plan and housing facility. *Payment plans:* installment, deferred payment. *Waivers:* senior citizens and employees or children of employees.

Financial Aid Of all full-time matriculated undergraduates who enrolled in 2010, 888 applied for aid, 822 were judged to have need, 70 had their need fully met. In 2010, 105 non-need-based awards were made. *Average percent of need met:* 59%. *Average financial aid package:* $14,850. *Average need-based loan:* $4378. *Average need-based gift aid:* $10,806. *Average non-need-based aid:* $5066. *Average indebtedness upon graduation:* $43,189.

Applying *Options:* electronic application, deferred entrance. *Application fee:* $25. *Required:* essay or personal statement, high school transcript, 1 letter of recommendation. *Required for some:* interview. *Recommended:* minimum 2.3 GPA, interview. *Application deadlines:* rolling (freshmen), rolling (transfers). *Notification:* continuous (freshmen), continuous (transfers).

Freshman Application Contact Karen Schedin, Vice President for Enrollment Management, Rivier University, 420 South Main Street, Nashua, NH 03060. *Phone:* 603-897-8507. *Toll-free phone:* 800-44RIVIER. *Fax:* 603-891-1799. *E-mail:* rivadmit@rivier.edu.
Website: http://www.rivier.edu/.

See previous page for display ad and page 1456 for the College Close-Up.

Saint Anselm College

Manchester, New Hampshire

- **Independent Roman Catholic** 4-year, founded 1889
- **Suburban** 450-acre campus with easy access to Boston
- **Endowment** $85.3 million
- **Coed** 1,954 undergraduate students, 97% full-time, 59% women, 41% men
- **Moderately difficult** entrance level, 75% of applicants were admitted

Undergraduates 1,900 full-time, 54 part-time. Students come from 24 states and territories; 3 other countries; 77% are from out of state; 1% Black or African American, non-Hispanic/Latino; 3% Hispanic/Latino; 0.9% Asian, non-Hispanic/Latino; 0.1% Native Hawaiian or other Pacific Islander, non-Hispanic/Latino; 0.3% American Indian or Alaska Native, non-Hispanic/Latino; 1% Two or more races, non-Hispanic/Latino; 19% Race/ethnicity unknown; 0.5% international; 0.9% transferred in; 90% live on campus. *Retention:* 88% of full-time freshmen returned.

Freshmen *Admission:* 4,089 applied, 3,056 admitted, 527 enrolled. *Average high school GPA:* 3.22. *Test scores:* SAT critical reading scores over 500: 81%; SAT math scores over 500: 87%; SAT writing scores over 500: 83%; ACT scores over 18: 97%; SAT critical reading scores over 600: 28%; SAT math scores over 600: 35%; SAT writing scores over 600: 25%; ACT scores over 24: 70%; SAT critical reading scores over 700: 4%; SAT math scores over 700: 2%; SAT writing scores over 700: 3%; ACT scores over 30: 2%.

Faculty *Total:* 217, 66% full-time, 67% with terminal degrees. *Student/faculty ratio:* 11:1.

Academics *Calendar:* semesters. *Degree:* bachelor's. *Special study options:* advanced placement credit, double majors, honors programs, independent study, internships, off-campus study, part-time degree program, services for LD students, study abroad, summer session for credit. *ROTC:* Army (c), Air Force (c). *Unusual degree programs:* 3-2 engineering with University of Massachusetts Lowell, Catholic University of America, University of Notre Dame, Manhattan College.

Computers on Campus 400 computers/terminals are available on campus for general student use. Students can access the following: campus intranet, computer help desk, free student e-mail accounts, online (class) registration, online (class) schedules. Campuswide network is available. 100% of college-owned or -operated housing units are wired for high-speed Internet access. Wireless service is available via classrooms, computer centers, computer labs, dorm rooms, learning centers, libraries, student centers.

Student Life *Housing options:* coed, men-only, women-only. Campus housing is university owned. Freshman campus housing is guaranteed. *Activities and organizations:* drama/theater group, student-run newspaper, radio station, choral group, Center for Volunteers, Anselmian Abbey Players, Knights of Columbus, spring break alternative, International Relations Club. *Campus security:* 24-hour emergency response devices and patrols, late-night transport/escort service, controlled dormitory access. *Student services:* health clinic, personal/psychological counseling.

Athletics Member NCAA. All Division II. *Intercollegiate sports:* baseball M(s), basketball M(s)/W(s), cheerleading W(c), cross-country running M(s)/W(s), field hockey W(s), football M(s), golf M(s), ice hockey M/W, lacrosse M(s)/W(s), rugby M(c)/W(c), skiing (downhill) M(s)/W(s), soccer M(s)/W(s), softball W(s), tennis M(s)/W(s), volleyball W(s). *Intramural sports:* basketball M/W, football M/W, ice hockey M/W, racquetball M/W, skiing (cross-country) M/W, soccer M/W, softball M/W, swimming and diving M(c)/W(c), tennis M/W, track and field M(c)/W(c), ultimate Frisbee M/W, volleyball M/W, weight lifting M/W.

Standardized Tests *Required for some:* SAT or ACT (for admission).

Costs (2013–14) *Comprehensive fee:* $48,324 includes full-time tuition ($34,084), mandatory fees ($1550), and room and board ($12,690). *College room only:* $7636. Room and board charges vary according to housing facility. *Payment plan:* installment. *Waivers:* employees or children of employees.

Financial Aid Of all full-time matriculated undergraduates who enrolled in 2012, 1,635 applied for aid, 1,434 were judged to have need, 281 had their need fully met. 1,180 Federal Work-Study jobs (averaging $1482). 9 state and other part-time jobs (averaging $2000). In 2012, 367 non-need-based awards were made. *Average percent of need met:* 81%. *Average financial aid package:* $25,424. *Average need-based loan:* $5712. *Average need-based gift aid:* $19,351. *Average non-need-based aid:* $10,366. *Average indebtedness upon graduation:* $42,631. *Financial aid deadline:* 3/15.

Applying *Options:* electronic application, early admission, early action, deferred entrance. *Application fee:* $55. *Required:* essay or personal statement, high school transcript, 2 letters of recommendation. *Recommended:* interview. *Application deadlines:* 2/1 (freshmen), rolling (transfers), 11/15 (early action). *Notification:* continuous (freshmen), continuous (transfers), 1/15 (early action).

Freshman Application Contact Saint Anselm College, 100 Saint Anselm Drive, Manchester, NH 03102-1310. *Phone:* 603-641-7500. *Toll-free phone:* 888-4ANSELM.
Website: http://www.anselm.edu/.

Southern New Hampshire University

Manchester, New Hampshire

- **Independent** university, founded 1932
- **Suburban** 317-acre campus with easy access to Boston
- **Coed** 11,253 undergraduate students, 52% full-time, 58% women, 42% men
- **Moderately difficult** entrance level, 81% of applicants were admitted

Undergraduates 5,805 full-time, 5,448 part-time. 0.6% Black or African American, non-Hispanic/Latino; 0.7% Hispanic/Latino; 0.4% Asian, non-Hispanic/Latino; 0.1% American Indian or Alaska Native, non-Hispanic/Latino; 78% Race/ethnicity unknown; 2% international; 73% live on campus. *Retention:* 73% of full-time freshmen returned.

Freshmen *Admission:* 4,386 applied, 3,541 admitted, 1,343 enrolled. *Average high school GPA:* 3.07. *Test scores:* SAT critical reading scores over 500: 45%; SAT math scores over 500: 55%; SAT writing scores over 500: 41%; SAT critical reading scores over 600: 9%; SAT math scores over 600: 13%; SAT writing scores over 600: 7%; SAT math scores over 700: 1%.

Faculty *Total:* 1,167, 11% full-time, 33% with terminal degrees. *Student/faculty ratio:* 24:1.

Academics *Calendar:* semesters. *Degrees:* certificates, associate, bachelor's, master's, doctoral, post-master's, and postbachelor's certificates. *Special study options:* academic remediation for entering students, accelerated degree program, adult/continuing education programs, advanced placement credit, cooperative education, distance learning, double majors, English as a second language, honors programs, independent study, internships, off-campus study, part-time degree program, services for LD students, study abroad, summer session for credit. *ROTC:* Army (c), Air Force (c). *Unusual degree programs:* 3-2 business administration.

Computers on Campus 557 computers/terminals and 1,500 ports are available on campus for general student use. Students can access the following: campus intranet, computer help desk, free student e-mail accounts, online (class) grades, online (class) registration, online (class) schedules. Campus-wide network is available. 100% of college-owned or -operated housing units

are wired for high-speed Internet access. Wireless service is available via entire campus.

Student Life *Housing options:* coed, disabled students. Campus housing is university owned. *Activities and organizations:* drama/theater group, student-run newspaper, radio and television station, choral group, Coordinators of Activities and Programming Events (CAPE), International Student Association, Radio SNHU, Outing Club, Outreach Association, national fraternities, national sororities. *Campus security:* 24-hour emergency response devices and patrols, student patrols, late-night transport/escort service, controlled dormitory access. *Student services:* health clinic, personal/psychological counseling.

Athletics Member NCAA. All Division II. *Intercollegiate sports:* baseball M(s), basketball M(s)/W(s), cheerleading M/W, cross-country running M(s)/W(s), golf M, ice hockey M, lacrosse M(s)/W(s), soccer M(s)/W(s), softball W(s), tennis M(s)/W(s), volleyball W(s). *Intramural sports:* badminton M/W, basketball M/W, crew M(c)/W(c), field hockey M(c)/W(c), football M, ice hockey M(c), racquetball M/W, skiing (cross-country) M/W, soccer M/W, softball W, table tennis M/W, tennis M/W, ultimate Frisbee M/W, volleyball W.

Standardized Tests *Recommended:* SAT or ACT (for admission).

Costs (2013–14) *Comprehensive fee:* $40,504 includes full-time tuition ($28,554), mandatory fees ($330), and room and board ($11,620). Full-time tuition and fees vary according to class time and course load. Part-time tuition: $1190 per credit. Part-time tuition and fees vary according to class time, location, and program. *College room only:* $7720. Room and board charges vary according to board plan and housing facility. *Payment plan:* installment. *Waivers:* senior citizens and employees or children of employees.

Financial Aid Of all full-time matriculated undergraduates who enrolled in 2007, 1,560 applied for aid, 1,392 were judged to have need, 173 had their need fully met. In 2007, 330 non-need-based awards were made. *Average percent of need met:* 69%. *Average financial aid package:* $15,514. *Average need-based loan:* $5174. *Average need-based gift aid:* $10,223. *Average non-need-based aid:* $3599.

Applying *Options:* electronic application, early action, deferred entrance. *Application fee:* $40. *Required:* essay or personal statement, high school transcript, minimum 2.0 GPA, 1 letter of recommendation. *Recommended:* interview. *Application deadlines:* rolling (freshmen), rolling (transfers), 11/15 (early action). *Notification:* continuous (freshmen), continuous (transfers), 12/15 (early action).

Freshman Application Contact Mr. Steve Soba, Assistant VP for Undergraduate Day Admission, Southern New Hampshire University, 2500

How Much Does a Great Education Cost?

Southern New Hampshire University

North River Road, Manchester, NH 03106-1045. *Phone:* 603-645-9611. *Toll-free phone:* 888-327-7648. *Fax:* 603-645-9693. *E-mail:* s.soba@snhu.edu. *Website:* http://www.snhu.edu/.

See previous page for display ad and page 1510 for the College Close-Up.

Thomas More College of Liberal Arts
Merrimack, New Hampshire

- **Independent** 4-year, founded 1978, affiliated with Roman Catholic Church
- **Small-town** 14-acre campus with easy access to Boston
- **Coed**
- **Moderately difficult** entrance level

Faculty *Student/faculty ratio:* 12:1.
Academics *Calendar:* semesters. *Degree:* bachelor's.
Student Life *Campus security:* student patrols, late-night transport/escort service.
Standardized Tests *Recommended:* SAT or ACT (for admission).
Financial Aid *Of all full-time matriculated undergraduates who enrolled in 2012,* 87 applied for aid, 78 were judged to have need, 7 had their need fully met. 53 state and other part-time jobs (averaging $1425). *In 2012,* 15 non-need-based awards were made. *Average percent of need met:* 76. *Average financial aid package:* $17,808. *Average need-based loan:* $3713. *Average need-based gift aid:* $8651. *Average non-need-based aid:* $4853. *Average indebtedness upon graduation:* $20,107.
Applying *Options:* electronic application. *Required:* essay or personal statement, high school transcript, 2 letters of recommendation. *Required for some:* interview.
Freshman Application Contact Teddy Sifert, Director of Admissions, Thomas More College of Liberal Arts, 6 Manchester Street, Merrimack, NH 03054-4818. *Toll-free phone:* 800-880-8308. *Fax:* 603-880-9280. *E-mail:* admissions@thomasmorecollege.edu.
Website: http://www.thomasmorecollege.edu/.

University of New Hampshire
Durham, New Hampshire

- **State-supported** university, founded 1866, part of University System of New Hampshire
- **Small-town** 2600-acre campus with easy access to Boston
- **Endowment** $177.6 million
- **Coed** 12,811 undergraduate students, 96% full-time, 54% women, 46% men
- **Moderately difficult** entrance level, 78% of applicants were admitted

Undergraduates 12,335 full-time, 476 part-time. Students come from 45 states and territories; 30 other countries; 40% are from out of state; 1% Black or African American, non-Hispanic/Latino; 2% Hispanic/Latino; 2% Asian, non-Hispanic/Latino; 0.3% American Indian or Alaska Native, non-Hispanic/Latino; 2% Two or more races, non-Hispanic/Latino; 8% Race/ethnicity unknown; 0.8% international; 4% transferred in; 57% live on campus. *Retention:* 86% of full-time freshmen returned.
Freshmen *Admission:* 17,234 applied, 13,433 admitted, 2,999 enrolled. *Test scores:* SAT critical reading scores over 500: 70%; SAT math scores over 500: 77%; SAT writing scores over 500: 73%; ACT scores over 18: 96%; SAT critical reading scores over 600: 21%; SAT math scores over 600: 30%; SAT writing scores over 600: 22%; ACT scores over 24: 51%; SAT critical reading scores over 700: 3%; SAT math scores over 700: 3%; SAT writing scores over 700: 2%; ACT scores over 30: 6%.
Faculty *Total:* 987, 60% full-time, 63% with terminal degrees. *Student/faculty ratio:* 20:1.
Academics *Calendar:* semesters. *Degrees:* associate, bachelor's, master's, doctoral, post-master's, and postbachelor's certificates. *Special study options:* accelerated degree program, advanced placement credit, cooperative education, distance learning, double majors, English as a second language, honors programs, independent study, internships, off-campus study, part-time degree program, services for LD students, student-designed majors, study abroad, summer session for credit. *ROTC:* Army (b), Air Force (b). *Unusual degree programs:* 3-2 business administration; social work; accounting, biochemistry, occupational therapy.
Computers on Campus 464 computers/terminals are available on campus for general student use. Students can access the following: campus intranet, computer help desk, free student e-mail accounts, online (class) grades, online

UNH has a well-earned reputation for attracting talented students from all corners of the United States and the world. They come to UNH because of our invigorating seacoast setting; our proximity to the ocean, mountains, and Boston; and for the opportunity to work with our prize-winning faculty in nearly 100 fields of study.

For more information, contact:
Office of Admissions
University of New Hampshire
3 Garrison Avenue
Durham, New Hampshire 03824
Phone: 603-862-1360
Fax: 603-862-0077
E-mail @admissions @unh.edu

www.unh.edu/admissions

(class) registration, online (class) schedules. Campuswide network is available. 100% of college-owned or -operated housing units are wired for high-speed Internet access. Wireless service is available via classrooms, computer centers, computer labs, dorm rooms, libraries, student centers.

Student Life *Housing options:* coed, disabled students. Campus housing is university owned. Freshman campus housing is guaranteed. *Activities and organizations:* drama/theater group, student-run newspaper, radio station, choral group, marching band, Campus Activity Board, The Outing Club, Resident Hall Association, Best Buddies, Memorial Union Student Organization, national fraternities, national sororities. *Campus security:* 24-hour emergency response devices and patrols, student patrols, late-night transport/escort service, controlled dormitory access, lighted pathways and sidewalks. *Student services:* health clinic, personal/psychological counseling, women's center, legal services.

Athletics Member NCAA. All Division I except football (Division I-AA). *Intercollegiate sports:* archery M(c)/W(c), baseball M(c), basketball M(s)/W(s), crew M(c)/W(c), cross-country running M(s)/W(s), fencing M(c)/W(c), field hockey W(s), golf M(c)/W(c), gymnastics W(s), ice hockey M(s)/W(s), lacrosse M(c)/W(s), riflery M(c)/W(c), rock climbing M(c)/W(c), rugby M(c)/W(c), sailing M(c)/W(c), skiing (cross-country) M(s)/W(s), skiing (downhill) M(s)/W(s), soccer M(s)/W(s), softball W(c), swimming and diving W(s), tennis M(c)/W(c), track and field M(s)/W(s), ultimate Frisbee M(c)/W(c), volleyball M(c)/W(c), wrestling M(c)/W(c). *Intramural sports:* basketball M/W, field hockey W, football M/W, ice hockey M/W, racquetball M/W, soccer M/W, softball M/W, table tennis M/W, tennis M/W, volleyball M/W, water polo M/W.

Standardized Tests *Required:* SAT or ACT (for admission).

Costs (2012–13) *Tuition:* state resident $13,670 full-time, $570 per credit hour part-time; nonresident $26,130 full-time, $1089 per credit hour part-time. Full-time tuition and fees vary according to degree level and program. Part-time tuition and fees vary according to course load, degree level, and program. *Required fees:* $2752 full-time, $688 per term part-time. *Room and board:* $9764; room only: $6090. Room and board charges vary according to board plan and housing facility. *Payment plan:* installment. *Waivers:* employees or children of employees.

Financial Aid Of all full-time matriculated undergraduates who enrolled in 2011, 9,462 applied for aid, 7,909 were judged to have need, 1,430 had their need fully met. 5,358 Federal Work-Study jobs (averaging $2520). 3,851 state and other part-time jobs (averaging $1161). In 2011, 1954 non-need-based awards were made. *Average percent of need met:* 78%. *Average financial aid package:* $20,939. *Average need-based loan:* $3341. *Average need-based gift aid:* $4647. *Average non-need-based aid:* $8460. *Average indebtedness upon graduation:* $35,168.

Applying *Options:* electronic application, early action, deferred entrance. *Application fee:* $50. *Required:* essay or personal statement, high school transcript, 1 letter of recommendation. *Recommended:* minimum 3.0 GPA. *Application deadlines:* 2/1 (freshmen), 2/1 (out-of-state freshmen), 3/1 (transfers), 11/15 (early action). *Notification:* 4/15 (freshmen), 4/15 (out-of-state freshmen), 4/15 (transfers), 1/15 (early action). **Freshman Application Contact** Admissions Office, University of New Hampshire, 3 Garrison Avenue, Durham, NH 03824. *Phone:* 603-862-1360. *Fax:* 603-862-0077. *E-mail:* admissions@unh.edu. *Website:* http://www.unh.edu/.

See previous page for display ad and page 1586 for the College Close-Up.

University of New Hampshire at Manchester

Manchester, New Hampshire

- **State-supported** comprehensive, founded 1967, part of University System of New Hampshire
- **Urban** campus with easy access to Boston
- **Coed** 777 undergraduate students, 75% full-time, 50% women, 50% men
- **Moderately difficult** entrance level, 48% of applicants were admitted

Undergraduates 586 full-time, 191 part-time. 2% Black or African American, non-Hispanic/Latino; 4% Hispanic/Latino; 2% Asian, non-Hispanic/Latino; 0.1% Native Hawaiian or other Pacific Islander, non-Hispanic/Latino; 0.1% American Indian or Alaska Native, non-Hispanic/Latino; 0.8% Two or more races, non-Hispanic/Latino; 13% Race/ethnicity unknown; 0.1% international. **Freshmen** *Admission:* 157 applied, 76 admitted, 76 enrolled. **Faculty** *Total:* 109, 35% full-time. *Student/faculty ratio:* 13:1. **Academics** *Calendar:* semesters. *Degrees:* certificates, associate, bachelor's, and master's. *Special study options:* academic remediation for entering students, adult/continuing education programs, advanced placement credit, double majors, independent study, internships, off-campus study, part-time degree

program, services for LD students, student-designed majors, study abroad, summer session for credit. *ROTC:* Army (c), Air Force (c). *Unusual degree programs:* 3-2 Pharmacy program with Massachusetts College of Pharmacy and Health Sciences.

Computers on Campus 108 computers/terminals are available on campus for general student use. Students can access the following: online (class) registration. Campuswide network is available. Wireless service is available via entire campus.

Student Life *Housing:* college housing not available. *Activities and organizations:* student-run radio station, Student Council. *Campus security:* 24-hour emergency response devices, late-night transport/escort service.

Standardized Tests *Required:* SAT or ACT (for admission).

Costs (2012–13) *Tuition:* state resident $13,350 full-time, $556 per credit hour part-time; nonresident $25,810 full-time, $1075 per credit hour part-time. Full-time tuition and fees vary according to course load and program. Part-time tuition and fees vary according to course load and program. *Required fees:* $407 full-time. *Payment plan:* installment. *Waivers:* senior citizens and employees or children of employees.

Financial Aid Of all full-time matriculated undergraduates who enrolled in 2011, 655 applied for aid, 532 were judged to have need, 56 had their need fully met. 229 Federal Work-Study jobs (averaging $2389). In 2011, 11 non-need-based awards were made. *Average percent of need met:* 60%. *Average financial aid package:* $12,051. *Average need-based loan:* $3856. *Average need-based gift aid:* $864. *Average non-need-based aid:* $655. *Average indebtedness upon graduation:* $25,411.

Applying *Options:* electronic application, deferred entrance. *Application fee:* $45. *Required:* essay or personal statement, high school transcript, 1 letter of recommendation. *Recommended:* interview. *Application deadlines:* 6/15 (freshmen), 6/15 (transfers). *Notification:* continuous (freshmen), continuous (transfers). **Freshman Application Contact** Ms. Donna Lukasiak, Senior Assistant Director Admissions, University of New Hampshire at Manchester, 400 Commercial Street, Manchester, NH 03101. *Phone:* 603-641-4150. *Fax:* 603-641-4342. *E-mail:* unhm@unh.edu. *Website:* http://www.unhm.unh.edu/.

NEW JERSEY

Berkeley College

Woodland Park, New Jersey

Freshman Application Contact Berkeley College, 44 Rifle Camp Road, Woodland Park, NJ 07424-3353. *Phone:* 973-278-5400. *Toll-free phone:* 800-446-5400.
Website: http://www.berkeleycollege.edu/.

Beth Medrash Govoha

Lakewood, New Jersey

Director of Admissions Director of Admissions, Beth Medrash Govoha, 617 Sixth Street, Lakewood, NJ 08701-2797. *Phone:* 908-367-1060 Ext. 4224.

Bloomfield College

Bloomfield, New Jersey

- **Independent** comprehensive, founded 1868, affiliated with Presbyterian Church (U.S.A.)
- **Suburban** 12-acre campus with easy access to New York City
- **Endowment** $9.5 million
- **Coed** 2,036 undergraduate students, 89% full-time, 64% women, 36% men
- **Moderately difficult** entrance level, 55% of applicants were admitted

Undergraduates 1,810 full-time, 226 part-time. Students come from 18 states and territories; 29 other countries; 5% are from out of state; 51% Black or African American, non-Hispanic/Latino; 20% Hispanic/Latino; 3% Asian, non-Hispanic/Latino; 0.3% American Indian or Alaska Native, non-Hispanic/Latino; 0.4% Two or more races, non-Hispanic/Latino; 9% Race/ethnicity unknown; 3% international; 11% transferred in; 24% live on campus. *Retention:* 64% of full-time freshmen returned.

Freshmen *Admission:* 3,115 applied, 1,702 admitted, 382 enrolled. *Average high school GPA:* 2.6. *Test scores:* SAT critical reading scores over 500: 10%; SAT math scores over 500: 13%; SAT critical reading scores over 600: 2%; SAT math scores over 600: 2%.

Faculty *Total:* 226, 31% full-time, 31% with terminal degrees. *Student/faculty ratio:* 15:1.

Academics *Calendar:* semesters. *Degrees:* certificates, bachelor's, master's, and postbachelor's certificates. *Special study options:* academic remediation for entering students, accelerated degree program, advanced placement credit, distance learning, double majors, honors programs, independent study, internships, off-campus study, part-time degree program, services for LD students, student-designed majors, study abroad, summer session for credit. *ROTC:* Army (c).

Computers on Campus 363 computers/terminals are available on campus for general student use. Students can access the following: computer help desk, free student e-mail accounts, online (class) grades, online (class) schedules. Campuswide network is available. Wireless service is available via entire campus.

Student Life *Housing options:* coed. Campus housing is university owned and is provided by a third party. *Activities and organizations:* drama/theater group, student-run radio station, First Ladies, Team Infinite, Lambda Theta Alpha, Gentlemen's Club, Iota Phi Theta/ Chi Phi Sigma/Zeta Phi Beta, national fraternities, national sororities. *Campus security:* 24-hour emergency response devices and patrols, late-night transport/escort service, security cameras in high-traffic areas. *Student services:* health clinic, personal/psychological counseling.

Athletics Member NCAA. All Division II. *Intercollegiate sports:* baseball M(s), basketball M(s)/W(s), cross-country running M(s)/W(s), soccer M(s)/W(s), softball W(s), tennis M(s), volleyball W(s). *Intramural sports:* basketball M/W, volleyball M/W.

Standardized Tests *Required:* SAT or ACT (for admission).

Costs (2012–13) *Comprehensive fee:* $35,750 includes full-time tuition ($23,850), mandatory fees ($1200), and room and board ($10,700). Part-time tuition: $2980 per course. Part-time tuition and fees vary according to course load. *College room only:* $5350. Room and board charges vary according to housing facility. *Payment plans:* installment, deferred payment. *Waivers:* senior citizens and employees or children of employees.

Financial Aid Of all full-time matriculated undergraduates who enrolled in 2011, 1,714 applied for aid, 1,626 were judged to have need, 33 had their need fully met. 579 Federal Work-Study jobs (averaging $2177). In 2011, 66 non-need-based awards were made. *Average percent of need met:* 51%. *Average financial aid package:* $20,690. *Average need-based loan:* $4051. *Average need-based gift aid:* $14,453. *Average non-need-based aid:* $13,616. *Average indebtedness upon graduation:* $32,698. *Financial aid deadline:* 6/1.

Applying *Options:* electronic application, early action, deferred entrance. *Application fee:* $40. *Required:* essay or personal statement, high school transcript, minimum 2.5 GPA, 2 letters of recommendation, graded essay/term paper or personal essay. *Recommended:* interview. *Application deadlines:* 8/1 (freshmen), 8/1 (out-of-state freshmen), 8/1 (transfers), 12/1 (early action). *Notification:* continuous until 10/1 (freshmen), continuous until 10/1 (out-of-state freshmen), continuous until 10/1 (transfers), 12/23 (early action).

Freshman Application Contact Ms. Nicole Cibelli, Director of Admissions, Bloomfield College, Office of Enrollment Management and Admission, Bloomfield, NJ 07003-9981. *Phone:* 973-748-9000 Ext. 1390. *Toll-free phone:* 800-848-4555 Ext. 230. *Fax:* 973-748-0916. *E-mail:* nicole_cibelli@bloomfield.edu.

Website: http://www.bloomfield.edu/.

Caldwell College

Caldwell, New Jersey

- **Independent Roman Catholic** comprehensive, founded 1939
- **Suburban** 70-acre campus with easy access to New York City
- **Endowment** $5.8 million
- **Coed** 1,591 undergraduate students, 79% full-time, 67% women, 33% men
- **Moderately difficult** entrance level, 61% of applicants were admitted

Undergraduates 1,260 full-time, 331 part-time. Students come from 19 states and territories; 24 other countries; 8% are from out of state; 16% Black or African American, non-Hispanic/Latino; 15% Hispanic/Latino; 3% Asian, non-Hispanic/Latino; 0.2% Native Hawaiian or other Pacific Islander, non-Hispanic/Latino; 0.2% American Indian or Alaska Native, non-Hispanic/Latino; 1% Two or more races, non-Hispanic/Latino; 15% Race/ethnicity unknown; 4% international; 3% transferred in; 31% live on campus. *Retention:* 82% of full-time freshmen returned.

Freshmen *Admission:* 2,598 applied, 1,591 admitted, 292 enrolled. *Test scores:* SAT critical reading scores over 500: 27%; SAT math scores over 500: 33%; SAT writing scores over 500: 31%; ACT scores over 18: 72%; SAT critical reading scores over 600: 4%; SAT math scores over 600: 8%; SAT writing scores over 600: 6%; ACT scores over 24: 13%; SAT math scores over 700: 1%; SAT writing scores over 700: 1%; ACT scores over 30: 3%.

Faculty *Total:* 227, 39% full-time. *Student/faculty ratio:* 12:1.

Academics *Calendar:* semesters. *Degrees:* bachelor's, master's, doctoral, post-master's, and postbachelor's certificates. *Special study options:* academic remediation for entering students, accelerated degree program, adult/continuing education programs, advanced placement credit, cooperative education, distance learning, double majors, English as a second language, external degree program, honors programs, independent study, internships, off-campus study, part-time degree program, services for LD students, student-designed majors, study abroad, summer session for credit. *ROTC:* Army (c). *Unusual degree programs:* 3-2 business administration; social work with Rutgers University; BA Psychology/MA Counseling Psychology, BA Psychology/MA ABA, BA Education/MA Curriculum and Instruction, BA Biology or BA Psychology/MS in Occupational Therapy (Columbia University), BA Biology/MS in Athletic Training (Seton Hall University).

Computers on Campus 286 computers/terminals and 796 ports are available on campus for general student use. Students can access the following: campus intranet, computer help desk, free student e-mail accounts, online (class) grades, online (class) registration, online (class) schedules. Campuswide network is available. 100% of college-owned or -operated housing units are wired for high-speed Internet access. Wireless service is available via classrooms, dorm rooms, learning centers, libraries.

Student Life *Housing options:* coed. Campus housing is university owned. Freshman applicants given priority for college housing. *Activities and organizations:* drama/theater group, student-run newspaper, choral group, Black Student Union, Latino American Student Organization, Autism Awareness Club, Martial Arts Club, Marketing Club, national fraternities, national sororities. *Campus security:* 24-hour patrols, late-night transport/escort service, controlled dormitory access, dusk-to-dawn patrols by trained security personnel. *Student services:* health clinic, personal/psychological counseling.

Athletics Member NCAA. All Division II. *Intercollegiate sports:* baseball M(s), basketball M(s)/W(s), cross-country running W(s), soccer M(s)/W(s), softball W(s), tennis M(s)/W(s), track and field W(s), volleyball W(s). *Intramural sports:* basketball M/W, cheerleading W(c), football M/W, soccer M/W, softball M/W, tennis M/W, ultimate Frisbee M/W, volleyball M/W.

Standardized Tests *Required:* SAT or ACT (for admission).

Costs (2013–14) *Comprehensive fee:* $40,000 includes full-time tuition ($27,900), mandatory fees ($1100), and room and board ($11,000). Full-time tuition and fees vary according to course load and location. Part-time tuition: $738 per credit hour. Part-time tuition and fees vary according to course load and location. *Required fees:* $150 per semester part-time. *Room and board:* Room and board charges vary according to housing facility. *Payment plan:* installment. *Waivers:* children of alumni, adult students, senior citizens, and employees or children of employees.

Financial Aid Of all full-time matriculated undergraduates who enrolled in 2011, 1,063 applied for aid, 979 were judged to have need, 93 had their need fully met. 168 Federal Work-Study jobs (averaging $696). 104 state and other part-time jobs (averaging $4562). In 2011, 206 non-need-based awards were made. *Average percent of need met:* 70%. *Average financial aid package:* $19,853. *Average need-based loan:* $3936. *Average need-based gift aid:* $16,494. *Average non-need-based aid:* $14,511. *Average indebtedness upon graduation:* $24,196.

Applying *Options:* electronic application, early admission, early action, deferred entrance. *Application fee:* $40. *Required:* essay or personal statement, high school transcript, 2 letters of recommendation, SAT or ACT Scores. *Required for some:* interview. *Recommended:* minimum 3.0 GPA, interview. *Application deadlines:* rolling (freshmen), rolling (out-of-state freshmen), rolling (transfers), 12/1 (early action). *Notification:* continuous (freshmen), continuous (out-of-state freshmen), continuous (transfers), 12/31 (early action).

Freshman Application Contact Mr. Stephen Quinn, Executive Director of Undergraduate Admissions, Caldwell College, 120 Bloomfield Avenue, Caldwell, NJ 07006. *Phone:* 973-618-3320. *Fax:* 973-618-3600. *E-mail:* squinn@caldwell.edu.

Website: http://www.caldwell.edu/.

Centenary College

Hackettstown, New Jersey

- **Independent** comprehensive, founded 1867, affiliated with United Methodist Church
- **Suburban** campus
- **Coed**
- **Moderately difficult** entrance level

Faculty *Student/faculty ratio:* 19:1.

Academics *Calendar:* semesters. *Degrees:* associate, bachelor's, master's, and postbachelor's certificates.

Student Life *Campus security:* 24-hour emergency response devices and patrols, late-night transport/escort service, controlled dormitory access.

Athletics Member NCAA. All Division III.

Standardized Tests *Required:* SAT or ACT (for admission).

Costs (2012–13) *Comprehensive fee:* $38,616 includes full-time tuition ($28,500) and room and board ($10,116). Full-time tuition and fees vary according to program. Part-time tuition and fees vary according to program. *Room and board:* Room and board charges vary according to board plan.

Financial Aid *Of all full-time matriculated undergraduates who enrolled in 2010,* 1,219 applied for aid, 1,094 were judged to have need, 121 had their need fully met. *In 2010,* 303 non-need-based awards were made. *Average percent of need met:* 72. *Average financial aid package:* $19,967. *Average need-based loan:* $5414. *Average need-based gift aid:* $15,457. *Average non-need-based aid:* $9157. *Average indebtedness upon graduation:* $40,588.

Applying *Options:* electronic application, deferred entrance. *Application fee:* $30. *Required:* essay or personal statement, high school transcript. *Required for some:* interview. *Recommended:* interview.

Freshman Application Contact Centenary College, 400 Jefferson Street, Hackettstown, NJ 07840-2100. *Phone:* 908-852-1400. *Toll-free phone:* 800-236-8679.

Website: http://www.centenarycollege.edu/.

The College of New Jersey

Ewing, New Jersey

- **State-supported** comprehensive, founded 1855
- **Suburban** 255-acre campus with easy access to Philadelphia
- **Coed** 6,545 undergraduate students, 97% full-time, 57% women, 43% men
- **Very difficult** entrance level, 46% of applicants were admitted

Undergraduates 6,340 full-time, 205 part-time. Students come from 19 states and territories; 9 other countries; 6% are from out of state; 6% Black or African American, non-Hispanic/Latino; 10% Hispanic/Latino; 9% Asian, non-Hispanic/Latino; 0.4% Native Hawaiian or other Pacific Islander, non-Hispanic/Latino; 0.1% American Indian or Alaska Native, non-Hispanic/Latino; 1% Two or more races, non-Hispanic/Latino; 8% Race/ethnicity unknown; 0.2% international; 4% transferred in; 60% live on campus. *Retention:* 94% of full-time freshmen returned.

Freshmen *Admission:* 10,295 applied, 4,750 admitted, 1,363 enrolled. *Test scores:* SAT critical reading scores over 500: 92%; SAT math scores over 500: 95%; SAT writing scores over 500: 93%; SAT critical reading scores over 600: 53%; SAT math scores over 600: 69%; SAT writing scores over 600: 57%; SAT critical reading scores over 700: 11%; SAT math scores over 700: 19%; SAT writing scores over 700: 14%.

Faculty *Total:* 754, 47% full-time, 55% with terminal degrees. *Student/faculty ratio:* 13:1.

Academics *Calendar:* semesters. *Degrees:* bachelor's, master's, post-master's, and postbachelor's certificates. *Special study options:* academic remediation for entering students, accelerated degree program, advanced placement credit, double majors, honors programs, independent study, internships, off-campus study, part-time degree program, services for LD students, student-designed majors, study abroad, summer session for credit. *ROTC:* Army (c), Air Force (c). *Unusual degree programs:* 3-2 education of the deaf and hard of hearing and elementary education; special education and liberal arts.

Computers on Campus 631 computers/terminals are available on campus for general student use. Students can access the following: campus intranet, computer help desk, free student e-mail accounts, online (class) grades, online (class) registration, online (class) schedules. Campuswide network is available. 100% of college-owned or -operated housing units are wired for high-speed

Internet access. Wireless service is available via classrooms, computer labs, learning centers, libraries, student centers.

Student Life *Housing:* on-campus residence required for freshman year. *Options:* coed, disabled students. Campus housing is university owned. Freshman campus housing is guaranteed. *Activities and organizations:* drama/theater group, student-run newspaper, radio and television station, choral group, Student Government Association, College Union Board, Inter-Greek Council, The Signal, national fraternities, national sororities. *Campus security:* 24-hour emergency response devices and patrols, student patrols, late-night transport/escort service, controlled dormitory access. *Student services:* health clinic, personal/psychological counseling, women's center, legal services.

Athletics Member NCAA. All Division III. *Intercollegiate sports:* baseball M, basketball M/W, cross-country running M/W, field hockey W, football M, lacrosse W, soccer M/W, softball W, swimming and diving M/W, tennis M/W, track and field M/W, wrestling M. *Intramural sports:* baseball M(c), basketball M(c)/W, bowling M(c)/W(c), cheerleading M(c)/W(c), crew M(c)/W(c), fencing M(c)/W(c), field hockey M/W, football M/W, golf M(c)/W(c), ice hockey M(c), lacrosse M(c)/W(c), racquetball M/W, rugby M(c)/W(c), skiing (cross-country) M(c)/W(c), skiing (downhill) M(c)/W(c), soccer M(c)/W(c), softball M/W(c), swimming and diving M(c)/W(c), table tennis M(c)/W(c), tennis M(c)/W(c), ultimate Frisbee M(c)/W(c), volleyball M(c)/W(c), water polo M(c)/W(c).

Standardized Tests *Required:* SAT or ACT (for admission).

Costs (2012–13) *Tuition:* state resident $10,102 full-time, $358 per credit hour part-time; nonresident $20,254 full-time, $717 per credit hour part-time. Part-time tuition and fees vary according to course load. *Required fees:* $4276 full-time, $170 per credit hour part-time. *Room and board:* $10,998; room only: $8006. Room and board charges vary according to board plan. *Payment plan:* installment. *Waivers:* senior citizens and employees or children of employees.

Financial Aid Of all full-time matriculated undergraduates who enrolled in 2012, 4,643 applied for aid, 3,408 were judged to have need, 466 had their need fully met. In 2012, 635 non-need-based awards were made. *Average percent of need met:* 47%. *Average financial aid package:* $10,647. *Average need-based loan:* $4603. *Average need-based gift aid:* $11,219. *Average non-need-based aid:* $4609. *Average indebtedness upon graduation:* $33,889.

Applying *Options:* electronic application, early decision, deferred entrance. *Application fee:* $75. *Required:* essay or personal statement, high school transcript. *Required for some:* interview, art portfolio or music audition. *Recommended:* minimum 2.5 GPA, 3 letters of recommendation. *Application deadlines:* 1/15 (freshmen), 1/15 (transfers). *Early decision deadline:* 11/15. *Notification:* continuous until 1/15 (freshmen), continuous until 1/15 (transfers), 12/15 (early decision).

Freshman Application Contact Ms. Grecia Montero, Director of Admissions, The College of New Jersey, PO Box 7718, Ewing, NJ 08628. *Phone:* 609-771-2131. *Fax:* 609-637-5174. *E-mail:* admiss@tcnj.edu. *Website:* http://www.tcnj.edu/.

See previous page for display ad and page 1246 for the College Close-Up.

College of Saint Elizabeth

Morristown, New Jersey

- **Independent Roman Catholic** comprehensive, founded 1899
- **Suburban** 188-acre campus with easy access to New York City
- **Endowment** $19.4 million
- **Coed, primarily women** 1,079 undergraduate students, 54% full-time, 93% women, 7% men
- **Moderately difficult** entrance level, 58% of applicants were admitted

Undergraduates 583 full-time, 496 part-time. Students come from 8 states and territories; 25 other countries; 3% are from out of state; 21% Black or African American, non-Hispanic/Latino; 15% Hispanic/Latino; 3% Asian, non-Hispanic/Latino; 0.2% Native Hawaiian or other Pacific Islander, non-Hispanic/Latino; 0.3% American Indian or Alaska Native, non-Hispanic/Latino; 0.6% Two or more races, non-Hispanic/Latino; 11% Race/ethnicity unknown; 4% international; 2% transferred in; 63% live on campus. *Retention:* 70% of full-time freshmen returned.

Freshmen *Admission:* 1,386 applied, 798 admitted, 146 enrolled. *Test scores:* SAT critical reading scores over 500: 22%; SAT math scores over 500: 20%; SAT writing scores over 500: 21%; SAT critical reading scores over 600: 5%; SAT math scores over 600: 3%; SAT writing scores over 600: 4%; SAT critical reading scores over 700: 1%; SAT math scores over 700: 1%.

Faculty *Total:* 289, 24% full-time, 47% with terminal degrees. *Student/faculty ratio:* 7:1.

Academics *Calendar:* semesters. *Degrees:* certificates, bachelor's, master's, doctoral, and postbachelor's certificates (also offers coed adult undergraduate degree program and coed graduate programs). *Special study options:* academic remediation for entering students, accelerated degree program, advanced

placement credit, distance learning, double majors, English as a second language, honors programs, independent study, internships, off-campus study, part-time degree program, services for LD students, student-designed majors, study abroad, summer session for credit. *Unusual degree programs:* 3-2 business administration; nursing; counseling psychology.

Computers on Campus 127 computers/terminals and 20 ports are available on campus for general student use. Students can access the following: campus intranet, computer help desk, free student e-mail accounts, online (class) grades, online (class) registration, online (class) schedules. Campuswide network is available. 100% of college-owned or -operated housing units are wired for high-speed Internet access. Wireless service is available via entire campus.

Student Life *Housing options:* women-only. Campus housing is university owned. Freshman campus housing is guaranteed. *Activities and organizations:* drama/theater group, student-run newspaper, choral group, Student Government Association, Students Take Action Committee, International/Intercultural Club, College Activities Board, Campus Ministry. *Campus security:* 24-hour emergency response devices and patrols, late-night transport/escort service, controlled dormitory access. *Student services:* health clinic, personal/psychological counseling.

Athletics Member NCAA. All Division III. *Intercollegiate sports:* basketball W, equestrian sports W, soccer W, softball W, swimming and diving W, tennis W, volleyball W. *Intramural sports:* volleyball W.

Standardized Tests *Required:* SAT or ACT (for admission).

Costs (2012–13) *Comprehensive fee:* $42,161 includes full-time tuition ($28,026), mandatory fees ($1881), and room and board ($12,254). Full-time tuition and fees vary according to class time and location. Part-time tuition: $806 per credit hour. Part-time tuition and fees vary according to class time, course load, location, program, and reciprocity agreements. *Room and board:* Room and board charges vary according to board plan. *Payment plan:* installment. *Waivers:* children of alumni, senior citizens, and employees or children of employees.

Financial Aid Of all full-time matriculated undergraduates who enrolled in 2010, 557 applied for aid, 557 were judged to have need, 61 had their need fully met. 379 Federal Work-Study jobs (averaging $290). In 2010, 306 non-need-based awards were made. *Average percent of need met:* 72%. *Average financial aid package:* $23,720. *Average need-based loan:* $4942. *Average need-based gift aid:* $16,498. *Average non-need-based aid:* $13,128. *Average indebtedness upon graduation:* $7746.

Applying *Options:* electronic application, deferred entrance. *Application fee:* $35. *Required:* high school transcript, minimum 2.0 GPA, 2 letters of recommendation. *Recommended:* essay or personal statement, interview. *Application deadlines:* 8/15 (freshmen), rolling (transfers). *Notification:* 11/15 (freshmen), continuous (transfers).

Freshman Application Contact Ms. Donna Tatarka, Dean of Admissions, College of Saint Elizabeth, 2 Convent Road, Morristown, NJ 07960-6989. *Phone:* 973-290-4700. *Toll-free phone:* 800-210-7900. *Fax:* 973-290-4710. *E-mail:* apply@cse.edu. *Website:* http://www.cse.edu/.

DeVry University

North Brunswick, New Jersey

- **Proprietary** comprehensive, founded 1969, part of DeVry University
- **Urban** campus
- **Coed** 1,213 undergraduate students, 46% full-time, 28% women, 72% men
- **Minimally difficult** entrance level

Undergraduates 556 full-time, 657 part-time. 9% are from out of state; 16% Black or African American, non-Hispanic/Latino; 20% Hispanic/Latino; 5% Asian, non-Hispanic/Latino; 0.4% Native Hawaiian or other Pacific Islander, non-Hispanic/Latino; 0.4% American Indian or Alaska Native, non-Hispanic/Latino; 0.3% Two or more races, non-Hispanic/Latino; 22% Race/ethnicity unknown; 2% international; 14% transferred in.

Freshmen *Admission:* 113 enrolled.

Faculty *Total:* 159, 21% full-time. *Student/faculty ratio:* 12:1.

Academics *Calendar:* semesters. *Degrees:* associate, bachelor's, and master's. *Special study options:* adult/continuing education programs, part-time degree program.

Computers on Campus Students can access the following: online (class) registration.

Student Life *Housing:* college housing not available.

Costs (2013–14) *Tuition:* $16,076 full-time, $609 per credit hour part-time. *Required fees:* $80 full-time.

Financial Aid Of all full-time matriculated undergraduates who enrolled in 2007, 449 applied for aid, 430 were judged to have need, 9 had their need fully met. In 2007, 50 non-need-based awards were made. *Average percent of need* *met:* 34%. *Average financial aid package:* $12,399. *Average need-based loan:* $6629. *Average need-based gift aid:* $8242. *Average non-need-based aid:* $11,630. *Average indebtedness upon graduation:* $24,045.

Applying *Application fee:* $40. *Required:* high school transcript, interview. *Application deadlines:* rolling (freshmen), rolling (transfers). *Notification:* continuous (freshmen), continuous (transfers).

Freshman Application Contact DeVry University, 630 US Highway 1, North Brunswick, NJ 08902-3362. *Phone:* 732-729-3532. *Toll-free phone:* 866-338-7941.

Website: http://www.devry.edu/.

DeVry University

Paramus, New Jersey

Admissions Office Contact DeVry University, 35 Plaza, 81 East State Route 4, Suite 102, Paramus, NJ 07652. *Toll-free phone:* 866-338-7941.
Website: http://www.devry.edu/.

Drew University

Madison, New Jersey

- **Independent** university, founded 1867, affiliated with United Methodist Church
- **Suburban** 186-acre campus with easy access to New York City
- **Endowment** $210.0 million
- **Coed** 1,640 undergraduate students, 96% full-time, 60% women, 40% men
- **Moderately difficult** entrance level, 85% of applicants were admitted

Undergraduates 1,568 full-time, 72 part-time. Students come from 35 states and territories; 24 other countries; 35% are from out of state; 10% Black or African American, non-Hispanic/Latino; 14% Hispanic/Latino; 5% Asian, non-Hispanic/Latino; 0.1% American Indian or Alaska Native, non-Hispanic/Latino; 2% Two or more races, non-Hispanic/Latino; 10% Race/ethnicity unknown; 2% international; 3% transferred in; 82% live on campus. *Retention:* 75% of full-time freshmen returned.

Freshmen *Admission:* 3,872 applied, 3,294 admitted, 363 enrolled. *Average high school GPA:* 3.32. *Test scores:* SAT critical reading scores over 500: 73%; SAT math scores over 500: 69%; SAT writing scores over 500: 72%; ACT scores over 18: 92%; SAT critical reading scores over 600: 32%; SAT math scores over 600: 31%; SAT writing scores over 600: 30%; ACT scores over 24: 53%; SAT critical reading scores over 700: 7%; SAT math scores over 700: 6%; SAT writing scores over 700: 5%; ACT scores over 30: 11%.

Faculty *Total:* 300, 53% full-time. *Student/faculty ratio:* 10:1.

Academics *Calendar:* semesters. *Degrees:* master's, doctoral, post-master's, and postbachelor's certificates. *Special study options:* academic remediation for entering students, accelerated degree program, adult/continuing education programs, advanced placement credit, double majors, external degree program, honors programs, independent study, internships, off-campus study, part-time degree program, services for LD students, student-designed majors, study abroad, summer session for credit.

Computers on Campus Students can access the following: campus intranet, computer help desk, free student e-mail accounts, online (class) grades, online (class) registration, online (class) schedules. Campuswide network is available. 100% of college-owned or -operated housing units are wired for high-speed Internet access. Wireless service is available via entire campus.

Student Life *Housing options:* coed, disabled students. Campus housing is university owned. Freshman campus housing is guaranteed. *Activities and organizations:* drama/theater group, student-run newspaper, radio and television station, choral group, New Social Engine, Student Government Association, D.U.D.S.-Drew University Dramatic Society, University Program Board, Kuumba Pan African Student Association. *Campus security:* 24-hour emergency response devices and patrols, late-night transport/escort service, controlled dormitory access. *Student services:* health clinic, personal/psychological counseling.

Athletics Member NCAA. All Division III. *Intercollegiate sports:* baseball M, basketball M/W, cross-country running M/W, equestrian sports M/W, fencing M/W, field hockey W, lacrosse M/W, rugby M(c)/W(c), soccer M/W, softball W, swimming and diving M/W, tennis M/W. *Intramural sports:* basketball M/W, football M/W, racquetball M/W, soccer M/W, softball M/W, squash M/W, table tennis M/W, ultimate Frisbee M/W, volleyball M/W.

Standardized Tests *Recommended:* SAT and ACT scores are optional and are considered if submitted. SAT subject tests are not used.

Costs (2013–14) *Comprehensive fee:* $56,012 includes full-time tuition ($42,936), mandatory fees ($1132), and room and board ($11,944). Full-time

tuition and fees vary according to course load. Part-time tuition: $1789 per credit hour. Part-time tuition and fees vary according to course load. *College room only:* $7684. Room and board charges vary according to board plan and housing facility. *Payment plans:* tuition prepayment, installment, deferred payment. *Waivers:* senior citizens and employees or children of employees.

Financial Aid Of all full-time matriculated undergraduates who enrolled in 2011, 1,248 applied for aid, 1,129 were judged to have need, 129 had their need fully met. In 2011, 429 non-need-based awards were made. *Average percent of need met:* 72%. *Average financial aid package:* $30,732. *Average need-based loan:* $4740. *Average need-based gift aid:* $25,930. *Average non-need-based aid:* $11,778. *Average indebtedness upon graduation:* $24,470. *Financial aid deadline:* 2/15.

Applying *Options:* electronic application, early admission, early decision, early action, deferred entrance. *Application fee:* $60. *Required:* essay or personal statement, high school transcript, 1 letter of recommendation. *Recommended:* interview. *Application deadlines:* 2/1 (freshmen), 8/1 (transfers), 1/15 (early action). *Early decision deadline:* 11/1 (for plan 1), 1/15 (for plan 2). *Notification:* continuous until 11/15 (freshmen), continuous until 4/1 (transfers), 1/15 (early decision plan 1), 2/15 (early decision plan 2).

Freshman Application Contact Drew University, 36 Madison Avenue, Madison, NJ 07940-1493. *Phone:* 973-408-3739.

Website: http://www.drew.edu/.

Fairleigh Dickinson University, College at Florham

Madison, New Jersey

- **Independent** comprehensive, founded 1942
- **Suburban** 178-acre campus with easy access to New York City
- **Coed** 2,396 undergraduate students, 92% full-time, 55% women, 45% men
- **Moderately difficult** entrance level, 78% of applicants were admitted

Undergraduates 2,213 full-time, 183 part-time. Students come from 26 states and territories; 11 other countries; 16% are from out of state; 11% Black or African American, non-Hispanic/Latino; 13% Hispanic/Latino; 4% Asian, non-Hispanic/Latino; 0.9% American Indian or Alaska Native, non-Hispanic/Latino; 0.8% Two or more races, non-Hispanic/Latino; 8% Race/ethnicity unknown; 0.6% international; 5% transferred in; 63% live on campus. *Retention:* 76% of full-time freshmen returned.

Freshmen *Admission:* 3,647 applied, 2,835 admitted, 586 enrolled. *Average high school GPA:* 3.1. *Test scores:* SAT critical reading scores over 500: 56%; SAT math scores over 500: 60%; SAT writing scores over 500: 55%; SAT critical reading scores over 600: 13%; SAT math scores over 600: 19%; SAT writing scores over 600: 14%; SAT critical reading scores over 700: 1%; SAT math scores over 700: 1%; SAT writing scores over 700: 1%.

Faculty *Total:* 378, 37% full-time. *Student/faculty ratio:* 12:1.

Academics *Calendar:* semesters. *Degrees:* bachelor's, master's, doctoral, post-master's, and postbachelor's certificates. *Special study options:* academic remediation for entering students, accelerated degree program, adult/continuing education programs, advanced placement credit, cooperative education, distance learning, double majors, honors programs, independent study, internships, off-campus study, part-time degree program, services for LD students, student-designed majors, study abroad, summer session for credit. *ROTC:* Army (c), Air Force (c).

Computers on Campus 150 computers/terminals are available on campus for general student use. Students can access the following: computer help desk, free student e-mail accounts, online (class) grades, online (class) registration, online (class) schedules. Campuswide network is available. 100% of college-owned or -operated housing units are wired for high-speed Internet access. Wireless service is available via entire campus.

Student Life *Housing options:* coed. Campus housing is university owned. Freshman applicants given priority for college housing. *Activities and organizations:* drama/theater group, student-run newspaper, choral group, College Panhellenic Council, Association of Black Collegians, Latin American Student Organization, Florham Programming Committee, InterFraternity Council, national fraternities, national sororities. *Campus security:* 24-hour emergency response devices and patrols, late-night transport/escort service, controlled dormitory access, trained law enforcement personnel on staff. *Student services:* health clinic, personal/psychological counseling.

Athletics Member NCAA. All Division III. *Intercollegiate sports:* baseball M, basketball M/W, cross-country running M/W, field hockey W, football M, golf M/W, lacrosse M/W, soccer M/W, softball W, swimming and diving M/W, tennis M/W, volleyball W. *Intramural sports:* basketball M/W, football M/W, soccer M/W, softball M/W, volleyball M/W, weight lifting M/W.

Standardized Tests *Required:* SAT or ACT (for admission).

Costs (2012–13) *Comprehensive fee:* $48,324 includes full-time tuition ($35,412), mandatory fees ($940), and room and board ($11,972). Part-time tuition: $1054 per credit hour. *College room only:* $7902. Room and board charges vary according to board plan and housing facility. *Payment plans:* installment, deferred payment. *Waivers:* senior citizens and employees or children of employees.

Financial Aid Of all full-time matriculated undergraduates who enrolled in 2007, 1,788 applied for aid, 1,568 were judged to have need. In 2007, 213 non-need-based awards were made. *Average financial aid package:* $17,400. *Average need-based loan:* $4001. *Average need-based gift aid:* $9956. *Average non-need-based aid:* $6501.

Applying *Options:* electronic application. *Application fee:* $40. *Required:* high school transcript, 2 letters of recommendation. *Application deadlines:* rolling (freshmen), rolling (transfers). *Notification:* continuous (freshmen), continuous (transfers).

Freshman Application Contact Fairleigh Dickinson University, College at Florham, 285 Madison Avenue, Madison, NJ 07940-1099. *Toll-free phone:* 800-338-8803.

Website: http://www.fdu.edu/.

Fairleigh Dickinson University, Metropolitan Campus

Teaneck, New Jersey

- **Independent** comprehensive, founded 1942
- **Suburban** 88-acre campus with easy access to New York City
- **Coed** 6,775 undergraduate students, 43% full-time, 60% women, 40% men
- **Moderately difficult** entrance level, 73% of applicants were admitted

Undergraduates 2,882 full-time, 3,893 part-time. Students come from 30 states and territories; 45 other countries; 14% are from out of state; 14% Black or African American, non-Hispanic/Latino; 34% Hispanic/Latino; 5% Asian, non-Hispanic/Latino; 0.1% Native Hawaiian or other Pacific Islander, non-Hispanic/Latino; 0.2% American Indian or Alaska Native, non-Hispanic/Latino; 0.7% Two or more races, non-Hispanic/Latino; 11% Race/ethnicity unknown; 7% international; 6% transferred in; 19% live on campus. *Retention:* 70% of full-time freshmen returned.

Freshmen *Admission:* 5,193 applied, 3,812 admitted, 757 enrolled. *Average high school GPA:* 3.2. *Test scores:* SAT critical reading scores over 500: 41%; SAT math scores over 500: 52%; SAT writing scores over 500: 41%; SAT critical reading scores over 600: 10%; SAT math scores over 600: 13%; SAT writing scores over 600: 9%; SAT math scores over 700: 2%; SAT writing scores over 700: 1%.

Faculty *Total:* 753, 25% full-time. *Student/faculty ratio:* 15:1.

Academics *Calendar:* semesters. *Degrees:* certificates, associate, bachelor's, master's, doctoral, post-master's, and postbachelor's certificates. *Special study options:* academic remediation for entering students, accelerated degree program, adult/continuing education programs, advanced placement credit, cooperative education, distance learning, double majors, English as a second language, honors programs, independent study, internships, off-campus study, part-time degree program, services for LD students, student-designed majors, study abroad, summer session for credit. *ROTC:* Army (c), Air Force (c).

Computers on Campus 225 computers/terminals are available on campus for general student use. Students can access the following: computer help desk, free student e-mail accounts, online (class) grades, online (class) registration, online (class) schedules. Campuswide network is available. 100% of college-owned or -operated housing units are wired for high-speed Internet access. Wireless service is available via entire campus.

Student Life *Housing options:* coed, men-only, women-only. Campus housing is university owned. *Activities and organizations:* drama/theater group, student-run newspaper, radio station, choral group, Student Programming Board, Student Government Association, Greek Life, Residence Hall Association, Spectrum (LGBT), national fraternities, national sororities. *Campus security:* 24-hour emergency response devices and patrols, late-night transport/escort service, controlled dormitory access, trained law enforcement personnel on staff. *Student services:* health clinic, personal/psychological counseling, women's center.

Athletics Member NCAA. All Division I. *Intercollegiate sports:* baseball M(s), basketball M(s)/W(s), bowling W(s), cross-country running M(s)/W(s), fencing W(s), golf M(s)/W(s), soccer M(s)/W(s), softball W(s), tennis M(s)/W(s), track and field M(s)/W(s), volleyball W(s). *Intramural sports:* badminton M/W, basketball M/W, football M/W, rugby M(c)/W(c), soccer M/W, table tennis M/W, tennis M/W, volleyball M/W.

Standardized Tests *Required:* SAT or ACT (for admission).

Costs (2012–13) *Comprehensive fee:* $46,198 includes full-time tuition ($32,852), mandatory fees ($940), and room and board ($12,406). Part-time tuition: $1054 per credit hour. *College room only:* $8336. Room and board charges vary according to board plan and housing facility. *Payment plans:* installment, deferred payment. *Waivers:* senior citizens and employees or children of employees.

Financial Aid Of all full-time matriculated undergraduates who enrolled in 2007, 1,671 applied for aid, 1,549 were judged to have need. In 2007, 117 non-need-based awards were made. *Average financial aid package:* $18,283. *Average need-based loan:* $3808. *Average need-based gift aid:* $8702. *Average non-need-based aid:* $6403.

Applying *Options:* electronic application, early admission. *Application fee:* $40. *Required:* high school transcript, 2 letters of recommendation. *Required for some:* interview. *Application deadlines:* rolling (freshmen), rolling (transfers). *Notification:* continuous (freshmen), continuous (transfers).

Freshman Application Contact Fairleigh Dickinson University, Metropolitan Campus, 1000 River Road, Teaneck, NJ 07666-1914. *Toll-free phone:* 800-338-8803.

Website: http://www.fdu.edu/.

Felician College

Lodi, New Jersey

- **Independent Roman Catholic** comprehensive, founded 1942
- **Suburban** 37-acre campus with easy access to New York City
- **Endowment** $4.8 million
- **Coed** 1,775 undergraduate students, 84% full-time, 74% women, 26% men
- **Moderately difficult** entrance level, 90% of applicants were admitted

Undergraduates 1,485 full-time, 290 part-time. Students come from 12 states and territories; 20 other countries; 6% are from out of state; 15% Black or African American, non-Hispanic/Latino; 22% Hispanic/Latino; 7% Asian, non-Hispanic/Latino; 0.4% Native Hawaiian or other Pacific Islander, non-Hispanic/Latino; 0.5% American Indian or Alaska Native, non-Hispanic/Latino; 0.7% Two or more races, non-Hispanic/Latino; 21% Race/ethnicity unknown; 2% international; 5% transferred in; 18% live on campus. *Retention:* 73% of full-time freshmen returned.

Freshmen *Admission:* 2,206 applied, 1,980 admitted, 229 enrolled. *Average high school GPA:* 2.9. *Test scores:* SAT critical reading scores over 500: 15%; SAT math scores over 500: 23%; SAT writing scores over 500: 15%; ACT scores over 18: 52%; SAT critical reading scores over 600: 2%; SAT math scores over 600: 2%; SAT writing scores over 600: 2%; ACT scores over 24: 12%.

Faculty *Total:* 241, 48% full-time. *Student/faculty ratio:* 12:1.

Academics *Calendar:* semesters. *Degrees:* certificates, associate, bachelor's, master's, doctoral, post-master's, and postbachelor's certificates. *Special study options:* academic remediation for entering students, accelerated degree program, adult/continuing education programs, advanced placement credit, cooperative education, distance learning, double majors, English as a second language, honors programs, independent study, internships, off-campus study, part-time degree program, services for LD students, student-designed majors, study abroad, summer session for credit.

Computers on Campus 100 computers/terminals are available on campus for general student use. Students can access the following: computer help desk, free student e-mail accounts, online (class) grades, online (class) registration, online (class) schedules. Campuswide network is available. 100% of college-owned or -operated housing units are wired for high-speed Internet access. Wireless service is available via dorm rooms, learning centers, libraries, student centers.

Student Life *Housing options:* coed, men-only, women-only, disabled students. Campus housing is university owned. Freshman applicants given priority for college housing. *Activities and organizations:* drama/theater group, student-run radio station, choral group, Student Nurses Association, Zeta Alpha Zeta teaching sorority, Campus Activity Board, Students In Free Enterprise (SIFE), Student Government Association. *Campus security:* 24-hour patrols, student patrols, late-night transport/escort service. *Student services:* health clinic, personal/psychological counseling.

Athletics Member NCAA, NAIA. All NCAA Division II. *Intercollegiate sports:* baseball M(s), basketball M(s)/W(s), cross-country running M(s)/W(s), golf M(s), soccer M(s)/W(s), softball W(s), volleyball W(s). *Intramural sports:* soccer M/W, softball W, volleyball M/W, weight lifting M/W.

Standardized Tests *Required:* SAT or ACT (for admission). *Required for some:* ACT (for admission), SAT Subject Tests (for admission).

Costs (2013–14) *Comprehensive fee:* $41,640 includes full-time tuition ($28,360), mandatory fees ($1630), and room and board ($11,650). Full-time tuition and fees vary according to program. Part-time tuition: $935 per credit

hour. Part-time tuition and fees vary according to course load and program. *Room and board:* Room and board charges vary according to housing facility. *Payment plan:* installment. *Waivers:* employees or children of employees.
Financial Aid Of all full-time matriculated undergraduates in 2012, 1,334 applied for aid, 1,275 were judged to have need, 63 had their need fully met. In 2012, 44 non-need-based awards were made. *Average financial aid package:* $23,662. *Average need-based loan:* $4131. *Average need-based gift aid:* $12,202. *Average non-need-based aid:* $11,324. *Average indebtedness upon graduation:* $32,532.
Applying *Options:* deferred entrance. *Application fee:* $30. *Required:* high school transcript, minimum 2.0 GPA. *Required for some:* essay or personal statement, interview. *Application deadlines:* rolling (freshmen), rolling (transfers). *Notification:* continuous (freshmen), continuous (transfers).
Freshman Application Contact College Admissions Office, Felician College, 262 South Main Street, Lodi, NJ 07644-2117. *Phone:* 201-559-6131. *Fax:* 201-559-6138. *E-mail:* admissions@felician.edu. *Website:* http://www.felician.edu/.

Georgian Court University
Lakewood, New Jersey

- **Independent Roman Catholic** comprehensive, founded 1908
- **Suburban** 156-acre campus with easy access to New York City, Philadelphia
- **Coed, primarily women**
- **Moderately difficult** entrance level

Faculty *Student/faculty ratio:* 13:1.
Academics *Calendar:* semesters. *Degrees:* certificates, bachelor's, master's, post-master's, and postbachelor's certificates.
Student Life *Campus security:* 24-hour emergency response devices and patrols, late-night transport/escort service, controlled dormitory access.
Athletics Member NCAA. All Division II.
Standardized Tests *Required:* SAT or ACT (for admission).
Costs (2012–13) *Comprehensive fee:* $39,600 includes full-time tuition ($26,740) and room and board ($12,860). Part-time tuition and fees vary according to location.
Financial Aid *Of all full-time matriculated undergraduates who enrolled in 2011,* 1,295 applied for aid, 1,201 were judged to have need, 334 had their need fully met. *In 2011,* 102 non-need-based awards were made. *Average percent of need met:* 83. *Average financial aid package:* $24,201. *Average need-based loan:* $7936. *Average need-based gift aid:* $14,817. *Average non-need-based aid:* $8996. *Average indebtedness upon graduation:* $33,888. *Financial aid deadline:* 8/1.
Applying *Options:* electronic application, early action, deferred entrance. *Application fee:* $40. *Required:* high school transcript, minimum 2.5 GPA, 2 letters of recommendation. *Recommended:* essay or personal statement, interview.
Freshman Application Contact Ms. Maria Colon, Assistant Director of Undergraduate Admissions, Georgian Court University, 900 Lakewood Avenue. *Phone:* 732-987-2760. *Toll-free phone:* 800-458-8422. *Fax:* 732-987-2000. *E-mail:* admissions@georgian.edu. *Website:* http://www.georgian.edu/.

Kean University
Union, New Jersey

- **State-supported** comprehensive, founded 1855, part of New Jersey State College System
- **Suburban** 186-acre campus with easy access to New York City
- **Endowment** $13.1 million
- **Coed** 12,895 undergraduate students, 77% full-time, 61% women, 39% men
- **Moderately difficult** entrance level, 68% of applicants were admitted

Undergraduates 9,899 full-time, 2,996 part-time. Students come from 21 states and territories; 50 other countries; 2% are from out of state; 17% Black or African American, non-Hispanic/Latino; 22% Hispanic/Latino; 5% Asian, non-Hispanic/Latino; 0.4% Native Hawaiian or other Pacific Islander, non-Hispanic/Latino; 0.1% American Indian or Alaska Native, non-Hispanic/Latino; 1% Two or more races, non-Hispanic/Latino; 15% Race/ethnicity unknown; 1% international; 12% transferred in; 14% live on campus. *Retention:* 72% of full-time freshmen returned.
Freshmen *Admission:* 6,015 applied, 4,114 admitted, 1,410 enrolled. *Average high school GPA:* 3.05. *Test scores:* SAT critical reading scores over 500: 26%;

SAT math scores over 500: 36%; SAT critical reading scores over 600: 3%; SAT math scores over 600: 5%; SAT math scores over 700: 1%.
Faculty *Total:* 1,481, 23% full-time. *Student/faculty ratio:* 17:1.
Academics *Calendar:* semesters. *Degrees:* bachelor's, master's, doctoral, and post-master's certificates. *Special study options:* academic remediation for entering students, accelerated degree program, adult/continuing education programs, advanced placement credit, cooperative education, distance learning, double majors, English as a second language, honors programs, independent study, internships, off-campus study, part-time degree program, services for LD students, study abroad, summer session for credit. *ROTC:* Army (c), Air Force (c). *Unusual degree programs:* 3-2 business administration; engineering; public administration; occupational therapy; science and technology; instruction & curriculum; biology/physician's assistant; health information management or psychology/psychiatric rehabilitation; DPT: UMDNJ; MD: Drexel University; DPM: New York College of Podiatric Medicine.
Computers on Campus 1,700 computers/terminals and 2,000 ports are available on campus for general student use. Students can access the following: free student e-mail accounts, online (class) grades, online (class) registration, online (class) schedules. Campuswide network is available. 100% of college-owned or -operated housing units are wired for high-speed Internet access. Wireless service is available via entire campus.
Student Life *Housing options:* coed, disabled students. Campus housing is university owned. Freshman applicants given priority for college housing. *Activities and organizations:* drama/theater group, student-run newspaper, radio station, choral group, Association for Computing Machinery, Student Occupational Therapy Association, Accounting Club, American Sign Language, Association of Latin American Students, national fraternities, national sororities. *Campus security:* 24-hour emergency response devices and patrols, student patrols, late-night transport/escort service, controlled dormitory access, 24-hour patrols by campus police. *Student services:* health clinic, personal/psychological counseling.
Athletics Member NCAA. All Division III. *Intercollegiate sports:* baseball M, basketball M/W, field hockey W, football M, lacrosse M/W, soccer M/W, softball W, tennis W, volleyball M/W. *Intramural sports:* basketball M/W, soccer M/W, softball M/W, tennis M/W, ultimate Frisbee M/W, volleyball M/W, weight lifting M/W.
Standardized Tests *Required:* SAT or ACT (for admission).
Costs (2012–13) *Tuition:* state resident $6925 full-time, $270 per credit part-time; nonresident $12,967 full-time, $457 per credit part-time. Part-time tuition and fees vary according to course load. *Required fees:* $3676 full-time, $135 per credit part-time. *Room and board:* $13,934; room only: $10,804. Room and board charges vary according to board plan, housing facility, and student level. *Payment plan:* installment. *Waivers:* senior citizens and employees or children of employees.
Financial Aid Of all full-time matriculated undergraduates who enrolled in 2012, 8,061 applied for aid, 6,985 were judged to have need, 558 had their need fully met. 229 Federal Work-Study jobs (averaging $1844). In 2012, 70 non-need-based awards were made. *Average percent of need met:* 82%. *Average financial aid package:* $9623. *Average need-based loan:* $4495. *Average need-based gift aid:* $7267. *Average non-need-based aid:* $3583. *Average indebtedness upon graduation:* $30,335.
Applying *Options:* electronic application. *Application fee:* $75. *Required:* essay or personal statement, high school transcript, minimum 2.8 GPA, 2 letters of recommendation, SAT or ACT. *Required for some:* interview. *Application deadlines:* 5/31 (freshmen), 7/6 (transfers). *Notification:* continuous (freshmen), continuous (transfers).
Freshman Application Contact Ms. Valerie Winslow, Director of Undergraduate Admissions, Kean University, 1000 Morris Avenue, Union, NJ 07083. *Phone:* 908-737-7100. *Fax:* 908-737-7105. *E-mail:* admitme@kean.edu. *Website:* http://www.kean.edu/.

Monmouth University
West Long Branch, New Jersey

- **Independent** comprehensive, founded 1933
- **Suburban** 156-acre campus with easy access to New York City, Philadelphia
- **Endowment** $61.6 million
- **Coed** 4,738 undergraduate students, 94% full-time, 59% women, 41% men
- **Moderately difficult** entrance level, 71% of applicants were admitted

Undergraduates 4,437 full-time, 301 part-time. Students come from 29 states and territories; 23 other countries; 12% are from out of state; 4% Black or African American, non-Hispanic/Latino; 9% Hispanic/Latino; 2% Asian, non-Hispanic/Latino; 0.1% Native Hawaiian or other Pacific Islander, non-Hispanic/

Latino; 0.1% American Indian or Alaska Native, non-Hispanic/Latino; 2% Two or more races, non-Hispanic/Latino; 4% Race/ethnicity unknown; 0.7% international; 7% transferred in; 46% live on campus. *Retention:* 79% of full-time freshmen returned.

Freshmen *Admission:* 6,127 applied, 4,358 admitted, 1,006 enrolled. *Average high school GPA:* 3.38. *Test scores:* SAT critical reading scores over 500: 61%; SAT math scores over 500: 73%; SAT writing scores over 500: 71%; ACT scores over 18: 100%; SAT critical reading scores over 600: 13%; SAT math scores over 600: 20%; SAT writing scores over 600: 17%; ACT scores over 24: 50%; SAT critical reading scores over 700: 1%; SAT math scores over 700: 1%; SAT writing scores over 700: 1%; ACT scores over 30: 2%.

Faculty *Total:* 597, 45% full-time, 51% with terminal degrees. *Student/faculty ratio:* 15:1.

Academics *Calendar:* semesters. *Degrees:* certificates, associate, bachelor's, master's, doctoral, post-master's, and postbachelor's certificates. *Special study options:* academic remediation for entering students, accelerated degree program, advanced placement credit, cooperative education, distance learning, double majors, honors programs, independent study, internships, part-time degree program, services for LD students, student-designed majors, study abroad, summer session for credit. *ROTC:* Army (c), Air Force (c).

Computers on Campus 423 computers/terminals are available on campus for general student use. Students can access the following: computer help desk, free student e-mail accounts, online (class) grades, online (class) registration, online (class) schedules. Campuswide network is available. 85% of college-owned or -operated housing units are wired for high-speed Internet access. Wireless service is available via classrooms, computer centers, computer labs, dorm rooms, learning centers, libraries, student centers.

Student Life *Housing options:* coed. Campus housing is university owned and leased by the school. Freshman campus housing is guaranteed. *Activities and organizations:* drama/theater group, student-run newspaper, radio and television station, choral group, radio station WMCX 88.9 FM, Student Government Association, student newspaper (Outlook), Student Activities Board, Shadows (yearbook), national fraternities, national sororities. *Campus security:* 24-hour emergency response devices and patrols, late-night transport/escort service, controlled dormitory access. *Student services:* health clinic, personal/psychological counseling, women's center, legal services.

Athletics Member NCAA. All Division I except football (Division I-AA). *Intercollegiate sports:* baseball M(s), basketball M(s)/W(s), bowling M(c)/W(s), cross-country running M(s)/W(s), field hockey W(s), golf M(s)/W(s), ice hockey M(c), lacrosse M(s)/W(s), sailing M(c)/W(c), soccer M(s)/W(s), softball W(s), tennis M(s)/W(s), track and field M(s)/W(s). *Intramural sports:* badminton M/W, basketball M/W, cheerleading M(c)/W(c), field hockey W(c), football W, soccer M/W, softball M/W, volleyball M/W.

Standardized Tests *Required:* SAT or ACT (for admission).

Costs (2012–13) *One-time required fee:* $200. *Comprehensive fee:* $40,512 includes full-time tuition ($29,082), mandatory fees ($628), and room and board ($10,802). Part-time tuition: $842 per credit hour. Part-time tuition and fees vary according to course load. *Required fees:* $157 per term part-time. *College room only:* $6169. Room and board charges vary according to board plan and housing facility. *Payment plan:* installment. *Waivers:* senior citizens and employees or children of employees.

Financial Aid Of all full-time matriculated undergraduates who enrolled in 2012, 3,616 applied for aid, 3,096 were judged to have need, 509 had their need fully met. 955 Federal Work-Study jobs (averaging $1968). In 2012, 1199 non-need-based awards were made. *Average percent of need met:* 66%. *Average financial aid package:* $21,477. *Average need-based loan:* $4940. *Average need-based gift aid:* $12,554. *Average non-need-based aid:* $7678. *Average indebtedness upon graduation:* $34,810.

Applying *Options:* electronic application, early action, deferred entrance. *Application fee:* $50. *Required:* essay or personal statement, high school transcript, 1 letter of recommendation. *Required for some:* essay or personal statement, interview. *Recommended:* resume of activities including community involvement and leadership positions. *Application deadlines:* 3/1 (freshmen), 7/15 (transfers), 12/1 (early action). *Notification:* 4/1 (freshmen), continuous (transfers), 1/15 (early action).

Freshman Application Contact Ms. Victoria Bobik, Director of Undergraduate Admission, Monmouth University, 400 Cedar Avenue, West Long Branch, NJ 07764-1898. *Phone:* 732-571-3456. *Toll-free phone:* 800-543-9671. *Fax:* 732-263-5166. *E-mail:* admission@monmouth.edu. *Website:* http://www.monmouth.edu/.

See this page for display ad and page 1400 for the College Close-Up.

Montclair State University

Montclair, New Jersey

- **State-supported** comprehensive, founded 1908
- **Suburban** 275-acre campus with easy access to New York City
- **Endowment** $53.2 million
- **Coed** 14,432 undergraduate students, 86% full-time, 61% women, 39% men
- **Moderately difficult** entrance level, 55% of applicants were admitted

Undergraduates 12,380 full-time, 2,052 part-time. Students come from 33 states and territories; 70 other countries; 3% are from out of state; 9% Black or African American, non-Hispanic/Latino; 22% Hispanic/Latino; 5% Asian, non-Hispanic/Latino; 0.1% Native Hawaiian or other Pacific Islander, non-Hispanic/Latino; 0.1% American Indian or Alaska Native, non-Hispanic/Latino; 3% Two or more races, non-Hispanic/Latino; 9% Race/ethnicity unknown; 2% international; 10% transferred in; 26% live on campus. *Retention:* 82% of full-time freshmen returned.

Freshmen *Admission:* 12,319 applied, 6,716 admitted, 2,213 enrolled. *Average high school GPA:* 3.24. *Test scores:* SAT critical reading scores over 500: 42%; SAT math scores over 500: 52%; SAT writing scores over 500: 48%; SAT critical reading scores over 600: 8%; SAT math scores over 600: 10%; SAT writing scores over 600: 9%; SAT critical reading scores over 700: 1%; SAT math scores over 700: 1%; SAT writing scores over 700: 1%.

Faculty *Total:* 1,589, 36% full-time, 36% with terminal degrees. *Student/faculty ratio:* 17:1.

Academics *Calendar:* semesters. *Degrees:* bachelor's, master's, doctoral, and postbachelor's certificates. *Special study options:* academic remediation for entering students, accelerated degree program, adult/continuing education programs, advanced placement credit, cooperative education, double majors, English as a second language, freshman honors college, honors programs, independent study, internships, off-campus study, part-time degree program, services for LD students, study abroad, summer session for credit. *ROTC:* Army (b), Navy (b), Air Force (b). *Unusual degree programs:* BA/MAT, BMus/MAT, BS/MS Aquatic & Coastal Science, Chemistry, Mathematics, Statistics.

Computers on Campus 300 computers/terminals are available on campus for general student use. Students can access the following: campus intranet, computer help desk, free student e-mail accounts, online (class) grades, online (class) registration, online (class) schedules. Campuswide network is available. 60% of college-owned or -operated housing units are wired for high-speed Internet access. Wireless service is available via entire campus.

Student Life *Housing options:* coed, women-only. Campus housing is university owned and is provided by a third party. Freshman campus housing is guaranteed. *Activities and organizations:* drama/theater group, student-run newspaper, radio station, choral group, Latin American Student Organization, Campus Recreation, MSU Gamers, Unified Asian American Student Organization, Human Relations and Leadership Association, national fraternities, national sororities. *Campus security:* 24-hour emergency response devices and patrols, late-night transport/escort service, controlled dormitory access, video surveillance, student escorts. *Student services:* health clinic, personal/psychological counseling, women's center.

Athletics Member NCAA. All Division III. *Intercollegiate sports:* baseball M, basketball M/W, field hockey W, football M, lacrosse M/W, soccer M/W, softball W, swimming and diving M/W, track and field W, volleyball W. *Intramural sports:* badminton M(c)/W(c), baseball M, basketball M/W, bowling M/W, football M, golf M/W, ice hockey M(c), racquetball M/W, rugby M(c)/W(c), soccer M/W, softball M/W, swimming and diving M(c)/W(c), tennis M/W, volleyball M/W, water polo M/W, wrestling M(c)/W(c).

Standardized Tests *Required:* SAT or ACT (for admission).

Costs (2012–13) *Tuition:* state resident $7982 full-time, $266 per credit part-time; nonresident $17,060 full-time, $569 per credit part-time. *Required fees:* $3076 full-time, $103 per credit part-time. *Room and board:* $13,443; room only: $9543. Room and board charges vary according to board plan, housing facility, and student level. *Payment plan:* installment. *Waivers:* senior citizens and employees or children of employees.

Financial Aid Of all full-time matriculated undergraduates who enrolled in 2011, 9,977 applied for aid, 8,597 were judged to have need, 812 had their need fully met. 399 Federal Work-Study jobs (averaging $1029). In 2011, 192 non-need-based awards were made. *Average percent of need met:* 72%. *Average financial aid package:* $9202. *Average need-based loan:* $4534. *Average need-based gift aid:* $8271. *Average non-need-based aid:* $12,179. *Average indebtedness upon graduation:* $28,070.

Applying *Options:* electronic application, deferred entrance. *Application fee:* $65. *Required:* essay or personal statement, high school transcript. *Required for some:* interview. *Application deadlines:* 3/1 (freshmen), 6/15 (transfers). *Notification:* continuous (freshmen), continuous (transfers).

Freshman Application Contact Lisa Kasper, Director of Admissions, Montclair State University, One Normal Avenue, Montclair, NJ 07043-1624. *Phone:* 973-655-6911. *Fax:* 973-655-7700.
E-mail: undergraduate.admissions@montclair.edu.
Website: http://www.montclair.edu/.

New Jersey City University

Jersey City, New Jersey

- **State-supported** comprehensive, founded 1927
- **Urban** 51-acre campus with easy access to New York City
- **Endowment** $3.3 million
- **Coed** 6,587 undergraduate students, 73% full-time, 60% women, 40% men
- **Moderately difficult** entrance level, 44% of applicants were admitted

Undergraduates 4,834 full-time, 1,753 part-time. Students come from 13 states and territories; 23 other countries; 1% are from out of state; 20% Black or African American, non-Hispanic/Latino; 35% Hispanic/Latino; 8% Asian, non-Hispanic/Latino; 0.2% American Indian or Alaska Native, non-Hispanic/Latino; 1% Two or more races, non-Hispanic/Latino; 9% Race/ethnicity unknown; 0.8% international; 15% transferred in; 4% live on campus. *Retention:* 64% of full-time freshmen returned.

Freshmen *Admission:* 4,971 applied, 2,171 admitted, 797 enrolled. *Average high school GPA:* 3.2. *Test scores:* SAT critical reading scores over 500: 14%; SAT math scores over 500: 79%; SAT critical reading scores over 600: 2%; SAT math scores over 600: 26%; SAT math scores over 700: 1%.

Faculty *Total:* 752, 32% full-time, 29% with terminal degrees. *Student/faculty ratio:* 16:1.

Academics *Calendar:* semesters. *Degrees:* certificates, bachelor's, master's, post-master's, and postbachelor's certificates. *Special study options:* academic remediation for entering students, accelerated degree program, adult/continuing education programs, advanced placement credit, cooperative education, distance learning, double majors, English as a second language, honors programs, independent study, internships, off-campus study, part-time degree program, services for LD students, study abroad, summer session for credit.

Computers on Campus 704 computers/terminals are available on campus for general student use. Students can access the following: free student e-mail accounts, online (class) grades, online (class) registration, online (class) schedules. Campuswide network is available. Wireless service is available via learning centers, student centers.

Student Life *Housing options:* coed. Campus housing is university owned. *Activities and organizations:* drama/theater group, student-run newspaper, radio station, choral group, International Student Association, Black Freedom Society, Latin Power Association, national fraternities. *Campus security:* 24-hour emergency response devices and patrols, late-night transport/escort service. *Student services:* health clinic, personal/psychological counseling, women's center, legal services.

Athletics Member NCAA. All Division III. *Intercollegiate sports:* baseball M, basketball M/W, bowling W, cross-country running W, golf M, soccer M/W, softball W, track and field M/W, volleyball M/W. *Intramural sports:* baseball M, basketball M/W, bowling W, cross-country running W, golf M, soccer M/W, softball W, track and field M/W, volleyball M/W.

Standardized Tests *Required:* SAT (for admission).

Costs (2013–14) *Tuition:* state resident $245 per credit hour part-time; nonresident $518 per credit hour part-time. Full-time tuition and fees vary according to program. Part-time tuition and fees vary according to course load. *Payment plan:* deferred payment. *Waivers:* senior citizens and employees or children of employees.

Financial Aid Of all full-time matriculated undergraduates who enrolled in 2011, 4,407 applied for aid, 4,218 were judged to have need, 237 had their need fully met. In 2011, 54 non-need-based awards were made. *Average percent of need met:* 59%. *Average financial aid package:* $20,515. *Average need-based loan:* $12,190. *Average need-based gift aid:* $7603. *Average non-need-based aid:* $6398. *Average indebtedness upon graduation:* $19,233.

Applying *Options:* electronic application, early admission, deferred entrance. *Application fee:* $50. *Required:* essay or personal statement, high school transcript, minimum 2.0 GPA. *Required for some:* interview. *Recommended:* 1 letter of recommendation. *Application deadlines:* 4/1 (freshmen), rolling (transfers). *Notification:* continuous (freshmen).

Freshman Application Contact Mr. Jose Balda, Director of Admissions, New Jersey City University, 2039 Kennedy Boulevard, Jersey City, NJ 07305. *Phone:* 201-200-3234. *Toll-free phone:* 888-441-NJCU. *E-mail:* admissions@njcu.edu.
Website: http://www.njcu.edu/.

New Jersey Institute of Technology

Newark, New Jersey

- **State-supported** university, founded 1881
- **Urban** 48-acre campus with easy access to New York City
- **Endowment** $67.5 million
- **Coed** 7,111 undergraduate students, 78% full-time, 24% women, 76% men
- **Moderately difficult** entrance level, 64% of applicants were admitted

Undergraduates 5,529 full-time, 1,582 part-time. Students come from 23 states and territories; 86 other countries; 9% are from out of state; 9% Black or African American, non-Hispanic/Latino; 15% Hispanic/Latino; 21% Asian, non-Hispanic/Latino; 0.1% Native Hawaiian or other Pacific Islander, non-Hispanic/Latino; 0.1% American Indian or Alaska Native, non-Hispanic/Latino; 9% Two or more races, non-Hispanic/Latino; 5% Race/ethnicity unknown; 5% international; 9% transferred in; 26% live on campus. *Retention:* 82% of full-time freshmen returned.

Freshmen *Admission:* 4,216 applied, 2,684 admitted, 1,020 enrolled. *Test scores:* SAT critical reading scores over 500: 66%; SAT math scores over 500: 96%; SAT writing scores over 500: 63%; SAT critical reading scores over 600: 26%; SAT math scores over 600: 53%; SAT writing scores over 600: 22%; SAT critical reading scores over 700: 5%; SAT math scores over 700: 13%; SAT writing scores over 700: 4%.

Faculty *Total:* 691, 60% full-time, 60% with terminal degrees. *Student/faculty ratio:* 16:1.

Academics *Calendar:* semesters. *Degrees:* bachelor's, master's, doctoral, and postbachelor's certificates. *Special study options:* academic remediation for entering students, accelerated degree program, adult/continuing education programs, advanced placement credit, cooperative education, distance learning, double majors, English as a second language, freshman honors college, honors programs, independent study, internships, off-campus study, part-time degree program, services for LD students, study abroad, summer session for credit. *ROTC:* Army (c), Air Force (b). *Unusual degree programs:* 3-2 business administration; engineering.

Computers on Campus 1,938 computers/terminals are available on campus for general student use. Students can access the following: campus intranet, computer help desk, free student e-mail accounts, online (class) grades, online (class) registration, online (class) schedules. Campuswide network is available. 100% of college-owned or -operated housing units are wired for high-speed Internet access. Wireless service is available via entire campus.

Student Life *Housing options:* coed. Campus housing is university owned. *Activities and organizations:* drama/theater group, student-run newspaper, radio station, marching band, Student Senate, Student Activities Council, Vector, Institute of Industrial Engineers, WJTB Geek Radio, national fraternities, national sororities. *Campus security:* 24-hour emergency response devices and patrols, late-night transport/escort service, controlled dormitory access, bicycle patrols. *Student services:* health clinic, personal/psychological counseling, women's center.

Athletics Member NCAA. All Division I. *Intercollegiate sports:* baseball M(s), basketball M(s)/W(s), bowling M(c), cross-country running M(s)/W(s), fencing M(s)/W(s), ice hockey M(c), soccer M(s)/W(s), swimming and diving M(s)/W(s), tennis M(s)/W(s), track and field M/W, volleyball M(s)/W(s). *Intramural sports:* basketball M/W, bowling M/W, cheerleading M/W, ice hockey M, racquetball M/W, soccer M/W, softball M, swimming and diving M/W, tennis M/W, track and field M/W, ultimate Frisbee M/W, volleyball M/W, water polo M/W.

Standardized Tests *Required:* SAT or ACT (for admission).

Costs (2012–13) *Tuition:* state resident $12,400 full-time, $472 per credit part-time; nonresident $24,800 full-time, $1060 per credit part-time. Full-time tuition and fees vary according to course load and degree level. Part-time tuition and fees vary according to course load and degree level. *Required fees:* $2340 full-time, $116 per credit part-time. *Room and board:* $11,750. Room and board charges vary according to board plan and housing facility. *Payment plans:* installment, deferred payment. *Waivers:* employees or children of employees.

Financial Aid Of all full-time matriculated undergraduates who enrolled in 2011, 4,045 applied for aid, 3,691 were judged to have need, 133 had their need fully met. 264 Federal Work-Study jobs (averaging $1205). 704 state and other part-time jobs (averaging $2043). In 2011, 549 non-need-based awards were made. *Average percent of need met:* 50%. *Average financial aid package:* $12,201. *Average need-based loan:* $4344. *Average need-based gift aid:* $10,748. *Average non-need-based aid:* $12,252. *Average indebtedness upon graduation:* $34,867.

Applying *Options:* electronic application, early admission, deferred entrance. *Application fee:* $70. *Required:* high school transcript. *Required for some:* essay or personal statement, interview. *Recommended:* 1 letter of recommendation, Standardized test scores recommended for some. *Application dead-*

lines: 3/1 (freshmen), 6/1 (transfers). *Notification:* continuous (freshmen), continuous (transfers).
Freshman Application Contact Mr. Stephen M. Eck, Director of University Admissions, New Jersey Institute of Technology, University Heights, Newark, NJ 07102. *Phone:* 973-596-3306. *Toll-free phone:* 800-925-NJIT. *Fax:* 973-596-3461. *E-mail:* admissions@njit.edu.
Website: http://www.njit.edu/.

Pillar College
Zarephath, New Jersey

Freshman Application Contact Ms. Linda Aarni, Senior Admissions Counselor, Pillar College, 10 College Way, PO Box 9035, Zarephath, NJ 08890-9035. *Phone:* 732-356-1595. *Toll-free phone:* 800-234-9305. *Fax:* 732-356-4846. *E-mail:* info@pillar.edu.
Website: http://www.pillar.edu.

See previous page for display ad and page 1438 for the College Close-Up.

Princeton University
Princeton, New Jersey

- **Independent** university, founded 1746
- **Suburban** 600-acre campus with easy access to New York City, Philadelphia
- **Endowment** $17.0 billion
- **Coed** 5,336 undergraduate students, 99% full-time, 49% women, 51% men
- **Most difficult** entrance level, 8% of applicants were admitted

Undergraduates 5,264 full-time, 72 part-time. Students come from 52 states and territories; 91 other countries; 83% are from out of state; 7% Black or African American, non-Hispanic/Latino; 7% Hispanic/Latino; 19% Asian, non-Hispanic/Latino; 0.1% Native Hawaiian or other Pacific Islander, non-Hispanic/Latino; 0.2% American Indian or Alaska Native, non-Hispanic/Latino; 4% Two or more races, non-Hispanic/Latino; 2% Race/ethnicity unknown; 11% international; 97% live on campus. *Retention:* 98% of full-time freshmen returned.
Freshmen *Admission:* 26,664 applied, 2,094 admitted, 1,357 enrolled. *Average high school GPA:* 3.87. *Test scores:* SAT critical reading scores over 500: 100%; SAT math scores over 500: 100%; SAT writing scores over 500: 100%; ACT scores over 18: 100%; SAT critical reading scores over 600: 97%; SAT math scores over 600: 99%; SAT writing scores over 600: 98%; ACT scores over 24: 100%; SAT critical reading scores over 700: 76%; SAT math scores over 700: 81%; SAT writing scores over 700: 81%; ACT scores over 30: 84%.
Faculty *Total:* 1,098, 79% full-time, 88% with terminal degrees. *Student/faculty ratio:* 6:1.
Academics *Calendar:* semesters. *Degrees:* bachelor's, master's, and doctoral. *Special study options:* adult/continuing education programs, advanced placement credit, independent study, off-campus study, services for LD students, student-designed majors, study abroad. *ROTC:* Army (b), Navy (c), .
Computers on Campus 500 computers/terminals and 17,000 ports are available on campus for general student use. Students can access the following: campus intranet, computer help desk, free student e-mail accounts, online (class) grades, online (class) registration, online (class) schedules, academic applications and courseware, printing, network file space, Web site hosting, media lab, broadcast center. Campuswide network is available. 100% of college-owned or -operated housing units are wired for high-speed Internet access. Wireless service is available via entire campus.
Student Life *Housing:* on-campus residence required through sophomore year. *Options:* coed, men-only, women-only, disabled students. Campus housing is university owned. Freshman campus housing is guaranteed. *Activities and organizations:* drama/theater group, student-run newspaper, radio station, choral group, marching band. *Campus security:* 24-hour emergency response devices and patrols, student patrols, late-night transport/escort service, controlled dormitory access. *Student services:* health clinic, personal/psychological counseling, women's center, legal services.
Athletics Member NCAA. All Division I except football (Division I-AA). *Intercollegiate sports:* baseball M, basketball M/W, crew M/W, cross-country running M/W, fencing M/W, field hockey W, golf M/W, ice hockey M/W, lacrosse M/W, soccer M/W, softball W, squash M/W, swimming and diving M/W, tennis M/W, track and field M/W, volleyball M/W, water polo M/W, wrestling M. *Intramural sports:* badminton M(c)/W(c), baseball M(c), basketball M(c)/W(c), cheerleading M(c)/W(c), cross-country running M(c)/W(c), equestrian sports M(c)/W(c), fencing M(c)/W(c), field hockey W(c), ice hockey M(c)/W(c), lacrosse M(c)/W(c), rugby M(c)/W(c), sailing M(c)/W(c), skiing

(downhill) M(c)/W(c), soccer M(c)/W(c), softball W(c), squash M(c)/W(c), swimming and diving M(c)/W(c), table tennis M(c)/W(c), tennis M(c)/W(c), ultimate Frisbee M(c)/W(c), volleyball M(c)/W(c).
Standardized Tests *Required:* SAT or ACT (for admission).
Costs (2013–14) *Comprehensive fee:* $53,795 includes full-time tuition ($40,170), mandatory fees ($545), and room and board ($13,080). *College room only:* $7220. Room and board charges vary according to board plan. *Payment plans:* installment, deferred payment. *Waivers:* employees or children of employees.
Financial Aid Of all full-time matriculated undergraduates who enrolled in 2011, 3,334 applied for aid, 3,072 were judged to have need, 3,072 had their need fully met. 696 Federal Work-Study jobs (averaging $884). 1,559 state and other part-time jobs (averaging $1286). *Average percent of need met:* 100%. *Average financial aid package:* $36,989. *Average need-based gift aid:* $35,664. *Average indebtedness upon graduation:* $5096.
Applying *Options:* electronic application, early action, deferred entrance. *Application fee:* $65. *Required:* essay or personal statement, high school transcript, 3 letters of recommendation. *Recommended:* interview. *Application deadlines:* 1/1 (freshmen), 11/1 (early action). *Notification:* 3/31 (freshmen).
Freshman Application Contact Ms. Janet Rapelye, Dean of Admission, Princeton University, PO Box 430, Princeton, NJ 08542-0430. *Phone:* 609-258-3060. *Fax:* 609-258-6743. *E-mail:* uaoffice@princeton.edu.
Website: http://www.princeton.edu/.

Rabbi Jacob Joseph School
Edison, New Jersey

Admissions Office Contact Rabbi Jacob Joseph School, One Plainfield Ave, Edison, NJ 08817.

Rabbinical College of America
Morristown, New Jersey

Director of Admissions Sharon Miller, Registrar, Rabbinical College of America, 226 Sussex Avenue, PO Box 1996, Morristown, NJ 07962-1996. *Phone:* 973-267-9404. *E-mail:* rca079@aol.com.
Website: http://www.rca.edu/.

Ramapo College of New Jersey
Mahwah, New Jersey

- **State-supported** comprehensive, founded 1969, part of New Jersey State College System
- **Suburban** 300-acre campus with easy access to New York City
- **Coed** 5,624 undergraduate students, 90% full-time, 58% women, 42% men
- **Moderately difficult** entrance level, 47% of applicants were admitted

Undergraduates 5,052 full-time, 572 part-time. 5% are from out of state; 4% Black or African American, non-Hispanic/Latino; 12% Hispanic/Latino; 5% Asian, non-Hispanic/Latino; 0.4% Native Hawaiian or other Pacific Islander, non-Hispanic/Latino; 0.2% American Indian or Alaska Native, non-Hispanic/Latino; 1% Two or more races, non-Hispanic/Latino; 6% Race/ethnicity unknown; 1% international; 11% transferred in; 51% live on campus. *Retention:* 88% of full-time freshmen returned.
Freshmen *Admission:* 6,299 applied, 2,933 admitted, 871 enrolled. *Average high school GPA:* 3.27. *Test scores:* SAT critical reading scores over 500: 73%; SAT math scores over 500: 80%; SAT writing scores over 500: 75%; SAT critical reading scores over 600: 28%; SAT math scores over 600: 36%; SAT writing scores over 600: 28%; SAT critical reading scores over 700: 4%; SAT math scores over 700: 6%; SAT writing scores over 700: 4%.
Faculty *Total:* 503, 43% full-time. *Student/faculty ratio:* 17:1.
Academics *Calendar:* semesters. *Degrees:* certificates, bachelor's, master's, post-master's, and postbachelor's certificates. *Special study options:* academic remediation for entering students, accelerated degree program, adult/continuing education programs, advanced placement credit, cooperative education, distance learning, double majors, external degree program, freshman honors college, honors programs, independent study, internships, off-campus study, part-time degree program, services for LD students, student-designed majors, study abroad, summer session for credit. *ROTC:* Air Force (c). *Unusual degree programs:* 3-2 biology, and chemistry with Rutgers, The State University of New Jersey; NY University College of Dentistry; SUNY State College of Optometry. RCNJ confers BSN & MSN degrees here on campus (with clinical

internships at Valley Hospital, Englewood Hospital & Medical Center, and other state hospitals).

Computers on Campus Students can access the following: campus intranet, computer help desk, free student e-mail accounts, online (class) grades, online (class) registration, online (class) schedules. Campuswide network is available. 100% of college-owned or -operated housing units are wired for high-speed Internet access. Wireless service is available via classrooms, computer centers, computer labs, learning centers, libraries, student centers.

Student Life *Housing options:* coed, disabled students. Campus housing is university owned. Freshman campus housing is guaranteed. *Activities and organizations:* drama/theater group, student-run newspaper, radio and television station, choral group, NORML, 1 Step, Biology & BioChemistry Club, Campus Crusade for Christ, Culture Club, national fraternities, national sororities. *Campus security:* 24-hour emergency response devices and patrols, late-night transport/escort service, controlled dormitory access, surveillance cameras, patrols by trained security personnel. *Student services:* health clinic, personal/psychological counseling, women's center.

Athletics Member NCAA. All Division III. *Intercollegiate sports:* baseball M, basketball M/W, cross-country running M/W, field hockey W, lacrosse W, soccer M/W, softball W, swimming and diving M/W, tennis M/W, track and field M/W, volleyball M/W. *Intramural sports:* basketball M/W, bowling M/W, football M/W, rock climbing M/W, soccer M/W, softball M/W, table tennis M/W, ultimate Frisbee M/W, volleyball M/W.

Standardized Tests *Required:* SAT (for admission).

Costs (2013–14) *Tuition:* state resident $8480 full-time, $265 per credit hour part-time; nonresident $16,960 full-time, $530 per credit hour part-time. *Required fees:* $4664 full-time. *Room and board:* $11,370; room only: $1940.

Financial Aid Of all full-time matriculated undergraduates who enrolled in 2012, 3,899 applied for aid, 2,991 were judged to have need, 423 had their need fully met. 109 Federal Work-Study jobs (averaging $1976). 748 state and other part-time jobs (averaging $2008). In 2012, 345 non-need-based awards were made. *Average percent of need met:* 59%. *Average financial aid package:* $10,999. *Average need-based loan:* $4397. *Average need-based gift aid:* $8902. *Average non-need-based aid:* $10,272. *Average indebtedness upon graduation:* $30,053.

Applying *Options:* electronic application, early admission, early action, deferred entrance. *Application fee:* $60. *Required:* essay or personal statement, high school transcript. *Recommended:* minimum 3.0 GPA. *Application deadlines:* 3/1 (freshmen), 5/1 (transfers). *Notification:* continuous until 3/15 (freshmen), continuous until 7/1 (transfers).

Freshman Application Contact Michael DiBartolomeo, Associate Director for Freshmen Admissions, Ramapo College of New Jersey, Office of Admissions, 505 Ramapo Valley Road, Mahwah, NJ 07430-1680. *Phone:* 201-684-7300. *Toll-free phone:* 800-9RAMAPO. *Fax:* 201-684-7964. *E-mail:* admissions@ramapo.edu. *Website:* http://www.ramapo.edu/.

The Richard Stockton College of New Jersey

Galloway, New Jersey

- **State-supported** comprehensive, founded 1969, part of New Jersey State College System
- **Suburban** 2000-acre campus with easy access to Philadelphia
- **Endowment** $21.0 million
- **Coed** 7,516 undergraduate students, 91% full-time, 58% women, 42% men
- **Very difficult** entrance level, 57% of applicants were admitted

Undergraduates 6,820 full-time, 696 part-time. Students come from 13 states and territories; 6 other countries; 1% are from out of state; 7% Black or African American, non-Hispanic/Latino; 9% Hispanic/Latino; 5% Asian, non-Hispanic/Latino; 0.2% Native Hawaiian or other Pacific Islander, non-Hispanic/Latino; 0.2% American Indian or Alaska Native, non-Hispanic/Latino; 3% Two or more races, non-Hispanic/Latino; 0.9% Race/ethnicity unknown; 0.2% international; 14% transferred in; 35% live on campus. *Retention:* 84% of full-time freshmen returned.

Freshmen *Admission:* 6,195 applied, 3,551 admitted, 1,003 enrolled. *Test scores:* SAT critical reading scores over 500: 64%; SAT math scores over 500: 79%; SAT writing scores over 500: 63%; ACT scores over 18: 92%; SAT critical reading scores over 600: 17%; SAT math scores over 600: 27%; SAT writing scores over 600: 17%; ACT scores over 24: 5%; SAT critical reading scores over 700: 2%; SAT math scores over 700: 2%; SAT writing scores over 700: 2%.

Faculty *Total:* 626, 45% full-time, 64% with terminal degrees. *Student/faculty ratio:* 18:1.

Academics *Calendar:* semesters. *Degrees:* bachelor's, master's, doctoral, and postbachelor's certificates. *Special study options:* academic remediation for

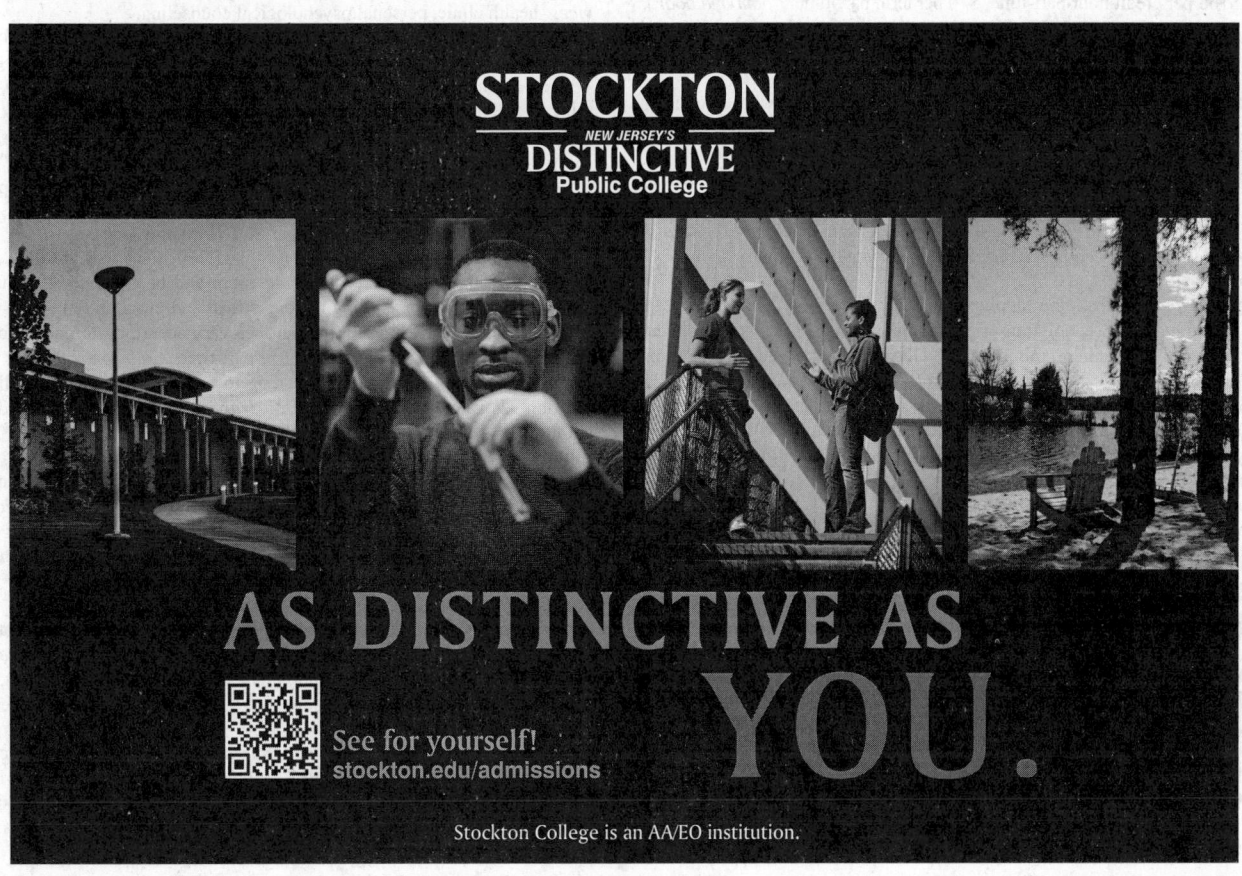

entering students, accelerated degree program, adult/continuing education programs, advanced placement credit, distance learning, honors programs, independent study, internships, off-campus study, part-time degree program, services for LD students, student-designed majors, study abroad, summer session for credit. *ROTC:* Army (c). *Unusual degree programs:* 3-2 business administration; engineering with New Jersey Institute of Technology; Rutgers, The State University of New Jersey; criminal justice/public health with University of Medicine and Dentistry of NJ; medical technology with University of Delaware.

Computers on Campus 930 computers/terminals and 2,400 ports are available on campus for general student use. Students can access the following: campus intranet, computer help desk, free student e-mail accounts, online (class) grades, online (class) registration, online (class) schedules. Campuswide network is available. 100% of college-owned or -operated housing units are wired for high-speed Internet access. Wireless service is available via entire campus.

Student Life *Housing options:* coed, disabled students. Campus housing is university owned. Freshman campus housing is guaranteed. *Activities and organizations:* drama/theater group, student-run newspaper, radio and television station, choral group, Multi-Cultural Connection, Stockton Entertainment Team, Los Latinos Unidos, Unified Black Student Society, Stockton Action Volunteers for the Environment, national fraternities, national sororities. *Campus security:* 24-hour emergency response devices and patrols, late-night transport/escort service, controlled dormitory access, on-campus sworn/commissioned police force. *Student services:* health clinic, personal/psychological counseling, women's center.

Athletics Member NCAA. All Division III. *Intercollegiate sports:* baseball M, basketball M/W, cheerleading M/W, crew W, cross-country running M/W, field hockey W, lacrosse M, soccer M/W, softball W, tennis M, track and field M/W, volleyball W. *Intramural sports:* basketball M/W, bowling M(c)/W(c), crew M(c), fencing M(c)/W(c), golf M(c)/W(c), ice hockey M(c), lacrosse W, soccer M/W, softball M/W, table tennis M/W, ultimate Frisbee M(c)/W(c), volleyball M(c)/W(c).

Standardized Tests *Required:* SAT or ACT (for admission).

Costs (2012–13) *Tuition:* state resident $7948 full-time, $306 per credit hour part-time; nonresident $14,341 full-time, $552 per credit hour part-time. Part-time tuition and fees vary according to course load. *Required fees:* $4374 full-time, $168 per credit hour part-time, $70 per term part-time. *Room and board:* $10,796; room only: $7381. Room and board charges vary according to board plan and housing facility. *Payment plans:* installment, deferred payment. *Waivers:* senior citizens and employees or children of employees.

Financial Aid Of all full-time matriculated undergraduates who enrolled in 2012, 5,806 applied for aid, 5,075 were judged to have need, 1,208 had their need fully met. 158 Federal Work-Study jobs (averaging $1664). 699 state and other part-time jobs (averaging $1677). In 2012, 350 non-need-based awards were made. *Average percent of need met:* 64%. *Average financial aid package:* $15,774. *Average need-based loan:* $4586. *Average need-based gift aid:* $8034. *Average non-need-based aid:* $6716. *Average indebtedness upon graduation:* $34,287.

Applying *Options:* electronic application, early admission. *Application fee:* $50. *Required:* high school transcript, minimum 2.0 GPA. *Recommended:* essay or personal statement, minimum 3.0 GPA, 3 letters of recommendation. *Application deadlines:* 5/1 (freshmen), 6/1 (transfers). *Notification:* 5/15 (freshmen), continuous until 6/15 (transfers).

Freshman Application Contact The Richard Stockton College of New Jersey, 101 Vera King Farris Drive, Galloway, NJ 08205-9441. *Phone:* 609-652-4261.
Website: http://www.stockton.edu/.

See previous page for display ad and page 1450 for the College Close-Up.

Rider University

Lawrenceville, New Jersey

- **Independent** comprehensive, founded 1865
- **Suburban** 280-acre campus with easy access to New York City, Philadelphia
- **Endowment** $50.3 million
- **Coed** 4,549 undergraduate students, 86% full-time, 58% women, 42% men
- **Moderately difficult** entrance level, 72% of applicants were admitted

Undergraduates 3,928 full-time, 621 part-time. Students come from 44 states and territories; 64 other countries; 22% are from out of state; 10% Black or African American, non-Hispanic/Latino; 9% Hispanic/Latino; 4% Asian, non-Hispanic/Latino; 0.2% Native Hawaiian or other Pacific Islander, non-Hispanic/Latino; 0.2% American Indian or Alaska Native, non-Hispanic/Latino; 2% Two or more races, non-Hispanic/Latino; 7% Race/ethnicity unknown; 2% international; 5% transferred in; 57% live on campus. *Retention:* 77% of full-time freshmen returned.

Freshmen *Admission:* 7,903 applied, 5,701 admitted, 920 enrolled. *Average high school GPA:* 3.3. *Test scores:* SAT critical reading scores over 500: 56%; SAT math scores over 500: 64%; SAT writing scores over 500: 56%; ACT scores over 18: 89%; SAT critical reading scores over 600: 14%; SAT math scores over 600: 20%; SAT writing scores over 600: 16%; ACT scores over 24: 34%; SAT critical reading scores over 700: 2%; SAT math scores over 700: 2%; SAT writing scores over 700: 2%; ACT scores over 30: 5%.

Faculty *Total:* 626, 41% full-time, 69% with terminal degrees. *Student/faculty ratio:* 12:1.

Academics *Calendar:* semesters. *Degrees:* certificates, associate, bachelor's, master's, post-master's, and postbachelor's certificates. *Special study options:* academic remediation for entering students, adult/continuing education programs, advanced placement credit, cooperative education, distance learning, double majors, English as a second language, honors programs, independent study, internships, part-time degree program, services for LD students, study abroad, summer session for credit. *ROTC:* Army (c).

Computers on Campus 300 computers/terminals are available on campus for general student use. Students can access the following: computer help desk, free student e-mail accounts, online (class) grades, online (class) registration, online (class) schedules. Campuswide network is available. 100% of college-owned or -operated housing units are wired for high-speed Internet access. Wireless service is available via entire campus.

Student Life *Housing options:* coed, women-only, disabled students. Campus housing is university owned. Freshman applicants given priority for college housing. *Activities and organizations:* drama/theater group, student-run newspaper, radio and television station, choral group, Student Government Association, Greek Council, Association of Commuter Students, Black Student Union, Residence Hall Association, national fraternities, national sororities. *Campus security:* 24-hour emergency response devices and patrols, student patrols, late-night transport/escort service, controlled dormitory access. *Student services:* health clinic, personal/psychological counseling.

Athletics Member NCAA. All Division I. *Intercollegiate sports:* baseball M(s), basketball M(s)/W(s), cheerleading M/W, cross-country running M(s)/W(s), field hockey W(s), golf M(s), soccer M(s)/W(s), softball W(s), swimming and diving M(s)/W(s), tennis M(s)/W(s), track and field M(s)/W(s), volleyball W(s), wrestling M(s). *Intramural sports:* basketball M/W, cheerleading M/W, equestrian sports W(c), golf M, ice hockey M(c), lacrosse M(c)/W, soccer M/W, softball M/W, track and field M/W, volleyball M/W, water polo M/W.

Standardized Tests *Required:* SAT or ACT (for admission).

Costs (2012–13) *Comprehensive fee:* $45,760 includes full-time tuition ($32,820), mandatory fees ($600), and room and board ($12,340). Full-time tuition and fees vary according to course load and program. Part-time tuition: $597 per credit. Part-time tuition and fees vary according to course load and program. *Required fees:* $35 per course part-time. *College room only:* $7770. Room and board charges vary according to board plan, housing facility, and location. *Payment plan:* installment. *Waivers:* employees or children of employees.

Financial Aid Of all full-time matriculated undergraduates who enrolled in 2012, 3,215 applied for aid, 2,806 were judged to have need, 407 had their need fully met. In 2012, 828 non-need-based awards were made. *Average percent of need met:* 70%. *Average financial aid package:* $22,352. *Average need-based loan:* $3919. *Average need-based gift aid:* $18,157. *Average non-need-based aid:* $12,657. *Average indebtedness upon graduation:* $32,718.

Applying *Options:* electronic application, early admission, early action, deferred entrance. *Application fee:* $50. *Required:* essay or personal statement, high school transcript, 2 letters of recommendation. *Required for some:* interview. *Application deadlines:* rolling (freshmen), rolling (transfers), 11/15 (early action). *Notification:* continuous (freshmen), continuous (transfers), 12/15 (early action).

Freshman Application Contact Mr. William Larrousse, Director of Admissions, Rider University, 2083 Lawrenceville Road, Lawrenceville, NJ 08648. *Phone:* 609-896-5177. *Toll-free phone:* 800-257-9026. *Fax:* 609-895-6645. *E-mail:* wlarrousse@rider.edu.
Website: http://www.rider.edu/.

Rowan University

Glassboro, New Jersey

- **State-supported** comprehensive, founded 1923, part of New Jersey State College System
- **Suburban** 800-acre campus with easy access to Philadelphia
- **Endowment** $140.5 million
- **Coed** 10,750 undergraduate students, 86% full-time, 51% women, 49% men
- **Moderately difficult** entrance level, 62% of applicants were admitted

Undergraduates 9,254 full-time, 1,496 part-time. 4% are from out of state; 9% Black or African American, non-Hispanic/Latino; 9% Hispanic/Latino; 4% Asian, non-Hispanic/Latino; 0.2% Native Hawaiian or other Pacific Islander, non-Hispanic/Latino; 1% American Indian or Alaska Native, non-Hispanic/Latino; 0.7% Two or more races, non-Hispanic/Latino; 1% Race/ethnicity unknown; 12% transferred in; 35% live on campus. *Retention:* 85% of full-time freshmen returned.

Freshmen *Admission:* 7,346 applied, 4,553 admitted, 1,484 enrolled. *Average high school GPA:* 3.3. *Test scores:* SAT critical reading scores over 500: 69%; SAT math scores over 500: 82%; SAT writing scores over 500: 67%; SAT critical reading scores over 600: 21%; SAT math scores over 600: 38%; SAT writing scores over 600: 19%; SAT critical reading scores over 700: 2%; SAT math scores over 700: 7%; SAT writing scores over 700: 2%.

Faculty *Total:* 1,125, 34% full-time, 39% with terminal degrees. *Student/faculty ratio:* 16:1.

Academics *Calendar:* semesters. *Degrees:* certificates, bachelor's, master's, and doctoral. *Special study options:* academic remediation for entering students, adult/continuing education programs, advanced placement credit, cooperative education, distance learning, double majors, English as a second language, freshman honors college, honors programs, independent study, internships, off-campus study, part-time degree program, services for LD students, study abroad, summer session for credit. *ROTC:* Army (c). *Unusual degree programs:* 3-2 mathematics and computer science.

Computers on Campus 1,200 computers/terminals and 2,500 ports are available on campus for general student use. Students can access the following: campus intranet, computer help desk, free student e-mail accounts, online (class) grades, online (class) registration, online (class) schedules, online library. Campuswide network is available. 100% of college-owned or -operated housing units are wired for high-speed Internet access. Wireless service is available via entire campus.

Student Life *Housing:* on-campus residence required through sophomore year. *Options:* coed, disabled students. Campus housing is university owned and leased by the school. Freshman campus housing is guaranteed. *Activities and organizations:* drama/theater group, student-run newspaper, radio and television station, choral group, Kappa Delta Pi, Public Relations Student Society of America, Student University Programmes, Rowan Television Network, Elementary Education Club, national fraternities, national sororities. *Campus security:* 24-hour emergency response devices and patrols, student patrols, late-night transport/escort service, controlled dormitory access, EMS Service including 2 ambulances, Security and Campus Police trained as Police Officers in NJ. *Student services:* health clinic, personal/psychological counseling, legal services.

Athletics Member NCAA. All Division III. *Intercollegiate sports:* baseball M, basketball M/W, cross-country running M/W, field hockey W, football M, lacrosse W, soccer M/W, softball W, swimming and diving M/W, track and field M/W, volleyball W. *Intramural sports:* basketball M/W, bowling M/W, cheerleading W(c), field hockey W(c), football M/W, golf M/W, ice hockey M(c), lacrosse M(c)/W, racquetball M/W, rock climbing M(c), rugby M, skiing (downhill) M(c)/W(c), soccer M/W, softball M/W, table tennis M/W, tennis M(c)/W(c), ultimate Frisbee M(c)/W(c), volleyball M/W, water polo M/W, wrestling M(c).

Standardized Tests *Required:* SAT or ACT (for admission).

Costs (2013–14) *Tuition:* state resident $8906 full-time, $342 per credit hour part-time; nonresident $16,712 full-time, $644 per credit hour part-time. Full-time tuition and fees vary according to course load, degree level, and program. Part-time tuition and fees vary according to course load, degree level, and program. *Required fees:* $3474 full-time. *Room and board:* $10,972; room only: $6892. Room and board charges vary according to board plan and housing facility. *Payment plan:* deferred payment. *Waivers:* employees or children of employees.

Financial Aid Of all full-time matriculated undergraduates who enrolled in 2011, 7,350 applied for aid, 5,876 were judged to have need, 374 had their need fully met. 332 Federal Work-Study jobs (averaging $1500). 341 state and other part-time jobs (averaging $1400). In 2011, 527 non-need-based awards were made. *Average percent of need met:* 82%. *Average financial aid package:* $9312. *Average need-based loan:* $4347. *Average need-based gift aid:* $8659.

Average non-need-based aid: $5623. *Average indebtedness upon graduation:* $35,027.

Applying *Options:* electronic application, early admission, deferred entrance. *Application fee:* $65. *Required:* high school transcript. *Required for some:* interview. *Recommended:* minimum 2.0 GPA. *Application deadlines:* 3/1 (freshmen), 3/1 (transfers). *Notification:* continuous (freshmen), continuous (transfers).

Freshman Application Contact Mr. Albert Betts, Director of Admissions, Rowan University, 201 Mullica Hill Road, Glassboro, NJ 08028. *Phone:* 856-256-4200. *Toll-free phone:* 800-447-1165 (in-state); 800-447-1165N (out-of-state). *Fax:* 856-256-4430. *E-mail:* admissions@rowan.edu. *Website:* http://www.rowan.edu/.

Rutgers, The State University of New Jersey, Camden

Camden, New Jersey

- **State-supported** university, founded 1927, part of Rutgers, The State University of New Jersey
- **Urban** 34-acre campus with easy access to Philadelphia
- **Endowment** $508.8 million
- **Coed** 4,708 undergraduate students, 81% full-time, 55% women, 45% men
- **Moderately difficult** entrance level, 62% of applicants were admitted

Undergraduates 3,833 full-time, 875 part-time. Students come from 18 states and territories; 12 other countries; 2% are from out of state; 17% Black or African American, non-Hispanic/Latino; 10% Hispanic/Latino; 8% Asian, non-Hispanic/Latino; 0.2% Native Hawaiian or other Pacific Islander, non-Hispanic/Latino; 0.1% American Indian or Alaska Native, non-Hispanic/Latino; 3% Two or more races, non-Hispanic/Latino; 2% Race/ethnicity unknown; 1% international; 18% transferred in; 20% live on campus. *Retention:* 82% of full-time freshmen returned.

Freshmen *Admission:* 5,686 applied, 3,553 admitted, 485 enrolled. *Test scores:* SAT critical reading scores over 500: 56%; SAT math scores over 500: 67%; SAT writing scores over 500: 55%; SAT critical reading scores over 600: 13%; SAT math scores over 600: 19%; SAT writing scores over 600: 14%; SAT critical reading scores over 700: 2%; SAT math scores over 700: 3%; SAT writing scores over 700: 2%.

Faculty *Total:* 537, 53% full-time, 99% with terminal degrees. *Student/faculty ratio:* 11:1.

Academics *Calendar:* semesters. *Degrees:* bachelor's, master's, and doctoral. *Special study options:* academic remediation for entering students, accelerated degree program, advanced placement credit, cooperative education, distance learning, double majors, English as a second language, freshman honors college, honors programs, independent study, internships, part-time degree program, services for LD students, student-designed majors, study abroad, summer session for credit. *ROTC:* Army (c), Air Force (c). *Unusual degree programs:* 3-2 business administration; engineering; medical technology with approved hospital; African-American studies, general science, childhood studies, English, history, liberal studies, psychology; biology, chemistry and mathematics with the Graduate School-Camden.

Computers on Campus 184 computers/terminals are available on campus for general student use. Students can access the following: campus intranet, computer help desk, free student e-mail accounts, online (class) grades, online (class) registration, online (class) schedules, online grade reports. Campuswide network is available. 100% of college-owned or -operated housing units are wired for high-speed Internet access. Wireless service is available via classrooms, computer centers, computer labs, dorm rooms, learning centers, libraries, student centers.

Student Life *Housing options:* coed, disabled students. Campus housing is university owned. *Activities and organizations:* drama/theater group, student-run radio station. *Campus security:* 24-hour emergency response devices and patrols, student patrols, late-night transport/escort service, controlled dormitory access.

Athletics Member NCAA. All Division III. *Intercollegiate sports:* baseball M, basketball M/W, crew M/W, cross-country running W, golf M, lacrosse W, soccer M/W, softball W, track and field M/W, volleyball W. *Intramural sports:* baseball M, basketball M/W, cheerleading W, crew M, golf M, ice hockey M, lacrosse M, racquetball M, soccer M, tennis M, track and field M, ultimate Frisbee M/W, volleyball M/W.

Standardized Tests *Required:* SAT or ACT (for admission).

Costs (2012–13) *Tuition:* state resident $10,356 full-time, $333 per credit part-time; nonresident $23,232 full-time, $754 per credit part-time. Part-time tuition and fees vary according to course load. *Required fees:* $2567 full-time,

$1004 per year part-time. *Room and board:* $11,206; room only: $7906. Room and board charges vary according to board plan and housing facility.

Financial Aid Of all full-time matriculated undergraduates who enrolled in 2012, 3,173 applied for aid, 2,829 were judged to have need, 206 had their need fully met. 254 Federal Work-Study jobs (averaging $1420). 533 state and other part-time jobs (averaging $2347). In 2012, 47 non-need-based awards were made. *Average percent of need met:* 55%. *Average financial aid package:* $11,535. *Average need-based loan:* $4473. *Average need-based gift aid:* $9216. *Average non-need-based aid:* $7548. *Average indebtedness upon graduation:* $27,535.

Applying *Options:* electronic application. *Application fee:* $65. *Required:* high school transcript. *Application deadlines:* 12/1 (freshmen), 1/15 (transfers). *Notification:* 2/28 (freshmen), 5/15 (transfers).

Freshman Application Contact Rutgers, The State University of New Jersey, Camden, 406 Penn Street, Camden, NJ 08102-1401. *Phone:* 856-225-6104. *Website:* http://www.rutgers.edu/.

Rutgers, The State University of New Jersey, Newark

Newark, New Jersey

- **State-supported** university, founded 1892, part of Rutgers, The State University of New Jersey
- **Urban** 38-acre campus
- **Endowment** $508.8 million
- **Coed** 7,666 undergraduate students, 81% full-time, 53% women, 47% men
- **Moderately difficult** entrance level, 58% of applicants were admitted

Undergraduates 6,220 full-time, 1,446 part-time. Students come from 25 states and territories; 45 other countries; 16% are from out of state; 18% Black or African American, non-Hispanic/Latino; 22% Hispanic/Latino; 23% Asian, non-Hispanic/Latino; 0.7% Native Hawaiian or other Pacific Islander, non-Hispanic/Latino; 0.1% American Indian or Alaska Native, non-Hispanic/Latino; 3% Two or more races, non-Hispanic/Latino; 5% Race/ethnicity unknown; 3% international; 12% transferred in; 20% live on campus. *Retention:* 89% of full-time freshmen returned.

Freshmen *Admission:* 11,863 applied, 6,824 admitted, 1,052 enrolled. *Test scores:* SAT critical reading scores over 500: 52%; SAT math scores over 500: 72%; SAT writing scores over 500: 61%; SAT critical reading scores over 600: 11%; SAT math scores over 600: 25%; SAT writing scores over 600: 14%; SAT critical reading scores over 700: 2%; SAT math scores over 700: 4%; SAT writing scores over 700: 2%.

Faculty *Total:* 819, 60% full-time, 99% with terminal degrees. *Student/faculty ratio:* 11:1.

Academics *Calendar:* semesters. *Degrees:* bachelor's, master's, and doctoral. *Special study options:* academic remediation for entering students, accelerated degree program, adult/continuing education programs, advanced placement credit, cooperative education, distance learning, double majors, English as a second language, freshman honors college, honors programs, independent study, internships, off-campus study, part-time degree program, services for LD students, student-designed majors, study abroad, summer session for credit. *ROTC:* Army (b), Navy (b), Air Force (b). *Unusual degree programs:* 3-2 business administration; engineering; nursing.

Computers on Campus 708 computers/terminals are available on campus for general student use. Students can access the following: computer help desk, free student e-mail accounts, online (class) grades, online (class) schedules, online grade reports. Campuswide network is available. Wireless service is available via classrooms, computer centers, computer labs, dorm rooms, learning centers, libraries, student centers.

Student Life *Housing options:* coed. Campus housing is university owned. *Activities and organizations:* drama/theater group, student-run newspaper, radio station, choral group. *Campus security:* 24-hour emergency response devices and patrols, student patrols, late-night transport/escort service, controlled dormitory access.

Athletics Member NCAA. All Division III except volleyball (Division I). *Intercollegiate sports:* baseball M, basketball M/W, cross-country running M/W, soccer M/W, tennis M/W, track and field M, volleyball M/W. *Intramural sports:* baseball M/W, basketball M/W, racquetball M/W, rock climbing M/W, soccer M/W, swimming and diving M/W, weight lifting M/W.

Standardized Tests *Required:* SAT or ACT (for admission).

Costs (2012–13) *Tuition:* state resident $10,356 full-time, $333 per credit part-time; nonresident $23,676 full-time, $768 per credit part-time. Part-time tuition and fees vary according to course load. *Required fees:* $2234 full-time, $632 per year part-time. *Room and board:* $12,285; room only: $7613. Room

and board charges vary according to board plan and housing facility. *Payment plan:* installment.

Financial Aid Of all full-time matriculated undergraduates who enrolled in 2012, 4,672 applied for aid, 4,362 were judged to have need, 4,307 had their need fully met. 472 Federal Work-Study jobs (averaging $1355). 785 state and other part-time jobs (averaging $1852). In 2012, 36 non-need-based awards were made. *Average percent of need met:* 56%. *Average financial aid package:* $12,795. *Average need-based loan:* $4605. *Average need-based gift aid:* $10,206. *Average non-need-based aid:* $9219. *Average indebtedness upon graduation:* $24,837.

Applying *Options:* electronic application. *Application fee:* $65. *Required:* high school transcript. *Application deadlines:* 12/1 (freshmen), 1/15 (transfers). *Notification:* 2/28 (freshmen), 5/15 (transfers).

Freshman Application Contact Mr. Jason Hand, Director of Admissions, Rutgers, The State University of New Jersey, Newark, 249 University Avenue, Newark, NJ 07102. *Phone:* 973-353-5205. *Fax:* 973-353-1440. *E-mail:* admissions@ugadm.rutgers.edu. *Website:* http://www.rutgers.edu/.

Rutgers, The State University of New Jersey, New Brunswick

Piscataway, New Jersey

- **State-supported** university, founded 1766, part of Rutgers, The State University of New Jersey
- **Urban** 2683-acre campus with easy access to New York City
- **Endowment** $508.8 million
- **Coed** 31,593 undergraduate students, 95% full-time, 49% women, 51% men
- **Moderately difficult** entrance level, 61% of applicants were admitted

Undergraduates 30,038 full-time, 1,555 part-time. Students come from 52 states and territories; 72 other countries; 6% are from out of state; 8% Black or African American, non-Hispanic/Latino; 12% Hispanic/Latino; 25% Asian, non-Hispanic/Latino; 0.3% Native Hawaiian or other Pacific Islander, non-Hispanic/Latino; 0.1% American Indian or Alaska Native, non-Hispanic/Latino; 3% Two or more races, non-Hispanic/Latino; 2% Race/ethnicity unknown; 3% international; 7% transferred in; 53% live on campus. *Retention:* 92% of full-time freshmen returned.

Freshmen *Admission:* 28,635 applied, 17,436 admitted, 6,170 enrolled. *Test scores:* SAT critical reading scores over 500: 85%; SAT math scores over 500: 93%; SAT writing scores over 500: 90%; SAT critical reading scores over 600: 40%; SAT math scores over 600: 62%; SAT writing scores over 600: 49%; SAT critical reading scores over 700: 9%; SAT math scores over 700: 21%; SAT writing scores over 700: 13%.

Faculty *Total:* 2,890, 61% full-time, 99% with terminal degrees. *Student/faculty ratio:* 14:1.

Academics *Calendar:* semesters. *Degrees:* bachelor's, master's, doctoral, post-master's, and postbachelor's certificates. *Special study options:* academic remediation for entering students, accelerated degree program, advanced placement credit, cooperative education, distance learning, double majors, English as a second language, honors programs, independent study, internships, part-time degree program, student-designed majors, study abroad. *ROTC:* Army (b), Air Force (b). *Unusual degree programs:* 3-2 business administration; engineering; University of Medicine and Dentistry of New Jersey, Robert Wood Johnson Medical School.

Computers on Campus 1,450 computers/terminals are available on campus for general student use. Students can access the following: campus intranet, computer help desk, free student e-mail accounts, online (class) grades, online (class) registration, online (class) schedules, online grade reports. Campuswide network is available. Wireless service is available via entire campus.

Student Life *Housing options:* coed, men-only, women-only, cooperative. Campus housing is university owned. *Activities and organizations:* drama/theater group, student-run newspaper, radio and television station, choral group, marching band, national fraternities, national sororities. *Campus security:* 24-hour emergency response devices and patrols, student patrols, late-night transport/escort service, controlled dormitory access. *Student services:* health clinic, personal/psychological counseling, women's center.

Athletics Member NCAA. All Division I except football (Division I-A). *Intercollegiate sports:* baseball M, basketball M/W, crew M/W, cross-country running M/W, fencing M/W, golf M/W, gymnastics W, lacrosse M/W, soccer M/W, softball W, swimming and diving M/W, tennis M/W, track and field M/W, volleyball W, wrestling M. *Intramural sports:* badminton M/W, baseball M(c), basketball M/W, bowling M/W, cross-country running M/W, equestrian sports M(c)/W(c), field hockey W(c), football M, golf M/W, ice hockey M(c), lacrosse M/W, racquetball M/W, rugby M(c)/W(c), sailing M(c)/W(c), skiing (cross-country) M(c)/W(c), skiing (downhill) M(c)/W(c), soccer M/W, softball M/W, squash M(c)/W(c), swimming and diving M/W, table tennis M(c)/W(c), tennis M/W, track and field M/W, volleyball M/W, water polo M/W, wrestling M.

Standardized Tests *Required:* SAT or ACT (for admission).

Costs (2012–13) *Tuition:* state resident $10,356 full-time, $333 per credit part-time; nonresident $23,676 full-time, $768 per credit part-time. *Required fees:* $2717 full-time, $658 per year part-time. *Room and board:* $11,412; room only: $7042. Room and board charges vary according to board plan and housing facility. *Payment plan:* installment. *Waivers:* employees or children of employees.

Financial Aid Of all full-time matriculated undergraduates who enrolled in 2012, 20,240 applied for aid, 17,507 were judged to have need, 1,468 had their need fully met. 2,410 Federal Work-Study jobs (averaging $1240). 6,129 state and other part-time jobs (averaging $1929). In 2012, 498 non-need-based awards were made. *Average percent of need met:* 52%. *Average financial aid package:* $12,393. *Average need-based loan:* $4548. *Average need-based gift aid:* $10,009. *Average non-need-based aid:* $8901. *Average indebtedness upon graduation:* $26,656.

Applying *Options:* electronic application. *Application fee:* $65. *Required:* high school transcript. *Required for some:* interview. *Recommended:* essay or personal statement. *Application deadlines:* 12/1 (freshmen), 1/15 (transfers). *Notification:* 2/28 (freshmen), 5/15 (transfers).

Freshman Application Contact Rutgers, The State University of New Jersey, New Brunswick, 65 Davidson Road, Room 202, Piscataway, NJ 08854-8097. *Phone:* 732-445-4636.

Website: http://www.rutgers.edu/.

Saint Peter's University

Jersey City, New Jersey

- **Independent Roman Catholic (Jesuit)** comprehensive, founded 1872
- **Urban** 15-acre campus with easy access to New York City
- **Coed**
- **Moderately difficult** entrance level

Faculty *Student/faculty ratio:* 12:1.

Academics *Calendar:* semesters. *Degrees:* certificates, associate, bachelor's, master's, and doctoral.

Student Life *Campus security:* 24-hour emergency response devices and patrols, late-night transport/escort service, controlled dormitory access, ID checks at residence halls and library.

Athletics Member NCAA. All Division I.

Standardized Tests *Required:* SAT or ACT (for admission).

Costs (2012–13) *One-time required fee:* $290. *Comprehensive fee:* $44,240 includes full-time tuition ($30,320), mandatory fees ($900), and room and board ($13,020). Full-time tuition and fees vary according to class time and course load. Part-time tuition: $990 per credit. Part-time tuition and fees vary according to class time and course load. *Required fees:* $8 per credit hour part-time. *College room only:* $7824. Room and board charges vary according to board plan, housing facility, and student level.

Financial Aid Of all full-time matriculated undergraduates who enrolled in 2008, 1,999 applied for aid, 1,698 were judged to have need, 255 had their need fully met. 244 Federal Work-Study jobs (averaging $1976). In 2008, 272 non-need-based awards were made. *Average percent of need met:* 77. *Average financial aid package:* $22,083. *Average need-based loan:* $3932. *Average need-based gift aid:* $16,453. *Average non-need-based aid:* $13,962. *Average indebtedness upon graduation:* $19,553.

Applying *Options:* early admission, deferred entrance. *Required:* essay or personal statement, high school transcript, minimum 2.0 GPA, 2 letters of recommendation. *Required for some:* interview. *Recommended:* interview.

Freshman Application Contact Saint Peter's University, 2641 Kennedy Boulevard, Jersey City, NJ 07306-5997. *Phone:* 201-761-7106. *Toll-free phone:* 888-SPC-9933.

Website: http://www.spcollege.edu/.

Seton Hall University

South Orange, New Jersey

Freshman Application Contact Mr. Peter Nacy, Assistant Vice President for Admissions, Seton Hall University, Enrollment Management, South Orange, NJ 07079-2697. *Phone:* 973-275-2498. *Toll-free phone:* 800-THE HALL. *Fax:* 973-275-2040. *E-mail:* thehall@shu.edu. *Website:* http://www.shu.edu/.

Stevens Institute of Technology

Hoboken, New Jersey

- **Independent** university, founded 1870
- **Urban** 55-acre campus with easy access to New York City
- **Endowment** $144.0 million
- **Coed**
- **Very difficult** entrance level

Faculty *Student/faculty ratio:* 8:1.

Academics *Calendar:* semesters. *Degrees:* bachelor's, master's, doctoral, and postbachelor's certificates.

Student Life *Campus security:* 24-hour emergency response devices and patrols, late-night transport/escort service, controlled dormitory access.

Athletics Member NCAA. All Division III.

Standardized Tests *Required:* SAT or ACT (for admission). *Required for some:* SAT Subject Tests (for admission).

Costs (2012–13) *Comprehensive fee:* $55,742 includes full-time tuition ($41,670), mandatory fees ($272), and room and board ($13,800). *Room and board:* Room and board charges vary according to board plan and housing facility.

Financial Aid *Of all full-time matriculated undergraduates who enrolled in 2005,* 1,645 applied for aid, 1,431 were judged to have need, 245 had their need fully met. 818 Federal Work-Study jobs (averaging $1269). *In 2005,* 296 non-need-based awards were made. *Average percent of need met:* 85. *Average financial aid package:* $21,139. *Average need-based loan:* $4203. *Average need-based gift aid:* $12,871. *Average non-need-based aid:* $9973. *Average indebtedness upon graduation:* $14,113.

Applying *Options:* electronic application, early admission, early decision, deferred entrance. *Application fee:* $55. *Required:* essay or personal statement, high school transcript, 2 letters of recommendation, interview.

Freshman Application Contact Mr. Daniel Gallagher, Dean of University Admissions, Stevens Institute of Technology, Castle Point on Hudson, Hoboken, NJ 07030. *Phone:* 201-216-5197. *Toll-free phone:* 800-458-5323. *E-mail:* admissions@stevens.edu.

Website: http://www.stevens.edu/.

Strayer University—Cherry Hill Campus

Cherry Hill, New Jersey

Freshman Application Contact Strayer University—Cherry Hill Campus, 2201 Route 38, Suite 100, Cherry Hill, NJ 08002.

Website: http://www.strayer.edu/campus/cherry-hill/.

Strayer University— Lawrenceville Campus

Lawrenceville, New Jersey

Freshman Application Contact Strayer University—Lawrenceville Campus, 3150 Brunswick Pike, Suite 100, Lawrenceville, NJ 08648.

Website: http://www.strayer.edu/campus/lawrenceville.

Strayer University—Piscataway Campus

Piscataway, New Jersey

Freshman Application Contact Strayer University—Piscataway Campus, 242 Old New Brunswick Road, Suite 220, Piscataway, NJ 08854.

Website: http://www.strayer.edu/campus/piscataway.

Strayer University—Willingboro Campus

Willingboro, New Jersey

Freshman Application Contact Strayer University—Willingboro Campus, 300 Willingboro Parkway, Willingboro Town Center, Suite 125, Willingboro, NJ 08046.
Website: http://www.strayer.edu/campus/willingboro.

Talmudical Academy of New Jersey

Adelphia, New Jersey

Director of Admissions Director of Admissions, Talmudical Academy of New Jersey, 868 Route 524, Adelphia, NJ 07710. *Phone:* 201-431-1600.

Thomas Edison State College

Trenton, New Jersey

- **State-supported** comprehensive, founded 1972
- **Urban** 2-acre campus with easy access to Philadelphia
- **Coed** 19,406 undergraduate students, 45% women, 55% men
- **Noncompetitive** entrance level

Undergraduates 19,406 part-time. Students come from 56 states and territories; 68 other countries; 60% are from out of state; 16% Black or African American, non-Hispanic/Latino; 8% Hispanic/Latino; 4% Asian, non-Hispanic/Latino; 0.7% Native Hawaiian or other Pacific Islander, non-Hispanic/Latino; 0.7% American Indian or Alaska Native, non-Hispanic/Latino; 1% Two or more races, non-Hispanic/Latino; 9% Race/ethnicity unknown; 0.9% international.
Academics *Calendar:* continuous. *Degrees:* certificates, associate, bachelor's, master's, post-master's, and postbachelor's certificates (offers only distance learning degree programs). *Special study options:* accelerated degree program, adult/continuing education programs, advanced placement credit, distance learning, double majors, external degree program, independent study, part-time degree program, services for LD students, student-designed majors, summer session for credit.
Computers on Campus Students can access the following: online (class) grades, online (class) registration, online (class) schedules, undergraduate and Nursing students are able to schedule appointments online with their advisors. Campuswide network is available. Wireless service is available via entire campus.
Student Life *Housing:* college housing not available. *Campus security:* 24-hour emergency response devices and patrols, late-night transport/escort service, security officer from 7 am to 11 pm, local police patrol.
Costs (2012–13) *Tuition:* state resident $5508 full-time, $164 per credit hour part-time; nonresident $8111 full-time, $221 per credit hour part-time. Part-time tuition and fees vary according to program and student level. There are two tuition plans available. Students may choose either the Comprehensive Plan: $5322 per year (state residents and military personnel), $7837 (non-resident), which covers up to 36 credits per year for all credit-earning options, or the Enrolled Options Plan: $1533 per year (state residents and military personnel), $2858 (non-resident) and $4011 (international) for annual enrollment tuition and a technology services fee($113); tests, portfolios, courses and other fees at additional cost. *Required fees:* $117 per year part-time. *Waivers:* employees or children of employees.
Applying *Options:* electronic application. *Application fee:* $75. *Required:* age 21 or older and a high school graduate. *Application deadlines:* rolling (freshmen), rolling (out-of-state freshmen), rolling (transfers).
Freshman Application Contact Mr. David Hoftiezer, Director of Admissions, Thomas Edison State College, 101 West State Street, Trenton, NJ 08608. *Phone:* 888-442-8372. *Toll-free phone:* 888-442-8372. *Fax:* 609-984-8447. *E-mail:* admissions@tesc.edu. *Website:* http://www.tesc.edu/.

University of Medicine and Dentistry of New Jersey

Newark, New Jersey

- **State-supported** comprehensive, founded 1970, part of The School of Health Related Professions is one of 8 schools within the University of Medicine and Dentistry of New Jersey
- **Rural** campus with easy access to New York City, Philadelphia, Newark
- **Coed** 548 undergraduate students, 44% full-time, 80% women, 20% men

Undergraduates 241 full-time, 307 part-time. Students come from 29 states and territories; 10 other countries; 17% are from out of state; 18% Black or African American, non-Hispanic/Latino; 13% Hispanic/Latino; 12% Asian, non-Hispanic/Latino; 0.9% Native Hawaiian or other Pacific Islander, non-Hispanic/Latino; 0.2% American Indian or Alaska Native, non-Hispanic/Latino; 8% Race/ethnicity unknown; 2% international.
Faculty *Total:* 448, 34% full-time, 40% with terminal degrees. *Student/faculty ratio:* 10:1.
Academics *Calendar:* semesters. *Degrees:* certificates, diplomas, associate, bachelor's, master's, doctoral, post-master's, and postbachelor's certificates. *Special study options:* academic remediation for entering students, accelerated degree program, distance learning, external degree program, honors programs, independent study, internships, off-campus study, part-time degree program, services for LD students, summer session for credit. *Unusual degree programs:* 3-2 health professions.
Computers on Campus 120 computers/terminals are available on campus for general student use. Students can access the following: campus intranet, computer help desk, free student e-mail accounts, online (class) grades, online (class) registration, online (class) schedules. Campuswide network is available. Wireless service is available via entire campus.
Student Life *Housing options:* coed. Campus housing is university owned. *Activities and organizations:* Student Leadership Council, Student Senate. *Campus security:* 24-hour emergency response devices and patrols, late-night transport/escort service, controlled dormitory access. *Student services:* health clinic, personal/psychological counseling.
Costs (2013–14) *Tuition:* state resident $7658 full-time, $319 per credit hour part-time; nonresident $11,844 full-time, $494 per credit hour part-time. Full-time tuition and fees vary according to class time, course load, location, and program. Part-time tuition and fees vary according to class time, course load, location, and program. *Payment plan:* installment.
Applying *Required for some:* essay or personal statement, interview.
Freshman Application Contact Student Contact, University of Medicine and Dentistry of New Jersey, 65 Bergen Street, PO Box 1709, Newark, NJ 07107-1709. *Phone:* 973-972-5454.
Website: http://www.umdnj.edu/.

University of Phoenix–Jersey City Campus

Jersey City, New Jersey

Admissions Office Contact University of Phoenix–Jersey City Campus, 100 Town Square Place, Jersey City, NJ 07310. *Toll-free phone:* 866-766-0766. *Website:* http://www.phoenix.edu/.

William Paterson University of New Jersey

Wayne, New Jersey

- **State-supported** comprehensive, founded 1855, part of New Jersey State College System
- **Suburban** 370-acre campus with easy access to New York City
- **Endowment** $6.2 million
- **Coed** 10,089 undergraduate students, 83% full-time, 54% women, 46% men
- **Moderately difficult** entrance level, 61% of applicants were admitted

Undergraduates 8,381 full-time, 1,708 part-time. Students come from 41 states and territories; 41 other countries; 2% are from out of state; 14% Black or African American, non-Hispanic/Latino; 23% Hispanic/Latino; 7% Asian, non-Hispanic/Latino; 0.2% American Indian or Alaska Native, non-Hispanic/

Latino; 2% Two or more races, non-Hispanic/Latino; 5% Race/ethnicity unknown; 0.8% international; 14% transferred in; 23% live on campus. *Retention:* 77% of full-time freshmen returned.

Freshmen *Admission:* 6,941 applied, 4,214 admitted, 1,240 enrolled. *Average high school GPA:* 3.08. *Test scores:* SAT critical reading scores over 500: 50%; SAT math scores over 500: 58%; SAT critical reading scores over 600: 11%; SAT math scores over 600: 12%; SAT critical reading scores over 700: 2%.

Faculty *Total:* 1,060, 38% full-time. *Student/faculty ratio:* 16:1.

Academics *Calendar:* semesters. *Degrees:* bachelor's, master's, doctoral, post-master's, and postbachelor's certificates. *Special study options:* academic remediation for entering students, accelerated degree program, adult/continuing education programs, advanced placement credit, distance learning, double majors, English as a second language, freshman honors college, honors programs, independent study, internships, off-campus study, part-time degree program, services for LD students, study abroad, summer session for credit. *ROTC:* Air Force (c).

Computers on Campus 700 computers/terminals are available on campus for general student use. Students can access the following: campus intranet, computer help desk, free student e-mail accounts, online (class) grades, online (class) registration, online (class) schedules. Campuswide network is available. 100% of college-owned or -operated housing units are wired for high-speed Internet access. Wireless service is available via entire campus.

Student Life *Housing options:* coed, disabled students. Campus housing is university owned, leased by the school and is provided by a third party. *Activities and organizations:* drama/theater group, student-run newspaper, radio and television station, choral group, 720 Modeling Group, Organization of Latin American Students (OLAS), Young Democratic Socialists, WPBN (TV Club), Honors College Club, national fraternities, national sororities. *Campus security:* 24-hour emergency response devices and patrols, student patrols, controlled dormitory access. *Student services:* health clinic, personal/psychological counseling, women's center, legal services.

Athletics Member NCAA. All Division III. *Intercollegiate sports:* baseball M, basketball M/W, bowling M(c), cheerleading M/W, field hockey W, football M, golf M, ice hockey M(c), rugby M, skiing (downhill) M(c)/W(c), soccer M/W, softball W, swimming and diving M/W, track and field M/W, volleyball W. *Intramural sports:* basketball M, bowling M(c), cheerleading M(c)/W(c), equestrian sports M(c)/W(c), golf M, ice hockey M(c), racquetball M/W, rugby M(c), softball M/W, tennis M(c)/W(c), track and field M(c)/W(c), volleyball M/W, wrestling M.

Standardized Tests *Required:* SAT or ACT (for admission).

Costs (2012–13) *Tuition:* state resident $7197 full-time, $230 per credit hour part-time; nonresident $14,597 full-time, $473 per credit hour part-time. Full-time tuition and fees vary according to course load and location. Part-time tuition and fees vary according to course load and location. *Required fees:* $4497 full-time, $145 per credit hour part-time. *Room and board:* $10,540; room only: $6700. Room and board charges vary according to board plan and housing facility. *Payment plan:* installment. *Waivers:* senior citizens and employees or children of employees.

Financial Aid *Average indebtedness upon graduation:* $29,314.

Applying *Options:* electronic application, early admission, deferred entrance. *Application fee:* $50. *Required:* high school transcript. *Required for some:* essay or personal statement, interview, portfolio for art, audition for music. *Recommended:* minimum 2.0 GPA. *Application deadlines:* 6/1 (freshmen), 6/1 (transfers), 12/1 (early action). *Notification:* continuous (freshmen), continuous (transfers), 1/15 (early action).

Freshman Application Contact Mr. Anthony Leckey, Senior Associate Director of Admissions, William Paterson University of New Jersey, 300 Pompton Road, Wayne, NJ 07470-8420. *Phone:* 973-720-2903. *Toll-free phone:* 877-WPU-EXCEL. *Fax:* 973-720-2910. *E-mail:* leckeya@wpunj.edu. *Website:* http://www.wpunj.edu/.

See below for display ad and page 1652 for the College Close-Up.

NEW MEXICO

Brookline College
Albuquerque, New Mexico

Freshman Application Contact Mr. Andrew Webb, Campus Director, Brookline College, 4201 Central Avenue NW, Suite J, Albuquerque, NM 87105. *Phone:* 505-880-2877. *Toll-free phone:* 888-660-2428. *Fax:* 505-352-0199. *E-mail:* awebb@brooklinecollege.edu. *Website:* http://brooklinecollege.edu/.

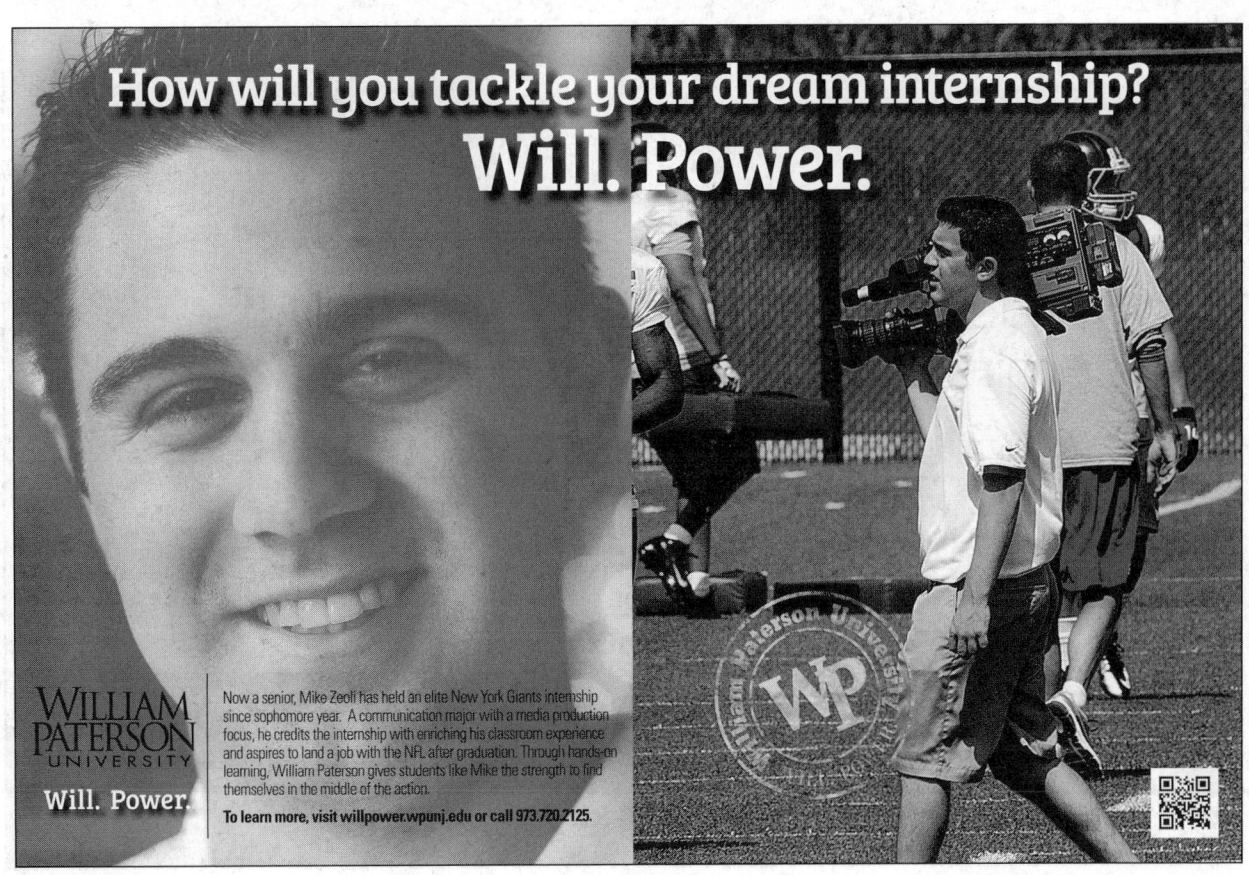

Brown Mackie College–Albuquerque

Albuquerque, New Mexico

Freshman Application Contact Brown Mackie College–Albuquerque, 10500 Copper Avenue NE, Albuquerque, NM 87123. *Phone:* 505-559-5200. *Toll-free phone:* 877-271-3488.
Website: http://www.brownmackie.edu/albuquerque/.

See below for display ad and page 1170 for the College Close-Up.

Eastern New Mexico University

Portales, New Mexico

- **State-supported** comprehensive, founded 1934
- **Rural** 400-acre campus
- **Endowment** $7.3 million
- **Coed** 4,586 undergraduate students, 62% full-time, 56% women, 44% men
- **Noncompetitive** entrance level, 66% of applicants were admitted

Undergraduates 2,845 full-time, 1,741 part-time. Students come from 49 states and territories; 20 other countries; 24% are from out of state; 0.5% Black or African American, non-Hispanic/Latino; 34% Hispanic/Latino; 0.9% Asian, non-Hispanic/Latino; 0.3% Native Hawaiian or other Pacific Islander, non-Hispanic/Latino; 2% American Indian or Alaska Native, non-Hispanic/Latino; 2% Two or more races, non-Hispanic/Latino; 6% Race/ethnicity unknown; 3% international; 11% transferred in; 26% live on campus. *Retention:* 63% of full-time freshmen returned.
Freshmen *Admission:* 2,291 applied, 1,515 admitted, 709 enrolled. *Average high school GPA:* 3.25. *Test scores:* SAT critical reading scores over 500: 32%; SAT math scores over 500: 43%; ACT scores over 18: 69%; SAT critical reading scores over 600: 9%; SAT math scores over 600: 10%; ACT scores over 24: 19%; SAT math scores over 700: 1%; ACT scores over 30: 1%.
Faculty *Total:* 378, 40% full-time, 39% with terminal degrees. *Student/faculty ratio:* 17:1.

Academics *Calendar:* semesters. *Degrees:* associate, bachelor's, and master's. *Special study options:* academic remediation for entering students, accelerated degree program, adult/continuing education programs, advanced placement credit, cooperative education, distance learning, double majors, English as a second language, independent study, internships, part-time degree program, services for LD students, student-designed majors, summer session for credit. *Unusual degree programs:* 3-2 Chemistry (qualified undergraduate students entering the chemistry program will be allowed to apply to the Graduate School during the last semester of the junior year to take a limited number of graduate courses for credit at the 500 level leading to a B.S. and an M.S. in 5-5.5 years total).
Computers on Campus 208 computers/terminals are available on campus for general student use. Students can access the following: campus intranet, computer help desk, free student e-mail accounts, online (class) grades, online (class) registration, online (class) schedules, WIFI in most buildings. Campus-wide network is available. 100% of college-owned or -operated housing units are wired for high-speed Internet access. Wireless service is available via entire campus.
Student Life *Housing:* on-campus residence required for freshman year. *Options:* coed, women-only, disabled students. Campus housing is university owned. Freshman campus housing is guaranteed. *Activities and organizations:* drama/theater group, student-run newspaper, radio and television station, choral group, marching band, Student Government, Student Activities Board, Residence Hall Association, IFC (Inter-Fraternity Council)Panhellenic Council, national fraternities, national sororities. *Campus security:* 24-hour emergency response devices and patrols, late-night transport/escort service, controlled dormitory access, University Emergency Notification System; security cameras; security lights. *Student services:* health clinic, personal/psychological counseling.
Athletics Member NCAA. All Division II. *Intercollegiate sports:* baseball M(s), basketball M(s)/W(s), cross-country running M(s)/W(s), football M(s), soccer M(s)/W(s), softball W(s), track and field M(s)/W(s), volleyball W(s). *Intramural sports:* badminton M/W, basketball M/W, cross-country running M/W, football M/W, racquetball M/W, soccer M/W, softball M/W, tennis M/W, volleyball M/W, water polo M/W.
Standardized Tests *Required for some:* SAT or ACT (for admission).
Costs (2013–14) *One-time required fee:* $120. *Tuition:* state resident $4350 full-time, $122 per credit hour part-time; nonresident $9860 full-time, $351 per credit hour part-time. Full-time tuition and fees vary according to course load and reciprocity agreements. Part-time tuition and fees vary according to course load. *Required fees:* $1426 full-time, $59 per credit hour part-time.

Room and board: $6090; room only: $2930. Room and board charges vary according to gender, housing facility, location, and student level. *Payment plan:* installment. *Waivers:* senior citizens and employees or children of employees.

Financial Aid Of all full-time matriculated undergraduates who enrolled in 2011, 1,635 applied for aid, 1,634 were judged to have need, 1,619 had their need fully met. In 2011, 219 non-need-based awards were made. *Average percent of need met:* 44%. *Average financial aid package:* $11,015. *Average need-based loan:* $4130. *Average need-based gift aid:* $4575. *Average non-need-based aid:* $4213. *Average indebtedness upon graduation:* $14,821.

Applying *Options:* electronic application. *Required:* Official transcripts from any post-secondary institution attended—must be in good standing with all institutions. *Required for some:* high school transcript, minimum 2.5 GPA. *Application deadlines:* 8/24 (freshmen), 8/24 (out-of-state freshmen), 8/24 (transfers). *Notification:* continuous until 8/1 (freshmen), continuous until 8/1 (out-of-state freshmen), continuous until 8/1 (transfers).

Freshman Application Contact Mr. Cody Spitz, Director, Enrollment Services, Eastern New Mexico University, Station #7 ENMU, Portales, NM 88130. *Phone:* 575-562-2178. *Toll-free phone:* 800-367-3668. *Fax:* 575-562-2118. *E-mail:* cody.spitz@enmu.edu.
Website: http://www.enmu.edu/.

Institute of American Indian Arts

Santa Fe, New Mexico

- **Federally supported** comprehensive, founded 1962
- **Urban** 140-acre campus
- **Coed** 414 students

Faculty *Student/faculty ratio:* 15:1.

Academics *Calendar:* semesters. *Degrees:* associate, bachelor's, and master's. *Special study options:* academic remediation for entering students, distance learning, double majors, independent study, internships, off-campus study, services for LD students, summer session for credit.

Student Life *Housing options:* coed. Campus housing is university owned. *Activities and organizations:* drama/theater group, student-run newspaper. *Campus security:* 24-hour patrols, late-night transport/escort service. *Student services:* personal/psychological counseling.

Athletics *Intramural sports:* cross-country running M/W.

Standardized Tests *Required:* SAT or ACT (for admission), ACCUPLACER, Compass, ASSET (for admission).

Financial Aid Of all full-time matriculated undergraduates who enrolled in 2011, 263 applied for aid, 261 were judged to have need, 201 had their need fully met. 2 Federal Work-Study jobs (averaging $2300). 3 state and other part-time jobs (averaging $2300). In 2011, 58 non-need-based awards were made. *Average percent of need met:* 71%. *Average financial aid package:* $5005. *Average need-based gift aid:* $2500. *Average non-need-based aid:* $2500.

Applying *Required:* high school transcript, 2 letters of recommendation. *Required for some:* essay or personal statement, interview. *Recommended:* interview.

Freshman Application Contact Institute of American Indian Arts, 83 Avan Nu Po Road, Santa Fe, NM 87508. *Phone:* 505-4242307.
Website: http://www.iaia.edu/.

ITT Technical Institute

Albuquerque, New Mexico

- **Proprietary** primarily 2-year, founded 1989, part of ITT Educational Services, Inc.
- **Coed**
- **Minimally difficult** entrance level

Academics *Calendar:* quarters. *Degrees:* associate and bachelor's.

Freshman Application Contact Director of Recruitment, ITT Technical Institute, 5100 Masthead Street, NE, Albuquerque, NM 87109. *Phone:* 505-828-1114. *Toll-free phone:* 800-636-1114.
Website: http://www.itt-tech.edu/.

National American University

Albuquerque, New Mexico

Freshman Application Contact National American University, 4775 Indian School, NE, Suite 200, Albuquerque, NM 87110. *Phone:* 505-265-7517. *Toll-free phone:* 800-895-9904.
Website: http://www.national.edu/.

National College of Midwifery

Taos, New Mexico

Director of Admissions Ms. Beth Enson, Dean of Students, National College of Midwifery, 209 State Road 240, Taos, NM 87571. *Phone:* 505-758-8914.
E-mail: info@midwiferycollege.org.
Website: http://www.midwiferycollege.org/.

New Mexico Highlands University

Las Vegas, New Mexico

- **State-supported** comprehensive, founded 1893
- **Small-town** campus
- **Endowment** $1.8 million
- **Coed** 2,416 undergraduate students, 71% full-time, 59% women, 41% men
- **Minimally difficult** entrance level, 100% of applicants were admitted

Undergraduates 1,724 full-time, 692 part-time. 23% are from out of state; 6% Black or African American, non-Hispanic/Latino; 57% Hispanic/Latino; 0.4% Asian, non-Hispanic/Latino; 0.5% Native Hawaiian or other Pacific Islander, non-Hispanic/Latino; 7% American Indian or Alaska Native, non-Hispanic/Latino; 2% Two or more races, non-Hispanic/Latino; 2% Race/ethnicity unknown; 7% international; 16% transferred in; 29% live on campus. *Retention:* 55% of full-time freshmen returned.

Freshmen *Admission:* 2,649 applied, 2,649 admitted, 436 enrolled. *Average high school GPA:* 2.93. *Test scores:* SAT critical reading scores over 500: 18%; SAT math scores over 500: 33%; SAT writing scores over 500: 23%; ACT scores over 18: 44%; SAT critical reading scores over 600: 3%; SAT math scores over 600: 10%; SAT writing scores over 600: 3%; ACT scores over 24: 4%.

Faculty *Total:* 331, 43% full-time, 37% with terminal degrees. *Student/faculty ratio:* 14:1.

Academics *Calendar:* semesters. *Degrees:* bachelor's, master's, post-master's, and postbachelor's certificates. *Special study options:* academic remediation for entering students, accelerated degree program, advanced placement credit, cooperative education, distance learning, double majors, honors programs, independent study, internships, off-campus study, part-time degree program, services for LD students, summer session for credit.

Computers on Campus 500 computers/terminals are available on campus for general student use. Students can access the following: online (class) registration. Campuswide network is available.

Student Life *Housing options:* coed, men-only, women-only, disabled students. Campus housing is university owned. *Activities and organizations:* drama/theater group, student-run radio station, choral group, marching band, Vatos Rugby, Fire Escape Club, MeChA, NMHU Cheerleaders, NMHU Student Ambassadors, national fraternities, national sororities. *Campus security:* 24-hour emergency response devices and patrols, late-night transport/escort service, controlled dormitory access. *Student services:* health clinic, personal/psychological counseling, women's center.

Athletics Member NCAA. All Division II. *Intercollegiate sports:* baseball M(s), basketball M(s)/W(s), cross-country running M(s)/W(s), football M(s), soccer W(s), softball W(s), track and field M/W, volleyball W(s). *Intramural sports:* badminton M/W, basketball M/W, football M, golf M/W, racquetball M/W, rugby M, skiing (cross-country) M/W, skiing (downhill) M/W, softball W, swimming and diving M/W, table tennis M/W, tennis M/W, volleyball M/W, weight lifting M/W.

Standardized Tests *Recommended:* SAT or ACT (for admission), COMPASS.

Costs (2013–14) *Tuition:* state resident $2653 full-time, $221 per credit hour part-time; nonresident $5671 full-time, $402 per credit hour part-time. Full-time tuition and fees vary according to course load and location. Part-time tuition and fees vary according to course load and location. *Required fees:* $851 full-time. *Room and board:* $5920. Room and board charges vary according to board plan and housing facility. *Payment plan:* installment. *Waivers:* senior citizens and employees or children of employees.

Financial Aid Of all full-time matriculated undergraduates who enrolled in 2011, 1,399 applied for aid, 1,245 were judged to have need, 46 had their need fully met. *Average financial aid package:* $1747. *Average need-based loan:* $2056. *Average need-based gift aid:* $1889.

Applying *Options:* electronic application, early admission, deferred entrance. *Required:* high school transcript, minimum 2.0 GPA. *Required for some:* 2 letters of recommendation, interview. *Application deadlines:* rolling (freshmen), rolling (out-of-state freshmen), rolling (transfers). *Notification:* continuous (freshmen), continuous (out-of-state freshmen), continuous (transfers).

Freshman Application Contact Mr. Fidel Trujillo, Vice President for Student Affairs, New Mexico Highlands University, Box 9000, Las Vegas, NM 87701. *Phone:* 505-454-3566. *Toll-free phone:* 800-338-6648. *E-mail:* admission@nmhu.edu.

Website: http://www.nmhu.edu/.

New Mexico Institute of Mining and Technology

Socorro, New Mexico

- **State-supported** university, founded 1889
- **Small-town** 320-acre campus with easy access to Albuquerque
- **Endowment** $25.3 million
- **Coed** 1,565 undergraduate students, 87% full-time, 30% women, 70% men
- **Moderately difficult** entrance level, 31% of applicants were admitted

Undergraduates 1,359 full-time, 206 part-time. Students come from 38 states and territories; 10 other countries; 17% are from out of state; 2% Black or African American, non-Hispanic/Latino; 26% Hispanic/Latino; 2% Asian, non-Hispanic/Latino; 0.1% Native Hawaiian or other Pacific Islander, non-Hispanic/Latino; 3% American Indian or Alaska Native, non-Hispanic/Latino; 3% Two or more races, non-Hispanic/Latino; 0.1% Race/ethnicity unknown; 3% international; 7% transferred in; 48% live on campus. *Retention:* 74% of full-time freshmen returned.

Freshman *Admission:* 1,188 applied, 369 admitted, 348 enrolled. *Average high school GPA:* 3.65. *Test scores:* SAT critical reading scores over 500: 92%; SAT math scores over 500: 95%; ACT scores over 18: 100%; SAT critical reading scores over 600: 59%; SAT math scores over 600: 72%; ACT scores over 24: 71%; SAT critical reading scores over 700: 13%; SAT math scores over 700: 25%; ACT scores over 30: 21%.

Faculty *Total:* 162, 77% full-time, 82% with terminal degrees. *Student/faculty ratio:* 12:1.

Academics *Calendar:* semesters. *Degrees:* associate, bachelor's, master's, and doctoral. *Special study options:* accelerated degree program, advanced placement credit, cooperative education, distance learning, double majors, independent study, internships, services for LD students, student-designed majors, summer session for credit. *Unusual degree programs:* 3-2 earth sciences.

Computers on Campus 225 computers/terminals are available on campus for general student use. Students can access the following: computer help desk, free student e-mail accounts, online (class) registration, online (class) schedules. Campuswide network is available. Wireless service is available via computer centers, learning centers, student centers.

Student Life *Housing options:* coed, men-only, women-only. Campus housing is university owned. *Activities and organizations:* drama/theater group, student-run newspaper, radio station, choral group. *Campus security:* 24-hour emergency response devices and patrols, late-night transport/escort service. *Student services:* health clinic, personal/psychological counseling.

Athletics *Intercollegiate sports:* golf M(c)/W(c), rugby M(c)/W(c), soccer M(c)/W(c). *Intramural sports:* badminton M/W, basketball M/W, soccer M/W, softball M/W, volleyball M/W.

Standardized Tests *Required:* SAT or ACT (for admission). *Recommended:* ACT (for admission).

Costs (2012–13) *Tuition:* state resident $4828 full-time, $201 per credit hour part-time; nonresident $15,699 full-time, $654 per credit hour part-time. Full-time tuition and fees vary according to reciprocity agreements. Part-time tuition and fees vary according to course load. *Required fees:* $668 full-time, $18 per credit hour part-time, $72 per term part-time. *Room and board:* $6304. Room and board charges vary according to board plan and housing facility. *Waivers:* senior citizens and employees or children of employees.

Financial Aid Of all full-time matriculated undergraduates who enrolled in 2012, 1,216 applied for aid, 712 were judged to have need, 150 had their need fully met. In 2012, 454 non-need-based awards were made. *Average percent of need met:* 82%. *Average financial aid package:* $12,026. *Average need-based loan:* $4293. *Average need-based gift aid:* $6046. *Average non-need-based aid:* $6707. *Average indebtedness upon graduation:* $18,834.

Applying *Options:* electronic application, deferred entrance. *Application fee:* $15. *Required:* high school transcript, minimum 2.5 GPA. *Required for some:* 2 letters of recommendation. *Recommended:* interview. *Application deadlines:* 8/1 (freshmen), 8/1 (transfers). *Notification:* continuous (freshmen), continuous (transfers).

Freshman Application Contact Mr. Mike Kloeppel, Director of Admissions, New Mexico Institute of Mining and Technology, 801 Leroy Place, Socorro, NM 87801. *Phone:* 575-835-5424. *Toll-free phone:* 800-428-TECH. *Fax:* 575-835-5989. *E-mail:* admission@admin.nmt.edu.

Website: http://www.nmt.edu/.

New Mexico State University

Las Cruces, New Mexico

- **State-supported** university, founded 1888, part of New Mexico State University System
- **Suburban** 900-acre campus with easy access to El Paso
- **Endowment** $77.9 million
- **Coed** 14,276 undergraduate students, 82% full-time, 54% women, 46% men
- **Moderately difficult** entrance level, 80% of applicants were admitted

Undergraduates 11,673 full-time, 2,603 part-time. Students come from 50 states and territories; 62 other countries; 21% are from out of state; 3% Black or African American, non-Hispanic/Latino; 51% Hispanic/Latino; 1% Asian, non-Hispanic/Latino; 0.2% Native Hawaiian or other Pacific Islander, non-Hispanic/Latino; 2% American Indian or Alaska Native, non-Hispanic/Latino; 1% Two or more races, non-Hispanic/Latino; 4% Race/ethnicity unknown; 4% international; 5% transferred in; 18% live on campus. *Retention:* 72% of full-time freshmen returned.

Freshman *Admission:* 5,928 applied, 4,746 admitted, 2,061 enrolled. *Average high school GPA:* 3.37. *Test scores:* SAT critical reading scores over 500: 47%; SAT math scores over 500: 51%; SAT writing scores over 500: 59%; ACT scores over 18: 80%; SAT critical reading scores over 600: 16%; SAT math scores over 600: 12%; SAT writing scores over 600: 19%; ACT scores over 24: 28%; SAT critical reading scores over 700: 2%; SAT math scores over 700: 1%; SAT writing scores over 700: 1%; ACT scores over 30: 3%.

Faculty *Total:* 833, 74% full-time, 72% with terminal degrees. *Student/faculty ratio:* 22:1.

Academics *Calendar:* semesters. *Degrees:* associate, bachelor's, master's, doctoral, post-master's, and postbachelor's certificates. *Special study options:* academic remediation for entering students, accelerated degree program, adult/continuing education programs, advanced placement credit, cooperative education, distance learning, double majors, English as a second language, honors programs, independent study, internships, off-campus study, part-time degree program, services for LD students, student-designed majors, study abroad, summer session for credit. *ROTC:* Army (b), Air Force (b).

Computers on Campus 369 computers/terminals and 600 ports are available on campus for general student use. Students can access the following: campus intranet, computer help desk, free student e-mail accounts, online (class) grades, online (class) registration, online (class) schedules, dialup internet, antivirus software, student portal online (Microsoft products, file share/storage space, student employee clock-in, payments system, emergency notification signup) PC/laptop/equipment rentals, short-term iPad checkout, software discounts. Campuswide network is available. 100% of college-owned or -operated housing units are wired for high-speed Internet access. Wireless service is available via entire campus.

Student Life *Housing options:* coed, disabled students. Campus housing is university owned. *Activities and organizations:* drama/theater group, student-run newspaper, radio and television station, choral group, marching band, Pride Marching Band, Kappa Sigma (Social Fraternity), Blue Wings, Gamma Beta Phi, Chi Omega (social sorority), national fraternities, national sororities. *Campus security:* 24-hour emergency response devices and patrols, late-night transport/escort service, controlled dormitory access. *Student services:* health clinic, personal/psychological counseling, legal services.

Athletics Member NCAA. All Division I except football (Division I-A). *Intercollegiate sports:* baseball M(s), basketball M(s)/W(s), cross-country running M(s)/W(s), equestrian sports M/W, golf M(s)/W(s), softball W(s), swimming and diving W(s), tennis M(s)/W(s), track and field W(s), volleyball W(s). *Intramural sports:* archery M/W, badminton M/W, baseball M, basketball M/W, bowling M(c)/W(c), cheerleading M/W, football M/W, golf M/W, racquetball M/W, rock climbing M(c)/W(c), rugby M(c)/W(c), skiing (downhill) M(c)/W(c), soccer M(c)/W(c), softball M/W, tennis M/W, ultimate Frisbee M(c)/W(c), volleyball M(c)/W(c), water polo M/W, weight lifting M(c)/W(c), wrestling M.

Standardized Tests *Required:* SAT or ACT (for admission).

Costs (2012–13) *One-time required fee:* $40. *Tuition:* state resident $4766 full-time, $199 per credit hour part-time; nonresident $17,794 full-time, $741 per credit hour part-time. *Required fees:* $1274 full-time, $53 per credit hour part-time. *Room and board:* $7182; room only: $3946. Room and board charges vary according to board plan and housing facility. *Payment plans:* installment, deferred payment. *Waivers:* senior citizens and employees or children of employees.

Financial Aid Of all full-time matriculated undergraduates who enrolled in 2012, 9,092 applied for aid, 7,705 were judged to have need, 932 had their need fully met. 330 Federal Work-Study jobs (averaging $3018). 314 state and other part-time jobs (averaging $3179). In 2012, 620 non-need-based awards were made. *Average percent of need met:* 69%. *Average financial aid package:* $9715. *Average need-based loan:* $3754. *Average need-based gift aid:* $8313. *Average non-need-based aid:* $1872. *Average indebtedness upon graduation:* $18,922.

Applying *Options:* electronic application, early admission, deferred entrance. *Application fee:* $20. *Required:* high school transcript, minimum 2.0 GPA, Applicants must score 20 on the ACT or may take the SAT (accepted, but not recommended) and submit a composite score of 780. The GED is accepted. Minimum high school participation includes 4 units of English, 3 of math, 2 beyond general science, and 1 foreign language/fine arts. *Application deadlines:* 8/19 (freshmen), 8/14 (transfers). *Notification:* continuous (freshmen), continuous (transfers).

Freshman Application Contact Valerie Pickett, Director of Admissions, New Mexico State University, Box 30001, MSC 3A, Las Cruces, NM 88003-8001. *Phone:* 575-646-3121. *Toll-free phone:* 800-662-6678. *Fax:* 575-646-6330. *E-mail:* admssions@nmsu.edu. *Website:* http://www.nmsu.edu/.

Northern New Mexico College

Española, New Mexico

Freshman Application Contact Mr. Mike L. Costello, Registrar, Northern New Mexico College, 921 Paseo de Oñate, Española, NM 87532. *Phone:* 505-747-2193. *Fax:* 505-747-2191. *E-mail:* dms@nnmc.edu. *Website:* http://www.nnmc.edu/.

Pima Medical Institute

Albuquerque, New Mexico

Freshman Application Contact Admissions Office, Pima Medical Institute, 4400 Cutler Avenue NE, Albuquerque, NM 87110. *Phone:* 505-881-1234. *Toll-free phone:* 800-477-PIMA (in-state); 888-477-PIMA (out-of-state). *Fax:* 505-881-5329. *Website:* http://www.pmi.edu/.

St. John's College

Santa Fe, New Mexico

- **Independent** comprehensive, founded 1964
- **Suburban** 250-acre campus with easy access to Albuquerque
- **Endowment** $129.9 million
- **Coed** 349 undergraduate students, 99% full-time, 43% women, 57% men
- **Very difficult** entrance level, 84% of applicants were admitted

Undergraduates 345 full-time, 4 part-time. Students come from 18 states and territories; 24 other countries; 79% are from out of state; 0.6% Black or African American, non-Hispanic/Latino; 11% Hispanic/Latino; 3% Asian, non-Hispanic/Latino; 0.6% American Indian or Alaska Native, non-Hispanic/Latino; 6% Two or more races, non-Hispanic/Latino; 2% Race/ethnicity unknown; 14% international; 6% transferred in; 82% live on campus. *Retention:* 70% of full-time freshmen returned.

Freshmen *Admission:* 251 applied, 211 admitted, 99 enrolled. *Test scores:* SAT critical reading scores over 500: 92%; SAT math scores over 500: 83%; SAT writing scores over 500: 90%; ACT scores over 18: 100%; SAT critical reading scores over 600: 72%; SAT math scores over 600: 65%; SAT writing scores over 600: 57%; ACT scores over 24: 96%; SAT critical reading scores over 700: 39%; SAT math scores over 700: 22%; SAT writing scores over 700: 16%; ACT scores over 30: 21%.

Faculty *Total:* 60, 97% full-time, 80% with terminal degrees. *Student/faculty ratio:* 7:1.

Academics *Calendar:* semesters. *Degrees:* diplomas, bachelor's, and master's. *Special study options:* internships, off-campus study, summer session for credit.

Computers on Campus 21 computers/terminals are available on campus for general student use. Students can access the following: computer help desk, free student e-mail accounts. Campuswide network is available. 100% of college-owned or -operated housing units are wired for high-speed Internet access. Wireless service is available via classrooms, computer centers, computer labs, dorm rooms, learning centers, student centers.

Student Life *Housing:* on-campus residence required through senior year. *Options:* coed, men-only, women-only, disabled students. Campus housing is university owned. Freshman campus housing is guaranteed. *Activities and organizations:* drama/theater group, student-run newspaper, Iron Bookworm Workout, Chrysostomos (Theater), Jazz Dance, Student Government/Student Committee on Instruction, Intramural Sports. *Campus security:* 24-hour emergency response devices and patrols, late-night transport/escort service, controlled dormitory access. *Student services:* health clinic, personal/psychological counseling.

Athletics *Intercollegiate sports:* fencing M/W. *Intramural sports:* badminton M/W, basketball M/W, cross-country running M/W, fencing M/W, ice hockey M/W, racquetball M/W, rock climbing M/W, skiing (cross-country) M/W, skiing (downhill) M/W, soccer M/W, softball M/W, squash M/W, table tennis M/W, tennis M/W, ultimate Frisbee M/W, volleyball M/W.

Standardized Tests *Required for some:* SAT (for admission).

Costs (2013–14) *Comprehensive fee:* $54,998 includes full-time tuition ($44,554), mandatory fees ($450), and room and board ($9994). Part-time tuition: $1311 per credit hour. *College room only:* $4997. Room and board charges vary according to board plan. *Payment plans:* tuition prepayment, installment. *Waivers:* employees or children of employees.

Financial Aid Of all full-time matriculated undergraduates who enrolled in 2011, 342 applied for aid, 321 were judged to have need, 285 had their need fully met. 121 Federal Work-Study jobs (averaging $2920). 8 state and other part-time jobs (averaging $2930). *Average percent of need met:* 90%. *Average financial aid package:* $34,220. *Average need-based loan:* $59,800. *Average need-based gift aid:* $25,580. *Average indebtedness upon graduation:* $28,563.

Applying *Options:* electronic application, early action. *Required:* essay or personal statement, high school transcript, 2 letters of recommendation. *Required for some:* interview. *Recommended:* 3 letters of recommendation, interview. *Application deadline:* 11/15 (early action). *Notification:* 12/15 (early action).

Freshman Application Contact Mr. Larry Clendenin, Director of Admissions, St. John's College, 1160 Camino Cruz Blanca, Santa Fe, NM 87505. *Phone:* 505-984-6060. *Toll-free phone:* 800-331-5232. *Fax:* 505-984-6162. *E-mail:* admissions@sjcsf.edu. *Website:* http://www.stjohnscollege.edu/.

See page 380 for display ad and page 1470 for the College Close-Up.

Santa Fe University of Art and Design

Santa Fe, New Mexico

- **Independent** 4-year, founded 1947
- **Suburban** 100-acre campus with easy access to Albuquerque
- **Coed** 544 undergraduate students, 99% full-time, 53% women, 47% men
- **Moderately difficult** entrance level, 100% of applicants were admitted

Undergraduates 541 full-time, 3 part-time. Students come from 40 states and territories; 12 other countries; 66% are from out of state; 7% Black or African American, non-Hispanic/Latino; 22% Hispanic/Latino; 1% Asian, non-Hispanic/Latino; 1% Native Hawaiian or other Pacific Islander, non-Hispanic/Latino; 3% American Indian or Alaska Native, non-Hispanic/Latino; 4% Two or more races, non-Hispanic/Latino; 5% Race/ethnicity unknown; 12% international; 12% transferred in; 66% live on campus. *Retention:* 55% of full-time freshmen returned.

Freshmen *Admission:* 347 applied, 347 admitted, 166 enrolled. *Average high school GPA:* 3.12. *Test scores:* SAT critical reading scores over 500: 68%; SAT math scores over 500: 54%; SAT writing scores over 500: 52%; ACT scores over 18: 80%; SAT critical reading scores over 600: 19%; SAT math scores over 600: 21%; SAT writing scores over 600: 17%; ACT scores over 24: 28%; SAT critical reading scores over 700: 2%; SAT math scores over 700: 1%; ACT scores over 30: 3%.

Faculty *Total:* 99, 27% full-time. *Student/faculty ratio:* 10:1.

Academics *Calendar:* semesters. *Degree:* bachelor's. *Special study options:* academic remediation for entering students, accelerated degree program, advanced placement credit, cooperative education, double majors, English as a second language, independent study, internships, off-campus study, services for LD students, student-designed majors, study abroad, summer session for credit.

Computers on Campus 84 computers/terminals are available on campus for general student use. Students can access the following: campus intranet, free student e-mail accounts, online (class) grades, online (class) registration, online (class) schedules. Campuswide network is available. 100% of college-owned or -operated housing units are wired for high-speed Internet access. Wireless service is available via entire campus.

Student Life *Housing:* on-campus residence required through sophomore year. *Options:* coed, disabled students. Campus housing is university owned. *Activities and organizations:* drama/theater group, student-run newspaper, choral group, Student Writer's Association, Performing Arts Collective, Colors: Queer Identity Group, Cluster, Film Clubs. *Campus security:* 24-hour patrols, late-night transport/escort service, controlled dormitory access. *Student services:* health clinic, personal/psychological counseling.

Athletics *Intramural sports:* racquetball M/W.

Standardized Tests *Required:* SAT or ACT (for admission).

Costs (2013–14) *Tuition:* $28,836 full-time, $1081 per credit hour part-time.

Applying *Options:* electronic application, deferred entrance. *Application fee:* $50. *Required:* essay or personal statement, high school transcript. *Required for some:* portfolio or audition for visual and performing arts programs. *Recommended:* minimum 2.0 GPA. *Application deadlines:* rolling (freshmen), rolling (out-of-state freshmen), rolling (transfers). *Notification:* continuous (freshmen), continuous (out-of-state freshmen), continuous (transfers).

Freshman Application Contact Ms. Christine Lyn Guevara, Executive Director of Student Operations, Santa Fe University of Art and Design, 1600 Saint Michael's Drive, Santa Fe, NM 87505-7634. *Phone:* 505-473-6652. *Toll-free phone:* 800-456-2673. *Fax:* 505-473-6127. *E-mail:* christine.guevara@santafeuniversity.edu.
Website: http://www.santafeuniversity.edu/.

University of New Mexico
Albuquerque, New Mexico

- **State-supported** university, founded 1889
- **Urban** 769-acre campus with easy access to Albuquerque
- **Endowment** $336.0 million
- **Coed**
- **Moderately difficult** entrance level, 65% of applicants were admitted

Undergraduates Students come from 52 states and territories; 63 other countries. *Retention:* 77% of full-time freshmen returned.

Freshmen *Admission:* 11,467 applied, 7,405 admitted. *Average high school GPA:* 3.24. *Test scores:* SAT critical reading scores over 500: 68%; SAT math scores over 500: 67%; ACT scores over 18: 88%; SAT critical reading scores over 600: 30%; SAT math scores over 600: 27%; ACT scores over 24: 37%; SAT critical reading scores over 700: 8%; SAT math scores over 700: 5%; ACT scores over 30: 5%.

Faculty *Total:* 1,548, 66% full-time, 62% with terminal degrees. *Student/faculty ratio:* 23:1.

Academics *Calendar:* semesters. *Degrees:* certificates, associate, bachelor's, master's, doctoral, and post-master's certificates. *Special study options:* academic remediation for entering students, accelerated degree program, adult/continuing education programs, advanced placement credit, cooperative education, distance learning, double majors, English as a second language, freshman honors college, honors programs, independent study, internships, off-campus study, part-time degree program, services for LD students, student-designed majors, study abroad, summer session for credit. *ROTC:* Army (b), Navy (b), Air Force (b). *Unusual degree programs:* 3-2 business administration; engineering; Latin American studies, business.

Computers on Campus 766 computers/terminals are available on campus for general student use. Students can access the following: computer help desk, free student e-mail accounts, online (class) grades, online (class) registration, online (class) schedules. Campuswide network is available. 100% of college-owned or -operated housing units are wired for high-speed Internet access. Wireless service is available via entire campus.

Student Life *Housing options:* coed, disabled students. Campus housing is university owned and is provided by a third party. *Activities and organizations:* drama/theater group, student-run newspaper, radio and television station, choral group, marching band, Associated Students of UNM, Graduate and Professional Students Association, Golden Key National Honor Society, national fraternities, national sororities. *Campus security:* 24-hour emergency response devices and patrols, student patrols, late-night transport/escort service, controlled dormitory access. *Student services:* health clinic, personal/psychological counseling, women's center.

Athletics Member NCAA. All Division I except football (Division I-A). *Intercollegiate sports:* baseball M, basketball M(s)/W(s), cross-country running

M(s)/W(s), golf M(s)/W(s), skiing (cross-country) M(s)/W(s), skiing (downhill) M(s)/W(s), soccer M(s)/W(s), softball W(s), swimming and diving W(s), tennis M(s)/W(s), track and field M(s)/W(s), volleyball W(s). *Intramural sports:* basketball M/W, bowling M/W, cheerleading W(c), cross-country running M/W, fencing M/W, football M/W, golf M/W, ice hockey M(c)/W(c), racquetball M/W, rugby M(c)/W(c), skiing (downhill) M/W, soccer M/W, softball M/W, swimming and diving W, table tennis M/W, tennis M/W, ultimate Frisbee M(c)/W(c), volleyball M/W, water polo M/W, wrestling M(c).

Standardized Tests *Required:* SAT or ACT (for admission).

Costs (2012–13) *Tuition:* state resident $6049 full-time; nonresident $20,688 full-time. Full-time tuition and fees vary according to program. Part-time tuition and fees vary according to course load and program. *Required fees:* $612 full-time. *Room and board:* Room and board charges vary according to board plan and housing facility. *Payment plan:* installment. *Waivers:* senior citizens and employees or children of employees.

Applying *Options:* electronic application, early admission, deferred entrance. *Application fee:* $20. *Required:* high school transcript, minimum 2.5 GPA. *Required for some:* essay or personal statement, interview. *Application deadlines:* rolling (freshmen), rolling (transfers). *Notification:* continuous (freshmen), continuous (transfers).

Freshman Application Contact Mr. Matthew Hulett, Director of Admissions and Recruitment Services, University of New Mexico, Office of Admissions, PO Box 4895, Albuquerque, NM 87196-4895. *Phone:* 505-277-8900. *Toll-free phone:* 800-CALL-UNM. *Fax:* 505-277-6686. *E-mail:* apply@unm.edu. *Website:* http://www.unm.edu/.

University of New Mexico–Gallup
Gallup, New Mexico

Director of Admissions Ms. Pearl A. Morris, Admissions Representative, University of New Mexico–Gallup, 200 College Road, Gallup, NM 87301-5603. *Phone:* 505-863-7576.
Website: http://www.gallup.unm.edu/.

University of Phoenix–New Mexico Campus
Albuquerque, New Mexico

Freshman Application Contact Marc Booker, Sr. Director, Office of Admissions and Evaluation, University of Phoenix–New Mexico Campus, 4035 South Riverpoint Parkway, Mail Stop CF-L101, Phoenix, AZ 85040. *Phone:* 602-557-4609. *Toll-free phone:* 866-766-0766. *Fax:* 480-643-1156. *Website:* http://www.phoenix.edu/.

University of the Southwest
Hobbs, New Mexico

- **Independent Christian** comprehensive, founded 1962
- **Small-town** 162-acre campus
- **Endowment** $4.5 million
- **Coed**
- **Moderately difficult** entrance level

Faculty *Student/faculty ratio:* 15:1.

Academics *Calendar:* semesters. *Degrees:* bachelor's and master's.

Student Life *Campus security:* student patrols, controlled dormitory access, night Security.

Athletics Member NAIA.

Standardized Tests *Required:* SAT or ACT (for admission).

Costs (2012–13) *One-time required fee:* $300. *Comprehensive fee:* $18,905 includes full-time tuition ($12,240), mandatory fees ($25), and room and board ($6640). Full-time tuition and fees vary according to course load. Part-time tuition: $510 per semester hour. Part-time tuition and fees vary according to course load. *College room only:* $3720. Room and board charges vary according to board plan and housing facility.

Financial Aid *Of all full-time matriculated undergraduates who enrolled in 2011,* 282 applied for aid, 234 were judged to have need, 38 had their need fully met. 22 Federal Work-Study jobs (averaging $1663). 18 state and other part-time jobs (averaging $1751). *In 2011,* 48 non-need-based awards were made. *Average percent of need met:* 70. *Average financial aid package:* $6687. *Average need-based loan:* $3815. *Average need-based gift aid:* $3948. *Aver-*

age *non-need-based aid:* $1219. *Average indebtedness upon graduation:* $23,159.

Applying *Options:* electronic application, early admission, deferred entrance. *Application fee:* $25. *Required:* high school transcript, minimum 2.0 GPA.

Freshman Application Contact Ashley Taylor, Admissions Coordinator, University of the Southwest, 6610 North Lovington Highway, Hobbs, NM 88240. *Phone:* 575-492-2121. *Toll-free phone:* 800-530-4400. *Fax:* 575-392-6006. *E-mail:* ataylor@usw.edu. *Website:* http://www.usw.edu/.

Western New Mexico University

Silver City, New Mexico

Freshman Application Contact Mr. Dan Tressler, Director of Admissions, Western New Mexico University, PO Box 680, Silver City, NM 88062-0680. *Phone:* 505-538-6106. *Toll-free phone:* 800-872-WNMU. *Fax:* 505-538-6127. *E-mail:* tresslerd@wnmu.edu. *Website:* http://www.wnmu.edu/.

NEW YORK

Adelphi University

Garden City, New York

- **Independent** university, founded 1896
- **Suburban** 75-acre campus with easy access to New York City
- **Endowment** $131.3 million
- **Coed** 5,103 undergraduate students, 89% full-time, 70% women, 30% men
- **Moderately difficult** entrance level, 66% of applicants were admitted

Undergraduates 4,525 full-time, 578 part-time. Students come from 36 states and territories; 39 other countries; 8% are from out of state; 10% Black or African American, non-Hispanic/Latino; 13% Hispanic/Latino; 7% Asian, non-Hispanic/Latino; 0.3% Native Hawaiian or other Pacific Islander, non-Hispanic/Latino; 0.2% American Indian or Alaska Native, non-Hispanic/Latino; 3% Two or more races, non-Hispanic/Latino; 10% Race/ethnicity unknown; 3% international; 11% transferred in; 24% live on campus. *Retention:* 82% of full-time freshmen returned.

Freshmen *Admission:* 9,184 applied, 6,104 admitted, 999 enrolled. *Average high school GPA:* 3.5. *Test scores:* SAT critical reading scores over 500: 75%; SAT math scores over 500: 82%; SAT writing scores over 500: 81%; ACT scores over 18: 98%; SAT critical reading scores over 600: 26%; SAT math scores over 600: 34%; SAT writing scores over 600: 34%; ACT scores over 24: 63%; SAT critical reading scores over 700: 5%; SAT math scores over 700: 5%; SAT writing scores over 700: 5%; ACT scores over 30: 12%.

Faculty *Total:* 999, 32% full-time. *Student/faculty ratio:* 12:1.

Academics *Calendar:* semesters. *Degrees:* associate, bachelor's, master's, doctoral, post-master's, and postbachelor's certificates. *Special study options:* accelerated degree program, advanced placement credit, cooperative education, distance learning, double majors, English as a second language, freshman honors college, honors programs, independent study, internships, part-time degree program, services for LD students, student-designed majors, study abroad, summer session for credit. *ROTC:* Army (c), Air Force (c). *Unusual degree programs:* 3-2 engineering with Columbia University; Physical Therapy: New York Medical Coll, New York Institute of Tech; Dentistry: NYU Coll of Dentistry; Environmental Studies: Columbia University; Medicine: Philadelphia Coll of Osteopathic Medicine, Lake Erie Coll of Osteopathic Medicine; Optometry: SUNY State Coll of Optometry; Podiatry: NYCPM.

Computers on Campus 880 computers/terminals are available on campus for general student use. Students can access the following: computer help desk, free student e-mail accounts, online (class) grades, online (class) registration, online (class) schedules, payment, drop/add classes, check application status. Campuswide network is available. 100% of college-owned or -operated housing units are wired for high-speed Internet access. Wireless service is available via entire campus.

Student Life *Housing options:* coed, disabled students. Campus housing is university owned. Freshman applicants given priority for college housing. *Activities and organizations:* student-run newspaper, radio station, choral group, Student Activities Board, C. A. L. I. B. E. R. (Cause to Achieve Leadership, Intelligence, Brotherhood, Excellence, and Respect), Circle K International, Commuter Student Organization, S.N.A.P. Student Nurses Acting for Progress, national fraternities, national sororities. *Campus security:* 24-hour emergency response devices and patrols, late-night transport/escort service,

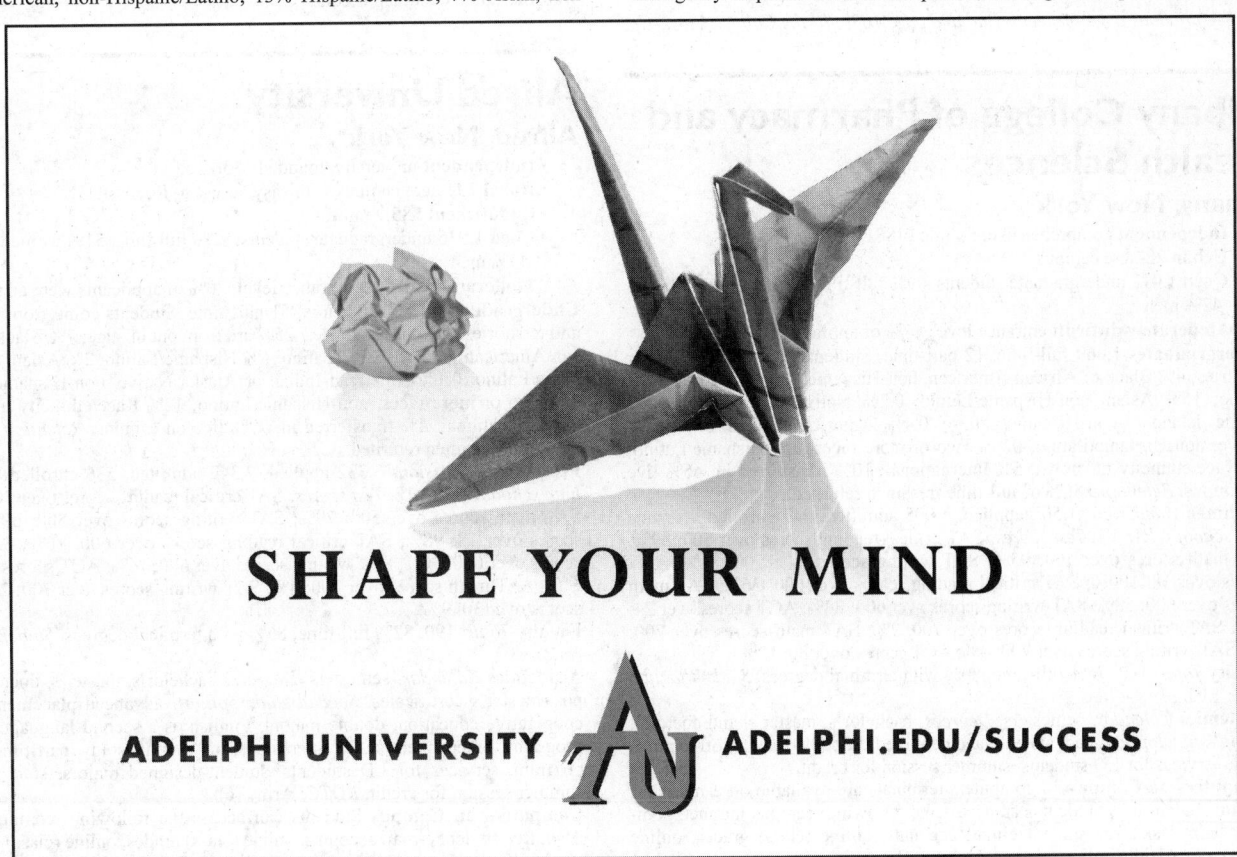

controlled dormitory access. *Student services:* health clinic, personal/psychological counseling.

Athletics Member NCAA. All Division II. *Intercollegiate sports:* baseball M(s), basketball M(s)/W(s), bowling W(s), cross-country running M(s)/W(s), field hockey W(s), golf M(s), lacrosse M(s)/W(s), soccer M(s)/W(s), softball W(s), swimming and diving M(s), tennis M(s)/W(s), track and field M(s)/W(s), volleyball W(s). *Intramural sports:* badminton M/W, basketball M/W, cheerleading W, equestrian sports M(c)/W(c), fencing M(c)/W(c), football M/W, soccer M/W, ultimate Frisbee M(c)/W(c), volleyball M/W, water polo M(c)/W.

Standardized Tests *Required for some:* SAT or ACT (for admission).

Costs (2012–13) *Comprehensive fee:* $41,220 includes full-time tuition ($27,870), mandatory fees ($1450), and room and board ($11,900). Full-time tuition and fees vary according to course level, course load, location, program, and student level. Part-time tuition: $860 per credit hour. Part-time tuition and fees vary according to course level, course load, location, program, and student level. *College room only:* $8420. Room and board charges vary according to board plan and housing facility. *Payment plans:* tuition prepayment, installment, deferred payment. *Waivers:* children of alumni, senior citizens, and employees or children of employees.

Financial Aid Of all full-time matriculated undergraduates who enrolled in 2012, 3,654 applied for aid, 3,275 were judged to have need, 22 had their need fully met. 343 Federal Work-Study jobs (averaging $1680). 996 state and other part-time jobs (averaging $2216). In 2012, 922 non-need-based awards were made. *Average percent of need met:* 32%. *Average financial aid package:* $19,000. *Average need-based loan:* $4581. *Average need-based gift aid:* $6685. *Average non-need-based aid:* $11,471. *Average indebtedness upon graduation:* $35,429.

Applying *Options:* electronic application, early action, deferred entrance. *Application fee:* $40. *Required:* essay or personal statement, high school transcript. *Required for some:* 2 letters of recommendation, interview, auditions/portfolios for performing and fine arts. *Recommended:* minimum 3.4 GPA. *Application deadlines:* rolling (freshmen), rolling (transfers), 12/1 (early action). *Notification:* continuous (freshmen), continuous (transfers), 12/31 (early action).

Freshman Application Contact Ms. Kristen Collins, Director of Undergraduate Admissions, Adelphi University, Levermore Hall 110, 1 South Avenue, PO Box 701, Garden City, NY 11530-0701. *Phone:* 516-877-3050. *Toll-free phone:* 800-ADELPHI. *Fax:* 516-877-3039. *E-mail:* admissions@adelphi.edu.

Website: http://www.adelphi.edu/.

See previous page for display ad and page 1036 for the College Close-Up.

Albany College of Pharmacy and Health Sciences

Albany, New York

- **Independent** comprehensive, founded 1881
- **Urban** 28-acre campus
- **Coed** 1,072 undergraduate students, 99% full-time, 58% women, 42% men
- **Moderately difficult** entrance level, 67% of applicants were admitted

Undergraduates 1,060 full-time, 12 part-time. Students come from 18 other countries; 4% Black or African American, non-Hispanic/Latino; 4% Hispanic/Latino; 15% Asian, non-Hispanic/Latino; 0.2% Native Hawaiian or other Pacific Islander, non-Hispanic/Latino; 0.4% American Indian or Alaska Native, non-Hispanic/Latino; 0.7% Two or more races, non-Hispanic/Latino; 5% Race/ethnicity unknown; 5% international; 10% transferred in; 65% live on campus. *Retention:* 86% of full-time freshmen returned.

Freshmen *Admission:* 1,507 applied, 1,005 admitted, 247 enrolled. *Average high school GPA:* 3.7. *Test scores:* SAT critical reading scores over 500: 89%; SAT math scores over 500: 95%; SAT writing scores over 500: 81%; ACT scores over 18: 100%; SAT critical reading scores over 600: 36%; SAT math scores over 600: 58%; SAT writing scores over 600: 24%; ACT scores over 24: 80%; SAT critical reading scores over 700: 2%; SAT math scores over 700: 7%; SAT writing scores over 700: 4%; ACT scores over 30: 12%.

Faculty *Total:* 142, 76% full-time, 80% with terminal degrees. *Student/faculty ratio:* 13:1.

Academics *Calendar:* semesters. *Degrees:* bachelor's, master's, and doctoral. *Special study options:* advanced placement credit, double majors, off-campus study, services for LD students, summer session for credit.

Computers on Campus 30 computers/terminals are available on campus for general student use. Students can access the following: campus intranet, computer help desk, free student e-mail accounts, online (class) grades, online (class) registration, online (class) schedules. Campuswide network is available.

100% of college-owned or -operated housing units are wired for high-speed Internet access. Wireless service is available via entire campus.

Student Life *Housing:* on-campus residence required through sophomore year. *Options:* coed. Campus housing is university owned and is provided by a third party. Freshman campus housing is guaranteed. *Activities and organizations:* student-run newspaper, American Pharmacy Association-Student Chapter, Orthodox Christian Student Association, Student Government Association, Colleges Against Cancer, national fraternities, national sororities. *Campus security:* 24-hour emergency response devices and patrols, controlled dormitory access. *Student services:* health clinic, personal/psychological counseling.

Athletics Member USCAA. *Intercollegiate sports:* basketball M/W, cross-country running M/W, soccer M/W. *Intramural sports:* basketball M/W, football M/W, golf M(c)/W(c), lacrosse M(c), tennis M(c)/W(c), ultimate Frisbee M/W, volleyball M/W.

Standardized Tests *Required:* SAT or ACT (for admission).

Costs (2012–13) *Comprehensive fee:* $37,390 includes full-time tuition ($26,900), mandatory fees ($730), and room and board ($9760). Full-time tuition and fees vary according to degree level, program, and student level. Part-time tuition: $900 per credit hour. Part-time tuition and fees vary according to degree level, program, and student level. *College room only:* $6400. Room and board charges vary according to board plan, housing facility, and location. *Payment plan:* installment. *Waivers:* employees or children of employees.

Financial Aid Of all full-time matriculated undergraduates who enrolled in 2012, 999 applied for aid, 904 were judged to have need, 80 had their need fully met. In 2012, 114 non-need-based awards were made. *Average percent of need met:* 39%. *Average financial aid package:* $12,568. *Average need-based loan:* $4615. *Average need-based gift aid:* $9719. *Average non-need-based aid:* $8338. *Average indebtedness upon graduation:* $29,160. *Financial aid deadline:* 5/1.

Applying *Options:* electronic application, early decision. *Application fee:* $75. *Required:* essay or personal statement, high school transcript, 2 letters of recommendation. *Required for some:* interview. *Recommended:* minimum 3.0 GPA. *Application deadlines:* 2/1 (freshmen), 2/1 (transfers). *Early decision deadline:* 11/1. *Notification:* 3/15 (freshmen), 3/15 (transfers), 12/16 (early decision).

Freshman Application Contact Mr. Matthew Stever, Director of Admissions, Albany College of Pharmacy and Health Sciences, 106 New Scotland Avenue, Albany, NY 12208. *Phone:* 518-694-7221. *Toll-free phone:* 888-203-8010. *Fax:* 518-694-7322. *E-mail:* admissions@acphs.edu.

Website: http://www.acphs.edu/.

Alfred University

Alfred, New York

- **Independent** university, founded 1836
- **Rural** 232-acre campus with easy access to Rochester, NY
- **Endowment** $85.9 million
- **Coed** 1,935 undergraduate students, 97% full-time, 51% women, 49% men
- **Moderately difficult** entrance level, 70% of applicants were admitted

Undergraduates 1,884 full-time, 51 part-time. Students come from 37 states and territories; 16 other countries; 25% are from out of state; 7% Black or African American, non-Hispanic/Latino; 6% Hispanic/Latino; 2% Asian, non-Hispanic/Latino; 0.1% American Indian or Alaska Native, non-Hispanic/Latino; 2% Two or more races, non-Hispanic/Latino; 12% Race/ethnicity unknown; 3% international; 4% transferred in; 77% live on campus. *Retention:* 68% of full-time freshmen returned.

Freshmen *Admission:* 3,332 applied, 2,342 admitted, 536 enrolled. *Average high school GPA:* 3.18. *Test scores:* SAT critical reading scores over 500: 65%; SAT math scores over 500: 79%; SAT writing scores over 500: 60%; ACT scores over 18: 98%; SAT critical reading scores over 600: 16%; SAT math scores over 600: 30%; SAT writing scores over 600: 16%; ACT scores over 24: 51%; SAT math scores over 700: 4%; SAT writing scores over 700: 2%; ACT scores over 30: 9%.

Faculty *Total:* 190, 82% full-time, 85% with terminal degrees. *Student/faculty ratio:* 13:1.

Academics *Calendar:* semesters. *Degrees:* bachelor's, master's, doctoral, and post-master's certificates. *Special study options:* advanced placement credit, cooperative education, double majors, English as a second language, honors programs, independent study, internships, off-campus study, part-time degree program, services for LD students, student-designed majors, study abroad, summer session for credit. *ROTC:* Army (c).

Computers on Campus Students can access the following: computer help desk, free student e-mail accounts, online (class) grades, online (class) registration, online (class) schedules, online bill pay. Campuswide network is avail-

able. 100% of college-owned or -operated housing units are wired for high-speed Internet access. Wireless service is available via entire campus.
Student Life *Housing:* on-campus residence required through junior year. *Options:* coed, cooperative. Campus housing is university owned. Freshman campus housing is guaranteed. *Activities and organizations:* drama/theater group, student-run newspaper, radio and television station, choral group, Student Senate, Habitat for Humanity, Drawn to Diversity, Student Activities Board. *Campus security:* 24-hour emergency response devices, student patrols, late-night transport/escort service, all dormitories are key-only access, but not electronic. *Student services:* health clinic, personal/psychological counseling, women's center.
Athletics Member NCAA. All Division III. *Intercollegiate sports:* basketball M/W, cross-country running M/W, equestrian sports M/W, football M, lacrosse M/W, skiing (downhill) M/W, soccer M/W, softball W, swimming and diving M/W, tennis M/W, track and field M/W, volleyball W. *Intramural sports:* baseball M(c), basketball M/W, cheerleading W(c), football M/W, golf M/W, ice hockey M(c), lacrosse M/W, racquetball M/W, rugby M(c)/W(c), skiing (cross-country) M/W, soccer M/W, softball M/W, squash M/W, tennis M/W, ultimate Frisbee M(c)/W(c), volleyball M/W.
Standardized Tests *Required:* SAT or ACT (for admission).
Costs (2013–14) *Comprehensive fee:* $40,272 includes full-time tuition ($27,824), mandatory fees ($950), and room and board ($11,498). Full-time tuition and fees vary according to program. Part-time tuition: $902 per credit hour. *Required fees:* $160 per year part-time. *Room and board:* Room and board charges vary according to board plan and housing facility. *Payment plans:* tuition prepayment, installment, deferred payment. *Waivers:* employees or children of employees.
Financial Aid Of all full-time matriculated undergraduates who enrolled in 2011, 1,700 applied for aid, 1,528 were judged to have need, 227 had their need fully met. In 2011, 126 non-need-based awards were made. *Average percent of need met:* 83%. *Average financial aid package:* $23,774. *Average need-based loan:* $5611. *Average need-based gift aid:* $17,387. *Average non-need-based aid:* $8290. *Average indebtedness upon graduation:* $34,494. *Financial aid deadline:* 3/15.
Applying *Options:* electronic application, early admission, early decision, deferred entrance. *Application fee:* $50. *Required:* essay or personal statement, high school transcript, 1 letter of recommendation. *Required for some:* interview, portfolio for applicants to the School of Art & Design. *Recommended:* interview. *Application deadlines:* 8/1 (freshmen), 8/1 (transfers). *Early decision deadline:* 12/1. *Notification:* continuous (freshmen), continuous (transfers), 12/15 (early decision).
Freshman Application Contact Mr. Corry D. Unis, Director of Admissions, Alfred University, Alumni Hall, Alfred, NY 14802-1205. *Phone:* 607-871-2115. *Toll-free phone:* 800-541-9229. *Fax:* 607-871-2198. *E-mail:* admissions@alfred.edu.
Website: http://www.alfred.edu/.

Bard College
Annandale-on-Hudson, New York
- **Independent** comprehensive, founded 1860
- **Rural** 600-acre campus
- **Coed** 2,051 undergraduate students, 95% full-time, 56% women, 44% men
- **Very difficult** entrance level, 35% of applicants were admitted

Undergraduates 1,958 full-time, 93 part-time. Students come from 48 states and territories; 65 other countries; 57% are from out of state; 5% Black or African American, non-Hispanic/Latino; 3% Hispanic/Latino; 3% Asian, non-Hispanic/Latino; 0.6% American Indian or Alaska Native, non-Hispanic/Latino; 14% Race/ethnicity unknown; 12% international; 3% transferred in; 73% live on campus. *Retention:* 86% of full-time freshmen returned.
Freshmen *Admission:* 5,410 applied, 1,902 admitted, 537 enrolled. *Average high school GPA:* 3.5.
Faculty *Total:* 265, 56% full-time, 92% with terminal degrees. *Student/faculty ratio:* 10:1.
Academics *Calendar:* semesters. *Degrees:* bachelor's, master's, and doctoral. *Special study options:* adult/continuing education programs, advanced placement credit, double majors, independent study, internships, off-campus study, part-time degree program, services for LD students, student-designed majors, study abroad. *Unusual degree programs:* 3-2 business administration; engineering with Columbia University, Washington University in St. Louis, Dartmouth College; forestry with Duke University; social work; teaching.
Computers on Campus 425 computers/terminals are available on campus for general student use. Students can access the following: campus intranet, computer help desk, free student e-mail accounts, online (class) grades, online (class) registration, online (class) schedules. Campuswide network is available.

100% of college-owned or -operated housing units are wired for high-speed Internet access. Wireless service is available via classrooms, computer centers, computer labs, dorm rooms, learning centers, libraries, student centers.
Student Life *Housing:* on-campus residence required through sophomore year. *Options:* coed, women-only, cooperative. Campus housing is university owned. Freshman campus housing is guaranteed. *Activities and organizations:* drama/theater group, student-run newspaper, radio station, choral group, Student government, Debate Team, Queer-Straight Alliance, International Student Organization / Black Student Organization, Free Press (student newspaper). *Campus security:* 24-hour emergency response devices and patrols, student patrols, late-night transport/escort service, controlled dormitory access. *Student services:* health clinic, personal/psychological counseling, legal services.
Athletics Member NCAA, NAIA. All NCAA Division III. *Intercollegiate sports:* baseball M, basketball M/W, cross-country running M/W, lacrosse M/W, soccer M/W, squash M, swimming and diving M/W, tennis M/W, track and field M/W, ultimate Frisbee M(c)/W(c), volleyball M/W. *Intramural sports:* badminton M/W, basketball M/W, bowling M/W, equestrian sports M(c)/W(c), fencing M(c)/W(c), golf M/W, rugby M(c)/W(c), softball M/W, squash M/W, table tennis M/W, tennis M/W, ultimate Frisbee M(c)/W(c), volleyball M/W.
Costs (2013–14) *One-time required fee:* $1574. *Comprehensive fee:* $59,872 includes full-time tuition ($45,730), mandatory fees ($640), and room and board ($13,502). Full-time tuition and fees vary according to degree level. Part-time tuition: $1429 per credit hour. Part-time tuition and fees vary according to degree level. *Payment plans:* tuition prepayment, installment. *Waivers:* employees or children of employees.
Financial Aid Of all full-time matriculated undergraduates who enrolled in 2012, 1,374 applied for aid, 1,327 were judged to have need, 649 had their need fully met. 806 Federal Work-Study jobs (averaging $1565). 82 state and other part-time jobs (averaging $1650). In 2012, 21 non-need-based awards were made. *Average percent of need met:* 80%. *Average financial aid package:* $36,279. *Average need-based loan:* $5746. *Average need-based gift aid:* $31,912. *Average non-need-based aid:* $17,030. *Average indebtedness upon graduation:* $24,913. *Financial aid deadline:* 2/15.
Applying *Options:* electronic application, early admission, early action, deferred entrance. *Application fee:* $50. *Required:* essay or personal statement, high school transcript, minimum 3.0 GPA, 3 letters of recommendation. *Application deadlines:* 1/1 (freshmen), 3/15 (transfers), 11/1 (early action). *Notification:* 4/1 (freshmen), 5/15 (transfers), 1/1 (early action).
Freshman Application Contact Ms. Mary Backlund, Director of Admissions, Bard College, PO Box 5000, 51 Ravine Road, Annandale-on-Hudson, NY 12504-5000. *Phone:* 845-758-7472. *Fax:* 845-758-5208. *E-mail:* admission@bard.edu.
Website: http://www.bard.edu/.

Barnard College
New York, New York
- **Independent** 4-year, founded 1889, part of Columbia University
- **Urban** 4-acre campus
- **Women only**
- **Most difficult** entrance level

Faculty *Student/faculty ratio:* 10:1.
Academics *Calendar:* semesters. *Degree:* bachelor's.
Student Life *Campus security:* 24-hour emergency response devices and patrols, late-night transport/escort service, gated campus with permanent security posts.
Athletics Member NCAA. All Division I.
Standardized Tests *Required:* SAT with writing and two subject tests or ACT with writing (for admission).
Costs (2012–13) *Comprehensive fee:* $57,312 includes full-time tuition ($41,850), mandatory fees ($1652), and room and board ($13,810). *College room only:* $8240. Room and board charges vary according to board plan and housing facility. *Payment plans:* tuition prepayment, installment, deferred payment.
Financial Aid *Of all full-time matriculated undergraduates who enrolled in 2012,* 1,107 applied for aid, 962 were judged to have need, 962 had their need fully met. 191 Federal Work-Study jobs (averaging $2020). 527 state and other part-time jobs (averaging $2013). *Average percent of need met:* 100. *Average financial aid package:* $41,408. *Average need-based loan:* $4547. *Average need-based gift aid:* $42,572. *Average indebtedness upon graduation:* $19,931. *Financial aid deadline:* 2/15.
Applying *Options:* early admission, early decision, deferred entrance. *Application fee:* $55. *Required:* essay or personal statement, high school transcript, 3 letters of recommendation, Common Application with Barnard supplement. *Recommended:* interview.

Freshman Application Contact Ms. Jennifer Gill Fondiller, Dean of Admissions, Barnard College, 3009 Broadway, New York, NY 10027-6598. *Phone:* 212-854-2014. *Fax:* 212-854-6220. *E-mail:* admissions@barnard.edu. *Website:* http://www.barnard.edu/.

See below for display ad and page 1148 for the College Close-Up.

Baruch College of the City University of New York

New York, New York

- **State and locally supported** comprehensive, founded 1919, part of City University of New York System
- **Urban** campus
- **Coed**
- **Very difficult** entrance level

Faculty *Student/faculty ratio:* 18:1.
Academics *Calendar:* semesters. *Degrees:* bachelor's, master's, and post-master's certificates.
Student Life *Campus security:* 24-hour emergency response devices and patrols, late-night transport/escort service, controlled access by ID card.
Athletics Member NCAA. All Division III.
Standardized Tests *Required:* SAT or ACT (for admission).
Costs (2012–13) *Tuition:* state resident $5430 full-time; nonresident $14,550 full-time. Full-time tuition and fees vary according to course load. Part-time tuition and fees vary according to course load. *Room only:* $11,590. Room and board charges vary according to housing facility. *Payment plans:* installment, deferred payment.
Financial Aid *Of all full-time matriculated undergraduates who enrolled in 2011,* 9,760 applied for aid, 7,419 were judged to have need, 1,598 had their need fully met. 2,000 Federal Work-Study jobs (averaging $1400). 500 state and other part-time jobs (averaging $1000). *In 2011,* 301 non-need-based awards were made. *Average percent of need met:* 54. *Average financial aid package:* $5262. *Average need-based loan:* $4536. *Average need-based gift aid:* $6296. *Average non-need-based aid:* $5610. *Average indebtedness upon graduation:* $15,822.

Applying *Options:* electronic application, early admission, deferred entrance. *Application fee:* $65. *Required:* high school transcript, minimum 2.5 GPA, 16 academic units. *Required for some:* interview.
Freshman Application Contact Baruch College of the City University of New York, 1 Bernard Baruch Way, New York, NY 10010-5585. *Phone:* 646-312-1400.
Website: http://www.baruch.cuny.edu/.

Beis Medrash Heichal Dovid

Far Rockaway, New York

Admissions Office Contact Beis Medrash Heichal Dovid, 257 Beach 17th Street, Far Rockaway, NY 11691.

Berkeley College–New York City Campus

New York, New York

Freshman Application Contact Berkeley College–New York City Campus, 3 East 43rd Street, New York, NY 10017-4604. *Phone:* 212-986-4343. *Toll-free phone:* 800-446-5400.
Website: http://www.berkeleycollege.edu/.

Berkeley College–Westchester Campus

White Plains, New York

Freshman Application Contact Director of Admissions, Berkeley College–Westchester Campus, White Plains, NY 10601. *Phone:* 914-694-1122. *Toll-*

free phone: 800-446-5400. *Fax:* 914-328-9469. *E-mail:* info@berkeleycollege.edu.
Website: http://www.berkeleycollege.edu/.

Beth HaMedrash Shaarei Yosher Institute

Brooklyn, New York

Director of Admissions Director of Admissions, Beth HaMedrash Shaarei Yosher Institute, 4102-10 Sixteenth Avenue, Brooklyn, NY 11204. *Phone:* 718-854-2290.

Beth Hatalmud Rabbinical College

Brooklyn, New York

Director of Admissions Rabbi Osina, Director of Admissions, Beth Hatalmud Rabbinical College, 2127 Eighty-second Street, Brooklyn, NY 11214. *Phone:* 718-259-2525.

Binghamton University, State University of New York

Binghamton, New York

- **State-supported** university, founded 1946, part of State University of New York System
- **Suburban** 930-acre campus
- **Endowment** $62.0 million
- **Coed** 12,356 undergraduate students, 96% full-time, 47% women, 53% men
- **Very difficult** entrance level, 43% of applicants were admitted

Undergraduates 11,904 full-time, 452 part-time. Students come from 46 states and territories; 102 other countries; 12% are from out of state; 5% Black or African American, non-Hispanic/Latino; 9% Hispanic/Latino; 13% Asian, non-Hispanic/Latino; 0.1% Native Hawaiian or other Pacific Islander, non-Hispanic/Latino; 0.1% American Indian or Alaska Native, non-Hispanic/Latino; 2% Two or more races, non-Hispanic/Latino; 6% Race/ethnicity unknown; 12% international; 9% transferred in; 61% live on campus. *Retention:* 91% of full-time freshmen returned.
Freshmen *Admission:* 28,232 applied, 12,104 admitted, 2,664 enrolled. *Average high school GPA:* 3.6. *Test scores:* SAT critical reading scores over 500: 97%; SAT math scores over 500: 100%; SAT writing scores over 500: 99%; ACT scores over 18: 100%; SAT critical reading scores over 600: 70%; SAT math scores over 600: 90%; SAT writing scores over 600: 77%; ACT scores over 24: 98%; SAT critical reading scores over 700: 15%; SAT math scores over 700: 32%; SAT writing scores over 700: 21%; ACT scores over 30: 37%.
Faculty *Total:* 866, 70% full-time. *Student/faculty ratio:* 20:1.
Academics *Calendar:* semesters. *Degrees:* bachelor's, master's, doctoral, and post-master's certificates. *Special study options:* accelerated degree program, adult/continuing education programs, advanced placement credit, distance learning, double majors, English as a second language, honors programs, independent study, internships, off-campus study, part-time degree program, services for LD students, student-designed majors, study abroad, summer session for credit. *ROTC:* Army (c), Air Force (c). *Unusual degree programs:* 3-2 business administration; engineering; anthropology; art history; Asian & Asian American studies; biology; chemistry; computer science; economics; education; French; geography; geology; Italian; mathematics; materials science; philosophy, politics, & law; physics; political science; public administration; Spanish; systems science;theatre.
Computers on Campus 1,300 computers/terminals and 40,000 ports are available on campus for general student use. Students can access the following: campus intranet, computer help desk, free student e-mail accounts, online (class) grades, online (class) registration, online (class) schedules, course management system, personal Web space, wiki, virtual desktop. Campuswide network is available. 100% of college-owned or -operated housing units are wired for high-speed Internet access. Wireless service is available via entire campus.
Student Life *Housing:* on-campus residence required for freshman year. *Options:* coed, disabled students. Campus housing is university owned and is provided by a third party. Freshman campus housing is guaranteed. *Activities and organizations:* drama/theater group, student-run newspaper, radio and television station, choral group, intramurals, club sports, Student Association, cultural organizations, Peer Counseling/Mentoring/Volunteering Program, national fraternities, national sororities. *Campus security:* 24-hour emergency response devices and patrols, student patrols, late-night transport/escort service, controlled dormitory access, well-lit campus, self-defense/safety education, secured entrances 12 am-5 am, emergency phones, emergency text messages, safety escorts. *Student services:* health clinic, personal/psychological counseling, women's center, legal services.
Athletics Member NCAA. All Division I. *Intercollegiate sports:* baseball M(s), basketball M(s)/W(s), cross-country running M(s)/W(s), golf M(s), lacrosse M(s)/W(s), soccer M(s)/W(s), softball W(s), swimming and diving M(s)/W(s), tennis M(s)/W(s), track and field M(s)/W(s), volleyball W(s), wrestling M(s). *Intramural sports:* badminton M(c)/W(c), baseball M(c), basketball M/W, bowling M/W, cheerleading M/W, crew M(c)/W(c), cross-country running M(c)/W(c), equestrian sports M(c)/W(c), fencing M(c)/W(c), field hockey M(c)/W(c), golf M(c)/W(c), gymnastics M(c)/W(c), ice hockey M(c)/W(c), lacrosse M(c)/W(c), racquetball M/W, rugby M(c)/W(c), skiing (downhill) M(c)/W(c), soccer M/W, softball M/W, swimming and diving M(c)/W(c), table tennis M(c)/W(c), tennis M/W, ultimate Frisbee M(c)/W(c), volleyball M/W, water polo M(c)/W(c).
Standardized Tests *Required:* SAT or ACT (for admission).
Costs (2012–13) *Tuition:* state resident $5570 full-time, $232 per credit hour part-time; nonresident $14,720 full-time, $613 per credit hour part-time. Full-time tuition and fees vary according to program. Part-time tuition and fees vary according to course load and program. *Required fees:* $2075 full-time, $84 per credit hour part-time, $25 per term part-time. *Room and board:* $12,446. Room and board charges vary according to board plan and housing facility. *Payment plan:* installment.
Financial Aid Of all full-time matriculated undergraduates who enrolled in 2012, 8,109 applied for aid, 5,704 were judged to have need, 1,121 had their need fully met. 353 Federal Work-Study jobs (averaging $1417). In 2012, 244 non-need-based awards were made. *Average percent of need met:* 74%. *Average financial aid package:* $11,783. *Average need-based loan:* $5482. *Average need-based gift aid:* $7230. *Average non-need-based aid:* $6709. *Average indebtedness upon graduation:* $23,710.
Applying *Options:* electronic application, early admission, early action, deferred entrance. *Application fee:* $50. *Required:* essay or personal statement, high school transcript, 1 letter of recommendation. *Required for some:* portfolio, audition. *Application deadlines:* 1/15 (freshmen), 1/15 (out-of-state freshmen), rolling (transfers), 11/15 (early action). *Notification:* 4/1 (freshmen), 4/1 (out-of-state freshmen), continuous (transfers), 1/15 (early action).
Freshman Application Contact Townsend Plant, Assistant Provost for Undergraduate Admissions, Binghamton University, State University of New York, Binghamton University, PO Box 6001, Binghamton, NY 13902-6001. *Phone:* 607-777-2171. *Fax:* 607-777-4445. *E-mail:* admit@binghamton.edu. *Website:* http://www.binghamton.edu/.

Boricua College

New York, New York

Freshman Application Contact Mrs. Miriam Pfeffer, Director of Student Services, Boricua College, 186 North 6th Street, Brooklyn, NY 11211. *Phone:* 718-782-2200. *Fax:* 718-782-2025. *E-mail:* mpfeffer@boricuacollege.edu. *Website:* http://www.boricuacollege.edu/.

Briarcliffe College

Bethpage, New York

Freshman Application Contact Admissions Office, Briarcliffe College, 1055 Stewart Avenue, Bethpage, NY 11714. *Phone:* 516-918-3600. *Toll-free phone:* 888-349-4999 (in-state); 888-348-4999 (out-of-state). *Fax:* 516-470-6020. *Website:* http://www.briarcliffe.edu/.

Brooklyn College of the City University of New York

Brooklyn, New York

Freshman Application Contact Office of Admissions, Brooklyn College of the City University of New York, 2900 Bedford Avenue, West Quad Building,

Room 222, Brooklyn, NY 11210-2889. *Phone:* 718-951-5001. *Fax:* 718-951-4506. *E-mail:* adminqry@brooklyn.cuny.edu. *Website:* http://www.brooklyn.cuny.edu/.

Bryant & Stratton College— Amherst Campus

Clarence, New York

Freshman Application Contact Mr. Brian K. Dioguardi, Director of Admissions, Bryant & Stratton College—Amherst Campus, Audubon Business Center, 40 Hazelwood Drive, Amherst, NY 14228. *Phone:* 716-691-0012. *Fax:* 716-691-0012. *E-mail:* bkdioguardi@bryantstratton.edu. *Website:* http://www.bryantstratton.edu/.

Bryant & Stratton College— Buffalo Campus

Buffalo, New York

Freshman Application Contact Mr. Philip J. Struebel, Director of Admissions, Bryant & Stratton College—Buffalo Campus, 465 Main Street, Suite 400, Buffalo, NY 14203. *Phone:* 716-884-9120. *Fax:* 716-884-0091. *E-mail:* pjstruebel@bryantstratton.edu. *Website:* http://www.bryantstratton.edu/.

Bryant & Stratton College— Southtowns Campus

Orchard Park, New York

Freshman Application Contact Bryant & Stratton College—Southtowns Campus, 200 Redtail, Orchard Park, NY 14127. *Phone:* 716-677-9500. *Website:* http://www.bryantstratton.edu/.

Buffalo State College, State University of New York

Buffalo, New York

- **State-supported** comprehensive, founded 1867, part of State University of New York System
- **Urban** 115-acre campus
- **Endowment** $24.1 million
- **Coed** 9,731 undergraduate students, 89% full-time, 57% women, 43% men
- **Moderately difficult** entrance level, 46% of applicants were admitted

Undergraduates 8,616 full-time, 1,115 part-time. Students come from 27 states and territories; 18 other countries; 1% are from out of state; 18% Black or African American, non-Hispanic/Latino; 8% Hispanic/Latino; 2% Asian, non-Hispanic/Latino; 0.1% Native Hawaiian or other Pacific Islander, non-Hispanic/Latino; 0.4% American Indian or Alaska Native, non-Hispanic/Latino; 3% Two or more races, non-Hispanic/Latino; 0.5% Race/ethnicity unknown; 1% international; 26% live on campus. *Retention:* 74% of full-time freshmen returned.

Freshmen *Admission:* 11,856 applied, 5,439 admitted. *Average high school GPA:* 3.15. *Test scores:* SAT critical reading scores over 500: 36%; SAT math scores over 500: 43%; SAT writing scores over 500: 30%; SAT critical reading scores over 600: 6%; SAT math scores over 600: 8%; SAT writing scores over 600: 4%.

Faculty *Total:* 842, 49% full-time, 53% with terminal degrees. *Student/faculty ratio:* 17:1.

Academics *Calendar:* semesters. *Degrees:* bachelor's, master's, and post-master's certificates. *Special study options:* academic remediation for entering students, adult/continuing education programs, advanced placement credit, cooperative education, distance learning, double majors, English as a second language, freshman honors college, honors programs, independent study, internships, off-campus study, part-time degree program, services for LD students, study abroad, summer session for credit. *ROTC:* Army (c). *Unusual*

degree programs: 3-2 engineering with State University of New York at Binghamton, Clarkson University, State University of New York at Buffalo.

Computers on Campus 1,700 computers/terminals are available on campus for general student use. Students can access the following: computer help desk, free student e-mail accounts, online (class) registration, online (class) schedules. Campuswide network is available. Wireless service is available via classrooms, libraries, student centers.

Student Life *Housing:* on-campus residence required through sophomore year. *Options:* coed. Campus housing is university owned. Freshman campus housing is guaranteed. *Activities and organizations:* drama/theater group, student-run newspaper, radio station, choral group, United Student Government, African-American Student Organization, Caribbean Student Organization, The Record, WBNY radio, national fraternities, national sororities. *Campus security:* 24-hour emergency response devices and patrols, student patrols, late-night transport/escort service, controlled dormitory access. *Student services:* health clinic, personal/psychological counseling, women's center, legal services.

Athletics Member NCAA. All Division III. *Intercollegiate sports:* baseball M(c), basketball M/W, bowling M(c)/W(c), cheerleading W(c), cross-country running M/W, fencing M(c), football M, ice hockey M/W, lacrosse M(c)/W, rugby M(c)/W(c), skiing (cross-country) M(c)/W(c), skiing (downhill) M(c)/W(c), soccer M/W, softball W, swimming and diving M/W, tennis W, track and field M/W, volleyball M(c)/W. *Intramural sports:* basketball M, football M, racquetball M/W, softball M/W, volleyball M/W, water polo M(c)/W(c).

Standardized Tests *Required:* SAT and SAT Subject Tests or ACT (for admission). *Recommended:* SAT (for admission).

Costs (2012–13) *Tuition:* state resident $5570 full-time; nonresident $14,820 full-time. Part-time tuition and fees vary according to course load. *Required fees:* $1124 full-time. *Room and board:* $11,192; room only: $6592. Room and board charges vary according to board plan, housing facility, and student level. *Payment plan:* installment. *Waivers:* employees or children of employees.

Financial Aid Of all full-time matriculated undergraduates who enrolled in 2011, 8,624 applied for aid, 7,548 were judged to have need, 1,395 had their need fully met. 331 Federal Work-Study jobs (averaging $2137). In 2011, 575 non-need-based awards were made. *Average percent of need met:* 25%. *Average financial aid package:* $11,433. *Average need-based loan:* $4269. *Average need-based gift aid:* $5540. *Average non-need-based aid:* $2265. *Average indebtedness upon graduation:* $22,565. *Financial aid deadline:* 5/1.

Applying *Options:* electronic application, early admission, early decision, deferred entrance. *Application fee:* $40. *Required:* high school transcript, minimum 3.0 GPA. *Required for some:* essay or personal statement, interview. *Application deadlines:* rolling (freshmen), rolling (transfers). *Early decision deadline:* 11/15. *Notification:* continuous (freshmen), continuous (transfers), 12/15 (early decision).

Freshman Application Contact Ms. Carmella Thompson, Director of Admissions, Buffalo State College, State University of New York, 110 Moot Hall, Buffalo, NY 14222. *Phone:* 716-878-4017. *Fax:* 716-878-6100. *E-mail:* admissions@buffalostate.edu. *Website:* http://www.buffalostate.edu/.

Canisius College

Buffalo, New York

- **Independent Roman Catholic (Jesuit)** comprehensive, founded 1870
- **Urban** 72-acre campus
- **Endowment** $86.7 million
- **Coed** 3,280 undergraduate students, 90% full-time, 50% women, 50% men
- **Moderately difficult** entrance level, 74% of applicants were admitted

Undergraduates 2,954 full-time, 326 part-time. Students come from 32 states and territories; 27 other countries; 8% are from out of state; 7% Black or African American, non-Hispanic/Latino; 3% Hispanic/Latino; 2% Asian, non-Hispanic/Latino; 0.3% American Indian or Alaska Native, non-Hispanic/Latino; 1% Two or more races, non-Hispanic/Latino; 7% Race/ethnicity unknown; 4% international; 5% transferred in; 49% live on campus. *Retention:* 82% of full-time freshmen returned.

Freshmen *Admission:* 4,361 applied, 3,222 admitted, 713 enrolled. *Average high school GPA:* 3.5. *Test scores:* SAT critical reading scores over 500: 71%; SAT math scores over 500: 78%; ACT scores over 18: 100%; SAT critical reading scores over 600: 25%; SAT math scores over 600: 32%; ACT scores over 24: 61%; SAT critical reading scores over 700: 3%; SAT math scores over 700: 3%; ACT scores over 30: 17%.

Faculty *Total:* 519, 43% full-time, 56% with terminal degrees. *Student/faculty ratio:* 11:1.

Academics *Calendar:* semesters. *Degrees:* associate, bachelor's, master's, and post-master's certificates. *Special study options:* academic remediation for entering students, adult/continuing education programs, advanced placement credit, cooperative education, distance learning, double majors, English as a second language, honors programs, independent study, internships, off-campus study, part-time degree program, services for LD students, study abroad, summer session for credit. *ROTC:* Army (b). *Unusual degree programs:* 3-2 business administration with BA/BS MBA program enables a qualified student in most majors to earn an undergraduate degree and an MBA within a five-year period; engineering with Physics Engineering with SUNY Buffalo (UB).

Computers on Campus 700 computers/terminals are available on campus for general student use. Students can access the following: computer help desk, free student e-mail accounts, online (class) grades, online (class) registration, online (class) schedules, online accounts. Campuswide network is available. 100% of college-owned or -operated housing units are wired for high-speed Internet access. Wireless service is available via entire campus.

Student Life *Housing:* on-campus residence required through sophomore year. *Options:* coed, disabled students. Campus housing is university owned. Freshman applicants given priority for college housing. *Activities and organizations:* drama/theater group, student-run newspaper, radio and television station, choral group, Campus Programming Board, Undergraduate Student Association, Afro-American Society, Residence Hall Association, Student Association, national fraternities, national sororities. *Campus security:* 24-hour emergency response devices and patrols, late-night transport/escort service, controlled dormitory access, crime prevention programs, closed-circuit television monitors, emergency call boxes across campus. *Student services:* health clinic, personal/psychological counseling.

Athletics Member NCAA. All Division I. *Intercollegiate sports:* baseball M(s), basketball M(s)/W(s), cross-country running M(s)/W(s), equestrian sports W(c), golf M(s), ice hockey M(s), lacrosse M(s)/W(s), rugby M(c)/W(c), soccer M(s)/W(s), softball W(s), swimming and diving M(s)/W(s), volleyball M(c)/W(s). *Intramural sports:* basketball M/W, bowling M(c)/W(c), cheerleading M(c)/W(c), crew M(c)/W(c), field hockey W(c), golf M, ice hockey M(c)/W(c), lacrosse M(c), racquetball M/W, riflery M(c)/W(c), skiing (downhill) M(c)/W(c), soccer M/W, softball M(c)/W(c), tennis M/W, track and field M(c)/W(c), ultimate Frisbee M(c)/W(c), volleyball M/W, wrestling M(c).

Standardized Tests *Required:* SAT or ACT (for admission).

Costs (2012–13) *Comprehensive fee:* $43,850 includes full-time tuition ($30,780), mandatory fees ($1250), and room and board ($11,820). Full-time tuition and fees vary according to course load and degree level. Part-time tuition: $879 per credit. Part-time tuition and fees vary according to course load and degree level. *Required fees:* $21 per credit hour part-time, $63 per credit part-time. *College room only:* $6940. Room and board charges vary according to board plan and housing facility. *Payment plans:* installment, deferred payment. *Waivers:* employees or children of employees.

Financial Aid Of all full-time matriculated undergraduates who enrolled in 2012, 2,451 applied for aid, 2,294 were judged to have need, 590 had their need fully met. 556 Federal Work-Study jobs (averaging $1777). In 2012, 559 non-need-based awards were made. *Average percent of need met:* 81%. *Average financial aid package:* $27,009. *Average need-based loan:* $4363. *Average need-based gift aid:* $20,666. *Average non-need-based aid:* $15,361. *Average indebtedness upon graduation:* $36,383.

Applying *Options:* electronic application, early admission, deferred entrance. *Application fee:* $40. *Required:* high school transcript, minimum 2.0 GPA. *Required for some:* interview. *Recommended:* essay or personal statement, 1 letter of recommendation, interview. *Application deadlines:* 5/1 (freshmen), rolling (transfers). *Notification:* continuous (freshmen), continuous (transfers).

Freshman Application Contact Ms. Molly Ballaro, Director of Admissions, Canisius College, 2001 Main Street, Buffalo, NY 14208-1098. *Phone:* 716-888-2200. *Toll-free phone:* 800-843-1517. *Fax:* 716-888-3230. *E-mail:* admissions@canisius.edu. *Website:* http://www.canisius.edu/.

Cazenovia College

Cazenovia, New York

Freshman Application Contact Office of Admission and Enrollment Services, Cazenovia College, 3 Sullivan Street, Cazenovia, NY 13035. *Phone:* 315-655-7208. *Toll-free phone:* 800-654-3210. *Fax:* 315-655-4860. *E-mail:* admission@cazenovia.edu. *Website:* http://www.cazenovia.edu/.

Central Yeshiva Tomchei Tmimim-Lubavitch

Brooklyn, New York

Director of Admissions Director of Admissions, Central Yeshiva Tomchei Tmimim-Lubavitch, 841-853 Ocean Parkway, Brooklyn, NY 11230. *Phone:* 718-859-7600.

City College of the City University of New York

New York, New York

- **State and locally supported** comprehensive, founded 1847, part of City University of New York System
- **Urban** 35-acre campus with easy access to New York City
- **Coed** 13,113 undergraduate students, 73% full-time, 52% women, 48% men
- **Moderately difficult** entrance level, 33% of applicants were admitted

Undergraduates 9,524 full-time, 3,589 part-time. Students come from 140 other countries; 4% are from out of state; 20% Black or African American, non-Hispanic/Latino; 32% Hispanic/Latino; 22% Asian, non-Hispanic/Latino; 0.1% American Indian or Alaska Native, non-Hispanic/Latino; 8% international; 11% transferred in; 1% live on campus. *Retention:* 83% of full-time freshmen returned.

Freshmen *Admission:* 28,183 applied, 9,160 admitted, 1,397 enrolled. *Test scores:* SAT critical reading scores over 500: 58%; SAT math scores over 500: 90%; SAT critical reading scores over 600: 23%; SAT math scores over 600: 43%; SAT critical reading scores over 700: 8%; SAT math scores over 700: 13%.

Faculty *Total:* 1,922, 27% full-time, 36% with terminal degrees. *Student/faculty ratio:* 13:1.

Academics *Calendar:* semesters. *Degrees:* bachelor's, master's, doctoral, and post-master's certificates. *Special study options:* accelerated degree program, adult/continuing education programs, advanced placement credit, English as a second language, freshman honors college, honors programs, independent study, internships, off-campus study, part-time degree program, services for LD students, student-designed majors, study abroad, summer session for credit. *ROTC:* Army (b). *Unusual degree programs:* 3-2 optometry with State University of New York Optometry.

Computers on Campus 3,000 computers/terminals are available on campus for general student use. Students can access the following: campus intranet, computer help desk, free student e-mail accounts, online (class) grades, online (class) registration, online (class) schedules. Campuswide network is available. 100% of college-owned or -operated housing units are wired for high-speed Internet access. Wireless service is available via entire campus.

Student Life *Housing options:* coed. Campus housing is provided by a third party. *Activities and organizations:* drama/theater group, student-run newspaper, radio station, choral group, LAESA-SHPE, NSBE, BSA, Salsa-Mambo, IVCF, national fraternities. *Campus security:* 24-hour patrols, late-night transport/escort service, controlled dormitory access. *Student services:* health clinic, personal/psychological counseling.

Athletics Member NCAA. All Division III. *Intercollegiate sports:* baseball M, basketball M/W, cross-country running M/W, fencing W, lacrosse M, soccer M/W, softball W, tennis M/W, track and field M/W, volleyball W. *Intramural sports:* basketball M/W, fencing W, soccer M, softball W, tennis M/W, track and field M/W, volleyball W.

Standardized Tests *Required:* SAT or ACT (for admission).

Costs (2012–13) *Tuition:* state resident $5131 full-time; nonresident $13,800 full-time. Full-time tuition and fees vary according to course load and program. Part-time tuition and fees vary according to course load and program. *Room and board:* Room and board charges vary according to housing facility. *Payment plan:* deferred payment. *Waivers:* senior citizens.

Financial Aid Of all full-time matriculated undergraduates who enrolled in 2011, 8,872 applied for aid, 8,699 were judged to have need, 6,907 had their need fully met. In 2011, 780 non-need-based awards were made. *Average percent of need met:* 82%. *Average financial aid package:* $8978. *Average need-based loan:* $4115. *Average need-based gift aid:* $7801. *Average non-need-based aid:* $4085. *Average indebtedness upon graduation:* $16,944.

Applying *Options:* early admission, deferred entrance. *Application fee:* $65. *Required:* high school transcript. *Required for some:* essay or personal statement, creative challenge for Architecture, supplemental application for Engineering. *Application deadlines:* 2/1 (freshmen), 2/1 (transfers). *Notification:* continuous until 2/1 (freshmen), continuous until 3/1 (transfers).

Freshman Application Contact City College of the City University of New York, 160 Convent Avenue, New York, NY 10031-9198. *Phone:* 212-650-6977.

Website: http://www.ccny.cuny.edu/.

Clarkson University

Potsdam, New York

- **Independent** university, founded 1896
- **Small-town** 640-acre campus
- **Endowment** $158.3 million
- **Coed** 3,072 undergraduate students, 99% full-time, 28% women, 72% men
- **Very difficult** entrance level, 76% of applicants were admitted

Undergraduates 3,050 full-time, 22 part-time. Students come from 38 states and territories; 29 other countries; 26% are from out of state; 3% Black or African American, non-Hispanic/Latino; 4% Hispanic/Latino; 3% Asian, non-Hispanic/Latino; 0.2% American Indian or Alaska Native, non-Hispanic/Latino; 2% Two or more races, non-Hispanic/Latino; 1% Race/ethnicity unknown; 3% international; 3% transferred in; 83% live on campus. *Retention:* 86% of full-time freshmen returned.

Freshmen *Admission:* 4,199 applied, 3,195 admitted, 778 enrolled. *Average high school GPA:* 3.56. *Test scores:* SAT critical reading scores over 500: 80%; SAT math scores over 500: 93%; SAT writing scores over 500: 68%; ACT scores over 18: 98%; SAT critical reading scores over 600: 31%; SAT math scores over 600: 59%; SAT writing scores over 600: 22%; ACT scores over 24: 72%; SAT critical reading scores over 700: 5%; SAT math scores over 700: 10%; SAT writing scores over 700: 3%; ACT scores over 30: 18%.

Faculty *Total:* 273, 81% full-time, 78% with terminal degrees. *Student/faculty ratio:* 15:1.

Academics *Calendar:* semesters. *Degrees:* bachelor's, master's, and doctoral. *Special study options:* accelerated degree program, advanced placement credit, cooperative education, distance learning, double majors, English as a second language, honors programs, independent study, off-campus study, part-time degree program, services for LD students, student-designed majors, study abroad, summer session for credit. *ROTC:* Army (b), Air Force (b). *Unusual degree programs:* 3-2 engineering.

Computers on Campus 350 computers/terminals and 6,000 ports are available on campus for general student use. Students can access the following: campus intranet, computer help desk, free student e-mail accounts, online (class) grades, online (class) registration, online (class) schedules. Campuswide network is available. 100% of college-owned or -operated housing units are wired for high-speed Internet access. Wireless service is available via classrooms, computer centers, computer labs, learning centers, libraries, student centers.

Student Life *Housing:* on-campus residence required through senior year. *Options:* coed, men-only, women-only, disabled students. Campus housing is university owned. Freshman campus housing is guaranteed. *Activities and organizations:* drama/theater group, student-run newspaper, radio and television station, choral group, Ski Club, Outing Club, Pep Band, Ultimate Frisbee Club, Sports Car Club, national fraternities, national sororities. *Campus security:* 24-hour emergency response devices and patrols, late-night transport/escort service, controlled dormitory access. *Student services:* health clinic, personal/psychological counseling, legal services.

Athletics Member NCAA. All Division III except men's and women's ice hockey (Division I). *Intercollegiate sports:* baseball M, basketball M/W, cross-country running M/W, golf M, ice hockey M(s)/W(s), lacrosse M/W, skiing (cross-country) M/W, skiing (downhill) M/W, soccer M/W, softball W, swimming and diving M/W, volleyball W. *Intramural sports:* basketball M/W, bowling M(c)/W(c), crew M(c)/W(c), football M/W, golf M(c), ice hockey M/W, lacrosse M(c)/W(c), racquetball M(c)/W(c), rugby M(c)/W(c), skiing (cross-country) M(c)/W(c), skiing (downhill) M(c)/W(c), soccer M/W, softball M/W, tennis M(c)/W(c), ultimate Frisbee M(c)/W(c), volleyball M/W.

Standardized Tests *Required:* SAT or ACT (for admission). *Recommended:* SAT Subject Tests (for admission).

Costs (2013–14) *Comprehensive fee:* $53,608 includes full-time tuition ($39,770), mandatory fees ($840), and room and board ($12,998). Full-time tuition and fees vary according to course load. Part-time tuition: $1324 per credit. Part-time tuition and fees vary according to course load. *College room only:* $6886. Room and board charges vary according to board plan and housing facility. *Payment plans:* tuition prepayment, installment. *Waivers:* employees or children of employees.

Financial Aid Of all full-time matriculated undergraduates who enrolled in 2012, 2,725 applied for aid, 2,594 were judged to have need, 437 had their need fully met. 1,919 Federal Work-Study jobs (averaging $1600). 71 state and other part-time jobs (averaging $9587). In 2012, 376 non-need-based awards were made. *Average percent of need met:* 89%. *Average financial aid package:* $36,967. *Average need-based loan:* $4685. *Average need-based gift aid:* $26,790. *Average non-need-based aid:* $15,548. *Average indebtedness upon graduation:* $27,866. *Financial aid deadline:* 3/1.

Applying *Options:* electronic application, early admission, early decision, deferred entrance. *Application fee:* $50. *Required:* essay or personal statement, high school transcript, 2 letters of recommendation, SAT or ACT. *Recommended:* interview. *Application deadline:* 1/15 (freshmen). *Early decision deadline:* 12/1. *Notification:* continuous (freshmen), continuous (transfers), 1/1 (early decision).

Freshman Application Contact Mr. Brian T. Grant, Dean of Admissions, Clarkson University, 8 Clarkson Ave, Box 5605, CU Box 5605, Potsdam, NY 13699. *Phone:* 315-268-6480. *Toll-free phone:* 800-527-6577. *Fax:* 315-268-7647. *E-mail:* admission@clarkson.edu.

Website: http://www.clarkson.edu/.

Colgate University

Hamilton, New York

- **Independent** comprehensive, founded 1819
- **Rural** 515-acre campus with easy access to Syracuse, Utica
- **Endowment** $693.4 million
- **Coed** 2,850 undergraduate students, 100% full-time, 54% women, 46% men
- **Most difficult** entrance level, 29% of applicants were admitted

Undergraduates 2,850 full-time. Students come from 48 states and territories; 45 other countries; 75% are from out of state; 4% Black or African American, non-Hispanic/Latino; 8% Hispanic/Latino; 4% Asian, non-Hispanic/Latino; 0.1% Native Hawaiian or other Pacific Islander, non-Hispanic/Latino; 0.3% American Indian or Alaska Native, non-Hispanic/Latino; 3% Two or more races, non-Hispanic/Latino; 4% Race/ethnicity unknown; 8% international; 0.3% transferred in; 92% live on campus. *Retention:* 95% of full-time freshmen returned.

Freshmen *Admission:* 7,798 applied, 2,289 admitted, 756 enrolled. *Average high school GPA:* 3.64. *Test scores:* SAT math scores over 500: 99%; ACT scores over 18: 100%; SAT math scores over 600: 89%; ACT scores over 24: 98%; SAT math scores over 700: 42%; ACT scores over 30: 75%.

Faculty *Total:* 349, 84% full-time, 93% with terminal degrees. *Student/faculty ratio:* 9:1.

Academics *Calendar:* semesters. *Degrees:* bachelor's and master's. *Special study options:* advanced placement credit, double majors, honors programs, independent study, internships, off-campus study, services for LD students, student-designed majors, study abroad. *ROTC:* Army (c). *Unusual degree programs:* 3-2 engineering with Rensselaer Polytechnic Institute, Columbia University, Washington University in St. Louis.

Computers on Campus 780 computers/terminals are available on campus for general student use. Students can access the following: campus intranet, computer help desk, free student e-mail accounts, online (class) registration, online (class) schedules, software applications. Campuswide network is available. 100% of college-owned or -operated housing units are wired for high-speed Internet access. Wireless service is available via entire campus.

Student Life *Housing:* on-campus residence required through junior year. *Options:* coed, cooperative, disabled students. Campus housing is university owned. Freshman campus housing is guaranteed. *Activities and organizations:* drama/theater group, student-run newspaper, radio and television station, choral group, COVE, student government, cultural/ethnic interest groups, student publications, Outdoor Education, national fraternities, national sororities. *Campus security:* 24-hour emergency response devices and patrols, student patrols, late-night transport/escort service, controlled dormitory access. *Student services:* health clinic, personal/psychological counseling, women's center, legal services.

Athletics Member NCAA. All Division I except football (Division I-AA). *Intercollegiate sports:* badminton M(c)/W(c), baseball M(c), basketball M(s)/W(s), cheerleading M(c)/W(c), crew M/W, cross-country running M/W, equestrian sports M(c)/W(c), fencing M(c)/W(c), field hockey W(s), golf M/W(c), ice hockey M(s)/W(s), lacrosse M(s)/W(s), rugby M(c)/W(c), sailing M(c)/W(c), skiing (downhill) M(c)/W(c), soccer M(s)/W(s), softball W(s), squash M(c)/W(c), swimming and diving M/W, table tennis M(c)/W(c), tennis M/W, track and field M/W, volleyball M(c)/W(s), water polo M(c)/W(c). *Intramural sports:* basketball M/W, bowling M/W, cross-country running M(c)/W(c), football M/W, golf M(c)/W(c), ice hockey M/W, lacrosse M(c)/W(c), racquetball M/W, riflery M/W, soccer M/W, softball M/W, squash M/W, tennis M/W, ultimate Frisbee M/W, volleyball M/W.

Standardized Tests *Required:* SAT or ACT (for admission).

Costs (2012–13) *One-time required fee:* $50. *Comprehensive fee:* $55,715 includes full-time tuition ($44,330), mandatory fees ($310), and room and board ($11,075). Full-time tuition and fees vary according to course load. Part-time tuition: $5541 per course. Part-time tuition and fees vary according to course load. *College room only:* $5345. Room and board charges vary according to board plan and housing facility. *Payment plans:* tuition prepayment, installment, deferred payment. *Waivers:* employees or children of employees.

Financial Aid Of all full-time matriculated undergraduates who enrolled in 2012, 1,145 applied for aid, 1,020 were judged to have need, 1,020 had their need fully met. 539 Federal Work-Study jobs (averaging $2080). 283 state and other part-time jobs (averaging $1811). *Average percent of need met:* 100%. *Average financial aid package:* $42,522. *Average need-based loan:* $3861. *Average need-based gift aid:* $38,288. *Average indebtedness upon graduation:* $20,751. *Financial aid deadline:* 1/15.

Applying *Options:* electronic application, early decision, deferred entrance. *Application fee:* $60. *Required:* essay or personal statement, high school transcript, 3 letters of recommendation, Colgate supplement. *Application deadlines:* 1/15 (freshmen), 1/15 (out-of-state freshmen), 3/15 (transfers). *Early decision deadline:* 11/15 (for plan 1), 1/15 (for plan 2). *Notification:* 4/1 (freshmen), 4/1 (out-of-state freshmen), 5/1 (transfers), 12/15 (early decision plan 1), rolling (early decision plan 2).

Freshman Application Contact Mr. Gary L. Ross, Dean of Admission, Colgate University, Colgate Office of Admission, 13 Oak Drive, Hamilton, NY 13346-1383. *Phone:* 315-228-7401. *Fax:* 315-228-7544. *E-mail:* admission@colgate.edu.
Website: http://www.colgate.edu/.

The College at Brockport, State University of New York

Brockport, New York

- **State-supported** comprehensive, founded 1867, part of State University of New York System
- **Small-town** 454-acre campus with easy access to Rochester
- **Coed** 7,133 undergraduate students, 90% full-time, 55% women, 45% men
- **Moderately difficult** entrance level, 48% of applicants were admitted

Undergraduates 6,444 full-time, 689 part-time. 2% are from out of state; 7% Black or African American, non-Hispanic/Latino; 5% Hispanic/Latino; 1% Asian, non-Hispanic/Latino; 0.1% Native Hawaiian or other Pacific Islander, non-Hispanic/Latino; 0.3% American Indian or Alaska Native, non-Hispanic/Latino; 2% Two or more races, non-Hispanic/Latino; 9% Race/ethnicity unknown; 14% transferred in; 38% live on campus. *Retention:* 81% of full-time freshmen returned.

Freshmen *Admission:* 8,570 applied, 4,091 admitted, 1,084 enrolled. *Test scores:* SAT critical reading scores over 500: 63%; SAT math scores over 500: 72%; ACT scores over 18: 97%; SAT critical reading scores over 600: 14%; SAT math scores over 600: 21%; ACT scores over 24: 45%; SAT critical reading scores over 700: 1%; SAT math scores over 700: 2%; ACT scores over 30: 3%.

Faculty *Total:* 604, 54% full-time, 60% with terminal degrees. *Student/faculty ratio:* 18:1.

Academics *Calendar:* semesters. *Degrees:* bachelor's, master's, and post-master's certificates. *Special study options:* academic remediation for entering students, accelerated degree program, advanced placement credit, cooperative education, distance learning, double majors, English as a second language, freshman honors college, honors programs, independent study, internships, off-campus study, part-time degree program, services for LD students, student-designed majors, study abroad, summer session for credit. *ROTC:* Army (b), Navy (c), Air Force (c).

Computers on Campus Students can access the following: campus intranet, computer help desk, free student e-mail accounts, online (class) registration, online (class) schedules. Campuswide network is available. 100% of college-owned or -operated housing units are wired for high-speed Internet access. Wireless service is available via entire campus.

Student Life *Housing:* on-campus residence required through sophomore year. *Options:* coed, disabled students. Campus housing is university owned. Freshman campus housing is guaranteed. *Activities and organizations:* drama/theater group, student-run newspaper, radio and television station, choral group, fine arts clubs, Organization for Students of African Descent, Communication

Club, student radio station, sports clubs, national fraternities, national sororities. *Campus security:* 24-hour emergency response devices and patrols, student patrols, late-night transport/escort service, controlled dormitory access. *Student services:* health clinic, personal/psychological counseling, women's center, legal services.

Athletics Member NCAA. All Division III. *Intercollegiate sports:* baseball M, basketball M/W, cross-country running M/W, field hockey W, football M, gymnastics W, ice hockey M, lacrosse M/W, soccer M/W, softball W, swimming and diving M/W, tennis W, track and field M/W, volleyball W, wrestling M. *Intramural sports:* badminton M/W, basketball M/W, bowling M/W, cheerleading M/W, football M/W, golf M(c), ice hockey W(c), racquetball M/W, rugby M/W, soccer M/W, softball M/W, table tennis M/W, tennis M/W, ultimate Frisbee M/W, volleyball M/W.

Standardized Tests *Required:* SAT or ACT (for admission).

Costs (2013–14) *Tuition:* state resident $5870 full-time; nonresident $14,820 full-time. Part-time tuition and fees vary according to course load. *Required fees:* $1340 full-time. *Room and board:* $11,386. Room and board charges vary according to board plan and housing facility. *Payment plans:* installment, deferred payment. *Waivers:* senior citizens and employees or children of employees.

Financial Aid Of all full-time matriculated undergraduates who enrolled in 2012, 4,808 applied for aid, 3,966 were judged to have need, 422 had their need fully met. 531 Federal Work-Study jobs (averaging $2072). 1,580 state and other part-time jobs (averaging $1423). In 2012, 149 non-need-based awards were made. *Average percent of need met:* 69%. *Average financial aid package:* $9821. *Average need-based loan:* $4927. *Average need-based gift aid:* $5357. *Average non-need-based aid:* $4350. *Average indebtedness upon graduation:* $27,844.

Applying *Options:* electronic application, deferred entrance. *Application fee:* $50. *Required:* essay or personal statement, high school transcript, 1 letter of recommendation, SAT or ACT. *Required for some:* interview. *Recommended:* minimum 3.1 GPA. *Application deadlines:* rolling (freshmen), 8/1 (transfers). *Notification:* continuous (freshmen), continuous (transfers).

Freshman Application Contact The College at Brockport, State University of New York, 350 New Campus Drive, Brockport, NY 14420-2997. *Phone:* 585-395-2751.
Website: http://www.brockport.edu/.

College of Mount Saint Vincent

Riverdale, New York

- **Independent** comprehensive, founded 1911
- **Suburban** 70-acre campus with easy access to New York City
- **Coed**
- **Moderately difficult** entrance level

Faculty *Student/faculty ratio:* 13:1.

Academics *Calendar:* semesters. *Degrees:* bachelor's, master's, and post-master's certificates.

Student Life *Campus security:* 24-hour emergency response devices and patrols, late-night transport/escort service, controlled dormitory access, emergency call boxes.

Athletics Member NCAA. All Division III.

Standardized Tests *Required:* SAT or ACT (for admission).

Costs (2012–13) *Comprehensive fee:* $40,820 includes full-time tuition ($27,860), mandatory fees ($1310), and room and board ($11,650). Part-time tuition: $860 per credit. *Required fees:* $250 per term part-time. *Room and board:* Room and board charges vary according to housing facility.

Financial Aid *Of all full-time matriculated undergraduates who enrolled in 2004,* 1,019 applied for aid, 881 were judged to have need. *Average percent of need met:* 74. *Average financial aid package:* $17,000. *Average need-based loan:* $4100. *Average need-based gift aid:* $7500. *Average indebtedness upon graduation:* $17,000.

Applying *Options:* electronic application, early admission, early action, deferred entrance. *Application fee:* $35. *Required:* essay or personal statement, high school transcript, minimum 2.0 GPA. *Required for some:* interview. *Recommended:* 2 letters of recommendation, interview.

Freshman Application Contact Ms. Brenda Nelson, Associate Director of Admissions, College of Mount Saint Vincent, 6301 Riverdale Avenue, Riverdale, NY 10471-1093. *Phone:* 718-405-3223. *Toll-free phone:* 800-665-CMSV. *Fax:* 718-549-7945. *E-mail:* brenda.nelson@mountsaintvincent.edu.
Website: http://www.mountsaintvincent.edu/.

The College of New Rochelle
New Rochelle, New York

- **Independent** comprehensive, founded 1904
- **Suburban** 20-acre campus with easy access to New York City
- **Coed, primarily women** 840 undergraduate students, 63% full-time, 92% women, 8% men
- **Moderately difficult** entrance level, 37% of applicants were admitted

Undergraduates 526 full-time, 314 part-time. Students come from 16 states and territories; 10% are from out of state; 33% Black or African American, non-Hispanic/Latino; 19% Hispanic/Latino; 6% Asian, non-Hispanic/Latino; 0.2% Native Hawaiian or other Pacific Islander, non-Hispanic/Latino; 0.2% American Indian or Alaska Native, non-Hispanic/Latino; 1% Two or more races, non-Hispanic/Latino; 25% Race/ethnicity unknown; 1% international; 13% transferred in; 23% live on campus. *Retention:* 80% of full-time freshmen returned.

Freshmen *Admission:* 1,114 applied, 407 admitted, 84 enrolled. *Average high school GPA:* 3.1. *Test scores:* SAT critical reading scores over 500: 36%; SAT math scores over 500: 25%; ACT scores over 18: 79%; SAT critical reading scores over 600: 6%; SAT math scores over 600: 3%; ACT scores over 24: 21%.

Faculty *Student/faculty ratio:* 10:1.

Academics *Calendar:* semesters. *Degrees:* bachelor's, master's, post-master's, and postbachelor's certificates (also offers a non-traditional adult program with significant enrollment not reflected in profile). *Special study options:* academic remediation for entering students, accelerated degree program, adult/continuing education programs, advanced placement credit, cooperative education, double majors, honors programs, independent study, internships, off-campus study, part-time degree program, services for LD students, student-designed majors, study abroad, summer session for credit.

Computers on Campus 120 computers/terminals are available on campus for general student use. Students can access the following: campus intranet, computer help desk, free student e-mail accounts, online (class) registration. Campuswide network is available. 100% of college-owned or -operated housing units are wired for high-speed Internet access. Wireless service is available via entire campus.

Student Life *Housing options:* women-only. Campus housing is university owned. Freshman campus housing is guaranteed. *Activities and organizations:* drama/theater group, student-run newspaper, choral group, Drama Club, CNR Model United Nations, Student Nurses Association. *Campus security:* 24-hour emergency response devices and patrols, late-night transport/escort service, controlled dormitory access, 24-hour monitored security cameras at residence hall entrances. *Student services:* health clinic, personal/psychological counseling, women's center.

Athletics Member NCAA. All Division III. *Intercollegiate sports:* basketball W, cross-country running W, softball W, swimming and diving W, tennis W, volleyball W. *Intramural sports:* badminton M/W, basketball M/W, cheerleading W(c), cross-country running M/W(c), table tennis M/W, ultimate Frisbee M/W, volleyball M/W.

Standardized Tests *Required:* SAT or ACT (for admission).

Costs (2013–14) *Comprehensive fee:* $42,950 includes full-time tuition ($30,210), mandatory fees ($1050), and room and board ($11,690). Full-time tuition and fees vary according to course load, location, and program. Part-time tuition: $896 per credit. Part-time tuition and fees vary according to course load, location, and program. *Required fees:* $450 per term part-time. *Room and board:* Room and board charges vary according to housing facility. *Payment plan:* installment. *Waivers:* employees or children of employees.

Financial Aid Of all full-time matriculated undergraduates who enrolled in 2011, 535 applied for aid, 507 were judged to have need, 11 had their need fully met. 391 Federal Work-Study jobs (averaging $2529). In 2011, 26 non-need-based awards were made. *Average percent of need met:* 64%. *Average financial aid package:* $22,319. *Average need-based loan:* $5586. *Average need-based gift aid:* $10,056. *Average non-need-based aid:* $14,044. *Average indebtedness upon graduation:* $22,923.

Applying *Options:* electronic application, early admission, early decision, deferred entrance. *Application fee:* $35. *Required:* high school transcript. *Recommended:* essay or personal statement, 1 letter of recommendation, interview. *Application deadlines:* rolling (freshmen), rolling (transfers). *Early decision deadline:* 11/1. *Notification:* continuous (freshmen), continuous (transfers), 12/15 (early decision).

Freshman Application Contact Ms. Danielle Robinson, Assistant Director, Undergraduate Admission SAS/SON, The College of New Rochelle, 29 Castle Place, New Rochelle, NY 10805-2339. *Phone:* 914-654-5452. *Toll-free phone:* 800-933-5923. *Fax:* 914-654-5464. *E-mail:* admission@cnr.edu. *Website:* http://www.cnr.edu/.

The College of Saint Rose
Albany, New York

- **Independent** comprehensive, founded 1920
- **Urban** 46-acre campus
- **Endowment** $31.7 million
- **Coed** 2,881 undergraduate students, 94% full-time, 67% women, 33% men
- **Moderately difficult** entrance level, 66% of applicants were admitted

Undergraduates 2,721 full-time, 160 part-time. Students come from 24 states and territories; 27 other countries; 10% are from out of state; 6% Black or African American, non-Hispanic/Latino; 5% Hispanic/Latino; 2% Asian, non-Hispanic/Latino; 0.1% Native Hawaiian or other Pacific Islander, non-Hispanic/Latino; 0.5% American Indian or Alaska Native, non-Hispanic/Latino; 4% Two or more races, non-Hispanic/Latino; 6% Race/ethnicity unknown; 1% international; 9% transferred in; 47% live on campus. *Retention:* 81% of full-time freshmen returned.

Freshmen *Admission:* 5,353 applied, 3,544 admitted, 590 enrolled. *Average high school GPA:* 3.5. *Test scores:* SAT critical reading scores over 500: 59%; SAT math scores over 500: 62%; ACT scores over 18: 88%; SAT critical reading scores over 600: 18%; SAT math scores over 600: 18%; ACT scores over 24: 44%; SAT critical reading scores over 700: 2%; SAT math scores over 700: 3%; ACT scores over 30: 6%.

Faculty *Total:* 426, 48% full-time. *Student/faculty ratio:* 14:1.

Academics *Calendar:* semesters. *Degrees:* certificates, bachelor's, master's, post-master's, and postbachelor's certificates. *Special study options:* academic remediation for entering students, accelerated degree program, advanced placement credit, double majors, external degree program, independent study, internships, off-campus study, part-time degree program, services for LD students, student-designed majors, study abroad, summer session for credit. *ROTC:* Army (c), Navy (c), Air Force (c). *Unusual degree programs:* 3-2 engineering with Alfred University, Clarkson University, Union College (NY), Rensselaer Polytechnic Institute.

Computers on Campus 733 computers/terminals and 4,418 ports are available on campus for general student use. Students can access the following: computer help desk, free student e-mail accounts, online (class) grades, online (class) registration, online (class) schedules. Campuswide network is available. 100% of college-owned or -operated housing units are wired for high-speed Internet access. Wireless service is available via entire campus.

Student Life *Housing options:* coed, men-only, women-only, disabled students. Campus housing is university owned and leased by the school. Freshman applicants given priority for college housing. *Activities and organizations:* drama/theater group, student-run newspaper, radio and television station, choral group, Student Association, Student Events Board, Spectrum-ALANA Student Union, Colleges Against Cancer, Music & Entertainment Industry Student Association. *Campus security:* 24-hour emergency response devices and patrols, late-night transport/escort service, controlled dormitory access. *Student services:* health clinic, personal/psychological counseling.

Athletics Member NCAA. All Division II. *Intercollegiate sports:* baseball M(s), basketball M(s)/W(s), cross-country running M/W, golf M, lacrosse M(s), soccer M(s)/W(s), softball W(s), swimming and diving M(s)/W(s), tennis W, track and field M(s)/W(s), volleyball W(s). *Intramural sports:* basketball M/W, cheerleading M(c)/W(c), soccer M/W, softball M/W, ultimate Frisbee M/W, volleyball M/W.

Standardized Tests *Required for some:* SAT or ACT (for admission).

Costs (2013–14) *Comprehensive fee:* $38,934 includes full-time tuition ($26,750), mandatory fees ($934), and room and board ($11,250). Full-time tuition and fees vary according to class time and course load. Part-time tuition: $894 per credit hour. Part-time tuition and fees vary according to class time and course load. *Required fees:* $30 per credit hour part-time, $78 per semester part-time. *College room only:* $5630. Room and board charges vary according to board plan and housing facility. *Payment plan:* installment. *Waivers:* employees or children of employees.

Financial Aid Of all full-time matriculated undergraduates who enrolled in 2011, 2,554 applied for aid, 2,311 were judged to have need, 373 had their need fully met. In 2011, 344 non-need-based awards were made. *Average percent of need met:* 80%. *Average financial aid package:* $16,599. *Average need-based loan:* $4107. *Average need-based gift aid:* $12,673. *Average non-need-based aid:* $9683. *Average indebtedness upon graduation:* $23,920. *Financial aid deadline:* 4/1.

Applying *Options:* electronic application, early admission, early action, deferred entrance. *Application fee:* $40. *Required:* essay or personal statement, high school transcript, 1 letter of recommendation. *Required for some:* interview. *Recommended:* minimum 3.0 GPA. *Application deadlines:* 2/1 (freshmen), 2/1 (transfers), 12/1 (early action). *Notification:* continuous (freshmen), continuous (transfers), 12/15 (early action).

Freshman Application Contact Mr. Jeremy Bogan, Assistant Vice President of Undergraduate Admissions, The College of Saint Rose, 1001 Madison Avenue, Albany, NY 12203. *Phone:* 518-454-5154. *Toll-free phone:* 800-637-8556. *Fax:* 518-454-2013. *E-mail:* admit@strose.edu. *Website:* http://www.strose.edu/.

College of Staten Island of the City University of New York

Staten Island, New York

- **State and locally supported** comprehensive, founded 1955, part of City University of New York
- **Urban** 204-acre campus with easy access to New York City
- **Endowment** $5.0 million
- **Coed** 13,364 undergraduate students, 74% full-time, 55% women, 45% men
- **Noncompetitive** entrance level, 100% of applicants were admitted

Undergraduates 9,917 full-time, 3,447 part-time. Students come from 11 states and territories; 67 other countries; 0.6% are from out of state; 9% Black or African American, non-Hispanic/Latino; 15% Hispanic/Latino; 9% Asian, non-Hispanic/Latino; 0.2% Native Hawaiian or other Pacific Islander, non-Hispanic/Latino; 0.2% American Indian or Alaska Native, non-Hispanic/Latino; 1% Two or more races, non-Hispanic/Latino; 23% Race/ethnicity unknown; 3% international; 5% transferred in. *Retention:* 84% of full-time freshmen returned.

Freshmen *Admission:* 11,630 applied, 11,630 admitted, 2,556 enrolled. *Average high school GPA:* 2.98. *Test scores:* SAT critical reading scores over 500: 42%; SAT math scores over 500: 58%; SAT writing scores over 500: 39%; SAT critical reading scores over 600: 6%; SAT math scores over 600: 13%; SAT writing scores over 600: 6%; SAT critical reading scores over 700: 1%; SAT math scores over 700: 1%; SAT writing scores over 700: 1%.

Faculty *Total:* 1,219, 27% full-time, 51% with terminal degrees. *Student/faculty ratio:* 19:1.

Academics *Calendar:* semesters. *Degrees:* certificates, associate, bachelor's, master's, doctoral, and post-master's certificates. *Special study options:* academic remediation for entering students, accelerated degree program, adult/continuing education programs, advanced placement credit, cooperative education, distance learning, double majors, English as a second language, freshman honors college, honors programs, independent study, internships, off-campus study, services for LD students, student-designed majors, study abroad, summer session for credit.

Computers on Campus 1,408 computers/terminals and 1,000 ports are available on campus for general student use. Students can access the following: campus intranet, computer help desk, free student e-mail accounts, online (class) grades, online (class) registration, online (class) schedules, zero balance confirmation. Campuswide network is available. Wireless service is available via entire campus.

Student Life *Activities and organizations:* drama/theater group, student-run newspaper, radio station, choral group, Japanese Visual Culture Club, Hillel Club, International Business Society, Psychology Club, Love Your Neighbor Club. *Student services:* health clinic, personal/psychological counseling, women's center.

Athletics Member NCAA. All Division III. *Intercollegiate sports:* baseball M, basketball M/W, cheerleading M(c)/W(c), soccer M/W, softball W, swimming and diving M/W, tennis M/W, volleyball W. *Intramural sports:* basketball M/W, racquetball M/W, soccer M/W, swimming and diving M/W, table tennis M/W, tennis M/W, track and field M(c)/W(c), volleyball M/W.

Standardized Tests *Required:* SAT or ACT (for admission).

Costs (2012–13) *Tuition:* state resident $5430 full-time, $230 per credit part-time; nonresident $14,550 full-time, $485 per credit part-time. *Required fees:* $428 full-time, $128 per term part-time. *Payment plan:* installment. *Waivers:* senior citizens and employees or children of employees.

Financial Aid Of all full-time matriculated undergraduates who enrolled in 2012, 7,775 applied for aid, 6,624 were judged to have need, 150 had their need fully met. 350 Federal Work-Study jobs (averaging $1400). In 2012, 339 non-need-based awards were made. *Average percent of need met:* 55%. *Average financial aid package:* $8074. *Average need-based loan:* $4751. *Average need-based gift aid:* $7244. *Average non-need-based aid:* $1703.

Applying *Options:* electronic application, deferred entrance. *Application fee:* $65. *Required:* high school transcript. *Required for some:* essay or personal statement, letters of recommendation, interview. *Application deadlines:* rolling (freshmen), rolling (transfers). *Notification:* continuous (freshmen), continuous (transfers).

Freshman Application Contact Mr. Emmanuel Esperance Jr., Director of Recruitment and Admissions, College of Staten Island of the City University of New York, 2800 Victory Boulevard, 2A-103, Staten Island, NY 10314. *Phone:* 718-982-2190. *Fax:* 718-982-2500. *E-mail:* admissions@csi.cuny.edu. *Website:* http://www.csi.cuny.edu/.

See previous page for display ad and page 1248 for the College Close-Up.

Columbia University
New York, New York

- **Independent** university, founded 1754
- **Urban** 36-acre campus
- **Endowment** $7.8 billion
- **Coed** 6,068 undergraduate students, 100% full-time, 47% women, 53% men
- **Most difficult** entrance level, 7% of applicants were admitted

Undergraduates 6,068 full-time. 73% are from out of state; 12% Black or African American, non-Hispanic/Latino; 15% Hispanic/Latino; 20% Asian, non-Hispanic/Latino; 2% American Indian or Alaska Native, non-Hispanic/Latino; 6% Race/ethnicity unknown; 12% international; 2% transferred in; 94% live on campus. *Retention:* 99% of full-time freshmen returned.

Freshmen *Admission:* 31,851 applied, 2,362 admitted, 1,415 enrolled. *Test scores:* SAT critical reading scores over 500: 100%; SAT math scores over 500: 100%; SAT writing scores over 500: 100%; SAT critical reading scores over 600: 97%; SAT math scores over 600: 98%; SAT writing scores over 600: 97%; ACT scores over 24: 100%; SAT critical reading scores over 700: 73%; SAT math scores over 700: 76%; SAT writing scores over 700: 73%; ACT scores over 30: 85%.

Faculty *Total:* 1,965, 76% full-time, 100% with terminal degrees. *Student/faculty ratio:* 6:1.

Academics *Calendar:* semesters. *Degrees:* bachelor's, master's, and doctoral. *Special study options:* accelerated degree program, advanced placement credit, double majors, independent study, internships, off-campus study, services for LD students, student-designed majors, study abroad, summer session for credit. *ROTC:* Army (c), Navy (b), Air Force (c). *Unusual degree programs:* 3-2 engineering with Combined Plan Program with over 100 liberal arts colleges.

Computers on Campus 400 computers/terminals are available on campus for general student use. Students can access the following: campus intranet, computer help desk, free student e-mail accounts, online (class) grades, online (class) registration, online (class) schedules. Campuswide network is available. Wireless service is available via entire campus.

Student Life *Housing:* on-campus residence required for freshman year. *Options:* coed, men-only, women-only, disabled students. Campus housing is university owned. Freshman campus housing is guaranteed. *Activities and organizations:* drama/theater group, student-run newspaper, radio and television station, choral group, marching band, community service, cultural organizations, performing arts, athletics, publications, national fraternities, national sororities. *Campus security:* 24-hour emergency response devices and patrols, late-night transport/escort service, controlled dormitory access. *Student services:* health clinic, personal/psychological counseling, women's center.

Athletics Member NCAA. All Division I except football (Division I-AA). *Intercollegiate sports:* archery M(c)/W, badminton M(c)/W(c), baseball M, basketball M/W, crew M/W, cross-country running M/W, fencing M/W, field hockey W, golf M, ice hockey W(c), lacrosse M(c)/W, racquetball M(c)/W(c), riflery M(c)/W(c), rugby M(c)/W(c), skiing (cross-country) M(c)/W(c), skiing (downhill) M(c)/W(c), soccer M(c)/W(c), softball W, squash M(c)/W(c), swimming and diving M/W, table tennis M(c)/W(c), tennis M(c)/W(c), track and field M/W, ultimate Frisbee M(c)/W(c), volleyball M(c)/W(c), water polo M(c)/W(c), wrestling M. *Intramural sports:* archery W(c), badminton M/W, basketball M(c)/W(c), cross-country running M(c)/W(c), field hockey W, lacrosse W(c), racquetball M/W, soccer M/W, softball M/W, squash M/W, swimming and diving M/W, tennis M/W, volleyball M/W, water polo W.

Standardized Tests *Required:* SAT and SAT Subject Tests or ACT (for admission).

Costs (2012–13) *One-time required fee:* $511. *Comprehensive fee:* $58,842 includes full-time tuition ($45,028), mandatory fees ($2318), and room and board ($11,496). *Payment plan:* installment. *Waivers:* employees or children of employees.

Financial Aid Of all full-time matriculated undergraduates who enrolled in 2011, 3,468 applied for aid, 3,159 were judged to have need, 3,159 had their need fully met. *Average percent of need met:* 100%. *Average financial aid package:* $40,441. *Average need-based loan:* $3352. *Average need-based gift aid:* $39,075. *Financial aid deadline:* 3/1.

Applying *Options:* electronic application, early admission, early decision, deferred entrance. *Application fee:* $80. *Required:* essay or personal statement, high school transcript, 3 letters of recommendation, SAT and 2 SAT Subject Tests or ACT. *Application deadlines:* 1/1 (freshmen), 3/1 (transfers). *Early decision deadline:* 11/1. *Notification:* 4/1 (freshmen), 5/15 (transfers), 12/15 (early decision).

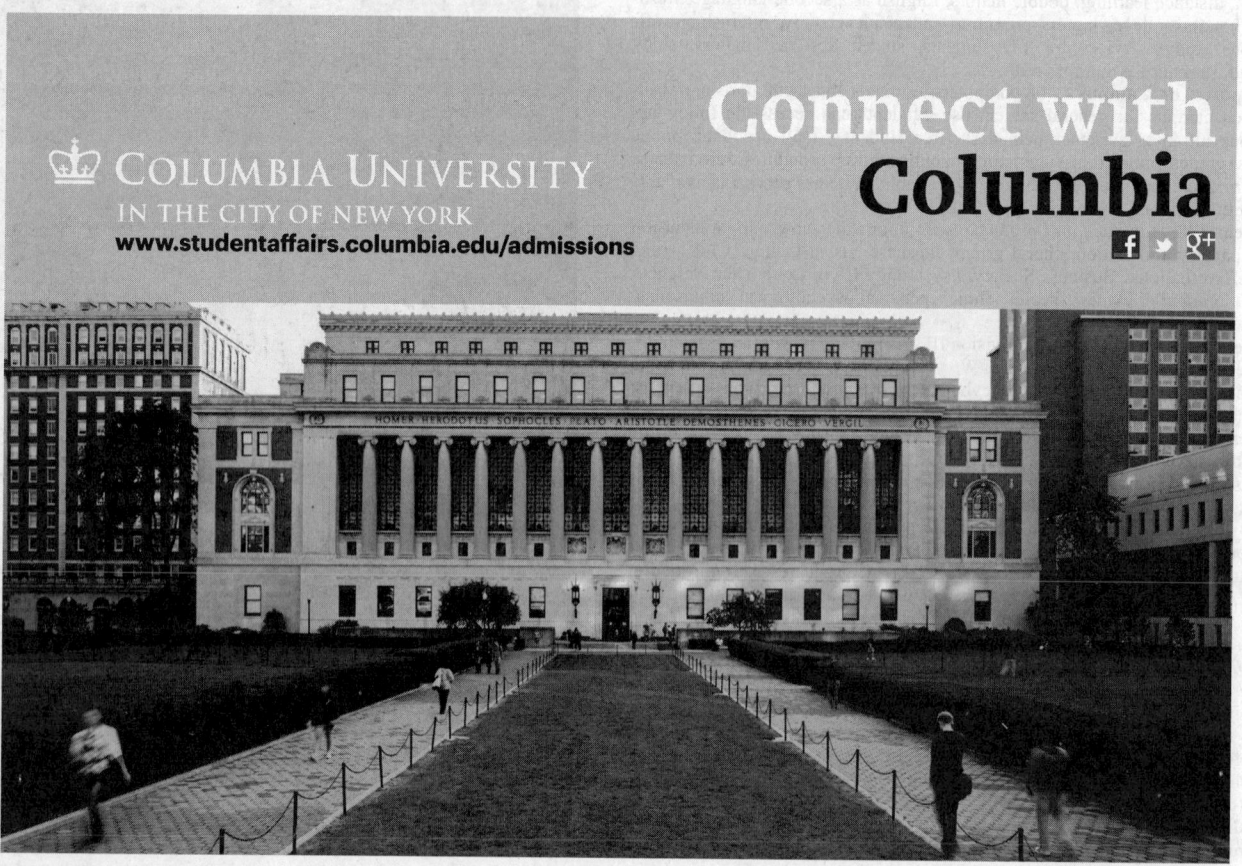

Freshman Application Contact Columbia University, 116th Street and Broadway, New York, NY 10027. *Phone:* 212-854-1222. *Website:* http://www.columbia.edu/.

See previous page for display ad and page 1254 for the College Close-Up.

Columbia University, School of General Studies

New York, New York

- **Independent** 4-year, founded 1754, part of Columbia University
- **Urban** 36-acre campus
- **Endowment** $6.5 billion
- **Coed** 1,632 undergraduate students, 68% full-time, 43% women, 57% men
- **Most difficult** entrance level, 34% of applicants were admitted

Undergraduates 1,108 full-time, 524 part-time. 45% are from out of state; 5% Black or African American, non-Hispanic/Latino; 10% Hispanic/Latino; 7% Asian, non-Hispanic/Latino; 0.7% Native Hawaiian or other Pacific Islander, non-Hispanic/Latino; 0.2% American Indian or Alaska Native, non-Hispanic/Latino; 2% Two or more races, non-Hispanic/Latino; 7% Race/ethnicity unknown; 16% international; 28% transferred in; 24% live on campus.

Freshmen *Admission:* 601 applied, 203 admitted, 119 enrolled.

Academics *Calendar:* semesters. *Degrees:* bachelor's and postbachelor's certificates. *Special study options:* adult/continuing education programs, advanced placement credit, double majors, external degree program, independent study, internships, off-campus study, part-time degree program, services for LD students, student-designed majors, study abroad, summer session for credit. *ROTC:* Army (c), Navy (b), Air Force (c). *Unusual degree programs:* 3-2 business administration with Columbia University, Graduate School of Business; engineering with Columbia University, School of Engineering and Applied Science; social work with Columbia University School of Social Work; international affairs, public policy and administration with Columbia University, School of International and Public Affairs; public health with Columbia University, School of Public Health.

Computers on Campus 768 computers/terminals are available on campus for general student use. Students can access the following: campus intranet, computer help desk, free student e-mail accounts, online (class) grades, online (class) registration, online (class) schedules. Campuswide network is available. 100% of college-owned or -operated housing units are wired for high-speed Internet access. Wireless service is available via entire campus.

Student Life *Housing options:* coed, cooperative. Campus housing is university owned, leased by the school and is provided by a third party. *Activities and organizations:* drama/theater group, student-run newspaper, radio and television station, choral group, marching band, General Studies Student Council, national fraternities, national sororities. *Campus security:* 24-hour emergency response devices and patrols, late-night transport/escort service. *Student services:* health clinic, personal/psychological counseling, women's center.

Athletics Member NCAA. All Division I except football (Division I-AA). *Intercollegiate sports:* archery W, badminton M(c)/W(c), baseball M, basketball M/W, crew M/W, cross-country running M/W, equestrian sports W(c), fencing M/W, field hockey W(c), golf M, gymnastics W, ice hockey M(c)/W(c), lacrosse M(c), racquetball M(c)/W(c), rugby M(c)/W(c), sailing M(c)/W(c), skiing (downhill) M(c)/W(c), soccer M/W, squash M(c)/W(c), swimming and diving M/W, table tennis M(c)/W(c), tennis M/W, track and field M/W, volleyball W, water polo M(c)/W(c), wrestling M. *Intramural sports:* football M/W, soccer M/W, volleyball M/W.

Standardized Tests *Required:* SAT or ACT (for admission).

Costs (2012–13) *Comprehensive fee:* $55,932 includes full-time tuition ($43,620), mandatory fees ($2079), and room and board ($10,233). Full-time tuition and fees vary according to course load, program, and student level. Part-time tuition: $1454 per credit hour. Part-time tuition and fees vary according to course load, program, and student level. *College room only:* $5823. Room and board charges vary according to board plan and housing facility. *Payment plans:* tuition prepayment, installment. *Waivers:* employees or children of employees.

Financial Aid *Financial aid deadline:* 6/1.

Applying *Options:* electronic application, early action, deferred entrance. *Application fee:* $80. *Required:* essay or personal statement, high school transcript, 2 letters of recommendation. *Required for some:* interview. *Application deadlines:* 6/1 (freshmen), 6/1 (transfers), 3/1 (early action). *Notification:* continuous (freshmen), continuous (transfers), 5/1 (early action).

Freshman Application Contact Mr. Curtis M. Rodgers, Dean of Enrollment Management, Columbia University, School of General Studies, 2970 Broadway, 408 Lewisohn Hall, MC 4101, New York, NY 10027. *Phone:* 212-

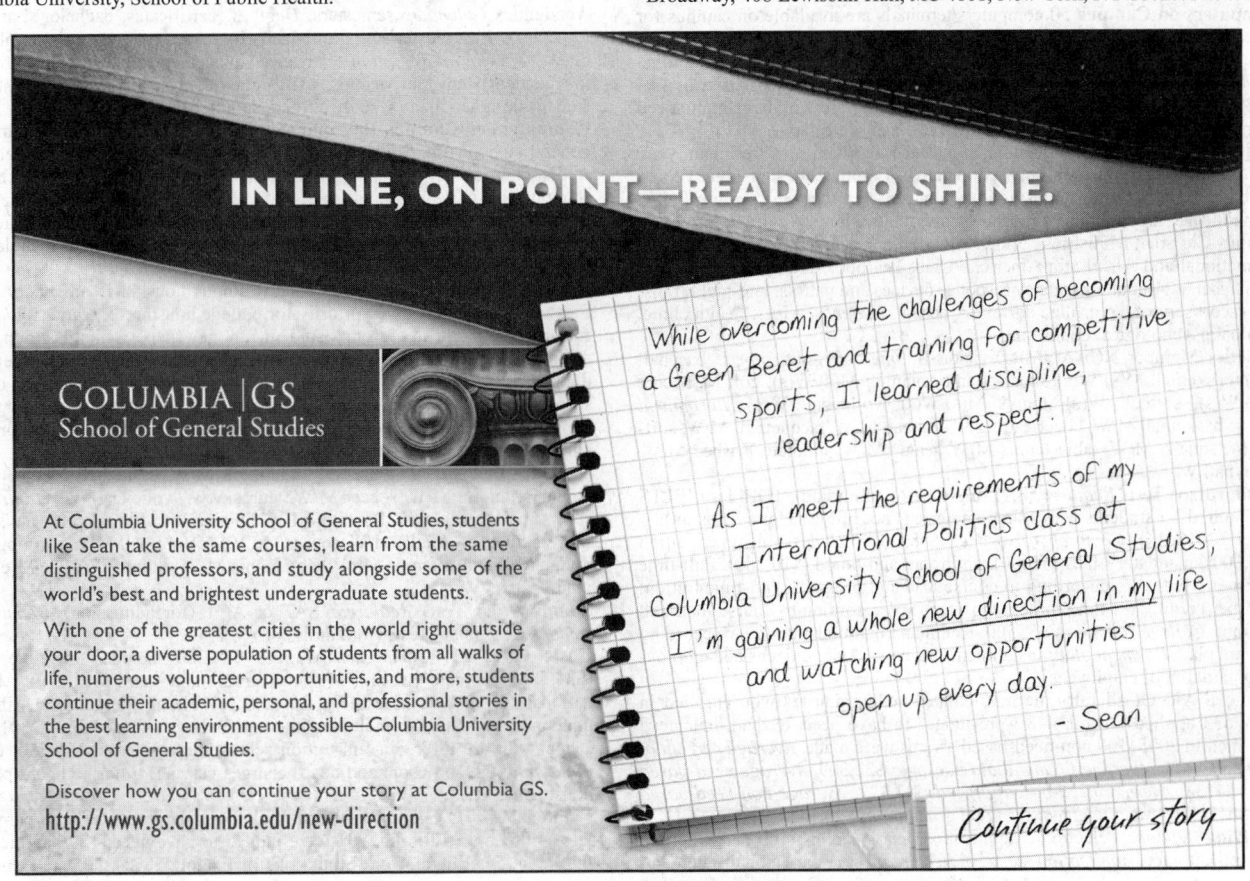

854-2772. *Toll-free phone:* 800-895-1169. *Fax:* 212-854-6316. *E-mail:* gsdegree@columbia.edu.
Website: http://www.gs.columbia.edu/.

See previous page for display ad and page 1256 for the College Close-Up.

Concordia College–New York

Bronxville, New York

- **Independent Lutheran** 4-year, founded 1881, part of Concordia University System
- **Suburban** 33-acre campus with easy access to New York City
- **Endowment** $6.4 million
- **Coed** 715 undergraduate students, 82% full-time, 65% women, 35% men
- **Moderately difficult** entrance level, 71% of applicants were admitted

Undergraduates 587 full-time, 128 part-time. Students come from 46 states and territories; 35 other countries; 29% are from out of state; 16% Black or African American, non-Hispanic/Latino; 16% Hispanic/Latino; 1% Asian, non-Hispanic/Latino; 0.4% Native Hawaiian or other Pacific Islander, non-Hispanic/Latino; 1% American Indian or Alaska Native, non-Hispanic/Latino; 3% Two or more races, non-Hispanic/Latino; 5% Race/ethnicity unknown; 11% international; 6% transferred in; 68% live on campus. *Retention:* 73% of full-time freshmen returned.

Freshmen *Admission:* 1,206 applied, 857 admitted, 138 enrolled. *Average high school GPA:* 2.86. *Test scores:* SAT critical reading scores over 500: 36%; SAT math scores over 500: 40%; SAT writing scores over 500: 35%; ACT scores over 18: 66%; SAT critical reading scores over 600: 8%; SAT math scores over 600: 9%; SAT writing scores over 600: 6%; ACT scores over 24: 21%; SAT critical reading scores over 700: 1%; SAT math scores over 700: 1%; ACT scores over 30: 3%.

Faculty *Total:* 77, 43% full-time, 79% with terminal degrees. *Student/faculty ratio:* 12:1.

Academics *Calendar:* semesters. *Degrees:* associate, bachelor's, and master's. *Special study options:* academic remediation for entering students, accelerated degree program, adult/continuing education programs, advanced placement credit, distance learning, double majors, English as a second language, honors programs, independent study, internships, off-campus study, part-time degree program, services for LD students, student-designed majors, study abroad. *ROTC:* Army (c), Air Force (c).

Computers on Campus 50 computers/terminals are available on campus for general student use. Students can access the following: campus intranet, computer help desk, free student e-mail accounts, online (class) grades, online (class) registration, online (class) schedules. Campuswide network is available. 100% of college-owned or -operated housing units are wired for high-speed Internet access. Wireless service is available via entire campus.

Student Life *Housing:* on-campus residence required for freshman year. *Options:* men-only, women-only, cooperative. Campus housing is university owned. Freshman campus housing is guaranteed. *Activities and organizations:* drama/theater group, student-run newspaper, television station, choral group, Campus Christian Ministries, Drama Club, Student Government Association, International and Afro/Latin American Club, Yearbook and newspaper. *Campus security:* 24-hour emergency response devices and patrols, late-night transport/escort service, controlled dormitory access. *Student services:* health clinic, personal/psychological counseling.

Athletics Member NCAA. All Division II. *Intercollegiate sports:* baseball M(s), basketball M(s)/W(s), cross-country running M(s)/W(s), golf M, soccer M(s)/W(s), softball W(s), tennis M(s)/W(s), volleyball W(s). *Intramural sports:* basketball M/W, cheerleading W, football M/W, racquetball M/W, softball W, squash M/W, table tennis M/W, tennis M/W, ultimate Frisbee M/W, volleyball W.

Standardized Tests *Required:* SAT or ACT (for admission), TOEFL or IELTS are required for students who's first language is not English (for admission).

Costs (2013–14) *Comprehensive fee:* $38,280 includes full-time tuition ($27,000), mandatory fees ($1000), and room and board ($10,280). Full-time tuition and fees vary according to course load and program. Part-time tuition: $775 per credit. Part-time tuition and fees vary according to course load and program. *College room only:* $5500. Room and board charges vary according to board plan. *Payment plan:* installment. *Waivers:* senior citizens and employees or children of employees.

Financial Aid Of all full-time matriculated undergraduates who enrolled in 2008, 533 applied for aid, 448 were judged to have need, 89 had their need fully met. In 2008, 100 non-need-based awards were made. *Average percent of need met:* 71%. *Average financial aid package:* $22,309. *Average need-based loan:* $4133. *Average need-based gift aid:* $11,129. *Average non-need-based aid:* $6170. *Average indebtedness upon graduation:* $24,153.

Applying *Options:* electronic application, early admission, early action, deferred entrance. *Application fee:* $50. *Required:* essay or personal statement,

high school transcript, 1 letter of recommendation, Common Application Supplement. *Required for some:* interview. *Recommended:* minimum 2.7 GPA. *Application deadlines:* 3/15 (freshmen), 7/15 (transfers), 11/15 (early action). *Notification:* continuous until 4/15 (freshmen), continuous until 8/15 (transfers), 12/1 (early action).

Freshman Application Contact Mr. Robert C. Piurowski, Director of Admission, Concordia College–New York, 171 White Plains Rd, Bronxville, NY 10708. *Phone:* 914-337-9300 Ext. 2155. *Toll-free phone:* 800-YES-COLLEGE. *Fax:* 914-395-4636. *E-mail:* admission@concordia-ny.edu. *Website:* http://www.concordia-ny.edu/.

Cooper Union for the Advancement of Science and Art

New York, New York

- **Independent** comprehensive, founded 1859
- **Urban** campus with easy access to New York City
- **Endowment** $640.5 million
- **Coed** 927 undergraduate students, 97% full-time, 38% women, 62% men
- **Most difficult** entrance level, 8% of applicants were admitted

Undergraduates 902 full-time, 25 part-time. Students come from 38 states and territories; 30 other countries; 46% are from out of state; 6% Black or African American, non-Hispanic/Latino; 9% Hispanic/Latino; 18% Asian, non-Hispanic/Latino; 0.2% Native Hawaiian or other Pacific Islander, non-Hispanic/Latino; 0.9% American Indian or Alaska Native, non-Hispanic/Latino; 5% Two or more races, non-Hispanic/Latino; 9% Race/ethnicity unknown; 15% international; 4% transferred in; 20% live on campus. *Retention:* 96% of full-time freshmen returned.

Freshmen *Admission:* 3,415 applied, 264 admitted, 201 enrolled. *Average high school GPA:* 3.6. *Test scores:* SAT critical reading scores over 500: 96%; SAT math scores over 500: 95%; SAT writing scores over 500: 93%; SAT critical reading scores over 600: 82%; SAT math scores over 600: 83%; SAT writing scores over 600: 79%; ACT scores over 24: 100%; SAT critical reading scores over 700: 37%; SAT math scores over 700: 61%; SAT writing scores over 700: 37%; ACT scores over 30: 60%.

Faculty *Total:* 229, 23% full-time, 49% with terminal degrees. *Student/faculty ratio:* 9:1.

Academics *Calendar:* semesters. *Degrees:* certificates, bachelor's, and master's (also offers master's program primarily made up of currently-enrolled students). *Special study options:* advanced placement credit, honors programs, independent study, internships, off-campus study, services for LD students, student-designed majors, study abroad, summer session for credit.

Computers on Campus 100 computers/terminals are available on campus for general student use. Students can access the following: computer help desk, free student e-mail accounts, online (class) grades, online (class) schedules. Campuswide network is available. 100% of college-owned or -operated housing units are wired for high-speed Internet access. Wireless service is available via classrooms, computer centers, computer labs, learning centers, student centers.

Student Life *Housing options:* coed. Campus housing is university owned. Freshman applicants given priority for college housing. *Activities and organizations:* drama/theater group, student-run newspaper, choral group, South Asian Society, Pro Musica, Chinese Student Association, Drama Society, Outdoors Club; Intervarsity Christian Fellowship, national fraternities, national sororities. *Campus security:* 24-hour emergency response devices and patrols, controlled dormitory access, security guards. *Student services:* personal/psychological counseling.

Athletics *Intercollegiate sports:* badminton M/W, basketball M/W(c), cross-country running M/W, soccer M/W, tennis M/W, volleyball M/W. *Intramural sports:* basketball M/W, bowling M/W, fencing M(c)/W(c), golf M/W, sailing M/W, skiing (downhill) M/W, soccer M(c)/W(c), softball M/W, swimming and diving M/W, table tennis M(c)/W(c), tennis M/W, ultimate Frisbee M(c)/W(c), volleyball M/W.

Standardized Tests *Required:* SAT or ACT (for admission). *Required for some:* SAT Subject Tests (for admission).

Costs (2012–13) *Comprehensive fee:* $54,220 includes full-time tuition ($38,550), mandatory fees ($1700), and room and board ($13,970). All international students are assessed a fee of $ 1,910/year. Please note: All of our undergraduate students (including international) specifically for the 2012-2013 school year are offered a full-tuition scholarship valued at $38.550. *College room only:* $9970. Room and board charges vary according to board plan and housing facility.

Financial Aid Of all full-time matriculated undergraduates who enrolled in 2011, 406 applied for aid, 291 were judged to have need, 129 had their need fully met. 54 Federal Work-Study jobs (averaging $872). 505 state and other

part-time jobs (averaging $1619). In 2011, 596 non-need-based awards were made. *Average percent of need met:* 91%. *Average financial aid package:* $37,500. *Average need-based loan:* $3887. *Average need-based gift aid:* $43,208. *Average non-need-based aid:* $37,500. *Average indebtedness upon graduation:* $15,864. *Financial aid deadline:* 6/1.
Applying *Options:* electronic application, early admission, early decision, deferred entrance. *Application fee:* $65. *Required:* essay or personal statement, high school transcript, minimum 2.0 GPA. *Required for some:* minimum 3.5 GPA, 3 letters of recommendation, interview, portfolio, home examination for art and architecture applicants. *Recommended:* minimum 3.0 GPA. *Application deadlines:* 1/1 (freshmen), 1/1 (transfers). *Early decision deadline:* 12/1 (for plan 1), 12/1 (for plan 2). *Notification:* 4/1 (freshmen), 5/1 (transfers), 12/24 (early decision plan 1), 2/1 (early decision plan 2).
Freshman Application Contact Mr. Mitchell L. Lipton, Dean of Admissions and Records and Registrar, Cooper Union for the Advancement of Science and Art, 30 Cooper Square, New York, NY 10003. *Phone:* 212-353-4120. *Fax:* 212-353-4342. *E-mail:* admissions@cooper.edu. *Website:* http://www.cooper.edu/.

Cornell University

Ithaca, New York

- **Independent** university, founded 1865
- **Small-town** 745-acre campus with easy access to Syracuse
- **Endowment** $5.1 million
- **Coed**
- **Most difficult** entrance level

Faculty *Student/faculty ratio:* 9:1.
Academics *Calendar:* semesters. *Degrees:* bachelor's, master's, and doctoral.
Student Life *Campus security:* 24-hour emergency response devices and patrols, late-night transport/escort service, controlled dormitory access, indoor and outdoor emergency phones.
Athletics Member NCAA. All Division I except football (Division I-AA).
Standardized Tests *Required:* SAT or ACT (for admission). *Required for some:* SAT Subject Tests (for admission).
Costs (2012–13) *Comprehensive fee:* $57,091 includes full-time tuition ($43,185), mandatory fees ($228), and room and board ($13,678). Full-time tuition and fees vary according to degree level. *College room only:* $8112. Room and board charges vary according to board plan and housing facility.
Financial Aid *Of all full-time matriculated undergraduates who enrolled in 2012,* 8,035 applied for aid, 7,045 were judged to have need, 7,045 had their need fully met. 5,213 Federal Work-Study jobs (averaging $1800). 1,338 state and other part-time jobs (averaging $1540). *Average percent of need met:* 100. *Average financial aid package:* $40,942. *Average need-based loan:* $3549. *Average need-based gift aid:* $35,752. *Average indebtedness upon graduation:* $20,490. *Financial aid deadline:* 2/15.
Applying *Options:* electronic application, early decision, deferred entrance. *Application fee:* $75. *Required:* essay or personal statement, high school transcript, 2 letters of recommendation. *Required for some:* interview.
Freshman Application Contact Mr. Jason C. Locke, Director of Undergraduate Admissions, Cornell University, Ithaca, NY 14853-0001. *Phone:* 607-255-1446. *Fax:* 607-255-0659. *E-mail:* admissions@cornell.edu. *Website:* http://www.cornell.edu/.

The Culinary Institute of America

Hyde Park, New York

- **Independent** 4-year, founded 1946
- **Suburban** 170-acre campus
- **Endowment** $101.1 million
- **Coed** 2,827 undergraduate students, 100% full-time, 47% women, 53% men
- **Moderately difficult** entrance level, 84% of applicants were admitted

Undergraduates 2,827 full-time. Students come from 55 states and territories; 39 other countries; 77% are from out of state; 4% Black or African American, non-Hispanic/Latino; 11% Hispanic/Latino; 7% Asian, non-Hispanic/Latino; 0.8% Native Hawaiian or other Pacific Islander, non-Hispanic/Latino; 0.7% American Indian or Alaska Native, non-Hispanic/Latino; 1% Two or more races, non-Hispanic/Latino; 4% Race/ethnicity unknown; 8% international; 79% live on campus.

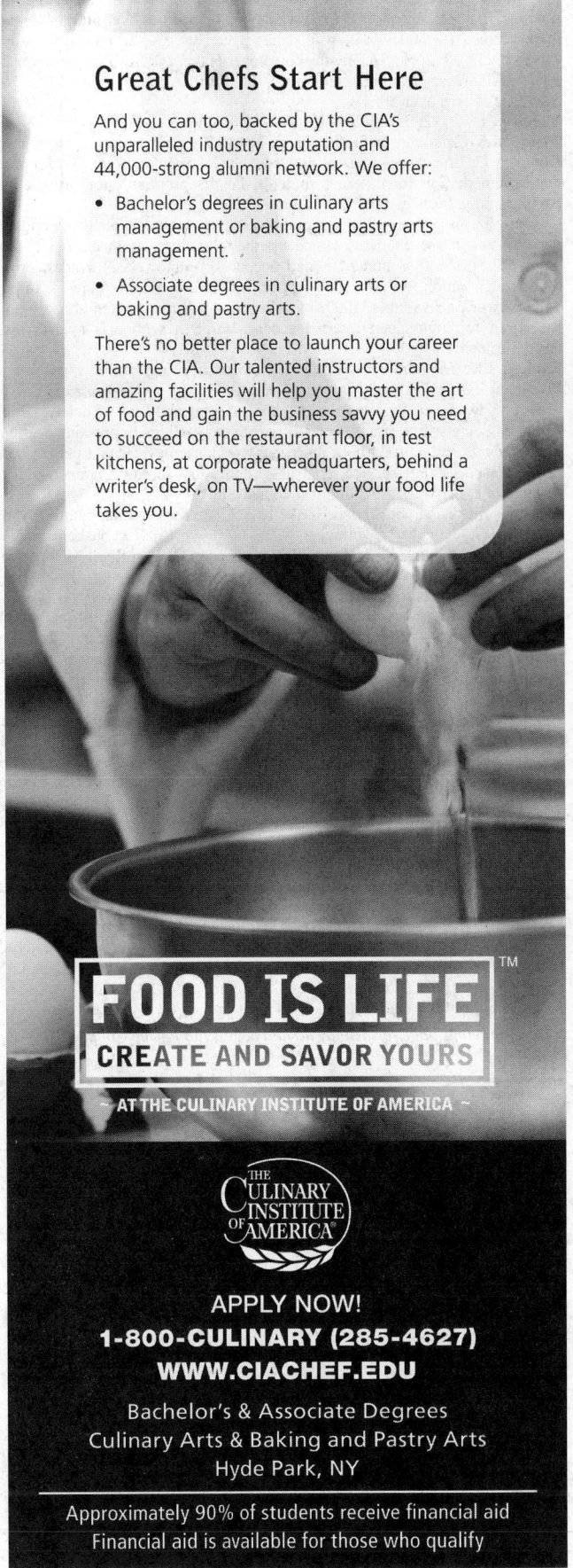

Freshmen *Admission:* 951 applied, 803 admitted, 534 enrolled. *Average high school GPA:* 3.2. *Test scores:* SAT critical reading scores over 500: 64%; SAT math scores over 500: 66%; ACT scores over 18: 86%; SAT critical reading scores over 600: 20%; SAT math scores over 600: 22%; ACT scores over 24: 34%; SAT critical reading scores over 700: 3%; SAT math scores over 700: 5%; ACT scores over 30: 1%.

Faculty *Total:* 192, 79% full-time. *Student/faculty ratio:* 17:1.

Academics *Calendar:* semesters plus 18 or 21 week externship program. *Degrees:* certificates, associate, and bachelor's. *Special study options:* academic remediation for entering students, honors programs, internships, off-campus study, services for LD students.

Computers on Campus 218 computers/terminals are available on campus for general student use. Students can access the following: campus intranet, computer help desk, free student e-mail accounts, online (class) grades, online (class) registration, online (class) schedules, online course guides. Campus-wide network is available. 100% of college-owned or -operated housing units are wired for high-speed Internet access. Wireless service is available via entire campus.

Student Life *Housing options:* coed. Campus housing is university owned. Freshman campus housing is guaranteed. *Activities and organizations:* student-run newspaper, choral group, Alliance, Baking and Pastry Society, Global Culinary Society, Eta Sigma Delta Honor Society, Chips Supporting Agriculture. *Campus security:* 24-hour emergency response devices and patrols, late-night transport/escort service, controlled dormitory access. *Student services:* health clinic, personal/psychological counseling.

Athletics *Intercollegiate sports:* basketball M/W, cross-country running M/W, soccer M/W, tennis M/W, volleyball M/W. *Intramural sports:* basketball M/W, cross-country running M/W, football M/W, soccer M/W, softball M/W, swimming and diving M/W, tennis M/W, volleyball M/W.

Standardized Tests *Recommended:* SAT or ACT (for admission).

Costs (2012–13) *Comprehensive fee:* $35,710 includes full-time tuition ($25,900), mandatory fees ($1230), and room and board ($8580). Full-time tuition and fees vary according to degree level. *College room only:* $5920. Room and board charges vary according to board plan and housing facility.

Financial Aid Of all full-time matriculated undergraduates who enrolled in 2008, 2,600 applied for aid, 2,340 were judged to have need, 134 had their need fully met. 900 Federal Work-Study jobs (averaging $435). In 2008, 238 non-need-based awards were made. *Average percent of need met:* 44%. *Average financial aid package:* $13,805. *Average need-based loan:* $4032. *Average need-based gift aid:* $3500. *Average non-need-based aid:* $2500. *Average indebtedness upon graduation:* $29,351. *Financial aid deadline:* 2/15.

Applying *Options:* electronic application, deferred entrance. *Application fee:* $50. *Required:* essay or personal statement, high school transcript, 1 letter of recommendation. *Required for some:* Affidavit of Support. *Application deadline:* rolling (freshmen). *Notification:* continuous (transfers).

Freshman Application Contact Ms. Rachel Birchwood, Director of Admissions, The Culinary Institute of America, 1946 Campus Drive, Hyde Park, NY 12538. *Phone:* 845-451-1459. *Toll-free phone:* 800-CULINARY. *Fax:* 845-451-1068. *E-mail:* admissions@culinary.edu. *Website:* http://www.ciachef.edu/.

See previous page for display ad and page 1258 for the College Close-Up.

Daemen College

Amherst, New York

- **Independent** comprehensive, founded 1947
- **Suburban** 35-acre campus with easy access to Buffalo
- **Endowment** $7.1 million
- **Coed**
- **Moderately difficult** entrance level

Faculty *Student/faculty ratio:* 14:1.

Academics *Calendar:* semesters. *Degrees:* certificates, bachelor's, master's, doctoral, and post-master's certificates.

Student Life *Campus security:* 24-hour emergency response devices and patrols, late-night transport/escort service, 24-hour security cameras.

Athletics Member NAIA.

Standardized Tests *Recommended:* SAT or ACT (for admission).

Costs (2012–13) *Comprehensive fee:* $33,830 includes full-time tuition ($22,620), mandatory fees ($510), and room and board ($10,700). Full-time tuition and fees vary according to location and reciprocity agreements. Part-time tuition: $750 per credit hour. Part-time tuition and fees vary according to course load, location, and reciprocity agreements. *Required fees:* $6 per credit hour part-time, $80 per term part-time. *Room and board:* Room and board charges vary according to board plan and housing facility. *Payment plans:* installment, deferred payment.

Financial Aid *Of all full-time matriculated undergraduates who enrolled in 2009,* 1,380 applied for aid, 1,205 were judged to have need, 421 had their need fully met. 265 Federal Work-Study jobs (averaging $1456). 327 state and other part-time jobs (averaging $1464). *In 2009,* 241 non-need-based awards were made. *Average percent of need met:* 80. *Average financial aid package:* $16,217. *Average need-based loan:* $4837. *Average need-based gift aid:* $16,528. *Average non-need-based aid:* $9388. *Average indebtedness upon graduation:* $27,444.

Applying *Options:* electronic application, early admission, deferred entrance. *Application fee:* $25. *Required:* essay or personal statement, high school transcript, minimum 2.0 GPA, 1 letter of recommendation. *Required for some:* 3 letters of recommendation, interview, high school transcript, class rank, writing sample-test optional.

Freshman Application Contact Daemen College, 4380 Main Street, Amherst, NY 14226-3592. *Phone:* 716-839-8225. *Toll-free phone:* 800-462-7652. *Fax:* 716-839-8229. *E-mail:* admissions@daemen.edu. *Website:* http://www.daemen.edu/.

See previous page for display ad and page 1262 for the College Close-Up.

Darkei Noam Rabbinical College

Brooklyn, New York

Director of Admissions Rabbi Pinchas Horowitz, Director of Admissions, Darkei Noam Rabbinical College, 2822 Avenue J, Brooklyn, NY 11210. *Phone:* 718-338-6464.

Davis College

Johnson City, New York

Freshman Application Contact Admissions Coordinator, Davis College, 400 Riverside Drive, Johnson City, NY 13790. *Phone:* 607-729-1581 Ext. 406. *Toll-free phone:* 877-949-3248. *Fax:* 607-798-7754. *E-mail:* admissions@davisny.edu. *Website:* http://www.davisny.edu/.

DeVry College of New York

New York, New York

- **Proprietary** comprehensive, founded 1998, part of DeVry University
- **Urban** campus
- **Coed** 1,239 undergraduate students, 57% full-time, 28% women, 72% men
- **Minimally difficult** entrance level

Undergraduates 711 full-time, 528 part-time. 15% are from out of state; 27% Black or African American, non-Hispanic/Latino; 28% Hispanic/Latino; 6% Asian, non-Hispanic/Latino; 0.5% Native Hawaiian or other Pacific Islander, non-Hispanic/Latino; 0.2% American Indian or Alaska Native, non-Hispanic/Latino; 0.6% Two or more races, non-Hispanic/Latino; 24% Race/ethnicity unknown; 3% international; 21% transferred in.

Freshmen *Admission:* 145 enrolled.

Faculty *Total:* 68, 40% full-time. *Student/faculty ratio:* 31:1.

Academics *Calendar:* semesters. *Degrees:* associate, bachelor's, master's, and postbachelor's certificates. *Special study options:* adult/continuing education programs, part-time degree program.

Student Life *Housing:* college housing not available.

Costs (2013–14) *Tuition:* $16,076 full-time, $609 per credit hour part-time. *Required fees:* $80 full-time.

Financial Aid *Of all full-time matriculated undergraduates who enrolled in 2007,* 387 applied for aid, 371 were judged to have need, 8 had their need fully met. In 2007, 19 non-need-based awards were made. *Average percent of need met:* 5%. *Average financial aid package:* $15,942. *Average need-based loan:* $8712. *Average need-based gift aid:* $7343. *Average non-need-based aid:* $11,806. *Average indebtedness upon graduation:* $29,136.

Applying *Application fee:* $40. *Required:* high school transcript, interview. *Application deadlines:* rolling (freshmen), rolling (transfers). *Notification:* continuous (freshmen), continuous (transfers).

Freshman Application Contact DeVry College of New York, 180 Madison Avenue, Suite 900, New York, NY 10016-5267. *Phone:* 212-312-4300. *Toll-free phone:* 866-338-7941. *Website:* http://www.devry.edu/.

Dominican College

Orangeburg, New York

- **Independent** comprehensive, founded 1952
- **Suburban** 70-acre campus with easy access to New York City
- **Endowment** $3.2 million
- **Coed** 1,595 undergraduate students, 85% full-time, 67% women, 33% men
- **Noncompetitive** entrance level, 69% of applicants were admitted

Undergraduates 1,357 full-time, 238 part-time. Students come from 23 states and territories; 13 other countries; 24% are from out of state; 16% Black or African American, non-Hispanic/Latino; 24% Hispanic/Latino; 8% Asian, non-Hispanic/Latino; 0.3% American Indian or Alaska Native, non-Hispanic/Latino; 8% Two or more races, non-Hispanic/Latino; 8% Race/ethnicity unknown; 1% international; 13% transferred in; 51% live on campus. *Retention:* 64% of full-time freshmen returned.

Freshmen *Admission:* 1,850 applied, 1,277 admitted, 293 enrolled. *Average high school GPA:* 2.76. *Test scores:* ACT scores over 18: 58%; ACT scores over 24: 5%.

Faculty *Total:* 237, 32% full-time, 36% with terminal degrees. *Student/faculty ratio:* 15:1.

Academics *Calendar:* semesters. *Degrees:* certificates, associate, bachelor's, master's, and doctoral. *Special study options:* academic remediation for entering students, accelerated degree program, adult/continuing education programs, advanced placement credit, cooperative education, distance learning, double majors, freshman honors college, honors programs, independent study, internships, off-campus study, part-time degree program, services for LD students, summer session for credit. *Unusual degree programs:* 3-2 occupational therapy.

Computers on Campus 150 computers/terminals are available on campus for general student use. Students can access the following: campus intranet, free student e-mail accounts, online (class) registration, online (class) schedules, Web portal, Black Board. Campuswide network is available. 100% of college-owned or -operated housing units are wired for high-speed Internet access. Wireless service is available via entire campus.

Student Life *Housing options:* coed. Campus housing is university owned. Freshman campus housing is guaranteed. *Activities and organizations:* drama/theater group, student-run newspaper, radio station, choral group, Student Government Association, Business Club, Aquin Players, school newspaper, Nursing Association. *Campus security:* 24-hour emergency response devices and patrols, student patrols, late-night transport/escort service, controlled dormitory access. *Student services:* health clinic, personal/psychological counseling.

Athletics Member NCAA, NAIA. All NCAA Division II. *Intercollegiate sports:* baseball M(s), basketball M(s)/W(s), cross-country running W(s), golf M(s), lacrosse M(s)/W(s), soccer M(s)/W(s), softball W(s), track and field W(s), volleyball W(s). *Intramural sports:* basketball M/W, crew M(c)/W(c), volleyball M/W.

Standardized Tests *Required:* SAT or ACT (for admission).

Costs (2012–13) *Comprehensive fee:* $35,950 includes full-time tuition ($23,200), mandatory fees ($770), and room and board ($11,980). Full-time tuition and fees vary according to degree level. Part-time tuition: $700 per credit hour. Part-time tuition and fees vary according to degree level and program. *Room and board:* Room and board charges vary according to board plan and housing facility. *Payment plans:* installment, deferred payment. *Waivers:* senior citizens and employees or children of employees.

Financial Aid Of all full-time matriculated undergraduates who enrolled in 2012, 1,296 applied for aid, 1,196 were judged to have need, 122 had their need fully met. 262 Federal Work-Study jobs (averaging $2000). In 2012, 138 non-need-based awards were made. *Average percent of need met:* 56%. *Average financial aid package:* $15,358. *Average need-based loan:* $4033. *Average need-based gift aid:* $12,358. *Average non-need-based aid:* $7041. *Average indebtedness upon graduation:* $17,930.

Applying *Options:* electronic application, deferred entrance. *Application fee:* $35. *Required:* high school transcript. *Required for some:* essay or personal statement, interview. *Recommended:* interview. *Application deadlines:* rolling (freshmen), rolling (transfers). *Notification:* continuous (freshmen), continuous (transfers).

Freshman Application Contact Ms. Joyce Elbe, Director of Admissions, Dominican College, 470 Western Highway, Orangeburg, NY 10962-1210. *Phone:* 845-359-7901. *Toll-free phone:* 866-432-4636. *Fax:* 845-365-3150. *E-mail:* admissions@dc.edu. *Website:* http://www.dc.edu/.

Dowling College

Oakdale, New York

- **Independent** comprehensive, founded 1955
- **Suburban** 157-acre campus with easy access to New York City
- **Coed**
- **Moderately difficult** entrance level

Faculty *Student/faculty ratio:* 15:1.

Academics *Calendar:* semesters. *Degrees:* bachelor's, master's, doctoral, post-master's, and postbachelor's certificates.

Student Life *Campus security:* 24-hour emergency response devices and patrols, late-night transport/escort service, controlled dormitory access.

Athletics Member NCAA. All Division II.

Standardized Tests *Recommended:* SAT or ACT (for admission).

Costs (2012–13) *Comprehensive fee:* $37,714 includes full-time tuition ($25,324), mandatory fees ($1800), and room and board ($10,590). Full-time tuition and fees vary according to course load and degree level. Part-time tuition: $849 per credit. Part-time tuition and fees vary according to course load and degree level. *Required fees:* $566 per term part-time. *Room and board:* Room and board charges vary according to housing facility and location. *Payment plans:* installment, deferred payment.

Financial Aid *Of all full-time matriculated undergraduates who enrolled in 2010,* 1,543 applied for aid, 1,543 were judged to have need, 168 had their need fully met. 313 Federal Work-Study jobs (averaging $1599). 59 state and other part-time jobs (averaging $1536). *In 2010,* 239 non-need-based awards were made. *Average percent of need met:* 94. *Average financial aid package:* $15,570. *Average need-based loan:* $4200. *Average need-based gift aid:* $8270. *Average non-need-based aid:* $5770. *Average indebtedness upon graduation:* $22,177.

Applying *Options:* electronic application, early action, deferred entrance. *Application fee:* $35. *Required:* essay or personal statement, high school transcript, minimum 2.0 GPA, 1 letter of recommendation. *Recommended:* minimum 2.5 GPA.

Freshman Application Contact Ms. Ronnie Lee Macdonald, Vice President for Enrollment and Student Services, Dowling College, 150 Idle Hour Boulevard, Oakdale, NY 11769. *Phone:* 631-244-3480. *Toll-free phone:* 800-DOWLING. *Fax:* 631-244-1059. *Website:* http://www.dowling.edu/.

See below for display ad and page 1272 for the College Close-Up.

D'Youville College

Buffalo, New York

Freshman Application Contact D'Youville College, 320 Porter Avenue, Buffalo, NY 14201-1084. *Phone:* 716-829-7600. *Toll-free phone:* 800-777-3921. *Website:* http://www.dyc.edu/.

See next page for display ad and page 1276 for the College Close-Up.

Elmira College

Elmira, New York

- **Independent** comprehensive, founded 1855
- **Suburban** 55-acre campus
- **Coed** 1,386 undergraduate students, 87% full-time, 71% women, 29% men
- **Moderately difficult** entrance level, 89% of applicants were admitted

Undergraduates 1,199 full-time, 187 part-time. Students come from 35 states and territories; 31 other countries; 50% are from out of state; 3% Black or African American, non-Hispanic/Latino; 3% Hispanic/Latino; 0.8% Asian, non-Hispanic/Latino; 0.2% American Indian or Alaska Native, non-Hispanic/Latino; 3% Two or more races, non-Hispanic/Latino; 9% Race/ethnicity unknown; 6% international; 3% transferred in; 94% live on campus. *Retention:* 75% of full-time freshmen returned.

Freshmen *Admission:* 2,056 applied, 1,828 admitted, 356 enrolled. *Average high school GPA:* 3.34. *Test scores:* SAT critical reading scores over 500: 68%; SAT math scores over 500: 72%; ACT scores over 18: 96%; SAT critical reading scores over 600: 27%; SAT math scores over 600: 30%; ACT scores over 24: 50%; SAT critical reading scores over 700: 4%; SAT math scores over 700: 5%; ACT scores over 30: 13%.

Faculty *Total:* 192, 49% full-time. *Student/faculty ratio:* 10:1.

Academics *Calendar:* 4-4-1. *Degrees:* associate, bachelor's, and master's. *Special study options:* accelerated degree program, adult/continuing education programs, advanced placement credit, distance learning, double majors, English as a second language, independent study, internships, off-campus study, part-time degree program, services for LD students, student-designed majors, study abroad, summer session for credit. *ROTC:* Army (b), Air Force (c).

Computers on Campus 173 computers/terminals are available on campus for general student use. Students can access the following: campus intranet, computer help desk, free student e-mail accounts, online (class) grades, online (class) schedules. Campuswide network is available. 100% of college-owned or -operated housing units are wired for high-speed Internet access. Wireless service is available via classrooms, computer centers, computer labs, dorm rooms, libraries, student centers.

Student Life *Housing:* on-campus residence required through senior year. *Options:* coed, women-only, cooperative, disabled students. Campus housing is university owned. Freshman campus housing is guaranteed. *Activities and organizations:* drama/theater group, student-run newspaper, radio station, choral group, student radio station, Student Activities Board, College Republicans and Democrats, Ski Club, Habitat for Humanity. *Campus security:* 24-hour patrols, late-night transport/escort service, 24-hour locked residence hall entrances. *Student services:* health clinic, personal/psychological counseling.

Athletics Member NCAA. All Division III. *Intercollegiate sports:* basketball M/W, cheerleading W, field hockey W, golf M/W, ice hockey M/W, lacrosse M/W, soccer M/W, softball W, tennis M/W, volleyball M/W. *Intramural sports:* badminton M/W, basketball M/W, equestrian sports M/W, football M/W, ice hockey M/W, lacrosse M/W, racquetball M/W, rock climbing M/W, skiing (cross-country) M/W, skiing (downhill) M/W, soccer M/W, softball M/W, swimming and diving M/W, table tennis M/W, tennis M/W, ultimate Frisbee M/W, volleyball M/W.

Standardized Tests *Required:* SAT or ACT (for admission).

Costs (2013–14) *Comprehensive fee:* $49,950 includes full-time tuition ($36,600), mandatory fees ($1550), and room and board ($11,800). Part-time tuition and fees vary according to course load and degree level. *College room only:* $6300. Room and board charges vary according to housing facility. *Payment plans:* tuition prepayment, installment. *Waivers:* employees or children of employees.

Financial Aid Of all full-time matriculated undergraduates who enrolled in 2012, 1,037 applied for aid, 976 were judged to have need, 161 had their need fully met. 298 Federal Work-Study jobs (averaging $1200). 224 state and other part-time jobs (averaging $1200). In 2012, 205 non-need-based awards were made. *Average percent of need met:* 76%. *Average financial aid package:* $29,374. *Average need-based loan:* $4220. *Average need-based gift aid:* $25,512. *Average non-need-based aid:* $23,117. *Average indebtedness upon graduation:* $28,586.

Applying *Options:* electronic application, early decision, deferred entrance. *Application fee:* $50. *Required:* essay or personal statement, high school transcript, minimum 2.0 GPA, 1 letter of recommendation. *Required for some:* interview. *Recommended:* interview. *Application deadlines:* 3/31 (freshmen), rolling (transfers). *Early decision deadline:* 11/15 (for plan 1), 1/15 (for plan 2). *Notification:* continuous until 4/30 (freshmen), continuous (transfers), 12/15 (early decision plan 1), 1/31 (early decision plan 2).

Freshman Application Contact Mr. Brett Moore, Dean of Admissions, Elmira College, One Park Place, Elmira, NY 14901. *Phone:* 607-735-1724. *Toll-free phone:* 800-935-6472. *Fax:* 607-735-1718. *E-mail:* admissions@ elmira.edu.

Website: http://www.elmira.edu/.

See next page for display ad and page 1280 for the College Close-Up.

Eugene Lang College The New School for Liberal Arts

New York, New York

- **Independent** 4-year, founded 1978, part of The New School
- **Urban** 5-acre campus with easy access to New York City
- **Coed** 1,457 undergraduate students, 93% full-time, 68% women, 32% men
- **Very difficult** entrance level, 73% of applicants were admitted

Undergraduates 1,355 full-time, 102 part-time. 70% are from out of state; 6% Black or African American, non-Hispanic/Latino; 13% Hispanic/Latino; 5% Asian, non-Hispanic/Latino; 0.1% Native Hawaiian or other Pacific Islander, non-Hispanic/Latino; 0.1% American Indian or Alaska Native, non-Hispanic/Latino; 4% Two or more races, non-Hispanic/Latino; 10% Race/ethnicity unknown; 5% international; 50% transferred in; 27% live on campus. *Retention:* 80% of full-time freshmen returned.

Freshmen *Admission:* 1,543 applied, 1,126 admitted, 290 enrolled. *Average high school GPA:* 3.38. *Test scores:* SAT critical reading scores over 500: 89%;

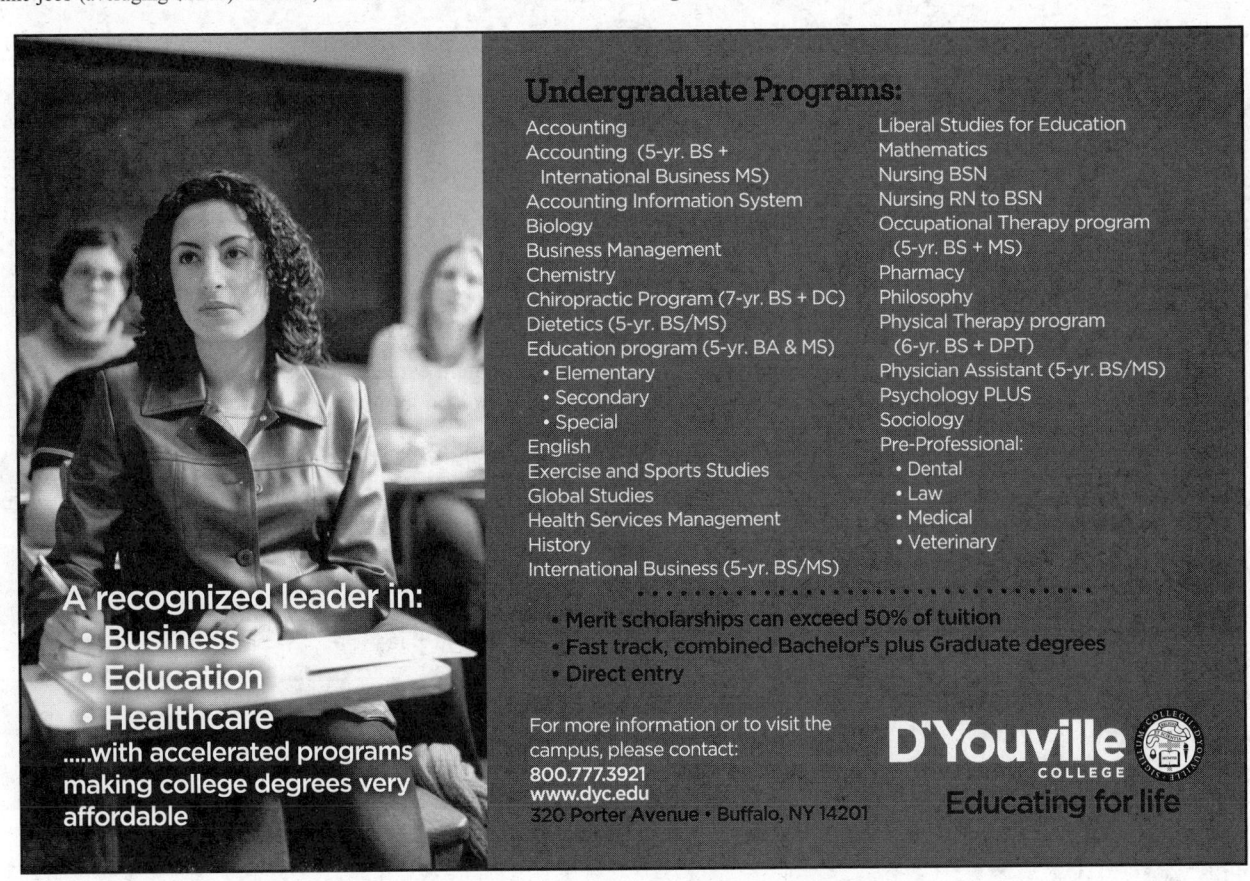

Undergraduate Programs:

Accounting
Accounting (5-yr. BS + International Business MS)
Accounting Information System
Biology
Business Management
Chemistry
Chiropractic Program (7-yr. BS + DC)
Dietetics (5-yr. BS/MS)
Education program (5-yr. BA & MS)
- Elementary
- Secondary
- Special
English
Exercise and Sports Studies
Global Studies
Health Services Management
History
International Business (5-yr. BS/MS)

Liberal Studies for Education
Mathematics
Nursing BSN
Nursing RN to BSN
Occupational Therapy program (5-yr. BS + MS)
Pharmacy
Philosophy
Physical Therapy program (6-yr. BS + DPT)
Physician Assistant (5-yr. BS/MS)
Psychology PLUS
Sociology
Pre-Professional:
- Dental
- Law
- Medical
- Veterinary

- Merit scholarships can exceed 50% of tuition
- Fast track, combined Bachelor's plus Graduate degrees
- Direct entry

For more information or to visit the campus, please contact:
800.777.3921
www.dyc.edu
320 Porter Avenue • Buffalo, NY 14201

A recognized leader in:
- Business
- Education
- Healthcare
.....with accelerated programs making college degrees very affordable

D'Youville
COLLEGE
Educating for life

SAT math scores over 500: 77%; SAT writing scores over 500: 91%; ACT scores over 18: 99%; SAT critical reading scores over 600: 51%; SAT math scores over 600: 37%; SAT writing scores over 600: 54%; ACT scores over 24: 76%; SAT critical reading scores over 700: 16%; SAT math scores over 700: 5%; SAT writing scores over 700: 11%; ACT scores over 30: 8%.

Faculty *Total:* 149, 43% full-time, 37% with terminal degrees. *Student/faculty ratio:* 15:1.

Academics *Calendar:* semesters. *Degree:* bachelor's. *Special study options:* accelerated degree program, advanced placement credit, distance learning, double majors, English as a second language, independent study, internships, off-campus study, services for LD students, student-designed majors, study abroad, summer session for credit.

Computers on Campus Students can access the following: campus intranet, computer help desk, free student e-mail accounts, online (class) grades, online (class) registration, online (class) schedules, online portal. Campuswide network is available. 100% of college-owned or -operated housing units are wired for high-speed Internet access. Wireless service is available via entire campus.

Student Life *Housing options:* coed, disabled students. Campus housing is university owned and leased by the school. Freshman applicants given priority for college housing. *Activities and organizations:* drama/theater group, student-run newspaper, radio station, choral group. *Campus security:* 24-hour emergency response devices, controlled dormitory access, 24-hour desk attendants in residence halls. *Student services:* health clinic, personal/psychological counseling.

Costs (2013–14) *Comprehensive fee:* $55,870 includes full-time tuition ($37,710), mandatory fees ($860), and room and board ($17,300). Part-time tuition: $1280 per credit hour. *College room only:* $13,900.

Financial Aid Of all full-time matriculated undergraduates who enrolled in 2011, 926 applied for aid, 839 were judged to have need, 100 had their need fully met. In 2011, 50 non-need-based awards were made. *Average percent of need met:* 64%. *Average financial aid package:* $28,480. *Average need-based loan:* $9620. *Average need-based gift aid:* $21,630. *Average non-need-based aid:* $7475. *Average indebtedness upon graduation:* $34,455.

Applying *Options:* electronic application, early decision, deferred entrance. *Application fee:* $50. *Required:* essay or personal statement, high school transcript, interview, counselor evaluation, teacher evaluation. *Recommended:* minimum 3.0 GPA. *Application deadlines:* 1/5 (freshmen), 4/1 (transfers).

Early decision deadline: 11/1. *Notification:* 4/1 (freshmen), 5/1 (transfers), 12/1 (early decision).

Freshman Application Contact Eugene Lang College The New School for Liberal Arts, 65 West 11th Street, New York, NY 10011-8601. *Phone:* 212-229-5665. *Toll-free phone:* 800-292-3040.

Website: http://www.newschool.edu/lang.

See next page for display ad and page 1414 for the College Close-Up.

Excelsior College
Albany, New York

- **Independent** comprehensive, founded 1970
- **Suburban** campus with easy access to Albany, NY
- **Coed** 35,302 undergraduate students, 59% women, 41% men

Undergraduates 35,302 part-time. Students come from 52 states and territories; 20 other countries; 86% are from out of state; 23% Black or African American, non-Hispanic/Latino; 8% Hispanic/Latino; 3% Asian, non-Hispanic/Latino; 0.5% Native Hawaiian or other Pacific Islander, non-Hispanic/Latino; 0.7% American Indian or Alaska Native, non-Hispanic/Latino; 2% Two or more races, non-Hispanic/Latino; 2% Race/ethnicity unknown; 0.7% international; 29% transferred in.

Faculty *Student/faculty ratio:* 8:1.

Academics *Calendar:* continuous. *Degrees:* certificates, associate, bachelor's, master's, post-master's, and postbachelor's certificates (offers only external degree programs). *Special study options:* accelerated degree program, adult/continuing education programs, advanced placement credit, distance learning, English as a second language, external degree program, honors programs, independent study, off-campus study, part-time degree program, services for LD students, student-designed majors. *Unusual degree programs:* 3-2 business administration; nursing; Bachelor of Science in Nuclear Engineering Technology/Master of Business Administration.

Computers on Campus Students can access the following: computer help desk, online (class) grades, online (class) registration, online (class) schedules. Campuswide network is available.

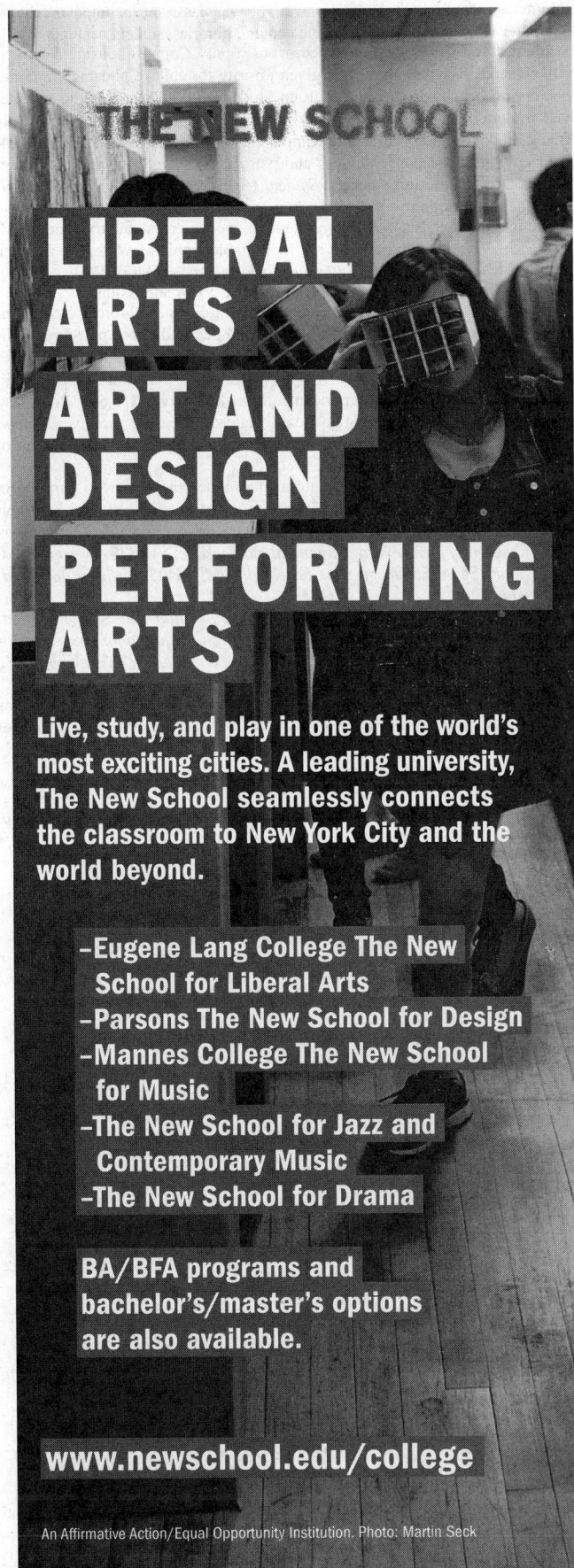

LIBERAL ARTS
ART AND DESIGN
PERFORMING ARTS

Live, study, and play in one of the world's most exciting cities. A leading university, The New School seamlessly connects the classroom to New York City and the world beyond.

- Eugene Lang College The New School for Liberal Arts
- Parsons The New School for Design
- Mannes College The New School for Music
- The New School for Jazz and Contemporary Music
- The New School for Drama

BA/BFA programs and bachelor's/master's options are also available.

www.newschool.edu/college

An Affirmative Action/Equal Opportunity Institution. Photo: Martin Seck

Costs (2013–14) *Tuition:* $390 per credit hour part-time. *Payment plan:* installment. *Waivers:* employees or children of employees.
Applying *Options:* electronic application. *Application fee:* $80. *Required for some:* college transcripts. *Application deadlines:* rolling (freshmen), rolling (transfers). *Notification:* continuous (freshmen), continuous (transfers).
Freshman Application Contact Admissions, Excelsior College, 7 Columbia Circle, Albany, NY 12203-5159. *Phone:* 518-464-8500. *Toll-free phone:* 888-647-2388. *Fax:* 518-464-8777. *E-mail:* admissions@excelsior.edu. *Website:* http://www.excelsior.edu/.

Farmingdale State College
Farmingdale, New York

- **State-supported** 4-year, founded 1912, part of State University of New York System
- **Small-town** 380-acre campus with easy access to New York City
- **Endowment** $6.5 million
- **Coed** 7,889 undergraduate students, 73% full-time, 42% women, 58% men
- **Moderately difficult** entrance level, 58% of applicants were admitted

Undergraduates 5,787 full-time, 2,102 part-time. Students come from 13 states and territories; 38 other countries; 1% are from out of state; 11% Black or African American, non-Hispanic/Latino; 14% Hispanic/Latino; 7% Asian, non-Hispanic/Latino; 0.5% Native Hawaiian or other Pacific Islander, non-Hispanic/Latino; 0.2% American Indian or Alaska Native, non-Hispanic/Latino; 2% Two or more races, non-Hispanic/Latino; 0.7% Race/ethnicity unknown; 3% international; 14% transferred in; 8% live on campus. *Retention:* 80% of full-time freshmen returned.
Freshmen *Admission:* 5,398 applied, 3,138 admitted, 1,190 enrolled. *Average high school GPA:* 3.27. *Test scores:* SAT critical reading scores over 500: 44%; SAT math scores over 500: 69%; SAT critical reading scores over 600: 5%; SAT math scores over 600: 15%.
Faculty *Total:* 592, 34% full-time. *Student/faculty ratio:* 20:1.
Academics *Calendar:* semesters. *Degrees:* certificates, associate, and bachelor's. *Special study options:* academic remediation for entering students, accelerated degree program, advanced placement credit, distance learning, double majors, English as a second language, independent study, internships, part-time degree program, services for LD students, student-designed majors, study abroad, summer session for credit. *ROTC:* Army (c), Navy (c), Air Force (c).
Computers on Campus 926 computers/terminals are available on campus for general student use. Students can access the following: free student e-mail accounts, online (class) registration, online (class) schedules. Campuswide network is available. Wireless service is available via entire campus.
Student Life *Housing options:* coed. Campus housing is university owned. *Activities and organizations:* drama/theater group, student-run newspaper, radio station, Campus Activities Board, Farmingdale Student Government, Student radio station, Rambler Newspaper, national fraternities, national sororities. *Campus security:* 24-hour emergency response devices and patrols, controlled dormitory access. *Student services:* health clinic, personal/psychological counseling.
Athletics Member NCAA. All Division III. *Intercollegiate sports:* baseball M, basketball M/W, cross-country running M/W, golf M, ice hockey M(c), lacrosse M/W, soccer M/W, softball W, tennis M/W, track and field M/W, volleyball W. *Intramural sports:* basketball M/W, football M, golf M/W, racquetball M/W, soccer M/W, softball M/W, squash M/W, swimming and diving M/W, table tennis M(c)/W(c), tennis M/W, ultimate Frisbee M(c)/W(c), volleyball M/W, weight lifting M(c)/W(c).
Standardized Tests *Required:* SAT or ACT (for admission).
Costs (2012–13) *Tuition:* state resident $5570 full-time, $232 per credit part-time; nonresident $14,820 full-time, $618 per credit part-time. Part-time tuition and fees vary according to course load. *Required fees:* $1223 full-time, $59 per credit part-time. *Room and board:* $11,790; room only: $7190. Room and board charges vary according to board plan and housing facility. *Payment plan:* installment.
Financial Aid Of all full-time matriculated undergraduates who enrolled in 2012, 3,884 applied for aid, 3,029 were judged to have need, 316 had their need fully met. 386 Federal Work-Study jobs (averaging $2636). In 2012, 14 non-need-based awards were made. *Average percent of need met:* 65%. *Average financial aid package:* $8502. *Average need-based loan:* $3978. *Average need-based gift aid:* $5990. *Average non-need-based aid:* $1046. *Average indebtedness upon graduation:* $18,867.
Applying *Options:* electronic application, early admission, deferred entrance. *Application fee:* $50. *Required:* high school transcript, minimum 2.5 GPA. *Required for some:* interview, Requirements vary by program. *Application deadlines:* rolling (freshmen), rolling (transfers). *Notification:* continuous (freshmen), continuous (transfers).

Freshman Application Contact Farmingdale State College, 2350 Broadhollow Road, Farmingdale, NY 11735. *Phone:* 631-420-2200. *Toll-free phone:* 877-4-FARMINGDALE.
Website: http://www.farmingdale.edu/.

Fashion Institute of Technology
New York, New York

- **State and locally supported** comprehensive, founded 1944, part of State University of New York System
- **Urban** 5-acre campus with easy access to New York City
- **Endowment** $25.9 million
- **Coed, primarily women** 9,848 undergraduate students, 73% full-time, 85% women, 15% men
- **Moderately difficult** entrance level, 45% of applicants were admitted

Undergraduates 7,154 full-time, 2,694 part-time. 35% are from out of state; 9% Black or African American, non-Hispanic/Latino; 15% Hispanic/Latino; 10% Asian, non-Hispanic/Latino; 0.4% Native Hawaiian or other Pacific Islander, non-Hispanic/Latino; 0.1% American Indian or Alaska Native, non-Hispanic/Latino; 3% Two or more races, non-Hispanic/Latino; 3% Race/ethnicity unknown; 13% international; 10% transferred in; 28% live on campus. *Retention:* 85% of full-time freshmen returned.
Freshmen *Admission:* 4,449 applied, 1,995 admitted, 1,233 enrolled.
Faculty *Total:* 977, 24% full-time. *Student/faculty ratio:* 17:1.
Academics *Calendar:* semesters. *Degrees:* certificates, associate, bachelor's, and master's. *Special study options:* academic remediation for entering students, adult/continuing education programs, advanced placement credit, distance learning, English as a second language, honors programs, internships, part-time degree program, services for LD students, study abroad, summer session for credit.
Computers on Campus 1,700 computers/terminals are available on campus for general student use. Students can access the following: campus intranet, computer help desk, free student e-mail accounts, online (class) grades, online (class) registration, online (class) schedules. Campuswide network is available. 100% of college-owned or -operated housing units are wired for high-speed Internet access. Wireless service is available via classrooms, computer centers, computer labs, dorm rooms, learning centers, libraries, student centers.
Student Life *Housing options:* coed, women-only. Campus housing is university owned. Freshman applicants given priority for college housing. *Activities and organizations:* drama/theater group, student-run newspaper, radio and television station, choral group, Asian Student Network, Fashion Show Club, Black Student Union, Phi Theta Kappa, Gospel Choir. *Campus security:* 24-hour emergency response devices and patrols, late-night transport/escort service, controlled dormitory access. *Student services:* health clinic, personal/psychological counseling.
Athletics Member NJCAA. *Intercollegiate sports:* cross-country running M/W, soccer W, swimming and diving M/W, table tennis M/W, tennis W, track and field M/W, volleyball W. *Intramural sports:* archery M(c)/W(c).
Standardized Tests *Recommended:* SAT or ACT (for admission).
Costs (2012–13) *Tuition:* state resident $5768 full-time, $240 per credit hour part-time; nonresident $15,430 full-time, $643 per credit hour part-time. Full-time tuition and fees vary according to degree level. Part-time tuition and fees vary according to degree level. *Required fees:* $590 full-time, $8 per credit hour part-time, $170 per term part-time. *Room and board:* $12,598. Room and board charges vary according to board plan and housing facility. *Payment plan:* installment. *Waivers:* senior citizens and employees or children of employees.
Financial Aid Of all full-time matriculated undergraduates who enrolled in 2010, 5,019 applied for aid, 3,858 were judged to have need, 535 had their need fully met. In 2010, 95 non-need-based awards were made. *Average percent of need met:* 75%. *Average financial aid package:* $13,577. *Average need-based loan:* $4248. *Average need-based gift aid:* $5405. *Average non-need-based aid:* $894.
Applying *Options:* electronic application. *Application fee:* $50. *Required:* essay or personal statement, high school transcript. *Required for some:* portfolio for art and design programs. *Application deadlines:* 1/1 (freshmen), 1/1 (transfers). *Notification:* 4/1 (freshmen), 4/1 (transfers).
Freshman Application Contact Ms. Laura Arbogast, Director of Admissions and Strategic Recruitment, Fashion Institute of Technology, Seventh Avenue at 27th Street, New York, NY 10001-5992. *Phone:* 212-217-3760. *Fax:* 212-217-3761. *E-mail:* fitinfo@fitnyc.edu.
Website: http://www.fitnyc.edu/.

See below for display ad and page 1288 for the College Close-Up.

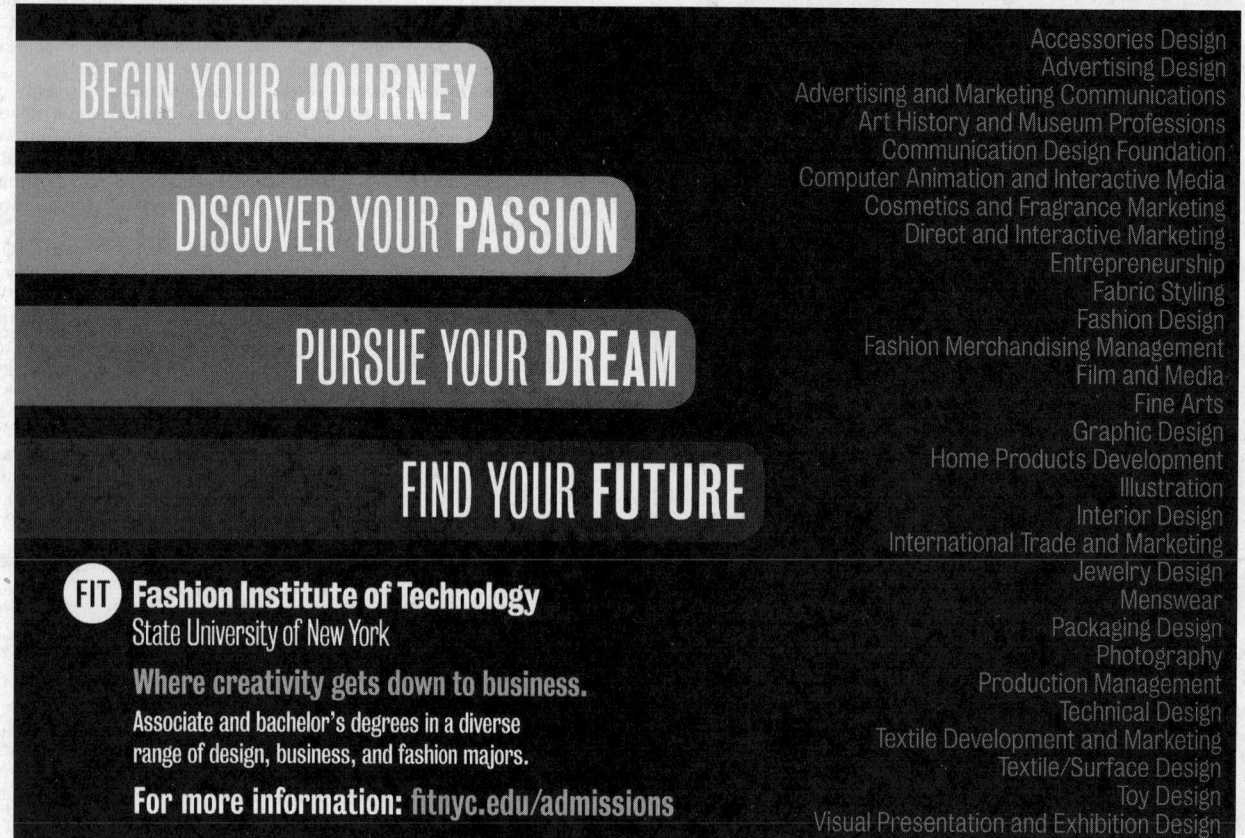

Five Towns College

Dix Hills, New York

- **Independent** comprehensive, founded 1972
- **Suburban** 35-acre campus with easy access to New York City
- **Coed** 869 undergraduate students, 96% full-time, 30% women, 70% men
- **Moderately difficult** entrance level, 41% of applicants were admitted

Undergraduates 835 full-time, 34 part-time. Students come from 12 states and territories; 2 other countries; 12% are from out of state; 26% Black or African American, non-Hispanic/Latino; 20% Hispanic/Latino; 5% Asian, non-Hispanic/Latino; 0.3% American Indian or Alaska Native, non-Hispanic/Latino; 2% Two or more races, non-Hispanic/Latino; 10% Race/ethnicity unknown; 0.1% international; 11% transferred in; 20% live on campus. *Retention:* 55% of full-time freshmen returned.

Freshmen *Admission:* 745 applied, 305 admitted, 189 enrolled. *Average high school GPA:* 2.7. *Test scores:* SAT critical reading scores over 500: 33%; SAT math scores over 500: 33%; SAT writing scores over 500: 22%; ACT scores over 18: 100%; SAT critical reading scores over 600: 3%; SAT math scores over 600: 10%; SAT writing scores over 600: 3%; ACT scores over 24: 50%; SAT critical reading scores over 700: 1%; SAT math scores over 700: 1%.

Faculty *Total:* 94, 40% full-time. *Student/faculty ratio:* 9:1.

Academics *Calendar:* semesters. *Degrees:* associate, bachelor's, master's, and doctoral. *Special study options:* academic remediation for entering students, adult/continuing education programs, advanced placement credit, independent study, internships, off-campus study, part-time degree program, services for LD students, summer session for credit.

Computers on Campus 110 computers/terminals are available on campus for general student use. Students can access the following: campus intranet, free student e-mail accounts, online (class) grades, online (class) schedules. Campuswide network is available. 100% of college-owned or -operated housing units are wired for high-speed Internet access. Wireless service is available via entire campus.

Student Life *Housing options:* coed. Campus housing is university owned. *Activities and organizations:* drama/theater group, student-run newspaper, radio station, choral group, Film Video Club, Audio Club, Music Business Club, Hip Hop Club, yearbook. *Campus security:* 24-hour emergency response devices and patrols, late-night transport/escort service, controlled dormitory access. *Student services:* personal/psychological counseling.

Standardized Tests *Required:* SAT or ACT (for admission).

Costs (2012–13) *One-time required fee:* $110. *Comprehensive fee:* $33,740 includes full-time tuition ($19,900), mandatory fees ($370), and room and board ($13,470). Full-time tuition and fees vary according to course level, degree level, program, and student level. Part-time tuition: $825 per credit hour. Part-time tuition and fees vary according to course level, course load, degree level, program, and student level. *Required fees:* $120 per term part-time, $70 per year part-time. *College room only:* $8100. *Payment plan:* installment. *Waivers:* employees or children of employees.

Financial Aid Of all full-time matriculated undergraduates who enrolled in 2009, 939 applied for aid, 791 were judged to have need, 466 had their need fully met. 95 Federal Work-Study jobs (averaging $1387). In 2009, 69 non-need-based awards were made. *Average percent of need met:* 48%. *Average financial aid package:* $8100. *Average need-based loan:* $3700. *Average need-based gift aid:* $5500. *Average non-need-based aid:* $2400. *Average indebtedness upon graduation:* $19,000.

Applying *Options:* electronic application, early decision, deferred entrance. *Application fee:* $35. *Required:* essay or personal statement, high school transcript, minimum 2.3 GPA, 2 letters of recommendation, Immunization records and an audition for Music or Theatre students. *Required for some:* interview. *Application deadlines:* rolling (freshmen), rolling (out-of-state freshmen), rolling (transfers). *Early decision deadline:* 12/1. *Notification:* continuous (freshmen), continuous (out-of-state freshmen), continuous (transfers), 12/15 (early decision).

Freshman Application Contact Mr. Jerry Cohen, Dean of Enrollment, Five Towns College, 305 North Service Road, Dix Hills, NY 11746-6055. *Phone:* 631-424-7000 Ext. 2110. *Fax:* 631-656-2172. *E-mail:* jerry.cohen@ftc.edu. *Website:* http://www.ftc.edu/.

See below for display ad and page 1294 for the College Close-Up.

Fordham University

New York, New York

- **Independent** Roman Catholic (Jesuit) university, founded 1841
- **Urban** 85-acre campus with easy access to New York City
- **Endowment** $458.0 million
- **Coed**
- **Very difficult** entrance level

Faculty *Student/faculty ratio:* 13:1.

Academics *Calendar:* semesters. *Degrees:* bachelor's, master's, doctoral, and post-master's certificates (branch locations at Rose Hill and Lincoln Center).

Student Life *Campus security:* 24-hour emergency response devices and patrols, student patrols, late-night transport/escort service, controlled dormitory access, security at each campus entrance and at residence halls.

Athletics Member NCAA. All Division I except football (Division I-AA).

Standardized Tests *Required:* SAT or ACT (for admission). *Recommended:* SAT Subject Tests (for admission).

Costs (2012–13) *Comprehensive fee:* $57,102 includes full-time tuition ($41,000), mandatory fees ($732), and room and board ($15,370). Full-time tuition and fees vary according to student level. Part-time tuition and fees vary according to course load. *College room only:* $10,205. Room and board charges vary according to board plan, housing facility, and location.

Financial Aid *Of all full-time matriculated undergraduates who enrolled in 2010,* 6,408 applied for aid, 5,041 were judged to have need, 1,222 had their need fully met. *In 2010,* 1346 non-need-based awards were made. *Average percent of need met:* 74. *Average financial aid package:* $26,539. *Average need-based loan:* $6471. *Average need-based gift aid:* $17,972. *Average non-need-based aid:* $11,179. *Average indebtedness upon graduation:* $38,150. *Financial aid deadline:* 2/1.

Applying *Options:* electronic application, early admission, early action, deferred entrance. *Application fee:* $70. *Required:* essay or personal statement, high school transcript, 1 letter of recommendation.

Freshman Application Contact Mr. John Buckley, Associate Vice President of Enrollment, Fordham University, 441 East Fordham Road, New York, NY 10458. *Phone:* 718-817-4000. *Toll-free phone:* 800-FORDHAM. *Fax:* 718-367-9404. *E-mail:* enroll@fordham.edu. *Website:* http://www.fordham.edu/.

Globe Institute of Technology

New York, New York

Freshman Application Contact Mr. Michael Scalice, Admissions Director, Globe Institute of Technology, 500 7th Avenue, New York, NY 10018. *Phone:* 212-349-4330 Ext. 1624. *Toll-free phone:* 888-51-GLOBE (in-state); 800-51-GLOBE (out-of-state). *Fax:* 212-227-5920. *E-mail:* admissions@globe.edu. *Website:* http://www.globe.edu/.

Hamilton College

Clinton, New York

- **Independent** 4-year, founded 1812
- **Small-town** 1300-acre campus
- **Endowment** $635.2 million
- **Coed** 1,884 undergraduate students, 99% full-time, 51% women, 49% men
- **Very difficult** entrance level, 27% of applicants were admitted

Undergraduates 1,868 full-time, 16 part-time. Students come from 47 states and territories; 39 other countries; 67% are from out of state; 4% Black or African American, non-Hispanic/Latino; 7% Hispanic/Latino; 8% Asian, non-Hispanic/Latino; 0.3% American Indian or Alaska Native, non-Hispanic/Latino; 2% Two or more races, non-Hispanic/Latino; 11% Race/ethnicity unknown; 5% international; 0.7% transferred in; 98% live on campus. *Retention:* 96% of full-time freshmen returned.

Freshmen *Admission:* 5,107 applied, 1,389 admitted, 469 enrolled. *Test scores:* SAT critical reading scores over 500: 99%; SAT math scores over 500: 100%; SAT writing scores over 500: 99%; ACT scores over 18: 100%; SAT critical reading scores over 600: 89%; SAT math scores over 600: 92%; SAT writing scores over 600: 88%; ACT scores over 24: 98%; SAT critical reading scores over 700: 50%; SAT math scores over 700: 50%; SAT writing scores over 700: 52%; ACT scores over 30: 74%.

Faculty *Total:* 223, 84% full-time, 87% with terminal degrees. *Student/faculty ratio:* 9:1.

Academics *Calendar:* semesters. *Degree:* bachelor's. *Special study options:* accelerated degree program, adult/continuing education programs, advanced placement credit, double majors, English as a second language, independent study, internships, off-campus study, part-time degree program, services for LD students, student-designed majors, study abroad. *ROTC:* Army (c), Air Force (c). *Unusual degree programs:* 3-2 engineering with Columbia University, Dartmouth College, Rensselaer Polytechnic Institute, Washington University in St. Louis.

Computers on Campus 811 computers/terminals and 5,000 ports are available on campus for general student use. Students can access the following: campus intranet, computer help desk, free student e-mail accounts, online

(class) grades, online (class) registration, online (class) schedules. Campus-wide network is available. 100% of college-owned or -operated housing units are wired for high-speed Internet access. Wireless service is available via entire campus.

Student Life *Housing:* on-campus residence required through senior year. *Options:* coed, cooperative, disabled students. Campus housing is university owned. Freshman campus housing is guaranteed. *Activities and organizations:* drama/theater group, student-run newspaper, radio and television station, choral group, WHCL (Hamilton College Radio), Culinary Society, AHI Undergraduate Fellows, Operation Smile, Slow Food, national fraternities, national sororities. *Campus security:* 24-hour emergency response devices and patrols, late-night transport/escort service, controlled dormitory access, student safety program. *Student services:* health clinic, personal/psychological counseling, women's center.

Athletics Member NCAA. All Division III. *Intercollegiate sports:* baseball M, basketball M/W, crew M/W, cross-country running M/W, equestrian sports M(c)/W(c), fencing M(c)/W(c), field hockey W, football M, golf M/W, ice hockey M/W, lacrosse M/W, rugby M(c)/W(c), sailing M(c)/W(c), skiing (cross-country) M(c)/W(c), skiing (downhill) M(c)/W(c), soccer M/W, softball W, squash M/W, swimming and diving M/W, tennis M/W, track and field M/W, ultimate Frisbee M(c)/W(c), volleyball M(c)/W, water polo M(c). *Intramural sports:* badminton M/W, basketball M/W, football M/W, golf M/W, ice hockey M/W, racquetball M/W, skiing (cross-country) M/W, soccer M/W, softball M/W, squash M/W, tennis M/W, volleyball M/W, water polo M/W.

Standardized Tests *Required:* SAT and SAT Subject Tests or ACT (for admission).

Costs (2012–13) *Comprehensive fee:* $55,620 includes full-time tuition ($43,910), mandatory fees ($440), and room and board ($11,270). Part-time tuition: $5489 per course. *College room only:* $6160. Room and board charges vary according to board plan. *Payment plan:* installment. *Waivers:* employees or children of employees.

Financial Aid Of all full-time matriculated undergraduates who enrolled in 2012, 1,154 applied for aid, 868 were judged to have need, 868 had their need fully met. 556 Federal Work-Study jobs (averaging $1508). 58 state and other part-time jobs (averaging $1821). In 2012, 5 non-need-based awards were made. *Average percent of need met:* 100%. *Average financial aid package:* $39,386. *Average need-based loan:* $3880. *Average need-based gift aid:* $35,441. *Average non-need-based aid:* $37,808. *Average indebtedness upon graduation:* $18,568. *Financial aid deadline:* 2/15.

Applying *Options:* electronic application, early decision, deferred entrance. *Application fee:* $60. *Required:* essay or personal statement, high school transcript, 1 letter of recommendation. *Recommended:* interview. *Application deadlines:* 1/1 (freshmen), 4/15 (transfers). *Early decision deadline:* 11/15 (for plan 1), 1/1 (for plan 2). *Notification:* 4/1 (freshmen), 5/15 (transfers), 12/15 (early decision plan 1), 2/15 (early decision plan 2).

Freshman Application Contact Ms. Monica Inzer, Vice President and Dean of Admission and Financial Aid, Hamilton College, 198 College Hill Road, Clinton, NY 13323. *Phone:* 800-843-2655. *Toll-free phone:* 800-843-2655. *Fax:* 315-859-4457. *E-mail:* admission@hamilton.edu. *Website:* http://www.hamilton.edu/.

Hartwick College

Oneonta, New York

- **Independent** 4-year, founded 1797
- **Small-town** 425-acre campus with easy access to Albany, NY
- **Endowment** $57.8 million
- **Coed** 1,558 undergraduate students, 96% full-time, 60% women, 40% men
- **Moderately difficult** entrance level, 77% of applicants were admitted

Undergraduates 1,503 full-time, 55 part-time. Students come from 32 states and territories; 18 other countries; 26% are from out of state; 5% Black or African American, non-Hispanic/Latino; 6% Hispanic/Latino; 1% Asian, non-Hispanic/Latino; 0.1% Native Hawaiian or other Pacific Islander, non-Hispanic/Latino; 0.8% American Indian or Alaska Native, non-Hispanic/Latino; 15% Race/ethnicity unknown; 3% international; 3% transferred in; 78% live on campus. *Retention:* 73% of full-time freshmen returned.

Freshmen *Admission:* 4,897 applied, 3,774 admitted, 447 enrolled. *Average high school GPA:* 3.2. *Test scores:* SAT critical reading scores over 500: 82%; SAT math scores over 500: 83%; SAT writing scores over 500: 73%; ACT scores over 18: 99%; SAT critical reading scores over 600: 30%; SAT math scores over 600: 33%; SAT writing scores over 600: 24%; ACT scores over 24: 68%; SAT critical reading scores over 700: 4%; SAT math scores over 700: 2%; SAT writing scores over 700: 4%; ACT scores over 30: 12%.

Faculty *Total:* 183, 57% full-time, 55% with terminal degrees. *Student/faculty ratio:* 11:1.

Academics *Calendar:* 4-1-4. *Degree:* bachelor's. *Special study options:* accelerated degree program, advanced placement credit, double majors, honors programs, independent study, internships, off-campus study, part-time degree program, services for LD students, student-designed majors, study abroad, summer session for credit. *Unusual degree programs:* 3-2 engineering with Clarkson University, Columbia University.

Computers on Campus 80 computers/terminals are available on campus for general student use. Students can access the following: computer help desk, free student e-mail accounts, online (class) grades, online (class) registration, online (class) schedules. Campuswide network is available. 100% of college-owned or -operated housing units are wired for high-speed Internet access. Wireless service is available via entire campus.

Student Life *Housing:* on-campus residence required through junior year. *Options:* coed. Campus housing is university owned. Freshman campus housing is guaranteed. *Activities and organizations:* drama/theater group, student-run newspaper, radio station, choral group, Student Union, student radio station, Student Senate, Hilltops campus newspaper, Cardboard Alley Players, national fraternities, national sororities. *Campus security:* 24-hour emergency response devices and patrols, late-night transport/escort service, controlled dormitory access. *Student services:* health clinic, personal/psychological counseling, women's center.

Athletics Member NCAA. All Division III except soccer (Division I), water polo (Division I). *Intercollegiate sports:* basketball M/W, cheerleading W, cross-country running M/W, equestrian sports W, field hockey W, football M, ice hockey M(c), lacrosse M/W, rugby M(c), soccer M(s)/W, swimming and diving M/W, tennis M/W, volleyball W, water polo M(c)/W(s). *Intramural sports:* basketball M/W, cross-country running M/W, football M, golf M/W, racquetball M/W, soccer M/W, squash M/W, swimming and diving M/W, table tennis M/W, tennis M/W, track and field M/W, volleyball M/W, water polo M/W.

Standardized Tests *Required for some:* SAT or ACT (for admission).

Costs (2013–14) *One-time required fee:* $400. *Comprehensive fee:* $49,415 includes full-time tuition ($38,120), mandatory fees ($810), and room and board ($10,485). Part-time tuition: $1217 per credit. *College room only:* $5515. Room and board charges vary according to board plan and housing facility. *Payment plan:* installment. *Waivers:* employees or children of employees.

Financial Aid Of all full-time matriculated undergraduates who enrolled in 2010, 586 Federal Work-Study jobs (averaging $1212).

Applying *Options:* electronic application, early admission, early decision, deferred entrance. *Required:* high school transcript, audition for music program; portfolio for Art majors; SAT scores required of Nursing majors. *Recommended:* minimum 2.5 GPA. *Application deadlines:* rolling (freshmen), 8/1 (transfers). *Early decision deadline:* 11/1. *Notification:* continuous (freshmen), continuous until 8/15 (transfers), 12/1 (early decision plan 1), rolling (early decision plan 2).

Freshman Application Contact Mr. Jonathan Kent, Director of Admissions, Hartwick College, PO Box 4022, Oneonta, NY 13820-4022. *Phone:* 607-431-4150. *Toll-free phone:* 888-HARTWICK. *Fax:* 607-431-4102. *E-mail:* admissions@hartwick.edu.
Website: http://www.hartwick.edu/.

Hilbert College
Hamburg, New York

- **Independent** comprehensive, founded 1957
- **Suburban** 40-acre campus with easy access to Buffalo
- **Endowment** $5.1 million
- **Coed** 1,033 undergraduate students, 85% full-time, 56% women, 44% men
- **Minimally difficult** entrance level, 77% of applicants were admitted

Undergraduates 878 full-time, 155 part-time. Students come from 13 states and territories; 2 other countries; 3% are from out of state; 11% Black or African American, non-Hispanic/Latino; 2% Hispanic/Latino; 0.4% Asian, non-Hispanic/Latino; 0.2% Native Hawaiian or other Pacific Islander, non-Hispanic/Latino; 2% American Indian or Alaska Native, non-Hispanic/Latino; 1% Two or more races, non-Hispanic/Latino; 10% Race/ethnicity unknown; 0.8% international; 10% transferred in; 28% live on campus. *Retention:* 67% of full-time freshmen returned.

Freshmen *Admission:* 1,035 applied, 793 admitted, 182 enrolled. *Test scores:* SAT critical reading scores over 500: 36%; SAT math scores over 500: 46%; SAT writing scores over 500: 20%; ACT scores over 18: 89%; SAT critical reading scores over 600: 5%; SAT math scores over 600: 10%; SAT writing scores over 600: 2%; ACT scores over 24: 20%; SAT critical reading scores over 700: 1%.

Faculty *Total:* 122, 43% full-time, 33% with terminal degrees. *Student/faculty ratio:* 12:1.

Academics *Calendar:* semesters. *Degrees:* associate, bachelor's, and master's. *Special study options:* academic remediation for entering students, advanced placement credit, cooperative education, distance learning, honors programs, independent study, internships, part-time degree program, services for LD students, study abroad, summer session for credit. *ROTC:* Army (c).

Computers on Campus 146 computers/terminals are available on campus for general student use. Students can access the following: campus intranet, computer help desk, free student e-mail accounts, online (class) grades, online (class) registration, online (class) schedules. Campuswide network is available. 100% of college-owned or -operated housing units are wired for high-speed Internet access. Wireless service is available via entire campus.

Student Life *Housing options:* coed. Campus housing is university owned and leased by the school. Freshman applicants given priority for college housing. *Activities and organizations:* drama/theater group, student-run newspaper, radio station, Student Government Association, Student Business and Accounting Association, SADD, Students in Free Enterprise (SIFE), Criminal Justice Association. *Campus security:* 24-hour emergency response devices and patrols, student patrols, late-night transport/escort service, controlled dormitory access. *Student services:* health clinic, personal/psychological counseling.

Athletics Member NCAA. All Division III. *Intercollegiate sports:* baseball M, basketball M/W, cross-country running M/W, golf M, lacrosse M/W, soccer M/W, softball W, volleyball M/W. *Intramural sports:* baseball M, basketball M/W, bowling M/W, cheerleading W, football M/W, golf M, ice hockey M(c), lacrosse W(c), skiing (downhill) M(c)/W(c), soccer M/W, softball W, table tennis M/W, ultimate Frisbee M/W, volleyball M/W.

Standardized Tests *Recommended:* SAT or ACT (for admission).

Costs (2013–14) *One-time required fee:* $50. *Comprehensive fee:* $29,150 includes full-time tuition ($19,900), mandatory fees ($600), and room and board ($8650). Full-time tuition and fees vary according to course load. Part-time tuition: $485 per credit. Part-time tuition and fees vary according to course load. *Required fees:* $13 per credit part-time, $55 per term part-time. *College room only:* $4450. Room and board charges vary according to board plan and housing facility. *Payment plan:* installment. *Waivers:* minority students, children of alumni, adult students, senior citizens, and employees or children of employees.

Financial Aid Of all full-time matriculated undergraduates who enrolled in 2012, 912 applied for aid, 823 were judged to have need, 147 had their need fully met. 61 Federal Work-Study jobs (averaging $1671). In 2012, 85 non-need-based awards were made. *Average percent of need met:* 68%. *Average financial aid package:* $13,118. *Average need-based loan:* $4706. *Average need-based gift aid:* $9081. *Average non-need-based aid:* $3516. *Average indebtedness upon graduation:* $16,608.

Applying *Options:* electronic application, deferred entrance. *Application fee:* $25. *Required:* high school transcript. *Required for some:* interview. *Recommended:* essay or personal statement, interview. *Application deadlines:* rolling (freshmen), rolling (transfers). *Notification:* continuous (freshmen), continuous (transfers).

Freshman Application Contact Mr. Justin Rogers, Director of Admissions, Hilbert College, 5200 South Park Avenue, Hamburg, NY 14075-1597. *Phone:* 716-649-7900. *Toll-free phone:* 800-649-8003. *Fax:* 716-649-0702. *E-mail:* jrogers@hilbert.edu.
Website: http://www.hilbert.edu/.

Hobart and William Smith Colleges
Geneva, New York

- **Independent** comprehensive, founded 1822
- **Small-town** 200-acre campus with easy access to Rochester, Syracuse
- **Endowment** $161.2 million
- **Coed** 2,292 undergraduate students, 99% full-time, 55% women, 45% men
- **Very difficult** entrance level, 53% of applicants were admitted

Undergraduates 2,267 full-time, 25 part-time. Students come from 45 states and territories; 27 other countries; 57% are from out of state; 4% Black or African American, non-Hispanic/Latino; 3% Hispanic/Latino; 2% Asian, non-Hispanic/Latino; 0.4% American Indian or Alaska Native, non-Hispanic/Latino; 16% Race/ethnicity unknown; 4% international; 0.8% transferred in; 90% live on campus. *Retention:* 88% of full-time freshmen returned.

Freshmen *Admission:* 4,465 applied, 2,370 admitted, 600 enrolled. *Average high school GPA:* 3.32. *Test scores:* SAT critical reading scores over 500: 94%; SAT math scores over 500: 95%; ACT scores over 18: 100%; SAT critical reading scores over 600: 59%; SAT math scores over 600: 64%; ACT scores over 24: 91%; SAT critical reading scores over 700: 12%; SAT math scores over 700: 12%; ACT scores over 30: 22%.

Faculty *Total:* 231, 94% full-time, 95% with terminal degrees. *Student/faculty ratio:* 11:1.

Academics *Calendar:* semesters. *Degrees:* bachelor's, master's, and postbachelor's certificates. *Special study options:* accelerated degree program, adult/continuing education programs, advanced placement credit, double majors, English as a second language, honors programs, independent study, internships, off-campus study, services for LD students, student-designed majors, study abroad. *ROTC:* Army (c), Air Force (c). *Unusual degree programs:* 3-2 business administration with Clarkson University, Rochester Institute of Technology; engineering with Columbia University, Rensselaer Polytechnic Institute, Dartmouth College; architecture with Washington University in St. Louis.

Computers on Campus 167 computers/terminals and 7,942 ports are available on campus for general student use. Students can access the following: campus intranet, computer help desk, free student e-mail accounts, online (class) grades, online (class) registration, online (class) schedules. Campuswide network is available. 100% of college-owned or -operated housing units are wired for high-speed Internet access. Wireless service is available via entire campus.

Student Life *Housing:* on-campus residence required through junior year. *Options:* coed, men-only, women-only, cooperative. Campus housing is university owned. Freshman campus housing is guaranteed. *Activities and organizations:* drama/theater group, student-run newspaper, radio station, choral group, Student Life and Leadership, student government, campus publications, Service Network, sports clubs, national fraternities. *Campus security:* 24-hour emergency response devices and patrols, late-night transport/escort service, controlled dormitory access. *Student services:* health clinic, personal/psychological counseling, women's center, legal services.

Athletics Member NCAA. All Division III except lacrosse (Division I). *Intercollegiate sports:* basketball M/W, crew M/W, cross-country running M/W, equestrian sports M(c)/W(c), field hockey W, football M, golf M/W, ice hockey M/W(c), lacrosse M/W, rock climbing M(c)/W(c), rugby M(c)/W(c), sailing M/W, skiing (downhill) M(c)/W(c), soccer M/W, squash M/W, swimming and diving W, tennis M/W, ultimate Frisbee M(c)/W(c). *Intramural sports:* badminton M/W, baseball M, basketball M/W, fencing M/W, football M, golf M/W, ice hockey M/W, lacrosse M/W, racquetball M/W, skiing (cross-country) M/W, skiing (downhill) M/W, soccer M/W, softball M/W, squash M/W, swimming and diving M/W, table tennis M/W, tennis M/W, track and field M/W, ultimate Frisbee M/W, volleyball M/W, water polo M/W, weight lifting M/W.

Standardized Tests *Required for some:* SAT or ACT (for admission).

Costs (2012–13) *Comprehensive fee:* $55,699 includes full-time tuition ($43,484), mandatory fees ($954), and room and board ($11,261). *Room and board:* Room and board charges vary according to board plan. *Payment plans:* tuition prepayment, installment. *Waivers:* employees or children of employees.

Financial Aid Of all full-time matriculated undergraduates who enrolled in 2011, 1,636 applied for aid, 1,406 were judged to have need, 829 had their need fully met. 1,030 Federal Work-Study jobs (averaging $1845). 519 state and other part-time jobs (averaging $1921). In 2011, 443 non-need-based awards were made. *Average percent of need met:* 79%. *Average financial aid package:* $30,891. *Average need-based loan:* $3933. *Average need-based gift aid:* $26,852. *Average non-need-based aid:* $15,339. *Average indebtedness upon graduation:* $34,463. *Financial aid deadline:* 2/15.

Applying *Options:* electronic application, early admission, early decision, deferred entrance. *Application fee:* $45. *Required:* essay or personal statement, high school transcript, 1 letter of recommendation. *Recommended:* interview. *Application deadlines:* 2/1 (freshmen), 7/1 (transfers). *Early decision deadline:* 11/15 (for plan 1), 1/1 (for plan 2). *Notification:* 4/1 (freshmen), continuous (transfers), 12/15 (early decision plan 1), 2/1 (early decision plan 2).

Freshman Application Contact Hobart and William Smith Colleges, Geneva, NY 14456-3397. *Phone:* 315-781-3622. *Toll-free phone:* 800-852-2256. *Website:* http://www.hws.edu/.

Hofstra University

Hempstead, New York

- **Independent** university, founded 1935
- **Suburban** 240-acre campus with easy access to New York City
- **Endowment** $311.0 million
- **Coed** 6,893 undergraduate students, 92% full-time, 53% women, 47% men
- **Moderately difficult** entrance level, 59% of applicants were admitted

Undergraduates 6,374 full-time, 519 part-time. Students come from 46 states and territories; 50 other countries; 35% are from out of state; 9% Black or African American, non-Hispanic/Latino; 11% Hispanic/Latino; 7% Asian, non-Hispanic/Latino; 0.7% Native Hawaiian or other Pacific Islander, non-Hispanic/Latino; 0.3% American Indian or Alaska Native, non-Hispanic/Latino; 3% Two or more races, non-Hispanic/Latino; 5% Race/ethnicity unknown; 2% international; 7% transferred in; 49% live on campus. *Retention:* 78% of full-time freshmen returned.

Freshmen *Admission:* 22,733 applied, 13,346 admitted, 1,488 enrolled. *Average high school GPA:* 3.48. *Test scores:* SAT critical reading scores over 500: 91%; SAT math scores over 500: 92%; ACT scores over 18: 100%; SAT critical reading scores over 600: 40%; SAT math scores over 600: 45%; ACT scores over 24: 74%; SAT critical reading scores over 700: 6%; SAT math scores over 700: 6%; ACT scores over 30: 11%.

Faculty *Total:* 1,135, 46% full-time, 65% with terminal degrees. *Student/faculty ratio:* 14:1.

Academics *Calendar:* 4-1-4. *Degrees:* certificates, bachelor's, master's, doctoral, post-master's, and postbachelor's certificates. *Special study options:* accelerated degree program, advanced placement credit, distance learning, double majors, English as a second language, external degree program, freshman honors college, honors programs, independent study, internships, off-campus study, part-time degree program, services for LD students, student-designed majors, study abroad, summer session for credit. *ROTC:* Army (b). *Unusual degree programs:* 3-2 business administration; BS/MS in Physician Assistant Studies; BA/MS and BS/MS in Computer Science; BA/JD LEAP Program.

Computers on Campus 1,628 computers/terminals and 1,900 ports are available on campus for general student use. Students can access the following: campus intranet, computer help desk, free student e-mail accounts, online (class) grades, online (class) registration, online (class) schedules, Gmail/Google Apps for students; Emergency Notification System; Online course management system; online card services balance update; online e-portfolio. Campuswide network is available. 100% of college-owned or -operated housing units are wired for high-speed Internet access. Wireless service is available via entire campus.

Student Life *Housing options:* coed, disabled students. Campus housing is university owned. Freshman applicants given priority for college housing. *Activities and organizations:* drama/theater group, student-run newspaper, radio and television station, choral group, Chinese Student Association (Graduate Club), Inter Fraternal and Sororal Council, Danceworks, Phi Eta Sigma Honor Society, Hofstra vs. Zombies, national fraternities, national sororities. *Campus security:* 24-hour emergency response devices and patrols, student patrols, late-night transport/escort service, controlled dormitory access, residence halls—security cameras/card access to entry (monitored 24/7); bike patrol; and motorist assistance program. *Student services:* health clinic, personal/psychological counseling, legal services.

Athletics Member NCAA. All Division I. *Intercollegiate sports:* baseball M(s), basketball M(s)/W(s), cross-country running M(s)/W(s), field hockey W(s), golf M(s)/W(s), lacrosse M(s)/W(s), soccer M(s)/W(s), softball W(s), tennis M(s)/W(s), volleyball W(s), wrestling M(s). *Intramural sports:* baseball M(c), basketball M/W, cheerleading M(c)/W(c), crew M(c)/W(c), cross-country running M(c)/W(c), equestrian sports M(c)/W(c), football M/W, ice hockey M(c), lacrosse M(c)/W(c), rugby M(c)/W(c), skiing (downhill) M(c)/W(c), soccer M/W, softball M/W, table tennis M(c)/W(c), tennis M(c)/W(c), ultimate Frisbee M(c)/W(c), volleyball M/W.

Standardized Tests *Required for some:* SAT or ACT (for admission). *Recommended:* SAT Subject Tests (for admission).

Costs (2012–13) *Comprehensive fee:* $48,320 includes full-time tuition ($34,900), mandatory fees ($1050), and room and board ($12,370). Full-time tuition and fees vary according to course load and program. Part-time tuition: $1100 per credit hour. Part-time tuition and fees vary according to course load and program. No tuition increase for student's term of enrollment. *Required fees:* $145 per term part-time. *College room only:* $8450. Room and board charges vary according to board plan and housing facility. *Payment plan:* installment. *Waivers:* senior citizens and employees or children of employees.

Financial Aid Of all full-time matriculated undergraduates who enrolled in 2011, 5,181 applied for aid, 4,398 were judged to have need, 845 had their need fully met. 1,403 Federal Work-Study jobs (averaging $3024). 1,514 state and other part-time jobs (averaging $2960). In 2011, 1302 non-need-based awards were made. *Average percent of need met:* 60%. *Average financial aid package:* $22,000. *Average need-based loan:* $5000. *Average need-based gift aid:* $13,000. *Average non-need-based aid:* $11,000.

Applying *Options:* electronic application, early admission, early action, deferred entrance. *Application fee:* $70. *Required:* essay or personal statement, high school transcript, 2 letters of recommendation, Proof of degree required for all; TOEFL required for international students. *Required for some:* interview. *Recommended:* minimum 2.5 GPA. *Application deadlines:* rolling (freshmen), 12/15 (early action). *Notification:* 2/1 (freshmen), continuous (transfers), 1/15 (early action).

Freshman Application Contact Sunil Samuel, Director of Admissions, Hofstra University, 100 Hofstra University, Hempstead, NY 11549. *Phone:*

516-463-6700. *Toll-free phone:* 800-HOFSTRA. *Fax:* 516-463-5100. *E-mail:* admission@hofstra.edu.
Website: http://www.hofstra.edu/.

See previous page for display ad and page 1324 for the College Close-Up.

Holy Trinity Orthodox Seminary

Jordanville, New York

- **Independent Russian Orthodox** 5-year, founded 1948
- **Rural** 900-acre campus
- **Men only** 29 undergraduate students, 100% full-time
- **Noncompetitive** entrance level, 100% of applicants were admitted

Undergraduates 29 full-time. 95% live on campus.

Freshmen *Admission:* 12 applied, 12 admitted, 11 enrolled.

Faculty *Total:* 15. *Student/faculty ratio:* 2:1.

Academics *Calendar:* semesters. *Degree:* certificates and bachelor's. *Special study options:* accelerated degree program, distance learning, English as a second language.

Computers on Campus 8 computers/terminals are available on campus for general student use. Campuswide network is available.

Student Life *Housing options:* men-only. Campus housing is university owned. *Activities and organizations:* student-run newspaper, choral group, Student Union. *Campus security:* 24-hour emergency response devices. *Student services:* health clinic, personal/psychological counseling.

Costs (2012–13) *Comprehensive fee:* $8000 includes full-time tuition ($5500) and room and board ($2500).

Applying *Options:* deferred entrance. *Required:* essay or personal statement, high school transcript, 1 letter of recommendation, interview, Orthodoxy/Orthodox baptism, entrance exam required. Recommendation from spiritual father or parish priest necessary. *Application deadlines:* 5/1 (freshmen), 5/1 (out-of-state freshmen), 5/1 (transfers).

Freshman Application Contact Ephraim Willmarth, Administrative Assistant, Holy Trinity Orthodox Seminary, PO Box 36, Jordanville, NY 13361. *Phone:* 315-858-0945. *Fax:* 315-858-0945. *E-mail:* ejwillmarth@hts.edu.
Website: http://www.hts.edu/.

Houghton College

Houghton, New York

- **Independent Wesleyan** comprehensive, founded 1883
- **Rural** 1300-acre campus with easy access to Buffalo, Rochester
- **Endowment** $38.1 million
- **Coed** 1,147 undergraduate students, 95% full-time, 66% women, 34% men
- **Moderately difficult** entrance level, 73% of applicants were admitted

Undergraduates 1,086 full-time, 61 part-time. Students come from 35 states and territories; 30 other countries; 39% are from out of state; 3% Black or African American, non-Hispanic/Latino; 2% Hispanic/Latino; 1% Asian, non-Hispanic/Latino; 0.4% American Indian or Alaska Native, non-Hispanic/Latino; 2% Two or more races, non-Hispanic/Latino; 0.2% Race/ethnicity unknown; 5% international; 4% transferred in; 87% live on campus. *Retention:* 88% of full-time freshmen returned.

Freshmen *Admission:* 830 applied, 609 admitted, 234 enrolled. *Average high school GPA:* 3.59. *Test scores:* SAT critical reading scores over 500: 86%; SAT math scores over 500: 79%; SAT writing scores over 500: 77%; ACT scores over 18: 96%; SAT critical reading scores over 600: 43%; SAT math scores over 600: 38%; SAT writing scores over 600: 36%; ACT scores over 24: 56%; SAT critical reading scores over 700: 13%; SAT math scores over 700: 7%; SAT writing scores over 700: 6%; ACT scores over 30: 8%.

Faculty *Total:* 125, 57% full-time, 70% with terminal degrees. *Student/faculty ratio:* 12:1.

Academics *Calendar:* semesters. *Degrees:* associate, bachelor's, and master's. *Special study options:* accelerated degree program, adult/continuing education programs, advanced placement credit, distance learning, double majors, honors programs, independent study, internships, off-campus study, services for LD students, student-designed majors, study abroad, summer session for credit. *ROTC:* Army (c). *Unusual degree programs:* 3-2 business administration; engineering with Clarkson University.

Computers on Campus 30 computers/terminals and 820 ports are available on campus for general student use. Students can access the following: campus intranet, computer help desk, free student e-mail accounts, online (class) grades, online (class) registration, online (class) schedules. Campuswide net-

work is available. 100% of college-owned or -operated housing units are wired for high-speed Internet access. Wireless service is available via entire campus. **Student Life** *Housing:* on-campus residence required through sophomore year. *Options:* men-only, women-only, cooperative. Campus housing is university owned. Freshman campus housing is guaranteed. *Activities and organizations:* drama/theater group, student-run newspaper, choral group, Student Government Association, Global Christian Fellowship, Allegany County Outreach, Drama Clubs, Intercultural Student Association. *Campus security:* 24-hour emergency response devices and patrols, late-night transport/escort service, controlled dormitory access, Emergency phone number rings directly to cell phone carried by officer on duty 24/7, automatic fire alarms throughout campus. *Student services:* health clinic, personal/psychological counseling.
Athletics Member NCCAA. *Intercollegiate sports:* baseball M, basketball M/W, cross-country running M/W, field hockey W, golf M/W, lacrosse M/W, soccer M/W, softball W, tennis M/W, track and field M/W, volleyball W. *Intramural sports:* baseball M, basketball M/W, equestrian sports M(c)/W(c), football M, racquetball M/W, rock climbing M(c)/W(c), skiing (cross-country) M(c)/W(c), skiing (downhill) M(c)/W(c), soccer M/W, swimming and diving M(c)/W(c), table tennis M/W, ultimate Frisbee M(c)/W(c), volleyball M/W, water polo M/W.
Standardized Tests *Required:* SAT or ACT (for admission).
Costs (2013–14) *Comprehensive fee:* $35,740 includes full-time tuition ($27,578), mandatory fees ($150), and room and board ($8012). Part-time tuition: $1159 per credit hour. *College room only:* $4298. Room and board charges vary according to board plan, gender, housing facility, and student level. *Payment plan:* installment. *Waivers:* employees or children of employees.
Financial Aid Of all full-time matriculated undergraduates who enrolled in 2012, 928 applied for aid, 876 were judged to have need, 114 had their need fully met. 614 Federal Work-Study jobs (averaging $1905). 4 state and other part-time jobs (averaging $2100). In 2012, 174 non-need-based awards were made. *Average percent of need met:* 78%. *Average financial aid package:* $22,532. *Average need-based loan:* $5394. *Average need-based gift aid:* $16,494. *Average non-need-based aid:* $10,775. *Average indebtedness upon graduation:* $22,197.
Applying *Options:* electronic application, early action, deferred entrance. *Application fee:* $40. *Required:* high school transcript, 1 letter of recommendation. *Required for some:* essay or personal statement. *Recommended:* essay or personal statement, minimum 3.0 GPA, interview. *Application deadlines:* rolling (freshmen), rolling (transfers). *Notification:* continuous (freshmen), continuous (transfers).

Freshman Application Contact Mr. Jeff Kirksey, Director of Admission, Houghton College, PO Box 128, Houghton, NY 14744. *Phone:* 585-567-9353. *Toll-free phone:* 800-777-2556. *Fax:* 585-567-9522. *E-mail:* admission@houghton.edu.
Website: http://www.houghton.edu/.

See below for display ad and page 1328 for the College Close-Up.

Hunter College of the City University of New York
New York, New York

- **State and locally supported** comprehensive, founded 1870, part of City University of New York System
- **Urban** campus
- **Endowment** $65.7 million
- **Coed** 16,708 undergraduate students, 72% full-time, 66% women, 34% men
- **Moderately difficult** entrance level, 30% of applicants were admitted

Undergraduates 11,956 full-time, 4,752 part-time. Students come from 37 states and territories; 140 other countries; 4% are from out of state; 11% Black or African American, non-Hispanic/Latino; 19% Hispanic/Latino; 25% Asian, non-Hispanic/Latino; 0.2% American Indian or Alaska Native, non-Hispanic/Latino; 7% international; 11% transferred in; 1% live on campus. *Retention:* 85% of full-time freshmen returned.
Freshmen *Admission:* 30,758 applied, 9,140 admitted, 1,971 enrolled. *Average high school GPA:* 3. *Test scores:* SAT critical reading scores over 500: 88%; SAT math scores over 500: 97%; SAT critical reading scores over 600: 34%; SAT math scores over 600: 47%; SAT critical reading scores over 700: 8%; SAT math scores over 700: 10%.
Faculty *Total:* 1,908, 37% full-time, 43% with terminal degrees. *Student/faculty ratio:* 15:1.
Academics *Calendar:* semesters. *Degrees:* bachelor's, master's, doctoral, post-master's, and postbachelor's certificates. *Special study options:* advanced placement credit, distance learning, double majors, English as a second language, freshman honors college, honors programs, independent study, internships, off-campus study, part-time degree program, services for LD students,

student-designed majors, study abroad, summer session for credit. *Unusual degree programs:* 3-2 anthropology, economics, English, history, mathematics, music, physics, sociology.

Computers on Campus 1,280 computers/terminals are available on campus for general student use. Students can access the following: computer help desk, free student e-mail accounts, online (class) registration, online (class) schedules. Campuswide network is available.

Student Life *Housing options:* coed. *Activities and organizations:* drama/theater group, student-run newspaper, radio and television station, choral group. *Campus security:* 24-hour emergency response devices and patrols. *Student services:* personal/psychological counseling, women's center.

Athletics Member NCAA. All Division III. *Intercollegiate sports:* basketball M/W, cross-country running M/W, fencing M/W, gymnastics W, soccer M, swimming and diving W, tennis M/W, track and field M/W, volleyball M/W, wrestling M. *Intramural sports:* basketball M/W, cross-country running M/W, gymnastics M/W, racquetball M/W, rugby M, soccer M/W, swimming and diving M/W, tennis M/W, volleyball M/W.

Standardized Tests *Required:* SAT or ACT (for admission).

Costs (2013–14) *Tuition:* state resident $5430 full-time, $230 per credit part-time; nonresident $14,550 full-time, $485 per credit part-time. Full-time tuition and fees vary according to degree level and program. Part-time tuition and fees vary according to degree level and program. *Required fees:* $399 full-time, $184 part-time. *Room only:* $5500. *Payment plan:* installment.

Financial Aid Of all full-time matriculated undergraduates who enrolled in 2011, 8,845 applied for aid, 7,641 were judged to have need, 1,330 had their need fully met. In 2011, 572 non-need-based awards were made. *Average percent of need met:* 76%. *Average financial aid package:* $6122. *Average need-based loan:* $5331. *Average need-based gift aid:* $5080. *Average non-need-based aid:* $3421. *Average indebtedness upon graduation:* $11,000.

Applying *Options:* early admission. *Application fee:* $65. *Required:* high school transcript. *Application deadlines:* 3/15 (freshmen), 3/15 (transfers). *Notification:* continuous (freshmen), continuous (transfers).

Freshman Application Contact Mr. William Zlata, Director of Admissions, Hunter College of the City University of New York, 695 Park Avenue, New York, NY 10065-5085. *Phone:* 212-772-4490. *Fax:* 212-650-3472. *E-mail:* bill.zlata@hunter.cuny.edu.
Website: http://www.hunter.cuny.edu/.

See this page for display ad and page 1330 for the College Close-Up.

Iona College

New Rochelle, New York

- **Independent** comprehensive, founded 1940, affiliated with Roman Catholic Church
- **Suburban** 35-acre campus with easy access to New York City
- **Endowment** $52.5 million
- **Coed** 3,462 undergraduate students, 85% full-time, 56% women, 44% men
- **Moderately difficult** entrance level, 86% of applicants were admitted

Undergraduates 2,927 full-time, 535 part-time. Students come from 33 states and territories; 32 other countries; 24% are from out of state; 6% Black or African American, non-Hispanic/Latino; 18% Hispanic/Latino; 2% Asian, non-Hispanic/Latino; 0.1% Native Hawaiian or other Pacific Islander, non-Hispanic/Latino; 0.2% American Indian or Alaska Native, non-Hispanic/Latino; 1% Two or more races, non-Hispanic/Latino; 8% Race/ethnicity unknown; 2% international; 3% transferred in; 43% live on campus. *Retention:* 81% of full-time freshmen returned.

Freshmen *Admission:* 8,741 applied, 7,556 admitted, 722 enrolled. *Average high school GPA:* 3.1. *Test scores:* SAT critical reading scores over 500: 51%; SAT math scores over 500: 57%; ACT scores over 18: 98%; SAT critical reading scores over 600: 10%; SAT math scores over 600: 15%; ACT scores over 24: 35%; SAT critical reading scores over 700: 1%; SAT math scores over 700: 2%; ACT scores over 30: 8%.

Faculty *Total:* 353, 50% full-time. *Student/faculty ratio:* 15:1.

Academics *Calendar:* semesters. *Degrees:* certificates, bachelor's, master's, post-master's, and postbachelor's certificates. *Special study options:* accelerated degree program, adult/continuing education programs, advanced placement credit, distance learning, double majors, external degree program, honors programs, independent study, internships, off-campus study, part-time degree program, services for LD students, study abroad, summer session for credit. *ROTC:* Army (c), Air Force (c). *Unusual degree programs:* 3-2 chemistry and education, chemistry and computer science, criminal justice, computer science, English, history, psychology.

Computers on Campus 745 computers/terminals and 10,000 ports are available on campus for general student use. Students can access the following: campus intranet, computer help desk, free student e-mail accounts, online

(class) grades, online (class) registration, online (class) schedules, bill payment. Campuswide network is available. 100% of college-owned or -operated housing units are wired for high-speed Internet access. Wireless service is available via entire campus.

Student Life *Housing options:* coed, disabled students. Campus housing is university owned and leased by the school. Freshman applicants given priority for college housing. *Activities and organizations:* drama/theater group, student-run newspaper, radio and television station, choral group, marching band, Student Government Association, Gaels Activities Board, Council for Greek Governance, Council of Multicultural Leaders, The Ionian—Student Newspaper, national fraternities, national sororities. *Campus security:* 24-hour emergency response devices and patrols, controlled dormitory access. *Student services:* health clinic, personal/psychological counseling.

Athletics Member NCAA. All Division I. *Intercollegiate sports:* baseball M(s), basketball M(s)/W(s), crew M/W, cross-country running M(s)/W(s), golf M(s), lacrosse W(s), soccer M(s)/W(s), softball W(s), swimming and diving M(s)/W(s), track and field M(s)/W(s), volleyball W(s), water polo M/W(s). *Intramural sports:* basketball M/W, cheerleading M(c)/W(c), football M/W, rugby M(c), soccer M/W, table tennis M/W, volleyball M/W.

Standardized Tests *Required:* SAT or ACT (for admission).

Costs (2013–14) *Comprehensive fee:* $45,945 includes full-time tuition ($30,670), mandatory fees ($2100), and room and board ($13,175). Part-time tuition: $1020 per credit. Part-time tuition and fees vary according to course load. *Required fees:* $520 per term part-time. *Room and board:* Room and board charges vary according to housing facility. *Payment plan:* installment. *Waivers:* children of alumni and employees or children of employees.

Financial Aid Of all full-time matriculated undergraduates who enrolled in 2011, 3,028 applied for aid, 2,452 were judged to have need, 473 had their need fully met. 479 Federal Work-Study jobs (averaging $1094). 300 state and other part-time jobs (averaging $1075). In 2011, 529 non-need-based awards were made. *Average percent of need met:* 27%. *Average financial aid package:* $19,091. *Average need-based loan:* $3204. *Average need-based gift aid:* $5812. *Average non-need-based aid:* $12,015. *Average indebtedness upon graduation:* $21,794. *Financial aid deadline:* 4/15.

Applying *Options:* electronic application, early action, deferred entrance. *Application fee:* $50. *Required:* essay or personal statement, high school transcript, 2 letters of recommendation, SAT or ACT required. *Required for some:* interview. *Application deadlines:* 2/15 (freshmen), 8/15 (transfers), 12/1 (early action). *Notification:* continuous (freshmen), continuous (transfers), 12/21 (early action).

Freshman Application Contact Ms. Kathy Reilly, Director of Undergraduate Admissions, Iona College, Admissions, 715 North Avenue, New Rochelle, NY 10801. *Phone:* 914-633-2439. *Toll-free phone:* 800-231-IONA. *Fax:* 914-633-2182. *E-mail:* admissions@iona.edu.
Website: http://www.iona.edu/.

Ithaca College

Ithaca, New York

- **Independent** comprehensive, founded 1892
- **Small-town** 669-acre campus with easy access to Syracuse
- **Endowment** $205.3 million
- **Coed** 6,276 undergraduate students, 98% full-time, 57% women, 43% men
- **Moderately difficult** entrance level, 68% of applicants were admitted

Undergraduates 6,173 full-time, 103 part-time. Students come from 52 states and territories; 67 other countries; 56% are from out of state; 4% Black or African American, non-Hispanic/Latino; 6% Hispanic/Latino; 3% Asian, non-Hispanic/Latino; 0.1% Native Hawaiian or other Pacific Islander, non-Hispanic/Latino; 0.2% American Indian or Alaska Native, non-Hispanic/Latino; 3% Two or more races, non-Hispanic/Latino; 13% Race/ethnicity unknown; 2% international; 2% transferred in; 69% live on campus. *Retention:* 83% of full-time freshmen returned.

Freshmen *Admission:* 13,436 applied, 9,163 admitted, 1,625 enrolled. *Test scores:* SAT critical reading scores over 500: 83%; SAT math scores over 500: 86%; SAT writing scores over 500: 86%; SAT critical reading scores over 600: 39%; SAT math scores over 600: 43%; SAT writing scores over 600: 40%; SAT critical reading scores over 700: 6%; SAT math scores over 700: 6%; SAT writing scores over 700: 6%.

Faculty *Total:* 701, 68% full-time, 86% with terminal degrees. *Student/faculty ratio:* 12:1.

Academics *Calendar:* semesters. *Degrees:* certificates, bachelor's, master's, and doctoral. *Special study options:* accelerated degree program, adult/continuing education programs, advanced placement credit, distance learning, double majors, freshman honors college, honors programs, independent study, internships, off-campus study, part-time degree program, services for LD students,

student-designed majors, study abroad, summer session for credit. *ROTC:* Army (c), Air Force (c). *Unusual degree programs:* 3-2 engineering with Cornell University, Rensselaer Polytechnic Institute, Clarkson University, State University of New York at Binghamton.

Computers on Campus 640 computers/terminals and 20 ports are available on campus for general student use. Students can access the following: campus intranet, computer help desk, free student e-mail accounts, online (class) grades, online (class) registration, online (class) schedules. Campuswide network is available. 100% of college-owned or -operated housing units are wired for high-speed Internet access. Wireless service is available via entire campus.

Student Life *Housing:* on-campus residence required through junior year. *Options:* coed, women-only, disabled students. Campus housing is university owned. Freshman campus housing is guaranteed. *Activities and organizations:* drama/theater group, student-run newspaper, radio and television station, choral group, Student Government Association, African-Latino Society, Residence Hall Association, Habitat for Humanity, Senior Class, national fraternities, national sororities. *Campus security:* 24-hour emergency response devices and patrols, student patrols, late-night transport/escort service, controlled dormitory access. *Student services:* health clinic, personal/psychological counseling.

Athletics Member NCAA. All Division III. *Intercollegiate sports:* baseball M, basketball M/W, crew M/W, cross-country running M/W, field hockey W, football M, golf W, gymnastics W, lacrosse M/W, soccer M/W, softball W, swimming and diving M/W, tennis M/W, track and field M/W, volleyball W, wrestling M. *Intramural sports:* basketball M/W, crew M(c)/W(c), equestrian sports M(c)/W(c), football M, golf M/W, ice hockey M(c), lacrosse M(c)/W(c), rugby W(c), skiing (downhill) M(c)/W(c), soccer M/W, softball M/W, squash M(c)/W(c), tennis M/W, ultimate Frisbee M(c)/W(c), volleyball M/W.

Standardized Tests *Required for some:* SAT or ACT (for admission).

Costs (2012–13) *Comprehensive fee:* $50,400 includes full-time tuition ($37,000) and room and board ($13,400). Part-time tuition: $1232 per credit hour. *College room only:* $7200. Room and board charges vary according to board plan and housing facility. *Payment plan:* installment. *Waivers:* children of alumni and employees or children of employees.

Financial Aid Of all full-time matriculated undergraduates who enrolled in 2012, 4,888 applied for aid, 4,276 were judged to have need, 1,907 had their need fully met. 3,332 Federal Work-Study jobs (averaging $2350). 1,580 state and other part-time jobs (averaging $2398). In 2012, 1191 non-need-based awards were made. *Average percent of need met:* 86%. *Average financial aid package:* $30,772. *Average need-based loan:* $6469. *Average need-based gift aid:* $21,169. *Average non-need-based aid:* $10,666.

Applying *Options:* electronic application, early admission, early decision, early action, deferred entrance. *Application fee:* $60. *Required:* essay or personal statement, high school transcript, 1 letter of recommendation. *Required for some:* audition for some programs. *Recommended:* minimum 3.0 GPA. *Application deadlines:* 2/1 (freshmen), 3/1 (transfers), 12/1 (early action). *Early decision deadline:* 11/1. *Notification:* 4/15 (freshmen), continuous (transfers), 12/15 (early decision), 2/1 (early action).

Freshman Application Contact Mr. Gerard Turbide, Director of Admission, Ithaca College, 953 Danby Road, Ithaca, NY 14850-7002. *Phone:* 607-274-3124. *Toll-free phone:* 800-429-4274. *Fax:* 607-274-1900. *E-mail:* admission@ithaca.edu.
Website: http://www.ithaca.edu/.

Jamestown Business College

Jamestown, New York

- **Proprietary** primarily 2-year, founded 1886
- **Small-town** 1-acre campus
- **Coed** 294 undergraduate students, 98% full-time, 73% women, 27% men
- **Minimally difficult** entrance level, 93% of applicants were admitted

Undergraduates 288 full-time, 6 part-time. Students come from 2 states and territories; 11% are from out of state; 2% Black or African American, non-Hispanic/Latino; 3% Hispanic/Latino; 0.7% Asian, non-Hispanic/Latino; 0.3% Native Hawaiian or other Pacific Islander, non-Hispanic/Latino; 2% American Indian or Alaska Native, non-Hispanic/Latino; 2% Two or more races, non-Hispanic/Latino; 2% Race/ethnicity unknown; 10% transferred in.

Freshmen *Admission:* 98 applied, 91 admitted, 70 enrolled.

Faculty *Total:* 24, 29% full-time, 8% with terminal degrees. *Student/faculty ratio:* 25:1.

Academics *Calendar:* quarters. *Degrees:* certificates, associate, and bachelor's. *Special study options:* advanced placement credit, double majors, internships, part-time degree program, summer session for credit.

Computers on Campus 100 computers/terminals are available on campus for general student use. Students can access the following: campus intranet, free

student e-mail accounts, online (class) grades, online (class) schedules. Campuswide network is available. Wireless service is available via entire campus.
Student Life *Housing:* college housing not available. *Campus security:* 24-hour emergency response devices.
Athletics *Intramural sports:* basketball M(c)/W(c), racquetball M(c)/W(c), softball M(c)/W(c), swimming and diving M(c)/W(c), table tennis M(c)/W(c), tennis M(c)/W(c), volleyball M(c)/W(c), weight lifting M(c)/W(c).
Costs (2013–14) *One-time required fee:* $25. *Tuition:* $10,500 full-time, $292 per credit hour part-time. *Required fees:* $900 full-time, $150 per term part-time. *Waivers:* employees or children of employees.
Financial Aid Of all full-time matriculated undergraduates who enrolled in 2011, 311 applied for aid, 311 were judged to have need. *Average need-based loan:* $6049. *Average need-based gift aid:* $8254.
Applying *Application fee:* $25. *Required:* essay or personal statement, high school transcript, interview. *Application deadlines:* rolling (freshmen), rolling (transfers).
Freshman Application Contact Mrs. Brenda Salemme, Director of Admissions and Placement, Jamestown Business College, 7 Fairmount Avenue, Box 429, Jamestown, NY 14702-0429. *Phone:* 716-664-5100. *Fax:* 716-664-3144. *E-mail:* brendasalemme@jamestownbusinesscollege.edu. *Website:* http://www.jbcny.org/.

The Jewish Theological Seminary

New York, New York

Freshman Application Contact Mr. Sergio Lineberge, List College Admissions Coordinator, The Jewish Theological Seminary, 3080 Broadway, New York, NY 10027. *Phone:* 212-678-8820. *E-mail:* lcadmissions@jtsa.edu. *Website:* http://www.jtsa.edu/.

John Jay College of Criminal Justice of the City University of New York

New York, New York

- **State and locally supported** comprehensive, founded 1964, part of City University of New York System
- **Urban** campus with easy access to New York City
- **Coed** 13,167 undergraduate students, 78% full-time, 56% women, 44% men
- **Moderately difficult** entrance level, 48% of applicants were admitted

Undergraduates 10,286 full-time, 2,881 part-time. Students come from 23 states and territories; 67 other countries; 3% are from out of state; 22% Black or African American, non-Hispanic/Latino; 39% Hispanic/Latino; 11% Asian, non-Hispanic/Latino; 0.3% American Indian or Alaska Native, non-Hispanic/Latino; 3% international; 12% transferred in. *Retention:* 78% of full-time freshmen returned.
Freshmen *Admission:* 13,753 applied, 6,576 admitted, 1,908 enrolled. *Average high school GPA:* 2.77. *Test scores:* SAT critical reading scores over 500: 29%; SAT math scores over 500: 41%; SAT critical reading scores over 600: 3%; SAT math scores over 600: 7%; SAT math scores over 700: 1%.
Academics *Calendar:* semesters. *Degrees:* certificates, associate, bachelor's, and master's. *Special study options:* academic remediation for entering students, advanced placement credit, cooperative education, distance learning, double majors, English as a second language, honors programs, independent study, internships, off-campus study, part-time degree program, services for LD students, student-designed majors, study abroad, summer session for credit. *Unusual degree programs:* 3-2 public management, law enforcement.
Computers on Campus 1,900 computers/terminals are available on campus for general student use. Students can access the following: campus intranet, computer help desk, free student e-mail accounts, online (class) grades, online (class) registration, online (class) schedules. Campuswide network is available. Wireless service is available via classrooms, computer centers, computer labs, learning centers, libraries, student centers.
Student Life *Housing:* college housing not available. *Activities and organizations:* drama/theater group, student-run newspaper, radio station, choral group, JJC Debate Team, Universal Image Dance Group, Environmental Club, Justice in Action Club, Artist United. *Campus security:* 24-hour emergency response

devices and patrols. *Student services:* health clinic, personal/psychological counseling, women's center, legal services.
Athletics Member NCAA. All Division III. *Intercollegiate sports:* baseball M, basketball M/W, cross-country running M/W, soccer M/W, softball W, swimming and diving W, tennis M/W, volleyball W. *Intramural sports:* baseball M, basketball M/W, cross-country running M/W, riflery M/W, soccer M/W, softball M/W, swimming and diving M/W, tennis M/W, track and field M/W, volleyball M/W, weight lifting M/W.
Standardized Tests *Required:* SAT or ACT (for admission).
Costs (2012–13) *Tuition:* state resident $5430 full-time; nonresident $14,550 full-time. Full-time tuition and fees vary according to course load and program. Part-time tuition and fees vary according to course load and program. *Required fees:* $330 full-time. *Payment plan:* installment. *Waivers:* senior citizens.
Financial Aid Of all full-time matriculated undergraduates who enrolled in 2011, 8,662 applied for aid, 7,393 were judged to have need. *Average percent of need met:* 85%. *Average financial aid package:* $10,150. *Average need-based loan:* $3500. *Average need-based gift aid:* $3175. *Average indebtedness upon graduation:* $11,890.
Applying *Application fee:* $65. *Required:* high school transcript, minimum 2.0 GPA, high school diploma and minimum SAT score of 1100. *Application deadlines:* 5/31 (freshmen), rolling (transfers). *Notification:* continuous until 1/15 (freshmen), continuous (transfers).
Freshman Application Contact Marisol Marrero, Interim Director of Admissions, John Jay College of Criminal Justice of the City University of New York, 524 West 59th Street, L.62.20NB, New York, NY 10019. *Phone:* 212-237-8006. *Toll-free phone:* 877-JOHNJAY. *E-mail:* mmarrero@jjay.cuny.edu. *Website:* http://www.jjay.cuny.edu/.

The Juilliard School

New York, New York

- **Independent** comprehensive, founded 1905
- **Urban** campus
- **Coed** 684 undergraduate students, 76% full-time, 46% women, 54% men
- **Most difficult** entrance level, 6% of applicants were admitted

Undergraduates 521 full-time, 163 part-time. 85% are from out of state; 6% Black or African American, non-Hispanic/Latino; 6% Hispanic/Latino; 12% Asian, non-Hispanic/Latino; 7% Two or more races, non-Hispanic/Latino; 1% Race/ethnicity unknown; 23% international; 4% transferred in; 55% live on campus.
Freshmen *Admission:* 2,566 applied, 153 admitted, 101 enrolled.
Faculty *Total:* 307, 40% full-time. *Student/faculty ratio:* 4:1.
Academics *Calendar:* semesters. *Degrees:* diplomas, bachelor's, master's, doctoral, post-master's, and postbachelor's certificates. *Special study options:* adult/continuing education programs.
Computers on Campus Campuswide network is available.
Student Life *Housing:* on-campus residence required for freshman year. *Options:* coed. Campus housing is university owned. Freshman campus housing is guaranteed. *Campus security:* 24-hour emergency response devices and patrols, controlled dormitory access, electronically operated main building entrances.
Costs (2013–14) *Comprehensive fee:* $46,400 includes full-time tuition ($33,630) and room and board ($12,770).
Financial Aid Of all full-time matriculated undergraduates who enrolled in 2011, 454 applied for aid, 395 were judged to have need, 88 had their need fully met. In 2011, 34 non-need-based awards were made. *Average percent of need met:* 74%. *Average financial aid package:* $30,300. *Average need-based loan:* $4991. *Average need-based gift aid:* $25,311. *Average non-need-based aid:* $17,187. *Average indebtedness upon graduation:* $24,117. *Financial aid deadline:* 3/1.
Applying *Options:* electronic application. *Application fee:* $110. *Required:* essay or personal statement, high school transcript, audition. *Application deadlines:* 12/1 (freshmen), 12/1 (transfers). *Notification:* 4/1 (freshmen), 4/1 (transfers).
Freshman Application Contact Ms. Lee Cioppa, Associate Dean for Admissions, The Juilliard School, 60 Lincoln Center Plaza, New York, NY 10023-6588. *Phone:* 212-799-5000. *Fax:* 212-724-0263. *E-mail:* admissions@julliard.edu.
Website: http://www.juilliard.edu/.

Kehilath Yakov Rabbinical Seminary

Ossining, New York

Director of Admissions Admissions Officer, Kehilath Yakov Rabbinical Seminary, 340 Illington Road, Ossining, NY 10562. *Phone:* 718-963-1212.

Keuka College

Keuka Park, New York

- **Independent** comprehensive, founded 1890, affiliated with American Baptist Churches in the U.S.A.
- **Rural** 173-acre campus with easy access to Rochester
- **Endowment** $8.2 million
- **Coed** 1,874 undergraduate students, 83% full-time, 75% women, 25% men
- **Moderately difficult** entrance level, 76% of applicants were admitted

Undergraduates 1,551 full-time, 323 part-time. Students come from 22 states and territories; 4 other countries; 6% are from out of state; 7% Black or African American, non-Hispanic/Latino; 0.8% Hispanic/Latino; 2% Asian, non-Hispanic/Latino; 0.2% Native Hawaiian or other Pacific Islander, non-Hispanic/Latino; 0.7% American Indian or Alaska Native, non-Hispanic/Latino; 15% Race/ethnicity unknown; 4% transferred in; 81% live on campus. *Retention:* 70% of full-time freshmen returned.

Freshmen *Admission:* 840 applied, 635 admitted, 244 enrolled. *Average high school GPA:* 3.1. *Test scores:* SAT critical reading scores over 500: 38%; SAT math scores over 500: 41%; SAT writing scores over 500: 27%; SAT critical reading scores over 600: 6%; SAT math scores over 600: 9%; SAT writing scores over 600: 5%; SAT math scores over 700: 1%.

Faculty *Total:* 153, 55% full-time, 52% with terminal degrees. *Student/faculty ratio:* 14:1.

Academics *Calendar:* 4-1-4. *Degrees:* bachelor's and master's. *Special study options:* academic remediation for entering students, accelerated degree program, adult/continuing education programs, advanced placement credit, cooperative education, double majors, independent study, internships, off-campus study, part-time degree program, services for LD students, student-designed majors, study abroad, summer session for credit. *Unusual degree programs:* 3-2 occupational therapy.

Computers on Campus 256 computers/terminals are available on campus for general student use. Campuswide network is available.

Student Life *Housing options:* coed, women-only, cooperative. Campus housing is university owned. Freshman campus housing is guaranteed. *Activities and organizations:* drama/theater group, student-run newspaper, radio station, choral group, Student Senate, Campus Activities Board, OTTERS (occupational therapy club), Education Club, BAKU. *Campus security:* 24-hour emergency response devices and patrols, late-night transport/escort service. *Student services:* health clinic, personal/psychological counseling.

Athletics Member NCAA. All Division III. *Intercollegiate sports:* baseball M, basketball M/W, cross-country running M/W, golf W, lacrosse M, soccer M/W, softball W, swimming and diving W, track and field M, volleyball W. *Intramural sports:* badminton M/W, basketball M/W, cheerleading M/W, crew M/W, lacrosse W, skiing (cross-country) M/W, skiing (downhill) M/W, soccer M/W, softball M/W, table tennis M/W, tennis M/W, volleyball W, water polo M/W.

Standardized Tests *Recommended:* SAT or ACT (for admission).

Costs (2012–13) *Comprehensive fee:* $36,600 includes full-time tuition ($25,530), mandatory fees ($790), and room and board ($10,280). Full-time tuition and fees vary according to degree level and program. Part-time tuition: $850 per credit hour. Part-time tuition and fees vary according to program. *Required fees:* $700 per year part-time. *College room only:* $4880. Room and board charges vary according to board plan and housing facility. *Payment plan:* installment. *Waivers:* employees or children of employees.

Financial Aid Of all full-time matriculated undergraduates who enrolled in 2012, 1,301 applied for aid, 1,297 were judged to have need, 45 had their need fully met. In 2012, 56 non-need-based awards were made. *Average percent of need met:* 68%. *Average financial aid package:* $17,472. *Average need-based loan:* $4259. *Average need-based gift aid:* $8906. *Average non-need-based aid:* $11,967. *Average indebtedness upon graduation:* $19,845.

Applying *Options:* electronic application, early admission, deferred entrance. *Application fee:* $30. *Required:* essay or personal statement, high school tran-

script, 1 letter of recommendation. *Required for some:* interview. *Recommended:* minimum 2.8 GPA, interview. *Application deadlines:* rolling (freshmen), rolling (transfers).

Freshman Application Contact Gary Boyer, Director of Admissions, Keuka College, Wagner House, Keuka Park, NY 14478. *Phone:* 315-279-5254. *Toll-free phone:* 800-33-KEUKA. *Fax:* 315-279-5386. *E-mail:* admissions@mail.keuka.edu.

Website: http://www.keuka.edu/.

The King's College

New York, New York

- **Independent nondenominational** 4-year, founded 1939
- **Urban** campus
- **Endowment** $755,106
- **Coed** 582 undergraduate students, 97% full-time, 59% women, 41% men
- **Moderately difficult** entrance level, 67% of applicants were admitted

Undergraduates 565 full-time, 17 part-time. Students come from 37 states and territories; 6 other countries; 93% are from out of state; 4% Black or African American, non-Hispanic/Latino; 8% Hispanic/Latino; 4% Asian, non-Hispanic/Latino; 0.9% American Indian or Alaska Native, non-Hispanic/Latino; 5% Two or more races, non-Hispanic/Latino; 2% international; 6% transferred in; 76% live on campus. *Retention:* 68% of full-time freshmen returned.

Freshmen *Admission:* 3,388 applied, 2,255 admitted, 203 enrolled. *Average high school GPA:* 3.5. *Test scores:* SAT critical reading scores over 500: 99%; SAT math scores over 500: 84%; ACT scores over 18: 100%; SAT critical reading scores over 600: 63%; SAT math scores over 600: 35%; ACT scores over 24: 78%; SAT critical reading scores over 700: 14%; SAT math scores over 700: 2%; ACT scores over 30: 15%.

Faculty *Total:* 43, 56% full-time, 77% with terminal degrees. *Student/faculty ratio:* 18:1.

Academics *Calendar:* semesters. *Degree:* bachelor's. *Special study options:* advanced placement credit, distance learning, independent study, internships, summer session for credit.

Computers on Campus 14 computers/terminals are available on campus for general student use. Students can access the following: computer help desk, free student e-mail accounts, online (class) grades, online (class) registration, online (class) schedules. Campuswide network is available. 100% of college-owned or -operated housing units are wired for high-speed Internet access. Wireless service is available via entire campus.

Student Life *Housing options:* men-only, women-only. Campus housing is leased by the school. Freshman campus housing is guaranteed. *Activities and organizations:* drama/theater group, student-run newspaper, choral group, King's Debate Society, King's Theater, sports clubs, King's Dancers, The Tent. *Campus security:* 24-hour emergency response devices. *Student services:* personal/psychological counseling.

Athletics *Intramural sports:* baseball M, basketball M/W, cross-country running M/W, golf M, soccer M/W, ultimate Frisbee M/W, volleyball W.

Standardized Tests *Required:* SAT or ACT (for admission).

Costs (2012–13) *Tuition:* $28,890 full-time, $1204 per credit hour part-time. Full-time tuition and fees vary according to course load. Part-time tuition and fees vary according to course load. *Required fees:* $350 full-time, $175 per term part-time. *Room only:* $11,600. Room and board charges vary according to location. *Payment plans:* installment, deferred payment. *Waivers:* employees or children of employees.

Financial Aid Of all full-time matriculated undergraduates who enrolled in 2011, 387 applied for aid, 369 were judged to have need, 39 had their need fully met. In 2011, 80 non-need-based awards were made. *Average percent of need met:* 64%. *Average financial aid package:* $24,333. *Average need-based loan:* $5238. *Average need-based gift aid:* $20,315. *Average non-need-based aid:* $14,311. *Average indebtedness upon graduation:* $23,270.

Applying *Options:* electronic application, early action, deferred entrance. *Application fee:* $30. *Required:* high school transcript. *Recommended:* high school transcript, minimum 3.0 GPA, interview. *Application deadlines:* rolling (freshmen), rolling (out-of-state freshmen), rolling (transfers), 11/15 (early action). *Notification:* continuous (freshmen), continuous (out-of-state freshmen), continuous (transfers), 12/15 (early action).

Freshman Application Contact The King's College, 52 Broadway 5th Floor, New York, NY 10004. *Phone:* 212-659-7217. *Toll-free phone:* 888-969-7200 Ext. 3610.

Website: http://www.tkc.edu/.

Lehman College of the City University of New York

Bronx, New York

- **State and locally supported** comprehensive, founded 1931, part of City University of New York System
- **Urban** 37-acre campus
- **Endowment** $7.1 million
- **Coed** 9,577 undergraduate students, 56% full-time, 68% women, 32% men
- **Moderately difficult** entrance level, 23% of applicants were admitted

Undergraduates 5,344 full-time, 4,233 part-time. Students come from 15 states and territories; 99 other countries; 1% are from out of state; 30% Black or African American, non-Hispanic/Latino; 50% Hispanic/Latino; 6% Asian, non-Hispanic/Latino; 0.1% American Indian or Alaska Native, non-Hispanic/Latino; 4% international; 13% transferred in. *Retention:* 82% of full-time freshmen returned.

Freshmen *Admission:* 15,518 applied, 3,612 admitted, 551 enrolled. *Test scores:* SAT critical reading scores over 500: 33%; SAT math scores over 500: 49%; SAT writing scores over 500: 30%; SAT critical reading scores over 600: 7%; SAT math scores over 600: 11%; SAT writing scores over 600: 7%; SAT critical reading scores over 700: 2%; SAT math scores over 700: 2%; SAT writing scores over 700: 2%.

Faculty *Total:* 912, 40% full-time, 42% with terminal degrees. *Student/faculty ratio:* 13:1.

Academics *Calendar:* semesters. *Degrees:* certificates, bachelor's, master's, and post-master's certificates. *Special study options:* adult/continuing education programs, advanced placement credit, cooperative education, distance learning, double majors, English as a second language, freshman honors college, honors programs, independent study, internships, off-campus study, part-time degree program, services for LD students, student-designed majors, study abroad, summer session for credit. *ROTC:* Army (c). *Unusual degree programs:* 3-2 mathematics.

Computers on Campus 800 computers/terminals are available on campus for general student use. Students can access the following: campus intranet, computer help desk, free student e-mail accounts, online (class) grades, online (class) registration, online (class) schedules. Campuswide network is available. Wireless service is available via entire campus.

Student Life *Housing options:* Campus housing is university owned. *Activities and organizations:* drama/theater group, student-run newspaper, radio and television station, choral group, Club Mac, African Students Association, Dominican Student Association, The Sociology Club, Club Live. *Campus security:* 24-hour emergency response devices and patrols, student patrols, late-night transport/escort service. *Student services:* health clinic, personal/psychological counseling, women's center.

Athletics Member NCAA. All Division III. *Intercollegiate sports:* baseball M, basketball M/W, cross-country running M/W, racquetball M/W, soccer M/W, softball M/W, swimming and diving M/W, table tennis M/W, tennis M/W, track and field M/W, volleyball M/W, water polo M, wrestling M. *Intramural sports:* badminton M/W, baseball M/W, basketball M/W, cross-country running M/W, racquetball M/W, soccer M, softball M/W, swimming and diving M/W, tennis M/W, volleyball M/W, wrestling M.

Standardized Tests *Required:* SAT or ACT (for admission).

Costs (2012–13) *Tuition:* state resident $5430 full-time, $230 per credit part-time; nonresident $11,640 full-time, $485 per credit part-time. *Required fees:* $378 full-time. *Room only:* $8085. *Payment plan:* installment.

Applying *Options:* deferred entrance. *Application fee:* $65. *Required:* high school transcript, minimum 3.0 GPA. *Required for some:* essay or personal statement, interview. *Application deadlines:* rolling (freshmen), rolling (transfers). *Notification:* continuous (freshmen), continuous (transfers).

Freshman Application Contact Ms. Laurie Austin, Director of Admissions, Lehman College of the City University of New York, 250 Bedford Park Boulevard West, Bronx, NY 10468. *Phone:* 718-960-8706. *Toll-free phone:* 877-LEHMAN1. *Fax:* 718-960-8712. *E-mail:* enroll@lehman.cuny.edu. *Website:* http://www.lehman.cuny.edu/.

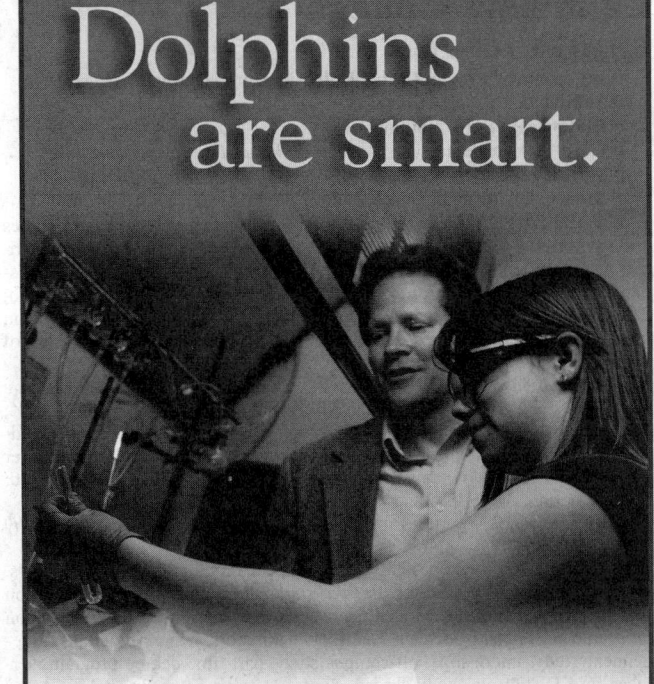

Dolphins are smart.

With incredible new facilities, top-notch faculty and a close-knit campus community, Le Moyne College seeks to develop our students' fullest potential as they live and learn together. Beyond the classroom, they have the opportunity to conduct original research, be mentored by successful professionals, study abroad, and work as interns for a wide array of prestigious organizations. They craft lives that are personally and professionally meaningful.

Le Moyne has won national acclaim for academic excellence and value in rankings compiled by *U.S. News and World Report* for 21 consecutive years, and has been named one of the best colleges and universities in the Northeast by The Princeton Review for the past four years. In addition to those honors, Le Moyne has also earned accolades from *Forbes, Kiplinger's Personal Finance* and *Washington Monthly.*

LE MOYNE

SPIRIT. INQUIRY. LEADERSHIP. *JESUIT.*

To arrange for a campus visit, contact us at (800) 333-4733 or admission@lemoyne.edu

Le Moyne College

Syracuse, New York

- **Independent Roman Catholic (Jesuit)** comprehensive, founded 1946
- **Suburban** 161-acre campus
- **Endowment** $114.7 million
- **Coed** 2,749 undergraduate students, 85% full-time, 60% women, 40% men
- **Moderately difficult** entrance level, 70% of applicants were admitted

Undergraduates 2,338 full-time, 411 part-time. Students come from 27 states and territories; 34 other countries; 6% are from out of state; 5% Black or African American, non-Hispanic/Latino; 5% Hispanic/Latino; 2% Asian, non-Hispanic/Latino; 0.5% American Indian or Alaska Native, non-Hispanic/Latino; 2% Two or more races, non-Hispanic/Latino; 5% Race/ethnicity unknown; 0.6% international; 7% transferred in; 59% live on campus. *Retention:* 85% of full-time freshmen returned.
Freshmen *Admission:* 4,304 applied, 2,999 admitted, 521 enrolled. *Average high school GPA:* 3.39. *Test scores:* SAT critical reading scores over 500: 66%; SAT math scores over 500: 74%; ACT scores over 18: 95%; SAT critical reading scores over 600: 19%; SAT math scores over 600: 31%; ACT scores over 24: 45%; SAT critical reading scores over 700: 3%; SAT math scores over 700: 5%; ACT scores over 30: 7%.
Faculty *Total:* 326, 46% full-time, 68% with terminal degrees. *Student/faculty ratio:* 13:1.
Academics *Calendar:* semesters. *Degrees:* bachelor's, master's, post-master's, and postbachelor's certificates. *Special study options:* academic remediation for entering students, accelerated degree program, adult/continuing education programs, advanced placement credit, double majors, honors programs, independent study, internships, off-campus study, part-time degree program, services for LD students, study abroad, summer session for credit. *ROTC:* Army (c), Air Force (c). *Unusual degree programs:* 3-2 engineering with Manhattan College, Clarkson University, University of Detroit Mercy, Syracuse University.
Computers on Campus 330 computers/terminals and 330 ports are available on campus for general student use. Students can access the following: campus intranet, computer help desk, free student e-mail accounts, online (class) grades, online (class) registration, online (class) schedules, ECHO (campuswide portal), some virtual access from off campus. Campuswide network is available. 100% of college-owned or -operated housing units are wired for high-speed Internet access. Wireless service is available via entire campus.
Student Life *Housing:* on-campus residence required through senior year. *Options:* coed, women-only, disabled students. Campus housing is university owned. Freshman campus housing is guaranteed. *Activities and organizations:* drama/theater group, student-run newspaper, radio and television station, choral group, Student Programming Board, Outing Club, performing arts groups, Student Dancers, New Student Orientation Committee. *Campus security:* 24-hour emergency response devices and patrols, late-night transport/escort service, controlled dormitory access, lighted pathways, closed-circuit security cameras, and emergency code blue phones. *Student services:* health clinic, personal/psychological counseling.
Athletics Member NCAA. All Division II. *Intercollegiate sports:* baseball M(s), basketball M(s)/W(s), cross-country running M(s)/W(s), golf M(s)/W(s), lacrosse M(s)/W(s), soccer M(s)/W(s), softball W(s), swimming and diving M(s)/W(s), tennis M(s)/W(s), volleyball W(s). *Intramural sports:* basketball M/W, field hockey W(c), football M/W, ice hockey M(c), lacrosse M(c), racquetball M/W, rugby M(c)/W(c), soccer M/W, softball M/W, volleyball M/W.
Standardized Tests *Required:* SAT or ACT (for admission).
Costs (2013–14) *Comprehensive fee:* $42,200 includes full-time tuition ($29,470), mandatory fees ($990), and room and board ($11,740). Part-time tuition: $618 per credit hour. Part-time tuition and fees vary according to class time and course load. *College room only:* $7430. Room and board charges vary according to board plan and housing facility. *Payment plans:* installment, deferred payment. *Waivers:* employees or children of employees.
Financial Aid Of all full-time matriculated undergraduates who enrolled in 2011, 2,173 applied for aid, 2,021 were judged to have need, 434 had their need fully met. 396 Federal Work-Study jobs (averaging $950). 375 state and other part-time jobs (averaging $1000). In 2011, 189 non-need-based awards were made. *Average percent of need met:* 74%. *Average financial aid package:* $21,106. *Average need-based loan:* $4521. *Average need-based gift aid:* $16,543. *Average non-need-based aid:* $5895. *Average indebtedness upon graduation:* $34,532.
Applying *Options:* electronic application, early admission, deferred entrance. *Application fee:* $35. *Required:* essay or personal statement, high school transcript, 2 letters of recommendation. *Recommended:* interview. *Application deadlines:* 2/1 (freshmen), 8/1 (transfers). *Notification:* continuous until 12/1 (freshmen), continuous (transfers).
Freshman Application Contact Mr. Dennis J. Nicholson, Dean of Admission, Le Moyne College, 1419 Salt Springs Road, Syracuse, NY 13214-1301. *Phone:* 315-445-4300. *Toll-free phone:* 800-333-4733. *Fax:* 315-445-4711. *E-mail:* admission@lemoyne.edu.
Website: http://www.lemoyne.edu/.

See previous page for display ad and page 1350 for the College Close-Up.

LIM College

New York, New York

Freshman Application Contact Ms. Kristina Ortiz, Assistant Dean of Admissions, LIM College, 12 East 53rd Street, New York, NY 10022. *Phone:* 212-752-1530 Ext. 217. *Toll-free phone:* 800-677-1323. *Fax:* 212-317-8602. *E-mail:* admissions@limcollege.edu.
Website: http://www.limcollege.edu/.

See next page for display ad and page 1356 for the College Close-Up.

LIU Global

Brooklyn, New York

Freshman Application Contact LIU Global, 9 Hanover Place, 4th Floor, Brooklyn, NY 11201. *Phone:* 718-780-4320. *Toll-free phone:* 800-LIU-PLAN. *Website:* http://www.liu.edu/globalcollege/.

Long Island University–Brentwood Campus

Brentwood, New York

- **Independent** upper-level, founded 1959, part of Long Island University
- **Suburban** 172-acre campus with easy access to Manhattan
- **Endowment** $74.0 million
- **Coed**

Faculty *Student/faculty ratio:* 6:1.
Academics *Calendar:* semesters. *Degrees:* bachelor's, master's, and post-master's certificates.
Student Life *Campus security:* evening security guards.
Applying *Options:* electronic application. *Application fee:* $30.
Application Contact Long Island University–Brentwood Campus, 100 Second Avenue, Brentwood, NY 11717. *Phone:* 631-273-5112 Ext. 202. *Website:* http://www.liu.edu/.

Long Island University–Brooklyn Campus

Brooklyn, New York

- **Independent** university, founded 1926
- **Urban** 10-acre campus
- **Coed** 5,109 undergraduate students, 84% full-time, 71% women, 29% men
- **Moderately difficult** entrance level, 83% of applicants were admitted

Undergraduates 4,307 full-time, 802 part-time. Students come from 42 states and territories; 41 other countries; 14% are from out of state; 33% Black or African American, non-Hispanic/Latino; 15% Hispanic/Latino; 15% Asian, non-Hispanic/Latino; 0.1% Native Hawaiian or other Pacific Islander, non-Hispanic/Latino; 0.4% American Indian or Alaska Native, non-Hispanic/Latino; 0.6% Two or more races, non-Hispanic/Latino; 14% Race/ethnicity unknown; 2% international; 13% transferred in; 15% live on campus. *Retention:* 65% of full-time freshmen returned.
Freshmen *Admission:* 5,071 applied, 4,199 admitted, 917 enrolled. *Average high school GPA:* 2.8. *Test scores:* SAT critical reading scores over 500: 23%; SAT math scores over 500: 34%; SAT writing scores over 500: 27%; ACT scores over 18: 70%; SAT critical reading scores over 600: 2%; SAT math scores over 600: 12%; SAT writing scores over 600: 4%; ACT scores over 24: 16%; SAT math scores over 700: 2%.
Faculty *Total:* 863, 35% full-time. *Student/faculty ratio:* 15:1.

Academics *Calendar:* semesters. *Degrees:* associate, bachelor's, master's, doctoral, post-master's, and postbachelor's certificates. *Special study options:* academic remediation for entering students, accelerated degree program, advanced placement credit, cooperative education, distance learning, double majors, English as a second language, honors programs, independent study, internships, part-time degree program, services for LD students, student-designed majors, study abroad, summer session for credit. *Unusual degree programs:* 3-2 nursing; physical therapy, Speech language pathology.

Computers on Campus 300 computers/terminals are available on campus for general student use. Students can access the following: campus intranet, computer help desk, free student e-mail accounts, online (class) grades, online (class) registration, online (class) schedules. Campuswide network is available. 100% of college-owned or -operated housing units are wired for high-speed Internet access. Wireless service is available via entire campus.

Student Life *Housing options:* coed, disabled students. Campus housing is university owned and leased by the school. Freshman applicants given priority for college housing. *Activities and organizations:* drama/theater group, student-run newspaper, radio and television station, choral group, The Student Government Association, The American Pharmacists Association—Academy of Student Pharmacists, Hillel Jewish Students Organization, Student Activities Board, The Society of Health Systems Pharmacists, national fraternities, national sororities. *Campus security:* 24-hour emergency response devices and patrols, controlled dormitory access, lighted pathways/sidewalks. *Student services:* health clinic, personal/psychological counseling.

Athletics Member NCAA. All Division I. *Intercollegiate sports:* baseball M(s), basketball M(s)/W(s), cross-country running M(s)/W(s), golf M(s)/W(s), lacrosse W(s), soccer M(s)/W(s), softball W(s), tennis W(s), track and field M(s)/W(s), volleyball W(s).

Standardized Tests *Required:* SAT or ACT (for admission).

Costs (2012–13) *Comprehensive fee:* $42,490 includes full-time tuition ($29,220), mandatory fees ($1570), and room and board ($11,700). Full-time tuition and fees vary according to program. Part-time tuition and fees vary according to program. *College room only:* $7220. Room and board charges vary according to board plan and housing facility. *Payment plan:* installment. *Waivers:* employees or children of employees.

Financial Aid Of all full-time matriculated undergraduates who enrolled in 2011, 4,126 applied for aid, 3,947 were judged to have need, 271 had their need fully met. In 2011, 215 non-need-based awards were made. *Average percent of need met:* 56%. *Average financial aid package:* $16,409. *Average need-based loan:* $4230. *Average need-based gift aid:* $9120. *Average non-need-based aid:* $5511.

Applying *Options:* electronic application, deferred entrance. *Application fee:* $40. *Required:* essay or personal statement, high school transcript, minimum 2.0 GPA, 3 letters of recommendation. *Required for some:* minimum 3.0 GPA. *Recommended:* minimum 2.5 GPA, interview. *Application deadlines:* rolling (freshmen), rolling (transfers). *Notification:* continuous (freshmen), continuous (transfers).

Freshman Application Contact Richard Sunday, Senior Associate Dean of Admissions, Long Island University–Brooklyn Campus, 1 University Plaza, Brooklyn, NY 11201. *Phone:* 718-488-1011. *Toll-free phone:* 800-LIU-PLAN. *Fax:* 718-797-2399. *E-mail:* admissions@brooklyn.liu.edu. *Website:* http://www.liu.edu/.

Long Island University–C. W. Post Campus

Brookville, New York

- **Independent** comprehensive, founded 1954
- **Suburban** 308-acre campus with easy access to New York City
- **Coed** 8,315 undergraduate students, 48% full-time, 75% women, 25% men
- **Moderately difficult** entrance level, 79% of applicants were admitted

Undergraduates 3,978 full-time, 4,337 part-time. Students come from 31 states and territories; 38 other countries; 7% are from out of state; 10% Black or African American, non-Hispanic/Latino; 12% Hispanic/Latino; 4% Asian, non-Hispanic/Latino; 0.2% American Indian or Alaska Native, non-Hispanic/Latino; 0.8% Two or more races, non-Hispanic/Latino; 15% Race/ethnicity unknown; 10% international; 6% transferred in; 36% live on campus. *Retention:* 68% of full-time freshmen returned.

Freshmen *Admission:* 7,215 applied, 5,687 admitted, 980 enrolled. *Average high school GPA:* 3. *Test scores:* SAT critical reading scores over 500: 47%; SAT math scores over 500: 52%; SAT writing scores over 500: 45%; ACT scores over 18: 91%; SAT critical reading scores over 600: 9%; SAT math scores over 600: 14%; SAT writing scores over 600: 11%; ACT scores over 24: 31%; SAT critical reading scores over 700: 1%; SAT math scores over 700: 1%; SAT writing scores over 700: 1%; ACT scores over 30: 1%.

Faculty *Total:* 798, 38% full-time. *Student/faculty ratio:* 13:1.

Academics *Calendar:* semesters. *Degrees:* associate, bachelor's, master's, doctoral, post-master's, and postbachelor's certificates. *Special study options:* academic remediation for entering students, accelerated degree program, adult/continuing education programs, advanced placement credit, cooperative education, distance learning, double majors, English as a second language, honors programs, independent study, internships, part-time degree program, services for LD students, student-designed majors, study abroad, summer session for credit. *ROTC:* Army (c). *Unusual degree programs:* 3-2 business administration; nursing; respiratory therapy and pharmacy with Long Island University, Brooklyn Campus.

Computers on Campus 500 computers/terminals are available on campus for general student use. Students can access the following: campus intranet, computer help desk, free student e-mail accounts, online (class) grades, online (class) registration, online (class) schedules. Campuswide network is available. 100% of college-owned or -operated housing units are wired for high-speed Internet access. Wireless service is available via entire campus.

Student Life *Housing options:* coed, disabled students. Campus housing is university owned. Freshman campus housing is guaranteed. *Activities and organizations:* drama/theater group, student-run newspaper, radio and television station, choral group, Student Government Association, Association for Campus Programming, African People's Organization, Resident Student Association, Post TV and Newman, national fraternities, national sororities. *Campus security:* 24-hour emergency response devices and patrols, late-night transport/escort service, controlled dormitory access, lighted pathways/sidewalks. *Student services:* health clinic, personal/psychological counseling.

Athletics Member NCAA. All Division II. *Intercollegiate sports:* baseball M(s), basketball M(s)/W(s), crew M(c)/W(c), cross-country running M(s)/W(s), equestrian sports M(c)/W(c), field hockey W(s), football M(s), lacrosse M(s)/W(s), soccer M(s)/W(s), softball W(s), swimming and diving W(s), tennis W(s), volleyball W(s).

Standardized Tests *Required:* SAT or ACT (for admission).

Costs (2012–13) *Comprehensive fee:* $45,102 includes full-time tuition ($31,202), mandatory fees ($1660), and room and board ($12,240). *College room only:* $7680. Room and board charges vary according to board plan and housing facility. *Payment plan:* installment. *Waivers:* employees or children of employees.

Financial Aid Of all full-time matriculated undergraduates who enrolled in 2011, 3,257 applied for aid, 2,744 were judged to have need, 713 had their need fully met. In 2011, 523 non-need-based awards were made. *Average percent of need met:* 68%. *Average financial aid package:* $18,043. *Average need-based loan:* $4439. *Average need-based gift aid:* $8324. *Average non-need-based aid:* $11,136. *Financial aid deadline:* 3/1.

Applying *Options:* electronic application, deferred entrance. *Application fee:* $40. *Required:* essay or personal statement, high school transcript, minimum 3.0 GPA, letters of recommendation. *Required for some:* interview. *Application deadlines:* rolling (freshmen), rolling (transfers). *Notification:* continuous (freshmen), continuous (transfers).

Freshman Application Contact Dr. Reginald Ross, Associate Provost/Dean of Admissions, Long Island University–C. W. Post Campus, 720 Northern Boulevard, Brookville, NY 11548-1300. *Phone:* 516-299-2900. *Toll-free phone:* 800-LIU-PLAN. *Fax:* 516-299-2137. *E-mail:* post-enroll@liu.edu. *Website:* http://www.liu.edu/.

Machzikei Hadath Rabbinical College

Brooklyn, New York

Director of Admissions Rabbi Abraham M. Lezerowitz, Director of Admissions, Machzikei Hadath Rabbinical College, 5407 Sixteenth Avenue, Brooklyn, NY 11204-1805. *Phone:* 718-854-8777.

Manhattan College

Riverdale, New York

- **Independent** comprehensive, founded 1853, affiliated with Roman Catholic Church
- **Urban** 31-acre campus with easy access to New York City
- **Endowment** $56.9 million
- **Coed** 3,351 undergraduate students, 94% full-time, 44% women, 56% men
- **Moderately difficult** entrance level, 70% of applicants were admitted

Undergraduates 3,141 full-time, 210 part-time. Students come from 36 states and territories; 46 other countries; 28% are from out of state; 4% Black or Afri-

can American, non-Hispanic/Latino; 17% Hispanic/Latino; 3% Asian, non-Hispanic/Latino; 0.1% American Indian or Alaska Native, non-Hispanic/Latino; 2% Two or more races, non-Hispanic/Latino; 11% Race/ethnicity unknown; 2% international; 4% transferred in; 67% live on campus. *Retention:* 88% of full-time freshmen returned.

Freshmen *Admission:* 6,545 applied, 4,555 admitted, 842 enrolled. *Average high school GPA:* 3.3. *Test scores:* SAT critical reading scores over 500: 63%; SAT math scores over 500: 71%; SAT writing scores over 500: 65%; ACT scores over 18: 98%; SAT critical reading scores over 600: 18%; SAT math scores over 600: 31%; SAT writing scores over 600: 21%; ACT scores over 24: 57%; SAT critical reading scores over 700: 2%; SAT math scores over 700: 4%; SAT writing scores over 700: 2%; ACT scores over 30: 10%.

Faculty *Total:* 408, 51% full-time, 68% with terminal degrees. *Student/faculty ratio:* 12:1.

Academics *Calendar:* semesters. *Degrees:* bachelor's, master's, and post-master's certificates. *Special study options:* accelerated degree program, adult/continuing education programs, advanced placement credit, cooperative education, distance learning, double majors, English as a second language, honors programs, independent study, internships, off-campus study, part-time degree program, services for LD students, student-designed majors, study abroad, summer session for credit. *ROTC:* Army (c), Air Force (b). *Unusual degree programs:* business administration; engineering; education.

Computers on Campus 350 computers/terminals and 600 ports are available on campus for general student use. Students can access the following: campus intranet, computer help desk, free student e-mail accounts, online (class) grades, online (class) registration, online (class) schedules, course management system. Campuswide network is available. 100% of college-owned or -operated housing units are wired for high-speed Internet access. Wireless service is available via entire campus.

Student Life *Housing options:* coed, disabled students. Campus housing is university owned. Freshman campus housing is guaranteed. *Activities and organizations:* drama/theater group, student-run newspaper, radio and television station, choral group, marching band, Society of Hispanic Professional Engineers, Gaelic Society, Student Government, LaSallian Collegians (Community Service Group), Manhattan College Players (Theater/Drama group), national fraternities, national sororities. *Campus security:* 24-hour emergency response devices and patrols, late-night transport/escort service, controlled dormitory access. *Student services:* health clinic, personal/psychological counseling.

Athletics Member NCAA. All Division I. *Intercollegiate sports:* baseball M(s), basketball M(s)/W(s), cheerleading M/W, crew M(c)/W(c), cross-country running M(s)/W(s), golf M(s), lacrosse M(s)/W(s), rugby M(c), soccer M(s)/W(s), softball W(s), swimming and diving M(s)/W(s), tennis W(s), track and field M(s)/W(s), volleyball W(s). *Intramural sports:* baseball M, basketball M/W, cross-country running M/W, equestrian sports M/W, soccer M/W, softball M/W, swimming and diving W, track and field M/W, volleyball M/W.

Standardized Tests *Required:* SAT or ACT (for admission).

Costs (2013–14) *Comprehensive fee:* $48,805 includes full-time tuition ($33,000), mandatory fees ($2725), and room and board ($13,080). Full-time tuition and fees vary according to course load, program, and student level. Part-time tuition and fees vary according to course load. *Room and board:* Room and board charges vary according to board plan. *Payment plans:* installment, deferred payment. *Waivers:* employees or children of employees.

Financial Aid Of all full-time matriculated undergraduates who enrolled in 2012, 2,605 applied for aid, 2,275 were judged to have need, 281 had their need fully met. In 2012, 848 non-need-based awards were made. *Average percent of need met:* 67%. *Average financial aid package:* $20,131. *Average need-based loan:* $4428. *Average need-based gift aid:* $15,837. *Average non-need-based aid:* $4993. *Average indebtedness upon graduation:* $34,189.

Applying *Options:* electronic application, early admission, early decision, deferred entrance. *Application fee:* $60. *Required:* essay or personal statement, high school transcript, minimum 2.5 GPA, 1 letter of recommendation, SAT or ACT scores. *Required for some:* interview. *Recommended:* minimum 3.0 GPA, interview. *Application deadlines:* 4/15 (freshmen), 7/1 (transfers). *Early decision deadline:* 11/15. *Notification:* continuous until 4/15 (freshmen), continuous until 8/15 (transfers), 12/1 (early decision).

Freshman Application Contact Mr. William Bisset, Vice President for Enrollment Management, Manhattan College, 4513 Manhattan College Parkway, Riverdale, NY 10471. *Phone:* 718-862-7200. *Toll-free phone:* 800-622-9235. *Fax:* 718-862-8019. *E-mail:* admit@manhattan.edu. *Website:* http://www.manhattan.edu/.

See previous page for display ad and page 1374 for the College Close-Up.

Manhattan School of Music
New York, New York

Freshman Application Contact Amy Anderson, Associate Dean for Enrollment Management, Manhattan School of Music, 120 Claremont Avenue, New York, NY 10027-4698. *Phone:* 917-493-4501. *Fax:* 212-749-3025. *E-mail:* admission@msmnyc.edu. *Website:* http://www.msmnyc.edu/.

Manhattanville College
Purchase, New York

- **Independent** comprehensive, founded 1841
- **Suburban** 100-acre campus with easy access to New York City
- **Endowment** $10.9 million
- **Coed** 1,767 undergraduate students, 94% full-time, 63% women, 37% men
- **Moderately difficult** entrance level, 69% of applicants were admitted

Undergraduates 1,659 full-time, 108 part-time. Students come from 39 states and territories; 53 other countries; 39% are from out of state; 10% Black or African American, non-Hispanic/Latino; 17% Hispanic/Latino; 3% Asian, non-Hispanic/Latino; 0.5% American Indian or Alaska Native, non-Hispanic/Latino; 15% Race/ethnicity unknown; 11% international; 3% transferred in; 78% live on campus. *Retention:* 73% of full-time freshmen returned.

Freshmen *Admission:* 4,148 applied, 2,874 admitted, 535 enrolled. *Average high school GPA:* 3.

Faculty *Total:* 352, 30% full-time. *Student/faculty ratio:* 12:1.

Academics *Calendar:* semesters. *Degrees:* bachelor's, master's, doctoral, post-master's, and postbachelor's certificates. *Special study options:* academic remediation for entering students, accelerated degree program, adult/continuing education programs, advanced placement credit, distance learning, double majors, English as a second language, honors programs, independent study, internships, off-campus study, part-time degree program, services for LD students, student-designed majors, study abroad, summer session for credit. *Unusual degree programs:* 3-2 business administration; education.

Computers on Campus 240 computers/terminals are available on campus for general student use. Students can access the following: computer help desk, free student e-mail accounts, online (class) grades, online (class) registration, online (class) schedules. Campuswide network is available. 100% of college-owned or -operated housing units are wired for high-speed Internet access. Wireless service is available via classrooms, computer centers, computer labs, libraries, student centers.

Student Life *Housing options:* coed, disabled students. Campus housing is university owned. Freshman campus housing is guaranteed. *Activities and organizations:* drama/theater group, student-run newspaper, radio and television station, choral group, Latin American Student Organization, International Student Organization, Black Student Union, WMVL (radio station), Connie Hogarth Center. *Campus security:* 24-hour emergency response devices and patrols, late-night transport/escort service, controlled dormitory access. *Student services:* health clinic, personal/psychological counseling, women's center.

Athletics Member NCAA. All Division III. *Intercollegiate sports:* baseball M, basketball M/W, field hockey W, golf M, ice hockey M/W, lacrosse M/W, soccer M/W, softball W, swimming and diving W, tennis M/W, volleyball W. *Intramural sports:* basketball M/W, cheerleading M/W.

Costs (2013–14) *Comprehensive fee:* $49,710 includes full-time tuition ($34,020), mandatory fees ($1350), and room and board ($14,340). Part-time tuition: $790 per credit. Part-time tuition and fees vary according to program. *Required fees:* $60 per term part-time. *College room only:* $8680. Room and board charges vary according to board plan. *Payment plans:* installment, deferred payment. *Waivers:* senior citizens and employees or children of employees.

Financial Aid Of all full-time matriculated undergraduates who enrolled in 2010, 1,234 applied for aid, 1,131 were judged to have need, 111 had their need fully met. 275 Federal Work-Study jobs (averaging $1300). 265 state and other part-time jobs (averaging $1300). In 2010, 480 non-need-based awards were made. *Average percent of need met:* 96%. *Average financial aid package:* $26,779. *Average need-based loan:* $4523. *Average need-based gift aid:* $17,427. *Average non-need-based aid:* $18,753.

Applying *Options:* electronic application, early admission, early decision, deferred entrance. *Application fee:* $75. *Required:* essay or personal statement, high school transcript, minimum 2.0 GPA, 2 letters of recommendation. *Recommended:* minimum 3.0 GPA, interview. *Application deadlines:* 3/1 (freshmen), 3/1 (transfers). *Notification:* continuous (freshmen), continuous (transfers).

Freshman Application Contact Mr. Kevin O'Sullivan, Director of Admissions, Manhattanville College, 2900 Purchase Street, Purchase, NY 10577. *Phone:* 914-323-5125. *Toll-free phone:* 800-328-4553. *Fax:* 914-694-1732. *E-mail:* admissions@mville.edu.
Website: http://www.manhattanville.edu/.

See below for display ad and page 1376 for the College Close-Up.

Mannes College The New School for Music

New York, New York

- **Independent** comprehensive, founded 1916, part of The New School
- **Urban** campus with easy access to Manhattan
- **Coed** 205 undergraduate students, 88% full-time, 55% women, 45% men
- **Very difficult** entrance level, 41% of applicants were admitted

Undergraduates 180 full-time, 25 part-time. 64% are from out of state; 1% Black or African American, non-Hispanic/Latino; 5% Hispanic/Latino; 8% Asian, non-Hispanic/Latino; 0.5% Two or more races, non-Hispanic/Latino; 7% Race/ethnicity unknown; 44% international; 87% transferred in; 10% live on campus. *Retention:* 83% of full-time freshmen returned.
Freshmen *Admission:* 393 applied, 160 admitted, 39 enrolled. *Average high school GPA:* 3.56.
Faculty *Total:* 233, 8% full-time, 0.9% with terminal degrees. *Student/faculty ratio:* 4:1.
Academics *Calendar:* semesters. *Degrees:* diplomas, bachelor's, master's, post-master's, and postbachelor's certificates. *Special study options:* academic remediation for entering students, advanced placement credit, English as a second language, independent study, internships, services for LD students, summer session for credit.
Computers on Campus Students can access the following: campus intranet, computer help desk, free student e-mail accounts, online (class) grades, online (class) registration, online (class) schedules, online portal. Campuswide network is available. 100% of college-owned or -operated housing units are wired for high-speed Internet access. Wireless service is available via entire campus.

Student Life *Housing options:* coed, disabled students. Campus housing is university owned and leased by the school. Freshman applicants given priority for college housing. *Activities and organizations:* drama/theater group, student-run newspaper, radio station, choral group. *Campus security:* 24-hour emergency response devices, controlled dormitory access. *Student services:* health clinic, personal/psychological counseling.
Costs (2013–14) *Comprehensive fee:* $54,820 includes full-time tuition ($36,660), mandatory fees ($860), and room and board ($17,300). Part-time tuition: $1200 per credit hour. *College room only:* $13,900.
Financial Aid Of all full-time matriculated undergraduates who enrolled in 2011, 55 applied for aid, 48 were judged to have need, 9 had their need fully met. In 2011, 5 non-need-based awards were made. *Average percent of need met:* 59%. *Average financial aid package:* $23,700. *Average need-based loan:* $9260. *Average need-based gift aid:* $16,515. *Average non-need-based aid:* $15,850. *Average indebtedness upon graduation:* $34,455.
Applying *Options:* electronic application. *Application fee:* $100. *Required:* essay or personal statement, high school transcript, 1 letter of recommendation, interview, audition, written test. *Application deadlines:* 12/1 (freshmen), 4/1 (transfers). *Notification:* 4/1 (freshmen).
Freshman Application Contact Mannes College The New School for Music, 150 West 85th Street, New York, NY 10024-4402. *Phone:* 212-580-0210 Ext. 4862. *Toll-free phone:* 800-292-3040.
Website: http://www.mannes.edu/.

See page 575 for display ad and page 1414 for the College Close-Up.

Maria College

Albany, New York

- **Independent** 4-year, founded 1958
- **Urban** 9-acre campus
- **Coed**
- **Minimally difficult** entrance level

Faculty *Student/faculty ratio:* 12:1.
Academics *Calendar:* semesters. *Degrees:* certificates, associate, and bachelor's.
Student Life *Campus security:* late-night transport/escort service.
Standardized Tests *Required:* SAT or ACT (for admission).

Financial Aid *Of all full-time matriculated undergraduates who enrolled in 2011,* 25 Federal Work-Study jobs (averaging $1000).

Applying *Options:* electronic application, early admission. *Application fee:* $35. *Required:* essay or personal statement, high school transcript, minimum 2.0 GPA, 1 letter of recommendation, interview.

Freshmen Application Contact Ms. Laurie A. Gilmore, Director of Admissions, Maria College, 700 New Scotland Avenue, Albany, NY 12208-1798. *Phone:* 518-438-3111. *Fax:* 518-453-1366. *E-mail:* admissions@mariacollege.edu.

Website: http://www.mariacollege.edu/.

Marist College

Poughkeepsie, New York

- **Independent** comprehensive, founded 1929
- **Suburban** 210-acre campus with easy access to Albany, New York City
- **Endowment** $147.1 million
- **Coed** 5,560 undergraduate students, 86% full-time, 58% women, 42% men
- **Very difficult** entrance level, 31% of applicants were admitted

Undergraduates 4,768 full-time, 792 part-time. 45% are from out of state; 4% Black or African American, non-Hispanic/Latino; 8% Hispanic/Latino; 2% Asian, non-Hispanic/Latino; 0.2% Native Hawaiian or other Pacific Islander, non-Hispanic/Latino; 0.2% American Indian or Alaska Native, non-Hispanic/Latino; 2% Two or more races, non-Hispanic/Latino; 5% Race/ethnicity unknown; 1% international; 6% transferred in; 67% live on campus. *Retention:* 89% of full-time freshmen returned.

Freshmen *Admission:* 11,466 applied, 3,597 admitted, 1,098 enrolled. *Average high school GPA:* 3.3. *Test scores:* SAT critical reading scores over 500: 91%; SAT math scores over 500: 95%; SAT writing scores over 500: 91%; ACT scores over 18: 99%; SAT critical reading scores over 600: 40%; SAT math scores over 600: 53%; SAT writing scores over 600: 43%; ACT scores over 24: 85%; SAT critical reading scores over 700: 6%; SAT math scores over 700: 5%; SAT writing scores over 700: 7%; ACT scores over 30: 15%.

Faculty *Total:* 558, 39% full-time, 45% with terminal degrees. *Student/faculty ratio:* 16:1.

Academics *Calendar:* semesters. *Degrees:* certificates, bachelor's, master's, and postbachelor's certificates. *Special study options:* academic remediation for entering students, accelerated degree program, adult/continuing education programs, advanced placement credit, cooperative education, distance learning, double majors, English as a second language, external degree program, honors programs, independent study, internships, off-campus study, part-time degree program, services for LD students, study abroad, summer session for credit. *ROTC:* Army (b).

Computers on Campus 804 computers/terminals and 650 ports are available on campus for general student use. Students can access the following: campus intranet, computer help desk, free student e-mail accounts, online (class) grades, online (class) registration, online (class) schedules, Admissions, Billing, Transcript, Degree Audit, Financial Aid Application, Financial Aid Award Review, Student Account Summary, Payment, Library Database Search, Campus OneCard Account. Campuswide network is available. 100% of college-owned or -operated housing units are wired for high-speed Internet access. Wireless service is available via entire campus.

Student Life *Housing options:* coed, disabled students. Campus housing is university owned. Freshman campus housing is guaranteed. *Activities and organizations:* drama/theater group, student-run newspaper, radio and television station, choral group, marching band, Marist Singers, Dance Club, student government, Theater Club, Community Service and Campus Ministry, national fraternities. *Campus security:* 24-hour emergency response devices and patrols, student patrols, late-night transport/escort service, controlled dormitory access, night residence hall monitors. *Student services:* health clinic, personal/psychological counseling.

Athletics Member NCAA. All Division I except football (Division I-AA). *Intercollegiate sports:* baseball M(s), basketball M(s)/W(s), bowling M(c)/W(c), cheerleading M(c)/W(c), crew M/W(s), cross-country running M(s)/W(s), equestrian sports M(c)/W(c), fencing M(c)/W(c), ice hockey M(c), lacrosse M(s)/W(s), rugby M(c)/W(c), skiing (downhill) M(c)/W(c), soccer M(s)/W(s), softball W(s), swimming and diving M(s)/W(s), tennis M(s)/W(s), track and field M(s)/W(s), volleyball M(c)/W(s), water polo W(s). *Intramural sports:* basketball M/W, soccer M/W, softball M/W, ultimate Frisbee M(c)/W(c), volleyball M/W.

Costs (2012–13) *One-time required fee:* $90. *Comprehensive fee:* $42,600 includes full-time tuition ($29,500), mandatory fees ($500), and room and board ($12,600). Full-time tuition and fees vary according to course load and location. Part-time tuition: $634 per credit hour. Part-time tuition and fees vary according to course load. *Required fees:* $40 per term part-time. *College room*

only: $8100. Room and board charges vary according to board plan, housing facility, and location. *Payment plan:* installment. *Waivers:* adult students and employees or children of employees.

Financial Aid Of all full-time matriculated undergraduates who enrolled in 2012, 3,495 applied for aid, 2,839 were judged to have need, 444 had their need fully met. 1,370 Federal Work-Study jobs (averaging $2441). 701 state and other part-time jobs (averaging $1478). In 2012, 1106 non-need-based awards were made. *Average financial aid package:* $17,754. *Average need-based loan:* $4811. *Average need-based gift aid:* $14,182. *Average non-need-based aid:* $7400. *Average indebtedness upon graduation:* $33,707. *Financial aid deadline:* 5/1.

Applying *Options:* electronic application, early admission, early decision, early action, deferred entrance. *Application fee:* $50. *Required:* essay or personal statement, high school transcript, 2 letters of recommendation. *Application deadlines:* 2/1 (freshmen), 6/1 (transfers), 11/15 (early action). *Early decision deadline:* 11/1. *Notification:* 3/30 (freshmen), continuous (transfers), 12/15 (early decision), 1/30 (early action).

Freshman Application Contact Mr. Kenton Rinehart, Dean of Undergraduate Admissions, Marist College, 3399 North Road, Poughkeepsie, NY 12601. *Phone:* 845-575-3226. *Toll-free phone:* 800-436-5483. *Fax:* 845-575-3215. *E-mail:* admission@marist.edu.

Website: http://www.marist.edu/.

Marymount Manhattan College

New York, New York

- **Independent** 4-year, founded 1936
- **Urban** 3-acre campus
- **Endowment** $14.0 million
- **Coed** 1,908 undergraduate students, 82% full-time, 84% women, 16% men
- **Moderately difficult** entrance level, 72% of applicants were admitted

Undergraduates 1,563 full-time, 345 part-time. 57% are from out of state; 10% Black or African American, non-Hispanic/Latino; 17% Hispanic/Latino; 5% Asian, non-Hispanic/Latino; 0.2% Native Hawaiian or other Pacific Islander, non-Hispanic/Latino; 1% American Indian or Alaska Native, non-Hispanic/Latino; 2% Race/ethnicity unknown; 3% international; 7% transferred in; 39% live on campus. *Retention:* 68% of full-time freshmen returned.

Freshmen *Admission:* 4,174 applied, 2,995 admitted, 462 enrolled. *Average high school GPA:* 3.36. *Test scores:* SAT critical reading scores over 500: 86%; SAT math scores over 500: 78%; SAT writing scores over 500: 78%; ACT scores over 18: 93%; SAT critical reading scores over 600: 52%; SAT math scores over 600: 34%; SAT writing scores over 600: 37%; ACT scores over 24: 60%; SAT critical reading scores over 700: 10%; SAT math scores over 700: 2%; SAT writing scores over 700: 7%; ACT scores over 30: 9%.

Faculty *Total:* 293, 35% full-time, 72% with terminal degrees. *Student/faculty ratio:* 11:1.

Academics *Calendar:* semesters plus summer and January mini-semesters. *Degrees:* associate, bachelor's, and post-master's certificates. *Special study options:* academic remediation for entering students, accelerated degree program, adult/continuing education programs, advanced placement credit, distance learning, double majors, honors programs, independent study, internships, off-campus study, part-time degree program, services for LD students, study abroad, summer session for credit. *Unusual degree programs:* computer science with Polytechnic University.

Computers on Campus 152 computers/terminals are available on campus for general student use. Students can access the following: campus intranet, computer help desk, free student e-mail accounts, online (class) grades, online (class) registration, online (class) schedules. Campuswide network is available. 100% of college-owned or -operated housing units are wired for high-speed Internet access. Wireless service is available via classrooms, computer centers, computer labs, dorm rooms, learning centers, libraries, student centers.

Student Life *Housing options:* coed. Campus housing is university owned and leased by the school. Freshman applicants given priority for college housing. *Activities and organizations:* drama/theater group, student-run newspaper, radio station, choral group, Education Club, African-American Heritage Club, Asian-American Heritage Club, Latino Heritage Club, Business Club. *Campus security:* 24-hour emergency response devices and patrols, student patrols, 24-hour security in residence halls. *Student services:* personal/psychological counseling.

Athletics *Intramural sports:* softball M/W.

Standardized Tests *Required:* SAT or ACT (for admission).

Costs (2013–14) *Comprehensive fee:* $40,118 includes full-time tuition ($24,482), mandatory fees ($1206), and room and board ($14,430). Part-time tuition: $816 per credit hour. *College room only:* $11,930. *Payment plan:* installment. *Waivers:* senior citizens and employees or children of employees.

Financial Aid Of all full-time matriculated undergraduates who enrolled in 2009, 1,303 applied for aid, 1,073 were judged to have need, 32 had their need fully met. In 2009, 294 non-need-based awards were made. *Average percent of need met:* 47%. *Average financial aid package:* $13,251. *Average need-based loan:* $4236. *Average need-based gift aid:* $9454. *Average non-need-based aid:* $5119. *Average indebtedness upon graduation:* $15,988.

Applying *Options:* electronic application, deferred entrance. *Application fee:* $60. *Required:* essay or personal statement, high school transcript, minimum 2.0 GPA, 2 letters of recommendation. *Required for some:* audition for dance and theater programs. *Recommended:* interview. *Application deadlines:* rolling (freshmen), rolling (transfers). *Notification:* continuous (freshmen), continuous (transfers).

Freshman Application Contact Mr. James Rogers, Dean of Admissions, Marymount Manhattan College, 221 East 71st Street, New York, NY 10021. *Phone:* 212-517-0430. *Toll-free phone:* 800-MARYMOUNT. *Fax:* 212-517-0448. *E-mail:* admissions@mmm.edu. *Website:* http://www.mmm.edu/.

See below for display ad and page 1378 for the College Close-Up.

Medaille College

Buffalo, New York

- **Independent** comprehensive, founded 1875
- **Urban** 13-acre campus
- **Coed** 1,844 undergraduate students, 89% full-time, 66% women, 34% men
- **Moderately difficult** entrance level, 60% of applicants were admitted

Undergraduates 1,650 full-time, 194 part-time. Students come from 19 states and territories; 4 other countries; 3% are from out of state; 18% Black or African American, non-Hispanic/Latino; 5% Hispanic/Latino; 3% Asian, non-Hispanic/Latino; 2% Native Hawaiian or other Pacific Islander, non-Hispanic/Latino; 0.8% American Indian or Alaska Native, non-Hispanic/Latino; 7% Race/ethnicity unknown; 0.1% international; 11% transferred in; 23% live on campus.

Freshmen *Admission:* 1,497 applied, 895 admitted, 400 enrolled. *Test scores:* SAT critical reading scores over 500: 24%; SAT math scores over 500: 27%; SAT critical reading scores over 600: 3%; SAT math scores over 600: 5%.

Faculty *Total:* 281, 29% full-time. *Student/faculty ratio:* 16:1.

Academics *Calendar:* semesters (modular courses available for evening studies and weekend college program). *Degrees:* certificates, associate, bachelor's, master's, doctoral, and post-master's certificates. *Special study options:* academic remediation for entering students, accelerated degree program, adult/continuing education programs, advanced placement credit, double majors, honors programs, independent study, internships, off-campus study, part-time degree program, services for LD students, student-designed majors, summer session for credit. *ROTC:* Army (c). *Unusual degree programs:* 3-2 business administration; sport management.

Computers on Campus 120 computers/terminals are available on campus for general student use. Students can access the following: campus intranet, computer help desk, free student e-mail accounts, online (class) grades, online (class) registration, online (class) schedules. Campuswide network is available. 100% of college-owned or -operated housing units are wired for high-speed Internet access. Wireless service is available via entire campus.

Student Life *Housing options:* coed, men-only, women-only, disabled students. Campus housing is university owned. *Activities and organizations:* drama/theater group, student-run newspaper, radio and television station, student government, Club Green, Dance Team, WMCB The Lizard (college radio station), ice hockey club. *Campus security:* 24-hour emergency response devices and patrols, late-night transport/escort service, controlled dormitory access. *Student services:* health clinic, personal/psychological counseling.

Athletics Member NCAA. All Division III. *Intercollegiate sports:* baseball M, basketball M/W, bowling W, cross-country running M/W, golf M, lacrosse M/W, soccer M/W, softball W, volleyball M/W. *Intramural sports:* basketball M/W, soccer M/W, softball M/W, table tennis M/W, tennis M/W, volleyball M/W, weight lifting M/W.

Standardized Tests *Required:* SAT or ACT (for admission). *Recommended:* SAT (for admission).

Costs (2012–13) *Comprehensive fee:* $33,438 includes full-time tuition ($22,678) and room and board ($10,760). Full-time tuition and fees vary according to location. Part-time tuition: $799 per credit hour. Part-time tuition and fees vary according to course load. *Room and board:* Room and board charges vary according to housing facility. *Payment plan:* installment. *Waivers:* adult students, senior citizens, and employees or children of employees.

Financial Aid Of all full-time matriculated undergraduates who enrolled in 2010, 1,722 applied for aid, 1,586 were judged to have need, 43 had their need fully met. 234 Federal Work-Study jobs (averaging $1451). In 2010, 52 non-need-based awards were made. *Average percent of need met:* 58%. *Average financial aid package:* $14,241. *Average need-based loan:* $4882. *Average need-based gift aid:* $8500. *Average non-need-based aid:* $7529.

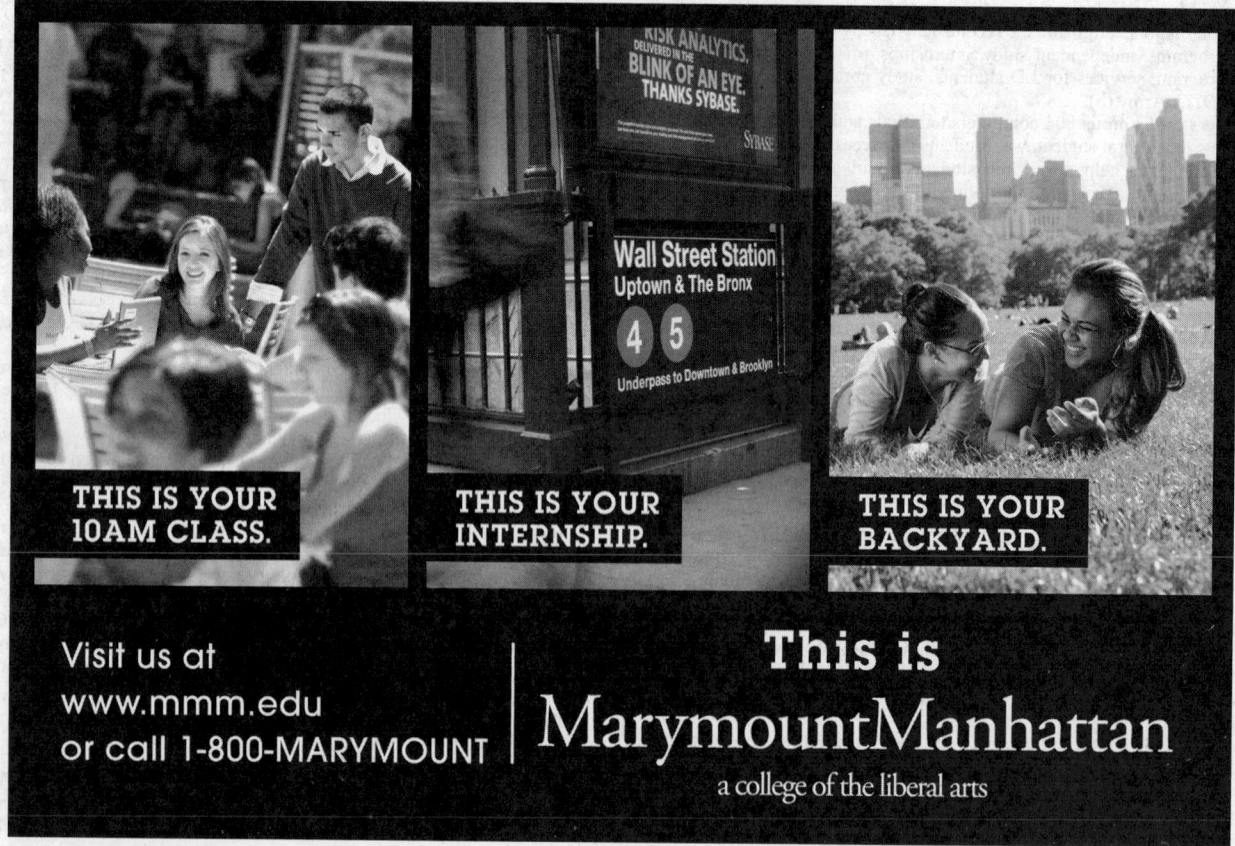

THIS IS YOUR 10AM CLASS.

THIS IS YOUR INTERNSHIP.

THIS IS YOUR BACKYARD.

Visit us at www.mmm.edu or call 1-800-MARYMOUNT

This is MarymountManhattan

a college of the liberal arts

Applying *Options:* electronic application, early admission, deferred entrance. *Application fee:* $25. *Required:* high school transcript, interview. *Required for some:* essay or personal statement, 2.5 high school GPA for veterinary technology and elementary teacher education majors. *Recommended:* essay or personal statement, minimum 2.0 GPA, 1 letter of recommendation. *Application deadlines:* 8/1 (freshmen), rolling (transfers). *Notification:* continuous (freshmen), continuous (transfers).

Freshman Application Contact Mrs. Karen McGrath, Vice President for Enrollment Management & UG Admissions, Medaille College, Office of Admissions, Buffalo, NY 14214. *Phone:* 716-880-2200. *Toll-free phone:* 800-292-1582. *Fax:* 716-880-2007. *E-mail:* admissionsug@medaille.edu. *Website:* http://www.medaille.edu/.

Medgar Evers College of the City University of New York

Brooklyn, New York

- **State and locally supported** 4-year, founded 1969, part of City University of New York System
- **Urban** 8-acre campus
- **Endowment** $515,142
- **Coed**
- **Noncompetitive** entrance level

Faculty *Student/faculty ratio:* 19:1.

Academics *Calendar:* semesters. *Degrees:* certificates, associate, and bachelor's.

Student Life *Campus security:* 24-hour patrols.

Athletics Member NCAA. All Division III.

Standardized Tests *Recommended:* SAT and SAT Subject Tests or ACT (for admission).

Costs (2012–13) *Tuition:* state resident $5130 full-time, $215 per credit part-time; nonresident $13,800 full-time, $460 per credit part-time. Full-time tuition and fees vary according to course load. Part-time tuition and fees vary according to course load. *Required fees:* $302 full-time, $101 per term part-time. *Payment plans:* installment, deferred payment.

Financial Aid *Of all full-time matriculated undergraduates who enrolled in 2010,* 302 Federal Work-Study jobs (averaging $1012). *Average financial aid package:* $4033. *Average need-based loan:* $1865. *Average need-based gift aid:* $3706.

Applying *Options:* electronic application, deferred entrance. *Application fee:* $65. *Required:* high school transcript.

Freshman Application Contact Ms. Julie M. Augustin, Director of Admissions, Medgar Evers College of the City University of New York, 1650 Bedford Avenue, Brooklyn, NY 11225. *Phone:* 718-270-6021. *Fax:* 718-270-6411. *E-mail:* jaugustin@mec.cuny.edu. *Website:* http://www.mec.cuny.edu/.

Mercy College

Dobbs Ferry, New York

- **Independent** comprehensive, founded 1951
- **Suburban** 45-acre campus with easy access to New York City
- **Coed** 8,029 undergraduate students, 69% full-time, 68% women, 32% men
- **Moderately difficult** entrance level, 65% of applicants were admitted

Undergraduates 5,505 full-time, 2,524 part-time. Students come from 19 states and territories; 43 other countries; 7% are from out of state; 25% Black or African American, non-Hispanic/Latino; 30% Hispanic/Latino; 3% Asian, non-Hispanic/Latino; 0.1% Native Hawaiian or other Pacific Islander, non-Hispanic/Latino; 0.3% American Indian or Alaska Native, non-Hispanic/Latino; 2% Two or more races, non-Hispanic/Latino; 12% Race/ethnicity unknown; 0.5% international; 14% transferred in; 8% live on campus. *Retention:* 69% of full-time freshmen returned.

Freshmen *Admission:* 5,766 applied, 3,746 admitted, 833 enrolled. *Average high school GPA:* 2.9.

Faculty *Total:* 893, 21% full-time. *Student/faculty ratio:* 18:1.

Academics *Calendar:* semesters. *Degrees:* certificates, bachelor's, master's, doctoral, post-master's, and postbachelor's certificates. *Special study options:* academic remediation for entering students, accelerated degree program, adult/continuing education programs, advanced placement credit, cooperative education, distance learning, double majors, honors programs, independent study, internships, off-campus study, part-time degree program, services for LD students, study abroad, summer session for credit. *ROTC:* Army (c), Air Force (c). *Unusual degree programs:* 3-2 education, accounting.

Computers on Campus 186 computers/terminals are available on campus for general student use. Students can access the following: campus intranet, computer help desk, free student e-mail accounts, online (class) grades, online (class) registration, online (class) schedules. Campuswide network is available. 100% of college-owned or -operated housing units are wired for high-speed Internet access. Wireless service is available via entire campus.

Student Life *Housing options:* coed, disabled students. Campus housing is university owned and leased by the school. Freshman applicants given priority for college housing. *Activities and organizations:* student-run newspaper, PACT, Honors, Mercy Gives Back, Model United Nations. *Campus security:* 24-hour emergency response devices and patrols, late-night transport/escort service, controlled dormitory access. *Student services:* health clinic, personal/psychological counseling.

Athletics Member NCAA. All Division II. *Intercollegiate sports:* baseball M(s), basketball M(s)/W(s), field hockey W(s), lacrosse M(s)/W(s), soccer M(s)/W(s), softball W(s), volleyball W(s). *Intramural sports:* baseball M, basketball M/W, softball W.

Standardized Tests *Recommended:* SAT (for admission), ACT (for admission), SAT or ACT (for admission), SAT and SAT Subject Tests or ACT (for admission), SAT Subject Tests (for admission).

Costs (2012–13) *Comprehensive fee:* $29,740 includes full-time tuition ($16,996), mandatory fees ($560), and room and board ($12,184). Full-time tuition and fees vary according to course load. Part-time tuition: $715 per credit. Part-time tuition and fees vary according to course load. *Required fees:* $140 per term part-time. *College room only:* $8734. Room and board charges vary according to board plan and housing facility. *Payment plan:* installment. *Waivers:* employees or children of employees.

Financial Aid Of all full-time matriculated undergraduates who enrolled in 2011, 5,073 applied for aid, 4,853 were judged to have need, 104 had their need fully met. In 2011, 49 non-need-based awards were made. *Average percent of need met:* 53%. *Average financial aid package:* $13,245. *Average need-based loan:* $3955. *Average need-based gift aid:* $9656. *Average non-need-based aid:* $3036. *Average indebtedness upon graduation:* $24,138.

Applying *Options:* electronic application, deferred entrance. *Application fee:* $40. *Required:* high school transcript, minimum 2.5 GPA. *Required for some:* essay or personal statement, interview. *Application deadlines:* rolling (freshmen), rolling (out-of-state freshmen), rolling (transfers). *Notification:* continuous (freshmen), continuous (out-of-state freshmen), continuous (transfers).

Freshman Application Contact Mrs. Tara Fay-Reilly, Senior Director of Admissions, Mercy College, 555 Broadway, Dobbs Ferry, NY 10522-1189. *Phone:* 914-674-7762 Ext. 7762. *Toll-free phone:* 800-MERCY-NY. *Fax:* 914-674-7608. *E-mail:* admissions@mercy.edu. *Website:* http://www.mercy.edu/.

Mesivta of Eastern Parkway–Yeshiva Zichron Meilech

Brooklyn, New York

Director of Admissions Rabbi Joseph Halberstadt, Dean, Mesivta of Eastern Parkway–Yeshiva Zichron Meilech, 510 Dahill Road, Brooklyn, NY 11218-5559. *Phone:* 718-438-1002.

Mesivta Tifereth Jerusalem of America

New York, New York

Director of Admissions Rabbi Fishellis, Director of Admissions, Mesivta Tifereth Jerusalem of America, 145 East Broadway, New York, NY 10002-6301. *Phone:* 212-964-2830.

Mesivta Torah Vodaath Rabbinical Seminary

Brooklyn, New York

Director of Admissions Rabbi Issac Braun, Administrator, Mesivta Torah Vodaath Rabbinical Seminary, 425 East Ninth Street, Brooklyn, NY 11218-5299. *Phone:* 718-941-8000.
Website: http://www.torahvodaath.org/.

Metropolitan College of New York

New York, New York

Freshman Application Contact Metropolitan College of New York, 431 Canal Street, New York, NY 10013. *Phone:* 212-343-1234 Ext. 2700. *Toll-free phone:* 800-33-THINK Ext. 5001. *Fax:* 212-343-8470.
Website: http://www.metropolitan.edu/.

Mirrer Yeshiva

Brooklyn, New York

Director of Admissions Director of Admissions, Mirrer Yeshiva, 1795 Ocean Parkway, Brooklyn, NY 11223-2010. *Phone:* 718-645-0536.

Molloy College

Rockville Centre, New York

- **Independent** comprehensive, founded 1955
- **Suburban** 30-acre campus with easy access to New York City
- **Endowment** $28.0 million
- **Coed** 3,444 undergraduate students, 77% full-time, 75% women, 25% men
- **Moderately difficult** entrance level, 74% of applicants were admitted

Undergraduates 2,642 full-time, 802 part-time. Students come from 13 states and territories; 6 other countries; 1% are from out of state; 13% Black or African American, non-Hispanic/Latino; 14% Hispanic/Latino; 7% Asian, non-Hispanic/Latino; 0.6% Native Hawaiian or other Pacific Islander, non-Hispanic/Latino; 0.2% American Indian or Alaska Native, non-Hispanic/Latino; 1% Two or more races, non-Hispanic/Latino; 0.7% Race/ethnicity unknown; 0.1% international; 11% transferred in; 5% live on campus. *Retention:* 88% of full-time freshmen returned.

Freshmen *Admission:* 2,304 applied, 1,698 admitted, 455 enrolled. *Average high school GPA:* 3. *Test scores:* SAT critical reading scores over 500: 60%; SAT math scores over 500: 70%; SAT writing scores over 500: 61%; ACT scores over 18: 100%; SAT critical reading scores over 600: 17%; SAT math scores over 600: 23%; SAT writing scores over 600: 15%; ACT scores over 24: 73%; SAT critical reading scores over 700: 1%; SAT math scores over 700: 1%; SAT writing scores over 700: 2%; ACT scores over 30: 17%.

Faculty *Total:* 674, 27% full-time, 33% with terminal degrees. *Student/faculty ratio:* 10:1.

Academics *Calendar:* 4-1-4. *Degrees:* associate, bachelor's, master's, doctoral, and post-master's certificates. *Special study options:* academic remediation for entering students, adult/continuing education programs, advanced placement credit, double majors, English as a second language, honors programs, independent study, internships, part-time degree program, services for LD students, student-designed majors, study abroad, summer session for credit. *ROTC:* Army (c), Navy (c), .

Computers on Campus 457 computers/terminals are available on campus for general student use. Students can access the following: computer help desk, free student e-mail accounts, online (class) grades, online (class) registration, online (class) schedules. Campuswide network is available. 100% of college-

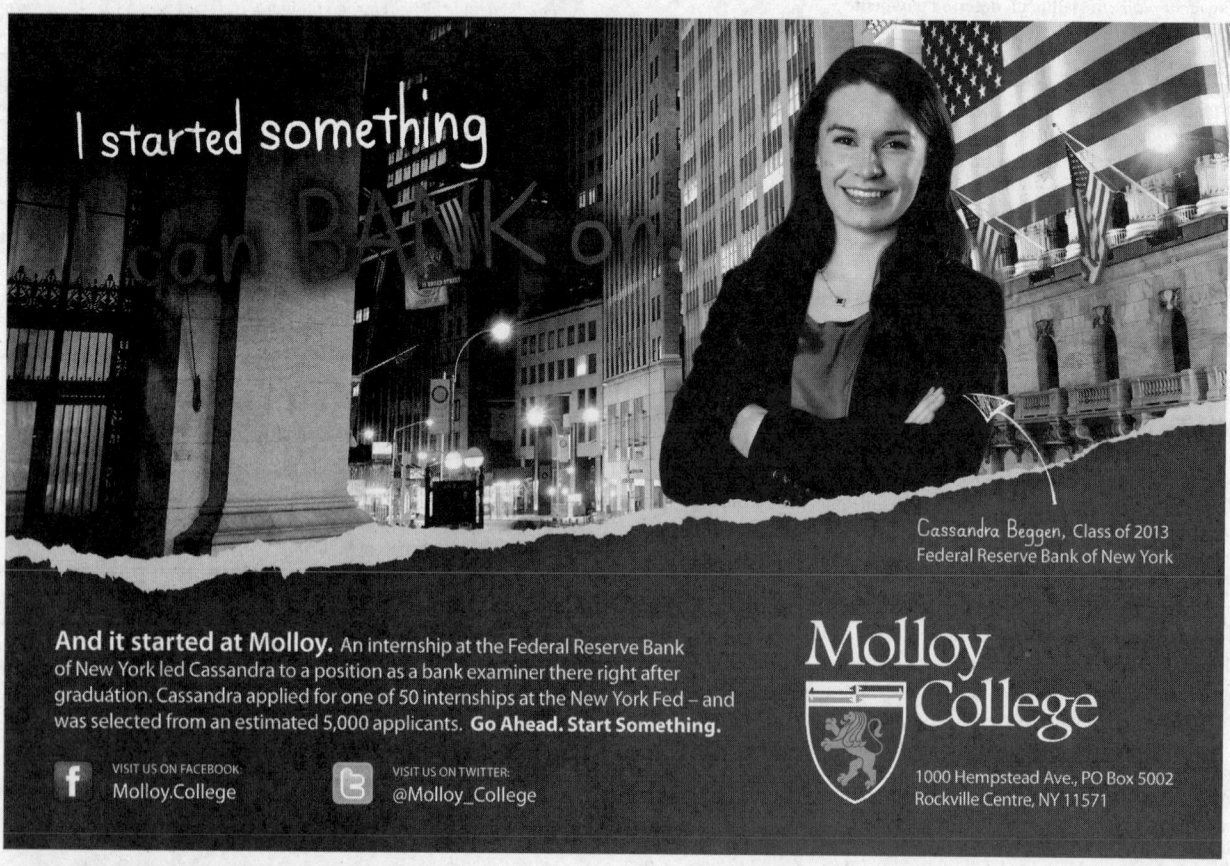

owned or -operated housing units are wired for high-speed Internet access. Wireless service is available via entire campus.

Student Life *Housing options:* coed. Campus housing is university owned. Freshman applicants given priority for college housing. *Activities and organizations:* drama/theater group, student-run newspaper, choral group, Men's Rugby, Women's Rugby, Molloy Student Government, Molloy Nursing Student Association, Student Media. *Campus security:* 24-hour emergency response devices and patrols, late-night transport/escort service. *Student services:* health clinic, personal/psychological counseling, women's center, legal services.

Athletics Member NCAA. All Division II. *Intercollegiate sports:* baseball M(s), basketball M(s)/W(s), cross-country running M(s)/W(s), lacrosse M(s)/W(s), soccer M(s)/W(s), softball W(s), tennis W(s), track and field M(s)/W(s), volleyball W(s). *Intramural sports:* cheerleading W(c), equestrian sports W(c), rugby M(c)/W(c), ultimate Frisbee M(c)/W.

Standardized Tests *Required:* SAT or ACT (for admission).

Costs (2012–13) *Comprehensive fee:* $36,500 includes full-time tuition ($23,410), mandatory fees ($1010), and room and board ($12,080). Full-time tuition and fees vary according to degree level. Part-time tuition: $770 per credit hour. Part-time tuition and fees vary according to degree level. *College room only:* $9090. Room and board charges vary according to board plan. *Payment plan:* installment. *Waivers:* employees or children of employees.

Financial Aid Of all full-time matriculated undergraduates who enrolled in 2011, 2,583 applied for aid, 2,319 were judged to have need, 224 had their need fully met. In 2011, 163 non-need-based awards were made. *Average percent of need met:* 50%. *Average financial aid package:* $13,818. *Average need-based loan:* $5988. *Average need-based gift aid:* $9438. *Average non-need-based aid:* $8006. *Average indebtedness upon graduation:* $29,823. *Financial aid deadline:* 5/1.

Applying *Options:* electronic application, early admission, early action, deferred entrance. *Application fee:* $30. *Required for some:* essay or personal statement, high school transcript, 1 letter of recommendation. *Recommended:* interview. *Application deadlines:* rolling (freshmen), rolling (transfers). *Notification:* continuous (freshmen), continuous (transfers).

Freshman Application Contact Ms. Marguerite Lane, Dean of Admissions, Molloy College, 1000 Hempstead Avenue, PO Box 5002, Rockville Centre, NY 11571-5002. *Phone:* 516-678-5000 Ext. 6240. *Toll-free phone:* 888-4MOLLOY. *Fax:* 516-256-2247. *E-mail:* admissions@molloy.edu. *Website:* http://www.molloy.edu/.

See previous page for display ad and page 1398 for the College Close-Up.

Monroe College

Bronx, New York

Freshman Application Contact Monroe College, Monroe College Way, Bronx, NY 10468-5407. *Phone:* 718-933-6700 Ext. 8246. *Toll-free phone:* 800-55MONROE.
Website: http://www.monroecollege.edu/.

Monroe College

New Rochelle, New York

Freshman Application Contact Ms. Lisa Scorca, High School Admissions, Monroe College, 434 Main Street, New Rochelle, NY 10801. *Phone:* 914-654-3200. *Toll-free phone:* 800-55MONROE. *E-mail:* lscorca@monroecollege.edu.
Website: http://www.monroecollege.edu/.

Morrisville State College

Morrisville, New York

- **State-supported** 4-year, founded 1908, part of State University of New York System
- **Rural** 185-acre campus with easy access to Syracuse
- **Coed** 3,095 undergraduate students, 87% full-time, 48% women, 52% men
- **Moderately difficult** entrance level, 64% of applicants were admitted

Undergraduates 2,708 full-time, 387 part-time. Students come from 18 states and territories; 8 other countries; 5% are from out of state; 21% Black or African American, non-Hispanic/Latino; 0.5% Hispanic/Latino; 1% Asian, non-Hispanic/Latino; 0.1% Native Hawaiian or other Pacific Islander, non-His-

panic/Latino; 0.8% American Indian or Alaska Native, non-Hispanic/Latino; 4% Two or more races, non-Hispanic/Latino; 7% Race/ethnicity unknown; 8% transferred in; 66% live on campus. *Retention:* 57% of full-time freshmen returned.

Freshmen *Admission:* 4,251 applied, 2,721 admitted, 905 enrolled. *Average high school GPA:* 2.9. *Test scores:* SAT critical reading scores over 500: 28%; SAT math scores over 500: 20%; SAT critical reading scores over 600: 4%; SAT math scores over 600: 2%.

Faculty *Total:* 252, 57% full-time, 38% with terminal degrees. *Student/faculty ratio:* 17:1.

Academics *Calendar:* semesters. *Degrees:* certificates, associate, and bachelor's. *Special study options:* academic remediation for entering students, advanced placement credit, cooperative education, distance learning, double majors, independent study, internships, off-campus study, part-time degree program, services for LD students, student-designed majors, summer session for credit. *ROTC:* Army (c), Air Force (c).

Computers on Campus 150 computers/terminals and 9,120 ports are available on campus for general student use. Students can access the following: campus intranet, computer help desk, free student e-mail accounts, online (class) grades, online (class) registration, online (class) schedules. Campus-wide network is available. 100% of college-owned or -operated housing units are wired for high-speed Internet access. Wireless service is available via entire campus.

Student Life *Housing:* on-campus residence required through sophomore year. *Options:* coed, disabled students. Campus housing is university owned. Freshman campus housing is guaranteed. *Activities and organizations:* drama/theater group, student-run newspaper, radio station, choral group, African Student Union Black Alliance, Student Government Organization, Agriculture Club, Latino-American Student Association, WCVM (student radio station). *Campus security:* 24-hour emergency response devices and patrols, student patrols, late-night transport/escort service, controlled dormitory access. *Student services:* health clinic, personal/psychological counseling, legal services.

Athletics Member NCAA. All Division III. *Intercollegiate sports:* basketball M/W, cross-country running M/W, equestrian sports M/W, field hockey W, football M, ice hockey M, lacrosse M/W, soccer M/W, softball W, volleyball W. *Intramural sports:* badminton M/W, basketball M/W, ice hockey M/W, skiing (downhill) M/W, soccer M/W, softball M/W, table tennis M/W, tennis M/W, ultimate Frisbee M/W, volleyball M/W.

Standardized Tests *Required for some:* SAT (for admission), ACT (for admission), SAT or ACT (for admission).

Costs (2013–14) *Tuition:* state resident $5570 full-time, $232 per credit hour part-time; nonresident $9740 full-time, $406 per credit hour part-time. Full-time tuition and fees vary according to degree level. Part-time tuition and fees vary according to course load and degree level. *Required fees:* $2222 full-time, $175 per credit hour part-time. *Room and board:* $10,720; room only: $6160. Room and board charges vary according to board plan and housing facility. *Payment plans:* installment, deferred payment.

Financial Aid Of all full-time matriculated undergraduates who enrolled in 2009, 2,785 applied for aid, 2,515 were judged to have need, 32 had their need fully met. 160 Federal Work-Study jobs (averaging $1740). In 2009, 60 non-need-based awards were made. *Average financial aid package:* $9249. *Average need-based loan:* $3659. *Average need-based gift aid:* $5900. *Average non-need-based aid:* $1597. *Average indebtedness upon graduation:* $21,067.

Applying *Options:* electronic application, deferred entrance. *Application fee:* $50. *Required:* essay or personal statement, high school transcript, 1 letter of recommendation. *Recommended:* minimum 2.0 GPA, interview. *Application deadlines:* rolling (freshmen), rolling (out-of-state freshmen), rolling (transfers). *Notification:* continuous (freshmen), continuous (out-of-state freshmen), continuous (transfers).

Freshman Application Contact Morrisville State College, PO Box 901, Morrisville, NY 13408-0901. *Phone:* 315-684-6046. *Toll-free phone:* 800-258-0111.
Website: http://www.morrisville.edu/.

Mount Saint Mary College

Newburgh, New York

- **Independent** comprehensive, founded 1960
- **Suburban** 86-acre campus with easy access to New York City
- **Endowment** $4.8 million
- **Coed** 2,286 undergraduate students, 81% full-time, 72% women, 28% men
- **Moderately difficult** entrance level, 81% of applicants were admitted

Undergraduates 1,863 full-time, 423 part-time. Students come from 13 states and territories; 11% are from out of state; 6% Black or African American, non-Hispanic/Latino; 11% Hispanic/Latino; 3% Asian, non-Hispanic/Latino; 0.2%

Native Hawaiian or other Pacific Islander, non-Hispanic/Latino; 0.8% American Indian or Alaska Native, non-Hispanic/Latino; 1% Two or more races, non-Hispanic/Latino; 19% Race/ethnicity unknown; 0.1% international; 8% transferred in; 44% live on campus. *Retention:* 70% of full-time freshmen returned.

Freshmen *Admission:* 3,472 applied, 2,817 admitted, 442 enrolled. *Average high school GPA:* 3.1. *Test scores:* SAT critical reading scores over 500: 51%; SAT math scores over 500: 53%; SAT writing scores over 500: 50%; ACT scores over 18: 91%; SAT critical reading scores over 600: 8%; SAT math scores over 600: 13%; SAT writing scores over 600: 9%; ACT scores over 24: 32%; SAT critical reading scores over 700: 1%; ACT scores over 30: 1%.

Faculty *Total:* 279, 32% full-time, 42% with terminal degrees. *Student/faculty ratio:* 14:1.

Academics *Calendar:* semesters. *Degrees:* certificates, bachelor's, master's, and post-master's certificates. *Special study options:* academic remediation for entering students, accelerated degree program, adult/continuing education programs, advanced placement credit, cooperative education, distance learning, double majors, freshman honors college, honors programs, independent study, internships, off-campus study, part-time degree program, services for LD students, student-designed majors, study abroad, summer session for credit. *ROTC:* Army (c). *Unusual degree programs:* 3-2 social work with Fordham University; publishing, counseling with Pace University.

Computers on Campus 576 computers/terminals are available on campus for general student use. Students can access the following: campus intranet, computer help desk, free student e-mail accounts, online (class) grades, online (class) registration, online (class) schedules, Intranet. Campuswide network is available. 100% of college-owned or -operated housing units are wired for high-speed Internet access. Wireless service is available via entire campus.

Student Life *Housing:* on-campus residence required through junior year. *Options:* coed, men-only, women-only, disabled students. Campus housing is university owned. Freshman applicants given priority for college housing. *Activities and organizations:* drama/theater group, student-run newspaper, radio station, choral group, Student Government Association, Different Stages, Big Brothers/Big Sisters, Dance Team and Cheerleading, Habitat for Humanity. *Campus security:* 24-hour emergency response devices and patrols, student patrols, late-night transport/escort service, controlled dormitory access, monitored surveillance cameras in all residence halls. *Student services:* health clinic, personal/psychological counseling.

Athletics Member NCAA. All Division III. *Intercollegiate sports:* baseball M, basketball M/W, cross-country running M/W, lacrosse M/W, soccer M/W, softball W, swimming and diving M/W, tennis M/W, track and field M/W, volleyball W. *Intramural sports:* basketball M/W, bowling M/W, cheerleading W(c), football M, golf M/W, soccer M/W, softball M/W, swimming and diving M/W, table tennis M/W, volleyball M/W.

Standardized Tests *Required:* SAT or ACT (for admission).

Costs (2013–14) *Comprehensive fee:* $39,540 includes full-time tuition ($25,300), mandatory fees ($950), and room and board ($13,290). Full-time tuition and fees vary according to class time, location, and program. Part-time tuition: $843 per credit hour. Part-time tuition and fees vary according to class time, location, and program. *College room only:* $7698. Room and board charges vary according to board plan and housing facility. *Payment plan:* installment. *Waivers:* employees or children of employees.

Financial Aid Of all full-time matriculated undergraduates who enrolled in 2012, 1,705 applied for aid, 1,502 were judged to have need, 272 had their need fully met. 273 Federal Work-Study jobs (averaging $1396). In 2012, 232 non-need-based awards were made. *Average percent of need met:* 60%. *Average financial aid package:* $15,564. *Average need-based loan:* $4269. *Average need-based gift aid:* $11,839. *Average non-need-based aid:* $8243. *Average indebtedness upon graduation:* $28,716. *Financial aid deadline:* 3/1.

Applying *Options:* electronic application, early admission, deferred entrance. *Application fee:* $45. *Required:* essay or personal statement, high school transcript. *Required for some:* 2 letters of recommendation, interview. *Recommended:* minimum 3.0 GPA, 2 letters of recommendation. *Application deadline:* 8/15 (freshmen). *Notification:* continuous (freshmen).

Freshman Application Contact Ms. Nancy Scaffidi-Clark, Director of Admissions, Mount Saint Mary College, 330 Powell Avenue, Newburgh, NY 12550-3494. *Phone:* 845-569-3254. *Toll-free phone:* 888-937-6762. *Fax:* 845-562-6762. *E-mail:* admissions@msmc.edu. *Website:* http://www.msmc.edu/.

Nazareth College of Rochester
Rochester, New York

- **Independent** comprehensive, founded 1924
- **Suburban** 150-acre campus
- **Endowment** $53.9 million
- **Coed** 2,456 undergraduate students, 95% full-time, 77% women, 23% men
- **Moderately difficult** entrance level, 71% of applicants were admitted

Undergraduates 2,321 full-time, 135 part-time. Students come from 28 states and territories; 21 other countries; 7% are from out of state; 5% Black or African American, non-Hispanic/Latino; 4% Hispanic/Latino; 2% Asian, non-Hispanic/Latino; 0.5% American Indian or Alaska Native, non-Hispanic/Latino; 0.9% Two or more races, non-Hispanic/Latino; 13% Race/ethnicity unknown; 2% international; 6% transferred in; 56% live on campus. *Retention:* 82% of full-time freshmen returned.

Freshmen *Admission:* 3,109 applied, 2,212 admitted, 472 enrolled. *Average high school GPA:* 3.45. *Test scores:* SAT critical reading scores over 500: 79%; SAT math scores over 500: 81%; ACT scores over 18: 99%; SAT critical reading scores over 600: 30%; SAT math scores over 600: 41%; ACT scores over 24: 66%; SAT critical reading scores over 700: 5%; SAT math scores over 700: 4%; ACT scores over 30: 4%.

Faculty *Total:* 461, 38% full-time, 46% with terminal degrees. *Student/faculty ratio:* 10:1.

Academics *Calendar:* semesters. *Degrees:* bachelor's, master's, doctoral, and post-master's certificates. *Special study options:* academic remediation for entering students, adult/continuing education programs, advanced placement credit, cooperative education, double majors, English as a second language, honors programs, independent study, internships, off-campus study, part-time degree program, services for LD students, study abroad, summer session for credit. *ROTC:* Army (c), Air Force (c).

Computers on Campus 240 computers/terminals are available on campus for general student use. Students can access the following: computer help desk, free student e-mail accounts, online (class) grades, online (class) registration, online (class) schedules. Campuswide network is available. 100% of college-owned or -operated housing units are wired for high-speed Internet access. Wireless service is available via classrooms, computer centers, dorm rooms, libraries, student centers.

Student Life *Housing:* on-campus residence required through sophomore year. *Options:* coed, disabled students. Campus housing is university owned. Freshman campus housing is guaranteed. *Activities and organizations:* drama/theater group, student-run newspaper, radio station, choral group, Student Activities Council, intramurals and recreation, Theater League, Center for Spirituality Council, NAZ Ultimate Frisbee. *Campus security:* 24-hour emergency response devices and patrols, student patrols, late-night transport/escort service, controlled dormitory access, alarm system, security beeper, lighted pathways. *Student services:* health clinic, personal/psychological counseling, women's center.

Athletics Member NCAA. All Division III. *Intercollegiate sports:* basketball M/W, cross-country running M/W, equestrian sports M/W, field hockey W, golf M/W, ice hockey M, lacrosse M/W, soccer M/W, softball W, swimming and diving M/W, tennis M/W, track and field M/W, volleyball M/W. *Intramural sports:* basketball M/W, racquetball M/W, soccer M/W, ultimate Frisbee M/W, volleyball M/W.

Costs (2012–13) *Comprehensive fee:* $38,366 includes full-time tuition ($26,048), mandatory fees ($1174), and room and board ($11,144). Full-time tuition and fees vary according to course load and program. Part-time tuition: $621 per credit hour. *Required fees:* $25 per term part-time. *Room and board:* Room and board charges vary according to board plan and housing facility. *Payment plan:* installment. *Waivers:* minority students, children of alumni, and employees or children of employees.

Financial Aid Of all full-time matriculated undergraduates who enrolled in 2012, 1,748 applied for aid, 1,589 were judged to have need, 451 had their need fully met. 1,008 Federal Work-Study jobs (averaging $2021). In 2012, 155 non-need-based awards were made. *Average percent of need met:* 79%. *Average financial aid package:* $23,635. *Average need-based loan:* $4362. *Average need-based gift aid:* $14,509. *Average non-need-based aid:* $17,470. *Average indebtedness upon graduation:* $30,500.

Applying *Options:* electronic application, early admission, early decision, early action, deferred entrance. *Application fee:* $45. *Required:* essay or personal statement, high school transcript, 1 letter of recommendation. *Required for some:* audition/portfolio review. *Recommended:* interview. *Application deadlines:* 2/15 (freshmen), 5/15 (transfers), 12/1 (early action). *Early decision deadline:* 11/1. *Notification:* continuous until 3/1 (freshmen), continuous until 2/15 (transfers), 12/1 (early decision), 1/15 (early action).

Freshman Application Contact Mr. Thomas DaRin, Vice President for Enrollment Management, Nazareth College of Rochester, 4245 East Avenue,

Rochester, NY 14618-3790. *Phone:* 585-389-2830. *Toll-free phone:* 800-462-3944. *Fax:* 585-389-2826. *E-mail:* admissions@naz.edu. *Website:* http://www.naz.edu/.

The New School for Jazz and Contemporary Music

New York, New York

- **Independent** 4-year, founded 1986, part of The New School
- **Urban** campus with easy access to Manhattan
- **Coed** 269 undergraduate students, 96% full-time, 19% women, 81% men
- **Very difficult** entrance level, 73% of applicants were admitted

Undergraduates 257 full-time, 12 part-time. 51% are from out of state; 9% Black or African American, non-Hispanic/Latino; 7% Hispanic/Latino; 3% Asian, non-Hispanic/Latino; 5% Two or more races, non-Hispanic/Latino; 3% Race/ethnicity unknown; 33% international; 14% transferred in; 27% live on campus. *Retention:* 80% of full-time freshmen returned.

Freshmen *Admission:* 416 applied, 304 admitted, 49 enrolled.

Faculty *Total:* 59, 5% full-time. *Student/faculty ratio:* 11:1.

Academics *Calendar:* semesters. *Degree:* bachelor's. *Special study options:* academic remediation for entering students, advanced placement credit, double majors, English as a second language, independent study, internships, services for LD students.

Computers on Campus Students can access the following: campus intranet, computer help desk, free student e-mail accounts, online (class) grades, online (class) registration, online (class) schedules, online portal. Campuswide network is available. 100% of college-owned or -operated housing units are wired for high-speed Internet access. Wireless service is available via entire campus.

Student Life *Housing options:* coed, disabled students. Campus housing is university owned and leased by the school. Freshman applicants given priority for college housing. *Activities and organizations:* drama/theater group, student-run newspaper, radio station, choral group. *Campus security:* 24-hour emergency response devices, controlled dormitory access. *Student services:* health clinic, personal/psychological counseling.

Costs (2013–14) *Comprehensive fee:* $55,526 includes full-time tuition ($37,950), mandatory fees ($276), and room and board ($17,300). Part-time tuition: $1245 per credit.

Applying *Options:* electronic application, deferred entrance. *Application fee:* $100. *Required:* essay or personal statement, high school transcript, 1 letter of recommendation, audition, pre-screen tape/CD. *Application deadlines:* 1/1 (freshmen), 1/1 (transfers). *Notification:* continuous (freshmen), 4/1 (transfers).

Freshman Application Contact Ms. Terri Lucas, Jazz Admissions, The New School for Jazz and Contemporary Music, 55 West 13th Street, 5th Floor, New York, NY 10011. *Phone:* 212-229-5896. *Toll-free phone:* 800-292-3040. *Fax:* 212-229-8936. *E-mail:* jazzadm@newschool.edu. *Website:* http://www.jazz.newschool.edu/.

See page 575 for display ad and page 1414 for the College Close-Up.

The New School for Public Engagement

New York, New York

- **Independent** comprehensive, founded 1919, part of The New School
- **Urban** campus with easy access to Manhattan
- **Coed** 594 undergraduate students, 46% full-time, 61% women, 39% men
- **Moderately difficult** entrance level, 91% of applicants were admitted

Undergraduates 275 full-time, 319 part-time. Students come from 91 other countries; 36% are from out of state; 10% Black or African American, non-Hispanic/Latino; 12% Hispanic/Latino; 4% Asian, non-Hispanic/Latino; 0.2% Native Hawaiian or other Pacific Islander, non-Hispanic/Latino; 0.3% American Indian or Alaska Native, non-Hispanic/Latino; 4% Two or more races, non-Hispanic/Latino; 7% Race/ethnicity unknown; 8% international; 20% transferred in. *Retention:* 67% of full-time freshmen returned.

Freshmen *Admission:* 11 applied, 10 admitted, 4 enrolled.

Faculty *Total:* 385, 17% full-time.

Academics *Calendar:* semesters. *Degrees:* certificates, bachelor's, master's, and postbachelor's certificates. *Special study options:* adult/continuing education programs, advanced placement credit, distance learning, English as a second language, independent study, internships, part-time degree program,

services for LD students, student-designed majors, study abroad, summer session for credit.

Computers on Campus Students can access the following: campus intranet, computer help desk, free student e-mail accounts, online (class) grades, online (class) registration, online (class) schedules, online portal, unlimited wireless. Campuswide network is available. 100% of college-owned or -operated housing units are wired for high-speed Internet access. Wireless service is available via entire campus.

Student Life *Housing options:* coed, disabled students. Campus housing is university owned and leased by the school. *Activities and organizations:* drama/theater group, student-run newspaper, radio station, choral group. *Campus security:* 24-hour emergency response devices, controlled dormitory access, trained security personnel in central buildings. *Student services:* health clinic, personal/psychological counseling.

Financial Aid Of all full-time matriculated undergraduates who enrolled in 2010, 264 applied for aid, 246 were judged to have need, 8 had their need fully met. In 2010, 4 non-need-based awards were made. *Average percent of need met:* 67%. *Average financial aid package:* $23,660. *Average need-based loan:* $11,430. *Average need-based gift aid:* $10,805. *Average non-need-based aid:* $6625.

Applying *Options:* electronic application, deferred entrance. *Application fee:* $50. *Required:* essay or personal statement, resume and college transcripts. *Required for some:* high school transcript, interview. *Application deadline:* 6/1 (transfers). *Notification:* continuous (transfers).

Freshman Application Contact Ms. Cory Meyers, Assistant Director of Admissions, The New School for Public Engagement, 72 Fifth Avenue, Room 304, New York, NY 10011. *Phone:* 212-229-5630. *Toll-free phone:* 800-292-3040. *Fax:* 212-627-2695. *E-mail:* nsadmissions@newschool.edu. *Website:* http://www.newschool.edu/public-engagement/.

See page 575 for display ad and page 1414 for the College Close-Up.

New York City College of Technology of the City University of New York

Brooklyn, New York

- **State and locally supported** 4-year, founded 1946, part of City University of New York System
- **Urban** campus
- **Coed** 16,207 undergraduate students, 62% full-time, 45% women, 55% men
- **Noncompetitive** entrance level, 77% of applicants were admitted

Undergraduates 10,018 full-time, 6,189 part-time. Students come from 14 states and territories; 138 other countries; 34% Black or African American, non-Hispanic/Latino; 29% Hispanic/Latino; 17% Asian, non-Hispanic/Latino; 0.4% Native Hawaiian or other Pacific Islander, non-Hispanic/Latino; 0.4% American Indian or Alaska Native, non-Hispanic/Latino; 0.6% Two or more races, non-Hispanic/Latino; 5% international; 8% transferred in. *Retention:* 77% of full-time freshmen returned.

Freshmen *Admission:* 16,870 applied, 12,957 admitted, 2,861 enrolled.

Faculty *Total:* 1,350, 32% full-time. *Student/faculty ratio:* 16:1.

Academics *Calendar:* semesters. *Degrees:* certificates, associate, and bachelor's. *Special study options:* academic remediation for entering students, accelerated degree program, adult/continuing education programs, advanced placement credit, distance learning, English as a second language, freshman honors college, honors programs, independent study, internships, off-campus study, part-time degree program, services for LD students, student-designed majors, study abroad, summer session for credit.

Computers on Campus 340 computers/terminals are available on campus for general student use. Students can access the following: campus intranet, computer help desk, free student e-mail accounts, online (class) grades, online (class) registration, online (class) schedules. Campuswide network is available. Wireless service is available via classrooms, computer centers, computer labs, learning centers, libraries, student centers.

Student Life *Housing:* college housing not available. *Activities and organizations:* drama/theater group, student-run newspaper, choral group, International Business Organization (IBO), NYCCT—Mock Trial Club, Chess Club, Women in Islam, ASCE-Student Chapter of American Society of Civil Engineering. *Campus security:* 24-hour emergency response devices and patrols. *Student services:* health clinic, personal/psychological counseling, women's center.

Athletics *Intramural sports:* badminton M/W, basketball M/W, soccer M/W, table tennis M/W, tennis M/W, volleyball M/W, weight lifting M/W.

Standardized Tests *Required for some:* SAT or ACT (for admission).

Costs (2013–14) *Tuition:* state resident $5430 full-time, $230 per credit part-time; nonresident $14,550 full-time, $485 per credit part-time. *Required fees:* $339 full-time, $85 per term part-time. *Payment plan:* installment. *Waivers:* employees or children of employees.

Financial Aid Of all full-time matriculated undergraduates who enrolled in 2012, 8,718 applied for aid, 8,272 were judged to have need, 350 had their need fully met. In 2012, 128 non-need-based awards were made. *Average percent of need met:* 57%. *Average financial aid package:* $8867. *Average need-based loan:* $4267. *Average need-based gift aid:* $8356. *Average non-need-based aid:* $233.

Applying *Options:* electronic application, deferred entrance. *Application fee:* $65. *Required:* high school transcript. *Application deadlines:* 2/1 (freshmen), 2/1 (transfers). *Notification:* continuous until 2/1 (freshmen), 4/1 (transfers).

Freshman Application Contact Alexis Chaconis, Director of Admissions, New York City College of Technology of the City University of New York, 300 Jay Street, Brooklyn, NY 11201-2983. *Phone:* 718-260-5500. *E-mail:* achaconis@citytech.cuny.edu.
Website: http://www.citytech.cuny.edu/.

New York College of Health Professions

Syosset, New York

Director of Admissions Ms. Mary Rodas, Associate Director of Admissions, New York College of Health Professions, 6801 Jericho Turnpike, Syosset, NY 11791-4413. *Toll-free phone:* 800-922-7337 Ext. 351. *E-mail:* rdodas@nycollege.edu.
Website: http://www.nycollege.edu/.

New York Institute of Technology

Old Westbury, New York

- **Independent** university, founded 1955
- **Suburban** 1050-acre campus with easy access to New York City
- **Endowment** $54.8 million
- **Coed** 4,796 undergraduate students, 84% full-time, 39% women, 61% men
- **Moderately difficult** entrance level, 66% of applicants were admitted

Undergraduates 4,017 full-time, 779 part-time. Students come from 32 states and territories; 86 other countries; 11% are from out of state; 8% Black or African American, non-Hispanic/Latino; 12% Hispanic/Latino; 14% Asian, non-Hispanic/Latino; 0.1% Native Hawaiian or other Pacific Islander, non-Hispanic/Latino; 0.3% American Indian or Alaska Native, non-Hispanic/Latino; 0.9% Two or more races, non-Hispanic/Latino; 30% Race/ethnicity unknown; 12% international; 10% transferred in; 15% live on campus. *Retention:* 70% of full-time freshmen returned.

Freshmen *Admission:* 6,546 applied, 4,314 admitted, 898 enrolled. *Average high school GPA:* 3.47. *Test scores:* SAT critical reading scores over 500: 69%; SAT math scores over 500: 92%; ACT scores over 18: 98%; SAT critical reading scores over 600: 21%; SAT math scores over 600: 47%; ACT scores over 24: 56%; SAT critical reading scores over 700: 4%; SAT math scores over 700: 11%; ACT scores over 30: 14%.

Faculty *Total:* 1,248, 23% full-time. *Student/faculty ratio:* 11:1.

Academics *Calendar:* semesters. *Degrees:* certificates, associate, bachelor's, master's, doctoral, post-master's, and postbachelor's certificates. *Special study options:* academic remediation for entering students, accelerated degree program, adult/continuing education programs, advanced placement credit, cooperative education, distance learning, double majors, English as a second language, external degree program, honors programs, independent study, internships, off-campus study, part-time degree program, services for LD students, student-designed majors, study abroad, summer session for credit. *ROTC:* Army (b), Air Force (b). *Unusual degree programs:* 3-2 Occupational therapy, physical therapy, communication arts, architectural technology/energy management, architectural technology/MBA, mechanical engineering/energy management.

Computers on Campus 1,386 computers/terminals are available on campus for general student use. Students can access the following: e-mail. Campuswide network is available. 100% of college-owned or -operated housing units are wired for high-speed Internet access. Wireless service is available via classrooms, computer centers, computer labs, libraries.

Student Life *Housing options:* coed. Campus housing is university owned and is provided by a third party. Freshman campus housing is guaranteed. *Activities and organizations:* drama/theater group, student-run newspaper, radio and tele-

vision station, choral group, national fraternities, national sororities. *Campus security:* 24-hour emergency response devices and patrols, late-night transport/escort service, controlled dormitory access. *Student services:* health clinic, personal/psychological counseling, women's center.

Athletics Member NCAA. All Division II except baseball (Division I). *Intercollegiate sports:* baseball M(s), basketball M(s)/W(s), cross-country running M(s)/W(s), lacrosse M(s), soccer M(s)/W(s), softball W(s), tennis M(s)/W(s), volleyball W(s). *Intramural sports:* basketball M/W, soccer M/W, softball W, tennis M/W, volleyball W.

Standardized Tests *Required:* SAT or ACT (for admission).

Costs (2012–13) *Comprehensive fee:* $40,590 includes full-time tuition ($28,020), mandatory fees ($920), and room and board ($11,650). Full-time tuition and fees vary according to course load and program. Part-time tuition: $950 per credit hour. Part-time tuition and fees vary according to course load. *Required fees:* $400 per term part-time. *College room only:* $7320. Room and board charges vary according to board plan, housing facility, and location. *Payment plan:* installment. *Waivers:* senior citizens and employees or children of employees.

Financial Aid Of all full-time matriculated undergraduates who enrolled in 2012, 3,124 applied for aid, 2,917 were judged to have need. In 2012, 433 non-need-based awards were made. *Average financial aid package:* $22,693. *Average need-based loan:* $5375. *Average need-based gift aid:* $6468. *Average non-need-based aid:* $14,333.

Applying *Options:* electronic application, early admission, early decision, deferred entrance. *Application fee:* $50. *Required:* essay or personal statement, high school transcript, 2 letters of recommendation. *Required for some:* interview, Occupational Therapy and Physical Therapy requires 100 volunteer hours. *Recommended:* minimum 3.0 GPA. *Application deadlines:* rolling (freshmen), rolling (out-of-state freshmen), rolling (transfers). *Notification:* continuous (freshmen), continuous (out-of-state freshmen), continuous (transfers).

Freshman Application Contact Ms. Doreen Meyer, Director of Financial Aid, New York Institute of Technology, PO Box 8000, Old Westbury, NY 11568. *Phone:* 516-686-1083. *Toll-free phone:* 800-345-NYIT. *Fax:* 516-686-7613. *E-mail:* admissions@nyit.edu.
Website: http://www.nyit.edu/.

New York School of Interior Design

New York, New York

- **Independent** comprehensive, founded 1916
- **Urban** 1-acre campus
- **Endowment** $3.1 million
- **Coed, primarily women** 556 undergraduate students, 30% full-time, 87% women, 13% men
- **Moderately difficult** entrance level, 38% of applicants were admitted

Undergraduates 166 full-time, 390 part-time. Students come from 24 states and territories; 28 other countries; 33% are from out of state; 3% Black or African American, non-Hispanic/Latino; 8% Hispanic/Latino; 6% Asian, non-Hispanic/Latino; 1% Two or more races, non-Hispanic/Latino; 17% Race/ethnicity unknown; 16% international; 8% transferred in; 1% live on campus. *Retention:* 75% of full-time freshmen returned.

Freshmen *Admission:* 156 applied, 59 admitted, 40 enrolled. *Average high school GPA:* 3.14. *Test scores:* SAT critical reading scores over 500: 50%; SAT math scores over 500: 54%; SAT writing scores over 500: 47%; SAT critical reading scores over 600: 9%; SAT math scores over 600: 27%; SAT writing scores over 600: 4%.

Faculty *Total:* 109, 7% full-time, 61% with terminal degrees. *Student/faculty ratio:* 6:1.

Academics *Calendar:* semesters. *Degrees:* certificates, associate, bachelor's, and master's. *Special study options:* adult/continuing education programs, advanced placement credit, English as a second language, external degree program, independent study, internships, part-time degree program, services for LD students, summer session for credit.

Computers on Campus 135 computers/terminals are available on campus for general student use. Students can access the following: free student e-mail accounts, online (class) grades, online (class) registration, online (class) schedules. Campuswide network is available. Wireless service is available via classrooms, libraries.

Student Life *Housing options:* coed. Campus housing is leased by the school and is provided by a third party. *Activities and organizations:* American Society of Interior Designers, Contract Club, Student Council. *Campus security:* security during school hours.

Standardized Tests *Required for some:* SAT or ACT (for admission).

Costs (2013–14) *Tuition:* $27,324 full-time, $828 per credit part-time. Full-time tuition and fees vary according to course load. Part-time tuition and fees vary according to course load. *Required fees:* $570 full-time, $570 per term part-time. *Room only:* $14,400. *Payment plan:* installment. *Waivers:* employees or children of employees.

Financial Aid Of all full-time matriculated undergraduates who enrolled in 2011, 110 applied for aid, 106 were judged to have need, 1 had their need fully met. 24 Federal Work-Study jobs (averaging $1800). In 2011, 6 non-need-based awards were made. *Average percent of need met:* 29%. *Average financial aid package:* $9590. *Average need-based loan:* $3825. *Average need-based gift aid:* $7394. *Average non-need-based aid:* $8390. *Average indebtedness upon graduation:* $35,502.

Applying *Options:* electronic application, deferred entrance. *Application fee:* $60. *Required:* essay or personal statement, high school transcript, minimum 2.8 GPA, 2 letters of recommendation, portfolio. *Application deadlines:* 2/1 (freshmen), 2/1 (transfers). *Notification:* 4/1 (freshmen), 4/1 (transfers).

Freshman Application Contact Audrey Zahor, Admissions Associate, New York School of Interior Design, 170 East 70th Street, New York, NY 10021-5110. *Phone:* 212-472-1500 Ext. 204. *Toll-free phone:* 800-336-9743 Ext. 204. *Fax:* 212-472-1867. *E-mail:* admissions@nysid.edu. *Website:* http://www.nysid.edu/.

New York University

New York, New York

- **Independent** university, founded 1831
- **Urban** campus
- **Endowment** $2.8 billion
- **Coed** 22,498 undergraduate students, 94% full-time, 60% women, 40% men
- **Most difficult** entrance level, 35% of applicants were admitted

Undergraduates 21,247 full-time, 1,251 part-time. Students come from 52 states and territories; 94 other countries; 65% are from out of state; 5% Black or African American, non-Hispanic/Latino; 10% Hispanic/Latino; 19% Asian, non-Hispanic/Latino; 0.3% American Indian or Alaska Native, non-Hispanic/Latino; 3% Two or more races, non-Hispanic/Latino; 12% Race/ethnicity unknown; 12% international; 3% transferred in; 50% live on campus. *Retention:* 92% of full-time freshmen returned.

Freshmen *Admission:* 42,807 applied, 14,998 admitted, 5,140 enrolled. *Average high school GPA:* 3.6. *Test scores:* SAT critical reading scores over 500: 99%; SAT math scores over 500: 99%; SAT writing scores over 500: 99%; ACT scores over 18: 100%; SAT critical reading scores over 600: 85%; SAT math scores over 600: 87%; SAT writing scores over 600: 90%; ACT scores over 24: 98%; SAT critical reading scores over 700: 33%; SAT math scores over 700: 41%; SAT writing scores over 700: 43%; ACT scores over 30: 54%.

Faculty *Total:* 6,574, 38% full-time, 65% with terminal degrees. *Student/faculty ratio:* 10:1.

Academics *Calendar:* semesters. *Degrees:* certificates, associate, bachelor's, master's, doctoral, post-master's, and postbachelor's certificates. *Special study options:* accelerated degree program, adult/continuing education programs, advanced placement credit, double majors, honors programs, independent study, internships, off-campus study, part-time degree program, services for LD students, student-designed majors, study abroad, summer session for credit. *ROTC:* Army (c), Air Force (c). *Unusual degree programs:* 3-2 engineering with NYU-Polytechnic.

Computers on Campus 4,500 computers/terminals are available on campus for general student use. Students can access the following: computer help desk, free student e-mail accounts, online (class) grades, online (class) registration, online (class) schedules. Campuswide network is available. 100% of college-owned or -operated housing units are wired for high-speed Internet access. Wireless service is available via classrooms, computer labs, learning centers, libraries, student centers.

Student Life *Housing options:* coed, disabled students. Campus housing is university owned and leased by the school. Freshman campus housing is guaranteed. *Activities and organizations:* drama/theater group, student-run newspaper, radio and television station, choral group, Inter-Varsity Christian Fellowship, Asian Cultural Union, Hillel, Latinos Unidos Con Honor y Amistad (LUCHA), South Asian Student Association (SHRUTI), national fraternities, national sororities. *Campus security:* 24-hour emergency response devices and patrols, student patrols, late-night transport/escort service, controlled dormitory access, 24-hour security in residence halls. *Student services:* health clinic, personal/psychological counseling, women's center.

Athletics Member NCAA. All Division III. *Intercollegiate sports:* baseball M(c), basketball M/W, cheerleading M/W, crew M(c)/W(c), cross-country running M/W, equestrian sports M(c)/W(c), fencing M/W, golf M/W, ice hockey M(c), lacrosse M(c)/W(c), soccer M/W, softball W(c), swimming and diving M/W, tennis M/W, track and field M/W, ultimate Frisbee M(c)/W(c), volleyball M/W, wrestling M. *Intramural sports:* badminton M(c)/W(c), basketball M/W, bowling M/W, ice hockey M(c), lacrosse M(c)/W(c), racquetball M/W, soccer M/W, softball M(c)/W(c), squash M/W, table tennis M(c)/W(c), tennis M/W, volleyball M/W, water polo M/W(c).

Standardized Tests *Required:* SAT and SAT Subject Tests or ACT (for admission), Three SAT subject tests or three Advanced Placement Exam scores. These scores must be submitted in the form of: one in literature or the humanities; one in math or science; and one test of the student's choice in any subject (for admission).

Costs (2012–13) *Comprehensive fee:* $59,337 includes full-time tuition ($40,878), mandatory fees ($2326), and room and board ($16,133). Full-time tuition and fees vary according to course load and program. Part-time tuition: $1204 per credit. Part-time tuition and fees vary according to program. *Required fees:* $63 per credit part-time, $434 per term part-time. *Room and board:* Room and board charges vary according to board plan and housing facility. *Payment plans:* tuition prepayment, installment, deferred payment. *Waivers:* employees or children of employees.

Financial Aid Of all full-time matriculated undergraduates who enrolled in 2011, 13,081 applied for aid, 11,515 were judged to have need, 495 had their need fully met. 6,625 Federal Work-Study jobs (averaging $2882). In 2011, 1091 non-need-based awards were made. *Average percent of need met:* 55%. *Average financial aid package:* $29,367. *Average need-based loan:* $5555. *Average need-based gift aid:* $19,497. *Average non-need-based aid:* $7841. *Average indebtedness upon graduation:* $35,104. *Financial aid deadline:* 2/15.

Applying *Options:* electronic application, early decision, deferred entrance. *Application fee:* $70. *Required:* essay or personal statement, high school transcript, 1 letter of recommendation. *Required for some:* An audition or a portfolio is required for some specific programs. *Application deadlines:* 1/1 (freshmen), 1/1 (out-of-state freshmen), 4/1 (transfers). *Early decision deadline:* 11/1 (for plan 1), 1/1 (for plan 2). *Notification:* 4/1 (freshmen), 4/1 (out-of-state freshmen), 12/15 (early decision plan 1), 2/15 (early decision plan 2).

Freshman Application Contact Kristy Materasso, Undergraduate Admissions Processing Center, New York University, 665 Broadway, 11th Floor, New York, NY 10011. *Phone:* 212-998-4500. *Fax:* 212-995-4902. *E-mail:* admissions@nyu.edu. *Website:* http://www.nyu.edu/.

Niagara University

Niagara Falls, New York

- **Independent** comprehensive, founded 1856, affiliated with Roman Catholic Church
- **Suburban** 160-acre campus with easy access to Buffalo, Toronto
- **Endowment** $72.2 million
- **Coed** 3,175 undergraduate students, 89% full-time, 60% women, 40% men
- **Moderately difficult** entrance level, 69% of applicants were admitted

Undergraduates 2,810 full-time, 365 part-time. Students come from 31 states and territories; 12 other countries; 8% are from out of state; 5% Black or African American, non-Hispanic/Latino; 3% Hispanic/Latino; 1% Asian, non-Hispanic/Latino; 0.8% American Indian or Alaska Native, non-Hispanic/Latino; 0.6% Two or more races, non-Hispanic/Latino; 8% Race/ethnicity unknown; 16% international; 6% transferred in; 51% live on campus. *Retention:* 81% of full-time freshmen returned.

Freshmen *Admission:* 3,703 applied, 2,544 admitted, 641 enrolled. *Average high school GPA:* 3.4. *Test scores:* SAT critical reading scores over 500: 59%; SAT math scores over 500: 63%; ACT scores over 18: 94%; SAT critical reading scores over 600: 13%; SAT math scores over 600: 20%; ACT scores over 24: 36%; SAT critical reading scores over 700: 1%; SAT math scores over 700: 1%; ACT scores over 30: 3%.

Faculty *Total:* 333, 47% full-time, 44% with terminal degrees. *Student/faculty ratio:* 11:1.

Academics *Calendar:* semesters. *Degrees:* associate, bachelor's, master's, doctoral, post-master's, and postbachelor's certificates. *Special study options:* academic remediation for entering students, accelerated degree program, advanced placement credit, cooperative education, double majors, English as a second language, freshman honors college, honors programs, independent study, internships, off-campus study, part-time degree program, services for LD students, study abroad, summer session for credit. *ROTC:* Army (b).

Computers on Campus 175 computers/terminals are available on campus for general student use. Students can access the following: campus intranet, computer help desk, free student e-mail accounts, online (class) grades, online (class) registration, online (class) schedules. Campuswide network is available. 100% of college-owned or -operated housing units are wired for high-speed

Internet access. Wireless service is available via classrooms, computer centers, computer labs, libraries, student centers.

Student Life *Housing:* on-campus residence required through sophomore year. *Options:* coed. Campus housing is university owned. Freshman campus housing is guaranteed. *Activities and organizations:* drama/theater group, student-run newspaper, radio station, choral group, Niagara University Community Action Program, student government, Programming Board, national fraternities. *Campus security:* 24-hour emergency response devices and patrols, late-night transport/escort service, controlled dormitory access, 24-hour escort service. *Student services:* health clinic, personal/psychological counseling.

Athletics Member NCAA. All Division I. *Intercollegiate sports:* baseball M(s), basketball M(s)/W(s), cross-country running M(s)/W(s), golf M(s)/W(s), ice hockey M(s), lacrosse M/W(s), soccer M(s)/W(s), softball W(s), swimming and diving M(s)/W(s), tennis M(s)/W(s), track and field W(s), volleyball W(s). *Intramural sports:* basketball M/W, ice hockey M/W, lacrosse M/W, racquetball M/W, rugby M(c)/W(c), skiing (downhill) M(c)/W(c), soccer M/W, softball M/W, volleyball M/W, water polo M/W.

Standardized Tests *Required:* SAT or ACT (for admission).

Costs (2012–13) *Comprehensive fee:* $38,530 includes full-time tuition ($26,100), mandatory fees ($1130), and room and board ($11,300). Part-time tuition: $870 per credit hour. *Payment plans:* installment, deferred payment. *Waivers:* senior citizens and employees or children of employees.

Financial Aid Of all full-time matriculated undergraduates who enrolled in 2012, 2,251 applied for aid, 2,093 were judged to have need, 1,065 had their need fully met. 366 Federal Work-Study jobs (averaging $2910). 41 state and other part-time jobs (averaging $5350). In 2012, 435 non-need-based awards were made. *Average percent of need met:* 83%. *Average financial aid package:* $22,337. *Average need-based loan:* $4819. *Average need-based gift aid:* $17,961. *Average non-need-based aid:* $11,523. *Average indebtedness upon graduation:* $32,114.

Applying *Options:* electronic application, early admission, deferred entrance. *Application fee:* $30. *Required:* high school transcript. *Recommended:* minimum 3.0 GPA, 3 letters of recommendation, interview. *Application deadlines:* 8/1 (freshmen), 8/15 (transfers).

Freshman Application Contact Ms. Christine M. McDermott, Associate Director of Admissions, Niagara University, Niagara University, NY 14109. *Phone:* 716-286-8700 Ext. 8715. *Toll-free phone:* 800-462-2111. *Fax:* 716-286-8733. *E-mail:* admissions@niagara.edu. *Website:* http://www.niagara.edu/.

See this page for display ad and page 1416 for the College Close-Up.

Nyack College

Nyack, New York

- **Independent** comprehensive, founded 1882, affiliated with The Christian and Missionary Alliance
- **Suburban** 125-acre campus with easy access to New York City
- **Coed** 2,040 undergraduate students, 83% full-time, 61% women, 39% men
- **Minimally difficult** entrance level, 93% of applicants were admitted

Undergraduates 1,693 full-time, 347 part-time. Students come from 36 states and territories; 44 other countries; 31% are from out of state; 33% Black or African American, non-Hispanic/Latino; 25% Hispanic/Latino; 10% Asian, non-Hispanic/Latino; 0.4% Native Hawaiian or other Pacific Islander, non-Hispanic/Latino; 0.3% American Indian or Alaska Native, non-Hispanic/Latino; 3% Two or more races, non-Hispanic/Latino; 2% Race/ethnicity unknown; 5% international; 11% transferred in; 70% live on campus. *Retention:* 66% of full-time freshmen returned.

Freshmen *Admission:* 638 applied, 592 admitted, 297 enrolled. *Average high school GPA:* 2.74. *Test scores:* SAT critical reading scores over 500: 34%; SAT math scores over 500: 34%; ACT scores over 18: 70%; SAT critical reading scores over 600: 10%; SAT math scores over 600: 11%; ACT scores over 24: 29%; SAT critical reading scores over 700: 3%; ACT scores over 30: 3%.

Faculty *Total:* 315, 37% full-time, 42% with terminal degrees. *Student/faculty ratio:* 13:1.

Academics *Calendar:* semesters. *Degrees:* associate, bachelor's, master's, and doctoral. *Special study options:* academic remediation for entering students, accelerated degree program, adult/continuing education programs, advanced placement credit, distance learning, double majors, English as a second language, honors programs, independent study, internships, off-campus study, part-time degree program, services for LD students, study abroad, summer session for credit. *Unusual degree programs:* 3-2 Education (BS/MS Childhood Special Education).

Computers on Campus 130 computers/terminals are available on campus for general student use. Students can access the following: campus intranet, computer help desk, free student e-mail accounts, online (class) grades, online

(class) registration, online (class) schedules. Campuswide network is available. 100% of college-owned or -operated housing units are wired for high-speed Internet access. Wireless service is available via entire campus.

Student Life *Housing:* on-campus residence required through sophomore year. *Options:* men-only, women-only, disabled students. Campus housing is university owned. Freshman campus housing is guaranteed. *Activities and organizations:* drama/theater group, student-run newspaper, radio station, choral group. *Campus security:* 24-hour emergency response devices and patrols, late-night transport/escort service. *Student services:* health clinic, personal/psychological counseling.

Athletics Member NCAA, NCCAA. All NCAA Division II. *Intercollegiate sports:* baseball M(s), basketball M(s)/W(s), cheerleading M(s)/W(s), cross-country running M(s)/W(s), golf M(s), lacrosse W(s), soccer M(s)/W(s), softball W(s), volleyball W(s).

Standardized Tests *Required for some:* SAT or ACT (for admission).

Costs (2013–14) *One-time required fee:* $100. *Comprehensive fee:* $31,900 includes full-time tuition ($23,000), mandatory fees ($250), and room and board ($8650). Part-time tuition: $960 per credit hour. *Required fees:* $75 per term part-time. *Room and board:* Room and board charges vary according to board plan and housing facility. *Payment plan:* installment. *Waivers:* employees or children of employees.

Financial Aid Of all full-time matriculated undergraduates who enrolled in 2011, 1,403 applied for aid, 1,343 were judged to have need, 140 had their need fully met. 193 Federal Work-Study jobs (averaging $1084). 53 state and other part-time jobs (averaging $1692). In 2011, 159 non-need-based awards were made. *Average percent of need met:* 64%. *Average financial aid package:* $18,553. *Average need-based loan:* $4643. *Average need-based gift aid:* $13,144. *Average non-need-based aid:* $7668. *Average indebtedness upon graduation:* $32,003.

Applying *Options:* electronic application, deferred entrance. *Application fee:* $25. *Required:* essay or personal statement, high school transcript, minimum 2.0 GPA, 1 letter of recommendation, Signed statement of faith and community life form. *Required for some:* interview. *Application deadlines:* rolling (freshmen), rolling (out-of-state freshmen), rolling (transfers). *Notification:* continuous (freshmen), continuous (out-of-state freshmen), continuous (transfers).

Freshman Application Contact Dinesh Mahtani, Director of Admissions, Nyack College, 1 South Boulevard, Nyack, NY 10960-3698. *Phone:* 845-675-4401. *Toll-free phone:* 800-33-NYACK. *Fax:* 845-358-3047. *E-mail:* admissions@nyack.edu.
Website: http://www.nyack.edu/.

Ohr Hameir Theological Seminary

Cortlandt Manor, New York

Director of Admissions Director of Admissions, Ohr Hameir Theological Seminary, 141 Furnace Woods Road, Cortlandt Manor, NY 10567. *Phone:* 914-736-1500.

Ohr Somayach/Joseph Tanenbaum Educational Center

Monsey, New York

- **Independent Jewish** comprehensive, founded 1979
- **Small-town** 7-acre campus with easy access to New York City
- **Men only**
- **Moderately difficult** entrance level

Academics *Calendar:* semesters. *Degree:* bachelor's and doctoral.

Student Life *Campus security:* 24-hour emergency response devices and patrols, controlled dormitory access.

Applying *Options:* early admission. *Required:* interview. *Required for some:* essay or personal statement. *Recommended:* high school transcript.

Freshman Application Contact Ohr Somayach/Joseph Tanenbaum Educational Center, PO Box 334, 244 Route 306, Monsey, NY 10952-0334. *Phone:* 845-425-1370 Ext. 22.
Website: http://ohr.edu/.

Pace University

New York, New York

- **Independent** university, founded 1906
- **Urban** campus with easy access to New York City
- **Endowment** $121.8 million
- **Coed** 8,336 undergraduate students, 85% full-time, 59% women, 41% men
- **Moderately difficult** entrance level, 77% of applicants were admitted

Undergraduates 7,107 full-time, 1,229 part-time. Students come from 50 states and territories; 103 other countries; 37% are from out of state; 11% Black or African American, non-Hispanic/Latino; 16% Hispanic/Latino; 9% Asian, non-Hispanic/Latino; 0.2% Native Hawaiian or other Pacific Islander, non-Hispanic/Latino; 0.3% American Indian or Alaska Native, non-Hispanic/Latino; 3% Two or more races, non-Hispanic/Latino; 7% Race/ethnicity unknown; 7% international; 8% transferred in; 45% live on campus. *Retention:* 76% of full-time freshmen returned.

Freshmen *Admission:* 12,885 applied, 9,900 admitted, 1,848 enrolled. *Average high school GPA:* 3.2. *Test scores:* SAT critical reading scores over 500: 73%; SAT math scores over 500: 78%; ACT scores over 18: 100%; SAT critical reading scores over 600: 21%; SAT math scores over 600: 26%; ACT scores over 24: 57%; SAT critical reading scores over 700: 2%; SAT math scores over 700: 3%; ACT scores over 30: 4%.

Faculty *Total:* 1,324, 35% full-time, 46% with terminal degrees. *Student/faculty ratio:* 14:1.

Academics *Calendar:* semesters. *Degrees:* certificates, associate, bachelor's, master's, doctoral, post-master's, and postbachelor's certificates. *Special study options:* accelerated degree program, adult/continuing education programs, advanced placement credit, cooperative education, distance learning, double majors, English as a second language, freshman honors college, honors programs, independent study, internships, part-time degree program, study abroad, summer session for credit. *ROTC:* Army (c), Air Force (c). *Unusual degree programs:* 3-2 engineering with Manhattan College, Rensselaer Polytechnic Institute; occupational therapy with Columbia University College of Physicians and Surgeons, physical therapy with New York Medical College, podiatry with the New York College of Podiatric Medicine.

Computers on Campus 268 computers/terminals are available on campus for general student use. Students can access the following: computer help desk, free student e-mail accounts, online (class) registration, online (class) schedules, administrative functions—pay tuition, view student records, update personal information, view financial aid and complete health insurance waiver. Campuswide network is available. 100% of college-owned or -operated housing units are wired for high-speed Internet access. Wireless service is available via classrooms, computer centers, computer labs, libraries, student centers.

Student Life *Housing options:* coed. Campus housing is university owned and leased by the school. *Activities and organizations:* drama/theater group, student-run newspaper, radio and television station, choral group, Black Student Union, Beta Alpha Psi, OLAS (Organization of Latin American Students), Pace Board, Lubin Business Association, national fraternities, national sororities. *Campus security:* 24-hour emergency response devices and patrols, late-night transport/escort service, controlled dormitory access. *Student services:* health clinic, personal/psychological counseling.

Athletics Member NCAA. All Division II. *Intercollegiate sports:* baseball M(s), basketball M(s)/W(s), cross-country running M(s)/W(s), football M(s), lacrosse M(s), soccer W(s), softball W(s), swimming and diving M(s)/W(s), volleyball W(s). *Intramural sports:* badminton M/W, basketball M/W, soccer M/W, ultimate Frisbee M/W, volleyball M/W.

Standardized Tests *Required:* SAT or ACT (for admission).

Costs (2012–13) *Comprehensive fee:* $49,154 includes full-time tuition ($35,320), mandatory fees ($1244), and room and board ($12,590). Part-time tuition: $1013 per credit. Part-time tuition and fees vary according to course load. *Room and board:* Room and board charges vary according to board plan, housing facility, location, and student level. *Payment plan:* installment. *Waivers:* senior citizens and employees or children of employees.

Financial Aid Of all full-time matriculated undergraduates who enrolled in 2012, 5,772 applied for aid, 5,395 were judged to have need, 472 had their need fully met. 1,176 Federal Work-Study jobs (averaging $3623). In 2012, 1320 non-need-based awards were made. *Average percent of need met:* 70%. *Average financial aid package:* $28,354. *Average need-based loan:* $4644. *Average need-based gift aid:* $23,746. *Average non-need-based aid:* $12,438. *Average indebtedness upon graduation:* $35,895.

Applying *Options:* electronic application, early action, deferred entrance. *Application fee:* $50. *Required:* essay or personal statement, high school transcript, 2 letters of recommendation. *Recommended:* minimum 3.0 GPA, interview. *Application deadlines:* 2/15 (freshmen), rolling (transfers), 11/30 (early action). *Notification:* continuous (freshmen), continuous (transfers), 1/1 (early action).

Freshman Application Contact Ms. Donna J. Grand Pre, Dean of Admissions, Pace University, One Pace Plaza, 163 William Street, New York, NY 10038. *Phone:* 212-346-1794. *Toll-free phone:* 800-874-7223. *Fax:* 212-346-1821. *E-mail:* dgrandpre@pace.edu. *Website:* http://www.pace.edu/.

See below for display ad and page 1432 for the College Close-Up.

Parsons The New School for Design

New York, New York

- **Independent** comprehensive, founded 1896, part of The New School
- **Urban** 2-acre campus with easy access to Manhattan
- **Coed** 4,260 undergraduate students, 90% full-time, 79% women, 21% men
- **Very difficult** entrance level, 63% of applicants were admitted

Undergraduates 3,813 full-time, 447 part-time. 73% are from out of state; 4% Black or African American, non-Hispanic/Latino; 9% Hispanic/Latino; 15% Asian, non-Hispanic/Latino; 0.2% Native Hawaiian or other Pacific Islander, non-Hispanic/Latino; 0.1% American Indian or Alaska Native, non-Hispanic/Latino; 2% Two or more races, non-Hispanic/Latino; 3% Race/ethnicity unknown; 39% international; 73% transferred in; 21% live on campus. *Retention:* 85% of full-time freshmen returned.

Freshmen *Admission:* 2,634 applied, 1,672 admitted, 717 enrolled. *Average high school GPA:* 3.3. *Test scores:* SAT critical reading scores over 500: 68%; SAT math scores over 500: 72%; SAT writing scores over 500: 72%; ACT scores over 18: 95%; SAT critical reading scores over 600: 24%; SAT math scores over 600: 40%; SAT writing scores over 600: 32%; ACT scores over 24: 51%; SAT critical reading scores over 700: 4%; SAT math scores over 700: 12%; SAT writing scores over 700: 7%; ACT scores over 30: 6%.

Faculty *Total:* 1,046, 15% full-time, 9% with terminal degrees. *Student/faculty ratio:* 10:1.

Academics *Calendar:* semesters. *Degrees:* certificates, associate, bachelor's, and master's. *Special study options:* advanced placement credit, cooperative education, distance learning, English as a second language, independent study, internships, off-campus study, services for LD students, student-designed majors, study abroad, summer session for credit.

Computers on Campus Students can access the following: campus intranet, computer help desk, free student e-mail accounts, online (class) grades, online (class) registration, online (class) schedules, online portal. Campuswide network is available. 100% of college-owned or -operated housing units are wired for high-speed Internet access. Wireless service is available via entire campus.

Student Life *Housing options:* coed, disabled students. Campus housing is university owned and leased by the school. Freshman applicants given priority for college housing. *Activities and organizations:* drama/theater group, student-run newspaper, radio station, choral group. *Campus security:* 24-hour emergency response devices, controlled dormitory access. *Student services:* health clinic, personal/psychological counseling.

Standardized Tests *Required:* SAT or ACT (for admission).

Costs (2013–14) *Comprehensive fee:* $55,240 includes full-time tuition ($39,280), mandatory fees ($860), and room and board ($15,100). Part-time tuition: $1335 per credit hour.

Financial Aid Of all full-time matriculated undergraduates who enrolled in 2011, 2,175 applied for aid, 1,981 were judged to have need, 242 had their need fully met. In 2011, 114 non-need-based awards were made. *Average percent of need met:* 59%. *Average financial aid package:* $25,665. *Average need-based loan:* $9190. *Average need-based gift aid:* $16,265. *Average non-need-based aid:* $6695. *Average indebtedness upon graduation:* $32,715.

Applying *Options:* electronic application, early action, deferred entrance. *Application fee:* $50. *Required:* high school transcript, portfolio, home examination. *Required for some:* essay or personal statement, interview. *Recommended:* minimum 3.0 GPA. *Application deadlines:* rolling (freshmen), 4/1 (transfers). *Notification:* continuous (freshmen), continuous (transfers).

Freshman Application Contact Director of Admissions, Parsons The New School for Design, 65 Fifth Avenue, New York, NY 10011-8878. *Phone:* 212-229-8989. *Toll-free phone:* 800-292-3040. *Fax:* 212-229-8975. *E-mail:* thinkparsons@newschool.edu. *Website:* http://www.parsons.edu/.

See page 575 for display ad and page 1414 for the College Close-Up.

Paul Smith's College

Paul Smiths, New York

Freshman Application Contact Admissions Office, Paul Smith's College, Routes 86 and 30, PO Box 265, Paul Smiths, NY 12970. *Phone:* 518-327-

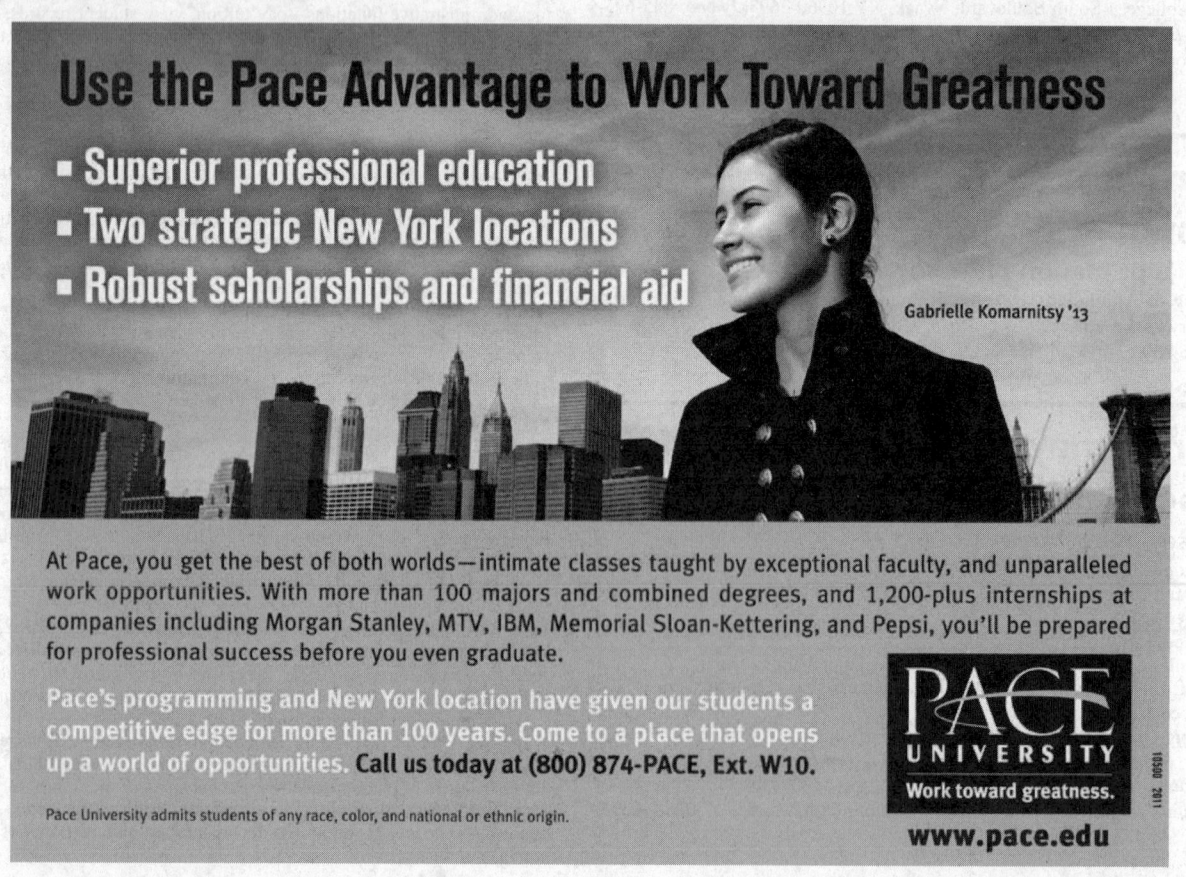

6227. *Toll-free phone:* 800-421-2605. *Fax:* 518-327-6016. *E-mail:* admissions@paulsmiths.edu. *Website:* http://www.paulsmiths.edu/.

Plaza College

Jackson Heights, New York

Freshman Application Contact Dean Rose Ann Black, Dean of Administration, Plaza College, 74-09 37th Avenue, Jackson Heights, NY 11372. *Phone:* 718-779-1430. *E-mail:* info@plazacollege.edu. *Website:* http://www.plazacollege.edu/.

Polytechnic Institute of New York University

Brooklyn, New York

- **Independent** university, founded 1854
- **Urban** 3-acre campus
- **Endowment** $107.0 million
- **Coed** 2,071 undergraduate students, 94% full-time, 23% women, 79% men
- **Very difficult** entrance level, 75% of applicants were admitted

Undergraduates 1,952 full-time, 154 part-time. Students come from 38 states and territories; 33 other countries; 19% are from out of state; 6% Black or African American, non-Hispanic/Latino; 10% Hispanic/Latino; 35% Asian, non-Hispanic/Latino; 0.2% American Indian or Alaska Native, non-Hispanic/Latino; 9% Race/ethnicity unknown; 10% international; 4% transferred in; 24% live on campus. *Retention:* 85% of full-time freshmen returned.
Freshmen *Admission:* 3,284 applied, 2,453 admitted, 495 enrolled. *Average high school GPA:* 3.52. *Test scores:* SAT critical reading scores over 500: 89%; SAT math scores over 500: 99%; SAT writing scores over 500: 91%; SAT critical reading scores over 600: 51%; SAT math scores over 600: 89%; SAT writing scores over 600: 51%; SAT critical reading scores over 700: 11%; SAT math scores over 700: 44%; SAT writing scores over 700: 10%.
Faculty *Total:* 396, 40% full-time, 73% with terminal degrees. *Student/faculty ratio:* 14:1.
Academics *Calendar:* semesters. *Degrees:* bachelor's, master's, doctoral, and postbachelor's certificates. *Special study options:* academic remediation for entering students, accelerated degree program, advanced placement credit, cooperative education, distance learning, double majors, honors programs, internships, part-time degree program, study abroad, summer session for credit. *ROTC:* Army (c), Air Force (c).
Computers on Campus 1,334 computers/terminals are available on campus for general student use. Students can access the following: campus intranet, computer help desk, free student e-mail accounts, online (class) grades, online (class) registration, online (class) schedules. Campuswide network is available. 100% of college-owned or -operated housing units are wired for high-speed Internet access. Wireless service is available via entire campus.
Student Life *Housing options:* coed. Campus housing is university owned. Freshman applicants given priority for college housing. *Activities and organizations:* student-run newspaper, National Society of Black Engineers, Society of Hispanic Professional Engineers, Association for Computing Machinery, Alpha Phi Omega, Chinese Student Society, national fraternities, national sororities. *Campus security:* 24-hour patrols, controlled dormitory access. *Student services:* health clinic, personal/psychological counseling, women's center.
Athletics Member NCAA. All Division III. *Intercollegiate sports:* baseball M, basketball M/W, cross-country running M/W, soccer M/W, softball W, tennis M/W, volleyball M/W. *Intramural sports:* badminton M/W, basketball M/W, bowling M/W, football M/W, golf M(c)/W(c), soccer M/W, table tennis M(c)/W(c), volleyball M/W, weight lifting M(c)/W(c).
Standardized Tests *Required:* SAT or ACT (for admission). *Recommended:* SAT Subject Tests (for admission).
Financial Aid Of all full-time matriculated undergraduates who enrolled in 2011, 1,720 applied for aid, 1,387 were judged to have need, 519 had their need fully met. In 2011, 319 non-need-based awards were made. *Average percent of need met:* 87%. *Average financial aid package:* $28,035. *Average need-based loan:* $4597. *Average need-based gift aid:* $15,812. *Average non-need-based aid:* $16,827. *Average indebtedness upon graduation:* $30,560.
Applying *Options:* electronic application, early admission, deferred entrance. *Application fee:* $65. *Required:* essay or personal statement, high school tran-

script, 2 letters of recommendation. *Recommended:* interview. *Application deadlines:* 2/1 (freshmen), rolling (transfers).
Freshman Application Contact Joy Colelli, Dean of Admissions and New Students, Polytechnic Institute of New York University, Six Metrotech Center, Brooklyn, NY 11201-2990. *Phone:* 718-260-5917. *Toll-free phone:* 800-POLYTECH. *Fax:* 718-260-3446. *E-mail:* uadmit@poly.edu. *Website:* http://www.poly.edu/.

Pratt Institute

Brooklyn, New York

- **Independent** comprehensive, founded 1887
- **Urban** 25-acre campus
- **Coed**
- **Very difficult** entrance level

Faculty *Student/faculty ratio:* 11:1.
Academics *Calendar:* semesters plus optional May term and summer session. *Degrees:* associate, bachelor's, master's, and post-master's certificates.
Student Life *Campus security:* 24-hour emergency response devices and patrols, late-night transport/escort service.
Athletics Member NCAA. All Division III.
Standardized Tests *Required:* SAT or ACT (for admission). *Required for some:* SAT Subject Tests (for admission).
Costs (2012–13) *Comprehensive fee:* $51,598 includes full-time tuition ($39,282), mandatory fees ($1810), and room and board ($10,506). Full-time tuition and fees vary according to program. Part-time tuition: $1267 per credit. Part-time tuition and fees vary according to program. *College room only:* $6726. Room and board charges vary according to board plan and housing facility.
Financial Aid *Of all full-time matriculated undergraduates who enrolled in 2011,* 1,786 applied for aid, 1,645 were judged to have need. *In 2011,* 698 non-need-based awards were made. *Average financial aid package:* $20,905. *Average need-based loan:* $5036. *Average need-based gift aid:* $10,189. *Average non-need-based aid:* $11,529. *Financial aid deadline:* 2/1.
Applying *Options:* electronic application, early action, deferred entrance. *Application fee:* $50. *Required:* essay or personal statement, high school transcript, 1 letter of recommendation. *Required for some:* portfolio. *Recommended:* minimum 3.0 GPA.
Freshman Application Contact Ms. Olga Burger, Visit Coordinator, Pratt Institute, 200 Willoughby Avenue, DeKalb Hall, Brooklyn, NY 11205. *Phone:* 718-636-3779. *Toll-free phone:* 800-331-0834. *Fax:* 718-636-3670. *E-mail:* visit@pratt.edu.
Website: http://www.pratt.edu/.

See previous page for display ad and page 1442 for the College Close-Up.

Purchase College, State University of New York

Purchase, New York

- **State-supported** comprehensive, founded 1967, part of State University of New York System
- **Small-town** 500-acre campus with easy access to New York City
- **Coed** 4,155 undergraduate students, 90% full-time, 56% women, 44% men
- **Moderately difficult** entrance level, 33% of applicants were admitted

Undergraduates 3,740 full-time, 415 part-time. Students come from 43 states and territories; 31 other countries; 17% are from out of state; 7% Black or African American, non-Hispanic/Latino; 16% Hispanic/Latino; 2% Asian, non-Hispanic/Latino; 0.1% American Indian or Alaska Native, non-Hispanic/Latino; 8% Two or more races, non-Hispanic/Latino; 12% Race/ethnicity unknown; 2% international; 11% transferred in; 67% live on campus. *Retention:* 83% of full-time freshmen returned.
Freshmen *Admission:* 8,907 applied, 2,971 admitted, 694 enrolled. *Average high school GPA:* 3.2. *Test scores:* SAT critical reading scores over 500: 78%; SAT math scores over 500: 66%; SAT writing scores over 500: 71%; ACT scores over 18: 98%; SAT critical reading scores over 600: 33%; SAT math scores over 600: 17%; SAT writing scores over 600: 25%; ACT scores over 24: 53%; SAT critical reading scores over 700: 5%; SAT math scores over 700: 1%; SAT writing scores over 700: 2%; ACT scores over 30: 8%.
Faculty *Total:* 403, 39% full-time, 67% with terminal degrees. *Student/faculty ratio:* 16:1.

Academics *Calendar:* semesters. *Degrees:* certificates, bachelor's, master's, and post-master's certificates. *Special study options:* academic remediation for entering students, adult/continuing education programs, advanced placement credit, double majors, English as a second language, independent study, internships, off-campus study, part-time degree program, services for LD students, student-designed majors, study abroad, summer session for credit.
Computers on Campus 600 computers/terminals and 3,500 ports are available on campus for general student use. Students can access the following: campus intranet, computer help desk, free student e-mail accounts, online (class) grades, online (class) registration, online (class) schedules. Campus-wide network is available. 100% of college-owned or -operated housing units are wired for high-speed Internet access. Wireless service is available via classrooms, computer centers, computer labs, learning centers, libraries, student centers.
Student Life *Housing options:* coed. Campus housing is university owned. Freshman applicants given priority for college housing. *Activities and organizations:* drama/theater group, student-run newspaper, radio and television station, choral group, Student Union, WPUR radio station, Latinos Unidos, Gay/Lesbian/Bisexual/Transgender Union, Organization of African People in America. *Campus security:* 24-hour emergency response devices and patrols, late-night transport/escort service, controlled dormitory access, 24-hour patrols by police officers. *Student services:* health clinic, personal/psychological counseling, women's center, legal services.
Athletics Member NCAA. All Division III. *Intercollegiate sports:* baseball M, basketball M/W, cross-country running M/W, golf M, lacrosse W, soccer M/W, softball W, swimming and diving M/W, tennis M/W, volleyball M/W. *Intramural sports:* badminton M/W, basketball M/W, bowling M/W, cross-country running M/W, fencing M/W, football M/W, golf M/W, racquetball M/W, skiing (cross-country) M/W, skiing (downhill) M/W, soccer M/W, softball M/W, squash M/W, swimming and diving M/W, table tennis M/W, tennis M/W, volleyball M/W, water polo M/W, weight lifting M/W.
Standardized Tests *Required:* SAT or ACT (for admission). *Recommended:* SAT (for admission).
Costs (2013–14) *One-time required fee:* $200. *Tuition:* state resident $5570 full-time, $232 per credit part-time; nonresident $14,820 full-time, $618 per credit part-time. Full-time tuition and fees vary according to program. Part-time tuition and fees vary according to course load and program. *Required fees:* $1660 full-time, $68 per credit part-time. *Room and board:* $11,566; room only: $7378. Room and board charges vary according to board plan and housing facility. *Payment plan:* installment. *Waivers:* employees or children of employees.
Financial Aid Of all full-time matriculated undergraduates who enrolled in 2012, 2,894 applied for aid, 2,313 were judged to have need, 92 had their need fully met. In 2012, 122 non-need-based awards were made. *Average percent of need met:* 53%. *Average financial aid package:* $10,079. *Average need-based loan:* $4714. *Average need-based gift aid:* $6305. *Average non-need-based aid:* $2231. *Average indebtedness upon graduation:* $26,684.
Applying *Options:* electronic application, early admission, early action, deferred entrance. *Application fee:* $40. *Required:* high school transcript, minimum 3.0 GPA. *Required for some:* essay or personal statement, 1 letter of recommendation, interview, audition, portfolio. *Application deadlines:* 7/15 (freshmen), rolling (transfers), 11/15 (early action). *Notification:* continuous until 5/1 (freshmen), continuous (transfers), 12/15 (early action).
Freshman Application Contact Stephanie McCaine, Director of Admissions, Purchase College, State University of New York, 735 Anderson Hill Road, Purchase, NY 10577-1400. *Phone:* 914-251-6300. *Fax:* 914-251-6314. *E-mail:* admission@purchase.edu.
Website: http://www.purchase.edu/.

Queens College of the City University of New York

Flushing, New York

- **State and locally supported** comprehensive, founded 1937, part of City University of New York System
- **Urban** 77-acre campus with easy access to New York City
- **Coed**
- **Very difficult** entrance level

Faculty *Student/faculty ratio:* 16:1.
Academics *Calendar:* semesters. *Degrees:* bachelor's, master's, post-master's, and postbachelor's certificates.
Student Life *Campus security:* 24-hour emergency response devices and patrols.
Athletics Member NCAA. All Division II.

Standardized Tests *Required:* SAT or ACT (for admission). *Required for some:* SAT Subject Tests (for admission). *Recommended:* SAT Subject Tests (for admission).

Costs (2012–13) *Tuition:* state resident $5130 full-time, $215 per credit part-time; nonresident $13,800 full-time, $460 per credit part-time. *Required fees:* $477 full-time. *Room and board:* $11,840. Room and board charges vary according to board plan and housing facility.

Financial Aid *Of all full-time matriculated undergraduates who enrolled in 2012,* 11,207 applied for aid, 8,648 were judged to have need, 7,000 had their need fully met. 456 Federal Work-Study jobs (averaging $1033). *In 2012,* 177 non-need-based awards were made. *Average percent of need met:* 95. *Average financial aid package:* $8000. *Average need-based loan:* $4500. *Average need-based gift aid:* $4800. *Average non-need-based aid:* $7800. *Average indebtedness upon graduation:* $20,624.

Applying *Options:* electronic application, deferred entrance. *Application fee:* $65. *Required:* high school transcript, minimum 3.0 GPA.

Freshman Application Contact Queens College of the City University of New York, 65-30 Kissena Boulevard, Flushing, NY 11367-1597. *Phone:* 718-997-5600.

Website: http://www.qc.cuny.edu/.

See below for display ad and page 1444 for the College Close-Up.

Rabbinical Academy Mesivta Rabbi Chaim Berlin

Brooklyn, New York

Director of Admissions Executive Administrator, Rabbinical Academy Mesivta Rabbi Chaim Berlin, 1605 Coney Island Avenue, Brooklyn, NY 11230-4715. *Phone:* 718-377-0777. *Fax:* 718-338-5578.

Rabbinical College Beth Shraga

Monsey, New York

Director of Admissions Rabbi Sydney Schiff, Director of Admissions, Rabbinical College Beth Shraga, 28 Saddle River Road, Monsey, NY 10952-3035.

Rabbinical College Bobover Yeshiva B'nei Zion

Brooklyn, New York

Director of Admissions Director of Admissions, Rabbinical College Bobover Yeshiva B'nei Zion, 1577 Forty-eighth Street, Brooklyn, NY 11219. *Phone:* 718-438-2018.

Rabbinical College Ch'san Sofer

Brooklyn, New York

Director of Admissions Director of Admissions, Rabbinical College Ch'san Sofer, 1876 Fiftieth Street, Brooklyn, NY 11204. *Phone:* 718-236-1171.

Rabbinical College of Long Island

Long Beach, New York

Director of Admissions Director of Admissions, Rabbinical College of Long Island, 205 West Beech Street, Long Beach, NY 11561-3305. *Phone:* 516-431-7414.

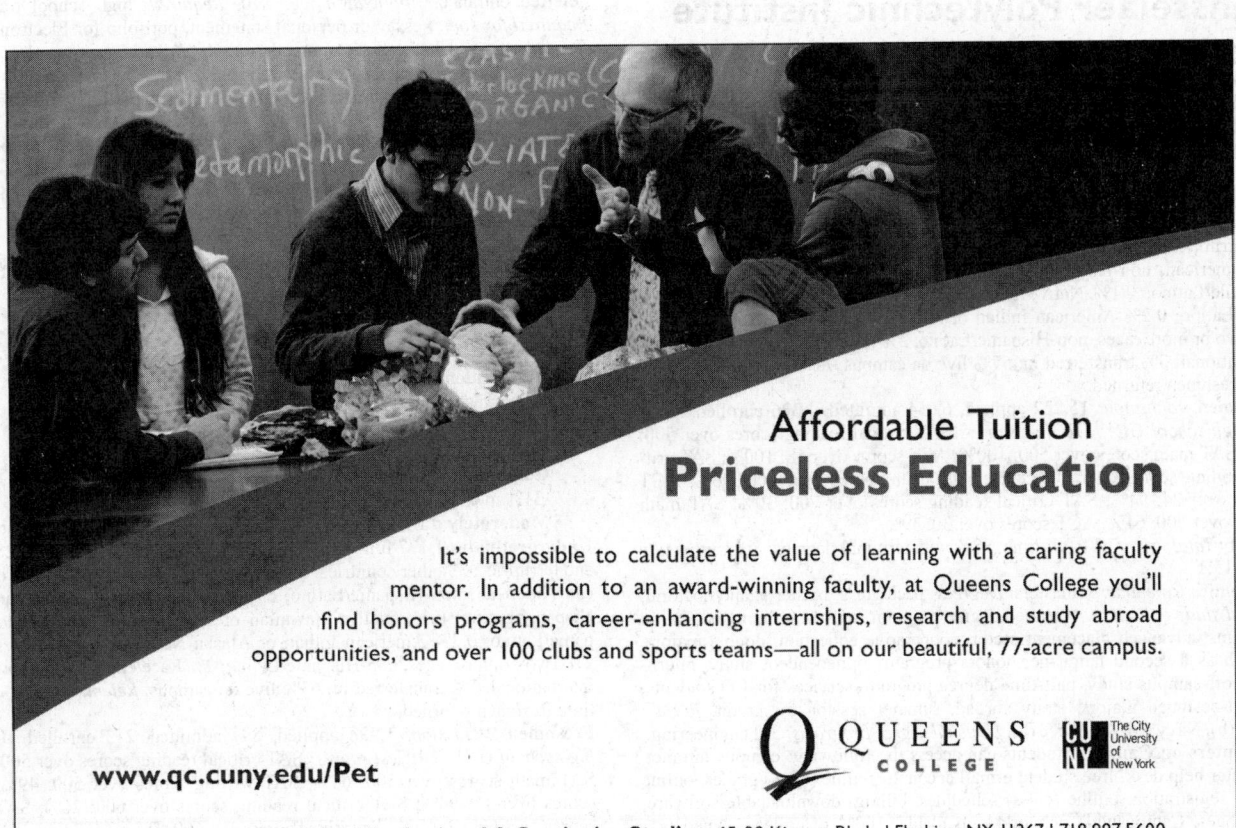

Rabbinical College of Ohr Shimon Yisroel

Brooklyn, New York

Admissions Office Contact Rabbinical College of Ohr Shimon Yisroel, 215-217 Hewes Street, Brooklyn, NY 11211.

Rabbinical Seminary Adas Yereim

Brooklyn, New York

Director of Admissions Director of Admissions, Rabbinical Seminary Adas Yereim, 185 Wilson Street, Brooklyn, NY 11211-7206. *Phone:* 718-388-1751.

Rabbinical Seminary M'kor Chaim

Brooklyn, New York

Director of Admissions Director of Admissions, Rabbinical Seminary M'kor Chaim, 1571 Fifty-fifth Street, Brooklyn, NY 11219. *Phone:* 718-851-0183.

Rabbinical Seminary of America

Flushing, New York

Director of Admissions Rabbi Abraham Semmel, Director of Admissions, Rabbinical Seminary of America, 76-01 147th Street, Flushing, NY 11367. *Phone:* 718-268-4700.

Rensselaer Polytechnic Institute

Troy, New York

- **Independent** university, founded 1824
- **Suburban** 284-acre campus with easy access to Albany, NY
- **Endowment** $583.4 million
- **Coed** 5,391 undergraduate students, 100% full-time, 29% women, 71% men
- **Very difficult** entrance level, 44% of applicants were admitted

Undergraduates 5,371 full-time, 20 part-time. Students come from 50 states and territories; 31 other countries; 66% are from out of state; 2% Black or African American, non-Hispanic/Latino; 6% Hispanic/Latino; 10% Asian, non-Hispanic/Latino; 0.1% Native Hawaiian or other Pacific Islander, non-Hispanic/Latino; 0.2% American Indian or Alaska Native, non-Hispanic/Latino; 6% Two or more races, non-Hispanic/Latino; 2% Race/ethnicity unknown; 6% international; 3% transferred in; 57% live on campus. *Retention:* 94% of full-time freshmen returned.

Freshmen *Admission:* 15,222 applied, 6,634 admitted, 1,326 enrolled. *Average high school GPA:* 3.7. *Test scores:* SAT critical reading scores over 500: 98%; SAT math scores over 500: 100%; ACT scores over 18: 100%; SAT critical reading scores over 600: 80%; SAT math scores over 600: 96%; ACT scores over 24: 94%; SAT critical reading scores over 700: 30%; SAT math scores over 700: 61%; ACT scores over 30: 39%.

Faculty *Total:* 500, 76% full-time, 88% with terminal degrees. *Student/faculty ratio:* 15:1.

Academics *Calendar:* semesters. *Degrees:* bachelor's, master's, and doctoral. *Special study options:* accelerated degree program, adult/continuing education programs, advanced placement credit, cooperative education, double majors, English as a second language, honors programs, independent study, internships, off-campus study, part-time degree program, services for LD students, student-designed majors, study abroad, summer session for credit. *ROTC:* Army (b), Navy (b), Air Force (b). *Unusual degree programs:* 3-2 engineering.

Computers on Campus Students can access the following: campus intranet, computer help desk, free student e-mail accounts, online (class) grades, online (class) registration, online (class) schedules, billing, downloadable software, web pages. Campuswide network is available. 100% of college-owned or -operated housing units are wired for high-speed Internet access. Wireless service is available via entire campus.

Student Life *Housing:* on-campus residence required through sophomore year. *Options:* coed, disabled students. Campus housing is university owned. Freshman campus housing is guaranteed. *Activities and organizations:* drama/theater group, student-run newspaper, radio and television station, choral group, Red Army Spirit Club, Outing Club, Indian Student Association, Chinese American Student Association, pep band, national fraternities, national sororities. *Campus security:* 24-hour emergency response devices and patrols, late-night transport/escort service, controlled dormitory access, campus foot patrols at night. *Student services:* health clinic, personal/psychological counseling, women's center, legal services.

Athletics Member NCAA. All Division III except men's and women's ice hockey (Division I). *Intercollegiate sports:* archery M(c)/W(c), badminton M(c)/W(c), baseball M/W(c), basketball M/W, crew M(c)/W(c), cross-country running M/W, equestrian sports M(c)/W(c), fencing M(c)/W(c), field hockey W, football M, golf M, ice hockey M(s)/W(s), lacrosse M/W, racquetball M(c)/W(c), riflery M(c)/W(c), rugby M(c)/W(c), sailing M(c)/W(c), skiing (cross-country) M(c)/W(c), soccer M/W, softball W, squash M(c)/W(c), swimming and diving M/W, table tennis M(c)/W(c), tennis M/W, track and field M/W, ultimate Frisbee M(c)/W(c), volleyball M(c)/W(c), water polo M(c)/W(c), weight lifting M(c)/W(c). *Intramural sports:* basketball M/W, bowling M(c)/W(c), cheerleading W, ice hockey M/W, lacrosse M(c), racquetball M/W, rock climbing M(c)/W(c), skiing (downhill) M/W, soccer M/W, softball M/W, swimming and diving M(c)/W(c), table tennis M/W, tennis M(c)/W(c), ultimate Frisbee M/W, volleyball M/W, wrestling M.

Standardized Tests *Required:* SAT or ACT (for admission). *Required for some:* SAT and SAT Subject Tests or ACT (for admission).

Costs (2012–13) *Comprehensive fee:* $56,925 includes full-time tuition ($43,350), mandatory fees ($1125), and room and board ($12,450). Part-time tuition: $1805 per credit hour. *College room only:* $7110. Room and board charges vary according to board plan and location. *Payment plan:* installment. *Waivers:* employees or children of employees.

Financial Aid Of all full-time matriculated undergraduates who enrolled in 2012, 3,834 applied for aid, 3,450 were judged to have need, 858 had their need fully met. 1,110 Federal Work-Study jobs (averaging $1917). In 2012, 1544 non-need-based awards were made. *Average percent of need met:* 79%. *Average financial aid package:* $30,208. *Average need-based loan:* $4996. *Average need-based gift aid:* $24,799. *Average non-need-based aid:* $13,334. *Average indebtedness upon graduation:* $31,000.

Applying *Options:* electronic application, early admission, early decision, deferred entrance. *Application fee:* $70. *Required:* high school transcript. *Required for some:* essay or personal statement, portfolio for Electronic Arts. *Recommended:* 1 letter of recommendation. *Application deadline:* 1/15 (freshmen). *Early decision deadline:* 11/15 (for plan 1), 12/15 (for plan 2). *Notification:* 3/9 (freshmen), continuous (transfers), 12/4 (early decision plan 1), 1/18 (early decision plan 2).

Freshman Application Contact Mr. Paul Marthers, Vice President for Enrollment, Rensselaer Polytechnic Institute, 110 8th Street, Troy, NY 12180. *Phone:* 518-276-6216. *Fax:* 518-276-4072. *E-mail:* admissions@rpi.edu. *Website:* http://www.rpi.edu/.

Roberts Wesleyan College

Rochester, New York

- **Independent** comprehensive, founded 1866, affiliated with Free Methodist Church of North America
- **Suburban** 188-acre campus
- **Endowment** $16.4 million
- **Coed** 1,323 undergraduate students, 89% full-time, 69% women, 31% men
- **Moderately difficult** entrance level, 47% of applicants were admitted

Undergraduates 1,177 full-time, 146 part-time. Students come from 28 states and territories; 33 other countries; 8% are from out of state; 12% Black or African American, non-Hispanic/Latino; 5% Hispanic/Latino; 0.8% Asian, non-Hispanic/Latino; 0.1% Native Hawaiian or other Pacific Islander, non-Hispanic/Latino; 0.3% American Indian or Alaska Native, non-Hispanic/Latino; 2% Two or more races, non-Hispanic/Latino; 2% Race/ethnicity unknown; 4% international; 7% transferred in; 63% live on campus. *Retention:* 80% of full-time freshmen returned.

Freshmen *Admission:* 1,928 applied, 897 admitted, 213 enrolled. *Average high school GPA:* 3.4. *Test scores:* SAT critical reading scores over 500: 65%; SAT math scores over 500: 60%; SAT writing scores over 500: 49%; ACT scores over 18: 94%; SAT critical reading scores over 600: 26%; SAT math scores over 600: 21%; SAT writing scores over 600: 18%; ACT scores over 24: 50%; SAT critical reading scores over 700: 5%; SAT math scores over 700: 4%; SAT writing scores over 700: 4%; ACT scores over 30: 11%.

Faculty *Total:* 259, 36% full-time, 38% with terminal degrees. *Student/faculty ratio:* 11:1.

Academics *Calendar:* semesters. *Degrees:* associate, bachelor's, and master's. *Special study options:* academic remediation for entering students, accelerated degree program, advanced placement credit, cooperative education, double majors, English as a second language, honors programs, independent study, internships, off-campus study, services for LD students, student-designed majors, study abroad, summer session for credit. *ROTC:* Army (b), Air Force (c). *Unusual degree programs:* 3-2 engineering with Clarkson University, Rensselaer Polytechnic Institute, Rochester Institute of Technology.

Computers on Campus 250 computers/terminals are available on campus for general student use. Students can access the following: campus intranet, computer help desk, free student e-mail accounts, online (class) grades, online (class) registration, online (class) schedules. Campuswide network is available. 100% of college-owned or -operated housing units are wired for high-speed Internet access. Wireless service is available via student centers.

Student Life *Housing:* on-campus residence required through senior year. *Options:* men-only, women-only. Campus housing is university owned. Freshman campus housing is guaranteed. *Activities and organizations:* drama/theater group, student-run newspaper, choral group, Intramurals, Foot of the Cross, Fellowship of Christian Athletes, Nursing Club, Drama Club. *Campus security:* 24-hour emergency response devices and patrols, student patrols, late-night transport/escort service, controlled dormitory access, 24-hour Resident Life staff on-call. *Student services:* health clinic, personal/psychological counseling.

Athletics Member NCAA, NCCAA. All NCAA Division II. *Intercollegiate sports:* basketball M(s)/W(s), cross-country running M(s)/W(s), golf M(s), soccer M(s)/W(s), tennis M(s)/W(s), track and field M(s)/W(s), volleyball W(s). *Intramural sports:* basketball M/W, football M/W, racquetball M/W, skiing (downhill) M/W, soccer M/W, softball M/W, table tennis M/W, tennis M/W, ultimate Frisbee M/W, volleyball M/W, water polo M/W.

Standardized Tests *Required:* SAT or ACT (for admission).

Costs (2013–14) *One-time required fee:* $375. *Comprehensive fee:* $37,094 includes full-time tuition ($26,352), mandatory fees ($1112), and room and board ($9630). Part-time tuition and fees vary according to course load. *College room only:* $6166. Room and board charges vary according to board plan and housing facility. *Payment plan:* installment. *Waivers:* senior citizens and employees or children of employees.

Financial Aid Of all full-time matriculated undergraduates who enrolled in 2012, 1,323 applied for aid, 1,262 were judged to have need, 144 had their need fully met. 732 Federal Work-Study jobs (averaging $1847). 37 state and other part-time jobs (averaging $1803). In 2012, 160 non-need-based awards were made. *Average percent of need met:* 67%. *Average financial aid package:* $17,512. *Average need-based loan:* $4878. *Average need-based gift aid:* $12,663. *Average non-need-based aid:* $7025. *Average indebtedness upon graduation:* $33,528.

Applying *Options:* electronic application, early admission, deferred entrance. *Application fee:* $35. *Required:* essay or personal statement, high school transcript, 1 letter of recommendation. *Recommended:* minimum 2.7 GPA, 2 letters of recommendation, interview. *Application deadlines:* 2/1 (freshmen), rolling (transfers).

Freshman Application Contact Mr. John Paul Anderson, Associate Vice President of Undergraduate Admissions & Seminary, Roberts Wesleyan College, 2301 Westside Drive, Rochester, NY 14624-1997. *Phone:* 585-594-6400. *Toll-free phone:* 800-777-4RWC. *Fax:* 585-594-6371. *E-mail:* admissions@roberts.edu.

Website: http://www.roberts.edu/.

See below for display ad and page 1460 for the College Close-Up.

Rochester Institute of Technology
Rochester, New York

- **Independent** comprehensive, founded 1829
- **Suburban** 1300-acre campus with easy access to Rochester
- **Endowment** $628.1 million
- **Coed** 13,711 undergraduate students, 90% full-time, 32% women, 68% men
- **Moderately difficult** entrance level, 58% of applicants were admitted

Undergraduates 12,393 full-time, 1,318 part-time. Students come from 52 states and territories; 102 other countries; 45% are from out of state; 5% Black or African American, non-Hispanic/Latino; 6% Hispanic/Latino; 5% Asian, non-Hispanic/Latino; 0.1% Native Hawaiian or other Pacific Islander, non-Hispanic/Latino; 0.2% American Indian or Alaska Native, non-Hispanic/Latino; 2% Two or more races, non-Hispanic/Latino; 17% Race/ethnicity unknown; 5% international; 5% transferred in; 68% live on campus. *Retention:* 89% of full-time freshmen returned.

Freshmen *Admission:* 16,353 applied, 9,562 admitted, 2,736 enrolled. *Average high school GPA:* 3.7. *Test scores:* SAT critical reading scores over 500: 89%; SAT math scores over 500: 96%; SAT writing scores over 500: 83%;

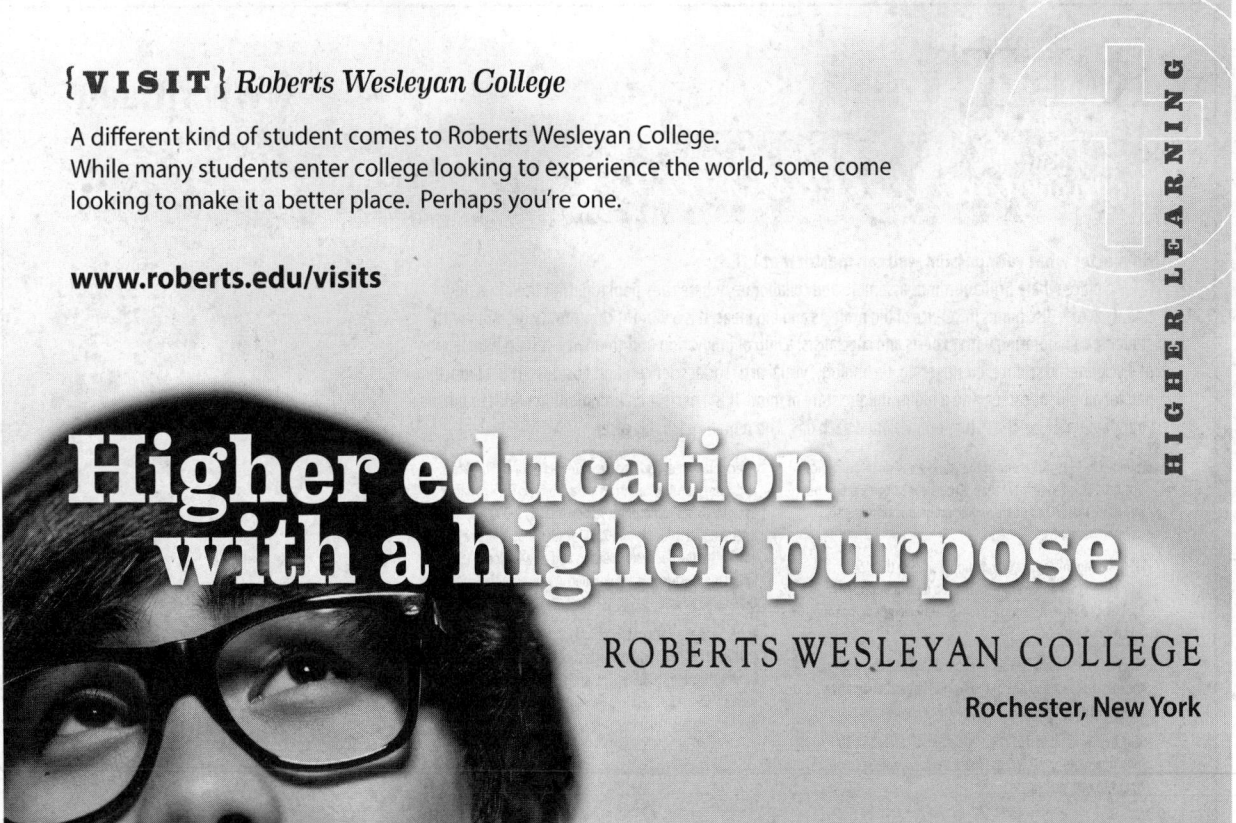

ACT scores over 18: 100%; SAT critical reading scores over 600: 48%; SAT math scores over 600: 68%; SAT writing scores over 600: 39%; ACT scores over 24: 86%; SAT critical reading scores over 700: 10%; SAT math scores over 700: 20%; SAT writing scores over 700: 7%; ACT scores over 30: 34%. **Faculty** *Total:* 1,475, 66% full-time, 47% with terminal degrees. *Student/faculty ratio:* 13:1.

Academics *Calendar:* quarters. *Degrees:* certificates, associate, bachelor's, master's, doctoral, post-master's, and postbachelor's certificates. *Special study options:* accelerated degree program, adult/continuing education programs, advanced placement credit, cooperative education, distance learning, double majors, English as a second language, freshman honors college, honors programs, independent study, internships, off-campus study, part-time degree program, services for LD students, student-designed majors, study abroad, summer session for credit. *ROTC:* Army (b), Navy (c), Air Force (b).

Computers on Campus 2,500 computers/terminals are available on campus for general student use. Students can access the following: campus intranet, computer help desk, free student e-mail accounts, online (class) grades, online (class) registration, student account information. Campuswide network is available. 100% of college-owned or -operated housing units are wired for high-speed Internet access. Wireless service is available via classrooms, computer centers, computer labs, learning centers, libraries, student centers.

Student Life *Housing:* on-campus residence required for freshman year. *Options:* coed, men-only, women-only, disabled students. Campus housing is university owned. Freshman campus housing is guaranteed. *Activities and organizations:* drama/theater group, student-run newspaper, radio station, choral group, national fraternities, national sororities. *Campus security:* 24-hour emergency response devices and patrols, student patrols, late-night transport/ escort service. *Student services:* health clinic, personal/psychological counseling, women's center, legal services.

Athletics Member NCAA. All Division III except ice hockey (Division I). *Intercollegiate sports:* baseball M, basketball M/W, bowling M(c)/W(c), cheerleading M(c)/W(c), crew M/W, cross-country running M/W, equestrian sports M(c)/W(c), fencing M(c)/W(c), field hockey W(c), ice hockey M/W, lacrosse M/W, skiing (downhill) M(c)/W(c), soccer M/W, softball W, swimming and diving M/W, tennis M/W, track and field M/W, ultimate Frisbee M(c)/W(c), volleyball M(c)/W, water polo M(c)/W(c), wrestling M. *Intramural sports:* badminton M/W, basketball M/W, bowling M/W, football M, golf M/W, ice hockey M/W, lacrosse M(c), racquetball M/W, rock climbing M(c)/ W(c), soccer M/W, softball M/W, table tennis M/W, tennis M/W, volleyball M/W.

Standardized Tests *Required:* SAT or ACT (for admission).

Costs (2013–14) *Comprehensive fee:* $46,164 includes full-time tuition ($33,932), mandatory fees ($492), and room and board ($11,740). Full-time tuition and fees vary according to course load. Part-time tuition: $1191 per credit. Part-time tuition and fees vary according to class time and course load. *College room only:* $6530. Room and board charges vary according to board plan and housing facility. *Payment plans:* installment, deferred payment. *Waivers:* employees or children of employees.

Financial Aid Of all full-time matriculated undergraduates who enrolled in 2011, 9,329 applied for aid, 8,507 were judged to have need, 6,980 had their need fully met. In 2011, 1500 non-need-based awards were made. *Average percent of need met:* 87%. *Average financial aid package:* $23,800. *Average need-based loan:* $5400. *Average need-based gift aid:* $1800. *Average non-need-based aid:* $10,000.

Applying *Options:* electronic application, early admission, early decision, deferred entrance. *Application fee:* $60. *Required:* essay or personal statement, high school transcript. *Required for some:* portfolio of original artwork required for applicants to the School of Art and the School of Design. *Recommended:* minimum 3.3 GPA, 1 letter of recommendation, interview. *Application deadline:* 2/1 (freshmen). *Early decision deadline:* 12/1. *Notification:* 3/15 (freshmen), continuous (transfers), 1/15 (early decision).

Freshman Application Contact Dr. Daniel Shelley, Assistant Vice President, Rochester Institute of Technology, 60 Lomb Memorial Drive, Rochester, NY 14623-5604. *Phone:* 585-475-6631. *Fax:* 585-475-7424. *E-mail:* admissions@ rit.edu.

Website: http://www.rit.edu/.

See below for display ad and page 1462 for the College Close-Up.

Russell Sage College

Troy, New York

- **Independent** 4-year, founded 1916, part of The Sage Colleges
- **Urban** 8-acre campus
- **Endowment** $24.8 million
- **Women only** 827 undergraduate students, 94% full-time
- **Moderately difficult** entrance level, 59% of applicants were admitted

Undergraduates 780 full-time, 47 part-time. Students come from 17 states and territories; 1 other country; 8% are from out of state; 10% Black or African American, non-Hispanic/Latino; 6% Hispanic/Latino; 4% Asian, non-Hispanic/Latino; 0.3% Native Hawaiian or other Pacific Islander, non-Hispanic/Latino; 0.4% American Indian or Alaska Native, non-Hispanic/Latino; 2% Two or more races, non-Hispanic/Latino; 13% Race/ethnicity unknown; 0.5% international; 13% transferred in; 48% live on campus. *Retention:* 73% of full-time freshmen returned.

Freshmen *Admission:* 851 applied, 500 admitted, 158 enrolled. *Average high school GPA:* 3.23. *Test scores:* SAT critical reading scores over 500: 43%; SAT math scores over 500: 44%; ACT scores over 18: 82%; SAT critical reading scores over 600: 15%; SAT math scores over 600: 9%; ACT scores over 24: 37%; SAT critical reading scores over 700: 4%; ACT scores over 30: 9%.

Faculty *Total:* 114, 64% full-time, 60% with terminal degrees. *Student/faculty ratio:* 9:1.

Academics *Calendar:* semesters. *Degree:* bachelor's. *Special study options:* academic remediation for entering students, accelerated degree program, advanced placement credit, cooperative education, distance learning, double majors, honors programs, independent study, internships, off-campus study, services for LD students, student-designed majors, study abroad, summer session for credit. *ROTC:* Army (c), Air Force (c). *Unusual degree programs:* 3-2 business administration with Sage Graduate School; engineering with Rensselaer Polytechnic Institute; nursing with Sage Graduate School; occupational therapy and physical therapy with Sage Graduate School.

Computers on Campus 165 computers/terminals are available on campus for general student use. Students can access the following: campus intranet, computer help desk, free student e-mail accounts, online (class) grades, online (class) registration, online (class) schedules. Campuswide network is available. 100% of college-owned or -operated housing units are wired for high-speed Internet access. Wireless service is available via classrooms, computer labs, learning centers, libraries.

Student Life *Housing options:* women-only. Campus housing is university owned. Freshman campus housing is guaranteed. *Activities and organizations:* drama/theater group, student-run newspaper, choral group, Student government, Sage Recreation Association, Physical Therapy Club, Crew Club, Black-Latin Student Alliance. *Campus security:* 24-hour emergency response devices and patrols, late-night transport/escort service, controlled dormitory access. *Student services:* health clinic, personal/psychological counseling, women's center.

Athletics Member NCAA. All Division III. *Intercollegiate sports:* basketball W, lacrosse W, soccer W, softball W, tennis W, volleyball W. *Intramural sports:* cheerleading W(c), crew W(c), ice hockey W, track and field W(c).

Standardized Tests *Required for some:* SAT or ACT (for admission).

Costs (2012–13) *Comprehensive fee:* $38,995 includes full-time tuition ($27,000), mandatory fees ($1000), and room and board ($10,995). Part-time tuition: $900 per credit hour. *College room only:* $5795. Room and board charges vary according to board plan. *Payment plans:* installment, deferred payment. *Waivers:* senior citizens and employees or children of employees.

Financial Aid Of all full-time matriculated undergraduates who enrolled in 2012, 754 applied for aid, 716 were judged to have need. 258 Federal Work-Study jobs (averaging $1937). 17 state and other part-time jobs (averaging $5893). In 2012, 29 non-need-based awards were made. *Average need-based loan:* $3963. *Average need-based gift aid:* $13,542. *Average non-need-based aid:* $10,479. *Average indebtedness upon graduation:* $27,907.

Applying *Options:* electronic application, early admission, early action, deferred entrance. *Application fee:* $30. *Required:* essay or personal statement, high school transcript, minimum 2.5 GPA, 2 letters of recommendation. *Recommended:* interview. *Application deadlines:* rolling (freshmen), rolling (transfers). *Notification:* continuous (freshmen), continuous (transfers).

Freshman Application Contact Mr. Thomas Breen, Senior Director of Undergraduate Admission, Russell Sage College, 140 New Scotland Avenue, Albany, NY 12208. *Phone:* 518-292-1928. *Toll-free phone:* 888-VERY-SAGE (in-state); 888-VERY SAGE (out-of-state). *Fax:* 518-292-1912. *E-mail:* breent@sage.edu.

Website: http://www.sage.edu/rsc/.

Sage College of Albany

Albany, New York

- **Independent** 4-year, founded 1957, part of The Sage Colleges
- **Urban** 15-acre campus
- **Endowment** $24.8 million
- **Coed** 911 undergraduate students, 74% full-time, 62% women, 38% men
- **Minimally difficult** entrance level, 51% of applicants were admitted

Undergraduates 678 full-time, 233 part-time. Students come from 16 states and territories; 2 other countries; 5% are from out of state; 17% Black or African American, non-Hispanic/Latino; 9% Hispanic/Latino; 2% Asian, non-Hispanic/Latino; 0.3% Native Hawaiian or other Pacific Islander, non-Hispanic/Latino; 0.2% American Indian or Alaska Native, non-Hispanic/Latino; 3%

Two or more races, non-Hispanic/Latino; 11% Race/ethnicity unknown; 0.6% international; 17% transferred in; 51% live on campus. *Retention:* 75% of full-time freshmen returned.

Freshmen *Admission:* 1,241 applied, 638 admitted, 127 enrolled. *Average high school GPA:* 3.1. *Test scores:* SAT critical reading scores over 500: 33%; SAT math scores over 500: 36%; ACT scores over 18: 83%; SAT critical reading scores over 600: 9%; SAT math scores over 600: 3%; ACT scores over 24: 33%.

Faculty *Total:* 69, 61% full-time, 68% with terminal degrees. *Student/faculty ratio:* 16:1.

Academics *Calendar:* semesters. *Degree:* bachelor's. *Special study options:* academic remediation for entering students, accelerated degree program, adult/continuing education programs, advanced placement credit, cooperative education, distance learning, honors programs, independent study, internships, off-campus study, part-time degree program, services for LD students, student-designed majors, study abroad, summer session for credit. *ROTC:* Army (c), Air Force (c). *Unusual degree programs:* 3-2 business administration with Sage Graduate School; clinical biology and cytotechnology with Albany College of Pharmacy.

Computers on Campus 205 computers/terminals are available on campus for general student use. Students can access the following: campus intranet, computer help desk, free student e-mail accounts, online (class) grades, online (class) registration. Campuswide network is available. 100% of college-owned or -operated housing units are wired for high-speed Internet access. Wireless service is available via classrooms, computer labs, learning centers, libraries, student centers.

Student Life *Housing options:* coed, women-only. Campus housing is university owned. Freshman applicants given priority for college housing. *Activities and organizations:* Sage African, Latino, Asian, and Native American, VIBE, College Republicans, Love Your College Experience, Sage GEMS. *Campus security:* 24-hour emergency response devices and patrols, late-night transport/escort service, controlled dormitory access, 24-hour security cameras. *Student services:* health clinic, personal/psychological counseling.

Athletics Member NCAA. All Division III. *Intercollegiate sports:* basketball M/W, cross-country running M, golf M, lacrosse W, soccer M/W, softball W, tennis M/W, volleyball M/W. *Intramural sports:* badminton M/W, cheerleading W(c), crew M(c)/W(c), football M/W, ice hockey M(c)/W(c), skiing (cross-country) M(c).

Standardized Tests *Required for some:* SAT or ACT (for admission).

Costs (2012–13) *Comprehensive fee:* $38,995 includes full-time tuition ($27,000), mandatory fees ($1000), and room and board ($10,995). Part-time tuition: $900 per credit hour. *College room only:* $5795. Room and board charges vary according to board plan. *Payment plans:* installment, deferred payment. *Waivers:* employees or children of employees.

Financial Aid Of all full-time matriculated undergraduates who enrolled in 2012, 624 applied for aid, 606 were judged to have need. 253 Federal Work-Study jobs (averaging $2003). 11 state and other part-time jobs (averaging $5864). In 2012, 9 non-need-based awards were made. *Average need-based loan:* $4421. *Average need-based gift aid:* $14,673. *Average non-need-based aid:* $7056. *Average indebtedness upon graduation:* $28,971.

Applying *Options:* electronic application, deferred entrance. *Application fee:* $30. *Required:* essay or personal statement, high school transcript, minimum 2.5 GPA, 2 letters of recommendation, portfolio for fine arts program. *Recommended:* interview. *Application deadlines:* rolling (freshmen), 8/1 (transfers). *Notification:* 8/15 (freshmen), continuous until 8/15 (transfers).

Freshman Application Contact Mr. Thomas Breen, Senior Director of Undergraduate Admission, Sage College of Albany, 140 New Scotland Avenue, Albany, NY 12208. *Phone:* 518-292-1928. *Toll-free phone:* 888-VERY-SAGE. *Fax:* 518-292-1912. *E-mail:* scaadm@sage.edu.

Website: http://www.sage.edu/.

St. Bonaventure University

St. Bonaventure, New York

- **Independent** comprehensive, founded 1858, affiliated with Roman Catholic Church
- **Small-town** 500-acre campus
- **Endowment** $50.6 million
- **Coed** 1,908 undergraduate students, 96% full-time, 52% women, 48% men
- **Moderately difficult** entrance level, 79% of applicants were admitted

Undergraduates 1,839 full-time, 69 part-time. Students come from 33 states and territories; 32 other countries; 76% are from out of state; 5% Black or African American, non-Hispanic/Latino; 5% Hispanic/Latino; 3% Asian, non-Hispanic/Latino; 0.7% Native Hawaiian or other Pacific Islander, non-Hispanic/Latino; 0.6% American Indian or Alaska Native, non-Hispanic/Latino; 0.8%

ST. BONAVENTURE
UNIVERSITY
Founded 1858

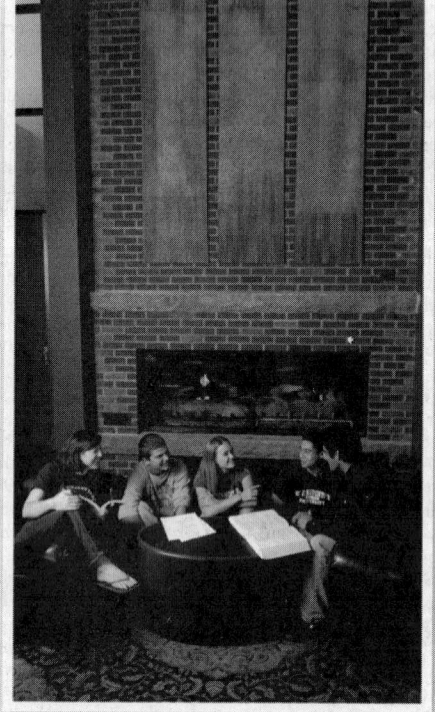

For more than 150 years, we've been helping

good students
become
extraordinary

Arts & Sciences | Business | Education
Journalism/Mass Communication
Combined degree Pre-Health Programs

To learn more about SBU, visit **www.sbu.edu**

Two or more races, non-Hispanic/Latino; 15% Race/ethnicity unknown; 2% international; 4% transferred in; 76% live on campus. *Retention:* 81% of full-time freshmen returned.

Freshmen *Admission:* 2,456 applied, 1,942 admitted, 486 enrolled. *Average high school GPA:* 3.31. *Test scores:* SAT critical reading scores over 500: 57%; SAT math scores over 500: 64%; SAT writing scores over 500: 48%; ACT scores over 18: 91%; SAT critical reading scores over 600: 18%; SAT math scores over 600: 26%; SAT writing scores over 600: 13%; ACT scores over 24: 51%; SAT critical reading scores over 700: 2%; SAT math scores over 700: 5%; SAT writing scores over 700: 2%; ACT scores over 30: 9%.

Faculty *Total:* 220, 70% full-time, 61% with terminal degrees. *Student/faculty ratio:* 12:1.

Academics *Calendar:* semesters. *Degrees:* bachelor's, master's, post-master's, and postbachelor's certificates. *Special study options:* accelerated degree program, advanced placement credit, distance learning, double majors, honors programs, independent study, internships, off-campus study, part-time degree program, services for LD students, student-designed majors, study abroad, summer session for credit. *ROTC:* Army (b). *Unusual degree programs:* 3-2 business administration.

Computers on Campus 220 computers/terminals and 2,500 ports are available on campus for general student use. Students can access the following: campus intranet, computer help desk, free student e-mail accounts, online (class) grades, online (class) registration, online (class) schedules. Campus-wide network is available. 100% of college-owned or -operated housing units are wired for high-speed Internet access. Wireless service is available via entire campus.

Student Life *Housing:* on-campus residence required for freshman year. *Options:* coed, disabled students. Campus housing is university owned. Freshman campus housing is guaranteed. *Activities and organizations:* drama/theater group, student-run newspaper, radio and television station, choral group, Student Government Association, Bona Responds, BV newspaper, Students for the Mountain, Student Ambassadors. *Campus security:* 24-hour emergency response devices and patrols, late-night transport/escort service, controlled dormitory access. *Student services:* health clinic, personal/psychological counseling.

Athletics Member NCAA. All Division I. *Intercollegiate sports:* baseball M(s), basketball M(s)/W(s), cross-country running M(s)/W(s), field hockey W(c), golf M(s), lacrosse M(c)/W(s), rugby M(c)/W(c), soccer M(s)/W(s), softball W(s), swimming and diving M(s)/W(s), tennis M(s)/W(s). *Intramural sports:* basketball M/W, football M/W, golf M/W, ice hockey M(c), racquetball M/W, soccer M(c)/W(c), softball M/W, table tennis M/W, tennis M/W, volleyball M/W.

Standardized Tests *Required:* SAT or ACT (for admission). *Required for some:* SAT Subject Tests (for admission).

Costs (2013–14) *Comprehensive fee:* $39,431 includes full-time tuition ($27,762), mandatory fees ($965), and room and board ($10,704). Part-time tuition: $830 per credit hour. Part-time tuition and fees vary according to course load. *College room only:* $5294. Room and board charges vary according to board plan and housing facility. *Waivers:* senior citizens and employees or children of employees.

Financial Aid Of all full-time matriculated undergraduates who enrolled in 2011, 1,609 applied for aid, 1,420 were judged to have need, 254 had their need fully met. 313 Federal Work-Study jobs (averaging $834). 340 state and other part-time jobs (averaging $854). In 2011, 408 non-need-based awards were made. *Average percent of need met:* 74%. *Average financial aid package:* $25,378. *Average need-based loan:* $4483. *Average need-based gift aid:* $17,472. *Average non-need-based aid:* $11,697. *Average indebtedness upon graduation:* $37,102.

Applying *Options:* electronic application, deferred entrance. *Required:* high school transcript, 1 letter of recommendation. *Required for some:* essay or personal statement. *Recommended:* essay or personal statement, minimum 3.0 GPA, 3 letters of recommendation, interview. *Application deadlines:* 7/1 (freshmen), 8/15 (transfers). *Notification:* continuous until 10/15 (freshmen), continuous until 10/1 (transfers).

Freshman Application Contact Monica Emery, Director of Recruitment, St. Bonaventure University, 3261 West State Road, St. Bonaventure, NY 14778. *Phone:* 716-375-2400. *Toll-free phone:* 800-462-5050. *Fax:* 716-375-4005. *E-mail:* memery@sbu.edu. *Website:* http://www.sbu.edu/.

See this page for display ad and page 1464 for the College Close-Up.

St. Francis College
Brooklyn Heights, New York

- **Independent Roman Catholic** comprehensive, founded 1884
- **Urban** 1-acre campus with easy access to New York City
- **Coed** 2,837 undergraduate students, 90% full-time, 57% women, 43% men
- **Moderately difficult** entrance level, 74% of applicants were admitted

Undergraduates 2,541 full-time, 296 part-time. Students come from 20 states and territories; 53 other countries; 3% are from out of state; 20% Black or African American, non-Hispanic/Latino; 21% Hispanic/Latino; 4% Asian, non-Hispanic/Latino; 0.3% Native Hawaiian or other Pacific Islander, non-Hispanic/Latino; 0.2% American Indian or Alaska Native, non-Hispanic/Latino; 2% Two or more races, non-Hispanic/Latino; 10% Race/ethnicity unknown; 5% international; 6% transferred in; 5% live on campus. *Retention:* 78% of full-time freshmen returned.

Freshmen *Admission:* 2,577 applied, 1,896 admitted, 695 enrolled. *Test scores:* SAT critical reading scores over 500: 33%; SAT math scores over 500: 34%; SAT writing scores over 500: 31%; SAT critical reading scores over 600: 4%; SAT math scores over 600: 6%; SAT writing scores over 600: 5%.

Faculty *Total:* 281, 30% full-time, 44% with terminal degrees. *Student/faculty ratio:* 18:1.

Academics *Calendar:* semesters. *Degrees:* associate, bachelor's, master's, and postbachelor's certificates. *Special study options:* academic remediation for entering students, accelerated degree program, advanced placement credit, cooperative education, double majors, English as a second language, honors programs, independent study, internships, part-time degree program, student-designed majors, study abroad, summer session for credit. *ROTC:* Army (c), Air Force (c). *Unusual degree programs:* business administration with Dual-degree BS and MS in Accounting; social work with Dual-degree BA and MA in Psychology.

Computers on Campus 354 computers/terminals are available on campus for general student use. Students can access the following: campus intranet, computer help desk, free student e-mail accounts, online (class) registration, wireless zones. Campuswide network is available. Wireless service is available via classrooms, computer labs, libraries, student centers.

Student Life *Housing options:* cooperative. Campus housing is provided by a third party. *Activities and organizations:* drama/theater group, student-run newspaper, radio station, choral group, Latin American Society, Fine Arts Society, Power Lifting Club, Games Club, Haitian American Students Alliance, national fraternities, national sororities. *Campus security:* ID checks, crime awareness workshops, pamphlets, posters, films, emergency notification system. *Student services:* personal/psychological counseling.

Athletics Member NCAA. All Division I. *Intercollegiate sports:* basketball M(s)/W(s), cross-country running M(s)/W(s), golf M(s)/W(s), soccer M(s), swimming and diving M(s)/W(s), tennis M(s)/W(s), track and field M(s)/W(s), volleyball W(s), water polo M(s)/W(s). *Intramural sports:* basketball M/W, football M, soccer M/W, table tennis M/W, volleyball M/W.

Standardized Tests *Required:* SAT (for admission).

Costs (2012–13) *Tuition:* $18,500 full-time, $620 per credit part-time. Full-time tuition and fees vary according to course level, course load, degree level, and program. Part-time tuition and fees vary according to course level, course load, and degree level. *Required fees:* $700 full-time, $175 per term part-time. *Room only:* $13,000. Room and board charges vary according to housing facility. *Payment plans:* installment, deferred payment. *Waivers:* employees or children of employees.

Financial Aid Of all full-time matriculated undergraduates who enrolled in 2006, 1,747 applied for aid, 1,683 were judged to have need, 443 had their need fully met. 161 Federal Work-Study jobs (averaging $2200). *Average percent of need met:* 64%. *Average financial aid package:* $9300. *Average need-based loan:* $7700. *Average need-based gift aid:* $6640.

Applying *Options:* electronic application, deferred entrance. *Application fee:* $35. *Required:* essay or personal statement, high school transcript, minimum 2.0 GPA, 1 letter of recommendation. *Recommended:* interview. *Application deadlines:* rolling (freshmen), rolling (transfers). *Notification:* continuous (freshmen), continuous (transfers).

Freshman Application Contact Mrs. Lisa Randazzo, Associate Director of Admissions, St. Francis College, 180 Remsen Street, Brooklyn Heights, NY 11201-4398. *Phone:* 718-489-5336. *Fax:* 718-802-0453. *E-mail:* lrandazzo@sfc.edu. *Website:* http://www.sfc.edu/.

St. John Fisher College
Rochester, New York

- **Independent** comprehensive, founded 1948, affiliated with Roman Catholic Church
- **Suburban** 154-acre campus
- **Endowment** $50.5 million
- **Coed** 2,960 undergraduate students, 93% full-time, 59% women, 41% men
- **Moderately difficult** entrance level, 64% of applicants were admitted

Undergraduates 2,753 full-time, 207 part-time. Students come from 25 states and territories; 2 other countries; 3% are from out of state; 4% Black or African American, non-Hispanic/Latino; 4% Hispanic/Latino; 3% Asian, non-Hispanic/Latino; 0.1% Native Hawaiian or other Pacific Islander, non-Hispanic/Latino; 0.3% American Indian or Alaska Native, non-Hispanic/Latino; 1% Two or more races, non-Hispanic/Latino; 3% Race/ethnicity unknown; 0.1% international; 10% transferred in; 49% live on campus. *Retention:* 84% of full-time freshmen returned.

Freshmen *Admission:* 3,769 applied, 2,419 admitted, 578 enrolled. *Average high school GPA:* 3.5. *Test scores:* SAT critical reading scores over 500: 64%; SAT math scores over 500: 77%; SAT writing scores over 500: 54%; ACT scores over 18: 98%; SAT critical reading scores over 600: 13%; SAT math scores over 600: 28%; SAT writing scores over 600: 12%; ACT scores over 24: 59%; SAT critical reading scores over 700: 2%; SAT math scores over 700: 2%; SAT writing scores over 700: 1%; ACT scores over 30: 5%.

Faculty *Total:* 415, 54% full-time, 47% with terminal degrees. *Student/faculty ratio:* 13:1.

Academics *Calendar:* semesters. *Degrees:* certificates, bachelor's, master's, doctoral, post-master's, and postbachelor's certificates. *Special study options:* academic remediation for entering students, accelerated degree program, adult/continuing education programs, advanced placement credit, distance learning, double majors, honors programs, independent study, internships, off-campus study, part-time degree program, services for LD students, student-designed majors, study abroad, summer session for credit. *ROTC:* Army (c), Navy (c), Air Force (c). *Unusual degree programs:* 3-2 engineering with Clarkson University, Manhattan College, Rensselaer Polytechnic Institute, Columbia University, University of Detroit Mercy, University of Rochester, S.U.N.Y. at Buffalo.

Computers on Campus 550 computers/terminals and 1,875 ports are available on campus for general student use. Students can access the following: campus intranet, computer help desk, free student e-mail accounts, online (class) grades, online (class) registration, online (class) schedules. Campuswide network is available. 100% of college-owned or -operated housing units are wired for high-speed Internet access. Wireless service is available via entire campus.

Student Life *Housing options:* coed, women-only, disabled students. Campus housing is university owned. Freshman campus housing is guaranteed. *Activities and organizations:* drama/theater group, student-run newspaper, television station, choral group, Student Government, Student Activities Board, Commuter Council, Resident Student Association, Teddi Dance for Love. *Campus security:* 24-hour emergency response devices and patrols, late-night transport/escort service, controlled dormitory access. *Student services:* health clinic, personal/psychological counseling.

Athletics Member NCAA. All Division III. *Intercollegiate sports:* baseball M, basketball M/W, crew M, cross-country running M/W, field hockey W, football M, golf M/W, lacrosse M/W, soccer M/W, softball W, tennis M/W, track and field M/W, volleyball W. *Intramural sports:* basketball M/W, cheerleading W(c), crew M(c)/W(c), equestrian M(c)/W(c), ice hockey M(c)/W(c), rugby M(c)/W(c), soccer M/W, volleyball M.

Standardized Tests *Required:* SAT or ACT (for admission).

Costs (2013–14) *Comprehensive fee:* $39,370 includes full-time tuition ($27,870), mandatory fees ($560), and room and board ($10,940). Part-time tuition: $730 per credit hour. Part-time tuition and fees vary according to course load. *College room only:* $7090. Room and board charges vary according to board plan. *Payment plans:* installment, deferred payment. *Waivers:* employees or children of employees.

Financial Aid Of all full-time matriculated undergraduates who enrolled in 2012, 2,523 applied for aid, 2,296 were judged to have need, 891 had their need fully met. 1,366 Federal Work-Study jobs (averaging $1448). In 2012, 423 non-need-based awards were made. *Average percent of need met:* 78%. *Average financial aid package:* $19,460. *Average need-based loan:* $4704. *Average need-based gift aid:* $14,561. *Average non-need-based aid:* $9876. *Average indebtedness upon graduation:* $32,157.

Applying *Options:* electronic application, early decision, deferred entrance. *Application fee:* $30. *Required:* essay or personal statement, high school transcript, minimum 3.0 GPA, 1 letter of recommendation. *Recommended:* interview. *Application deadlines:* rolling (freshmen), rolling (transfers). *Early* *decision deadline:* 12/1. *Notification:* continuous until 12/1 (freshmen), continuous until 9/1 (transfers), 12/15 (early decision).

Freshman Application Contact Mrs. Stacy A. Ledermann, Director of Freshmen Admissions, St. John Fisher College, 3690 East Avenue, Rochester, NY 14618. *Phone:* 585-385-8064. *Toll-free phone:* 800-444-4640. *Fax:* 585-385-8386. *E-mail:* admissions@sjfc.edu.
Website: http://www.sjfc.edu/.

See below for display ad and page 1468 for the College Close-Up.

St. John's University

Queens, New York

- **Independent** university, founded 1870, affiliated with Roman Catholic Church
- **Urban** 105-acre campus with easy access to New York City
- **Endowment** $350.5 million
- **Coed** 15,840 undergraduate students, 69% full-time, 54% women, 46% men
- **Moderately difficult** entrance level, 53% of applicants were admitted

Undergraduates 10,956 full-time, 4,884 part-time. Students come from 48 states and territories; 92 other countries; 29% are from out of state; 19% Black or African American, non-Hispanic/Latino; 16% Hispanic/Latino; 18% Asian, non-Hispanic/Latino; 0.3% Native Hawaiian or other Pacific Islander, non-Hispanic/Latino; 0.2% American Indian or Alaska Native, non-Hispanic/Latino; 4% Two or more races, non-Hispanic/Latino; 2% Race/ethnicity unknown; 5% international; 3% transferred in; 31% live on campus. *Retention:* 76% of full-time freshmen returned.

Freshmen *Admission:* 51,634 applied, 27,449 admitted, 2,792 enrolled. *Average high school GPA:* 3.3. *Test scores:* SAT critical reading scores over 500: 69%; SAT math scores over 500: 73%; ACT scores over 18: 96%; SAT critical reading scores over 600: 22%; SAT math scores over 600: 33%; ACT scores over 24: 52%; SAT critical reading scores over 700: 3%; SAT math scores over 700: 9%; ACT scores over 30: 11%.

Faculty *Total:* 1,467, 44% full-time, 54% with terminal degrees. *Student/faculty ratio:* 17:1.

Academics *Calendar:* semesters. *Degrees:* certificates, associate, bachelor's, master's, doctoral, post-master's, and postbachelor's certificates. *Special study options:* accelerated degree program, adult/continuing education programs, advanced placement credit, distance learning, double majors, English as a second language, honors programs, independent study, internships, off-campus study, part-time degree program, services for LD students, study abroad, summer session for credit. *ROTC:* Army (b). *Unusual degree programs:* 3-2 engineering with Manhattan College.

Computers on Campus 13,025 computers/terminals and 302 ports are available on campus for general student use. Students can access the following: campus intranet, computer help desk, free student e-mail accounts, online (class) grades, online (class) registration, online (class) schedules. Campuswide network is available. 100% of college-owned or -operated housing units are wired for high-speed Internet access. Wireless service is available via entire campus.

Student Life *Housing options:* coed. Campus housing is university owned and leased by the school. Freshman applicants given priority for college housing. *Activities and organizations:* drama/theater group, student-run newspaper, radio and television station, choral group, Student Government, Incorporated, Student Programming Board, Haraya (Pan-African Students Coalition), American Pharmaceutical Association, Muslim Student Organization, national fraternities, national sororities. *Campus security:* 24-hour emergency response devices and patrols, student patrols, late-night transport/escort service, controlled dormitory access, Emergency Notification System. *Student services:* health clinic, personal/psychological counseling.

Athletics Member NCAA. All Division I. *Intercollegiate sports:* baseball M(s), basketball M(s)/W(s), cross-country running W(s), fencing M(s)/W(s), golf M(s)/W(s), lacrosse M(s), soccer M(s)/W(s), softball W(s), tennis M(s)/W(s), track and field W(s), volleyball W(s). *Intramural sports:* badminton M/W, basketball M/W, bowling M(c)/W(c), cheerleading M/W, fencing M/W, football M/W, racquetball M/W, soccer M/W, softball M/W, table tennis M/W, tennis M/W, ultimate Frisbee M/W, volleyball M(c)/W(c), weight lifting M/W.

Standardized Tests *Required:* SAT or ACT (for admission).

Costs (2012–13) *Comprehensive fee:* $50,790 includes full-time tuition ($34,750), mandatory fees ($770), and room and board ($15,270). Full-time tuition and fees vary according to course load, program, and student level. Part-time tuition: $1158 per credit. Part-time tuition and fees vary according to course load, program, and student level. *Required fees:* $288 per term part-time. *College room only:* $9550. Room and board charges vary according to board plan, housing facility, and location. *Payment plan:* installment. *Waivers:* senior citizens and employees or children of employees.

Financial Aid Of all full-time matriculated undergraduates who enrolled in 2011, 9,814 applied for aid, 9,340 were judged to have need, 896 had their need fully met. 835 Federal Work-Study jobs (averaging $2512). In 2011, 342

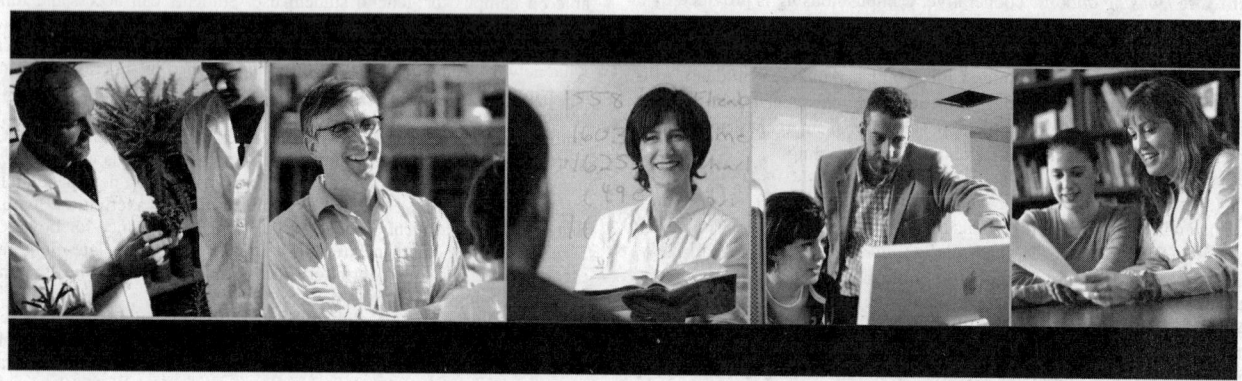

Teaching is what we do best.

St. John Fisher College in Rochester, NY, offers students access to an outstanding faculty—caring and competent men and women who help students develop critical-thinking skills, a foundation in the liberal arts, and proficiency in a major. Our goal is to help students reach their goals.

Visit our impressive campus and see for yourself!

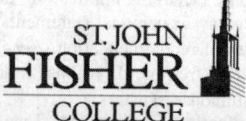

ST. JOHN
FISHER
COLLEGE

www.sjfc.edu/freshman

non-need-based awards were made. *Average percent of need met:* 70%. *Average financial aid package:* $23,468. *Average need-based loan:* $4682. *Average need-based gift aid:* $13,255. *Average non-need-based aid:* $12,133. *Average indebtedness upon graduation:* $29,199.

Applying *Options:* electronic application, early admission, deferred entrance. *Application fee:* $50. *Required:* high school transcript. *Required for some:* essay or personal statement, 2 letters of recommendation, interview, PharmD requires signed Doctor of Pharmacy Technical Standards. *Recommended:* essay or personal statement, minimum 3.0 GPA. *Application deadlines:* rolling (freshmen), rolling (out-of-state freshmen), rolling (transfers). *Notification:* continuous (freshmen), continuous (out-of-state freshmen), continuous (transfers).

Freshman Application Contact Mr. Bryan J. Gross, Associate Vice President of Enrollment Management, St. John's University, 8000 Utopia Parkway, Queens, NY 11439. *Phone:* 718-990-2000. *Toll-free phone:* 888-9STJOHNS. *Fax:* 718-990-2096. *E-mail:* admhelp@stjohns.edu. *Website:* http://www.stjohns.edu/.

St. Joseph's College, Long Island Campus

Patchogue, New York

- **Independent** comprehensive, founded 1916
- **Suburban** 51-acre campus with easy access to New York City
- **Endowment** $25.5 million
- **Coed** 3,522 undergraduate students, 81% full-time, 71% women, 29% men
- **Moderately difficult** entrance level, 72% of applicants were admitted

Undergraduates 2,847 full-time, 675 part-time. Students come from 13 states and territories; 35 other countries; 1% are from out of state; 5% Black or African American, non-Hispanic/Latino; 7% Hispanic/Latino; 2% Asian, non-Hispanic/Latino; 0.2% Native Hawaiian or other Pacific Islander, non-Hispanic/Latino; 0.4% American Indian or Alaska Native, non-Hispanic/Latino; 2% Two or more races, non-Hispanic/Latino; 13% Race/ethnicity unknown; 13% transferred in. *Retention:* 85% of full-time freshmen returned.

Freshmen *Admission:* 1,609 applied, 1,165 admitted, 378 enrolled. *Average high school GPA:* 3.5. *Test scores:* SAT critical reading scores over 500: 76%; SAT math scores over 500: 76%; SAT writing scores over 500: 72%; ACT scores over 18: 97%; SAT critical reading scores over 600: 18%; SAT math scores over 600: 30%; SAT writing scores over 600: 15%; ACT scores over 24: 40%; SAT critical reading scores over 700: 1%; SAT math scores over 700: 3%; SAT writing scores over 700: 2%; ACT scores over 30: 2%.

Faculty *Total:* 453, 26% full-time, 30% with terminal degrees. *Student/faculty ratio:* 14:1.

Academics *Calendar:* 4-1-4. *Degrees:* certificates, bachelor's, master's, and postbachelor's certificates. *Special study options:* accelerated degree program, adult/continuing education programs, advanced placement credit, cooperative education, distance learning, double majors, honors programs, independent study, internships, off-campus study, part-time degree program, services for LD students, study abroad, summer session for credit. *Unusual degree programs:* 3-2 business administration; Math Education; Special Education.

Computers on Campus 269 computers/terminals are available on campus for general student use. Students can access the following: campus intranet, computer help desk, free student e-mail accounts, online (class) grades, online (class) registration, online (class) schedules. Campuswide network is available. Wireless service is available via classrooms, computer centers, computer labs, learning centers, libraries, student centers.

Student Life *Housing:* college housing not available. *Activities and organizations:* drama/theater group, student-run newspaper, choral group, Student Leadership Experience, Biology Club, Diversity Union, Child Study Club, Stars, national fraternities, national sororities. *Campus security:* 24-hour emergency response devices and patrols, late-night transport/escort service, Emergency Notification System via cell phones. *Student services:* health clinic, personal/psychological counseling.

Athletics Member NCAA. All Division III. *Intercollegiate sports:* baseball M, basketball M/W, cross-country running M/W, equestrian sports W, golf M, lacrosse W, soccer M/W, softball W, swimming and diving W, tennis M/W, track and field M/W, volleyball W. *Intramural sports:* basketball M/W, bowling M(c)/W(c), cheerleading M(c)/W(c), equestrian sports M(c)/W(c), field hockey M/W, golf M(c)/W(c), lacrosse M/W, soccer M/W, table tennis M/W, tennis M/W, ultimate Frisbee M/W, volleyball M/W.

Standardized Tests *Required:* SAT or ACT (for admission). *Recommended:* SAT Subject Tests (for admission).

Costs (2012–13) *Tuition:* $19,500 full-time, $635 per credit hour part-time. Full-time tuition and fees vary according to course load, degree level, and pro-

gram. Part-time tuition and fees vary according to course load, degree level, and program. *Required fees:* $625 full-time. *Payment plans:* installment, deferred payment. *Waivers:* senior citizens and employees or children of employees.

Financial Aid Of all full-time matriculated undergraduates who enrolled in 2011, 2,811 applied for aid, 2,116 were judged to have need, 510 had their need fully met. 83 Federal Work-Study jobs (averaging $2342). 131 state and other part-time jobs (averaging $2940). In 2011, 508 non-need-based awards were made. *Average percent of need met:* 67%. *Average financial aid package:* $11,309. *Average need-based loan:* $4237. *Average need-based gift aid:* $8006. *Average non-need-based aid:* $7797. *Average indebtedness upon graduation:* $25,137.

Applying *Options:* electronic application, early admission, deferred entrance. *Application fee:* $25. *Required:* essay or personal statement, high school transcript, minimum 2.8 GPA, Standardized test scores required for most. Midyear grades required for some. *Recommended:* 2 letters of recommendation, interview. *Application deadlines:* 8/15 (freshmen), 8/15 (transfers). *Notification:* continuous until 11/1 (freshmen), continuous until 11/1 (transfers).

Freshman Application Contact Ms. Gigi Lamens, Associate Vice President for Enrollment Management, St. Joseph's College, Long Island Campus, 155 West Roe Boulevard, Patchogue, NY 11772-2399. *Phone:* 631-687-4500. *E-mail:* glamens@sjcny.edu. *Website:* http://www.sjcny.edu/.

St. Joseph's College, New York

Brooklyn, New York

- **Independent** comprehensive, founded 1916
- **Urban** 5-acre campus
- **Endowment** $7.6 million
- **Coed** 1,299 undergraduate students, 75% full-time, 72% women, 28% men
- **Moderately difficult** entrance level, 69% of applicants were admitted

Undergraduates 970 full-time, 329 part-time. Students come from 14 states and territories; 35 other countries; 3% are from out of state; 30% Black or African American, non-Hispanic/Latino; 16% Hispanic/Latino; 7% Asian, non-Hispanic/Latino; 0.2% Native Hawaiian or other Pacific Islander, non-Hispanic/Latino; 0.2% American Indian or Alaska Native, non-Hispanic/Latino; 3% Two or more races, non-Hispanic/Latino; 6% Race/ethnicity unknown; 0.2% international; 8% transferred in; 1% live on campus. *Retention:* 84% of full-time freshmen returned.

Freshmen *Admission:* 1,572 applied, 1,090 admitted, 211 enrolled. *Average high school GPA:* 3.25. *Test scores:* SAT critical reading scores over 500: 45%; SAT math scores over 500: 50%; SAT writing scores over 500: 45%; ACT scores over 18: 80%; SAT critical reading scores over 600: 10%; SAT math scores over 600: 13%; SAT writing scores over 600: 12%; ACT scores over 24: 35%; SAT critical reading scores over 700: 1%; SAT math scores over 700: 1%; SAT writing scores over 700: 2%; ACT scores over 30: 3%.

Faculty *Total:* 189, 32% full-time, 36% with terminal degrees. *Student/faculty ratio:* 11:1.

Academics *Calendar:* semesters. *Degrees:* certificates, bachelor's, master's, and postbachelor's certificates. *Special study options:* adult/continuing education programs, advanced placement credit, cooperative education, distance learning, double majors, honors programs, independent study, internships, part-time degree program, study abroad, summer session for credit. *Unusual degree programs:* 3-2 business administration.

Computers on Campus 214 computers/terminals are available on campus for general student use. Students can access the following: campus intranet, computer help desk, free student e-mail accounts, online (class) grades, online (class) registration, online (class) schedules. Campuswide network is available. Wireless service is available via classrooms, computer centers, computer labs, learning centers, libraries, student centers.

Student Life *Housing:* college housing not available. *Options:* coed. Campus housing is leased by the school. *Activities and organizations:* drama/theater group, student-run newspaper, choral group, Black Student Association, Student Leadership Experience, Chapel Players, Child Study Club, Dance Team, national sororities. *Campus security:* 24-hour emergency response devices and patrols, late-night transport/escort service, Emergency Notification System via cell phones. *Student services:* health clinic, personal/psychological counseling.

Athletics Member NCAA, USCAA. All Division III. *Intercollegiate sports:* baseball M, basketball M/W, cross-country running M/W, soccer M/W, softball W, swimming and diving W, tennis M/W, volleyball M/W. *Intramural sports:* basketball M/W, bowling M/W, golf M(c), swimming and diving M(c), table tennis M/W, ultimate Frisbee M/W, wrestling M(c).

Standardized Tests *Required:* SAT or ACT (for admission).

Costs (2012–13) *Tuition:* $19,500 full-time, $635 per credit hour part-time. Full-time tuition and fees vary according to course load, degree level, and program. Part-time tuition and fees vary according to course load, degree level, and program. *Required fees:* $615 full-time. *Payment plans:* installment, deferred payment. *Waivers:* senior citizens and employees or children of employees.

Financial Aid Of all full-time matriculated undergraduates who enrolled in 2011, 880 applied for aid, 742 were judged to have need, 109 had their need fully met. 112 Federal Work-Study jobs (averaging $1804). 23 state and other part-time jobs (averaging $1939). In 2011, 153 non-need-based awards were made. *Average percent of need met:* 66%. *Average financial aid package:* $13,853. *Average need-based loan:* $3742. *Average need-based gift aid:* $10,680. *Average non-need-based aid:* $9013. *Average indebtedness upon graduation:* $25,836.

Applying *Options:* electronic application, early admission, deferred entrance. *Application fee:* $25. *Required:* high school transcript, minimum 2.5 GPA. *Required for some:* interview. *Recommended:* essay or personal statement, 2 letters of recommendation. *Application deadlines:* 8/15 (freshmen), 8/15 (transfers).

Freshman Application Contact Mr. Michael Learmond, Director of Admissions Operation, St. Joseph's College, New York, 245 Clinton Avenue, Brooklyn, NY 11205-3688. *Phone:* 718-940-5828. *E-mail:* mlearmond@sjcny.edu.

Website: http://www.sjcny.edu/.

See below for display ad and page 1472 for the College Close-Up.

St. Lawrence University

Canton, New York

- **Independent** comprehensive, founded 1856
- **Small-town** 1000-acre campus
- **Endowment** $230.3 million
- **Coed** 2,398 undergraduate students, 99% full-time, 55% women, 45% men
- **Very difficult** entrance level, 48% of applicants were admitted

Undergraduates 2,374 full-time, 24 part-time. Students come from 42 states and territories; 50 other countries; 53% are from out of state; 3% Black or African American, non-Hispanic/Latino; 4% Hispanic/Latino; 2% Asian, non-Hispanic/Latino; 0.1% Native Hawaiian or other Pacific Islander, non-Hispanic/Latino; 0.3% American Indian or Alaska Native, non-Hispanic/Latino; 2% Two or more races, non-Hispanic/Latino; 1% Race/ethnicity unknown; 7% international; 0.8% transferred in; 97% live on campus. *Retention:* 93% of full-time freshmen returned.

Freshmen *Admission:* 4,067 applied, 1,962 admitted, 642 enrolled. *Average high school GPA:* 3.48. *Test scores:* SAT critical reading scores over 500: 93%; SAT math scores over 500: 96%; SAT writing scores over 500: 91%; ACT scores over 18: 100%; SAT critical reading scores over 600: 56%; SAT math scores over 600: 60%; SAT writing scores over 600: 55%; ACT scores over 24: 87%; SAT critical reading scores over 700: 10%; SAT math scores over 700: 11%; SAT writing scores over 700: 7%; ACT scores over 30: 18%.

Faculty *Total:* 201, 84% full-time, 90% with terminal degrees. *Student/faculty ratio:* 12:1.

Academics *Calendar:* semesters. *Degrees:* bachelor's, master's, and post-master's certificates. *Special study options:* advanced placement credit, double majors, independent study, internships, off-campus study, part-time degree program, services for LD students, student-designed majors, study abroad, summer session for credit. *ROTC:* Army (c), Air Force (c). *Unusual degree programs:* 3-2 business administration with Clarkson University, Union College, Rochester Institute of Technology; engineering with Columbia University, Clarkson University, Rensselaer Polytechnic Institute, University of Rochester, University of Southern California, Dartmouth College; nursing with New York University; physician assistant program at Clarkson University, early assurance program for medical school at Syracuse, SUNY Buffalo, SUNY Buffalo School of Dentistry.

Computers on Campus 681 computers/terminals are available on campus for general student use. Students can access the following: computer help desk, free student e-mail accounts, online (class) grades, online (class) registration, online (class) schedules. Campuswide network is available. 100% of college-owned or -operated housing units are wired for high-speed Internet access. Wireless service is available via entire campus.

Student Life *Housing:* on-campus residence required through senior year. *Options:* coed, women-only, disabled students. Campus housing is university owned. Freshman campus housing is guaranteed. *Activities and organizations:* drama/theater group, student-run newspaper, radio station, choral group, Outing Club, student newspaper, student government, Circle K, Habitat for Humanity, national fraternities, national sororities. *Campus security:* 24-hour emergency response devices and patrols, student patrols, late-night transport/escort service, controlled dormitory access. *Student services:* health clinic, personal/psychological counseling, women's center.

Athletics Member NCAA. All Division III except men's and women's ice hockey (Division I). *Intercollegiate sports:* baseball M, basketball M/W, crew M/W, cross-country running M/W, equestrian sports M/W, field hockey W, football M, golf M/W, ice hockey M(s)/W(s), lacrosse M/W, skiing (cross-country) M/W, skiing (downhill) M/W, soccer M/W, softball W, squash M/W, swimming and diving M/W, tennis M/W, track and field M/W, volleyball W. *Intramural sports:* basketball M/W, football M, ice hockey M/W, skiing (cross-country) M/W, soccer M/W, softball W, ultimate Frisbee M/W, volleyball M/W.

Costs (2012–13) *Comprehensive fee:* $55,825 includes full-time tuition ($44,075), mandatory fees ($315), and room and board ($11,435). *College room only:* $6155. Room and board charges vary according to board plan. *Payment plan:* installment. *Waivers:* employees or children of employees.

Financial Aid Of all full-time matriculated undergraduates who enrolled in 2011, 1,696 applied for aid, 1,504 were judged to have need, 565 had their need fully met. 875 Federal Work-Study jobs (averaging $1569). 353 state and other part-time jobs (averaging $1536). In 2011, 504 non-need-based awards were made. *Average percent of need met:* 89%. *Average financial aid package:* $37,945. *Average need-based loan:* $4541. *Average need-based gift aid:* $28,278. *Average non-need-based aid:* $17,381. *Average indebtedness upon graduation:* $26,270. *Financial aid deadline:* 2/1.

Applying *Options:* electronic application, early admission, early decision, deferred entrance. *Application fee:* $60. *Required:* essay or personal statement, high school transcript, 2 letters of recommendation. *Recommended:* minimum 2.0 GPA, interview. *Application deadlines:* 2/1 (freshmen), 4/1 (transfers). *Early decision deadline:* 11/1 (for plan 1), 2/1 (for plan 2). *Notification:* 3/31 (freshmen), 5/1 (transfers), 12/15 (early decision).

Freshman Application Contact Jeff Rickey, Vice President and Dean of Admissions and Financial Aid, St. Lawrence University, 23 Romoda Drive, Canton, NY 13617-1455. *Phone:* 315-229-5261. *Toll-free phone:* 800-285-1856. *Fax:* 315-229-5818. *E-mail:* jrickey@stlawu.edu. *Website:* http://www.stlawu.edu/.

See next page for display ad and page 1476 for the College Close-Up.

St. Thomas Aquinas College

Sparkill, New York

- **Independent** comprehensive, founded 1952
- **Suburban** 46-acre campus with easy access to New York City
- **Endowment** $23.1 million
- **Coed** 1,796 undergraduate students, 69% full-time, 53% women, 47% men
- **Moderately difficult** entrance level, 78% of applicants were admitted

Undergraduates 1,241 full-time, 555 part-time. Students come from 1 other state; 10 other countries; 21% are from out of state; 6% Black or African American, non-Hispanic/Latino; 15% Hispanic/Latino; 2% Asian, non-Hispanic/Latino; 0.3% American Indian or Alaska Native, non-Hispanic/Latino; 1% Two or more races, non-Hispanic/Latino; 9% Race/ethnicity unknown; 1% international; 6% transferred in; 33% live on campus. *Retention:* 75% of full-time freshmen returned.

Freshmen *Admission:* 1,723 applied, 1,338 admitted, 270 enrolled. *Test scores:* SAT critical reading scores over 500: 35%; SAT writing scores over 500: 37%; ACT scores over 18: 78%; SAT critical reading scores over 600: 13%; SAT writing scores over 600: 9%; ACT scores over 24: 33%; SAT critical reading scores over 700: 1%; SAT writing scores over 700: 2%.

Faculty *Total:* 143, 44% full-time, 49% with terminal degrees. *Student/faculty ratio:* 14:1.

Academics *Calendar:* semesters. *Degrees:* associate, bachelor's, master's, post-master's, and postbachelor's certificates. *Special study options:* academic remediation for entering students, accelerated degree program, adult/continuing education programs, advanced placement credit, double majors, freshman honors college, honors programs, independent study, internships, off-campus study, part-time degree program, services for LD students, study abroad, summer session for credit. *ROTC:* Air Force (c). *Unusual degree programs:* 3-2 engineering with George Washington University, Manhattan College; social work with New York University School of Social Work; physical therapy with New York Medical College.

Computers on Campus 200 computers/terminals are available on campus for general student use. Students can access the following: campus intranet, computer help desk, free student e-mail accounts, online (class) grades, online (class) registration, online (class) schedules. Campuswide network is available.

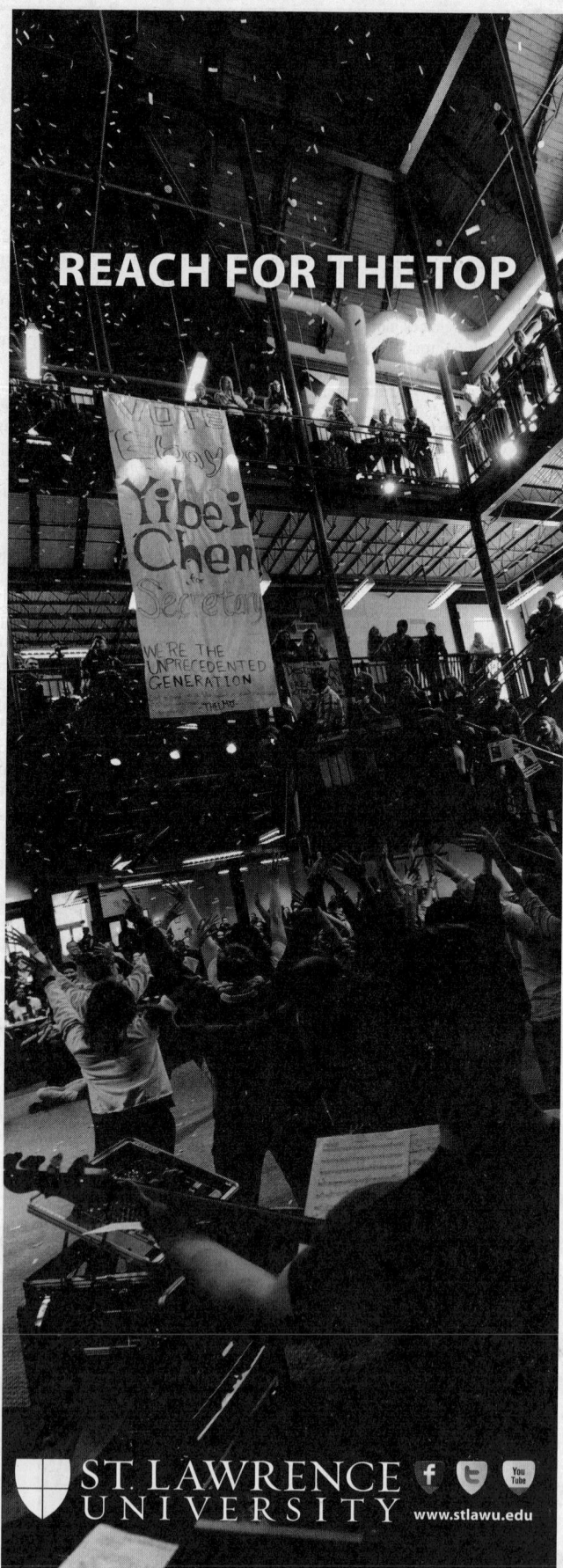

REACH FOR THE TOP

ST. LAWRENCE UNIVERSITY

www.stlawu.edu

100% of college-owned or -operated housing units are wired for high-speed Internet access. Wireless service is available via entire campus.
Student Life *Housing options:* men-only, women-only, disabled students. Campus housing is university owned. Freshman campus housing is guaranteed. *Activities and organizations:* drama/theater group, student-run newspaper, radio station, choral group, Spartan Volunteers, Campus Activities Board, WSTK campus radio, Bowling Club, Laetare Players, national fraternities. *Campus security:* 24-hour emergency response devices and patrols, student patrols, late-night transport/escort service, controlled dormitory access. *Student services:* health clinic, personal/psychological counseling.
Athletics Member NCAA, NAIA. All NCAA Division II. *Intercollegiate sports:* baseball M(s), basketball M(s)/W(s), cross-country running M(s)/W(s), golf M/W, lacrosse W, soccer M(s)/W(s), softball W(s), tennis M/W, volleyball W(s). *Intramural sports:* basketball M/W, volleyball M/W.
Standardized Tests *Required:* SAT or ACT (for admission).
Costs (2013–14) *Comprehensive fee:* $38,140 includes full-time tuition ($25,840), mandatory fees ($1000), and room and board ($11,300). Part-time tuition: $825 per credit. *College room only:* $6090. Room and board charges vary according to board plan and housing facility. *Payment plan:* installment. *Waivers:* employees or children of employees.
Financial Aid Of all full-time matriculated undergraduates who enrolled in 2011, 1,165 applied for aid, 924 were judged to have need, 157 had their need fully met. 200 Federal Work-Study jobs (averaging $1717). In 2011, 176 non-need-based awards were made. *Average percent of need met:* 62%. *Average financial aid package:* $15,233. *Average need-based loan:* $4351. *Average need-based gift aid:* $12,303. *Average non-need-based aid:* $9047. *Average indebtedness upon graduation:* $29,420.
Applying *Options:* electronic application, early decision, early action, deferred entrance. *Application fee:* $30. *Required:* high school transcript, minimum 2.0 GPA. *Required for some:* 3 letters of recommendation. *Recommended:* essay or personal statement, 2 letters of recommendation, interview. *Application deadlines:* rolling (freshmen), rolling (transfers), 12/15 (early action). *Early decision deadline:* 12/1. *Notification:* 10/1 (freshmen), continuous (transfers), 1/15 (early decision), 1/15 (early action).
Freshman Application Contact Ms. Danielle Mac Kay, Director of Admissions, St. Thomas Aquinas College, 125 Route 340, Sparkill, NY 10976. *Phone:* 845-398-4100. *Toll-free phone:* 800-999-STAC. *Fax:* 845-398-4114. *E-mail:* dmackay@stac.edu. *Website:* http://www.stac.edu/.

See previous page for display ad and page 1488 for the College Close-Up.

Sarah Lawrence College

Bronxville, New York

- **Independent** comprehensive, founded 1926
- **Suburban** 44-acre campus with easy access to New York City
- **Coed**
- **Very difficult** entrance level

Faculty *Student/faculty ratio:* 9:1.
Academics *Calendar:* semesters. *Degrees:* bachelor's, master's, and post-master's certificates.
Student Life *Campus security:* 24-hour emergency response devices and patrols, late-night transport/escort service, controlled dormitory access.
Costs (2012–13) *Tuition:* $45,900 full-time. Full-time tuition and fees vary according to course load. Part-time tuition and fees vary according to course load. *Required fees:* $1024 full-time. *Room only:* $9324. Room and board charges vary according to board plan.
Financial Aid *Of all full-time matriculated undergraduates who enrolled in 2012,* 1,061 applied for aid, 955 were judged to have need, 575 had their need fully met. 686 Federal Work-Study jobs (averaging $1682). 46 state and other part-time jobs (averaging $1892). *In 2012,* 109 non-need-based awards were made. *Average percent of need met:* 84. *Average financial aid package:* $36,266. *Average need-based loan:* $4546. *Average need-based gift aid:* $32,825. *Average non-need-based aid:* $6821. *Average indebtedness upon graduation:* $15,309. *Financial aid deadline:* 2/1.
Applying *Options:* early admission, early decision, deferred entrance. *Required:* essay or personal statement, high school transcript, 3 letters of recommendation. *Recommended:* minimum 3.0 GPA, interview.
Freshman Application Contact Mr. Stephen M. Schierloh, Director of Admission, Sarah Lawrence College, 1 Mead Way, Bronxville, NY 10708-5999. *Phone:* 914-395-2510. *Toll-free phone:* 800-888-2858. *Fax:* 914-395-2515. *E-mail:* slcadmit@sarahlawrence.edu. *Website:* http://www.sarahlawrence.edu/.

School of Visual Arts

New York, New York

Freshman Application Contact Admissions Office, School of Visual Arts, 209 East 23rd Street, New York, NY 10010. *Phone:* 212-592-2100. *Toll-free phone:* 800-436-4204. *Fax:* 212-592-2116. *E-mail:* admissions@sva.edu. *Website:* http://www.sva.edu/.

Sh'or Yoshuv Rabbinical College

Lawrence, New York

Director of Admissions Rabbi Moshe Rubin, Registrar, Sh'or Yoshuv Rabbinical College, 1 Cedarlawn Avenue, Lawrence, NY 11559-1714. *Phone:* 516-239-9002 Ext. 124. *Fax:* 516-977-1282. *E-mail:* mrubin@shoryoshuv.org. *Website:* http://www.shoryoshuv.org/.

Siena College

Loudonville, New York

- **Independent Roman Catholic** comprehensive, founded 1937
- **Suburban** 175-acre campus
- **Endowment** $120.7 million
- **Coed** 3,236 undergraduate students, 94% full-time, 52% women, 48% men
- **Moderately difficult** entrance level, 57% of applicants were admitted

Undergraduates 3,047 full-time, 189 part-time. Students come from 33 states and territories; 13 other countries; 19% are from out of state; 3% Black or African American, non-Hispanic/Latino; 6% Hispanic/Latino; 4% Asian, non-Hispanic/Latino; 0.1% Native Hawaiian or other Pacific Islander, non-Hispanic/Latino; 0.3% American Indian or Alaska Native, non-Hispanic/Latino; 2% Two or more races, non-Hispanic/Latino; 0.8% Race/ethnicity unknown; 2% international; 4% transferred in; 77% live on campus. *Retention:* 89% of full-time freshmen returned.
Freshmen *Admission:* 9,577 applied, 5,502 admitted, 734 enrolled. *Average high school GPA:* 3.5. *Test scores:* SAT critical reading scores over 500: 76%; SAT math scores over 500: 83%; SAT writing scores over 500: 71%; ACT scores over 18: 95%; SAT critical reading scores over 600: 27%; SAT math scores over 600: 39%; SAT writing scores over 600: 22%; ACT scores over 24: 63%; SAT critical reading scores over 700: 4%; SAT math scores over 700: 5%; SAT writing scores over 700: 4%; ACT scores over 30: 10%.
Faculty *Total:* 354, 59% full-time, 71% with terminal degrees. *Student/faculty ratio:* 12:1.
Academics *Calendar:* semesters. *Degrees:* certificates, bachelor's, and master's. *Special study options:* accelerated degree program, advanced placement credit, double majors, English as a second language, honors programs, independent study, internships, off-campus study, part-time degree program, services for LD students, study abroad, summer session for credit. *ROTC:* Army (b), Navy (c), Air Force (c).
Computers on Campus 361 computers/terminals and 5,291 ports are available on campus for general student use. Students can access the following: campus intranet, computer help desk, free student e-mail accounts, online (class) grades, online (class) registration, online (class) schedules. Campuswide network is available. 100% of college-owned or -operated housing units are wired for high-speed Internet access. Wireless service is available via classrooms, computer centers, computer labs, dorm rooms, learning centers, libraries, student centers.
Student Life *Housing:* on-campus residence required through senior year. *Options:* coed, disabled students. Campus housing is university owned. Freshman applicants given priority for college housing. *Activities and organizations:* drama/theater group, student-run newspaper, radio and television station, choral group, Dog Pound (sports spirit group), Mentoring Program, Outing Club, READ for the Stars, Accounting student Association, national fraternities, national sororities. *Campus security:* 24-hour emergency response devices and patrols, late-night transport/escort service, controlled dormitory access, call boxes in parking lots and on roadways. *Student services:* health clinic, personal/psychological counseling, women's center, legal services.
Athletics Member NCAA. All Division I. *Intercollegiate sports:* baseball M(s), basketball M(s)/W(s), cheerleading W(c), cross-country running M(s)/W(s), equestrian sports M(c)/W(c), field hockey W(s), golf M(s)/W(s), ice hockey M(c), lacrosse M(s)/W(s), rugby M(c)/W(c), soccer M(s)/W(s), softball W(s), swimming and diving W(s), tennis M(s)/W(s), volleyball M(c)/W(s), water polo W(s). *Intramural sports:* basketball M/W, football M, racquetball M/W, soccer M/W, softball M/W, squash M/W, volleyball M/W.
Standardized Tests *Required:* SAT or ACT (for admission).
Costs (2013–14) *One-time required fee:* $250. *Comprehensive fee:* $43,863 includes full-time tuition ($31,118), mandatory fees ($250), and room and board ($12,495). Full-time tuition and fees vary according to course load and student level. Part-time tuition: $500 per credit. Part-time tuition and fees vary according to course load and student level. *College room only:* $7365. Room and board charges vary according to board plan and housing facility. *Payment plan:* installment. *Waivers:* employees or children of employees.
Financial Aid Of all full-time matriculated undergraduates who enrolled in 2010, 2,641 applied for aid, 2,271 were judged to have need, 335 had their need fully met. 500 Federal Work-Study jobs (averaging $712). In 2010, 223 non-need-based awards were made. *Average percent of need met:* 70%. *Average financial aid package:* $18,100. *Average need-based loan:* $4622. *Average need-based gift aid:* $13,800. *Average non-need-based aid:* $6900. *Average indebtedness upon graduation:* $29,700.
Applying *Options:* electronic application, early admission, early decision, early action, deferred entrance. *Application fee:* $50. *Required:* essay or personal statement, high school transcript, 1 letter of recommendation. *Required for some:* interview. *Recommended:* interview. *Application deadlines:* 2/15 (freshmen), 8/15 (transfers), 12/1 (early action). *Early decision deadline:* 12/1. *Notification:* 3/15 (freshmen), continuous (transfers), 12/15 (early decision), 1/1 (early action).
Freshman Application Contact Ms. Heather Renault, Director of Admissions, Siena College, 515 Loudon Road, Loudonville, NY 12211-1462. *Phone:* 518-783-2426. *Toll-free phone:* 888-AT-SIENA. *Fax:* 518-783-2436. *E-mail:* admit@siena.edu. *Website:* http://www.siena.edu/.

Skidmore College

Saratoga Springs, New York

- **Independent** 4-year, founded 1903
- **Small-town** 800-acre campus with easy access to Albany, NY
- **Endowment** $283.1 million
- **Coed** 2,663 undergraduate students, 99% full-time, 61% women, 39% men
- **Very difficult** entrance level, 42% of applicants were admitted

Undergraduates 2,624 full-time, 39 part-time. Students come from 46 states and territories; 51 other countries; 67% are from out of state; 4% Black or African American, non-Hispanic/Latino; 8% Hispanic/Latino; 6% Asian, non-Hispanic/Latino; 0.3% Native Hawaiian or other Pacific Islander, non-Hispanic/Latino; 5% Two or more races, non-Hispanic/Latino; 7% Race/ethnicity unknown; 6% international; 1% transferred in; 86% live on campus. *Retention:* 92% of full-time freshmen returned.
Freshmen *Admission:* 5,702 applied, 2,389 admitted, 647 enrolled. *Test scores:* SAT critical reading scores over 500: 89%; SAT math scores over 500: 94%; SAT writing scores over 500: 92%; ACT scores over 18: 99%; SAT critical reading scores over 600: 60%; SAT math scores over 600: 63%; SAT writing scores over 600: 61%; ACT scores over 24: 93%; SAT critical reading scores over 700: 17%; SAT math scores over 700: 14%; SAT writing scores over 700: 17%; ACT scores over 30: 30%.
Faculty *Total:* 335, 73% full-time, 71% with terminal degrees. *Student/faculty ratio:* 9:1.
Academics *Calendar:* semesters plus optional 6-week internship period. *Degrees:* bachelor's and master's. *Special study options:* accelerated degree program, adult/continuing education programs, advanced placement credit, double majors, honors programs, independent study, internships, off-campus study, services for LD students, student-designed majors, study abroad, summer session for credit. *ROTC:* Army (c), Air Force (c). *Unusual degree programs:* 3-2 business administration with Clarkson University, Union College, Rochester Institute of Technology, Syracuse University; engineering with Dartmouth College, Clarkson University, Rensselaer Polytechnic Institute; nursing with New York University; MALS at Skidmore College, MSF with Syracuse University, MSA with Syracuse University, DPT and MS in Occupational Therapy with Sage Graduate School.
Computers on Campus 600 computers/terminals are available on campus for general student use. Students can access the following: campus intranet, computer help desk, free student e-mail accounts, online (class) grades, online (class) registration, online (class) schedules. Campuswide network is available. 100% of college-owned or -operated housing units are wired for high-speed Internet access. Wireless service is available via classrooms, computer centers, computer labs, dorm rooms, learning centers, libraries, student centers.
Student Life *Housing:* on-campus residence required through sophomore year. *Options:* coed, women-only, disabled students. Campus housing is university

" Creative Thought Matters *actually* has *sentimental* value to *me*. I asked my *Mother* if she remembered **THE SLOGAN** from SKIDMORE, **Creative Thought Matters**. She answered as if it was the **stupidest** question I'd ever asked, '*Of course! It's why you went to Skidmore.*' **"**

2008 Skidmore graduate

" Creative Thought Matters is *more* than just a theme for me. It really **captures** what makes SKIDMORE *unique*.... SKIDMORE understands that learning does not *(and should not) exist* in neat little **silos**, which I think helps GRADUATES **thrive** in a **complex**, *INTERCONNECTED* WORLD. **"**

2007 Skidmore graduate

Skidmore College Office of Admissions
Saratoga Springs, New York
www.skidmore.edu

Creative Thought Matters

owned. Freshman campus housing is guaranteed. *Activities and organizations:* drama/theater group, student-run newspaper, radio and television station, choral group, Student Government Association, student radio station, Student Volunteer Bureau, Outing Club, Skidmore News. *Campus security:* 24-hour emergency response devices and patrols, late-night transport/escort service, controlled dormitory access, well-lit campus. *Student services:* health clinic, personal/psychological counseling.

Athletics Member NCAA. All Division III. *Intercollegiate sports:* baseball M, basketball M/W, crew M/W, equestrian sports W, field hockey W, golf M, ice hockey M, lacrosse M/W, soccer M/W, softball W, swimming and diving M/W, tennis M/W, volleyball W. *Intramural sports:* basketball M/W, football M/W, racquetball M/W, soccer M/W, softball M/W, tennis M/W, volleyball M/W.

Standardized Tests *Required:* SAT or ACT (for admission). *Recommended:* SAT Subject Tests (for admission).

Costs (2012–13) *Comprehensive fee:* $55,764 includes full-time tuition ($43,138), mandatory fees ($882), and room and board ($11,744). Full-time tuition and fees vary according to course load. Part-time tuition: $1438 per credit. Part-time tuition and fees vary according to course load. *Required fees:* $25 per term part-time. *College room only:* $6944. Room and board charges vary according to board plan and housing facility. *Payment plans:* tuition prepayment, installment. *Waivers:* senior citizens and employees or children of employees.

Financial Aid Of all full-time matriculated undergraduates who enrolled in 2012, 1,269 applied for aid, 1,152 were judged to have need, 1,020 had their need fully met. In 2012, 10 non-need-based awards were made. *Average percent of need met:* 95%. *Average financial aid package:* $37,824. *Average need-based loan:* $3634. *Average need-based gift aid:* $34,926. *Average non-need-based aid:* $11,700. *Average indebtedness upon graduation:* $22,753. *Financial aid deadline:* 2/1.

Applying *Options:* electronic application, early admission, early decision, deferred entrance. *Application fee:* $65. *Required:* essay or personal statement, high school transcript, 2 letters of recommendation. *Recommended:* interview. *Application deadlines:* 1/15 (freshmen), 4/1 (transfers). *Early decision deadline:* 11/15 (for plan 1), 1/15 (for plan 2). *Notification:* 4/1 (freshmen), 12/15 (early decision plan 1), 2/15 (early decision plan 2).

Freshman Application Contact Ms. Mary Lou Bates, Dean of Admissions and Financial Aid, Skidmore College, 815 North Broadway, Saratoga Springs, NY 12866-1632. *Phone:* 518-580-5570. *Toll-free phone:* 800-867-6007. *Fax:* 518-580-5584. *E-mail:* admissions@skidmore.edu.
Website: http://www.skidmore.edu/.

See this page for display ad and page 1504 for the College Close-Up.

State University of New York at Fredonia

Fredonia, New York

- **State-supported** comprehensive, founded 1826, part of State University of New York System
- **Small-town** 249-acre campus with easy access to Buffalo
- **Endowment** $24.5 million
- **Coed** 5,231 undergraduate students, 97% full-time, 56% women, 44% men
- **Moderately difficult** entrance level, 52% of applicants were admitted

Undergraduates 5,071 full-time, 160 part-time. Students come from 26 states and territories; 12 other countries; 2% are from out of state; 4% Black or African American, non-Hispanic/Latino; 4% Hispanic/Latino; 1% Asian, non-Hispanic/Latino; 0.1% Native Hawaiian or other Pacific Islander, non-Hispanic/Latino; 0.4% American Indian or Alaska Native, non-Hispanic/Latino; 2% Two or more races, non-Hispanic/Latino; 4% Race/ethnicity unknown; 3% international; 8% transferred in; 53% live on campus. *Retention:* 78% of full-time freshmen returned.

Freshmen *Admission:* 5,883 applied, 3,032 admitted, 1,003 enrolled. *Average high school GPA:* 3.3. *Test scores:* SAT critical reading scores over 500: 61%; SAT math scores over 500: 66%; ACT scores over 18: 95%; SAT critical reading scores over 600: 16%; SAT math scores over 600: 20%; ACT scores over 24: 47%; SAT critical reading scores over 700: 2%; SAT math scores over 700: 2%; ACT scores over 30: 4%.

Faculty *Total:* 482, 52% full-time, 54% with terminal degrees. *Student/faculty ratio:* 16:1.

Academics *Calendar:* semesters. *Degrees:* bachelor's, master's, and post-master's certificates. *Special study options:* accelerated degree program, adult/continuing education programs, advanced placement credit, distance learning, double majors, honors programs, independent study, internships, off-campus study, part-time degree program, services for LD students, student-designed majors, study abroad, summer session for credit. *Unusual degree programs:* 3-

2 engineering with Clarkson University, State University of New York at Buffalo, Case Western Reserve, Columbia University, Cornell University, Louisiana Technical University, New York State College of Ceramics at Alfred, Ohio State University.

Computers on Campus 500 computers/terminals are available on campus for general student use. Students can access the following: campus intranet, computer help desk, free student e-mail accounts, online (class) grades, online (class) registration, online (class) schedules. Campuswide network is available. 100% of college-owned or -operated housing units are wired for high-speed Internet access. Wireless service is available via entire campus.

Student Life *Housing:* on-campus residence required through sophomore year. *Options:* coed, men-only, women-only. Campus housing is university owned. Freshman campus housing is guaranteed. *Activities and organizations:* drama/theater group, student-run newspaper, radio and television station, choral group, Student Association, Undergraduate Alumni Council, Communication Club, ethnic organizations, spectrum entertainment board, national fraternities, national sororities. *Campus security:* 24-hour emergency response devices and patrols, late-night transport/escort service, controlled dormitory access. *Student services:* health clinic, personal/psychological counseling, legal services.

Athletics Member NCAA. All Division III. *Intercollegiate sports:* baseball M, basketball M/W, cheerleading M/W, cross-country running M/W, field hockey M(c)/W(c), ice hockey M, lacrosse M(c)/W, rugby M(c)/W(c), soccer M/W, softball W, swimming and diving M/W, tennis M/W, track and field M/W, volleyball M/W. *Intramural sports:* basketball M/W, cross-country running M/W, fencing M(c)/W(c), ice hockey M(c), racquetball M/W, rock climbing M/W, skiing (cross-country) M/W, skiing (downhill) M/W, soccer M/W, softball M/W, squash M/W, tennis M/W, ultimate Frisbee M/W, volleyball M(c)/W, water polo M/W.

Standardized Tests *Required:* SAT or ACT (for admission).

Costs (2012–13) *Tuition:* state resident $5570 full-time, $232 per credit hour part-time; nonresident $14,820 full-time, $618 per credit hour part-time. *Required fees:* $1488 full-time, $62 per credit part-time. *Room and board:* $11,100; room only: $6550. Room and board charges vary according to board plan and housing facility. *Payment plan:* installment.

Financial Aid Of all full-time matriculated undergraduates who enrolled in 2012, 4,230 applied for aid, 3,417 were judged to have need, 367 had their need fully met. 240 Federal Work-Study jobs (averaging $1704). In 2012, 302 non-need-based awards were made. *Average percent of need met:* 59%. *Average financial aid package:* $9530. *Average need-based loan:* $5120. *Average need-based gift aid:* $4798. *Average non-need-based aid:* $2338. *Average indebtedness upon graduation:* $27,431.

Applying *Options:* electronic application, early admission, early decision, deferred entrance. *Application fee:* $50. *Required:* essay or personal statement, high school transcript, 1 letter of recommendation. *Required for some:* interview, Audition for music, dance and theater programs; portfolio for visual arts and technical theatre programs. *Application deadlines:* rolling (freshmen), rolling (transfers). *Early decision deadline:* 11/1. *Notification:* continuous (freshmen), continuous (transfers), 12/1 (early decision).

Freshman Application Contact Office of Admissions, State University of New York at Fredonia, 178 Central Avenue, Fredonia, NY 14063. *Phone:* 716-673-3251. *Toll-free phone:* 800-252-1212. *Fax:* 716-673-3249. *E-mail:* admissions@fredonia.edu. *Website:* http://www.fredonia.edu/.

State University of New York at New Paltz

New Paltz, New York

- **State-supported** comprehensive, founded 1828, part of State University of New York System
- **Small-town** 216-acre campus
- **Endowment** $13.5 million
- **Coed** 6,685 undergraduate students, 93% full-time, 62% women, 38% men
- **Very difficult** entrance level, 44% of applicants were admitted

Undergraduates 6,194 full-time, 491 part-time. Students come from 74 other countries; 4% are from out of state; 5% Black or African American, non-Hispanic/Latino; 12% Hispanic/Latino; 4% Asian, non-Hispanic/Latino; 0.1% Native Hawaiian or other Pacific Islander, non-Hispanic/Latino; 0.1% American Indian or Alaska Native, non-Hispanic/Latino; 2% Two or more races, non-Hispanic/Latino; 8% Race/ethnicity unknown; 3% international; 10% transferred in; 42% live on campus. *Retention:* 88% of full-time freshmen returned.

Freshmen *Admission:* 12,892 applied, 5,620 admitted, 1,119 enrolled. *Test scores:* SAT critical reading scores over 500: 82%; SAT writing scores over

500: 79%; ACT scores over 18: 98%; SAT critical reading scores over 600: 31%; SAT writing scores over 600: 30%; ACT scores over 24: 72%; SAT critical reading scores over 700: 3%; SAT writing scores over 700: 2%; ACT scores over 30: 8%.

Faculty *Total:* 634, 53% full-time, 55% with terminal degrees. *Student/faculty ratio:* 16:1.

Academics *Calendar:* semesters. *Degrees:* bachelor's, master's, and post-master's certificates. *Special study options:* academic remediation for entering students, adult/continuing education programs, advanced placement credit, cooperative education, distance learning, double majors, English as a second language, honors programs, independent study, internships, off-campus study, part-time degree program, services for LD students, student-designed majors, study abroad, summer session for credit. *Unusual degree programs:* 3-2 forestry with State University of New York College of Environmental Science and Forestry.

Computers on Campus Students can access the following: campus intranet, computer help desk, free student e-mail accounts, online (class) grades, online (class) registration, online (class) schedules. Campuswide network is available. 100% of college-owned or -operated housing units are wired for high-speed Internet access. Wireless service is available via classrooms, dorm rooms, libraries, student centers.

Student Life *Housing:* on-campus residence required for freshman year. *Options:* coed, men-only, women-only, disabled students. Campus housing is university owned. Freshman campus housing is guaranteed. *Activities and organizations:* drama/theater group, student-run newspaper, radio and television station, choral group, Student Association, Residence Hall Student Association, intramurals and club sports, Outing Club, national fraternities, national sororities. *Campus security:* 24-hour emergency response devices and patrols, late-night transport/escort service, controlled dormitory access, safety seminars, RAD Women's Self Defense. *Student services:* health clinic, personal/psychological counseling, legal services.

Athletics Member NCAA. All Division III. *Intercollegiate sports:* baseball M, basketball M/W, cross-country running M/W, equestrian sports W(c), fencing M(c)/W(c), field hockey W, ice hockey M(c), lacrosse M(c)/W, racquetball M(c)/W(c), rugby M(c)/W(c), skiing (cross-country) M/W, soccer M/W, softball W, squash W, swimming and diving M/W, tennis M/W, track and field M(c)/W(c), ultimate Frisbee M(c)/W(c), volleyball M/W. *Intramural sports:* badminton M/W, basketball M/W, cheerleading M(c)/W(c), field hockey M/W, golf M/W, racquetball M/W, soccer M/W, softball M/W, swimming and diving M(c)/W(c), tennis M/W, volleyball W.

Standardized Tests *Required:* SAT or ACT (for admission).

Financial Aid Of all full-time matriculated undergraduates who enrolled in 2012, 4,626 applied for aid, 3,333 were judged to have need, 203 had their need fully met. 1,166 Federal Work-Study jobs (averaging $1000). 1,023 state and other part-time jobs (averaging $1108). In 2012, 175 non-need-based awards were made. *Average percent of need met:* 55%. *Average financial aid package:* $9493. *Average need-based loan:* $4428. *Average need-based gift aid:* $4655. *Average non-need-based aid:* $1856. *Average indebtedness upon graduation:* $24,445.

Applying *Options:* electronic application, early admission, early action. *Application fee:* $50. *Required:* essay or personal statement, high school transcript, 1 letter of recommendation. *Required for some:* portfolio for art program, audition for music and theater programs. *Application deadlines:* 4/1 (freshmen), 4/1 (transfers), 11/15 (early action). *Notification:* continuous (freshmen), continuous (transfers), 12/15 (early action).

Freshman Application Contact Ms. Kimberly A. Strano, Director of Freshman Admissions, State University of New York at New Paltz, 1 Hawk Drive, New Paltz, NY 12561-2499. *Phone:* 845-257-3200. *Fax:* 845-257-3209. *E-mail:* admissions@newpaltz.edu. *Website:* http://www.newpaltz.edu/.

State University of New York at Oswego

Oswego, New York

- **State-supported** comprehensive, founded 1861, part of State University of New York System
- **Small-town** 696-acre campus with easy access to Syracuse
- **Endowment** $12.1 million
- **Coed** 7,151 undergraduate students, 95% full-time, 52% women, 48% men
- **Moderately difficult** entrance level, 48% of applicants were admitted

Undergraduates 6,815 full-time, 336 part-time. Students come from 26 states and territories; 17 other countries; 2% are from out of state; 5% Black or African American, non-Hispanic/Latino; 8% Hispanic/Latino; 2% Asian, non-His-

panic/Latino; 0.1% Native Hawaiian or other Pacific Islander, non-Hispanic/Latino; 0.2% American Indian or Alaska Native, non-Hispanic/Latino; 2% Two or more races, non-Hispanic/Latino; 0.3% Race/ethnicity unknown; 1% international; 11% transferred in; 56% live on campus. *Retention:* 80% of full-time freshmen returned.

Freshmen *Admission:* 9,746 applied, 4,719 admitted, 1,271 enrolled. *Average high school GPA:* 3.5. *Test scores:* SAT critical reading scores over 500: 80%; ACT scores over 18: 100%; SAT critical reading scores over 600: 20%; ACT scores over 24: 49%; SAT critical reading scores over 700: 2%; ACT scores over 30: 3%.

Faculty *Total:* 576, 59% full-time, 61% with terminal degrees. *Student/faculty ratio:* 18:1.

Academics *Calendar:* semesters. *Degrees:* bachelor's, master's, and post-master's certificates. *Special study options:* accelerated degree program, adult/continuing education programs, advanced placement credit, cooperative education, distance learning, double majors, English as a second language, freshman honors college, honors programs, independent study, internships, off-campus study, part-time degree program, services for LD students, study abroad, summer session for credit. *ROTC:* Army (c). *Unusual degree programs:* 3-2 engineering with Clarkson University, Case Western Reserve University, State University of New York at Binghamton.

Computers on Campus 1,050 computers/terminals are available on campus for general student use. Students can access the following: campus intranet, computer help desk, free student e-mail accounts, online (class) grades, online (class) registration, online (class) schedules. Campuswide network is available. 100% of college-owned or -operated housing units are wired for high-speed Internet access. Wireless service is available via classrooms, computer centers, computer labs, dorm rooms, learning centers, libraries, student centers.

Student Life *Housing:* on-campus residence required through sophomore year. *Options:* coed, disabled students. Campus housing is university owned. Freshman campus housing is guaranteed. *Activities and organizations:* drama/theater group, student-run newspaper, radio and television station, choral group, club/intramural sports, student radio/television stations (WNYO and WTOP), Outing/Recreation Club, Dance Organization (Del Sarte), Financial Management Association, national fraternities, national sororities. *Campus security:* 24-hour emergency response devices and patrols, controlled dormitory access. *Student services:* health clinic, personal/psychological counseling, women's center, legal services.

Athletics Member NCAA. All Division III. *Intercollegiate sports:* baseball M, basketball M/W, crew M(c)/W(c), cross-country running M/W, field hockey W, golf M, ice hockey M/W, lacrosse M/W, soccer M/W, softball W, swimming and diving M/W, tennis M/W, track and field M/W, volleyball W, wrestling M. *Intramural sports:* badminton M/W, basketball M/W, cheerleading W(c), equestrian sports M(c)/W(c), fencing M(c)/W(c), field hockey W(c), football M/W, golf M/W, gymnastics M(c)/W(c), ice hockey M(c)/W(c), lacrosse M(c), racquetball M/W, rock climbing M(c)/W(c), rugby M(c)/W(c), skiing (cross-country) M(c)/W(c), skiing (downhill) M(c)/W(c), soccer M/W, softball M/W, swimming and diving M/W, table tennis M/W, tennis M/W, ultimate Frisbee M(c)/W(c), volleyball M(c)/W, water polo M/W.

Standardized Tests *Required:* SAT or ACT (for admission).

Costs (2012–13) *Tuition:* state resident $5570 full-time, $232 per credit hour part-time; nonresident $14,820 full-time, $618 per credit hour part-time. Full-time tuition and fees vary according to degree level. Part-time tuition and fees vary according to course load and degree level. *Required fees:* $1271 full-time, $53 per credit hour part-time. *Room and board:* $12,510. Room and board charges vary according to board plan and housing facility. *Payment plan:* installment.

Financial Aid Of all full-time matriculated undergraduates who enrolled in 2012, 5,876 applied for aid, 4,719 were judged to have need, 670 had their need fully met. 468 Federal Work-Study jobs (averaging $1136). 1,541 state and other part-time jobs (averaging $1713). In 2012, 642 non-need-based awards were made. *Average percent of need met:* 81%. *Average financial aid package:* $8138. *Average need-based loan:* $4565. *Average need-based gift aid:* $6150. *Average non-need-based aid:* $2999. *Average indebtedness upon graduation:* $27,004.

Applying *Options:* electronic application, early admission, early decision, deferred entrance. *Application fee:* $50. *Required:* high school transcript. *Recommended:* essay or personal statement, interview. *Application deadlines:* rolling (freshmen), rolling (transfers). *Early decision deadline:* 11/15. *Notification:* 1/15 (freshmen), 1/15 (transfers), 12/15 (early decision).

Freshman Application Contact Mr. Daniel Griffin, Interim Director of Admissions, State University of New York at Oswego, 7060 State Route 104, Oswego, NY 13126. *Phone:* 315-312-2250. *Fax:* 315-312-3260. *E-mail:* admiss@oswego.edu.

Website: http://www.oswego.edu/.

See below for display ad and page 1514 for the College Close-Up.

State University of New York at Plattsburgh

Plattsburgh, New York

- **State-supported** comprehensive, founded 1889, part of State University of New York System
- **Small-town** 265-acre campus with easy access to Montreal
- **Endowment** $13.8 million
- **Coed** 5,706 undergraduate students, 93% full-time, 55% women, 45% men
- **Moderately difficult** entrance level, 46% of applicants were admitted

Undergraduates 5,318 full-time, 388 part-time. Students come from 29 states and territories; 65 other countries; 4% are from out of state; 6% Black or African American, non-Hispanic/Latino; 8% Hispanic/Latino; 2% Asian, non-Hispanic/Latino; 0.1% Native Hawaiian or other Pacific Islander, non-Hispanic/Latino; 0.3% American Indian or Alaska Native, non-Hispanic/Latino; 2% Two or more races, non-Hispanic/Latino; 4% Race/ethnicity unknown; 6% international; 12% transferred in; 46% live on campus. *Retention:* 78% of full-time freshmen returned.

Freshmen *Admission:* 7,939 applied, 3,622 admitted, 970 enrolled. *Average high school GPA:* 3.2. *Test scores:* SAT critical reading scores over 500: 68%; SAT math scores over 500: 77%; ACT scores over 18: 98%; SAT critical reading scores over 600: 16%; SAT math scores over 600: 22%; ACT scores over 24: 39%; SAT critical reading scores over 700: 2%; SAT math scores over 700: 2%; ACT scores over 30: 3%.

Faculty *Total:* 519, 55% full-time, 58% with terminal degrees. *Student/faculty ratio:* 16:1.

Academics *Calendar:* semesters plus 2 5-week summer sessions and 1 winter session. *Degrees:* certificates, bachelor's, master's, and post-master's certificates. *Special study options:* academic remediation for entering students, accelerated degree program, adult/continuing education programs, advanced placement credit, cooperative education, distance learning, double majors, English as a second language, honors programs, independent study, internships, off-campus study, part-time degree program, services for LD students, student-designed majors, study abroad, summer session for credit. *ROTC:* Army (b).

Computers on Campus 450 computers/terminals and 8 ports are available on campus for general student use. Students can access the following: campus intranet, computer help desk, free student e-mail accounts, online (class) grades, online (class) registration, online (class) schedules. Campuswide network is available. 100% of college-owned or -operated housing units are wired for high-speed Internet access. Wireless service is available via classrooms, computer labs, dorm rooms, learning centers, libraries, student centers.

Student Life *Housing:* on-campus residence required through sophomore year. *Options:* coed, disabled students. Campus housing is university owned. Freshman campus housing is guaranteed. *Activities and organizations:* drama/theater group, student-run newspaper, radio and television station, choral group, Student Association, Honor Societies, Student Media Organizations, service/leadership organizations, intramural and recreational sports, national fraternities, national sororities. *Campus security:* 24-hour emergency response devices and patrols, late-night transport/escort service, controlled dormitory access. *Student services:* health clinic, personal/psychological counseling, women's center, legal services.

Athletics Member NCAA. All Division III. *Intercollegiate sports:* baseball M, basketball M/W, cross-country running M/W, ice hockey M/W, lacrosse M, soccer M/W, softball W, tennis M, track and field M/W, volleyball W. *Intramural sports:* basketball M/W, cheerleading M(c)/W(c), field hockey M/W, football M, ice hockey M(c)/W(c), racquetball M/W, rock climbing M(c)/W(c), rugby M(c)/W(c), soccer M/W, softball M/W, tennis M/W, ultimate Frisbee M/W, volleyball M/W.

Standardized Tests *Required:* SAT or ACT (for admission).

Costs (2012–13) *Tuition:* state resident $5570 full-time, $232 per credit hour part-time; nonresident $14,820 full-time, $618 per credit hour part-time. Part-time tuition and fees vary according to course load. *Required fees:* $1238 full-time, $51 per credit hour part-time. *Room and board:* $10,582; room only: $6682. Room and board charges vary according to board plan and housing facility. *Payment plans:* installment, deferred payment. *Waivers:* employees or children of employees.

Financial Aid Of all full-time matriculated undergraduates who enrolled in 2012, 4,357 applied for aid, 3,503 were judged to have need, 712 had their need fully met. 353 Federal Work-Study jobs (averaging $1993). In 2012, 1228 non-need-based awards were made. *Average percent of need met:* 80%. *Average financial aid package:* $12,058. *Average need-based loan:* $7602. *Average need-based gift aid:* $6230. *Average non-need-based aid:* $6533. *Average indebtedness upon graduation:* $25,297.

Applying *Options:* electronic application, early admission, early decision, deferred entrance. *Application fee:* $50. *Required:* essay or personal statement, high school transcript, minimum 2.5 GPA, 1 letter of recommendation. *Required for some:* minimum 3.4 GPA. *Recommended:* minimum 3.0 GPA, interview. *Application deadline:* rolling (transfers). *Notification:* continuous (freshmen), continuous (transfers).

Freshman Application Contact Mrs. Carrie Woodward, Assistant Director for Freshman Admissions, State University of New York at Plattsburgh, 101 Broad Street, Plattsburgh, NY 12901. *Phone:* 888-673-0012. *Toll-free phone:* 888-673-0012. *Fax:* 518-564-2045. *E-mail:* carrie.woodward@plattsburgh.edu.
Website: http://www.plattsburgh.edu/.

State University of New York College at Cortland

Cortland, New York

- **State-supported** comprehensive, founded 1868, part of State University of New York System
- **Small-town** 191-acre campus with easy access to Syracuse
- **Coed** 6,345 undergraduate students, 98% full-time, 57% women, 43% men
- **Moderately difficult** entrance level, 44% of applicants were admitted

Undergraduates 6,228 full-time, 117 part-time. 4% Black or African American, non-Hispanic/Latino; 9% Hispanic/Latino; 1% Asian, non-Hispanic/Latino; 0.2% American Indian or Alaska Native, non-Hispanic/Latino; 2% Two or more races, non-Hispanic/Latino; 10% Race/ethnicity unknown; 0.4% international; 10% transferred in. *Retention:* 85% of full-time freshmen returned.

Freshmen *Admission:* 11,687 applied, 5,200 admitted, 1,210 enrolled. *Test scores:* SAT critical reading scores over 500: 77%; SAT math scores over 500: 61%; ACT scores over 18: 91%; SAT critical reading scores over 600: 20%; SAT math scores over 600: 8%; ACT scores over 24: 31%; SAT critical reading scores over 700: 1%; ACT scores over 30: 2%.

Faculty *Total:* 641, 43% full-time, 41% with terminal degrees. *Student/faculty ratio:* 17:1.

Academics *Calendar:* semesters. *Degrees:* bachelor's, master's, post-master's, and postbachelor's certificates. *Special study options:* adult/continuing education programs, off-campus study. *ROTC:* Army (c), Air Force (c). *Unusual degree programs:* 3-2 engineering with State University of New York at Buffalo, State University of New York at Stony Brook, Alfred University, Clarkson University, State University of New York at Binghamton, Case Western Reserve University; forestry with Duke University, State University of New York College of Environmental Science and Forestry.

Computers on Campus Campuswide network is available.

Student Life *Housing options:* coed, cooperative, disabled students. Campus housing is university owned. *Campus security:* 24-hour emergency response devices and patrols, late-night transport/escort service.

Athletics Member NCAA. All Division III. *Intercollegiate sports:* baseball M, basketball M/W, cross-country running M/W, field hockey W, football M/W(c), golf W, gymnastics W, ice hockey M/W(c), lacrosse M/W, racquetball M(c)/W(c), rugby M(c)/W(c), soccer M/W, softball W, swimming and diving M/W, tennis W, track and field M/W, volleyball M(c)/W, wrestling M. *Intramural sports:* archery M/W, badminton M/W, baseball M, basketball M/W, bowling M/W, cross-country running M/W, fencing M/W, field hockey W, football M/W, golf M/W, gymnastics W, ice hockey M, lacrosse M/W, racquetball M/W, rugby M/W, skiing (cross-country) M/W, skiing (downhill) M/W, soccer M/W, softball M/W, squash M/W, swimming and diving M/W, table tennis M/W, tennis M/W, track and field M/W, volleyball M/W, weight lifting M/W, wrestling M.

Standardized Tests *Required:* SAT or ACT (for admission).

Costs (2013–14) *Tuition:* state resident $5570 full-time, $232 per credit hour part-time; nonresident $14,820 full-time, $618 per credit hour part-time. Full-time tuition and fees vary according to degree level. Part-time tuition and fees vary according to degree level. *Required fees:* $1372 full-time. *Room and board:* $11,430; room only: $7070. Room and board charges vary according to board plan and housing facility. *Payment plan:* installment.

Financial Aid Of all full-time matriculated undergraduates who enrolled in 2011, 5,214 applied for aid, 3,874 were judged to have need, 359 had their need fully met. In 2011, 194 non-need-based awards were made. *Average percent of need met:* 69%. *Average financial aid package:* $12,801. *Average need-based loan:* $4198. *Average need-based gift aid:* $5277. *Average non-need-based aid:* $2896. *Average indebtedness upon graduation:* $27,534.

Applying *Options:* early admission, early action, deferred entrance. *Application fee:* $50. *Required:* essay or personal statement, high school transcript, minimum 2.3 GPA, 1 letter of recommendation. *Recommended:* minimum 3.0 GPA, 3 letters of recommendation, interview. *Application deadlines:* rolling (freshmen), rolling (transfers), 11/15 (early action). *Notification:* continuous (freshmen), continuous (transfers), 1/1 (early action).

Freshman Application Contact Director of Admission, State University of New York College at Cortland, PO Box 2000, Cortland, NY 13045. *Phone:* 607-753-4711. *Fax:* 607-753-5998. *E-mail:* admissions@cortland.edu. *Website:* http://www.cortland.edu/.

State University of New York College at Geneseo

Geneseo, New York

- **State-supported** comprehensive, founded 1871, part of State University of New York System
- **Small-town** 220-acre campus with easy access to Rochester
- **Endowment** $18.2 million
- **Coed** 5,388 undergraduate students, 98% full-time, 58% women, 42% men
- **Very difficult** entrance level, 46% of applicants were admitted

Undergraduates 5,277 full-time, 111 part-time. Students come from 34 states and territories; 42 other countries; 2% are from out of state; 2% Black or African American, non-Hispanic/Latino; 6% Hispanic/Latino; 7% Asian, non-Hispanic/Latino; 0.2% American Indian or Alaska Native, non-Hispanic/Latino; 2% Two or more races, non-Hispanic/Latino; 4% Race/ethnicity unknown; 3% international; 7% transferred in; 54% live on campus. *Retention:* 90% of full-time freshmen returned.

Freshmen *Admission:* 9,164 applied, 4,184 admitted, 997 enrolled. *Average high school GPA:* 3.6. *Test scores:* SAT critical reading scores over 500: 89%; SAT math scores over 500: 93%; ACT scores over 18: 100%; SAT critical reading scores over 600: 72%; SAT math scores over 600: 78%; ACT scores over 24: 97%; SAT critical reading scores over 700: 23%; SAT math scores over 700: 26%; ACT scores over 30: 24%.

Faculty *Total:* 359, 71% full-time, 65% with terminal degrees. *Student/faculty ratio:* 19:1.

Academics *Calendar:* semesters. *Degrees:* bachelor's and master's. *Special study options:* advanced placement credit, distance learning, double majors, English as a second language, honors programs, independent study, internships, off-campus study, part-time degree program, services for LD students, study abroad, summer session for credit. *ROTC:* Army (c), Air Force (c). *Unusual degree programs:* 3-2 business administration with Syracuse University, State University of New York at Buffalo, State University of New York at Binghamton, Rochester Institute of Technology, Clarkson University, Alfred University, Union College; engineering with Columbia University, Case Western Reserve University, Alfred University, Clarkson University, Syracuse University, The Pennsylvania State University, University of Rochester, SUNY Binghamton, SUNY Buffalo, Rochester Institute of Technology; nursing with Johns Hopkins School of Nursing; optometry with State University of New York College of Optometry; dental with State University of New York at Buffalo, physical therapy degree with SUNY Upstate Medical University, osteopathy program with New York Institute of Technology College of Osteopathic Medicine.

Computers on Campus 503 computers/terminals and 96 ports are available on campus for general student use. Students can access the following: campus intranet, computer help desk, free student e-mail accounts, online (class) grades, online (class) registration, online (class) schedules. Campuswide network is available. 100% of college-owned or -operated housing units are wired for high-speed Internet access. Wireless service is available via entire campus.

Student Life *Housing:* on-campus residence required through sophomore year. *Options:* coed, disabled students. Campus housing is university owned. Freshman campus housing is guaranteed. *Activities and organizations:* drama/theater group, student-run newspaper, radio and television station, choral group, Alpha Phi Omega, Inter-Varsity Christian Fellowship, Inter-Residence Council, Colleges Against Cancer, Geneseo Area Gaming Group, national fraternities, national sororities. *Campus security:* 24-hour emergency response devices and patrols, student patrols, late-night transport/escort service, controlled dormitory access. *Student services:* health clinic, personal/psychological counseling, legal services.

Athletics Member NCAA. All Division III. *Intercollegiate sports:* badminton M(c)/W(c), baseball M(c)/W(c), basketball M/W, cheerleading M(c)/W(c), crew M(c)/W(c), cross-country running M/W, equestrian sports W, fencing M(c)/W(c), field hockey W, ice hockey M/W(c), lacrosse M/W, rugby M(c)/W(c), skiing (downhill) M(c)/W(c), soccer M/W, softball W, swimming and diving M/W, tennis M(c)/W, track and field M/W, ultimate Frisbee M(c)/W(c), volleyball M(c)/W. *Intramural sports:* basketball M/W.

Standardized Tests *Required:* SAT or ACT (for admission).

Costs (2012–13) *Tuition:* state resident $5570 full-time; nonresident $14,820 full-time. Part-time tuition and fees vary according to course load. *Required fees:* $1525 full-time. *Room and board:* $10,960; room only: $6950. Room and board charges vary according to board plan and housing facility. *Payment plans:* installment, deferred payment.

Financial Aid Of all full-time matriculated undergraduates who enrolled in 2011, 4,028 applied for aid, 2,340 were judged to have need, 1,534 had their need fully met. In 2011, 538 non-need-based awards were made. *Average percent of need met:* 68%. *Average financial aid package:* $8886. *Average need-based loan:* $4690. *Average need-based gift aid:* $4472. *Average non-need-based aid:* $2082. *Average indebtedness upon graduation:* $21,000. *Financial aid deadline:* 2/15.

Applying *Options:* electronic application, early admission, early decision, deferred entrance. *Application fee:* $50. *Required:* essay or personal statement, high school transcript. *Recommended:* 1 letter of recommendation. *Application deadlines:* 1/1 (freshmen), rolling (transfers). *Early decision deadline:* 11/15. *Notification:* 3/1 (freshmen), 5/1 (transfers), 12/15 (early decision).

Freshman Application Contact Ms. Kris Shay, Director of Admissions, State University of New York College at Geneseo, 1 College Circle, Geneseo, NY 14454-1401. *Phone:* 585-245-5571. *Toll-free phone:* 866-245-5211. *Fax:* 585-245-5550. *E-mail:* admissions@geneseo.edu. *Website:* http://www.geneseo.edu/.

State University of New York College at Old Westbury

Old Westbury, New York

- **State-supported** comprehensive, founded 1965, part of State University of New York System
- **Suburban** 604-acre campus with easy access to New York City
- **Coed** 4,217 undergraduate students, 86% full-time, 59% women, 41% men
- **Moderately difficult** entrance level, 52% of applicants were admitted

Undergraduates 3,609 full-time, 608 part-time. Students come from 13 states and territories; 58 other countries; 1% are from out of state; 30% Black or African American, non-Hispanic/Latino; 21% Hispanic/Latino; 9% Asian, non-Hispanic/Latino; 0.4% Native Hawaiian or other Pacific Islander, non-Hispanic/Latino; 0.7% American Indian or Alaska Native, non-Hispanic/Latino; 2% Two or more races, non-Hispanic/Latino; 3% Race/ethnicity unknown; 1% international; 17% transferred in; 22% live on campus. *Retention:* 80% of full-time freshmen returned.

Freshmen *Admission:* 3,855 applied, 2,005 admitted, 414 enrolled. *Average high school GPA:* 3.1. *Test scores:* SAT critical reading scores over 500: 44%; SAT math scores over 500: 60%; SAT writing scores over 500: 38%; ACT scores over 18: 97%; SAT critical reading scores over 600: 5%; SAT math scores over 600: 10%; SAT writing scores over 600: 6%; ACT scores over 24: 24%; SAT critical reading scores over 700: 1%; SAT math scores over 700: 1%; ACT scores over 30: 3%.

Faculty *Total:* 311, 48% full-time, 52% with terminal degrees. *Student/faculty ratio:* 18:1.

Academics *Calendar:* semesters. *Degrees:* certificates, bachelor's, master's, and post-master's certificates. *Special study options:* academic remediation for entering students, advanced placement credit, distance learning, double majors, English as a second language, freshman honors college, honors programs, independent study, internships, off-campus study, part-time degree program, services for LD students, study abroad, summer session for credit. *ROTC:* Army (c), Air Force (c). *Unusual degree programs:* 3-2 engineering with State University of New York at Stony Brook; biological sciences/Doctor of Osteopathic Medicine with NY College of Osteopathic Medicine.

Computers on Campus 640 computers/terminals and 700 ports are available on campus for general student use. Students can access the following: campus intranet, free student e-mail accounts, online (class) grades, online (class) registration, financial aid, billing information, grades. Campuswide network is available. 100% of college-owned or -operated housing units are wired for high-speed Internet access. Wireless service is available via entire campus.

Student Life *Housing options:* coed. Campus housing is university owned. Freshman campus housing is guaranteed. *Activities and organizations:* drama/theater group, student-run newspaper, radio station, choral group, Student Government Association, Alianza Latina, PRIDE, Step Tunes, Anime Magna Games Club, national fraternities, national sororities. *Campus security:* 24-hour emergency response devices and patrols, student patrols, late-night transport/escort service, controlled dormitory access. *Student services:* health clinic, personal/psychological counseling, women's center.

Athletics Member NCAA. All Division III. *Intercollegiate sports:* baseball M, basketball M/W, cross-country running M/W, golf M, lacrosse W, soccer M/W, softball W, swimming and diving M/W, volleyball W. *Intramural sports:* badminton M/W, basketball M/W, cheerleading M(c)/W(c), equestrian sports M(c)/W(c), football M/W, racquetball M/W, soccer M/W, softball W, squash M/W, ultimate Frisbee M/W, weight lifting M/W.

Standardized Tests *Required:* SAT or ACT (for admission).

Costs (2012–13) *Tuition:* state resident $5570 full-time, $232 per credit part-time; nonresident $14,820 full-time, $618 per credit part-time. Part-time tuition and fees vary according to course load. *Required fees:* $1054 full-time, $21 per credit part-time, $148 per term part-time. *Room and board:* $9700; room only: $6600. Room and board charges vary according to board plan. *Payment plan:* installment. *Waivers:* senior citizens.

Financial Aid Of all full-time matriculated undergraduates who enrolled in 2011, 2,231 applied for aid, 2,228 were judged to have need, 2,228 had their need fully met. 337 Federal Work-Study jobs (averaging $887). *Average percent of need met:* 50%. *Average financial aid package:* $8265. *Average need-based loan:* $4415. *Average need-based gift aid:* $5616. *Average indebtedness upon graduation:* $17,722.

Applying *Options:* electronic application, early admission, early decision, deferred entrance. *Application fee:* $50. *Required:* essay or personal statement, high school transcript, 2 letters of recommendation. *Required for some:* interview. *Application deadlines:* rolling (freshmen), 12/15 (transfers). *Early decision deadline:* 11/1. *Notification:* continuous (freshmen), continuous (transfers), 12/15 (early decision).

Freshman Application Contact State University of New York College at Old Westbury, PO Box 307, Old Westbury, NY 11568. *Phone:* 516-876-3073. *Fax:* 516-876-3307. *E-mail:* enroll@oldwestbury.edu. *Website:* http://www.oldwestbury.edu/.

State University of New York College at Oneonta

Oneonta, New York

- **State-supported** comprehensive, founded 1889, part of State University of New York
- **Small-town** 250-acre campus
- **Endowment** $37.8 million
- **Coed**
- **Very difficult** entrance level

Faculty *Student/faculty ratio:* 18:1.

Academics *Calendar:* semesters. *Degrees:* bachelor's, master's, post-master's, and postbachelor's certificates.

Student Life *Campus security:* 24-hour emergency response devices and patrols, late-night transport/escort service, controlled dormitory access, Oneonta Emergency Squad: an organization of student volunteers with first responder credentials, e.g., EMT training, CPR certification.

Athletics Member NCAA. All Division III.

Standardized Tests *Required:* SAT or ACT (for admission).

Costs (2012–13) *Tuition:* state resident $5570 full-time, $232 per semester hour part-time; nonresident $14,820 full-time, $618 per semester hour part-time. Part-time tuition and fees vary according to course load. *Required fees:* $1317 full-time, $37 per semester hour part-time. *Room and board:* $10,540; room only: $6740. Room and board charges vary according to housing facility.

Financial Aid *Of all full-time matriculated undergraduates who enrolled in 2011,* 4,577 applied for aid, 3,361 were judged to have need, 1,540 had their need fully met. 343 Federal Work-Study jobs (averaging $1133). *In 2011,* 690 non-need-based awards were made. *Average percent of need met:* 36. *Average financial aid package:* $15,540. *Average need-based loan:* $2022. *Average need-based gift aid:* $5320. *Average non-need-based aid:* $2618. *Average indebtedness upon graduation:* $13,697.

Applying *Options:* electronic application, early admission, early action, deferred entrance. *Application fee:* $50. *Required:* essay or personal statement, high school transcript. *Recommended:* minimum 3.0 GPA, 3 letters of recommendation.

Freshman Application Contact Ms. Karen Brown, Director of Admissions, State University of New York College at Oneonta, Alumni Hall 116, Oneonta, NY 13820-4015. *Phone:* 607-436-2524. *Toll-free phone:* 800-SUNY-123. *Fax:* 607-436-3074. *E-mail:* admissions@oneonta.edu. *Website:* http://www.oneonta.edu/.

State University of New York College at Potsdam

Potsdam, New York

- **State-supported** comprehensive, founded 1816, part of State University of New York System
- **Small-town** 240-acre campus
- **Endowment** $18.5 million
- **Coed** 3,868 undergraduate students, 97% full-time, 58% women, 42% men
- **Moderately difficult** entrance level, 65% of applicants were admitted

Undergraduates 3,762 full-time, 106 part-time. Students come from 54 states and territories; 20 other countries; 3% are from out of state; 5% Black or African American, non-Hispanic/Latino; 7% Hispanic/Latino; 1% Asian, non-Hispanic/Latino; 0.1% Native Hawaiian or other Pacific Islander, non-Hispanic/Latino; 0.9% American Indian or Alaska Native, non-Hispanic/Latino; 2% Two or more races, non-Hispanic/Latino; 6% Race/ethnicity unknown; 1% international; 9% transferred in; 97% live on campus. *Retention:* 75% of full-time freshmen returned.

Freshmen *Admission:* 5,022 applied, 3,279 admitted, 888 enrolled.

Faculty *Total:* 362, 72% full-time, 68% with terminal degrees. *Student/faculty ratio:* 14:1.

Academics *Calendar:* semesters. *Degrees:* bachelor's and master's. *Special study options:* advanced placement credit, distance learning, double majors, honors programs, independent study, internships, off-campus study, part-time degree program, services for LD students, student-designed majors, study abroad, summer session for credit. *ROTC:* Army (c), Air Force (c). *Unusual degree programs:* 3-2 engineering with Clarkson University, SUNY IT; geology, physics, computer science, chemistry and mathematics with Clarkson University.

Computers on Campus 608 computers/terminals and 80 ports are available on campus for general student use. Students can access the following: campus intranet, computer help desk, free student e-mail accounts, online (class) grades, online (class) registration, online (class) schedules, online access to financial aid status, unofficial transcripts, billing, meal plan and housing sign ups,225 wireless hot spots with 95 on campus and 130 in the residence halls. Campuswide network is available. 100% of college-owned or -operated housing units are wired for high-speed Internet access. Wireless service is available via classrooms, computer centers, computer labs, dorm rooms, learning centers, libraries, student centers.

Student Life *Housing:* on-campus residence required through sophomore year. *Options:* coed, disabled students. Campus housing is university owned. Freshman campus housing is guaranteed. *Activities and organizations:* drama/theater group, student-run newspaper, radio station, choral group, Student Government Association, Crane Student Association, Student Entertainment Services (Programming Board), WALH Radio, The Racquette Student Newspaper, national fraternities, national sororities. *Campus security:* 24-hour emergency response devices and patrols, late-night transport/escort service, controlled dormitory access, educational programs, campus rescue squad, portable jump start packets, vehicle lock outs and parking management. *Student services:* health clinic, personal/psychological counseling, women's center, legal services.

Athletics Member NCAA. All Division III. *Intercollegiate sports:* basketball M/W, cross-country running M/W, equestrian sports W, golf M, ice hockey M/W, lacrosse M/W, soccer M/W, swimming and diving M/W, volleyball W. *Intramural sports:* basketball M, racquetball M, soccer M/W, softball M/W.

Standardized Tests *Required for some:* SAT or ACT (for admission).

Costs (2012–13) *Tuition:* state resident $5570 full-time, $232 per credit hour part-time; nonresident $14,820 full-time, $618 per credit hour part-time. *Required fees:* $1272 full-time. *Room and board:* $10,180; room only: $5970. Room and board charges vary according to board plan and housing facility. *Payment plan:* installment. *Waivers:* employees or children of employees.

Financial Aid Of all full-time matriculated undergraduates who enrolled in 2012, 3,441 applied for aid, 2,736 were judged to have need, 1,267 had their need fully met. 246 Federal Work-Study jobs (averaging $1090). In 2012, 296 non-need-based awards were made. *Average percent of need met:* 88%. *Average financial aid package:* $13,076. *Average need-based loan:* $4635. *Average need-based gift aid:* $6571. *Average non-need-based aid:* $2366. *Average indebtedness upon graduation:* $20,734. *Financial aid deadline:* 5/1.

Applying *Options:* electronic application, early admission, deferred entrance. *Application fee:* $50. *Required:* high school transcript, minimum 2.5 GPA, audition for music program. *Required for some:* essay or personal statement, minimum 2.0 GPA, interview. *Application deadlines:* rolling (freshmen), rolling (transfers). *Notification:* continuous (freshmen), continuous (transfers).

Freshman Application Contact Mr. Thomas Nesbitt, Director of Admissions, State University of New York College at Potsdam, 44 Pierrepont Avenue,

Potsdam, NY 13676. *Phone:* 315-267-2180. *Toll-free phone:* 877-POTSDAM. *Fax:* 315-267-2163. *E-mail:* admissions@potsdam.edu. *Website:* http://www.potsdam.edu/.

State University of New York College of Agriculture and Technology at Cobleskill
Cobleskill, New York

- **State-supported** 4-year, founded 1916, part of State University of New York System
- **Rural** 75,775-acre campus with easy access to Albany, NY
- **Endowment** $2.1 million
- **Coed** 2,519 undergraduate students, 93% full-time, 52% women, 48% men
- **Minimally difficult** entrance level, 74% of applicants were admitted

Undergraduates 2,340 full-time, 179 part-time. Students come from 16 states and territories; 13 other countries; 7% are from out of state; 10% Black or African American, non-Hispanic/Latino; 5% Hispanic/Latino; 1% Asian, non-Hispanic/Latino; 0.4% American Indian or Alaska Native, non-Hispanic/Latino; 5% Race/ethnicity unknown; 2% international; 8% transferred in; 76% live on campus. *Retention:* 74% of full-time freshmen returned.

Freshmen *Admission:* 2,635 applied, 1,955 admitted, 758 enrolled. *Average high school GPA:* 82. *Test scores:* SAT critical reading scores over 500: 24%; SAT math scores over 500: 26%; ACT scores over 18: 62%; SAT critical reading scores over 600: 3%; SAT math scores over 600: 6%; ACT scores over 24: 11%; SAT critical reading scores over 700: 1%; SAT math scores over 700: 1%; ACT scores over 30: 1%.

Faculty *Total:* 150, 75% full-time, 31% with terminal degrees. *Student/faculty ratio:* 19:1.

Academics *Calendar:* semesters. *Degrees:* certificates, associate, and bachelor's. *Special study options:* academic remediation for entering students, advanced placement credit, cooperative education, distance learning, honors programs, independent study, internships, off-campus study, part-time degree program, services for LD students, study abroad, summer session for credit.

Computers on Campus 360 computers/terminals and 255 ports are available on campus for general student use. Students can access the following: campus intranet, computer help desk, free student e-mail accounts, online (class) grades, online (class) registration, online (class) schedules. Campuswide network is available. 100% of college-owned or -operated housing units are wired for high-speed Internet access. Wireless service is available via entire campus.

Student Life *Housing:* on-campus residence required through sophomore year. *Options:* coed, men-only, women-only, disabled students. Campus housing is university owned. Freshman campus housing is guaranteed. *Activities and organizations:* drama/theater group, student-run newspaper, choral group, Post-Secondary Agricultural Students, Woodsmen's Team, Society for Agricultural Engineers, Council for Student Activities. *Campus security:* 24-hour emergency response devices and patrols, student patrols, late-night transport/escort service, controlled dormitory access, bicycle patrols, horse-mounted patrols. *Student services:* health clinic, personal/psychological counseling.

Athletics Member NCAA. All Division III. *Intercollegiate sports:* basketball M/W, cheerleading M/W, cross-country running M/W, golf M/W, lacrosse M, soccer M/W, softball W, swimming and diving M/W, tennis M/W, track and field M/W, volleyball W. *Intramural sports:* baseball M(c), bowling M/W, football M/W, soccer M/W, softball M/W.

Standardized Tests *Required for some:* SAT or ACT (for admission).

Costs (2012–13) *One-time required fee:* $55. *Tuition:* state resident $5570 full-time, $232 per credit hour part-time; nonresident $14,820 full-time, $618 per credit hour part-time. *Required fees:* $2692 full-time, $73 per credit hour part-time. *Room and board:* $10,866; room only: $6600. Room and board charges vary according to board plan. *Payment plans:* installment, deferred payment. *Waivers:* senior citizens and employees or children of employees.

Financial Aid Of all full-time matriculated undergraduates who enrolled in 2007, 2,297 applied for aid, 1,789 were judged to have need, 248 had their need fully met. 160 Federal Work-Study jobs (averaging $1064). In 2007, 371 non-need-based awards were made. *Average percent of need met:* 63%. *Average financial aid package:* $5842. *Average need-based loan:* $3626. *Average need-based gift aid:* $4124. *Average indebtedness upon graduation:* $22,475. *Financial aid deadline:* 3/1.

Applying *Options:* electronic application, early admission, deferred entrance. *Application fee:* $50. *Required:* high school transcript. *Required for some:* essay or personal statement, minimum 2.0 GPA, 3 letters of recommendation, interview. *Recommended:* minimum 1.8 GPA. *Application deadlines:* rolling

(freshmen), rolling (transfers). *Notification:* continuous (freshmen), continuous (transfers).

Freshman Application Contact State University of New York College of Agriculture and Technology at Cobleskill, Cobleskill, NY 12043. *Phone:* 518-255-5525. *Toll-free phone:* 800-295-8988. *Website:* http://www.cobleskill.edu/.

State University of New York College of Environmental Science and Forestry
Syracuse, New York

- **State-supported** university, founded 1911, part of State University of New York System
- **Urban** 17-acre campus
- **Endowment** $18.9 million
- **Coed**
- **Very difficult** entrance level

Faculty *Student/faculty ratio:* 13:1.

Academics *Calendar:* semesters. *Degrees:* associate, bachelor's, master's, doctoral, and postbachelor's certificates.

Student Life *Campus security:* 24-hour emergency response devices and patrols, late-night transport/escort service, controlled dormitory access.

Athletics Member USCAA.

Standardized Tests *Required:* SAT or ACT (for admission). *Recommended:* SAT Subject Tests (for admission).

Costs (2012–13) *Tuition:* state resident $5270 full-time, $220 per credit hour part-time; nonresident $14,320 full-time, $597 per credit hour part-time. Full-time tuition and fees vary according to location. Part-time tuition and fees vary according to course load and location. *Required fees:* $971 full-time, $43 per credit hour part-time. *Room and board:* $14,032. Room and board charges vary according to board plan, housing facility, and location. *Payment plans:* installment, deferred payment.

Financial Aid *Of all full-time matriculated undergraduates who enrolled in 2011,* 1,389 applied for aid, 975 were judged to have need, 887 had their need fully met. 190 Federal Work-Study jobs (averaging $1750). 175 state and other part-time jobs (averaging $1500). *In 2011,* 85 non-need-based awards were made. *Average percent of need met:* 90. *Average financial aid package:* $13,000. *Average need-based loan:* $5500. *Average need-based gift aid:* $5000. *Average non-need-based aid:* $2820. *Average indebtedness upon graduation:* $23,982.

Applying *Options:* electronic application, early admission, early decision, deferred entrance. *Application fee:* $50. *Required:* essay or personal statement, high school transcript, minimum 3.0 GPA, supplemental application. *Recommended:* 1 letter of recommendation, interview.

Freshman Application Contact Ms. Susan Sanford, Director of Admissions, State University of New York College of Environmental Science and Forestry, Office of Undergraduate Admissions, 106 Bray Hall, 1 Forestry Drive, Syracuse, NY 13210-2779. *Phone:* 315-470-6600. *Fax:* 315-470-6933. *E-mail:* esfinfo@esf.edu. *Website:* http://www.esf.edu/.

See next page for display ad and page 1516 for the College Close-Up.

State University of New York College of Technology at Alfred
Alfred, New York

- **State-supported** primarily 2-year, founded 1908, part of The State University of New York System
- **Rural** 1084-acre campus with easy access to Rochester, Buffalo
- **Endowment** $3.6 million
- **Coed** 3,527 undergraduate students, 91% full-time, 38% women, 62% men
- **Moderately difficult** entrance level, 55% of applicants were admitted

Undergraduates 3,211 full-time, 316 part-time. Students come from 35 states and territories; 19 other countries; 7% are from out of state; 9% Black or African American, non-Hispanic/Latino; 6% Hispanic/Latino; 2% Asian, non-Hispanic/Latino; 0.1% Native Hawaiian or other Pacific Islander, non-Hispanic/Latino; 0.3% American Indian or Alaska Native, non-Hispanic/Latino; 2% Two or more races, non-Hispanic/Latino; 5% Race/ethnicity unknown; 7%

transferred in; 74% live on campus. *Retention:* 81% of full-time freshmen returned.

Freshmen *Admission:* 3,890 applied, 2,136 admitted, 1,109 enrolled. *Average high school GPA:* 2.9.

Faculty *Total:* 219, 83% full-time, 21% with terminal degrees. *Student/faculty ratio:* 18:1.

Academics *Calendar:* semesters. *Degrees:* certificates, associate, and bachelor's. *Special study options:* academic remediation for entering students, adult/continuing education programs, advanced placement credit, cooperative education, distance learning, double majors, English as a second language, honors programs, independent study, internships, off-campus study, part-time degree program, services for LD students, student-designed majors, study abroad, summer session for credit. *ROTC:* Army (c).

Computers on Campus 100 computers/terminals are available on campus for general student use. Students can access the following: campus intranet, computer help desk, free student e-mail accounts, online (class) grades, online (class) registration, online (class) schedules. Campuswide network is available. 100% of college-owned or -operated housing units are wired for high-speed Internet access. Wireless service is available via entire campus.

Student Life *Housing options:* coed, men-only, women-only, disabled students. Campus housing is university owned. Freshman campus housing is guaranteed. *Activities and organizations:* drama/theater group, student-run newspaper, radio station, choral group, Outdoor Recreation Club, International Club, intramural sports, Pioneer Woodsmen Team, Black Student Union. *Campus security:* 24-hour emergency response devices and patrols, late-night transport/escort service, controlled dormitory access, residence hall entrance guards. *Student services:* health clinic, personal/psychological counseling.

Athletics Member NJCAA. *Intercollegiate sports:* baseball M, basketball M(s)/W(s), cross-country running M/W, equestrian sports M/W, football M(s), lacrosse M(s), soccer M/W, softball W, swimming and diving M/W, track and field M/W, volleyball W, wrestling M. *Intramural sports:* basketball M/W, football M(c), golf M/W, ice hockey M(c)/W(c), lacrosse M(c)/W(c), rock climbing M/W, soccer M/W, softball M/W, swimming and diving M(c)/W(c), tennis M/W, ultimate Frisbee M/W, volleyball M/W.

Standardized Tests *Required for some:* SAT or ACT (for admission). *Recommended:* SAT or ACT (for admission).

Costs (2013–14) *One-time required fee:* $100. *Tuition:* state resident $5570 full-time, $232 per credit hour part-time; nonresident $9740 full-time, $406 per credit hour part-time. Full-time tuition and fees vary according to course load and degree level. Part-time tuition and fees vary according to course load and degree level. *Required fees:* $1304 full-time, $53 per credit hour part-time, $10 per credit hour part-time. *Room and board:* $11,160; room only: $6650. Room and board charges vary according to board plan and housing facility. *Payment plan:* installment. *Waivers:* employees or children of employees.

Financial Aid Of all full-time matriculated undergraduates who enrolled in 2010, 3,084 applied for aid, 2,722 were judged to have need, 256 had their need fully met. 228 Federal Work-Study jobs (averaging $861). In 2010, 99 non-need-based awards were made. *Average percent of need met:* 57%. *Average financial aid package:* $9568. *Average need-based loan:* $3760. *Average need-based gift aid:* $5759. *Average non-need-based aid:* $4307. *Average indebtedness upon graduation:* $29,772.

Applying *Options:* electronic application. *Application fee:* $50. *Required:* high school transcript, minimum 2.0 GPA. *Recommended:* essay or personal statement, interview. *Application deadlines:* rolling (freshmen), rolling (out-of-state freshmen), rolling (transfers). *Notification:* continuous (freshmen), continuous (out-of-state freshmen), continuous (transfers).

Freshman Application Contact Mrs. Deborah Goodrich, Associate Vice President for Enrollment Management, State University of New York College of Technology at Alfred, Huntington Administration Building, 10 Upper College Drive, Alfred, NY 14802. *Phone:* 607-587-4215. *Toll-free phone:* 800-4-ALFRED. *Fax:* 607-587-4299. *E-mail:* admissions@alfredstate.edu. *Website:* http://www.alfredstate.edu/.

State University of New York College of Technology at Canton

Canton, New York

- **State-supported** comprehensive, founded 1906, part of State University of New York System
- **Small-town** 555-acre campus
- **Endowment** $8.1 million
- **Coed** 3,780 undergraduate students, 82% full-time, 54% women, 46% men
- **Minimally difficult** entrance level, 67% of applicants were admitted

Undergraduates 3,087 full-time, 693 part-time. Students come from 33 states and territories; 9 other countries; 3% are from out of state; 18% Black or African American, non-Hispanic/Latino; 9% Hispanic/Latino; 1% Asian, non-Hispanic/Latino; 0.1% Native Hawaiian or other Pacific Islander, non-Hispanic/Latino; 2% American Indian or Alaska Native, non-Hispanic/Latino; 1% Two or more races, non-Hispanic/Latino; 4% Race/ethnicity unknown; 0.8% international; 9% transferred in; 35% live on campus. *Retention:* 75% of full-time freshmen returned.

Freshmen *Admission:* 4,884 applied, 3,281 admitted, 1,003 enrolled. *Test scores:* SAT critical reading scores over 500: 27%; SAT math scores over 500: 35%; SAT writing scores over 500: 18%; ACT scores over 18: 75%; SAT critical reading scores over 600: 3%; SAT math scores over 600: 7%; SAT writing scores over 600: 1%; ACT scores over 24: 14%; ACT scores over 30: 1%.

Faculty *Total:* 220, 54% full-time, 28% with terminal degrees. *Student/faculty ratio:* 22:1.

Academics *Calendar:* semesters. *Degrees:* certificates, associate, bachelor's, and master's. *Special study options:* academic remediation for entering students, advanced placement credit, distance learning, honors programs, independent study, internships, off-campus study, services for LD students, student-designed majors, study abroad, summer session for credit. *ROTC:* Army (c), Air Force (c).

Computers on Campus 635 computers/terminals are available on campus for general student use. Students can access the following: campus intranet, computer help desk, free student e-mail accounts, online (class) grades, online (class) registration, online (class) schedules, bill payment. Campuswide network is available. 100% of college-owned or -operated housing units are wired for high-speed Internet access. Wireless service is available via classrooms, computer labs, dorm rooms, libraries, student centers.

Student Life *Housing:* on-campus residence required through junior year. *Options:* coed, disabled students. Campus housing is university owned. Freshman campus housing is guaranteed. *Activities and organizations:* drama/theater group, choral group, Criminal Justice, Student Cooperative Alliance, Automotive Club, Gaming Club, African Student Union, national fraternities, national sororities. *Campus security:* 24-hour emergency response devices and patrols, late-night transport/escort service, controlled dormitory access. *Student services:* health clinic, personal/psychological counseling.

Athletics Member NAIA, USCAA. *Intercollegiate sports:* baseball M, basketball M/W, cross-country running M/W, golf M, ice hockey M/W, lacrosse M/W, soccer M/W, softball W, volleyball W. *Intramural sports:* basketball M/W, football M/W, soccer M/W, softball M/W.

Standardized Tests *Required for some:* SAT or ACT (for admission).

Costs (2012–13) *One-time required fee:* $90. *Tuition:* state resident $5570 full-time, $220 per credit hour part-time; nonresident $10,324 full-time, $597 per credit hour part-time. Full-time tuition and fees vary according to degree level, location, and program. Part-time tuition and fees vary according to degree level, location, and program. *Required fees:* $1400 full-time, $58 per credit hour part-time, $5 per term part-time. *Room and board:* $10,952; room only: $6510. Room and board charges vary according to board plan and housing facility. *Payment plans:* installment, deferred payment. *Waivers:* employees or children of employees.

Applying *Options:* electronic application, early admission, deferred entrance. *Application fee:* $40. *Required:* high school transcript. *Required for some:* essay or personal statement, interview. *Recommended:* minimum 2.0 GPA. *Application deadlines:* rolling (freshmen), rolling (out-of-state freshmen), rolling (transfers). *Notification:* continuous (freshmen), continuous (out-of-state freshmen), continuous (transfers).

Freshman Application Contact Mr. Michael Perry, Interim Director of Admissions, State University of New York College of Technology at Canton, Cornell Drive, Canton, NY 13617. *Phone:* 315-386-7123. *Toll-free phone:* 800-388-7123. *Fax:* 315-386-7929. *E-mail:* admissions@canton.edu. *Website:* http://www.canton.edu/.

State University of New York College of Technology at Delhi
Delhi, New York

- **State-supported** 4-year, founded 1913, part of State University of New York System
- **Rural** 405-acre campus
- **Endowment** $3.5 million
- **Coed** 3,151 undergraduate students, 83% full-time, 52% women, 48% men
- **Moderately difficult** entrance level, 57% of applicants were admitted

Undergraduates 2,605 full-time, 546 part-time. Students come from 22 states and territories; 6 other countries; 4% are from out of state; 14% Black or African American, non-Hispanic/Latino; 11% Hispanic/Latino; 2% Asian, non-Hispanic/Latino; 0.1% Native Hawaiian or other Pacific Islander, non-Hispanic/Latino; 0.2% American Indian or Alaska Native, non-Hispanic/Latino; 2% Two or more races, non-Hispanic/Latino; 5% Race/ethnicity unknown; 1% international; 17% transferred in; 48% live on campus. *Retention:* 72% of full-time freshmen returned.

Freshmen *Admission:* 5,012 applied, 2,873 admitted, 922 enrolled. *Average high school GPA:* 2.7. *Test scores:* SAT critical reading scores over 500: 25%; SAT math scores over 500: 25%; SAT writing scores over 500: 28%; ACT scores over 18: 75%; SAT critical reading scores over 600: 5%; SAT math scores over 600: 5%; SAT writing scores over 600: 5%; ACT scores over 24: 6%; SAT critical reading scores over 700: 1%; SAT math scores over 700: 1%; SAT writing scores over 700: 1%; ACT scores over 30: 2%.

Faculty *Total:* 227, 57% full-time, 20% with terminal degrees. *Student/faculty ratio:* 17:1.

Academics *Calendar:* semesters. *Degrees:* certificates, associate, and bachelor's. *Special study options:* academic remediation for entering students, advanced placement credit, distance learning, English as a second language, honors programs, internships, off-campus study, part-time degree program, services for LD students, student-designed majors, summer session for credit.

Computers on Campus 350 computers/terminals are available on campus for general student use. Students can access the following: campus intranet, computer help desk, free student e-mail accounts, online (class) grades, online (class) registration, online (class) schedules. Campuswide network is available. 100% of college-owned or -operated housing units are wired for high-speed Internet access. Wireless service is available via entire campus.

Student Life *Housing:* on-campus residence required through sophomore year. *Options:* coed, women-only. Campus housing is university owned and is provided by a third party. *Activities and organizations:* drama/theater group, student-run newspaper, radio and television station, Latin American Student Organization, Hotel Sales Management Association, student radio station, Phi Theta Kappa, Student Programming Board, national fraternities. *Campus security:* 24-hour emergency response devices and patrols, late-night transport/escort service, controlled dormitory access. *Student services:* health clinic, personal/psychological counseling.

Athletics Member NAIA, NJCAA. *Intercollegiate sports:* basketball M/W, cross-country running M/W, golf M/W, lacrosse M, soccer M/W, softball W, swimming and diving M/W, tennis M/W, track and field M/W, volleyball W. *Intramural sports:* badminton M/W(c), basketball M, bowling M(c)/W(c), equestrian sports M(c)/W(c), football M, racquetball M/W, skiing (downhill) M(c)/W(c), softball M/W, ultimate Frisbee M/W, volleyball M/W.

Standardized Tests *Recommended:* SAT or ACT (for admission).

Costs (2012–13) *Tuition:* state resident $5570 full-time, $232 per credit hour part-time; nonresident $9740 full-time, $406 per credit hour part-time. Full-time tuition and fees vary according to degree level. Part-time tuition and fees vary according to degree level. *Required fees:* $1520 full-time, $76 per credit hour part-time, $76 per credit hour part-time. *Room and board:* $10,346; room only: $5936. Room and board charges vary according to board plan and housing facility. *Payment plan:* installment.

Financial Aid Of all full-time matriculated undergraduates who enrolled in 2011, 2,501 applied for aid. 92 Federal Work-Study jobs (averaging $1016).

Applying *Options:* electronic application, early admission, deferred entrance. *Application fee:* $50. *Required:* high school transcript. *Required for some:* minimum 2.0 GPA, some Bachelor degree programs require Associate degree for admission; BSN program requires RN license. *Recommended:* interview. *Application deadlines:* rolling (freshmen), rolling (transfers). *Notification:* continuous (freshmen), continuous (transfers).

Freshman Application Contact Mr., State University of New York College of Technology at Delhi, 2 Main St—Stop 2, Delhi, NY 13753. *Phone:* 607-746-4550. *Toll-free phone:* 800-96-DELHI. *Fax:* 607-746-4104. *E-mail:* enroll@delhi.edu. *Website:* http://www.delhi.edu/.

State University of New York Downstate Medical Center
Brooklyn, New York

Application Contact Admissions Office, State University of New York Downstate Medical Center, 450 Clarkson Avenue, Brooklyn, NY 11203-2446. *Phone:* 718-270-2446. *Fax:* 718-270-7592. *E-mail:* admissions@downstate.edu. *Website:* http://www.downstate.edu/.

State University of New York Empire State College

Saratoga Springs, New York

- **State-supported** comprehensive, founded 1971, part of State University of New York System
- **Small-town** campus
- **Endowment** $13.8 million
- **Coed** 11,121 undergraduate students, 39% full-time, 62% women, 38% men
- **Minimally difficult** entrance level, 79% of applicants were admitted

Undergraduates 4,352 full-time, 6,769 part-time. Students come from 52 states and territories; 13 other countries; 8% are from out of state; 18% Black or African American, non-Hispanic/Latino; 5% Hispanic/Latino; 2% Asian, non-Hispanic/Latino; 0.8% Native Hawaiian or other Pacific Islander, non-Hispanic/Latino; 1% American Indian or Alaska Native, non-Hispanic/Latino; 7% Race/ethnicity unknown; 16% transferred in.

Freshmen *Admission:* 1,536 applied, 1,221 admitted, 469 enrolled.

Faculty *Total:* 1,400, 14% full-time. *Student/faculty ratio:* 8:1.

Academics *Calendar:* continuous. *Degrees:* certificates, associate, bachelor's, master's, and postbachelor's certificates (branch locations at 7 regional centers with 35 auxiliary units). *Special study options:* adult/continuing education programs, advanced placement credit, cooperative education, distance learning, external degree program, independent study, off-campus study, part-time degree program, services for LD students, student-designed majors, summer session for credit.

Computers on Campus 100 computers/terminals are available on campus for general student use. Students can access the following: online (class) registration. Campuswide network is available.

Student Life *Housing:* college housing not available.

Costs (2012–13) *Tuition:* state resident $5570 full-time, $232 per credit hour part-time; nonresident $14,820 full-time, $618 per credit hour part-time. Full-time tuition and fees vary according to course level, course load, location, and program. Part-time tuition and fees vary according to course level, location, and program. *Required fees:* $345 full-time, $7 per credit hour part-time, $115 per term part-time. *Payment plan:* installment.

Applying *Options:* electronic application, early admission. *Required:* essay or personal statement, high school transcript. *Required for some:* interview. *Application deadlines:* rolling (freshmen), rolling (transfers). *Notification:* continuous (transfers).

Freshman Application Contact Ms. Jennifer D'Agostino, Director of Admissions, State University of New York Empire State College, Two Union Avenue, Saratoga Springs, NY 12866. *Phone:* 518-587-2100 Ext. 2214. *Toll-free phone:* 800-847-3000. *Fax:* 518-587-9759. *E-mail:* Jennifer.D'Agostino@esc.edu.

Website: http://www.esc.edu/.

State University of New York Institute of Technology

Utica, New York

- **State-supported** comprehensive, founded 1966, part of State University of New York System
- **Suburban** 850-acre campus
- **Endowment** $2.4 million
- **Coed** 1,693 undergraduate students, 75% full-time, 46% women, 54% men
- **Moderately difficult** entrance level, 39% of applicants were admitted

Undergraduates 1,272 full-time, 421 part-time. Students come from 22 states and territories; 12 other countries; 1% are from out of state; 8% Black or African American, non-Hispanic/Latino; 5% Hispanic/Latino; 2% Asian, non-Hispanic/Latino; 0.2% American Indian or Alaska Native, non-Hispanic/Latino; 8% Race/ethnicity unknown; 0.7% international; 18% transferred in; 30% live on campus. *Retention:* 70% of full-time freshmen returned.

Freshmen *Admission:* 1,884 applied, 732 admitted, 198 enrolled. *Average high school GPA:* 3.5. *Test scores:* SAT critical reading scores over 500: 55%; SAT math scores over 500: 77%; ACT scores over 18: 95%; SAT critical reading scores over 600: 15%; SAT math scores over 600: 28%; ACT scores over 24: 37%; SAT critical reading scores over 700: 1%; SAT math scores over 700: 3%; ACT scores over 30: 3%.

Faculty *Total:* 180, 41% full-time, 49% with terminal degrees. *Student/faculty ratio:* 18:1.

Academics *Calendar:* semesters. *Degrees:* bachelor's, master's, and post-master's certificates. *Special study options:* accelerated degree program, advanced placement credit, cooperative education, distance learning, double majors, English as a second language, independent study, internships, part-time degree program, services for LD students, study abroad, summer session for credit. *ROTC:* Army (c), Air Force (c).

Computers on Campus 244 computers/terminals and 144 ports are available on campus for general student use. Students can access the following: campus intranet, computer help desk, free student e-mail accounts, online (class) grades, online (class) registration, online (class) schedules. Campuswide network is available. 100% of college-owned or -operated housing units are wired for high-speed Internet access.

Student Life *Housing:* on-campus residence required through sophomore year. *Options:* coed, disabled students. Campus housing is university owned. Freshman campus housing is guaranteed. *Activities and organizations:* student-run newspaper, radio and television station, SUNYIT Gamers Club, Soccer Club, Black and Latino Student Union, Psychology and Sociology Club, Anime Club. *Campus security:* 24-hour emergency response devices and patrols, student patrols, late-night transport/escort service, controlled dormitory access, closed-circuit TV monitors, 24 hour police department. *Student services:* health clinic, personal/psychological counseling, legal services.

Athletics Member NCAA. All Division III. *Intercollegiate sports:* baseball M, basketball M/W, cross-country running M/W, lacrosse M/W, soccer M/W, softball W, volleyball W. *Intramural sports:* badminton M/W, basketball M/W, bowling M/W, racquetball M/W, soccer M/W, softball M/W, tennis M/W, volleyball M/W.

Standardized Tests *Required:* SAT or ACT (for admission). *Recommended:* SAT Subject Tests (for admission).

Costs (2013–14) *Tuition:* state resident $5570 full-time, $232 per credit hour part-time; nonresident $14,820 full-time, $618 per credit hour part-time. Part-time tuition and fees vary according to course load. *Required fees:* $1194 full-time, $50 per credit hour part-time, $50 per credit hour part-time. *Room and board:* $10,290. Room and board charges vary according to board plan. *Payment plan:* installment.

Financial Aid Of all full-time matriculated undergraduates who enrolled in 2009, 1,289 applied for aid, 1,074 were judged to have need. In 2009, 40 non-need-based awards were made. *Average need-based loan:* $4168. *Average need-based gift aid:* $5604. *Average non-need-based aid:* $1747.

Applying *Options:* electronic application, early admission, early action, deferred entrance. *Application fee:* $50. *Required:* essay or personal statement, high school transcript, minimum 3.0 GPA, 2 letters of recommendation. *Recommended:* interview. *Application deadlines:* rolling (freshmen), rolling (out-of-state freshmen), 8/1 (transfers), 11/1 (early action). *Notification:* continuous until 1/15 (freshmen), continuous until 1/15 (out-of-state freshmen), continuous until 12/1 (transfers), 12/15 (early action).

Freshman Application Contact Ms. Jennifer Phelan-Ninh, Director of Admissions, State University of New York Institute of Technology, 100 Seymour Road, Utica, NY 13502. *Phone:* 315-792-7500. *Toll-free phone:* 866-2-SUNYIT. *Fax:* 315-792-7837. *E-mail:* admissions@sunyit.edu. *Website:* http://www.sunyit.edu/.

See previous page for display ad and page 1518 for the College Close-Up.

State University of New York Maritime College

Throggs Neck, New York

- **State-supported** comprehensive, founded 1874, part of State University of New York System
- **Suburban** 56-acre campus with easy access to New York City
- **Endowment** $5.0 million
- **Coed, primarily men** 1,614 undergraduate students, 96% full-time, 10% women, 90% men
- **Very difficult** entrance level, 58% of applicants were admitted

Undergraduates 1,553 full-time, 61 part-time. Students come from 32 states and territories; 21 other countries; 27% are from out of state; 3% Black or African American, non-Hispanic/Latino; 8% Hispanic/Latino; 3% Asian, non-Hispanic/Latino; 0.1% American Indian or Alaska Native, non-Hispanic/Latino; 28% Race/ethnicity unknown; 3% international; 5% transferred in; 78% live on campus. *Retention:* 81% of full-time freshmen returned.

Freshmen *Admission:* 1,317 applied, 759 admitted, 327 enrolled. *Test scores:* SAT critical reading scores over 500: 70%; SAT math scores over 500: 87%; ACT scores over 18: 95%; SAT critical reading scores over 600: 14%; SAT math scores over 600: 34%; ACT scores over 24: 42%; SAT critical reading scores over 700: 2%; SAT math scores over 700: 2%; ACT scores over 30: 4%.

Faculty *Total:* 149, 65% full-time, 32% with terminal degrees. *Student/faculty ratio:* 14:1.

Academics *Calendar:* semesters plus 2-month summer sea term. *Degrees:* associate, bachelor's, and master's. *Special study options:* academic remediation for entering students, adult/continuing education programs, advanced placement credit, cooperative education, distance learning, double majors, English as a second language, honors programs, independent study, internships, services for LD students, summer session for credit. *ROTC:* Army (c), Navy (b), .

Computers on Campus 110 computers/terminals are available on campus for general student use. Students can access the following: computer help desk, free student e-mail accounts, online (class) grades, online (class) registration, online (class) schedules. Campuswide network is available. Wireless service is available via classrooms, computer centers, dorm rooms, libraries.

Student Life *Housing:* on-campus residence required through senior year. *Options:* coed. Campus housing is university owned. *Activities and organizations:* choral group, marching band, student government, Maritime Activities and Programs, Campus Crusade for Christ, The Propeller Club, Chorale. *Campus security:* 24-hour emergency response devices and patrols, student patrols, late-night transport/escort service, controlled dormitory access. *Student services:* health clinic, personal/psychological counseling.

Athletics Member NCAA. All Division III. *Intercollegiate sports:* baseball M, basketball M/W, crew W, cross-country running M/W, football M, ice hockey M, lacrosse M/W, riflery M/W, soccer M/W, softball W, swimming and diving M/W, volleyball W. *Intramural sports:* basketball M/W, cross-country running M/W, football M, rugby M, sailing M/W, soccer M/W, softball M/W, volleyball M/W.

Standardized Tests *Required:* SAT or ACT (for admission).

Costs (2012–13) *Tuition:* state resident $5570 full-time, $232 per credit hour part-time; nonresident $14,820 full-time, $618 per credit hour part-time. Full-time tuition and fees vary according to degree level and program. Part-time tuition and fees vary according to course load, degree level, and program. *Required fees:* $1212 full-time, $51 per credit hour part-time. *Room and board:* $10,444; room only: $6594. Room and board charges vary according to board plan, gender, and housing facility. *Payment plan:* installment. *Waivers:* employees or children of employees.

Financial Aid Of all full-time matriculated undergraduates who enrolled in 2011, 903 applied for aid, 862 were judged to have need. In 2011, 45 non-need-based awards were made. *Average non-need-based aid:* $1994. *Financial aid deadline:* 7/15.

Applying *Options:* electronic application, early decision, deferred entrance. *Application fee:* $50. *Required:* essay or personal statement. *Recommended:* high school transcript, interview. *Application deadlines:* rolling (freshmen), rolling (transfers). *Notification:* continuous (freshmen), continuous (transfers).

Freshman Application Contact Ms. Yamiley Saintvil, Dean of Admissions, State University of New York Maritime College, 6 Pennyfield Avenue, Throggs Neck, NY 10465. *Phone:* 718-409-7222. *Fax:* 718-409-7465. *E-mail:* ysaintvil@sunymaritime.edu. *Website:* http://www.sunymaritime.edu/.

State University of New York Upstate Medical University

Syracuse, New York

- **State-supported** upper-level, founded 1950, part of State University of New York System
- **Urban** 25-acre campus
- **Endowment** $60.1 million
- **Coed**
- **Moderately difficult** entrance level

Academics *Calendar:* semesters. *Degrees:* bachelor's, master's, doctoral, and post-master's certificates.

Student Life *Campus security:* 24-hour emergency response devices and patrols, late-night transport/escort service, controlled dormitory access.

Financial Aid *Of all full-time matriculated undergraduates who enrolled in 2009,* 227 applied for aid, 227 were judged to have need. *Average percent of need met:* 86. *Average financial aid package:* $11,847. *Average need-based loan:* $11,128. *Average need-based gift aid:* $1608.

Applying *Options:* electronic application, early admission, deferred entrance. *Application fee:* $50.

Application Contact Mrs. Donna L. Vavonese, Associate Director of Admissions, State University of New York Upstate Medical University, Weiskotten Hall, 766 Irving Avenue, Syracuse, NY 13210. *Phone:* 315-464-

4570. *Toll-free phone:* 800-736-2171. *Fax:* 315-464-8867. *E-mail:* admiss@upstate.edu.
Website: http://www.upstate.edu/.

Stony Brook University, State University of New York

Stony Brook, New York

- **State-supported** university, founded 1957, part of State University of New York
- **Suburban** 1450-acre campus with easy access to New York City
- **Endowment** $125.4 million
- **Coed** 16,003 undergraduate students, 92% full-time, 47% women, 53% men
- **Very difficult** entrance level, 40% of applicants were admitted

Undergraduates 14,689 full-time, 1,314 part-time. Students come from 48 states and territories; 110 other countries; 8% are from out of state; 6% Black or African American, non-Hispanic/Latino; 10% Hispanic/Latino; 25% Asian, non-Hispanic/Latino; 0.1% Native Hawaiian or other Pacific Islander, non-Hispanic/Latino; 0.1% American Indian or Alaska Native, non-Hispanic/Latino; 2% Two or more races, non-Hispanic/Latino; 10% Race/ethnicity unknown; 9% international; 9% transferred in; 61% live on campus. *Retention:* 90% of full-time freshmen returned.

Freshmen *Admission:* 27,513 applied, 11,023 admitted, 2,676 enrolled. *Average high school GPA:* 3.68. *Test scores:* SAT critical reading scores over 500: 86%; SAT math scores over 500: 96%; SAT writing scores over 500: 87%; ACT scores over 18: 99%; SAT critical reading scores over 600: 46%; SAT math scores over 600: 75%; SAT writing scores over 600: 46%; ACT scores over 24: 90%; SAT critical reading scores over 700: 10%; SAT math scores over 700: 26%; SAT writing scores over 700: 10%; ACT scores over 30: 24%.

Faculty *Total:* 1,467, 65% full-time, 91% with terminal degrees. *Student/faculty ratio:* 18:1.

Academics *Calendar:* semesters. *Degrees:* bachelor's, master's, doctoral, post-master's, and postbachelor's certificates. *Special study options:* academic remediation for entering students, adult/continuing education programs, advanced placement credit, cooperative education, distance learning, double majors, English as a second language, freshman honors college, honors programs, independent study, internships, off-campus study, part-time degree program, services for LD students, student-designed majors, study abroad, summer session for credit. *ROTC:* Army (b), Navy (c), Air Force (c). *Unusual degree programs:* 3-2 business administration; engineering; applied math and statistics BS/MPH, pharmacology BS/MPH, women's students BA/MPH, earth and space sciences BA/MPH, occupational therapy BS/MS, linguistics BA/TESOL MA, political science BA/public policy MA, Masters in Adolescent Ed in combination with a variety of academic programs.

Computers on Campus 2,600 computers/terminals are available on campus for general student use. Students can access the following: campus intranet, computer help desk, free student e-mail accounts, online (class) grades, online (class) registration, online (class) schedules. Campuswide network is available. 100% of college-owned or -operated housing units are wired for high-speed Internet access. Wireless service is available via entire campus.

Student Life *Housing options:* coed. Campus housing is university owned. Freshman campus housing is guaranteed. *Activities and organizations:* drama/theater group, student-run newspaper, radio and television station, choral group, marching band, Inter Fraternity and Sorority Council, Residence Hall Association, Commuter Student Association, Undergraduate Student Government—Student Activities Board, Chinese Association at Stony Brook, national fraternities, national sororities. *Campus security:* 24-hour emergency response devices and patrols, late-night transport/escort service, controlled dormitory access. *Student services:* health clinic, personal/psychological counseling, women's center, legal services.

Athletics Member NCAA. All Division I. *Intercollegiate sports:* baseball M(s), basketball M(s)/W(s), cross-country running M(s)/W(s), football M(s), lacrosse M(s)/W(s), soccer M(s)/W(s), softball W(s), swimming and diving M/W(s), tennis M(s)/W(s), track and field M(s)/W(s), volleyball W(s). *Intramural sports:* badminton M(c)/W(c), basketball M/W, bowling M(c)/W(c), cheerleading M(c)/W, crew M(c)/W(c), equestrian sports M(c)/W(c), fencing M(c)/W(c), ice hockey M(c), lacrosse M(c)/W(c), racquetball M/W, riflery M(c)/W(c), rugby M(c)/W(c), soccer M/W, softball M/W, squash M(c)/W(c), table tennis M(c)/W(c), tennis M(c)/W(c), ultimate Frisbee M(c)/W(c), volleyball M/W, weight lifting M(c), wrestling M(c).

Standardized Tests *Required:* SAT or ACT (for admission).

Costs (2012–13) *Tuition:* state resident $5570 full-time, $232 per credit hour part-time; nonresident $16,190 full-time, $675 per credit hour part-time. Full-time tuition and fees vary according to course load. Part-time tuition and fees vary according to course load. *Required fees:* $1990 full-time, $98 per credit hour part-time. *Room and board:* $10,934; room only: $6968. Room and board charges vary according to board plan and housing facility. *Payment plan:* installment.

Financial Aid Of all full-time matriculated undergraduates who enrolled in 2012, 10,424 applied for aid, 8,682 were judged to have need, 1,171 had their need fully met. 392 Federal Work-Study jobs (averaging $2119). 1,669 state and other part-time jobs (averaging $1986). In 2012, 1196 non-need-based awards were made. *Average percent of need met:* 65%. *Average financial aid package:* $11,473. *Average need-based loan:* $4692. *Average need-based gift aid:* $6905. *Average non-need-based aid:* $3926. *Average indebtedness upon graduation:* $20,954.

Applying *Options:* electronic application, deferred entrance. *Application fee:* $50. *Required:* essay or personal statement, high school transcript, minimum 3.0 GPA, 1 letter of recommendation. *Required for some:* audition. *Recommended:* interview. *Application deadlines:* 1/15 (freshmen), 3/1 (transfers). *Notification:* 4/1 (freshmen), continuous (transfers).

Freshman Application Contact Ms. Judith Burke-Berhanan, Dean of Undergraduate Admissions, Stony Brook University, State University of New York, Admissions Office, 118 Administration Building, Stony Brook, NY 11794-1901. *Phone:* 631-632-6868. *Fax:* 631-632-9898. *E-mail:* enroll@stonybrook.edu.
Website: http://www.sunysb.edu/.

See previous page for display ad and page 1526 for the College Close-Up.

Swedish Institute, College of Health Sciences

New York, New York

Freshman Application Contact Admissions Advisor, Swedish Institute, College of Health Sciences, 226 West 26th Street, New York, NY 10001. *Phone:* 212-914-5900 Ext. 125. *E-mail:* admissions@swedishinstitute.edu. *Website:* http://www.swedishinstitute.org/.

Syracuse University

Syracuse, New York

- **Independent** university, founded 1870
- **Urban** 200-acre campus with easy access to Syracuse
- **Endowment** $940.1 million
- **Coed** 14,798 undergraduate students, 96% full-time, 56% women, 44% men
- **Very difficult** entrance level, 51% of applicants were admitted

Undergraduates 14,169 full-time, 629 part-time. Students come from 49 states and territories; 82 other countries; 55% are from out of state; 9% Black or African American, non-Hispanic/Latino; 10% Hispanic/Latino; 8% Asian, non-Hispanic/Latino; 0.1% Native Hawaiian or other Pacific Islander, non-Hispanic/Latino; 0.7% American Indian or Alaska Native, non-Hispanic/Latino; 2% Two or more races, non-Hispanic/Latino; 5% Race/ethnicity unknown; 8% international; 3% transferred in; 75% live on campus. *Retention:* 92% of full-time freshmen returned.

Freshmen *Admission:* 25,790 applied, 13,240 admitted, 3,392 enrolled. *Average high school GPA:* 3.6. *Test scores:* SAT critical reading scores over 500: 81%; SAT math scores over 500: 90%; SAT writing scores over 500: 84%; ACT scores over 18: 99%; SAT critical reading scores over 600: 34%; SAT math scores over 600: 53%; SAT writing scores over 600: 40%; ACT scores over 24: 74%; SAT critical reading scores over 700: 5%; SAT math scores over 700: 10%; SAT writing scores over 700: 7%; ACT scores over 30: 13%.

Faculty *Total:* 1,563, 65% full-time, 63% with terminal degrees. *Student/faculty ratio:* 16:1.

Academics *Calendar:* semesters. *Degrees:* certificates, bachelor's, master's, doctoral, post-master's, and postbachelor's certificates. *Special study options:* academic remediation for entering students, accelerated degree program, adult/continuing education programs, advanced placement credit, cooperative education, distance learning, double majors, English as a second language, freshman honors college, honors programs, independent study, internships, off-campus study, part-time degree program, services for LD students, student-designed majors, study abroad, summer session for credit. *ROTC:* Army (b), Air Force (b).

Computers on Campus 3,500 computers/terminals and 678 ports are available on campus for general student use. Students can access the following: campus intranet, computer help desk, free student e-mail accounts, online (class) grades, online (class) registration, online (class) schedules, Library; web conferencing; learning management system (Blackboard); blogging service; personal websites; Advising Reports; digital asset management system (Collage). Campuswide network is available. 100% of college-owned or -operated housing units are wired for high-speed Internet access. Wireless service is available via classrooms, computer centers, computer labs, dorm rooms, learning centers, libraries, student centers.

Student Life *Housing:* on-campus residence required through sophomore year. *Options:* coed, disabled students. Campus housing is university owned. Freshman campus housing is guaranteed. *Activities and organizations:* drama/theater group, student-run newspaper, radio and television station, choral group, marching band, University Union, Student Association, Student Leadership Conference, Habitat for Humanity, national fraternities, national sororities. *Campus security:* 24-hour emergency response devices and patrols, student patrols, late-night transport/escort service, controlled dormitory access, crisis alert notification system, outdoor emergency sirens, off-campus patrols in student rental neighborhoods. *Student services:* health clinic, personal/psychological counseling, women's center, legal services.

Athletics Member NCAA. All Division I except football (Division I-A). *Intercollegiate sports:* badminton M(c)/W(c), baseball M(c), basketball M(s)/W(s), bowling M(c)/W(c), cheerleading M/W, crew M(s)/W(s), cross-country running M(s)/W(s), equestrian sports M(c)/W(c), fencing M(c)/W(c), field hockey W(s), gymnastics M(c)/W(c), ice hockey M(c)/W(s), lacrosse M(s)/W(s), rugby M(c)/W(c), sailing M(c)/W(c), skiing (downhill) M(c)/W(c), soccer M(s)/W(s), softball W(s), tennis M(c)/W(s), track and field M(s)/W(s), volleyball M(c)/W(s), water polo M(c)/W(c), wrestling M(c). *Intramural sports:* basketball M/W, field hockey W(c), golf M(c)/W(c), ice hockey M/W, lacrosse M(c)/W(c), racquetball M/W, soccer M/W, softball M/W, swimming and diving M(c)/W(c), tennis M/W, ultimate Frisbee M(c)/W(c), volleyball M/W.

Standardized Tests *Required:* SAT or ACT (for admission).

Costs (2012–13) *Comprehensive fee:* $52,696 includes full-time tuition ($37,610), mandatory fees ($1394), and room and board ($13,692). Full-time tuition and fees vary according to course load. Part-time tuition: $1637 per credit hour. Part-time tuition and fees vary according to course load. *College room only:* $7212. Room and board charges vary according to board plan and housing facility. *Payment plan:* installment. *Waivers:* employees or children of employees.

Financial Aid Of all full-time matriculated undergraduates who enrolled in 2012, 9,666 applied for aid, 8,241 were judged to have need, 4,940 had their need fully met. In 2012, 1404 non-need-based awards were made. *Average percent of need met:* 93%. *Average financial aid package:* $34,000. *Average need-based loan:* $7300. *Average need-based gift aid:* $24,740. *Average non-need-based aid:* $9030. *Average indebtedness upon graduation:* $33,504. *Financial aid deadline:* 2/1.

Applying *Options:* electronic application, early admission, early decision, deferred entrance. *Application fee:* $70. *Required:* essay or personal statement, high school transcript, 2 letters of recommendation. *Application deadline:* 1/1 (freshmen). *Early decision deadline:* 11/15.

Freshman Application Contact Office of Admissions, Syracuse University, 100 Crouse-Hinds Hall, 900 South Crouse Avenue, Syracuse, NY 13244-2130. *Phone:* 315-443-3611. *Fax:* 315-443-4226. *E-mail:* orange@syr.edu. *Website:* http://www.syr.edu/.

See previous page for display ad and page 1532 for the College Close-Up.

Talmudical Institute of Upstate New York

Rochester, New York

Director of Admissions Rabbi Menachem Davidowitz, Director of Admissions, Talmudical Institute of Upstate New York, 769 Park Avenue, Rochester, NY 14607-3046. *Phone:* 716-473-2810. *E-mail:* yeshiva@tiuny.org. *Website:* http://www.tiuny.org/.

Talmudical Seminary Oholei Torah

Brooklyn, New York

Director of Admissions Rabbi Yisroel Friedman, Director of Academic Affairs, Talmudical Seminary Oholei Torah, 667 Eastern Parkway, Brooklyn, NY 11213-3310. *Phone:* 718-363-2034. *E-mail:* info@oholeitorah.com.

Torah Temimah Talmudical Seminary

Brooklyn, New York

Director of Admissions Principal, Torah Temimah Talmudical Seminary, 507 Ocean Parkway, Brooklyn, NY 11218-5913. *Phone:* 718-853-8500.

Touro College

New York, New York

- **Independent** comprehensive, founded 1971
- **Urban** campus
- **Coed**
- **Moderately difficult** entrance level

Academics *Calendar:* semesters. *Degrees:* certificates, associate, bachelor's, master's, doctoral, and post-master's certificates.

Student Life *Campus security:* 24-hour emergency response devices and patrols.

Standardized Tests *Recommended:* SAT or ACT (for admission).

Costs (2012–13) *Comprehensive fee:* $25,770 includes full-time tuition ($14,800), mandatory fees ($570), and room and board ($10,400). Full-time tuition and fees vary according to course load, degree level, location, and program. Part-time tuition: $610 per credit hour. Part-time tuition and fees vary according to course load, degree level, location, and program. *College room only:* $7300. Room and board charges vary according to housing facility and location.

Financial Aid Of all full-time matriculated undergraduates who enrolled in 2002, 5,940 applied for aid, 5,940 were judged to have need. *Average percent of need met:* 90. *Average financial aid package:* $9000. *Average need-based loan:* $4275. *Average non-need-based aid:* $1500. *Average indebtedness upon graduation:* $17,000.

Applying *Options:* early admission, deferred entrance. *Application fee:* $50. *Required:* high school transcript. *Required for some:* minimum 3.0 GPA, 2 letters of recommendation, interview. *Recommended:* essay or personal statement, 1 letter of recommendation.

Freshman Application Contact Mr. David Luk, Associate Director of Admissions, Touro College, 27-33 West 23rd Street, New York, NY 10010. *Phone:* 212-463-0400 Ext. 5644. *Fax:* 212-627-9542. *E-mail:* david.luk@touro.edu. *Website:* http://www.touro.edu/.

Union College

Schenectady, New York

- **Independent** 4-year, founded 1795
- **Urban** 100-acre campus
- **Endowment** $327.8 million
- **Coed**
- **Very difficult** entrance level

Faculty *Student/faculty ratio:* 10:1.

Academics *Calendar:* trimesters. *Degree:* bachelor's.

Student Life *Campus security:* 24-hour emergency response devices and patrols, late-night transport/escort service, controlled dormitory access, awareness programs, bicycle patrol, shuttle service.

Athletics Member NCAA. All Division III except men's and women's ice hockey (Division I).

Standardized Tests *Required for some:* SAT or ACT (for admission), SAT and SAT Subject Tests or ACT (for admission).

Costs (2012–13) *Comprehensive fee:* $56,289 includes full-time tuition ($44,748), mandatory fees ($471), and room and board ($11,070). *College room only:* $6069.

Financial Aid Of all full-time matriculated undergraduates who enrolled in 2012, 1,295 applied for aid, 1,060 were judged to have need, 1,029 had their need fully met. In 2012, 455 non-need-based awards were made. *Average percent of need met:* 98. *Average financial aid package:* $36,295. *Average need-based loan:* $5103. *Average need-based gift aid:* $30,926. *Average non-need-based aid:* $9196. *Financial aid deadline:* 2/1.

Applying *Options:* electronic application, early admission, early decision, deferred entrance. *Application fee:* $50. *Required:* essay or personal statement, high school transcript, 2 letters of recommendation. *Recommended:* interview.

Freshman Application Contact Union College, Grant Hall, 807 Union Street, Schenectady, NY 12308. *Phone:* 518-388-6112. *Toll-free phone:* 888-843-6688. *Fax:* 518-388-6986. *E-mail:* admissions@union.edu. *Website:* http://www.union.edu/.

See below for display ad and page 1544 for the College Close-Up.

United States Merchant Marine Academy

Kings Point, New York

- **Federally supported** comprehensive, founded 1943
- **Suburban** 82-acre campus with easy access to New York City
- **Coed** 987 undergraduate students, 100% full-time, 14% women, 86% men
- **Very difficult** entrance level, 12% of applicants were admitted

Undergraduates 987 full-time. Students come from 59 states and territories; 2 other countries; 88% are from out of state; 2% Black or African American, non-Hispanic/Latino; 7% Hispanic/Latino; 5% Asian, non-Hispanic/Latino; 0.7% American Indian or Alaska Native, non-Hispanic/Latino; 1% Race/ethnicity unknown; 2% international; 3% transferred in; 100% live on campus. *Retention:* 85% of full-time freshmen returned.

Freshmen *Admission:* 2,211 applied, 273 admitted, 225 enrolled. *Average high school GPA:* 3.6. *Test scores:* SAT critical reading scores over 500: 99%; SAT math scores over 500: 100%; ACT scores over 18: 100%; SAT critical reading scores over 600: 58%; SAT math scores over 600: 84%; ACT scores over 24: 98%; SAT critical reading scores over 700: 16%; SAT math scores over 700: 18%; ACT scores over 30: 24%.

Faculty *Total:* 79.

Academics *Calendar:* trimesters. *Degrees:* bachelor's and master's. *Special study options:* honors programs, internships.

Computers on Campus Students can access the following: campus intranet, computer help desk, free student e-mail accounts, engineering and economics software. Campuswide network is available.

Student Life *Housing:* on-campus residence required through senior year. *Options:* coed. Campus housing is university owned. Freshman campus housing is guaranteed. *Activities and organizations:* drama/theater group, student-run newspaper, choral group, marching band, Regimental Band, CFC, Neuman Club, Honor Guard. *Campus security:* 24-hour emergency response devices and patrols. *Student services:* health clinic, personal/psychological counseling.

Athletics Member NCAA. All Division III. *Intercollegiate sports:* baseball M, basketball M/W, crew M/W, cross-country running M/W, football M, ice hockey M(c), lacrosse M/W, riflery M(c), rugby M(c), sailing M/W, soccer M, swimming and diving M/W, tennis M, track and field M/W, volleyball W, wrestling M. *Intramural sports:* basketball M/W, golf M(c), ice hockey M(c), racquetball M/W, riflery M(c), rugby M(c), sailing M/W, soccer W(c), ultimate Frisbee M(c), volleyball M(c), water polo M(c), weight lifting M(c).

Standardized Tests *Required:* SAT or ACT (for admission).

Costs (2012–13) *Tuition:* Full-time tuition and fees vary according to student level. Tuition, room and board, and medical and dental care are provided by the U.S. government. Each midshipman receives a monthly stipend while assigned aboard ship for training. Entering freshmen are required to pay fees for laptop, equipment, and activity fees. *Required fees:* $1054 full-time.

Applying *Options:* electronic application. *Required:* essay or personal statement, high school transcript, 3 letters of recommendation, SAT or ACT. *Recommended:* interview. *Application deadlines:* 3/1 (freshmen), 3/1 (transfers). *Notification:* continuous until 4/1 (freshmen), continuous until 4/1 (transfers).

Freshman Application Contact Capt. Robert E. Johnson, Director of Admissions and Financial Aid, United States Merchant Marine Academy, 300 Steamboat Road, Kings Point, NY 11024-1699. *Phone:* 516-726-5641. *Toll-free phone:* 866-546-4778. *Fax:* 516-773-5390. *E-mail:* admissions@usmma.edu. *Website:* http://www.usmma.edu/.

See next page for display ad and page 1550 for the College Close-Up.

United States Military Academy

West Point, New York

- **Federally supported** 4-year, founded 1802
- **Small-town** 16,080-acre campus with easy access to New York City
- **Endowment** $201.1 million
- **Coed** 4,592 undergraduate students, 100% full-time, 16% women, 84% men
- **Most difficult** entrance level, 9% of applicants were admitted

Undergraduates 4,592 full-time. Students come from 55 states and territories; 35 other countries; 93% are from out of state; 7% Black or African American,

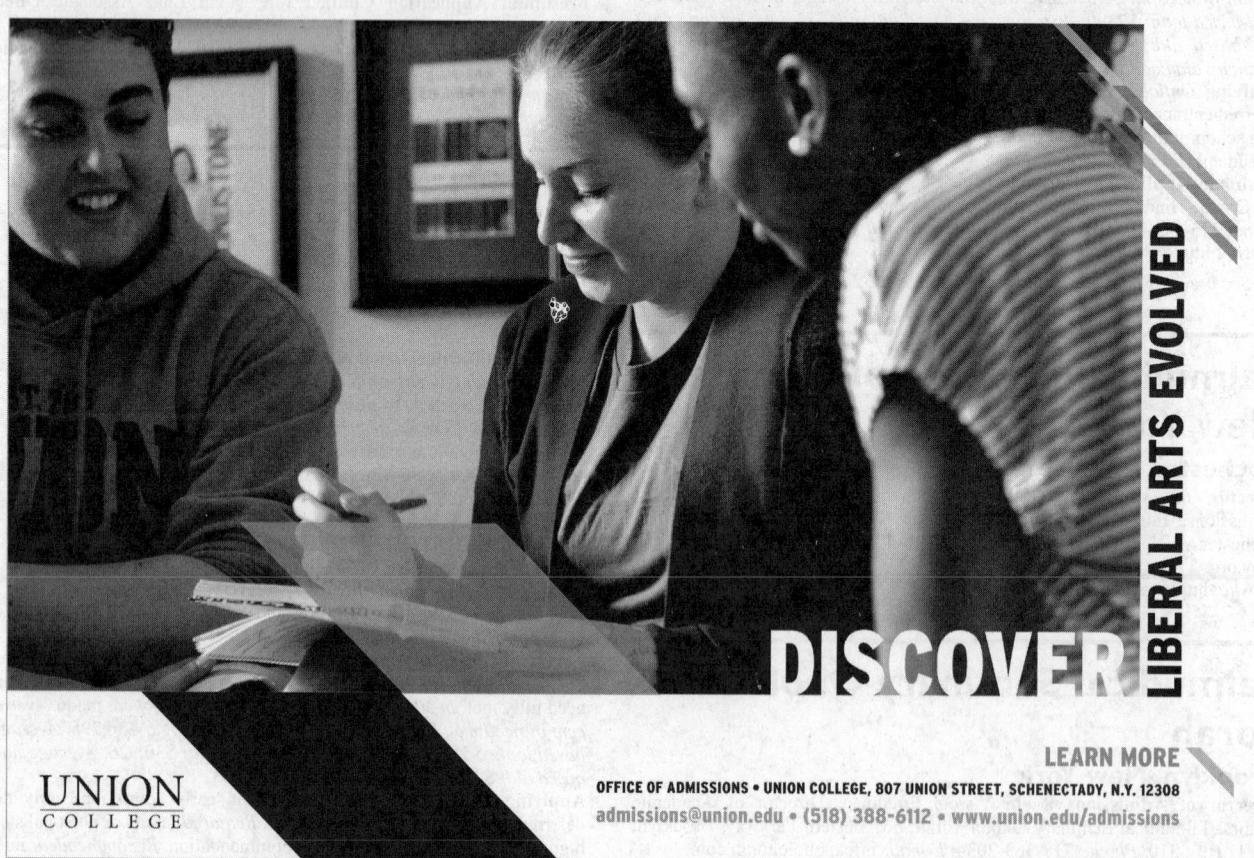

non-Hispanic/Latino; 9% Hispanic/Latino; 5% Asian, non-Hispanic/Latino; 0.5% Native Hawaiian or other Pacific Islander, non-Hispanic/Latino; 0.9% American Indian or Alaska Native, non-Hispanic/Latino; 4% Two or more races, non-Hispanic/Latino; 1% Race/ethnicity unknown; 1% international; 100% live on campus. *Retention:* 96% of full-time freshmen returned.

Freshmen *Admission:* 15,171 applied, 1,358 admitted, 1,164 enrolled. *Test scores:* SAT critical reading scores over 500: 95%; SAT math scores over 500: 98%; SAT writing scores over 500: 93%; ACT scores over 18: 100%; SAT critical reading scores over 600: 63%; SAT math scores over 600: 72%; SAT writing scores over 600: 53%; ACT scores over 24: 91%; SAT critical reading scores over 700: 18%; SAT math scores over 700: 22%; SAT writing scores over 700: 13%; ACT scores over 30: 36%.

Faculty *Total:* 617, 100% full-time, 45% with terminal degrees. *Student/faculty ratio:* 7:1.

Academics *Calendar:* semesters. *Degree:* bachelor's. *Special study options:* academic remediation for entering students, advanced placement credit, double majors, honors programs, independent study, off-campus study, study abroad, summer session for credit.

Computers on Campus Students can access the following: computer help desk, free student e-mail accounts, online (class) grades, online (class) registration, online (class) schedules, All cadets will receive a laptop, printer, PDA, and portable memory device. All courses have a Blackboard presence so that once cadets log into Blackboard, they can access all their academic courses from a single interface. Campuswide network is available. 100% of college-owned or -operated housing units are wired for high-speed Internet access. Wireless service is available via entire campus.

Student Life *Housing:* on-campus residence required through senior year. *Options:* coed. Campus housing is university owned. Freshman campus housing is guaranteed. *Activities and organizations:* drama/theater group, student-run radio station, choral group, Asian-Pacific Club, Big Brothers and Big Sisters, Spirit Support Group, Film Forum, Philosophy Forum. *Campus security:* 24-hour emergency response devices and patrols, late-night transport/escort service. *Student services:* health clinic, personal/psychological counseling, legal services.

Athletics Member NCAA. All Division I except football (Division I-A). *Intercollegiate sports:* baseball M, basketball M/W, cheerleading M/W, crew M(c)/W(c), cross-country running M/W, equestrian sports M(c)/W(c), fencing M(c)/W(c), golf M, gymnastics M, ice hockey M, lacrosse M/W(c), racquetball M(c)/W(c), riflery M/W, rock climbing M(c)/W(c), rugby M(c)/W(c), sailing M(c)/W(c), skiing (cross-country) M(c)/W(c), skiing (downhill) M(c)/W(c), soccer M/W, softball W, swimming and diving M/W, tennis M/W, track and field M/W, volleyball M(c)/W, water polo M(c), weight lifting M(c)/W(c), wrestling M. *Intramural sports:* basketball M/W, bowling M(c)/W(c), football M, rugby M/W, soccer M/W, squash M/W, swimming and diving M/W, ultimate Frisbee M/W, wrestling M.

Standardized Tests *Required:* SAT or ACT (for admission).

Costs (2012–13) *Comprehensive fee:* All students receive a full scholarship, including room and board, and medical and dental-care are provided by the US Army. Cadets are on Active Duty Status as members of the US Army and receive an annual salary. A portion of the cadet pay is deposited into a personal checking account. Another portion of cadet pay is deposited to a Cadet Account that is used to help a cadet pay for expenses such as uniforms, books, a computer, activity fees, etc. The only cost for students is a one-time deposit upon admission to defray the initial costs of uniforms, books, supplies, and equipment. If needed, loans for the deposit are available from $100-2,000.

Applying *Options:* electronic application. *Required:* essay or personal statement, high school transcript, 4 letters of recommendation, You must obtain nominations from an approved source, pass a Department of Defense qualifying medical examination, must be at least 17 but not yet 23 years of age by July 1 of year of entry, and be an unmarried U.S. citizen (foreign nationals with approval) with no parental obligations. *Recommended:* interview. *Application deadline:* 2/28 (freshmen). *Notification:* 5/1 (freshmen).

Freshman Application Contact Col. Deborah J. McDonald, Director of Admissions, United States Military Academy, 600 Thayer Road, West Point, NY 10996. *Phone:* 845-938-4041. *E-mail:* 8dad@sunams.usma.army.mil. *Website:* http://www.usma.edu/.

United Talmudical Seminary

Brooklyn, New York

Director of Admissions Director of Admissions, United Talmudical Seminary, 191 Rodney Street, Brooklyn, NY 11211. *Phone:* 718-963-9770.

University at Albany, State University of New York

Albany, New York

- **State-supported** university, founded 1844, part of State University of New York System
- **Suburban** 560-acre campus
- **Endowment** $35.2 million
- **Coed** 12,875 undergraduate students, 94% full-time, 48% women, 52% men
- **Very difficult** entrance level, 55% of applicants were admitted

Undergraduates 12,068 full-time, 807 part-time. Students come from 38 states and territories; 53 other countries; 5% are from out of state; 13% Black or African American, non-Hispanic/Latino; 12% Hispanic/Latino; 7% Asian, non-Hispanic/Latino; 0.2% Native Hawaiian or other Pacific Islander, non-Hispanic/Latino; 0.3% American Indian or Alaska Native, non-Hispanic/Latino; 2% Two or more races, non-Hispanic/Latino; 4% Race/ethnicity unknown; 4% international; 11% transferred in; 57% live on campus. *Retention:* 83% of full-time freshmen returned.

Freshmen *Admission:* 21,178 applied, 11,744 admitted, 2,568 enrolled. *Average high school GPA:* 3.5. *Test scores:* SAT critical reading scores over 500: 74%; SAT math scores over 500: 84%; ACT scores over 18: 100%; SAT critical reading scores over 600: 18%; SAT math scores over 600: 31%; ACT scores over 24: 52%; SAT critical reading scores over 700: 1%; SAT math scores over 700: 3%; ACT scores over 30: 6%.

Faculty *Total:* 1,198, 49% full-time, 66% with terminal degrees. *Student/faculty ratio:* 20:1.

Academics *Calendar:* semesters. *Degrees:* bachelor's, master's, doctoral, post-master's, and postbachelor's certificates. *Special study options:* accelerated degree program, advanced placement credit, distance learning, double majors, English as a second language, freshman honors college, honors programs, independent study, internships, off-campus study, part-time degree program, services for LD students, student-designed majors, study abroad, summer session for credit. *ROTC:* Army (b), Air Force (c). *Unusual degree programs:* 3-2 business administration; engineering with Rensselaer Polytechnic Institute, State University of New York at Binghamton, State University of New York at New Paltz, Clarkson University.

Computers on Campus 500 computers/terminals are available on campus for general student use. Students can access the following: campus intranet, computer help desk, free student e-mail accounts, online (class) grades, online (class) registration, online (class) schedules. Campuswide network is available. 100% of college-owned or -operated housing units are wired for high-speed Internet access. Wireless service is available via classrooms, computer centers, computer labs, dorm rooms, libraries, student centers.

Student Life *Housing:* on-campus residence required through sophomore year. *Options:* coed. Campus housing is university owned. Freshman campus housing is guaranteed. *Activities and organizations:* drama/theater group, student-run newspaper, radio and television station, choral group, intramural athletics, cultural organizations, political organizations, community service, honor societies, national fraternities, national sororities. *Campus security:* 24-hour emergency response devices and patrols, late-night transport/escort service, controlled dormitory access, Five Quad Ambulance Service; On-Campus Dead Car Battery Assistance. *Student services:* health clinic, personal/psychological counseling, legal services.

Athletics Member NCAA. All Division I. *Intercollegiate sports:* baseball M(s), basketball M(s)/W(s), crew M/W, cross-country running M(s)/W(s), field hockey W(s), football M(s), golf W(s), lacrosse M(s)/W(s), rock climbing M/W, soccer M(s)/W(s), softball W(s), tennis W(s), track and field M(s)/W(s), volleyball W(s). *Intramural sports:* badminton M/W, baseball M, basketball M/W, equestrian sports W, fencing M/W, football M(c), ice hockey M, lacrosse M, racquetball M/W, rugby M/W, skiing (cross-country) M/W, skiing (downhill) M/W, soccer M/W, softball W, tennis M/W, track and field M/W, ultimate Frisbee M/W, volleyball M/W, wrestling M.

Standardized Tests *Required:* SAT or ACT (for admission).

Costs (2013–14) *Tuition:* state resident $5570 full-time, $232 per credit hour part-time; nonresident $14,050 full-time, $613 per credit hour part-time. Part-time tuition and fees vary according to course load. *Required fees:* $1993 full-time. *Room and board:* $11,276; room only: $6976. Room and board charges vary according to board plan and housing facility.

Financial Aid Of all full-time matriculated undergraduates who enrolled in 2012, 9,606 applied for aid, 7,555 were judged to have need, 498 had their need fully met. 733 Federal Work-Study jobs (averaging $1545). 215 state and other part-time jobs (averaging $6679). In 2012, 620 non-need-based awards were made. *Average percent of need met:* 63%. *Average financial aid package:* $9723. *Average need-based loan:* $4444. *Average need-based gift aid:* $6424.

Average non-need-based aid: $2821. *Average indebtedness upon graduation:* $24,126.

Applying *Options:* electronic application, early admission, early action, deferred entrance. *Application fee:* $50. *Required:* essay or personal statement, high school transcript, 1 letter of recommendation. *Required for some:* portfolio, audition. *Application deadlines:* 3/1 (freshmen), 3/1 (out-of-state freshmen), 7/1 (transfers), 11/15 (early action). *Notification:* continuous (freshmen), continuous (transfers), 1/15 (early action).

Freshman Application Contact University at Albany, State University of New York, Office of Undergraduate Admissions, 1400 Washington Avenue, Albany, NY 12222. *Phone:* 518-442-5435. *Fax:* 518-442-5383. *E-mail:* ugadmissions@albany.edu. *Website:* http://www.albany.edu/.

University at Buffalo, the State University of New York

Buffalo, New York

- **State-supported** university, founded 1846, part of State University of New York System
- **Suburban** 1350-acre campus
- **Endowment** $511.0 million
- **Coed** 19,505 undergraduate students, 92% full-time, 46% women, 54% men
- **Moderately difficult** entrance level, 57% of applicants were admitted

Undergraduates 17,903 full-time, 1,602 part-time. Students come from 46 states and territories; 80 other countries; 4% are from out of state; 7% Black or African American, non-Hispanic/Latino; 7% Hispanic/Latino; 11% Asian, non-Hispanic/Latino; 0.1% Native Hawaiian or other Pacific Islander, non-Hispanic/Latino; 0.3% American Indian or Alaska Native, non-Hispanic/Latino; 2% Two or more races, non-Hispanic/Latino; 5% Race/ethnicity unknown; 16% international; 10% transferred in; 35% live on campus. *Retention:* 87% of full-time freshmen returned.

Freshmen *Admission:* 22,009 applied, 12,525 admitted, 3,650 enrolled. *Average high school GPA:* 3.2. *Test scores:* SAT critical reading scores over 500: 77%; SAT math scores over 500: 92%; ACT scores over 18: 100%; SAT critical reading scores over 600: 27%; SAT math scores over 600: 52%; ACT scores over 24: 70%; SAT critical reading scores over 700: 4%; SAT math scores over 700: 12%; ACT scores over 30: 15%.

Faculty *Total:* 1,719, 68% full-time, 84% with terminal degrees. *Student/faculty ratio:* 14:1.

Academics *Calendar:* semesters. *Degrees:* certificates, bachelor's, master's, doctoral, and post-master's certificates. *Special study options:* academic remediation for entering students, accelerated degree program, advanced placement credit, cooperative education, distance learning, double majors, English as a second language, freshman honors college, honors programs, independent study, internships, off-campus study, part-time degree program, services for LD students, student-designed majors, study abroad, summer session for credit. *ROTC:* Army (c). *Unusual degree programs:* 3-2 business administration; engineering; nursing; social work; law.

Computers on Campus 2,700 computers/terminals are available on campus for general student use. Students can access the following: campus intranet, computer help desk, free student e-mail accounts, online (class) grades, online (class) registration, online (class) schedules. Campuswide network is available. 100% of college-owned or -operated housing units are wired for high-speed Internet access. Wireless service is available via entire campus.

Student Life *Housing options:* coed, disabled students. Campus housing is university owned. Freshman campus housing is guaranteed. *Activities and organizations:* drama/theater group, student-run newspaper, radio and television station, choral group, marching band, national fraternities, national sororities. *Campus security:* 24-hour emergency response devices and patrols, student patrols, late-night transport/escort service, controlled dormitory access, self-defense and awareness programs, security cameras. *Student services:* health clinic, personal/psychological counseling, legal services.

Athletics Member NCAA. All Division I except football (Division I-A). *Intercollegiate sports:* baseball M(s), basketball M(s)/W(s), crew W(s), cross-country running M(s)/W(s), soccer M(s)/W(s), softball W(s), swimming and diving M(s)/W(s), tennis M(s)/W(s), track and field M(s)/W(s), volleyball W(s), wrestling M(s). *Intramural sports:* badminton M(c)/W(c), baseball M(c), basketball M/W, crew M(c), cross-country running M(c)/W(c), equestrian sports M(c)/W(c), field hockey W(c), gymnastics M(c)/W(c), ice hockey M(c)/W(c), lacrosse M(c)/W(c), racquetball M/W, rock climbing M(c)/W(c), rugby M(c)/W(c), skiing (cross-country) M(c)/W(c), skiing (downhill) M(c)/W(c), soccer M(c)/W(c), softball M/W, tennis M(c)/W(c), track and field M(c)/W(c), ultimate Frisbee M(c)/W(c), volleyball M(c)/W(c), wrestling M(c).

Standardized Tests *Required:* SAT or ACT (for admission).
Costs (2012–13) *Tuition:* state resident $5570 full-time, $232 per credit hour part-time; nonresident $16,190 full-time, $675 per credit hour part-time. Part-time tuition and fees vary according to course load. *Required fees:* $2419 full-time, $94 per credit hour part-time. *Room and board:* $11,310; room only: $6540. Room and board charges vary according to board plan and housing facility. *Payment plan:* installment. *Waivers:* minority students.
Financial Aid Of all full-time matriculated undergraduates who enrolled in 2011, 15,403 applied for aid, 14,483 were judged to have need, 9,510 had their need fully met. 1,070 Federal Work-Study jobs (averaging $1376). 2,300 state and other part-time jobs (averaging $3500). In 2011, 225 non-need-based awards were made. *Average percent of need met:* 65%. *Average financial aid package:* $7261. *Average need-based loan:* $4425. *Average need-based gift aid:* $5140. *Average non-need-based aid:* $5474. *Average indebtedness upon graduation:* $16,025.
Applying *Options:* electronic application, early admission, early decision. *Application fee:* $50. *Required:* essay or personal statement, high school transcript, 1 letter of recommendation. *Required for some:* Architecture requires a portfolio and Dance, Music Theatre, Theatre and Music require an audition. *Early decision deadline:* 11/1. *Notification:* continuous (freshmen), continuous (transfers), 12/15 (early decision).
Freshman Application Contact Ms. Regina Toomey, Interim Director of Admissions, University at Buffalo, the State University of New York, 12 Capen Hall, North Campus, Buffalo, NY 14260-1660. *Phone:* 716-645-6900. *Toll-free phone:* 888-UB-ADMIT. *Fax:* 716-645-6411. *E-mail:* ub-admissions@buffalo.edu.
Website: http://www.buffalo.edu/.

University of Rochester

Rochester, New York

- **Independent** university, founded 1850
- **Suburban** 655-acre campus
- **Endowment** $1.6 billion
- **Coed** 5,785 undergraduate students, 95% full-time, 52% women, 48% men
- **Very difficult** entrance level, 36% of applicants were admitted

Undergraduates 5,512 full-time, 273 part-time. Students come from 52 states and territories; 94 other countries; 64% are from out of state; 5% Black or African American, non-Hispanic/Latino; 6% Hispanic/Latino; 11% Asian, non-Hispanic/Latino; 0.1% Native Hawaiian or other Pacific Islander, non-Hispanic/Latino; 0.3% American Indian or Alaska Native, non-Hispanic/Latino; 3% Two or more races, non-Hispanic/Latino; 7% Race/ethnicity unknown; 13% international; 2% transferred in; 83% live on campus. *Retention:* 96% of full-time freshmen returned.
Freshmen *Admission:* 14,987 applied, 5,370 admitted, 1,343 enrolled. *Average high school GPA:* 3.8. *Test scores:* SAT critical reading scores over 500: 99%; SAT math scores over 500: 99%; SAT writing scores over 500: 98%; ACT scores over 18: 100%; SAT critical reading scores over 600: 76%; SAT math scores over 600: 89%; SAT writing scores over 600: 78%; ACT scores over 24: 99%; SAT critical reading scores over 700: 28%; SAT math scores over 700: 46%; SAT writing scores over 700: 27%; ACT scores over 30: 63%.
Faculty *Total:* 762, 74% full-time, 83% with terminal degrees. *Student/faculty ratio:* 10:1.
Academics *Calendar:* semesters plus optional summer term. *Degrees:* bachelor's, master's, doctoral, post-master's, and postbachelor's certificates. *Special study options:* accelerated degree program, advanced placement credit, cooperative education, double majors, English as a second language, honors programs, independent study, internships, off-campus study, part-time degree program, services for LD students, student-designed majors, study abroad, summer session for credit. *ROTC:* Army (c), Navy (b), Air Force (c). *Unusual degree programs:* 3-2 business administration; engineering; nursing; business, computer science, engineering, public health, optics, human development, neuroscience, medical physics, and physics and astronomy.
Computers on Campus 512 computers/terminals and 4,000 ports are available on campus for general student use. Students can access the following: computer help desk, free student e-mail accounts, online (class) grades, online (class) registration, online (class) schedules. Campuswide network is available. 100% of college-owned or -operated housing units are wired for high-speed Internet access. Wireless service is available via classrooms, computer centers, computer labs, learning centers, libraries, student centers.
Student Life *Housing:* on-campus residence required through sophomore year. *Options:* coed. Campus housing is university owned and leased by the school. Freshman campus housing is guaranteed. *Activities and organizations:* drama/theater group, student-run newspaper, radio and television station, choral group, marching band, Campus Activities Board, Black Students' Union,

Grassroots (environmental group), Women's Caucus, American Sign Language Club, national fraternities, national sororities. *Campus security:* 24-hour emergency response devices and patrols, student patrols, late-night transport/escort service, controlled dormitory access. *Student services:* health clinic, personal/psychological counseling, women's center, legal services.
Athletics Member NCAA. All Division III except squash (Division I). *Intercollegiate sports:* badminton M(c)/W(c), baseball M, basketball M/W, crew M(c)/W, cross-country running M/W, equestrian sports M(c)/W(c), field hockey W, football M, golf M, ice hockey M(c)/W(c), lacrosse M(c)/W, rugby M(c)/W(c), skiing (downhill) M(c)/W(c), soccer M/W, softball W, squash M, swimming and diving M/W, tennis M/W, track and field M/W, ultimate Frisbee M(c)/W(c), volleyball M(c)/W, water polo M(c)/W(c). *Intramural sports:* archery M(c)/W(c), basketball M/W, cheerleading M(c)/W(c), fencing M(c)/W(c), football M/W, gymnastics M(c)/W(c), sailing M(c)/W(c), soccer M/W, softball M/W, tennis M/W, ultimate Frisbee M/W, volleyball M/W.
Standardized Tests *Required for some:* SAT and SAT Subject Tests or ACT (for admission). *Recommended:* SAT or ACT (for admission), SAT Subject Tests (for admission).
Costs (2012–13) *Comprehensive fee:* $56,284 includes full-time tuition ($42,890), mandatory fees ($776), and room and board ($12,618). Full-time tuition and fees vary according to student level. Part-time tuition: $1340 per credit hour. Part-time tuition and fees vary according to course load. *College room only:* $7682. Room and board charges vary according to board plan. *Payment plans:* tuition prepayment, installment. *Waivers:* employees or children of employees.
Financial Aid Of all full-time matriculated undergraduates who enrolled in 2012, 3,038 applied for aid, 2,659 were judged to have need, 2,383 had their need fully met. 1,769 Federal Work-Study jobs (averaging $2314). In 2012, 1330 non-need-based awards were made. *Average percent of need met:* 90%. *Average financial aid package:* $36,815. *Average need-based loan:* $5057. *Average need-based gift aid:* $31,541. *Average non-need-based aid:* $13,001. *Average indebtedness upon graduation:* $27,601.
Applying *Options:* electronic application, early admission, early decision, deferred entrance. *Application fee:* $70. *Required:* essay or personal statement, high school transcript. *Required for some:* Audition is required for music programs at Eastman School of Music. *Recommended:* 2 letters of recommendation, interview. *Application deadlines:* 1/1 (freshmen), 1/1 (out-of-state freshmen), 3/15 (transfers). *Early decision deadline:* 11/1. *Notification:* 4/1 (freshmen), 4/1 (out-of-state freshmen), 3/1 (transfers), 12/15 (early decision).
Freshman Application Contact Office of Admissions, University of Rochester, PO Box 270251, 300 Wilson Boulevard, Rochester, NY 14627-0251. *Phone:* 585-275-3221. *Toll-free phone:* 888-822-2256. *Fax:* 585-461-4595. *E-mail:* admit@admissions.rochester.edu.
Website: http://www.rochester.edu/.

U.T.A. Mesivta of Kiryas Joel

Monroe, New York

Admissions Office Contact U.T.A. Mesivta of Kiryas Joel, 9 Nickelsburg Road, Unit 312, Monroe, NY 10950.

Utica College

Utica, New York

- **Independent** comprehensive, founded 1946
- **Suburban** 128-acre campus
- **Endowment** $20.1 million
- **Coed** 2,768 undergraduate students, 77% full-time, 60% women, 40% men
- **Moderately difficult** entrance level, 81% of applicants were admitted

Undergraduates 2,126 full-time, 642 part-time. Students come from 42 states and territories; 27 other countries; 16% are from out of state; 10% Black or African American, non-Hispanic/Latino; 8% Hispanic/Latino; 2% Asian, non-Hispanic/Latino; 0.2% Native Hawaiian or other Pacific Islander, non-Hispanic/Latino; 0.4% American Indian or Alaska Native, non-Hispanic/Latino; 2% Two or more races, non-Hispanic/Latino; 3% Race/ethnicity unknown; 3% international; 6% transferred in; 47% live on campus. *Retention:* 67% of full-time freshmen returned.
Freshmen *Admission:* 3,260 applied, 2,652 admitted, 505 enrolled. *Average high school GPA:* 3.02. *Test scores:* SAT critical reading scores over 500: 38%; SAT math scores over 500: 42%; SAT writing scores over 500: 32%; ACT scores over 18: 68%; SAT critical reading scores over 600: 6%; SAT math scores over 600: 10%; SAT writing scores over 600: 3%; ACT scores over 24: 21%; ACT scores over 30: 4%.

Faculty *Total:* 378, 38% full-time. *Student/faculty ratio:* 11:1.
Academics *Calendar:* semesters. *Degrees:* certificates, bachelor's, master's, doctoral, and postbachelor's certificates. *Special study options:* academic remediation for entering students, accelerated degree program, adult/continuing education programs, advanced placement credit, distance learning, double majors, honors programs, independent study, internships, off-campus study, part-time degree program, services for LD students, study abroad, summer session for credit. *ROTC:* Army (b), Air Force (c). *Unusual degree programs:* 3-2 engineering with Syracuse University.
Computers on Campus 430 computers/terminals are available on campus for general student use. Students can access the following: computer help desk, free student e-mail accounts, online (class) grades, online (class) registration, online (class) schedules. Campuswide network is available. 100% of college-owned or -operated housing units are wired for high-speed Internet access. Wireless service is available via classrooms, libraries, student centers.
Student Life *Housing:* on-campus residence required through sophomore year. *Options:* coed, disabled students. Campus housing is university owned. Freshman campus housing is guaranteed. *Activities and organizations:* drama/theater group, student-run newspaper, radio station, choral group, Physical Therapy Society, Student Nurses Association, Kappa Delta Pi, Student Senate, Utica College Honor Association, national fraternities, national sororities. *Campus security:* 24-hour emergency response devices and patrols, late-night transport/escort service, controlled dormitory access. *Student services:* health clinic, personal/psychological counseling, women's center.
Athletics Member NCAA. All Division III except track and field (Division II). *Intercollegiate sports:* baseball M, basketball M/W, field hockey W, football M, golf M/W, ice hockey M/W, lacrosse M/W, soccer M/W, softball W, swimming and diving M/W, tennis M/W, track and field M/W, volleyball W, water polo W. *Intramural sports:* basketball M/W, bowling M/W, cheerleading M(c)/W(c), fencing M(c)/W(c), racquetball M/W, soccer M/W, softball M/W, tennis M/W, volleyball M/W, water polo M/W.
Standardized Tests *Required for some:* SAT or ACT (for admission).
Financial Aid Of all full-time matriculated undergraduates who enrolled in 2012, 1,952 applied for aid, 1,863 were judged to have need, 164 had their need fully met. In 2012, 107 non-need-based awards were made. *Average percent of need met:* 69%. *Average financial aid package:* $24,203. *Average need-based loan:* $4403. *Average need-based gift aid:* $6793. *Average non-need-based aid:* $12,857. *Average indebtedness upon graduation:* $42,303.
Applying *Options:* electronic application, deferred entrance. *Application fee:* $40. *Required:* essay or personal statement, high school transcript, minimum 2.0 GPA, 1 letter of recommendation. *Required for some:* minimum 3.0 GPA.

Recommended: interview. *Application deadlines:* rolling (freshmen), rolling (transfers). *Notification:* 9/1 (freshmen), continuous (transfers).
Freshman Application Contact Utica College, 1600 Burrstone Road, Utica, NY 13502-4892. *Phone:* 315-792-3006. *Toll-free phone:* 800-782-8884. *Website:* http://www.utica.edu/.

See below for display ad and page 1618 for the College Close-Up.

Vassar College

Poughkeepsie, New York

- **Independent** 4-year, founded 1861
- **Suburban** 1000-acre campus with easy access to New York City
- **Endowment** $804.9 million
- **Coed** 2,406 undergraduate students, 99% full-time, 56% women, 44% men
- **Very difficult** entrance level, 23% of applicants were admitted

Undergraduates 2,370 full-time, 36 part-time. Students come from 52 states and territories; 60 other countries; 73% are from out of state; 6% Black or African American, non-Hispanic/Latino; 11% Hispanic/Latino; 9% Asian, non-Hispanic/Latino; 5% Two or more races, non-Hispanic/Latino; 0.2% Race/ethnicity unknown; 7% international; 0.4% transferred in; 94% live on campus. *Retention:* 96% of full-time freshmen returned.
Freshmen *Admission:* 7,908 applied, 1,806 admitted, 658 enrolled. *Average high school GPA:* 3.8. *Test scores:* SAT critical reading scores over 500: 100%; SAT math scores over 500: 100%; SAT writing scores over 500: 100%; ACT scores over 18: 100%; SAT critical reading scores over 600: 93%; SAT math scores over 600: 95%; SAT writing scores over 600: 93%; ACT scores over 24: 100%; SAT critical reading scores over 700: 58%; SAT math scores over 700: 47%; SAT writing scores over 700: 54%; ACT scores over 30: 72%.
Faculty *Total:* 320, 87% full-time, 84% with terminal degrees. *Student/faculty ratio:* 8:1.
Academics *Calendar:* semesters. *Degrees:* bachelor's and master's. *Special study options:* advanced placement credit, cooperative education, double majors, independent study, internships, off-campus study, part-time degree program, services for LD students, student-designed majors, study abroad. *Unusual degree programs:* 3-2 engineering with Dartmouth College.
Computers on Campus 509 computers/terminals are available on campus for general student use. Students can access the following: campus intranet, com-

puter help desk, free student e-mail accounts, online (class) grades, online (class) registration, online (class) schedules, Ethernet. Campuswide network is available. 100% of college-owned or -operated housing units are wired for high-speed Internet access. Wireless service is available via entire campus.

Student Life *Housing:* on-campus residence required through senior year. *Options:* coed, women-only, cooperative. Campus housing is university owned. Freshman campus housing is guaranteed. *Activities and organizations:* drama/theater group, student-run newspaper, radio station, choral group, Student Association, WVKR radio station, VICE (programming social events), Vassar Greens, Ultimate Frisbee. *Campus security:* 24-hour emergency response devices and patrols, student patrols, late-night transport/escort service, controlled dormitory access. *Student services:* health clinic, personal/psychological counseling, women's center.

Athletics Member NCAA. All Division III. *Intercollegiate sports:* baseball M, basketball M/W, crew M(c)/W(c), cross-country running M/W, fencing M/W, field hockey W, golf W, lacrosse M/W, rugby M(c)/W(c), soccer M/W, squash M(c)/W(c), swimming and diving M/W, tennis M/W, track and field M/W, volleyball M/W. *Intramural sports:* badminton M(c)/W(c), equestrian sports M(c)/W(c), sailing M(c)/W(c), skiing (cross-country) M(c)/W(c), skiing (downhill) M(c)/W(c), ultimate Frisbee M(c)/W(c).

Standardized Tests *Required:* SAT and SAT Subject Tests or ACT (for admission).

Costs (2012–13) *One-time required fee:* $75. *Comprehensive fee:* $57,070 includes full-time tuition ($45,580), mandatory fees ($690), and room and board ($10,800). Part-time tuition: $5410 per unit. Part-time tuition and fees vary according to course load. *College room only:* $5860. Room and board charges vary according to board plan and housing facility. *Payment plan:* installment. *Waivers:* employees or children of employees.

Financial Aid Of all full-time matriculated undergraduates who enrolled in 2012, 1,729 applied for aid, 1,559 were judged to have need, 1,559 had their need fully met. 1,186 Federal Work-Study jobs (averaging $1733). 490 state and other part-time jobs (averaging $1754). *Average percent of need met:* 100%. *Average financial aid package:* $44,285. *Average need-based loan:* $2544. *Average need-based gift aid:* $40,045. *Average indebtedness upon graduation:* $17,234. *Financial aid deadline:* 2/15.

Applying *Options:* electronic application, early decision, deferred entrance. *Application fee:* $70. *Required:* essay or personal statement, high school transcript, 2 letters of recommendation. *Application deadlines:* 1/1 (freshmen), 3/15 (transfers). *Early decision deadline:* 11/15. *Notification:* 4/1 (freshmen), 5/10 (transfers), 12/15 (early decision).

Freshman Application Contact Dr. David M. Borus, Dean of Admission and Financial Aid, Vassar College, 124 Raymond Avenue, Poughkeepsie, NY 12604. *Phone:* 845-437-7300. *Toll-free phone:* 800-827-7270. *Fax:* 845-437-7063. *E-mail:* admissions@vassar.edu. *Website:* http://www.vassar.edu/.

Vaughn College of Aeronautics and Technology

Flushing, New York

- **Independent** comprehensive, founded 1932
- **Urban** 6-acre campus with easy access to New York City
- **Endowment** $21.5 million
- **Coed, primarily men** 1,799 undergraduate students, 76% full-time, 13% women, 87% men
- **Moderately difficult** entrance level, 85% of applicants were admitted

Undergraduates 1,362 full-time, 437 part-time. Students come from 31 states and territories; 10 other countries; 11% are from out of state; 19% Black or African American, non-Hispanic/Latino; 38% Hispanic/Latino; 8% Asian, non-Hispanic/Latino; 5% Native Hawaiian or other Pacific Islander, non-Hispanic/Latino; 0.7% American Indian or Alaska Native, non-Hispanic/Latino; 5% Two or more races, non-Hispanic/Latino; 6% Race/ethnicity unknown; 2% international; 14% transferred in; 10% live on campus. *Retention:* 80% of full-time freshmen returned.

Freshmen *Admission:* 723 applied, 618 admitted, 321 enrolled. *Test scores:* SAT critical reading scores over 500: 46%; SAT math scores over 500: 75%; ACT scores over 18: 84%; SAT critical reading scores over 600: 9%; SAT math scores over 600: 27%; ACT scores over 24: 17%; SAT critical reading scores over 700: 1%; SAT math scores over 700: 3%.

Faculty *Total:* 216, 19% full-time, 18% with terminal degrees. *Student/faculty ratio:* 15:1.

Academics *Calendar:* semesters. *Degrees:* certificates, associate, bachelor's, and master's. *Special study options:* academic remediation for entering students, advanced placement credit, cooperative education, distance learning,

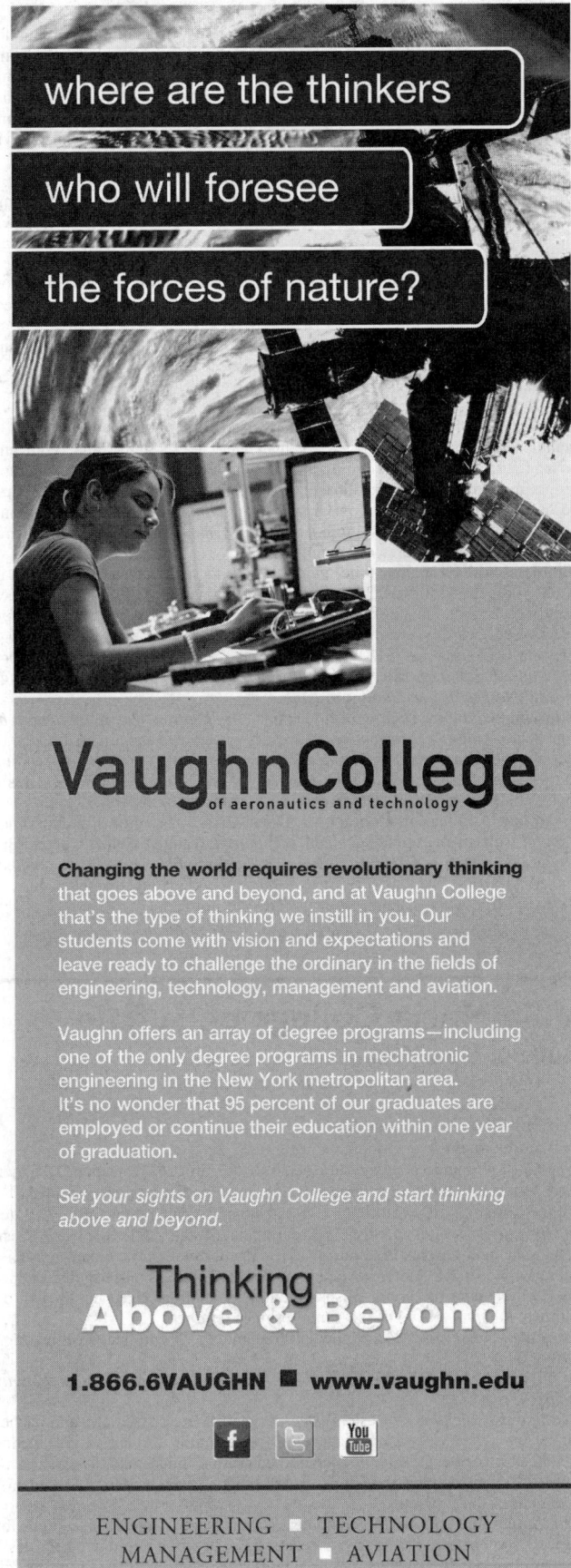

double majors, independent study, internships, part-time degree program, summer session for credit. *ROTC:* Army (c), Air Force (c).

Computers on Campus 50 computers/terminals are available on campus for general student use. Students can access the following: campus intranet, computer help desk, free student e-mail accounts, online (class) grades, online (class) registration, online (class) schedules, Vaughn Student Portal. Campuswide network is available. 100% of college-owned or -operated housing units are wired for high-speed Internet access. Wireless service is available via entire campus.

Student Life *Housing options:* coed, disabled students. Campus housing is university owned. Freshman applicants given priority for college housing. *Activities and organizations:* American Association of Airport Executives, Women in Aviation-International, Institute of Electrical and Electronics Engineers, Robotics Club, Red Tail Pilots Club. *Campus security:* 24-hour emergency response devices and patrols, student patrols, late-night transport/escort service, controlled dormitory access. *Student services:* personal/psychological counseling.

Athletics *Intercollegiate sports:* basketball M, soccer M, tennis W, track and field M/W. *Intramural sports:* basketball M, soccer M, tennis W.

Standardized Tests *Required for some:* SAT and SAT Subject Tests or ACT (for admission).

Costs (2013–14) *One-time required fee:* $160. *Comprehensive fee:* $32,330 includes full-time tuition ($19,850), mandatory fees ($600), and room and board ($11,880). Full-time tuition and fees vary according to course load and program. Part-time tuition: $665 per credit. Part-time tuition and fees vary according to course load and program. *College room only:* $9480. Room and board charges vary according to board plan. *Payment plan:* installment. *Waivers:* employees or children of employees.

Financial Aid Of all full-time matriculated undergraduates who enrolled in 2008, 704 applied for aid, 704 were judged to have need, 476 had their need fully met. 25 Federal Work-Study jobs (averaging $3000). In 2008, 145 non-need-based awards were made. *Average percent of need met:* 82%. *Average financial aid package:* $18,030. *Average need-based loan:* $1770. *Average need-based gift aid:* $2950. *Average non-need-based aid:* $2000. *Average indebtedness upon graduation:* $17,125.

Applying *Options:* electronic application. *Application fee:* $40. *Required:* high school transcript. *Recommended:* essay or personal statement, 2 letters of recommendation, interview. *Application deadlines:* rolling (freshmen), rolling (out-of-state freshmen), rolling (transfers). *Notification:* continuous (freshmen), continuous (out-of-state freshmen), continuous (transfers).

Freshman Application Contact Mr. David Griffey, Director of Admissions, Vaughn College of Aeronautics and Technology, Vaughn College, 8601 23rd Avenue, Flushing, NY 11369. *Phone:* 718-429.6600 Ext. 117. *Toll-free phone:* 866-6VAUGHN. *Fax:* 718-779.2231. *E-mail:* David.griffey@vaughn.edu. *Website:* http://www.vaughn.edu/.

See previous page for display ad and page 1622 for the College Close-Up.

Villa Maria College of Buffalo

Buffalo, New York

- **Independent** 4-year, founded 1960, affiliated with Roman Catholic Church
- **Suburban** 15-acre campus
- **Endowment** $1.2 million
- **Coed** 470 undergraduate students, 77% full-time, 63% women, 37% men
- **Minimally difficult** entrance level, 81% of applicants were admitted

Undergraduates 364 full-time, 106 part-time. Students come from 6 states and territories; 1 other country; 2% are from out of state; 17% Black or African American, non-Hispanic/Latino; 5% Hispanic/Latino; 0.7% Asian, non-Hispanic/Latino; 0.2% American Indian or Alaska Native, non-Hispanic/Latino; 4% Two or more races, non-Hispanic/Latino; 10% transferred in; 7% live on campus. *Retention:* 70% of full-time freshmen returned.

Freshmen *Admission:* 243 applied, 196 admitted, 75 enrolled. *Average high school GPA:* 2.5.

Faculty *Total:* 74, 41% full-time, 45% with terminal degrees. *Student/faculty ratio:* 8:1.

Academics *Calendar:* semesters. *Degrees:* certificates, associate, and bachelor's. *Special study options:* academic remediation for entering students, advanced placement credit, cooperative education, independent study, internships, off-campus study, part-time degree program, services for LD students, summer session for credit.

Computers on Campus 250 computers/terminals are available on campus for general student use. Students can access the following: computer help desk, free student e-mail accounts, online (class) grades, online (class) registration, online (class) schedules. Campuswide network is available. Wireless service is available via entire campus.

Student Life *Housing:* college housing not available. *Options:* Campus housing is provided by a third party. *Activities and organizations:* choral group, Design and Beyond, Teachers Love Children, Multicultural Club, Phi Theta Kappa, Helping Adults New Dreams Succeed. *Campus security:* late-night transport/escort service, security guard during hours of operation. *Student services:* health clinic, personal/psychological counseling.

Costs (2013–14) *Tuition:* $17,640 full-time. Full-time tuition and fees vary according to program. Part-time tuition and fees vary according to course load and program. *Required fees:* $370 full-time, $590 part-time, $280 part-time. *Payment plan:* installment. *Waivers:* employees or children of employees.

Financial Aid Of all full-time matriculated undergraduates who enrolled in 2010, 470 applied for aid, 468 were judged to have need, 18 had their need fully met. 59 Federal Work-Study jobs (averaging $535). In 2010, 11 non-need-based awards were made. *Average percent of need met:* 54%. *Average financial aid package:* $7965. *Average need-based gift aid:* $941. *Average non-need-based aid:* $1868. *Average indebtedness upon graduation:* $30,353.

Applying *Options:* electronic application, deferred entrance. *Required:* essay or personal statement, high school transcript, interview, Admission to music programs require audition; Arts programs require portfolio review. *Required for some:* Admission to music programs require audition; Arts programs require portfolio review. *Application deadlines:* rolling (freshmen), rolling (out-of-state freshmen), rolling (transfers). *Notification:* continuous (freshmen), continuous (out-of-state freshmen), continuous (transfers).

Freshman Application Contact Mr. Kevin Donovan, Director of Admissions, Villa Maria College of Buffalo, Buffalo, NY 14211. *Phone:* 716-896-0700 Ext. 1802. *Fax:* 716-896-0705. *E-mail:* admissions@villa.edu. *Website:* http://www.villa.edu/.

Wagner College

Staten Island, New York

- **Independent** comprehensive, founded 1883
- **Urban** 105-acre campus with easy access to New York City
- **Endowment** $64.4 million
- **Coed** 1,821 undergraduate students, 96% full-time, 65% women, 35% men

Undergraduates 1,744 full-time, 77 part-time. Students come from 40 states and territories; 30 other countries; 48% are from out of state; 6% Black or African American, non-Hispanic/Latino; 9% Hispanic/Latino; 2% Asian, non-Hispanic/Latino; 0.2% Native Hawaiian or other Pacific Islander, non-Hispanic/Latino; 0.1% American Indian or Alaska Native, non-Hispanic/Latino; 2% Two or more races, non-Hispanic/Latino; 11% Race/ethnicity unknown; 2% international; 5% transferred in; 67% live on campus. *Retention:* 83% of full-time freshmen returned.

Freshmen *Admission:* 426 enrolled. *Average high school GPA:* 3.6. *Test scores:* SAT critical reading scores over 500: 91%; SAT math scores over 500: 89%; SAT writing scores over 500: 88%; ACT scores over 18: 99%; SAT critical reading scores over 600: 49%; SAT math scores over 600: 49%; SAT writing scores over 600: 49%; ACT scores over 24: 87%; SAT critical reading scores over 700: 7%; SAT math scores over 700: 7%; SAT writing scores over 700: 7%; ACT scores over 30: 5%.

Faculty *Total:* 275, 37% full-time, 35% with terminal degrees. *Student/faculty ratio:* 13:1.

Academics *Calendar:* semesters. *Degrees:* bachelor's, master's, and post-master's certificates. *Special study options:* adult/continuing education programs, advanced placement credit, double majors, honors programs, independent study, internships, off-campus study, part-time degree program, services for LD students, student-designed majors, study abroad, summer session for credit. *ROTC:* Army (c). *Unusual degree programs:* 3-2 accounting.

Computers on Campus 230 computers/terminals are available on campus for general student use. Students can access the following: campus intranet, computer help desk, free student e-mail accounts, online (class) grades, online (class) registration, online (class) schedules. Campuswide network is available. 100% of college-owned or -operated housing units are wired for high-speed Internet access. Wireless service is available via entire campus.

Student Life *Housing options:* coed. Campus housing is university owned and leased by the school. Freshman campus housing is guaranteed. *Activities and organizations:* drama/theater group, student-run newspaper, radio station, choral group, Student Government Association, Student Activities Board, Wagner College Theatre, Wagner College Choir, student newspaper, national fraternities, national sororities. *Campus security:* 24-hour emergency response devices and patrols, late-night transport/escort service, controlled dormitory access. *Student services:* health clinic, personal/psychological counseling.

Athletics Member NCAA. All Division I except football (Division I-AA). *Intercollegiate sports:* baseball M(s), basketball M(s)/W(s), cross-country running M(s)/W(s), golf M(s)/W(s), ice hockey M(c), lacrosse M(s)/W(s), soccer

W(s), softball W(s), swimming and diving W(s), tennis M(s)/W(s), track and field M(s)/W(s), water polo W(s). *Intramural sports:* basketball M/W, bowling M/W, football M, rugby M, soccer M/W, softball M/W, table tennis M/W, tennis M/W, ultimate Frisbee M/W, volleyball M/W.

Standardized Tests *Required for some:* SAT or ACT (for admission), SAT Subject Tests (for admission).

Costs (2013–14) *Comprehensive fee:* $50,880 includes full-time tuition ($38,920), mandatory fees ($300), and room and board ($11,660). Part-time tuition: $4865 per unit. *Waivers:* employees or children of employees.

Financial Aid Of all full-time matriculated undergraduates who enrolled in 2012, 1,347 applied for aid, 1,156 were judged to have need, 255 had their need fully met. In 2012, 238 non-need-based awards were made. *Average percent of need met:* 70%. *Average financial aid package:* $24,303. *Average need-based loan:* $4915. *Average need-based gift aid:* $19,209. *Average non-need-based aid:* $13,042. *Financial aid deadline:* 4/15.

Applying *Required:* essay or personal statement, high school transcript, minimum 2.5 GPA, 2 letters of recommendation. *Required for some:* interview. *Recommended:* minimum 3.0 GPA, interview.

Freshman Application Contact Mr. Robert Herr, Dean of Admissions, Wagner College, One Campus Road, Pape Admissions Building, Staten Island, NY 10301. *Phone:* 718-420-4242. *Toll-free phone:* 800-221-1010. *Fax:* 718-390-3105. *E-mail:* robert.herr@wagner.edu. *Website:* http://www.wagner.edu/.

Webb Institute

Glen Cove, New York

- **Independent** 4-year, founded 1889
- **Suburban** 26-acre campus with easy access to New York City
- **Endowment** $50.2 million
- **Coed** 79 undergraduate students, 100% full-time, 19% women, 81% men
- **Most difficult** entrance level, 38% of applicants were admitted

Undergraduates 79 full-time. Students come from 20 states and territories; 3 other countries; 70% are from out of state; 4% Hispanic/Latino; 6% Asian, non-Hispanic/Latino; 4% Two or more races, non-Hispanic/Latino; 3% trans-

ferred in; 100% live on campus. *Retention:* 83% of full-time freshmen returned.

Freshmen *Admission:* 82 applied, 31 admitted, 22 enrolled. *Average high school GPA:* 4. *Test scores:* SAT critical reading scores over 500: 100%; SAT math scores over 500: 100%; SAT writing scores over 500: 100%; SAT critical reading scores over 600: 95%; SAT math scores over 600: 100%; SAT writing scores over 600: 86%; SAT critical reading scores over 700: 45%; SAT math scores over 700: 77%; SAT writing scores over 700: 27%.

Faculty *Total:* 14, 79% full-time, 50% with terminal degrees. *Student/faculty ratio:* 7:1.

Academics *Calendar:* semesters. *Degree:* bachelor's. *Special study options:* cooperative education, double majors, independent study, internships, services for LD students, study abroad.

Computers on Campus 25 computers/terminals are available on campus for general student use. Students can access the following: campus intranet, computer help desk, free student e-mail accounts. Campuswide network is available. 100% of college-owned or -operated housing units are wired for high-speed Internet access. Wireless service is available via entire campus.

Student Life *Housing:* on-campus residence required through senior year. *Options:* coed, men-only, women-only. Campus housing is university owned. Freshman campus housing is guaranteed. *Activities and organizations:* choral group, Student Organization, Society of Naval Architects and Marine Engineers, American Society of Naval Engineers, Society of Women Engineers, Marine Technology Society. *Campus security:* 24-hour emergency response devices and patrols, controlled dormitory access. *Student services:* personal/psychological counseling.

Athletics *Intercollegiate sports:* basketball M/W, cross-country running M/W, sailing M/W, soccer M/W, tennis M/W, volleyball M/W. *Intramural sports:* ultimate Frisbee M/W.

Standardized Tests *Required:* SAT (for admission), SAT Subject Tests (for admission).

Costs (2013–14) *Comprehensive fee:* includes room and board ($13,750). Full-tuition scholarship covering all four years are awarded to all accepted students who are U.S. citizens or Green Card holders.

Financial Aid Of all full-time matriculated undergraduates who enrolled in 2012, 19 applied for aid, 19 were judged to have need. *Average financial aid package:* $4500. *Average need-based gift aid:* $5500. *Average indebtedness upon graduation:* $4500.

WEBB INSTITUTE

For more information, contact:

William G. Murray, Director of Enrollment Management
Office of Admissions
298 Crescent Beach Road
Glen Cove, New York 11542
E-mail: admissions@webb-institute.edu

Web site: www.webb-institute.edu

Applying *Options:* early decision. *Application fee:* $25. *Required:* high school transcript, minimum 3.5 GPA, 2 letters of recommendation, interview, proof of U.S. citizenship or permanent residency status. *Application deadlines:* 2/15 (freshmen), 2/15 (transfers). *Early decision deadline:* 10/15. *Notification:* 4/30 (freshmen), 4/30 (transfers), 12/15 (early decision).

Freshman Application Contact Webb Institute, Crescent Beach Road, Glen Cove, NY 11542-1398. *Phone:* 516-671-2213. *Fax:* 516-674-9838. *E-mail:* admissions@webb-institute.edu.
Website: http://www.webb-institute.edu/.

See previous page for display ad and page 1632 for the College Close-Up.

Wells College

Aurora, New York

- **Independent** 4-year, founded 1868
- **Rural** 365-acre campus with easy access to Syracuse
- **Endowment** $23.5 million
- **Coed, primarily women** 532 undergraduate students, 98% full-time, 67% women, 33% men
- **Moderately difficult** entrance level, 45% of applicants were admitted

Undergraduates 523 full-time, 9 part-time. Students come from 30 states and territories; 6 other countries; 27% are from out of state; 11% Black or African American, non-Hispanic/Latino; 5% Hispanic/Latino; 2% Asian, non-Hispanic/Latino; 0.4% Native Hawaiian or other Pacific Islander, non-Hispanic/Latino; 0.6% American Indian or Alaska Native, non-Hispanic/Latino; 2% Two or more races, non-Hispanic/Latino; 11% Race/ethnicity unknown; 2% international; 4% transferred in; 84% live on campus. *Retention:* 70% of full-time freshmen returned.

Freshmen *Admission:* 1,803 applied, 810 admitted, 224 enrolled.

Faculty *Total:* 68, 57% full-time, 60% with terminal degrees. *Student/faculty ratio:* 10:1.

Academics *Calendar:* semesters. *Degree:* bachelor's. *Special study options:* accelerated degree program, adult/continuing education programs, advanced placement credit, double majors, English as a second language, independent study, internships, off-campus study, part-time degree program, services for LD students, student-designed majors, study abroad. *ROTC:* Army (c), Air Force (c). *Unusual degree programs:* 3-2 business administration with Clarkson University; engineering with Columbia University, Clarkson University, and Cornell University; community health with University of Rochester, education with University of Rochester.

Computers on Campus 96 computers/terminals and 1,224 ports are available on campus for general student use. Students can access the following: campus intranet, computer help desk, free student e-mail accounts, online (class) grades, online (class) registration, online (class) schedules. Campuswide network is available. 100% of college-owned or -operated housing units are wired for high-speed Internet access. Wireless service is available via classrooms, dorm rooms, learning centers, libraries, student centers.

Student Life *Housing:* on-campus residence required through senior year. *Options:* coed, women-only. Campus housing is university owned. Freshman campus housing is guaranteed. *Activities and organizations:* drama/theater group, student-run newspaper, choral group, Praising Our Work Ethnicity and Race (POWER), Women's Resource Center (WRC), Dance Collective, Model UN, Red Cross Club. *Campus security:* 24-hour emergency response devices and patrols, late-night transport/escort service, controlled dormitory access. *Student services:* health clinic, personal/psychological counseling, women's center.

Athletics Member NCAA. All Division III. *Intercollegiate sports:* basketball M/W, cross-country running M/W, field hockey W, golf M/W, lacrosse M/W, soccer M/W, softball W, swimming and diving M/W, tennis W, volleyball M/W.

Standardized Tests *Required:* SAT or ACT (for admission).

Costs (2012–13) *Comprehensive fee:* $46,600 includes full-time tuition ($33,200), mandatory fees ($1500), and room and board ($11,900). *Payment plan:* installment. *Waivers:* senior citizens and employees or children of employees.

Financial Aid Of all full-time matriculated undergraduates who enrolled in 2012, 486 applied for aid, 469 were judged to have need, 94 had their need fully met. 63 Federal Work-Study jobs (averaging $1600). 232 state and other part-time jobs (averaging $1600). In 2012, 41 non-need-based awards were made. *Average percent of need met:* 81%. *Average financial aid package:* $32,524. *Average need-based loan:* $4151. *Average need-based gift aid:* $26,844. *Average non-need-based aid:* $16,455. *Average indebtedness upon graduation:* $30,933.

Applying *Options:* electronic application, early admission, early decision, early action, deferred entrance. *Application fee:* $40. *Required:* essay or per-

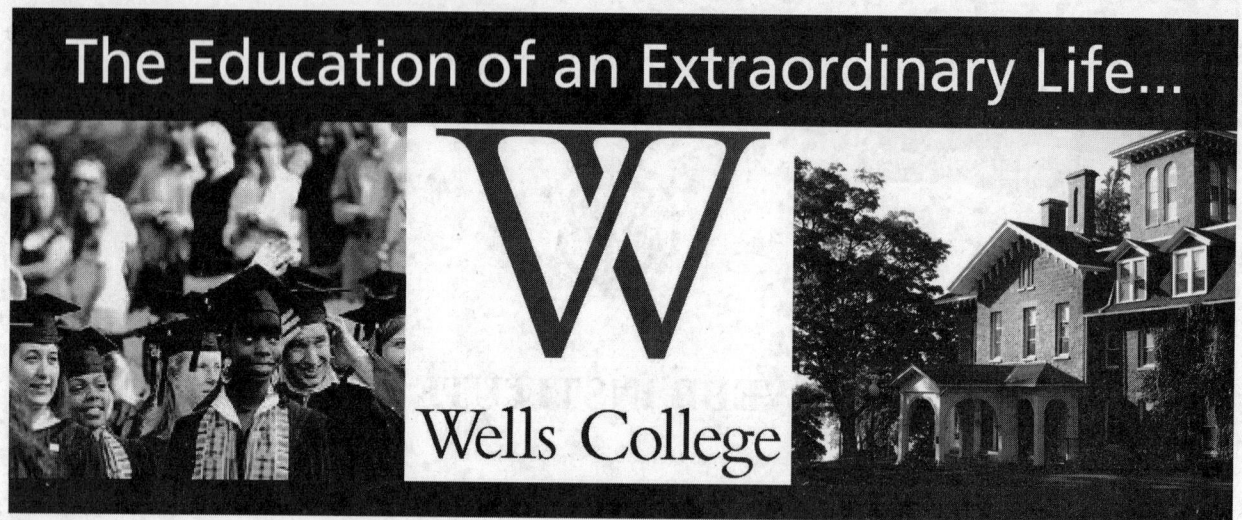

sonal statement, high school transcript, 2 letters of recommendation. *Recommended:* minimum 3.0 GPA, interview. *Application deadlines:* 3/1 (freshmen), rolling (transfers), 12/15 (early action). *Early decision deadline:* 12/15. *Notification:* 4/1 (freshmen), continuous (transfers), 1/15 (early decision), 2/1 (early action).

Freshman Application Contact Ms. Susan Raith Sloan, Director of Admissions, Wells College, 170 Main Street, Aurora, NY 13026. *Phone:* 315-364-3264. *Toll-free phone:* 800-952-9355. *Fax:* 315-364-3227. *E-mail:* admissions@wells.edu. *Website:* http://www.wells.edu/.

See previous page for display ad and page 1634 for the College Close-Up.

Yeshiva and Kolel Bais Medrash Elyon

Monsey, New York

Admissions Office Contact Yeshiva and Kolel Bais Medrash Elyon, 73 Main Street, Monsey, NY 10952.

Yeshiva and Kollel Harbotzas Torah

Brooklyn, New York

Admissions Office Contact Yeshiva and Kollel Harbotzas Torah, 1049 East 15th Street, Brooklyn, NY 11230.

Yeshiva Derech Chaim

Brooklyn, New York

Director of Admissions Administrator, Yeshiva Derech Chaim, 1573 39th Street, Brooklyn, NY 11218. *Phone:* 718-438-5476.

Yeshiva D'Monsey Rabbinical College

Monsey, New York

Admissions Office Contact Yeshiva D'Monsey Rabbinical College, 2 Roman Boulevard, Monsey, NY 10952.

Yeshiva Gedolah Imrei Yosef D'Spinka

Brooklyn, New York

Admissions Office Contact Yeshiva Gedolah Imrei Yosef D'Spinka, 1466 56th Street, Brooklyn, NY 11219.

Yeshiva Karlin Stolin Rabbinical Institute

Brooklyn, New York

Director of Admissions Director of Admissions, Yeshiva Karlin Stolin Rabbinical Institute, 1818 Fifty-fourth Street, Brooklyn, NY 11204. *Phone:* 718-232-7800 Ext. 26.

Yeshiva of Nitra Rabbinical College

Mount Kisco, New York

Director of Admissions Administrator, Yeshiva of Nitra Rabbinical College, Pines Bridge Road, Mount Kisco, NY 10549. *Phone:* 718-384-5460. *Fax:* 718-387-9400.

Yeshiva of the Telshe Alumni

Riverdale, New York

Admissions Office Contact Yeshiva of the Telshe Alumni, 4904 Independence Avenue, Riverdale, NY 10471.

Yeshiva Shaarei Torah of Rockland

Suffern, New York

Admissions Office Contact Yeshiva Shaarei Torah of Rockland, 91 West Carlton Road, Suffern, NY 10901.

Yeshiva Shaar Hatorah Talmudic Research Institute

Kew Gardens, New York

Director of Admissions Assistant Dean, Yeshiva Shaar Hatorah Talmudic Research Institute, 117-06 84th Avenue, Kew Gardens, NY 11418-1469. *Phone:* 718-846-1940.

Yeshivas Novominsk

Brooklyn, New York

Admissions Office Contact Yeshivas Novominsk, 1569 47th Street, Brooklyn, NY 11219.

Yeshivath Viznitz

Monsey, New York

Director of Admissions Registrar, Yeshivath Viznitz, 25 Phyllis Terrace, Monsey, NY 10952. *Phone:* 914-356-1010.

Yeshivath Zichron Moshe

South Fallsburg, New York

Director of Admissions Rabbi Abba Gorelick, Dean, Yeshivath Zichron Moshe, Laurel Park Road, South Fallsburg, NY 12779. *Phone:* 914-434-5240.

Yeshivat Mikdash Melech

Brooklyn, New York

Director of Admissions Rabbi S. Beyda, Director of Admissions, Yeshivat Mikdash Melech, 1326 Ocean Parkway, Brooklyn, NY 11230-5601. *Phone:* 718-339-1090. *E-mail:* mikdashmelech@verizon.net.

Yeshiva University

New York, New York

- **Independent** university, founded 1886
- **Urban** campus
- **Coed**
- **Moderately difficult** entrance level

Faculty *Student/faculty ratio:* 6:1.

Academics *Calendar:* semesters. *Degrees:* associate, bachelor's, master's, doctoral, post-master's, and postbachelor's certificates (Yeshiva College and Stern College for Women are coordinate undergraduate colleges of arts and sciences for men and women, respectively. Sy Syms School of Business offers programs at both campuses).

Student Life *Campus security:* 24-hour emergency response devices and patrols, late-night transport/escort service.

Athletics Member NCAA. All Division III.

Standardized Tests *Required:* SAT or ACT (for admission).

Costs (2012–13) *Comprehensive fee:* $47,250 includes full-time tuition ($35,500), mandatory fees ($1000), and room and board ($10,750). Full-time tuition and fees vary according to student level. Part-time tuition: $1240 per credit hour.

Financial Aid *Of all full-time matriculated undergraduates who enrolled in 2011,* 1,924 applied for aid, 1,604 were judged to have need, 381 had their need fully met. *Average percent of need met:* 89. *Average financial aid package:* $30,650. *Average need-based loan:* $6222. *Average need-based gift aid:* $26,206. *Average non-need-based aid:* $21,511. *Average indebtedness upon graduation:* $22,705.

Applying *Options:* early admission, deferred entrance. *Application fee:* $65. *Required:* essay or personal statement, high school transcript, 2 letters of recommendation, interview.

Freshman Application Contact Yeshiva University, 500 West 185th Street, New York, NY 10033-3201. *Phone:* 212-960-5277.
Website: http://www.yu.edu/.

York College of the City University of New York

Jamaica, New York

- **State and locally supported** comprehensive, founded 1967, part of City University of New York System
- **Urban** 50-acre campus with easy access to New York City
- **Coed** 8,350 undergraduate students, 64% full-time, 66% women, 34% men
- **Moderately difficult** entrance level, 60% of applicants were admitted

Undergraduates 5,327 full-time, 3,023 part-time. Students come from 4 states and territories; 131 other countries; 0.1% are from out of state; 34% Black or African American, non-Hispanic/Latino; 18% Hispanic/Latino; 16% Asian, non-Hispanic/Latino; 0.9% American Indian or Alaska Native, non-Hispanic/Latino; 27% Race/ethnicity unknown; 9% transferred in. *Retention:* 77% of full-time freshmen returned.

Freshmen *Admission:* 13,319 applied, 8,038 admitted, 1,110 enrolled. *Test scores:* SAT math scores over 500: 29%; SAT math scores over 600: 4%.

Faculty *Total:* 553, 36% full-time. *Student/faculty ratio:* 19:1.

Academics *Calendar:* semesters. *Degrees:* bachelor's and master's. *Special study options:* adult/continuing education programs, advanced placement credit, cooperative education, double majors, English as a second language, honors programs, independent study, internships, off-campus study, part-time degree program, services for LD students, study abroad, summer session for credit. *ROTC:* Army (b). *Unusual degree programs:* 3-2 occupational therapy.

Computers on Campus 650 computers/terminals and 844 ports are available on campus for general student use. Students can access the following: computer help desk, free student e-mail accounts, online (class) registration, online (class) schedules. Campuswide network is available. Wireless service is available via entire campus.

Student Life *Housing:* college housing not available. *Activities and organizations:* drama/theater group, student-run newspaper, television station, choral group, Haitian Students Association, Caribbean Students Association, Haitian Cultural Association, Latin Caucus, Muslim Student Association. *Campus security:* 24-hour emergency response devices and patrols, late-night transport/escort service. *Student services:* health clinic, personal/psychological counseling, women's center.

Athletics Member NCAA. All Division III. *Intercollegiate sports:* baseball M/W, basketball M/W, cross-country running M/W, soccer M, softball W, swimming and diving M/W, tennis M, track and field M/W, volleyball M/W. *Intramural sports:* basketball M/W, cross-country running M/W, soccer M, softball W, swimming and diving M/W, table tennis M/W, tennis M, track and field M/W, volleyball M/W.

Standardized Tests *Required:* SAT or ACT (for admission).

Costs (2013–14) *Tuition:* state resident $5730 full-time, $245 per credit part-time; nonresident $12,240 full-time, $510 per credit part-time. Full-time tuition and fees vary according to degree level and student level. Part-time tuition and fees vary according to degree level and student level. *Required fees:* $366 full-time, $113 per term part-time. *Payment plan:* installment. *Waivers:* senior citizens and employees or children of employees.

Financial Aid Of all full-time matriculated undergraduates who enrolled in 2011, 4,335 applied for aid, 3,896 were judged to have need, 16 had their need fully met. 1,737 Federal Work-Study jobs (averaging $1160). In 2011, 52 non-need-based awards were made. *Average percent of need met:* 10%. *Average financial aid package:* $1819. *Average need-based loan:* $2225. *Average need-based gift aid:* $800. *Average non-need-based aid:* $1084. *Average indebtedness upon graduation:* $2996. *Financial aid deadline:* 6/30.

Applying *Options:* electronic application, early admission, deferred entrance. *Application fee:* $65. *Required:* high school transcript, minimum 2.5 GPA. *Required for some:* minimum 2.8 GPA. *Recommended:* minimum 3.0 GPA. *Application deadlines:* rolling (freshmen), rolling (out-of-state freshmen), rolling (transfers). *Notification:* continuous (freshmen), continuous (out-of-state freshmen), continuous (transfers).

Freshman Application Contact York College of the City University of New York, 94-20 Guy R. Brewer Boulevard, Jamaica, NY 11451. *Phone:* 718-262-2165. *Fax:* 718-262-2601. *E-mail:* lbruno@york.cuny.edu.
Website: http://www.york.cuny.edu/.

NORTH CAROLINA

Apex School of Theology

Durham, North Carolina

- **Independent interdenominational** comprehensive, founded 1995
- **Suburban** campus
- **Coed**
- **Moderately difficult** entrance level

Faculty *Student/faculty ratio:* 17:1.

Academics *Calendar:* semesters. *Degrees:* associate, bachelor's, master's, and doctoral.

Costs (2012–13) *Tuition:* $4800 full-time, $200 per credit hour part-time. No tuition increase for student's term of enrollment. *Required fees:* $200 full-time.

Applying *Options:* electronic application. *Application fee:* $25. *Required:* essay or personal statement, high school transcript, 1 letter of recommendation.

Freshman Application Contact Dr. Henry D. Wells Jr., Registrar, Apex School of Theology, 2945 South Miami Boulevard, Suite 114, Durham, NC 27703. *Phone:* 919-572-1625. *Fax:* 919-572-1762. *E-mail:* registrar@apexsot.edu.
Website: http://www.apexsot.edu/.

Appalachian State University

Boone, North Carolina

- **State-supported** comprehensive, founded 1899, part of University of North Carolina System
- **Small-town** 411-acre campus
- **Endowment** $72.2 million
- **Coed** 15,712 undergraduate students, 94% full-time, 53% women, 47% men
- **Moderately difficult** entrance level, 63% of applicants were admitted

Undergraduates 14,837 full-time, 875 part-time. Students come from 44 states and territories; 60 other countries; 8% are from out of state; 3% Black or African American, non-Hispanic/Latino; 4% Hispanic/Latino; 1% Asian, non-Hispanic/Latino; 0.1% Native Hawaiian or other Pacific Islander, non-Hispanic/Latino; 0.2% American Indian or Alaska Native, non-Hispanic/Latino; 2% Two or more races, non-Hispanic/Latino; 2% Race/ethnicity unknown; 0.5% international; 7% transferred in; 37% live on campus. *Retention:* 88% of full-time freshmen returned.

Freshmen *Admission:* 12,248 applied, 7,744 admitted, 3,028 enrolled. *Average high school GPA:* 3.99. *Test scores:* SAT critical reading scores over 500:

89%; SAT writing scores over 500: 78%; ACT scores over 18: 99%; SAT critical reading scores over 600: 34%; SAT writing scores over 600: 23%; ACT scores over 24: 83%; SAT critical reading scores over 700: 4%; SAT writing scores over 700: 2%; ACT scores over 30: 10%.

Faculty *Total:* 1,256, 71% full-time, 94% with terminal degrees. *Student/faculty ratio:* 16:1.

Academics *Calendar:* semesters. *Degrees:* bachelor's, master's, doctoral, post-master's, and postbachelor's certificates. *Special study options:* academic remediation for entering students, adult/continuing education programs, advanced placement credit, distance learning, double majors, English as a second language, honors programs, independent study, internships, off-campus study, part-time degree program, services for LD students, student-designed majors, study abroad, summer session for credit. *ROTC:* Army (b). *Unusual degree programs:* 3-2 engineering with Auburn University, Clemson University.

Computers on Campus 2,422 computers/terminals are available on campus for general student use. Students can access the following: campus intranet, computer help desk, free student e-mail accounts, online (class) grades, online (class) registration, online (class) schedules. Campuswide network is available. 100% of college-owned or -operated housing units are wired for high-speed Internet access. Wireless service is available via entire campus.

Student Life *Housing:* on-campus residence required for freshman year. *Options:* coed, men-only, women-only, disabled students. Campus housing is university owned. Freshman campus housing is guaranteed. *Activities and organizations:* drama/theater group, student-run newspaper, radio station, choral group, marching band, Appalachian Intramural Recreation Sports Association, Appalachian State Fly-Fishing Club, Health Professions Club, Invisible Children at Appalachian State, APPS Special Events, national fraternities, national sororities. *Campus security:* 24-hour emergency response devices and patrols, late-night transport/escort service, controlled dormitory access. *Student services:* health clinic, personal/psychological counseling, women's center, legal services.

Athletics Member NCAA, NAIA. All NCAA Division I except football (Division I-AA). *Intercollegiate sports:* baseball M(s), basketball M(s)/W(s), cross-country running M(s)/W(s), equestrian sports M(c)/W(c), fencing M(c)/W(c), field hockey W(s), golf M(s)/W(s), ice hockey M(c)/W(c), lacrosse M(c)/W(c), racquetball M(c)/W(c), rugby M(c)/W(c), skiing (downhill) M(c)/W(c), soccer M(s)/W(s), softball W(s), swimming and diving M(c)/W(c), tennis M(s)/W(s), track and field M(s)/W(s), ultimate Frisbee M(c)/W(c), volleyball W(s), wrestling M(s). *Intramural sports:* badminton M/W, basketball M/W, bowling M/W, cross-country running M/W, golf M/W, racquetball M/W, soccer M/W, softball M/W, table tennis M/W, tennis M/W, ultimate Frisbee M/W, volleyball M/W.

Standardized Tests *Required:* SAT or ACT (for admission).

Costs (2012–13) *Tuition:* state resident $3542 full-time, $107 per credit hour part-time; nonresident $15,590 full-time, $514 per credit hour part-time. Part-time tuition and fees vary according to course load. *Required fees:* $2317 full-time, $13 per credit hour part-time. *Room and board:* $7060; room only: $3900. Room and board charges vary according to board plan and housing facility. *Payment plan:* installment. *Waivers:* employees or children of employees.

Financial Aid Of all full-time matriculated undergraduates who enrolled in 2012, 7,574 applied for aid, 7,355 were judged to have need, 2,320 had their need fully met. 306 Federal Work-Study jobs (averaging $1685). In 2012, 411 non-need-based awards were made. *Average percent of need met:* 70%. *Average financial aid package:* $9104. *Average need-based loan:* $5773. *Average need-based gift aid:* $7394. *Average non-need-based aid:* $2510. *Average indebtedness upon graduation:* $20,016.

Applying *Options:* electronic application, deferred entrance. *Application fee:* $55. *Required:* high school transcript. *Application deadlines:* 11/15 (freshmen), 11/15 (out-of-state freshmen), rolling (transfers). *Notification:* 3/1 (freshmen), 3/1 (out-of-state freshmen), continuous (transfers).

Freshman Application Contact Mr. Lloyd M Scott, Director of Admissions, Appalachian State University, ASU Box 32004, Boone, NC 28608. *Phone:* 828-262-2120. *Fax:* 828-262-3296. *E-mail:* admissions@appstate.edu. *Website:* http://www.appstate.edu/.

The Art Institute of Charlotte

Charlotte, North Carolina

- **Proprietary** 4-year, founded 1973, part of Education Management Corporation
- **Suburban** campus
- **Coed**

Academics *Calendar:* quarters. *Degrees:* certificates, associate, and bachelor's.

Freshman Application Contact The Art Institute of Charlotte, Three LakePointe Plaza, 2110 Water Ridge Parkway, Charlotte, NC 28217. *Phone:* 704-357-8020. *Toll-free phone:* 800-872-4417. *Website:* http://www.artinstitutes.edu/charlotte/.

See full-page ad on page 54 and page 1074 for the College Close-Up.

The Art Institute of Raleigh-Durham

Durham, North Carolina

- **Proprietary** 4-year, founded 2008, part of Education Management Corporation
- **Coed**

Academics *Degrees:* certificates, associate, and bachelor's.

Freshman Application Contact The Art Institute of Raleigh-Durham, 410 Blackwell Street, Suite 200, Durham, NC 27701. *Phone:* 919-317-3050. *Toll-free phone:* 888-245-9593. *Website:* http://www.artinstitutes.edu/raleigh-durham.

See full-page ad on page 54 and page 1108 for the College Close-Up.

Barton College

Wilson, North Carolina

- **Independent** comprehensive, founded 1902, affiliated with Christian Church (Disciples of Christ)
- **Small-town** 76-acre campus with easy access to Raleigh-Durham
- **Coed** 1,094 undergraduate students, 80% full-time, 69% women, 31% men
- **Minimally difficult** entrance level, 44% of applicants were admitted

Undergraduates 879 full-time, 215 part-time. Students come from 26 states and territories; 9 other countries; 14% are from out of state; 27% Black or African American, non-Hispanic/Latino; 3% Hispanic/Latino; 0.5% Asian, non-Hispanic/Latino; 0.5% Native Hawaiian or other Pacific Islander, non-Hispanic/Latino; 0.7% American Indian or Alaska Native, non-Hispanic/Latino; 4% Two or more races, non-Hispanic/Latino; 2% Race/ethnicity unknown; 3% international. *Retention:* 71% of full-time freshmen returned.

Freshmen *Admission:* 3,017 applied, 1,340 admitted, 202 enrolled. *Average high school GPA:* 3.07. *Test scores:* SAT critical reading scores over 500: 36%; SAT math scores over 500: 45%; SAT writing scores over 500: 30%; ACT scores over 18: 64%; SAT critical reading scores over 600: 6%; SAT math scores over 600: 9%; SAT writing scores over 600: 5%; ACT scores over 24: 10%; SAT critical reading scores over 700: 1%; SAT math scores over 700: 2%; SAT writing scores over 700: 1%.

Faculty *Total:* 111, 62% full-time, 47% with terminal degrees. *Student/faculty ratio:* 12:1.

Academics *Calendar:* 4-1-4. *Degrees:* bachelor's and master's. *Special study options:* academic remediation for entering students, adult/continuing education programs, advanced placement credit, cooperative education, double majors, English as a second language, honors programs, independent study, internships, part-time degree program, services for LD students, summer session for credit.

Computers on Campus 125 computers/terminals are available on campus for general student use. Students can access the following: campus intranet, computer help desk, free student e-mail accounts, student picture directory. Campuswide network is available. 100% of college-owned or -operated housing units are wired for high-speed Internet access. Wireless service is available via computer centers, computer labs, learning centers, libraries, student centers.

Student Life *Housing:* on-campus residence required through sophomore year. *Options:* coed, women-only. Campus housing is university owned. Freshman campus housing is guaranteed. *Activities and organizations:* drama/theater group, student-run newspaper, television station, choral group, Barton College Association of Nurses, Students in Free Enterprise (SIFE), Stage and Script, Campus Activities Board, College Habitat for Humanity, national fraternities, national sororities. *Campus security:* 24-hour emergency response devices, late-night transport/escort service, controlled dormitory access, city police substation on campus. *Student services:* health clinic, personal/psychological counseling.

Athletics Member NCAA. All Division II. *Intercollegiate sports:* baseball M(s), basketball M(s)/W(s), cross-country running M(s)/W(s), golf M(s)/W(s), soccer M(s)/W(s), softball W(s), tennis M(s)/W(s), track and field M(s)/W(s), volleyball M(s)/W(s). *Intramural sports:* archery M/W, badminton M/W, baseball M/W, basketball M/W, cheerleading M/W, football M/W, golf M/W, soc-

cer M/W, softball M/W, swimming and diving M/W, table tennis M/W, tennis M/W, volleyball M/W, weight lifting M/W.
Standardized Tests *Required:* SAT or ACT (for admission).
Costs (2012–13) *Comprehensive fee:* $32,120 includes full-time tuition ($22,278), mandatory fees ($1902), and room and board ($7940). Full-time tuition and fees vary according to class time, course load, and program. Part-time tuition: $941 per credit hour. Part-time tuition and fees vary according to class time, course load, and program. *College room only:* $3600. Room and board charges vary according to board plan and housing facility. *Payment plan:* installment. *Waivers:* children of alumni, adult students, senior citizens, and employees or children of employees.
Financial Aid Of all full-time matriculated undergraduates who enrolled in 2011, 991 applied for aid, 913 were judged to have need, 77 had their need fully met. In 2011, 105 non-need-based awards were made. *Average percent of need met:* 58%. *Average financial aid package:* $16,475. *Average need-based loan:* $4188. *Average need-based gift aid:* $12,688. *Average non-need-based aid:* $6317.
Applying *Options:* electronic application, deferred entrance. *Application fee:* $25. *Required:* high school transcript. *Recommended:* minimum 2.3 GPA, interview. *Application deadlines:* rolling (freshmen), rolling (transfers). *Notification:* continuous (freshmen), continuous (transfers).
Freshman Application Contact Barton College, PO Box 5000, Wilson, NC 27893-7000. *Phone:* 800-345-4973. *Toll-free phone:* 800-345-4973. *Website:* http://www.barton.edu/.

Belmont Abbey College

Belmont, North Carolina

- **Independent Roman Catholic** 4-year, founded 1876
- **Small-town** 650-acre campus with easy access to Charlotte
- **Endowment** $8.4 million
- **Coed** 1,706 undergraduate students, 93% full-time, 59% women, 41% men
- **Moderately difficult** entrance level, 64% of applicants were admitted

Undergraduates 1,590 full-time, 116 part-time. Students come from 45 states and territories; 24 other countries; 28% are from out of state; 27% Black or African American, non-Hispanic/Latino; 2% Hispanic/Latino; 0.8% Asian, non-Hispanic/Latino; 0.1% Native Hawaiian or other Pacific Islander, non-Hispanic/Latino; 0.2% American Indian or Alaska Native, non-Hispanic/Latino; 0.4% Two or more races, non-Hispanic/Latino; 31% Race/ethnicity unknown; 3% international; 11% transferred in; 43% live on campus. *Retention:* 63% of full-time freshmen returned.
Freshmen *Admission:* 1,842 applied, 1,185 admitted, 303 enrolled. *Average high school GPA:* 3.11. *Test scores:* SAT critical reading scores over 500: 44%; SAT math scores over 500: 58%; ACT scores over 18: 89%; SAT critical reading scores over 600: 16%; SAT math scores over 600: 19%; ACT scores over 24: 33%; SAT critical reading scores over 700: 3%; SAT math scores over 700: 2%.
Faculty *Total:* 157, 48% full-time, 45% with terminal degrees. *Student/faculty ratio:* 16:1.
Academics *Calendar:* semesters. *Degree:* bachelor's. *Special study options:* accelerated degree program, adult/continuing education programs, advanced placement credit, cooperative education, double majors, external degree program, freshman honors college, honors programs, independent study, internships, off-campus study, part-time degree program, services for LD students, study abroad, summer session for credit. *ROTC:* Army (c), Air Force (c).
Computers on Campus 125 computers/terminals are available on campus for general student use. Students can access the following: computer help desk, free student e-mail accounts, online (class) grades, online (class) schedules. Campuswide network is available. 100% of college-owned or -operated housing units are wired for high-speed Internet access. Wireless service is available via classrooms, computer labs, libraries, student centers.
Student Life *Housing:* on-campus residence required through senior year. *Options:* coed, men-only, women-only. Campus housing is university owned and leased by the school. Freshman campus housing is guaranteed. *Activities and organizations:* drama/theater group, student-run newspaper, radio station, choral group, Abbey Ambassadors, Abbey Players, The Crusader, Greek Life (fraternities and sororities), national fraternities, national sororities. *Campus security:* 24-hour emergency response devices and patrols, late-night transport/escort service. *Student services:* health clinic, personal/psychological counseling.
Athletics Member NCAA. All Division II. *Intercollegiate sports:* baseball M(s), basketball M(s)/W(s), cheerleading M/W, cross-country running M(s)/W(s), golf M(s)/W(s), lacrosse M(s)/W(s), soccer M(s)/W(s), softball W(s), tennis M(s)/W(s), track and field M(s)/W(s), volleyball M(s)/W(s), wrestling M(s). *Intramural sports:* badminton M/W, basketball M/W, crew M/W, cross-

country running M/W, football M/W, rugby M(c), soccer M/W, softball M/W, table tennis M/W, tennis M/W, ultimate Frisbee M/W, volleyball M/W, weight lifting M, wrestling M.
Standardized Tests *Required for some:* SAT or ACT (for admission).
Costs (2012–13) *One-time required fee:* $400. *Comprehensive fee:* $38,025 includes full-time tuition ($27,622) and room and board ($10,403). Full-time tuition and fees vary according to class time, course load, location, program, and reciprocity agreements. Part-time tuition: $921 per credit hour. Part-time tuition and fees vary according to class time, course load, location, and reciprocity agreements. *College room only:* $6137. Room and board charges vary according to board plan, housing facility, and location. *Payment plans:* installment, deferred payment. *Waivers:* senior citizens and employees or children of employees.
Financial Aid Of all full-time matriculated undergraduates who enrolled in 2011, 1,124 applied for aid, 1,049 were judged to have need, 74 had their need fully met. 109 Federal Work-Study jobs (averaging $2000). In 2011, 156 non-need-based awards were made. *Average percent of need met:* 54%. *Average financial aid package:* $15,085. *Average need-based loan:* $4484. *Average need-based gift aid:* $10,867. *Average non-need-based aid:* $12,734. *Average indebtedness upon graduation:* $21,004.
Applying *Options:* electronic application, deferred entrance. *Application fee:* $35. *Required:* high school transcript, minimum 2.3 GPA. *Required for some:* essay or personal statement, 2 letters of recommendation. *Recommended:* interview. *Application deadlines:* 8/1 (freshmen), 8/15 (transfers). *Notification:* continuous (freshmen), continuous (transfers).
Freshman Application Contact Roger Jones, Director of Admission, Belmont Abbey College, 100 Belmont-Mt. Holly Road, Belmont, NC 28012-1802. *Phone:* 704-461-6214. *Toll-free phone:* 888-BAC-0110. *Fax:* 704-461-6214. *E-mail:* rogerjones@bac.edu. *Website:* http://www.belmontabbeycollege.edu/.

Bennett College

Greensboro, North Carolina

- **Independent United Methodist** 4-year, founded 1873
- **Urban** 55-acre campus
- **Endowment** $12.3 million
- **Women only**
- **Moderately difficult** entrance level

Faculty *Student/faculty ratio:* 10:1.
Academics *Calendar:* semesters. *Degree:* bachelor's.
Student Life *Campus security:* 24-hour patrols, late-night transport/escort service, controlled dormitory access.
Athletics Member USCAA.
Standardized Tests *Recommended:* SAT or ACT (for admission).
Costs (2012–13) *One-time required fee:* $225. *Comprehensive fee:* $24,222 includes full-time tuition ($14,614), mandatory fees ($2180), and room and board ($7428). Part-time tuition: $609 per credit hour. Part-time tuition and fees vary according to course load. *Required fees:* $900 per term part-time. *College room only:* $3698.
Financial Aid *Of all full-time matriculated undergraduates who enrolled in 2011,* 664 applied for aid, 643 were judged to have need, 22 had their need fully met. *In 2011,* 7 non-need-based awards were made. *Average percent of need met:* 47. *Average financial aid package:* $13,092. *Average need-based loan:* $4170. *Average need-based gift aid:* $9402. *Average non-need-based aid:* $4714. *Financial aid deadline:* 3/15.
Applying *Options:* electronic application, deferred entrance. *Application fee:* $35. *Required:* essay or personal statement, high school transcript, minimum 2.0 GPA, 2 letters of recommendation. *Required for some:* interview.
Freshman Application Contact Ms. Taunya Monroe, Interim Director of Admissions, Bennett College, 900 East Washington Street, Campus Box H, Greensboro, NC 27401. *Phone:* 336-517-2161. *Toll-free phone:* 800-413-5323. *E-mail:* tmonroe@bennett.edu. *Website:* http://www.bennett.edu/.

Brevard College

Brevard, North Carolina

- **Independent United Methodist** 4-year, founded 1853
- **Small-town** 120-acre campus
- **Endowment** $21.8 million
- **Coed** 633 undergraduate students, 98% full-time, 41% women, 59% men
- **Minimally difficult** entrance level, 54% of applicants were admitted

Undergraduates 621 full-time, 12 part-time. Students come from 30 states and territories; 17 other countries; 42% are from out of state; 11% Black or African American, non-Hispanic/Latino; 0.2% Hispanic/Latino; 0.6% Asian, non-Hispanic/Latino; 1% American Indian or Alaska Native, non-Hispanic/Latino; 2% Two or more races, non-Hispanic/Latino; 7% Race/ethnicity unknown; 5% international; 7% transferred in; 76% live on campus. *Retention:* 52% of full-time freshmen returned.
Freshmen *Admission:* 1,591 applied, 855 admitted, 220 enrolled. *Average high school GPA:* 3.03. *Test scores:* SAT critical reading scores over 500: 44%; SAT math scores over 500: 49%; ACT scores over 18: 72%; SAT critical reading scores over 600: 9%; SAT math scores over 600: 11%; ACT scores over 24: 20%; SAT critical reading scores over 700: 1%; SAT math scores over 700: 2%; ACT scores over 30: 1%.
Faculty *Total:* 84, 62% full-time, 58% with terminal degrees. *Student/faculty ratio:* 10:1.
Academics *Calendar:* semesters. *Degree:* bachelor's. *Special study options:* academic remediation for entering students, advanced placement credit, double majors, honors programs, independent study, internships, part-time degree program, services for LD students, student-designed majors, study abroad.
Computers on Campus 100 computers/terminals are available on campus for general student use. Students can access the following: campus intranet, computer help desk, free student e-mail accounts, online (class) grades, online (class) schedules. Campuswide network is available. 100% of college-owned or -operated housing units are wired for high-speed Internet access. Wireless service is available via learning centers, libraries, student centers.
Student Life *Housing:* on-campus residence required through senior year. *Options:* coed, men-only, women-only, disabled students. Campus housing is university owned. Freshman campus housing is guaranteed. *Activities and organizations:* drama/theater group, student-run newspaper, choral group, Fine Arts organizations, Omicron Delta Kappa, Fellowship of Christian Athletes, BC Greens, Business Club. *Campus security:* 24-hour emergency response devices and patrols. *Student services:* health clinic, personal/psychological counseling, women's center.
Athletics Member NCAA. All Division II. *Intercollegiate sports:* baseball M(s), basketball M(s)/W(s), cheerleading W(s), cross-country running M(s)/W(s), football M(s), golf M(s)/W(s), lacrosse M(s), soccer M(s)/W(s), softball W(s), tennis M(s)/W(s), track and field M(s)/W(s), volleyball W(s). *Intramural sports:* badminton M/W, basketball M/W, bowling M/W, fencing M(c)/W(c), football M/W, soccer M/W, softball M/W, tennis M/W, track and field M/W, ultimate Frisbee M/W, volleyball M/W, weight lifting M/W.
Standardized Tests *Required:* SAT or ACT (for admission).
Costs (2012–13) *Comprehensive fee:* $32,100 includes full-time tuition ($23,900) and room and board ($8200). Full-time tuition and fees vary according to course load. Part-time tuition: $850 per credit hour. Part-time tuition and fees vary according to course load. *Room and board:* Room and board charges vary according to board plan and housing facility. *Payment plan:* installment. *Waivers:* senior citizens and employees or children of employees.
Financial Aid Of all full-time matriculated undergraduates who enrolled in 2011, 493 applied for aid, 431 were judged to have need, 70 had their need fully met. 66 Federal Work-Study jobs (averaging $1430). In 2011, 182 non-need-based awards were made. *Average percent of need met:* 73%. *Average financial aid package:* $19,367. *Average need-based loan:* $3532. *Average need-based gift aid:* $15,928. *Average non-need-based aid:* $5241. *Average indebtedness upon graduation:* $29,002.
Applying *Options:* electronic application, deferred entrance. *Application fee:* $30. *Required:* essay or personal statement, high school transcript, minimum 2.0 GPA. *Required for some:* interview, students in music require auditions, music tests; students in art require portfolio. *Application deadlines:* rolling (freshmen), rolling (out-of-state freshmen), rolling (transfers). *Notification:* continuous (freshmen), continuous (out-of-state freshmen), continuous (transfers).
Freshman Application Contact Mr. David Volrath, Admissions, Brevard College, One Brevard College Drive, Brevard, NC 28712. *Phone:* 828-884-8367. *Toll-free phone:* 800-527-9090. *Fax:* 828-884-3790. *E-mail:* admissions@brevard.edu.
Website: http://www.brevard.edu/.

Cabarrus College of Health Sciences
Concord, North Carolina
Freshman Application Contact Mr. Mark Ellison, Director of Admissions, Cabarrus College of Health Sciences, 401 Medical Park Drive, Concord, NC 28025-2077. *Phone:* 704-403-1616. *Fax:* 704-403-2077. *E-mail:* mellison@cabarruscollege.edu.
Website: http://www.cabarruscollege.edu/.

Campbell University
Buies Creek, North Carolina
Freshman Application Contact Ms. Peggy Mason, Director of Admissions, Campbell University, PO Box 546, 450 Leslie Campbell Avenue, Buies Creek, NC 27506. *Phone:* 910-893-1290. *Toll-free phone:* 800-334-4111. *Fax:* 910-893-1288. *E-mail:* adm@mailcenter.campbell.edu.
Website: http://www.campbell.edu/.

Carolina Christian College
Winston-Salem, North Carolina
- **Independent nondenominational** comprehensive, founded 1949
- **Small-town** 2-acre campus
- **Endowment** $250,000
- **Coed**
- **Noncompetitive** entrance level
Faculty *Student/faculty ratio:* 13:1.
Academics *Calendar:* semesters. *Degrees:* associate, bachelor's, and master's.
Student Life *Campus security:* 24-hour emergency response devices.
Costs (2012–13) *Tuition:* $7500 full-time, $938 per course part-time. *Required fees:* $200 full-time.
Financial Aid Of all full-time matriculated undergraduates who enrolled in 2011, 64 applied for aid, 60 were judged to have need, 50 had their need fully met. In 2011, 4 non-need-based awards were made. *Average percent of need met:* 85. *Average financial aid package:* $9500. *Average need-based gift aid:* $1500. *Average non-need-based aid:* $3500. *Average indebtedness upon graduation:* $6500.
Applying *Options:* electronic application. *Application fee:* $50. *Required:* essay or personal statement, high school transcript, 2 letters of recommendation, interview.
Freshman Application Contact Carolina Christian College, 4209 Indiana Avenue, PO Box 777, Winston-Salem, NC 27102-0777. *Phone:* 336-744-0900 Ext. 106.
Website: http://www.carolina.edu/.

Carolina College of Biblical Studies
Fayetteville, North Carolina
Admissions Office Contact Carolina College of Biblical Studies, 817 South McPherson Church Road, Fayetteville, NC 28303.
Website: http://carolinabiblecollege.org/.

Catawba College
Salisbury, North Carolina
- **Independent** comprehensive, founded 1851, affiliated with United Church of Christ
- **Small-town** 210-acre campus with easy access to Charlotte
- **Coed** 1,279 undergraduate students, 94% full-time, 52% women, 48% men
- **Moderately difficult** entrance level, 45% of applicants were admitted
Undergraduates 1,202 full-time, 77 part-time. Students come from 29 states and territories; 13 other countries; 30% are from out of state; 19% Black or African American, non-Hispanic/Latino; 3% Hispanic/Latino; 0.6% Asian, non-Hispanic/Latino; 0.8% American Indian or Alaska Native, non-Hispanic/Latino; 1% Two or more races, non-Hispanic/Latino; 0.2% Race/ethnicity unknown; 3% international; 9% transferred in; 50% live on campus. *Retention:* 67% of full-time freshmen returned.
Freshmen *Admission:* 3,448 applied, 1,547 admitted, 296 enrolled. *Average high school GPA:* 3.34. *Test scores:* SAT critical reading scores over 500: 45%; SAT math scores over 500: 52%; SAT critical reading scores over 600: 13%; SAT math scores over 600: 14%; SAT critical reading scores over 700: 3%; SAT math scores over 700: 1%.
Faculty *Total:* 129, 50% full-time, 57% with terminal degrees. *Student/faculty ratio:* 15:1.

Academics *Calendar:* semesters. *Degrees:* bachelor's and master's. *Special study options:* advanced placement credit, double majors, honors programs, independent study, internships, part-time degree program, services for LD students, student-designed majors, study abroad, summer session for credit. *ROTC:* Army (c), Air Force (c).

Computers on Campus 97 computers/terminals are available on campus for general student use. Students can access the following: campus intranet, computer help desk, free student e-mail accounts, online (class) grades, online (class) registration, online (class) schedules. Campuswide network is available. 100% of college-owned or -operated housing units are wired for high-speed Internet access. Wireless service is available via entire campus.

Student Life *Housing:* on-campus residence required through senior year. *Options:* coed, men-only, women-only. Campus housing is university owned. Freshman campus housing is guaranteed. *Activities and organizations:* drama/theater group, student-run newspaper, radio station, choral group, marching band, Volunteer Catawba, Catawba Ambassadors (admissions guides), Blue Masque (drama), Fellowship of Christian Athletes, Wigwam Productions (student activities board). *Campus security:* 24-hour emergency response devices and patrols, late-night transport/escort service, controlled dormitory access. *Student services:* health clinic, personal/psychological counseling.

Athletics Member NCAA. All Division II. *Intercollegiate sports:* baseball M(s), basketball M(s)/W(s), cheerleading M(s)/W(s), cross-country running M(s)/W(s), football M(s), golf M(s)/W(s), lacrosse M(s)/W(s), soccer M(s)/W(s), softball W(s), swimming and diving M(s)/W(s), tennis M(s)/W(s), volleyball W(s). *Intramural sports:* basketball M/W, football M/W, racquetball M/W, soccer M/W, tennis M/W, volleyball M/W, weight lifting M/W.

Standardized Tests *Required:* SAT or ACT (for admission).

Costs (2013–14) *Comprehensive fee:* $36,230 includes full-time tuition ($26,820) and room and board ($9410). Full-time tuition and fees vary according to class time and course load. Part-time tuition: $680 per credit hour. Part-time tuition and fees vary according to class time and course load. *Required fees:* $50 per term part-time. *Payment plan:* installment. *Waivers:* employees or children of employees.

Financial Aid Of all full-time matriculated undergraduates who enrolled in 2011, 1,108 applied for aid, 1,015 were judged to have need, 145 had their need fully met. In 2011, 149 non-need-based awards were made. *Average financial aid package:* $19,761. *Average need-based loan:* $4477. *Average need-based gift aid:* $6324. *Average non-need-based aid:* $8472. *Average indebtedness upon graduation:* $31,966.

Applying *Options:* electronic application, early admission, deferred entrance. *Application fee:* $25. *Required:* essay or personal statement, high school transcript, minimum 2.0 GPA, 2 letters of recommendation. *Recommended:* interview. *Application deadlines:* rolling (freshmen), rolling (transfers). *Notification:* continuous (freshmen), continuous (transfers).

Freshman Application Contact Catawba College, 2300 West Innes Street, Salisbury, NC 28144-2488. *Phone:* 704-637-4414. *Toll-free phone:* 800-CATAWBA.

Website: http://www.catawba.edu/.

Chowan University

Murfreesboro, North Carolina

- **Independent Baptist** comprehensive, founded 1848
- **Small-town** 300-acre campus with easy access to Norfolk
- **Coed** 1,308 undergraduate students, 95% full-time, 54% women, 46% men
- **Minimally difficult** entrance level, 58% of applicants were admitted

Undergraduates 1,239 full-time, 69 part-time. Students come from 21 states and territories; 12 other countries; 52% are from out of state; 67% Black or African American, non-Hispanic/Latino; 3% Hispanic/Latino; 0.1% Asian, non-Hispanic/Latino; 0.6% American Indian or Alaska Native, non-Hispanic/Latino; 3% Two or more races, non-Hispanic/Latino; 2% Race/ethnicity unknown; 1% international; 6% transferred in; 80% live on campus. *Retention:* 43% of full-time freshmen returned.

Freshmen *Admission:* 4,330 applied, 2,505 admitted, 516 enrolled. *Average high school GPA:* 2.63. *Test scores:* SAT critical reading scores over 500: 10%; SAT math scores over 500: 12%; ACT scores over 18: 24%; SAT critical reading scores over 600: 2%; SAT math scores over 600: 2%; ACT scores over 24: 1%; SAT critical reading scores over 700: 1%; SAT math scores over 700: 1%.

Faculty *Total:* 105, 60% full-time, 42% with terminal degrees. *Student/faculty ratio:* 16:1.

Academics *Calendar:* semesters. *Degrees:* associate, bachelor's, and master's. *Special study options:* advanced placement credit, cooperative education, double majors, freshman honors college, honors programs, independent study, internships, part-time degree program, services for LD students, student-designed majors, study abroad, summer session for credit.

Computers on Campus 215 computers/terminals are available on campus for general student use. Students can access the following: campus intranet, computer help desk, free student e-mail accounts, online (class) grades, online (class) registration, online (class) schedules. Campuswide network is available. 100% of college-owned or -operated housing units are wired for high-speed Internet access. Wireless service is available via entire campus.

Student Life *Housing:* on-campus residence required through sophomore year. *Options:* men-only, women-only. Campus housing is university owned. Freshman campus housing is guaranteed. *Activities and organizations:* drama/theater group, student-run newspaper, choral group, national fraternities, national sororities. *Campus security:* 24-hour emergency response devices and patrols, late-night transport/escort service, controlled dormitory access. *Student services:* health clinic, personal/psychological counseling.

Athletics Member NCAA, NCCAA. All NCAA Division II. *Intercollegiate sports:* baseball M(s), basketball M(s)/W(s), bowling W, cheerleading M/W, cross-country running M(s)/W(s), football M(s), golf M(s), lacrosse W(s), soccer M(s)/W(s), softball W(s), tennis M(s)/W(s), volleyball W(s). *Intramural sports:* basketball M/W, football M/W, racquetball M/W, soccer M/W, softball M/W, table tennis M/W, tennis M/W, volleyball M/W.

Standardized Tests *Required:* SAT or ACT (for admission).

Costs (2013–14) *Comprehensive fee:* $30,030 includes full-time tuition ($22,160) and room and board ($7870). Full-time tuition and fees vary according to class time, course load, and program. Part-time tuition and fees vary according to class time and program. *College room only:* $3900. Room and board charges vary according to board plan and housing facility. *Payment plan:* installment. *Waivers:* senior citizens and employees or children of employees.

Financial Aid Of all full-time matriculated undergraduates who enrolled in 2012, 1,338 applied for aid, 1,292 were judged to have need, 244 had their need fully met. 292 Federal Work-Study jobs (averaging $1563). 218 state and other part-time jobs (averaging $1209). In 2012, 84 non-need-based awards were made. *Average percent of need met:* 77%. *Average financial aid package:* $16,142. *Average need-based loan:* $3759. *Average need-based gift aid:* $8447. *Average non-need-based aid:* $7562. *Average indebtedness upon graduation:* $38,932.

Applying *Options:* electronic application. *Application fee:* $20. *Required:* high school transcript. *Required for some:* essay or personal statement, interview. *Recommended:* minimum 2.0 GPA, 2 letters of recommendation. *Application deadlines:* rolling (freshmen), rolling (out-of-state freshmen), rolling (transfers). *Notification:* continuous (freshmen), continuous (out-of-state freshmen), continuous (transfers).

Freshman Application Contact Kimberly Sherman, Associate Dean of Admissions, Chowan University, One University Place, Murfreesboro, NC 27855. *Phone:* 252-398-1236. *Toll-free phone:* 888-4-CHOWAN. *Fax:* 252-398-1190. *E-mail:* shermk@chowan.edu.

Website: http://www.chowan.edu/.

Davidson College

Davidson, North Carolina

- **Independent Presbyterian** 4-year, founded 1837
- **Small-town** 665-acre campus with easy access to Charlotte
- **Endowment** $511.4 million
- **Coed** 1,790 undergraduate students, 100% full-time, 50% women, 50% men
- **Very difficult** entrance level, 25% of applicants were admitted

Undergraduates 1,790 full-time. Students come from 47 states and territories; 39 other countries; 76% are from out of state; 7% Black or African American, non-Hispanic/Latino; 6% Hispanic/Latino; 5% Asian, non-Hispanic/Latino; 0.1% Native Hawaiian or other Pacific Islander, non-Hispanic/Latino; 0.6% American Indian or Alaska Native, non-Hispanic/Latino; 3% Two or more races, non-Hispanic/Latino; 4% Race/ethnicity unknown; 5% international; 0.4% transferred in; 92% live on campus. *Retention:* 97% of full-time freshmen returned.

Freshmen *Admission:* 4,770 applied, 1,184 admitted, 490 enrolled. *Average high school GPA:* 4.1. *Test scores:* SAT critical reading scores over 500: 100%; SAT math scores over 500: 100%; SAT writing scores over 500: 99%; ACT scores over 18: 100%; SAT critical reading scores over 600: 85%; SAT math scores over 600: 88%; SAT writing scores over 600: 84%; ACT scores over 24: 97%; SAT critical reading scores over 700: 38%; SAT math scores over 700: 38%; SAT writing scores over 700: 41%; ACT scores over 30: 63%.

Faculty *Total:* 176, 96% full-time, 95% with terminal degrees. *Student/faculty ratio:* 10:1.

Academics *Calendar:* semesters. *Degree:* bachelor's. *Special study options:* advanced placement credit, double majors, honors programs, independent study, internships, off-campus study, services for LD students, student-designed majors, study abroad. *ROTC:* Army (b), Air Force (c). *Unusual degree programs:* 3-2 engineering with Columbia University, Washington University in St. Louis.

Computers on Campus 180 computers/terminals are available on campus for general student use. Students can access the following: campus intranet, computer help desk, free student e-mail accounts, online (class) grades, online (class) registration, online (class) schedules. Campuswide network is available. 100% of college-owned or -operated housing units are wired for high-speed Internet access. Wireless service is available via entire campus.

Student Life *Housing:* on-campus residence required through senior year. *Options:* coed, cooperative. Campus housing is university owned. Freshman campus housing is guaranteed. *Activities and organizations:* drama/theater group, student-run newspaper, radio station, choral group, Inter-Varsity Christian Fellowship, Dean Rusk Program Student Advisory Council, music organizations, Community Service Council, Student Government Association, national fraternities, national sororities. *Campus security:* 24-hour emergency response devices and patrols, late-night transport/escort service, controlled dormitory access. *Student services:* health clinic, personal/psychological counseling, women's center.

Athletics Member NCAA. All Division I except football (Division I-AA). *Intercollegiate sports:* baseball M(s), basketball M(s)/W(s), crew M(c)/W(c), cross-country running M(s)/W(s), fencing M(c)/W(c), field hockey W(s), golf M(s), lacrosse W(s), rugby M(c), sailing M(c)/W(c), soccer M(s)/W(s), swimming and diving M(s)/W(s), tennis M(s)/W(s), track and field M(s)/W(s), ultimate Frisbee M(c)/W(c), volleyball W(s), weight lifting M(c)/W(c), wrestling M(s). *Intramural sports:* basketball M/W, equestrian sports W(c), field hockey M(c)/W(c), football M/W, lacrosse M(c)/W(c), soccer M(c)/W(c), softball M/W, swimming and diving M(c)/W(c), tennis M(c)/W(c), volleyball M/W(c), water polo M(c).

Standardized Tests *Required:* SAT or ACT (for admission). *Recommended:* SAT and SAT Subject Tests or ACT (for admission).

Costs (2013–14) *Comprehensive fee:* $54,683 includes full-time tuition ($42,425), mandatory fees ($424), and room and board ($11,834). *College room only:* $6249. Room and board charges vary according to board plan. *Waivers:* employees or children of employees.

Financial Aid Of all full-time matriculated undergraduates who enrolled in 2011, 876 applied for aid, 831 were judged to have need, 831 had their need fully met. 302 Federal Work-Study jobs (averaging $1538). 137 state and other part-time jobs (averaging $1695). In 2011, 113 non-need-based awards were made. *Average percent of need met:* 100%. *Average financial aid package:* $34,121. *Average need-based loan:* $3303. *Average need-based gift aid:* $29,064. *Average non-need-based aid:* $21,747. *Average indebtedness upon graduation:* $23,904. *Financial aid deadline:* 3/1.

Applying *Options:* electronic application, early admission, early decision, deferred entrance. *Application fee:* $50. *Required:* essay or personal statement, high school transcript, 3 letters of recommendation. *Recommended:* interview. *Application deadlines:* 1/2 (freshmen), 3/15 (transfers). *Early decision deadline:* 11/15 (for plan 1), 1/2 (for plan 2). *Notification:* 4/1 (freshmen), 5/15 (transfers), 12/15 (early decision plan 1), 2/1 (early decision plan 2).

Freshman Application Contact Mr. Christopher J. Gruber, Vice President and Dean of Admission and Financial Aid, Davidson College, Box 7156, Davidson, NC 28035-7156. *Phone:* 704-894-2230. *Toll-free phone:* 800-768-0380. *Fax:* 704-894-2016. *E-mail:* admission@davidson.edu. *Website:* http://www.davidson.edu/.

DeVry University
Charlotte, North Carolina
Freshman Application Contact DeVry University, 2015 Ayrsley Town Boulevard, Suite 109, Charlotte, NC 28273-4068. *Toll-free phone:* 866-338-7941.
Website: http://www.devry.edu/.

Duke University
Durham, North Carolina
Freshman Application Contact Mr. Christoph Guttentag, Director of Admissions, Duke University, Durham, NC 27708-0586. *Phone:* 919-684-3214. *E-mail:* askduke@admiss.duke.edu.
Website: http://www.duke.edu/.

East Carolina University
Greenville, North Carolina
- **State-supported** university, founded 1907, part of University of North Carolina System
- **Urban** 1401-acre campus
- **Endowment** $128.7 million
- **Coed** 21,298 undergraduate students, 86% full-time, 59% women, 41% men
- **Moderately difficult** entrance level, 62% of applicants were admitted

Undergraduates 18,317 full-time, 2,981 part-time. Students come from 42 states and territories; 54 other countries; 12% are from out of state; 15% Black or African American, non-Hispanic/Latino; 3% Hispanic/Latino; 2% Asian, non-Hispanic/Latino; 0.1% Native Hawaiian or other Pacific Islander, non-Hispanic/Latino; 0.5% American Indian or Alaska Native, non-Hispanic/Latino; 2% Two or more races, non-Hispanic/Latino; 3% Race/ethnicity unknown; 0.6% international; 7% transferred in; 24% live on campus. *Retention:* 78% of full-time freshmen returned.

Freshmen *Admission:* 15,535 applied, 9,658 admitted, 4,015 enrolled. *Average high school GPA:* 3.58. *Test scores:* SAT critical reading scores over 500: 51%; SAT math scores over 500: 68%; SAT writing scores over 500: 43%; ACT scores over 18: 96%; SAT critical reading scores over 600: 8%; SAT math scores over 600: 12%; SAT writing scores over 600: 6%; ACT scores over 24: 25%; SAT critical reading scores over 700: 1%; SAT math scores over 700: 1%; ACT scores over 30: 1%.

Faculty *Total:* 1,491, 78% full-time, 72% with terminal degrees. *Student/faculty ratio:* 18:1.

Academics *Calendar:* semesters. *Degrees:* certificates, bachelor's, master's, doctoral, post-master's, and postbachelor's certificates. *Special study options:* accelerated degree program, adult/continuing education programs, advanced placement credit, cooperative education, distance learning, double majors, honors programs, independent study, internships, off-campus study, part-time degree program, services for LD students, student-designed majors, study abroad, summer session for credit. *ROTC:* Army (b), Air Force (b). *Unusual degree programs:* 3-2 business administration.

Computers on Campus 2,625 computers/terminals and 2,625 ports are available on campus for general student use. Students can access the following: campus intranet, computer help desk, free student e-mail accounts, online (class) grades, online (class) registration, online (class) schedules. Campuswide network is available. 100% of college-owned or -operated housing units are wired for high-speed Internet access. Wireless service is available via entire campus.

Student Life *Housing options:* coed, women-only, disabled students. Campus housing is university owned. *Activities and organizations:* drama/theater group, student-run newspaper, radio and television station, choral group, marching band, Student Government Association, Student Union, Residence Hall Association, Student Pirate Club, Black Student Union, national fraternities, national sororities. *Campus security:* 24-hour emergency response devices and patrols, student patrols, late-night transport/escort service, controlled dormitory access, Operation ID, Staff and Faculty Eyes, Campus Community Watch program. *Student services:* health clinic, personal/psychological counseling, legal services.

Athletics Member NCAA. All Division I except football (Division I-A). *Intercollegiate sports:* baseball M(s), basketball M(s)/W(s), cross-country running M(s)/W(s), golf M(s)/W(s), soccer M(s)/W(s), softball W(s), swimming and diving M(s)/W(s), tennis M(s)/W(s), track and field M(s)/W(s), volleyball W(s). *Intramural sports:* badminton M(c)/W(c), baseball M(c), basketball M/W, bowling M(c)/W(c), equestrian sports M(c)/W(c), fencing M(c)/W(c), field hockey M(c)/W(c), football M/W, golf M/W, ice hockey M(c), lacrosse M(c)/W(c), racquetball M/W, rugby M(c)/W(c), skiing (downhill) M(c)/W(c), soccer M/W, softball M/W, swimming and diving M(c)/W(c), table tennis M/W, tennis M/W, ultimate Frisbee M/W, volleyball M(c)/W(c).

Standardized Tests *Required:* SAT or ACT (for admission).

Costs (2012–13) *Tuition:* state resident $3758 full-time, $470 per course part-time; nonresident $17,572 full-time, $2197 per course part-time. Full-time tuition and fees vary according to location. Part-time tuition and fees vary according to course load and location. *Required fees:* $2111 full-time, $264 per course part-time. *Room and board:* $8300; room only: $4774. Room and board charges vary according to board plan and housing facility. *Payment plans:* installment, deferred payment. *Waivers:* senior citizens and employees or children of employees.

Financial Aid Of all full-time matriculated undergraduates who enrolled in 2012, 13,387 applied for aid, 10,966 were judged to have need, 949 had their need fully met. 445 Federal Work-Study jobs (averaging $2510). 1,213 state and other part-time jobs (averaging $1100). In 2012, 501 non-need-based awards were made. *Average percent of need met:* 66%. *Average financial aid package:* $9718. *Average need-based loan:* $4053. *Average need-based gift *aid:* $7529. *Average non-need-based aid:* $3467. *Average indebtedness upon graduation:* $25,983.

Applying *Options:* electronic application, early admission, deferred entrance. *Application fee:* $70. *Required:* high school transcript, minimum 2.0 GPA. *Application deadlines:* 3/15 (freshmen), 3/15 (out-of-state freshmen), 4/15 (transfers). *Notification:* continuous (freshmen), continuous (out-of-state freshmen), continuous (transfers).

Freshman Application Contact Undergraduate Admission, East Carolina University, Whichard Building 106, East Fifth St., Greenville, NC 27858-4353. *Phone:* 252-328-6640. *E-mail:* admis@ecu.edu. *Website:* http://www.ecu.edu/.

ECPI College of Technology

Charlotte, North Carolina

Admissions Office Contact ECPI College of Technology, 4800 Airport Center Parkway, Charlotte, NC 28208. *Toll-free phone:* 866-708-6167. *Website:* http://www.ecpi.edu/.

ECPI College of Technology

Greensboro, North Carolina

Admissions Office Contact ECPI College of Technology, 7802 Airport Center Drive, Greensboro, NC 27409. *Toll-free phone:* 866-708-6170. *Website:* http://www.ecpi.edu/.

ECPI College of Technology

Raleigh, North Carolina

Freshman Application Contact Ms. Susan Wells, Campus President, ECPI College of Technology, 4101 Doie Cope Road, Raleigh, NC 27613. *Phone:* 919-571-0057. *Toll-free phone:* 800-986-1200. *Fax:* 919-571-0780. *E-mail:* swells@ecpi.edu. *Website:* http://www.ecpi.edu/.

Elizabeth City State University

Elizabeth City, North Carolina

- **State-supported** comprehensive, founded 1891, part of University of North Carolina System
- **Small-town** 200-acre campus with easy access to Norfolk
- **Coed** 2,760 undergraduate students, 91% full-time, 60% women, 40% men
- **Moderately difficult** entrance level, 57% of applicants were admitted

Undergraduates 2,509 full-time, 251 part-time. 13% are from out of state; 73% Black or African American, non-Hispanic/Latino; 0.8% Hispanic/Latino; 0.4% Asian, non-Hispanic/Latino; 0.5% American Indian or Alaska Native, non-Hispanic/Latino; 12% Race/ethnicity unknown; 7% transferred in; 52% live on campus. *Retention:* 79% of full-time freshmen returned.

Freshmen *Admission:* 3,925 applied, 2,243 admitted, 472 enrolled. *Average high school GPA:* 3.02. *Test scores:* SAT critical reading scores over 500: 11%; SAT math scores over 500: 17%; SAT writing scores over 500: 8%; ACT scores over 18: 41%; SAT critical reading scores over 600: 1%; SAT math scores over 600: 1%; ACT scores over 24: 1%.

Faculty *Total:* 218, 77% full-time, 56% with terminal degrees. *Student/faculty ratio:* 14:1.

Academics *Calendar:* semesters. *Degrees:* bachelor's and master's. *Special study options:* academic remediation for entering students, adult/continuing education programs, advanced placement credit, cooperative education, distance learning, double majors, honors programs, independent study, internships, off-campus study, part-time degree program, services for LD students, study abroad, summer session for credit. *ROTC:* Army (b).

Computers on Campus 1,035 computers/terminals and 1,200 ports are available on campus for general student use. Students can access the following: campus intranet, computer help desk, free student e-mail accounts, online (class) registration, online (class) schedules. Campuswide network is available. 100% of college-owned or -operated housing units are wired for high-speed Internet access. Wireless service is available via entire campus.

Student Life *Housing options:* coed, men-only, women-only. Campus housing is university owned and leased by the school. Freshman campus housing is guaranteed. *Activities and organizations:* drama/theater group, student-run newspaper, choral group, marching band, Vans (Vikings Assisting New Students), Student Activities Committee, Vike Nu' Fashion Troupe, Pep Squad, Essence of Praise, national fraternities, national sororities. *Campus security:* 24-hour emergency response devices and patrols. *Student services:* health clinic, personal/psychological counseling.

Athletics Member NCAA. All Division II. *Intercollegiate sports:* baseball M(s), basketball M(s)/W(s), bowling W(s), cheerleading W, cross-country running M/W, football M(s), golf M(s), softball W(s), tennis W(s), volleyball W(s).

Standardized Tests *Required:* SAT or ACT (for admission).

Costs (2013–14) *Tuition:* $347 per credit hour part-time; state resident $2776 full-time; nonresident $13,633 full-time, $1704 per credit hour part-time. *Required fees:* $1652 full-time. *Room and board:* $7213; room only: $4440. Room and board charges vary according to housing facility. *Payment plan:* installment.

Financial Aid Of all full-time matriculated undergraduates who enrolled in 2011, 2,836 applied for aid, 2,643 were judged to have need. *Average need-based loan:* $3633. *Average need-based gift aid:* $5882.

Applying *Options:* electronic application, deferred entrance. *Application fee:* $30. *Required:* high school transcript, minimum 2.3 GPA. *Application deadlines:* 5/8 (freshmen), 5/8 (transfers). *Notification:* continuous (freshmen), continuous (transfers).

Freshman Application Contact Elizabeth City State University, 1704 Weeksville Road, Elizabeth City, NC 27909-7806. *Toll-free phone:* 800-347-3278. *Website:* http://www.ecsu.edu/.

Elon University

Elon, North Carolina

- **Independent** comprehensive, founded 1889, affiliated with United Church of Christ
- **Suburban** 620-acre campus with easy access to Raleigh
- **Endowment** $132.0 million
- **Coed** 5,357 undergraduate students, 97% full-time, 59% women, 41% men
- **Moderately difficult** entrance level, 52% of applicants were admitted

Undergraduates 5,209 full-time, 148 part-time. Students come from 48 states and territories; 48 other countries; 75% are from out of state; 6% Black or African American, non-Hispanic/Latino; 4% Hispanic/Latino; 2% Asian, non-Hispanic/Latino; 0.1% Native Hawaiian or other Pacific Islander, non-Hispanic/Latino; 0.3% American Indian or Alaska Native, non-Hispanic/Latino; 1% Two or more races, non-Hispanic/Latino; 3% Race/ethnicity unknown; 2% international; 2% transferred in; 60% live on campus. *Retention:* 90% of full-time freshmen returned.

Freshmen *Admission:* 10,241 applied, 5,293 admitted, 1,425 enrolled. *Average high school GPA:* 3.99. *Test scores:* SAT critical reading scores over 500: 95%; SAT math scores over 500: 94%; SAT writing scores over 500: 95%; ACT scores over 18: 99%; SAT critical reading scores over 600: 62%; SAT math scores over 600: 63%; SAT writing scores over 600: 64%; ACT scores over 24: 88%; SAT critical reading scores over 700: 15%; SAT math scores over 700: 13%; SAT writing scores over 700: 14%; ACT scores over 30: 23%.

Faculty *Total:* 535, 72% full-time, 76% with terminal degrees. *Student/faculty ratio:* 13:1.

Academics *Calendar:* semesters 3-week winter term. *Degrees:* bachelor's, master's, and doctoral. *Special study options:* accelerated degree program, advanced placement credit, double majors, English as a second language, honors programs, independent study, internships, off-campus study, part-time degree program, services for LD students, student-designed majors, study abroad, summer session for credit. *ROTC:* Army (b), Air Force (c). *Unusual degree programs:* 3-2 engineering with North Carolina State University, Georgia Tech, Penn State, Virginia Tech, University of Notre Dame, Columbia University, Washington University in St. Louis, North Carolina A&T State University, University of South Carolina.

Computers on Campus 1,169 computers/terminals and 10,000 ports are available on campus for general student use. Students can access the following: computer help desk, free student e-mail accounts, online (class) grades, online (class) registration, online (class) schedules. Campuswide network is available. 100% of college-owned or -operated housing units are wired for high-speed Internet access. Wireless service is available via entire campus.

Student Life *Housing:* on-campus residence required through sophomore year. *Options:* coed, men-only, women-only. Campus housing is university owned and leased by the school. Freshman campus housing is guaranteed. *Activities* *and organizations:* drama/theater group, student-run newspaper, radio and television station, choral group, marching band, Elon volunteers, student media, intramural athletics, religious life, Habitat for Humanity, national fraternities, national sororities. *Campus security:* 24-hour emergency response devices and patrols, late-night transport/escort service, controlled dormitory access. *Student services:* health clinic, personal/psychological counseling, women's center.

Athletics Member NCAA. All Division I except football (Division I-AA). *Intercollegiate sports:* baseball M(s), basketball M(s)/W(s), cheerleading M/W, cross-country running M(s)/W(s), equestrian sports M(c)/W(c), field hockey W(c), golf M(s)/W(s), lacrosse M(c)/W(s)(c), rugby M(c)/W(c), skiing (downhill) M(c)/W(c), soccer M(s)/W(s), softball W(s), swimming and diving M(c)/W(c), tennis M(s)/W(s), track and field W(s), ultimate Frisbee M(c)/W(c), volleyball W(s). *Intramural sports:* basketball M/W, bowling M/W, football M/W, golf M/W, racquetball M/W, soccer M/W, softball M/W, table tennis M/W, tennis M/W, volleyball M/W.

Standardized Tests *Required:* SAT or ACT (for admission).

Costs (2012–13) *Comprehensive fee:* $38,460 includes full-time tuition ($28,633), mandatory fees ($347), and room and board ($9480). Part-time tuition: $898 per hour. Part-time tuition and fees vary according to course load. *College room only:* $4690. Room and board charges vary according to board plan and housing facility. *Payment plan:* installment. *Waivers:* employees or children of employees.

Financial Aid Of all full-time matriculated undergraduates who enrolled in 2012, 2,563 applied for aid, 1,834 were judged to have need. 1,308 Federal Work-Study jobs (averaging $2306). In 2012, 1067 non-need-based awards were made. *Average percent of need met:* 63%. *Average financial aid package:* $17,378. *Average need-based loan:* $4402. *Average need-based gift aid:* $13,628. *Average non-need-based aid:* $5882. *Average indebtedness upon graduation:* $28,183.

Applying *Options:* electronic application, early admission, early decision, early action, deferred entrance. *Application fee:* $50. *Required:* essay or personal statement, high school transcript. *Required for some:* interview. *Application deadlines:* 1/10 (freshmen), rolling (transfers), 11/10 (early action). *Early decision deadline:* 11/1. *Notification:* 3/15 (freshmen), continuous (transfers), 12/1 (early decision), 12/20 (early action).

Freshman Application Contact Ms. Melinda Wood, Associate Director of Admissions and Director of Applications, Elon University, 100 Campus Box, Elon, NC 27244. *Phone:* 336-278-3566. *Toll-free phone:* 800-334-8448. *Fax:* 336-278-7699. *E-mail:* admissions@elon.edu.
Website: http://www.elon.edu/.

Fayetteville State University

Fayetteville, North Carolina

- **State-supported** comprehensive, founded 1867, part of University of North Carolina System
- **Urban** 156-acre campus with easy access to Raleigh
- **Endowment** $13.6 million
- **Coed** 5,287 undergraduate students, 74% full-time, 69% women, 31% men
- **Minimally difficult** entrance level, 55% of applicants were admitted

Undergraduates 3,916 full-time, 1,371 part-time. Students come from 30 states and territories; 7 other countries; 5% are from out of state; 68% Black or African American, non-Hispanic/Latino; 6% Hispanic/Latino; 1% Asian, non-Hispanic/Latino; 0.1% Native Hawaiian or other Pacific Islander, non-Hispanic/Latino; 2% American Indian or Alaska Native, non-Hispanic/Latino; 0.6% Two or more races, non-Hispanic/Latino; 6% Race/ethnicity unknown; 0.7% international; 14% transferred in; 29% live on campus. *Retention:* 76% of full-time freshmen returned.

Freshmen *Admission:* 4,010 applied, 2,204 admitted, 612 enrolled. *Average high school GPA:* 2.94. *Test scores:* SAT critical reading scores over 500: 11%; SAT math scores over 500: 15%; SAT writing scores over 500: 7%; SAT critical reading scores over 600: 2%; SAT math scores over 600: 3%; SAT writing scores over 600: 1%.

Faculty *Total:* 334, 83% full-time, 77% with terminal degrees. *Student/faculty ratio:* 16:1.

Academics *Calendar:* semesters. *Degrees:* bachelor's, master's, and doctoral. *Special study options:* academic remediation for entering students, accelerated degree program, adult/continuing education programs, advanced placement credit, cooperative education, distance learning, double majors, honors programs, independent study, internships, part-time degree program, services for LD students, study abroad, summer session for credit. *ROTC:* Army (c), Air Force (b). *Unusual degree programs:* 3-2 engineering with North Carolina State University.

Computers on Campus 600 computers/terminals and 2,400 ports are available on campus for general student use. Students can access the following: campus intranet, computer help desk, free student e-mail accounts, online (class) grades, online (class) registration, online (class) schedules. Campus-wide network is available. 100% of college-owned or -operated housing units are wired for high-speed Internet access. Wireless service is available via classrooms, computer centers, computer labs, learning centers, libraries, student centers.

Student Life *Housing options:* coed, men-only, women-only, disabled students. Campus housing is university owned. Freshman applicants given priority for college housing. *Activities and organizations:* drama/theater group, student-run newspaper, radio station, choral group, marching band, Student Government Association, Student Activities Council, Pan-Hellenic Council, Residence Hall Association, Illusions and Black Millennium Modeling Clubs, national fraternities, national sororities. *Campus security:* 24-hour emergency response devices and patrols, late-night transport/escort service, controlled dormitory access. *Student services:* health clinic, personal/psychological counseling.

Athletics Member NCAA. All Division II. *Intercollegiate sports:* basketball M(s)/W(s), bowling W, cross-country running M(s)/W(s), football M(s), golf M(s), softball W(s), tennis M/W(s), track and field M/W(s), volleyball W(s). *Intramural sports:* basketball M/W, bowling M/W, football M, golf M/W, gymnastics M/W, tennis M, volleyball M/W.

Standardized Tests *Required:* SAT or ACT (for admission).

Costs (2012–13) *Tuition:* state resident $2585 full-time; nonresident $13,289 full-time. Full-time tuition and fees vary according to course level, course load, degree level, location, and program. Part-time tuition and fees vary according to course level, course load, degree level, location, and program. *Required fees:* $3086 full-time. *Room and board:* $6142; room only: $3392. Room and board charges vary according to board plan and housing facility. *Payment plan:* installment. *Waivers:* senior citizens and employees or children of employees.

Financial Aid Of all full-time matriculated undergraduates who enrolled in 2011, 3,746 applied for aid, 3,516 were judged to have need, 839 had their need fully met. In 2011, 147 non-need-based awards were made. *Average percent of need met:* 82%. *Average financial aid package:* $9791. *Average need-based loan:* $4294. *Average need-based gift aid:* $6195. *Average non-need-based aid:* $604. *Financial aid deadline:* 3/1.

Applying *Options:* electronic application, early admission, early decision, early action, deferred entrance. *Application fee:* $35. *Required:* high school transcript, minimum 2.0 GPA. *Recommended:* essay or personal statement. *Application deadlines:* 6/30 (freshmen), 6/30 (transfers). *Notification:* continuous (freshmen), continuous (transfers).

Freshman Application Contact Fayetteville State University, 1200 Murchison Road, Fayetteville, NC 28301-4298. *Phone:* 910-672-1371. *Toll-free phone:* 800-222-2594. *Fax:* 910-672-1414.
Website: http://www.uncfsu.edu/.

Gardner-Webb University

Boiling Springs, North Carolina

- **Independent Baptist** university, founded 1905
- **Small-town** 250-acre campus with easy access to Charlotte, NC
- **Endowment** $51.1 million
- **Coed** 2,677 undergraduate students, 82% full-time, 65% women, 35% men
- **Moderately difficult** entrance level, 54% of applicants were admitted

Undergraduates 2,192 full-time, 485 part-time. Students come from 43 states and territories; 13 other countries; 22% are from out of state; 19% Black or African American, non-Hispanic/Latino; 2% Hispanic/Latino; 0.9% Asian, non-Hispanic/Latino; 0.6% American Indian or Alaska Native, non-Hispanic/Latino; 9% Race/ethnicity unknown; 2% international; 17% transferred in; 51% live on campus. *Retention:* 67% of full-time freshmen returned.

Freshmen *Admission:* 5,232 applied, 2,843 admitted, 493 enrolled. *Average high school GPA:* 3.62. *Test scores:* SAT critical reading scores over 500: 51%; SAT math scores over 500: 55%; ACT scores over 18: 84%; SAT critical reading scores over 600: 16%; SAT math scores over 600: 17%; ACT scores over 24: 31%; SAT critical reading scores over 700: 1%; SAT math scores over 700: 2%; ACT scores over 30: 2%.

Faculty *Total:* 258, 48% full-time. *Student/faculty ratio:* 13:1.

Academics *Calendar:* semesters. *Degrees:* certificates, associate, bachelor's, master's, and doctoral. *Special study options:* academic remediation for entering students, accelerated degree program, adult/continuing education programs, advanced placement credit, cooperative education, distance learning, double majors, English as a second language, honors programs, independent study, internships, off-campus study, part-time degree program, services for

LD students, study abroad, summer session for credit. *ROTC:* Army (b), Air Force (c). *Unusual degree programs:* 3-2 Bachelor of Music/MBA.

Computers on Campus 121 computers/terminals are available on campus for general student use. Students can access the following: campus intranet, free student e-mail accounts, online (class) grades, online (class) registration, online (class) schedules. Campuswide network is available. 100% of college-owned or -operated housing units are wired for high-speed Internet access. Wireless service is available via entire campus.

Student Life *Housing:* on-campus residence required through junior year. *Options:* men-only, women-only, disabled students. Campus housing is university owned. Freshman campus housing is guaranteed. *Activities and organizations:* drama/theater group, student-run newspaper, radio station, choral group, marching band, Campus Ministries United, Student Government Association, Dawg Pound, Honors Student Association, International Club. *Campus security:* 24-hour emergency response devices and patrols, student patrols, late-night transport/escort service, controlled dormitory access. *Student services:* personal/psychological counseling.

Athletics Member NCAA. All Division I except football (Division I-AA). *Intercollegiate sports:* baseball M(s), basketball M(s)/W(s), cheerleading M(s)/W(s), cross-country running M(s)/W(s), golf M(s)/W(s), soccer M(s)/W(s), softball W(s), swimming and diving M(s)/W(s), tennis M(s)/W(s), track and field M(s)/W(s), volleyball W(s), wrestling M(s). *Intramural sports:* badminton M/W, baseball M/W, basketball M/W, football M/W, racquetball M/W, soccer M/W, softball M/W, swimming and diving M/W, table tennis M/W, tennis M/W, ultimate Frisbee M/W, volleyball M/W.

Standardized Tests *Required:* SAT or ACT (for admission).

Costs (2012–13) *One-time required fee:* $100. *Comprehensive fee:* $32,580 includes full-time tuition ($24,250), mandatory fees ($390), and room and board ($7940). Full-time tuition and fees vary according to degree level. Part-time tuition: $387 per credit hour. Part-time tuition and fees vary according to course load. *College room only:* $4080. Room and board charges vary according to board plan and housing facility. *Payment plan:* installment. *Waivers:* employees or children of employees.

Financial Aid Of all full-time matriculated undergraduates who enrolled in 2012, 1,394 applied for aid, 1,239 were judged to have need, 269 had their need fully met. 210 Federal Work-Study jobs (averaging $1421). 23 state and other part-time jobs (averaging $1317). In 2012, 256 non-need-based awards were made. *Average percent of need met:* 74%. *Average financial aid package:* $19,032. *Average need-based loan:* $4248. *Average need-based gift aid:* $7091. *Average non-need-based aid:* $9202. *Average indebtedness upon graduation:* $27,261.

Applying *Options:* electronic application. *Application fee:* $40. *Required:* high school transcript, minimum 2.5 GPA, SAT or ACT. *Required for some:* 2 letters of recommendation, interview. *Recommended:* essay or personal statement, 2 letters of recommendation. *Application deadlines:* rolling (freshmen), rolling (out-of-state freshmen), rolling (transfers). *Notification:* continuous (freshmen), continuous (out-of-state freshmen), continuous (transfers).

Freshman Application Contact Mrs. Kristen Setzer, Associate Vice President of Undergraduate Admissions, Gardner-Webb University, PO Box 817, 110 South Main Street, Boiling Springs, NC 28017. *Phone:* 704-406-4491. *Toll-free phone:* 800-253-6472. *Fax:* 704-406-4488. *E-mail:* admissions@gardner-webb.edu.

Website: http://www.gardner-webb.edu/.

Grace College of Divinity

Fayetteville, North Carolina

Admissions Office Contact Grace College of Divinity, 5117 Cliffdale Road, Fayetteville, NC 28314.
Website: http://www.gcdivinity.org/.

Greensboro College

Greensboro, North Carolina

Freshman Application Contact Ms. Colleen Murphy, Vice President for Enrollment Management and Marketing, Greensboro College, 815 West Market Street, Greensboro, NC 27401-1875. *Phone:* 336-272-7102. *Toll-free phone:* 800-346-8226. *Fax:* 336-378-0154. *E-mail:* admissions@greensborocollege.edu.
Website: http://www.greensboro.edu/.

Guilford College

Greensboro, North Carolina

- **Independent** 4-year, founded 1837, affiliated with Society of Friends
- **Suburban** 340-acre campus with easy access to Winston Salem, Raleigh
- **Endowment** $65.9 million
- **Coed** 2,462 undergraduate students, 84% full-time, 58% women, 42% men
- **Moderately difficult** entrance level, 80% of applicants were admitted

Undergraduates 2,056 full-time, 406 part-time. Students come from 43 states and territories; 13 other countries; 52% are from out of state; 25% Black or African American, non-Hispanic/Latino; 5% Hispanic/Latino; 3% Asian, non-Hispanic/Latino; 0.4% American Indian or Alaska Native, non-Hispanic/Latino; 3% Two or more races, non-Hispanic/Latino; 1% Race/ethnicity unknown; 0.9% international; 1% transferred in; 77% live on campus. *Retention:* 71% of full-time freshmen returned.

Freshmen *Admission:* 2,549 applied, 2,040 admitted, 322 enrolled. *Average high school GPA:* 3.23. *Test scores:* SAT critical reading scores over 500: 71%; SAT math scores over 500: 71%; SAT writing scores over 500: 64%; ACT scores over 18: 93%; SAT critical reading scores over 600: 30%; SAT math scores over 600: 24%; SAT writing scores over 600: 27%; ACT scores over 24: 48%; SAT critical reading scores over 700: 5%; SAT math scores over 700: 3%; SAT writing scores over 700: 4%; ACT scores over 30: 7%.

Faculty *Total:* 190, 65% full-time, 77% with terminal degrees. *Student/faculty ratio:* 15:1.

Academics *Calendar:* semesters. *Degree:* certificates and bachelor's. *Special study options:* academic remediation for entering students, accelerated degree program, adult/continuing education programs, advanced placement credit, cooperative education, double majors, English as a second language, honors programs, independent study, internships, off-campus study, part-time degree program, services for LD students, student-designed majors, study abroad, summer session for credit. *Unusual degree programs:* 3-2 engineering with Engineering; Environment Management.

Computers on Campus 275 computers/terminals are available on campus for general student use. Students can access the following: computer help desk, free student e-mail accounts, online (class) grades, online (class) registration, online (class) schedules, network storage. Campuswide network is available. 100% of college-owned or -operated housing units are wired for high-speed Internet access. Wireless service is available via entire campus.

Student Life *Housing:* on-campus residence required through junior year. *Options:* coed, men-only, women-only, cooperative, disabled students. Campus housing is university owned. Freshman campus housing is guaranteed. *Activities and organizations:* drama/theater group, student-run newspaper, radio station, choral group, student government, student radio station, student newspaper, Project Community, African-American Cultural Society. *Campus security:* 24-hour emergency response devices and patrols, student patrols, late-night transport/escort service, controlled dormitory access. *Student services:* health clinic, personal/psychological counseling, women's center.

Athletics Member NCAA. All Division III. *Intercollegiate sports:* baseball M, basketball M/W, cross-country running M/W, football M, golf M, lacrosse M/W, rugby M/W, soccer M/W, softball W, swimming and diving W, tennis M/W, volleyball W. *Intramural sports:* archery M(c)/W(c), badminton M(c)/W(c), basketball M(c), bowling M(c)/W(c), cheerleading W(c), football M(c), rugby M(c)/W(c), soccer M(c)/W(c), softball W(c), table tennis M(c)/W(c), tennis M(c)/W(c), ultimate Frisbee M(c)/W(c), volleyball M(c)/W(c), water polo M(c)/W(c).

Standardized Tests *Recommended:* SAT or ACT (for admission).

Costs (2013–14) *Comprehensive fee:* $41,270 includes full-time tuition ($32,090), mandatory fees ($380), and room and board ($8800). Part-time tuition and fees vary according to course load. *Room and board:* Room and board charges vary according to board plan and housing facility. *Payment plan:* installment. *Waivers:* employees or children of employees.

Financial Aid Of all full-time matriculated undergraduates who enrolled in 2012, 1,781 applied for aid, 1,595 were judged to have need, 74 had their need fully met. 235 Federal Work-Study jobs (averaging $1620). 270 state and other part-time jobs (averaging $1463). In 2012, 198 non-need-based awards were made. *Average financial aid package:* $17,587. *Average need-based loan:* $7240. *Average need-based gift aid:* $18,681. *Average non-need-based aid:* $12,594. *Average indebtedness upon graduation:* $25,025.

Applying *Options:* electronic application, early admission, early action, deferred entrance. *Application fee:* $25. *Required:* essay or personal statement, high school transcript, minimum 2.0 GPA. *Recommended:* minimum 3.0 GPA, 2 letters of recommendation, interview. *Application deadlines:* 2/15 (freshmen), 6/1 (transfers), 1/15 (early action). *Notification:* 4/1 (freshmen), continuous (transfers), 2/15 (early action).

Freshman Application Contact Andrew Strickler, Associate Director of Admissions, Guilford College, 5800 West Friendly Avenue, Greensboro, NC

27410. *Phone:* 336-316-2100. *Toll-free phone:* 800-992-7759. *Fax:* 336-316-2954. *E-mail:* admission@guilford.edu. *Website:* http://www.guilford.edu/.

Heritage Bible College

Dunn, North Carolina

Freshman Application Contact Mrs. Traci Newton, Director of Recruitment and Marketing, Heritage Bible College, PO Box 1628, Dunn, NC 28335-1628. *Phone:* 910-892-3178 Ext. 239. *Toll-free phone:* 800-297-6351. *Fax:* 910-891-1660. *E-mail:* tnewton@heritagebiblecollege.edu. *Website:* http://www.heritagebiblecollege.edu/.

High Point University

High Point, North Carolina

- **Independent United Methodist** comprehensive, founded 1924
- **Suburban** 320-acre campus with easy access to Charlotte
- **Endowment** $36.4 million
- **Coed** 4,070 undergraduate students, 98% full-time, 59% women, 41% men
- **Moderately difficult** entrance level, 64% of applicants were admitted

Undergraduates 3,996 full-time, 74 part-time. Students come from 46 states and territories; 29 other countries; 74% are from out of state; 6% Black or African American, non-Hispanic/Latino; 2% Hispanic/Latino; 1% Asian, non-Hispanic/Latino; 2% American Indian or Alaska Native, non-Hispanic/Latino; 0.7% Two or more races, non-Hispanic/Latino; 5% Race/ethnicity unknown; 0.9% international; 1% transferred in; 93% live on campus. *Retention:* 75% of full-time freshmen returned.

Freshmen *Admission:* 7,663 applied, 4,918 admitted, 1,257 enrolled. *Average high school GPA:* 3.23. *Test scores:* SAT critical reading scores over 500: 72%; SAT math scores over 500: 78%; SAT writing scores over 500: 70%; ACT scores over 18: 97%; SAT critical reading scores over 600: 20%; SAT math scores over 600: 29%; SAT writing scores over 600: 21%; ACT scores over 24: 54%; SAT critical reading scores over 700: 4%; SAT math scores over 700: 4%; SAT writing scores over 700: 3%; ACT scores over 30: 7%.

Faculty *Total:* 338, 68% full-time, 58% with terminal degrees. *Student/faculty ratio:* 15:1.

Academics *Calendar:* semesters. *Degrees:* bachelor's, master's, doctoral, and postbachelor's certificates. *Special study options:* academic remediation for entering students, accelerated degree program, advanced placement credit, cooperative education, double majors, English as a second language, honors programs, independent study, internships, off-campus study, services for LD students, student-designed majors, study abroad, summer session for credit. *ROTC:* Army (c), Air Force (c). *Unusual degree programs:* 3-2 Elementary Education, Strategic Communication.

Computers on Campus 1,100 computers/terminals and 1,100 ports are available on campus for general student use. Students can access the following: campus intranet, computer help desk, free student e-mail accounts, online (class) grades, online (class) registration, online (class) schedules. Campus-wide network is available. 100% of college-owned or -operated housing units are wired for high-speed Internet access. Wireless service is available via entire campus.

Student Life *Housing:* on-campus residence required through sophomore year. *Options:* coed, men-only, women-only, cooperative, disabled students. Campus housing is university owned and leased by the school. Freshman campus housing is guaranteed. *Activities and organizations:* drama/theater group, student-run newspaper, radio and television station, choral group, Student Government, Habitat for Humanity, International Club, Student Activities Board, Honors Club, national fraternities, national sororities. *Campus security:* 24-hour emergency response devices and patrols, student patrols, late-night transport/escort service, controlled dormitory access. *Student services:* health clinic, personal/psychological counseling.

Athletics Member NCAA. All Division I. *Intercollegiate sports:* baseball M(s), basketball M(s)/W(s), cross-country running M(s)/W(s), golf M(s), lacrosse M/W, soccer M(s)/W(s), tennis M(s)/W(s), track and field M(s)/W(s), volleyball W(s). *Intramural sports:* basketball M/W, bowling M/W, football M/W, racquetball M/W, soccer M/W, softball M/W, swimming and diving M/W, table tennis W, tennis M/W, track and field M/W, volleyball M/W, water polo M.

Standardized Tests *Required:* SAT or ACT (for admission).

Costs (2012–13) *Comprehensive fee:* $39,800. Full-time tuition and fees vary according to course load and reciprocity agreements. Part-time tuition: $800 per credit hour. Part-time tuition and fees vary according to course load and reciprocity agreements. *Room and board:* Room and board charges vary according to board plan and housing facility. *Payment plan:* installment. *Waivers:* employees or children of employees.

Financial Aid Of all full-time matriculated undergraduates who enrolled in 2011, 2,404 applied for aid, 1,958 were judged to have need, 196 had their need fully met. 252 Federal Work-Study jobs (averaging $952). In 2011, 632 non-need-based awards were made. *Average percent of need met:* 49%. *Average financial aid package:* $13,054. *Average need-based loan:* $4250. *Average need-based gift aid:* $4958. *Average non-need-based aid:* $6139. *Average indebtedness upon graduation:* $9567.

Applying *Options:* electronic application, early decision, early action, deferred entrance. *Application fee:* $50. *Required:* high school transcript, minimum 2.0 GPA, 2 letters of recommendation. *Recommended:* essay or personal statement, minimum 3.0 GPA, interview. *Application deadlines:* 8/15 (freshmen), 8/15 (transfers), 11/8 (early action). *Early decision deadline:* 11/1. *Notification:* continuous until 8/15 (freshmen), continuous (transfers), 11/23 (early decision), 12/9 (early action).

Freshman Application Contact Mr. Kevin Sellers, Director of Admissions, High Point University, University Station, Montlieu Avenue, High Point, NC 27262-3598. *Phone:* 336-841-9148. *Toll-free phone:* 800-345-6993. *Fax:* 336-888-6382. *E-mail:* jmcilrat@highpoint.edu. *Website:* http://www.highpoint.edu/.

ITT Technical Institute

Cary, North Carolina

- **Proprietary** primarily 2-year, part of ITT Educational Services, Inc.
- **Coed**
- **Minimally difficult** entrance level

Academics *Degrees:* associate and bachelor's.

Freshman Application Contact Director of Recruitment, ITT Technical Institute, 5520 Dillard Drive, Suite 100, Cary, NC 27518. *Phone:* 919-233-2520. *Toll-free phone:* 877-203-5533. *Website:* http://www.itt-tech.edu/.

ITT Technical Institute

Charlotte, North Carolina

- **Proprietary** 4-year, part of ITT Educational Services, Inc.
- **Coed**
- **Minimally difficult** entrance level

Academics *Calendar:* quarters. *Degrees:* associate and bachelor's.

Freshman Application Contact Director of Recruitment, ITT Technical Institute, 10926 David Taylor Drive, Suite 100, Charlotte, NC 28262. *Phone:* 704-548-2300. *Toll-free phone:* 877-243-7685. *Website:* http://www.itt-tech.edu/.

ITT Technical Institute

Charlotte, North Carolina

- **Proprietary** primarily 2-year
- **Coed**
- **Minimally difficult** entrance level

Academics *Degrees:* associate and bachelor's.

Freshman Application Contact Director of Recruitment, ITT Technical Institute, 4135 Southstream Boulevard, Suite 200, Charlotte, NC 28217. *Phone:* 704-423-3100. *Toll-free phone:* 800-488-0173. *Website:* http://www.itt-tech.edu/.

ITT Technical Institute

Durham, North Carolina

- **Proprietary** 4-year
- **Coed**
- **Minimally difficult** entrance level

Academics *Degrees:* associate and bachelor's.

Freshman Application Contact Director of Recruitment, ITT Technical Institute, 3518 Westgate Drive, Suite 150, Durham, NC 27707. *Phone:* 919-401-1400. *Toll-free phone:* 877-452-8662.
Website: http://www.itt-tech.edu/.

ITT Technical Institute
High Point, North Carolina

- **Proprietary** primarily 2-year, founded 2007, part of ITT Educational Services, Inc.
- **Coed**
- **Minimally difficult** entrance level

Academics *Calendar:* quarters. *Degrees:* associate and bachelor's.
Freshman Application Contact Director of Recruitment, ITT Technical Institute, 4050 Piedmont Parkway, Suite 110, High Point, NC 27265. *Phone:* 336-819-5900. *Toll-free phone:* 877-536-5231.
Website: http://www.itt-tech.edu/.

Johnson & Wales University— Charlotte Campus
Charlotte, North Carolina

Freshman Application Contact Joseph Campos, Director of Admissions, Johnson & Wales University—Charlotte Campus, 801 West Trade Street, Charlotte, NC 28202. *Phone:* 980-598-1100. *Toll-free phone:* 866-598-2427. *Fax:* 980-598-1111. *E-mail:* clt@admissions.jwu.edu.
Website: http://www.jwu.edu/charlotte/.

Johnson C. Smith University
Charlotte, North Carolina

- **Independent** 4-year, founded 1867
- **Urban** 100-acre campus with easy access to Atlanta
- **Endowment** $50.3 million
- **Coed** 1,669 undergraduate students, 96% full-time, 61% women, 39% men
- **Moderately difficult** entrance level, 38% of applicants were admitted

Undergraduates 1,606 full-time, 63 part-time. Students come from 34 states and territories; 8 other countries; 48% are from out of state; 74% Black or African American, non-Hispanic/Latino; 5% Hispanic/Latino; 0.4% Asian, non-Hispanic/Latino; 0.1% Native Hawaiian or other Pacific Islander, non-Hispanic/Latino; 0.1% American Indian or Alaska Native, non-Hispanic/Latino; 1% Two or more races, non-Hispanic/Latino; 15% Race/ethnicity unknown; 3% international; 8% transferred in; 61% live on campus. *Retention:* 72% of full-time freshmen returned.
Freshmen *Admission:* 5,064 applied, 1,928 admitted, 386 enrolled. *Average high school GPA:* 3.07. *Test scores:* SAT critical reading scores over 500: 16%; SAT math scores over 500: 20%; ACT scores over 18: 56%; SAT critical reading scores over 600: 3%; SAT math scores over 600: 3%; ACT scores over 24: 4%; SAT critical reading scores over 700: 1%.
Faculty *Total:* 159, 65% full-time, 58% with terminal degrees. *Student/faculty ratio:* 13:1.
Academics *Calendar:* semesters. *Degree:* bachelor's. *Special study options:* adult/continuing education programs, advanced placement credit, cooperative education, double majors, honors programs, independent study, internships, off-campus study, part-time degree program, services for LD students, student-designed majors, study abroad, summer session for credit. *ROTC:* Army (b), Air Force (c).
Computers on Campus 293 computers/terminals are available on campus for general student use. Students can access the following: campus intranet, computer help desk, free student e-mail accounts, online (class) grades, online (class) registration, online (class) schedules. Campuswide network is available. 100% of college-owned or -operated housing units are wired for high-speed Internet access. Wireless service is available via entire campus.
Student Life *Housing:* on-campus residence required for freshman year. *Options:* coed, men-only, women-only. Campus housing is university owned and leased by the school. Freshman campus housing is guaranteed. *Activities and organizations:* drama/theater group, student-run newspaper, choral group, marching band, International Club, Math Club, Karibbean Vybz, Student Orientation Leaders, Unparalleled Production Evolution, national fraternities,

national sororities. *Campus security:* 24-hour emergency response devices and patrols, late-night transport/escort service, controlled dormitory access. *Student services:* health clinic, personal/psychological counseling.
Athletics Member NCAA. All Division II. *Intercollegiate sports:* basketball M(s)/W(s), bowling W(s), cheerleading W(c), cross-country running M(s)/W(s), football M(s), golf M(s), softball W(s), tennis M(s)/W(s), track and field M(s)/W(s), volleyball W(s).
Standardized Tests *Required:* SAT or ACT (for admission).
Costs (2012–13) *Comprehensive fee:* $25,336 includes full-time tuition ($15,466), mandatory fees ($2770), and room and board ($7100). Full-time tuition and fees vary according to course load. Part-time tuition: $418 per credit hour. Part-time tuition and fees vary according to course load. *Required fees:* $292 per term part-time. *College room only:* $4086. Room and board charges vary according to board plan and housing facility. *Payment plan:* installment. *Waivers:* children of alumni and employees or children of employees.
Financial Aid Of all full-time matriculated undergraduates who enrolled in 2012, 1,450 applied for aid, 1,416 were judged to have need, 75 had their need fully met. 287 Federal Work-Study jobs (averaging $2017). In 2012, 115 non-need-based awards were made. *Average percent of need met:* 55%. *Average financial aid package:* $15,437. *Average need-based loan:* $4723. *Average need-based gift aid:* $11,103. *Average non-need-based aid:* $19,783. *Average indebtedness upon graduation:* $32,621.
Applying *Options:* electronic application, early admission, deferred entrance. *Application fee:* $25. *Required:* high school transcript. *Recommended:* essay or personal statement, 2 letters of recommendation. *Notification:* continuous (freshmen), continuous (out-of-state freshmen), continuous (transfers).
Freshman Application Contact Mrs. Catherine Hurd, Dean of Enrollment Services, Johnson C. Smith University, 100 Beatties Ford Road, Charlotte, NC 28216. *Phone:* 704-378-1181. *Toll-free phone:* 800-782-7303. *Fax:* 704-378-1242. *E-mail:* churd@jcsu.edu.
Website: http://www.jcsu.edu/.

Laurel University
High Point, North Carolina

- **Independent interdenominational** comprehensive, founded 1932
- **Urban** 24-acre campus
- **Coed** 278 undergraduate students, 51% full-time, 45% women, 55% men
- **Minimally difficult** entrance level, 39% of applicants were admitted

Undergraduates 142 full-time, 136 part-time. Students come from 17 states and territories; 12% are from out of state; 22% Black or African American, non-Hispanic/Latino; 1% Hispanic/Latino; 0.3% American Indian or Alaska Native, non-Hispanic/Latino; 2% Two or more races, non-Hispanic/Latino; 44% Race/ethnicity unknown; 11% transferred in. *Retention:* 63% of full-time freshmen returned.
Freshmen *Admission:* 161 applied, 63 admitted, 39 enrolled. *Average high school GPA:* 3.1.
Faculty *Total:* 37, 8% full-time, 49% with terminal degrees. *Student/faculty ratio:* 10:1.
Academics *Calendar:* semesters. *Degrees:* certificates, associate, bachelor's, master's, and doctoral. *Special study options:* academic remediation for entering students, adult/continuing education programs, advanced placement credit, distance learning, double majors, independent study, internships, off-campus study, part-time degree program, summer session for credit.
Computers on Campus 7 computers/terminals and 7 ports are available on campus for general student use. Students can access the following: free student e-mail accounts, online (class) grades, online (class) registration, online (class) schedules. 100% of college-owned or -operated housing units are wired for high-speed Internet access. Wireless service is available via classrooms, computer labs, libraries, student centers.
Student Life *Housing options:* men-only, women-only. Campus housing is university owned. *Activities and organizations:* student government, Travel Team, Praise Band.
Standardized Tests *Required for some:* College Board ACCUPLACER Test for English.
Financial Aid Of all full-time matriculated undergraduates who enrolled in 2011, 3 Federal Work-Study jobs (averaging $2500).
Applying *Options:* electronic application, early admission, deferred entrance. *Application fee:* $30. *Required:* high school transcript, 2 letters of recommendation, interview. *Recommended:* minimum 2.0 GPA. *Application deadlines:* 8/1 (freshmen), 8/1 (transfers). *Notification:* 8/10 (freshmen), continuous until 8/10 (transfers).
Freshman Application Contact Jeremy Reese, Admissions Officer, Laurel University, 1215 Eastchester Drive, High Point, NC 27265-3197. *Phone:* 336-

887-3000 Ext. 127. *Toll-free phone:* 855-LaurelU. *E-mail:* admissions@ laureluniversity.edu.
Website: http://www.laureluniversity.edu/.

Lees-McRae College

Banner Elk, North Carolina

- **Independent** 4-year, founded 1900, affiliated with Presbyterian Church (U.S.A.)
- **Rural** 460-acre campus
- **Coed** 837 undergraduate students, 99% full-time, 59% women, 41% men
- **Minimally difficult** entrance level, 68% of applicants were admitted

Undergraduates 830 full-time, 7 part-time. Students come from 39 states and territories; 11 other countries; 32% are from out of state; 2% Black or African American, non-Hispanic/Latino; 0.5% Hispanic/Latino; 0.1% Asian, non-Hispanic/Latino; 0.1% Two or more races, non-Hispanic/Latino; 80% Race/ethnicity unknown; 3% international; 20% transferred in; 63% live on campus. *Retention:* 55% of full-time freshmen returned.
Freshmen *Admission:* 1,266 applied, 855 admitted, 182 enrolled. *Average high school GPA:* 3.25. *Test scores:* SAT critical reading scores over 500: 33%; SAT math scores over 500: 41%; SAT critical reading scores over 600: 9%; SAT math scores over 600: 11%; SAT critical reading scores over 700: 2%; SAT math scores over 700: 1%.
Faculty *Total:* 88, 49% full-time, 38% with terminal degrees. *Student/faculty ratio:* 14:1.
Academics *Calendar:* semesters. *Degree:* bachelor's. *Special study options:* academic remediation for entering students, accelerated degree program, adult/continuing education programs, advanced placement credit, cooperative education, double majors, honors programs, independent study, internships, off-campus study, part-time degree program, services for LD students, study abroad, summer session for credit.
Computers on Campus Students can access the following: computer help desk, free student e-mail accounts, online (class) schedules. 100% of college-owned or -operated housing units are wired for high-speed Internet access.
Student Life *Housing options:* coed, men-only, women-only, disabled students. Campus housing is university owned. Freshman campus housing is guaranteed. *Activities and organizations:* drama/theater group, choral group, Student Government Association, Order of the Tower. *Campus security:* 24-hour patrols. *Student services:* health clinic, personal/psychological counseling.
Athletics Member NCAA. All Division II. *Intercollegiate sports:* basketball M(s)/W(s), cross-country running M(s)/W(s), lacrosse M(s)/W(s), soccer M(s)/W(s), softball W(s), tennis M(s)/W(s), track and field M(s)/W(s), volleyball M(s)/W(s). *Intramural sports:* basketball M/W.
Standardized Tests *Required for some:* SAT or ACT (for admission).
Costs (2012–13) *Comprehensive fee:* $32,950 includes full-time tuition ($23,950), mandatory fees ($500), and room and board ($8500). Full-time tuition and fees vary according to course load, location, and reciprocity agreements. Part-time tuition: $650 per credit hour. Part-time tuition and fees vary according to course load, location, and reciprocity agreements. *Required fees:* $650 per credit hour part-time. *Room and board:* Room and board charges vary according to housing facility. *Payment plan:* installment. *Waivers:* employees or children of employees.
Financial Aid Of all full-time matriculated undergraduates who enrolled in 2012, 658 applied for aid, 629 were judged to have need, 3 had their need fully met. In 2012, 149 non-need-based awards were made. *Average percent of need met:* 75%. *Average financial aid package:* $13,523. *Average need-based loan:* $5000. *Average need-based gift aid:* $8840. *Average non-need-based aid:* $9500.
Applying *Options:* electronic application, early action. *Application fee:* $35. *Required:* high school transcript, minimum 2.0 GPA. *Required for some:* essay or personal statement, interview. *Application deadlines:* rolling (freshmen), rolling (out-of-state freshmen), rolling (transfers). *Notification:* continuous (freshmen), continuous (out-of-state freshmen), continuous (transfers).
Freshman Application Contact Mrs. Ginger Hansen, Lees-McRae College, PO Box 128, Banner Elk, NC 28604. *Phone:* 800-280-4562. *Toll-free phone:* 800-280-4562. *Fax:* 828-898-8707. *E-mail:* admissions@lmc.edu.
Website: http://www.lmc.edu/.

Lenoir-Rhyne University

Hickory, North Carolina

- **Independent Lutheran** comprehensive, founded 1891
- **Small-town** campus
- **Coed**
- **Moderately difficult** entrance level

Faculty *Student/faculty ratio:* 14:1.
Academics *Calendar:* semesters. *Degrees:* bachelor's, master's, and postbachelor's certificates.
Student Life *Campus security:* 24-hour emergency response devices and patrols, late-night transport/escort service, controlled dormitory access.
Athletics Member NCAA. All Division II.
Standardized Tests *Required:* SAT or ACT (for admission).
Costs (2012–13) *Comprehensive fee:* $37,514 includes full-time tuition ($27,718) and room and board ($9796). Part-time tuition: $1100 per credit hour. Part-time tuition and fees vary according to class time.
Financial Aid *Of all full-time matriculated undergraduates who enrolled in 2011,* 1,371 applied for aid, 1,280 were judged to have need, 334 had their need fully met. *In 2011,* 146 non-need-based awards were made. *Average percent of need met:* 82. *Average financial aid package:* $26,212. *Average need-based loan:* $4338. *Average need-based gift aid:* $21,803. *Average non-need-based aid:* $10,887. *Average indebtedness upon graduation:* $23,600.
Applying *Options:* early admission, early action, deferred entrance. *Application fee:* $35. *Required:* high school transcript, minimum 2.5 GPA. *Recommended:* interview. .
Freshman Application Contact Lenoir-Rhyne University, 625 7th Avenue NE, Hickory, NC 28601. *Phone:* 828-328-7300. *Toll-free phone:* 800-277-5721.
Website: http://www.lr.edu/.

Livingstone College

Salisbury, North Carolina

Freshman Application Contact Livingstone College, 701 West Monroe Street, Salifbury, NC 28144. *Phone:* 704-216-6001. *Toll-free phone:* 800-835-3435. *Fax:* 704-216-6215. *E-mail:* admissions@livingstone.edu.
Website: http://www.livingstone.edu/.

Mars Hill College

Mars Hill, North Carolina

- **Independent Baptist** 4-year, founded 1856
- **Small-town** 194-acre campus
- **Endowment** $42.0 million
- **Coed** 1,351 undergraduate students, 93% full-time, 49% women, 51% men
- **Moderately difficult** entrance level, 69% of applicants were admitted

Undergraduates 1,255 full-time, 96 part-time. Students come from 34 states and territories; 15 other countries; 29% are from out of state; 19% Black or African American, non-Hispanic/Latino; 2% Hispanic/Latino; 0.4% Asian, non-Hispanic/Latino; 2% American Indian or Alaska Native, non-Hispanic/Latino; 3% Race/ethnicity unknown; 2% international; 8% transferred in; 68% live on campus. *Retention:* 55% of full-time freshmen returned.
Freshmen *Admission:* 2,970 applied, 2,039 admitted, 437 enrolled. *Average high school GPA:* 3.22. *Test scores:* SAT critical reading scores over 500: 31%; SAT math scores over 500: 38%; ACT scores over 18: 63%; SAT critical reading scores over 600: 8%; SAT math scores over 600: 8%; ACT scores over 24: 21%; SAT critical reading scores over 700: 1%; ACT scores over 30: 1%.
Faculty *Total:* 184, 46% full-time. *Student/faculty ratio:* 11:1.
Academics *Calendar:* semesters. *Degrees:* bachelor's and master's. *Special study options:* academic remediation for entering students, accelerated degree program, adult/continuing education programs, advanced placement credit, cooperative education, double majors, English as a second language, honors programs, independent study, internships, part-time degree program, services for LD students, student-designed majors, study abroad, summer session for credit.
Computers on Campus 188 computers/terminals are available on campus for general student use. Students can access the following: campus intranet, computer help desk, free student e-mail accounts, online (class) grades, online (class) registration, online (class) schedules. Campuswide network is available.

100% of college-owned or -operated housing units are wired for high-speed Internet access. Wireless service is available via entire campus.

Student Life *Housing:* on-campus residence required through sophomore year. *Options:* men-only, women-only. Campus housing is university owned. Freshman campus housing is guaranteed. *Activities and organizations:* drama/theater group, choral group, marching band, Student Government Association, Fellowship of Christian Athletes, Christian Student Movement, Fraternity/Sorority, Athletic Trainers Association, national fraternities, national sororities. *Campus security:* 24-hour emergency response devices and patrols, late-night transport/escort service, controlled dormitory access. *Student services:* health clinic, personal/psychological counseling.

Athletics Member NCAA. All Division II. *Intercollegiate sports:* baseball M(s), basketball M(s)/W(s), cheerleading M(s)/W(s), cross-country running M(s)/W(s), football M(s), golf M(s)/W(s), lacrosse M(s), soccer M(s)/W(s), softball W(s), swimming and diving M(s)/W(s), tennis M(s)/W(s), track and field M(s)/W(s), volleyball W(s). *Intramural sports:* basketball M/W, football M/W, rock climbing M/W, skiing (downhill) M(c)/W(c), soccer M/W, track and field M(c)/W(c), ultimate Frisbee M/W, volleyball M/W, water polo M/W, weight lifting M/W.

Standardized Tests *Required:* SAT or ACT (for admission).

Costs (2013–14) *Comprehensive fee:* $34,824 includes full-time tuition ($23,152), mandatory fees ($2484), and room and board ($9188). Part-time tuition: $295 per credit. Part-time tuition and fees vary according to course load. *College room only:* $4948. *Waivers:* employees or children of employees.

Financial Aid Of all full-time matriculated undergraduates who enrolled in 2010, 2,256 applied for aid, 1,007 were judged to have need, 164 had their need fully met. 252 Federal Work-Study jobs (averaging $1354). In 2010, 141 non-need-based awards were made. *Average percent of need met:* 73%. *Average financial aid package:* $17,195. *Average need-based loan:* $3988. *Average need-based gift aid:* $13,790. *Average non-need-based aid:* $8631. *Average indebtedness upon graduation:* $27,775.

Applying *Options:* electronic application, early admission, deferred entrance. *Application fee:* $25. *Required:* high school transcript, minimum 2.0 GPA. *Required for some:* interview. *Recommended:* essay or personal statement, minimum 3.0 GPA. *Application deadlines:* rolling (freshmen), rolling (transfers).

Freshman Application Contact Dr. Craig Goforth, Dean of Admissions and Financial Aid, Mars Hill College, PO Box 370, Mars Hill, NC 28754. *Phone:* 828-689-1201. *Toll-free phone:* 866-MHC-4-YOU. *Fax:* 828-689-1473. *E-mail:* ehoffmeyer@mhc.edu. *Website:* http://www.mhc.edu/.

Meredith College

Raleigh, North Carolina

- **Independent** comprehensive, founded 1891
- **Urban** 225-acre campus
- **Endowment** $80.4 million
- **Undergraduate: women only; graduate: coed**
- **Moderately difficult** entrance level

Faculty *Student/faculty ratio:* 11:1.

Academics *Calendar:* semesters. *Degrees:* bachelor's, master's, and postbachelor's certificates.

Student Life *Campus security:* 24-hour emergency response devices and patrols, late-night transport/escort service, controlled dormitory access, self-defense instruction.

Athletics Member NCAA. All Division III.

Standardized Tests *Required:* SAT or ACT (for admission). *Required for some:* SAT Subject Tests (for admission).

Costs (2012–13) *Comprehensive fee:* $37,454 includes full-time tuition ($29,106) and room and board ($8348). Full-time tuition and fees vary according to course load. Part-time tuition and fees vary according to course load.

Financial Aid *Of all full-time matriculated undergraduates who enrolled in 2011,* 1,332 applied for aid, 1,174 were judged to have need, 139 had their need fully met. *In 2011,* 129 non-need-based awards were made. *Average percent of need met:* 70. *Average financial aid package:* $19,850. *Average need-based loan:* $4270. *Average need-based gift aid:* $15,938. *Average non-need-based aid:* $8058. *Average indebtedness upon graduation:* $34,549.

Applying *Options:* electronic application, early admission, early decision, deferred entrance. *Application fee:* $40. *Required:* high school transcript, minimum 2.0 GPA, 2 letters of recommendation. *Required for some:* essay or personal statement, interview.

Freshman Application Contact Shery Boyles, Director of Admissions, Meredith College, 3800 Hillsborough Street, Raleigh, NC 27807-5298. *Phone:*

919-760-8026. *Toll-free phone:* 800-MEREDITH. *Fax:* 919-760-2298. *E-mail:* admissions@meredith.edu. *Website:* http://www.meredith.edu/.

Methodist University

Fayetteville, North Carolina

Freshman Application Contact Mr. Jamie Legg, Director of Admissions, Methodist University, 5400 Ramset Street, Fayetteville, NC 28311-1496. *Phone:* 910-630-7027. *Toll-free phone:* 800-488-7110 Ext. 7027. *Fax:* 910-630-7285. *E-mail:* admissions@methodist.edu. *Website:* http://www.methodist.edu/.

Mid-Atlantic Christian University

Elizabeth City, North Carolina

- **Independent Christian** 4-year, founded 1948
- **Small-town** 19-acre campus with easy access to Norfolk
- **Endowment** $2.3 million
- **Coed** 165 undergraduate students, 76% full-time, 49% women, 51% men
- **Minimally difficult** entrance level, 41% of applicants were admitted

Undergraduates 126 full-time, 39 part-time. Students come from 17 states and territories; 1 other country; 37% are from out of state; 35% Black or African American, non-Hispanic/Latino; 4% Hispanic/Latino; 2% Race/ethnicity unknown; 15% transferred in; 55% live on campus. *Retention:* 57% of full-time freshmen returned.

Freshmen *Admission:* 168 applied, 69 admitted, 37 enrolled. *Average high school GPA:* 2.69. *Test scores:* SAT critical reading scores over 500: 36%; SAT math scores over 500: 28%; ACT scores over 18: 43%; SAT critical reading scores over 600: 4%; SAT math scores over 600: 8%; ACT scores over 24: 11%.

Faculty *Total:* 43, 14% full-time, 28% with terminal degrees. *Student/faculty ratio:* 10:1.

Academics *Calendar:* semesters. *Degrees:* certificates, associate, and bachelor's. *Special study options:* academic remediation for entering students, adult/continuing education programs, advanced placement credit, distance learning, double majors, internships, part-time degree program, summer session for credit. *ROTC:* Army (c).

Computers on Campus 24 computers/terminals are available on campus for general student use. Students can access the following: free student e-mail accounts, online (class) grades, online (class) registration, online (class) schedules. Campuswide network is available. 100% of college-owned or -operated housing units are wired for high-speed Internet access. Wireless service is available via entire campus.

Student Life *Housing:* on-campus residence required through senior year. *Options:* men-only, women-only. Campus housing is university owned. Freshman campus housing is guaranteed. *Activities and organizations:* Student Advisory Council, Counseling Club. *Campus security:* 24-hour emergency response devices, controlled dormitory access. *Student services:* personal/psychological counseling.

Athletics Member USCAA. *Intercollegiate sports:* basketball M/W, golf M/W, volleyball W. *Intramural sports:* basketball M/W, golf M/W, soccer M/W, softball M/W, table tennis M/W, tennis M/W, volleyball M/W.

Standardized Tests *Required:* SAT or ACT (for admission).

Costs (2013–14) *Comprehensive fee:* $19,940 includes full-time tuition ($12,160) and room and board ($7780). Full-time tuition and fees vary according to program. Part-time tuition: $380 per credit hour. Part-time tuition and fees vary according to program. *Room and board:* Room and board charges vary according to housing facility. *Payment plan:* deferred payment. *Waivers:* children of alumni, senior citizens, and employees or children of employees.

Financial Aid Of all full-time matriculated undergraduates who enrolled in 2011, 148 applied for aid, 144 were judged to have need, 4 had their need fully met. 12 Federal Work-Study jobs (averaging $824). In 2011, 6 non-need-based awards were made. *Average percent of need met:* 52%. *Average financial aid package:* $9387. *Average need-based loan:* $4158. *Average need-based gift aid:* $5701. *Average non-need-based aid:* $3064. *Average indebtedness upon graduation:* $37,108.

Applying *Options:* electronic application, early admission, deferred entrance. *Application fee:* $50. *Required:* essay or personal statement, high school transcript, minimum 2.0 GPA, 1 letter of recommendation, reference from church or character reference. *Required for some:* interview. *Application deadlines:* 8/1 (freshmen), 8/1 (transfers). *Notification:* continuous (freshmen), continuous (transfers).

Freshman Application Contact Mrs. Julie A. Fields, Mid-Atlantic Christian University, 715 North Poindexter Street, Elizabeth City, NC 27909-4054. *Phone:* 252-334-2028. *Toll-free phone:* 866-996-MACU. *Fax:* 252-334-2064. *E-mail:* julie.fields@macuniversity.edu.
Website: http://www.macuniversity.edu/.

Montreat College

Montreat, North Carolina

- **Independent** comprehensive, founded 1916, affiliated with Presbyterian Church (U.S.A.)
- **Small-town** 112-acre campus
- **Coed** 766 undergraduate students, 55% full-time, 54% women, 46% men
- **Moderately difficult** entrance level, 51% of applicants were admitted

Undergraduates 422 full-time, 344 part-time. 25% are from out of state; 21% Black or African American, non-Hispanic/Latino; 3% Hispanic/Latino; 0.5% Asian, non-Hispanic/Latino; 1% American Indian or Alaska Native, non-Hispanic/Latino; 2% Two or more races, non-Hispanic/Latino; 15% Race/ethnicity unknown; 3% international; 6% transferred in; 72% live on campus. *Retention:* 50% of full-time freshmen returned.
Freshmen *Admission:* 854 applied, 438 admitted, 102 enrolled. *Average high school GPA:* 3.16. *Test scores:* SAT critical reading scores over 500: 54%; SAT math scores over 500: 51%; ACT scores over 18: 72%; SAT critical reading scores over 600: 20%; SAT math scores over 600: 15%; ACT scores over 24: 40%; SAT critical reading scores over 700: 1%; SAT math scores over 700: 1%; ACT scores over 30: 2%.
Faculty *Total:* 90, 29% full-time, 50% with terminal degrees. *Student/faculty ratio:* 11:1.
Academics *Calendar:* semesters. *Degrees:* certificates, associate, bachelor's, and master's. *Special study options:* adult/continuing education programs, part-time degree program.
Computers on Campus Students can access the following: campus intranet, computer help desk, free student e-mail accounts, online (class) grades, online (class) schedules. Campuswide network is available. 100% of college-owned or -operated housing units are wired for high-speed Internet access. Wireless service is available via entire campus.
Student Life *Housing:* on-campus residence required through sophomore year. *Options:* men-only, women-only. Campus housing is university owned. Freshman campus housing is guaranteed. *Activities and organizations:* drama/theater group, student-run newspaper, choral group. *Campus security:* 24-hour emergency response devices and patrols, controlled dormitory access. *Student services:* health clinic, personal/psychological counseling.
Athletics Member NAIA. *Intercollegiate sports:* baseball M(s), basketball M(s)/W(s), cross-country running M(s)/W(s), golf M(s), soccer M(s)/W(s), softball W(s), tennis M(s)/W(s), track and field M(s)/W(s), volleyball W(s). *Intramural sports:* basketball M/W, football M, softball M/W, table tennis M/W, tennis M/W, ultimate Frisbee M/W, volleyball M/W.
Standardized Tests *Required:* SAT or ACT (for admission).
Costs (2013–14) *Comprehensive fee:* $30,278 includes full-time tuition ($22,684), mandatory fees ($100), and room and board ($7494). Part-time tuition: $600 per credit hour. *Room and board:* Room and board charges vary according to board plan.
Financial Aid Of all full-time matriculated undergraduates who enrolled in 2012, 468 applied for aid, 425 were judged to have need, 75 had their need fully met. 50 Federal Work-Study jobs (averaging $1820). 30 state and other part-time jobs (averaging $870). In 2012, 61 non-need-based awards were made. *Average percent of need met:* 74%. *Average financial aid package:* $17,314. *Average need-based loan:* $4113. *Average need-based gift aid:* $12,932. *Average non-need-based aid:* $7232. *Average indebtedness upon graduation:* $18,147.
Applying *Options:* early admission, deferred entrance. *Required:* essay or personal statement, high school transcript, minimum 2.8 GPA. *Required for some:* 1 letter of recommendation, interview. *Application deadlines:* 8/15 (freshmen), 8/15 (out-of-state freshmen), rolling (transfers). *Notification:* continuous (freshmen), continuous (out-of-state freshmen), continuous (transfers).
Freshman Application Contact Mr. Joey Higgins, Director of Admissions, Montreat College, PO Box 1267, Montreat, NC 28757. *Phone:* 828-669-8012 Ext. 3782. *Toll-free phone:* 800-622-6968. *Fax:* 828-669-0120. *E-mail:* admissions@montreat.edu.
Website: http://www.montreat.edu/.

Mount Olive College

Mount Olive, North Carolina

Freshman Application Contact Mount Olive College, 634 Henderson Street, Mount Olive, NC 28365. *Phone:* 919-658-2502 Ext. 3009. *Toll-free phone:* 800-653-0854.
Website: http://www.moc.edu/.

New Life Theological Seminary

Charlotte, North Carolina

Freshman Application Contact New Life Theological Seminary, PO Box 790106, Charlotte, NC 28206-7901. *Phone:* 704-334-6882 Ext. 08.
Website: http://www.nlts.org/.

North Carolina Agricultural and Technical State University

Greensboro, North Carolina

- **State-supported** university, founded 1891, part of University of North Carolina System
- **Suburban** 200-acre campus with easy access to Charlotte
- **Coed**
- **Moderately difficult** entrance level

Academics *Calendar:* semesters. *Degrees:* bachelor's, master's, and doctoral.
Student Life *Campus security:* 24-hour emergency response devices and patrols, late-night transport/escort service, controlled dormitory access.
Athletics Member NCAA. All Division I.
Standardized Tests *Required:* SAT or ACT (for admission).
Costs (2012–13) *Tuition:* state resident $5058 full-time; nonresident $15,657 full-time. Full-time tuition and fees vary according to course load and student level. Part-time tuition and fees vary according to course load and student level. *Room and board:* $7349. Room and board charges vary according to board plan and housing facility.
Financial Aid *Of all full-time matriculated undergraduates who enrolled in 2010,* 7,701 applied for aid, 6,954 were judged to have need, 365 had their need fully met. *In 2010,* 307 non-need-based awards were made. *Average percent of need met:* 82. *Average financial aid package:* $13,583. *Average need-based loan:* $3939. *Average need-based gift aid:* $5741. *Average non-need-based aid:* $4610. *Average indebtedness upon graduation:* $20,389.
Applying *Options:* early admission, deferred entrance. *Application fee:* $45. *Required:* high school transcript, minimum 2.0 GPA.
Freshman Application Contact Ms. Keyana Scales, Director of Admissions, North Carolina Agricultural and Technical State University, North Carolina Agricultural & Technical State University (Webb Hall), 1601 East Market Street, Greensboro, NC 27411. *Phone:* 336-334-7946. *Toll-free phone:* 800-443-8964. *Fax:* 336-334-7478. *E-mail:* uadmit@ncat.edu.
Website: http://www.ncat.edu/.

North Carolina Central University

Durham, North Carolina

- **State-supported** comprehensive, founded 1910, part of University of North Carolina System
- **Urban** 115-acre campus with easy access to Raleigh
- **Endowment** $20.0 million
- **Coed** 6,658 undergraduate students, 84% full-time, 67% women, 33% men
- **Minimally difficult** entrance level, 50% of applicants were admitted

Undergraduates 5,602 full-time, 1,056 part-time. Students come from 40 states and territories; 30 other countries; 10% are from out of state; 84% Black or African American, non-Hispanic/Latino; 2% Hispanic/Latino; 1% Asian, non-Hispanic/Latino; 0.3% American Indian or Alaska Native, non-Hispanic/Latino; 2% Two or more races, non-Hispanic/Latino; 4% Race/ethnicity unknown; 0.5% international; 7% transferred in; 40% live on campus. *Retention:* 72% of full-time freshmen returned.

Freshmen *Admission:* 8,886 applied, 4,472 admitted, 1,407 enrolled. *Average high school GPA:* 2.99. *Test scores:* SAT critical reading scores over 500: 12%; SAT math scores over 500: 15%; SAT writing scores over 500: 9%; ACT scores over 18: 39%; SAT critical reading scores over 600: 2%; SAT math scores over 600: 1%; SAT writing scores over 600: 1%; ACT scores over 24: 8%.

Faculty *Total:* 598, 75% full-time, 66% with terminal degrees. *Student/faculty ratio:* 15:1.

Academics *Calendar:* semesters. *Degrees:* bachelor's, master's, and doctoral. *Special study options:* academic remediation for entering students, accelerated degree program, adult/continuing education programs, advanced placement credit, cooperative education, distance learning, double majors, English as a second language, external degree program, honors programs, independent study, internships, off-campus study, part-time degree program, services for LD students, study abroad, summer session for credit. *ROTC:* Army (b), Air Force (b).

Computers on Campus 1,262 computers/terminals and 3,700 ports are available on campus for general student use. Students can access the following: campus intranet, computer help desk, free student e-mail accounts, online (class) grades, online (class) registration, online (class) schedules. Campuswide network is available. 100% of college-owned or -operated housing units are wired for high-speed Internet access. Wireless service is available via entire campus.

Student Life *Housing options:* coed. Campus housing is university owned and leased by the school. Freshman applicants given priority for college housing. *Activities and organizations:* drama/theater group, student-run newspaper, choral group, marching band, national fraternities, national sororities. *Campus security:* 24-hour emergency response devices and patrols, student patrols, late-night transport/escort service, controlled dormitory access. *Student services:* health clinic, personal/psychological counseling, women's center.

Athletics Member NCAA, NAIA. All NCAA Division I. *Intercollegiate sports:* baseball M(s), basketball M(s)/W(s), bowling W(s), cross-country running M(s)/W(s), football M(s), golf M(s), softball W(s), tennis M(s)/W(s), track and field M(s)/W(s), volleyball W(s). *Intramural sports:* basketball M/W, football M, golf M, soccer M, volleyball W.

Standardized Tests *Required:* SAT or ACT (for admission).

Costs (2012–13) *Tuition:* state resident $3244 full-time; nonresident $13,817 full-time. Part-time tuition and fees vary according to course load. *Room and board:* $9923; room only: $6791. Room and board charges vary according to board plan, housing facility, and location. *Payment plan:* installment. *Waivers:* employees or children of employees.

Financial Aid Of all full-time matriculated undergraduates who enrolled in 2011, 5,049 applied for aid, 4,771 were judged to have need, 199 had their need fully met. In 2011, 40 non-need-based awards were made. *Average percent of need met:* 61%. *Average financial aid package:* $11,956. *Average need-based loan:* $4034. *Average need-based gift aid:* $6213. *Average non-need-based aid:* $4446.

Applying *Options:* electronic application, deferred entrance. *Application fee:* $40. *Required:* high school transcript, minimum 2.3 GPA, University of North Carolina System minimum course requirements. *Application deadlines:* 8/1 (freshmen), 8/1 (transfers). *Notification:* continuous until 10/15 (freshmen), continuous until 10/15 (transfers).

Freshman Application Contact Mr. Anthony Brooks, Undergraduate Director of Admissions, North Carolina Central University, 1801 Fayetteville Street, McDougald House, Durham, NC 27707. *Phone:* 919-530-6298. *Toll-free phone:* 877-667-7533. *Fax:* 919-530-7625. *E-mail:* admissions@nccu.edu.

Website: http://www.nccu.edu/.

North Carolina State University

Raleigh, North Carolina

- **State-supported** university, founded 1887, part of University of North Carolina System
- **Urban** 2110-acre campus
- **Endowment** $635.3 million
- **Coed** 24,833 undergraduate students, 88% full-time, 44% women, 56% men
- **Very difficult** entrance level, 50% of applicants were admitted

Undergraduates 21,821 full-time, 3,012 part-time. Students come from 52 states and territories; 67 other countries; 10% are from out of state; 8% Black or African American, non-Hispanic/Latino; 4% Hispanic/Latino; 5% Asian, non-Hispanic/Latino; 0.5% American Indian or Alaska Native, non-Hispanic/Latino; 2% Two or more races, non-Hispanic/Latino; 3% Race/ethnicity unknown; 2% international; 5% transferred in; 27% live on campus. *Retention:* 92% of full-time freshmen returned.

Freshmen *Admission:* 20,435 applied, 10,137 admitted, 4,398 enrolled. *Average high school GPA:* 4.37. *Test scores:* SAT critical reading scores over 500: 93%; SAT math scores over 500: 97%; SAT writing scores over 500: 87%; ACT scores over 18: 99%; SAT critical reading scores over 600: 45%; SAT math scores over 600: 70%; SAT writing scores over 600: 35%; ACT scores over 24: 82%; SAT critical reading scores over 700: 8%; SAT math scores over 700: 16%; SAT writing scores over 700: 5%; ACT scores over 30: 21%.

Faculty *Total:* 1,821, 91% full-time, 86% with terminal degrees. *Student/faculty ratio:* 18:1.

Academics *Calendar:* semesters. *Degrees:* certificates, associate, bachelor's, master's, doctoral, post-master's, and postbachelor's certificates. *Special study options:* academic remediation for entering students, accelerated degree program, adult/continuing education programs, advanced placement credit, cooperative education, distance learning, double majors, English as a second language, honors programs, independent study, internships, off-campus study, part-time degree program, services for LD students, student-designed majors, study abroad, summer session for credit. *ROTC:* Army (b), Navy (b), Air Force (b).

Computers on Campus 3,024 computers/terminals are available on campus for general student use. Students can access the following: campus intranet, computer help desk, free student e-mail accounts, online (class) grades, online (class) registration, online (class) schedules, course materials, online homework submission, online testing/quizzes, financial aid/cashier's office account balances, wiki space, blogging service, Web space, online storage space, on-site OS and virus removal, online/hybrid courses. Campuswide network is available. 100% of college-owned or -operated housing units are wired for high-speed Internet access. Wireless service is available via classrooms, computer centers, computer labs, dorm rooms, learning centers, libraries, student centers.

Student Life *Housing options:* coed, men-only, women-only, disabled students. Campus housing is university owned. Freshman applicants given priority for college housing. *Activities and organizations:* drama/theater group, student-run newspaper, radio and television station, choral group, marching band, Student Wolfpack Club, Inter-Fraternity Council, Panhellenic Association, Campus Crusade for Christ, Mechanical and Aerospace Engineering Graduate Student Association, national fraternities, national sororities. *Campus security:* 24-hour emergency response devices and patrols, student patrols, late-night transport/escort service, controlled dormitory access. *Student services:* health clinic, personal/psychological counseling, women's center, legal services.

Athletics Member NCAA. All Division I except football (Division I-A), riflery (Division II). *Intercollegiate sports:* badminton M(c)/W(c), baseball M(s), basketball M(s)/W(s), bowling M(c)/W(c), cheerleading M(s)/W(s), crew M(c)/W(c), cross-country running M(s)/W(s), equestrian sports M(c)/W(c), fencing M/W, field hockey M(c)/W(c), golf M(s)/W(s), gymnastics W(s), ice hockey M(c)/W(c), lacrosse M(c)/W(c), racquetball M(c)/W(c), riflery M(s)/W(s), rugby M(c)/W(c), sailing M(c)/W(c), skiing (downhill) M(c)/W(c), soccer M(s)/W(s), softball W(s), swimming and diving M(s)/W(s), table tennis M(c)/W(c), tennis M(s)/W(s), track and field M(s)/W(s), ultimate Frisbee M(c)/W(c), volleyball M(c)/W(c), water polo M(c)/W(c), wrestling M(s). *Intramural sports:* badminton M/W, baseball M, basketball M/W, bowling M/W, cheerleading W(c), crew M/W, cross-country running M/W, equestrian sports M/W, fencing M/W, field hockey W, football M/W, golf M/W, gymnastics W, ice hockey M, lacrosse M/W, racquetball M/W, rugby M/W, sailing M/W, skiing (downhill) M/W, soccer M/W, softball M/W, swimming and diving M/W, table tennis M/W, tennis M/W, track and field M/W, volleyball M/W, water polo M/W, wrestling M.

Standardized Tests *Required:* SAT or ACT (for admission). *Recommended:* SAT Subject Tests (for admission).

Costs (2012–13) *Tuition:* state resident $5748 full-time; nonresident $18,913 full-time. Full-time tuition and fees vary according to degree level, location, and program. Part-time tuition and fees vary according to course load, degree level, location, and program. *Required fees:* $2040 full-time. *Room and board:* $8414; room only: $5434. Room and board charges vary according to board plan and housing facility. *Payment plan:* installment. *Waivers:* employees or children of employees.

Financial Aid Of all full-time matriculated undergraduates who enrolled in 2012, 14,206 applied for aid, 10,853 were judged to have need, 3,466 had their need fully met. In 2012, 863 non-need-based awards were made. *Average percent of need met:* 84%. *Average financial aid package:* $12,652. *Average need-based loan:* $3907. *Average need-based gift aid:* $9360. *Average non-need-based aid:* $5587. *Average indebtedness upon graduation:* $22,626.

Applying *Options:* electronic application, early action, deferred entrance. *Application fee:* $70. *Required:* high school transcript. *Required for some:* interview. *Recommended:* essay or personal statement. *Application deadlines:* 2/1 (freshmen), 4/1 (transfers). *Notification:* continuous (freshmen), continuous (transfers).

Freshman Application Contact Mr. Thomas Griffin, Director of Undergraduate Admissions, North Carolina State University, Box 7103,

Raleigh, NC 27695. *Phone:* 919-515-2434. *Fax:* 919-515-5039. *E-mail:* undergrad_admissions@ncsu.edu.
Website: http://www.ncsu.edu/.

North Carolina Wesleyan College
Rocky Mount, North Carolina

- **Independent** 4-year, founded 1956, affiliated with United Methodist Church
- **Suburban** 200-acre campus
- **Endowment** $9.4 million
- **Coed** 1,522 undergraduate students, 76% full-time, 61% women, 39% men
- **Moderately difficult** entrance level, 47% of applicants were admitted

Undergraduates 1,154 full-time, 368 part-time. Students come from 24 states and territories; 18 other countries; 12% are from out of state; 52% Black or African American, non-Hispanic/Latino; 2% Hispanic/Latino; 0.3% Asian, non-Hispanic/Latino; 0.1% Native Hawaiian or other Pacific Islander, non-Hispanic/Latino; 1% American Indian or Alaska Native, non-Hispanic/Latino; 1% Two or more races, non-Hispanic/Latino; 10% Race/ethnicity unknown; 3% international; 3% transferred in; 41% live on campus. *Retention:* 56% of full-time freshmen returned.
Freshmen *Admission:* 1,634 applied, 764 admitted, 222 enrolled. *Average high school GPA:* 2.94. *Test scores:* SAT critical reading scores over 500: 17%; SAT math scores over 500: 27%; ACT scores over 18: 46%; SAT critical reading scores over 600: 4%; SAT math scores over 600: 4%; ACT scores over 24: 5%.
Faculty *Total:* 213, 21% full-time. *Student/faculty ratio:* 15:1.
Academics *Calendar:* semesters. *Degrees:* bachelor's (also offers adult part-time degree program with significant enrollment not reflected in profile). *Special study options:* academic remediation for entering students, accelerated degree program, adult/continuing education programs, advanced placement credit, cooperative education, distance learning, double majors, honors programs, independent study, internships, part-time degree program, services for LD students, summer session for credit. *ROTC:* Army (b).
Computers on Campus 199 computers/terminals are available on campus for general student use. Students can access the following: campus intranet, computer help desk, free student e-mail accounts, online (class) grades, online (class) schedules. Campuswide network is available.
Student Life *Housing:* on-campus residence required through sophomore year. *Options:* coed, men-only, women-only, disabled students. Campus housing is university owned. Freshman campus housing is guaranteed. *Activities and organizations:* drama/theater group, student-run newspaper, choral group, marching band, Refuge Campus Ministry, NCWC Cheerleaders, Voices of Triumph, Campus Crusade for Christ, Visions of Beauty, national fraternities, national sororities. *Campus security:* 24-hour emergency response devices and patrols, late-night transport/escort service, controlled dormitory access. *Student services:* health clinic, personal/psychological counseling.
Athletics Member NCAA. All Division III. *Intercollegiate sports:* baseball M, basketball M/W, football M, golf M, lacrosse W, soccer M/W, softball W, tennis M/W, volleyball W. *Intramural sports:* basketball M/W, football M/W, lacrosse M/W, softball M/W, table tennis M/W, tennis M/W, volleyball M/W.
Standardized Tests *Required:* SAT or ACT (for admission).
Costs (2013–14) *Comprehensive fee:* $35,660 includes full-time tuition ($26,481), mandatory fees ($500), and room and board ($8679). Full-time tuition and fees vary according to location. Part-time tuition and fees vary according to course load and location. *College room only:* $4159. Room and board charges vary according to housing facility. *Payment plan:* installment. *Waivers:* employees or children of employees.
Financial Aid Of all full-time matriculated undergraduates who enrolled in 2008, 956 applied for aid, 788 were judged to have need, 360 had their need fully met. 323 Federal Work-Study jobs (averaging $1438). 67 state and other part-time jobs (averaging $565). In 2008, 46 non-need-based awards were made. *Average percent of need met:* 70%. *Average financial aid package:* $12,524. *Average need-based loan:* $3898. *Average need-based gift aid:* $6696. *Average non-need-based aid:* $7876. *Average indebtedness upon graduation:* $7269.
Applying *Options:* electronic application. *Application fee:* $45. *Required:* high school transcript. *Required for some:* essay or personal statement, interview. *Recommended:* minimum 2.0 GPA, 2 letters of recommendation, interview. *Application deadlines:* rolling (freshmen), 7/15 (transfers). *Notification:* continuous (freshmen), continuous (transfers).
Freshman Application Contact Ms. Heather Johnson, Associate Director of Admissions, North Carolina Wesleyan College, 3400 North Wesleyan

Boulevard, Rocky Mount, NC 27804. *Phone:* 252-985-5200. *Toll-free phone:* 800-488-6292. *Fax:* 252-985-5295. *E-mail:* hjohnson@ncwc.edu.
Website: http://www.ncwc.edu/.

Pfeiffer University
Misenheimer, North Carolina

Freshman Application Contact Ms. Diane Martin, Associate Director of Admissions, Pfeiffer University, PO Box 960, Highway 52 North, Misenheimer, NC 28109. *Phone:* 704-463-3052. *Toll-free phone:* 800-338-2060. *Fax:* 704-463-1363. *E-mail:* admiss@pfeiffer.edu.
Website: http://www.pfeiffer.edu/.

Piedmont International University
Winston-Salem, North Carolina

- **Independent Baptist** comprehensive, founded 1947
- **Urban** 12-acre campus
- **Coed**
- **Noncompetitive** entrance level

Academics *Calendar:* semesters. *Degrees:* certificates, associate, bachelor's, master's, and doctoral.
Student Life *Campus security:* 24-hour emergency response devices, student patrols, late-night transport/escort service, controlled dormitory access, security guards on duty from dusk until dawn.
Athletics Member NCCAA.
Standardized Tests *Required:* SAT or ACT (for admission).
Costs (2012–13) *Comprehensive fee:* $19,605 includes full-time tuition ($12,340), mandatory fees ($855), and room and board ($6410). Part-time tuition and fees vary according to course load.
Financial Aid *Financial aid deadline:* 8/31.
Applying *Options:* electronic application, early admission, early action, deferred entrance. *Application fee:* $55. *Required:* essay or personal statement, high school transcript, 2 letters of recommendation, medical history, proof of immunization. *Recommended:* minimum 2.0 GPA, interview.
Freshman Application Contact Ms. Samantha Stevenson, Undergraduate Admissions Counselor, Piedmont International University, 420 South Broad Street, Winston-Salem, NC 27101. *Phone:* 336-714-7963. *Toll-free phone:* 800-937-5097. *Fax:* 336-725-5522. *E-mail:* stevensons@piedmontU.edu.
Website: http://www.pbc.edu/.

Queens University of Charlotte
Charlotte, North Carolina

- **Independent Presbyterian** comprehensive, founded 1857
- **Suburban** 30-acre campus
- **Endowment** $84.0 million
- **Coed** 1,869 undergraduate students, 78% full-time, 74% women, 26% men
- **Moderately difficult** entrance level, 53% of applicants were admitted

Undergraduates 1,450 full-time, 419 part-time. Students come from 30 states and territories; 19 other countries; 40% are from out of state; 19% Black or African American, non-Hispanic/Latino; 7% Hispanic/Latino; 3% Asian, non-Hispanic/Latino; 0.6% American Indian or Alaska Native, non-Hispanic/Latino; 3% Two or more races, non-Hispanic/Latino; 7% Race/ethnicity unknown; 1% international; 9% transferred in; 80% live on campus. *Retention:* 69% of full-time freshmen returned.
Freshmen *Admission:* 3,472 applied, 1,831 admitted, 359 enrolled. *Average high school GPA:* 3.57. *Test scores:* SAT critical reading scores over 500: 65%; SAT math scores over 500: 62%; SAT writing scores over 500: 57%; ACT scores over 18: 94%; SAT critical reading scores over 600: 23%; SAT math scores over 600: 20%; SAT writing scores over 600: 18%; ACT scores over 24: 42%; SAT critical reading scores over 700: 3%; SAT math scores over 700: 1%; SAT writing scores over 700: 2%; ACT scores over 30: 2%.
Faculty *Total:* 254, 49% full-time, 49% with terminal degrees. *Student/faculty ratio:* 12:1.
Academics *Calendar:* semesters. *Degrees:* bachelor's, master's, and postbachelor's certificates. *Special study options:* adult/continuing education programs, advanced placement credit, double majors, honors programs, independent

study, internships, off-campus study, part-time degree program, study abroad, summer session for credit. *ROTC:* Army (c), Air Force (c).

Computers on Campus 125 computers/terminals are available on campus for general student use. Students can access the following: campus intranet, computer help desk, free student e-mail accounts, online (class) grades, online (class) registration, online (class) schedules. Campuswide network is available. 100% of college-owned or -operated housing units are wired for high-speed Internet access. Wireless service is available via entire campus.

Student Life *Housing:* on-campus residence required through junior year. *Options:* coed, disabled students. Campus housing is university owned. Freshman campus housing is guaranteed. *Activities and organizations:* drama/theater group, student-run newspaper, choral group, Senate, College Union Board, Royal Ambassadors, Students for Black Awareness, International Club, national fraternities, national sororities. *Campus security:* 24-hour emergency response devices and patrols, late-night transport/escort service, controlled dormitory access, Emergency Alert System. *Student services:* health clinic, personal/psychological counseling.

Athletics Member NCAA. All Division II. *Intercollegiate sports:* basketball M(s)/W(s), cheerleading M(s)/W(s), cross-country running M(s)/W(s), golf M(s)/W(s), lacrosse M(s)/W(s), soccer M(s)/W(s), softball W(s), swimming and diving M(s)/W(s), tennis M(s)/W(s), volleyball W(s). *Intramural sports:* basketball M/W, soccer M/W, softball M/W, tennis M/W, volleyball M/W.

Standardized Tests *Required:* SAT or ACT (for admission).

Costs (2012–13) *Comprehensive fee:* $36,988 includes full-time tuition ($27,576) and room and board ($9412). *College room only:* $5514. Room and board charges vary according to board plan and housing facility. *Payment plan:* installment. *Waivers:* employees or children of employees.

Financial Aid Of all full-time matriculated undergraduates who enrolled in 2011, 1,111 applied for aid, 966 were judged to have need, 217 had their need fully met. In 2011, 360 non-need-based awards were made. *Average percent of need met:* 67%. *Average financial aid package:* $18,055. *Average need-based loan:* $4193. *Average need-based gift aid:* $14,332. *Average non-need-based aid:* $9773. *Average indebtedness upon graduation:* $27,832.

Applying *Options:* electronic application, deferred entrance. *Application fee:* $40. *Required:* high school transcript, minimum 2.5 GPA. *Required for some:* essay or personal statement, letters of recommendation. *Recommended:* interview. *Application deadlines:* rolling (freshmen), rolling (out-of-state freshmen), rolling (transfers). *Notification:* continuous (freshmen), continuous (out-of-state freshmen), continuous (transfers).

Freshman Application Contact Queens University of Charlotte, 1900 Selwyn Avenue, Harris Welcome Center—MSC 1428, Charlotte, NC 28274. *Phone:* 704-337-2212. *Toll-free phone:* 800-849-0202. *Fax:* 704-337-2403. *E-mail:* admissions@queens.edu. *Website:* http://www.queens.edu/.

St. Andrews University
Laurinburg, North Carolina

- **Independent Presbyterian** comprehensive, founded 1958
- **Small-town** 600-acre campus
- **Coed** 460 undergraduate students, 95% full-time, 55% women, 45% men
- **Moderately difficult** entrance level, 69% of applicants were admitted

Undergraduates 438 full-time, 22 part-time. 51% are from out of state; 19% Black or African American, non-Hispanic/Latino; 1% Hispanic/Latino; 1% Asian, non-Hispanic/Latino; 1% American Indian or Alaska Native, non-Hispanic/Latino; 1% Race/ethnicity unknown; 7% international; 16% transferred in; 85% live on campus. *Retention:* 64% of full-time freshmen returned.

Freshmen *Admission:* 826 applied, 566 admitted, 146 enrolled. *Average high school GPA:* 3. *Test scores:* SAT critical reading scores over 500: 33%; SAT math scores over 500: 34%; SAT critical reading scores over 600: 5%; SAT math scores over 600: 5%; SAT critical reading scores over 700: 1%.

Faculty *Total:* 53, 51% full-time, 58% with terminal degrees. *Student/faculty ratio:* 13:1.

Academics *Calendar:* semesters. *Degrees:* bachelor's and master's. *Special study options:* adult/continuing education programs, part-time degree program. *Unusual degree programs:* 3-2 engineering with North Carolina State University and St. Andrews University.

Computers on Campus Students can access the following: campus intranet, computer help desk, free student e-mail accounts. Campuswide network is available. Wireless service is available via classrooms, libraries, student centers.

Student Life *Housing:* on-campus residence required through senior year. *Options:* coed, men-only, women-only. Campus housing is university owned. *Campus security:* 24-hour emergency response devices and patrols, late-night transport/escort service.

Athletics Member NCAA, NAIA. All NCAA Division II. *Intercollegiate sports:* baseball M(s), basketball M(s)/W(s), cross-country running M(s)/W(s), equestrian sports M(s)/W(s), golf M(s)/W(s), lacrosse M(s)/W(s), soccer M(s)/W(s), softball W(s), wrestling M. *Intramural sports:* basketball M/W, football M/W, rugby M(c)/W(c), softball M/W, table tennis M/W, volleyball M/W.

Standardized Tests *Required:* SAT or ACT (for admission).

Costs (2012–13) *Comprehensive fee:* $32,050 includes full-time tuition ($22,674) and room and board ($9376). Full-time tuition and fees vary according to course load and location. Part-time tuition and fees vary according to location. *Room and board:* Room and board charges vary according to housing facility. *Payment plan:* installment. *Waivers:* adult students, senior citizens, and employees or children of employees.

Financial Aid Of all full-time matriculated undergraduates who enrolled in 2012, 446 applied for aid, 410 were judged to have need, 48 had their need fully met. In 2012, 88 non-need-based awards were made. *Average percent of need met:* 67%. *Average financial aid package:* $17,947. *Average need-based loan:* $4307. *Average need-based gift aid:* $14,093. *Average non-need-based aid:* $5661. *Average indebtedness upon graduation:* $31,684.

Applying *Options:* electronic application, deferred entrance. *Application fee:* $30. *Required:* high school transcript. *Required for some:* essay or personal statement, interview. *Recommended:* minimum 2.0 GPA. *Application deadlines:* rolling (freshmen), rolling (transfers). *Notification:* continuous (freshmen), continuous (transfers).

Freshman Application Contact Erin Balduf, Director of Admissions, St. Andrews University, 1700 Dogwood Mile, Laurinburg, NC 28352. *Phone:* 910-277-5555. *Toll-free phone:* 800-763-0198. *Fax:* 910-277-5087. *E-mail:* admission@sapc.edu. *Website:* http://www.sapc.edu/.

Saint Augustine's College
Raleigh, North Carolina

- **Independent Episcopal** 4-year, founded 1867
- **Urban** 122-acre campus
- **Endowment** $17.7 million
- **Coed**
- **Moderately difficult** entrance level

Faculty *Student/faculty ratio:* 14:1.

Academics *Calendar:* semesters. *Degree:* bachelor's.

Student Life *Campus security:* 24-hour emergency response devices and patrols, RAVE—Emergency Notification System.

Athletics Member NCAA. All Division II.

Standardized Tests *Required:* SAT or ACT (for admission).

Costs (2012–13) *Comprehensive fee:* $24,722 includes full-time tuition ($12,364), mandatory fees ($4796), and room and board ($7562). Full-time tuition and fees vary according to course load. Part-time tuition: $515 per credit hour. Part-time tuition and fees vary according to course load. *Required fees:* $200 per credit hour part-time. *College room only:* $3128. Room and board charges vary according to housing facility.

Financial Aid *Of all full-time matriculated undergraduates who enrolled in 2011,* 1,432 applied for aid, 1,355 were judged to have need, 40 had their need fully met. 327 Federal Work-Study jobs (averaging $2500). 4 state and other part-time jobs (averaging $2500). *In 2011,* 34 non-need-based awards were made. *Average percent of need met:* 96. *Average financial aid package:* $3850. *Average need-based loan:* $2167. *Average need-based gift aid:* $2069. *Average non-need-based aid:* $2028. *Average indebtedness upon graduation:* $12,652.

Applying *Options:* electronic application, deferred entrance. *Application fee:* $25. *Required:* high school transcript, minimum 2.0 GPA, 2 letters of recommendation, medical history, social security card, background check. *Required for some:* essay or personal statement, interview. *Recommended:* minimum 2.5 GPA.

Freshman Application Contact Mr. Jorge E. Sousa, Director of Admissions, Saint Augustine's College, 1315 Oakwood Avenue, Raleigh, NC 27610-2298. *Phone:* 919-516-4012. *Toll-free phone:* 800-948-1126. *Fax:* 919-516-5804. *E-mail:* jesousa@st-aug.edu. *Website:* http://www.st-aug.edu/.

Salem College
Winston-Salem, North Carolina

Freshman Application Contact Dean Katherine Knapp Watts, Dean of Admissions and Financial Aid, Salem College, Single Sisters House, 601 South Church Street, Winston-Salem, NC 27101. *Phone:* 336-721-2621. *Toll-*

free phone: 800-327-2536. *Fax:* 336-917-5572. *E-mail:* admissions@
salem.edu.
Website: http://www.salem.edu/.

Shaw University

Raleigh, North Carolina

- **Independent Baptist** comprehensive, founded 1865
- **Urban** 30-acre campus
- **Coed** 2,031 undergraduate students, 93% full-time, 58% women, 42% men
- **Minimally difficult** entrance level, 54% of applicants were admitted

Undergraduates 1,879 full-time, 152 part-time. Students come from 30 states and territories; 16 other countries; 32% are from out of state; 86% Black or African American, non-Hispanic/Latino; 0.4% Hispanic/Latino; 0.0% Asian, non-Hispanic/Latino; 0.0% American Indian or Alaska Native, non-Hispanic/Latino; 11% Race/ethnicity unknown; 2% international; 8% transferred in; 40% live on campus.
Freshmen *Admission:* 6,207 applied, 3,382 admitted, 507 enrolled. *Average high school GPA:* 2.31.
Faculty *Total:* 187, 58% full-time, 59% with terminal degrees. *Student/faculty ratio:* 15:1.
Academics *Calendar:* semesters. *Degrees:* associate, bachelor's, and master's. *Special study options:* academic remediation for entering students, accelerated degree program, adult/continuing education programs, advanced placement credit, distance learning, double majors, honors programs, independent study, internships, off-campus study, part-time degree program, services for LD students, student-designed majors, study abroad, summer session for credit. *ROTC:* Army (c).
Computers on Campus Students can access the following: computer help desk, free student e-mail accounts, online (class) grades, online (class) registration, online (class) schedules. Campuswide network is available. Wireless service is available via classrooms, computer centers, computer labs, learning centers, libraries, student centers.
Student Life *Housing:* on-campus residence required for freshman year. *Options:* men-only, women-only. Campus housing is university owned. *Activities and organizations:* drama/theater group, student-run newspaper, radio station, choral group, marching band, Student Government Association, choir, University band, Shaw Players, academic clubs, national fraternities, national sororities. *Campus security:* 24-hour emergency response devices and patrols, late-night transport/escort service, 24-hour electronic surveillance cameras. *Student services:* health clinic, personal/psychological counseling.
Athletics Member NCAA. All Division II. *Intercollegiate sports:* baseball M(s), basketball M(s)/W(s), bowling W(s), cross-country running M(s)/W(s), football M(s), softball W(s), tennis M(s)/W(s), track and field M(s)/W(s), volleyball W(s). *Intramural sports:* basketball M/W, football M, tennis M/W, volleyball M/W.
Standardized Tests *Recommended:* SAT or ACT (for admission).
Financial Aid Of all full-time matriculated undergraduates who enrolled in 2005, 2,197 applied for aid, 2,068 were judged to have need, 201 had their need fully met. 347 Federal Work-Study jobs (averaging $1120). In 2005, 117 non-need-based awards were made. *Average percent of need met:* 63%. *Average financial aid package:* $8992. *Average need-based loan:* $3394. *Average need-based gift aid:* $5898. *Average non-need-based aid:* $9333. *Average indebtedness upon graduation:* $15,982. *Financial aid deadline:* 6/1.
Applying *Options:* electronic application, early admission, deferred entrance. *Application fee:* $25. *Required:* high school transcript, minimum 2.0 GPA. *Application deadline:* 7/30 (freshmen). *Notification:* continuous (freshmen).
Freshman Application Contact Mr. Sherlock McDougald, Director of Admissions and Recruitment, Shaw University, 118 East South Street, Raleigh, NC 27601-2399. *Phone:* 919-546-8423. *Toll-free phone:* 800-214-6683. *Fax:* 919-546-8271. *E-mail:* sherlock@shawu.edu.
Website: http://www.shawu.edu/.

Shepherds Theological Seminary

Cary, North Carolina

Admissions Office Contact Shepherds Theological Seminary, 6051 Tyron Road, Cary, NC 27518.
Website: http://shepherds.edu/.

South College–Asheville

Asheville, North Carolina

Freshman Application Contact Director of Admissions, South College–Asheville, 1567 Patton Avenue, Asheville, NC 28806. *Phone:* 828-277-5521. *Fax:* 828-277-6151.
Website: http://www.southcollegenc.edu/.

Southeastern Baptist Theological Seminary

Wake Forest, North Carolina

- **Independent Southern Baptist** comprehensive, founded 1950
- **Small-town** 300-acre campus with easy access to Raleigh
- **Coed**
- **Minimally difficult** entrance level

Faculty *Student/faculty ratio:* 17:1.
Academics *Calendar:* semesters. *Degrees:* certificates, associate, bachelor's, and master's.
Student Life *Campus security:* 24-hour emergency response devices and patrols, late-night transport/escort service.
Standardized Tests *Required:* SAT or ACT (for admission).
Applying *Application fee:* $25. *Required:* essay or personal statement, high school transcript. *Required for some:* interview.
Freshman Application Contact Mrs. Audrey Greeson, Admissions Counselor, Southeastern Baptist Theological Seminary, PO Box 1889, Wake Forest, NC 27588-1889. *Phone:* 800-284-6317. *Toll-free phone:* 800-284-6317.
Website: http://www.sebts.edu/.

South University

High Point, North Carolina

Admissions Office Contact South University, 3975 Premier Drive, High Point, NC 27265. *Toll-free phone:* 855-268-2187.
Website: http://www.southuniversity.edu/high-point.aspx.

Strayer University—Greensboro Campus

Greensboro, North Carolina

Freshman Application Contact Strayer University—Greensboro Campus, 4900 Koger Boulevard, Suite 400, Greensboro, NC 27407.
Website: http://www.strayer.edu/campus/greensboro.

Strayer University—Huntersville Campus

Huntersville, North Carolina

Freshman Application Contact Strayer University—Huntersville Campus, 13620 Reese Boulevard, Suite 130, Huntersville, NC 28078.
Website: http://www.strayer.edu/campus/huntersville/.

Strayer University—North Charlotte Campus

Concord, North Carolina

Freshman Application Contact Strayer University—North Charlotte Campus, 7870 Commons Park Circle NW, Concord, NC 28027.
Website: http://www.strayer.edu/campus/north-charlotte.

Strayer University—North Raleigh Campus

Raleigh, North Carolina

Freshman Application Contact Strayer University—North Raleigh Campus, 8701 Wadford Drive, Raleigh, NC 27616.
Website: http://www.strayer.edu/campus/north-raleigh.

Strayer University—RTP Campus

Morrisville, North Carolina

Freshman Application Contact Strayer University—RTP Campus, 4 Copley Parkway, Morrisville, NC 27560.
Website: http://www.strayer.edu/campus/rtp.

Strayer University—South Charlotte Campus

Charlotte, North Carolina

Freshman Application Contact Strayer University—South Charlotte Campus, 9101 Kings Parade Boulevard, Suite 200, Charlotte, NC 28273.
Website: http://www.strayer.edu/campus/south-charlotte.

Strayer University—South Raleigh Campus

Raleigh, North Carolina

Freshman Application Contact Strayer University—South Raleigh Campus, 3421 Olympia Drive, Raleigh, NC 27603.
Website: http://www.strayer.edu/campus/south-raleigh.

University of North Carolina at Asheville

Asheville, North Carolina

- **State-supported** comprehensive, founded 1927, part of University of North Carolina System
- **Urban** 365-acre campus
- **Endowment** $28.6 million
- **Coed** 3,693 undergraduate students, 83% full-time, 58% women, 42% men
- **Moderately difficult** entrance level, 64% of applicants were admitted

Undergraduates 3,054 full-time, 639 part-time. Students come from 40 states and territories; 23 other countries; 12% are from out of state; 3% Black or African American, non-Hispanic/Latino; 4% Hispanic/Latino; 1% Asian, non-Hispanic/Latino; 0.1% Native Hawaiian or other Pacific Islander, non-Hispanic/Latino; 0.1% American Indian or Alaska Native, non-Hispanic/Latino; 3% Two or more races, non-Hispanic/Latino; 3% Race/ethnicity unknown; 1% international; 9% transferred in; 38% live on campus. *Retention:* 78% of full-time freshmen returned.
Freshmen *Admission:* 3,018 applied, 1,926 admitted, 553 enrolled. *Average high school GPA:* 4.05. *Test scores:* SAT critical reading scores over 500: 93%; SAT math scores over 500: 96%; SAT writing scores over 500: 85%; ACT scores over 18: 99%; SAT critical reading scores over 600: 53%; SAT math scores over 600: 50%; SAT writing scores over 600: 38%; ACT scores over 24: 74%; SAT critical reading scores over 700: 11%; SAT math scores over 700: 7%; SAT writing scores over 700: 6%; ACT scores over 30: 8%.
Faculty *Total:* 270, 79% full-time, 76% with terminal degrees. *Student/faculty ratio:* 14:1.
Academics *Calendar:* semesters. *Degrees:* bachelor's, master's, and postbachelor's certificates. *Special study options:* academic remediation for entering students, adult/continuing education programs, advanced placement credit, distance learning, double majors, honors programs, independent study, intern-

ships, off-campus study, part-time degree program, services for LD students, student-designed majors, study abroad, summer session for credit. *Unusual degree programs:* 3-2 chemistry and textile chemistry with North Carolina State University.
Computers on Campus 477 computers/terminals are available on campus for general student use. Students can access the following: computer help desk, free student e-mail accounts, online (class) grades, online (class) registration, online (class) schedules. Campuswide network is available. 100% of college-owned or -operated housing units are wired for high-speed Internet access. Wireless service is available via entire campus.
Student Life *Housing:* on-campus residence required for freshman year. *Options:* coed, men-only, women-only, disabled students. Campus housing is university owned. Freshman campus housing is guaranteed. *Activities and organizations:* drama/theater group, student-run newspaper, radio station, choral group, Student Government Association, Underdog Productions, Resident Student Association, Black Student Association, Active Students for a Healthy Environment, national fraternities, national sororities. *Campus security:* 24-hour emergency response devices and patrols, late-night transport/escort service, controlled dormitory access. *Student services:* health clinic, personal/psychological counseling, women's center.
Athletics Member NCAA. All Division I. *Intercollegiate sports:* baseball M(s), basketball M(s)/W(s), cheerleading M/W, cross-country running M(s)/W(s), soccer M(s)/W(s), swimming and diving W(s), tennis M(s)/W(s), track and field M(s)/W(s), volleyball W(s). *Intramural sports:* archery M(c)/W(c), badminton M/W, basketball M/W, equestrian sports M(c)/W(c), fencing M(c)/W(c), football M/W, racquetball M/W, rugby M(c)/W(c), soccer M/W, ultimate Frisbee M(c)/W(c), volleyball M/W, water polo M/W.
Standardized Tests *Required:* SAT or ACT (for admission).
Costs (2012–13) *Tuition:* state resident $3476 full-time; nonresident $17,292 full-time. Full-time tuition and fees vary according to course load. Part-time tuition and fees vary according to course load. *Required fees:* $2390 full-time. *Room and board:* $7584; room only: $4348. Room and board charges vary according to housing facility. *Payment plan:* installment. *Waivers:* employees or children of employees.
Financial Aid Of all full-time matriculated undergraduates who enrolled in 2011, 2,292 applied for aid, 1,688 were judged to have need, 618 had their need fully met. 46 Federal Work-Study jobs (averaging $2354). In 2011, 124 non-need-based awards were made. *Average percent of need met:* 79%. *Average financial aid package:* $11,490. *Average need-based loan:* $4483. *Average need-based gift aid:* $6096. *Average non-need-based aid:* $2910. *Average indebtedness upon graduation:* $17,696.
Applying *Options:* electronic application, early action, deferred entrance. *Application fee:* $50. *Required:* essay or personal statement, high school transcript, 1 letter of recommendation, minimum course requirement. *Required for some:* interview. *Application deadlines:* 2/15 (freshmen), 2/15 (out-of-state freshmen), 4/15 (transfers), 11/15 (early action). *Notification:* continuous until 12/15 (freshmen), continuous (transfers), 12/15 (early action).
Freshman Application Contact Ms. Shannon Earle, Director of Admissions, University of North Carolina at Asheville, Brown Hall, CPO # 1320, Asheville, NC 28804-8510. *Phone:* 828-251-6481. *Toll-free phone:* 800-531-9842. *Fax:* 828-251-6482. *E-mail:* admissions@unca.edu.
Website: http://www.unca.edu/.

The University of North Carolina at Chapel Hill

Chapel Hill, North Carolina

- **State-supported** university, founded 1789, part of University of North Carolina System
- **Suburban** 729-acre campus with easy access to Raleigh-Durham
- **Endowment** $2.2 billion
- **Coed** 18,503 undergraduate students, 95% full-time, 58% women, 42% men
- **Very difficult** entrance level, 28% of applicants were admitted

Undergraduates 17,562 full-time, 941 part-time. Students come from 50 states and territories; 94 other countries; 18% are from out of state; 9% Black or African American, non-Hispanic/Latino; 8% Hispanic/Latino; 8% Asian, non-Hispanic/Latino; 0.6% American Indian or Alaska Native, non-Hispanic/Latino; 3% Two or more races, non-Hispanic/Latino; 2% Race/ethnicity unknown; 3% international; 5% transferred in; 46% live on campus. *Retention:* 97% of full-time freshmen returned.
Freshmen *Admission:* 28,437 applied, 7,847 admitted, 3,915 enrolled. *Average high school GPA:* 4.53. *Test scores:* SAT critical reading scores over 500: 96%; SAT math scores over 500: 98%; SAT writing scores over 500: 96%; ACT scores over 18: 100%; SAT critical reading scores over 600: 74%; SAT

math scores over 600: 82%; SAT writing scores over 600: 70%; ACT scores over 24: 92%; SAT critical reading scores over 700: 25%; SAT math scores over 700: 32%; SAT writing scores over 700: 24%; ACT scores over 30: 49%.
Faculty *Total:* 1,936, 86% full-time, 87% with terminal degrees. *Student/faculty ratio:* 14:1.
Academics *Calendar:* semesters. *Degrees:* certificates, bachelor's, master's, doctoral, post-master's, and postbachelor's certificates. *Special study options:* advanced placement credit, distance learning, double majors, English as a second language, honors programs, independent study, internships, off-campus study, part-time degree program, services for LD students, student-designed majors, study abroad, summer session for credit. *ROTC:* Army (b), Navy (b), Air Force (b).
Computers on Campus 867 computers/terminals and 9,999 ports are available on campus for general student use. Students can access the following: computer help desk, free student e-mail accounts, online (class) grades, online (class) registration, online (class) schedules. Campuswide network is available. 100% of college-owned or -operated housing units are wired for high-speed Internet access. Wireless service is available via entire campus.
Student Life *Housing:* on-campus residence required for freshman year. *Options:* coed, men-only, women-only, disabled students. Campus housing is university owned. Freshman campus housing is guaranteed. *Activities and organizations:* drama/theater group, student-run newspaper, radio and television station, choral group, marching band, Campus Y, Carolina Athletic Association, Campus Crusade for Christ (Cornerstone), Residence Hall Association, Black Student Movement, national fraternities, national sororities. *Campus security:* 24-hour emergency response devices and patrols, late-night transport/escort service, controlled dormitory access, crime prevention initiatives (date rape, violence, larceny, etc.), campus-wide emergency alert system, cell phone/GPS security options. *Student services:* health clinic, personal/psychological counseling, women's center, legal services.
Athletics Member NCAA. All Division I except football (Division I-A). *Intercollegiate sports:* baseball M(s), basketball M(s)/W(s), cheerleading W(c), crew M(c)/W(s), cross-country running M(s)/W(s), equestrian sports M(c)/W(c), fencing M/W, field hockey M(c)/W(s), golf M(s)/W(s), gymnastics M(c)/W(s), ice hockey M(c), lacrosse M(s)/W(s), racquetball M(c)/W(c), rugby M(c)/W(c), sailing M(c)/W(c), skiing (downhill) M(c)/W(c), soccer M(s)/W(s), softball W(s), swimming and diving M(s)/W(s), tennis M(s)/W(s), track and field M(s)/W(s), ultimate Frisbee M(c)/W(c), volleyball M(c)/W(s), water polo M(c)/W(c), wrestling M(s). *Intramural sports:* badminton M/W, baseball M(c), basketball M(c)/W(c), cross-country running M(c)/W(c), field hockey W(c), football M(c), golf M(c)/W(c), gymnastics W(c), lacrosse M(c)/W(c), racquetball M/W, soccer M(c)/W(c), softball M/W(c), swimming and diving M(c)/W(c), table tennis M/W, tennis M(c)/W(c), track and field M(c)/W(c), ultimate Frisbee M/W, volleyball M/W(c), water polo M/W, wrestling M(c).
Standardized Tests *Required:* SAT or ACT (for admission).
Costs (2012–13) *Tuition:* state resident $5823 full-time; nonresident $26,575 full-time. Full-time tuition and fees vary according to program. Part-time tuition and fees vary according to course load and program. *Required fees:* $1867 full-time. *Room and board:* $9734; room only: $5630. Room and board charges vary according to board plan, housing facility, and location. *Payment plan:* installment. *Waivers:* employees or children of employees.
Financial Aid Of all full-time matriculated undergraduates who enrolled in 2011, 9,941 applied for aid, 7,393 were judged to have need, 5,980 had their need fully met. 1,800 Federal Work-Study jobs (averaging $1849). In 2011, 702 non-need-based awards were made. *Average percent of need met:* 100%. *Average financial aid package:* $15,983. *Average need-based loan:* $4529. *Average need-based gift aid:* $13,222. *Average non-need-based aid:* $6249. *Average indebtedness upon graduation:* $16,983.
Applying *Options:* electronic application, early action, deferred entrance. *Application fee:* $80. *Required:* essay or personal statement, high school transcript, 1 letter of recommendation, counselor's statement. *Application deadlines:* 1/7 (freshmen), 2/15 (transfers), 11/3 (early action). *Notification:* 3/20 (freshmen), 4/30 (transfers), 1/30 (early action).
Freshman Application Contact The University of North Carolina at Chapel Hill, Chapel Hill, NC 27599. *Phone:* 919-966-3621.
Website: http://www.unc.edu/.

The University of North Carolina at Charlotte
Charlotte, North Carolina

- **State-supported** university, founded 1946, part of University of North Carolina System
- **Suburban** 1000-acre campus with easy access to Charlotte, NC
- **Endowment** $140.2 million
- **Coed** 21,179 undergraduate students, 85% full-time, 49% women, 51% men
- **Moderately difficult** entrance level, 80% of applicants were admitted

Undergraduates 18,039 full-time, 3,140 part-time. Students come from 46 states and territories; 136 other countries; 7% are from out of state; 17% Black or African American, non-Hispanic/Latino; 7% Hispanic/Latino; 5% Asian, non-Hispanic/Latino; 0.1% Native Hawaiian or other Pacific Islander, non-Hispanic/Latino; 0.5% American Indian or Alaska Native, non-Hispanic/Latino; 3% Two or more races, non-Hispanic/Latino; 4% Race/ethnicity unknown; 2% international; 12% transferred in; 25% live on campus. *Retention:* 77% of full-time freshmen returned.
Freshmen *Admission:* 5,087 applied, 4,046 admitted, 3,541 enrolled. *Average high school GPA:* 3.71. *Test scores:* SAT critical reading scores over 500: 64%; SAT math scores over 500: 79%; SAT writing scores over 500: 56%; ACT scores over 18: 95%; SAT critical reading scores over 600: 14%; SAT math scores over 600: 26%; SAT writing scores over 600: 10%; ACT scores over 24: 37%; SAT critical reading scores over 700: 1%; SAT math scores over 700: 3%; SAT writing scores over 700: 1%; ACT scores over 30: 3%.
Faculty *Total:* 1,412, 72% full-time, 69% with terminal degrees. *Student/faculty ratio:* 19:1.
Academics *Calendar:* semesters. *Degrees:* bachelor's, master's, doctoral, post-master's, and postbachelor's certificates. *Special study options:* accelerated degree program, adult/continuing education programs, advanced placement credit, cooperative education, distance learning, double majors, English as a second language, freshman honors college, honors programs, independent study, internships, off-campus study, part-time degree program, services for LD students, study abroad, summer session for credit. *ROTC:* Army (b), Air Force (b).
Computers on Campus 1,500 computers/terminals are available on campus for general student use. Students can access the following: computer help desk, free student e-mail accounts, online (class) grades, online (class) registration, online (class) schedules. Campuswide network is available. 100% of college-owned or -operated housing units are wired for high-speed Internet access. Wireless service is available via classrooms, computer centers, computer labs, learning centers, libraries, student centers.
Student Life *Housing options:* coed, men-only, women-only, disabled students. Campus housing is university owned. *Activities and organizations:* drama/theater group, student-run newspaper, radio and television station, choral group, Student Government Association, Student Alumni Ambassadors, Black Student Union, 49er Social and Ballroom Dance, Feminist Student Union, national fraternities, national sororities. *Campus security:* 24-hour emergency response devices and patrols, late-night transport/escort service, controlled dormitory access. *Student services:* health clinic, personal/psychological counseling.
Athletics Member NCAA. All Division I. *Intercollegiate sports:* baseball M(s), basketball M(s)/W(s), cheerleading M/W, cross-country running M(s)/W(s), football M, golf M(s), soccer M(s)/W(s), softball W(s), tennis M(s)/W(s), track and field M(s)/W(s), volleyball W(s). *Intramural sports:* archery M(c)/W(c), badminton M(c)/W(c), baseball M(c)/W(c), basketball M/W, bowling M(c)/W(c), fencing M(c)/W(c), football M/W, golf M/W, ice hockey M(c)/W(c), lacrosse M(c)/W(c), racquetball M(c)/W(c), rock climbing M/W, rugby M(c)/W(c), soccer M(c)/W(c), softball M(c)/W(c), swimming and diving M(c)/W(c), table tennis M/W, tennis M(c)/W(c), track and field M/W, ultimate Frisbee M(c)/W(c), volleyball M(c)/W(c), water polo M/W, wrestling M(c)/W(c).
Standardized Tests *Required:* SAT or ACT (for admission).
Costs (2012–13) *Tuition:* state resident $3453 full-time; nonresident $15,982 full-time. Full-time tuition and fees vary according to course load and program. Part-time tuition and fees vary according to course load and program. *Required fees:* $2420 full-time. *Room and board:* $8130; room only: $4480. Room and board charges vary according to board plan and housing facility. *Payment plan:* installment. *Waivers:* senior citizens and employees or children of employees.
Financial Aid Of all full-time matriculated undergraduates who enrolled in 2010, 11,301 applied for aid, 8,557 were judged to have need, 1,493 had their need fully met. In 2010, 263 non-need-based awards were made. *Average percent of need met:* 71%. *Average financial aid package:* $9203. *Average need-*

based loan: $4000. *Average need-based gift aid:* $6234. *Average non-need-based aid:* $2190. *Average indebtedness upon graduation:* $17,472.

Applying *Options:* electronic application, early admission, early action. *Application fee:* $60. *Required:* high school transcript, minimum 2.0 GPA, medical history, no criminal record. *Required for some:* interview. *Application deadlines:* 7/1 (freshmen), 7/1 (out-of-state freshmen), 7/1 (transfers), 10/15 (early action). *Notification:* continuous (freshmen), continuous (out-of-state freshmen), continuous (transfers), 12/15 (early action).

Freshman Application Contact Ms. Claire Kirby, Director of Admissions, The University of North Carolina at Charlotte, 9201 University City Boulevard, 1st Floor, Cato Hall, Charlotte, NC 28223-0001. *Phone:* 704-687-5507. *Fax:* 704-687-6483. *E-mail:* unccadm@uncc.edu. *Website:* http://www.uncc.edu/.

The University of North Carolina at Greensboro

Greensboro, North Carolina

- **State-supported** university, founded 1891, part of University of North Carolina System
- **Urban** 210-acre campus
- **Endowment** $192.5 million
- **Coed** 14,674 undergraduate students, 88% full-time, 66% women, 34% men
- **Moderately difficult** entrance level, 60% of applicants were admitted

Undergraduates 12,910 full-time, 1,764 part-time. Students come from 40 states and territories; 46 other countries; 6% are from out of state; 25% Black or African American, non-Hispanic/Latino; 6% Hispanic/Latino; 4% Asian, non-Hispanic/Latino; 0.1% Native Hawaiian or other Pacific Islander, non-Hispanic/Latino; 0.3% American Indian or Alaska Native, non-Hispanic/Latino; 4% Two or more races, non-Hispanic/Latino; 0.3% Race/ethnicity unknown; 1% international; 11% transferred in; 30% live on campus. *Retention:* 76% of full-time freshmen returned.

Freshmen *Admission:* 10,108 applied, 6,065 admitted, 2,516 enrolled. *Average high school GPA:* 3.51. *Test scores:* SAT critical reading scores over 500: 56%; SAT math scores over 500: 60%; SAT writing scores over 500: 46%; SAT critical reading scores over 600: 13%; SAT math scores over 600: 14%; SAT writing scores over 600: 10%; SAT critical reading scores over 700: 2%; SAT math scores over 700: 2%; SAT writing scores over 700: 1%.

Faculty *Total:* 1,006, 78% full-time, 66% with terminal degrees. *Student/faculty ratio:* 18:1.

Academics *Calendar:* semesters. *Degrees:* bachelor's, master's, doctoral, post-master's, and postbachelor's certificates. *Special study options:* academic remediation for entering students, accelerated degree program, adult/continuing education programs, advanced placement credit, distance learning, double majors, freshman honors college, honors programs, independent study, internships, off-campus study, part-time degree program, services for LD students, student-designed majors, study abroad, summer session for credit. *ROTC:* Army (c), Air Force (c). *Unusual degree programs:* 3-2 BS/MS Accounting, BS Biology/MS Chemistry, BS/MS Chemistry, BS/MS Computer Science, BA Economics/MPA Public Affairs, BS Kinesiology/MS in Athletic Training (MSAT), BA Political Science/Master of Public Affairs (MPA).

Computers on Campus 360 computers/terminals are available on campus for general student use. Students can access the following: computer help desk, free student e-mail accounts, online (class) grades, online (class) registration, online (class) schedules. Campuswide network is available. 100% of college-owned or -operated housing units are wired for high-speed Internet access. Wireless service is available via classrooms, computer centers, computer labs, dorm rooms, learning centers, libraries, student centers.

Student Life *Housing options:* coed, disabled students. Campus housing is university owned. Freshman campus housing is guaranteed. *Activities and organizations:* drama/theater group, student-run newspaper, radio station, choral group, marching band, national fraternities, national sororities. *Campus security:* 24-hour emergency response devices and patrols, student patrols, late-night transport/escort service, controlled dormitory access. *Student services:* health clinic, personal/psychological counseling, women's center.

Athletics Member NCAA. All Division I. *Intercollegiate sports:* baseball M(s), basketball M(s)/W(s), cross-country running M(s)/W(s), golf M(s)/W(s), soccer M(s)/W(s), softball W(s), tennis M(s)/W(s), track and field M(s)/W(s), volleyball W(s). *Intramural sports:* basketball M(c)/W(c), cross-country running M(c)/W(c), equestrian sports M(c)/W(c), football W(c), lacrosse M(c), racquetball M(c)/W(c), rugby M(c)/W(c), soccer M(c)/W(c), swimming and diving M(c)/W(c), tennis M(c)/W(c), ultimate Frisbee M(c)/W(c), volleyball W(c).

Standardized Tests *Required:* SAT or ACT (for admission).

Costs (2013–14) *Tuition:* state resident $3779 full-time, $492 per unit part-time; nonresident $17,577 full-time, $2216 per unit part-time. Part-time tuition and fees vary according to course load. *Required fees:* $2450 full-time, $91 per hour part-time. *Room and board:* $8948; room only: $5950. Room and board charges vary according to board plan and housing facility. *Payment plan:* installment. *Waivers:* employees or children of employees.

Financial Aid Of all full-time matriculated undergraduates who enrolled in 2012, 10,677 applied for aid, 10,352 were judged to have need, 1,815 had their need fully met. In 2012, 322 non-need-based awards were made. *Average percent of need met:* 54%. *Average financial aid package:* $9827. *Average need-based loan:* $4088. *Average need-based gift aid:* $5731. *Average non-need-based aid:* $3206. *Average indebtedness upon graduation:* $24,199.

Applying *Options:* electronic application, early admission. *Application fee:* $55. *Required:* high school transcript, minimum 2.0 GPA. *Application deadlines:* 3/1 (freshmen), 7/15 (transfers). *Notification:* continuous (freshmen), continuous (transfers).

Freshman Application Contact The University of North Carolina at Greensboro, Armfield-Preyer Admissions and Visitor Center, 1400 Spring Garden Street, Greensboro, NC 27412. *Phone:* 336-334-5243. *Fax:* 336-334-4180. *E-mail:* admissions@uncg.edu. *Website:* http://www.uncg.edu/.

The University of North Carolina at Pembroke

Pembroke, North Carolina

- **State-supported** 4-year, founded 1887, part of University of North Carolina System
- **Rural** 200-acre campus
- **Endowment** $15.9 million
- **Coed** 5,504 undergraduate students, 81% full-time, 61% women, 39% men
- **Moderately difficult** entrance level, 72% of applicants were admitted

Undergraduates 4,432 full-time, 1,072 part-time. Students come from 19 states and territories; 18 other countries; 3% are from out of state; 34% Black or African American, non-Hispanic/Latino; 4% Hispanic/Latino; 2% Asian, non-Hispanic/Latino; 0.1% Native Hawaiian or other Pacific Islander, non-Hispanic/Latino; 16% American Indian or Alaska Native, non-Hispanic/Latino; 2% Two or more races, non-Hispanic/Latino; 3% Race/ethnicity unknown; 1% international; 9% transferred in; 28% live on campus. *Retention:* 64% of full-time freshmen returned.

Freshmen *Admission:* 3,087 applied, 2,224 admitted, 1,020 enrolled. *Average high school GPA:* 3.29. *Test scores:* SAT math scores over 500: 27%; SAT writing scores over 500: 13%; ACT scores over 18: 61%; SAT math scores over 600: 5%; SAT writing scores over 600: 2%; ACT scores over 24: 10%; SAT math scores over 700: 1%; SAT writing scores over 700: 1%; ACT scores over 30: 1%.

Faculty *Total:* 402, 81% full-time, 68% with terminal degrees. *Student/faculty ratio:* 15:1.

Academics *Calendar:* semesters. *Degrees:* bachelor's and master's. *Special study options:* academic remediation for entering students, accelerated degree program, adult/continuing education programs, advanced placement credit, cooperative education, distance learning, double majors, English as a second language, honors programs, internships, off-campus study, part-time degree program, services for LD students, study abroad, summer session for credit. *ROTC:* Army (b), Air Force (b).

Computers on Campus 875 computers/terminals are available on campus for general student use. Students can access the following: campus intranet, computer help desk, free student e-mail accounts, online (class) grades, online (class) registration, online (class) schedules, wireless network, online library, commuter/off campus connection to network, discounted computer software/hardware. Campuswide network is available. 100% of college-owned or -operated housing units are wired for high-speed Internet access. Wireless service is available via classrooms, computer centers, computer labs, dorm rooms, learning centers, libraries, student centers.

Student Life *Housing options:* coed, men-only, women-only. Campus housing is university owned and is provided by a third party. Freshman applicants given priority for college housing. *Activities and organizations:* drama/theater group, student-run newspaper, radio and television station, choral group, marching band, NAACP, African Student Organization, English Club, International Student Organization, Voices of Serenity and Disabled Student Organization, national fraternities, national sororities. *Campus security:* 24-hour emergency response devices and patrols, late-night transport/escort service, controlled dormitory access. *Student services:* health clinic, personal/psychological counseling.

Athletics Member NCAA. All Division II. *Intercollegiate sports:* baseball M(s), basketball M(s)/W(s), cheerleading M/W, cross-country running M(s)/W(s), football M(s), golf M(s)/W(s), soccer M(s)/W(s), softball W(s), tennis W(s), track and field M(s)/W(s), volleyball W(s), wrestling M(s). *Intramural sports:* basketball M/W, bowling M/W, football M, golf M, racquetball M/W, soccer M, softball M/W, volleyball M/W, wrestling M.

Standardized Tests *Required:* SAT or ACT (for admission).

Costs (2012–13) *Tuition:* state resident $3012 full-time; nonresident $12,219 full-time. Full-time tuition and fees vary according to course load and location. Part-time tuition and fees vary according to course load and location. *Required fees:* $1845 full-time. *Room and board:* $7010; room only: $5500. Room and board charges vary according to board plan, housing facility, and location. *Payment plan:* installment. *Waivers:* employees or children of employees.

Financial Aid Of all full-time matriculated undergraduates who enrolled in 2012, 3,901 applied for aid, 3,479 were judged to have need, 371 had their need fully met. 118 Federal Work-Study jobs (averaging $1748). In 2012, 36 non-need-based awards were made. *Average percent of need met:* 71%. *Average financial aid package:* $9676. *Average need-based loan:* $4135. *Average need-based gift aid:* $6239. *Average non-need-based aid:* $737. *Average indebtedness upon graduation:* $23,760.

Applying *Options:* electronic application, deferred entrance. *Application fee:* $45. *Required:* high school transcript. *Required for some:* 1 letter of recommendation, interview. *Recommended:* essay or personal statement, minimum 2.0 GPA. *Application deadlines:* rolling (freshmen), rolling (transfers). *Notification:* continuous (freshmen), continuous (transfers).

Freshman Application Contact Ms. Jennifer McNeil, Associate Director of Admissions, The University of North Carolina at Pembroke, PO Box 1510, Pembroke, NC 28372-1510. *Phone:* 910-521-6262. *Toll-free phone:* 800-949-UNCP. *Fax:* 910-521-6497. *E-mail:* jennifer.mcneill@uncp.edu. *Website:* http://www.uncp.edu/.

University of North Carolina School of the Arts

Winston-Salem, North Carolina

- **State-supported** comprehensive, founded 1963, part of University of North Carolina System
- **Urban** 57-acre campus
- **Endowment** $31.6 million
- **Coed** 760 undergraduate students, 97% full-time, 41% women, 59% men

Undergraduates 738 full-time, 22 part-time. Students come from 50 states and territories; 16 other countries; 52% are from out of state; 8% Black or African American, non-Hispanic/Latino; 8% Hispanic/Latino; 1% Asian, non-Hispanic/Latino; 0.1% Native Hawaiian or other Pacific Islander, non-Hispanic/Latino; 0.5% American Indian or Alaska Native, non-Hispanic/Latino; 4% Two or more races, non-Hispanic/Latino; 4% Race/ethnicity unknown; 1% international; 6% transferred in; 58% live on campus. *Retention:* 85% of full-time freshmen returned.

Freshmen *Admission:* 172 enrolled. *Average high school GPA:* 3.52. *Test scores:* SAT critical reading scores over 500: 78%; SAT math scores over 500: 74%; SAT writing scores over 500: 76%; ACT scores over 18: 98%; SAT critical reading scores over 600: 44%; SAT math scores over 600: 32%; SAT writing scores over 600: 32%; ACT scores over 24: 50%; SAT critical reading scores over 700: 7%; SAT math scores over 700: 4%; SAT writing scores over 700: 3%; ACT scores over 30: 11%.

Faculty *Total:* 170, 76% full-time, 36% with terminal degrees. *Student/faculty ratio:* 6:1.

Academics *Calendar:* trimesters. *Degrees:* diplomas, bachelor's, master's, and post-master's certificates. *Special study options:* advanced placement credit, English as a second language, independent study, internships, services for LD students, summer session for credit.

Computers on Campus 30 computers/terminals and 40 ports are available on campus for general student use. Students can access the following: campus intranet, computer help desk, free student e-mail accounts, online (class) grades, online (class) schedules. Campuswide network is available. 100% of college-owned or -operated housing units are wired for high-speed Internet access. Wireless service is available via entire campus.

Student Life *Housing:* on-campus residence required through sophomore year. *Options:* coed. Campus housing is university owned. Freshman campus housing is guaranteed. *Activities and organizations:* drama/theater group, student-run newspaper, choral group, Students for Sustainability, Arts & Soul [faith based], Young Americans for Liberty (YAL) [political awareness]. *Campus security:* 24-hour emergency response devices and patrols, late-night transport/escort service, controlled dormitory access. *Student services:* health clinic, personal/psychological counseling.

Standardized Tests *Required:* SAT or ACT (for admission).

Costs (2013–14) *Tuition:* state resident $5870 full-time; nonresident $19,015 full-time. *Required fees:* $2401 full-time. *Room and board:* $8410; room only: $4018. Room and board charges vary according to board plan and housing facility. *Waivers:* employees or children of employees.

Financial Aid Of all full-time matriculated undergraduates who enrolled in 2009, 519 applied for aid, 405 were judged to have need, 67 had their need fully met. 108 Federal Work-Study jobs (averaging $460). In 2009, 108 non-need-based awards were made. *Average percent of need met:* 89%. *Average financial aid package:* $15,093. *Average need-based loan:* $4167. *Average need-based gift aid:* $7404. *Average non-need-based aid:* $3960. *Average indebtedness upon graduation:* $22,173.

Applying *Required:* essay or personal statement, high school transcript, minimum 2.5 GPA, 2 letters of recommendation, audition. *Required for some:* interview.

Freshman Application Contact University of North Carolina School of the Arts, 1533 South Main Street, PO Box 12189, Winston-Salem, NC 27127-2188. *Phone:* 336-770-3290. *Website:* http://www.uncsa.edu/.

The University of North Carolina Wilmington

Wilmington, North Carolina

- **State-supported** comprehensive, founded 1947, part of University of North Carolina System
- **Urban** 656-acre campus
- **Endowment** $62.8 million
- **Coed** 12,348 undergraduate students, 91% full-time, 60% women, 40% men
- **Moderately difficult** entrance level, 54% of applicants were admitted

Undergraduates 11,295 full-time, 1,053 part-time. Students come from 45 states and territories; 54 other countries; 16% are from out of state; 5% Black or African American, non-Hispanic/Latino; 6% Hispanic/Latino; 2% Asian, non-Hispanic/Latino; 0.1% Native Hawaiian or other Pacific Islander, non-Hispanic/Latino; 0.5% American Indian or Alaska Native, non-Hispanic/Latino; 2% Two or more races, non-Hispanic/Latino; 2% Race/ethnicity unknown; 0.6% international; 13% transferred in; 33% live on campus. *Retention:* 86% of full-time freshmen returned.

Freshmen *Admission:* 11,184 applied, 6,061 admitted, 2,053 enrolled. *Average high school GPA:* 3.99. *Test scores:* SAT critical reading scores over 500: 95%; SAT math scores over 500: 97%; SAT writing scores over 500: 86%; ACT scores over 18: 100%; SAT critical reading scores over 600: 39%; SAT math scores over 600: 50%; SAT writing scores over 600: 28%; ACT scores over 24: 59%; SAT critical reading scores over 700: 5%; SAT math scores over 700: 3%; SAT writing scores over 700: 3%; ACT scores over 30: 4%.

Faculty *Total:* 1,027, 62% full-time, 66% with terminal degrees. *Student/faculty ratio:* 16:1.

Academics *Calendar:* semesters. *Degrees:* bachelor's, master's, doctoral, post-master's, and postbachelor's certificates. *Special study options:* academic remediation for entering students, accelerated degree program, advanced placement credit, cooperative education, distance learning, double majors, English as a second language, honors programs, independent study, internships, off-campus study, services for LD students, study abroad, summer session for credit.

Computers on Campus 1,650 computers/terminals and 3,481 ports are available on campus for general student use. Students can access the following: campus intranet, computer help desk, free student e-mail accounts, online (class) grades, online (class) registration, online (class) schedules. Campuswide network is available. 100% of college-owned or -operated housing units are wired for high-speed Internet access. Wireless service is available via entire campus.

Student Life *Housing options:* coed, women-only, disabled students. Campus housing is university owned and is provided by a third party. Freshman applicants given priority for college housing. *Activities and organizations:* drama/theater group, student-run newspaper, radio and television station, choral group, Student Government Association, Association of Campus Entertainment, Residence Hall Association, national fraternities, national sororities. *Campus security:* 24-hour emergency response devices and patrols, late-night transport/escort service, controlled dormitory access. *Student services:* health clinic, personal/psychological counseling, women's center, legal services.

Athletics Member NCAA. All Division I. *Intercollegiate sports:* baseball M(s), basketball M(s)/W(s), cheerleading M/W(s), cross-country running M(s)/W(s), golf M(s)/W(s), soccer M(s)/W(s), softball W(s), swimming and diving M(s)/W(s), tennis M(s)/W(s), track and field M(s)/W(s), volleyball

W(s). *Intramural sports:* baseball M(c), basketball W, crew M(c)/W(c), field hockey W(c), golf M/W, gymnastics W(c), ice hockey M, lacrosse M(c)/W(c), sailing M(c)/W(c), soccer M/W, softball M/W, swimming and diving M(c)/W(c), tennis M(c)/W(c), ultimate Frisbee M(c)/W(c), volleyball M/W.
Standardized Tests *Required:* SAT or ACT (for admission).
Costs (2012–13) *Tuition:* state resident $3742 full-time; nonresident $15,845 full-time. Full-time tuition and fees vary according to course load. Part-time tuition and fees vary according to course load. *Required fees:* $2058 full-time. *Room and board:* $8016; room only: $4620. Room and board charges vary according to board plan and housing facility. *Payment plan:* installment. *Waivers:* employees or children of employees.
Financial Aid Of all full-time matriculated undergraduates who enrolled in 2012, 8,100 applied for aid, 5,729 were judged to have need, 1,966 had their need fully met. 151 Federal Work-Study jobs (averaging $2310). In 2012, 292 non-need-based awards were made. *Average percent of need met:* 70%. *Average financial aid package:* $9668. *Average need-based loan:* $4326. *Average need-based gift aid:* $4911. *Average non-need-based aid:* $2464. *Average indebtedness upon graduation:* $25,821.
Applying *Options:* electronic application, early admission, early action, deferred entrance. *Application fee:* $60. *Required:* essay or personal statement, high school transcript, letters of recommendation. *Application deadlines:* 2/1 (freshmen), 3/1 (transfers), 11/1 (early action). *Notification:* 4/1 (freshmen), continuous (transfers), 1/20 (early action).
Freshman Application Contact Dr. Terrence M. Curran, Associate Provost, The University of North Carolina Wilmington, 601 South College Road, Wilmington, NC 28403-3297. *Phone:* 910-962-3876. *Fax:* 910-962-3922. *E-mail:* admissions@uncw.edu.
Website: http://www.uncw.edu/.

University of Phoenix–Charlotte Campus

Charlotte, North Carolina

Freshman Application Contact Marc Booker, Sr. Director, Office of Admissions and Evaluation, University of Phoenix–Charlotte Campus, 4035 South Riverpoint Parkway, Mail Stop CF-L101, Phoenix, AZ 85040. *Phone:* 602-557-4609. *Toll-free phone:* 866-766-0766. *Fax:* 480-643-1156.
Website: http://www.phoenix.edu/.

University of Phoenix–Raleigh Campus

Raleigh, North Carolina

Freshman Application Contact Marc Booker, Sr. Director, Office of Admissions and Evaluation, University of Phoenix–Raleigh Campus, 4035 South Riverpoint Parkway, Mail Stop CF-L101, Phoenix, AZ 85040. *Phone:* 602-557-4609. *Toll-free phone:* 866-766-0766. *Fax:* 480-643-1156.
Website: http://www.phoenix.edu/.

Wake Forest University

Winston-Salem, North Carolina

- **Independent** university, founded 1834
- **Suburban** 340-acre campus
- **Coed** 4,815 undergraduate students, 99% full-time, 52% women, 48% men
- **Very difficult** entrance level, 34% of applicants were admitted

Undergraduates 4,746 full-time, 69 part-time. 77% are from out of state; 7% Black or African American, non-Hispanic/Latino; 5% Hispanic/Latino; 5% Asian, non-Hispanic/Latino; 0.3% American Indian or Alaska Native, non-Hispanic/Latino; 2% Two or more races, non-Hispanic/Latino; 0.3% Race/ethnicity unknown; 3% international; 0.7% transferred in; 68% live on campus. *Retention:* 94% of full-time freshmen returned.
Freshmen *Admission:* 11,407 applied, 3,875 admitted, 1,234 enrolled. *Test scores:* SAT critical reading scores over 500: 96%; SAT math scores over 500: 98%; ACT scores over 18: 100%; SAT critical reading scores over 600: 83%; SAT math scores over 600: 88%; ACT scores over 24: 95%; SAT critical reading scores over 700: 28%; SAT math scores over 700: 35%; ACT scores over 30: 64%.

Faculty *Total:* 690, 77% full-time. *Student/faculty ratio:* 11:1.
Academics *Calendar:* semesters. *Degrees:* bachelor's, master's, and doctoral. *Special study options:* advanced placement credit, double majors, honors programs, independent study, internships, part-time degree program, services for LD students, study abroad, summer session for credit. *ROTC:* Army (b). *Unusual degree programs:* 3-2 engineering.
Computers on Campus Students can access the following: campus intranet, computer help desk, free student e-mail accounts, online (class) grades, online (class) registration, online (class) schedules, financial information online, drop-add, transcript requests. Campuswide network is available. Wireless service is available via entire campus.
Student Life *Housing:* on-campus residence required through sophomore year. *Options:* coed. Campus housing is university owned. Freshman campus housing is guaranteed. *Activities and organizations:* drama/theater group, student-run newspaper, radio and television station, choral group, marching band, national fraternities, national sororities. *Campus security:* 24-hour emergency response devices and patrols, late-night transport/escort service, controlled dormitory access. *Student services:* health clinic, personal/psychological counseling.
Athletics Member NCAA. All Division I except football (Division I-A). *Intercollegiate sports:* baseball M(s), basketball M(s)/W(s), cross-country running M(s)/W(s), field hockey W(s), golf M(s)/W(s), soccer M(s)/W(s), tennis M(s)/W(s), track and field M(s)/W(s), volleyball W(s). *Intramural sports:* archery M(c)/W(c), baseball M(c), basketball M/W, bowling M/W, cheerleading M(c)/W(c), crew M(c)/W(c), cross-country running M(c)/W(c), equestrian sports M(c)/W(c), fencing M(c)/W(c), field hockey W(c), football M, golf M(c)/W(c), ice hockey M(c)/W(c), lacrosse M(c)/W(c), racquetball M/W, rugby M(c)/W(c), skiing (cross-country) M(c)/W(c), skiing (downhill) M(c)/W(c), soccer M(c)/W(c), softball M/W(c), swimming and diving M/W, table tennis M/W, tennis M/W, ultimate Frisbee M/W, volleyball M/W, water polo M(c)/W(c), wrestling M(c).
Costs (2013–14) *Comprehensive fee:* $56,742 includes full-time tuition ($44,200), mandatory fees ($542), and room and board ($12,000). Part-time tuition: $1832 per credit hour. *College room only:* $8000.
Financial Aid Of all full-time matriculated undergraduates who enrolled in 2012, 2,146 applied for aid, 1,932 were judged to have need, 1,287 had their need fully met. In 2012, 517 non-need-based awards were made. *Average percent of need met:* 99%. *Average financial aid package:* $32,015. *Average need-based loan:* $7476. *Average need-based gift aid:* $29,732. *Average non-need-based aid:* $16,702. *Average indebtedness upon graduation:* $33,262. *Financial aid deadline:* 3/1.
Applying *Options:* electronic application, early admission, early decision. *Application fee:* $50. *Required:* essay or personal statement, high school transcript, 1 letter of recommendation. *Recommended:* interview. *Application deadline:* 1/1 (freshmen). *Early decision deadline:* 1/1. *Notification:* 4/1 (freshmen), rolling (early decision).
Freshman Application Contact Wake Forest University, PO Box 7373 Reynolda Station, Winston-Salem, NC 27109. *Phone:* 336-758-5201.
Website: http://www.wfu.edu/.

Warren Wilson College

Swannanoa, North Carolina

- **Independent** comprehensive, founded 1894, affiliated with Presbyterian Church (U.S.A.)
- **Small-town** 1135-acre campus
- **Endowment** $51.9 million
- **Coed**
- **Moderately difficult** entrance level

Faculty *Student/faculty ratio:* 13:1.
Academics *Calendar:* semesters. *Degrees:* bachelor's and master's.
Student Life *Campus security:* 24-hour emergency response devices and patrols, student patrols, late-night transport/escort service, controlled dormitory access.
Standardized Tests *Required:* SAT or ACT (for admission).
Costs (2012–13) *Comprehensive fee:* $36,660 includes full-time tuition ($27,740), mandatory fees ($354), and room and board ($8566). Full-time tuition and fees vary according to course load. Part-time tuition and fees vary according to course load. *Room and board:* Room and board charges vary according to board plan.
Financial Aid *Of all full-time matriculated undergraduates who enrolled in 2012,* 657 applied for aid, 594 were judged to have need, 65 had their need fully met. 538 Federal Work-Study jobs (averaging $3480). 400 state and other part-time jobs (averaging $3480). *In 2012,* 122 non-need-based awards were made. *Average percent of need met:* 71. *Average financial aid package:* $23,653. *Average need-based loan:* $4020. *Average need-based gift aid:*

$16,189. *Average non-need-based aid:* $6234. *Average indebtedness upon graduation:* $23,239.

Applying *Options:* electronic application, early admission, early decision, deferred entrance. *Required:* essay or personal statement, high school transcript, minimum 2.5 GPA, 2 letters of recommendation. *Recommended:* interview.

Freshman Application Contact Mr. Richard Blomgren, Dean of Admission, Warren Wilson College, PO Box 9000, Asheville, NC 28815-9000. *Phone:* 828-771-2073. *Toll-free phone:* 800-934-3536. *Fax:* 828-298-1440. *E-mail:* admit@warren-wilson.edu.

Website: http://www.warren-wilson.edu/.

See below for display ad and page 1630 for the College Close-Up.

Western Carolina University

Cullowhee, North Carolina

- **State-supported** comprehensive, founded 1889, part of University of North Carolina System
- **Rural** 682-acre campus
- **Coed** 7,979 undergraduate students, 85% full-time, 53% women, 47% men
- **Moderately difficult** entrance level, 38% of applicants were admitted

Undergraduates 6,795 full-time, 1,184 part-time. Students come from 40 states and territories; 15 other countries; 7% are from out of state; 7% Black or African American, non-Hispanic/Latino; 3% Hispanic/Latino; 1% Asian, non-Hispanic/Latino; 0.1% Native Hawaiian or other Pacific Islander, non-Hispanic/Latino; 0.9% American Indian or Alaska Native, non-Hispanic/Latino; 3% Two or more races, non-Hispanic/Latino; 1% Race/ethnicity unknown; 0.7% international; 10% transferred in; 49% live on campus. *Retention:* 74% of full-time freshmen returned.

Freshmen *Admission:* 15,234 applied, 5,739 admitted, 1,560 enrolled. *Average high school GPA:* 3.63. *Test scores:* SAT critical reading scores over 500: 57%; SAT math scores over 500: 64%; SAT writing scores over 500: 39%; ACT scores over 18: 98%; SAT critical reading scores over 600: 14%; SAT math scores over 600: 16%; SAT writing scores over 600: 8%; ACT scores over 24: 29%; SAT critical reading scores over 700: 1%; SAT math scores over 700: 1%; SAT writing scores over 700: 1%; ACT scores over 30: 3%.

Faculty *Total:* 657, 74% full-time, 59% with terminal degrees. *Student/faculty ratio:* 15:1.

Academics *Calendar:* semesters. *Degrees:* bachelor's, master's, doctoral, post-master's, and postbachelor's certificates. *Special study options:* advanced placement credit, cooperative education, distance learning, double majors, English as a second language, honors programs, independent study, internships, part-time degree program, services for LD students, student-designed majors, study abroad, summer session for credit.

Computers on Campus 115 computers/terminals and 6,110 ports are available on campus for general student use. Students can access the following: campus intranet, computer help desk, free student e-mail accounts, online (class) grades, online (class) registration, online (class) schedules. Campus-wide network is available. 100% of college-owned or -operated housing units are wired for high-speed Internet access. Wireless service is available via entire campus.

Student Life *Housing:* on-campus residence required for freshman year. *Options:* coed, men-only, women-only, disabled students. Campus housing is university owned, leased by the school and is provided by a third party. Freshman campus housing is guaranteed. *Activities and organizations:* drama/theater group, student-run newspaper, radio and television station, choral group, marching band, WCU Leadership Institute, Physical Therapy Club, UNITY, WCU Gaming Club, WCU Climbing Team, national fraternities, national sororities. *Campus security:* 24-hour emergency response devices and patrols, late-night transport/escort service, controlled dormitory access. *Student services:* health clinic, personal/psychological counseling, women's center.

Athletics Member NCAA. All Division I except football (Division I-AA). *Intercollegiate sports:* baseball M(s), basketball M(s)/W(s), cheerleading M/W, cross-country running M(s)/W(s), equestrian sports M(c)/W(c), fencing M(c)/W(c), golf M(s)/W(s), rock climbing M(c)/W(c), rugby M(c), soccer W(s), softball W(s), swimming and diving M(c)/W(c), tennis M(c)/W(s), track and field M(s)/W(s), ultimate Frisbee M(c)/W(c), volleyball W(s), wrestling M(c). *Intramural sports:* badminton M/W, basketball M/W, bowling M/W, cross-country running M/W, racquetball M/W, soccer M/W, softball M/W, swimming and diving M/W, table tennis M/W, tennis M/W, ultimate Frisbee M/W, volleyball M/W, water polo M/W, weight lifting M/W, wrestling M/W.

Standardized Tests *Required:* SAT or ACT (for admission). *Recommended:* SAT (for admission).

Costs (2013–14) *Tuition:* state resident $3669 full-time; nonresident $13,266 full-time. Full-time tuition and fees vary according to degree level. Part-time tuition and fees vary according to course load and degree level. *Required fees:*

$2810 full-time. *Room and board:* $7477; room only: $4429. Room and board charges vary according to board plan and housing facility.

Financial Aid Of all full-time matriculated undergraduates who enrolled in 2011, 5,286 applied for aid, 4,245 were judged to have need, 995 had their need fully met. In 2011, 226 non-need-based awards were made. *Average percent of need met:* 75%. *Average financial aid package:* $9168. *Average need-based loan:* $3691. *Average need-based gift aid:* $6241. *Average non-need-based aid:* $2214.

Applying *Options:* electronic application, early admission, early action. *Application fee:* $55. *Required:* high school transcript. *Application deadlines:* 3/1 (freshmen), 6/1 (transfers), 11/15 (early action). *Notification:* continuous (freshmen), continuous (transfers), 12/15 (early action).

Freshman Application Contact Mr. Chris Parrish, Senior Assistant Director of Admissions, Western Carolina University, 102 Cordelia Camp Building, Cullowhee, NC 28723. *Phone:* 828-227-7317. *Toll-free phone:* 877-WCU4YOU. *E-mail:* admiss@email.wcu.edu. *Website:* http://www.wcu.edu/.

William Peace University

Raleigh, North Carolina

- **Independent** 4-year, founded 1857, affiliated with Presbyterian Church (U.S.A.)
- **Urban** 21-acre campus with easy access to Raleigh-Cary
- **Endowment** $40.2 million
- **Coed** 791 undergraduate students, 88% full-time, 83% women, 17% men
- **Moderately difficult** entrance level, 61% of applicants were admitted

Undergraduates 700 full-time, 91 part-time. Students come from 18 states and territories; 1 other country; 6% are from out of state; 36% Black or African American, non-Hispanic/Latino; 5% Hispanic/Latino; 2% Asian, non-Hispanic/Latino; 2% American Indian or Alaska Native, non-Hispanic/Latino; 13% Race/ethnicity unknown; 8% transferred in; 51% live on campus. *Retention:* 65% of full-time freshmen returned.

Freshmen *Admission:* 1,238 applied, 755 admitted, 232 enrolled. *Average high school GPA:* 3.07. *Test scores:* SAT critical reading scores over 500: 27%; SAT math scores over 500: 27%; ACT scores over 18: 62%; SAT critical reading scores over 600: 5%; SAT math scores over 600: 3%; ACT scores over 24: 26%; ACT scores over 30: 5%.

Faculty *Total:* 106, 24% full-time, 49% with terminal degrees. *Student/faculty ratio:* 14:1.

Academics *Calendar:* semesters. *Degree:* bachelor's. *Special study options:* academic remediation for entering students, accelerated degree program, adult/continuing education programs, advanced placement credit, distance learning, double majors, honors programs, independent study, internships, off-campus study, part-time degree program, services for LD students, study abroad, summer session for credit. *ROTC:* Army (c), Navy (c), Air Force (c).

Computers on Campus 92 computers/terminals are available on campus for general student use. Students can access the following: campus intranet, computer help desk, free student e-mail accounts, online (class) grades, online (class) registration, online (class) schedules. Campuswide network is available. 100% of college-owned or -operated housing units are wired for high-speed Internet access. Wireless service is available via entire campus.

Student Life *Housing:* on-campus residence required through sophomore year. *Options:* coed, women-only. Campus housing is university owned, leased by the school and is provided by a third party. Freshman applicants given priority for college housing. *Activities and organizations:* drama/theater group, student-run newspaper, choral group, Campus Activities Board, Phi Beta Lamda, Gamma Sigma Sigma, Ambassadors for Christ, Class Councils. *Campus security:* 24-hour emergency response devices and patrols, late-night transport/escort service, controlled dormitory access. *Student services:* health clinic, personal/psychological counseling.

Athletics Member NCAA. All Division III. *Intercollegiate sports:* baseball M, basketball M/W, cross-country running M/W, golf M, soccer M/W, softball W, tennis W, volleyball W. *Intramural sports:* basketball M/W, football M/W, tennis M/W, volleyball M/W.

Standardized Tests *Required:* SAT or ACT (for admission). *Recommended:* SAT and SAT Subject Tests or ACT (for admission), SAT Subject Tests (for admission).

Costs (2013–14) *Comprehensive fee:* $33,041 includes full-time tuition ($23,700), mandatory fees ($200), and room and board ($9141). Full-time tuition and fees vary according to class time, course load, and program. Part-time tuition: $790 per credit. Part-time tuition and fees vary according to class time, course load, and program. *College room only:* $6186. Room and board charges vary according to board plan and housing facility. *Payment plan:* installment. *Waivers:* senior citizens and employees or children of employees.

Financial Aid Of all full-time matriculated undergraduates who enrolled in 2012, 673 applied for aid, 623 were judged to have need, 60 had their need fully met. 75 Federal Work-Study jobs (averaging $1790). 1 state and other part-time job (averaging $3000). In 2012, 83 non-need-based awards were

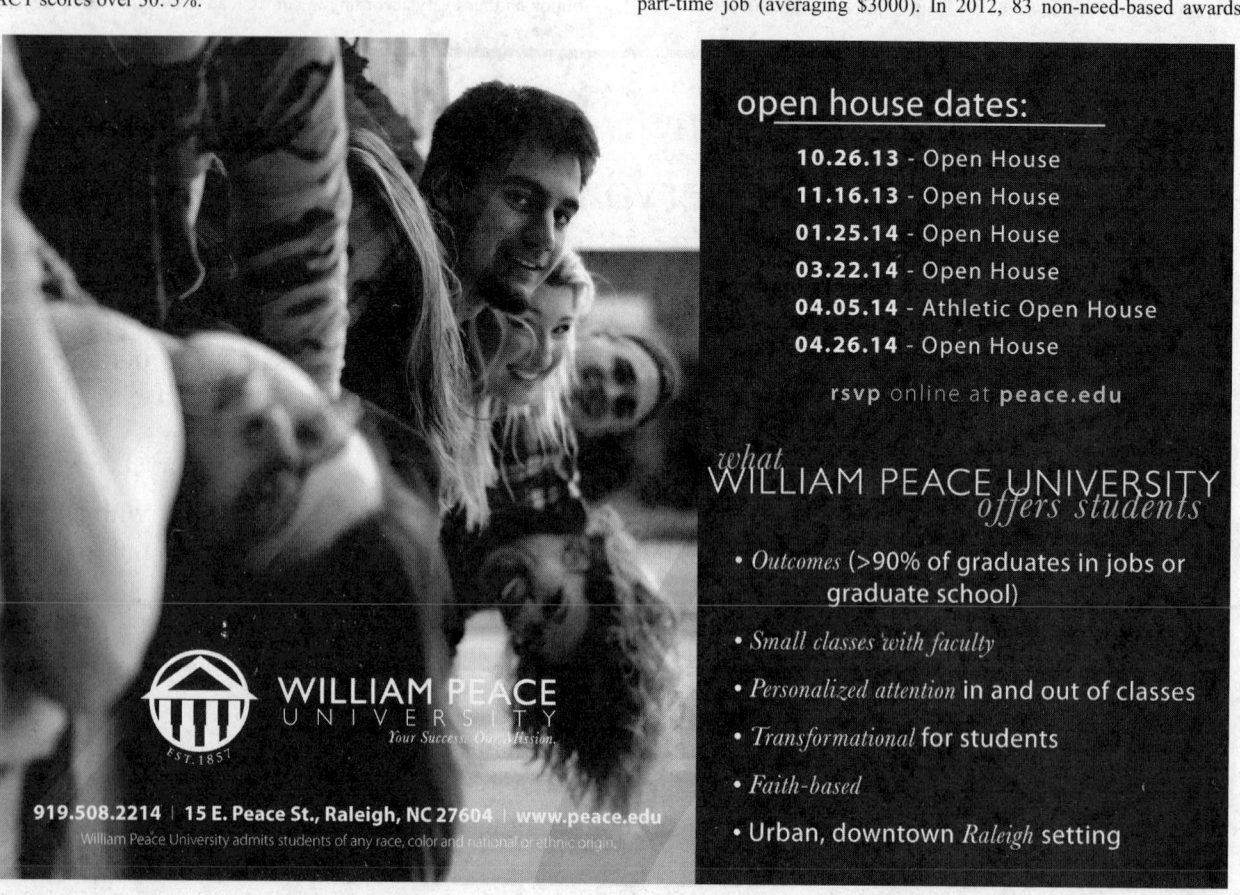

made. *Average percent of need met: 71%. Average financial aid package:* $20,637. *Average need-based loan:* $4189. *Average need-based gift aid:* $17,217. *Average non-need-based aid:* $8192. *Average indebtedness upon graduation:* $33,147.
Applying *Options:* electronic application, early admission, early action, deferred entrance. *Application fee:* $25. *Required:* high school transcript, minimum 2.0 GPA, Dean's Evaluation (transfers). *Recommended:* essay or personal statement, 2 letters of recommendation, interview. *Application deadlines:* rolling (freshmen), rolling (out-of-state freshmen), rolling (transfers), 11/1 (early action). *Notification:* continuous (freshmen), continuous (out-of-state freshmen), continuous (transfers), rolling (early action).
Freshman Application Contact Office of Admissions, William Peace University, 15 East Peace Street, Raleigh, NC 27604. *Phone:* 919-508-2214. *Toll-free phone:* 800-PEACE-47. *Fax:* 919-508-2326.
Website: http://www.peace.edu/.

See previous page for display ad and page 1654 for the College Close-Up.

Wingate University
Wingate, North Carolina
- **Independent Baptist** comprehensive, founded 1896
- **Small-town** 330-acre campus with easy access to Charlotte
- **Coed**
- **Moderately difficult** entrance level

Faculty *Student/faculty ratio:* 14:1.
Academics *Calendar:* semesters. *Degrees:* bachelor's, master's, doctoral, and post-master's certificates.
Student Life *Campus security:* 24-hour emergency response devices and patrols, late-night transport/escort service, controlled dormitory access.
Athletics Member NCAA. All Division II.
Standardized Tests *Required:* SAT or ACT (for admission).
Costs (2012–13) *Comprehensive fee:* $33,165 includes full-time tuition ($22,540), mandatory fees ($1305), and room and board ($9320). Part-time tuition: $750 per hour. Part-time tuition and fees vary according to course load. *Room and board:* Room and board charges vary according to board plan.
Financial Aid *Of all full-time matriculated undergraduates who enrolled in 2011,* 1,507 applied for aid, 1,375 were judged to have need, 380 had their need fully met. 293 Federal Work-Study jobs (averaging $900). 330 state and other part-time jobs (averaging $1019). *In 2011,* 357 non-need-based awards were made. *Average percent of need met:* 83. *Average financial aid package:* $20,367. *Average need-based loan:* $3946. *Average need-based gift aid:* $16,479. *Average non-need-based aid:* $10,766. *Average indebtedness upon graduation:* $24,298.
Applying *Options:* electronic application, early admission, deferred entrance. *Application fee:* $30. *Required:* high school transcript, minimum 2.0 GPA. *Recommended:* minimum 3.0 GPA, interview.
Freshman Application Contact Director of Student Recruitment, Wingate University, PO Box 159, Wingate, NC 28174. *Phone:* 704-233-8000. *Toll-free phone:* 800-755-5550. *Fax:* 704-233-8110. *E-mail:* admit@wingate.edu.
Website: http://www.wingate.edu/.

Winston-Salem State University
Winston-Salem, North Carolina
Freshman Application Contact Ms. Tomikia LeGrande, Assistant Vice Chancellor for Enrollment Services, Winston-Salem State University, 601 Martin Luther King, Jr. Drive, Thompson Center, Winston-Salem, NC 27110. *Phone:* 336-750-2070. *Toll-free phone:* 800-257-4052. *Fax:* 336-750-2079. *E-mail:* Legrandet@wssu.edu.
Website: http://www.wssu.edu/.

NORTH DAKOTA

Bismarck State College
Bismarck, North Dakota
- **State-supported** primarily 2-year, founded 1939, part of North Dakota University System
- **Urban** 100-acre campus
- **Coed** 4,109 undergraduate students, 59% full-time, 45% women, 55% men
- **Noncompetitive** entrance level

Undergraduates 2,416 full-time, 1,693 part-time. 3% Black or African American, non-Hispanic/Latino; 2% Hispanic/Latino; 0.4% Asian, non-Hispanic/Latino; 0.2% Native Hawaiian or other Pacific Islander, non-Hispanic/Latino; 2% American Indian or Alaska Native, non-Hispanic/Latino; 2% Two or more races, non-Hispanic/Latino; 2% Race/ethnicity unknown; 0.5% international. **Freshmen** *Admission:* 807 enrolled.
Faculty *Total:* 370, 34% full-time. *Student/faculty ratio:* 16:1.
Academics *Calendar:* semesters. *Degrees:* certificates, diplomas, associate, and bachelor's. *Special study options:* academic remediation for entering students, adult/continuing education programs, advanced placement credit, cooperative education, distance learning, internships, part-time degree program, study abroad, summer session for credit. *ROTC:* Army (c), Air Force (c).
Computers on Campus Students can access the following: computer help desk, free student e-mail accounts, online (class) grades, online (class) registration, online (class) schedules. Campuswide network is available.
Student Life *Housing options:* men-only, women-only. Campus housing is university owned. *Activities and organizations:* drama/theater group, student-run newspaper, radio station, choral group. *Campus security:* 24-hour emergency response devices and patrols, late-night transport/escort service, controlled dormitory access.
Athletics Member NJCAA.
Standardized Tests *Required:* SAT or ACT (for admission).
Financial Aid Of all full-time matriculated undergraduates who enrolled in 2011, 60 Federal Work-Study jobs (averaging $1367).
Applying *Options:* electronic application, early admission. *Application fee:* $35. *Required:* high school transcript. *Required for some:* interview. *Application deadlines:* rolling (freshmen), 8/1 (transfers). *Notification:* continuous (freshmen), continuous (transfers).
Freshman Application Contact Karen Erickson, Director of Admissions and Enrollment Services, Bismarck State College, PO Box 5587, Bismarck, ND 58506-5587. *Phone:* 701-224-5424. *Toll-free phone:* 800-445-5073. *Fax:* 701-224-5643. *E-mail:* karen.erickson@bismarckstate.edu.
Website: http://www.bismarckstate.edu/.

Dickinson State University
Dickinson, North Dakota
- **State-supported** 4-year, founded 1918, part of North Dakota University System
- **Small-town** 132-acre campus
- **Endowment** $9.9 million
- **Coed**
- **Minimally difficult** entrance level

Faculty *Student/faculty ratio:* 17:1.
Academics *Calendar:* semesters. *Degrees:* certificates, associate, and bachelor's.
Student Life *Campus security:* 24-hour emergency response devices and patrols, late-night transport/escort service.
Athletics Member NAIA.
Standardized Tests *Required:* SAT or ACT (for admission).
Costs (2012–13) *Tuition:* state resident $5717 full-time; nonresident $11,784 full-time. Full-time tuition and fees vary according to course load and reciprocity agreements. Part-time tuition and fees vary according to course load and reciprocity agreements. *Room and board:* $4950. Room and board charges vary according to board plan.
Financial Aid *Of all full-time matriculated undergraduates who enrolled in 2011,* 1,042 applied for aid, 792 were judged to have need, 763 had their need fully met. *In 2011,* 516 non-need-based awards were made. *Average percent of need met:* 31. *Average financial aid package:* $7499. *Average need-based loan:* $3789. *Average need-based gift aid:* $3972. *Average non-need-based aid:* $1388. *Average indebtedness upon graduation:* $22,193.

Applying *Options:* electronic application, early admission, deferred entrance. *Application fee:* $35. *Required:* high school transcript, medical history, proof of measles-rubella shot.
Freshman Application Contact Miss Marie Moe, Director of University Relations, Dickinson State University, Campus Box 169, Dickinson, ND 58601. *Phone:* 701-483-2175. *Toll-free phone:* 800-279-4295. *Fax:* 701-483-2409. *E-mail:* dsu.hawk@dickinsonstate.edu.
Website: http://www.dickinsonstate.edu/.

Jamestown College

Jamestown, North Dakota

- **Independent Presbyterian** comprehensive, founded 1883
- **Small-town** 110-acre campus
- **Endowment** $27.1 million
- **Coed** 939 undergraduate students, 93% full-time, 51% women, 49% men
- **Minimally difficult** entrance level, 56% of applicants were admitted

Undergraduates 872 full-time, 67 part-time. Students come from 35 states and territories; 14 other countries; 52% are from out of state; 4% Black or African American, non-Hispanic/Latino; 5% Hispanic/Latino; 2% Asian, non-Hispanic/Latino; 0.5% Native Hawaiian or other Pacific Islander, non-Hispanic/Latino; 0.9% American Indian or Alaska Native, non-Hispanic/Latino; 0.1% Race/ethnicity unknown; 7% international; 8% transferred in; 76% live on campus. *Retention:* 68% of full-time freshmen returned.
Freshmen *Admission:* 1,031 applied, 580 admitted, 223 enrolled. *Average high school GPA:* 3.29. *Test scores:* SAT critical reading scores over 500: 30%; SAT math scores over 500: 39%; ACT scores over 18: 92%; SAT math scores over 600: 9%; ACT scores over 24: 37%; ACT scores over 30: 5%.
Faculty *Total:* 80, 75% full-time, 44% with terminal degrees. *Student/faculty ratio:* 13:1.
Academics *Calendar:* semesters. *Degrees:* bachelor's and master's. *Special study options:* adult/continuing education programs, advanced placement credit, cooperative education, double majors, honors programs, independent study, internships, part-time degree program, services for LD students, student-designed majors, study abroad, summer session for credit. *Unusual degree programs:* 3-2 engineering with North Dakota State University, University of North Dakota, South Dakota State University, Washington University in St. Louis.
Computers on Campus 300 computers/terminals and 600 ports are available on campus for general student use. Students can access the following: campus intranet, computer help desk, free student e-mail accounts, online (class) grades, online (class) registration, online (class) schedules. Campuswide network is available. 100% of college-owned or -operated housing units are wired for high-speed Internet access. Wireless service is available via entire campus.
Student Life *Housing:* on-campus residence required through sophomore year. *Options:* coed. Campus housing is university owned. Freshman campus housing is guaranteed. *Activities and organizations:* drama/theater group, student-run newspaper, radio and television station, choral group, Science Club, International Student Organization, Student Media Center, Jimmie Ambassadors, Roots. *Campus security:* late-night transport/escort service, controlled dormitory access. *Student services:* personal/psychological counseling.
Athletics Member NAIA. *Intercollegiate sports:* baseball M(s), basketball M(s)/W(s), cross-country running M(s)/W(s), football M(s), golf M(s)/W(s), soccer M(s)/W(s), softball W(s), track and field M(s)/W(s), volleyball W(s), wrestling M(s)/W(s). *Intramural sports:* basketball M/W, football M/W, volleyball M/W.
Standardized Tests *Required:* SAT or ACT (for admission).
Costs (2013–14) *Comprehensive fee:* $24,668 includes full-time tuition ($17,974), mandatory fees ($450), and room and board ($6244). Full-time tuition and fees vary according to course load, degree level, and program. Part-time tuition: $435 per credit. Part-time tuition and fees vary according to course load, degree level, and program. *College room only:* $2754. Room and board charges vary according to housing facility. *Payment plan:* installment. *Waivers:* employees or children of employees.
Financial Aid Of all full-time matriculated undergraduates who enrolled in 2011, 916 applied for aid, 625 were judged to have need, 128 had their need fully met. 243 Federal Work-Study jobs (averaging $913). 73 state and other part-time jobs (averaging $784). In 2011, 273 non-need-based awards were made. *Average percent of need met:* 75%. *Average financial aid package:* $12,763. *Average need-based loan:* $4004. *Average need-based gift aid:* $9475. *Average non-need-based aid:* $6022. *Average indebtedness upon graduation:* $28,726.
Applying *Options:* electronic application, deferred entrance. *Application fee:* $35. *Required:* high school transcript, 1 letter of recommendation. *Recommended:* minimum 2.5 GPA. *Application deadlines:* rolling (freshmen), rolling (out-of-state freshmen), rolling (transfers).

Freshman Application Contact Jamestown College, 6000 College Lane, Jamestown, ND 58405. *Phone:* 701-252-3467 Ext. 5512. *Toll-free phone:* 800-336-2554.
Website: http://www.jc.edu/.

Mayville State University

Mayville, North Dakota

- **State-supported** 4-year, founded 1889, part of North Dakota University System
- **Rural** 60-acre campus
- **Coed** 990 undergraduate students, 62% full-time, 57% women, 43% men
- **Noncompetitive** entrance level, 60% of applicants were admitted

Undergraduates 614 full-time, 376 part-time. Students come from 38 states and territories; 5 other countries; 38% are from out of state; 6% Black or African American, non-Hispanic/Latino; 4% Hispanic/Latino; 0.7% Asian, non-Hispanic/Latino; 0.2% Native Hawaiian or other Pacific Islander, non-Hispanic/Latino; 2% American Indian or Alaska Native, non-Hispanic/Latino; 2% Two or more races, non-Hispanic/Latino; 0.6% Race/ethnicity unknown; 4% international; 12% transferred in; 48% live on campus. *Retention:* 53% of full-time freshmen returned.
Freshmen *Admission:* 311 applied, 186 admitted, 157 enrolled. *Average high school GPA:* 3.05. *Test scores:* ACT scores over 18: 76%; ACT scores over 24: 13%.
Faculty *Total:* 81, 51% full-time, 23% with terminal degrees. *Student/faculty ratio:* 14:1.
Academics *Calendar:* semesters. *Degrees:* associate and bachelor's. *Special study options:* academic remediation for entering students, accelerated degree program, adult/continuing education programs, advanced placement credit, cooperative education, distance learning, double majors, internships, off-campus study, part-time degree program, services for LD students, student-designed majors, summer session for credit. *ROTC:* Army (c), Air Force (c).
Computers on Campus Students can access the following: campus intranet, computer help desk, free student e-mail accounts, online (class) grades, online (class) registration, online (class) schedules. Campuswide network is available. 100% of college-owned or -operated housing units are wired for high-speed Internet access. Wireless service is available via entire campus.
Student Life *Housing:* on-campus residence required through sophomore year. *Options:* coed, men-only, women-only. Campus housing is university owned and is provided by a third party. Freshman campus housing is guaranteed. *Activities and organizations:* drama/theater group, student-run newspaper, radio station, choral group, Student Activities Council, Student Education Association, Health and Physical Education Club, Campus Crusade, Student Ambassadors. *Campus security:* controlled dormitory access. *Student services:* health clinic, personal/psychological counseling.
Athletics Member NAIA. *Intercollegiate sports:* baseball M(s), basketball M(s)/W(s), football M(s), softball W(s), volleyball W(s). *Intramural sports:* basketball M/W, bowling M/W, football M/W, golf M/W, ice hockey M, racquetball M/W, soccer M/W, softball M/W, table tennis M/W, tennis M/W, track and field M/W, volleyball M/W.
Standardized Tests *Required:* SAT or ACT (for admission).
Costs (2012–13) *One-time required fee:* $35. *Tuition:* state resident $4484 full-time, $187 per credit hour part-time; nonresident $6727 full-time, $280 per credit hour part-time. Full-time tuition and fees vary according to course load and reciprocity agreements. Part-time tuition and fees vary according to course load and reciprocity agreements. *Required fees:* $1709 full-time, $71 per credit hour part-time. *Room and board:* $4854; room only: $1874. Room and board charges vary according to board plan and housing facility. *Payment plan:* installment. *Waivers:* minority students, senior citizens, and employees or children of employees.
Financial Aid Of all full-time matriculated undergraduates who enrolled in 2012, 513 applied for aid, 393 were judged to have need, 47 had their need fully met. 52 Federal Work-Study jobs (averaging $1000). In 2012, 165 non-need-based awards were made. *Average percent of need met:* 1%. *Average financial aid package:* $8207. *Average need-based loan:* $4076. *Average need-based gift aid:* $4117. *Average non-need-based aid:* $1109. *Average indebtedness upon graduation:* $30,351.
Applying *Options:* electronic application, deferred entrance. *Application fee:* $35. *Required:* high school transcript, minimum 2.0 GPA. *Application deadlines:* rolling (freshmen), rolling (out-of-state freshmen), rolling (transfers). *Notification:* continuous until 1/1 (freshmen), continuous (out-of-state freshmen), continuous until 1/1 (transfers).
Freshman Application Contact Jim Morowski, Director of Freshmen Enrollment Services, Mayville State University, 330 3rd Street, NE, Mayville,

ND 58257-1299. *Phone:* 701-788-4842. *Toll-free phone:* 800-437-4104. *Fax:* 701-788-4748. *E-mail:* james.morowski@mayvillestate.edu. *Website:* http://www.mayvillestate.edu/.

Minot State University
Minot, North Dakota

- **State-supported** comprehensive, founded 1913, part of North Dakota University System
- **Small-town** 103-acre campus
- **Coed** 3,298 undergraduate students, 66% full-time, 61% women, 39% men
- **Moderately difficult** entrance level, 54% of applicants were admitted

Undergraduates 2,178 full-time, 1,120 part-time. 15% are from out of state; 2% Black or African American, non-Hispanic/Latino; 4% Hispanic/Latino; 74% Asian, non-Hispanic/Latino; 0.4% Native Hawaiian or other Pacific Islander, non-Hispanic/Latino; 3% American Indian or Alaska Native, non-Hispanic/Latino; 2% Two or more races, non-Hispanic/Latino; 3% Race/ethnicity unknown; 10% international; 9% transferred in; 20% live on campus. *Retention:* 65% of full-time freshmen returned.

Freshmen *Admission:* 1,003 applied, 538 admitted, 398 enrolled. *Average high school GPA:* 3.27. *Test scores:* ACT scores over 18: 92%; ACT scores over 24: 37%; ACT scores over 30: 4%.

Faculty *Total:* 276, 63% full-time, 38% with terminal degrees. *Student/faculty ratio:* 13:1.

Academics *Calendar:* semesters. *Degrees:* certificates, associate, bachelor's, master's, and postbachelor's certificates. *Special study options:* academic remediation for entering students, accelerated degree program, advanced placement credit, cooperative education, distance learning, double majors, English as a second language, honors programs, independent study, internships, part-time degree program, services for LD students, student-designed majors, study abroad, summer session for credit.

Computers on Campus 450 computers/terminals are available on campus for general student use. Students can access the following: campus intranet, computer help desk, free student e-mail accounts, online (class) grades, online (class) registration, online (class) schedules. Campuswide network is available. Wireless service is available via entire campus.

Student Life *Housing:* on-campus residence required for freshman year. *Options:* coed, men-only, women-only, disabled students. Campus housing is university owned. Freshman campus housing is guaranteed. *Activities and organizations:* drama/theater group, student-run newspaper, radio and television station, choral group, marching band, Residence Hall Association, Student Government Association, Beavers on Business, Student Social Work Organization, National Student Speech and Hearing Association. *Campus security:* controlled dormitory access, patrols by trained security personnel. *Student services:* health clinic, personal/psychological counseling, women's center.

Athletics Member NCAA, NAIA, NCCAA. All NCAA Division II. *Intercollegiate sports:* baseball M(s), basketball M(s)/W(s), cheerleading W, cross-country running M(s)/W(s), football M(s), golf M/W, ice hockey M(c), soccer W, softball W(s), track and field M(s)/W(s), volleyball W(s), wrestling M. *Intramural sports:* basketball M/W, racquetball M/W, softball M/W, volleyball M/W.

Standardized Tests *Required:* SAT or ACT (for admission).

Costs (2013–14) *Tuition:* state resident $4702 full-time, $247 per credit hour part-time; nonresident $4702 full-time, $247 per credit hour part-time. Full-time tuition and fees vary according to class time, course load, degree level, location, program, and reciprocity agreements. Part-time tuition and fees vary according to class time, course load, degree level, location, program, and reciprocity agreements. *Required fees:* $1219 full-time. *Room and board:* $4994. Room and board charges vary according to board plan and housing facility. *Payment plan:* installment. *Waivers:* minority students, children of alumni, senior citizens, and employees or children of employees.

Financial Aid Of all full-time matriculated undergraduates who enrolled in 2011, 1,426 applied for aid, 1,033 were judged to have need, 1,004 had their need fully met. In 2011, 299 non-need-based awards were made. *Average percent of need met:* 48%. *Average financial aid package:* $7847. *Average need-based loan:* $4160. *Average need-based gift aid:* $4154. *Average non-need-based aid:* $978. *Average indebtedness upon graduation:* $25,117.

Applying *Options:* electronic application, deferred entrance. *Application fee:* $35. *Required:* high school transcript. *Required for some:* minimum 2.5 GPA. *Application deadlines:* rolling (freshmen), rolling (out-of-state freshmen), rolling (transfers). *Notification:* continuous (freshmen), continuous (out-of-state freshmen), continuous (transfers).

Freshman Application Contact Mr. Kevin Harmon, Vice President of Enrollment Management, Minot State University, 500 University Avenue

West, Minot, ND 58707-0002. *Phone:* 701-858-3126. *Toll-free phone:* 800-777-0750 Ext. 3350. *Fax:* 701-858-3825. *E-mail:* askmsu@minotstateu.edu. *Website:* http://www.minotstateu.edu/.

North Dakota State University
Fargo, North Dakota

- **State-supported** university, founded 1890, part of North Dakota University System
- **Urban** 2100-acre campus
- **Endowment** $372,771
- **Coed** 12,332 undergraduate students, 90% full-time, 45% women, 55% men
- **Moderately difficult** entrance level, 84% of applicants were admitted

Undergraduates 11,059 full-time, 1,273 part-time. Students come from 47 states and territories; 79 other countries; 55% are from out of state; 2% Black or African American, non-Hispanic/Latino; 1% Hispanic/Latino; 1% Asian, non-Hispanic/Latino; 0.6% American Indian or Alaska Native, non-Hispanic/Latino; 1% Two or more races, non-Hispanic/Latino; 1% Race/ethnicity unknown; 4% international; 6% transferred in; 26% live on campus. *Retention:* 80% of full-time freshmen returned.

Freshmen *Admission:* 5,562 applied, 4,647 admitted, 2,442 enrolled. *Average high school GPA:* 3.39. *Test scores:* SAT critical reading scores over 500: 69%; SAT math scores over 500: 75%; ACT scores over 18: 97%; SAT critical reading scores over 600: 31%; SAT math scores over 600: 37%; ACT scores over 24: 50%; SAT critical reading scores over 700: 7%; SAT math scores over 700: 11%; ACT scores over 30: 8%.

Faculty *Total:* 833, 77% full-time, 71% with terminal degrees. *Student/faculty ratio:* 18:1.

Academics *Calendar:* semesters. *Degrees:* certificates, bachelor's, master's, doctoral, post-master's, and postbachelor's certificates. *Special study options:* advanced placement credit, cooperative education, distance learning, double majors, honors programs, independent study, internships, part-time degree program, services for LD students, student-designed majors, study abroad, summer session for credit. *ROTC:* Army (b), Air Force (b).

Computers on Campus 500 computers/terminals are available on campus for general student use. Students can access the following: computer help desk, free student e-mail accounts, online (class) grades, online (class) registration, online (class) schedules. Campuswide network is available. Wireless service is available via classrooms, computer centers, computer labs, dorm rooms, libraries, student centers.

Student Life *Housing:* on-campus residence required for freshman year. *Options:* coed, men-only, women-only, disabled students. Campus housing is university owned. Freshman campus housing is guaranteed. *Activities and organizations:* drama/theater group, student-run newspaper, radio and television station, choral group, marching band, Saddle and Sirloin, Students Today, Leaders Forever, International Student Association, Chi Alpha Christian Organization, fraternities/sororities, national fraternities, national sororities. *Campus security:* 24-hour emergency response devices and patrols, student patrols, late-night transport/escort service, controlled dormitory access. *Student services:* health clinic, personal/psychological counseling.

Athletics Member NCAA. All Division I. *Intercollegiate sports:* baseball M(s), basketball M(s)/W(s), bowling M(c)/W(c), cheerleading M(c)/W(c), cross-country running M(s)/W(s), equestrian sports M(c)/W(c), football M(s), golf M/W(s), ice hockey M(c)/W(c), lacrosse M(c)/W(c), riflery M(c)/W(c), rugby M(c)/W(c), soccer M(c)/W(s), softball W(s), track and field M(s)/W(s), volleyball M(c)/W(s), wrestling M(s). *Intramural sports:* basketball M/W, football M/W, softball M/W, volleyball M/W, wrestling M.

Standardized Tests *Required:* SAT or ACT (for admission).

Costs (2012–13) *One-time required fee:* $120. *Tuition:* state resident $6135 full-time, $270 per credit hour part-time; nonresident $16,381 full-time, $721 per credit hour part-time. Full-time tuition and fees vary according to program, reciprocity agreements, and student level. Part-time tuition and fees vary according to course load, program, reciprocity agreements, and student level. *Required fees:* $1098 full-time, $46 per credit hour part-time. *Room and board:* $6910; room only: $3226. Room and board charges vary according to board plan and housing facility. *Payment plan:* installment. *Waivers:* minority students, children of alumni, senior citizens, and employees or children of employees.

Financial Aid Of all full-time matriculated undergraduates who enrolled in 2007, 7,109 applied for aid, 4,917 were judged to have need, 980 had their need fully met. In 2007, 1763 non-need-based awards were made. *Average percent of need met:* 3%. *Average financial aid package:* $7030. *Average need-based loan:* $4378. *Average need-based gift aid:* $3419. *Average non-need-based aid:* $1533.

Applying *Options:* electronic application. *Application fee:* $35. *Required:* high school transcript, minimum 2.5 GPA. *Application deadlines:* 8/15 (freshmen), 8/15 (transfers). *Notification:* continuous (freshmen), continuous (transfers).

Freshman Application Contact Jobey Lichtblau, Director of Admission, North Dakota State University, NDSU Department 5230, PO Box 6050, Fargo, ND 58105-5454. *Phone:* 701-231-8643. *Toll-free phone:* 800-488-NDSU. *Fax:* 701-231-8802. *E-mail:* ndsu.admission@ndsu.edu. *Website:* http://www.ndsu.edu/.

Rasmussen College Bismarck

Bismarck, North Dakota

- **Proprietary** primarily 2-year, part of Rasmussen College System
- **Suburban** campus
- **Coed** 222 undergraduate students
- **Minimally difficult** entrance level

Faculty *Student/faculty ratio:* 22:1.

Academics *Degrees:* certificates, diplomas, associate, and bachelor's. *Special study options:* academic remediation for entering students, accelerated degree program, adult/continuing education programs, distance learning, double majors, internships, part-time degree program, summer session for credit.

Computers on Campus 67 computers/terminals are available on campus for general student use. Students can access the following: computer help desk, free student e-mail accounts, online (class) grades, online (class) schedules. Campuswide network is available. Wireless service is available via entire campus.

Student Life *Housing:* college housing not available.

Standardized Tests *Required:* Internal Exam (for admission).

Costs (2013–14) *Tuition:* $12,600 full-time. Full-time tuition and fees vary according to course level, course load, degree level, location, and program. Part-time tuition and fees vary according to course level, course load, degree level, location, and program. *Required fees:* $1800 full-time. *Payment plans:* installment, deferred payment. *Waivers:* employees or children of employees.

Applying *Options:* electronic application, early admission, deferred entrance. *Required:* high school transcript, minimum 2.0 GPA. *Required for some:* interview. *Application deadlines:* rolling (freshmen), rolling (transfers).

Freshman Application Contact Susan Hammerstrom, Director of Admissions, Rasmussen College Bismarck, 1701 East Century Avenue, Bismarck, ND 58503. *Phone:* 701-530-9600. *Toll-free phone:* 888-549-6755. *E-mail:* susan.hammerstrom@rasmussen.edu. *Website:* http://www.rasmussen.edu/.

Rasmussen College Fargo

Fargo, North Dakota

- **Proprietary** primarily 2-year, founded 1902, part of Rasmussen College System
- **Suburban** campus
- **Coed** 400 undergraduate students
- **Minimally difficult** entrance level

Faculty *Student/faculty ratio:* 22:1.

Academics *Calendar:* quarters. *Degrees:* certificates, diplomas, associate, and bachelor's. *Special study options:* academic remediation for entering students, accelerated degree program, adult/continuing education programs, distance learning, double majors, internships, part-time degree program, summer session for credit.

Computers on Campus 87 computers/terminals are available on campus for general student use. Students can access the following: computer help desk, free student e-mail accounts, online (class) grades, online (class) schedules. Campuswide network is available. Wireless service is available via entire campus.

Student Life *Housing:* college housing not available.

Standardized Tests *Required:* Internal Exam (for admission).

Costs (2013–14) *Tuition:* $12,600 full-time. Full-time tuition and fees vary according to course level, course load, degree level, location, and program. Part-time tuition and fees vary according to course level, course load, degree level, location, and program. *Required fees:* $1800 full-time. *Payment plans:* installment, deferred payment. *Waivers:* employees or children of employees.

Applying *Options:* electronic application, early admission, deferred entrance. *Required:* high school transcript, minimum 2.0 GPA. *Required for some:* interview. *Application deadlines:* rolling (freshmen), rolling (transfers).

Freshman Application Contact Susan Hammerstrom, Director of Admissions, Rasmussen College Fargo, 4012 19th Avenue, SW, Fargo, ND

58103. *Phone:* 701-277-3889. *Toll-free phone:* 888-549-6755. *E-mail:* susan.hammerstrom@rasmussen.edu. *Website:* http://www.rasmussen.edu/.

Sanford College of Nursing

Bismarck, North Dakota

- **Independent** upper-level, founded 1988
- **Small-town** 15-acre campus
- **Coed, primarily women** 109 undergraduate students, 100% full-time, 89% women, 11% men
- **Moderately difficult** entrance level, 58% of applicants were admitted

Undergraduates 109 full-time. Students come from 5 states and territories; 10% are from out of state; 5% Black or African American, non-Hispanic/Latino; 2% Hispanic/Latino; 0.9% Asian, non-Hispanic/Latino; 2% American Indian or Alaska Native, non-Hispanic/Latino; 6% Race/ethnicity unknown; 59% transferred in.

Freshmen *Admission:* 127 applied, 74 admitted.

Faculty *Total:* 13, 77% full-time, 8% with terminal degrees. *Student/faculty ratio:* 8:1.

Academics *Calendar:* semesters. *Degree:* bachelor's. *Special study options:* independent study, internships.

Computers on Campus 25 computers/terminals are available on campus for general student use. Students can access the following: campus intranet, free student e-mail accounts. Campuswide network is available. Wireless service is available via entire campus.

Student Life *Housing:* college housing not available. *Activities and organizations:* Student Body Organization, Student Nurses Association. *Campus security:* late-night transport/escort service. *Student services:* personal/psychological counseling, legal services.

Costs (2013–14) *One-time required fee:* $275. *Tuition:* $10,724 full-time, $447 per credit part-time. Part-time tuition and fees vary according to course load. *Required fees:* $855 full-time, $71 per credit part-time. *Waivers:* employees or children of employees.

Financial Aid Of all full-time matriculated undergraduates who enrolled in 2011, 78 applied for aid, 60 were judged to have need, 40 had their need fully met. 6 Federal Work-Study jobs (averaging $1200). In 2011, 4 non-need-based awards were made. *Average percent of need met:* 92%. *Average financial aid package:* $13,553. *Average need-based loan:* $4467. *Average need-based gift aid:* $3881. *Average non-need-based aid:* $650.

Applying *Options:* early admission, early action. *Application fee:* $40. *Application deadline:* 11/1 (transfers). *Notification:* continuous (transfers).

Application Contact Ms. Mary Smith, Director of Student Services, Sanford College of Nursing, 512 North 7th Street, Bismarck, ND 58501-4494. *Phone:* 701-323-6271. *Fax:* 701-323-6289. *E-mail:* mary.j.smith@sanfordcollege.edu. *Website:* http://bismarck.sanfordhealth.org/collegeofnursing/index.asp.

Trinity Bible College

Ellendale, North Dakota

Director of Admissions Rev. Steve Tvedt, Vice President of College Relations, Trinity Bible College, 50 South 6th Avenue, Ellendale, ND 58436-7150. *Phone:* 701-349-3621 Ext. 2045. *Toll-free phone:* 800-523-1603. *Website:* http://www.trinitybiblecollege.edu/.

University of Mary

Bismarck, North Dakota

- **Independent Roman Catholic** comprehensive, founded 1959
- **Rural** 107-acre campus
- **Endowment** $23.4 million
- **Coed**
- **Minimally difficult** entrance level

Faculty *Student/faculty ratio:* 17:1.

Academics *Calendar:* 4-4-1. *Degrees:* bachelor's, master's, and doctoral.

Student Life *Campus security:* 24-hour emergency response devices and patrols, late-night transport/escort service, controlled dormitory access.

Athletics Member NCAA. All Division II.

Standardized Tests *Required:* SAT or ACT (for admission).

Costs (2012–13) *Comprehensive fee:* $19,890 includes full-time tuition ($13,600) and room and board ($6290). Full-time tuition and fees vary according to course load, degree level, and program. Part-time tuition and fees vary according to course load, degree level, and program. *College room only:* $3330. Room and board charges vary according to board plan and housing facility.

Financial Aid *Of all full-time matriculated undergraduates who enrolled in 2010,* 1,513 applied for aid, 1,264 were judged to have need, 640 had their need fully met. 155 Federal Work-Study jobs (averaging $1224). 60 state and other part-time jobs (averaging $1725). *In 2010,* 414 non-need-based awards were made. *Average percent of need met:* 70. *Average financial aid package:* $11,057. *Average need-based loan:* $4418. *Average need-based gift aid:* $3904. *Average non-need-based aid:* $4163. *Average indebtedness upon graduation:* $24,749.

Applying *Options:* electronic application, early admission, deferred entrance. *Application fee:* $25. *Required:* high school transcript, 2.0 College Prep GPA. *Required for some:* essay or personal statement, interview. *Recommended:* minimum 2.5 GPA, 2 letters of recommendation.

Freshman Application Contact Mike Heitkamp, University of Mary, 7500 University Drive, Bismarck, ND 58504-9652. *Phone:* 701-355-8191. *Toll-free phone:* 800-288-6279. *Fax:* 701-255-7687. *E-mail:* mcheitkamp@umary.edu. *Website:* http://www.umary.edu/.

University of North Dakota

Grand Forks, North Dakota

- **State-supported** university, founded 1883, part of North Dakota University System
- **Urban** 550-acre campus
- **Endowment** $13.1 million
- **Coed** 11,522 undergraduate students, 81% full-time, 45% women, 55% men
- **Minimally difficult** entrance level, 43% of applicants were admitted

Undergraduates 9,334 full-time, 2,188 part-time. Students come from 44 other countries; 57% are from out of state; 2% Black or African American, non-Hispanic/Latino; 2% Hispanic/Latino; 1% Asian, non-Hispanic/Latino; 0.1% Native Hawaiian or other Pacific Islander, non-Hispanic/Latino; 2% American Indian or Alaska Native, non-Hispanic/Latino; 2% Two or more races, non-Hispanic/Latino; 4% Race/ethnicity unknown; 6% international; 8% transferred in; 32% live on campus. *Retention:* 77% of full-time freshmen returned.

Freshmen *Admission:* 4,857 applied, 2,091 admitted, 2,091 enrolled. *Average high school GPA:* 3.36. *Test scores:* ACT scores over 18: 95%; ACT scores over 24: 45%; ACT scores over 30: 6%.

Faculty *Total:* 703, 91% full-time, 74% with terminal degrees.

Academics *Calendar:* semesters. *Degrees:* certificates, diplomas, bachelor's, master's, doctoral, and postbachelor's certificates. *Special study options:* accelerated degree program, adult/continuing education programs, advanced placement credit, cooperative education, distance learning, double majors, English as a second language, honors programs, independent study, internships, off-campus study, part-time degree program, services for LD students, student-designed majors, study abroad, summer session for credit. *ROTC:* Army (b), Air Force (b). *Unusual degree programs:* 3-2 engineering; applied economics, counseling, chemistry, public administration.

Computers on Campus 1,500 computers/terminals and 400 ports are available on campus for general student use. Students can access the following: campus intranet, computer help desk, free student e-mail accounts, online (class) grades, online (class) registration, online (class) schedules. Campuswide network is available. 100% of college-owned or -operated housing units are wired for high-speed Internet access. Wireless service is available via classrooms, computer centers, computer labs, dorm rooms, learning centers, libraries, student centers.

Student Life *Housing options:* coed, men-only, women-only, disabled students. Campus housing is university owned and leased by the school. *Activities and organizations:* drama/theater group, student-run newspaper, radio and television station, choral group, marching band, Student Government, Greek Life, Association of Residence Halls, University of North Dakota Indian Association, NoDak Nation Student Athletic Boosters, national fraternities, national sororities. *Campus security:* 24-hour emergency response devices and patrols, student patrols, late-night transport/escort service, controlled dormitory access, emergency telephones. *Student services:* health clinic, personal/psychological counseling, women's center, legal services.

Athletics Member NCAA. All Division I. *Intercollegiate sports:* baseball M(s), basketball M(s)/W(s), cross-country running M(s)/W(s), football M(s), golf M(s)/W(s), ice hockey M(s)/W(s), soccer W(s), softball W(s), swimming and diving M(s)/W(s), tennis W(s), track and field M(s)/W(s), volleyball W(s). *Intramural sports:* basketball M/W, ice hockey M/W, soccer M/W, softball M/W, ultimate Frisbee M/W, volleyball M/W.

Standardized Tests *Required:* SAT or ACT (for admission). *Recommended:* ACT (for admission).

Costs (2012–13) *Tuition:* state resident $5938 full-time, $247 per credit hour part-time; nonresident $15,854 full-time, $661 per credit hour part-time. Full-time tuition and fees vary according to degree level, program, and reciprocity agreements. Part-time tuition and fees vary according to course load, degree level, program, and reciprocity agreements. *Required fees:* $1316 full-time. *Room and board:* $6332; room only: $2482. Room and board charges vary according to board plan and housing facility. *Payment plan:* deferred payment. *Waivers:* minority students, adult students, senior citizens, and employees or children of employees.

Financial Aid Of all full-time matriculated undergraduates who enrolled in 2010, 6,878 applied for aid, 5,256 were judged to have need, 5,108 had their need fully met. In 2010, 2719 non-need-based awards were made. *Average percent of need met:* 39%. *Average financial aid package:* $9651. *Average need-based loan:* $5349. *Average need-based gift aid:* $4076. *Average non-need-based aid:* $1602. *Average indebtedness upon graduation:* $31,764.

Applying *Options:* electronic application, deferred entrance. *Application fee:* $35. *Required:* high school transcript. *Recommended:* minimum 2.5 GPA. *Application deadline:* rolling (transfers). *Notification:* continuous (transfers).

Freshman Application Contact Deborah Melby, Director of Admissions, University of North Dakota, Stop 8357, 205 Twamley Hall, 264 Centennial Drive, Grand Forks, ND 58202. *Phone:* 701-777-3821. *Toll-free phone:* 800-CALL-UND. *Fax:* 701-777-2721. *E-mail:* und.enrollmentservices@und.edu. *Website:* http://www.und.nodak.edu/.

Valley City State University

Valley City, North Dakota

- **State-supported** comprehensive, founded 1890, part of North Dakota University System
- **Small-town** 55-acre campus
- **Coed** 1,214 undergraduate students, 65% full-time, 55% women, 45% men
- **Noncompetitive** entrance level, 81% of applicants were admitted

Undergraduates 795 full-time, 419 part-time. Students come from 43 states and territories; 11 other countries; 43% are from out of state; 4% Black or African American, non-Hispanic/Latino; 4% Hispanic/Latino; 0.7% Asian, non-Hispanic/Latino; 0.4% Native Hawaiian or other Pacific Islander, non-Hispanic/Latino; 1% American Indian or Alaska Native, non-Hispanic/Latino; 2% Two or more races, non-Hispanic/Latino; 1% Race/ethnicity unknown; 4% international; 9% transferred in; 24% live on campus. *Retention:* 54% of full-time freshmen returned.

Freshmen *Admission:* 351 applied, 285 admitted, 190 enrolled. *Average high school GPA:* 3.07. *Test scores:* SAT critical reading scores over 500: 30%; SAT math scores over 500: 30%; ACT scores over 18: 82%; SAT math scores over 600: 5%; ACT scores over 24: 18%.

Faculty *Total:* 109, 61% full-time, 54% with terminal degrees. *Student/faculty ratio:* 12:1.

Academics *Calendar:* semesters. *Degrees:* bachelor's and master's. *Special study options:* academic remediation for entering students, cooperative education, distance learning, double majors, internships, off-campus study, part-time degree program, services for LD students, student-designed majors, study abroad, summer session for credit.

Computers on Campus 995 computers/terminals are available on campus for general student use. Students can access the following: campus intranet, computer help desk, free student e-mail accounts, online (class) grades, online (class) registration, online (class) schedules. Campuswide network is available. 100% of college-owned or -operated housing units are wired for high-speed Internet access. Wireless service is available via entire campus.

Student Life *Housing:* on-campus residence required for freshman year. *Options:* coed, men-only, women-only. Campus housing is university owned. Freshman campus housing is guaranteed. *Activities and organizations:* drama/theater group, choral group, departmental clubs, Fellowship of Christian Athletes, intramural sports, VCAB, Viking Ambassadors. *Campus security:* controlled dormitory access, security cameras throughout campus. *Student services:* health clinic, personal/psychological counseling.

Athletics Member NAIA. *Intercollegiate sports:* baseball M(s), basketball M(s)/W(s), cross-country running M(s)/W(s), football M(s), golf M(s)/W(s), softball W(s), tennis M(c)/W(c), track and field M(s)/W(s), volleyball W(s). *Intramural sports:* basketball M/W, bowling M/W, cross-country running M/W, football M/W, golf M/W, ice hockey M/W, racquetball M/W, skiing (cross-country) M/W, soccer M/W, softball M/W, tennis M/W, track and field M/W, volleyball M/W.

Standardized Tests *Required for some:* SAT or ACT (for admission).

Costs (2013–14) *Tuition:* state resident $4657 full-time, $155 per semester hour part-time; nonresident $12,435 full-time, $155 per semester hour part-time. Full-time tuition and fees vary according to course load, location, program, and reciprocity agreements. Part-time tuition and fees vary according to course load, location, program, and reciprocity agreements. *Required fees:* $1667 full-time. *Room and board:* $5480; room only: $2040. Room and board charges vary according to board plan and housing facility. *Payment plan:* installment. *Waivers:* employees or children of employees.
Financial Aid Of all full-time matriculated undergraduates who enrolled in 2012, 635 applied for aid, 509 were judged to have need, 111 had their need fully met. 53 Federal Work-Study jobs (averaging $1921). In 2012, 91 non-need-based awards were made. *Average percent of need met:* 61%. *Average financial aid package:* $8178. *Average need-based loan:* $3693. *Average need-based gift aid:* $4357. *Average non-need-based aid:* $1693. *Average indebtedness upon graduation:* $27,884.
Applying *Options:* electronic application, early admission, deferred entrance. *Application fee:* $35. *Required:* high school transcript. *Application deadlines:* rolling (freshmen), rolling (transfers). *Notification:* continuous (freshmen), continuous (transfers).
Freshman Application Contact Ms. Kaleen Peterson, Admission Counselor, Valley City State University, 101 College Street Southwest, Valley City, ND 58072. *Phone:* 701-845-7115. *Toll-free phone:* 800-532-8641 Ext. 7101. *Fax:* 701-845-7299. *E-mail:* kaleen.peterson@vcsu.edu.
Website: http://www.vcsu.edu/.

OHIO

Akron Institute of Herzing University
Akron, Ohio
Admissions Office Contact Akron Institute of Herzing University, 1600 South Arlington Street, Suite 100, Akron, OH 44306. *Toll-free phone:* 800-311-0512.
Website: http://www.akroninstitute.com/.

Allegheny Wesleyan College
Salem, Ohio
Director of Admissions Admissions Office, Allegheny Wesleyan College, 2161 Woodsdale Road, Salem, OH 44460. *Phone:* 330-337-6403. *Toll-free phone:* 800-292-3153. *E-mail:* college@awc.edu.
Website: http://www.awc.edu/.

Antioch University Midwest
Yellow Springs, Ohio
- **Independent** upper-level, founded 1988, part of Antioch University
- **Small-town** 100-acre campus with easy access to Dayton
- **Coed** 116 undergraduate students, 47% full-time, 74% women, 26% men
- **Noncompetitive** entrance level

Undergraduates 55 full-time, 61 part-time. Students come from 1 other state; 21% Black or African American, non-Hispanic/Latino; 0.9% Hispanic/Latino; 2% Asian, non-Hispanic/Latino; 4% American Indian or Alaska Native, non-Hispanic/Latino; 6% Race/ethnicity unknown; 27% transferred in.
Faculty *Total:* 55, 33% full-time. *Student/faculty ratio:* 7:1.
Academics *Calendar:* quarters. *Degrees:* certificates, bachelor's, master's, post-master's, and postbachelor's certificates. *Special study options:* accelerated degree program, adult/continuing education programs, advanced placement credit, cooperative education, distance learning, double majors, independent study, internships, off-campus study, part-time degree program, student-designed majors, summer session for credit.
Computers on Campus 32 computers/terminals are available on campus for general student use. Students can access the following: campus intranet, computer help desk, free student e-mail accounts, online (class) grades, online (class) registration, online (class) schedules, online bill pay, and online view of financial aid award letter. Campuswide network is available. Wireless service is available via entire campus.

Student Life *Housing:* college housing not available. *Campus security:* 24-hour emergency response devices. *Student services:* personal/psychological counseling.
Financial Aid Of all full-time matriculated undergraduates who enrolled in 2011, 35 applied for aid, 34 were judged to have need. 5 Federal Work-Study jobs (averaging $7000). *Average percent of need met:* 30%. *Average financial aid package:* $8800. *Average need-based loan:* $7000. *Average need-based gift aid:* $5000. *Average indebtedness upon graduation:* $40,000.
Applying *Options:* electronic application, deferred entrance. *Application fee:* $45. *Application deadline:* rolling (transfers).
Application Contact Antioch University Midwest, 900 Dayton Street, Yellow Springs, OH 45387-1609. *Phone:* 937-769-1814.
Website: http://midwest.antioch.edu/.

Art Academy of Cincinnati
Cincinnati, Ohio
Freshman Application Contact Mr. John J. Wadell, Director of Admissions, Art Academy of Cincinnati, 1212 Jackson Street, Cincinnati, OH 45202-7106. *Phone:* 513-562-8744. *Toll-free phone:* 800-323-5692. *Fax:* 513-562-8778. *E-mail:* admissions@artacademy.edu.
Website: http://www.artacademy.edu/.

The Art Institute of Ohio–Cincinnati
Cincinnati, Ohio
- **Proprietary** primarily 2-year, part of Education Management Corporation
- **Urban** campus
- **Coed**

Academics *Calendar:* continuous. *Degrees:* diplomas, associate, and bachelor's.
Freshman Application Contact The Art Institute of Ohio–Cincinnati, 8845 Governors Hill Drive, Cincinnati, OH 45249-3317. *Phone:* 513-833-2400. *Toll-free phone:* 866-613-5184.
Website: http://www.artinstitutes.edu/cincinnati/.

See full-page ad on page 54 and page 1098 for the College Close-Up.

Ashland University
Ashland, Ohio
- **Independent** comprehensive, founded 1878, affiliated with Brethren Church
- **Small-town** 135-acre campus with easy access to Cleveland
- **Endowment** $39.4 million
- **Coed** 3,146 undergraduate students, 83% full-time, 54% women, 46% men
- **Moderately difficult** entrance level, 77% of applicants were admitted

Undergraduates 2,622 full-time, 524 part-time. Students come from 31 states and territories; 19 other countries; 10% are from out of state; 3% transferred in; 72% live on campus. *Retention:* 69% of full-time freshmen returned.
Freshmen *Admission:* 3,530 applied, 2,722 admitted, 675 enrolled. *Average high school GPA:* 3.37. *Test scores:* SAT critical reading scores over 500: 59%; SAT math scores over 500: 58%; ACT scores over 18: 96%; SAT critical reading scores over 600: 18%; SAT math scores over 600: 22%; ACT scores over 24: 40%; SAT critical reading scores over 700: 1%; SAT math scores over 700: 2%; ACT scores over 30: 4%.
Faculty *Total:* 591, 46% full-time, 56% with terminal degrees. *Student/faculty ratio:* 13:1.
Academics *Calendar:* semesters. *Degrees:* certificates, diplomas, bachelor's, master's, doctoral, post-master's, and postbachelor's certificates. *Special study options:* academic remediation for entering students, accelerated degree program, adult/continuing education programs, advanced placement credit, cooperative education, distance learning, double majors, English as a second language, honors programs, independent study, internships, off-campus study, part-time degree program, services for LD students, student-designed majors, study abroad, summer session for credit. *ROTC:* Army (c), Air Force (c).
Computers on Campus 760 computers/terminals are available on campus for general student use. Students can access the following: campus intranet, com-

puter help desk, free student e-mail accounts, online (class) grades, online (class) registration, online (class) schedules. Campuswide network is available. 100% of college-owned or -operated housing units are wired for high-speed Internet access. Wireless service is available via classrooms, computer centers, computer labs, learning centers, libraries, student centers.

Student Life *Housing:* on-campus residence required through junior year. *Options:* coed, men-only, women-only, disabled students. Campus housing is university owned. Freshman campus housing is guaranteed. *Activities and organizations:* drama/theater group, student-run newspaper, radio and television station, choral group, marching band, Campus Activity Board, Fellowship of Christian Athletes, The Well, Intramurals, Sororities, national fraternities, national sororities. *Campus security:* 24-hour emergency response devices and patrols, student patrols, late-night transport/escort service, controlled dormitory access. *Student services:* health clinic, personal/psychological counseling.

Athletics Member NCAA. All Division II. *Intercollegiate sports:* baseball M(s), basketball M(s)/W(s), cross-country running M(s)/W(s), football M(s), golf M(s)/W(s), soccer M(s)/W(s), softball M/W(s), swimming and diving M(s)/W(s), tennis W, track and field M(s)/W(s), volleyball W(s), wrestling M(s). *Intramural sports:* badminton M/W, baseball M(c), basketball M/W, bowling M/W, cross-country running M/W, field hockey M/W, football M, golf M/W, lacrosse M(c), racquetball M/W, rock climbing M/W, rugby M(c)/W(c), skiing (downhill) M(c)/W(c), soccer M/W, softball M(c)/W(c), swimming and diving M/W, table tennis M/W, tennis M/W, track and field M/W, ultimate Frisbee M/W, volleyball M(c)/W(c), weight lifting M(c)/W(c), wrestling M.

Standardized Tests *Required:* SAT or ACT (for admission).

Costs (2012–13) *Comprehensive fee:* $38,360 includes full-time tuition ($27,930), mandatory fees ($928), and room and board ($9502). Full-time tuition and fees vary according to location and program. Part-time tuition and fees vary according to course load, location, and program. *College room only:* $5172. Room and board charges vary according to board plan and housing facility. *Payment plan:* installment. *Waivers:* children of alumni, senior citizens, and employees or children of employees.

Financial Aid Of all full-time matriculated undergraduates who enrolled in 2012, 1,947 applied for aid, 1,947 were judged to have need. 1,380 Federal Work-Study jobs (averaging $2589). In 2012, 220 non-need-based awards were made. *Average financial aid package:* $25,115. *Average need-based loan:* $4648. *Average need-based gift aid:* $18,414. *Average non-need-based aid:* $11,236. *Average indebtedness upon graduation:* $36,058.

Applying *Options:* electronic application, deferred entrance. *Required:* high school transcript, minimum 2.5 GPA, Standardized test score for Freshmen applicants, 18 ACT or 870 SAT (Critical Reading and Math). *Application*

deadlines: rolling (freshmen), rolling (out-of-state freshmen), rolling (transfers). *Notification:* continuous (freshmen), continuous (transfers).

Freshman Application Contact Mr. W.C. Vance, Director of Admission, Ashland University, 401 College Avenue, Ashland, OH 44805. *Phone:* 419-289-5052. *Toll-free phone:* 800-882-1548. *Fax:* 419-289-5999. *E-mail:* enrollme@ashland.edu.

Website: http://www.exploreashland.com/.

Baldwin Wallace University

Berea, Ohio

- **Independent Methodist** comprehensive, founded 1845
- **Suburban** 120-acre campus with easy access to Cleveland
- **Endowment** $113.9 million
- **Coed** 3,512 undergraduate students, 86% full-time, 55% women, 45% men
- **Moderately difficult** entrance level, 70% of applicants were admitted

Undergraduates 3,036 full-time, 476 part-time. Students come from 39 states and territories; 13 other countries; 15% are from out of state; 8% Black or African American, non-Hispanic/Latino; 4% Hispanic/Latino; 0.8% Asian, non-Hispanic/Latino; 0.1% American Indian or Alaska Native, non-Hispanic/Latino; 3% Two or more races, non-Hispanic/Latino; 0.6% Race/ethnicity unknown; 1% international; 6% transferred in; 60% live on campus. *Retention:* 82% of full-time freshmen returned.

Freshmen *Admission:* 3,573 applied, 2,502 admitted, 712 enrolled. *Average high school GPA:* 3.54. *Test scores:* SAT critical reading scores over 500: 66%; SAT math scores over 500: 67%; ACT scores over 18: 94%; SAT critical reading scores over 600: 22%; SAT math scores over 600: 26%; ACT scores over 24: 50%; SAT critical reading scores over 700: 2%; SAT math scores over 700: 4%; ACT scores over 30: 6%.

Faculty *Total:* 424, 40% full-time, 40% with terminal degrees. *Student/faculty ratio:* 15:1.

Academics *Calendar:* semesters. *Degrees:* certificates, bachelor's, and master's. *Special study options:* academic remediation for entering students, accelerated degree program, adult/continuing education programs, advanced placement credit, distance learning, double majors, English as a second language, honors programs, independent study, internships, off-campus study, part-time degree program, services for LD students, student-designed majors,

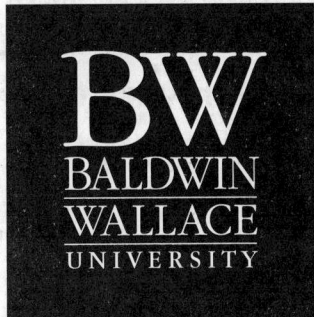

study abroad, summer session for credit. *ROTC:* Army (c), Air Force (c). *Unusual degree programs:* 3-2 engineering with Case Western Reserve University and Columbia University; social work with Case Western Reserve University; MBA programs in accounting, computer information systems, computer science, and human resources.

Computers on Campus 583 computers/terminals and 100 ports are available on campus for general student use. Students can access the following: campus intranet, computer help desk, free student e-mail accounts, online (class) grades, online (class) registration, online (class) schedules. Campuswide network is available. 100% of college-owned or -operated housing units are wired for high-speed Internet access. Wireless service is available via entire campus.

Student Life *Housing:* on-campus residence required through sophomore year. *Options:* coed, disabled students. Campus housing is university owned. Freshman campus housing is guaranteed. *Activities and organizations:* drama/theater group, student-run newspaper, radio station, choral group, marching band, Circle K, Habitat for Humanity, Dance Marathon, Campus Crusade, Black Student Alliance, national fraternities, national sororities. *Campus security:* 24-hour emergency response devices and patrols, student patrols, late-night transport/escort service, controlled dormitory access. *Student services:* health clinic, personal/psychological counseling.

Athletics Member NCAA. All Division III. *Intercollegiate sports:* baseball M, basketball M/W, cross-country running M/W, football M, golf M/W, lacrosse M/W, soccer M/W, softball W, swimming and diving M/W, tennis M/W, track and field M/W, volleyball W, wrestling M. *Intramural sports:* archery M(c)/W(c), badminton M/W, basketball M/W, cheerleading W(c), crew M(c)/W(c), football M/W, golf M/W, gymnastics W(c), lacrosse M(c)/W(c), racquetball M/W, rugby M(c), skiing (cross-country) M(c)/W(c), skiing (downhill) M(c)/W(c), soccer M/W, softball M/W, table tennis M(c)/W(c), tennis M/W, volleyball M/W, water polo M(c)/W(c), wrestling M.

Standardized Tests *Required for some:* SAT or ACT (for admission).

Costs (2012–13) *Comprehensive fee:* $34,580 includes full-time tuition ($27,060) and room and board ($7520). Full-time tuition and fees vary according to class time, course level, course load, degree level, program, and reciprocity agreements. Part-time tuition: $840 per semester hour. Part-time tuition and fees vary according to class time, course level, course load, degree level, program, and reciprocity agreements. *College room only:* $4340. Room and board charges vary according to housing facility. *Payment plans:* installment, deferred payment. *Waivers:* children of alumni and employees or children of employees.

Financial Aid Of all full-time matriculated undergraduates who enrolled in 2012, 2,701 applied for aid, 2,416 were judged to have need, 823 had their need fully met. 875 Federal Work-Study jobs (averaging $969). 351 state and other part-time jobs (averaging $700). In 2012, 521 non-need-based awards were made. *Average percent of need met:* 85%. *Average financial aid package:* $21,205. *Average need-based loan:* $4557. *Average need-based gift aid:* $16,134. *Average non-need-based aid:* $10,327. *Average indebtedness upon graduation:* $31,022. *Financial aid deadline:* 9/1.

Applying *Options:* electronic application, deferred entrance. *Application fee:* $25. *Required:* essay or personal statement, high school transcript, 1 letter of recommendation. *Recommended:* minimum 3.0 GPA, interview. *Application deadlines:* 3/1 (freshmen), 8/1 (transfers). *Notification:* continuous (freshmen), continuous (transfers).

Freshman Application Contact Patricia Skrha, Director of Undergraduate Admission, Baldwin Wallace University, Bonds Administration Building, 275 Eastland Road, Berea, OH 44017. *Phone:* 440-826-2222. *Toll-free phone:* 877-BW-APPLY. *Fax:* 440-826-3830. *E-mail:* admission@bw.edu. *Website:* http://www.bw.edu/.

See previous page for display ad and page 1142 for the College Close-Up.

Bluffton University

Bluffton, Ohio

- **Independent Mennonite** 4-year, founded 1899
- **Small-town** 65-acre campus with easy access to Toledo
- **Endowment** $19.3 million
- **Coed** 1,077 undergraduate students, 77% full-time, 52% women, 48% men
- **Moderately difficult** entrance level, 58% of applicants were admitted

Undergraduates 833 full-time, 244 part-time. Students come from 21 states and territories; 8 other countries; 18% are from out of state; 7% Black or African American, non-Hispanic/Latino; 3% Hispanic/Latino; 0.3% Asian, non-Hispanic/Latino; 0.1% American Indian or Alaska Native, non-Hispanic/Latino; 1% Two or more races, non-Hispanic/Latino; 2% Race/ethnicity unknown; 1% international; 6% transferred in; 72% live on campus. *Retention:* 68% of full-time freshmen returned.

Freshmen *Admission:* 1,807 applied, 1,057 admitted, 239 enrolled. *Average high school GPA:* 3.3. *Test scores:* SAT critical reading scores over 500: 57%; SAT math scores over 500: 73%; ACT scores over 18: 89%; SAT critical reading scores over 600: 17%; SAT math scores over 600: 23%; ACT scores over 24: 29%; SAT critical reading scores over 700: 4%; SAT math scores over 700: 3%; ACT scores over 30: 4%.

Faculty *Total:* 107, 53% full-time, 63% with terminal degrees. *Student/faculty ratio:* 12:1.

Academics *Calendar:* semesters. *Degrees:* bachelor's and master's. *Special study options:* academic remediation for entering students, accelerated degree program, adult/continuing education programs, advanced placement credit, distance learning, double majors, honors programs, independent study, internships, off-campus study, part-time degree program, services for LD students, student-designed majors, study abroad, summer session for credit.

Computers on Campus 170 computers/terminals and 1,300 ports are available on campus for general student use. Students can access the following: campus intranet, computer help desk, free student e-mail accounts, online (class) grades, online (class) registration, online (class) schedules. Campuswide network is available. 100% of college-owned or -operated housing units are wired for high-speed Internet access. Wireless service is available via classrooms, computer centers, computer labs, dorm rooms, libraries, student centers.

Student Life *Housing:* on-campus residence required through senior year. *Options:* coed, men-only, women-only. Campus housing is university owned. Freshman campus housing is guaranteed. *Activities and organizations:* drama/theater group, student-run newspaper, radio station, choral group, Intramurals, Student Senate, Marbeck Center Board, Music Groups/Chorale, Campus Ministries. *Campus security:* 24-hour emergency response devices, controlled dormitory access, night security guards. *Student services:* health clinic, personal/psychological counseling.

Athletics Member NCAA. All Division III. *Intercollegiate sports:* baseball M, basketball M/W, cheerleading W, cross-country running M/W, football M, soccer M/W, softball W, tennis M/W, track and field M/W, volleyball W. *Intramural sports:* basketball M/W, bowling M/W, football M/W, softball M/W, ultimate Frisbee M, volleyball M/W.

Standardized Tests *Required:* SAT or ACT (for admission).

Costs (2012–13) *Comprehensive fee:* $36,436 includes full-time tuition ($26,976), mandatory fees ($450), and room and board ($9010). Full-time tuition and fees vary according to course load and reciprocity agreements. Part-time tuition: $1124 per credit hour. Part-time tuition and fees vary according to course load. *Required fees:* $113 per term part-time. *Room and board:* Room and board charges vary according to board plan and housing facility. *Payment plan:* installment. *Waivers:* employees or children of employees.

Financial Aid Of all full-time matriculated undergraduates who enrolled in 2012, 708 applied for aid, 668 were judged to have need, 282 had their need fully met. 557 Federal Work-Study jobs (averaging $2225). 182 state and other part-time jobs (averaging $2265). In 2012, 84 non-need-based awards were made. *Average percent of need met:* 88%. *Average financial aid package:* $24,591. *Average need-based loan:* $4832. *Average need-based gift aid:* $17,939. *Average non-need-based aid:* $13,071. *Average indebtedness upon graduation:* $37,879. *Financial aid deadline:* 10/1.

Applying *Options:* electronic application, deferred entrance. *Application fee:* $20. *Required:* high school transcript, minimum 2.3 GPA, 1 letter of recommendation, rank in upper 50% of high school class or 19 on ACT. *Required for some:* essay or personal statement. *Recommended:* interview. *Application deadlines:* 8/15 (freshmen), rolling (transfers). *Notification:* continuous (freshmen), continuous (transfers).

Freshman Application Contact Mr. Ronald Headings, Vice President for Enrollment Management and Marketing, Bluffton University, 1 University Drive, Bluffton, OH 45817. *Phone:* 419-358-3660. *Toll-free phone:* 800-488-3257. *Fax:* 419-358-3081. *E-mail:* admissions@bluffton.edu. *Website:* http://www.bluffton.edu/.

Bowling Green State University

Bowling Green, Ohio

- **State-supported** university, founded 1910
- **Small-town** 1338-acre campus with easy access to Toledo
- **Endowment** $129.4 million
- **Coed** 14,815 undergraduate students, 93% full-time, 56% women, 44% men
- **Moderately difficult** entrance level, 74% of applicants were admitted

Undergraduates 13,735 full-time, 1,080 part-time. Students come from 52 states and territories; 45 other countries; 12% are from out of state; 11% Black or African American, non-Hispanic/Latino; 4% Hispanic/Latino; 0.9% Asian, non-Hispanic/Latino; 0.1% Native Hawaiian or other Pacific Islander, non-

Hispanic/Latino; 0.4% American Indian or Alaska Native, non-Hispanic/Latino; 2% Two or more races, non-Hispanic/Latino; 3% Race/ethnicity unknown; 2% international; 4% transferred in; 44% live on campus. *Retention:* 69% of full-time freshmen returned.

Freshmen *Admission:* 16,108 applied, 11,848 admitted, 3,621 enrolled. *Average high school GPA:* 3.2. *Test scores:* SAT critical reading scores over 500: 52%; SAT math scores over 500: 54%; SAT writing scores over 500: 44%; ACT scores over 18: 90%; SAT critical reading scores over 600: 15%; SAT math scores over 600: 17%; SAT writing scores over 600: 9%; ACT scores over 24: 32%; SAT critical reading scores over 700: 2%; SAT math scores over 700: 1%; SAT writing scores over 700: 1%; ACT scores over 30: 3%.

Faculty *Total:* 1,067, 76% full-time, 65% with terminal degrees. *Student/faculty ratio:* 18:1.

Academics *Calendar:* semesters. *Degrees:* bachelor's, master's, doctoral, post-master's, and postbachelor's certificates. *Special study options:* academic remediation for entering students, accelerated degree program, adult/continuing education programs, advanced placement credit, cooperative education, distance learning, double majors, English as a second language, honors programs, independent study, internships, off-campus study, part-time degree program, services for LD students, student-designed majors, study abroad, summer session for credit. *ROTC:* Army (b), Air Force (b).

Computers on Campus 1,500 computers/terminals and 500 ports are available on campus for general student use. Students can access the following: computer help desk, free student e-mail accounts, online (class) grades, online (class) registration, online (class) schedules, wireless networking, ePortfolio, MyFiles, Bursar billing information and payment, online mid-term grade reporting, view and change personal information, order official and unofficial transcripts, check meal plan balance, apply for graduation. Campuswide network is available. 100% of college-owned or -operated housing units are wired for high-speed Internet access. Wireless service is available via classrooms, computer centers, computer labs, dorm rooms, learning centers, libraries, student centers.

Student Life *Housing:* on-campus residence required through sophomore year. *Options:* coed, disabled students. Campus housing is university owned. Freshman campus housing is guaranteed. *Activities and organizations:* drama/theater group, student-run newspaper, radio and television station, choral group, marching band, Dance Marathon, University Activities Organization, BG Undead, H2O, Black Student Union, national fraternities, national sororities. *Campus security:* 24-hour emergency response devices and patrols, student patrols, late-night transport/escort service, controlled dormitory access. *Student services:* health clinic, personal/psychological counseling, women's center, legal services.

Athletics Member NCAA. All Division I. *Intercollegiate sports:* baseball M(s), basketball M(s)/W(s), cross-country running M(s)/W(s), football M(s), golf M(s)/W(s), gymnastics W(s), ice hockey M(s), soccer M(s)/W(s), softball W(s), swimming and diving W(s), tennis W(s), track and field W(s), volleyball W(s). *Intramural sports:* badminton M/W, baseball M, basketball M/W, bowling M(c)/W(c), cross-country running M(c)/W(c), equestrian sports M(c)/W(c), football M/W, golf M/W, gymnastics M(c)/W(c), ice hockey M(c), lacrosse M(c)/W(c), racquetball M/W, rugby M(c)/W(c), sailing M(c)/W(c), skiing (downhill) M(c)/W(c), soccer M/W, softball W, swimming and diving M(c)/W(c), tennis M(c)/W, track and field M(c)/W, ultimate Frisbee M/W, volleyball M/W, water polo M/W, wrestling M(c)/W(c).

Standardized Tests *Required:* SAT or ACT (for admission).

Costs (2012–13) *Tuition:* state resident $8913 full-time, $371 per credit hour part-time; nonresident $16,222 full-time, $676 per credit hour part-time. Full-time tuition and fees vary according to course load and location. Part-time tuition and fees vary according to course load and location. *Required fees:* $1600 full-time, $66 per credit hour part-time. *Room and board:* $8064. Room and board charges vary according to board plan and housing facility. *Payment plan:* installment. *Waivers:* senior citizens and employees or children of employees.

Financial Aid Of all full-time matriculated undergraduates who enrolled in 2012, 11,212 applied for aid, 9,422 were judged to have need, 1,236 had their need fully met. 512 Federal Work-Study jobs (averaging $1930). In 2012, 2368 non-need-based awards were made. *Average percent of need met:* 75%. *Average financial aid package:* $13,285. *Average need-based loan:* $7303. *Average need-based gift aid:* $5948. *Average non-need-based aid:* $4012. *Average indebtedness upon graduation:* $31,262.

Applying *Options:* electronic application, deferred entrance. *Application fee:* $45. *Required:* high school transcript. *Required for some:* interview. *Application deadlines:* 7/15 (freshmen), 7/15 (out-of-state freshmen), 7/15 (transfers). *Notification:* continuous (freshmen), continuous (out-of-state freshmen), continuous (transfers).

Freshman Application Contact Mr. Gary Swegan, Assistant Vice President/Director of Admissions, Bowling Green State University, Admissions Office, 110 McFall, Bowling Green, OH 43403. *Phone:* 419-372-BGSU. *Fax:* 419-372-6955. *E-mail:* choosebgsu@bgsu.edu.

Website: http://www.bgsu.edu/.

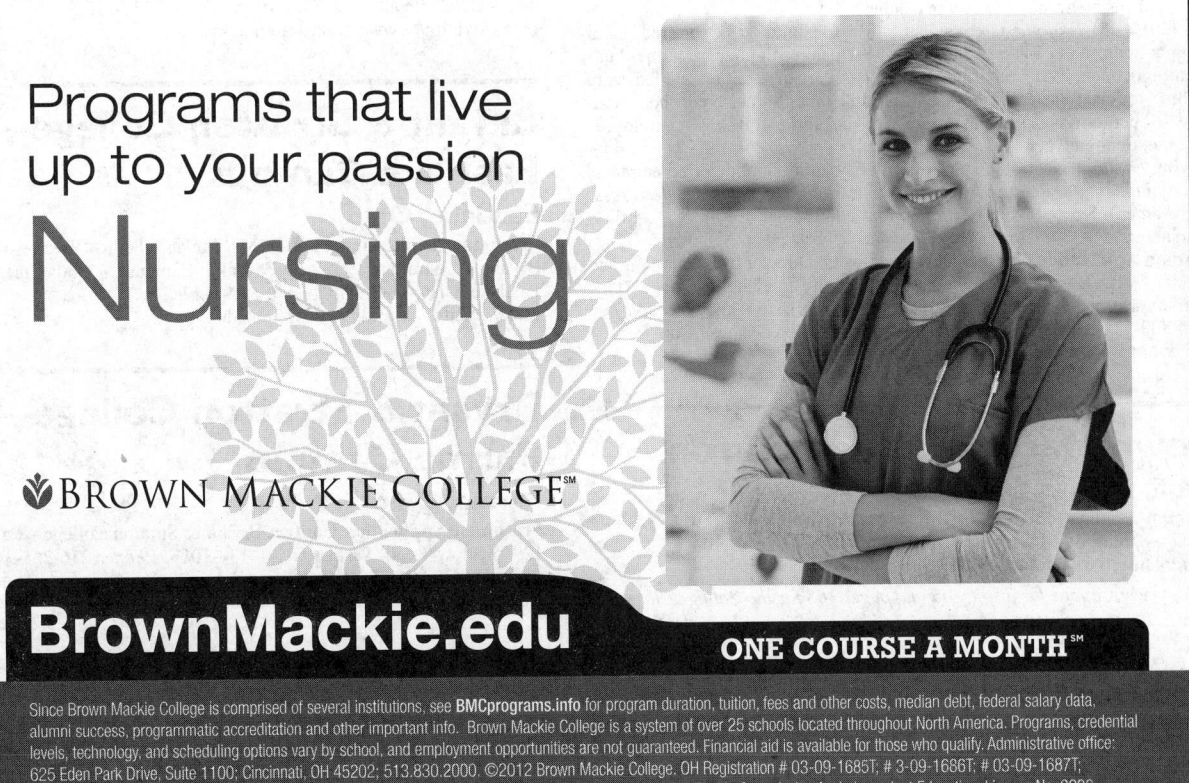

Bowling Green State University-Firelands College

Huron, Ohio

- **State-supported** primarily 2-year, founded 1968, part of Bowling Green State University System
- **Rural** 216-acre campus with easy access to Cleveland, Toledo
- **Coed** 2,397 undergraduate students, 54% full-time, 65% women, 35% men
- **Noncompetitive** entrance level, 78% of applicants were admitted

Undergraduates 1,285 full-time, 1,112 part-time. Students come from 2 states and territories; 7% Black or African American, non-Hispanic/Latino; 4% Hispanic/Latino; 0.6% Asian, non-Hispanic/Latino; 0.2% Native Hawaiian or other Pacific Islander, non-Hispanic/Latino; 0.5% American Indian or Alaska Native, non-Hispanic/Latino; 3% Two or more races, non-Hispanic/Latino; 3% Race/ethnicity unknown; 6% transferred in. *Retention:* 54% of full-time freshmen returned.

Freshmen *Admission:* 711 applied, 555 admitted, 393 enrolled. *Average high school GPA:* 2.69. *Test scores:* ACT scores over 18: 75%; ACT scores over 24: 15%; ACT scores over 30: 1%.

Faculty *Total:* 154, 36% full-time, 27% with terminal degrees. *Student/faculty ratio:* 19:1.

Academics *Calendar:* semesters. *Degrees:* certificates, associate, and bachelor's (also offers some upper-level and graduate courses). *Special study options:* academic remediation for entering students, adult/continuing education programs, advanced placement credit, distance learning, double majors, honors programs, independent study, internships, part-time degree program, services for LD students, student-designed majors, summer session for credit. *ROTC:* Army (c), Air Force (c).

Computers on Campus 300 computers/terminals are available on campus for general student use. Students can access the following: computer help desk, free student e-mail accounts, online (class) grades, online (class) registration, online (class) schedules. Campuswide network is available. Wireless service is available via entire campus.

Student Life *Housing:* college housing not available. *Activities and organizations:* drama/theater group, Humanity Organized for Peace through Education-H.O.P.E., Science and Environment Club, Speech Activities Organization—Theatre, Visual Communication Technology Organization, intramurals. *Campus security:* 24-hour emergency response devices, late-night transport/escort service, patrols by trained security personnel.

Costs (2012–13) *Tuition:* state resident $4614 full-time, $192 per credit hour part-time; nonresident $11,922 full-time, $497 per credit hour part-time. Full-time tuition and fees vary according to location. Part-time tuition and fees vary according to location. *Required fees:* $236 full-time, $9 per credit hour part-time, $118 per term part-time. *Payment plan:* installment. *Waivers:* employees or children of employees.

Applying *Options:* electronic application, early admission, deferred entrance. *Application fee:* $45. *Required:* high school transcript. *Application deadlines:* 8/6 (freshmen), 8/6 (transfers). *Notification:* continuous (freshmen), continuous (transfers).

Freshman Application Contact Debralee Divers, Director of Admissions and Financial Aid, Bowling Green State University-Firelands College, One University Drive, Huron, OH 44839-9791. *Phone:* 419-433-5560. *Toll-free phone:* 800-322-4787. *Fax:* 419-372-0604. *E-mail:* divers@bgsu.edu. *Website:* http://www.firelands.bgsu.edu/.

Brown Mackie College–Akron

Akron, Ohio

Freshman Application Contact Brown Mackie College–Akron, 755 White Pond Drive, Suite 101, Akron, OH 44320. *Phone:* 330-869-3600. *Website:* http://www.brownmackie.edu/akron/.

See previous page for display ad and page 1168 for the College Close-Up.

Brown Mackie College–Cincinnati

Cincinnati, Ohio

Freshman Application Contact Brown Mackie College–Cincinnati, 1011 Glendale-Milford Road, Cincinnati, OH 45215. *Phone:* 513-771-2424. *Toll-free phone:* 800-888-1445. *Website:* http://www.brownmackie.edu/cincinnati/.

See previous page for display ad and page 1176 for the College Close-Up.

Brown Mackie College–Findlay

Findlay, Ohio

Freshman Application Contact Brown Mackie College–Findlay, 1700 Fostoria Avenue, Suite 100, Findlay, OH 45840. *Phone:* 419-423-2211. *Toll-free phone:* 800-842-3687. *Website:* http://www.brownmackie.edu/findlay/.

See next page for display ad and page 1180 for the College Close-Up.

Brown Mackie College–North Canton

Canton, Ohio

Freshman Application Contact Brown Mackie College–North Canton, 4300 Munson Street NW, Canton, OH 44718-3674. *Phone:* 330-494-1214. *Website:* http://www.brownmackie.edu/northcanton/.

See next page for display ad and page 1198 for the College Close-Up.

Bryant & Stratton College

Cleveland, Ohio

Freshman Application Contact Bryant & Stratton College, Cleveland, OH 44114-3203. *Phone:* 216-771-1700. *Fax:* 216-771-7787. *Website:* http://www.bryantstratton.edu/.

Bryant & Stratton College—Eastlake Campus

Eastlake, Ohio

Freshman Application Contact Ms. Melanie Pettit, Director of Admissions, Bryant & Stratton College—Eastlake Campus, 35350 Curtis Boulevard, Eastlake, OH 44095. *Phone:* 440-510-1112. *Website:* http://www.bryantstratton.edu/.

Bryant & Stratton College—Parma Campus

Parma, Ohio

Freshman Application Contact Bryant & Stratton College—Parma Campus, 12955 Snow Road, Parma, OH 44130-1013. *Phone:* 216-265-3151. *Toll-free phone:* 866-948-0571. *Website:* http://www.bryantstratton.edu/.

Capital University

Columbus, Ohio

- **Independent** comprehensive, founded 1830, affiliated with Evangelical Lutheran Church in America
- **Suburban** 48-acre campus with easy access to Columbus
- **Endowment** $60.6 million
- **Coed** 2,720 undergraduate students, 90% full-time, 57% women, 43% men
- **Moderately difficult** entrance level, 75% of applicants were admitted

Undergraduates 2,448 full-time, 272 part-time. Students come from 33 states and territories; 12 other countries; 10% are from out of state; 10% Black or African American, non-Hispanic/Latino; 3% Hispanic/Latino; 1% Asian, non-Hispanic/Latino; 0.1% Native Hawaiian or other Pacific Islander, non-Hispanic/Latino; 4% Two or more races, non-Hispanic/Latino; 2% Race/ethnicity unknown; 0.8% international; 3% transferred in; 57% live on campus. *Retention:* 75% of full-time freshmen returned.

Freshmen *Admission:* 3,844 applied, 2,880 admitted, 670 enrolled. *Average high school GPA:* 3.44. *Test scores:* SAT critical reading scores over 500: 67%; SAT math scores over 500: 70%; SAT writing scores over 500: 56%; ACT scores over 18: 96%; SAT critical reading scores over 600: 28%; SAT math scores over 600: 30%; SAT writing scores over 600: 20%; ACT scores over 24: 54%; SAT critical reading scores over 700: 7%; SAT math scores over 700: 6%; SAT writing scores over 700: 4%; ACT scores over 30: 11%.

Faculty *Total:* 450, 40% full-time, 50% with terminal degrees. *Student/faculty ratio:* 11:1.

Academics *Calendar:* semesters. *Degrees:* bachelor's, master's, and doctoral. *Special study options:* accelerated degree program, adult/continuing education programs, advanced placement credit, cooperative education, double majors, English as a second language, external degree program, freshman honors college, honors programs, independent study, internships, off-campus study, part-time degree program, services for LD students, student-designed majors, study abroad, summer session for credit. *ROTC:* Army (b), Air Force (c). *Unusual degree programs:* 3-2 engineering with Washington University in St. Louis, Case Western Reserve University; occupational therapy with Washington University in St. Louis, University of Indianapolis.

Computers on Campus 415 computers/terminals and 1,400 ports are available on campus for general student use. Students can access the following: campus intranet, computer help desk, free student e-mail accounts, online (class) grades, online (class) registration, online (class) schedules. Campus-wide network is available. 100% of college-owned or -operated housing units are wired for high-speed Internet access. Wireless service is available via entire campus.

Student Life *Housing:* on-campus residence required through sophomore year. *Options:* coed, disabled students. Campus housing is university owned. Freshman campus housing is guaranteed. *Activities and organizations:* drama/theater group, student-run newspaper, radio station, choral group, Campus Crusade for Christ, student government, University Programming, College Republicans, American Marketing Association, national fraternities, national sororities. *Campus security:* 24-hour emergency response devices and patrols, late-night transport/escort service, controlled dormitory access. *Student services:* health clinic, personal/psychological counseling.

Athletics Member NCAA. All Division III. *Intercollegiate sports:* baseball M, basketball M/W, cross-country running M/W, football M, golf M/W, soccer M/W, softball W, tennis M/W, track and field M/W, volleyball W. *Intramural sports:* basketball M/W, bowling M/W, cheerleading M(c)/W(c), football M/W, lacrosse M(c)/W(c), skiing (downhill) M(c)/W(c), softball M/W, swimming and diving M(c)/W(c), volleyball M/W.

Standardized Tests *Required:* SAT or ACT (for admission).

Costs (2012–13) *Comprehensive fee:* $39,824 includes full-time tuition ($31,364) and room and board ($8460). Full-time tuition and fees vary according to course load. Part-time tuition: $1045 per credit hour. Part-time tuition and fees vary according to course load. *Room and board:* Room and board charges vary according to board plan and housing facility. *Payment plan:* installment. *Waivers:* senior citizens and employees or children of employees.

Financial Aid Of all full-time matriculated undergraduates who enrolled in 2011, 2,103 applied for aid, 1,954 were judged to have need, 338 had their need fully met. In 2011, 142 non-need-based awards were made. *Average percent of need met:* 76%. *Average financial aid package:* $22,845. *Average need-based loan:* $4355. *Average need-based gift aid:* $17,683. *Average non-need-based aid:* $16,387. *Average indebtedness upon graduation:* $33,200.

Applying *Options:* electronic application, deferred entrance. *Application fee:* $25. *Required:* high school transcript, minimum 2.6 GPA. *Required for some:* 1 letter of recommendation, audition for Conservatory of Music. *Recommended:* interview. *Application deadlines:* 5/1 (freshmen), rolling (transfers). *Notification:* 9/30 (freshmen), continuous (transfers).

Freshman Application Contact Ms. Amanda Sohl, Director of Admission, Capital University, 1 College and Main, Columbus, OH 43209. *Phone:* 614-

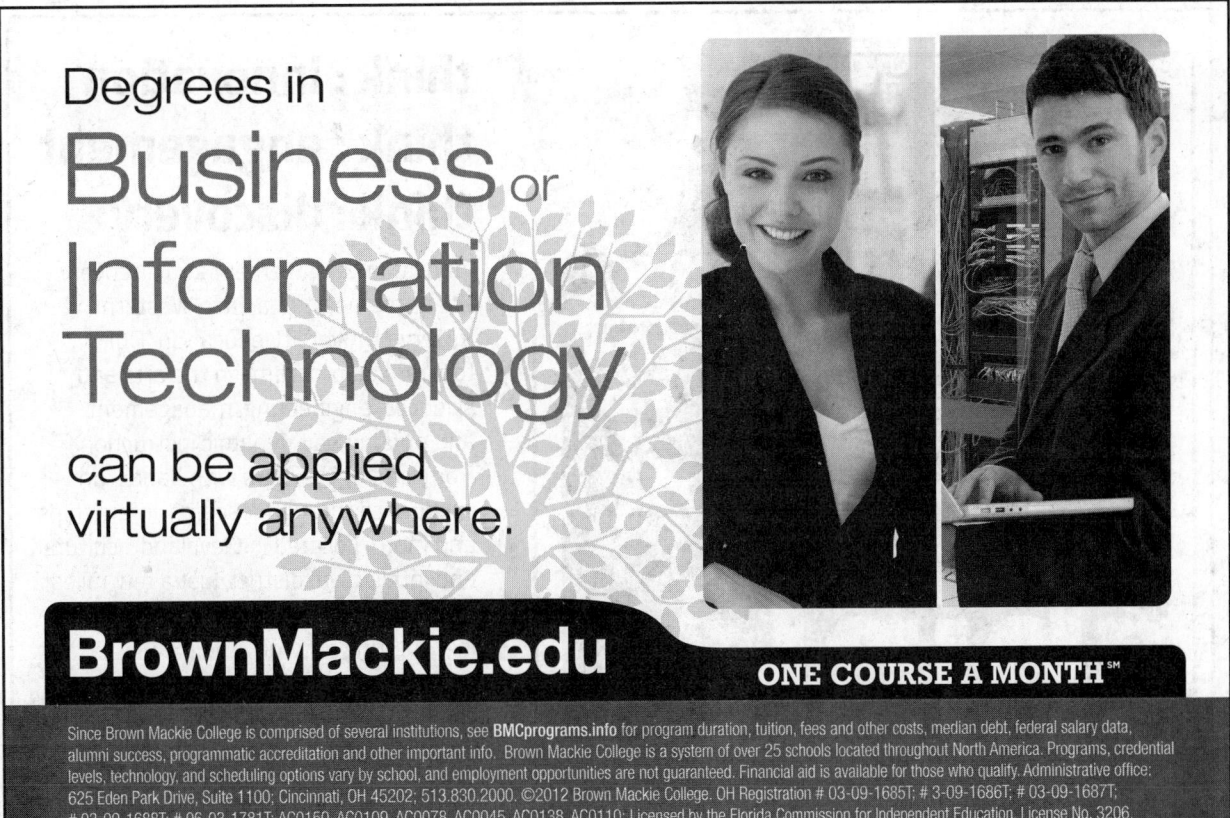

236-6574. *Toll-free phone:* 866-544-6175. *Fax:* 614-236-6926. *E-mail:* asohl@capital.edu.
Website: http://www.capital.edu/.

Case Western Reserve University

Cleveland, Ohio

- **Independent** university, founded 1826
- **Urban** 155-acre campus
- **Endowment** $1.6 billion
- **Coed** 4,386 undergraduate students, 97% full-time, 44% women, 56% men
- **Very difficult** entrance level, 54% of applicants were admitted

Undergraduates 4,260 full-time, 126 part-time. Students come from 49 states and territories; 36 other countries; 59% are from out of state; 4% Black or African American, non-Hispanic/Latino; 5% Hispanic/Latino; 19% Asian, non-Hispanic/Latino; 0.2% American Indian or Alaska Native, non-Hispanic/Latino; 3% Two or more races, non-Hispanic/Latino; 8% Race/ethnicity unknown; 7% international; 1% transferred in; 77% live on campus. *Retention:* 92% of full-time freshmen returned.

Freshmen *Admission:* 14,778 applied, 8,027 admitted, 1,372 enrolled. *Test scores:* SAT critical reading scores over 500: 98%; SAT math scores over 500: 100%; SAT writing scores over 500: 98%; ACT scores over 18: 100%; SAT critical reading scores over 600: 79%; SAT math scores over 600: 93%; SAT writing scores over 600: 78%; ACT scores over 24: 99%; SAT critical reading scores over 700: 34%; SAT math scores over 700: 60%; SAT writing scores over 700: 29%; ACT scores over 30: 70%.

Faculty *Total:* 932, 81% full-time, 86% with terminal degrees. *Student/faculty ratio:* 10:1.

Academics *Calendar:* semesters. *Degrees:* bachelor's, master's, doctoral, and postbachelor's certificates. *Special study options:* accelerated degree program, adult/continuing education programs, advanced placement credit, cooperative education, double majors, English as a second language, honors programs, independent study, internships, off-campus study, part-time degree program, services for LD students, student-designed majors, study abroad, summer session for credit. *ROTC:* Army (b), Air Force (c). *Unusual degree programs:* 3-2 engineering.

Computers on Campus 298 computers/terminals and 48,000 ports are available on campus for general student use. Students can access the following: campus intranet, computer help desk, free student e-mail accounts, online (class) grades, online (class) registration, online (class) schedules, software library, online reference databases, electronic books and journals, research computing, training. Campuswide network is available. 100% of college-owned or -operated housing units are wired for high-speed Internet access. Wireless service is available via entire campus.

Student Life *Housing:* on-campus residence required through sophomore year. *Options:* coed. Campus housing is university owned. Freshman campus housing is guaranteed. *Activities and organizations:* drama/theater group, student-run newspaper, radio station, choral group, marching band, CASE EMS, Habitat for Humanity, international student groups, music/dance groups, Alpha Phi Omega (national service organization), national fraternities, national sororities. *Campus security:* 24-hour emergency response devices and patrols, student patrols, late-night transport/escort service, controlled dormitory access, crime prevention programs. *Student services:* health clinic, personal/psychological counseling, women's center, legal services.

Athletics Member NCAA. All Division III. *Intercollegiate sports:* archery M(c)/W(c), baseball M, basketball M/W, cheerleading M(c)/W(c), crew M(c)/W(c), cross-country running M/W, fencing M(c)/W(c), football M, ice hockey M(c)/W(c), soccer M/W, softball W, swimming and diving M/W, tennis M/W, track and field M/W, ultimate Frisbee M(c)/W(c), volleyball M(c)/W, wrestling M. *Intramural sports:* badminton M/W, basketball M/W, bowling M/W, cross-country running M/W, football M/W, golf M/W, racquetball M/W, soccer M/W, softball M/W, squash M/W, swimming and diving M/W, table tennis M/W, tennis M/W, track and field M/W, ultimate Frisbee M/W, volleyball M/W, water polo M/W, weight lifting M/W, wrestling M.

Standardized Tests *Required:* SAT or ACT (for admission).

Costs (2012–13) *One-time required fee:* $465. *Comprehensive fee:* $52,926 includes full-time tuition ($40,120), mandatory fees ($370), and room and board ($12,436). Part-time tuition: $1672 per credit hour. Part-time tuition and fees vary according to course load. *College room only:* $7140. Room and board charges vary according to board plan, housing facility, and student level. *Payment plan:* installment. *Waivers:* employees or children of employees.

Financial Aid Of all full-time matriculated undergraduates who enrolled in 2012, 3,090 applied for aid, 2,675 were judged to have need, 1,265 had their need fully met. 1,711 Federal Work-Study jobs (averaging $2297). In 2012, 917 non-need-based awards were made. *Average percent of need met:* 82%. *Average financial aid package:* $33,214. *Average need-based loan:* $4906.

Average need-based gift aid: $27,174. *Average non-need-based aid:* $21,117. *Average indebtedness upon graduation:* $37,610.

Applying *Options:* electronic application, early admission, early action, deferred entrance. *Required:* essay or personal statement, high school transcript, 1 letter of recommendation. *Recommended:* interview. *Application deadlines:* 1/15 (freshmen), 5/15 (transfers), 11/1 (early action). *Notification:* 3/20 (freshmen), continuous until 7/1 (transfers), 12/15 (early action).

Freshman Application Contact Mr. Robert McCullough, Director of Undergraduate Admission, Case Western Reserve University, 10900 Euclid Avenue, Cleveland, OH 44106. *Phone:* 216-368-4450. *Fax:* 216-368-5111. *E-mail:* admission@case.edu. *Website:* http://www.case.edu/.

See previous page for display ad and page 1228 for the College Close-Up.

Cedarville University

Cedarville, Ohio

- **Independent Baptist** comprehensive, founded 1887
- **Rural** 400-acre campus with easy access to Columbus, Dayton
- **Endowment** $19.8 million
- **Coed** 3,220 undergraduate students, 95% full-time, 53% women, 47% men
- **Moderately difficult** entrance level, 75% of applicants were admitted

Undergraduates 3,047 full-time, 173 part-time. Students come from 48 states and territories; 16 other countries; 61% are from out of state; 2% Black or African American, non-Hispanic/Latino; 2% Hispanic/Latino; 1% Asian, non-Hispanic/Latino; 0.1% Native Hawaiian or other Pacific Islander, non-Hispanic/Latino; 0.4% American Indian or Alaska Native, non-Hispanic/Latino; 0.8% Two or more races, non-Hispanic/Latino; 5% Race/ethnicity unknown; 1% international; 3% transferred in; 76% live on campus. *Retention:* 85% of full-time freshmen returned.

Freshmen *Admission:* 3,347 applied, 2,523 admitted, 832 enrolled. *Average high school GPA:* 3.65. *Test scores:* SAT critical reading scores over 500: 90%; SAT math scores over 500: 87%; SAT writing scores over 500: 84%; ACT scores over 18: 100%; SAT critical reading scores over 600: 49%; SAT math scores over 600: 50%; SAT writing scores over 600: 43%; ACT scores over 24: 74%; SAT critical reading scores over 700: 14%; SAT math scores over 700: 10%; SAT writing scores over 700: 11%; ACT scores over 30: 19%.

Faculty *Total:* 311, 58% full-time, 46% with terminal degrees. *Student/faculty ratio:* 14:1.

Academics *Calendar:* semesters. *Degrees:* certificates, bachelor's, master's, and doctoral. *Special study options:* academic remediation for entering students, accelerated degree program, adult/continuing education programs, advanced placement credit, distance learning, double majors, honors programs, independent study, internships, off-campus study, part-time degree program, services for LD students, study abroad, summer session for credit. *ROTC:* Army (c), Air Force (c).

Computers on Campus 2,030 computers/terminals are available on campus for general student use. Students can access the following: campus intranet, computer help desk, free student e-mail accounts, online (class) grades, online (class) registration, online (class) schedules, over 150 software packages. Campuswide network is available. Wireless service is available via entire campus.

Student Life *Housing:* on-campus residence required through senior year. *Options:* men-only, women-only, disabled students. Campus housing is university owned. Freshman campus housing is guaranteed. *Activities and organizations:* drama/theater group, student-run newspaper, radio station, choral group, Students in Free Enterprise, Christian Pharmacist Association, Society of Automotive Engineers—SAE, Christian Nursing Association, Cedarville Men's Rugby. *Campus security:* 24-hour emergency response devices and patrols, student patrols, late-night transport/escort service, controlled dormitory access. *Student services:* health clinic, personal/psychological counseling.

Athletics Member NCAA. All Division II. *Intercollegiate sports:* baseball M(s), basketball M(s)/W(s), cheerleading M/W, cross-country running M(s)/W(s), golf M(s), soccer M(s)/W(s), softball W(s), tennis M(s)/W(s), track and field M(s)/W(s), volleyball W(s). *Intramural sports:* badminton M/W, basketball M/W, bowling M/W, cross-country running M/W, football M/W, golf M/W, racquetball M/W, rock climbing M/W, skiing (downhill) M/W, soccer M/W, softball M/W, table tennis M/W, tennis M/W, ultimate Frisbee M/W, volleyball M/W.

Standardized Tests *Required:* SAT or ACT (for admission). *Recommended:* SAT and SAT Subject Tests or ACT (for admission).

Costs (2012–13) *Comprehensive fee:* $31,036 includes full-time tuition ($25,496) and room and board ($5540). Part-time tuition: $965 per credit. Part-time tuition and fees vary according to course load. *College room only:* $3140.

Room and board charges vary according to board plan. *Payment plan:* installment. *Waivers:* senior citizens and employees or children of employees.

Financial Aid Of all full-time matriculated undergraduates who enrolled in 2011, 2,353 applied for aid, 2,005 were judged to have need, 317 had their need fully met. 479 Federal Work-Study jobs (averaging $802). 1,608 state and other part-time jobs (averaging $1046). In 2011, 501 non-need-based awards were made. *Average percent of need met:* 36%. *Average financial aid package:* $23,356. *Average need-based loan:* $5869. *Average need-based gift aid:* $4078. *Average non-need-based aid:* $18,113. *Average indebtedness upon graduation:* $28,251.

Applying *Options:* electronic application, early admission, deferred entrance. *Application fee:* $30. *Required:* essay or personal statement, high school transcript, minimum 3.0 GPA, 1 letter of recommendation, Clear testimony of faith in Jesus Christ and evidence of consistent Christian lifestyle. *Required for some:* interview. *Application deadlines:* rolling (freshmen), rolling (transfers). *Notification:* continuous (freshmen), continuous (transfers).

Freshman Application Contact Ms. Amy Holderby, Director of Admissions, Cedarville University, 251 North Main Street, Cedarville, OH 45314-0601. *Phone:* 937-766-7700. *Toll-free phone:* 800-CEDARVILLE. *Fax:* 937-766-7575. *E-mail:* admiss@cedarville.edu. *Website:* http://www.cedarville.edu/.

Central State University

Wilberforce, Ohio

- **State-supported** comprehensive, founded 1887, part of Ohio Board of Regents
- **Rural** 60-acre campus with easy access to Dayton
- **Endowment** $2.0 million
- **Coed** 2,116 undergraduate students, 89% full-time, 53% women, 47% men
- **Minimally difficult** entrance level, 37% of applicants were admitted

Undergraduates 1,878 full-time, 238 part-time. Students come from 29 states and territories; 2 other countries; 57% are from out of state; 96% Black or African American, non-Hispanic/Latino; 0.7% Hispanic/Latino; 0.1% Asian, non-Hispanic/Latino; 0.2% American Indian or Alaska Native, non-Hispanic/Latino; 0.4% Two or more races, non-Hispanic/Latino; 1% Race/ethnicity unknown; 0.1% international; 6% transferred in; 52% live on campus. *Retention:* 43% of full-time freshmen returned.

Freshmen *Admission:* 7,959 applied, 2,923 admitted, 516 enrolled. *Average high school GPA:* 2.4. *Test scores:* SAT critical reading scores over 500: 5%; SAT math scores over 500: 10%; ACT scores over 18: 28%; SAT math scores over 600: 1%; ACT scores over 24: 2%.

Faculty *Total:* 243, 46% full-time, 42% with terminal degrees. *Student/faculty ratio:* 13:1.

Academics *Calendar:* semesters. *Degrees:* bachelor's and master's. *Special study options:* adult/continuing education programs, cooperative education, double majors, honors programs, independent study, internships, off-campus study, part-time degree program, services for LD students, study abroad, summer session for credit. *ROTC:* Army (b).

Computers on Campus 555 computers/terminals and 160 ports are available on campus for general student use. Students can access the following: campus intranet, computer help desk, free student e-mail accounts, online (class) grades, online (class) registration, online (class) schedules. Campuswide network is available. 100% of college-owned or -operated housing units are wired for high-speed Internet access. Wireless service is available via classrooms, computer centers, computer labs, dorm rooms, learning centers, libraries, student centers.

Student Life *Housing:* on-campus residence required for freshman year. *Options:* coed, men-only, women-only. Campus housing is university owned and leased by the school. Freshman campus housing is guaranteed. *Activities and organizations:* drama/theater group, student-run newspaper, radio and television station, choral group, marching band, Student Ambassadors, student government, Make it Happen (Inter-Faith), Daughters of Nia Anaya (Social Group), Evolutions (Modeling Troupe), national fraternities, national sororities. *Campus security:* 24-hour emergency response devices and patrols, controlled dormitory access. *Student services:* health clinic, personal/psychological counseling.

Athletics Member NCAA. All Division II. *Intercollegiate sports:* basketball M(s)/W(s), cheerleading M(s)/W(s), cross-country running M(s)/W(s), golf M(s)/W(s), tennis M(s)/W(s), track and field M(s)/W(s), volleyball W(s). *Intramural sports:* basketball M/W, bowling M/W, softball M/W, tennis M/W.

Standardized Tests *Required:* SAT or ACT (for admission). *Recommended:* ACT (for admission).

Costs (2012–13) *Tuition:* state resident $3550 full-time; nonresident $10,770 full-time. Full-time tuition and fees vary according to course load. Part-time tuition and fees vary according to course load. *Required fees:* $2320 full-time. *Room and board:* $8782; room only: $4720. Room and board charges vary according to board plan. *Payment plans:* installment, deferred payment. *Waivers:* senior citizens and employees or children of employees.

Financial Aid Of all full-time matriculated undergraduates who enrolled in 2008, 1,899 applied for aid, 1,799 were judged to have need. 408 Federal Work-Study jobs (averaging $1720). In 2008, 33 non-need-based awards were made. *Average non-need-based aid:* $5125.

Applying *Options:* electronic application. *Application fee:* $20. *Required:* high school transcript. *Required for some:* essay or personal statement, minimum 2.0 GPA, 2 letters of recommendation, 2.5 high school GPA for nonresidents. *Recommended:* interview. *Application deadlines:* 6/15 (freshmen), 6/15 (transfers). *Notification:* continuous (freshmen), continuous (transfers).

Freshman Application Contact Ms. Robin Rucker, Director, Admissions, Central State University, PO Box 1004, 1400 Blush Row Road, Wilberforce, OH 45384. *Phone:* 937-376-6580. *Toll-free phone:* 800-388-CSU1 (in-state); 800-388-2781 (out-of-state). *Fax:* 937-376-6648. *E-mail:* admissions@centralstate.edu.

Website: http://www.centralstate.edu/.

Chamberlain College of Nursing

Cleveland, Ohio

- Proprietary 4-year
- Coed

Academics *Degree:* bachelor's.

Standardized Tests *Required:* SAT or ACT (for admission).

Costs (2013–14) *Tuition:* $16,360 full-time, $665 per credit hour part-time. *Required fees:* $600 full-time.

Applying *Application fee:* $95.

Freshman Application Contact Chamberlain College of Nursing, 6700 Euclid Avenue, Suite 201, Cleveland, OH 44103.

Website: http://www.chamberlain.edu/.

Chamberlain College of Nursing

Columbus, Ohio

- Proprietary 4-year
- Coed

Faculty *Student/faculty ratio:* 9:1.

Academics *Calendar:* semesters. *Degrees:* associate and bachelor's.

Standardized Tests *Required:* SAT or ACT (for admission).

Costs (2013–14) *Tuition:* $16,360 full-time, $665 per credit hour part-time. Full-time tuition and fees vary according to course load. Part-time tuition and fees vary according to course load. *Required fees:* $600 full-time.

Freshman Application Contact Admissions, Chamberlain College of Nursing, 1350 Alum Creek Drive, Columbus, OH 43209. *Phone:* 614-252-8890. *Toll-free phone:* 888-556-8CCN.

Website: http://www.chamberlain.edu/.

Chancellor University

Cleveland, Ohio

Director of Admissions Vice President for Enrollment Management, Chancellor University, 3921 Chester Avenue, Cleveland, OH 44114-4624. *Phone:* 216-523-3806 Ext. 805. *Toll-free phone:* 888-316-9377. *E-mail:* admissions@myers.edu.

Website: http://www.chancelloru.edu/.

Cincinnati Christian University

Cincinnati, Ohio

- **Independent** upper-level, founded 1924, affiliated with Church of Christ
- **Urban** 40-acre campus with easy access to Cincinnati
- **Coed** 677 undergraduate students
- **Minimally difficult** entrance level, 94% of applicants were admitted

Undergraduates Students come from 12 states and territories; 33% are from out of state; 13% Black or African American, non-Hispanic/Latino; 0.6% Hispanic/Latino; 0.3% American Indian or Alaska Native, non-Hispanic/Latino;

0.9% Two or more races, non-Hispanic/Latino; 13% Race/ethnicity unknown; 1% international; 39% live on campus.

Freshmen *Admission:* 215 applied, 203 admitted.

Faculty *Total:* 82, 41% full-time. *Student/faculty ratio:* 15:1.

Academics *Calendar:* semesters. *Degrees:* associate, bachelor's, and master's. *Special study options:* academic remediation for entering students, accelerated degree program, adult/continuing education programs, advanced placement credit, cooperative education, distance learning, double majors, independent study, internships, off-campus study, part-time degree program, services for LD students, summer session for credit.

Computers on Campus 45 computers/terminals are available on campus for general student use. Students can access the following: campus intranet, computer help desk, free student e-mail accounts, online (class) grades, online (class) registration, online (class) schedules. Campuswide network is available. 100% of college-owned or -operated housing units are wired for high-speed Internet access. Wireless service is available via entire campus.

Student Life *Housing:* on-campus residence required in junior year. *Options:* men-only, women-only. Campus housing is university owned. Freshman campus housing is guaranteed. *Activities and organizations:* drama/theater group, choral group. *Campus security:* 24-hour emergency response devices and patrols, student patrols, late-night transport/escort service, controlled dormitory access. *Student services:* personal/psychological counseling.

Athletics Member NAIA. *Intercollegiate sports:* basketball M(s)/W(s), cross-country running M(s)/W(s), golf M(s), soccer M(s)/W(s), volleyball M(s)/W(s). *Intramural sports:* basketball M/W, soccer M/W, volleyball M/W.

Standardized Tests *Required:* SAT or ACT (for admission).

Costs (2013–14) *Comprehensive fee:* $21,938 includes full-time tuition ($14,766), mandatory fees ($500), and room and board ($6672). Full-time tuition and fees vary according to course load and student level. Part-time tuition: $600 per credit. Part-time tuition and fees vary according to course load and student level. *Required fees:* $500 per year part-time. *College room only:* $2820. Room and board charges vary according to board plan, housing facility, and student level. *Payment plan:* installment. *Waivers:* employees or children of employees.

Financial Aid Of all full-time matriculated undergraduates who enrolled in 2011, 555 applied for aid, 514 were judged to have need, 40 had their need fully met. 235 Federal Work-Study jobs (averaging $1555). In 2011, 54 non-need-based awards were made. *Average percent of need met:* 50%. *Average financial aid package:* $11,279. *Average need-based loan:* $3916. *Average need-based gift aid:* $7893. *Average non-need-based aid:* $5145. *Average indebtedness upon graduation:* $32,280.

Applying *Options:* electronic application, deferred entrance. *Application fee:* $40. *Application deadline:* 7/1 (transfers). *Notification:* continuous (transfers).

Application Contact Cincinnati Christian University, 2700 Glenway Avenue, PO Box 04320, Cincinnati, OH 45204-3200. *Phone:* 513-244-8110. *Toll-free phone:* 800-949-4228 (in-state); 800-949-4CCU (out-of-state).

Website: http://www.ccuniversity.edu/.

Cincinnati College of Mortuary Science

Cincinnati, Ohio

Freshman Application Contact Cincinnati College of Mortuary Science, 645 West North Bend Road, Cincinnati, OH 45224-1462. *Phone:* 513-761-2020. *Toll-free phone:* 888-377-8433. *Fax:* 513-761-3333.

Website: http://www.ccms.edu/.

Cleveland Institute of Art

Cleveland, Ohio

- **Independent** 4-year, founded 1882
- **Urban** 5-acre campus
- **Endowment** $24.3 million
- **Coed** 556 undergraduate students, 99% full-time, 58% women, 42% men
- **Moderately difficult** entrance level, 71% of applicants were admitted

Undergraduates 550 full-time, 6 part-time. Students come from 31 states and territories; 10 other countries; 30% are from out of state; 10% Black or African American, non-Hispanic/Latino; 4% Hispanic/Latino; 3% Asian, non-Hispanic/Latino; 0.2% American Indian or Alaska Native, non-Hispanic/Latino; 3% Two or more races, non-Hispanic/Latino; 4% international; 5% transferred in; 21% live on campus. *Retention:* 79% of full-time freshmen returned.

Freshmen *Admission:* 584 applied, 415 admitted, 138 enrolled. *Average high school GPA:* 3.3. *Test scores:* SAT critical reading scores over 500: 68%; SAT math scores over 500: 73%; SAT writing scores over 500: 63%; ACT scores over 18: 88%; SAT critical reading scores over 600: 34%; SAT math scores over 600: 25%; SAT writing scores over 600: 21%; ACT scores over 24: 40%; SAT critical reading scores over 700: 11%; SAT writing scores over 700: 5%; ACT scores over 30: 5%.

Faculty *Total:* 108, 46% full-time, 61% with terminal degrees. *Student/faculty ratio:* 9:1.

Academics *Calendar:* semesters. *Degree:* bachelor's. *Special study options:* academic remediation for entering students, advanced placement credit, double majors, independent study, internships, off-campus study, part-time degree program, services for LD students, study abroad.

Computers on Campus 80 computers/terminals are available on campus for general student use. Students can access the following: campus intranet, free student e-mail accounts, online (class) grades, online (class) registration, online (class) schedules, Wireless Internet access available throughout campus. Campuswide network is available. 100% of college-owned or -operated housing units are wired for high-speed Internet access. Wireless service is available via entire campus.

Student Life *Housing:* on-campus residence required for freshman year. *Options:* coed. Campus housing is leased by the school. Freshman applicants given priority for college housing. *Activities and organizations:* drama/theater group, choral group, marching band, Campus Activities Board, Student Independent Exhibition, International Interior Design Association, Student Leadership Council, Community Service Club, national fraternities, national sororities. *Campus security:* 24-hour emergency response devices and patrols, late-night transport/escort service, controlled dormitory access. *Student services:* health clinic, personal/psychological counseling, women's center, legal services.

Athletics *Intramural sports:* basketball M/W, cross-country running M/W, football M/W, golf M/W, racquetball M/W, soccer M/W, softball M/W, swimming and diving M/W, tennis M/W, track and field M/W, ultimate Frisbee M/W, volleyball M/W.

Standardized Tests *Required:* SAT or ACT (for admission).

Costs (2013–14) *Comprehensive fee:* $48,641 includes full-time tuition ($34,270), mandatory fees ($2239), and room and board ($12,132). Full-time tuition and fees vary according to program, reciprocity agreements, and student level. Part-time tuition: $1430 per credit. Part-time tuition and fees vary according to course load, program, reciprocity agreements, and student level. *Required fees:* $150 per credit part-time, $115 per term part-time. *College room only:* $6912. Room and board charges vary according to board plan. *Payment plan:* installment. *Waivers:* employees or children of employees.

Financial Aid Of all full-time matriculated undergraduates who enrolled in 2011, 488 applied for aid, 470 were judged to have need, 26 had their need fully met. 381 Federal Work-Study jobs (averaging $2461). In 2011, 59 non-need-based awards were made. *Average percent of need met:* 61%. *Average financial aid package:* $24,550. *Average need-based loan:* $4642. *Average need-based gift aid:* $18,521. *Average non-need-based aid:* $10,426. *Average indebtedness upon graduation:* $38,259.

Applying *Options:* electronic application, early admission, early action. *Application fee:* $30. *Required:* essay or personal statement, high school transcript, minimum 2.0 GPA, 1 letter of recommendation, portfolio. *Recommended:* interview. *Application deadlines:* 3/1 (freshmen), 6/1 (transfers). *Notification:* continuous (freshmen), continuous (transfers).

Freshman Application Contact Office of Admissions, Cleveland Institute of Art, 11141 East Boulevard, Cleveland, OH 44106-1700. *Phone:* 216-421-7418. *Toll-free phone:* 800-223-4700. *Fax:* 216-754-3634. *E-mail:* admissions@cia.edu. *Website:* http://www.cia.edu/.

Cleveland Institute of Music

Cleveland, Ohio

Freshman Application Contact Mr. William Fay, Director of Admission, Cleveland Institute of Music, 11021 East Boulevard, Cleveland, OH 44106-1776. *Phone:* 216-795-3107. *Fax:* 216-791-1530. *E-mail:* william.fay@case.edu. *Website:* http://www.cim.edu/.

Cleveland State University

Cleveland, Ohio

- **State-supported** university, founded 1964, part of University System of Ohio
- **Urban** 82-acre campus with easy access to Cleveland, Ohio metro area
- **Endowment** $47.7 million
- **Coed** 12,038 undergraduate students, 71% full-time, 54% women, 46% men
- **Moderately difficult** entrance level, 63% of applicants were admitted

Undergraduates 8,590 full-time, 3,448 part-time. Students come from 41 states and territories; 8 other countries; 3% are from out of state; 21% Black or African American, non-Hispanic/Latino; 4% Hispanic/Latino; 2% Asian, non-Hispanic/Latino; 0.1% Native Hawaiian or other Pacific Islander, non-Hispanic/Latino; 0.3% American Indian or Alaska Native, non-Hispanic/Latino; 2% Two or more races, non-Hispanic/Latino; 4% Race/ethnicity unknown; 4% international; 15% transferred in; 8% live on campus. *Retention:* 65% of full-time freshmen returned.

Freshmen *Admission:* 5,938 applied, 3,750 admitted, 1,588 enrolled. *Average high school GPA:* 3.19. *Test scores:* SAT critical reading scores over 500: 53%; SAT math scores over 500: 55%; ACT scores over 18: 84%; SAT critical reading scores over 600: 18%; SAT math scores over 600: 21%; ACT scores over 24: 33%; SAT critical reading scores over 700: 3%; SAT math scores over 700: 4%; ACT scores over 30: 3%.

Faculty *Total:* 1,041, 50% full-time, 49% with terminal degrees. *Student/faculty ratio:* 19:1.

Academics *Calendar:* semesters. *Degrees:* bachelor's, master's, doctoral, post-master's, and postbachelor's certificates. *Special study options:* academic remediation for entering students, accelerated degree program, adult/continuing education programs, advanced placement credit, cooperative education, distance learning, double majors, English as a second language, freshman honors college, honors programs, independent study, internships, off-campus study, part-time degree program, services for LD students, student-designed majors, study abroad, summer session for credit. *ROTC:* Army (c), Air Force (c).

Computers on Campus 736 computers/terminals are available on campus for general student use. Students can access the following: campus intranet, computer help desk, free student e-mail accounts, online (class) grades, online (class) registration, online (class) schedules, each general purpose computer lab has a scanner and printer, and students are allowed free black and white printing up to 2,000 pages per semester. Campuswide network is available. 100% of college-owned or -operated housing units are wired for high-speed Internet access. Wireless service is available via entire campus.

Student Life *Housing options:* coed, disabled students. Campus housing is university owned. Freshman campus housing is guaranteed. *Activities and organizations:* drama/theater group, student-run newspaper, radio station, choral group, Friends of India, Chinese Students and Scholars Association, Chi Sigma Iota, Student Nurses Association, Engineers Without Borders, national fraternities, national sororities. *Campus security:* 24-hour emergency response devices and patrols, student patrols, late-night transport/escort service, controlled dormitory access, Campus Watch, CSU Alert Notification System, Community Emergency and Response Team (CERT). *Student services:* health clinic, personal/psychological counseling, women's center.

Athletics Member NCAA. All Division I. *Intercollegiate sports:* basketball M(s)/W(s), cheerleading M/W, cross-country running W(s), fencing M(s)/W(s), golf M(s)/W, soccer M(s)/W, softball W(s), swimming and diving M(s)/W(s), tennis M/W(s), track and field W(s), volleyball W(s), wrestling M(s). *Intramural sports:* baseball M(c), basketball M/W, crew M(c)/W(c), cross-country running M/W, fencing M/W, golf M/W, ice hockey M(c), rock climbing M(c)/W(c), rugby M(c), soccer M(c)/W(c), track and field M/W, ultimate Frisbee M/W, volleyball W, wrestling M.

Standardized Tests *Required:* SAT or ACT (for admission).

Costs (2013–14) *Tuition:* state resident $9264 full-time, $386 per credit hour part-time; nonresident $12,386 full-time, $516 per credit hour part-time. Full-time tuition and fees vary according to course load, degree level, and program. Part-time tuition and fees vary according to course load, degree level, and program. *Required fees:* $50 full-time, $25 per term part-time. *Room and board:* $11,848; room only: $7648. Room and board charges vary according to board plan and housing facility. *Payment plan:* installment. *Waivers:* senior citizens and employees or children of employees.

Financial Aid Of all full-time matriculated undergraduates who enrolled in 2012, 7,157 applied for aid, 6,598 were judged to have need, 416 had their need fully met. 416 Federal Work-Study jobs (averaging $3697). In 2012, 398 non-need-based awards were made. *Average percent of need met:* 45%. *Average financial aid package:* $8821. *Average need-based loan:* $4240. *Average need-based gift aid:* $6090. *Average non-need-based aid:* $5013. *Average indebtedness upon graduation:* $23,436.

Applying *Options:* electronic application, early action, deferred entrance. *Application fee:* $30. *Required:* high school transcript, minimum 2.3 GPA, minimum ACT score of 16 or SAT of 770 (combined critical reading and math). *Application deadlines:* 5/15 (freshmen), 5/15 (transfers), 5/1 (early action). *Notification:* continuous (freshmen), continuous (transfers).
Freshman Application Contact Undergraduate Admissions Office, Cleveland State University, 2121 Euclid Avenue, RW 204, Cleveland, OH 44115. *Phone:* 216-687-2100. *Toll-free phone:* 888-CSU-OHIO. *E-mail:* admissions@csuohio.edu.
Website: http://www.csuohio.edu/.

College of Mount St. Joseph
Cincinnati, Ohio

- **Independent Roman Catholic** comprehensive, founded 1920
- **Suburban** 92-acre campus
- **Endowment** $29.1 million
- **Coed** 1,840 undergraduate students, 67% full-time, 64% women, 36% men
- **Moderately difficult** entrance level, 70% of applicants were admitted

Undergraduates 1,227 full-time, 613 part-time. Students come from 20 states and territories; 3 other countries; 17% are from out of state; 9% Black or African American, non-Hispanic/Latino; 3% Hispanic/Latino; 0.4% Asian, non-Hispanic/Latino; 0.2% American Indian or Alaska Native, non-Hispanic/Latino; 2% Two or more races, non-Hispanic/Latino; 2% Race/ethnicity unknown; 0.2% international; 5% transferred in; 21% live on campus. *Retention:* 77% of full-time freshmen returned.
Freshmen *Admission:* 1,235 applied, 862 admitted, 281 enrolled. *Average high school GPA:* 3.2. *Test scores:* SAT critical reading scores over 500: 36%; SAT math scores over 500: 46%; ACT scores over 18: 92%; SAT critical reading scores over 600: 3%; SAT math scores over 600: 8%; ACT scores over 24: 32%; ACT scores over 30: 1%.
Faculty *Total:* 233, 51% full-time, 51% with terminal degrees. *Student/faculty ratio:* 11:1.
Academics *Calendar:* semesters, *Degrees:* certificates, associate, bachelor's, master's, doctoral, and postbachelor's certificates. *Special study options:* academic remediation for entering students, accelerated degree program, advanced placement credit, cooperative education, distance learning, double majors, honors programs, independent study, internships, off-campus study, part-time degree program, services for LD students, study abroad, summer session for credit. *ROTC:* Army (c), Air Force (c).
Computers on Campus 202 computers/terminals are available on campus for general student use. Students can access the following: computer help desk, free student e-mail accounts, online (class) grades, online (class) registration, online (class) schedules. Campuswide network is available. 100% of college-owned or -operated housing units are wired for high-speed Internet access. Wireless service is available via entire campus.
Student Life *Housing:* on-campus residence required through sophomore year. *Options:* coed, disabled students. Campus housing is university owned. Freshman applicants given priority for college housing. *Activities and organizations:* drama/theater group, student-run newspaper, choral group, Student Government Association, Black Student Union, Campus Ministry Leadership Team, Campus Activities Board, Campus Ambassadors. *Campus security:* 24-hour emergency response devices and patrols, late-night transport/escort service. *Student services:* health clinic, personal/psychological counseling.
Athletics Member NCAA. All Division III. *Intercollegiate sports:* baseball M, basketball M/W, cheerleading W, cross-country running M/W, football M, golf M/W, lacrosse M/W, soccer M/W, softball W, tennis M/W, track and field M/W, volleyball M/W, wrestling M. *Intramural sports:* basketball M/W, football M/W, racquetball M/W, soccer M/W, softball M/W, tennis M/W, volleyball M/W.
Standardized Tests *Required:* SAT or ACT (for admission).
Costs (2013–14) *One-time required fee:* $200. *Comprehensive fee:* $33,880 includes full-time tuition ($24,900), mandatory fees ($900), and room and board ($8080). Full-time tuition and fees vary according to course load and reciprocity agreements. Part-time tuition: $500 per credit hour. Part-time tuition and fees vary according to course load and reciprocity agreements. *College room only:* $3990. Room and board charges vary according to board plan and housing facility. *Payment plans:* installment, deferred payment. *Waivers:* senior citizens and employees or children of employees.
Financial Aid Of all full-time matriculated undergraduates who enrolled in 2012, 1,082 applied for aid, 964 were judged to have need, 205 had their need fully met. 32 Federal Work-Study jobs (averaging $1425). 109 state and other part-time jobs (averaging $1482). In 2012, 219 non-need-based awards were made. *Average percent of need met:* 76%. *Average financial aid package:*

$18,744. *Average need-based loan:* $4569. *Average need-based gift aid:* $14,102. *Average non-need-based aid:* $10,341.
Applying *Options:* electronic application, deferred entrance. *Application fee:* $25. *Required:* high school transcript. *Required for some:* essay or personal statement, 2 letters of recommendation, interview. *Recommended:* minimum 2.0 GPA. *Application deadlines:* 8/15 (freshmen), 8/1 (transfers). *Notification:* continuous (freshmen), continuous (transfers).
Freshman Application Contact Peggy Minnich, Director of Admission, College of Mount St. Joseph, 5701 Delhi Road, Cincinnati, OH 45233-1670. *Phone:* 513-244-4531. *Toll-free phone:* 800-654-9314. *Fax:* 513-244-4629. *E-mail:* admissions@mail.msj.edu.
Website: http://www.msj.edu/.

The College of Wooster
Wooster, Ohio

- **Independent** 4-year, founded 1866, affiliated with Presbyterian Church (U.S.A.)
- **Small-town** 240-acre campus with easy access to Cleveland
- **Endowment** $232.0 million
- **Coed** 2,080 undergraduate students, 98% full-time, 55% women, 45% men
- **Moderately difficult** entrance level, 58% of applicants were admitted

Undergraduates 2,043 full-time, 37 part-time. Students come from 51 states and territories; 50 other countries; 62% are from out of state; 9% Black or African American, non-Hispanic/Latino; 4% Hispanic/Latino; 3% Asian, non-Hispanic/Latino; 1% American Indian or Alaska Native, non-Hispanic/Latino; 13% Race/ethnicity unknown; 6% international; 0.6% transferred in; 99% live on campus. *Retention:* 85% of full-time freshmen returned.
Freshmen *Admission:* 5,208 applied, 3,024 admitted, 573 enrolled. *Average high school GPA:* 3.64. *Test scores:* SAT critical reading scores over 500: 92%; SAT math scores over 500: 90%; SAT writing scores over 500: 87%; ACT scores over 18: 100%; SAT critical reading scores over 600: 54%; SAT math scores over 600: 55%; SAT writing scores over 600: 47%; ACT scores over 24: 81%; SAT critical reading scores over 700: 17%; SAT math scores over 700: 15%; SAT writing scores over 700: 9%; ACT scores over 30: 24%.
Faculty *Total:* 213, 81% full-time, 88% with terminal degrees. *Student/faculty ratio:* 12:1.
Academics *Calendar:* semesters. *Degree:* bachelor's. *Special study options:* advanced placement credit, double majors, independent study, internships, off-campus study, services for LD students, student-designed majors, study abroad. *Unusual degree programs:* 3-2 engineering with Case Western Reserve University, Washington University in St. Louis, University of Michigan; forestry with Duke University; nursing with Case Western Reserve University; social work with Case Western Reserve University; dentistry with Case Western Reserve University, architecture with Washington University in St. Louis.
Computers on Campus 450 computers/terminals and 3,000 ports are available on campus for general student use. Students can access the following: campus intranet, computer help desk, free student e-mail accounts, online (class) grades, online (class) registration, online (class) schedules, learning management system, campus blogging site, campus wiki site. Campuswide network is available. 100% of college-owned or -operated housing units are wired for high-speed Internet access. Wireless service is available via entire campus.
Student Life *Housing:* on-campus residence required through senior year. *Options:* coed, women-only. Campus housing is university owned. Freshman campus housing is guaranteed. *Activities and organizations:* drama/theater group, student-run newspaper, radio station, choral group, marching band, Volunteer Network, International Student Association, Inter-Greek Council, Wooster Activities Crew, Women's Athletic and Recreation Association. *Campus security:* 24-hour emergency response devices and patrols, student patrols, late-night transport/escort service, controlled dormitory access. *Student services:* health clinic, personal/psychological counseling, women's center.
Athletics Member NCAA. All Division III. *Intercollegiate sports:* baseball M, basketball M/W, cheerleading W(c), cross-country running M/W, equestrian sports M(c)/W(c), field hockey W, football M, golf M/W, lacrosse M/W, rugby M(c)/W(c), soccer M/W, softball W, swimming and diving M/W, tennis M/W, track and field M/W, ultimate Frisbee M(c)/W(c), volleyball M(c)/W. *Intramural sports:* badminton M/W, ice hockey M(c)/W(c), table tennis M/W.
Standardized Tests *Required:* SAT or ACT (for admission).
Costs (2012–13) *Comprehensive fee:* $49,400 includes full-time tuition ($39,500), mandatory fees ($310), and room and board ($9590). Full-time tuition and fees vary according to course load. Part-time tuition: $1230 per credit. Part-time tuition and fees vary according to course load. *College room only:* $4440. Room and board charges vary according to board plan and hous-

ing facility. *Payment plan:* installment. *Waivers:* employees or children of employees.

Financial Aid Of all full-time matriculated undergraduates who enrolled in 2012, 1,345 applied for aid, 1,202 were judged to have need, 722 had their need fully met. 886 Federal Work-Study jobs (averaging $1662). 68 state and other part-time jobs (averaging $2000). In 2012, 772 non-need-based awards were made. *Average percent of need met:* 94%. *Average financial aid package:* $35,763. *Average need-based loan:* $6142. *Average need-based gift aid:* $27,300. *Average non-need-based aid:* $18,482. *Average indebtedness upon graduation:* $26,750.

Applying *Options:* electronic application, early admission, early decision, early action, deferred entrance. *Application fee:* $40. *Required:* essay or personal statement, high school transcript, SAT or ACT. *Recommended:* interview. *Application deadlines:* 2/15 (freshmen), 7/15 (transfers), 11/15 (early action). *Early decision deadline:* 11/1 (for plan 1), 1/15 (for plan 2). *Notification:* 4/1 (freshmen), continuous (transfers), 11/15 (early decision plan 1), 2/1 (early decision plan 2), 12/31 (early action).

Freshman Application Contact Ms. Jennifer Winge, Dean of Admissions, The College of Wooster, 1189 Beall Avenue, Wooster, OH 44691-2363. *Phone:* 330-263-2270. *Toll-free phone:* 800-877-9905. *Fax:* 330-263-2621. *E-mail:* admissions@wooster.edu. *Website:* http://www.wooster.edu/.

See below for display ad and page 1250 for the College Close-Up.

Columbus College of Art & Design

Columbus, Ohio

- **Independent** 4-year, founded 1879
- **Urban** 17-acre campus
- **Endowment** $8.3 million
- **Coed** 1,375 undergraduate students, 92% full-time, 61% women, 39% men
- **Moderately difficult** entrance level, 87% of applicants were admitted

Undergraduates 1,261 full-time, 114 part-time. Students come from 41 states and territories; 16 other countries; 24% are from out of state; 8% Black or African American, non-Hispanic/Latino; 4% Hispanic/Latino; 2% Asian, non-His-panic/Latino; 0.1% Native Hawaiian or other Pacific Islander, non-Hispanic/Latino; 0.1% American Indian or Alaska Native, non-Hispanic/Latino; 4% Two or more races, non-Hispanic/Latino; 3% Race/ethnicity unknown; 7% international; 0.4% transferred in; 32% live on campus. *Retention:* 81% of full-time freshmen returned.

Freshmen *Admission:* 563 applied, 488 admitted, 260 enrolled. *Average high school GPA:* 3.12. *Test scores:* SAT critical reading scores over 500: 61%; SAT math scores over 500: 47%; SAT writing scores over 500: 41%; ACT scores over 18: 85%; SAT critical reading scores over 600: 15%; SAT math scores over 600: 8%; SAT writing scores over 600: 11%; ACT scores over 24: 29%; SAT critical reading scores over 700: 1%; SAT math scores over 700: 1%; ACT scores over 30: 2%.

Faculty *Total:* 193, 33% full-time, 46% with terminal degrees. *Student/faculty ratio:* 11:1.

Academics *Calendar:* semesters. *Degrees:* bachelor's and master's. *Special study options:* academic remediation for entering students, advanced placement credit, distance learning, double majors, English as a second language, honors programs, independent study, internships, off-campus study, services for LD students, study abroad, summer session for credit.

Computers on Campus 485 computers/terminals are available on campus for general student use. Students can access the following: campus intranet, computer help desk, free student e-mail accounts, online (class) grades, online (class) registration, online (class) schedules, online library. Campuswide network is available. 100% of college-owned or -operated housing units are wired for high-speed Internet access. Wireless service is available via classrooms, computer centers, computer labs, dorm rooms, learning centers, libraries, student centers.

Student Life *Housing:* on-campus residence required for freshman year. *Options:* coed, disabled students. Campus housing is university owned. Freshman campus housing is guaranteed. *Activities and organizations:* Student Government Association, Gay Straight Student Alliance, Sanctuary, Environmental Awareness Society, Student Programming Board. *Campus security:* 24-hour emergency response devices and patrols, late-night transport/escort service, controlled dormitory access. *Student services:* personal/psychological counseling.

Athletics *Intramural sports:* basketball M/W, ultimate Frisbee M/W.

Standardized Tests *Required:* SAT or ACT (for admission).

Costs (2012–13) *Comprehensive fee:* $36,014 includes full-time tuition ($27,504), mandatory fees ($1020), and room and board ($7490). Full-time tuition and fees vary according to course load. Part-time tuition: $1146 per credit hour. Part-time tuition and fees vary according to course load. *Required*

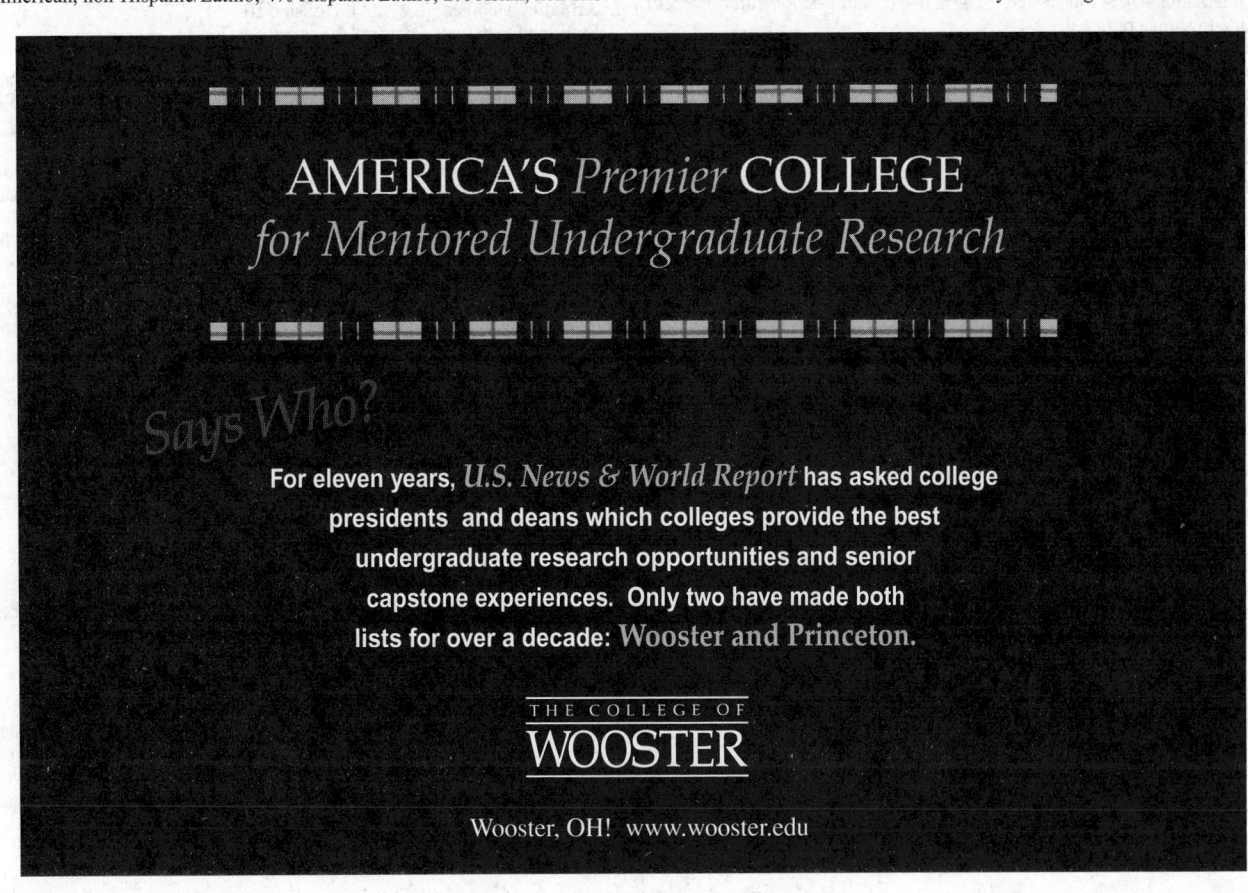

fees: $180 per semester part-time. *Room and board:* Room and board charges vary according to board plan, housing facility, and student level. *Payment plans:* installment, deferred payment. *Waivers:* children of alumni and employees or children of employees.

Financial Aid Of all full-time matriculated undergraduates who enrolled in 2012, 1,218 applied for aid, 1,132 were judged to have need, 96 had their need fully met. 187 Federal Work-Study jobs (averaging $3465). 210 state and other part-time jobs (averaging $3465). In 2012, 201 non-need-based awards were made. *Average percent of need met:* 52%. *Average financial aid package:* $18,296. *Average need-based loan:* $6092. *Average need-based gift aid:* $12,773. *Average non-need-based aid:* $10,071. *Average indebtedness upon graduation:* $36,100.

Applying *Options:* electronic application, deferred entrance. *Application fee:* $30. *Required:* essay or personal statement, high school transcript, minimum 2.0 GPA, 1 letter of recommendation, portfolio. *Recommended:* interview. *Application deadlines:* rolling (freshmen), rolling (transfers). *Notification:* continuous (freshmen), continuous (transfers).

Freshman Application Contact Columbus College of Art & Design, 60 Cleveland Avenue, Columbus, OH 43215-1758. *Phone:* 614-224-9101. *Toll-free phone:* 877-997-2223. *Fax:* 614-232-8344. *E-mail:* admissions@ccad.edu.

Website: http://www.ccad.edu/.

Defiance College

Defiance, Ohio

- **Independent** comprehensive, founded 1850, affiliated with United Church of Christ
- **Small-town** 150-acre campus with easy access to Toledo
- **Endowment** $14.7 million
- **Coed** 932 undergraduate students, 79% full-time, 51% women, 49% men
- **Moderately difficult** entrance level, 67% of applicants were admitted

Undergraduates 735 full-time, 197 part-time. Students come from 26 states and territories; 4 other countries; 27% are from out of state; 11% Black or African American, non-Hispanic/Latino; 5% Hispanic/Latino; 0.5% Asian, non-Hispanic/Latino; 2% American Indian or Alaska Native, non-Hispanic/Latino; 0.1% Two or more races, non-Hispanic/Latino; 2% Race/ethnicity unknown; 0.9% international; 4% transferred in; 44% live on campus. *Retention:* 59% of full-time freshmen returned.

Freshmen *Admission:* 1,854 applied, 1,248 admitted, 241 enrolled. *Average high school GPA:* 3.02. *Test scores:* SAT critical reading scores over 500: 37%; SAT math scores over 500: 43%; SAT writing scores over 500: 26%; ACT scores over 18: 81%; SAT critical reading scores over 600: 4%; SAT math scores over 600: 7%; SAT writing scores over 600: 3%; ACT scores over 24: 23%; ACT scores over 30: 1%.

Faculty *Total:* 107, 38% full-time, 56% with terminal degrees. *Student/faculty ratio:* 12:1.

Academics *Calendar:* semesters. *Degrees:* associate, bachelor's, and master's. *Special study options:* academic remediation for entering students, adult/continuing education programs, advanced placement credit, cooperative education, distance learning, double majors, honors programs, independent study, internships, off-campus study, part-time degree program, services for LD students, student-designed majors, study abroad, summer session for credit.

Computers on Campus 200 computers/terminals are available on campus for general student use. Students can access the following: campus intranet, computer help desk, free student e-mail accounts, online (class) grades, online (class) schedules. Campuswide network is available. 100% of college-owned or -operated housing units are wired for high-speed Internet access. Wireless service is available via classrooms, computer centers, computer labs, learning centers, libraries, student centers.

Student Life *Housing:* on-campus residence required through junior year. *Options:* coed. Campus housing is university owned. Freshman campus housing is guaranteed. *Activities and organizations:* drama/theater group, student-run newspaper, choral group, Campus Activities Board, Criminal Justice Society, Student Senate, Black Action Student Association, DC Players, national sororities. *Campus security:* late-night transport/escort service, controlled dormitory access. *Student services:* health clinic, personal/psychological counseling.

Athletics Member NCAA. All Division III. *Intercollegiate sports:* baseball M, basketball M/W, cross-country running M/W, football M, golf M/W, lacrosse M/W, soccer M/W, softball W, swimming and diving M/W, tennis M/W, track and field M/W, volleyball W. *Intramural sports:* baseball M, basketball M/W, cheerleading M/W, field hockey M/W, football M/W, racquetball M/W, soccer M/W, softball M/W, volleyball M/W, weight lifting M, wrestling M(c).

Standardized Tests *Required:* SAT or ACT (for admission).

Costs (2012–13) *Comprehensive fee:* $36,210 includes full-time tuition ($26,740), mandatory fees ($620), and room and board ($8850). Full-time tuition and fees vary according to program. Part-time tuition and fees vary according to course load. *Room and board:* Room and board charges vary according to board plan and housing facility. *Payment plan:* installment. *Waivers:* senior citizens and employees or children of employees.

Financial Aid Of all full-time matriculated undergraduates who enrolled in 2011, 783 applied for aid, 759 were judged to have need, 74 had their need fully met. 591 Federal Work-Study jobs (averaging $2445). 16 state and other part-time jobs (averaging $2675). In 2011, 45 non-need-based awards were made. *Average percent of need met:* 71%. *Average financial aid package:* $21,720. *Average need-based loan:* $4407. *Average need-based gift aid:* $7433. *Average non-need-based aid:* $12,078. *Average indebtedness upon graduation:* $36,659.

Applying *Options:* electronic application, deferred entrance. *Application fee:* $25. *Required:* high school transcript, minimum 2.3 GPA. *Required for some:* essay or personal statement, interview. *Recommended:* interview. *Application deadlines:* 8/15 (freshmen), 8/15 (transfers). *Notification:* continuous (freshmen), continuous (transfers).

Freshman Application Contact Mr. Brad Harsha, Director of Admissions, Defiance College, 701 North Clinton Street, Defiance, OH 43512. *Phone:* 419-783-2365. *Toll-free phone:* 800-520-4632. *Fax:* 419-783-2468. *E-mail:* bharsha@defiance.edu.

Website: http://www.defiance.edu/.

Denison University

Granville, Ohio

- **Independent** 4-year, founded 1831
- **Small-town** 800-acre campus with easy access to Columbus
- **Endowment** $585.0 million
- **Coed**
- **Very difficult** entrance level

Faculty *Student/faculty ratio:* 10:1.

Academics *Calendar:* semesters plus optional May term. *Degree:* bachelor's.

Student Life *Campus security:* 24-hour emergency response devices and patrols, student patrols, late-night transport/escort service, controlled dormitory access, security lighting, escort service.

Athletics Member NCAA. All Division III.

Standardized Tests *Required for some:* SAT or ACT (for admission).

Costs (2012–13) *Comprehensive fee:* $52,640 includes full-time tuition ($41,380), mandatory fees ($900), and room and board ($10,360). Part-time tuition: $1290 per credit. Part-time tuition and fees vary according to course load. *Required fees:* $660 per term part-time. *College room only:* $5700. Room and board charges vary according to board plan and housing facility.

Financial Aid *Of all full-time matriculated undergraduates who enrolled in 2012,* 1,384 applied for aid, 1,194 were judged to have need, 335 had their need fully met. 488 Federal Work-Study jobs (averaging $2550). *In 2012,* 1006 non-need-based awards were made. *Average percent of need met:* 96. *Average financial aid package:* $36,688. *Average need-based loan:* $4626. *Average need-based gift aid:* $30,749. *Average non-need-based aid:* $16,450.

Applying *Options:* early admission, early decision, deferred entrance. *Application fee:* $40. *Required:* essay or personal statement, high school transcript, 2 letters of recommendation. *Recommended:* interview.

Freshman Application Contact Mr. Perry Robinson, Director of Admissions, Denison University, Granville, OH 43023. *Phone:* 740-587-6276. *Toll-free phone:* 800-DENISON. *E-mail:* admissions@denison.edu.

Website: http://www.denison.edu/.

DeVry University

Columbus, Ohio

- **Proprietary** comprehensive, founded 1952, part of DeVry University
- **Urban** campus
- **Coed** 2,198 undergraduate students, 36% full-time, 46% women, 54% men
- **Minimally difficult** entrance level

Undergraduates 789 full-time, 1,409 part-time. 8% are from out of state; 17% Black or African American, non-Hispanic/Latino; 2% Hispanic/Latino; 1% Asian, non-Hispanic/Latino; 0.6% American Indian or Alaska Native, non-Hispanic/Latino; 2% Two or more races, non-Hispanic/Latino; 17% Race/ethnicity unknown; 0.4% international; 19% transferred in.

Freshmen *Admission:* 185 enrolled.

Faculty *Total:* 107, 34% full-time. *Student/faculty ratio:* 23:1.

Academics *Calendar:* semesters. *Degrees:* associate, bachelor's, master's, and postbachelor's certificates. *Special study options:* adult/continuing education programs, part-time degree program. *ROTC:* Army (b).
Student Life *Housing:* college housing not available.
Costs (2013–14) *Tuition:* $16,076 full-time, $609 per credit hour part-time. *Required fees:* $80 full-time.
Financial Aid Of all full-time matriculated undergraduates who enrolled in 2007, 853 applied for aid, 826 were judged to have need, 35 had their need fully met. In 2007, 53 non-need-based awards were made. *Average percent of need met:* 46%. *Average financial aid package:* $14,130. *Average need-based loan:* $7868. *Average need-based gift aid:* $7762. *Average non-need-based aid:* $13,228. *Average indebtedness upon graduation:* $40,467.
Applying *Application fee:* $40. *Required:* high school transcript, interview. *Application deadlines:* rolling (freshmen), rolling (transfers). *Notification:* continuous (freshmen), continuous (transfers).
Freshman Application Contact DeVry University, 1350 Alum Creek Drive, Columbus, OH 43209-2705. *Phone:* 614-253-7291. *Toll-free phone:* 866-338-7941.
Website: http://www.devry.edu/.

DeVry University

Columbus, Ohio

Admissions Office Contact DeVry University, 8800 Lyra Drive, Columbus, OH 43240. *Toll-free phone:* 866-338-7941.
Website: http://www.devry.edu/.

DeVry University

Seven Hills, Ohio

Admissions Office Contact DeVry University, The Genesis Building, 6000 Lombardo Center, Suite 200, Seven Hills, OH 44131. *Toll-free phone:* 866-338-7941.
Website: http://www.devry.edu/.

Franciscan University of Steubenville

Steubenville, Ohio

- **Independent Roman Catholic** comprehensive, founded 1946
- **Suburban** campus
- **Coed**
- **Moderately difficult** entrance level

Faculty *Student/faculty ratio:* 15:1.
Academics *Calendar:* semesters. *Degrees:* associate, bachelor's, and master's.
Student Life *Campus security:* 24-hour emergency response devices and patrols, student patrols, late-night transport/escort service.
Athletics Member NCAA. All Division III.
Standardized Tests *Required:* SAT or ACT (for admission).
Costs (2012–13) *Comprehensive fee:* $29,580 includes full-time tuition ($21,740), mandatory fees ($440), and room and board ($7400). Part-time tuition: $725 per credit hour. Part-time tuition and fees vary according to class time and course load. *College room only:* $4280. Room and board charges vary according to board plan.
Financial Aid *Of all full-time matriculated undergraduates who enrolled in 2011,* 1,601 applied for aid, 1,353 were judged to have need, 175 had their need fully met. *In 2011,* 370 non-need-based awards were made. *Average percent of need met:* 60. *Average financial aid package:* $13,355. *Average need-based loan:* $4410. *Average need-based gift aid:* $8931. *Average non-need-based aid:* $4435. *Average indebtedness upon graduation:* $29,354.
Applying *Options:* deferred entrance. *Application fee:* $20. *Required:* essay or personal statement, high school transcript, minimum 2.4 GPA. *Required for some:* 3 letters of recommendation. *Recommended:* interview.
Freshman Application Contact Mrs. Margaret Weber, Director of Admissions, Franciscan University of Steubenville, 1235 University

Boulevard, Steubenville, OH 43952-1763. *Phone:* 740-283-6226. *Toll-free phone:* 800-783-6220. *Fax:* 740-284-5456. *E-mail:* admissions@franciscan.edu.
Website: http://www.franciscan.edu/.

Franklin University

Columbus, Ohio

- **Independent** comprehensive, founded 1902
- **Urban** 14-acre campus
- **Endowment** $66.8 million
- **Coed** 5,838 undergraduate students, 34% full-time, 58% women, 42% men
- **Noncompetitive** entrance level, 74% of applicants were admitted

Undergraduates 1,973 full-time, 3,865 part-time. Students come from 48 states and territories; 85 other countries; 21% are from out of state; 23% Black or African American, non-Hispanic/Latino; 3% Hispanic/Latino; 3% Asian, non-Hispanic/Latino; 0.1% Native Hawaiian or other Pacific Islander, non-Hispanic/Latino; 0.3% American Indian or Alaska Native, non-Hispanic/Latino; 2% Two or more races, non-Hispanic/Latino; 3% Race/ethnicity unknown; 0.4% international; 21% transferred in. *Retention:* 30% of full-time freshmen returned.
Freshmen *Admission:* 1,016 applied, 755 admitted, 115 enrolled.
Faculty *Total:* 843, 7% full-time, 23% with terminal degrees. *Student/faculty ratio:* 12:1.
Academics *Calendar:* trimesters. *Degrees:* associate, bachelor's, and master's. *Special study options:* academic remediation for entering students, accelerated degree program, adult/continuing education programs, advanced placement credit, cooperative education, distance learning, double majors, English as a second language, independent study, internships, off-campus study, part-time degree program, services for LD students, student-designed majors, study abroad, summer session for credit. *ROTC:* Army (c), Air Force (c).
Computers on Campus 500 computers/terminals are available on campus for general student use. Students can access the following: campus intranet, computer help desk, free student e-mail accounts, online (class) grades, online (class) registration, online (class) schedules. Campuswide network is available. Wireless service is available via entire campus.
Student Life *Housing:* college housing not available. *Campus security:* 24-hour emergency response devices, late-night transport/escort service, Franklin University has video monitoring capabilities of all public/customer facing locations.
Costs (2012–13) *One-time required fee:* $25. *Tuition:* $12,450 full-time, $415 per credit hour part-time. Full-time tuition and fees vary according to degree level and program. Part-time tuition and fees vary according to degree level and program. *Payment plans:* installment, deferred payment. *Waivers:* employees or children of employees.
Financial Aid Of all full-time matriculated undergraduates who enrolled in 2003, 1,135 applied for aid, 1,071 were judged to have need. 29 Federal Work-Study jobs (averaging $7702). In 2003, 108 non-need-based awards were made. *Average need-based loan:* $5091. *Average need-based gift aid:* $4436. *Average non-need-based aid:* $2211.
Applying *Options:* electronic application, deferred entrance. *Required for some:* high school transcript. *Application deadlines:* rolling (freshmen), rolling (transfers). *Notification:* continuous (freshmen), continuous (transfers).
Freshman Application Contact Lynne Hull, Director of New Student Enrollment, Franklin University, 201 South Grant Avenue, Columbus, OH 43215. *Phone:* 614-947-6046. *Toll-free phone:* 877-341-6300. *E-mail:* hulll@franklin.edu.
Website: http://www.franklin.edu/.

God's Bible School and College

Cincinnati, Ohio

Freshman Application Contact Steve Buckland, Director of Financial Aid and Admissions, God's Bible School and College, 1810 Young Street, Cincinnati, OH 45202-6838. *Phone:* 513-721-7944 Ext. 1161. *Toll-free phone:* 800-486-4637. *Fax:* 513-763-6649. *E-mail:* sbuckland@gbs.edu.
Website: http://www.gbs.edu/.

Heidelberg University

Tiffin, Ohio

- **Independent** comprehensive, founded 1850, affiliated with United Church of Christ
- **Small-town** 115-acre campus with easy access to Cleveland, Columbus, Detroit
- **Endowment** $32.1 million
- **Coed**
- **Moderately difficult** entrance level

Faculty *Student/faculty ratio:* 13:1.

Academics *Calendar:* semesters. *Degrees:* bachelor's and master's.

Student Life *Campus security:* 24-hour emergency response devices and patrols, student patrols, late-night transport/escort service, controlled dormitory access.

Athletics Member NCAA. All Division III.

Standardized Tests *Required:* SAT or ACT (for admission).

Costs (2012–13) *Comprehensive fee:* $33,556 includes full-time tuition ($24,000), mandatory fees ($582), and room and board ($8974). Full-time tuition and fees vary according to course load, degree level, and location. Part-time tuition and fees vary according to course load, degree level, and location. *College room only:* $4248. Room and board charges vary according to housing facility and location.

Financial Aid *Of all full-time matriculated undergraduates who enrolled in 2011,* 953 applied for aid, 898 were judged to have need, 164 had their need fully met. 623 Federal Work-Study jobs (averaging $1867). 89 state and other part-time jobs (averaging $1911). *In 2011,* 118 non-need-based awards were made. *Average percent of need met:* 74. *Average financial aid package:* $19,960. *Average need-based loan:* $4666. *Average need-based gift aid:* $14,400. *Average non-need-based aid:* $13,871. *Average indebtedness upon graduation:* $36,706.

Applying *Options:* electronic application, deferred entrance. *Application fee:* $25. *Required:* high school transcript, minimum 2.5 GPA. *Recommended:* essay or personal statement, interview.

Freshman Application Contact Mr. Jason Miller, Interim Director of Admission, Heidelberg University, 310 East Market Street, Tiffin, OH 44883. *Phone:* 419-448-2330. *Toll-free phone:* 800-434-3352. *Fax:* 419-448-2334. *E-mail:* jmiller7@heidelberg.edu. *Website:* http://www.heidelberg.edu/.

Herzing University

Toledo, Ohio

Admissions Office Contact Herzing University, 5212 Hill Avenue, Toledo, OH 43615. *Toll-free phone:* 800-596-0724. *Website:* http://www.herzing.edu/toledo.

Hiram College

Hiram, Ohio

- **Independent** comprehensive, founded 1850, affiliated with Christian Church (Disciples of Christ)
- **Rural** 110-acre campus with easy access to Cleveland
- **Endowment** $60.8 million
- **Coed** 1,313 undergraduate students, 89% full-time, 56% women, 44% men
- **Moderately difficult** entrance level, 62% of applicants were admitted

Undergraduates 1,164 full-time, 149 part-time. Students come from 39 states and territories; 25 other countries; 14% are from out of state; 12% Black or African American, non-Hispanic/Latino; 3% Hispanic/Latino; 1% Asian, non-Hispanic/Latino; 0.1% Native Hawaiian or other Pacific Islander, non-Hispanic/Latino; 0.2% American Indian or Alaska Native, non-Hispanic/Latino; 1% Two or more races, non-Hispanic/Latino; 3% Race/ethnicity unknown; 6% international; 6% transferred in; 82% live on campus. *Retention:* 75% of full-time freshmen returned.

Freshmen *Admission:* 2,378 applied, 1,476 admitted, 308 enrolled. *Average high school GPA:* 3.29. *Test scores:* SAT critical reading scores over 500: 60%; SAT math scores over 500: 60%; ACT scores over 18: 95%; SAT critical reading scores over 600: 25%; SAT math scores over 600: 24%; ACT scores over 24: 40%; SAT critical reading scores over 700: 4%; SAT math scores over 700: 2%; ACT scores over 30: 5%.

Faculty *Total:* 139, 57% full-time, 67% with terminal degrees. *Student/faculty ratio:* 13:1.

Academics *Calendar:* semesters. *Degrees:* bachelor's and master's. *Special study options:* accelerated degree program, adult/continuing education programs, advanced placement credit, double majors, English as a second language, independent study, internships, off-campus study, part-time degree program, services for LD students, student-designed majors, study abroad, summer session for credit. *ROTC:* Army (c). *Unusual degree programs:* 3-2 engineering with Case Western Reserve University, Washington University in St. Louis.

Computers on Campus 100 computers/terminals and 12,960 ports are available on campus for general student use. Students can access the following: campus intranet, computer help desk, free student e-mail accounts, online (class) grades, online (class) registration, online (class) schedules. Campus-wide network is available. Wireless service is available via entire campus.

Student Life *Housing:* on-campus residence required through junior year. *Options:* coed, women-only, cooperative, disabled students. Campus housing is university owned. Freshman campus housing is guaranteed. *Activities and organizations:* drama/theater group, student-run newspaper, radio station, choral group, marching band, Student Senate, African American Students United, Outdoors Club, Resident Student Association, Christian Outreach. *Campus security:* 24-hour emergency response devices and patrols, late-night transport/escort service, controlled dormitory access. *Student services:* health clinic, personal/psychological counseling.

Athletics Member NCAA. All Division III. *Intercollegiate sports:* baseball M, basketball M/W, cheerleading M(c)/W(c), cross-country running M/W, equestrian sports M(c)/W(c), football M, golf M/W, lacrosse M/W, rugby M(c)/W(c), sailing M(c)/W(c), soccer M/W, softball W, swimming and diving M/W, table tennis M(c)/W(c), tennis M/W, track and field M/W, ultimate Frisbee M/W, volleyball M/W. *Intramural sports:* basketball M/W, cheerleading M/W, football M/W, racquetball M/W, soccer M/W, softball M/W, tennis M/W, ultimate Frisbee M/W, volleyball M/W, water polo M/W.

Standardized Tests *Required:* SAT or ACT (for admission).

Financial Aid Of all full-time matriculated undergraduates who enrolled in 2002, 790 applied for aid, 736 were judged to have need, 699 had their need fully met. 587 Federal Work-Study jobs (averaging $1600). 18 state and other part-time jobs (averaging $1580). In 2002, 114 non-need-based awards were made. *Average percent of need met:* 95%. *Average financial aid package:* $21,218. *Average need-based loan:* $6960. *Average need-based gift aid:* $8163. *Average non-need-based aid:* $8635. *Average indebtedness upon graduation:* $17,125.

Applying *Options:* electronic application, deferred entrance. *Required:* high school transcript. *Recommended:* essay or personal statement, minimum 2.8 GPA, 1 letter of recommendation, interview. *Application deadlines:* rolling (freshmen), rolling (out-of-state freshmen), rolling (transfers). *Notification:* continuous (freshmen), continuous (out-of-state freshmen), continuous (transfers).

Freshman Application Contact Mr. Sherman C. Dean II, Director of Admission, Hiram College, PO Box 96, Hiram, OH 44234. *Phone:* 330-569-5169. *Toll-free phone:* 800-362-5280. *Fax:* 330-569-5944. *E-mail:* admission@hiram.edu. *Website:* http://www.hiram.edu/.

ITT Technical Institute

Akron, Ohio

- **Proprietary** primarily 2-year
- **Coed**
- **Minimally difficult** entrance level

Academics *Degrees:* associate and bachelor's.

Freshman Application Contact Director of Recruitment, ITT Technical Institute, 3428 West Market Street, Akron, OH 44333. *Phone:* 330-865-8600. *Toll-free phone:* 877-818-0154. *Website:* http://www.itt-tech.edu/.

ITT Technical Institute

Columbus, Ohio

- **Proprietary** primarily 2-year, part of ITT Educational Services, Inc.
- **Coed**
- **Minimally difficult** entrance level

Academics *Calendar:* quarters. *Degrees:* associate and bachelor's.

Freshman Application Contact Director of Recruitment, ITT Technical Institute, 4717 Hilton Corporate Drive, Columbus, OH 43232. *Phone:* 614-868-2000. *Toll-free phone:* 877-233-8864.
Website: http://www.itt-tech.edu/.

ITT Technical Institute

Dayton, Ohio

- **Proprietary** primarily 2-year, founded 1935, part of ITT Educational Services, Inc.
- **Suburban** campus
- **Coed**
- **Minimally difficult** entrance level

Academics *Calendar:* quarters. *Degrees:* associate and bachelor's.
Freshman Application Contact Director of Recruitment, ITT Technical Institute, 3325 Stop 8 Road, Dayton, OH 45414. *Phone:* 937-264-7700. *Toll-free phone:* 800-568-3241.
Website: http://www.itt-tech.edu/.

ITT Technical Institute

Hilliard, Ohio

- **Proprietary** primarily 2-year, founded 2003, part of ITT Educational Services, Inc.
- **Coed**
- **Minimally difficult** entrance level

Academics *Calendar:* quarters. *Degrees:* associate and bachelor's.
Freshman Application Contact Director of Recruitment, ITT Technical Institute, 3781 Park Mill Run Drive, Hilliard, OH 43026. *Phone:* 614-771-4888. *Toll-free phone:* 888-483-4888.
Website: http://www.itt-tech.edu/.

ITT Technical Institute

Maumee, Ohio

- **Proprietary** primarily 2-year
- **Coed**

Academics *Degrees:* associate and bachelor's.
Freshman Application Contact Director of Recruitment, ITT Technical Institute, 1656 Henthorne Drive, Suite B, Maumee, OH 43537. *Phone:* 419-861-6500. *Toll-free phone:* 877-205-4639.
Website: http://www.itt-tech.edu/.

ITT Technical Institute

Norwood, Ohio

- **Proprietary** primarily 2-year, founded 1995, part of ITT Educational Services, Inc.
- **Coed**
- **Minimally difficult** entrance level

Academics *Calendar:* quarters. *Degrees:* associate and bachelor's.
Freshman Application Contact Director of Recruitment, ITT Technical Institute, 4750 Wesley Avenue, Norwood, OH 45212. *Phone:* 513-531-8300.
Toll-free phone: 800-314-8324.
Website: http://www.itt-tech.edu/.

ITT Technical Institute

Strongsville, Ohio

- **Proprietary** primarily 2-year, founded 1994, part of ITT Educational Services, Inc.
- **Coed**
- **Minimally difficult** entrance level

Academics *Calendar:* quarters. *Degrees:* associate and bachelor's.

Freshman Application Contact Director of Recruitment, ITT Technical Institute, 14955 Sprague Road, Strongsville, OH 44136. *Phone:* 440-234-9091. *Toll-free phone:* 800-331-1488.
Website: http://www.itt-tech.edu/.

ITT Technical Institute

Warrensville Heights, Ohio

- **Proprietary** primarily 2-year, founded 2005
- **Coed**
- **Minimally difficult** entrance level

Academics *Calendar:* quarters. *Degrees:* associate and bachelor's.
Freshman Application Contact Director of Recruitment, ITT Technical Institute, 4700 Richmond Road, Warrensville Heights, OH 44128. *Phone:* 216-896-6500. *Toll-free phone:* 800-741-3494.
Website: http://www.itt-tech.edu/.

ITT Technical Institute

Youngstown, Ohio

- **Proprietary** primarily 2-year, founded 1967, part of ITT Educational Services, Inc.
- **Suburban** campus
- **Coed**
- **Minimally difficult** entrance level

Academics *Calendar:* quarters. *Degrees:* associate and bachelor's.
Financial Aid *Of all full-time matriculated undergraduates who enrolled in 2011,* 5 Federal Work-Study jobs (averaging $3979).
Freshman Application Contact Director of Recruitment, ITT Technical Institute, 1030 North Meridian Road, Youngstown, OH 44509-4098. *Phone:* 330-270-1600. *Toll-free phone:* 800-832-5001.
Website: http://www.itt-tech.edu/.

John Carroll University

University Heights, Ohio

- **Independent Roman Catholic (Jesuit)** comprehensive, founded 1886
- **Suburban** 60-acre campus with easy access to Cleveland
- **Coed** 2,949 undergraduate students, 97% full-time, 49% women, 51% men
- **Moderately difficult** entrance level, 81% of applicants were admitted

Undergraduates 2,859 full-time, 90 part-time. Students come from 39 states and territories; 13 other countries; 30% are from out of state; 4% Black or African American, non-Hispanic/Latino; 4% Hispanic/Latino; 2% Asian, non-Hispanic/Latino; 0.1% American Indian or Alaska Native, non-Hispanic/Latino; 2% Two or more races, non-Hispanic/Latino; 4% Race/ethnicity unknown; 2% international; 3% transferred in; 59% live on campus. *Retention:* 87% of full-time freshmen returned.
Freshmen *Admission:* 3,490 applied, 2,843 admitted, 681 enrolled. *Average high school GPA:* 3.46. *Test scores:* SAT critical reading scores over 500: 75%; SAT math scores over 500: 78%; SAT writing scores over 500: 74%; ACT scores over 18: 97%; SAT critical reading scores over 600: 28%; SAT math scores over 600: 33%; SAT writing scores over 600: 24%; ACT scores over 24: 58%; SAT critical reading scores over 700: 4%; SAT math scores over 700: 4%; SAT writing scores over 700: 3%; ACT scores over 30: 8%.
Faculty *Total:* 366, 53% full-time, 69% with terminal degrees. *Student/faculty ratio:* 13:1.
Academics *Calendar:* semesters. *Degrees:* bachelor's, master's, and post-master's certificates. *Special study options:* advanced placement credit, cooperative education, double majors, honors programs, independent study, internships, off-campus study, part-time degree program, services for LD students, student-designed majors, study abroad, summer session for credit. *ROTC:* Army (b). *Unusual degree programs:* 3-2 engineering with Case Western Reserve University; nursing with Joint BA/BSN degree program with Ursuline College.
Computers on Campus 411 computers/terminals and 500 ports are available on campus for general student use. Students can access the following: campus intranet, computer help desk, free student e-mail accounts, online (class) grades, online (class) registration, online (class) schedules, campus portal, course management site, online financial aid and billing; online course sites; online housing selection. Campuswide network is available. 100% of college-

owned or -operated housing units are wired for high-speed Internet access. Wireless service is available via entire campus.

Student Life *Housing:* on-campus residence required through sophomore year. *Options:* coed, cooperative, disabled students. Campus housing is university owned. Freshman campus housing is guaranteed. *Activities and organizations:* drama/theater group, student-run newspaper, radio and television station, choral group, Community Outreach/Volunteer Service Organization, Student Union, Club Sports, Fraternities and Sororities, Carroll News, national fraternities, national sororities. *Campus security:* 24-hour emergency response devices and patrols, late-night transport/escort service, Distinctive Student EMS program fully staffed. *Student services:* health clinic, personal/psychological counseling, women's center.

Athletics Member NCAA. All Division III. *Intercollegiate sports:* baseball M, basketball M/W, cheerleading W(c), crew M(c)/W(c), cross-country running M/W, field hockey W(c), football M, golf M/W, ice hockey M(c), lacrosse M/W, rugby M(c)/W(c), sailing M(c)/W(c), skiing (cross-country) M(c)/W(c), skiing (downhill) M(c)/W(c), soccer M/W, softball W, swimming and diving M/W, tennis M/W, track and field M/W, ultimate Frisbee M(c), volleyball M(c)/W, wrestling M. *Intramural sports:* basketball M/W, football M/W, golf M/W, racquetball M/W, rock climbing M/W, soccer M/W, softball M/W, swimming and diving M/W, table tennis M/W, tennis M/W, ultimate Frisbee M/W, volleyball M/W, water polo M/W.

Standardized Tests *Required:* SAT or ACT (for admission).

Costs (2013–14) *One-time required fee:* $325. *Comprehensive fee:* $44,520 includes full-time tuition ($33,330), mandatory fees ($1150), and room and board ($10,040). Part-time tuition: $1016 per credit. Part-time tuition and fees vary according to course load. *Room and board:* Room and board charges vary according to board plan and housing facility. *Payment plans:* installment, deferred payment. *Waivers:* senior citizens and employees or children of employees.

Financial Aid Of all full-time matriculated undergraduates who enrolled in 2010, 2,479 applied for aid, 2,217 were judged to have need, 988 had their need fully met. 744 Federal Work-Study jobs (averaging $2200). 209 state and other part-time jobs (averaging $1188). In 2010, 539 non-need-based awards were made. *Average percent of need met:* 81%. *Average financial aid package:* $24,817. *Average need-based loan:* $3935. *Average need-based gift aid:* $19,554. *Average non-need-based aid:* $10,222. *Average indebtedness upon graduation:* $30,422. *Financial aid deadline:* 3/15.

Applying *Options:* electronic application, early admission, early action, deferred entrance. *Required:* essay or personal statement, high school transcript, 1 letter of recommendation. *Required for some:* 2 letters of recommendation, interview. *Application deadlines:* 2/1 (freshmen), rolling (transfers), 12/1 (early action). *Notification:* continuous (freshmen), 12/20 (early action).

Freshman Application Contact Mr. Steven P. Vitatoe, Executive Director of Enrollment, John Carroll University, 1 John Carroll Boulevard, University Heights, OH 44118. *Phone:* 216-397-4294. *Toll-free phone:* 888-335-6800. *Fax:* 216-397-4981. *E-mail:* svitatoe@jcu.edu.
Website: http://www.jcu.edu/.

Kent State University

Kent, Ohio

- **State-supported** university, founded 1910, part of Kent State University System
- **Suburban** 1347-acre campus with easy access to Cleveland
- **Endowment** $85.2 million
- **Coed** 22,436 undergraduate students, 87% full-time, 58% women, 42% men
- **Moderately difficult** entrance level, 83% of applicants were admitted

Undergraduates 19,489 full-time, 2,947 part-time. Students come from 50 states and territories; 64 other countries; 11% are from out of state; 9% Black or African American, non-Hispanic/Latino; 3% Hispanic/Latino; 1% Asian, non-Hispanic/Latino; 0.1% Native Hawaiian or other Pacific Islander, non-Hispanic/Latino; 0.3% American Indian or Alaska Native, non-Hispanic/Latino; 2% Two or more races, non-Hispanic/Latino; 3% Race/ethnicity unknown; 6% international; 6% transferred in; 29% live on campus. *Retention:* 77% of full-time freshmen returned.

Freshmen *Admission:* 15,970 applied, 13,259 admitted, 4,124 enrolled. *Average high school GPA:* 3.27. *Test scores:* SAT critical reading scores over 500: 60%; SAT math scores over 500: 63%; SAT writing scores over 500: 51%;

ACT scores over 18: 97%; SAT critical reading scores over 600: 17%; SAT math scores over 600: 18%; SAT writing scores over 600: 15%; ACT scores over 24: 34%; SAT critical reading scores over 700: 3%; SAT math scores over 700: 2%; SAT writing scores over 700: 2%; ACT scores over 30: 4%.

Faculty *Total:* 1,688, 54% full-time. *Student/faculty ratio:* 21:1.

Academics *Calendar:* semesters. *Degrees:* certificates, associate, bachelor's, master's, doctoral, post-master's, and postbachelor's certificates. *Special study options:* academic remediation for entering students, accelerated degree program, adult/continuing education programs, advanced placement credit, cooperative education, distance learning, double majors, English as a second language, external degree program, freshman honors college, honors programs, independent study, internships, off-campus study, part-time degree program, services for LD students, student-designed majors, study abroad, summer session for credit. *ROTC:* Army (b), Air Force (b). *Unusual degree programs:* 3-2 business administration; nursing; Speech Pathology & Audiology; International Relations & Business Administration; Fashion Merchandising & Business Administration; Visual Communication Design; Human Development & Family Services with concentration in Gerontology and Nursing Home Administration & Business Administration.

Computers on Campus 2,000 computers/terminals and 1,200 ports are available on campus for general student use. Students can access the following: computer help desk, free student e-mail accounts, online (class) grades, online (class) registration, online (class) schedules. Campuswide network is available. 100% of college-owned or -operated housing units are wired for high-speed Internet access. Wireless service is available via entire campus.

Student Life *Housing:* on-campus residence required through sophomore year. *Options:* coed, men-only, women-only, disabled students. Campus housing is university owned. Freshman campus housing is guaranteed. *Activities and organizations:* drama/theater group, student-run newspaper, radio and television station, choral group, marching band, Commuter & Off-Campus Student Organization (COSO), Fashion Student Organization (FSO), Public Relations Students Society of America (PRSSA), Habitat for Humanity, Relay for Life, national fraternities, national sororities. *Campus security:* 24-hour emergency response devices and patrols, student patrols, late-night transport/escort service, controlled dormitory access, campus police and fire department, electronic locks on computer labs, studios and laboratory research areas. *Student services:* health clinic, personal/psychological counseling, women's center, legal services.

Athletics Member NCAA. All Division I. *Intercollegiate sports:* baseball M(s), basketball M(s)/W(s), cross-country running M(s)/W(s), field hockey W(s), football M(s), golf M(s)/W(s), gymnastics W(s), soccer W(s), softball W(s), track and field M(s)/W(s), volleyball W(s), wrestling M(s). *Intramural sports:* badminton M(c)/W(c), baseball M(c), basketball M/W, bowling M(c)/W(c), equestrian sports M(c)/W(c), fencing M(c)/W(c), field hockey W(c), football M/W, golf M(c)/W(c), gymnastics M(c)/W(c), ice hockey M(c), lacrosse M(c), racquetball M(c)/W(c), rugby M(c)/W(c), sailing M(c)/W(c), skiing (downhill) M(c)/W(c), soccer M(c)/W(c), softball M/W, swimming and diving M(c)/W(c), table tennis M/W, tennis M/W, ultimate Frisbee M/W, volleyball M(c)/W(c), water polo M/W, wrestling M.

Standardized Tests *Required:* SAT or ACT (for admission).

Costs (2012–13) *Tuition:* state resident $9672 full-time; nonresident $17,632 full-time. Full-time tuition and fees vary according to course load. Part-time tuition and fees vary according to course load. *Room and board:* $9176. Room and board charges vary according to board plan and housing facility. *Payment plans:* installment, deferred payment. *Waivers:* senior citizens and employees or children of employees.

Financial Aid Of all full-time matriculated undergraduates who enrolled in 2012, 14,474 applied for aid, 12,539 were judged to have need, 4,522 had their need fully met. 358 Federal Work-Study jobs (averaging $2942). In 2012, 2239 non-need-based awards were made. *Average percent of need met:* 50%. *Average financial aid package:* $9082. *Average need-based loan:* $4327. *Average need-based gift aid:* $5604. *Average non-need-based aid:* $4235. *Average indebtedness upon graduation:* $31,954.

Applying *Options:* electronic application, early admission. *Application fee:* $40. *Required:* high school transcript, minimum 2.5 GPA. *Application deadlines:* rolling (freshmen), rolling (transfers). *Notification:* continuous (freshmen), continuous (transfers).

Freshman Application Contact Mr. Christopher Buttenschon, Assistant Director of Admissions, Kent State University, 161 Michael Schwartz Center, Kent, OH 44242-0001. *Phone:* 330-672-2444. *Toll-free phone:* 800-988-KENT. *Fax:* 330-672-2499. *E-mail:* admissions@kent.edu.
Website: http://www.kent.edu/.

Kent State University at Ashtabula

Ashtabula, Ohio

- **State-supported** primarily 2-year, founded 1958, part of Kent State University System
- **Small-town** 120-acre campus with easy access to Cleveland
- **Coed** 2,511 undergraduate students, 50% full-time, 65% women, 35% men
- **Noncompetitive** entrance level, 99% of applicants were admitted

Undergraduates 1,268 full-time, 1,243 part-time. Students come from 12 states and territories; 1 other country; 2% are from out of state; 5% Black or African American, non-Hispanic/Latino; 3% Hispanic/Latino; 0.6% Asian, non-Hispanic/Latino; 0.5% American Indian or Alaska Native, non-Hispanic/Latino; 1% Two or more races, non-Hispanic/Latino; 3% Race/ethnicity unknown; 0.2% international; 7% transferred in. *Retention:* 49% of full-time freshmen returned.

Freshmen *Admission:* 565 applied, 562 admitted, 348 enrolled. *Average high school GPA:* 2.74. *Test scores:* SAT critical reading scores over 500: 29%; ACT scores over 18: 67%; ACT scores over 24: 11%; ACT scores over 30: 2%.

Faculty *Total:* 126, 42% full-time. *Student/faculty ratio:* 22:1.

Academics *Calendar:* semesters. *Degrees:* certificates, associate, and bachelor's (also offers some upper-level and graduate courses). *Special study options:* academic remediation for entering students, advanced placement credit, distance learning, double majors, independent study, internships, part-time degree program, services for LD students, student-designed majors, study abroad, summer session for credit. *ROTC:* Army (c), Navy (c), Air Force (c).

Computers on Campus 70 computers/terminals and 175 ports are available on campus for general student use. Students can access the following: computer help desk, free student e-mail accounts, online (class) grades, online (class) registration, online (class) schedules. Campuswide network is available. Wireless service is available via entire campus.

Student Life *Housing:* college housing not available. *Activities and organizations:* student government, student veterans association, Student Nurses Association, Student Occupational Therapy Association (SOTA), Media Club. *Campus security:* 24-hour emergency response devices.

Standardized Tests *Required for some:* SAT or ACT (for admission). *Recommended:* SAT or ACT (for admission).

Financial Aid Of all full-time matriculated undergraduates who enrolled in 2012, 846 applied for aid, 814 were judged to have need, 169 had their need fully met. In 2012, 3 non-need-based awards were made. *Average percent of need met:* 42%. *Average financial aid package:* $7513. *Average need-based loan:* $3764. *Average need-based gift aid:* $4675. *Average non-need-based aid:* $1333.

Applying *Options:* electronic application, early admission, deferred entrance. *Application fee:* $30. *Required:* high school transcript. *Application deadlines:* rolling (freshmen), rolling (transfers). *Notification:* continuous (freshmen), continuous (transfers).

Freshman Application Contact Kent State University at Ashtabula, 3300 Lake Road West, Ashtabula, OH 44004-2299. *Phone:* 440-964-4217. *Website:* http://www.ashtabula.kent.edu/.

Kent State University at East Liverpool

East Liverpool, Ohio

- **State-supported** primarily 2-year, founded 1967, part of Kent State University System
- **Small-town** 4-acre campus with easy access to Pittsburgh
- **Coed** 1,504 undergraduate students, 54% full-time, 69% women, 31% men
- **Noncompetitive** entrance level, 96% of applicants were admitted

Undergraduates 818 full-time, 686 part-time. Students come from 8 states and territories; 2 other countries; 5% are from out of state; 4% Black or African American, non-Hispanic/Latino; 2% Hispanic/Latino; 0.6% Asian, non-Hispanic/Latino; 0.3% American Indian or Alaska Native, non-Hispanic/Latino; 1% Two or more races, non-Hispanic/Latino; 2% Race/ethnicity unknown; 0.1% international; 5% transferred in. *Retention:* 52% of full-time freshmen returned.

Freshmen *Admission:* 179 applied, 171 admitted, 130 enrolled. *Average high school GPA:* 2.89. *Test scores:* SAT math scores over 500: 50%; ACT scores over 18: 53%; ACT scores over 24: 7%.

Faculty *Total:* 75, 36% full-time. *Student/faculty ratio:* 24:1.

Academics *Calendar:* semesters. *Degrees:* certificates, associate, and bachelor's (also offers some upper-level and graduate courses). *Special study options:* academic remediation for entering students, accelerated degree program, adult/continuing education programs, advanced placement credit, distance learning, double majors, freshman honors college, honors programs, independent study, internships, part-time degree program, services for LD students, student-designed majors, study abroad, summer session for credit. *ROTC:* Army (c), Navy (c), Air Force (c).

Computers on Campus 72 computers/terminals are available on campus for general student use. Students can access the following: computer help desk, free student e-mail accounts, online (class) grades, online (class) registration, online (class) schedules. Campuswide network is available. Wireless service is available via entire campus.

Student Life *Housing:* college housing not available. *Activities and organizations:* student-run newspaper, Student Government, Student Nurses Association, Environmental Club, Occupational Therapist Assistant Club, Physical Therapist Assistant Club. *Campus security:* student patrols, late-night transport/escort service.

Standardized Tests *Required for some:* SAT or ACT (for admission). *Recommended:* SAT or ACT (for admission).

Financial Aid Of all full-time matriculated undergraduates who enrolled in 2012, 398 applied for aid, 372 were judged to have need, 97 had their need fully met. In 2012, 2 non-need-based awards were made. *Average percent of need met:* 45%. *Average financial aid package:* $7555. *Average need-based loan:* $3821. *Average need-based gift aid:* $4655. *Average non-need-based aid:* $750.

Applying *Options:* electronic application, early admission, deferred entrance. *Application fee:* $30. *Required:* high school transcript. *Application deadlines:* rolling (freshmen), rolling (transfers). *Notification:* continuous (freshmen), continuous (transfers).

Freshman Application Contact Kent State University at East Liverpool, OH. *Phone:* 330-385-3805. *Website:* http://www.eliv.kent.edu/.

Kent State University at Geauga

Burton, Ohio

- **State-supported** 4-year, founded 1964, part of Kent State University System
- **Rural** 87-acre campus with easy access to Cleveland
- **Coed** 2,533 undergraduate students, 59% full-time, 66% women, 34% men
- **Noncompetitive** entrance level, 98% of applicants were admitted

Undergraduates 1,490 full-time, 1,043 part-time. Students come from 12 states and territories; 6 other countries; 1% are from out of state; 10% Black or African American, non-Hispanic/Latino; 2% Hispanic/Latino; 1% Asian, non-Hispanic/Latino; 0.1% Native Hawaiian or other Pacific Islander, non-Hispanic/Latino; 0.4% American Indian or Alaska Native, non-Hispanic/Latino; 1% Two or more races, non-Hispanic/Latino; 4% Race/ethnicity unknown; 0.5% international; 7% transferred in. *Retention:* 53% of full-time freshmen returned.

Freshmen *Admission:* 419 applied, 412 admitted, 271 enrolled. *Average high school GPA:* 2.6. *Test scores:* SAT critical reading scores over 500: 45%; SAT math scores over 500: 40%; SAT writing scores over 500: 33%; ACT scores over 18: 67%; SAT critical reading scores over 600: 10%; SAT math scores over 600: 13%; SAT writing scores over 600: 5%; ACT scores over 24: 12%; ACT scores over 30: 2%.

Faculty *Total:* 125, 26% full-time. *Student/faculty ratio:* 29:1.

Academics *Calendar:* semesters. *Degrees:* certificates, associate, and bachelor's. *Special study options:* academic remediation for entering students, accelerated degree program, advanced placement credit, distance learning, double majors, independent study, internships, part-time degree program, services for LD students, student-designed majors, study abroad, summer session for credit. *ROTC:* Army (c), Air Force (c).

Computers on Campus Students can access the following: computer help desk, free student e-mail accounts, online (class) grades, online (class) registration, online (class) schedules. Campuswide network is available. Wireless service is available via entire campus.

Student Life *Housing:* college housing not available. *Activities and organizations:* Student Ambassadors, Campus Crusade for Christ, Gaia Society. *Campus security:* 24-hour emergency response devices.

Standardized Tests *Required for some:* SAT or ACT (for admission). *Recommended:* SAT or ACT (for admission).

Costs (2012–13) *Tuition:* state resident $5472 full-time; nonresident $13,432 full-time. Full-time tuition and fees vary according to course level and course load. Part-time tuition and fees vary according to course level and course load. *Payment plans:* installment, deferred payment. *Waivers:* senior citizens and employees or children of employees.

Financial Aid Of all full-time matriculated undergraduates who enrolled in 2012, 578 applied for aid, 520 were judged to have need, 150 had their need fully met. In 2012, 6 non-need-based awards were made. *Average percent of need met:* 45%. *Average financial aid package:* $6824. *Average need-based loan:* $3777. *Average need-based gift aid:* $4425. *Average non-need-based aid:* $503.

Applying *Options:* electronic application, deferred entrance. *Application fee:* $30. *Required:* high school transcript. *Application deadlines:* rolling (freshmen), rolling (out-of-state freshmen), rolling (transfers). *Notification:* continuous (freshmen), continuous (out-of-state freshmen), continuous (transfers).

Freshman Application Contact Kent State University at Geauga, 14111 Claridon-Troy Road, Burton, OH 44021. *Phone:* 440-834-4187. *Fax:* 440-834-3786. *E-mail:* geaugaadmissions@kent.edu.

Website: http://www.geauga.kent.edu/.

Kent State University at Salem

Salem, Ohio

- **State-supported** primarily 2-year, founded 1966, part of Kent State University System
- **Rural** 98-acre campus
- **Coed** 1,878 undergraduate students, 67% full-time, 70% women, 30% men
- **Noncompetitive** entrance level, 98% of applicants were admitted

Undergraduates 1,266 full-time, 612 part-time. Students come from 11 states and territories; 4 other countries; 1% are from out of state; 3% Black or African American, non-Hispanic/Latino; 1% Hispanic/Latino; 0.6% Asian, non-Hispanic/Latino; 0.4% American Indian or Alaska Native, non-Hispanic/Latino; 1% Two or more races, non-Hispanic/Latino; 3% Race/ethnicity unknown; 0.1% international; 7% transferred in. *Retention:* 59% of full-time freshmen returned.

Freshmen *Admission:* 446 applied, 439 admitted, 262 enrolled. *Average high school GPA:* 2.92. *Test scores:* SAT math scores over 500: 50%; ACT scores over 18: 71%; ACT scores over 24: 13%.

Faculty *Total:* 123, 37% full-time. *Student/faculty ratio:* 20:1.

Academics *Calendar:* semesters. *Degrees:* certificates, associate, and bachelor's (also offers some upper-level and graduate courses). *Special study options:* academic remediation for entering students, accelerated degree program, adult/continuing education programs, advanced placement credit, cooperative education, distance learning, double majors, freshman honors college, honors programs, independent study, internships, part-time degree program, services for LD students, student-designed majors, study abroad, summer session for credit. *ROTC:* Army (c), Air Force (c).

Computers on Campus Students can access the following: computer help desk, free student e-mail accounts, online (class) grades, online (class) registration, online (class) schedules. Campuswide network is available. Wireless service is available via entire campus.

Student Life *Housing:* college housing not available. *Activities and organizations:* choral group, Honors Club, Human Services Technology Club, Radiologic Technology Club, Student Government Organization, Students for Professional Nursing. *Campus security:* 24-hour emergency response devices, late-night transport/escort service. *Student services:* personal/psychological counseling.

Athletics *Intramural sports:* basketball M/W, skiing (downhill) M/W, table tennis M/W, tennis M/W, volleyball M/W.

Standardized Tests *Required for some:* SAT or ACT (for admission). *Recommended:* SAT or ACT (for admission).

Financial Aid Of all full-time matriculated undergraduates who enrolled in 2012, 889 applied for aid, 815 were judged to have need, 246 had their need fully met. In 2012, 9 non-need-based awards were made. *Average percent of need met:* 46%. *Average financial aid package:* $7145. *Average need-based loan:* $3786. *Average need-based gift aid:* $4536. *Average non-need-based aid:* $1448.

Applying *Options:* electronic application, early admission, deferred entrance. *Application fee:* $30. *Required:* high school transcript. *Required for some:* essay or personal statement. *Application deadlines:* rolling (freshmen), rolling (out-of-state freshmen), rolling (transfers). *Notification:* continuous (freshmen), continuous (out-of-state freshmen), continuous (transfers).

Freshman Application Contact Kent State University at Salem, 2491 State Route 45 South, Salem, OH 44460-9412. *Phone:* 330-382-7415.

Website: http://www.salem.kent.edu/.

Kent State University at Stark

Canton, Ohio

- **State-supported** comprehensive, founded 1967, part of Kent State University System
- **Suburban** 200-acre campus with easy access to Cleveland
- **Coed** 4,816 undergraduate students, 65% full-time, 61% women, 39% men
- **Noncompetitive** entrance level, 96% of applicants were admitted

Undergraduates 3,146 full-time, 1,670 part-time. Students come from 14 states and territories; 5 other countries; 1% are from out of state; 8% Black or African American, non-Hispanic/Latino; 2% Hispanic/Latino; 0.9% Asian, non-Hispanic/Latino; 0.1% Native Hawaiian or other Pacific Islander, non-Hispanic/Latino; 0.6% American Indian or Alaska Native, non-Hispanic/Latino; 2% Two or more races, non-Hispanic/Latino; 3% Race/ethnicity unknown; 0.2% international; 10% transferred in. *Retention:* 59% of full-time freshmen returned.

Freshmen *Admission:* 1,019 applied, 981 admitted, 682 enrolled. *Average high school GPA:* 2.78. *Test scores:* SAT critical reading scores over 500: 24%; SAT math scores over 500: 29%; SAT writing scores over 500: 29%; ACT scores over 18: 74%; SAT critical reading scores over 600: 6%; SAT writing scores over 600: 6%; ACT scores over 24: 14%; ACT scores over 30: 1%.

Faculty *Total:* 255, 43% full-time. *Student/faculty ratio:* 23:1.

Academics *Calendar:* semesters. *Degrees:* certificates, associate, bachelor's, and master's. *Special study options:* academic remediation for entering students, adult/continuing education programs, advanced placement credit, distance learning, double majors, honors programs, independent study, internships, off-campus study, part-time degree program, services for LD students, student-designed majors, study abroad, summer session for credit. *ROTC:* Army (c), Navy (c), Air Force (c).

Computers on Campus 575 computers/terminals are available on campus for general student use. Students can access the following: campus intranet, computer help desk, free student e-mail accounts, online (class) grades, online (class) registration, online (class) schedules. Campuswide network is available. Wireless service is available via entire campus.

Student Life *Housing:* college housing not available. *Activities and organizations:* drama/theater group, choral group, Club Sunaarashi (Japanese Animation, Magic the Gathering, and Dungeons and Dragons), Rooted in Faith-Bible Club (non-denominational), Kent State Stark Education Association (KSSEA), SCRUBS (nursing organization), Ohio Collegiate Music Education Association (OCMEA). *Campus security:* 24-hour emergency response devices, late-night transport/escort service. *Student services:* personal/psychological counseling.

Standardized Tests *Required for some:* SAT or ACT (for admission). *Recommended:* SAT or ACT (for admission).

Costs (2012–13) *Tuition:* state resident $5472 full-time; nonresident $13,432 full-time. Full-time tuition and fees vary according to course level and course load. Part-time tuition and fees vary according to course level and course load. *Payment plans:* installment, deferred payment. *Waivers:* senior citizens and employees or children of employees.

Financial Aid Of all full-time matriculated undergraduates who enrolled in 2012, 2,291 applied for aid, 2,067 were judged to have need, 617 had their need fully met. In 2012, 52 non-need-based awards were made. *Average percent of need met:* 49%. *Average financial aid package:* $7272. *Average need-based loan:* $3933. *Average need-based gift aid:* $4375. *Average non-need-based aid:* $2851.

Applying *Options:* electronic application, early admission, deferred entrance. *Application fee:* $30. *Required:* high school transcript. *Application deadlines:* rolling (freshmen), rolling (out-of-state freshmen), rolling (transfers). *Notification:* continuous (freshmen), continuous (out-of-state freshmen), continuous (transfers).

Freshman Application Contact Office of Admissions, Kent State University at Stark, Kent State University at Stark, 6000 Frank Avenue NW, North Canton, OH 44720. *Phone:* 330-244-3251. *Fax:* 330-499-0301. *E-mail:* starkadmissions@kent.edu.

Website: http://www.stark.kent.edu/.

Kent State University at Trumbull

Warren, Ohio

- **State-supported** primarily 2-year, founded 1954, part of Kent State University System
- **Suburban** 200-acre campus with easy access to Cleveland
- **Coed** 3,103 undergraduate students, 61% full-time, 63% women, 37% men
- **Noncompetitive** entrance level, 99% of applicants were admitted

Undergraduates 1,892 full-time, 1,211 part-time. Students come from 16 states and territories; 3 other countries; 1% are from out of state; 10% Black or African American, non-Hispanic/Latino; 3% Hispanic/Latino; 0.5% Asian, non-Hispanic/Latino; 0.2% American Indian or Alaska Native, non-Hispanic/Latino; 2% Two or more races, non-Hispanic/Latino; 2% Race/ethnicity unknown; 0.4% international; 7% transferred in. *Retention:* 47% of full-time freshmen returned.

Freshmen *Admission:* 485 applied, 481 admitted, 375 enrolled. *Average high school GPA:* 2.69. *Test scores:* SAT math scores over 500: 50%; SAT writing scores over 500: 25%; ACT scores over 18: 74%; ACT scores over 24: 10%; ACT scores over 30: 1%.

Faculty *Total:* 121, 48% full-time. *Student/faculty ratio:* 29:1.

Academics *Calendar:* semesters. *Degrees:* certificates, associate, and bachelor's (also offers some upper-level and graduate courses). *Special study options:* academic remediation for entering students, adult/continuing education programs, advanced placement credit, distance learning, double majors, freshman honors college, honors programs, independent study, internships, part-time degree program, services for LD students, student-designed majors, study abroad, summer session for credit. *ROTC:* Army (c), Air Force (c).

Computers on Campus 300 computers/terminals are available on campus for general student use. Students can access the following: computer help desk, free student e-mail accounts, online (class) grades, online (class) registration, online (class) schedules. Campuswide network is available. Wireless service is available via entire campus.

Student Life *Housing:* college housing not available. *Activities and organizations:* drama/theater group, National Student Nurses Association, Spot On Improv Group, ENACTUS, GLOW (Gay, Lesbian, or Whatever), If These Hands Could Talk—ASL. *Campus security:* 24-hour emergency response devices, late-night transport/escort service, patrols by trained security personnel during open hours. *Student services:* personal/psychological counseling.

Standardized Tests *Required for some:* SAT or ACT (for admission). *Recommended:* SAT or ACT (for admission).

Financial Aid Of all full-time matriculated undergraduates who enrolled in 2012, 1,119 applied for aid, 1,058 were judged to have need, 254 had their need fully met. In 2012, 7 non-need-based awards were made. *Average percent of need met:* 45%. *Average financial aid package:* $7497. *Average need-based loan:* $3869. *Average need-based gift aid:* $4614. *Average non-need-based aid:* $1500.

Applying *Options:* electronic application, deferred entrance. *Application fee:* $30. *Required:* high school transcript. *Application deadlines:* rolling (freshmen), rolling (out-of-state freshmen), rolling (transfers). *Notification:* continuous (freshmen), continuous (out-of-state freshmen), continuous (transfers).

Freshman Application Contact Kent State University at Trumbull, Warren, OH 44483. *Phone:* 330-675-8935.

Website: http://www.trumbull.kent.edu/.

Kent State University at Tuscarawas

New Philadelphia, Ohio

- **State-supported** primarily 2-year, founded 1962, part of Kent State University System
- **Small-town** 172-acre campus with easy access to Cleveland
- **Coed** 2,983 undergraduate students, 50% full-time, 54% women, 46% men
- **Noncompetitive** entrance level, 95% of applicants were admitted

Undergraduates 1,484 full-time, 1,499 part-time. 1% are from out of state; 2% Black or African American, non-Hispanic/Latino; 0.9% Hispanic/Latino; 0.6% Asian, non-Hispanic/Latino; 0.1% Native Hawaiian or other Pacific Islander, non-Hispanic/Latino; 0.1% American Indian or Alaska Native, non-Hispanic/Latino; 1% Two or more races, non-Hispanic/Latino; 3% Race/ethnicity unknown; 0.2% international; 6% transferred in. *Retention:* 59% of full-time freshmen returned.

Freshmen *Admission:* 470 applied, 448 admitted, 348 enrolled. *Average high school GPA:* 2.81. *Test scores:* SAT critical reading scores over 500: 25%; SAT math scores over 500: 50%; SAT writing scores over 500: 25%; ACT scores over 18: 77%; SAT critical reading scores over 600: 25%; ACT scores over 24: 19%; ACT scores over 30: 2%.

Faculty *Total:* 139, 37% full-time. *Student/faculty ratio:* 23:1.

Academics *Calendar:* semesters. *Degrees:* certificates, associate, and bachelor's (also offers some upper-level and graduate courses). *Special study options:* academic remediation for entering students, accelerated degree program, adult/continuing education programs, advanced placement credit, distance learning, double majors, freshman honors college, honors programs, independent study, internships, part-time degree program, services for LD students, student-designed majors, study abroad, summer session for credit.

Computers on Campus 194 computers/terminals are available on campus for general student use. Students can access the following: computer help desk, free student e-mail accounts, online (class) grades, online (class) registration, online (class) schedules. Campuswide network is available. Wireless service is available via entire campus.

Student Life *Housing:* college housing not available. *Activities and organizations:* drama/theater group, choral group, Society of Manufacturing Engineers, IEEE, Animation Imagineers, Justice Studies Club, Student Activities Council. *Campus security:* 24-hour emergency response devices.

Athletics *Intramural sports:* basketball M/W, volleyball M/W.

Standardized Tests *Required for some:* SAT or ACT (for admission). *Recommended:* SAT or ACT (for admission).

Financial Aid Of all full-time matriculated undergraduates who enrolled in 2012, 1,002 applied for aid, 928 were judged to have need, 262 had their need fully met. In 2012, 15 non-need-based awards were made. *Average percent of need met:* 47%. *Average financial aid package:* $7249. *Average need-based loan:* $3860. *Average need-based gift aid:* $4382. *Average non-need-based aid:* $1265.

Applying *Options:* electronic application, deferred entrance. *Application fee:* $30. *Required:* high school transcript. *Application deadlines:* rolling (freshmen), rolling (out-of-state freshmen), rolling (transfers). *Notification:* continuous (freshmen), continuous (out-of-state freshmen), continuous (transfers).

Freshman Application Contact Kent State University at Tuscarawas, Kent State University at Tuscarawas, 330 University Drive Northeast, New Philadelphia, OH 44663-9403. *Phone:* 330-339-3391 Ext. 47425. *Fax:* 330-339-3321. *E-mail:* info@tusc.kent.edu.

Website: http://www.tusc.kent.edu/.

Kenyon College

Gambier, Ohio

- **Independent** 4-year, founded 1824
- **Rural** 1200-acre campus with easy access to Columbus
- **Endowment** $187.8 million
- **Coed** 1,667 undergraduate students, 99% full-time, 53% women, 47% men
- **Very difficult** entrance level, 36% of applicants were admitted

Undergraduates 1,658 full-time, 9 part-time. Students come from 50 states and territories; 41 other countries; 85% are from out of state; 3% Black or African American, non-Hispanic/Latino; 5% Hispanic/Latino; 7% Asian, non-Hispanic/Latino; 1% American Indian or Alaska Native, non-Hispanic/Latino; 0.5% Two or more races, non-Hispanic/Latino; 2% Race/ethnicity unknown; 4% international; 0.8% transferred in; 98% live on campus. *Retention:* 91% of full-time freshmen returned.

Freshmen *Admission:* 3,947 applied, 1,421 admitted, 446 enrolled. *Average high school GPA:* 3.9. *Test scores:* SAT critical reading scores over 500: 99%; SAT math scores over 500: 99%; SAT writing scores over 500: 98%; ACT scores over 18: 100%; SAT critical reading scores over 600: 86%; SAT math scores over 600: 84%; SAT writing scores over 600: 85%; ACT scores over 24: 100%; SAT critical reading scores over 700: 44%; SAT math scores over 700: 22%; SAT writing scores over 700: 41%; ACT scores over 30: 61%.

Faculty *Total:* 201, 80% full-time, 88% with terminal degrees. *Student/faculty ratio:* 10:1.

Academics *Calendar:* semesters. *Degree:* bachelor's. *Special study options:* accelerated degree program, advanced placement credit, double majors, honors programs, independent study, off-campus study, services for LD students, student-designed majors, study abroad. *Unusual degree programs:* 3-2 engineering with Washington University in St. Louis, Case Western Reserve University, Rensselaer Polytechnic Institute; environmental science with Duke University, education with The Bank Street College of Education.

Computers on Campus 450 computers/terminals are available on campus for general student use. Students can access the following: campus intranet, computer help desk, free student e-mail accounts, online (class) grades, online

COLLEGES AT-A-GLANCE

(class) schedules, commercial databases. Campuswide network is available. 99% of college-owned or -operated housing units are wired for high-speed Internet access. Wireless service is available via entire campus.

Student Life *Housing:* on-campus residence required through senior year. *Options:* coed, women-only, disabled students. Campus housing is university owned. Freshman campus housing is guaranteed. *Activities and organizations:* drama/theater group, student-run newspaper, radio station, choral group, student theater organizations, student radio station, musical groups, intramural sports and clubs, national fraternities, national sororities. *Campus security:* 24-hour emergency response devices and patrols, student patrols, late-night transport/escort service, controlled dormitory access. *Student services:* health clinic, personal/psychological counseling, women's center.

Athletics Member NCAA. All Division III. *Intercollegiate sports:* baseball M, basketball M/W, cross-country running M/W, field hockey W, football M, golf M, lacrosse M/W, soccer M/W, softball W, swimming and diving M/W, tennis M/W, track and field M/W, volleyball W. *Intramural sports:* archery M(c)/W(c), basketball M/W, equestrian sports M(c)/W(c), fencing M(c)/W(c), football M, racquetball M/W, rugby M(c)/W(c), soccer M(c)/W(c), squash M(c)/W(c), tennis M(c)/W(c), ultimate Frisbee M(c)/W(c), volleyball M/W.

Standardized Tests *Required:* SAT or ACT (for admission).

Costs (2013–14) *Comprehensive fee:* $56,810 includes full-time tuition ($43,900), mandatory fees ($1740), and room and board ($11,170). *Payment plan:* installment. *Waivers:* employees or children of employees.

Financial Aid Of all full-time matriculated undergraduates who enrolled in 2012, 870 applied for aid, 720 were judged to have need, 466 had their need fully met. 199 Federal Work-Study jobs (averaging $1360). 128 state and other part-time jobs (averaging $1366). In 2012, 223 non-need-based awards were made. *Average percent of need met:* 95%. *Average financial aid package:* $37,283. *Average need-based loan:* $4119. *Average need-based gift aid:* $34,245. *Average non-need-based aid:* $12,094. *Average indebtedness upon graduation:* $20,992.

Applying *Options:* electronic application, early admission, early decision, deferred entrance. *Application fee:* $50. *Required:* essay or personal statement, high school transcript, counselor recommendation. *Recommended:* 2 letters of recommendation, interview. *Application deadlines:* 1/15 (freshmen), 4/1 (transfers). *Early decision deadline:* 11/15 (for plan 1), 1/15 (for plan 2). *Notification:* 4/1 (freshmen), 5/15 (transfers), 12/15 (early decision plan 1), 2/1 (early decision plan 2).

Freshman Application Contact Ms. Jennifer Delahunty, Dean of Admissions, Kenyon College, Ransom Hall, Gambier, OH 43022. *Phone:* 740-427-5776. *Toll-free phone:* 800-848-2468. *Fax:* 740-427-5770. *E-mail:* admissions@kenyon.edu.
Website: http://www.kenyon.edu/.

Kettering College

Kettering, Ohio

Freshman Application Contact Mrs. Becky McDonald, Director of Enrollment Services, Kettering College, 3737 Southern Boulevard, Kettering, OH 45429-1299. *Phone:* 937-395-8628. *Toll-free phone:* 800-433-5262. *Fax:* 937-296-4238.
Website: http://www.kc.edu/.

Lake Erie College

Painesville, Ohio

- **Independent** comprehensive, founded 1856
- **Suburban** 48-acre campus with easy access to Cleveland
- **Endowment** $27.4 million
- **Coed** 1,032 undergraduate students, 91% full-time, 50% women, 50% men
- **Moderately difficult** entrance level, 63% of applicants were admitted

Undergraduates 944 full-time, 88 part-time. Students come from 27 states and territories; 14 other countries; 24% are from out of state; 8% Black or African American, non-Hispanic/Latino; 2% Hispanic/Latino; 0.5% Asian, non-Hispanic/Latino; ####% American Indian or Alaska Native, non-Hispanic/Latino; 3% Two or more races, non-Hispanic/Latino; 0.9% Race/ethnicity unknown; 4% international; 5% transferred in; 56% live on campus. *Retention:* 64% of full-time freshmen returned.

Freshmen *Admission:* 1,509 applied, 953 admitted, 275 enrolled. *Average high school GPA:* 3.15. *Test scores:* SAT critical reading scores over 500: 48%; SAT math scores over 500: 58%; SAT writing scores over 500: 37%; ACT scores over 18: 85%; SAT critical reading scores over 600: 14%; SAT math scores over 600: 8%; SAT writing scores over 600: 10%; ACT scores over 24:

22%; SAT critical reading scores over 700: 5%; SAT math scores over 700: 2%; SAT writing scores over 700: 1%; ACT scores over 30: 4%.

Faculty *Total:* 114, 36% full-time, 40% with terminal degrees. *Student/faculty ratio:* 16:1.

Academics *Calendar:* semesters. *Degrees:* bachelor's, master's, and postbachelor's certificates. *Special study options:* accelerated degree program, advanced placement credit, double majors, honors programs, independent study, internships, off-campus study, part-time degree program, services for LD students, student-designed majors, study abroad, summer session for credit.

Computers on Campus 78 computers/terminals are available on campus for general student use. Students can access the following: campus intranet, computer help desk, free student e-mail accounts, online (class) grades, online (class) registration, online (class) schedules. Campuswide network is available. 100% of college-owned or -operated housing units are wired for high-speed Internet access. Wireless service is available via entire campus.

Student Life *Housing:* on-campus residence required through sophomore year. *Options:* coed, women-only. Campus housing is university owned and leased by the school. Freshman applicants given priority for college housing. *Activities and organizations:* drama/theater group, choral group, marching band, Student Athlete Advisory Committee, Intercollegiate Horse Show Association, Gamma Phi Beta Sorority, Spanish Club, Student Government Association, national fraternities, national sororities. *Campus security:* 24-hour emergency response devices and patrols, late-night transport/escort service.

Athletics Member NCAA. All Division II. *Intercollegiate sports:* baseball M(s), basketball M(s)/W(s), cross-country running M(s)/W(s), football M(s), golf M(s)/W(s), lacrosse M(s)/W(s), soccer M(s)/W(s), softball W(s), swimming and diving M(s)/W(s), tennis M(s)/W(s), track and field M(s)/W(s), volleyball W(s), wrestling M(s). *Intramural sports:* basketball M/W, cheerleading W(c), equestrian sports M(c)/W(c), football M/W, soccer M/W, softball M/W, ultimate Frisbee M/W, volleyball M/W.

Standardized Tests *Required:* SAT or ACT (for admission). *Recommended:* AP, CLEP, Institutional Exam.

Costs (2013–14) *One-time required fee:* $350. *Comprehensive fee:* $35,704 includes full-time tuition ($25,976), mandatory fees ($1392), and room and board ($8336). Full-time tuition and fees vary according to course load, degree level, and program. Part-time tuition: $688 per credit hour. Part-time tuition and fees vary according to course load, degree level, and program. *Required fees:* $51 per credit hour part-time. *College room only:* $4054. Room and board charges vary according to board plan. *Payment plan:* installment. *Waivers:* senior citizens and employees or children of employees.

Financial Aid Of all full-time matriculated undergraduates who enrolled in 2012, 808 applied for aid, 755 were judged to have need, 128 had their need fully met. In 2012, 5 non-need-based awards were made. *Average percent of need met:* 72%. *Average financial aid package:* $20,606. *Average need-based loan:* $4162. *Average need-based gift aid:* $16,822. *Average non-need-based aid:* $7355. *Average indebtedness upon graduation:* $34,758.

Applying *Options:* electronic application, deferred entrance. *Application fee:* $30. *Required:* essay or personal statement, high school transcript, minimum 2.5 GPA, SAT or ACT Tests. *Required for some:* high school transcript. *Recommended:* interview. *Application deadlines:* 8/1 (freshmen), 8/1 (out-of-state freshmen), rolling (transfers). *Notification:* continuous (freshmen), continuous (out-of-state freshmen), continuous (transfers).

Freshman Application Contact Mr. Chris Harris, Dean of Admissions and Financial Aid, Lake Erie College, 391 West Washington Street, Painesville, OH 44077-3389. *Phone:* 800-916-0904. *Toll-free phone:* 800-916-0904. *Fax:* 440-375-7058. *E-mail:* admissions@lec.edu.
Website: http://www.lec.edu/.

Lourdes University

Sylvania, Ohio

- **Independent Roman Catholic** comprehensive, founded 1958
- **Suburban** 113-acre campus with easy access to Toledo
- **Endowment** $7.9 million
- **Coed** 2,118 undergraduate students, 61% full-time, 74% women, 26% men
- **Minimally difficult** entrance level, 71% of applicants were admitted

Undergraduates 1,295 full-time, 823 part-time. Students come from 17 states and territories; 12% are from out of state; 14% Black or African American, non-Hispanic/Latino; 6% Hispanic/Latino; 0.5% Asian, non-Hispanic/Latino; 0.1% Native Hawaiian or other Pacific Islander, non-Hispanic/Latino; 0.3% American Indian or Alaska Native, non-Hispanic/Latino; 1% Two or more races, non-Hispanic/Latino; 24% Race/ethnicity unknown; 0.3% international; 11% transferred in; 16% live on campus. *Retention:* 62% of full-time freshmen returned.

Freshmen *Admission:* 1,231 applied, 879 admitted, 264 enrolled. *Average high school GPA:* 3.09.
Faculty *Total:* 280, 35% full-time, 32% with terminal degrees. *Student/faculty ratio:* 11:1.
Academics *Calendar:* semesters. *Degrees:* certificates, associate, bachelor's, master's, and postbachelor's certificates. *Special study options:* academic remediation for entering students, adult/continuing education programs, advanced placement credit, distance learning, double majors, independent study, internships, part-time degree program, services for LD students, student-designed majors, study abroad, summer session for credit. *ROTC:* Army (c), Air Force (c).
Computers on Campus 242 computers/terminals are available on campus for general student use. Students can access the following: computer help desk, free student e-mail accounts, online (class) grades, online (class) registration, online (class) schedules, Sakai/eLearning, LiveText ePortfolio system, RRS news feeds, Facebook, Twitter, online polls, webcasting, panopto, ploycom. Campuswide network is available. 100% of college-owned or -operated housing units are wired for high-speed Internet access. Wireless service is available via entire campus.
Student Life *Housing:* on-campus residence required through junior year. *Options:* coed. Campus housing is university owned. Freshman applicants given priority for college housing. *Activities and organizations:* drama/theater group, choral group, Student Government Association, Drama Society, Student Nurses Association, Orbis Ars, Pre-Art Therapy Association. *Campus security:* 24-hour emergency response devices and patrols, late-night transport/escort service, controlled dormitory access. *Student services:* personal/psychological counseling.
Athletics Member NAIA. *Intercollegiate sports:* baseball M(s), basketball M(s)/W(s), cheerleading M(s)/W(s), cross-country running M(s), golf M(s)/W(s), lacrosse M(s), softball W(s), volleyball M(s)/W(s). *Intramural sports:* basketball M/W, bowling M/W, golf M/W, ice hockey M/W, soccer M/W, tennis M/W, volleyball M/W.
Costs (2013–14) *Tuition:* $17,455 full-time, $582 per credit part-time. Full-time tuition and fees vary according to course load and location. Part-time tuition and fees vary according to course load and location. *Room only:* Room and board charges vary according to board plan and housing facility. *Payment plans:* installment, deferred payment. *Waivers:* senior citizens and employees or children of employees.
Financial Aid Of all full-time matriculated undergraduates who enrolled in 2012, 1,219 applied for aid, 1,074 were judged to have need. 100 Federal Work-Study jobs (averaging $1754). 230 state and other part-time jobs (averaging $935). *Average financial aid package:* $12,127. *Average need-based loan:* $3928. *Average need-based gift aid:* $6180.
Applying *Options:* electronic application, early admission, deferred entrance. *Application fee:* $25. *Required:* high school transcript. *Application deadlines:* rolling (freshmen), rolling (out-of-state freshmen), rolling (transfers). *Notification:* continuous (freshmen), continuous (out-of-state freshmen), continuous (transfers).
Freshman Application Contact Ms. Amy Mergen, Dean of Enrollment, Lourdes University, 6832 Convent Boulevard, Sylvania, OH 43560. *Phone:* 419-885-5291. *Toll-free phone:* 800-878-3210. *Fax:* 419-824-3916. *E-mail:* AdmissionsLCAdmits@lourdes.edu.
Website: http://www.lourdes.edu/.

Malone University

Canton, Ohio

- **Independent** comprehensive, founded 1892, affiliated with Evangelical Friends Church–Eastern Region
- **Suburban** 96-acre campus with easy access to Cleveland
- **Endowment** $14.7 million
- **Coed** 1,897 undergraduate students, 88% full-time, 58% women, 42% men
- **Moderately difficult** entrance level, 70% of applicants were admitted

Undergraduates 1,669 full-time, 228 part-time. Students come from 35 states and territories; 17 other countries; 13% are from out of state; 8% Black or African American, non-Hispanic/Latino; 2% Hispanic/Latino; 0.6% Asian, non-Hispanic/Latino; 0.2% Native Hawaiian or other Pacific Islander, non-Hispanic/Latino; 0.2% American Indian or Alaska Native, non-Hispanic/Latino; 2% Two or more races, non-Hispanic/Latino; 0.3% Race/ethnicity unknown; 1% international; 6% transferred in; 55% live on campus. *Retention:* 64% of full-time freshmen returned.
Freshmen *Admission:* 1,546 applied, 1,075 admitted, 353 enrolled. *Average high school GPA:* 3.3. *Test scores:* SAT critical reading scores over 500: 53%; SAT math scores over 500: 54%; ACT scores over 18: 94%; SAT critical reading scores over 600: 19%; SAT math scores over 600: 19%; ACT scores over

24: 40%; SAT critical reading scores over 700: 5%; SAT math scores over 700: 2%; ACT scores over 30: 7%.
Faculty *Total:* 223, 48% full-time, 43% with terminal degrees. *Student/faculty ratio:* 13:1.
Academics *Calendar:* semesters. *Degrees:* bachelor's, master's, and postbachelor's certificates. *Special study options:* academic remediation for entering students, accelerated degree program, adult/continuing education programs, advanced placement credit, distance learning, double majors, honors programs, independent study, internships, off-campus study, part-time degree program, services for LD students, student-designed majors, study abroad, summer session for credit. *ROTC:* Army (c), Air Force (c).
Computers on Campus 207 computers/terminals and 250 ports are available on campus for general student use. Students can access the following: campus intranet, computer help desk, free student e-mail accounts, online (class) grades, online (class) registration, online (class) schedules, online advising, online financial aid information, and online credit card payments. Campuswide network is available. 100% of college-owned or -operated housing units are wired for high-speed Internet access. Wireless service is available via entire campus.
Student Life *Housing:* on-campus residence required through junior year. *Options:* men-only, women-only, disabled students. Campus housing is university owned. Freshman applicants given priority for college housing. *Activities and organizations:* drama/theater group, student-run newspaper, radio and television station, choral group, marching band, Celebration Worship Services, Student Activities Council, Student Senate, be: Justice, intramural athletics. *Campus security:* 24-hour emergency response devices and patrols, late-night transport/escort service, controlled dormitory access. *Student services:* health clinic, personal/psychological counseling.
Athletics Member NCAA, NCCAA. All NCAA Division II. *Intercollegiate sports:* baseball M(s), basketball M(s)/W(s), cheerleading M/W, cross-country running M(s)/W(s), football M(s), golf M(s)/W(s), soccer M(s)/W(s), softball W(s), swimming and diving M(s)/W(s), tennis M(s)/W(s), track and field M(s)/W(s), volleyball W(s). *Intramural sports:* basketball M/W, bowling M/W, football M/W, lacrosse M(c)/W(c), skiing (cross-country) M/W, soccer M/W, softball M/W, table tennis M/W, ultimate Frisbee M(c)/W(c), volleyball M(c)/W, weight lifting M/W.
Standardized Tests *Required:* SAT or ACT (for admission).
Costs (2013–14) *Comprehensive fee:* $34,334 includes full-time tuition ($24,934), mandatory fees ($744), and room and board ($8656). Part-time tuition: $445 per hour. Part-time tuition and fees vary according to course load. *College room only:* $4412. Room and board charges vary according to board plan. *Payment plan:* installment. *Waivers:* senior citizens and employees or children of employees.
Financial Aid Of all full-time matriculated undergraduates who enrolled in 2012, 1,400 applied for aid, 1,332 were judged to have need, 196 had their need fully met. 337 Federal Work-Study jobs (averaging $1970). In 2012, 189 non-need-based awards were made. *Average percent of need met:* 72%. *Average financial aid package:* $19,284. *Average need-based loan:* $4366. *Average need-based gift aid:* $15,450. *Average non-need-based aid:* $9167. *Average indebtedness upon graduation:* $33,263. *Financial aid deadline:* 7/31.
Applying *Options:* electronic application, early admission, deferred entrance. *Application fee:* $20. *Required:* high school transcript, minimum 2.0 GPA. *Required for some:* essay or personal statement. *Recommended:* interview. *Application deadlines:* rolling (freshmen), rolling (out-of-state freshmen), rolling (transfers). *Notification:* continuous (freshmen), continuous (out-of-state freshmen), continuous (transfers).
Freshman Application Contact Mrs. Missy A. Paciorek, Admissions Office Manager, Malone University, Malone University, 2600 Cleveland Avenue NW, Canton, OH 44709-3897. *Phone:* 330-471-8142. *Toll-free phone:* 800-521-1146. *Fax:* 330-471-8149. *E-mail:* admissions@malone.edu.
Website: http://www.malone.edu/.

Marietta College

Marietta, Ohio

- **Independent** comprehensive, founded 1835
- **Small-town** 90-acre campus
- **Endowment** $61.0 million
- **Coed** 1,487 undergraduate students, 95% full-time, 43% women, 57% men
- **Moderately difficult** entrance level, 68% of applicants were admitted

Undergraduates 1,418 full-time, 69 part-time. Students come from 40 states and territories; 15 other countries; 36% are from out of state; 6% Black or African American, non-Hispanic/Latino; 2% Hispanic/Latino; 0.6% Asian, non-Hispanic/Latino; 0.1% American Indian or Alaska Native, non-Hispanic/Latino; 1% Two or more races, non-Hispanic/Latino; 7% Race/ethnicity

unknown; 12% international; 3% transferred in; 76% live on campus. *Retention:* 75% of full-time freshmen returned.

Freshmen *Admission:* 4,157 applied, 2,811 admitted, 393 enrolled. *Average high school GPA:* 3.41. *Test scores:* SAT critical reading scores over 500: 67%; SAT math scores over 500: 73%; SAT writing scores over 500: 60%; ACT scores over 18: 97%; SAT critical reading scores over 600: 27%; SAT math scores over 600: 37%; SAT writing scores over 600: 18%; ACT scores over 24: 49%; SAT critical reading scores over 700: 2%; SAT math scores over 700: 3%; SAT writing scores over 700: 1%; ACT scores over 30: 6%.

Faculty *Total:* 173, 64% full-time, 67% with terminal degrees. *Student/faculty ratio:* 12:1.

Academics *Calendar:* semesters. *Degrees:* certificates, associate, bachelor's, and master's. *Special study options:* academic remediation for entering students, accelerated degree program, adult/continuing education programs, advanced placement credit, double majors, English as a second language, honors programs, independent study, internships, off-campus study, part-time degree program, services for LD students, student-designed majors, study abroad, summer session for credit. *Unusual degree programs:* 3-2 engineering with Columbia University, Case Western Reserve University, Ohio University.

Computers on Campus 400 computers/terminals are available on campus for general student use. Students can access the following: campus intranet, computer help desk, free student e-mail accounts, online (class) grades, online (class) schedules. Campuswide network is available. 100% of college-owned or -operated housing units are wired for high-speed Internet access. Wireless service is available via classrooms, computer centers, computer labs, dorm rooms, learning centers, libraries, student centers.

Student Life *Housing:* on-campus residence required through senior year. *Options:* coed, men-only, women-only, disabled students. Campus housing is university owned, leased by the school and is provided by a third party. Freshman campus housing is guaranteed. *Activities and organizations:* drama/theater group, student-run newspaper, radio and television station, choral group, Student Programming Board, student government, Society of Petroleum Engineers, Inter-Varsity Christian Fellowship, Arts and Humanities Council, national fraternities, national sororities. *Campus security:* 24-hour emergency response devices and patrols, student patrols, late-night transport/escort service, controlled dormitory access. *Student services:* health clinic, personal/psychological counseling.

Athletics Member NCAA. All Division III. *Intercollegiate sports:* baseball M, basketball M/W, cheerleading W(c), crew M/W, cross-country running M/W, football M, soccer M/W, softball W, tennis M/W, track and field M/W, volleyball W, wrestling M(c)/W(c). *Intramural sports:* badminton M/W, basketball M/W, bowling M/W, cross-country running M/W, football M/W, golf M/W, racquetball M/W, rock climbing M/W, soccer M/W, softball M/W, swimming and diving M/W, tennis M/W, ultimate Frisbee M/W, volleyball M/W, weight lifting M.

Standardized Tests *Required:* SAT or ACT (for admission). *Recommended:* SAT Subject Tests (for admission).

Costs (2013–14) *Comprehensive fee:* $40,500 includes full-time tuition ($30,090), mandatory fees ($850), and room and board ($9560). Part-time tuition: $990 per credit. *College room only:* $5500.

Financial Aid Of all full-time matriculated undergraduates who enrolled in 2011, 1,168 applied for aid, 1,060 were judged to have need, 327 had their need fully met. 914 Federal Work-Study jobs (averaging $1977). In 2011, 206 non-need-based awards were made. *Average percent of need met:* 87%. *Average financial aid package:* $24,703. *Average need-based loan:* $4178. *Average need-based gift aid:* $14,372. *Average non-need-based aid:* $11,215. *Average indebtedness upon graduation:* $32,127.

Applying *Options:* electronic application, early admission, deferred entrance. *Application fee:* $25. *Required:* essay or personal statement, high school transcript, minimum 2.0 GPA, 1 letter of recommendation. *Recommended:* minimum 3.0 GPA, interview. *Application deadlines:* 5/1 (freshmen), rolling (transfers). *Notification:* continuous until 5/1 (freshmen), continuous (transfers).

Freshman Application Contact Mr. Jason Turley, Director of Admission, Marietta College, 215 Fifth Street, Marietta, OH 45750. *Phone:* 740-376-4600. *Toll-free phone:* 800-331-7896. *Fax:* 740-376-8888. *E-mail:* admit@marietta.edu.

Website: http://www.marietta.edu/.

Mercy College of Ohio

Toledo, Ohio

- **Independent** 4-year, founded 1993, affiliated with Roman Catholic Church
- **Urban** campus with easy access to Detroit
- **Endowment** $9.3 million
- **Coed, primarily women** 1,206 undergraduate students, 37% full-time, 87% women, 13% men
- **Moderately difficult** entrance level, 74% of applicants were admitted

Undergraduates 446 full-time, 759 part-time. Students come from 9 states and territories; 26% are from out of state; 7% Black or African American, non-Hispanic/Latino; 3% Hispanic/Latino; 1% Asian, non-Hispanic/Latino; 0.4% American Indian or Alaska Native, non-Hispanic/Latino; 2% Two or more races, non-Hispanic/Latino; 3% Race/ethnicity unknown; 26% transferred in; 4% live on campus. *Retention:* 100% of full-time freshmen returned.

Freshmen *Admission:* 68 applied, 50 admitted, 49 enrolled.

Faculty *Total:* 166, 39% full-time, 14% with terminal degrees. *Student/faculty ratio:* 11:1.

Academics *Calendar:* semesters. *Degrees:* certificates, associate, and bachelor's. *Special study options:* academic remediation for entering students, advanced placement credit, distance learning, double majors, independent study, internships, part-time degree program, services for LD students, summer session for credit.

Computers on Campus 76 computers/terminals are available on campus for general student use. Students can access the following: computer help desk, free student e-mail accounts, online (class) grades, online (class) registration, online (class) schedules, billing and payment, degree audit, and transcripts. Campuswide network is available. Wireless service is available via classrooms, computer centers, computer labs, learning centers, libraries.

Student Life *Housing options:* coed. Campus housing is leased by the school. *Activities and organizations:* Student Senate, intramural sports, Student Nurses Association, Phi Theta Kappa. *Campus security:* 24-hour patrols, late-night transport/escort service, controlled dormitory access. *Student services:* personal/psychological counseling.

Standardized Tests *Required for some:* SAT or ACT (for admission), SAT and SAT Subject Tests or ACT (for admission).

Financial Aid Of all full-time matriculated undergraduates who enrolled in 2011, 416 applied for aid, 381 were judged to have need, 7 had their need fully met. 34 Federal Work-Study jobs (averaging $1337). In 2011, 7 non-need-based awards were made. *Average percent of need met:* 36%. *Average financial aid package:* $8416. *Average need-based loan:* $4600. *Average need-based gift aid:* $5726. *Average non-need-based aid:* $1000. *Average indebtedness upon graduation:* $24,127.

Applying *Options:* electronic application, deferred entrance. *Application fee:* $25. *Required:* high school transcript, minimum 2.3 GPA. *Application deadlines:* rolling (freshmen), rolling (transfers). *Notification:* continuous (freshmen), continuous (transfers).

Freshman Application Contact Mercy College of Ohio, OH. *Phone:* 419-251-1313 Ext. 1802. *Toll-free phone:* 888-80-MERCY.

Website: http://www.mercycollege.edu/.

Miami University

Oxford, Ohio

- **State-related** university, founded 1809, part of Miami University System
- **Small-town** 2000-acre campus with easy access to Cincinnati
- **Endowment** $387.4 million
- **Coed** 15,081 undergraduate students, 97% full-time, 52% women, 48% men
- **Moderately difficult** entrance level, 73% of applicants were admitted

Undergraduates 14,657 full-time, 424 part-time. Students come from 51 states and territories; 73 other countries; 30% are from out of state; 4% Black or African American, non-Hispanic/Latino; 3% Hispanic/Latino; 2% Asian, non-Hispanic/Latino; 0.1% Native Hawaiian or other Pacific Islander, non-Hispanic/Latino; 0.3% American Indian or Alaska Native, non-Hispanic/Latino; 2% Two or more races, non-Hispanic/Latino; 1% Race/ethnicity unknown; 6% international; 1% transferred in; 52% live on campus. *Retention:* 89% of full-time freshmen returned.

Freshmen *Admission:* 20,314 applied, 14,788 admitted, 3,734 enrolled. *Average high school GPA:* 3.63. *Test scores:* SAT critical reading scores over 500: 89%; SAT math scores over 500: 93%; ACT scores over 18: 99%; SAT critical reading scores over 600: 43%; SAT math scores over 600: 58%; ACT scores over 24: 84%; SAT critical reading scores over 700: 9%; SAT math scores over 700: 13%; ACT scores over 30: 20%.

Faculty *Total:* 1,114, 75% full-time, 76% with terminal degrees. *Student/faculty ratio:* 18:1.

Academics *Calendar:* semesters. *Degrees:* certificates, associate, bachelor's, master's, doctoral, and post-master's certificates. *Special study options:* advanced placement credit, cooperative education, distance learning, double majors, English as a second language, honors programs, independent study, internships, off-campus study, services for LD students, student-designed majors, study abroad, summer session for credit. *ROTC:* Army (c), Navy (b), Air Force (b). *Unusual degree programs:* 3-2 engineering with Case Western Reserve University, Columbia University; forestry with Duke University.

Computers on Campus 1,200 computers/terminals and 11,200 ports are available on campus for general student use. Students can access the following: campus intranet, computer help desk, free student e-mail accounts, online (class) grades, online (class) registration, online (class) schedules. Campus-wide network is available. 100% of college-owned or -operated housing units are wired for high-speed Internet access. Wireless service is available via entire campus.

Student Life *Housing:* on-campus residence required through sophomore year. *Options:* coed, men-only, women-only, disabled students. Campus housing is university owned. Freshman campus housing is guaranteed. *Activities and organizations:* drama/theater group, student-run newspaper, radio and television station, choral group, marching band, College Republicans, CRU (formerly Campus Crusade for Christ), Culinary Association, Pistol Club, Stage Left, national fraternities, national sororities. *Campus security:* 24-hour emergency response devices and patrols, student patrols, late-night transport/escort service, controlled dormitory access. *Student services:* health clinic, personal/psychological counseling, women's center.

Athletics Member NCAA. All Division I except football (Division I-A). *Intercollegiate sports:* baseball M(s)/W(c), basketball M(s)/W(s), cross-country running M(s)/W(s), equestrian sports M(c)/W(c), fencing M(c)/W(c), field hockey M(c)/W(s), golf M(s), gymnastics M(c)/W(c), ice hockey M(s)/W(c), lacrosse M(c)/W(c), rugby M(c)/W(c), sailing M(c)/W(c), soccer M(c)/W(s), softball M(c)/W(s), swimming and diving M(s)/W(s), tennis M(c)/W(s), track and field M(s)/W(s), ultimate Frisbee M(c)/W(c), volleyball M(c)/W(s), water polo M(c)/W(c), weight lifting M(c)/W(c), wrestling M(c)/W(c). *Intramural sports:* badminton M(c)/W(c), baseball M/W, basketball M/W, golf M(c)/W(c), ice hockey M/W, racquetball M/W, soccer M/W, softball M/W, ultimate Frisbee M/W, volleyball M/W.

Standardized Tests *Required:* SAT or ACT (for admission).

Costs (2012–13) *Tuition:* state resident $13,067 full-time; nonresident $28,631 full-time. Full-time tuition and fees vary according to location and program. Part-time tuition and fees vary according to course load, location, and program. *Required fees:* $528 full-time. *Room and board:* $10,596; room only: $5250. Room and board charges vary according to board plan and housing facility. *Payment plan:* installment. *Waivers:* employees or children of employees.

Financial Aid Of all full-time matriculated undergraduates who enrolled in 2012, 8,694 applied for aid, 6,334 were judged to have need, 976 had their need fully met. 687 Federal Work-Study jobs (averaging $2360). In 2012, 3079 non-need-based awards were made. *Average percent of need met:* 56%. *Average financial aid package:* $11,437. *Average need-based loan:* $4424. *Average need-based gift aid:* $5231. *Average non-need-based aid:* $5910. *Average indebtedness upon graduation:* $27,817.

Applying *Options:* electronic application, early decision, early action, deferred entrance. *Application fee:* $50. *Required:* essay or personal statement, high school transcript, 1 letter of recommendation. *Application deadlines:* 2/1 (freshmen), 6/1 (transfers), 12/1 (early action). *Early decision deadline:* 11/15. *Notification:* 3/15 (freshmen), continuous (transfers), 12/15 (early decision), 2/1 (early action).

Freshman Application Contact Office of Admissions, Miami University, 301 South Campus Avenue, Oxford, OH 45056. *Phone:* 513-529-2531. *Fax:* 513-529-1550. *E-mail:* admission@miamioh.edu.

Website: http://www.muohio.edu/.

Miami University Hamilton
Hamilton, Ohio

Freshman Application Contact Mr. Archie Nelson, Director of Admission and Financial Aid, Miami University Hamilton, 1601 Peck Boulevard, Hamilton, OH 45011-3399. *Phone:* 513-785-3111. *Fax:* 513-785-1807. *E-mail:* nelsona3@muohio.edu.

Website: http://www.ham.muohio.edu/.

Miami University–Middletown Campus
Middletown, Ohio

Freshman Application Contact Diane Cantonwine, Assistant Director of Admission and Financial Aid, Miami University–Middletown Campus, 4200 East University Boulevard, Middletown, OH 45042-3497. *Phone:* 513-727-3346. *Toll-free phone:* 866-426-4643. *Fax:* 513-727-3223. *E-mail:* cantondm@muohio.edu.

Website: http://www.mid.muohio.edu/.

Mount Carmel College of Nursing
Columbus, Ohio

- **Independent** comprehensive, founded 1903
- **Urban** campus with easy access to Columbus
- **Endowment** $824,552
- **Coed, primarily women**
- **Moderately difficult** entrance level

Faculty *Student/faculty ratio:* 15:1.

Academics *Calendar:* semesters. *Degrees:* bachelor's, master's, and post-master's certificates.

Student Life *Campus security:* 24-hour emergency response devices and patrols, late-night transport/escort service, controlled dormitory access.

Standardized Tests *Required for some:* SAT or ACT (for admission).

Costs (2012–13) *One-time required fee:* $225. *Tuition:* $10,633 full-time, $343 per semester hour part-time. Full-time tuition and fees vary according to course level, course load, and student level. Part-time tuition and fees vary according to course level, course load, and student level. *Required fees:* $732 full-time, $276 per term part-time. *Room only:* $5000.

Financial Aid Of all full-time matriculated undergraduates who enrolled in 2012, 722 applied for aid, 722 were judged to have need. In 2012, 6 non-need-based awards were made. *Average percent of need met:* 65. *Average financial aid package:* $13,500. *Average need-based loan:* $4427. *Average need-based gift aid:* $1700. *Average non-need-based aid:* $2300. *Average indebtedness upon graduation:* $8985.

Applying *Application fee:* $30. *Required:* essay or personal statement, high school transcript, activities/interests resume. *Required for some:* interview. *Recommended:* minimum 3.0 GPA.

Freshman Application Contact Kim Campbell, Direct, Admissions and Recruitment, Mount Carmel College of Nursing, 127 South Davis Avenue, Columbus, OH 43222-1504. *Phone:* 614-234-1085. *Toll-free phone:* 800-556-6942. *Fax:* 614-234-5427. *E-mail:* kcampbell@mccn.edu.

Website: http://www.mccn.edu/.

Mount Vernon Nazarene University
Mount Vernon, Ohio

- **Independent Nazarene** comprehensive, founded 1964
- **Small-town** 406-acre campus with easy access to Columbus
- **Endowment** $14.7 million
- **Coed** 1,756 undergraduate students, 82% full-time, 65% women, 35% men
- **Moderately difficult** entrance level, 73% of applicants were admitted

Undergraduates 1,448 full-time, 308 part-time. Students come from 33 states and territories; 5 other countries; 8% are from out of state; 3% Black or African American, non-Hispanic/Latino; 2% Hispanic/Latino; 0.5% Asian, non-Hispanic/Latino; 0.1% Native Hawaiian or other Pacific Islander, non-Hispanic/Latino; 0.3% American Indian or Alaska Native, non-Hispanic/Latino; 1% Two or more races, non-Hispanic/Latino; 0.6% Race/ethnicity unknown; 0.6% international; 2% transferred in; 80% live on campus. *Retention:* 76% of full-time freshmen returned.

Freshmen *Admission:* 1,000 applied, 733 admitted, 290 enrolled. *Average high school GPA:* 3.34. *Test scores:* SAT critical reading scores over 500: 47%; SAT math scores over 500: 55%; ACT scores over 18: 89%; SAT critical reading scores over 600: 20%; SAT math scores over 600: 20%; ACT scores over 24: 45%; SAT critical reading scores over 700: 8%; SAT math scores over 700: 4%; ACT scores over 30: 7%.

Faculty *Total:* 235, 43% full-time, 40% with terminal degrees. *Student/faculty ratio:* 13:1.

Academics *Calendar:* 4-1-4. *Degrees:* associate, bachelor's, and master's. *Special study options:* academic remediation for entering students, adult/continuing education programs, advanced placement credit, distance learning, double majors, honors programs, independent study, internships, off-campus study, part-time degree program, services for LD students, study abroad, summer session for credit. *Unusual degree programs:* 3-2 engineering with Olivet Nazarene University; pre-occupational therapy/physician assistant with Chatham University.

Computers on Campus 186 computers/terminals and 1,200 ports are available on campus for general student use. Students can access the following: campus intranet, computer help desk, free student e-mail accounts, online (class) grades, online (class) schedules. Campuswide network is available. 100% of college-owned or -operated housing units are wired for high-speed Internet access. Wireless service is available via entire campus.

Student Life *Housing:* on-campus residence required through senior year. *Options:* men-only, women-only, disabled students. Campus housing is university owned. Freshman campus housing is guaranteed. *Activities and organizations:* drama/theater group, student-run newspaper, radio station, choral group, Campus Ministry Groups, Student Government Association, Student Education Association, Drama Club, Music Department Ensembles. *Campus security:* 24-hour emergency response devices and patrols, late-night transport/escort service, controlled dormitory access. *Student services:* health clinic, personal/psychological counseling.

Athletics Member NAIA, NCCAA. *Intercollegiate sports:* baseball M(s), basketball M(s)/W(s), cross-country running M(s)/W(s), golf M(s)/W(s), soccer M(s)/W(s), softball W(s), volleyball W(s). *Intramural sports:* basketball M/W, bowling M/W, cheerleading M(c)/W(c), football M/W, soccer M/W, softball M/W, table tennis M/W, ultimate Frisbee M/W, volleyball M/W.

Standardized Tests *Required:* SAT or ACT (for admission).

Costs (2013–14) *Comprehensive fee:* $30,670 includes full-time tuition ($23,690) and room and board ($6980). Part-time tuition: $658 per credit hour. *College room only:* $3900. *Payment plan:* installment. *Waivers:* senior citizens and employees or children of employees.

Financial Aid Of all full-time matriculated undergraduates who enrolled in 2012, 1,333 applied for aid, 1,168 were judged to have need, 187 had their need fully met. 254 Federal Work-Study jobs (averaging $1752). 326 state and other part-time jobs (averaging $1683). In 2012, 62 non-need-based awards were made. *Average percent of need met:* 68%. *Average financial aid package:* $18,609. *Average need-based loan:* $3970. *Average need-based gift aid:* $11,449. *Average non-need-based aid:* $7899. *Average indebtedness upon graduation:* $25,462.

Applying *Options:* electronic application, deferred entrance. *Application fee:* $25. *Required:* essay or personal statement, high school transcript, minimum 2.5 GPA, 2 letters of recommendation. *Application deadline:* 7/15 (freshmen). *Notification:* 9/1 (freshmen), continuous (transfers).

Freshman Application Contact Mr. James Smith, Director of Admissions and Student Recruitment, Mount Vernon Nazarene University, 800 Martinsburg Road, Mount Vernon, OH 43050. *Phone:* 740-392-6868 Ext. 4516. *Toll-free phone:* 866-462-6868. *Fax:* 740-393-0511. *E-mail:* admissions@mvnu.edu.

Website: http://www.mvnu.edu/.

Muskingum University

New Concord, Ohio

Freshman Application Contact Mrs. Beth DaLonzo, Director of Admission, Muskingum University, 163 Stormont Street, New Concord, OH 43762. *Phone:* 740-826-8137. *Toll-free phone:* 800-752-6082. *Fax:* 740-826-8100. *E-mail:* adminfo@muskingum.edu.

Website: http://www.muskingum.edu/.

Notre Dame College

South Euclid, Ohio

Freshman Application Contact Mr. David Armstrong, Dean of Admissions, Notre Dame College, 4545 College Road, South Euclid, OH 44121-4293. *Phone:* 216-373-5214. *Toll-free phone:* 877-NDC-OHIO. *Fax:* 216-381-3802. *E-mail:* admissinos@ndc.edu.

Website: http://www.notredamecollege.edu/.

See below for display ad and page 1424 for the College Close-Up.

Oberlin College

Oberlin, Ohio

Freshman Application Contact Ms. Debra Chermonte, Dean of Admissions and Financial Aid, Oberlin College, Admissions Office, Carnegie Building, Oberlin, OH 44074-1090. *Phone:* 440-775-8411. *Toll-free phone:* 800-622-OBIE. *Fax:* 440-775-6905. *E-mail:* college.admissions@oberlin.edu. *Website:* http://www.oberlin.edu/.

Ohio Christian University

Circleville, Ohio

Director of Admissions Mike Egenreider, Associate Vice President for Enrollment, Ohio Christian University, 1476 Lancaster Pike, PO Box 458, Circleville, OH 43113-9487. *Phone:* 740-477-7741. *Toll-free phone:* 877-762-8669. *E-mail:* enroll@ohiochristian.edu. *Website:* http://www.ohiochristian.edu/.

Ohio Dominican University

Columbus, Ohio

- **Independent Roman Catholic** comprehensive, founded 1911
- **Urban** 71-acre campus
- **Endowment** $23.2 million
- **Coed** 2,280 undergraduate students, 68% full-time, 60% women, 40% men
- **Moderately difficult** entrance level, 59% of applicants were admitted

Undergraduates 1,547 full-time, 733 part-time. Students come from 17 states and territories; 11 other countries; 3% are from out of state; 5% transferred in; 76% live on campus. *Retention:* 61% of full-time freshmen returned.
Freshmen *Admission:* 2,367 applied, 1,404 admitted, 283 enrolled. *Average high school GPA:* 3.04. *Test scores:* ACT scores over 18: 92%; ACT scores over 24: 25%; ACT scores over 30: 1%.
Faculty *Total:* 170, 44% full-time, 55% with terminal degrees. *Student/faculty ratio:* 14:1.
Academics *Calendar:* semesters. *Degrees:* certificates, associate, bachelor's, and master's. *Special study options:* academic remediation for entering students, advanced placement credit, distance learning, honors programs, independent study, internships, off-campus study, part-time degree program, student-designed majors, study abroad, summer session for credit. *ROTC:* Army (c). *Unusual degree programs:* business administration.
Computers on Campus 198 computers/terminals and 1,900 ports are available on campus for general student use. Students can access the following: campus intranet, computer help desk, free student e-mail accounts, online (class) grades, online (class) registration, online (class) schedules. Campus-wide network is available. 100% of college-owned or -operated housing units are wired for high-speed Internet access. Wireless service is available via classrooms, computer centers, computer labs, dorm rooms, learning centers, libraries, student centers.
Student Life *Housing:* on-campus residence required through junior year. *Options:* coed. Campus housing is university owned. *Activities and organizations:* drama/theater group, student-run newspaper, radio station, choral group, Delta Sigma Pi, student government, Panther Activities Council, Black Student Union, Panther Players. *Campus security:* 24-hour emergency response devices and patrols, late-night transport/escort service, controlled dormitory access. *Student services:* health clinic, personal/psychological counseling.
Athletics Member NAIA. *Intercollegiate sports:* baseball M(s), basketball M(s)/W(s), cheerleading M/W, cross-country running M/W, football M(s), golf M(s)/W(s), soccer M(s)/W(s), softball W(s), tennis M(s)/W(s), volleyball W(s). *Intramural sports:* badminton M/W, basketball M/W, bowling M/W, golf M/W, lacrosse M/W, soccer M/W, table tennis M/W, tennis M/W, volleyball M/W.
Standardized Tests *Required:* SAT or ACT (for admission).
Financial Aid Of all full-time matriculated undergraduates who enrolled in 2011, 200 Federal Work-Study jobs (averaging $2000). *Average percent of need met:* 92%. *Average financial aid package:* $12,467. *Average indebtedness upon graduation:* $13,500.
Applying *Options:* electronic application, deferred entrance. *Application fee:* $25. *Required:* high school transcript, minimum 2.0 GPA, interview. *Required for some:* essay or personal statement. *Application deadlines:* rolling (freshmen), rolling (transfers). *Notification:* continuous (freshmen), continuous (transfers).

Freshman Application Contact Ms. Nicole A. Evans, Director of Admissions, Ohio Dominican University, 1216 Sunbury Road, Columbus, OH 43219. *Phone:* 614-251-4500. *Toll-free phone:* 800-955-6446. *Fax:* 614-251-0156. *E-mail:* admissions@ohiodominican.edu. *Website:* http://www.ohiodominican.edu/.

Ohio Mid-Western College

Sharonville, Ohio

Admissions Office Contact Ohio Mid-Western College, 19 Triangle Park Drive, Sharonville, OH 45246. *Website:* http://omw.edu/.

Ohio Northern University

Ada, Ohio

- **Independent** comprehensive, founded 1871, affiliated with United Methodist Church
- **Small-town** 340-acre campus
- **Endowment** $143.1 million
- **Coed**
- **Moderately difficult** entrance level

Faculty *Student/faculty ratio:* 12:1.
Academics *Calendar:* quarters. *Degrees:* bachelor's, master's, doctoral, and postbachelor's certificates.
Student Life *Campus security:* 24-hour emergency response devices and patrols, late-night transport/escort service, controlled dormitory access.
Athletics Member NCAA. All Division III.
Standardized Tests *Required:* SAT or ACT (for admission).
Costs (2012–13) *Comprehensive fee:* $45,898 includes full-time tuition ($35,438), mandatory fees ($240), and room and board ($10,220). Full-time tuition and fees vary according to course load, degree level, and program. Part-time tuition and fees vary according to course load, degree level, and program. *Required fees:* $1477 per semester hour part-time. *Room and board:* Room and board charges vary according to board plan, housing facility, and student level.
Applying *Options:* electronic application, deferred entrance. *Application fee:* $30. *Required:* essay or personal statement, high school transcript, 1 letter of recommendation. *Recommended:* minimum 2.5 GPA, 2 letters of recommendation, interview.
Freshman Application Contact Ms. Deborah Miller, Director of Admissions, Ohio Northern University, 525 South Main Street, Ada, OH 45810-1599. *Phone:* 419-772-2260 Ext. 2464. *Toll-free phone:* 888-408-4ONU. *Fax:* 419-772-2821. *E-mail:* admissions-ug@onu.edu. *Website:* http://www.onu.edu/.

See next page for display ad and page 1426 for the College Close-Up.

The Ohio State University

Columbus, Ohio

- **State-supported** university, founded 1870, part of Ohio State University System
- **Urban** 3469-acre campus with easy access to Columbus
- **Endowment** $2.4 billion
- **Coed** 43,058 undergraduate students, 90% full-time, 47% women, 53% men
- **Very difficult** entrance level, 64% of applicants were admitted

Undergraduates 38,884 full-time, 4,174 part-time. Students come from 55 states and territories; 72 other countries; 12% are from out of state; 6% Black or African American, non-Hispanic/Latino; 3% Hispanic/Latino; 5% Asian, non-Hispanic/Latino; 0.1% Native Hawaiian or other Pacific Islander, non-Hispanic/Latino; 0.2% American Indian or Alaska Native, non-Hispanic/Latino; 2% Two or more races, non-Hispanic/Latino; 2% Race/ethnicity unknown; 8% international; 6% transferred in; 25% live on campus. *Retention:* 92% of full-time freshmen returned.
Freshmen *Admission:* 25,816 applied, 16,521 admitted, 7,215 enrolled. *Test scores:* SAT critical reading scores over 500: 86%; SAT math scores over 500: 97%; SAT writing scores over 500: 90%; ACT scores over 18: 100%; SAT critical reading scores over 600: 54%; SAT math scores over 600: 80%; SAT writing scores over 600: 50%; ACT scores over 24: 93%; SAT critical reading scores over 700: 12%; SAT math scores over 700: 33%; SAT writing scores over 700: 9%; ACT scores over 30: 33%.

Faculty *Total:* 4,974, 70% full-time, 69% with terminal degrees. *Student/faculty ratio:* 19:1.

Academics *Calendar:* quarters. *Degrees:* certificates, bachelor's, master's, doctoral, post-master's, and postbachelor's certificates. *Special study options:* academic remediation for entering students, accelerated degree program, adult/continuing education programs, advanced placement credit, cooperative education, distance learning, double majors, English as a second language, freshman honors college, honors programs, independent study, internships, off-campus study, part-time degree program, services for LD students, student-designed majors, study abroad, summer session for credit. *ROTC:* Army (b), Navy (b), Air Force (b). *Unusual degree programs:* 3-2 business administration.

Computers on Campus 295 computers/terminals are available on campus for general student use. Students can access the following: campus intranet, computer help desk, free student e-mail accounts, online (class) grades, online (class) registration, online (class) schedules, students can apply for admission, register, check grades, pay fees and obtain library resources, including books, online. Campuswide network is available. 100% of college-owned or -operated housing units are wired for high-speed Internet access. Wireless service is available via entire campus.

Student Life *Housing:* on-campus residence required for freshman year. *Options:* coed, women-only, cooperative, disabled students. Campus housing is university owned. Freshman campus housing is guaranteed. *Activities and organizations:* drama/theater group, student-run newspaper, radio and television station, choral group, marching band, African Student Union, Bisexual, Gay and Lesbian Alliance, Campus Crusade for Christ, University Wide Council of Hispanic Organizations, Asian-American Association, national fraternities, national sororities. *Campus security:* 24-hour emergency response devices and patrols, student patrols, late-night transport/escort service, controlled dormitory access, dorm entrances locked after 9 pm, lighted pathways and sidewalks, self-defense education. *Student services:* health clinic, personal/psychological counseling, women's center, legal services.

Athletics Member NCAA. All Division I except football (Division I-A). *Intercollegiate sports:* baseball M(s), basketball M(s)/W(s), cheerleading M/W, cross-country running M(s)/W(s), fencing M(s)/W(s), field hockey W(s), golf M(s)/W(s), gymnastics M(s)/W(s), ice hockey M(s)/W(s), lacrosse M(s)/W(s), riflery M/W, soccer M(s)/W(s), softball W(s), swimming and diving M(s)/W(s), tennis M(s)/W(s), track and field M(s)/W(s), volleyball M(s)/W(s), wrestling M(s). *Intramural sports:* badminton M(c)/W(c), baseball M(c), basketball M/W, bowling M(c)/W(c), crew M(c)/W, cross-country running M/W, equestrian sports M(c)/W(c), fencing M(c)/W(c), field hockey W, football M/W, golf M/W, gymnastics M(c)/W(c), ice hockey M(c)/W(c), lacrosse M(c)/W(c), racquetball M(c)/W(c), riflery M(c)/W(c), rock climbing M/W, rugby M(c)/W(c), sailing M(c)/W(c), skiing (downhill) M(c)/W(c), soccer M(c)/W(c), softball W(c), squash M(c)/W(c), swimming and diving M(c)/W(c), table tennis M/W, tennis M/W, track and field M(c)/W(c), ultimate Frisbee M(c)/W(c), volleyball M(c)/W(c), water polo M(c)/W(c), weight lifting M(c), wrestling M/W.

Standardized Tests *Required:* SAT or ACT (for admission).

Costs (2012–13) *Tuition:* state resident $10,037 full-time; nonresident $25,445 full-time. Full-time tuition and fees vary according to course load, location, program, and reciprocity agreements. Part-time tuition and fees vary according to course load, location, program, and reciprocity agreements. *Room and board:* $10,392. Room and board charges vary according to board plan, housing facility, and location. *Payment plan:* installment. *Waivers:* senior citizens and employees or children of employees.

Financial Aid Of all full-time matriculated undergraduates who enrolled in 2012, 26,697 applied for aid, 20,575 were judged to have need, 3,371 had their need fully met. 4,321 Federal Work-Study jobs (averaging $2250). 172 state and other part-time jobs (averaging $2342). In 2012, 7215 non-need-based awards were made. *Average percent of need met:* 64%. *Average financial aid package:* $11,671. *Average need-based loan:* $4675. *Average need-based gift aid:* $8795. *Average non-need-based aid:* $5336. *Average indebtedness upon graduation:* $26,409.

Applying *Options:* electronic application. *Application fee:* $60. *Required:* essay or personal statement, high school transcript. *Application deadlines:* 2/1 (freshmen), 2/1 (out-of-state freshmen), 5/1 (transfers). *Notification:* continuous (freshmen), continuous (out-of-state freshmen), continuous (transfers).

Freshman Application Contact The Ohio State University, Student Academic Services Building, 281 West Lane Avenue, Columbus, OH 43210. *Phone:* 614-292-3980. *Fax:* 614-292-4818. *E-mail:* askabuckeye@osu.edu. *Website:* http://www.osu.edu/.

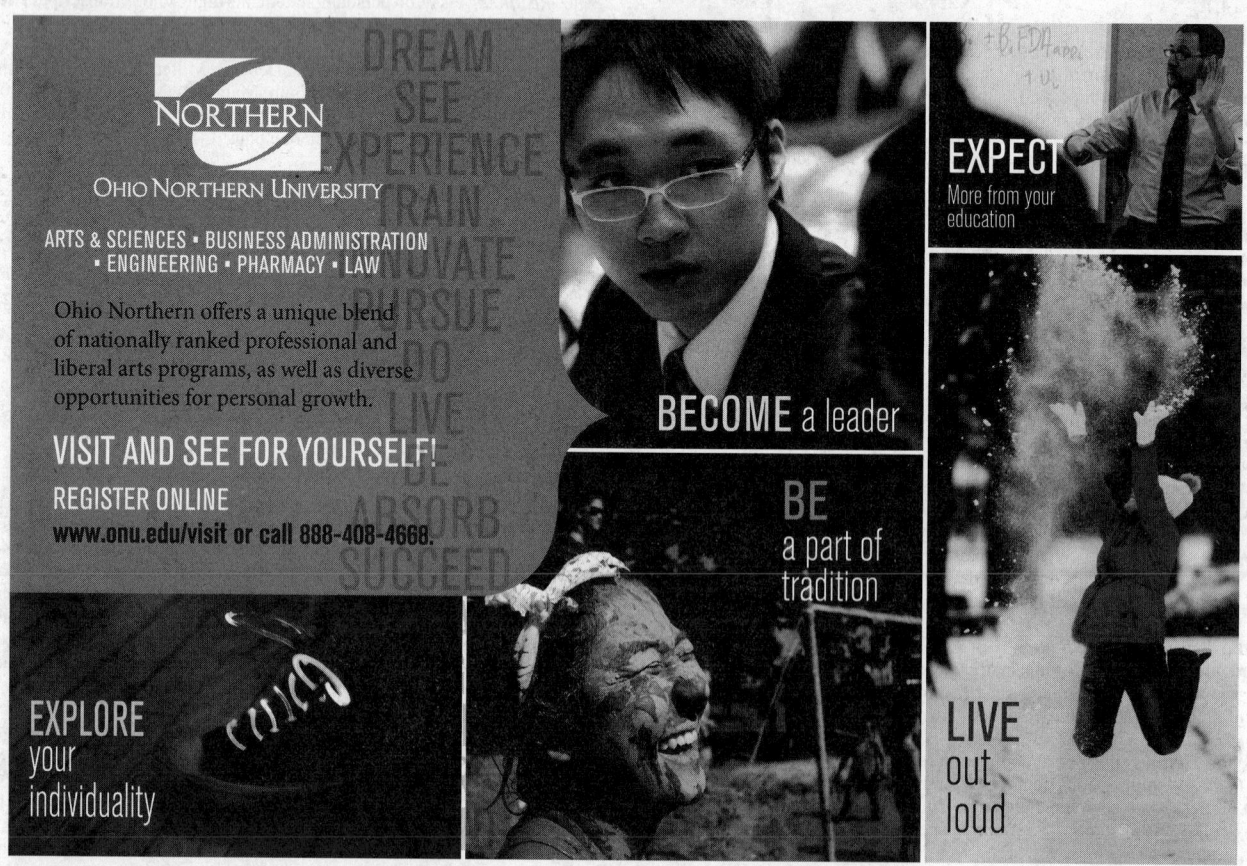

The Ohio State University at Lima

Lima, Ohio

- **State-supported** comprehensive, founded 1960, part of The Ohio State University
- **Suburban** 565-acre campus
- **Coed** 1,068 undergraduate students, 86% full-time, 55% women, 45% men
- **Noncompetitive** entrance level, 99% of applicants were admitted

Undergraduates 915 full-time, 153 part-time. Students come from 3 states and territories; 2 other countries; 1% are from out of state; 5% Black or African American, non-Hispanic/Latino; 3% Hispanic/Latino; 1% Asian, non-Hispanic/Latino; 0.3% American Indian or Alaska Native, non-Hispanic/Latino; 2% Two or more races, non-Hispanic/Latino; 1% Race/ethnicity unknown; 0.2% international; 5% transferred in. *Retention:* 62% of full-time freshmen returned.

Freshmen *Admission:* 1,068 applied, 1,055 admitted, 427 enrolled. *Test scores:* SAT critical reading scores over 500: 66%; SAT math scores over 500: 83%; SAT writing scores over 500: 56%; ACT scores over 18: 91%; SAT critical reading scores over 600: 11%; SAT math scores over 600: 22%; SAT writing scores over 600: 17%; ACT scores over 24: 42%; ACT scores over 30: 2%.

Faculty *Total:* 89, 40% full-time. *Student/faculty ratio:* 18:1.

Academics *Calendar:* quarters. *Degrees:* associate, bachelor's, and master's. *Special study options:* academic remediation for entering students, accelerated degree program, adult/continuing education programs, advanced placement credit, cooperative education, distance learning, double majors, English as a second language, freshman honors college, honors programs, independent study, internships, off-campus study, part-time degree program, services for LD students, student-designed majors, study abroad, summer session for credit. *ROTC:* Army (c), Navy (c), Air Force (c).

Computers on Campus 150 computers/terminals are available on campus for general student use. Students can access the following: campus intranet, computer help desk, free student e-mail accounts, online (class) grades, online (class) registration, online (class) schedules. Campuswide network is available. Wireless service is available via entire campus.

Student Life *Housing:* college housing not available. *Activities and organizations:* choral group, Student Senate, Psychology Club, Honors Club, Aggies, Newman Catholic Association. *Campus security:* 24-hour emergency response devices and patrols, student patrols, late-night transport/escort service, lighted pathways/sidewalks. *Student services:* personal/psychological counseling.

Athletics *Intramural sports:* baseball M(c), basketball M(c)/W(c), football M/W, golf M(c)/W(c), soccer M/W, volleyball M(c)/W(c).

Standardized Tests *Required:* SAT or ACT (for admission).

Applying *Options:* electronic application. *Application fee:* $60. *Required:* essay or personal statement, high school transcript. *Application deadlines:* 6/1 (freshmen), 6/1 (out-of-state freshmen), 6/1 (transfers). *Notification:* continuous (freshmen), continuous (out-of-state freshmen), continuous (transfers).

Freshman Application Contact The Ohio State University at Lima, OH. *Phone:* 419-995-8434. *Fax:* 419-995-8483. *E-mail:* admissions@lima.ohio-state.edu.

Website: http://lima.osu.edu/.

The Ohio State University at Marion

Marion, Ohio

- **State-supported** comprehensive, founded 1958, part of The Ohio State University
- **Small-town** 188-acre campus with easy access to Columbus
- **Coed** 1,224 undergraduate students, 78% full-time, 54% women, 46% men
- **Noncompetitive** entrance level, 98% of applicants were admitted

Undergraduates 951 full-time, 273 part-time. Students come from 4 states and territories; 1 other country; 6% Black or African American, non-Hispanic/Latino; 2% Hispanic/Latino; 4% Asian, non-Hispanic/Latino; 0.2% Native Hawaiian or other Pacific Islander, non-Hispanic/Latino; 0.4% American Indian or Alaska Native, non-Hispanic/Latino; 2% Two or more races, non-Hispanic/Latino; 1% Race/ethnicity unknown; 0.1% international; 6% transferred in. *Retention:* 67% of full-time freshmen returned.

Freshmen *Admission:* 853 applied, 840 admitted, 409 enrolled. *Test scores:* SAT critical reading scores over 500: 55%; ACT scores over 18: 91%; SAT

critical reading scores over 600: 9%; ACT scores over 24: 35%; ACT scores over 30: 2%.

Faculty *Total:* 103, 34% full-time, 33% with terminal degrees. *Student/faculty ratio:* 18:1.

Academics *Calendar:* quarters. *Degrees:* associate, bachelor's, and master's. *Special study options:* academic remediation for entering students, accelerated degree program, adult/continuing education programs, advanced placement credit, cooperative education, distance learning, double majors, English as a second language, freshman honors college, honors programs, independent study, internships, off-campus study, part-time degree program, services for LD students, student-designed majors, study abroad, summer session for credit. *ROTC:* Army (c), Navy (c), Air Force (c).

Computers on Campus 128 computers/terminals are available on campus for general student use. Students can access the following: campus intranet, computer help desk, free student e-mail accounts, online (class) grades, online (class) registration, online (class) schedules. Campuswide network is available. Wireless service is available via classrooms, libraries.

Student Life *Activities and organizations:* choral group. *Campus security:* 24-hour emergency response devices. *Student services:* personal/psychological counseling.

Athletics Member USCAA. *Intercollegiate sports:* basketball M, golf M, volleyball W. *Intramural sports:* cheerleading M(c)/W(c), rugby M(c)/W(c), skiing (downhill) M(c)/W(c), soccer M(c)/W(c), softball M(c)/W(c), table tennis M/W.

Standardized Tests *Required:* SAT or ACT (for admission).

Costs (2012–13) *Tuition:* state resident $7140 full-time; nonresident $22,548 full-time. Full-time tuition and fees vary according to course load and student level. Part-time tuition and fees vary according to course load and student level. *Payment plan:* installment. *Waivers:* senior citizens and employees or children of employees.

Applying *Options:* electronic application. *Application fee:* $60. *Required:* essay or personal statement, high school transcript. *Application deadlines:* 6/1 (freshmen), 6/1 (out-of-state freshmen), 6/1 (transfers). *Notification:* continuous (freshmen), continuous (out-of-state freshmen), continuous (transfers).

Freshman Application Contact Mr. Matthew Moreau, Admissions and Financial Aid Coordinator, The Ohio State University at Marion, 1465 Mount Vernon Avenue, Marion, OH 43302. *Phone:* 740-725-6337. *Fax:* 740-386-2439. *E-mail:* moreau.1@osu.edu.

Website: http://osumarion.osu.edu/.

The Ohio State University–Mansfield Campus

Mansfield, Ohio

- **State-supported** comprehensive, founded 1958, part of The Ohio State University
- **Small-town** 640-acre campus with easy access to Columbus, Cleveland
- **Coed** 1,204 undergraduate students, 83% full-time, 54% women, 46% men
- **Noncompetitive** entrance level, 99% of applicants were admitted

Undergraduates 1,002 full-time, 202 part-time. Students come from 6 states and territories; 1 other country; 1% are from out of state; 7% Black or African American, non-Hispanic/Latino; 2% Hispanic/Latino; 0.4% Asian, non-Hispanic/Latino; 0.2% American Indian or Alaska Native, non-Hispanic/Latino; 2% Two or more races, non-Hispanic/Latino; 2% Race/ethnicity unknown; 0.1% international; 6% transferred in; 17% live on campus. *Retention:* 70% of full-time freshmen returned.

Freshmen *Admission:* 1,366 applied, 1,347 admitted, 485 enrolled. *Test scores:* SAT critical reading scores over 500: 45%; SAT math scores over 500: 45%; SAT writing scores over 500: 39%; ACT scores over 18: 89%; SAT critical reading scores over 600: 8%; SAT math scores over 600: 16%; SAT writing scores over 600: 4%; ACT scores over 24: 34%; SAT critical reading scores over 700: 2%; SAT math scores over 700: 4%; ACT scores over 30: 2%.

Faculty *Total:* 92, 43% full-time, 42% with terminal degrees. *Student/faculty ratio:* 19:1.

Academics *Calendar:* quarters. *Degrees:* associate, bachelor's, and master's. *Special study options:* academic remediation for entering students, accelerated degree program, adult/continuing education programs, advanced placement credit, cooperative education, distance learning, double majors, English as a second language, freshman honors college, honors programs, independent study, internships, off-campus study, part-time degree program, services for LD students, student-designed majors, study abroad, summer session for credit. *ROTC:* Army (c), Navy (c), Air Force (c).

Computers on Campus 235 computers/terminals are available on campus for general student use. Students can access the following: campus intranet, com-

puter help desk, free student e-mail accounts, online (class) grades, online (class) registration, online (class) schedules. Campuswide network is available. 100% of college-owned or -operated housing units are wired for high-speed Internet access. Wireless service is available via computer centers, libraries, student centers.

Student Life *Housing options:* coed, disabled students. Campus housing is university owned. *Activities and organizations:* drama/theater group, choral group, Campus Activities Board, Campus Crusader for Christ, Club Ed, Multicultural Student Association, Psychology Student Association. *Campus security:* 24-hour emergency response devices and patrols. *Student services:* personal/psychological counseling.

Athletics *Intramural sports:* baseball M(c), basketball M(c)/W(c), bowling M/W, cheerleading M(c)/W(c), football M/W, golf M/W, soccer M(c), softball M/W, table tennis M/W, tennis M/W, volleyball M/W(c).

Standardized Tests *Required:* SAT or ACT (for admission).

Applying *Options:* electronic application. *Application fee:* $60. *Required:* essay or personal statement, high school transcript. *Application deadlines:* 6/1 (freshmen), 6/1 (out-of-state freshmen), 6/1 (transfers). *Notification:* continuous (freshmen), continuous (out-of-state freshmen), continuous (transfers).

Freshman Application Contact The Ohio State University–Mansfield Campus, OH. *Phone:* 419-755-4225. *Fax:* 419-755-4241. *E-mail:* admissions@mansfield.ohio-state.edu.
Website: http://www.mansfield.osu.edu/.

The Ohio State University–Newark Campus

Newark, Ohio

- **State-supported** comprehensive, founded 1957, part of The Ohio State University
- **Small-town** 106-acre campus with easy access to Columbus
- **Coed** 2,301 undergraduate students, 83% full-time, 53% women, 47% men
- **Noncompetitive** entrance level, 99% of applicants were admitted

Undergraduates 1,918 full-time, 383 part-time. Students come from 7 states and territories; 14% Black or African American, non-Hispanic/Latino; 2% Hispanic/Latino; 3% Asian, non-Hispanic/Latino; 0.1% Native Hawaiian or other Pacific Islander, non-Hispanic/Latino; 0.3% American Indian or Alaska Native, non-Hispanic/Latino; 4% Two or more races, non-Hispanic/Latino; 2% Race/ethnicity unknown; 5% transferred in; 8% live on campus. *Retention:* 61% of full-time freshmen returned.

Freshmen *Admission:* 2,764 applied, 2,726 admitted, 1,136 enrolled. *Test scores:* SAT critical reading scores over 500: 52%; SAT math scores over 500: 58%; SAT writing scores over 500: 40%; ACT scores over 18: 84%; SAT critical reading scores over 600: 11%; SAT math scores over 600: 22%; SAT writing scores over 600: 7%; ACT scores over 24: 28%; SAT critical reading scores over 700: 1%; ACT scores over 30: 1%.

Faculty *Total:* 151, 33% full-time, 32% with terminal degrees. *Student/faculty ratio:* 24:1.

Academics *Calendar:* quarters. *Degrees:* associate, bachelor's, and master's. *Special study options:* academic remediation for entering students, accelerated degree program, adult/continuing education programs, advanced placement credit, cooperative education, distance learning, double majors, English as a second language, freshman honors college, honors programs, independent study, internships, off-campus study, part-time degree program, services for LD students, student-designed majors, study abroad, summer session for credit. *ROTC:* Army (b), Navy (c), Air Force (c).

Computers on Campus 132 computers/terminals are available on campus for general student use. Students can access the following: campus intranet, computer help desk, free student e-mail accounts, online (class) grades, online (class) registration, online (class) schedules. Campuswide network is available. 100% of college-owned or -operated housing units are wired for high-speed Internet access. Wireless service is available via entire campus.

Student Life *Housing options:* coed. Campus housing is university owned. *Activities and organizations:* choral group. *Campus security:* 24-hour emergency response devices and patrols, late-night transport/escort service, self-defense education. *Student services:* personal/psychological counseling.

Athletics *Intramural sports:* baseball M(c), basketball M(c)/W(c), football M(c)/W(c), golf M(c)/W(c), soccer M(c)/W(c), softball W(c), volleyball M(c)/W(c), weight lifting M(c)/W(c).

Standardized Tests *Required:* SAT or ACT (for admission).

Applying *Options:* electronic application. *Application fee:* $60. *Required:* essay or personal statement, high school transcript. *Application deadlines:* 6/1 (freshmen), 6/1 (out-of-state freshmen), 6/1 (transfers). *Notification:* continuous (freshmen), continuous (out-of-state freshmen), continuous (transfers).

Freshman Application Contact Ms. Ann Donahue, Director of Enrollment, The Ohio State University–Newark Campus, 1179 University Drive, Newark, OH 43055. *Phone:* 740-366-9333. *Fax:* 740-364-9645. *E-mail:* barclay.3@osu.edu.
Website: http://www.newark.osu.edu/.

Ohio University

Athens, Ohio

- **State-supported** university, founded 1804, part of Ohio Board of Regents, University System of Ohio
- **Small-town** 1774-acre campus
- **Endowment** $409.0 million
- **Coed** 22,685 undergraduate students, 74% full-time, 60% women, 40% men
- **Moderately difficult** entrance level, 78% of applicants were admitted

Undergraduates 16,862 full-time, 5,823 part-time. Students come from 49 states and territories; 61 other countries; 13% are from out of state; 5% Black or African American, non-Hispanic/Latino; 2% Hispanic/Latino; 0.9% Asian, non-Hispanic/Latino; 0.1% Native Hawaiian or other Pacific Islander, non-Hispanic/Latino; 0.2% American Indian or Alaska Native, non-Hispanic/Latino; 2% Two or more races, non-Hispanic/Latino; 1% Race/ethnicity unknown; 4% international; 3% transferred in; 40% live on campus. *Retention:* 79% of full-time freshmen returned.

Freshmen *Admission:* 17,466 applied, 13,571 admitted, 3,886 enrolled. *Average high school GPA:* 3.4. *Test scores:* SAT critical reading scores over 500: 72%; SAT math scores over 500: 75%; SAT writing scores over 500: 63%; ACT scores over 18: 99%; SAT critical reading scores over 600: 25%; SAT math scores over 600: 31%; SAT writing scores over 600: 20%; ACT scores over 24: 52%; SAT critical reading scores over 700: 6%; SAT math scores over 700: 4%; SAT writing scores over 700: 3%; ACT scores over 30: 9%.

Faculty *Total:* 1,229, 69% full-time, 66% with terminal degrees. *Student/faculty ratio:* 19:1.

Academics *Calendar:* quarters. *Degrees:* associate, bachelor's, master's, and doctoral. *Special study options:* academic remediation for entering students, accelerated degree program, adult/continuing education programs, advanced placement credit, cooperative education, distance learning, double majors, English as a second language, external degree program, freshman honors college, honors programs, independent study, internships, off-campus study, part-time degree program, services for LD students, student-designed majors, study abroad, summer session for credit. *ROTC:* Army (b), Air Force (b).

Computers on Campus 1,000 computers/terminals and 22,000 ports are available on campus for general student use. Students can access the following: campus intranet, computer help desk, free student e-mail accounts, online (class) grades, online (class) registration, online (class) schedules. Campuswide network is available. 100% of college-owned or -operated housing units are wired for high-speed Internet access. Wireless service is available via entire campus.

Student Life *Housing:* on-campus residence required through sophomore year. *Options:* coed, women-only, disabled students. Campus housing is university owned. Freshman campus housing is guaranteed. *Activities and organizations:* drama/theater group, student-run newspaper, radio and television station, choral group, marching band, Alpha Phi Omega, Golden Key Honor Society, International Student Union, Kappa Delta Pi, Campus Crusade for Christ, national fraternities, national sororities. *Campus security:* 24-hour emergency response devices and patrols, student patrols, late-night transport/escort service, controlled dormitory access, electronic dormitory access is being phased in gradually as part of renovations. OU has a fully sworn, 24/7 police department. *Student services:* health clinic, personal/psychological counseling, women's center, legal services.

Athletics Member NCAA. All Division I except football (Division I-A). *Intercollegiate sports:* baseball M(s), basketball M(s)/W(s), cheerleading M/W, cross-country running M(s)/W(s), field hockey W(s), golf M(s)/W(s), ice hockey M(c), soccer W(s), softball W(s), swimming and diving W(s), track and field W(s), volleyball W(s), wrestling M(s). *Intramural sports:* badminton M/W, basketball M/W, crew M(c)/W(c), equestrian sports M(c)/W(c), fencing M(c)/W(c), golf M/W, gymnastics M(c)/W(c), lacrosse W(c), racquetball M/W, rugby M(c)/W(c), soccer M(c)/W(c), softball M/W(c), tennis M(c)/W(c), ultimate Frisbee M(c)/W(c), volleyball M(c)/W(c), water polo M(c)/W, wrestling M(c)/W(c).

Standardized Tests *Required:* SAT or ACT (for admission).

Costs (2012–13) *Tuition:* state resident $10,282 full-time, $487 per semester hour part-time; nonresident $19,246 full-time, $929 per semester hour part-time. Full-time tuition and fees vary according to degree level, location, program, and reciprocity agreements. Part-time tuition and fees vary according to course load, degree level, location, program, and reciprocity agreements. *Room* *and board:* $10,010; room only: $5648. Room and board charges vary according to board plan. *Payment plan:* installment. *Waivers:* senior citizens and employees or children of employees.

Financial Aid Of all full-time matriculated undergraduates who enrolled in 2012, 11,659 applied for aid, 9,271 were judged to have need, 1,041 had their need fully met. 800 Federal Work-Study jobs (averaging $1672). In 2012, 1824 non-need-based awards were made. *Average percent of need met:* 53%. *Average financial aid package:* $8458. *Average need-based loan:* $4044. *Average need-based gift aid:* $5797. *Average non-need-based aid:* $4331. *Average indebtedness upon graduation:* $27,060.

Applying *Options:* electronic application, early admission, deferred entrance. *Application fee:* $45. *Required:* high school transcript. *Required for some:* essay or personal statement, 2 letters of recommendation, interview, Auditions required for music and dance; interview and portfolio reviews for visual communication, and application supplement for Honors Tutorial College. *Recommended:* 2 letters of recommendation. *Application deadlines:* 2/1 (freshmen), 2/1 (out-of-state freshmen), 6/15 (transfers). *Notification:* continuous (freshmen), continuous (out-of-state freshmen), continuous (transfers).

Freshman Application Contact Undergraduate Admissions, Ohio University, Athens, OH 45701-2979. *Phone:* 740-593-4100. *Fax:* 740-593-0560. *E-mail:* admissions@ohio.edu.

Website: http://www.ohio.edu/.

Ohio University–Chillicothe

Chillicothe, Ohio

- **State-supported** 4-year, founded 1946, part of Ohio Board of Regents
- **Small-town** 124-acre campus with easy access to Columbus
- **Coed** 2,200 undergraduate students
- **Noncompetitive** entrance level

Undergraduates Students come from 1 other state.

Academics *Calendar:* quarters. *Degrees:* associate, bachelor's, and master's (offers first 2 years of most bachelor's degree programs available at the main campus in Athens; also offers several bachelor's degree programs that can be completed at this campus and several programs exclusive to this campus; also offers some graduate programs). *Special study options:* academic remediation for entering students, adult/continuing education programs, advanced placement credit, distance learning, external degree program, internships, part-time degree program, services for LD students, study abroad, summer session for credit.

Computers on Campus Students can access the following: online (class) registration. Campuswide network is available.

Student Life *Housing:* college housing not available. *Activities and organizations:* drama/theater group. *Campus security:* 24-hour emergency response devices, patrols by city police. *Student services:* personal/psychological counseling.

Athletics *Intramural sports:* baseball M(c), basketball M(c)/W(c), golf M(c), softball W(c), tennis M(c)/W(c), volleyball M(c)/W(c).

Standardized Tests *Required:* COMPASS (for admission).

Costs (2012–13) *Tuition:* state resident $4956 full-time, $222 per credit hour part-time; nonresident $6802 full-time, $308 per credit hour part-time. Full-time tuition and fees vary according to course load, location, program, and student level. Part-time tuition and fees vary according to course load, location, program, and student level. *Payment plan:* installment. *Waivers:* senior citizens and employees or children of employees.

Financial Aid Of all full-time matriculated undergraduates who enrolled in 2012, 1,149 applied for aid, 1,068 were judged to have need, 46 had their need fully met. 20 Federal Work-Study jobs (averaging $1763). In 2012, 10 non-need-based awards were made. *Average percent of need met:* 50%. *Average financial aid package:* $7729. *Average need-based loan:* $3614. *Average need-based gift aid:* $4979. *Average non-need-based aid:* $4151. *Average indebtedness upon graduation:* $27,060.

Applying *Options:* electronic application, early admission, deferred entrance. *Application fee:* $20. *Required:* high school transcript. *Application deadlines:* 9/1 (freshmen), 9/1 (transfers). *Notification:* continuous (freshmen), continuous (transfers).

Freshman Application Contact Neeley Allen, Coordinator, Recruitment, Ohio University–Chillicothe, 101 University Drive, Chillicothe, OH 45601. *Phone:* 740-774-7241. *Toll-free phone:* 877-462-6824. *Fax:* 740-774-7214. *E-mail:* evelandt@ohio.edu.

Website: http://www.chillicothe.ohiou.edu/.

Ohio University–Eastern

St. Clairsville, Ohio

Director of Admissions N. Kip Howard, Assistant Vice President for Enrollment Services/Director of Admissions, Ohio University–Eastern, 45425 National Road, St. Clairsville, OH 43950-9724. *Phone:* 740-593-4120. *Toll-free phone:* 800-648-3331. *E-mail:* howardn@ohio.edu.

Website: http://www.eastern.ohiou.edu/.

Ohio University–Lancaster

Lancaster, Ohio

Director of Admissions Pat Fox, Enrollment Manager, Ohio University–Lancaster, 1570 Granville Pike, Lancaster, OH 43130-1097. *Phone:* 740-654-6711 Ext. 215. *Toll-free phone:* 888-446-4468. *E-mail:* fox@ohio.edu.

Website: http://www.ohiou.edu/lancaster/.

Ohio University–Southern Campus

Ironton, Ohio

Director of Admissions Linda Harlow, Admission, Registration and Records Coordinator, Ohio University–Southern Campus, 1804 Liberty Avenue, Ironton, OH 45638-2214. *Phone:* 740-533-4584. *Toll-free phone:* 800-626-0513. *E-mail:* harlow@ohio.edu.

Website: http://www.ohiou.edu/.

Ohio University–Zanesville

Zanesville, Ohio

- **State-supported** 4-year, founded 1946
- **Rural** 179-acre campus with easy access to Columbus
- **Coed** 1,972 undergraduate students, 55% full-time, 69% women, 31% men
- **Noncompetitive** entrance level, 91% of applicants were admitted

Undergraduates 1,090 full-time, 882 part-time. 1% are from out of state; 3% Black or African American, non-Hispanic/Latino; 2% Hispanic/Latino; 0.4% Asian, non-Hispanic/Latino; 0.1% Native Hawaiian or other Pacific Islander, non-Hispanic/Latino; 0.3% American Indian or Alaska Native, non-Hispanic/Latino; 5% Two or more races, non-Hispanic/Latino; 2% Race/ethnicity unknown; 0.7% international. *Retention:* 55% of full-time freshmen returned.

Freshmen *Admission:* 546 applied, 497 admitted, 290 enrolled.

Faculty *Total:* 130, 24% full-time, 25% with terminal degrees. *Student/faculty ratio:* 23:1.

Academics *Calendar:* quarters. *Degrees:* associate and bachelor's (offers first 2 years of most bachelor's degree programs available at the main campus in Athens; also offers several bachelor's degree programs that can be completed at this campus; also offers some graduate courses). *Special study options:* academic remediation for entering students, adult/continuing education programs, advanced placement credit, distance learning, double majors, external degree program, independent study, off-campus study, part-time degree program, services for LD students, student-designed majors, study abroad, summer session for credit.

Computers on Campus 200 computers/terminals are available on campus for general student use. Students can access the following: computer help desk, free student e-mail accounts, online (class) grades, online (class) registration, online (class) schedules. Campuswide network is available.

Student Life *Activities and organizations:* drama/theater group, student-run newspaper, radio station, Student Senate, Student Nurses Association, Good Intentions Group, Green Bobcats, Habitat for Humanity Club. *Campus security:* student patrols, late-night transport/escort service, night security. *Student services:* personal/psychological counseling.

Athletics *Intercollegiate sports:* baseball M, basketball M/W, golf M/W, softball W, volleyball W.

Standardized Tests *Required for some:* SAT or ACT (for admission).

Costs (2012–13) *Tuition:* state resident $5038 full-time, $219 per semester hour part-time; nonresident $6884 full-time, $307 per semester hour part-time. *Required fees:* $66 full-time. *Payment plan:* installment. *Waivers:* senior citizens and employees or children of employees.

Financial Aid Of all full-time matriculated undergraduates who enrolled in 2012, 934 applied for aid, 838 were judged to have need, 90 had their need fully met. 17 Federal Work-Study jobs (averaging $1524). In 2012, 51 non-need-based awards were made. *Average percent of need met:* 57%. *Average financial aid package:* $7437. *Average need-based loan:* $3555. *Average need-based gift aid:* $4851. *Average non-need-based aid:* $3288. *Average indebtedness upon graduation:* $27,060.

Applying *Options:* electronic application. *Application fee:* $20. *Required:* high school transcript. *Application deadlines:* rolling (freshmen), rolling (transfers).

Freshman Application Contact Mrs., Ohio University–Zanesville, Office of Student Services, 1425 Newark Road, Zanesville, OH 43701. *Phone:* 740-588-1440. *Fax:* 740-588-1444. *E-mail:* ouzservices@ohio.edu. *Website:* http://www.zanesville.ohiou.edu/.

Ohio Wesleyan University

Delaware, Ohio

- **Independent United Methodist** 4-year, founded 1842
- **Small-town** 200-acre campus with easy access to Columbus
- **Coed** 1,821 undergraduate students, 99% full-time, 55% women, 45% men
- **Very difficult** entrance level, 74% of applicants were admitted

Undergraduates 1,806 full-time, 15 part-time. 47% are from out of state; 5% Black or African American, non-Hispanic/Latino; 3% Hispanic/Latino; 2% Asian, non-Hispanic/Latino; 0.1% Native Hawaiian or other Pacific Islander, non-Hispanic/Latino; 0.3% American Indian or Alaska Native, non-Hispanic/Latino; 3% Two or more races, non-Hispanic/Latino; 3% Race/ethnicity unknown; 8% international; 2% transferred in; 90% live on campus. *Retention:* 83% of full-time freshmen returned.

Freshmen *Admission:* 3,835 applied, 2,823 admitted, 537 enrolled. *Average high school GPA:* 3.49. *Test scores:* SAT critical reading scores over 500: 80%; SAT math scores over 500: 87%; SAT writing scores over 500: 76%; ACT scores over 18: 99%; SAT critical reading scores over 600: 36%; SAT math scores over 600: 45%; SAT writing scores over 600: 36%; ACT scores over 24: 68%; SAT critical reading scores over 700: 10%; SAT math scores over 700: 10%; SAT writing scores over 700: 7%; ACT scores over 30: 16%.

Faculty *Total:* 219, 65% full-time. *Student/faculty ratio:* 11:1.

Academics *Calendar:* semesters. *Degree:* bachelor's. *Special study options:* double majors, honors programs, internships, off-campus study, services for LD students, student-designed majors, study abroad, summer session for credit.

Computers on Campus Students can access the following: campus intranet, computer help desk, free student e-mail accounts, online (class) grades, online (class) registration, online (class) schedules. Campuswide network is available.

Student Life *Housing:* on-campus residence required through senior year. *Options:* coed, women-only. Campus housing is university owned. Freshman campus housing is guaranteed. *Activities and organizations:* drama/theater group, student-run newspaper, radio station, choral group, national fraternities, national sororities. *Campus security:* 24-hour emergency response devices and patrols, late-night transport/escort service, controlled dormitory access. *Student services:* health clinic.

Athletics Member NCAA. All Division III. *Intercollegiate sports:* baseball M, basketball M/W, cross-country running M/W, equestrian sports M(c)/W(c), field hockey W, football M, golf M, ice hockey M(c)/W(c), lacrosse M/W, rugby M(c)/W(c), sailing M(c)/W(c), soccer M/W, softball W, swimming and diving M/W, tennis M/W, track and field M/W, ultimate Frisbee M(c)/W(c), volleyball M(c)/W. *Intramural sports:* badminton M/W, basketball M/W, football M/W, golf M/W, lacrosse M/W, racquetball M/W, skiing (cross-country) M/W, skiing (downhill) M/W, soccer M/W, softball M/W, squash M/W, swimming and diving M/W, tennis M/W, track and field M/W, volleyball M/W, water polo M/W.

Standardized Tests *Required:* SAT or ACT (for admission).

Costs (2012–13) *Comprehensive fee:* $49,460 includes full-time tuition ($38,890), mandatory fees ($260), and room and board ($10,310). *College room only:* $5500. Room and board charges vary according to board plan. *Payment plan:* installment.

Financial Aid Of all full-time matriculated undergraduates who enrolled in 2011, 1,337 applied for aid, 1,185 were judged to have need, 334 had their need fully met. In 2011, 574 non-need-based awards were made. *Average percent of need met:* 80%. *Average financial aid package:* $27,376. *Average need-based loan:* $4542. *Average need-based gift aid:* $22,956. *Average non-need-based aid:* $19,780. *Average indebtedness upon graduation:* $30,900.

Applying *Options:* electronic application, early admission, early decision, early action, deferred entrance. *Application fee:* $35. *Required:* essay or personal statement, high school transcript, minimum 2.5 GPA, 1 letter of recommendation. *Recommended:* 2 letters of recommendation, interview. *Application deadlines:* 3/1 (freshmen), 3/1 (out-of-state freshmen), rolling

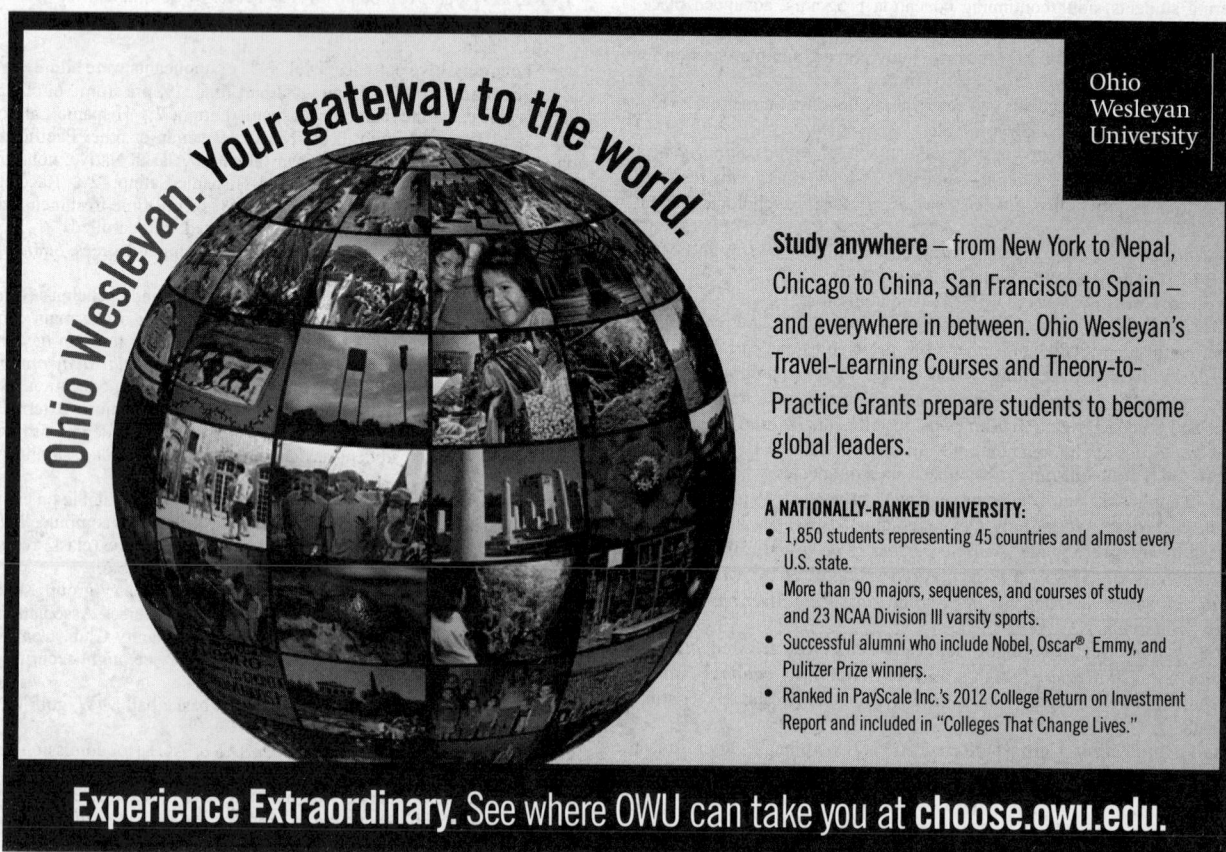

(transfers), 12/15 (early action). *Early decision deadline:* 11/15. *Notification:* continuous (transfers), 1/15 (early action).
Freshman Application Contact Ms. Alisha Couch, Director of Admission, Ohio Wesleyan University, 61 South Sandusky Street, Delaware, OH 43015. *Phone:* 740-368-3099. *Toll-free phone:* 800-922-8953. *Fax:* 740-368-3314. *E-mail:* amcouch@owu.edu.
Website: http://www.owu.edu/.

See previous page for display ad and page 1428 for the College Close-Up.

Otterbein University
Westerville, Ohio
- **Independent United Methodist** comprehensive, founded 1847
- **Suburban** 142-acre campus with easy access to Columbus
- **Endowment** $70.0 million
- **Coed**
- **Moderately difficult** entrance level

Faculty *Student/faculty ratio:* 11:1.
Academics *Calendar:* quarters. *Degrees:* bachelor's, master's, doctoral, and post-master's certificates.
Student Life *Campus security:* 24-hour emergency response devices and patrols, student patrols, late-night transport/escort service, controlled dormitory access, 24-hour locked residence hall entrances.
Athletics Member NCAA. All Division III.
Standardized Tests *Required:* SAT or ACT (for admission).
Costs (2012–13) *Comprehensive fee:* $39,342 includes full-time tuition ($30,658) and room and board ($8684). Full-time tuition and fees vary according to course load and program. Part-time tuition: $557 per credit hour. Part-time tuition and fees vary according to course load and program. *College room only:* $4576. Room and board charges vary according to housing facility.
Financial Aid *Of all full-time matriculated undergraduates who enrolled in 2011,* 1,983 applied for aid, 1,789 were judged to have need, 325 had their need fully met. 500 Federal Work-Study jobs (averaging $1000). 250 state and other part-time jobs (averaging $1000). *In 2011,* 411 non-need-based awards were made. *Average percent of need met:* 73. *Average financial aid package:* $25,300. *Average need-based loan:* $8610. *Average need-based gift aid:* $15,206. *Average non-need-based aid:* $11,411. *Average indebtedness upon graduation:* $27,924.
Applying *Options:* electronic application, deferred entrance. *Application fee:* $25. *Required:* high school transcript. *Required for some:* essay or personal statement, 1 letter of recommendation. *Recommended:* minimum 2.5 GPA, interview.
Freshman Application Contact Mr. Ben Shoemaker, Interim Director of Admissions, Otterbein University, 1 South Grove Street, Office Of Admission, Westerville, OH 43081-9924. *Phone:* 614-823-1500. *Toll-free phone:* 800-488-8144. *Fax:* 614-823-1200. *E-mail:* uotterb@otterbein.edu.
Website: http://www.otterbein.edu/.

Pontifical College Josephinum
Columbus, Ohio
Freshman Application Contact Mrs. Arminda Crawford, Secretary for Admissions, Pontifical College Josephinum, 7825 North High Street, Columbus, OH 43235. *Phone:* 614-985-2241. *Toll-free phone:* 888-252-5812. *Fax:* 614-885-2307. *E-mail:* acrawford@pcj.edu.
Website: http://www.pcj.edu/.

Rabbinical College of Telshe
Wickliffe, Ohio
Freshman Application Contact Admissions Office, Rabbinical College of Telshe, 28400 Euclid Avenue, Wickliffe, OH 44092-2523. *Phone:* 440-943-5300.

Shawnee State University
Portsmouth, Ohio
- **State-supported** comprehensive, founded 1986
- **Small-town** 52-acre campus
- **Endowment** $13.2 million
- **Coed** 4,554 undergraduate students, 85% full-time, 58% women, 42% men
- **Noncompetitive** entrance level, 82% of applicants were admitted

Undergraduates 3,862 full-time, 692 part-time. Students come from 17 states and territories; 21 other countries; 11% are from out of state; 6% Black or African American, non-Hispanic/Latino; 0.6% Hispanic/Latino; 0.4% Asian, non-Hispanic/Latino; 0.7% American Indian or Alaska Native, non-Hispanic/Latino; 1% Two or more races, non-Hispanic/Latino; 6% Race/ethnicity unknown; 0.7% international; 7% transferred in; 23% live on campus. *Retention:* 49% of full-time freshmen returned.
Freshmen *Admission:* 4,340 applied, 3,568 admitted, 1,167 enrolled. *Test scores:* SAT critical reading scores over 500: 43%; SAT math scores over 500: 52%; SAT writing scores over 500: 29%; ACT scores over 18: 71%; SAT critical reading scores over 600: 11%; SAT math scores over 600: 18%; SAT writing scores over 600: 9%; ACT scores over 24: 21%; SAT critical reading scores over 700: 2%; SAT math scores over 700: 4%; ACT scores over 30: 1%.
Faculty *Total:* 328, 46% full-time. *Student/faculty ratio:* 19:1.
Academics *Calendar:* semesters. *Degrees:* certificates, associate, bachelor's, and master's. *Special study options:* academic remediation for entering students, accelerated degree program, adult/continuing education programs, advanced placement credit, distance learning, double majors, English as a second language, honors programs, independent study, internships, off-campus study, part-time degree program, services for LD students, student-designed majors, study abroad, summer session for credit. *Unusual degree programs:* 3-2 psychology (MOT).
Computers on Campus 620 computers/terminals are available on campus for general student use. Students can access the following: campus intranet, computer help desk, free student e-mail accounts, online (class) grades, online (class) registration, online (class) schedules, financial aid, student billing, courses, student service portal. Campuswide network is available. 100% of college-owned or -operated housing units are wired for high-speed Internet access. Wireless service is available via entire campus.
Student Life *Housing:* on-campus residence required for freshman year. *Options:* coed. Campus housing is university owned and leased by the school. Freshman applicants given priority for college housing. *Activities and organizations:* drama/theater group, student-run newspaper, choral group, campus ministry, Health Executives and Administrators Learning Society, Student Programming Board, Student Government Association, national fraternities. *Campus security:* 24-hour emergency response devices and patrols. *Student services:* health clinic, personal/psychological counseling, women's center.
Athletics Member NAIA. *Intercollegiate sports:* baseball M(s), basketball M(s)/W(s), cross-country running M(s)/W(s), golf M(s), soccer M(s)/W(s), softball W, tennis W(s), volleyball W(s). *Intramural sports:* basketball M/W, bowling M/W, golf M/W, racquetball M/W, softball M, swimming and diving M/W, table tennis M/W, tennis M/W, volleyball M/W.
Standardized Tests *Required for some:* ACT (for admission), SAT or ACT (for admission). *Recommended:* ACT (for admission), SAT or ACT (for admission).
Costs (2012–13) *Tuition:* state resident $5918 full-time, $247 per credit hour part-time; nonresident $10,893 full-time, $454 per credit hour part-time. Full-time tuition and fees vary according to course load and reciprocity agreements. Part-time tuition and fees vary according to course load and reciprocity agreements. *Required fees:* $1070 full-time, $45 per credit hour part-time. *Room and board:* $9012; room only: $5478. Room and board charges vary according to board plan and housing facility. *Payment plan:* installment. *Waivers:* senior citizens and employees or children of employees.
Applying *Options:* electronic application, deferred entrance. *Required:* high school transcript. *Required for some:* interview. *Application deadlines:* rolling (freshmen), rolling (out-of-state freshmen), rolling (transfers). *Notification:* continuous (freshmen), continuous (out-of-state freshmen), continuous (transfers).
Freshman Application Contact Shawnee State University, 940 Second Street, Portsmouth, OH 45662-4344. *Phone:* 740-351-3610 Ext. 610. *Toll-free phone:* 800-959-2SSU.
Website: http://www.shawnee.edu/.

South University

Cleveland, Ohio

Admissions Office Contact South University, 4743 Richmond Road, Cleveland, OH 44128. *Toll-free phone:* 855-398-9280. *Website:* http://www.southuniversity.edu/cleveland.aspx.

Strayer University—Akron Campus

Akron, Ohio

Freshman Application Contact Strayer University—Akron Campus, 51 Park West Boulevard, Akron, OH 44320. *Website:* http://www.strayer.edu/campus/akron.

Strayer University—Cincinnati Campus

Cincinnati, Ohio

Freshman Application Contact Strayer University—Cincinnati Campus, 2135 Dana Avenue, Suite 300, Cincinnati, OH 45207. *Website:* http://www.strayer.edu/campus/cincinnati.

Strayer University—Columbus Campus

Columbus, Ohio

Freshman Application Contact Strayer University—Columbus Campus, 8425 Pulsar Place, Suite 400, Columbus, OH 43240. *Website:* http://www.strayer.edu/campus/columbus/.

Strayer University—Fairborn Campus

Fairborn, Ohio

Freshman Application Contact Strayer University—Fairborn Campus, 2600 Paramount Place, Suite 300, Fairborn, OH 45324. *Website:* http://www.strayer.edu/campus/fairborn.

Strayer University—Fairview Park Campus

Fairview Park, Ohio

Freshman Application Contact Strayer University—Fairview Park Campus, 22730 Fairview Center Drive, Suite 150, Fairview Park, OH 44126-3616. *Website:* http://www.strayer.edu/campus/fairview-park.

Strayer University—Mason Campus

Mason, Ohio

Freshman Application Contact Strayer University—Mason Campus, 4605 Duke Drive, Suite 700, Mason, OH 45040. *Website:* http://www.strayer.edu/campus/mason/.

Tiffin University

Tiffin, Ohio

- **Independent** comprehensive, founded 1888
- **Small-town** 110-acre campus with easy access to Toledo
- **Coed** 5,728 undergraduate students, 48% full-time, 63% women, 37% men
- **Moderately difficult** entrance level, 39% of applicants were admitted

Undergraduates 2,766 full-time, 2,962 part-time. Students come from 50 states and territories; 29 other countries; 51% are from out of state; 27% Black or African American, non-Hispanic/Latino; 1% Hispanic/Latino; 0.3% Asian, non-Hispanic/Latino; 0.1% Native Hawaiian or other Pacific Islander, non-Hispanic/Latino; 0.6% American Indian or Alaska Native, non-Hispanic/Latino; 46% Race/ethnicity unknown; 1% international; 5% transferred in; 20% live on campus. *Retention:* 66% of full-time freshmen returned.

Freshmen *Admission:* 5,228 applied, 2,016 admitted, 1,313 enrolled. *Average high school GPA:* 3.04. *Test scores:* SAT critical reading scores over 500: 35%; SAT math scores over 500: 48%; ACT scores over 18: 82%; SAT critical reading scores over 600: 7%; SAT math scores over 600: 9%; ACT scores over 24: 24%; SAT critical reading scores over 700: 1%; SAT math scores over 700: 1%; ACT scores over 30: 1%.

Faculty *Total:* 506, 17% full-time, 32% with terminal degrees. *Student/faculty ratio:* 19:1.

Academics *Calendar:* semesters. *Degrees:* certificates, associate, bachelor's, master's, post-master's, and postbachelor's certificates. *Special study options:* academic remediation for entering students, accelerated degree program, adult/continuing education programs, advanced placement credit, distance learning, double majors, English as a second language, external degree program, freshman honors college, honors programs, independent study, internships, off-campus study, services for LD students, study abroad, summer session for credit. *ROTC:* Army (c), Air Force (c).

Computers on Campus 280 computers/terminals are available on campus for general student use. Students can access the following: campus intranet, computer help desk, free student e-mail accounts, online (class) grades, online (class) registration, online (class) schedules. Campuswide network is available. 100% of college-owned or -operated housing units are wired for high-speed Internet access. Wireless service is available via classrooms, computer centers, computer labs, dorm rooms, learning centers, libraries, student centers.

Student Life *Housing:* on-campus residence required through sophomore year. *Options:* coed, men-only, women-only, disabled students. Campus housing is university owned and leased by the school. Freshman campus housing is guaranteed. *Activities and organizations:* drama/theater group, student-run newspaper, choral group, marching band, Student Government Association, H2O, International Student Association, Global Affairs Organization, Circle K, national fraternities, national sororities. *Campus security:* 24-hour emergency response devices, student patrols, late-night transport/escort service, controlled dormitory access. *Student services:* health clinic, personal/psychological counseling, women's center.

Athletics Member NCAA. All Division II. *Intercollegiate sports:* baseball M(s), basketball M(s)/W(s), cheerleading M(s)/W(s), cross-country running M(s)/W(s), equestrian sports M(s)/W(s), football M(s), golf M(s)/W(s), lacrosse W(s), soccer M(s)/W(s), softball W(s), swimming and diving M(s)/W(s), tennis M(s)/W(s), track and field M(s)/W(s), volleyball W(s), wrestling M(s). *Intramural sports:* basketball M/W, bowling M/W, equestrian sports M(c)/W(c), football M, rugby M(c), soccer M/W, softball M/W, table tennis M/W, tennis M/W, ultimate Frisbee M/W, volleyball M/W, weight lifting M/W.

Standardized Tests *Required for some:* SAT or ACT (for admission).

Costs (2013–14) *Comprehensive fee:* $30,273 includes full-time tuition ($20,700) and room and board ($9573). Full-time tuition and fees vary according to course load, degree level, location, and program. Part-time tuition: $690 per credit. Part-time tuition and fees vary according to course load, degree level, location, and program. *College room only:* $4973. Room and board charges vary according to board plan and housing facility. *Payment plans:* installment, deferred payment. *Waivers:* senior citizens and employees or children of employees.

Financial Aid Of all full-time matriculated undergraduates who enrolled in 2012, 2,157 applied for aid, 2,079 were judged to have need, 147 had their need fully met. 221 Federal Work-Study jobs (averaging $1234). *Average percent of need met:* 56%. *Average financial aid package:* $14,571. *Average need-based loan:* $4807. *Average need-based gift aid:* $10,363. *Average indebtedness upon graduation:* $30,119.

Applying *Options:* electronic application. *Application fee:* $20. *Required:* high school transcript. *Required for some:* essay or personal statement, interview. *Recommended:* minimum 3.0 GPA. *Application deadline:* rolling (freshmen). *Notification:* continuous (transfers).

Freshman Application Contact Mr. Joe Borich, Director of Undergraduate Admissions, Tiffin University, 155 Miami Street, Tiffin, OH 44883. *Phone:*

419-448-3014. *Toll-free phone:* 800-968-6446. *Fax:* 419-443-5006. *E-mail:* borichj@tiffin.edu.
Website: http://www.tiffin.edu/.

Tri-State Bible College

South Point, Ohio

- **Independent nondenominational** comprehensive, founded 1970
- **Suburban** 4-acre campus
- **Coed**

Academics *Calendar:* semesters. *Degrees:* associate, bachelor's, and master's.
Applying *Application fee:* $25.
Freshman Application Contact Tri-State Bible College, 506 Margaret Street, PO Box 445, South Point, OH 45680-8402. *Phone:* 740-377-2520.
Website: http://www.tsbc.edu/.

Union Institute & University

Cincinnati, Ohio

- **Independent** university, founded 1969
- **Urban** 5-acre campus with easy access to Cincinnati
- **Endowment** $696,114
- **Coed**
- **Noncompetitive** entrance level

Faculty *Student/faculty ratio:* 9:1.
Academics *Calendar:* trimesters some programs offer split (8wk) sessions. *Degrees:* bachelor's, master's, doctoral, and post-master's certificates.
Student Life *Campus security:* 24-hour emergency response devices, late-night transport/escort service, security personnel on site during business and class hours.
Applying *Options:* electronic application, deferred entrance. *Required:* essay or personal statement, recommendation from program faculty. *Required for some:* high school transcript, 1 letter of recommendation. *Recommended:* interview.
Freshman Application Contact Union Institute & University, 440 East McMillan Street, Cincinnati, OH 45206-1925. *Phone:* 513-487-1173. *Toll-free phone:* 800-486-3116.
Website: http://www.myunion.edu/.

The University of Akron

Akron, Ohio

- **State-supported** university, founded 1870
- **Urban** 223-acre campus with easy access to Cleveland
- **Endowment** $188.4 million
- **Coed** 22,122 undergraduate students, 77% full-time, 48% women, 52% men
- **Moderately difficult** entrance level, 97% of applicants were admitted

Undergraduates 17,045 full-time, 5,077 part-time. Students come from 43 states and territories; 52 other countries; 3% are from out of state; 16% Black or African American, non-Hispanic/Latino; 2% Hispanic/Latino; 2% Asian, non-Hispanic/Latino; 0.2% Native Hawaiian or other Pacific Islander, non-Hispanic/Latino; 0.3% American Indian or Alaska Native, non-Hispanic/Latino; 2% Two or more races, non-Hispanic/Latino; 3% Race/ethnicity unknown; 1% international; 5% transferred in; 15% live on campus. *Retention:* 67% of full-time freshmen returned.
Freshman *Admission:* 10,854 applied, 10,501 admitted, 4,178 enrolled. *Average high school GPA:* 3. *Test scores:* SAT critical reading scores over 500: 55%; SAT math scores over 500: 60%; ACT scores over 18: 79%; SAT critical reading scores over 600: 19%; SAT math scores over 600: 25%; ACT scores over 24: 32%; SAT critical reading scores over 700: 3%; SAT math scores over 700: 7%; ACT scores over 30: 5%.
Faculty *Total:* 1,706, 46% full-time, 53% with terminal degrees. *Student/faculty ratio:* 21:1.
Academics *Calendar:* semesters. *Degrees:* certificates, associate, bachelor's, master's, doctoral, post-master's, and postbachelor's certificates. *Special study options:* academic remediation for entering students, accelerated degree program, adult/continuing education programs, advanced placement credit, cooperative education, distance learning, double majors, English as a second language, external degree program, freshman honors college, honors programs, independent study, internships, part-time degree program, services for

LD students, student-designed majors, study abroad, summer session for credit. *ROTC:* Army (b), Air Force (c). *Unusual degree programs:* 3-2 accounting, BSMD (NEOUCOM), mathematics.
Computers on Campus 3,100 computers/terminals and 16,000 ports are available on campus for general student use. Students can access the following: campus intranet, computer help desk, free student e-mail accounts, online (class) grades, online (class) registration, online (class) schedules, library laptops for student checkout. Campuswide network is available. 100% of college-owned or -operated housing units are wired for high-speed Internet access. Wireless service is available via entire campus.
Student Life *Housing:* on-campus residence required for freshman year. *Options:* coed, men-only, women-only. Campus housing is university owned. Freshman applicants given priority for college housing. *Activities and organizations:* drama/theater group, student-run newspaper, radio and television station, choral group, marching band, Associated Student Government, Residence Hall Program Board, American Society of Mechanical Engineers, AK-Rowdies, national fraternities, national sororities. *Campus security:* 24-hour emergency response devices and patrols, student patrols, late-night transport/escort service, controlled dormitory access. *Student services:* health clinic, personal/psychological counseling, women's center, legal services.
Athletics Member NCAA. All Division I except football (Division I-A). *Intercollegiate sports:* baseball M(s), basketball M(s)/W(s), cheerleading M/W, cross-country running M(s)/W(s), golf M(s)/W(s), riflery M/W(s), soccer M(s)/W(s), softball W(s), swimming and diving W(s), tennis W(s), track and field M(s)/W(s), volleyball W(s). *Intramural sports:* badminton M/W, basketball M/W, bowling M/W, cross-country running M/W, golf M/W, racquetball M/W, skiing (cross-country) M/W, skiing (downhill) M/W, soccer M/W, softball M/W, swimming and diving M/W, table tennis M/W, track and field M/W, volleyball W, wrestling M.
Standardized Tests *Required:* SAT or ACT (for admission).
Costs (2012–13) *Tuition:* state resident $8284 full-time, $345 per credit hour part-time; nonresident $16,484 full-time, $687 per credit hour part-time. Full-time tuition and fees vary according to course load, degree level, and location. Part-time tuition and fees vary according to course load, degree level, and location. *Required fees:* $1579 full-time. *Room and board:* $9878; room only: $6306. Room and board charges vary according to board plan and housing facility. *Payment plan:* installment. *Waivers:* senior citizens and employees or children of employees.
Financial Aid Of all full-time matriculated undergraduates who enrolled in 2012, 14,613 applied for aid, 12,013 were judged to have need, 906 had their need fully met. In 2012, 1642 non-need-based awards were made. *Average percent of need met:* 49%. *Average financial aid package:* $7522. *Average need-based loan:* $3112. *Average need-based gift aid:* $2856. *Average non-need-based aid:* $4408. *Average indebtedness upon graduation:* $23,392.
Applying *Options:* electronic application, early action, deferred entrance. *Application fee:* $40. *Required:* high school transcript. *Required for some:* essay or personal statement, 3 letters of recommendation, interview. *Application deadlines:* 8/11 (freshmen), rolling (transfers), 11/1 (early action). *Notification:* 9/15 (freshmen), continuous (transfers).
Freshman Application Contact The University of Akron, 302 Buchtel Common, Akron, OH 44325. *Phone:* 330-972-7100. *Toll-free phone:* 800-655-4884.
Website: http://www.uakron.edu/.

The University of Akron–Wayne College

Orrville, Ohio

- **State-supported** primarily 2-year, founded 1972, part of The University of Akron
- **Rural** 157-acre campus
- **Coed** 2,415 undergraduate students, 49% full-time, 59% women, 41% men
- **Noncompetitive** entrance level, 85% of applicants were admitted

Undergraduates 1,185 full-time, 1,230 part-time. Students come from 2 states and territories; 3% Black or African American, non-Hispanic/Latino; 1% Hispanic/Latino; 0.8% Asian, non-Hispanic/Latino; 0.3% American Indian or Alaska Native, non-Hispanic/Latino; 4% Two or more races, non-Hispanic/Latino; 3% Race/ethnicity unknown; 3% transferred in. *Retention:* 49% of full-time freshmen returned.
Freshmen *Admission:* 983 applied, 838 admitted, 394 enrolled. *Average high school GPA:* 2.97. *Test scores:* ACT scores over 18: 80%; ACT scores over 24: 20%; ACT scores over 30: 1%.
Faculty *Total:* 202, 13% full-time, 24% with terminal degrees. *Student/faculty ratio:* 19:1.

Academics *Calendar:* semesters. *Degrees:* certificates, associate, and bachelor's. *Special study options:* academic remediation for entering students, adult/continuing education programs, advanced placement credit, cooperative education, distance learning, double majors, honors programs, independent study, internships, off-campus study, part-time degree program, services for LD students, summer session for credit. *ROTC:* Army (c), Air Force (c).

Computers on Campus 280 computers/terminals are available on campus for general student use. Students can access the following: campus intranet, computer help desk, free student e-mail accounts, online (class) grades, online (class) registration, online (class) schedules. Campuswide network is available. Wireless service is available via entire campus.

Student Life *Housing:* college housing not available. *Campus security:* 24-hour emergency response devices, late-night transport/escort service. *Student services:* personal/psychological counseling.

Athletics *Intercollegiate sports:* basketball M/W, cheerleading W, golf M, volleyball W. *Intramural sports:* basketball M/W, golf M, volleyball M/W.

Standardized Tests *Required for some:* SAT or ACT (for admission), ACT COMPASS. *Recommended:* SAT or ACT (for admission), ACT COMPASS.

Costs (2012–13) *Tuition:* state resident $5940 full-time, $248 per semester hour part-time; nonresident $14,281 full-time, $526 per semester hour part-time. Full-time tuition and fees vary according to course load and location. Part-time tuition and fees vary according to course load and location. *Required fees:* $176 full-time, $7 per semester hour part-time. *Payment plan:* installment. *Waivers:* employees or children of employees.

Financial Aid Of all full-time matriculated undergraduates who enrolled in 2011, 8 Federal Work-Study jobs (averaging $2200).

Applying *Options:* electronic application, early admission, deferred entrance. *Application fee:* $40. *Required for some:* high school transcript. *Application deadlines:* 8/13 (freshmen), 8/13 (transfers). *Notification:* continuous (freshmen), continuous (transfers).

Freshman Application Contact Ms. Alicia Broadus, Student Services Counselor, The University of Akron–Wayne College, Orrville, OH 44667. *Phone:* 800-221-8308 Ext. 8901. *Toll-free phone:* 800-221-8308. *Fax:* 330-684-8989. *E-mail:* wayneadmissions@uakron.edu.
Website: http://www.wayne.uakron.edu/.

University of Cincinnati

Cincinnati, Ohio

- **State-supported** university, founded 1819
- **Urban** 137-acre campus with easy access to Cincinnati
- **Endowment** $900.1 million
- **Coed** 23,096 undergraduate students, 85% full-time, 51% women, 49% men
- **Moderately difficult** entrance level, 67% of applicants were admitted

Undergraduates 19,667 full-time, 3,429 part-time. Students come from 51 states and territories; 81 other countries; 13% are from out of state; 8% Black or African American, non-Hispanic/Latino; 3% Hispanic/Latino; 3% Asian, non-Hispanic/Latino; 0.1% Native Hawaiian or other Pacific Islander, non-Hispanic/Latino; 0.2% American Indian or Alaska Native, non-Hispanic/Latino; 2% Two or more races, non-Hispanic/Latino; 4% Race/ethnicity unknown; 3% international; 6% transferred in; 19% live on campus. *Retention:* 86% of full-time freshmen returned.

Freshmen *Admission:* 17,104 applied, 11,469 admitted, 4,160 enrolled. *Average high school GPA:* 3.46. *Test scores:* SAT critical reading scores over 500: 80%; SAT math scores over 500: 84%; SAT writing scores over 500: 70%; ACT scores over 18: 100%; SAT critical reading scores over 600: 36%; SAT math scores over 600: 44%; SAT writing scores over 600: 29%; ACT scores over 24: 63%; SAT critical reading scores over 700: 8%; SAT math scores over 700: 12%; SAT writing scores over 700: 6%; ACT scores over 30: 12%.

Faculty *Total:* 1,195, 98% full-time, 75% with terminal degrees. *Student/faculty ratio:* 18:1.

Academics *Calendar:* quarters. *Degrees:* certificates, associate, bachelor's, master's, doctoral, post-master's, and postbachelor's certificates. *Special study options:* academic remediation for entering students, accelerated degree program, adult/continuing education programs, advanced placement credit, cooperative education, distance learning, double majors, English as a second language, honors programs, independent study, internships, off-campus study, part-time degree program, services for LD students, study abroad, summer session for credit. *ROTC:* Army (b), Air Force (b).

Computers on Campus Students can access the following: campus intranet, computer help desk, free student e-mail accounts, online (class) grades, online (class) registration, online (class) schedules. Campuswide network is available. 100% of college-owned or -operated housing units are wired for high-speed Internet access. Wireless service is available via entire campus.

Student Life *Housing:* on-campus residence required for freshman year. *Options:* coed, men-only, women-only, disabled students. Campus housing is university owned, leased by the school and is provided by a third party. Freshman campus housing is guaranteed. *Activities and organizations:* drama/theater group, student-run newspaper, radio station, choral group, marching band, Navigators, Criminal Justice Society, Serve Beyond Cincinnati, United Black Student Association, Engineering Tribunal, national fraternities, national sororities. *Campus security:* 24-hour emergency response devices and patrols, late-night transport/escort service, controlled dormitory access. *Student services:* health clinic, personal/psychological counseling, women's center.

Athletics Member NCAA. All Division I except football (Division I-A). *Intercollegiate sports:* baseball M(s), basketball M(s)/W(s), cheerleading M/W, cross-country running M(s)/W(s), golf M(s)/W(s), lacrosse W(s), soccer M(s)/W(s), swimming and diving M(s)/W(s), tennis W(s), track and field M(s)/W(s), volleyball W(s). *Intramural sports:* badminton M(c)/W(c), baseball M(c)/W(c), basketball M/W, bowling M(c)/W(c), crew M/W, fencing M(c)/W(c), football M(c)/W(c), golf M(c)/W(c), gymnastics W, ice hockey M(c), lacrosse M(c)/W(c), racquetball M/W, riflery M(c)/W(c), rugby M, soccer M/W, softball M/W, squash M/W, swimming and diving M/W, table tennis M(c)/W(c), tennis M(c)/W(c), track and field M(c)/W(c), ultimate Frisbee M(c)/W(c), volleyball M/W, water polo M(c)/W(c), weight lifting M, wrestling M(c)/W(c).

Standardized Tests *Required:* SAT or ACT (for admission).

Costs (2012–13) *Tuition:* state resident $9124 full-time, $381 per credit hour part-time; nonresident $24,156 full-time, $1017 per credit hour part-time. Full-time tuition and fees vary according to course load, degree level, location, program, and reciprocity agreements. Part-time tuition and fees vary according to course load, degree level, location, program, and reciprocity agreements. *Required fees:* $1660 full-time, $69 per credit hour part-time. *Room and board:* $10,170; room only: $6030. Room and board charges vary according to board plan and housing facility. *Payment plan:* installment. *Waivers:* employees or children of employees.

Financial Aid Of all full-time matriculated undergraduates who enrolled in 2012, 14,148 applied for aid, 11,739 were judged to have need, 1,090 had their need fully met. 913 Federal Work-Study jobs (averaging $3169). In 2012, 2445 non-need-based awards were made. *Average percent of need met:* 47%. *Average financial aid package:* $8650. *Average need-based loan:* $4387. *Average need-based gift aid:* $5561. *Average non-need-based aid:* $5243. *Average indebtedness upon graduation:* $30,078.

Applying *Options:* electronic application, deferred entrance. *Application fee:* $50. *Required:* essay or personal statement, high school transcript, minimum 2.7 GPA. *Required for some:* 2 letters of recommendation, audition. *Application deadlines:* 7/1 (freshmen), rolling (transfers). *Notification:* continuous (freshmen), continuous (transfers).

Freshman Application Contact Dr. Thomas Canepa EdD, Associate Vice President, Admissions, University of Cincinnati, Office of Admissions, PO Box210091, Cincinnati, OH 45221-0091. *Phone:* 513-556-1100. *Fax:* 513-556-1105. *E-mail:* admissions@uc.edu.
Website: http://www.uc.edu/.

University of Dayton

Dayton, Ohio

- **Independent Roman Catholic** university, founded 1850
- **Suburban** 373-acre campus with easy access to Cincinnati
- **Endowment** $423.4 million
- **Coed**
- **Moderately difficult** entrance level

Faculty *Student/faculty ratio:* 15:1.

Academics *Calendar:* semesters plus 2 6-week summer terms. *Degrees:* bachelor's, master's, doctoral, post-master's, and postbachelor's certificates.

Student Life *Campus security:* 24-hour emergency response devices and patrols, student patrols, late-night transport/escort service, controlled dormitory access.

Athletics Member NCAA. All Division I except football (Division I-AA).

Standardized Tests *Required:* SAT or ACT (for admission).

Costs (2012–13) *Comprehensive fee:* $43,750 includes full-time tuition ($32,000), mandatory fees ($1400), and room and board ($10,350). Full-time tuition and fees vary according to program. Part-time tuition: $1067 per credit hour. Part-time tuition and fees vary according to course load and program. *College room only:* $6450. Room and board charges vary according to board plan and housing facility. *Payment plans:* tuition prepayment, installment, deferred payment.

Financial Aid *Of all full-time matriculated undergraduates who enrolled in 2012,* 5,325 applied for aid, 4,014 were judged to have need, 1,363 had their need fully met. 1,430 Federal Work-Study jobs (averaging $2567). 3,658 state and other part-time jobs (averaging $2634). *In 2012, 2802 non-need-based awards were made. Average percent of need met:* 77. *Average financial aid package:* $23,137. *Average need-based loan:* $4938. *Average need-based gift aid:* $24,633. *Average non-need-based aid:* $11,387. *Average indebtedness upon graduation:* $40,628.

Applying *Options:* electronic application, early action, deferred entrance. *Required:* essay or personal statement, high school transcript, 1 letter of recommendation. *Required for some:* audition required for music, music therapy, music education programs. *Recommended:* interview.

Freshman Application Contact Mr. Robert Durkle, Assistant Vice President of Enrollment Management, University of Dayton, 300 College Park, Dayton, OH 45469-1300. *Phone:* 937-229-4411. *Toll-free phone:* 800-837-7433. *Fax:* 937-229-4729. *E-mail:* admission@udayton.edu. *Website:* http://www.udayton.edu/.

The University of Findlay

Findlay, Ohio

- **Independent** comprehensive, founded 1882, affiliated with Church of God
- **Urban** 390-acre campus with easy access to Toledo
- **Endowment** $24.8 million
- **Coed** 3,898 undergraduate students, 64% full-time, 64% women, 36% men
- **Moderately difficult** entrance level, 68% of applicants were admitted

Undergraduates 2,496 full-time, 1,402 part-time. Students come from 45 states and territories; 34 other countries; 19% are from out of state; 3% Black or African American, non-Hispanic/Latino; 2% Hispanic/Latino; 1% Asian, non-Hispanic/Latino; 0.3% American Indian or Alaska Native, non-Hispanic/Latino; 1% Two or more races, non-Hispanic/Latino; 5% Race/ethnicity unknown; 4% international; 5% transferred in; 40% live on campus. *Retention:* 74% of full-time freshmen returned.

Freshmen *Admission:* 2,655 applied, 1,814 admitted, 575 enrolled. *Average high school GPA:* 3.51. *Test scores:* SAT critical reading scores over 500: 72%; SAT math scores over 500: 54%; SAT writing scores over 500: 59%; ACT scores over 18: 95%; SAT critical reading scores over 600: 15%; SAT math scores over 600: 12%; SAT writing scores over 600: 7%; ACT scores over 24: 63%; SAT critical reading scores over 700: 3%; SAT math scores over 700: 2%; SAT writing scores over 700: 3%; ACT scores over 30: 4%.

Faculty *Total:* 293, 69% full-time, 56% with terminal degrees. *Student/faculty ratio:* 15:1.

Academics *Calendar:* semesters. *Degrees:* certificates, associate, bachelor's, master's, and doctoral. *Special study options:* academic remediation for entering students, accelerated degree program, adult/continuing education programs, advanced placement credit, cooperative education, distance learning, double majors, English as a second language, honors programs, independent study, internships, off-campus study, part-time degree program, services for LD students, student-designed majors, study abroad, summer session for credit. *ROTC:* Army (c), Air Force (c). *Unusual degree programs:* 3-2 nursing with Mount Carmel College of Nursing.

Computers on Campus 324 computers/terminals are available on campus for general student use. Students can access the following: campus intranet, computer help desk, free student e-mail accounts, online (class) grades, online (class) registration, online (class) schedules. Campuswide network is available. 100% of college-owned or -operated housing units are wired for high-speed Internet access. Wireless service is available via entire campus.

Student Life *Housing:* on-campus residence required through sophomore year. *Options:* coed, men-only, women-only, disabled students. Campus housing is university owned. Freshman campus housing is guaranteed. *Activities and organizations:* drama/theater group, student-run newspaper, radio and television station, choral group, marching band, Campus Program Board, Pre-Vet Club, Horse Club, Circle K, International Club, national fraternities, national sororities. *Campus security:* 24-hour emergency response devices and patrols, late-night transport/escort service, controlled dormitory access. *Student services:* health clinic, personal/psychological counseling, women's center.

Athletics Member NCAA. All Division II. *Intercollegiate sports:* baseball M(s), basketball M(s)/W(s), cross-country running M(s)/W(s), equestrian sports W, football M(s), golf M(s)/W(s), lacrosse W(s), soccer M(s)/W(s), softball W(s), swimming and diving M(s)/W(s), tennis M(s)/W(s), track and field M(s)/W(s), volleyball W(s), wrestling M(s). *Intramural sports:* basketball M/W, bowling M/W, cheerleading M/W, equestrian sports M(c)/W(c), football M/W, golf M/W, racquetball M/W, soccer M/W, softball W, tennis M/W, volleyball M/W.

Standardized Tests *Required:* SAT or ACT (for admission).

Costs (2013–14) *Comprehensive fee:* $39,056 includes full-time tuition ($28,894), mandatory fees ($904), and room and board ($9258). Part-time tuition: $641 per semester hour. Part-time tuition and fees vary according to course load and program. *Required fees:* $387 per term part-time. *College*

room only: $4620. *Payment plan:* installment. *Waivers:* children of alumni, senior citizens, and employees or children of employees.

Financial Aid Of all full-time matriculated undergraduates who enrolled in 2011, 2,235 applied for aid, 1,970 were judged to have need, 31 had their need fully met. In 2011, 273 non-need-based awards were made. *Average percent of need met:* 57%. *Average financial aid package:* $20,859. *Average need-based loan:* $5055. *Average need-based gift aid:* $2635. *Average non-need-based aid:* $11,850. *Average indebtedness upon graduation:* $38,022.

Applying *Options:* electronic application, deferred entrance. *Required:* essay or personal statement, high school transcript, minimum 2.3 GPA, . *Required for some:* interview. *Application deadlines:* rolling (freshmen), rolling (transfers). *Notification:* continuous (freshmen), continuous (transfers).

Freshman Application Contact Dr. Donna Gruber, Director of Undergraduate Admissions, The University of Findlay, 1000 North Main Street, Findlay, OH 45840-3653. *Phone:* 419-434-4540. *Toll-free phone:* 800-548-0932. *Fax:* 419-434-4898. *E-mail:* admissions@findlay.edu. *Website:* http://www.findlay.edu/.

See previous page for display ad and page 1562 for the College Close-Up.

University of Mount Union

Alliance, Ohio

- **Independent United Methodist** comprehensive, founded 1846
- **Suburban** 122-acre campus with easy access to Cleveland
- **Endowment** $133.2 million
- **Coed** 2,175 undergraduate students, 99% full-time, 49% women, 51% men
- **Moderately difficult** entrance level, 72% of applicants were admitted

Undergraduates 2,148 full-time, 27 part-time. Students come from 31 states and territories; 21 other countries; 13% are from out of state; 6% Black or African American, non-Hispanic/Latino; 1% Hispanic/Latino; 0.5% Asian, non-Hispanic/Latino; 0.1% American Indian or Alaska Native, non-Hispanic/Latino; 3% Two or more races, non-Hispanic/Latino; 2% Race/ethnicity unknown; 3% international; 2% transferred in; 76% live on campus. *Retention:* 72% of full-time freshmen returned.

Freshmen *Admission:* 2,774 applied, 2,005 admitted, 647 enrolled. *Average high school GPA:* 3.19. *Test scores:* SAT critical reading scores over 500: 51%; SAT math scores over 500: 69%; ACT scores over 18: 94%; SAT critical reading scores over 600: 16%; SAT math scores over 600: 24%; ACT scores over 24: 35%; SAT critical reading scores over 700: 3%; SAT math scores over 700: 2%; ACT scores over 30: 3%.

Faculty *Total:* 236, 54% full-time, 57% with terminal degrees. *Student/faculty ratio:* 14:1.

Academics *Calendar:* semesters. *Degrees:* bachelor's and master's. *Special study options:* accelerated degree program, adult/continuing education programs, advanced placement credit, cooperative education, distance learning, double majors, English as a second language, honors programs, independent study, internships, off-campus study, part-time degree program, services for LD students, student-designed majors, study abroad, summer session for credit. *ROTC:* Army (b), Air Force (c).

Computers on Campus 265 computers/terminals and 6,000 ports are available on campus for general student use. Students can access the following: campus intranet, computer help desk, free student e-mail accounts, online (class) grades, online (class) registration, online (class) schedules. Campus-wide network is available. 100% of college-owned or -operated housing units are wired for high-speed Internet access. Wireless service is available via entire campus.

Student Life *Housing:* on-campus residence required through sophomore year. *Options:* coed, men-only, women-only, disabled students. Campus housing is university owned. Freshman campus housing is guaranteed. *Activities and organizations:* drama/theater group, student-run newspaper, radio and television station, choral group, marching band, Alpha Phi Omega, Student Senate, FCA Fellowship of Christian Athletes, Black Student Union, Raider Programming Board, national fraternities, national sororities. *Campus security:* 24-hour emergency response devices and patrols, late-night transport/escort service, controlled dormitory access, 24-hour locked residence hall entrances, outside phones. *Student services:* health clinic, personal/psychological counseling.

Athletics Member NCAA. All Division III. *Intercollegiate sports:* baseball M, basketball M/W, cheerleading W, cross-country running M/W, football M, golf M/W, soccer M/W, softball W, swimming and diving M/W, tennis M/W, track and field M/W, volleyball W, wrestling M. *Intramural sports:* archery M/W, badminton M/W, basketball M/W, bowling M/W, football M, golf M/W, gymnastics M/W, lacrosse M/W, racquetball M/W, soccer M/W, softball M/W, swimming and diving M/W, tennis M/W, track and field M/W, volleyball M/W, weight lifting M/W.

Standardized Tests *Required:* SAT or ACT (for admission).

Costs (2012–13) *Comprehensive fee:* $35,130 includes full-time tuition ($26,350), mandatory fees ($300), and room and board ($8480). Full-time tuition and fees vary according to course load and degree level. Part-time tuition: $1110 per credit hour. Part-time tuition and fees vary according to course load. *Room and board:* Room and board charges vary according to board plan and housing facility. *Payment plans:* tuition prepayment, installment. *Waivers:* children of alumni, senior citizens, and employees or children of employees.

Financial Aid Of all full-time matriculated undergraduates who enrolled in 2012, 1,911 applied for aid, 1,764 were judged to have need, 189 had their need fully met. 1,440 Federal Work-Study jobs (averaging $1304). 264 state and other part-time jobs (averaging $1568). In 2012, 352 non-need-based awards were made. *Average percent of need met:* 76%. *Average financial aid package:* $20,548. *Average need-based loan:* $5547. *Average need-based gift aid:* $14,863. *Average non-need-based aid:* $9625. *Average indebtedness upon graduation:* $33,568.

Applying *Options:* electronic application, early admission, deferred entrance. *Required:* essay or personal statement, high school transcript, minimum 2.0 GPA, 1 letter of recommendation. *Recommended:* interview. *Application deadlines:* rolling (freshmen), rolling (transfers). *Notification:* continuous (freshmen), continuous (transfers).

Freshman Application Contact Ms. Grace Chalker, Director of Admissions, University of Mount Union, 1972 Clark Avenue, Alliance, OH 44601. *Phone:* 330-823-2587. *Toll-free phone:* 800-334-6682 (in-state); 800-992-6682 (out-of-state). *Fax:* 330-823-5097. *E-mail:* admission@mountunion.edu. *Website:* http://www.mountunion.edu/.

University of Northwestern Ohio

Lima, Ohio

Freshman Application Contact Mr. Dan Klopp, Vice President for Enrollment Management, University of Northwestern Ohio, 1441 North Cable Road, Lima, OH 45805-1498. *Phone:* 419-227-3141. *Fax:* 419-229-6926. *E-mail:* klopp_d@unoh.edu. *Website:* http://www.unoh.edu/.

University of Phoenix–Cincinnati Campus

West Chester, Ohio

Freshman Application Contact Marc Booker, Sr. Director, Office of Admissions and Evaluation, University of Phoenix–Cincinnati Campus, 4035 South Riverpoint Parkway, Mail Stop CF-L101, Phoenix, AZ 85040. *Phone:* 602-557-4609. *Toll-free phone:* 866-766-0766. *Fax:* 480-643-1156. *Website:* http://www.phoenix.edu/.

University of Phoenix–Cleveland Campus

Independence, Ohio

Freshman Application Contact Marc Booker, Sr. Director, Office of Admissions and Evaluation, University of Phoenix–Cleveland Campus, 4035 South Riverpoint Parkway, Mail Stop CF-L101, Phoenix, AZ 85040. *Phone:* 602-557-4609. *Toll-free phone:* 866-766-0766. *Fax:* 480-643-1156. *Website:* http://www.phoenix.edu/.

University of Phoenix–Columbus Ohio Campus

Columbus, Ohio

Freshman Application Contact Marc Booker, Sr. Director, Office of Admissions and Evaluation, University of Phoenix–Columbus Ohio Campus, 4035 South Riverpoint Parkway, Mall Stop CF-L101, Phoenix, AZ 85040. *Phone:* 602-557-4609. *Toll-free phone:* 866-766-0766. *Fax:* 480-643-1156. *Website:* http://www.phoenix.edu/.

University of Rio Grande

Rio Grande, Ohio

- **Independent** comprehensive, founded 1876
- **Rural** 170-acre campus
- **Endowment** $18.1 million
- **Coed**
- **Noncompetitive** entrance level

Faculty *Student/faculty ratio:* 15:1.

Academics *Calendar:* semesters. *Degrees:* certificates, associate, bachelor's, and master's.

Student Life *Campus security:* 24-hour emergency response devices and patrols, late-night transport/escort service, controlled dormitory access.

Athletics Member NAIA.

Standardized Tests *Recommended:* ACT (for admission).

Financial Aid *Of all full-time matriculated undergraduates who enrolled in 2011,* 1,129 applied for aid, 1,124 were judged to have need, 808 had their need fully met. *In 2011,* 83 non-need-based awards were made. *Average percent of need met:* 73. *Average financial aid package:* $6648. *Average need-based loan:* $4065. *Average need-based gift aid:* $3423. *Average non-need-based aid:* $3749. *Average indebtedness upon graduation:* $22,633.

Applying *Options:* electronic application. *Application fee:* $25. *Required:* high school transcript, medical history.

Freshman Application Contact Ms. Alicia Martin, Director of Admissions, University of Rio Grande, PO Box 500, Rio Grande, OH 45674. *Phone:* 740-245-7208. *Toll-free phone:* 800-282-7201. *Fax:* 740-245-7260. *E-mail:* admissions@rio.edu.

Website: http://www.rio.edu/.

The University of Toledo

Toledo, Ohio

- **State-supported** university, founded 1872
- **Urban** 813-acre campus with easy access to Detroit
- **Endowment** $47.0 million
- **Coed** 16,877 undergraduate students, 80% full-time, 49% women, 51% men
- **Noncompetitive** entrance level, 95% of applicants were admitted

Undergraduates 13,538 full-time, 3,339 part-time. Students come from 55 states and territories; 90 other countries; 15% are from out of state; 15% Black or African American, non-Hispanic/Latino; 4% Hispanic/Latino; 2% Asian, non-Hispanic/Latino; 0.1% Native Hawaiian or other Pacific Islander, non-Hispanic/Latino; 0.2% American Indian or Alaska Native, non-Hispanic/Latino; 2% Two or more races, non-Hispanic/Latino; 3% Race/ethnicity unknown; 4% international; 6% transferred in; 15% live on campus. *Retention:* 62% of full-time freshmen returned.

Freshmen *Admission:* 11,040 applied, 10,465 admitted, 3,431 enrolled. *Average high school GPA:* 3.15. *Test scores:* ACT scores over 18: 81%; ACT scores over 24: 35%; ACT scores over 30: 4%.

Faculty *Total:* 1,249, 72% full-time, 54% with terminal degrees. *Student/faculty ratio:* 19:1.

Academics *Calendar:* semesters. *Degrees:* certificates, bachelor's, master's, doctoral, post-master's, and postbachelor's certificates. *Special study options:* academic remediation for entering students, accelerated degree program, adult/continuing education programs, advanced placement credit, cooperative education, distance learning, double majors, English as a second language, freshman honors college, honors programs, independent study, internships, off-campus study, part-time degree program, services for LD students, student-designed majors, study abroad, summer session for credit. *ROTC:* Army (b), Air Force (c). *Unusual degree programs:* 3-2 BS Environmental Sciences—Masters in Public Health (MPH).

Computers on Campus 5,000 computers/terminals and 7,450 ports are available on campus for general student use. Students can access the following: campus intranet, computer help desk, free student e-mail accounts, online (class) grades, online (class) registration, online (class) schedules, online transcripts, student account. Campuswide network is available. 100% of college-owned or -operated housing units are wired for high-speed Internet access. Wireless service is available via entire campus.

Student Life *Housing:* on-campus residence required for freshman year. *Options:* coed, disabled students. Campus housing is university owned. *Activities and organizations:* drama/theater group, student-run newspaper, radio and television station, choral group, marching band, student government, University YMCA, Newman Club, International Student Association, Campus Activities and Programming, national fraternities, national sororities. *Campus*

security: 24-hour emergency response devices and patrols, student patrols, late-night transport/escort service, controlled dormitory access, bicycle patrols by security staff, crime prevention officer. *Student services:* health clinic, personal/psychological counseling, women's center, legal services.

Athletics Member NCAA. All Division I except football (Division I-A). *Intercollegiate sports:* baseball M(s), basketball M(s)/W(s), cross-country running M(s)/W(s), golf M(s)/W(s), soccer W(s), softball W(s), swimming and diving W(s), tennis M(s)/W(s), track and field W(s), volleyball W(s). *Intramural sports:* badminton M/W, basketball M/W, bowling M/W, cheerleading W, crew M(c)/W(c), fencing M(c)/W(c), football M/W, golf M/W, lacrosse M/W, racquetball M/W, sailing M(c)/W(c), skiing (cross-country) M(c)/W(c), skiing (downhill) M(c)/W(c), soccer M(c)/W(c), softball M/W, swimming and diving M/W, table tennis M/W, tennis M/W, track and field M/W, volleyball M/W, water polo M/W, weight lifting M/W, wrestling M.

Standardized Tests *Required:* SAT or ACT (for admission).

Costs (2012–13) *Tuition:* state resident $7864 full-time, $328 per credit hour part-time; nonresident $16,984 full-time, $708 per credit hour part-time. Full-time tuition and fees vary according to course load, program, and reciprocity agreements. Part-time tuition and fees vary according to course load, program, and reciprocity agreements. *Required fees:* $1411 full-time, $58 per credit hour part-time. *Room and board:* $9738; room only: $6338. Room and board charges vary according to board plan and housing facility. *Payment plan:* installment. *Waivers:* employees or children of employees.

Financial Aid Of all full-time matriculated undergraduates who enrolled in 2012, 11,435 applied for aid, 9,694 were judged to have need, 1,180 had their need fully met. 273 Federal Work-Study jobs (averaging $1748). In 2012, 2546 non-need-based awards were made. *Average percent of need met:* 55%. *Average financial aid package:* $10,265. *Average need-based loan:* $4220. *Average need-based gift aid:* $7701. *Average non-need-based aid:* $5922. *Average indebtedness upon graduation:* $30,421.

Applying *Options:* electronic application, deferred entrance. *Application fee:* $40. *Required:* high school transcript. *Required for some:* minimum 2.0 GPA, CORE high school curriculum. *Application deadlines:* rolling (freshmen), rolling (transfers). *Notification:* continuous (freshmen), continuous (transfers).

Freshman Application Contact Billy L Pierce, Director of Undergraduate Admissions, The University of Toledo, 2801 West Bancroft, Toledo, OH 43606-3390. *Phone:* 419-530-5445. *Toll-free phone:* 800-5TOLEDO. *Fax:* 419-530-5713. *E-mail:* william.pierce@utoledo.edu.

Website: http://www.utoledo.edu/.

Urbana University

Urbana, Ohio

Freshman Application Contact Ms. Paula Brown, Director of Admissions, Urbana University, 579 College Way, Urbana, OH 43078. *Phone:* 937-484-1356. *Toll-free phone:* 800-7-URBANA. *Fax:* 937-652-6871. *E-mail:* admiss@urbana.edu.

Website: http://www.urbana.edu/.

Ursuline College

Pepper Pike, Ohio

- **Independent Roman Catholic** comprehensive, founded 1871
- **Suburban** 112-acre campus with easy access to Cleveland
- **Endowment** $33.0 million
- **Coed, primarily women** 879 undergraduate students, 65% full-time, 91% women, 9% men
- **Minimally difficult** entrance level, 58% of applicants were admitted

Undergraduates 573 full-time, 306 part-time. Students come from 15 states and territories; 6 other countries; 5% are from out of state; 30% Black or African American, non-Hispanic/Latino; 2% Hispanic/Latino; 0.6% Asian, non-Hispanic/Latino; 0.3% American Indian or Alaska Native, non-Hispanic/Latino; 3% Two or more races, non-Hispanic/Latino; 0.6% Race/ethnicity unknown; 2% international; 13% transferred in; 17% live on campus. *Retention:* 71% of full-time freshmen returned.

Freshmen *Admission:* 470 applied, 273 admitted, 90 enrolled. *Average high school GPA:* 3.19. *Test scores:* SAT critical reading scores over 500: 25%; SAT math scores over 500: 21%; SAT writing scores over 500: 29%; ACT scores over 18: 82%; ACT scores over 24: 18%; ACT scores over 30: 4%.

Faculty *Total:* 202, 35% full-time, 32% with terminal degrees. *Student/faculty ratio:* 11:1.

Academics *Calendar:* semesters. *Degrees:* certificates, bachelor's, master's, doctoral, post-master's, and postbachelor's certificates (applications from men are also accepted). *Special study options:* academic remediation for entering students, accelerated degree program, adult/continuing education programs, advanced placement credit, cooperative education, distance learning, double majors, independent study, internships, off-campus study, part-time degree program, services for LD students, student-designed majors, summer session for credit. *ROTC:* Army (c). *Unusual degree programs:* 3-2 pharmacy with University of Toledo.

Computers on Campus 72 computers/terminals are available on campus for general student use. Students can access the following: campus intranet, computer help desk, free student e-mail accounts, online (class) grades, online (class) registration, online (class) schedules. Campuswide network is available. 100% of college-owned or -operated housing units are wired for high-speed Internet access. Wireless service is available via classrooms, computer centers, computer labs, libraries.

Student Life *Housing options:* coed, women-only. Campus housing is university owned. *Activities and organizations:* drama/theater group, choral group, Student Government Association, Student Nurses of Ursuline College, Fashion Focus, Students United for Black Awareness, Drama Club. *Campus security:* 24-hour emergency response devices and patrols, late-night transport/escort service, controlled dormitory access. *Student services:* personal/psychological counseling.

Athletics Member NCAA. All Division II. *Intercollegiate sports:* basketball W(s), bowling W(s), cross-country running W(s), golf W(s), lacrosse W(s), soccer W(s), softball W(s), swimming and diving W(s), tennis W(s), track and field W(s), volleyball W(s).

Standardized Tests *Required:* SAT or ACT (for admission).

Costs (2013–14) *Comprehensive fee:* \$35,660 includes full-time tuition (\$26,490), mandatory fees (\$270), and room and board (\$8900). Full-time tuition and fees vary according to location. Part-time tuition: \$546 per credit. Part-time tuition and fees vary according to location. *Required fees:* \$90 per term part-time. *College room only:* \$4546. Room and board charges vary according to board plan and housing facility. *Payment plan:* installment. *Waivers:* employees or children of employees.

Financial Aid Of all full-time matriculated undergraduates who enrolled in 2011, 663 applied for aid, 635 were judged to have need, 40 had their need fully met. In 2011, 37 non-need-based awards were made. *Average percent of need met:* 63%. *Average financial aid package:* \$15,930. *Average need-based loan:* \$5366. *Average need-based gift aid:* \$12,092. *Average non-need-based aid:* \$5611. *Average indebtedness upon graduation:* \$25,963.

Applying *Options:* electronic application, deferred entrance. *Application fee:* \$25. *Required:* essay or personal statement, high school transcript, 1 letter of recommendation. *Recommended:* minimum 2.5 GPA, interview. *Application*

deadlines: 2/1 (freshmen), 2/1 (out-of-state freshmen), rolling (transfers). *Notification:* continuous (freshmen), continuous (out-of-state freshmen), continuous (transfers).

Freshman Application Contact Ursuline College, 2550 Lander Road, Pepper Pike, OH 44124-4398. *Phone:* 440-449-4203. *Toll-free phone:* 888-URSULINE.
Website: http://www.ursuline.edu/.

Walsh University
North Canton, Ohio

- **Independent Roman Catholic** comprehensive, founded 1958
- **Small-town** 134-acre campus with easy access to Cleveland
- **Endowment** \$13.3 million
- **Coed** 2,371 undergraduate students, 81% full-time, 63% women, 37% men
- **Moderately difficult** entrance level, 78% of applicants were admitted

Undergraduates 1,922 full-time, 449 part-time. Students come from 20 states and territories; 20 other countries; 3% are from out of state; 5% Black or African American, non-Hispanic/Latino; 2% Hispanic/Latino; 0.5% Asian, non-Hispanic/Latino; 0.3% American Indian or Alaska Native, non-Hispanic/Latino; 2% Two or more races, non-Hispanic/Latino; 10% Race/ethnicity unknown; 2% international; 8% transferred in; 53% live on campus. *Retention:* 74% of full-time freshmen returned.

Freshmen *Admission:* 1,621 applied, 1,259 admitted, 494 enrolled. *Average high school GPA:* 3.35. *Test scores:* SAT critical reading scores over 500: 57%; SAT math scores over 500: 64%; ACT scores over 18: 97%; SAT critical reading scores over 600: 14%; SAT math scores over 600: 15%; ACT scores over 24: 36%; SAT critical reading scores over 700: 4%; SAT math scores over 700: 3%; ACT scores over 30: 2%.

Faculty *Total:* 254, 50% full-time, 41% with terminal degrees. *Student/faculty ratio:* 14:1.

Academics *Calendar:* semesters. *Degrees:* associate, bachelor's, master's, and doctoral. *Special study options:* academic remediation for entering students, accelerated degree program, adult/continuing education programs, advanced placement credit, distance learning, double majors, English as a second language, external degree program, honors programs, independent study, internships, off-campus study, part-time degree program, services for LD students,

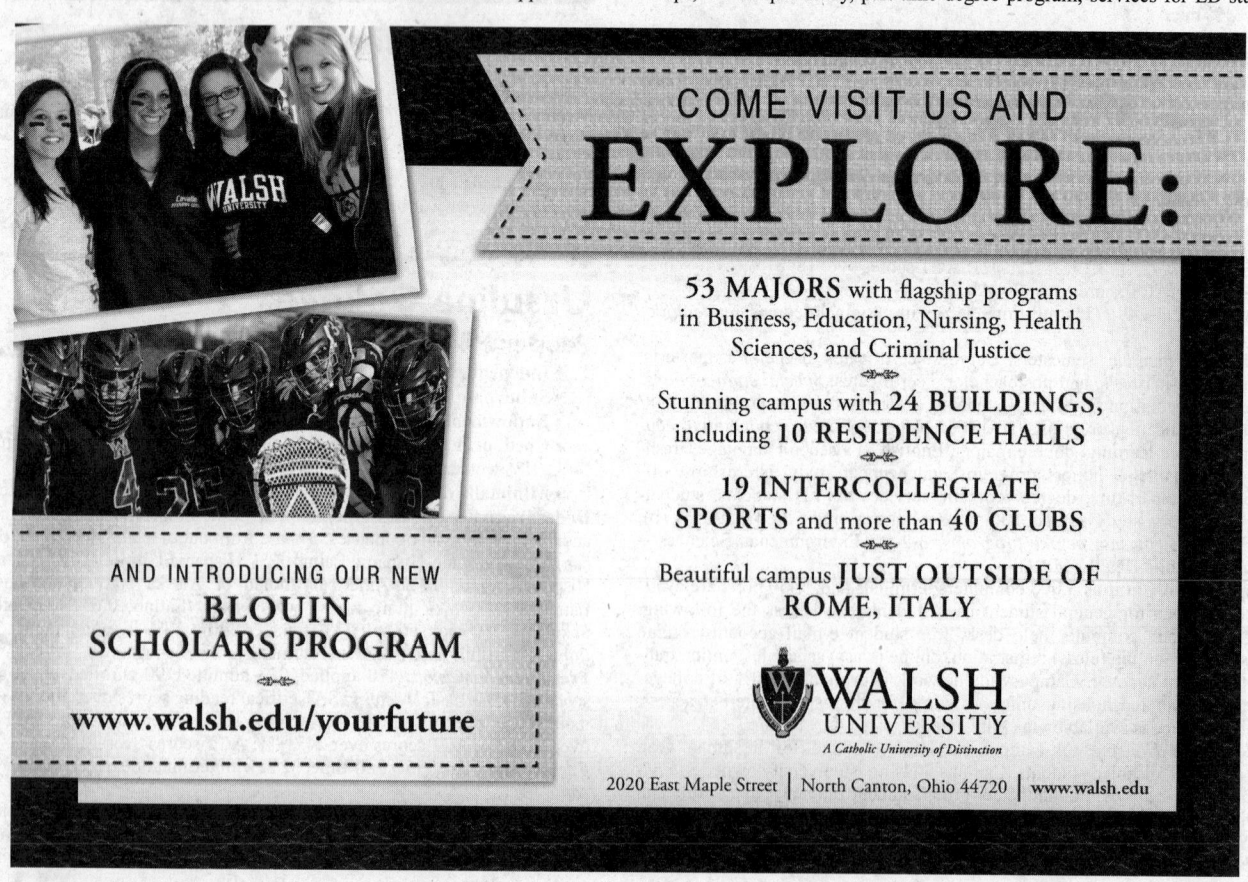

study abroad, summer session for credit. *Unusual degree programs:* 3-2 behavioral science/counseling; biology/physical therapy, theology.

Computers on Campus 371 computers/terminals and 1,050 ports are available on campus for general student use. Students can access the following: campus intranet, computer help desk, free student e-mail accounts, online (class) grades, online (class) registration, online (class) schedules. Campuswide network is available. 100% of college-owned or -operated housing units are wired for high-speed Internet access. Wireless service is available via entire campus.

Student Life *Housing:* on-campus residence required through senior year. *Options:* coed, men-only, women-only, disabled students. Campus housing is university owned. Freshman campus housing is guaranteed. *Activities and organizations:* drama/theater group, student-run newspaper, radio station, choral group, marching band, student government, University Programming Board, Business and Communication Club, Behavioral Science Club, Education Club. *Campus security:* 24-hour emergency response devices and patrols, late-night transport/escort service, controlled dormitory access. *Student services:* health clinic, personal/psychological counseling.

Athletics Member NCAA, NAIA. All NCAA Division II. *Intercollegiate sports:* baseball M(s), basketball M(s)/W(s), cheerleading W(c), cross-country running M(s)/W(s), football M(s), golf M(s)/W(s), lacrosse M(s)/W(s), soccer M(s)/W(s), softball W(s), tennis M(s)/W(s), track and field M(s)/W(s), volleyball W(s). *Intramural sports:* basketball M/W, bowling M/W, football M, golf M/W, skiing (downhill) M(c)/W(c), soccer M/W, table tennis M/W, tennis M/W, ultimate Frisbee M(c)/W(c), volleyball M/W.

Standardized Tests *Required:* SAT or ACT (for admission).

Costs (2012–13) *Comprehensive fee:* $33,630 includes full-time tuition ($23,550), mandatory fees ($1140), and room and board ($8940). Full-time tuition and fees vary according to location. Part-time tuition: $785 per credit hour. Part-time tuition and fees vary according to course load and location. *Required fees:* $38 per credit hour part-time. *College room only:* $4730. Room and board charges vary according to board plan and housing facility. *Payment plan:* installment. *Waivers:* children of alumni, senior citizens, and employees or children of employees.

Financial Aid Of all full-time matriculated undergraduates who enrolled in 2010, 1,726 applied for aid, 1,661 were judged to have need, 798 had their need fully met. In 2010, 180 non-need-based awards were made. *Average percent of need met:* 71%. *Average financial aid package:* $18,133. *Average need-based loan:* $4850. *Average need-based gift aid:* $6844. *Average non-need-based aid:* $9372. *Average indebtedness upon graduation:* $24,753.

Applying *Options:* electronic application, early admission, deferred entrance. *Application fee:* $25. *Required:* high school transcript, minimum 2.4 GPA. *Required for some:* essay or personal statement, minimum 3.0 GPA, 2 letters of recommendation. *Recommended:* interview. *Application deadlines:* rolling (freshmen), rolling (out-of-state freshmen), rolling (transfers). *Notification:* continuous (freshmen), continuous (out-of-state freshmen), continuous (transfers).

Freshman Application Contact Mr. Brett Freshour, Vice President for Enrollment Management, Walsh University, 2020 East Maple, North Canton, OH 44720. *Phone:* 330-490-7171. *Toll-free phone:* 800-362-9846 (in-state); 800-362-8846 (out-of-state). *Fax:* 330-490-7165. *E-mail:* admissions@walsh.edu.
Website: http://www.walsh.edu/.

See previous page for display ad and page 1628 for the College Close-Up.

Wilberforce University

Wilberforce, Ohio

- **Independent** comprehensive, founded 1856, affiliated with African Methodist Episcopal Church
- **Rural** 125-acre campus with easy access to Dayton
- **Coed** 534 undergraduate students
- **Minimally difficult** entrance level, 43% of applicants were admitted

Undergraduates Students come from 14 states and territories; 3 other countries; 60% are from out of state; 95% Black or African American, non-Hispanic/Latino; 0.6% Hispanic/Latino; 0.6% American Indian or Alaska Native, non-Hispanic/Latino; 3% Race/ethnicity unknown.

Freshmen *Admission:* 2,321 applied, 987 admitted.

Academics *Calendar:* semesters. *Degrees:* bachelor's and master's. *Special study options:* academic remediation for entering students, adult/continuing education programs, advanced placement credit, cooperative education, distance learning, double majors, external degree program, freshman honors college, honors programs, independent study, internships, off-campus study, study abroad. *ROTC:* Army (c), Air Force (c).

Computers on Campus Students can access the following: free student e-mail accounts, online (class) grades, online (class) registration, online (class) sched-

ules. Campuswide network is available. Wireless service is available via entire campus.

Student Life *Housing:* on-campus residence required through junior year. *Options:* coed, men-only, women-only. Campus housing is university owned. Freshman campus housing is guaranteed. *Activities and organizations:* drama/theater group, student-run newspaper, radio station, choral group, national fraternities, national sororities. *Campus security:* 24-hour emergency response devices and patrols, controlled dormitory access. *Student services:* health clinic, personal/psychological counseling.

Athletics Member NAIA. *Intercollegiate sports:* basketball M/W, cross-country running M/W. *Intramural sports:* basketball M/W, soccer M/W, softball M/W, tennis M/W, volleyball M/W.

Standardized Tests *Required:* SAT or ACT (for admission).

Costs (2013–14) *Comprehensive fee:* $20,946 includes full-time tuition ($14,330) and room and board ($6616). Full-time tuition and fees vary according to course load, location, and program. Part-time tuition: $500 per credit hour. Part-time tuition and fees vary according to course load, location, and program. *College room only:* $3746. *Payment plans:* installment, deferred payment.

Financial Aid *Financial aid deadline:* 6/1.

Applying *Options:* electronic application, early admission, early decision, deferred entrance. *Application fee:* $25. *Required:* essay or personal statement, high school transcript, minimum 2.5 GPA, 2 letters of recommendation. *Application deadlines:* 7/1 (freshmen), 7/1 (transfers). *Notification:* continuous until 8/1 (freshmen), continuous until 8/1 (transfers).

Freshman Application Contact Mr. John Johnson, Director, Office of Admissions, Wilberforce University, 1055 N. Bickett Road, Wolfe Administration, Wilberforce, OH 45384. *Phone:* 937-708-5720. *Toll-free phone:* 800-367-8568. *E-mail:* jjohnson@wilberforce.edu. *Website:* http://www.wilberforce.edu/.

Wilmington College

Wilmington, Ohio

- **Independent Friends** comprehensive, founded 1870
- **Small-town** campus
- **Coed**
- **Moderately difficult** entrance level

Faculty *Student/faculty ratio:* 14:1.

Academics *Calendar:* semesters. *Degrees:* bachelor's and master's.

Student Life *Campus security:* 24-hour emergency response devices and patrols, late-night transport/escort service, controlled dormitory access.

Athletics Member NCAA. All Division III.

Standardized Tests *Recommended:* SAT or ACT (for admission).

Financial Aid *Of all full-time matriculated undergraduates who enrolled in 2008,* 1,096 applied for aid, 1,021 were judged to have need, 306 had their need fully met. *In 2008,* 138 non-need-based awards were made. *Average percent of need met:* 81. *Average financial aid package:* $21,500. *Average need-based loan:* $6000. *Average need-based gift aid:* $14,300. *Average non-need-based aid:* $7300.

Applying *Options:* deferred entrance. *Required:* high school transcript. *Recommended:* minimum 2.5 GPA, 1 letter of recommendation, interview.

Freshman Application Contact Ms. Tina Garland, Director of Admission and Financial Aid, Wilmington College, 1870 Quaker Way, Wilmington, OH 45177. *Phone:* 937-382-6661 Ext. 426. *Toll-free phone:* 800-341-9318. *Fax:* 937-383-8542. *E-mail:* admissions@wilmington.edu. *Website:* http://www.wilmington.edu/.

Wittenberg University

Springfield, Ohio

- **Independent** comprehensive, founded 1845, affiliated with Evangelical Lutheran Church
- **Suburban** 114-acre campus with easy access to Columbus, Dayton
- **Endowment** $90.9 million
- **Coed** 1,881 undergraduate students, 95% full-time, 55% women, 45% men
- **Moderately difficult** entrance level, 91% of applicants were admitted

Undergraduates 1,784 full-time, 97 part-time. Students come from 43 states and territories; 22 other countries; 27% are from out of state; 7% Black or African American, non-Hispanic/Latino; 3% Hispanic/Latino; 0.8% Asian, non-Hispanic/Latino; 0.2% American Indian or Alaska Native, non-Hispanic/Latino; 3% Two or more races, non-Hispanic/Latino; 3% Race/ethnicity

unknown; 2% international; 2% transferred in; 83% live on campus. *Retention:* 78% of full-time freshmen returned.

Freshmen *Admission:* 4,887 applied, 4,455 admitted, 489 enrolled. *Average high school GPA:* 3.42. *Test scores:* SAT critical reading scores over 500: 78%; SAT math scores over 500: 77%; ACT scores over 18: 99%; SAT critical reading scores over 600: 35%; SAT math scores over 600: 41%; ACT scores over 24: 71%; SAT critical reading scores over 700: 6%; SAT math scores over 700: 5%; ACT scores over 30: 16%.

Faculty *Total:* 194, 73% full-time, 80% with terminal degrees. *Student/faculty ratio:* 11:1.

Academics *Calendar:* semesters. *Degrees:* bachelor's and master's. *Special study options:* academic remediation for entering students, adult/continuing education programs, advanced placement credit, cooperative education, double majors, English as a second language, freshman honors college, honors programs, independent study, internships, off-campus study, part-time degree program, student-designed majors, study abroad, summer session for credit. *ROTC:* Army (c), Air Force (c). *Unusual degree programs:* 3-2 engineering with Georgia Institute of Technology, Washington University in St. Louis, Case Western Reserve University; forestry with Duke University; nursing with Case Western Reserve University, Johns Hopkins University; Occupational therapy with Washington University in St. Louis.

Computers on Campus 900 computers/terminals and 1,200 ports are available on campus for general student use. Students can access the following: computer help desk, free student e-mail accounts, online (class) grades, online (class) registration, online (class) schedules. Campuswide network is available. Wireless service is available via entire campus.

Student Life *Housing:* on-campus residence required through sophomore year. *Options:* coed, women-only. Campus housing is university owned, leased by the school and is provided by a third party. Freshman campus housing is guaranteed. *Activities and organizations:* drama/theater group, student-run newspaper, radio station, choral group, Student Senate, Union Board, Choirs, Weaver Chapel Association, national fraternities, national sororities. *Campus security:* 24-hour emergency response devices and patrols, student patrols, late-night transport/escort service, controlled dormitory access, crime prevention programs. *Student services:* health clinic, personal/psychological counseling, women's center.

Athletics Member NCAA. All Division III. *Intercollegiate sports:* baseball M, basketball M/W, crew M(c)/W(c), cross-country running M/W, field hockey W, football M, golf M/W, lacrosse M/W, rugby M(c)/W(c), soccer M/W, softball W, swimming and diving M/W, tennis M/W, track and field M/W, volleyball M(c)/W. *Intramural sports:* basketball M/W, football M, golf M/W, sailing M/W, soccer M/W, softball M/W, swimming and diving M/W, tennis M/W, track and field M/W, volleyball M/W.

Standardized Tests *Recommended:* test scores are optional.

Costs (2013–14) *Comprehensive fee:* $47,766 includes full-time tuition ($37,230), mandatory fees ($800), and room and board ($9736). Part-time tuition: $1241 per credit. Part-time tuition and fees vary according to course load. *College room only:* $5056. Room and board charges vary according to board plan and housing facility. *Payment plan:* installment. *Waivers:* minority students, children of alumni, adult students, senior citizens, and employees or children of employees.

Financial Aid Of all full-time matriculated undergraduates who enrolled in 2012, 1,581 applied for aid, 1,408 were judged to have need, 30 had their need fully met. In 2012, 358 non-need-based awards were made. *Average percent of need met:* 80%. *Average financial aid package:* $30,154. *Average need-based loan:* $4521. *Average need-based gift aid:* $24,927. *Average non-need-based aid:* $15,668. *Average indebtedness upon graduation:* $31,712.

Applying *Options:* electronic application, early admission, early decision, early action, deferred entrance. *Application fee:* $40. *Required:* essay or personal statement, high school transcript, interview. *Application deadlines:* rolling (transfers), 12/1 (early action). *Early decision deadline:* 11/15. *Notification:* continuous (freshmen), continuous (transfers), 12/15 (early decision), 1/1 (early action).

Freshman Application Contact Ms. Karen Hunt, Director of Admission, Wittenberg University, PO Box 720, Springfield, OH 45501-0720. *Phone:* 877-206-0332 Ext. 6377. *Toll-free phone:* 800-677-7558 Ext. 6314. *Fax:* 937-327-6379. *E-mail:* admission@wittenberg.edu. *Website:* http://www.wittenberg.edu/.

Wright State University
Dayton, Ohio

- **State-supported** university, founded 1964, part of University System of Ohio
- **Suburban** 557-acre campus with easy access to Columbus
- **Endowment** $77.0 million
- **Coed** 13,143 undergraduate students, 79% full-time, 52% women, 48% men
- **Minimally difficult** entrance level, 69% of applicants were admitted

Undergraduates 10,324 full-time, 2,819 part-time. Students come from 51 states and territories; 40 other countries; 3% are from out of state; 13% Black or African American, non-Hispanic/Latino; 3% Hispanic/Latino; 2% Asian, non-Hispanic/Latino; 0.1% Native Hawaiian or other Pacific Islander, non-Hispanic/Latino; 0.2% American Indian or Alaska Native, non-Hispanic/Latino; 3% Two or more races, non-Hispanic/Latino; 0.6% Race/ethnicity unknown; 5% international; 8% transferred in; 19% live on campus. *Retention:* 56% of full-time freshmen returned.

Freshmen *Admission:* 8,112 applied, 5,569 admitted, 2,311 enrolled. *Average high school GPA:* 3.1. *Test scores:* SAT critical reading scores over 500: 51%; SAT math scores over 500: 53%; SAT writing scores over 500: 47%; ACT scores over 18: 81%; SAT critical reading scores over 600: 16%; SAT math scores over 600: 21%; SAT writing scores over 600: 13%; ACT scores over 24: 29%; SAT critical reading scores over 700: 4%; SAT math scores over 700: 3%; SAT writing scores over 700: 1%; ACT scores over 30: 4%.

Faculty *Total:* 647, 99% full-time. *Student/faculty ratio:* 22:1.

Academics *Calendar:* quarters. *Degrees:* associate, bachelor's, master's, doctoral, post-master's, and postbachelor's certificates. *Special study options:* academic remediation for entering students, adult/continuing education programs, advanced placement credit, cooperative education, distance learning, double majors, English as a second language, freshman honors college, honors programs, independent study, internships, off-campus study, part-time degree program, services for LD students, student-designed majors, study abroad, summer session for credit. *ROTC:* Army (b), Air Force (b).

Computers on Campus 1,700 computers/terminals are available on campus for general student use. Students can access the following: campus intranet, computer help desk, free student e-mail accounts, online (class) grades, online (class) registration, online (class) schedules, Student web pages permitted. Campuswide network is available. 100% of college-owned or -operated housing units are wired for high-speed Internet access. Wireless service is available via entire campus.

Student Life *Housing options:* coed, disabled students. Campus housing is university owned and leased by the school. *Activities and organizations:* drama/theater group, student-run newspaper, radio and television station, choral group, Student government, National Association for the Advancement of Colored People, Interfraternity Council, Panhellenic Council, Golden Key International Honor Society, national fraternities, national sororities. *Campus security:* 24-hour emergency response devices and patrols, student patrols, late-night transport/escort service, controlled dormitory access. *Student services:* health clinic, personal/psychological counseling, women's center, legal services.

Athletics Member NCAA. All Division I. *Intercollegiate sports:* baseball M(s), basketball M(s)/W(s), cross-country running M(s)/W(s), golf M(s), soccer M(s)/W(s), softball W(s), swimming and diving M(s)/W(s), tennis M(s)/W(s), track and field W(s), volleyball W(s). *Intramural sports:* badminton M/W, baseball M/W, basketball M/W, bowling M/W, cheerleading M/W, football M/W, gymnastics M/W, ice hockey M, lacrosse M, racquetball M(c)/W(c), rugby M(c)/W(c), skiing (downhill) M(c)/W(c), soccer M/W, softball M/W, squash M(c)/W(c), table tennis M(c), tennis M/W, ultimate Frisbee M/W, volleyball M(c)/W, wrestling M.

Standardized Tests *Required:* SAT or ACT (for admission).

Costs (2012–13) *Tuition:* state resident $8354 full-time, $378 per credit hour part-time; nonresident $16,182 full-time, $738 per credit hour part-time. Full-time tuition and fees vary according to course load. Part-time tuition and fees vary according to course load. *Room and board:* $8629; room only: $5689. Room and board charges vary according to housing facility and location. *Payment plan:* installment. *Waivers:* senior citizens and employees or children of employees.

Financial Aid Of all full-time matriculated undergraduates who enrolled in 2012, 8,236 applied for aid, 7,146 were judged to have need, 704 had their need fully met. 1,247 Federal Work-Study jobs (averaging $3553). In 2012, 779 non-need-based awards were made. *Average percent of need met:* 57%. *Average financial aid package:* $10,186. *Average need-based loan:* $4584. *Average need-based gift aid:* $5995. *Average non-need-based aid:* $3997. *Average indebtedness upon graduation:* $28,349.

Applying *Options:* electronic application, early admission, deferred entrance. *Application fee:* $30. *Required:* high school transcript. *Recommended:* minimum 2.0 GPA. *Application deadlines:* rolling (freshmen), rolling (transfers). *Notification:* continuous (freshmen), continuous (out-of-state freshmen), continuous (transfers).

Freshman Application Contact Ms. Cathy Davis, Assistant Vice President for Undergraduate Admissions, Wright State University, 3640 Colonel Glenn Highway, E148 Student Union, Dayton, OH 45435. *Phone:* 937-775-5700. *Toll-free phone:* 800-247-1770. *Fax:* 937-775-5795. *E-mail:* admissions@ wright.edu.
Website: http://www.wright.edu/.

Xavier University

Cincinnati, Ohio

- **Independent Roman Catholic** comprehensive, founded 1831
- **Urban** 180-acre campus
- **Endowment** $117.0 million
- **Coed** 4,485 undergraduate students, 91% full-time, 54% women, 46% men
- **Moderately difficult** entrance level, 68% of applicants were admitted

Undergraduates 4,066 full-time, 419 part-time. Students come from 49 states and territories; 38 other countries; 44% are from out of state; 9% Black or African American, non-Hispanic/Latino; 4% Hispanic/Latino; 2% Asian, non-Hispanic/Latino; 0.1% Native Hawaiian or other Pacific Islander, non-Hispanic/Latino; 0.4% American Indian or Alaska Native, non-Hispanic/Latino; 2% Two or more races, non-Hispanic/Latino; 2% Race/ethnicity unknown; 3% international; 3% transferred in; 50% live on campus. *Retention:* 80% of full-time freshmen returned.

Freshmen *Admission:* 11,232 applied, 7,604 admitted, 1,066 enrolled. *Average high school GPA:* 3.57. *Test scores:* SAT critical reading scores over 500: 76%; SAT math scores over 500: 77%; SAT writing scores over 500: 72%; ACT scores over 18: 99%; SAT critical reading scores over 600: 28%; SAT math scores over 600: 29%; SAT writing scores over 600: 26%; ACT scores over 24: 67%; SAT critical reading scores over 700: 5%; SAT math scores over 700: 4%; SAT writing scores over 700: 4%; ACT scores over 30: 13%.

Faculty *Total:* 677, 51% full-time, 49% with terminal degrees. *Student/faculty ratio:* 12:1.

Academics *Calendar:* semesters. *Degrees:* certificates, associate, bachelor's, master's, and doctoral. *Special study options:* academic remediation for entering students, adult/continuing education programs, advanced placement credit, cooperative education, double majors, English as a second language, honors programs, independent study, internships, off-campus study, part-time degree program, services for LD students, study abroad, summer session for credit. *ROTC:* Army (b), Air Force (c). *Unusual degree programs:* 3-2 forestry with Duke University; environmental management, accounting.

Computers on Campus 340 computers/terminals and 10,128 ports are available on campus for general student use. Students can access the following: campus intranet, computer help desk, free student e-mail accounts, online (class) grades, online (class) registration, online (class) schedules. Campuswide network is available. 100% of college-owned or -operated housing units are wired for high-speed Internet access. Wireless service is available via entire campus.

Student Life *Housing:* on-campus residence required through sophomore year. *Options:* coed, disabled students. Campus housing is university owned. Freshman campus housing is guaranteed. *Activities and organizations:* drama/theater group, student-run newspaper, television station, choral group, Student Government Association, Black Student Association, X-treme Fans, Alternative Spring Break, Club Sports. *Campus security:* 24-hour emergency response devices and patrols, late-night transport/escort service, controlled dormitory access, campus-wide shuttle service. *Student services:* health clinic, personal/psychological counseling, women's center.

Athletics Member NCAA. All Division I. *Intercollegiate sports:* baseball M(s), basketball M(s)/W(s), cheerleading M(c)/W(c), crew M(c)/W(c), cross-country running M(s)/W(s), equestrian sports M(c)/W(c), fencing M(c)/W(c), field hockey M(c)/W(c), football M(c), golf M(s)/W(s), gymnastics M(c)/W(c), ice hockey M(c)/W(c), lacrosse M(c)/W(c), racquetball M(c)/W(c), rugby M(c)/W(c), soccer M(s)/W(s), softball M(c)/W(c), swimming and diving M(s)/W(s), tennis M(s)/W(s), track and field M(s)/W(s), ultimate Frisbee M(c)/W(c), volleyball M(c)/W(c), water polo M(c)/W(c). *Intramural sports:* baseball M(c), basketball M/W, bowling M/W, cross-country running M(c)/W(c), football M/W, golf M(c), racquetball M/W, soccer M(c)/W(c), softball W, swimming and diving M(c)/W(c), tennis M/W, volleyball M/W.

Standardized Tests *Required:* SAT or ACT (for admission).

Costs (2013–14) *Comprehensive fee:* $43,740 includes full-time tuition ($32,070), mandatory fees ($930), and room and board ($10,740). Full-time tuition and fees vary according to class time, course load, degree level, location, and program. Part-time tuition and fees vary according to class time, course load, degree level, location, and program. *College room only:* $5940. Room and board charges vary according to board plan and housing facility. *Payment plans:* installment, deferred payment. *Waivers:* senior citizens and employees or children of employees.

Financial Aid Of all full-time matriculated undergraduates who enrolled in 2012, 2,926 applied for aid, 2,434 were judged to have need, 468 had their need fully met. 630 Federal Work-Study jobs (averaging $2225). 25 state and other part-time jobs (averaging $1900). In 2012, 1415 non-need-based awards were made. *Average percent of need met:* 72%. *Average financial aid package:* $20,355. *Average need-based loan:* $3509. *Average need-based gift aid:* $15,307. *Average non-need-based aid:* $12,836. *Average indebtedness upon graduation:* $32,155.

Applying *Options:* electronic application, deferred entrance. *Application fee:* $35. *Required:* essay or personal statement, high school transcript, 1 letter of recommendation. *Required for some:* minimum 3.0 GPA, interview. *Application deadlines:* rolling (freshmen), rolling (transfers). *Notification:* continuous until 10/15 (freshmen), continuous (transfers).

Freshman Application Contact Xavier University, 3800 Victory Parkway, Cincinnati, OH 45207-5311. *Phone:* 513-745-3301. *Toll-free phone:* 877-XUADMIT. *E-mail:* xuadmit@xavier.edu.
Website: http://www.xu.edu/.

Youngstown State University

Youngstown, Ohio

- **State-supported** comprehensive, founded 1908
- **Urban** 200-acre campus with easy access to Cleveland, Pittsburgh
- **Endowment** $191.1 million
- **Coed** 12,644 undergraduate students, 78% full-time, 52% women, 48% men
- **Noncompetitive** entrance level, 87% of applicants were admitted

Undergraduates 9,906 full-time, 2,738 part-time. Students come from 38 states and territories; 60 other countries; 11% are from out of state; 16% Black or African American, non-Hispanic/Latino; 3% Hispanic/Latino; 0.9% Asian, non-Hispanic/Latino; 0.0% Native Hawaiian or other Pacific Islander, non-Hispanic/Latino; 0.3% American Indian or Alaska Native, non-Hispanic/Latino; 1% Two or more races, non-Hispanic/Latino; 5% Race/ethnicity unknown; 0.9% international; 5% transferred in; 10% live on campus. *Retention:* 65% of full-time freshmen returned.

Freshmen *Admission:* 4,458 applied, 3,867 admitted, 2,220 enrolled. *Average high school GPA:* 2.88. *Test scores:* SAT critical reading scores over 500: 34%; SAT math scores over 500: 40%; SAT writing scores over 500: 29%; ACT scores over 18: 71%; SAT critical reading scores over 600: 12%; SAT math scores over 600: 15%; SAT writing scores over 600: 8%; ACT scores over 24: 23%; SAT critical reading scores over 700: 2%; SAT math scores over 700: 4%; SAT writing scores over 700: 2%; ACT scores over 30: 3%.

Faculty *Total:* 1,054, 41% full-time, 47% with terminal degrees. *Student/faculty ratio:* 18:1.

Academics *Calendar:* semesters. *Degrees:* certificates, diplomas, associate, bachelor's, master's, doctoral, post-master's, and postbachelor's certificates. *Special study options:* academic remediation for entering students, accelerated degree program, adult/continuing education programs, advanced placement credit, cooperative education, distance learning, double majors, English as a second language, honors programs, independent study, internships, off-campus study, part-time degree program, services for LD students, student-designed majors, study abroad, summer session for credit. *ROTC:* Army (b), Air Force (c). *Unusual degree programs:* 3-2 BS/MS Program in Chemistry; BS/MD Program.

Computers on Campus 170 computers/terminals are available on campus for general student use. Students can access the following: campus intranet, computer help desk, free student e-mail accounts, online (class) grades, online (class) registration, online (class) schedules. Campuswide network is available. 100% of college-owned or -operated housing units are wired for high-speed Internet access. Wireless service is available via entire campus.

Student Life *Housing options:* coed, women-only. Campus housing is university owned and is provided by a third party. *Activities and organizations:* drama/theater group, student-run newspaper, radio station, choral group, marching band, Student Government Association, Omicron Delta Kappa, Golden Key Society, Fraternities/Sororities (IFC, NPHC and Panhellenic Council), History Club, national fraternities, national sororities. *Campus security:* 24-hour emergency response devices and patrols, student patrols, late-night transport/escort service, controlled dormitory access, residence hall patrols. *Student services:* health clinic, personal/psychological counseling.

Athletics Member NCAA. All Division I except football (Division I-AA). *Intercollegiate sports:* baseball M(s), basketball M(s)/W(s), cross-country running M(s)/W(s), golf M(s)/W(s), soccer W(s), softball W(s), swimming and diving W(s), tennis M(s)/W(s), track and field M(s)/W(s), volleyball W(s). *Intramural sports:* badminton M/W, basketball M/W, bowling M(c)/W(c), football M/W, ice hockey M(c), lacrosse M(c)/W(c), racquetball M/W, rock climbing M/W, soccer M/W, softball M/W, table tennis M/W, tennis M/W, ultimate Frisbee M/W, volleyball M/W, weight lifting M/W.

Standardized Tests *Required:* SAT or ACT (for admission).

Costs (2012–13) *Tuition:* state resident $7483 full-time, $312 per credit hour part-time; nonresident $13,440 full-time, $560 per credit hour part-time. Full-time tuition and fees vary according to course load. Part-time tuition and fees vary according to course load. *Required fees:* $229 full-time, $10 per credit hour part-time. *Room and board:* $8150. Room and board charges vary according to board plan and housing facility. *Payment plan:* installment. *Waivers:* senior citizens and employees or children of employees.

Financial Aid Of all full-time matriculated undergraduates who enrolled in 2011, 9,097 applied for aid, 8,112 were judged to have need, 542 had their need fully met. In 2011, 659 non-need-based awards were made. *Average percent of need met:* 29%. *Average financial aid package:* $8522. *Average need-based loan:* $3865. *Average need-based gift aid:* $5163. *Average non-need-based aid:* $2841. *Average indebtedness upon graduation:* $24,209.

Applying *Options:* electronic application, early admission, deferred entrance. *Application fee:* $40. *Required:* high school transcript. *Required for some:* interview. *Application deadlines:* 8/1 (freshmen), 8/1 (out-of-state freshmen), 8/1 (transfers). *Notification:* continuous (freshmen), continuous (out-of-state freshmen), continuous (transfers).

Freshman Application Contact Ms. Sue Davis, Director of Admissions, Youngstown State University, One University Plaza, Youngstown, OH 44555-0001. *Phone:* 330-941-2000. *Toll-free phone:* 877-468-6978. *Fax:* 330-941-3674. *E-mail:* enroll@ysu.edu. *Website:* http://www.ysu.edu/.

OKLAHOMA

Bacone College
Muskogee, Oklahoma

Freshman Application Contact Bacone College, 2299 Old Bacone Road, Muskogee, OK 74403-1597. *Phone:* 918-781-7342. *Toll-free phone:* 888-682-5514 Ext. 7340.
Website: http://www.bacone.edu/.

Brown Mackie College–Oklahoma City
Oklahoma City, Oklahoma

Admissions Office Contact Brown Mackie College–Oklahoma City, 7101 Northwest Expressway, Suite 800, Oklahoma City, OK 73132. *Toll-free phone:* 888-229-3280.
Website: http://www.brownmackie.edu/oklahoma-city/.

See below for display ad and page 1202 for the College Close-Up.

Brown Mackie College–Tulsa
Tulsa, Oklahoma

Freshman Application Contact Brown Mackie College–Tulsa, 4608 South Garnett, Suite 110, Tulsa, OK 74146. *Phone:* 918-628-3700. *Toll-free phone:* 888-794-8411.
Website: http://www.brownmackie.edu/tulsa/.

See below for display ad and page 1214 for the College Close-Up.

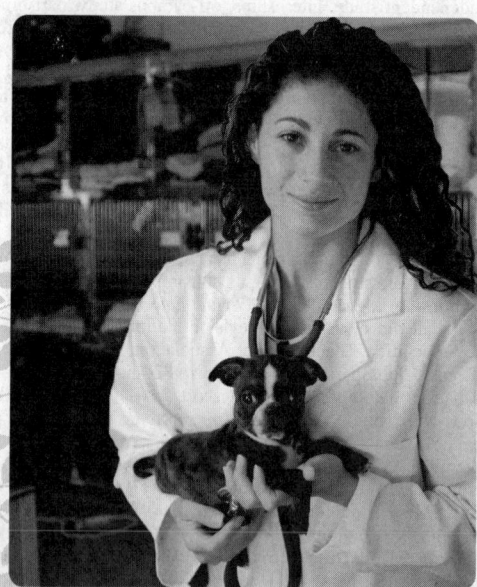

Cameron University

Lawton, Oklahoma

- **State-supported** comprehensive, founded 1908, part of Oklahoma State Regents for Higher Education
- **Small-town** 360-acre campus
- **Endowment** $15.7 million
- **Coed** 5,567 undergraduate students, 67% full-time, 61% women, 39% men
- **Noncompetitive** entrance level, 100% of applicants were admitted

Undergraduates 3,734 full-time, 1,833 part-time. Students come from 39 states and territories; 42 other countries; 5% are from out of state; 16% Black or African American, non-Hispanic/Latino; 10% Hispanic/Latino; 2% Asian, non-Hispanic/Latino; 0.7% Native Hawaiian or other Pacific Islander, non-Hispanic/Latino; 6% American Indian or Alaska Native, non-Hispanic/Latino; 6% Race/ethnicity unknown; 5% international; 8% transferred in; 10% live on campus. *Retention:* 57% of full-time freshmen returned.
Freshmen *Admission:* 1,336 applied, 1,331 admitted, 921 enrolled. *Average high school GPA:* 3.14. *Test scores:* ACT scores over 18: 68%; ACT scores over 24: 18%; ACT scores over 30: 3%.
Faculty *Total:* 319, 55% full-time, 46% with terminal degrees. *Student/faculty ratio:* 20:1.
Academics *Calendar:* semesters. *Degrees:* associate, bachelor's, master's, and post-master's certificates. *Special study options:* academic remediation for entering students, accelerated degree program, adult/continuing education programs, advanced placement credit, distance learning, double majors, honors programs, independent study, internships, off-campus study, part-time degree program, services for LD students, student-designed majors, study abroad, summer session for credit. *ROTC:* Army (b).
Computers on Campus 277 computers/terminals are available on campus for general student use. Students can access the following: computer help desk, free student e-mail accounts, online (class) grades, online (class) schedules, online courses, student information system, library, computer labs, mobile app. Campuswide network is available. 100% of college-owned or -operated housing units are wired for high-speed Internet access. Wireless service is available via classrooms, computer centers, computer labs, dorm rooms, learning centers, libraries, student centers.
Student Life *Housing options:* coed, men-only, women-only. Campus housing is university owned. *Activities and organizations:* drama/theater group, student-run newspaper, television station, choral group, Student Government Association, Programming Activities Council, Nigerian Student Association, International Club, Greek Life, national fraternities, national sororities. *Campus security:* 24-hour emergency response devices and patrols, late-night transport/escort service, controlled dormitory access. *Student services:* health clinic, personal/psychological counseling.
Athletics Member NCAA. All Division II. *Intercollegiate sports:* baseball M(s), basketball M(s)/W(s), cross-country running M(s), golf M(s)/W(s), softball W(s), tennis M(s)/W(s), volleyball W(s). *Intramural sports:* archery M/W, basketball M/W, bowling M/W, racquetball M/W, soccer M/W, swimming and diving M/W, table tennis M/W, tennis M/W, volleyball M/W.
Standardized Tests *Required:* SAT or ACT (for admission).
Costs (2012–13) *Tuition:* state resident $3225 full-time, $108 per credit hour part-time; nonresident $10,200 full-time, $340 per credit hour part-time. Full-time tuition and fees vary according to course load, location, and program. Part-time tuition and fees vary according to course load, location, and program. *Required fees:* $1545 full-time, $52 per credit hour part-time. *Room and board:* $3884; room only: $1504. Room and board charges vary according to board plan and housing facility. *Payment plan:* installment. *Waivers:* employees or children of employees.
Financial Aid Of all full-time matriculated undergraduates who enrolled in 2011, 3,006 applied for aid, 2,643 were judged to have need, 88 had their need fully met. 78 Federal Work-Study jobs (averaging $1899). 245 state and other part-time jobs (averaging $4716). In 2011, 221 non-need-based awards were made. *Average percent of need met:* 56%. *Average financial aid package:* $8936. *Average need-based loan:* $3691. *Average need-based gift aid:* $5456. *Average non-need-based aid:* $1154. *Average indebtedness upon graduation:* $15,020.
Applying *Options:* electronic application, deferred entrance. *Application fee:* $15. *Required for some:* high school transcript, Baccalaureate degree: Minimum composite ACT of 20 or SAT of 890 or rank in the top 50% of high school graduation class and have a high school GPA of at least 2.7; AS degree: Meet minimum high school curricular requirements and completed the ACT or SAT; AAS degree: completed ACT or SAT. *Application deadlines:* rolling (freshmen), rolling (out-of-state freshmen), rolling (transfers). *Notification:* continuous (freshmen), continuous (out-of-state freshmen), continuous (transfers).

Freshman Application Contact Ms. Heather Young, Prospective Students Services Coordinator, Cameron University, Admissions, 2800 West Gore Boulevard, Lawton, OK 73505-6377. *Phone:* 580-581-2798. *Toll-free phone:* 888-454-7600. *Fax:* 580-581-5416. *E-mail:* admissions@cameron.edu. *Website:* http://www.cameron.edu/.

DeVry University

Oklahoma City, Oklahoma

Freshman Application Contact DeVry University, Lakepointe Towers, 4013 Northwest Expressway Street, Suite 100, Oklahoma City, OK 73116. *Toll-free phone:* 866-338-7941.
Website: http://www.devry.edu/.

East Central University

Ada, Oklahoma

- **State-supported** comprehensive, founded 1909, part of Oklahoma State Regents for Higher Education
- **Small-town** 140-acre campus with easy access to Oklahoma City
- **Endowment** $26.4 million
- **Coed** 3,804 undergraduate students, 80% full-time, 59% women, 41% men
- **Minimally difficult** entrance level, 95% of applicants were admitted

Undergraduates 3,039 full-time, 765 part-time. Students come from 37 states and territories; 39 other countries; 8% are from out of state; 4% Black or African American, non-Hispanic/Latino; 4% Hispanic/Latino; 0.4% Asian, non-Hispanic/Latino; 0.2% Native Hawaiian or other Pacific Islander, non-Hispanic/Latino; 17% American Indian or Alaska Native, non-Hispanic/Latino; 8% Two or more races, non-Hispanic/Latino; 2% Race/ethnicity unknown; 5% international; 10% transferred in; 28% live on campus. *Retention:* 59% of full-time freshmen returned.
Freshmen *Admission:* 999 applied, 953 admitted, 627 enrolled. *Average high school GPA:* 3.37. *Test scores:* SAT critical reading scores over 500: 22%; SAT math scores over 500: 57%; ACT scores over 18: 80%; SAT critical reading scores over 600: 4%; SAT math scores over 600: 11%; ACT scores over 24: 23%; ACT scores over 30: 2%.
Faculty *Total:* 277, 60% full-time, 45% with terminal degrees. *Student/faculty ratio:* 19:1.
Academics *Calendar:* semesters. *Degrees:* bachelor's and master's. *Special study options:* academic remediation for entering students, adult/continuing education programs, advanced placement credit, distance learning, double majors, honors programs, independent study, internships, off-campus study, part-time degree program, services for LD students, study abroad, summer session for credit.
Computers on Campus 677 computers/terminals are available on campus for general student use. Students can access the following: campus intranet, computer help desk, free student e-mail accounts, online (class) grades, online (class) registration, online (class) schedules. Campuswide network is available. Wireless service is available via entire campus.
Student Life *Housing:* on-campus residence required for freshman year. *Options:* coed, women-only, disabled students. Campus housing is university owned. *Activities and organizations:* drama/theater group, student-run newspaper, choral group, marching band, BACCHUS, Fellowship of Christian Athletes, Human Resources, national fraternities, national sororities. *Campus security:* 24-hour emergency response devices and patrols, student patrols, late-night transport/escort service, agreements with all local, state, federal, and tribal police departments for added crime and violation prevention. *Student services:* health clinic, personal/psychological counseling.
Athletics Member NCAA, NAIA. All NCAA Division II. *Intercollegiate sports:* baseball M(s), basketball M(s)/W(s), cheerleading M/W, cross-country running M(s)/W(s), football M(s), golf M(s)/W, soccer W(s), softball W(s), tennis M(s)/W(s), track and field M/W, volleyball W(s). *Intramural sports:* basketball M/W, football M/W, racquetball M/W, soccer M/W, softball M/W, tennis M/W, volleyball M/W.
Standardized Tests *Required:* SAT or ACT (for admission). *Recommended:* ACT (for admission).
Costs (2012–13) *Tuition:* state resident $3608 full-time, $120 per semester hour part-time; nonresident $10,604 full-time, $353 per semester hour part-time. No tuition increase for student's term of enrollment. *Required fees:* $1349 full-time, $42 per semester hour part-time, $48 per term part-time. *Room and board:* $4824; room only: $1900. Room and board charges vary according to board plan and housing facility. *Waivers:* senior citizens and employees or children of employees.

Financial Aid Of all full-time matriculated undergraduates who enrolled in 2006, 2,396 applied for aid, 2,085 were judged to have need, 756 had their need fully met. 175 Federal Work-Study jobs (averaging $2349). 232 state and other part-time jobs (averaging $572). In 2006, 542 non-need-based awards were made. *Average percent of need met:* 70%. *Average financial aid package:* $7597. *Average need-based loan:* $3835. *Average need-based gift aid:* $3420. *Average non-need-based aid:* $1567. *Average indebtedness upon graduation:* $19,190.

Applying *Options:* electronic application, early admission. *Application fee:* $20. *Required:* high school transcript. *Required for some:* minimum 2.7 GPA, rank in upper 50% of high school class. *Notification:* continuous (freshmen), continuous (transfers).

Freshman Application Contact Ms. Kristen Kelley, Freshman Admissions Officer, East Central University, PMBJ8, 1100 East 14th Street, Ada, OK 74820-6999. *Phone:* 580-310-5233 Ext. 233. *Fax:* 580-310-5432. *E-mail:* KKelley@ecok.edu.
Website: http://www.ecok.edu/.

Family of Faith College

Shawnee, Oklahoma

Admissions Office Contact Family of Faith College, 30 Kinville, Shawnee, OK 74802.
Website: http://www.familyoffaithcollege.edu/.

Hillsdale Free Will Baptist College

Moore, Oklahoma

- **Independent Free Will Baptist** comprehensive, founded 1959
- **Suburban** 41-acre campus with easy access to Oklahoma City
- **Coed** 202 undergraduate students, 91% full-time, 36% women, 64% men
- **Noncompetitive** entrance level, 45% of applicants were admitted

Undergraduates 184 full-time, 18 part-time. 16% Black or African American, non-Hispanic/Latino; 7% Hispanic/Latino; 0.5% Asian, non-Hispanic/Latino; 9% American Indian or Alaska Native, non-Hispanic/Latino; 0.5% Two or more races, non-Hispanic/Latino; 0.5% Race/ethnicity unknown; 2% international. *Retention:* 60% of full-time freshmen returned.

Freshmen *Admission:* 167 applied, 75 admitted, 53 enrolled.

Faculty *Total:* 47, 28% full-time. *Student/faculty ratio:* 11:1.

Academics *Calendar:* semesters. *Degrees:* associate, bachelor's, and master's. *Special study options:* academic remediation for entering students, accelerated degree program, adult/continuing education programs, advanced placement credit, English as a second language, independent study, internships, part-time degree program, summer session for credit.

Computers on Campus 22 computers/terminals are available on campus for general student use. Students can access the following: campus intranet, free student e-mail accounts. Campuswide network is available.

Student Life *Housing:* on-campus residence required through sophomore year. *Options:* men-only, women-only. Campus housing is university owned. *Activities and organizations:* drama/theater group, choral group. *Campus security:* 24-hour emergency response devices, controlled dormitory access. *Student services:* personal/psychological counseling.

Athletics Member NCCAA. *Intercollegiate sports:* baseball M, basketball M/W, cross-country running M/W, soccer M, softball W, volleyball W. *Intramural sports:* basketball M/W, volleyball M/W.

Standardized Tests *Required:* SAT or ACT (for admission).

Costs (2013–14) *Comprehensive fee:* $17,350 includes full-time tuition ($9000), mandatory fees ($1880), and room and board ($6470). Full-time tuition and fees vary according to course load. Part-time tuition: $375 per credit. Part-time tuition and fees vary according to course load. *College room only:* $3020. Room and board charges vary according to board plan and housing facility. *Payment plan:* installment. *Waivers:* children of alumni, senior citizens, and employees or children of employees.

Financial Aid Of all full-time matriculated undergraduates who enrolled in 2011, 179 applied for aid, 154 were judged to have need. 49 Federal Work-Study jobs (averaging $1015). In 2011, 21 non-need-based awards were made. *Average percent of need met:* 50%. *Average financial aid package:* $11,749. *Average need-based loan:* $3911. *Average need-based gift aid:* $6174. *Average non-need-based aid:* $2611. *Average indebtedness upon graduation:* $22,313.

Applying *Options:* electronic application, early admission, deferred entrance. *Application fee:* $20. *Required:* high school transcript, 2 letters of recommendation. *Required for some:* interview. *Recommended:* minimum 2.0 GPA.

Freshman Application Contact Hillsdale Free Will Baptist College, PO Box 7208, Moore, OK 73160. *Phone:* 405-912-9007. *Fax:* 405-912-9050. *E-mail:* recruitment@hc.edu.
Website: http://www.hc.edu/.

ITT Technical Institute

Oklahoma City, Oklahoma

- **Proprietary** 4-year, founded 2006, part of ITT Educational Services, Inc.
- **Coed**
- **Minimally difficult** entrance level

Academics *Calendar:* quarters. *Degrees:* associate and bachelor's.

Freshman Application Contact Director of Recruitment, ITT Technical Institute, 50 Penn Place Office Tower, 1900 Northwest Expressway, Suite 305R, Oklahoma City, OK 73118. *Phone:* 405-810-4100. *Toll-free phone:* 800-518-1612.
Website: http://www.itt-tech.edu/.

ITT Technical Institute

Tulsa, Oklahoma

- **Proprietary** primarily 2-year, founded 2005
- **Coed**
- **Minimally difficult** entrance level

Academics *Calendar:* quarters. *Degrees:* associate and bachelor's.

Freshman Application Contact Director of Recruitment, ITT Technical Institute, 4500 South 129th East Avenue, Suite 152, Tulsa, OK 74134. *Phone:* 918-615-3900. *Toll-free phone:* 800-514-6535.
Website: http://www.itt-tech.edu/.

Langston University

Langston, Oklahoma

- **State-supported** comprehensive, founded 1897, part of Oklahoma State Regents for Higher Education
- **Rural** 40-acre campus with easy access to Oklahoma City
- **Coed** 1,976 undergraduate students, 87% full-time, 59% women, 41% men
- **Minimally difficult** entrance level, 63% of applicants were admitted

Undergraduates 1,718 full-time, 258 part-time. Students come from 36 states and territories; 29 other countries; 40% are from out of state; 87% Black or African American, non-Hispanic/Latino; 0.1% Hispanic/Latino; 0.8% Native Hawaiian or other Pacific Islander, non-Hispanic/Latino; 1% American Indian or Alaska Native, non-Hispanic/Latino; 0.8% Two or more races, non-Hispanic/Latino; 3% Race/ethnicity unknown.

Freshmen *Admission:* 3,113 applied, 1,966 admitted, 405 enrolled.

Faculty *Total:* 205, 68% full-time. *Student/faculty ratio:* 30:1.

Academics *Calendar:* semesters. *Degrees:* associate, bachelor's, and master's. *Special study options:* academic remediation for entering students, accelerated degree program, adult/continuing education programs, advanced placement credit, cooperative education, distance learning, double majors, English as a second language, external degree program, honors programs, independent study, internships, part-time degree program, services for LD students, study abroad, summer session for credit. *ROTC:* Army (c).

Computers on Campus 300 computers/terminals are available on campus for general student use. Students can access the following: campus intranet, computer help desk, free student e-mail accounts, online (class) grades, online (class) registration, online (class) schedules. Campuswide network is available. Wireless service is available via entire campus.

Student Life *Housing:* on-campus residence required through sophomore year. *Options:* coed, disabled students. Campus housing is university owned and is provided by a third party. Freshman campus housing is guaranteed. *Activities and organizations:* drama/theater group, student-run newspaper, radio station, choral group, marching band, Student Government Association, Student Senate, Sorority and Fraternity (Greek Letter), NAACP, Pre- Alumni Council, national fraternities, national sororities. *Campus security:* 24-hour emergency response devices and patrols, student patrols, late-night transport/escort service, controlled dormitory access. *Student services:* health clinic, personal/psychological counseling, women's center.

Athletics Member NAIA. *Intercollegiate sports:* basketball M(s)/W(s), cheerleading W, cross-country running M/W, football M(s), softball W, track and

field M(s)/W(s), volleyball W. *Intramural sports:* archery M/W, badminton M/W, basketball M/W, football M/W, golf M/W, soccer M, swimming and diving M/W, table tennis M/W, tennis M/W, track and field M/W, volleyball M/W.
Standardized Tests *Required:* SAT or ACT (for admission).
Costs (2013–14) *Tuition:* state resident $3030 full-time, $102 per credit part-time; nonresident $9510 full-time, $317 per credit part-time. Full-time tuition and fees vary according to location and program. Part-time tuition and fees vary according to location and program. *Required fees:* $1255 full-time, $35 per term part-time. *Room and board:* $8690; room only: $5930. Room and board charges vary according to board plan, housing facility, and location.
Financial Aid Of all full-time matriculated undergraduates who enrolled in 2009, 2,599 applied for aid, 2,015 were judged to have need, 638 had their need fully met. In 2009, 733 non-need-based awards were made. *Average percent of need met:* 59%. *Average financial aid package:* $8855. *Average need-based loan:* $4956. *Average need-based gift aid:* $4727. *Average non-need-based aid:* $1884. *Average indebtedness upon graduation:* $33,875.
Applying *Options:* electronic application, deferred entrance. *Application fee:* $35. *Required:* high school transcript, minimum 2.7 GPA. *Application deadlines:* rolling (freshmen), rolling (transfers).
Freshman Application Contact Langston University, OK.
Website: http://www.langston.edu/.

Mid-America Christian University

Oklahoma City, Oklahoma

Freshman Application Contact Mid-America Christian University, 3500 Southwest 119th Street, Oklahoma City, OK 73170-4504. *Phone:* 405-392-3180. *Toll-free phone:* 888-436-3035.
Website: http://www.macu.edu/.

National American University

Tulsa, Oklahoma

Admissions Office Contact National American University, 8040 South Sheridan Road, Tulsa, OK 74133.
Website: http://www.national.edu/.

Northeastern State University

Tahlequah, Oklahoma

- **State-supported** comprehensive, founded 1846, part of Regional University System of Oklahoma
- **Small-town** 160-acre campus with easy access to Tulsa
- **Endowment** $12.8 million
- **Coed**
- **Moderately difficult** entrance level
Faculty *Student/faculty ratio:* 20:1.
Academics *Calendar:* semesters. *Degrees:* bachelor's, master's, doctoral, post-master's, and postbachelor's certificates.
Student Life *Campus security:* 24-hour emergency response devices and patrols, late-night transport/escort service, controlled dormitory access.
Athletics Member NCAA. All Division II.
Standardized Tests *Required:* ACT (for admission).
Costs (2012–13) *Tuition:* state resident $3750 full-time, $125 per credit hour part-time; nonresident $10,500 full-time, $350 per credit hour part-time. Full-time tuition and fees vary according to course load and program. Part-time tuition and fees vary according to course load and program. *Required fees:* $1107 full-time, $37 per credit hour part-time. *Room and board:* $5914. Room and board charges vary according to board plan and housing facility.
Financial Aid *Of all full-time matriculated undergraduates who enrolled in 2012,* 4,555 applied for aid, 3,645 were judged to have need, 2,610 had their need fully met. 115 Federal Work-Study jobs (averaging $1179). 550 state and other part-time jobs (averaging $1886). *In 2012,* 209 non-need-based awards were made. *Average percent of need met:* 96. *Average financial aid package:* $11,270. *Average need-based loan:* $6438. *Average need-based gift aid:* $6082. *Average non-need-based aid:* $2692. *Average indebtedness upon graduation:* $20,503.
Applying *Options:* deferred entrance. *Application fee:* $25. *Required:* high school transcript, minimum 2.7 GPA, upper 50% of class or minimum ACT composite of 20. *Required for some:* interview.
Freshman Application Contact Ms. Dawn Cain, Director of Admissions, Northeastern State University, 600 N Grand Ave, Tahlequah, OK 74464.

Phone: 918-444-2211. *Toll-free phone:* 800-722-9614. *Fax:* 918-458-2342.
E-mail: cain@nsuok.edu.
Website: http://www.nsuok.edu/.

Northwestern Oklahoma State University

Alva, Oklahoma

- **State-supported** comprehensive, founded 1897, part of Oklahoma State Regents for Higher Education
- **Rural** 70-acre campus
- **Endowment** $21.6 million
- **Coed** 2,066 undergraduate students, 66% full-time, 53% women, 47% men
- **Moderately difficult** entrance level, 69% of applicants were admitted
Undergraduates 1,367 full-time, 699 part-time. Students come from 38 states and territories; 18 other countries; 23% are from out of state; 7% Black or African American, non-Hispanic/Latino; 6% Hispanic/Latino; 0.9% Asian, non-Hispanic/Latino; 0.4% Native Hawaiian or other Pacific Islander, non-Hispanic/Latino; 6% American Indian or Alaska Native, non-Hispanic/Latino; 8% Race/ethnicity unknown; 2% international; 13% transferred in; 35% live on campus. *Retention:* 65% of full-time freshmen returned.
Freshmen *Admission:* 975 applied, 669 admitted, 419 enrolled. *Average high school GPA:* 3.16.
Faculty *Total:* 182, 45% full-time, 33% with terminal degrees. *Student/faculty ratio:* 14:1.
Academics *Calendar:* semesters. *Degrees:* bachelor's and master's. *Special study options:* academic remediation for entering students, adult/continuing education programs, advanced placement credit, cooperative education, distance learning, honors programs, independent study, internships, off-campus study, part-time degree program, services for LD students, study abroad, summer session for credit.
Computers on Campus 260 computers/terminals are available on campus for general student use. Students can access the following: campus intranet, computer help desk, free student e-mail accounts, online (class) grades, online (class) registration, online (class) schedules. Campuswide network is available. 100% of college-owned or -operated housing units are wired for high-speed Internet access. Wireless service is available via classrooms, computer centers, computer labs, learning centers, libraries, student centers.
Student Life *Housing:* on-campus residence required for freshman year. *Options:* men-only, women-only. Campus housing is university owned. Freshman campus housing is guaranteed. *Activities and organizations:* drama/theater group, student-run newspaper, radio and television station, choral group, marching band, Student Government Association, Aggie Club, Phi Beta Lambda, Baptist Student Union. *Campus security:* 24-hour emergency response devices and patrols, late-night transport/escort service. *Student services:* personal/psychological counseling.
Athletics Member NCAA. All Division II. *Intercollegiate sports:* baseball M(s), basketball M(s)/W(s), cheerleading M(s)/W(s), cross-country running M(s)/W(s), football M(s), golf M(s)/W(s), soccer W(s), softball W(s), volleyball W(s). *Intramural sports:* basketball M/W, football M, racquetball M/W, softball M/W, ultimate Frisbee M/W, volleyball M/W.
Standardized Tests *Required:* SAT or ACT (for admission).
Costs (2012–13) *Tuition:* state resident $4253 full-time; nonresident $10,185 full-time. Full-time tuition and fees vary according to course load, degree level, location, and program. Part-time tuition and fees vary according to course load, degree level, location, and program. *Required fees:* $945 full-time. *Room and board:* $3780; room only: $1300. Room and board charges vary according to board plan. *Payment plan:* installment. *Waivers:* senior citizens and employees or children of employees.
Financial Aid Of all full-time matriculated undergraduates who enrolled in 2012, 1,172 applied for aid, 983 were judged to have need. 110 Federal Work-Study jobs (averaging $1672). 190 state and other part-time jobs (averaging $1348). *Average indebtedness upon graduation:* $14,975.
Applying *Options:* electronic application, early admission. *Application fee:* $15. *Required:* high school transcript. *Required for some:* essay or personal statement, minimum 2.7 GPA, 3 letters of recommendation. *Application deadlines:* rolling (freshmen), rolling (transfers). *Notification:* continuous (freshmen), continuous (transfers).
Freshman Application Contact Mrs. Carly Williams, Director of Recruitment, Northwestern Oklahoma State University, 709 Oklahoma Boulevard, Alva, OK 73717-2799. *Phone:* 580-327-8545. *Fax:* 580-327-8699.
E-mail: wmadair@nwosu.edu.
Website: http://www.nwosu.edu/.

Oklahoma Baptist University

Shawnee, Oklahoma

- **Independent Southern Baptist** comprehensive, founded 1910
- **Small-town** 125-acre campus with easy access to Oklahoma City
- **Coed** 1,903 undergraduate students, 91% full-time, 58% women, 42% men
- **Moderately difficult** entrance level, 62% of applicants were admitted

Undergraduates 1,731 full-time, 172 part-time. Students come from 39 states and territories; 14 other countries; 36% are from out of state; 5% Black or African American, non-Hispanic/Latino; 4% Hispanic/Latino; 1% Asian, non-Hispanic/Latino; 0.1% Native Hawaiian or other Pacific Islander, non-Hispanic/Latino; 6% American Indian or Alaska Native, non-Hispanic/Latino; 6% Two or more races, non-Hispanic/Latino; 5% Race/ethnicity unknown; 5% international; 6% transferred in; 80% live on campus. *Retention:* 75% of full-time freshmen returned.

Freshmen *Admission:* 4,909 applied, 3,042 admitted, 506 enrolled. *Average high school GPA:* 3.64. *Test scores:* SAT critical reading scores over 500: 68%; SAT math scores over 500: 66%; ACT scores over 18: 95%; SAT critical reading scores over 600: 29%; SAT math scores over 600: 22%; ACT scores over 24: 48%; SAT critical reading scores over 700: 3%; SAT math scores over 700: 4%; ACT scores over 30: 9%.

Faculty *Total:* 192, 61% full-time, 48% with terminal degrees. *Student/faculty ratio:* 14:1.

Academics *Calendar:* 4-1-4. *Degrees:* associate, bachelor's, and master's. *Special study options:* academic remediation for entering students, advanced placement credit, cooperative education, double majors, honors programs, independent study, internships, off-campus study, part-time degree program, services for LD students, student-designed majors, study abroad, summer session for credit. *ROTC:* Air Force (c). *Unusual degree programs:* 3-2 engineering; medicine.

Computers on Campus 175 computers/terminals are available on campus for general student use. Students can access the following: campus intranet, computer help desk, free student e-mail accounts, online (class) grades, online (class) registration, online (class) schedules, campus portal, online course work. Campuswide network is available. 100% of college-owned or -operated housing units are wired for high-speed Internet access. Wireless service is available via classrooms, computer labs, dorm rooms, learning centers, libraries, student centers.

Student Life *Housing:* on-campus residence required through junior year. *Options:* men-only, women-only. Campus housing is university owned. Freshman campus housing is guaranteed. *Activities and organizations:* drama/theater group, student-run newspaper, television station, choral group, Campus Activities Board, University Concert Series, Student Foundation, Blitz Week Activities, Canterbury. *Campus security:* 24-hour emergency response devices and patrols, late-night transport/escort service, controlled dormitory access. *Student services:* health clinic, personal/psychological counseling.

Athletics Member NAIA. *Intercollegiate sports:* baseball M(s), basketball M(s)/W(s), cross-country running M(s)/W(s), golf M(s)/W(s), soccer M/W, softball W(s), tennis M(s)/W(s), track and field M(s)/W(s). *Intramural sports:* badminton M/W, basketball M/W, bowling M/W, football M/W, racquetball M/W, soccer M/W, softball M/W, swimming and diving M/W, table tennis M/W, tennis M/W, volleyball M/W.

Standardized Tests *Required:* SAT or ACT (for admission).

Costs (2012–13) *One-time required fee:* $50. *Comprehensive fee:* $27,056 includes full-time tuition ($18,954), mandatory fees ($1902), and room and board ($6200). Full-time tuition and fees vary according to course load. Part-time tuition: $614 per credit hour. Part-time tuition and fees vary according to course load. *Room and board:* Room and board charges vary according to housing facility. *Payment plan:* installment. *Waivers:* senior citizens and employees or children of employees.

Financial Aid Of all full-time matriculated undergraduates who enrolled in 2011, 1,338 applied for aid, 1,241 were judged to have need, 340 had their need fully met. 204 Federal Work-Study jobs (averaging $1389). In 2011, 97 non-need-based awards were made. *Average percent of need met:* 83%. *Average financial aid package:* $19,333. *Average need-based loan:* $3921. *Average need-based gift aid:* $4666. *Average non-need-based aid:* $6285. *Average indebtedness upon graduation:* $23,039.

Applying *Options:* early admission, deferred entrance. *Required:* high school transcript, minimum 2.5 GPA. *Required for some:* essay or personal statement, interview. *Application deadlines:* rolling (freshmen), 8/1 (transfers). *Notification:* continuous until 9/1 (freshmen), continuous until 9/1 (transfers).

Freshman Application Contact Oklahoma Baptist University, 500 West University, Shawnee, OK 74804. *Phone:* 405-585-5120. *Toll-free phone:* 800-654-3285.

Website: http://www.okbu.edu/.

Oklahoma Christian University

Oklahoma City, Oklahoma

- **Independent** comprehensive, founded 1950, affiliated with Church of Christ
- **Suburban** 200-acre campus
- **Endowment** $59.7 million
- **Coed** 1,910 undergraduate students, 96% full-time, 49% women, 51% men
- **Noncompetitive** entrance level, 45% of applicants were admitted

Undergraduates 1,833 full-time, 77 part-time. Students come from 45 states and territories; 38 other countries; 63% are from out of state; 3% Black or African American, non-Hispanic/Latino; 3% Hispanic/Latino; 1% Asian, non-Hispanic/Latino; 4% American Indian or Alaska Native, non-Hispanic/Latino; 14% Race/ethnicity unknown; 11% international; 7% transferred in; 80% live on campus. *Retention:* 76% of full-time freshmen returned.

Freshmen *Admission:* 2,156 applied, 964 admitted, 446 enrolled. *Average high school GPA:* 3.49. *Test scores:* SAT critical reading scores over 500: 66%; SAT math scores over 500: 70%; ACT scores over 18: 90%; SAT critical reading scores over 600: 34%; SAT math scores over 600: 36%; ACT scores over 24: 55%; SAT critical reading scores over 700: 10%; SAT math scores over 700: 10%; ACT scores over 30: 13%.

Faculty *Total:* 194, 60% full-time, 52% with terminal degrees. *Student/faculty ratio:* 13:1.

Academics *Calendar:* semesters. *Degrees:* bachelor's and master's. *Special study options:* academic remediation for entering students, accelerated degree program, advanced placement credit, distance learning, double majors, English as a second language, honors programs, independent study, internships, off-campus study, services for LD students, study abroad, summer session for credit. *ROTC:* Army (c), Air Force (c).

Computers on Campus 101 computers/terminals and 450 ports are available on campus for general student use. Students can access the following: campus intranet, computer help desk, free student e-mail accounts, online (class) grades, online (class) registration, online (class) schedules. Campuswide network is available. 100% of college-owned or -operated housing units are wired for high-speed Internet access. Wireless service is available via entire campus.

Student Life *Housing:* on-campus residence required through senior year. *Options:* men-only, women-only, disabled students. Campus housing is university owned. Freshman campus housing is guaranteed. *Activities and organizations:* drama/theater group, student-run newspaper, radio and television station, choral group, Outreach, Wishing Well Project, Acting on Aids, Young Republicans, College Democrats. *Campus security:* 24-hour emergency response devices and patrols, late-night transport/escort service, controlled dormitory access. *Student services:* health clinic, personal/psychological counseling.

Athletics Member NCAA, NCCAA. All NCAA Division II. *Intercollegiate sports:* baseball M(s), basketball M(s)/W(s), cross-country running M(s)/W(s), golf M(s), soccer M(s)/W(s), softball W(s), tennis M(s)/W(s), track and field M(s)/W(s). *Intramural sports:* baseball M/W, basketball M/W, bowling M/W, cheerleading M/W, cross-country running M/W, football M/W, golf M/W, soccer M/W, softball M/W, swimming and diving M/W, table tennis M/W, tennis M/W, track and field M/W, volleyball M/W.

Standardized Tests *Required:* SAT or ACT (for admission).

Costs (2013–14) *Comprehensive fee:* $24,975 includes full-time tuition ($18,800) and room and board ($6175). Full-time tuition and fees vary according to course load. Part-time tuition: $783 per credit hour. Part-time tuition and fees vary according to course load. *College room only:* $3575. Room and board charges vary according to board plan and housing facility. *Payment plan:* installment. *Waivers:* employees or children of employees.

Financial Aid Of all full-time matriculated undergraduates who enrolled in 2012, 1,364 applied for aid, 1,148 were judged to have need, 513 had their need fully met. 851 Federal Work-Study jobs (averaging $1614). In 2012, 430 non-need-based awards were made. *Average percent of need met:* 84%. *Average financial aid package:* $21,593. *Average need-based loan:* $2246. *Average need-based gift aid:* $2951. *Average non-need-based aid:* $5492. *Average indebtedness upon graduation:* $29,388. *Financial aid deadline:* 8/31.

Applying *Options:* electronic application, early admission, deferred entrance. *Application fee:* $25. *Required:* high school transcript, 1 letter of recommendation. *Application deadlines:* rolling (freshmen), rolling (transfers). *Notification:* continuous (freshmen), continuous (transfers).

Freshman Application Contact Mr. Michael Mitchell, Director, Admissions and Recruiting, Oklahoma Christian University, Box 11000, Oklahoma City, OK 73136-1100. *Phone:* 405-425-5065. *Toll-free phone:* 800-877-5010. *Fax:* 405-425-5208. *E-mail:* info@oc.edu.

Website: http://www.oc.edu/.

Oklahoma City University

Oklahoma City, Oklahoma

- **Independent United Methodist** comprehensive, founded 1904
- **Urban** campus
- **Coed**

Undergraduates 58% live on campus.

Faculty *Total:* 342.

Academics *Calendar:* semesters. *Degrees:* bachelor's, master's, and doctoral. *Special study options:* accelerated degree program, adult/continuing education programs, advanced placement credit, distance learning, double majors, English as a second language, honors programs, independent study, internships, off-campus study, part-time degree program, services for LD students, study abroad, summer session for credit. *ROTC:* Army (c), Navy (c), Air Force (c).

Computers on Campus 368 computers/terminals are available on campus for general student use. Students can access the following: campus intranet, computer help desk, free student e-mail accounts, online (class) grades, online (class) registration, online (class) schedules. Campuswide network is available. Wireless service is available via entire campus.

Student Life *Housing options:* coed, men-only, women-only. Campus housing is university owned. Freshman applicants given priority for college housing. *Activities and organizations:* drama/theater group, choral group, Tri-Beta, Multicultural Student Association, Student Nursing Associate, Fellowship of Christian Athletes, national fraternities, national sororities. *Campus security:* 24-hour emergency response devices and patrols, late-night transport/escort service, controlled dormitory access. *Student services:* health clinic, personal/psychological counseling.

Athletics Member NAIA. *Intercollegiate sports:* baseball M(s), basketball M(s)/W(s), cheerleading M(s)/W(s), crew M(s)/W(s), golf M(s)/W(s), sailing M(c)/W(c), soccer M(s)/W(s), softball W(s), track and field M(s)/W(s), volleyball W(s), wrestling M(s)/W(s). *Intramural sports:* basketball M/W, fencing M/W, football M, golf M/W, softball M/W, table tennis M/W, volleyball M/W.

Standardized Tests *Required:* SAT or ACT (for admission).

Costs (2012–13) *Comprehensive fee:* $37,360 includes full-time tuition ($24,740), mandatory fees ($3450), and room and board ($9170). Part-time tuition: $840 per credit hour. No tuition increase for student's term of enrollment. *College room only:* $5090. Room and board charges vary according to board plan and housing facility. *Payment plans:* installment, deferred payment. *Waivers:* employees or children of employees.

Financial Aid Of all full-time matriculated undergraduates who enrolled in 2012, 1,321 applied for aid, 1,137 were judged to have need, 230 had their need fully met. 326 Federal Work-Study jobs (averaging $2196). 327 state and other part-time jobs (averaging $1669). In 2012, 473 non-need-based awards were made. *Average percent of need met:* 78%. *Average financial aid package:* $23,737. *Average need-based loan:* $5166. *Average need-based gift aid:* $16,100. *Average non-need-based aid:* $12,524. *Average indebtedness upon graduation:* $25,557.

Applying *Required:* essay or personal statement, high school transcript. *Required for some:* interview.

Freshman Application Contact Ms. Michelle cook, Senior Director of Admissions, Oklahoma City University, 2501 North Blackwelder, Oklahoma City, OK 73106. *Phone:* 405-208-5050. *Toll-free phone:* 800-633-7242. *Fax:* 405-208-5916. *E-mail:* michelle.cook@okcu.edu.

Website: http://www.okcu.edu/.

Oklahoma Panhandle State University

Goodwell, Oklahoma

Freshman Application Contact Mr. Bobby Jenkins, Registrar and Director of Admissions, Oklahoma Panhandle State University, PO Box 430, 323 Eagle Boulevard, Goodwell, OK 73939-0430. *Phone:* 580-349-1376. *Toll-free phone:* 800-664-6778. *Fax:* 580-349-1371. *E-mail:* opsu@opsu.edu. *Website:* http://www.opsu.edu/.

Oklahoma State University

Stillwater, Oklahoma

- **State-supported** university, founded 1890, part of Oklahoma State University
- **Small-town** 840-acre campus with easy access to Oklahoma City, Tulsa
- **Endowment** $557.7 million
- **Coed** 20,130 undergraduate students, 87% full-time, 48% women, 52% men
- **Moderately difficult** entrance level, 78% of applicants were admitted

Undergraduates 17,549 full-time, 2,581 part-time. Students come from 49 states and territories; 64 other countries; 24% are from out of state; 5% Black or African American, non-Hispanic/Latino; 4% Hispanic/Latino; 1% Asian, non-Hispanic/Latino; 6% American Indian or Alaska Native, non-Hispanic/Latino; 7% Two or more races, non-Hispanic/Latino; 0.9% Race/ethnicity unknown; 2% international; 9% transferred in; 45% live on campus. *Retention:* 79% of full-time freshmen returned.

Freshmen *Admission:* 12,056 applied, 9,351 admitted, 4,289 enrolled. *Average high school GPA:* 3.51. *Test scores:* SAT critical reading scores over 500: 73%; SAT math scores over 500: 81%; ACT scores over 18: 98%; SAT critical reading scores over 600: 25%; SAT math scores over 600: 38%; ACT scores over 24: 64%; SAT critical reading scores over 700: 4%; SAT math scores over 700: 6%; ACT scores over 30: 15%.

Faculty *Total:* 1,344, 77% full-time, 74% with terminal degrees. *Student/faculty ratio:* 20:1.

Academics *Calendar:* semesters. *Degrees:* bachelor's, master's, doctoral, post-master's, and postbachelor's certificates. *Special study options:* academic remediation for entering students, accelerated degree program, advanced placement credit, distance learning, double majors, English as a second language, freshman honors college, honors programs, independent study, internships, off-campus study, part-time degree program, services for LD students, student-designed majors, study abroad, summer session for credit. *ROTC:* Army (b), Air Force (b).

Computers on Campus Students can access the following: campus intranet, computer help desk, free student e-mail accounts, online (class) grades, online (class) registration, online (class) schedules. Campuswide network is available. Wireless service is available via classrooms, computer centers, computer labs, libraries, student centers.

Student Life *Housing:* on-campus residence required for freshman year. *Options:* coed, men-only, women-only, disabled students. Campus housing is university owned. Freshman campus housing is guaranteed. *Activities and organizations:* drama/theater group, student-run newspaper, radio and television station, choral group, marching band, national fraternities, national sororities. *Campus security:* 24-hour emergency response devices and patrols, student patrols, controlled dormitory access. *Student services:* health clinic, personal/psychological counseling, women's center.

Athletics Member NCAA. All Division I. *Intercollegiate sports:* baseball M(s), basketball M(s)/W(s), cross-country running M(s)/W(s), equestrian sports W(s), football M(s), golf M(s)/W(s), soccer W(s), softball W(s), tennis M(s)/W(s), track and field M(s)/W(s), wrestling M(s).

Standardized Tests *Required:* SAT or ACT (for admission).

Costs (2013–14) *One-time required fee:* $95. *Tuition:* state resident $4425 full-time, $148 per credit hour part-time; nonresident $16,440 full-time, $548 per credit hour part-time. Full-time tuition and fees vary according to program and student level. Part-time tuition and fees vary according to program and student level. *Required fees:* $3017 full-time, $101 per credit hour part-time. *Room and board:* $6868; room only: $3710. Room and board charges vary according to board plan and housing facility. *Payment plan:* installment. *Waivers:* children of alumni.

Financial Aid Of all full-time matriculated undergraduates who enrolled in 2011, 11,159 applied for aid, 8,768 were judged to have need, 1,128 had their need fully met. 388 Federal Work-Study jobs (averaging $2410). 3,623 state and other part-time jobs (averaging $2647). In 2011, 4193 non-need-based awards were made. *Average percent of need met:* 77%. *Average financial aid package:* $12,601. *Average need-based loan:* $4081. *Average need-based gift aid:* $6297. *Average non-need-based aid:* $5049. *Average indebtedness upon graduation:* $22,736.

Applying *Options:* electronic application, deferred entrance. *Application fee:* $40. *Required:* high school transcript, minimum 3.0 GPA, class rank. *Required for some:* essay or personal statement, interview. *Application deadlines:* rolling (freshmen), rolling (out-of-state freshmen), rolling (transfers). *Notification:* continuous (freshmen), continuous (out-of-state freshmen), continuous (transfers).

Freshman Application Contact Oklahoma State University, Stillwater, OK 74078. *Phone:* 405-744-3087. *Toll-free phone:* 800-233-5019 Ext. 1 (in-state); 800-852-1255 (out-of-state).

Website: http://www.okstate.edu/.

Oklahoma State University, Oklahoma City

Oklahoma City, Oklahoma

- **State-supported** primarily 2-year, founded 1961, part of Oklahoma State University
- **Urban** 110-acre campus
- **Coed** 7,585 undergraduate students, 33% full-time, 61% women, 39% men
- **Noncompetitive** entrance level, 100% of applicants were admitted

Undergraduates 2,510 full-time, 5,075 part-time. Students come from 18 states and territories; 8 other countries; 2% are from out of state; 17% Black or African American, non-Hispanic/Latino; 8% Hispanic/Latino; 2% Asian, non-Hispanic/Latino; 4% American Indian or Alaska Native, non-Hispanic/Latino; 6% Two or more races, non-Hispanic/Latino; 2% Race/ethnicity unknown; 0.2% international; 11% transferred in. *Retention:* 40% of full-time freshmen returned.

Freshmen *Admission:* 562 applied, 562 admitted, 606 enrolled.

Faculty *Total:* 389, 22% full-time. *Student/faculty ratio:* 20:1.

Academics *Calendar:* semesters. *Degrees:* certificates, associate, and bachelor's. *Special study options:* academic remediation for entering students, advanced placement credit, cooperative education, distance learning, double majors, honors programs, independent study, part-time degree program, services for LD students, study abroad, summer session for credit.

Computers on Campus 800 computers/terminals are available on campus for general student use. Campuswide network is available.

Student Life *Housing:* college housing not available. *Activities and organizations:* Phi Theta Kappa, Deaf/Hearing Social Club, American Criminal Justice Association, Horticulture Club, Vet-Tech Club. *Campus security:* 24-hour patrols, late-night transport/escort service.

Applying *Options:* electronic application, early admission. *Required:* high school transcript. *Application deadlines:* rolling (freshmen), rolling (transfers). *Notification:* continuous (freshmen), continuous (transfers).

Freshman Application Contact Mr. Kyle Williams, Director, Enrollment Management, Oklahoma State University, Oklahoma City, 900 North Portland, AD202, Oklahoma City, OK 73107. *Phone:* 405-945-9152. *Toll-free phone:* 800-560-4099. *E-mail:* wilkylw@osuokc.edu.
Website: http://www.osuokc.edu/.

Oklahoma Wesleyan University

Bartlesville, Oklahoma

- **Independent** comprehensive, founded 1909, affiliated with Wesleyan Church
- **Small-town** 127-acre campus with easy access to Tulsa
- **Endowment** $3.1 million
- **Coed**
- **Minimally difficult** entrance level

Faculty *Student/faculty ratio:* 10:1.

Academics *Calendar:* semesters. *Degrees:* associate, bachelor's, and master's.

Student Life *Campus security:* student patrols.

Athletics Member NAIA, NCCAA.

Standardized Tests *Required:* SAT or ACT (for admission).

Costs (2012–13) *Comprehensive fee:* $28,380 includes full-time tuition ($19,940), mandatory fees ($1200), and room and board ($7240). Full-time tuition and fees vary according to course load. Part-time tuition: $795 per credit hour. *Required fees:* $55 per credit hour part-time, $60 per term part-time. *College room only:* $3820. Room and board charges vary according to board plan and housing facility. *Payment plans:* installment, deferred payment.

Financial Aid *Of all full-time matriculated undergraduates who enrolled in 2012,* 688 applied for aid, 603 were judged to have need, 76 had their need fully met. 123 Federal Work-Study jobs (averaging $1744). 24 state and other part-time jobs (averaging $1734). In 2012, 96 non-need-based awards were made. *Average percent of need met:* 59. *Average financial aid package:* $12,544. *Average need-based loan:* $4171. *Average need-based gift aid:* $9809. *Average non-need-based aid:* $5100. *Average indebtedness upon graduation:* $20,060.

Applying *Options:* electronic application. *Application fee:* $25. *Required:* high school transcript, ACT score 18 or higher. *Required for some:* interview. *Recommended:* minimum 2.0 GPA.

Freshman Application Contact Jennifer Weaver, Enrollment Counselor, Oklahoma Wesleyan University, 2201 Silver Lake Road, Bartlesville, OK

74006. *Phone:* 866-222-8226. *Toll-free phone:* 866-222-8226. *Fax:* 918-335-6229. *E-mail:* admissions@okwu.edu.
Website: http://www.okwu.edu/.

Oral Roberts University

Tulsa, Oklahoma

- **Independent interdenominational** comprehensive, founded 1963
- **Urban** 263-acre campus
- **Coed** 2,782 undergraduate students, 91% full-time, 57% women, 43% men
- **Moderately difficult** entrance level, 52% of applicants were admitted

Undergraduates 2,545 full-time, 237 part-time. 41% are from out of state; 14% Black or African American, non-Hispanic/Latino; 7% Hispanic/Latino; 2% Asian, non-Hispanic/Latino; 3% American Indian or Alaska Native, non-Hispanic/Latino; 4% Two or more races, non-Hispanic/Latino; 10% Race/ethnicity unknown; 5% international; 50% transferred in; 72% live on campus.

Freshmen *Admission:* 1,557 applied, 811 admitted, 480 enrolled. *Average high school GPA:* 3.45. *Test scores:* SAT critical reading scores over 500: 61%; SAT math scores over 500: 59%; ACT scores over 18: 93%; SAT critical reading scores over 600: 24%; SAT math scores over 600: 22%; ACT scores over 24: 42%; SAT critical reading scores over 700: 6%; SAT math scores over 700: 3%; ACT scores over 30: 7%.

Faculty *Total:* 273, 60% full-time, 47% with terminal degrees. *Student/faculty ratio:* 15:1.

Academics *Calendar:* semesters. *Degrees:* bachelor's, master's, and doctoral. *Special study options:* adult/continuing education programs, external degree program, part-time degree program. *ROTC:* Air Force (c).

Computers on Campus Students can access the following: free student e-mail accounts, online (class) registration. Campuswide network is available.

Student Life *Housing:* on-campus residence required through senior year. *Options:* men-only, women-only. *Campus security:* 24-hour emergency response devices and patrols, late-night transport/escort service.

Athletics Member NCAA. All Division I. *Intercollegiate sports:* baseball M(s), basketball M(s)/W(s), cross-country running M(s)/W(s), golf M(s)/W(s), soccer M(s)/W(s), tennis M(s)/W(s), track and field M(s)/W(s), volleyball W(s), wrestling M. *Intramural sports:* badminton M/W, basketball M/W, bowling M/W, cross-country running M/W, football M/W, golf M/W, racquetball M/W, softball M/W, swimming and diving M/W, table tennis M/W, tennis M/W, volleyball M/W.

Costs (2013–14) *Comprehensive fee:* $31,734 includes full-time tuition ($21,696), mandatory fees ($742), and room and board ($9296). Full-time tuition and fees vary according to degree level. Part-time tuition: $906 per credit hour. Part-time tuition and fees vary according to degree level. *College room only:* $4534. Room and board charges vary according to board plan and housing facility.

Financial Aid Of all full-time matriculated undergraduates who enrolled in 2008, 1,978 applied for aid, 1,738 were judged to have need, 643 had their need fully met. In 2008, 501 non-need-based awards were made. *Average percent of need met:* 86%. *Average financial aid package:* $18,229. *Average need-based loan:* $10,159. *Average need-based gift aid:* $9304. *Average non-need-based aid:* $7151. *Average indebtedness upon graduation:* $34,555.

Applying *Options:* deferred entrance. *Application fee:* $35. *Required:* essay or personal statement, high school transcript, minimum 2.0 GPA, 1 letter of recommendation, proof of immunization. *Required for some:* interview. *Recommended:* interview. *Application deadlines:* rolling (freshmen), rolling (transfers). *Notification:* continuous (freshmen), continuous (transfers).

Freshman Application Contact Chris Belcher, Director of Admissions, Oral Roberts University, 7777 South Lewis Avenue, Tulsa, OK 74171. *Phone:* 918-495-6529. *Toll-free phone:* 800-678-8876. *Fax:* 918-495-6222. *E-mail:* admissions@oru.edu.
Website: http://www.oru.edu/.

Rogers State University

Claremore, Oklahoma

- **State-supported** 4-year, founded 1909, part of Oklahoma State Regents for Higher Education
- **Small-town** 40-acre campus with easy access to Tulsa
- **Endowment** $7.6 million
- **Coed** 4,646 undergraduate students, 61% full-time, 63% women, 37% men
- **Noncompetitive** entrance level, 55% of applicants were admitted

Undergraduates 2,856 full-time, 1,790 part-time. Students come from 26 states and territories; 29 other countries; 3% are from out of state; 3% Black or African American, non-Hispanic/Latino; 4% Hispanic/Latino; 1% Asian, non-Hispanic/Latino; 0.1% Native Hawaiian or other Pacific Islander, non-Hispanic/Latino; 13% American Indian or Alaska Native, non-Hispanic/Latino; 17% Two or more races, non-Hispanic/Latino; 0.3% Race/ethnicity unknown; 1% international; 9% transferred in; 6% live on campus. *Retention:* 61% of full-time freshmen returned.

Freshmen *Admission:* 1,988 applied, 1,090 admitted, 834 enrolled. *Average high school GPA:* 3.13. *Test scores:* ACT scores over 18: 75%; ACT scores over 24: 18%; ACT scores over 30: 2%.

Faculty *Total:* 281, 38% full-time, 34% with terminal degrees. *Student/faculty ratio:* 21:1.

Academics *Calendar:* semesters. *Degrees:* associate and bachelor's. *Special study options:* academic remediation for entering students, adult/continuing education programs, advanced placement credit, cooperative education, distance learning, double majors, honors programs, independent study, internships, off-campus study, part-time degree program, services for LD students, study abroad, summer session for credit.

Computers on Campus 237 computers/terminals are available on campus for general student use. Students can access the following: computer help desk, free student e-mail accounts, online (class) grades, online (class) registration, online (class) schedules, software to support courses. Campuswide network is available. 100% of college-owned or -operated housing units are wired for high-speed Internet access. Wireless service is available via classrooms, computer labs, dorm rooms, learning centers, libraries, student centers.

Student Life *Housing options:* coed. Campus housing is university owned. *Activities and organizations:* drama/theater group, student-run newspaper, radio station, choral group, Community Counseling and Psychology Student Association, Baptist Collegiate Ministry, Native American Student Association, Psychology Students for Social Responsibility, Pre-Professional Health Club, national fraternities, national sororities. *Campus security:* 24-hour emergency response devices and patrols, student patrols, late-night transport/escort service, controlled dormitory access, RSU employs only State certified law enforcement officers and has a comprehensive camera surveillance system. *Student services:* health clinic, personal/psychological counseling.

Athletics Member NAIA. *Intercollegiate sports:* baseball M(s), basketball M(s)/W(s), cheerleading M(s)/W(s), cross-country running M(s)/W(s), golf M(s)/W(s), soccer M(s)/W(s), softball W(s). *Intramural sports:* basketball M/W, soccer M/W, softball M/W, table tennis M/W, volleyball M/W.

Standardized Tests *Required:* SAT or ACT (for admission). *Required for some:* ACT COMPASS. *Recommended:* ACT (for admission).

Costs (2013–14) *Tuition:* state resident $3263 full-time, $109 per hour part-time; nonresident $9788 full-time, $326 per hour part-time. Full-time tuition and fees vary according to course level, course load, location, program, and student level. Part-time tuition and fees vary according to course level, course load, location, program, and student level. *Required fees:* $1784 full-time, $58 per hour part-time, $15 per term part-time. *Room and board:* $6425. Room and board charges vary according to housing facility. *Payment plan:* installment. *Waivers:* senior citizens and employees or children of employees.

Financial Aid Of all full-time matriculated undergraduates who enrolled in 2012, 2,375 applied for aid, 2,038 were judged to have need, 73 had their need fully met. 65 Federal Work-Study jobs (averaging $1742). 244 state and other part-time jobs (averaging $1696). In 2012, 52 non-need-based awards were made. *Average percent of need met:* 44%. *Average financial aid package:* $8723. *Average need-based loan:* $4126. *Average need-based gift aid:* $5610. *Average non-need-based aid:* $5296. *Average indebtedness upon graduation:* $19,019.

Applying *Options:* electronic application. *Required:* high school transcript. *Required for some:* minimum 2.8 GPA, Baccalaureate degree programs require 20 ACT composite or 2.75 GPA and top 50% rank for admission; Associate degree programs have an open admission policy. *Application deadlines:* rolling (freshmen), rolling (out-of-state freshmen), rolling (transfers).

Freshman Application Contact Ms. Joy Lin Husted, Director of Admissions, Rogers State University, 1701 West Will Rogers Boulevard, Claremore, OK 74017. *Phone:* 918-343-7546. *Toll-free phone:* 800-256-7511. *Fax:* 918-343-7595. *E-mail:* info@rsu.edu. *Website:* http://www.rsu.edu/.

St. Gregory's University
Shawnee, Oklahoma

- **Independent Roman Catholic** comprehensive, founded 1875
- **Small-town** 640-acre campus with easy access to Oklahoma City
- **Endowment** $9.6 million
- **Coed** 628 undergraduate students, 54% full-time, 56% women, 44% men
- **Minimally difficult** entrance level, 31% of applicants were admitted

Undergraduates 337 full-time, 291 part-time. Students come from 11 states and territories; 15 other countries; 6% are from out of state; 12% Black or African American, non-Hispanic/Latino; 10% Hispanic/Latino; 1% Asian, non-Hispanic/Latino; 8% American Indian or Alaska Native, non-Hispanic/Latino; 9% Two or more races, non-Hispanic/Latino; 11% Race/ethnicity unknown; 8% international; 11% transferred in; 36% live on campus. *Retention:* 41% of full-time freshmen returned.

Freshmen *Admission:* 306 applied, 96 admitted, 86 enrolled. *Average high school GPA:* 3.23. *Test scores:* SAT critical reading scores over 500: 29%; SAT math scores over 500: 25%; SAT writing scores over 500: 17%; ACT scores over 18: 83%; SAT critical reading scores over 600: 4%; SAT math scores over 600: 8%; ACT scores over 24: 23%; ACT scores over 30: 2%.

Faculty *Total:* 136, 21% full-time, 16% with terminal degrees. *Student/faculty ratio:* 11:1.

Academics *Calendar:* semesters. *Degrees:* certificates, associate, bachelor's, and master's. *Special study options:* accelerated degree program, adult/continuing education programs, advanced placement credit, cooperative education, distance learning, double majors, external degree program, honors programs, independent study, internships, off-campus study, part-time degree program, services for LD students, summer session for credit.

Computers on Campus 35 computers/terminals and 100 ports are available on campus for general student use. Students can access the following: campus intranet, computer help desk, free student e-mail accounts, online (class) grades, online (class) registration, online (class) schedules. Campuswide network is available. 100% of college-owned or -operated housing units are wired for high-speed Internet access. Wireless service is available via entire campus.

Student Life *Housing:* on-campus residence required through senior year. *Options:* men-only, women-only, disabled students. Campus housing is university owned. Freshman campus housing is guaranteed. *Activities and organizations:* drama/theater group, choral group, Greek Life, Student Government Association, Pro-Life, Hispanic American Student Association, Campus Ministry. *Campus security:* 24-hour emergency response devices and patrols, late-night transport/escort service, controlled dormitory access. *Student services:* personal/psychological counseling.

Athletics Member NAIA. *Intercollegiate sports:* baseball M(s), basketball M(s)/W(s), cheerleading M/W, soccer M(s)/W(s), softball W(s), track and field M(s)/W(s), volleyball W(s). *Intramural sports:* basketball M/W, football M/W, racquetball M/W, soccer M/W, softball M/W, swimming and diving M/W, table tennis M/W, tennis M/W, volleyball M/W.

Standardized Tests *Required:* SAT or ACT (for admission).

Financial Aid Of all full-time matriculated undergraduates who enrolled in 2005, 555 applied for aid, 521 were judged to have need, 60 had their need fully met. 38 Federal Work-Study jobs (averaging $867). 24 state and other part-time jobs (averaging $2551). In 2005, 61 non-need-based awards were made. *Average percent of need met:* 69%. *Average financial aid package:* $10,686. *Average need-based loan:* $3720. *Average need-based gift aid:* $6883. *Average non-need-based aid:* $1500. *Average indebtedness upon graduation:* $10,160.

Applying *Options:* electronic application, deferred entrance. *Required:* minimum 2.8 GPA. *Required for some:* essay or personal statement, high school transcript, interview. *Application deadlines:* rolling (freshmen), rolling (transfers). *Notification:* continuous (freshmen), continuous (transfers).

Freshman Application Contact William Kuehl, Vice President for Enrollment Management, St. Gregory's University, 1900 West MacArthur Drive, Shawnee, OK 74804. *Phone:* 405-878-5161. *Toll-free phone:* 888-STGREGS. *Fax:* 405-878-5198. *E-mail:* admissions@stgregorys.edu. *Website:* http://www.stgregorys.edu/.

Southeastern Oklahoma State University

Durant, Oklahoma

- **State-supported** comprehensive, founded 1909, part of Oklahoma State Regents for Higher Education
- **Small-town** 177-acre campus
- **Endowment** $12.0 million
- **Coed** 3,676 undergraduate students, 77% full-time, 54% women, 46% men
- **Moderately difficult** entrance level, 78% of applicants were admitted

Undergraduates 2,822 full-time, 854 part-time. Students come from 36 states and territories; 40 other countries; 26% are from out of state; 7% Black or African American, non-Hispanic/Latino; 3% Hispanic/Latino; 0.7% Asian, non-Hispanic/Latino; 0.4% Native Hawaiian or other Pacific Islander, non-Hispanic/Latino; 30% American Indian or Alaska Native, non-Hispanic/Latino; 3% international; 11% transferred in; 19% live on campus. *Retention:* 57% of full-time freshmen returned.

Freshmen *Admission:* 1,143 applied, 886 admitted, 600 enrolled. *Average high school GPA:* 3.29. *Test scores:* ACT scores over 18: 75%; ACT scores over 24: 16%; ACT scores over 30: 2%.

Faculty *Total:* 262, 54% full-time, 52% with terminal degrees. *Student/faculty ratio:* 19:1.

Academics *Calendar:* semesters. *Degrees:* bachelor's, master's, and post-master's certificates. *Special study options:* academic remediation for entering students, accelerated degree program, adult/continuing education programs, advanced placement credit, distance learning, double majors, honors programs, independent study, internships, off-campus study, part-time degree program, services for LD students, summer session for credit.

Computers on Campus 598 computers/terminals and 598 ports are available on campus for general student use. Students can access the following: campus intranet, computer help desk, free student e-mail accounts, online (class) grades, online (class) registration, online (class) schedules, campus Blackboard classes. Campuswide network is available. 100% of college-owned or -operated housing units are wired for high-speed Internet access. Wireless service is available via classrooms, computer labs, dorm rooms, learning centers, libraries, student centers.

Student Life *Housing:* on-campus residence required for freshman year. *Options:* coed, men-only, women-only, disabled students. Campus housing is university owned. Freshman campus housing is guaranteed. *Activities and organizations:* drama/theater group, student-run newspaper, radio station, choral group, marching band, Baptist Collegiate Ministries, Greek Community, Wesley Center, Resident Hall Association, national fraternities, national sororities. *Campus security:* 24-hour emergency response devices and patrols, late-night transport/escort service, controlled dormitory access. *Student services:* health clinic, personal/psychological counseling.

Athletics Member NCAA. All Division II. *Intercollegiate sports:* baseball M(s), basketball M(s)/W(s), cross-country running W(s), football M(s), golf M(s), softball W(s), tennis M(s)/W(s), volleyball W(s). *Intramural sports:* basketball M/W, football M.

Standardized Tests *Required:* SAT or ACT (for admission).

Costs (2012–13) *Tuition:* state resident $4427 full-time, $148 per credit hour part-time; nonresident $12,162 full-time, $258 per credit hour part-time. Full-time tuition and fees vary according to course level. Part-time tuition and fees vary according to course level and course load. *Required fees:* $633 full-time, $21 per credit hour part-time. *Room and board:* $4970; room only: $2200. Room and board charges vary according to board plan and housing facility. *Payment plan:* installment. *Waivers:* minority students, children of alumni, senior citizens, and employees or children of employees.

Financial Aid Of all full-time matriculated undergraduates who enrolled in 2010, 2,459 applied for aid, 2,229 were judged to have need, 649 had their need fully met. 657 Federal Work-Study jobs (averaging $1666). 712 state and other part-time jobs (averaging $1260). In 2010, 5 non-need-based awards were made. *Average percent of need met:* 34%. *Average financial aid package:* $9769. *Average need-based loan:* $1796. *Average need-based gift aid:* $1503. *Average non-need-based aid:* $550. *Average indebtedness upon graduation:* $14,808.

Applying *Application fee:* $20. *Required:* high school transcript. *Required for some:* interview. *Application deadlines:* rolling (freshmen), rolling (transfers). *Notification:* continuous (freshmen), continuous (transfers).

Freshman Application Contact Southeastern Oklahoma State University, 1405 North 4th Avenue, Durant, OK 74701-0609. *Phone:* 580-745-2060. *Toll-free phone:* 800-435-1327.
Website: http://www.se.edu/.

Southern Nazarene University

Bethany, Oklahoma

- **Independent Nazarene** comprehensive, founded 1899
- **Suburban** 40-acre campus with easy access to Oklahoma City
- **Endowment** $21.6 million
- **Coed** 1,702 undergraduate students, 97% full-time, 53% women, 47% men
- **Noncompetitive** entrance level, 49% of applicants were admitted

Undergraduates 1,643 full-time, 59 part-time. Students come from 33 states and territories; 33 other countries; 23% are from out of state; 15% Black or African American, non-Hispanic/Latino; 6% Hispanic/Latino; 3% Asian, non-Hispanic/Latino; 0.5% Native Hawaiian or other Pacific Islander, non-Hispanic/Latino; 6% American Indian or Alaska Native, non-Hispanic/Latino; 0.1% Race/ethnicity unknown; 3% international; 5% transferred in; 71% live on campus. *Retention:* 58% of full-time freshmen returned.

Freshmen *Admission:* 988 applied, 484 admitted, 287 enrolled. *Average high school GPA:* 3.3. *Test scores:* ACT scores over 18: 81%; ACT scores over 24: 34%; ACT scores over 30: 3%.

Faculty *Total:* 189, 37% full-time, 56% with terminal degrees. *Student/faculty ratio:* 18:1.

Academics *Calendar:* semesters. *Degrees:* associate, bachelor's, and master's. *Special study options:* academic remediation for entering students, accelerated degree program, adult/continuing education programs, advanced placement credit, distance learning, double majors, English as a second language, external degree program, honors programs, independent study, internships, off-campus study, part-time degree program, services for LD students, student-designed majors, study abroad, summer session for credit. *ROTC:* Army (c), Air Force (c).

Computers on Campus 120 computers/terminals are available on campus for general student use. Students can access the following: campus intranet, computer help desk, free student e-mail accounts, online (class) grades, online (class) schedules. Campuswide network is available. 100% of college-owned or -operated housing units are wired for high-speed Internet access. Wireless service is available via entire campus.

Student Life *Housing:* on-campus residence required through senior year. *Options:* men-only, women-only. Campus housing is university owned. Freshman campus housing is guaranteed. *Activities and organizations:* drama/theater group, student-run newspaper, choral group, Business Gaming Team, Campus Social Life Committee, intramural sports societies, Choral Society, Inter-Club. *Campus security:* 24-hour emergency response devices, student patrols, late-night transport/escort service, controlled dormitory access. *Student services:* health clinic, personal/psychological counseling.

Athletics Member NAIA. *Intercollegiate sports:* baseball M(s), basketball M(s)/W(s), cheerleading M(s)/W(s), cross-country running M(s)/W(s), equestrian sports M/W, football M(s), golf M(s)/W(s), soccer M(s)/W(s), softball W(s), tennis M(s)/W(s), track and field M(s)/W(s), volleyball W(s). *Intramural sports:* basketball M/W, football M/W, golf M/W, racquetball M/W, soccer M/W, softball M/W, swimming and diving M/W, table tennis M/W, tennis M/W, volleyball M/W, weight lifting M/W.

Standardized Tests *Required:* SAT or ACT (for admission). *Recommended:* ACT (for admission).

Costs (2013–14) *Comprehensive fee:* $28,774 includes full-time tuition ($20,550), mandatory fees ($624), and room and board ($7600). Part-time tuition: $639 per credit hour. Part-time tuition and fees vary according to course load. *Room and board:* Room and board charges vary according to board plan and housing facility. *Payment plans:* tuition prepayment, installment, deferred payment. *Waivers:* employees or children of employees.

Financial Aid Of all full-time matriculated undergraduates who enrolled in 2009, 1,485 applied for aid, 1,366 were judged to have need. 104 Federal Work-Study jobs (averaging $2125). 115 state and other part-time jobs (averaging $3000).

Applying *Options:* electronic application, deferred entrance. *Application fee:* $35. *Required:* high school transcript, minimum 2.0 GPA, 2 letters of recommendation, interview. *Application deadlines:* 8/15 (freshmen), 8/15 (transfers). *Notification:* continuous (freshmen), continuous (transfers).

Freshman Application Contact Dr. Linda Cantwell, Director of Recruitment, Southern Nazarene University, 6729 Northwest 39th Expressway, Bethany, OK 73008. *Phone:* 405-491-6324. *Toll-free phone:* 800-648-9899. *Fax:* 405-491-6320. *E-mail:* admiss@snu.edu.
Website: http://www.snu.edu/.

Southwestern Christian University

Bethany, Oklahoma

- **Independent** comprehensive, founded 1946, affiliated with Pentecostal Holiness Church
- **Suburban** 7-acre campus with easy access to Oklahoma City
- **Coed**
- **Minimally difficult** entrance level

Faculty *Student/faculty ratio:* 15:1.

Academics *Calendar:* semesters. *Degrees:* certificates, associate, bachelor's, and master's.

Student Life *Campus security:* 24-hour emergency response devices and patrols, student patrols.

Athletics Member NAIA, NCCAA.

Standardized Tests *Required:* SAT or ACT (for admission).

Costs (2012–13) *Comprehensive fee:* $16,560 includes full-time tuition ($11,060), mandatory fees ($500), and room and board ($5000). Full-time tuition and fees vary according to class time, course load, location, and program. Part-time tuition: $395 per credit hour. Part-time tuition and fees vary according to class time, course load, location, and program. *Required fees:* $250 per term part-time. *Room and board:* Room and board charges vary according to housing facility.

Financial Aid *Of all full-time matriculated undergraduates who enrolled in 2008,* 177 applied for aid, 170 were judged to have need, 61 had their need fully met. 60 Federal Work-Study jobs (averaging $1500). 10 state and other part-time jobs (averaging $1000). *In 2008,* 12 non-need-based awards were made. *Average percent of need met:* 71. *Average financial aid package:* $9000. *Average need-based loan:* $4000. *Average need-based gift aid:* $2500. *Average non-need-based aid:* $2000. *Average indebtedness upon graduation:* $17,000.

Applying *Options:* electronic application, early admission, deferred entrance. *Required:* essay or personal statement, high school transcript, minimum 2.5 GPA, 19 ACT or 900 SAT, top 50% rank in class. *Recommended:* interview.

Freshman Application Contact Jessie Burpo, Admissions Counselor, Southwestern Christian University, PO Box 340, Bethany, OK 73008-0340. *Phone:* 405-789-7661 Ext. 3432. *Fax:* 405-495-0078. *E-mail:* admissions@swcu.edu.

Website: http://www.swcu.edu/.

Southwestern Oklahoma State University

Weatherford, Oklahoma

- **State-supported** comprehensive, founded 1901
- **Small-town** campus
- **Coed**
- **Minimally difficult** entrance level

Faculty *Student/faculty ratio:* 21:1.

Academics *Calendar:* semesters. *Degrees:* associate, bachelor's, master's, and doctoral.

Student Life *Campus security:* late-night transport/escort service, controlled dormitory access, 20-hour campus emergency security.

Athletics Member NCAA. All Division II.

Standardized Tests *Required:* SAT or ACT (for admission). *Recommended:* ACT (for admission).

Costs (2012–13) *Tuition:* state resident $4755 full-time; nonresident $11,265 full-time. Full-time tuition and fees vary according to program. Part-time tuition and fees vary according to program. *Room and board:* $4240; room only: $1800. Room and board charges vary according to board plan.

Financial Aid *Of all full-time matriculated undergraduates who enrolled in 2011,* 2,888 applied for aid, 2,462 were judged to have need, 898 had their need fully met. *In 2011,* 1388 non-need-based awards were made. *Average percent of need met:* 92. *Average financial aid package:* $5290. *Average need-based loan:* $1855. *Average need-based gift aid:* $1645. *Average non-need-based aid:* $465. *Average indebtedness upon graduation:* $18,190. *Financial aid deadline:* 3/1.

Applying *Options:* deferred entrance. *Application fee:* $15. *Required:* high school transcript, minimum 2.0 GPA.

Freshman Application Contact Ms. Connie Phillips, Admission Counselor, Southwestern Oklahoma State University, 100 Campus Drive, Weatherford,

OK 73096-3098. *Phone:* 580-774-3009. *Fax:* 580-774-3795. *E-mail:* ropers@swosu.edu.

Website: http://www.swosu.edu/.

Spartan College of Aeronautics and Technology

Tulsa, Oklahoma

Freshman Application Contact Mr. Mark Fowler, Vice President of Student Records and Finance, Spartan College of Aeronautics and Technology, 8820 East Pine Street, PO Box 582833, Tulsa, OK 74158-2833. *Phone:* 918-836-6886. *Toll-free phone:* 800-331-1204 (in-state); 800-331-124 (out-of-state). *Website:* http://www.spartan.edu/.

University of Central Oklahoma

Edmond, Oklahoma

- **State-supported** comprehensive, founded 1890, part of Oklahoma State Regents for Higher Education
- **Suburban** 200-acre campus with easy access to Oklahoma City
- **Endowment** $8.6 million
- **Coed** 15,379 undergraduate students, 72% full-time, 56% women, 44% men
- **Minimally difficult** entrance level, 79% of applicants were admitted

Undergraduates 11,010 full-time, 4,369 part-time. Students come from 50 states and territories; 91 other countries; 4% are from out of state; 9% Black or African American, non-Hispanic/Latino; 7% Hispanic/Latino; 3% Asian, non-Hispanic/Latino; 0.2% Native Hawaiian or other Pacific Islander, non-Hispanic/Latino; 4% American Indian or Alaska Native, non-Hispanic/Latino; 6% Two or more races, non-Hispanic/Latino; 3% Race/ethnicity unknown; 7% international; 12% transferred in; 12% live on campus. *Retention:* 65% of full-time freshmen returned.

Freshmen *Admission:* 4,784 applied, 3,774 admitted, 2,348 enrolled. *Average high school GPA:* 3.57. *Test scores:* ACT scores over 18: 82%; ACT scores over 24: 22%; ACT scores over 30: 3%.

Faculty *Total:* 1,024, 45% full-time, 33% with terminal degrees. *Student/faculty ratio:* 19:1.

Academics *Calendar:* semesters. *Degrees:* certificates, associate, bachelor's, and master's. *Special study options:* accelerated degree program, advanced placement credit, distance learning, double majors, English as a second language, honors programs, independent study, internships, part-time degree program, services for LD students, summer session for credit. *ROTC:* Army (b).

Computers on Campus 88 computers/terminals are available on campus for general student use. Students can access the following: computer help desk, free student e-mail accounts, online (class) grades, online (class) registration, online (class) schedules. Campuswide network is available. Wireless service is available via entire campus.

Student Life *Housing options:* coed, men-only, women-only. Campus housing is university owned and leased by the school. *Activities and organizations:* drama/theater group, student-run newspaper, radio and television station, choral group, marching band, Student Government Association, Student Programming Board, International Student Council, Panhellenic Council, Interfraternity Council, national fraternities, national sororities. *Campus security:* 24-hour emergency response devices and patrols, late-night transport/escort service. *Student services:* health clinic, personal/psychological counseling.

Athletics Member NCAA. All Division II. *Intercollegiate sports:* baseball M(s), basketball M(s)/W(s), cross-country running M(s)/W(s), football M(s), golf M(s)/W(s), soccer W(s), softball W(s), tennis M(s)/W(s), volleyball W(s), wrestling M(s). *Intramural sports:* badminton M/W, baseball M, basketball M/W, bowling M/W, football M/W, golf M/W, soccer M/W, softball M/W, swimming and diving M/W, table tennis M/W, tennis M/W, track and field M/W, ultimate Frisbee M/W, volleyball M/W, wrestling M.

Standardized Tests *Required:* SAT or ACT (for admission). *Required for some:* SAT and SAT Subject Tests or ACT (for admission). *Recommended:* SAT (for admission), ACT (for admission).

Costs (2012–13) *Tuition:* state resident $4460 full-time, $149 per credit hour part-time; nonresident $12,135 full-time, $405 per credit hour part-time. Full-time tuition and fees vary according to course load, degree level, and program. Part-time tuition and fees vary according to course load, degree level, and program. No tuition increase for student's term of enrollment. *Required fees:* $632 full-time, $21 per credit hour part-time. *Room and board:* $6708. Room and board charges vary according to board plan and housing facility. *Payment plan:* deferred payment. *Waivers:* employees or children of employees.

Financial Aid Of all full-time matriculated undergraduates who enrolled in 2010, 4,073 applied for aid, 3,449 were judged to have need, 349 had their need fully met. In 2010, 644 non-need-based awards were made. *Average percent of need met:* 68%. *Average financial aid package:* $7904. *Average need-based loan:* $5136. *Average need-based gift aid:* $8043. *Average non-need-based aid:* $3222. *Average indebtedness upon graduation:* $19,820.

Applying *Options:* electronic application, deferred entrance. *Application fee:* $40. *Required:* high school transcript, minimum 2.7 GPA, rank in upper 50% of high school class. *Application deadlines:* rolling (freshmen), rolling (out-of-state freshmen), rolling (transfers). *Notification:* continuous (freshmen), continuous (out-of-state freshmen), continuous (transfers).

Freshman Application Contact Ms. Stephanie Kahne, Director, Admissions and Records Processing, University of Central Oklahoma, Office of Enrollment Services, 100 North University Drive, Box 151, Edmond, OK 73034-5209. *Phone:* 405-974-2338 Ext. 2338. *Fax:* 405-341-4964. *E-mail:* admituco@uco.edu.
Website: http://www.uco.edu/.

University of Oklahoma

Norman, Oklahoma

- **State-supported** university, founded 1890
- **Suburban** 3153-acre campus with easy access to Oklahoma City
- **Endowment** $784.8 million
- **Coed** 21,109 undergraduate students, 86% full-time, 50% women, 50% men
- **Moderately difficult** entrance level, 79% of applicants were admitted

Undergraduates 18,104 full-time, 3,005 part-time. Students come from 54 states and territories; 111 other countries; 31% are from out of state; 5% Black or African American, non-Hispanic/Latino; 7% Hispanic/Latino; 5% Asian, non-Hispanic/Latino; 0.2% Native Hawaiian or other Pacific Islander, non-Hispanic/Latino; 5% American Indian or Alaska Native, non-Hispanic/Latino; 5% Two or more races, non-Hispanic/Latino; 5% Race/ethnicity unknown; 5% international; 6% transferred in; 32% live on campus. *Retention:* 85% of full-time freshmen returned.

Freshmen *Admission:* 11,650 applied, 9,220 admitted, 4,138 enrolled. *Average high school GPA:* 3.59. *Test scores:* SAT critical reading scores over 500: 80%; SAT math scores over 500: 88%; ACT scores over 18: 99%; SAT critical reading scores over 600: 39%; SAT math scores over 600: 50%; ACT scores over 24: 70%; SAT critical reading scores over 700: 13%; SAT math scores over 700: 14%; ACT scores over 30: 20%.

Faculty *Total:* 1,403, 82% full-time, 79% with terminal degrees. *Student/faculty ratio:* 19:1.

Academics *Calendar:* semesters. *Degrees:* bachelor's, master's, doctoral, and postbachelor's certificates. *Special study options:* academic remediation for entering students, accelerated degree program, adult/continuing education programs, advanced placement credit, cooperative education, distance learning, double majors, English as a second language, external degree program, freshman honors college, honors programs, independent study, internships, off-campus study, part-time degree program, services for LD students, student-designed majors, study abroad, summer session for credit. *ROTC:* Army (b), Navy (b), Air Force (b). *Unusual degree programs:* 3-2 business administration; engineering; English, mathematics/biostatistics, computer science.

Computers on Campus 4,500 computers/terminals and 2,200 ports are available on campus for general student use. Students can access the following: campus intranet, computer help desk, free student e-mail accounts, online (class) grades, online (class) registration, online (class) schedules. Campuswide network is available. 100% of college-owned or -operated housing units are wired for high-speed Internet access. Wireless service is available via entire campus.

Student Life *Housing:* on-campus residence required for freshman year. *Options:* coed, men-only, women-only, disabled students. Campus housing is university owned. Freshman campus housing is guaranteed. *Activities and organizations:* drama/theater group, student-run newspaper, radio and television station, choral group, marching band, Campus Activities Council, University of Oklahoma Student Association, OU Cousins, Fraternities/Sororities, The Big Event, national fraternities, national sororities. *Campus security:* 24-hour emergency response devices and patrols, student patrols, late-night transport/escort service, controlled dormitory access, crime prevention programs, police bicycle patrols, self-defense classes. *Student services:* health clinic, personal/psychological counseling, women's center, legal services.

Athletics Member NCAA. All Division I except football (Division I-A). *Intercollegiate sports:* baseball M(s), basketball M(s)/W(s), cheerleading M(s)/W(s), crew W(s), cross-country running M(s)/W(s), golf M(s)/W(s), gymnas-

tics M(s)/W(s), soccer W(s), softball W(s), tennis M(s)/W(s), track and field M(s)/W(s), volleyball W(s), wrestling M(s). *Intramural sports:* badminton M(c)/W(c), basketball M/W, crew M(c)/W(c), cross-country running M/W, equestrian sports M(c)/W(c), field hockey M(c)/W(c), golf M/W, ice hockey M(c), lacrosse M(c)/W(c), racquetball M/W, rugby M(c)/W(c), sailing M(c)/W(c), soccer M(c)/W, softball M/W, table tennis M/W, tennis M(c)/W(c), ultimate Frisbee M(c)/W(c), volleyball M(c)/W(c).

Standardized Tests *Required:* SAT or ACT (for admission).

Costs (2012–13) *Tuition:* state resident $3957 full-time, $132 per credit hour part-time; nonresident $15,594 full-time, $520 per credit hour part-time. Full-time tuition and fees vary according to course load, location, program, and reciprocity agreements. Part-time tuition and fees vary according to course load, location, program, and reciprocity agreements. No tuition increase for student's term of enrollment. *Required fees:* $3384 full-time, $104 per credit hour part-time, $127 per term part-time. *Room and board:* $8382; room only: $4588. Room and board charges vary according to board plan and housing facility. *Payment plan:* installment. *Waivers:* senior citizens and employees or children of employees.

Financial Aid Of all full-time matriculated undergraduates who enrolled in 2011, 11,305 applied for aid, 8,896 were judged to have need, 7,540 had their need fully met. 531 Federal Work-Study jobs (averaging $3320). 111 state and other part-time jobs (averaging $7404). In 2011, 1813 non-need-based awards were made. *Average percent of need met:* 88%. *Average financial aid package:* $11,896. *Average need-based loan:* $4365. *Average need-based gift aid:* $5522. *Average non-need-based aid:* $2069. *Average indebtedness upon graduation:* $26,005.

Applying *Options:* electronic application. *Application fee:* $40. *Required:* essay or personal statement, high school transcript, 15 specified curricular units. *Recommended:* letters of recommendation. *Application deadlines:* 4/1 (freshmen), 4/1 (out-of-state freshmen), 4/1 (transfers). *Notification:* continuous (freshmen), continuous (out-of-state freshmen), continuous (transfers).

Freshman Application Contact Mr. Andy Roop, Executive Director of Recruitment Services, University of Oklahoma, 550 Parrington Oval, Norman, OK 73019-3032. *Phone:* 405-325-2151. *Toll-free phone:* 800-234-6868. *Fax:* 405-325-7478. *E-mail:* ou-pss@ou.edu.
Website: http://www.ou.edu/.

University of Oklahoma Health Sciences Center

Oklahoma City, Oklahoma

- **State-supported** upper-level, founded 1890, part of University of Oklahoma
- **Urban** 200-acre campus with easy access to Oklahoma City
- **Endowment** $377.5 million
- **Coed** 875 undergraduate students, 95% full-time, 87% women, 13% men

Undergraduates 827 full-time, 48 part-time. Students come from 47 states and territories; 15 other countries; 13% are from out of state; 3% Black or African American, non-Hispanic/Latino; 7% Hispanic/Latino; 4% Asian, non-Hispanic/Latino; 5% American Indian or Alaska Native, non-Hispanic/Latino; 9% Two or more races, non-Hispanic/Latino; 0.9% Race/ethnicity unknown; 0.5% international; 46% transferred in; 16% live on campus.

Faculty *Total:* 448, 71% full-time, 56% with terminal degrees. *Student/faculty ratio:* 8:1.

Academics *Calendar:* semesters. *Degrees:* bachelor's, master's, doctoral, post-master's, and postbachelor's certificates. *Special study options:* advanced placement credit, distance learning, honors programs, internships, part-time degree program, summer session for credit. *ROTC:* Army (c), Air Force (c).

Computers on Campus 140 computers/terminals are available on campus for general student use. Students can access the following: campus intranet, computer help desk, free student e-mail accounts, online (class) grades, online (class) registration, online (class) schedules, online bursar bill and payment. Campuswide network is available. 100% of college-owned or -operated housing units are wired for high-speed Internet access. Wireless service is available via classrooms, computer centers, computer labs, learning centers, libraries, student centers.

Student Life *Housing options:* coed, disabled students. Campus housing is university owned. *Activities and organizations:* student-run newspaper, Health Sciences Center Student Association, College of Nursing Student Association, College of Medicine Student Association, Pharmacy Student Counsel, College of Allied Health Student Association. *Campus security:* 24-hour emergency response devices and patrols, late-night transport/escort service. *Student services:* health clinic, personal/psychological counseling, women's center.

Costs (2012–13) *Tuition:* state resident $3957 full-time, $132 per credit hour part-time; nonresident $15,594 full-time, $520 per semester hour part-time.

Full-time tuition and fees vary according to course level, course load, degree level, location, program, and student level. Part-time tuition and fees vary according to course level, course load, degree level, location, program, and student level. *Required fees:* $2095 full-time, $54 per credit hour part-time, $238 per term part-time. *Room and board:* Room and board charges vary according to location. *Payment plan:* installment. *Waivers:* employees or children of employees.
Applying *Options:* electronic application, deferred entrance. *Application deadline:* rolling (transfers). *Notification:* continuous (transfers).
Application Contact University of Oklahoma Health Sciences Center, PO Box 26901, Oklahoma City, OK 73190. *Phone:* 405-271-2359 Ext. 48916. *Website:* http://www.ouhsc.edu/.

University of Phoenix–Oklahoma City Campus

Oklahoma City, Oklahoma

Freshman Application Contact Marc Booker, Sr. Director, Office of Admissions and Evaluation, University of Phoenix–Oklahoma City Campus, 4035 South Riverpoint Parkway, Mail Stop CF-L101, Phoenix, AZ 85040-1958. *Phone:* 602-557-4609. *Toll-free phone:* 866-766-0766. *Fax:* 480-643-1156.
Website: http://www.phoenix.edu/.

University of Phoenix–Tulsa Campus

Tulsa, Oklahoma

Freshman Application Contact Marc Booker, Sr. Director, Office of Admissions and Evaluation, University of Phoenix–Tulsa Campus, 4615 East Elwood Street, Mail Stop AA-K101, Phoenix, AZ 85040-1958. *Phone:* 602-557-4609. *Toll-free phone:* 866-766-0766. *Fax:* 480-643-1156.
Website: http://www.phoenix.edu/.

University of Science and Arts of Oklahoma

Chickasha, Oklahoma

- **State-supported** 4-year, founded 1908, part of Oklahoma State Regents for Higher Education
- **Small-town** 75-acre campus with easy access to Oklahoma City
- **Coed** 983 undergraduate students, 88% full-time, 65% women, 35% men
- **Moderately difficult** entrance level, 39% of applicants were admitted

Undergraduates 863 full-time, 120 part-time. Students come from 24 states and territories; 19 other countries; 8% are from out of state; 4% Black or African American, non-Hispanic/Latino; 5% Hispanic/Latino; 0.8% Asian, non-Hispanic/Latino; 13% American Indian or Alaska Native, non-Hispanic/Latino; 6% international; 11% transferred in; 44% live on campus. *Retention:* 60% of full-time freshmen returned.
Freshmen *Admission:* 597 applied, 230 admitted, 187 enrolled. *Average high school GPA:* 3.44. *Test scores:* ACT scores over 18: 97%; ACT scores over 24: 42%; ACT scores over 30: 6%.
Faculty *Total:* 89, 62% full-time, 61% with terminal degrees. *Student/faculty ratio:* 13:1.
Academics *Calendar:* trimesters. *Degree:* bachelor's. *Special study options:* academic remediation for entering students, accelerated degree program, advanced placement credit, double majors, independent study, internships, off-campus study, part-time degree program, services for LD students, student-designed majors, summer session for credit.
Computers on Campus 175 computers/terminals are available on campus for general student use. Students can access the following: computer help desk, free student e-mail accounts, online (class) schedules. Campuswide network is available. 100% of college-owned or -operated housing units are wired for high-speed Internet access. Wireless service is available via entire campus.
Student Life *Housing:* on-campus residence required for freshman year. *Options:* coed. Campus housing is university owned. Freshman campus housing is guaranteed. *Activities and organizations:* drama/theater group, student-run newspaper, television station, choral group, Student Activities Board, Vol-

unteer Action Council, Psychology Club, Young Democrats, Young Conservatives, national fraternities. *Campus security:* 24-hour emergency response devices and patrols, controlled dormitory access. *Student services:* health clinic, personal/psychological counseling.
Athletics Member NAIA. *Intercollegiate sports:* baseball M(s), basketball M(s)/W(s), cheerleading M(s)/W(s), cross-country running M/W, soccer M(s)/W(s), softball W(s). *Intramural sports:* basketball M/W, football M/W, golf M/W, softball M/W, volleyball M/W.
Standardized Tests *Required:* SAT or ACT (for admission).
Costs (2012–13) *Tuition:* state resident $4230 full-time, $141 per credit hour part-time; nonresident $11,550 full-time, $385 per credit hour part-time. No tuition increase for student's term of enrollment. *Required fees:* $1170 full-time, $39 per credit hour part-time. *Room and board:* $5160; room only: $2680. Room and board charges vary according to board plan and housing facility. *Payment plan:* installment. *Waivers:* senior citizens and employees or children of employees.
Financial Aid Of all full-time matriculated undergraduates who enrolled in 2012, 677 applied for aid, 614 were judged to have need, 76 had their need fully met. 170 Federal Work-Study jobs (averaging $1732). In 2012, 78 non-need-based awards were made. *Average percent of need met:* 61%. *Average financial aid package:* $9418. *Average need-based loan:* $3281. *Average need-based gift aid:* $7467. *Average non-need-based aid:* $2129. *Average indebtedness upon graduation:* $18,378.
Applying *Options:* electronic application, deferred entrance. *Application fee:* $40. *Required for some:* high school transcript, minimum 3.0 GPA, Option 1: ACT of 24 and (3.0 GPA or top 50% HS Class), Option 2: 3.0 GPA and top 25% HS Class, Option 3: 3.0 GPA in 15-unit HS core and ACT of 22. *Recommended:* Option 1: ACT of 24 and (3.0 GPA or top 50% HS Class), Option 2: 3.0 GPA and top 25% HS Class, Option 3: 3.0 GPA in 15-unit HS core and ACT of 22. *Application deadlines:* 9/2 (freshmen), 9/2 (out-of-state freshmen), 9/2 (transfers). *Notification:* continuous until 1/2 (freshmen), continuous until 1/2 (out-of-state freshmen), continuous (transfers).
Freshman Application Contact Ms. Monica Trevino, Director of Admissions, University of Science and Arts of Oklahoma, 1727 West Alabama, Chickasha, OK 73018-5322. *Phone:* 405-574-1356. *Toll-free phone:* 800-933-8726. *Fax:* 405-574-1220. *E-mail:* usao-admissions@usao.edu. *Website:* http://www.usao.edu/.

University of Tulsa

Tulsa, Oklahoma

- **Independent** university, founded 1894, affiliated with Presbyterian Church (U.S.A.)
- **Urban** 209-acre campus with easy access to Oklahoma City
- **Endowment** $802.5 million
- **Coed** 3,160 undergraduate students, 95% full-time, 43% women, 57% men
- **Very difficult** entrance level, 41% of applicants were admitted

Undergraduates 3,007 full-time, 153 part-time. Students come from 42 states and territories; 53 other countries; 47% are from out of state; 5% Black or African American, non-Hispanic/Latino; 4% Hispanic/Latino; 3% Asian, non-Hispanic/Latino; 4% American Indian or Alaska Native, non-Hispanic/Latino; 2% Two or more races, non-Hispanic/Latino; 2% Race/ethnicity unknown; 22% international; 4% transferred in; 74% live on campus. *Retention:* 86% of full-time freshmen returned.
Freshmen *Admission:* 6,984 applied, 2,844 admitted, 806 enrolled. *Average high school GPA:* 3.75. *Test scores:* SAT critical reading scores over 500: 96%; SAT math scores over 500: 96%; ACT scores over 18: 100%; SAT critical reading scores over 600: 67%; SAT math scores over 600: 72%; ACT scores over 24: 84%; SAT critical reading scores over 700: 31%; SAT math scores over 700: 29%; ACT scores over 30: 37%.
Faculty *Total:* 404, 79% full-time, 96% with terminal degrees. *Student/faculty ratio:* 11:1.
Academics *Calendar:* semesters. *Degrees:* bachelor's, master's, doctoral, and postbachelor's certificates. *Special study options:* accelerated degree program, adult/continuing education programs, advanced placement credit, double majors, English as a second language, honors programs, independent study, internships, part-time degree program, services for LD students, student-designed majors, study abroad, summer session for credit. *ROTC:* Air Force (c). *Unusual degree programs:* 3-2 business administration.
Computers on Campus 900 computers/terminals are available on campus for general student use. Students can access the following: campus intranet, computer help desk, free student e-mail accounts, online (class) grades, online (class) registration, online (class) schedules. Campuswide network is available. 100% of college-owned or -operated housing units are wired for high-speed Internet access. Wireless service is available via entire campus.

Student Life *Housing:* on-campus residence required through sophomore year. *Options:* coed, men-only, women-only, disabled students. Campus housing is university owned. Freshman campus housing is guaranteed. *Activities and organizations:* drama/theater group, student-run newspaper, radio and television station, choral group, marching band, Student Association, Residence Hall Association, Pre-Professional organizations, Intramural sports, Greek life, national fraternities, national sororities. *Campus security:* 24-hour emergency response devices and patrols, late-night transport/escort service, controlled dormitory access. *Student services:* health clinic, personal/psychological counseling, women's center.

Athletics Member NCAA. All Division I except football (Division I-A). *Intercollegiate sports:* basketball M(s)/W(s), crew W(s), cross-country running M(s)/W(s), golf M(s)/W(s), soccer M(s)/W(s), softball W(s), tennis M(s)/W(s), track and field M(s)/W(s), volleyball W(s). *Intramural sports:* badminton M/W, basketball M/W, bowling M/W, crew M(c), cross-country running M/W, fencing M(c)/W(c), football M/W, golf M/W, racquetball M/W, rugby M(c), soccer M/W, softball M/W, squash M/W, swimming and diving M/W, table tennis M/W, tennis M/W, track and field M/W, volleyball M/W, water polo M/W, weight lifting M/W.

Standardized Tests *Required:* SAT or ACT (for admission).

Costs (2013–14) *One-time required fee:* $485. *Comprehensive fee:* $44,826 includes full-time tuition ($34,030), mandatory fees ($320), and room and board ($10,476). Full-time tuition and fees vary according to course load. Part-time tuition: $1221 per credit. Part-time tuition and fees vary according to course load. *College room only:* $5800. Room and board charges vary according to board plan and housing facility. *Payment plans:* tuition prepayment, installment. *Waivers:* employees or children of employees.

Financial Aid Of all full-time matriculated undergraduates who enrolled in 2012, 2,635 applied for aid, 1,252 were judged to have need, 603 had their need fully met. In 2012, 1260 non-need-based awards were made. *Average percent of need met:* 82%. *Average financial aid package:* $24,613. *Average need-based loan:* $5888. *Average need-based gift aid:* $6826. *Average non-need-based aid:* $15,555. *Average indebtedness upon graduation:* $34,574.

Applying *Options:* electronic application, early admission, early action, deferred entrance. *Application fee:* $50. *Required:* essay or personal statement, high school transcript, 1 letter of recommendation, interview. *Recommended:* minimum 3.0 GPA. *Application deadlines:* rolling (freshmen), rolling (out-of-state freshmen), rolling (transfers), 11/1 (early action). *Notification:* continuous (freshmen), continuous (out-of-state freshmen), continuous (transfers), 11/22 (early action).

Freshman Application Contact Mr. Earl Johnson, Dean of Admission, University of Tulsa, 800 South Tucker Drive, Tulsa, OK 74104. *Phone:* 918-631-2307. *Toll-free phone:* 800-331-3050. *Fax:* 918-631-5003. *E-mail:* admission@utulsa.edu.
Website: http://www.utulsa.edu/.

See below for display ad and page 1612 for the College Close-Up.

OREGON

The Art Institute of Portland
Portland, Oregon

- **Proprietary** 4-year, founded 1963, part of Education Management Corporation
- **Urban** campus
- **Coed**

Academics *Calendar:* quarters. *Degrees:* diplomas, associate, and bachelor's.
Freshman Application Contact The Art Institute of Portland, 1122 NW Davis Street, Portland, OR 97209. *Phone:* 503-228-6528. *Toll-free phone:* 888-228-6528.
Website: http://www.artinstitutes.edu/portland/.

See full-page ad on page 54 and page 1106 for the College Close-Up.

Birthingway College of Midwifery
Portland, Oregon

Director of Admissions Director of Admission, Birthingway College of Midwifery, 12113 SE Foster Road, Portland, OR 97299. *Phone:* 503-760-3131. *E-mail:* info@birthingway.edu.
Website: http://www.birthingway.edu/.

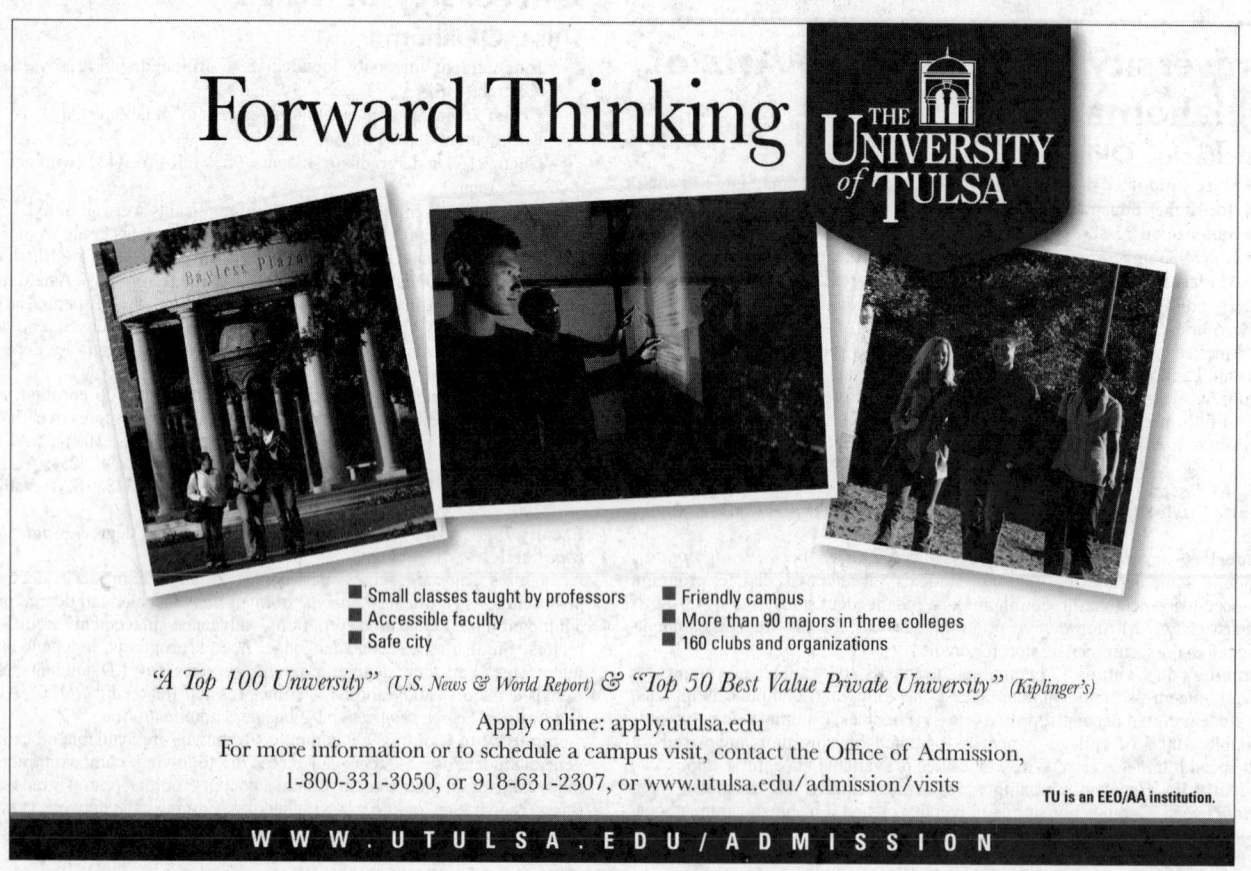

Concordia University

Portland, Oregon

- **Independent** comprehensive, founded 1905, affiliated with Lutheran Church–Missouri Synod, part of Concordia University System
- **Urban** 13-acre campus
- **Endowment** $7.2 million
- **Coed** 1,369 undergraduate students, 84% full-time, 67% women, 33% men
- **Moderately difficult** entrance level, 54% of applicants were admitted

Undergraduates 1,147 full-time, 222 part-time. Students come from 36 states and territories; 13 other countries; 42% are from out of state; 7% Black or African American, non-Hispanic/Latino; 8% Hispanic/Latino; 4% Asian, non-Hispanic/Latino; 2% Native Hawaiian or other Pacific Islander, non-Hispanic/Latino; 0.9% American Indian or Alaska Native, non-Hispanic/Latino; 4% Two or more races, non-Hispanic/Latino; 13% Race/ethnicity unknown; 1% international; 21% transferred in; 36% live on campus. *Retention:* 70% of full-time freshmen returned.

Freshmen *Admission:* 1,961 applied, 1,055 admitted, 247 enrolled. *Average high school GPA:* 3.42. *Test scores:* SAT critical reading scores over 500: 54%; SAT math scores over 500: 57%; ACT scores over 18: 78%; SAT critical reading scores over 600: 13%; SAT math scores over 600: 14%; ACT scores over 24: 29%; SAT critical reading scores over 700: 1%; SAT math scores over 700: 1%; ACT scores over 30: 1%.

Faculty *Total:* 259, 25% full-time, 42% with terminal degrees. *Student/faculty ratio:* 19:1.

Academics *Calendar:* semesters. *Degrees:* certificates, associate, bachelor's, master's, and postbachelor's certificates. *Special study options:* academic remediation for entering students, accelerated degree program, adult/continuing education programs, advanced placement credit, distance learning, double majors, English as a second language, honors programs, independent study, internships, off-campus study, part-time degree program, services for LD students, student-designed majors, study abroad, summer session for credit. *ROTC:* Air Force (c).

Computers on Campus 100 computers/terminals are available on campus for general student use. Students can access the following: campus intranet, computer help desk, free student e-mail accounts, online (class) grades, online (class) registration, online (class) schedules, campus wide wifi. Campuswide network is available. 100% of college-owned or -operated housing units are wired for high-speed Internet access. Wireless service is available via entire campus.

Student Life *Housing:* on-campus residence required through sophomore year. *Options:* coed. Campus housing is university owned. Freshman applicants given priority for college housing. *Activities and organizations:* drama/theater group, student-run newspaper, choral group, Hawaiian Club, The Navy—athletic boosters, Soccer Club, Ultimate Frisbee Club, Volunteer Corps (Teacher, Service, Athlete). *Campus security:* 24-hour emergency response devices and patrols, late-night transport/escort service, controlled dormitory access, Extensive video camera security of main campus areas. *Student services:* health clinic, personal/psychological counseling.

Athletics Member NAIA. *Intercollegiate sports:* baseball M(s), basketball M(s)/W(s), cross-country running M(s)/W(s), golf M(s)/W(s), soccer M(s)/W(s), softball W(s), track and field M(s)/W(s), volleyball W(s). *Intramural sports:* basketball M/W, ultimate Frisbee M(c)/W(c), volleyball M/W.

Standardized Tests *Required:* SAT or ACT (for admission).

Financial Aid Of all full-time matriculated undergraduates who enrolled in 2011, 999 applied for aid, 905 were judged to have need, 57 had their need fully met. In 2011, 129 non-need-based awards were made. *Average financial aid package:* $17,414. *Average need-based loan:* $4814. *Average need-based gift aid:* $5826. *Average non-need-based aid:* $7683. *Average indebtedness upon graduation:* $32,888.

Applying *Options:* electronic application, deferred entrance. *Required:* essay or personal statement, high school transcript, minimum 2.5 GPA, 1 letter of recommendation. *Required for some:* interview. *Recommended:* interview. *Application deadlines:* rolling (freshmen), rolling (transfers). *Notification:* continuous (freshmen), continuous (transfers).

Freshman Application Contact Ms. Bobi Swan, Dean of Admission, Concordia University, 2811 Northeast Holman, Portland, OR 97211-6099. *Phone:* 503-493-6526. *Toll-free phone:* 800-321-9371. *Fax:* 503-280-8531. *E-mail:* admissions@cu-portland.edu. *Website:* http://www.cu-portland.edu/.

Corban University

Salem, Oregon

- **Independent Christian** comprehensive, founded 1935
- **Suburban** 145-acre campus with easy access to Portland
- **Endowment** $1.6 million
- **Coed** 954 undergraduate students, 93% full-time, 62% women, 38% men
- **Moderately difficult** entrance level, 34% of applicants were admitted

Undergraduates 886 full-time, 68 part-time. Students come from 20 states and territories; 5 other countries; 44% are from out of state; 2% Black or African American, non-Hispanic/Latino; 6% Hispanic/Latino; 5% Asian, non-Hispanic/Latino; 2% Native Hawaiian or other Pacific Islander, non-Hispanic/Latino; 3% American Indian or Alaska Native, non-Hispanic/Latino; 5% Race/ethnicity unknown; 0.8% international; 5% transferred in; 63% live on campus. *Retention:* 68% of full-time freshmen returned.

Freshmen *Admission:* 2,688 applied, 915 admitted, 218 enrolled. *Average high school GPA:* 3.57. *Test scores:* SAT critical reading scores over 500: 66%; SAT math scores over 500: 58%; SAT writing scores over 500: 55%; ACT scores over 18: 89%; SAT critical reading scores over 600: 25%; SAT math scores over 600: 20%; SAT writing scores over 600: 16%; ACT scores over 24: 37%; SAT critical reading scores over 700: 5%; SAT math scores over 700: 1%; SAT writing scores over 700: 2%; ACT scores over 30: 7%.

Faculty *Total:* 107, 48% full-time, 49% with terminal degrees. *Student/faculty ratio:* 13:1.

Academics *Calendar:* semesters. *Degrees:* certificates, associate, bachelor's, master's, doctoral, and postbachelor's certificates. *Special study options:* accelerated degree program, adult/continuing education programs, advanced placement credit, cooperative education, distance learning, double majors, freshman honors college, honors programs, independent study, internships, off-campus study, services for LD students, student-designed majors, study abroad, summer session for credit. *ROTC:* Army (c), Air Force (c).

Computers on Campus 64 computers/terminals are available on campus for general student use. Students can access the following: computer help desk, free student e-mail accounts, online (class) grades, online (class) schedules. Campuswide network is available. 100% of college-owned or -operated housing units are wired for high-speed Internet access. Wireless service is available via entire campus.

Student Life *Housing:* on-campus residence required through sophomore year. *Options:* men-only, women-only, disabled students. Campus housing is university owned. Freshman campus housing is guaranteed. *Activities and organizations:* drama/theater group, student-run newspaper, choral group, Student Fellowship Groups, Poetry Club, Worship Teams, Drama Club, Westrek Hiking Club. *Campus security:* 24-hour emergency response devices and patrols, student patrols, late-night transport/escort service, controlled dormitory access. *Student services:* health clinic, personal/psychological counseling.

Athletics Member NAIA, NCCAA. *Intercollegiate sports:* baseball M(s), basketball M(s)/W(s), cross-country running M(s)/W(s), golf M(s)/W(s), soccer M(s)/W(s), softball W(s), track and field M(s)/W(s), volleyball W(s). *Intramural sports:* basketball M/W, football M, soccer M/W, table tennis M/W, volleyball M/W.

Standardized Tests *Required:* SAT or ACT (for admission).

Costs (2012–13) *One-time required fee:* $100. *Comprehensive fee:* $34,575 includes full-time tuition ($25,975), mandatory fees ($455), and room and board ($8145). Full-time tuition and fees vary according to course level, degree level, program, and reciprocity agreements. Part-time tuition: $1082 per credit hour. Part-time tuition and fees vary according to course level, course load, degree level, program, and reciprocity agreements. *College room only:* $2375. Room and board charges vary according to board plan. *Payment plan:* installment. *Waivers:* senior citizens and employees or children of employees.

Financial Aid Of all full-time matriculated undergraduates who enrolled in 2012, 740 applied for aid, 705 were judged to have need, 79 had their need fully met. 200 Federal Work-Study jobs (averaging $1806). In 2012, 98 non-need-based awards were made. *Average percent of need met:* 64%. *Average financial aid package:* $19,467. *Average need-based loan:* $4498. *Average need-based gift aid:* $15,974. *Average non-need-based aid:* $7487. *Average indebtedness upon graduation:* $23,853.

Applying *Options:* electronic application. *Application fee:* $35. *Required:* essay or personal statement, high school transcript, minimum 2.7 GPA, 2 letters of recommendation. *Application deadlines:* 8/1 (freshmen), 8/1 (transfers). *Notification:* continuous (freshmen).

Freshman Application Contact Ms. Heidi Stowman, Director of Admissions, Corban University, 5000 Deer Park Drive, SE, Salem, OR 97301-9392. *Phone:* 503-375-7115. *Toll-free phone:* 800-845-3005. *Fax:* 503-585-4316. *E-mail:* admissions@corban.edu. *Website:* http://www.corban.edu/.

DeVry University

Portland, Oregon

Freshman Application Contact DeVry University, 9755 Southwest Barnes Road, Suite 150, Portland, OR 97225-6651. *Toll-free phone:* 866-338-7941. *Website:* http://www.devry.edu/.

Eastern Oregon University

La Grande, Oregon

- **State-supported** comprehensive, founded 1929, part of Oregon University System
- **Rural** 121-acre campus
- **Coed**
- **Moderately difficult** entrance level

Faculty *Student/faculty ratio:* 24:1.
Academics *Calendar:* quarters. *Degrees:* certificates, associate, bachelor's, and master's.
Student Life *Campus security:* controlled dormitory access.
Athletics Member NCAA, NAIA. All NCAA Division III.
Standardized Tests *Required:* SAT or ACT (for admission).
Financial Aid *Of all full-time matriculated undergraduates who enrolled in 2011,* 2,062 applied for aid, 1,844 were judged to have need, 374 had their need fully met. *In 2011,* 37 non-need-based awards were made. *Average percent of need met:* 49. *Average financial aid package:* $9456. *Average need-based loan:* $3741. *Average need-based gift aid:* $5247. *Average non-need-based aid:* $1434. *Average indebtedness upon graduation:* $21,973.
Applying *Options:* electronic application, early admission, early action, deferred entrance. *Required:* high school transcript, minimum 3.0 GPA. *Required for some:* essay or personal statement, 2 letters of recommendation.
Freshman Application Contact Tyler Dubsky, Assistant Director of Admissions, Eastern Oregon University, Eastern Oregon University, La Grande, OR. *Phone:* 541-962-3085. *Toll-free phone:* 800-452-8639. *Fax:* 541-962-3418. *E-mail:* admissions@eou.edu.
Website: http://www.eou.edu/.

George Fox University

Newberg, Oregon

- **Independent Friends** university, founded 1891
- **Small-town** 108-acre campus with easy access to Portland
- **Endowment** $18.0 million
- **Coed** 2,184 undergraduate students, 88% full-time, 59% women, 41% men
- **Moderately difficult** entrance level, 75% of applicants were admitted

Undergraduates 1,928 full-time, 256 part-time. Students come from 35 states and territories; 31 other countries; 35% are from out of state; 2% Black or African American, non-Hispanic/Latino; 7% Hispanic/Latino; 4% Asian, non-Hispanic/Latino; 0.5% Native Hawaiian or other Pacific Islander, non-Hispanic/Latino; 0.6% American Indian or Alaska Native, non-Hispanic/Latino; 4% Two or more races, non-Hispanic/Latino; 5% Race/ethnicity unknown; 6% international; 4% transferred in; 52% live on campus. *Retention:* 82% of full-time freshmen returned.
Freshmen *Admission:* 2,215 applied, 1,672 admitted, 422 enrolled. *Average high school GPA:* 3.62. *Test scores:* SAT critical reading scores over 500: 74%; SAT math scores over 500: 77%; SAT writing scores over 500: 66%; ACT scores over 18: 93%; SAT critical reading scores over 600: 37%; SAT math scores over 600: 34%; SAT writing scores over 600: 28%; ACT scores over 24: 49%; SAT critical reading scores over 700: 10%; SAT math scores over 700: 5%; SAT writing scores over 700: 6%; ACT scores over 30: 9%.
Faculty *Total:* 377, 43% full-time, 50% with terminal degrees. *Student/faculty ratio:* 13:1.
Academics *Calendar:* semesters. *Degrees:* bachelor's, master's, doctoral, post-master's, and postbachelor's certificates. *Special study options:* academic remediation for entering students, accelerated degree program, adult/continuing education programs, advanced placement credit, distance learning, double majors, English as a second language, honors programs, independent study, internships, off-campus study, part-time degree program, services for LD students, student-designed majors, study abroad, summer session for credit. *ROTC:* Air Force (c). *Unusual degree programs:* 3-2 engineering.

Computers on Campus 186 computers/terminals are available on campus for general student use. Students can access the following: campus intranet, computer help desk, free student e-mail accounts, online (class) grades, online (class) registration, online (class) schedules, online acceptance of financial aid. Campuswide network is available. 100% of college-owned or -operated housing units are wired for high-speed Internet access. Wireless service is available via classrooms, computer centers, computer labs, dorm rooms, learning centers, libraries, student centers.
Student Life *Housing:* on-campus residence required through junior year. *Options:* men-only, women-only, disabled students. Campus housing is university owned. Freshman applicants given priority for college housing. *Activities and organizations:* drama/theater group, student-run newspaper, radio station, choral group, student government, Christian Ministries, Orientation Committee, Outdoor Club and Bruin Ambassadors, Blue Zone. *Campus security:* 24-hour emergency response devices and patrols, student patrols, late-night transport/escort service, controlled dormitory access, parking lot cameras, and video surveillance of key buildings. *Student services:* health clinic, personal/psychological counseling.
Athletics Member NCAA. All Division III. *Intercollegiate sports:* baseball M, basketball M/W, cross-country running M/W, football M, golf M/W, lacrosse W, soccer M/W, softball W, tennis M/W, track and field M/W, volleyball W. *Intramural sports:* badminton M/W, basketball M/W, football M/W, golf M/W, racquetball M/W, rock climbing M/W, soccer M/W, table tennis M/W, tennis M/W, volleyball M/W.
Standardized Tests *Required:* SAT or ACT (for admission).
Costs (2012–13) *Comprehensive fee:* $39,590 includes full-time tuition ($29,900), mandatory fees ($330), and room and board ($9360). Part-time tuition: $905 per semester hour. Part-time tuition and fees vary according to course load. *College room only:* $5460. Room and board charges vary according to board plan. *Payment plan:* installment. *Waivers:* senior citizens and employees or children of employees.
Financial Aid *Of all full-time matriculated undergraduates who enrolled in 2012,* 1,651 applied for aid, 1,523 were judged to have need, 498 had their need fully met. In 2012, 107 non-need-based awards were made. *Average percent of need met:* 85%. *Average financial aid package:* $26,429. *Average need-based loan:* $3633. *Average need-based gift aid:* $9787. *Average non-need-based aid:* $8812. *Average indebtedness upon graduation:* $23,512.
Applying *Options:* electronic application, early action, deferred entrance. *Application fee:* $40. *Required:* essay or personal statement, high school transcript, 2 letters of recommendation. *Required for some:* interview. *Recommended:* minimum 2.6 GPA, interview. *Application deadlines:* rolling (freshmen), 6/1 (transfers), 11/15 (early action). *Notification:* continuous until 10/1 (freshmen), continuous (transfers), 12/15 (early action).
Freshman Application Contact Ms. Lindsay Peterson, Director of Undergraduate Admissions, George Fox University, 414 North Meridian Street, Newberg, OR 97132. *Phone:* 503-554-2240. *Toll-free phone:* 800-765-4369. *Fax:* 503-554-3110. *E-mail:* admissions@georgefox.edu.
Website: http://www.georgefox.edu/.

Gutenberg College

Eugene, Oregon

Freshman Application Contact Mr. Terry Stollar, Director of Admissions and Development, Gutenberg College, 1883 University Street, Eugene, OR 97403. *Phone:* 541-736-9071. *Fax:* 541-683-6997. *E-mail:* tstollar@gutenberg.edu.
Website: http://www.gutenberg.edu/.

ITT Technical Institute

Portland, Oregon

- **Proprietary** primarily 2-year, founded 1971, part of ITT Educational Services, Inc.
- **Urban** campus
- **Coed**
- **Minimally difficult** entrance level

Academics *Calendar:* quarters. *Degrees:* associate and bachelor's.
Financial Aid *Of all full-time matriculated undergraduates who enrolled in 2011,* 15 Federal Work-Study jobs (averaging $5000).
Freshman Application Contact Director of Recruitment, ITT Technical Institute, 9500 Northeast Cascades Parkway, Portland, OR 97220. *Phone:* 503-255-6500. *Toll-free phone:* 800-234-5488.
Website: http://www.itt-tech.edu/.

ITT Technical Institute

Salem, Oregon

- **Proprietary** 4-year
- **Coed**
- **Minimally difficult** entrance level

Academics *Degrees:* associate and bachelor's.

Freshman Application Contact Director of Recruiting, ITT Technical Institute, 4825 Commercial Street SE, Suite 100, Salem, OR 97302-2177. *Phone:* 503-579-2300. *Toll-free phone:* 877-273-7397. *Website:* http://www.itt-tech.edu/.

Lewis & Clark College

Portland, Oregon

- **Independent** comprehensive, founded 1867
- **Suburban** 137-acre campus with easy access to Portland
- **Endowment** $201.6 million
- **Coed**
- **Very difficult** entrance level

Faculty *Student/faculty ratio:* 12:1.

Academics *Calendar:* semesters. *Degrees:* bachelor's, master's, doctoral, and post-master's certificates.

Student Life *Campus security:* 24-hour emergency response devices and patrols, student patrols, late-night transport/escort service, controlled dormitory access.

Athletics Member NCAA. All Division III.

Standardized Tests *Required:* SAT or ACT, or academic portfolio. Students may apply via Portfolio Path where test scores are optional (for admission). *Required for some:* SAT or ACT (for admission).

Costs (2012–13) *Comprehensive fee:* $50,688 includes full-time tuition ($39,970), mandatory fees ($360), and room and board ($10,358). *College room only:* $5450. Room and board charges vary according to board plan and housing facility.

Financial Aid *Of all full-time matriculated undergraduates who enrolled in 2011,* 1,383 applied for aid, 1,240 were judged to have need, 466 had their need fully met. *In 2011,* 314 non-need-based awards were made. *Average percent of need met:* 89. *Average financial aid package:* $31,841. *Average need-based loan:* $4980. *Average need-based gift aid:* $26,166. *Average non-need-based aid:* $10,631. *Average indebtedness upon graduation:* $22,956.

Applying *Options:* electronic application, early action, deferred entrance. *Application fee:* $50. *Required:* essay or personal statement, high school transcript, minimum 2.0 GPA, "portfolio path" applicants submit samples of writing. *Required for some:* 4 letters of recommendation. *Recommended:* minimum 3.0 GPA, interview.

Freshman Application Contact Lisa Meyer, Dean of Admissions and Financial Aid, Lewis & Clark College, 0615 SW Palatine Hill Road, Portland, OR 97219. *Phone:* 503-768-7040. *Toll-free phone:* 800-444-4111. *Fax:* 503-768-7055. *E-mail:* admissions@lclark.edu. *Website:* http://www.lclark.edu/.

See below for display ad and page 1352 for the College Close-Up.

Linfield College

McMinnville, Oregon

- **Independent American Baptist Churches in the USA** 4-year, founded 1849, part of Linfield College includes the Linfield College McMinnville Campus (209065); the School of Nursing in Portland, Oregon (437316); and the Linfield College Adult Degree Program (437325)
- **Small-town** 193-acre campus with easy access to Portland
- **Endowment** $78.1 million
- **Coed** 1,663 undergraduate students, 98% full-time, 60% women, 40% men
- **Moderately difficult** entrance level, 83% of applicants were admitted

Undergraduates 1,633 full-time, 30 part-time. Students come from 21 states and territories; 20 other countries; 46% are from out of state; 2% Black or African American, non-Hispanic/Latino; 8% Hispanic/Latino; 6% Asian, non-Hispanic/Latino; 0.5% Native Hawaiian or other Pacific Islander, non-Hispanic/Latino; 1% American Indian or Alaska Native, non-Hispanic/Latino; 8% Two or more races, non-Hispanic/Latino; 5% Race/ethnicity unknown; 6% international; 3% transferred in; 75% live on campus. *Retention:* 88% of full-time freshmen returned.

LEWIS & CLARK COLLEGE

For more information, contact:

Emily A. Decker
Office of Admissions
0615 SW Palatine Hill Road
Portland, Oregon 97219
E-mail: admiss@lclark.edu

www.lclark.edu

Freshmen *Admission:* 2,338 applied, 1,936 admitted, 443 enrolled. *Average high school GPA:* 3.5. *Test scores:* SAT critical reading scores over 500: 67%; SAT math scores over 500: 74%; SAT writing scores over 500: 58%; ACT scores over 18: 94%; SAT critical reading scores over 600: 23%; SAT math scores over 600: 29%; SAT writing scores over 600: 18%; ACT scores over 24: 52%; SAT critical reading scores over 700: 3%; SAT math scores over 700: 3%; SAT writing scores over 700: 1%; ACT scores over 30: 9%.
Faculty *Total:* 196, 61% full-time, 68% with terminal degrees. *Student/faculty ratio:* 11:1.
Academics *Calendar:* 4-1-4. *Degree:* bachelor's. *Special study options:* accelerated degree program, adult/continuing education programs, advanced placement credit, distance learning, double majors, English as a second language, external degree program, independent study, internships, off-campus study, part-time degree program, services for LD students, student-designed majors, study abroad, summer session for credit. *ROTC:* Air Force (c). *Unusual degree programs:* 3-2 engineering with Washington State University, Oregon State University, University of Southern California.
Computers on Campus 250 computers/terminals are available on campus for general student use. Students can access the following: computer help desk, free student e-mail accounts, online (class) grades, online (class) registration, online (class) schedules. Campuswide network is available. 100% of college-owned or -operated housing units are wired for high-speed Internet access. Wireless service is available via classrooms, computer centers, computer labs, dorm rooms, learning centers, libraries, student centers.
Student Life *Housing:* on-campus residence required through junior year. *Options:* coed, men-only, women-only, disabled students. Campus housing is university owned. Freshman campus housing is guaranteed. *Activities and organizations:* drama/theater group, student-run newspaper, radio station, choral group, Fellowship of Christian Athletes, Linfield Ultimate Players Association, Hawaiian Club, International Club, Outdoor Club, national fraternities, national sororities. *Campus security:* 24-hour emergency response devices and patrols, late-night transport/escort service, controlled dormitory access. *Student services:* health clinic, personal/psychological counseling.
Athletics Member NCAA. All Division III. *Intercollegiate sports:* baseball M, basketball M/W, cross-country running M/W, football M, golf M/W, lacrosse W, soccer M/W, softball W, swimming and diving M/W, tennis M/W, track and field M/W, volleyball W. *Intramural sports:* basketball M/W, bowling M/W, soccer M/W, softball M/W, ultimate Frisbee M/W, volleyball M/W.
Standardized Tests *Required:* SAT or ACT (for admission).
Costs (2012–13) *Comprehensive fee:* $43,828 includes full-time tuition ($34,000), mandatory fees ($328), and room and board ($9500). Full-time

tuition and fees vary according to location. Part-time tuition: $1059 per semester hour. Part-time tuition and fees vary according to course load and location. *College room only:* $5180. Room and board charges vary according to board plan, housing facility, and location. *Payment plan:* installment. *Waivers:* senior citizens and employees or children of employees.
Financial Aid Of all full-time matriculated undergraduates who enrolled in 2012, 1,337 applied for aid, 1,165 were judged to have need, 335 had their need fully met. 531 Federal Work-Study jobs (averaging $2427). 398 state and other part-time jobs (averaging $2234). In 2012, 340 non-need-based awards were made. *Average percent of need met:* 82%. *Average financial aid package:* $27,068. *Average need-based loan:* $4607. *Average need-based gift aid:* $9439. *Average non-need-based aid:* $14,337. *Average indebtedness upon graduation:* $29,751.
Applying *Options:* electronic application, early action, deferred entrance. *Required:* essay or personal statement, high school transcript, 1 letter of recommendation. *Recommended:* interview. *Application deadlines:* 2/15 (freshmen), 4/15 (transfers), 11/15 (early action). *Notification:* 4/1 (freshmen), 5/15 (transfers), 1/15 (early action).
Freshman Application Contact Ms. Lisa Knodle-Bragiel, Director of Admission, Linfield College, 900 SE Baker Street, McMinnville, OR 97128. *Phone:* 503-883-2213. *Toll-free phone:* 800-640-2287. *Fax:* 503-883-2472. *E-mail:* admission@linfield.edu.
Website: http://www.linfield.edu/.

See below for display ad and page 1360 for the College Close-Up.

Marylhurst University
Marylhurst, Oregon

- **Independent Roman Catholic** comprehensive, founded 1893
- **Suburban** 63-acre campus with easy access to Portland
- **Endowment** $15.2 million
- **Coed, primarily women**
- **Noncompetitive** entrance level

Faculty *Student/faculty ratio:* 7:1.
Academics *Calendar:* quarters. *Degrees:* bachelor's, master's, post-master's, and postbachelor's certificates.
Student Life *Campus security:* security is available during campus hours.

Financial Aid *Of all full-time matriculated undergraduates who enrolled in 2011,* 320 applied for aid, 299 were judged to have need, 12 had their need fully met. 61 Federal Work-Study jobs (averaging $3250). *In 2011,* 33 non-need-based awards were made. *Average percent of need met:* 44. *Average financial aid package:* $10,214. *Average need-based loan:* $4187. *Average need-based gift aid:* $7395. *Average non-need-based aid:* $2220. *Average indebtedness upon graduation:* $24,269.

Applying *Options:* electronic application, deferred entrance. *Application fee:* $40. *Required:* essay or personal statement, high school transcript, minimum 2.5 GPA. *Required for some:* 2 letters of recommendation, interview.

Freshman Application Contact Chris Sweet, Director of Admissions, Marylhurst University, 17600 Pacific Highway, PO Box 261, Marylhurst, OR 97036-0261. *Phone:* 503-699-6267. *Toll-free phone:* 800-634-9982. *Fax:* 503-699-6320. *E-mail:* admissions@marylhurst.edu.
Website: http://www.marylhurst.edu/.

Mount Angel Seminary

Saint Benedict, Oregon

Director of Admissions Registrar/Admissions Officer, Mount Angel Seminary, Saint Benedict, OR 97373. *Phone:* 503-845-3951 Ext. 14. *E-mail:* admissions@mtangel.edu.
Website: http://www.mountangelabbey.org/seminary/.

Multnomah University

Portland, Oregon

- **Independent interdenominational** comprehensive, founded 1936
- **Urban** 22-acre campus
- **Endowment** $6.8 million
- **Coed** 503 undergraduate students, 82% full-time, 40% women, 60% men
- **Moderately difficult** entrance level, 64% of applicants were admitted

Undergraduates 414 full-time, 89 part-time. Students come from 25 states and territories; 4 other countries; 50% are from out of state; 3% Black or African American, non-Hispanic/Latino; 6% Hispanic/Latino; 2% Asian, non-Hispanic/Latino; 1% Native Hawaiian or other Pacific Islander, non-Hispanic/Latino; 0.4% American Indian or Alaska Native, non-Hispanic/Latino; 4% Two or more races, non-Hispanic/Latino; 3% Race/ethnicity unknown; 0.6% international; 15% transferred in; 42% live on campus. *Retention:* 60% of full-time freshmen returned.

Freshmen *Admission:* 118 applied, 75 admitted, 32 enrolled. *Average high school GPA:* 3.07. *Test scores:* SAT critical reading scores over 500: 71%; SAT math scores over 500: 67%; SAT writing scores over 500: 62%; ACT scores over 18: 100%; SAT critical reading scores over 600: 24%; SAT math scores over 600: 19%; SAT writing scores over 600: 14%; ACT scores over 24: 50%; SAT critical reading scores over 700: 10%; SAT math scores over 700: 5%; ACT scores over 30: 13%.

Faculty *Total:* 89, 37% full-time, 54% with terminal degrees. *Student/faculty ratio:* 15:1.

Academics *Calendar:* semesters. *Degrees:* bachelor's and master's. *Special study options:* academic remediation for entering students, adult/continuing education programs, advanced placement credit, double majors, internships, part-time degree program, services for LD students, summer session for credit.

Computers on Campus 36 computers/terminals are available on campus for general student use. Students can access the following: campus intranet, computer help desk, free student e-mail accounts, online (class) grades, online (class) registration, online (class) schedules. Campuswide network is available. 80% of college-owned or -operated housing units are wired for high-speed Internet access. Wireless service is available via entire campus.

Student Life *Housing:* on-campus residence required through junior year. *Options:* men-only, women-only. Campus housing is university owned. Freshman campus housing is guaranteed. *Activities and organizations:* drama/theater group, choral group, Day of Outreach, Prayer for the Persecuted, Multnomah Soccer Club, The Beautiful Response, Student World Outreach Team. *Campus security:* 24-hour emergency response devices and patrols, late-night transport/escort service, controlled dormitory access. *Student services:* health clinic, personal/psychological counseling.

Athletics Member NCCAA. *Intercollegiate sports:* basketball M, volleyball W. *Intramural sports:* basketball M/W, soccer M/W, ultimate Frisbee M/W, volleyball M/W.

Standardized Tests *Required:* SAT or ACT (for admission).

Costs (2012–13) *Comprehensive fee:* $28,440 includes full-time tuition ($20,990), mandatory fees ($250), and room and board ($7200). Full-time tuition and fees vary according to course load, location, and program. Part-time

tuition: $655 per semester hour. Part-time tuition and fees vary according to course load, location, and program. *Required fees:* $110 part-time. *Room and board:* Room and board charges vary according to housing facility. *Payment plan:* installment. *Waivers:* employees or children of employees.

Financial Aid *Of all full-time matriculated undergraduates who enrolled in 2009,* 503 applied for aid, 441 were judged to have need, 11 had their need fully met. 75 Federal Work-Study jobs (averaging $1500). In 2009, 36 non-need-based awards were made. *Average percent of need met:* 50%. *Average financial aid package:* $9211. *Average need-based loan:* $4094. *Average need-based gift aid:* $5846. *Average non-need-based aid:* $1848. *Average indebtedness upon graduation:* $21,020.

Applying *Options:* electronic application, deferred entrance. *Application fee:* $40. *Required:* essay or personal statement, high school transcript, minimum 2.5 GPA, 2 letters of recommendation. *Notification:* continuous (freshmen), continuous (transfers).

Freshman Application Contact Ms. Erin Kascel, Admissions Assistant, Multnomah University, 8435 Northeast Glisan Street, Portland, OR 97220-5898. *Phone:* 503-251-6489. *Toll-free phone:* 877-251-6560. *Fax:* 503-254-1268. *E-mail:* admiss@multnomah.edu.
Website: http://www.multnomah.edu/.

New Hope Christian College

Eugene, Oregon

- **Independent** 4-year, founded 1925, affiliated with Open Bible Standard Churches
- **Suburban** 40-acre campus
- **Coed**
- **Minimally difficult** entrance level

Faculty *Student/faculty ratio:* 11:1.

Academics *Calendar:* semesters. *Degree:* bachelor's.

Student Life *Campus security:* 24-hour emergency response devices, student patrols, controlled dormitory access.

Financial Aid *Of all full-time matriculated undergraduates who enrolled in 2011,* 80 applied for aid, 80 were judged to have need. *In 2011,* 8 non-need-based awards were made. *Average percent of need met:* 50. *Average financial aid package:* $14,000. *Average need-based loan:* $3500. *Average need-based gift aid:* $6500. *Average non-need-based aid:* $1900. *Financial aid deadline:* 9/1.

Applying *Options:* electronic application, deferred entrance. *Application fee:* $35. *Required:* essay or personal statement, high school transcript, minimum 2.0 GPA, 2 letters of recommendation.

Freshman Application Contact Sarah Slater, Director of Admissions, New Hope Christian College, 2155 Bailey Hill Road, Eugene, OR 97405. *Phone:* 541-485-1780 Ext. 3115. *Toll-free phone:* 800-322-2638. *Fax:* 541-343-5801. *E-mail:* sarahslater@newhope.edu.
Website: http://www.newhope.edu/.

Northwest Christian University

Eugene, Oregon

- **Independent Christian** comprehensive, founded 1895
- **Urban** 8-acre campus with easy access to Portland
- **Endowment** $10.0 million
- **Coed** 456 undergraduate students, 78% full-time, 62% women, 38% men
- **Moderately difficult** entrance level, 66% of applicants were admitted

Undergraduates 356 full-time, 100 part-time. Students come from 15 states and territories; 19% are from out of state; 1% Black or African American, non-Hispanic/Latino; 6% Hispanic/Latino; 2% Asian, non-Hispanic/Latino; 0.7% Native Hawaiian or other Pacific Islander, non-Hispanic/Latino; 1% American Indian or Alaska Native, non-Hispanic/Latino; 3% Two or more races, non-Hispanic/Latino; 1% Race/ethnicity unknown; 11% transferred in; 31% live on campus. *Retention:* 71% of full-time freshmen returned.

Freshmen *Admission:* 273 applied, 181 admitted, 68 enrolled. *Average high school GPA:* 3.41. *Test scores:* SAT critical reading scores over 500: 45%; SAT math scores over 500: 59%; SAT writing scores over 500: 40%; ACT scores over 18: 86%; SAT critical reading scores over 600: 10%; SAT math scores over 600: 7%; SAT writing scores over 600: 9%; ACT scores over 24: 25%; SAT critical reading scores over 700: 2%; SAT math scores over 700: 2%; SAT writing scores over 700: 2%.

Faculty *Total:* 75, 33% full-time, 21% with terminal degrees. *Student/faculty ratio:* 13:1.

Academics *Calendar:* quarters. *Degrees:* certificates, associate, bachelor's, master's, and postbachelor's certificates. *Special study options:* academic remediation for entering students, accelerated degree program, adult/continuing education programs, advanced placement credit, distance learning, double majors, independent study, internships, off-campus study, part-time degree program, services for LD students, student-designed majors, study abroad, summer session for credit.

Computers on Campus 60 computers/terminals are available on campus for general student use. Students can access the following: campus intranet, computer help desk, free student e-mail accounts, online (class) grades, online (class) registration, online (class) schedules. Campuswide network is available. 100% of college-owned or -operated housing units are wired for high-speed Internet access. Wireless service is available via entire campus.

Student Life *Housing:* on-campus residence required for freshman year. *Options:* men-only, women-only. Campus housing is university owned. Freshman campus housing is guaranteed. *Activities and organizations:* drama/theater group, student-run newspaper, choral group, Community Life Groups, Circle K, Believers Building Bonds through Boardgames, Parable. *Campus security:* 24-hour emergency response devices and patrols, late-night transport/escort service, controlled dormitory access, Late-night patrols by trained security personnel. *Student services:* personal/psychological counseling.

Athletics Member NAIA. *Intercollegiate sports:* basketball M(s)/W(s), cross-country running M(s)/W(s), golf M(s)/W(s), soccer M(s)/W(s), softball W(s), track and field M(s)/W(s), volleyball W(s). *Intramural sports:* basketball M/W, football W, volleyball M/W.

Standardized Tests *Required:* SAT or ACT (for admission).

Costs (2013–14) *Comprehensive fee:* $32,480 includes full-time tuition ($24,780), mandatory fees ($100), and room and board ($7600). Full-time tuition and fees vary according to course load. Part-time tuition: $825 per credit. Part-time tuition and fees vary according to course load. *Required fees:* $100 per year part-time. *Room and board:* Room and board charges vary according to board plan and housing facility. *Payment plans:* installment, deferred payment. *Waivers:* employees or children of employees.

Financial Aid Of all full-time matriculated undergraduates who enrolled in 2011, 334 applied for aid, 306 were judged to have need, 44 had their need fully met. 62 Federal Work-Study jobs (averaging $993). 60 state and other part-time jobs (averaging $1386). In 2011, 29 non-need-based awards were made. *Average percent of need met:* 68%. *Average financial aid package:* $19,056. *Average need-based loan:* $4560. *Average need-based gift aid:* $14,917. *Average non-need-based aid:* $7046. *Average indebtedness upon graduation:* $32,045.

Applying *Options:* electronic application, deferred entrance. *Required:* essay or personal statement, minimum 2.5 GPA. *Required for some:* high school transcript. *Recommended:* interview. *Application deadlines:* rolling (freshmen), rolling (out-of-state freshmen), rolling (transfers). *Notification:* continuous (freshmen), continuous (out-of-state freshmen), continuous (transfers).

Freshman Application Contact Kassia Galick, Admissions Counselor, Northwest Christian University, 828 E. 11th Ave., Eugene, OR 97401-3745. *Phone:* 541-684-7201. *Toll-free phone:* 877-463-6622. *Fax:* 541-684-7317. *E-mail:* admissions@nwcu.edu. *Website:* http://www.nwcu.edu/.

Oregon College of Art & Craft

Portland, Oregon

- **Independent** comprehensive, founded 1907
- **Urban** 10-acre campus with easy access to Portland
- **Endowment** $3.7 million
- **Coed** 164 undergraduate students, 81% full-time, 76% women, 24% men
- **Moderately difficult** entrance level, 27% of applicants were admitted

Undergraduates 133 full-time, 31 part-time. Students come from 21 states and territories; 3 other countries; 35% are from out of state; 7% Hispanic/Latino; 0.6% Asian, non-Hispanic/Latino; 1% Native Hawaiian or other Pacific Islander, non-Hispanic/Latino; 2% American Indian or Alaska Native, non-Hispanic/Latino; 10% Two or more races, non-Hispanic/Latino; 15% Race/ethnicity unknown; 2% international; 16% transferred in; 10% live on campus. *Retention:* 86% of full-time freshmen returned.

Freshmen *Admission:* 71 applied, 19 admitted, 18 enrolled. *Average high school GPA:* 3.53.

Faculty *Total:* 37, 22% full-time, 95% with terminal degrees. *Student/faculty ratio:* 9:1.

Academics *Calendar:* semesters. *Degrees:* certificates, bachelor's, and post-bachelor's certificates. *Special study options:* adult/continuing education pro-

grams, advanced placement credit, independent study, internships, off-campus study, part-time degree program, services for LD students, study abroad.

Computers on Campus 15 computers/terminals are available on campus for general student use. Students can access the following: free student e-mail accounts. Campuswide network is available. 100% of college-owned or -operated housing units are wired for high-speed Internet access. Wireless service is available via entire campus.

Student Life *Housing options:* coed. Campus housing is university owned. Freshman applicants given priority for college housing. *Activities and organizations:* Student Commonwealth. *Campus security:* 24-hour emergency response devices, late-night transport/escort service. *Student services:* personal/psychological counseling.

Standardized Tests *Recommended:* SAT (for admission), ACT (for admission).

Financial Aid Of all full-time matriculated undergraduates who enrolled in 2012, 116 applied for aid, 112 were judged to have need, 8 had their need fully met. In 2012, 15 non-need-based awards were made. *Average percent of need met:* 73%. *Average financial aid package:* $22,239. *Average need-based loan:* $4332. *Average need-based gift aid:* $6986. *Average non-need-based aid:* $7533. *Average indebtedness upon graduation:* $22,500.

Applying *Options:* electronic application, deferred entrance. *Application fee:* $35. *Required:* essay or personal statement, high school transcript, minimum 2.0 GPA, 2 letters of recommendation, A portfolio that includes 12 to 20 pieces of studio artwork. *Required for some:* interview. *Application deadlines:* rolling (freshmen), rolling (out-of-state freshmen), rolling (transfers). *Notification:* continuous (freshmen), continuous (out-of-state freshmen), continuous (transfers).

Freshman Application Contact Oregon College of Art & Craft, 8245 Southwest Barnes Road, Portland, OR 97225. *Phone:* 971-255-4192. *Toll-free phone:* 800-390-0632. *Website:* http://www.ocac.edu/.

Oregon Health & Science University

Portland, Oregon

- **State-related** upper-level, founded 1974
- **Urban** 120-acre campus
- **Coed** 825 undergraduate students, 17% full-time, 83% women, 17% men

Undergraduates 141 full-time, 684 part-time. 2% Black or African American, non-Hispanic/Latino; 6% Hispanic/Latino; 5% Asian, non-Hispanic/Latino; 0.1% Native Hawaiian or other Pacific Islander, non-Hispanic/Latino; 0.7% American Indian or Alaska Native, non-Hispanic/Latino; 4% Two or more races, non-Hispanic/Latino; 4% Race/ethnicity unknown; 0.5% international.

Faculty *Total:* 111, 66% full-time, 23% with terminal degrees. *Student/faculty ratio:* 7:1.

Academics *Calendar:* quarters. *Degrees:* certificates, bachelor's, master's, doctoral, post-master's, and postbachelor's certificates. *Special study options:* accelerated degree program, advanced placement credit, distance learning, off-campus study, part-time degree program, summer session for credit.

Computers on Campus Students can access the following: campus intranet, computer help desk, free student e-mail accounts, online (class) grades, online (class) registration, online (class) schedules. Campuswide network is available. Wireless service is available via entire campus.

Student Life *Housing:* college housing not available. *Activities and organizations:* student-run newspaper, choral group, national fraternities. *Campus security:* 24-hour emergency response devices and patrols, late-night transport/escort service. *Student services:* health clinic, personal/psychological counseling.

Athletics *Intramural sports:* basketball M/W, soccer M/W, volleyball M/W.

Financial Aid Of all full-time matriculated undergraduates who enrolled in 2012, 290 applied for aid, 281 were judged to have need, 14 had their need fully met. 15 Federal Work-Study jobs (averaging $1367). In 2012, 1 non-need-based awards were made. *Average percent of need met:* 29%. *Average financial aid package:* $9971. *Average need-based loan:* $4943. *Average need-based gift aid:* $7903. *Average non-need-based aid:* $400.

Applying *Options:* electronic application. *Application fee:* $120. *Application deadline:* 2/15 (transfers). *Notification:* 6/1 (transfers).

Application Contact Oregon Health & Science University, 3181 Southwest Sam Jackson Park Road, Portland, OR 97239-3098. *Phone:* 503-494-0647. *Website:* http://www.ohsu.edu/.

Oregon Institute of Technology

Klamath Falls, Oregon

- **State-supported** comprehensive, founded 1947, part of Oregon University System
- **Small-town** 173-acre campus
- **Coed**
- **Moderately difficult** entrance level

Faculty *Student/faculty ratio:* 20:1.

Academics *Calendar:* quarters. *Degrees:* certificates, associate, bachelor's, master's, and postbachelor's certificates.

Student Life *Campus security:* 24-hour emergency response devices and patrols, late-night transport/escort service.

Athletics Member NAIA.

Standardized Tests *Required:* SAT or ACT (for admission).

Financial Aid *Of all full-time matriculated undergraduates who enrolled in 2011,* 1,851 applied for aid, 1,642 were judged to have need, 501 had their need fully met. *Average percent of need met:* 21. *Average financial aid package:* $7722. *Average need-based loan:* $4402. *Average need-based gift aid:* $5611. *Average indebtedness upon graduation:* $28,546.

Applying *Options:* electronic application, deferred entrance. *Application fee:* $50. *Required:* high school transcript, minimum 3.0 GPA.

Freshman Application Contact Oregon Institute of Technology, 3201 Campus Drive, Klamath Falls, OR 97601-8801. *Phone:* 541-885-1151. *Toll-free phone:* 800-422-2017.

Website: http://www.oit.edu/.

Oregon State University

Corvallis, Oregon

- **State-supported** university, founded 1868, part of Oregon University System
- **Small-town** 422-acre campus
- **Endowment** $403.6 million
- **Coed** 21,812 undergraduate students, 82% full-time, 47% women, 53% men
- **Moderately difficult** entrance level, 79% of applicants were admitted

Undergraduates 17,795 full-time, 4,017 part-time. Students come from 50 states and territories; 62 other countries; 21% are from out of state; 1% Black or African American, non-Hispanic/Latino; 7% Hispanic/Latino; 7% Asian, non-Hispanic/Latino; 0.5% Native Hawaiian or other Pacific Islander, non-Hispanic/Latino; 0.9% American Indian or Alaska Native, non-Hispanic/Latino; 5% Two or more races, non-Hispanic/Latino; 4% Race/ethnicity unknown; 5% international; 8% transferred in; 20% live on campus. *Retention:* 81% of full-time freshmen returned.

Freshmen *Admission:* 12,330 applied, 9,720 admitted, 3,333 enrolled. *Average high school GPA:* 3.56. *Test scores:* SAT critical reading scores over 500: 68%; SAT math scores over 500: 74%; SAT writing scores over 500: 61%; ACT scores over 18: 94%; SAT critical reading scores over 600: 27%; SAT math scores over 600: 37%; SAT writing scores over 600: 20%; ACT scores over 24: 57%; SAT critical reading scores over 700: 5%; SAT math scores over 700: 7%; SAT writing scores over 700: 3%; ACT scores over 30: 12%.

Faculty *Total:* 1,345, 70% full-time, 77% with terminal degrees. *Student/faculty ratio:* 21:1.

Academics *Calendar:* quarters. *Degrees:* certificates, bachelor's, master's, doctoral, post-master's, and postbachelor's certificates. *Special study options:* academic remediation for entering students, accelerated degree program, advanced placement credit, cooperative education, distance learning, double majors, English as a second language, external degree program, freshman honors college, honors programs, independent study, internships, off-campus study, part-time degree program, services for LD students, student-designed majors, study abroad, summer session for credit. *ROTC:* Army (b), Navy (b), Air Force (b).

Computers on Campus 2,179 computers/terminals are available on campus for general student use. Students can access the following: campus intranet, computer help desk, free student e-mail accounts, online (class) grades, online (class) registration, online (class) schedules. Campuswide network is available. 100% of college-owned or -operated housing units are wired for high-speed Internet access. Wireless service is available via entire campus.

Student Life *Housing options:* coed, cooperative, disabled students. Campus housing is university owned. Freshman applicants given priority for college housing. *Activities and organizations:* drama/theater group, student-run newspaper, radio and television station, choral group, marching band, Associated Students of OSU, International Students of OSU, Graduate Students Organiza-

tion, Campus Crusade, MECHA, national fraternities, national sororities. *Campus security:* 24-hour emergency response devices and patrols, student patrols, late-night transport/escort service, controlled dormitory access, crime prevention office. *Student services:* health clinic, personal/psychological counseling, women's center, legal services.

Athletics Member NCAA. All Division I except football (Division I-A). *Intercollegiate sports:* baseball M(s), basketball M(s)/W(s), crew M/W, golf M(s)/W(s), gymnastics W(s), soccer M(s)/W(s), softball W(s), swimming and diving W(s), volleyball W(s), wrestling M(s). *Intramural sports:* archery M/W, badminton M/W, baseball M, basketball M/W, bowling M/W, crew M/W, cross-country running M/W, equestrian sports M(c)/W(c), fencing M(c)/W(c), football M, golf M/W, lacrosse M(c)/W(c), racquetball M/W, riflery M(c)/W(c), rugby M(c)/W(c), sailing M(c)/W(c), skiing (cross-country) M(c)/W(c), skiing (downhill) M(c)/W(c), soccer M/W, softball M/W, squash M(c), swimming and diving M/W, table tennis M(c)/W(c), tennis M/W, track and field M/W, ultimate Frisbee M/W, volleyball M/W, water polo M/W, wrestling M.

Standardized Tests *Required:* SAT or ACT (for admission). *Required for some:* SAT Subject Tests (for admission).

Costs (2012–13) *One-time required fee:* $300. *Tuition:* state resident $6660 full-time, $185 per credit hour part-time; nonresident $20,844 full-time, $579 per credit hour part-time. Full-time tuition and fees vary according to course load and program. Part-time tuition and fees vary according to course load and program. *Required fees:* $1478 full-time, $451 per term part-time. *Room and board:* $10,563; room only: $7130. Room and board charges vary according to board plan and housing facility. *Waivers:* employees or children of employees.

Financial Aid Of all full-time matriculated undergraduates who enrolled in 2012, 12,514 applied for aid, 10,216 were judged to have need, 1,132 had their need fully met. In 2012, 2228 non-need-based awards were made. *Average percent of need met:* 53%. *Average financial aid package:* $10,515. *Average need-based loan:* $3750. *Average need-based gift aid:* $3220. *Average non-need-based aid:* $3568.

Applying *Options:* electronic application, early action, deferred entrance. *Application fee:* $50. *Required:* essay or personal statement, high school transcript, minimum 3.0 GPA. *Application deadlines:* 9/1 (freshmen), 9/1 (transfers), 11/1 (early action). *Notification:* continuous (freshmen), continuous (transfers).

Freshman Application Contact Oregon State University, Corvallis, OR 97331. *Phone:* 541-737-4411. *Toll-free phone:* 800-291-4192.

Website: http://www.oregonstate.edu/.

Oregon State University–Cascades

Bend, Oregon

Freshman Application Contact Admissions Department, Oregon State University–Cascades, 2600 Northwest College Way, Bend, OR 97701. *Phone:* 541-322-3150. *E-mail:* cascadeadmit@osucascades.edu.

Website: http://www.osucascades.edu/.

Pacific Northwest College of Art

Portland, Oregon

- **Independent** comprehensive, founded 1909
- **Urban** 2-acre campus with easy access to Portland
- **Endowment** $14.8 million
- **Coed** 446 undergraduate students, 88% full-time, 67% women, 33% men
- **Minimally difficult** entrance level

Undergraduates 392 full-time, 54 part-time. Students come from 27 states and territories; 4 other countries; 73% are from out of state; 2% Black or African American, non-Hispanic/Latino; 5% Hispanic/Latino; 5% Asian, non-Hispanic/Latino; 0.2% Native Hawaiian or other Pacific Islander, non-Hispanic/Latino; 2% American Indian or Alaska Native, non-Hispanic/Latino; 10% Two or more races, non-Hispanic/Latino; 2% Race/ethnicity unknown; 0.4% international; 17% transferred in; 21% live on campus. *Retention:* 56% of full-time freshmen returned.

Freshmen *Admission:* 78 enrolled.

Faculty *Total:* 101, 26% full-time, 87% with terminal degrees. *Student/faculty ratio:* 9:1.

Academics *Calendar:* semesters. *Degrees:* bachelor's and master's. *Special study options:* advanced placement credit, cooperative education, independent study, internships, off-campus study, part-time degree program, services for LD students, student-designed majors, study abroad, summer session for credit.

Computers on Campus 300 computers/terminals are available on campus for general student use. Students can access the following: campus intranet, computer help desk, free student e-mail accounts, online (class) grades, online (class) registration, online (class) schedules. Campuswide network is available. Wireless service is available via entire campus.

Student Life *Housing:* on-campus residence required for freshman year. *Options:* coed. Campus housing is leased by the school. Freshman campus housing is guaranteed. *Campus security:* 24-hour emergency response devices, late-night transport/escort service, controlled dormitory access, entrance security guards during open hours. *Student services:* personal/psychological counseling.

Costs (2013–14) *Tuition:* $29,442 full-time, $1227 per credit part-time. Part-time tuition and fees vary according to course load. *Required fees:* $1150 full-time, $43 per credit part-time. *Room only:* $10,890. *Payment plans:* installment, deferred payment. *Waivers:* employees or children of employees.

Financial Aid Of all full-time matriculated undergraduates who enrolled in 2006, 264 applied for aid, 238 were judged to have need, 13 had their need fully met. 33 Federal Work-Study jobs (averaging $1200). 33 state and other part-time jobs (averaging $1200). In 2006, 10 non-need-based awards were made. *Average percent of need met:* 54%. *Average financial aid package:* $11,845. *Average need-based loan:* $4040. *Average need-based gift aid:* $4699. *Average non-need-based aid:* $2442. *Average indebtedness upon graduation:* $22,155.

Applying *Options:* electronic application, deferred entrance. *Required:* essay or personal statement, high school transcript, portfolio of artwork. *Recommended:* minimum 2.0 GPA, interview. *Application deadlines:* rolling (freshmen), rolling (out-of-state freshmen), rolling (transfers). *Notification:* continuous (freshmen), continuous (out-of-state freshmen), continuous (transfers).

Freshman Application Contact Pacific Northwest College of Art, 1241 NW Johnson Street, Portland, OR 97209. *Phone:* 503-821-8926. *Website:* http://www.pnca.edu/.

Pacific University

Forest Grove, Oregon

- **Independent** comprehensive, founded 1849
- **Small-town** 60-acre campus with easy access to Portland
- **Coed** 1,716 undergraduate students, 97% full-time, 57% women, 43% men
- **Moderately difficult** entrance level, 85% of applicants were admitted

Undergraduates 1,658 full-time, 58 part-time. 49% are from out of state; 1% Black or African American, non-Hispanic/Latino; 9% Hispanic/Latino; 13% Asian, non-Hispanic/Latino; 2% Native Hawaiian or other Pacific Islander, non-Hispanic/Latino; 0.9% American Indian or Alaska Native, non-Hispanic/Latino; 9% Two or more races, non-Hispanic/Latino; 6% Race/ethnicity unknown; 2% international; 5% transferred in. *Retention:* 82% of full-time freshmen returned.

Freshmen *Admission:* 2,618 applied, 2,214 admitted, 460 enrolled. *Average high school GPA:* 3.59. *Test scores:* SAT critical reading scores over 500: 75%; SAT math scores over 500: 81%; ACT scores over 18: 98%; SAT critical reading scores over 600: 28%; SAT math scores over 600: 31%; ACT scores over 24: 50%; SAT critical reading scores over 700: 5%; SAT math scores over 700: 6%; ACT scores over 30: 8%.

Academics *Calendar:* semesters. *Degrees:* bachelor's, master's, doctoral, post-master's, and postbachelor's certificates. *ROTC:* Army (c), Air Force (c).

Computers on Campus Students can access the following: campus intranet, computer help desk, free student e-mail accounts, online (class) grades, online (class) schedules, Web space, printing, student and academic information, WebCT, computer peripherals. Campuswide network is available. 100% of college-owned or -operated housing units are wired for high-speed Internet access. Wireless service is available via entire campus.

Student Life *Housing:* on-campus residence required through sophomore year. *Options:* coed, disabled students. Campus housing is university owned. Freshman campus housing is guaranteed. *Campus security:* 24-hour emergency response devices and patrols, late-night transport/escort service, controlled dormitory access.

Athletics Member NCAA, NAIA. All NCAA Division III. *Intercollegiate sports:* baseball M, basketball M/W, cross-country running M/W, football M, golf M/W, lacrosse W, soccer M/W, softball W, swimming and diving M/W, tennis M/W, track and field M/W, volleyball W, wrestling M/W. *Intramural*

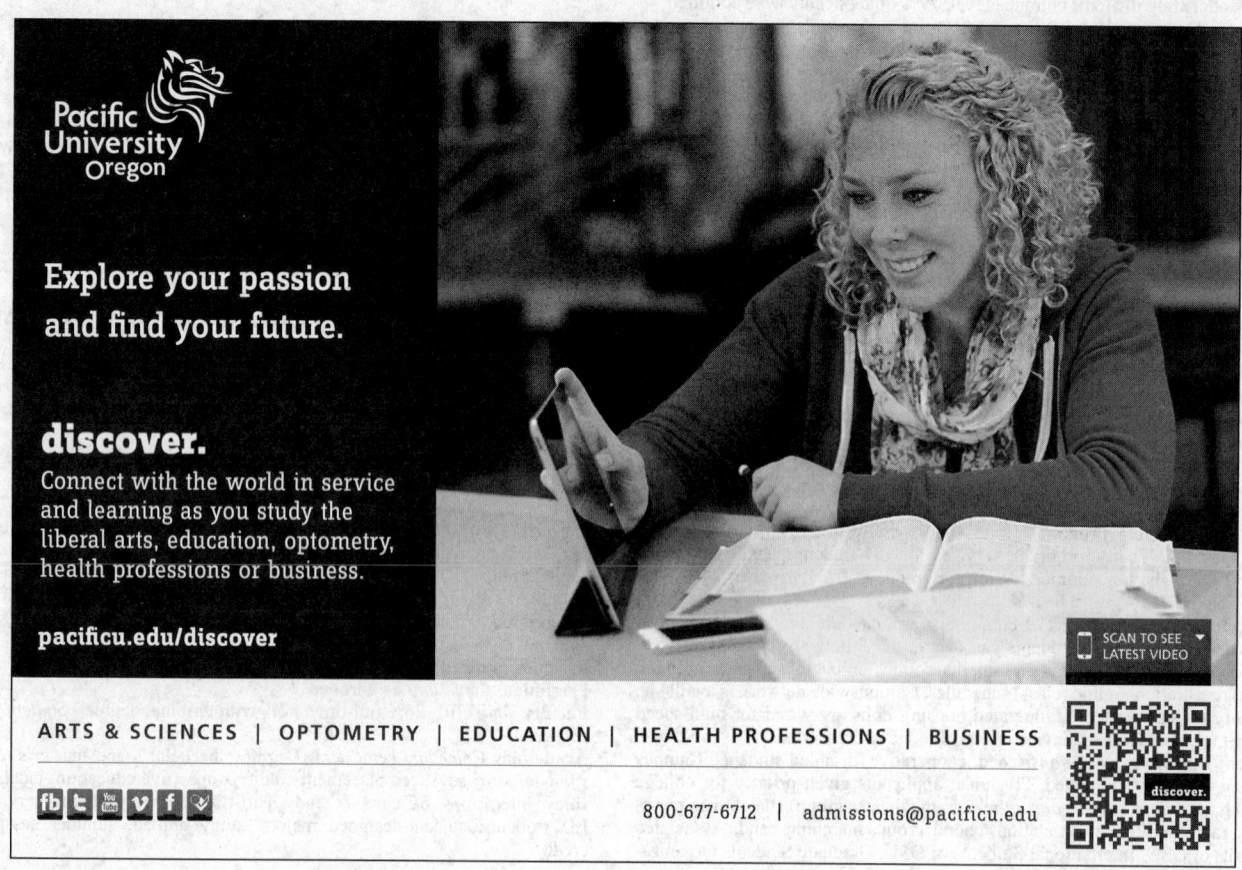

sports: basketball M/W, cheerleading M/W, crew M/W, football M/W, racquetball W, softball M/W, volleyball M/W.

Standardized Tests *Required:* SAT or ACT (for admission).

Costs (2012–13) *Comprehensive fee:* $45,252 includes full-time tuition ($35,260) and room and board ($9992). Part-time tuition and fees vary according to course load. *Room and board:* Room and board charges vary according to board plan and housing facility. *Payment plans:* installment, deferred payment. *Waivers:* employees or children of employees.

Financial Aid Of all full-time matriculated undergraduates who enrolled in 2012, 1,481 applied for aid, 1,367 were judged to have need, 206 had their need fully met. In 2012, 254 non-need-based awards were made. *Average percent of need met:* 80%. *Average financial aid package:* $27,799. *Average need-based loan:* $5266. *Average need-based gift aid:* $21,234. *Average non-need-based aid:* $12,982. *Average indebtedness upon graduation:* $30,880.

Applying *Options:* electronic application, deferred entrance. *Application fee:* $40. *Required:* essay or personal statement, high school transcript, minimum 3.0 GPA, 1 letter of recommendation. *Recommended:* interview. *Application deadlines:* 8/15 (freshmen), 8/15 (transfers). *Notification:* continuous (freshmen), continuous (transfers).

Freshman Application Contact Ms. Karen Dunston, Executive Director, Pacific University, 2043 College Way, Forest Grove, OR 97116-1797. *Phone:* 503-352-2218. *Toll-free phone:* 877-722-8648. *Fax:* 503-352-2975. *E-mail:* admissions@pacificu.edu. *Website:* http://www.pacificu.edu/.

See previous page for display ad and page 1434 for the College Close-Up.

Pioneer Pacific College

Clackamas, Oregon

Freshman Application Contact Admissions Office, Pioneer Pacific College, 8800 SE Sunnyside Road, Clackamas, OR 97015. *Phone:* 503-654-8000. *Toll-free phone:* 866-772-4636. *E-mail:* inquiries@pioneerpacific.edu. *Website:* http://www.pioneerpacific.edu/.

Pioneer Pacific College

Wilsonville, Oregon

Freshman Application Contact Ms. Kristin Lynn, Director of Admissions, Pioneer Pacific College, 27501 Southwest Parkway Avenue, Wilsonville, OR 97070. *Phone:* 866-772-4636. *Toll-free phone:* 866-PPC-INFO. *Fax:* 503-682-1514. *E-mail:* inquiries@pioneerpacific.edu. *Website:* http://www.pioneerpacific.edu/.

Pioneer Pacific College–Eugene/ Springfield Branch

Springfield, Oregon

Freshman Application Contact Admissions Office, Pioneer Pacific College–Eugene/Springfield Branch, 3800 Sports Way, Springfield, OR 97477. *Phone:* 541-684-4644. *Toll-free phone:* 866-772-4636. *E-mail:* inquiries@pioneerpacific.edu. *Website:* http://www.pioneerpacific.edu/.

Portland State University

Portland, Oregon

- **State-supported** university, founded 1946, part of Oregon University System
- **Urban** 49-acre campus with easy access to Portland
- **Coed** 23,170 undergraduate students, 63% full-time, 52% women, 48% men
- **Moderately difficult** entrance level

Undergraduates 14,517 full-time, 8,653 part-time. 12% are from out of state; 3% Black or African American, non-Hispanic/Latino; 8% Hispanic/Latino; 8% Asian, non-Hispanic/Latino; 0.6% Native Hawaiian or other Pacific Islander, non-Hispanic/Latino; 1% American Indian or Alaska Native, non-Hispanic/Latino; 4% Two or more races, non-Hispanic/Latino; 4% Race/ethnicity unknown; 6% international. *Retention:* 74% of full-time freshmen returned.

Freshmen *Admission:* 1,418 enrolled. *Test scores:* SAT critical reading scores over 500: 59%; SAT writing scores over 500: 50%; ACT scores over 18: 77%; SAT critical reading scores over 600: 18%; SAT writing scores over 600: 14%; ACT scores over 24: 33%; SAT critical reading scores over 700: 3%; SAT writing scores over 700: 1%; ACT scores over 30: 2%.

Faculty *Total:* 1,734, 54% full-time. *Student/faculty ratio:* 15:1.

Academics *Calendar:* quarters. *Degrees:* certificates, bachelor's, master's, doctoral, and postbachelor's certificates. *Special study options:* academic remediation for entering students, accelerated degree program, adult/continuing education programs, advanced placement credit, cooperative education, distance learning, double majors, English as a second language, freshman honors college, honors programs, independent study, internships, off-campus study, part-time degree program, services for LD students, study abroad, summer session for credit. *ROTC:* Army (b), Air Force (c).

Computers on Campus Students can access the following: campus intranet, computer help desk, free student e-mail accounts, online (class) grades, online (class) registration, online (class) schedules. Campuswide network is available. Wireless service is available via entire campus.

Student Life *Housing options:* coed, disabled students. Campus housing is university owned. Freshman campus housing is guaranteed. *Activities and organizations:* drama/theater group, student-run newspaper, radio station, choral group, national fraternities, national sororities. *Campus security:* 24-hour emergency response devices and patrols, late-night transport/escort service, controlled dormitory access. *Student services:* health clinic, personal/psychological counseling, women's center, legal services.

Athletics Member NCAA. All Division I except football (Division I-AA). *Intercollegiate sports:* basketball M/W, cross-country running M/W, golf W, soccer W, softball W, tennis M/W, track and field M/W, volleyball W.

Standardized Tests *Required:* SAT or ACT (for admission).

Costs (2012–13) *One-time required fee:* $300. *Tuition:* state resident $6390 full-time, $142 per credit hour part-time; nonresident $21,600 full-time, $480 per credit hour part-time. Full-time tuition and fees vary according to program and reciprocity agreements. Part-time tuition and fees vary according to program. *Required fees:* $1263 full-time, $17 per credit hour part-time, $98 per term part-time. *Room and board:* $11,019; room only: $7650. Room and board charges vary according to board plan and housing facility. *Payment plan:* installment. *Waivers:* senior citizens and employees or children of employees.

Financial Aid Of all full-time matriculated undergraduates who enrolled in 2010, 9,885 applied for aid, 8,737 were judged to have need, 539 had their need fully met. 1,421 Federal Work-Study jobs (averaging $2876). In 2010, 76 non-need-based awards were made. *Average percent of need met:* 80%. *Average financial aid package:* $12,986. *Average need-based loan:* $4505. *Average need-based gift aid:* $5447. *Average non-need-based aid:* $1176. *Average indebtedness upon graduation:* $26,287.

Applying *Options:* electronic application, early admission, deferred entrance. *Application fee:* $50. *Required:* high school transcript, minimum 3.0 GPA. *Application deadlines:* rolling (freshmen), rolling (out-of-state freshmen), rolling (transfers). *Notification:* continuous (freshmen), continuous (out-of-state freshmen), continuous (transfers).

Freshman Application Contact Melissa Trifiletti, Director of New Student Programs, Portland State University, PO Box 751, Portland, OR 97207. *Phone:* 503-725-5504. *Toll-free phone:* 800-547-8887. *Fax:* 503-725-5525. *E-mail:* mtrifi@pdx.edu. *Website:* http://www.pdx.edu/.

Reed College

Portland, Oregon

- **Independent** 4-year, founded 1908
- **Urban** 116-acre campus
- **Endowment** $450.1 million
- **Coed** 1,432 undergraduate students, 97% full-time, 54% women, 46% men
- **Most difficult** entrance level, 36% of applicants were admitted

Undergraduates 1,395 full-time, 37 part-time. Students come from 50 states and territories; 44 other countries; 87% are from out of state; 3% Black or African American, non-Hispanic/Latino; 9% Hispanic/Latino; 8% Asian, non-Hispanic/Latino; 0.1% Native Hawaiian or other Pacific Islander, non-Hispanic/Latino; 1% American Indian or Alaska Native, non-Hispanic/Latino; 1% Two or more races, non-Hispanic/Latino; 12% Race/ethnicity unknown; 6% international; 2% transferred in; 67% live on campus. *Retention:* 92% of full-time freshmen returned.

Freshmen *Admission:* 3,131 applied, 1,125 admitted, 320 enrolled. *Average high school GPA:* 3.9. *Test scores:* SAT critical reading scores over 500: 100%; SAT math scores over 500: 99%; SAT writing scores over 500: 100%; ACT scores over 18: 100%; SAT critical reading scores over 600: 95%; SAT math scores over 600: 88%; SAT writing scores over 600: 93%; ACT scores over 24: 98%; SAT critical reading scores over 700: 63%; SAT math scores over 700: 37%; SAT writing scores over 700: 49%; ACT scores over 30: 63%.

Faculty *Total:* 139, 94% full-time, 92% with terminal degrees. *Student/faculty ratio:* 10:1.

Academics *Calendar:* semesters. *Degrees:* bachelor's and master's. *Special study options:* academic remediation for entering students, advanced placement credit, cooperative education, double majors, independent study, internships, off-campus study, part-time degree program, services for LD students, study abroad. *Unusual degree programs:* 3-2 engineering with California Institute of Technology, Rensselaer Polytechnic Institute, Columbia University School of Engineering and Applied Sciences; forestry with Nicholas School of the Environment of Duke University; computer science at University of Washington; visual arts at Pacific Northwest College of Art.

Computers on Campus 434 computers/terminals are available on campus for general student use. Students can access the following: campus intranet, computer help desk, free student e-mail accounts, online (class) registration, online (class) schedules. Campuswide network is available. 100% of college-owned or -operated housing units are wired for high-speed Internet access. Wireless service is available via entire campus.

Student Life *Housing:* on-campus residence required for freshman year. *Options:* coed, women-only, cooperative, disabled students. Campus housing is university owned. Freshman campus housing is guaranteed. *Activities and organizations:* drama/theater group, student-run newspaper, radio station, choral group, GreenBoard, Canyon Day, Reed Outing Club, Bike Co-op, Comic Book Reading Room. *Campus security:* 24-hour emergency response devices and patrols, student patrols, late-night transport/escort service, controlled dormitory access, 24-hour emergency dispatch. *Student services:* health clinic, personal/psychological counseling, women's center.

Athletics *Intramural sports:* basketball M/W, rugby M/W, soccer M, squash M/W, ultimate Frisbee M/W.

Standardized Tests *Required:* SAT or ACT (for admission). *Recommended:* SAT Subject Tests (for admission), International citizens who have an SAT critical reading score below 600 are strongly recommended to submit TOEFL or IELTS scores.

Costs (2012–13) *Comprehensive fee:* $55,920 includes full-time tuition ($44,200), mandatory fees ($260), and room and board ($11,460). Part-time tuition: $1903 per semester hour. Part-time tuition and fees vary according to course load. *College room only:* $5960. Room and board charges vary according to board plan and housing facility. *Payment plan:* installment. *Waivers:* employees or children of employees.

Financial Aid Of all full-time matriculated undergraduates who enrolled in 2011, 810 applied for aid, 719 were judged to have need, 719 had their need fully met. 490 Federal Work-Study jobs (averaging $1441). 78 state and other part-time jobs (averaging $1462). *Average percent of need met:* 100%. *Average financial aid package:* $35,990. *Average need-based loan:* $4165. *Average need-based gift aid:* $33,921. *Average indebtedness upon graduation:* $20,840. *Financial aid deadline:* 2/1.

Applying *Options:* electronic application, early admission, early decision, deferred entrance. *Application fee:* $50. *Required:* essay or personal statement, high school transcript, 2 letters of recommendation. *Recommended:* interview. *Application deadlines:* 1/15 (freshmen), 3/1 (transfers). *Early decision deadline:* 11/15 (for plan 1), 12/20 (for plan 2). *Notification:* 4/1 (freshmen), 5/15 (transfers), 12/15 (early decision plan 1), 2/1 (early decision plan 2).

Freshman Application Contact Mr. Keith Todd, Dean of Admission, Reed College, 3203 Southeast Woodstock Boulevard, Portland, OR 97202-8199. *Phone:* 503-777-7511. *Toll-free phone:* 800-547-4750. *Fax:* 503-777-7553. *E-mail:* admission@reed.edu. *Website:* http://www.reed.edu/.

See below for display ad and page 1448 for the College Close-Up.

Southern Oregon University

Ashland, Oregon

- **State-supported** comprehensive, founded 1926, part of Oregon University System
- **Small-town** 175-acre campus
- **Endowment** $20.1 million
- **Coed** 5,660 undergraduate students, 68% full-time, 57% women, 43% men
- **Moderately difficult** entrance level, 92% of applicants were admitted

Undergraduates 3,874 full-time, 1,786 part-time. Students come from 45 states and territories; 18 other countries; 31% are from out of state; 2% Black or African American, non-Hispanic/Latino; 9% Hispanic/Latino; 2% Asian, non-Hispanic/Latino; 0.7% Native Hawaiian or other Pacific Islander, non-Hispanic/Latino; 2% American Indian or Alaska Native, non-Hispanic/Latino; 5% Two or more races, non-Hispanic/Latino; 9% Race/ethnicity unknown; 2% international; 11% transferred in; 24% live on campus. *Retention:* 68% of full-time freshmen returned.

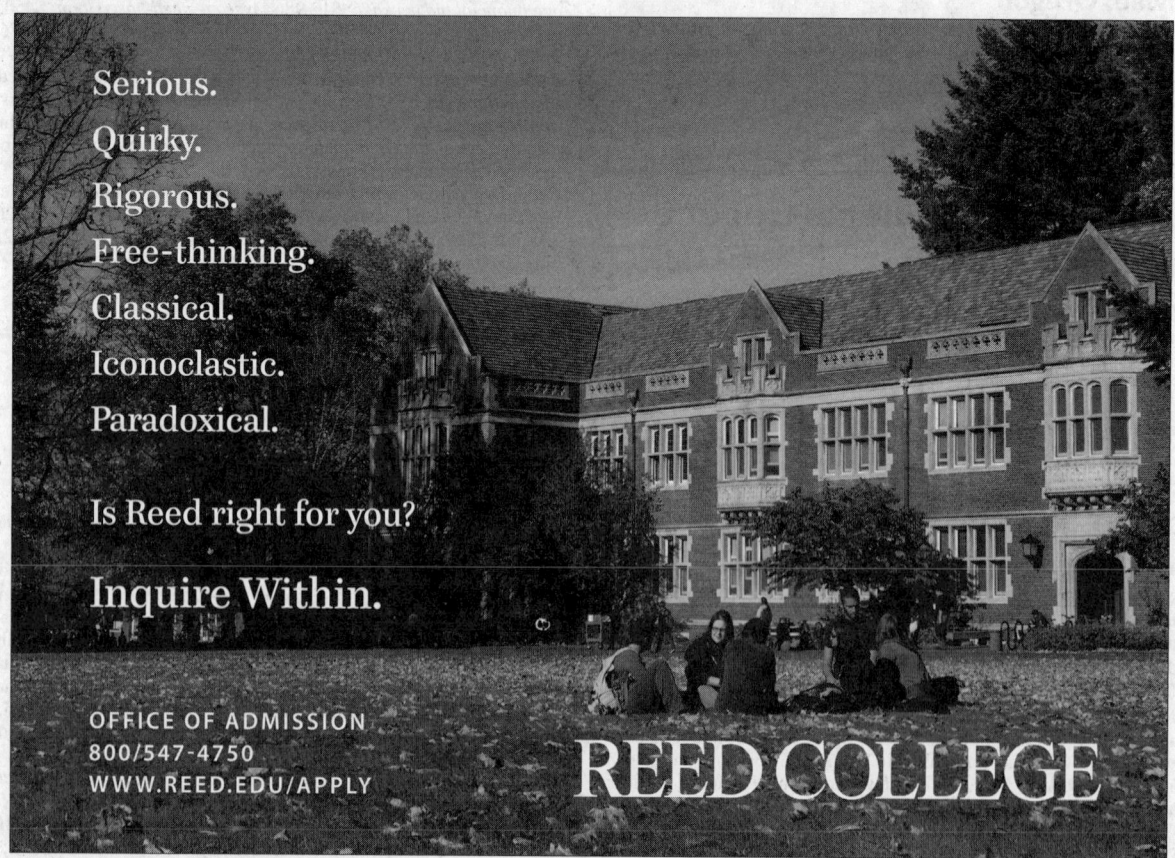

Freshmen *Admission:* 2,063 applied, 1,899 admitted, 704 enrolled. *Average high school GPA:* 3.25. *Test scores:* SAT critical reading scores over 500: 59%; SAT math scores over 500: 54%; SAT writing scores over 500: 43%; ACT scores over 18: 89%; SAT critical reading scores over 600: 18%; SAT math scores over 600: 14%; SAT writing scores over 600: 11%; ACT scores over 24: 41%; SAT critical reading scores over 700: 3%; SAT math scores over 700: 1%; SAT writing scores over 700: 1%; ACT scores over 30: 3%.

Faculty *Total:* 334, 60% full-time, 49% with terminal degrees. *Student/faculty ratio:* 20:1.

Academics *Calendar:* quarters. *Degrees:* bachelor's, master's, post-master's, and postbachelor's certificates. *Special study options:* academic remediation for entering students, accelerated degree program, adult/continuing education programs, advanced placement credit, cooperative education, distance learning, double majors, English as a second language, freshman honors college, honors programs, independent study, internships, off-campus study, part-time degree program, services for LD students, student-designed majors, study abroad, summer session for credit. *ROTC:* Army (b). *Unusual degree programs:* 3-2 engineering with Oregon State University.

Computers on Campus 750 computers/terminals are available on campus for general student use. Students can access the following: campus intranet, computer help desk, free student e-mail accounts, online (class) grades, online (class) registration, online (class) schedules, Online account information including bill payment, online employee records for student workers. Campuswide network is available. 100% of college-owned or -operated housing units are wired for high-speed Internet access. Wireless service is available via classrooms, computer centers, computer labs, dorm rooms, learning centers, libraries, student centers.

Student Life *Housing:* on-campus residence required for freshman year. *Options:* coed, disabled students. Campus housing is university owned. Freshman campus housing is guaranteed. *Activities and organizations:* drama/theater group, student-run newspaper, radio and television station, choral group, Native American Student Union, International Student Association, Impact (religious club), Ho`opa`a Hawaii Club, Omicron Delta Kappa. *Campus security:* 24-hour emergency response devices and patrols, student patrols, late-night transport/escort service, controlled dormitory access. *Student services:* health clinic, personal/psychological counseling, women's center, legal services.

Athletics Member NAIA. *Intercollegiate sports:* basketball M(s)/W(s), cheerleading W, football M(s), lacrosse M(c), rugby M(c)/W(c), soccer M(c)/W(s), softball W(s), tennis M(c)/W(c), track and field M(s)/W(s), volleyball W(s), wrestling M(s). *Intramural sports:* basketball M/W, football M, soccer M/W, softball M/W, volleyball M/W.

Standardized Tests *Required:* SAT or ACT (for admission). *Required for some:* SAT Subject Tests (for admission).

Costs (2013–14) *Tuition:* state resident $6183 full-time; nonresident $18,900 full-time. Full-time tuition and fees vary according to course load, program, and reciprocity agreements. Part-time tuition and fees vary according to course load, program, and reciprocity agreements. *Required fees:* $1338 full-time. *Room and board:* $9918; room only: $5400. Room and board charges vary according to board plan and housing facility. *Payment plans:* installment, deferred payment. *Waivers:* senior citizens and employees or children of employees.

Financial Aid Of all full-time matriculated undergraduates who enrolled in 2009, 3,272 applied for aid, 2,860 were judged to have need, 273 had their need fully met. 316 Federal Work-Study jobs (averaging $1047). In 2009, 297 non-need-based awards were made. *Average percent of need met:* 60%. *Average financial aid package:* $10,226. *Average need-based loan:* $4003. *Average need-based gift aid:* $7816. *Average non-need-based aid:* $8905. *Average indebtedness upon graduation:* $24,132.

Applying *Options:* electronic application, early admission, deferred entrance. *Application fee:* $50. *Required:* high school transcript, minimum 2.8 GPA. *Required for some:* essay or personal statement. *Application deadlines:* rolling (freshmen), rolling (transfers). *Notification:* continuous (freshmen), continuous (transfers).

Freshman Application Contact Mr. Kelly Moutsatson, Director of Admissions, Southern Oregon University, 1250 Siskiyou Boulevard, Ashland, OR 97520. *Phone:* 541-552-6411. *Fax:* 541-552-6614. *E-mail:* admissions@sou.edu.

Website: http://www.sou.edu/.

University of Oregon
Eugene, Oregon

- **State-supported** university, founded 1872, part of Oregon University System
- **Urban** 295-acre campus
- **Endowment** $493.5 million
- **Coed** 20,809 undergraduate students, 91% full-time, 52% women, 48% men
- **Moderately difficult** entrance level, 74% of applicants were admitted

Undergraduates 18,847 full-time, 1,962 part-time. Students come from 53 states and territories; 75 other countries; 35% are from out of state; 2% Black or African American, non-Hispanic/Latino; 7% Hispanic/Latino; 5% Asian, non-Hispanic/Latino; 0.6% Native Hawaiian or other Pacific Islander, non-Hispanic/Latino; 0.6% American Indian or Alaska Native, non-Hispanic/Latino; 5% Two or more races, non-Hispanic/Latino; 2% Race/ethnicity unknown; 11% international; 7% transferred in; 20% live on campus. *Retention:* 85% of full-time freshmen returned.

Freshmen *Admission:* 21,263 applied, 15,770 admitted, 4,031 enrolled. *Average high school GPA:* 3.57. *Test scores:* SAT critical reading scores over 500: 73%; SAT math scores over 500: 77%; SAT critical reading scores over 600: 29%; SAT math scores over 600: 36%; SAT critical reading scores over 700: 5%; SAT math scores over 700: 5%.

Faculty *Total:* 1,505, 69% full-time, 92% with terminal degrees. *Student/faculty ratio:* 19:1.

Academics *Calendar:* quarters. *Degrees:* bachelor's, master's, doctoral, and postbachelor's certificates. *Special study options:* advanced placement credit, cooperative education, distance learning, double majors, English as a second language, honors programs, independent study, internships, off-campus study, part-time degree program, services for LD students, student-designed majors, study abroad, summer session for credit. *ROTC:* Army (b), Air Force (c). *Unusual degree programs:* 3-2 engineering with Oregon State University.

Computers on Campus 1,118 computers/terminals and 1,000 ports are available on campus for general student use. Students can access the following: campus intranet, computer help desk, free student e-mail accounts, online (class) grades, online (class) registration, online (class) schedules. Campuswide network is available. 100% of college-owned or -operated housing units are wired for high-speed Internet access. Wireless service is available via entire campus.

Student Life *Housing options:* coed, cooperative. Campus housing is university owned. Freshman applicants given priority for college housing. *Activities and organizations:* drama/theater group, student-run newspaper, radio station, choral group, marching band, political and environmental action, cultural organizations, major-specific organizations, community service organizations, club sports, national fraternities, national sororities. *Campus security:* 24-hour emergency response devices and patrols, late-night transport/escort service, controlled dormitory access. *Student services:* health clinic, personal/psychological counseling, women's center, legal services.

Athletics Member NCAA. All Division I except football (Division I-A). *Intercollegiate sports:* baseball M(s), basketball M(s)/W(s), cross-country running M(s)/W(s), golf M(s)/W(s), lacrosse W(s), soccer W(s), softball W(s), tennis M(s)/W(s), track and field M(s)/W(s), volleyball W(s). *Intramural sports:* archery M(c)/W(c), badminton M/W, baseball M(c), basketball M/W, crew M(c)/W(c), cross-country running M/W, equestrian sports M(c)/W(c), fencing M(c)/W(c), football M/W, golf M/W, ice hockey M(c)/W(c), lacrosse M(c)/W(c), racquetball M/W, rugby M(c)/W(c), sailing M(c)/W(c), skiing (downhill) M(c)/W(c), soccer M(c)/W(c), softball W(c), swimming and diving M/W, table tennis M(c)/W(c), tennis M/W, track and field M(c)/W(c), ultimate Frisbee M(c)/W(c), volleyball M(c)/W(c), water polo M(c)/W(c).

Standardized Tests *Required:* SAT or ACT (for admission). *Required for some:* SAT and SAT Subject Tests or ACT (for admission).

Costs (2012–13) *One-time required fee:* $347. *Tuition:* state resident $8010 full-time, $178 per credit hour part-time; nonresident $27,360 full-time, $608 per credit hour part-time. Full-time tuition and fees vary according to course load. Part-time tuition and fees vary according to course load. *Required fees:* $1300 full-time. *Room and board:* $10,580. Room and board charges vary according to board plan and housing facility. *Payment plan:* installment. *Waivers:* employees or children of employees.

Financial Aid Of all full-time matriculated undergraduates who enrolled in 2012, 11,284 applied for aid, 8,799 were judged to have need, 764 had their need fully met. 2,771 Federal Work-Study jobs (averaging $1474). 151 state and other part-time jobs (averaging $2208). In 2012, 806 non-need-based awards were made. *Average percent of need met:* 47%. *Average financial aid package:* $9848. *Average need-based loan:* $4742. *Average need-based gift aid:* $5955. *Average non-need-based aid:* $3280. *Average indebtedness upon graduation:* $24,528.

Applying *Options:* electronic application, early action. *Application fee:* $50. *Required:* essay or personal statement, high school transcript, 15 college preparatory units required. *Required for some:* 2 letters of recommendation. *Recommended:* minimum 3.0 GPA. *Application deadlines:* 1/15 (freshmen), 5/15 (transfers), 11/1 (early action). *Notification:* 10/1 (freshmen), 12/15 (early action).

Freshman Application Contact University of Oregon, Eugene, OR 97403. *Phone:* 541-346-3201. *Toll-free phone:* 800-232-3825. *Website:* http://www.uoregon.edu/.

See below for display ad and page 1590 for the College Close-Up.

University of Phoenix–Oregon Campus

Tigard, Oregon

Freshman Application Contact Marc Booker, Sr. Director, Office of Admissions and Evaluation, University of Phoenix–Oregon Campus, 4035 South Riverpoint Parkway, Mail Stop CF-L101, Phoenix, AZ 85040. *Phone:* 602-557-4609. *Toll-free phone:* 866-766-0766. *Fax:* 480-643-1156. *Website:* http://www.phoenix.edu/.

University of Portland

Portland, Oregon

- **Independent Roman Catholic** comprehensive, founded 1901
- **Urban** 125-acre campus
- **Endowment** $80.0 million
- **Coed** 3,402 undergraduate students, 98% full-time, 59% women, 41% men
- **Moderately difficult** entrance level, 67% of applicants were admitted

Undergraduates 3,320 full-time, 82 part-time. 65% are from out of state; 1% Black or African American, non-Hispanic/Latino; 9% Hispanic/Latino; 10% Asian, non-Hispanic/Latino; 1% Native Hawaiian or other Pacific Islander, non-Hispanic/Latino; 0.3% American Indian or Alaska Native, non-Hispanic/ Latino; 7% Two or more races, non-Hispanic/Latino; 2% Race/ethnicity unknown; 3% international; 2% transferred in; 55% live on campus. *Retention:* 89% of full-time freshmen returned.

Freshmen *Admission:* 8,696 applied, 5,785 admitted, 874 enrolled. *Average high school GPA:* 3.64. *Test scores:* SAT critical reading scores over 500: 91%; SAT math scores over 500: 91%; SAT critical reading scores over 600: 48%; SAT math scores over 600: 54%; SAT critical reading scores over 700: 15%; SAT math scores over 700: 9%.

Faculty *Total:* 335, 64% full-time, 59% with terminal degrees. *Student/faculty ratio:* 13:1.

Academics *Calendar:* semesters. *Degrees:* bachelor's, master's, doctoral, and post-master's certificates. *Special study options:* adult/continuing education programs, advanced placement credit, double majors, honors programs, independent study, internships, off-campus study, part-time degree program, services for LD students, study abroad, summer session for credit. *ROTC:* Army (b), Air Force (b).

Computers on Campus 575 computers/terminals and 1,950 ports are available on campus for general student use. Students can access the following: campus intranet, computer help desk, free student e-mail accounts, online (class) grades, online (class) registration, online (class) schedules. Campus-wide network is available. 100% of college-owned or -operated housing units are wired for high-speed Internet access. Wireless service is available via entire campus.

Student Life *Housing:* on-campus residence required for freshman year. *Options:* coed, men-only, women-only. Campus housing is university owned. Freshman campus housing is guaranteed. *Activities and organizations:* drama/ theater group, student-run newspaper, radio station, choral group, English Society, International Club, Hawaiian Club, rugby club, Social Science Club. *Campus security:* 24-hour emergency response devices and patrols, student patrols, late-night transport/escort service, controlled dormitory access. *Student services:* health clinic, personal/psychological counseling.

Athletics Member NCAA. All Division I. *Intercollegiate sports:* baseball M(s), basketball M(s)/W(s), crew W, cross-country running M(s)/W(s), rugby M(c), soccer M(s)/W(s), tennis M(s)/W(s), track and field M(s)/W(s), volleyball W(s). *Intramural sports:* basketball M/W, crew M/W, cross-country running M/W, football M/W, rugby M, skiing (cross-country) M/W, skiing (downhill) M/W, soccer M(c)/W, softball M/W, swimming and diving M/W, tennis M/W, track and field M/W, volleyball M/W, water polo M/W, weight lifting M/W.

Standardized Tests *Required:* SAT or ACT (for admission). *Recommended:* SAT (for admission), ACT (for admission).

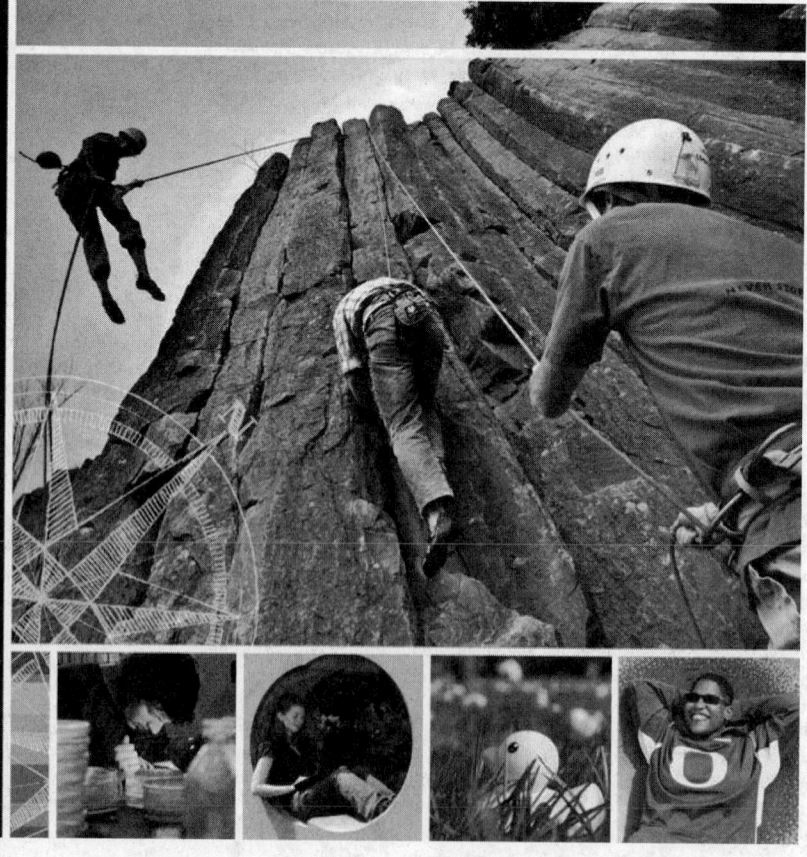

Costs (2013–14) *Tuition:* $35,120 full-time, $1100 per credit hour part-time. Full-time tuition and fees vary according to program. Part-time tuition and fees vary according to course load and program. *Required fees:* $140 full-time. *Room only:* $7290. Room and board charges vary according to board plan and housing facility. *Payment plans:* installment, deferred payment. *Waivers:* employees or children of employees.
Financial Aid Of all full-time matriculated undergraduates who enrolled in 2012, 2,499 applied for aid, 2,132 were judged to have need, 135 had their need fully met. 353 Federal Work-Study jobs (averaging $1305). 1,216 state and other part-time jobs (averaging $1350). In 2012, 918 non-need-based awards were made. *Average percent of need met:* 71%. *Average financial aid package:* $26,238. *Average need-based loan:* $4817. *Average need-based gift aid:* $20,703. *Average non-need-based aid:* $13,281. *Average indebtedness upon graduation:* $27,544.
Applying *Options:* electronic application, deferred entrance. *Application fee:* $50. *Required:* essay or personal statement, high school transcript, 1 letter of recommendation. *Application deadlines:* 6/1 (freshmen), 6/1 (transfers). *Notification:* continuous (freshmen), continuous (transfers).
Freshman Application Contact Mr. Jason McDonald, Dean of Admissions, University of Portland, 5000 North Willamette Boulevard, Portland, OR 97203-5798. *Phone:* 503-943-7147. *Toll-free phone:* 888-627-5601. *Fax:* 503-943-7315. *E-mail:* admissions@up.edu.
Website: http://www.up.edu/.

Warner Pacific College
Portland, Oregon

- **Independent** 4-year, founded 1937, affiliated with Church of God
- **Urban** 15-acre campus with easy access to Portland
- **Endowment** $7.7 million
- **Coed** 1,181 undergraduate students, 99% full-time, 62% women, 38% men
- **Moderately difficult** entrance level, 61% of applicants were admitted

Undergraduates 1,166 full-time, 15 part-time. Students come from 26 states and territories; 18 other countries; 42% are from out of state; 10% transferred in; 19% live on campus. *Retention:* 60% of full-time freshmen returned.
Freshmen *Admission:* 514 applied, 311 admitted, 101 enrolled. *Average high school GPA:* 3.1. *Test scores:* SAT critical reading scores over 500: 61%; SAT math scores over 500: 63%; SAT writing scores over 500: 55%; SAT critical reading scores over 600: 19%; SAT math scores over 600: 14%; SAT writing scores over 600: 11%; SAT critical reading scores over 700: 1%; SAT math scores over 700: 1%; SAT writing scores over 700: 2%.
Faculty *Total:* 116, 21% full-time, 20% with terminal degrees. *Student/faculty ratio:* 22:1.
Academics *Calendar:* semesters. *Degrees:* associate, bachelor's, master's, and postbachelor's certificates. *Special study options:* academic remediation for entering students, accelerated degree program, adult/continuing education programs, advanced placement credit, cooperative education, double majors, honors programs, independent study, internships, off-campus study, part-time degree program, services for LD students, student-designed majors, study abroad, summer session for credit. *ROTC:* Air Force (c).
Computers on Campus 90 computers/terminals are available on campus for general student use. Students can access the following: campus intranet, computer help desk, free student e-mail accounts, online (class) grades, online (class) registration, online (class) schedules. Campuswide network is available. 100% of college-owned or -operated housing units are wired for high-speed Internet access. Wireless service is available via classrooms, computer centers, computer labs, dorm rooms, learning centers, libraries, student centers.
Student Life *Housing:* on-campus residence required through junior year. *Options:* men-only, women-only. Campus housing is university owned. Freshman applicants given priority for college housing. *Activities and organizations:* drama/theater group, student-run newspaper, choral group, Associated Students of Warner Pacific College, yearbook, College Activities Board, Fellowship of Christian Athletes. *Campus security:* 24-hour emergency response devices and patrols, student patrols, late-night transport/escort service, controlled dormitory access. *Student services:* health clinic, personal/psychological counseling.
Athletics Member NAIA, NCCAA. *Intercollegiate sports:* basketball M(s)/W(s), cross-country running M(s)/W(s), golf M(s)/W(s), soccer M(s)/W(s), track and field M(s)/W(s), volleyball W(s). *Intramural sports:* basketball M/W, volleyball M/W.
Standardized Tests *Required:* SAT or ACT (for admission). *Recommended:* SAT Subject Tests (for admission).
Financial Aid Of all full-time matriculated undergraduates who enrolled in 2012, 500 applied for aid, 465 were judged to have need, 58 had their need fully met. 391 Federal Work-Study jobs (averaging $1987). In 2012, 53 non-

need-based awards were made. *Average percent of need met:* 65%. *Average financial aid package:* $15,617. *Average need-based loan:* $4502. *Average need-based gift aid:* $5118. *Average non-need-based aid:* $5434. *Average indebtedness upon graduation:* $33,035.
Applying *Options:* electronic application. *Application fee:* $50. *Required:* essay or personal statement, high school transcript, minimum 2.5 GPA. *Required for some:* 1 letter of recommendation, interview. *Recommended:* minimum 3.0 GPA, interview. *Application deadlines:* rolling (freshmen), rolling (transfers). *Notification:* continuous (freshmen), continuous (transfers).
Freshman Application Contact Dale Seipp, Vice President for Enrollment Management, Warner Pacific College, 2219 Southeast 68th Avenue, Portland, OR 97215. *Phone:* 503-517-1020. *Toll-free phone:* 800-804-1510. *Fax:* 503-517-1540. *E-mail:* admiss@warnerpacific.edu.
Website: http://www.warnerpacific.edu/.

Western Oregon University
Monmouth, Oregon

- **State-supported** comprehensive, founded 1856, part of Oregon University System
- **Rural** 157-acre campus with easy access to Portland
- **Coed** 5,497 undergraduate students, 87% full-time, 60% women, 40% men
- **Moderately difficult** entrance level, 88% of applicants were admitted

Undergraduates 4,797 full-time, 700 part-time. Students come from 33 states and territories; 22 other countries; 12% are from out of state; 4% Black or African American, non-Hispanic/Latino; 6% Hispanic/Latino; 3% Asian, non-Hispanic/Latino; 3% Native Hawaiian or other Pacific Islander, non-Hispanic/Latino; 2% American Indian or Alaska Native, non-Hispanic/Latino; 0.4% Two or more races, non-Hispanic/Latino; 5% Race/ethnicity unknown; 5% international; 11% transferred in. *Retention:* 70% of full-time freshmen returned.
Freshmen *Admission:* 2,841 applied, 2,510 admitted, 1,031 enrolled. *Average high school GPA:* 3.2. *Test scores:* SAT critical reading scores over 500: 11%; SAT math scores over 500: 46%; SAT writing scores over 500: 31%; ACT scores over 18: 69%; SAT critical reading scores over 600: 1%; SAT math scores over 600: 12%; SAT writing scores over 600: 7%; ACT scores over 24: 23%.
Faculty *Total:* 406, 47% full-time, 49% with terminal degrees. *Student/faculty ratio:* 20:1.
Academics *Calendar:* quarters. *Degrees:* bachelor's, master's, and postbachelor's certificates. *Special study options:* academic remediation for entering students, advanced placement credit, distance learning, double majors, English as a second language, freshman honors college, honors programs, independent study, internships, off-campus study, part-time degree program, services for LD students, student-designed majors, study abroad, summer session for credit. *ROTC:* Army (b), Navy (c). *Unusual degree programs:* nursing.
Computers on Campus 411 computers/terminals are available on campus for general student use. Students can access the following: computer help desk, free student e-mail accounts, online (class) grades, online (class) registration, online (class) schedules. Campuswide network is available. Wireless service is available via entire campus.
Student Life *Housing:* on-campus residence required for freshman year. *Options:* coed, disabled students. Campus housing is university owned. Freshman applicants given priority for college housing. *Activities and organizations:* drama/theater group, student-run newspaper, television station, choral group, Model United Nations, Multicultural Student Union, Oregon Student Association, Alternative Spring Break (community service), M.E.Ch.A. *Campus security:* 24-hour emergency response devices and patrols, student patrols, late-night transport/escort service, controlled dormitory access. *Student services:* health clinic, personal/psychological counseling, women's center.
Athletics Member NCAA. All Division II. *Intercollegiate sports:* baseball M(s), basketball M(s)/W(s), cross-country running M(s)/W(s), football M(s), soccer W(s), softball W(s), track and field M(s)/W(s), volleyball W(s). *Intramural sports:* badminton M/W, basketball M/W, bowling M/W, cross-country running M(c)/W(c), football M/W, golf M/W, lacrosse M(c), racquetball M(c)/W(c), riflery M/W, rugby M(c)/W(c), skiing (downhill) M/W, soccer M(c)/W(c), softball M/W, swimming and diving M(c)/W(c), table tennis M/W, tennis M/W, track and field M/W, volleyball M(c)/W(c), water polo M(c)/W(c), weight lifting M/W, wrestling M.
Costs (2013–14) *Tuition:* state resident $8529 full-time; nonresident $21,114 full-time. No tuition increase for student's term of enrollment. *Room and board:* Room and board charges vary according to board plan and housing facility.
Financial Aid Of all full-time matriculated undergraduates who enrolled in 2012, 3,994 applied for aid, 3,487 were judged to have need, 302 had their

need fully met. 963 Federal Work-Study jobs (averaging $908). In 2012, 187 non-need-based awards were made. *Average percent of need met:* 57%. *Average financial aid package:* $9078. *Average need-based loan:* $4009. *Average need-based gift aid:* $6363. *Average non-need-based aid:* $2486. *Average indebtedness upon graduation:* $28,774.

Applying *Options:* electronic application, deferred entrance. *Application fee:* $50. *Required:* high school transcript, minimum 2.8 GPA, general college preparatory program completion. *Application deadlines:* rolling (freshmen), rolling (transfers). *Notification:* continuous (freshmen), continuous (transfers).

Freshman Application Contact Mr. Rob Findtner, Assistant Director of Admissions, Western Oregon University, 345 North Monmouth Avenue, Monmouth, OR 97361. *Phone:* 503-838-8211. *Toll-free phone:* 877-877-1593. *Fax:* 503-838-8067. *E-mail:* wolfgram@wou.edu. *Website:* http://www.wou.edu/.

Willamette University
Salem, Oregon

- **Independent United Methodist** comprehensive, founded 1842
- **Urban** 72-acre campus with easy access to Portland
- **Endowment** $205.2 million
- **Coed** 2,103 undergraduate students, 94% full-time, 55% women, 45% men
- **Very difficult** entrance level, 83% of applicants were admitted

Undergraduates 1,968 full-time, 135 part-time. Students come from 43 states and territories; 20 other countries; 73% are from out of state; 2% Black or African American, non-Hispanic/Latino; 9% Hispanic/Latino; 7% Asian, non-Hispanic/Latino; 0.6% Native Hawaiian or other Pacific Islander, non-Hispanic/Latino; 1% American Indian or Alaska Native, non-Hispanic/Latino; 7% Two or more races, non-Hispanic/Latino; 8% Race/ethnicity unknown; 0.9% international; 2% transferred in; 68% live on campus. *Retention:* 86% of full-time freshmen returned.

Freshmen *Admission:* 6,462 applied, 5,370 admitted, 525 enrolled. *Average high school GPA:* 3.66. *Test scores:* SAT critical reading scores over 500: 95%; SAT math scores over 500: 94%; SAT writing scores over 500: 92%; ACT scores over 18: 100%; SAT critical reading scores over 600: 58%; SAT math scores over 600: 58%; SAT writing scores over 600: 50%; ACT scores over 24: 89%; SAT critical reading scores over 700: 18%; SAT math scores over 700: 11%; SAT writing scores over 700: 13%; ACT scores over 30: 28%.

Faculty *Total:* 320, 76% full-time, 85% with terminal degrees. *Student/faculty ratio:* 10:1.

Academics *Calendar:* semesters. *Degrees:* bachelor's, master's, and doctoral. *Special study options:* accelerated degree program, advanced placement credit, double majors, independent study, internships, off-campus study, part-time degree program, services for LD students, student-designed majors, study abroad. *ROTC:* Army (c), Air Force (c). *Unusual degree programs:* 3-2 engineering with University of Southern California, Washington University in St. Louis, Columbia University; forestry with Duke University.

Computers on Campus Students can access the following: online (class) registration. Campuswide network is available. 100% of college-owned or -operated housing units are wired for high-speed Internet access.

Student Life *Housing:* on-campus residence required through sophomore year. *Options:* coed. Campus housing is university owned. Freshman campus housing is guaranteed. *Activities and organizations:* drama/theater group, student-run newspaper, radio station, choral group, national fraternities, national sororities. *Campus security:* 24-hour emergency response devices and patrols, student patrols, late-night transport/escort service, controlled dormitory access. *Student services:* health clinic, personal/psychological counseling, women's center.

Athletics Member NCAA. All Division III. *Intercollegiate sports:* baseball M, basketball M/W, crew M/W, cross-country running M/W, football M, golf M/W, lacrosse M(c), soccer M/W, softball W, swimming and diving M/W, tennis M/W, track and field M/W, volleyball W. *Intramural sports:* badminton M/W, basketball M/W, bowling M/W, cross-country running M/W, football M/W, golf M/W, racquetball M/W, skiing (cross-country) M(c)/W(c), skiing (downhill) M(c)/W(c), soccer M/W, softball M/W, table tennis M/W, tennis M/W, ultimate Frisbee M/W, volleyball M/W, water polo M/W, weight lifting M/W.

Standardized Tests *Required:* SAT or ACT (for admission).

Costs (2012–13) *Comprehensive fee:* $50,694 includes full-time tuition ($40,560), mandatory fees ($314), and room and board ($9820). Full-time tuition and fees vary according to course load. Part-time tuition: $5070 per course. Part-time tuition and fees vary according to course load. *Room and board:* Room and board charges vary according to board plan and housing facility. *Payment plans:* tuition prepayment, installment. *Waivers:* employees or children of employees.

Financial Aid Of all full-time matriculated undergraduates who enrolled in 2012, 1,465 applied for aid, 1,281 were judged to have need, 539 had their need fully met. In 2012, 597 non-need-based awards were made. *Average percent of need met:* 87%. *Average financial aid package:* $32,296. *Average need-based loan:* $5203. *Average need-based gift aid:* $25,099. *Average non-need-based aid:* $15,128. *Average indebtedness upon graduation:* $26,740.

Applying *Options:* electronic application, early action, deferred entrance. *Application fee:* $50. *Required:* essay or personal statement, high school transcript, minimum 2.0 GPA, 1 letter of recommendation. *Required for some:* interview. *Recommended:* interview. *Application deadlines:* 2/1 (freshmen), 2/1 (transfers), 11/1 (early action). *Notification:* continuous until 4/1 (freshmen), 3/15 (transfers), 12/15 (early action).

Freshman Application Contact Teresa Hudkins, Director of Admission, Willamette University, 900 State Street, Salem, OR 97301. *Phone:* 877-542-2787. *Toll-free phone:* 877-542-2787. *Fax:* 503-375-5363. *E-mail:* libarts@willamette.edu. *Website:* http://www.willamette.edu/.

PENNSYLVANIA

Albright College
Reading, Pennsylvania

- **Independent** comprehensive, founded 1856, affiliated with United Methodist Church
- **Suburban** 118-acre campus with easy access to Philadelphia
- **Endowment** $51.3 million
- **Coed** 1,625 undergraduate students, 98% full-time, 56% women, 44% men
- **Moderately difficult** entrance level, 49% of applicants were admitted

Undergraduates 1,589 full-time, 36 part-time. Students come from 23 states and territories; 17 other countries; 36% are from out of state; 20% Black or African American, non-Hispanic/Latino; 10% Hispanic/Latino; 4% Asian, non-Hispanic/Latino; 0.9% American Indian or Alaska Native, non-Hispanic/Latino; 2% Two or more races, non-Hispanic/Latino; 2% Race/ethnicity unknown; 5% international; 3% transferred in; 65% live on campus. *Retention:* 75% of full-time freshmen returned.

Freshmen *Admission:* 6,132 applied, 3,011 admitted, 410 enrolled. *Average high school GPA:* 3.33. *Test scores:* SAT critical reading scores over 500: 68%; SAT math scores over 500: 68%; SAT critical reading scores over 600: 17%; SAT math scores over 600: 20%; SAT critical reading scores over 700: 3%; SAT math scores over 700: 3%.

Faculty *Total:* 173, 65% full-time, 56% with terminal degrees. *Student/faculty ratio:* 12:1.

Academics *Calendar:* 4-1-4. *Degrees:* certificates, bachelor's, and master's. *Special study options:* accelerated degree program, adult/continuing education programs, advanced placement credit, double majors, English as a second language, honors programs, independent study, internships, off-campus study, part-time degree program, services for LD students, student-designed majors, study abroad, summer session for credit. *ROTC:* Army (c).

Computers on Campus 372 computers/terminals are available on campus for general student use. Students can access the following: campus intranet, computer help desk, free student e-mail accounts, online (class) grades, online (class) registration, online (class) schedules, online financial statements, housing choices, course management systems. Campuswide network is available. 100% of college-owned or -operated housing units are wired for high-speed Internet access. Wireless service is available via entire campus.

Student Life *Housing:* on-campus residence required through sophomore year. *Options:* coed, men-only, women-only. Campus housing is university owned. Freshman campus housing is guaranteed. *Activities and organizations:* drama/theater group, student-run newspaper, radio station, choral group, Greek Organizations (combined), Alpha Phi Omega (service organization), Albright College Activities Council, Student Government Association, Newspaper, national fraternities, national sororities. *Campus security:* 24-hour emergency response devices and patrols, student patrols, late-night transport/escort service, controlled dormitory access, E2 Campus Text messaging, Rape Aggression Defense Training, Marked Patrol Cars, Partnership with Reading PD, PA State Police. *Student services:* health clinic, personal/psychological counseling, women's center.

Athletics Member NCAA. All Division III. *Intercollegiate sports:* badminton W(c), baseball M, basketball M/W, cheerleading M/W, cross-country running M/W, field hockey W, football M, golf M/W, lacrosse M(c)/W(c), rugby M(c)/W(c), soccer M/W, softball W, swimming and diving M/W, tennis M/W, track and field M/W, ultimate Frisbee M(c)/W(c), volleyball W. *Intramural sports:* badminton W, basketball M/W, football M, racquetball M/W, soccer M/W, softball M/W, volleyball M/W.

Standardized Tests *Required:* students applying tests optional, must complete an on-campus admission interview (for admission). *Recommended:* SAT (for admission), ACT (for admission), SAT or ACT (for admission).

Costs (2013–14) *Comprehensive fee:* $46,660 includes full-time tuition ($35,860), mandatory fees ($800), and room and board ($10,000). Full-time tuition and fees vary according to degree level. Part-time tuition: $4483 per course. Part-time tuition and fees vary according to degree level. *College room only:* $5550. Room and board charges vary according to board plan and housing facility. *Payment plan:* installment. *Waivers:* adult students, senior citizens, and employees or children of employees.

Financial Aid Of all full-time matriculated undergraduates who enrolled in 2011, 1,426 applied for aid, 1,272 were judged to have need, 332 had their need fully met. 592 Federal Work-Study jobs (averaging $1996). In 2011, 426 non-need-based awards were made. *Average percent of need met: 71%. Average financial aid package: $28,528. Average need-based loan: $6051. Average need-based gift aid: $13,726. Average non-need-based aid: $14,388. Average indebtedness upon graduation: $23,265.*

Applying *Options:* electronic application, early admission, deferred entrance. *Application fee:* $25. *Required:* essay or personal statement, high school transcript, 1 letter of recommendation, secondary school report (guidance department). *Recommended:* interview. *Application deadlines:* rolling (freshmen), rolling (transfers). *Notification:* continuous (freshmen), continuous (transfers).

Freshman Application Contact Mr. Gregory Eichhorn, Vice President for Enrollment Management, Albright College, PO Box 15234, 13th and Bern Streets, Reading, PA 19612-5234. *Phone:* 610-921-7260. *Toll-free phone:* 800-252-1856. *Fax:* 610-921-7294. *E-mail:* admission@albright.edu. *Website:* http://www.albright.edu/.

Allegheny College

Meadville, Pennsylvania

- **Independent** 4-year, founded 1815
- **Suburban** 565-acre campus
- **Endowment** $153.5 million
- **Coed**
- **Very difficult** entrance level

Faculty *Student/faculty ratio:* 12:1.
Academics *Calendar:* semesters. *Degree:* bachelor's.
Student Life *Campus security:* 24-hour emergency response devices and patrols, late-night transport/escort service, controlled dormitory access, local police patrol, emergency alert system, self defense education, TIPS Hotline—discriminatory harassment reporting.
Athletics Member NCAA. All Division III.
Standardized Tests *Required:* SAT or ACT (for admission).
Costs (2012–13) *Comprehensive fee:* $47,150 includes full-time tuition ($37,260), mandatory fees ($350), and room and board ($9540). Part-time tuition: $1553 per credit hour. Part-time tuition and fees vary according to course load. *Required fees:* $175 per term part-time. *College room only:* $5020. Room and board charges vary according to board plan and housing facility.
Financial Aid *Of all full-time matriculated undergraduates who enrolled in 2012,* 1,695 applied for aid, 1,506 were judged to have need, 466 had their need fully met. 1,232 Federal Work-Study jobs (averaging $2000). 109 state and other part-time jobs (averaging $4500). *In 2012,* 553 non-need-based awards were made. *Average percent of need met:* 88. *Average financial aid package:* $30,739. *Average need-based loan:* $5009. *Average need-based gift aid:* $23,731. *Average non-need-based aid:* $14,359.
Applying *Options:* electronic application, early admission, early decision, deferred entrance. *Application fee:* $35. *Required:* essay or personal statement, high school transcript, 2 letters of recommendation, college preparatory program, standardized test scores, health examination. *Recommended:* interview.
Freshman Application Contact Ms. Linda Clune, Senior Associate Director of Admissions, Allegheny College, 520 North Main Street, Box 5, Meadville, PA 16335. *Phone:* 814-332-4351. *Toll-free phone:* 800-521-5293. *Fax:* 814-337-0431. *E-mail:* admissions@allegheny.edu. *Website:* http://www.allegheny.edu/.

Alvernia University

Reading, Pennsylvania

- **Independent Roman Catholic** comprehensive, founded 1958
- **Suburban** 121-acre campus with easy access to Philadelphia
- **Endowment** $19.7 million
- **Coed** 2,347 undergraduate students, 72% full-time, 71% women, 29% men
- **Moderately difficult** entrance level, 80% of applicants were admitted

Undergraduates 1,689 full-time, 658 part-time. Students come from 18 states and territories; 4 other countries; 24% are from out of state; 12% Black or African American, non-Hispanic/Latino; 8% Hispanic/Latino; 1% Asian, non-Hispanic/Latino; 0.1% Native Hawaiian or other Pacific Islander, non-Hispanic/Latino; 0.1% American Indian or Alaska Native, non-Hispanic/Latino; 1% Two or more races, non-Hispanic/Latino; 4% Race/ethnicity unknown; 0.2% international; 4% transferred in; 57% live on campus. *Retention:* 75% of full-time freshmen returned.
Freshmen *Admission:* 1,864 applied, 1,500 admitted, 412 enrolled. *Average high school GPA:* 3.22. *Test scores:* SAT critical reading scores over 500: 37%; SAT math scores over 500: 44%; SAT writing scores over 500: 35%; ACT scores over 18: 78%; SAT critical reading scores over 600: 5%; SAT math scores over 600: 7%; SAT writing scores over 600: 6%; ACT scores over 24: 16%; SAT critical reading scores over 700: 1%; ACT scores over 30: 1%.
Faculty *Total:* 292, 35% full-time, 39% with terminal degrees. *Student/faculty ratio:* 12:1.
Academics *Calendar:* semesters. *Degrees:* associate, bachelor's, master's, and doctoral. *Special study options:* academic remediation for entering students, accelerated degree program, adult/continuing education programs, advanced placement credit, distance learning, double majors, English as a second language, honors programs, independent study, internships, off-campus study, part-time degree program, services for LD students, student-designed majors, study abroad, summer session for credit. *ROTC:* Army (c). *Unusual degree programs:* 3-2 Occupational Therapy.
Computers on Campus 426 computers/terminals and 1,020 ports are available on campus for general student use. Students can access the following: computer help desk, free student e-mail accounts, online (class) grades, online (class) registration, online (class) schedules. Campuswide network is available. 100% of college-owned or -operated housing units are wired for high-speed Internet access. Wireless service is available via classrooms, computer centers, computer labs, dorm rooms, learning centers, libraries, student centers.
Student Life *Housing:* on-campus residence required for freshman year. *Options:* coed. Campus housing is university owned. Freshman campus housing is guaranteed. *Activities and organizations:* drama/theater group, student-run newspaper, choral group, Student Government Association, Student Nurses Association of Alvernia (ASNA), Criminal Justice Association (CJA), Sport Management Association (SMA), Science Association. *Campus security:* 24-hour patrols, late-night transport/escort service, controlled dormitory access. *Student services:* health clinic, personal/psychological counseling.
Athletics Member NCAA. All Division III. *Intercollegiate sports:* baseball M, basketball M/W, cross-country running M/W, field hockey W, golf M, ice hockey M(c), lacrosse M/W, soccer M/W, softball W, tennis M/W, track and field M/W, volleyball W. *Intramural sports:* basketball M/W, cheerleading W(c), soccer M/W.
Standardized Tests *Required:* SAT or ACT (for admission).
Costs (2013–14) *Comprehensive fee:* $39,250 includes full-time tuition ($28,500), mandatory fees ($560), and room and board ($10,190). Full-time tuition and fees vary according to class time and reciprocity agreements. Part-time tuition: $780 per credit hour. Part-time tuition and fees vary according to class time and course load. *College room only:* $5070. Room and board charges vary according to board plan and housing facility. *Payment plan:* installment. *Waivers:* senior citizens and employees or children of employees.
Financial Aid Of all full-time matriculated undergraduates who enrolled in 2010, 1,588 applied for aid, 1,464 were judged to have need, 141 had their need fully met. 213 Federal Work-Study jobs (averaging $968). 27 state and other part-time jobs (averaging $2677). In 2010, 163 non-need-based awards were made. *Average percent of need met: 58%. Average financial aid package: $16,241. Average need-based loan: $4196. Average need-based gift aid: $12,182. Average non-need-based aid: $7785. Average indebtedness upon graduation: $37,773.*
Applying *Options:* electronic application, deferred entrance. *Application fee:* $25. *Required:* essay or personal statement, high school transcript. *Required for some:* 2 letters of recommendation, interview. *Recommended:* minimum 2.0 GPA, 1 letter of recommendation. *Application deadlines:* rolling (freshmen), rolling (transfers). *Notification:* continuous (freshmen).
Freshman Application Contact Ms. Stacey Adams Perry, Dean of Admissions, Alvernia University, 400 Saint Bernardine Street, Reading, PA

19607-1799. *Phone:* 610-796-8221. *Toll-free phone:* 888-ALVERNIA. *Fax:* 610-796-2873. *E-mail:* admissions@alvernia.edu.
Website: http://www.alvernia.edu/.

See below for display ad and page 1038 for the College Close-Up.

Arcadia University

Glenside, Pennsylvania

- **Independent** comprehensive, founded 1853, affiliated with Presbyterian Church (U.S.A.)
- **Suburban** 71-acre campus with easy access to Philadelphia
- **Endowment** $55.5 million
- **Coed**
- **Moderately difficult** entrance level

Faculty *Student/faculty ratio:* 11:1.

Academics *Calendar:* semesters. *Degrees:* bachelor's, master's, doctoral, and postbachelor's certificates.

Student Life *Campus security:* 24-hour emergency response devices and patrols, student patrols, late-night transport/escort service, controlled dormitory access.

Athletics Member NCAA. All Division III.

Standardized Tests *Required:* SAT or ACT (for admission).

Costs (2012–13) *Comprehensive fee:* $47,770 includes full-time tuition ($34,960), mandatory fees ($660), and room and board ($12,150). Full-time tuition and fees vary according to course load, degree level, and program. *Room and board:* Room and board charges vary according to board plan.

Financial Aid *Of all full-time matriculated undergraduates who enrolled in 2011,* 1,966 applied for aid, 1,765 were judged to have need, 234 had their need fully met. 1,289 Federal Work-Study jobs (averaging $1645). 150 state and other part-time jobs (averaging $1541). *In 2011,* 321 non-need-based awards were made. *Average percent of need met:* 70. *Average financial aid package:* $23,875. *Average need-based loan:* $4164. *Average need-based gift aid:* $19,587. *Average non-need-based aid:* $14,367. *Average indebtedness upon graduation:* $40,287.

Applying *Options:* electronic application, deferred entrance. *Application fee:* $30. *Required:* essay or personal statement, high school transcript, 2 letters of recommendation. *Required for some:* portfolio, audition. *Recommended:* minimum 3.0 GPA, interview.

Freshman Application Contact Colleen Pernicello, Director of Undergraduate Admissions, Arcadia University, 450 South Easton Road, Glenside, PA 19038. *Phone:* 215-572-2910. *Toll-free phone:* 877-ARCADIA. *Fax:* 215-572-4049. *E-mail:* admiss@arcadia.edu.
Website: http://www.arcadia.edu/.

See next page for display ad and page 1048 for the College Close-Up.

The Art Institute of Philadelphia

Philadelphia, Pennsylvania

- **Proprietary** 4-year, founded 1966, part of Education Management Corporation
- **Urban** campus
- **Coed**

Academics *Calendar:* quarters. *Degrees:* diplomas, associate, and bachelor's.

Freshman Application Contact The Art Institute of Philadelphia, 1622 Chestnut Street, Philadelphia, PA 19103. *Phone:* 215-567-7080. *Toll-free phone:* 800-275-2474.
Website: http://www.artinstitutes.edu/philadelphia/.

See full-page ad on page 54 and page 1100 for the College Close-Up.

The Art Institute of Pittsburgh

Pittsburgh, Pennsylvania

- **Proprietary** 4-year, founded 1921, part of Education Management Corporation
- **Urban** campus
- **Coed**

Academics *Calendar:* quarters. *Degrees:* certificates, diplomas, associate, and bachelor's.

Freshman Application Contact The Art Institute of Pittsburgh, 420 Boulevard of the Allies, Pittsburgh, PA 15219. *Phone:* 412-263-6600. *Toll-free phone:* 800-275-2470.
Website: http://www.artinstitutes.edu/pittsburgh/.

See full-page ad on page 54 and page 1104 for the College Close-Up.

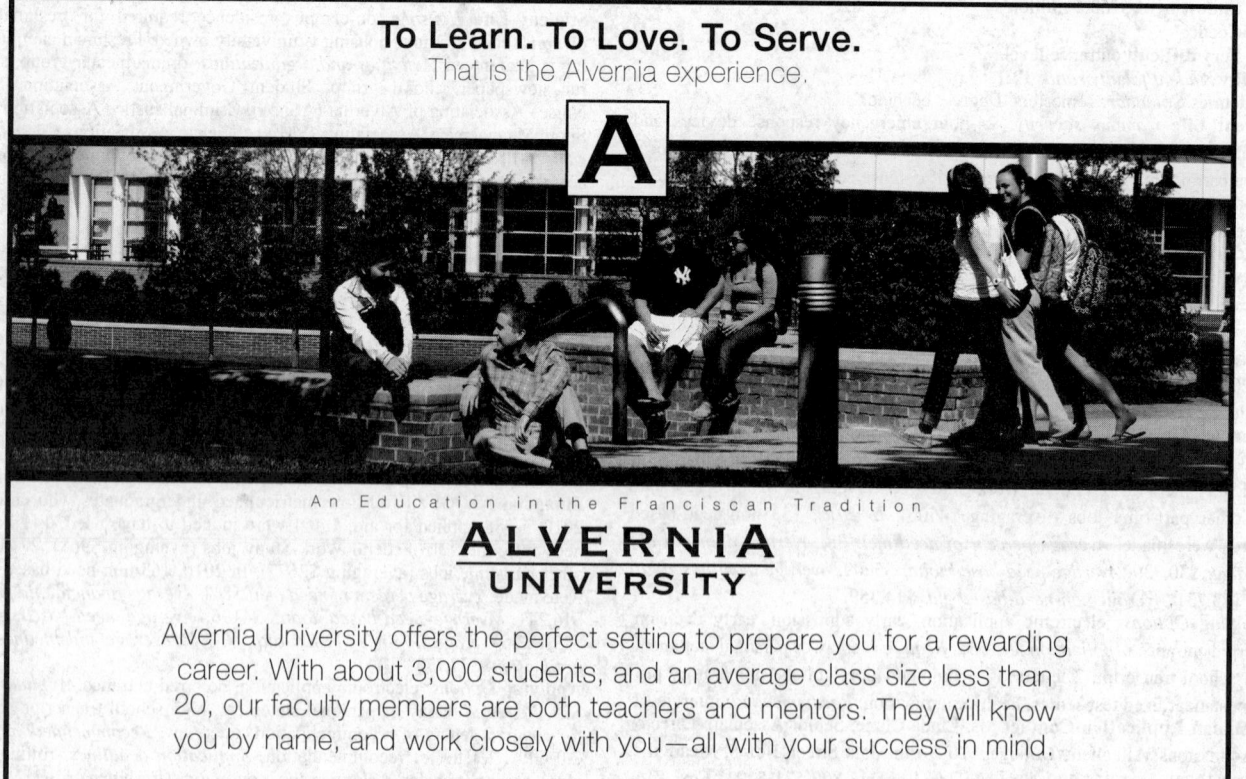

The Art Institute of York–Pennsylvania

York, Pennsylvania

- **Proprietary** primarily 2-year, founded 1952, part of Education Management Corporation
- **Suburban** campus
- **Coed**

Academics *Calendar:* quarters. *Degrees:* associate and bachelor's.

Freshman Application Contact The Art Institute of York–Pennsylvania, 1409 Williams Road, York, PA 17402-9012. *Phone:* 717-755-2300. *Toll-free phone:* 800-864-7725.

Website: http://www.artinstitutes.edu/york/.

See full-page ad on page 54 and page 1132 for the College Close-Up.

Baptist Bible College of Pennsylvania

Clarks Summit, Pennsylvania

- **Independent Baptist** comprehensive, founded 1932
- **Suburban** 124-acre campus
- **Endowment** $2.1 million
- **Coed**
- **Minimally difficult** entrance level

Faculty *Student/faculty ratio:* 11:1.

Academics *Calendar:* semesters. *Degrees:* certificates, associate, bachelor's, master's, and doctoral.

Student Life *Campus security:* 24-hour patrols, student patrols, controlled dormitory access.

Athletics Member NCAA, NCCAA. All NCAA Division III.

Standardized Tests *Required:* SAT or ACT (for admission).

Costs (2012–13) *Comprehensive fee:* $25,981 includes full-time tuition ($17,771), mandatory fees ($1260), and room and board ($6950). Part-time tuition: $592 per credit. *Required fees:* $42 per credit part-time. *College room only:* $2500. Room and board charges vary according to board plan.

Financial Aid *Of all full-time matriculated undergraduates who enrolled in 2011,* 492 applied for aid, 453 were judged to have need, 31 had their need fully met. *In 2011,* 72 non-need-based awards were made. *Average percent of need met:* 64. *Average financial aid package:* $13,779. *Average need-based loan:* $4341. *Average need-based gift aid:* $5813. *Average non-need-based aid:* $4644. *Average indebtedness upon graduation:* $23,677.

Applying *Options:* electronic application, early admission, deferred entrance. *Application fee:* $40. *Required:* essay or personal statement, high school transcript, 3 letters of recommendation, Christian testimony. *Required for some:* interview.

Freshman Application Contact Ms. Kellyn Lovell, Supervisor, Support Services, Baptist Bible College of Pennsylvania, 538 Venard Road, Clarks Summit, PA 18411-1297. *Phone:* 800-451-7664. *Toll-free phone:* 800-451-7664. *Fax:* 570-585-9271. *E-mail:* admissions@bbc.edu.

Website: http://www.bbc.edu/.

Bloomsburg University of Pennsylvania

Bloomsburg, Pennsylvania

- **State-supported** comprehensive, founded 1839, part of Pennsylvania State System of Higher Education
- **Rural** 282-acre campus
- **Endowment** $21.3 million
- **Coed** 9,201 undergraduate students, 94% full-time, 57% women, 43% men
- **Moderately difficult** entrance level, 68% of applicants were admitted

Undergraduates 8,642 full-time, 559 part-time. Students come from 31 states and territories; 19 other countries; 11% are from out of state; 7% Black or African American, non-Hispanic/Latino; 4% Hispanic/Latino; 0.9% Asian, non-Hispanic/Latino; 0.1% Native Hawaiian or other Pacific Islander, non-Hispanic/Latino; 0.1% American Indian or Alaska Native, non-Hispanic/Latino; 2% Two or more races, non-Hispanic/Latino; 3% Race/ethnicity unknown; 2% international; 5% transferred in; 42% live on campus. *Retention:* 78% of full-time freshmen returned.

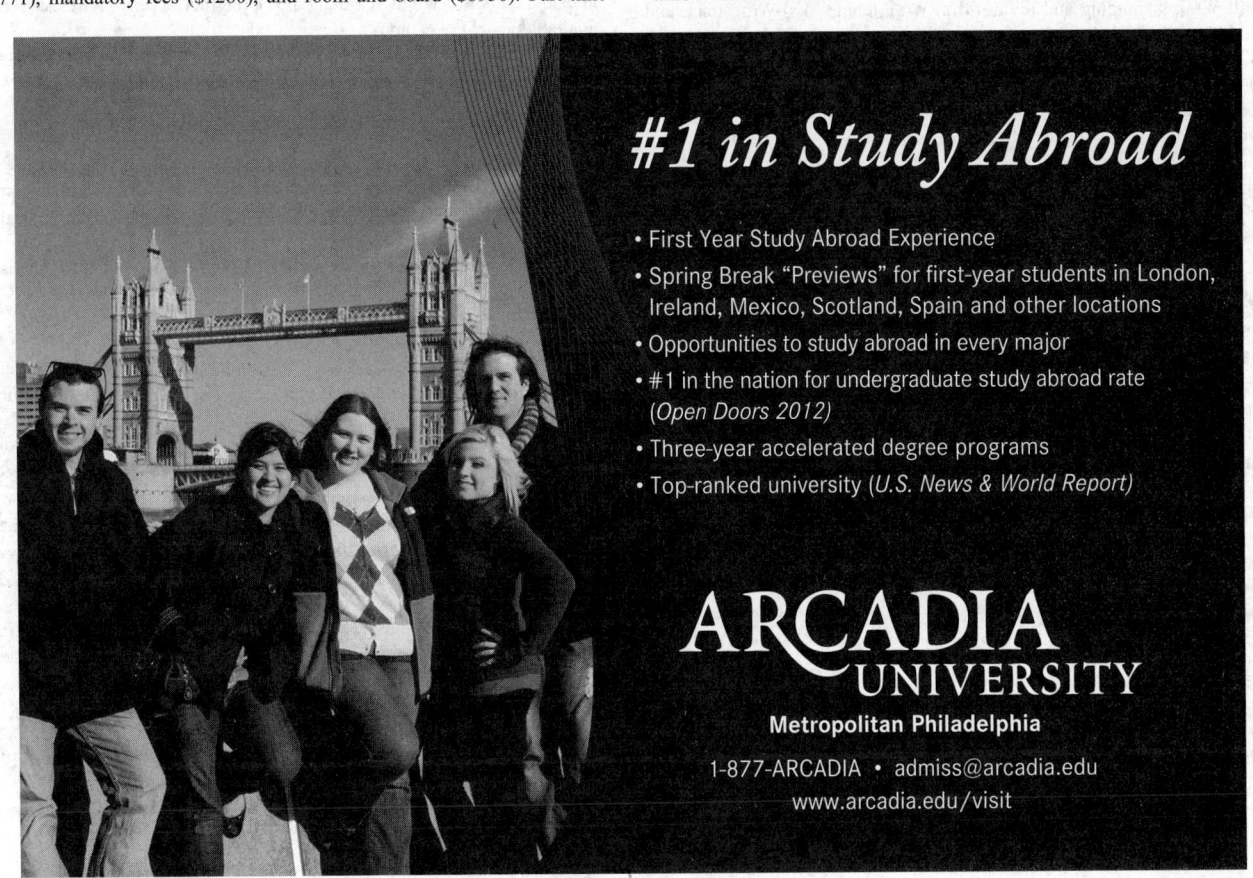

Freshmen *Admission:* 10,379 applied, 7,015 admitted, 1,924 enrolled. *Average high school GPA:* 3.3. *Test scores:* SAT critical reading scores over 500: 46%; SAT math scores over 500: 55%; SAT writing scores over 500: 42%; ACT scores over 18: 89%; SAT critical reading scores over 600: 7%; SAT math scores over 600: 11%; SAT writing scores over 600: 5%; ACT scores over 24: 23%; SAT critical reading scores over 700: 1%; SAT math scores over 700: 1%; SAT writing scores over 700: 1%; ACT scores over 30: 3%.

Faculty *Total:* 519, 80% full-time, 66% with terminal degrees. *Student/faculty ratio:* 21:1.

Academics *Calendar:* semesters. *Degrees:* bachelor's, master's, doctoral, and postbachelor's certificates. *Special study options:* academic remediation for entering students, advanced placement credit, cooperative education, distance learning, double majors, English as a second language, honors programs, independent study, internships, off-campus study, part-time degree program, services for LD students, study abroad, summer session for credit. *ROTC:* Army (b), Air Force (c). *Unusual degree programs:* 3-2 engineering with Pennsylvania State University (College of Engineering, College of Earth and Mineral Sciences).

Computers on Campus 1,567 computers/terminals are available on campus for general student use. Students can access the following: computer help desk, free student e-mail accounts, online (class) grades, online (class) registration, online (class) schedules. Campuswide network is available. 100% of college-owned or -operated housing units are wired for high-speed Internet access. Wireless service is available via entire campus.

Student Life *Housing:* on-campus residence required for freshman year. *Options:* coed. Campus housing is university owned and leased by the school. Freshman campus housing is guaranteed. *Activities and organizations:* drama/theater group, student-run newspaper, radio and television station, choral group, marching band, Living and Learning Communities, Band and Music Groups, Greek Organizations, Residence Hall Councils, national fraternities, national sororities. *Campus security:* 24-hour emergency response devices and patrols, late-night transport/escort service, controlled dormitory access, monitored surveillance cameras. *Student services:* health clinic, personal/psychological counseling, women's center.

Athletics Member NCAA. All Division II except wrestling (Division I). *Intercollegiate sports:* baseball M(s), basketball M(s)/W(s), cross-country running M(s)/W(s), field hockey W(s), football M(s), lacrosse W(s), soccer M(s)/W(s), softball W(s), swimming and diving M(s)/W(s), tennis M(s)/W(s), track and field M(s)/W(s), wrestling M(s). *Intramural sports:* baseball M(c), basketball M/W, bowling M(c)/W(c), cheerleading M(c)/W(c), cross-country running M(c)/W(c), equestrian sports M(c)/W(c), field hockey W, football M, ice hockey M(c), lacrosse M(c), racquetball M/W, rugby M(c)/W(c), skiing (downhill) M(c)/W(c), soccer M(c)/W(c), softball M/W, table tennis M(c)/W(c), tennis M(c)/W(c), ultimate Frisbee M(c)/W(c), volleyball M(c)/W(c), water polo M(c)/W(c), weight lifting M(c).

Standardized Tests *Required:* SAT or ACT (for admission).

Costs (2012–13) *Tuition:* state resident $6428 full-time, $268 per credit part-time; nonresident $16,070 full-time, $670 per credit part-time. Full-time tuition and fees vary according to course load and location. Part-time tuition and fees vary according to course load and location. *Required fees:* $1915 full-time, $70 per credit part-time, $55 per term part-time. *Room and board:* $7498; room only: $4598. Room and board charges vary according to board plan and housing facility. *Payment plan:* installment. *Waivers:* minority students, senior citizens, and employees or children of employees.

Financial Aid Of all full-time matriculated undergraduates who enrolled in 2012, 7,421 applied for aid, 5,555 were judged to have need, 684 had their need fully met. 669 Federal Work-Study jobs (averaging $2475). 1,143 state and other part-time jobs (averaging $3724). In 2012, 135 non-need-based awards were made. *Average percent of need met:* 56%. *Average financial aid package:* $8391. *Average need-based loan:* $4224. *Average need-based gift aid:* $5474. *Average non-need-based aid:* $1553. *Average indebtedness upon graduation:* $27,223.

Applying *Options:* electronic application, early admission, early action, deferred entrance. *Application fee:* $35. *Required:* high school transcript. *Application deadlines:* rolling (freshmen), rolling (out-of-state freshmen), rolling (transfers), 10/31 (early action). *Notification:* continuous until 10/1 (freshmen), continuous until 10/1 (out-of-state freshmen), continuous (transfers).

Freshman Application Contact Mr. Christopher Keller, Director of Admissions, Bloomsburg University of Pennsylvania, 104 Student Services Center, Bloomsburg, PA 17815-1905. *Phone:* 570-389-4316. *Fax:* 570-389-4741. *E-mail:* buadmiss@bloomu.edu. *Website:* http://www.bloomu.edu/.

Bryn Athyn College of the New Church

Bryn Athyn, Pennsylvania

- **Independent Christian** comprehensive, founded 1876, affiliated with Church of the New Jerusalem, part of The Academy of the New Church
- **Suburban** 130-acre campus with easy access to Philadelphia
- **Endowment** $59.3 million
- **Coed** 242 undergraduate students, 97% full-time, 55% women, 45% men
- **Minimally difficult** entrance level, 45% of applicants were admitted

Undergraduates 235 full-time, 7 part-time. Students come from 20 states and territories; 10 other countries; 40% are from out of state; 15% Black or African American, non-Hispanic/Latino; 5% Hispanic/Latino; 3% Asian, non-Hispanic/Latino; 0.4% Native Hawaiian or other Pacific Islander, non-Hispanic/Latino; 0.4% American Indian or Alaska Native, non-Hispanic/Latino; 11% international; 2% transferred in. *Retention:* 80% of full-time freshmen returned.

Freshmen *Admission:* 456 applied, 207 admitted, 55 enrolled. *Average high school GPA:* 3.15. *Test scores:* SAT math scores over 500: 51%; ACT scores over 18: 100%; SAT math scores over 600: 18%; ACT scores over 24: 40%; SAT math scores over 700: 7%; ACT scores over 30: 20%.

Faculty *Total:* 63, 43% full-time, 46% with terminal degrees. *Student/faculty ratio:* 6:1.

Academics *Calendar:* trimesters. *Degrees:* associate, bachelor's, master's, and doctoral. *Special study options:* academic remediation for entering students, accelerated degree program, advanced placement credit, cooperative education, English as a second language, independent study, internships, part-time degree program, services for LD students, student-designed majors, study abroad. *ROTC:* Army (c), Air Force (c).

Computers on Campus 18 computers/terminals are available on campus for general student use. Students can access the following: computer help desk, free student e-mail accounts, online (class) registration, online (class) schedules. Campuswide network is available. 100% of college-owned or -operated housing units are wired for high-speed Internet access. Wireless service is available via entire campus.

Student Life *Housing options:* men-only, women-only. Campus housing is university owned. Freshman campus housing is guaranteed. *Activities and organizations:* drama/theater group, student-run newspaper, choral group, C.A.R.E. (Community Service), Social council, International Student Organization, Peer Advisory Council, Student government. *Campus security:* 24-hour emergency response devices, controlled dormitory access, 18-hour patrols by trained personnel. *Student services:* health clinic, personal/psychological counseling.

Athletics *Intramural sports:* ice hockey M, lacrosse M, soccer M, tennis M/W, volleyball W.

Standardized Tests *Required:* SAT or ACT (for admission).

Costs (2013–14) *Comprehensive fee:* $27,982 includes full-time tuition ($16,498), mandatory fees ($1224), and room and board ($10,260). Part-time tuition: $635 per credit hour. *Required fees:* $45 per credit hour part-time. *Payment plan:* installment. *Waivers:* senior citizens.

Financial Aid Of all full-time matriculated undergraduates who enrolled in 2008, 92 applied for aid, 66 were judged to have need, 30 had their need fully met. In 2008, 22 non-need-based awards were made. *Average percent of need met:* 95%. *Average financial aid package:* $9987. *Average need-based loan:* $3329. *Average need-based gift aid:* $8358. *Average non-need-based aid:* $2232. *Average indebtedness upon graduation:* $8299. *Financial aid deadline:* 7/1.

Applying *Options:* electronic application, deferred entrance. *Required:* essay or personal statement, high school transcript, minimum 2.0 GPA, 1 letter of recommendation, interest in the writings of Emanuel Swedenborg. *Required for some:* interview. *Notification:* continuous (freshmen), continuous (transfers).

Freshman Application Contact Admissions Office, Bryn Athyn College of the New Church, 2945 College Drive, Box 462, Bryn Athyn, PA 19009. *Phone:* 267-502-6000. *Toll-free phone:* 800-767-9552. *Fax:* 267-502-2593. *E-mail:* admissions@brynathyn.edu. *Website:* http://www.brynathyn.edu/.

Bryn Mawr College

Bryn Mawr, Pennsylvania

- **Independent** university, founded 1885
- **Suburban** 135-acre campus with easy access to Philadelphia
- **Endowment** $671.1 million
- **Undergraduate: women only; graduate: coed**
- **Most difficult** entrance level

Faculty *Student/faculty ratio:* 8:1.

Academics *Calendar:* semesters. *Degrees:* bachelor's, master's, doctoral, and postbachelor's certificates.

Student Life *Campus security:* 24-hour emergency response devices and patrols, late-night transport/escort service, controlled dormitory access, shuttle bus service, awareness programs, bicycle registration, security Web site.

Athletics Member NCAA. All Division III.

Standardized Tests *Required:* SAT and SAT Subject Tests or ACT (for admission).

Costs (2012–13) *Comprehensive fee:* $55,586 includes full-time tuition ($41,260), mandatory fees ($986), and room and board ($13,340). Part-time tuition: $5160 per course. *College room only:* $7620.

Financial Aid *Of all full-time matriculated undergraduates who enrolled in 2011,* 822 applied for aid, 760 were judged to have need, 760 had their need fully met. 549 Federal Work-Study jobs (averaging $1956). 155 state and other part-time jobs (averaging $2041). *In 2011,* 99 non-need-based awards were made. *Average percent of need met:* 100. *Average financial aid package:* $37,817. *Average need-based loan:* $4781. *Average need-based gift aid:* $32,303. *Average non-need-based aid:* $12,550. *Average indebtedness upon graduation:* $22,830. *Financial aid deadline:* 3/1.

Applying *Options:* electronic application, early admission, early decision, deferred entrance. *Application fee:* $50. *Required:* essay or personal statement, high school transcript, 3 letters of recommendation. *Recommended:* interview.

Freshman Application Contact Ms. Laurie Koehler, Dean of Admissions, Bryn Mawr College, 101 North Merion Avenue, Bryn Mawr, PA 19010. *Phone:* 610-526-5152. *Toll-free phone:* 800-BMC-1885. *Fax:* 610-526-7471. *E-mail:* admissions@brynmawr.edu. *Website:* http://www.brynmawr.edu/.

Bucknell University

Lewisburg, Pennsylvania

- **Independent** comprehensive, founded 1846
- **Small-town** 446-acre campus
- **Endowment** $599.2 million
- **Coed** 3,536 undergraduate students, 99% full-time, 52% women, 48% men
- **Most difficult** entrance level, 27% of applicants were admitted

Undergraduates 3,515 full-time, 21 part-time. Students come from 45 states and territories; 66 other countries; 76% are from out of state; 3% Black or African American, non-Hispanic/Latino; 5% Hispanic/Latino; 3% Asian, non-Hispanic/Latino; 3% Two or more races, non-Hispanic/Latino; 0.9% Race/ethnicity unknown; 5% international; 0.8% transferred in; 86% live on campus. *Retention:* 95% of full-time freshmen returned.

Freshmen *Admission:* 8,291 applied, 2,238 admitted, 918 enrolled. *Average high school GPA:* 3.5. *Test scores:* SAT critical reading scores over 500: 96%; SAT math scores over 500: 99%; SAT writing scores over 500: 97%; ACT scores over 18: 100%; SAT critical reading scores over 600: 69%; SAT math scores over 600: 83%; SAT writing scores over 600: 72%; ACT scores over 24: 95%; SAT critical reading scores over 700: 17%; SAT math scores over 700: 31%; SAT writing scores over 700: 21%; ACT scores over 30: 49%.

Faculty *Total:* 386, 94% full-time, 94% with terminal degrees. *Student/faculty ratio:* 10:1.

Academics *Calendar:* semesters. *Degrees:* bachelor's and master's. *Special study options:* advanced placement credit, double majors, honors programs, independent study, internships, off-campus study, part-time degree program, services for LD students, student-designed majors, study abroad, summer session for credit. *ROTC:* Army (b). *Unusual degree programs:* 3-2 engineering; biology, chemistry.

Computers on Campus 970 computers/terminals and 153 ports are available on campus for general student use. Students can access the following: campus intranet, computer help desk, free student e-mail accounts, online (class) grades, online (class) registration, online (class) schedules. Campuswide network is available. 100% of college-owned or -operated housing units are wired for high-speed Internet access. Wireless service is available via entire campus.

Student Life *Housing:* on-campus residence required through senior year. *Options:* coed, men-only, cooperative, disabled students. Campus housing is

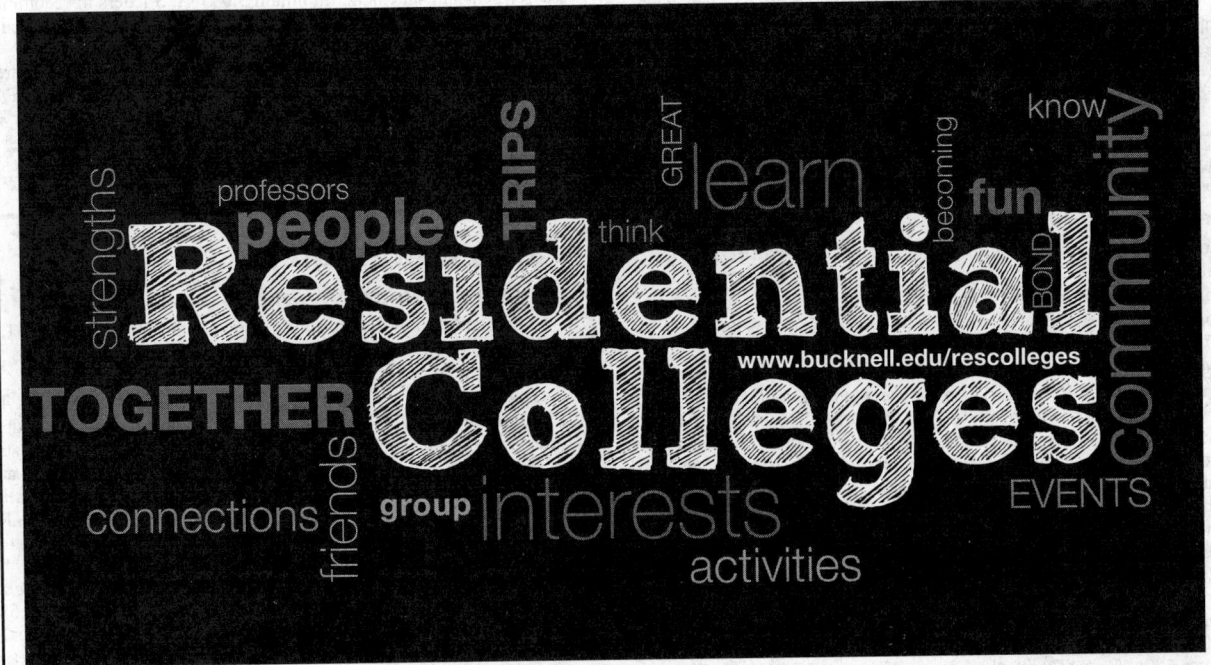

university owned. Freshman campus housing is guaranteed. *Activities and organizations:* drama/theater group, student-run newspaper, radio station, choral group, Alpha Phi Omega, Outing Club, Activities and Campus Events, Catholic Campus Ministries, CALVIN and HOBBES, national fraternities, national sororities. *Campus security:* 24-hour emergency response devices and patrols, student patrols, late-night transport/escort service, controlled dormitory access, well-lit pathways, self-defense education, safety/security orientation. *Student services:* health clinic, personal/psychological counseling, women's center.

Athletics Member NCAA. All Division I except football (Division I-AA). *Intercollegiate sports:* baseball M, basketball M(s)/W(s), cheerleading M(c)/W(c), crew M(c)/W, cross-country running M/W(s), equestrian sports M(c)/W(c), field hockey W, golf M/W, ice hockey M(c), lacrosse M(s)/W(s), rock climbing M(c)/W(c), rugby M(c)/W(c), sailing M(c)/W(c), skiing (downhill) M(c)/W(c), soccer M(s)/W(s), softball W, squash M(c)/W(c), swimming and diving M(s)/W(s), tennis M/W, track and field M/W, ultimate Frisbee M(c)/W(c), volleyball M(c)/W, water polo M/W, weight lifting M(c)/W(c), wrestling M(s). *Intramural sports:* badminton M/W, basketball M/W, bowling M/W, cross-country running M/W, golf M/W, racquetball M/W, soccer M/W, softball M/W, squash M/W, table tennis M/W, tennis M/W, ultimate Frisbee M/W, volleyball M/W, weight lifting M, wrestling M.

Standardized Tests *Required:* SAT or ACT (for admission).

Costs (2013–14) *Comprehensive fee:* $58,160 includes full-time tuition ($46,646), mandatory fees ($256), and room and board ($11,258). Part-time tuition: $5121 per course. *College room only:* $6622. Room and board charges vary according to board plan and housing facility. *Payment plans:* tuition prepayment, installment. *Waivers:* employees or children of employees.

Financial Aid Of all full-time matriculated undergraduates who enrolled in 2012, 1,847 applied for aid, 1,585 were judged to have need, 1,506 had their need fully met. 600 Federal Work-Study jobs (averaging $1500). 50 state and other part-time jobs (averaging $1500). In 2012, 207 non-need-based awards were made. *Average percent of need met:* 95%. *Average financial aid package:* $27,000. *Average need-based loan:* $4816. *Average need-based gift aid:* $23,150. *Average non-need-based aid:* $13,562. *Average indebtedness upon graduation:* $21,163. *Financial aid deadline:* 1/15.

Applying *Options:* electronic application, early decision, deferred entrance. *Application fee:* $60. *Required:* essay or personal statement, high school transcript, 1 letter of recommendation. *Application deadlines:* 1/15 (freshmen), 3/15 (transfers). *Early decision deadline:* 11/15 (for plan 1), 1/15 (for plan 2). *Notification:* 4/1 (freshmen), 5/1 (transfers), 12/15 (early decision plan 1), 2/15 (early decision plan 2).

Freshman Application Contact Dean Robert Springall, Dean of Admissions, Bucknell University, Bucknell University, 1 Dent Drive, Lewisburg, PA 17837. *Phone:* 570-577-1101. *Fax:* 570-577-3538. *E-mail:* admissions@bucknell.edu.

Website: http://www.bucknell.edu/.

See previous page for display ad and page 1216 for the College Close-Up.

Cabrini College

Radnor, Pennsylvania

- **Independent Roman Catholic** comprehensive, founded 1957
- **Suburban** 112-acre campus with easy access to Philadelphia
- **Endowment** $12.7 million
- **Coed** 1,405 undergraduate students, 92% full-time, 63% women, 37% men
- **Moderately difficult** entrance level, 73% of applicants were admitted

Undergraduates 1,298 full-time, 107 part-time. Students come from 21 states and territories; 16 other countries; 39% are from out of state; 10% Black or African American, non-Hispanic/Latino; 5% Hispanic/Latino; 2% Asian, non-Hispanic/Latino; 0.6% Native Hawaiian or other Pacific Islander, non-Hispanic/Latino; 0.1% American Indian or Alaska Native, non-Hispanic/Latino; 2% Two or more races, non-Hispanic/Latino; 6% Race/ethnicity unknown; 0.3% international; 4% transferred in; 59% live on campus. *Retention:* 74% of full-time freshmen returned.

Freshmen *Admission:* 2,608 applied, 1,895 admitted, 385 enrolled. *Average high school GPA:* 3.01. *Test scores:* SAT critical reading scores over 500: 27%; SAT math scores over 500: 29%; SAT writing scores over 500: 29%; SAT critical reading scores over 600: 4%; SAT math scores over 600: 6%; SAT writing scores over 600: 4%; SAT critical reading scores over 700: 1%; SAT writing scores over 700: 1%.

Faculty *Total:* 293, 26% full-time, 36% with terminal degrees. *Student/faculty ratio:* 13:1.

Academics *Calendar:* semesters. *Degrees:* bachelor's and master's. *Special study options:* academic remediation for entering students, adult/continuing education programs, advanced placement credit, cooperative education, double

majors, honors programs, independent study, internships, off-campus study, part-time degree program, services for LD students, student-designed majors, study abroad, summer session for credit. *ROTC:* Army (c), Air Force (c). *Unusual degree programs:* 3-2 physical therapy, occupational therapy with Thomas Jefferson University.

Computers on Campus 575 computers/terminals and 2,922 ports are available on campus for general student use. Students can access the following: campus intranet, computer help desk, free student e-mail accounts, online (class) grades, online (class) registration, online (class) schedules, account balances and other services. Campuswide network is available. 100% of college-owned or -operated housing units are wired for high-speed Internet access. Wireless service is available via entire campus.

Student Life *Housing options:* coed, women-only, disabled students. Campus housing is university owned and leased by the school. Freshman applicants given priority for college housing. *Activities and organizations:* drama/theater group, student-run newspaper, radio station, choral group, Student Government Association, Campus Activities and Programming Board, Colleges Against Cancer/Relay for Life, Psychology Club, Habitat for Humanity. *Campus security:* 24-hour emergency response devices and patrols, student patrols, late-night transport/escort service, controlled dormitory access, resident assistants and directors on nightly duty. *Student services:* health clinic, personal/psychological counseling.

Athletics Member NCAA. All Division III. *Intercollegiate sports:* basketball M/W, cross-country running M/W, field hockey W, golf M, lacrosse M/W, soccer M/W, softball W, swimming and diving M/W, tennis M/W, volleyball W. *Intramural sports:* basketball M/W, cheerleading M(c)/W(c), football M/W, soccer M/W, squash M/W, ultimate Frisbee M/W, volleyball M/W.

Standardized Tests *Required:* SAT or ACT (for admission).

Costs (2013–14) *Tuition:* $28,090 full-time. Part-time tuition and fees vary according to course load. *Required fees:* $910 full-time. *Room only:* Room and board charges vary according to board plan and housing facility. *Payment plan:* installment. *Waivers:* children of alumni, senior citizens, and employees or children of employees.

Financial Aid Of all full-time matriculated undergraduates who enrolled in 2012, 1,117 applied for aid, 1,019 were judged to have need, 299 had their need fully met. 287 Federal Work-Study jobs (averaging $1446). In 2012, 287 non-need-based awards were made. *Average percent of need met:* 58%. *Average financial aid package:* $20,553. *Average need-based loan:* $3876. *Average need-based gift aid:* $10,591. *Average non-need-based aid:* $10,876. *Average indebtedness upon graduation:* $39,665.

Applying *Options:* electronic application, deferred entrance. *Application fee:* $35. *Required:* high school transcript, minimum 2.0 GPA. *Recommended:* essay or personal statement, minimum 3.0 GPA, 3 letters of recommendation, interview. *Application deadlines:* rolling (freshmen), rolling (out-of-state freshmen), rolling (transfers).

Freshman Application Contact Ms. Shannon Zottola, Director of Enrollment, Cabrini College, 610 King of Prussia Road, Radnor, PA 19087-3698. *Phone:* 610-902-1027. *Toll-free phone:* 800-848-1003. *Fax:* 610-902-8508. *E-mail:* admit@cabrini.edu.

Website: http://www.cabrini.edu/.

Cairn University

Langhorne, Pennsylvania

- **Independent nondenominational** comprehensive, founded 1913
- **Suburban** 105-acre campus with easy access to Philadelphia
- **Endowment** $9.6 million
- **Coed** 952 undergraduate students, 92% full-time, 52% women, 48% men
- **Moderately difficult** entrance level, 72% of applicants were admitted

Undergraduates 877 full-time, 75 part-time. 45% are from out of state; 16% Black or African American, non-Hispanic/Latino; 4% Hispanic/Latino; 4% Asian, non-Hispanic/Latino; 0.6% American Indian or Alaska Native, non-Hispanic/Latino; 2% Two or more races, non-Hispanic/Latino; 0.9% Race/ethnicity unknown; 2% international; 10% transferred in; 55% live on campus. *Retention:* 75% of full-time freshmen returned.

Freshmen *Admission:* 466 applied, 336 admitted, 173 enrolled. *Average high school GPA:* 3.23. *Test scores:* SAT critical reading scores over 500: 58%; SAT math scores over 500: 54%; ACT scores over 18: 81%; SAT critical reading scores over 600: 24%; SAT math scores over 600: 13%; ACT scores over 24: 48%; SAT critical reading scores over 700: 2%.

Faculty *Total:* 115, 40% full-time, 37% with terminal degrees. *Student/faculty ratio:* 15:1.

Academics *Calendar:* semesters. *Degrees:* certificates, bachelor's, master's, and postbachelor's certificates. *Special study options:* academic remediation for entering students, accelerated degree program, adult/continuing education programs, advanced placement credit, double majors, honors programs, internships, off-campus study, part-time degree program, services for LD students, study abroad, summer session for credit. *ROTC:* Air Force (c).

Computers on Campus 79 computers/terminals are available on campus for general student use. Students can access the following: campus intranet, computer help desk, free student e-mail accounts, online (class) grades, online (class) registration, online (class) schedules. Campuswide network is available. 100% of college-owned or -operated housing units are wired for high-speed Internet access. Wireless service is available via classrooms, computer labs, dorm rooms, learning centers, libraries.

Student Life *Housing:* on-campus residence required through senior year. *Options:* men-only, women-only, disabled students. Campus housing is university owned and leased by the school. Freshman campus housing is guaranteed. *Activities and organizations:* drama/theater group, student-run newspaper, choral group, Student Senate, Chi Beta Sigma (Social Work Club), Students in Free Enterprise, Student Missionary Fellowship, Culture & Arts Association. *Campus security:* 24-hour emergency response devices and patrols, student patrols, late-night transport/escort service, controlled dormitory access. *Student services:* health clinic, personal/psychological counseling.

Athletics Member NCAA, NCCAA. All NCAA Division III. *Intercollegiate sports:* baseball M, basketball M/W, cross-country running M/W, golf M, soccer M/W, softball W, tennis W, volleyball M/W. *Intramural sports:* basketball M/W, soccer M/W, tennis M/W, ultimate Frisbee M/W, volleyball M/W.

Standardized Tests *Required:* SAT or ACT (for admission).

Costs (2013–14) *Tuition:* $22,250 full-time, $660 per credit part-time. Full-time tuition and fees vary according to course load and location. Part-time tuition and fees vary according to course load and location. *Required fees:* $205 full-time. *Room only:* $4625. Room and board charges vary according to board plan and location. *Payment plan:* installment. *Waivers:* employees or children of employees.

Financial Aid Of all full-time matriculated undergraduates who enrolled in 2012, 772 applied for aid, 720 were judged to have need, 78 had their need fully met. In 2012, 114 non-need-based awards were made. *Average percent of need met:* 70%. *Average financial aid package:* $17,074. *Average need-based loan:* $4949. *Average need-based gift aid:* $12,557. *Average non-need-based aid:* $7665. *Average indebtedness upon graduation:* $30,633.

Applying *Options:* electronic application, early admission, deferred entrance. *Application fee:* $25. *Required:* essay or personal statement, high school transcript, minimum 2.0 GPA. *Required for some:* interview. *Recommended:* interview. *Application deadlines:* rolling (freshmen), rolling (out-of-state freshmen), rolling (transfers). *Notification:* continuous (freshmen), continuous (out-of-state freshmen), continuous (transfers).

Freshman Application Contact Mr. Eric Rivera, Interim Director of Undergraduate Admissions, Cairn University, 200 Manor Avenue, Langhorne, PA 19047. *Phone:* 215-702-4250. *Toll-free phone:* 800-RUN-2-PBU. *Fax:* 215-702-4248. *E-mail:* admissions@pbu.edu. *Website:* http://cairn.edu/.

California University of Pennsylvania

California, Pennsylvania

- **State-supported** comprehensive, founded 1852, part of Pennsylvania State System of Higher Education
- **Small-town** 188-acre campus with easy access to Pittsburgh
- **Coed**
- **Moderately difficult** entrance level

Faculty *Student/faculty ratio:* 19:1.

Academics *Calendar:* semesters. *Degrees:* certificates, associate, bachelor's, master's, post-master's, and postbachelor's certificates.

Student Life *Campus security:* 24-hour emergency response devices and patrols, student patrols, late-night transport/escort service, residence hall entrances staffed 24/7, fire suppression and smoke detection systems, security staff are trained police officers.

Athletics Member NCAA. All Division II.

Standardized Tests *Required:* SAT or ACT (for admission).

Costs (2012–13) *Tuition:* state resident $6240 full-time, $260 per credit hour part-time; nonresident $9984 full-time, $416 per credit hour part-time. Full-time tuition and fees vary according to location and student level. Part-time tuition and fees vary according to location and student level. *Required fees:* $2774 full-time. *Room and board:* $9934; room only: $6592. Room and board charges vary according to board plan and housing facility.

Financial Aid Of all full-time matriculated undergraduates who enrolled in 2011, 5,090 applied for aid, 3,907 were judged to have need, 3,750 had their need fully met. In 2011, 81 non-need-based awards were made. *Average percent of need met:* 77. *Average financial aid package:* $7212. *Average need-*

based loan: $7212. *Average need-based gift aid:* $8645. *Average non-need-based aid:* $4500. *Average indebtedness upon graduation:* $24,251.

Applying *Options:* early admission, deferred entrance. *Application fee:* $25. *Required:* high school transcript.

Freshman Application Contact Mr. William Edmonds, Dean of Enrollment Management and Academic Services, California University of Pennsylvania, 250 University Avenue, California, PA 15419. *Phone:* 724-938-4404. *Toll-free phone:* 888-412-0479. *Fax:* 724-938-4564. *Website:* http://www.calu.edu/.

Carlow University

Pittsburgh, Pennsylvania

- **Independent Roman Catholic** comprehensive, founded 1929
- **Urban** 14-acre campus with easy access to Pittsburgh
- **Endowment** $16.6 million
- **Coed, primarily women** 1,955 undergraduate students, 53% full-time, 83% women, 17% men
- **Moderately difficult** entrance level, 61% of applicants were admitted

Undergraduates 1,040 full-time, 915 part-time. Students come from 17 states and territories; 11 other countries; 4% are from out of state; 19% Black or African American, non-Hispanic/Latino; 2% Hispanic/Latino; 0.9% Asian, non-Hispanic/Latino; 0.6% American Indian or Alaska Native, non-Hispanic/Latino; 2% Two or more races, non-Hispanic/Latino; 20% Race/ethnicity unknown; 0.4% international; 10% transferred in; 27% live on campus. *Retention:* 70% of full-time freshmen returned.

Freshmen *Admission:* 1,169 applied, 715 admitted, 219 enrolled. *Average high school GPA:* 3.63. *Test scores:* SAT critical reading scores over 500: 36%; SAT math scores over 500: 37%; SAT writing scores over 500: 32%; ACT scores over 18: 71%; SAT critical reading scores over 600: 3%; SAT math scores over 600: 7%; SAT writing scores over 600: 5%; ACT scores over 24: 13%; SAT critical reading scores over 700: 1%; SAT math scores over 700: 1%; SAT writing scores over 700: 1%.

Faculty *Total:* 280, 35% full-time, 41% with terminal degrees. *Student/faculty ratio:* 11:1.

Academics *Calendar:* semesters. *Degrees:* bachelor's, master's, doctoral, post-master's, and postbachelor's certificates. *Special study options:* academic remediation for entering students, accelerated degree program, adult/continuing education programs, advanced placement credit, cooperative education, distance learning, double majors, honors programs, independent study, internships, off-campus study, part-time degree program, services for LD students, study abroad, summer session for credit. *ROTC:* Army (c), Navy (c), Air Force (c). *Unusual degree programs:* 3-2 engineering with Carnegie Mellon University (Math/Engineering, Chemistry/Chemical Engineering, Biology/Environmental Engineering); Duquesne University (Biology/Environmental Science & Management).

Computers on Campus 162 computers/terminals are available on campus for general student use. Students can access the following: campus intranet, computer help desk, free student e-mail accounts, online (class) grades, online (class) registration, online (class) schedules. Campuswide network is available. 100% of college-owned or -operated housing units are wired for high-speed Internet access. Wireless service is available via entire campus.

Student Life *Housing options:* men-only, women-only. Campus housing is university owned. *Activities and organizations:* drama/theater group, choral group, Student Government Association, Campus Activities, SPiRiT (Student Ambassadors), SNAP (Student Nursing Association), PSEA (School Education Association). *Campus security:* 24-hour emergency response devices and patrols, late-night transport/escort service, controlled dormitory access. *Student services:* health clinic, personal/psychological counseling.

Athletics Member NAIA, USCAA. *Intercollegiate sports:* basketball W(s), cross-country running M(s)/W(s), soccer W(s), softball W(s), tennis W(s), volleyball W(s).

Standardized Tests *Required:* SAT or ACT (for admission).

Costs (2012–13) *Comprehensive fee:* $34,068 includes full-time tuition ($24,230), mandatory fees ($208), and room and board ($9630). Full-time tuition and fees vary according to course load, program, and reciprocity agreements. Part-time tuition: $770 per credit hour. Part-time tuition and fees vary according to course load, program, and reciprocity agreements. *College room only:* $4924. Room and board charges vary according to board plan. *Payment plans:* installment, deferred payment. *Waivers:* children of alumni, adult students, and employees or children of employees.

Financial Aid Of all full-time matriculated undergraduates who enrolled in 2003, 431 Federal Work-Study jobs (averaging $776).

Applying *Options:* electronic application, deferred entrance. *Application fee:* $20. *Required:* high school transcript. *Recommended:* essay or personal state-

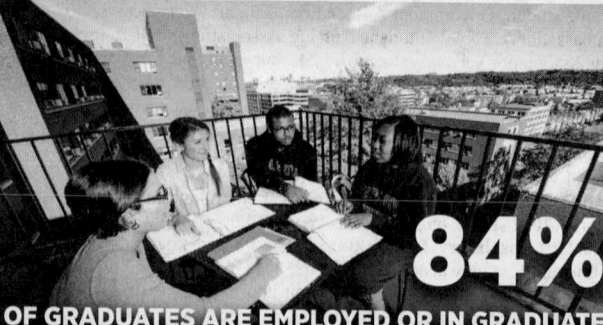
ment, minimum 2.5 GPA, interview. *Application deadlines:* rolling (freshmen), rolling (transfers). *Notification:* continuous (freshmen), continuous (transfers). **Freshman Application Contact** Ms. Susan Winstel, Director of Admissions, Carlow University, 3333 Fifth Avenue, Pittsburgh, PA 15213. *Phone:* 412-578-6059. *Toll-free phone:* 800-333-CARLOW. *Fax:* 412-578-6668. *E-mail:* admissions@carlow.edu.
Website: http://www.carlow.edu/.

See this page for display ad and page 1224 for the College Close-Up.

Carnegie Mellon University

Pittsburgh, Pennsylvania

- **Independent** university, founded 1900
- **Urban** 145-acre campus
- **Endowment** $987.1 million
- **Coed** 6,279 undergraduate students, 97% full-time, 43% women, 57% men
- **Most difficult** entrance level, 28% of applicants were admitted

Undergraduates 6,083 full-time, 196 part-time. Students come from 49 states and territories; 78 other countries; 82% are from out of state; 5% Black or African American, non-Hispanic/Latino; 7% Hispanic/Latino; 22% Asian, non-Hispanic/Latino; 0.1% American Indian or Alaska Native, non-Hispanic/Latino; 4% Two or more races, non-Hispanic/Latino; 5% Race/ethnicity unknown; 18% international; 0.7% transferred in; 64% live on campus. *Retention:* 95% of full-time freshmen returned.
Freshmen *Admission:* 17,313 applied, 4,807 admitted, 1,408 enrolled. *Average high school GPA:* 3.69. *Test scores:* SAT critical reading scores over 500: 99%; SAT math scores over 500: 99%; SAT writing scores over 500: 99%; ACT scores over 18: 100%; SAT critical reading scores over 600: 88%; SAT math scores over 600: 96%; SAT writing scores over 600: 91%; ACT scores over 24: 99%; SAT critical reading scores over 700: 40%; SAT math scores over 700: 73%; SAT writing scores over 700: 50%; ACT scores over 30: 74%.
Academics *Calendar:* semesters. *Degrees:* bachelor's, master's, doctoral, and post-master's certificates. *Special study options:* advanced placement credit, cooperative education, distance learning, double majors, independent study, internships, off-campus study, part-time degree program, services for LD students, student-designed majors, study abroad, summer session for credit. *ROTC:* Army (b), Navy (b), Air Force (b). *Unusual degree programs:* 3-2 business administration; engineering; public management and policy.
Computers on Campus 421 computers/terminals are available on campus for general student use. Students can access the following: campus intranet, computer help desk, free student e-mail accounts, online (class) grades, online (class) registration, online (class) schedules. Campuswide network is available. 100% of college-owned or -operated housing units are wired for high-speed Internet access. Wireless service is available via entire campus.
Student Life *Housing:* on-campus residence required for freshman year. *Options:* coed, men-only, women-only, disabled students. Campus housing is university owned and leased by the school. Freshman campus housing is guaranteed. *Activities and organizations:* drama/theater group, student-run newspaper, radio and television station, choral group, marching band, Student Senate, Alpha Phi Omega, Tartan Club, Spirit Club, Greek Community, national fraternities, national sororities. *Campus security:* 24-hour emergency response devices and patrols, late-night transport/escort service, controlled dormitory access. *Student services:* health clinic, personal/psychological counseling, women's center, legal services.
Athletics Member NCAA. All Division III. *Intercollegiate sports:* badminton W(c), baseball M(c), basketball M/W, cheerleading M/W, crew M(c)/W(c), cross-country running M/W, fencing M(c)/W(c), football M, golf M, ice hockey M(c)/W(c), lacrosse M(c)/W(c), racquetball M(c)/W(c), rugby M(c)/W(c), soccer M/W, softball W(c), squash M(c)/W(c), swimming and diving M/W, tennis M/W, track and field M/W, ultimate Frisbee M(c)/W(c), volleyball M(c)/W, water polo M(c)/W(c). *Intramural sports:* badminton M/W, basketball M/W, bowling M/W, cross-country running M/W, fencing M/W, football M/W, golf M/W, racquetball M/W, soccer M/W, softball M/W, squash M/W, swimming and diving M/W, table tennis M/W, tennis M/W, track and field M/W, ultimate Frisbee M/W, volleyball M/W, water polo M/W.
Standardized Tests *Required:* SAT or ACT (for admission), SAT Subject Tests (for admission).
Costs (2013–14) *Comprehensive fee:* $59,632 includes full-time tuition ($46,670), mandatory fees ($972), and room and board ($11,990). Full-time tuition and fees vary according to student level. Part-time tuition and fees vary according to student level. *College room only:* $7070. Room and board charges vary according to board plan and housing facility.
Financial Aid Of all full-time matriculated undergraduates who enrolled in 2012, 3,413 applied for aid, 2,882 were judged to have need, 825 had their need fully met. In 2012, 428 non-need-based awards were made. *Average per-*

cent of need met: 83%. *Average financial aid package:* $32,077. *Average need-based loan:* $5721. *Average need-based gift aid:* $26,305. *Average non-need-based aid:* $9040. *Average indebtedness upon graduation:* $31,747.

Applying *Options:* electronic application, early admission, early decision, deferred entrance. *Application fee:* $70. *Required:* essay or personal statement, high school transcript, 2 letters of recommendation. *Required for some:* audition/portfolio required for certain majors/BFA. *Recommended:* interview. *Application deadlines:* 1/1 (freshmen), 3/1 (transfers). *Early decision deadline:* 11/1 (for plan 1), 12/1 (for plan 2). *Notification:* 4/15 (freshmen), 6/30 (transfers), 12/15 (early decision plan 1), 1/15 (early decision plan 2).

Freshman Application Contact Mr. Michael Steidel, Director of Admissions, Carnegie Mellon University, 5000 Forbes Avenue, Pittsburgh, PA 15213. *Phone:* 412-268-2082. *Fax:* 412-268-7838. *E-mail:* undergraduate-admissions@andrew.cmu.edu. *Website:* http://www.cmu.edu/.

Cedar Crest College

Allentown, Pennsylvania

- **Independent** comprehensive, founded 1867, affiliated with United Church of Christ
- **Suburban** 84-acre campus with easy access to Philadelphia
- **Endowment** $18.9 million
- **Coed, primarily women** 1,359 undergraduate students, 52% full-time, 94% women, 6% men
- **Moderately difficult** entrance level, 61% of applicants were admitted

Undergraduates 700 full-time, 659 part-time. 14% are from out of state; 5% transferred in; 30% live on campus. *Retention:* 70% of full-time freshmen returned.

Freshmen *Admission:* 1,155 applied, 707 admitted, 145 enrolled. *Average high school GPA:* 3.29. *Test scores:* SAT critical reading scores over 500: 49%; SAT math scores over 500: 52%; SAT writing scores over 500: 43%; ACT scores over 18: 82%; SAT critical reading scores over 600: 13%; SAT math scores over 600: 8%; SAT writing scores over 600: 9%; ACT scores over 24: 23%; SAT critical reading scores over 700: 2%; ACT scores over 30: 9%.

Faculty *Total:* 156, 47% full-time, 49% with terminal degrees. *Student/faculty ratio:* 10:1.

Academics *Calendar:* semesters. *Degrees:* certificates, bachelor's, master's, and postbachelor's certificates. *Special study options:* academic remediation for entering students, advanced placement credit, double majors, honors programs, independent study, internships, off-campus study, part-time degree program, services for LD students, student-designed majors, summer session for credit. *ROTC:* Army (c).

Computers on Campus 285 computers/terminals and 587 ports are available on campus for general student use. Students can access the following: campus intranet, computer help desk, free student e-mail accounts, online (class) grades, online (class) registration, online (class) schedules. Campuswide network is available. 100% of college-owned or -operated housing units are wired for high-speed Internet access. Wireless service is available via entire campus.

Student Life *Housing options:* women-only, disabled students. Campus housing is university owned. Freshman campus housing is guaranteed. *Activities and organizations:* drama/theater group, student-run newspaper, radio station, choral group, Alpha Phi Omega, Forensic Science Student Organization, Crestiad Student Newspaper, Student Activities Board, Student Government Association. *Campus security:* 24-hour emergency response devices and patrols, late-night transport/escort service, controlled dormitory access, crime prevention programs. *Student services:* health clinic, personal/psychological counseling.

Athletics Member NCAA. All Division III. *Intercollegiate sports:* basketball W, cross-country running W, equestrian sports W(c), field hockey W, lacrosse W, soccer W, softball W, tennis W, track and field W(c), volleyball W. *Intramural sports:* badminton W, basketball W, soccer W, softball W, tennis W, volleyball W.

Standardized Tests *Required:* SAT or ACT (for admission).

Costs (2012–13) *Comprehensive fee:* $41,186 includes full-time tuition ($31,196) and room and board ($9990). Full-time tuition and fees vary according to class time, course load, and program. Part-time tuition and fees vary according to class time, course load, and program. *College room only:* $5160. Room and board charges vary according to board plan and housing facility. *Payment plans:* installment, deferred payment. *Waivers:* children of alumni and employees or children of employees.

Financial Aid Of all full-time matriculated undergraduates who enrolled in 2012, 531 applied for aid, 510 were judged to have need, 44 had their need fully met. In 2012, 32 non-need-based awards were made. *Average percent of need met:* 74%. *Average financial aid package:* $24,153. *Average need-based loan:* $4476. *Average need-based gift aid:* $19,819. *Average non-need-based aid:* $10,893. *Average indebtedness upon graduation:* $31,933.

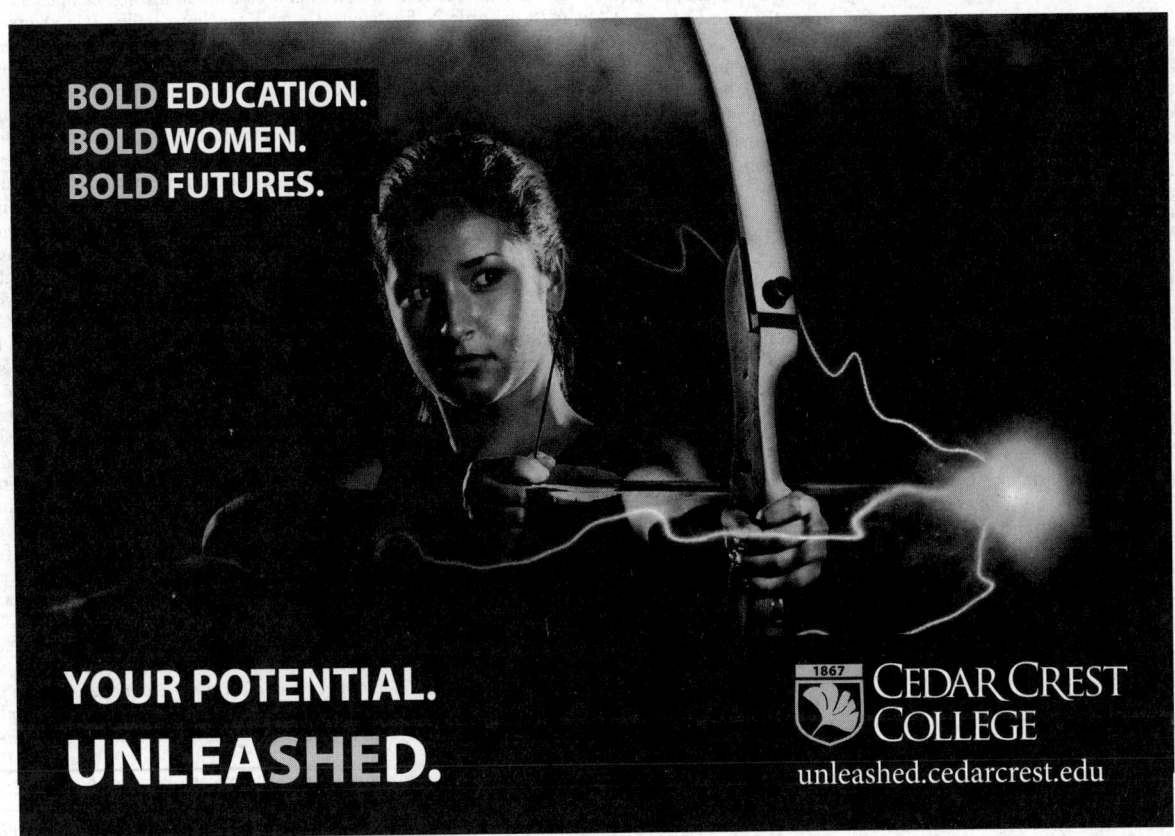

Applying *Options:* electronic application, early admission, deferred entrance. *Required:* essay or personal statement, high school transcript. *Required for some:* 2 letters of recommendation. *Recommended:* minimum 2.0 GPA, interview. *Application deadlines:* rolling (freshmen), rolling (transfers). *Notification:* continuous (freshmen), continuous (transfers).
Freshman Application Contact Andrea Stewart, Associate Director of Admissions, Cedar Crest College, 100 College Drive, Allentown, PA 18104. *Phone:* 610-606-4666. *Toll-free phone:* 800-360-1222. *E-mail:* astewart@cedarcrest.edu.
Website: http://www.cedarcrest.edu/.

See previous page for display ad and page 1232 for the College Close-Up.

Central Penn College

Summerdale, Pennsylvania

- **Proprietary** 4-year, founded 1881
- **Small-town** 35-acre campus with easy access to Harrisburg
- **Coed** 1,342 undergraduate students, 47% full-time, 65% women, 35% men
- **Minimally difficult** entrance level, 35% of applicants were admitted

Undergraduates 636 full-time, 706 part-time. Students come from 19 states and territories; 1 other country; 5% are from out of state; 19% Black or African American, non-Hispanic/Latino; 3% Hispanic/Latino; 1% Asian, non-Hispanic/Latino; 0.1% American Indian or Alaska Native, non-Hispanic/Latino; 14% Race/ethnicity unknown; 18% live on campus. *Retention:* 55% of full-time freshmen returned.
Freshmen *Admission:* 1,182 applied, 412 admitted, 121 enrolled.
Faculty *Total:* 133, 20% full-time, 31% with terminal degrees. *Student/faculty ratio:* 14:1.
Academics *Calendar:* quarters. *Degrees:* associate and bachelor's. *Special study options:* academic remediation for entering students, adult/continuing education programs, advanced placement credit, distance learning, double majors, honors programs, independent study, internships, part-time degree program, study abroad, summer session for credit.
Computers on Campus 100 computers/terminals are available on campus for general student use. Students can access the following: campus intranet, computer help desk, free student e-mail accounts, online (class) grades, online (class) registration, online (class) schedules. Campuswide network is available. 100% of college-owned or -operated housing units are wired for high-speed Internet access. Wireless service is available via entire campus.
Student Life *Housing options:* men-only, women-only. Campus housing is university owned. Freshman applicants given priority for college housing. *Activities and organizations:* student-run newspaper, choral group, International Travel Club, Student Government Association, Toastmasters, Student Ambassadors. *Campus security:* 24-hour emergency response devices and patrols, late-night transport/escort service. *Student services:* personal/psychological counseling.
Athletics Member USCAA. *Intercollegiate sports:* baseball M, basketball M/W, cross-country running M/W, volleyball W. *Intramural sports:* basketball M/W, football M/W, tennis M/W, volleyball M/W.
Standardized Tests *Recommended:* SAT or ACT (for admission).
Costs (2013–14) *Comprehensive fee:* $23,127 includes full-time tuition ($15,372), mandatory fees ($795), and room and board ($6960). Full-time tuition and fees vary according to course load and program. Part-time tuition: $427 per credit hour. Part-time tuition and fees vary according to course load and program. *Required fees:* $265 per term part-time. *College room only:* $5220. Room and board charges vary according to board plan and housing facility. *Payment plans:* installment, deferred payment. *Waivers:* employees or children of employees.
Financial Aid Of all full-time matriculated undergraduates who enrolled in 2006, 50 Federal Work-Study jobs (averaging $1500). *Financial aid deadline:* 5/1.
Applying *Options:* electronic application. *Required:* essay or personal statement, high school transcript, minimum 2.0 GPA, interview. *Required for some:* some majors have special requirements. *Application deadlines:* rolling (freshmen), rolling (out-of-state freshmen), rolling (transfers). *Notification:* continuous (freshmen), continuous (out-of-state freshmen), continuous (transfers).
Freshman Application Contact Ms. Rebecca Cummins, Director of Traditional Admissions, Central Penn College, College Hill and Valley Roads, Mechanicsburg, PA 17093. *Phone:* 717-728-2267. *Toll-free phone:* 800-759-2727. *Fax:* 717-728-2505. *E-mail:* rebeccacummins@centralpenn.edu.
Website: http://www.centralpenn.edu/.

Chatham University

Pittsburgh, Pennsylvania

- **Independent** university, founded 1869
- **Urban** 427-acre campus
- **Endowment** $58.9 million
- **Undergraduate: women only; graduate: coed** 922 undergraduate students, 68% full-time, 94% women, 6% men
- **Moderately difficult** entrance level, 60% of applicants were admitted

Undergraduates 629 full-time, 293 part-time. Students come from 31 states and territories; 29 other countries; 19% are from out of state; 10% Black or African American, non-Hispanic/Latino; 2% Hispanic/Latino; 2% Asian, non-Hispanic/Latino; 2% Two or more races, non-Hispanic/Latino; 16% Race/ethnicity unknown; 9% international; 21% transferred in; 53% live on campus. *Retention:* 76% of full-time freshmen returned.
Freshmen *Admission:* 727 applied, 433 admitted, 117 enrolled. *Average high school GPA:* 3.59. *Test scores:* SAT critical reading scores over 500: 82%; SAT math scores over 500: 61%; SAT writing scores over 500: 70%; ACT scores over 18: 96%; SAT critical reading scores over 600: 24%; SAT math scores over 600: 19%; SAT writing scores over 600: 19%; ACT scores over 24: 68%; SAT critical reading scores over 700: 6%; SAT math scores over 700: 1%; SAT writing scores over 700: 4%; ACT scores over 30: 7%.
Faculty *Total:* 323, 31% full-time, 50% with terminal degrees. *Student/faculty ratio:* 10:1.
Academics *Calendar:* 4-4-1. *Degrees:* bachelor's, master's, doctoral, postmaster's, and postbachelor's certificates. *Special study options:* accelerated degree program, adult/continuing education programs, advanced placement credit, cooperative education, distance learning, double majors, English as a second language, honors programs, independent study, internships, off-campus study, part-time degree program, services for LD students, student-designed majors, study abroad, summer session for credit. *ROTC:* Army (c), Navy (c), Air Force (c). *Unusual degree programs:* 3-2 business administration; engineering with Carnegie Mellon University, Pennsylvania State University, University of Pittsburgh; arts management with Carnegie Mellon, biology, counseling psychology, film/digital technology, leadership/organizational transformation, occupational therapy, physician assistant studies, business, teaching, writing and creative writing, architecture (landscape and interior), global/public policy.
Computers on Campus 250 computers/terminals are available on campus for general student use. Students can access the following: campus intranet, computer help desk, free student e-mail accounts, online (class) grades, online (class) registration, online (class) schedules. Campuswide network is available. Wireless service is available via classrooms, computer centers, computer labs, learning centers, libraries.
Student Life *Housing:* on-campus residence required through sophomore year. *Options:* women-only. Campus housing is university owned. Freshman campus housing is guaranteed. *Activities and organizations:* drama/theater group, student-run newspaper, choral group, Chatham Student Government, Residence Hall Council, Chatham University Dance Team, Creative Writing Club & MFA Writing Council, Graduate Student Assembly. *Campus security:* 24-hour emergency response devices and patrols, late-night transport/escort service, controlled dormitory access, self-defense education, well-lighted pathways and sidewalks. *Student services:* health clinic, personal/psychological counseling.
Athletics Member NCAA. All Division III. *Intercollegiate sports:* basketball W, cross-country running W, ice hockey W, soccer W, softball W, swimming and diving W, tennis W, track and field W, volleyball W, water polo W. *Intramural sports:* badminton W, basketball W, bowling W, cross-country running W, football W, golf W, rock climbing W, skiing (downhill) W, soccer W, softball W, squash W, swimming and diving W, volleyball W, water polo W.
Standardized Tests *Recommended:* Consider SAT or ACT if submitted.
Costs (2013–14) *Comprehensive fee:* $42,440 includes full-time tuition ($31,294), mandatory fees ($1160), and room and board ($9986). Part-time tuition: $759 per credit. Part-time tuition and fees vary according to course load. *College room only:* $5061. Room and board charges vary according to board plan and housing facility. *Payment plan:* installment. *Waivers:* employees or children of employees.
Financial Aid Of all full-time matriculated undergraduates who enrolled in 2009, 552 applied for aid, 517 were judged to have need, 80 had their need fully met. In 2009, 25 non-need-based awards were made. *Average percent of need met:* 66%. *Average financial aid package:* $15,515. *Average need-based loan:* $9265. *Average need-based gift aid:* $8645. *Average non-need-based aid:* $13,107.
Applying *Options:* electronic application, early admission, deferred entrance. *Application fee:* $35. *Required:* essay or personal statement, high school transcript, minimum 2.0 GPA, 1 letter of recommendation. *Recommended:* inter-

view. *Application deadlines:* 8/1 (freshmen), rolling (transfers). *Notification:* continuous (freshmen), continuous (transfers).

Freshman Application Contact Ms. Marylyn Scott, Director of Admissions, Chatham University, Woodland Road, Pittsburgh, PA 15232. *Phone:* 412-365-1295. *Toll-free phone:* 800-837-1290. *Fax:* 412-365-1609. *E-mail:* MSCOTT2@chatham.edu.
Website: http://www.chatham.edu/.

Chestnut Hill College

Philadelphia, Pennsylvania

- **Independent Roman Catholic** comprehensive, founded 1924
- **Suburban** 75-acre campus with easy access to Philadelphia
- **Coed** 1,581 undergraduate students, 79% full-time, 70% women, 30% men
- **Moderately difficult** entrance level, 66% of applicants were admitted

Undergraduates 1,249 full-time, 332 part-time. Students come from 24 states and territories; 41 other countries; 23% are from out of state; 36% Black or African American, non-Hispanic/Latino; 7% Hispanic/Latino; 1% Asian, non-Hispanic/Latino; 0.6% Native Hawaiian or other Pacific Islander, non-Hispanic/Latino; 0.1% American Indian or Alaska Native, non-Hispanic/Latino; 2% Two or more races, non-Hispanic/Latino; 7% Race/ethnicity unknown; 2% international; 5% transferred in; 32% live on campus. *Retention:* 74% of full-time freshmen returned.

Freshmen *Admission:* 2,173 applied, 1,439 admitted, 211 enrolled. *Average high school GPA:* 3.24. *Test scores:* SAT critical reading scores over 500: 49%; SAT math scores over 500: 43%; SAT writing scores over 500: 44%; ACT scores over 18: 89%; SAT critical reading scores over 600: 11%; SAT math scores over 600: 12%; SAT writing scores over 600: 9%; ACT scores over 24: 23%; SAT critical reading scores over 700: 1%; SAT math scores over 700: 1%; SAT writing scores over 700: 2%; ACT scores over 30: 3%.

Faculty *Total:* 354, 25% full-time, 38% with terminal degrees. *Student/faculty ratio:* 9:1.

Academics *Calendar:* semesters. *Degrees:* certificates, associate, bachelor's, master's, doctoral, post-master's, and postbachelor's certificates (profile includes figures from both traditional and accelerated (part-time) programs). *Special study options:* academic remediation for entering students, adult/continuing education programs, advanced placement credit, double majors, English as a second language, honors programs, independent study, internships, off-campus study, part-time degree program, services for LD students, student-designed majors, study abroad, summer session for credit. *Unusual degree programs:* 3-2 Computer Science/Instructional Technology; Early Education; Biology/Chemistry and various medical areas of study (Thomas Jefferson University), Biology/Chemistry and Physician Asst (Arcadia University). Human Services Admin; Counseling Psychology; International Business, Language, and Culture.

Computers on Campus 70 computers/terminals and 150 ports are available on campus for general student use. Students can access the following: campus intranet, computer help desk, free student e-mail accounts, online (class) grades, online (class) registration, online (class) schedules. Campuswide network is available. 90% of college-owned or -operated housing units are wired for high-speed Internet access. Wireless service is available via classrooms, dorm rooms.

Student Life *Housing options:* coed. Campus housing is university owned and leased by the school. Freshman campus housing is guaranteed. *Activities and organizations:* drama/theater group, student-run newspaper, radio and television station, choral group, Student Government, Mask and Foil Drama Club, African American Awareness Society, Campus Ministry Community Service Group, Business Club. *Campus security:* 24-hour emergency response devices and patrols, late-night transport/escort service, controlled dormitory access. *Student services:* health clinic, personal/psychological counseling.

Athletics Member NCAA. All Division II. *Intercollegiate sports:* baseball M(s), basketball M(s)/W(s), cross-country running M(s)/W(s), golf M(s), lacrosse M(s)/W(s), soccer M(s)/W(s), softball W(s), tennis M(s)/W(s), volleyball W(s).

Standardized Tests *Required:* SAT or ACT (for admission).

Costs (2013–14) *Comprehensive fee:* $41,045 includes full-time tuition ($31,000), mandatory fees ($170), and room and board ($9875). Part-time tuition: $665 per credit hour. *Room and board:* Room and board charges vary according to housing facility. *Payment plans:* installment, deferred payment. *Waivers:* senior citizens and employees or children of employees.

Financial Aid Of all full-time matriculated undergraduates who enrolled in 2012, 1,089 applied for aid, 1,018 were judged to have need, 114 had their need fully met. 334 Federal Work-Study jobs (averaging $1000). 92 state and other part-time jobs (averaging $1000). In 2012, 66 non-need-based awards were made. *Average percent of need met:* 68%. *Average financial aid package:*

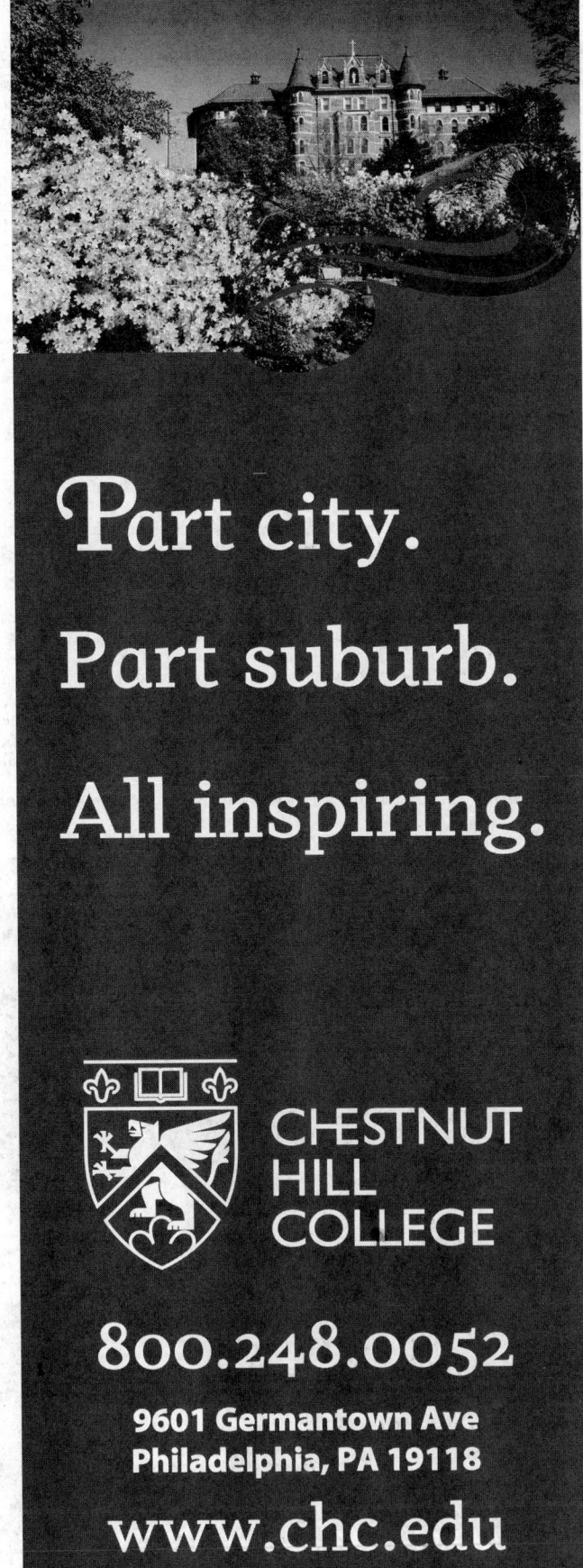

$21,349. *Average need-based loan:* $4398. *Average need-based gift aid:* $14,291. *Average non-need-based aid:* $12,546. *Average indebtedness upon graduation:* $10,688.

Applying *Options:* electronic application, deferred entrance. *Application fee:* $35. *Required:* high school transcript. *Required for some:* interview. *Recommended:* essay or personal statement, minimum 2.0 GPA. *Application deadlines:* rolling (freshmen), rolling (out-of-state freshmen), rolling (transfers). *Notification:* continuous (freshmen), continuous (out-of-state freshmen), continuous (transfers).

Freshman Application Contact Ms. Stephanie Williams, Chestnut Hill College, 9601 Germantown Avenue, Philadelphia, PA 19118-2693. *Phone:* 215-248-7001. *Toll-free phone:* 800-248-0052. *Fax:* 215-248-7082. *E-mail:* williamss@chc.edu.
Website: http://www.chc.edu/.

See previous page for display ad and page 1238 for the College Close-Up.

Cheyney University of Pennsylvania

Cheyney, Pennsylvania

- **State-supported** comprehensive, founded 1837, part of Pennsylvania State System of Higher Education
- **Suburban** 275-acre campus with easy access to Philadelphia
- **Coed** 1,224 undergraduate students, 95% full-time, 51% women, 49% men
- **Minimally difficult** entrance level, 87% of applicants were admitted

Undergraduates 1,160 full-time, 64 part-time. Students come from 15 states and territories; 21% are from out of state; 93% Black or African American, non-Hispanic/Latino; 3% Hispanic/Latino; 0.2% Two or more races, non-Hispanic/Latino; 3% Race/ethnicity unknown; 8% transferred in; 74% live on campus. *Retention:* 65% of full-time freshmen returned.

Freshmen *Admission:* 1,582 applied, 1,379 admitted, 317 enrolled. *Average high school GPA:* 2.5. *Test scores:* SAT critical reading scores over 500: 6%; SAT math scores over 500: 6%; SAT writing scores over 500: 4%; SAT critical reading scores over 600: 1%; SAT writing scores over 600: 1%.

Faculty *Total:* 107, 65% full-time, 57% with terminal degrees. *Student/faculty ratio:* 14:1.

Academics *Calendar:* semesters. *Degrees:* associate, bachelor's, master's, and postbachelor's certificates. *Special study options:* academic remediation for entering students, adult/continuing education programs, cooperative education, distance learning, double majors, honors programs, independent study, internships, off-campus study, part-time degree program, services for LD students, study abroad, summer session for credit. *ROTC:* Army (c).

Computers on Campus Students can access the following: free student e-mail accounts, online (class) grades, online (class) registration, online (class) schedules, online tutorials, various software packages, online payment/online Praxis study guide. Campuswide network is available. Wireless service is available via classrooms, computer centers, computer labs, learning centers, libraries, student centers.

Student Life *Housing options:* coed, men-only, women-only. Campus housing is university owned. Freshman applicants given priority for college housing. *Activities and organizations:* drama/theater group, student-run newspaper, radio and television station, choral group, marching band, NAACP, Student Government Association, Alpha Kappa Alpha, Kappa Alpha Psi, Alpha Phi Alpha, national fraternities, national sororities. *Campus security:* 24-hour emergency response devices and patrols. *Student services:* health clinic, personal/psychological counseling.

Athletics Member NCAA. All Division II. *Intercollegiate sports:* basketball M(s)/W(s), bowling W(s), cross-country running M(s)/W(s), football M(s), track and field M(s)/W(s), volleyball W(s). *Intramural sports:* basketball M/W, football M.

Standardized Tests *Required:* SAT (for admission), ACT (for admission), SAT and SAT Subject Tests or ACT (for admission).

Costs (2013–14) *One-time required fee:* $150. *Tuition:* state resident $6600 full-time, $275 per credit hour part-time; nonresident $10,872 full-time, $453 per credit hour part-time. Full-time tuition and fees vary according to course load. Part-time tuition and fees vary according to course load. *Required fees:* $2436 full-time, $15 per credit hour part-time, $454 per credit hour part-time. *Room and board:* $11,552; room only: $7552. Room and board charges vary according to board plan and housing facility. *Payment plan:* deferred payment. *Waivers:* senior citizens and employees or children of employees.

Financial Aid Of all full-time matriculated undergraduates who enrolled in 2003, 1,030 applied for aid, 1,005 were judged to have need, 451 had their need fully met. 215 Federal Work-Study jobs (averaging $1300). 133 state and other part-time jobs (averaging $600). *Average percent of need met:* 87%. *Average financial aid package:* $11,789. *Average need-based loan:* $3700. *Average need-based gift aid:* $1975. *Average non-need-based aid:* $10,000. *Average indebtedness upon graduation:* $21,000.

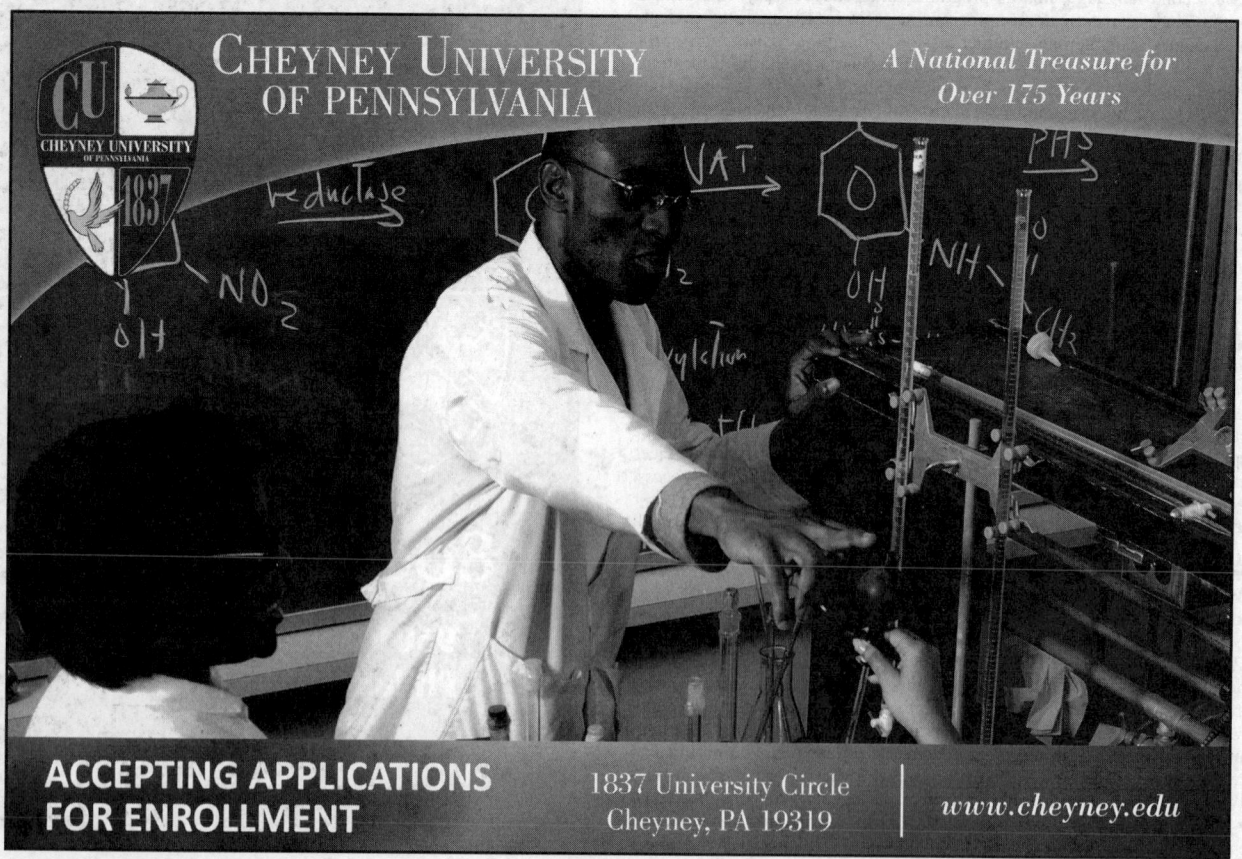

Applying *Options:* electronic application, deferred entrance. *Application fee:* $20. *Required:* essay or personal statement, high school transcript. *Required for some:* 3 letters of recommendation. *Recommended:* interview. *Application deadline:* 3/31 (freshmen). *Notification:* continuous (freshmen).

Freshman Application Contact Cheyney University of Pennsylvania, 1837 University Circle, PO Box 200, Cheyney, PA 19319. *Phone:* 610-399-2100. *Toll-free phone:* 800-CHEYNEY.
Website: http://www.cheyney.edu/.

See previous page for display ad and page 1240 for the College Close-Up.

Clarion University of Pennsylvania

Clarion, Pennsylvania

- **State-supported** comprehensive, founded 1867, part of Pennsylvania State System of Higher Education
- **Rural** 100-acre campus
- **Coed** 5,518 undergraduate students, 84% full-time, 63% women, 37% men
- **Minimally difficult** entrance level, 77% of applicants were admitted

Undergraduates 4,609 full-time, 909 part-time. 5% are from out of state; 6% Black or African American, non-Hispanic/Latino; 1% Hispanic/Latino; 0.4% Asian, non-Hispanic/Latino; 0.1% Native Hawaiian or other Pacific Islander, non-Hispanic/Latino; 0.1% American Indian or Alaska Native, non-Hispanic/Latino; 2% Two or more races, non-Hispanic/Latino; 3% Race/ethnicity unknown; 0.5% international; 6% transferred in; 25% live on campus. *Retention:* 70% of full-time freshmen returned.

Freshmen *Admission:* 3,408 applied, 2,614 admitted, 1,132 enrolled. *Average high school GPA:* 3.21. *Test scores:* SAT critical reading scores over 500: 64%; SAT math scores over 500: 62%; SAT writing scores over 500: 70%; ACT scores over 18: 72%; SAT critical reading scores over 600: 16%; SAT math scores over 600: 14%; SAT writing scores over 600: 20%; ACT scores over 24: 20%; SAT writing scores over 700: 1%.

Faculty *Total:* 387, 71% full-time, 52% with terminal degrees. *Student/faculty ratio:* 17:1.

Academics *Calendar:* semesters. *Degrees:* certificates, associate, bachelor's, master's, post-master's, and postbachelor's certificates. *Special study options:* academic remediation for entering students, accelerated degree program, adult/continuing education programs, advanced placement credit, cooperative education, distance learning, double majors, English as a second language, honors programs, independent study, internships, off-campus study, part-time degree program, services for LD students, study abroad, summer session for credit. *ROTC:* Army (c). *Unusual degree programs:* 3-2 engineering with University of Pittsburgh, Case Western Reserve University.

Computers on Campus 386 computers/terminals and 117 ports are available on campus for general student use. Students can access the following: campus intranet, computer help desk, free student e-mail accounts, online (class) grades, online (class) registration, online (class) schedules, Online Learning Management System, web-based personal disk space, other online student services (financial aid, billing etc.). Campuswide network is available. 100% of college-owned or -operated housing units are wired for high-speed Internet access. Wireless service is available via classrooms, computer centers, computer labs, learning centers, libraries, student centers.

Student Life *Housing:* on-campus residence required for freshman year. *Options:* coed, men-only, women-only, disabled students. Campus housing is university owned. Freshman campus housing is guaranteed. *Activities and organizations:* drama/theater group, student-run newspaper, radio and television station, choral group, marching band, Circle K, Psychology Club, Council for Exceptional Children, Animae Club, Allies, national fraternities, national sororities. *Campus security:* 24-hour emergency response devices and patrols, student patrols, controlled dormitory access. *Student services:* health clinic, personal/psychological counseling, women's center.

Athletics Member NCAA. All Division II except wrestling (Division I). *Intercollegiate sports:* baseball M(s), basketball M(s)/W(s), cross-country running W(s), football M(s), golf M(s), soccer W(s), softball W(s), swimming and diving M(s)/W(s), tennis W(s), track and field W(s), volleyball W(s), wrestling M(s). *Intramural sports:* badminton M/W, basketball M/W, bowling M/W, cheerleading M/W, cross-country running W, equestrian sports M(c)/W(c), football M/W, golf M/W, racquetball M/W, rock climbing M/W, rugby M/W, soccer M/W, softball M/W, swimming and diving M/W, table tennis M/W, tennis M/W, track and field M/W, ultimate Frisbee M/W, volleyball M(c)/W, weight lifting M/W, wrestling M.

Standardized Tests *Required:* SAT or ACT (for admission). *Required for some:* International TOEFL or TSE or IELTS students.

Costs (2012–13) *Tuition:* state resident $9141 full-time; nonresident $12,861 full-time. Full-time tuition and fees vary according to course level and course load. Part-time tuition and fees vary according to course level and course load. *Room and board:* $7186. Room and board charges vary according to board plan, housing facility, and location. *Payment plan:* installment. *Waivers:* senior citizens and employees or children of employees.

Financial Aid Of all full-time matriculated undergraduates who enrolled in 2011, 4,566 applied for aid, 4,023 were judged to have need, 216 had their need fully met. In 2011, 138 non-need-based awards were made. *Average percent of need met:* 55%. *Average financial aid package:* $8044. *Average need-based loan:* $3994. *Average need-based gift aid:* $5459. *Average non-need-based aid:* $1936. *Average indebtedness upon graduation:* $29,410.

Applying *Options:* deferred entrance. *Application fee:* $30. *Required:* high school transcript. *Required for some:* essay or personal statement, interview, NLN Test for ASN Program. *Recommended:* essay or personal statement, 2 letters of recommendation, interview. *Application deadlines:* rolling (freshmen), rolling (out-of-state freshmen), rolling (transfers). *Notification:* continuous (freshmen), continuous (out-of-state freshmen), continuous (transfers).

Freshman Application Contact Clarion University of Pennsylvania, 890 Wood Street, Clarion, PA 16214. *Phone:* 814-393-2306. *Toll-free phone:* 800-672-7171.
Website: http://www.clarion.edu/.

Curtis Institute of Music

Philadelphia, Pennsylvania

Director of Admissions Mr. Christopher Hodges, Admissions Officer, Curtis Institute of Music, 1726 Locust Street, Philadelphia, PA 19103-6107. *Phone:* 215-893-5262. *E-mail:* chris.hodges@curtis.edu.
Website: http://www.curtis.edu/.

Delaware Valley College

Doylestown, Pennsylvania

- **Independent** comprehensive, founded 1896
- **Suburban** 600-acre campus with easy access to Philadelphia
- **Endowment** $33.1 million
- **Coed**
- **Moderately difficult** entrance level

Faculty *Student/faculty ratio:* 15:1.

Academics *Calendar:* semesters. *Degrees:* certificates, associate, bachelor's, and master's.

Student Life *Campus security:* 24-hour patrols, late-night transport/escort service, controlled dormitory access.

Athletics Member NCAA. All Division III.

Standardized Tests *Required:* SAT or ACT (for admission).

Costs (2012–13) *Comprehensive fee:* $43,008 includes full-time tuition ($29,696), mandatory fees ($2050), and room and board ($11,262). Part-time tuition: $818 per credit. *College room only:* $5106.

Financial Aid *Of all full-time matriculated undergraduates who enrolled in 2011, 1,474 applied for aid, 1,375 were judged to have need, 221 had their need fully met. In 2011, 281 non-need-based awards were made. Average percent of need met: 67. Average financial aid package: $22,135. Average need-based loan: $4498. Average need-based gift aid: $14,498. Average non-need-based aid: $10,806. Average indebtedness upon graduation: $34,998. Financial aid deadline: 4/1.*

Applying *Options:* electronic application, deferred entrance. *Application fee:* $50. *Required:* high school transcript, 1 letter of recommendation. *Required for some:* minimum 3.0 GPA. *Recommended:* minimum 2.8 GPA, interview.

Freshman Application Contact Mr. Dwayne Walker, Director of Admissions, Delaware Valley College, 700 East Butler Avenue, Doylestown, PA 18901-2697. *Phone:* 215-489-2372. *Toll-free phone:* 800-2DELVAL. *Fax:* 215-230-2968. *E-mail:* admitme@devalcol.edu.
Website: http://www.delval.edu/.

See next page for display ad and page 1266 for the College Close-Up.

DeSales University

Center Valley, Pennsylvania

- **Independent Roman Catholic** comprehensive, founded 1964
- **Suburban** 480-acre campus
- **Endowment** $48.1 million
- **Coed** 2,468 undergraduate students, 72% full-time, 61% women, 39% men
- **Moderately difficult** entrance level, 72% of applicants were admitted

Undergraduates 1,782 full-time, 686 part-time. Students come from 31 states and territories; 5 other countries; 64% are from out of state; 4% Black or African American, non-Hispanic/Latino; 8% Hispanic/Latino; 2% Asian, non-Hispanic/Latino; 0.1% Native Hawaiian or other Pacific Islander, non-Hispanic/Latino; 0.6% American Indian or Alaska Native, non-Hispanic/Latino; 11% Race/ethnicity unknown; 4% transferred in; 67% live on campus. *Retention:* 83% of full-time freshmen returned.

Freshmen *Admission:* 2,353 applied, 1,684 admitted, 389 enrolled. *Average high school GPA:* 3.2. *Test scores:* SAT critical reading scores over 500: 70%; SAT math scores over 500: 69%; ACT scores over 18: 92%; SAT critical reading scores over 600: 23%; SAT math scores over 600: 26%; ACT scores over 24: 47%; SAT critical reading scores over 700: 3%; SAT math scores over 700: 3%; ACT scores over 30: 9%.

Faculty *Total:* 308, 34% full-time, 44% with terminal degrees. *Student/faculty ratio:* 14:1.

Academics *Calendar:* semesters. *Degrees:* certificates, bachelor's, master's, doctoral, post-master's, and postbachelor's certificates. *Special study options:* academic remediation for entering students, accelerated degree program, advanced placement credit, cooperative education, distance learning, double majors, external degree program, honors programs, independent study, internships, off-campus study, part-time degree program, services for LD students, student-designed majors, study abroad, summer session for credit. *ROTC:* Army (c). *Unusual degree programs:* 3-2 Physician Assistant Studies, MACJ, MBA/Accounting.

Computers on Campus 200 computers/terminals and 200 ports are available on campus for general student use. Students can access the following: computer help desk, free student e-mail accounts, online (class) grades, online (class) registration, online (class) schedules. Campuswide network is available. 100% of college-owned or -operated housing units are wired for high-speed Internet access. Wireless service is available via classrooms, computer centers, computer labs, learning centers, libraries, student centers.

Student Life *Housing:* on-campus residence required for freshman year. *Options:* men-only, women-only, disabled students. Campus housing is university owned. Freshman campus housing is guaranteed. *Activities and organizations:* drama/theater group, student-run newspaper, radio and television station, choral group, marching band, DSU Equestrian Team, PA Student Society, Colleges Against Cancer, Colleges Against Cancer, CEO (Creative Exploration Organization), SHARE. *Campus security:* 24-hour emergency response devices and patrols, late-night transport/escort service, controlled dormitory access. *Student services:* personal/psychological counseling.

Athletics Member NCAA. All Division III. *Intercollegiate sports:* baseball M, basketball M, cross-country running M, field hockey W, golf M, lacrosse M, soccer M/W, softball W, track and field M/W, volleyball W. *Intramural sports:* basketball M/W, cheerleading W(c), fencing M(c), ice hockey M(c), lacrosse M/W(c), rugby M(c), soccer M/W, softball M/W, swimming and diving M(c)/W(c), tennis M(c), ultimate Frisbee M/W, volleyball M(c)/W.

Standardized Tests *Required:* SAT or ACT (for admission).

Costs (2012–13) *Comprehensive fee:* $41,120 includes full-time tuition ($29,000), mandatory fees ($1150), and room and board ($10,970). Full-time tuition and fees vary according to course load, degree level, and program. Part-time tuition: $1210 per credit hour. Part-time tuition and fees vary according to course load, degree level, and program. *Room and board:* Room and board charges vary according to board plan and housing facility. *Payment plans:* installment, deferred payment. *Waivers:* adult students, senior citizens, and employees or children of employees.

Financial Aid Of all full-time matriculated undergraduates who enrolled in 2012, 1,585 applied for aid, 1,445 were judged to have need, 262 had their need fully met. 530 Federal Work-Study jobs (averaging $1942). 275 state and other part-time jobs (averaging $1995). In 2012, 273 non-need-based awards were made. *Average percent of need met:* 69%. *Average financial aid package:* $19,577. *Average need-based loan:* $4492. *Average need-based gift aid:* $16,572. *Average non-need-based aid:* $10,653. *Average indebtedness upon graduation:* $28,875. *Financial aid deadline:* 5/1.

Applying *Options:* electronic application. *Required:* essay or personal statement, high school transcript, . *Recommended:* interview. *Application deadline:* 8/1 (freshmen).

Freshman Application Contact Mr. Derrick Wetzel, Director of Admissions, DeSales University, 2755 Station Avenue, Center Valley, PA 18034-9568.

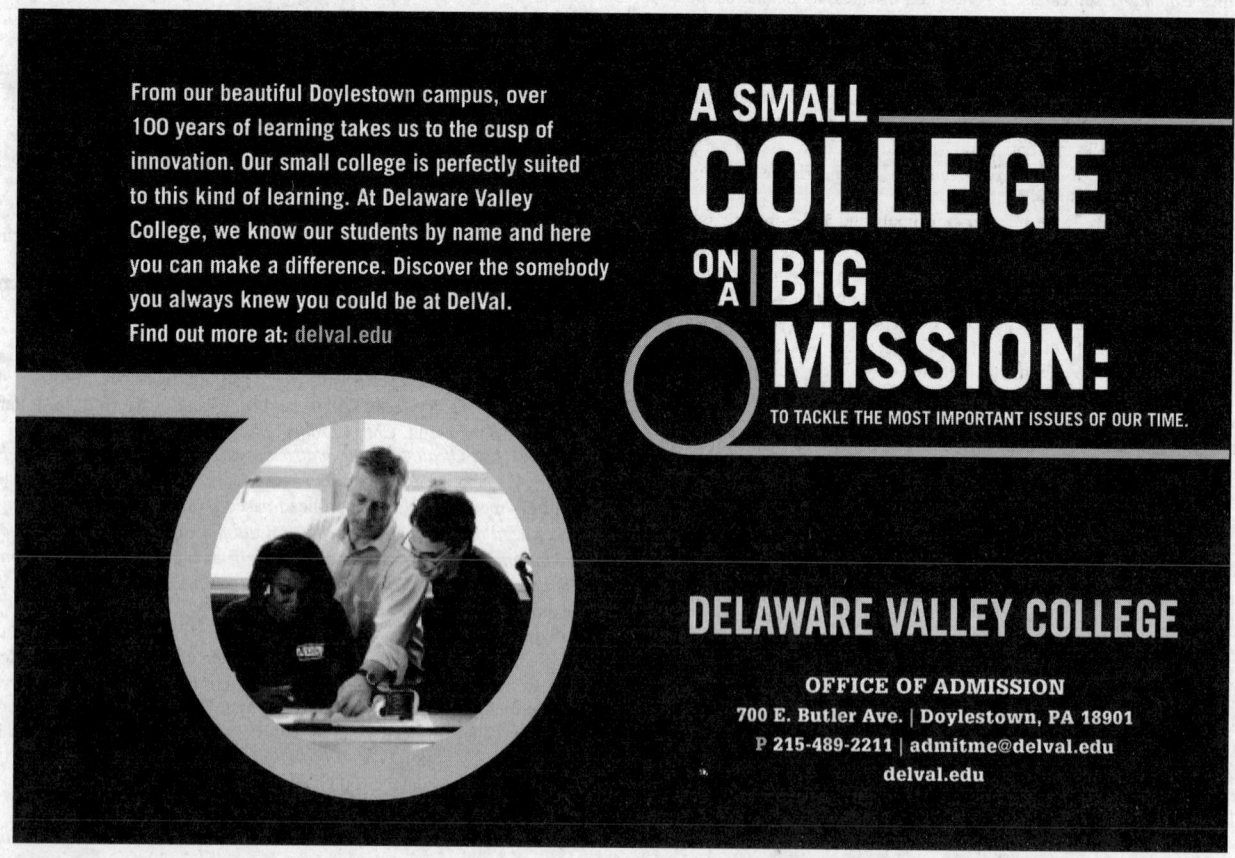

Phone: 610-282-4443. *Fax:* 610-282-0131. *E-mail:* derrick.wetzell@desales.edu.
Website: http://www.desales.edu/.

> See below for display ad and page 1268 for the College Close-Up.

DeVry University
Fort Washington, Pennsylvania

- **Proprietary** comprehensive, founded 2002, part of DeVry University
- **Coed** 660 undergraduate students, 39% full-time, 35% women, 65% men
- **Minimally difficult** entrance level

Undergraduates 257 full-time, 403 part-time. 17% are from out of state; 26% Black or African American, non-Hispanic/Latino; 9% Hispanic/Latino; 4% Asian, non-Hispanic/Latino; 0.8% American Indian or Alaska Native, non-Hispanic/Latino; 0.6% Two or more races, non-Hispanic/Latino; 19% Race/ethnicity unknown; 0.9% international; 14% transferred in.
Freshmen *Admission:* 68 enrolled.
Faculty *Total:* 150, 13% full-time. *Student/faculty ratio:* 7:1.
Academics *Calendar:* semesters. *Degrees:* associate, bachelor's, master's, and postbachelor's certificates. *Special study options:* adult/continuing education programs, part-time degree program.
Student Life *Housing:* college housing not available.
Costs (2013–14) *Tuition:* $16,076 full-time, $609 per credit hour part-time. *Required fees:* $80 full-time.
Financial Aid Of all full-time matriculated undergraduates who enrolled in 2007, 254 applied for aid, 244 were judged to have need, 2 had their need fully met. In 2007, 23 non-need-based awards were made. *Average percent of need met:* 34%. *Average financial aid package:* $12,114. *Average need-based loan:* $6836. *Average need-based gift aid:* $6835. *Average non-need-based aid:* $13,057. *Average indebtedness upon graduation:* $15,638.
Applying *Application fee:* $40. *Required:* high school transcript, interview. *Application deadlines:* rolling (freshmen), rolling (transfers). *Notification:* continuous (freshmen), continuous (transfers).

Freshman Application Contact DeVry University, 1140 Virginia Drive, Fort Washington, PA 19034. *Phone:* 215-591-5700. *Toll-free phone:* 866-338-7941. *Website:* http://www.devry.edu/.

DeVry University
King of Prussia, Pennsylvania

Admissions Office Contact DeVry University, 150 Allendale Road, Buillding 3, Suite 3201, King of Prussia, PA 19406-2926. *Toll-free phone:* 866-338-7941.
Website: http://www.devry.edu/.

DeVry University
Philadelphia, Pennsylvania

Admissions Office Contact DeVry University, Philadelphia Downtown Center, 1800 JFK Boulevard, Suite 104, Philadelphia, PA 19103-7421. *Toll-free phone:* 866-338-7941.
Website: http://www.devry.edu/.

DeVry University
Pittsburgh, Pennsylvania

Admissions Office Contact DeVry University, FreeMarkets Center, 210 Sixth Avenue, Suite 200, Pittsburgh, PA 15222-2606. *Toll-free phone:* 866-338-7941.
Website: http://www.devry.edu/.

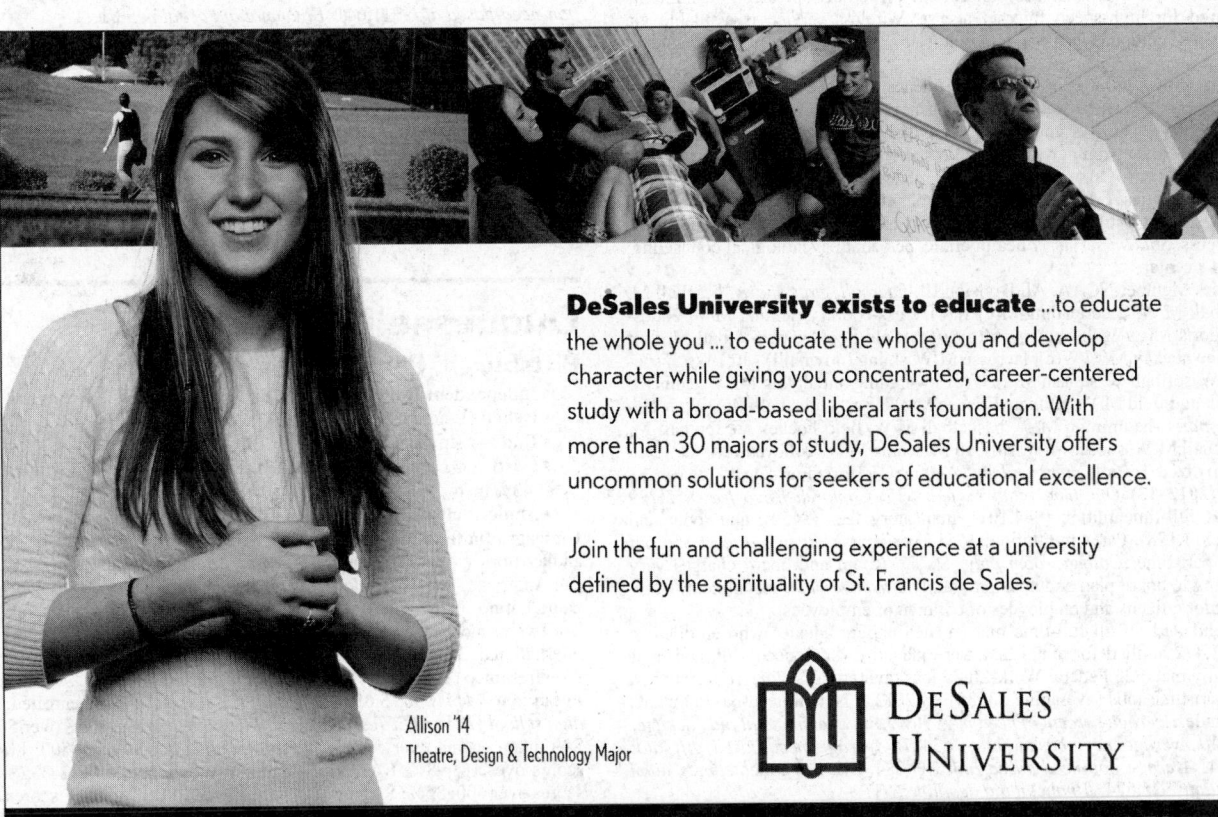

Dickinson College

Carlisle, Pennsylvania

- **Independent** 4-year, founded 1773
- **Suburban** 180-acre campus with easy access to Harrisburg
- **Endowment** $325.7 million
- **Coed** 2,386 undergraduate students, 98% full-time, 55% women, 45% men
- **Very difficult** entrance level, 40% of applicants were admitted

Undergraduates 2,341 full-time, 45 part-time. Students come from 43 states and territories; 48 other countries; 77% are from out of state; 3% Black or African American, non-Hispanic/Latino; 6% Hispanic/Latino; 2% Asian, non-Hispanic/Latino; 2% Two or more races, non-Hispanic/Latino; 1% Race/ethnicity unknown; 7% international; 0.8% transferred in; 95% live on campus. *Retention:* 91% of full-time freshmen returned.

Freshmen *Admission:* 5,818 applied, 2,340 admitted, 602 enrolled. *Test scores:* SAT critical reading scores over 500: 99%; SAT math scores over 500: 99%; SAT writing scores over 500: 98%; ACT scores over 18: 100%; SAT critical reading scores over 600: 71%; SAT math scores over 600: 80%; SAT writing scores over 600: 74%; ACT scores over 24: 98%; SAT critical reading scores over 700: 21%; SAT math scores over 700: 24%; SAT writing scores over 700: 22%; ACT scores over 30: 38%.

Faculty *Total:* 253, 83% full-time, 84% with terminal degrees. *Student/faculty ratio:* 10:1.

Academics *Calendar:* semesters. *Degree:* bachelor's. *Special study options:* accelerated degree program, adult/continuing education programs, advanced placement credit, double majors, English as a second language, independent study, internships, off-campus study, part-time degree program, services for LD students, student-designed majors, study abroad, summer session for credit. *ROTC:* Army (b). *Unusual degree programs:* 3-2 engineering with Case Western Reserve University; Rensselaer Polytechnic Institute, Columbia University's Fu Foundation School of Engineering and Applied Science; nursing with Johns Hopkins University School of Nursing; pre-law with the Dickinson School of Law of the Pennsylvania State University 3/3.

Computers on Campus 1,081 computers/terminals and 5,000 ports are available on campus for general student use. Students can access the following: campus intranet, computer help desk, free student e-mail accounts, online (class) grades, online (class) registration, online (class) schedules. Campus-wide network is available. 100% of college-owned or -operated housing units are wired for high-speed Internet access. Wireless service is available via classrooms, computer centers, computer labs, dorm rooms, libraries, student centers.

Student Life *Housing:* on-campus residence required through senior year. *Options:* coed, disabled students. Campus housing is university owned. Freshman campus housing is guaranteed. *Activities and organizations:* drama/theater group, student-run newspaper, radio station, choral group, Student Senate, CommServ, Multi-Organization Board, Hillel, Spectrum, national fraternities, national sororities. *Campus security:* 24-hour emergency response devices and patrols, student patrols, late-night transport/escort service, controlled dormitory access. *Student services:* health clinic, personal/psychological counseling, women's center.

Athletics Member NCAA. All Division III. *Intercollegiate sports:* baseball M, basketball M/W, cheerleading M(c)/W(c), cross-country running M/W, equestrian sports M(c)/W(c), fencing M(c)/W(c), field hockey W, football M, golf M/W, ice hockey M(c)/W(c), lacrosse M/W, skiing (downhill) M(c)/W(c), soccer M/W, softball W, squash M(c)/W(c), swimming and diving M/W, tennis M/W, track and field M/W, ultimate Frisbee M(c)/W(c), volleyball M(c)/W. *Intramural sports:* badminton M/W, basketball M/W, field hockey W, football M, racquetball M/W, soccer M/W, softball M, tennis M/W, volleyball M/W.

Standardized Tests *Recommended:* SAT or ACT (for admission).

Costs (2012–13) *One-time required fee:* $25. *Comprehensive fee:* $55,729 includes full-time tuition ($44,101), mandatory fees ($450), and room and board ($11,178). Part-time tuition: $5515 per course. *Required fees:* $56 per course part-time. *College room only:* $5765. Room and board charges vary according to board plan and housing facility. *Payment plan:* installment. *Waivers:* senior citizens and employees or children of employees.

Financial Aid Of all full-time matriculated undergraduates who enrolled in 2012, 1,472 applied for aid, 1,324 were judged to have need, 908 had their need fully met. 925 Federal Work-Study jobs (averaging $2248). 179 state and other part-time jobs (averaging $3535). In 2012, 274 non-need-based awards were made. *Average percent of need met:* 96%. *Average financial aid package:* $36,221. *Average need-based loan:* $5487. *Average need-based gift aid:* $30,004. *Average non-need-based aid:* $11,084. *Average indebtedness upon graduation:* $25,574. *Financial aid deadline:* 2/1.

Applying *Options:* electronic application, early decision, early action, deferred entrance. *Application fee:* $65. *Required:* essay or personal statement, high school transcript, 2 letters of recommendation. *Recommended:* minimum 3.0 GPA, interview. *Application deadlines:* 2/1 (freshmen), 2/1 (out-of-state freshmen), 4/1 (transfers), 12/1 (early action). *Early decision deadline:* 11/15 (for plan 1), 1/15 (for plan 2). *Notification:* 3/20 (freshmen), 3/20 (out-of-state freshmen), continuous until 5/1 (transfers), 12/15 (early decision plan 1), 2/15 (early decision plan 2), 2/1 (early action).

Freshman Application Contact Stephanie Balmer, Vice President for Enrollment, Marketing and Communications and Dean of Admissions, Dickinson College, PO Box 1773, Admissions Office, Carlisle, PA 17013-2896. *Phone:* 717-245-1231. *Toll-free phone:* 800-644-1773. *Fax:* 717-245-1442. *E-mail:* admit@dickinson.edu.
Website: http://www.dickinson.edu/.

Drexel University

Philadelphia, Pennsylvania

- **Independent** university, founded 1891
- **Urban** 96-acre campus with easy access to Philadelphia
- **Coed**
- **Moderately difficult** entrance level

Faculty *Student/faculty ratio:* 11:1.

Academics *Calendar:* quarters. *Degrees:* certificates, associate, bachelor's, master's, doctoral, post-master's, and postbachelor's certificates.

Student Life *Campus security:* 24-hour emergency response devices and patrols, late-night transport/escort service, controlled dormitory access.

Athletics Member NCAA. All Division I.

Standardized Tests *Required:* SAT or ACT (for admission). *Recommended:* SAT (for admission).

Costs (2012–13) *Comprehensive fee:* $50,275 includes full-time tuition ($33,800), mandatory fees ($2300), and room and board ($14,175). Full-time tuition and fees vary according to course load, location, program, and student level. Part-time tuition: $930 per credit. Part-time tuition and fees vary according to course load and program. *College room only:* $8430. Room and board charges vary according to board plan and housing facility.

Financial Aid *Of all full-time matriculated undergraduates who enrolled in 2008,* 5,878 applied for aid, 5,833 were judged to have need, 1,826 had their need fully met. *In 2008,* 2086 non-need-based awards were made. *Average percent of need met:* 56. *Average financial aid package:* $21,488. *Average need-based loan:* $12,875. *Average need-based gift aid:* $13,204. *Average non-need-based aid:* $11,641. *Financial aid deadline:* 3/1.

Applying *Options:* electronic application, deferred entrance. *Application fee:* $75. *Required:* essay or personal statement, high school transcript, minimum 2.0 GPA. *Recommended:* 2 letters of recommendation, interview.

Freshman Application Contact Ms. Margaret Sparzani, Director of Freshman Admissions, Drexel University, 3141 Chestnut Street, Philadelphia, PA 19104-2875. *Phone:* 215-895-2400. *Toll-free phone:* 800-2-DREXEL. *Fax:* 215-895-5939. *E-mail:* enroll@drexel.edu.
Website: http://www.drexel.edu/.

See next page for display ad and page 1274 for the College Close-Up.

Duquesne University

Pittsburgh, Pennsylvania

- **Independent Roman Catholic** university, founded 1878
- **Urban** 50-acre campus with easy access to Pittsburgh
- **Endowment** $177.2 million
- **Coed** 5,832 undergraduate students, 97% full-time, 57% women, 43% men
- **Moderately difficult** entrance level, 75% of applicants were admitted

Undergraduates 5,650 full-time, 182 part-time. Students come from 43 states and territories; 49 other countries; 25% are from out of state; 4% Black or African American, non-Hispanic/Latino; 3% Hispanic/Latino; 2% Asian, non-Hispanic/Latino; 0.2% American Indian or Alaska Native, non-Hispanic/Latino; 2% Two or more races, non-Hispanic/Latino; 2% Race/ethnicity unknown; 4% international; 3% transferred in; 59% live on campus. *Retention:* 89% of full-time freshmen returned.

Freshmen *Admission:* 6,659 applied, 4,975 admitted, 1,526 enrolled. *Average high school GPA:* 3.65. *Test scores:* SAT critical reading scores over 500: 83%; SAT math scores over 500: 87%; SAT writing scores over 500: 80%; ACT scores over 18: 98%; SAT critical reading scores over 600: 24%; SAT math scores over 600: 35%; SAT writing scores over 600: 27%; ACT scores over 24: 61%; SAT critical reading scores over 700: 2%; SAT math scores over 700: 3%; SAT writing scores over 700: 2%; ACT scores over 30: 7%.

Faculty *Total:* 987, 49% full-time. *Student/faculty ratio:* 14:1.

Academics *Calendar:* semesters. *Degrees:* bachelor's, master's, doctoral, post-master's, and postbachelor's certificates. *Special study options:* academic remediation for entering students, accelerated degree program, adult/continuing education programs, advanced placement credit, distance learning, double majors, English as a second language, external degree program, freshman honors college, honors programs, independent study, internships, off-campus study, part-time degree program, services for LD students, student-designed majors, study abroad, summer session for credit. *ROTC:* Army (b), Navy (c), Air Force (c). *Unusual degree programs:* 3-2 engineering with Case Western Reserve University, University of Pittsburgh.

Computers on Campus 1,000 computers/terminals are available on campus for general student use. Students can access the following: campus intranet, computer help desk, free student e-mail accounts, online (class) grades, online (class) registration, online (class) schedules. Campuswide network is available. 100% of college-owned or -operated housing units are wired for high-speed Internet access. Wireless service is available via classrooms, computer centers, computer labs, dorm rooms, learning centers, libraries, student centers.

Student Life *Housing:* on-campus residence required through sophomore year. *Options:* coed, men-only, women-only, disabled students. Campus housing is university owned. Freshman campus housing is guaranteed. *Activities and organizations:* drama/theater group, student-run newspaper, radio and television station, choral group, marching band, Duquesne University Volunteers (DUV), Red and Blue Crew, Student Government Association, Duquesne Program Council, Residence Hall Association, national fraternities, national sororities. *Campus security:* 24-hour emergency response devices and patrols, late-night transport/escort service, controlled dormitory access, cameras monitor exterior 24 hours/day; card access for buildings; 8 Code Blue Emergency service stations; outside warning siren system. *Student services:* health clinic, personal/psychological counseling.

Athletics Member NCAA. All Division I except football (Division I-AA). *Intercollegiate sports:* basketball M(s)/W(s), crew W(s), cross-country running M(s)/W(s), lacrosse W(s), soccer M(s)/W(s), swimming and diving W(s), tennis M(s)/W(s), track and field M(s)/W(s), volleyball W(s). *Intramural sports:* basketball M/W, crew M(c)/W(c), equestrian sports M(c)/W(c), football M/W, golf M(c)/W(c), ice hockey M(c)/W(c), racquetball M/W, rugby M(c)/W(c), soccer M/W, tennis M(c)/W(c), volleyball M(c)/W(c).

Standardized Tests *Required:* SAT or ACT (for admission).

Costs (2013–14) *Comprehensive fee:* $40,232 includes full-time tuition ($27,668), mandatory fees ($2366), and room and board ($10,198). Full-time tuition and fees vary according to program. Part-time tuition: $902 per credit. Part-time tuition and fees vary according to program. *Required fees:* $92 per credit part-time. *College room only:* $5562. Room and board charges vary according to board plan and housing facility. *Payment plans:* installment, deferred payment. *Waivers:* senior citizens and employees or children of employees.

Financial Aid Of all full-time matriculated undergraduates who enrolled in 2011, 4,586 applied for aid, 3,920 were judged to have need, 997 had their need fully met. 3,332 Federal Work-Study jobs (averaging $2913). In 2011, 1308 non-need-based awards were made. *Average percent of need met:* 78%. *Average financial aid package:* $22,520. *Average need-based loan:* $3081. *Average need-based gift aid:* $15,343. *Average non-need-based aid:* $8990. *Average indebtedness upon graduation:* $25,228. *Financial aid deadline:* 5/1.

Applying *Options:* electronic application, early decision, early admission, early action, deferred entrance. *Application fee:* $50. *Required:* essay or personal statement, high school transcript, 1 letter of recommendation. *Required for some:* audition for School of Music applicants; Physical Therapy freshman-40 hours of volunteer, paid, or shadowing experience before start of freshman year. *Recommended:* minimum 3.0 GPA, interview. *Application deadlines:* 7/1 (freshmen), 7/1 (transfers), 12/1 (early action). *Early decision deadline:* 11/1. *Notification:* continuous until 10/1 (freshmen), 12/15 (early decision), 1/15 (early action).

Freshman Application Contact Ms. Debra Zugates, Director of Admissions, Duquesne University, Administration Building, 600 Forbes Avenue, Pittsburgh, PA 15282-0201. *Phone:* 412-396-5211. *Toll-free phone:* 800-456-0590. *Fax:* 412-396-5644. *E-mail:* admissions@duq.edu. *Website:* http://www.duq.edu/.

Eastern University
St. Davids, Pennsylvania

- **Independent Christian** comprehensive, founded 1952
- **Suburban** 92-acre campus with easy access to Philadelphia
- **Coed**
- **Moderately difficult** entrance level

Faculty *Student/faculty ratio:* 13:1.

Academics *Calendar:* semesters. *Degrees:* associate, bachelor's, master's, and doctoral.

Student Life *Campus security:* 24-hour emergency response devices and patrols, late-night transport/escort service, controlled dormitory access, emergency call boxes.

Athletics Member NCAA. All Division III.

Standardized Tests *Required:* SAT or ACT (for admission).

Costs (2012–13) *Comprehensive fee:* $36,264 includes full-time tuition ($26,934) and room and board ($9330). Full-time tuition and fees vary according to course load, degree level, and program. Part-time tuition and fees vary according to course load, degree level, and program. *College room only:* $5080. Room and board charges vary according to board plan, housing facility, and location.

Applying *Options:* electronic application, early admission, deferred entrance. *Required:* essay or personal statement, high school transcript, minimum 2.0 GPA, 1 letter of recommendation. *Recommended:* minimum 3.0 GPA, 2 letters of recommendation, interview.

Freshman Application Contact Mr. Michael Dziedziak, Director of Undergraduate Admissions, Eastern University, 1300 Eagle Road, St. Davids, PA 19087-3696. *Phone:* 610-341-1376. *Toll-free phone:* 800-452-0996. *Fax:* 610-341-1723. *E-mail:* ugadm@eastern.edu.

Website: http://www.eastern.edu/.

East Stroudsburg University of Pennsylvania

East Stroudsburg, Pennsylvania

- **State-supported** comprehensive, founded 1893, part of Pennsylvania State System of Higher Education
- **Small-town** 256-acre campus
- **Endowment** $10.3 million
- **Coed**
- **Moderately difficult** entrance level

Faculty *Student/faculty ratio:* 24:1.

Academics *Calendar:* semesters. *Degrees:* associate, bachelor's, and master's.

Student Life *Campus security:* 24-hour emergency response devices and patrols, late-night transport/escort service, controlled dormitory access.

Athletics Member NCAA. All Division II.

Standardized Tests *Required:* SAT or ACT (for admission).

Costs (2012–13) *Tuition:* state resident $6428 full-time; nonresident $16,070 full-time. Full-time tuition and fees vary according to course load. Part-time tuition and fees vary according to course load. *Required fees:* $1887 full-time. *Room and board:* $9176; room only: $6718. Room and board charges vary according to board plan and housing facility.

Financial Aid *Of all full-time matriculated undergraduates who enrolled in 2010,* 4,597 applied for aid, 3,624 were judged to have need, 1,936 had their need fully met. *In 2010,* 900 non-need-based awards were made. *Average percent of need met:* 81. *Average financial aid package:* $6584. *Average need-based loan:* $4146. *Average need-based gift aid:* $4707. *Average non-need-based aid:* $10,538. *Average indebtedness upon graduation:* $22,333. *Financial aid deadline:* 3/1.

Applying *Options:* electronic application. *Application fee:* $45. *Required for some:* high school transcript.

Freshman Application Contact Mr. Jeff Jones, Director of Admissions, East Stroudsburg University of Pennsylvania, 200 Prospect Street, East Stroudsburg, PA 18301. *Phone:* 570-422-3542. *Toll-free phone:* 877-230-5547. *Fax:* 570-422-3933. *E-mail:* undergrads@po-box.esu.edu.

Website: http://www.esu.edu/.

Edinboro University of Pennsylvania

Edinboro, Pennsylvania

- **State-supported** comprehensive, founded 1857, part of Pennsylvania State System of Higher Education
- **Small-town** 585-acre campus
- **Endowment** $8.3 million
- **Coed** 6,090 undergraduate students, 91% full-time, 58% women, 42% men
- **Moderately difficult** entrance level, 75% of applicants were admitted

Undergraduates 5,565 full-time, 525 part-time. Students come from 32 states and territories; 33 other countries; 14% are from out of state; 7% Black or African American, non-Hispanic/Latino; 3% Hispanic/Latino; 0.8% Asian, non-Hispanic/Latino; 0.1% Native Hawaiian or other Pacific Islander, non-Hispanic/Latino; 0.2% American Indian or Alaska Native, non-Hispanic/Latino; 2% Two or more races, non-Hispanic/Latino; 0.3% Race/ethnicity unknown; 1% international; 4% transferred in; 37% live on campus. *Retention:* 68% of full-time freshmen returned.

Freshmen *Admission:* 3,992 applied, 3,006 admitted, 1,235 enrolled. *Average high school GPA:* 3.2. *Test scores:* SAT critical reading scores over 500: 37%; SAT math scores over 500: 38%; ACT scores over 18: 67%; SAT critical reading scores over 600: 8%; SAT math scores over 600: 8%; ACT scores over 24: 14%; SAT critical reading scores over 700: 1%; SAT math scores over 700: 1%; ACT scores over 30: 1%.

Faculty *Total:* 410, 82% full-time, 71% with terminal degrees. *Student/faculty ratio:* 18:1.

Academics *Calendar:* semesters. *Degrees:* associate, bachelor's, master's, post-master's, and postbachelor's certificates. *Special study options:* academic remediation for entering students, adult/continuing education programs, advanced placement credit, distance learning, double majors, freshman honors college, honors programs, independent study, internships, off-campus study, part-time degree program, services for LD students, student-designed majors, study abroad, summer session for credit. *ROTC:* Army (b). *Unusual degree programs:* 3-2 business administration with Pennsylvania State-Behrend, Rochester Institute of Technology; engineering with Pennsylvania State University, University of Pittsburgh, Case Western Reserve University; pre-pharmacy (2+3 at Lake Erie College of Osteopathic Medicine and School of Pharmacy), MA Counseling (3-2 program for Criminal Justice Majors).

Computers on Campus 4,420 computers/terminals and 2,000 ports are available on campus for general student use. Students can access the following: campus intranet, computer help desk, free student e-mail accounts, online (class) grades, online (class) registration, online (class) schedules, software. Campuswide network is available. 100% of college-owned or -operated housing units are wired for high-speed Internet access. Wireless service is available via classrooms, computer centers, computer labs, dorm rooms, learning centers, libraries, student centers.

Student Life *Housing:* on-campus residence required through sophomore year. *Options:* coed, disabled students. Campus housing is university owned and is provided by a third party. Freshman campus housing is guaranteed. *Activities and organizations:* drama/theater group, student-run newspaper, radio and television station, choral group, marching band, Student Government Association, University Programming Board, Greek Life, Recreational Sports, Student Concert Series, national fraternities, national sororities. *Campus security:* 24-hour emergency response devices and patrols, controlled dormitory access, self-defense education. *Student services:* health clinic, personal/psychological counseling, women's center, legal services.

Athletics Member NCAA. All Division II except wrestling (Division I). *Intercollegiate sports:* basketball M(s)/W(s), cross-country running M(s)/W(s), football M(s), lacrosse W(s), soccer W(s), softball W(s), swimming and diving M(s)/W(s), tennis M/W, track and field M(s)/W(s), volleyball W(s), wrestling M(s). *Intramural sports:* basketball M/W, bowling M/W, cheerleading W, equestrian sports M/W, fencing M/W, golf M/W, ice hockey M/W, riflery M/W, soccer M/W, ultimate Frisbee M/W, volleyball M/W.

Standardized Tests *Required:* SAT or ACT (for admission).

Costs (2012–13) *Tuition:* state resident $6428 full-time, $268 per credit part-time; nonresident $9642 full-time, $402 per credit part-time. Part-time tuition and fees vary according to course load. *Required fees:* $2150 full-time, $90 per credit part-time. *Room and board:* $7362; room only: $5200. Room and board charges vary according to board plan. *Payment plan:* installment. *Waivers:* minority students, senior citizens, and employees or children of employees.

Financial Aid Of all full-time matriculated undergraduates who enrolled in 2011, 5,468 applied for aid, 4,935 were judged to have need, 171 had their need fully met. 347 Federal Work-Study jobs (averaging $1505). 648 state and other part-time jobs (averaging $1829). In 2011, 60 non-need-based awards were made. *Average percent of need met:* 48%. *Average financial aid package:* $8407. *Average need-based loan:* $3841. *Average need-based gift aid:* $4148. *Average non-need-based aid:* $2213. *Average indebtedness upon graduation:* $23,633.

Applying *Options:* electronic application, deferred entrance. *Application fee:* $30. *Required:* high school transcript. *Required for some:* essay or personal statement, 1 letter of recommendation, interview, music auditions. *Recommended:* minimum 2.5 GPA. *Application deadline:* rolling (transfers). *Notification:* continuous (freshmen), continuous (transfers).

Freshman Application Contact Mr. Craig Grooms, Director of Undergraduate Admissions, Edinboro University of Pennsylvania, Academy Hall, Edinboro, PA 16444. *Phone:* 814-732-2761. *Toll-free phone:* 888-846-2676. *Fax:* 814-732-2420. *E-mail:* eup_admissions@edinboro.edu.

Website: http://www.edinboro.edu/.

Elizabethtown College

Elizabethtown, Pennsylvania

- **Independent** 4-year, founded 1899, affiliated with Church of the Brethren
- **Small-town** 201-acre campus with easy access to Baltimore, Philadelphia
- **Endowment** $54.8 million
- **Coed** 1,885 undergraduate students, 99% full-time, 65% women, 35% men
- **Moderately difficult** entrance level, 70% of applicants were admitted

Undergraduates 1,858 full-time, 27 part-time. Students come from 27 states and territories; 26 other countries; 31% are from out of state; 3% Black or African American, non-Hispanic/Latino; 2% Hispanic/Latino; 2% Asian, non-Hispanic/Latino; 0.2% Native Hawaiian or other Pacific Islander, non-Hispanic/Latino; 0.3% American Indian or Alaska Native, non-Hispanic/Latino; 1% Two or more races, non-Hispanic/Latino; 0.1% Race/ethnicity unknown; 4% international; 1% transferred in; 88% live on campus. *Retention:* 86% of full-time freshmen returned.

Freshmen *Admission:* 3,732 applied, 2,598 admitted, 505 enrolled. *Test scores:* SAT critical reading scores over 500: 75%; SAT math scores over 500: 77%; ACT scores over 18: 94%; SAT critical reading scores over 600: 28%; SAT math scores over 600: 37%; ACT scores over 24: 48%; SAT critical reading scores over 700: 3%; SAT math scores over 700: 5%; ACT scores over 30: 12%.

Faculty *Total:* 212, 62% full-time, 66% with terminal degrees. *Student/faculty ratio:* 12:1.

Academics *Calendar:* semesters. *Degrees:* bachelor's and master's. *Special study options:* advanced placement credit, distance learning, double majors, English as a second language, honors programs, independent study, internships, off-campus study, services for LD students, study abroad, summer session for credit. *Unusual degree programs:* 3-2 engineering with Pennsylvania State University–University Park Campus; forestry with Duke University; allied health programs with Thomas Jefferson University, Widener University, University of Maryland at Baltimore.

Computers on Campus 200 computers/terminals and 200 ports are available on campus for general student use. Students can access the following: campus intranet, computer help desk, free student e-mail accounts, online (class) grades, online (class) registration, online (class) schedules, file space, personal web page, financial aid, student billing, residence hall selection, personal and group blogs. Campuswide network is available. 100% of college-owned or -operated housing units are wired for high-speed Internet access. Wireless service is available via classrooms, computer centers, computer labs, dorm rooms, learning centers, libraries, student centers.

Student Life *Housing:* on-campus residence required through senior year. *Options:* coed, women-only, disabled students. Campus housing is university owned and leased by the school. Freshman campus housing is guaranteed. *Activities and organizations:* drama/theater group, student-run newspaper, radio and television station, choral group, Students in Free Enterprise (SIFE), Emotion Dance Club, Student Senate, Acappella groups, religious groups. *Campus security:* 24-hour emergency response devices and patrols, student patrols, late-night transport/escort service, controlled dormitory access, self-defense workshops, crime prevention program. *Student services:* personal/psychological counseling.

Athletics Member NCAA. All Division III. *Intercollegiate sports:* baseball M, basketball M/W, cross-country running M/W, field hockey W, golf M, lacrosse M/W, soccer M/W, softball W, swimming and diving M/W, tennis M/W, track and field M/W, volleyball W, wrestling M. *Intramural sports:* badminton M/W, basketball M/W, cheerleading M(c)/W(c), equestrian sports M(c)/W(c), ice hockey M(c), racquetball M/W, soccer M/W, softball M/W, tennis M/W, volleyball M(c)/W(c), water polo M/W.

Standardized Tests *Required:* SAT or ACT (for admission).

Costs (2013–14) *Comprehensive fee:* $47,600 includes full-time tuition ($38,200) and room and board ($9400). Full-time tuition and fees vary according to course load. Part-time tuition: $925 per credit hour. Part-time tuition and fees vary according to course load. *Required fees:* $525 part-time. *College room only:* $4650. Room and board charges vary according to board plan and housing facility. *Payment plan:* installment. *Waivers:* employees or children of employees.

Financial Aid Of all full-time matriculated undergraduates who enrolled in 2012, 1,565 applied for aid, 1,423 were judged to have need, 261 had their need fully met. 968 Federal Work-Study jobs (averaging $1325). In 2012, 397 non-need-based awards were made. *Average percent of need met:* 78%. *Average financial aid package:* $25,493. *Average need-based loan:* $4433. *Average need-based gift aid:* $20,942. *Average non-need-based aid:* $16,032.

Applying *Options:* electronic application, deferred entrance. *Application fee:* $30. *Required:* essay or personal statement, high school transcript, minimum

2.0 GPA, 2 letters of recommendation. *Required for some:* interview. *Recommended:* minimum 3.0 GPA, interview. *Application deadlines:* 3/1 (freshmen), 8/1 (transfers). *Notification:* continuous (freshmen), continuous (transfers).
Freshman Application Contact Ms. Debra Murray, Director of Admissions, Elizabethtown College, One Alpha Drive, Elizabethtown, PA 17022. *Phone:* 717-361-1400. *Fax:* 717-361-1365. *E-mail:* admissions@etown.edu. *Website:* http://www.etown.edu/.

See previous page for display ad and page 1278 for the College Close-Up.

Elizabethtown College School of Continuing and Professional Studies

Elizabethtown, Pennsylvania

Admissions Office Contact Elizabethtown College School of Continuing and Professional Studies, One Alpha Drive, Elizabethtown, PA 17022.

Franklin & Marshall College

Lancaster, Pennsylvania

- **Independent** 4-year, founded 1787
- **Suburban** 209-acre campus with easy access to Philadelphia
- **Coed** 2,365 undergraduate students, 98% full-time, 52% women, 48% men
- **Very difficult** entrance level, 39% of applicants were admitted

Undergraduates 2,307 full-time, 58 part-time. Students come from 42 states and territories; 41 other countries; 70% are from out of state; 4% Black or African American, non-Hispanic/Latino; 6% Hispanic/Latino; 4% Asian, non-Hispanic/Latino; 0.1% American Indian or Alaska Native, non-Hispanic/Latino; 2% Two or more races, non-Hispanic/Latino; 6% Race/ethnicity unknown; 10% international; 0.7% transferred in; 99% live on campus. *Retention:* 92% of full-time freshmen returned.
Freshmen *Admission:* 5,174 applied, 2,034 admitted, 599 enrolled. *Test scores:* SAT critical reading scores over 500: 98%; SAT math scores over 500: 99%; SAT critical reading scores over 600: 76%; SAT math scores over 600: 88%; SAT critical reading scores over 700: 23%; SAT math scores over 700: 30%.
Faculty *Total:* 288, 80% full-time, 86% with terminal degrees. *Student/faculty ratio:* 9:1.
Academics *Calendar:* semesters. *Degree:* bachelor's. *Special study options:* accelerated degree program, advanced placement credit, double majors, independent study, internships, off-campus study, services for LD students, student-designed majors, study abroad, summer session for credit. *ROTC:* Army (c). *Unusual degree programs:* 3-2 engineering with Rensselaer Polytechnic Institute, Washington University in St. Louis, Columbia University, Case Western Reserve University, Penn State University College of Engineering; forestry with Duke University; environmental studies with Duke University.
Computers on Campus 125 computers/terminals are available on campus for general student use. Students can access the following: campus intranet, computer help desk, free student e-mail accounts, online (class) grades, online (class) registration, online (class) schedules, online degree audit, unofficial transcripts, course material. Campuswide network is available. 100% of college-owned or -operated housing units are wired for high-speed Internet access. Wireless service is available via entire campus.
Student Life *Housing:* on-campus residence required through senior year. *Options:* coed, disabled students. Campus housing is university owned and is provided by a third party. Freshman campus housing is guaranteed. *Activities and organizations:* drama/theater group, student-run newspaper, radio station, choral group, Intervarsity, Hillel, Mi Gente Latina, Cia Bella, F&M Players, national fraternities, national sororities. *Campus security:* 24-hour emergency response devices and patrols, late-night transport/escort service, controlled dormitory access, residence hall security, campus security connected to city police and fire company. *Student services:* health clinic, personal/psychological counseling, women's center.
Athletics Member NCAA. All Division III except wrestling (Division I). *Intercollegiate sports:* baseball M, basketball M/W, crew M(c)/W, cross-country running M/W, equestrian sports W(c), field hockey W, football M, golf M/W, ice hockey M(c), lacrosse M/W, rugby M(c)/W(c), soccer M/W, softball W, squash M/W, swimming and diving M/W, tennis M/W, track and field M/W, ultimate Frisbee M(c)/W(c), volleyball M(c)/W, wrestling M. *Intramural*

sports: basketball M/W, football M, soccer M/W, softball M/W, squash M/W, tennis M/W, volleyball M/W, wrestling M.
Costs (2013–14) *One-time required fee:* $200. *Comprehensive fee:* $56,110 includes full-time tuition ($44,260), mandatory fees ($100), and room and board ($11,750). *Part-time tuition:* $5533 per course. *College room only:* $7330. Room and board charges vary according to board plan and housing facility. *Payment plans:* installment, deferred payment. *Waivers:* employees or children of employees.
Financial Aid Of all full-time matriculated undergraduates who enrolled in 2011, 1,306 applied for aid, 1,071 were judged to have need, 897 had their need fully met. In 2011, 177 non-need-based awards were made. *Average percent of need met:* 98%. *Average financial aid package:* $34,998. *Average need-based loan:* $4236. *Average need-based gift aid:* $30,597. *Average non-need-based aid:* $11,222. *Average indebtedness upon graduation:* $31,617. *Financial aid deadline:* 2/15.
Applying *Options:* electronic application, early admission, early decision, deferred entrance. *Application fee:* $60. *Required:* essay or personal statement, high school transcript, 2 letters of recommendation, Common Application Supplement. *Required for some:* interview. *Application deadlines:* 2/1 (freshmen), 2/1 (out-of-state freshmen), 5/15 (transfers). *Early decision deadline:* 11/15 (for plan 1), 1/15 (for plan 2). *Notification:* 4/1 (freshmen), 4/1 (out-of-state freshmen), 12/15 (early decision plan 1), 2/15 (early decision plan 2).
Freshman Application Contact Julie Kerich, Director of Admissions, Franklin & Marshall College, PO Box 3003, Lancaster, PA 17604-3003. *Phone:* 717-358-47433. *Toll-free phone:* 877-678-9111. *Fax:* 717-291-4389. *E-mail:* julie.kerich@fandm.edu. *Website:* http://www.fandm.edu/.

Gannon University

Erie, Pennsylvania

- **Independent Roman Catholic** university, founded 1925
- **Urban** 37-acre campus with easy access to Cleveland, Buffalo, Pittsburgh
- **Endowment** $41.3 million
- **Coed** 3,008 undergraduate students, 84% full-time, 58% women, 42% men
- **Moderately difficult** entrance level, 83% of applicants were admitted

Undergraduates 2,525 full-time, 483 part-time. Students come from 35 states and territories; 24 other countries; 24% are from out of state; 6% Black or African American, non-Hispanic/Latino; 2% Hispanic/Latino; 1% Asian, non-Hispanic/Latino; 0.1% Native Hawaiian or other Pacific Islander, non-Hispanic/Latino; 0.4% American Indian or Alaska Native, non-Hispanic/Latino; 0.7% Two or more races, non-Hispanic/Latino; 5% Race/ethnicity unknown; 5% international; 4% transferred in; 45% live on campus. *Retention:* 80% of full-time freshmen returned.
Freshmen *Admission:* 3,859 applied, 3,208 admitted, 629 enrolled. *Average high school GPA:* 3.52. *Test scores:* SAT critical reading scores over 500: 55%; SAT math scores over 500: 62%; ACT scores over 18: 91%; SAT critical reading scores over 600: 13%; SAT math scores over 600: 22%; ACT scores over 24: 35%; SAT critical reading scores over 700: 1%; SAT math scores over 700: 2%; ACT scores over 30: 6%.
Faculty *Total:* 363, 56% full-time, 46% with terminal degrees. *Student/faculty ratio:* 13:1.
Academics *Calendar:* semesters plus 2 summer sessions. *Degrees:* certificates, bachelor's, master's, doctoral, post-master's, and postbachelor's certificates. *Special study options:* academic remediation for entering students, accelerated degree program, adult/continuing education programs, advanced placement credit, cooperative education, distance learning, double majors, English as a second language, honors programs, independent study, internships, off-campus study, part-time degree program, services for LD students, study abroad, summer session for credit. *ROTC:* Army (b). *Unusual degree programs:* 3-2 business administration; engineering with University of Pittsburgh; occupational therapy, physician assistant.
Computers on Campus 380 computers/terminals and 1,425 ports are available on campus for general student use. Students can access the following: campus intranet, computer help desk, free student e-mail accounts, online (class) grades, online (class) registration, online (class) schedules. Campuswide network is available. 100% of college-owned or -operated housing units are wired for high-speed Internet access. Wireless service is available via entire campus.
Student Life *Housing:* on-campus residence required through sophomore year. *Options:* coed, disabled students. Campus housing is university owned and leased by the school. Freshman campus housing is guaranteed. *Activities and organizations:* drama/theater group, student-run newspaper, radio station, choral group, Student Occupational Therapy Association, GU Habitat for Human-

...ity, Phi Eta Sigma, Activities Programming Board, GU Society of Physician Assistants, national fraternities, national sororities. *Campus security:* 24-hour emergency response devices and patrols, student patrols, late-night transport/escort service, controlled dormitory access, security cameras. *Student services:* health clinic, personal/psychological counseling.

Athletics Member NCAA. All Division II. *Intercollegiate sports:* baseball M(s), basketball M(s)/W(s), cheerleading M/W, cross-country running M(s)/W(s), football M(s), golf M(s)/W(s), lacrosse W(s), soccer M(s)/W(s), softball W(s), swimming and diving M(s)/W(s), volleyball W(s), water polo M(s)/W(s), wrestling M(s). *Intramural sports:* badminton M/W, basketball M/W, football M/W, racquetball M/W, soccer M/W, ultimate Frisbee M/W, volleyball M(c)/W, water polo M, weight lifting M, wrestling M.

Standardized Tests *Required:* SAT or ACT (for admission).

Costs (2013–14) *Comprehensive fee:* $38,486 includes full-time tuition ($27,000), mandatory fees ($546), and room and board ($10,940). Full-time tuition and fees vary according to class time, course load, and program. Part-time tuition: $650 per credit hour. Part-time tuition and fees vary according to class time, course load, and program. *Required fees:* $18 per credit hour part-time. *College room only:* $5740. Room and board charges vary according to board plan and housing facility. *Payment plans:* installment, deferred payment. *Waivers:* senior citizens and employees or children of employees.

Financial Aid Of all full-time matriculated undergraduates who enrolled in 2012, 2,284 applied for aid, 2,088 were judged to have need, 447 had their need fully met. 514 Federal Work-Study jobs (averaging $2300). 160 state and other part-time jobs (averaging $2300). In 2012, 366 non-need-based awards were made. *Average percent of need met:* 71%. *Average financial aid package:* $21,641. *Average need-based loan:* $4504. *Average need-based gift aid:* $17,346. *Average non-need-based aid:* $10,877.

Applying *Options:* electronic application, early admission, deferred entrance. *Application fee:* $25. *Required:* high school transcript, minimum 2.0 GPA. *Required for some:* minimum 3.0 GPA, 3 letters of recommendation, interview. *Recommended:* essay or personal statement, counselor's recommendation. *Application deadlines:* rolling (freshmen), rolling (transfers).

Freshman Application Contact Office of Admissions, Gannon University, 109 University Square, Erie, PA 16541. *Phone:* 814-871-7240. *Toll-free phone:* 800-GANNONU. *Fax:* 814-871-5803. *E-mail:* admissions@gannon.edu.

Website: http://www.gannon.edu/.

See below for display ad and page 1304 for the College Close-Up.

Geneva College

Beaver Falls, Pennsylvania

- **Independent** comprehensive, founded 1848, affiliated with Reformed Presbyterian Church of North America
- **Small-town** 55-acre campus with easy access to Pittsburgh
- **Endowment** $31.9 million
- **Coed** 1,342 undergraduate students, 98% full-time, 48% women, 52% men
- **Moderately difficult** entrance level, 72% of applicants were admitted

Undergraduates 1,312 full-time, 30 part-time. Students come from 39 states and territories; 5 other countries; 29% are from out of state; 3% Black or African American, non-Hispanic/Latino; 0.8% Hispanic/Latino; 1% Asian, non-Hispanic/Latino; 0.2% American Indian or Alaska Native, non-Hispanic/Latino; 2% Two or more races, non-Hispanic/Latino; 0.7% international; 3% transferred in; 71% live on campus. *Retention:* 79% of full-time freshmen returned.

Freshmen *Admission:* 1,588 applied, 1,148 admitted, 340 enrolled. *Average high school GPA:* 3.52. *Test scores:* SAT critical reading scores over 500: 65%; SAT math scores over 500: 67%; SAT writing scores over 500: 57%; ACT scores over 18: 93%; SAT critical reading scores over 600: 27%; SAT math scores over 600: 28%; SAT writing scores over 600: 18%; ACT scores over 24: 43%; SAT critical reading scores over 700: 5%; SAT math scores over 700: 4%; SAT writing scores over 700: 5%; ACT scores over 30: 11%.

Faculty *Total:* 202, 43% full-time. *Student/faculty ratio:* 13:1.

Academics *Calendar:* semesters. *Degrees:* associate, bachelor's, and master's (also offers non-traditional programs in Philadelphia and western Pennsylvania with significant enrollment not reflected in profile). *Special study options:* academic remediation for entering students, accelerated degree program, adult/continuing education programs, advanced placement credit, cooperative education, double majors, English as a second language, honors programs, independent study, internships, off-campus study, part-time degree program, services for LD students, student-designed majors, study abroad, summer session for credit. *ROTC:* Army (c). *Unusual degree programs:* 3-2 nursing with Roberts Wesleyan College; Master's of Divinity with Reformed Presbyterian Theological Seminary.

Computers on Campus 150 computers/terminals and 400 ports are available on campus for general student use. Students can access the following: campus

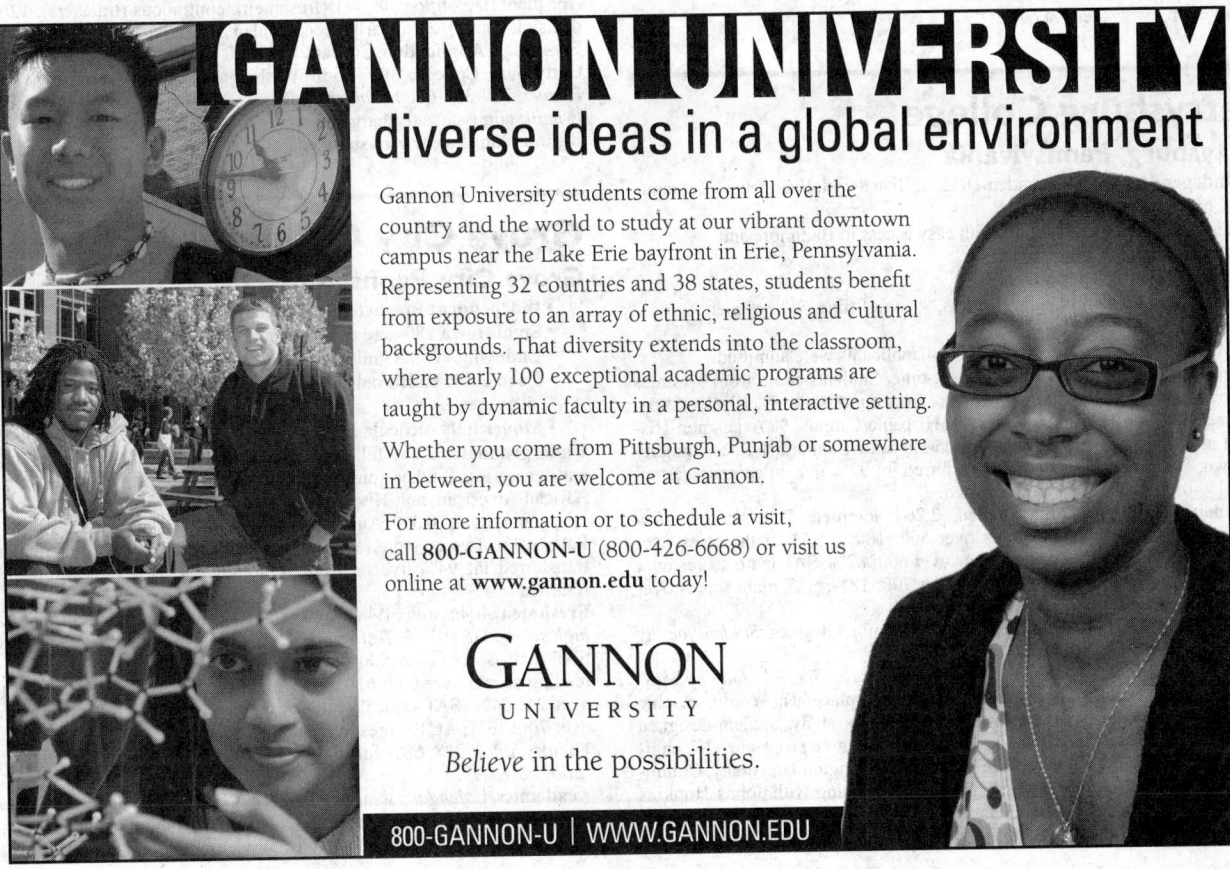

intranet, computer help desk, free student e-mail accounts, online (class) grades, online (class) registration, online (class) schedules. Campuswide network is available. 50% of college-owned or -operated housing units are wired for high-speed Internet access. Wireless service is available via entire campus.

Student Life *Housing:* on-campus residence required through senior year. *Options:* men-only, women-only. Campus housing is university owned. Freshman campus housing is guaranteed. *Activities and organizations:* drama/theater group, student-run newspaper, radio station, choral group, marching band, marching band, Genevans Choir, ministry groups, intermurals, discipleship groups. *Campus security:* 24-hour emergency response devices and patrols, late-night transport/escort service, controlled dormitory access. *Student services:* health clinic, personal/psychological counseling.

Athletics Member NCAA, NCCAA. All NCAA Division III. *Intercollegiate sports:* baseball M, basketball M/W, cross-country running M/W, football M, soccer M/W, softball W, tennis W, track and field M/W, volleyball M(c)/W. *Intramural sports:* basketball M/W, football M/W, golf M/W, ice hockey M(c), racquetball M/W, rugby M(c)/W(c), skiing (downhill) M(c)/W(c), soccer M/W, softball M/W, table tennis M/W, ultimate Frisbee M/W, volleyball M/W.

Standardized Tests *Required:* SAT or ACT (for admission).

Costs (2013–14) *Comprehensive fee:* $34,470 includes full-time tuition ($25,220) and room and board ($9250). Full-time tuition and fees vary according to course load. Part-time tuition: $850 per credit. Part-time tuition and fees vary according to course load. *Room and board:* Room and board charges vary according to board plan. *Payment plan:* installment. *Waivers:* employees or children of employees.

Financial Aid Of all full-time matriculated undergraduates who enrolled in 2012, 1,275 applied for aid, 1,170 were judged to have need, 193 had their need fully met. 260 Federal Work-Study jobs (averaging $2000). In 2012, 194 non-need-based awards were made. *Average percent of need met:* 75%. *Average financial aid package:* $19,077. *Average need-based loan:* $4076. *Average need-based gift aid:* $14,897. *Average non-need-based aid:* $9510. *Average indebtedness upon graduation:* $26,883.

Applying *Options:* electronic application, early admission, early action, deferred entrance. *Application fee:* $40. *Required:* essay or personal statement, high school transcript, minimum 2.0 GPA. *Required for some:* interview. *Recommended:* minimum 3.0 GPA, 2 letters of recommendation, interview. *Application deadlines:* rolling (freshmen), rolling (transfers). *Notification:* continuous (freshmen), continuous (transfers).

Freshman Application Contact Mr. David Layton, Associate Vice President for Enrollment, Geneva College, 3200 College Avenue, Beaver Falls, PA 15010-3599. *Phone:* 724-847-6500. *Toll-free phone:* 800-847-8255. *E-mail:* admissions@geneva.edu.
Website: http://www.geneva.edu/.

Gettysburg College

Gettysburg, Pennsylvania

- **Independent** 4-year, founded 1832, affiliated with Evangelical Lutheran Church in America
- **Suburban** 200-acre campus with easy access to Baltimore and Washington, DC
- **Endowment** $231.5 million
- **Coed** 2,597 undergraduate students, 99% full-time, 53% women, 47% men
- **Most difficult** entrance level, 40% of applicants were admitted

Undergraduates 2,573 full-time, 24 part-time. Students come from 37 states and territories; 31 other countries; 73% are from out of state; 3% Black or African American, non-Hispanic/Latino; 4% Hispanic/Latino; 2% Asian, non-Hispanic/Latino; 2% Two or more races, non-Hispanic/Latino; 6% Race/ethnicity unknown; 2% international; 0.5% transferred in; 92% live on campus. *Retention:* 91% of full-time freshmen returned.

Freshmen *Admission:* 5,620 applied, 2,264 admitted, 769 enrolled. *Test scores:* SAT critical reading scores over 500: 100%; SAT math scores over 500: 100%; SAT critical reading scores over 600: 82%; SAT math scores over 600: 84%; SAT critical reading scores over 700: 18%; SAT math scores over 700: 15%.

Faculty *Total:* 312, 71% full-time, 78% with terminal degrees. *Student/faculty ratio:* 10:1.

Academics *Calendar:* semesters. *Degree:* bachelor's. *Special study options:* adult/continuing education programs, advanced placement credit, double majors, independent study, internships, off-campus study, student-designed majors, study abroad. *ROTC:* Army (c). *Unusual degree programs:* 3-2 engineering with Rensselaer Polytechnic Institute, Washington University, Columbia University; forestry with Duke University; nursing with Johns Hopkins University; Optometry with State University of New York College of Optometry, Pennsylvania College of Optometry; physical therapy at Drexel University.

Computers on Campus 291 computers/terminals are available on campus for general student use. Students can access the following: campus intranet, computer help desk, free student e-mail accounts, online (class) grades, online (class) registration, online (class) schedules. Campuswide network is available. 100% of college-owned or -operated housing units are wired for high-speed Internet access. Wireless service is available via entire campus.

Student Life *Housing:* on-campus residence required through senior year. *Options:* coed, men-only, women-only. Campus housing is university owned. Freshman campus housing is guaranteed. *Activities and organizations:* drama/theater group, student-run newspaper, radio and television station, choral group, marching band, community service, music, athletics, student government, national fraternities, national sororities. *Campus security:* 24-hour emergency response devices and patrols, late-night transport/escort service, controlled dormitory access. *Student services:* health clinic, personal/psychological counseling, women's center.

Athletics Member NCAA. All Division III. *Intercollegiate sports:* baseball M, basketball M/W, cheerleading M/W, cross-country running M/W, equestrian sports M(c)/W(c), field hockey W, football M, golf M/W, ice hockey M(c), lacrosse M/W, rugby M(c)/W(c), soccer M/W, softball W, swimming and diving M/W, tennis M/W, track and field M/W, ultimate Frisbee M(c)/W(c), volleyball W, wrestling M. *Intramural sports:* basketball M/W, fencing M(c)/W(c), football M/W, soccer M/W, softball M/W, tennis M/W, volleyball M/W, water polo M/W.

Standardized Tests *Required:* SAT or ACT (for admission). *Recommended:* SAT Subject Tests (for admission).

Costs (2012–13) *Comprehensive fee:* $54,770 includes full-time tuition ($44,210) and room and board ($10,560). *Room and board:* Room and board charges vary according to board plan and housing facility.

Financial Aid Of all full-time matriculated undergraduates who enrolled in 2012, 1,804 applied for aid, 1,570 were judged to have need, 1,436 had their need fully met. 549 Federal Work-Study jobs (averaging $670). 804 state and other part-time jobs (averaging $1553). In 2012, 364 non-need-based awards were made. *Average percent of need met:* 95%. *Average financial aid package:* $33,215. *Average need-based loan:* $5392. *Average need-based gift aid:* $27,550. *Average non-need-based aid:* $13,444. *Average indebtedness upon graduation:* $25,530. *Financial aid deadline:* 2/15.

Applying *Options:* electronic application, early admission, early decision, deferred entrance. *Application fee:* $60. *Required:* essay or personal statement, high school transcript, 2 letters of recommendation. *Recommended:* minimum 3.0 GPA, interview, extracurricular activities. *Application deadlines:* 2/1 (freshmen), 11/1 (transfers). *Early decision deadline:* 11/15 (for plan 1), 1/15 (for plan 2). *Notification:* 4/1 (freshmen), continuous (transfers), 12/15 (early decision plan 1), 2/15 (early decision plan 2).

Freshman Application Contact Ms. Gail Sweezey, Director of Admissions, Gettysburg College, 300 North Washington Street, Gettysburg, PA 17325. *Phone:* 717-337-6100. *Toll-free phone:* 800-431-0803. *Fax:* 717-337-6145. *E-mail:* admiss@gettysburg.edu.
Website: http://www.gettysburg.edu/.

Grove City College

Grove City, Pennsylvania

- **Independent Presbyterian** 4-year, founded 1876
- **Small-town** 180-acre campus with easy access to Pittsburgh
- **Endowment** $92.3 million
- **Coed** 2,506 undergraduate students, 99% full-time, 50% women, 50% men
- **Moderately difficult** entrance level, 84% of applicants were admitted

Undergraduates 2,469 full-time, 37 part-time. Students come from 45 states and territories; 8 other countries; 54% are from out of state; 0.8% Black or African American, non-Hispanic/Latino; 1% Hispanic/Latino; 2% Asian, non-Hispanic/Latino; 0.3% American Indian or Alaska Native, non-Hispanic/Latino; 1% Two or more races, non-Hispanic/Latino; 0.8% international; 1% transferred in; 94% live on campus. *Retention:* 91% of full-time freshmen returned.

Freshmen *Admission:* 1,481 applied, 1,247 admitted, 670 enrolled. *Average high school GPA:* 3.76. *Test scores:* SAT critical reading scores over 500: 94%; SAT math scores over 500: 94%; ACT scores over 18: 100%; SAT critical reading scores over 600: 61%; SAT math scores over 600: 59%; ACT scores over 24: 84%; SAT critical reading scores over 700: 15%; SAT math scores over 700: 13%; ACT scores over 30: 24%.

Faculty *Total:* 228, 58% full-time, 64% with terminal degrees. *Student/faculty ratio:* 15:1.

Academics *Calendar:* semesters. *Degree:* bachelor's. *Special study options:* advanced placement credit, distance learning, double majors, independent study, internships, off-campus study, services for LD students, study abroad, summer session for credit. *ROTC:* Army (c). *Unusual degree programs:* 3-2 Lake Erie College of Osteopathic Medicine: Doctor of Osteopathy Program.

Computers on Campus 50 computers/terminals and 8,000 ports are available on campus for general student use. Students can access the following: campus intranet, computer help desk, free student e-mail accounts, online (class) grades, online (class) registration, online (class) schedules. Campuswide network is available. 100% of college-owned or -operated housing units are wired for high-speed Internet access. Wireless service is available via entire campus.

Student Life *Housing:* on-campus residence required through senior year. *Options:* men-only, women-only. Campus housing is university owned. Freshman campus housing is guaranteed. *Activities and organizations:* drama/theater group, student-run newspaper, radio and television station, choral group, marching band, Salt Company, Warriors for Christ, Orientation Board, Orchesis, Touring Choir. *Campus security:* 24-hour emergency response devices and patrols, student patrols, late-night transport/escort service, controlled dormitory access, security cameras located around campus and in parking lots. *Student services:* health clinic, personal/psychological counseling.

Athletics Member NCAA. All Division III. *Intercollegiate sports:* baseball M, basketball M/W, cheerleading W, cross-country running M/W, fencing M(c)/W(c), field hockey M(c)/W(c), football M, golf M/W, lacrosse M(c)/W(c), rugby M(c)/W(c), soccer M/W, softball W, swimming and diving M/W, tennis M/W, track and field M/W, volleyball M(c)/W(c), water polo M(c)/W. *Intramural sports:* badminton M/W, basketball M/W, bowling M/W, football M, golf M/W, racquetball M/W, soccer M/W, softball M/W, table tennis M/W, tennis M/W, ultimate Frisbee M/W, volleyball M/W.

Standardized Tests *Required:* SAT or ACT (for admission).

Costs (2013–14) *Comprehensive fee:* $22,988 includes full-time tuition ($14,880) and room and board ($8108). Full-time tuition and fees vary according to course load. Part-time tuition: $465 per credit. *Room and board:* Room and board charges vary according to housing facility. *Payment plan:* installment. *Waivers:* employees or children of employees.

Financial Aid Of all full-time matriculated undergraduates who enrolled in 2012, 1,321 applied for aid, 1,066 were judged to have need, 83 had their need fully met. In 2012, 289 non-need-based awards were made. *Average percent of need met:* 46%. *Average financial aid package:* $6122. *Average need-based gift aid:* $6122. *Average non-need-based aid:* $2034. *Average indebtedness upon graduation:* $28,767. *Financial aid deadline:* 4/15.

Applying *Options:* electronic application, early admission, early decision, deferred entrance. *Application fee:* $50. *Required:* essay or personal statement, high school transcript, 2 letters of recommendation. *Recommended:* interview. *Application deadlines:* 2/1 (freshmen), 8/15 (transfers). *Early decision deadline:* 11/15. *Notification:* 3/15 (freshmen), continuous (transfers), 12/15 (early decision).

Freshman Application Contact Sarah E. Gibbs, Director of Admissions, Grove City College, 100 Campus Drive, Grove City, PA 16127-2104. *Phone:* 724-458-2100. *Fax:* 724-458-3395. *E-mail:* admissions@gcc.edu. *Website:* http://www.gcc.edu/.

See below for display ad and page 1310 for the College Close-Up.

Gwynedd-Mercy College

Gwynedd Valley, Pennsylvania

- **Independent Roman Catholic** comprehensive, founded 1948
- **Suburban** 170-acre campus with easy access to Philadelphia
- **Endowment** $7.4 million
- **Coed**
- **Moderately difficult** entrance level

Faculty *Student/faculty ratio:* 16:1.

Academics *Calendar:* semesters. *Degrees:* certificates, associate, bachelor's, master's, post-master's, and postbachelor's certificates.

Student Life *Campus security:* 24-hour emergency response devices and patrols, late-night transport/escort service.

Athletics Member NCAA. All Division III.

Standardized Tests *Required:* SAT or ACT (for admission).

Costs (2012–13) *Comprehensive fee:* $38,190 includes full-time tuition ($27,740), mandatory fees ($600), and room and board ($9850). Full-time tuition and fees vary according to program. Part-time tuition: $600 per credit hour. Part-time tuition and fees vary according to program. *Room and board:* Room and board charges vary according to board plan and housing facility.

Financial Aid Of all full-time matriculated undergraduates who enrolled in 2012, 1,390 applied for aid, 1,208 were judged to have need, 201 had their need fully met. In 2012, 186 non-need-based awards were made. *Average percent of need met:* 65. *Average financial aid package:* $18,628. *Average need-based loan:* $4073. *Average need-based gift aid:* $15,288. *Average non-need-based aid:* $10,165. *Average indebtedness upon graduation:* $36,067. *Financial aid deadline:* 5/1.

Applying *Options:* electronic application, deferred entrance. *Application fee:* $25. *Required:* high school transcript. *Required for some:* essay or personal statement, interview.

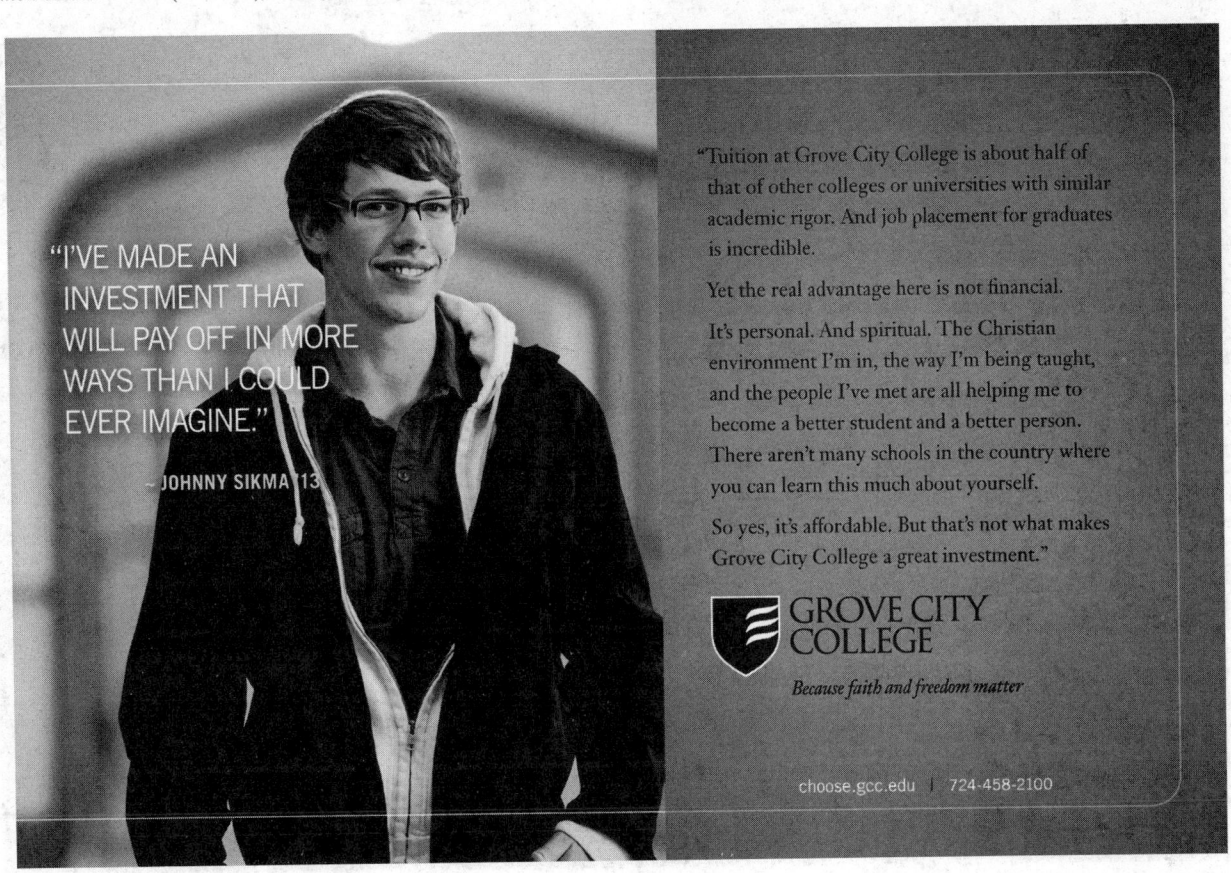

Freshman Application Contact Ms. Michelle Diehl, Director of Admissions, Gwynedd-Mercy College, 1325 Sumneytown Pike, Gwynedd Valley, PA 19437-0901. *Phone:* 215-646-7300. *Toll-free phone:* 800-DIAL-GMC. *Fax:* 215-641-5556. *E-mail:* admissions@gmc.edu.
Website: http://www.gmc.edu/.

See below for display ad and page 1312 for the College Close-Up.

Harrisburg University of Science and Technology

Harrisburg, Pennsylvania

- **Independent** comprehensive, founded 2005
- **Urban** campus
- **Coed**
- **Minimally difficult** entrance level

Faculty *Student/faculty ratio:* 11:1.

Academics *Calendar:* semesters. *Degrees:* certificates, bachelor's, master's, and postbachelor's certificates.

Student Life *Campus security:* 24-hour emergency response devices and patrols, trained security personnel during all university operating hours.

Standardized Tests *Recommended:* SAT or ACT (for admission).

Costs (2012–13) *Tuition:* $23,900 full-time, $1000 per credit hour part-time. Full-time tuition and fees vary according to degree level. Part-time tuition and fees vary according to course load and degree level. *Room only:* $6340. Room and board charges vary according to housing facility. *Payment plans:* installment, deferred payment.

Financial Aid *Of all full-time matriculated undergraduates who enrolled in 2012,* 267 applied for aid, 251 were judged to have need, 13 had their need fully met. 16 Federal Work-Study jobs (averaging $1500). *In 2012,* 13 non-need-based awards were made. *Average percent of need met:* 57. *Average financial aid package:* $17,502. *Average need-based loan:* $5075. *Average need-based gift aid:* $13,330. *Average non-need-based aid:* $10,473. *Average indebtedness upon graduation:* $38,779.

Applying *Options:* electronic application. *Required:* high school transcript. *Recommended:* essay or personal statement, interview.

Freshman Application Contact Harrisburg University of Science and Technology, 326 Market Street, Harrisburg, PA 17101. *Phone:* 717-901-5158. *Toll-free phone:* 866-HBG-UNIV.
Website: http://www.HarrisburgU.edu/.

Haverford College

Haverford, Pennsylvania

- **Independent** 4-year, founded 1833
- **Suburban** 200-acre campus with easy access to Philadelphia
- **Endowment** $387.6 million
- **Coed** 1,205 undergraduate students, 100% full-time, 53% women, 47% men
- **Most difficult** entrance level, 23% of applicants were admitted

Undergraduates 1,205 full-time. Students come from 44 states and territories; 42 other countries; 86% are from out of state; 6% Black or African American, non-Hispanic/Latino; 9% Hispanic/Latino; 7% Asian, non-Hispanic/Latino; 0.2% American Indian or Alaska Native, non-Hispanic/Latino; 6% Two or more races, non-Hispanic/Latino; 4% international; 0.4% transferred in; 99% live on campus. *Retention:* 96% of full-time freshmen returned.

Freshmen *Admission:* 3,626 applied, 830 admitted, 323 enrolled. *Test scores:* SAT critical reading scores over 500: 100%; SAT math scores over 500: 100%; SAT writing scores over 500: 100%; SAT critical reading scores over 600: 92%; SAT math scores over 600: 92%; SAT writing scores over 600: 94%; SAT critical reading scores over 700: 53%; SAT math scores over 700: 55%; SAT writing scores over 700: 60%.

Faculty *Total:* 138, 86% full-time, 93% with terminal degrees. *Student/faculty ratio:* 8:1.

Academics *Calendar:* semesters. *Degree:* bachelor's. *Special study options:* advanced placement credit, double majors, independent study, internships, off-campus study, services for LD students, student-designed majors, study abroad. *Unusual degree programs:* 3-2 engineering with California Institute of Technology, University of Pennsylvania.

Computers on Campus 300 computers/terminals and 1,600 ports are available on campus for general student use. Students can access the following: campus intranet, computer help desk, free student e-mail accounts, online (class) grades, online (class) registration, online (class) schedules. Campuswide network is available. 100% of college-owned or -operated housing units

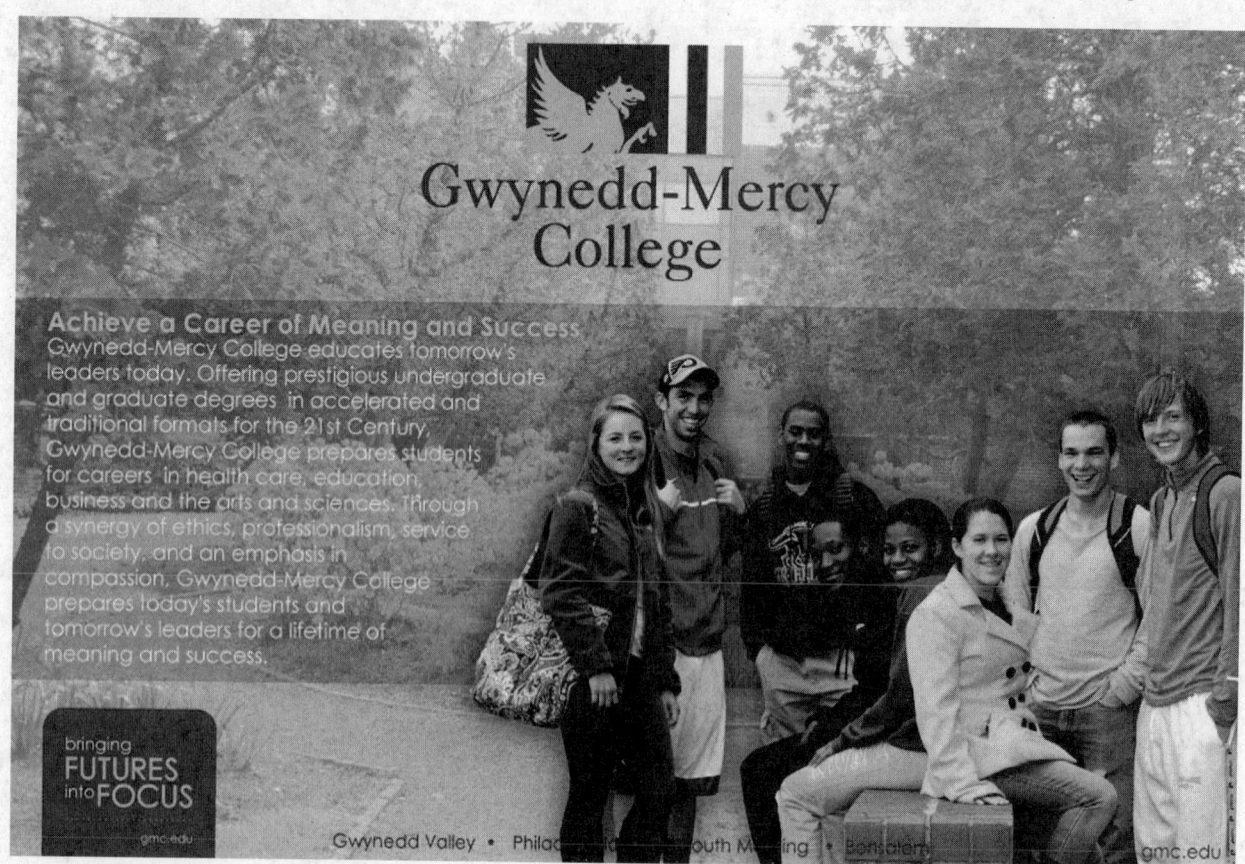

are wired for high-speed Internet access. Wireless service is available via entire campus.

Student Life *Housing:* on-campus residence required for freshman year. *Options:* coed, disabled students. Campus housing is university owned. Freshman campus housing is guaranteed. *Activities and organizations:* drama/theater group, student-run newspaper, radio station, choral group, Volunteer Programs, Student government, Choral groups, Multicultural Groups, Orientation Team/Residential Life Leaders. *Campus security:* 24-hour emergency response devices and patrols, late-night transport/escort service, controlled dormitory access. *Student services:* health clinic, personal/psychological counseling, women's center.

Athletics Member NCAA. All Division III. *Intercollegiate sports:* badminton W(c), baseball M, basketball M/W, crew M(c)/W(c), cross-country running M/W, fencing M/W, field hockey W, golf M(c)/W(c), lacrosse M/W, rugby M(c), soccer M/W, softball W, squash M/W, tennis M/W, track and field M/W, ultimate Frisbee M(c)/W(c), volleyball M(c)/W, wrestling M(c). *Intramural sports:* basketball M/W, ice hockey M(c)/W(c), sailing M(c)/W(c), soccer M/W, softball M/W, tennis M/W, volleyball W.

Standardized Tests *Required:* SAT and SAT Subject Tests or ACT (for admission).

Costs (2012–13) *One-time required fee:* $210. *Comprehensive fee:* $56,992 includes full-time tuition ($43,310), mandatory fees ($392), and room and board ($13,290). *College room only:* $7570. *Payment plans:* tuition prepayment, installment. *Waivers:* employees or children of employees.

Financial Aid Of all full-time matriculated undergraduates who enrolled in 2012, 620 applied for aid, 604 were judged to have need, 604 had their need fully met. *Average percent of need met:* 100%. *Average financial aid package:* $40,321. *Average need-based loan:* $955. *Average need-based gift aid:* $39,702. *Average indebtedness upon graduation:* $14,171. *Financial aid deadline:* 2/1.

Applying *Options:* electronic application, early admission, early decision, deferred entrance. *Application fee:* $60. *Required:* essay or personal statement, 2 letters of recommendation. *Required for some:* high school transcript. *Recommended:* interview. *Application deadlines:* 1/15 (freshmen), 3/31 (transfers). *Early decision deadline:* 11/15. *Notification:* 4/15 (freshmen), 6/1 (transfers), 12/15 (early decision).

Freshman Application Contact Mr. Jess Lord, Dean of Admissions and Financial Aid, Haverford College, 370 Lancaster Avenue, Haverford, PA 19041-1392. *Phone:* 610-896-1350. *Fax:* 610-896-1338. *E-mail:* admitme@haverford.edu.
Website: http://www.haverford.edu/.

See below for display ad and page 1316 for the College Close-Up.

Holy Family University

Philadelphia, Pennsylvania

- **Independent Roman Catholic** comprehensive, founded 1954
- **Suburban** 47-acre campus with easy access to Philadelphia
- **Endowment** $11.5 million
- **Coed** 2,139 undergraduate students, 72% full-time, 75% women, 25% men
- **Minimally difficult** entrance level, 67% of applicants were admitted

Undergraduates 1,544 full-time, 595 part-time. Students come from 16 states and territories; 9 other countries; 18% are from out of state; 8% Black or African American, non-Hispanic/Latino; 6% Hispanic/Latino; 4% Asian, non-Hispanic/Latino; 0.2% American Indian or Alaska Native, non-Hispanic/Latino; 18% Race/ethnicity unknown; 0.5% international; 8% transferred in; 17% live on campus. *Retention:* 76% of full-time freshmen returned.

Freshmen *Admission:* 1,400 applied, 940 admitted, 312 enrolled. *Average high school GPA:* 3.06. *Test scores:* SAT critical reading scores over 500: 29%; SAT math scores over 500: 36%; SAT writing scores over 500: 33%; ACT scores over 18: 88%; SAT critical reading scores over 600: 4%; SAT math scores over 600: 5%; SAT writing scores over 600: 4%; ACT scores over 24: 6%.

Faculty *Total:* 375, 25% full-time, 36% with terminal degrees. *Student/faculty ratio:* 12:1.

Academics *Calendar:* semesters. *Degrees:* certificates, associate, bachelor's, master's, doctoral, post-master's, and postbachelor's certificates. *Special study options:* academic remediation for entering students, accelerated degree program, adult/continuing education programs, advanced placement credit, cooperative education, double majors, English as a second language, freshman honors college, honors programs, independent study, internships, part-time degree program, services for LD students, study abroad, summer session for credit. *Unusual degree programs:* 3-2 Criminal Justice BA/MA Program; Psychology BA/Criminal Justice MA Program; Sociology BA/Criminal Justice

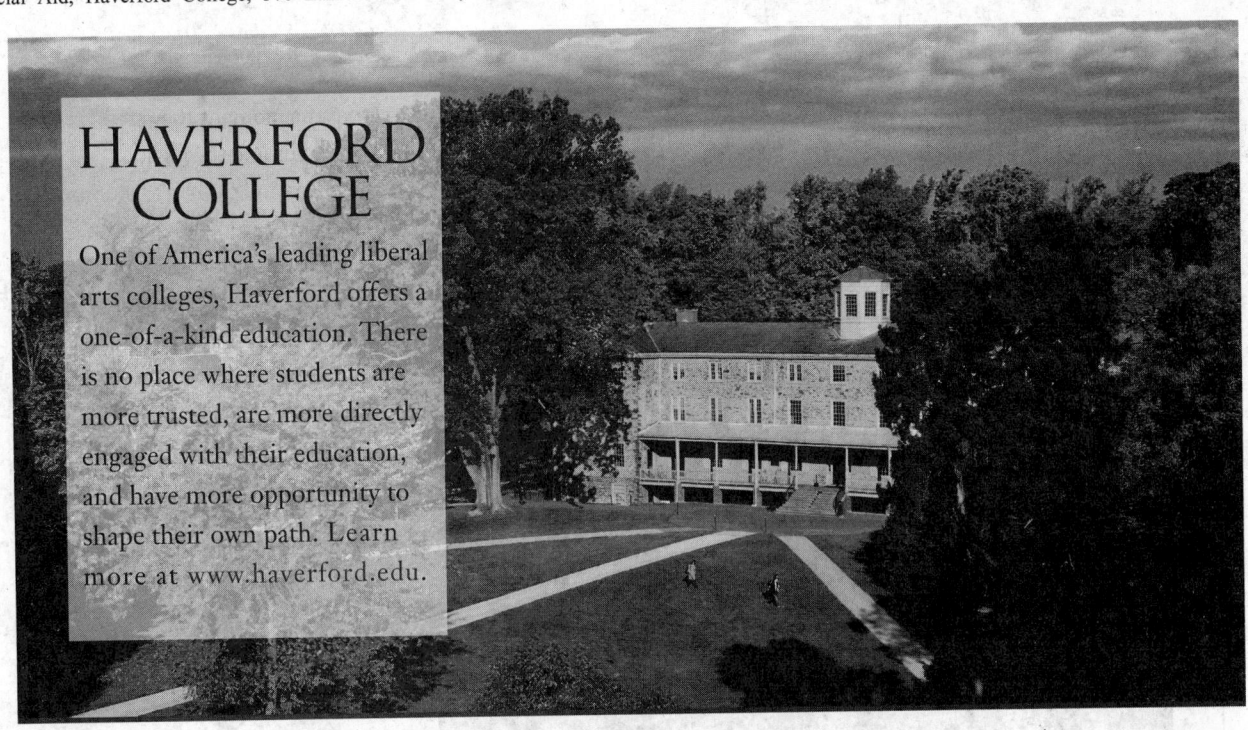

Program; Business Administration BA/Human Resources Management or Information Systems Management MS.

Computers on Campus 350 computers/terminals are available on campus for general student use. Students can access the following: campus intranet, computer help desk, free student e-mail accounts, online (class) grades, online (class) registration, online (class) schedules. Campuswide network is available. 100% of college-owned or -operated housing units are wired for high-speed Internet access. Wireless service is available via entire campus.

Student Life *Housing options:* coed, cooperative, disabled students. Campus housing is university owned. Freshman applicants given priority for college housing. *Activities and organizations:* drama/theater group, student-run newspaper, television station, choral group, Students at Your Service (S.A.Y.S.), student government, Campus Ministry Team, Habitat for Humanity, Tri-lite. *Campus security:* 24-hour emergency response devices and patrols, late-night transport/escort service, controlled dormitory access, video surveillance. *Student services:* health clinic, personal/psychological counseling.

Athletics Member NCAA. All Division II. *Intercollegiate sports:* basketball M(s)/W(s), cheerleading W(c), cross-country running M(s)/W(s), golf M(s), lacrosse W(s), rugby M(c), skiing (downhill) M(c)/W(c), soccer M(s)(c)/W(s)(c), softball W(s), swimming and diving M(c)/W(c), tennis W(s), track and field M(s)/W(s), volleyball W(s). *Intramural sports:* basketball M/W, football M, volleyball M/W.

Standardized Tests *Required:* SAT or ACT (for admission).

Costs (2012–13) *Comprehensive fee:* $37,940 includes full-time tuition ($24,940), mandatory fees ($650), and room and board ($12,350). Full-time tuition and fees vary according to course load and program. Part-time tuition: $535 per credit hour. Part-time tuition and fees vary according to course load and program. *Required fees:* $60 per term part-time. *College room only:* $6650. Room and board charges vary according to board plan and housing facility. *Payment plans:* installment, deferred payment. *Waivers:* senior citizens and employees or children of employees.

Financial Aid Of all full-time matriculated undergraduates who enrolled in 2011, 1,491 applied for aid, 1,365 were judged to have need, 250 had their need fully met. 291 Federal Work-Study jobs (averaging $1252). In 2011, 73 non-need-based awards were made. *Average percent of need met:* 71%. *Average financial aid package:* $17,079. *Average need-based loan:* $4444. *Average need-based gift aid:* $12,694. *Average non-need-based aid:* $7254. *Average indebtedness upon graduation:* $33,962.

Applying *Options:* electronic application, deferred entrance. *Application fee:* $25. *Required:* essay or personal statement, high school transcript, minimum 2.0 GPA, 2 letters of recommendation. *Recommended:* interview. *Application*

deadlines: rolling (freshmen), rolling (out-of-state freshmen), rolling (transfers). *Notification:* continuous (freshmen), continuous (out-of-state freshmen), continuous (transfers).

Freshman Application Contact Ms. Lauren Campbell, Director of Admissions, Holy Family University, 9801 Frankford Avenue, Philadelphia, PA 19114-2009. *Phone:* 215-637-3050. *Fax:* 215-281-1022. *E-mail:* admissions@holyfamily.edu.
Website: http://www.holyfamily.edu/.

See below for display ad and page 1326 for the College Close-Up.

Immaculata University
Immaculata, Pennsylvania

- **Independent Roman Catholic** comprehensive, founded 1920
- **Suburban** 400-acre campus with easy access to Philadelphia
- **Coed, primarily women** 2,883 undergraduate students, 41% full-time, 79% women, 21% men
- **Moderately difficult** entrance level, 80% of applicants were admitted

Undergraduates 1,175 full-time, 1,708 part-time. 21% are from out of state; 16% Black or African American, non-Hispanic/Latino; 4% Hispanic/Latino; 3% Asian, non-Hispanic/Latino; 0.1% Native Hawaiian or other Pacific Islander, non-Hispanic/Latino; 0.1% American Indian or Alaska Native, non-Hispanic/Latino; 2% Two or more races, non-Hispanic/Latino; 2% Race/ethnicity unknown; 0.5% international; 2% transferred in; 19% live on campus. *Retention:* 80% of full-time freshmen returned.

Freshmen *Admission:* 1,650 applied, 1,314 admitted, 247 enrolled. *Average high school GPA:* 3.23. *Test scores:* SAT critical reading scores over 500: 39%; SAT math scores over 500: 40%; SAT writing scores over 500: 39%; ACT scores over 18: 76%; SAT critical reading scores over 600: 5%; SAT math scores over 600: 9%; SAT writing scores over 600: 8%; ACT scores over 24: 17%; SAT writing scores over 700: 1%.

Faculty *Total:* 426, 24% full-time. *Student/faculty ratio:* 10:1.

Academics *Calendar:* semesters. *Degrees:* certificates, associate, bachelor's, master's, and doctoral. *ROTC:* Army (c).

Computers on Campus Campuswide network is available.

Student Life *Housing options:* coed, men-only, women-only, disabled students. Campus housing is university owned. Freshman campus housing is guaranteed. *Campus security:* 24-hour emergency response devices and patrols, late-night transport/escort service, controlled dormitory access.

Athletics Member NCAA. All Division III. *Intercollegiate sports:* basketball W, cross-country running W, field hockey W, lacrosse W, soccer W, softball W, tennis W, volleyball W. *Intramural sports:* archery W, badminton W, cheerleading W(c), equestrian sports W(c), fencing W, swimming and diving W.

Standardized Tests *Required:* SAT or ACT (for admission).

Costs (2012–13) *Comprehensive fee:* $40,740 includes full-time tuition ($29,000) and room and board ($11,740). Full-time tuition and fees vary according to student level. Part-time tuition: $470 per credit hour. No tuition increase for student's term of enrollment. *College room only:* $6280. Room and board charges vary according to board plan and housing facility. *Payment plan:* installment. *Waivers:* senior citizens and employees or children of employees.

Financial Aid Of all full-time matriculated undergraduates who enrolled in 2007, 810 applied for aid, 697 were judged to have need, 201 had their need fully met. *Average percent of need met:* 24%. *Average financial aid package:* $15,657. *Average need-based loan:* $4132. *Average need-based gift aid:* $5516. *Average non-need-based aid:* $6508.

Applying *Options:* electronic application. *Application fee:* $35. *Required:* high school transcript, minimum 2.0 GPA. *Required for some:* essay or personal statement. *Recommended:* minimum 3.0 GPA, interview. *Application deadlines:* rolling (freshmen), rolling (transfers). *Notification:* continuous (freshmen), continuous (transfers).

Freshman Application Contact Director of Admissions, Immaculata University, PO Box 642, Immaculata, PA 19345-0702. *Phone:* 610-647-4400 Ext. 3046. *Toll-free phone:* 877-428-6329. *Fax:* 610-640-0836. *E-mail:* admiss@immaculata.edu.
Website: http://www.immaculata.edu/.

Indiana University of Pennsylvania

Indiana, Pennsylvania

- **State-supported** university, founded 1875, part of Pennsylvania State System of Higher Education
- **Small-town** 374-acre campus with easy access to Pittsburgh
- **Endowment** $47.9 million
- **Coed** 13,058 undergraduate students, 93% full-time, 55% women, 45% men
- **Moderately difficult** entrance level, 61% of applicants were admitted

Undergraduates 12,195 full-time, 863 part-time. Students come from 38 states and territories; 43 other countries; 7% are from out of state; 11% Black or African American, non-Hispanic/Latino; 3% Hispanic/Latino; 0.9% Asian, non-Hispanic/Latino; 0.1% American Indian or Alaska Native, non-Hispanic/Latino; 2% Two or more races, non-Hispanic/Latino; 2% Race/ethnicity unknown; 2% international; 5% transferred in; 83% live on campus. *Retention:* 75% of full-time freshmen returned.

Freshmen *Admission:* 12,333 applied, 7,527 admitted, 2,934 enrolled. *Test scores:* SAT critical reading scores over 500: 45%; SAT math scores over 500: 50%; SAT writing scores over 500: 39%; SAT critical reading scores over 600: 8%; SAT math scores over 600: 10%; SAT writing scores over 600: 6%; SAT critical reading scores over 700: 1%; SAT math scores over 700: 1%.

Faculty *Total:* 708, 88% full-time. *Student/faculty ratio:* 18:1.

Academics *Calendar:* semesters. *Degrees:* certificates, associate, bachelor's, master's, doctoral, post-master's, and postbachelor's certificates. *Special study options:* academic remediation for entering students, accelerated degree program, adult/continuing education programs, advanced placement credit, cooperative education, distance learning, double majors, English as a second language, external degree program, freshman honors college, honors programs, independent study, internships, off-campus study, part-time degree program, services for LD students, study abroad, summer session for credit. *ROTC:* Army (b). *Unusual degree programs:* 3-2 engineering with Drexel University, University of Pittsburgh; Chiropractic with Logan College of Chiropractic, New York Chiropractic College, Parker College, Sherman College of Straight Chiropractic & Palmer College of Chiropractic; Dentistry with Temple University School of Dentistry; optometry with Pennsylvania College of Optometry.

Computers on Campus 2,363 computers/terminals and 2,047 ports are available on campus for general student use. Students can access the following: computer help desk, free student e-mail accounts, online (class) grades, online (class) registration, online (class) schedules. Campuswide network is available. 100% of college-owned or -operated housing units are wired for high-speed Internet access. Wireless service is available via entire campus.

Student Life *Housing:* on-campus residence required for freshman year. *Options:* coed, women-only, disabled students. Campus housing is university owned and is provided by a third party. Freshman campus housing is guaranteed. *Activities and organizations:* drama/theater group, student-run newspaper, radio and television station, choral group, marching band, Student Government Association, Panhellenic Association, Interfraternity Council, Amplify, NAACP, national fraternities, national sororities. *Campus security:* 24-hour emergency response devices and patrols, late-night transport/escort service, controlled dormitory access. *Student services:* health clinic, personal/psychological counseling, legal services.

Athletics Member NCAA. All Division II. *Intercollegiate sports:* baseball M(s), basketball M(s)/W(s), cross-country running M(s)/W(s), field hockey W(s), football M(s), golf M(s), lacrosse W(s), soccer W(s), softball W(s), swimming and diving M(s)/W(s), tennis W(s), track and field M(s)/W(s), volleyball W(s). *Intramural sports:* basketball M/W, bowling M/W, cheerleading M(c)/W(c), equestrian sports M(c)/W(c), fencing M(c)/W(c), golf M/W, gymnastics M(c)/W(c), ice hockey M(c)/W(c), lacrosse M(c), racquetball M/W, riflery M(c)/W(c), rugby M(c)/W(c), sailing M(c)/W(c), skiing (downhill) M(c)/W(c), soccer M/W, softball M/W, swimming and diving M(c)/W(c), tennis M(c)/W(c), track and field M/W, ultimate Frisbee M(c)/W(c), volleyball M(c)/W, wrestling M(c)/W(c).

Standardized Tests *Required:* SAT or ACT (for admission).

Costs (2012–13) *Tuition:* state resident $6428 full-time, $268 per credit hour part-time; nonresident $16,070 full-time, $670 per credit hour part-time. Full-time tuition and fees vary according to course load and reciprocity agreements. Part-time tuition and fees vary according to course load and reciprocity agreements. *Required fees:* $2244 full-time, $52 per credit hour part-time, $203 per term part-time. *Room and board:* $10,466; room only: $7740. Room and board charges vary according to board plan, housing facility, and location. *Payment plans:* installment, deferred payment. *Waivers:* senior citizens and employees or children of employees.

Financial Aid Of all full-time matriculated undergraduates who enrolled in 2011, 10,488 applied for aid, 8,789 were judged to have need, 389 had their need fully met. 1,003 Federal Work-Study jobs (averaging $2063). 1,650 state and other part-time jobs (averaging $2625). In 2011, 202 non-need-based awards were made. *Average percent of need met:* 57%. *Average financial aid package:* $9083. *Average need-based loan:* $4146. *Average need-based gift aid:* $5547. *Average non-need-based aid:* $1640. *Average indebtedness upon graduation:* $35,229. *Financial aid deadline:* 4/25.

Applying *Options:* electronic application, early admission, deferred entrance. *Application fee:* $50. *Required:* high school transcript. *Recommended:* essay or personal statement, 2 letters of recommendation. *Application deadlines:* rolling (freshmen), rolling (transfers). *Notification:* 9/1 (freshmen), continuous (transfers).

Freshman Application Contact Office of Admissions, Indiana University of Pennsylvania, 1011 South Drive, Sutton Hall 214, Indiana, PA 15705. *Phone:* 724-357-2230. *Toll-free phone:* 800-442-6830. *Fax:* 724-357-6281. *E-mail:* admissions-inquiry@iup.edu.
Website: http://www.iup.edu/.

Juniata College

Huntingdon, Pennsylvania

- **Independent** comprehensive, founded 1876, affiliated with Church of the Brethren
- **Small-town** 110-acre campus
- **Endowment** $77.4 million
- **Coed** 1,558 undergraduate students, 96% full-time, 55% women, 45% men
- **Moderately difficult** entrance level, 66% of applicants were admitted

Undergraduates 1,500 full-time, 58 part-time. Students come from 30 states and territories; 43 other countries; 30% are from out of state; 3% Black or African American, non-Hispanic/Latino; 4% Hispanic/Latino; 2% Asian, non-Hispanic/Latino; 0.3% American Indian or Alaska Native, non-Hispanic/Latino; 2% Two or more races, non-Hispanic/Latino; 2% Race/ethnicity unknown; 9% international; 2% transferred in; 81% live on campus. *Retention:* 90% of full-time freshmen returned.

Freshmen *Admission:* 2,418 applied, 1,605 admitted, 402 enrolled. *Average high school GPA:* 3.81. *Test scores:* SAT critical reading scores over 500: 90%; SAT math scores over 500: 90%; SAT critical reading scores over 600: 48%; SAT math scores over 600: 49%; SAT critical reading scores over 700: 7%; SAT math scores over 700: 11%.

Faculty *Total:* 143, 73% full-time, 69% with terminal degrees. *Student/faculty ratio:* 13:1.

Academics *Calendar:* semesters. *Degrees:* bachelor's and master's. *Special study options:* accelerated degree program, advanced placement credit, double majors, English as a second language, independent study, internships, off-campus study, part-time degree program, services for LD students, student-designed majors, study abroad, summer session for credit. *Unusual degree programs:* 3-2 engineering with Columbia University, Penn State University, Washington University-St. Louis, Clarkson University; nursing with Case Western University, Johns Hopkins University.

Computers on Campus 340 computers/terminals and 500 ports are available on campus for general student use. Students can access the following: computer help desk, free student e-mail accounts, online (class) grades, online (class) registration, online (class) schedules. Campuswide network is available. 100% of college-owned or -operated housing units are wired for high-speed Internet access. Wireless service is available via classrooms, computer centers, computer labs, dorm rooms, learning centers, libraries, student centers.

Student Life *Housing:* on-campus residence required through senior year. *Options:* coed, women-only. Campus housing is university owned. Freshman campus housing is guaranteed. *Activities and organizations:* drama/theater group, student-run newspaper, radio and television station, choral group, Student Government Association, Juniata Activities Board (JAB), Colleges Against Cancer, Habitat for Humanity, Model UN. *Campus security:* 24-hour emergency response devices and patrols, student patrols, late-night transport/escort service, controlled dormitory access, fire safety training, adopt-an-officer program, security web site, weather/terror alerts, travel forecast, crime statistics. *Student services:* health clinic, personal/psychological counseling, women's center.

Athletics Member NCAA. All Division III. *Intercollegiate sports:* baseball M, basketball M/W, cross-country running M/W, equestrian sports M(c)/W(c), field hockey W, football M, golf M(c)/W(c), lacrosse M(c), rugby M(c)/W(c), soccer M/W, softball W, swimming and diving W, tennis M/W, track and field M/W, ultimate Frisbee M(c)/W(c), volleyball M/W. *Intramural sports:* basketball M/W, cheerleading W(c), field hockey M(c)/W(c), lacrosse W(c), racquetball M(c)/W(c), skiing (downhill) M(c)/W(c), soccer M/W, volleyball M(c)/W(c).

Standardized Tests *Recommended:* SAT or ACT (for admission).

Costs (2013–14) *Comprehensive fee:* $47,370 includes full-time tuition ($36,410), mandatory fees ($760), and room and board ($10,200). Full-time tuition and fees vary according to course load and program. Part-time tuition: $1500 per credit hour. *College room only:* $5380. Room and board charges vary according to board plan. *Payment plan:* installment. *Waivers:* senior citizens and employees or children of employees.

Financial Aid Of all full-time matriculated undergraduates who enrolled in 2011, 1,184 applied for aid, 1,062 were judged to have need, 223 had their need fully met. 340 Federal Work-Study jobs (averaging $567). 368 state and other part-time jobs (averaging $965). In 2011, 406 non-need-based awards were made. *Average percent of need met:* 83%. *Average financial aid package:* $26,506. *Average need-based loan:* $4838. *Average need-based gift aid:* $21,165. *Average non-need-based aid:* $15,016. *Average indebtedness upon graduation:* $30,109. *Financial aid deadline:* 3/1.

Applying *Options:* electronic application, early admission, early decision, early action, deferred entrance. *Application fee:* $30. *Required:* essay or personal statement, high school transcript, minimum 3.0 GPA, 1 letter of recommendation. *Recommended:* interview. *Application deadlines:* 3/15 (freshmen), 6/15 (transfers), 1/1 (early action). *Early decision deadline:* 11/15. *Notification:* continuous (freshmen), continuous (transfers), 12/23 (early decision), 1/30 (early action).

Freshman Application Contact Terri Bollman-Dalansky, Director of Admissions, Juniata College, 1700 Moore Street, Huntingdon, PA 16652-2119. *Phone:* 814-641-3424. *Toll-free phone:* 877-JUNIATA. *Fax:* 814-641-3100. *E-mail:* admissions@juniata.edu. *Website:* http://www.juniata.edu/.

Keystone College

La Plume, Pennsylvania

- **Independent 4-year,** founded 1868
- **Small-town** 270-acre campus
- **Endowment** $6.7 million
- **Coed** 1,670 undergraduate students, 83% full-time, 59% women, 41% men
- **Minimally difficult** entrance level, 70% of applicants were admitted

Undergraduates 1,388 full-time, 282 part-time. Students come from 11 other countries; 13% are from out of state; 4% Black or African American, non-Hispanic/Latino; 3% Hispanic/Latino; 1% Asian, non-Hispanic/Latino; 0.1% Native Hawaiian or other Pacific Islander, non-Hispanic/Latino; 0.2% American Indian or Alaska Native, non-Hispanic/Latino; 2% Two or more races, non-Hispanic/Latino; 16% Race/ethnicity unknown; 0.8% international; 8%

transferred in; 29% live on campus. *Retention:* 61% of full-time freshmen returned.

Freshmen *Admission:* 1,192 applied, 837 admitted, 363 enrolled. *Average high school GPA:* 2.92. *Test scores:* SAT critical reading scores over 500: 26%; SAT math scores over 500: 29%; SAT writing scores over 500: 19%; ACT scores over 18: 59%; SAT critical reading scores over 600: 4%; SAT math scores over 600: 4%; SAT writing scores over 600: 3%; ACT scores over 24: 6%.

Faculty *Total:* 244, 28% full-time, 23% with terminal degrees. *Student/faculty ratio:* 12:1.

Academics *Calendar:* semesters. *Degrees:* certificates, associate, bachelor's, and postbachelor's certificates. *Special study options:* academic remediation for entering students, adult/continuing education programs, advanced placement credit, cooperative education, distance learning, double majors, English as a second language, honors programs, independent study, internships, part-time degree program, services for LD students, study abroad, summer session for credit. *ROTC:* Army (c), Air Force (c).

Computers on Campus 100 computers/terminals are available on campus for general student use. Students can access the following: campus intranet, computer help desk, free student e-mail accounts, online (class) grades, online (class) registration, online (class) schedules. Campuswide network is available. 100% of college-owned or -operated housing units are wired for high-speed Internet access. Wireless service is available via entire campus.

Student Life *Housing:* on-campus residence required for freshman year. *Options:* coed, women-only, disabled students. Campus housing is university owned. Freshman campus housing is guaranteed. *Activities and organizations:* drama/theater group, student-run newspaper, radio station, choral group, Art Society, Inter-Hall Council, O.P.E.N. (Opposing Prejudice Ending Negativity), S.M.A.R.T. (Sports Management and Recreation Team), Eco Club. *Campus security:* 24-hour emergency response devices and patrols, student patrols, late-night transport/escort service, controlled dormitory access. *Student services:* health clinic, personal/psychological counseling.

Athletics Member NCAA. All Division III. *Intercollegiate sports:* baseball M, basketball M/W, cross-country running M/W, field hockey W, golf M, soccer M/W, softball W, tennis M/W, track and field M/W, volleyball W. *Intramural sports:* basketball M/W, cheerleading M(c)/W(c), football M/W, skiing (downhill) M/W, soccer M/W, volleyball M/W, wrestling M(c).

Standardized Tests *Required:* SAT or ACT (for admission).

Costs (2013–14) *One-time required fee:* $500. *Comprehensive fee:* $31,000 includes full-time tuition ($20,300), mandatory fees ($900), and room and board ($9800). Part-time tuition: $400 per credit. Part-time tuition and fees vary according to course load. *Required fees:* $225 per term part-time. *College room only:* $4950. Room and board charges vary according to board plan and housing facility. *Payment plans:* installment, deferred payment. *Waivers:* senior citizens and employees or children of employees.

Financial Aid Of all full-time matriculated undergraduates who enrolled in 2010, 1,123 applied for aid, 1,123 were judged to have need, 352 had their need fully met. 202 Federal Work-Study jobs (averaging $1450). 50 state and other part-time jobs (averaging $1450). In 2010, 39 non-need-based awards were made. *Average percent of need met:* 77%. *Average financial aid package:* $22,554. *Average need-based loan:* $6500. *Average need-based gift aid:* $20,719. *Average non-need-based aid:* $11,868. *Average indebtedness upon graduation:* $24,750.

Applying *Options:* electronic application, early admission, deferred entrance. *Application fee:* $30. *Required:* essay or personal statement, high school transcript, 1 letter of recommendation. *Required for some:* interview, art portfolio for visual arts and art education. *Recommended:* interview. *Application deadlines:* 6/1 (freshmen), 8/1 (transfers). *Notification:* continuous (freshmen), continuous (transfers).

Freshman Application Contact Jessica Lopez, Senior Administrative Assistant, Keystone College, One College Green, PO Box 50, La Plume, PA 18440-1099. *Phone:* 570-945-8111. *Toll-free phone:* 877-4-COLLEGE. *Fax:* 570-945-7916. *E-mail:* admissions@keystone.edu. *Website:* http://www.keystone.edu/.

King's College

Wilkes-Barre, Pennsylvania

- **Independent Roman Catholic** comprehensive, founded 1946
- **Urban** 48-acre campus
- **Endowment** $49.5 million
- **Coed** 2,218 undergraduate students, 89% full-time, 49% women, 51% men
- **Moderately difficult** entrance level, 70% of applicants were admitted

Undergraduates 1,981 full-time, 237 part-time. Students come from 19 states and territories; 2 other countries; 28% are from out of state; 3% Black or Afri-

can American, non-Hispanic/Latino; 6% Hispanic/Latino; 2% Asian, non-Hispanic/Latino; 0.1% Native Hawaiian or other Pacific Islander, non-Hispanic/Latino; 0.2% American Indian or Alaska Native, non-Hispanic/Latino; 1% Two or more races, non-Hispanic/Latino; 8% Race/ethnicity unknown; 0.1% international; 4% transferred in; 52% live on campus. *Retention:* 78% of full-time freshmen returned.

Freshmen *Admission:* 2,967 applied, 2,072 admitted, 514 enrolled. *Average high school GPA:* 3.3. *Test scores:* SAT critical reading scores over 500: 62%; SAT math scores over 500: 62%; SAT writing scores over 500: 55%; SAT critical reading scores over 600: 15%; SAT math scores over 600: 20%; SAT writing scores over 600: 13%; SAT critical reading scores over 700: 2%; SAT math scores over 700: 2%; SAT writing scores over 700: 2%.

Faculty *Total:* 237, 57% full-time, 59% with terminal degrees. *Student/faculty ratio:* 13:1.

Academics *Calendar:* semesters. *Degrees:* certificates, associate, bachelor's, master's, and postbachelor's certificates. *Special study options:* accelerated degree program, adult/continuing education programs, advanced placement credit, distance learning, double majors, honors programs, independent study, internships, off-campus study, part-time degree program, services for LD students, student-designed majors, study abroad, summer session for credit. *ROTC:* Army (b), Air Force (c). *Unusual degree programs:* 3-2 engineering with The 3+2 Engineering Dual Degree Program with the University of Notre Dame will provide students with the opportunity to take math, science, and CORE courses at King's and then transfer to complete engineering courses in their chosen field.

Computers on Campus 470 computers/terminals are available on campus for general student use. Students can access the following: computer help desk, free student e-mail accounts, online (class) grades, online (class) registration, online (class) schedules. Campuswide network is available. 100% of college-owned or -operated housing units are wired for high-speed Internet access. Wireless service is available via classrooms, computer labs, libraries, student centers.

Student Life *Housing:* on-campus residence required through sophomore year. *Options:* coed, men-only, women-only, cooperative, disabled students. Campus housing is university owned. Freshman campus housing is guaranteed. *Activities and organizations:* drama/theater group, student-run newspaper, radio station, choral group, Association of Campus Events, Student Government Association, Accounting Association, International/Multicultural Club, Biology Club. *Campus security:* 24-hour emergency response devices and patrols, late-night transport/escort service, controlled dormitory access. *Student services:* health clinic, personal/psychological counseling, women's center.

Athletics Member NCAA. All Division III. *Intercollegiate sports:* baseball M, basketball M/W, cheerleading M/W, cross-country running M/W, field hockey W, football M, golf M, lacrosse M/W, soccer M/W, softball W, swimming and diving M/W, tennis M/W, volleyball W, wrestling M. *Intramural sports:* basketball M/W, ice hockey M(c), soccer M/W, track and field M(c)/W(c).

Standardized Tests *Recommended:* SAT or ACT (for admission).

Costs (2012–13) *Comprehensive fee:* $40,194 includes full-time tuition ($29,174) and room and board ($11,020). Part-time tuition: $530 per credit hour. *College room only:* $5380. Room and board charges vary according to board plan. *Payment plan:* installment. *Waivers:* senior citizens and employees or children of employees.

Financial Aid Of all full-time matriculated undergraduates who enrolled in 2012, 1,817 applied for aid, 1,678 were judged to have need, 269 had their need fully met. 427 Federal Work-Study jobs (averaging $657). 168 state and other part-time jobs (averaging $2146). In 2012, 274 non-need-based awards were made. *Average percent of need met:* 73%. *Average financial aid package:* $21,336. *Average need-based loan:* $4518. *Average need-based gift aid:* $16,188. *Average non-need-based aid:* $12,668. *Average indebtedness upon graduation:* $36,538.

Applying *Options:* electronic application, deferred entrance. *Application fee:* $30. *Required:* essay or personal statement, high school transcript. *Recommended:* interview. *Application deadlines:* rolling (freshmen), rolling (out-of-state freshmen), rolling (transfers). *Notification:* continuous (freshmen), continuous (out-of-state freshmen), continuous (transfers).

Freshman Application Contact Mr. James Anderson, Director of Admission, King's College, 133 North River Street, Wilkes-Barre, PA 18711-0801. *Phone:* 570-208-5858. *Toll-free phone:* 888-KINGSPA. *Fax:* 570-208-5971. *E-mail:* admissions@kings.edu.

Website: http://www.kings.edu/.

See below for display ad and page 1344 for the College Close-Up.

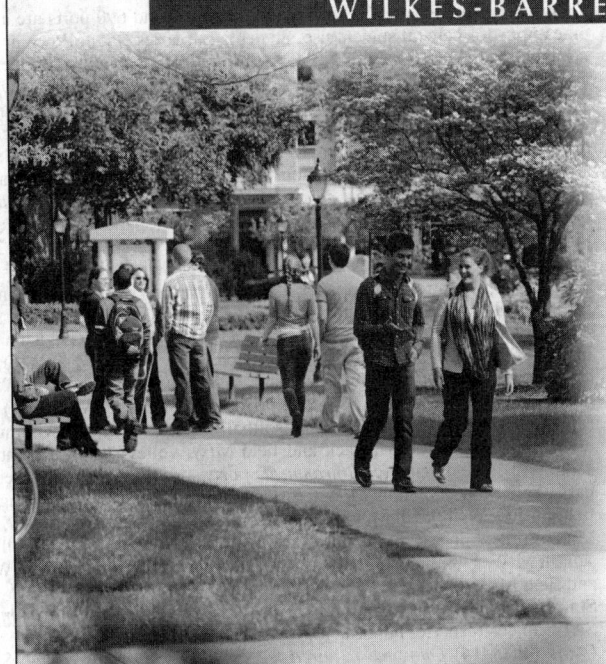

Kutztown University of Pennsylvania

Kutztown, Pennsylvania

- **State-supported** comprehensive, founded 1866, part of Pennsylvania State System of Higher Education
- **Rural** 289-acre campus with easy access to Philadelphia
- **Endowment** $15.3 million
- **Coed** 9,135 undergraduate students, 95% full-time, 57% women, 43% men
- **Moderately difficult** entrance level, 68% of applicants were admitted

Undergraduates 8,641 full-time, 494 part-time. Students come from 22 states and territories; 24 other countries; 11% are from out of state; 7% Black or African American, non-Hispanic/Latino; 6% Hispanic/Latino; 1% Asian, non-Hispanic/Latino; 0.1% Native Hawaiian or other Pacific Islander, non-Hispanic/Latino; 0.2% American Indian or Alaska Native, non-Hispanic/Latino; 2% Two or more races, non-Hispanic/Latino; 2% Race/ethnicity unknown; 0.7% international; 8% transferred in; 46% live on campus. *Retention:* 71% of full-time freshmen returned.

Freshmen *Admission:* 9,730 applied, 6,570 admitted, 1,997 enrolled. *Average high school GPA:* 3.1. *Test scores:* SAT critical reading scores over 500: 37%; SAT math scores over 500: 39%; SAT writing scores over 500: 32%; ACT scores over 18: 72%; SAT critical reading scores over 600: 6%; SAT math scores over 600: 7%; SAT writing scores over 600: 5%; ACT scores over 24: 15%; SAT critical reading scores over 700: 1%; SAT writing scores over 700: 1%; ACT scores over 30: 1%.

Faculty *Total:* 464, 91% full-time, 75% with terminal degrees. *Student/faculty ratio:* 20:1.

Academics *Calendar:* semesters. *Degrees:* bachelor's, master's, and postbachelor's certificates. *Special study options:* academic remediation for entering students, accelerated degree program, adult/continuing education programs, advanced placement credit, distance learning, double majors, honors programs, independent study, internships, off-campus study, part-time degree program, services for LD students, student-designed majors, study abroad, summer session for credit. *ROTC:* Army (c). *Unusual degree programs:* 3-2 engineering with Pennsylvania State University–University Park Campus.

Computers on Campus 1,075 computers/terminals and 100 ports are available on campus for general student use. Students can access the following: computer help desk, free student e-mail accounts, online (class) grades, online (class) registration, online (class) schedules. Campuswide network is available. 100% of college-owned or -operated housing units are wired for high-speed Internet access. Wireless service is available via classrooms, computer centers, computer labs, dorm rooms, learning centers, libraries, student centers.

Student Life *Housing options:* coed, women-only, cooperative. Campus housing is university owned and leased by the school. Freshman campus housing is guaranteed. *Activities and organizations:* drama/theater group, student-run newspaper, radio and television station, choral group, marching band, Student Government Board, Student Pennsylvania State Education Association, National Art Education Association, Residence Hall Association, Association of Campus Events, national fraternities, national sororities. *Campus security:* 24-hour emergency response devices and patrols, student patrols, late-night transport/escort service, secondary door electronic alarm system in residence halls, 24-hour student desk personnel at main entrance of residence halls. *Student services:* health clinic, personal/psychological counseling, women's center.

Athletics Member NCAA. All Division II. *Intercollegiate sports:* baseball M(s), basketball M(s)/W(s), bowling W(s), cheerleading W(c), cross-country running M(s)/W(s), equestrian sports M(c)/W(c), fencing M(c)/W(c), field hockey W(s), football M(s), golf W(s), ice hockey M(c), lacrosse M(c)/W(s), rugby M(c)/W(c), soccer M(c)/W(s), softball W(s), swimming and diving W(s), tennis M(s)/W(s), track and field M(s)/W(s), ultimate Frisbee M(c)/W(c), volleyball M(c)/W(s), wrestling M(s). *Intramural sports:* basketball M/W, racquetball M/W, rock climbing M/W, soccer M/W, softball M/W, swimming and diving M/W, table tennis M/W, tennis M/W, volleyball M/W.

Standardized Tests *Required:* SAT or ACT (for admission). *Required for some:* SAT Subject Tests (for admission).

Costs (2012–13) *One-time required fee:* $238. *Tuition:* state resident $6428 full-time, $268 per credit hour part-time; nonresident $16,070 full-time, $670 per credit hour part-time. Part-time tuition and fees vary according to course load. *Required fees:* $2168 full-time, $90 per credit hour part-time. *Room and board:* $8890; room only: $5552. Room and board charges vary according to board plan and housing facility. *Payment plans:* installment, deferred payment. *Waivers:* senior citizens and employees or children of employees.

Financial Aid Of all full-time matriculated undergraduates who enrolled in 2011, 7,325 applied for aid, 6,063 were judged to have need, 452 had their need fully met. In 2011, 78 non-need-based awards were made. *Average per-cent of need met:* 50%. *Average financial aid package:* $7743. *Average need-based loan:* $4026. *Average need-based gift aid:* $5191. *Average non-need-based aid:* $866. *Average indebtedness upon graduation:* $30,831.

Applying *Options:* electronic application, early admission, deferred entrance. *Application fee:* $35. *Required:* high school transcript, minimum 2.0 GPA. *Required for some:* audition for music; portfolio and/or art test for arts. *Application deadlines:* rolling (freshmen), rolling (transfers). *Notification:* continuous (freshmen), continuous (transfers).

Freshman Application Contact Kutztown University of Pennsylvania, 15200 Kutztown Road, Kutztown, PA 19530-0730. *Phone:* 610-683-4060. *Toll-free phone:* 877-628-1915.

Website: http://www.kutztown.edu/.

Lafayette College

Easton, Pennsylvania

- **Independent** 4-year, founded 1826, affiliated with Presbyterian Church (U.S.A.)
- **Suburban** 340-acre campus with easy access to New York City, Philadelphia
- **Endowment** $700.0 million
- **Coed** 2,488 undergraduate students, 98% full-time, 47% women, 53% men

Undergraduates 2,438 full-time, 50 part-time. Students come from 47 states and territories; 37 other countries; 78% are from out of state; 5% Black or African American, non-Hispanic/Latino; 6% Hispanic/Latino; 3% Asian, non-Hispanic/Latino; 0.1% Native Hawaiian or other Pacific Islander, non-Hispanic/Latino; 0.2% American Indian or Alaska Native, non-Hispanic/Latino; 2% Two or more races, non-Hispanic/Latino; 12% Race/ethnicity unknown; 5% international; 0.5% transferred in; 92% live on campus. *Retention:* 95% of full-time freshmen returned.

Freshmen *Admission:* 629 enrolled. *Average high school GPA:* 3.46. *Test scores:* SAT critical reading scores over 500: 97%; SAT math scores over 500: 97%; SAT writing scores over 500: 97%; ACT scores over 18: 99%; SAT critical reading scores over 600: 68%; SAT math scores over 600: 82%; SAT writing scores over 600: 70%; ACT scores over 24: 93%; SAT critical reading scores over 700: 20%; SAT math scores over 700: 31%; SAT writing scores over 700: 20%; ACT scores over 30: 36%.

Faculty *Total:* 258, 84% full-time, 91% with terminal degrees. *Student/faculty ratio:* 11:1.

Academics *Calendar:* semesters plus interim January program. *Degree:* bachelor's. *Special study options:* academic remediation for entering students, accelerated degree program, advanced placement credit, double majors, honors programs, independent study, internships, off-campus study, part-time degree program, services for LD students, student-designed majors, study abroad, summer session for credit. *ROTC:* Army (c).

Computers on Campus 690 computers/terminals and 690 ports are available on campus for general student use. Students can access the following: campus intranet, computer help desk, free student e-mail accounts, online (class) grades, online (class) registration, online (class) schedules. Campuswide network is available. 100% of college-owned or -operated housing units are wired for high-speed Internet access. Wireless service is available via entire campus.

Student Life *Housing:* on-campus residence required through senior year. *Options:* coed, men-only, women-only, disabled students. Campus housing is university owned. Freshman campus housing is guaranteed. *Activities and organizations:* drama/theater group, student-run newspaper, radio station, choral group, national fraternities, national sororities. *Campus security:* 24-hour emergency response devices and patrols, student patrols, late-night transport/escort service, controlled dormitory access. *Student services:* health clinic, personal/psychological counseling, women's center.

Athletics Member NCAA. All Division I except football (Division I-AA). *Intercollegiate sports:* baseball M, basketball M/W, crew M(c)/W(c), cross-country running M/W, equestrian sports M(c)/W(c), fencing M/W, field hockey W, golf M, ice hockey M(c), lacrosse M/W, rugby M(c)/W(c), skiing (downhill) M(c)/W(c), soccer M/W, softball W, squash M(c), swimming and diving M/W, tennis M/W, track and field M/W, volleyball W, weight lifting M(c)/W(c), wrestling M(c). *Intramural sports:* badminton M/W, baseball M, basketball M/W, bowling M/W, cross-country running M/W, fencing M/W, field hockey W, football M, golf M/W, lacrosse M/W, racquetball M/W, sailing M(c)/W(c), skiing (cross-country) M(c)/W(c), soccer M/W, softball M/W, squash M/W, swimming and diving M/W, table tennis M/W, tennis M/W, track and field M/W, volleyball M/W, weight lifting M/W, wrestling M.

Standardized Tests *Required:* SAT or ACT (for admission). *Recommended:* SAT Subject Tests (for admission).

Costs (2013–14) *One-time required fee:* $700. *Comprehensive fee:* $57,050 includes full-time tuition ($43,580), mandatory fees ($390), and room and board ($13,080). Full-time tuition and fees vary according to course load. Part-time tuition: $5450 per course. Part-time tuition and fees vary according to course load. *College room only:* $8090. Room and board charges vary according to board plan, housing facility, and student level. *Payment plans:* tuition prepayment, installment. *Waivers:* employees or children of employees.

Financial Aid Of all full-time matriculated undergraduates who enrolled in 2011, 1,402 applied for aid, 1,016 were judged to have need, 877 had their need fully met. In 2011, 177 non-need-based awards were made. *Average percent of need met:* 98%. *Average financial aid package:* $38,323. *Average need-based loan:* $4326. *Average need-based gift aid:* $32,709. *Average non-need-based aid:* $20,842. *Average indebtedness upon graduation:* $26,717. *Financial aid deadline:* 3/1.

Applying *Required:* essay or personal statement, high school transcript, 1 letter of recommendation. *Recommended:* interview.

Freshman Application Contact Mr. Matthew Hyde, Director of Admissions, Lafayette College, 118 Markle Hall, Easton, PA 18042-1798. *Phone:* 610-330-5100. *Fax:* 610-330-5355. *E-mail:* hydem@lafayette.edu. *Website:* http://www.lafayette.edu/.

Lancaster Bible College

Lancaster, Pennsylvania

Freshman Application Contact Mrs. Joanne M. Roper, Associate Vice President for Admissions, Lancaster Bible College, PO Box 83403, Lancaster, PA 17608. *Phone:* 717-560-8271. *Toll-free phone:* 800-544-7335. *Fax:* 717-560-8213. *E-mail:* admissions@lbc.edu. *Website:* http://www.lbc.edu/.

Lancaster General College of Nursing & Health Sciences

Lancaster, Pennsylvania

- **Independent** primarily 2-year, founded 1903
- **Urban** campus with easy access to Harrisburg, PA
- **Endowment** $1.0 million
- **Coed** 1,375 undergraduate students, 37% full-time, 85% women, 15% men
- **Moderately difficult** entrance level, 28% of applicants were admitted

Undergraduates 503 full-time, 872 part-time. 2% are from out of state; 5% Black or African American, non-Hispanic/Latino; 4% Hispanic/Latino; 3% Asian, non-Hispanic/Latino; 0.3% Native Hawaiian or other Pacific Islander, non-Hispanic/Latino; 0.1% American Indian or Alaska Native, non-Hispanic/Latino; 0.1% Two or more races, non-Hispanic/Latino; 3% Race/ethnicity unknown; 25% transferred in.

Freshmen *Admission:* 517 applied, 145 admitted, 367 enrolled. *Test scores:* SAT critical reading scores over 500: 44%; SAT math scores over 500: 57%; SAT critical reading scores over 600: 13%; SAT math scores over 600: 8%; SAT math scores over 700: 1%.

Faculty *Total:* 168, 38% full-time. *Student/faculty ratio:* 8:1.

Academics *Degrees:* certificates, associate, and bachelor's. *Special study options:* accelerated degree program, adult/continuing education programs, advanced placement credit, distance learning, part-time degree program, services for LD students, summer session for credit.

Computers on Campus 98 computers/terminals are available on campus for general student use. Students can access the following: campus intranet, free student e-mail accounts, online (class) grades, online (class) registration, online (class) schedules. Campuswide network is available. Wireless service is available via entire campus.

Student Life *Housing:* college housing not available. *Activities and organizations:* Student Government Association, Soccer Club, Distance Running. *Campus security:* 24-hour emergency response devices and patrols, late-night transport/escort service. *Student services:* health clinic, personal/psychological counseling.

Athletics *Intramural sports:* cross-country running M(c)/W(c), soccer M(c)/W(c).

Standardized Tests *Required:* SAT or ACT (for admission).

Costs (2013–14) *Tuition:* $18,800 full-time, $425 per credit part-time. Full-time tuition and fees vary according to program. Part-time tuition and fees vary according to program. *Required fees:* $1350 full-time, $250 per term part-time. *Payment plan:* installment. *Waivers:* employees or children of employees.

Applying *Options:* electronic application. *Application fee:* $60. *Required:* minimum 3.0 GPA, 2 letters of recommendation, Official GED transcript may be substituted in lieu of high school transcript. SAT or ACT scores required if

graduated from high school within last 2 years. Official transcripts of all institutions attended. *Required for some:* essay or personal statement, high school transcript. *Application deadline:* 2/1 (freshmen). *Notification:* continuous (freshmen).

Freshman Application Contact Admissions Office, Lancaster General College of Nursing & Health Sciences, 410 Lime Street, Lancaster, PA 17602. *Phone:* 800-622-5443. *Toll-free phone:* 800-622-5443. *E-mail:* lgc_admissions@lancastergeneral.org. *Website:* http://www.lancastergeneralcollege.edu/content/.

La Roche College

Pittsburgh, Pennsylvania

- **Independent** comprehensive, founded 1963, affiliated with Roman Catholic Church
- **Suburban** 43-acre campus
- **Endowment** $4.4 million
- **Coed** 1,345 undergraduate students, 82% full-time, 58% women, 42% men
- **Minimally difficult** entrance level, 52% of applicants were admitted

Undergraduates 1,103 full-time, 242 part-time. Students come from 13 states and territories; 29 other countries; 8% are from out of state; 6% Black or African American, non-Hispanic/Latino; 2% Hispanic/Latino; 0.8% Asian, non-Hispanic/Latino; 1% Two or more races, non-Hispanic/Latino; 15% Race/ethnicity unknown; 11% international; 15% transferred in; 47% live on campus. *Retention:* 66% of full-time freshmen returned.

Freshmen *Admission:* 1,587 applied, 825 admitted, 249 enrolled. *Average high school GPA:* 3.17. *Test scores:* ACT scores over 18: 75%; ACT scores over 24: 20%.

Faculty *Total:* 194, 30% full-time, 26% with terminal degrees. *Student/faculty ratio:* 12:1.

Academics *Calendar:* semesters plus summer term. *Degrees:* certificates, associate, bachelor's, master's, and postbachelor's certificates. *Special study options:* academic remediation for entering students, accelerated degree program, adult/continuing education programs, advanced placement credit, distance learning, double majors, English as a second language, honors programs, independent study, internships, part-time degree program, services for LD students, student-designed majors, study abroad, summer session for credit. *ROTC:* Army (c), Air Force (c). *Unusual degree programs:* 3-2 engineering with University of Pittsburgh; physical therapy, physician's assistant, speech language pathologist, athletic trainer, occupational therapy with Duquesne University.

Computers on Campus 164 computers/terminals are available on campus for general student use. Students can access the following: campus intranet, computer help desk, free student e-mail accounts, online (class) grades, online (class) registration, online (class) schedules. Campuswide network is available. 100% of college-owned or -operated housing units are wired for high-speed Internet access. Wireless service is available via classrooms, computer labs, learning centers, libraries, student centers.

Student Life *Housing options:* coed. Campus housing is university owned. Freshman campus housing is guaranteed. *Activities and organizations:* drama/theater group, student-run newspaper, radio station, choral group, American Society of Interior Design, student government, Visions (environmental club), Helping Hands. *Campus security:* 24-hour emergency response devices and patrols, student patrols, late-night transport/escort service, controlled dormitory access. *Student services:* health clinic, personal/psychological counseling.

Athletics Member NCAA. All Division III. *Intercollegiate sports:* baseball M, basketball M/W, cross-country running M/W, golf M, lacrosse M, soccer M/W, softball W, tennis W, volleyball W. *Intramural sports:* basketball M/W, weight lifting M/W.

Standardized Tests *Required:* SAT or ACT (for admission).

Costs (2012–13) *Comprehensive fee:* $33,790 includes full-time tuition ($23,328), mandatory fees ($730), and room and board ($9732). Full-time tuition and fees vary according to student level. Part-time tuition: $595 per credit hour. *College room only:* $6160. Room and board charges vary according to board plan and housing facility. *Payment plan:* installment. *Waivers:* senior citizens and employees or children of employees.

Financial Aid Of all full-time matriculated undergraduates who enrolled in 2012, 905 applied for aid, 864 were judged to have need, 286 had their need fully met. 169 Federal Work-Study jobs (averaging $1402). In 2012, 56 non-need-based awards were made. *Average percent of need met:* 94%. *Average financial aid package:* $24,869. *Average need-based loan:* $4642. *Average need-based gift aid:* $7778. *Average non-need-based aid:* $16,799. *Average indebtedness upon graduation:* $26,296.

Applying *Options:* electronic application, early admission, deferred entrance. *Application fee:* $50. *Required:* high school transcript, minimum 2.0 GPA, 2 letters of recommendation. *Recommended:* essay or personal statement, minimum 3.0 GPA, interview. *Application deadlines:* rolling (freshmen), rolling (transfers). *Notification:* 9/15 (freshmen).

Freshman Application Contact Mr., Director of Admissions, La Roche College, 9000 Babcock Boulevard, Pittsburgh, PA 15237. *Phone:* 412-536-1275. *Toll-free phone:* 800-838-4LRC. *Fax:* 412-536-1048. *E-mail:* admissions@laroche.edu. *Website:* http://www.laroche.edu/.

La Salle University

Philadelphia, Pennsylvania

- **Independent Roman Catholic** comprehensive, founded 1863
- **Urban** 130-acre campus with easy access to Philadelphia
- **Endowment** $71.7 million
- **Coed** 4,516 undergraduate students, 79% full-time, 64% women, 36% men
- **Moderately difficult** entrance level, 73% of applicants were admitted

Undergraduates 3,557 full-time, 959 part-time. Students come from 40 states and territories; 27 other countries; 38% are from out of state; 18% Black or African American, non-Hispanic/Latino; 10% Hispanic/Latino; 5% Asian, non-Hispanic/Latino; 0.1% Native Hawaiian or other Pacific Islander, non-Hispanic/Latino; 0.4% American Indian or Alaska Native, non-Hispanic/Latino; 4% Two or more races, non-Hispanic/Latino; 6% Race/ethnicity unknown; 1% international; 3% transferred in; 54% live on campus. *Retention:* 80% of full-time freshmen returned.

Freshmen *Admission:* 6,101 applied, 4,460 admitted, 926 enrolled. *Average high school GPA:* 3.35. *Test scores:* SAT critical reading scores over 500: 46%; SAT math scores over 500: 49%; ACT scores over 18: 89%; SAT critical reading scores over 600: 11%; SAT math scores over 600: 14%; ACT scores over 24: 21%; SAT critical reading scores over 700: 1%; SAT math scores over 700: 1%; ACT scores over 30: 2%.

Faculty *Total:* 457, 54% full-time. *Student/faculty ratio:* 12:1.

Academics *Calendar:* semesters. *Degrees:* associate, bachelor's, master's, doctoral, post-master's, and postbachelor's certificates. *Special study options:* academic remediation for entering students, accelerated degree program, adult/continuing education programs, advanced placement credit, cooperative education, distance learning, double majors, English as a second language, freshman honors college, honors programs, independent study, internships, off-campus study, part-time degree program, services for LD students, student-designed majors, study abroad, summer session for credit. *ROTC:* Army (c), Air Force (c). *Unusual degree programs:* 3-2 business administration; 5-year BS/MS in speech-language-hearing science, 5-year BA/BS/MS in computer information science, 5-year BA/MA in history, and an occupational therapy program with Thomas Jefferson University.

Computers on Campus 1,100 computers/terminals are available on campus for general student use. Students can access the following: campus intranet, computer help desk, free student e-mail accounts, online (class) grades, online (class) registration, online (class) schedules, Blackboard Course Management System. Campuswide network is available. 100% of college-owned or -operated housing units are wired for high-speed Internet access. Wireless service is available via classrooms, computer centers, computer labs, dorm rooms, learning centers, libraries, student centers.

Student Life *Housing options:* coed, men-only, women-only, disabled students. Campus housing is university owned. Freshman campus housing is guaranteed. *Activities and organizations:* drama/theater group, student-run newspaper, radio and television station, choral group, Student Government Association, Community service organization, La Salle Entertainment Organization, The Explorer (yearbook), The Masque (theater group), national fraternities, national sororities. *Campus security:* 24-hour emergency response devices and patrols, student patrols, late-night transport/escort service, controlled dormitory access. *Student services:* health clinic, personal/psychological counseling, women's center.

Athletics Member NCAA. All Division I. *Intercollegiate sports:* baseball M(s), basketball M(s)/W(s), cheerleading M/W, crew M(s)/W(s), cross-country running M(s)/W(s), field hockey W(s), golf M(s)/W(s), lacrosse W(s), soccer M(s)/W(s), softball W(s), swimming and diving M(s)/W(s), tennis M(s)/W(s), track and field M(s)/W(s), volleyball W(s). *Intramural sports:* cross-country running M(c)/W(c), equestrian sports W(c), ice hockey M(c), lacrosse M(c), rugby M(c)/W(c), swimming and diving M(c)/W(c), tennis M(c)/W(c), track and field M(c)/W(c), ultimate Frisbee M(c)/W(c), water polo M(c)/W(c).

Standardized Tests *Required:* SAT or ACT (for admission).

Costs (2012–13) *One-time required fee:* $150. *Comprehensive fee:* $48,860 includes full-time tuition ($36,250), mandatory fees ($400), and room and board ($12,210). Full-time tuition and fees vary according to course load and program. Part-time tuition: $500 per credit hour. Part-time tuition and fees vary

according to course load and program. *Required fees:* $125 per term part-time. *College room only:* $6430. Room and board charges vary according to board plan and housing facility. *Payment plans:* installment, deferred payment. *Waivers:* employees or children of employees.

Financial Aid Of all full-time matriculated undergraduates who enrolled in 2011, 3,039 applied for aid, 2,817 were judged to have need, 442 had their need fully met. 377 Federal Work-Study jobs (averaging $1324). In 2011, 597 non-need-based awards were made. *Average percent of need met:* 74%. *Average financial aid package:* $25,451. *Average need-based loan:* $4761. *Average need-based gift aid:* $19,593. *Average non-need-based aid:* $14,496. *Average indebtedness upon graduation:* $37,225.

Applying *Options:* electronic application, early admission, early decision, early action, deferred entrance. *Application fee:* $35. *Required:* essay or personal statement, high school transcript, 1 letter of recommendation, SAT or ACT. *Recommended:* interview. *Application deadlines:* 8/15 (transfers), 11/15 (early action). *Notification:* continuous (freshmen), continuous (transfers), 12/15 (early action).

Freshman Application Contact Mr. James Plunkett, Executive Director of Undergraduate Admission, La Salle University, 1900 West Olney Avenue, Philadelphia, PA 19141-1199. *Phone:* 215-951-1500. *Toll-free phone:* 800-328-1910. *Fax:* 215-951-1656. *E-mail:* admiss@lasalle.edu. *Website:* http://www.lasalle.edu/.

Lebanon Valley College

Annville, Pennsylvania

- **Independent United Methodist** comprehensive, founded 1866
- **Small-town** 340-acre campus
- **Endowment** $51.0 million
- **Coed** 1,744 undergraduate students, 93% full-time, 55% women, 45% men
- **Moderately difficult** entrance level, 66% of applicants were admitted

Undergraduates 1,618 full-time, 126 part-time. Students come from 22 states and territories; 3 other countries; 21% are from out of state; 2% Black or African American, non-Hispanic/Latino; 4% Hispanic/Latino; 1% Asian, non-Hispanic/Latino; 0.1% Native Hawaiian or other Pacific Islander, non-Hispanic/Latino; 0.2% American Indian or Alaska Native, non-Hispanic/Latino; 2% Two or more races, non-Hispanic/Latino; 3% Race/ethnicity unknown; 0.2% international; 3% transferred in; 76% live on campus. *Retention:* 86% of full-time freshmen returned.

Freshmen *Admission:* 3,012 applied, 1,981 admitted, 404 enrolled. *Test scores:* SAT critical reading scores over 500: 74%; SAT math scores over 500: 79%; SAT writing scores over 500: 64%; ACT scores over 18: 92%; SAT critical reading scores over 600: 20%; SAT math scores over 600: 41%; SAT writing scores over 600: 19%; ACT scores over 24: 46%; SAT critical reading scores over 700: 2%; SAT math scores over 700: 6%; SAT writing scores over 700: 3%; ACT scores over 30: 5%.

Faculty *Total:* 219, 47% full-time, 58% with terminal degrees. *Student/faculty ratio:* 12:1.

Academics *Calendar:* semesters. *Degrees:* certificates, associate, bachelor's, master's, doctoral, and postbachelor's certificates. *Special study options:* academic remediation for entering students, adult/continuing education programs, advanced placement credit, double majors, independent study, internships, off-campus study, part-time degree program, services for LD students, student-designed majors, study abroad, summer session for credit. *Unusual degree programs:* 3-2 engineering with Case Western Reserve University, The Pennsylvania State University.

Computers on Campus 192 computers/terminals are available on campus for general student use. Students can access the following: campus intranet, computer help desk, free student e-mail accounts, online (class) grades, online (class) registration, online (class) schedules. Campuswide network is available. 100% of college-owned or -operated housing units are wired for high-speed Internet access. Wireless service is available via entire campus.

Student Life *Housing:* on-campus residence required through senior year. *Options:* coed, disabled students. Campus housing is university owned. Freshman campus housing is guaranteed. *Activities and organizations:* drama/theater group, student-run newspaper, radio station, choral group, marching band, LVC PSEA, Corner Stone, College Against Cancer, Wig and Buckle Theater Group, Habitat for Humanity, national fraternities, national sororities. *Campus security:* 24-hour emergency response devices and patrols, late-night transport/escort service, controlled dormitory access, residence hall entrances locked 24 hours a day. *Student services:* health clinic, personal/psychological counseling, women's center.

Athletics Member NCAA. All Division III. *Intercollegiate sports:* baseball M, basketball M/W, cross-country running M/W, field hockey W, football M, golf M/W, ice hockey M(c), lacrosse M/W, soccer M/W, softball W, swimming and diving M/W, tennis M/W, track and field M/W, volleyball M/W. *Intramural sports:* basketball M/W, equestrian sports M(c)/W(c), football M/W, racquetball M/W, rugby W(c), soccer M(c), softball M/W, table tennis M/W, ultimate Frisbee M(c)/W(c), volleyball M(c)/W.

Costs (2012–13) *Comprehensive fee:* $43,650 includes full-time tuition ($33,670), mandatory fees ($800), and room and board ($9180). Part-time tuition: $575 per credit. Part-time tuition and fees vary according to class time and degree level. *College room only:* $4480. Room and board charges vary according to board plan and housing facility. *Payment plans:* tuition prepayment, installment. *Waivers:* senior citizens and employees or children of employees.

Financial Aid Of all full-time matriculated undergraduates who enrolled in 2012, 1,479 applied for aid, 1,472 were judged to have need, 379 had their need fully met. 1,020 Federal Work-Study jobs (averaging $1483). In 2012, 209 non-need-based awards were made. *Average percent of need met:* 79%. *Average financial aid package:* $24,546. *Average need-based loan:* $4459. *Average need-based gift aid:* $21,751. *Average non-need-based aid:* $14,149. *Average indebtedness upon graduation:* $34,561.

Applying *Options:* electronic application. *Application fee:* $30. *Required:* high school transcript. *Required for some:* essay or personal statement, audition for music majors. *Recommended:* 2 letters of recommendation, interview. *Application deadlines:* rolling (freshmen), rolling (transfers). *Notification:* continuous (freshmen), continuous (transfers).

Freshman Application Contact Ms. Erin Sanno, Associate Director of Admission, Lebanon Valley College, 101 North College Avenue, Annville, PA 17003. *Phone:* 717-867-6181. *Toll-free phone:* 866-LVC-4ADM. *Fax:* 717-867-6026. *E-mail:* admission@lvc.edu.
Website: http://www.lvc.edu/.

See below for display ad and page 1348 for the College Close-Up.

Lehigh University
Bethlehem, Pennsylvania

- **Independent** university, founded 1865
- **Suburban** 1600-acre campus with easy access to Philadelphia
- **Endowment** $1.0 billion
- **Coed** 4,883 undergraduate students, 99% full-time, 43% women, 57% men
- **Most difficult** entrance level, 33% of applicants were admitted

Undergraduates 4,824 full-time, 59 part-time. Students come from 52 states and territories; 50 other countries; 74% are from out of state; 4% Black or African American, non-Hispanic/Latino; 8% Hispanic/Latino; 6% Asian, non-Hispanic/Latino; 3% Two or more races, non-Hispanic/Latino; 4% Race/ethnicity unknown; 6% international; 1% transferred in; 69% live on campus. *Retention:* 94% of full-time freshmen returned.

Freshmen *Admission:* 11,529 applied, 3,756 admitted, 1,217 enrolled. *Test scores:* SAT critical reading scores over 500: 95%; SAT math scores over 500: 98%; ACT scores over 18: 100%; SAT critical reading scores over 600: 66%; SAT math scores over 600: 86%; ACT scores over 24: 97%; SAT critical reading scores over 700: 17%; SAT math scores over 700: 41%; ACT scores over 30: 54%.

Faculty *Total:* 691, 71% full-time, 69% with terminal degrees. *Student/faculty ratio:* 10:1.

Academics *Calendar:* semesters. *Degrees:* bachelor's, master's, doctoral, post-master's, and postbachelor's certificates. *Special study options:* accelerated degree program, advanced placement credit, cooperative education, distance learning, double majors, English as a second language, external degree program, honors programs, independent study, internships, off-campus study, services for LD students, study abroad, summer session for credit. *ROTC:* Army (b). *Unusual degree programs:* 3-2 engineering; education.

Computers on Campus 605 computers/terminals are available on campus for general student use. Students can access the following: campus intranet, computer help desk, free student e-mail accounts, online (class) grades, online (class) registration, online (class) schedules. Campuswide network is available. 100% of college-owned or -operated housing units are wired for high-speed Internet access. Wireless service is available via classrooms, computer centers, computer labs, dorm rooms, learning centers, libraries, student centers.

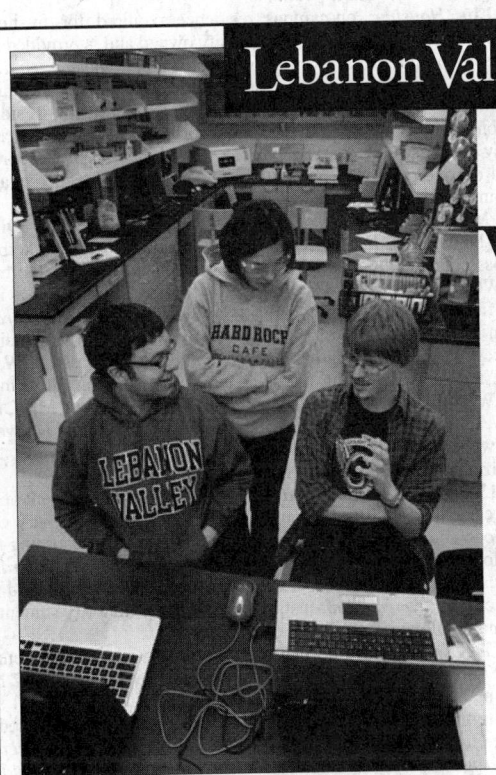

Student Life *Housing:* on-campus residence required through sophomore year. *Options:* coed, disabled students. Campus housing is university owned. Freshman campus housing is guaranteed. *Activities and organizations:* drama/theater group, student-run newspaper, radio station, choral group, marching band, WLVR Radio Station, Association of Student Alumni, University Productions, Accounting Club, Phi Sigma Pi, national fraternities, national sororities. *Campus security:* 24-hour emergency response devices and patrols, student patrols, late-night transport/escort service, controlled dormitory access. *Student services:* health clinic, personal/psychological counseling, women's center.

Athletics Member NCAA. All Division I except football (Division I-AA). *Intercollegiate sports:* baseball M, basketball M(s)/W(s), crew M(c)/W(s), cross-country running M(s)/W(s), equestrian sports M(c)/W(c), fencing M(c)/W(c), field hockey W(s), golf M(s)/W(s), ice hockey M(c), lacrosse M(s)/W(s), rugby M(c)/W(c), skiing (downhill) M(c)/W(c), soccer M/W, softball W(s), squash M(c)/W(c), swimming and diving M(s)/W(s), tennis M(s)/W(s), track and field M(s)/W(s), ultimate Frisbee M(c)/W(c), volleyball M(c)/W(s), water polo M(c)/W(c), wrestling M(s). *Intramural sports:* badminton M(c)/W(c), basketball M/W, cheerleading M(c)/W(c), cross-country running M/W, football M/W, golf M(c)/W(c), gymnastics M(c)/W(c), skiing (downhill) M(c)/W(c), soccer M/W, table tennis M(c)/W(c), volleyball M/W.

Standardized Tests *Required:* SAT or ACT (for admission).

Costs (2012–13) *Comprehensive fee:* $53,450 includes full-time tuition ($41,920), mandatory fees ($300), and room and board ($11,230). Part-time tuition: $1750 per credit hour. *College room only:* $6450. Room and board charges vary according to board plan and housing facility. *Payment plans:* tuition prepayment, installment. *Waivers:* employees or children of employees.

Financial Aid Of all full-time matriculated undergraduates who enrolled in 2012, 2,798 applied for aid, 2,105 were judged to have need, 1,478 had their need fully met. 1,349 Federal Work-Study jobs (averaging $1750). 33 state and other part-time jobs (averaging $1811). In 2012, 286 non-need-based awards were made. *Average percent of need met:* 95%. *Average financial aid package:* $36,771. *Average need-based loan:* $4603. *Average need-based gift aid:* $30,904. *Average non-need-based aid:* $10,259. *Average indebtedness upon graduation:* $31,122. *Financial aid deadline:* 2/15.

Applying *Options:* electronic application, early admission, early decision, deferred entrance. *Application fee:* $70. *Required:* essay or personal statement, high school transcript, 2 letters of recommendation. *Application deadlines:* 1/1 (freshmen), 4/1 (transfers). *Early decision deadline:* 11/15 (for plan 1), 1/15 (for plan 2). *Notification:* 4/1 (freshmen), 5/1 (transfers), 12/15 (early decision plan 1), 2/15 (early decision plan 2).

Freshman Application Contact Bruce Bunnick, Director of Admissions, Lehigh University, 27 Memorial Drive West, Bethlehem, PA 18015. *Phone:* 610-758-3100. *Fax:* 610-758-4361. *E-mail:* admissions@lehigh.edu. *Website:* http://www.lehigh.edu/.

Lincoln University

Lincoln University, Pennsylvania

- **State-related** comprehensive, founded 1854
- **Rural** 422-acre campus with easy access to Philadelphia
- **Endowment** $21.7 million
- **Coed**
- **Moderately difficult** entrance level

Faculty *Student/faculty ratio:* 16:1.

Academics *Calendar:* semesters. *Degrees:* bachelor's and master's.

Student Life *Campus security:* 24-hour emergency response devices and patrols, late-night transport/escort service, controlled dormitory access.

Athletics Member NCAA. All Division II.

Standardized Tests *Required:* SAT or ACT (for admission).

Costs (2012–13) *Tuition:* state resident $6866 full-time; nonresident $11,352 full-time. Full-time tuition and fees vary according to student level. Part-time tuition and fees vary according to course load. *Required fees:* $3112 full-time. *Room and board:* $8404; room only: $4564. Room and board charges vary according to board plan and housing facility.

Financial Aid *Financial aid deadline:* 5/1.

Applying *Options:* electronic application, early admission, deferred entrance. *Application fee:* $20. *Required:* essay or personal statement, high school transcript, minimum 2.0 GPA, 2 letters of recommendation. *Recommended:* interview.

Freshman Application Contact Ms. Germel Eaton-Clarke, Interim Director of Admissions, Lincoln University, PO Box 179, Lincoln University, PA 19352. *Phone:* 484-365-7218. *Toll-free phone:* 800-790-0191. *Fax:* 484-365-8109. *E-mail:* admiss@lincoln.edu. *Website:* http://www.lincoln.edu/.

Lock Haven University of Pennsylvania

Lock Haven, Pennsylvania

- **State-supported** comprehensive, founded 1870, part of Pennsylvania State System of Higher Education
- **Rural** 165-acre campus
- **Endowment** $9.3 million
- **Coed** 4,969 undergraduate students, 93% full-time, 57% women, 43% men
- **Moderately difficult** entrance level, 56% of applicants were admitted

Undergraduates 4,638 full-time, 331 part-time. Students come from 26 states and territories; 22 other countries; 7% are from out of state; 8% Black or African American, non-Hispanic/Latino; 2% Hispanic/Latino; 0.7% Asian, non-Hispanic/Latino; 0.3% American Indian or Alaska Native, non-Hispanic/Latino; 0.5% Two or more races, non-Hispanic/Latino; 0.7% Race/ethnicity unknown; 0.8% international; 6% transferred in; 37% live on campus. *Retention:* 69% of full-time freshmen returned.

Freshmen *Admission:* 4,498 applied, 2,522 admitted, 1,155 enrolled. *Average high school GPA:* 3.28. *Test scores:* SAT critical reading scores over 500: 31%; SAT math scores over 500: 38%; SAT writing scores over 500: 73%; ACT scores over 18: 62%; SAT critical reading scores over 600: 6%; SAT math scores over 600: 7%; SAT writing scores over 600: 19%; ACT scores over 24: 15%; SAT writing scores over 700: 1%.

Faculty *Total:* 245, 94% full-time, 66% with terminal degrees. *Student/faculty ratio:* 21:1.

Academics *Calendar:* semesters. *Degrees:* associate, bachelor's, and master's. *Special study options:* academic remediation for entering students, adult/continuing education programs, advanced placement credit, cooperative education, distance learning, double majors, English as a second language, freshman honors college, honors programs, independent study, internships, off-campus study, part-time degree program, services for LD students, student-designed majors, study abroad, summer session for credit. *ROTC:* Army (b). *Unusual degree programs:* 3-2 engineering with Pennsylvania State University–University Park Campus; nursing with Clarion University of Pennsylvania.

Computers on Campus 290 computers/terminals are available on campus for general student use. Students can access the following: online (class) registration. Campuswide network is available.

Student Life *Housing:* on-campus residence required for freshman year. *Options:* coed. Campus housing is university owned and is provided by a third party. Freshman applicants given priority for college housing. *Activities and organizations:* drama/theater group, student-run newspaper, radio and television station, choral group, marching band, student government, Residence Hall Association, national fraternities, national sororities. *Campus security:* 24-hour emergency response devices and patrols, late-night transport/escort service, controlled dormitory access. *Student services:* health clinic, personal/psychological counseling, women's center.

Athletics Member NCAA. All Division II except field hockey (Division I), wrestling (Division I). *Intercollegiate sports:* baseball M(s), basketball M(s)/W(s), cross-country running M(s)/W(s), field hockey W(s), football M(s), lacrosse W(s), soccer M(s)/W(s), softball W(s), swimming and diving W(s), track and field M(s)/W(s), volleyball W(s), wrestling M(s). *Intramural sports:* badminton M/W, basketball M/W, cross-country running M/W, fencing M/W, field hockey W, football M, golf M/W, ice hockey M, lacrosse M/W, racquetball M/W, rugby M/W, skiing (cross-country) M/W, skiing (downhill) M/W, soccer M/W, softball M/W, swimming and diving M/W, tennis M/W, track and field M/W, ultimate Frisbee M/W, volleyball M/W, water polo M, weight lifting M/W, wrestling M.

Standardized Tests *Required:* SAT or ACT (for admission).

Costs (2013–14) *One-time required fee:* $25. *Tuition:* state resident $6428 full-time; nonresident $14,070 full-time. Full-time tuition and fees vary according to course load and location. Part-time tuition and fees vary according to course load and location. *Required fees:* $2136 full-time. *Room and board:* $8016; room only: $4712. Room and board charges vary according to board plan and housing facility. *Payment plan:* installment. *Waivers:* minority students, senior citizens, and employees or children of employees.

Financial Aid Of all full-time matriculated undergraduates who enrolled in 2012, 4,327 applied for aid, 3,331 were judged to have need, 1,832 had their need fully met. 269 Federal Work-Study jobs (averaging $1044). 731 state and other part-time jobs (averaging $1257). In 2012, 78 non-need-based awards were made. *Average percent of need met:* 75%. *Average financial aid package:* $8662. *Average need-based loan:* $4241. *Average need-based gift aid:* $7622. *Average non-need-based aid:* $1129. *Average indebtedness upon graduation:* $23,840. *Financial aid deadline:* 3/15.

Applying *Options:* electronic application, deferred entrance. *Application fee:* $25. *Required:* high school transcript. *Required for some:* essay or personal statement. *Recommended:* interview. *Application deadlines:* rolling (freshmen), rolling (transfers). *Notification:* continuous (freshmen), continuous (transfers).

Freshman Application Contact Ms. Robin Rockey, Interim Director of Admissions, Lock Haven University of Pennsylvania, Office of Admission, DACC, Lock Haven, PA 17745. *Phone:* 570-484-2027. *Toll-free phone:* 800-332-8900 (in-state); 800-233-8978 (out-of-state). *Fax:* 570-484-2201. *E-mail:* admissions@lhup.edu.
Website: http://www.lhup.edu/.

Lycoming College
Williamsport, Pennsylvania

- **Independent United Methodist** 4-year, founded 1812
- **Small-town** 35-acre campus
- **Endowment** $152.3 million
- **Coed**
- **Moderately difficult** entrance level

Faculty *Student/faculty ratio:* 14:1.

Academics *Calendar:* semesters. *Degree:* bachelor's.

Student Life *Campus security:* 24-hour emergency response devices and patrols, student patrols, late-night transport/escort service, controlled dormitory access.

Athletics Member NCAA. All Division III.

Standardized Tests *Recommended:* SAT or ACT (for admission).

Costs (2012–13) *One-time required fee:* $225. *Comprehensive fee:* $42,176 includes full-time tuition ($32,096), mandatory fees ($660), and room and board ($9420). Part-time tuition: $1003 per contact hour. Part-time tuition and fees vary according to course load. *Room and board:* Room and board charges vary according to board plan and housing facility.

Financial Aid *Of all full-time matriculated undergraduates who enrolled in 2012,* 1,205 applied for aid, 1,117 were judged to have need, 309 had their need fully met. 306 Federal Work-Study jobs (averaging $619). *In 2012,* 204 non-need-based awards were made. *Average percent of need met:* 77. *Average financial aid package:* $27,007. *Average need-based loan:* $4680. *Average need-based gift aid:* $21,559. *Average non-need-based aid:* $15,868. *Average indebtedness upon graduation:* $35,990.

Applying *Options:* electronic application, deferred entrance. *Application fee:* $35. *Required:* essay or personal statement, high school transcript, 2 letters of recommendation. *Recommended:* minimum 2.3 GPA, interview.

Freshman Application Contact Mr. James Spencer, Vice President of Admissions and Financial Aid, Lycoming College, 700 College Place, Williamsport, PA 17701. *Phone:* 570-321-4026. *Toll-free phone:* 800-345-3920 Ext. 4026. *Fax:* 570-321-4317. *E-mail:* admissions@lycoming.edu.
Website: http://www.lycoming.edu/.

Mansfield University of Pennsylvania
Mansfield, Pennsylvania

- **State-supported** comprehensive, founded 1857, part of Pennsylvania State System of Higher Education
- **Small-town** 174-acre campus
- **Coed** 2,824 undergraduate students, 91% full-time, 59% women, 41% men
- **Moderately difficult** entrance level, 94% of applicants were admitted

Undergraduates 2,557 full-time, 267 part-time. 20% are from out of state; 8% Black or African American, non-Hispanic/Latino; 3% Hispanic/Latino; 1% Asian, non-Hispanic/Latino; 0.1% Native Hawaiian or other Pacific Islander, non-Hispanic/Latino; 0.6% American Indian or Alaska Native, non-Hispanic/Latino; 2% Two or more races, non-Hispanic/Latino; 4% Race/ethnicity unknown; 1% international; 9% transferred in; 52% live on campus. *Retention:* 72% of full-time freshmen returned.

Freshmen *Admission:* 1,995 applied, 1,878 admitted, 595 enrolled. *Average high school GPA:* 3.25. *Test scores:* SAT critical reading scores over 500: 39%; SAT math scores over 500: 39%; SAT writing scores over 500: 29%; SAT critical reading scores over 600: 8%; SAT math scores over 600: 9%; SAT writing scores over 600: 5%; SAT critical reading scores over 700: 1%; SAT math scores over 700: 1%.

Faculty *Total:* 188, 73% full-time, 65% with terminal degrees. *Student/faculty ratio:* 17:1.

Academics *Calendar:* semesters. *Degrees:* associate, bachelor's, and master's. *Special study options:* adult/continuing education programs, part-time degree program. *ROTC:* Army (c).

Computers on Campus Students can access the following: campus intranet, computer help desk, free student e-mail accounts, online (class) grades, online (class) registration, online (class) schedules. Campuswide network is available. 100% of college-owned or -operated housing units are wired for high-speed Internet access. Wireless service is available via classrooms, computer centers, computer labs, dorm rooms, learning centers, libraries, student centers.

Student Life *Housing:* on-campus residence required through sophomore year. *Options:* coed. Campus housing is university owned. Freshman campus housing is guaranteed. *Campus security:* 24-hour emergency response devices and patrols, student patrols, late-night transport/escort service, controlled dormitory access.

Athletics Member NCAA. All Division II. *Intercollegiate sports:* baseball M(s), basketball M(s)/W(s), cross-country running M(s)/W(s), field hockey W(s), football M(c), soccer W(s), softball W(s), swimming and diving W, track and field M(s)/W(s). *Intramural sports:* badminton M/W, basketball M/W, bowling M/W, cheerleading W, cross-country running M/W, equestrian sports M/W, football M/W, golf M/W, racquetball M/W, skiing (cross-country) M/W, skiing (downhill) M/W, soccer M/W, softball M/W, swimming and diving M/W, tennis M/W, track and field M/W, volleyball M/W, water polo M/W, weight lifting M/W.

Standardized Tests *Required:* SAT or ACT (for admission).

Costs (2013–14) *Tuition:* state resident $6428 full-time, $268 per credit hour part-time; nonresident $16,070 full-time, $670 per credit hour part-time. Part-time tuition and fees vary according to course load. *Required fees:* $2498 full-time. *Room and board:* $8592; room only: $5780. Room and board charges vary according to board plan and housing facility. *Payment plans:* installment, deferred payment. *Waivers:* senior citizens and employees or children of employees.

Financial Aid Of all full-time matriculated undergraduates who enrolled in 2010, 2,454 applied for aid, 2,234 were judged to have need, 134 had their need fully met. *Average percent of need met:* 54%. *Average financial aid package:* $9305. *Average need-based loan:* $4331. *Average need-based gift aid:* $5612. *Average indebtedness upon graduation:* $23,216.

Applying *Options:* electronic application, early admission, deferred entrance. *Application fee:* $25. *Required:* high school transcript. *Required for some:* interview. *Recommended:* essay or personal statement, minimum 2.5 GPA. *Application deadlines:* rolling (freshmen), rolling (transfers). *Notification:* continuous (freshmen), continuous (transfers).

Freshman Application Contact Mr. Brian Barden, Director of Admissions, Mansfield University of Pennsylvania, Academy Street, Mansfield, PA 16933. *Phone:* 570-662-4813. *Toll-free phone:* 800-577-6826. *E-mail:* admissions@mnsfld.edu.
Website: http://www.mansfield.edu/.

Marywood University
Scranton, Pennsylvania

- **Independent Roman Catholic** comprehensive, founded 1915
- **Suburban** 122-acre campus
- **Endowment** $39.6 million
- **Coed** 2,267 undergraduate students, 93% full-time, 70% women, 30% men
- **Moderately difficult** entrance level, 69% of applicants were admitted

Undergraduates 2,106 full-time, 161 part-time. Students come from 32 states and territories; 21 other countries; 27% are from out of state; 1% Black or African American, non-Hispanic/Latino; 3% Hispanic/Latino; 2% Asian, non-Hispanic/Latino; 0.1% American Indian or Alaska Native, non-Hispanic/Latino; 0.1% Two or more races, non-Hispanic/Latino; 6% Race/ethnicity unknown; 0.7% international; 6% transferred in; 49% live on campus. *Retention:* 81% of full-time freshmen returned.

Freshmen *Admission:* 2,284 applied, 1,578 admitted, 458 enrolled. *Average high school GPA:* 3.21. *Test scores:* SAT critical reading scores over 500: 66%; SAT math scores over 500: 64%; SAT writing scores over 500: 63%; ACT scores over 18: 97%; SAT critical reading scores over 600: 14%; SAT math scores over 600: 16%; SAT writing scores over 600: 14%; ACT scores over 24: 29%; SAT critical reading scores over 700: 1%; SAT math scores over 700: 1%; SAT writing scores over 700: 3%; ACT scores over 30: 4%.

Faculty *Total:* 398, 38% full-time. *Student/faculty ratio:* 13:1.

Academics *Calendar:* semesters. *Degrees:* certificates, bachelor's, master's, doctoral, post-master's, and postbachelor's certificates. *Special study options:* adult/continuing education programs, advanced placement credit, double majors, English as a second language, honors programs, independent study, internships, off-campus study, part-time degree program, services for LD students, student-designed majors, study abroad, summer session for credit. *ROTC:* Army (c), Air Force (c). *Unusual degree programs:* 3-2 physician assistant, communication sciences disorders, criminal justice, biotechnology, health services administration.

Computers on Campus 460 computers/terminals are available on campus for general student use. Students can access the following: computer help desk, free student e-mail accounts, online (class) grades, online (class) registration, online (class) schedules, degree audit, student account management. Campus-wide network is available. 100% of college-owned or -operated housing units are wired for high-speed Internet access. Wireless service is available via entire campus.

Student Life *Housing:* on-campus residence required through sophomore year. *Options:* coed, men-only, women-only, disabled students. Campus housing is university owned. Freshman campus housing is guaranteed. *Activities and organizations:* drama/theater group, student-run newspaper, radio and television station, choral group, Anime and Japanese Club, Diversity United, Marywood Aviators, Marywood Players, International Club. *Campus security:* 24-hour emergency response devices and patrols, late-night transport/escort service, controlled dormitory access, apartments with deadbolts, self-defense education, lighted pathways, seminars on safety. *Student services:* health clinic, personal/psychological counseling.

Athletics Member NCAA. All Division III. *Intercollegiate sports:* baseball M, basketball M/W, cross-country running M/W, field hockey W, golf M, lacrosse M/W, skiing (cross-country) M(c)/W(c), soccer M/W, softball W, swimming and diving M/W, tennis M/W, track and field M(c)/W(c), volleyball W. *Intramural sports:* badminton M/W, basketball M/W, cheerleading M(c)/W(c), cross-country running M(c)/W(c), racquetball M/W, soccer M/W, softball M/W, swimming and diving M/W, table tennis M/W, tennis M/W, track and field M(c)/W(c), volleyball M/W.

Standardized Tests *Required:* SAT or ACT (for admission).

Costs (2013–14) *Comprehensive fee:* $44,006 includes full-time tuition ($29,340), mandatory fees ($1100), and room and board ($13,566). Full-time tuition and fees vary according to course load. Part-time tuition and fees vary according to course load. *College room only:* $7634. Room and board charges vary according to board plan and housing facility. *Payment plans:* installment, deferred payment. *Waivers:* senior citizens and employees or children of employees.

Financial Aid Of all full-time matriculated undergraduates who enrolled in 2012, 1,873 applied for aid, 1,765 were judged to have need, 86 had their need fully met. 502 Federal Work-Study jobs (averaging $1981). In 2012, 260 non-need-based awards were made. *Average percent of need met:* 73%. *Average financial aid package:* $20,979. *Average need-based loan:* $4358. *Average need-based gift aid:* $17,612. *Average non-need-based aid:* $13,271. *Average indebtedness upon graduation:* $41,198.

Applying *Options:* electronic application, early admission, deferred entrance. *Application fee:* $35. *Required:* essay or personal statement, high school transcript, 1 letter of recommendation. *Required for some:* interview, art majors require portfolio, music majors require audition. *Recommended:* interview. *Application deadlines:* rolling (freshmen), rolling (transfers). *Notification:* continuous (freshmen), continuous (transfers).

Freshman Application Contact Mr. Christian DiGregorio, Director of University Admissions, Marywood University, 2300 Adams Avenue, Scranton, PA 18509. *Phone:* 570-348-6234. *Toll-free phone:* 866-279-9663. *Fax:* 570-961-4763. *E-mail:* yourfuture@marywood.edu. *Website:* http://www.marywood.edu/.

See below for display ad and page 1380 for the College Close-Up.

Mercyhurst North East
North East, Pennsylvania

Director of Admissions Travis Lindahl, Director of Admissions, Mercyhurst North East, 16 West Division Street, North East, PA 16428. *Phone:* 814-725-6217. *Toll-free phone:* 866-846-6042. *Fax:* 814-725-6251. *E-mail:* neadmiss@mercyhurst.edu. *Website:* http://northeast.mercyhurst.edu/.

Mercyhurst University
Erie, Pennsylvania

- **Independent Roman Catholic** comprehensive, founded 1926
- **Suburban** 88-acre campus with easy access to Buffalo
- **Endowment** $26.9 million
- **Coed** 2,790 undergraduate students, 93% full-time, 57% women, 43% men
- **Moderately difficult** entrance level, 77% of applicants were admitted

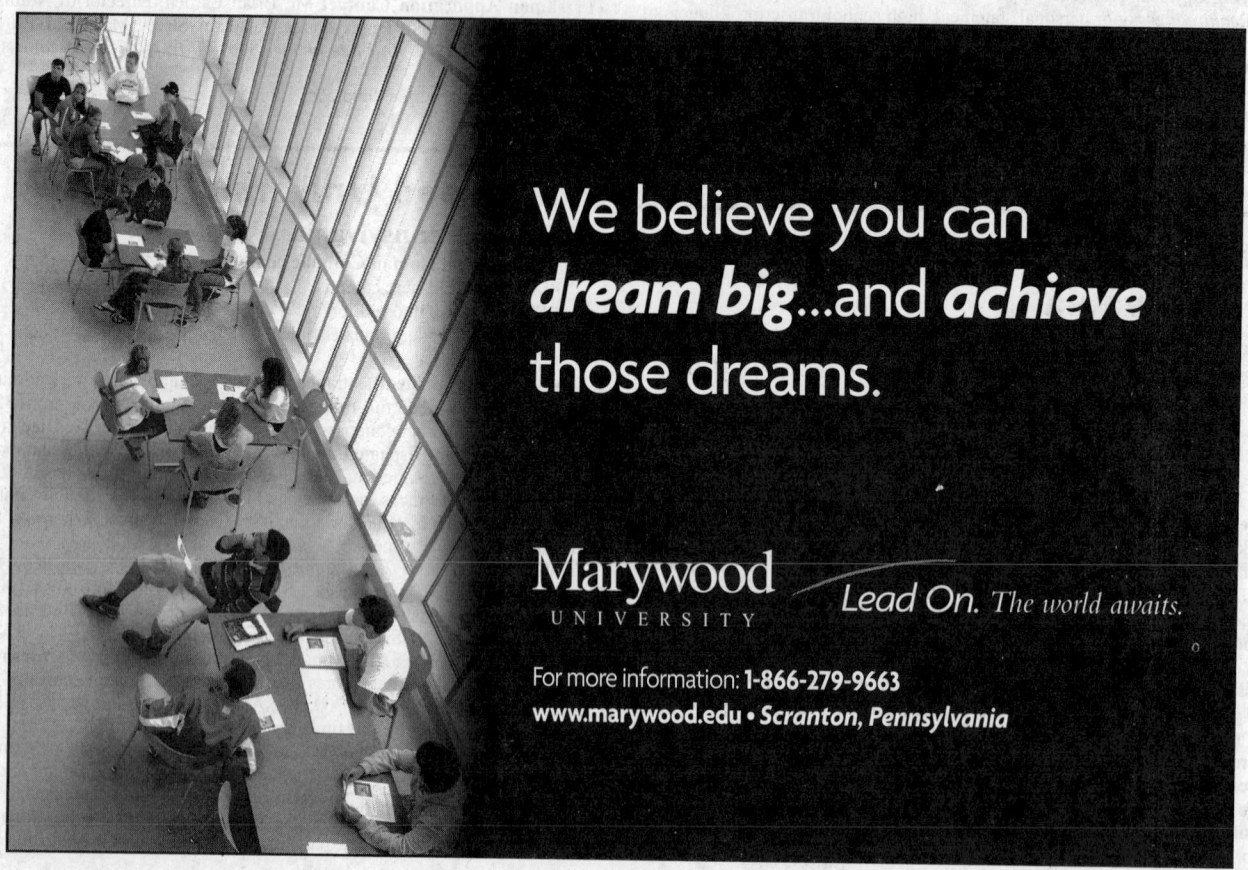

Undergraduates 2,607 full-time, 183 part-time. Students come from 41 states and territories; 31 other countries; 48% are from out of state; 4% Black or African American, non-Hispanic/Latino; 2% Hispanic/Latino; 1% Asian, non-Hispanic/Latino; 0.4% American Indian or Alaska Native, non-Hispanic/Latino; 8% Race/ethnicity unknown; 7% international; 3% transferred in; 68% live on campus. *Retention:* 81% of full-time freshmen returned.
Freshmen *Admission:* 2,961 applied, 2,270 admitted, 672 enrolled. *Average high school GPA:* 3.4. *Test scores:* SAT critical reading scores over 500: 68%; SAT math scores over 500: 69%; ACT scores over 18: 96%; SAT critical reading scores over 600: 22%; SAT math scores over 600: 25%; ACT scores over 24: 47%; SAT critical reading scores over 700: 2%; SAT math scores over 700: 2%; ACT scores over 30: 4%.
Faculty *Total:* 249, 63% full-time, 46% with terminal degrees. *Student/faculty ratio:* 14:1.
Academics *Calendar:* 4-3-3. *Degrees:* associate, bachelor's, master's, and postbachelor's certificates. *Special study options:* academic remediation for entering students, accelerated degree program, adult/continuing education programs, advanced placement credit, cooperative education, distance learning, double majors, honors programs, independent study, internships, off-campus study, part-time degree program, services for LD students, student-designed majors, study abroad, summer session for credit. *ROTC:* Army (c), Air Force (c). *Unusual degree programs:* 3-2 business administration.
Computers on Campus 350 computers/terminals and 150 ports are available on campus for general student use. Students can access the following: campus intranet, computer help desk, free student e-mail accounts, online (class) grades, online (class) registration, online (class) schedules. Campuswide network is available. 100% of college-owned or -operated housing units are wired for high-speed Internet access. Wireless service is available via entire campus.
Student Life *Housing:* on-campus residence required through sophomore year. *Options:* coed, men-only, women-only. Campus housing is university owned and leased by the school. Freshman campus housing is guaranteed. *Activities and organizations:* drama/theater group, student-run newspaper, radio and television station, choral group, student government, chorus, Admission Ambassadors, Amnesty International, The Merciad. *Campus security:* 24-hour emergency response devices and patrols, campus-wide camera system. *Student services:* health clinic, personal/psychological counseling.
Athletics Member NCAA. All Division II except men's and women's ice hockey (Division I). *Intercollegiate sports:* baseball M(s), basketball M(s)/W(s), crew M(s)/W(s), cross-country running M(s)/W(s), field hockey W(s), football M(s), golf M(s)/W(s), ice hockey M(s)/W(s), lacrosse M(s)/W(s), soccer M(s)/W(s), softball W(s), tennis M(s)/W(s), volleyball W(s), water polo M(s)/W(s), wrestling M(s). *Intramural sports:* basketball M/W, football M, skiing (cross-country) M/W, skiing (downhill) M/W, volleyball M/W.
Standardized Tests *Required:* SAT or ACT (for admission). *Recommended:* SAT Subject Tests (for admission).
Costs (2012–13) *Comprehensive fee:* $39,141 includes full-time tuition ($27,150), mandatory fees ($1887), and room and board ($10,104). Full-time tuition and fees vary according to class time, course load, degree level, location, and program. Part-time tuition: $905 per semester hour. Part-time tuition and fees vary according to class time, course load, degree level, location, and program. *College room only:* $5118. Room and board charges vary according to board plan, housing facility, and location. *Payment plan:* installment. *Waivers:* adult students and employees or children of employees.
Financial Aid Of all full-time matriculated undergraduates who enrolled in 2011, 1,976 applied for aid, 1,802 were judged to have need, 527 had their need fully met. 553 Federal Work-Study jobs (averaging $1211). 372 state and other part-time jobs (averaging $1257). In 2011, 492 non-need-based awards were made. *Average percent of need met:* 83%. *Average financial aid package:* $23,673. *Average need-based loan:* $3706. *Average need-based gift aid:* $19,051. *Average non-need-based aid:* $14,360. *Average indebtedness upon graduation:* $24,728. *Financial aid deadline:* 5/1.
Applying *Options:* electronic application, deferred entrance. *Application fee:* $30. *Required:* essay or personal statement, high school transcript. *Required for some:* 1 letter of recommendation. *Recommended:* interview. *Application deadlines:* rolling (freshmen), rolling (out-of-state freshmen), rolling (transfers). *Notification:* continuous until 11/1 (freshmen), continuous until 11/1 (out-of-state freshmen), continuous until 12/1 (transfers).
Freshman Application Contact Christopher Coons, Director of Undergraduate Admissions, Mercyhurst University, 501 East 38th Street, Erie, PA 16546-0001. *Phone:* 814-824-2202. *Toll-free phone:* 800-825-1926. *Fax:* 814-824-2071. *E-mail:* ccoons@mercyhurst.edu. *Website:* http://www.mercyhurst.edu/.

Messiah College
Mechanicsburg, Pennsylvania
- **Independent interdenominational** comprehensive, founded 1909
- **Small-town** 485-acre campus
- **Endowment** $120.3 million
- **Coed** 2,798 undergraduate students, 97% full-time, 61% women, 39% men
- **Moderately difficult** entrance level, 64% of applicants were admitted

Undergraduates 2,710 full-time, 88 part-time. Students come from 37 states and territories; 27 other countries; 40% are from out of state; 2% Black or African American, non-Hispanic/Latino; 3% Hispanic/Latino; 2% Asian, non-Hispanic/Latino; 0.1% Native Hawaiian or other Pacific Islander, non-Hispanic/Latino; 0.1% American Indian or Alaska Native, non-Hispanic/Latino; 2% Two or more races, non-Hispanic/Latino; 2% Race/ethnicity unknown; 2% international; 3% transferred in; 87% live on campus. *Retention:* 87% of full-time freshmen returned.
Freshmen *Admission:* 3,149 applied, 2,023 admitted, 708 enrolled. *Average high school GPA:* 3.68. *Test scores:* SAT critical reading scores over 500: 79%; SAT math scores over 500: 81%; SAT writing scores over 500: 75%; ACT scores over 18: 96%; SAT critical reading scores over 600: 35%; SAT math scores over 600: 39%; SAT writing scores over 600: 33%; ACT scores over 24: 57%; SAT critical reading scores over 700: 7%; SAT math scores over 700: 7%; SAT writing scores over 700: 7%; ACT scores over 30: 16%.
Faculty *Total:* 312, 56% full-time, 59% with terminal degrees. *Student/faculty ratio:* 13:1.
Academics *Calendar:* semesters. *Degrees:* bachelor's, master's, post-master's, and postbachelor's certificates. *Special study options:* accelerated degree program, adult/continuing education programs, advanced placement credit, cooperative education, distance learning, double majors, English as a second language, freshman honors college, honors programs, independent study, internships, off-campus study, part-time degree program, services for LD students, student-designed majors, study abroad, summer session for credit. *Unusual degree programs:* 3-2 Biopsychology (BS)/EMOT in Occupational Therapy with Thomas Jefferson University; Health and Exercise Science (BA)/MSOT in Occupational Therapy with Thomas Jefferson University; Politics (BA)/MS in Public Policy and Management with Carnegie Mellon University.
Computers on Campus 571 computers/terminals are available on campus for general student use. Students can access the following: campus intranet, computer help desk, free student e-mail accounts, online (class) grades, online (class) registration, online (class) schedules, access to software. Campuswide network is available. 100% of college-owned or -operated housing units are wired for high-speed Internet access. Wireless service is available via entire campus.
Student Life *Housing:* on-campus residence required through senior year. *Options:* coed, men-only, women-only, disabled students. Campus housing is university owned. Freshman campus housing is guaranteed. *Activities and organizations:* drama/theater group, student-run newspaper, radio station, choral group, Outreach teams, student government, choral groups and ensembles, Small Group Program, Outdoors Club. *Campus security:* 24-hour emergency response devices and patrols, student patrols, late-night transport/escort service, controlled dormitory access, bicycle patrols, security lighting, self-defense classes, prevention/awareness programs. *Student services:* health clinic, personal/psychological counseling.
Athletics Member NCAA. All Division III. *Intercollegiate sports:* baseball M, basketball M/W, cross-country running M/W, field hockey W, golf M, lacrosse M/W, soccer M/W, softball W, swimming and diving M/W, tennis M/W, track and field M/W, volleyball W, wrestling M. *Intramural sports:* basketball M/W, football M/W, ice hockey M(c), racquetball M/W, soccer M/W, softball M/W, ultimate Frisbee M/W, volleyball M/W.
Standardized Tests *Required for some:* SAT or ACT (for admission). *Recommended:* SAT or ACT (for admission).
Costs (2013–14) *Comprehensive fee:* $39,540 includes full-time tuition ($29,650), mandatory fees ($820), and room and board ($9070). Part-time tuition: $1235 per credit hour. *College room only:* $4800. Room and board charges vary according to board plan, housing facility, and location. *Payment plan:* installment. *Waivers:* minority students, children of alumni, adult students, senior citizens, and employees or children of employees.
Financial Aid Of all full-time matriculated undergraduates who enrolled in 2012, 2,254 applied for aid, 1,992 were judged to have need, 352 had their need fully met. 893 Federal Work-Study jobs (averaging $2087). 779 state and other part-time jobs (averaging $1941). In 2012, 686 non-need-based awards were made. *Average percent of need met:* 70%. *Average financial aid package:* $20,782. *Average need-based loan:* $4790. *Average need-based gift aid:* $15,077. *Average non-need-based aid:* $11,434. *Average indebtedness upon graduation:* $35,306.

Applying *Options:* electronic application, deferred entrance. *Application fee:* $30. *Required:* essay or personal statement, high school transcript, 1 letter of recommendation. *Recommended:* interview. *Application deadlines:* rolling (freshmen), rolling (transfers). *Notification:* continuous (freshmen), continuous (transfers).

Freshman Application Contact Mr. John Chopka, Vice President for Enrollment Management, Messiah College, One College Avenue, Suite 3005, Mechanicsburg, PA 17055. *Phone:* 717-691-6000. *Toll-free phone:* 800-233-4220. *Fax:* 717-791-2307. *E-mail:* admiss@messiah.edu. *Website:* http://www.messiah.edu/.

Millersville University of Pennsylvania

Millersville, Pennsylvania

- **State-supported** comprehensive, founded 1855, part of Pennsylvania State System of Higher Education
- **Small-town** 250-acre campus
- **Endowment** $2.0 million
- **Coed** 7,424 undergraduate students, 90% full-time, 55% women, 45% men
- **Moderately difficult** entrance level, 63% of applicants were admitted

Undergraduates 6,675 full-time, 749 part-time. Students come from 23 states and territories; 57 other countries; 4% are from out of state; 8% Black or African American, non-Hispanic/Latino; 7% Hispanic/Latino; 2% Asian, non-Hispanic/Latino; 0.1% Native Hawaiian or other Pacific Islander, non-Hispanic/Latino; 0.2% American Indian or Alaska Native, non-Hispanic/Latino; 2% Two or more races, non-Hispanic/Latino; 0.7% Race/ethnicity unknown; 0.5% international; 8% transferred in; 30% live on campus. *Retention:* 79% of full-time freshmen returned.

Freshmen *Admission:* 6,665 applied, 4,192 admitted, 1,318 enrolled. *Test scores:* SAT critical reading scores over 500: 55%; SAT math scores over 500: 62%; SAT writing scores over 500: 47%; ACT scores over 18: 87%; SAT critical reading scores over 600: 13%; SAT math scores over 600: 15%; SAT writing scores over 600: 10%; ACT scores over 24: 26%; SAT critical reading scores over 700: 1%; SAT math scores over 700: 1%.

Faculty *Total:* 442, 64% full-time, 73% with terminal degrees. *Student/faculty ratio:* 22:1.

Academics *Calendar:* 4-1-4. *Degrees:* associate, bachelor's, master's, post-master's, and postbachelor's certificates. *Special study options:* academic remediation for entering students, accelerated degree program, adult/continuing education programs, advanced placement credit, cooperative education, distance learning, double majors, honors programs, independent study, internships, off-campus study, part-time degree program, services for LD students, study abroad, summer session for credit. *ROTC:* Army (b). *Unusual degree programs:* engineering with Pennsylvania State University.

Computers on Campus 430 computers/terminals are available on campus for general student use. Students can access the following: computer help desk, free student e-mail accounts, online (class) grades, online (class) registration, online (class) schedules. Campuswide network is available. 100% of college-owned or -operated housing units are wired for high-speed Internet access. Wireless service is available via entire campus.

Student Life *Housing:* on-campus residence required through sophomore year. *Options:* coed, disabled students. Campus housing is university owned. Freshman campus housing is guaranteed. *Activities and organizations:* drama/theater group, student-run newspaper, radio and television station, choral group, marching band, MUTV 99, University Christian Fellowship, Marching Band, University Activities Board (UAB), Student Senate, national fraternities, national sororities. *Campus security:* 24-hour emergency response devices and patrols, student patrols, late-night transport/escort service, controlled dormitory access, crime awareness programs, self-defense education, shuttle buses, lighted pathways / sidewalks. *Student services:* health clinic, personal/psychological counseling, women's center.

Athletics Member NCAA. All Division II except wrestling (Division I). *Intercollegiate sports:* baseball M(s), basketball M(s)/W(s), cheerleading W, cross-country running M(s)/W(s), field hockey W(s), football M(s), golf M(s), lacrosse W(s), soccer M(s)/W(s), softball W(s), swimming and diving W(s), tennis M(s)/W(s), track and field M(s)/W(s), volleyball W(s), wrestling M(s). *Intramural sports:* badminton M/W, basketball M/W, bowling M(c)/W(c), fencing M(c)/W(c), golf M/W, ice hockey M(c), lacrosse M(c), racquetball M/W, rock climbing M/W, rugby M(c)/W(c), soccer M/W, softball M/W, tennis M/W, ultimate Frisbee M/W, volleyball M(c)/W, water polo M(c)/W(c).

Standardized Tests *Required:* SAT or ACT (for admission).

Costs (2012–13) *Tuition:* state resident $6428 full-time, $268 per credit part-time; nonresident $16,070 full-time, $670 per credit part-time. Part-time tuition and fees vary according to course load. *Required fees:* $2172 full-time, $76 per credit part-time, $15 per credit part-time. *Room and board:* $9234;

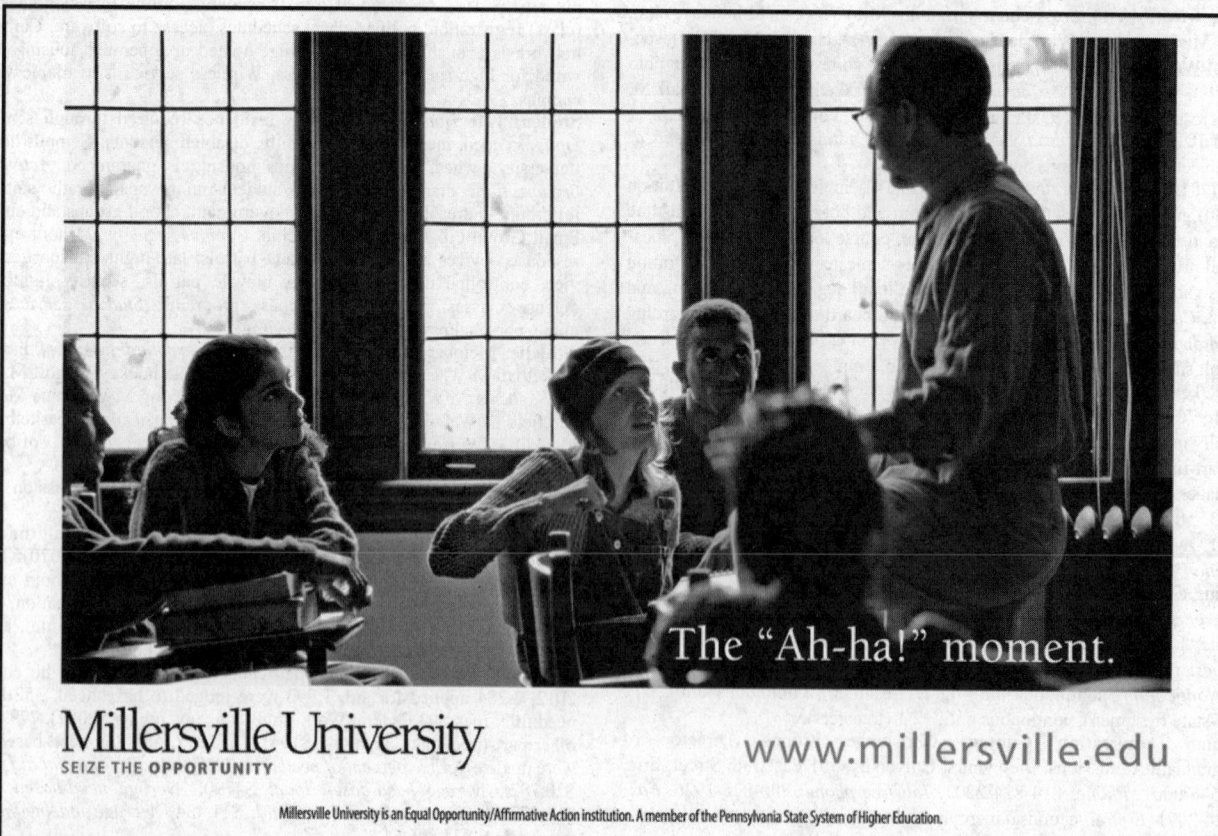

The "Ah-ha!" moment.

Millersville University
SEIZE THE OPPORTUNITY

www.millersville.edu

Millersville University is an Equal Opportunity/Affirmative Action institution. A member of the Pennsylvania State System of Higher Education.

room only: $5378. Room and board charges vary according to board plan and housing facility. *Payment plan:* installment. *Waivers:* senior citizens and employees or children of employees.

Financial Aid Of all full-time matriculated undergraduates who enrolled in 2011, 5,680 applied for aid, 4,516 were judged to have need, 429 had their need fully met. 260 Federal Work-Study jobs (averaging $1086). 1,844 state and other part-time jobs (averaging $1564). In 2011, 141 non-need-based awards were made. *Average percent of need met:* 70%. *Average financial aid package:* $8185. *Average need-based loan:* $4236. *Average need-based gift aid:* $5395. *Average non-need-based aid:* $3113. *Average indebtedness upon graduation:* $30,210.

Applying *Options:* electronic application, early admission, deferred entrance. *Application fee:* $50. *Required:* high school transcript, minimum 2.0 GPA. *Required for some:* essay or personal statement, 1 letter of recommendation, interview. *Recommended:* essay or personal statement, 1 letter of recommendation. *Application deadlines:* rolling (freshmen), rolling (out-of-state freshmen), rolling (transfers). *Notification:* continuous (freshmen), continuous (out-of-state freshmen), continuous (transfers).

Freshman Application Contact Mr. Brian Hazlett, Director of Admissions, Millersville University of Pennsylvania, PO Box 1002, Millersville, PA 17551-0302. *Phone:* 717-872-3371. *Toll-free phone:* 800-MU-ADMIT. *Fax:* 717-871-2147. *E-mail:* admissions@millersville.edu. *Website:* http://www.millersville.edu/

See previous page for display ad and page 1390 for the College Close-Up.

Misericordia University

Dallas, Pennsylvania

- **Independent Roman Catholic** comprehensive, founded 1924
- **Small-town** 120-acre campus
- **Endowment** $25.4 million
- **Coed, primarily women** 2,427 undergraduate students, 73% full-time, 68% women, 32% men
- **Moderately difficult** entrance level, 58% of applicants were admitted

Undergraduates 1,767 full-time, 660 part-time. Students come from 21 states and territories; 1 other country; 21% are from out of state; 1% Black or African American, non-Hispanic/Latino; 3% Hispanic/Latino; 0.8% Asian, non-Hispanic/Latino; 0.1% American Indian or Alaska Native, non-Hispanic/Latino; 0.3% Two or more races, non-Hispanic/Latino; 5% transferred in; 45% live on campus. *Retention:* 86% of full-time freshmen returned.

Freshmen *Admission:* 2,526 applied, 1,476 admitted, 511 enrolled. *Average high school GPA:* 3.27. *Test scores:* SAT critical reading scores over 500: 59%; SAT math scores over 500: 67%; ACT scores over 18: 98%; SAT critical reading scores over 600: 11%; SAT math scores over 600: 17%; ACT scores over 24: 55%; SAT critical reading scores over 700: 1%; SAT math scores over 700: 2%; ACT scores over 30: 4%.

Faculty *Total:* 323, 34% full-time, 37% with terminal degrees. *Student/faculty ratio:* 12:1.

Academics *Calendar:* semesters. *Degrees:* certificates, bachelor's, master's, doctoral, post-master's, and postbachelor's certificates. *Special study options:* accelerated degree program, adult/continuing education programs, advanced placement credit, cooperative education, distance learning, double majors, external degree program, honors programs, independent study, internships, off-campus study, part-time degree program, services for LD students, student-designed majors, study abroad, summer session for credit. *ROTC:* Army (c), Air Force (c). *Unusual degree programs:* 3-2 occupational therapy, speech-language pathology.

Computers on Campus 150 computers/terminals and 1,000 ports are available on campus for general student use. Students can access the following: campus intranet, computer help desk, free student e-mail accounts, online (class) grades, online (class) registration, online (class) schedules, student leadership transcript. Campuswide network is available. 100% of college-owned or -operated housing units are wired for high-speed Internet access. Wireless service is available via entire campus.

Student Life *Housing options:* coed. Freshman applicants given priority for college housing. *Activities and organizations:* drama/theater group, student-run newspaper, radio and television station, choral group, MSOTA, Peer Associates, Physical Therapy club, Varsity 'M' Club, Education Club. *Campus security:* 24-hour emergency response devices and patrols, late-night transport/escort service, controlled dormitory access. *Student services:* health clinic, personal/psychological counseling, women's center.

Athletics Member NCAA. All Division III except tennis (Division II). *Intercollegiate sports:* baseball M, basketball M/W, cross-country running M/W, field hockey W, football M, golf M/W, lacrosse M/W, soccer M/W, softball W, swimming and diving M/W, tennis M/W, track and field M/W, volleyball W. *Intramural sports:* basketball M/W, football M/W, soccer M/W, softball M/W, tennis M/W, ultimate Frisbee M/W, volleyball M/W.

Standardized Tests *Required:* SAT or ACT (for admission).

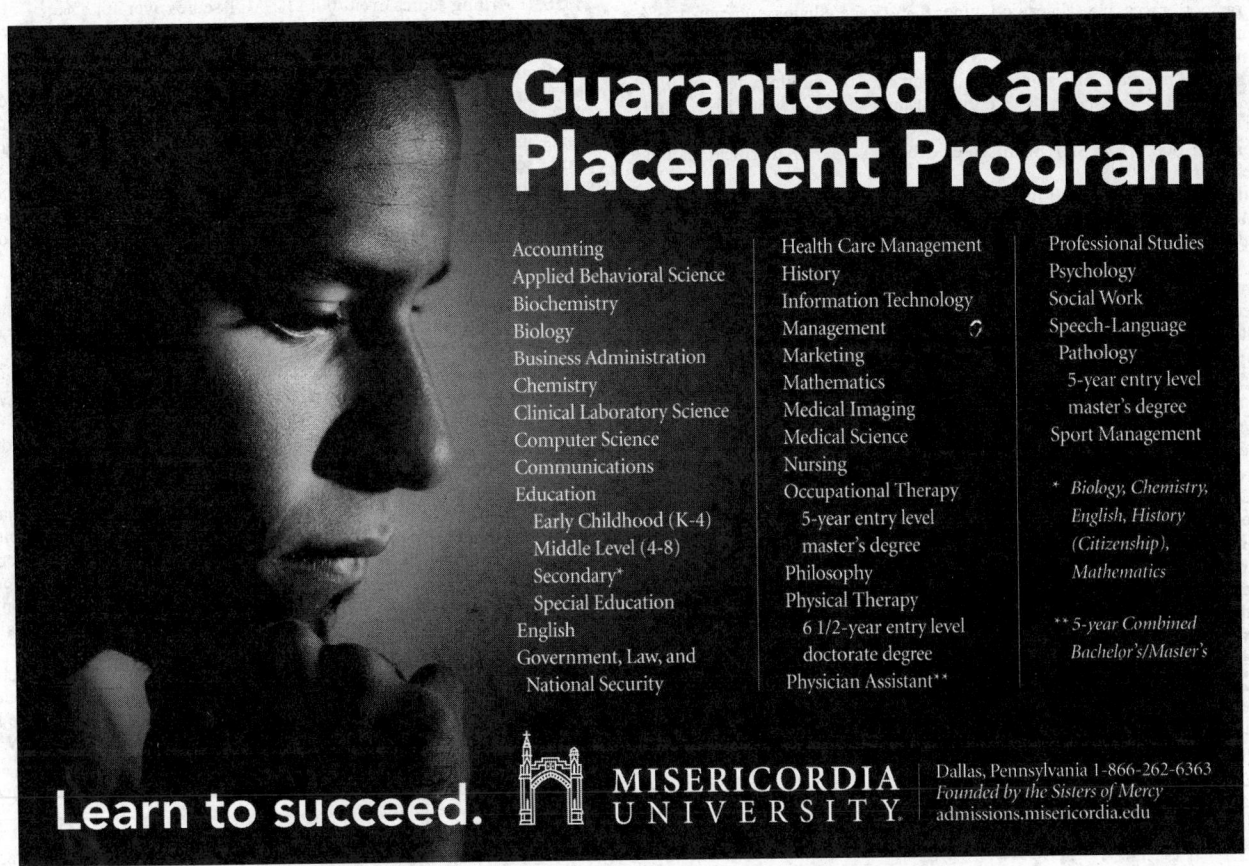

Costs (2012–13) *Comprehensive fee:* $38,420 includes full-time tuition ($25,890), mandatory fees ($1340), and room and board ($11,190). Part-time tuition: $495 per credit. Part-time tuition and fees vary according to class time, degree level, and location. *College room only:* $6530. Room and board charges vary according to board plan and housing facility. *Payment plans:* installment, deferred payment. *Waivers:* employees or children of employees.
Financial Aid Of all full-time matriculated undergraduates who enrolled in 2012, 1,656 applied for aid, 1,462 were judged to have need, 308 had their need fully met. In 2012, 190 non-need-based awards were made. *Average percent of need met:* 75%. *Average financial aid package:* $19,070. *Average need-based loan:* $8237. *Average need-based gift aid:* $13,496. *Average non-need-based aid:* $8631.
Applying *Options:* electronic application, early admission, deferred entrance. *Application fee:* $25. *Required:* high school transcript. *Required for some:* essay or personal statement, minimum 2.5 GPA, 2 letters of recommendation. *Recommended:* interview. *Application deadlines:* rolling (freshmen), rolling (out-of-state freshmen), rolling (transfers). *Notification:* continuous (freshmen), continuous (out-of-state freshmen), continuous (transfers).
Freshman Application Contact Mr. Glenn Bozinski, Director of Admissions, Misericordia University, 301 Lake Street, Dallas, PA 18612-1098. *Phone:* 570-675-6264. *Toll-free phone:* 866-262-6363. *Fax:* 570-674-6232. *E-mail:* admiss@misericordia.edu.
Website: http://www.misericordia.edu/.

See previous page for display ad and page 1396 for the College Close-Up.

Moore College of Art & Design
Philadelphia, Pennsylvania
- **Independent** 4-year, founded 1848
- **Urban** 3-acre campus with easy access to Philadelphia
- **Endowment** $13.7 million
- **Women only** 482 undergraduate students, 94% full-time
- **Moderately difficult** entrance level, 54% of applicants were admitted

Undergraduates 451 full-time, 31 part-time. Students come from 29 states and territories; 12 other countries; 42% are from out of state; 16% Black or African American, non-Hispanic/Latino; 5% Hispanic/Latino; 4% Asian, non-Hispanic/Latino; 0.8% Native Hawaiian or other Pacific Islander, non-Hispanic/Latino; 1% American Indian or Alaska Native, non-Hispanic/Latino; 5% Two or more races, non-Hispanic/Latino; 0.8% Race/ethnicity unknown; 3% international; 9% transferred in. *Retention:* 73% of full-time freshmen returned.
Freshmen *Admission:* 607 applied, 330 admitted, 105 enrolled. *Average high school GPA:* 3.2. *Test scores:* SAT critical reading scores over 500: 52%; SAT math scores over 500: 42%; ACT scores over 18: 78%; SAT critical reading scores over 600: 15%; SAT math scores over 600: 9%; SAT critical reading scores over 700: 2%.
Faculty *Total:* 136, 18% full-time. *Student/faculty ratio:* 8:1.
Academics *Calendar:* semesters. *Degrees:* certificates, bachelor's, master's, and postbachelor's certificates. *Special study options:* academic remediation for entering students, advanced placement credit, cooperative education, double majors, external degree program, independent study, internships, part-time degree program, services for LD students, study abroad, summer session for credit.
Computers on Campus Students can access the following: computer help desk, free student e-mail accounts, online (class) grades, online (class) registration, online (class) schedules, Free iPads for all first year students. Campuswide network is available. Wireless service is available via entire campus.
Student Life *Housing options:* women-only. Campus housing is university owned. Freshman campus housing is guaranteed. *Activities and organizations:* Student Government Association, Student Orientation Staff, yearbook, Residence Life Staff, Business Scholars in the Arts. *Campus security:* 24-hour patrols, late-night transport/escort service, controlled dormitory access. *Student services:* health clinic, personal/psychological counseling.
Athletics *Intramural sports:* volleyball W.
Standardized Tests *Required for some:* SAT or ACT (for admission).
Costs (2013–14) *One-time required fee:* $241. *Tuition:* $31,654 full-time, $1321 per credit part-time. Full-time tuition and fees vary according to course load. Part-time tuition and fees vary according to course load. *Required fees:* $1084 full-time, $543 per year part-time. *Room only:* $12,298. Room and board charges vary according to board plan. *Payment plan:* installment.
Financial Aid Of all full-time matriculated undergraduates who enrolled in 2006, 383 applied for aid, 357 were judged to have need, 9 had their need fully met. 87 Federal Work-Study jobs (averaging $1500). In 2006, 93 non-need-based awards were made. *Average percent of need met:* 45%. *Average financial aid package:* $14,823. *Average need-based loan:* $4355. *Average need-based gift aid:* $10,180. *Average non-need-based aid:* $9729. *Average indebtedness upon graduation:* $36,778.
Applying *Options:* electronic application, deferred entrance. *Application fee:* $40. *Required:* high school transcript, minimum 2.5 GPA, 1 letter of recommendation, portfolio review required. *Required for some:* minimum 3.0 GPA. *Recommended:* essay or personal statement, interview. *Application deadlines:* 8/15 (freshmen), rolling (transfers). *Notification:* continuous (freshmen), continuous (transfers).
Freshman Application Contact Ms. Jasmine Zateeny, Assistant Director of Admissions, Recruitment Coordinator, Moore College of Art & Design, 20th and The Parkway, Philadelphia, PA 19103. *Phone:* 215-965-4015. *Toll-free phone:* 800-523-2025. *Fax:* 215-965-8544. *E-mail:* enroll@moore.edu. *Website:* http://www.moore.edu/.

Moravian College
Bethlehem, Pennsylvania
- **Independent** comprehensive, founded 1742, affiliated with Moravian Church
- **Suburban** 60-acre campus with easy access to Philadelphia
- **Endowment** $91.6 million
- **Coed** 1,582 undergraduate students, 92% full-time, 61% women, 39% men
- **Moderately difficult** entrance level, 79% of applicants were admitted

Undergraduates 1,459 full-time, 123 part-time. Students come from 20 states and territories; 7 other countries; 32% are from out of state; 3% Black or African American, non-Hispanic/Latino; 7% Hispanic/Latino; 2% Asian, non-Hispanic/Latino; 0.2% Native Hawaiian or other Pacific Islander, non-Hispanic/Latino; 0.1% American Indian or Alaska Native, non-Hispanic/Latino; 3% Two or more races, non-Hispanic/Latino; 0.4% Race/ethnicity unknown; 0.3% international; 5% transferred in; 73% live on campus. *Retention:* 76% of full-time freshmen returned.
Freshmen *Admission:* 2,034 applied, 1,597 admitted, 378 enrolled. *Average high school GPA:* 3.32. *Test scores:* SAT critical reading scores over 500: 60%; SAT math scores over 500: 63%; SAT writing scores over 500: 59%; ACT scores over 18: 100%; SAT critical reading scores over 600: 21%; SAT math scores over 600: 24%; SAT writing scores over 600: 14%; ACT scores over 24: 39%; SAT critical reading scores over 700: 3%; SAT math scores over 700: 2%; SAT writing scores over 700: 2%; ACT scores over 30: 8%.
Faculty *Total:* 167, 60% full-time, 72% with terminal degrees. *Student/faculty ratio:* 12:1.
Academics *Calendar:* semesters. *Degrees:* bachelor's, master's, and postbachelor's certificates. *Special study options:* adult/continuing education programs, advanced placement credit, cooperative education, double majors, honors programs, independent study, internships, off-campus study, part-time degree program, services for LD students, student-designed majors, study abroad, summer session for credit. *ROTC:* Army (c). *Unusual degree programs:* 3-2 business administration with Accounting; engineering with Washington University in St. Louis; Lehigh University; forestry with Duke University; occupational therapy with Thomas Jefferson University, Dental School, Temple University.
Computers on Campus 180 computers/terminals are available on campus for general student use. Students can access the following: campus intranet, computer help desk, free student e-mail accounts, online (class) grades, online (class) schedules. Campuswide network is available. 100% of college-owned or -operated housing units are wired for high-speed Internet access. Wireless service is available via entire campus.
Student Life *Housing:* on-campus residence required through senior year. *Options:* coed, men-only, women-only. Campus housing is university owned. Freshman campus housing is guaranteed. *Activities and organizations:* drama/theater group, student-run newspaper, radio station, choral group, marching band, United Student Government, Moravian College Choir, Habitat for Humanity, Student Nurses Association, Moravian College Theatre Company, national fraternities, national sororities. *Campus security:* 24-hour emergency response devices and patrols, late-night transport/escort service, controlled dormitory access. *Student services:* health clinic, personal/psychological counseling.
Athletics Member NCAA. All Division III. *Intercollegiate sports:* baseball M, basketball M/W, cheerleading W(c), cross-country running M/W, equestrian sports M(c)/W(c), field hockey W, football M, golf M, ice hockey M(c)/W(c), soccer M/W, softball W, tennis M/W, track and field M/W, volleyball W. *Intramural sports:* basketball M/W, volleyball M/W.
Standardized Tests *Recommended:* SAT (for admission), ACT (for admission), SAT or ACT (for admission).
Costs (2012–13) *Comprehensive fee:* $44,630 includes full-time tuition ($33,919), mandatory fees ($565), and room and board ($10,146). Part-time

tuition: $942 per credit hour. Part-time tuition and fees vary according to class time. *College room only:* $5676. Room and board charges vary according to board plan and housing facility. *Payment plan:* installment. *Waivers:* employees or children of employees.

Financial Aid Of all full-time matriculated undergraduates who enrolled in 2012, 1,321 applied for aid, 1,227 were judged to have need, 152 had their need fully met. 997 Federal Work-Study jobs (averaging $1858). 173 state and other part-time jobs (averaging $870). In 2012, 169 non-need-based awards were made. *Average percent of need met:* 74%. *Average financial aid package:* $25,753. *Average need-based loan:* $4715. *Average need-based gift aid:* $19,876. *Average non-need-based aid:* $10,271.

Applying *Options:* electronic application, deferred entrance. *Application fee:* $40. *Required:* essay or personal statement, high school transcript, 2 letters of recommendation. *Recommended:* interview. *Application deadlines:* 3/1 (freshmen), 3/1 (transfers). *Notification:* 3/15 (freshmen), continuous (transfers).

Freshman Application Contact Kenneth Huus, Vice President for Enrollment, Moravian College, 1200 Main Street, Bethlehem, PA 18018. *Phone:* 610-861-1645. *Toll-free phone:* 800-441-3191. *Fax:* 610-625-7930. *E-mail:* admissions@moravian.edu. *Website:* http://www.moravian.edu/.

Mount Aloysius College

Cresson, Pennsylvania

- **Independent Roman Catholic** comprehensive, founded 1939
- **Small-town** 193-acre campus
- **Coed** 1,706 undergraduate students, 73% full-time, 72% women, 28% men
- **Minimally difficult** entrance level, 69% of applicants were admitted

Undergraduates 1,241 full-time, 465 part-time. 3% are from out of state; 1% Black or African American, non-Hispanic/Latino; 0.9% Hispanic/Latino; 0.2% Asian, non-Hispanic/Latino; 0.2% American Indian or Alaska Native, non-Hispanic/Latino; 23% Race/ethnicity unknown; 1% international; 9% transferred in; 33% live on campus. *Retention:* 66% of full-time freshmen returned.

Freshmen *Admission:* 1,546 applied, 1,063 admitted, 379 enrolled. *Average high school GPA:* 3.2. *Test scores:* SAT critical reading scores over 500: 25%; SAT math scores over 500: 31%; SAT writing scores over 500: 21%; ACT scores over 18: 76%; SAT critical reading scores over 600: 1%; SAT math scores over 600: 3%; SAT writing scores over 600: 1%; ACT scores over 24: 11%.

Faculty *Total:* 184, 36% full-time, 25% with terminal degrees. *Student/faculty ratio:* 13:1.

Academics *Calendar:* semesters. *Degrees:* certificates, associate, bachelor's, and master's. *Special study options:* academic remediation for entering students, accelerated degree program, advanced placement credit, distance learning, double majors, external degree program, honors programs, independent study, internships, part-time degree program, student-designed majors, study abroad, summer session for credit.

Computers on Campus 120 computers/terminals and 20 ports are available on campus for general student use. Students can access the following: campus intranet, computer help desk, free student e-mail accounts, online (class) grades, online (class) registration, online (class) schedules. Campuswide network is available. 100% of college-owned or -operated housing units are wired for high-speed Internet access. Wireless service is available via entire campus.

Student Life *Housing:* on-campus residence required through sophomore year. *Options:* coed. Campus housing is university owned. Freshman campus housing is guaranteed. *Activities and organizations:* drama/theater group, student-run newspaper, choral group, Student Government, Campus Activity Board, Student Athletic Advisory Committee, Spirit Team, Dance Team. *Campus security:* 24-hour emergency response devices and patrols, student patrols, late-night transport/escort service, controlled dormitory access. *Student services:* health clinic, personal/psychological counseling.

Athletics Member NCAA. All Division III. *Intercollegiate sports:* baseball M, basketball M/W, cross-country running M/W, golf M/W, soccer M/W, softball W, tennis M/W, volleyball W. *Intramural sports:* basketball M/W, bowling M/W, cheerleading M(c)/W(c), football M/W, skiing (cross-country) M/W, skiing (downhill) M/W, table tennis M/W, ultimate Frisbee M/W, volleyball M/W, weight lifting M/W.

Standardized Tests *Required:* SAT or ACT (for admission). *Recommended:* SAT (for admission), ACT (for admission).

Financial Aid Of all full-time matriculated undergraduates who enrolled in 2012, 1,240 applied for aid, 1,194 were judged to have need. 253 Federal Work-Study jobs (averaging $1400). In 2012, 46 non-need-based awards were made. *Average percent of need met:* 35%. *Average financial aid package:* $13,250. *Average need-based loan:* $4030. *Average need-based gift aid:* $4300. *Average non-need-based aid:* $4370. *Average indebtedness upon graduation:* $33,793.

Applying *Options:* electronic application, early admission, deferred entrance. *Application fee:* $30. *Required:* high school transcript. *Required for some:*

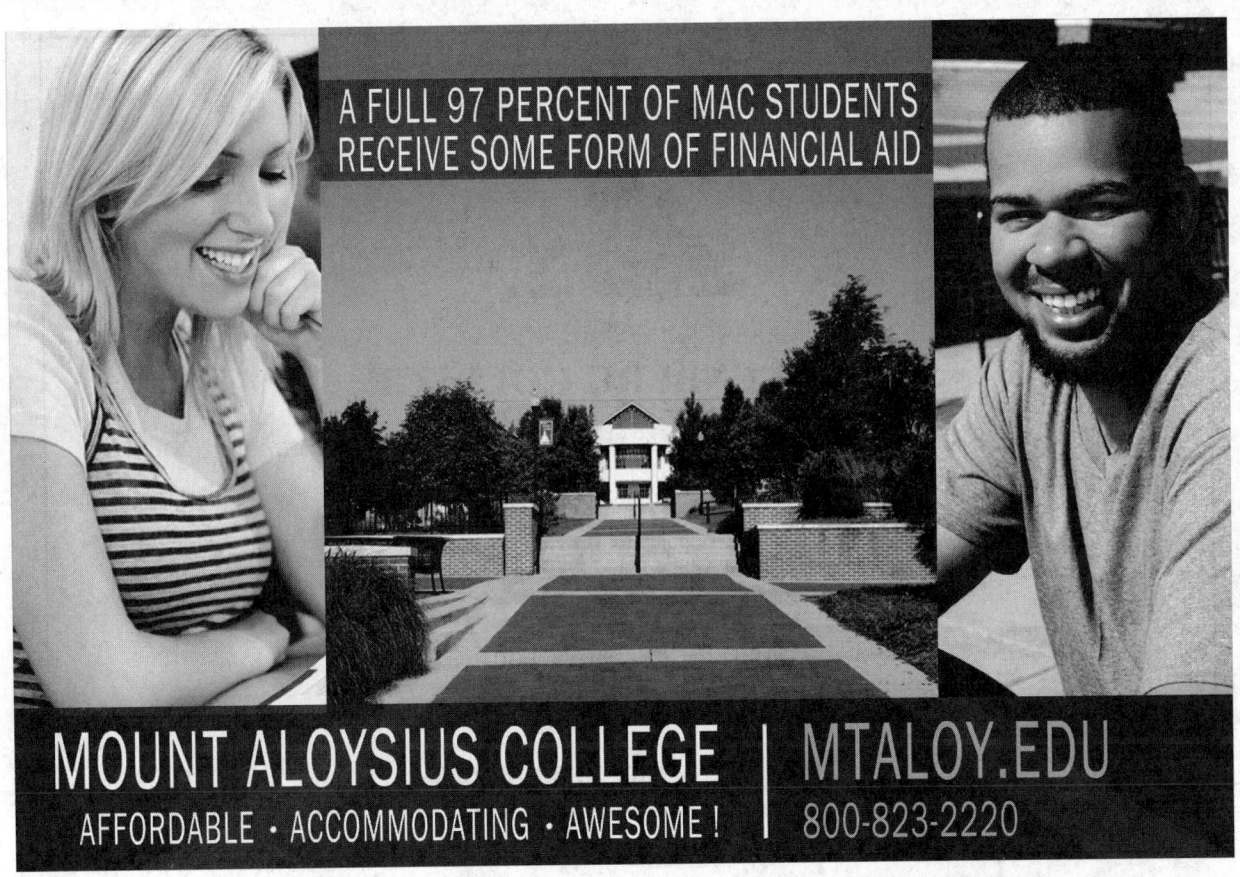

essay or personal statement, interview. *Recommended:* interview. *Application deadlines:* rolling (freshmen), rolling (transfers). *Notification:* continuous (freshmen), continuous (transfers).

Freshman Application Contact Mr. Frank C. Crouse Jr., Vice President for Enrollment Management/Dean of Admissions, Mount Aloysius College, 7373 Admiral Peary Highway, Cresson, PA 16630-1999. *Phone:* 814-886-6383. *Toll-free phone:* 888-823-2220. *Fax:* 814-886-6441. *E-mail:* admissions@ mtaloy.edu.
Website: http://www.mtaloy.edu/.

See previous page for display ad and page 1404 for the College Close-Up.

Muhlenberg College
Allentown, Pennsylvania

- **Independent** 4-year, founded 1848, affiliated with Lutheran Church
- **Suburban** 75-acre campus with easy access to Philadelphia
- **Endowment** $149.4 million
- **Coed** 2,422 undergraduate students, 95% full-time, 59% women, 41% men
- **Very difficult** entrance level, 46% of applicants were admitted

Undergraduates 2,301 full-time, 121 part-time. Students come from 39 states and territories; 9 other countries; 79% are from out of state; 3% Black or African American, non-Hispanic/Latino; 3% Hispanic/Latino; 2% Asian, non-Hispanic/Latino; 0.1% Native Hawaiian or other Pacific Islander, non-Hispanic/Latino; 0.2% American Indian or Alaska Native, non-Hispanic/Latino; 3% Two or more races, non-Hispanic/Latino; 10% Race/ethnicity unknown; 0.4% international; 0.4% transferred in; 91% live on campus. *Retention:* 94% of full-time freshmen returned.

Freshmen *Admission:* 5,023 applied, 2,316 admitted, 581 enrolled. *Average high school GPA:* 3.29. *Test scores:* SAT critical reading scores over 500: 96%; SAT math scores over 500: 97%; SAT writing scores over 500: 93%; ACT scores over 18: 100%; SAT critical reading scores over 600: 60%; SAT math scores over 600: 66%; SAT writing scores over 600: 64%; ACT scores over 24: 93%; SAT critical reading scores over 700: 15%; SAT math scores over 700: 16%; SAT writing scores over 700: 16%; ACT scores over 30: 19%.

Faculty *Total:* 262, 63% full-time, 68% with terminal degrees. *Student/faculty ratio:* 12:1.

Academics *Calendar:* semesters. *Degrees:* certificates, associate, and bachelor's. *Special study options:* accelerated degree program, adult/continuing education programs, advanced placement credit, double majors, honors programs, independent study, internships, off-campus study, part-time degree program, services for LD students, student-designed majors, study abroad, summer session for credit. *ROTC:* Army (c). *Unusual degree programs:* 3-2 engineering with Columbia University; forestry with Duke University.

Computers on Campus 471 computers/terminals and 100 ports are available on campus for general student use. Students can access the following: campus intranet, computer help desk, free student e-mail accounts, online (class) grades, online (class) registration, online (class) schedules. Campuswide network is available. 100% of college-owned or -operated housing units are wired for high-speed Internet access. Wireless service is available via classrooms, dorm rooms, libraries, student centers.

Student Life *Housing:* on-campus residence required through senior year. *Options:* coed, women-only, disabled students. Campus housing is university owned and leased by the school. Freshman campus housing is guaranteed. *Activities and organizations:* drama/theater group, student-run newspaper, radio and television station, choral group, Theater Association, Environmental Action Team, Jefferson School Partnership, Select Choir, Habitat for Humanity, national fraternities, national sororities. *Campus security:* 24-hour emergency response devices and patrols, late-night transport/escort service, controlled dormitory access. *Student services:* health clinic, personal/psychological counseling.

Athletics Member NCAA. All Division III. *Intercollegiate sports:* baseball M, basketball M/W, cheerleading M/W, cross-country running M/W, field hockey W, football M, golf M/W, lacrosse M/W, soccer M/W, softball W, tennis M/W, track and field M/W, volleyball W, wrestling M. *Intramural sports:* basketball M/W, cross-country running M/W, football M/W, ice hockey M, racquetball M/W, rugby M/W, soccer M/W, softball M, swimming and diving M/W, tennis M/W, ultimate Frisbee M, volleyball M/W.

Standardized Tests *Required for some:* SAT or ACT (for admission).

Costs (2012–13) *Comprehensive fee:* $52,650 includes full-time tuition ($41,225), mandatory fees ($285), and room and board ($11,140). Part-time tuition and fees vary according to program. *College room only:* $7175. Room and board charges vary according to board plan, housing facility, and location. *Payment plan:* installment. *Waivers:* employees or children of employees.

Financial Aid Of all full-time matriculated undergraduates who enrolled in 2011, 1,486 applied for aid, 1,207 were judged to have need, 1,102 had their need fully met. In 2011, 687 non-need-based awards were made. *Average percent of need met:* 94%. *Average financial aid package:* $25,143. *Average need-*

based loan: $4662. *Average need-based gift aid:* $22,081. *Average non-need-based aid:* $10,806. *Average indebtedness upon graduation:* $26,270. *Financial aid deadline:* 2/15.

Applying *Options:* electronic application, early admission, early decision, deferred entrance. *Application fee:* $50. *Required:* essay or personal statement, high school transcript, 2 letters of recommendation. *Required for some:* interview, graded paper. *Recommended:* interview. *Application deadlines:* 2/15 (freshmen), 6/15 (transfers). *Early decision deadline:* 2/1. *Notification:* 3/15 (freshmen), continuous until 7/1 (transfers), rolling (early decision).

Freshman Application Contact Mr. Christopher Hooker-Haring, Director of Undergraduate Admissions, Muhlenberg College, 2400 Chew Street, Allentown, PA 18104. *Phone:* 484-664-3245. *Fax:* 484-664-3234. *E-mail:* adm@muhlenberg.edu.
Website: http://www.muhlenberg.edu/.

See previous page for display ad and page 1406 for the College Close-Up.

Neumann University

Aston, Pennsylvania

- **Independent Roman Catholic** comprehensive, founded 1965
- **Suburban** 50-acre campus with easy access to Philadelphia
- **Endowment** $22.3 million
- **Coed** 2,674 undergraduate students, 81% full-time, 65% women, 35% men
- **Minimally difficult** entrance level, 71% of applicants were admitted

Undergraduates 2,166 full-time, 508 part-time. Students come from 24 states and territories; 33% are from out of state; 19% Black or African American, non-Hispanic/Latino; 3% Hispanic/Latino; 1% Asian, non-Hispanic/Latino; 0.1% Native Hawaiian or other Pacific Islander, non-Hispanic/Latino; 0.3% American Indian or Alaska Native, non-Hispanic/Latino; 2% Two or more races, non-Hispanic/Latino; 22% Race/ethnicity unknown; 2% international; 5% transferred in; 40% live on campus. *Retention:* 74% of full-time freshmen returned.

Freshmen *Admission:* 3,567 applied, 2,542 admitted, 574 enrolled. *Average high school GPA:* 2.88. *Test scores:* SAT critical reading scores over 500: 17%; SAT writing scores over 500: 17%; ACT scores over 18: 69%; SAT critical reading scores over 600: 1%; SAT writing scores over 600: 1%; ACT scores over 24: 7%.

Faculty *Total:* 308, 31% full-time, 41% with terminal degrees. *Student/faculty ratio:* 14:1.

Academics *Calendar:* semesters. *Degrees:* associate, bachelor's, master's, doctoral, post-master's, and postbachelor's certificates. *Special study options:* academic remediation for entering students, accelerated degree program, adult/continuing education programs, advanced placement credit, cooperative education, distance learning, double majors, freshman honors college, honors programs, independent study, internships, off-campus study, part-time degree program, services for LD students, student-designed majors, study abroad, summer session for credit. *ROTC:* Army (c).

Computers on Campus 400 computers/terminals and 1,500 ports are available on campus for general student use. Students can access the following: campus intranet, computer help desk, free student e-mail accounts, online (class) grades, online (class) schedules. Campuswide network is available. 100% of college-owned and -operated housing units are wired for high-speed Internet access. Wireless service is available via entire campus.

Student Life *Housing options:* coed. Campus housing is university owned and leased by the school. Freshman applicants given priority for college housing. *Activities and organizations:* drama/theater group, student-run newspaper, radio station, choral group, Student Government, Student Activities Board, Black Student Union, Boogie Knights, Neumann Media. *Campus security:* 24-hour emergency response devices and patrols, late-night transport/escort service, controlled dormitory access. *Student services:* health clinic, personal/psychological counseling.

Athletics Member NCAA. All Division III. *Intercollegiate sports:* baseball M, basketball M/W, cross-country running M/W, field hockey W, golf M, ice hockey M/W, lacrosse M/W, rugby M(c), soccer M/W, softball W, tennis M/W, track and field M/W, volleyball W. *Intramural sports:* basketball M/W, cheerleading W(c), ice hockey M(c), lacrosse M, soccer M/W, softball W, tennis M/W, track and field M/W, volleyball W.

Standardized Tests *Required:* SAT or ACT (for admission).

Costs (2012–13) *Comprehensive fee:* $35,302 includes full-time tuition ($23,262), mandatory fees ($970), and room and board ($11,070). Part-time tuition: $531 per credit hour. *Required fees:* $50 per semester hour part-time. *College room only:* $6510. Room and board charges vary according to board plan. *Payment plan:* installment. *Waivers:* employees or children of employees.

Financial Aid Of all full-time matriculated undergraduates who enrolled in 2009, 1,820 applied for aid, 1,820 were judged to have need, 1,100 had their need fully met. 180 Federal Work-Study jobs (averaging $1400). *Average percent of need met:* 65%. *Average financial aid package:* $19,000. *Average need-*

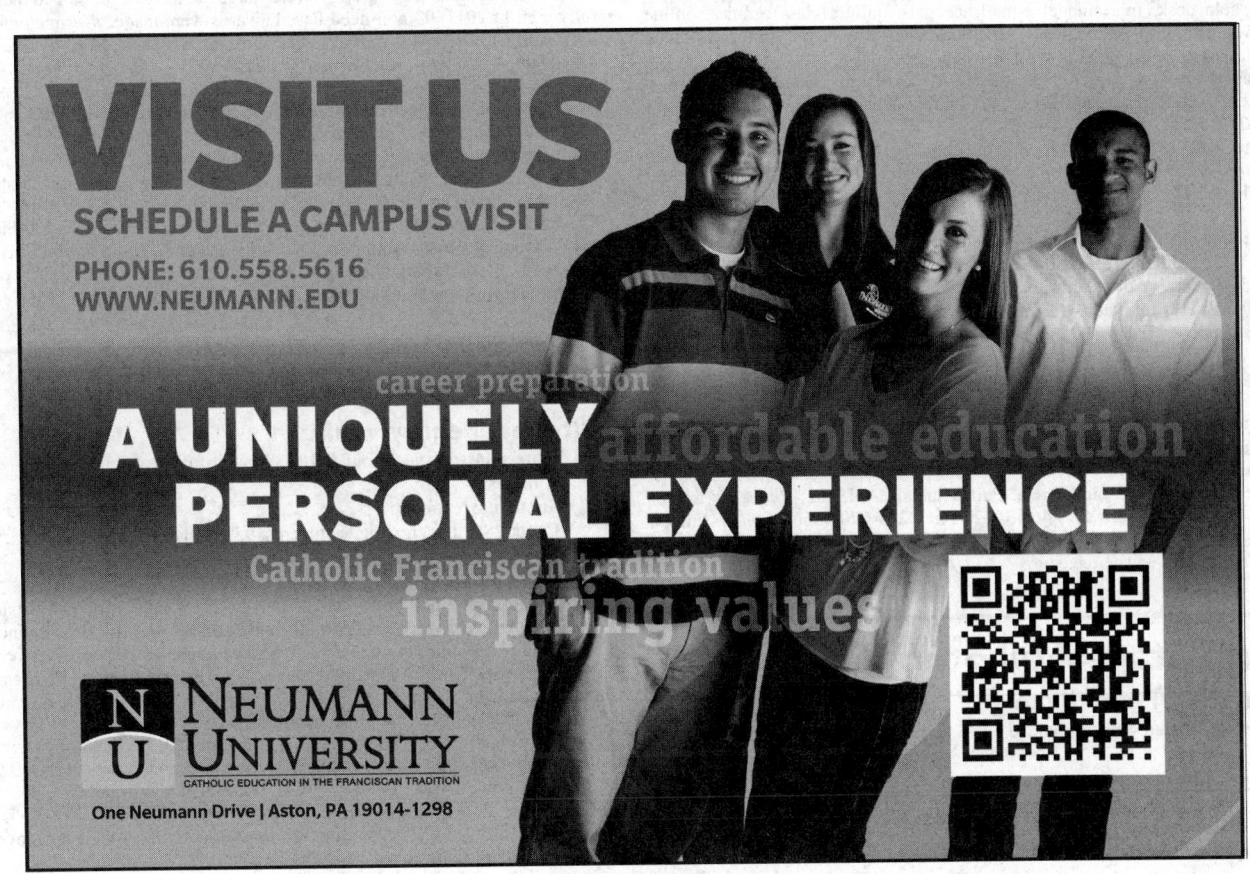

based loan: $5000. *Average need-based gift aid:* $11,000. *Average indebtedness upon graduation:* $30,000.

Applying *Options:* electronic application, deferred entrance. *Application fee:* $40. *Required:* high school transcript, minimum 2.0 GPA. *Recommended:* interview. *Application deadlines:* 4/1 (freshmen), rolling (transfers). *Notification:* continuous (freshmen), continuous (transfers).

Freshman Application Contact Mr. Dennis J. Murphy, Vice President for Enrollment Management, Neumann University, One Neumann Drive, Aston, PA 19014-1298. *Phone:* 610-361-2448. *Toll-free phone:* 800-963-8626. *Fax:* 610-558-5652. *E-mail:* neumann@neumann.edu.
Website: http://www.neumann.edu/.

See previous page for display ad and page 1408 for the College Close-Up.

Peirce College

Philadelphia, Pennsylvania

- **Independent** 4-year, founded 1865
- **Urban** 1-acre campus
- **Endowment** $17.3 million
- **Coed, primarily women** 2,261 undergraduate students, 36% full-time, 73% women, 27% men
- **Noncompetitive** entrance level

Undergraduates 817 full-time, 1,444 part-time. Students come from 27 states and territories; 22 other countries; 11% are from out of state; 68% Black or African American, non-Hispanic/Latino; 7% Hispanic/Latino; 1% Asian, non-Hispanic/Latino; 0.4% American Indian or Alaska Native, non-Hispanic/Latino; 0.4% Two or more races, non-Hispanic/Latino; 1% Race/ethnicity unknown; 0.3% international.

Freshmen *Admission:* 135 enrolled.

Faculty *Total:* 149, 25% full-time, 35% with terminal degrees. *Student/faculty ratio:* 17:1.

Academics *Calendar:* semesters. *Degrees:* certificates, associate, and bachelor's. *Special study options:* accelerated degree program, adult/continuing education programs, advanced placement credit, cooperative education, distance learning, internships, part-time degree program, services for LD students, summer session for credit.

Computers on Campus 46 computers/terminals are available on campus for general student use. Students can access the following: campus intranet, computer help desk, free student e-mail accounts, online (class) grades, online (class) registration, online (class) schedules. Campuswide network is available. Wireless service is available via entire campus.

Student Life *Housing:* college housing not available. *Campus security:* 24-hour emergency response devices and patrols, late-night transport/escort service, 24-hour security cameras.

Costs (2012–13) *Tuition:* $15,450 full-time, $515 per credit hour part-time. *Required fees:* $1050 full-time, $105 per course part-time. *Payment plan:* installment. *Waivers:* children of alumni and employees or children of employees.

Financial Aid Of all full-time matriculated undergraduates who enrolled in 2011, 675 applied for aid, 660 were judged to have need, 4 had their need fully met. 54 Federal Work-Study jobs (averaging $2626). In 2011, 26 non-need-based awards were made. *Average percent of need met:* 39%. *Average financial aid package:* $9438. *Average need-based loan:* $5013. *Average need-based gift aid:* $5026. *Average non-need-based aid:* $2290.

Applying *Options:* electronic application. *Application fee:* $50. *Required:* high school transcript. *Application deadlines:* rolling (freshmen), rolling (out-of-state freshmen), rolling (transfers). *Notification:* continuous (freshmen), continuous (out-of-state freshmen), continuous (transfers).

Freshman Application Contact Mr. Paul Ballentine, Manager, Admissions, Peirce College, 1420 Pine Street, Philadelphia, PA 19102. *Phone:* 215-670-9214. *Toll-free phone:* 888-467-3472. *Fax:* 215-670-9366. *E-mail:* info@peirce.edu.
Website: http://www.peirce.edu/.

Penn State Abington

Abington, Pennsylvania

- **State-related** 4-year, founded 1950, part of Pennsylvania State University
- **Small-town** campus
- **Coed** 3,506 undergraduate students, 78% full-time, 51% women, 49% men
- **Very difficult** entrance level, 78% of applicants were admitted

Undergraduates 2,728 full-time, 778 part-time. 7% are from out of state; 15% Black or African American, non-Hispanic/Latino; 8% Hispanic/Latino; 16% Asian, non-Hispanic/Latino; 0.1% Native Hawaiian or other Pacific Islander, non-Hispanic/Latino; 0.2% American Indian or Alaska Native, non-Hispanic/Latino; 2% Two or more races, non-Hispanic/Latino; 3% Race/ethnicity unknown; 2% international; 5% transferred in. *Retention:* 74% of full-time freshmen returned.

Freshmen *Admission:* 3,221 applied, 2,504 admitted, 691 enrolled. *Average high school GPA:* 3.12. *Test scores:* SAT critical reading scores over 500: 30%; SAT math scores over 500: 45%; SAT writing scores over 500: 32%; ACT scores over 18: 75%; SAT critical reading scores over 600: 6%; SAT math scores over 600: 13%; SAT writing scores over 600: 6%; ACT scores over 24: 25%; SAT critical reading scores over 700: 1%; SAT math scores over 700: 1%; ACT scores over 30: 3%.

Faculty *Total:* 226, 48% full-time, 45% with terminal degrees. *Student/faculty ratio:* 20:1.

Academics *Calendar:* semesters. *Degrees:* certificates, associate, and bachelor's (enrollment figures include students enrolled at The Graduate School at Penn State who are taking courses at this location). *Special study options:* adult/continuing education programs, external degree program, part-time degree program. *ROTC:* Army (b), Air Force (c).

Computers on Campus Students can access the following: campus intranet, computer help desk, free student e-mail accounts, online (class) grades, online (class) registration, online (class) schedules. Campuswide network is available.

Student Life *Housing:* college housing not available. *Campus security:* 24-hour emergency response devices and patrols.

Athletics *Intercollegiate sports:* baseball M, basketball M/W, golf M, soccer M/W, softball W, tennis M/W, volleyball W. *Intramural sports:* basketball M/W, cross-country running M/W, football M, soccer M/W, softball M, tennis M/W, volleyball M/W.

Standardized Tests *Required:* SAT or ACT (for admission).

Costs (2013–14) *Tuition:* area resident $12,474 full-time, $504 per credit hour part-time; state resident $12,474 full-time, $504 per credit hour part-time; non-resident $19,030 full-time, $793 per credit hour part-time. Full-time tuition and fees vary according to course level, degree level, location, program, and student level. Part-time tuition and fees vary according to course level, course load, degree level, location, program, and student level. *Required fees:* $882 full-time. *Payment plans:* installment, deferred payment. *Waivers:* senior citizens and employees or children of employees.

Financial Aid Of all full-time matriculated undergraduates who enrolled in 2011, 2,305 applied for aid, 1,954 were judged to have need, 63 had their need fully met. In 2011, 93 non-need-based awards were made. *Average percent of need met:* 61%. *Average financial aid package:* $10,042. *Average need-based loan:* $4054. *Average need-based gift aid:* $7090. *Average non-need-based aid:* $1645. *Average indebtedness upon graduation:* $35,100.

Applying *Options:* electronic application, early admission, deferred entrance. *Application fee:* $50. *Required:* high school transcript. *Required for some:* interview. *Recommended:* essay or personal statement. *Application deadlines:* rolling (freshmen), rolling (transfers). *Notification:* continuous (freshmen), continuous (transfers).

Freshman Application Contact Admissions Office, Penn State Abington, 1600 Woodland Road, Abington, PA 19001. *Phone:* 215-881-7600. *Fax:* 215-881-7655. *E-mail:* abingtonadmissions@psu.edu.
Website: http://www.abington.psu.edu/.

Penn State Altoona

Altoona, Pennsylvania

- **State-related** 4-year, founded 1939, part of Pennsylvania State University
- **Suburban** campus
- **Coed** 3,863 undergraduate students, 95% full-time, 47% women, 53% men
- **Very difficult** entrance level, 85% of applicants were admitted

Undergraduates 3,660 full-time, 203 part-time. 19% are from out of state; 8% Black or African American, non-Hispanic/Latino; 4% Hispanic/Latino; 2% Asian, non-Hispanic/Latino; 0.1% American Indian or Alaska Native, non-Hispanic/Latino; 2% Two or more races, non-Hispanic/Latino; 1% Race/ethnicity unknown; 2% international; 2% transferred in; 24% live on campus. *Retention:* 84% of full-time freshmen returned.

Freshmen *Admission:* 5,700 applied, 4,856 admitted, 1,379 enrolled. *Average high school GPA:* 3.04. *Test scores:* SAT critical reading scores over 500: 44%; SAT math scores over 500: 55%; SAT writing scores over 500: 44%; ACT scores over 18: 84%; SAT critical reading scores over 600: 7%; SAT math scores over 600: 15%; SAT writing scores over 600: 5%; ACT scores over 24: 24%; SAT math scores over 700: 1%.

Faculty *Total:* 292, 60% full-time, 51% with terminal degrees. *Student/faculty ratio:* 18:1.

Academics *Calendar:* semesters. *Degrees:* certificates, associate, and bachelor's (enrollment figures include students enrolled at The Graduate School at Penn State who are taking courses at this location). *ROTC:* Army (b), Air Force (b).

Computers on Campus Students can access the following: campus intranet, computer help desk, free student e-mail accounts, online (class) grades, online (class) registration, online (class) schedules.

Student Life *Housing options:* coed, disabled students. Campus housing is university owned. *Campus security:* 24-hour emergency response devices and patrols, late-night transport/escort service.

Athletics Member NCAA. All Division III. *Intercollegiate sports:* baseball M, basketball M/W, cross-country running M/W, golf M/W, soccer M/W, softball W, swimming and diving M/W, tennis M/W. *Intramural sports:* badminton M/W, baseball M/W, basketball M/W, football M/W, golf M/W, racquetball M/W, soccer M/W, softball M/W, table tennis M/W, tennis M/W, track and field M/W, volleyball M/W, weight lifting M/W.

Standardized Tests *Required:* SAT or ACT (for admission).

Costs (2013–14) *Tuition:* area resident $13,018 full-time, $542 per credit hour part-time; state resident $13,018 full-time, $542 per credit hour part-time; non-resident $19,912 full-time, $830 per credit hour part-time. Full-time tuition and fees vary according to course level, degree level, location, program, and student level. Part-time tuition and fees vary according to course level, course load, degree level, location, program, and student level. *Required fees:* $882 full-time. *Room and board:* $9690; room only: $4910. Room and board charges vary according to board plan, housing facility, and location. *Payment plans:* installment, deferred payment. *Waivers:* employees or children of employees.

Financial Aid Of all full-time matriculated undergraduates who enrolled in 2011, 3,255 applied for aid, 2,754 were judged to have need, 140 had their need fully met. In 2011, 111 non-need-based awards were made. *Average percent of need met:* 60%. *Average financial aid package:* $9636. *Average need-based loan:* $4015. *Average need-based gift aid:* $6001. *Average non-need-based aid:* $1322. *Average indebtedness upon graduation:* $35,100.

Applying *Options:* electronic application, early admission, deferred entrance. *Application fee:* $50. *Required:* high school transcript. *Required for some:* interview. *Recommended:* essay or personal statement. *Application deadlines:* rolling (freshmen), rolling (transfers). *Notification:* continuous (freshmen), continuous (transfers).

Freshman Application Contact Admissions Office, Penn State Altoona, 3000 Ivyside Park, Altoona, PA 16601-3760. *Phone:* 814-949-5466. *Toll-free phone:* 800-848-9843. *Fax:* 814-949-5564. *E-mail:* aaadmit@psu.edu. *Website:* http://www.aa.psu.edu/.

Penn State Beaver

Monaca, Pennsylvania

- **State-related** primarily 2-year, founded 1964, part of Pennsylvania State University
- **Small-town** campus
- **Coed** 759 undergraduate students, 84% full-time, 45% women, 55% men
- **Moderately difficult** entrance level, 87% of applicants were admitted

Undergraduates 634 full-time, 125 part-time. 8% are from out of state; 11% Black or African American, non-Hispanic/Latino; 4% Hispanic/Latino; 2% Asian, non-Hispanic/Latino; 0.3% Native Hawaiian or other Pacific Islander, non-Hispanic/Latino; 0.2% American Indian or Alaska Native, non-Hispanic/Latino; 2% Two or more races, non-Hispanic/Latino; 2% Race/ethnicity unknown; 1% international; 4% transferred in; 22% live on campus. *Retention:* 71% of full-time freshmen returned.

Freshmen *Admission:* 670 applied, 585 admitted, 208 enrolled. *Average high school GPA:* 2.94. *Test scores:* SAT critical reading scores over 500: 37%; SAT math scores over 500: 46%; SAT writing scores over 500: 28%; ACT scores over 18: 71%; SAT critical reading scores over 600: 10%; SAT math scores over 600: 15%; SAT writing scores over 600: 7%; ACT scores over 24: 29%; SAT critical reading scores over 700: 1%; SAT math scores over 700: 2%; SAT writing scores over 700: 2%.

Faculty *Total:* 64, 53% full-time, 41% with terminal degrees. *Student/faculty ratio:* 15:1.

Academics *Calendar:* semesters. *Degrees:* certificates, associate, and bachelor's. *Special study options:* adult/continuing education programs.

Student Life *Housing options:* coed, disabled students. Campus housing is university owned. Freshman campus housing is guaranteed.

Athletics Member NJCAA. *Intercollegiate sports:* baseball M, basketball M, softball M/W, volleyball W. *Intramural sports:* basketball M/W, cheerleading

M(c)/W(c), cross-country running M/W, football M, golf M/W, soccer M/W, softball M/W, table tennis M/W.

Standardized Tests *Required:* SAT or ACT (for admission).

Costs (2013–14) *Tuition:* area resident $12,474 full-time, $504 per credit hour part-time; state resident $12,474 full-time, $504 per credit hour part-time; non-resident $19,030 full-time, $793 per credit hour part-time. Full-time tuition and fees vary according to course level, degree level, location, program, and student level. Part-time tuition and fees vary according to course level, course load, degree level, location, program, and student level. *Required fees:* $876 full-time. *Room and board:* $9690; room only: $4910. Room and board charges vary according to board plan, housing facility, and location. *Payment plans:* installment, deferred payment. *Waivers:* employees or children of employees.

Financial Aid Of all full-time matriculated undergraduates who enrolled in 2011, 624 applied for aid, 534 were judged to have need, 29 had their need fully met. In 2011, 33 non-need-based awards were made. *Average percent of need met:* 66%. *Average financial aid package:* $10,703. *Average need-based loan:* $4065. *Average need-based gift aid:* $6659. *Average non-need-based aid:* $2144. *Average indebtedness upon graduation:* $35,100.

Applying *Options:* electronic application, early admission, deferred entrance. *Application fee:* $50. *Required:* high school transcript. *Required for some:* interview. *Recommended:* essay or personal statement. *Application deadlines:* rolling (freshmen), rolling (transfers). *Notification:* continuous (freshmen), continuous (transfers).

Freshman Application Contact Admissions Office, Penn State Beaver, 100 University Drive, Monaca, PA 15061. *Phone:* 724-773-3800. *Fax:* 724-773-3658. *E-mail:* br-admissions@psu.edu. *Website:* http://www.br.psu.edu/.

Penn State Berks

Reading, Pennsylvania

- **State-related** 4-year, founded 1924, part of Pennsylvania State University
- **Suburban** campus
- **Coed** 2,743 undergraduate students, 89% full-time, 45% women, 55% men
- **Very difficult** entrance level, 83% of applicants were admitted

Undergraduates 2,432 full-time, 311 part-time. 8% are from out of state; 9% Black or African American, non-Hispanic/Latino; 9% Hispanic/Latino; 4% Asian, non-Hispanic/Latino; 0.1% American Indian or Alaska Native, non-Hispanic/Latino; 2% Two or more races, non-Hispanic/Latino; 1% Race/ethnicity unknown; 1% international; 4% transferred in; 29% live on campus. *Retention:* 80% of full-time freshmen returned.

Freshmen *Admission:* 2,570 applied, 2,135 admitted, 814 enrolled. *Average high school GPA:* 3.02. *Test scores:* SAT critical reading scores over 500: 44%; SAT math scores over 500: 53%; SAT writing scores over 500: 36%; ACT scores over 18: 84%; SAT critical reading scores over 600: 8%; SAT math scores over 600: 15%; SAT writing scores over 600: 3%; ACT scores over 24: 31%; SAT critical reading scores over 700: 1%; SAT math scores over 700: 1%; ACT scores over 30: 2%.

Faculty *Total:* 217, 56% full-time, 45% with terminal degrees. *Student/faculty ratio:* 17:1.

Academics *Calendar:* semesters. *Degrees:* certificates, associate, and bachelor's (enrollment figures include students enrolled at The Graduate School at Penn State who are taking courses at this location). *Special study options:* adult/continuing education programs, part-time degree program. *ROTC:* Army (c).

Computers on Campus Students can access the following: campus intranet, computer help desk, free student e-mail accounts, online (class) grades, online (class) registration, online (class) schedules. Campuswide network is available.

Student Life *Housing options:* coed, disabled students. Campus housing is university owned. *Campus security:* 24-hour emergency response devices and patrols, late-night transport/escort service, controlled dormitory access.

Athletics Member NJCAA. *Intercollegiate sports:* baseball M, basketball M/W, cheerleading M/W, cross-country running M/W, golf M/W, soccer M/W, softball M/W, tennis M/W, volleyball M/W. *Intramural sports:* badminton M/W, basketball M/W, football M/W, golf M/W, table tennis M/W, volleyball M/W.

Standardized Tests *Required:* SAT or ACT (for admission).

Costs (2013–14) *Tuition:* area resident $13,018 full-time, $542 per credit hour part-time; state resident $13,018 full-time, $542 per credit hour part-time; non-resident $19,912 full-time, $830 per credit hour part-time. Full-time tuition and fees vary according to course level, degree level, location, program, and student level. Part-time tuition and fees vary according to course level, course load, degree level, location, program, and student level. *Required fees:* $882 full-time. *Room and board:* $10,560; room only: $5780. Room and board charges vary according to board plan, housing facility, and location. *Payment plans:* installment, deferred payment. *Waivers:* employees or children of employees.

Financial Aid Of all full-time matriculated undergraduates who enrolled in 2011, 2,118 applied for aid, 1,786 were judged to have need, 69 had their need fully met. In 2011, 57 non-need-based awards were made. *Average percent of need met:* 60%. *Average financial aid package:* $9395. *Average need-based loan:* $4095. *Average need-based gift aid:* $6351. *Average non-need-based aid:* $2214. *Average indebtedness upon graduation:* $35,100.

Applying *Options:* electronic application, early admission, deferred entrance. *Application fee:* $50. *Required:* high school transcript. *Required for some:* interview. *Recommended:* essay or personal statement. *Application deadlines:* rolling (freshmen), rolling (transfers). *Notification:* continuous (freshmen), continuous (transfers).

Freshman Application Contact Admissions Office, Penn State Berks, Tulpehocken Road, PO Box 7009, Reading, PA 19610-6009. *Phone:* 610-396-6060. *Fax:* 610-396-6077. *E-mail:* admissionsbk@psu.edu. *Website:* http://www.bk.psu.edu/.

Penn State Brandywine

Media, Pennsylvania

- **State-related** primarily 2-year, founded 1966, part of Pennsylvania State University
- **Small-town** campus
- **Coed** 1,581 undergraduate students, 85% full-time, 44% women, 56% men
- **Moderately difficult** entrance level, 79% of applicants were admitted

Undergraduates 1,338 full-time, 243 part-time. 6% are from out of state; 13% Black or African American, non-Hispanic/Latino; 5% Hispanic/Latino; 9% Asian, non-Hispanic/Latino; 0.1% Native Hawaiian or other Pacific Islander, non-Hispanic/Latino; 0.2% American Indian or Alaska Native, non-Hispanic/Latino; 2% Two or more races, non-Hispanic/Latino; 2% Race/ethnicity unknown; 0.9% international; 4% transferred in. *Retention:* 71% of full-time freshmen returned.

Freshmen *Admission:* 1,279 applied, 1,011 admitted, 368 enrolled. *Average high school GPA:* 3. *Test scores:* SAT critical reading scores over 500: 36%; SAT math scores over 500: 50%; SAT writing scores over 500: 35%; ACT scores over 18: 68%; SAT critical reading scores over 600: 9%; SAT math scores over 600: 15%; SAT writing scores over 600: 6%; ACT scores over 24: 11%; SAT critical reading scores over 700: 1%; SAT math scores over 700: 1%; SAT writing scores over 700: 1%; ACT scores over 30: 4%.

Faculty *Total:* 131, 46% full-time, 47% with terminal degrees. *Student/faculty ratio:* 17:1.

Academics *Calendar:* semesters. *Degrees:* certificates, associate, and bachelor's. *Special study options:* adult/continuing education programs. *ROTC:* Army (c), Air Force (c).

Computers on Campus Students can access the following: online (class) registration. Campuswide network is available.

Student Life *Housing:* college housing not available. *Campus security:* late-night transport/escort service, part-time trained security personnel.

Athletics Member NJCAA. *Intercollegiate sports:* baseball M, basketball M/W, soccer M/W, tennis M/W, volleyball W. *Intramural sports:* basketball M/W, cheerleading M(c)/W(c), golf M/W, ice hockey M(c)/W(c), lacrosse M/W, soccer M/W, softball W(c), tennis M/W, volleyball M(c)/W.

Standardized Tests *Required:* SAT or ACT (for admission).

Costs (2013–14) *Tuition:* area resident $12,474 full-time, $504 per credit hour part-time; state resident $12,474 full-time, $504 per credit hour part-time; nonresident $19,030 full-time, $793 per credit hour part-time. Full-time tuition and fees vary according to course level, degree level, location, program, and student level. Part-time tuition and fees vary according to course level, course load, degree level, location, program, and student level. *Required fees:* $882 full-time. *Payment plans:* installment, deferred payment. *Waivers:* employees or children of employees.

Financial Aid Of all full-time matriculated undergraduates who enrolled in 2011, 1,038 applied for aid, 807 were judged to have need, 30 had their need fully met. In 2011, 101 non-need-based awards were made. *Average percent of need met:* 61%. *Average financial aid package:* $9345. *Average need-based loan:* $3960. *Average need-based gift aid:* $6338. *Average non-need-based aid:* $2237. *Average indebtedness upon graduation:* $35,100.

Applying *Options:* electronic application, early admission, deferred entrance. *Application fee:* $50. *Required:* high school transcript. *Required for some:* interview. *Recommended:* essay or personal statement. *Application deadlines:* rolling (freshmen), rolling (transfers). *Notification:* continuous (freshmen), continuous (transfers).

Freshman Application Contact Admissions Office, Penn State Brandywine, 25 Yearsley Mill Road, Media, PA 19063-5596. *Phone:* 610-892-1200. *Fax:* 610-892-1320. *E-mail:* bwadmissions@psu.edu. *Website:* http://www.brandywine.psu.edu/.

Penn State DuBois

DuBois, Pennsylvania

- **State-related** primarily 2-year, founded 1935, part of Pennsylvania State University
- **Small-town** campus
- **Coed** 704 undergraduate students, 79% full-time, 52% women, 48% men
- **Moderately difficult** entrance level, 88% of applicants were admitted

Undergraduates 554 full-time, 150 part-time. 2% are from out of state; 2% Black or African American, non-Hispanic/Latino; 1% Hispanic/Latino; 0.7% Asian, non-Hispanic/Latino; 0.3% American Indian or Alaska Native, non-Hispanic/Latino; 1% Two or more races, non-Hispanic/Latino; 0.7% Race/ethnicity unknown; 0.5% international; 2% transferred in. *Retention:* 71% of full-time freshmen returned.

Freshmen *Admission:* 439 applied, 386 admitted, 183 enrolled. *Average high school GPA:* 3.06. *Test scores:* SAT critical reading scores over 500: 35%; SAT math scores over 500: 46%; SAT writing scores over 500: 28%; ACT scores over 18: 100%; SAT critical reading scores over 600: 5%; SAT math scores over 600: 13%; SAT writing scores over 600: 6%; SAT critical reading scores over 700: 1%; SAT math scores over 700: 1%; SAT writing scores over 700: 1%.

Faculty *Total:* 79, 58% full-time, 43% with terminal degrees. *Student/faculty ratio:* 11:1.

Academics *Calendar:* semesters. *Degrees:* certificates, associate, and bachelor's. *Special study options:* adult/continuing education programs.

Computers on Campus Students can access the following: online (class) registration. Campuswide network is available.

Student Life *Housing:* college housing not available.

Athletics Member NJCAA. *Intercollegiate sports:* basketball M, cross-country running M/W, golf M/W, volleyball W. *Intramural sports:* basketball M/W, football M, soccer M/W, table tennis M/W, volleyball M/W.

Standardized Tests *Required:* SAT or ACT (for admission).

Costs (2013–14) *Tuition:* area resident $12,474 full-time, $504 per credit hour part-time; state resident $12,474 full-time, $504 per credit hour part-time; nonresident $19,030 full-time, $793 per credit hour part-time. Full-time tuition and fees vary according to course level, degree level, location, program, and student level. Part-time tuition and fees vary according to course level, course load, degree level, location, program, and student level. *Required fees:* $770 full-time. *Payment plans:* installment, deferred payment. *Waivers:* employees or children of employees.

Financial Aid Of all full-time matriculated undergraduates who enrolled in 2011, 529 applied for aid, 482 were judged to have need, 16 had their need fully met. In 2011, 12 non-need-based awards were made. *Average percent of need met:* 63%. *Average financial aid package:* $11,410. *Average need-based loan:* $3919. *Average need-based gift aid:* $6353. *Average non-need-based aid:* $1474. *Average indebtedness upon graduation:* $35,100.

Applying *Options:* electronic application, early admission, deferred entrance. *Application fee:* $50. *Required:* high school transcript. *Required for some:* interview. *Recommended:* essay or personal statement. *Application deadlines:* rolling (freshmen), rolling (transfers). *Notification:* continuous (freshmen), continuous (transfers).

Freshman Application Contact Admissions Office, Penn State DuBois, College Place, DuBois, PA 15801-3199. *Phone:* 814-375-4720. *Toll-free phone:* 800-346-7627. *Fax:* 814-375-4784. *E-mail:* duboisinfo@psi.edu. *Website:* http://www.ds.psu.edu/.

Penn State Erie, The Behrend College

Erie, Pennsylvania

- **State-related** comprehensive, founded 1948, part of Pennsylvania State University
- **Suburban** 725-acre campus
- **Coed** 4,065 undergraduate students, 92% full-time, 36% women, 64% men
- **Very difficult** entrance level, 84% of applicants were admitted

Undergraduates 3,723 full-time, 342 part-time. 10% are from out of state; 4% Black or African American, non-Hispanic/Latino; 3% Hispanic/Latino; 2%

Asian, non-Hispanic/Latino; 0.1% Native Hawaiian or other Pacific Islander, non-Hispanic/Latino; 0.1% American Indian or Alaska Native, non-Hispanic/Latino; 1% Two or more races, non-Hispanic/Latino; 1% Race/ethnicity unknown; 3% international; 3% transferred in; 41% live on campus. *Retention:* 82% of full-time freshmen returned.

Freshmen *Admission:* 3,437 applied, 2,890 admitted, 1,080 enrolled. *Average high school GPA:* 3.25. *Test scores:* SAT critical reading scores over 500: 58%; SAT math scores over 500: 72%; SAT writing scores over 500: 48%; ACT scores over 18: 85%; SAT critical reading scores over 600: 13%; SAT math scores over 600: 26%; SAT writing scores over 600: 9%; ACT scores over 24: 44%; SAT critical reading scores over 700: 1%; SAT math scores over 700: 4%; ACT scores over 30: 3%.

Faculty *Total:* 299, 81% full-time, 53% with terminal degrees. *Student/faculty ratio:* 15:1.

Academics *Calendar:* semesters. *Degrees:* certificates, associate, bachelor's, and master's. *Special study options:* adult/continuing education programs, part-time degree program. *ROTC:* Army (b).

Computers on Campus Students can access the following: campus intranet, computer help desk, free student e-mail accounts, online (class) grades, online (class) registration, online (class) schedules. Campuswide network is available.

Student Life *Housing options:* coed, men-only, women-only, disabled students. Campus housing is university owned. *Campus security:* 24-hour emergency response devices and patrols, student patrols, late-night transport/escort service, controlled dormitory access.

Athletics Member NCAA. All Division III. *Intercollegiate sports:* baseball M, basketball M/W, cheerleading M/W, cross-country running M/W, golf M/W, ice hockey M(c), lacrosse M(c), skiing (downhill) M(c)/W(c), soccer M/W, softball W, swimming and diving M/W, tennis M/W, track and field M/W, volleyball M(c)/W, water polo M/W. *Intramural sports:* badminton M/W, basketball M/W, bowling M/W, cross-country running M/W, football M/W, golf M/W, skiing (downhill) M/W, soccer M/W, softball M/W, swimming and diving M/W, table tennis M/W, tennis M/W, volleyball M/W.

Standardized Tests *Required:* SAT or ACT (for admission).

Costs (2013–14) *Tuition:* area resident $13,018 full-time, $542 per credit hour part-time; state resident $13,018 full-time, $542 per credit hour part-time; nonresident $19,912 full-time, $830 per credit hour part-time. Full-time tuition and fees vary according to course level, degree level, location, program, and student level. Part-time tuition and fees vary according to course level, course load, degree level, location, program, and student level. *Required fees:* $882 full-time. *Room and board:* $9690; room only: $4910. Room and board charges vary according to board plan, housing facility, and location. *Payment plans:* installment, deferred payment. *Waivers:* employees or children of employees.

Financial Aid Of all full-time matriculated undergraduates who enrolled in 2011, 3,236 applied for aid, 2,816 were judged to have need, 124 had their need fully met. In 2011, 96 non-need-based awards were made. *Average percent of need met:* 61%. *Average financial aid package:* $9771. *Average need-based loan:* $4323. *Average need-based gift aid:* $6129. *Average non-need-based aid:* $3860. *Average indebtedness upon graduation:* $35,100.

Applying *Options:* electronic application, early admission, deferred entrance. *Application fee:* $50. *Required:* high school transcript. *Required for some:* interview. *Recommended:* essay or personal statement. *Application deadlines:* rolling (freshmen), rolling (transfers). *Notification:* continuous (freshmen), continuous (transfers).

Freshman Application Contact Admissions Office, Penn State Erie, The Behrend College, 4701 College Drive, Erie, PA 16563-0001. *Phone:* 814-898-6100. *Toll-free phone:* 866-374-3378. *Fax:* 814-898-6044. *E-mail:* behrend.admissions@psu.edu. *Website:* http://www.pserie.psu.edu/.

Penn State Fayette, The Eberly Campus

Uniontown, Pennsylvania

- **State-related** primarily 2-year, founded 1934, part of Pennsylvania State University
- **Small-town** campus
- **Coed** 867 undergraduate students, 78% full-time, 55% women, 45% men
- **Moderately difficult** entrance level, 89% of applicants were admitted

Undergraduates 680 full-time, 187 part-time. 5% are from out of state; 3% Black or African American, non-Hispanic/Latino; 1% Hispanic/Latino; 0.6% Asian, non-Hispanic/Latino; 0.1% Native Hawaiian or other Pacific Islander, non-Hispanic/Latino; 0.2% American Indian or Alaska Native, non-Hispanic/Latino; 2% Two or more races, non-Hispanic/Latino; 0.9% Race/ethnicity

unknown; 2% international; 4% transferred in. *Retention:* 69% of full-time freshmen returned.

Freshmen *Admission:* 610 applied, 544 admitted, 224 enrolled. *Average high school GPA:* 3.09. *Test scores:* SAT critical reading scores over 500: 36%; SAT math scores over 500: 45%; SAT writing scores over 500: 26%; ACT scores over 18: 75%; SAT critical reading scores over 600: 6%; SAT math scores over 600: 11%; SAT writing scores over 600: 4%; SAT critical reading scores over 700: 1%; SAT math scores over 700: 2%.

Faculty *Total:* 96, 55% full-time, 35% with terminal degrees. *Student/faculty ratio:* 11:1.

Academics *Calendar:* semesters. *Degrees:* certificates, associate, and bachelor's. *Special study options:* adult/continuing education programs. *ROTC:* Army (b).

Computers on Campus Students can access the following: online (class) registration. Campuswide network is available.

Student Life *Housing:* college housing not available. *Campus security:* student patrols, 8-hour patrols by trained security personnel.

Athletics Member NJCAA. *Intercollegiate sports:* baseball M, basketball M, softball W, volleyball W. *Intramural sports:* badminton M/W, basketball M/W, cheerleading M(c)/W(c), equestrian sports M(c)/W(c), football M/W, golf M(c)/W(c), softball M/W, tennis M/W, volleyball M/W, weight lifting M/W.

Standardized Tests *Required:* SAT or ACT (for admission).

Costs (2013–14) *Tuition:* area resident $12,474 full-time, $504 per credit hour part-time; state resident $12,474 full-time, $504 per credit hour part-time; nonresident $19,030 full-time, $793 per credit hour part-time. Full-time tuition and fees vary according to course level, degree level, location, program, and student level. Part-time tuition and fees vary according to course level, course load, degree level, location, program, and student level. *Required fees:* $826 full-time. *Payment plans:* installment, deferred payment. *Waivers:* employees or children of employees.

Financial Aid Of all full-time matriculated undergraduates who enrolled in 2011, 698 applied for aid, 629 were judged to have need, 32 had their need fully met. In 2011, 31 non-need-based awards were made. *Average percent of need met:* 63%. *Average financial aid package:* $10,156. *Average need-based loan:* $3959. *Average need-based gift aid:* $6396. *Average non-need-based aid:* $2479. *Average indebtedness upon graduation:* $35,100.

Applying *Options:* electronic application, early admission, deferred entrance. *Application fee:* $50. *Required:* high school transcript. *Required for some:* interview. *Recommended:* essay or personal statement. *Application deadlines:* rolling (freshmen), rolling (transfers). *Notification:* continuous (freshmen), continuous (transfers).

Freshman Application Contact Admissions Office, Penn State Fayette, The Eberly Campus, 1 University Drive, PO Box 519, Uniontown, PA 15401-0519. *Phone:* 724-430-4130. *Toll-free phone:* 877-568-4130. *Fax:* 724-430-4175. *E-mail:* feadm@psu.edu. *Website:* http://www.fe.psu.edu/.

Penn State Greater Allegheny

McKeesport, Pennsylvania

- **State-related** primarily 2-year, founded 1947, part of Pennsylvania State University
- **Small-town** campus
- **Coed** 635 undergraduate students, 92% full-time, 43% women, 57% men
- **Moderately difficult** entrance level, 80% of applicants were admitted

Undergraduates 582 full-time, 53 part-time. 9% are from out of state; 24% Black or African American, non-Hispanic/Latino; 4% Hispanic/Latino; 2% Asian, non-Hispanic/Latino; 0.2% Native Hawaiian or other Pacific Islander, non-Hispanic/Latino; 3% Two or more races, non-Hispanic/Latino; 1% Race/ethnicity unknown; 5% international; 4% transferred in; 27% live on campus. *Retention:* 75% of full-time freshmen returned.

Freshmen *Admission:* 699 applied, 558 admitted, 201 enrolled. *Average high school GPA:* 3.04. *Test scores:* SAT critical reading scores over 500: 32%; SAT math scores over 500: 47%; SAT writing scores over 500: 25%; ACT scores over 18: 89%; SAT critical reading scores over 600: 6%; SAT math scores over 600: 18%; SAT writing scores over 600: 5%; ACT scores over 24: 44%; SAT critical reading scores over 700: 1%; SAT math scores over 700: 3%.

Faculty *Total:* 62, 61% full-time, 45% with terminal degrees. *Student/faculty ratio:* 13:1.

Academics *Calendar:* semesters. *Degrees:* certificates, associate, bachelor's, and master's. *Special study options:* adult/continuing education programs.

Computers on Campus Students can access the following: online (class) registration. Campuswide network is available.

Student Life *Housing options:* coed, disabled students. Campus housing is university owned. Freshman campus housing is guaranteed. *Campus security:* 24-hour patrols, controlled dormitory access.

Athletics Member NJCAA. *Intercollegiate sports:* baseball M, basketball M, softball W, volleyball W. *Intramural sports:* basketball M/W, cheerleading M(c)/W(c), football M/W, ice hockey M(c), racquetball M/W, skiing (cross-country) M(c)/W(c), skiing (downhill) M(c)/W(c), soccer M(c)/W(c), softball M/W, tennis M/W, volleyball M/W.

Standardized Tests *Required:* SAT or ACT (for admission).

Costs (2013–14) *Tuition:* area resident $12,474 full-time, $504 per credit hour part-time; state resident $12,474 full-time, $504 per credit hour part-time; non-resident $19,030 full-time, $793 per credit hour part-time. Full-time tuition and fees vary according to course level, degree level, location, program, and student level. Part-time tuition and fees vary according to course level, course load, degree level, location, program, and student level. *Required fees:* $882 full-time. *Room and board:* $9690; room only: $4910. Room and board charges vary according to board plan, housing facility, and location. *Payment plans:* installment, deferred payment. *Waivers:* employees or children of employees.

Financial Aid Of all full-time matriculated undergraduates who enrolled in 2011, 544 applied for aid, 498 were judged to have need, 24 had their need fully met. In 2011, 24 non-need-based awards were made. *Average percent of need met:* 67%. *Average financial aid package:* $12,082. *Average need-based loan:* $3916. *Average need-based gift aid:* $7587. *Average non-need-based aid:* $2627. *Average indebtedness upon graduation:* $35,100.

Applying *Options:* electronic application, early admission, deferred entrance. *Application fee:* $50. *Required:* high school transcript. *Required for some:* interview. *Recommended:* essay or personal statement. *Application deadlines:* rolling (freshmen), rolling (transfers). *Notification:* continuous (freshmen), continuous (transfers).

Freshman Application Contact Admissions Office, Penn State Greater Allegheny, 4000 University Drive, McKeesport, PA 15132-7698. *Phone:* 412-675-9010. *Fax:* 412-675-9046. *E-mail:* psuga@psu.edu. *Website:* http://www.ga.psu.edu/.

Penn State Harrisburg

Middletown, Pennsylvania

- **State-related** comprehensive, founded 1966, part of Pennsylvania State University
- **Small-town** campus
- **Coed** 3,426 undergraduate students, 85% full-time, 44% women, 56% men
- **Very difficult** entrance level, 80% of applicants were admitted

Undergraduates 2,905 full-time, 521 part-time. 13% are from out of state; 10% Black or African American, non-Hispanic/Latino; 5% Hispanic/Latino; 7% Asian, non-Hispanic/Latino; 0.1% Native Hawaiian or other Pacific Islander, non-Hispanic/Latino; 0.3% American Indian or Alaska Native, non-Hispanic/Latino; 2% Two or more races, non-Hispanic/Latino; 2% Race/ethnicity unknown; 5% international; 10% transferred in; 12% live on campus. *Retention:* 81% of full-time freshmen returned.

Freshmen *Admission:* 2,792 applied, 2,232 admitted, 628 enrolled. *Average high school GPA:* 3.08. *Test scores:* SAT critical reading scores over 500: 47%; SAT math scores over 500: 62%; SAT writing scores over 500: 44%; ACT scores over 18: 90%; SAT critical reading scores over 600: 11%; SAT math scores over 600: 25%; SAT writing scores over 600: 8%; ACT scores over 24: 37%; SAT critical reading scores over 700: 1%; SAT math scores over 700: 6%.

Faculty *Total:* 341, 64% full-time, 64% with terminal degrees. *Student/faculty ratio:* 14:1.

Academics *Calendar:* semesters. *Degrees:* certificates, associate, bachelor's, master's, and doctoral. *Special study options:* adult/continuing education programs, part-time degree program. *ROTC:* Army (c).

Computers on Campus Students can access the following: campus intranet, computer help desk, free student e-mail accounts, online (class) grades, online (class) registration, online (class) schedules. Campuswide network is available.

Student Life *Housing options:* disabled students. Campus housing is university owned. *Campus security:* 24-hour emergency response devices and patrols, student patrols, late-night transport/escort service, controlled dormitory access.

Athletics *Intercollegiate sports:* baseball M, basketball M/W, cross-country running M/W, golf M/W, soccer M/W, softball W, tennis M/W, volleyball W. *Intramural sports:* badminton M/W, basketball M/W, racquetball M/W, tennis M/W.

Standardized Tests *Required:* SAT or ACT (for admission).

Costs (2013–14) *Tuition:* area resident $13,018 full-time, $542 per credit hour part-time; state resident $13,018 full-time, $542 per credit hour part-time; non-resident $19,912 full-time, $830 per credit hour part-time. Full-time tuition and fees vary according to course level, degree level, location, program, and student level. Part-time tuition and fees vary according to course level, course load, degree level, location, program, and student level. *Required fees:* $882 full-time. *Room and board:* $11,000; room only: $6220. Room and board charges vary according to board plan, housing facility, and location. *Payment plans:* installment, deferred payment. *Waivers:* employees or children of employees.

Financial Aid Of all full-time matriculated undergraduates who enrolled in 2011, 2,128 applied for aid, 1,863 were judged to have need, 117 had their need fully met. In 2011, 65 non-need-based awards were made. *Average percent of need met:* 59%. *Average financial aid package:* $10,542. *Average need-based loan:* $4505. *Average need-based gift aid:* $6432. *Average non-need-based aid:* $1522. *Average indebtedness upon graduation:* $35,100.

Applying *Options:* electronic application, early admission, deferred entrance. *Application fee:* $50. *Required:* high school transcript. *Required for some:* interview. *Recommended:* essay or personal statement. *Application deadlines:* rolling (freshmen), rolling (transfers). *Notification:* continuous (freshmen), continuous (transfers).

Freshman Application Contact Admissions Office, Penn State Harrisburg, 777 West Harrisburg Pike, Middletown, PA 17057-4898. *Phone:* 717-948-6250. *Toll-free phone:* 800-222-2056. *Fax:* 717-948-6325. *E-mail:* hbgadmit@psu.edu. *Website:* http://www.hbg.psu.edu/.

Penn State Hazleton

Hazleton, Pennsylvania

- **State-related** primarily 2-year, founded 1934, part of Pennsylvania State University
- **Small-town** campus
- **Coed** 1,060 undergraduate students, 94% full-time, 45% women, 55% men
- **Moderately difficult** entrance level, 86% of applicants were admitted

Undergraduates 1,000 full-time, 60 part-time. 28% are from out of state; 16% Black or African American, non-Hispanic/Latino; 15% Hispanic/Latino; 4% Asian, non-Hispanic/Latino; 0.1% Native Hawaiian or other Pacific Islander, non-Hispanic/Latino; 0.3% American Indian or Alaska Native, non-Hispanic/Latino; 3% Two or more races, non-Hispanic/Latino; 1% Race/ethnicity unknown; 0.9% international; 4% transferred in; 45% live on campus. *Retention:* 78% of full-time freshmen returned.

Freshmen *Admission:* 1,179 applied, 1,018 admitted, 433 enrolled. *Average high school GPA:* 2.89. *Test scores:* SAT critical reading scores over 500: 35%; SAT math scores over 500: 41%; SAT writing scores over 500: 25%; ACT scores over 18: 93%; SAT critical reading scores over 600: 6%; SAT math scores over 600: 10%; SAT writing scores over 600: 3%; ACT scores over 24: 40%; ACT scores over 30: 7%.

Faculty *Total:* 80, 68% full-time, 45% with terminal degrees. *Student/faculty ratio:* 16:1.

Academics *Calendar:* semesters. *Degrees:* certificates, associate, and bachelor's. *Special study options:* adult/continuing education programs. *ROTC:* Army (b), Air Force (c).

Computers on Campus Students can access the following: online (class) registration. Campuswide network is available.

Student Life *Housing options:* coed. Campus housing is university owned. Freshman campus housing is guaranteed. *Campus security:* 24-hour patrols, late-night transport/escort service, controlled dormitory access.

Athletics Member NJCAA. *Intercollegiate sports:* baseball M, basketball M/W, cheerleading M/W, soccer M, softball W(s), tennis M/W, volleyball M/W. *Intramural sports:* basketball M/W, skiing (downhill) M(c)/W(c), soccer M/W, volleyball M/W.

Standardized Tests *Required:* SAT or ACT (for admission).

Costs (2013–14) *Tuition:* area resident $12,474 full-time, $504 per credit hour part-time; state resident $12,474 full-time, $504 per credit hour part-time; non-resident $19,030 full-time, $793 per credit hour part-time. Full-time tuition and fees vary according to course level, degree level, location, program, and student level. Part-time tuition and fees vary according to course level, course load, degree level, location, program, and student level. *Required fees:* $826 full-time. *Room and board:* $9690; room only: $4910. Room and board charges vary according to board plan, housing facility, and location. *Payment plans:* installment, deferred payment. *Waivers:* employees or children of employees.

Financial Aid Of all full-time matriculated undergraduates who enrolled in 2011, 978 applied for aid, 852 were judged to have need, 26 had their need fully met. In 2011, 61 non-need-based awards were made. *Average percent of need met:* 61%. *Average financial aid package:* $9823. *Average need-based loan:* $3819. *Average need-based gift aid:* $6462. *Average non-need-based aid:* $2301. *Average indebtedness upon graduation:* $35,100.

Applying *Options:* electronic application, early admission, deferred entrance. *Application fee:* $50. *Required:* high school transcript. *Required for some:* interview. *Recommended:* essay or personal statement. *Application deadlines:* rolling (freshmen), rolling (transfers). *Notification:* continuous (freshmen), continuous (transfers).
Freshman Application Contact Admissions Office, Penn State Hazleton, Hazleton, PA 18202-1291. *Phone:* 570-450-3142. *Toll-free phone:* 800-279-8495. *Fax:* 570-450-3182. *E-mail:* admissions-hn@psu.edu.
Website: http://www.hn.psu.edu/.

Penn State Lehigh Valley

Fogelsville, Pennsylvania

- **State-related** primarily 2-year, founded 1912, part of Pennsylvania State University
- **Rural** campus
- **Coed** 907 undergraduate students, 80% full-time, 44% women, 56% men
- **Moderately difficult** entrance level, 85% of applicants were admitted

Undergraduates 728 full-time, 179 part-time. 4% are from out of state; 5% Black or African American, non-Hispanic/Latino; 15% Hispanic/Latino; 10% Asian, non-Hispanic/Latino; 0.1% Native Hawaiian or other Pacific Islander, non-Hispanic/Latino; 2% Two or more races, non-Hispanic/Latino; 2% Race/ethnicity unknown; 0.5% international; 5% transferred in. *Retention:* 81% of full-time freshmen returned.
Freshmen *Admission:* 909 applied, 777 admitted, 225 enrolled. *Average high school GPA:* 2.98. *Test scores:* SAT critical reading scores over 500: 43%; SAT math scores over 500: 58%; SAT writing scores over 500: 43%; ACT scores over 18: 90%; SAT critical reading scores over 600: 11%; SAT math scores over 600: 16%; SAT writing scores over 600: 6%; ACT scores over 24: 30%; SAT critical reading scores over 700: 1%; SAT math scores over 700: 1%; SAT writing scores over 700: 1%; ACT scores over 30: 10%.
Faculty *Total:* 90, 39% full-time, 46% with terminal degrees. *Student/faculty ratio:* 15:1.
Academics *Calendar:* semesters. *Degrees:* certificates, associate, and bachelor's (enrollment figures include students enrolled at The Graduate School at Penn State who are taking courses at this location). *Special study options:* adult/continuing education programs. *ROTC:* Army (c).
Computers on Campus Students can access the following: online (class) registration. Campuswide network is available.
Student Life *Housing:* college housing not available.
Athletics Member NJCAA. *Intercollegiate sports:* baseball M, basketball M/W, bowling M(c)/W(c), cheerleading M/W, cross-country running M/W, football M(c), golf M(c)/W(c), ice hockey M(c)/W(c), skiing (downhill) M(c)/W(c), soccer M(c)/W, tennis M/W, volleyball M(c)/W. *Intramural sports:* badminton M/W, basketball M/W, football M/W, golf M/W, soccer M/W, volleyball M/W.
Standardized Tests *Required:* SAT or ACT (for admission).
Costs (2013–14) *Tuition:* area resident $12,474 full-time, $504 per credit hour part-time; state resident $12,474 full-time, $504 per credit hour part-time; nonresident $19,030 full-time, $793 per credit hour part-time. Full-time tuition and fees vary according to course level, degree level, location, program, and student level. Part-time tuition and fees vary according to course level, course load, degree level, location, program, and student level. *Required fees:* $876 full-time. *Payment plans:* installment, deferred payment. *Waivers:* employees or children of employees.
Financial Aid Of all full-time matriculated undergraduates who enrolled in 2011, 584 applied for aid, 504 were judged to have need, 14 had their need fully met. In 2011, 44 non-need-based awards were made. *Average percent of need met:* 61%. *Average financial aid package:* $9723. *Average need-based loan:* $4101. *Average need-based gift aid:* $6442. *Average non-need-based aid:* $1838. *Average indebtedness upon graduation:* $35,100.
Applying *Options:* electronic application, early admission, deferred entrance. *Application fee:* $50. *Required:* high school transcript. *Application deadlines:* rolling (freshmen), rolling (transfers). *Notification:* continuous (freshmen), continuous (transfers).
Freshman Application Contact Admissions Office, Penn State Lehigh Valley, 2809 Saucon Valley Road, Fogelsville, PA 18051-9999. *Phone:* 610-285-5000. *Fax:* 610-285-5220. *E-mail:* admissions-lv@psu.edu.
Website: http://www.lv.psu.edu/.

Penn State Mont Alto

Mont Alto, Pennsylvania

- **State-related** primarily 2-year, founded 1929, part of Pennsylvania State University
- **Small-town** campus
- **Coed** 1,106 undergraduate students, 75% full-time, 56% women, 44% men
- **Moderately difficult** entrance level, 83% of applicants were admitted

Undergraduates 831 full-time, 275 part-time. 17% are from out of state; 11% Black or African American, non-Hispanic/Latino; 4% Hispanic/Latino; 2% Asian, non-Hispanic/Latino; 3% Two or more races, non-Hispanic/Latino; 1% Race/ethnicity unknown; 0.7% international; 4% transferred in; 29% live on campus. *Retention:* 74% of full-time freshmen returned.
Freshmen *Admission:* 827 applied, 684 admitted, 325 enrolled. *Average high school GPA:* 2.97. *Test scores:* SAT critical reading scores over 500: 36%; SAT math scores over 500: 47%; SAT writing scores over 500: 29%; ACT scores over 18: 91%; SAT critical reading scores over 600: 6%; SAT math scores over 600: 17%; SAT writing scores over 600: 6%; ACT scores over 24: 18%; SAT math scores over 700: 2%.
Faculty *Total:* 108, 53% full-time, 35% with terminal degrees. *Student/faculty ratio:* 13:1.
Academics *Calendar:* semesters. *Degrees:* certificates, associate, and bachelor's. *Special study options:* adult/continuing education programs. *ROTC:* Army (c).
Computers on Campus Students can access the following: online (class) registration. Campuswide network is available.
Student Life *Housing options:* coed, disabled students. Campus housing is university owned. Freshman campus housing is guaranteed. *Campus security:* 24-hour patrols, controlled dormitory access.
Athletics Member NJCAA. *Intercollegiate sports:* basketball M/W, cheerleading M/W, cross-country running M/W, golf M/W, soccer M/W, softball W, tennis M/W, volleyball W. *Intramural sports:* badminton M/W, basketball M/W, cheerleading M(c)/W(c), racquetball M/W, soccer M/W, softball W, volleyball M/W.
Standardized Tests *Required:* SAT or ACT (for admission).
Costs (2013–14) *Tuition:* area resident $12,474 full-time, $504 per credit hour part-time; state resident $12,474 full-time, $504 per credit hour part-time; nonresident $19,030 full-time, $793 per credit hour part-time. Full-time tuition and fees vary according to course level, degree level, location, program, and student level. Part-time tuition and fees vary according to course level, course load, degree level, location, program, and student level. *Required fees:* $882 full-time. *Room and board:* $9690; room only: $4910. Room and board charges vary according to board plan, housing facility, and location. *Payment plans:* installment, deferred payment. *Waivers:* employees or children of employees.
Financial Aid Of all full-time matriculated undergraduates who enrolled in 2011, 852 applied for aid, 754 were judged to have need, 40 had their need fully met. In 2011, 46 non-need-based awards were made. *Average percent of need met:* 64%. *Average financial aid package:* $10,829. *Average need-based loan:* $3849. *Average need-based gift aid:* $6401. *Average non-need-based aid:* $2946. *Average indebtedness upon graduation:* $35,100.
Applying *Options:* electronic application, early admission, deferred entrance. *Application fee:* $50. *Required:* high school transcript. *Required for some:* interview. *Recommended:* essay or personal statement. *Application deadlines:* rolling (freshmen), rolling (transfers). *Notification:* continuous (freshmen), continuous (transfers).
Freshman Application Contact Admissions Office, Penn State Mont Alto, 1 Campus Drive, Mont Alto, PA 17237-9703. *Phone:* 717-749-6130. *Toll-free phone:* 800-392-6173. *Fax:* 717-749-6132. *E-mail:* psuma@psu.edu.
Website: http://www.ma.psu.edu/.

Penn State New Kensington

New Kensington, Pennsylvania

- **State-related** primarily 2-year, founded 1958, part of Pennsylvania State University
- **Small-town** campus
- **Coed** 715 undergraduate students, 78% full-time, 40% women, 60% men
- **Moderately difficult** entrance level, 74% of applicants were admitted

Undergraduates 558 full-time, 157 part-time. 2% are from out of state; 3% Black or African American, non-Hispanic/Latino; 2% Hispanic/Latino; 1% Asian, non-Hispanic/Latino; 0.2% American Indian or Alaska Native, non-Hispanic/Latino; 1% Two or more races, non-Hispanic/Latino; 2% Race/ethnicity unknown; 0.9% international; 7% transferred in. *Retention:* 71% of full-time freshmen returned.

Freshmen *Admission:* 477 applied, 352 admitted, 154 enrolled. *Average high school GPA:* 3.03. *Test scores:* SAT critical reading scores over 500: 44%; SAT math scores over 500: 56%; SAT writing scores over 500: 35%; ACT scores over 18: 67%; SAT critical reading scores over 600: 13%; SAT math scores over 600: 18%; SAT writing scores over 600: 9%; ACT scores over 24: 50%; SAT critical reading scores over 700: 1%; SAT math scores over 700: 5%; SAT writing scores over 700: 1%.

Faculty *Total:* 78, 47% full-time, 44% with terminal degrees. *Student/faculty ratio:* 12:1.

Academics *Calendar:* semesters. *Degrees:* certificates, associate, bachelor's, and master's. *Special study options:* adult/continuing education programs, external degree program. *ROTC:* Air Force (c).

Computers on Campus Students can access the following: online (class) registration. Campuswide network is available.

Student Life *Campus security:* part-time trained security personnel.

Athletics Member NJCAA. *Intercollegiate sports:* baseball M, basketball M/W, cheerleading M/W, golf M/W, softball W, volleyball W. *Intramural sports:* badminton M/W, basketball M/W, bowling M/W, cheerleading M(c)/W(c), football M/W, ice hockey M(c)/W(c), racquetball M/W, skiing (downhill) M(c)/W(c), soccer M/W, softball W, volleyball M/W.

Standardized Tests *Required:* SAT or ACT (for admission).

Costs (2013–14) *Tuition:* state resident $504 per credit part-time; nonresident $793 per credit part-time. Full-time tuition and fees vary according to course level, degree level, location, program, and student level. Part-time tuition and fees vary according to course level, course load, degree level, location, program, and student level. *Payment plans:* installment, deferred payment. *Waivers:* employees or children of employees.

Financial Aid Of all full-time matriculated undergraduates who enrolled in 2011, 521 applied for aid, 447 were judged to have need, 17 had their need fully met. In 2011, 28 non-need-based awards were made. *Average percent of need met:* 64%. *Average financial aid package:* $9992. *Average need-based loan:* $3993. *Average need-based gift aid:* $5931. *Average non-need-based aid:* $1979. *Average indebtedness upon graduation:* $35,100.

Applying *Options:* electronic application, early admission, deferred entrance. *Application fee:* $50. *Required:* high school transcript. *Required for some:* interview. *Recommended:* essay or personal statement. *Application deadlines:* rolling (freshmen), rolling (transfers). *Notification:* continuous (freshmen), continuous (transfers).

Freshman Application Contact Admissions Office, Penn State New Kensington, 3550 Seventh Street Road, New Kensington, PA 15068. *Phone:* 724-334-5466. *Toll-free phone:* 888-968-7297. *Fax:* 724-334-6111. *E-mail:* nkadmissions@psu.edu.
Website: http://www.nk.psu.edu/.

Penn State Schuylkill

Schuylkill Haven, Pennsylvania

- **State-related** primarily 2-year, founded 1934, part of Pennsylvania State University
- **Small-town** campus
- **Coed** 867 undergraduate students, 80% full-time, 58% women, 42% men
- **Moderately difficult** entrance level, 81% of applicants were admitted

Undergraduates 696 full-time, 171 part-time. 18% are from out of state; 29% Black or African American, non-Hispanic/Latino; 6% Hispanic/Latino; 1% Asian, non-Hispanic/Latino; 0.2% Native Hawaiian or other Pacific Islander, non-Hispanic/Latino; 0.2% American Indian or Alaska Native, non-Hispanic/Latino; 2% Two or more races, non-Hispanic/Latino; 2% Race/ethnicity unknown; 1% international; 5% transferred in; 32% live on campus. *Retention:* 69% of full-time freshmen returned.

Freshmen *Admission:* 693 applied, 562 admitted, 248 enrolled. *Average high school GPA:* 2.75. *Test scores:* SAT critical reading scores over 500: 21%; SAT math scores over 500: 23%; SAT writing scores over 500: 19%; ACT scores over 18: 75%; SAT critical reading scores over 600: 3%; SAT math scores over 600: 5%; SAT writing scores over 600: 2%; ACT scores over 24: 13%.

Faculty *Total:* 68, 65% full-time, 56% with terminal degrees. *Student/faculty ratio:* 15:1.

Academics *Calendar:* semesters. *Degrees:* certificates, associate, and bachelor's (bachelor's degree programs completed at the Harrisburg campus). *Special study options:* adult/continuing education programs, external degree program.

Computers on Campus Students can access the following: online (class) registration. Campuswide network is available.

Student Life *Housing options:* disabled students. *Campus security:* 24-hour patrols, controlled dormitory access.

Athletics Member NJCAA. *Intercollegiate sports:* basketball M, cross-country running M/W, golf M, soccer M, softball W, volleyball W. *Intramural sports:* basketball M/W, football M, soccer M/W, softball M/W, table tennis M/W, volleyball M/W.

Standardized Tests *Required:* SAT or ACT (for admission).

Costs (2012–13) *Tuition:* state resident $12,474 full-time, $504 per credit part-time; nonresident $19,030 full-time, $793 per credit part-time. Full-time tuition and fees vary according to course level, degree level, location, program, and student level. Part-time tuition and fees vary according to course level, course load, degree level, location, program, and student level. *Required fees:* $770 full-time. *Payment plans:* installment, deferred payment. *Waivers:* employees or children of employees.

Financial Aid Of all full-time matriculated undergraduates who enrolled in 2011, 775 applied for aid, 719 were judged to have need, 28 had their need fully met. In 2011, 20 non-need-based awards were made. *Average percent of need met:* 64%. *Average financial aid package:* $10,749. *Average need-based loan:* $3912. *Average need-based gift aid:* $6796. *Average non-need-based aid:* $2001. *Average indebtedness upon graduation:* $35,100.

Applying *Options:* electronic application, early admission, deferred entrance. *Application fee:* $50. *Required:* high school transcript. *Application deadlines:* rolling (freshmen), rolling (transfers). *Notification:* continuous (freshmen), continuous (transfers).

Freshman Application Contact Admissions Office, Penn State Schuylkill, 200 University Drive, Schuylkill Haven, PA 17972-2208. *Phone:* 570-385-6252. *Fax:* 570-385-6272. *E-mail:* sl-admissions@psu.edu.
Website: http://www.sl.psu.edu/.

Penn State Shenango

Sharon, Pennsylvania

- **State-related** 4-year, founded 1965, part of Pennsylvania State University
- **Small-town** campus
- **Coed** 578 undergraduate students, 58% full-time, 66% women, 34% men
- **Moderately difficult** entrance level, 69% of applicants were admitted

Undergraduates 336 full-time, 242 part-time. 19% are from out of state; 9% Black or African American, non-Hispanic/Latino; 2% Hispanic/Latino; 0.2% Asian, non-Hispanic/Latino; 0.4% Native Hawaiian or other Pacific Islander, non-Hispanic/Latino; 2% Two or more races, non-Hispanic/Latino; 3% Race/ethnicity unknown; 9% transferred in. *Retention:* 56% of full-time freshmen returned.

Freshmen *Admission:* 229 applied, 159 admitted, 90 enrolled. *Average high school GPA:* 2.95. *Test scores:* SAT critical reading scores over 500: 22%; SAT math scores over 500: 31%; SAT writing scores over 500: 12%; ACT scores over 18: 57%; SAT critical reading scores over 600: 8%; SAT math scores over 600: 4%; SAT writing scores over 600: 2%; ACT scores over 24: 7%; ACT scores over 30: 7%.

Faculty *Total:* 68, 44% full-time, 38% with terminal degrees. *Student/faculty ratio:* 10:1.

Academics *Calendar:* semesters. *Degrees:* certificates, associate, and bachelor's. *Special study options:* adult/continuing education programs.

Computers on Campus Students can access the following: online (class) registration. Campuswide network is available.

Student Life *Housing:* college housing not available.

Athletics *Intramural sports:* basketball M(c)/W, bowling M/W, football M(c), golf M/W, softball M/W, tennis M/W, volleyball M/W.

Standardized Tests *Required:* SAT or ACT (for admission).

Costs (2012–13) *Tuition:* state resident $12,474 full-time, $504 per credit part-time; nonresident $19,030 full-time, $793 per credit part-time. Full-time tuition and fees vary according to course level, degree level, location, program, and student level. Part-time tuition and fees vary according to course level, course load, degree level, location, program, and student level. *Required fees:* $770 full-time. *Payment plans:* installment, deferred payment. *Waivers:* employees or children of employees.

Financial Aid Of all full-time matriculated undergraduates who enrolled in 2011, 354 applied for aid, 339 were judged to have need, 10 had their need fully met. In 2011, 12 non-need-based awards were made. *Average percent of need met:* 63%. *Average financial aid package:* $12,880. *Average need-based loan:* $4145. *Average need-based gift aid:* $6864. *Average non-need-based aid:* $2060. *Average indebtedness upon graduation:* $35,100.

Applying *Options:* electronic application, early admission, deferred entrance. *Application fee:* $50. *Required:* high school transcript. *Required for some:* interview. *Recommended:* essay or personal statement. *Application deadlines:* rolling (freshmen), rolling (transfers). *Notification:* continuous (freshmen), continuous (transfers).

Freshman Application Contact Admissions Office, Penn State Shenango, 147 Shenango Avenue, Sharon, PA 16146-1537. *Phone:* 724-983-2803. *Fax:* 724-983-2820. *E-mail:* psushenango@psu.edu. *Website:* http://www.shenango.psu.edu/.

Penn State University Park

State College, Pennsylvania

- **State-related** university, founded 1855, part of Pennsylvania State University
- **Small-town** 8556-acre campus with easy access to Harrisburg
- **Endowment** $1.9 billion
- **Coed** 39,192 undergraduate students, 97% full-time, 46% women, 54% men
- **Very difficult** entrance level, 54% of applicants were admitted

Undergraduates 37,917 full-time, 1,275 part-time. Students come from 53 states and territories; 98 other countries; 30% are from out of state; 4% Black or African American, non-Hispanic/Latino; 5% Hispanic/Latino; 5% Asian, non-Hispanic/Latino; 0.1% Native Hawaiian or other Pacific Islander, non-Hispanic/Latino; 0.1% American Indian or Alaska Native, non-Hispanic/Latino; 2% Two or more races, non-Hispanic/Latino; 1% Race/ethnicity unknown; 8% international; 1% transferred in; 36% live on campus. *Retention:* 92% of full-time freshmen returned.

Freshmen *Admission:* 47,552 applied, 25,772 admitted, 7,649 enrolled. *Average high school GPA:* 3.59. *Test scores:* SAT critical reading scores over 500: 86%; SAT math scores over 500: 93%; SAT writing scores over 500: 89%; SAT critical reading scores over 600: 40%; SAT math scores over 600: 62%; SAT writing scores over 600: 46%; SAT critical reading scores over 700: 7%; SAT math scores over 700: 15%; SAT writing scores over 700: 8%.

Faculty *Total:* 2,910, 87% full-time, 73% with terminal degrees. *Student/faculty ratio:* 17:1.

Academics *Calendar:* semesters. *Degrees:* certificates, associate, bachelor's, master's, doctoral, and postbachelor's certificates. *Special study options:* academic remediation for entering students, accelerated degree program, adult/continuing education programs, advanced placement credit, cooperative education, distance learning, double majors, English as a second language, external degree program, freshman honors college, honors programs, independent study, internships, off-campus study, part-time degree program, services for LD students, student-designed majors, study abroad, summer session for credit. *ROTC:* Army (b), Navy (b), Air Force (b). *Unusual degree programs:* 3-2 engineering; geoscience.

Computers on Campus 6,150 computers/terminals and 23,225 ports are available on campus for general student use. Students can access the following: campus intranet, computer help desk, free student e-mail accounts, online (class) grades, online (class) registration, online (class) schedules. Campuswide network is available. 100% of college-owned or -operated housing units are wired for high-speed Internet access. Wireless service is available via classrooms, computer centers, computer labs, dorm rooms, learning centers, libraries, student centers.

Student Life *Housing:* on-campus residence required for freshman year. *Options:* coed, men-only, women-only, disabled students. Campus housing is university owned. Freshman campus housing is guaranteed. *Activities and organizations:* drama/theater group, student-run newspaper, radio and television station, choral group, marching band, national fraternities, national sororities. *Campus security:* 24-hour emergency response devices and patrols, student patrols, late-night transport/escort service, controlled dormitory access. *Student services:* health clinic, personal/psychological counseling, women's center.

Athletics Member NCAA, USCAA. All Division I except football (Division I-A). *Intercollegiate sports:* baseball M(s), basketball M(s)/W(s), cheerleading M(s)/W(s), cross-country running M(s)/W(s), fencing M(s)/W(s), field hockey W(s), golf M(s)/W(s), gymnastics M(s)/W(s), ice hockey M(s)(c)/W(s)(c), lacrosse M(s)/W(s), soccer M(s)/W(s), softball W(s), swimming and diving M(s)/W(s), tennis M(s)/W(s), track and field M(s)/W(s), volleyball M(s)/W(s), wrestling M(s). *Intramural sports:* archery M(c)/W(c), badminton M(c)/W, baseball M(c)/W(c), basketball M(c)/W(c), bowling M(c)/W(c), cheerleading M(c)/W(c), crew M(c)/W(c), cross-country running M/W, equestrian sports M(c)/W(c), fencing M(c)/W(c), field hockey M(c)/W(c), football M, golf M(c)/W(c), gymnastics M(c)/W(c), lacrosse M(c)/W(c), racquetball M(c)/W(c), riflery M(c)/W(c), rugby M(c)/W(c), sailing M(c)/W(c), skiing (downhill) M(c)/W(c), soccer M(c)/W(c), softball M(c)/W(c), squash M(c)/W(c), swimming and diving M(c)/W(c), table tennis M(c)/W(c), tennis M(c)/W(c), track and field M(c)/W(c), ultimate Frisbee M(c)/W(c), volleyball M(c)/W(c), water polo M(c)/W(c), weight lifting M(c)/W(c), wrestling M/W.

Standardized Tests *Required:* SAT or ACT (for admission).

Costs (2012–13) *Tuition:* state resident $15,562 full-time, $648 per credit part-time; nonresident $27,864 full-time, $1161 per credit part-time. Full-time tuition and fees vary according to course level, degree level, location, program, and student level. Part-time tuition and fees vary according to course level, course load, degree level, location, program, and student level. *Required fees:* $882 full-time. *Room and board:* $9690; room only: $4910. Room and board charges vary according to board plan, housing facility, and location. *Payment plans:* installment, deferred payment. *Waivers:* employees or children of employees.

Financial Aid Of all full-time matriculated undergraduates who enrolled in 2011, 24,671 applied for aid, 19,662 were judged to have need, 1,522 had their need fully met. 869 Federal Work-Study jobs (averaging $1911). In 2011, 2963 non-need-based awards were made. *Average percent of need met:* 61%. *Average financial aid package:* $10,552. *Average need-based loan:* $4693. *Average need-based gift aid:* $6524. *Average non-need-based aid:* $3153. *Average indebtedness upon graduation:* $35,100.

Applying *Options:* electronic application, early admission, deferred entrance. *Application fee:* $50. *Required:* high school transcript. *Required for some:* interview. *Recommended:* essay or personal statement. *Application deadlines:* rolling (freshmen), rolling (transfers). *Notification:* continuous (freshmen), continuous (transfers).

Freshman Application Contact Anne L. Rohrbach, Director for Undergraduate Admissions, Penn State University Park, 201 Shields Building, Box 3000, University Park, PA 16804-3000. *Phone:* 814-865-4700. *Fax:* 814-863-7590. *E-mail:* admissions@psu.edu. *Website:* http://www.psu.edu/.

Penn State Wilkes-Barre

Lehman, Pennsylvania

- **State-related** primarily 2-year, founded 1916, part of Pennsylvania State University
- **Rural** campus
- **Coed** 617 undergraduate students, 87% full-time, 31% women, 69% men
- **Moderately difficult** entrance level, 82% of applicants were admitted

Undergraduates 539 full-time, 78 part-time. 6% are from out of state; 5% Black or African American, non-Hispanic/Latino; 5% Hispanic/Latino; 1% Asian, non-Hispanic/Latino; 0.2% Native Hawaiian or other Pacific Islander, non-Hispanic/Latino; 0.2% American Indian or Alaska Native, non-Hispanic/Latino; 1% Two or more races, non-Hispanic/Latino; 1% Race/ethnicity unknown; 0.7% international; 4% transferred in. *Retention:* 84% of full-time freshmen returned.

Freshmen *Admission:* 472 applied, 387 admitted, 148 enrolled. *Average high school GPA:* 3. *Test scores:* SAT critical reading scores over 500: 44%; SAT math scores over 500: 54%; SAT writing scores over 500: 30%; ACT scores over 18: 83%; SAT critical reading scores over 600: 13%; SAT math scores over 600: 19%; SAT writing scores over 600: 6%; ACT scores over 24: 17%; SAT math scores over 700: 2%.

Faculty *Total:* 58, 57% full-time, 43% with terminal degrees. *Student/faculty ratio:* 14:1.

Academics *Calendar:* semesters. *Degrees:* certificates, associate, and bachelor's (enrollment figures include students enrolled at The Graduate School at Penn State who are taking courses at this location). *Special study options:* adult/continuing education programs. *ROTC:* Army (c), Air Force (c).

Computers on Campus Students can access the following: online (class) registration. Campuswide network is available.

Student Life *Housing:* college housing not available.

Athletics Member NJCAA. *Intercollegiate sports:* baseball M, basketball M, cross-country running M/W, golf M/W, soccer M/W, volleyball W. *Intramural sports:* basketball M/W, bowling M(c)/W(c), cheerleading M(c)/W(c), football M, racquetball M/W, softball W, volleyball M(c)/W.

Standardized Tests *Required:* SAT or ACT (for admission).

Costs (2013–14) *Tuition:* area resident $12,474 full-time, $504 per credit hour part-time; state resident $12,474 full-time, $504 per credit hour part-time; nonresident $19,030 full-time, $793 per credit hour part-time. Full-time tuition and fees vary according to course level, degree level, location, program, and student level. Part-time tuition and fees vary according to course level, course load, degree level, location, program, and student level. *Required fees:* $764 full-time. *Payment plans:* installment, deferred payment. *Waivers:* employees or children of employees.

Financial Aid Of all full-time matriculated undergraduates who enrolled in 2011, 491 applied for aid, 420 were judged to have need, 26 had their need fully met. In 2011, 39 non-need-based awards were made. *Average percent of need met:* 65%. *Average financial aid package:* $10,042. *Average need-based loan:* $4051. *Average need-based gift aid:* $6492. *Average non-need-based aid:* $2715. *Average indebtedness upon graduation:* $35,100.

Applying *Options:* electronic application, early admission, deferred entrance. *Application fee:* $50. *Required:* high school transcript. *Required for some:* interview. *Recommended:* essay or personal statement. *Application deadlines:* rolling (freshmen), rolling (transfers). *Notification:* continuous (freshmen), continuous (transfers).

Freshman Application Contact Admissions Office, Penn State Wilkes-Barre, PO PSU, Lehman, PA 18627-0217. *Phone:* 570-675-9238. *Fax:* 570-675-9113. *E-mail:* wbadmissions@psu.edu. *Website:* http://www.wb.psu.edu/.

Penn State Worthington Scranton

Dunmore, Pennsylvania

- **State-related** primarily 2-year, founded 1923, part of Pennsylvania State University
- **Small-town** campus
- **Coed** 1,234 undergraduate students, 80% full-time, 54% women, 46% men
- **Moderately difficult** entrance level, 82% of applicants were admitted

Undergraduates 990 full-time, 244 part-time. 3% are from out of state; 2% Black or African American, non-Hispanic/Latino; 5% Hispanic/Latino; 5% Asian, non-Hispanic/Latino; 0.1% Native Hawaiian or other Pacific Islander, non-Hispanic/Latino; 0.3% American Indian or Alaska Native, non-Hispanic/Latino; 2% Two or more races, non-Hispanic/Latino; 2% Race/ethnicity unknown; 0.4% international; 4% transferred in. *Retention:* 69% of full-time freshmen returned.

Freshmen *Admission:* 722 applied, 591 admitted, 282 enrolled. *Average high school GPA:* 2.84. *Test scores:* SAT critical reading scores over 500: 34%; SAT math scores over 500: 42%; SAT writing scores over 500: 26%; ACT scores over 18: 80%; SAT critical reading scores over 600: 6%; SAT math scores over 600: 9%; SAT writing scores over 600: 5%; ACT scores over 24: 20%.

Faculty *Total:* 99, 52% full-time, 40% with terminal degrees. *Student/faculty ratio:* 16:1.

Academics *Calendar:* semesters. *Degrees:* certificates, associate, and bachelor's. *Special study options:* adult/continuing education programs. *ROTC:* Army (c), Air Force (c).

Computers on Campus Students can access the following: online (class) registration. Campuswide network is available.

Student Life *Housing:* college housing not available.

Athletics Member NJCAA. *Intercollegiate sports:* baseball M, basketball M/W, cheerleading M/W, cross-country running M/W, soccer M, softball W, volleyball W. *Intramural sports:* basketball M/W, bowling M(c)/W(c), skiing (downhill) M(c)/W(c), soccer M/W, softball M/W, volleyball M/W(c), weight lifting M(c)/W(c).

Standardized Tests *Required:* SAT or ACT (for admission).

Costs (2013–14) *Tuition:* area resident $12,474 full-time, $504 per credit hour part-time; state resident $12,474 full-time, $504 per credit hour part-time; nonresident $19,030 full-time, $793 per credit hour part-time. Full-time tuition and fees vary according to course level, degree level, location, program, and student level. Part-time tuition and fees vary according to course level, course load, degree level, location, program, and student level. *Required fees:* $756 full-time. *Payment plans:* installment, deferred payment. *Waivers:* employees or children of employees.

Financial Aid Of all full-time matriculated undergraduates who enrolled in 2011, 880 applied for aid, 770 were judged to have need, 30 had their need fully met. In 2011, 27 non-need-based awards were made. *Average percent of need met:* 62%. *Average financial aid package:* $9815. *Average need-based loan:* $4047. *Average need-based gift aid:* $6305. *Average non-need-based aid:* $2258. *Average indebtedness upon graduation:* $35,100.

Applying *Options:* electronic application, early admission, deferred entrance. *Application fee:* $50. *Required:* high school transcript. *Required for some:* interview. *Recommended:* essay or personal statement. *Application deadlines:* rolling (freshmen), rolling (transfers). *Notification:* continuous (freshmen), continuous (transfers).

Freshman Application Contact Admissions Office, Penn State Worthington Scranton, 120 Ridge View Drive, Dunmore, PA 18512-1699. *Phone:* 570-963-2500. *Fax:* 570-963-2524. *E-mail:* wsadmissions@psu.edu. *Website:* http://www.sn.psu.edu/.

Penn State York

York, Pennsylvania

- **State-related** primarily 2-year, founded 1926, part of Pennsylvania State University
- **Suburban** campus
- **Coed** 1,155 undergraduate students, 72% full-time, 43% women, 57% men
- **Moderately difficult** entrance level, 84% of applicants were admitted

Undergraduates 829 full-time, 326 part-time. 10% are from out of state; 9% Black or African American, non-Hispanic/Latino; 7% Hispanic/Latino; 5% Asian, non-Hispanic/Latino; 0.1% American Indian or Alaska Native, non-Hispanic/Latino; 3% Two or more races, non-Hispanic/Latino; 2% Race/ethnicity unknown; 5% international; 4% transferred in. *Retention:* 76% of full-time freshmen returned.

Freshmen *Admission:* 1,329 applied, 1,123 admitted, 300 enrolled. *Average high school GPA:* 2.95. *Test scores:* SAT critical reading scores over 500: 43%; SAT math scores over 500: 54%; SAT writing scores over 500: 33%; ACT scores over 18: 91%; SAT critical reading scores over 600: 10%; SAT math scores over 600: 18%; SAT writing scores over 600: 6%; ACT scores over 24: 36%; SAT critical reading scores over 700: 2%; SAT math scores over 700: 3%.

Faculty *Total:* 103, 50% full-time, 47% with terminal degrees. *Student/faculty ratio:* 14:1.

Academics *Calendar:* semesters. *Degrees:* certificates, associate, bachelor's, and master's (also offers up to 2 years of most bachelor's degree programs offered at University Park campus). *Special study options:* adult/continuing education programs.

Computers on Campus Students can access the following: online (class) registration. Campuswide network is available.

Student Life *Housing:* college housing not available.

Athletics Member NJCAA.

Standardized Tests *Required:* SAT or ACT (for admission).

Costs (2013–14) *Tuition:* area resident $12,474 full-time, $504 per credit hour part-time; state resident $12,474 full-time, $504 per credit hour part-time; nonresident $19,030 full-time, $793 per credit hour part-time. Full-time tuition and fees vary according to course level, degree level, location, program, and student level. Part-time tuition and fees vary according to course level, course load, degree level, location, program, and student level. *Required fees:* $764 full-time. *Payment plans:* installment, deferred payment. *Waivers:* employees or children of employees.

Financial Aid Of all full-time matriculated undergraduates who enrolled in 2011, 695 applied for aid, 570 were judged to have need, 37 had their need fully met. In 2011, 61 non-need-based awards were made. *Average percent of need met:* 61%. *Average financial aid package:* $9745. *Average need-based loan:* $3912. *Average need-based gift aid:* $6385. *Average non-need-based aid:* $2555. *Average indebtedness upon graduation:* $35,100.

Applying *Options:* electronic application, early admission, deferred entrance. *Application fee:* $50. *Required:* high school transcript. *Required for some:* interview. *Recommended:* essay or personal statement. *Application deadlines:* rolling (freshmen), rolling (transfers). *Notification:* continuous (freshmen), continuous (transfers).

Freshman Application Contact Admissions Office, Penn State York, 1031 Edgecomb Avenue, York, PA 17403-3398. *Phone:* 717-771-4040. *Toll-free phone:* 800-778-6227. *Fax:* 717-771-4005. *E-mail:* ykadmission@psu.edu. *Website:* http://www.yk.psu.edu/.

Pennsylvania Academy of the Fine Arts

Philadelphia, Pennsylvania

Freshman Application Contact Andre F. van de Putte, Dean of Enrollment, Pennsylvania Academy of the Fine Arts, 128 North Broad Street, Philadelphia, PA 19102. *Phone:* 215-972-7625. *E-mail:* admissions@pafa.edu. *Website:* http://www.pafa.edu/.

Pennsylvania College of Art & Design

Lancaster, Pennsylvania

- **Independent** 4-year, founded 1982
- **Urban** campus with easy access to Philadelphia, Baltimore
- **Coed** 248 undergraduate students, 91% full-time, 67% women, 33% men
- **Moderately difficult** entrance level, 40% of applicants were admitted

Undergraduates 225 full-time, 23 part-time. Students come from 12 states and territories; 26% are from out of state; 5% Black or African American, non-Hispanic/Latino; 6% Hispanic/Latino; 2% Asian, non-Hispanic/Latino; 4% Two or more races, non-Hispanic/Latino; 6% Race/ethnicity unknown; 8% transferred in. *Retention:* 59% of full-time freshmen returned.

Freshmen *Admission:* 375 applied, 151 admitted, 63 enrolled. *Average high school GPA:* 3.01.

Faculty *Total:* 54, 26% full-time. *Student/faculty ratio:* 9:1.

Academics *Calendar:* semesters. *Degree:* certificates and bachelor's. *Special study options:* advanced placement credit, internships.

Computers on Campus 86 computers/terminals are available on campus for general student use. Students can access the following: campus intranet, computer help desk, free student e-mail accounts, online (class) grades, online (class) schedules. Campuswide network is available. Wireless service is available via entire campus.

Student Life *Housing:* college housing not available. *Activities and organizations:* Student Council, Anime Club, Student AIGA, Society of Illustrators—Student Group. *Campus security:* late-night transport/escort service, trained evening/weekend security personnel.

Standardized Tests *Recommended:* SAT (for admission), ACT (for admission).

Costs (2012–13) *Tuition:* $18,700 full-time, $779 per credit part-time. Part-time tuition and fees vary according to course load. *Required fees:* $980 full-time. *Payment plan:* installment. *Waivers:* employees or children of employees.

Applying *Options:* electronic application, deferred entrance. *Application fee:* $40. *Required:* essay or personal statement, high school transcript, minimum 2.5 GPA, interview, portfolio. *Required for some:* 2 letters of recommendation. *Application deadlines:* rolling (freshmen), rolling (transfers). *Notification:* continuous (freshmen), continuous (transfers).

Freshman Application Contact Admissions Department, Pennsylvania College of Art & Design, 204 North Prince Street, PO Box 59, Lancaster, PA 17608. *Phone:* 717-396-7833. *Fax:* 717-396-1339. *E-mail:* admissions@pcad.edu.
Website: http://www.pcad.edu/.

Pennsylvania College of Technology

Williamsport, Pennsylvania

- **State-related** 4-year, founded 1965
- **Small-town** 997-acre campus
- **Coed** 5,671 undergraduate students, 84% full-time, 38% women, 62% men
- **Noncompetitive** entrance level, 88% of applicants were admitted

Undergraduates 4,764 full-time, 907 part-time. Students come from 36 states and territories; 11 other countries; 11% are from out of state; 4% Black or African American, non-Hispanic/Latino; 3% Hispanic/Latino; 0.7% Asian, non-Hispanic/Latino; 0.1% Native Hawaiian or other Pacific Islander, non-Hispanic/Latino; 0.2% American Indian or Alaska Native, non-Hispanic/Latino; 1% Two or more races, non-Hispanic/Latino; 6% Race/ethnicity unknown; 1% international; 9% transferred in; 30% live on campus. *Retention:* 66% of full-time freshmen returned.

Freshmen *Admission:* 3,598 applied, 3,152 admitted, 1,235 enrolled.

Faculty *Total:* 477, 62% full-time. *Student/faculty ratio:* 17:1.

Academics *Calendar:* semesters. *Degrees:* certificates, associate, and bachelor's. *Special study options:* academic remediation for entering students, advanced placement credit, cooperative education, distance learning, English as a second language, independent study, internships, off-campus study, part-time degree program, services for LD students, student-designed majors, study abroad, summer session for credit. *ROTC:* Army (b).

Computers on Campus 1,785 computers/terminals are available on campus for general student use. Students can access the following: campus intranet, computer help desk, free student e-mail accounts, online (class) grades, online

(class) registration, online (class) schedules. Campuswide network is available. 100% of college-owned or -operated housing units are wired for high-speed Internet access. Wireless service is available via entire campus.

Student Life *Housing options:* coed, disabled students. Campus housing is university owned. *Activities and organizations:* student-run radio station, Student Government Association, Residence Hall Association, Wildcats Event Board, Association of Computing Machinery, Campus Ministry International, national fraternities. *Campus security:* 24-hour emergency response devices and patrols, late-night transport/escort service, controlled dormitory access. *Student services:* health clinic, personal/psychological counseling.

Athletics Member USCAA. *Intercollegiate sports:* archery M/W, baseball M, basketball M/W, bowling M/W, cross-country running M/W, golf M/W, soccer M/W, softball W, tennis M/W, volleyball M/W, wrestling M. *Intramural sports:* archery M/W, badminton M/W, basketball M/W, bowling M/W, football M/W, golf M/W, lacrosse M, soccer M/W, softball M/W, table tennis M/W, tennis M/W, ultimate Frisbee M/W, volleyball M/W, weight lifting M/W.

Standardized Tests *Required for some:* SAT (for admission).

Costs (2012–13) *Tuition:* state resident $12,000 full-time, $400 per credit hour part-time; nonresident $15,630 full-time, $521 per credit hour part-time. Full-time tuition and fees vary according to course load and program. Part-time tuition and fees vary according to course load and program. *Required fees:* $2370 full-time, $79 per credit hour part-time. *Room and board:* $10,500; room only: $5994. Room and board charges vary according to board plan and housing facility. *Payment plan:* deferred payment. *Waivers:* employees or children of employees.

Financial Aid Of all full-time matriculated undergraduates who enrolled in 2011, 4,318 applied for aid, 4,298 were judged to have need. 141 Federal Work-Study jobs (averaging $1816). *Average financial aid package:* $15,034. *Average need-based loan:* $3608. *Average need-based gift aid:* $7289.

Applying *Options:* electronic application, early admission, deferred entrance. *Application fee:* $50. *Required for some:* high school transcript, college transcripts if transfer applicant. *Application deadlines:* 7/1 (freshmen), rolling (transfers).

Freshman Application Contact Mr. Dennis L. Correll, Associate Dean for Admissions/Financial Aid, Pennsylvania College of Technology, One College Avenue, DIF #119, Williamsport, PA 17701. *Phone:* 570-327-4761 Ext. 7337. *Toll-free phone:* 800-367-9222. *Fax:* 570-321-5551. *E-mail:* admissions@pct.edu.
Website: http://www.pct.edu/.

Philadelphia University

Philadelphia, Pennsylvania

- **Independent** comprehensive, founded 1884
- **Suburban** 100-acre campus
- **Coed** 2,888 undergraduate students, 93% full-time, 65% women, 35% men
- **Moderately difficult** entrance level, 72% of applicants were admitted

Undergraduates 2,679 full-time, 209 part-time. 12% Black or African American, non-Hispanic/Latino; 6% Hispanic/Latino; 4% Asian, non-Hispanic/Latino; 0.1% Native Hawaiian or other Pacific Islander, non-Hispanic/Latino; 0.1% American Indian or Alaska Native, non-Hispanic/Latino; 2% Two or more races, non-Hispanic/Latino; 10% Race/ethnicity unknown; 3% international; 8% transferred in. *Retention:* 71% of full-time freshmen returned.

Freshmen *Admission:* 3,602 applied, 2,590 admitted, 604 enrolled. *Average high school GPA:* 3.43. *Test scores:* SAT critical reading scores over 500: 67%; SAT math scores over 500: 72%; SAT writing scores over 500: 58%; SAT critical reading scores over 600: 16%; SAT math scores over 600: 20%; SAT writing scores over 600: 15%; SAT critical reading scores over 700: 2%; SAT math scores over 700: 2%; SAT writing scores over 700: 1%.

Faculty *Total:* 488, 23% full-time. *Student/faculty ratio:* 13:1.

Academics *Calendar:* semesters. *Degrees:* certificates, associate, bachelor's, master's, doctoral, post-master's, and postbachelor's certificates. *Special study options:* adult/continuing education programs, part-time degree program.

Computers on Campus Students can access the following: online (class) registration. Campuswide network is available.

Student Life *Housing options:* coed, women-only, disabled students. Campus housing is university owned and leased by the school. Freshman campus housing is guaranteed. *Campus security:* 24-hour emergency response devices and patrols, late-night transport/escort service, controlled dormitory access.

Athletics Member NCAA. All Division II except soccer (Division I). *Intercollegiate sports:* baseball M(s), basketball M(s)/W(s), field hockey W(s), golf M(s), lacrosse W(s), soccer M(s)/W(s), softball W(s), tennis M(s)/W(s), volleyball W(s). *Intramural sports:* basketball M/W, cross-country running M/W, football M, skiing (downhill) M(c)/W(c), soccer M/W, softball M/W, swimming and diving M/W, table tennis M/W, tennis M/W, volleyball M/W, weight lifting M/W.

Standardized Tests *Required:* SAT or ACT (for admission).

Costs (2012–13) *Comprehensive fee:* $42,052 includes full-time tuition ($31,874) and room and board ($10,178). Full-time tuition and fees vary according to degree level and program. Part-time tuition and fees vary according to class time, course load, degree level, program, and reciprocity agreements. *College room only:* $5032. Room and board charges vary according to board plan and housing facility. *Payment plans:* installment, deferred payment. *Waivers:* employees or children of employees.

Financial Aid Of all full-time matriculated undergraduates who enrolled in 2011, 2,345 applied for aid, 2,132 were judged to have need, 203 had their need fully met. In 2011, 515 non-need-based awards were made. *Average percent of need met:* 76%. *Average financial aid package:* $25,490. *Average need-based loan:* $4663. *Average need-based gift aid:* $21,691. *Average non-need-based aid:* $7091. *Average indebtedness upon graduation:* $38,923. *Financial aid deadline:* 4/15.

Applying *Options:* electronic application, deferred entrance. *Application fee:* $40. *Required:* high school transcript. *Recommended:* essay or personal statement, 2 letters of recommendation, interview. *Application deadlines:* rolling (freshmen), rolling (transfers). *Notification:* continuous (freshmen).

Freshman Application Contact Ms. Christine Greb, Director of Admissions, Philadelphia University, School House Lane and Henry Avenue, Philadelphia, PA 19144-5497. *Phone:* 215-951-2800. *Fax:* 215-951-2907. *E-mail:* admissions@philau.edu.

Website: http://www.philau.edu/.

Point Park University

Pittsburgh, Pennsylvania

- **Independent** comprehensive, founded 1960
- **Urban** campus
- **Endowment** $26.7 million
- **Coed** 3,225 undergraduate students, 79% full-time, 58% women, 42% men
- **Moderately difficult** entrance level, 76% of applicants were admitted

Undergraduates 2,537 full-time, 688 part-time. Students come from 26 states and territories; 23 other countries; 21% are from out of state; 17% Black or African American, non-Hispanic/Latino; 3% Hispanic/Latino; 0.8% Asian, non-Hispanic/Latino; 0.1% American Indian or Alaska Native, non-Hispanic/Latino; 3% Two or more races, non-Hispanic/Latino; 2% international; 14% transferred in; 25% live on campus. *Retention:* 74% of full-time freshmen returned.

Freshmen *Admission:* 3,673 applied, 2,799 admitted, 523 enrolled. *Average high school GPA:* 3.21. *Test scores:* SAT critical reading scores over 500: 60%; SAT math scores over 500: 53%; SAT writing scores over 500: 58%; ACT scores over 18: 89%; SAT critical reading scores over 600: 18%; SAT math scores over 600: 14%; SAT writing scores over 600: 15%; ACT scores over 24: 43%; SAT critical reading scores over 700: 1%; SAT writing scores over 700: 1%; ACT scores over 30: 3%.

Faculty *Total:* 442, 30% full-time. *Student/faculty ratio:* 13:1.

Academics *Calendar:* semesters. *Degrees:* certificates, associate, bachelor's, master's, and postbachelor's certificates. *Special study options:* academic remediation for entering students, accelerated degree program, adult/continuing education programs, advanced placement credit, cooperative education, distance learning, double majors, English as a second language, honors programs, independent study, internships, off-campus study, part-time degree program, services for LD students, student-designed majors, study abroad, summer session for credit. *ROTC:* Army (c), Air Force (c).

Computers on Campus 309 computers/terminals and 112 ports are available on campus for general student use. Students can access the following: campus intranet, computer help desk, free student e-mail accounts, online (class) grades, online (class) registration, online (class) schedules. Campuswide network is available. 100% of college-owned or -operated housing units are wired for high-speed Internet access. Wireless service is available via classrooms, computer labs, libraries, student centers.

Student Life *Housing options:* coed, women-only, disabled students. Campus housing is university owned and leased by the school. Freshman campus housing is guaranteed. *Activities and organizations:* drama/theater group, student-run newspaper, radio and television station, student radio station, The Body Christian Fellowship, Dance Club, Campus Activities Board, Action Sports Club. *Campus security:* 24-hour emergency response devices and patrols, late-night transport/escort service, controlled dormitory access, 24-hour security desk, video security. *Student services:* personal/psychological counseling.

Athletics *Intercollegiate sports:* baseball M(s), basketball M(s)/W(s), cross-country running M(s)/W(s), golf M(s)/W(s), soccer M(s)/W(s), softball W(s),

volleyball W(s). *Intramural sports:* basketball M, bowling M/W, football M, golf M, tennis M/W, volleyball M/W, weight lifting M/W.

Standardized Tests *Required:* SAT or ACT (for admission).

Costs (2012–13) *Comprehensive fee:* $33,190 includes full-time tuition ($24,020), mandatory fees ($1170), and room and board ($8000). Full-time tuition and fees vary according to program. Part-time tuition and fees vary according to program. *College room only:* $4720. Room and board charges vary according to board plan and housing facility. *Payment plans:* installment, deferred payment. *Waivers:* employees or children of employees.

Financial Aid Of all full-time matriculated undergraduates who enrolled in 2012, 2,440 applied for aid, 2,249 were judged to have need, 312 had their need fully met. 235 Federal Work-Study jobs (averaging $1795). 214 state and other part-time jobs (averaging $3180). In 2012, 155 non-need-based awards were made. *Average percent of need met:* 67%. *Average financial aid package:* $18,384. *Average need-based loan:* $5122. *Average need-based gift aid:* $13,081. *Average non-need-based aid:* $8376. *Average indebtedness upon graduation:* $26,526. *Financial aid deadline:* 3/15.

Applying *Options:* electronic application, deferred entrance. *Application fee:* $40. *Required:* high school transcript. *Required for some:* 2 letters of recommendation, interview, audition. *Recommended:* essay or personal statement, minimum 2.5 GPA. *Application deadlines:* rolling (freshmen), rolling (transfers). *Notification:* continuous (freshmen), continuous (transfers).

Freshman Application Contact Point Park University, 201 Wood Street, Pittsburgh, PA 15222-1984. *Phone:* 412-392-3430. *Toll-free phone:* 800-321-0129.

Website: http://www.pointpark.edu/.

The Restaurant School at Walnut Hill College

Philadelphia, Pennsylvania

- **Proprietary** primarily 2-year, founded 1974
- **Urban** 2-acre campus
- **Coed**
- 97% of applicants were admitted

Faculty *Student/faculty ratio:* 22:1.

Academics *Calendar:* quarters. *Degrees:* associate and bachelor's.

Student Life *Campus security:* 24-hour emergency response devices and patrols, student patrols, controlled dormitory access.

Standardized Tests *Recommended:* SAT or ACT (for admission).

Costs (2012–13) *One-time required fee:* $200. *Tuition:* $19,050 full-time. *Required fees:* $3675 full-time. *Room only:* $4600. Room and board charges vary according to housing facility. *Payment plans:* installment, deferred payment.

Applying *Options:* electronic application, early admission, early decision, deferred entrance. *Application fee:* $50. *Required:* essay or personal statement, high school transcript, 2 letters of recommendation, interview. *Required for some:* entrance exam. *Recommended:* minimum 2.0 GPA.

Freshman Application Contact Miss Toni Morelli, Director of Admissions, The Restaurant School at Walnut Hill College, 4207 Walnut Street, Philadelphia, PA 19104-3518. *Phone:* 267-295-2353. *Fax:* 215-222-4219. *E-mail:* tmorelli@walnuthillcollege.edu.

Website: http://www.walnuthillcollege.edu/.

Robert Morris University

Moon Township, Pennsylvania

- **Independent** university, founded 1921
- **Suburban** 230-acre campus with easy access to Pittsburgh
- **Endowment** $26.4 million
- **Coed** 4,144 undergraduate students, 88% full-time, 46% women, 54% men
- **Minimally difficult** entrance level, 82% of applicants were admitted

Undergraduates 3,643 full-time, 501 part-time. Students come from 38 states and territories; 39 other countries; 16% are from out of state; 7% Black or African American, non-Hispanic/Latino; 2% Hispanic/Latino; 1% Asian, non-Hispanic/Latino; 0.1% Native Hawaiian or other Pacific Islander, non-Hispanic/Latino; 0.2% American Indian or Alaska Native, non-Hispanic/Latino; 1% Two or more races, non-Hispanic/Latino; 5% Race/ethnicity unknown; 4% international; 10% transferred in; 43% live on campus. *Retention:* 76% of full-time freshmen returned.

Freshmen *Admission:* 5,220 applied, 4,298 admitted, 853 enrolled. *Average high school GPA:* 34. *Test scores:* SAT critical reading scores over 500: 55%;

SAT math scores over 500: 64%; SAT writing scores over 500: 50%; ACT scores over 18: 93%; SAT critical reading scores over 600: 14%; SAT math scores over 600: 23%; SAT writing scores over 600: 10%; ACT scores over 24: 29%; SAT critical reading scores over 700: 1%; SAT math scores over 700: 3%; SAT writing scores over 700: 1%; ACT scores over 30: 2%.

Faculty *Total:* 469, 42% full-time, 52% with terminal degrees. *Student/faculty ratio:* 15:1.

Academics *Calendar:* semesters. *Degrees:* certificates, bachelor's, master's, doctoral, and postbachelor's certificates. *Special study options:* academic remediation for entering students, accelerated degree program, adult/continuing education programs, cooperative education, distance learning, double majors, honors programs, independent study, internships, off-campus study, part-time degree program, services for LD students, study abroad, summer session for credit. *ROTC:* Army (b), Air Force (c).

Computers on Campus 300 computers/terminals are available on campus for general student use. Students can access the following: campus intranet, computer help desk, free student e-mail accounts, online (class) grades, online (class) registration, online (class) schedules, online payment. Campuswide network is available. 100% of college-owned or -operated housing units are wired for high-speed Internet access. Wireless service is available via classrooms, computer centers, computer labs, learning centers, libraries, student centers.

Student Life *Housing:* on-campus residence required for freshman year. *Options:* coed, men-only, women-only, disabled students. Campus housing is university owned. Freshman applicants given priority for college housing. *Activities and organizations:* drama/theater group, student-run newspaper, radio and television station, choral group, marching band, Student Government Association, Residence Hall Association, R-MOVE, National Society of Collegiate Scholars, Black Student Union, national fraternities, national sororities. *Campus security:* 24-hour emergency response devices and patrols, late-night transport/escort service, controlled dormitory access. *Student services:* health clinic, personal/psychological counseling.

Athletics Member NCAA. All Division I. *Intercollegiate sports:* baseball M(c), basketball M(s)/W(s), cheerleading M(c)/W(c), crew W(s), field hockey W(s), football M(s), golf M(s)/W(s), ice hockey M(s)/W(s), lacrosse M(s)/W(s), soccer M(s)/W(s), softball W(s), tennis M(s)/W(s), track and field M(s)/W(s), volleyball W(s). *Intramural sports:* basketball M/W, bowling M(c)/W(c), football M, ice hockey M(c), rugby M(c), softball M/W, volleyball M(c)/W.

Standardized Tests *Required:* SAT or ACT (for admission).

Costs (2012–13) *Comprehensive fee:* $35,424 includes full-time tuition ($23,410), mandatory fees ($654), and room and board ($11,360). Full-time tuition and fees vary according to degree level and program. Part-time tuition: $760 per credit hour. Part-time tuition and fees vary according to course load, degree level, and program. *Required fees:* $30 per credit hour part-time. *College room only:* $5370. Room and board charges vary according to board plan and housing facility. *Payment plans:* installment, deferred payment. *Waivers:* employees or children of employees.

Financial Aid Of all full-time matriculated undergraduates who enrolled in 2012, 3,230 applied for aid, 2,904 were judged to have need, 354 had their need fully met. In 2012, 577 non-need-based awards were made. *Average percent of need met:* 68%. *Average financial aid package:* $17,807. *Average need-based loan:* $5732. *Average need-based gift aid:* $11,768. *Average non-need-based aid:* $9119. *Average indebtedness upon graduation:* $41,093.

Applying *Options:* electronic application, deferred entrance. *Application fee:* $30. *Required:* high school transcript, minimum 2.5 GPA. *Required for some:* interview. *Recommended:* essay or personal statement, minimum 3.0 GPA, interview. *Application deadlines:* 7/1 (freshmen), 7/1 (transfers). *Notification:* continuous until 9/1 (freshmen), continuous (transfers).

Freshman Application Contact Enrollment Services Department, Robert Morris University, 6001 University Boulevard, Moon Township, PA 15108-1189. *Phone:* 412-397-5200. *Toll-free phone:* 800-762-0097. *Fax:* 412-397-2425. *E-mail:* admissionsoffice@rmu.edu.

Website: http://www.rmu.edu/.

See below for display ad and page 1458 for the College Close-Up.

Rosemont College
Rosemont, Pennsylvania

- **Independent Roman Catholic** comprehensive, founded 1921
- **Suburban** 56-acre campus with easy access to Philadelphia
- **Endowment** $13.6 million
- **Coed** 524 undergraduate students, 81% full-time, 68% women, 32% men
- **Moderately difficult** entrance level, 50% of applicants were admitted

Undergraduates 426 full-time, 98 part-time. Students come from 11 states and territories; 14 other countries; 20% are from out of state; 35% Black or African American, non-Hispanic/Latino; 7% Hispanic/Latino; 4% Asian, non-Hispanic/Latino; 2% Two or more races, non-Hispanic/Latino; 10% Race/ethnicity unknown; 2% international; 5% transferred in; 70% live on campus. *Retention:* 80% of full-time freshmen returned.

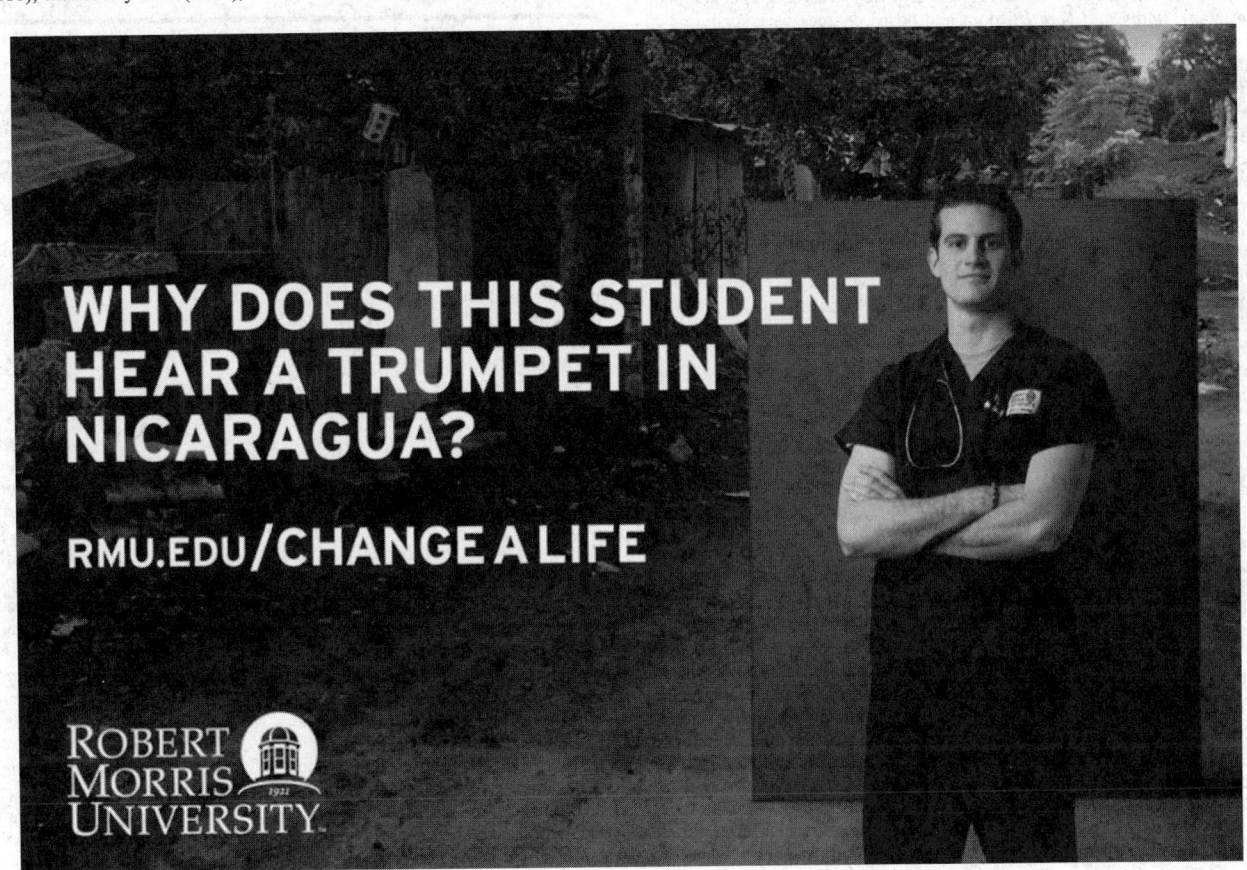

Freshmen *Admission:* 941 applied, 470 admitted, 75 enrolled. *Average high school GPA:* 3.4. *Test scores:* SAT critical reading scores over 500: 39%; SAT math scores over 500: 35%; SAT critical reading scores over 600: 14%; SAT math scores over 600: 13%; SAT critical reading scores over 700: 1%.

Faculty *Total:* 139, 20% full-time, 80% with terminal degrees. *Student/faculty ratio:* 10:1.

Academics *Calendar:* semesters. *Degrees:* bachelor's, master's, and postbachelor's certificates. *Special study options:* academic remediation for entering students, accelerated degree program, adult/continuing education programs, advanced placement credit, double majors, English as a second language, honors programs, independent study, internships, off-campus study, part-time degree program, services for LD students, student-designed majors, study abroad, summer session for credit. *ROTC:* Army (c). *Unusual degree programs:* 3-2 nursing with Villanova University, Drexel University; counseling psychology, dentistry, art therapy, physical therapy, creative arts in therapy, nursing with Drexel University.

Computers on Campus 100 computers/terminals and 250 ports are available on campus for general student use. Students can access the following: campus intranet, computer help desk, free student e-mail accounts, online (class) grades, online (class) registration, online (class) schedules. Campuswide network is available. 100% of college-owned or -operated housing units are wired for high-speed Internet access. Wireless service is available via classrooms, computer centers, computer labs, dorm rooms, learning centers, libraries, student centers.

Student Life *Housing:* on-campus residence required through junior year. *Options:* coed, women-only. Campus housing is university owned. Freshman campus housing is guaranteed. *Activities and organizations:* drama/theater group, student-run newspaper, choral group, student government, Triad, Jest and Gesture, Best Buddies, Political Science Club. *Campus security:* 24-hour emergency response devices and patrols, late-night transport/escort service, controlled dormitory access. *Student services:* health clinic, personal/psychological counseling, women's center, legal services.

Athletics Member NCAA. All Division III. *Intercollegiate sports:* basketball M/W, cross-country running M/W, golf M, lacrosse M/W, soccer M/W, softball W, tennis M/W, volleyball W.

Standardized Tests *Required:* SAT or ACT (for admission).

Costs (2013–14) *Comprehensive fee:* $43,330 includes full-time tuition ($30,000), mandatory fees ($950), and room and board ($12,380). Full-time tuition and fees vary according to course load and program. Part-time tuition: $1140 per credit hour. Part-time tuition and fees vary according to course load and program. *Room and board:* Room and board charges vary according to board plan and housing facility. *Payment plan:* installment. *Waivers:* senior citizens and employees or children of employees.

Financial Aid Of all full-time matriculated undergraduates who enrolled in 2011, 404 applied for aid, 383 were judged to have need, 29 had their need fully met. 65 Federal Work-Study jobs (averaging $1550). In 2011, 13 non-need-based awards were made. *Average percent of need met:* 69%. *Average financial aid package:* $26,263. *Average need-based loan:* $3698. *Average need-based gift aid:* $23,199. *Average non-need-based aid:* $11,865. *Average indebtedness upon graduation:* $21,490.

Applying *Options:* electronic application, early admission, deferred entrance. *Required:* essay or personal statement, high school transcript, 2 letters of recommendation. *Recommended:* minimum 3.0 GPA, interview. *Application deadlines:* rolling (freshmen), rolling (transfers). *Notification:* 8/1 (freshmen), continuous until 8/1 (transfers).

Freshman Application Contact Mr. Kevin McIntyre, Vice President for Enrollment Management, Rosemont College, 1400 Montgomery Avenue, Main Building, Rosemont, PA 19010. *Phone:* 610-527-0200 Ext. 2905. *Toll-free phone:* 888-2-ROSEMONT. *Fax:* 610-520-4399. *E-mail:* admissions@rosemont.edu.

Website: http://www.rosemont.edu/.

Saint Charles Borromeo Seminary, Overbrook

Wynnewood, Pennsylvania

- **Independent Roman Catholic** comprehensive, founded 1832
- **Suburban** 77-acre campus with easy access to Philadelphia
- **Coed, primarily men** 98 undergraduate students, 76% full-time, 17% women, 83% men
- **Moderately difficult** entrance level, 100% of applicants were admitted

Undergraduates 74 full-time, 24 part-time. Students come from 6 states and territories; 13% are from out of state; 9% Hispanic/Latino; 2% Asian, non-Hispanic/Latino; 5% transferred in; 100% live on campus. *Retention:* 78% of full-time freshmen returned.

Freshmen *Admission:* 8 applied, 8 admitted, 7 enrolled. *Test scores:* SAT critical reading scores over 500: 100%; SAT math scores over 500: 75%; SAT writing scores over 500: 50%; SAT critical reading scores over 600: 50%; SAT math scores over 600: 25%.

Faculty *Total:* 33, 48% full-time, 48% with terminal degrees. *Student/faculty ratio:* 6:1.

Academics *Calendar:* semesters. *Degrees:* certificates, bachelor's, master's, and postbachelor's certificates (also offers coed part-time programs). *Special study options:* academic remediation for entering students, accelerated degree program, adult/continuing education programs, advanced placement credit, English as a second language, independent study, summer session for credit.

Computers on Campus 60 computers/terminals are available on campus for general student use. Students can access the following: campus intranet, free student e-mail accounts. Campuswide network is available. Wireless service is available via classrooms, computer centers, computer labs, libraries.

Student Life *Housing:* on-campus residence required through senior year. *Options:* men-only. Campus housing is university owned. Freshman campus housing is guaranteed. *Activities and organizations:* drama/theater group, student-run newspaper, choral group, Seminarians for Life, Student Council. *Campus security:* 24-hour emergency response devices and patrols. *Student services:* health clinic, personal/psychological counseling.

Athletics *Intramural sports:* basketball M, football M, soccer M, volleyball M.

Standardized Tests *Recommended:* SAT or ACT (for admission).

Costs (2012–13) *Comprehensive fee:* $31,210 includes full-time tuition ($17,950), mandatory fees ($1200), and room and board ($12,060). Part-time tuition: $880 per course. *Payment plan:* installment. *Waivers:* employees or children of employees.

Financial Aid *Average indebtedness upon graduation:* $19,000.

Applying *Options:* deferred entrance. *Required:* essay or personal statement, high school transcript, minimum 2.0 GPA, 3 letters of recommendation, interview, sponsorship by diocese or religious community. *Application deadlines:* 7/15 (freshmen), 7/15 (transfers). *Notification:* continuous (freshmen), continuous (transfers).

Freshman Application Contact Rev. Joseph W. Bongard, Vice Rector, Saint Charles Borromeo Seminary, Overbrook, 100 East Wynnewood Road, Wynnewood, PA 19096. *Phone:* 610-785-6271. *Fax:* 610-617-9267. *Website:* http://www.scs.edu/.

Saint Francis University

Loretto, Pennsylvania

- **Independent Roman Catholic** comprehensive, founded 1847
- **Rural** 600-acre campus
- **Endowment** $34.2 million
- **Coed**
- **Moderately difficult** entrance level

Faculty *Student/faculty ratio:* 15:1.

Academics *Calendar:* semesters. *Degrees:* certificates, associate, bachelor's, master's, and doctoral.

Student Life *Campus security:* 24-hour emergency response devices and patrols, late-night transport/escort service, controlled dormitory access.

Athletics Member NCAA. All Division I.

Standardized Tests *Required:* SAT or ACT (for admission).

Costs (2012–13) *One-time required fee:* $60. *Comprehensive fee:* $38,778 includes full-time tuition ($27,828), mandatory fees ($1050), and room and board ($9900). Full-time tuition and fees vary according to course load, degree level, program, and student level. Part-time tuition: $874 per credit hour. Part-time tuition and fees vary according to class time, degree level, and program. *Required fees:* $412 per credit hour part-time. *College room only:* $4970. Room and board charges vary according to board plan and housing facility.

Financial Aid *Of all full-time matriculated undergraduates who enrolled in 2012,* 1,502 applied for aid, 1,190 were judged to have need, 160 had their need fully met. 271 Federal Work-Study jobs (averaging $1000). 746 state and other part-time jobs (averaging $1000). *In 2012,* 130 non-need-based awards were made. *Average percent of need met:* 62. *Average financial aid package:* $18,343. *Average need-based loan:* $4506. *Average need-based gift aid:* $15,307. *Average non-need-based aid:* $11,494. *Average indebtedness upon graduation:* $9677.

Applying *Options:* electronic application, deferred entrance. *Application fee:* $30. *Required:* essay or personal statement, high school transcript, 1 letter of recommendation. *Required for some:* interview. *Recommended:* interview.

Freshman Application Contact Robert Beener, Dean for Enrollment Management, Saint Francis University, PO Box 600, 117 Evergreen Drive,

Loretto, PA 15940-0600. *Phone:* 814-472-3100. *Toll-free phone:* 866-DIAL-SFU. *E-mail:* rbeener@francis.edu. *Website:* http://www.francis.edu/.

See below for display ad and page 1466 for the College Close-Up.

Saint Joseph's University

Philadelphia, Pennsylvania

- **Independent Roman Catholic (Jesuit)** comprehensive, founded 1851
- **Suburban** 105-acre campus
- **Endowment** $168.8 million
- **Coed** 5,342 undergraduate students, 83% full-time, 53% women, 47% men
- **Moderately difficult** entrance level, 78% of applicants were admitted

Undergraduates 4,433 full-time, 909 part-time. Students come from 37 states and territories; 29 other countries; 53% are from out of state; 7% Black or African American, non-Hispanic/Latino; 5% Hispanic/Latino; 2% Asian, non-Hispanic/Latino; 0.1% Native Hawaiian or other Pacific Islander, non-Hispanic/Latino; 0.1% American Indian or Alaska Native, non-Hispanic/Latino; 1% Two or more races, non-Hispanic/Latino; 3% Race/ethnicity unknown; 1% international; 1% transferred in; 59% live on campus. *Retention:* 89% of full-time freshmen returned.

Freshmen *Admission:* 7,386 applied, 5,783 admitted, 1,231 enrolled. *Average high school GPA:* 3.46. *Test scores:* SAT critical reading scores over 500: 80%; SAT math scores over 500: 84%; ACT scores over 18: 100%; SAT critical reading scores over 600: 26%; SAT math scores over 600: 37%; ACT scores over 24: 58%; SAT critical reading scores over 700: 3%; SAT math scores over 700: 4%; ACT scores over 30: 9%.

Faculty *Total:* 786, 39% full-time. *Student/faculty ratio:* 13:1.

Academics *Calendar:* semesters. *Degrees:* certificates, associate, bachelor's, master's, doctoral, post-master's, and postbachelor's certificates. *Special study options:* accelerated degree program, adult/continuing education programs, advanced placement credit, cooperative education, distance learning, double majors, English as a second language, honors programs, independent study, internships, off-campus study, part-time degree program, services for LD students, student-designed majors, study abroad, summer session for credit. *ROTC:* Army (c), Navy (c), Air Force (b).

Computers on Campus 825 computers/terminals are available on campus for general student use. Students can access the following: campus intranet, computer help desk, free student e-mail accounts, online (class) grades, online (class) registration, online (class) schedules. Campuswide network is available. 100% of college-owned or -operated housing units are wired for high-speed Internet access. Wireless service is available via entire campus.

Student Life *Housing:* on-campus residence required through sophomore year. *Options:* coed, men-only, women-only, disabled students. Campus housing is university owned, leased by the school and is provided by a third party. Freshman campus housing is guaranteed. *Activities and organizations:* drama/theater group, student-run newspaper, radio station, choral group, Student Union Board, Hand-in-Hand, 54th Airborne / Booster Club, Appalachian Experience, Weekly Service, national fraternities, national sororities. *Campus security:* 24-hour emergency response devices and patrols, late-night transport/escort service, controlled dormitory access, 24-hour shuttle/escort service, bicycle patrols. *Student services:* health clinic, personal/psychological counseling.

Athletics Member NCAA. All Division I. *Intercollegiate sports:* baseball M(s), basketball M(s)/W(s), cheerleading M(c)/W(c), crew M(s)/W(s), cross-country running M(s)/W(s), field hockey W(s), golf M(s), lacrosse M(s)/W(s), soccer M(s)/W(s), softball W(s), tennis M(s)/W(s), track and field M(s)/W(s). *Intramural sports:* baseball M(c), basketball M(c)/W(c), field hockey W(c), football M/W, golf M(c)/W(c), ice hockey M(c), lacrosse M(c)/W(c), racquetball M/W, rugby M(c)/W(c), soccer M(c)/W(c), softball M/W, swimming and diving M(c)/W(c), tennis M(c)/W(c), ultimate Frisbee M(c)/W(c), volleyball M(c)/W(c), water polo M(c)/W(c).

Standardized Tests *Required:* SAT or ACT (for admission).

Costs (2012–13) *Comprehensive fee:* $50,630 includes full-time tuition ($37,670), mandatory fees ($160), and room and board ($12,800). Full-time tuition and fees vary according to course load. Part-time tuition: $500 per credit. *College room only:* $8105. Room and board charges vary according to board plan and housing facility. *Payment plans:* tuition prepayment, installment. *Waivers:* employees or children of employees.

Financial Aid Of all full-time matriculated undergraduates who enrolled in 2012, 3,245 applied for aid, 2,640 were judged to have need, 598 had their need fully met. In 2012, 1714 non-need-based awards were made. *Average percent of need met:* 76%. *Average financial aid package:* $22,124. *Average need-based loan:* $5500. *Average need-based gift aid:* $17,323. *Average non-need-based aid:* $11,330.

Applying *Options:* electronic application, early action, deferred entrance. *Application fee:* $60. *Required:* essay or personal statement, high school transcript. *Application deadlines:* 2/1 (freshmen), 3/1 (transfers), 11/15 (early action). *Notification:* 3/15 (freshmen), continuous (transfers), 12/25 (early action).

Freshman Application Contact Office of Admissions, Saint Joseph's University, 5600 City Avenue, Philadelphia, PA 19131-1395. *Phone:* 610-660-1300. *Toll-free phone:* 888-BE-A-HAWK (in-state); 800-BE-A-HAWK (out-of-state). *Fax:* 610-660-1314. *E-mail:* admit@sju.edu. *Website:* http://www.sju.edu/.

See below for display ad and page 1474 for the College Close-Up.

Saint Vincent College

Latrobe, Pennsylvania

- **Independent Roman Catholic** comprehensive, founded 1846
- **Suburban** 200-acre campus with easy access to Pittsburgh
- **Coed** 1,566 undergraduate students, 95% full-time, 48% women, 52% men
- **Moderately difficult** entrance level, 66% of applicants were admitted

Undergraduates 1,481 full-time, 85 part-time. 16% are from out of state; 5% Black or African American, non-Hispanic/Latino; 3% Hispanic/Latino; 0.9% Asian, non-Hispanic/Latino; 0.1% Native Hawaiian or other Pacific Islander, non-Hispanic/Latino; 0.2% American Indian or Alaska Native, non-Hispanic/Latino; 1% Two or more races, non-Hispanic/Latino; 1% Race/ethnicity unknown; 0.7% international; 2% transferred in; 67% live on campus. *Retention:* 81% of full-time freshmen returned.

Freshmen *Admission:* 1,696 applied, 1,116 admitted, 339 enrolled. *Average high school GPA:* 3.56. *Test scores:* SAT critical reading scores over 500: 61%; SAT math scores over 500: 69%; SAT writing scores over 500: 56%; SAT critical reading scores over 600: 15%; SAT math scores over 600: 28%; SAT writing scores over 600: 16%; SAT critical reading scores over 700: 4%; SAT math scores over 700: 2%; SAT writing scores over 700: 3%.

Academics *Calendar:* semesters. *Degrees:* certificates, bachelor's, master's, and postbachelor's certificates. *Special study options:* external degree program, part-time degree program. *ROTC:* Army (c), Air Force (c).

Computers on Campus Students can access the following: campus intranet, computer help desk, free student e-mail accounts, online (class) grades, online (class) registration, online (class) schedules. Campuswide network is available. 100% of college-owned or -operated housing units are wired for high-speed Internet access. Wireless service is available via entire campus.

Student Life *Housing:* on-campus residence required for freshman year. *Options:* coed. Campus housing is university owned. Freshman applicants given priority for college housing. *Campus security:* 24-hour emergency response devices and patrols, late-night transport/escort service, controlled dormitory access, limited access to residence halls on weekends.

Athletics Member NCAA. All Division III. *Intercollegiate sports:* baseball M, basketball M/W, cheerleading M(c)/W(c), cross-country running M/W, equestrian sports M(c)/W(c), fencing M(c)/W(c), field hockey W, golf M/W, ice hockey M(c), lacrosse M/W, soccer M/W, softball W, swimming and diving M/W, tennis M/W, track and field M, volleyball W. *Intramural sports:* football M/W, ultimate Frisbee M/W, volleyball M/W.

Standardized Tests *Required:* SAT or ACT (for admission).

Costs (2012–13) *Comprehensive fee:* $38,738 includes full-time tuition ($28,542), mandatory fees ($602), and room and board ($9594). *College room only:* $5098. Room and board charges vary according to board plan and housing facility.

Financial Aid Of all full-time matriculated undergraduates who enrolled in 2009, 1,492 applied for aid, 1,282 were judged to have need, 315 had their need fully met. In 2009, 386 non-need-based awards were made. *Average percent of need met:* 81%. *Average financial aid package:* $21,705. *Average need-based loan:* $4662. *Average need-based gift aid:* $16,506. *Average non-need-based aid:* $12,349. *Financial aid deadline:* 5/1.

Applying *Options:* electronic application, early admission, deferred entrance. *Application fee:* $25. *Required:* essay or personal statement, high school transcript, minimum 2.5 GPA. *Required for some:* interview. *Recommended:* minimum 3.2 GPA, 3 letters of recommendation, interview. *Application deadlines:* 4/1 (freshmen), 7/1 (transfers). *Notification:* continuous until 10/1 (freshmen), continuous (transfers).

Freshman Application Contact Mr. David Collins, Assistant Vice President of Admission and Financial Aid, Saint Vincent College, 300 Fraser Purchase Road, Latrobe, PA 15650-2690. *Phone:* 800-782-5549. *Toll-free phone:* 800-782-5549. *Fax:* 724-532-5069. *E-mail:* admission@stvincent.edu. *Website:* http://www.stvincent.edu/.

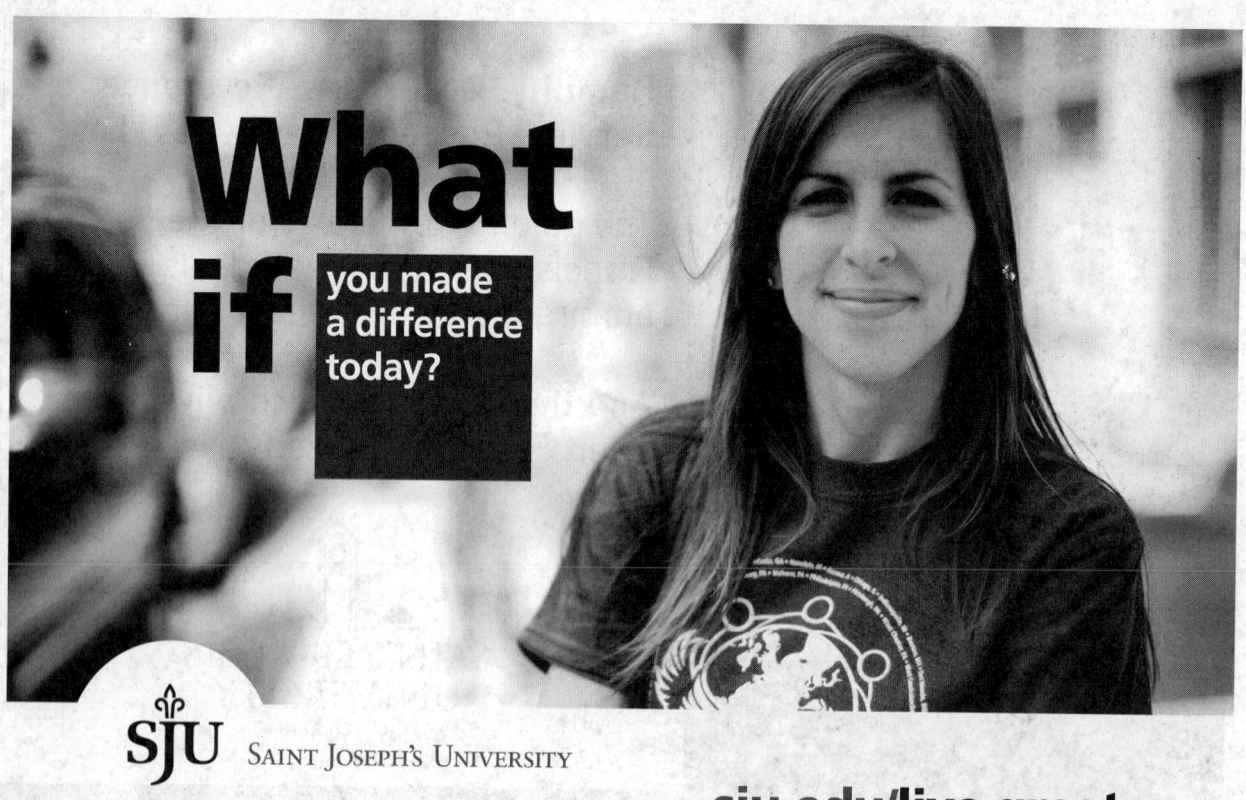

What if you made a difference today?

SJU SAINT JOSEPH'S UNIVERSITY

sju.edu/live greater

Seton Hill University

Greensburg, Pennsylvania

- **Independent Roman Catholic** comprehensive, founded 1883
- **Small-town** 200-acre campus with easy access to Pittsburgh
- **Endowment** $30.0 million
- **Coed** 1,680 undergraduate students, 88% full-time, 64% women, 36% men
- **Moderately difficult** entrance level, 66% of applicants were admitted

Undergraduates 1,482 full-time, 198 part-time. Students come from 32 states and territories; 13 other countries; 23% are from out of state; 10% Black or African American, non-Hispanic/Latino; 3% Hispanic/Latino; 0.3% Asian, non-Hispanic/Latino; 0.2% American Indian or Alaska Native, non-Hispanic/Latino; 4% Race/ethnicity unknown; 2% international; 5% transferred in; 46% live on campus. *Retention:* 78% of full-time freshmen returned.

Freshmen *Admission:* 2,150 applied, 1,424 admitted, 350 enrolled. *Average high school GPA:* 3.52. *Test scores:* SAT critical reading scores over 500: 54%; SAT math scores over 500: 63%; SAT writing scores over 500: 51%; ACT scores over 18: 92%; SAT critical reading scores over 600: 16%; SAT math scores over 600: 18%; SAT writing scores over 600: 11%; ACT scores over 24: 49%; SAT critical reading scores over 700: 1%; SAT math scores over 700: 3%; SAT writing scores over 700: 1%; ACT scores over 30: 3%.

Faculty *Total:* 196, 50% full-time, 58% with terminal degrees. *Student/faculty ratio:* 14:1.

Academics *Calendar:* semesters. *Degrees:* certificates, bachelor's, master's, post-master's, and postbachelor's certificates. *Special study options:* academic remediation for entering students, adult/continuing education programs, advanced placement credit, distance learning, double majors, English as a second language, honors programs, independent study, internships, off-campus study, part-time degree program, services for LD students, student-designed majors, study abroad, summer session for credit. *ROTC:* Army (b). *Unusual degree programs:* 3-2 engineering with University of Pittsburgh, Pennsylvania State University- University Park Campus, Georgia Institute of Technology; physician assistant with Seton Hill University, BS/DO and BS/DPharm with Lake Erie College of Osteopathic Medicine.

Computers on Campus 50 computers/terminals and 50 ports are available on campus for general student use. Students can access the following: campus intranet, computer help desk, free student e-mail accounts, online (class) grades, online (class) registration, online (class) schedules. Campuswide network is available. 100% of college-owned or -operated housing units are wired for high-speed Internet access. Wireless service is available via entire campus.

Student Life *Housing:* on-campus residence required for freshman year. *Options:* coed, men-only, women-only, disabled students. Campus housing is university owned and leased by the school. Freshman campus housing is guaranteed. *Activities and organizations:* drama/theater group, student-run newspaper, choral group, marching band, Student Body Activities Council, Future Greek leaders, Peer Ministry Council, Biology Club, Intramurals. *Campus security:* 24-hour emergency response devices and patrols, late-night transport/escort service, controlled dormitory access, emergency phones throughout camps, campus alert system, safety committee. *Student services:* health clinic, personal/psychological counseling.

Athletics Member NCAA. All Division II. *Intercollegiate sports:* baseball M(s), basketball M(s)/W(s), cross-country running M(s)/W(s), equestrian sports W(s), field hockey W(s), football M(s), golf W(s), lacrosse M(s)/W(s), soccer M(s)/W(s), softball W(s), tennis M(s)/W(s), track and field M(s)/W(s), volleyball W(s), wrestling M(s).

Standardized Tests *Recommended:* SAT or ACT (for admission).

Costs (2012–13) *Comprehensive fee:* $39,394 includes full-time tuition ($28,350), mandatory fees ($1100), and room and board ($9944). Full-time tuition and fees vary according to course load and program. Part-time tuition: $760 per credit hour. Part-time tuition and fees vary according to course load and program. *Required fees:* $25 per credit hour part-time, $50 per term part-time. *Room and board:* Room and board charges vary according to board plan and housing facility. *Payment plan:* installment. *Waivers:* employees or children of employees.

Financial Aid Of all full-time matriculated undergraduates who enrolled in 2012, 1,258 applied for aid, 1,183 were judged to have need, 196 had their need fully met. In 2012, 135 non-need-based awards were made. *Average percent of need met:* 74%. *Average financial aid package:* $23,392. *Average need-based loan:* $5605. *Average need-based gift aid:* $18,123. *Average non-need-based aid:* $10,668. *Average indebtedness upon graduation:* $32,290.

Applying *Options:* electronic application, deferred entrance. *Application fee:* $35. *Required:* essay or personal statement, high school transcript, 1 letter of recommendation, portfolio for art, audition for music and theatre. *Recommended:* interview. *Application deadlines:* rolling (freshmen), rolling (out-of-state freshmen), rolling (transfers). *Notification:* continuous (freshmen), continuous (out-of-state freshmen), continuous (transfers).

Freshman Application Contact Mrs. Allison Sasso, Assistant Director of Admissions, Seton Hill University, Seton Hill Drive, Greensburg, PA 15601. *Phone:* 724-838-4255. *Toll-free phone:* 800-826-6234. *Fax:* 724-830-1294. *E-mail:* admit@setonhill.edu. *Website:* http://www.setonhill.edu/.

Shippensburg University of Pennsylvania

Shippensburg, Pennsylvania

- **State-supported** comprehensive, founded 1871, part of Pennsylvania State System of Higher Education
- **Rural** 200-acre campus
- **Endowment** $27.4 million
- **Coed** 6,712 undergraduate students, 95% full-time, 50% women, 50% men
- **Moderately difficult** entrance level, 81% of applicants were admitted

Undergraduates 6,363 full-time, 349 part-time. Students come from 21 states and territories; 15 other countries; 6% are from out of state; 8% Black or African American, non-Hispanic/Latino; 3% Hispanic/Latino; 0.9% Asian, non-Hispanic/Latino; 0.1% Native Hawaiian or other Pacific Islander, non-Hispanic/Latino; 0.2% American Indian or Alaska Native, non-Hispanic/Latino; 3% Two or more races, non-Hispanic/Latino; 3% Race/ethnicity unknown; 0.3% international; 5% transferred in; 33% live on campus. *Retention:* 70% of full-time freshmen returned.

Freshmen *Admission:* 6,402 applied, 5,158 admitted, 1,485 enrolled. *Average high school GPA:* 3.16. *Test scores:* SAT critical reading scores over 500: 44%; SAT math scores over 500: 48%; SAT writing scores over 500: 35%; ACT scores over 18: 75%; SAT critical reading scores over 600: 9%; SAT math scores over 600: 11%; SAT writing scores over 600: 6%; ACT scores over 24: 16%; SAT critical reading scores over 700: 1%; SAT math scores over 700: 1%; ACT scores over 30: 1%.

Faculty *Total:* 397, 83% full-time, 78% with terminal degrees. *Student/faculty ratio:* 20:1.

Academics *Calendar:* semesters. *Degrees:* certificates, bachelor's, master's, post-master's, and postbachelor's certificates. *Special study options:* academic remediation for entering students, accelerated degree program, advanced placement credit, cooperative education, distance learning, double majors, honors programs, independent study, internships, off-campus study, part-time degree program, services for LD students, study abroad, summer session for credit. *ROTC:* Army (b). *Unusual degree programs:* 3-2 engineering with Pennsylvania State University–University Park and Harrisburg Campus, University of Maryland College Park.

Computers on Campus 1,100 computers/terminals are available on campus for general student use. Students can access the following: campus intranet, computer help desk, free student e-mail accounts, online (class) grades, online (class) registration, online (class) schedules, personal Web pages. Campuswide network is available. 100% of college-owned or -operated housing units are wired for high-speed Internet access. Wireless service is available via classrooms, computer centers, computer labs, learning centers, libraries, student centers.

Student Life *Housing:* on-campus residence required for freshman year. *Options:* coed. Campus housing is university owned and leased by the school. Freshman campus housing is guaranteed. *Activities and organizations:* drama/theater group, student-run newspaper, radio and television station, choral group, marching band, national fraternities, national sororities. *Campus security:* 24-hour emergency response devices and patrols, late-night transport/escort service, controlled dormitory access, surveillance cameras in certain parking lots and buildings, foot, vehicular and bicycle patrols by security officers. *Student services:* health clinic, personal/psychological counseling, women's center.

Athletics Member NCAA. All Division II. *Intercollegiate sports:* baseball M(s), basketball M(s)/W(s), cross-country running M(s)/W(s), field hockey W(s), football M(s), lacrosse W(s), soccer M(s)/W(s), softball W(s), swimming and diving M(s)/W(s), tennis W(s), track and field M(s)/W(s), volleyball W(s), wrestling M(s). *Intramural sports:* basketball M/W, ice hockey M(c), lacrosse M(c), rugby M(c)/W(c), soccer M/W, softball M/W, tennis M(c)/W(c), ultimate Frisbee M/W, volleyball M/W.

Standardized Tests *Required:* SAT or ACT (for admission).

Costs (2012–13) *Tuition:* state resident $6428 full-time, $268 per credit hour part-time; nonresident $14,464 full-time, $603 per credit hour part-time. *Required fees:* $2726 full-time, $113 per credit hour part-time. *Room and board:* $7910; room only: $4180. Room and board charges vary according to board plan and housing facility. *Payment plan:* installment. *Waivers:* senior citizens and employees or children of employees.

Financial Aid Of all full-time matriculated undergraduates who enrolled in 2012, 5,349 applied for aid, 4,256 were judged to have need, 553 had their need fully met. 122 Federal Work-Study jobs (averaging $1684). 603 state and other part-time jobs (averaging $2045). In 2012, 418 non-need-based awards were made. *Average percent of need met:* 60%. *Average financial aid package:* $8168. *Average need-based loan:* $3957. *Average need-based gift aid:* $5872. *Average non-need-based aid:* $4837. *Average indebtedness upon graduation:* $27,661.

Applying *Options:* electronic application, early admission, early action, deferred entrance. *Application fee:* $30. *Required:* high school transcript. *Required for some:* interview. *Recommended:* essay or personal statement, class rank, letters of recommendation optional. *Application deadlines:* rolling (freshmen), rolling (transfers). *Notification:* continuous (freshmen), continuous (transfers).

Freshman Application Contact Mr. William Washabaugh, Acting Dean of Enrollment Management, Shippensburg University of Pennsylvania, 1871 Old Main Drive, Shippensburg, PA 17257-2299. *Phone:* 717-477-1231. *Toll-free phone:* 800-822-8028. *Fax:* 717-477-4016. *E-mail:* admiss@ship.edu. *Website:* http://www.ship.edu/.

See below for display ad and page 1496 for the College Close-Up.

Slippery Rock University of Pennsylvania

Slippery Rock, Pennsylvania

- **State-supported** comprehensive, founded 1889, part of Pennsylvania State System of Higher Education
- **Small-town** 650-acre campus with easy access to Pittsburgh
- **Endowment** $18.5 million
- **Coed** 7,860 undergraduate students, 93% full-time, 57% women, 43% men
- **Moderately difficult** entrance level, 63% of applicants were admitted

Undergraduates 7,308 full-time, 552 part-time. Students come from 36 states and territories; 37 other countries; 11% are from out of state; 5% Black or African American, non-Hispanic/Latino; 2% Hispanic/Latino; 0.5% Asian, non-Hispanic/Latino; 0.1% American Indian or Alaska Native, non-Hispanic/Latino; 2% Two or more races, non-Hispanic/Latino; 4% Race/ethnicity unknown; 0.7% international; 8% transferred in; 36% live on campus. *Retention:* 81% of full-time freshmen returned.

Freshmen *Admission:* 6,276 applied, 3,966 admitted, 1,546 enrolled. *Average high school GPA:* 3.41. *Test scores:* SAT critical reading scores over 500: 48%; SAT math scores over 500: 59%; SAT writing scores over 500: 42%; ACT scores over 18: 90%; SAT critical reading scores over 600: 8%; SAT math scores over 600: 11%; SAT writing scores over 600: 7%; ACT scores over 24: 24%; SAT critical reading scores over 700: 1%; ACT scores over 30: 2%.

Faculty *Total:* 407, 87% full-time, 82% with terminal degrees. *Student/faculty ratio:* 20:1.

Academics *Calendar:* semesters. *Degrees:* certificates, bachelor's, master's, doctoral, and postbachelor's certificates. *Special study options:* academic remediation for entering students, adult/continuing education programs, advanced placement credit, distance learning, double majors, honors programs, independent study, internships, off-campus study, part-time degree program, services for LD students, student-designed majors, study abroad, summer session for credit. *ROTC:* Army (b). *Unusual degree programs:* 3-2 engineering with Pennsylvania State University–University Park Campus; Youngstown State University, West Virginia University.

Computers on Campus 1,305 computers/terminals and 75 ports are available on campus for general student use. Students can access the following: computer help desk, free student e-mail accounts, online (class) grades, online (class) registration, online (class) schedules. Campuswide network is available. 100% of college-owned or -operated housing units are wired for high-speed Internet access. Wireless service is available via classrooms, computer labs, dorm rooms, libraries, student centers.

Student Life *Housing:* on-campus residence required for freshman year. *Options:* coed, disabled students. Campus housing is university owned. Freshman campus housing is guaranteed. *Activities and organizations:* drama/theater group, student-run newspaper, radio and television station, choral group, marching band, Exercise Science Society, Down Hill Ski and Snowboard Club, Pre Physical Therapy Club, Interfraternity Council, Panhellenic Council, national fraternities, national sororities. *Campus security:* 24-hour emergency response devices and patrols, late-night transport/escort service, controlled dormitory access. *Student services:* health clinic, personal/psychological counseling, women's center, legal services.

Athletics Member NCAA. All Division II. *Intercollegiate sports:* baseball M(s), basketball M(s)/W(s), cheerleading M(c)/W(c), cross-country running M(s)/W(s), equestrian sports M(c)/W(c), field hockey W(s), football M(s), golf M(c)/W(c), ice hockey M(c)/W(c), lacrosse M(c)/W(s), racquetball M(c)/W(c), rugby M(c)/W(c), soccer M(s)/W(s), softball W(s), swimming and div-

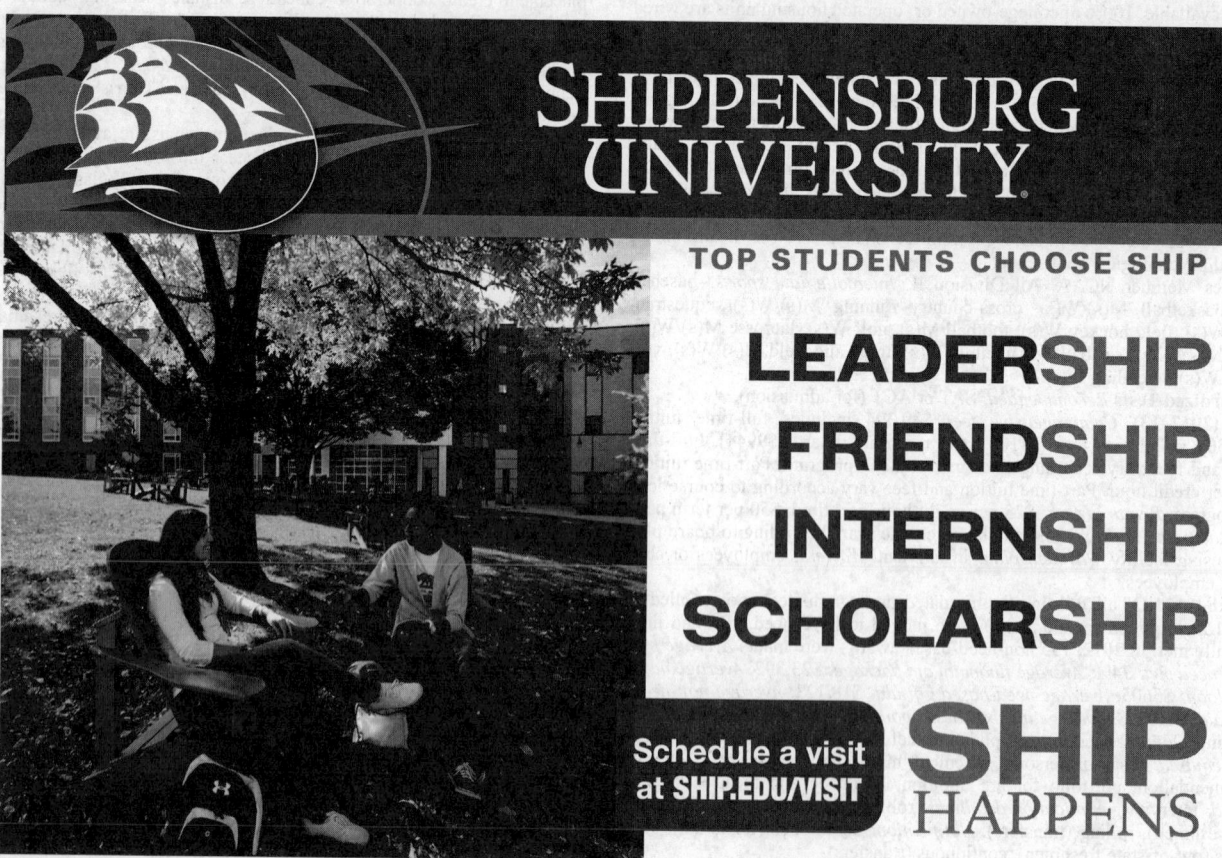

ing M(c)/W(c), tennis M(c)/W(s), track and field M(s)/W(s), volleyball M(c)/W(s), water polo M(c)/W(c), wrestling M(c)/W(c). *Intramural sports:* badminton M/W, basketball M/W, football M/W, gymnastics M(c)/W(c), skiing (downhill) M(c)/W(c), soccer M/W, softball M/W, table tennis M/W, ultimate Frisbee M(c)/W(c).

Standardized Tests *Required:* SAT or ACT (for admission).

Costs (2012–13) *Tuition:* state resident $6428 full-time, $268 per credit hour part-time; nonresident $9642 full-time, $536 per credit hour part-time. Full-time tuition and fees vary according to course load and degree level. Part-time tuition and fees vary according to course load and degree level. *Required fees:* $2319 full-time, $97 per credit hour part-time. *Room and board:* $9364; room only: $6206. Room and board charges vary according to board plan and housing facility. *Payment plan:* installment. *Waivers:* minority students, senior citizens, and employees or children of employees.

Financial Aid Of all full-time matriculated undergraduates who enrolled in 2012, 6,345 applied for aid, 5,164 were judged to have need, 669 had their need fully met. 645 Federal Work-Study jobs (averaging $1588). 843 state and other part-time jobs (averaging $1869). In 2012, 353 non-need-based awards were made. *Average percent of need met:* 62%. *Average financial aid package:* $8598. *Average need-based loan:* $4327. *Average need-based gift aid:* $5443. *Average non-need-based aid:* $2674. *Average indebtedness upon graduation:* $28,959.

Applying *Options:* electronic application, deferred entrance. *Application fee:* $30. *Required:* high school transcript, minimum 2.0 GPA. *Application deadline:* rolling (freshmen). *Notification:* continuous until 6/15 (freshmen).

Freshman Application Contact Slippery Rock University of Pennsylvania, 1 Morrow Way, Slippery Rock, PA 16057-1383. *Phone:* 724-738-2015. *Toll-free phone:* 800-SRU-9111.

Website: http://www.sru.edu/.

Strayer University—Allentown Campus

Center Valley, Pennsylvania

Freshman Application Contact Strayer University—Allentown Campus, 3800 Sierra Circle, Suite 300, Center Valley, PA 18034.
Website: http://www.strayer.edu/campus/allentown/.

Strayer University—Center City Campus

Philadelphia, Pennsylvania

Freshman Application Contact Strayer University—Center City Campus, 1601 Cherry Street, Suite 100, Philadelphia, PA 19102.
Website: http://www.strayer.edu/campus/center-city.

Strayer University—Delaware County Campus

Springfield, Pennsylvania

Freshman Application Contact Strayer University—Delaware County Campus, 760 West Sproul Road, Suite 200, Springfield, PA 19064-1215.
Website: http://www.strayer.edu/campus/delaware-county.

Strayer University—King of Prussia Campus

King of Prussia, Pennsylvania

Freshman Application Contact Strayer University—King of Prussia Campus, 234 Mall Boulevard, Suite G-50, King of Prussia, PA 19406.
Website: http://www.strayer.edu/campus/king-prussia.

Strayer University—Lower Bucks County Campus

Trevose, Pennsylvania

Freshman Application Contact Strayer University—Lower Bucks County Campus, 3800 Horizon Boulevard, Suite 100, Trevose, PA 19053.
Website: http://www.strayer.edu/campus/lower-bucks-county/.

Strayer University—Penn Center West Campus

Pittsburgh, Pennsylvania

Freshman Application Contact Strayer University—Penn Center West Campus, One Penn Center West, Suite 320, Pittsburgh, PA 15276.
Website: http://www.strayer.edu/campus/penn-center-west/.

Strayer University—Warrendale Campus

Warrendale, Pennsylvania

Freshman Application Contact Strayer University—Warrendale Campus, 802 Warrendale Village Drive, Warrendale, PA 15086.
Website: http://www.strayer.edu/campus/warrendale.

Susquehanna University

Selinsgrove, Pennsylvania

- **Independent** 4-year, founded 1858, affiliated with Evangelical Lutheran Church in America
- **Small-town** 306-acre campus with easy access to Harrisburg
- **Endowment** $121.2 million
- **Coed** 2,197 undergraduate students, 97% full-time, 54% women, 46% men
- **Moderately difficult** entrance level, 76% of applicants were admitted

Undergraduates 2,142 full-time, 55 part-time. Students come from 35 states and territories; 17 other countries; 49% are from out of state; 5% Black or African American, non-Hispanic/Latino; 5% Hispanic/Latino; 1% Asian, non-Hispanic/Latino; 0.2% Native Hawaiian or other Pacific Islander, non-Hispanic/Latino; 0.1% American Indian or Alaska Native, non-Hispanic/Latino; 2% Two or more races, non-Hispanic/Latino; 1% international; 2% transferred in; 77% live on campus. *Retention:* 84% of full-time freshmen returned.

Freshmen *Admission:* 3,458 applied, 2,612 admitted, 631 enrolled. *Average high school GPA:* 3.33. *Test scores:* SAT critical reading scores over 500: 81%; SAT math scores over 500: 81%; SAT writing scores over 500: 70%; ACT scores over 18: 99%; SAT critical reading scores over 600: 28%; SAT math scores over 600: 29%; SAT writing scores over 600: 23%; ACT scores over 24: 65%; SAT critical reading scores over 700: 6%; SAT math scores over 700: 4%; SAT writing scores over 700: 4%; ACT scores over 30: 14%.

Faculty *Total:* 254, 56% full-time, 65% with terminal degrees. *Student/faculty ratio:* 12:1.

Academics *Calendar:* semesters. *Degrees:* bachelor's (also offers evening associate degree program limited to local adult students). *Special study options:* accelerated degree program, advanced placement credit, distance learning, double majors, honors programs, independent study, internships, off-campus study, part-time degree program, services for LD students, student-designed majors, study abroad, summer session for credit. *ROTC:* Army (c). *Unusual degree programs:* forestry with Duke University.

Computers on Campus 300 computers/terminals and 60 ports are available on campus for general student use. Students can access the following: campus intranet, computer help desk, free student e-mail accounts, online (class) grades, online (class) registration, online (class) schedules, class listings and assignments, online voting booth. Campuswide network is available. 100% of college-owned or -operated housing units are wired for high-speed Internet access. Wireless service is available via classrooms, computer centers, computer labs, dorm rooms, learning centers, libraries, student centers.

Student Life *Housing:* on-campus residence required through junior year. *Options:* coed. Campus housing is university owned. Freshman campus housing is guaranteed. *Activities and organizations:* drama/theater group, student-run newspaper, radio and television station, choral group, Student Government Association, community service organizations, music performance groups, theater performance groups, intramurals and outdoor recreation, national fraternities, national sororities. *Campus security:* 24-hour emergency response devices and patrols, late-night transport/escort service, controlled dormitory access. *Student services:* health clinic, personal/psychological counseling.

Athletics Member NCAA. All Division III. *Intercollegiate sports:* baseball M, basketball M/W, cheerleading M(c)/W(c), crew M(c)/W(c), cross-country running M/W, equestrian sports M(c)/W(c), field hockey W, football M, golf M/W, lacrosse M/W, rugby M(c)/W(c), soccer M/W, softball W, swimming and diving M/W, tennis M/W, track and field M/W, volleyball M(c)/W. *Intramural sports:* basketball M/W, racquetball M/W, soccer M/W, softball M/W, tennis M/W, volleyball M/W.

Standardized Tests *Recommended:* SAT or ACT (for admission).

Costs (2012–13) *Comprehensive fee:* $47,280 includes full-time tuition ($36,800), mandatory fees ($480), and room and board ($10,000). Part-time tuition: $1170 per semester hour. *College room only:* $5250. Room and board charges vary according to board plan and housing facility. *Payment plans:* tuition prepayment, installment. *Waivers:* employees or children of employees.

Financial Aid Of all full-time matriculated undergraduates who enrolled in 2011, 1,741 applied for aid, 1,554 were judged to have need, 289 had their need fully met. In 2011, 557 non-need-based awards were made. *Average percent of need met:* 80%. *Average financial aid package:* $26,079. *Average need-based loan:* $4257. *Average need-based gift aid:* $21,359. *Average non-need-based aid:* $12,094. *Average indebtedness upon graduation:* $29,356.

Applying *Options:* electronic application, early admission, early decision, deferred entrance. *Application fee:* $35. *Required:* essay or personal statement, high school transcript, minimum 2.5 GPA, 1 letter of recommendation. *Required for some:* writing portfolio, auditions for music programs. *Recommended:* minimum 3.0 GPA, interview. *Application deadlines:* 3/1 (freshmen), 7/1 (transfers). *Early decision deadline:* 12/1. *Notification:* continuous until 12/15 (freshmen), continuous until 8/1 (transfers), 12/15 (early decision).

Freshman Application Contact Mr. Chris Markle, Director of Admissions, Susquehanna University, 514 University Avenue, Selinsgrove, PA 17870.

Phone: 570-372-4260. *Toll-free phone:* 800-326-9672. *Fax:* 570-372-2722. *E-mail:* suadmiss@susqu.edu. *Website:* http://www.susqu.edu/.

See below for display ad and page 1528 for the College Close-Up.

Swarthmore College
Swarthmore, Pennsylvania

- **Independent** 4-year, founded 1864
- **Suburban** 425-acre campus with easy access to Philadelphia
- **Endowment** $1.5 billion
- **Coed** 1,552 undergraduate students, 99% full-time, 51% women, 49% men
- **Most difficult** entrance level, 14% of applicants were admitted

Undergraduates 1,537 full-time, 15 part-time. Students come from 53 states and territories; 44 other countries; 88% are from out of state; 6% Black or African American, non-Hispanic/Latino; 13% Hispanic/Latino; 14% Asian, non-Hispanic/Latino; 0.3% American Indian or Alaska Native, non-Hispanic/Latino; 8% Two or more races, non-Hispanic/Latino; 7% Race/ethnicity unknown; 8% international; 0.6% transferred in; 93% live on campus. *Retention:* 97% of full-time freshmen returned.

Freshmen *Admission:* 6,589 applied, 935 admitted, 378 enrolled. *Test scores:* SAT critical reading scores over 500: 100%; SAT math scores over 500: 100%; SAT writing scores over 500: 100%; ACT scores over 18: 100%; SAT critical reading scores over 600: 96%; SAT math scores over 600: 94%; SAT writing scores over 600: 96%; ACT scores over 24: 100%; SAT critical reading scores over 700: 67%; SAT math scores over 700: 64%; SAT writing scores over 700: 71%; ACT scores over 30: 79%.

Faculty *Total:* 205, 83% full-time, 94% with terminal degrees. *Student/faculty ratio:* 8:1.

Academics *Calendar:* semesters. *Degree:* bachelor's. *Special study options:* accelerated degree program, advanced placement credit, cooperative education, double majors, honors programs, independent study, internships, off-campus study, services for LD students, student-designed majors, study abroad. *ROTC:* Army (c), Navy (c), Air Force (c).

Computers on Campus 332 computers/terminals and 3,300 ports are available on campus for general student use. Students can access the following: computer help desk, free student e-mail accounts, online (class) grades, online

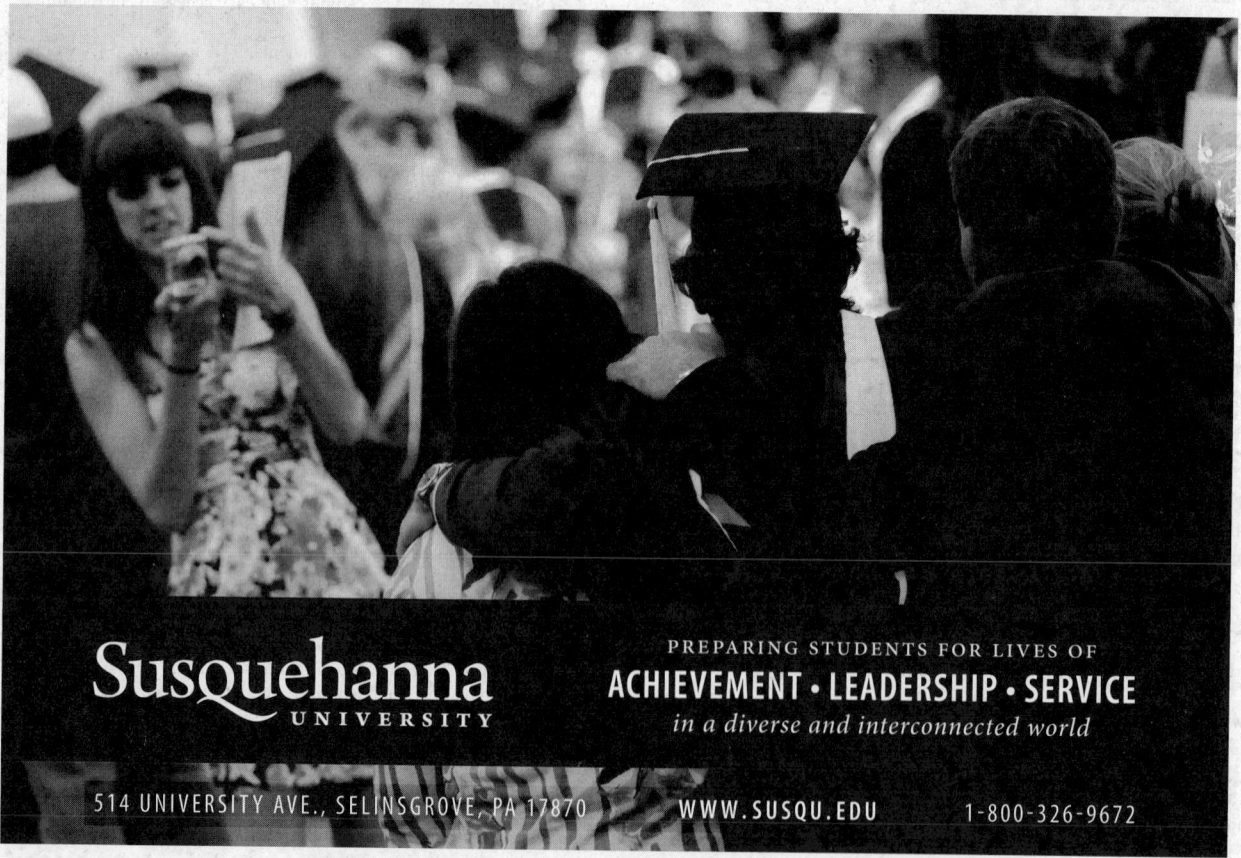

(class) registration, online (class) schedules, Course materials and academic software are available online for many courses. Campuswide network is available. 100% of college-owned or -operated housing units are wired for high-speed Internet access. Wireless service is available via entire campus.

Student Life *Housing:* on-campus residence required for freshman year. *Options:* coed, men-only, women-only, disabled students. Campus housing is university owned. Freshman campus housing is guaranteed. *Activities and organizations:* drama/theater group, student-run newspaper, radio station, choral group, community service and activist groups, club sports and intramurals, social/cultural clubs, music/acappella groups, political and debate clubs, national fraternities. *Campus security:* 24-hour emergency response devices and patrols, late-night transport/escort service. *Student services:* health clinic, personal/psychological counseling, women's center.

Athletics Member NCAA. All Division III. *Intercollegiate sports:* badminton M(c)/W, baseball M, basketball M/W, cross-country running M/W, fencing M(c)/W(c), field hockey W, golf M, ice hockey M(c)/W(c), lacrosse M/W, rugby M(c)/W(c), soccer M/W, softball W, squash M(c)/W(c), swimming and diving M/W, tennis M/W, track and field M/W, ultimate Frisbee M(c)/W(c), volleyball M(c)/W, water polo M(c)/W(c). *Intramural sports:* basketball M/W, football M/W, soccer M/W, softball M/W, table tennis M/W, tennis M/W, volleyball M/W.

Standardized Tests *Required:* SAT and SAT Subject Tests or ACT (for admission).

Costs (2012–13) *Comprehensive fee:* $55,750 includes full-time tuition ($42,744), mandatory fees ($336), and room and board ($12,670). *College room only:* $6500. Room and board charges vary according to board plan. *Payment plan:* installment.

Financial Aid Of all full-time matriculated undergraduates who enrolled in 2012, 890 applied for aid, 788 were judged to have need, 788 had their need fully met. 707 Federal Work-Study jobs (averaging $1788). In 2012, 12 non-need-based awards were made. *Average percent of need met:* 100%. *Average financial aid package:* $39,255. *Average need-based gift aid:* $37,651. *Average non-need-based aid:* $42,744. *Average indebtedness upon graduation:* $20,020. *Financial aid deadline:* 2/15.

Applying *Options:* electronic application, early decision, deferred entrance. *Application fee:* $60. *Required:* essay or personal statement, high school transcript, 3 letters of recommendation. *Required for some:* Statement of good standing from prior institution(s) for transfer applicants. *Application deadlines:* 1/1 (freshmen), 1/1 (out-of-state freshmen), 4/1 (transfers). *Early decision deadline:* 11/15 (for plan 1), 1/1 (for plan 2). *Notification:* 4/1 (freshmen), 4/1 (out-of-state freshmen), 5/30 (transfers), 12/15 (early decision plan 1), 2/15 (early decision plan 2).

Freshman Application Contact Mr. James L. Bock, Dean of Admissions and Financial Aid, Swarthmore College, 500 College Avenue, Swarthmore, PA 19081. *Phone:* 610-328-8300. *Toll-free phone:* 800-667-3110. *Fax:* 610-328-8580. *E-mail:* admissions@swarthmore.edu. *Website:* http://www.swarthmore.edu/.

Talmudical Yeshiva of Philadelphia

Philadelphia, Pennsylvania

Freshman Application Contact Rabbi Shmuel Kamenetsky, Co-Dean, Talmudical Yeshiva of Philadelphia, 6063 Drexel Road, Philadelphia, PA 19131-1296. *Phone:* 215-473-1212.

Temple University

Philadelphia, Pennsylvania

- **State-related** university, founded 1884
- **Urban** 330-acre campus with easy access to Philadelphia
- **Endowment** $277.5 million
- **Coed** 27,567 undergraduate students, 88% full-time, 51% women, 49% men
- **Moderately difficult** entrance level, 67% of applicants were admitted

Undergraduates 24,382 full-time, 3,185 part-time. Students come from 52 states and territories; 66 other countries; 18% are from out of state; 13% Black or African American, non-Hispanic/Latino; 5% Hispanic/Latino; 10% Asian, non-Hispanic/Latino; 0.1% Native Hawaiian or other Pacific Islander, non-Hispanic/Latino; 0.2% American Indian or Alaska Native, non-Hispanic/Latino; 2% Two or more races, non-Hispanic/Latino; 6% Race/ethnicity unknown; 3% international; 10% transferred in; 14% live on campus. *Retention:* 87% of full-time freshmen returned.

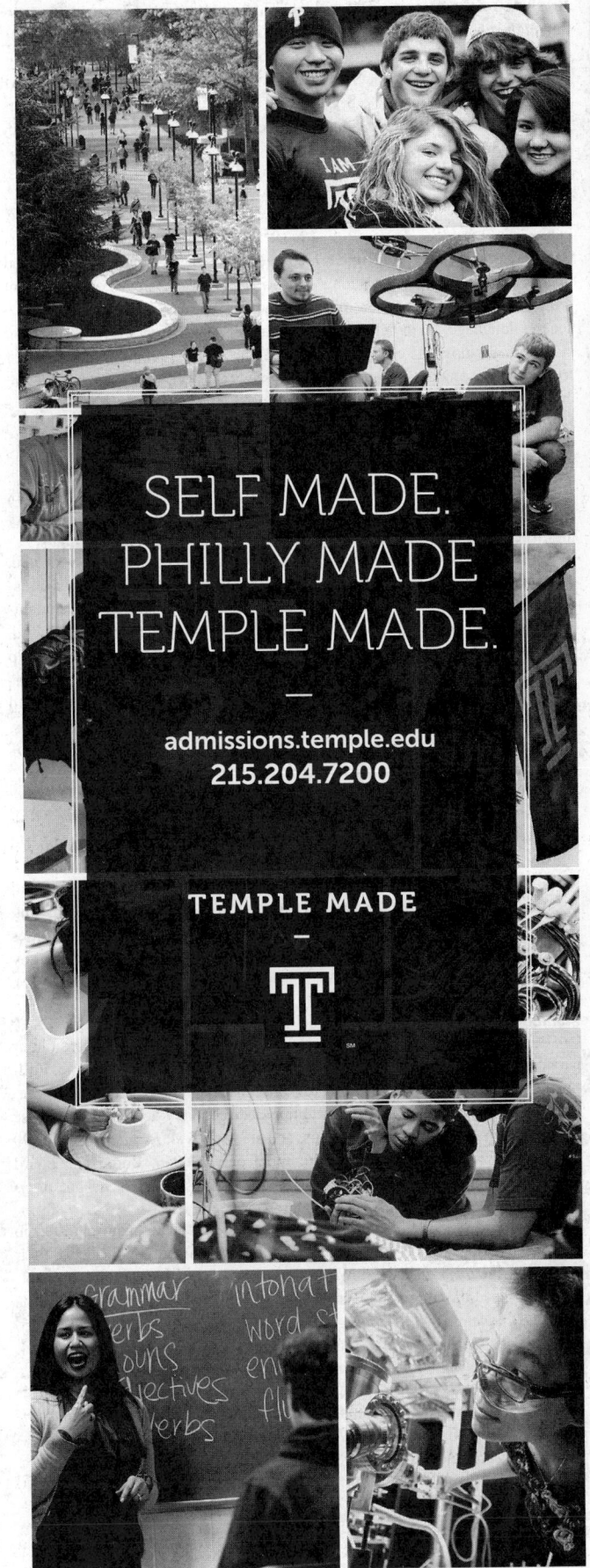

Freshmen *Admission:* 18,731 applied, 12,593 admitted, 4,132 enrolled. *Average high school GPA:* 3.41. *Test scores:* SAT critical reading scores over 500: 75%; SAT math scores over 500: 83%; SAT writing scores over 500: 74%; ACT scores over 18: 93%; SAT critical reading scores over 600: 26%; SAT math scores over 600: 34%; SAT writing scores over 600: 24%; ACT scores over 24: 48%; SAT critical reading scores over 700: 3%; SAT math scores over 700: 4%; SAT writing scores over 700: 3%; ACT scores over 30: 5%.
Faculty *Total:* 2,888, 50% full-time, 41% with terminal degrees. *Student/faculty ratio:* 15:1.
Academics *Calendar:* semesters. *Degrees:* certificates, diplomas, associate, bachelor's, master's, doctoral, post-master's, and postbachelor's certificates. *Special study options:* academic remediation for entering students, accelerated degree program, adult/continuing education programs, advanced placement credit, cooperative education, distance learning, double majors, English as a second language, external degree program, honors programs, independent study, internships, off-campus study, part-time degree program, services for LD students, student-designed majors, study abroad, summer session for credit. *ROTC:* Army (b), Navy (c), Air Force (c).
Computers on Campus 3,670 computers/terminals are available on campus for general student use. Students can access the following: computer help desk, free student e-mail accounts, online (class) grades, online (class) registration, online (class) schedules, student accounts, Web hosting. Campuswide network is available. 100% of college-owned or -operated housing units are wired for high-speed Internet access. Wireless service is available via entire campus.
Student Life *Housing options:* coed. Campus housing is university owned, leased by the school and is provided by a third party. Freshman campus housing is guaranteed. *Activities and organizations:* drama/theater group, student-run newspaper, radio and television station, choral group, marching band, Temple Film Collective, Habitat for Humanity, Feminist Majority Leadership Alliance, Alpha Epsilon Delta (Pre-professional students with interests in pursuing careers in healthcare), The Spanish Club, national fraternities, national sororities. *Campus security:* 24-hour emergency response devices and patrols, late-night transport/escort service, controlled dormitory access. *Student services:* health clinic, personal/psychological counseling, legal services.
Athletics Member NCAA. All Division I except football (Division I-A). *Intercollegiate sports:* baseball M(s), basketball M(s)/W(s), cheerleading M(s)/W(s), crew M(s)/W(s), cross-country running M(s)/W(s), fencing W(s), field hockey W(s), golf M(s), gymnastics M(s)/W(s), lacrosse W(s), soccer M(s)/W(s), softball M/W(s), tennis M(s)/W(s), track and field M(s)/W(s), volleyball W(s). *Intramural sports:* badminton M(c)/W(c), basketball M/W, bowling M(c)/W(c), equestrian sports M(c)/W(c), fencing M(c)/W(c), gymnastics M(c)/W(c), ice hockey M(c), lacrosse M(c)/W(c), racquetball M/W, rugby M(c)/W(c), soccer M/W, softball W, tennis M/W, ultimate Frisbee M(c)/W(c), volleyball M/W.
Standardized Tests *Required:* SAT or ACT (for admission).
Costs (2012–13) *Tuition:* state resident $13,006 full-time, $502 per credit hour part-time; nonresident $22,832 full-time, $813 per credit hour part-time. Full-time tuition and fees vary according to course load, program, reciprocity agreements, and student level. Part-time tuition and fees vary according to course load, program, reciprocity agreements, and student level. *Required fees:* $590 full-time. *Room and board:* $10,276; room only: $6956. Room and board charges vary according to board plan and housing facility. *Payment plan:* installment. *Waivers:* employees or children of employees.
Financial Aid Of all full-time matriculated undergraduates who enrolled in 2011, 20,194 applied for aid, 17,393 were judged to have need, 4,273 had their need fully met. 1,835 Federal Work-Study jobs (averaging $1057). In 2011, 1908 non-need-based awards were made. *Average percent of need met:* 68%. *Average financial aid package:* $15,957. *Average need-based loan:* $4513. *Average need-based gift aid:* $6734. *Average non-need-based aid:* $4474. *Average indebtedness upon graduation:* $33,500.
Applying *Options:* electronic application, deferred entrance. *Application fee:* $55. *Required:* essay or personal statement, high school transcript. *Recommended:* minimum 3.0 GPA. *Application deadlines:* 3/1 (freshmen), 6/1 (transfers). *Notification:* continuous (freshmen), continuous (transfers).
Freshman Application Contact Temple University, 1801 North Broad Street, Philadelphia, PA 19122-6096. *Phone:* 215-204-7200. *Toll-free phone:* 888-340-2222.
Website: http://www.temple.edu/.

See previous page for display ad and page 1534 for the College Close-Up.

Thiel College
Greenville, Pennsylvania

- **Independent** 4-year, founded 1866, affiliated with Evangelical Lutheran Church in America
- **Rural** 135-acre campus with easy access to Cleveland, Pittsburgh
- **Endowment** $20.9 million
- **Coed**
- **Moderately difficult** entrance level

Faculty *Student/faculty ratio:* 14:1.
Academics *Calendar:* semesters. *Degrees:* associate and bachelor's.
Student Life *Campus security:* 24-hour emergency response devices and patrols, late-night transport/escort service, controlled dormitory access.
Athletics Member NCAA. All Division III.
Standardized Tests *Required:* SAT or ACT (for admission).
Costs (2012–13) *One-time required fee:* $300. *Comprehensive fee:* $36,108 includes full-time tuition ($24,208), mandatory fees ($1780), and room and board ($10,120). Part-time tuition: $808 per credit. Part-time tuition and fees vary according to course load. *Required fees:* $890 per term part-time. *College room only:* $5060. Room and board charges vary according to board plan and housing facility.
Financial Aid *Of all full-time matriculated undergraduates who enrolled in 2012,* 1,047 applied for aid, 1,008 were judged to have need, 64 had their need fully met. 42 Federal Work-Study jobs (averaging $1472). 271 state and other part-time jobs (averaging $1472). *In 2012,* 72 non-need-based awards were made. *Average percent of need met:* 66. *Average financial aid package:* $20,877. *Average need-based loan:* $4303. *Average need-based gift aid:* $16,660. *Average non-need-based aid:* $9508. *Average indebtedness upon graduation:* $28,401.
Applying *Options:* electronic application, deferred entrance. *Application fee:* $35. *Required:* essay or personal statement, high school transcript, minimum 2.0 GPA, 1 letter of recommendation. *Required for some:* interview.
Freshman Application Contact Ms. Amy Becker, Chief Admissions Officer, Thiel College, 75 College Avenue, Greenville, PA 16125. *Phone:* 724-589-2182. *Toll-free phone:* 800-248-4435. *Fax:* 724-589-2013. *E-mail:* admissions@thiel.edu.
Website: http://www.thiel.edu/.

Thomas Jefferson University
Philadelphia, Pennsylvania

Freshman Application Contact Ms. Karen Jacobs, Director of Admissions, Thomas Jefferson University, Edison Building, 130 South Ninth Street, Philadelphia, PA 19107. *Phone:* 215-503-8890. *Toll-free phone:* 877-533-3247. *Fax:* 215-503-7241. *E-mail:* chpadmissions@mail.tju.edu. *Website:* http://www.jefferson.edu/.

University of Pennsylvania
Philadelphia, Pennsylvania

- **Independent** university, founded 1740
- **Urban** 302-acre campus
- **Endowment** $6.8 billion
- **Coed** 9,682 undergraduate students, 97% full-time, 50% women, 50% men
- **Most difficult** entrance level, 13% of applicants were admitted

Undergraduates 9,374 full-time, 308 part-time. Students come from 54 states and territories; 101 other countries; 84% are from out of state; 7% Black or African American, non-Hispanic/Latino; 9% Hispanic/Latino; 19% Asian, non-Hispanic/Latino; 0.1% Native Hawaiian or other Pacific Islander, non-Hispanic/Latino; 0.2% American Indian or Alaska Native, non-Hispanic/Latino; 3% Two or more races, non-Hispanic/Latino; 4% Race/ethnicity unknown; 12% international; 1% transferred in; 56% live on campus. *Retention:* 98% of full-time freshmen returned.
Freshmen *Admission:* 31,218 applied, 3,935 admitted, 2,397 enrolled. *Average high school GPA:* 3.9. *Test scores:* SAT critical reading scores over 500: 101%; SAT math scores over 500: 100%; SAT writing scores over 500: 100%; ACT scores over 18: 100%; SAT critical reading scores over 600: 95%; SAT math scores over 600: 97%; SAT writing scores over 600: 96%; ACT scores over 24: 99%; SAT critical reading scores over 700: 62%; SAT math scores over 700: 73%; SAT writing scores over 700: 68%; ACT scores over 30: 80%.

Faculty *Total:* 2,250, 64% full-time, 100% with terminal degrees. *Student/faculty ratio:* 6:1.

Academics *Calendar:* semesters plus 2 5-week summer sessions. *Degrees:* certificates, associate, bachelor's, master's, doctoral, post-master's, and post-bachelor's certificates (also offers evening program with significant enrollment not reflected in profile). *Special study options:* academic remediation for entering students, accelerated degree program, adult/continuing education programs, advanced placement credit, cooperative education, distance learning, double majors, English as a second language, honors programs, independent study, internships, off-campus study, part-time degree program, services for LD students, student-designed majors, study abroad, summer session for credit. *ROTC:* Army (c), Navy (b), Air Force (c).

Computers on Campus Students can access the following: campus intranet, computer help desk, free student e-mail accounts, online (class) grades, online (class) registration, online (class) schedules, billing information, financial aid application, status, academic records, student services. Campuswide network is available. 100% of college-owned or -operated housing units are wired for high-speed Internet access. Wireless service is available via entire campus.

Student Life *Housing options:* coed, disabled students. Campus housing is university owned. Freshman campus housing is guaranteed. *Activities and organizations:* drama/theater group, student-run newspaper, radio and television station, choral group, marching band, Kite and Key Society, Social Planning and Events Committee, Hillel at Penn, Sports Club Council, Interfraternity Council, national fraternities, national sororities. *Campus security:* 24-hour emergency response devices and patrols, late-night transport/escort service, controlled dormitory access. *Student services:* health clinic, personal/psychological counseling, women's center, legal services.

Athletics Member NCAA. All Division I except football (Division I-AA). *Intercollegiate sports:* baseball M, basketball M/W, crew M/W, cross-country running M/W, fencing M/W, field hockey W, golf M/W, gymnastics W, lacrosse M/W, soccer M/W, softball W, squash M/W, swimming and diving M/W, tennis M/W, track and field M/W, volleyball W, wrestling M. *Intramural sports:* badminton M(c)/W(c), baseball M(c)/W(c), basketball M(c)/W(c), cheerleading M/W, equestrian sports M(c)/W(c), field hockey M(c)/W(c), golf M(c)/W(c), gymnastics M(c)/W(c), ice hockey M(c)/W(c), lacrosse M/W, rugby M(c)/W(c), sailing M(c)/W(c), skiing (downhill) M(c)/W(c), soccer M/W, softball M/W, squash M/W, swimming and diving M/W, table tennis M/W, tennis M/W, ultimate Frisbee M(c)/W(c), volleyball M/W, water polo M(c)/W(c).

Standardized Tests *Required:* SAT and SAT Subject Tests or ACT (for admission).

Costs (2012–13) *Comprehensive fee:* $56,106 includes full-time tuition ($39,088), mandatory fees ($4650), and room and board ($12,368). Part-time tuition: $4989 per course. Part-time tuition and fees vary according to course load. *Required fees:* $543 per course part-time. *College room only:* $7952. Room and board charges vary according to board plan and housing facility. *Payment plans:* tuition prepayment, installment. *Waivers:* employees or children of employees.

Financial Aid Of all full-time matriculated undergraduates who enrolled in 2011, 5,187 applied for aid, 4,681 were judged to have need, 4,681 had their need fully met. 3,621 Federal Work-Study jobs (averaging $3078). 654 state and other part-time jobs (averaging $2400). *Average percent of need met:* 100%. *Average financial aid package:* $39,011. *Average need-based loan:* $428. *Average need-based gift aid:* $36,048. *Average indebtedness upon graduation:* $21,190.

Applying *Options:* electronic application, early admission, early decision, deferred entrance. *Application fee:* $75. *Required:* essay or personal statement, high school transcript, 2 letters of recommendation. *Application deadlines:* 1/1 (freshmen), 3/15 (transfers). *Early decision deadline:* 11/1. *Notification:* 4/1 (freshmen), 5/15 (transfers), 12/15 (early decision).

Freshman Application Contact The Office of Undergraduate Admissions, University of Pennsylvania, 1 College Hall, Room 1, Philadelphia, PA 19104. *Phone:* 215-898-7507. *Website:* http://www.upenn.edu/.

University of Phoenix–Harrisburg Campus

Harrisburg, Pennsylvania

Admissions Office Contact University of Phoenix–Harrisburg Campus, 4050 Crums Mill Road, Harrisburg, PA 17112. *Toll-free phone:* 866-766-0766. *Website:* http://www.phoenix.edu/.

University of Phoenix– Philadelphia Campus

Wayne, Pennsylvania

Freshman Application Contact Marc Booker, Sr. Director, Office of Admissions and Evaluation, University of Phoenix–Philadelphia Campus, 4035 South Riverpoint Parkway, Mail Stop CF-L101, Phoenix, AZ 85040. *Phone:* 602-557-4609. *Toll-free phone:* 866-766-0766. *Fax:* 480-643-1156. *Website:* http://www.phoenix.edu/.

University of Phoenix–Pittsburgh Campus

Pittsburgh, Pennsylvania

Freshman Application Contact Marc Booker, Sr. Director, Office of Admissions and Evaluation, University of Phoenix–Pittsburgh Campus, 4035 South Riverpoint Parkway, Mail Stop CF-L101, Phoenix, AZ 85040. *Phone:* 602-557-4609. *Toll-free phone:* 866-766-0766. *Fax:* 480-643-1156. *Website:* http://www.phoenix.edu/.

University of Pittsburgh

Pittsburgh, Pennsylvania

- **State-related** university, founded 1787, part of Commonwealth System of Higher Education
- **Urban** 132-acre campus with easy access to Pittsburgh
- **Endowment** $2.6 billion
- **Coed** 18,429 undergraduate students, 94% full-time, 50% women, 50% men
- **Moderately difficult** entrance level, 56% of applicants were admitted

Undergraduates 17,256 full-time, 1,173 part-time. Students come from 52 states and territories; 45 other countries; 25% are from out of state; 6% Black or African American, non-Hispanic/Latino; 2% Hispanic/Latino; 6% Asian, non-Hispanic/Latino; 0.1% Native Hawaiian or other Pacific Islander, non-Hispanic/Latino; 0.1% American Indian or Alaska Native, non-Hispanic/Latino; 3% Two or more races, non-Hispanic/Latino; 2% Race/ethnicity unknown; 3% international; 5% transferred in; 44% live on campus. *Retention:* 93% of full-time freshmen returned.

Freshmen *Admission:* 24,871 applied, 13,959 admitted, 3,640 enrolled. *Average high school GPA:* 3.93. *Test scores:* SAT critical reading scores over 500: 98%; SAT math scores over 500: 99%; SAT writing scores over 500: 95%; ACT scores over 18: 100%; SAT critical reading scores over 600: 62%; SAT math scores over 600: 78%; SAT writing scores over 600: 57%; ACT scores over 24: 95%; SAT critical reading scores over 700: 14%; SAT math scores over 700: 21%; SAT writing scores over 700: 12%; ACT scores over 30: 33%.

Faculty *Total:* 2,334, 73% full-time. *Student/faculty ratio:* 14:1.

Academics *Calendar:* semesters plus summer term. *Degrees:* certificates, bachelor's, master's, doctoral, post-master's, and postbachelor's certificates. *Special study options:* academic remediation for entering students, accelerated degree program, adult/continuing education programs, advanced placement credit, cooperative education, distance learning, double majors, English as a second language, external degree program, freshman honors college, honors programs, independent study, internships, off-campus study, part-time degree program, services for LD students, student-designed majors, study abroad, summer session for credit. *ROTC:* Army (b), Navy (c), Air Force (b). *Unusual degree programs:* 3-2 engineering; statistics with graduate school of public and international affairs.

Computers on Campus 2,000 computers/terminals and 2,000 ports are available on campus for general student use. Students can access the following: campus intranet, computer help desk, free student e-mail accounts, online (class) grades, online (class) registration, online (class) schedules, online class listings, online tuition payment. Campuswide network is available. 100% of college-owned or -operated housing units are wired for high-speed Internet access. Wireless service is available via entire campus.

Student Life *Housing options:* coed, women-only, disabled students. Campus housing is university owned. Freshman campus housing is guaranteed. *Activities and organizations:* drama/theater group, student-run newspaper, radio and television station, choral group, marching band, Resident Student Association, Black Action Society, Engineering Student Council, Interfraternity Council, Panhellenic Association, national fraternities, national sororities. *Campus* *security:* 24-hour emergency response devices and patrols, late-night transport/escort service, controlled dormitory access, on-call van transportation. *Student services:* health clinic, personal/psychological counseling.

Athletics Member NCAA. All Division I except football (Division I-A). *Intercollegiate sports:* baseball M(s), basketball M(s)/W(s), cross-country running M(s)/W(s), gymnastics W(s), soccer M(s)/W(s), softball W(s), swimming and diving M(s)/W(s), tennis W(s), track and field M(s)/W(s), volleyball W(s), wrestling M(s). *Intramural sports:* badminton M/W, baseball M(c), basketball M/W, equestrian sports M(c)/W(c), fencing M(c)/W(c), field hockey M(c)/W(c), football M, gymnastics M(c)/W(c), ice hockey M(c)/W(c), lacrosse M(c)/W(c), racquetball M/W, rugby M(c)/W(c), sailing M(c)/W(c), skiing (downhill) M(c)/W(c), soccer M/W, softball M(c)/W(c), squash M/W, swimming and diving M(c)/W(c), tennis M(c)/W(c), ultimate Frisbee M/W, volleyball M/W, water polo M(c)/W(c), wrestling M(c).

Standardized Tests *Required:* SAT or ACT (for admission). *Recommended:* SAT and SAT Subject Tests or ACT (for admission), SAT Subject Tests (for admission).

Costs (2012–13) *Tuition:* state resident $15,730 full-time, $655 per credit part-time; nonresident $25,420 full-time, $1059 per credit part-time. Full-time tuition and fees vary according to location and program. Part-time tuition and fees vary according to location and program. *Required fees:* $860 full-time, $214 per credit part-time. *Room and board:* $9870; room only: $5950. Room and board charges vary according to board plan, housing facility, and location. *Payment plans:* installment, deferred payment. *Waivers:* employees or children of employees.

Financial Aid Of all full-time matriculated undergraduates who enrolled in 2011, 12,212 applied for aid, 9,695 were judged to have need, 925 had their need fully met. In 2011, 399 non-need-based awards were made. *Average percent of need met:* 56%. *Average financial aid package:* $12,338. *Average need-based loan:* $4855. *Average need-based gift aid:* $7774. *Average non-need-based aid:* $11,543. *Average indebtedness upon graduation:* $33,662.

Applying *Options:* electronic application. *Application fee:* $45. *Required:* high school transcript. *Recommended:* essay or personal statement, interview. *Application deadlines:* rolling (freshmen), rolling (transfers). *Notification:* continuous (freshmen), continuous (transfers).

Freshman Application Contact Marc L. Harding, Chief Enrollment Officer, University of Pittsburgh, 4227 Fifth Avenue, First Floor, Alumni Hall, Pittsburgh, PA 15260. *Phone:* 412-624-7488. *Fax:* 412-648-8815. *E-mail:* oafa@pitt.edu.

Website: http://www.pitt.edu/.

University of Pittsburgh at Bradford

Bradford, Pennsylvania

- **State-related** 4-year, founded 1963
- **Small-town** 317-acre campus with easy access to Buffalo
- **Endowment** $18.5 million
- **Coed** 1,518 undergraduate students, 91% full-time, 55% women, 45% men
- **Minimally difficult** entrance level, 45% of applicants were admitted

Undergraduates 1,378 full-time, 140 part-time. Students come from 25 states and territories; 12 other countries; 16% are from out of state; 9% Black or African American, non-Hispanic/Latino; 3% Hispanic/Latino; 3% Asian, non-Hispanic/Latino; 0.5% American Indian or Alaska Native, non-Hispanic/Latino; 5% Race/ethnicity unknown; 3% international; 7% transferred in; 62% live on campus. *Retention:* 72% of full-time freshmen returned.

Freshmen *Admission:* 940 applied, 422 admitted, 379 enrolled. *Average high school GPA:* 3.25. *Test scores:* SAT critical reading scores over 500: 44%; SAT math scores over 500: 53%; SAT writing scores over 500: 39%; ACT scores over 18: 81%; SAT critical reading scores over 600: 8%; SAT math scores over 600: 15%; SAT writing scores over 600: 7%; ACT scores over 24: 21%; SAT critical reading scores over 700: 1%; SAT math scores over 700: 3%; SAT writing scores over 700: 1%.

Faculty *Total:* 155, 46% full-time, 40% with terminal degrees. *Student/faculty ratio:* 17:1.

Academics *Calendar:* semesters. *Degrees:* associate and bachelor's. *Special study options:* academic remediation for entering students, accelerated degree program, adult/continuing education programs, advanced placement credit, distance learning, double majors, independent study, internships, off-campus study, part-time degree program, services for LD students, study abroad, summer session for credit. *ROTC:* Army (c).

Computers on Campus 120 computers/terminals and 1,056 ports are available on campus for general student use. Students can access the following: computer help desk, free student e-mail accounts, online (class) grades, online (class) registration, online (class) schedules, online bills. Campuswide network is available. 100% of college-owned or -operated housing units are wired for high-speed Internet access. Wireless service is available via entire campus.

Student Life *Housing:* on-campus residence required for freshman year. *Options:* coed, disabled students. Campus housing is university owned. Freshman campus housing is guaranteed. *Activities and organizations:* drama/theater group, student-run newspaper, radio station, choral group, Student Government Association, Student Activities Board, The Source (student newspaper), Alpha Phi Omega, WDRQ (student radio station), national fraternities, national sororities. *Campus security:* 24-hour emergency response devices and patrols, late-night transport/escort service, controlled dormitory access. *Student services:* health clinic, personal/psychological counseling.

Athletics Member NCAA. All Division III. *Intercollegiate sports:* baseball M, basketball M/W, cross-country running M/W, golf M, soccer M/W, softball W, swimming and diving M/W, tennis M/W, volleyball W. *Intramural sports:* basketball M/W, bowling W, cheerleading W(c), football M/W, golf M/W, ice hockey M/W, rock climbing M/W, skiing (cross-country) M/W, soccer M/W, softball M/W, swimming and diving M/W, table tennis M/W, ultimate Frisbee M/W, volleyball M/W, water polo M/W.

Standardized Tests *Required:* SAT or ACT (for admission).

Costs (2012–13) *One-time required fee:* $90. *Tuition:* state resident $11,970 full-time, $498 per credit hour part-time; nonresident $22,366 full-time, $931 per credit hour part-time. Full-time tuition and fees vary according to course load and program. Part-time tuition and fees vary according to course load and program. *Required fees:* $840 full-time, $135 per term part-time. *Room and board:* $7960; room only: $4920. Room and board charges vary according to board plan and housing facility. *Payment plan:* installment. *Waivers:* employees or children of employees.

Financial Aid Of all full-time matriculated undergraduates who enrolled in 2010, 1,371 applied for aid, 1,239 were judged to have need, 597 had their need fully met. 184 Federal Work-Study jobs (averaging $1740). 2 state and other part-time jobs (averaging $1740). In 2010, 95 non-need-based awards were made. *Average percent of need met:* 83%. *Average financial aid package:* $12,332. *Average need-based loan:* $4204. *Average need-based gift aid:* $8255. *Average non-need-based aid:* $5841. *Average indebtedness upon graduation:* $20,757.

Applying *Options:* electronic application, deferred entrance. *Application fee:* $45. *Required:* high school transcript, minimum 2.0 GPA. *Required for some:* minimum 3.0 GPA. *Recommended:* essay or personal statement, 2 letters of recommendation, interview. *Application deadlines:* rolling (freshmen), rolling (out-of-state freshmen), rolling (transfers). *Notification:* continuous (freshmen), continuous (out-of-state freshmen), continuous (transfers).

Freshman Application Contact Ms. Vicky Pingie, Associate Director of Admissions, University of Pittsburgh at Bradford, 300 Campus Drive, Bradford, PA 16701. *Phone:* 814-362-7552. *Toll-free phone:* 800-872-1787. *Fax:* 814-362-5150. *E-mail:* monti@pitt.edu. *Website:* http://www.upb.pitt.edu/.

See previous page for display ad and page 1592 for the College Close-Up.

University of Pittsburgh at Greensburg

Greensburg, Pennsylvania

- **State-related** 4-year, founded 1963, part of University of Pittsburgh system
- **Small-town** 219-acre campus with easy access to Pittsburgh
- **Coed** 1,733 undergraduate students, 93% full-time, 50% women, 50% men
- **Moderately difficult** entrance level, 93% of applicants were admitted

Undergraduates 1,606 full-time, 127 part-time. Students come from 20 states and territories; 6 other countries; 2% are from out of state; 5% Black or African American, non-Hispanic/Latino; 3% Hispanic/Latino; 3% Asian, non-Hispanic/Latino; 0.1% American Indian or Alaska Native, non-Hispanic/Latino; 2% Two or more races, non-Hispanic/Latino; 6% Race/ethnicity unknown; 2% international; 8% transferred in; 40% live on campus. *Retention:* 74% of full-time freshmen returned.

Freshmen *Admission:* 1,262 applied, 1,175 admitted, 394 enrolled. *Average high school GPA:* 3.46. *Test scores:* SAT critical reading scores over 500: 52%; SAT math scores over 500: 66%; SAT writing scores over 500: 46%; ACT scores over 18: 88%; SAT critical reading scores over 600: 9%; SAT math scores over 600: 16%; SAT writing scores over 600: 6%; ACT scores over 24: 31%; SAT critical reading scores over 700: 1%; SAT math scores over 700: 2%.

Faculty *Total:* 133, 55% full-time. *Student/faculty ratio:* 18:1.

Academics *Calendar:* semesters. *Degree:* certificates and bachelor's. *Special study options:* academic remediation for entering students, accelerated degree program, adult/continuing education programs, advanced placement credit, distance learning, double majors, independent study, internships, off-campus study, part-time degree program, services for LD students, student-designed majors, study abroad, summer session for credit. *ROTC:* Army (c), Air Force (c).

Computers on Campus 174 computers/terminals are available on campus for general student use. Students can access the following: campus intranet, computer help desk, free student e-mail accounts, online (class) grades, online (class) registration, online (class) schedules. Campuswide network is available. 100% of college-owned or -operated housing units are wired for high-speed Internet access. Wireless service is available via classrooms, computer centers, computer labs, learning centers, libraries, student centers.

Student Life *Housing options:* coed. Campus housing is university owned. *Activities and organizations:* drama/theater group, student-run newspaper, radio station, choral group, Habitat for Humanity, Student Government Association, Student Activities Board, Outdoor Adventure and Community Service, Freshmen Honor Society—Phi Eta Sigma. *Campus security:* 24-hour emergency response devices and patrols, late-night transport/escort service, controlled dormitory access. *Student services:* health clinic, personal/psychological counseling.

Athletics Member NCAA. All Division III. *Intercollegiate sports:* baseball M, basketball M/W, cross-country running M/W, golf M, soccer M/W, softball W, tennis M/W, volleyball W. *Intramural sports:* baseball M, basketball M/W, bowling M/W, football M/W, golf M/W, racquetball M/W, skiing (cross-country) M/W, skiing (downhill) M/W, soccer M/W, softball M/W, table tennis M/W, tennis M/W, volleyball M/W, weight lifting M/W.

Standardized Tests *Required:* SAT or ACT (for admission).

Costs (2012–13) *Tuition:* state resident $11,970 full-time, $498 per credit hour part-time; nonresident $22,366 full-time, $931 per credit hour part-time. *Required fees:* $920 full-time, $174 per term part-time. *Room and board:* $8730. Room and board charges vary according to board plan and housing facility. *Payment plan:* installment. *Waivers:* senior citizens and employees or children of employees.

Financial Aid Of all full-time matriculated undergraduates who enrolled in 2011, 1,407 applied for aid, 1,266 were judged to have need, 125 had their need fully met. In 2011, 35 non-need-based awards were made. *Average percent of need met:* 38%. *Average financial aid package:* $10,212. *Average need-based loan:* $4173. *Average need-based gift aid:* $6411. *Average non-need-based aid:* $4401. *Average indebtedness upon graduation:* $33,095.

Applying *Options:* electronic application, early admission, deferred entrance. *Application fee:* $45. *Required:* high school transcript, minimum 2.5 GPA. *Recommended:* essay or personal statement, interview. *Application deadlines:* 8/1 (freshmen), 8/1 (out-of-state freshmen), 8/1 (transfers). *Notification:* continuous (freshmen), continuous (transfers).

Freshman Application Contact Ms. Heather Kabala, Director of Admissions, University of Pittsburgh at Greensburg, 150 Finoli Drive, Greensburg, PA 15601. *Phone:* 724-836-9880. *Fax:* 724-836-7471. *E-mail:* upgadmit@pitt.edu. *Website:* http://www.greensburg.pitt.edu/.

University of Pittsburgh at Johnstown

Johnstown, Pennsylvania

- **State-related** 4-year, founded 1927, part of University of Pittsburgh System
- **Suburban** 655-acre campus with easy access to Pittsburgh
- **Coed**
- **Moderately difficult** entrance level

Academics *Calendar:* semesters. *Degrees:* certificates, associate, and bachelor's.

Student Life *Campus security:* 24-hour emergency response devices and patrols, late-night transport/escort service, controlled dormitory access.

Athletics Member NCAA. All Division II.

Standardized Tests *Required:* SAT or ACT (for admission).

Costs (2012–13) *Tuition:* state resident $11,970 full-time, $498 per credit hour part-time; nonresident $22,366 full-time, $931 per credit hour part-time. Full-time tuition and fees vary according to program. Part-time tuition and fees vary according to program. *Required fees:* $922 full-time. *Room and board:* $8230; room only: $5180. Room and board charges vary according to board plan and housing facility.

Financial Aid Of all full-time matriculated undergraduates who enrolled in 2010, 2,540 applied for aid, 2,198 were judged to have need, 217 had their

need fully met. 138 Federal Work-Study jobs (averaging $2737). 270 state and other part-time jobs (averaging $2880). *In 2010,* 36 non-need-based awards were made. *Average percent of need met:* 55. *Average financial aid package:* $10,364. *Average need-based loan:* $4329. *Average need-based gift aid:* $5041. *Average non-need-based aid:* $2765. *Average indebtedness upon graduation:* $27,905.

Applying *Options:* electronic application, early admission, deferred entrance. *Application fee:* $45. *Required:* high school transcript, minimum 2.0 GPA. *Required for some:* interview. *Recommended:* essay or personal statement, 3 letters of recommendation.

Freshman Application Contact Office of Admissions, University of Pittsburgh at Johnstown, 157 Blackington Hall, Johnstown, PA 15904. *Phone:* 814-269-7050. *Toll-free phone:* 800-765-4875. *E-mail:* upjadmit@pitt.edu. *Website:* http://www.upj.pitt.edu/.

The University of Scranton
Scranton, Pennsylvania

- **Independent Roman Catholic (Jesuit)** comprehensive, founded 1888
- **Urban** 50-acre campus
- **Endowment** $125.2 million
- **Coed** 4,041 undergraduate students, 95% full-time, 55% women, 45% men
- **Moderately difficult** entrance level, 69% of applicants were admitted

Undergraduates 3,847 full-time, 194 part-time. Students come from 24 states and territories; 12 other countries; 58% are from out of state; 2% Black or African American, non-Hispanic/Latino; 7% Hispanic/Latino; 3% Asian, non-Hispanic/Latino; 0.2% American Indian or Alaska Native, non-Hispanic/Latino; 2% Two or more races, non-Hispanic/Latino; 6% Race/ethnicity unknown; 0.4% international; 2% transferred in; 64% live on campus. *Retention:* 87% of full-time freshmen returned.

Freshmen *Admission:* 9,672 applied, 6,655 admitted, 961 enrolled. *Average high school GPA:* 3.39. *Test scores:* SAT critical reading scores over 500: 85%; SAT math scores over 500: 88%; ACT scores over 18: 97%; SAT critical reading scores over 600: 29%; SAT math scores over 600: 37%; ACT scores over 24: 61%; SAT critical reading scores over 700: 4%; SAT math scores over 700: 6%; ACT scores over 30: 6%.

Faculty *Total:* 522, 52% full-time, 48% with terminal degrees. *Student/faculty ratio:* 11:1.

Academics *Calendar:* 4-1-4. *Degrees:* certificates, bachelor's, master's, doctoral, post-master's, and postbachelor's certificates. *Special study options:* academic remediation for entering students, accelerated degree program, adult/continuing education programs, advanced placement credit, distance learning, double majors, honors programs, independent study, internships, off-campus study, part-time degree program, services for LD students, student-designed majors, study abroad, summer session for credit. *ROTC:* Army (b), Air Force (c).

Computers on Campus 973 computers/terminals are available on campus for general student use. Students can access the following: computer help desk, free student e-mail accounts, online (class) grades, online (class) registration, online (class) schedules. Campuswide network is available. 100% of college-owned or -operated housing units are wired for high-speed Internet access. Wireless service is available via classrooms, computer centers, computer labs, dorm rooms, learning centers, libraries, student centers.

Student Life *Housing:* on-campus residence required through sophomore year. *Options:* coed, men-only, women-only, disabled students. Campus housing is university owned. Freshman campus housing is guaranteed. *Activities and organizations:* drama/theater group, student-run newspaper, radio and television station, choral group, Service-oriented student clubs, United Colors, Retreat Programs, Biology/Pre-Medicine clubs, Pre-Law Society. *Campus security:* 24-hour emergency response devices and patrols, student patrols, late-night transport/escort service, controlled dormitory access, Sprinkler Systems in all University-owned housing. *Student services:* health clinic, personal/psychological counseling, women's center.

Athletics Member NCAA. All Division III. *Intercollegiate sports:* baseball M, basketball M/W, crew M(c)/W(c), cross-country running M/W, equestrian sports M(c)/W(c), fencing M(c)/W(c), field hockey W, golf M, ice hockey M(c), lacrosse M/W, rugby M(c)/W(c), soccer M/W, softball W, swimming and diving M/W, tennis M/W, ultimate Frisbee M(c)/W(c), volleyball M(c)/W, wrestling M. *Intramural sports:* badminton M/W, basketball M/W, cheerleading M(c)/W(c), football M/W, racquetball M/W, rock climbing M(c)/W(c), soccer M/W, softball M/W, table tennis M/W, tennis M/W, ultimate Frisbee M/W, volleyball M/W.

Standardized Tests *Required:* SAT or ACT (for admission).

Costs (2012–13) *Comprehensive fee:* $50,260 includes full-time tuition ($37,106), mandatory fees ($350), and room and board ($12,804). Part-time

tuition: $955 per credit. *College room only:* $7500. Room and board charges vary according to board plan and housing facility. *Payment plan:* installment. *Waivers:* senior citizens and employees or children of employees.

Financial Aid Of all full-time matriculated undergraduates who enrolled in 2010, 3,140 applied for aid, 2,738 were judged to have need, 270 had their need fully met. In 2010, 663 non-need-based awards were made. *Average percent of need met:* 70%. *Average financial aid package:* $22,597. *Average need-based loan:* $7833. *Average need-based gift aid:* $18,242. *Average non-need-based aid:* $11,107. *Average indebtedness upon graduation:* $32,582.

Applying *Options:* electronic application, early admission, early action, deferred entrance. *Required:* essay or personal statement, high school transcript, 1 letter of recommendation. *Required for some:* interview. *Application deadlines:* 3/1 (freshmen), rolling (transfers), 11/15 (early action). *Notification:* continuous until 1/15 (freshmen), continuous (transfers), 12/15 (early action).

Freshman Application Contact Mr. Joseph Roback, Associate Vice President, Admissions and Enrollment, The University of Scranton, The Estate Room 208, The University of Scranton, Scranton, PA 18510-4501. *Phone:* 570-941-7540. *Toll-free phone:* 888-SCRANTON. *Fax:* 570-941-5928. *E-mail:* admissions@scranton.edu. *Website:* http://www.scranton.edu/.

The University of the Arts
Philadelphia, Pennsylvania

- **Independent** comprehensive, founded 1870
- **Urban** 21-acre campus
- **Coed** 1,909 undergraduate students, 98% full-time, 57% women, 43% men
- **Moderately difficult** entrance level, 69% of applicants were admitted

Undergraduates 1,867 full-time, 42 part-time. Students come from 41 states and territories; 16 other countries; 63% are from out of state; 13% Black or African American, non-Hispanic/Latino; 7% Hispanic/Latino; 3% Asian, non-Hispanic/Latino; 0.6% Native Hawaiian or other Pacific Islander, non-Hispanic/Latino; 0.4% American Indian or Alaska Native, non-Hispanic/Latino; 3% Two or more races, non-Hispanic/Latino; 5% Race/ethnicity unknown; 6% international; 6% transferred in; 33% live on campus. *Retention:* 81% of full-time freshmen returned.

Freshmen *Admission:* 1,634 applied, 1,132 admitted, 417 enrolled. *Average high school GPA:* 2.9. *Test scores:* SAT critical reading scores over 500: 55%; SAT math scores over 500: 44%; SAT writing scores over 500: 53%; ACT scores over 18: 82%; SAT critical reading scores over 600: 18%; SAT math scores over 600: 14%; SAT writing scores over 600: 17%; ACT scores over 24: 38%; SAT critical reading scores over 700: 3%; SAT math scores over 700: 1%; SAT writing scores over 700: 3%; ACT scores over 30: 13%.

Faculty *Total:* 505, 24% full-time. *Student/faculty ratio:* 8:1.

Academics *Calendar:* semesters. *Degrees:* certificates, diplomas, bachelor's, master's, and postbachelor's certificates. *Special study options:* academic remediation for entering students, accelerated degree program, advanced placement credit, double majors, English as a second language, honors programs, independent study, internships, off-campus study, part-time degree program, services for LD students, study abroad, summer session for credit.

Computers on Campus 368 computers/terminals are available on campus for general student use. Students can access the following: campus intranet, computer help desk, free student e-mail accounts, online (class) grades, online (class) registration, online (class) schedules. Campuswide network is available. 100% of college-owned or -operated housing units are wired for high-speed Internet access. Wireless service is available via entire campus.

Student Life *Housing options:* coed. Campus housing is university owned and leased by the school. Freshman applicants given priority for college housing. *Activities and organizations:* drama/theater group, choral group, Student Council, Gallery One, African Diaspora Collective, UArts Literary Society, The Fifth Circle (fencing). *Campus security:* 24-hour emergency response devices and patrols, late-night transport/escort service, crime prevention workshops and seminars. *Student services:* health clinic, personal/psychological counseling.

Athletics *Intramural sports:* fencing M/W.

Standardized Tests *Required for some:* SAT or ACT (for admission).

Costs (2012–13) *Comprehensive fee:* $47,540 includes full-time tuition ($34,840) and room and board ($12,700). Part-time tuition and fees vary according to course load. *College room only:* $8200. Room and board charges vary according to board plan and housing facility. *Payment plan:* installment. *Waivers:* children of alumni and employees or children of employees.

Financial Aid In 2002, 561 non-need-based awards were made. *Average percent of need met:* 65%. *Average financial aid package:* $16,500. *Average indebtedness upon graduation:* $17,000.

Applying *Options:* electronic application, deferred entrance. *Application fee:* $60. *Required:* essay or personal statement, high school transcript, 1 letter of recommendation, Interview recommended for all; audition or portfolio required for performing arts programs; portfolio required for design, visual arts, film programs, essay required for all programs. *Required for some:* interview. *Recommended:* minimum 2.0 GPA, interview. *Application deadlines:* rolling (freshmen), rolling (out-of-state freshmen), rolling (transfers). *Notification:* continuous (freshmen), continuous (out-of-state freshmen), continuous (transfers).

Freshman Application Contact Mr. Dan O'Neil, Assistant Director, Admissions, The University of the Arts, 320 South Broad Street, Philadelphia, PA 19102-4944. *Phone:* 215-717-6041. *Toll-free phone:* 800-616-ARTS. *Fax:* 215-717-6045. *E-mail:* admissions@uarts.edu. *Website:* http://www.uarts.edu/.

See below for display ad and page 1606 for the College Close-Up.

University of the Sciences

Philadelphia, Pennsylvania

- **Independent** university, founded 1821
- **Urban** 35-acre campus
- **Endowment** $154.2 million
- **Coed** 2,436 undergraduate students, 99% full-time, 61% women, 39% men
- **Moderately difficult** entrance level, 56% of applicants were admitted

Undergraduates 2,406 full-time, 30 part-time. Students come from 34 states and territories; 13 other countries; 56% are from out of state; 5% Black or African American, non-Hispanic/Latino; 3% Hispanic/Latino; 36% Asian, non-Hispanic/Latino; 0.4% Native Hawaiian or other Pacific Islander, non-Hispanic/Latino; 0.2% American Indian or Alaska Native, non-Hispanic/Latino; 1% Two or more races, non-Hispanic/Latino; 6% Race/ethnicity unknown; 2% international; 4% transferred in; 32% live on campus. *Retention:* 84% of full-time freshmen returned.

Freshmen *Admission:* 4,307 applied, 2,427 admitted, 483 enrolled. *Average high school GPA:* 3.61. *Test scores:* SAT critical reading scores over 500: 87%; SAT math scores over 500: 95%; SAT writing scores over 500: 85%; ACT scores over 18: 99%; SAT critical reading scores over 600: 30%; SAT math scores over 600: 57%; SAT writing scores over 600: 38%; ACT scores over 24: 70%; SAT critical reading scores over 700: 3%; SAT math scores over 700: 12%; SAT writing scores over 700: 6%; ACT scores over 30: 6%.

Faculty *Total:* 323, 58% full-time. *Student/faculty ratio:* 10:1.

Academics *Calendar:* semesters. *Degrees:* bachelor's, master's, doctoral, and postbachelor's certificates. *Special study options:* academic remediation for entering students, adult/continuing education programs, advanced placement credit, cooperative education, distance learning, double majors, honors programs, internships, off-campus study, part-time degree program, services for LD students, study abroad, summer session for credit. *ROTC:* Army (c), Air Force (c).

Computers on Campus 350 computers/terminals are available on campus for general student use. Students can access the following: campus intranet, computer help desk, free student e-mail accounts, online (class) grades, online (class) registration, online (class) schedules. Campuswide network is available. 100% of college-owned or -operated housing units are wired for high-speed Internet access. Wireless service is available via classrooms, computer centers, computer labs, dorm rooms, learning centers, libraries, student centers.

Student Life *Housing:* on-campus residence required through sophomore year. *Options:* coed. Campus housing is university owned and leased by the school. Freshman campus housing is guaranteed. *Activities and organizations:* drama/theater group, student-run newspaper, choral group, student government, Bharat, Academy of Students of Pharmacy, Student Physical Therapy Association, Asian Student Association, national fraternities, national sororities. *Campus security:* 24-hour emergency response devices and patrols, late-night transport/escort service, controlled dormitory access. *Student services:* health clinic, personal/psychological counseling.

Athletics Member NCAA, NAIA. All NCAA Division II. *Intercollegiate sports:* baseball M(s), basketball M(s)/W(s), cross-country running M/W, golf M/W, riflery M/W, softball W(s), tennis M/W, volleyball W(s). *Intramural sports:* archery M/W, basketball M/W, bowling M/W, riflery M/W, softball M/W, table tennis M/W, volleyball M/W.

Standardized Tests *Required:* SAT or ACT (for admission). *Recommended:* SAT (for admission).

Financial Aid Of all full-time matriculated undergraduates who enrolled in 2009, 2,227 applied for aid, 2,075 were judged to have need, 928 had their need fully met. In 2009, 485 non-need-based awards were made. *Average percent of need met:* 88%. *Average financial aid package:* $32,647. *Average need-based loan:* $5576. *Average need-based gift aid:* $7155. *Average non-need-based aid:* $8328. *Average indebtedness upon graduation:* $12,005.

Applying *Options:* electronic application, deferred entrance. *Application fee:* $45. *Required:* high school transcript. *Recommended:* minimum 3.0 GPA.

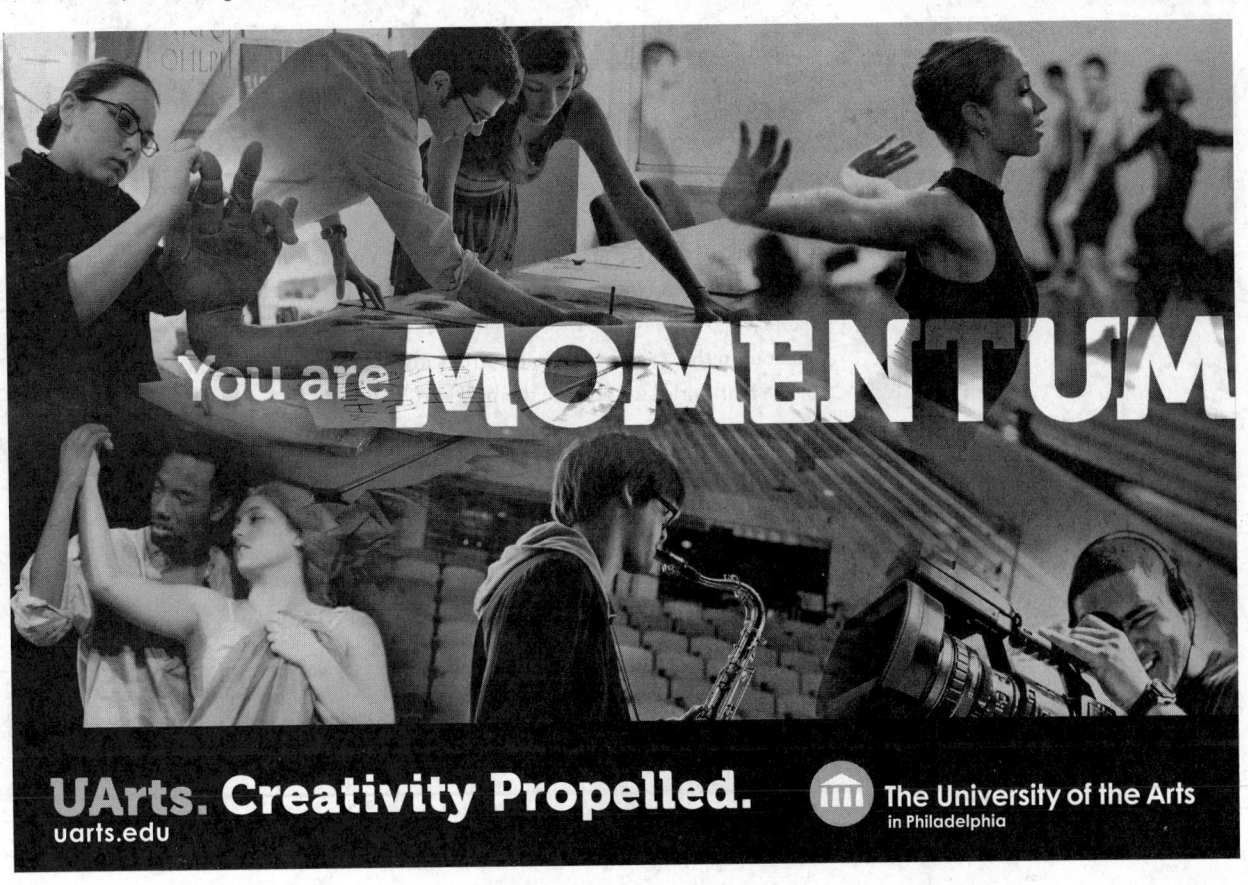

Application deadline: rolling (freshmen). *Notification:* continuous (freshmen), continuous (transfers).

Freshman Application Contact Ms. Dianna Collins, Executive Director of Admission and Enrollment Services, University of the Sciences, 600 South 43rd Street, Philadelphia, PA 19104-4495. *Phone:* 888-996-8747. *Toll-free phone:* 888-996-8747. *Fax:* 215-596-8821. *E-mail:* admit@usciences.edu. *Website:* http://www.usciences.edu/.

See below for display ad and page 1610 for the College Close-Up.

Ursinus College

Collegeville, Pennsylvania

Freshman Application Contact Mr. Richard Floyd, Dean of Admission, Ursinus College, PO Box 1000, Main Street, Collegeville, PA 19426. *Phone:* 610-409-3200. *Fax:* 610-409-3197. *E-mail:* admissions@ursinus.edu. *Website:* http://www.ursinus.edu/.

Valley Forge Christian College

Phoenixville, Pennsylvania

Freshman Application Contact Rev. William Chenco, Director of Admissions, Valley Forge Christian College, 1401 Charlestown Road, Phoenixville, PA 19460. *Phone:* 610-935-0450 Ext. 1430. *Toll-free phone:* 800-432-8322. *Fax:* 610-917-2069. *E-mail:* admissions@vfcc.edu. *Website:* http://www.vfcc.edu/.

Villanova University

Villanova, Pennsylvania

- **Independent Roman Catholic** comprehensive, founded 1842
- **Suburban** 254-acre campus with easy access to Philadelphia
- **Endowment** $370.3 million
- **Coed** 7,111 undergraduate students, 93% full-time, 51% women, 49% men
- **Very difficult** entrance level, 44% of applicants were admitted

Undergraduates 6,603 full-time, 508 part-time. Students come from 51 states and territories; 50 other countries; 76% are from out of state; 5% Black or African American, non-Hispanic/Latino; 7% Hispanic/Latino; 6% Asian, non-Hispanic/Latino; 0.1% Native Hawaiian or other Pacific Islander, non-Hispanic/Latino; 2% Two or more races, non-Hispanic/Latino; 2% Race/ethnicity unknown; 3% international; 2% transferred in; 70% live on campus. *Retention:* 94% of full-time freshmen returned.

Freshmen *Admission:* 15,394 applied, 6,768 admitted, 1,644 enrolled. *Average high school GPA:* 3.86. *Test scores:* SAT critical reading scores over 500: 96%; SAT math scores over 500: 98%; ACT scores over 18: 100%; SAT critical reading scores over 600: 73%; SAT math scores over 600: 84%; ACT scores over 24: 97%; SAT critical reading scores over 700: 19%; SAT math scores over 700: 37%; ACT scores over 30: 64%.

Faculty *Total:* 951, 62% full-time, 68% with terminal degrees. *Student/faculty ratio:* 11:1.

Academics *Calendar:* semesters. *Degrees:* bachelor's, master's, doctoral, post-master's, and postbachelor's certificates. *Special study options:* accelerated degree program, adult/continuing education programs, advanced placement credit, cooperative education, distance learning, double majors, English as a second language, honors programs, independent study, internships, off-campus study, part-time degree program, services for LD students, study abroad, summer session for credit. *ROTC:* Army (b), Navy (b), Air Force (c). *Unusual degree programs:* 3-2 engineering with Civil Engineering, Chemical Engineering, Computer Engineering, Electrical Engineering, and Mechanical Engineering; arts/liberal studies; classical studies; communication; criminal justice; political science; psychology; Spanish; religious studies; computer science; biology; chemistry; mathematics; mathematics/applied statistics; human resources development; business information systems/software engineering.

Computers on Campus 6,609 computers/terminals and 20,000 ports are available on campus for general student use. Students can access the following: campus intranet, computer help desk, free student e-mail accounts, online (class) grades, online (class) registration, online (class) schedules, learning management system with anti-plagiarism software, testing software, online faculty hours, videoconferencing; electronic portfolios; data vaulting/backup service; emergency notification system; Citrix-based library of advanced software. Campuswide network is available. 100% of college-owned or -operated housing units are wired for high-speed Internet access. Wireless service is available via classrooms, computer centers, computer labs, dorm rooms, learning centers, libraries, student centers.

Student Life *Housing options:* coed, men-only, women-only, disabled students. Campus housing is university owned. Freshman campus housing is guaranteed. *Activities and organizations:* drama/theater group, student-run newspaper, radio and television station, choral group, marching band, Blue Key Society, New Student Orientation Counselor Program, Special Olympics, Campus Activities Team, Student Government Association, national fraternities, national sororities. *Campus security:* 24-hour emergency response devices and patrols, late-night transport/escort service, controlled dormitory access, Nova Alert—email, text messaging re: emergency situations. *Student services:* health clinic, personal/psychological counseling.

Athletics Member NCAA. All Division I except football (Division I-AA). *Intercollegiate sports:* baseball M(s), basketball M(s)/W(s), cheerleading M/W, crew M(c)/W, cross-country running M(s)/W(s), equestrian sports W(c), field hockey W(s), golf M, ice hockey M(c)/W(c), lacrosse M(s)/W(s), sailing M(c)/W(c), skiing (downhill) M(c)/W(c), soccer M(s)/W(s), softball W(s), swimming and diving M/W(s), tennis M/W, track and field M(s)/W(s), volleyball M(c)/W(s), water polo M(c)/W. *Intramural sports:* badminton M(c)/W(c), baseball M(c), basketball M(c)/W(c), crew M(c), cross-country running M(c)/W(c), equestrian sports W(c), field hockey W(c), football M/W, golf M(c)/W(c), ice hockey M(c)/W(c), lacrosse M(c)/W(c), rugby M(c), sailing M(c)/W(c), skiing (downhill) M(c)/W(c), soccer M(c)/W(c), softball M/W, swimming and diving M(c)/W(c), tennis M(c)/W(c), ultimate Frisbee M(c)/W(c), volleyball M(c)/W(c), water polo M(c).

Standardized Tests *Required:* SAT or ACT (for admission).

Costs (2012–13) *Comprehensive fee:* $54,110 includes full-time tuition ($42,150), mandatory fees ($590), and room and board ($11,370). Part-time tuition: $1760 per credit. Part-time tuition and fees vary according to class time and program. *Required fees:* $30 per year part-time. *College room only:* $6020. Room and board charges vary according to board plan and housing facility.

Payment plan: installment. *Waivers:* senior citizens and employees or children of employees.

Financial Aid Of all full-time matriculated undergraduates who enrolled in 2011, 3,829 applied for aid, 3,100 were judged to have need, 471 had their need fully met. 2,542 Federal Work-Study jobs (averaging $2799). 41 state and other part-time jobs (averaging $2915). In 2011, 479 non-need-based awards were made. *Average percent of need met:* 81%. *Average financial aid package:* $29,762. *Average need-based loan:* $4460. *Average need-based gift aid:* $24,340. *Average non-need-based aid:* $11,076. *Average indebtedness upon graduation:* $38,055. *Financial aid deadline:* 2/7.

Applying *Options:* electronic application, early admission, early action, deferred entrance. *Application fee:* $80. *Required:* essay or personal statement, high school transcript, 1 letter of recommendation, Test Scores (SAT or ACT). *Application deadlines:* 1/7 (freshmen), 1/7 (out-of-state freshmen), 6/1 (transfers), 11/1 (early action). *Notification:* 4/1 (freshmen), 4/1 (out-of-state freshmen), continuous (transfers), 12/20 (early action).

Freshman Application Contact Mr. Michael Gaynor, Director of University Admission, Villanova University, 800 Lancaster Avenue, Villanova, PA 19085-1672. *Phone:* 610-519-4000. *Fax:* 610-519-6450. *E-mail:* gotovu@villanova.edu.
Website: http://www.villanova.edu/.

See below for display ad and page 1626 for the College Close-Up.

Washington & Jefferson College

Washington, Pennsylvania

- **Independent** 4-year, founded 1781
- **Suburban** 60-acre campus with easy access to Pittsburgh
- **Endowment** $103.8 million
- **Coed** 1,429 undergraduate students, 99% full-time, 51% women, 49% men
- **Very difficult** entrance level, 41% of applicants were admitted

Undergraduates 1,419 full-time, 10 part-time. Students come from 35 states and territories; 18 other countries; 27% are from out of state; 3% Black or African American, non-Hispanic/Latino; 3% Hispanic/Latino; 2% Asian, non-Hispanic/Latino; 0.1% Native Hawaiian or other Pacific Islander, non-Hispanic/Latino; 0.6% American Indian or Alaska Native, non-Hispanic/Latino; 2%

Two or more races, non-Hispanic/Latino; 5% Race/ethnicity unknown; 3% international; 2% transferred in; 91% live on campus.

Freshmen *Admission:* 6,504 applied, 2,651 admitted, 376 enrolled. *Average high school GPA:* 3.34. *Test scores:* SAT critical reading scores over 500: 85%; SAT math scores over 500: 87%; ACT scores over 18: 100%; SAT critical reading scores over 600: 30%; SAT math scores over 600: 40%; ACT scores over 24: 70%; SAT critical reading scores over 700: 5%; SAT math scores over 700: 4%; ACT scores over 30: 8%.

Faculty *Total:* 151, 75% full-time, 77% with terminal degrees. *Student/faculty ratio:* 11:1.

Academics *Calendar:* 4-1-4. *Degree:* bachelor's. *Special study options:* academic remediation for entering students, accelerated degree program, advanced placement credit, double majors, honors programs, independent study, internships, off-campus study, part-time degree program, services for LD students, student-designed majors, study abroad, summer session for credit. *ROTC:* Army (b), Air Force (c). *Unusual degree programs:* 3-2 engineering with Columbia University in New York City; Case Western Reserve University in Ohio, Washington University in St. Louis.

Computers on Campus 450 computers/terminals and 2,000 ports are available on campus for general student use. Students can access the following: campus intranet, computer help desk, free student e-mail accounts, online (class) grades, online (class) registration, online (class) schedules. Campus-wide network is available. 100% of college-owned or -operated housing units are wired for high-speed Internet access. Wireless service is available via entire campus.

Student Life *Housing:* on-campus residence required through senior year. *Options:* coed, men-only, women-only, disabled students. Campus housing is university owned. Freshman campus housing is guaranteed. *Activities and organizations:* drama/theater group, student-run newspaper, radio station, choral group, Student Government Association, Student Activities Board, Black Student Union, The Newman Club, W&J American Mock Trial Association, national fraternities, national sororities. *Campus security:* 24-hour emergency response devices and patrols, late-night transport/escort service, controlled dormitory access, security cameras monitored 24/7 throughout campus, card access to buildings. *Student services:* health clinic, personal/psychological counseling, women's center.

Athletics Member NCAA. All Division III. *Intercollegiate sports:* baseball M, basketball M/W, cheerleading M(c)/W(c), cross-country running M/W, equestrian sports M(c)/W(c), fencing M(c)/W(c), field hockey W, football M, golf M/W, ice hockey M(c), lacrosse M/W, rugby M(c)/W(c), soccer M/W, softball W, swimming and diving M/W, tennis M/W, track and field M/W, ultimate Frisbee M(c)/W(c), volleyball M(c)/W, water polo M/W, wrestling M. *Intramural sports:* basketball M/W, bowling M/W, racquetball M/W, soccer M/W, softball M/W, squash M/W, table tennis M/W, tennis M/W, ultimate Frisbee M/W, volleyball M/W, water polo M/W.

Costs (2012–13) *Comprehensive fee:* $48,270 includes full-time tuition ($37,850), mandatory fees ($460), and room and board ($9960). Full-time tuition and fees according to reciprocity agreements. Part-time tuition: $950 per credit hour. Part-time tuition and fees vary according to course load. *College room only:* $5970. Room and board charges vary according to board plan and housing facility. *Payment plans:* installment, deferred payment. *Waivers:* employees or children of employees.

Financial Aid Of all full-time matriculated undergraduates who enrolled in 2012, 1,174 applied for aid, 1,071 were judged to have need, 191 had their need fully met. 608 Federal Work-Study jobs (averaging $1700). 200 state and other part-time jobs (averaging $800). In 2012, 294 non-need-based awards were made. *Average percent of need met:* 76%. *Average financial aid package:* $27,800. *Average need-based loan:* $4553. *Average need-based gift aid:* $11,206. *Average non-need-based aid:* $13,238.

Applying *Options:* electronic application, early admission, early decision, early action, deferred entrance. *Application fee:* $25. *Required:* essay or personal statement, high school transcript, 1 letter of recommendation. *Required for some:* interview. *Recommended:* interview. *Application deadlines:* 3/1 (freshmen), rolling (transfers), 1/15 (early action). *Early decision deadline:* 12/1. *Notification:* 3/15 (freshmen), 12/15 (early decision), 2/15 (early action).

Freshman Application Contact Mr. Alton E. Newell, Vice President for Enrollment, Washington & Jefferson College, 60 South Lincoln Street, Washington, PA 15301. *Phone:* 724-223-6025. *Toll-free phone:* 888-WANDJAY. *Fax:* 724-223-6534. *E-mail:* admission@washjeff.edu. *Website:* http://www.washjeff.edu/.

Waynesburg University
Waynesburg, Pennsylvania

- **Independent** comprehensive, founded 1849, affiliated with Presbyterian Church (U.S.A.)
- **Small-town** 30-acre campus with easy access to Pittsburgh
- **Coed** 1,630 undergraduate students, 90% full-time, 61% women, 39% men
- **Moderately difficult** entrance level, 76% of applicants were admitted

Undergraduates 1,464 full-time, 166 part-time. Students come from 33 states and territories; 4 other countries; 18% are from out of state; 4% Black or African American, non-Hispanic/Latino; 1% Hispanic/Latino; 0.5% Asian, non-Hispanic/Latino; 0.5% American Indian or Alaska Native, non-Hispanic/Latino; 0.2% Two or more races, non-Hispanic/Latino; 1% Race/ethnicity unknown; 0.2% international; 3% transferred in; 64% live on campus. *Retention:* 83% of full-time freshmen returned.

Freshmen *Admission:* 1,827 applied, 1,396 admitted, 352 enrolled. *Average high school GPA:* 3.53.

Faculty *Total:* 278, 27% full-time, 50% with terminal degrees. *Student/faculty ratio:* 14:1.

Academics *Calendar:* semesters. *Degrees:* bachelor's, master's, and doctoral. *Special study options:* accelerated degree program, adult/continuing education programs, advanced placement credit, distance learning, double majors, honors programs, independent study, internships, part-time degree program, services for LD students, study abroad, summer session for credit. *ROTC:* Army (c). *Unusual degree programs:* 3-2 engineering with Washington University in St. Louis, Pennsylvania State University—University Park Campus.

Computers on Campus 150 computers/terminals are available on campus for general student use. Students can access the following: campus intranet, computer help desk, free student e-mail accounts, online (class) grades, online (class) registration, online (class) schedules. Campuswide network is available. 100% of college-owned or -operated housing units are wired for high-speed Internet access. Wireless service is available via classrooms, computer labs, libraries.

Student Life *Housing:* on-campus residence required through junior year. *Options:* men-only, women-only. Campus housing is university owned. Freshman campus housing is guaranteed. *Activities and organizations:* drama/theater group, student-run newspaper, radio and television station, choral group, marching band, Student Senate, Student Activities Board, Student Nurses Association, Christian Fellowship. *Campus security:* 24-hour emergency response devices and patrols, late-night transport/escort service, controlled dormitory access. *Student services:* health clinic, personal/psychological counseling.

Athletics Member NCAA. All Division III. *Intercollegiate sports:* baseball M, basketball M/W, cross-country running M/W, football M, golf M/W, lacrosse W, soccer M/W, softball W, tennis M/W, track and field M/W, volleyball W, wrestling M. *Intramural sports:* basketball M/W, bowling M/W, racquetball M/W, softball M/W, table tennis M/W, volleyball M/W.

Standardized Tests *Required:* SAT or ACT (for admission).

Costs (2012–13) *Comprehensive fee:* $28,060 includes full-time tuition ($19,450), mandatory fees ($360), and room and board ($8250). Full-time tuition and fees vary according to class time. Part-time tuition: $820 per credit hour. Part-time tuition and fees vary according to class time, course load, and location. *Required fees:* $16 per credit hour part-time. *College room only:* $4170. Room and board charges vary according to board plan. *Payment plan:* installment. *Waivers:* employees or children of employees.

Financial Aid Of all full-time matriculated undergraduates who enrolled in 2012, 1,360 applied for aid, 1,223 were judged to have need, 325 had their need fully met. 300 Federal Work-Study jobs (averaging $1200). In 2012, 160 non-need-based awards were made. *Average percent of need met:* 75%. *Average financial aid package:* $15,052. *Average need-based loan:* $4623. *Average need-based gift aid:* $10,937. *Average non-need-based aid:* $8250. *Average indebtedness upon graduation:* $29,000.

Applying *Options:* electronic application, early admission. *Application fee:* $20. *Required:* high school transcript, minimum 2.8 GPA. *Required for some:* essay or personal statement, 2 letters of recommendation. *Recommended:* minimum 3.0 GPA, interview. *Application deadlines:* rolling (freshmen), rolling (transfers). *Notification:* continuous (freshmen), continuous (transfers).

Freshman Application Contact Ms. Robin L. King, Senior Vice President for Enrollment and Marketing, Waynesburg University, 51 West College Street, Waynesburg, PA 15370. *Phone:* 724-852-3333. *Toll-free phone:* 800-225-7393. *Fax:* 724-627-8124. *E-mail:* admissions@waynesburg.edu. *Website:* http://www.waynesburg.edu/.

West Chester University of Pennsylvania

West Chester, Pennsylvania

- **State-supported** comprehensive, founded 1871, part of Pennsylvania State System of Higher Education
- **Suburban** 409-acre campus with easy access to Philadelphia
- **Endowment** $16.6 million
- **Coed** 13,297 undergraduate students, 91% full-time, 59% women, 41% men
- **Moderately difficult** entrance level, 50% of applicants were admitted

Undergraduates 12,133 full-time, 1,164 part-time. Students come from 28 states and territories; 66 other countries; 12% are from out of state; 9% Black or African American, non-Hispanic/Latino; 5% Hispanic/Latino; 2% Asian, non-Hispanic/Latino; 0.1% Native Hawaiian or other Pacific Islander, non-Hispanic/Latino; 0.1% American Indian or Alaska Native, non-Hispanic/Latino; 2% Two or more races, non-Hispanic/Latino; 0.6% Race/ethnicity unknown; 0.4% international; 10% transferred in; 40% live on campus. *Retention:* 85% of full-time freshmen returned.

Freshmen *Admission:* 14,356 applied, 7,161 admitted, 2,334 enrolled. *Average high school GPA:* 3.52. *Test scores:* SAT critical reading scores over 500: 72%; SAT math scores over 500: 80%; SAT writing scores over 500: 70%; SAT critical reading scores over 600: 18%; SAT math scores over 600: 22%; SAT writing scores over 600: 16%; SAT critical reading scores over 700: 1%; SAT math scores over 700: 1%; SAT writing scores over 700: 1%.

Faculty *Total:* 890, 68% full-time, 66% with terminal degrees. *Student/faculty ratio:* 18:1.

Academics *Calendar:* semesters. *Degrees:* bachelor's, master's, post-master's, and postbachelor's certificates. *Special study options:* academic remediation for entering students, accelerated degree program, adult/continuing education programs, advanced placement credit, distance learning, double majors, freshman honors college, honors programs, independent study, internships, off-campus study, part-time degree program, services for LD students, student-designed majors, study abroad, summer session for credit. *ROTC:* Army (b), Air Force (c). *Unusual degree programs:* 3-2 engineering with Pennsylvania State University, Philadelphia University.

Computers on Campus 1,900 computers/terminals are available on campus for general student use. Students can access the following: campus intranet, computer help desk, free student e-mail accounts, online (class) grades, online (class) registration, online (class) schedules. Campuswide network is available. 100% of college-owned or -operated housing units are wired for high-speed Internet access. Wireless service is available via classrooms, computer centers, computer labs, learning centers, libraries, student centers.

Student Life *Housing options:* coed, disabled students. Campus housing is university owned and is provided by a third party. Freshman applicants given priority for college housing. *Activities and organizations:* drama/theater group, student-run newspaper, radio and television station, choral group, marching band, Student Government Association, Residence Hall Association, Inter-Greek Council, Sports Club Council, Campus Crusade for Christ, national fraternities, national sororities. *Campus security:* 24-hour emergency response devices and patrols, late-night transport/escort service, controlled dormitory access, officers are on site 24/7, 365. Camera systems in campus residence halls, recreational and classroom facilities and outdoor areas. *Student services:* health clinic, personal/psychological counseling, women's center, legal services.

Athletics Member NCAA. All Division II. *Intercollegiate sports:* baseball M(s), basketball M(s)/W(s), bowling M(c)/W(c), cheerleading W, equestrian sports M(c)/W(c), fencing M(c)/W(c), field hockey W(s), football M(s), golf M(s)/W(s), gymnastics W(s), ice hockey M(c)/W(c), lacrosse M(c)/W(s), rugby M(c)/W(s), skiing (downhill) M(c)/W(c), soccer M(s)/W(s), softball W(s), swimming and diving M(s)/W(s), tennis M(s)/W(s), track and field M(s)/W(s), volleyball M(c)/W(s), water polo W(c), wrestling M(c). *Intramural sports:* badminton M/W, basketball M/W, football M/W, racquetball M/W, rock climbing M/W, soccer M/W, softball M/W, squash M/W, tennis M/W, volleyball M/W.

Standardized Tests *Required:* SAT or ACT (for admission).

Costs (2012–13) *Tuition:* state resident $6428 full-time, $268 per credit hour part-time; nonresident $16,070 full-time, $670 per credit hour part-time. Full-time tuition and fees vary according to course load. Part-time tuition and fees vary according to course load. *Required fees:* $2192 full-time, $80 per credit hour part-time, $11 per credit hour part-time. *Room and board:* $6786; room only: $4848. Room and board charges vary according to board plan and housing facility. *Payment plan:* installment. *Waivers:* senior citizens and employees or children of employees.

Financial Aid Of all full-time matriculated undergraduates who enrolled in 2012, 9,473 applied for aid, 7,458 were judged to have need, 615 had their need fully met. In 2012, 143 non-need-based awards were made. *Average per-*

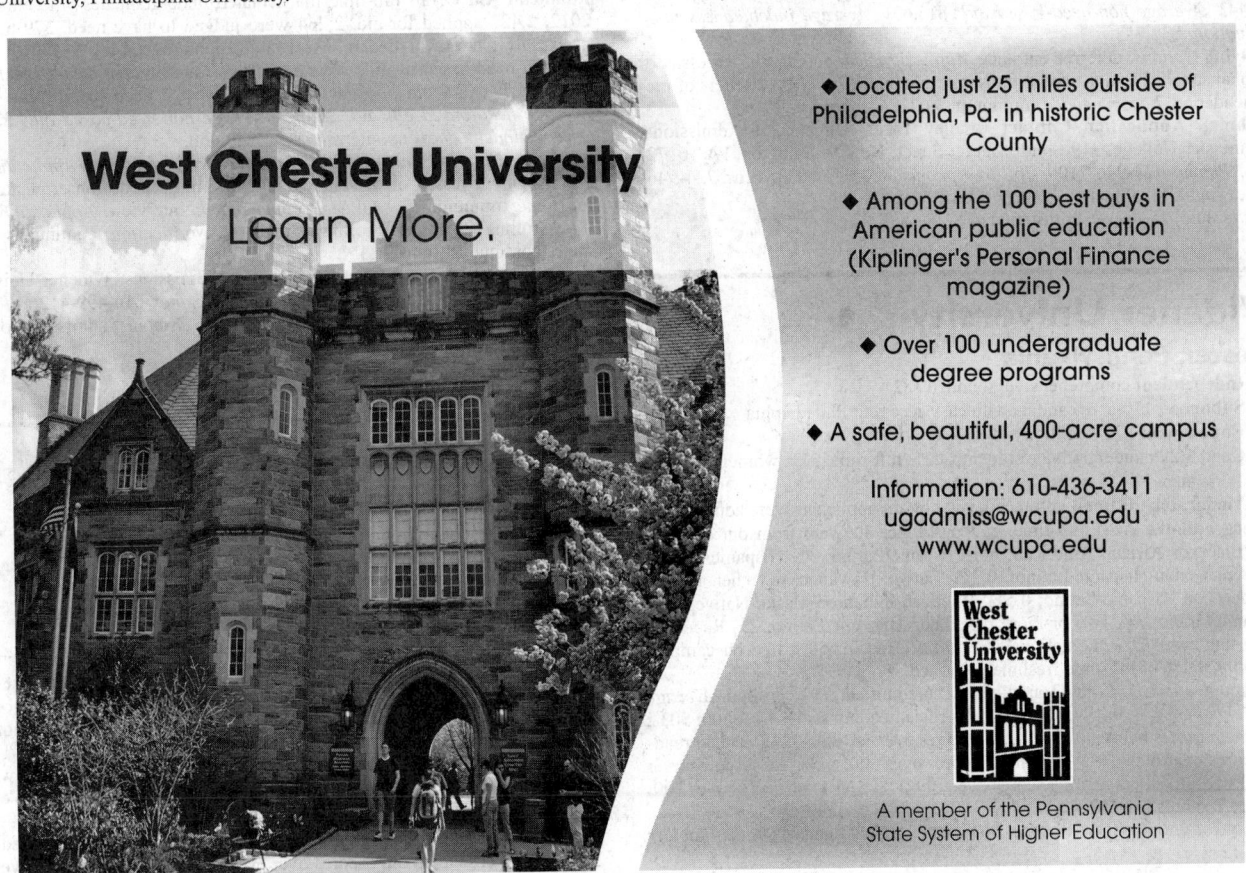

cent of need met: 48%. *Average financial aid package:* $7235. *Average need-based loan:* $4183. *Average need-based gift aid:* $5300. *Average non-need-based aid:* $3941. *Average indebtedness upon graduation:* $30,345.

Applying *Options:* electronic application, deferred entrance. *Application fee:* $45. *Required:* essay or personal statement, high school transcript, SAT or ACT. *Required for some:* interview. *Recommended:* minimum 3.0 GPA. *Application deadlines:* rolling (freshmen), rolling (transfers). *Notification:* continuous (freshmen), continuous (transfers).

Freshman Application Contact West Chester University of Pennsylvania, University Avenue and High Street, West Chester, PA 19383. *Phone:* 610-436-3414. *Toll-free phone:* 877-315-2165.
Website: http://www.wcupa.edu/.

See previous page for display ad and page 1638 for the College Close-Up.

Westminster College
New Wilmington, Pennsylvania

- **Independent** comprehensive, founded 1852, affiliated with Presbyterian Church (U.S.A.)
- **Small-town** 350-acre campus with easy access to Pittsburgh
- **Coed**
- **Moderately difficult** entrance level

Faculty *Student/faculty ratio:* 12:1.
Academics *Calendar:* semesters. *Degrees:* bachelor's and master's.
Student Life *Campus security:* 24-hour patrols, late-night transport/escort service.
Athletics Member NCAA. All Division III.
Standardized Tests *Required:* SAT or ACT (for admission).
Costs (2012–13) *Comprehensive fee:* $40,980 includes full-time tuition ($30,320), mandatory fees ($1090), and room and board ($9570). Part-time tuition: $970 per credit hour. *Room and board:* Room and board charges vary according to board plan and housing facility.
Financial Aid *Of all full-time matriculated undergraduates who enrolled in 2011,* 1,238 applied for aid, 1,150 were judged to have need, 194 had their need fully met. 392 Federal Work-Study jobs (averaging $1699). 68 state and other part-time jobs (averaging $1449). *In 2011,* 241 non-need-based awards were made. *Average percent of need met:* 80. *Average financial aid package:* $25,130. *Average need-based loan:* $4513. *Average need-based gift aid:* $20,443. *Average non-need-based aid:* $15,671. *Average indebtedness upon graduation:* $32,753.
Applying *Options:* deferred entrance. *Application fee:* $35. *Required:* essay or personal statement, high school transcript, minimum 2.0 GPA, 2 letters of recommendation. *Recommended:* minimum 3.0 GPA, interview.
Freshman Application Contact Bradley Tokar, Director of Admissions, Westminster College, 319 South Market Street, New Wilmington, PA 16172-0001. *Phone:* 724-946-7100. *Toll-free phone:* 800-942-8033. *Fax:* 724-946-7171. *E-mail:* tokarbp@westminster.edu.
Website: http://www.westminster.edu/.

Widener University
Chester, Pennsylvania

- **Independent** comprehensive, founded 1821
- **Suburban** 110-acre campus with easy access to Philadelphia
- **Endowment** $72.8 million
- **Coed** 3,298 undergraduate students, 83% full-time, 57% women, 43% men
- **Moderately difficult** entrance level, 66% of applicants were admitted

Undergraduates 2,741 full-time, 557 part-time. 40% are from out of state; 16% Black or African American, non-Hispanic/Latino; 3% Hispanic/Latino; 3% Asian, non-Hispanic/Latino; 0.2% Native Hawaiian or other Pacific Islander, non-Hispanic/Latino; 0.5% American Indian or Alaska Native, non-Hispanic/Latino; 3% Two or more races, non-Hispanic/Latino; 2% Race/ethnicity unknown; 5% international; 5% transferred in; 50% live on campus. *Retention:* 71% of full-time freshmen returned.
Freshmen *Admission:* 4,863 applied, 3,186 admitted, 717 enrolled. *Average high school GPA:* 3.36. *Test scores:* SAT critical reading scores over 500: 50%; SAT math scores over 500: 57%; ACT scores over 18: 88%; SAT critical reading scores over 600: 10%; SAT math scores over 600: 21%; ACT scores over 24: 29%; SAT critical reading scores over 700: 1%; SAT math scores over 700: 2%; ACT scores over 30: 4%.
Faculty *Total:* 656, 48% full-time, 66% with terminal degrees. *Student/faculty ratio:* 12:1.

Academics *Calendar:* semesters. *Degrees:* associate, bachelor's, master's, and doctoral. *Special study options:* academic remediation for entering students, accelerated degree program, adult/continuing education programs, advanced placement credit, cooperative education, distance learning, double majors, English as a second language, honors programs, independent study, internships, off-campus study, part-time degree program, services for LD students, student-designed majors, study abroad, summer session for credit. *ROTC:* Army (b), Navy (c), Air Force (c). *Unusual degree programs:* 3-2 business administration; engineering; social work; physical therapy, education.
Computers on Campus 710 computers/terminals are available on campus for general student use. Students can access the following: campus intranet, computer help desk, free student e-mail accounts, online (class) grades, online (class) registration, online (class) schedules. Campuswide network is available. 100% of college-owned or -operated housing units are wired for high-speed Internet access. Wireless service is available via classrooms, computer centers, computer labs, dorm rooms, learning centers, libraries, student centers.
Student Life *Housing:* on-campus residence required through sophomore year. *Options:* coed, men-only, women-only, cooperative. Campus housing is university owned. Freshman campus housing is guaranteed. *Activities and organizations:* drama/theater group, student-run newspaper, radio and television station, choral group, WDNR Radio, Black Student Union, volunteer services, rugby club, Theatre Widener, national fraternities, national sororities. *Campus security:* 24-hour emergency response devices and patrols, late-night transport/escort service, controlled dormitory access, blue light emergency phones located throughout campus. *Student services:* health clinic, personal/psychological counseling.
Athletics Member NCAA. All Division III. *Intercollegiate sports:* baseball M, basketball M/W, cheerleading W, cross-country running M/W, field hockey W, football M, golf M, lacrosse M/W, soccer M/W, softball W, swimming and diving M/W, track and field M/W, volleyball W. *Intramural sports:* crew M, ice hockey M(c), rock climbing M(c)/W(c), rugby M(c), skiing (downhill) M(c)/W(c), soccer M, volleyball M(c).
Standardized Tests *Required:* SAT or ACT (for admission).
Costs (2012–13) *Comprehensive fee:* $48,630 includes full-time tuition ($35,764), mandatory fees ($618), and room and board ($12,248). Full-time tuition and fees vary according to class time, course load, and program. Part-time tuition: $1190 per credit hour. *College room only:* $6300. Room and board charges vary according to board plan and housing facility. *Payment plan:* installment. *Waivers:* senior citizens and employees or children of employees.
Financial Aid *Of all full-time matriculated undergraduates who enrolled in 2012,* 2,427 applied for aid, 2,264 were judged to have need, 379 had their need fully met. 1,617 Federal Work-Study jobs (averaging $1480). In 2012, 313 non-need-based awards were made. *Average percent of need met:* 73%. *Average financial aid package:* $26,380. *Average need-based loan:* $4640. *Average need-based gift aid:* $8490. *Average non-need-based aid:* $15,500. *Average indebtedness upon graduation:* $40,460.
Applying *Options:* electronic application, deferred entrance. *Application fee:* $35. *Required:* essay or personal statement, high school transcript. *Required for some:* minimum 2.9 GPA. *Recommended:* interview. *Application deadlines:* rolling (freshmen), rolling (transfers). *Notification:* continuous (freshmen), continuous (transfers).
Freshman Application Contact Office of Admissions, Widener University, One University Place, Chester, PA 19013. *Phone:* 610-499-4126. *Toll-free phone:* 888-WIDENER. *Fax:* 610-499-4676. *E-mail:* admissions.office@widener.edu.
Website: http://www.widener.edu/.

Wilkes University
Wilkes-Barre, Pennsylvania

- **Independent** comprehensive, founded 1933
- **Urban** 25-acre campus
- **Endowment** $35.7 million
- **Coed** 2,302 undergraduate students, 91% full-time, 49% women, 51% men
- **Moderately difficult** entrance level, 76% of applicants were admitted

Undergraduates 2,095 full-time, 207 part-time. Students come from 18 states and territories; 10 other countries; 17% are from out of state; 4% Black or African American, non-Hispanic/Latino; 4% Hispanic/Latino; 3% Asian, non-Hispanic/Latino; 0.1% American Indian or Alaska Native, non-Hispanic/Latino; 3% Two or more races, non-Hispanic/Latino; 5% Race/ethnicity unknown; 5% international; 7% transferred in; 37% live on campus. *Retention:* 80% of full-time freshmen returned.
Freshmen *Admission:* 2,998 applied, 2,278 admitted, 596 enrolled. *Test scores:* SAT critical reading scores over 500: 61%; SAT math scores over 500:

70%; SAT writing scores over 500: 59%; SAT critical reading scores over 600: 14%; SAT math scores over 600: 25%; SAT writing scores over 600: 12%; SAT critical reading scores over 700: 1%; SAT math scores over 700: 2%; SAT writing scores over 700: 1%.

Faculty *Total:* 407, 39% full-time. *Student/faculty ratio:* 14:1.

Academics *Calendar:* semesters. *Degrees:* bachelor's, master's, and doctoral. *Special study options:* academic remediation for entering students, accelerated degree program, adult/continuing education programs, advanced placement credit, cooperative education, distance learning, double majors, English as a second language, external degree program, honors programs, independent study, internships, off-campus study, part-time degree program, services for LD students, student-designed majors, study abroad, summer session for credit. *ROTC:* Army (c), Air Force (b).

Computers on Campus 868 computers/terminals are available on campus for general student use. Students can access the following: campus intranet, computer help desk, free student e-mail accounts, online (class) grades, online (class) registration, online (class) schedules. Campuswide network is available. Wireless service is available via libraries, student centers.

Student Life *Housing:* on-campus residence required through sophomore year. *Options:* coed, men-only, women-only. Campus housing is university owned. Freshman campus housing is guaranteed. *Activities and organizations:* drama/theater group, student-run newspaper, radio and television station, choral group. *Campus security:* 24-hour emergency response devices and patrols, late-night transport/escort service, controlled dormitory access. *Student services:* health clinic, personal/psychological counseling.

Athletics Member NCAA. All Division III. *Intercollegiate sports:* baseball M, basketball M/W, cross-country running M/W, field hockey W, football M, golf M, lacrosse W, soccer M/W, softball W, tennis M/W, volleyball W, wrestling M. *Intramural sports:* basketball M/W, football M, racquetball M/W, volleyball M/W, weight lifting M/W.

Standardized Tests *Required:* SAT or ACT (for admission).

Costs (2012–13) *Comprehensive fee:* $41,360 includes full-time tuition ($27,908), mandatory fees ($1418), and room and board ($12,034). Part-time tuition: $775 per credit hour. *Required fees:* $64 per credit hour part-time. *College room only:* $7228. Room and board charges vary according to board plan and housing facility. *Payment plans:* installment, deferred payment. *Waivers:* employees or children of employees.

Financial Aid Of all full-time matriculated undergraduates who enrolled in 2012, 1,829 applied for aid, 1,700 were judged to have need, 187 had their need fully met. In 2012, 226 non-need-based awards were made. *Average percent of need met:* 69%. *Average financial aid package:* $21,066. *Average need-*

based loan: $4306. *Average need-based gift aid:* $17,400. *Average non-need-based aid:* $10,670. *Average indebtedness upon graduation:* $38,442.

Applying *Options:* electronic application, early admission, deferred entrance. *Application fee:* $40. *Required:* high school transcript. *Required for some:* 2 letters of recommendation. *Recommended:* interview. *Application deadlines:* rolling (freshmen), rolling (transfers). *Notification:* 8/30 (freshmen), continuous until 8/30 (transfers).

Freshman Application Contact Ms. Melanie Wade, Vice President of Enrollment Services, Wilkes University, 84 West South Street, Wilkes-Barre, PA 18766. *Phone:* 570-408-4400. *Toll-free phone:* 800-945-5378 Ext. 4400. *Fax:* 570-408-4904. *E-mail:* admissions@wilkes.edu. *Website:* http://www.wilkes.edu/.

See below for display ad and page 1650 for the College Close-Up.

Wilson College

Chambersburg, Pennsylvania

- **Independent** comprehensive, founded 1869, affiliated with Presbyterian Church (U.S.A.)
- **Small-town** 300-acre campus
- **Endowment** $60.5 million
- **Coed, primarily women**
- **Moderately difficult** entrance level

Faculty *Student/faculty ratio:* 10:1.

Academics *Calendar:* 4-1-4. *Degrees:* associate, bachelor's, and master's.

Student Life *Campus security:* 24-hour emergency response devices and patrols, late-night transport/escort service, controlled dormitory access.

Athletics Member NCAA. All Division III.

Standardized Tests *Required for some:* SAT or ACT (for admission), SAT/ACT optional for students with high school GPA of 3.0 and specified college prep curriculum from regionally accredited schools; TOEFL/IELTS/STEP for international students.

Financial Aid *Of all full-time matriculated undergraduates who enrolled in 2011,* 316 applied for aid, 297 were judged to have need, 38 had their need fully met. 23 Federal Work-Study jobs (averaging $2000). 121 state and other part-time jobs (averaging $2000). *In 2011,* 39 non-need-based awards were made. *Average percent of need met:* 77. *Average financial aid package:* $23,609. *Average need-based loan:* $4954. *Average need-based gift aid:*

$19,235. *Average non-need-based aid:* $13,341. *Average indebtedness upon graduation:* $33,862.

Applying *Options:* electronic application, early admission, deferred entrance. *Required:* essay or personal statement, high school transcript, 1 letter of recommendation, college preparatory program that includes 4 units of English, 4 units of History/Civics, 3 units of Mathematics (preferably Algebra I, II or Geometry), 2 units of same Foreign Language, and 2 units of Natural Sciences with lab. *Recommended:* minimum 2.8 GPA, interview.

Freshman Application Contact Ms. Nancy Myers, Admissions Administrator, Wilson College, 1015 Philadelphia Avenue, Chambersburg, PA 17201. *Phone:* 717-262-2002. *Toll-free phone:* 800-421-8402. *Fax:* 717-262-2546. *E-mail:* admissions@wilson.edu. *Website:* http://www.wilson.edu/.

Yeshiva Beth Moshe

Scranton, Pennsylvania

Director of Admissions Dean, Yeshiva Beth Moshe, 930 Hickory Street, PO Box 1141, Scranton, PA 18505-2124. *Phone:* 717-346-1747.

York College of Pennsylvania

York, Pennsylvania

- **Independent** comprehensive, founded 1787
- **Suburban** 190-acre campus with easy access to Baltimore
- **Endowment** $61.7 million
- **Coed** 5,182 undergraduate students, 89% full-time, 56% women, 44% men
- **Moderately difficult** entrance level, 74% of applicants were admitted

Undergraduates 4,595 full-time, 587 part-time. Students come from 31 states and territories; 5 other countries; 40% are from out of state; 5% Black or African American, non-Hispanic/Latino; 5% Hispanic/Latino; 1% Asian, non-Hispanic/Latino; 0.1% Native Hawaiian or other Pacific Islander, non-Hispanic/Latino; 0.1% American Indian or Alaska Native, non-Hispanic/Latino; 2% Two or more races, non-Hispanic/Latino; 5% Race/ethnicity unknown; 0.2% international; 5% transferred in; 55% live on campus. *Retention:* 73% of full-time freshmen returned.

Freshmen *Admission:* 9,283 applied, 6,860 admitted, 1,142 enrolled. *Average high school GPA:* 3.49. *Test scores:* SAT critical reading scores over 500: 72%; SAT math scores over 500: 81%; SAT writing scores over 500: 62%; ACT scores over 18: 94%; SAT critical reading scores over 600: 16%; SAT math scores over 600: 26%; SAT writing scores over 600: 11%; ACT scores over 24: 32%; SAT critical reading scores over 700: 1%; SAT math scores over 700: 1%; SAT writing scores over 700: 1%; ACT scores over 30: 1%.

Faculty *Total:* 550, 34% full-time, 38% with terminal degrees. *Student/faculty ratio:* 16:1.

Academics *Calendar:* semesters. *Degrees:* bachelor's, master's, doctoral, and post-master's certificates. *Special study options:* advanced placement credit, cooperative education, double majors, independent study, internships, part-time degree program, services for LD students, student-designed majors, study abroad, summer session for credit. *ROTC:* Army (c). *Unusual degree programs:* 3-2 business administration.

Computers on Campus 1,054 computers/terminals are available on campus for general student use. Students can access the following: campus intranet, computer help desk, free student e-mail accounts, online (class) grades, online (class) registration, online (class) schedules. Campuswide network is available. 100% of college-owned or -operated housing units are wired for high-speed Internet access. Wireless service is available via entire campus.

Student Life *Housing:* on-campus residence required through senior year. *Options:* coed, disabled students. Campus housing is university owned. Freshman campus housing is guaranteed. *Activities and organizations:* drama/theater group, student-run newspaper, radio station, choral group, Pre-Med Society, Ski and Outdoor Club, Habitat for Humanity, Students in Free Enterprise (SIFE), WVYC Radio Station, national fraternities, national sororities. *Campus security:* 24-hour emergency response devices and patrols, student patrols, late-night transport/escort service, controlled dormitory access. *Student services:* health clinic, personal/psychological counseling.

Athletics Member NCAA. All Division III. *Intercollegiate sports:* baseball M, basketball M/W, cheerleading M/W, cross-country running M/W, field hockey W, golf M, lacrosse M/W, soccer M/W, softball W, swimming and diving M/W, tennis M/W, track and field M/W, volleyball W, wrestling M. *Intramural sports:* basketball M/W, cheerleading W(c), equestrian sports M(c)/W(c), football M/W, lacrosse M(c)/W(c), racquetball M/W, rugby M(c)/W(c), soccer M/

W, softball W, swimming and diving M/W, table tennis M/W, tennis M/W, track and field M/W, ultimate Frisbee M(c)/W(c), volleyball M.

Standardized Tests *Required:* SAT or ACT (for admission).

Costs (2013–14) *Comprehensive fee:* $26,590 includes full-time tuition ($15,350), mandatory fees ($1660), and room and board ($9580). Full-time tuition and fees vary according to program. Part-time tuition: $475 per credit. *Required fees:* $360 per term part-time. *College room only:* $5380. Room and board charges vary according to board plan and housing facility. *Payment plan:* installment. *Waivers:* employees or children of employees.

Financial Aid Of all full-time matriculated undergraduates who enrolled in 2012, 3,921 applied for aid, 3,125 were judged to have need, 710 had their need fully met. 311 Federal Work-Study jobs (averaging $1989). 10 state and other part-time jobs (averaging $1980). In 2012, 949 non-need-based awards were made. *Average percent of need met:* 65%. *Average financial aid package:* $12,134. *Average need-based loan:* $6658. *Average need-based gift aid:* $5098. *Average non-need-based aid:* $3593. *Average indebtedness upon graduation:* $35,297.

Applying *Options:* electronic application, deferred entrance. *Required:* high school transcript, minimum 2.0 GPA. *Required for some:* interview. *Recommended:* essay or personal statement, 1 letter of recommendation. *Application deadlines:* 8/15 (freshmen), 8/15 (out-of-state freshmen), rolling (transfers). *Notification:* continuous (freshmen), continuous (out-of-state freshmen), continuous (transfers).

Freshman Application Contact York College of Pennsylvania, York, PA 17405-7199. *Phone:* 717-849-1600. *Toll-free phone:* 800-455-8018. *Website:* http://www.ycp.edu/.

RHODE ISLAND

Brown University

Providence, Rhode Island

- **Independent** university, founded 1764
- **Urban** 140-acre campus with easy access to Boston
- **Endowment** $2.5 billion
- **Coed** 6,435 undergraduate students, 95% full-time, 53% women, 47% men
- **Most difficult** entrance level, 10% of applicants were admitted

Undergraduates 6,117 full-time, 318 part-time. Students come from 52 states and territories; 95% are from out of state; 6% Black or African American, non-Hispanic/Latino; 10% Hispanic/Latino; 12% Asian, non-Hispanic/Latino; 0.1% Native Hawaiian or other Pacific Islander, non-Hispanic/Latino; 0.3% American Indian or Alaska Native, non-Hispanic/Latino; 5% Two or more races, non-Hispanic/Latino; 10% Race/ethnicity unknown; 12% international. *Retention:* 97% of full-time freshmen returned.

Freshmen *Admission:* 28,742 applied, 2,759 admitted, 1,536 enrolled. *Test scores:* SAT critical reading scores over 500: 100%; SAT math scores over 500: 100%; SAT writing scores over 500: 99%; ACT scores over 18: 100%; SAT critical reading scores over 600: 91%; SAT math scores over 600: 93%; SAT writing scores over 600: 93%; ACT scores over 24: 98%; SAT critical reading scores over 700: 62%; SAT math scores over 700: 65%; SAT writing scores over 700: 66%; ACT scores over 30: 72%.

Faculty *Total:* 977, 81% full-time, 88% with terminal degrees. *Student/faculty ratio:* 9:1.

Academics *Calendar:* semesters. *Degrees:* bachelor's, master's, and doctoral. *Special study options:* adult/continuing education programs, advanced placement credit, double majors, honors programs, independent study, internships, off-campus study, services for LD students, student-designed majors, study abroad, summer session for credit. *ROTC:* Army (c).

Computers on Campus Students can access the following: campus intranet, computer help desk, free student e-mail accounts, online (class) grades, online (class) registration, online (class) schedules. Campuswide network is available. 100% of college-owned or -operated housing units are wired for high-speed Internet access. Wireless service is available via entire campus.

Student Life *Housing:* on-campus residence required through junior year. *Options:* coed, women-only, cooperative, disabled students. Campus housing is university owned. Freshman campus housing is guaranteed. *Activities and organizations:* drama/theater group, student-run newspaper, radio and television station, choral group, marching band, national fraternities, national sororities. *Campus security:* 24-hour emergency response devices and patrols, late-night transport/escort service, controlled dormitory access. *Student services:* health clinic, personal/psychological counseling, women's center.

Athletics Member NCAA. All Division I except football (Division I-AA). *Intercollegiate sports:* baseball M, basketball M/W, crew M/W, cross-country running M/W, equestrian sports W, fencing M/W, field hockey W, golf M/W, gymnastics W, ice hockey M/W, lacrosse M/W, rugby M(c)/W(c), sailing M(c)/W(c), skiing (downhill) M(c)/W, soccer M/W, softball W, squash M/W, swimming and diving M/W, tennis M/W, track and field M/W, volleyball M(c)/W, water polo M/W, wrestling M. *Intramural sports:* badminton M(c)/W(c), basketball M/W, cheerleading M/W, fencing M/W, field hockey W, football M, ice hockey M/W, lacrosse M/W, racquetball M(c)/W(c), rugby M/W, skiing (downhill) M/W, soccer M/W, softball M/W, squash M/W, swimming and diving M/W, table tennis M(c)/W(c), tennis M/W, ultimate Frisbee M(c)/W(c), volleyball M/W, water polo M/W.

Standardized Tests *Required:* SAT and SAT Subject Tests or ACT (for admission).

Costs (2012–13) *Comprehensive fee:* $55,016 includes full-time tuition ($42,808), mandatory fees ($950), and room and board ($11,258). *College room only:* $6974. Room and board charges vary according to board plan. *Payment plan:* installment. *Waivers:* employees or children of employees.

Financial Aid Of all full-time matriculated undergraduates who enrolled in 2012, 2,943 applied for aid, 2,710 were judged to have need, 2,710 had their need fully met. 1,544 Federal Work-Study jobs (averaging $2288). 367 state and other part-time jobs (averaging $2354). In 2012, 8 non-need-based awards were made. *Average percent of need met:* 100%. *Average financial aid package:* $39,526. *Average need-based loan:* $5579. *Average need-based gift aid:* $36,541. *Average non-need-based aid:* $9615. *Average indebtedness upon graduation:* $23,521. *Financial aid deadline:* 3/1.

Applying *Options:* electronic application, early decision, deferred entrance. *Application fee:* $75. *Required:* essay or personal statement, high school transcript, 2 letters of recommendation, Common application; Brown University supplement. *Recommended:* interview. *Application deadlines:* 1/1 (freshmen), 3/1 (transfers). *Early decision deadline:* 11/1. *Notification:* 4/1 (freshmen), 5/15 (transfers), 12/15 (early decision).

Freshman Application Contact Mr. James Miller, Dean of Admission, Brown University, Box 1876, Providence, RI 02912. *Phone:* 401-863-2378. *Fax:* 401-863-9300. *E-mail:* admission_undergraduate@brown.edu. *Website:* http://www.brown.edu/.

Bryant University

Smithfield, Rhode Island

- **Independent** comprehensive, founded 1863
- **Suburban** 428-acre campus with easy access to Boston, Providence
- **Endowment** $141.8 million
- **Coed** 3,180 undergraduate students, 97% full-time, 42% women, 58% men
- **Moderately difficult** entrance level, 62% of applicants were admitted

Undergraduates 3,078 full-time, 102 part-time. Students come from 31 states and territories; 65 other countries; 87% are from out of state; 4% Black or African American, non-Hispanic/Latino; 5% Hispanic/Latino; 3% Asian, non-Hispanic/Latino; 0.1% Native Hawaiian or other Pacific Islander, non-Hispanic/Latino; 0.5% American Indian or Alaska Native, non-Hispanic/Latino; 0.1% Two or more races, non-Hispanic/Latino; 4% Race/ethnicity unknown; 8% international; 3% transferred in; 81% live on campus. *Retention:* 88% of full-time freshmen returned.

Freshmen *Admission:* 5,997 applied, 3,718 admitted, 772 enrolled. *Average high school GPA:* 3.3. *Test scores:* SAT critical reading scores over 500: 81%; SAT math scores over 500: 91%; SAT writing scores over 500: 80%; ACT scores over 18: 98%; SAT critical reading scores over 600: 26%; SAT math scores over 600: 49%; SAT writing scores over 600: 28%; ACT scores over 24: 73%; SAT critical reading scores over 700: 4%; SAT math scores over 700: 7%; SAT writing scores over 700: 3%; ACT scores over 30: 7%.

Faculty *Total:* 308, 55% full-time, 54% with terminal degrees. *Student/faculty ratio:* 15:1.

Academics *Calendar:* semesters. *Degrees:* bachelor's and master's. *Special study options:* adult/continuing education programs, advanced placement credit, double majors, English as a second language, honors programs, independent study, internships, part-time degree program, services for LD students, study abroad, summer session for credit. *ROTC:* Army (b).

Computers on Campus 559 computers/terminals and 9,000 ports are available on campus for general student use. Students can access the following: campus intranet, computer help desk, free student e-mail accounts, online (class) grades, online (class) registration, online (class) schedules, e-mail, online library, wireless network, student Web hosts. Campuswide network is available. 100% of college-owned or -operated housing units are wired for high-speed Internet access. Wireless service is available via entire campus.

Student Life *Housing options:* coed, women-only, disabled students. Campus housing is university owned. Freshman campus housing is guaranteed. *Activities and organizations:* drama/theater group, student-run newspaper, radio and television station, choral group, Bryant Outdoor Activities Club, Student Programming Board, Rhythm and Pride Dance Team, WJMF Radio, Bryant Players (drama club), national fraternities, national sororities. *Campus security:* 24-hour emergency response devices and patrols, late-night transport/escort service, controlled dormitory access, 24 full-time staff; 20 patrol officers on foot, bike, golf cart, and car; Entry Control Station staffed 24/7 at only campus entry point. *Student services:* health clinic, personal/psychological counseling, women's center.

Athletics Member NCAA. All Division I except football (Division I-AA). *Intercollegiate sports:* baseball M(s), basketball M(s)/W(s), bowling M(c)/W(c), cheerleading W(c), crew W(c), cross-country running M(s)/W(s), field hockey W(s), golf M(s), ice hockey M(c), lacrosse M(s)/W(s), racquetball M(c)/W(c), rugby M(c)/W(c), soccer M(s)/W(s), softball W(s), squash M(c), swimming and diving M(s)/W(s), tennis M(s)/W(s), track and field M(s)/W(s), ultimate Frisbee M(c), volleyball M(c)/W(s), wrestling M(c). *Intramural sports:* basketball M/W, football M, soccer M, softball M/W, volleyball M/W.

Costs (2013–14) *Comprehensive fee:* $50,898 includes full-time tuition ($36,872), mandatory fees ($362), and room and board ($13,664). Part-time tuition: $807 per credit hour. Part-time tuition and fees vary according to course load. *College room only:* $8020. Room and board charges vary according to board plan and housing facility. *Payment plan:* installment. *Waivers:* employees or children of employees.

Financial Aid Of all full-time matriculated undergraduates who enrolled in 2012, 2,240 applied for aid, 2,003 were judged to have need, 1,002 had their need fully met. In 2012, 405 non-need-based awards were made. *Average percent of need met:* 53%. *Average financial aid package:* $22,549. *Average need-based loan:* $5044. *Average need-based gift aid:* $12,758. *Average non-need-based aid:* $12,781. *Average indebtedness upon graduation:* $44,580.

Applying *Options:* electronic application, early decision, early action, deferred entrance. *Application fee:* $50. *Required:* essay or personal statement, high school transcript, 1 letter of recommendation, senior year first-quarter grades; SAT Reasoning Test or ACT results. *Recommended:* minimum 3.3 GPA, 2 letters of recommendation, interview. *Application deadlines:* 2/15 (freshmen), 2/15 (out-of-state freshmen), rolling (transfers), 12/1 (early action). *Early decision deadline:* 11/15 (for plan 1), 1/15 (for plan 2). *Notification:* 3/21 (freshmen), 3/21 (out-of-state freshmen), continuous (transfers), 12/15 (early decision plan 1), 2/15 (early decision plan 2), 1/15 (early action).

Freshman Application Contact Ms. Michelle Cloutier, Executive Director of Admission, Bryant University, 1150 Douglas Pike, Smithfield, RI 02917. *Phone:* 401-232-6100. *Toll-free phone:* 800-622-7001. *Fax:* 401-232-6741. *E-mail:* admission@bryant.edu. *Website:* http://www.bryant.edu/.

Johnson & Wales University

Providence, Rhode Island

Freshman Application Contact Amy Podbelski, Dean of Undergraduate Admissions, Johnson & Wales University, 8 Abbott Park Place, Providence, RI 02903-3703. *Phone:* 401-598-2310. *Toll-free phone:* 800-342-5598. *Fax:* 401-598-2948. *E-mail:* pvd@admissions.jwu.edu. *Website:* http://www.jwu.edu/providence/.

See next page for display ad and page 1340 for the College Close-Up.

Mater Ecclesiae College

Greenville, Rhode Island

Freshman Application Contact Admissions, Mater Ecclesiae College, 60 Austin Avenue, Greenville, RI 02828. *Phone:* 401-949-2820. *E-mail:* info@mecollege.org. *Website:* http://www.mecollege.edu/.

New England Institute of Technology

East Greenwich, Rhode Island

- **Independent** 4-year, founded 1940
- **Suburban** 225-acre campus with easy access to Boston
- **Coed** 2,713 undergraduate students, 86% full-time, 28% women, 72% men
- **Noncompetitive** entrance level

Undergraduates 2,320 full-time, 393 part-time. Students come from 8 states and territories; 13 other countries; 5% Black or African American, non-Hispanic/Latino; 7% Hispanic/Latino; 2% Asian, non-Hispanic/Latino; 0.1% Native Hawaiian or other Pacific Islander, non-Hispanic/Latino; 0.6% American Indian or Alaska Native, non-Hispanic/Latino; 0.8% Two or more races, non-Hispanic/Latino; 11% Race/ethnicity unknown; 3% international.
Freshmen *Admission:* 444 enrolled.
Faculty *Total:* 294, 40% full-time, 11% with terminal degrees.
Academics *Calendar:* quarters. *Degrees:* associate, bachelor's, and master's. *Special study options:* academic remediation for entering students, accelerated degree program, adult/continuing education programs, advanced placement credit, cooperative education, distance learning, double majors, internships, part-time degree program, services for LD students, student-designed majors, summer session for credit.
Computers on Campus 1,000 computers/terminals are available on campus for general student use. Students can access the following: computer help desk, free student e-mail accounts, online (class) grades, online (class) registration, online (class) schedules. Campuswide network is available. Wireless service is available via entire campus.
Student Life *Housing:* college housing not available. *Activities and organizations:* Skills USA, Game Developers Network, Vet Tech, Student Occupational Therapy Association, Phi Theta Kappa (International Honor Society). *Campus security:* security personnel during open hours. *Student services:* personal/psychological counseling.
Costs (2013–14) *Tuition:* $20,870 full-time, $390 per credit hour part-time. Full-time tuition and fees vary according to degree level and program. Part-time tuition and fees vary according to degree level and program. No tuition increase for student's term of enrollment. *Required fees:* $1125 full-time. *Payment plans:* tuition prepayment, installment. *Waivers:* employees or children of employees.
Financial Aid Of all full-time matriculated undergraduates who enrolled in 2011, 250 Federal Work-Study jobs (averaging $2290).
Applying *Options:* electronic application, early admission, deferred entrance. *Application fee:* $25. *Required:* high school transcript, interview, basic skills testing, Ronald P. Carver reading test used for placement. Portfolios required for advanced standing. *Application deadlines:* rolling (freshmen), rolling (transfers).
Freshman Application Contact Mr. James Jessup, Director of Admissions, New England Institute of Technology, One New England Tech Boulevard, East Greenwich, RI 02818. *Phone:* 401-739-5000. *Toll-free phone:* 800-736-7744. *Fax:* 401-886-0868. *E-mail:* jjessup@neit.edu. *Website:* http://www.neit.edu/.

Providence College
Providence, Rhode Island

- **Independent Roman Catholic** comprehensive, founded 1917
- **Suburban** 105-acre campus with easy access to Boston
- **Endowment** $166.0 million
- **Coed** 3,810 undergraduate students, 100% full-time, 57% women, 43% men

Undergraduates 3,802 full-time, 8 part-time. Students come from 38 states and territories; 26 other countries; 88% are from out of state; 4% Black or African American, non-Hispanic/Latino; 5% Hispanic/Latino; 1% Asian, non-Hispanic/Latino; 0.2% Native Hawaiian or other Pacific Islander, non-Hispanic/Latino; 0.2% American Indian or Alaska Native, non-Hispanic/Latino; 1% Two or more races, non-Hispanic/Latino; 9% Race/ethnicity unknown; 2% international; 1% transferred in; 78% live on campus. *Retention:* 90% of full-time freshmen returned.
Freshmen *Admission:* 998 enrolled. *Average high school GPA:* 3.39. *Test scores:* SAT critical reading scores over 500: 85%; SAT math scores over 500: 86%; SAT writing scores over 500: 87%; ACT scores over 18: 99%; SAT critical reading scores over 600: 36%; SAT math scores over 600: 44%; SAT writing scores over 600: 45%; ACT scores over 24: 65%; SAT critical reading scores over 700: 6%; SAT math scores over 700: 7%; SAT writing scores over 700: 8%; ACT scores over 30: 7%.
Faculty *Total:* 395, 78% full-time, 85% with terminal degrees. *Student/faculty ratio:* 12:1.
Academics *Calendar:* semesters. *Degrees:* certificates, associate, bachelor's, and master's. *Special study options:* adult/continuing education programs, advanced placement credit, cooperative education, distance learning, double majors, honors programs, independent study, internships, part-time degree program, services for LD students, student-designed majors, study abroad, summer session for credit. *ROTC:* Army (b). *Unusual degree programs:* 3-2 engineering with Columbia University, Washington University in St. Louis.
Computers on Campus 390 computers/terminals and 5,000 ports are available on campus for general student use. Students can access the following:

campus intranet, computer help desk, free student e-mail accounts, online (class) grades, online (class) registration, online (class) schedules. Campuswide network is available. 100% of college-owned or -operated housing units are wired for high-speed Internet access. Wireless service is available via entire campus.

Student Life *Housing:* on-campus residence required through sophomore year. *Options:* coed, men-only, women-only, disabled students. Campus housing is university owned. Freshman campus housing is guaranteed. *Activities and organizations:* drama/theater group, student-run newspaper, radio and television station, choral group, Board of Multicultural Student Activities, Board of Programmers, Student Congress, Campus Ministry, Future Friar Executives. *Campus security:* 24-hour emergency response devices and patrols, student patrols, late-night transport/escort service, controlled dormitory access. *Student services:* health clinic, personal/psychological counseling.

Athletics Member NCAA. All Division I. *Intercollegiate sports:* basketball M(s)/W(s), cheerleading M/W, cross-country running M(s)/W(s), field hockey W(s), golf M(c)/W(c), ice hockey M(s)/W(s), lacrosse M(s), racquetball M(c)/W(c), rugby M(c)/W(c), sailing M(c)/W(c), soccer M(s)/W(s), softball W(s), swimming and diving M(s)/W(s), tennis W(s), track and field M(s)/W(s), ultimate Frisbee M(c)/W(c), volleyball M(c)/W(s), wrestling M(c). *Intramural sports:* basketball M/W, field hockey M/W, football M/W, ice hockey M/W, lacrosse M/W, racquetball M/W, soccer M/W, softball M/W, tennis M/W, volleyball M/W, water polo M/W, weight lifting M/W.

Standardized Tests *Recommended:* Test scores are considered if submitted.

Costs (2012–13) *Comprehensive fee:* $54,646 includes full-time tuition ($41,350), mandatory fees ($856), and room and board ($12,440). Full-time tuition and fees vary according to degree level and student level. Part-time tuition: $1477 per credit. Part-time tuition and fees vary according to degree level. *College room only:* $7170. Room and board charges vary according to board plan and housing facility. *Payment plan:* installment. *Waivers:* employees or children of employees.

Financial Aid Of all full-time matriculated undergraduates who enrolled in 2012, 2,610 applied for aid, 2,125 were judged to have need, 759 had their need fully met. 1,148 Federal Work-Study jobs (averaging $1800). In 2012, 460 non-need-based awards were made. *Average percent of need met:* 84%. *Average financial aid package:* $26,379. *Average need-based loan:* $5070. *Average need-based gift aid:* $22,045. *Average non-need-based aid:* $19,925. *Average indebtedness upon graduation:* $26,832. *Financial aid deadline:* 2/1.

Applying *Required:* essay or personal statement, high school transcript, 2 letters of recommendation.

Freshman Application Contact Providence College, 1 Cunningham Square, Providence, RI 02918. *Phone:* 401-865-2535. *Toll-free phone:* 800-721-6444. *Website:* http://www.providence.edu/.

Rhode Island College

Providence, Rhode Island

- **State-supported** comprehensive, founded 1854
- **Suburban** 180-acre campus with easy access to Boston
- **Endowment** $15.7 million
- **Coed** 7,553 undergraduate students, 73% full-time, 66% women, 34% men
- **Moderately difficult** entrance level, 69% of applicants were admitted

Undergraduates 5,533 full-time, 2,020 part-time. Students come from 29 states and territories; 14% are from out of state; 7% Black or African American, non-Hispanic/Latino; 11% Hispanic/Latino; 2% Asian, non-Hispanic/Latino; 0.1% Native Hawaiian or other Pacific Islander, non-Hispanic/Latino; 0.2% American Indian or Alaska Native, non-Hispanic/Latino; 2% Two or more races, non-Hispanic/Latino; 12% Race/ethnicity unknown; 0.1% international; 10% transferred in; 14% live on campus. *Retention:* 75% of full-time freshmen returned.

Freshmen *Admission:* 4,492 applied, 3,106 admitted, 1,071 enrolled. *Average high school GPA:* 2.98. *Test scores:* SAT critical reading scores over 500: 37%; SAT math scores over 500: 34%; SAT writing scores over 500: 35%; ACT scores over 18: 73%; SAT critical reading scores over 600: 6%; SAT math scores over 600: 6%; SAT writing scores over 600: 6%; ACT scores over 24: 16%; SAT critical reading scores over 700: 1%; ACT scores over 30: 1%.

Faculty *Total:* 743, 44% full-time. *Student/faculty ratio:* 14:1.

Academics *Calendar:* semesters. *Degrees:* certificates, bachelor's, master's, doctoral, post-master's, and postbachelor's certificates. *Special study options:* academic remediation for entering students, adult/continuing education programs, advanced placement credit, double majors, honors programs, independent study, internships, off-campus study, part-time degree program, services for LD students, student-designed majors, study abroad, summer session for credit. *ROTC:* Army (c). *Unusual degree programs:* 3-2 public administration with University of Rhode Island.

Computers on Campus 220 computers/terminals are available on campus for general student use. Students can access the following: campus intranet, computer help desk, free student e-mail accounts, online (class) grades, online (class) registration, online (class) schedules. Campuswide network is available. 100% of college-owned or -operated housing units are wired for high-speed Internet access. Wireless service is available via classrooms, computer centers, computer labs, dorm rooms, learning centers, libraries, student centers.

Student Life *Housing options:* coed, women-only, disabled students. Campus housing is university owned. Freshman applicants given priority for college housing. *Activities and organizations:* drama/theater group, student-run newspaper, radio and television station, choral group, student government, newspaper (The Anchor), campus radio station (WXIN), Programming Board, Resident Student Association, national fraternities, national sororities. *Campus security:* 24-hour emergency response devices and patrols, late-night transport/escort service, controlled dormitory access. *Student services:* health clinic, personal/psychological counseling, women's center.

Athletics Member NCAA. All Division III. *Intercollegiate sports:* baseball M, basketball M/W, cross-country running M/W, golf M/W, gymnastics W, lacrosse W, soccer M/W, softball W, swimming and diving W, tennis M/W, track and field M/W, volleyball W, wrestling M. *Intramural sports:* badminton M/W, basketball M/W, football M, soccer M/W, softball M/W, swimming and diving M/W, tennis M/W, volleyball M/W, water polo M/W.

Standardized Tests *Required:* SAT or ACT (for admission).

Costs (2012–13) *Tuition:* state resident $6530 full-time, $272 per credit part-time; nonresident $17,228 full-time, $670 per credit part-time. Part-time tuition and fees vary according to course load. *Required fees:* $1068 full-time, $32 per credit part-time, $72 per term part-time. *Room and board:* $9534; room only: $5424. Room and board charges vary according to housing facility. *Payment plan:* installment. *Waivers:* employees or children of employees.

Financial Aid Of all full-time matriculated undergraduates who enrolled in 2011, 4,635 applied for aid, 3,773 were judged to have need, 877 had their need fully met. In 2011, 129 non-need-based awards were made. *Average percent of need met:* 72%. *Average financial aid package:* $8960. *Average need-based loan:* $4001. *Average need-based gift aid:* $5476. *Average non-need-based aid:* $2185. *Average indebtedness upon graduation:* $21,384.

Applying *Options:* electronic application, early admission. *Application fee:* $50. *Required:* essay or personal statement, high school transcript, 1 letter of recommendation, one letter from guidance counselor. *Required for some:* interview. *Recommended:* minimum 3.0 GPA. *Application deadlines:* 3/15 (freshmen), 3/15 (out-of-state freshmen), 6/1 (transfers). *Notification:* continuous (freshmen), continuous (out-of-state freshmen), continuous (transfers).

Freshman Application Contact John McLaughlin, Director of Admissions, Rhode Island College, 600 Mount Pleasant Avenue, Providence, RI 02908-1927. *Phone:* 401-456-8234. *Toll-free phone:* 800-669-5760. *Fax:* 401-456-8817. *E-mail:* admissions@ric.edu. *Website:* http://www.ric.edu/.

Rhode Island School of Design

Providence, Rhode Island

- **Independent** comprehensive, founded 1877
- **Urban** 13-acre campus with easy access to Boston
- **Endowment** $283.5 million
- **Coed** 1,971 undergraduate students, 100% full-time, 67% women, 33% men
- **Very difficult** entrance level, 25% of applicants were admitted

Undergraduates 1,971 full-time. Students come from 35 states and territories; 56 other countries; 93% are from out of state; 2% Black or African American, non-Hispanic/Latino; 7% Hispanic/Latino; 18% Asian, non-Hispanic/Latino; 0.1% Native Hawaiian or other Pacific Islander, non-Hispanic/Latino; 0.2% American Indian or Alaska Native, non-Hispanic/Latino; 3% Two or more races, non-Hispanic/Latino; 15% Race/ethnicity unknown; 21% international; 4% transferred in; 70% live on campus. *Retention:* 93% of full-time freshmen returned.

Freshmen *Admission:* 3,113 applied, 790 admitted, 434 enrolled. *Average high school GPA:* 3.5. *Test scores:* SAT critical reading scores over 500: 93%; SAT math scores over 500: 94%; SAT writing scores over 500: 95%; ACT scores over 18: 97%; SAT critical reading scores over 600: 54%; SAT math scores over 600: 67%; SAT writing scores over 600: 62%; ACT scores over 24: 82%; SAT critical reading scores over 700: 16%; SAT math scores over 700: 25%; SAT writing scores over 700: 20%; ACT scores over 30: 40%.

Faculty *Total:* 530, 28% full-time, 63% with terminal degrees. *Student/faculty ratio:* 9:1.

Academics *Calendar:* 4-1-4. *Degrees:* bachelor's and master's. *Special study options:* academic remediation for entering students, advanced placement credit, cooperative education, double majors, English as a second language, honors programs, independent study, internships, off-campus study, services for LD students, study abroad.

Computers on Campus 400 computers/terminals are available on campus for general student use. Students can access the following: campus intranet, computer help desk, free student e-mail accounts, online (class) grades, online (class) registration, online (class) schedules. Campuswide network is available. 100% of college-owned or -operated housing units are wired for high-speed Internet access. Wireless service is available via entire campus.

Student Life *Housing:* on-campus residence required through sophomore year. *Options:* coed. Campus housing is university owned. Freshman campus housing is guaranteed. *Activities and organizations:* drama/theater group, student-run newspaper, choral group, athletic clubs, Industrial Design Club, Korean Students Association, Lesbian/Gay/Bisexual Alliance. *Campus security:* 24-hour emergency response devices and patrols, late-night transport/escort service, controlled dormitory access. *Student services:* health clinic, personal/psychological counseling, legal services.

Athletics *Intramural sports:* basketball M/W, bowling M(c)/W(c), fencing M(c)/W(c), football M(c)/W(c), ice hockey M/W, sailing M(c)/W(c), skiing (downhill) M(c)/W(c), soccer M/W, softball M/W, volleyball M/W.

Standardized Tests *Required:* SAT or ACT (for admission).

Costs (2013–14) *Comprehensive fee:* $53,312 includes full-time tuition ($41,022), mandatory fees ($310), and room and board ($11,980). *College room only:* $6280. Room and board charges vary according to board plan and housing facility. *Payment plan:* installment. *Waivers:* employees or children of employees.

Financial Aid Of all full-time matriculated undergraduates who enrolled in 2004, 1,120 applied for aid, 915 were judged to have need, 85 had their need fully met. 511 Federal Work-Study jobs (averaging $1408). 350 state and other part-time jobs (averaging $1400). In 2004, 34 non-need-based awards were made. *Average percent of need met:* 69%. *Average financial aid package:* $17,000. *Average need-based loan:* $5900. *Average need-based gift aid:* $11,100. *Average non-need-based aid:* $4700. *Average indebtedness upon graduation:* $22,500.

Applying *Options:* electronic application, early admission, early decision, deferred entrance. *Application fee:* $60. *Required:* essay or personal statement, high school transcript, portfolio, drawing assignments. *Recommended:* 3 letters of recommendation. *Application deadlines:* 2/1 (freshmen), 3/15 (transfers). *Early decision deadline:* 11/1. *Notification:* 3/15 (freshmen), 5/1 (transfers), 12/1 (early decision).

Freshman Application Contact Mr. Edward Newhall, Director of Admissions, Rhode Island School of Design, 2 College Street, Providence, RI 02905-2791. *Phone:* 401-454-6307. *Toll-free phone:* 800-364-7473. *Fax:* 401-454-6309. *E-mail:* admissions@risd.edu.
Website: http://www.risd.edu/.

Roger Williams University

Bristol, Rhode Island

- **Independent** comprehensive, founded 1956
- **Small-town** 140-acre campus with easy access to Boston
- **Endowment** $58.6 million
- **Coed** 4,451 undergraduate students, 86% full-time, 49% women, 51% men
- **Moderately difficult** entrance level, 78% of applicants were admitted

Undergraduates 3,833 full-time, 618 part-time. Students come from 46 states and territories; 50 other countries; 84% are from out of state; 1% Black or African American, non-Hispanic/Latino; 3% Hispanic/Latino; 1% Asian, non-Hispanic/Latino; 0.1% American Indian or Alaska Native, non-Hispanic/Latino; 1% Two or more races, non-Hispanic/Latino; 29% Race/ethnicity unknown; 1% international; 4% transferred in. *Retention:* 80% of full-time freshmen returned.

Freshmen *Admission:* 8,853 applied, 6,876 admitted, 1,323 enrolled. *Average high school GPA:* 3.2. *Test scores:* SAT critical reading scores over 500: 77%; SAT math scores over 500: 73%; ACT scores over 18: 99%; SAT critical reading scores over 600: 22%; SAT math scores over 600: 21%; ACT scores over 24: 54%; SAT critical reading scores over 700: 2%; SAT math scores over 700: 1%; ACT scores over 30: 5%.

Faculty *Total:* 541, 37% full-time. *Student/faculty ratio:* 14:1.

Academics *Calendar:* semesters. *Degrees:* certificates, associate, bachelor's, master's, doctoral, and postbachelor's certificates. *Special study options:* adult/continuing education programs, advanced placement credit, cooperative education, distance learning, double majors, English as a second language, freshman honors college, honors programs, independent study, internships, part-time degree program, services for LD students, student-designed majors, study abroad, summer session for credit. *ROTC:* Army (c).

Computers on Campus Students can access the following: campus intranet, computer help desk, free student e-mail accounts, online (class) registration, online (class) schedules. Campuswide network is available. 100% of college-owned or -operated housing units are wired for high-speed Internet access. Wireless service is available via classrooms, computer centers, computer labs, dorm rooms, learning centers, libraries, student centers.

Student Life *Housing options:* coed, disabled students. Campus housing is university owned and leased by the school. Freshman campus housing is guaranteed. *Activities and organizations:* drama/theater group, student-run newspaper, radio station, choral group, Entertainment Network, Student Senate, American Institute of Architects, John Jay Society, residence hall councils. *Campus security:* 24-hour emergency response devices and patrols, student patrols, late-night transport/escort service, controlled dormitory access. *Student services:* health clinic, personal/psychological counseling, women's center.

Athletics Member NCAA. All Division III. *Intercollegiate sports:* baseball M, basketball M/W, cheerleading W(c), crew M(c)/W(c), cross-country running M/W, equestrian sports M/W, lacrosse M/W, rugby M(c), sailing M/W, soccer M/W, softball W, swimming and diving M/W, tennis M/W, track and field M(c)/W(c), volleyball M(c)/W, wrestling M. *Intramural sports:* badminton M/W, basketball M/W, field hockey M/W, football M/W, golf M/W, lacrosse M/W, racquetball M/W, soccer M/W, softball M/W, squash M/W, swimming and diving M/W, table tennis M/W, tennis M/W, ultimate Frisbee M/W, volleyball M/W.

Standardized Tests *Required:* SAT or ACT (for admission).

Costs (2012–13) *Comprehensive fee:* $45,308 includes full-time tuition ($29,976), mandatory fees ($1642), and room and board ($13,690). Full-time tuition and fees vary according to class time, course load, and program. Part-time tuition: $939 per course. Part-time tuition and fees vary according to class time. *College room only:* $7370. Room and board charges vary according to board plan and housing facility. *Payment plans:* installment, deferred payment. *Waivers:* employees or children of employees.

Financial Aid Of all full-time matriculated undergraduates who enrolled in 2011, 2,791 applied for aid, 2,246 were judged to have need, 167 had their need fully met. 405 Federal Work-Study jobs (averaging $1700). In 2011, 433 non-need-based awards were made. *Average percent of need met:* 88%. *Average financial aid package:* $19,970. *Average need-based loan:* $4638. *Average need-based gift aid:* $13,214. *Average non-need-based aid:* $9755. *Average indebtedness upon graduation:* $38,365. *Financial aid deadline:* 2/1.

Applying *Options:* electronic application, early action, deferred entrance. *Application fee:* $50. *Required:* essay or personal statement, high school transcript, 1 letter of recommendation. *Required for some:* portfolio/audition. *Application deadlines:* 2/1 (freshmen), 2/1 (out-of-state freshmen), rolling (transfers), 11/7 (early action). *Notification:* 3/15 (freshmen), continuous (transfers), 12/5 (early action).

Freshman Application Contact Office of Undergraduate Admission, Roger Williams University, 1 Old Ferry Road, Bristol, RI 02809. *Phone:* 401-254-3500. *Toll-free phone:* 800-458-7144. *Fax:* 401-254-3557. *E-mail:* admit@rwu.edu.
Website: http://www.rwu.edu/.

Salve Regina University

Newport, Rhode Island

- **Independent Roman Catholic** comprehensive, founded 1934
- **Suburban** 75-acre campus with easy access to Boston, Providence
- **Endowment** $44.3 million
- **Coed** 2,053 undergraduate students, 96% full-time, 70% women, 30% men
- **Moderately difficult** entrance level, 70% of applicants were admitted

Undergraduates 1,974 full-time, 79 part-time. Students come from 38 states and territories; 19 other countries; 78% are from out of state; 2% Black or African American, non-Hispanic/Latino; 6% Hispanic/Latino; 1% Asian, non-Hispanic/Latino; 0.0% Native Hawaiian or other Pacific Islander, non-Hispanic/Latino; 0.3% American Indian or Alaska Native, non-Hispanic/Latino; 2% Two or more races, non-Hispanic/Latino; 12% Race/ethnicity unknown; 2% international; 2% transferred in; 60% live on campus. *Retention:* 82% of full-time freshmen returned.

Freshmen *Admission:* 4,824 applied, 3,360 admitted, 545 enrolled. *Average high school GPA:* 3.2. *Test scores:* SAT critical reading scores over 500: 83%; SAT math scores over 500: 86%; SAT writing scores over 500: 83%; ACT scores over 18: 100%; SAT critical reading scores over 600: 24%; SAT math scores over 600: 26%; SAT writing scores over 600: 28%; ACT scores over 24: 65%; SAT critical reading scores over 700: 2%; SAT math scores over 700: 1%; SAT writing scores over 700: 3%; ACT scores over 30: 4%.

Faculty *Total:* 236, 49% full-time, 50% with terminal degrees. *Student/faculty ratio:* 15:1.

Academics *Calendar:* semesters. *Degrees:* certificates, associate, bachelor's, master's, doctoral, post-master's, and postbachelor's certificates. *Special study options:* accelerated degree program, adult/continuing education programs, advanced placement credit, double majors, English as a second language, honors programs, independent study, internships, off-campus study, part-time degree program, services for LD students, study abroad, summer session for credit. *ROTC:* Army (c). *Unusual degree programs:* 3-2 business administration; administration of justice, business administration, holistic counseling, international relations, management, rehabilitation counseling.

Computers on Campus 163 computers/terminals are available on campus for general student use. Students can access the following: campus intranet, computer help desk, free student e-mail accounts, online (class) grades, online (class) registration, online (class) schedules. Campuswide network is available. 95% of college-owned or -operated housing units are wired for high-speed Internet access. Wireless service is available via entire campus.

Student Life *Housing:* on-campus residence required through sophomore year. *Options:* coed, men-only, women-only, disabled students. Campus housing is university owned and leased by the school. Freshman campus housing is guaranteed. *Activities and organizations:* drama/theater group, student-run newspaper, radio station, choral group, Orpheus Musical Society, Student Government Association, Student Outdoor Adventures, Student Nurse Organization, Stagefright Theatre Company. *Campus security:* 24-hour emergency response devices and patrols, late-night transport/escort service, controlled dormitory access. *Student services:* health clinic, personal/psychological counseling.

Athletics Member NCAA. All Division III. *Intercollegiate sports:* baseball M, basketball M/W, cross-country running M/W, field hockey W, football M, ice hockey M/W, lacrosse M/W, rugby M(c)/W(c), sailing M/W, soccer M/W, softball W, tennis M/W, track and field W, volleyball W. *Intramural sports:* baseball M, basketball M/W, cheerleading W(c), field hockey W, football M/W, soccer M/W, softball M/W, tennis M/W, track and field M/W, volleyball M/W, weight lifting M/W.

Standardized Tests *Required for some:* SAT or ACT (for admission).

Costs (2012–13) *Comprehensive fee:* $45,850 includes full-time tuition ($33,450), mandatory fees ($500), and room and board ($11,900). Full-time tuition and fees vary according to course load and location. Part-time tuition: $1115 per credit. Part-time tuition and fees vary according to course load and location. *Required fees:* $40 per term part-time. *Room and board:* Room and board charges vary according to board plan and housing facility. *Payment plan:* installment. *Waivers:* employees or children of employees.

Financial Aid Of all full-time matriculated undergraduates who enrolled in 2012, 1,738 applied for aid, 1,563 were judged to have need, 123 had their need fully met. 409 Federal Work-Study jobs (averaging $691). 111 state and other part-time jobs (averaging $1281). In 2012, 286 non-need-based awards were made. *Average percent of need met:* 65%. *Average financial aid package:* $22,619. *Average need-based loan:* $4455. *Average need-based gift aid:* $17,824. *Average non-need-based aid:* $10,358. *Average indebtedness upon graduation:* $39,996.

Applying *Options:* electronic application, early action, deferred entrance. *Application fee:* $50. *Required:* essay or personal statement, high school transcript, 2 letters of recommendation. *Recommended:* minimum 2.7 GPA. *Application deadlines:* 2/1 (freshmen), rolling (transfers), 11/1 (early action). *Notification:* 12/25 (freshmen), continuous (transfers), 12/25 (early action).

Freshman Application Contact Dean Colleen Emerson, Dean of Undergraduate Admissions, Salve Regina University, 100 Ochre Point Avenue, Newport, RI 02840-4192. *Phone:* 401-341-2908. *Toll-free phone:* 888-GO SALVE. *Fax:* 401-848-2823. *E-mail:* sruadmis@salve.edu. *Website:* http://www.salve.edu/.

University of Rhode Island

Kingston, Rhode Island

- **State-supported** university, founded 1892
- **Small-town** 1200-acre campus
- **Coed** 13,398 undergraduate students, 89% full-time, 54% women, 46% men
- **Moderately difficult** entrance level, 77% of applicants were admitted

Undergraduates 11,945 full-time, 1,453 part-time. Students come from 43 states and territories; 40 other countries; 39% are from out of state; 5% Black or African American, non-Hispanic/Latino; 8% Hispanic/Latino; 3% Asian, non-Hispanic/Latino; 0.1% Native Hawaiian or other Pacific Islander, non-Hispanic/Latino; 0.3% American Indian or Alaska Native, non-Hispanic/Latino; 2% Two or more races, non-Hispanic/Latino; 11% Race/ethnicity unknown; 0.9% international; 5% transferred in; 44% live on campus. *Retention:* 81% of full-time freshmen returned.

Freshmen *Admission:* 20,637 applied, 15,875 admitted, 2,994 enrolled. *Average high school GPA:* 3.3. *Test scores:* SAT critical reading scores over 500: 70%; SAT math scores over 500: 77%; SAT writing scores over 500: 70%;

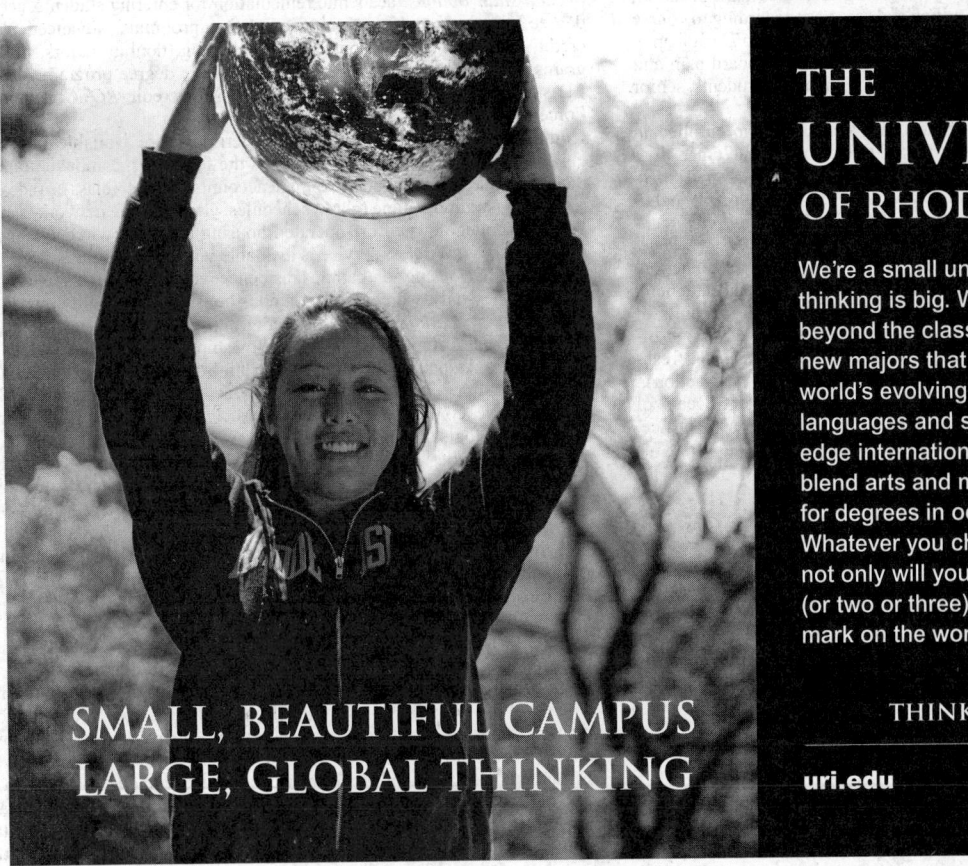

ACT scores over 18: 99%; SAT critical reading scores over 600: 18%; SAT math scores over 600: 29%; SAT writing scores over 600: 19%; ACT scores over 24: 52%; SAT critical reading scores over 700: 1%; SAT math scores over 700: 3%; SAT writing scores over 700: 1%; ACT scores over 30: 4%.

Faculty *Total:* 1,169, 55% full-time, 49% with terminal degrees. *Student/faculty ratio:* 16:1.

Academics *Calendar:* semesters. *Degrees:* bachelor's, master's, doctoral, and postbachelor's certificates. *Special study options:* academic remediation for entering students, accelerated degree program, adult/continuing education programs, advanced placement credit, cooperative education, distance learning, double majors, English as a second language, honors programs, independent study, internships, off-campus study, part-time degree program, services for LD students, study abroad, summer session for credit. *ROTC:* Army (b). *Unusual degree programs:* 3-2 engineering; nursing; accounting, pharmacy, chemistry, education, psychology.

Computers on Campus 2,500 computers/terminals are available on campus for general student use. Students can access the following: campus intranet, computer help desk, free student e-mail accounts, online (class) grades, online (class) registration, online (class) schedules. Campuswide network is available. 100% of college-owned or -operated housing units are wired for high-speed Internet access. Wireless service is available via entire campus.

Student Life *Housing options:* coed, cooperative, disabled students. Campus housing is university owned and leased by the school. Freshman campus housing is guaranteed. *Activities and organizations:* drama/theater group, student-run newspaper, radio and television station, choral group, marching band, Student Entertainment Committee, Student radio station, Intramural sport clubs, Student Alumni Association, student newspaper, national fraternities, national sororities. *Campus security:* 24-hour emergency response devices and patrols, student patrols, late-night transport/escort service, controlled dormitory access. *Student services:* health clinic, personal/psychological counseling, women's center.

Athletics Member NCAA. All Division I. *Intercollegiate sports:* baseball M(s), basketball M(s), crew M(s), cross-country running M(s)/W(s), football M(s), golf M(s), soccer M(s)/W(s), softball W(s), swimming and diving W(s), tennis W(s), track and field M(s)/W(s), volleyball W(s). *Intramural sports:* equestrian sports M(c)/W(c), gymnastics W(c), ice hockey M(c)/W(c), lacrosse M(c)/W(c), rugby M(c)/W(c), sailing M(c)/W(c), skiing (downhill) M(c)/W(c), swimming and diving M(c), ultimate Frisbee M(c)/W(c), volleyball M(c), wrestling M(c).

Standardized Tests *Required:* SAT or ACT (for admission).

Costs (2012–13) *Tuition:* state resident $10,878 full-time; nonresident $26,444 full-time. Full-time tuition and fees vary according to course load, location, and reciprocity agreements. Part-time tuition and fees vary according to course load, location, and reciprocity agreements. *Required fees:* $1572 full-time. *Room and board:* Room and board charges vary according to board plan and housing facility. *Payment plan:* installment. *Waivers:* minority students, senior citizens, and employees or children of employees.

Financial Aid Of all full-time matriculated undergraduates who enrolled in 2012, 11,274 applied for aid, 9,697 were judged to have need, 6,676 had their need fully met. In 2012, 512 non-need-based awards were made. *Average percent of need met:* 58%. *Average financial aid package:* $14,901. *Average need-based loan:* $5396. *Average need-based gift aid:* $9219. *Average non-need-based aid:* $5793. *Average indebtedness upon graduation:* $30,387.

Applying *Options:* electronic application, early admission, early action, deferred entrance. *Application fee:* $65. *Required:* essay or personal statement, high school transcript, 1 letter of recommendation, minimum of 18 units of college preparatory work. *Application deadlines:* 2/1 (freshmen), 2/1 (out-of-state freshmen), 6/1 (transfers), 12/1 (early action). *Notification:* 3/31 (freshmen), 3/31 (out-of-state freshmen), continuous (transfers), 1/31 (early action).

Freshman Application Contact Ms. Joanne Lynch, Assistant Dean of Admissions, University of Rhode Island, Undergraduate Admission Office, Newman Hall, 14 Upper College Road, Kingston, RI 02881. *Phone:* 401-874-7110. *Fax:* 401-874-5523. *E-mail:* lynch@uri.edu. *Website:* http://www.uri.edu/.

See previous page for display ad and page 1598 for the College Close-Up.

SOUTH CAROLINA

Allen University
Columbia, South Carolina

Freshman Application Contact Terri Parker, Director of Admission, Allen University, 1530 Harden Street, Columbia, SC 29204. *Phone:* 803-376-5733. *Toll-free phone:* 877-625-5368. *E-mail:* tparker@allenuniversity.edu. *Website:* http://www.allenuniversity.edu/.

Anderson University
Anderson, South Carolina

- **Independent Baptist** comprehensive, founded 1911
- **Suburban** 271-acre campus with easy access to Greenville
- **Endowment** $32.2 million
- **Coed** 2,630 undergraduate students, 82% full-time, 65% women, 35% men
- **Moderately difficult** entrance level, 72% of applicants were admitted

Undergraduates 2,152 full-time, 478 part-time. Students come from 35 states and territories; 22 other countries; 18% are from out of state; 11% Black or African American, non-Hispanic/Latino; 3% Hispanic/Latino; 0.9% Asian, non-Hispanic/Latino; 0.9% Native Hawaiian or other Pacific Islander, non-Hispanic/Latino; 0.7% American Indian or Alaska Native, non-Hispanic/Latino; 1% international; 4% transferred in; 54% live on campus. *Retention:* 77% of full-time freshmen returned.

Freshmen *Admission:* 2,060 applied, 1,476 admitted, 538 enrolled. *Average high school GPA:* 3.37. *Test scores:* SAT math scores over 500: 67%; SAT writing scores over 500: 57%; ACT scores over 18: 93%; SAT math scores over 600: 23%; SAT writing scores over 600: 20%; ACT scores over 24: 39%; SAT math scores over 700: 2%; SAT writing scores over 700: 2%; ACT scores over 30: 4%.

Faculty *Total:* 302, 38% full-time, 45% with terminal degrees. *Student/faculty ratio:* 15:1.

Academics *Calendar:* semesters. *Degrees:* bachelor's, master's, and doctoral. *Special study options:* academic remediation for entering students, accelerated degree program, adult/continuing education programs, advanced placement credit, cooperative education, distance learning, double majors, honors programs, independent study, internships, part-time degree program, services for LD students, study abroad, summer session for credit. *ROTC:* Army (c), Air Force (c).

Computers on Campus 192 computers/terminals are available on campus for general student use. Students can access the following: campus intranet, computer help desk, free student e-mail accounts, online (class) grades, online (class) registration, online (class) schedules. Campuswide network is available. 100% of college-owned or -operated housing units are wired for high-speed Internet access. Wireless service is available via entire campus.

Student Life *Housing:* on-campus residence required through sophomore year. *Options:* men-only, women-only. Campus housing is university owned. *Activities and organizations:* drama/theater group, student-run newspaper, choral group, Baptist Campus Ministries, Fellowship of Christian Athletes, Student Government Association, Gamma Beta Phi, Student Alumni Council. *Campus security:* 24-hour emergency response devices and patrols, late-night transport/escort service, controlled dormitory access. *Student services:* health clinic, personal/psychological counseling.

Athletics Member NCAA. All Division II. *Intercollegiate sports:* baseball M(s), basketball M(s)/W(s), cheerleading W(s), cross-country running M(s)/W(s), golf M(s)/W(s), soccer M(s)/W(s), softball W(s), tennis M(s)/W(s), track and field M(s)/W(s), volleyball W(s), wrestling M(s). *Intramural sports:* basketball M/W, football M/W, racquetball M/W, softball M/W, table tennis M/W, ultimate Frisbee M/W, volleyball M/W, weight lifting M.

Standardized Tests *Required:* SAT or ACT (for admission).

Costs (2013–14) *Comprehensive fee:* $31,138 includes full-time tuition ($20,820), mandatory fees ($1970), and room and board ($8348). Full-time tuition and fees vary according to course load and program. Part-time tuition: $515 per credit hour. Part-time tuition and fees vary according to program. *College room only:* $4316. Room and board charges vary according to board plan and housing facility. *Payment plan:* installment. *Waivers:* employees or children of employees.

Financial Aid Of all full-time matriculated undergraduates who enrolled in 2012, 2,030 applied for aid, 1,793 were judged to have need, 461 had their need fully met. 204 Federal Work-Study jobs (averaging $1898). 296 state and other part-time jobs (averaging $489). In 2012, 303 non-need-based awards

were made. *Average percent of need met:* 70%. *Average financial aid package:* $17,029. *Average need-based loan:* $4891. *Average need-based gift aid:* $13,714. *Average non-need-based aid:* $9971. *Average indebtedness upon graduation:* $27,187. *Financial aid deadline:* 7/30.

Applying *Options:* electronic application, deferred entrance. *Application fee:* $25. *Required:* high school transcript. *Required for some:* essay or personal statement, 2 letters of recommendation, interview. *Recommended:* minimum 2.9 GPA. *Application deadline:* 7/1 (freshmen). *Notification:* continuous (freshmen), continuous (transfers).

Freshman Application Contact Mrs. Pam Bryant-Ross, Anderson University, 316 Boulevard, Anderson, SC 29621-4035. *Phone:* 864-231-2030. *Toll-free phone:* 800-542-3594.

Website: http://www.andersonuniversity.edu/.

The Art Institute of Charleston

Charleston, South Carolina

- **Proprietary** 4-year, founded 2007, part of Education Management Corporation
- **Urban** campus
- **Coed**

Academics *Calendar:* quarters. *Degrees:* certificates, associate, and bachelor's.

Freshman Application Contact The Art Institute of Charleston, 24 North Market Street, Charleston, SC 29401. *Phone:* 843-727-3500. *Toll-free phone:* 866-211-0107.

Website: http://www.artinstitutes.edu/charleston/.

See full-page ad on page 54 and page 1072 for the College Close-Up.

Benedict College

Columbia, South Carolina

Freshman Application Contact Benedict College, 1600 Harden Street, Columbia, SC 29204. *Phone:* 803-705-4491. *Toll-free phone:* 800-868-6598. *Website:* http://www.benedict.edu/.

Bob Jones University

Greenville, South Carolina

- **Independent Christian** university, founded 1927
- **Urban** 225-acre campus
- **Coed** 2,976 undergraduate students, 94% full-time, 57% women, 43% men
- **Minimally difficult** entrance level, 73% of applicants were admitted

Undergraduates 2,802 full-time, 174 part-time. Students come from 52 states and territories; 90 other countries; 75% are from out of state; 1% Black or African American, non-Hispanic/Latino; 2% Hispanic/Latino; 2% Asian, non-Hispanic/Latino; 0.3% Native Hawaiian or other Pacific Islander, non-Hispanic/Latino; 0.2% American Indian or Alaska Native, non-Hispanic/Latino; 6% Two or more races, non-Hispanic/Latino; 4% Race/ethnicity unknown; 5% international; 3% transferred in; 74% live on campus. *Retention:* 83% of full-time freshmen returned.

Freshmen *Admission:* 1,437 applied, 1,056 admitted, 695 enrolled. *Average high school GPA:* 3.42. *Test scores:* ACT scores over 18: 100%; ACT scores over 24: 46%; ACT scores over 30: 7%.

Faculty *Total:* 260, 76% full-time, 45% with terminal degrees. *Student/faculty ratio:* 15:1.

Academics *Calendar:* semesters. *Degrees:* associate, bachelor's, master's, doctoral, and post-master's certificates. *Special study options:* accelerated degree program, adult/continuing education programs, advanced placement credit, distance learning, English as a second language, internships, off-campus study, part-time degree program, services for LD students, summer session for credit.

Computers on Campus 450 computers/terminals and 500 ports are available on campus for general student use. Students can access the following: campus intranet, computer help desk, free student e-mail accounts, online (class) grades, online (class) registration, online (class) schedules. Campuswide network is available. 100% of college-owned or -operated housing units are wired for high-speed Internet access. Wireless service is available via classrooms, computer labs, dorm rooms, learning centers, libraries, student centers.

Student Life *Housing:* on-campus residence required through senior year. *Options:* men-only, women-only, disabled students. Campus housing is university owned. Freshman campus housing is guaranteed. *Activities and organizations:* drama/theater group, student-run newspaper, radio and television station, choral group, Community Relations Council, Extension Ministries, Societies, Mission Prayer Band, University Business Association. *Campus security:* 24-hour patrols, student patrols, late-night transport/escort service, controlled dormitory access, 24/7 emergency dispatcher. *Student services:* health clinic, personal/psychological counseling.

Athletics Member NCCAA. *Intercollegiate sports:* basketball M/W, cross-country running M/W, golf M/W, soccer M/W. *Intramural sports:* badminton M/W, basketball M/W, cheerleading W, racquetball M, soccer M/W, softball M/W, table tennis M/W, tennis M/W, volleyball M/W, water polo W.

Standardized Tests *Required:* ACT (for admission).

Costs (2013–14) *Comprehensive fee:* $19,220 includes full-time tuition ($12,820), mandatory fees ($610), and room and board ($5790). Full-time tuition and fees vary according to program. Part-time tuition: $624 per credit hour. Part-time tuition and fees vary according to program. *Payment plan:* installment. *Waivers:* senior citizens and employees or children of employees.

Financial Aid Of all full-time matriculated undergraduates who enrolled in 2011, 2,210 applied for aid, 2,047 were judged to have need. *Average percent of need met:* 46%. *Average financial aid package:* $12,000. *Average need-based loan:* $3936. *Average need-based gift aid:* $6500.

Applying *Options:* electronic application. *Required:* essay or personal statement, high school transcript, 3 letters of recommendation. *Application deadlines:* 8/1 (freshmen), 8/1 (transfers).

Freshman Application Contact Mr. Gary Deedrick, Director of Admissions, Bob Jones University, 1700 Wade Hampton Boulevard, Greenville, SC 29614. *Phone:* 864-242-5100. *Toll-free phone:* 800-BJANDME. *Fax:* 800-232-9258. *E-mail:* admission@bju.edu.

Website: http://www.bju.edu/.

Brown Mackie College–Greenville

Greenville, South Carolina

Freshman Application Contact Brown Mackie College–Greenville, Two Liberty Square, 75 Beattie Place, Suite 100, Greenville, SC 29601. *Phone:* 864-239-5300. *Toll-free phone:* 877-479-8465.

Website: http://www.brownmackie.edu/greenville/.

See next page for display ad and page 1184 for the College Close-Up.

Charleston Southern University

Charleston, South Carolina

Freshman Application Contact Mr. Jim Rhoden, Director of Enrollment Management, Charleston Southern University, Charleston, SC 29423-8087. *Phone:* 843-863-7050. *Toll-free phone:* 800-947-7474. *E-mail:* enroll@csuniv.edu.

Website: http://www.charlestonsouthern.edu/.

The Citadel, The Military College of South Carolina

Charleston, South Carolina

- **State-supported** comprehensive, founded 1842
- **Suburban** 300-acre campus
- **Endowment** $58.2 million
- **Coed, primarily men** 2,629 undergraduate students, 93% full-time, 10% women, 90% men
- **Moderately difficult** entrance level, 80% of applicants were admitted

Undergraduates 2,438 full-time, 191 part-time. Students come from 44 states and territories; 8 other countries; 44% are from out of state; 8% Black or African American, non-Hispanic/Latino; 6% Hispanic/Latino; 2% Asian, non-Hispanic/Latino; 0.2% Native Hawaiian or other Pacific Islander, non-Hispanic/Latino; 1% American Indian or Alaska Native, non-Hispanic/Latino; 1% Two or more races, non-Hispanic/Latino; 0.1% Race/ethnicity unknown; 1% international; 4% transferred in; 100% live on campus. *Retention:* 84% of full-time freshmen returned.

Freshmen *Admission:* 2,557 applied, 2,056 admitted, 676 enrolled. *Average high school GPA:* 3.5. *Test scores:* SAT critical reading scores over 500: 69%;

SAT math scores over 500: 76%; ACT scores over 18: 99%; SAT critical reading scores over 600: 23%; SAT math scores over 600: 27%; ACT scores over 24: 41%; SAT critical reading scores over 700: 3%; SAT math scores over 700: 2%; ACT scores over 30: 4%.

Faculty *Total:* 266, 68% full-time, 76% with terminal degrees. *Student/faculty ratio:* 13:1.

Academics *Calendar:* semesters. *Degrees:* bachelor's, master's, and post-master's certificates. *Special study options:* advanced placement credit, cooperative education, distance learning, double majors, English as a second language, honors programs, independent study, internships, off-campus study, part-time degree program, services for LD students, study abroad, summer session for credit. *ROTC:* Army (b), Navy (b), Air Force (b).

Computers on Campus 350 computers/terminals are available on campus for general student use. Students can access the following: campus intranet, computer help desk, free student e-mail accounts, online (class) grades, online (class) registration, online (class) schedules. Campuswide network is available. Wireless service is available via classrooms, dorm rooms, libraries, student centers.

Student Life *Housing:* on-campus residence required through senior year. *Options:* coed. Campus housing is university owned. Freshman campus housing is guaranteed. *Activities and organizations:* student-run newspaper, choral group, marching band, The Republican Society, Semper Fi Society, HESS Majors, Rod & Gun Club, Cordell Airborne Rangers. *Campus security:* 24-hour patrols. *Student services:* health clinic, personal/psychological counseling.

Athletics Member NCAA. All Division I except football (Division I-AA). *Intercollegiate sports:* baseball M(s), basketball M(s), cross-country running M(s)/W(s), golf W(s), ice hockey M(c), lacrosse M(c), riflery M(s)/W(s), rugby M(c)/W(c), soccer M(c)/W(s), tennis M(s), track and field M(s)/W(s), volleyball W(s), wrestling M(s). *Intramural sports:* badminton M/W, basketball M/W, football M, golf M/W, racquetball M/W, soccer M/W, softball M/W, swimming and diving M/W, table tennis M/W, tennis M/W, track and field M/W, ultimate Frisbee M/W, volleyball M/W, weight lifting M/W, wrestling M/W.

Standardized Tests *Required:* SAT or ACT (for admission).

Costs (2012–13) *Tuition:* state resident $10,523 full-time, $410 per credit part-time; nonresident $28,776 full-time, $743 per credit part-time. *Required fees:* $1249 full-time. *Room and board:* $6115. *Waivers:* senior citizens and employees or children of employees.

Financial Aid Of all full-time matriculated undergraduates who enrolled in 2012, 1,792 applied for aid, 1,418 were judged to have need, 344 had their need fully met. 83 Federal Work-Study jobs (averaging $1500). In 2012, 464 non-need-based awards were made. *Average percent of need met:* 62%. *Average financial aid package:* $14,436. *Average need-based loan:* $4322. *Average need-based gift aid:* $14,157. *Average non-need-based aid:* $13,984. *Average indebtedness upon graduation:* $31,217.

Applying *Options:* electronic application. *Application fee:* $40. *Required:* high school transcript. *Recommended:* interview. *Application deadlines:* rolling (freshmen), rolling (transfers). *Notification:* continuous (freshmen), continuous (transfers).

Freshman Application Contact Lt. Col. John W. Powell Jr., Director of Admissions, The Citadel, The Military College of South Carolina, 171 Moultrie Street, Charleston, SC 29409. *Phone:* 843-953-5230. *Toll-free phone:* 800-868-1842. *Fax:* 843-953-7036. *E-mail:* john.powell@citadel.edu. *Website:* http://www.citadel.edu/.

Claflin University
Orangeburg, South Carolina

- **Independent United Methodist** comprehensive, founded 1869
- **Small-town** 46-acre campus with easy access to Columbia
- **Endowment** $19.0 million
- **Coed** 1,883 undergraduate students, 97% full-time, 65% women, 35% men
- **Minimally difficult** entrance level, 53% of applicants were admitted

Undergraduates 1,830 full-time, 53 part-time. Students come from 27 states and territories; 15 other countries; 19% are from out of state; 92% Black or African American, non-Hispanic/Latino; 2% Hispanic/Latino; 0.2% Asian, non-Hispanic/Latino; 0.3% American Indian or Alaska Native, non-Hispanic/Latino; 0.5% Two or more races, non-Hispanic/Latino; 3% international; 6% transferred in; 71% live on campus. *Retention:* 74% of full-time freshmen returned.

Freshmen *Admission:* 4,394 applied, 2,310 admitted, 442 enrolled. *Average high school GPA:* 3. *Test scores:* SAT critical reading scores over 500: 22%; SAT math scores over 500: 29%; ACT scores over 18: 46%; SAT critical reading scores over 600: 4%; SAT math scores over 600: 10%; ACT scores over 24: 9%; SAT math scores over 700: 2%.

Faculty *Total:* 153, 79% full-time, 69% with terminal degrees. *Student/faculty ratio:* 14:1.

Academics *Calendar:* semesters. *Degrees:* bachelor's and master's. *Special study options:* academic remediation for entering students, adult/continuing education programs, advanced placement credit, cooperative education, freshman honors college, honors programs, independent study, internships, off-campus study, part-time degree program, summer session for credit. *ROTC:* Army (c). *Unusual degree programs:* 3-2 engineering with Clemson University, South Carolina State University.

Computers on Campus 530 computers/terminals are available on campus for general student use. Students can access the following: computer help desk, free student e-mail accounts, online (class) grades, online (class) registration, online (class) schedules. Campuswide network is available. 100% of college-owned or -operated housing units are wired for high-speed Internet access. Wireless service is available via entire campus.

Student Life *Housing options:* men-only, women-only. Campus housing is university owned. Freshman applicants given priority for college housing. *Activities and organizations:* drama/theater group, student-run newspaper, television station, choral group, national fraternities, national sororities. *Campus security:* 24-hour emergency response devices and patrols, student patrols, controlled dormitory access. *Student services:* health clinic, personal/psychological counseling.

Athletics Member NCAA. All Division II. *Intercollegiate sports:* baseball M(s)/W(s), basketball M(s)/W(s), cross-country running M(s)/W(s), softball W(s), track and field M(s)/W(s), volleyball W(s).

Standardized Tests *Required:* SAT or ACT (for admission). *Recommended:* SAT Subject Tests (for admission).

Costs (2012–13) *Comprehensive fee:* $22,464 includes full-time tuition ($13,974), mandatory fees ($450), and room and board ($8040). Full-time tuition and fees vary according to class time. Part-time tuition: $582 per credit hour. Part-time tuition and fees vary according to class time. *College room only:* $3420. Room and board charges vary according to housing facility. *Payment plans:* installment, deferred payment. *Waivers:* employees or children of employees.

Financial Aid Of all full-time matriculated undergraduates who enrolled in 2006, 1,517 applied for aid, 1,475 were judged to have need, 144 had their need fully met. In 2006, 300 non-need-based awards were made. *Average percent of need met:* 56%. *Average financial aid package:* $10,917. *Average need-based loan:* $3734. *Average need-based gift aid:* $8220. *Average non-need-based aid:* $17,712. *Average indebtedness upon graduation:* $19,993.

Applying *Options:* electronic application, deferred entrance. *Application fee:* $30. *Required:* essay or personal statement, high school transcript, minimum 2.0 GPA. *Application deadlines:* rolling (freshmen), rolling (transfers). *Notification:* continuous (freshmen), continuous (transfers).

Freshman Application Contact Claflin University, 400 Magnolia Street, Orangeburg, SC 29115. *Phone:* 803-5355340. *Toll-free phone:* 800-922-1276. *Website:* http://www.claflin.edu/.

Clemson University
Clemson, South Carolina

- **State-supported** university, founded 1889
- **Small-town** 1400-acre campus
- **Endowment** $453.5 million
- **Coed** 16,562 undergraduate students, 94% full-time, 46% women, 54% men
- **Moderately difficult** entrance level, 58% of applicants were admitted

Undergraduates 15,643 full-time, 919 part-time. Students come from 53 states and territories; 84 other countries; 29% are from out of state; 6% Black or African American, non-Hispanic/Latino; 3% Hispanic/Latino; 2% Asian, non-Hispanic/Latino; 0.1% Native Hawaiian or other Pacific Islander, non-Hispanic/Latino; 0.2% American Indian or Alaska Native, non-Hispanic/Latino; 2% Two or more races, non-Hispanic/Latino; 1% Race/ethnicity unknown; 1% international; 7% transferred in; 37% live on campus. *Retention:* 91% of full-time freshmen returned.

Freshmen *Admission:* 18,500 applied, 10,706 admitted, 3,463 enrolled. *Average high school GPA:* 4.23. *Test scores:* SAT critical reading scores over 500: 93%; SAT math scores over 500: 97%; ACT scores over 18: 100%; SAT critical reading scores over 600: 59%; SAT math scores over 600: 75%; ACT scores over 24: 92%; SAT critical reading scores over 700: 14%; SAT math scores over 700: 20%; ACT scores over 30: 34%.

Faculty *Total:* 1,157, 91% full-time, 86% with terminal degrees. *Student/faculty ratio:* 18:1.

Academics *Calendar:* semesters. *Degrees:* bachelor's, master's, doctoral, and post-master's certificates. *Special study options:* academic remediation for entering students, advanced placement credit, cooperative education, distance learning, double majors, English as a second language, freshman honors college, honors programs, independent study, internships, off-campus study, part-time degree program, services for LD students, study abroad, summer session for credit. *ROTC:* Army (b), Air Force (b).

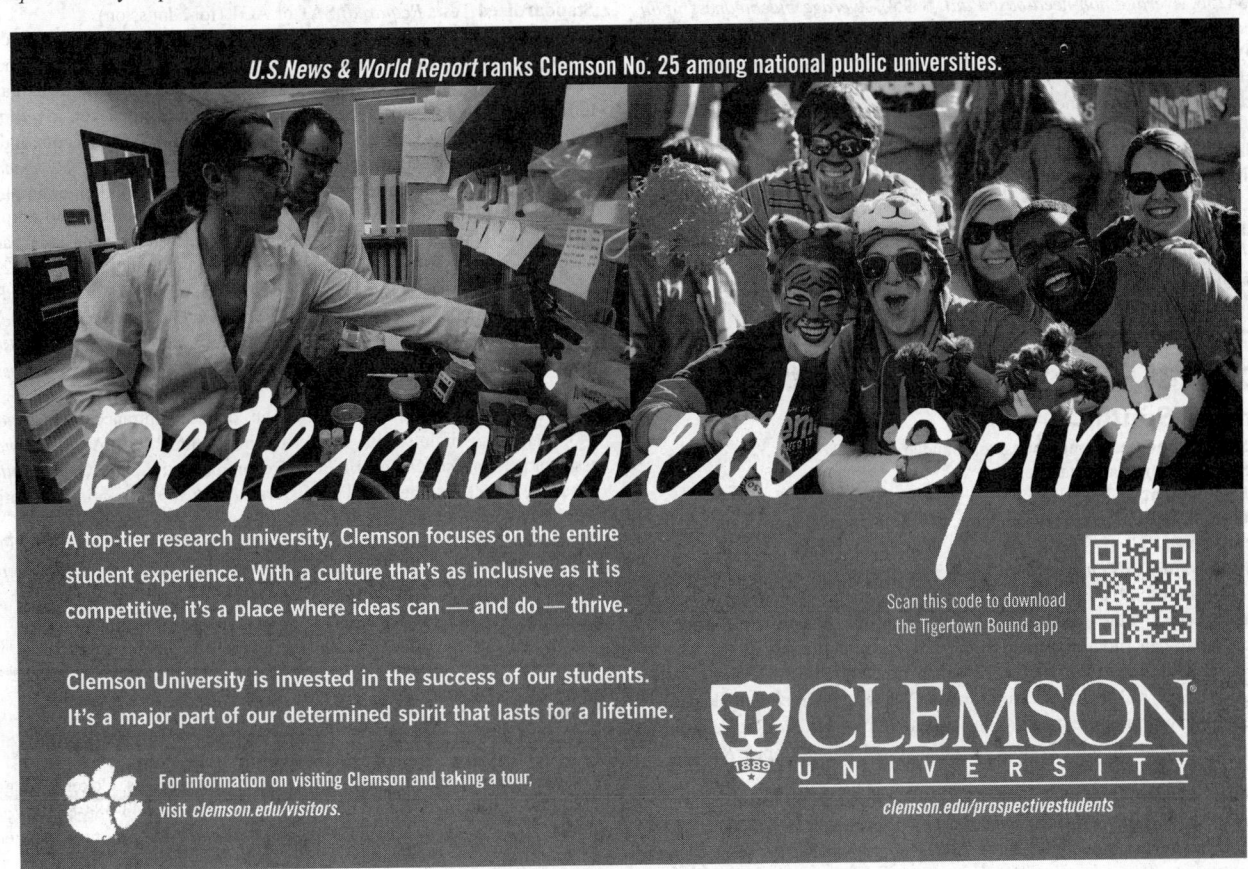

U.S. News & World Report ranks Clemson No. 25 among national public universities.

Determined spirit

A top-tier research university, Clemson focuses on the entire student experience. With a culture that's as inclusive as it is competitive, it's a place where ideas can — and do — thrive.

Clemson University is invested in the success of our students. It's a major part of our determined spirit that lasts for a lifetime.

Scan this code to download the Tigertown Bound app

CLEMSON
UNIVERSITY
1889

For information on visiting Clemson and taking a tour, visit clemson.edu/visitors.

clemson.edu/prospectivestudents

Computers on Campus 1,250 computers/terminals are available on campus for general student use. Students can access the following: online (class) registration. Campuswide network is available. 100% of college-owned or -operated housing units are wired for high-speed Internet access. Wireless service is available via entire campus.

Student Life *Housing:* on-campus residence required for freshman year. *Options:* coed, men-only, women-only. Campus housing is university owned. Freshman campus housing is guaranteed. *Activities and organizations:* drama/theater group, student-run newspaper, radio and television station, choral group, marching band, student government, Fellowship of Christian Athletes, Tiger Band, national fraternities, national sororities. *Campus security:* 24-hour emergency response devices and patrols, late-night transport/escort service, controlled dormitory access. *Student services:* health clinic, personal/psychological counseling, legal services.

Athletics Member NCAA. All Division I except football (Division I-A). *Intercollegiate sports:* baseball M, basketball M(s)/W(s), bowling M(c)/W(c), cheerleading M/W, crew M(c)/W(s), cross-country running M(s)/W(s), equestrian sports M(c)/W(c), fencing M(c)/W(c), field hockey M(c)/W(c), golf M(s), ice hockey M(c)/W(c), lacrosse M(c)/W(c), riflery M(c)/W(c), rugby M(c)/W(c), sailing M(c)/W(c), soccer M(s)/W(s), softball W(c), tennis M(s)/W(s), track and field M(s)/W(s), ultimate Frisbee M(c)/W(c), volleyball M(c)/W(s), weight lifting M(c)/W(c), wrestling M(c). *Intramural sports:* basketball M/W, golf M/W, racquetball M/W, soccer M/W, softball M/W, swimming and diving M(c)/W(c), table tennis M/W, tennis M(c)/W(c), volleyball M/W, water polo M/W.

Standardized Tests *Required:* SAT or ACT (for admission).

Costs (2012–13) *Tuition:* state resident $13,076 full-time; nonresident $29,720 full-time. Full-time tuition and fees vary according to course load, location, and program. Part-time tuition and fees vary according to program. *Room and board:* $7552. Room and board charges vary according to board plan, housing facility, and location. *Payment plan:* installment. *Waivers:* senior citizens.

Financial Aid Of all full-time matriculated undergraduates who enrolled in 2012, 11,655 applied for aid, 9,125 were judged to have need, 965 had their need fully met. 715 Federal Work-Study jobs (averaging $2322). 2,162 state and other part-time jobs (averaging $3700). In 2012, 3197 non-need-based awards were made. *Average percent of need met:* 50%. *Average financial aid package:* $9578. *Average need-based loan:* $4372. *Average need-based gift aid:* $4256. *Average non-need-based aid:* $5950. *Average indebtedness upon graduation:* $31,172.

Applying *Options:* electronic application. *Application fee:* $70. *Required:* high school transcript. *Recommended:* essay or personal statement. *Application deadlines:* 5/1 (freshmen), 7/1 (transfers). *Notification:* continuous (freshmen), continuous (transfers).

Freshman Application Contact Ms. Audrey R. Bodell, Associate Director of Admissions, Clemson University, PO Box 345124, 105 Sikes Hall, Clemson, SC 29634. *Phone:* 864-656-2287. *Fax:* 864-656-2464. *E-mail:* cuadmissions@clemson.edu.
Website: http://www.clemson.edu/.

See previous page for display ad and page 1242 for the College Close-Up.

Coastal Carolina University

Conway, South Carolina

- **State-supported** comprehensive, founded 1954
- **Suburban** 630-acre campus
- **Endowment** $30.1 million
- **Coed** 8,746 undergraduate students, 91% full-time, 54% women, 46% men
- **Moderately difficult** entrance level, 74% of applicants were admitted

Undergraduates 7,916 full-time, 830 part-time. Students come from 45 states and territories; 51 other countries; 47% are from out of state; 20% Black or African American, non-Hispanic/Latino; 3% Hispanic/Latino; 0.8% Asian, non-Hispanic/Latino; 0.1% Native Hawaiian or other Pacific Islander, non-Hispanic/Latino; 0.3% American Indian or Alaska Native, non-Hispanic/Latino; 3% Two or more races, non-Hispanic/Latino; 0.2% Race/ethnicity unknown; 2% international; 9% transferred in; 38% live on campus. *Retention:* 60% of full-time freshmen returned.

Freshmen *Admission:* 10,993 applied, 8,139 admitted, 2,206 enrolled. *Average high school GPA:* 3.32. *Test scores:* SAT critical reading scores over 500: 44%; SAT math scores over 500: 54%; ACT scores over 18: 93%; SAT critical reading scores over 600: 8%; SAT math scores over 600: 12%; ACT scores over 24: 22%; SAT critical reading scores over 700: 1%; SAT math scores over 700: 1%; ACT scores over 30: 1%.

Faculty *Total:* 645, 59% full-time, 56% with terminal degrees. *Student/faculty ratio:* 17:1.

Academics *Calendar:* semesters. *Degrees:* certificates, bachelor's, master's, post-master's, and postbachelor's certificates. *Special study options:* accelerated degree program, adult/continuing education programs, advanced placement credit, cooperative education, distance learning, double majors, honors programs, independent study, internships, part-time degree program, services for LD students, student-designed majors, study abroad, summer session for credit. *ROTC:* Army (b).

Computers on Campus 987 computers/terminals are available on campus for general student use. Students can access the following: computer help desk, free student e-mail accounts, online (class) grades, online (class) registration, online (class) schedules. Campuswide network is available. Wireless service is available via classrooms, computer centers, computer labs, dorm rooms, learning centers, libraries, student centers.

Student Life *Housing:* on-campus residence required through sophomore year. *Options:* coed, disabled students. Campus housing is university owned. Freshman campus housing is guaranteed. *Activities and organizations:* drama/theater group, student-run newspaper, radio station, choral group, marching band, Student Government Association, Campus Activities Board, STAR (Students Taking Active Responsibility), SCREAM (Student Spirit Organization), Leadership Challenge, national fraternities, national sororities. *Campus security:* 24-hour emergency response devices and patrols, late-night transport/escort service. *Student services:* health clinic, personal/psychological counseling, women's center.

Athletics Member NCAA. All Division I. *Intercollegiate sports:* baseball M(s), basketball M(s)/W(s), cheerleading M(c)/W(c), cross-country running M(s)/W(s), equestrian sports M(c)/W(c), field hockey M(c)/W(c), football M(s), golf M(s)/W(s), lacrosse M(c)/W(s), rugby M(c)/W(c), soccer M(s)/W(s), softball W(s), swimming and diving M(c)/W(c), tennis M(s)/W(s), track and field M(s)/W(s), volleyball M(c)/W(s), weight lifting M(c), wrestling M(c). *Intramural sports:* badminton M/W, basketball M/W, football M/W, golf M/W, soccer M/W, softball M/W, table tennis M/W, tennis M/W, volleyball M/W, water polo M/W.

Standardized Tests *Required:* SAT or ACT (for admission).

Costs (2012–13) *Tuition:* state resident $9680 full-time, $407 per credit hour part-time; nonresident $21,970 full-time, $920 per credit hour part-time. Full-time tuition and fees vary according to course load and degree level. Part-time tuition and fees vary according to course load and degree level. *Required fees:* $80 full-time. *Room and board:* $7700; room only: $5000. Room and board charges vary according to board plan and housing facility. *Payment plan:* installment. *Waivers:* senior citizens and employees or children of employees.

Financial Aid Of all full-time matriculated undergraduates who enrolled in 2011, 6,741 applied for aid, 5,633 were judged to have need, 481 had their need fully met. 140 Federal Work-Study jobs (averaging $2242). 1,022 state and other part-time jobs (averaging $2410). In 2011, 1195 non-need-based awards were made. *Average percent of need met:* 47%. *Average financial aid package:* $9283. *Average need-based loan:* $8176. *Average need-based gift aid:* $4661. *Average non-need-based aid:* $12,396. *Average indebtedness upon graduation:* $34,040.

Applying *Options:* electronic application, deferred entrance. *Application fee:* $45. *Required:* high school transcript, minimum 2.0 GPA. *Recommended:* essay or personal statement, 1 letter of recommendation, interview. *Application deadlines:* 6/1 (freshmen), 6/1 (transfers). *Notification:* continuous until 10/1 (freshmen), continuous until 10/1 (transfers).

Freshman Application Contact Coastal Carolina University, PO Box 261954, Conway, SC 29528-6054. *Phone:* 843-349-2037. *Toll-free phone:* 800-277-7000.
Website: http://www.coastal.edu/.

Coker College

Hartsville, South Carolina

Freshman Application Contact Director of Admissions, Coker College, 300 East College Avenue, Hartsville, SC 29550. *Phone:* 843-383-8050. *Toll-free phone:* 800-950-1908. *Fax:* 843-383-8056. *E-mail:* admissions@coker.edu. *Website:* http://www.coker.edu/.

College of Charleston

Charleston, South Carolina

- **State-supported** comprehensive, founded 1770
- **Urban** 52-acre campus
- **Endowment** $55.9 million
- **Coed** 10,506 undergraduate students, 93% full-time, 62% women, 38% men
- **Moderately difficult** entrance level, 68% of applicants were admitted

Undergraduates 9,760 full-time, 746 part-time. Students come from 51 states and territories; 63 other countries; 38% are from out of state; 6% Black or African American, non-Hispanic/Latino; 4% Hispanic/Latino; 2% Asian, non-Hispanic/Latino; 0.2% Native Hawaiian or other Pacific Islander, non-Hispanic/Latino; 0.1% American Indian or Alaska Native, non-Hispanic/Latino; 3% Two or more races, non-Hispanic/Latino; 1% Race/ethnicity unknown; 0.7% international; 7% transferred in; 31% live on campus. *Retention:* 82% of full-time freshmen returned.

Freshmen *Admission:* 11,962 applied, 8,092 admitted, 2,138 enrolled. *Average high school GPA:* 3.9. *Test scores:* SAT critical reading scores over 500: 96%; SAT math scores over 500: 95%; ACT scores over 18: 100%; SAT critical reading scores over 600: 55%; SAT math scores over 600: 55%; ACT scores over 24: 72%; SAT critical reading scores over 700: 11%; SAT math scores over 700: 9%; ACT scores over 30: 6%.

Faculty *Total:* 957, 57% full-time, 65% with terminal degrees. *Student/faculty ratio:* 16:1.

Academics *Calendar:* semesters. *Degrees:* bachelor's, master's, post-master's, and postbachelor's certificates (also offers graduate degree programs through University of Charleston, South Carolina). *Special study options:* accelerated degree program, adult/continuing education programs, advanced placement credit, cooperative education, distance learning, double majors, English as a second language, honors programs, independent study, internships, off-campus study, part-time degree program, services for LD students, study abroad, summer session for credit. *ROTC:* Air Force (c).

Computers on Campus 750 computers/terminals and 1,200 ports are available on campus for general student use. Students can access the following: computer help desk, free student e-mail accounts, online (class) grades, online (class) registration, online (class) schedules. Campuswide network is available. 100% of college-owned or -operated housing units are wired for high-speed Internet access. Wireless service is available via entire campus.

Student Life *Housing options:* coed, men-only, women-only. Campus housing is university owned. Freshman campus housing is guaranteed. *Activities and organizations:* drama/theater group, student-run newspaper, radio station, choral group, Student Government Association, Cougar Activities Board, Intramural basketball, Black Student Union, Cisternyard Student Media, national fraternities, national sororities. *Campus security:* 24-hour emergency response devices and patrols, student patrols, late-night transport/escort service, controlled dormitory access. *Student services:* health clinic, personal/psychological counseling, women's center, legal services.

Athletics Member NCAA. All Division I. *Intercollegiate sports:* baseball M(s), basketball M(s)/W(s), cheerleading W, cross-country running M(s)/W(s), equestrian sports W, golf M(s)/W(s), sailing M/W, soccer M(s)/W(s), softball M/W, swimming and diving M(s)/W(s), tennis M(s)/W(s), track and field W, volleyball W(s). *Intramural sports:* badminton M/W, basketball M/W, crew M(c)/W(c), golf M(c)/W(c), gymnastics M(c)/W(c), ice hockey M(c)/W(c), lacrosse M(c)/W(c), racquetball M/W, rugby M(c)/W(c), soccer M/W, softball W, squash M(c)/W(c), swimming and diving M(c)/W(c), table tennis M/W, tennis M(c)/W(c), ultimate Frisbee M(c)/W(c), volleyball M/W(c), weight lifting M/W.

Standardized Tests *Required:* SAT or ACT (for admission).

Costs (2012–13) *Tuition:* state resident $9918 full-time, $413 per semester hour part-time; nonresident $25,304 full-time, $1054 per semester hour part-time. Full-time tuition and fees vary according to degree level. Part-time tuition and fees vary according to course load and degree level. *Room and board:* $10,461; room only: $7111. Room and board charges vary according to board plan and housing facility. *Payment plan:* installment. *Waivers:* senior citizens.

Financial Aid Of all full-time matriculated undergraduates who enrolled in 2012, 6,090 applied for aid, 4,690 were judged to have need, 897 had their need fully met. In 2012, 1712 non-need-based awards were made. *Average percent of need met:* 57%. *Average financial aid package:* $12,724. *Average need-based loan:* $3578. *Average need-based gift aid:* $3030. *Average non-need-based aid:* $10,788. *Average indebtedness upon graduation:* $32,880.

Applying *Options:* electronic application, early action, deferred entrance. *Application fee:* $50. *Required:* essay or personal statement, high school transcript, SAT or ACT. *Application deadlines:* 4/1 (freshmen), 5/1 (transfers), 11/1 (early action). *Notification:* 5/15 (freshmen), 6/1 (transfers), 12/15 (early action).

Freshman Application Contact Ms. Suzette Stille, Director of Undergraduate Admissions, College of Charleston, 66 George Street, Charleston, SC 29424-0001. *Phone:* 843-953-5670. *Fax:* 843-953-6322. *E-mail:* admissions@cofc.edu.
Website: http://www.cofc.edu/.

Columbia College

Columbia, South Carolina

- **Independent United Methodist** comprehensive, founded 1854
- **Suburban** 33-acre campus
- **Endowment** $19.0 million
- **Undergraduate: women only; graduate: coed** 1,088 undergraduate students, 76% full-time, 97% women, 3% men
- **Moderately difficult** entrance level, 65% of applicants were admitted

Undergraduates 828 full-time, 260 part-time. Students come from 24 states and territories; 6 other countries; 10% are from out of state; 41% Black or African American, non-Hispanic/Latino; 3% Hispanic/Latino; 1% Asian, non-Hispanic/Latino; 0.4% American Indian or Alaska Native, non-Hispanic/Latino; 4% Race/ethnicity unknown; 0.6% international; 13% transferred in; 44% live on campus. *Retention:* 60% of full-time freshmen returned.

Freshmen *Admission:* 771 applied, 499 admitted, 188 enrolled. *Average high school GPA:* 3.6. *Test scores:* SAT critical reading scores over 500: 56%; SAT writing scores over 500: 44%; ACT scores over 18: 89%; SAT critical reading scores over 600: 17%; SAT writing scores over 600: 11%; ACT scores over 24: 30%; SAT critical reading scores over 700: 3%; SAT writing scores over 700: 1%; ACT scores over 30: 4%.

Faculty *Total:* 134, 54% full-time, 57% with terminal degrees. *Student/faculty ratio:* 12:1.

Academics *Calendar:* semesters. *Degrees:* bachelor's, master's, and doctoral. *Special study options:* academic remediation for entering students, adult/continuing education programs, advanced placement credit, distance learning, double majors, honors programs, independent study, internships, off-campus study, part-time degree program, student-designed majors, study abroad, summer session for credit. *ROTC:* Army (c), Navy (c), Air Force (c).

Computers on Campus 165 computers/terminals are available on campus for general student use. Students can access the following: campus intranet, computer help desk, free student e-mail accounts, online (class) grades, online (class) registration, online (class) schedules. Campuswide network is available. 100% of college-owned or -operated housing units are wired for high-speed Internet access. Wireless service is available via student centers.

Student Life *Housing:* on-campus residence required through sophomore year. *Options:* women-only. Campus housing is university owned. Freshman campus housing is guaranteed. *Activities and organizations:* drama/theater group, student-run newspaper, choral group, Student Government Association, African-American Student Association, Columbia College Activities Board, Heavenly Creations Gospel Choir, Student Christian Association. *Campus security:* 24-hour emergency response devices and patrols, late-night transport/escort service, controlled dormitory access. *Student services:* health clinic, personal/psychological counseling, women's center.

Athletics Member NAIA. *Intercollegiate sports:* basketball W(s), golf W(s), soccer W(s), softball W(s), tennis W(s), volleyball W(s).

Standardized Tests *Required:* SAT or ACT (for admission).

Costs (2013–14) *Comprehensive fee:* $34,228 includes full-time tuition ($26,800), mandatory fees ($450), and room and board ($6978). Full-time tuition and fees vary according to class time. Part-time tuition: $710 per semester hour. Part-time tuition and fees vary according to course load. *College room only:* $3496. Room and board charges vary according to board plan and housing facility. *Payment plan:* installment. *Waivers:* employees or children of employees.

Financial Aid Of all full-time matriculated undergraduates who enrolled in 2005, 794 applied for aid, 698 were judged to have need, 310 had their need fully met. 200 Federal Work-Study jobs (averaging $1000). In 2005, 152 non-need-based awards were made. *Average percent of need met:* 70%. *Average financial aid package:* $20,052. *Average need-based loan:* $3810. *Average need-based gift aid:* $8495. *Average non-need-based aid:* $7775. *Average indebtedness upon graduation:* $25,333.

Applying *Options:* electronic application. *Application fee:* $25. *Required:* high school transcript, minimum 2.0 GPA, 1 letter of recommendation. *Required for some:* interview. *Recommended:* essay or personal statement. *Application deadlines:* 8/1 (freshmen), 8/1 (transfers).

Freshman Application Contact Ms. Julie King, Director of Admissions, Columbia College, 1301 Columbia College Drive, Columbia, SC 29203. *Phone:* 803-786-3765. *Toll-free phone:* 800-277-1301. *Fax:* 803-786-3674. *E-mail:* admissions@colacoll.edu.
Website: http://www.columbiasc.edu/.

Columbia International University

Columbia, South Carolina

- **Independent nondenominational** university, founded 1923
- **Suburban** 450-acre campus
- **Endowment** $12.7 million
- **Coed** 534 undergraduate students, 92% full-time, 51% women, 49% men
- **Minimally difficult** entrance level, 64% of applicants were admitted

Undergraduates 489 full-time, 45 part-time. Students come from 35 states and territories; 9 other countries; 47% are from out of state; 7% Black or African American, non-Hispanic/Latino; 4% Hispanic/Latino; 2% Asian, non-Hispanic/Latino; 0.4% Native Hawaiian or other Pacific Islander, non-Hispanic/Latino; 0.2% American Indian or Alaska Native, non-Hispanic/Latino; 1% Two or more races, non-Hispanic/Latino; 2% Race/ethnicity unknown; 2% international; 7% transferred in; 77% live on campus. *Retention:* 80% of full-time freshmen returned.

Freshmen *Admission:* 320 applied, 206 admitted, 106 enrolled. *Average high school GPA:* 3.73. *Test scores:* SAT critical reading scores over 500: 78%; SAT math scores over 500: 67%; SAT writing scores over 500: 65%; ACT scores over 18: 95%; SAT critical reading scores over 600: 40%; SAT math scores over 600: 26%; SAT writing scores over 600: 24%; ACT scores over 24: 44%; SAT critical reading scores over 700: 6%; SAT math scores over 700: 3%; SAT writing scores over 700: 6%; ACT scores over 30: 5%.

Faculty *Total:* 84, 55% full-time, 62% with terminal degrees. *Student/faculty ratio:* 14:1.

Academics *Calendar:* semesters. *Degrees:* certificates, associate, bachelor's, master's, doctoral, and postbachelor's certificates. *Special study options:* academic remediation for entering students, advanced placement credit, cooperative education, distance learning, double majors, independent study, internships, off-campus study, services for LD students, study abroad, summer session for credit.

Computers on Campus 106 computers/terminals and 374 ports are available on campus for general student use. Students can access the following: campus intranet, computer help desk, free student e-mail accounts, online (class) grades, online (class) registration, online (class) schedules. Campuswide network is available. 100% of college-owned or -operated housing units are wired for high-speed Internet access. Wireless service is available via classrooms, computer centers, computer labs, dorm rooms, learning centers, libraries, student centers.

Student Life *Housing:* on-campus residence required through senior year. *Options:* men-only, women-only, disabled students. Campus housing is university owned and leased by the school. Freshman campus housing is guaranteed. *Activities and organizations:* drama/theater group, student-run newspaper, choral group, Student Union, Mu Kappa, Student Missions Connection, GradLife, African American Fellowship Ministries. *Campus security:* 24-hour emergency response devices and patrols, late-night transport/escort service. *Student services:* health clinic, personal/psychological counseling.

Athletics Member NCCAA. *Intercollegiate sports:* cross-country running M/W, soccer M. *Intramural sports:* basketball M/W, football M/W, soccer M/W, ultimate Frisbee M/W, volleyball M/W.

Standardized Tests *Required:* SAT or ACT (for admission).

Costs (2013–14) *One-time required fee:* $825. *Comprehensive fee:* $25,836 includes full-time tuition ($18,200), mandatory fees ($540), and room and board ($7096). Full-time tuition and fees vary according to course load, program, and reciprocity agreements. Part-time tuition: $750 per credit hour. Part-time tuition and fees vary according to course load, program, and reciprocity agreements. *Required fees:* $10 per credit part-time, $120 per term part-time. *College room only:* $3548. Room and board charges vary according to board plan and housing facility. *Payment plan:* installment. *Waivers:* employees or children of employees.

Financial Aid Of all full-time matriculated undergraduates who enrolled in 2009, 433 applied for aid, 411 were judged to have need, 24 had their need fully met. 67 Federal Work-Study jobs (averaging $2000). 274 state and other part-time jobs (averaging $2000). In 2009, 61 non-need-based awards were made. *Average percent of need met:* 72%. *Average financial aid package:* $16,042. *Average need-based loan:* $3966. *Average indebtedness upon graduation:* $21,057.

Applying *Options:* electronic application, deferred entrance. *Application fee:* $45. *Required:* essay or personal statement, minimum 2.0 GPA, 3 letters of recommendation. *Required for some:* high school transcript, interview, SAT or ACT Scores. *Application deadlines:* 7/1 (freshmen), 7/1 (out-of-state freshmen), 7/1 (transfers), 7/1 (early action). *Early decision deadline:* 7/1 (for plan 1), 7/1 (for plan 2). *Notification:* continuous (freshmen), continuous (out-of-state freshmen), continuous (transfers), rolling (early decision plan 1), rolling (early decision plan 2), rolling (early action).

Freshman Application Contact Dori Beach, Columbia International University, PO Box 3122, Columbia, SC 29230-3122. *Phone:* 803-807-5088. *Toll-free phone:* 800-777-2227 Ext. 5024. *Fax:* 803-786-4041. *E-mail:* yesciu@ciu.edu. *Website:* http://www.ciu.edu/.

Converse College

Spartanburg, South Carolina

- **Independent** comprehensive, founded 1889
- **Urban** 70-acre campus
- **Endowment** $76.9 million
- **Undergraduate: women only; graduate: coed** 690 undergraduate students, 88% full-time, 100% women
- **Moderately difficult** entrance level, 51% of applicants were admitted

Undergraduates 608 full-time, 82 part-time. Students come from 26 states and territories; 11 other countries; 24% are from out of state; 8% Black or African American, non-Hispanic/Latino; 3% Hispanic/Latino; 0.9% Asian, non-Hispanic/Latino; 0.1% Native Hawaiian or other Pacific Islander, non-Hispanic/Latino; 0.1% American Indian or Alaska Native, non-Hispanic/Latino; 3% Two or more races, non-Hispanic/Latino; 39% Race/ethnicity unknown; 0.9% international; 2% transferred in; 80% live on campus. *Retention:* 76% of full-time freshmen returned.

Freshmen *Admission:* 1,383 applied, 710 admitted, 186 enrolled. *Average high school GPA:* 3.81. *Test scores:* SAT critical reading scores over 500: 71%; SAT math scores over 500: 65%; ACT scores over 18: 98%; SAT critical reading scores over 600: 28%; SAT math scores over 600: 15%; ACT scores over 24: 45%; SAT critical reading scores over 700: 3%; SAT math scores over 700: 1%; ACT scores over 30: 2%.

Faculty *Total:* 83, 92% full-time, 90% with terminal degrees. *Student/faculty ratio:* 11:1.

Academics *Calendar:* 4-2-4. *Degrees:* bachelor's, master's, and post-master's certificates. *Special study options:* adult/continuing education programs, advanced placement credit, cooperative education, distance learning, double majors, English as a second language, honors programs, independent study, internships, off-campus study, part-time degree program, services for LD students, student-designed majors, study abroad, summer session for credit. *ROTC:* Army (c). *Unusual degree programs:* engineering with Clemson University; nursing with Vanderbilt University.

Computers on Campus 140 computers/terminals are available on campus for general student use. Students can access the following: campus intranet, computer help desk, free student e-mail accounts, online (class) grades, online (class) registration, online (class) schedules. Campuswide network is available. 100% of college-owned or -operated housing units are wired for high-speed Internet access. Wireless service is available via entire campus.

Student Life *Housing:* on-campus residence required through senior year. *Options:* women-only. Campus housing is university owned. Freshman campus housing is guaranteed. *Activities and organizations:* drama/theater group, student-run newspaper, choral group, student government, student volunteer services, Student Christian Organization, Student Activities Committee, Athletic Association. *Campus security:* 24-hour emergency response devices and patrols, late-night transport/escort service, controlled dormitory access. *Student services:* health clinic, personal/psychological counseling, women's center.

Athletics Member NCAA. All Division II. *Intercollegiate sports:* basketball W(s), cross-country running W(s), equestrian sports W(s), golf W(s), lacrosse W(s), soccer W(s), swimming and diving W(s), tennis W(s), track and field W(s), volleyball W(s). *Intramural sports:* archery W, basketball W, bowling W, equestrian sports W, fencing W, field hockey W, soccer W, softball W, swimming and diving W, tennis W, volleyball W, weight lifting W.

Standardized Tests *Required:* SAT or ACT (for admission).

Costs (2012–13) *Comprehensive fee:* $37,130 includes full-time tuition ($28,276) and room and board ($8854). Full-time tuition and fees vary according to course load and program. Part-time tuition: $850 per credit hour. Part-time tuition and fees vary according to program. *Room and board:* Room and board charges vary according to board plan, housing facility, and student level. *Payment plan:* installment. *Waivers:* employees or children of employees.

Financial Aid Of all full-time matriculated undergraduates who enrolled in 2012, 590 applied for aid, 555 were judged to have need, 115 had their need fully met. 88 Federal Work-Study jobs (averaging $1511). 60 state and other part-time jobs (averaging $1000). In 2012, 72 non-need-based awards were made. *Average percent of need met:* 76%. *Average financial aid package:* $23,249. *Average need-based loan:* $4996. *Average need-based gift aid:* $19,470. *Average non-need-based aid:* $14,597. *Average indebtedness upon graduation:* $28,986.

Applying *Options:* electronic application. *Required:* high school transcript, 1 letter of recommendation. *Required for some:* interview. *Recommended:* essay or personal statement, minimum 3.0 GPA. *Application deadlines:* rolling (freshmen), rolling (out-of-state freshmen), rolling (transfers). *Notification:* continuous (freshmen), continuous (out-of-state freshmen), continuous (transfers).

Freshman Application Contact Ms. April Lewis, Director of Admissions, Converse College, 580 East Main Street, Spartanburg, SC 29302. *Phone:* 864-596-9040 Ext. 9746. *Toll-free phone:* 800-766-1125. *Fax:* 864-596-9225. *E-mail:* admissions@converse.edu.
Website: http://www.converse.edu/.

ECPI College of Technology

Columbia, South Carolina

Admissions Office Contact ECPI College of Technology, 250 Berryhill Road, #300, Columbia, SC 29210. *Toll-free phone:* 866-708-6168.
Website: http://www.ecpi.edu/.

ECPI College of Technology

Greenville, South Carolina

Admissions Office Contact ECPI College of Technology, 1001 Keys Drive, #100, Greenville, SC 29615. *Toll-free phone:* 866-708-6171.
Website: http://www.ecpi.edu/.

ECPI College of Technology

North Charleston, South Carolina

Admissions Office Contact ECPI College of Technology, 7410 Northside Drive, Suite 100, North Charleston, SC 29420. *Toll-free phone:* 866-708-6166.
Website: http://www.ecpi.edu/.

Erskine College

Due West, South Carolina

Freshman Application Contact Erskine College, 2 Washington Street, PO Box 338, Due West, SC 29639. *Phone:* 864-379-8838. *Toll-free phone:* 800-241-8721.
Website: http://www.erskine.edu/.

Francis Marion University

Florence, South Carolina

- **State-supported** comprehensive, founded 1970
- **Rural** 400-acre campus
- **Endowment** $25.0 million
- **Coed** 3,780 undergraduate students, 90% full-time, 67% women, 33% men
- **Moderately difficult** entrance level, 59% of applicants were admitted

Undergraduates 3,395 full-time, 385 part-time. Students come from 31 states and territories; 16 other countries; 4% are from out of state; 47% Black or African American, non-Hispanic/Latino; 0.9% Hispanic/Latino; 1% Asian, non-Hispanic/Latino; 0.1% Native Hawaiian or other Pacific Islander, non-Hispanic/Latino; 0.5% American Indian or Alaska Native, non-Hispanic/Latino; 0.1% Two or more races, non-Hispanic/Latino; 2% Race/ethnicity unknown; 1% international; 8% transferred in; 40% live on campus. *Retention:* 65% of full-time freshmen returned.
Freshmen *Admission:* 3,908 applied, 2,300 admitted, 814 enrolled. *Average high school GPA:* 3.56. *Test scores:* SAT critical reading scores over 500: 37%; SAT math scores over 500: 37%; SAT writing scores over 500: 28%; ACT scores over 18: 68%; SAT critical reading scores over 600: 8%; SAT math scores over 600: 8%; SAT writing scores over 600: 4%; ACT scores over 24: 16%; SAT critical reading scores over 700: 1%; SAT math scores over 700: 1%.
Faculty *Total:* 270, 76% full-time, 62% with terminal degrees. *Student/faculty ratio:* 16:1.

Academics *Calendar:* semesters. *Degrees:* bachelor's, master's, and post-master's certificates. *Special study options:* accelerated degree program, adult/continuing education programs, advanced placement credit, distance learning, double majors, honors programs, independent study, internships, off-campus study, part-time degree program, services for LD students, study abroad, summer session for credit. *ROTC:* Army (b). *Unusual degree programs:* 3-2 engineering with Clemson University; forestry with Clemson University.
Computers on Campus 634 computers/terminals are available on campus for general student use. Students can access the following: computer help desk, online (class) grades, online (class) registration, online (class) schedules, Blackboard. Campuswide network is available. 100% of college-owned or -operated housing units are wired for high-speed Internet access. Wireless service is available via classrooms, computer labs, dorm rooms, libraries.
Student Life *Housing options:* men-only, women-only, disabled students. Campus housing is university owned and is provided by a third party. Freshman applicants given priority for college housing. *Activities and organizations:* drama/theater group, student-run newspaper, choral group, Baptist Collegiate Ministries, University Programming Board, National Pan-Hellenic Association, Student Alumni Association, Student Government Association, national fraternities, national sororities. *Campus security:* 24-hour emergency response devices and patrols, late-night transport/escort service, controlled dormitory access. *Student services:* health clinic, personal/psychological counseling.
Athletics Member NCAA. All Division II except golf (Division I), soccer (Division I). *Intercollegiate sports:* baseball M(s), basketball M(s)/W(s), cross-country running M(s)/W(s), golf M(s), soccer M(s)/W(s), softball W(s), tennis M(s)/W(s), track and field M/W, volleyball W(s). *Intramural sports:* basketball M/W, bowling M/W, cheerleading M(c)/W(c), football M/W, golf M/W, racquetball M/W, soccer M/W, softball M/W, table tennis M/W, tennis M/W, track and field M/W, ultimate Frisbee M/W, volleyball M/W.
Standardized Tests *Required:* SAT or ACT (for admission).
Costs (2012–13) *Tuition:* state resident $8708 full-time, $435 per credit hour part-time; nonresident $17,416 full-time, $871 per credit hour part-time. Full-time tuition and fees vary according to program. Part-time tuition and fees vary according to course load and program. *Required fees:* $358 full-time. *Room and board:* $6820; room only: $3842. Room and board charges vary according to board plan and housing facility. *Payment plan:* installment. *Waivers:* senior citizens and employees or children of employees.
Financial Aid Of all full-time matriculated undergraduates who enrolled in 2011, 2,926 applied for aid, 2,766 were judged to have need. In 2011, 44 non-need-based awards were made. *Average financial aid package:* $9953. *Average need-based loan:* $4187. *Average need-based gift aid:* $4454. *Average non-need-based aid:* $1922. *Average indebtedness upon graduation:* $26,453. *Financial aid deadline:* 6/30.
Applying *Options:* electronic application, early admission, deferred entrance. *Application fee:* $32. *Required:* high school transcript, minimum 2.0 GPA. *Application deadlines:* 8/15 (freshmen), 8/15 (out-of-state freshmen), rolling (transfers). *Notification:* 9/1 (freshmen), 9/1 (out-of-state freshmen).
Freshman Application Contact Mrs. Perry Wilson, Director of Admissions, Francis Marion University, PO Box 100547, Florence, SC 29502-0547. *Phone:* 843-661-1231. *Toll-free phone:* 800-368-7551. *Fax:* 843-661-4635. *E-mail:* admission@fmarion.edu.
Website: http://www.fmarion.edu/.

Furman University

Greenville, South Carolina

- **Independent** comprehensive, founded 1826
- **Suburban** 800-acre campus
- **Endowment** $550.3 million
- **Coed** 2,753 undergraduate students, 95% full-time, 57% women, 43% men
- **Moderately difficult** entrance level, 77% of applicants were admitted

Undergraduates 2,623 full-time, 130 part-time. Students come from 46 states and territories; 53 other countries; 71% are from out of state; 5% Black or African American, non-Hispanic/Latino; 3% Hispanic/Latino; 2% Asian, non-Hispanic/Latino; 0.1% American Indian or Alaska Native, non-Hispanic/Latino; 2% Two or more races, non-Hispanic/Latino; 5% Race/ethnicity unknown; 3% international; 0.9% transferred in; 96% live on campus. *Retention:* 90% of full-time freshmen returned.
Freshmen *Admission:* 6,035 applied, 4,676 admitted, 695 enrolled. *Test scores:* SAT critical reading scores over 500: 88%; SAT math scores over 500: 92%; SAT writing scores over 500: 86%; ACT scores over 18: 98%; SAT critical reading scores over 600: 55%; SAT math scores over 600: 61%; SAT writing scores over 600: 54%; ACT scores over 24: 83%; SAT critical reading

scores over 700: 12%; SAT math scores over 700: 15%; SAT writing scores over 700: 12%; ACT scores over 30: 20%.

Faculty *Total:* 268, 90% full-time, 90% with terminal degrees. *Student/faculty ratio:* 11:1.

Academics *Calendar:* 3-2-3. *Degrees:* bachelor's and master's. *Special study options:* accelerated degree program, adult/continuing education programs, advanced placement credit, double majors, independent study, internships, part-time degree program, services for LD students, student-designed majors, study abroad, summer session for credit. *ROTC:* Army (b). *Unusual degree programs:* 3-2 engineering with Georgia Institute of Technology, Clemson University, Auburn University, North Carolina State University, Washington University in St. Louis; forestry with Duke University.

Computers on Campus 425 computers/terminals and 3,500 ports are available on campus for general student use. Students can access the following: campus intranet, computer help desk, free student e-mail accounts, online (class) grades, online (class) registration, online (class) schedules. Campus-wide network is available. 100% of college-owned or -operated housing units are wired for high-speed Internet access. Wireless service is available via entire campus.

Student Life *Housing:* on-campus residence required through senior year. *Options:* coed, men-only, women-only. Campus housing is university owned. Freshman campus housing is guaranteed. *Activities and organizations:* drama/theater group, student-run newspaper, radio and television station, choral group, marching band, Collegiate Educational Service Corps, Fellowship of Christian Athletes, Baptist Student Union, Student Activities Board, Furman Singers, national fraternities, national sororities. *Campus security:* 24-hour emergency response devices and patrols, student patrols, late-night transport/escort service, controlled dormitory access. *Student services:* health clinic, personal/psychological counseling, women's center.

Athletics Member NCAA. All Division I except football (Division I-AA). *Intercollegiate sports:* baseball M(s), basketball M(s)/W(s), cheerleading M/W, crew M(c)/W(c), cross-country running M(s)/W(s), equestrian sports W(c), fencing M(c)/W(c), golf M(s)/W(s), ice hockey M(c), lacrosse M/W, rugby M(c)/W(c), soccer M(s)/W(s), softball W(s), swimming and diving M(c)/W(c), tennis M(s)/W(s), track and field M(s)/W(s), ultimate Frisbee M(c)/W(c), volleyball W(s), weight lifting M(c)/W(c), wrestling M(c). *Intramural sports:* basketball M/W, bowling M/W, cross-country running M/W, football M/W, golf M/W, racquetball M/W, soccer M/W, softball M/W, swimming and diving M/W, tennis M/W, track and field M/W, volleyball M/W.

Standardized Tests *Recommended:* SAT or ACT (for admission).

Costs (2012–13) *Comprehensive fee:* $52,041 includes full-time tuition ($41,152), mandatory fees ($380), and room and board ($10,509). Part-time tuition: $1286 per credit. Part-time tuition and fees vary according to course load. *College room only:* $5704. Room and board charges vary according to board plan and housing facility. *Payment plan:* installment. *Waivers:* employees or children of employees.

Financial Aid Of all full-time matriculated undergraduates who enrolled in 2012, 1,397 applied for aid, 1,027 were judged to have need, 317 had their need fully met. 609 Federal Work-Study jobs (averaging $1462). In 2012, 941 non-need-based awards were made. *Average percent of need met:* 73%. *Average financial aid package:* $30,492. *Average need-based loan:* $4826. *Average need-based gift aid:* $24,227. *Average non-need-based aid:* $16,049. *Average indebtedness upon graduation:* $26,661. *Financial aid deadline:* 1/15.

Applying *Options:* electronic application, early decision, early action. *Application fee:* $50. *Required:* essay or personal statement, high school transcript. *Recommended:* interview. *Application deadlines:* 1/15 (freshmen), 1/15 (transfers), 11/15 (early action). *Early decision deadline:* 11/1. *Notification:* 4/2 (freshmen), 4/2 (transfers), 12/1 (early decision), 2/1 (early action).

Freshman Application Contact Mr. Brad Pochard, Associate Vice President of Admissions, Furman University, 3300 Poinsett Highway, Greenville, SC 29613. *Phone:* 864-294-2034. *Fax:* 864-294-2018. *E-mail:* admissions@furman.edu.

Website: http://www.furman.edu/.

ITT Technical Institute

Columbia, South Carolina

- **Proprietary** primarily 2-year, part of ITT Educational Services, Inc.
- **Coed**

Academics *Degrees:* associate and bachelor's.

Freshman Application Contact Director of Recruitment, ITT Technical Institute, 1628 Browning Road, Suite 180, Columbia, SC 29210. *Phone:* 803-216-6000. *Toll-free phone:* 800-242-5158.

Website: http://www.itt-tech.edu/.

ITT Technical Institute

Greenville, South Carolina

- **Proprietary** primarily 2-year, founded 1992, part of ITT Educational Services, Inc.
- **Coed**
- **Minimally difficult** entrance level

Academics *Calendar:* quarters. *Degrees:* associate and bachelor's.

Financial Aid *Of all full-time matriculated undergraduates who enrolled in 2011,* 3 Federal Work-Study jobs.

Freshman Application Contact Director of Recruitment, ITT Technical Institute, Independence Corporate Park, 6 Independence Pointe, Greenville, SC 29615. *Phone:* 864-288-0777. *Toll-free phone:* 800-932-4488.

Website: http://www.itt-tech.edu/.

ITT Technical Institute

Myrtle Beach, South Carolina

- **Proprietary** primarily 2-year, part of ITT Educational Services, Inc.
- **Coed**

Academics *Calendar:* quarters. *Degrees:* associate and bachelor's.

Freshman Application Contact Director of Recruitment, ITT Technical Institute, 9654 N. Kings Highway, Suite 101, Myrtle Beach, SC 29572. *Phone:* 843-497-7820. *Toll-free phone:* 877-316-7054.

Website: http://www.itt-tech.edu/.

ITT Technical Institute

North Charleston, South Carolina

- **Proprietary** primarily 2-year, part of ITT Educational Services, Inc.
- **Coed**

Academics *Calendar:* quarters. *Degrees:* associate and bachelor's.

Freshman Application Contact Director of Recruitment, ITT Technical Institute, 2431 W. Aviation Avenue, North Charleston, SC 29406. *Phone:* 843-745-5700. *Toll-free phone:* 877-291-0900.

Website: http://www.itt-tech.edu/.

Lander University

Greenwood, South Carolina

- **State-supported** comprehensive, founded 1872, part of South Carolina Commission on Higher Education
- **Small-town** 120-acre campus
- **Coed** 2,969 undergraduate students, 91% full-time, 69% women, 31% men
- **Moderately difficult** entrance level, 42% of applicants were admitted

Undergraduates 2,706 full-time, 263 part-time. Students come from 23 states and territories; 28 other countries; 5% are from out of state; 34% Black or African American, non-Hispanic/Latino; 1% Hispanic/Latino; 0.4% Asian, non-Hispanic/Latino; 0.2% Native Hawaiian or other Pacific Islander, non-Hispanic/Latino; 0.3% American Indian or Alaska Native, non-Hispanic/Latino; 2% Two or more races, non-Hispanic/Latino; 2% Race/ethnicity unknown; 3% international; 7% transferred in; 45% live on campus. *Retention:* 61% of full-time freshmen returned.

Freshmen *Admission:* 3,342 applied, 1,414 admitted, 569 enrolled. *Average high school GPA:* 3.66. *Test scores:* SAT critical reading scores over 500: 42%; SAT math scores over 500: 46%; ACT scores over 18: 81%; SAT critical reading scores over 600: 8%; SAT math scores over 600: 11%; ACT scores over 24: 19%; ACT scores over 30: 1%.

Faculty *Total:* 249, 66% full-time, 49% with terminal degrees. *Student/faculty ratio:* 16:1.

Academics *Calendar:* semesters plus 3 summer sessions. *Degrees:* certificates, bachelor's, and master's. *Special study options:* academic remediation for entering students, adult/continuing education programs, advanced placement credit, cooperative education, distance learning, double majors, honors programs, independent study, internships, off-campus study, part-time degree program, services for LD students, study abroad, summer session for credit. *ROTC:* Army (b). *Unusual degree programs:* 3-2 engineering with Clemson University.

Computers on Campus 300 computers/terminals are available on campus for general student use. Students can access the following: campus intranet, computer help desk, free student e-mail accounts, online (class) grades, online (class) registration, online (class) schedules. Campuswide network is available. 100% of college-owned or -operated housing units are wired for high-speed Internet access. Wireless service is available via entire campus.

Student Life *Housing options:* coed, women-only. Campus housing is university owned. Freshman applicants given priority for college housing. *Activities and organizations:* drama/theater group, student-run newspaper, radio station, choral group, Students Promoting Intelligent Choices and Experiences (S.P.I.C.E.), Lander Association of Biological Science, Minorities on the Move (MOM), Presidential Ambassadors, Lander Dance Company, national fraternities, national sororities. *Campus security:* 24-hour emergency response devices and patrols, late-night transport/escort service, controlled dormitory access. *Student services:* health clinic, personal/psychological counseling.

Athletics Member NCAA. All Division II except golf (Division I). *Intercollegiate sports:* baseball M(s), basketball M(s)/W(s), golf M(s)/W(s), soccer M(s)/W(s), softball W(s), tennis M(s)/W(s), volleyball W(s). *Intramural sports:* basketball M/W, equestrian sports M/W, golf M/W, racquetball M/W, soccer M/W, softball M/W, ultimate Frisbee M/W, volleyball M/W.

Standardized Tests *Required:* SAT or ACT (for admission).

Financial Aid Of all full-time matriculated undergraduates who enrolled in 2002, 1,548 applied for aid, 929 were judged to have need, 481 had their need fully met. 189 Federal Work-Study jobs (averaging $1529). 348 state and other part-time jobs (averaging $2021). In 2002, 419 non-need-based awards were made. *Average percent of need met:* 68%. *Average financial aid package:* $5105. *Average need-based loan:* $3870. *Average need-based gift aid:* $1903. *Average non-need-based aid:* $3417. *Average indebtedness upon graduation:* $16,450.

Applying *Options:* electronic application. *Application fee:* $35. *Required:* high school transcript, minimum 2.0 GPA. *Recommended:* interview. *Application deadlines:* rolling (freshmen), rolling (out-of-state freshmen), rolling (transfers). *Notification:* continuous (freshmen), continuous (out-of-state freshmen), continuous (transfers).

Freshman Application Contact Ms. Jennifer M. Mathis, Director of Admissions, Lander University, 320 Stanley Avenue, Greenwood, SC 29649. *Phone:* 864-388-8307. *Toll-free phone:* 888-452-6337. *Fax:* 864-388-8125. *E-mail:* admissions@lander.edu. *Website:* http://www.lander.edu/.

Limestone College

Gaffney, South Carolina

- **Independent** 4-year, founded 1845
- **Suburban** 123-acre campus with easy access to Charlotte
- **Endowment** $12.5 million
- **Coed** 902 undergraduate students, 97% full-time, 41% women, 59% men
- **Minimally difficult** entrance level, 55% of applicants were admitted

Undergraduates 879 full-time, 23 part-time. Students come from 36 states and territories; 21 other countries; 51% are from out of state; 22% Black or African American, non-Hispanic/Latino; 4% Hispanic/Latino; 0.4% Asian, non-Hispanic/Latino; 0.8% American Indian or Alaska Native, non-Hispanic/Latino; 0.7% Two or more races, non-Hispanic/Latino; 4% Race/ethnicity unknown; 9% international; 7% transferred in; 50% live on campus. *Retention:* 53% of full-time freshmen returned.

Freshmen *Admission:* 1,389 applied, 760 admitted, 245 enrolled. *Average high school GPA:* 3.1. *Test scores:* SAT critical reading scores over 500: 47%; SAT math scores over 500: 67%; ACT scores over 18: 98%; SAT critical reading scores over 600: 8%; SAT math scores over 600: 10%; ACT scores over 24: 27%; ACT scores over 30: 2%.

Faculty *Total:* 91, 75% full-time, 67% with terminal degrees. *Student/faculty ratio:* 12:1.

Academics *Calendar:* semesters. *Degrees:* associate, bachelor's, and master's. *Special study options:* academic remediation for entering students, accelerated degree program, adult/continuing education programs, advanced placement credit, distance learning, double majors, honors programs, independent study, internships, part-time degree program, services for LD students, student-designed majors, summer session for credit. *ROTC:* Army (c).

Computers on Campus 134 computers/terminals are available on campus for general student use. Students can access the following: computer help desk, free student e-mail accounts, online (class) grades, online (class) registration, online (class) schedules. Campuswide network is available. 100% of college-owned or -operated housing units are wired for high-speed Internet access.

Wireless service is available via classrooms, dorm rooms, learning centers, libraries, student centers.

Student Life *Housing:* on-campus residence required through junior year. *Options:* men-only, women-only. Campus housing is university owned. Freshman applicants given priority for college housing. *Activities and organizations:* drama/theater group, choral group, Fellowship of Christian Athletes, Student Government Association, Student Alumni Leadership Council, Students in Free Enterprise (SIFE), Limestone Activities Board, national fraternities. *Campus security:* 24-hour patrols, late-night transport/escort service, controlled dormitory access. *Student services:* health clinic, personal/psychological counseling.

Athletics Member NCAA. All Division II. *Intercollegiate sports:* baseball M(s), basketball M(s)/W(s), cross-country running M(s)/W(s), field hockey W(s), golf M(s)/W(s), lacrosse M(s)/W(s), soccer M(s)/W(s), softball W(s), swimming and diving M(s)/W(s), tennis M(s)/W(s), track and field M(s)/W(s), volleyball M(s)/W(s), wrestling M(s). *Intramural sports:* basketball M/W, bowling M/W, cheerleading M/W, softball M/W, table tennis M/W, volleyball M/W.

Standardized Tests *Required:* SAT or ACT (for admission).

Costs (2013–14) *Comprehensive fee:* $29,880 includes full-time tuition ($22,080) and room and board ($7800). Full-time tuition and fees vary according to class time and course load. Part-time tuition: $920 per semester hour. Part-time tuition and fees vary according to class time. *College room only:* $3900. Room and board charges vary according to housing facility. *Payment plan:* installment. *Waivers:* employees or children of employees.

Financial Aid Of all full-time matriculated undergraduates who enrolled in 2012, 777 applied for aid, 729 were judged to have need, 101 had their need fully met. 126 Federal Work-Study jobs (averaging $1413). 111 state and other part-time jobs (averaging $862). In 2012, 52 non-need-based awards were made. *Average percent of need met:* 62%. *Average financial aid package:* $16,498. *Average need-based loan:* $3962. *Average need-based gift aid:* $12,970. *Average non-need-based aid:* $5401. *Average indebtedness upon graduation:* $31,409.

Applying *Options:* electronic application. *Application fee:* $25. *Required:* high school transcript, minimum 2.0 GPA. *Recommended:* 2 letters of recommendation, interview. *Application deadlines:* rolling (freshmen), rolling (out-of-state freshmen), rolling (transfers). *Notification:* continuous (freshmen), continuous (out-of-state freshmen), continuous (transfers).

Freshman Application Contact Ms. Lisa Hobbs, Admissions Office Manager, Limestone College, 1115 College Drive, Gaffney, SC 29340-3799. *Phone:* 864-488-4554. *Toll-free phone:* 800-795-7151. *Fax:* 864-487-8706. *E-mail:* lhobbs@limestone.edu. *Website:* http://www.limestone.edu/.

Medical University of South Carolina

Charleston, South Carolina

- **State-supported** upper-level, founded 1824
- **Urban** 82-acre campus
- **Endowment** $230.3 million
- **Coed**
- **Very difficult** entrance level

Faculty *Student/faculty ratio:* 2:1.

Academics *Calendar:* semesters. *Degrees:* bachelor's, master's, doctoral, post-master's, and postbachelor's certificates.

Student Life *Campus security:* 24-hour emergency response devices and patrols, late-night transport/escort service.

Costs (2012–13) *One-time required fee:* $485. *Tuition:* state resident $14,298 full-time, $647 per semester hour part-time; nonresident $24,300 full-time, $1124 per semester hour part-time. Full-time tuition and fees vary according to program. Part-time tuition and fees vary according to course load and program. *Required fees:* $1140 full-time, $1296 per unit part-time.

Financial Aid Of all full-time matriculated undergraduates who enrolled in 2010, 162 applied for aid, 158 were judged to have need, 2 had their need fully met. *Average percent of need met:* 38. *Average financial aid package:* $12,997. *Average need-based loan:* $9334. *Average need-based gift aid:* $4374.

Applying *Options:* electronic application, deferred entrance. *Application fee:* $95.

Application Contact Lyla E. Hudson, Director of Admissions, Medical University of South Carolina, 41 Bee Street MSC203, Charleston, SC 29425-2030. *Phone:* 843-792-7408. *E-mail:* hudsonly@musc.edu. *Website:* http://www.musc.edu/.

Morris College

Sumter, South Carolina

- **Independent** 4-year, founded 1908, affiliated with Baptist Educational and Missionary Convention of South Carolina
- **Small-town** 34-acre campus
- **Endowment** $12.8 million
- **Coed** 874 undergraduate students, 99% full-time, 58% women, 42% men
- **Noncompetitive** entrance level, 85% of applicants were admitted

Undergraduates 863 full-time, 11 part-time. Students come from 19 states and territories; 21% are from out of state; 93% Black or African American, non-Hispanic/Latino; 0.1% Hispanic/Latino; 1% Two or more races, non-Hispanic/Latino; 6% Race/ethnicity unknown; 6% transferred in; 78% live on campus. *Retention:* 40% of full-time freshmen returned.
Freshmen *Admission:* 2,946 applied, 2,493 admitted, 264 enrolled. *Average high school GPA:* 2.49.
Faculty *Total:* 67, 73% full-time, 63% with terminal degrees. *Student/faculty ratio:* 16:1.
Academics *Calendar:* semesters. *Degree:* bachelor's. *Special study options:* academic remediation for entering students, accelerated degree program, adult/continuing education programs, advanced placement credit, cooperative education, double majors, honors programs, internships, study abroad, summer session for credit. *ROTC:* Army (b). *Unusual degree programs:* 3-2 engineering with North Carolina Agricultural and Technical State University.
Computers on Campus 252 computers/terminals and 688 ports are available on campus for general student use. Students can access the following: campus intranet, free student e-mail accounts, online (class) grades, online (class) registration, online (class) schedules. Campuswide network is available. 100% of college-owned or -operated housing units are wired for high-speed Internet access. Wireless service is available via entire campus.
Student Life *Housing options:* men-only, women-only. Campus housing is university owned. Freshman applicants given priority for college housing. *Activities and organizations:* drama/theater group, student-run newspaper, radio station, choral group, Student Government Association, New Emphasis on Nontraditional Students (NEONS), Block M Club, Pre Alumni Council, Baptist Student Union, national fraternities, national sororities. *Campus security:* 24-hour patrols, controlled dormitory access, cameras in select locations. *Student services:* health clinic, personal/psychological counseling.
Athletics Member NAIA. *Intercollegiate sports:* baseball M(s), basketball M(s)/W(s), cheerleading M(s)/W(s), cross-country running M(s)/W(s), softball W(s), track and field M(s)/W(s), volleyball W(s). *Intramural sports:* basketball M/W, table tennis M/W.
Costs (2012–13) *Comprehensive fee:* $15,606 includes full-time tuition ($10,520), mandatory fees ($320), and room and board ($4766). Part-time tuition: $438 per credit hour. *Required fees:* $320 per term part-time. *College room only:* $2030. *Payment plan:* installment.
Financial Aid Of all full-time matriculated undergraduates who enrolled in 2011, 887 applied for aid, 859 were judged to have need, 10 had their need fully met. 300 Federal Work-Study jobs (averaging $818). *Average percent of need met:* 85%. *Average financial aid package:* $12,100. *Average need-based loan:* $3900. *Average need-based gift aid:* $7400. *Average indebtedness upon graduation:* $17,125.
Applying *Options:* electronic application, deferred entrance. *Application fee:* $20. *Required:* high school transcript, minimum 2.0 GPA, medical examination. *Required for some:* interview. *Application deadlines:* rolling (freshmen), rolling (out-of-state freshmen), rolling (transfers). *Notification:* continuous (freshmen), continuous (out-of-state freshmen), continuous (transfers).
Freshman Application Contact Ms. Deborah C. Calhoun, Director of Admissions and Records, Morris College, 100 West College Street, Sumter, SC 29150-3599. *Phone:* 803-934-3225. *Toll-free phone:* 866-853-1345. *Fax:* 803-773-8241. *E-mail:* dcalhoun@morris.edu.
Website: http://www.morris.edu/.

Newberry College

Newberry, South Carolina

- **Independent Evangelical Lutheran** 4-year, founded 1856
- **Small-town** 90-acre campus with easy access to Columbia, Greenville
- **Endowment** $20.3 million
- **Coed** 1,042 undergraduate students, 97% full-time, 44% women, 56% men
- **Moderately difficult** entrance level, 61% of applicants were admitted

Undergraduates 1,012 full-time, 30 part-time. Students come from 28 states and territories; 19 other countries; 18% are from out of state; 25% Black or African American, non-Hispanic/Latino; 3% Hispanic/Latino; 0.9% Asian, non-Hispanic/Latino; 0.3% American Indian or Alaska Native, non-Hispanic/Latino; 3% Two or more races, non-Hispanic/Latino; 2% Race/ethnicity unknown; 3% international; 6% transferred in; 72% live on campus. *Retention:* 68% of full-time freshmen returned.
Freshmen *Admission:* 858 applied, 525 admitted, 221 enrolled. *Average high school GPA:* 3.41. *Test scores:* SAT critical reading scores over 500: 34%; SAT math scores over 500: 44%; SAT writing scores over 500: 25%; ACT scores over 18: 62%; SAT critical reading scores over 600: 6%; SAT math scores over 600: 16%; SAT writing scores over 600: 5%; ACT scores over 24: 21%; SAT critical reading scores over 700: 1%; SAT math scores over 700: 1%; ACT scores over 30: 3%.
Faculty *Total:* 121, 54% full-time, 46% with terminal degrees. *Student/faculty ratio:* 12:1.
Academics *Calendar:* semesters. *Degree:* bachelor's. *Special study options:* academic remediation for entering students, accelerated degree program, adult/continuing education programs, advanced placement credit, double majors, honors programs, independent study, internships, part-time degree program, services for LD students, student-designed majors, study abroad, summer session for credit. *ROTC:* Army (c). *Unusual degree programs:* 3-2 forestry with Forestry and Environmental Management Dual-Degree Program with Duke University. Students may earn the Bachelor's and Master's degrees in 5 years, spending 3 years at Newberry and 2 years at Duke University.
Computers on Campus 22 computers/terminals are available on campus for general student use. Students can access the following: campus intranet, computer help desk, free student e-mail accounts, online (class) grades, online (class) registration, online (class) schedules. Campuswide network is available. 100% of college-owned or -operated housing units are wired for high-speed Internet access. Wireless service is available via entire campus.
Student Life *Housing:* on-campus residence required through senior year. *Options:* coed, men-only, women-only. Campus housing is university owned. Freshman applicants given priority for college housing. *Activities and organizations:* drama/theater group, student-run newspaper, radio and television station, choral group, marching band, Future Educators Association, Multi Cultural Student Association, American Chemistry Society, Blue key Honor Club, Baptist Collegiate Ministry, national fraternities, national sororities. *Campus security:* 24-hour emergency response devices and patrols, late-night transport/escort service, controlled dormitory access. *Student services:* health clinic, personal/psychological counseling.
Athletics Member NCAA. All Division II. *Intercollegiate sports:* baseball M(s), basketball M(s)/W(s), cheerleading M(s)/W(s), cross-country running M(s)/W(s), football M(s), golf M(s)/W(s), lacrosse W(s), soccer M(s)/W(s), softball W(s), tennis M(s)/W(s), volleyball W(s), wrestling M(s). *Intramural sports:* basketball M/W, football M/W, ultimate Frisbee M/W.
Standardized Tests *Required:* SAT or ACT (for admission).
Costs (2013–14) *Comprehensive fee:* $32,800 includes full-time tuition ($22,050), mandatory fees ($1750), and room and board ($9000). Full-time tuition and fees vary according to class time, course load, and student level. Part-time tuition: $525 per hour. Part-time tuition and fees vary according to class time, course load, and student level. No tuition increase for student's term of enrollment. *College room only:* $4500. Room and board charges vary according to board plan and housing facility. *Payment plan:* installment. *Waivers:* employees or children of employees.
Financial Aid Of all full-time matriculated undergraduates who enrolled in 2009, 977 applied for aid, 895 were judged to have need, 219 had their need fully met. In 2009, 147 non-need-based awards were made. *Average percent of need met:* 76%. *Average financial aid package:* $20,440. *Average need-based loan:* $4474. *Average need-based gift aid:* $16,969. *Average non-need-based aid:* $11,552. *Average indebtedness upon graduation:* $30,693.
Applying *Options:* electronic application, deferred entrance. *Application fee:* $30. *Required:* essay or personal statement, high school transcript, minimum 2.0 GPA. *Recommended:* 1 letter of recommendation, interview. *Application deadlines:* rolling (freshmen), rolling (transfers). *Notification:* continuous (freshmen), continuous (transfers).
Freshman Application Contact Ms. Delsie Phillips, Dean of Enrollment Management, Newberry College, 2100 College Street, Newberry, SC 29108. *Phone:* 803-321-5131. *Toll-free phone:* 800-845-4955. *Fax:* 803-321-5138. *E-mail:* admissions@newberry.edu.
Website: http://www.newberry.edu/.

North Greenville University

Tigerville, South Carolina

- **Independent Southern Baptist** comprehensive, founded 1892
- **Rural** 330-acre campus with easy access to Greenville
- **Coed** 2,215 undergraduate students, 89% full-time, 51% women, 49% men
- **Minimally difficult** entrance level, 60% of applicants were admitted

Undergraduates 1,980 full-time, 235 part-time. Students come from 35 states and territories; 11 other countries; 29% are from out of state; 7% Black or African American, non-Hispanic/Latino; 2% Hispanic/Latino; 0.5% Asian, non-Hispanic/Latino; 0.2% American Indian or Alaska Native, non-Hispanic/Latino; 0.9% Two or more races, non-Hispanic/Latino; 9% Race/ethnicity unknown; 0.4% international; 7% transferred in; 68% live on campus. *Retention:* 69% of full-time freshmen returned.

Freshmen *Admission:* 1,392 applied, 842 admitted, 526 enrolled. *Average high school GPA:* 3.5. *Test scores:* SAT critical reading scores over 500: 88%; SAT math scores over 500: 85%; SAT writing scores over 500: 87%; ACT scores over 18: 92%; SAT critical reading scores over 600: 47%; SAT math scores over 600: 40%; SAT writing scores over 600: 44%; ACT scores over 24: 48%; SAT critical reading scores over 700: 13%; SAT math scores over 700: 12%; SAT writing scores over 700: 18%; ACT scores over 30: 18%.

Faculty *Total:* 183, 69% full-time, 52% with terminal degrees. *Student/faculty ratio:* 14:1.

Academics *Calendar:* semesters. *Degrees:* bachelor's, master's, and doctoral. *Special study options:* academic remediation for entering students, accelerated degree program, advanced placement credit, cooperative education, distance learning, double majors, English as a second language, freshman honors college, honors programs, independent study, internships, part-time degree program, services for LD students, student-designed majors, study abroad, summer session for credit. *ROTC:* Army (c).

Computers on Campus 95 computers/terminals and 6 ports are available on campus for general student use. Students can access the following: campus intranet, computer help desk, free student e-mail accounts, online (class) grades, online (class) registration, online (class) schedules. Campuswide network is available. 100% of college-owned or -operated housing units are wired for high-speed Internet access. Wireless service is available via entire campus.

Student Life *Housing:* on-campus residence required through sophomore year. *Options:* men-only, women-only. Campus housing is university owned. Freshman campus housing is guaranteed. *Activities and organizations:* drama/theater group, student-run newspaper, radio station, choral group, marching band, Baptist Student Union, Fellowship of Christians in Service, Fellowship of Christian Athletes, Black Student Fellowship, Education Club. *Campus security:* 24-hour emergency response devices and patrols, late-night transport/escort service, controlled dormitory access. *Student services:* health clinic, personal/psychological counseling.

Athletics Member NCAA, NCCAA. All NCAA Division II. *Intercollegiate sports:* baseball M(s), basketball M(s)/W(s), cheerleading M(s)/W(s), cross-country running M(s)/W(s), football M(s), golf M(s)/W(s), soccer M(s)/W(s), softball W(s), tennis M(s)/W(s), track and field M(s)/W(s), volleyball W(s). *Intramural sports:* basketball M/W, bowling M/W, football M, golf M/W, softball M/W, table tennis M/W, tennis M/W, ultimate Frisbee M/W, volleyball W, weight lifting M/W.

Standardized Tests *Required:* SAT or ACT (for admission). *Required for some:* CPT. *Recommended:* CPT.

Costs (2012–13) *Comprehensive fee:* $22,100 includes full-time tuition ($13,936) and room and board ($8164). Full-time tuition and fees vary according to course load. Part-time tuition: $240 per unit. *Room and board:* Room and board charges vary according to housing facility. *Payment plan:* installment. *Waivers:* employees or children of employees.

Financial Aid Of all full-time matriculated undergraduates who enrolled in 2009, 1,800 applied for aid, 1,782 were judged to have need, 1,603 had their need fully met. *Average percent of need met:* 96%. *Average indebtedness upon graduation:* $18,200.

Applying *Options:* electronic application, early admission, deferred entrance. *Application fee:* $25. *Required:* high school transcript. *Required for some:* interview. *Recommended:* minimum 2.0 GPA. *Application deadlines:* 8/22 (freshmen), 8/26 (transfers). *Notification:* continuous (freshmen), continuous (transfers).

Freshman Application Contact North Greenville University, PO Box 1892, Tigerville, SC 29688-1892. *Phone:* 864-977-7052. *Toll-free phone:* 800-468-6642 Ext. 7001.
Website: http://www.ngu.edu/.

Presbyterian College

Clinton, South Carolina

- **Independent** 4-year, founded 1880, affiliated with Presbyterian Church (U.S.A.)
- **Small-town** 240-acre campus with easy access to Greenville, Spartanburg
- **Endowment** $75.0 million
- **Coed** 1,172 undergraduate students, 98% full-time, 56% women, 44% men
- **Very difficult** entrance level, 58% of applicants were admitted

Undergraduates 1,149 full-time, 23 part-time. Students come from 35 states and territories; 27 other countries; 34% are from out of state; 10% Black or African American, non-Hispanic/Latino; 2% Hispanic/Latino; 1% Asian, non-Hispanic/Latino; 0.5% American Indian or Alaska Native, non-Hispanic/Latino; 2% Two or more races, non-Hispanic/Latino; 0.3% Race/ethnicity unknown; 2% international; 1% transferred in; 97% live on campus. *Retention:* 86% of full-time freshmen returned.

Freshmen *Admission:* 1,438 applied, 831 admitted, 282 enrolled. *Average high school GPA:* 3.47. *Test scores:* SAT critical reading scores over 500: 70%; SAT math scores over 500: 75%; ACT scores over 18: 98%; SAT critical reading scores over 600: 22%; SAT math scores over 600: 26%; ACT scores over 24: 64%; SAT critical reading scores over 700: 5%; SAT math scores over 700: 2%; ACT scores over 30: 8%.

Faculty *Total:* 126, 78% full-time, 85% with terminal degrees. *Student/faculty ratio:* 14:1.

Academics *Calendar:* semesters. *Degrees:* bachelor's and doctoral. *Special study options:* advanced placement credit, double majors, honors programs, independent study, internships, off-campus study, services for LD students, study abroad, summer session for credit. *ROTC:* Army (b). *Unusual degree programs:* 3-2 engineering with Auburn University, Clemson University, Vanderbilt University, University of South Carolina.

Computers on Campus 100 computers/terminals and 275 ports are available on campus for general student use. Students can access the following: campus intranet, free student e-mail accounts, online (class) grades, online (class) registration, online (class) schedules. Campuswide network is available. 25% of college-owned or -operated housing units are wired for high-speed Internet access. Wireless service is available via entire campus.

Student Life *Housing:* on-campus residence required through senior year. *Options:* coed, men-only, women-only, disabled students. Campus housing is university owned. Freshman campus housing is guaranteed. *Activities and organizations:* drama/theater group, student-run newspaper, radio station, choral group, Student Volunteer Services, Intramural sports, Student Union Board, Fellowship of Christian Athletes, Student Government Association, national fraternities, national sororities. *Campus security:* 24-hour emergency response devices and patrols, late-night transport/escort service, controlled dormitory access. *Student services:* health clinic, personal/psychological counseling.

Athletics Member NCAA. All Division I. *Intercollegiate sports:* baseball M(s), basketball M(s)/W(s), cheerleading M(s)/W(s), cross-country running M(s)/W(s), football M(s), golf M(s)/W(s), lacrosse W(s), soccer M(s)/W(s), softball W(s), tennis M(s)/W(s), volleyball W(s). *Intramural sports:* basketball M/W, football M/W, golf M/W, rock climbing M/W, skiing (cross-country) M/W, soccer M/W, softball M/W, table tennis M/W, tennis M/W, ultimate Frisbee M/W, volleyball M/W.

Standardized Tests *Required:* SAT or ACT (for admission).

Costs (2012–13) *Comprehensive fee:* $41,430 includes full-time tuition ($30,080), mandatory fees ($2600), and room and board ($8750). Full-time tuition and fees vary according to reciprocity agreements. Part-time tuition and fees vary according to course load and program. *College room only:* $4260. Room and board charges vary according to board plan and housing facility. *Payment plan:* installment. *Waivers:* senior citizens and employees or children of employees.

Financial Aid Of all full-time matriculated undergraduates who enrolled in 2011, 954 applied for aid, 846 were judged to have need, 365 had their need fully met. In 2011, 222 non-need-based awards were made. *Average percent of need met:* 89%. *Average financial aid package:* $31,984. *Average need-based loan:* $3838. *Average need-based gift aid:* $28,146. *Average non-need-based aid:* $15,969. *Average indebtedness upon graduation:* $23,192. *Financial aid deadline:* 6/30.

Applying *Options:* electronic application, early admission, early decision, early action, deferred entrance. *Required:* essay or personal statement, high school transcript, 1 letter of recommendation. *Recommended:* interview. *Application deadlines:* 6/30 (freshmen), 6/30 (out-of-state freshmen), 7/1 (transfers), 11/15 (early action). *Early decision deadline:* 11/1. *Notification:* 3/15 (freshmen), 3/15 (out-of-state freshmen), 7/15 (transfers), 12/1 (early decision), 12/15 (early action).

Freshman Application Contact Mr. Brian J. Fortman, Dean of Admissions, Presbyterian College, 503 South Broad Street, Clinton, SC 29325. *Phone:* 864-833-8258. *Toll-free phone:* 800-960-7583 (in-state); 800-930-7583 (out-of-state). *Fax:* 864-833-8481. *E-mail:* bjfortman@presby.edu. *Website:* http://www.presby.edu/.

South Carolina State University

Orangeburg, South Carolina

- **State-supported** comprehensive, founded 1896, part of South Carolina Commission on Higher Education
- **Small-town** 160-acre campus
- **Endowment** $766,537
- **Coed**
- **Minimally difficult** entrance level

Faculty *Student/faculty ratio:* 17:1.

Academics *Calendar:* semesters. *Degrees:* bachelor's, master's, doctoral, post-master's, and postbachelor's certificates.

Student Life *Campus security:* 24-hour emergency response devices and patrols, late-night transport/escort service, controlled dormitory access.

Athletics Member NCAA. All Division I except football (Division I-AA).

Standardized Tests *Required:* SAT or ACT (for admission). *Recommended:* SAT Subject Tests (for admission).

Costs (2012–13) *Tuition:* state resident $8688 full-time; nonresident $17,600 full-time. *Required fees:* $570 full-time. *Room and board:* $9286; room only: $6300. Room and board charges vary according to housing facility. *Payment plans:* installment, deferred payment.

Financial Aid *Of all full-time matriculated undergraduates who enrolled in 2007,* 343 Federal Work-Study jobs (averaging $1048). 360 state and other part-time jobs (averaging $2050). *Average indebtedness upon graduation:* $26,678.

Applying *Options:* electronic application, deferred entrance. *Application fee:* $25. *Required:* high school transcript, minimum 2.0 GPA.

Freshman Application Contact Mr. Antonio Boyle, Assistant Vice President of Enrollment Management, South Carolina State University, 300 College Street Northeast, Orangeburg, SC 29117-0001. *Phone:* 803-536-7186. *Toll-free phone:* 800-260-5956. *Fax:* 803-536-8990. *E-mail:* admissions@scsu.edu. *Website:* http://www.scsu.edu/.

Southern Methodist College

Orangeburg, South Carolina

- **Independent Southern Methodist** 4-year, founded 1956
- **Small-town** 50-acre campus
- **Coed** 236 undergraduate students
- **Minimally difficult** entrance level

Academics *Degrees:* certificates, associate, and bachelor's. *Special study options:* academic remediation for entering students, accelerated degree program, adult/continuing education programs, advanced placement credit, cooperative education, double majors, honors programs, independent study, internships, off-campus study, part-time degree program, services for LD students, summer session for credit.

Computers on Campus Campuswide network is available.

Student Life *Housing options:* men-only, women-only. Campus housing is university owned.

Standardized Tests *Required:* SAT or ACT (for admission).

Financial Aid Of all full-time matriculated undergraduates who enrolled in 2006, 44 applied for aid, 44 were judged to have need. 3 Federal Work-Study jobs (averaging $884). *Average percent of need met:* 75%. *Average financial aid package:* $2155. *Average need-based loan:* $4000. *Average indebtedness upon graduation:* $18,000. *Financial aid deadline:* 3/15.

Applying *Options:* early admission, early action, deferred entrance. *Application fee:* $35. *Required:* essay or personal statement, high school transcript, 3 letters of recommendation, interview, health certificate. *Application deadlines:* 7/15 (freshmen), 7/15 (transfers), 7/15 (early action). *Notification:* continuous until 7/22 (freshmen), 8/15 (transfers).

Freshman Application Contact Mr. John Courson, Southern Methodist College, 541 Broughton, Orangeburg, SC 29115. *Phone:* 803-534-7826. *Fax:* 803-534-7827. *E-mail:* jcourson@smcollege.edu. *Website:* http://www.smcollege.edu/.

Southern Wesleyan University

Central, South Carolina

Freshman Application Contact Mrs. Beth Roe, Director of First Year Experience, Southern Wesleyan University, PO Box 1020, 907 Wesleyan Drive, Central, SC 29630-1020. *Phone:* 864-644-5149. *Toll-free phone:* 800-CU-AT-SWU. *Fax:* 864-644-5901. *E-mail:* broe@swu.edu. *Website:* http://www.swu.edu/.

South University

Columbia, South Carolina

- **Proprietary** comprehensive, founded 1935, part of Education Management Corporation
- **Coed**

Academics *Calendar:* quarters. *Degrees:* associate, bachelor's, and master's.

Freshman Application Contact South University, 9 Science Court, Columbia, SC 29203. *Phone:* 803-799-9082. *Toll-free phone:* 866-629-3031. *Website:* http://www.southuniversity.edu/columbia/.

Strayer University—Charleston Campus

North Charleston, South Carolina

Freshman Application Contact Strayer University—Charleston Campus, 5010 Wetland Crossing, North Charleston, SC 29418. *Website:* http://www.strayer.edu/campus/charleston/.

Strayer University—Columbia Campus

Columbia, South Carolina

Freshman Application Contact Strayer University—Columbia Campus, 200 Center Point Circle, Suite 300, Columbia, SC 29210. *Website:* http://www.strayer.edu/campus/columbia.

Strayer University—Greenville Campus

Greenville, South Carolina

Freshman Application Contact Strayer University—Greenville Campus, 555 North Pleasantburg Drive, Suite 300, Greenville, SC 29607. *Website:* http://www.strayer.edu/campus/greenville.

University of Phoenix–Columbia Campus

Columbia, South Carolina

Admissions Office Contact University of Phoenix–Columbia Campus, 1001 Pinnacle Point Drive, Suite 200, Columbia, SC 29223. *Toll-free phone:* 866-766-0766. *Website:* http://www.phoenix.edu/.

University of South Carolina

Columbia, South Carolina

- **State-supported** university, founded 1801, part of University of South Carolina System
- **Urban** 444-acre campus
- **Endowment** $513.9 million
- **Coed** 23,363 undergraduate students, 93% full-time, 54% women, 46% men
- **Moderately difficult** entrance level, 61% of applicants were admitted

Undergraduates 21,646 full-time, 1,717 part-time. Students come from 53 states and territories; 115 other countries; 31% are from out of state; 11% Black or African American, non-Hispanic/Latino; 4% Hispanic/Latino; 3% Asian, non-Hispanic/Latino; 0.1% Native Hawaiian or other Pacific Islander, non-Hispanic/Latino; 0.3% American Indian or Alaska Native, non-Hispanic/Latino; 3% Two or more races, non-Hispanic/Latino; 0.2% Race/ethnicity unknown; 1% international; 8% transferred in; 36% live on campus. *Retention:* 87% of full-time freshmen returned.

Freshmen *Admission:* 23,429 applied, 14,199 admitted, 4,625 enrolled. *Average high school GPA:* 4. *Test scores:* SAT critical reading scores over 500: 91%; SAT math scores over 500: 96%; ACT scores over 18: 100%; SAT critical reading scores over 600: 46%; SAT math scores over 600: 59%; ACT scores over 24: 81%; SAT critical reading scores over 700: 10%; SAT math scores over 700: 11%; ACT scores over 30: 21%.

Academics *Calendar:* semesters. *Degrees:* bachelor's, master's, doctoral, post-master's, and postbachelor's certificates. *Special study options:* accelerated degree program, adult/continuing education programs, advanced placement credit, cooperative education, distance learning, double majors, English as a second language, freshman honors college, honors programs, independent study, internships, part-time degree program, services for LD students, student-designed majors, study abroad, summer session for credit. *ROTC:* Army (b), Navy (b), Air Force (b).

Computers on Campus 2,800 computers/terminals are available on campus for general student use. Students can access the following: computer help desk, free student e-mail accounts, online (class) grades, online (class) registration, online (class) schedules. Campuswide network is available. 100% of college-owned or -operated housing units are wired for high-speed Internet access. Wireless service is available via entire campus.

Student Life *Housing:* on-campus residence required for freshman year. *Options:* coed, men-only, women-only, disabled students. Campus housing is university owned. Freshman campus housing is guaranteed. *Activities and organizations:* drama/theater group, student-run newspaper, radio and television station, choral group, marching band, Social Work Student Association, Friendship Association of Chinese Students and Scholars, Alpha Lambda Delta, Residence Hall Association, Student Bar Association, national fraternities, national sororities. *Campus security:* 24-hour emergency response devices and patrols, student patrols, late-night transport/escort service, controlled dormitory access. *Student services:* health clinic, personal/psychological counseling, women's center.

Athletics Member NCAA. All Division I except football (Division I-A). *Intercollegiate sports:* baseball M(s), basketball M(s)/W(s), cross-country running W(s), equestrian sports W(s), golf M(s)/W(s), soccer M(s)/W(s), softball W(s), swimming and diving M(s)/W(s), tennis M(s)/W(s), track and field M(s)/W(s), volleyball W(s). *Intramural sports:* badminton M(c)/W(c), baseball M(c), basketball M/W, bowling M/W, equestrian sports M(c)/W(c), fencing M(c)/W(c), field hockey W(c), football M/W, golf M/W, gymnastics W(c), ice hockey M(c), lacrosse M(c)/W(c), racquetball M/W, rock climbing M(c)/W(c), rugby M(c)/W(c), sailing M(c)/W(c), soccer M/W, softball M/W, swimming and diving M/W, table tennis M/W, tennis M/W, ultimate Frisbee M(c)/W(c), volleyball M/W, water polo M(c)/W(c), weight lifting M/W, wrestling M(c).

Standardized Tests *Required:* SAT or ACT (for admission).

Costs (2012–13) *Tuition:* state resident $10,088 full-time, $421 per credit hour part-time; nonresident $27,244 full-time, $1136 per credit hour part-time. Full-time tuition and fees vary according to program and reciprocity agreements. Part-time tuition and fees vary according to course load. *Required fees:* $400 full-time. *Room and board:* $8459; room only: $5624. Room and board charges vary according to board plan, housing facility, and location. *Payment plan:* deferred payment. *Waivers:* senior citizens and employees or children of employees.

Financial Aid Of all full-time matriculated undergraduates who enrolled in 2012, 14,096 applied for aid, 10,509 were judged to have need, 2,846 had their need fully met. 554 Federal Work-Study jobs (averaging $2165). 2,948 state and other part-time jobs (averaging $1772). In 2012, 6648 non-need-based awards were made. *Average percent of need met:* 74%. *Average financial aid package:* $13,012. *Average need-based loan:* $3405. *Average need-based gift aid:* $4862. *Average non-need-based aid:* $6212. *Average indebtedness upon graduation:* $25,022.

Applying *Options:* electronic application, early action. *Application fee:* $50. *Required:* high school transcript, minimum 2.0 GPA. *Application deadlines:* 12/1 (freshmen), 6/1 (transfers), 10/15 (early action). *Notification:* continuous (transfers), 12/20 (early action).

Freshman Application Contact Dr. Mary Wagner, Senior Associate Director, Undergraduate Admissions, University of South Carolina, Columbia, SC 29208. *Phone:* 803-777-7700. *Toll-free phone:* 800-868-5872. *Fax:* 803-777-0101. *E-mail:* admissions-ugrad@sc.edu. *Website:* http://www.sc.edu/.

University of South Carolina Aiken

Aiken, South Carolina

- **State-supported** comprehensive, founded 1961, part of University of South Carolina System
- **Suburban** 453-acre campus with easy access to Columbia
- **Endowment** $18.3 million
- **Coed** 3,123 undergraduate students, 78% full-time, 65% women, 35% men
- **Moderately difficult** entrance level

Undergraduates 2,427 full-time, 696 part-time. Students come from 30 states and territories; 24 other countries; 10% are from out of state; 28% Black or African American, non-Hispanic/Latino; 4% Hispanic/Latino; 1% Asian, non-Hispanic/Latino; 0.1% Native Hawaiian or other Pacific Islander, non-Hispanic/Latino; 0.4% American Indian or Alaska Native, non-Hispanic/Latino; 3% Two or more races, non-Hispanic/Latino; 0.7% Race/ethnicity unknown; 2% international; 9% transferred in; 27% live on campus. *Retention:* 68% of full-time freshmen returned.

Freshmen *Admission:* 525 enrolled. *Average high school GPA:* 3.59. *Test scores:* SAT critical reading scores over 500: 48%; SAT math scores over 500: 49%; SAT writing scores over 500: 34%; ACT scores over 18: 83%; SAT critical reading scores over 600: 9%; SAT math scores over 600: 10%; SAT writing scores over 600: 5%; ACT scores over 24: 22%; SAT critical reading scores over 700: 1%; SAT math scores over 700: 1%; ACT scores over 30: 1%.

Faculty *Total:* 237, 60% full-time, 49% with terminal degrees. *Student/faculty ratio:* 16:1.

Academics *Calendar:* semesters. *Degrees:* bachelor's and master's. *Special study options:* adult/continuing education programs, advanced placement credit, cooperative education, distance learning, double majors, English as a second language, honors programs, independent study, internships, off-campus study, part-time degree program, services for LD students, student-designed majors, study abroad, summer session for credit.

Computers on Campus 550 computers/terminals and 796 ports are available on campus for general student use. Students can access the following: computer help desk, free student e-mail accounts, online (class) grades, online (class) registration, online (class) schedules. Campuswide network is available. 100% of college-owned or -operated housing units are wired for high-speed Internet access. Wireless service is available via entire campus.

Student Life *Housing options:* coed, disabled students. Campus housing is university owned. Freshman applicants given priority for college housing. *Activities and organizations:* drama/theater group, student-run newspaper, choral group, student government, Pacesetters, Student Alumni Ambassadors, African-American Student Alliance, Pacer Union Board, national fraternities, national sororities. *Campus security:* 24-hour emergency response devices and patrols, late-night transport/escort service, controlled dormitory access. *Student services:* health clinic, personal/psychological counseling.

Athletics Member NCAA. All Division II. *Intercollegiate sports:* baseball M(s), basketball M(s)/W(s), cross-country running W(s), golf M(s), soccer M(s)/W(s), softball W(s), tennis M(s)/W(s), volleyball W(s). *Intramural sports:* basketball M/W, cheerleading M(c)/W(c), equestrian sports M(c)/W(c), soccer M/W, ultimate Frisbee M/W, volleyball M/W.

Standardized Tests *Required:* SAT or ACT (for admission).

Costs (2012–13) *Tuition:* state resident $8734 full-time, $380 per credit hour part-time; nonresident $17,490 full-time, $760 per credit hour part-time. Full-time tuition and fees vary according to reciprocity agreements. Part-time tuition and fees vary according to course load and reciprocity agreements. *Required fees:* $290 full-time, $9 per credit hour part-time, $25 per term part-time. *Room and board:* $6780. Room and board charges vary according to board plan and housing facility. *Payment plan:* deferred payment. *Waivers:* senior citizens and employees or children of employees.

Financial Aid Of all full-time matriculated undergraduates who enrolled in 2011, 2,372 applied for aid, 1,736 were judged to have need, 429 had their need fully met. 141 Federal Work-Study jobs (averaging $2209). 372 state and other part-time jobs (averaging $1707). In 2011, 436 non-need-based awards

were made. *Average percent of need met:* 72%. *Average financial aid package:* $10,767. *Average need-based loan:* $4103. *Average need-based gift aid:* $6799. *Average non-need-based aid:* $6557. *Average indebtedness upon graduation:* $22,677.

Applying *Options:* electronic application, early admission, deferred entrance. *Application fee:* $45. *Required:* high school transcript. *Application deadlines:* 8/1 (freshmen), 8/1 (out-of-state freshmen), 8/1 (transfers). *Notification:* continuous (freshmen), continuous (out-of-state freshmen), continuous (transfers).

Freshman Application Contact Mr. Andrew Hendrix, Director of Admissions, University of South Carolina Aiken, 471 University Parkway, Aiken, SC 29801-6309. *Phone:* 803-641-3366. *Toll-free phone:* 888-WOW-USCA. *Fax:* 803-641-3727. *E-mail:* admit@usca.edu. *Website:* http://www.usca.edu/.

University of South Carolina Beaufort

Bluffton, South Carolina

- **State-supported** 4-year, founded 1959, part of University of South Carolina System
- **Suburban** 200-acre campus
- **Coed**
- **Minimally difficult** entrance level

Faculty *Student/faculty ratio:* 18:1.

Academics *Calendar:* semesters. *Degree:* bachelor's.

Student Life *Campus security:* 24-hour emergency response devices, evening security service.

Athletics Member NAIA.

Standardized Tests *Required:* SAT or ACT (for admission).

Costs (2012–13) *One-time required fee:* $150. *Tuition:* state resident $8172 full-time, $344 per credit hour part-time; nonresident $17,570 full-time, $734 per credit hour part-time. Full-time tuition and fees vary according to course load, program, reciprocity agreements, and student level. Part-time tuition and fees vary according to course load, program, reciprocity agreements, and student level. *Required fees:* $386 full-time, $14 per credit hour part-time, $25 per term part-time. *Room and board:* $6910; room only: $4850. Room and board charges vary according to board plan, housing facility, and student level.

Financial Aid *Of all full-time matriculated undergraduates who enrolled in 2011,* 23 Federal Work-Study jobs (averaging $2800).

Applying *Options:* electronic application, deferred entrance. *Application fee:* $40. *Required:* high school transcript, Specific college prep classes required from high school. *Recommended:* minimum 2.0 GPA.

Freshman Application Contact Ms. Monica Williams, University of South Carolina Beaufort, 1 University Boulevard, Bluffton, SC 29909. *Phone:* 843-208-8112. *Fax:* 843-208-8015. *E-mail:* mrwilli5@uscb.edu. *Website:* http://www.uscb.edu/.

University of South Carolina Upstate

Spartanburg, South Carolina

- **State-supported** comprehensive, founded 1967, part of University of South Carolina System
- **Urban** 300-acre campus with easy access to Charlotte
- **Endowment** $3.6 million
- **Coed** 5,427 undergraduate students, 78% full-time, 65% women, 35% men
- **Moderately difficult** entrance level, 65% of applicants were admitted

Undergraduates 4,225 full-time, 1,202 part-time. Students come from 29 states and territories; 26 other countries; 4% are from out of state; 27% Black or African American, non-Hispanic/Latino; 4% Hispanic/Latino; 2% Asian, non-Hispanic/Latino; 0.1% Native Hawaiian or other Pacific Islander, non-Hispanic/Latino; 0.3% American Indian or Alaska Native, non-Hispanic/Latino; 3% Two or more races, non-Hispanic/Latino; 1% Race/ethnicity unknown; 2% international; 18% live on campus. *Retention:* 67% of full-time freshmen returned.

Freshmen *Admission:* 3,012 applied, 1,946 admitted, 805 enrolled. *Average high school GPA:* 3.67. *Test scores:* SAT critical reading scores over 500: 38%; SAT math scores over 500: 43%; SAT writing scores over 500: 31%; ACT scores over 18: 86%; SAT critical reading scores over 600: 6%; SAT math scores over 600: 8%; SAT writing scores over 600: 4%; ACT scores over 24: 17%; SAT critical reading scores over 700: 1%.

Faculty *Total:* 406, 52% full-time, 55% with terminal degrees. *Student/faculty ratio:* 17:1.

Academics *Calendar:* semesters. *Degrees:* bachelor's, master's, and postbachelor's certificates. *Special study options:* academic remediation for entering students, accelerated degree program, adult/continuing education programs, advanced placement credit, cooperative education, distance learning, double majors, English as a second language, honors programs, independent study, internships, off-campus study, part-time degree program, services for LD students, student-designed majors, study abroad, summer session for credit. *ROTC:* Army (c).

Computers on Campus 430 computers/terminals are available on campus for general student use. Students can access the following: computer help desk, free student e-mail accounts, online (class) grades, online (class) registration. Campuswide network is available. Wireless service is available via classrooms, computer centers, computer labs, dorm rooms, libraries, student centers.

Student Life *Housing options:* coed, disabled students. Campus housing is university owned. Freshman applicants given priority for college housing. *Activities and organizations:* drama/theater group, student-run newspaper, choral group, African-American Association, Campus Activity Board, Student Nurses Association, Student Government Association, Impact, national fraternities, national sororities. *Campus security:* 24-hour emergency response devices and patrols, late-night transport/escort service, campus security cameras. *Student services:* health clinic, personal/psychological counseling, women's center.

Athletics Member NCAA. All Division I. *Intercollegiate sports:* baseball M(s), basketball M(s)/W(s), cheerleading M(s)/W(s), cross-country running M(s)/W(s), golf M(s)/W(s), soccer M(s)/W(s), softball W(s), tennis M(s)/W(s), track and field M(s)/W(s), volleyball W(s). *Intramural sports:* badminton M/W, baseball M, basketball M/W, bowling M/W, football M/W, golf M/W, racquetball M/W, soccer M/W, softball M/W, table tennis M/W, tennis M/W, track and field M/W, volleyball M/W.

Standardized Tests *Required:* SAT or ACT (for admission).

Costs (2012–13) *Tuition:* state resident $9442 full-time, $403 per semester hour part-time; nonresident $19,164 full-time, $815 per semester hour part-time. Full-time tuition and fees vary according to course load and program. Part-time tuition and fees vary according to course load and program. *Required fees:* $450 full-time, $165 per term part-time. *Room and board:* $7250; room only: $4450. Room and board charges vary according to board plan and housing facility. *Payment plan:* deferred payment. *Waivers:* senior citizens.

Financial Aid Of all full-time matriculated undergraduates who enrolled in 2010, 3,328 applied for aid, 2,782 were judged to have need, 408 had their need fully met. 97 Federal Work-Study jobs (averaging $1730). 439 state and other part-time jobs (averaging $1244). In 2010, 94 non-need-based awards were made. *Average percent of need met:* 53%. *Average financial aid package:* $8944. *Average need-based loan:* $4011. *Average need-based gift aid:* $4214. *Average non-need-based aid:* $2048. *Average indebtedness upon graduation:* $18,762.

Applying *Options:* electronic application, deferred entrance. *Application fee:* $40. *Required:* high school transcript, minimum 2.0 GPA, college preparatory courses. *Notification:* continuous (freshmen), continuous (transfers).

Freshman Application Contact Ms. Donette Stewart, Assistant Vice Chancellor for Enrollment Services, University of South Carolina Upstate, 800 University Way, Spartanburg, SC 29303. *Phone:* 864-503-5280. *Toll-free phone:* 800-277-8727. *Fax:* 864-503-5727. *E-mail:* dstewart@uscupstate.edu. *Website:* http://www.uscupstate.edu/.

Voorhees College

Denmark, South Carolina

Freshman Application Contact Dr. Willie Jefferson, Dean of Enrollment Management, Voorhees College, PO Box 678, Denmark, SC 29042. *Phone:* 803-703-1049. *Toll-free phone:* 866-685-9904. *E-mail:* williej@voorhees.edu. *Website:* http://www.voorhees.edu/.

Winthrop University

Rock Hill, South Carolina

- **State-supported** comprehensive, founded 1886, part of South Carolina Commission on Higher Education
- **Suburban** 448-acre campus with easy access to Charlotte
- **Endowment** $32.5 million
- **Coed** 5,029 undergraduate students, 89% full-time, 67% women, 33% men
- **Moderately difficult** entrance level, 71% of applicants were admitted

Undergraduates 4,462 full-time, 567 part-time. Students come from 34 states and territories; 37 other countries; 8% are from out of state; 30% Black or African American, non-Hispanic/Latino; 2% Hispanic/Latino; 1% Asian, non-Hispanic/Latino; 0.5% Native Hawaiian or other Pacific Islander, non-Hispanic/Latino; 0.5% American Indian or Alaska Native, non-Hispanic/Latino; 1% Two or more races, non-Hispanic/Latino; 0.1% Race/ethnicity unknown; 3% international; 8% transferred in; 47% live on campus. *Retention:* 73% of full-time freshmen returned.

Freshmen *Admission:* 4,316 applied, 3,051 admitted, 1,143 enrolled. *Average high school GPA:* 3.8. *Test scores:* SAT critical reading scores over 500: 60%; SAT math scores over 500: 61%; ACT scores over 18: 94%; SAT critical reading scores over 600: 21%; SAT math scores over 600: 18%; ACT scores over 24: 36%; SAT critical reading scores over 700: 3%; SAT math scores over 700: 1%; ACT scores over 30: 6%.

Faculty *Total:* 525, 54% full-time, 54% with terminal degrees. *Student/faculty ratio:* 15:1.

Academics *Calendar:* semesters. *Degrees:* bachelor's, master's, post-master's, and postbachelor's certificates. *Special study options:* adult/continuing education programs, advanced placement credit, cooperative education, distance learning, double majors, honors programs, independent study, internships, off-campus study, part-time degree program, services for LD students, study abroad, summer session for credit. *ROTC:* Army (c), Air Force (c).

Computers on Campus 620 computers/terminals are available on campus for general student use. Students can access the following: campus intranet, computer help desk, free student e-mail accounts, online (class) grades, online (class) registration, online (class) schedules, vast majority of university services are available online. Campuswide network is available. 100% of college-owned or -operated housing units are wired for high-speed Internet access. Wireless service is available via entire campus.

Student Life *Housing:* on-campus residence required for freshman year. *Options:* coed, men-only, women-only, disabled students. Campus housing is university owned. Freshman campus housing is guaranteed. *Activities and organizations:* drama/theater group, student-run newspaper, radio station, choral group, Association of Ebonites, WU Crew, Greek Life, DiGiorgio Student Union, Campus Ministries, national fraternities, national sororities. *Campus security:* 24-hour emergency response devices and patrols, late-night transport/escort service, controlled dormitory access. *Student services:* health clinic, personal/psychological counseling.

Athletics Member NCAA. All Division I. *Intercollegiate sports:* baseball M(s), basketball M(s)/W(s), cheerleading M(c)/W(c), cross-country running M(s)/W(s), fencing M(c)/W(c), golf M(s)/W(s), lacrosse M(c)/W, rugby M(c), soccer M(s)/W(s), softball W(s), tennis M(s)/W(s), track and field M(s)/W(s), volleyball W(s). *Intramural sports:* badminton M/W, basketball M/W, cross-country running M/W, equestrian sports M(c)/W(c), football M/W, golf M/W, racquetball M/W, soccer M/W, softball M/W, swimming and diving M/W, table tennis M/W, tennis M/W, ultimate Frisbee M/W, volleyball M/W, water polo M/W, weight lifting M/W.

Standardized Tests *Required:* SAT or ACT (for admission).

Costs (2012–13) *Tuition:* state resident $13,026 full-time, $543 per credit hour part-time; nonresident $24,476 full-time, $1020 per credit hour part-time. Full-time tuition and fees vary according to degree level and reciprocity agreements. Part-time tuition and fees vary according to degree level. *Room and board:* $7464; room only: $4674. Room and board charges vary according to board plan and housing facility. *Payment plan:* installment. *Waivers:* senior citizens and employees or children of employees.

Financial Aid Of all full-time matriculated undergraduates who enrolled in 2012, 3,737 applied for aid, 3,230 were judged to have need, 425 had their need fully met. 233 Federal Work-Study jobs (averaging $742). In 2012, 481 non-need-based awards were made. *Average percent of need met:* 60%. *Average financial aid package:* $11,532. *Average need-based loan:* $4187. *Average need-based gift aid:* $7767. *Average non-need-based aid:* $3270. *Average indebtedness upon graduation:* $22,521.

Applying *Options:* electronic application, deferred entrance. *Application fee:* $40. *Required:* high school transcript, minimum 3.0 GPA. *Required for some:* essay or personal statement. *Application deadlines:* 5/1 (freshmen), 5/1 (out-of-state freshmen), 5/1 (transfers). *Notification:* continuous (freshmen), continuous (transfers).

Freshman Application Contact Winthrop University, 701 Oakland Avenue, Rock Hill, SC 29733. *Phone:* 803-323-2191. *Toll-free phone:* 800-763-0230. *Website:* http://www.winthrop.edu/.

Wofford College

Spartanburg, South Carolina

- **Independent** 4-year, founded 1854, affiliated with United Methodist Church
- **Urban** 170-acre campus with easy access to Charlotte
- **Endowment** $161.9 million
- **Coed**
- **Very difficult** entrance level

Faculty *Student/faculty ratio:* 11:1.

Academics *Calendar:* 4-1-4. *Degree:* bachelor's.

Student Life *Campus security:* 24-hour emergency response devices and patrols, late-night transport/escort service, controlled dormitory access.

Athletics Member NCAA. All Division I except football (Division I-AA).

Standardized Tests *Required:* SAT or ACT (for admission).

Costs (2012–13) *Comprehensive fee:* $44,475 includes full-time tuition ($34,555) and room and board ($9920).

Financial Aid Of all full-time matriculated undergraduates who enrolled in 2012, 1,127 applied for aid, 958 were judged to have need, 421 had their need fully met. In 2012, 401 non-need-based awards were made. *Average percent of need met:* 83. *Average financial aid package:* $27,803. *Average need-based loan:* $4251. *Average need-based gift aid:* $28,915. *Average non-need-based aid:* $14,769. *Average indebtedness upon graduation:* $22,118.

Applying *Options:* electronic application, early admission, early decision, deferred entrance. *Application fee:* $35. *Required:* essay or personal statement, high school transcript. *Recommended:* 2 letters of recommendation, interview.

Freshman Application Contact Mr. S. Wells Shepard, Director of Admission, Wofford College, 429 North Church Street, Spartanburg, SC 29303-3663. *Phone:* 864-597-4130. *Fax:* 864-597-4147. *E-mail:* admission@wofford.edu. *Website:* http://www.wofford.edu/.

SOUTH DAKOTA

Augustana College

Sioux Falls, South Dakota

- **Independent** comprehensive, founded 1860, affiliated with Evangelical Lutheran Church in America
- **Urban** 100-acre campus
- **Endowment** $55.7 million
- **Coed** 1,771 undergraduate students, 96% full-time, 60% women, 40% men
- **Moderately difficult** entrance level, 76% of applicants were admitted

Undergraduates 1,694 full-time, 77 part-time. Students come from 31 states and territories; 43 other countries; 54% are from out of state; 1% Black or African American, non-Hispanic/Latino; 1% Hispanic/Latino; 0.9% Asian, non-Hispanic/Latino; 0.2% American Indian or Alaska Native, non-Hispanic/Latino; 1% Two or more races, non-Hispanic/Latino; 7% international; 4% transferred in; 78% live on campus. *Retention:* 83% of full-time freshmen returned.

Freshmen *Admission:* 1,415 applied, 1,070 admitted, 407 enrolled. *Average high school GPA:* 3.68. *Test scores:* ACT scores over 18: 100%; ACT scores over 24: 74%; ACT scores over 30: 14%.

Faculty *Total:* 206, 65% full-time, 59% with terminal degrees. *Student/faculty ratio:* 11:1.

Academics *Calendar:* 4-1-4. *Degrees:* bachelor's and master's. *Special study options:* academic remediation for entering students, advanced placement credit, cooperative education, distance learning, double majors, honors programs, independent study, internships, off-campus study, part-time degree program, services for LD students, student-designed majors, study abroad, summer session for credit. *ROTC:* Army (c), Air Force (c). *Unusual degree programs:* 3-2 engineering with Columbia University, University of Minnesota, Washington University (St. Louis); Medical Laboratory Scientist programs with Sanford Heath in Sioux Falls and St. Luke in Sioux City.

Computers on Campus 286 computers/terminals and 1,900 ports are available on campus for general student use. Students can access the following: campus intranet, computer help desk, free student e-mail accounts, online

(class) grades, online (class) registration, online (class) schedules. Campus-wide network is available. 100% of college-owned or -operated housing units are wired for high-speed Internet access. Wireless service is available via classrooms, computer centers, computer labs, dorm rooms, learning centers, libraries, student centers.

Student Life *Housing:* on-campus residence required through junior year. *Options:* coed, disabled students. Campus housing is university owned. Freshman campus housing is guaranteed. *Activities and organizations:* drama/theater group, student-run newspaper, choral group, Augieholics (student athletics support organization), Intramurals, Union Board of Governors (student union), Augie Green, Campus Ministries. *Campus security:* 24-hour emergency response devices and patrols, late-night transport/escort service, controlled dormitory access, Special 'day lighting' night lights throughout the campus grounds. *Student services:* health clinic, personal/psychological counseling.

Athletics Member NCAA. All Division II. *Intercollegiate sports:* baseball M(s), basketball M(s)/W(s), cheerleading W, cross-country running M(s)/W(s), football M(s), golf M(s)/W(s), rugby W(c), soccer M(c)/W(s), softball W(s), tennis M(s)/W(s), track and field M(s)/W(s), ultimate Frisbee M(c)/W(c), volleyball W(s), wrestling M(s). *Intramural sports:* basketball M/W, bowling M/W, cross-country running M/W, football M, golf M/W, racquetball M/W, rock climbing M/W, skiing (cross-country) M/W, soccer M/W, softball M/W, swimming and diving M/W, table tennis M/W, tennis M/W, ultimate Frisbee M/W, volleyball M/W, weight lifting M/W.

Standardized Tests *Required:* SAT or ACT (for admission), minimum ACT score of 20 (for admission).

Costs (2012–13) *Comprehensive fee:* $34,406 includes full-time tuition ($27,380), mandatory fees ($400), and room and board ($6626). Full-time tuition and fees vary according to course load and degree level. Part-time tuition: $420 per credit hour. Part-time tuition and fees vary according to course load and degree level. *College room only:* $3214. Room and board charges vary according to board plan and housing facility. *Payment plan:* installment. *Waivers:* employees or children of employees.

Financial Aid Of all full-time matriculated undergraduates who enrolled in 2012, 1,303 applied for aid, 1,115 were judged to have need, 227 had their need fully met. 372 Federal Work-Study jobs (averaging $1604). 131 state and other part-time jobs (averaging $976). In 2012, 553 non-need-based awards were made. *Average percent of need met:* 86%. *Average financial aid package:* $22,001. *Average need-based loan:* $4972. *Average need-based gift aid:* $17,566. *Average non-need-based aid:* $12,769. *Average indebtedness upon graduation:* $34,878.

Applying *Options:* electronic application, deferred entrance. *Required:* essay or personal statement, high school transcript, minimum 2.7 GPA, 1 letter of recommendation. *Recommended:* interview. *Application deadlines:* rolling (freshmen), rolling (out-of-state freshmen), rolling (transfers). *Notification:* continuous until 10/1 (freshmen), continuous until 10/1 (out-of-state freshmen), continuous (transfers).

Freshman Application Contact Nancy Davidson, Vice President for Enrollment, Augustana College, 2001 South Summit Avenue, Sioux Falls, SD 57197. *Phone:* 605-274-5516. *Toll-free phone:* 800-727-2844. *Fax:* 605-274-5518. *E-mail:* admission@augie.edu.
Website: http://www.augie.edu/.

Black Hills State University
Spearfish, South Dakota

- **State-supported** comprehensive, founded 1883, part of South Dakota State University System
- **Small-town** 123-acre campus
- **Coed**
- **Minimally difficult** entrance level

Academics *Calendar:* semesters. *Degrees:* associate, bachelor's, master's, post-master's, and postbachelor's certificates.

Student Life *Campus security:* 24-hour patrols, late-night transport/escort service, controlled dormitory access.

Athletics Member NAIA.

Standardized Tests *Required:* SAT or ACT (for admission).

Costs (2012–13) *Tuition:* state resident $7320 full-time; nonresident $9184 full-time. *Room and board:* $5641; room only: $2834.

Financial Aid *Of all full-time matriculated undergraduates who enrolled in 2010,* 239 Federal Work-Study jobs (averaging $1714). 414 state and other part-time jobs (averaging $4217). *Average indebtedness upon graduation:* $25,628.

Applying *Options:* electronic application. *Application fee:* $20. *Required:* high school transcript, minimum 2.0 high school GPA in core curriculum.

Freshman Application Contact Black Hills State University, 1200 University Station, USB 9502, Spearfish, SD 57799-9502. *Phone:* 605-642-6343. *Toll-*

free phone: 800-255-2478. *Fax:* 605-642-6254. *E-mail:* admissions@bhsu.edu.
Website: http://www.bhsu.edu/.

Colorado Technical University Sioux Falls
Sioux Falls, South Dakota

Freshman Application Contact Colorado Technical University Sioux Falls, 3901 West 59th Street, Sioux Falls, SD 57108. *Phone:* 605-361-0200.
Website: http://www.coloradotech.edu/Sioux-Falls.

Dakota State University
Madison, South Dakota

- **State-supported** comprehensive, founded 1881, part of South Dakota Board of Regents
- **Rural** 56-acre campus with easy access to Sioux Falls
- **Endowment** $7.7 million
- **Coed** 2,872 undergraduate students, 41% full-time, 51% women, 49% men
- **Minimally difficult** entrance level, 89% of applicants were admitted

Undergraduates 1,190 full-time, 1,682 part-time. Students come from 41 states and territories; 13 other countries; 26% are from out of state; 2% Black or African American, non-Hispanic/Latino; 3% Hispanic/Latino; 0.9% Asian, non-Hispanic/Latino; 0.2% Native Hawaiian or other Pacific Islander, non-Hispanic/Latino; 1% American Indian or Alaska Native, non-Hispanic/Latino; 2% Two or more races, non-Hispanic/Latino; 1% Race/ethnicity unknown; 3% international; 10% transferred in; 33% live on campus. *Retention:* 60% of full-time freshmen returned.

Freshmen *Admission:* 742 applied, 659 admitted, 313 enrolled. *Average high school GPA:* 3.11. *Test scores:* SAT critical reading scores over 500: 33%; SAT math scores over 500: 50%; ACT scores over 18: 87%; SAT critical reading scores over 600: 10%; SAT math scores over 600: 20%; ACT scores over 24: 35%; ACT scores over 30: 3%.

Faculty *Total:* 119, 77% full-time, 63% with terminal degrees. *Student/faculty ratio:* 18:1.

Academics *Calendar:* semesters. *Degrees:* certificates, associate, bachelor's, master's, and doctoral. *Special study options:* academic remediation for entering students, adult/continuing education programs, advanced placement credit, cooperative education, distance learning, double majors, English as a second language, honors programs, independent study, internships, off-campus study, part-time degree program, services for LD students, study abroad, summer session for credit. *ROTC:* Air Force (c).

Computers on Campus 165 computers/terminals and 356 ports are available on campus for general student use. Students can access the following: computer help desk, free student e-mail accounts, online (class) grades, online (class) registration, online (class) schedules, wireless computing initiative requires full-time students to have a tablet computer. Campuswide network is available. 100% of college-owned or -operated housing units are wired for high-speed Internet access. Wireless service is available via entire campus.

Student Life *Housing:* on-campus residence required through sophomore year. *Options:* coed, men-only. Campus housing is university owned and leased by the school. Freshman campus housing is guaranteed. *Activities and organizations:* drama/theater group, student-run newspaper, radio station, choral group, Gaming Club, Students in Free Enterprise (SIFE), Phi Beta Lambda Business Club, Student Senate, Student Activities Board. *Campus security:* late-night transport/escort service, controlled dormitory access, night watchman. *Student services:* health clinic, personal/psychological counseling.

Athletics Member NAIA. *Intercollegiate sports:* baseball M(s), basketball M(s)/W(s), cheerleading M/W, cross-country running M(s)/W(s), football M(s), softball W(s), track and field M(s)/W(s), volleyball W(s). *Intramural sports:* basketball M/W, softball M/W, volleyball M/W.

Standardized Tests *Required:* SAT or ACT (for admission).

Costs (2012–13) *Tuition:* state resident $3726 full-time, $124 per credit hour part-time; nonresident $5591 full-time, $186 per credit hour part-time. Full-time tuition and fees vary according to location and reciprocity agreements. Part-time tuition and fees vary according to location and reciprocity agreements. *Required fees:* $4224 full-time. *Room and board:* $5235; room only: $2770. Room and board charges vary according to board plan and housing facility. *Payment plans:* installment, deferred payment. *Waivers:* senior citizens and employees or children of employees.

Financial Aid Of all full-time matriculated undergraduates who enrolled in 2011, 1,054 applied for aid, 892 were judged to have need, 104 had their need fully met. 149 Federal Work-Study jobs (averaging $1780). 20 state and other part-time jobs (averaging $4878). In 2011, 82 non-need-based awards were made. *Average percent of need met:* 77%. *Average financial aid package:* $7784. *Average need-based loan:* $3931. *Average need-based gift aid:* $4532. *Average non-need-based aid:* $3291. *Average indebtedness upon graduation:* $25,926.

Applying *Options:* electronic application, deferred entrance. *Application fee:* $20. *Required:* high school transcript, minimum 2.6 GPA, rank in top 60% of high school class, 18 or higher ACT or 870 SAT (Combined Math and Critical Reading). *Application deadlines:* rolling (freshmen), rolling (out-of-state freshmen), rolling (transfers). *Notification:* continuous (freshmen), continuous (out-of-state freshmen), continuous (transfers).

Freshman Application Contact Ms. Tory Bickett, Admissions Secretary, Dakota State University, 820 North Washington, Madison, SD 57042-1799. *Phone:* 605-256-5139. *Toll-free phone:* 888-DSU-9988. *Fax:* 605-256-5020. *E-mail:* yourfuture@dsu.edu.
Website: http://www.dsu.edu/.

Dakota Wesleyan University

Mitchell, South Dakota

- **Independent United Methodist** comprehensive, founded 1885
- **Small-town** 50-acre campus
- **Endowment** $20.9 million
- **Coed** 759 undergraduate students, 91% full-time, 54% women, 46% men
- **Moderately difficult** entrance level, 73% of applicants were admitted

Undergraduates 688 full-time, 71 part-time. Students come from 29 states and territories; 2 other countries; 26% are from out of state; 3% Black or African American, non-Hispanic/Latino; 2% Hispanic/Latino; 1% Asian, non-Hispanic/Latino; 1% American Indian or Alaska Native, non-Hispanic/Latino; 3% Two or more races, non-Hispanic/Latino; 0.1% Race/ethnicity unknown; 1% international; 12% transferred in; 45% live on campus. *Retention:* 67% of full-time freshmen returned.

Freshmen *Admission:* 659 applied, 483 admitted, 202 enrolled. *Average high school GPA:* 3.36. *Test scores:* SAT critical reading scores over 500: 54%; SAT critical reading scores over 600: 8%.

Faculty *Total:* 70, 71% full-time, 66% with terminal degrees. *Student/faculty ratio:* 11:1.

Academics *Calendar:* semesters. *Degrees:* associate, bachelor's, and master's. *Special study options:* academic remediation for entering students, advanced placement credit, cooperative education, distance learning, double majors, honors programs, independent study, internships, off-campus study, part-time degree program, services for LD students, student-designed majors, study abroad, summer session for credit. *ROTC:* Army (b).

Computers on Campus 100 computers/terminals are available on campus for general student use. Students can access the following: computer help desk, free student e-mail accounts, online (class) grades, online (class) registration, portal, course management system. Campuswide network is available. 100% of college-owned or -operated housing units are wired for high-speed Internet access. Wireless service is available via entire campus.

Student Life *Housing:* on-campus residence required through sophomore year. *Options:* coed, men-only, women-only. Campus housing is university owned and leased by the school. Freshman campus housing is guaranteed. *Activities and organizations:* drama/theater group, student-run newspaper, choral group, Future Teachers Organization, Student Nurses Association, Multi-Culture Club, Human Services Club, Student Ministry Council. *Campus security:* 24-hour emergency response devices, student patrols, late-night transport/escort service, controlled dormitory access, campus patrol from 2am to 6am by special request only. *Student services:* health clinic, personal/psychological counseling.

Athletics Member NAIA. *Intercollegiate sports:* baseball M(s), basketball M(s)/W(s), cheerleading M(s)/W(s), cross-country running M(s)/W(s), football M(s), golf M(s)/W(s), softball W(s), track and field M(s)/W(s), volleyball W(s), wrestling M(s). *Intramural sports:* basketball M/W, softball M/W, volleyball M/W, weight lifting M/W.

Standardized Tests *Required:* SAT or ACT (for admission).

Costs (2012–13) *Comprehensive fee:* $28,550 includes full-time tuition ($21,750) and room and board ($6800). *College room only:* $2900. Room and board charges vary according to board plan and housing facility. *Waivers:* senior citizens.

Financial Aid Of all full-time matriculated undergraduates who enrolled in 2012, 649 applied for aid, 601 were judged to have need, 122 had their need fully met. 93 Federal Work-Study jobs (averaging $1400). In 2012, 84 non-need-based awards were made. *Average percent of need met:* 74%. *Average*

financial aid package: $18,000. *Average need-based loan:* $3900. *Average need-based gift aid:* $13,400. *Average non-need-based aid:* $9326. *Average indebtedness upon graduation:* $29,526.

Applying *Options:* electronic application. *Application fee:* $25. *Required:* high school transcript. *Recommended:* minimum 2.0 GPA. *Application deadlines:* 8/27 (freshmen), 8/27 (transfers). *Notification:* continuous (freshmen), continuous (transfers).

Freshman Application Contact Mrs. Melissa Herr-Valburg, Director of Admissions, Dakota Wesleyan University, 1200 West University Avenue, Mitchell, SD 57301-4398. *Phone:* 605-995-2600 Ext. 2652. *Toll-free phone:* 800-333-8506. *Fax:* 605-995-2699. *E-mail:* admissions@dwu.edu. *Website:* http://www.dwu.edu/.

Globe University–Sioux Falls

Sioux Falls, South Dakota

- **Proprietary** 4-year, part of Globe Education Network (GEN) which is composed of Globe University, Minnesota School of Business, Broadview University, The Institute of Production and Recording and Minnesota School of Cosmetology
- **Small-town** 3-acre campus
- **Coed**

Faculty *Student/faculty ratio:* 14:1.

Academics *Degrees:* diplomas, associate, and bachelor's.

Student Life *Campus security:* 24-hour emergency response devices, late-night transport/escort service.

Standardized Tests *Required:* ACCUPLACER is required of all applicants unless documentation of a minimum ACT composite score of 21 or documentation of a minimum composite score of 1485 on the SAT is presented (for admission).

Costs (2012–13) *Tuition:* $15,300 full-time, $460 per credit part-time. Full-time tuition and fees vary according to course level, course load, degree level, location, and program. Part-time tuition and fees vary according to course level, course load, degree level, location, and program. *Required fees:* $1548 full-time, $43 per credit part-time.

Applying *Options:* electronic application. *Application fee:* $50. *Required:* high school transcript, interview. *Required for some:* essay or personal statement, 2 letters of recommendation, GED certificate in lieu of high school transcript.

Freshman Application Contact Globe University–Sioux Falls, 5101 South Broadband Lane, Sioux Falls, SD 57108-2208. *Toll-free phone:* 866-437-0705. *Website:* http://www.globeuniversity.edu/.

Mount Marty College

Yankton, South Dakota

- **Independent Roman Catholic** comprehensive, founded 1936
- **Small-town** 80-acre campus
- **Endowment** $15.0 million
- **Coed** 1,036 undergraduate students, 53% full-time, 59% women, 41% men
- **Minimally difficult** entrance level, 71% of applicants were admitted

Undergraduates 553 full-time, 483 part-time. Students come from 15 states and territories; 2 other countries; 45% are from out of state; 3% Black or African American, non-Hispanic/Latino; 8% Hispanic/Latino; 0.6% Asian, non-Hispanic/Latino; 0.4% Native Hawaiian or other Pacific Islander, non-Hispanic/Latino; 4% American Indian or Alaska Native, non-Hispanic/Latino; 0.1% Two or more races, non-Hispanic/Latino; 1% Race/ethnicity unknown; 6% transferred in; 70% live on campus. *Retention:* 68% of full-time freshmen returned.

Freshmen *Admission:* 434 applied, 310 admitted, 116 enrolled. *Average high school GPA:* 3.28. *Test scores:* ACT scores over 18: 87%; ACT scores over 24: 34%; ACT scores over 30: 2%.

Faculty *Total:* 61, 80% full-time, 54% with terminal degrees. *Student/faculty ratio:* 10:1.

Academics *Calendar:* semesters. *Degrees:* certificates, associate, bachelor's, and master's. *Special study options:* academic remediation for entering students, accelerated degree program, adult/continuing education programs, advanced placement credit, cooperative education, distance learning, double majors, honors programs, independent study, internships, off-campus study, part-time degree program, services for LD students, student-designed majors, summer session for credit. *ROTC:* Army (c).

Computers on Campus 12 computers/terminals are available on campus for general student use. Students can access the following: campus intranet, com-

puter help desk, free student e-mail accounts, online (class) grades, online (class) registration, online (class) schedules. Campuswide network is available. 100% of college-owned or -operated housing units are wired for high-speed Internet access. Wireless service is available via entire campus.

Student Life *Housing:* on-campus residence required through senior year. *Options:* men-only, women-only. Campus housing is university owned. Freshman campus housing is guaranteed. *Activities and organizations:* drama/theater group, student-run newspaper, choral group, Campus Ministry, Student Government Association, Nursing Club, Education Club, Theater Club. *Campus security:* 24-hour emergency response devices and patrols, late-night transport/escort service. *Student services:* health clinic, personal/psychological counseling.

Athletics Member NAIA. *Intercollegiate sports:* archery M(c)/W(c), baseball M(s), basketball M(s)/W(s), cross-country running M(s)/W(s), golf M(s)/W(s), soccer M(s)/W(s), softball W(s), tennis W(s), track and field M(s)/W(s), volleyball W(s). *Intramural sports:* archery M/W, basketball M/W, soccer M/W, softball W, volleyball M/W.

Standardized Tests *Required:* SAT or ACT (for admission).

Costs (2012–13) *Comprehensive fee:* $28,520 includes full-time tuition ($20,300), mandatory fees ($1830), and room and board ($6390). Full-time tuition and fees vary according to location. Part-time tuition: $325 per credit hour. Part-time tuition and fees vary according to course load and location. *Room and board:* Room and board charges vary according to board plan. *Payment plan:* installment. *Waivers:* employees or children of employees.

Financial Aid Of all full-time matriculated undergraduates who enrolled in 2012, 508 applied for aid, 463 were judged to have need, 164 had their need fully met. 206 Federal Work-Study jobs (averaging $1478). 31 state and other part-time jobs (averaging $1500). In 2012, 17 non-need-based awards were made. *Average percent of need met:* 85%. *Average financial aid package:* $22,375. *Average need-based loan:* $4836. *Average need-based gift aid:* $5741. *Average non-need-based aid:* $7547. *Average indebtedness upon graduation:* $32,369.

Applying *Options:* electronic application, early admission, deferred entrance. *Application fee:* $35. *Required:* high school transcript, minimum 2.0 GPA. *Recommended:* interview. *Application deadlines:* rolling (freshmen), rolling (transfers). *Notification:* continuous (freshmen), continuous (transfers).

Freshman Application Contact Paula Tacke, Vice President for Marketing and Admissions, Mount Marty College, 1105 West 8th Street, Yankton, SD 57078. *Phone:* 605-668-1545. *Toll-free phone:* 800-658-4552. *E-mail:* paula.tacke@mtmc.edu. *Website:* http://www.mtmc.edu/.

National American University

Rapid City, South Dakota

Freshman Application Contact Ms. Angela Beck, Director of Enrollment Management, National American University, 321 Kansas City Street, Rapid City, SD 57701. *Phone:* 605-394-4902. *Toll-free phone:* 800-209-0490 (in-state); 800-209-4090 (out-of-state). *Fax:* 605-394-4871. *E-mail:* abeck@national.edu. *Website:* http://www.national.edu/.

National American University– Sioux Falls Branch

Sioux Falls, South Dakota

Freshman Application Contact Ms. Lisa Houtsma, Director of Admissions, National American University–Sioux Falls Branch, 2801 South Kiwanis Avenue, Suite 100, Sioux Falls, SD 57105-4293. *Phone:* 605-336-4600. *Toll-free phone:* 800-388-5430. *Fax:* 605-336-4605. *E-mail:* lhoutsma@national.edu. *Website:* http://www.national.edu/.

Northern State University

Aberdeen, South Dakota

- **State-supported** comprehensive, founded 1901, part of South Dakota Board of Regents
- **Small-town** 72-acre campus
- **Endowment** $18.4 million
- **Coed** 2,967 undergraduate students, 52% full-time, 59% women, 41% men
- **Minimally difficult** entrance level, 90% of applicants were admitted

Undergraduates 1,557 full-time, 1,410 part-time. Students come from 37 states and territories; 14 other countries; 19% are from out of state; 1% Black or African American, non-Hispanic/Latino; 2% Hispanic/Latino; 0.4% Asian, non-Hispanic/Latino; 0.4% Native Hawaiian or other Pacific Islander, non-Hispanic/Latino; 0.6% American Indian or Alaska Native, non-Hispanic/Latino; 2% Two or more races, non-Hispanic/Latino; 0.9% Race/ethnicity unknown; 8% international; 4% transferred in; 26% live on campus. *Retention:* 69% of full-time freshmen returned.

Freshmen *Admission:* 1,142 applied, 1,026 admitted, 405 enrolled. *Average high school GPA:* 3.13. *Test scores:* SAT critical reading scores over 500: 71%; SAT math scores over 500: 62%; ACT scores over 18: 76%; SAT critical reading scores over 600: 5%; SAT math scores over 600: 14%; ACT scores over 24: 29%; ACT scores over 30: 5%.

Faculty *Total:* 101, 88% full-time, 69% with terminal degrees. *Student/faculty ratio:* 19:1.

Academics *Calendar:* semesters. *Degrees:* certificates, associate, bachelor's, master's, and postbachelor's certificates. *Special study options:* academic remediation for entering students, accelerated degree program, adult/continuing education programs, advanced placement credit, cooperative education, distance learning, double majors, English as a second language, freshman honors college, honors programs, independent study, internships, off-campus study, part-time degree program, services for LD students, student-designed majors, study abroad, summer session for credit.

Computers on Campus 135 computers/terminals are available on campus for general student use. Students can access the following: campus intranet, computer help desk, free student e-mail accounts, online (class) grades, online (class) registration, online (class) schedules. Campuswide network is available. 100% of college-owned or -operated housing units are wired for high-speed Internet access. Wireless service is available via entire campus.

Student Life *Housing:* on-campus residence required through sophomore year. *Options:* coed, disabled students. Campus housing is university owned. *Activities and organizations:* drama/theater group, student-run newspaper, television station, choral group, marching band, Student Ambassadors, Choices, honor society, Native American Student Association, International Student Association. *Campus security:* 24-hour emergency response devices, controlled dormitory access, evening patrols. *Student services:* health clinic, personal/psychological counseling, women's center, legal services.

Athletics Member NCAA. All Division II. *Intercollegiate sports:* baseball M(s), basketball M(s)/W(s), cheerleading W(s), cross-country running M(s)/W(s), football M(s), golf M(s)/W(s), soccer W(s), softball W(s), swimming and diving W(s), tennis M(s)/W(s), track and field M(s)/W(s), volleyball W(s), wrestling M(s). *Intramural sports:* basketball M/W, football M/W, racquetball M/W, rugby M(c), soccer M/W, softball M/W, table tennis M/W, volleyball M/W.

Standardized Tests *Required:* SAT or ACT (for admission).

Costs (2013–14) *Tuition:* state resident $3726 full-time; nonresident $5590 full-time. Full-time tuition and fees vary according to course level, course load, and reciprocity agreements. Part-time tuition and fees vary according to course level, course load, and reciprocity agreements. *Required fees:* $3543 full-time. *Room and board:* $6147; room only: $2703. Room and board charges vary according to board plan. *Payment plan:* installment.

Financial Aid Of all full-time matriculated undergraduates who enrolled in 2011, 1,256 applied for aid, 1,003 were judged to have need, 198 had their need fully met. 300 Federal Work-Study jobs (averaging $2000). 335 state and other part-time jobs (averaging $1493). In 2011, 127 non-need-based awards were made. *Average percent of need met:* 69%. *Average financial aid package:* $7071. *Average need-based loan:* $4981. *Average need-based gift aid:* $3616. *Average non-need-based aid:* $1562.

Applying *Options:* electronic application, early admission, deferred entrance. *Application fee:* $20. *Required:* high school transcript, minimum 2.6 GPA. *Notification:* continuous (freshmen), continuous (transfers).

Freshman Application Contact Mr. Allan Vogel, Director of Admissions, Northern State University, 1200 South Jay Street, Aberdeen, SD 57401. *Phone:* 605-626-2544. *Toll-free phone:* 800-678-5330. *Fax:* 605-626-2587. *E-mail:* admission2@northern.edu. *Website:* http://www.northern.edu/.

Oglala Lakota College

Kyle, South Dakota

Director of Admissions Director of Admissions, Oglala Lakota College, 490 Piya Wiconi Road, Kyle, SD 57752-0490. *Phone:* 605-455-2321 Ext. 236. *E-mail:* lmeseteth@olc.edu. *Website:* http://www.olc.edu/.

Presentation College

Aberdeen, South Dakota

- **Independent Roman Catholic** 4-year, founded 1951
- **Small-town** 100-acre campus
- **Endowment** $7.6 million
- **Coed, primarily women** 748 undergraduate students, 62% full-time, 71% women, 29% men
- **Noncompetitive** entrance level, 74% of applicants were admitted

Undergraduates 465 full-time, 283 part-time. Students come from 23 states and territories; 3 other countries; 57% are from out of state; 8% Black or African American, non-Hispanic/Latino; 4% Hispanic/Latino; 1% Asian, non-Hispanic/Latino; 0.6% Native Hawaiian or other Pacific Islander, non-Hispanic/Latino; 6% American Indian or Alaska Native, non-Hispanic/Latino; 0.8% Two or more races, non-Hispanic/Latino; 5% Race/ethnicity unknown; 0.5% international; 19% transferred in; 21% live on campus. *Retention:* 49% of full-time freshmen returned.

Freshmen *Admission:* 340 applied, 250 admitted, 110 enrolled. *Average high school GPA:* 3.07. *Test scores:* ACT scores over 18: 73%; ACT scores over 24: 23%; ACT scores over 30: 1%.

Faculty *Total:* 73, 63% full-time, 29% with terminal degrees. *Student/faculty ratio:* 10:1.

Academics *Calendar:* semesters. *Degrees:* certificates, associate, and bachelor's. *Special study options:* academic remediation for entering students, accelerated degree program, adult/continuing education programs, advanced placement credit, cooperative education, distance learning, double majors, external degree program, internships, off-campus study, part-time degree program, summer session for credit.

Computers on Campus 35 computers/terminals are available on campus for general student use. Students can access the following: computer help desk, free student e-mail accounts, online (class) grades, online (class) registration, online (class) schedules, wireless network has 100% coverage for students. Campuswide network is available. 100% of college-owned or -operated housing units are wired for high-speed Internet access. Wireless service is available via entire campus.

Student Life *Housing:* on-campus residence required through sophomore year. *Options:* men-only, women-only, disabled students. Campus housing is university owned. Freshman campus housing is guaranteed. *Activities and organizations:* choral group, Wellness/athletics, National Student Nursing Association, Social Work Organization, Rad Tech Organization, Student Ambassadors. *Campus security:* 24-hour emergency response devices, late-night transport/escort service, controlled dormitory access. *Student services:* health clinic, personal/psychological counseling.

Athletics Member NCAA. All Division III. *Intercollegiate sports:* baseball M, basketball M/W, football M, golf M/W, soccer M/W, softball W, track and field M, volleyball W.

Standardized Tests *Required:* SAT or ACT (for admission).

Costs (2013–14) *One-time required fee:* $195. *Comprehensive fee:* $23,314 includes full-time tuition ($16,664), mandatory fees ($150), and room and board ($6500). Full-time tuition and fees vary according to course load, location, and program. Part-time tuition: $617 per credit hour. Part-time tuition and fees vary according to course load, location, and program. *College room only:* $5300. Room and board charges vary according to board plan. *Payment plan:* installment. *Waivers:* senior citizens and employees or children of employees.

Financial Aid Of all full-time matriculated undergraduates who enrolled in 2007, 494 applied for aid, 471 were judged to have need, 66 had their need fully met. 56 Federal Work-Study jobs (averaging $1874). 39 state and other part-time jobs (averaging $1950). In 2007, 23 non-need-based awards were made. *Average percent of need met:* 43%. *Average financial aid package:* $8737. *Average need-based loan:* $3741. *Average need-based gift aid:* $3769. *Average non-need-based aid:* $2814. *Average indebtedness upon graduation:* $27,430.

Applying *Options:* electronic application. *Application fee:* $25. *Required:* high school transcript. *Required for some:* 2 letters of recommendation, GED, if applicable; college transcripts. *Recommended:* minimum 2.0 GPA. *Applica-*

tion deadlines: rolling (freshmen), rolling (transfers). *Notification:* continuous (freshmen), continuous (transfers).

Freshman Application Contact Mr. Robert Schuchardt, Vice President for Student Services, Presentation College, 1500 North Main Street, Aberdeen, SD 57401. *Phone:* 605-229-8406. *Toll-free phone:* 800-437-6060. *Fax:* 605-229-8425. *E-mail:* admit@presentation.edu. *Website:* http://www.presentation.edu/.

Sinte Gleska University

Mission, South Dakota

Director of Admissions Mr. Jack Herman, Registrar and Director of Admissions, Sinte Gleska University, 101 Antelope Lake Circle, PO Box 105, Mission, SD 57555. *Phone:* 605-856-8100 Ext. 8479. *Website:* http://www.sintegleska.edu/.

South Dakota School of Mines and Technology

Rapid City, South Dakota

- **State-supported** university, founded 1885, part of South Dakota State Board of Regents University System
- **Suburban** 120-acre campus
- **Endowment** $42.5 million
- **Coed**
- **Moderately difficult** entrance level

Faculty *Student/faculty ratio:* 15:1.

Academics *Calendar:* semesters. *Degrees:* associate, bachelor's, master's, doctoral, and postbachelor's certificates.

Student Life *Campus security:* 24-hour emergency response devices and patrols, student patrols, late-night transport/escort service, controlled dormitory access.

Athletics Member NCAA. All Division II.

Standardized Tests *Required:* SAT or ACT (for admission). *Required for some:* SAT or ACT (for admission). *Recommended:* SAT or ACT (for admission).

Financial Aid *Of all full-time matriculated undergraduates who enrolled in 2012,* 1,516 applied for aid, 981 were judged to have need, 367 had their need fully met. 116 Federal Work-Study jobs (averaging $1810). *In 2012,* 294 non-need-based awards were made. *Average percent of need met:* 78. *Average financial aid package:* $13,246. *Average need-based loan:* $4115. *Average need-based gift aid:* $4246. *Average non-need-based aid:* $2790. *Average indebtedness upon graduation:* $18,331.

Applying *Options:* electronic application. *Application fee:* $20. *Required:* high school transcript. *Recommended:* minimum 2.8 GPA.

Freshman Application Contact Genene Sigler, Applications Processor, South Dakota School of Mines and Technology, 501 East Saint Joseph Street, Rapid City, SD 57701-3995. *Phone:* 605-394-2414 Ext. 5209. *Toll-free phone:* 800-544-8162. *Fax:* 605-394-1979. *E-mail:* admissions@sdsmt.edu. *Website:* http://www.sdsmt.edu/.

South Dakota State University

Brookings, South Dakota

- **State-supported** university, founded 1881, part of South Dakota Board of Regents
- **Small-town** 272-acre campus
- **Coed** 11,118 undergraduate students, 77% full-time, 52% women, 48% men
- **Minimally difficult** entrance level, 92% of applicants were admitted

Undergraduates 8,562 full-time, 2,556 part-time. Students come from 50 states and territories; 63 other countries; 30% are from out of state; 1% Black or African American, non-Hispanic/Latino; 2% Hispanic/Latino; 1% Asian, non-Hispanic/Latino; 0.1% Native Hawaiian or other Pacific Islander, non-Hispanic/Latino; 1% American Indian or Alaska Native, non-Hispanic/Latino; 2% Two or more races, non-Hispanic/Latino; 0.4% Race/ethnicity unknown; 2% international; 7% transferred in; 42% live on campus. *Retention:* 75% of full-time freshmen returned.

Freshmen *Admission:* 4,725 applied, 4,331 admitted, 2,223 enrolled. *Average high school GPA:* 3.34. *Test scores:* ACT scores over 18: 94%; ACT scores over 24: 45%; ACT scores over 30: 4%.

Faculty *Total:* 693, 77% full-time, 63% with terminal degrees. *Student/faculty ratio:* 17:1.

Academics *Calendar:* semesters. *Degrees:* certificates, associate, bachelor's, master's, doctoral, post-master's, and postbachelor's certificates. *Special study options:* academic remediation for entering students, accelerated degree program, adult/continuing education programs, advanced placement credit, cooperative education, distance learning, double majors, freshman honors college, honors programs, independent study, internships, off-campus study, part-time degree program, services for LD students, study abroad, summer session for credit. *ROTC:* Army (b), Air Force (b). *Unusual degree programs:* 3-2 economics.

Computers on Campus 437 computers/terminals and 750 ports are available on campus for general student use. Students can access the following: campus intranet, computer help desk, free student e-mail accounts, online (class) grades, online (class) registration, online (class) schedules. Campuswide network is available. 100% of college-owned or -operated housing units are wired for high-speed Internet access. Wireless service is available via entire campus.

Student Life *Housing:* on-campus residence required through sophomore year. *Options:* coed, disabled students. Campus housing is university owned. Freshman campus housing is guaranteed. *Activities and organizations:* drama/theater group, student-run newspaper, radio station, choral group, marching band, national fraternities, national sororities. *Campus security:* 24-hour emergency response devices and patrols, student patrols, late-night transport/escort service, controlled dormitory access. *Student services:* health clinic, personal/psychological counseling, women's center, legal services.

Athletics Member NCAA. All Division I. *Intercollegiate sports:* baseball M(s), basketball M(s)/W(s), bowling M(c)/W(c), cheerleading M(c)/W(c), cross-country running M(s)/W(s), equestrian sports W, football M(s), golf M(s)/W(s), ice hockey M(c)/W(c), racquetball M(c)/W(c), rugby M(c)/W(c), soccer M(c)/W(s), softball W(s), swimming and diving M(s)/W(s), tennis M(s)/W(s), track and field M(s)/W(s), ultimate Frisbee M(c), volleyball W(s), wrestling M(s). *Intramural sports:* badminton M/W, basketball M/W, football M/W, golf M/W, racquetball M/W, soccer W, softball M/W, swimming and diving M/W, table tennis M/W, tennis M/W, track and field M/W, ultimate Frisbee M/W, volleyball M/W, wrestling M.

Standardized Tests *Required:* SAT or ACT (for admission).

Costs (2012–13) *Tuition:* state resident $3897 full-time, $130 per credit hour part-time; nonresident $5843 full-time, $195 per credit hour part-time. Full-time tuition and fees vary according to course level, course load, degree level, location, program, and reciprocity agreements. Part-time tuition and fees vary according to course level, course load, degree level, location, program, and reciprocity agreements. *Required fees:* $3507 full-time. *Room and board:* $5586; room only: $2839. Room and board charges vary according to board plan and housing facility. *Payment plans:* installment, deferred payment. *Waivers:* senior citizens and employees or children of employees.

Financial Aid Of all full-time matriculated undergraduates who enrolled in 2011, 7,486 applied for aid, 6,530 were judged to have need, 5,176 had their need fully met. 458 Federal Work-Study jobs (averaging $1628). 1,848 state and other part-time jobs (averaging $1785). In 2011, 1634 non-need-based awards were made. *Average percent of need met:* 89%. *Average financial aid package:* $9686. *Average need-based loan:* $5016. *Average need-based gift aid:* $4852. *Average non-need-based aid:* $1500. *Average indebtedness upon graduation:* $20,860.

Applying *Options:* electronic application. *Application fee:* $20. *Required:* high school transcript, minimum 2.6 GPA. *Application deadlines:* rolling (freshmen), rolling (transfers). *Notification:* continuous (freshmen), continuous (transfers).

Freshman Application Contact Ms. Michelle Kuebler, Assistant Director of Admissions, South Dakota State University, PO Box 2201, Brookings, SD 57007. *Phone:* 605-688-4121. *Toll-free phone:* 800-952-3541. *Fax:* 605-688-6891. *E-mail:* sdsu.admissions@sdstate.edu.
Website: http://www.sdstate.edu/.

University of Sioux Falls
Sioux Falls, South Dakota

Freshman Application Contact Aimee Vander Feen, Director of Admissions, University of Sioux Falls, 1101 West 22nd Street, Sioux Falls, SD 57105. *Phone:* 605-331-6602. *Toll-free phone:* 800-888-1047. *Fax:* 605-331-6615. *E-mail:* admissions@usiouxfalls.edu.
Website: http://www.usiouxfalls.edu/.

The University of South Dakota
Vermillion, South Dakota

- **State-supported** university, founded 1862, part of South Dakota Board of Regents
- **Small-town** 275-acre campus
- **Endowment** $157.5 million
- **Coed** 7,690 undergraduate students, 60% full-time, 63% women, 37% men
- **Moderately difficult** entrance level, 89% of applicants were admitted

Undergraduates 4,629 full-time, 3,061 part-time. Students come from 50 states and territories; 86 other countries; 38% are from out of state; 2% Black or African American, non-Hispanic/Latino; 3% Hispanic/Latino; 1% Asian, non-Hispanic/Latino; 0.2% Native Hawaiian or other Pacific Islander, non-Hispanic/Latino; 2% American Indian or Alaska Native, non-Hispanic/Latino; 2% Two or more races, non-Hispanic/Latino; 0.9% Race/ethnicity unknown; 1% international; 9% transferred in; 26% live on campus. *Retention:* 75% of full-time freshmen returned.

Freshmen *Admission:* 3,443 applied, 3,049 admitted, 1,353 enrolled. *Average high school GPA:* 3.37. *Test scores:* SAT critical reading scores over 500: 57%; SAT math scores over 500: 61%; ACT scores over 18: 94%; SAT critical reading scores over 600: 34%; SAT math scores over 600: 29%; ACT scores over 24: 46%; SAT critical reading scores over 700: 5%; SAT math scores over 700: 12%; ACT scores over 30: 6%.

Faculty *Total:* 579, 75% full-time, 66% with terminal degrees. *Student/faculty ratio:* 17:1.

Academics *Calendar:* semesters. *Degrees:* certificates, associate, bachelor's, master's, doctoral, post-master's, and postbachelor's certificates. *Special study options:* academic remediation for entering students, accelerated degree program, adult/continuing education programs, advanced placement credit, cooperative education, distance learning, double majors, English as a second language, external degree program, honors programs, independent study, internships, off-campus study, part-time degree program, services for LD students, student-designed majors, study abroad, summer session for credit. *ROTC:* Army (b). *Unusual degree programs:* 3-2 business administration; social work; accounting, political science, public administration.

Computers on Campus 917 computers/terminals are available on campus for general student use. Students can access the following: campus intranet, computer help desk, free student e-mail accounts, online (class) registration. Campuswide network is available. Wireless service is available via computer centers, computer labs, learning centers, libraries, student centers.

Student Life *Housing:* on-campus residence required through sophomore year. *Options:* coed, men-only, women-only, disabled students. Campus housing is university owned. Freshman campus housing is guaranteed. *Activities and organizations:* drama/theater group, student-run newspaper, radio station, choral group, marching band, Program Council, Residence Hall Association, Student Ambassadors, Delta Sigma Pi, national fraternities, national sororities. *Campus security:* 24-hour emergency response devices and patrols, student patrols, late-night transport/escort service, controlled dormitory access. *Student services:* health clinic, personal/psychological counseling, legal services.

Athletics Member NCAA. All Division I. *Intercollegiate sports:* basketball M(s)/W(s), cross-country running M(s)/W(s), football M(s), golf M/W(s), soccer W(s), softball W(s), swimming and diving M(s)/W(s), tennis W(s), track and field M(s)/W(s), volleyball W(s). *Intramural sports:* baseball M(c), basketball M/W, bowling M/W, crew M(c)/W(c), fencing M(c)/W(c), football M, ice hockey M(c), lacrosse M(c)/W(c), rock climbing M(c)/W(c), rugby M(c)/W(c), soccer M(c)/W(c), softball M(c)/W(c), tennis M/W.

Standardized Tests *Required:* SAT or ACT (for admission).

Costs (2012–13) *Tuition:* state resident $3897 full-time, $129 per credit hour part-time; nonresident $5843 full-time, $195 per credit hour part-time. Full-time tuition and fees vary according to course load. Part-time tuition and fees vary according to course load. *Required fees:* $3807 full-time, $127 per credit hour part-time. *Room and board:* $6648; room only: $3433. Room and board charges vary according to board plan and housing facility. *Payment plan:* deferred payment. *Waivers:* children of alumni, senior citizens, and employees or children of employees.

Financial Aid Of all full-time matriculated undergraduates who enrolled in 2011, 4,328 applied for aid, 3,463 were judged to have need, 1,781 had their need fully met. In 2011, 867 non-need-based awards were made. *Average percent of need met:* 70%. *Average financial aid package:* $6477. *Average need-based loan:* $4138. *Average need-based gift aid:* $4096. *Average non-need-based aid:* $4483. *Average indebtedness upon graduation:* $25,033.

Applying *Options:* electronic application, early admission, deferred entrance. *Application fee:* $20. *Required:* high school transcript. *Recommended:* minimum 2.0 GPA. *Application deadlines:* rolling (freshmen), rolling (transfers). *Notification:* continuous (freshmen), continuous (transfers).

Freshman Application Contact Mr. Scott Pohlson, Director of Enrollment Services, The University of South Dakota, 414 East Clark Street, Vermillion, SD 57069-2390. *Phone:* 605-677-5434. *Toll-free phone:* 877-269-6837. *Fax:* 605-677-6753. *E-mail:* admiss@usd.edu.
Website: http://www.usd.edu/.

TENNESSEE

American Baptist College of American Baptist Theological Seminary
Nashville, Tennessee

- **Independent Baptist** 4-year, founded 1924
- **Urban** 52-acre campus
- **Endowment** $875,540
- **Coed** 109 undergraduate students, 83% full-time, 26% women, 74% men
- **Noncompetitive** entrance level, 69% of applicants were admitted

Undergraduates 90 full-time, 19 part-time. Students come from 11 states and territories; 9% are from out of state; 9% transferred in; 63% live on campus. *Retention:* 61% of full-time freshmen returned.
Freshmen *Admission:* 16 applied, 11 admitted, 4 enrolled.
Faculty *Total:* 12, 42% full-time, 50% with terminal degrees. *Student/faculty ratio:* 10:1.
Academics *Calendar:* semesters. *Degree:* bachelor's. *Special study options:* academic remediation for entering students, adult/continuing education programs, double majors, off-campus study, part-time degree program, summer session for credit.
Computers on Campus 10 computers/terminals and 32 ports are available on campus for general student use. Students can access the following: campus intranet, free student e-mail accounts, online (class) grades, online (class) registration, online (class) schedules, IT support person on campus during regular campus hours. Campuswide network is available. 100% of college-owned or -operated housing units are wired for high-speed Internet access. Wireless service is available via entire campus.
Student Life *Housing options:* coed, men-only, women-only. Campus housing is university owned. *Activities and organizations:* choral group, Student Government Association, Vespers Service, Baptist Student Union, Choir, Greek Letter Fraternity and Hoi Adelphoi Fraternity, national fraternities.
Costs (2013–14) *Tuition:* $8688 full-time. *Required fees:* $317 full-time. *Room only:* $2000. *Payment plan:* installment.
Financial Aid Of all full-time matriculated undergraduates who enrolled in 2009, 60 applied for aid, 60 were judged to have need. 1 Federal Work-Study job (averaging $6741). *Average percent of need met:* 75%. *Average financial aid package:* $2675. *Average need-based gift aid:* $1161. *Financial aid deadline:* 7/23.
Applying *Options:* electronic application, deferred entrance. *Application fee:* $30. *Required:* essay or personal statement, high school transcript, minimum 2.0 GPA, 2 letters of recommendation. *Required for some:* interview. *Application deadlines:* 8/5 (freshmen), 8/5 (out-of-state freshmen), 8/5 (transfers). *Notification:* 8/12 (freshmen), 8/12 (out-of-state freshmen), continuous until 8/12 (transfers).
Freshman Application Contact Ms. Brandi Taylor, Recruiter, American Baptist College of American Baptist Theological Seminary, 1800 Baptist World Center Drive, Nashville, TN 37207. *Phone:* 615-687-6907. *Fax:* 615-226-7855. *E-mail:* admissions@abcnash.edu.
Website: http://www.abcnash.edu/.

Aquinas College
Nashville, Tennessee

Freshman Application Contact Ms. Connie Hansom, Director of Admission, Aquinas College, 4210 Harding Road, Nashville, TN 37205-2005. *Phone:* 615-297-7545 Ext. 411. *Toll-free phone:* 800-649-9956. *Fax:* 615-279-3893. *E-mail:* hansomc@aquinascollege.edu.
Website: http://www.aquinascollege.edu/.

Argosy University, Nashville
Nashville, Tennessee

Freshman Application Contact Argosy University, Nashville, 100 Centerview Drive, Suite 225, Nashville, TN 37214. *Phone:* 615-525-2800. *Toll-free phone:* 866-833-6598.
Website: http://www.argosy.edu/nashville/.

The Art Institute of Tennessee–Nashville
Nashville, Tennessee

- **Proprietary** 4-year, founded 2006, part of Education Management Corporation
- **Urban** campus
- **Coed**

Academics *Degrees:* diplomas, associate, and bachelor's.
Freshman Application Contact The Art Institute of Tennessee–Nashville, 100 Centerview Drive, Suite 250, Nashville, TN 37214. *Phone:* 615-874-1067. *Toll-free phone:* 866-747-5770.
Website: http://www.artinstitutes.edu/nashville/.

See full-page ad on page 54 and page 1120 for the College Close-Up.

Austin Peay State University
Clarksville, Tennessee

- **State-supported** comprehensive, founded 1927, part of Tennessee Board of Regents
- **Suburban** 169-acre campus with easy access to Nashville
- **Endowment** $6.8 million
- **Coed** 9,735 undergraduate students, 72% full-time, 60% women, 40% men
- **Moderately difficult** entrance level, 86% of applicants were admitted

Undergraduates 6,994 full-time, 2,741 part-time. Students come from 40 states and territories; 23 other countries; 11% are from out of state; 19% Black or African American, non-Hispanic/Latino; 5% Hispanic/Latino; 2% Asian, non-Hispanic/Latino; 0.3% Native Hawaiian or other Pacific Islander, non-Hispanic/Latino; 0.5% American Indian or Alaska Native, non-Hispanic/Latino; 4% Two or more races, non-Hispanic/Latino; 2% Race/ethnicity unknown; 0.3% international; 9% transferred in; 14% live on campus. *Retention:* 67% of full-time freshmen returned.
Freshmen *Admission:* 3,453 applied, 2,959 admitted, 1,522 enrolled. *Average high school GPA:* 3.16. *Test scores:* SAT critical reading scores over 500: 49%; SAT math scores over 500: 51%; ACT scores over 18: 90%; SAT critical reading scores over 600: 15%; SAT math scores over 600: 13%; ACT scores over 24: 28%; ACT scores over 30: 3%.
Faculty *Total:* 615, 57% full-time. *Student/faculty ratio:* 19:1.
Academics *Calendar:* semesters. *Degrees:* certificates, associate, bachelor's, master's, post-master's, and postbachelor's certificates. *Special study options:* academic remediation for entering students, accelerated degree program, adult/continuing education programs, advanced placement credit, cooperative education, distance learning, double majors, English as a second language, honors programs, independent study, internships, part-time degree program, services for LD students, study abroad, summer session for credit. *ROTC:* Army (b), Air Force (c).
Computers on Campus 825 computers/terminals are available on campus for general student use. Students can access the following: campus intranet, computer help desk, free student e-mail accounts, online (class) grades, online (class) registration, online (class) schedules. Campuswide network is available. Wireless service is available via entire campus.
Student Life *Housing:* on-campus residence required for freshman year. *Options:* coed, men-only, women-only, disabled students. Campus housing is university owned. Freshman campus housing is guaranteed. *Activities and organizations:* drama/theater group, student-run newspaper, radio and television station, choral group, marching band, national fraternities, national sororities. *Campus security:* 24-hour emergency response devices and patrols, student patrols, late-night transport/escort service, controlled dormitory access. *Student services:* health clinic, personal/psychological counseling.
Athletics Member NCAA. All Division I except football (Division I-AA). *Intercollegiate sports:* baseball M(s), basketball M(s)/W(s), cheerleading

M(s)/W(s), cross-country running M(s)/W(s), golf M(s)/W(s), soccer W(s), softball W(s), tennis M(s)/W(s), track and field W(s), volleyball W(s). *Intramural sports:* badminton M/W, basketball M/W, football M/W, golf M/W, ice hockey M/W, racquetball M/W, soccer M/W, softball M/W, table tennis M/W, ultimate Frisbee M/W, volleyball M/W.

Standardized Tests *Required for some:* SAT or ACT (for admission).

Costs (2012–13) *One-time required fee:* $75. *Tuition:* state resident $5424 full-time, $226 per credit hour part-time; nonresident $19,512 full-time, $813 per credit hour part-time. Full-time tuition and fees vary according to location and program. Part-time tuition and fees vary according to location and program. *Required fees:* $1224 full-time. *Room and board:* $7380; room only: $4600. Room and board charges vary according to board plan and housing facility. *Payment plan:* installment. *Waivers:* senior citizens and employees or children of employees.

Financial Aid Of all full-time matriculated undergraduates who enrolled in 2011, 6,562 applied for aid, 5,768 were judged to have need. 171 Federal Work-Study jobs (averaging $2219). 420 state and other part-time jobs (averaging $1710). In 2011, 541 non-need-based awards were made. *Average financial aid package:* $9517. *Average need-based loan:* $3835. *Average need-based gift aid:* $7357. *Average non-need-based aid:* $4307. *Average indebtedness upon graduation:* $26,030.

Applying *Options:* electronic application, early admission, deferred entrance. *Application fee:* $15. *Required:* high school transcript. *Required for some:* minimum 2.8 GPA. *Application deadlines:* 8/1 (freshmen), rolling (transfers). *Notification:* continuous (freshmen), continuous (transfers).

Freshman Application Contact Ms. Amy Deaton, Director of Admissions, Austin Peay State University, 601 College Street, Clarksville, TN 37044. *Phone:* 931-221-7661. *Toll-free phone:* 800-844-2778. *Fax:* 931-221-6168. *E-mail:* admissions@apsu.edu.
Website: http://www.apsu.edu/.

Baptist College of Health Sciences

Memphis, Tennessee

- **Independent Southern Baptist** 4-year, founded 1994
- **Urban** campus
- **Coed, primarily women** 1,043 undergraduate students, 47% full-time, 90% women, 10% men
- **Moderately difficult** entrance level, 27% of applicants were admitted

Undergraduates 489 full-time, 554 part-time. 34% are from out of state; 37% Black or African American, non-Hispanic/Latino; 0.5% Hispanic/Latino; 2% Asian, non-Hispanic/Latino; 0.1% American Indian or Alaska Native, non-Hispanic/Latino; 1% Two or more races, non-Hispanic/Latino; 1% Race/ethnicity unknown; 24% transferred in; 10% live on campus. *Retention:* 83% of full-time freshmen returned.

Freshmen *Admission:* 490 applied, 132 admitted, 66 enrolled. *Average high school GPA:* 3.42. *Test scores:* ACT scores over 18: 100%; ACT scores over 24: 45%; ACT scores over 30: 10%.

Faculty *Total:* 107, 55% full-time, 23% with terminal degrees. *Student/faculty ratio:* 9:1.

Academics *Calendar:* trimesters. *Degree:* bachelor's. *Special study options:* accelerated degree program, advanced placement credit, distance learning, part-time degree program, services for LD students, summer session for credit.

Computers on Campus Students can access the following: campus intranet, computer help desk, free student e-mail accounts, online (class) grades, online (class) registration, online (class) schedules. Campuswide network is available. 100% of college-owned or -operated housing units are wired for high-speed Internet access. Wireless service is available via entire campus.

Student Life *Housing options:* coed. Campus housing is university owned. *Activities and organizations:* Student Government Association, Student Nursing Association, Allied Health Organization. *Campus security:* 24-hour emergency response devices, late-night transport/escort service, controlled dormitory access, trained security personnel. *Student services:* health clinic, personal/psychological counseling.

Standardized Tests *Required:* ACT (for admission).

Costs (2013–14) *Tuition:* $10,980 full-time, $366 per credit hour part-time. *Required fees:* $890 full-time. *Room only:* $2200. Room and board charges vary according to housing facility.

Applying *Options:* electronic application. *Application fee:* $25. *Required:* high school transcript, minimum 2.8 GPA, immunizations, health physical. *Required for some:* interview. *Application deadlines:* 5/1 (freshmen), 5/1 (transfers).

Freshman Application Contact Baptist College of Health Sciences, 1003 Monroe Avenue, Memphis, TN 38104. *Phone:* 901-572-2441. *Toll-free phone:* 866-575-2247.
Website: http://www.bchs.edu/.

Belhaven University

Memphis, Tennessee

Director of Admissions Don Jones, Director of Admission, Belhaven University, 5100 Poplar Avenue, Suite 200, Memphis, TN 38137. *Phone:* 901-888-3343. *Fax:* 901-888-0771. *E-mail:* memphisadmission@belhaven.edu. *Website:* http://memphis.belhaven.edu/.

Belmont University

Nashville, Tennessee

- **Independent Christian** university, founded 1951
- **Urban** 77-acre campus
- **Endowment** $73.8 million
- **Coed** 5,289 undergraduate students, 93% full-time, 59% women, 41% men
- **Moderately difficult** entrance level, 84% of applicants were admitted

Undergraduates 4,906 full-time, 383 part-time. Students come from 50 states and territories; 21 other countries; 63% are from out of state; 4% Black or African American, non-Hispanic/Latino; 4% Hispanic/Latino; 1% Asian, non-Hispanic/Latino; 0.2% American Indian or Alaska Native, non-Hispanic/Latino; 3% Two or more races, non-Hispanic/Latino; 2% Race/ethnicity unknown; 1% international; 10% transferred in; 50% live on campus. *Retention:* 82% of full-time freshmen returned.

Freshmen *Admission:* 4,046 applied, 3,401 admitted, 1,254 enrolled. *Average high school GPA:* 3.54. *Test scores:* SAT critical reading scores over 500: 92%; SAT math scores over 500: 87%; ACT scores over 18: 100%; SAT critical reading scores over 600: 43%; SAT math scores over 600: 43%; ACT scores over 24: 85%; SAT critical reading scores over 700: 9%; SAT math scores over 700: 6%; ACT scores over 30: 39%.

Faculty *Total:* 735, 42% full-time, 49% with terminal degrees. *Student/faculty ratio:* 13:1.

Academics *Calendar:* semesters. *Degrees:* bachelor's, master's, doctoral, and post-master's certificates. *Special study options:* accelerated degree program, adult/continuing education programs, advanced placement credit, cooperative education, distance learning, double majors, English as a second language, honors programs, independent study, internships, off-campus study, part-time degree program, student-designed majors, study abroad, summer session for credit. *ROTC:* Army (c), Navy (c), Air Force (c). *Unusual degree programs:* 3-2 engineering with Auburn University, Georgia Institute of Technology, University of Tennessee.

Computers on Campus 500 computers/terminals are available on campus for general student use. Students can access the following: campus intranet, free student e-mail accounts, online (class) grades, online (class) registration, online (class) schedules, individual student information via BANNER Web. Campuswide network is available. 100% of college-owned or -operated housing units are wired for high-speed Internet access. Wireless service is available via entire campus.

Student Life *Housing:* on-campus residence required through sophomore year. *Options:* men-only, women-only. Campus housing is university owned. Freshman campus housing is guaranteed. *Activities and organizations:* drama/theater group, student-run newspaper, radio and television station, choral group, marching band, Service Corp, Alpha Sigma Tau, Phi Mu, Phi Kappa Tau, MOB, national fraternities, national sororities. *Campus security:* 24-hour emergency response devices and patrols, late-night transport/escort service, controlled dormitory access, bicycle patrol. *Student services:* health clinic, personal/psychological counseling, women's center.

Athletics Member NCAA. All Division I. *Intercollegiate sports:* baseball M(s), basketball M(s)/W(s), cross-country running M(s)/W(s), golf M(s)/W(s), soccer M(s)/W(s), softball W(s), tennis M(s)/W(s), track and field M(s)/W(s), volleyball W(s). *Intramural sports:* baseball M, basketball M/W, bowling M/W, cheerleading M/W, football M, golf M, ice hockey M/W, racquetball M/W, soccer M/W, softball M/W, table tennis M/W, tennis M/W, volleyball M/W.

Standardized Tests *Required:* SAT or ACT (for admission).

Costs (2012–13) *Comprehensive fee:* $38,550 includes full-time tuition ($24,900), mandatory fees ($1230), and room and board ($12,420). Full-time tuition and fees vary according to class time, course load, and location. Part-time tuition: $950 per credit hour. Part-time tuition and fees vary according to course load. *Required fees:* $840 per year part-time. *College room only:* $8200.

Room and board charges vary according to board plan, housing facility, and location. *Payment plans:* installment, deferred payment. *Waivers:* senior citizens and employees or children of employees.

Financial Aid Of all full-time matriculated undergraduates who enrolled in 2009, 4,001 applied for aid, 2,599 were judged to have need, 648 had their need fully met. 534 Federal Work-Study jobs (averaging $6297). In 2009, 522 non-need-based awards were made. *Average percent of need met:* 79%. *Average financial aid package:* $12,214. *Average need-based loan:* $4434. *Average need-based gift aid:* $6896. *Average non-need-based aid:* $4434. *Average indebtedness upon graduation:* $29,058.

Applying *Options:* electronic application, early admission, deferred entrance. *Application fee:* $50. *Required:* essay or personal statement, high school transcript, minimum 3.0 GPA, 2 letters of recommendation, resume of activities. *Required for some:* interview. *Application deadlines:* 8/1 (freshmen), 8/1 (transfers). *Notification:* continuous (freshmen), continuous (transfers).

Freshman Application Contact Mr. David Mee, Associate Provost and Dean of Enrollment, Belmont University, 1900 Belmont Boulevard, Nashville, TN 37212-3757. *Phone:* 615-460-5479. *Fax:* 615-460-5434. *E-mail:* david.mee@belmont.edu. *Website:* http://www.belmont.edu/.

Bethel University

McKenzie, Tennessee

- **Independent Cumberland Presbyterian** comprehensive, founded 1842
- **Small-town** 100-acre campus
- **Endowment** $8.1 million
- **Coed**
- **Minimally difficult** entrance level

Faculty *Student/faculty ratio:* 19:1.
Academics *Calendar:* semesters. *Degrees:* bachelor's and master's.
Student Life *Campus security:* night patrols by trained security personnel.
Athletics Member NAIA.
Standardized Tests *Recommended:* SAT or ACT (for admission).
Costs (2012–13) *Comprehensive fee:* $22,884 includes full-time tuition ($13,870), mandatory fees ($650), and room and board ($8364). Full-time tuition and fees vary according to program. Part-time tuition: $433 per credit hour. Part-time tuition and fees vary according to course load and program.

Applying *Options:* electronic application, early admission, deferred entrance. *Application fee:* $30. *Required:* high school transcript, minimum 2.0 GPA. *Required for some:* essay or personal statement, interview.

Freshman Application Contact Tina Hodges, Enrollment Director of Admissions and Financial Aid, Bethel University, 325 Cherry Avenue, McKenzie, TN 38201. *Phone:* 731-352-4030. *Fax:* 731-352-4069. *E-mail:* hodgest@bethelu.edu. *Website:* http://www.bethelu.edu/.

Bryan College

Dayton, Tennessee

Freshman Application Contact Michael Sapienza, Vice President for Enrollment Management, Bryan College, PO Box 7000, Dayton, TN 37321-7000. *Phone:* 423-775-2041. *Toll-free phone:* 800-277-9522. *Fax:* 423-775-7199. *E-mail:* admissions@bryan.edu. *Website:* http://www.bryan.edu/.

Carson-Newman University

Jefferson City, Tennessee

- **Independent Southern Baptist** comprehensive, founded 1851
- **Small-town** 90-acre campus with easy access to Knoxville
- **Endowment** $45.8 million
- **Coed** 1,646 undergraduate students, 96% full-time, 53% women, 47% men
- **Moderately difficult** entrance level, 66% of applicants were admitted

Undergraduates 1,573 full-time, 73 part-time. Students come from 30 states and territories; 23 other countries; 22% are from out of state; 10% Black or African American, non-Hispanic/Latino; 2% Hispanic/Latino; 0.4% Asian, non-Hispanic/Latino; 0.1% Native Hawaiian or other Pacific Islander, non-Hispanic/Latino; 0.3% American Indian or Alaska Native, non-Hispanic/Latino; 2% Two or more races, non-Hispanic/Latino; 2% Race/ethnicity unknown; 3% international; 6% transferred in; 51% live on campus. *Retention:* 60% of full-time freshmen returned.

Freshmen *Admission:* 2,917 applied, 1,913 admitted, 453 enrolled. *Average high school GPA:* 3.4. *Test scores:* ACT scores over 18: 93%; ACT scores over 24: 36%; ACT scores over 30: 5%.

Faculty *Total:* 206, 54% full-time, 52% with terminal degrees. *Student/faculty ratio:* 12:1.

Academics *Calendar:* semesters. *Degrees:* associate, bachelor's, and master's. *Special study options:* academic remediation for entering students, accelerated degree program, adult/continuing education programs, advanced placement credit, English as a second language, honors programs, internships, off-campus study, part-time degree program, services for LD students, student-designed majors, study abroad, summer session for credit. *ROTC:* Army (b), Air Force (c). *Unusual degree programs:* 3-2 engineering with Georgia Institute of Technology, University of Tennessee, Tennessee Technological University; pharmacy with Campbell University, Mercer University, University of Georgia.

Computers on Campus 200 computers/terminals are available on campus for general student use. Campuswide network is available.

Student Life *Housing:* on-campus residence required through junior year. *Options:* men-only, women-only. Freshman campus housing is guaranteed. *Activities and organizations:* drama/theater group, student-run newspaper, choral group, marching band, Baptist Student Union, Fellowship of Christian Athletes, Student Government Association, Student Ambassadors Association, Columbians, national fraternities, national sororities. *Campus security:* 24-hour emergency response devices and patrols, late-night transport/escort service, controlled dormitory access. *Student services:* health clinic, personal/psychological counseling.

Athletics Member NCAA. All Division II. *Intercollegiate sports:* baseball M(s), basketball M(s)/W(s), cross-country running M(s)/W(s), football M(s), golf M(s), soccer M(s)/W(s), softball W(s), tennis M(s)/W(s), track and field M(s)/W(s), volleyball W(s), wrestling M(s). *Intramural sports:* badminton M/W, baseball M/W, basketball M/W, football M/W, golf M/W, racquetball M/W, skiing (downhill) M/W, soccer M/W, softball M/W, table tennis M/W, tennis M/W, volleyball M/W.

Standardized Tests *Required:* SAT or ACT (for admission).

Costs (2012–13) *Comprehensive fee:* $29,058 includes full-time tuition ($21,660), mandatory fees ($992), and room and board ($6406). Full-time tuition and fees vary according to class time and course load. Part-time tuition: $900 per credit hour. *Room and board:* Room and board charges vary according to board plan, gender, and housing facility. *Payment plans:* installment, deferred payment. *Waivers:* senior citizens and employees or children of employees.

Financial Aid Of all full-time matriculated undergraduates who enrolled in 2011, 1,576 applied for aid, 1,291 were judged to have need, 273 had their need fully met. 237 Federal Work-Study jobs (averaging $1497). 20 state and other part-time jobs (averaging $568). In 2011, 261 non-need-based awards were made. *Average percent of need met:* 73%. *Average financial aid package:* $17,820. *Average need-based loan:* $3714. *Average need-based gift aid:* $13,116. *Average non-need-based aid:* $8141. *Average indebtedness upon graduation:* $22,306.

Applying *Options:* electronic application, deferred entrance. *Application fee:* $25. *Required:* high school transcript, minimum 2.3 GPA, medical history. *Required for some:* essay or personal statement, interview. *Recommended:* interview. *Application deadlines:* 8/1 (freshmen), 8/1 (transfers). *Notification:* continuous (freshmen), continuous (transfers).

Freshman Application Contact Melanie Redding, Director of Admissions, Carson-Newman University, 1646 Russell Avenue, PO Box 557, Jefferson City, TN 37760. *Phone:* 865-471-3223. *Toll-free phone:* 800-678-9061. *Fax:* 865-471-3502. *E-mail:* cnadmiss@cn.edu.

Website: http://www.cn.edu/.

See previous page for display ad and page 1226 for the College Close-Up.

Christian Brothers University

Memphis, Tennessee

- **Independent Roman Catholic** comprehensive, founded 1871
- **Urban** 75-acre campus with easy access to Memphis
- **Endowment** $26.9 million
- **Coed** 1,237 undergraduate students, 87% full-time, 58% women, 42% men
- **Moderately difficult** entrance level, 48% of applicants were admitted

Undergraduates 1,079 full-time, 158 part-time. Students come from 27 states and territories; 25 other countries; 20% are from out of state; 36% Black or African American, non-Hispanic/Latino; 5% Hispanic/Latino; 5% Asian, non-Hispanic/Latino; 0.1% Native Hawaiian or other Pacific Islander, non-Hispanic/Latino; 0.3% American Indian or Alaska Native, non-Hispanic/Latino;

3% Two or more races, non-Hispanic/Latino; 0.8% Race/ethnicity unknown; 4% international; 6% transferred in; 40% live on campus. *Retention:* 72% of full-time freshmen returned.

Freshmen *Admission:* 1,943 applied, 939 admitted, 255 enrolled. *Average high school GPA:* 3.71. *Test scores:* ACT scores over 18: 100%; ACT scores over 24: 51%; ACT scores over 30: 7%.

Faculty *Total:* 153, 68% full-time, 71% with terminal degrees. *Student/faculty ratio:* 11:1.

Academics *Calendar:* semesters. *Degrees:* bachelor's, master's, and postbachelor's certificates. *Special study options:* accelerated degree program, adult/continuing education programs, advanced placement credit, distance learning, double majors, honors programs, independent study, internships, off-campus study, part-time degree program, services for LD students, study abroad, summer session for credit. *ROTC:* Army (c), Navy (c), Air Force (c). *Unusual degree programs:* 3-2 engineering.

Computers on Campus 310 computers/terminals are available on campus for general student use. Students can access the following: campus intranet, computer help desk, free student e-mail accounts, online (class) grades, online (class) registration, online (class) schedules, online class listings, course assignments. Campuswide network is available. 100% of college-owned or -operated housing units are wired for high-speed Internet access. Wireless service is available via entire campus.

Student Life *Housing:* on-campus residence required through sophomore year. *Options:* coed, men-only, women-only. Campus housing is university owned. Freshman applicants given priority for college housing. *Activities and organizations:* drama/theater group, choral group, Black Student Association, BACCHUS Alcohol Awareness Group, Intercultural Club, The Chosen Generation, Lasallian Collegians, national fraternities, national sororities. *Campus security:* 24-hour emergency response devices and patrols, student patrols, late-night transport/escort service, controlled dormitory access. *Student services:* health clinic, personal/psychological counseling.

Athletics Member NCAA. All Division II. *Intercollegiate sports:* baseball M(s), basketball M(s)/W(s), cross-country running M(s)/W(s), golf M(s)/W(s), soccer M(s)/W(s), softball W(s), tennis M(s)/W(s), volleyball W(s). *Intramural sports:* basketball M/W, bowling M/W, cross-country running M/W, football M/W, golf M, lacrosse M, racquetball M/W, soccer M/W, softball M/W, swimming and diving M/W, table tennis M/W, tennis M/W, ultimate Frisbee M/W, volleyball M/W, weight lifting M.

Standardized Tests *Required:* SAT or ACT (for admission).

Costs (2012–13) *Comprehensive fee:* $33,424 includes full-time tuition ($26,694), mandatory fees ($590), and room and board ($6140). Full-time tuition and fees vary according to class time and program. Part-time tuition: $936 per credit hour. Part-time tuition and fees vary according to class time, course load, and program. *Required fees:* $115 per term part-time. *Room and board:* Room and board charges vary according to board plan and housing facility.

Financial Aid Of all full-time matriculated undergraduates who enrolled in 2011, 1,185 applied for aid, 962 were judged to have need, 411 had their need fully met. 228 Federal Work-Study jobs (averaging $604). 202 state and other part-time jobs (averaging $733). In 2011, 206 non-need-based awards were made. *Average percent of need met:* 76%. *Average financial aid package:* $20,412. *Average need-based loan:* $4239. *Average need-based gift aid:* $16,782. *Average non-need-based aid:* $11,921. *Average indebtedness upon graduation:* $22,839.

Applying *Options:* electronic application, deferred entrance. *Application fee:* $25. *Required:* essay or personal statement, high school transcript, minimum 2.0 GPA. *Required for some:* 2 letters of recommendation. *Recommended:* interview. *Application deadlines:* 8/1 (freshmen), 8/23 (transfers). *Notification:* 12/1 (freshmen), continuous (transfers).

Freshman Application Contact Ms. Rebecca Johnson, Director of Admissions, Christian Brothers University, 650 East Parkway South, Memphis, TN 38104. *Phone:* 901-321-3205. *Toll-free phone:* 877-321-4CBU. *Fax:* 901-321-3202. *E-mail:* admissions@cbu.edu.

Website: http://www.cbu.edu/.

Cumberland University

Lebanon, Tennessee

Freshman Application Contact Ms. Beatrice LaChance, Director of Enrollment Services, Cumberland University, One Cumberland Square, Lebanon, TN 37087. *Phone:* 615-547-1244. *Toll-free phone:* 800-467-0562. *Fax:* 615-444-2569. *E-mail:* admissions@cumberland.edu. *Website:* http://www.cumberland.edu/.

Daymar Institute

Clarksville, Tennessee

Freshman Application Contact Daymar Institute, 1860 Wilma Rudolph Boulevard, Clarksville, TN 37040. *Phone:* 931-552-7600 Ext. 204. *Website:* http://www.daymarinstitute.edu/.

Daymar Institute

Murfreesboro, Tennessee

Admissions Office Contact Daymar Institute, 415 Golden Bear Court, Murfreesboro, TN 37128.
Website: http://www.daymarinstitute.edu/.

DeVry University

Memphis, Tennessee

Freshman Application Contact DeVry University, 6401 Poplar Avenue, Suite 600, Memphis, TN 38119. *Toll-free phone:* 866-338-7941. *Website:* http://www.devry.edu/.

DeVry University

Nashville, Tennessee

Admissions Office Contact DeVry University, 3343 Perimeter Hill Drive, Suite 200, Nashville, TN 37211-4147. *Toll-free phone:* 866-338-7941. *Website:* http://www.devry.edu/.

East Tennessee State University

Johnson City, Tennessee

- **State-supported** university, founded 1911, part of State University and Community College System of Tennessee; Tennessee Board of Regents
- **Small-town** 366-acre campus
- **Endowment** $100.1 million
- **Coed** 12,267 undergraduate students, 83% full-time, 57% women, 43% men
- **Moderately difficult** entrance level, 89% of applicants were admitted

Undergraduates 10,234 full-time, 2,033 part-time. Students come from 44 states and territories; 45 other countries; 12% are from out of state; 6% Black or African American, non-Hispanic/Latino; 2% Hispanic/Latino; 1% Asian, non-Hispanic/Latino; 0.1% Native Hawaiian or other Pacific Islander, non-Hispanic/Latino; 0.4% American Indian or Alaska Native, non-Hispanic/Latino; 2% Two or more races, non-Hispanic/Latino; 0.5% Race/ethnicity unknown; 2% international; 10% transferred in; 20% live on campus. *Retention:* 66% of full-time freshmen returned.
Freshmen *Admission:* 5,124 applied, 4,572 admitted, 2,082 enrolled. *Average high school GPA:* 3.3. *Test scores:* SAT critical reading scores over 500: 44%; SAT math scores over 500: 49%; ACT scores over 18: 86%; SAT critical reading scores over 600: 13%; SAT math scores over 600: 14%; ACT scores over 24: 35%; SAT math scores over 700: 1%; ACT scores over 30: 5%.
Faculty *Total:* 845, 67% full-time, 61% with terminal degrees. *Student/faculty ratio:* 19:1.
Academics *Calendar:* semesters. *Degrees:* certificates, bachelor's, master's, doctoral, post-master's, and postbachelor's certificates. *Special study options:* adult/continuing education programs, advanced placement credit, cooperative education, distance learning, double majors, English as a second language, external degree program, freshman honors college, honors programs, independent study, internships, off-campus study, part-time degree program, services for LD students, student-designed majors, study abroad, summer session for credit. *ROTC:* Army (b).
Computers on Campus 1,400 computers/terminals are available on campus for general student use. Students can access the following: computer help desk, free student e-mail accounts, online (class) grades, online (class) registration, online (class) schedules. Campuswide network is available. Wireless service is available via entire campus.
Student Life *Housing options:* coed, men-only, women-only, disabled students. Campus housing is university owned. *Activities and organizations:* drama/theater group, student-run newspaper, radio and television station, choral group, honor societies, Volunteer ETSU, religious groups, residence hall councils, national fraternities, national sororities. *Campus security:* 24-hour emergency response devices and patrols, student patrols, late-night transport/escort service, controlled dormitory access. *Student services:* health clinic, personal/psychological counseling, women's center.
Athletics Member NCAA. All Division I. *Intercollegiate sports:* baseball M(s), basketball M(s)/W(s), cross-country running M(s)/W(s), golf M(s)/W(s), soccer M(s)/W(s), softball W(s), tennis M(s)/W(s), track and field M(s)/W(s), volleyball W(s). *Intramural sports:* basketball M/W, cross-country running M/W, football M/W, golf M/W, racquetball M/W, softball M/W, tennis M/W, volleyball W, weight lifting M.
Standardized Tests *Required:* SAT or ACT (for admission).
Applying *Options:* electronic application, early admission. *Application fee:* $25. *Required:* high school transcript, minimum 2.3 GPA, 2.3 high school GPA or 19 ACT. *Application deadlines:* rolling (freshmen), rolling (out-of-state freshmen), rolling (transfers). *Notification:* continuous (freshmen), continuous (out-of-state freshmen), continuous (transfers).
Freshman Application Contact Director of Admissions, East Tennessee State University, PO Box 70731, Johnson City, TN 37614-0734. *Phone:* 423-439-4213. *Toll-free phone:* 800-462-3878. *Fax:* 423-439-4630. *E-mail:* go2etsu@etsu.edu.
Website: http://www.etsu.edu/.

Fisk University

Nashville, Tennessee

Freshman Application Contact Fisk University, 1000 17th Avenue North, Nashville, TN 37208-3051. *Phone:* 615-329-8665. *Toll-free phone:* 888-702-0022. *Fax:* 615-329-8774. *E-mail:* admit@fisk.edu. *Website:* http://www.fisk.edu/.

Fountainhead College of Technology

Knoxville, Tennessee

- **Proprietary** primarily 2-year, founded 1947
- **Suburban** 2-acre campus
- **Coed** 200 undergraduate students, 115% full-time, 15% women, 100% men
- **Noncompetitive** entrance level

Undergraduates 230 full-time. *Retention:* 82% of full-time freshmen returned.
Faculty *Total:* 23, 48% full-time. *Student/faculty ratio:* 9:1.
Academics *Calendar:* semesters. *Degrees:* associate and bachelor's. *Special study options:* accelerated degree program, distance learning, double majors, summer session for credit.
Computers on Campus Students can access the following: campus intranet, computer help desk, free student e-mail accounts. Campuswide network is available. Wireless service is available via entire campus.
Student Life *Housing:* college housing not available. *Campus security:* 24-hour emergency response devices.
Standardized Tests *Required for some:* SAT or ACT (for admission).
Costs (2012–13) *Tuition:* $485 per credit hour part-time. Full-time tuition and fees vary according to program. No tuition increase for student's term of enrollment. *Payment plans:* tuition prepayment, installment.
Applying *Required:* high school transcript, interview. *Application deadlines:* rolling (freshmen), rolling (transfers). *Notification:* continuous (freshmen), continuous (transfers).
Freshman Application Contact Mr. Joel B Southern, Director of Admissions, Fountainhead College of Technology, 10208 Technology Drive, Knoxville, TN 37932. *Phone:* 865-688-9422. *Toll-free phone:* 888-218-7335. *Fax:* 865-688-2419. *E-mail:* joel.southern@fountainheadcollege.edu.
Website: http://www.fountainheadcollege.edu/.

Freed-Hardeman University

Henderson, Tennessee

Freshman Application Contact Mr. Joseph Askew, Interim Director of Admissions, Freed-Hardeman University, 158 East Main Street, Henderson, TN 38340-2399. *Phone:* 731-989-6651. *Toll-free phone:* 800-FHU-FHU-1. *Fax:* 731-989-6047. *E-mail:* admissions@fhu.edu.
Website: http://www.fhu.edu/.

Huntington College of Health Sciences

Knoxville, Tennessee

Freshman Application Contact Kim Galyon, Director of Admissions, Huntington College of Health Sciences, 1204 Kenesaw Avenue, Suite D, Knoxville, TN 37919. *Phone:* 800-290-4226. *Toll-free phone:* 800-290-4226. *Fax:* 865-524-8339. *E-mail:* studentservices@hchs.edu.
Website: http://www.hchs.edu/.

ITT Technical Institute

Chattanooga, Tennessee

- **Proprietary** primarily 2-year, part of ITT Educational Services, Inc.
- **Coed**
- **Minimally difficult** entrance level

Academics *Degrees:* associate and bachelor's.
Freshman Application Contact Director of Recruitment, ITT Technical Institute, 5600 Brainerd Road, Suite G-1, Chattanooga, TN 37411. *Phone:* 423-510-6800. *Toll-free phone:* 877-474-8312.
Website: http://www.itt-tech.edu/.

ITT Technical Institute

Cordova, Tennessee

- **Proprietary** primarily 2-year, founded 1994, part of ITT Educational Services, Inc.
- **Suburban** campus
- **Coed**
- **Minimally difficult** entrance level

Academics *Calendar:* quarters. *Degrees:* associate and bachelor's.
Freshman Application Contact Director of Recruitment, ITT Technical Institute, 7260 Goodlett Farms Parkway, Cordova, TN 38016. *Phone:* 901-381-0200. *Toll-free phone:* 866-444-5141.
Website: http://www.itt-tech.edu/.

ITT Technical Institute

Johnson City, Tennessee

- **Proprietary** primarily 2-year
- **Coed**
- **Minimally difficult** entrance level

Academics *Degrees:* associate and bachelor's.
Freshman Application Contact Director of Recruitment, ITT Technical Institute, 4721 Lake Park Drive, Suite 100, Johnson City, TN 37615. *Phone:* 423-952-4400. *Toll-free phone:* 877-301-9691.
Website: http://www.itt-tech.edu/.

ITT Technical Institute

Knoxville, Tennessee

- **Proprietary** primarily 2-year, founded 1988, part of ITT Educational Services, Inc.
- **Suburban** campus
- **Coed**
- **Minimally difficult** entrance level

Academics *Calendar:* quarters. *Degrees:* associate and bachelor's.
Freshman Application Contact Director of Recruitment, ITT Technical Institute, 9123 Executive Park Drive, Knoxville, TN 37923. *Phone:* 865-671-2800. *Toll-free phone:* 800-671-2801.
Website: http://www.itt-tech.edu/.

ITT Technical Institute

Nashville, Tennessee

- **Proprietary** primarily 2-year, founded 1984, part of ITT Educational Services, Inc.
- **Urban** campus
- **Coed**
- **Minimally difficult** entrance level

Academics *Calendar:* quarters. *Degrees:* associate and bachelor's.
Freshman Application Contact Director of Recruitment, ITT Technical Institute, 2845 Elm Hill Pike, Nashville, TN 37214. *Phone:* 615-889-8700. *Toll-free phone:* 800-331-8386.
Website: http://www.itt-tech.edu/.

Johnson University

Knoxville, Tennessee

Freshman Application Contact Mr. Tim Wingfield, Director of Admissions, Johnson University, 7900 Johnson Drive, Knoxville, TN 37998-1001. *Phone:* 865-251-2346. *Toll-free phone:* 800-827-2122. *Fax:* 865-251-2336. *E-mail:* twingfield@jbc.edu.
Website: http://www.johnsonu.edu/.

King College

Bristol, Tennessee

- **Independent** comprehensive, founded 1867, affiliated with Presbyterian Church (U.S.A.)
- **Suburban** 135-acre campus
- **Endowment** $29.1 million
- **Coed** 1,963 undergraduate students, 94% full-time, 64% women, 36% men
- **Moderately difficult** entrance level, 72% of applicants were admitted

Undergraduates 1,843 full-time, 120 part-time. Students come from 31 states and territories; 29 other countries; 37% are from out of state; 5% Black or African American, non-Hispanic/Latino; 2% Hispanic/Latino; 0.5% Asian, non-Hispanic/Latino; 0.1% Native Hawaiian or other Pacific Islander, non-Hispanic/Latino; 0.3% American Indian or Alaska Native, non-Hispanic/Latino; 1% Two or more races, non-Hispanic/Latino; 8% Race/ethnicity unknown; 3% international; 5% transferred in; 42% live on campus. *Retention:* 75% of full-time freshmen returned.
Freshmen *Admission:* 1,090 applied, 787 admitted, 214 enrolled. *Average high school GPA:* 3.4. *Test scores:* SAT critical reading scores over 500: 51%; SAT math scores over 500: 55%; SAT writing scores over 500: 34%; ACT scores over 18: 92%; SAT critical reading scores over 600: 7%; SAT math scores over 600: 11%; SAT writing scores over 600: 7%; ACT scores over 24: 31%; SAT math scores over 700: 3%; SAT writing scores over 700: 3%; ACT scores over 30: 4%.
Faculty *Total:* 212, 41% full-time, 44% with terminal degrees. *Student/faculty ratio:* 16:1.
Academics *Calendar:* semesters. *Degrees:* bachelor's, master's, and post-master's certificates. *Special study options:* adult/continuing education programs, advanced placement credit, cooperative education, distance learning, double majors, honors programs, independent study, internships, off-campus study, part-time degree program, services for LD students, student-designed majors,

study abroad, summer session for credit. *ROTC:* Army (c). *Unusual degree programs:* 3-2 engineering with University of Tennessee, Vanderbilt University.

Computers on Campus 90 computers/terminals and 500 ports are available on campus for general student use. Students can access the following: campus intranet, computer help desk, free student e-mail accounts, online (class) grades, online (class) registration, online (class) schedules, student portal. Campuswide network is available. 100% of college-owned or -operated housing units are wired for high-speed Internet access. Wireless service is available via classrooms, computer centers, computer labs, learning centers, libraries, student centers.

Student Life *Housing:* on-campus residence required through junior year. *Options:* men-only, women-only, disabled students. Campus housing is university owned. Freshman campus housing is guaranteed. *Activities and organizations:* drama/theater group, student-run newspaper, choral group, Student Government Association, Campus Life Committee, World Christian Fellowship, Fellowship of Christian Athletes, Drama Club. *Campus security:* 24-hour patrols, late-night transport/escort service, controlled dormitory access. *Student services:* personal/psychological counseling.

Athletics Member NCAA. All Division II. *Intercollegiate sports:* baseball M(s), basketball M(s)/W(s), cheerleading M(s)/W(s), cross-country running M(s)/W(s), golf M(s)/W(s), soccer M(s)/W(s), softball W(s), swimming and diving M(s)/W(s), tennis M(s)/W(s), track and field M(s)/W(s), volleyball M(s)/W(s), wrestling M(s)/W(s). *Intramural sports:* badminton M/W, basketball M/W, soccer M/W, softball M/W, table tennis M/W, tennis M/W, ultimate Frisbee M/W, volleyball M/W, weight lifting M.

Standardized Tests *Required:* SAT or ACT (for admission).

Costs (2012–13) *Comprehensive fee:* $33,140 includes full-time tuition ($23,608), mandatory fees ($1352), and room and board ($8180). Full-time tuition and fees vary according to course load and program. Part-time tuition: $600 per credit hour. Part-time tuition and fees vary according to course load and program. *College room only:* $4108. Room and board charges vary according to board plan. *Payment plan:* installment. *Waivers:* senior citizens and employees or children of employees.

Financial Aid Of all full-time matriculated undergraduates who enrolled in 2011, 1,622 applied for aid, 1,475 were judged to have need, 228 had their need fully met. 86 Federal Work-Study jobs (averaging $1563). 144 state and other part-time jobs (averaging $1296). In 2011, 101 non-need-based awards were made. *Average percent of need met:* 69%. *Average financial aid package:* $15,356. *Average need-based loan:* $4772. *Average need-based gift aid:* $12,802. *Average non-need-based aid:* $8673. *Average indebtedness upon graduation:* $28,946.

Applying *Options:* electronic application, early admission, deferred entrance. *Application fee:* $20. *Required:* high school transcript, minimum 2.4 GPA. *Required for some:* essay or personal statement. *Application deadlines:* rolling (freshmen), rolling (out-of-state freshmen), rolling (transfers). *Notification:* continuous (freshmen), continuous (out-of-state freshmen), continuous (transfers).

Freshman Application Contact Mr. Elvin Brown, Director of Undergraduate Recruitment and Admissions, King College, 1350 King College Road, Bristol, TN 37620. *Phone:* 423-652-4769. *Toll-free phone:* 800-362-0014. *Fax:* 423-652-4727. *E-mail:* admissions@king.edu.
Website: http://www.king.edu/.

Lane College

Jackson, Tennessee

- **Independent** 4-year, founded 1882, affiliated with Christian Methodist Episcopal Church
- **Suburban** 25-acre campus with easy access to Memphis
- **Endowment** $4.1 million
- **Coed** 1,512 undergraduate students, 98% full-time, 51% women, 49% men
- **Minimally difficult** entrance level, 33% of applicants were admitted

Undergraduates 1,484 full-time, 28 part-time. Students come from 29 states and territories; 37% are from out of state; 100% Black or African American, non-Hispanic/Latino; 6% transferred in; 61% live on campus. *Retention:* 50% of full-time freshmen returned.

Freshmen *Admission:* 5,324 applied, 1,780 admitted, 325 enrolled. *Average high school GPA:* 2.3. *Test scores:* ACT scores over 18: 19%; ACT scores over 24: 1%.

Faculty *Total:* 91, 99% full-time. *Student/faculty ratio:* 17:1.

Academics *Calendar:* semesters. *Degree:* bachelor's. *Special study options:* academic remediation for entering students, accelerated degree program, adult/continuing education programs, advanced placement credit, cooperative edu-

cation, honors programs, independent study, internships, off-campus study, part-time degree program, study abroad, summer session for credit.

Computers on Campus 258 computers/terminals and 258 ports are available on campus for general student use. Students can access the following: campus intranet, computer help desk, free student e-mail accounts, online admissions and advising. Campuswide network is available. 100% of college-owned or -operated housing units are wired for high-speed Internet access. Wireless service is available via classrooms, computer centers, computer labs, dorm rooms, learning centers, libraries, student centers.

Student Life *Housing:* on-campus residence required for freshman year. *Options:* men-only, women-only. Campus housing is university owned. Freshman applicants given priority for college housing. *Activities and organizations:* drama/theater group, choral group, marching band, Student Government Association, Pre-Law Club, Student Christian Association, Drama Club, Sociology Club, national fraternities, national sororities. *Campus security:* 24-hour emergency response devices and patrols, late-night transport/escort service, surveillance cameras, lighted parking areas. *Student services:* health clinic, personal/psychological counseling.

Athletics Member NCAA. All Division II. *Intercollegiate sports:* baseball M(s), basketball M(s)/W(s), cheerleading W, cross-country running M(s)/W(s), football M(s), softball W(s), tennis M(s)/W(s), track and field M(s)/W(s), volleyball W(s).

Standardized Tests *Required:* SAT or ACT (for admission).

Costs (2012–13) *Comprehensive fee:* $14,600 includes full-time tuition ($7860), mandatory fees ($700), and room and board ($6040). Full-time tuition and fees vary according to course load. Part-time tuition: $330 per credit hour. Part-time tuition and fees vary according to course load. *Required fees:* $700 per year part-time. *Payment plans:* installment, deferred payment. *Waivers:* adult students and employees or children of employees.

Financial Aid Of all full-time matriculated undergraduates who enrolled in 2012, 1,470 applied for aid, 1,440 were judged to have need, 24 had their need fully met. In 2012, 11 non-need-based awards were made. *Average percent of need met:* 55%. *Average financial aid package:* $4422. *Average need-based loan:* $2049. *Average need-based gift aid:* $3677. *Average non-need-based aid:* $1773. *Average indebtedness upon graduation:* $12,348.

Applying *Options:* electronic application, deferred entrance. *Required:* high school transcript, 2 letters of recommendation. *Application deadlines:* rolling (freshmen), rolling (out-of-state freshmen), rolling (transfers). *Notification:* continuous (freshmen), continuous (transfers).

Freshman Application Contact Dr. Juanita Morris, Director of Enrollment Management, Lane College, 545 Lane Avenue, Jackson, TN 38301. *Phone:* 731-426-7533. *Toll-free phone:* 800-960-7533. *Fax:* 731-426-7559. *E-mail:* jmorris@lanecollege.edu.
Website: http://www.lanecollege.edu/.

Lee University

Cleveland, Tennessee

- **Independent** comprehensive, founded 1918, affiliated with Church of God
- **Small-town** 104-acre campus with easy access to Chattanooga
- **Endowment** $12.0 million
- **Coed** 4,565 undergraduate students, 84% full-time, 57% women, 43% men

Undergraduates 3,834 full-time, 731 part-time. Students come from 50 states and territories; 57 other countries; 56% are from out of state; 6% Black or African American, non-Hispanic/Latino; 4% Hispanic/Latino; 1% Asian, non-Hispanic/Latino; 0.2% Native Hawaiian or other Pacific Islander, non-Hispanic/Latino; 0.4% American Indian or Alaska Native, non-Hispanic/Latino; 1% Two or more races, non-Hispanic/Latino; 7% Race/ethnicity unknown; 5% international; 5% transferred in; 48% live on campus. *Retention:* 73% of full-time freshmen returned.

Freshmen *Admission:* 860 enrolled. *Average high school GPA:* 3.53. *Test scores:* SAT critical reading scores over 500: 63%; SAT math scores over 500: 62%; ACT scores over 18: 90%; SAT critical reading scores over 600: 31%; SAT math scores over 600: 27%; ACT scores over 24: 57%; SAT critical reading scores over 700: 8%; SAT math scores over 700: 5%; ACT scores over 30: 14%.

Faculty *Total:* 388, 40% full-time, 54% with terminal degrees. *Student/faculty ratio:* 18:1.

Academics *Calendar:* semesters. *Degrees:* certificates, bachelor's, master's, post-master's, and postbachelor's certificates. *Special study options:* academic remediation for entering students, adult/continuing education programs, advanced placement credit, cooperative education, distance learning, double majors, English as a second language, external degree program, honors programs, independent study, internships, off-campus study, part-time degree program, services for LD students, study abroad, summer session for credit.

Computers on Campus 410 computers/terminals and 410 ports are available on campus for general student use. Students can access the following: campus intranet, computer help desk, free student e-mail accounts, online (class) grades, online (class) registration, online (class) schedules. Campuswide network is available. 99% of college-owned or -operated housing units are wired for high-speed Internet access. Wireless service is available via entire campus.

Student Life *Housing:* on-campus residence required through sophomore year. *Options:* men-only, women-only. Campus housing is university owned and leased by the school. Freshman campus housing is guaranteed. *Activities and organizations:* drama/theater group, student-run newspaper, choral group, Student Leadership Council, Pioneers for Christ, International Student Fellowship, Big Pal Little Pal, Back Yard Ministry. *Campus security:* 24-hour emergency response devices and patrols, late-night transport/escort service, controlled dormitory access. *Student services:* health clinic, personal/psychological counseling.

Athletics Member NAIA. *Intercollegiate sports:* baseball M(s), basketball M(s)/W(s), cheerleading M(s)(c)/W(s)(c), cross-country running M(s)/W(s), golf M(s)/W(s), rugby M(s)(c)/W(s)(c), soccer M(s)/W(s), softball W(s), tennis M(s)/W(s), track and field M(s)/W(s), volleyball M(c)/W(s), wrestling M(c). *Intramural sports:* badminton M/W, basketball M/W, bowling M/W, football M/W, racquetball M/W, soccer M/W, softball M/W, table tennis M/W, tennis M/W, ultimate Frisbee M/W, volleyball W.

Standardized Tests *Required:* SAT or ACT (for admission).

Costs (2013–14) *Comprehensive fee:* $20,512 includes full-time tuition ($13,200), mandatory fees ($550), and room and board ($6762). Full-time tuition and fees vary according to course load, location, and program. Part-time tuition: $550 per credit hour. Part-time tuition and fees vary according to course load, location, and program. *Required fees:* $550 per credit hour part-time. *College room only:* $3502. Room and board charges vary according to board plan and housing facility. *Payment plan:* deferred payment. *Waivers:* senior citizens and employees or children of employees.

Financial Aid Of all full-time matriculated undergraduates who enrolled in 2011, 3,248 applied for aid, 2,743 were judged to have need, 387 had their need fully met. 243 Federal Work-Study jobs (averaging $1715). 624 state and other part-time jobs (averaging $1450). In 2011, 514 non-need-based awards were made. *Average percent of need met:* 49%. *Average financial aid package:* $10,358. *Average need-based loan:* $4118. *Average need-based gift aid:* $8020. *Average non-need-based aid:* $7241. *Average indebtedness upon graduation:* $27,882.

Applying *Required:* high school transcript, minimum 2.0 GPA, MMR immunization record. *Required for some:* 3 letters of recommendation.

Freshman Application Contact Mr. Phillip Cook, Vice President for Enrollment, Lee University, 1120 N. Ocoee Street, Cleveland, TN 37311. *Phone:* 423-614-8500. *Toll-free phone:* 800-533-9930. *Fax:* 423-614-8533. *E-mail:* admissions@leeuniversity.edu. *Website:* http://www.leeuniversity.edu/.

LeMoyne-Owen College

Memphis, Tennessee

Freshman Application Contact LeMoyne-Owen College, 807 Walker Avenue, Memphis, TN 38126-6595. *Phone:* 901-435-1500. *Toll-free phone:* 800-737-7778. *Website:* http://www.loc.edu/.

Lincoln Memorial University

Harrogate, Tennessee

- **Independent** comprehensive, founded 1897
- **Small-town** 1000-acre campus
- **Endowment** $14.0 million
- **Coed** 1,851 undergraduate students, 76% full-time, 71% women, 29% men
- **Moderately difficult** entrance level, 65% of applicants were admitted

Undergraduates 1,416 full-time, 435 part-time. Students come from 46 states and territories; 25 other countries; 36% are from out of state; 4% Black or African American, non-Hispanic/Latino; 2% Hispanic/Latino; 1% Asian, non-Hispanic/Latino; 0.2% American Indian or Alaska Native, non-Hispanic/Latino; 0.4% Two or more races, non-Hispanic/Latino; 11% Race/ethnicity unknown; 3% international; 16% transferred in; 36% live on campus. *Retention:* 67% of full-time freshmen returned.

Freshmen *Admission:* 990 applied, 644 admitted, 253 enrolled. *Average high school GPA:* 3.49. *Test scores:* SAT critical reading scores over 500: 60%; SAT math scores over 500: 49%; ACT scores over 18: 90%; SAT critical reading scores over 600: 20%; SAT math scores over 600: 23%; ACT scores over 24: 33%; ACT scores over 30: 7%.

Faculty *Total:* 275, 69% full-time, 52% with terminal degrees. *Student/faculty ratio:* 13:1.

Academics *Calendar:* semesters. *Degrees:* associate, bachelor's, master's, doctoral, post-master's, and postbachelor's certificates. *Special study options:* academic remediation for entering students, accelerated degree program, adult/continuing education programs, advanced placement credit, distance learning, double majors, English as a second language, honors programs, independent study, internships, part-time degree program, summer session for credit.

Computers on Campus Students can access the following: campus intranet, computer help desk, free student e-mail accounts, online (class) grades, online (class) registration, online (class) schedules. Campuswide network is available. 100% of college-owned or -operated housing units are wired for high-speed Internet access.

Student Life *Housing options:* coed, men-only, women-only, disabled students. Campus housing is university owned. *Activities and organizations:* drama/theater group, student-run radio and television station, choral group, Students in Free Enterprise (SIFE), Baptist Campus Ministries, Pre-Med Club, Fishing Club, Earth Club. *Campus security:* 24-hour emergency response devices and patrols. *Student services:* health clinic, personal/psychological counseling.

Athletics Member NCAA. All Division II. *Intercollegiate sports:* baseball M(s), basketball M(s)/W(s), cross-country running M(s)/W(s), golf M(s)/W(s), soccer M(s)/W(s), softball W(s), tennis M(s)/W(s), volleyball W(s). *Intramural sports:* basketball M/W, football M/W, soccer M/W, softball M/W, swimming and diving M/W, table tennis M/W, tennis M/W, ultimate Frisbee M/W, volleyball M/W.

Standardized Tests *Required:* SAT or ACT (for admission).

Costs (2013–14) *Comprehensive fee:* $26,200 includes full-time tuition ($18,960), mandatory fees ($500), and room and board ($6740). Part-time tuition: $790 per credit hour. Part-time tuition and fees vary according to course load. *Room and board:* Room and board charges vary according to board plan and housing facility. *Payment plan:* installment. *Waivers:* children of alumni, senior citizens, and employees or children of employees.

Financial Aid Of all full-time matriculated undergraduates who enrolled in 2010, 1,426 applied for aid, 1,257 were judged to have need, 240 had their need fully met. In 2010, 155 non-need-based awards were made. *Average percent of need met:* 74%. *Average financial aid package:* $17,321. *Average need-based loan:* $3872. *Average need-based gift aid:* $13,112. *Average non-need-based aid:* $8412. *Average indebtedness upon graduation:* $21,749.

Applying *Options:* electronic application. *Application fee:* $50. *Required:* high school transcript, minimum 2.3 GPA, immunization records, financial aid application. *Application deadlines:* rolling (freshmen), rolling (transfers). *Notification:* continuous (freshmen), continuous (transfers).

Freshman Application Contact Lincoln Memorial University, 6965 Cumberland Gap Parkway, Harrogate, TN 37752-1901. *Phone:* 423-869-6280. *Toll-free phone:* 800-325-0900. *Website:* http://www.lmunet.edu/.

Lipscomb University

Nashville, Tennessee

- **Independent** comprehensive, founded 1891, affiliated with Church of Christ
- **Suburban** 75-acre campus
- **Endowment** $56.7 million
- **Coed** 2,740 undergraduate students, 91% full-time, 59% women, 41% men
- **Moderately difficult** entrance level, 52% of applicants were admitted

Undergraduates 2,491 full-time, 249 part-time. Students come from 48 states and territories; 35 other countries; 30% are from out of state; 7% Black or African American, non-Hispanic/Latino; 6% Hispanic/Latino; 2% Asian, non-Hispanic/Latino; 0.1% Native Hawaiian or other Pacific Islander, non-Hispanic/Latino; 2% Two or more races, non-Hispanic/Latino; 3% Race/ethnicity unknown; 2% international; 5% transferred in; 52% live on campus. *Retention:* 76% of full-time freshmen returned.

Freshmen *Admission:* 3,022 applied, 1,578 admitted, 675 enrolled. *Average high school GPA:* 3.51. *Test scores:* SAT critical reading scores over 500: 77%; SAT math scores over 500: 76%; ACT scores over 18: 99%; SAT critical reading scores over 600: 36%; SAT math scores over 600: 34%; ACT scores over 24: 64%; SAT critical reading scores over 700: 10%; SAT math scores over 700: 9%; ACT scores over 30: 19%.

Faculty *Total:* 490, 39% full-time, 56% with terminal degrees. *Student/faculty ratio:* 12:1.

Academics *Calendar:* semesters. *Degrees:* associate, bachelor's, master's, doctoral, and postbachelor's certificates. *Special study options:* academic remediation for entering students, accelerated degree program, adult/continuing education programs, advanced placement credit, distance learning, double majors, freshman honors college, honors programs, independent study, internships, services for LD students, study abroad, summer session for credit. *ROTC:* Army (c), Air Force (c).

Computers on Campus 175 computers/terminals are available on campus for general student use. Students can access the following: campus intranet, computer help desk, free student e-mail accounts, online (class) grades, online (class) registration, online (class) schedules. Campuswide network is available. 100% of college-owned or -operated housing units are wired for high-speed Internet access. Wireless service is available via entire campus.

Student Life *Housing:* on-campus residence required through junior year. *Options:* men-only, women-only. Campus housing is university owned. Freshman applicants given priority for college housing. *Activities and organizations:* drama/theater group, student-run newspaper, radio and television station, choral group, Sigma Pi Beta, business fraternities, Multicultural Association, Alpha Phi Chi men's service club, Pi Kappa Sigma women's service club. *Campus security:* 24-hour emergency response devices and patrols, late-night transport/escort service, controlled dormitory access. *Student services:* health clinic, personal/psychological counseling.

Athletics Member NCAA. All Division I. *Intercollegiate sports:* baseball M(s), basketball M(s)/W(s), cross-country running M(s)/W(s), golf M(s)/W(s), soccer M(s)/W(s), softball W(s), tennis M(s)/W(s), track and field M(s)/W(s), volleyball W(s). *Intramural sports:* badminton M/W, basketball M/W, football M/W, racquetball M/W, soccer M/W, softball M/W, table tennis M/W, ultimate Frisbee M/W, volleyball M/W.

Standardized Tests *Required:* SAT or ACT (for admission).

Costs (2012–13) *Comprehensive fee:* $33,978 includes full-time tuition ($22,978), mandatory fees ($1776), and room and board ($9224). Full-time tuition and fees vary according to course load. Part-time tuition: $960 per hour. Part-time tuition and fees vary according to course load. *Required fees:* $75 per credit hour part-time. *College room only:* $5184. Room and board charges vary according to board plan and housing facility. *Payment plan:* installment. *Waivers:* adult students and employees or children of employees.

Financial Aid Of all full-time matriculated undergraduates who enrolled in 2012, 2,374 applied for aid, 1,699 were judged to have need, 477 had their need fully met. 224 Federal Work-Study jobs (averaging $1334). In 2012, 600 non-need-based awards were made. *Average percent of need met:* 63%. *Average financial aid package:* $20,467. *Average need-based loan:* $5548. *Average need-based gift aid:* $5509. *Average non-need-based aid:* $11,640. *Average indebtedness upon graduation:* $15,155.

Applying *Options:* electronic application, early admission, deferred entrance. *Application fee:* $50. *Required:* high school transcript, minimum 2.3 GPA, 1 letter of recommendation, interview. *Recommended:* essay or personal statement. *Application deadlines:* rolling (freshmen), rolling (transfers). *Notification:* continuous (freshmen), continuous (transfers).

Freshman Application Contact Office of Admissions, Lipscomb University, One University Park Drive, Nashville, TN 37204-3951. *Phone:* 615-966-1776. *Toll-free phone:* 877-582-4766. *Fax:* 615-966-1804. *E-mail:* admissions@lipscomb.edu. *Website:* http://www.lipscomb.edu/.

Martin Methodist College

Pulaski, Tennessee

Freshman Application Contact Lisa Smith, Director of Admissions, Martin Methodist College, 433 West Madison Street, Pulaski, TN 38478-2716. *Phone:* 931-363-9868. *Toll-free phone:* 800-467-1273. *Fax:* 931-363-9818. *E-mail:* admit@martinmethodist.edu. *Website:* http://www.martinmethodist.edu/.

Maryville College

Maryville, Tennessee

- **Independent Presbyterian** 4-year, founded 1819
- **Suburban** 350-acre campus
- **Coed** 1,093 undergraduate students, 96% full-time, 56% women, 44% men
- **Moderately difficult** entrance level, 66% of applicants were admitted

Undergraduates 1,050 full-time, 43 part-time. Students come from 31 states and territories; 24 other countries; 19% are from out of state; 5% Black or African American, non-Hispanic/Latino; 3% Hispanic/Latino; 0.9% Asian, non-Hispanic/Latino; 0.1% Native Hawaiian or other Pacific Islander, non-Hispanic/Latino; 0.5% American Indian or Alaska Native, non-Hispanic/Latino; 2% Two or more races, non-Hispanic/Latino; 2% Race/ethnicity unknown; 4% international; 5% transferred in; 66% live on campus. *Retention:* 72% of full-time freshmen returned.

Freshmen *Admission:* 2,114 applied, 1,388 admitted, 313 enrolled. *Average high school GPA:* 3.5. *Test scores:* SAT critical reading scores over 500: 53%; SAT math scores over 500: 48%; ACT scores over 18: 97%; SAT critical reading scores over 600: 20%; SAT math scores over 600: 9%; ACT scores over 24: 49%; SAT critical reading scores over 700: 1%; ACT scores over 30: 12%.

Faculty *Total:* 106, 63% full-time, 70% with terminal degrees. *Student/faculty ratio:* 12:1.

Academics *Calendar:* 4-1-4. *Degree:* bachelor's. *Special study options:* academic remediation for entering students, advanced placement credit, double majors, English as a second language, honors programs, independent study, internships, off-campus study, part-time degree program, services for LD students, student-designed majors, study abroad, summer session for credit. *Unusual degree programs:* 3-2 engineering with Vanderbilt University, Washington University in St. Louis, Auburn University, Tennessee Technological University; nursing with Vanderbilt University.

Computers on Campus 290 computers/terminals are available on campus for general student use. Students can access the following: campus intranet, computer help desk, free student e-mail accounts, online (class) grades, online (class) registration, online (class) schedules. Campuswide network is available. 100% of college-owned or -operated housing units are wired for high-speed Internet access. Wireless service is available via entire campus.

Student Life *Housing:* on-campus residence required through senior year. *Options:* coed, men-only, women-only, disabled students. Campus housing is university owned. Freshman campus housing is guaranteed. *Activities and organizations:* drama/theater group, student-run newspaper, choral group, Voices of Praise, student government, Student Programming Board, Global Citizenship, Peer Mentors. *Campus security:* 24-hour emergency response devices and patrols, late-night transport/escort service, controlled dormitory access, campus-wide emergency alert system via cell phones, home phones, and email. *Student services:* health clinic, personal/psychological counseling.

Athletics Member NCAA. All Division III. *Intercollegiate sports:* baseball M, basketball M/W, cheerleading M/W, cross-country running M/W, equestrian sports M(s)(c)/W(s)(c), football M, golf M/W, soccer M/W, softball W, swimming and diving M/W, tennis M/W, ultimate Frisbee M(c)/W(c), volleyball W. *Intramural sports:* archery M/W, badminton M/W, basketball M/W, bowling M/W, football M/W, racquetball M/W, rugby M/W, skiing (downhill) M/W, soccer M/W, softball M/W, table tennis M/W, tennis M/W, track and field M/W, ultimate Frisbee M/W, volleyball M/W, water polo M/W.

Standardized Tests *Required:* SAT or ACT (for admission).

Costs (2013–14) *Comprehensive fee:* $41,022 includes full-time tuition ($30,410), mandatory fees ($722), and room and board ($9890). Full-time tuition and fees vary according to course load. Part-time tuition: $800 per credit hour. Part-time tuition and fees vary according to course load. *College room only:* $4908. Room and board charges vary according to board plan and housing facility. *Payment plan:* installment. *Waivers:* employees or children of employees.

Financial Aid Of all full-time matriculated undergraduates who enrolled in 2012, 1,050 applied for aid, 900 were judged to have need, 225 had their need fully met. 550 Federal Work-Study jobs (averaging $1704). 66 state and other part-time jobs (averaging $1665). In 2012, 150 non-need-based awards were made. *Average financial aid package:* $29,187. *Average need-based loan:* $5677. *Average need-based gift aid:* $23,495. *Average non-need-based aid:* $16,966.

Applying *Options:* electronic application, early admission, deferred entrance. *Required:* high school transcript, minimum 2.5 GPA, letters of recommendation. *Required for some:* essay or personal statement, interview. *Recommended:* minimum 3.0 GPA. *Application deadlines:* 3/1 (freshmen), rolling (transfers). *Notification:* continuous until 4/1 (freshmen).

Freshman Application Contact Ms. Linda L. Moore, Administrative Assistant of Admissions, Maryville College, 502 East Lamar Alexander Parkway, Maryville, TN 37804-5907. *Phone:* 865-981-8096. *Toll-free phone:* 800-597-2687. *Fax:* 865-981-8005. *E-mail:* admissions@maryvillecollege.edu. *Website:* http://www.maryvillecollege.edu/.

Memphis College of Art

Memphis, Tennessee

- **Independent** comprehensive, founded 1936
- **Urban** 200-acre campus
- **Coed**
- **Moderately difficult** entrance level

Faculty *Student/faculty ratio:* 10:1.

Academics *Calendar:* semesters. *Degrees:* bachelor's and master's.

Student Life *Campus security:* 24-hour emergency response devices and patrols, late-night transport/escort service, controlled dormitory access.

Standardized Tests *Required:* SAT or ACT (for admission).

Costs (2012–13) *Comprehensive fee:* $34,250 includes full-time tuition ($25,600), mandatory fees ($650), and room and board ($8000). Full-time tuition and fees vary according to degree level and program. Part-time tuition: $1117 per credit. Part-time tuition and fees vary according to course load, degree level, and program. *Required fees:* $650 per year part-time. *College room only:* $6000. Room and board charges vary according to housing facility.

Financial Aid *Of all full-time matriculated undergraduates who enrolled in 2010,* 325 applied for aid, 286 were judged to have need, 22 had their need fully met. *In 2010,* 74 non-need-based awards were made. *Average percent of need met:* 72. *Average financial aid package:* $18,390. *Average need-based loan:* $4409. *Average need-based gift aid:* $14,632. *Average non-need-based aid:* $9105.

Applying *Options:* electronic application, deferred entrance. *Application fee:* $25. *Required:* high school transcript, minimum 2.0 GPA, portfolio. *Recommended:* essay or personal statement, interview.

Freshman Application Contact Memphis College of Art, Overton Park, 1930 Poplar Avenue, Memphis, TN 38104-2764. *Phone:* 901-272-5153. *Toll-free phone:* 800-727-1088.

Website: http://www.mca.edu/.

Mid-America Baptist Theological Seminary

Cordova, Tennessee

Freshman Application Contact Mr. Duffy Guyton, Director of Admissions, Mid-America Baptist Theological Seminary, PO Box 2350, Cordova, TN 38016. *Phone:* 901-751-8453 Ext. 3066. *Toll-free phone:* 800-968-4508. *Fax:* 901-751-8454. *E-mail:* info@mabts.edu.

Website: http://www.mabts.edu/.

Middle Tennessee State University

Murfreesboro, Tennessee

- **State-supported** university, founded 1911, part of Tennessee Board of Regents
- **Urban** 500-acre campus with easy access to Nashville
- **Endowment** $64.7 million
- **Coed** 22,371 undergraduate students, 82% full-time, 53% women, 47% men
- **Moderately difficult** entrance level, 67% of applicants were admitted

Undergraduates 18,403 full-time, 3,968 part-time. 4% are from out of state; 19% Black or African American, non-Hispanic/Latino; 4% Hispanic/Latino; 3% Asian, non-Hispanic/Latino; 0.1% Native Hawaiian or other Pacific Islander, non-Hispanic/Latino; 0.3% American Indian or Alaska Native, non-Hispanic/Latino; 2% Two or more races, non-Hispanic/Latino; 2% Race/ethnicity unknown; 9% transferred in; 17% live on campus.

Freshmen *Admission:* 9,405 applied, 6,289 admitted, 3,120 enrolled. *Average high school GPA:* 3.31. *Test scores:* SAT critical reading scores over 500: 63%; SAT math scores over 500: 64%; ACT scores over 18: 89%; SAT critical reading scores over 600: 23%; SAT math scores over 600: 23%; ACT scores over 24: 30%; SAT critical reading scores over 700: 6%; SAT math scores over 700: 3%; ACT scores over 30: 3%.

Academics *Calendar:* semesters. *Degrees:* bachelor's, master's, doctoral, post-master's, and postbachelor's certificates. *Special study options:* adult/continuing education programs, part-time degree program. *ROTC:* Army (b), Air Force (c). *Unusual degree programs:* 3-2 engineering with University of Tennessee, Knoxville; Georgia Institute of Technology; Tennessee Technological University; The University of Memphis; Tennessee State University; Vanderbilt University.

Computers on Campus Students can access the following: online (class) registration. Campuswide network is available.

Student Life *Housing options:* coed, men-only, women-only, disabled students. Campus housing is university owned. *Activities and organizations:* drama/theater group, student-run newspaper, radio and television station, choral group, marching band, national fraternities, national sororities. *Campus security:* 24-hour emergency response devices and patrols, student patrols, late-night transport/escort service, controlled dormitory access. *Student services:* health clinic, personal/psychological counseling, women's center, legal services.

Athletics Member NCAA. All Division I except football (Division I-A). *Intercollegiate sports:* baseball M(s), basketball M(s)/W(s), cheerleading M(s)/W(s), cross-country running M(s)/W(s), equestrian sports M/W, golf M(s), soccer W(s), softball W(s), tennis M(s)/W(s), track and field M(s)/W(s), volleyball W(s). *Intramural sports:* badminton M/W, basketball M/W, bowling M(c)/W(c), fencing M(c)/W(c), field hockey M(c)/W(c), football M, ice hockey M(c), lacrosse M(c)/W(c), racquetball M(c)/W(c), riflery M, rugby M(c)/W(c), soccer M(c)/W, softball M/W, swimming and diving M/W, tennis M/W, ultimate Frisbee M(c)/W(c), volleyball M(c)/W(c), wrestling M(c)/W(c).

Standardized Tests *Required:* SAT or ACT (for admission).

Costs (2012–13) *Tuition:* state resident $5616 full-time, $234 per credit hour part-time; nonresident $20,232 full-time, $843 per credit hour part-time. Full-time tuition and fees vary according to course load. Part-time tuition and fees vary according to course load. *Required fees:* $1594 full-time. *Room and board:* $7532. Room and board charges vary according to board plan and housing facility.

Financial Aid Of all full-time matriculated undergraduates who enrolled in 2012, 16,349 applied for aid, 12,939 were judged to have need, 1,669 had their need fully met. 255 Federal Work-Study jobs (averaging $2524). In 2012, 1000 non-need-based awards were made. *Average percent of need met:* 63%. *Average financial aid package:* $9176. *Average need-based loan:* $3963. *Average need-based gift aid:* $5168. *Average non-need-based aid:* $2582. *Average indebtedness upon graduation:* $22,039.

Applying *Application fee:* $25. *Required:* high school transcript, minimum 3.0 GPA. *Required for some:* essay or personal statement. *Application deadlines:* rolling (freshmen), rolling (transfers). *Notification:* continuous (freshmen), continuous (transfers).

Freshman Application Contact Director of Admissions, Middle Tennessee State University, 1301 East Main Street, Murfreesboro, TN 37132. *Phone:* 615-898-2111. *Toll-free phone:* 800-331-MTSU. *Fax:* 615-898-5478. *E-mail:* admissions@mtsu.edu.

Website: http://www.mtsu.edu/.

Milligan College

Milligan College, Tennessee

- **Independent Christian** comprehensive, founded 1866
- **Suburban** 181-acre campus
- **Endowment** $17.3 million
- **Coed**
- **Moderately difficult** entrance level

Faculty *Student/faculty ratio:* 13:1.

Academics *Calendar:* semesters. *Degrees:* bachelor's and master's.

Student Life *Campus security:* 24-hour emergency response devices and patrols, late-night transport/escort service.

Athletics Member NAIA.

Standardized Tests *Required:* SAT or ACT (for admission).

Costs (2012–13) *Comprehensive fee:* $32,610 includes full-time tuition ($25,735), mandatory fees ($1025), and room and board ($5850). Full-time tuition and fees vary according to course load. Part-time tuition and fees vary according to course load. *College room only:* $2850. Room and board charges vary according to housing facility.

Financial Aid *Of all full-time matriculated undergraduates who enrolled in 2012,* 804 applied for aid, 712 were judged to have need, 170 had their need fully met. 163 Federal Work-Study jobs (averaging $1200). 153 state and other part-time jobs (averaging $1551). *In 2012,* 106 non-need-based awards were made. *Average percent of need met:* 75. *Average financial aid package:* $19,698. *Average need-based loan:* $4451. *Average need-based gift aid:* $16,561. *Average non-need-based aid:* $8560. *Average indebtedness upon graduation:* $27,687.

Applying *Options:* electronic application, deferred entrance. *Application fee:* $30. *Required:* essay or personal statement, high school transcript, minimum

2.0 GPA, 2 letters of recommendation. *Required for some:* interview. *Recommended:* minimum 3.0 GPA.

Freshman Application Contact Ms. Tracy Brinn, Director of Enrollment Management, Milligan College, PO Box 210, Milligan College, TN 37682. *Phone:* 423-461-8730. *Toll-free phone:* 800-262-8337. *Fax:* 423-461-8982. *E-mail:* admissions@milligan.edu. *Website:* http://www.milligan.edu/.

See below for display ad and page 1392 for the College Close-Up.

National College of Business and Technology

Bristol, Tennessee

Freshman Application Contact National College of Business and Technology, 1328 Highway 11 West, Bristol, TN 37620. *Phone:* 423-878-4440. *Toll-free phone:* 888-9-JOBREADY. *Website:* http://www.national-college.edu/.

Nossi College of Art

Goodlettsville, Tennessee

Freshman Application Contact Ms. Mary Alexander, Admissions Director, Nossi College of Art, 590 Cheron Road, Madison, TN 37115. *Phone:* 615-514-2787 (ARTS). *Toll-free phone:* 888-986-ARTS. *Fax:* 615-514-2788. *E-mail:* admissions@nossi.edu. *Website:* http://www.nossi.edu/.

O'More College of Design

Franklin, Tennessee

- **Independent** 4-year, founded 1970
- **Small-town** 6-acre campus with easy access to Nashville
- **Coed, primarily women** 205 undergraduate students, 86% full-time, 87% women, 13% men
- **Moderately difficult** entrance level, 55% of applicants were admitted

Undergraduates 177 full-time, 28 part-time. Students come from 18 states and territories; 3 other countries; 16% are from out of state; 3% Black or African American, non-Hispanic/Latino; 2% Hispanic/Latino; 4% Asian, non-Hispanic/Latino; 2% American Indian or Alaska Native, non-Hispanic/Latino; 2% Race/ethnicity unknown; 2% international; 14% transferred in.

Freshmen *Admission:* 69 applied, 38 admitted, 50 enrolled. *Average high school GPA:* 3.28. *Test scores:* SAT critical reading scores over 500: 72%; SAT math scores over 500: 72%; ACT scores over 18: 80%; SAT critical reading scores over 600: 14%; SAT math scores over 600: 14%; ACT scores over 24: 33%; SAT math scores over 700: 14%.

Faculty *Total:* 46, 35% full-time, 9% with terminal degrees. *Student/faculty ratio:* 7:1.

Academics *Calendar:* semesters. *Degree:* bachelor's. *Special study options:* advanced placement credit, cooperative education, double majors, independent study, internships, off-campus study, part-time degree program, study abroad, summer session for credit.

Computers on Campus 20 computers/terminals and 16 ports are available on campus for general student use. Students can access the following: campus intranet, computer help desk, free student e-mail accounts, library card catalog. Campuswide network is available. Wireless service is available via entire campus.

Student Life *Housing:* college housing not available. *Options:* Campus housing is provided by a third party. *Activities and organizations:* American Society for Interior Design, Student Government Association, O'More Fashion Merchandising Association, Visual Communications Forum, International Interior Design Association. *Campus security:* 24-hour emergency response devices and patrols, security cards at The Factory campus (off-campus).

Standardized Tests *Required:* SAT or ACT (for admission).

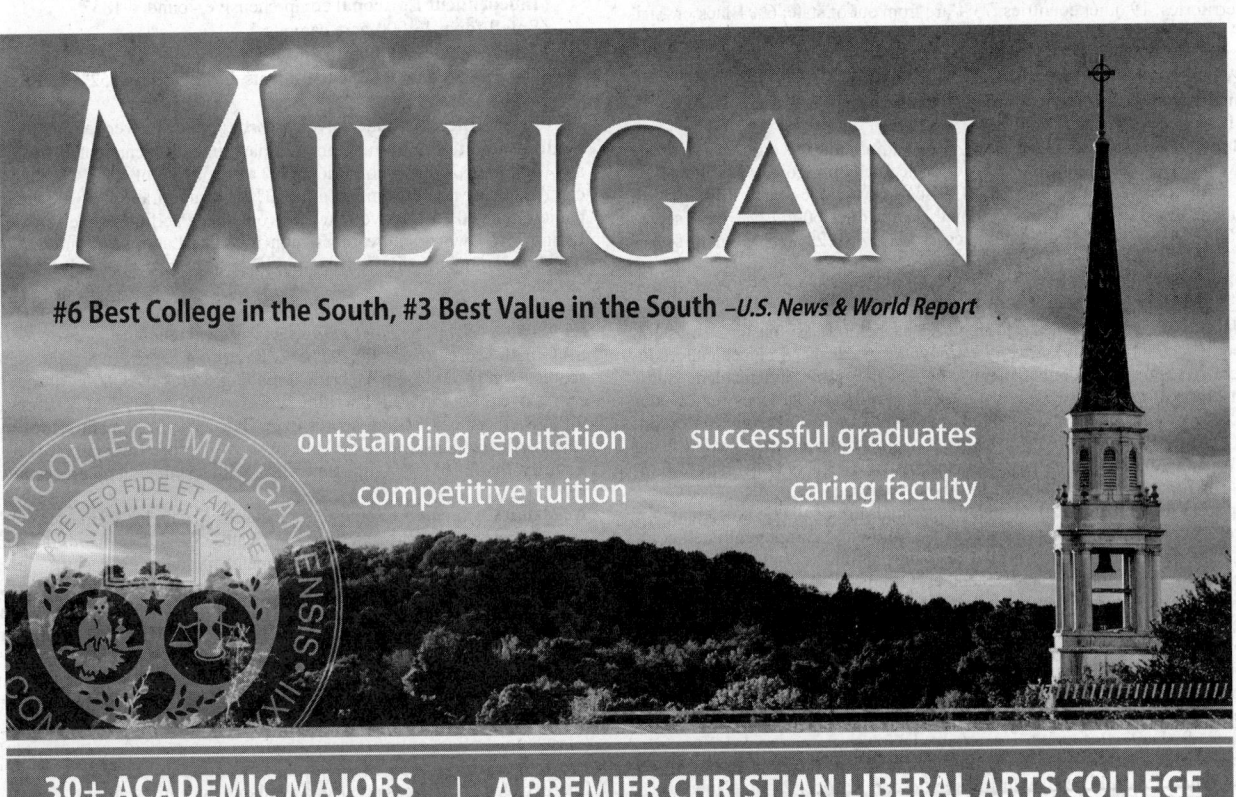

Costs (2013–14) *Tuition:* $25,000 full-time, $1041 per credit hour part-time. Part-time tuition and fees vary according to course load. *Payment plan:* installment. *Waivers:* employees or children of employees.
Applying *Options:* electronic application, deferred entrance. *Application fee:* $50. *Required:* minimum 2.7 GPA. *Required for some:* essay or personal statement, high school transcript, interview, Departmental Requirement for Admissions (Sewing Sample for Fashion Design). *Application deadlines:* 7/31 (freshmen), 7/31 (out-of-state freshmen), 7/31 (transfers). *Notification:* continuous (freshmen), continuous (out-of-state freshmen), continuous (transfers).
Freshman Application Contact Mrs. Tori Bagsby, Assistant Director of Admissions, O'More College of Design, 423 South Margin Street, Franklin, TN 37064-2816. *Phone:* 615-794-4254 Ext. 230. *Toll-free phone:* 888-662-1970. *Fax:* 615-790-1662. *E-mail:* tbagsby@omorecollege.edu. *Website:* http://www.omorecollege.edu/.

Remington College–Memphis Campus

Memphis, Tennessee

Director of Admissions Randal Hayes, Director of Recruitment, Remington College–Memphis Campus, 2710 Nonconnah Boulevard, Memphis, TN 38132. *Phone:* 901-345-1000. *Fax:* 901-396-8310. *E-mail:* randal.hayes@remingtoncollege.edu.
Website: http://www.remingtoncollege.edu/.

Rhodes College

Memphis, Tennessee

- **Independent** comprehensive, founded 1848
- **Urban** 100-acre campus with easy access to Memphis
- **Endowment** $271.5 million
- **Coed** 1,916 undergraduate students, 99% full-time, 59% women, 41% men
- **Very difficult** entrance level, 55% of applicants were admitted

Undergraduates 1,899 full-time, 17 part-time. Students come from 47 states and territories; 19 other countries; 73% are from out of state; 6% Black or African American, non-Hispanic/Latino; 3% Hispanic/Latino; 6% Asian, non-Hispanic/Latino; 0.6% American Indian or Alaska Native, non-Hispanic/Latino; 2% Two or more races, non-Hispanic/Latino; 6% Race/ethnicity unknown; 4% international; 0.8% transferred in; 71% live on campus. *Retention:* 90% of full-time freshmen returned.
Freshmen *Admission:* 4,138 applied, 2,258 admitted, 554 enrolled. *Average high school GPA:* 3.83. *Test scores:* SAT critical reading scores over 500: 96%; SAT math scores over 500: 98%; ACT scores over 18: 100%; SAT critical reading scores over 600: 67%; SAT math scores over 600: 72%; ACT scores over 24: 96%; SAT critical reading scores over 700: 23%; SAT math scores over 700: 19%; ACT scores over 30: 35%.
Faculty *Total:* 207, 83% full-time, 89% with terminal degrees. *Student/faculty ratio:* 10:1.
Academics *Calendar:* semesters. *Degrees:* bachelor's and master's (master's degree in accounting only). *Special study options:* advanced placement credit, cooperative education, double majors, honors programs, independent study, internships, off-campus study, part-time degree program, services for LD students, student-designed majors, study abroad, summer session for credit. *ROTC:* Army (c), Air Force (c). *Unusual degree programs:* 3-2 engineering with Washington University in St. Louis, Christian Brothers University (Memphis), University of Memphis/University of Tennessee.
Computers on Campus 220 computers/terminals are available on campus for general student use. Students can access the following: campus intranet, computer help desk, free student e-mail accounts, online (class) grades, online (class) registration, online (class) schedules. Campuswide network is available. Wireless service is available via entire campus.
Student Life *Housing:* on-campus residence required through sophomore year. *Options:* coed, men-only, women-only. Campus housing is university owned. Freshman campus housing is guaranteed. *Activities and organizations:* drama/theater group, student-run newspaper, radio and television station, choral group, Health Professions Society, Rhodes Outdoors Club, Kinney, RhodeKill (ultimate frisbee), Reformed University Fellowship, national fraternities, national sororities. *Campus security:* 24-hour emergency response devices and patrols, student patrols, late-night transport/escort service, 24-hour monitored security cameras in parking areas, fenced campus with monitored access at night. *Student services:* health clinic, personal/psychological counseling, women's center.

Athletics Member NCAA. All Division III. *Intercollegiate sports:* badminton M(c)/W(c), baseball M, basketball M/W, cheerleading W(c), crew M(c)/W(c), cross-country running M/W, fencing M(c)/W(c), field hockey W, football M, golf M/W, lacrosse M(c)/W(c), rugby M(c), soccer M/W, softball W, swimming and diving M/W, tennis M/W, track and field M/W, ultimate Frisbee M(c)/W(c), volleyball W. *Intramural sports:* basketball M/W, racquetball M/W, soccer M/W, squash M, volleyball M/W.
Standardized Tests *Required:* SAT or ACT (for admission).
Costs (2012–13) *Comprehensive fee:* $47,596 includes full-time tuition ($37,782), mandatory fees ($310), and room and board ($9504). Part-time tuition: $1590 per credit hour. *Room and board:* Room and board charges vary according to board plan and housing facility. *Payment plan:* installment. *Waivers:* employees or children of employees.
Financial Aid Of all full-time matriculated undergraduates who enrolled in 2012, 1,272 applied for aid, 938 were judged to have need, 436 had their need fully met. In 2012, 775 non-need-based awards were made. *Average percent of need met:* 90%. *Average financial aid package:* $34,042. *Average need-based loan:* $6627. *Average need-based gift aid:* $23,536. *Average non-need-based aid:* $16,385. *Average indebtedness upon graduation:* $26,372. *Financial aid deadline:* 3/1.
Applying *Options:* electronic application, early admission, early decision, early action, deferred entrance. *Application fee:* $45. *Required:* essay or personal statement, high school transcript, 2 letters of recommendation. *Recommended:* interview. *Application deadlines:* 1/15 (freshmen), 1/15 (out-of-state freshmen), 1/15 (transfers), 11/15 (early action). *Early decision deadline:* 11/1 (for plan 1), 1/1 (for plan 2). *Notification:* 4/1 (freshmen), 4/1 (out-of-state freshmen), 4/1 (transfers), 12/1 (early decision plan 1), 2/1 (early decision plan 2), 1/15 (early action).
Freshman Application Contact Rhodes College, 2000 North Parkway, Memphis, TN 38112-1690. *Phone:* 901-843-3700. *Toll-free phone:* 800-844-5969.
Website: http://www.rhodes.edu/.

Sewanee: The University of the South

Sewanee, Tennessee

- **Independent Episcopal** comprehensive, founded 1857
- **Small-town** 13,000-acre campus
- **Endowment** $319.0 million
- **Coed** 1,478 undergraduate students, 98% full-time, 52% women, 48% men
- **Very difficult** entrance level, 59% of applicants were admitted

Undergraduates 1,455 full-time, 23 part-time. Students come from 43 states and territories; 23 other countries; 74% are from out of state; 4% Black or African American, non-Hispanic/Latino; 3% Hispanic/Latino; 2% Asian, non-Hispanic/Latino; 0.1% Native Hawaiian or other Pacific Islander, non-Hispanic/Latino; 4% Two or more races, non-Hispanic/Latino; 3% international; 1% transferred in; 96% live on campus. *Retention:* 86% of full-time freshmen returned.
Freshmen *Admission:* 3,369 applied, 1,980 admitted, 453 enrolled. *Average high school GPA:* 3.59. *Test scores:* SAT critical reading scores over 500: 97%; SAT math scores over 500: 97%; SAT writing scores over 500: 95%; ACT scores over 18: 100%; SAT critical reading scores over 600: 70%; SAT math scores over 600: 68%; SAT writing scores over 600: 62%; ACT scores over 24: 97%; SAT critical reading scores over 700: 23%; SAT math scores over 700: 13%; SAT writing scores over 700: 16%; ACT scores over 30: 36%.
Faculty *Total:* 181, 75% full-time, 88% with terminal degrees. *Student/faculty ratio:* 10:1.
Academics *Calendar:* semesters. *Degrees:* bachelor's, master's, doctoral, post-master's, and postbachelor's certificates. *Special study options:* advanced placement credit, double majors, independent study, internships, services for LD students, student-designed majors, study abroad, summer session for credit. *Unusual degree programs:* 3-2 engineering with Washington University in St. Louis, Vanderbilt University, Rensselaer Polytechnic Institute, Columbia University; forestry with Duke University.
Computers on Campus 370 computers/terminals are available on campus for general student use. Students can access the following: campus intranet, computer help desk, free student e-mail accounts, online (class) grades, online (class) registration, online (class) schedules. Campuswide network is available. 100% of college-owned or -operated housing units are wired for high-speed Internet access. Wireless service is available via entire campus.
Student Life *Housing:* on-campus residence required through senior year. *Options:* coed, men-only, women-only, disabled students. Campus housing is university owned. Freshman campus housing is guaranteed. *Activities and*

organizations: drama/theater group, student-run newspaper, radio station, choral group, Sewanee Outing Program, Community Service Council, Student Activities Programming Board, student radio station, BACCHUS (alcohol and drug education), national fraternities, national sororities. *Campus security:* 24-hour emergency response devices and patrols, late-night transport/escort service, controlled dormitory access, security lighting. *Student services:* health clinic, personal/psychological counseling, women's center, legal services.
Athletics Member NCAA. All Division III. *Intercollegiate sports:* baseball M, basketball M/W, cheerleading M(c)/W(c), crew M(c)/W(c), cross-country running M/W, equestrian sports M(c)/W(c), fencing M(c)/W(c), field hockey W, football M, golf M/W, lacrosse M/W, rugby M(c)/W(c), soccer M/W, softball W, swimming and diving M/W, tennis M/W, track and field M/W, volleyball W. *Intramural sports:* badminton M/W, basketball M/W, cross-country running M/W, football M, golf M/W, racquetball M/W, soccer M/W, softball M/W, swimming and diving M/W, table tennis M/W, tennis M/W, track and field M/W, volleyball M/W.
Standardized Tests *Required for some:* TEOFL for International Students. *Recommended:* SAT or ACT (for admission).
Costs (2013–14) *Comprehensive fee:* $45,970 includes full-time tuition ($35,484), mandatory fees ($272), and room and board ($10,214). Full-time tuition and fees vary according to student level. Part-time tuition: $1250 per credit hour. No tuition increase for student's term of enrollment. *College room only:* $5302. Room and board charges vary according to student level. *Payment plans:* installment, deferred payment. *Waivers:* employees or children of employees.
Financial Aid Of all full-time matriculated undergraduates who enrolled in 2012, 898 applied for aid, 852 were judged to have need, 621 had their need fully met. 60 Federal Work-Study jobs (averaging $1609). 26 state and other part-time jobs (averaging $1650). In 2012, 378 non-need-based awards were made. *Average percent of need met:* 94%. *Average financial aid package:* $29,202. *Average need-based loan:* $9525. *Average need-based gift aid:* $20,795. *Average non-need-based aid:* $11,076. *Average indebtedness upon graduation:* $23,721. *Financial aid deadline:* 3/1.
Applying *Options:* electronic application, early admission, early decision, deferred entrance. *Application fee:* $45. *Required:* essay or personal statement, high school transcript, 2 letters of recommendation. *Recommended:* interview. *Application deadlines:* 2/1 (freshmen), 4/1 (transfers). *Early decision deadline:* 11/15 (for plan 1), 1/2 (for plan 2). *Notification:* 3/17 (freshmen), continuous (transfers), 12/17 (early decision plan 1), 2/8 (early decision plan 2).
Freshman Application Contact Ms. Lee Ann Afton, Dean of Admission and Financial Aid, Sewanee: The University of the South, 735 University Avenue, Sewanee, TN 37383-1000. *Phone:* 931-598-1238. *Toll-free phone:* 800-522-2234. *Fax:* 931-598-3248. *E-mail:* admiss@sewanee.edu.
Website: http://www.sewanee.edu/.

South College

Knoxville, Tennessee

Director of Admissions Mr. Walter Hosea, Director of Admissions, South College, 720 North Fifth Avenue, Knoxville, TN 37917. *Phone:* 865-524-3043 Ext. 1825. *E-mail:* whosea@southcollegetn.edu.
Website: http://www.southcollegetn.edu/.

Southern Adventist University

Collegedale, Tennessee

Freshman Application Contact Mr. Marc Grundy, Associate Vice President, Marketing and Enrollment Services, Southern Adventist University, PO Box 370, Collegedale, TN 37315-0370. *Phone:* 423-236-2844. *Toll-free phone:* 800-768-8437. *Fax:* 423-236-1844. *E-mail:* admissions@southern.edu.
Website: http://www.southern.edu/.

Strayer University—Knoxville Campus

Knoxville, Tennessee

Freshman Application Contact Strayer University—Knoxville Campus, 10118 Parkside Drive, Suite 200, Knoxville, TN 37922.
Website: http://www.strayer.edu/campus/knoxville/.

Strayer University—Nashville Campus

Nashville, Tennessee

Freshman Application Contact Strayer University—Nashville Campus, 1809 Dabbs Avenue, Nashville, TN 37210.
Website: http://www.strayer.edu/campus/nashville.

Strayer University—Shelby Campus

Memphis, Tennessee

Freshman Application Contact Strayer University—Shelby Campus, 7275 Appling Farms Parkway, Memphis, TN 38133.
Website: http://www.strayer.edu/campus/shelby.

Strayer University—Thousand Oaks Campus

Memphis, Tennessee

Freshman Application Contact Strayer University—Thousand Oaks Campus, 2620 Thousand Oaks Boulevard, Suite 1100, Memphis, TN 38118.
Website: http://www.strayer.edu/campus/thousand-oaks.

Tennessee State University

Nashville, Tennessee

- **State-supported** comprehensive, founded 1912, part of Tennessee Board of Regents
- **Urban** 450-acre campus
- **Coed** 6,780 undergraduate students, 78% full-time, 63% women, 37% men
- **Minimally difficult** entrance level, 58% of applicants were admitted

Undergraduates 5,277 full-time, 1,503 part-time. Students come from 46 states and territories; 11 other countries; 21% are from out of state; 77% Black or African American, non-Hispanic/Latino; 1% Hispanic/Latino; 1% Asian, non-Hispanic/Latino; 0.1% American Indian or Alaska Native, non-Hispanic/Latino; 0.9% Race/ethnicity unknown; 3% international; 10% transferred in; 39% live on campus. *Retention:* 55% of full-time freshmen returned.
Freshmen *Admission:* 5,307 applied, 3,090 admitted, 1,058 enrolled. *Average high school GPA:* 2.84. *Test scores:* SAT math scores over 500: 22%; SAT math scores over 600: 3%; SAT math scores over 700: 1%.
Faculty *Total:* 603, 72% full-time. *Student/faculty ratio:* 15:1.
Academics *Calendar:* semesters. *Degrees:* associate, bachelor's, master's, post-master's, and postbachelor's certificates. *Special study options:* academic remediation for entering students, accelerated degree program, adult/continuing education programs, cooperative education, external degree program, freshman honors college, honors programs, independent study, internships, off-campus study, part-time degree program, services for LD students, summer session for credit. *ROTC:* Army (c), Navy (c), Air Force (b).
Computers on Campus 1,025 computers/terminals are available on campus for general student use. Students can access the following: campus intranet, computer help desk, free student e-mail accounts, online (class) grades, online (class) registration, online (class) schedules. Campuswide network is available. Wireless service is available via entire campus.
Student Life *Housing options:* coed, men-only, women-only. Campus housing is university owned. Freshman applicants given priority for college housing. *Activities and organizations:* drama/theater group, student-run newspaper, radio and television station, choral group, marching band, Honda Civic Bowl, Jazz Ensemble, Honors Program, national fraternities, national sororities. *Campus security:* 24-hour patrols, controlled dormitory access. *Student services:* health clinic, personal/psychological counseling, women's center.
Athletics Member NCAA. All Division I except football (Division I-AA). *Intercollegiate sports:* basketball M(s)/W(s), cross-country running M(s)/W(s), golf M(s), softball W, tennis M(s)/W(s), track and field M(s)/W(s), vol-

leyball W. *Intramural sports:* baseball M, basketball M/W, cheerleading M/W, football M, softball W, track and field M/W, volleyball M/W.

Standardized Tests *Required:* SAT or ACT (for admission).

Financial Aid Of all full-time matriculated undergraduates who enrolled in 2012, 5,094 applied for aid, 4,787 were judged to have need, 42 had their need fully met. 715 Federal Work-Study jobs (averaging $2033). In 2012, 130 non-need-based awards were made. *Average financial aid package:* $14,393. *Average need-based loan:* $3663. *Average need-based gift aid:* $5564. *Average non-need-based aid:* $7315. *Average indebtedness upon graduation:* $30,477.

Applying *Options:* electronic application. *Application fee:* $25. *Required:* high school transcript. *Required for some:* 3 letters of recommendation. *Application deadlines:* 8/1 (freshmen), 8/1 (transfers). *Notification:* continuous until 8/15 (freshmen), continuous until 8/15 (transfers).

Freshman Application Contact Ms. Vernella Smith, Admissions Coordinator, Tennessee State University, 3500 John A Merritt Boulevard, Nashville, TN 37209-1561. *Phone:* 615-963-5104. *Fax:* 615-963-5108. *E-mail:* vsmith@tnstate.edu.

Website: http://www.tnstate.edu/.

Tennessee Technological University

Cookeville, Tennessee

Freshman Application Contact Ms. Vanessa Palmer, Director of Admissions, Tennessee Technological University, PO Box 5006, Cookeville, TN 38505. *Phone:* 931-372-3888. *Toll-free phone:* 800-255-8881. *Fax:* 931-372-6250. *E-mail:* admissions@tntech.edu.

Website: http://www.tntech.edu/.

Tennessee Temple University

Chattanooga, Tennessee

Director of Admissions Eric Lovett, Director of Recruitment, Tennessee Temple University, 1815 Union Avenue, Chattanooga, TN 37404-3587. *Phone:* 423-493-4371. *Toll-free phone:* 800-553-4050. *E-mail:* eric.lovett@tntemple.edu.

Website: http://www.tntemple.edu/.

Tennessee Wesleyan College

Athens, Tennessee

- **Independent United Methodist** comprehensive, founded 1857
- **Small-town** 40-acre campus with easy access to Knoxville, Chattanooga
- **Coed** 1,106 undergraduate students, 93% full-time, 64% women, 36% men
- **Minimally difficult** entrance level, 76% of applicants were admitted

Undergraduates 1,026 full-time, 80 part-time. Students come from 28 states and territories; 21 other countries; 9% are from out of state; 6% Black or African American, non-Hispanic/Latino; 1% Hispanic/Latino; 1% Asian, non-Hispanic/Latino; 0.2% Native Hawaiian or other Pacific Islander, non-Hispanic/Latino; 0.2% American Indian or Alaska Native, non-Hispanic/Latino; 2% Two or more races, non-Hispanic/Latino; 3% Race/ethnicity unknown; 4% international; 18% transferred in; 30% live on campus. *Retention:* 62% of full-time freshmen returned.

Freshmen *Admission:* 851 applied, 645 admitted, 220 enrolled. *Average high school GPA:* 3.28. *Test scores:* SAT critical reading scores over 500: 41%; SAT math scores over 500: 44%; ACT scores over 18: 85%; SAT critical reading scores over 600: 9%; SAT math scores over 600: 13%; ACT scores over 24: 25%; ACT scores over 30: 2%.

Faculty *Total:* 106, 52% full-time, 49% with terminal degrees. *Student/faculty ratio:* 15:1.

Academics *Calendar:* semesters. *Degrees:* bachelor's and master's (profile includes information for both the main and branch campuses). *Special study options:* academic remediation for entering students, accelerated degree program, adult/continuing education programs, advanced placement credit, double majors, honors programs, independent study, internships, off-campus study, part-time degree program, services for LD students, student-designed majors, study abroad, summer session for credit.

Computers on Campus 150 computers/terminals and 350 ports are available on campus for general student use. Students can access the following: campus intranet, computer help desk, free student e-mail accounts, online (class)

grades, online (class) registration, online (class) schedules. Campuswide network is available. 100% of college-owned or -operated housing units are wired for high-speed Internet access. Wireless service is available via entire campus.

Student Life *Housing:* on-campus residence required through senior year. *Options:* men-only, women-only. Campus housing is university owned. Freshman campus housing is guaranteed. *Activities and organizations:* drama/theater group, student-run newspaper, choral group, national sororities. *Campus security:* 24-hour patrols, late-night transport/escort service, controlled dormitory access, night patrols by trained security personnel.

Athletics Member NAIA. *Intercollegiate sports:* baseball M(s), basketball M(s)/W(s), cheerleading M(s)/W(s), cross-country running M(s)/W(s), golf M(s)/W(s), lacrosse M(s), soccer M(s)/W(s), softball W(s), tennis M(s)/W(s), track and field M(s)/W(s), volleyball W(s).

Standardized Tests *Required:* SAT or ACT (for admission).

Financial Aid Of all full-time matriculated undergraduates who enrolled in 2011, 1,029 applied for aid, 928 were judged to have need, 174 had their need fully met. In 2011, 78 non-need-based awards were made. *Average percent of need met:* 65%. *Average financial aid package:* $15,709. *Average need-based loan:* $3730. *Average need-based gift aid:* $13,454. *Average non-need-based aid:* $9012. *Average indebtedness upon graduation:* $27,011.

Applying *Options:* electronic application, deferred entrance. *Application fee:* $25. *Required:* essay or personal statement, high school transcript, minimum 2.3 GPA, 1 letter of recommendation. *Required for some:* interview.

Freshman Application Contact Stan Harrison, Vice President of Enrollment Services and Director of Athletics, Tennessee Wesleyan College, 204 East College Street, Athens, TN 37303. *Phone:* 423-746-5287. *Toll-free phone:* 800-PICK-TWC. *Fax:* 423-745-9335. *E-mail:* admissions@twcnet.edu. *Website:* http://www.twcnet.edu/.

Trevecca Nazarene University

Nashville, Tennessee

- **Independent Nazarene** comprehensive, founded 1901
- **Urban** 65-acre campus
- **Endowment** $20.1 million
- **Coed** 1,467 undergraduate students, 73% full-time, 55% women, 45% men
- **Moderately difficult** entrance level, 99% of applicants were admitted

Undergraduates 1,071 full-time, 396 part-time. Students come from 38 states and territories; 13 other countries; 34% are from out of state; 8% Black or African American, non-Hispanic/Latino; 2% Hispanic/Latino; 1% Asian, non-Hispanic/Latino; 0.1% Native Hawaiian or other Pacific Islander, non-Hispanic/Latino; 0.8% American Indian or Alaska Native, non-Hispanic/Latino; 2% Two or more races, non-Hispanic/Latino; 12% Race/ethnicity unknown; 2% international; 5% transferred in; 48% live on campus. *Retention:* 74% of full-time freshmen returned.

Freshmen *Admission:* 930 applied, 922 admitted, 239 enrolled. *Average high school GPA:* 3.3. *Test scores:* SAT critical reading scores over 500: 73%; SAT math scores over 500: 59%; ACT scores over 18: 89%; SAT critical reading scores over 600: 21%; SAT math scores over 600: 18%; ACT scores over 24: 42%; SAT critical reading scores over 700: 2%; SAT math scores over 700: 2%; ACT scores over 30: 6%.

Faculty *Total:* 223, 40% full-time, 65% with terminal degrees. *Student/faculty ratio:* 15:1.

Academics *Calendar:* semesters. *Degrees:* associate, bachelor's, master's, and doctoral. *Special study options:* academic remediation for entering students, adult/continuing education programs, advanced placement credit, distance learning, double majors, internships, services for LD students, study abroad, summer session for credit. *ROTC:* Army (c).

Computers on Campus 200 computers/terminals and 1,460 ports are available on campus for general student use. Students can access the following: campus intranet, computer help desk, free student e-mail accounts, online (class) grades, online (class) registration, online (class) schedules, Non-traditional and graduate student registered through Academic Records. Campuswide network is available. 100% of college-owned or -operated housing units are wired for high-speed Internet access. Wireless service is available via entire campus.

Student Life *Housing:* on-campus residence required through senior year. *Options:* men-only, women-only. Campus housing is university owned. *Activities and organizations:* drama/theater group, student-run newspaper, choral group, marching band. *Campus security:* 24-hour patrols, late-night transport/escort service, weather alert warning system (phone, email, siren). *Student services:* health clinic, personal/psychological counseling.

Athletics Member NCAA. All Division II. *Intercollegiate sports:* baseball M(s), basketball M(s)/W(s), golf M(s)/W(s), soccer M(s)/W(s), softball W(s), track and field M(s)/W(s), volleyball W(s). *Intramural sports:* badminton M/

W, basketball M/W, football M/W, golf M/W, racquetball M/W, softball M/W, table tennis M/W, track and field M/W, volleyball M/W.

Standardized Tests *Required:* SAT or ACT (for admission).

Costs (2012–13) *Comprehensive fee:* $28,778 includes full-time tuition ($20,790), mandatory fees ($500), and room and board ($7488). Full-time tuition and fees vary according to course load and program. Part-time tuition: $803 per credit hour. Part-time tuition and fees vary according to course load and program. *College room only:* $3744. Room and board charges vary according to board plan. *Payment plans:* tuition prepayment, installment. *Waivers:* senior citizens and employees or children of employees.

Financial Aid *Financial aid deadline:* 8/1.

Applying *Options:* electronic application, early admission, deferred entrance. *Application fee:* $25. *Required:* high school transcript, minimum 2.5 GPA, An ACT composite score of 18 or above, or SAT Critical Reading + Math score of 860 or above; enrollment fee; medical history and immunization records. *Application deadlines:* 8/1 (freshmen), rolling (transfers). *Notification:* continuous (freshmen), continuous (transfers).

Freshman Application Contact Ms. Melinda Miller, Director of Undergraduate Admissions, Trevecca Nazarene University, 333 Murfreesboro Road, Nashville, TN 37210-2834. *Phone:* 615-248-1320. *Toll-free phone:* 888-210-4TNU. *Fax:* 615-248-7406. *E-mail:* admissions_und@trevecca.edu. *Website:* http://www.trevecca.edu/.

Tusculum College

Greeneville, Tennessee

- **Independent Presbyterian** comprehensive, founded 1794
- **Small-town** 140-acre campus
- **Endowment** $16.8 million
- **Coed**
- **Moderately difficult** entrance level

Faculty *Student/faculty ratio:* 16:1.

Academics *Calendar:* semesters. *Degrees:* bachelor's and master's.

Student Life *Campus security:* 24-hour emergency response devices and patrols, student patrols, late-night transport/escort service, controlled dormitory access, trained security personnel on duty.

Athletics Member NCAA. All Division II.

Standardized Tests *Required:* SAT or ACT (for admission).

Financial Aid *Of all full-time matriculated undergraduates who enrolled in 2010,* 1,837 applied for aid, 1,678 were judged to have need. *Average financial aid package:* $14,025.

Applying *Options:* electronic application, early admission, deferred entrance. *Required:* essay or personal statement, high school transcript, minimum 2.0 GPA. *Required for some:* 3 letters of recommendation. *Recommended:* interview.

Freshman Application Contact Ms. Melissa Ripley, Director of Operations, Tusculum College, PO Box 5047, Greeneville, TN 37743-9997. *Phone:* 423-636-7300 Ext. 5374. *Toll-free phone:* 800-729-0256. *Fax:* 423-798-1622. *E-mail:* admissions@tusculum.edu. *Website:* http://www.tusculum.edu/.

Union University

Jackson, Tennessee

- **Independent Southern Baptist** comprehensive, founded 1823
- **Small-town** 360-acre campus with easy access to Memphis
- **Endowment** $30.2 million
- **Coed** 2,829 undergraduate students, 78% full-time, 59% women, 41% men
- **Moderately difficult** entrance level, 75% of applicants were admitted

Undergraduates 2,212 full-time, 617 part-time. Students come from 44 states and territories; 36 other countries; 32% are from out of state; 14% Black or African American, non-Hispanic/Latino; 2% Hispanic/Latino; 1% Asian, non-Hispanic/Latino; 0.1% Native Hawaiian or other Pacific Islander, non-Hispanic/Latino; 0.2% American Indian or Alaska Native, non-Hispanic/Latino; 0.8% Two or more races, non-Hispanic/Latino; 5% Race/ethnicity unknown; 2% international; 4% transferred in; 63% live on campus. *Retention:* 92% of full-time freshmen returned.

Freshmen *Admission:* 2,051 applied, 1,539 admitted, 457 enrolled. *Average high school GPA:* 3.69. *Test scores:* SAT critical reading scores over 500: 80%; SAT math scores over 500: 81%; ACT scores over 18: 95%; SAT critical reading scores over 600: 46%; SAT math scores over 600: 44%; ACT scores over 24: 62%; SAT critical reading scores over 700: 24%; SAT math scores over 700: 16%; ACT scores over 30: 24%.

Faculty *Total:* 248, 98% full-time, 79% with terminal degrees. *Student/faculty ratio:* 11:1.

Academics *Calendar:* 4-1-4. *Degrees:* certificates, diplomas, associate, bachelor's, master's, doctoral, and post-master's certificates. *Special study options:* academic remediation for entering students, accelerated degree program, adult/continuing education programs, advanced placement credit, cooperative education, distance learning, double majors, English as a second language, honors programs, independent study, internships, off-campus study, part-time degree program, services for LD students, study abroad, summer session for credit. *ROTC:* Army (c).

Computers on Campus 236 computers/terminals are available on campus for general student use. Students can access the following: campus intranet, computer help desk, free student e-mail accounts, online (class) grades, online (class) registration, online (class) schedules. Campuswide network is available. 100% of college-owned or -operated housing units are wired for high-speed Internet access. Wireless service is available via entire campus.

Student Life *Housing:* on-campus residence required through junior year. *Options:* men-only, women-only, disabled students. Campus housing is university owned. Freshman applicants given priority for college housing. *Activities and organizations:* drama/theater group, student-run newspaper, choral group, Campus Ministries, Student Government Association, Student Activities Council, Students in Free Enterprise (SIFE), national fraternities, national sororities. *Campus security:* 24-hour emergency response devices and patrols, student patrols, late-night transport/escort service. *Student services:* health clinic, personal/psychological counseling.

Athletics Member NCAA, NCCAA. All NCAA Division II. *Intercollegiate sports:* baseball M(s), basketball M(s)/W(s), cheerleading W(s), cross-country running M/W(s), golf M(s), soccer M(s)/W(s), softball W(s), track and field M/W, volleyball W(s). *Intramural sports:* basketball M/W, bowling M/W, cross-country running M/W, football M/W, golf M/W, racquetball M/W, soccer W, softball M/W, swimming and diving M/W, table tennis M/W, track and field M/W, ultimate Frisbee M/W, volleyball M/W.

Standardized Tests *Required:* SAT or ACT (for admission). *Recommended:* SAT Subject Tests (for admission).

Costs (2012–13) *Comprehensive fee:* $34,080 includes full-time tuition ($24,940), mandatory fees ($710), and room and board ($8430). Full-time tuition and fees vary according to class time, course load, degree level, location, and program. Part-time tuition: $845 per credit hour. Part-time tuition and fees vary according to class time, course load, degree level, location, and program. *Required fees:* $290 part-time. *Room and board:* Room and board charges vary according to board plan and housing facility. *Payment plans:* installment, deferred payment. *Waivers:* children of alumni and employees or children of employees.

Financial Aid Of all full-time matriculated undergraduates who enrolled in 2011, 1,577 applied for aid, 1,376 were judged to have need, 267 had their need fully met. 108 Federal Work-Study jobs (averaging $1618). 240 state and other part-time jobs (averaging $1851). In 2011, 409 non-need-based awards were made. *Average percent of need met:* 68%. *Average financial aid package:* $20,001. *Average need-based loan:* $4558. *Average need-based gift aid:* $5961. *Average non-need-based aid:* $9971. *Average indebtedness upon graduation:* $23,070.

Applying *Options:* electronic application, early admission, early action, deferred entrance. *Application fee:* $35. *Required:* high school transcript, minimum 2.5 GPA. *Required for some:* 3 letters of recommendation. *Recommended:* essay or personal statement, interview. *Application deadlines:* rolling (freshmen), rolling (transfers), 12/1 (early action). *Notification:* 8/1 (freshmen), continuous until 8/15 (transfers), 12/15 (early action).

Freshman Application Contact Mr. Robbie Graves, Director of Enrollment Services, Union University, 1050 Union University Drive, Jackson, TN 38305-3697. *Phone:* 731-661-5590. *Toll-free phone:* 800-33-UNION. *Fax:* 731-661-5017. *E-mail:* rgraves@uu.edu. *Website:* http://www.uu.edu/.

See previous page for display ad and page 1546 for the College Close-Up.

University of Memphis

Memphis, Tennessee

- **State-supported** university, founded 1912, part of Tennessee Board of Regents
- **Urban** 1160-acre campus
- **Coed** 17,647 undergraduate students, 72% full-time, 61% women, 39% men
- **Moderately difficult** entrance level, 62% of applicants were admitted

Undergraduates 12,728 full-time, 4,919 part-time. 10% are from out of state; 39% Black or African American, non-Hispanic/Latino; 3% Hispanic/Latino; 3% Asian, non-Hispanic/Latino; 0.1% Native Hawaiian or other Pacific Islander, non-Hispanic/Latino; 0.3% American Indian or Alaska Native, non-Hispanic/Latino; 3% Two or more races, non-Hispanic/Latino; 0.9% Race/ethnicity unknown; 0.9% international; 9% transferred in; 14% live on campus. *Retention:* 76% of full-time freshmen returned.

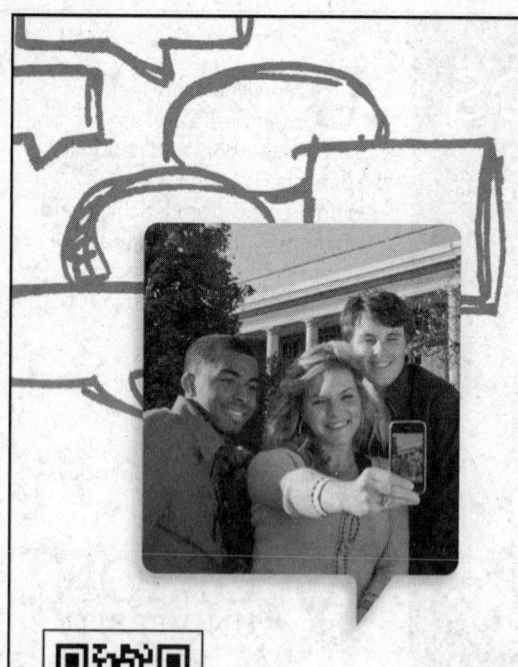

Freshmen *Admission:* 6,798 applied, 4,243 admitted, 2,252 enrolled. *Average high school GPA:* 3.33. *Test scores:* ACT scores over 18: 95%; ACT scores over 24: 40%; ACT scores over 30: 6%.
Faculty *Total:* 1,517, 57% full-time, 60% with terminal degrees. *Student/faculty ratio:* 14:1.
Academics *Calendar:* semesters. *Degrees:* bachelor's, master's, doctoral, post-master's, and postbachelor's certificates. *Special study options:* academic remediation for entering students, accelerated degree program, adult/continuing education programs, advanced placement credit, cooperative education, distance learning, double majors, English as a second language, external degree program, honors programs, independent study, internships, off-campus study, part-time degree program, services for LD students, student-designed majors, study abroad, summer session for credit. *ROTC:* Army (b), Navy (b), Air Force (b).
Computers on Campus 1,600 computers/terminals and 35 ports are available on campus for general student use. Students can access the following: campus intranet, computer help desk, free student e-mail accounts, online (class) grades, online (class) registration, online (class) schedules. Campuswide network is available. Wireless service is available via entire campus.
Student Life *Housing options:* coed, men-only, women-only, cooperative, disabled students. Campus housing is university owned. *Activities and organizations:* drama/theater group, student-run newspaper, radio station, choral group, marching band, Blue Crew, Up 'til Dawn, Black Student Association, national fraternities, national sororities. *Campus security:* 24-hour emergency response devices and patrols, student patrols, late-night transport/escort service, controlled dormitory access. *Student services:* health clinic, personal/psychological counseling, women's center.
Athletics Member NCAA. All Division I except football (Division I-A). *Intercollegiate sports:* baseball M(s), basketball M(s)/W(s), cheerleading M(s)/W(s), cross-country running M(s)/W(s), golf M(s)/W(s), racquetball M(c)/W(c), riflery M(s)/W(s), soccer M(s)/W(s), softball W, swimming and diving M(c)/W(c), tennis M(s)/W(s), track and field M(s)/W(s), volleyball W(s). *Intramural sports:* basketball M/W, bowling M/W, golf M/W, racquetball M/W, soccer M/W, softball M/W, table tennis M/W, tennis M/W, track and field M/W, ultimate Frisbee M/W, volleyball M/W, water polo M/W.
Standardized Tests *Required:* SAT or ACT (for admission).
Costs (2012–13) *Tuition:* state resident $6978 full-time, $277 per credit hour part-time; nonresident $22,428 full-time, $890 per credit hour part-time. Full-time tuition and fees vary according to course load, degree level, program, and reciprocity agreements. Part-time tuition and fees vary according to course load, degree level, and program. *Required fees:* $1256 full-time, $83 per credit hour part-time. *Room and board:* $6860. Room and board charges vary according to board plan and housing facility.
Financial Aid Of all full-time matriculated undergraduates who enrolled in 2012, 11,759 applied for aid, 9,966 were judged to have need, 1,292 had their need fully met. 207 Federal Work-Study jobs (averaging $2348). In 2012, 1290 non-need-based awards were made. *Average percent of need met:* 76%. *Average financial aid package:* $8783. *Average need-based loan:* $3143. *Average need-based gift aid:* $5351. *Average non-need-based aid:* $6109. *Average indebtedness upon graduation:* $22,214.
Applying *Options:* electronic application, early admission. *Application fee:* $25. *Required:* high school transcript. *Required for some:* minimum 2.0 GPA, 2 letters of recommendation, interview. *Application deadlines:* 7/1 (freshmen), 7/1 (transfers). *Notification:* continuous (freshmen), continuous (transfers).
Freshman Application Contact University of Memphis, Memphis, TN 38152. *Phone:* 901-678-2111. *Toll-free phone:* 800-669-2678. *Website:* http://www.memphis.edu/.

See previous page for display ad and page 1580 for the College Close-Up.

University of Phoenix–Chattanooga Campus

Chattanooga, Tennessee
Admissions Office Contact University of Phoenix–Chattanooga Campus, 1208 Pointe Centre Drive, Chattanooga, TN 37421-3707. *Toll-free phone:* 866-766-0766.
Website: http://www.phoenix.edu/.

University of Phoenix–Memphis Campus

Cordova, Tennessee
Admissions Office Contact University of Phoenix–Memphis Campus, 65 Germantown Court, Cordova, TN 38018. *Toll-free phone:* 866-766-0766. *Website:* http://www.phoenix.edu/.

University of Phoenix–Nashville Campus

Nashville, Tennessee
Freshman Application Contact Marc Booker, Sr. Director, Office of Admissions and Evaluation, University of Phoenix–Nashville Campus, 4035 South Riverpoint Parkway, Mail Stop CF-L101, Phoenix, AZ 85040. *Phone:* 602-557-4609. *Toll-free phone:* 866-766-0766. *Fax:* 480-643-1156. *Website:* http://www.phoenix.edu/.

The University of Tennessee

Knoxville, Tennessee
- **State-supported** university, founded 1794, part of University of Tennessee System
- **Urban** 560-acre campus
- **Endowment** $532.5 million
- **Coed** 20,916 undergraduate students, 94% full-time, 49% women, 51% men
- **Moderately difficult** entrance level, 67% of applicants were admitted

Undergraduates 19,588 full-time, 1,328 part-time. Students come from 48 states and territories; 103 other countries; 8% are from out of state; 7% Black or African American, non-Hispanic/Latino; 3% Hispanic/Latino; 3% Asian, non-Hispanic/Latino; 0.1% Native Hawaiian or other Pacific Islander, non-Hispanic/Latino; 0.3% American Indian or Alaska Native, non-Hispanic/Latino; 3% Two or more races, non-Hispanic/Latino; 2% Race/ethnicity unknown; 1% international; 6% transferred in; 37% live on campus. *Retention:* 85% of full-time freshmen returned.
Freshmen *Admission:* 14,398 applied, 9,693 admitted, 4,207 enrolled. *Average high school GPA:* 3.89. *Test scores:* SAT critical reading scores over 500: 88%; SAT math scores over 500: 87%; ACT scores over 18: 99%; SAT critical reading scores over 600: 42%; SAT math scores over 600: 48%; ACT scores over 24: 82%; SAT critical reading scores over 700: 10%; SAT math scores over 700: 10%; ACT scores over 30: 22%.
Faculty *Total:* 2,008, 84% full-time. *Student/faculty ratio:* 17:1.
Academics *Calendar:* semesters. *Degrees:* bachelor's, master's, doctoral, and postbachelor's certificates. *Special study options:* accelerated degree program, advanced placement credit, cooperative education, distance learning, double majors, English as a second language, external degree program, freshman honors college, honors programs, independent study, internships, off-campus study, part-time degree program, services for LD students, student-designed majors, study abroad, summer session for credit. *ROTC:* Army (b), Air Force (b).
Computers on Campus 1,000 computers/terminals are available on campus for general student use. Students can access the following: campus intranet, computer help desk, free student e-mail accounts, online (class) grades, online (class) registration, online (class) schedules, Blackboard Course Management System. Campuswide network is available. 100% of college-owned or -operated housing units are wired for high-speed Internet access. Wireless service is available via entire campus.
Student Life *Housing:* on-campus residence required for freshman year. *Options:* coed, men-only, women-only, disabled students. Campus housing is university owned. Freshman campus housing is guaranteed. *Activities and organizations:* drama/theater group, student-run newspaper, radio and television station, choral group, marching band, Fraternities/Sororities, Religious organizations, Central Program Council, Black Cultural Programming Committee, Student Government Association, national fraternities, national sororities. *Campus security:* 24-hour emergency response devices and patrols, late-night transport/escort service, controlled dormitory access, security cameras on all building entrances; card entry into the living sections of residence hall buildings. *Student services:* health clinic, personal/psychological counseling, women's center.

Athletics Member NCAA. All Division I. *Intercollegiate sports:* baseball M(s), basketball M(s)/W(s), crew W(s), cross-country running M/W, football M(s), golf M(s)/W(s), soccer W(s), softball W(s), swimming and diving M(s)/W(s), tennis M(s)/W(s), track and field M(s)/W(s), volleyball W(s). *Intramural sports:* badminton M/W, basketball M/W, bowling M/W, crew W, field hockey M/W, football M/W, racquetball M/W, soccer M/W, softball M/W, table tennis M/W, tennis M/W, ultimate Frisbee M/W, volleyball M/W, water polo M/W, weight lifting M/W.

Standardized Tests *Required:* SAT or ACT (for admission).

Costs (2012–13) *Tuition:* state resident $7802 full-time, $326 per hour part-time; nonresident $25,992 full-time, $1085 per hour part-time. Full-time tuition and fees vary according to course level, program, and reciprocity agreements. Part-time tuition and fees vary according to course level, program, and reciprocity agreements. *Required fees:* $1290 full-time, $62 per hour part-time. *Room and board:* $8752. Room and board charges vary according to board plan and housing facility. *Payment plan:* installment. *Waivers:* senior citizens and employees or children of employees.

Financial Aid Of all full-time matriculated undergraduates who enrolled in 2012, 17,489 applied for aid, 11,487 were judged to have need, 2,448 had their need fully met. 414 Federal Work-Study jobs (averaging $2568). In 2012, 2447 non-need-based awards were made. *Average percent of need met:* 62%. *Average financial aid package:* $11,410. *Average need-based loan:* $6187. *Average need-based gift aid:* $8182. *Average non-need-based aid:* $2200. *Average indebtedness upon graduation:* $22,860.

Applying *Options:* electronic application. *Application fee:* $40. *Required:* essay or personal statement, high school transcript, minimum 2.0 GPA, specific high school units. *Recommended:* 1 letter of recommendation. *Application deadlines:* 12/1 (freshmen), 6/1 (transfers). *Notification:* 3/31 (freshmen), continuous (transfers).

Freshman Application Contact Ms. Norma Harrington, Senior Associate Director, The University of Tennessee, 320 Student Services Building, Knoxville, TN 37996-0230. *Phone:* 865-974-2184. *Fax:* 865-974-4689. *E-mail:* admissions@utk.edu. *Website:* http://www.utk.edu/.

The University of Tennessee at Chattanooga
Chattanooga, Tennessee

- **State-supported** comprehensive, founded 1886, part of University of Tennessee System
- **Urban** 120-acre campus with easy access to Atlanta
- **Coed** 10,159 undergraduate students, 88% full-time, 55% women, 45% men
- **Moderately difficult** entrance level, 76% of applicants were admitted

Undergraduates 8,904 full-time, 1,255 part-time. 6% are from out of state; 12% Black or African American, non-Hispanic/Latino; 3% Hispanic/Latino; 2% Asian, non-Hispanic/Latino; 0.3% American Indian or Alaska Native, non-Hispanic/Latino; 8% Two or more races, non-Hispanic/Latino; 0.6% Race/ethnicity unknown; 0.9% international; 9% transferred in; 31% live on campus. *Retention:* 67% of full-time freshmen returned.

Freshmen *Admission:* 7,677 applied, 5,856 admitted, 2,290 enrolled. *Average high school GPA:* 3.37. *Test scores:* SAT critical reading scores over 500: 56%; SAT math scores over 500: 59%; ACT scores over 18: 99%; SAT critical reading scores over 600: 20%; SAT math scores over 600: 20%; ACT scores over 24: 39%; SAT critical reading scores over 700: 6%; SAT math scores over 700: 2%; ACT scores over 30: 4%.

Faculty *Total:* 751, 58% full-time, 49% with terminal degrees. *Student/faculty ratio:* 18:1.

Academics *Calendar:* semesters. *Degrees:* certificates, bachelor's, master's, doctoral, post-master's, and postbachelor's certificates. *Special study options:* academic remediation for entering students, adult/continuing education programs, advanced placement credit, cooperative education, distance learning, double majors, English as a second language, honors programs, independent study, internships, off-campus study, part-time degree program, services for LD students, study abroad, summer session for credit. *ROTC:* Army (b).

Computers on Campus 965 computers/terminals are available on campus for general student use. Students can access the following: campus intranet, computer help desk, free student e-mail accounts, online (class) grades, online (class) registration, online (class) schedules, pay fees. Campuswide network is available. 100% of college-owned or -operated housing units are wired for high-speed Internet access. Wireless service is available via classrooms, computer labs, dorm rooms, libraries.

Student Life *Housing:* on-campus residence required for freshman year. *Options:* coed. Campus housing is university owned. Freshman applicants

given priority for college housing. *Activities and organizations:* drama/theater group, student-run newspaper, radio station, choral group, marching band, Student Government Association, Black Student Association, Association for Campus Entertainment, International Student Association, Baptist Student Union, national fraternities, national sororities. *Campus security:* 24-hour emergency response devices and patrols, late-night transport/escort service, controlled dormitory access. *Student services:* health clinic, personal/psychological counseling.

Athletics Member NCAA. All Division I except football (Division I-AA). *Intercollegiate sports:* basketball M(s)/W(s), cross-country running M(s)/W(s), golf M(s)/W(s), soccer W(s), softball W(s), tennis M(s)/W(s), track and field M(s)/W(s), volleyball W(s), wrestling M(s). *Intramural sports:* badminton M/W, baseball M(c), basketball M/W, crew M(c)/W(c), cross-country running M/W, fencing M(c)/W(c), golf M/W, racquetball M/W, soccer M/W, swimming and diving M/W, tennis M/W, ultimate Frisbee M(c)/W(c), volleyball W, wrestling M.

Standardized Tests *Required:* SAT or ACT (for admission).

Costs (2012–13) *Tuition:* state resident $5722 full-time, $238 per credit hour part-time; nonresident $20,068 full-time, $836 per credit hour part-time. *Required fees:* $1490 full-time, $190 per credit hour part-time. *Room and board:* $8300. Room and board charges vary according to board plan and housing facility. *Payment plan:* installment. *Waivers:* senior citizens and employees or children of employees.

Financial Aid Of all full-time matriculated undergraduates who enrolled in 2012, 8,869 applied for aid, 5,524 were judged to have need, 1,134 had their need fully met. In 2012, 57 non-need-based awards were made. *Average percent of need met:* 79%. *Average financial aid package:* $7728. *Average need-based loan:* $4367. *Average need-based gift aid:* $7477. *Average non-need-based aid:* $3484. *Average indebtedness upon graduation:* $19,836.

Applying *Options:* electronic application, deferred entrance. *Application fee:* $30. *Required:* high school transcript. *Recommended:* essay or personal statement. *Application deadlines:* 8/1 (freshmen), 8/1 (out-of-state freshmen), 8/1 (transfers). *Notification:* continuous (freshmen), continuous (out-of-state freshmen), continuous (transfers).

Freshman Application Contact Ms. Lee Pierce, Director, Admissions and Recruitment, The University of Tennessee at Chattanooga, 615 McCallie Ave, University Center, Room 101, Dept. 5105, Chattanooga, TN 37403. *Phone:* 423-425-4662. *Toll-free phone:* 800-UTC-MOCS (in-state); 800-UTC.MOCS (out-of-state). *Fax:* 423-425-4157. *E-mail:* lee-pierce@utc.edu. *Website:* http://www.utc.edu/.

The University of Tennessee at Martin
Martin, Tennessee

- **State-supported** comprehensive, founded 1900, part of University of Tennessee System
- **Small-town** 250-acre campus
- **Endowment** $25.7 million
- **Coed** 7,326 undergraduate students, 83% full-time, 59% women, 41% men
- **Moderately difficult** entrance level, 76% of applicants were admitted

Undergraduates 6,082 full-time, 1,244 part-time. Students come from 58 states and territories; 18 other countries; 4% are from out of state; 16% Black or African American, non-Hispanic/Latino; 2% Hispanic/Latino; 0.5% Asian, non-Hispanic/Latino; 0.3% American Indian or Alaska Native, non-Hispanic/Latino; 1% Two or more races, non-Hispanic/Latino; 2% international; 7% transferred in; 32% live on campus. *Retention:* 76% of full-time freshmen returned.

Freshmen *Admission:* 3,730 applied, 2,838 admitted, 1,320 enrolled. *Average high school GPA:* 3.5. *Test scores:* ACT scores over 18: 93%; ACT scores over 24: 33%; ACT scores over 30: 4%.

Faculty *Total:* 563, 52% full-time, 45% with terminal degrees. *Student/faculty ratio:* 18:1.

Academics *Calendar:* semesters. *Degrees:* bachelor's and master's. *Special study options:* accelerated degree program, adult/continuing education programs, advanced placement credit, cooperative education, distance learning, double majors, English as a second language, honors programs, independent study, internships, off-campus study, part-time degree program, services for LD students, student-designed majors, study abroad, summer session for credit. *ROTC:* Army (b). *Unusual degree programs:* veterinary, medicine, dentistry, medicine, and pharmacy.

Computers on Campus 843 computers/terminals are available on campus for general student use. Students can access the following: campus intranet, computer help desk, free student e-mail accounts, online (class) grades, online

(class) registration, online (class) schedules, online fee payments, degree progress, financial aid data, housing applications, transcripts. Campuswide network is available. 100% of college-owned or -operated housing units are wired for high-speed Internet access. Wireless service is available via entire campus.

Student Life *Housing:* on-campus residence required for freshman year. *Options:* men-only, women-only, disabled students. Campus housing is university owned. Freshman applicants given priority for college housing. *Activities and organizations:* drama/theater group, student-run newspaper, radio and television station, choral group, marching band, Student Government Association, Student Activities Council, Sigma Theta Tau, Gamma Beta Phi, Student Tennessee Education Association, national fraternities, national sororities. *Campus security:* 24-hour emergency response devices and patrols, student patrols, controlled dormitory access. *Student services:* health clinic, personal/psychological counseling, women's center.

Athletics Member NCAA. All Division I except football (Division I-AA). *Intercollegiate sports:* baseball M(s), basketball M(s)/W(s), cheerleading W(s), cross-country running M(s)/W(s), equestrian sports W(s), golf M(s), riflery M(s)/W(s), soccer W(s), softball W(s), tennis W(s), volleyball W(s). *Intramural sports:* basketball M/W, football M/W, golf M/W, racquetball M/W, soccer M/W, softball M/W, tennis M/W, ultimate Frisbee M/W, volleyball M/W, water polo M/W.

Standardized Tests *Required:* SAT or ACT (for admission).

Costs (2012–13) *Tuition:* state resident $5978 full-time, $249 per credit hour part-time; nonresident $19,134 full-time, $798 per credit hour part-time. Part-time tuition and fees vary according to course load. *Required fees:* $1071 full-time, $46 per credit hour part-time. *Room and board:* $5593; room only: $2720. Room and board charges vary according to board plan and housing facility. *Payment plan:* deferred payment. *Waivers:* senior citizens and employees or children of employees.

Financial Aid Of all full-time matriculated undergraduates who enrolled in 2012, 4,890 applied for aid, 3,605 were judged to have need, 647 had their need fully met. 286 Federal Work-Study jobs (averaging $2500). In 2012, 591 non-need-based awards were made. *Average percent of need met:* 71%. *Average financial aid package:* $12,615. *Average need-based loan:* $4212. *Average need-based gift aid:* $5966. *Average non-need-based aid:* $6323. *Average indebtedness upon graduation:* $12,436.

Applying *Options:* electronic application, early admission, deferred entrance. *Application fee:* $30. *Required:* high school transcript, minimum 2.5 GPA. *Application deadlines:* rolling (freshmen), rolling (transfers). *Notification:* 8/1 (freshmen), continuous until 8/1 (transfers).

Freshman Application Contact Ms. Judy Rayburn, Director of Admissions, The University of Tennessee at Martin, 200 Hall-Moody Administration Building, Martin, TN 38238. *Phone:* 731-881-7032. *Toll-free phone:* 800-829-8861. *Fax:* 731-881-7029. *E-mail:* jrayburn@utm.edu.
Website: http://www.utm.edu/.

Vanderbilt University

Nashville, Tennessee

- **Independent** university, founded 1873
- **Urban** 330-acre campus
- **Endowment** $3.4 billion
- **Coed** 6,796 undergraduate students, 99% full-time, 50% women, 50% men
- **Most difficult** entrance level, 14% of applicants were admitted

Undergraduates 6,731 full-time, 65 part-time. Students come from 52 states and territories; 44 other countries; 87% are from out of state; 8% Black or African American, non-Hispanic/Latino; 8% Hispanic/Latino; 8% Asian, non-Hispanic/Latino; 0.3% American Indian or Alaska Native, non-Hispanic/Latino; 5% Two or more races, non-Hispanic/Latino; 3% Race/ethnicity unknown; 5% international; 3% transferred in; 86% live on campus. *Retention:* 96% of full-time freshmen returned.

Freshmen *Admission:* 28,348 applied, 4,034 admitted, 1,608 enrolled. *Average high school GPA:* 3.75. *Test scores:* SAT critical reading scores over 500: 98%; SAT math scores over 500: 99%; SAT writing scores over 500: 98%; ACT scores over 18: 100%; SAT critical reading scores over 600: 94%; SAT math scores over 600: 94%; SAT writing scores over 600: 93%; ACT scores over 24: 98%; SAT critical reading scores over 700: 73%; SAT math scores over 700: 79%; SAT writing scores over 700: 64%; ACT scores over 30: 88%.

Faculty *Total:* 1,148, 80% full-time. *Student/faculty ratio:* 8:1.

Academics *Calendar:* semesters. *Degrees:* bachelor's, master's, and doctoral. *Special study options:* accelerated degree program, advanced placement credit, cooperative education, double majors, English as a second language, honors programs, independent study, internships, off-campus study, services for LD students, student-designed majors, study abroad, summer session for credit. *ROTC:* Army (b), Navy (b), Air Force (c). *Unusual degree programs:* 3-2 business administration with Joint Five-Year Baccalaureate MBA Program. (one and one-half years of study in the Vanderbilt Owen Graduate School of Management, three and one-half years in Vanderbilt's College of Arts and Science); nursing with BS (human and organizational development or child development)/MSN through a senior-in-absentia program in the School of Nursing.

Computers on Campus Students can access the following: campus intranet, computer help desk, free student e-mail accounts, online (class) grades, online (class) registration, online (class) schedules, productivity and educational software. Campuswide network is available. Wireless service is available via entire campus.

Student Life *Housing:* on-campus residence required for freshman year. *Options:* coed, men-only, women-only, disabled students. Campus housing is university owned. Freshman campus housing is guaranteed. *Activities and organizations:* drama/theater group, student-run newspaper, radio and television station, choral group, marching band, national fraternities, national sororities. *Campus security:* 24-hour emergency response devices and patrols, student patrols, late-night transport/escort service, controlled dormitory access. *Student services:* health clinic, personal/psychological counseling, women's center.

Athletics Member NCAA. All Division I except football (Division I-A). *Intercollegiate sports:* baseball M(s), basketball M(s)/W(s), bowling W(s), cross-country running M(s)/W(s), golf M(s)/W(s), lacrosse W(s), soccer W(s), swimming and diving W(s), tennis M(s)/W(s), track and field W(s). *Intramural sports:* badminton M(c)/W(c), baseball M(c), basketball M(c)/W(c), bowling M(c)/W(c), crew M(c)/W(c), cross-country running M(c)/W(c), equestrian sports M(c)/W(c), fencing M(c)/W(c), field hockey M(c)/W(c), golf M(c)/W(c), ice hockey M(c), lacrosse M(c)/W(c), racquetball M(c)/W(c), rugby M(c), sailing M(c)/W(c), soccer M(c)/W, softball M(c)/W(c), squash M(c)/W(c), swimming and diving M(c)/W(c), tennis M(c)/W(c), track and field M(c)/W(c), ultimate Frisbee M(c)/W(c), volleyball M(c)/W(c), water polo M(c)/W(c), weight lifting M(c)/W(c), wrestling M(c).

Standardized Tests *Required:* SAT or ACT (for admission).

Costs (2012–13) *Comprehensive fee:* $55,936 includes full-time tuition ($41,088), mandatory fees ($1030), and room and board ($13,818). *College room only:* $9028. Room and board charges vary according to board plan. *Payment plans:* tuition prepayment, installment. *Waivers:* employees or children of employees.

Financial Aid Of all full-time matriculated undergraduates who enrolled in 2012, 3,631 applied for aid, 3,231 were judged to have need, 3,227 had their need fully met. 1,388 Federal Work-Study jobs (averaging $2342). In 2012, 653 non-need-based awards were made. *Average percent of need met:* 100%. *Average financial aid package:* $43,794. *Average need-based loan:* $3225. *Average need-based gift aid:* $38,577. *Average non-need-based aid:* $24,788. *Average indebtedness upon graduation:* $17,349.

Applying *Options:* electronic application, early admission, early decision, deferred entrance. *Application fee:* $50. *Required:* essay or personal statement, high school transcript, 3 letters of recommendation, 3 letters of recommendation (two from teachers in core subject areas and one from counselor). *Application deadlines:* 1/3 (freshmen), 3/15 (transfers). *Early decision deadline:* 11/1 (for plan 1), 1/3 (for plan 2). *Notification:* 4/1 (freshmen), 4/1 (transfers), 12/15 (early decision plan 1), 2/15 (early decision plan 2).

Freshman Application Contact Dr. John O. Gaines, Director of Undergraduate Admissions, Vanderbilt University, 2305 West End Avenue, Nashville, TN 37203. *Phone:* 615-936-2811. *Toll-free phone:* 800-288-0432. *Fax:* 615-343-8326. *E-mail:* admissions@vanderbilt.edu.
Website: http://www.vanderbilt.edu/.

See page 1620 for the College Close-Up.

Victory University

Memphis, Tennessee

Freshman Application Contact Ms. Shelley Dunn, Director of Admissions, Victory University, 255 North Highland, Memphis, TN 38111-1375. *Phone:* 901-320-9777. *Toll-free phone:* 800-960-9777. *Fax:* 901-320-9791. *E-mail:* admissions@victory.edu.
Website: http://www.victory.edu/.

Visible Music College

Memphis, Tennessee

Admissions Office Contact Visible Music College, 200 Madison Avenue, Memphis, TN 38103.
Website: http://visible.edu/.

Watkins College of Art, Design, & Film

Nashville, Tennessee

- **Independent** 4-year, founded 1885
- **Urban** 13-acre campus
- **Endowment** $1.8 million
- **Coed** 378 undergraduate students, 69% full-time, 52% women, 48% men
- **Moderately difficult** entrance level, 94% of applicants were admitted

Undergraduates 261 full-time, 117 part-time. Students come from 27 states and territories; 6 other countries; 25% are from out of state; 8% Black or African American, non-Hispanic/Latino; 5% Hispanic/Latino; 1% Asian, non-Hispanic/Latino; 0.5% Native Hawaiian or other Pacific Islander, non-Hispanic/Latino; 0.5% American Indian or Alaska Native, non-Hispanic/Latino; 4% Two or more races, non-Hispanic/Latino; 3% Race/ethnicity unknown; 2% international; 24% live on campus. *Retention:* 60% of full-time freshmen returned.
Freshmen *Admission:* 89 applied, 84 admitted. *Average high school GPA:* 3.01. *Test scores:* SAT critical reading scores over 500: 60%; ACT scores over 18: 89%; SAT critical reading scores over 600: 10%; ACT scores over 24: 38%; ACT scores over 30: 3%.
Faculty *Total:* 57, 35% full-time, 63% with terminal degrees. *Student/faculty ratio:* 10:1.
Academics *Calendar:* semesters. *Degree:* certificates and bachelor's. *Special study options:* advanced placement credit, cooperative education, independent study, internships, part-time degree program, services for LD students, summer session for credit.
Computers on Campus 200 computers/terminals and 175 ports are available on campus for general student use. Students can access the following: campus intranet, computer help desk, free student e-mail accounts, online (class) grades, online (class) registration, online (class) schedules. Campuswide network is available. 100% of college-owned or -operated housing units are wired for high-speed Internet access. Wireless service is available via entire campus.
Student Life *Housing:* on-campus residence required for freshman year. *Options:* men-only, women-only, disabled students. Campus housing is university owned. Freshman applicants given priority for college housing. *Activities and organizations:* Company Q (art society), Film club, sports club, Student Government. *Campus security:* 24-hour emergency response devices and patrols, late-night transport/escort service, controlled dormitory access, monitored 24 hour camera security. *Student services:* health clinic, personal/psychological counseling.
Standardized Tests *Required:* SAT or ACT (for admission).
Costs (2013–14) *Tuition:* $20,250 full-time, $675 per credit part-time. *Required fees:* $1650 full-time, $55 per credit part-time. *Room only:* $6380. *Payment plan:* installment. *Waivers:* employees or children of employees.
Financial Aid Of all full-time matriculated undergraduates who enrolled in 2008, 174 applied for aid, 174 were judged to have need, 30 had their need fully met. 17 Federal Work-Study jobs (averaging $1300). 25 state and other part-time jobs (averaging $2000). In 2008, 30 non-need-based awards were made. *Average percent of need met:* 45%. *Average financial aid package:* $11,150. *Average need-based loan:* $4750. *Average need-based gift aid:* $4000. *Average non-need-based aid:* $4000. *Average indebtedness upon graduation:* $15,000.
Applying *Options:* electronic application, early admission, deferred entrance. *Application fee:* $50. *Required:* essay or personal statement, high school transcript, minimum 2.6 GPA, 1 letter of recommendation. *Required for some:* high school transcript, artistic exercises, optional portfolio. *Recommended:* interview. *Application deadlines:* 7/15 (freshmen), 7/15 (transfers). *Notification:* 8/1 (freshmen), 8/1 (transfers).
Freshman Application Contact Ms. Linda E. Schwab, Director of Admissions, Watkins College of Art, Design, & Film, 2298 Rosa L. Parks Boulevard, Nashville, TN 37228. *Phone:* 615-383-4848 Ext. 7458. *Fax:* 615-383-4849. *E-mail:* admissions@watkins.edu.
Website: http://www.watkins.edu/.

Welch College

Nashville, Tennessee

- **Independent Free Will Baptist** 4-year, founded 1942
- **Urban** 10-acre campus with easy access to Nashville
- **Endowment** $1.3 million
- **Coed**
- **Noncompetitive** entrance level

Faculty *Student/faculty ratio:* 9:1.
Academics *Calendar:* semesters. *Degrees:* associate and bachelor's.
Student Life *Campus security:* 24-hour emergency response devices, student patrols, late-night transport/escort service, controlled dormitory access.
Athletics Member NCCAA.
Standardized Tests *Required:* SAT or ACT (for admission).
Costs (2012–13) *Comprehensive fee:* $21,584 includes full-time tuition ($14,250), mandatory fees ($948), and room and board ($6386). Part-time tuition: $475 per credit. *Room and board:* Room and board charges vary according to board plan. *Payment plans:* installment, deferred payment.
Financial Aid *Of all full-time matriculated undergraduates who enrolled in 2011,* 178 applied for aid, 172 were judged to have need. 7 Federal Work-Study jobs (averaging $1871). 101 state and other part-time jobs (averaging $1960). *Average percent of need met:* 71. *Average financial aid package:* $5331. *Average need-based loan:* $2195. *Average need-based gift aid:* $4214. *Average indebtedness upon graduation:* $19,688.
Applying *Options:* electronic application, early admission, deferred entrance. *Application fee:* $35. *Required:* essay or personal statement, high school transcript, 3 letters of recommendation, medical history.
Freshman Application Contact Mr. Rusty Campbell, Director of Enrollment Services, Welch College, 3606 West End Avenue, Nashville, TN 37205. *Phone:* 615-844-5269. *Toll-free phone:* 800-763-9222. *Fax:* 615-269-6028. *E-mail:* rcampbell@fwbbc.edu.
Website: http://www.fwbbc.edu/.

Williamson Christian College

Franklin, Tennessee

Freshman Application Contact Ms. Mary Newby, Recruiter, Williamson Christian College, 200 Seaboard Lane, Franklin, TN 37067. *Phone:* 615-771-7821. *Fax:* 615-771-7810. *E-mail:* mary@williamsoncc.edu.
Website: http://www.williamsoncc.edu/.

TEXAS

Abilene Christian University

Abilene, Texas

- **Independent** comprehensive, founded 1906, affiliated with Church of Christ
- **Urban** 208-acre campus
- **Endowment** $307.1 million
- **Coed** 3,626 undergraduate students, 94% full-time, 56% women, 44% men
- **Moderately difficult** entrance level, 45% of applicants were admitted

Undergraduates 3,408 full-time, 218 part-time. Students come from 52 states and territories; 43 other countries; 19% are from out of state; 7% Black or African American, non-Hispanic/Latino; 10% Hispanic/Latino; 0.9% Asian, non-Hispanic/Latino; 0.1% Native Hawaiian or other Pacific Islander, non-Hispanic/Latino; 0.3% American Indian or Alaska Native, non-Hispanic/Latino; 3% Two or more races, non-Hispanic/Latino; 5% international; 2% transferred in; 44% live on campus. *Retention:* 75% of full-time freshmen returned.
Freshmen *Admission:* 8,440 applied, 3,840 admitted, 957 enrolled. *Average high school GPA:* 3.58. *Test scores:* SAT critical reading scores over 500: 69%; SAT math scores over 500: 75%; SAT writing scores over 500: 60%; ACT scores over 18: 98%; SAT critical reading scores over 600: 26%; SAT math scores over 600: 29%; SAT writing scores over 600: 20%; ACT scores over 24: 55%; SAT critical reading scores over 700: 6%; SAT math scores over 700: 5%; SAT writing scores over 700: 2%; ACT scores over 30: 12%.
Faculty *Total:* 346, 70% full-time, 67% with terminal degrees. *Student/faculty ratio:* 14:1.
Academics *Calendar:* semesters. *Degrees:* certificates, associate, bachelor's, master's, doctoral, post-master's, and postbachelor's certificates. *Special study options:* adult/continuing education programs, advanced placement credit, distance learning, double majors, English as a second language, honors programs, independent study, internships, off-campus study, part-time degree program, services for LD students, student-designed majors, study abroad, summer session for credit. *Unusual degree programs:* 3-2 engineering with The University of Texas at Arlington.
Computers on Campus 860 computers/terminals and 3,900 ports are available on campus for general student use. Students can access the following:

campus intranet, computer help desk, free student e-mail accounts, online (class) grades, online (class) registration, online (class) schedules. Campuswide network is available. 100% of college-owned or -operated housing units are wired for high-speed Internet access. Wireless service is available via entire campus.

Student Life *Housing:* on-campus residence required through sophomore year. *Options:* men-only, women-only. Campus housing is university owned. Freshman campus housing is guaranteed. *Activities and organizations:* drama/theater group, student-run newspaper, radio and television station, choral group, marching band, Student Association, Graduate Students Association, Spring Break Campaigns, International Students Association, LYNAY. *Campus security:* 24-hour emergency response devices and patrols, student patrols, late-night transport/escort service, controlled dormitory access. *Student services:* health clinic, personal/psychological counseling.

Athletics Member NCAA. All Division II. *Intercollegiate sports:* baseball M(s), basketball M(s)/W(s), cross-country running M(s)/W(s), football M(s), golf M(s), soccer W(s), softball W(s), tennis M(s)/W(s), track and field M(s)/W(s), volleyball W(s). *Intramural sports:* basketball M/W, bowling M/W, football M/W, golf M/W, racquetball M/W, soccer M/W, softball M/W, tennis M/W, volleyball M/W, water polo M/W.

Standardized Tests *Required:* SAT or ACT (for admission).

Costs (2013–14) *Comprehensive fee:* $37,150 includes full-time tuition ($28,350) and room and board ($8800). Full-time tuition and fees vary according to course load. Part-time tuition: $950 per credit. Part-time tuition and fees vary according to course load. *College room only:* $3980. Room and board charges vary according to board plan and housing facility. *Payment plans:* tuition prepayment, installment. *Waivers:* employees or children of employees.

Financial Aid Of all full-time matriculated undergraduates who enrolled in 2011, 3,536 applied for aid, 2,330 were judged to have need, 492 had their need fully met. In 2011, 1127 non-need-based awards were made. *Average percent of need met:* 65%. *Average financial aid package:* $16,468. *Average need-based loan:* $4427. *Average need-based gift aid:* $12,357. *Average non-need-based aid:* $7174. *Average indebtedness upon graduation:* $39,508.

Applying *Options:* electronic application, early admission, early action. *Application fee:* $50. *Required:* high school transcript. *Required for some:* essay or personal statement. *Application deadlines:* 2/15 (freshmen), rolling (transfers). *Notification:* 3/15 (freshmen), continuous until 9/1 (transfers).

Freshman Application Contact Admissions, Abilene Christian University, ACU Box 29000, Abilene, TX 79699-9000. *Phone:* 325-674-2650. *Fax:* 325-674-2130. *E-mail:* info@admissions.acu.edu.

Website: http://www.acu.edu/.

Amberton University

Garland, Texas

- **Independent nondenominational** upper-level, founded 1971
- **Suburban** 5-acre campus with easy access to Dallas-Fort Worth
- **Endowment** $10.0 million
- **Coed**
- **Minimally difficult** entrance level

Faculty *Student/faculty ratio:* 25:1.

Academics *Calendar:* 4 10-week terms. *Degrees:* bachelor's and master's.

Student Life *Campus security:* 24-hour emergency response devices and patrols.

Costs (2012–13) *Tuition:* $5640 full-time.

Applying *Options:* electronic application, deferred entrance.

Application Contact Dr. Don Hebbard, Academic Dean, Amberton University, 1700 Eastgate Drive, Garland, TX 75041-5595. *Phone:* 972-279-6511. *E-mail:* advisor@amberton.edu.

Website: http://www.amberton.edu/.

American InterContinental University Houston

Houston, Texas

Freshman Application Contact American InterContinental University Houston, 9999 Richmond Avenue, Houston, TX 77042. *Phone:* 877-564-6248. *Toll-free phone:* 888-607-9888.

Website: http://www.aiuniv.edu/.

Angelo State University

San Angelo, Texas

- **State-supported** comprehensive, founded 1928, part of Texas Tech University System
- **Urban** 268-acre campus
- **Endowment** $119.1 million
- **Coed** 6,006 undergraduate students, 85% full-time, 54% women, 46% men
- **Moderately difficult** entrance level, 90% of applicants were admitted

Undergraduates 5,076 full-time, 930 part-time. Students come from 37 states and territories; 25 other countries; 3% are from out of state; 0.9% Black or African American, non-Hispanic/Latino; 28% Hispanic/Latino; 1% Asian, non-Hispanic/Latino; 0.1% Native Hawaiian or other Pacific Islander, non-Hispanic/Latino; 0.5% American Indian or Alaska Native, non-Hispanic/Latino; 2% Two or more races, non-Hispanic/Latino; 0.5% Race/ethnicity unknown; 2% international; 7% transferred in; 32% live on campus. *Retention:* 59% of full-time freshmen returned.

Freshmen *Admission:* 2,588 applied, 2,335 admitted, 1,402 enrolled. *Average high school GPA:* 3.47. *Test scores:* SAT critical reading scores over 500: 28%; SAT math scores over 500: 40%; ACT scores over 18: 78%; SAT critical reading scores over 600: 5%; SAT math scores over 600: 9%; ACT scores over 24: 21%; SAT math scores over 700: 1%; ACT scores over 30: 1%.

Faculty *Total:* 356, 77% full-time, 65% with terminal degrees. *Student/faculty ratio:* 20:1.

Academics *Calendar:* semesters. *Degrees:* bachelor's, master's, and doctoral. *Special study options:* academic remediation for entering students, advanced placement credit, distance learning, double majors, English as a second language, honors programs, independent study, internships, part-time degree program, study abroad, summer session for credit. *ROTC:* Air Force (b). *Unusual degree programs:* 3-2 accounting.

Computers on Campus 640 computers/terminals and 3,900 ports are available on campus for general student use. Students can access the following: campus intranet, computer help desk, free student e-mail accounts, online (class) grades, online (class) registration, online (class) schedules, online courses, tuition payments, purchase books, purchase parking permits, university calendar, library card catalog and library resources. Discounted hardware and software programs for personally owned computers. Campuswide network is available. 100% of college-owned or -operated housing units are wired for high-speed Internet access. Wireless service is available via entire campus.

Student Life *Housing:* on-campus residence required through sophomore year. *Options:* coed, disabled students. Campus housing is university owned. *Activities and organizations:* drama/theater group, student-run newspaper, radio and television station, choral group, marching band, Association of Mexican-American Students, Block and Bridle Club, Air force ROTC, University Center Program Council, Baptist Student Union, national fraternities, national sororities. *Campus security:* 24-hour emergency response devices and patrols, student patrols, late-night transport/escort service, controlled dormitory access. *Student services:* health clinic, personal/psychological counseling.

Athletics Member NCAA. All Division II. *Intercollegiate sports:* baseball M(s), basketball M(s)/W(s), cross-country running M(s)/W(s), football M(s), golf W(s), soccer W(s), softball W(s), track and field M(s)/W(s), volleyball W(s). *Intramural sports:* badminton M/W, basketball M/W, bowling M/W, football M/W, golf M/W, racquetball M/W, soccer M/W, softball M/W, swimming and diving M/W, table tennis M/W, tennis M/W, ultimate Frisbee M/W, volleyball M/W, weight lifting M/W.

Standardized Tests *Required:* SAT or ACT (for admission).

Costs (2012–13) *Tuition:* state resident $4994 full-time, $167 per credit hour part-time; nonresident $15,524 full-time, $518 per credit hour part-time. *Required fees:* $2499 full-time, $28 per credit hour part-time, $631 per term part-time. *Room and board:* $8026; room only: $5298. Room and board charges vary according to board plan and housing facility. *Payment plan:* installment. *Waivers:* senior citizens and employees or children of employees.

Financial Aid Of all full-time matriculated undergraduates who enrolled in 2011, 4,375 applied for aid, 3,739 were judged to have need, 438 had their need fully met. In 2011, 674 non-need-based awards were made. *Average percent of need met:* 69%. *Average financial aid package:* $9695. *Average need-based loan:* $4044. *Average need-based gift aid:* $3045. *Average non-need-based aid:* $3224. *Average indebtedness upon graduation:* $21,373.

Applying *Options:* electronic application, early admission, deferred entrance. *Application fee:* $35. *Required:* high school transcript, high school class rank. *Application deadlines:* rolling (freshmen), rolling (out-of-state freshmen), rolling (transfers). *Notification:* continuous (freshmen), continuous (out-of-state freshmen), continuous (transfers).

Freshman Application Contact Mr. Michael Loehring, Executive Director of Enrollment Management, Angelo State University, 2601 West Avenue N, San

Angelo, TX 76909. *Phone:* 325-942-2185. *Toll-free phone:* 800-946-8627. *Fax:* 325-942-2078. *E-mail:* admissions@angelo.edu. *Website:* http://www.angelo.edu/.

Argosy University, Dallas

Farmers Branch, Texas

Freshman Application Contact Argosy University, Dallas, 5001 Lyndon B. Johnson Freeway, Heritage Square, Farmers Branch, TX 75244. *Phone:* 214-890-9900. *Toll-free phone:* 866-954-9900. *Website:* http://www.argosy.edu/dallas/.

Arlington Baptist College

Arlington, Texas

- **Independent Baptist** comprehensive, founded 1939
- **Urban** 32-acre campus with easy access to Dallas-Fort Worth
- **Endowment** $17,000
- **Coed**
- **Noncompetitive** entrance level

Faculty *Student/faculty ratio:* 16:1.

Academics *Calendar:* semesters. *Degrees:* certificates, diplomas, bachelor's, and master's.

Student Life *Campus security:* controlled dormitory access, night security guards.

Athletics Member NCCAA.

Costs (2012–13) *Comprehensive fee:* $12,640 includes full-time tuition ($7100), mandatory fees ($740), and room and board ($4800). Full-time tuition and fees vary according to course load. Part-time tuition: $220 per credit hour. Part-time tuition and fees vary according to course load. *Required fees:* $740 per term part-time.

Financial Aid *Of all full-time matriculated undergraduates who enrolled in 2006,* 164 applied for aid, 118 were judged to have need, 93 had their need fully met. *Average financial aid package:* $6847. *Average indebtedness upon graduation:* $4838.

Applying *Options:* electronic application, early admission, deferred entrance. *Application fee:* $15. *Required:* essay or personal statement, high school transcript, 1 letter of recommendation, pastoral recommendation, medical examination. *Required for some:* interview.

Freshman Application Contact Ms. Janie Taylor, Registrar/Admissions, Arlington Baptist College, 3001 West Division, Arlington, TX 76012-3425. *Phone:* 817-461-8741 Ext. 105. *Fax:* 817-274-1138. *E-mail:* jtaylor@arlingtonbaptistcollege.edu. *Website:* http://www.arlingtonbaptistcollege.edu/.

The Art Institute of Austin

Austin, Texas

- **Proprietary** 4-year, part of Education Management Corporation
- **Coed**

Academics *Degrees:* associate and bachelor's.

Freshman Application Contact The Art Institute of Austin, 101 W. Louis Henna Boulevard, Suite 100, Austin, TX 78728. *Phone:* 512-691-1707. *Toll-free phone:* 866-583-7952. *Website:* http://www.artinstitutes.edu/austin.

See full-page ad on page 54 and page 1054 for the College Close-Up.

The Art Institute of Dallas

Dallas, Texas

- **Proprietary** comprehensive, founded 1978, part of Education Management Corporation
- **Urban** 2-acre campus
- **Coed**

Academics *Calendar:* quarters. *Degrees:* certificates, associate, bachelor's, and master's.

Freshman Application Contact The Art Institute of Dallas, 8080 Park Lane, Suite 100, Dallas, TX 75231-5993. *Phone:* 214-692-8080. *Toll-free phone:* 800-275-4243. *Website:* http://www.artinstitutes.edu/dallas/.

See full-page ad on page 54 and page 1078 for the College Close-Up.

The Art Institute of Fort Worth

Fort Worth, Texas

- **Proprietary** 4-year
- **Coed**

Academics *Degrees:* certificates, associate, and bachelor's.

Freshman Application Contact The Art Institute of Fort Worth, 7000 Calmont Avenue, Suite 150, Fort Worth, TX 76116. *Phone:* 817-210-0808. *Toll-free phone:* 888-422-9686. *Website:* http://www.artinstitutes.edu/fort-worth/.

See full-page ad on page 54 and page 1082 for the College Close-Up.

The Art Institute of Houston

Houston, Texas

- **Proprietary** 4-year, founded 1978, part of Education Management Corporation
- **Urban** campus
- **Coed**

Academics *Calendar:* quarters. *Degrees:* diplomas, associate, and bachelor's.

Freshman Application Contact The Art Institute of Houston, 1900 Yorktown Street, Houston, TX 77056. *Phone:* 713-623-2040. *Toll-free phone:* 800-275-4244. *Website:* http://www.artinstitutes.edu/houston/.

See full-page ad on page 54 and page 1084 for the College Close-Up.

The Art Institute of Houston— North

Houston, Texas

- **Proprietary** 4-year
- **Coed**

Academics *Degrees:* diplomas, associate, and bachelor's.

Freshman Application Contact The Art Institute of Houston—North, 10740 North Gessner Drive, Suite 190, Houston, TX 77064. *Phone:* 281-671-3381. *Toll-free phone:* 866-830-4450. *Website:* http://www.artinstitutes.edu/houston-north.

See full-page ad on page 54 and page 1086 for the College Close-Up.

The Art Institute of San Antonio

San Antonio, Texas

- **Proprietary** 4-year
- **Coed**

Academics *Degrees:* diplomas, associate, and bachelor's.

Freshman Application Contact The Art Institute of San Antonio, 1000 IH-10 West, Suite 200, San Antonio, TX 78230. *Phone:* 210-338-7320. *Toll-free phone:* 888-222-0040. *Website:* http://www.artinstitutes.edu/san-antonio/.

See full-page ad on page 54 and page 1114 for the College Close-Up.

Austin College

Sherman, Texas

- **Independent Presbyterian** comprehensive, founded 1849
- **Small-town** 60-acre campus with easy access to Dallas-Fort Worth
- **Endowment** $124.9 million
- **Coed**
- **Very difficult** entrance level

Faculty *Student/faculty ratio:* 12:1.

Academics *Calendar:* 4-1-4. *Degrees:* bachelor's and master's.

Student Life *Campus security:* 24-hour emergency response devices and patrols, late-night transport/escort service, controlled dormitory access.

Athletics Member NCAA. All Division III.

Standardized Tests *Required:* SAT or ACT (for admission).

Costs (2012–13) *One-time required fee:* $25. *Comprehensive fee:* $42,979 includes full-time tuition ($32,665), mandatory fees ($160), and room and board ($10,154). Full-time tuition and fees vary according to student level. *Room and board:* Room and board charges vary according to board plan.

Financial Aid *Of all full-time matriculated undergraduates who enrolled in 2011,* 1,283 applied for aid, 897 were judged to have need, 897 had their need fully met. *In 2011,* 371 non-need-based awards were made. *Average percent of need met:* 100. *Average financial aid package:* $32,280. *Average need-based loan:* $5126. *Average need-based gift aid:* $20,365. *Average non-need-based aid:* $15,057.

Applying *Options:* electronic application, early admission, deferred entrance. *Required:* essay or personal statement, high school transcript, 2 letters of recommendation. *Required for some:* interview. *Recommended:* minimum 3.0 GPA, interview.

Freshman Application Contact Ms. Nan Davis, Vice President for Institutional Enrollment, Austin College, 900 North Grand Avenue, Suite 6N, Sherman, TX 75090-4400. *Phone:* 903-813-3000. *Toll-free phone:* 800-596-4276 (in-state); 800-526.4276 (out-of-state). *Fax:* 903-813-3198. *E-mail:* admission@austincollege.edu.

Website: http://www.austincollege.edu/.

Austin Graduate School of Theology

Austin, Texas

Application Contact Mrs. Celeste Scarbrough, Director of Admissions, Austin Graduate School of Theology, 7640 Guadalupe Street, Austin, TX 78752. *Phone:* 512-476-2772. *Toll-free phone:* 866-AUS-GRAD. *Fax:* 512-476-3919. *E-mail:* registrar@austingrad.edu.

Website: http://www.austingrad.edu/.

Baptist Missionary Association Theological Seminary

Jacksonville, Texas

- **Independent Baptist** comprehensive, founded 1955
- **Small-town** 17-acre campus
- **Endowment** $1.2 million
- **Coed, primarily men** 56 undergraduate students, 41% full-time, 16% women, 84% men
- **Noncompetitive** entrance level

Undergraduates 23 full-time, 33 part-time. 29% live on campus.

Freshmen *Admission:* 9 applied.

Faculty *Total:* 11, 45% full-time, 82% with terminal degrees.

Academics *Calendar:* semesters. *Degrees:* associate, bachelor's, and master's. *Special study options:* adult/continuing education programs, distance learning, independent study, internships, part-time degree program, summer session for credit.

Computers on Campus 3 computers/terminals are available on campus for general student use. Students can access the following: free student e-mail accounts, online (class) schedules. Campuswide network is available. Wireless service is available via classrooms, computer centers, libraries, student centers.

Student Life *Housing options:* men-only, women-only. Campus housing is university owned. *Student services:* personal/psychological counseling.

Costs (2013–14) *Tuition:* $140 per hour part-time. Full-time tuition and fees vary according to course load and location. Part-time tuition and fees vary according to course load and location. *Required fees:* $75 per term part-time. *Room only:* Room and board charges vary according to housing facility. *Payment plan:* installment.

Financial Aid Of all full-time matriculated undergraduates who enrolled in 2001, 2 applied for aid, 2 were judged to have need. *Average percent of need met:* 50%. *Average financial aid package:* $1098.

Applying *Application fee:* $35. *Required:* 3 letters of recommendation, interview, Church approval statement. *Application deadlines:* 7/25 (freshmen), 8/1 (transfers). *Notification:* continuous (freshmen).

Freshman Application Contact Baptist Missionary Association Theological Seminary, 1530 East Pine Street, Jacksonville, TX 75766-5407. *Phone:* 903-586-2501 Ext. 229. *Toll-free phone:* 800-259-5673.

Website: http://www.bmats.edu/.

Baptist University of the Americas

San Antonio, Texas

- **Independent Baptist** 4-year, founded 1947
- **Urban** 90-acre campus with easy access to San Antonio
- **Endowment** $1.9 million
- **Coed** 175 undergraduate students, 14% full-time, 8% women, 7% men
- **Noncompetitive** entrance level, 53% of applicants were admitted

Undergraduates 25 full-time, 2 part-time. Students come from 12 states and territories; 16 other countries; 5% are from out of state; 6% Black or African American, non-Hispanic/Latino; 6% Hispanic/Latino; 1% American Indian or Alaska Native, non-Hispanic/Latino; 87% international; 96% transferred in. *Retention:* 31% of full-time freshmen returned.

Freshmen *Admission:* 66 applied, 35 admitted, 27 enrolled.

Faculty *Total:* 7, 100% full-time, 71% with terminal degrees. *Student/faculty ratio:* 12:1.

Academics *Calendar:* semesters. *Degrees:* certificates, diplomas, associate, bachelor's, and postbachelor's certificates (associate degree in Cross-Cultural Studies). *Special study options:* academic remediation for entering students, advanced placement credit, double majors, English as a second language, independent study, internships, part-time degree program, services for LD students.

Computers on Campus 22 computers/terminals are available on campus for general student use. Students can access the following: computer help desk, free student e-mail accounts. Campuswide network is available. 100% of college-owned or -operated housing units are wired for high-speed Internet access. Wireless service is available via entire campus.

Student Life *Housing options:* coed, men-only, women-only, disabled students. Campus housing is university owned. *Activities and organizations:* choral group, Communities In Schools, Missions Society, Navigators, Student Council/Embajadores, BSM. *Campus security:* 24-hour emergency response devices, student patrols, late-night transport/escort service, Gate code is required to enter the residence area. *Student services:* personal/psychological counseling.

Athletics *Intramural sports:* basketball M(c), football M(c), soccer M(c).

Standardized Tests *Required for some:* ACCUPLACER, THEA (Texas Higher Education Assessment). *Recommended:* SAT and SAT Subject Tests or ACT (for admission), ACCUPLACER, THEA (Texas Higher Education Assessment).

Costs (2013–14) *Comprehensive fee:* $8660 includes full-time tuition ($4800), mandatory fees ($480), and room and board ($3380). Part-time tuition: $200 per credit. *Required fees:* $20 per hour part-time. *College room only:* $2500. *Payment plan:* installment. *Waivers:* employees or children of employees.

Financial Aid Of all full-time matriculated undergraduates who enrolled in 2011, 3 Federal Work-Study jobs (averaging $4072). 81 state and other part-time jobs (averaging $2675).

Applying *Options:* electronic application. *Application fee:* $25. *Required:* essay or personal statement, high school transcript, 3 letters of recommendation. *Required for some:* interview. *Application deadlines:* 2/15 (freshmen), 2/15 (out-of-state freshmen). *Notification:* continuous (freshmen), continuous (transfers).

Freshman Application Contact Mr. David Natividad, Admissions Counselor, Baptist University of the Americas, 8019 Pan Am Expressway, San Antonio, TX 78224. *Phone:* 210-924-4338 Ext. 211. *Toll-free phone:* 800-721-1396. *Fax:* 210-924-2701. *E-mail:* david.natividad@bua.edu.

Website: http://www.bua.edu/.

Baylor University

Waco, Texas

- **Independent Baptist** university, founded 1845
- **Urban** 1000-acre campus with easy access to Dallas-Fort Worth
- **Endowment** $964.2 million
- **Coed** 12,918 undergraduate students, 98% full-time, 59% women, 41% men
- **Moderately difficult** entrance level, 61% of applicants were admitted

Undergraduates 12,615 full-time, 303 part-time. Students come from 51 states and territories; 73 other countries; 22% are from out of state; 7% Black or African American, non-Hispanic/Latino; 14% Hispanic/Latino; 6% Asian, non-Hispanic/Latino; 0.3% American Indian or Alaska Native, non-Hispanic/Latino; 5% Two or more races, non-Hispanic/Latino; 0.2% Race/ethnicity unknown; 3% international; 3% transferred in; 39% live on campus. *Retention:* 87% of full-time freshmen returned.

Freshmen *Admission:* 27,828 applied, 16,879 admitted, 3,254 enrolled. *Test scores:* SAT critical reading scores over 500: 94%; SAT math scores over 500: 98%; SAT writing scores over 500: 90%; ACT scores over 18: 100%; SAT critical reading scores over 600: 56%; SAT math scores over 600: 66%; SAT writing scores over 600: 46%; ACT scores over 24: 84%; SAT critical reading scores over 700: 15%; SAT math scores over 700: 18%; SAT writing scores over 700: 11%; ACT scores over 30: 23%.

Faculty *Total:* 1,238, 72% full-time. *Student/faculty ratio:* 15:1.

Academics *Calendar:* semesters. *Degrees:* certificates, bachelor's, master's, doctoral, and post-master's certificates. *Special study options:* accelerated degree program, advanced placement credit, double majors, honors programs, internships, part-time degree program, services for LD students, student-designed majors, study abroad, summer session for credit. *ROTC:* Army (b), Air Force (b). *Unusual degree programs:* 3-2 forestry with Duke University; clinical laboratory science.

Computers on Campus Students can access the following: campus intranet, computer help desk, free student e-mail accounts, online (class) grades, online (class) registration, online (class) schedules. Campuswide network is available. 99% of college-owned or -operated housing units are wired for high-speed Internet access. Wireless service is available via entire campus.

Student Life *Housing:* on-campus residence required for freshman year. *Options:* men-only, women-only, disabled students. Campus housing is university owned. Freshman campus housing is guaranteed. *Activities and organizations:* drama/theater group, student-run newspaper, radio and television station, choral group, marching band, The Bear Pit, Alpha Lambda Delta, Delta Epsilon Iota, National Society of Collegiate Scholars, American Medical Student Association, national fraternities, national sororities. *Campus security:* 24-hour emergency response devices and patrols, late-night transport/escort service, controlled dormitory access, bicycle patrols. *Student services:* health clinic, personal/psychological counseling, legal services.

Athletics Member NCAA. All Division I except football (Division I-A). *Intercollegiate sports:* baseball M(s), basketball M(s)/W(s), crew M(c)/W(c), cross-country running M(s)/W(s), equestrian sports W(s), fencing M(c)/W(c), golf M(s)/W(s), gymnastics M(c)/W(c), ice hockey M(c), lacrosse M(c)/W(c), rock climbing M(c)/W(c), rugby M(c), sailing M(c)/W(c), skiing (downhill) M(c)/W(c), soccer M(c)/W(s), softball W(s), tennis M(s)/W(s), track and field M(s)/W(s), ultimate Frisbee M(c), volleyball M(c)/W(s), water polo M(c)/W(c). *Intramural sports:* basketball M/W, cross-country running M/W, football M/W, racquetball M/W, soccer M/W, softball M/W, table tennis M/W, tennis M/W, ultimate Frisbee M/W, volleyball M/W.

Standardized Tests *Required:* SAT or ACT (for admission).

Costs (2013–14) *Comprehensive fee:* $46,885 includes full-time tuition ($32,574), mandatory fees ($3563), and room and board ($10,748). Part-time tuition: $1357 per semester hour. *Required fees:* $142 per semester hour part-time. *College room only:* $5312. Room and board charges vary according to board plan and housing facility. *Payment plan:* installment. *Waivers:* employees or children of employees.

Financial Aid Of all full-time matriculated undergraduates who enrolled in 2012, 8,522 applied for aid, 7,330 were judged to have need, 978 had their need fully met. 5,311 Federal Work-Study jobs (averaging $2837). In 2012, 3987 non-need-based awards were made. *Average percent of need met:* 62%. *Average financial aid package:* $23,851. *Average need-based loan:* $3782. *Average need-based gift aid:* $18,172. *Average non-need-based aid:* $12,130.

Applying *Options:* electronic application, early admission, early action. *Application fee:* $50. *Required:* high school transcript. *Required for some:* essay or personal statement, minimum 2.5 GPA, 2 letters of recommendation. *Recommended:* interview. *Application deadlines:* 2/1 (freshmen), rolling (transfers), 11/1 (early action). *Notification:* 3/15 (freshmen), continuous (transfers), 1/15 (early action).

Freshman Application Contact Ms. Jessica King Gereghty, Director of Admissions, Baylor University, PO Box 97056, Waco, TX 76798. *Phone:* 254-710-3435. *Toll-free phone:* 800-BAYLORU. *Fax:* 254-710-3436. *E-mail:* admissions@baylor.edu.
Website: http://www.baylor.edu/.

Brazosport College

Lake Jackson, Texas

Freshman Application Contact Brazosport College, 500 College Drive, Lake Jackson, TX 77566-3199. *Phone:* 979-230-3020.
Website: http://www.brazosport.edu/.

Brown Mackie College–Dallas/Fort Worth

Bedford, Texas

Admissions Office Contact Brown Mackie College–Dallas/Fort Worth, 2200 North Highway 121, Suite 270, Bedford, TX 76021.
Website: http://www.brownmackie.edu/dallas/.

See next page for display ad and page 1178 for the College Close-Up.

Brown Mackie College–San Antonio

San Antonio, Texas

Director of Admissions Director of Admissions, Brown Mackie College–San Antonio, 4715 Fredericksburg Road, Suite 100, San Antonio, TX 78229. *Phone:* 210-428-2210. *Toll-free phone:* 877-460-1714.
Website: http://www.brownmackie.edu/san-antonio.

See next page for display ad and page 1208 for the College Close-Up.

Career Point College

San Antonio, Texas

Admissions Office Contact Career Point College, 4522 Fredericksburg Road, San Antonio, TX 78201.
Website: http://www.careerpointcollege.edu/.

Chamberlain College of Nursing

Houston, Texas

- **Proprietary** 4-year
- **Coed** 231 undergraduate students, 45% full-time, 90% women, 10% men
- **Moderately difficult** entrance level

Undergraduates 103 full-time, 128 part-time. 4% are from out of state; 35% Black or African American, non-Hispanic/Latino; 11% Hispanic/Latino; 9% Asian, non-Hispanic/Latino; 0.9% Native Hawaiian or other Pacific Islander, non-Hispanic/Latino; 24% Race/ethnicity unknown; 0.4% international; 42% transferred in.

Freshmen *Admission:* 2 enrolled.

Faculty *Total:* 6, 50% full-time. *Student/faculty ratio:* 22:1.

Academics *Degree:* bachelor's.

Student Life *Housing:* college housing not available.

Standardized Tests *Required:* SAT or ACT (for admission).

Costs (2013–14) *Tuition:* $16,360 full-time, $665 per credit hour part-time. Full-time tuition and fees vary according to course load. Part-time tuition and fees vary according to course load. *Required fees:* $600 full-time. *Payment plan:* installment. *Waivers:* employees or children of employees.

Applying *Application fee:* $95. *Application deadlines:* rolling (freshmen), rolling (transfers). *Notification:* continuous (freshmen), continuous (transfers).

Freshman Application Contact Director of Recruitment, Chamberlain College of Nursing, 10025 Equity Drive, Houston, TX 77041. *Phone:* 713-277-9800.
Website: http://www.chamberlain.edu/.

College of Biblical Studies–Houston

Houston, Texas

- **Independent nondenominational** 4-year, founded 1979
- **Urban** 12-acre campus with easy access to Houston
- **Endowment** $1.4 million
- **Coed** 643 undergraduate students
- **Noncompetitive** entrance level

Academics *Calendar:* trimesters. *Degrees:* certificates, associate, and bachelor's. *Special study options:* accelerated degree program, adult/continuing education programs, English as a second language, honors programs, independent study, part-time degree program, services for LD students, summer session for credit.

Computers on Campus 25 computers/terminals and 14 ports are available on campus for general student use. Students can access the following: online (class) grades, online (class) registration, online (class) schedules. Wireless service is available via entire campus.

Student Life *Housing:* college housing not available. *Activities and organizations:* Student Ministries. *Campus security:* 24-hour emergency response devices, late-night transport/escort service, hourly patrols by trained security guards and police.

Applying *Options:* electronic application. *Application fee:* $40. *Required:* essay or personal statement, high school transcript.

Freshman Application Contact Admissions, College of Biblical Studies–Houston, 7000 Regency Square Boulevard, Houston, TX 77036. *Phone:* 832-252-3377. *Fax:* 713-532-8150. *E-mail:* admissions@cbshouston.edu. *Website:* http://www.cbshouston.edu/.

The College of Saints John Fisher & Thomas More

Fort Worth, Texas

- **Independent** 4-year, founded 1981, affiliated with Roman Catholic Church
- **Urban** 1-acre campus with easy access to Dallas-Fort Worth
- **Coed** 21 undergraduate students, 100% full-time, 48% women, 52% men
- **Very difficult** entrance level, 100% of applicants were admitted

Undergraduates 21 full-time. Students come from 9 states and territories; 67% are from out of state; 5% Black or African American, non-Hispanic/Latino; 10% Hispanic/Latino; 5% Native Hawaiian or other Pacific Islander, non-Hispanic/Latino; 5% Two or more races, non-Hispanic/Latino; 10% transferred in; 91% live on campus. *Retention:* 91% of full-time freshmen returned.

Freshmen *Admission:* 13 applied, 13 admitted, 13 enrolled. *Average high school GPA:* 3.35. *Test scores:* SAT critical reading scores over 500: 100%; SAT math scores over 500: 100%; SAT writing scores over 500: 100%; ACT scores over 18: 100%; SAT critical reading scores over 600: 75%; SAT math scores over 600: 80%; SAT writing scores over 600: 85%; ACT scores over 24: 92%; SAT critical reading scores over 700: 5%; SAT math scores over 700: 6%; SAT writing scores over 700: 8%; ACT scores over 30: 12%.

Faculty *Total:* 9, 89% full-time, 56% with terminal degrees. *Student/faculty ratio:* 8:1.

Academics *Calendar:* semesters. *Degrees:* associate and bachelor's. *Special study options:* distance learning. *ROTC:* Army (c).

Computers on Campus Students can access the following: free student e-mail accounts, online (class) grades, online (class) registration, online (class) schedules. Campuswide network is available. 100% of college-owned or -operated housing units are wired for high-speed Internet access. Wireless service is available via entire campus.

Student Life *Housing:* on-campus residence required through senior year. *Options:* men-only, women-only. Campus housing is university owned. *Activities and organizations:* student-run radio station, choral group. *Campus security:* 24-hour emergency response devices and patrols, late-night transport/escort service. *Student services:* health clinic, personal/psychological counseling.

Standardized Tests *Required:* SAT or ACT (for admission).

Costs (2013–14) *Comprehensive fee:* $10,000 includes full-time tuition ($8000) and room and board ($2000).

Financial Aid Of all full-time matriculated undergraduates who enrolled in 2012, 20 applied for aid, 20 were judged to have need, 6 had their need fully met. *Average percent of need met:* 88%. *Average financial aid package:* $15,800. *Average need-based gift aid:* $15,800. *Average indebtedness upon graduation:* $5474. *Financial aid deadline:* 6/15.

Applying *Options:* electronic application. *Application fee:* $25. *Required:* essay or personal statement, high school transcript, minimum 2.5 GPA, 2 letters of recommendation, interview, Transcripts of all post-secondary work attempted, ACT / SAT / GRE scores. *Application deadlines:* 6/22 (freshmen), 6/21 (out-of-state freshmen), 6/22 (transfers). *Notification:* 7/31 (freshmen), 7/31 (out-of-state freshmen), 7/31 (transfers).

Freshman Application Contact Mr. Peter Michael Capani, Director of Enrollment Management, The College of Saints John Fisher & Thomas More, 3020 Lubbock Avenue, Fort Worth, TX 76109-2323. *Phone:* 817-928-8459 Ext. 1. *E-mail:* peter.capani@fishermore.edu. *Website:* http://www.fishermore.edu/.

Concordia University Texas
Austin, Texas

- **Independent** comprehensive, founded 1926, affiliated with Lutheran Church–Missouri Synod, part of Concordia University System
- **Urban** 385-acre campus with easy access to Austin
- **Endowment** $12.1 million
- **Coed** 1,591 undergraduate students, 77% full-time, 63% women, 37% men
- **Moderately difficult** entrance level, 95% of applicants were admitted

Undergraduates 1,223 full-time, 368 part-time. Students come from 26 states and territories; 2 other countries; 13% are from out of state; 14% Black or African American, non-Hispanic/Latino; 20% Hispanic/Latino; 2% Asian, non-Hispanic/Latino; 0.8% American Indian or Alaska Native, non-Hispanic/Latino; 74% Race/ethnicity unknown; 0.7% international; 14% transferred in; 7% live on campus. *Retention:* 57% of full-time freshmen returned.

Freshmen *Admission:* 930 applied, 880 admitted, 259 enrolled. *Average high school GPA:* 3.29. *Test scores:* SAT critical reading scores over 500: 48%; SAT math scores over 500: 66%; SAT writing scores over 500: 41%; SAT critical reading scores over 600: 13%; SAT math scores over 600: 23%; SAT writing scores over 600: 11%; SAT critical reading scores over 700: 3%; SAT math scores over 700: 5%; SAT writing scores over 700: 2%.

Faculty *Total:* 278, 24% full-time, 61% with terminal degrees. *Student/faculty ratio:* 10:1.

Academics *Calendar:* semesters. *Degrees:* certificates, associate, bachelor's, master's, and postbachelor's certificates. *Special study options:* academic remediation for entering students, accelerated degree program, adult/continuing education programs, advanced placement credit, double majors, honors programs, independent study, internships, part-time degree program, services for LD students, study abroad, summer session for credit. *ROTC:* Army (c), Air Force (c).

Computers on Campus 25 computers/terminals and 50 ports are available on campus for general student use. Students can access the following: computer help desk, free student e-mail accounts, online (class) grades, online (class) registration, online (class) schedules. Campuswide network is available. 100% of college-owned or -operated housing units are wired for high-speed Internet access. Wireless service is available via entire campus.

Student Life *Housing:* on-campus residence required for freshman year. *Options:* coed. Campus housing is university owned. Freshman campus housing is guaranteed. *Activities and organizations:* drama/theater group, student-run newspaper, radio station, choral group, student government, Business Club (The Executives), Education Club, Student Nursing Association, Student Athlete Advisory Committee. *Campus security:* student patrols, late-night transport/escort service, controlled dormitory access. *Student services:* personal/psychological counseling.

Athletics Member NCAA. All Division III. *Intercollegiate sports:* baseball M, basketball M/W, cross-country running M/W, golf M/W, soccer M/W, softball W, track and field M/W, volleyball W. *Intramural sports:* badminton M/W, basketball M/W, football M/W, golf M/W, racquetball M/W, softball M/W, table tennis M/W, tennis M/W, volleyball M/W.

Standardized Tests *Required:* SAT or ACT (for admission).

Costs (2012–13) *Comprehensive fee:* $32,060 includes full-time tuition ($23,600) and room and board ($8460). Full-time tuition and fees vary according to course load, degree level, and program. Part-time tuition and fees vary according to course load, degree level, and program. *Room and board:* Room and board charges vary according to board plan. *Payment plan:* installment. *Waivers:* employees or children of employees.

Financial Aid Of all full-time matriculated undergraduates who enrolled in 2012, 955 applied for aid, 836 were judged to have need, 123 had their need fully met. 104 Federal Work-Study jobs (averaging $1577). 12 state and other part-time jobs (averaging $2102). In 2012, 206 non-need-based awards were made. *Average percent of need met:* 72%. *Average financial aid package:* $17,946. *Average need-based loan:* $4738. *Average need-based gift aid:* $13,802. *Average non-need-based aid:* $9671. *Average indebtedness upon graduation:* $30,587.

Applying *Options:* electronic application, early admission, deferred entrance. *Application fee:* $25. *Required:* high school transcript, minimum 2.5 GPA. *Required for some:* essay or personal statement, interview. *Application deadlines:* rolling (freshmen), rolling (transfers). *Notification:* continuous (freshmen), continuous (transfers).

Freshman Application Contact Ms. Kristin Coulter, Director of Admissions, Concordia University Texas, 11400 Concordia University Drive, Austin, TX 78726. *Phone:* 800-865-4282. *Toll-free phone:* 800-865-4282. *Fax:* 512-313-3999. *E-mail:* admissions@concordia.edu. *Website:* http://www.concordia.edu/.

The Criswell College
Dallas, Texas

- **Independent** comprehensive, founded 1970, affiliated with Southern Baptist Convention
- **Urban** 1-acre campus
- **Coed**
- **Minimally difficult** entrance level

Academics *Calendar:* semesters. *Degrees:* associate, bachelor's, and master's.

Student Life *Campus security:* 24-hour emergency response devices and patrols, late-night transport/escort service.

Financial Aid *Of all full-time matriculated undergraduates who enrolled in 2008,* 173 applied for aid, 173 were judged to have need. 24 state and other part-time jobs (averaging $2089). *Average financial aid package:* $1165. *Average non-need-based aid:* $1034.

Applying *Application fee:* $35.

Freshman Application Contact The Criswell College, 4010 Gaston Avenue, Dallas, TX 75246-1537. *Phone:* 214-821-5433. *Toll-free phone:* 800-899-0012. *Website:* http://www.criswell.edu/.

Dallas Baptist University
Dallas, Texas

- **Independent** comprehensive, founded 1965, affiliated with Baptist General Convention of Texas
- **Suburban** 293-acre campus with easy access to Dallas-Fort Worth
- **Endowment** $31.6 million
- **Coed** 3,513 undergraduate students, 69% full-time, 57% women, 43% men
- **Moderately difficult** entrance level, 41% of applicants were admitted

Undergraduates 2,437 full-time, 1,076 part-time. Students come from 46 states and territories; 43 other countries; 6% are from out of state; 17% Black or African American, non-Hispanic/Latino; 11% Hispanic/Latino; 2% Asian, non-Hispanic/Latino; 0.1% Native Hawaiian or other Pacific Islander, non-Hispanic/Latino; 1% American Indian or Alaska Native, non-Hispanic/Latino; 6% international; 8% transferred in; 49% live on campus. *Retention:* 71% of full-time freshmen returned.

Freshmen *Admission:* 2,692 applied, 1,111 admitted, 492 enrolled. *Average high school GPA:* 3.5. *Test scores:* SAT critical reading scores over 500: 78%; SAT math scores over 500: 83%; ACT scores over 18: 100%; SAT critical reading scores over 600: 29%; SAT math scores over 600: 30%; ACT scores over 24: 42%; SAT critical reading scores over 700: 4%; SAT math scores over 700: 3%; ACT scores over 30: 5%.

Faculty *Total:* 568, 23% full-time, 46% with terminal degrees. *Student/faculty ratio:* 15:1.

Academics *Calendar:* 4-1-4. *Degrees:* certificates, associate, bachelor's, master's, doctoral, post-master's, and postbachelor's certificates. *Special study options:* academic remediation for entering students, accelerated degree program, adult/continuing education programs, advanced placement credit, distance learning, double majors, English as a second language, honors programs, independent study, internships, off-campus study, part-time degree program, services for LD students, study abroad, summer session for credit. *ROTC:* Army (c), Air Force (c).

Computers on Campus 214 computers/terminals are available on campus for general student use. Students can access the following: computer help desk, free student e-mail accounts, online (class) grades, online (class) registration, online (class) schedules. Campuswide network is available. 100% of college-owned or -operated housing units are wired for high-speed Internet access. Wireless service is available via entire campus.

Student Life *Housing:* on-campus residence required through senior year. *Options:* men-only, women-only, disabled students. Campus housing is university owned and leased by the school. Freshman applicants given priority for college housing. *Activities and organizations:* drama/theater group, choral group, Ministry Fellowship, Baptist Student Ministry, Student Government Association, Student Education Association, International Student Organization. *Campus security:* 24-hour emergency response devices and patrols, late-night transport/escort service, controlled dormitory access. *Student services:* health clinic, personal/psychological counseling.

Athletics Member NCAA, NCCAA. All NCAA Division II except baseball (Division I). *Intercollegiate sports:* baseball M(s), basketball M(s), cheerleading W(c), cross-country running M/W(s), golf M/W(s), ice hockey M(c), soccer M/W(s), swimming and diving M(c)/W(c), tennis M/W(s), track and field M/W(s), volleyball W(s). *Intramural sports:* badminton M/W, basketball M/W, football M/W, golf M/W, softball M/W, table tennis M/W, tennis M/W, ultimate Frisbee M/W, volleyball M/W.

Standardized Tests *Required:* SAT or ACT (for admission).

Costs (2012–13) *Comprehensive fee:* $27,608 includes full-time tuition ($20,910), mandatory fees ($200), and room and board ($6498). Part-time tuition: $697 per credit hour. *Required fees:* $100 per term part-time. *College room only:* $2590. Room and board charges vary according to board plan and housing facility. *Payment plans:* installment, deferred payment. *Waivers:* employees or children of employees.

Financial Aid Of all full-time matriculated undergraduates who enrolled in 2012, 1,999 applied for aid, 1,614 were judged to have need, 679 had their need fully met. 88 Federal Work-Study jobs (averaging $2673). 22 state and other part-time jobs (averaging $1477). In 2012, 402 non-need-based awards were made. *Average percent of need met:* 64%. *Average financial aid package:* $15,939. *Average need-based loan:* $4139. *Average need-based gift aid:* $3698. *Average non-need-based aid:* $7991. *Average indebtedness upon graduation:* $18,943.

Applying *Options:* electronic application, early admission, deferred entrance. *Application fee:* $25. *Required:* essay or personal statement, high school transcript, minimum 2.5 GPA, rank in upper 50% of high school class. *Recommended:* interview. *Application deadlines:* rolling (freshmen), rolling (out-of-state freshmen), rolling (transfers). *Notification:* continuous (freshmen), continuous (out-of-state freshmen), continuous (transfers).

Freshman Application Contact Mr. Jason Williams, Assistant Vice President for Enrollment Services, Dallas Baptist University, 3000 Mountain Creek Parkway, Dallas, TX 75211-9299. *Phone:* 214-333-5360. *Toll-free phone:* 800-460-1328. *Fax:* 214-333-5447. *E-mail:* admiss@dbu.edu.
Website: http://www.dbu.edu/.

Dallas Christian College
Dallas, Texas
- **Independent** 4-year, founded 1950, affiliated with Christian Churches and Churches of Christ
- **Urban** 22-acre campus with easy access to Dallas-Fort Worth
- **Endowment** $169,907
- **Coed**
- **Minimally difficult** entrance level

Faculty *Student/faculty ratio:* 16:1.

Academics *Calendar:* semesters. *Degrees:* associate, bachelor's, and post-bachelor's certificates.

Student Life *Campus security:* controlled dormitory access.

Athletics Member NCCAA.

Standardized Tests *Required:* SAT or ACT (for admission).

Financial Aid *Of all full-time matriculated undergraduates who enrolled in 2005,* 189 applied for aid, 132 were judged to have need. 36 Federal Work-Study jobs (averaging $1404). *In 2005,* 26 non-need-based awards were made. *Average percent of need met:* 43. *Average financial aid package:* $3940. *Average need-based loan:* $3589. *Average need-based gift aid:* $1282. *Average non-need-based aid:* $3664. *Average indebtedness upon graduation:* $15,000.

Applying *Options:* electronic application, deferred entrance. *Application fee:* $25. *Required:* essay or personal statement, high school transcript, minimum 2.0 GPA, 2 letters of recommendation. *Required for some:* interview.

Freshman Application Contact Mr. Brett Vance, Admissions Counselor, Dallas Christian College, 2700 Christian Parkway, Dallas, TX 75234-7299. *Phone:* 972-241-3371 Ext. 134. *Toll-free phone:* 800-688-1029. *Fax:* 972-241-8021. *E-mail:* bvance@dallas.edu.
Website: http://www.dallas.edu/.

DeVry University
Houston, Texas
- **Proprietary** comprehensive
- **Coed** 1,070 undergraduate students, 40% full-time, 51% women, 49% men
- **Minimally difficult** entrance level

Undergraduates 431 full-time, 639 part-time. 8% are from out of state; 33% Black or African American, non-Hispanic/Latino; 29% Hispanic/Latino; 4% Asian, non-Hispanic/Latino; 0.3% Native Hawaiian or other Pacific Islander, non-Hispanic/Latino; 0.6% American Indian or Alaska Native, non-Hispanic/Latino; 0.6% Two or more races, non-Hispanic/Latino; 15% Race/ethnicity unknown; 1% international; 16% transferred in.

Freshmen *Admission:* 79 enrolled.

Faculty *Total:* 165, 15% full-time. *Student/faculty ratio:* 11:1.

Academics *Calendar:* semesters. *Degrees:* associate, bachelor's, master's, and postbachelor's certificates.

Costs (2013–14) *Tuition:* $16,076 full-time, $609 per credit hour part-time. *Required fees:* $80 full-time.

Financial Aid Of all full-time matriculated undergraduates who enrolled in 2007, 306 applied for aid, 299 were judged to have need, 3 had their need fully met. In 2007, 20 non-need-based awards were made. *Average percent of need met:* 39%. *Average financial aid package:* $12,662. *Average need-based loan:* $7855. *Average need-based gift aid:* $5374. *Average non-need-based aid:* $14,939. *Average indebtedness upon graduation:* $30,068.

Applying *Application fee:* $40. *Application deadlines:* rolling (freshmen), rolling (transfers). *Notification:* continuous (freshmen), continuous (transfers).

Freshman Application Contact DeVry University, 11125 Equity Drive, Houston, TX 77041. *Phone:* 713-973-3100. *Toll-free phone:* 866-338-7941.
Website: http://www.devry.edu/.

DeVry University
Irving, Texas
- **Proprietary** comprehensive, founded 1969, part of DeVry University
- **Suburban** campus
- **Coed** 926 undergraduate students, 36% full-time, 35% women, 65% men
- **Minimally difficult** entrance level

Undergraduates 337 full-time, 589 part-time. 13% are from out of state; 27% Black or African American, non-Hispanic/Latino; 22% Hispanic/Latino; 3% Asian, non-Hispanic/Latino; 0.1% Native Hawaiian or other Pacific Islander, non-Hispanic/Latino; 0.6% American Indian or Alaska Native, non-Hispanic/Latino; 0.8% Two or more races, non-Hispanic/Latino; 13% Race/ethnicity unknown; 1% international; 14% transferred in.

Freshmen *Admission:* 64 enrolled.

Faculty *Total:* 102, 37% full-time. *Student/faculty ratio:* 11:1.

Academics *Calendar:* semesters. *Degrees:* associate, bachelor's, master's, and postbachelor's certificates. *Special study options:* adult/continuing education programs, part-time degree program.

Student Life *Housing:* college housing not available.

Costs (2013–14) *Tuition:* $16,076 full-time, $609 per credit hour part-time. *Required fees:* $80 full-time.

Financial Aid Of all full-time matriculated undergraduates who enrolled in 2007, 354 applied for aid, 343 were judged to have need, 9 had their need fully met. In 2007, 33 non-need-based awards were made. *Average percent of need met:* 40%. *Average financial aid package:* $12,581. *Average need-based loan:* $8675. *Average need-based gift aid:* $5995. *Average non-need-based aid:* $17,309. *Average indebtedness upon graduation:* $31,895.

Applying *Application fee:* $40. *Required:* high school transcript, interview. *Application deadlines:* rolling (freshmen), rolling (transfers). *Notification:* continuous (freshmen), continuous (transfers).

Freshman Application Contact DeVry University, 4800 Regent Boulevard, Irving, TX 75063-2439. *Phone:* 972-929-6777. *Toll-free phone:* 866-338-7941.
Website: http://www.devry.edu/.

DeVry University

Richardson, Texas

Admissions Office Contact DeVry University, Richardson Center, 2201 North Central Expressway, Richardson, TX 75080. *Toll-free phone:* 866-338-7941.
Website: http://www.devry.edu/.

East Texas Baptist University

Marshall, Texas

- **Independent Baptist** comprehensive, founded 1912
- **Small-town** 200-acre campus
- **Endowment** $59.4 million
- **Coed** 1,241 undergraduate students, 87% full-time, 53% women, 47% men
- **Moderately difficult** entrance level, 58% of applicants were admitted

Undergraduates 1,085 full-time, 156 part-time. Students come from 20 states and territories; 5 other countries; 9% are from out of state; 19% Black or African American, non-Hispanic/Latino; 11% Hispanic/Latino; 0.5% Asian, non-Hispanic/Latino; 0.1% Native Hawaiian or other Pacific Islander, non-Hispanic/Latino; 0.9% American Indian or Alaska Native, non-Hispanic/Latino; 2% Two or more races, non-Hispanic/Latino; 1% international; 8% transferred in; 84% live on campus. *Retention:* 52% of full-time freshmen returned.
Freshmen *Admission:* 1,462 applied, 851 admitted, 350 enrolled. *Average high school GPA:* 3.33. *Test scores:* SAT critical reading scores over 500: 35%; SAT math scores over 500: 40%; ACT scores over 18: 84%; SAT critical reading scores over 600: 6%; SAT math scores over 600: 10%; ACT scores over 24: 17%; SAT critical reading scores over 700: 2%; SAT math scores over 700: 1%; ACT scores over 30: 1%.
Faculty *Total:* 118, 59% full-time, 59% with terminal degrees. *Student/faculty ratio:* 13:1.
Academics *Calendar:* semesters 4-4-1. *Degrees:* certificates, bachelor's, and master's. *Special study options:* accelerated degree program, adult/continuing education programs, advanced placement credit, distance learning, double majors, honors programs, independent study, internships, off-campus study, part-time degree program, services for LD students, student-designed majors, study abroad, summer session for credit.
Computers on Campus 200 computers/terminals and 720 ports are available on campus for general student use. Students can access the following: campus intranet, computer help desk, free student e-mail accounts, online (class) grades, online (class) registration, online (class) schedules. Campuswide network is available. 100% of college-owned or -operated housing units are wired for high-speed Internet access. Wireless service is available via entire campus.
Student Life *Housing:* on-campus residence required through senior year. *Options:* men-only, women-only. Campus housing is university owned. Freshman campus housing is guaranteed. *Activities and organizations:* drama/theater group, student-run newspaper, radio station, choral group, marching band, Baptist Student Ministry, Fellowship of Christian Athletes, Texas Nursing Students Association, Student Government Association, Spirit Program. *Campus security:* 24-hour emergency response devices and patrols, controlled dormitory access. *Student services:* personal/psychological counseling.
Athletics Member NCAA. All Division III. *Intercollegiate sports:* baseball M, basketball M/W, cross-country running M/W, football M, soccer M/W, softball W, tennis M/W, volleyball W. *Intramural sports:* basketball M/W, football M/W, racquetball M/W, soccer M/W, softball M/W, table tennis M/W, ultimate Frisbee M/W, volleyball M/W.
Standardized Tests *Required:* SAT or ACT (for admission).
Costs (2012–13) *Comprehensive fee:* $27,675 includes full-time tuition ($20,670), mandatory fees ($860), and room and board ($6145). Part-time tuition: $689 per credit hour. *Required fees:* $35 per credit hour part-time. *College room only:* $2540. Room and board charges vary according to board plan and housing facility. *Payment plan:* installment. *Waivers:* employees or children of employees.
Financial Aid Of all full-time matriculated undergraduates who enrolled in 2011, 1,028 applied for aid, 932 were judged to have need, 141 had their need fully met. 133 Federal Work-Study jobs (averaging $962). 302 state and other part-time jobs (averaging $1195). In 2011, 93 non-need-based awards were made. *Average percent of need met:* 40%. *Average financial aid package:* $15,408. *Average need-based loan:* $3958. *Average need-based gift aid:* $5696. *Average non-need-based aid:* $8975. *Average indebtedness upon graduation:* $23,458.
Applying *Options:* electronic application. *Application fee:* $25. *Required:* high school transcript. *Required for some:* interview. *Application deadlines:* 8/

17 (freshmen), 8/17 (out-of-state freshmen), 8/17 (transfers). *Notification:* continuous (freshmen), continuous (out-of-state freshmen), continuous (transfers).
Freshman Application Contact East Texas Baptist University, One Tiger Drive, Marshall, TX 75670-1498. *Phone:* 903-923-2000. *Toll-free phone:* 800-804-ETBU.
Website: http://www.etbu.edu/.

Hallmark College of Technology

San Antonio, Texas

- **Proprietary** primarily 2-year, founded 1969
- **Suburban** 3-acre campus
- **Coed** 356 undergraduate students, 100% full-time, 55% women, 45% men
- **Moderately difficult** entrance level

Undergraduates 356 full-time. Students come from 1 other state; 15% Black or African American, non-Hispanic/Latino; 55% Hispanic/Latino; 0.6% Asian, non-Hispanic/Latino; 0.3% Native Hawaiian or other Pacific Islander, non-Hispanic/Latino; 4% Two or more races, non-Hispanic/Latino; 1% Race/ethnicity unknown.
Freshmen *Admission:* 356 enrolled.
Faculty *Total:* 43, 47% full-time, 7% with terminal degrees. *Student/faculty ratio:* 8:1.
Academics *Calendar:* continuous. *Degrees:* certificates, associate, bachelor's, and master's. *Special study options:* accelerated degree program, advanced placement credit, distance learning, internships.
Computers on Campus 227 computers/terminals and 227 ports are available on campus for general student use. Students can access the following: campus intranet, computer help desk, free student e-mail accounts, online (class) grades, online (class) schedules. Campuswide network is available. Wireless service is available via classrooms, computer centers, computer labs, learning centers, libraries.
Student Life *Housing:* college housing not available. *Activities and organizations:* Alpha Beta Kappa Honor Society. *Campus security:* 24-hour emergency response devices.
Standardized Tests *Required:* Wonderlic aptitude test, SAT/ACT is used for entrance to some degree programs (for admission). *Required for some:* SAT or ACT (for admission).
Applying *Application fee:* $110. *Required:* high school transcript, interview, tour, application requirements differ depending on program of enrollment. *Required for some:* essay or personal statement, letters of recommendation. *Application deadlines:* rolling (freshmen), rolling (transfers). *Notification:* continuous (freshmen), continuous (transfers).
Freshman Application Contact Sal Ross, Vice President of Admissions, Hallmark College of Technology, 10401 IH-10 West, San Antonio, TX 78230. *Phone:* 210-690-9000 Ext. 214. *Fax:* 210-697-8225. *E-mail:* slross@hallmarkcollege.edu.
Website: http://www.hallmarkcollege.edu/.

Hardin-Simmons University

Abilene, Texas

- **Independent Baptist** comprehensive, founded 1891
- **Urban** 220-acre campus
- **Endowment** $120.4 million
- **Coed** 1,853 undergraduate students, 88% full-time, 51% women, 49% men
- **Moderately difficult** entrance level, 54% of applicants were admitted

Undergraduates 1,622 full-time, 231 part-time. Students come from 27 states and territories; 17 other countries; 4% are from out of state; 7% Black or African American, non-Hispanic/Latino; 14% Hispanic/Latino; 1% Asian, non-Hispanic/Latino; 0.1% Native Hawaiian or other Pacific Islander, non-Hispanic/Latino; 0.8% American Indian or Alaska Native, non-Hispanic/Latino; 2% Two or more races, non-Hispanic/Latino; 2% Race/ethnicity unknown; 2% international; 9% transferred in; 44% live on campus. *Retention:* 66% of full-time freshmen returned.
Freshmen *Admission:* 1,823 applied, 978 admitted, 395 enrolled. *Average high school GPA:* 3.61. *Test scores:* SAT critical reading scores over 500: 59%; SAT math scores over 500: 62%; SAT writing scores over 500: 46%; ACT scores over 18: 92%; SAT critical reading scores over 600: 20%; SAT math scores over 600: 25%; SAT writing scores over 600: 13%; ACT scores over 24: 38%; SAT critical reading scores over 700: 3%; SAT math scores over 700: 3%; SAT writing scores over 700: 3%; ACT scores over 30: 6%.

Faculty *Total:* 206, 67% full-time, 72% with terminal degrees. *Student/faculty ratio:* 13:1.

Academics *Calendar:* semesters. *Degrees:* bachelor's, master's, doctoral, post-master's, and postbachelor's certificates. *Special study options:* academic remediation for entering students, accelerated degree program, adult/continuing education programs, advanced placement credit, distance learning, double majors, honors programs, independent study, internships, off-campus study, part-time degree program, services for LD students, study abroad, summer session for credit.

Computers on Campus 258 computers/terminals and 1,100 ports are available on campus for general student use. Students can access the following: campus intranet, computer help desk, free student e-mail accounts, online (class) grades, online (class) registration, online (class) schedules. Campuswide network is available. 100% of college-owned or -operated housing units are wired for high-speed Internet access. Wireless service is available via entire campus.

Student Life *Housing:* on-campus residence required through sophomore year. *Options:* men-only, women-only, disabled students. Campus housing is university owned. Freshman campus housing is guaranteed. *Activities and organizations:* drama/theater group, student-run newspaper, choral group, marching band, Baptist Student Ministry, Alpha Phi Omega, Student Congress, Fellowship of Christian Athletes, Unity Group. *Campus security:* 24-hour emergency response devices and patrols, late-night transport/escort service, controlled dormitory access. *Student services:* health clinic, personal/psychological counseling.

Athletics Member NCAA. All Division III. *Intercollegiate sports:* baseball M, basketball M/W, cheerleading M(c)/W(c), cross-country running M/W, football M, golf M/W, soccer M/W, softball W, tennis M/W, track and field M/W, volleyball W. *Intramural sports:* badminton M/W, basketball M/W, bowling M/W, football M/W, golf M/W, racquetball M/W, rock climbing M(c)/W(c), soccer M/W, softball M/W, table tennis M(c)/W(c), tennis M(c)/W(c), ultimate Frisbee M/W, volleyball M/W.

Standardized Tests *Required:* SAT or ACT (for admission).

Costs (2013–14) *Comprehensive fee:* $30,252 includes full-time tuition ($22,350), mandatory fees ($1110), and room and board ($6792). Full-time tuition and fees vary according to program. Part-time tuition: $745 per credit hour. Part-time tuition and fees vary according to course load and program. No tuition increase for student's term of enrollment. *Required fees:* $200 per term part-time. *College room only:* $3400. Room and board charges vary according to board plan and housing facility. *Payment plan:* installment. *Waivers:* employees or children of employees.

Financial Aid Of all full-time matriculated undergraduates who enrolled in 2012, 1,578 applied for aid, 1,146 were judged to have need, 240 had their need fully met. 165 Federal Work-Study jobs (averaging $2400). 91 state and other part-time jobs (averaging $2400). In 2012, 446 non-need-based awards were made. *Average percent of need met:* 69%. *Average financial aid package:* $20,933. *Average need-based loan:* $4495. *Average need-based gift aid:* $7157. *Average non-need-based aid:* $9039. *Average indebtedness upon graduation:* $40,972.

Applying *Options:* electronic application, deferred entrance. *Application fee:* $50. *Required:* high school transcript, minimum 2.0 GPA. *Required for some:* 3 letters of recommendation. *Application deadlines:* rolling (freshmen), rolling (transfers). *Notification:* continuous (freshmen), continuous (transfers).

Freshman Application Contact Ms. Brynn Reynolds, Visitor Coordinator, Hardin-Simmons University, Box 16050, Abilene, TX 79698-0001. *Phone:* 325-670-5890. *Toll-free phone:* 877-464-7889. *Fax:* 325-671-2115. *E-mail:* breynolds@hsutx.edu.
Website: http://www.hsutx.edu/.

Houston Baptist University

Houston, Texas

- **Independent Baptist** comprehensive, founded 1960
- **Urban** 150-acre campus with easy access to Houston
- **Endowment** $85.5 million
- **Coed**
- **Moderately difficult** entrance level

Faculty *Student/faculty ratio:* 15:1.

Academics *Calendar:* semesters. *Degrees:* bachelor's and master's.

Student Life *Campus security:* 24-hour emergency response devices and patrols, late-night transport/escort service.

Athletics Member NCAA. All Division I.

Standardized Tests *Required:* SAT or ACT (for admission).

Costs (2012–13) *Comprehensive fee:* $33,085 includes full-time tuition ($25,245), mandatory fees ($1550), and room and board ($6290). Part-time tuition: $1000 per credit hour. Part-time tuition and fees vary according to

course load. *Required fees:* $775 per term part-time. *Room and board:* Room and board charges vary according to board plan and housing facility.

Financial Aid Of all full-time matriculated undergraduates who enrolled in 2011, 1,490 applied for aid, 1,421 were judged to have need, 262 had their need fully met. 897 Federal Work-Study jobs. In 2011, 429 non-need-based awards were made. *Average percent of need met:* 71. *Average financial aid package:* $22,745. *Average need-based loan:* $4029. *Average need-based gift aid:* $15,269. *Average non-need-based aid:* $7839. *Financial aid deadline:* 4/15.

Applying *Options:* electronic application, early admission. *Required:* high school transcript. *Required for some:* essay or personal statement, interview.

Freshman Application Contact Mr. Eduardo Borges, Director of Admissions, Houston Baptist University, 7502 Fondren Road, Houston, TX 77074-3298. *Phone:* 281-649-3299. *Toll-free phone:* 800-696-3210. *Fax:* 281-649-3217. *E-mail:* eborges@hbu.edu.
Website: http://www.hbu.edu/.

Howard Payne University

Brownwood, Texas

- **Independent** comprehensive, founded 1889, affiliated with Baptist General Convention of Texas
- **Small-town** 80-acre campus
- **Endowment** $45.5 million
- **Coed** 1,091 undergraduate students, 85% full-time, 50% women, 50% men
- **Moderately difficult** entrance level, 50% of applicants were admitted

Undergraduates 930 full-time, 161 part-time. Students come from 10 states and territories; 2% are from out of state; 8% Black or African American, non-Hispanic/Latino; 17% Hispanic/Latino; 0.4% Asian, non-Hispanic/Latino; 0.2% Native Hawaiian or other Pacific Islander, non-Hispanic/Latino; 0.6% American Indian or Alaska Native, non-Hispanic/Latino; 4% Two or more races, non-Hispanic/Latino; 2% Race/ethnicity unknown; 0.4% international; 5% transferred in; 62% live on campus. *Retention:* 61% of full-time freshmen returned.

Freshmen *Admission:* 1,554 applied, 781 admitted, 299 enrolled. *Average high school GPA:* 3.5. *Test scores:* SAT critical reading scores over 500: 34%; SAT math scores over 500: 49%; ACT scores over 18: 83%; SAT critical reading scores over 600: 12%; SAT math scores over 600: 16%; ACT scores over 24: 26%; SAT critical reading scores over 700: 2%; SAT math scores over 700: 1%; ACT scores over 30: 1%.

Faculty *Total:* 120, 68% full-time, 53% with terminal degrees. *Student/faculty ratio:* 11:1.

Academics *Calendar:* semesters. *Degrees:* certificates, associate, bachelor's, and master's. *Special study options:* academic remediation for entering students, advanced placement credit, distance learning, double majors, honors programs, independent study, internships, off-campus study, part-time degree program, services for LD students, study abroad, summer session for credit.

Computers on Campus 260 computers/terminals and 200 ports are available on campus for general student use. Students can access the following: campus intranet, computer help desk, free student e-mail accounts, online (class) grades, online (class) schedules. Campuswide network is available. 100% of college-owned or -operated housing units are wired for high-speed Internet access. Wireless service is available via entire campus.

Student Life *Housing:* on-campus residence required through sophomore year. *Options:* men-only, women-only. Campus housing is university owned. Freshman campus housing is guaranteed. *Activities and organizations:* drama/theater group, student-run newspaper, choral group, marching band, Baptist Student Ministry, Fellowship of Christian Athletes, Student Government Association, Student Foundation, Student Activities Council, national fraternities, national sororities. *Campus security:* 24-hour emergency response devices and patrols, late-night transport/escort service, controlled dormitory access. *Student services:* health clinic, personal/psychological counseling.

Athletics Member NCAA. All Division III. *Intercollegiate sports:* baseball M, basketball M/W, cheerleading M/W, football M, soccer M/W, softball W, tennis M/W, volleyball W. *Intramural sports:* basketball M/W, football M/W, soccer M/W, softball M/W, table tennis M/W, tennis M/W, ultimate Frisbee M/W, volleyball M/W.

Standardized Tests *Required:* SAT or ACT (for admission). *Required for some:* ACCUPLACER.

Costs (2013–14) *Comprehensive fee:* $30,000 includes full-time tuition ($21,800), mandatory fees ($1400), and room and board ($6800). Full-time tuition and fees vary according to course load, location, and program. Part-time tuition: $700 per credit hour. Part-time tuition and fees vary according to location and program. *Room and board:* Room and board charges vary according to board plan and housing facility. *Payment plan:* installment. *Waivers:* employees or children of employees.

Financial Aid Of all full-time matriculated undergraduates who enrolled in 2011, 884 applied for aid, 798 were judged to have need, 179 had their need fully met. 110 Federal Work-Study jobs (averaging $1412). 5 state and other part-time jobs (averaging $1953). In 2011, 156 non-need-based awards were made. *Average percent of need met:* 79%. *Average financial aid package:* $17,051. *Average need-based loan:* $4175. *Average need-based gift aid:* $11,861. *Average non-need-based aid:* $8047. *Average indebtedness upon graduation:* $24,086.

Applying *Options:* electronic application, early admission. *Required:* high school transcript, minimum 3.0 GPA. *Required for some:* 3 letters of recommendation, interview. *Recommended:* essay or personal statement. *Application deadlines:* rolling (freshmen), rolling (out-of-state freshmen), rolling (transfers). *Notification:* continuous (freshmen), continuous (out-of-state freshmen), continuous (transfers).

Freshman Application Contact Ms. Cheryl Mangrum, Associate Director of Admission, Howard Payne University, 1000 Fisk Street, Brownwood, TX 76801. *Phone:* 325-649-8027. *Toll-free phone:* 800-880-4478. *Fax:* 325-649-8901. *E-mail:* enroll@hputx.edu. *Website:* http://www.hputx.edu/.

Huston-Tillotson University

Austin, Texas

- **Independent interdenominational** 4-year, founded 1875
- **Urban** 23-acre campus
- **Endowment** $8.3 million
- **Coed**
- **Moderately difficult** entrance level

Faculty *Student/faculty ratio:* 14:1.

Academics *Calendar:* semesters. *Degrees:* bachelor's and postbachelor's certificates.

Student Life *Campus security:* 24-hour emergency response devices and patrols, late-night transport/escort service, controlled dormitory access.

Athletics Member NAIA.

Standardized Tests *Required:* SAT or ACT (for admission).

Costs (2012–13) *Comprehensive fee:* $20,000 includes full-time tuition ($11,020), mandatory fees ($2034), and room and board ($6946). Full-time tuition and fees vary according to course load. Part-time tuition: $368 per credit hour. Part-time tuition and fees vary according to course load. *College room only:* $2966. Room and board charges vary according to housing facility. *Payment plans:* installment, deferred payment.

Financial Aid *Of all full-time matriculated undergraduates who enrolled in 2009,* 775 applied for aid, 768 were judged to have need, 158 had their need fully met. *In 2009,* 4 non-need-based awards were made. *Average percent of need met:* 78. *Average financial aid package:* $14,885. *Average need-based loan:* $4875. *Average need-based gift aid:* $9772.

Applying *Options:* electronic application, deferred entrance. *Application fee:* $25. *Required:* high school transcript, minimum 2.3 GPA, university admission application. *Required for some:* essay or personal statement, interview.

Freshman Application Contact Ms. Shakitha Stinson, Director of Admission, Huston-Tillotson University, 900 Chicon Street, Austin, TX 78702. *Phone:* 512-505-3029. *Fax:* 512-505-3192. *E-mail:* slstinson@htu.edu. *Website:* http://www.htu.edu/.

ITT Technical Institute

Arlington, Texas

- **Proprietary** primarily 2-year, founded 1982, part of ITT Educational Services, Inc.
- **Suburban** campus
- **Coed**
- **Minimally difficult** entrance level

Academics *Calendar:* quarters. *Degrees:* associate and bachelor's.

Freshman Application Contact Director of Recruitment, ITT Technical Institute, 551 Ryan Plaza Drive, Arlington, TX 76011. *Phone:* 817-794-5100. *Toll-free phone:* 888-288-4950. *Fax:* 817-275-8446. *Website:* http://www.itt-tech.edu/.

ITT Technical Institute

Austin, Texas

- **Proprietary** primarily 2-year, founded 1985, part of ITT Educational Services, Inc.
- **Urban** campus
- **Coed**
- **Minimally difficult** entrance level

Academics *Calendar:* quarters. *Degrees:* associate and bachelor's.

Financial Aid *Of all full-time matriculated undergraduates who enrolled in 2011,* 1 Federal Work-Study job.

Freshman Application Contact Director of Recruitment, ITT Technical Institute, 6330 Highway 290 East, Austin, TX 78723. *Phone:* 512-467-6800. *Toll-free phone:* 800-431-0677. *Fax:* 512-467-6677. *Website:* http://www.itt-tech.edu/.

ITT Technical Institute

DeSoto, Texas

- **Proprietary** primarily 2-year
- **Coed**
- **Minimally difficult** entrance level

Academics *Degrees:* associate and bachelor's.

Freshman Application Contact Director of Recruitment, ITT Technical Institute, 921 West Belt Line Road, Suite 181, DeSoto, TX 75115. *Phone:* 972-274-8600. *Toll-free phone:* 877-854-5728. *Website:* http://www.itt-tech.edu/.

ITT Technical Institute

Houston, Texas

- **Proprietary** primarily 2-year, founded 1985, part of ITT Educational Services, Inc.
- **Suburban** campus
- **Coed**
- **Minimally difficult** entrance level

Academics *Calendar:* quarters. *Degrees:* associate and bachelor's.

Freshman Application Contact Director of Recruitment, ITT Technical Institute, 15651 North Freeway, Houston, TX 77090. *Phone:* 281-873-0512. *Toll-free phone:* 800-879-6486. *Website:* http://www.itt-tech.edu/.

ITT Technical Institute

Houston, Texas

- **Proprietary** primarily 2-year, founded 1983, part of ITT Educational Services, Inc.
- **Urban** campus
- **Coed**
- **Minimally difficult** entrance level

Academics *Calendar:* quarters. *Degrees:* associate and bachelor's.

Freshman Application Contact Director of Recruitment, ITT Technical Institute, 2950 South Gessner, Houston, TX 77063-3751. *Phone:* 713-952-2294. *Toll-free phone:* 800-235-4787. *Website:* http://www.itt-tech.edu/.

ITT Technical Institute

Richardson, Texas

- **Proprietary** primarily 2-year, founded 1989, part of ITT Educational Services, Inc.
- **Suburban** campus
- **Coed**
- **Minimally difficult** entrance level

Academics *Calendar:* quarters. *Degrees:* associate and bachelor's.

Financial Aid *Of all full-time matriculated undergraduates who enrolled in 2011,* 5 Federal Work-Study jobs (averaging $5000).
Freshman Application Contact Director of Recruitment, ITT Technical Institute, 2101 Waterview Parkway, Richardson, TX 75080. *Phone:* 972-690-9100. *Toll-free phone:* 888-488-5761.
Website: http://www.itt-tech.edu/.

ITT Technical Institute

San Antonio, Texas

- **Proprietary** primarily 2-year, founded 1988, part of ITT Educational Services, Inc.
- **Urban** campus
- **Coed**
- **Minimally difficult** entrance level

Academics *Calendar:* quarters. *Degrees:* associate and bachelor's.
Freshman Application Contact Director of Recruitment, ITT Technical Institute, 5700 Northwest Parkway, San Antonio, TX 78249-3303. *Phone:* 210-694-4612. *Toll-free phone:* 800-880-0570.
Website: http://www.itt-tech.edu/.

ITT Technical Institute

Waco, Texas

- **Proprietary** primarily 2-year, part of ITT Educational Services, Inc.
- **Coed**

Academics *Calendar:* quarters. *Degrees:* associate and bachelor's.
Freshman Application Contact Director of Recruitment, ITT Technical Institute, 3700 S. Jack Kultgen Expressway, Suite 100, Waco, TX 76706. *Phone:* 254-881-2200. *Toll-free phone:* 877-201-7143.
Website: http://www.itt-tech.edu/.

ITT Technical Institute

Webster, Texas

- **Proprietary** primarily 2-year, founded 1995, part of ITT Educational Services, Inc.
- **Coed**
- **Minimally difficult** entrance level

Academics *Calendar:* quarters. *Degrees:* associate and bachelor's.
Freshman Application Contact Director of Recruitment, ITT Technical Institute, 1001 Magnolia Avenue, Webster, TX 77598. *Phone:* 281-316-4700. *Toll-free phone:* 888-488-9347.
Website: http://www.itt-tech.edu/.

Jarvis Christian College

Hawkins, Texas

- **Independent** 4-year, founded 1912, affiliated with Christian Church (Disciples of Christ)
- **Rural** 465-acre campus
- **Endowment** $11.6 million
- **Coed** 603 undergraduate students, 93% full-time, 43% women, 57% men
- **Minimally difficult** entrance level, 100% of applicants were admitted

Undergraduates 560 full-time, 43 part-time. Students come from 20 states and territories; 11% are from out of state; 85% Black or African American, non-Hispanic/Latino; 7% Hispanic/Latino; 0.2% Native Hawaiian or other Pacific Islander, non-Hispanic/Latino; 0.3% American Indian or Alaska Native, non-Hispanic/Latino; 17% transferred in; 88% live on campus. *Retention:* 55% of full-time freshmen returned.
Freshmen *Admission:* 774 applied, 774 admitted, 177 enrolled. *Average high school GPA:* 2.5. *Test scores:* SAT critical reading scores over 500: 2%; SAT math scores over 500: 9%; SAT writing scores over 500: 6%; SAT critical reading scores over 600: 1%; SAT math scores over 600: 1%; SAT writing scores over 600: 1%; SAT writing scores over 700: 1%.
Faculty *Total:* 46, 70% full-time, 63% with terminal degrees. *Student/faculty ratio:* 16:1.
Academics *Calendar:* semesters. *Degree:* bachelor's. *Special study options:* academic remediation for entering students, advanced placement credit, coop-

erative education, double majors, English as a second language, honors programs, internships, off-campus study, student-designed majors, summer session for credit. *Unusual degree programs:* engineering with South Plains College, Blinn College, Lone Star College, Lon Morris College; nursing with Houston Community College, Cloud County Community, Lon Morris College.
Computers on Campus 100 computers/terminals and 200 ports are available on campus for general student use. Students can access the following: campus intranet, computer help desk, free student e-mail accounts, online (class) grades, online (class) registration, online (class) schedules. Campuswide network is available. 100% of college-owned or -operated housing units are wired for high-speed Internet access. Wireless service is available via entire campus.
Student Life *Housing options:* men-only, women-only, disabled students. Campus housing is university owned. *Activities and organizations:* drama/theater group, choral group, Student Government Association, Pre-Alumni Club, Student Ministers' Association, Women 2 Women, Panhellenic Council, national fraternities, national sororities. *Campus security:* 24-hour emergency response devices and patrols. *Student services:* health clinic.
Athletics Member NAIA. *Intercollegiate sports:* baseball M(s), basketball M(s)/W(s), cheerleading M/W, cross-country running M(s)/W(s). *Intramural sports:* baseball M, basketball M/W, volleyball M/W.
Costs (2013–14) *Comprehensive fee:* $19,552 includes full-time tuition ($10,090), mandatory fees ($1279), and room and board ($8183). Part-time tuition: $420 per semester hour. *Required fees:* $1279 per year part-time. *College room only:* $5174. Room and board charges vary according to housing facility. *Payment plans:* installment, deferred payment. *Waivers:* employees or children of employees.
Financial Aid Of all full-time matriculated undergraduates who enrolled in 2011, 476 applied for aid, 476 were judged to have need, 30 had their need fully met. 149 Federal Work-Study jobs (averaging $1538). 2 state and other part-time jobs (averaging $2315). In 2011, 5 non-need-based awards were made. *Average percent of need met:* 80%. *Average financial aid package:* $12,115. *Average need-based loan:* $5392. *Average need-based gift aid:* $8062. *Average non-need-based aid:* $17,192. *Average indebtedness upon graduation:* $29,296.
Applying *Options:* electronic application. *Application fee:* $50. *Required:* high school transcript. *Recommended:* minimum 2.0 GPA. *Application deadlines:* 8/1 (freshmen), 8/1 (out-of-state freshmen), rolling (transfers). *Notification:* 8/15 (freshmen), 8/15 (out-of-state freshmen).
Freshman Application Contact Mrs. Micheline Lambert, Director Admissions and Enrollment, Jarvis Christian College, PO Box 1470, Hawkins, TX 75765-9989. *Phone:* 903-730-4890 Ext. 2201. *Fax:* 903-769-4842. *E-mail:* mlambert@jarvis.edu.
Website: http://www.jarvis.edu/.

Lamar University

Beaumont, Texas

- **State-supported** university, founded 1923, part of Texas State University System
- **Suburban** 200-acre campus with easy access to Houston
- **Coed** 9,800 undergraduate students, 71% full-time, 58% women, 42% men
- **Minimally difficult** entrance level, 88% of applicants were admitted

Undergraduates 7,003 full-time, 2,797 part-time. Students come from 39 states and territories; 38 other countries; 2% are from out of state; 32% Black or African American, non-Hispanic/Latino; 10% Hispanic/Latino; 4% Asian, non-Hispanic/Latino; 0.6% American Indian or Alaska Native, non-Hispanic/Latino; 1% Two or more races, non-Hispanic/Latino; 3% Race/ethnicity unknown; 2% international; 7% transferred in. *Retention:* 56% of full-time freshmen returned.
Freshmen *Admission:* 4,929 applied, 4,351 admitted, 1,698 enrolled. *Test scores:* SAT critical reading scores over 500: 28%; SAT math scores over 500: 34%; SAT writing scores over 500: 21%; ACT scores over 18: 64%; SAT critical reading scores over 600: 6%; SAT math scores over 600: 8%; SAT writing scores over 600: 4%; ACT scores over 24: 14%; SAT critical reading scores over 700: 1%; SAT math scores over 700: 1%; SAT writing scores over 700: 1%; ACT scores over 30: 1%.
Faculty *Total:* 645, 62% full-time, 55% with terminal degrees. *Student/faculty ratio:* 20:1.
Academics *Calendar:* semesters. *Degrees:* associate, bachelor's, master's, and doctoral. *Special study options:* academic remediation for entering students, accelerated degree program, advanced placement credit, cooperative education, English as a second language, honors programs, internships, off-campus study, part-time degree program, services for LD students, student-designed majors, summer session for credit.

Computers on Campus 120 computers/terminals are available on campus for general student use. Campuswide network is available. Wireless service is available via entire campus.

Student Life *Housing options:* coed. *Activities and organizations:* drama/theater group, student-run newspaper, television station, choral group, national fraternities, national sororities. *Campus security:* 24-hour emergency response devices and patrols, student patrols, late-night transport/escort service. *Student services:* health clinic, personal/psychological counseling.

Athletics Member NCAA. All Division I except football (Division I-AA). *Intercollegiate sports:* baseball M(s), basketball M(s)/W(s), cheerleading M/W, cross-country running M(s)/W(s), golf M(s)/W(s), soccer W(s), tennis M(s)/W(s), track and field M(s)/W(s), volleyball W(s). *Intramural sports:* basketball M/W, cross-country running M/W, football M, golf M/W, gymnastics W, racquetball M/W, rugby M/W, sailing M/W, soccer M/W, swimming and diving M/W, table tennis M, tennis M/W, track and field M/W, volleyball M/W, weight lifting M/W.

Standardized Tests *Required:* SAT or ACT (for admission). *Required for some:* SAT Subject Tests (for admission).

Costs (2013–14) *Tuition:* state resident $6240 full-time, $208 per credit hour part-time; nonresident $18,270 full-time, $609 per credit hour part-time. Full-time tuition and fees vary according to course load. Part-time tuition and fees vary according to course load. *Required fees:* $2771 full-time. *Room and board:* $7966; room only: $5098. Room and board charges vary according to board plan. *Payment plan:* installment. *Waivers:* senior citizens and employees or children of employees.

Financial Aid Of all full-time matriculated undergraduates who enrolled in 2010, 4,827 applied for aid, 3,321 were judged to have need. 182 Federal Work-Study jobs (averaging $3159). 62 state and other part-time jobs (averaging $1228). *Average percent of need met:* 64%. *Average financial aid package:* $4618. *Average need-based loan:* $2107. *Average need-based gift aid:* $2134. *Average indebtedness upon graduation:* $8234.

Applying *Options:* electronic application, early admission. *Required:* high school transcript. *Required for some:* essay or personal statement. *Application deadlines:* 8/1 (freshmen), 8/1 (transfers). *Notification:* continuous (freshmen).

Freshman Application Contact Ms. Melissa Chesser, Director of Recruitment, Lamar University, PO Box 10009, Beaumont, TX 77710. *Phone:* 409-880-8888. *Fax:* 409-880-8463. *E-mail:* admissions@lamar.edu. *Website:* http://www.lamar.edu/.

LeTourneau University

Longview, Texas

- **Independent nondenominational** comprehensive, founded 1946
- **Suburban** 162-acre campus
- **Coed** 2,450 undergraduate students, 55% full-time, 49% women, 51% men
- **Moderately difficult** entrance level, 43% of applicants were admitted

Undergraduates 1,343 full-time, 1,107 part-time. 44% are from out of state; 12% Black or African American, non-Hispanic/Latino; 9% Hispanic/Latino; 0.9% Asian, non-Hispanic/Latino; 0.1% Native Hawaiian or other Pacific Islander, non-Hispanic/Latino; 0.5% American Indian or Alaska Native, non-Hispanic/Latino; 2% Two or more races, non-Hispanic/Latino; 8% Race/ethnicity unknown; 4% international; 4% transferred in; 72% live on campus. *Retention:* 78% of full-time freshmen returned.

Freshmen *Admission:* 1,684 applied, 730 admitted, 362 enrolled. *Average high school GPA:* 3.63. *Test scores:* SAT critical reading scores over 500: 80%; SAT math scores over 500: 87%; SAT writing scores over 500: 70%; ACT scores over 18: 99%; SAT critical reading scores over 600: 47%; SAT math scores over 600: 56%; SAT writing scores over 600: 31%; ACT scores over 24: 64%; SAT critical reading scores over 700: 14%; SAT math scores over 700: 13%; SAT writing scores over 700: 7%; ACT scores over 30: 19%.

Faculty *Total:* 232, 41% full-time. *Student/faculty ratio:* 15:1.

Academics *Calendar:* semesters. *Degrees:* associate, bachelor's, and master's. *Special study options:* adult/continuing education programs, part-time degree program.

Computers on Campus Students can access the following: campus intranet, computer help desk, free student e-mail accounts, online (class) grades, online (class) registration, online (class) schedules. Campuswide network is available. 100% of college-owned or -operated housing units are wired for high-speed Internet access. Wireless service is available via classrooms, computer centers, computer labs, dorm rooms, learning centers, libraries, student centers.

Student Life *Housing:* on-campus residence required through junior year. *Options:* coed, men-only, women-only, disabled students. Campus housing is university owned. Freshman campus housing is guaranteed. *Campus security:* 24-hour emergency response devices and patrols, late-night transport/escort service, controlled dormitory access, University police department.

Athletics Member NCAA, NCCAA. All NCAA Division III. *Intercollegiate sports:* baseball M, basketball M/W, cross-country running M/W, soccer M/W, softball W, tennis M/W, volleyball W. *Intramural sports:* badminton M/W, basketball M/W, bowling M/W, cross-country running M/W, football M/W, golf M/W, racquetball M/W, soccer M/W, softball M/W, swimming and diving M/W, table tennis M/W, tennis M/W, volleyball M/W.

Standardized Tests *Required:* SAT or ACT (for admission).

Costs (2012–13) *Comprehensive fee:* $33,480 includes full-time tuition ($24,050), mandatory fees ($490), and room and board ($8940). Part-time tuition: $959 per credit hour. Part-time tuition and fees vary according to course load. *Room and board:* Room and board charges vary according to board plan. *Payment plan:* installment. *Waivers:* employees or children of employees.

Financial Aid Of all full-time matriculated undergraduates who enrolled in 2011, 1,143 applied for aid, 1,038 were judged to have need, 112 had their need fully met. In 2011, 23 non-need-based awards were made. *Average percent of need met:* 60%. *Average financial aid package:* $16,772. *Average need-based loan:* $3924. *Average need-based gift aid:* $12,235. *Average non-need-based aid:* $7575. *Average indebtedness upon graduation:* $30,295.

Applying *Options:* electronic application, deferred entrance. *Application fee:* $35. *Application deadlines:* rolling (freshmen), rolling (transfers). *Notification:* continuous (freshmen), continuous (transfers).

Freshman Application Contact Mr. James Townsend, Director of Admissions, LeTourneau University, PO Box 7001, Longview, TX 75607-7001. *Phone:* 903-233-3400. *Toll-free phone:* 800-759-8811. *Fax:* 903-233-3411. *E-mail:* admissions@letu.edu. *Website:* http://www.letu.edu/.

Lubbock Christian University

Lubbock, Texas

- **Independent** comprehensive, founded 1957, affiliated with Church of Christ
- **Suburban** 120-acre campus
- **Endowment** $12.7 million
- **Coed** 1,640 undergraduate students, 81% full-time, 60% women, 40% men
- **Moderately difficult** entrance level, 93% of applicants were admitted

Undergraduates 1,334 full-time, 306 part-time. Students come from 28 states and territories; 20 other countries; 11% are from out of state; 7% Black or African American, non-Hispanic/Latino; 22% Hispanic/Latino; 0.3% Asian, non-Hispanic/Latino; 0.4% Native Hawaiian or other Pacific Islander, non-Hispanic/Latino; 0.9% American Indian or Alaska Native, non-Hispanic/Latino; 2% international; 13% transferred in; 65% live on campus. *Retention:* 65% of full-time freshmen returned.

Freshmen *Admission:* 979 applied, 909 admitted, 315 enrolled. *Average high school GPA:* 3.42. *Test scores:* SAT critical reading scores over 500: 41%; SAT math scores over 500: 57%; SAT writing scores over 500: 34%; ACT scores over 18: 89%; SAT critical reading scores over 600: 11%; SAT math scores over 600: 14%; SAT writing scores over 600: 5%; ACT scores over 24: 32%; SAT math scores over 700: 3%; ACT scores over 30: 3%.

Faculty *Total:* 187, 51% full-time, 51% with terminal degrees. *Student/faculty ratio:* 13:1.

Academics *Calendar:* semesters. *Degrees:* bachelor's and master's. *Special study options:* academic remediation for entering students, adult/continuing education programs, advanced placement credit, distance learning, double majors, English as a second language, honors programs, internships, part-time degree program, services for LD students, study abroad, summer session for credit. *ROTC:* Army (c), Air Force (c). *Unusual degree programs:* 3-2 engineering with Texas Tech University.

Computers on Campus 169 computers/terminals are available on campus for general student use. Students can access the following: campus intranet, computer help desk, free student e-mail accounts, online (class) grades, online (class) registration, online (class) schedules. Campuswide network is available. 100% of college-owned or -operated housing units are wired for high-speed Internet access. Wireless service is available via entire campus.

Student Life *Housing:* on-campus residence required through sophomore year. *Options:* men-only, women-only. Campus housing is university owned. Freshman campus housing is guaranteed. *Activities and organizations:* drama/theater group, student-run newspaper, choral group. *Campus security:* 24-hour patrols. *Student services:* health clinic, personal/psychological counseling.

Athletics Member NAIA. *Intercollegiate sports:* baseball M(s), basketball M(s)/W(s), cheerleading M/W, cross-country running M(s)/W(s), golf M(s)/W(s), soccer M(s)/W(s), softball W(s), track and field M/W, volleyball W(s). *Intramural sports:* badminton M/W, basketball M/W, cross-country running M/W, football M/W, golf M/W, racquetball M/W, rock climbing M/W, soccer

M/W, softball M/W, table tennis M/W, tennis M/W, track and field M/W, volleyball M/W.

Standardized Tests *Required:* SAT or ACT (for admission).

Costs (2012–13) *Comprehensive fee:* $24,434 includes full-time tuition ($16,350), mandatory fees ($1410), and room and board ($6674). Full-time tuition and fees vary according to degree level and program. Part-time tuition: $525 per semester hour. Part-time tuition and fees vary according to course load, degree level, and program. *Required fees:* $540 per term part-time. *Room and board:* Room and board charges vary according to board plan and housing facility. *Payment plan:* installment. *Waivers:* employees or children of employees.

Financial Aid Of all full-time matriculated undergraduates who enrolled in 2012, 1,139 applied for aid, 983 were judged to have need, 91 had their need fully met. 715 Federal Work-Study jobs (averaging $1797). 64 state and other part-time jobs (averaging $302). In 2012, 200 non-need-based awards were made. *Average percent of need met:* 64%. *Average financial aid package:* $13,738. *Average need-based loan:* $4418. *Average need-based gift aid:* $9371. *Average non-need-based aid:* $4707. *Average indebtedness upon graduation:* $29,053.

Applying *Options:* electronic application. *Application fee:* $25. *Required:* high school transcript. *Application deadlines:* 8/1 (freshmen), rolling (transfers). *Notification:* continuous (freshmen), continuous (transfers).

Freshman Application Contact Mr. Charles Webb, Director of Admissions, Lubbock Christian University, 5601 19th Street, Lubbock, TX 79407. *Phone:* 806-720-7156. *Toll-free phone:* 800-933-7601. *Fax:* 806-720-7162. *E-mail:* admissions@lcu.edu.
Website: http://www.lcu.edu/.

McMurry University

Abilene, Texas

- **Independent United Methodist** comprehensive, founded 1923
- **Suburban** 43-acre campus
- **Endowment** $61.4 million
- **Coed** 1,365 undergraduate students, 84% full-time, 48% women, 52% men
- **Moderately difficult** entrance level, 55% of applicants were admitted

Undergraduates 1,151 full-time, 214 part-time. Students come from 27 states and territories; 11 other countries; 6% are from out of state; 15% Black or African American, non-Hispanic/Latino; 18% Hispanic/Latino; 1% Asian, non-Hispanic/Latino; 0.2% Native Hawaiian or other Pacific Islander, non-Hispanic/Latino; 1% American Indian or Alaska Native, non-Hispanic/Latino; 3% Two or more races, non-Hispanic/Latino; 0.2% Race/ethnicity unknown; 2% international; 13% transferred in; 47% live on campus. *Retention:* 60% of full-time freshmen returned.

Freshmen *Admission:* 1,568 applied, 861 admitted, 303 enrolled. *Average high school GPA:* 3.45. *Test scores:* SAT critical reading scores over 500: 42%; SAT math scores over 500: 58%; ACT scores over 18: 77%; SAT critical reading scores over 600: 10%; SAT math scores over 600: 17%; ACT scores over 24: 21%; SAT critical reading scores over 700: 1%; SAT math scores over 700: 1%; ACT scores over 30: 1%.

Faculty *Total:* 126, 63% full-time, 52% with terminal degrees. *Student/faculty ratio:* 13:1.

Academics *Calendar:* semesters plus May term. *Degrees:* bachelor's and master's. *Special study options:* academic remediation for entering students, accelerated degree program, adult/continuing education programs, advanced placement credit, double majors, honors programs, independent study, internships, part-time degree program, services for LD students, student-designed majors, study abroad, summer session for credit.

Computers on Campus 130 computers/terminals and 705 ports are available on campus for general student use. Students can access the following: campus intranet, computer help desk, free student e-mail accounts, online (class) grades, online (class) registration, online (class) schedules, Moodle. Campuswide network is available. 100% of college-owned or -operated housing units are wired for high-speed Internet access. Wireless service is available via entire campus.

Student Life *Housing:* on-campus residence required through junior year. *Options:* coed, men-only, women-only. Campus housing is university owned and is provided by a third party. Freshman campus housing is guaranteed. *Activities and organizations:* drama/theater group, student-run newspaper, choral group, marching band, Alpha Phi Omega, Religious Life Council, McMurry Student Government, Campus Activity Board, Servant Leadership. *Campus security:* 24-hour emergency response devices and patrols, late-night transport/escort service, controlled dormitory access. *Student services:* health clinic, personal/psychological counseling.

Athletics Member NCAA, NCCAA. All NCAA Division II. *Intercollegiate sports:* baseball M, basketball M/W, cross-country running M/W, football M, golf M/W, soccer M/W, swimming and diving M/W, tennis M/W, track and field M/W, volleyball W. *Intramural sports:* basketball M/W, football M/W, golf M/W, racquetball M/W, soccer M/W, softball M/W, tennis M/W, ultimate Frisbee M/W, volleyball M/W.

Standardized Tests *Required:* SAT or ACT (for admission).

Costs (2012–13) *One-time required fee:* $175. *Comprehensive fee:* $30,765 includes full-time tuition ($23,305) and room and board ($7460). Full-time tuition and fees vary according to course load. Part-time tuition: $728 per credit hour. Part-time tuition and fees vary according to course load. *College room only:* $3636. Room and board charges vary according to board plan and housing facility. *Payment plan:* installment. *Waivers:* employees or children of employees.

Financial Aid Of all full-time matriculated undergraduates who enrolled in 2012, 1,044 applied for aid, 948 were judged to have need, 71 had their need fully met. 228 Federal Work-Study jobs (averaging $2184). 48 state and other part-time jobs (averaging $2291). In 2012, 70 non-need-based awards were made. *Average percent of need met:* 78%. *Average financial aid package:* $19,228. *Average need-based loan:* $4522. *Average need-based gift aid:* $9552. *Average non-need-based aid:* $6556. *Average indebtedness upon graduation:* $38,921.

Applying *Options:* electronic application, deferred entrance. *Application fee:* $25. *Required:* essay or personal statement, high school transcript, minimum 2.0 GPA, Official ACT or SAT score report. *Required for some:* 3 letters of recommendation, interview. *Application deadlines:* 8/15 (freshmen), 8/5 (out-of-state freshmen), 8/15 (transfers). *Notification:* continuous (freshmen), continuous (out-of-state freshmen), continuous (transfers).

Freshman Application Contact Ms. Kim Poligala, Admission and Recruitment Coordinator, McMurry University, 1 McMurry Station, Box 278, Abilene, TX 79697. *Phone:* 325-793-4700. *Toll-free phone:* 800-460-2392. *Fax:* 325-793-4701. *E-mail:* admissions@mcm.edu.
Website: http://www.mcm.edu/.

Messenger College

Euless, Texas

Freshman Application Contact Ron Cannon, Vice President of Academic Affairs, Messenger College, PO Box 1207, Euless, TX 76039. *Phone:* 417-624-7070 Ext. 108. *Toll-free phone:* 800-385-8940. *Fax:* 417-624-5070. *E-mail:* info@messengercollege.edu.
Website: http://www.messengercollege.edu/.

Midland College

Midland, Texas

- **State and locally supported** 4-year, founded 1969
- **Suburban** 163-acre campus
- **Endowment** $34.7 million
- **Coed** 5,530 undergraduate students, 29% full-time, 60% women, 40% men
- **Noncompetitive** entrance level

Undergraduates 1,627 full-time, 3,903 part-time. Students come from 28 states and territories; 39 other countries; 2% are from out of state; 7% Black or African American, non-Hispanic/Latino; 44% Hispanic/Latino; 1% Asian, non-Hispanic/Latino; 0.1% Native Hawaiian or other Pacific Islander, non-Hispanic/Latino; 0.3% American Indian or Alaska Native, non-Hispanic/Latino; 1% Two or more races, non-Hispanic/Latino; 7% Race/ethnicity unknown; 0.1% international; 4% transferred in.

Freshmen *Admission:* 754 enrolled.

Faculty *Total:* 271, 50% full-time, 13% with terminal degrees. *Student/faculty ratio:* 16:1.

Academics *Calendar:* semesters. *Degrees:* certificates, associate, and bachelor's. *Special study options:* academic remediation for entering students, adult/continuing education programs, advanced placement credit, distance learning, honors programs, services for LD students, summer session for credit.

Computers on Campus 950 computers/terminals are available on campus for general student use. Students can access the following: computer help desk, free student e-mail accounts, online (class) grades, online (class) registration, online (class) schedules. Campuswide network is available. 100% of college-owned or -operated housing units are wired for high-speed Internet access. Wireless service is available via entire campus.

Student Life *Housing options:* coed, men-only, women-only. Campus housing is university owned. *Activities and organizations:* drama/theater group, student-run newspaper, choral group, OIKOS, Midland College Latin American Student Society, Student Government Association, Student Nurses Association, Baptist Student Ministries. *Campus security:* 24-hour patrols, controlled dormitory access. *Student services:* personal/psychological counseling.

Athletics Member NJCAA. *Intercollegiate sports:* baseball M(s), basketball M(s)/W(s), cheerleading W, golf M(s), softball W(s), volleyball W(s). *Intramural sports:* basketball M/W, cheerleading W, volleyball M/W.

Costs (2013–14) *Tuition:* area resident $2160 full-time; state resident $3450 full-time; nonresident $4620 full-time. Full-time tuition and fees vary according to course level, course load, degree level, program, and reciprocity agreements. *Room and board:* $4650; room only: $2200. *Payment plans:* installment, deferred payment. *Waivers:* senior citizens and employees or children of employees.

Financial Aid Of all full-time matriculated undergraduates who enrolled in 2008, 75 Federal Work-Study jobs (averaging $2700). 5 state and other part-time jobs (averaging $2700).

Applying *Required:* high school transcript. *Application deadlines:* rolling (freshmen), rolling (out-of-state freshmen), rolling (transfers). *Notification:* continuous (freshmen), continuous (out-of-state freshmen), continuous (transfers).

Freshman Application Contact Mr. Jeremy Martinez, Director of Admissions, Midland College, 3600 North Garfield, Midland, TX 79705-6399. *Phone:* 432-685-5523. *Fax:* 432-685-6887. *E-mail:* jmartinez@midland.edu. *Website:* http://www.midland.edu/.

Midwestern State University

Wichita Falls, Texas

- **State-supported** comprehensive, founded 1922
- **Urban** 255-acre campus
- **Coed** 5,238 undergraduate students, 73% full-time, 57% women, 43% men
- **Moderately difficult** entrance level, 75% of applicants were admitted

Undergraduates 3,823 full-time, 1,415 part-time. Students come from 26 states and territories; 51 other countries; 8% are from out of state; 13% Black or African American, non-Hispanic/Latino; 13% Hispanic/Latino; 3% Asian, non-Hispanic/Latino; 0.3% Native Hawaiian or other Pacific Islander, non-Hispanic/Latino; 0.8% American Indian or Alaska Native, non-Hispanic/Latino; 2% Two or more races, non-Hispanic/Latino; 1% Race/ethnicity unknown; 7% international; 11% transferred in; 23% live on campus. *Retention:* 71% of full-time freshmen returned.

Freshmen *Admission:* 2,090 applied, 1,573 admitted, 623 enrolled. *Average high school GPA:* 3.44. *Test scores:* SAT critical reading scores over 500: 47%; SAT math scores over 500: 61%; SAT writing scores over 500: 36%; ACT scores over 18: 90%; SAT critical reading scores over 600: 9%; SAT math scores over 600: 14%; SAT writing scores over 600: 5%; ACT scores over 24: 24%; SAT critical reading scores over 700: 1%; SAT math scores over 700: 1%; ACT scores over 30: 2%.

Faculty *Total:* 342, 65% full-time, 62% with terminal degrees. *Student/faculty ratio:* 17:1.

Academics *Calendar:* semesters. *Degrees:* associate, bachelor's, master's, and postbachelor's certificates. *Special study options:* academic remediation for entering students, adult/continuing education programs, advanced placement credit, distance learning, double majors, English as a second language, honors programs, independent study, internships, part-time degree program, services for LD students, study abroad, summer session for credit. *ROTC:* Air Force (c). *Unusual degree programs:* 3-2 business administration.

Computers on Campus 405 computers/terminals are available on campus for general student use. Students can access the following: campus intranet, computer help desk, free student e-mail accounts, online (class) grades, online (class) registration, online (class) schedules. Campuswide network is available. 100% of college-owned or -operated housing units are wired for high-speed Internet access. Wireless service is available via entire campus.

Student Life *Housing:* on-campus residence required through sophomore year. *Options:* coed, men-only, women-only, disabled students. Campus housing is university owned. Freshman applicants given priority for college housing. *Activities and organizations:* drama/theater group, student-run newspaper, television station, choral group, marching band, Caribbean Students Organization, Baptist Student Ministry, Catholic Campus Ministry, African Students Organization, University Programming Board, national fraternities, national sororities. *Campus security:* 24-hour emergency response devices and patrols, controlled dormitory access. *Student services:* health clinic, personal/psychological counseling, legal services.

Athletics Member NCAA. All Division II. *Intercollegiate sports:* basketball M(s)/W(s), cheerleading M(s)(c)/W(s)(c), cross-country running W(s), fencing M(c)/W(c), football M(s), golf M(s)/W(s), soccer M(s)/W(s), softball W(s),

tennis M(s)/W(s), volleyball W(s). *Intramural sports:* archery M/W, badminton M/W, basketball M/W, bowling M/W, football M/W, golf M/W, rugby M(c), soccer M/W, softball M/W, table tennis M/W, tennis M/W, ultimate Frisbee M/W, volleyball M/W, weight lifting M/W.

Standardized Tests *Required:* SAT or ACT (for admission).

Costs (2013–14) *Tuition:* area resident $4845 full-time; state resident $4548 full-time, $162 per credit part-time; nonresident $6795 full-time, $227 per credit part-time. Full-time tuition and fees vary according to course load, location, and program. Part-time tuition and fees vary according to course load, location, and program. *Required fees:* $2393 full-time, $69 per credit part-time, $199 per term part-time. *Room and board:* $6350; room only: $3350. Room and board charges vary according to board plan and housing facility. *Payment plan:* installment. *Waivers:* senior citizens and employees or children of employees.

Financial Aid Of all full-time matriculated undergraduates who enrolled in 2011, 3,141 applied for aid, 2,283 were judged to have need, 343 had their need fully met. In 2011, 421 non-need-based awards were made. *Average percent of need met:* 67%. *Average financial aid package:* $9162. *Average need-based loan:* $7223. *Average need-based gift aid:* $5913. *Average non-need-based aid:* $1939. *Average indebtedness upon graduation:* $22,891.

Applying *Options:* electronic application, early action. *Application fee:* $25. *Required:* essay or personal statement, high school transcript. *Application deadlines:* 8/7 (freshmen), 8/7 (transfers). *Notification:* continuous (freshmen), continuous (transfers).

Freshman Application Contact Ms. Barbara Merkle, Director of Admissions, Midwestern State University, Wichita Falls, TX 76308. *Phone:* 940-397-4334. *Toll-free phone:* 800-842-1922. *Fax:* 940-397-4672. *E-mail:* admissions@mwsu.edu. *Website:* http://www.mwsu.edu/.

North American College

Houston, Texas

Admissions Office Contact North American College, 3203 North Sam Houston Parkway W., Houston, TX 77038. *Website:* http://www.northamerican.edu/.

Northwood University, Texas Campus

Cedar Hill, Texas

- **Independent** comprehensive, founded 1966
- **Small-town** 360-acre campus with easy access to Dallas-Fort Worth
- **Coed** 534 undergraduate students, 98% full-time, 42% women, 58% men
- **Moderately difficult** entrance level, 59% of applicants were admitted

Undergraduates 521 full-time, 13 part-time. Students come from 14 states and territories; 19 other countries; 6% are from out of state; 23% Black or African American, non-Hispanic/Latino; 49% Hispanic/Latino; 3% Asian, non-Hispanic/Latino; 0.6% American Indian or Alaska Native, non-Hispanic/Latino; 0.6% Two or more races, non-Hispanic/Latino; 39% international; 14% transferred in; 36% live on campus. *Retention:* 58% of full-time freshmen returned.

Freshmen *Admission:* 452 applied, 265 admitted, 172 enrolled. *Average high school GPA:* 3.32. *Test scores:* SAT critical reading scores over 500: 26%; SAT math scores over 500: 39%; SAT writing scores over 500: 15%; SAT critical reading scores over 600: 3%; SAT math scores over 600: 6%; SAT writing scores over 600: 1%.

Faculty *Total:* 44, 45% full-time, 27% with terminal degrees. *Student/faculty ratio:* 19:1.

Academics *Calendar:* quarters. *Degrees:* bachelor's and master's. *Special study options:* academic remediation for entering students, accelerated degree program, adult/continuing education programs, advanced placement credit, distance learning, double majors, external degree program, honors programs, internships, off-campus study, part-time degree program, study abroad, summer session for credit.

Computers on Campus 73 computers/terminals are available on campus for general student use. Students can access the following: campus intranet, computer help desk, free student e-mail accounts, online (class) grades, online (class) registration, online (class) schedules. Campuswide network is available. 100% of college-owned or -operated housing units are wired for high-speed Internet access. Wireless service is available via entire campus.

Student Life *Housing:* on-campus residence required for freshman year. *Options:* men-only, women-only. Campus housing is university owned. Freshman campus housing is guaranteed. *Activities and organizations:* drama/theater group, student-run newspaper, choral group, Association of Entertainment and Sports Management, In-Line Hockey Club, Alpha Nu Omega, Alpha Omega, Delta Epsilon Chi. *Campus security:* 24-hour emergency response devices and patrols, student patrols, late-night transport/escort service, controlled dormitory access. *Student services:* health clinic, personal/psychological counseling.

Athletics Member NAIA. *Intercollegiate sports:* baseball M(s), cross-country running M(s)/W(s), golf M(s)/W(s), soccer M(s)/W(s), softball W(s), track and field M(s)/W(s). *Intramural sports:* basketball M/W, soccer M/W, volleyball M/W.

Standardized Tests *Required:* SAT or ACT (for admission).

Costs (2012–13) *Comprehensive fee:* $30,103 includes full-time tuition ($20,040), mandatory fees ($956), and room and board ($9107). Part-time tuition: $776 per semester hour. *College room only:* $4907. Room and board charges vary according to board plan. *Payment plan:* installment. *Waivers:* employees or children of employees.

Financial Aid Of all full-time matriculated undergraduates who enrolled in 2012, 437 applied for aid, 411 were judged to have need, 64 had their need fully met. 66 Federal Work-Study jobs (averaging $1920). In 2012, 50 non-need-based awards were made. *Average percent of need met:* 65%. *Average financial aid package:* $21,625. *Average need-based loan:* $4131. *Average need-based gift aid:* $6995. *Average non-need-based aid:* $8340. *Average indebtedness upon graduation:* $24,254.

Applying *Options:* electronic application, early admission, deferred entrance. *Application fee:* $25. *Required:* essay or personal statement, high school transcript, minimum 2.0 GPA. *Recommended:* 1 letter of recommendation, interview. *Application deadlines:* 8/1 (freshmen), 8/1 (out-of-state freshmen), rolling (transfers). *Notification:* continuous (freshmen), continuous (out-of-state freshmen), continuous (transfers).

Freshman Application Contact Dr. Terry Silva, Director of Admissions, Northwood University, Texas Campus, 1114 West FM 1382, Cedar Hill, TX 75104. *Phone:* 972-293-5400. *Toll-free phone:* 800-927-9663. *Fax:* 972-291-3824. *E-mail:* txadmit@northwood.edu.
Website: http://www.northwood.edu/.

Our Lady of the Lake University of San Antonio

San Antonio, Texas

Freshman Application Contact Gilberto Becerra, Assistant Director of Undergraduate Admissions, Our Lady of the Lake University of San Antonio, 411 Southwest 24th Street, San Antonio, TX 78207-4689. *Phone:* 210-434-6711 Ext. 4129. *Toll-free phone:* 800-436-6558. *Fax:* 210-431-4036. *E-mail:* admission@lake.ollusa.edu.
Website: http://www.ollusa.edu/.

Paul Quinn College

Dallas, Texas

- **Independent African Methodist Episcopal** 4-year, founded 1872
- **Suburban** 132-acre campus
- **Endowment** $5.3 million
- **Coed** 193 undergraduate students, 75% full-time, 52% women, 48% men
- **Moderately difficult** entrance level, 96% of applicants were admitted

Undergraduates 145 full-time, 48 part-time. Students come from 21 states and territories; 1 other country; 19% are from out of state; 83% Black or African American, non-Hispanic/Latino; 11% Hispanic/Latino; 0.5% American Indian or Alaska Native, non-Hispanic/Latino; 1% Two or more races, non-Hispanic/Latino; 3% Race/ethnicity unknown; 0.5% international; 19% transferred in; 39% live on campus. *Retention:* 43% of full-time freshmen returned.

Freshmen *Admission:* 305 applied, 293 admitted, 50 enrolled. *Average high school GPA:* 2.74. *Test scores:* SAT critical reading scores over 500: 3%; SAT math scores over 500: 4%; SAT writing scores over 500: 4%; ACT scores over 18: 6%.

Faculty *Total:* 17, 59% full-time, 41% with terminal degrees. *Student/faculty ratio:* 11:1.

Academics *Calendar:* semesters. *Degree:* bachelor's. *Special study options:* academic remediation for entering students, adult/continuing education programs, cooperative education, external degree program, honors programs, independent study, internships, off-campus study, part-time degree program, services for LD students, summer session for credit.

Computers on Campus 50 computers/terminals are available on campus for general student use. Students can access the following: free student e-mail accounts, online (class) grades, online (class) registration, online (class) schedules. Campuswide network is available. 100% of college-owned or -operated housing units are wired for high-speed Internet access. Wireless service is available via entire campus.

Student Life *Housing:* on-campus residence required through sophomore year. *Options:* coed. Campus housing is university owned. Freshman applicants given priority for college housing. *Activities and organizations:* drama/theater group, choral group, marching band, Student Ambassadors, NAACP, Student Government Association, intramurals, Honda Campus All Star Challenge (academic quiz bowl), national fraternities, national sororities. *Campus security:* 24-hour patrols. *Student services:* health clinic, personal/psychological counseling.

Athletics Member NAIA. *Intercollegiate sports:* basketball M(s)/W(s). *Intramural sports:* basketball M/W, soccer M/W, track and field M/W.

Standardized Tests *Required:* SAT or ACT (for admission).

Costs (2012–13) *Comprehensive fee:* $18,800 includes full-time tuition ($9300), mandatory fees ($2150), and room and board ($7350). Full-time tuition and fees vary according to course load. Part-time tuition: $388 per semester hour. Part-time tuition and fees vary according to course load. *College room only:* $3600. Room and board charges vary according to board plan. *Payment plan:* installment.

Financial Aid Of all full-time matriculated undergraduates who enrolled in 2003, 743 applied for aid, 735 were judged to have need, 611 had their need fully met. 149 Federal Work-Study jobs (averaging $826). 16 state and other part-time jobs (averaging $607). *Average percent of need met:* 83%. *Average financial aid package:* $9900. *Average need-based loan:* $3875. *Average need-based gift aid:* $2954. *Average indebtedness upon graduation:* $2375.

Applying *Options:* electronic application. *Application fee:* $25. *Required:* essay or personal statement, high school transcript, minimum 2.5 GPA, interview, medical history, SAT or ACT scores. *Application deadlines:* 6/1 (freshmen), 6/1 (out-of-state freshmen), 6/1 (transfers). *Notification:* continuous (freshmen), continuous (out-of-state freshmen), continuous (transfers).

Freshman Application Contact Paul Quinn College, 3837 Simpson-Stuart Road, Dallas, TX 75241-4331. *Phone:* 214-379-5494. *Toll-free phone:* 877-346-1063.
Website: http://www.pqc.edu/.

Prairie View A&M University

Prairie View, Texas

- **State-supported** university, founded 1878, part of Texas A&M University System
- **Small-town** 1502-acre campus with easy access to Houston
- **Endowment** $54.1 million
- **Coed**
- **Moderately difficult** entrance level

Faculty *Student/faculty ratio:* 17:1.

Academics *Calendar:* semesters. *Degrees:* bachelor's, master's, and doctoral.

Student Life *Campus security:* 24-hour emergency response devices and patrols, late-night transport/escort service, controlled dormitory access.

Athletics Member NCAA, NAIA. All NCAA Division I except football (Division I-AA).

Standardized Tests *Required:* SAT or ACT (for admission).

Costs (2012–13) *Tuition:* state resident $5393 full-time, $180 per credit hour part-time; nonresident $15,923 full-time, $531 per credit hour part-time. Full-time tuition and fees vary according to course load, program, and reciprocity agreements. Part-time tuition and fees vary according to course load, program, and reciprocity agreements. *Required fees:* $2345 full-time, $78 per credit hour part-time. *Room and board:* $7467. Room and board charges vary according to board plan, housing facility, and student level.

Financial Aid *Of all full-time matriculated undergraduates who enrolled in 2010,* 5,744 applied for aid, 5,429 were judged to have need, 3,943 had their need fully met. 486 Federal Work-Study jobs (averaging $1504). 35 state and other part-time jobs (averaging $1103). *In 2010,* 1139 non-need-based awards were made. *Average financial aid package:* $10,867. *Average need-based gift aid:* $6538. *Average non-need-based aid:* $4718.

Applying *Options:* electronic application, deferred entrance. *Application fee:* $25. *Required:* high school transcript, minimum 2.5 GPA.

Freshman Application Contact Ms. Mary Gooch, Director of Admissions, Prairie View A&M University, PO Box 519, MS #1009, Prairie View, TX 77446-0188. *Phone:* 936-261-1066. *E-mail:* megooch@pvamu.edu.
Website: http://www.pvamu.edu/.

Rice University

Houston, Texas

- **Independent** university, founded 1912
- **Urban** 300-acre campus with easy access to Houston
- **Endowment** $4.4 billion
- **Coed** 7,866 undergraduate students, 99% full-time, 75% women, 25% men
- **Most difficult** entrance level, 17% of applicants were admitted

Undergraduates 7,821 full-time, 45 part-time. Students come from 53 states and territories; 51 other countries; 48% are from out of state; 7% Black or African American, non-Hispanic/Latino; 14% Hispanic/Latino; 21% Asian, non-Hispanic/Latino; 0.1% Native Hawaiian or other Pacific Islander, non-Hispanic/Latino; 0.2% American Indian or Alaska Native, non-Hispanic/Latino; 5% Two or more races, non-Hispanic/Latino; 1% Race/ethnicity unknown; 11% international; 0.7% transferred in; 72% live on campus. *Retention:* 96% of full-time freshmen returned.

Freshmen *Admission:* 15,133 applied, 2,528 admitted, 4,931 enrolled. *Test scores:* SAT critical reading scores over 500: 99%; SAT math scores over 500: 100%; SAT writing scores over 500: 98%; ACT scores over 18: 100%; SAT critical reading scores over 600: 93%; SAT math scores over 600: 95%; SAT writing scores over 600: 90%; ACT scores over 24: 97%; SAT critical reading scores over 700: 63%; SAT math scores over 700: 75%; SAT writing scores over 700: 61%; ACT scores over 30: 82%.

Faculty *Total:* 771, 88% full-time, 93% with terminal degrees. *Student/faculty ratio:* 6:1.

Academics *Calendar:* semesters. *Degrees:* bachelor's, master's, and doctoral. *Special study options:* accelerated degree program, advanced placement credit, double majors, English as a second language, honors programs, independent study, internships, off-campus study, services for LD students, student-designed majors, study abroad, summer session for credit. *ROTC:* Army (c), Navy (b), Air Force (c).

Computers on Campus 543 computers/terminals are available on campus for general student use. Students can access the following: campus intranet, computer help desk, free student e-mail accounts, online (class) grades, online (class) registration. Campuswide network is available. Wireless service is available via entire campus.

Student Life *Housing options:* coed. Campus housing is university owned. Freshman applicants given priority for college housing. *Activities and organizations:* drama/theater group, student-run newspaper, radio and television station, choral group, marching band, Drama Club, volunteer program, intramural sports, college government, Marching Owl Band. *Campus security:* 24-hour emergency response devices and patrols, late-night transport/escort service, controlled dormitory access. *Student services:* health clinic, personal/psychological counseling, women's center.

Athletics Member NCAA. All Division I except football (Division I-A). *Intercollegiate sports:* badminton M(c)/W(c), baseball M(s), basketball M(s)/W(s), cheerleading M(c)/W(c), crew M(c)/W(c), cross-country running M(s)/W(s), equestrian sports M(c)/W(c), fencing M(c)/W(c), field hockey W(c), golf M(s), lacrosse M(c)/W(c), riflery M(c)/W(c), rugby M(c)/W(c), sailing M(c)/W(c), soccer M(c)/W(s), softball W(c), swimming and diving W(s), tennis M(s)/W(s), track and field M(s)/W(s), ultimate Frisbee M(c)/W(c), volleyball M(c)/W(s), water polo M(c)/W(c). *Intramural sports:* badminton M/W, basketball M/W, cross-country running M/W, football M/W, racquetball M/W, soccer M/W, softball M/W, swimming and diving M/W, table tennis M/W, tennis M/W, track and field M/W, ultimate Frisbee M/W, volleyball M/W.

Standardized Tests *Required:* SAT and 2 SAT Subject Tests OR ACT with Writing (for admission).

Costs (2013–14) *One-time required fee:* $520. *Comprehensive fee:* $51,942 includes full-time tuition ($38,260), mandatory fees ($682), and room and board ($13,000). *College room only:* $8800. *Payment plan:* installment. *Waivers:* employees or children of employees.

Financial Aid Of all full-time matriculated undergraduates who enrolled in 2012, 2,391 applied for aid, 1,600 were judged to have need, 1,599 had their need fully met. In 2012, 595 non-need-based awards were made. *Average percent of need met:* 100%. *Average financial aid package:* $33,004. *Average need-based loan:* $1428. *Average need-based gift aid:* $31,820. *Average non-need-based aid:* $12,068. *Average indebtedness upon graduation:* $18,133.

Applying *Options:* electronic application, early decision, deferred entrance. *Application fee:* $75. *Required:* essay or personal statement, high school transcript, 2 letters of recommendation. *Required for some:* portfolio for architecture; audition for music. *Recommended:* interview. *Application deadlines:* 1/1 (freshmen), 3/15 (transfers). *Early decision deadline:* 11/1. *Notification:* 4/1 (freshmen), 5/15 (transfers), 12/15 (early decision).

Freshman Application Contact Office of Admission, Rice University, Office of Admission, PO Box 1892, MS 17, Houston, TX 77251-1892. *Phone:* 713-348-RICE. *Toll-free phone:* 800-527-OWLS. *E-mail:* admi@rice.edu. *Website:* http://www.rice.edu/.

Rio Grande Bible Institute

Edinburg, Texas

Director of Admissions David Loyola, Director of Admissions, Rio Grande Bible Institute, 4300 S US Hwy 281, Edinburg, TX 78539. *Phone:* 956-380-8100. *Fax:* 956-380-8256. *E-mail:* admisiones@riogrande.edu. *Website:* http://www.riogrande.edu/.

St. Edward's University

Austin, Texas

- **Independent Roman Catholic** comprehensive, founded 1885
- **Urban** 160-acre campus
- **Endowment** $54.2 million
- **Coed** 4,238 undergraduate students, 81% full-time, 61% women, 39% men
- **Moderately difficult** entrance level, 63% of applicants were admitted

Undergraduates 3,449 full-time, 789 part-time. Students come from 45 states and territories; 43 other countries; 11% are from out of state; 4% Black or African American, non-Hispanic/Latino; 35% Hispanic/Latino; 2% Asian, non-Hispanic/Latino; 0.2% Native Hawaiian or other Pacific Islander, non-Hispanic/Latino; 0.5% American Indian or Alaska Native, non-Hispanic/Latino; 3% Two or more races, non-Hispanic/Latino; 2% Race/ethnicity unknown; 7% international; 5% transferred in; 38% live on campus. *Retention:* 79% of full-time freshmen returned.

Freshmen *Admission:* 4,209 applied, 2,645 admitted, 788 enrolled. *Test scores:* SAT critical reading scores over 500: 82%; SAT math scores over 500: 84%; SAT writing scores over 500: 75%; ACT scores over 18: 100%; SAT critical reading scores over 600: 37%; SAT math scores over 600: 32%; SAT writing scores over 600: 29%; ACT scores over 24: 58%; SAT critical reading scores over 700: 6%; SAT math scores over 700: 2%; SAT writing scores over 700: 4%; ACT scores over 30: 9%.

Faculty *Total:* 532, 40% full-time, 64% with terminal degrees. *Student/faculty ratio:* 13:1.

Academics *Calendar:* semesters. *Degrees:* bachelor's, master's, and postbachelor's certificates. *Special study options:* academic remediation for entering students, adult/continuing education programs, advanced placement credit, double majors, honors programs, internships, part-time degree program, services for LD students, study abroad, summer session for credit. *ROTC:* Army (c), Air Force (c).

Computers on Campus 790 computers/terminals and 7,200 ports are available on campus for general student use. Students can access the following: computer help desk, free student e-mail accounts, online (class) grades, online (class) registration, online (class) schedules, online library, ability to change address and biographical data, look at transcripts, pull up statements of account, grades, online progress reports and degree audit, campus job postings, student timesheets, financial aid information. Campuswide network is available. 100% of college-owned or -operated housing units are wired for high-speed Internet access. Wireless service is available via classrooms, computer centers, computer labs, dorm rooms, learning centers, libraries, student centers.

Student Life *Housing:* on-campus residence required for freshman year. *Options:* coed, women-only, disabled students. Campus housing is university owned. Freshman campus housing is guaranteed. *Activities and organizations:* drama/theater group, student-run newspaper, radio and television station, choral group, Academy of Science, Promoting Respect, Inclusion, Diversity and Empowerment (PRIDE), Psychological Society, Outdoor Adventure Club, Students for Sustainability. *Campus security:* 24-hour emergency response devices and patrols, late-night transport/escort service, controlled dormitory access, self-defense education, informal discussions, pamphlets, posters, alcohol awareness meetings, lighted pathways and sidewalks. *Student services:* health clinic, personal/psychological counseling.

Athletics Member NCAA. All Division II. *Intercollegiate sports:* baseball M(s), basketball M(s)/W(s), golf M(s)/W(s), soccer M(s)/W(s), softball W(s), tennis M(s)/W(s), volleyball W(s). *Intramural sports:* basketball M(c)/W, crew M(c)/W(c), cross-country running M(c)/W(c), golf M/W, lacrosse M(c)/W(c), racquetball M/W, rugby M(c), soccer M(c)/W(c), swimming and diving M(c)/W(c), tennis M(c)/W(c), track and field M(c)/W(c), ultimate Frisbee M(c)/W(c), volleyball M(c)/W.

Standardized Tests *Required:* SAT or ACT (for admission).

Costs (2013–14) *Comprehensive fee:* $44,674 includes full-time tuition ($33,320), mandatory fees ($400), and room and board ($10,954). Full-time tuition and fees vary according to course load and degree level. Part-time tuition: $1112 per credit hour. Part-time tuition and fees vary according to course load and degree level. *Required fees:* $50 per term part-time. *College room only:* $6024. Room and board charges vary according to board plan and housing facility. *Payment plans:* installment, deferred payment. *Waivers:* employees or children of employees.

Financial Aid Of all full-time matriculated undergraduates who enrolled in 2012, 2,530 applied for aid, 2,132 were judged to have need, 200 had their need fully met. 240 Federal Work-Study jobs (averaging $1905). 16 state and other part-time jobs (averaging $2063). In 2012, 173 non-need-based awards were made. *Average percent of need met:* 63%. *Average financial aid package:* $23,013. *Average need-based loan:* $4590. *Average need-based gift aid:* $13,936. *Average non-need-based aid:* $10,003. *Average indebtedness upon graduation:* $34,314. *Financial aid deadline:* 5/1.

Applying *Options:* electronic application, deferred entrance. *Application fee:* $50. *Required:* essay or personal statement, high school transcript, 1 letter of recommendation. *Recommended:* interview. *Application deadlines:* 5/1 (freshmen), 5/1 (out-of-state freshmen), 7/1 (transfers). *Notification:* continuous (freshmen), continuous (out-of-state freshmen), continuous (transfers).

Freshman Application Contact Ms. Sol Cordova, Receptionist, St. Edward's University, 3001 South Congress Avenue, Austin, TX 78704. *Phone:* 512-448-8580. *Toll-free phone:* 800-555-0164. *Fax:* 512-464-8877. *E-mail:* seu.admit@stedwards.edu.
Website: http://www.gotostedwards.com/.

St. Mary's University

San Antonio, Texas

- **Independent Roman Catholic** comprehensive, founded 1852
- **Urban** 135-acre campus with easy access to San Antonio
- **Endowment** $134.4 million
- **Coed** 2,459 undergraduate students, 94% full-time, 58% women, 42% men
- **Moderately difficult** entrance level, 55% of applicants were admitted

Undergraduates 2,323 full-time, 136 part-time. Students come from 32 states and territories; 12 other countries; 8% are from out of state; 3% Black or African American, non-Hispanic/Latino; 73% Hispanic/Latino; 3% Asian, non-Hispanic/Latino; 0.2% Native Hawaiian or other Pacific Islander, non-Hispanic/Latino; 0.3% American Indian or Alaska Native, non-Hispanic/Latino; 0.1% Two or more races, non-Hispanic/Latino; 2% Race/ethnicity unknown; 3% international; 5% transferred in; 59% live on campus. *Retention:* 76% of full-time freshmen returned.

Freshmen *Admission:* 5,581 applied, 3,062 admitted, 584 enrolled. *Average high school GPA:* 3.45. *Test scores:* SAT critical reading scores over 500: 59%; SAT math scores over 500: 70%; SAT writing scores over 500: 50%; ACT scores over 18: 96%; SAT critical reading scores over 600: 14%; SAT math scores over 600: 18%; SAT writing scores over 600: 11%; ACT scores over 24: 38%; SAT critical reading scores over 700: 2%; SAT math scores over 700: 3%; SAT writing scores over 700: 1%; ACT scores over 30: 2%.

Faculty *Total:* 393, 52% full-time, 78% with terminal degrees. *Student/faculty ratio:* 13:1.

Academics *Calendar:* semesters. *Degrees:* bachelor's, master's, and doctoral. *Special study options:* academic remediation for entering students, adult/continuing education programs, advanced placement credit, cooperative education, distance learning, double majors, English as a second language, honors programs, independent study, internships, off-campus study, part-time degree program, services for LD students, study abroad, summer session for credit. *ROTC:* Army (b), Air Force (c).

Computers on Campus 200 computers/terminals and 125 ports are available on campus for general student use. Students can access the following: campus intranet, computer help desk, free student e-mail accounts, online (class) grades, online (class) registration, online (class) schedules. Campuswide network is available. 100% of college-owned or -operated housing units are wired for high-speed Internet access. Wireless service is available via entire campus.

Student Life *Housing:* on-campus residence required for freshman year. *Options:* coed, disabled students. Campus housing is university owned. Freshman applicants given priority for college housing. *Activities and organizations:* drama/theater group, student-run newspaper, choral group, Beta Beta Beta Biology Society, St. Mary's University Society of Honor Scholars, American Chemical Society of Students, Mexican Student Organization, Alpha Phi Omega, national fraternities, national sororities. *Campus security:* 24-hour emergency response devices and patrols, late-night transport/escort service, controlled dormitory access. *Student services:* health clinic, personal/psychological counseling.

Athletics Member NCAA. All Division II. *Intercollegiate sports:* baseball M(s), basketball M(s)/W(s), cheerleading M/W, cross-country running W, golf M(s)/W, rugby M(c), soccer M(s)/W(s), softball W, tennis M(s)/W(s), volleyball W(s). *Intramural sports:* basketball M/W, football M/W, racquetball M/W, soccer M/W, softball M/W, table tennis M/W, tennis M/W, volleyball M/W.

Standardized Tests *Required:* SAT or ACT (for admission).

Costs (2013–14) *Comprehensive fee:* $33,390 includes full-time tuition ($24,520) and room and board ($8870). Full-time tuition and fees vary according to course load. Part-time tuition and fees vary according to course load. *College room only:* $5210. Room and board charges vary according to board plan and housing facility. *Payment plan:* installment. *Waivers:* employees or children of employees.

Financial Aid Of all full-time matriculated undergraduates who enrolled in 2009, 1,747 applied for aid, 1,633 were judged to have need, 406 had their need fully met. In 2009, 509 non-need-based awards were made. *Average percent of need met:* 76%. *Average financial aid package:* $20,138. *Average need-based loan:* $6124. *Average need-based gift aid:* $14,206. *Average non-need-based aid:* $7292. *Average indebtedness upon graduation:* $22,592.

Applying *Options:* electronic application, deferred entrance. *Application fee:* $30. *Required:* high school transcript. *Recommended:* essay or personal statement, minimum 2.0 GPA, interview. *Application deadlines:* rolling (freshmen), rolling (transfers). *Notification:* continuous (freshmen), continuous (transfers).

Freshman Application Contact Mr. Nelson Delgado, Assistant Director of Undergraduate Admission, St. Mary's University, One Camino Santa Maria, Box #3, San Antonio, TX 78228. *Phone:* 210-436-3126. *Toll-free phone:* 800-FOR-STMU. *Fax:* 210-431-6742. *E-mail:* uadm@stmarytx.edu.
Website: http://www.stmarytx.edu/.

Sam Houston State University

Huntsville, Texas

- **State-supported** university, founded 1879, part of Texas State University System
- **Small-town** 1256-acre campus with easy access to Houston
- **Endowment** $49.7 million
- **Coed** 15,611 undergraduate students, 83% full-time, 58% women, 42% men
- **Moderately difficult** entrance level, 65% of applicants were admitted

Undergraduates 12,968 full-time, 2,643 part-time. Students come from 47 states and territories; 58 other countries; 1% are from out of state; 17% Black or African American, non-Hispanic/Latino; 17% Hispanic/Latino; 1% Asian, non-Hispanic/Latino; 0.1% Native Hawaiian or other Pacific Islander, non-Hispanic/Latino; 0.4% American Indian or Alaska Native, non-Hispanic/Latino; 2% Two or more races, non-Hispanic/Latino; 2% Race/ethnicity unknown; 1% international; 15% transferred in; 25% live on campus. *Retention:* 71% of full-time freshmen returned.

Freshmen *Admission:* 9,315 applied, 6,054 admitted, 2,415 enrolled. *Test scores:* SAT critical reading scores over 500: 47%; SAT math scores over 500: 60%; ACT scores over 18: 92%; SAT critical reading scores over 600: 9%; SAT math scores over 600: 12%; ACT scores over 24: 19%; SAT critical reading scores over 700: 1%; ACT scores over 30: 1%.

Faculty *Total:* 797, 78% full-time, 70% with terminal degrees. *Student/faculty ratio:* 25:1.

Academics *Calendar:* semesters. *Degrees:* bachelor's, master's, and doctoral. *Special study options:* academic remediation for entering students, accelerated degree program, distance learning, double majors, English as a second language, external degree program, honors programs, independent study, internships, off-campus study, part-time degree program, services for LD students, study abroad, summer session for credit. *ROTC:* Army (b).

Computers on Campus 1,600 computers/terminals are available on campus for general student use. Students can access the following: campus intranet, computer help desk, free student e-mail accounts, online (class) grades, online (class) registration, online (class) schedules. Campuswide network is available. 100% of college-owned or -operated housing units are wired for high-speed Internet access. Wireless service is available via entire campus.

Student Life *Housing:* on-campus residence required for freshman year. *Options:* coed, men-only, women-only, disabled students. Campus housing is university owned and is provided by a third party. Freshman campus housing is guaranteed. *Activities and organizations:* drama/theater group, student-run newspaper, radio and television station, choral group, marching band, Chi Alpha Christian Fellowship, Non-Traditional Student Organization, Sigma Alpha Pi Leadership Society, Baptist Student Ministry, Bearkats for Life, national fraternities, national sororities. *Campus security:* 24-hour emergency response devices and patrols, student patrols, late-night transport/escort service, controlled dormitory access. *Student services:* health clinic, personal/psychological counseling, legal services.

Athletics Member NCAA. All Division I except football (Division I-AA). *Intercollegiate sports:* baseball M(s), basketball M(s)/W(s), bowling W(s), cross-country running M(s)/W(s), golf M(s)/W(s), lacrosse M(c)/W(c), soccer W(s), softball W(s), tennis W(s), track and field M(s)/W(s), ultimate Frisbee M(c)/W(c), volleyball W(s). *Intramural sports:* basketball M/W, football M, lacrosse M, racquetball M/W, rugby M/W, soccer M/W, softball M/W, tennis M/W, volleyball M/W.

Standardized Tests *Required:* SAT or ACT (for admission).

Costs (2012–13) *Tuition:* state resident $5610 full-time; nonresident $16,140 full-time. Full-time tuition and fees vary according to course level, course load, location, and program. Part-time tuition and fees vary according to course level, course load, location, and program. *Required fees:* $2510 full-time. *Room and board:* $8092. Room and board charges vary according to board plan and housing facility. *Payment plan:* installment. *Waivers:* employees or children of employees.

Financial Aid Of all full-time matriculated undergraduates who enrolled in 2008, 8,023 applied for aid, 3,703 were judged to have need, 4 had their need fully met. 291 Federal Work-Study jobs (averaging $1563). 90 state and other part-time jobs (averaging $1206). In 2008, 708 non-need-based awards were made. *Average percent of need met:* 31%. *Average financial aid package:* $4340. *Average need-based loan:* $189. *Average need-based gift aid:* $906. *Average non-need-based aid:* $322. *Average indebtedness upon graduation:* $6196.

Applying *Options:* electronic application, early admission. *Application fee:* $45. *Required:* high school transcript. *Application deadlines:* 8/1 (freshmen), 8/1 (out-of-state freshmen), 8/1 (transfers). *Notification:* continuous (freshmen), continuous (out-of-state freshmen), continuous (transfers).

Freshman Application Contact Mr. Trevor B. Thorn, Director of Admissions and Recruitment, Sam Houston State University, PO Box 2418, Huntsville, TX 77341. *Phone:* 936-294-1828. *Toll-free phone:* 866-232-7528 Ext. 1828. *Fax:* 936-294-3758. *E-mail:* admissions@shsu.edu.
Website: http://www.shsu.edu/.

Schreiner University

Kerrville, Texas

- **Independent Presbyterian** comprehensive, founded 1923
- **Small-town** 175-acre campus with easy access to San Antonio, Austin
- **Endowment** $51.2 million
- **Coed** 1,068 undergraduate students, 95% full-time, 56% women, 44% men
- **Moderately difficult** entrance level, 63% of applicants were admitted

Undergraduates 1,015 full-time, 53 part-time. 3% are from out of state; 4% Black or African American, non-Hispanic/Latino; 28% Hispanic/Latino; 0.9% Asian, non-Hispanic/Latino; 0.1% Native Hawaiian or other Pacific Islander, non-Hispanic/Latino; 0.4% American Indian or Alaska Native, non-Hispanic/Latino; 3% Two or more races, non-Hispanic/Latino; 0.5% international; 7% transferred in; 66% live on campus. *Retention:* 71% of full-time freshmen returned.

Freshmen *Admission:* 1,153 applied, 731 admitted, 272 enrolled. *Average high school GPA:* 3.52. *Test scores:* SAT critical reading scores over 500: 46%; SAT math scores over 500: 55%; SAT writing scores over 500: 27%; SAT critical reading scores over 600: 11%; SAT math scores over 600: 14%; SAT writing scores over 600: 5%; SAT critical reading scores over 700: 1%; SAT math scores over 700: 1%.

Faculty *Total:* 119, 47% full-time, 46% with terminal degrees. *Student/faculty ratio:* 14:1.

Academics *Calendar:* semesters. *Degrees:* certificates, associate, bachelor's, and master's. *Special study options:* academic remediation for entering students, accelerated degree program, advanced placement credit, cooperative education, double majors, honors programs, independent study, internships, part-time degree program, services for LD students, student-designed majors, study abroad, summer session for credit. *Unusual degree programs:* 3-2 engineering with University of Texas at Austin, Texas A&M University.

Computers on Campus 120 computers/terminals are available on campus for general student use. Students can access the following: computer help desk, free student e-mail accounts, online (class) grades, online (class) registration, online (class) schedules. Campuswide network is available. 100% of college-owned or -operated housing units are wired for high-speed Internet access. Wireless service is available via classrooms, computer centers, computer labs, dorm rooms, learning centers, libraries, student centers.

Student Life *Housing:* on-campus residence required through junior year. *Options:* coed, disabled students. Campus housing is university owned. Freshman campus housing is guaranteed. *Activities and organizations:* drama/theater group, student-run newspaper, choral group, Student Senate, Greek Life, Campus Ministry, honor societies, Hall Councils, national fraternities, national

sororities. *Campus security:* 24-hour emergency response devices and patrols, late-night transport/escort service. *Student services:* health clinic, personal/psychological counseling.

Athletics Member NCAA. All Division III. *Intercollegiate sports:* baseball M, basketball M/W, cross-country running M/W, golf M/W, soccer M/W, softball W, tennis M/W, volleyball W. *Intramural sports:* cheerleading W.

Standardized Tests *Required:* SAT or ACT (for admission).

Costs (2012–13) *One-time required fee:* $25. *Comprehensive fee:* $31,602 includes full-time tuition ($20,940), mandatory fees ($600), and room and board ($10,062). Part-time tuition: $894 per credit hour. *Required fees:* $300 per term part-time. *Room and board:* Room and board charges vary according to board plan and housing facility. *Payment plan:* installment. *Waivers:* employees or children of employees.

Financial Aid Of all full-time matriculated undergraduates who enrolled in 2011, 874 applied for aid, 782 were judged to have need, 82 had their need fully met. In 2011, 79 non-need-based awards were made. *Average percent of need met:* 69%. *Average financial aid package:* $16,844. *Average need-based loan:* $3762. *Average need-based gift aid:* $13,600. *Average non-need-based aid:* $7332. *Average indebtedness upon graduation:* $20,900.

Applying *Options:* electronic application, deferred entrance. *Application fee:* $25. *Required:* essay or personal statement, high school transcript. *Recommended:* interview. *Application deadlines:* 5/1 (freshmen), 5/1 (transfers). *Notification:* continuous (freshmen), continuous (transfers).

Freshman Application Contact Dean of Admission and Financial Aid, Schreiner University, 2100 Memorial Boulevard, Kerrville, TX 78028. *Phone:* 830-792-7217. *Toll-free phone:* 800-343-4919. *E-mail:* admissions@schreiner.edu.
Website: http://www.schreiner.edu/.

Southern Methodist University

Dallas, Texas

- **Independent** university, founded 1911, affiliated with United Methodist Church
- **Suburban** 235-acre campus
- **Endowment** $1.2 billion
- **Coed** 6,249 undergraduate students, 96% full-time, 51% women, 49% men
- **Moderately difficult** entrance level, 54% of applicants were admitted

Undergraduates 5,999 full-time, 250 part-time. Students come from 50 states and territories; 66 other countries; 48% are from out of state; 6% Black or African American, non-Hispanic/Latino; 12% Hispanic/Latino; 7% Asian, non-Hispanic/Latino; 0.2% Native Hawaiian or other Pacific Islander, non-Hispanic/Latino; 0.4% American Indian or Alaska Native, non-Hispanic/Latino; 2% Two or more races, non-Hispanic/Latino; 0.5% Race/ethnicity unknown; 7% international; 5% transferred in; 32% live on campus. *Retention:* 91% of full-time freshmen returned.

Freshmen *Admission:* 11,217 applied, 6,031 admitted, 1,426 enrolled. *Average high school GPA:* 3.6. *Test scores:* SAT critical reading scores over 500: 96%; SAT math scores over 500: 98%; SAT writing scores over 500: 94%; ACT scores over 18: 99%; SAT critical reading scores over 600: 70%; SAT math scores over 600: 80%; SAT writing scores over 600: 66%; ACT scores over 24: 95%; SAT critical reading scores over 700: 18%; SAT math scores over 700: 24%; SAT writing scores over 700: 19%; ACT scores over 30: 39%.

Faculty *Total:* 1,155, 63% full-time, 71% with terminal degrees. *Student/faculty ratio:* 11:1.

Academics *Calendar:* semesters. *Degrees:* bachelor's, master's, doctoral, and postbachelor's certificates. *Special study options:* academic remediation for entering students, accelerated degree program, adult/continuing education programs, advanced placement credit, cooperative education, distance learning, double majors, English as a second language, honors programs, independent study, internships, part-time degree program, services for LD students, student-designed majors, study abroad, summer session for credit. *ROTC:* Army (b), Air Force (c).

Computers on Campus 758 computers/terminals are available on campus for general student use. Students can access the following: campus intranet, computer help desk, free student e-mail accounts, online (class) grades, online (class) registration, online (class) schedules, online billing/payment processing. Campuswide network is available. Wireless service is available via classrooms, computer centers, computer labs, dorm rooms, learning centers, libraries, student centers.

Student Life *Housing:* on-campus residence required for freshman year. *Options:* coed, disabled students. Campus housing is university owned. Freshman campus housing is guaranteed. *Activities and organizations:* drama/theater group, student-run newspaper, radio and television station, choral group, marching band, Program Council, Student Senate, Student Foundation, Residence Hall Association, SPARC (Students Promoting Awareness, Responsibility, and Citizenship), national fraternities, national sororities. *Campus security:* 24-hour emergency response devices and patrols, late-night transport/escort service, controlled dormitory access. *Student services:* health clinic, personal/psychological counseling, women's center.

Athletics Member NCAA. All Division I except football (Division I-A). *Intercollegiate sports:* baseball M(c), basketball M(s)/W(s), cheerleading M(s)(c)/W(s)(c), crew W(s), cross-country running W(s), equestrian sports W(s), fencing M(c)/W(c), golf M(s)/W(s), ice hockey M(c), lacrosse M(c), rugby M(c)/W(c), soccer M(s)/W(s), swimming and diving M(s)/W(s), tennis M(s)/W(s), track and field W, volleyball W(s), wrestling M(c). *Intramural sports:* basketball M/W, bowling M/W, football M, golf M/W, racquetball M/W, rock climbing M(c)/W(c), soccer M/W, softball M/W, swimming and diving M/W, table tennis M(c)/W(c), tennis M/W, ultimate Frisbee M/W, volleyball M/W, water polo M/W, weight lifting M(c)/W(c).

Standardized Tests *Required:* SAT or ACT (for admission). *Required for some:* SAT Subject Tests (for admission).

Costs (2013–14) *Comprehensive fee:* $57,755 includes full-time tuition ($38,870), mandatory fees ($4930), and room and board ($13,955). Part-time tuition: $1624 per credit hour. Part-time tuition and fees vary according to course load. *Room and board:* Room and board charges vary according to board plan and housing facility. *Payment plans:* tuition prepayment, installment. *Waivers:* employees or children of employees.

Financial Aid Of all full-time matriculated undergraduates who enrolled in 2011, 2,841 applied for aid, 2,426 were judged to have need, 792 had their need fully met. In 2011, 1853 non-need-based awards were made. *Average percent of need met:* 87%. *Average financial aid package:* $35,182. *Average need-based loan:* $4382. *Average need-based gift aid:* $18,730. *Average non-need-based aid:* $18,300. *Average indebtedness upon graduation:* $30,987.

Applying *Options:* electronic application, early action, deferred entrance. *Application fee:* $60. *Required:* high school transcript, minimum 2.0 GPA, 1 letter of recommendation, statement of good standing from prior institution(s). *Recommended:* essay or personal statement, minimum 2.7 GPA. *Application deadlines:* 3/15 (freshmen), 4/1 (transfers), 11/1 (early action). *Notification:* continuous (freshmen), 12/31 (early action).

Freshman Application Contact Mr. Wes Waggoner, Dean of Undergraduate Admission and Executive Director of Enrollment Services, Southern Methodist University, PO Box 750181, Dallas, TX 75275-0181. *Phone:* 214-768-3417. *Toll-free phone:* 800-323-0672. *Fax:* 214-768-1083. *E-mail:* ugadmission@smu.edu.

Website: http://www.smu.edu/.

South Texas College

McAllen, Texas

Freshman Application Contact Mr. Matthew Hebbard, Director of Enrollment Services and Registrar, South Texas College, 3201 West Pecan, McAllen, TX 78501. *Phone:* 956-872-2147. *Toll-free phone:* 800-742-7822. *E-mail:* mshebbar@southtexascollege.edu.

Website: http://www.southtexascollege.edu/.

South University

Austin, Texas

- **Proprietary** comprehensive
- **Coed**

Academics *Degrees:* associate, bachelor's, and master's.

Freshman Application Contact Director of Admissions, South University, 810 Hesters Crossing Road, Suite 220, Austin, TX 78681. *Phone:* 512-516-8800. *Fax:* 512-516-8680.

Website: http://www.southuniversity.edu/austin.aspx.

Southwestern Adventist University

Keene, Texas

- **Independent Seventh-day Adventist** comprehensive, founded 1894
- **Small-town** 150-acre campus with easy access to Dallas-Fort Worth
- **Endowment** $7.2 million
- **Coed** 781 undergraduate students, 80% full-time, 60% women, 40% men
- **Minimally difficult** entrance level, 56% of applicants were admitted

Undergraduates 625 full-time, 156 part-time. Students come from 31 states and territories; 42 other countries; 28% are from out of state; 14% Black or African American, non-Hispanic/Latino; 31% Hispanic/Latino; 3% Asian, non-Hispanic/Latino; 0.6% Native Hawaiian or other Pacific Islander, non-Hispanic/Latino; 3% Two or more races, non-Hispanic/Latino; 5% Race/ethnicity unknown; 19% international; 11% transferred in; 40% live on campus. *Retention:* 61% of full-time freshmen returned.

Freshmen *Admission:* 1,218 applied, 684 admitted, 120 enrolled. *Average high school GPA:* 3.21. *Test scores:* SAT critical reading scores over 500: 33%; SAT math scores over 500: 36%; ACT scores over 18: 55%; SAT critical reading scores over 600: 4%; SAT math scores over 600: 4%; ACT scores over 24: 20%; SAT critical reading scores over 700: 1%; ACT scores over 30: 2%.

Faculty *Total:* 78, 67% full-time, 53% with terminal degrees. *Student/faculty ratio:* 11:1.

Academics *Calendar:* semesters. *Degrees:* associate, bachelor's, and master's. *Special study options:* academic remediation for entering students, accelerated degree program, adult/continuing education programs, advanced placement credit, double majors, English as a second language, external degree program, honors programs, independent study, internships, off-campus study, part-time degree program, services for LD students, student-designed majors, study abroad, summer session for credit.

Computers on Campus 100 computers/terminals are available on campus for general student use. Students can access the following: campus intranet, computer help desk, free student e-mail accounts, online (class) grades, online (class) registration, online (class) schedules. Campuswide network is available. 100% of college-owned or -operated housing units are wired for high-speed Internet access. Wireless service is available via entire campus.

Student Life *Housing:* on-campus residence required through sophomore year. *Options:* men-only, women-only, cooperative. Campus housing is university owned. Freshman campus housing is guaranteed. *Activities and organizations:* drama/theater group, student-run newspaper, radio and television station, choral group, Student Association, Students in Free Enterprise (SIFE), Education/Psychology Club, Theology Club, Nursing Club. *Campus security:* 24-hour emergency response devices, student patrols. *Student services:* health clinic, personal/psychological counseling.

Athletics *Intramural sports:* basketball M(c)/W(c), football M/W, racquetball M/W, soccer M(c)/W(c), softball M/W, table tennis M/W, tennis M/W, volleyball M/W(c).

Standardized Tests *Required:* SAT or ACT (for admission).

Costs (2012–13) *Comprehensive fee:* $24,432 includes full-time tuition ($17,400) and room and board ($7032). Full-time tuition and fees vary according to course load and program. Part-time tuition: $725 per credit. Part-time tuition and fees vary according to course load and program. *College room only:* $3420. Room and board charges vary according to board plan. *Payment plans:* installment, deferred payment. *Waivers:* employees or children of employees.

Applying *Options:* electronic application, deferred entrance. *Application fee:* $25. *Required:* high school transcript, minimum 2.0 GPA. *Required for some:* essay or personal statement, 1 letter of recommendation, interview. *Application deadlines:* 8/31 (freshmen), 8/31 (transfers). *Notification:* 9/1 (freshmen), 9/1 (transfers).

Freshman Application Contact Ms. Rahneeka Hazelton, Associate Director of Admissions and Records, Southwestern Adventist University, 100 West Hillcrest, Keene, TX 76059. *Phone:* 817-202-6733. *Toll-free phone:* 800-433-2240. *E-mail:* rahneeka@swau.edu.

Website: http://www.swau.edu/.

Southwestern Assemblies of God University

Waxahachie, Texas

- **Independent** comprehensive, founded 1927, affiliated with Assemblies of God
- **Small-town** 70-acre campus with easy access to Dallas-Fort Worth
- **Endowment** $4.0 million
- **Coed**
- **Noncompetitive** entrance level

Faculty *Student/faculty ratio:* 16:1.

Academics *Calendar:* semesters. *Degrees:* associate, bachelor's, and master's.

Student Life *Campus security:* 24-hour patrols, late-night transport/escort service, controlled dormitory access, 2 dorms electronic access; 4 dorms key access to rooms, camera surveillance, 24 hour dispatch monitored fire alarm systems (offsite).

Athletics Member NAIA, NCCAA.

Standardized Tests *Required:* SAT or ACT (for admission).

Costs (2012–13) *Comprehensive fee:* $23,414 includes full-time tuition ($15,750), mandatory fees ($880), and room and board ($6784). Part-time tuition: $525 per credit. *College room only:* $3590. Room and board charges vary according to housing facility.

Financial Aid *Of all full-time matriculated undergraduates who enrolled in 2000,* 1,116 applied for aid, 1,002 were judged to have need, 110 had their need fully met. 178 Federal Work-Study jobs, 7 state and other part-time jobs (averaging $890). *In 2000,* 316 non-need-based awards were made. *Average percent of need met:* 64. *Average financial aid package:* $6728. *Average need-based loan:* $3177. *Average need-based gift aid:* $3511. *Average indebtedness upon graduation:* $13,938. *Financial aid deadline:* 7/1.

Applying *Options:* early admission, deferred entrance. *Application fee:* $35. *Required:* essay or personal statement, high school transcript, minimum 2.0 GPA, 1 letter of recommendation, medical history, evidence of approved Christian character.

Freshman Application Contact Mr. Bryan Brooks, Assistant Dean of Admissions, Southwestern Assemblies of God University, 1200 Sycamore Street, Waxahachie, TX 75165. *Phone:* 972-825-4821. *Toll-free phone:* 888-937-7248. *Fax:* 972-923-8131. *E-mail:* bbrooks@sagu.edu. *Website:* http://www.sagu.edu/.

Southwestern Christian College

Terrell, Texas

Freshman Application Contact Admissions Department, Southwestern Christian College, Box 10, 200 Bowser Street, Terrell, TX 75160. *Phone:* 214-524-3341.
Website: http://www.swcc.edu/.

Southwestern University

Georgetown, Texas

- **Independent Methodist** 4-year, founded 1840
- **Suburban** 700-acre campus with easy access to Austin
- **Endowment** $250.6 million
- **Coed** 1,394 undergraduate students, 99% full-time, 61% women, 39% men
- **Very difficult** entrance level, 61% of applicants were admitted

Undergraduates 1,376 full-time, 18 part-time. Students come from 33 states and territories; 6 other countries; 10% are from out of state; 3% Black or African American, non-Hispanic/Latino; 18% Hispanic/Latino; 4% Asian, non-Hispanic/Latino; 0.2% Native Hawaiian or other Pacific Islander, non-Hispanic/Latino; 0.8% American Indian or Alaska Native, non-Hispanic/Latino; 2% Two or more races, non-Hispanic/Latino; 0.6% Race/ethnicity unknown; 0.6% international; 3% transferred in; 78% live on campus. *Retention:* 86% of full-time freshmen returned.

Freshmen *Admission:* 2,795 applied, 1,692 admitted, 357 enrolled. *Test scores:* SAT critical reading scores over 500: 87%; SAT math scores over 500: 93%; ACT scores over 18: 100%; SAT critical reading scores over 600: 52%; SAT math scores over 600: 56%; ACT scores over 24: 81%; SAT critical reading scores over 700: 16%; SAT math scores over 700: 9%; ACT scores over 30: 24%.

Faculty *Total:* 165, 71% full-time, 87% with terminal degrees. *Student/faculty ratio:* 10:1.

Academics *Calendar:* semesters. *Degree:* bachelor's. *Special study options:* advanced placement credit, double majors, honors programs, independent study, internships, off-campus study, services for LD students, student-designed majors, study abroad, summer session for credit. *Unusual degree programs:* 3-2 engineering with Not limited to specific universities. however do have a contract with Washington University in St. Louis.

Computers on Campus 410 computers/terminals are available on campus for general student use. Students can access the following: campus intranet, computer help desk, free student e-mail accounts, online (class) grades, online (class) registration, online (class) schedules, transcripts. Campuswide network is available. 100% of college-owned or -operated housing units are wired for high-speed Internet access. Wireless service is available via entire campus.

Student Life *Housing:* on-campus residence required through sophomore year. *Options:* coed, men-only, women-only, disabled students. Campus housing is university owned. Freshman campus housing is guaranteed. *Activities and organizations:* drama/theater group, student-run newspaper, radio station, choral group, Student Peace Alliance (SPA), Students for Environmental Activism & Knowledge (SEAK), Alpha Phi Omega, Men's IFC, Women's Panhellenic, national fraternities, national sororities. *Campus security:* 24-hour emergency response devices and patrols, student patrols, late-night transport/escort service, controlled dormitory access. *Student services:* health clinic, personal/psychological counseling.

Athletics Member NCAA. All Division III. *Intercollegiate sports:* baseball M, basketball M/W, cross-country running M/W, golf M/W, lacrosse M, soccer M/W, softball W, swimming and diving M/W, tennis M/W, volleyball W. *Intramural sports:* basketball M/W, cheerleading M/W, fencing M/W, football M/W, racquetball M/W, rock climbing M/W, soccer M/W, table tennis M/W, tennis M/W, ultimate Frisbee M/W, volleyball M/W.

Standardized Tests *Required:* SAT or ACT (for admission).

Costs (2013–14) *Comprehensive fee:* $46,250 includes full-time tuition ($35,240) and room and board ($11,010). Part-time tuition: $1470 per credit hour. Part-time tuition and fees vary according to course load. *College room only:* $5650. Room and board charges vary according to board plan and housing facility. *Payment plan:* installment. *Waivers:* employees or children of employees.

Financial Aid Of all full-time matriculated undergraduates who enrolled in 2012, 971 applied for aid, 858 were judged to have need, 279 had their need fully met. In 2012, 461 non-need-based awards were made. *Average percent of need met:* 88%. *Average financial aid package:* $30,060. *Average need-based loan:* $4995. *Average need-based gift aid:* $24,309. *Average non-need-based aid:* $16,414. *Average indebtedness upon graduation:* $36,299. *Financial aid deadline:* 3/1.

Applying *Options:* electronic application, early admission, early action, deferred entrance. *Required:* essay or personal statement, high school transcript, 1 letter of recommendation, Counselor recommendation required; teacher and parent recommendation optional. *Required for some:* interview. *Recommended:* interview. *Application deadlines:* 2/1 (freshmen), rolling (out-of-state freshmen), 4/1 (transfers), 11/15 (early action). *Notification:* 4/1 (freshmen), 4/1 (out-of-state freshmen), 8/1 (transfers), 2/15 (early action).

Freshman Application Contact Ms. Christine Bowman, Director of Admissions, Southwestern University, 1001 East University Avenue, Georgetown, TX 78626. *Phone:* 512-863-1200. *Toll-free phone:* 800-252-3166. *Fax:* 512-863-9601. *E-mail:* admission@southwestern.edu. *Website:* http://www.southwestern.edu/.

Stephen F. Austin State University

Nacogdoches, Texas

- **State-supported** comprehensive, founded 1923
- **Small-town** 412-acre campus
- **Endowment** $50.2 million
- **Coed** 11,298 undergraduate students, 85% full-time, 63% women, 37% men
- **Moderately difficult** entrance level, 56% of applicants were admitted

Undergraduates 9,632 full-time, 1,666 part-time. Students come from 42 states and territories; 30 other countries; 2% are from out of state; 24% Black or African American, non-Hispanic/Latino; 13% Hispanic/Latino; 0.9% Asian, non-Hispanic/Latino; 0.5% American Indian or Alaska Native, non-Hispanic/Latino; 1% Two or more races, non-Hispanic/Latino; 2% Race/ethnicity unknown; 0.7% international; 9% transferred in; 42% live on campus. *Retention:* 63% of full-time freshmen returned.

Freshmen *Admission:* 11,463 applied, 6,374 admitted, 2,136 enrolled. *Test scores:* SAT critical reading scores over 500: 45%; SAT math scores over 500: 54%; SAT writing scores over 500: 36%; ACT scores over 18: 86%; SAT critical reading scores over 600: 9%; SAT math scores over 600: 14%; SAT writing scores over 600: 6%; ACT scores over 24: 24%; SAT critical reading scores over 700: 1%; SAT math scores over 700: 1%; ACT scores over 30: 2%.
Faculty *Total:* 673, 74% full-time, 63% with terminal degrees. *Student/faculty ratio:* 20:1.
Academics *Calendar:* semesters. *Degrees:* bachelor's, master's, and doctoral. *Special study options:* academic remediation for entering students, accelerated degree program, adult/continuing education programs, advanced placement credit, cooperative education, distance learning, double majors, freshman honors college, honors programs, independent study, internships, off-campus study, part-time degree program, services for LD students, student-designed majors, study abroad, summer session for credit. *ROTC:* Army (b). *Unusual degree programs:* 3-2 professional accountancy.
Computers on Campus 1,000 computers/terminals are available on campus for general student use. Students can access the following: campus intranet, computer help desk, free student e-mail accounts, online (class) grades, online (class) registration, online (class) schedules. Campuswide network is available. 100% of college-owned or -operated housing units are wired for high-speed Internet access. Wireless service is available via classrooms, computer centers, computer labs, dorm rooms, libraries, student centers.
Student Life *Housing:* on-campus residence required through sophomore year. *Options:* coed, men-only, women-only, disabled students. Campus housing is university owned. Freshman campus housing is guaranteed. *Activities and organizations:* drama/theater group, student-run newspaper, radio and television station, choral group, marching band, Residence Hall Association, Baptist Student Ministries, Greek Life, Student Activities Association, Student Government Association, national fraternities, national sororities. *Campus security:* 24-hour emergency response devices and patrols, student patrols, late-night transport/escort service, controlled dormitory access. *Student services:* health clinic, personal/psychological counseling, legal services.
Athletics Member NCAA. All Division I except football (Division I-AA). *Intercollegiate sports:* baseball M(s), basketball M(s)/W(s), bowling W(s), cross-country running M(s)/W(s), equestrian sports W, golf M(s)/W(s), soccer W(s), softball W(s), tennis W(s), track and field M(s)/W(s), volleyball W(s). *Intramural sports:* badminton M/W, baseball M(c), basketball M/W, football M/W, golf M/W, lacrosse M(c)/W(c), racquetball M(c)/W(c), rock climbing M/W, soccer M/W, softball M/W, table tennis M/W, tennis M/W, ultimate Frisbee M/W, volleyball M/W.
Standardized Tests *Required:* SAT or ACT (for admission).
Costs (2012–13) *Tuition:* state resident $5756 full-time, $192 per credit hour part-time; nonresident $16,286 full-time, $543 per credit hour part-time. Full-time tuition and fees vary according to course load, degree level, and location. Part-time tuition and fees vary according to course load, degree level, and location. *Required fees:* $2172 full-time, $154 per credit hour part-time. *Room and board:* $8476. Room and board charges vary according to board plan and housing facility. *Payment plan:* installment. *Waivers:* senior citizens and employees or children of employees.
Financial Aid Of all full-time matriculated undergraduates who enrolled in 2011, 8,278 applied for aid, 7,077 were judged to have need, 622 had their need fully met. In 2011, 726 non-need-based awards were made. *Average percent of need met:* 53%. *Average financial aid package:* $10,584. *Average need-based loan:* $4640. *Average need-based gift aid:* $5955. *Average non-need-based aid:* $2744. *Average indebtedness upon graduation:* $20,858.
Applying *Options:* electronic application. *Application fee:* $35. *Required:* high school transcript. *Application deadlines:* rolling (freshmen), rolling (out-of-state freshmen), rolling (transfers). *Notification:* continuous (freshmen), continuous (out-of-state freshmen), continuous (transfers).
Freshman Application Contact Mr. Kevin Davis, Associate Director of Admissions, Stephen F. Austin State University, PO Box 13051, SFA Station, Nacogdoches, TX 75962. *Phone:* 936-468-2504. *Toll-free phone:* 800-731-2902. *Fax:* 936-468-3849. *E-mail:* admissions@sfasu.edu. *Website:* http://www.sfasu.edu/.

Strayer University—Cedar Hill Campus
Cedar Hill, Texas
Freshman Application Contact Strayer University—Cedar Hill Campus, 610 Uptown Boulevard, Suite 3500, Cedar Hill, TX 75104.
Website: http://www.strayer.edu/campus/cedar-hill.

Strayer University—Irving Campus
Irving, Texas
Freshman Application Contact Strayer University—Irving Campus, 7701 Las Colinas Ridge, Suite 450, Irving, TX 75063.
Website: http://www.strayer.edu/campus/irving.

Strayer University—Katy Campus
Houston, Texas
Freshman Application Contact Strayer University—Katy Campus, 14511 Old Katy Road, Suite 200, Houston, TX 77079.
Website: http://www.strayer.edu/campus/katy.

Strayer University—North Austin Campus
Austin, Texas
Freshman Application Contact Strayer University—North Austin Campus, 8501 North Mo-pac Expressway, Suite 100, Austin, TX 78759.
Website: http://www.strayer.edu/campus/north-austin.

Strayer University—Northwest Houston Campus
Houston, Texas
Freshman Application Contact Strayer University—Northwest Houston Campus, 10940 W. Sam Houston Parkway N., Suite 200, Houston, TX 77064.
Website: http://www.strayer.edu/campus/northwest-houston.

Strayer University—Plano Campus
Plano, Texas
Freshman Application Contact Strayer University—Plano Campus, 2701 North Dallas Parkway, Suite 300, Plano, TX 75093.
Website: http://www.strayer.edu/campus/plano.

Sul Ross State University
Alpine, Texas
- **State-supported** comprehensive, founded 1920, part of Texas State University System
- **Rural** 640-acre campus
- **Coed** 1,236 undergraduate students, 81% full-time, 46% women, 54% men
- **Noncompetitive** entrance level, 97% of applicants were admitted

Undergraduates 1,003 full-time, 233 part-time. 2% are from out of state; 9% Black or African American, non-Hispanic/Latino; 51% Hispanic/Latino; 0.5% Asian, non-Hispanic/Latino; 0.2% Native Hawaiian or other Pacific Islander, non-Hispanic/Latino; 0.7% American Indian or Alaska Native, non-Hispanic/Latino; 0.1% Race/ethnicity unknown; 31% live on campus. *Retention:* 45% of full-time freshmen returned.
Freshmen *Admission:* 1,106 applied, 1,077 admitted, 252 enrolled. *Test scores:* SAT critical reading scores over 500: 12%; SAT math scores over 500: 21%; SAT writing scores over 500: 10%; ACT scores over 18: 52%; SAT critical reading scores over 600: 3%; SAT math scores over 600: 2%; ACT scores over 24: 8%; ACT scores over 30: 1%.
Faculty *Total:* 175, 69% full-time. *Student/faculty ratio:* 14:1.

Academics *Calendar:* semesters. *Degrees:* certificates, associate, bachelor's, master's, and postbachelor's certificates. *Special study options:* part-time degree program.

Computers on Campus Students can access the following: campus intranet, computer help desk, free student e-mail accounts, online (class) grades. Campuswide network is available.

Student Life *Housing:* on-campus residence required through sophomore year. *Options:* coed. Campus housing is university owned. Freshman campus housing is guaranteed. *Campus security:* 24-hour patrols, late-night transport/escort service.

Athletics Member NCAA. All Division III. *Intercollegiate sports:* baseball M, basketball M/W, cheerleading M/W, cross-country running W, football M, softball W, tennis M/W, track and field M/W, volleyball W. *Intramural sports:* basketball M/W, cheerleading M/W, equestrian sports M/W, football M/W, racquetball M/W, soccer M/W, softball M, tennis M/W, ultimate Frisbee M/W, volleyball M/W, water polo M/W, weight lifting M/W.

Standardized Tests *Required:* SAT or ACT (for admission).

Financial Aid Of all full-time matriculated undergraduates who enrolled in 2010, 1,239 applied for aid, 1,239 were judged to have need, 930 had their need fully met. In 2010, 127 non-need-based awards were made. *Average percent of need met:* 73%. *Average financial aid package:* $10,991. *Average need-based loan:* $3276. *Average need-based gift aid:* $5916. *Average non-need-based aid:* $3664. *Financial aid deadline:* 4/1.

Applying *Options:* early decision, deferred entrance. *Application fee:* $25. *Required:* high school transcript. *Recommended:* interview. *Application deadlines:* rolling (freshmen), rolling (transfers). *Notification:* continuous (freshmen), continuous (transfers).

Freshman Application Contact Sul Ross State University, PO Box C—114, Alpine, TX 79832. *Phone:* 432-837-8050. *Toll-free phone:* 888-722-7778. *Website:* http://www.sulross.edu/.

Tarleton State University

Stephenville, Texas

- **State-supported** comprehensive, founded 1899, part of Texas A&M University System
- **Small-town** 175-acre campus with easy access to Fort Worth
- **Endowment** $36.2 million
- **Coed** 8,917 undergraduate students, 79% full-time, 59% women, 41% men
- **Moderately difficult** entrance level, 76% of applicants were admitted

Undergraduates 7,057 full-time, 1,860 part-time. Students come from 40 states and territories; 22 other countries; 2% are from out of state; 6% Black or African American, non-Hispanic/Latino; 13% Hispanic/Latino; 0.9% Asian, non-Hispanic/Latino; 0.1% Native Hawaiian or other Pacific Islander, non-Hispanic/Latino; 0.6% American Indian or Alaska Native, non-Hispanic/Latino; 2% Two or more races, non-Hispanic/Latino; 0.6% Race/ethnicity unknown; 0.5% international; 14% transferred in; 30% live on campus. *Retention:* 67% of full-time freshmen returned.

Freshmen *Admission:* 4,643 applied, 3,536 admitted, 1,618 enrolled. *Test scores:* SAT critical reading scores over 500: 39%; SAT math scores over 500: 54%; SAT writing scores over 500: 29%; ACT scores over 18: 84%; SAT critical reading scores over 600: 7%; SAT math scores over 600: 10%; SAT writing scores over 600: 3%; ACT scores over 24: 24%; SAT critical reading scores over 700: 1%; SAT math scores over 700: 1%; ACT scores over 30: 2%.

Faculty *Total:* 601, 52% full-time. *Student/faculty ratio:* 19:1.

Academics *Calendar:* semesters. *Degrees:* associate, bachelor's, master's, and doctoral. *Special study options:* academic remediation for entering students, accelerated degree program, adult/continuing education programs, advanced placement credit, cooperative education, distance learning, double majors, honors programs, independent study, internships, off-campus study, part-time degree program, services for LD students, study abroad, summer session for credit. *ROTC:* Army (b).

Computers on Campus 1,000 computers/terminals are available on campus for general student use. Students can access the following: campus intranet, computer help desk, free student e-mail accounts, online (class) grades, online (class) registration, online (class) schedules. Campuswide network is available. 100% of college-owned or -operated housing units are wired for high-speed Internet access. Wireless service is available via entire campus.

Student Life *Housing:* on-campus residence required through sophomore year. *Options:* coed, men-only, women-only. Campus housing is university owned and leased by the school. Freshman campus housing is guaranteed. *Activities and organizations:* drama/theater group, student-run newspaper, radio station, choral group, marching band, Student Government Association, Student Programming Association, Kappa Delta Rho, Delta Zeta, Chi Alpha, national fraternities, national sororities. *Campus security:* 24-hour emergency response

devices and patrols, student patrols, late-night transport/escort service, controlled dormitory access. *Student services:* health clinic, personal/psychological counseling, legal services.

Athletics Member NCAA. All Division II. *Intercollegiate sports:* baseball M(s), basketball M(s)/W(s), cheerleading M(s)/W(s), cross-country running M(s)/W(s), football M(s), golf W(s), softball W(s), tennis W(s), track and field M(s)/W(s), volleyball W(s). *Intramural sports:* archery M/W, basketball M/W, football M/W, golf M/W, racquetball M/W, soccer M/W, softball M/W, table tennis M/W, tennis M/W, volleyball M/W.

Standardized Tests *Required:* SAT or ACT (for admission).

Costs (2012–13) *Tuition:* state resident $4619 full-time, $154 per credit hour part-time; nonresident $15,149 full-time, $505 per credit hour part-time. Full-time tuition and fees vary according to course load and degree level. Part-time tuition and fees vary according to course load and degree level. *Required fees:* $2320 full-time. *Room and board:* $7336; room only: $3972. Room and board charges vary according to board plan and housing facility. *Payment plan:* installment.

Financial Aid Of all full-time matriculated undergraduates who enrolled in 2011, 12,487 applied for aid, 11,768 were judged to have need, 2,849 had their need fully met. In 2011, 1765 non-need-based awards were made. *Average percent of need met:* 44%. *Average financial aid package:* $6985. *Average need-based loan:* $2451. *Average need-based gift aid:* $3003. *Average non-need-based aid:* $4062. *Average indebtedness upon graduation:* $15,548. *Financial aid deadline:* 11/1.

Applying *Options:* electronic application, early action. *Application fee:* $30. *Required:* high school transcript. *Application deadlines:* 7/22 (freshmen), 7/22 (transfers), 3/1 (early action).

Freshman Application Contact Ms. Cindy Hess, Director of Undergraduate Admissions, Tarleton State University, Box T-0030, Tarleton Station, Stephenville, TX 76402. *Phone:* 254-968-9123. *Toll-free phone:* 800-687-8236. *Fax:* 254-968-9951. *E-mail:* uadm@tarleton.edu. *Website:* http://www.tarleton.edu/.

Texas A&M Health Science Center

College Station, Texas

Application Contact Dr. Jack L. Long, Associate Dean for Student Services, Texas A&M Health Science Center, PO Box 660677, 3302 Gaston Avenue, Dallas, TX 75266-0677. *Phone:* 214-828-8232. *Fax:* 214-874-4567. *Website:* http://www.tamhsc.edu/.

Texas A&M International University

Laredo, Texas

- **State-supported** comprehensive, founded 1969, part of Texas A&M University System
- **Urban** 300-acre campus
- **Endowment** $34.3 million
- **Coed** 6,384 undergraduate students, 61% full-time, 58% women, 42% men
- **Moderately difficult** entrance level, 48% of applicants were admitted

Undergraduates 3,918 full-time, 2,466 part-time. Students come from 22 states and territories; 22 other countries; 0.9% are from out of state; 0.6% Black or African American, non-Hispanic/Latino; 94% Hispanic/Latino; 0.6% Asian, non-Hispanic/Latino; 0.1% Two or more races, non-Hispanic/Latino; 0.5% Race/ethnicity unknown; 2% international; 7% transferred in; 11% live on campus. *Retention:* 72% of full-time freshmen returned.

Freshmen *Admission:* 4,569 applied, 2,181 admitted, 837 enrolled. *Average high school GPA:* 3.7. *Test scores:* SAT critical reading scores over 500: 23%; SAT math scores over 500: 33%; SAT writing scores over 500: 20%; ACT scores over 18: 58%; SAT critical reading scores over 600: 3%; SAT math scores over 600: 7%; SAT writing scores over 600: 2%; ACT scores over 24: 9%; ACT scores over 30: 1%.

Faculty *Total:* 306, 55% full-time, 50% with terminal degrees. *Student/faculty ratio:* 21:1.

Academics *Calendar:* semesters. *Degrees:* bachelor's, master's, and doctoral. *Special study options:* academic remediation for entering students, advanced placement credit, distance learning, double majors, English as a second language, honors programs, independent study, internships, part-time degree program, services for LD students, study abroad, summer session for credit. *ROTC:* Army (b).

Computers on Campus 970 computers/terminals are available on campus for general student use. Students can access the following: campus intranet, computer help desk, free student e-mail accounts, online (class) grades, online (class) registration, online (class) schedules. Campuswide network is available. 100% of college-owned or -operated housing units are wired for high-speed Internet access. Wireless service is available via classrooms, computer centers, computer labs, learning centers, libraries, student centers.

Student Life *Housing options:* coed. Campus housing is university owned and is provided by a third party. *Activities and organizations:* drama/theater group, student-run newspaper, choral group, marching band, National Student Speech Language Hearing Association (NSSLHA), Association of International Students (AIS), Tri-Beta Biological Honor Society, Student Nurses' Association, STAR Club, national fraternities, national sororities. *Campus security:* 24-hour emergency response devices and patrols, late-night transport/escort service, controlled dormitory access, provide training to faculty, staff, a new students on active shooter. Interoperable communications with local, county, state, federal. *Student services:* health clinic, personal/psychological counseling, women's center.

Athletics Member NCAA. All Division II. *Intercollegiate sports:* baseball M(s), basketball M(s)/W(s), cross-country running M(s)/W(s), golf M(s)/W(s), soccer M(s)/W(s), softball W(s), volleyball W(s). *Intramural sports:* badminton M/W, basketball M/W, soccer M/W, softball M/W, table tennis M/W, ultimate Frisbee M/W, volleyball M/W.

Standardized Tests *Required:* SAT or ACT (for admission).

Costs (2012–13) *Tuition:* state resident $6838 full-time; nonresident $17,368 full-time. Full-time tuition and fees vary according to course load. Part-time tuition and fees vary according to course load and reciprocity agreements. *Room and board:* $6275. Room and board charges vary according to board plan and housing facility. *Payment plan:* installment. *Waivers:* senior citizens.

Financial Aid Of all full-time matriculated undergraduates who enrolled in 2011, 3,453 applied for aid, 3,405 were judged to have need, 331 had their need fully met. 105 Federal Work-Study jobs (averaging $3064). 17 state and other part-time jobs (averaging $3242). In 2011, 183 non-need-based awards were made. *Average percent of need met:* 66%. *Average financial aid package:* $10,646. *Average need-based loan:* $4655. *Average need-based gift aid:* $6294. *Average non-need-based aid:* $3493. *Average indebtedness upon graduation:* $15,941. *Financial aid deadline:* 8/1.

Applying *Options:* electronic application, early admission, deferred entrance. *Required:* high school transcript. *Application deadlines:* 7/1 (freshmen), 7/1 (transfers). *Notification:* 7/15 (freshmen), 7/15 (transfers).

Freshman Application Contact Ms. Rosa Dickinson, Director of Admissions, Texas A&M International University, 5201 University Boulevard, Laredo, TX 78041-1900. *Phone:* 956-326-2200. *Toll-free phone:* 888-489-2648. *E-mail:* adms@tamiu.edu. *Website:* http://www.tamiu.edu/.

Texas A&M University

College Station, Texas

- **State-supported** university, founded 1876, part of Texas A&M University System
- **Suburban** 5200-acre campus with easy access to Houston
- **Endowment** $7.6 billion
- **Coed** 40,103 undergraduate students, 90% full-time, 48% women, 52% men
- **Moderately difficult** entrance level, 67% of applicants were admitted

Undergraduates 36,219 full-time, 3,884 part-time. Students come from 53 states and territories; 87 other countries; 3% are from out of state; 3% Black or African American, non-Hispanic/Latino; 18% Hispanic/Latino; 5% Asian, non-Hispanic/Latino; 0.1% Native Hawaiian or other Pacific Islander, non-Hispanic/Latino; 0.3% American Indian or Alaska Native, non-Hispanic/Latino; 2% Two or more races, non-Hispanic/Latino; 0.2% Race/ethnicity unknown; 2% international; 5% transferred in; 25% live on campus. *Retention:* 92% of full-time freshmen returned.

Freshmen *Admission:* 27,798 applied, 18,663 admitted, 8,139 enrolled. *Test scores:* SAT critical reading scores over 500: 82%; SAT math scores over 500: 87%; SAT writing scores over 500: 76%; ACT scores over 18: 99%; SAT critical reading scores over 600: 45%; SAT math scores over 600: 62%; SAT writing scores over 600: 35%; ACT scores over 24: 78%; SAT critical reading scores over 700: 11%; SAT math scores over 700: 18%; SAT writing scores over 700: 7%; ACT scores over 30: 29%.

Faculty *Total:* 2,451, 83% full-time, 91% with terminal degrees. *Student/faculty ratio:* 22:1.

Academics *Calendar:* semesters. *Degrees:* bachelor's, master's, doctoral, and postbachelor's certificates. *Special study options:* academic remediation for entering students, accelerated degree program, advanced placement credit, cooperative education, distance learning, double majors, English as a second language, honors programs, independent study, internships, off-campus study, part-time degree program, services for LD students, study abroad, summer session for credit. *ROTC:* Army (b), Navy (b), Air Force (b).

Computers on Campus 1,961 computers/terminals and 5,000 ports are available on campus for general student use. Students can access the following: campus intranet, computer help desk, free student e-mail accounts, online (class) grades, online (class) registration, online (class) schedules. Campuswide network is available. 100% of college-owned or -operated housing units are wired for high-speed Internet access. Wireless service is available via classrooms, computer labs, learning centers, libraries, student centers.

Student Life *Housing options:* coed, men-only, women-only, disabled students. Campus housing is university owned. *Activities and organizations:* drama/theater group, student-run newspaper, radio and television station, choral group, marching band, Memorial Student Center, Corps of Cadets, Fish Camp, student government, national fraternities, national sororities. *Campus security:* 24-hour emergency response devices and patrols, late-night transport/escort service, controlled dormitory access, student escorts. *Student services:* health clinic, personal/psychological counseling, women's center, legal services.

Athletics Member NCAA. All Division I except football (Division I-A). *Intercollegiate sports:* archery W(s), baseball M(s), basketball M(s)/W(s), cross-country running M(s)/W(s), equestrian sports W(s), golf M(s)/W(s), soccer W(s), softball W(s), swimming and diving M(s)/W(s), tennis M(s)/W(s), track and field M(s)/W(s), volleyball W(s). *Intramural sports:* archery M/W, badminton M/W, basketball M/W, bowling M/W, cross-country running M/W, fencing M(c)/W(c), field hockey M(c)/W(c), football M/W, golf M/W, gymnastics M(c)/W(c), lacrosse M(c)/W(c), racquetball M(c)/W(c), riflery M/W, rugby M(c)/W(c), sailing M(c)/W(c), soccer M/W, softball M/W, squash M/W, swimming and diving M/W, table tennis M/W, tennis M/W, track and field M/W, ultimate Frisbee M(c)/W(c), volleyball M/W, water polo M/W, weight lifting M(c)/W(c), wrestling M(c).

Standardized Tests *Required:* SAT or ACT (for admission).

Costs (2012–13) *Tuition:* state resident $5297 full-time, $177 per credit hour part-time; nonresident $21,827 full-time, $728 per credit hour part-time. Full-time tuition and fees vary according to program. Part-time tuition and fees vary according to program. *Required fees:* $3209 full-time. *Room and board:* $8400. Room and board charges vary according to board plan, housing facility, and location. *Payment plan:* installment.

Financial Aid Of all full-time matriculated undergraduates who enrolled in 2012, 21,932 applied for aid, 15,430 were judged to have need, 6,202 had their need fully met. 640 Federal Work-Study jobs (averaging $2596). 201 state and other part-time jobs (averaging $2003). In 2012, 2170 non-need-based awards were made. *Average percent of need met:* 70%. *Average financial aid package:* $14,938. *Average need-based loan:* $6693. *Average need-based gift aid:* $9195. *Average non-need-based aid:* $3673. *Average indebtedness upon graduation:* $22,955.

Applying *Options:* electronic application. *Application fee:* $60. *Required:* essay or personal statement, high school transcript. *Application deadlines:* 1/15 (freshmen), 3/15 (transfers). *Notification:* continuous (freshmen), continuous (transfers).

Freshman Application Contact Mr. Scott McDonald, Director of Admissions, Texas A&M University, 217 John J. Koldus Building, College Station, TX 77843-1265. *Phone:* 979-845-3741. *Fax:* 979-845-8737. *E-mail:* admissions@tamu.edu. *Website:* http://www.tamu.edu/.

Texas A&M University at Galveston

Galveston, Texas

Freshman Application Contact Ms. Sarah Trombley, Associate Director of Admissions and Records, Texas A&M University at Galveston, PO Box 1675, Galveston, TX 77553-1675. *Phone:* 409-740-4448. *Fax:* 409-740-4731. *E-mail:* seaaggie@tamug.edu. *Website:* http://www.tamug.edu/.

Texas A&M University–Commerce

Commerce, Texas

- **State-supported** university, founded 1889, part of Texas A&M University System
- **Small-town** 1883-acre campus with easy access to Dallas-Fort Worth
- **Endowment** $14.7 million
- **Coed** 6,768 undergraduate students, 49% full-time, 59% women, 41% men
- **Moderately difficult** entrance level, 65% of applicants were admitted

Undergraduates 3,303 full-time, 3,465 part-time. Students come from 31 states and territories; 18 other countries; 1% are from out of state; 19% Black or African American, non-Hispanic/Latino; 14% Hispanic/Latino; 2% Asian, non-Hispanic/Latino; 0.1% Native Hawaiian or other Pacific Islander, non-Hispanic/Latino; 1% American Indian or Alaska Native, non-Hispanic/Latino; 1% Two or more races, non-Hispanic/Latino; 0.5% Race/ethnicity unknown; 4% international; 18% transferred in; 17% live on campus.
Freshmen *Admission:* 3,516 applied, 2,287 admitted, 786 enrolled. *Test scores:* SAT critical reading scores over 500: 44%; SAT math scores over 500: 50%; ACT scores over 18: 78%; SAT critical reading scores over 600: 12%; SAT math scores over 600: 14%; ACT scores over 24: 24%; SAT critical reading scores over 700: 2%; SAT math scores over 700: 2%; ACT scores over 30: 4%.
Faculty *Total:* 610, 55% full-time. *Student/faculty ratio:* 17:1.
Academics *Calendar:* semesters. *Degrees:* bachelor's, master's, and doctoral. *Special study options:* academic remediation for entering students, adult/continuing education programs, advanced placement credit, cooperative education, distance learning, double majors, honors programs, independent study, internships, off-campus study, part-time degree program, services for LD students, study abroad, summer session for credit. *Unusual degree programs:* 3-2 engineering with Texas A&M University.
Computers on Campus 313 computers/terminals and 800 ports are available on campus for general student use. Students can access the following: campus intranet, computer help desk, free student e-mail accounts, online (class) grades, online (class) registration, online (class) schedules. Campuswide network is available. 100% of college-owned or -operated housing units are wired for high-speed Internet access. Wireless service is available via computer centers, computer labs, dorm rooms, learning centers, libraries.
Student Life *Housing:* on-campus residence required for freshman year. *Options:* coed, men-only, women-only, disabled students. Campus housing is university owned. Freshman campus housing is guaranteed. *Activities and organizations:* drama/theater group, student-run newspaper, radio and television station, choral group, marching band, national fraternities, national sororities. *Campus security:* 24-hour emergency response devices and patrols, controlled dormitory access. *Student services:* health clinic, personal/psychological counseling, legal services.
Athletics Member NCAA. All Division II. *Intercollegiate sports:* basketball M(s)/W(s), cheerleading M(s)/W(s), cross-country running M(s)/W(s), football M(s), golf M(s)/W(s), soccer W(s), track and field M(s)/W(s), volleyball W(s). *Intramural sports:* badminton M/W, basketball M/W, cross-country running M/W, football M/W, racquetball M/W, soccer M/W, softball M/W, table tennis M/W, tennis M/W, track and field M/W, volleyball M/W.
Standardized Tests *Required:* SAT or ACT (for admission).
Costs (2013–14) *Tuition:* state resident $6583 full-time, $160 per semester hour part-time; nonresident $17,113 full-time. Full-time tuition and fees vary according to course load. Part-time tuition and fees vary according to course load. *Required fees:* $1793 full-time. *Room and board:* $3627; room only: $2062. Room and board charges vary according to board plan and housing facility.
Financial Aid Of all full-time matriculated undergraduates who enrolled in 2011, 4,096 applied for aid, 3,678 were judged to have need, 514 had their need fully met. In 2011, 214 non-need-based awards were made. *Average percent of need met:* 58%. *Average financial aid package:* $9901. *Average need-based loan:* $4077. *Average need-based gift aid:* $6995. *Average non-need-based aid:* $1762. *Average indebtedness upon graduation:* $28,839.
Applying *Options:* electronic application, early admission. *Required:* high school transcript. *Application deadlines:* 8/15 (freshmen), rolling (transfers). *Notification:* continuous (freshmen), continuous (transfers).
Freshman Application Contact Jody Todhunter, Director of Admissions, Texas A&M University–Commerce, PO Box 3011, Commerce, TX 75429. *Phone:* 903-886-5072. *Toll-free phone:* 888-868-2682. *Fax:* 903-886-5888. *E-mail:* admissions@tamu-commerce.edu. *Website:* http://www.tamuc.edu/.

Texas A&M University–Corpus Christi

Corpus Christi, Texas

- **State-supported** university, founded 1947, part of Texas A&M University System
- **Suburban** 240-acre campus
- **Endowment** $4.5 million
- **Coed**
- **Moderately difficult** entrance level

Faculty *Student/faculty ratio:* 21:1.
Academics *Calendar:* semesters. *Degrees:* bachelor's, master's, and doctoral.
Student Life *Campus security:* 24-hour emergency response devices and patrols, late-night transport/escort service, controlled dormitory access.
Athletics Member NCAA. All Division I.
Standardized Tests *Required:* SAT or ACT (for admission).
Financial Aid *Of all full-time matriculated undergraduates who enrolled in 2012,* 4,544 applied for aid, 3,796 were judged to have need, 351 had their need fully met. 108 Federal Work-Study jobs (averaging $3694). 167 state and other part-time jobs (averaging $3865). *In 2012,* 548 non-need-based awards were made. *Average percent of need met:* 58. *Average financial aid package:* $9140. *Average need-based loan:* $4049. *Average need-based gift aid:* $5649. *Average non-need-based aid:* $2087. *Average indebtedness upon graduation:* $24,168.
Applying *Options:* electronic application. *Application fee:* $25. *Required:* high school transcript, minimum 2.0 GPA.
Freshman Application Contact Mrs. Monica Martinez, Assistant Director of Admissions, Texas A&M University–Corpus Christi, SSC 107, 6300 Ocean Drive, Unit 5774, Corpus Christi, TX 78412-5774. *Phone:* 361-825-2624. *Toll-free phone:* 800-482-6822. *Fax:* 361-825-5887. *E-mail:* monica.martinez@tamucc.edu.
Website: http://www.tamucc.edu/.

Texas A&M University–Kingsville

Kingsville, Texas

- **State-supported** university, founded 1925, part of Texas A&M University System
- **Small-town** 255-acre campus
- **Endowment** $15.0 million
- **Coed** 5,967 undergraduate students, 82% full-time, 49% women, 51% men
- **Moderately difficult** entrance level, 93% of applicants were admitted

Undergraduates 4,864 full-time, 1,103 part-time. Students come from 32 states and territories; 28 other countries; 2% are from out of state; 6% Black or African American, non-Hispanic/Latino; 67% Hispanic/Latino; 0.8% Asian, non-Hispanic/Latino; 0.1% Native Hawaiian or other Pacific Islander, non-Hispanic/Latino; 0.3% American Indian or Alaska Native, non-Hispanic/Latino; 1% Two or more races, non-Hispanic/Latino; 2% Race/ethnicity unknown; 1% international; 9% transferred in. *Retention:* 62% of full-time freshmen returned.
Freshmen *Admission:* 4,920 applied, 4,599 admitted, 1,298 enrolled. *Average high school GPA:* 3.21. *Test scores:* SAT critical reading scores over 500: 21%; SAT math scores over 500: 37%; SAT writing scores over 500: 15%; ACT scores over 18: 58%; SAT critical reading scores over 600: 4%; SAT math scores over 600: 8%; SAT writing scores over 600: 3%; ACT scores over 24: 10%; SAT critical reading scores over 700: 1%; SAT math scores over 700: 1%; ACT scores over 30: 1%.
Faculty *Total:* 399, 67% full-time. *Student/faculty ratio:* 20:1.
Academics *Calendar:* semesters. *Degrees:* bachelor's, master's, doctoral, and postbachelor's certificates. *Special study options:* academic remediation for entering students, advanced placement credit, cooperative education, distance learning, double majors, English as a second language, honors programs, internships, off-campus study, part-time degree program, services for LD students, study abroad, summer session for credit. *ROTC:* Army (b). *Unusual degree programs:* 3-2 business administration.
Computers on Campus 170 computers/terminals are available on campus for general student use. Students can access the following: campus intranet, computer help desk, free student e-mail accounts, online (class) grades, online (class) registration, online (class) schedules, Blackboard. Campuswide network is available. Wireless service is available via classrooms, computer centers, computer labs, dorm rooms, learning centers, libraries.

Student Life *Housing:* on-campus residence required for freshman year. *Options:* coed, men-only, women-only. Campus housing is university owned. Freshman campus housing is guaranteed. *Activities and organizations:* drama/theater group, student-run newspaper, radio and television station, choral group, marching band, Catholic Student Organization, Baptist Student Ministry, Gamerz Elite, Javelina Students for Sustainability, Aggie Club, national fraternities, national sororities. *Campus security:* 24-hour emergency response devices and patrols, late-night transport/escort service, controlled dormitory access. *Student services:* health clinic, personal/psychological counseling, women's center.

Athletics Member NCAA. All Division II. *Intercollegiate sports:* baseball M(s), basketball M(s)/W(s), cross-country running M/W, football M(s), golf W(s), softball W(s), tennis M(s)/W(s), track and field M(s)/W(s), volleyball W(s). *Intramural sports:* archery M/W, bowling M/W, equestrian sports M/W, golf M/W, racquetball M/W, soccer M/W, softball W, volleyball M/W.

Standardized Tests *Required:* SAT or ACT (for admission).

Costs (2013–14) *Tuition:* state resident $6940 full-time; nonresident $17,560 full-time. Full-time tuition and fees vary according to course load and degree level. Part-time tuition and fees vary according to course load and degree level. *Room and board:* $7484; room only: $3674. Room and board charges vary according to board plan and housing facility. *Payment plans:* tuition prepayment, installment, deferred payment. *Waivers:* senior citizens and employees or children of employees.

Financial Aid Of all full-time matriculated undergraduates who enrolled in 2005, 4,449 applied for aid, 4,214 were judged to have need, 2,899 had their need fully met. *Average financial aid package:* $6500. *Average need-based loan:* $3875. *Average need-based gift aid:* $6500. *Average indebtedness upon graduation:* $2867.

Applying *Options:* electronic application, early admission, deferred entrance. *Application fee:* $15. *Required:* high school transcript. *Required for some:* interview. *Recommended:* minimum 2.0 GPA. *Application deadlines:* rolling (freshmen), rolling (transfers). *Notification:* continuous (freshmen), continuous (transfers).

Freshman Application Contact Laura Knippers, Associate Director of Admissions and Enrollment Management, Texas A&M University–Kingsville, MSC 116, 700 University Boulevard, Kingsville, TX 78363. *Phone:* 361-593-3907. *Toll-free phone:* 800-687-6000. *Fax:* 361-593-2991. *E-mail:* laura.knippers@tamuk.edu.
Website: http://www.tamuk.edu/.

Texas A&M University–San Antonio

San Antonio, Texas

Freshman Application Contact Jennifer Zamarripa, Director of Admissions and Registrar, Texas A&M University–San Antonio, One University Way, San Antonio, TX 78224. *Phone:* 210-932-6201. *E-mail:* jennifer.zamarripa@tamusa.tamus.edu.
Website: http://www.tamusa.tamus.edu/.

Texas A&M University–Texarkana

Texarkana, Texas

Application Contact Mrs. Patricia Black, Director of Admissions and Registrar, Texas A&M University–Texarkana, PO Box 5518, Texarkana, TX 75505-5518. *Phone:* 903-223-3068. *Fax:* 903-223-3140. *E-mail:* admissions@tamut.edu.
Website: http://www.tamut.edu/.

Texas Christian University

Fort Worth, Texas

- **Independent** university, founded 1873, affiliated with Christian Church (Disciples of Christ)
- **Suburban** 277-acre campus with easy access to Dallas-Fort Worth
- **Endowment** $1.1 billion
- **Coed** 8,456 undergraduate students, 96% full-time, 59% women, 41% men
- **Very difficult** entrance level, 41% of applicants were admitted

Undergraduates 8,145 full-time, 311 part-time. Students come from 51 states and territories; 66 other countries; 33% are from out of state; 5% Black or African American, non-Hispanic/Latino; 10% Hispanic/Latino; 2% Asian, non-Hispanic/Latino; 0.2% Native Hawaiian or other Pacific Islander, non-Hispanic/Latino; 0.9% American Indian or Alaska Native, non-Hispanic/Latino; 0.9% Two or more races, non-Hispanic/Latino; 1% Race/ethnicity unknown; 4% international; 5% transferred in; 47% live on campus. *Retention:* 90% of full-time freshmen returned.

Freshmen *Admission:* 19,335 applied, 7,901 admitted, 1,854 enrolled.

Faculty *Total:* 886, 65% full-time, 66% with terminal degrees. *Student/faculty ratio:* 13:1.

Academics *Calendar:* semesters. *Degrees:* certificates, diplomas, bachelor's, master's, doctoral, post-master's, and postbachelor's certificates. *Special study options:* accelerated degree program, advanced placement credit, distance learning, double majors, English as a second language, freshman honors college, honors programs, independent study, internships, part-time degree program, services for LD students, study abroad, summer session for credit. *ROTC:* Army (b), Air Force (b).

Computers on Campus 1,400 computers/terminals and 10,000 ports are available on campus for general student use. Students can access the following: campus intranet, computer help desk, free student e-mail accounts, online (class) grades, online (class) registration, online (class) schedules. Campus-wide network is available. 100% of college-owned or -operated housing units are wired for high-speed Internet access. Wireless service is available via entire campus.

Student Life *Housing:* on-campus residence required through sophomore year. *Options:* coed, men-only, women-only, disabled students. Campus housing is university owned. Freshman campus housing is guaranteed. *Activities and organizations:* drama/theater group, student-run newspaper, radio and television station, choral group, marching band, national fraternities, national sororities. *Campus security:* 24-hour emergency response devices and patrols, late-night transport/escort service, controlled dormitory access, emergency call boxes, video surveillance in parking lots, self-defense education, lighted sidewalks, emergency notification system. *Student services:* health clinic, personal/psychological counseling, women's center.

Athletics Member NCAA. All Division I. *Intercollegiate sports:* baseball M(s), basketball M(s)/W(s), cross-country running M(s)/W(s), equestrian sports W(s), football M(s), golf M(s)/W(s), riflery W(s), soccer W(s), swimming and diving M(s)/W(s), tennis M(s)/W(s), track and field M(s)/W(s), volleyball W(s). *Intramural sports:* baseball M(c), basketball M/W, bowling M/W, golf M(c)/W(c), gymnastics W(c), ice hockey M(c), lacrosse M(c)/W(c), racquetball M/W, rugby M(c)/W(c), soccer M(c)/W(c), table tennis M(c)/W(c), tennis M(c)/W(c), ultimate Frisbee M(c)/W(c), volleyball M(c)/W(c), wrestling M(c).

Standardized Tests *Required:* SAT or ACT (for admission).

Costs (2013–14) *Tuition:* $36,500 full-time. Part-time tuition and fees vary according to course load. *Required fees:* $90 full-time. *Room only:* Room and board charges vary according to board plan and housing facility. *Payment plan:* installment. *Waivers:* employees or children of employees.

Financial Aid Of all full-time matriculated undergraduates who enrolled in 2012, 4,352 applied for aid, 3,554 were judged to have need, 822 had their need fully met. 1,491 Federal Work-Study jobs (averaging $1761). 25 state and other part-time jobs (averaging $1729). In 2012, 1846 non-need-based awards were made. *Average percent of need met:* 62%. *Average financial aid package:* $21,185. *Average need-based loan:* $4758. *Average need-based gift aid:* $17,990. *Average non-need-based aid:* $12,263. *Average indebtedness upon graduation:* $38,516. *Financial aid deadline:* 5/1.

Applying *Options:* electronic application, early action, deferred entrance. *Application fee:* $40. *Required:* essay or personal statement, high school transcript, 1 letter of recommendation. *Recommended:* 2 letters of recommendation, interview. *Application deadlines:* 2/15 (freshmen), 8/1 (transfers), 11/1 (early action). *Notification:* 4/1 (freshmen), continuous (transfers), 1/1 (early action).

Freshman Application Contact Mr. Heath Einstein, Director of Freshman Admission, Texas Christian University, 2800 South University Drive, Fort Worth, TX 76129-0002. *Phone:* 817-257-7490. *Toll-free phone:* 800-828-3764. *Fax:* 817-257-7268. *E-mail:* frogmail@tcu.edu.
Website: http://www.tcu.edu/.

Texas College

Tyler, Texas

- **Independent** 4-year, founded 1894, affiliated with Christian Methodist Episcopal Church
- **Urban** 25-acre campus
- **Endowment** $1.3 million
- **Coed**
- **Noncompetitive** entrance level

Faculty *Student/faculty ratio:* 25:1.

Academics *Calendar:* semesters. *Degrees:* associate, bachelor's, and post-bachelor's certificates.

Student Life *Campus security:* 24-hour emergency response devices and patrols, late-night transport/escort service.

Athletics Member NAIA.

Standardized Tests *Required:* SAT or ACT (for admission).

Costs (2012–13) *Comprehensive fee:* $16,686 includes full-time tuition ($7996), mandatory fees ($1690), and room and board ($7000). *College room only:* $3600.

Financial Aid *Of all full-time matriculated undergraduates who enrolled in 2010,* 897 applied for aid, 880 were judged to have need, 35 had their need fully met. 151 Federal Work-Study jobs (averaging $1527). 21 state and other part-time jobs (averaging $1220). *In 2010,* 17 non-need-based awards were made. *Average percent of need met:* 61. *Average financial aid package:* $10,095. *Average need-based loan:* $3349. *Average need-based gift aid:* $7040. *Average non-need-based aid:* $3349. *Average indebtedness upon graduation:* $26,292.

Applying *Options:* electronic application, early admission. *Application fee:* $20. *Required:* high school transcript, minimum 2.0 GPA.

Freshman Application Contact Mr. John Roberts, Interim Dean for Enrollment Services, Texas College, 2404 North Grand Avenue, Tyler, TX 75702. *Phone:* 903-593-8311 Ext. 2297. *Toll-free phone:* 800-306-6299. *Fax:* 903-363-1854. *E-mail:* jroberts@texascollege.edu. *Website:* http://www.texascollege.edu/.

Texas Lutheran University

Seguin, Texas

- **Independent** comprehensive, founded 1891, affiliated with Evangelical Lutheran Church
- **Suburban** 196-acre campus with easy access to San Antonio, Austin
- **Endowment** $79.0 million
- **Coed** 1,311 undergraduate students, 95% full-time, 53% women, 47% men
- **Moderately difficult** entrance level, 53% of applicants were admitted

Undergraduates 1,246 full-time, 65 part-time. Students come from 19 states and territories; 6 other countries; 3% are from out of state; 9% Black or African American, non-Hispanic/Latino; 28% Hispanic/Latino; 1% Asian, non-Hispanic/Latino; 0.1% Native Hawaiian or other Pacific Islander, non-Hispanic/Latino; 0.5% American Indian or Alaska Native, non-Hispanic/Latino; 0.4% Two or more races, non-Hispanic/Latino; 3% Race/ethnicity unknown; 0.5% international; 5% transferred in; 56% live on campus. *Retention:* 67% of full-time freshmen returned.

Freshmen *Admission:* 1,852 applied, 974 admitted, 355 enrolled. *Average high school GPA:* 3.56. *Test scores:* SAT critical reading scores over 500: 44%; SAT math scores over 500: 83%; SAT writing scores over 500: 36%; ACT scores over 18: 86%; SAT critical reading scores over 600: 11%; SAT math scores over 600: 40%; SAT writing scores over 600: 8%; ACT scores over 24: 26%; SAT critical reading scores over 700: 2%; SAT math scores over 700: 4%; SAT writing scores over 700: 1%; ACT scores over 30: 3%.

Faculty *Total:* 129, 57% full-time, 57% with terminal degrees. *Student/faculty ratio:* 14:1.

Academics *Calendar:* semesters. *Degrees:* bachelor's and master's. *Special study options:* advanced placement credit, double majors, honors programs, independent study, internships, part-time degree program, services for LD students, study abroad, summer session for credit. *ROTC:* Army (c), Air Force (c). *Unusual degree programs:* 3-2 engineering with Texas A&M University, Texas Tech University, Texas State University.

Computers on Campus 243 computers/terminals and 374 ports are available on campus for general student use. Students can access the following: campus intranet, computer help desk, free student e-mail accounts, online (class) grades, online (class) registration, online (class) schedules, free printing. Campuswide network is available. 100% of college-owned or -operated housing

units are wired for high-speed Internet access. Wireless service is available via entire campus.

Student Life *Housing:* on-campus residence required through senior year. *Options:* coed, men-only, women-only. Campus housing is university owned. Freshman campus housing is guaranteed. *Activities and organizations:* drama/theater group, student-run newspaper, choral group, Campus Ministry, Mexican American Student Association, Student Government Association, Black Student Union. *Campus security:* 24-hour emergency response devices and patrols, late-night transport/escort service, controlled dormitory access. *Student services:* health clinic, personal/psychological counseling, women's center.

Athletics Member NCAA. All Division III. *Intercollegiate sports:* baseball M, basketball M/W, cross-country running W, football M, golf M/W, soccer M/W, softball W, tennis M/W, track and field W, volleyball W. *Intramural sports:* basketball M/W, bowling M/W, football M, racquetball M/W, softball M/W, tennis M/W, volleyball M/W.

Standardized Tests *Required:* SAT or ACT (for admission).

Costs (2012–13) *Comprehensive fee:* $32,330 includes full-time tuition ($24,860), mandatory fees ($130), and room and board ($7340). *Part-time tuition:* $825 per semester hour. *College room only:* $3800. Room and board charges vary according to board plan and housing facility. *Payment plan:* installment. *Waivers:* children of alumni and employees or children of employees.

Financial Aid Of all full-time matriculated undergraduates who enrolled in 2012, 1,139 applied for aid, 1,020 were judged to have need, 208 had their need fully met. 604 Federal Work-Study jobs (averaging $2015). 9 state and other part-time jobs (averaging $1990). In 2012, 208 non-need-based awards were made. *Average percent of need met:* 78%. *Average financial aid package:* $20,997. *Average need-based loan:* $4955. *Average need-based gift aid:* $15,641. *Average non-need-based aid:* $11,092. *Average indebtedness upon graduation:* $37,145.

Applying *Options:* electronic application, deferred entrance. *Application fee:* $40. *Required:* essay or personal statement, high school transcript, 2 letters of recommendation. *Required for some:* minimum 2.0 GPA. *Recommended:* interview. *Application deadlines:* rolling (freshmen), rolling (transfers). *Notification:* 8/1 (freshmen), continuous until 8/1 (transfers).

Freshman Application Contact Mr. Tom Oliver, Vice President for Enrollment Services, Texas Lutheran University, 1000 West Court Street, Seguin, TX 78155-5999. *Phone:* 830-372-8053. *Toll-free phone:* 800-771-8521. *Fax:* 830-372-8096. *E-mail:* toliver@tlu.edu. *Website:* http://www.tlu.edu/.

Texas Southern University

Houston, Texas

- **State-supported** university, founded 1947, part of Texas Higher Education Coordinating Board
- **Urban** 147-acre campus
- **Endowment** $35.4 million
- **Coed** 7,021 undergraduate students, 84% full-time, 57% women, 43% men
- **Noncompetitive** entrance level, 53% of applicants were admitted

Undergraduates 5,905 full-time, 1,116 part-time. Students come from 42 states and territories; 23 other countries; 11% are from out of state; 86% Black or African American, non-Hispanic/Latino; 5% Hispanic/Latino; 2% Asian, non-Hispanic/Latino; 0.3% American Indian or Alaska Native, non-Hispanic/Latino; 0.1% Race/ethnicity unknown; 4% international; 11% transferred in; 24% live on campus. *Retention:* 61% of full-time freshmen returned.

Freshmen *Admission:* 9,393 applied, 4,991 admitted, 1,349 enrolled. *Average high school GPA:* 2.96. *Test scores:* SAT critical reading scores over 500: 10%; SAT math scores over 500: 14%; SAT writing scores over 500: 8%; ACT scores over 18: 40%; SAT critical reading scores over 600: 1%; SAT math scores over 600: 1%; ACT scores over 24: 3%.

Faculty *Total:* 602, 61% full-time. *Student/faculty ratio:* 19:1.

Academics *Calendar:* semesters. *Degrees:* bachelor's, master's, and doctoral. *Special study options:* academic remediation for entering students, accelerated degree program, adult/continuing education programs, cooperative education, distance learning, English as a second language, external degree program, honors programs, independent study, internships, off-campus study, part-time degree program, services for LD students, study abroad, summer session for credit. *ROTC:* Army (b), Navy (c), Air Force (c).

Computers on Campus Students can access the following: computer help desk, free student e-mail accounts, online (class) grades, online (class) registration, online (class) schedules, Blackboard Learning and Community Portal System (E-education). Campuswide network is available. Wireless service is available via entire campus.

Student Life *Housing options:* coed, men-only, women-only. Campus housing is university owned, leased by the school and is provided by a third party. Freshman campus housing is guaranteed. *Activities and organizations:* drama/theater group, student-run newspaper, radio station, choral group, marching band, Debate Team, University Program Council, Student Government Association, Band, national fraternities, national sororities. *Campus security:* 24-hour emergency response devices and patrols, student patrols, late-night transport/escort service. *Student services:* health clinic, personal/psychological counseling, legal services.

Athletics Member NCAA. All Division I except football (Division I-AA). *Intercollegiate sports:* baseball M(s), basketball M(s)/W(s), bowling W(s), cross-country running M(s)/W(s), golf M(s), soccer M/W(s), softball W(s), tennis M(s)/W(s), track and field M(s)/W(s), volleyball M/W(s). *Intramural sports:* softball M/W, swimming and diving M/W, tennis M/W, volleyball M/W.

Standardized Tests *Required for some:* SAT or ACT (for admission).

Costs (2012–13) *Tuition:* state resident $7646 full-time; nonresident $16,946 full-time. Full-time tuition and fees vary according to course level, course load, degree level, and program. Part-time tuition and fees vary according to course level, course load, degree level, and program. *Room and board:* $10,566. Room and board charges vary according to board plan, housing facility, and location. *Payment plans:* installment, deferred payment. *Waivers:* minority students and senior citizens.

Financial Aid Of all full-time matriculated undergraduates who enrolled in 2012, 5,498 applied for aid, 5,483 were judged to have need, 4,639 had their need fully met. 283 Federal Work-Study jobs (averaging $4000). 20 state and other part-time jobs (averaging $4000). *Average percent of need met:* 85%. *Average financial aid package:* $22,266. *Average need-based loan:* $4099. *Average need-based gift aid:* $15,125. *Average indebtedness upon graduation:* $39,197.

Applying *Options:* electronic application, early admission, early decision. *Application fee:* $42. *Required:* high school transcript, minimum 2.0 GPA. *Application deadlines:* 8/15 (freshmen), 8/15 (transfers). *Notification:* 8/28 (freshmen), continuous until 8/28 (transfers).

Freshman Application Contact Enrollment Services Customer Service Center, Texas Southern University, 3100 Cleburne Street, Houston, TX 77004-4598. *Phone:* 713-313-7071. *Fax:* 713-313-7851. *E-mail:* eservices@em.tsu.edu.
Website: http://www.tsu.edu/.

Texas State University–San Marcos

San Marcos, Texas

- **State-supported** university, founded 1899, part of Texas State University System
- **Suburban** 423-acre campus with easy access to San Antonio, Austin
- **Endowment** $111.4 million
- **Coed** 29,458 undergraduate students, 82% full-time, 55% women, 45% men
- **Moderately difficult** entrance level, 66% of applicants were admitted

Undergraduates 24,223 full-time, 5,235 part-time. Students come from 49 states and territories; 42 other countries; 1% are from out of state; 6% Black or African American, non-Hispanic/Latino; 29% Hispanic/Latino; 2% Asian, non-Hispanic/Latino; 0.1% Native Hawaiian or other Pacific Islander, non-Hispanic/Latino; 0.4% American Indian or Alaska Native, non-Hispanic/Latino; 2% Two or more races, non-Hispanic/Latino; 2% Race/ethnicity unknown; 0.5% international; 13% transferred in; 20% live on campus. *Retention:* 77% of full-time freshmen returned.

Freshmen *Admission:* 10,418 applied, 6,889 admitted, 4,251 enrolled. *Test scores:* SAT critical reading scores over 500: 59%; SAT math scores over 500: 71%; SAT writing scores over 500: 49%; ACT scores over 18: 99%; SAT critical reading scores over 600: 15%; SAT math scores over 600: 19%; SAT writing scores over 600: 9%; ACT scores over 24: 42%; SAT critical reading scores over 700: 2%; SAT math scores over 700: 1%; SAT writing scores over 700: 1%; ACT scores over 30: 4%.

Faculty *Total:* 1,590, 75% full-time, 64% with terminal degrees. *Student/faculty ratio:* 20:1.

Academics *Calendar:* semesters. *Degrees:* bachelor's, master's, doctoral, and postbachelor's certificates. *Special study options:* academic remediation for entering students, accelerated degree program, adult/continuing education programs, advanced placement credit, distance learning, double majors, English as a second language, freshman honors college, honors programs, independent study, internships, off-campus study, part-time degree program, services for LD students, study abroad, summer session for credit. *ROTC:* Army (b), Air

Force (b). *Unusual degree programs:* 3-2 engineering with University of Texas at Austin, Texas A&M University, Texas Tech University, University of Texas at San Antonio.

Computers on Campus 1,792 computers/terminals are available on campus for general student use. Students can access the following: computer help desk, free student e-mail accounts, online (class) grades, online (class) registration, online (class) schedules. Campuswide network is available. 100% of college-owned or -operated housing units are wired for high-speed Internet access. Wireless service is available via entire campus.

Student Life *Housing:* on-campus residence required through sophomore year. *Options:* coed, men-only, women-only. Campus housing is university owned. Freshman campus housing is guaranteed. *Activities and organizations:* drama/theater group, student-run newspaper, radio station, choral group, marching band, Non-traditional Students Association, Student Association for Campus Activities, Association Student Government, Annual Martin Luther King Jr. Commemoration, national fraternities, national sororities. *Campus security:* 24-hour emergency response devices and patrols, late-night transport/escort service, controlled dormitory access. *Student services:* health clinic, personal/psychological counseling, legal services.

Athletics Member NCAA. All Division I except football (Division I-AA). *Intercollegiate sports:* baseball M(s), basketball M(s)/W(s), cheerleading M/W, cross-country running M(s)/W(s), equestrian sports M(c)/W(c), fencing M(c)/W(c), golf M(s)/W(s), gymnastics M(c)/W(c), lacrosse M(c)/W(c), rugby M(c)/W(c), soccer M(c)/W(s), softball M(c)/W(s), tennis M(c)/W(s), track and field M(s)/W(s), ultimate Frisbee M(c)/W(c), volleyball W(s), water polo M(c)/W(c), weight lifting M(c)/W(c), wrestling M(c)/W(c). *Intramural sports:* basketball M/W, bowling M/W, cross-country running M/W, football M/W, golf M/W, racquetball M/W, soccer M/W, softball M/W, tennis M/W, ultimate Frisbee M, volleyball M/W.

Standardized Tests *Required:* SAT or ACT (for admission). *Recommended:* SAT (for admission), ACT (for admission).

Costs (2012–13) *Tuition:* state resident $6510 full-time, $217 per credit hour part-time; nonresident $17,040 full-time, $568 per credit hour part-time. Full-time tuition and fees vary according to course load and degree level. Part-time tuition and fees vary according to course load and degree level. *Required fees:* $2262 full-time, $52 per credit hour part-time, $396 per term part-time. *Room and board:* $7070; room only: $4670. Room and board charges vary according to board plan and housing facility. *Payment plan:* installment. *Waivers:* employees or children of employees.

Financial Aid Of all full-time matriculated undergraduates who enrolled in 2012, 19,786 applied for aid, 13,931 were judged to have need, 3,785 had their need fully met. 735 Federal Work-Study jobs (averaging $3920). 54 state and other part-time jobs (averaging $4403). In 2012, 278 non-need-based awards were made. *Average percent of need met:* 72%. *Average financial aid package:* $12,568. *Average need-based loan:* $6843. *Average need-based gift aid:* $6689. *Average non-need-based aid:* $3363. *Average indebtedness upon graduation:* $23,575.

Applying *Options:* electronic application, early admission, deferred entrance. *Application fee:* $60. *Required:* essay or personal statement, high school transcript. *Application deadlines:* 5/1 (freshmen), 5/1 (out-of-state freshmen), 7/1 (transfers). *Notification:* continuous (freshmen), continuous (transfers).

Freshman Application Contact Texas State University–San Marcos, 601 University Drive, San Marcos, TX 78666. *Phone:* 512-245-2364 Ext. 2803. *Website:* http://www.txstate.edu/.

Texas Tech University

Lubbock, Texas

- **State-supported** university, founded 1923, part of Texas Tech University System
- **Urban** 1839-acre campus
- **Endowment** $491.6 million
- **Coed**
- **Moderately difficult** entrance level

Faculty *Student/faculty ratio:* 24:1.

Academics *Calendar:* semesters. *Degrees:* bachelor's, master's, doctoral, and postbachelor's certificates.

Student Life *Campus security:* 24-hour emergency response devices and patrols, late-night transport/escort service, controlled dormitory access.

Athletics Member NCAA. All Division I except football (Division I-A).

Standardized Tests *Required:* SAT or ACT (for admission).

Costs (2012–13) *Tuition:* state resident $6077 full-time, $203 per credit hour part-time; nonresident $16,607 full-time, $554 per credit hour part-time. Full-time tuition and fees vary according to course load, location, and reciprocity agreements. Part-time tuition and fees vary according to course load, location, and reciprocity agreements. *Required fees:* $2865 full-time, $35 per credit hour part-time, $908 per credit hour part-time. *Room and board:* $8275; room only: $4380. Room and board charges vary according to board plan and housing facility.

Financial Aid *Of all full-time matriculated undergraduates who enrolled in 2011,* 14,181 applied for aid, 13,671 were judged to have need, 1,264 had their need fully met. *In 2011,* 992 non-need-based awards were made. *Average percent of need met:* 44. *Average financial aid package:* $10,031. *Average need-based loan:* $4425. *Average need-based gift aid:* $7430. *Average non-need-based aid:* $2130. *Average indebtedness upon graduation:* $18,358.

Applying *Options:* electronic application, early admission. *Application fee:* $60. *Required:* high school transcript. *Recommended:* essay or personal statement.

Freshman Application Contact Texas Tech University, Lubbock, TX 79409. *Phone:* 806-742-1480.

Website: http://www.ttu.edu/.

Texas Wesleyan University

Fort Worth, Texas

- **Independent United Methodist** comprehensive, founded 1890
- **Urban** 74-acre campus with easy access to Dallas-Fort Worth
- **Endowment** $47.9 million
- **Coed** 1,794 undergraduate students, 69% full-time, 58% women, 42% men
- **Moderately difficult** entrance level, 55% of applicants were admitted

Undergraduates 1,233 full-time, 561 part-time. Students come from 22 states and territories; 29 other countries; 4% are from out of state; 17% Black or African American, non-Hispanic/Latino; 21% Hispanic/Latino; 2% Asian, non-Hispanic/Latino; 0.1% Native Hawaiian or other Pacific Islander, non-Hispanic/Latino; 0.8% American Indian or Alaska Native, non-Hispanic/Latino; 3% Two or more races, non-Hispanic/Latino; 13% Race/ethnicity unknown; 8% international; 15% transferred in; 25% live on campus. *Retention:* 65% of full-time freshmen returned.

Freshmen *Admission:* 2,107 applied, 1,160 admitted, 282 enrolled. *Average high school GPA:* 3.3. *Test scores:* SAT critical reading scores over 500: 48%; SAT math scores over 500: 61%; SAT writing scores over 500: 32%; ACT scores over 18: 95%; SAT critical reading scores over 600: 12%; SAT math scores over 600: 16%; SAT writing scores over 600: 3%; ACT scores over 24: 29%; SAT critical reading scores over 700: 3%; SAT writing scores over 700: 2%; ACT scores over 30: 4%.

Faculty *Total:* 274, 63% full-time, 58% with terminal degrees. *Student/faculty ratio:* 15:1.

Academics *Calendar:* semesters. *Degrees:* bachelor's, master's, and doctoral. *Special study options:* academic remediation for entering students, accelerated degree program, advanced placement credit, distance learning, double majors, external degree program, honors programs, independent study, internships, off-campus study, part-time degree program, services for LD students, study abroad, summer session for credit. *ROTC:* Army (b), Air Force (c).

Computers on Campus 478 computers/terminals and 530 ports are available on campus for general student use. Students can access the following: campus intranet, computer help desk, free student e-mail accounts, online (class) grades, online (class) registration, online (class) schedules. Campuswide network is available. 100% of college-owned or -operated housing units are wired for high-speed Internet access. Wireless service is available via entire campus.

Student Life *Housing options:* coed, disabled students. Campus housing is university owned. *Activities and organizations:* drama/theater group, student-run newspaper, television station, choral group, Gamma Phi Beta, Alpha Xi Delta, Kappa Alpha Order, Lambda Kappa Kappa, Burleson BLUE, national fraternities, national sororities. *Campus security:* 24-hour emergency response devices and patrols, student patrols, late-night transport/escort service, controlled dormitory access. *Student services:* health clinic, personal/psychological counseling.

Athletics Member NAIA. *Intercollegiate sports:* baseball M(s), basketball M(s)/W(s), cross-country running M(s)/W(s), golf M(s)/W(s), soccer M(s)/W(s), softball W(s), table tennis M(s)/W(s), track and field M(s)/W(s), volleyball W(s). *Intramural sports:* badminton M/W, basketball M/W, bowling M/W, golf M, softball M/W, table tennis M/W, tennis W, volleyball M/W.

Standardized Tests *Required:* SAT or ACT (for admission).

Costs (2012–13) *Comprehensive fee:* $28,310 includes full-time tuition ($18,722), mandatory fees ($2118), and room and board ($7470). Full-time tuition and fees vary according to course load. Part-time tuition: $635 per credit hour. Part-time tuition and fees vary according to course load. *Required fees:* $80 per credit hour part-time. *College room only:* $4380. Room and board charges vary according to housing facility. *Payment plans:* installment, deferred payment. *Waivers:* employees or children of employees.

Financial Aid Of all full-time matriculated undergraduates who enrolled in 2011, 1,088 applied for aid, 1,079 were judged to have need, 62 had their need fully met. In 2011, 132 non-need-based awards were made. *Average percent of need met:* 64%. *Average financial aid package:* $16,198. *Average need-based loan:* $4129. *Average need-based gift aid:* $10,779. *Average non-need-based aid:* $6439.

Applying *Options:* electronic application, deferred entrance. *Required:* minimum 2.0 GPA. *Required for some:* essay or personal statement, high school transcript. *Application deadlines:* rolling (freshmen), rolling (transfers). *Notification:* continuous (freshmen), continuous (transfers).

Freshman Application Contact Texas Wesleyan University, 1201 Wesleyan Street, Fort Worth, TX 76105-1536. *Phone:* 817-531-4422. *Toll-free phone:* 800-580-8980. *Fax:* 817-531-7515. *E-mail:* admissions@txwes.edu. *Website:* http://www.txwes.edu/.

Texas Woman's University

Denton, Texas

- **State-supported** university, founded 1901
- **Suburban** 270-acre campus with easy access to Dallas-Fort Worth
- **Endowment** $10.7 million
- **Coed, primarily women** 9,443 undergraduate students, 70% full-time, 90% women, 10% men
- **Minimally difficult** entrance level, 86% of applicants were admitted

Undergraduates 6,575 full-time, 2,868 part-time. 1% are from out of state; 21% Black or African American, non-Hispanic/Latino; 22% Hispanic/Latino; 8% Asian, non-Hispanic/Latino; 0.1% Native Hawaiian or other Pacific Islander, non-Hispanic/Latino; 0.6% American Indian or Alaska Native, non-Hispanic/Latino; 2% Two or more races, non-Hispanic/Latino; 0.8% Race/ethnicity unknown; 1% international; 16% transferred in; 20% live on campus. *Retention:* 68% of full-time freshmen returned.

Freshmen *Admission:* 4,268 applied, 3,679 admitted, 1,159 enrolled. *Average high school GPA:* 3.27. *Test scores:* SAT critical reading scores over 500: 30%; SAT math scores over 500: 39%; SAT writing scores over 500: 31%; ACT scores over 18: 50%; SAT critical reading scores over 600: 7%; SAT math scores over 600: 9%; SAT writing scores over 600: 9%; SAT critical reading scores over 700: 1%; SAT writing scores over 700: 3%.

Faculty *Total:* 886, 47% full-time. *Student/faculty ratio:* 21:1.

Academics *Calendar:* semesters. *Degrees:* certificates, bachelor's, master's, doctoral, post-master's, and postbachelor's certificates. *Special study options:* academic remediation for entering students, accelerated degree program, adult/continuing education programs, advanced placement credit, cooperative education, distance learning, double majors, honors programs, independent study, internships, off-campus study, part-time degree program, services for LD students, study abroad, summer session for credit. *ROTC:* Army (c), Air Force (c).

Computers on Campus 1,380 computers/terminals and 2,143 ports are available on campus for general student use. Students can access the following: campus intranet, computer help desk, free student e-mail accounts, online (class) grades, online (class) registration, online (class) schedules. Campuswide network is available. 100% of college-owned or -operated housing units are wired for high-speed Internet access. Wireless service is available via classrooms, computer centers, computer labs, learning centers, libraries, student centers.

Student Life *Housing:* on-campus residence required through sophomore year. *Options:* coed, women-only, disabled students. Campus housing is university owned and leased by the school. Freshman campus housing is guaranteed. *Activities and organizations:* drama/theater group, student-run newspaper, choral group, Helping Hands, Athenian Honor Society, Campus Activities Board, Nursing Student Organization, Graduate Library and Information Studies Association, national fraternities, national sororities. *Campus security:* 24-hour emergency response devices and patrols, late-night transport/escort service, controlled dormitory access. *Student services:* health clinic, personal/psychological counseling.

Athletics Member NCAA. All Division II. *Intercollegiate sports:* basketball W(s), gymnastics W(s), soccer W(s), softball W(s), volleyball W(s). *Intramural sports:* badminton M/W, basketball M(c)/W(c), football M/W, golf M(c)/W(c), soccer M(c)/W(c), softball M(c)/W(c), tennis M/W, track and field M(c)/W(c), volleyball M/W, weight lifting M(c)/W(c), wrestling M(c)/W(c).

Standardized Tests *Required for some:* SAT or ACT (for admission).

Costs (2013–14) *Tuition:* state resident $5156 full-time, $172 per credit hour part-time; nonresident $15,685 full-time, $523 per credit hour part-time. Full-time tuition and fees vary according to course load, program, and reciprocity agreements. Part-time tuition and fees vary according to course load, program, and reciprocity agreements. *Required fees:* $1547 full-time. *Room and board:*

$6930; room only: $3582. Room and board charges vary according to board plan and housing facility. *Payment plan:* installment. *Waivers:* senior citizens.
Financial Aid Of all full-time matriculated undergraduates who enrolled in 2011, 4,886 applied for aid, 4,263 were judged to have need, 600 had their need fully met. In 2011, 58 non-need-based awards were made. *Average percent of need met:* 72%. *Average financial aid package:* $3705. *Average need-based loan:* $2164. *Average need-based gift aid:* $2900. *Average non-need-based aid:* $1241.
Applying *Options:* electronic application, early admission, deferred entrance. *Application fee:* $50. *Required:* high school transcript, minimum 2.0 GPA. *Application deadlines:* 7/15 (freshmen), 7/15 (transfers). *Notification:* 8/15 (freshmen), continuous until 8/15 (transfers).
Freshman Application Contact Ms. Erma Nieto-Brecht, Director of Admissions, Texas Woman's University, 304 Administration Drive, Denton, TX 76201. *Phone:* 940-898-3188. *Toll-free phone:* 866-809-6130. *Fax:* 940-898-3081. *E-mail:* admissions@twu.edu.
Website: http://www.twu.edu/.

Trinity University

San Antonio, Texas

- **Independent** comprehensive, founded 1869, affiliated with Presbyterian Church
- **Urban** 113-acre campus
- **Endowment** $915.9 million
- **Coed** 2,353 undergraduate students, 98% full-time, 54% women, 46% men
- **Very difficult** entrance level, 64% of applicants were admitted

Undergraduates 2,317 full-time, 36 part-time. Students come from 46 states and territories; 70 other countries; 29% are from out of state; 4% Black or African American, non-Hispanic/Latino; 15% Hispanic/Latino; 8% Asian, non-Hispanic/Latino; 0.5% American Indian or Alaska Native, non-Hispanic/Latino; 2% Two or more races, non-Hispanic/Latino; 4% Race/ethnicity unknown; 7% international; 1% transferred in; 74% live on campus. *Retention:* 89% of full-time freshmen returned.
Freshmen *Admission:* 4,402 applied, 2,831 admitted, 580 enrolled. *Average high school GPA:* 3.73. *Test scores:* SAT math scores over 500: 98%; SAT writing scores over 500: 91%; ACT scores over 18: 100%; SAT math scores over 600: 71%; SAT writing scores over 600: 56%; ACT scores over 24: 93%; SAT math scores over 700: 17%; SAT writing scores over 700: 14%; ACT scores over 30: 43%.
Faculty *Total:* 309, 78% full-time, 82% with terminal degrees. *Student/faculty ratio:* 9:1.
Academics *Calendar:* semesters. *Degrees:* bachelor's and master's. *Special study options:* accelerated degree program, advanced placement credit, double majors, honors programs, independent study, internships, part-time degree program, services for LD students, study abroad, summer session for credit. *ROTC:* Air Force (c).
Computers on Campus 450 computers/terminals are available on campus for general student use. Students can access the following: campus intranet, computer help desk, free student e-mail accounts, online (class) grades, online (class) registration, online (class) schedules. Campuswide network is available. 100% of college-owned or -operated housing units are wired for high-speed Internet access. Wireless service is available via entire campus.
Student Life *Housing:* on-campus residence required through junior year. *Options:* coed. Campus housing is university owned. Freshman campus housing is guaranteed. *Activities and organizations:* drama/theater group, student-run newspaper, radio and television station, choral group, Voluntary Action Center, Alpha Phi Omega, Association of Student Representatives, Activities Council, Multicultural Network. *Campus security:* 24-hour emergency response devices and patrols, late-night transport/escort service, controlled dormitory access. *Student services:* health clinic, personal/psychological counseling.
Athletics Member NCAA. All Division III. *Intercollegiate sports:* baseball M, basketball M/W, cross-country running M/W, fencing M(c)/W(c), football M, golf M/W, lacrosse M(c)/W(c), riflery M(c)/W(c), soccer M/W, softball W, swimming and diving M/W, tennis M/W, track and field M/W, volleyball M(c)/W, water polo M(c)/W(c). *Intramural sports:* basketball M/W, cross-country running M/W, equestrian sports M(c)/W(c), football M, racquetball M/W, soccer M/W, softball M/W, swimming and diving M/W, table tennis M/W, tennis M/W, ultimate Frisbee M/W, volleyball M/W, wrestling M/W.
Standardized Tests *Required:* SAT or ACT (for admission).
Costs (2012–13) *Comprehensive fee:* $44,184 includes full-time tuition ($32,578), mandatory fees ($1110), and room and board ($10,496). Full-time tuition and fees vary according to course load. Part-time tuition: $1357 per credit hour. Part-time tuition and fees vary according to course load. *College*

room only: $6520. Room and board charges vary according to board plan. *Payment plan:* installment. *Waivers:* employees or children of employees.
Financial Aid Of all full-time matriculated undergraduates who enrolled in 2012, 1,340 applied for aid, 1,118 were judged to have need, 391 had their need fully met. In 2012, 898 non-need-based awards were made. *Average percent of need met:* 88%. *Average financial aid package:* $28,521. *Average need-based loan:* $6121. *Average need-based gift aid:* $22,377. *Average non-need-based aid:* $13,979. *Average indebtedness upon graduation:* $42,987.
Applying *Options:* electronic application, early decision, early action, deferred entrance. *Application fee:* $50. *Required:* essay or personal statement, high school transcript, 2 letters of recommendation. *Recommended:* interview. *Application deadlines:* 2/1 (freshmen), 3/1 (transfers), 11/1 (early action). *Early decision deadline:* 11/1. *Notification:* 4/1 (freshmen), 4/1 (transfers), 12/1 (early decision), 12/15 (early action).
Freshman Application Contact Mr. Christopher Ellertson, Dean of Admissions and Financial Aid, Trinity University, One Trinity Place, San Antonio, TX 78212-7200. *Phone:* 210-999-7207. *Toll-free phone:* 800-TRINITY. *Fax:* 210-999-8164. *E-mail:* admissions@trinity.edu.
Website: http://www.trinity.edu/.

University of Dallas

Irving, Texas

- **Independent Roman Catholic** university, founded 1955
- **Suburban** 215-acre campus with easy access to Dallas-Fort Worth
- **Endowment** $45.6 million
- **Coed** 1,356 undergraduate students, 98% full-time, 51% women, 49% men
- **Moderately difficult** entrance level, 88% of applicants were admitted

Undergraduates 1,332 full-time, 24 part-time. Students come from 49 states and territories; 12 other countries; 55% are from out of state; 1% Black or African American, non-Hispanic/Latino; 16% Hispanic/Latino; 4% Asian, non-Hispanic/Latino; 0.1% Native Hawaiian or other Pacific Islander, non-Hispanic/Latino; 0.4% American Indian or Alaska Native, non-Hispanic/Latino; 3% Two or more races, non-Hispanic/Latino; 3% Race/ethnicity unknown; 3% international; 3% transferred in; 63% live on campus. *Retention:* 80% of full-time freshmen returned.
Freshmen *Admission:* 1,082 applied, 947 admitted, 371 enrolled. *Average high school GPA:* 3.64. *Test scores:* SAT critical reading scores over 500: 89%; SAT math scores over 500: 87%; SAT writing scores over 500: 85%; ACT scores over 18: 100%; SAT critical reading scores over 600: 61%; SAT math scores over 600: 46%; SAT writing scores over 600: 54%; ACT scores over 24: 76%; SAT critical reading scores over 700: 25%; SAT math scores over 700: 11%; SAT writing scores over 700: 15%; ACT scores over 30: 29%.
Faculty *Total:* 235, 54% full-time. *Student/faculty ratio:* 12:1.
Academics *Calendar:* semesters. *Degrees:* bachelor's, master's, doctoral, post-master's, and postbachelor's certificates. *Special study options:* advanced placement credit, double majors, independent study, internships, off-campus study, part-time degree program, services for LD students, student-designed majors, study abroad, summer session for credit. *ROTC:* Army (c), Air Force (c). *Unusual degree programs:* 3-2 nursing with Texas Woman's University-College of Nursing.
Computers on Campus 125 computers/terminals are available on campus for general student use. Students can access the following: campus intranet, computer help desk, free student e-mail accounts, online (class) grades, online (class) registration, online (class) schedules. Campuswide network is available. 100% of college-owned or -operated housing units are wired for high-speed Internet access. Wireless service is available via entire campus.
Student Life *Housing:* on-campus residence required through junior year. *Options:* men-only, women-only. Campus housing is university owned. Freshman campus housing is guaranteed. *Activities and organizations:* drama/theater group, student-run newspaper, choral group, SPUD (Programming Board), Residence Hall Association, student government, Best Buddies, Alpha Phi Omega. *Campus security:* 24-hour emergency response devices and patrols, late-night transport/escort service, controlled dormitory access. *Student services:* health clinic, personal/psychological counseling.
Athletics Member NCAA. All Division III. *Intercollegiate sports:* baseball M, basketball M/W, cross-country running M/W, golf M, lacrosse M/W, soccer M/W, softball W, track and field M/W, volleyball W. *Intramural sports:* basketball M, equestrian sports M(c)/W(c), football M/W, rugby M(c)/W(c), sailing M(c)/W(c), soccer M/W, softball M/W, tennis M(c)/W(c), ultimate Frisbee M(c)/W(c), volleyball M/W.
Standardized Tests *Required:* SAT or ACT (for admission).
Costs (2012–13) *Comprehensive fee:* $40,960 includes full-time tuition ($29,140), mandatory fees ($1930), and room and board ($9890). Part-time tuition: $1210 per credit. *Required fees:* $1930 per year part-time. *College*

room only: $5690. Room and board charges vary according to board plan and housing facility. *Payment plan:* installment. *Waivers:* employees or children of employees.

Financial Aid Of all full-time matriculated undergraduates who enrolled in 2012, 912 applied for aid, 812 were judged to have need, 128 had their need fully met. 185 Federal Work-Study jobs (averaging $1597). 55 state and other part-time jobs (averaging $1830). In 2012, 517 non-need-based awards were made. *Average percent of need met:* 72%. *Average financial aid package:* $25,041. *Average need-based loan:* $5974. *Average need-based gift aid:* $19,741. *Average non-need-based aid:* $11,506. *Average indebtedness upon graduation:* $31,466.

Applying *Options:* electronic application, early action, deferred entrance. *Application fee:* $40. *Required:* essay or personal statement, high school transcript, 2 letters of recommendation. *Required for some:* interview. *Application deadlines:* 3/1 (freshmen), 3/1 (out-of-state freshmen), 8/1 (transfers), 12/1 (early action). *Notification:* continuous (freshmen), continuous (transfers), 1/15 (early action).

Freshman Application Contact Mr. Andrew Klein, Campus Visit Coordinator, University of Dallas, 1845 East Northgate Drive, Irving, TX 75062-4736. *Phone:* 800-628-6999. *Toll-free phone:* 800-628-6999. *Fax:* 972-721-5017. *E-mail:* ugadmis@udallas.edu.
Website: http://www.udallas.edu/.

See below for display ad and page 1556 for the College Close-Up.

University of Houston

Houston, Texas

- **State-supported** university, founded 1927, part of University of Houston System
- **Urban** 594-acre campus
- **Endowment** $359.0 million
- **Coed** 32,639 undergraduate students, 72% full-time, 49% women, 51% men
- **Moderately difficult** entrance level, 56% of applicants were admitted

Undergraduates 23,578 full-time, 9,061 part-time. Students come from 52 states and territories; 119 other countries; 2% are from out of state; 12% Black or African American, non-Hispanic/Latino; 28% Hispanic/Latino; 21% Asian, non-Hispanic/Latino; 0.3% Native Hawaiian or other Pacific Islander, non-Hispanic/Latino; 0.2% American Indian or Alaska Native, non-Hispanic/Latino; 3% Two or more races, non-Hispanic/Latino; 0.6% Race/ethnicity unknown; 4% international; 13% transferred in; 16% live on campus. *Retention:* 83% of full-time freshmen returned.

Freshmen *Admission:* 17,020 applied, 9,565 admitted, 3,492 enrolled. *Test scores:* SAT critical reading scores over 500: 75%; SAT math scores over 500: 88%; ACT scores over 18: 95%; SAT critical reading scores over 600: 27%; SAT math scores over 600: 47%; ACT scores over 24: 57%; SAT critical reading scores over 700: 5%; SAT math scores over 700: 9%; ACT scores over 30: 10%.

Faculty *Total:* 1,966, 70% full-time, 74% with terminal degrees. *Student/faculty ratio:* 22:1.

Academics *Calendar:* semesters. *Degrees:* bachelor's, master's, and doctoral. *Special study options:* academic remediation for entering students, adult/continuing education programs, advanced placement credit, cooperative education, distance learning, double majors, English as a second language, freshman honors college, honors programs, independent study, internships, off-campus study, part-time degree program, services for LD students, student-designed majors, study abroad, summer session for credit. *ROTC:* Army (b), Navy (c), Air Force (b). *Unusual degree programs:* 3-2 business administration.

Computers on Campus 997 computers/terminals and 25,000 ports are available on campus for general student use. Students can access the following: campus intranet, computer help desk, free student e-mail accounts, online (class) grades, online (class) registration, online (class) schedules. Campus-wide network is available. 100% of college-owned or -operated housing units are wired for high-speed Internet access. Wireless service is available via entire campus.

Student Life *Housing options:* coed, disabled students. Campus housing is university owned and is provided by a third party. *Activities and organizations:* drama/theater group, student-run newspaper, television station, choral group, marching band, Student Government Association, Residence Hall Association, Metropolitan Volunteer Program, Student Governing Board- Honors College, Student Alumni Connection, national fraternities, national sororities. *Campus security:* 24-hour emergency response devices and patrols, student patrols, late-night transport/escort service, controlled dormitory access, vehicle assistance. *Student services:* health clinic, personal/psychological counseling, women's center, legal services.

Athletics Member NCAA. All Division I except football (Division I-A). *Intercollegiate sports:* baseball M(s), basketball M(s)/W(s), cross-country running M(s)/W(s), golf M(s)/W(s), soccer W(s), softball W(s), swimming and diving W(s), tennis W(s), track and field M(s)/W(s), volleyball W(s). *Intramural*

sports: badminton M/W, basketball M/W, bowling M(c)/W, fencing M(c)/W(c), golf M/W, racquetball M/W, rock climbing M/W, soccer M/W, softball M/W, swimming and diving M/W, table tennis M/W, tennis M/W, track and field M/W, ultimate Frisbee M(c)/W(c), volleyball M/W(c), water polo M(c)/W(c), weight lifting M/W.

Standardized Tests *Required:* SAT or ACT (for admission).

Costs (2013–14) *Tuition:* state resident $8970 full-time; nonresident $19,500 full-time. Full-time tuition and fees vary according to course level, course load, degree level, program, and student level. Part-time tuition and fees vary according to course level, course load, degree level, program, and student level. *Required fees:* $918 full-time. *Room and board:* Room and board charges vary according to board plan and housing facility. *Payment plans:* installment, deferred payment. *Waivers:* employees or children of employees.

Financial Aid Of all full-time matriculated undergraduates who enrolled in 2011, 16,292 applied for aid, 14,759 were judged to have need, 2,501 had their need fully met. In 2011, 308 non-need-based awards were made. *Average percent of need met:* 71%. *Average financial aid package:* $12,558. *Average need-based loan:* $7588. *Average need-based gift aid:* $6306. *Average non-need-based aid:* $4795. *Average indebtedness upon graduation:* $15,613.

Applying *Options:* electronic application. *Application fee:* $50. *Required:* high school transcript, SAT or ACT Scores. *Application deadlines:* 4/1 (freshmen), 6/1 (transfers). *Notification:* continuous (freshmen), continuous (transfers).

Freshman Application Contact Jeff Fuller, Director, Student Recruitment, University of Houston, Welcome Center, 4400 University Boulevard, Houston, TX 77204-2023. *Phone:* 713-743-1010. *Fax:* 713-743-9633. *E-mail:* jdfuller@central.uh.edu.
Website: http://www.uh.edu/.

University of Houston–Clear Lake
Houston, Texas

- **State-supported** upper-level, founded 1971, part of University of Houston System
- **Suburban** 524-acre campus with easy access to Houston
- **Coed** 4,790 undergraduate students, 45% full-time, 68% women, 32% men
- **Minimally difficult** entrance level, 73% of applicants were admitted

Undergraduates 2,143 full-time, 2,647 part-time. Students come from 9 states and territories; 27 other countries; 9% Black or African American, non-Hispanic/Latino; 32% Hispanic/Latino; 6% Asian, non-Hispanic/Latino; 0.2% Native Hawaiian or other Pacific Islander, non-Hispanic/Latino; 0.3% American Indian or Alaska Native, non-Hispanic/Latino; 0.4% Two or more races, non-Hispanic/Latino; 1% Race/ethnicity unknown; 2% international; 22% transferred in.

Freshmen *Admission:* 2,177 applied, 1,596 admitted.

Faculty *Total:* 484, 51% full-time, 64% with terminal degrees. *Student/faculty ratio:* 17:1.

Academics *Calendar:* semesters. *Degrees:* certificates, bachelor's, master's, doctoral, post-master's, and postbachelor's certificates. *Special study options:* academic remediation for entering students, advanced placement credit, cooperative education, distance learning, double majors, English as a second language, independent study, internships, off-campus study, part-time degree program, services for LD students, study abroad, summer session for credit.

Computers on Campus 800 computers/terminals are available on campus for general student use. Students can access the following: campus intranet, computer help desk, free student e-mail accounts, online (class) grades, online (class) registration, online (class) schedules. Campuswide network is available. Wireless service is available via entire campus.

Student Life *Housing options:* coed. Campus housing is provided by a third party. *Activities and organizations:* student-run newspaper, Beta Alpha Psi, National Society of Leadership and Success, Applied Behavior Student Analysis Student Organization, Student Government Association, Accounting Association. *Campus security:* 24-hour emergency response devices and patrols, student patrols, late-night transport/escort service. *Student services:* health clinic, personal/psychological counseling, women's center.

Costs (2012–13) *Tuition:* state resident $5326 full-time, $178 per credit hour part-time; nonresident $17,110 full-time, $572 per credit hour part-time. Full-time tuition and fees vary according to course load and program. Part-time tuition and fees vary according to course load and program. *Required fees:* $1254 full-time, $486 per term part-time. *Room only:* $8354. Room and board charges vary according to housing facility. *Payment plans:* installment, deferred payment. *Waivers:* senior citizens.

Financial Aid Of all full-time matriculated undergraduates who enrolled in 2012, 1,666 applied for aid, 1,550 were judged to have need, 383 had their need fully met. 55 Federal Work-Study jobs (averaging $2619). 17 state and other part-time jobs (averaging $2807). In 2012, 62 non-need-based awards were made. *Average percent of need met:* 44%. *Average financial aid package:* $7651. *Average need-based loan:* $4527. *Average need-based gift aid:* $3154. *Average non-need-based aid:* $755.

Applying *Options:* electronic application, early admission, deferred entrance. *Application fee:* $45. *Application deadline:* 8/11 (transfers). *Notification:* continuous (transfers).

Application Contact Ms. Rauchelle Jones, Executive Director of Admissions, University of Houston–Clear Lake, 2700 Bay Area Boulevard, Box 13, Houston, TX 77058-1098. *Phone:* 281-283-2518. *Fax:* 281-283-2530. *E-mail:* admissions@uhcl.edu.
Website: http://www.uhcl.edu/.

University of Houston–Downtown
Houston, Texas

- **State-supported** comprehensive, founded 1974, part of University of Houston System
- **Urban** 24-acre campus
- **Endowment** $35.5 million
- **Coed** 13,709 undergraduate students, 49% full-time, 60% women, 40% men
- **Noncompetitive** entrance level, 91% of applicants were admitted

Undergraduates 6,768 full-time, 6,941 part-time. Students come from 28 states and territories; 65 other countries; 27% Black or African American, non-Hispanic/Latino; 38% Hispanic/Latino; 8% Asian, non-Hispanic/Latino; 0.2% Native Hawaiian or other Pacific Islander, non-Hispanic/Latino; 0.4% American Indian or Alaska Native, non-Hispanic/Latino; 1% Two or more races, non-Hispanic/Latino; 0.9% Race/ethnicity unknown; 5% international; 16% transferred in. *Retention:* 67% of full-time freshmen returned.

Freshmen *Admission:* 4,194 applied, 3,837 admitted, 1,442 enrolled. *Test scores:* SAT critical reading scores over 500: 16%; SAT math scores over 500: 31%; ACT scores over 18: 56%; SAT critical reading scores over 600: 2%; SAT math scores over 600: 4%; ACT scores over 24: 8%.

Faculty *Total:* 673, 50% full-time, 62% with terminal degrees. *Student/faculty ratio:* 20:1.

Academics *Calendar:* semesters. *Degrees:* bachelor's and master's. *Special study options:* academic remediation for entering students, advanced placement credit, distance learning, double majors, English as a second language, independent study, internships, off-campus study, part-time degree program, services for LD students, study abroad, summer session for credit. *ROTC:* Army (c), Air Force (c).

Computers on Campus 583 computers/terminals are available on campus for general student use. Students can access the following: computer help desk, free student e-mail accounts, online (class) grades, online (class) registration, online (class) schedules. Campuswide network is available. Wireless service is available via entire campus.

Student Life *Housing:* college housing not available. *Activities and organizations:* drama/theater group, student-run newspaper, Bilingual Education Student Organization, Student Government Association, Alpha Phi Sigma, American Marketing Association, Professional Accounting Society, national fraternities, national sororities. *Campus security:* 24-hour emergency response devices and patrols, late-night transport/escort service. *Student services:* health clinic, personal/psychological counseling, legal services.

Athletics *Intramural sports:* badminton M/W, baseball M(c), basketball M(c)/W(c), bowling M/W, cheerleading M(c)/W(c), soccer M(c)/W(c), tennis M/W, volleyball M(c)/W(c), weight lifting M(c)/W(c).

Standardized Tests *Required for some:* SAT or ACT (for admission). *Recommended:* SAT or ACT (for admission).

Costs (2012–13) *Tuition:* state resident $4875 full-time, $163 per credit hour part-time; nonresident $15,405 full-time, $514 per credit hour part-time. Full-time tuition and fees vary according to course load and program. Part-time tuition and fees vary according to course load and program. *Required fees:* $1122 full-time, $163 per credit hour part-time. *Payment plan:* installment. *Waivers:* senior citizens.

Financial Aid Of all full-time matriculated undergraduates who enrolled in 2010, 3,946 applied for aid, 3,775 were judged to have need, 128 had their need fully met. 199 Federal Work-Study jobs (averaging $3312). 27 state and other part-time jobs (averaging $2893). In 2010, 128 non-need-based awards were made. *Average percent of need met:* 49%. *Average financial aid package:* $8441. *Average need-based loan:* $3686. *Average need-based gift aid:* $6222. *Average non-need-based aid:* $2668. *Average indebtedness upon graduation:* $15,484.

Applying *Options:* electronic application. *Application fee:* $35. *Required:* high school transcript. *Application deadlines:* 6/1 (freshmen), 8/1 (transfers). *Notification:* continuous (freshmen), continuous (transfers).

Freshman Application Contact Ms. Kecia Osbourne, Assistant Director of Admissions-Outreach Services, University of Houston–Downtown, One Main Street, Suite 350-S, Houston, TX 77002. *Phone:* 713-221-8522. *Fax:* 713-221-8157. *E-mail:* uhdadmit@uhd.edu.
Website: http://www.uhd.edu/.

University of Houston–Victoria

Victoria, Texas

- **State-supported** upper-level, founded 1973, part of University of Houston System
- **Small-town** 20-acre campus
- **Endowment** $14.5 million
- **Coed** 2,664 undergraduate students, 47% full-time, 67% women, 33% men
- **Minimally difficult** entrance level, 51% of applicants were admitted

Undergraduates 1,254 full-time, 1,410 part-time. 16% Black or African American, non-Hispanic/Latino; 29% Hispanic/Latino; 6% Asian, non-Hispanic/Latino; 0.3% Native Hawaiian or other Pacific Islander, non-Hispanic/Latino; 0.1% American Indian or Alaska Native, non-Hispanic/Latino; 3% Two or more races, non-Hispanic/Latino; 0.8% Race/ethnicity unknown; 1% international; 16% transferred in; 12% live on campus.
Freshmen *Admission:* 2,455 applied, 1,244 admitted.
Faculty *Total:* 212, 60% full-time, 70% with terminal degrees. *Student/faculty ratio:* 18:1.
Academics *Calendar:* semesters. *Degrees:* bachelor's, master's, post-master's, and postbachelor's certificates. *Special study options:* accelerated degree program, adult/continuing education programs, distance learning, double majors, honors programs, independent study, internships, part-time degree program, study abroad. *ROTC:* Air Force (c).
Computers on Campus Students can access the following: campus intranet, computer help desk, free student e-mail accounts, online (class) grades, online (class) registration, online (class) schedules. Campuswide network is available. 100% of college-owned or -operated housing units are wired for high-speed Internet access. Wireless service is available via entire campus.
Student Life *Housing options:* coed. Campus housing is university owned. Freshman applicants given priority for college housing. *Campus security:* 24-hour emergency response devices and patrols, controlled dormitory access. *Student services:* personal/psychological counseling.
Athletics Member NAIA. *Intercollegiate sports:* baseball M, golf M/W, soccer M/W, softball W.
Costs (2012–13) *Tuition:* state resident $4809 full-time, $160 per credit hour part-time; nonresident $15,338 full-time, $511 per credit hour part-time. Full-time tuition and fees vary according to course level and course load. Part-time tuition and fees vary according to course level and course load. *Required fees:* $1308 full-time, $61 per credit hour part-time. *Room and board:* $7042. Room and board charges vary according to board plan and housing facility. *Payment plan:* installment. *Waivers:* senior citizens and employees or children of employees.
Financial Aid Of all full-time matriculated undergraduates who enrolled in 2010, 804 applied for aid, 740 were judged to have need. In 2010, 29 non-need-based awards were made. *Average financial aid package:* $8649. *Average need-based loan:* $4082. *Average need-based gift aid:* $5557. *Average non-need-based aid:* $1574.
Applying *Options:* electronic application, deferred entrance. *Application deadline:* rolling (transfers). *Notification:* continuous (transfers).
Application Contact Mrs. Trudy Wortham, Registrar, University of Houston–Victoria, 3007 North Ben Wilson, Victoria, TX 77901. *Phone:* 361-485-4521 Ext. 4184. *Toll-free phone:* 877-970-4848 Ext. 110. *E-mail:* worthamt@uhv.edu.
Website: http://www.uhv.edu/.

University of Mary Hardin-Baylor

Belton, Texas

- **Independent Southern Baptist** comprehensive, founded 1845
- **Small-town** 100-acre campus with easy access to Austin
- **Endowment** $63.1 million
- **Coed**
- **Moderately difficult** entrance level

Faculty *Student/faculty ratio:* 16:1.

Academics *Calendar:* semesters. *Degrees:* bachelor's, master's, and doctoral.
Student Life *Campus security:* 24-hour emergency response devices and patrols, late-night transport/escort service, controlled dormitory access, campus police force, lighted pathways and sidewalks.
Athletics Member NCAA. All Division III.
Standardized Tests *Required:* SAT or ACT (for admission).
Costs (2012–13) *Comprehensive fee:* $30,370 includes full-time tuition ($21,900), mandatory fees ($2250), and room and board ($6220). Full-time tuition and fees vary according to course load and degree level. Part-time tuition: $730 per credit hour. Part-time tuition and fees vary according to course load and degree level. *Required fees:* $75 per credit hour part-time, $50 per term part-time. *Room and board:* Room and board charges vary according to board plan and housing facility.
Financial Aid Of all full-time matriculated undergraduates who enrolled in 2012, 2,355 applied for aid, 2,158 were judged to have need, 165 had their need fully met. 210 Federal Work-Study jobs (averaging $2395). 349 state and other part-time jobs (averaging $2406). *In 2012,* 330 non-need-based awards were made. *Average percent of need met:* 58. *Average financial aid package:* $15,419. *Average need-based loan:* $4520. *Average need-based gift aid:* $11,412. *Average non-need-based aid:* $5720. *Average indebtedness upon graduation:* $34,655.
Applying *Options:* electronic application, early admission, deferred entrance. *Application fee:* $35. *Required:* high school transcript. *Required for some:* essay or personal statement, interview.
Freshman Application Contact Mr. Brent Burks, Director of Admissions, University of Mary Hardin-Baylor, UMHB Station Box 8004, 900 College Street, Belton, TX 76513-2599. *Phone:* 254-295-4520. *Toll-free phone:* 800-727-8642. *Fax:* 254-295-5049. *E-mail:* admission@umhb.edu.
Website: http://www.umhb.edu/.

University of North Texas

Denton, Texas

- **State-supported** university, founded 1890, part of University of North Texas System
- **Suburban** 875-acre campus with easy access to Dallas-Fort Worth
- **Endowment** $113.0 million
- **Coed** 28,956 undergraduate students, 81% full-time, 52% women, 48% men
- **Moderately difficult** entrance level, 64% of applicants were admitted

Undergraduates 23,346 full-time, 5,610 part-time. 4% are from out of state; 13% Black or African American, non-Hispanic/Latino; 19% Hispanic/Latino; 5% Asian, non-Hispanic/Latino; 0.1% Native Hawaiian or other Pacific Islander, non-Hispanic/Latino; 0.5% American Indian or Alaska Native, non-Hispanic/Latino; 3% Two or more races, non-Hispanic/Latino; 1% Race/ethnicity unknown; 3% international; 13% transferred in; 19% live on campus. *Retention:* 79% of full-time freshmen returned.
Freshmen *Admission:* 14,853 applied, 9,503 admitted, 4,453 enrolled. *Test scores:* SAT critical reading scores over 500: 70%; SAT math scores over 500: 77%; SAT writing scores over 500: 58%; ACT scores over 18: 95%; SAT critical reading scores over 600: 26%; SAT math scores over 600: 30%; SAT writing scores over 600: 18%; ACT scores over 24: 45%; SAT critical reading scores over 700: 5%; SAT math scores over 700: 7%; SAT writing scores over 700: 3%; ACT scores over 30: 5%.
Faculty *Total:* 1,489, 66% full-time, 54% with terminal degrees. *Student/faculty ratio:* 23:1.
Academics *Calendar:* semesters. *Degrees:* bachelor's, master's, doctoral, and postbachelor's certificates. *Special study options:* academic remediation for entering students, accelerated degree program, advanced placement credit, cooperative education, distance learning, double majors, English as a second language, freshman honors college, honors programs, independent study, internships, off-campus study, part-time degree program, services for LD students, study abroad, summer session for credit. *ROTC:* Army (b), Air Force (b).
Computers on Campus Students can access the following: campus intranet, computer help desk, free student e-mail accounts, online (class) grades, online (class) registration, online (class) schedules. Campuswide network is available. 100% of college-owned or -operated housing units are wired for high-speed Internet access. Wireless service is available via entire campus.
Student Life *Housing:* on-campus residence required for freshman year. *Options:* coed, women-only, disabled students. Campus housing is university owned. Freshman applicants given priority for college housing. *Activities and organizations:* drama/theater group, student-run newspaper, radio and television station, choral group, marching band, Student Government Association, Residence Hall Association, Panhellenic Association, Interfraternity Council, College Life, national fraternities, national sororities. *Campus security:* 24-

hour emergency response devices and patrols, late-night transport/escort service, controlled dormitory access. *Student services:* health clinic, personal/psychological counseling, women's center, legal services.

Athletics Member NCAA. All Division I except football (Division I-A). *Intercollegiate sports:* baseball M(c), basketball M(s)/W(s), bowling M(c)/W(c), cross-country running M(s)/W(s), fencing M(c)/W(s), golf M(s)/W(s), ice hockey M(c), lacrosse M(c)/W(c), racquetball M(c)/W(c), sailing M(c)/W(c), soccer M(c)/W(s), softball M/W(s), swimming and diving M(c)/W(s), tennis M(c)/W, track and field M(s)/W(s), ultimate Frisbee M(c)/W(c), volleyball W(s). *Intramural sports:* basketball M/W, bowling M/W, football M, golf M/W, racquetball M/W, soccer M/W, softball M/W, table tennis M/W, tennis M/W, volleyball M/W.

Standardized Tests *Required:* SAT or ACT (for admission).

Costs (2013–14) *Tuition:* state resident $6488 full-time; nonresident $17,018 full-time. *Required fees:* $2590 full-time. *Room and board:* $7150. Room and board charges vary according to board plan and housing facility. *Payment plan:* installment. *Waivers:* senior citizens and employees or children of employees.

Financial Aid Of all full-time matriculated undergraduates who enrolled in 2011, 16,413 applied for aid, 13,466 were judged to have need, 2,325 had their need fully met. In 2011, 2382 non-need-based awards were made. *Average percent of need met:* 63%. *Average financial aid package:* $10,412. *Average need-based loan:* $4539. *Average need-based gift aid:* $6617. *Average non-need-based aid:* $4403.

Applying *Options:* electronic application, early admission, deferred entrance. *Application fee:* $60. *Required:* high school transcript. *Required for some:* essay or personal statement. *Application deadlines:* 8/1 (freshmen), rolling (transfers). *Notification:* continuous (freshmen), continuous (transfers).

Freshman Application Contact Mr. Jasiel Perez, Associate Director of Admissions, University of North Texas, Denton, TX 76203. *Phone:* 940-369-7664. *Toll-free phone:* 800-868-8211. *E-mail:* jasiel.perez@unt.edu. *Website:* http://www.unt.edu/.

University of Phoenix–Austin Campus

Austin, Texas

Admissions Office Contact University of Phoenix–Austin Campus, 10801 North Mopac, Austin, TX 78759. *Toll-free phone:* 866-766-0766. *Website:* http://www.phoenix.edu/.

University of Phoenix–Dallas Campus

Dallas, Texas

Freshman Application Contact Marc Booker, Sr. Director, Office of Admissions and Evaluation, University of Phoenix–Dallas Campus, 4035 South Riverpoint Parkway, Mail Stop CF-L101, Phoenix, AZ 85040. *Phone:* 602-557-4609. *Toll-free phone:* 866-766-0766. *Fax:* 480-643-1156. *Website:* http://www.phoenix.edu/.

University of Phoenix–Houston Campus

Houston, Texas

Freshman Application Contact Marc Booker, Sr. Director, Office of Admissions and Evaluation, University of Phoenix–Houston Campus, 4305 South Riverpoint Parkway, Mail Stop CF-L101, Phoenix, AZ 85040. *Phone:* 602-557-4609. *Toll-free phone:* 866-766-0766. *Fax:* 480-643-1156. *Website:* http://www.phoenix.edu/.

University of Phoenix–San Antonio Campus

San Antonio, Texas

Admissions Office Contact University of Phoenix–San Antonio Campus, 8200 IH-10 West, Suite 900, San Antonio, TX 78230. *Toll-free phone:* 866-766-0766.
Website: http://www.phoenix.edu/.

University of St. Thomas

Houston, Texas

- **Independent Roman Catholic** comprehensive, founded 1947
- **Urban** 20-acre campus
- **Endowment** $64.7 million
- **Coed** 1,626 undergraduate students, 77% full-time, 62% women, 38% men
- **Moderately difficult** entrance level, 80% of applicants were admitted

Undergraduates 1,255 full-time, 371 part-time. Students come from 31 states and territories; 38 other countries; 4% are from out of state; 5% Black or African American, non-Hispanic/Latino; 37% Hispanic/Latino; 12% Asian, non-Hispanic/Latino; 0.1% Native Hawaiian or other Pacific Islander, non-Hispanic/Latino; 0.3% American Indian or Alaska Native, non-Hispanic/Latino; 2% Two or more races, non-Hispanic/Latino; 1% Race/ethnicity unknown; 8% international; 9% transferred in; 17% live on campus. *Retention:* 79% of full-time freshmen returned.

Freshmen *Admission:* 863 applied, 690 admitted, 271 enrolled. *Average high school GPA:* 3.61. *Test scores:* SAT critical reading scores over 500: 79%; SAT math scores over 500: 83%; SAT writing scores over 500: 72%; ACT scores over 18: 100%; SAT critical reading scores over 600: 27%; SAT math scores over 600: 40%; SAT writing scores over 600: 29%; ACT scores over 24: 67%; SAT critical reading scores over 700: 5%; SAT math scores over 700: 5%; SAT writing scores over 700: 5%; ACT scores over 30: 10%.

Faculty *Total:* 335, 46% full-time, 80% with terminal degrees. *Student/faculty ratio:* 11:1.

Academics *Calendar:* semesters. *Degrees:* diplomas, bachelor's, master's, and doctoral. *Special study options:* accelerated degree program, adult/continuing education programs, advanced placement credit, distance learning, double majors, honors programs, independent study, internships, off-campus study, part-time degree program, services for LD students, student-designed majors, study abroad, summer session for credit. *ROTC:* Army (c), Air Force (c). *Unusual degree programs:* 3-2 business administration; engineering with University of Notre Dame, University of Houston, Texas A&M University.

Computers on Campus 316 computers/terminals and 400 ports are available on campus for general student use. Students can access the following: campus intranet, computer help desk, free student e-mail accounts, online (class) grades, online (class) registration, online (class) schedules. Campuswide network is available. 95% of college-owned or -operated housing units are wired for high-speed Internet access. Wireless service is available via entire campus.

Student Life *Housing options:* coed, disabled students. Campus housing is university owned. Freshman applicants given priority for college housing. *Activities and organizations:* drama/theater group, student-run newspaper, choral group, Health Occupations Students of America (HOSA), Nursing Student Association, Student Activities Board (SAB), American Chemical Society, Soccer. *Campus security:* 24-hour emergency response devices and patrols, late-night transport/escort service, controlled dormitory access. *Student services:* personal/psychological counseling.

Athletics Member NAIA. *Intercollegiate sports:* basketball M(s)/W(s), cheerleading M(c)/W(c), fencing M(c)/W(c), golf M(s)/W(s), rugby M(c), soccer M(s), table tennis M(c)/W(c), tennis M(c)/W(c), ultimate Frisbee M(c)/W(c), volleyball W(s). *Intramural sports:* basketball M/W, bowling M/W, racquetball M/W, rock climbing M/W, soccer M(c)/W(c), table tennis M/W, tennis M/W, ultimate Frisbee M/W, volleyball M/W.

Standardized Tests *Required:* SAT or ACT (for admission).

Costs (2012–13) *Comprehensive fee:* $34,790 includes full-time tuition ($26,550), mandatory fees ($340), and room and board ($7900). Full-time tuition and fees vary according to course load. Part-time tuition: $885 per credit hour. Part-time tuition and fees vary according to course load. *College room only:* $4800. Room and board charges vary according to board plan and housing facility. *Payment plans:* installment, deferred payment. *Waivers:* senior citizens and employees or children of employees.

Financial Aid Of all full-time matriculated undergraduates who enrolled in 2012, 816 applied for aid, 743 were judged to have need, 91 had their need

fully met. 50 Federal Work-Study jobs (averaging $3843). In 2012, 362 non-need-based awards were made. *Average percent of need met:* 64%. *Average financial aid package:* $17,805. *Average need-based loan:* $4806. *Average need-based gift aid:* $14,135. *Average non-need-based aid:* $8963. *Average indebtedness upon graduation:* $33,936.

Applying *Options:* electronic application, early action, deferred entrance. *Application fee:* $25. *Required:* essay or personal statement, high school transcript, minimum 2.8 GPA, 1070 SAT (Critical Reading and Math) or 23 ACT. *Application deadlines:* 5/1 (freshmen), 5/1 (out-of-state freshmen), rolling (transfers), 11/1 (early action). *Notification:* continuous until 11/15 (freshmen), continuous until 11/15 (out-of-state freshmen), continuous (transfers), 12/15 (early action).

Freshman Application Contact Mr. Arthur Ortiz, Assistant Vice President of Enrollment, University of St. Thomas, 3800 Montrose Boulevard, Houston, TX 77006-4696. *Phone:* 713-525-3848. *Toll-free phone:* 800-856-8565. *Fax:* 713-525-3558. *E-mail:* admissions@stthom.edu.
Website: http://www.stthom.edu/.

The University of Texas at Arlington

Arlington, Texas

- **State-supported** university, founded 1895, part of University of Texas System
- **Urban** 420-acre campus with easy access to Dallas-Fort Worth
- **Endowment** $83.3 million
- **Coed** 25,761 undergraduate students, 63% full-time, 56% women, 44% men
- **Moderately difficult** entrance level, 59% of applicants were admitted

Undergraduates 16,164 full-time, 9,597 part-time. Students come from 49 states and territories; 65 other countries; 23% are from out of state; 15% Black or African American, non-Hispanic/Latino; 24% Hispanic/Latino; 11% Asian, non-Hispanic/Latino; 0.2% Native Hawaiian or other Pacific Islander, non-Hispanic/Latino; 0.4% American Indian or Alaska Native, non-Hispanic/Latino; 3% Two or more races, non-Hispanic/Latino; 1% Race/ethnicity unknown; 4% international; 34% transferred in; 11% live on campus. *Retention:* 76% of full-time freshmen returned.

Freshmen *Admission:* 10,280 applied, 6,017 admitted, 2,473 enrolled. *Test scores:* SAT critical reading scores over 500: 62%; SAT math scores over 500: 79%; SAT writing scores over 500: 55%; ACT scores over 18: 90%; SAT critical reading scores over 600: 21%; SAT math scores over 600: 35%; SAT writing scores over 600: 15%; ACT scores over 24: 45%; SAT critical reading scores over 700: 3%; SAT math scores over 700: 6%; SAT writing scores over 700: 1%; ACT scores over 30: 4%.

Faculty *Total:* 1,399, 60% full-time. *Student/faculty ratio:* 23:1.

Academics *Calendar:* semesters. *Degrees:* bachelor's, master's, doctoral, post-master's, and postbachelor's certificates. *Special study options:* academic remediation for entering students, adult/continuing education programs, advanced placement credit, cooperative education, distance learning, double majors, English as a second language, freshman honors college, honors programs, independent study, internships, off-campus study, part-time degree program, services for LD students, student-designed majors, study abroad, summer session for credit. *ROTC:* Army (b), Air Force (c). *Unusual degree programs:* 3-2 business administration; psychology, health care administration.

Computers on Campus 500 computers/terminals and 6,000 ports are available on campus for general student use. Students can access the following: campus intranet, computer help desk, free student e-mail accounts, online (class) grades, online (class) registration, online (class) schedules. Campus-wide network is available. 90% of college-owned or -operated housing units are wired for high-speed Internet access. Wireless service is available via classrooms, computer labs, learning centers, libraries, student centers.

Student Life *Housing options:* coed, men-only, women-only. Campus housing is university owned and leased by the school. *Activities and organizations:* drama/theater group, student-run newspaper, radio station, choral group, marching band, Baptist Student Ministry, Association of Mexican American Students, Latin American Student Association, Asian Student Association, African Student Association, national fraternities, national sororities. *Campus security:* 24-hour emergency response devices and patrols, late-night transport/escort service, controlled dormitory access, remote emergency telephones, bicycle patrols, crime prevention program, student shuttle service. *Student services:* health clinic, personal/psychological counseling, legal services.

Athletics Member NCAA. All Division I. *Intercollegiate sports:* baseball M(s), basketball M(s)/W(s), golf M, softball W(s), tennis M(s)/W(s), track and field M(s)/W(s), volleyball W(s). *Intramural sports:* badminton M/W, basket-

ball M/W, bowling M/W, golf M, racquetball M/W, soccer M/W, softball M/W, table tennis M/W, tennis M/W, volleyball M/W.

Standardized Tests *Required:* SAT or ACT (for admission).

Costs (2012–13) *Tuition:* state resident $8878 full-time; nonresident $19,408 full-time. Full-time tuition and fees vary according to course level, course load, and program. Part-time tuition and fees vary according to course level, course load, and program. *Room and board:* $7708; room only: $4028. Room and board charges vary according to board plan and housing facility. *Payment plan:* installment. *Waivers:* employees or children of employees.

Financial Aid Of all full-time matriculated undergraduates who enrolled in 2012, 12,158 applied for aid, 11,097 were judged to have need, 1,221 had their need fully met. 1,605 Federal Work-Study jobs (averaging $2926). 272 state and other part-time jobs (averaging $982). In 2012, 168 non-need-based awards were made. *Average percent of need met:* 77%. *Average financial aid package:* $12,673. *Average need-based loan:* $4244. *Average need-based gift aid:* $6907. *Average non-need-based aid:* $5179. *Average indebtedness upon graduation:* $22,137.

Applying *Options:* electronic application, deferred entrance. *Application fee:* $50. *Required:* high school transcript, class rank. *Application deadlines:* 6/1 (freshmen), rolling (transfers). *Notification:* continuous (freshmen), continuous (transfers).

Freshman Application Contact Dr. Hans Gatterdam, Executive Director of Admissions, Records and Registration, The University of Texas at Arlington, UTA Box 19088, 701 South Nedderman Drive, Arlington, TX 76019-0088. *Phone:* 817-272-3275. *Fax:* 817-272-3435. *E-mail:* admissions@uta.edu. *Website:* http://www.uta.edu/.

The University of Texas at Austin

Austin, Texas

- **State-supported** university, founded 1883, part of University of Texas System
- **Urban** 431-acre campus with easy access to San Antonio
- **Endowment** $2.9 billion
- **Coed** 39,955 undergraduate students, 93% full-time, 51% women, 49% men
- **Very difficult** entrance level, 47% of applicants were admitted

Undergraduates 37,083 full-time, 2,872 part-time. Students come from 53 states and territories; 99 other countries; 5% are from out of state; 4% Black or African American, non-Hispanic/Latino; 21% Hispanic/Latino; 18% Asian, non-Hispanic/Latino; 0.1% Native Hawaiian or other Pacific Islander, non-Hispanic/Latino; 0.3% American Indian or Alaska Native, non-Hispanic/Latino; 2% Two or more races, non-Hispanic/Latino; 0.3% Race/ethnicity unknown; 5% international; 7% transferred in; 19% live on campus. *Retention:* 93% of full-time freshmen returned.

Freshmen *Admission:* 35,431 applied, 16,563 admitted, 8,092 enrolled. *Test scores:* SAT critical reading scores over 500: 88%; SAT math scores over 500: 95%; SAT writing scores over 500: 87%; ACT scores over 18: 99%; SAT critical reading scores over 600: 57%; SAT math scores over 600: 71%; SAT writing scores over 600: 55%; ACT scores over 24: 84%; SAT critical reading scores over 700: 17%; SAT math scores over 700: 30%; SAT writing scores over 700: 18%; ACT scores over 30: 38%.

Faculty *Total:* 3,034, 90% full-time, 88% with terminal degrees. *Student/faculty ratio:* 18:1.

Academics *Calendar:* semesters. *Degrees:* certificates, bachelor's, master's, doctoral, and postbachelor's certificates. *Special study options:* academic remediation for entering students, accelerated degree program, advanced placement credit, cooperative education, distance learning, double majors, English as a second language, honors programs, independent study, internships, off-campus study, part-time degree program, services for LD students, student-designed majors, study abroad, summer session for credit. *ROTC:* Army (b), Navy (b), Air Force (b). *Unusual degree programs:* 3-2 business administration; engineering; computer science.

Computers on Campus 3,150 computers/terminals and 1,375 ports are available on campus for general student use. Students can access the following: campus intranet, computer help desk, free student e-mail accounts, online (class) grades, online (class) registration, online (class) schedules. Campus-wide network is available. 100% of college-owned or -operated housing units are wired for high-speed Internet access. Wireless service is available via entire campus.

Student Life *Housing options:* coed, men-only, women-only, disabled students. Campus housing is university owned. Freshman applicants given priority for college housing. *Activities and organizations:* drama/theater group, student-run newspaper, radio and television station, choral group, marching band, Alpha Phi Omega, Student Events Center, Texas Exes-Student Chapter, Longhorn Band Student Organization, Student Volunteer Board, national fraternities, national sororities. *Campus security:* 24-hour emergency response devices and patrols, late-night transport/escort service, controlled dormitory access. *Student services:* health clinic, personal/psychological counseling, women's center, legal services.

Athletics Member NCAA. All Division I except football (Division I-A). *Intercollegiate sports:* archery M(c)/W(c), badminton M(c)/W(c), baseball M(s)/W(c), basketball M/W(s), crew M(c)/W(s), cross-country running M(s)/W(s), fencing M(c)/W(c), golf M(s)/W(s), gymnastics M(c)/W(c), ice hockey M(c)/W(c), lacrosse M(c)/W(c), racquetball M(c)/W(c), rugby M(c)/W(c), sailing M(c)/W(c), soccer M(c)/W(s), softball W(s), swimming and diving M(s)/W(s), table tennis M(c)/W(c), tennis M(s)/W(s), track and field M(s)/W(s), ultimate Frisbee M(c)/W(c), volleyball M(c)/W(s), water polo M(c)/W(c), weight lifting M(c)/W(c), wrestling M(c)/W(c). *Intramural sports:* badminton M/W, basketball M/W, football M/W, golf M/W, racquetball M/W, soccer M/W, softball M/W, swimming and diving M/W, table tennis M/W, tennis M/W, track and field M/W, ultimate Frisbee M/W, volleyball M/W.

Standardized Tests *Required:* SAT or ACT (for admission).

Costs (2012–13) *Tuition:* state resident $9792 full-time; nonresident $33,060 full-time. Full-time tuition and fees vary according to course load and program. Part-time tuition and fees vary according to course load and program. *Room and board:* $10,946. Room and board charges vary according to housing facility. *Payment plan:* installment. *Waivers:* senior citizens and employees or children of employees.

Financial Aid Of all full-time matriculated undergraduates who enrolled in 2011, 21,849 applied for aid, 16,345 were judged to have need, 2,969 had their need fully met. In 2011, 396 non-need-based awards were made. *Average percent of need met:* 67%. *Average financial aid package:* $12,045. *Average need-based loan:* $4959. *Average need-based gift aid:* $7959. *Average non-need-based aid:* $3151. *Average indebtedness upon graduation:* $25,227.

Applying *Options:* electronic application. *Application fee:* $75. *Required:* essay or personal statement, high school transcript. *Application deadlines:* 12/1 (freshmen), 3/1 (transfers). *Notification:* continuous (freshmen), continuous (transfers).

Freshman Application Contact Dr. Kedra B. Ishop, Vice Provost and Director of Admissions, The University of Texas at Austin, Office of Admissions, Freshman Admissions Center, PO Box 8058, Austin, TX 78713-8058. *Phone:* 512-475-7440. *Fax:* 512-475-7475. *E-mail:* kedra.ishop@austin.utexas.edu.

Website: http://www.utexas.edu/.

The University of Texas at Brownsville

Brownsville, Texas

- **State-supported** comprehensive, founded 1973, part of University of Texas System
- **Urban** 380-acre campus
- **Endowment** $8.7 million
- **Coed** 12,547 undergraduate students
- **Noncompetitive** entrance level, 100% of applicants were admitted

Undergraduates 5% are from out of state; 2% live on campus. *Retention:* 57% of full-time freshmen returned.

Freshmen *Admission:* 2,341 applied, 2,341 admitted. *Average high school GPA:* 2.82.

Faculty *Total:* 642, 59% full-time. *Student/faculty ratio:* 21:1.

Academics *Calendar:* semesters. *Degrees:* certificates, associate, bachelor's, master's, and doctoral. *Special study options:* academic remediation for entering students, advanced placement credit, cooperative education, distance learning, double majors, English as a second language, independent study, internships, off-campus study, part-time degree program, services for LD students, study abroad, summer session for credit. *ROTC:* Army (b).

Computers on Campus 332 computers/terminals are available on campus for general student use. Students can access the following: computer help desk, free student e-mail accounts, online (class) grades, online (class) registration, online (class) schedules. Campuswide network is available. 100% of college-owned or -operated housing units are wired for high-speed Internet access. Wireless service is available via entire campus.

Student Life *Housing options:* coed. Campus housing is university owned. *Activities and organizations:* student-run newspaper, choral group, Alpha Chi, Anime Viewing Club, Counseling and Guidance Student Association, Gorgas Science, Alpha Chi Psi. *Campus security:* 24-hour emergency response devices and patrols, late-night transport/escort service. *Student services:* health clinic, personal/psychological counseling, legal services.

Athletics Member NAIA. *Intercollegiate sports:* cross-country running M(s)/W(s), golf M(s)/W(s), soccer M(s)/W(s), volleyball W(s).

Costs (2012–13) *Tuition:* state resident $3743 full-time, $156 per credit hour part-time; nonresident $12,167 full-time, $507 per credit hour part-time. Full-time tuition and fees vary according to class time, course level, course load, location, and program. Part-time tuition and fees vary according to class time, course level, course load, location, and program. *Required fees:* $1373 full-time, $469 per term part-time. *Room and board:* $6602. Room and board charges vary according to board plan. *Payment plan:* installment.

Financial Aid Of all full-time matriculated undergraduates who enrolled in 2012, 4,229 applied for aid, 4,022 were judged to have need. 127 Federal Work-Study jobs (averaging $4128). 28 state and other part-time jobs (averaging $3586). In 2012, 61 non-need-based awards were made. *Average percent of need met:* 44%. *Average financial aid package:* $7891. *Average need-based loan:* $3773. *Average need-based gift aid:* $5268. *Average non-need-based aid:* $6698.

Applying *Options:* electronic application, early admission. *Required:* high school transcript, minimum 2.0 GPA. *Application deadlines:* 7/1 (freshmen), 8/1 (transfers). *Notification:* continuous (transfers).

Freshman Application Contact Mr. Carlo Tamayo, Director of Admissions and Recruitment, The University of Texas at Brownsville, 80 Fort Brown, Tandy 115, Brownsville, TX 78520-4991. *Phone:* 956-882-8295. *Toll-free phone:* 877-UTBTSC1. *Fax:* 956-882-7810. *E-mail:* admissions@utb.edu. *Website:* http://www.utb.edu/.

The University of Texas at Dallas

Richardson, Texas

- **State-supported** university, founded 1969, part of University of Texas System
- **Suburban** 500-acre campus with easy access to Dallas-Fort Worth
- **Endowment** $273.6 million
- **Coed** 12,029 undergraduate students, 79% full-time, 44% women, 56% men
- **Very difficult** entrance level, 52% of applicants were admitted

Undergraduates 9,505 full-time, 2,524 part-time. Students come from 47 states and territories; 73 other countries; 4% are from out of state; 6% Black or African American, non-Hispanic/Latino; 16% Hispanic/Latino; 25% Asian, non-Hispanic/Latino; 0.1% Native Hawaiian or other Pacific Islander, non-Hispanic/Latino; 0.3% American Indian or Alaska Native, non-Hispanic/Latino; 3% Two or more races, non-Hispanic/Latino; 1% Race/ethnicity unknown; 5% international; 14% transferred in; 25% live on campus. *Retention:* 85% of full-time freshmen returned.

Freshmen *Admission:* 7,079 applied, 3,679 admitted, 1,545 enrolled. *Average high school GPA:* 3.9. *Test scores:* SAT critical reading scores over 500: 93%; SAT math scores over 500: 98%; SAT writing scores over 500: 89%; ACT scores over 18: 99%; SAT critical reading scores over 600: 59%; SAT math scores over 600: 79%; SAT writing scores over 600: 50%; ACT scores over 24: 89%; SAT critical reading scores over 700: 20%; SAT math scores over 700: 33%; SAT writing scores over 700: 14%; ACT scores over 30: 38%.

Faculty *Total:* 940, 71% full-time, 84% with terminal degrees. *Student/faculty ratio:* 21:1.

Academics *Calendar:* semesters. *Degrees:* bachelor's, master's, doctoral, and postbachelor's certificates. *Special study options:* academic remediation for entering students, accelerated degree program, adult/continuing education programs, advanced placement credit, cooperative education, distance learning, double majors, freshman honors college, honors programs, independent study, internships, part-time degree program, services for LD students, student-designed majors, study abroad, summer session for credit. *ROTC:* Army (c), Air Force (c). *Unusual degree programs:* 3-2 engineering with Abilene Christian University, Austin College, Paul Quinn College, Texas Woman's University.

Computers on Campus 168 computers/terminals are available on campus for general student use. Students can access the following: computer help desk, free student e-mail accounts, online (class) grades, online (class) registration, online (class) schedules. Campuswide network is available. 100% of college-owned or -operated housing units are wired for high-speed Internet access. Wireless service is available via classrooms, computer centers, dorm rooms, libraries, student centers.

Student Life *Housing options:* coed. Campus housing is university owned and is provided by a third party. Freshman applicants given priority for college housing. *Activities and organizations:* drama/theater group, student-run newspaper, radio and television station, choral group, Student Government Association, Golden Key National Honor Society, Muslim Students Association, Indian Student Association, Friendship Association of Chinese Students and Scholars, national fraternities, national sororities. *Campus security:* 24-hour emergency response devices and patrols, student patrols, late-night transport/

escort service, controlled dormitory access. *Student services:* health clinic, personal/psychological counseling, women's center, legal services.

Athletics Member NCAA. All Division III. *Intercollegiate sports:* baseball M, basketball M/W, cross-country running M/W, golf M/W, soccer M/W, softball W, tennis M/W, volleyball W. *Intramural sports:* archery M(c)/W(c), badminton M(c)/W(c), basketball M(c)/W(c), bowling M(c)/W(c), cheerleading M/W, cross-country running M(c)/W(c), fencing M(c)/W(c), football M(c)/W(c), gymnastics M(c)/W(c), lacrosse M(c), racquetball M(c)/W(c), rock climbing M(c)/W(c), rugby M(c)/W(c), soccer M(c)/W(c), squash M(c)/W(c), swimming and diving M(c)/W(c), table tennis M(c)/W(c), tennis M(c)/W(c), ultimate Frisbee M(c)/W(c), volleyball M(c)/W(c).

Standardized Tests *Required:* SAT or ACT (for admission). *Required for some:* THEA.

Costs (2012–13) *Tuition:* state resident $11,592 full-time, $386 per credit hour part-time; nonresident $29,266 full-time, $976 per credit hour part-time. Full-time tuition and fees vary according to course load and degree level. Part-time tuition and fees vary according to course load and degree level. No tuition increase for student's term of enrollment. *Room and board:* $9050. Room and board charges vary according to board plan and housing facility. *Payment plan:* installment. *Waivers:* senior citizens and employees or children of employees.

Financial Aid Of all full-time matriculated undergraduates who enrolled in 2011, 5,728 applied for aid, 4,958 were judged to have need, 778 had their need fully met. 249 Federal Work-Study jobs (averaging $3769). 21 state and other part-time jobs (averaging $3428). In 2011, 1942 non-need-based awards were made. *Average percent of need met:* 64%. *Average financial aid package:* $11,620. *Average need-based loan:* $4435. *Average need-based gift aid:* $7821. *Average non-need-based aid:* $10,478. *Average indebtedness upon graduation:* $17,516.

Applying *Options:* electronic application, deferred entrance. *Application fee:* $50. *Required:* essay or personal statement, high school transcript. *Required for some:* interview. *Recommended:* 3 letters of recommendation. *Application deadline:* 7/1 (freshmen). *Notification:* continuous (freshmen), continuous (transfers).

Freshman Application Contact Enrollment Services, The University of Texas at Dallas, 800 West Campbell Road, Mail Station ROC11, Richardson, TX 75083-0688. *Phone:* 972-883-2270. *Toll-free phone:* 800-889-2443. *Fax:* 972-883-2599. *E-mail:* interest@utdallas.edu. *Website:* http://www.utdallas.edu/.

The University of Texas at El Paso

El Paso, Texas

- **State-supported** university, founded 1913, part of University of Texas System
- **Urban** 360-acre campus
- **Coed** 19,217 undergraduate students, 66% full-time, 54% women, 46% men
- **Minimally difficult** entrance level, 100% of applicants were admitted

Undergraduates 12,681 full-time, 6,536 part-time. Students come from 53 states and territories; 41 other countries; 3% are from out of state; 3% Black or African American, non-Hispanic/Latino; 81% Hispanic/Latino; 0.7% Asian, non-Hispanic/Latino; 0.1% Native Hawaiian or other Pacific Islander, non-Hispanic/Latino; 0.2% American Indian or Alaska Native, non-Hispanic/Latino; 0.5% Two or more races, non-Hispanic/Latino; 2% Race/ethnicity unknown; 5% international; 10% transferred in. *Retention:* 72% of full-time freshmen returned.

Freshmen *Admission:* 6,240 applied, 6,228 admitted, 2,722 enrolled. *Average high school GPA:* 3.15. *Test scores:* SAT critical reading scores over 500: 26%; SAT math scores over 500: 40%; ACT scores over 18: 67%; SAT critical reading scores over 600: 5%; SAT math scores over 600: 9%; ACT scores over 24: 15%; SAT math scores over 700: 1%; ACT scores over 30: 1%.

Faculty *Total:* 1,215, 58% full-time. *Student/faculty ratio:* 21:1.

Academics *Calendar:* semesters. *Degrees:* bachelor's, master's, doctoral, and post-master's certificates. *Special study options:* academic remediation for entering students, accelerated degree program, adult/continuing education programs, advanced placement credit, cooperative education, distance learning, double majors, English as a second language, honors programs, independent study, internships, off-campus study, part-time degree program, services for LD students, study abroad, summer session for credit. *ROTC:* Army (b), Air Force (b).

Computers on Campus Students can access the following: computer help desk, free student e-mail accounts, online (class) grades, online (class) registration, online (class) schedules. Campuswide network is available.

Student Life *Housing options:* coed, disabled students. Campus housing is university owned. *Activities and organizations:* drama/theater group, student-

run newspaper, radio station, choral group, marching band, national fraternities, national sororities. *Campus security:* 24-hour emergency response devices and patrols, late-night transport/escort service. *Student services:* health clinic, personal/psychological counseling, women's center, legal services.

Athletics Member NCAA. All Division I except football (Division I-A). *Intercollegiate sports:* basketball M(s)/W(s), cross-country running M(s)/W(s), golf M(s), riflery M/W, tennis W(s), track and field M(s)/W(s), volleyball W(s). *Intramural sports:* archery M/W, badminton M/W, basketball M/W, bowling M/W, fencing M/W, field hockey M, golf M/W, gymnastics M/W, racquetball M/W, skiing (downhill) M, soccer M/W, squash M/W, swimming and diving M/W, tennis M/W, track and field M/W, volleyball M/W, water polo M/W, weight lifting M, wrestling M/W.

Standardized Tests *Required for some:* SAT or ACT (for admission).

Financial Aid Of all full-time matriculated undergraduates who enrolled in 2011, 11,448 applied for aid, 10,106 were judged to have need, 1,016 had their need fully met. 443 Federal Work-Study jobs (averaging $2826). 168 state and other part-time jobs (averaging $1540). In 2011, 592 non-need-based awards were made. *Average percent of need met:* 68%. *Average financial aid package:* $12,559. *Average need-based loan:* $6186. *Average need-based gift aid:* $7276. *Average non-need-based aid:* $3442. *Average indebtedness upon graduation:* $20,913.

Applying *Options:* deferred entrance. *Required:* high school transcript. *Application deadlines:* 7/31 (freshmen), 7/31 (transfers). *Notification:* continuous (transfers).

Freshman Application Contact Dr. Luisa S. Havens, Executive Director of Admissions, The University of Texas at El Paso, Academic Services Building, Room 102, El Paso, TX 779968. *Phone:* 915-747-5890. *Toll-free phone:* 877-74MINER. *Fax:* 915-747-5890. *E-mail:* futureminer@utep.edu. *Website:* http://www.utep.edu/.

The University of Texas at San Antonio

San Antonio, Texas

- **State-supported** university, founded 1969, part of University of Texas System
- **Suburban** 600-acre campus
- **Coed** 25,979 undergraduate students, 82% full-time, 47% women, 53% men
- 73% of applicants were admitted

Undergraduates 21,186 full-time, 4,793 part-time. 3% are from out of state; 10% Black or African American, non-Hispanic/Latino; 47% Hispanic/Latino; 5% Asian, non-Hispanic/Latino; 0.2% Native Hawaiian or other Pacific Islander, non-Hispanic/Latino; 0.2% American Indian or Alaska Native, non-Hispanic/Latino; 3% Two or more races, non-Hispanic/Latino; 1% Race/ethnicity unknown; 4% international; 9% transferred in; 12% live on campus. *Retention:* 63% of full-time freshmen returned.

Freshmen *Admission:* 15,239 applied, 11,165 admitted, 4,489 enrolled. *Test scores:* SAT critical reading scores over 500: 56%; SAT math scores over 500: 72%; SAT writing scores over 500: 45%; ACT scores over 18: 90%; SAT critical reading scores over 600: 15%; SAT math scores over 600: 24%; SAT writing scores over 600: 10%; ACT scores over 24: 36%; SAT critical reading scores over 700: 1%; SAT math scores over 700: 3%; SAT writing scores over 700: 1%; ACT scores over 30: 3%.

Faculty *Student/faculty ratio:* 23:1.

Academics *Calendar:* semesters. *Degrees:* bachelor's, master's, and doctoral. *Special study options:* academic remediation for entering students, adult/continuing education programs, advanced placement credit, cooperative education, distance learning, double majors, English as a second language, honors programs, independent study, internships, off-campus study, part-time degree program, services for LD students, study abroad, summer session for credit. *ROTC:* Army (b), Air Force (b).

Computers on Campus 542 computers/terminals are available on campus for general student use. Students can access the following: campus intranet, computer help desk, free student e-mail accounts, online (class) grades, online (class) registration, online (class) schedules. Campuswide network is available. 100% of college-owned or -operated housing units are wired for high-speed Internet access. Wireless service is available via entire campus.

Student Life *Housing options:* coed. Campus housing is university owned and is provided by a third party. *Activities and organizations:* student-run newspaper, radio station, choral group, marching band, Student Government Association, Hispanic Student Association, Black Student Union, GLBTQ, Marching Band, national fraternities, national sororities. *Campus security:* 24-hour emergency response devices and patrols, late-night transport/escort service, controlled dormitory access, close to 1,000 security cameras, Reverse 911 emergency telephone notification system, and Giant Voice speaker arrays. *Student services:* health clinic, personal/psychological counseling, women's center.

Athletics Member NCAA. All Division I except football (Division I-AA). *Intercollegiate sports:* baseball M(s), basketball M(s)/W(s), cross-country running M(s)/W(s), golf M(s)/W(s), soccer W(s), softball W(s), tennis M(s)/W(s), track and field M(s)/W(s), volleyball W(s). *Intramural sports:* badminton M/W, baseball M(c), basketball M/W, cross-country running M/W, fencing M(c)/W(c), football M/W, golf M/W, ice hockey M(c), lacrosse M(c), racquetball M/W, rugby M(c), soccer M/W, softball M/W, table tennis M/W, tennis M/W, track and field M/W, ultimate Frisbee M/W, volleyball M/W, weight lifting M(c)/W(c), wrestling M(c)/W(c).

Standardized Tests *Required:* SAT or ACT (for admission).

Costs (2012–13) *Tuition:* state resident $5928 full-time, $198 per hour part-time; nonresident $16,458 full-time, $549 per hour part-time. Full-time tuition and fees vary according to course load and degree level. Part-time tuition and fees vary according to course load and degree level. *Required fees:* $2491 full-time. *Room and board:* $9693; room only: $6651. Room and board charges vary according to board plan and housing facility. *Payment plans:* installment, deferred payment. *Waivers:* employees or children of employees.

Financial Aid Of all full-time matriculated undergraduates who enrolled in 2011, 16,205 applied for aid, 13,920 were judged to have need, 2,286 had their need fully met. 539 Federal Work-Study jobs (averaging $1725). 1,101 state and other part-time jobs (averaging $1510). In 2011, 902 non-need-based awards were made. *Average percent of need met:* 52%. *Average financial aid package:* $9388. *Average need-based loan:* $4164. *Average need-based gift aid:* $5935. *Average non-need-based aid:* $1889. *Average indebtedness upon graduation:* $25,140.

Applying *Options:* electronic application. *Application fee:* $40. *Required:* high school transcript. *Recommended:* essay or personal statement, 1 letter of recommendation. *Application deadlines:* 6/1 (freshmen), 6/1 (out-of-state freshmen), 7/1 (transfers). *Notification:* continuous (freshmen), continuous (out-of-state freshmen), continuous (transfers).

Freshman Application Contact Ms. Jennifer Ehlers, Director of Admissions, The University of Texas at San Antonio, One UTSA Circle, San Antonio, TX 78249-0617. *Phone:* 210-458-4536. *Toll-free phone:* 800-669-0919. *Fax:* 210-458-2001. *E-mail:* prospects@utsa.edu. *Website:* http://www.utsa.edu/.

The University of Texas at Tyler

Tyler, Texas

- **State-supported** comprehensive, founded 1971, part of University of Texas System
- **Urban** 200-acre campus
- **Coed**
- **Moderately difficult** entrance level

Faculty *Student/faculty ratio:* 17:1.

Academics *Calendar:* semesters. *Degrees:* bachelor's, master's, doctoral, and postbachelor's certificates.

Student Life *Campus security:* 24-hour emergency response devices and patrols, late-night transport/escort service, controlled dormitory access.

Athletics Member NCAA. All Division III.

Standardized Tests *Required:* SAT or ACT (for admission).

Costs (2012–13) *Tuition:* state resident $5370 full-time, $50 per semester hour part-time; nonresident $15,900 full-time, $401 per semester hour part-time. Full-time tuition and fees vary according to course load. Part-time tuition and fees vary according to course load. *Required fees:* $1852 full-time. *Room and board:* $8979; room only: $5679. Room and board charges vary according to board plan and housing facility.

Financial Aid Of all full-time matriculated undergraduates who enrolled in 2010, 2,639 applied for aid, 2,328 were judged to have need, 230 had their need fully met. In 2010, 332 non-need-based awards were made. *Average percent of need met:* 54. *Average financial aid package:* $8613. *Average need-based loan:* $6635. *Average need-based gift aid:* $6570. *Average non-need-based aid:* $2351. *Average indebtedness upon graduation:* $19,181.

Applying *Options:* electronic application, deferred entrance. *Application fee:* $40. *Required:* high school transcript.

Freshman Application Contact Ms. Sarah Bowdin, Director of Admissions, The University of Texas at Tyler, 3900 University Boulevard, Tyler, TX 75799-0001. *Phone:* 903-566-7057. *Toll-free phone:* 800-UTTYLER. *Fax:* 903-566-7068. *E-mail:* admissions@uttyler.edu. *Website:* http://www.uttyler.edu/.

The University of Texas Health Science Center at Houston

Houston, Texas

- **State-supported** upper-level, founded 1972, part of University of Texas System
- **Urban** campus with easy access to Houston
- **Coed**
- **Moderately difficult** entrance level

Faculty *Student/faculty ratio:* 6:1.

Academics *Calendar:* semesters. *Degrees:* certificates, bachelor's, master's, doctoral, post-master's, and postbachelor's certificates.

Student Life *Campus security:* 24-hour emergency response devices and patrols, late-night transport/escort service, controlled access to all buildings.

Standardized Tests *Required:* HESI A2-Nursing Entrance Test for BSN programs (for admission).

Financial Aid Of all full-time matriculated undergraduates who enrolled in 2011, 325 applied for aid, 302 were judged to have need, 101 had their need fully met. In 2011, 4 non-need-based awards were made. *Average percent of need met:* 72. *Average financial aid package:* $9838. *Average need-based loan:* $6215. *Average need-based gift aid:* $6154. *Average non-need-based aid:* $6751.

Applying *Options:* electronic application. *Application fee:* $30.

Application Contact The University of Texas Health Science Center at Houston, PO Box 20036, Houston, TX 77225-0036. *Phone:* 713-500-3361. *Website:* http://www.uthouston.edu/.

The University of Texas Health Science Center at San Antonio

San Antonio, Texas

Application Contact The University of Texas Health Science Center at San Antonio, 7703 Floyd Curl Drive, San Antonio, TX 78229-3900. *Phone:* 210-567-2659. *Website:* http://www.uthscsa.edu/.

The University of Texas Medical Branch

Galveston, Texas

Freshman Application Contact The University of Texas Medical Branch, 301 University Boulevard, Galveston, TX 77555. *Phone:* 409-772-1215. *Website:* http://www.utmb.edu/.

The University of Texas of the Permian Basin

Odessa, Texas

- **State-supported** comprehensive, founded 1969, part of University of Texas System
- **Urban** 600-acre campus
- **Endowment** $32.8 million
- **Coed** 3,852 undergraduate students, 65% full-time, 57% women, 43% men
- **Moderately difficult** entrance level, 86% of applicants were admitted

Undergraduates 2,507 full-time, 1,345 part-time. Students come from 33 states and territories; 20 other countries; 3% are from out of state; 5% Black or African American, non-Hispanic/Latino; 47% Hispanic/Latino; 3% Asian, non-Hispanic/Latino; 0.3% Native Hawaiian or other Pacific Islander, non-Hispanic/Latino; 0.8% American Indian or Alaska Native, non-Hispanic/Latino; 0.9% Two or more races, non-Hispanic/Latino; 0.1% Race/ethnicity unknown; 0.7% international; 13% transferred in; 15% live on campus. *Retention:* 66% of full-time freshmen returned.

Freshmen *Admission:* 1,007 applied, 870 admitted, 351 enrolled. *Test scores:* SAT critical reading scores over 500: 49%; SAT math scores over 500: 66%;

ACT scores over 18: 92%; SAT critical reading scores over 600: 10%; SAT math scores over 600: 16%; ACT scores over 24: 20%; SAT critical reading scores over 700: 1%; SAT math scores over 700: 1%; ACT scores over 30: 3%. **Faculty** *Total:* 186, 58% full-time, 62% with terminal degrees. *Student/faculty ratio:* 21:1.

Academics *Calendar:* semesters. *Degrees:* bachelor's and master's. *Special study options:* academic remediation for entering students, advanced placement credit, distance learning, double majors, English as a second language, honors programs, independent study, internships, part-time degree program, services for LD students, study abroad, summer session for credit.

Computers on Campus 170 computers/terminals are available on campus for general student use. Students can access the following: campus intranet, computer help desk, free student e-mail accounts, online (class) grades, online (class) registration, online (class) schedules. Campuswide network is available. 100% of college-owned or -operated housing units are wired for high-speed Internet access. Wireless service is available via entire campus.

Student Life *Housing options:* coed. Campus housing is university owned. *Activities and organizations:* drama/theater group, student-run newspaper, choral group, National Society of Leadership and Success (NSLS), Baptist Student Ministries (BSM), Students In Philanthropy (SIP), Catholic Student Association (CSA), Black Leadership Council (BLC), national fraternities. *Campus security:* 24-hour patrols, late-night transport/escort service. *Student services:* health clinic, personal/psychological counseling.

Athletics Member NCAA. All Division II. *Intercollegiate sports:* baseball M(s), basketball M(s)/W(s), cheerleading M(s)/W(s), cross-country running M(s)/W(s), soccer M(s)/W(s), softball W(s), swimming and diving M(s)/W(s), tennis M/W, volleyball W(s). *Intramural sports:* basketball M/W, racquetball M/W, ultimate Frisbee M(c)/W(c), volleyball M/W, water polo M/W.

Standardized Tests *Required:* SAT or ACT (for admission).

Costs (2012–13) *Tuition:* state resident $5037 full-time, $168 per credit hour part-time; nonresident $15,566 full-time, $519 per credit hour part-time. Full-time tuition and fees vary according to course load and location. Part-time tuition and fees vary according to course load and location. *Required fees:* $1422 full-time, $52 per credit hour part-time, $577 per term part-time. *Room and board:* $7616; room only: $4532. Room and board charges vary according to board plan and housing facility. *Payment plan:* installment. *Waivers:* senior citizens and employees or children of employees.

Financial Aid Of all full-time matriculated undergraduates who enrolled in 2010, 1,592 applied for aid, 1,411 were judged to have need, 75 had their need fully met. 44 Federal Work-Study jobs (averaging $1718). 30 state and other part-time jobs (averaging $7550). In 2010, 374 non-need-based awards were made. *Average percent of need met:* 47%. *Average financial aid package:* $8452. *Average need-based loan:* $3727. *Average need-based gift aid:* $5322. *Average non-need-based aid:* $2995. *Average indebtedness upon graduation:* $15,796.

Applying *Options:* electronic application, early admission, deferred entrance. *Required:* high school transcript. *Application deadlines:* 7/14 (freshmen), rolling (transfers). *Notification:* continuous (freshmen), continuous (transfers).

Freshman Application Contact The University of Texas of the Permian Basin, 4901 East University Boulevard, Odessa, TX 79762-0001. *Phone:* 432-552-2605. *Toll-free phone:* 866-552-UTPB. *Website:* http://www.utpb.edu/.

The University of Texas–Pan American

Edinburg, Texas

- **State-supported** comprehensive, founded 1927, part of University of Texas System
- **Small-town** 331-acre campus with easy access to McAllen-Edinburg-Mission
- **Endowment** $61.2 million
- **Coed** 16,966 undergraduate students, 74% full-time, 55% women, 45% men
- **Noncompetitive** entrance level, 62% of applicants were admitted

Undergraduates 12,491 full-time, 4,475 part-time. Students come from 35 states and territories; 52 other countries; 0.5% are from out of state; 0.6% Black or African American, non-Hispanic/Latino; 91% Hispanic/Latino; 1% Asian, non-Hispanic/Latino; 0.1% Native Hawaiian or other Pacific Islander, non-Hispanic/Latino; 0.1% American Indian or Alaska Native, non-Hispanic/Latino; 0.3% Two or more races, non-Hispanic/Latino; 1% Race/ethnicity unknown; 2% international; 7% transferred in; 4% live on campus. *Retention:* 75% of full-time freshmen returned.

Freshmen *Admission:* 9,313 applied, 5,790 admitted, 3,102 enrolled. *Test scores:* SAT critical reading scores over 500: 33%; SAT math scores over 500:

48%; SAT writing scores over 500: 28%; ACT scores over 18: 81%; SAT critical reading scores over 600: 6%; SAT math scores over 600: 9%; SAT writing scores over 600: 4%; ACT scores over 24: 11%; SAT math scores over 700: 1%; ACT scores over 30: 1%.

Faculty *Total:* 775, 83% full-time, 76% with terminal degrees. *Student/faculty ratio:* 22:1.

Academics *Calendar:* semesters. *Degrees:* bachelor's, master's, doctoral, and postbachelor's certificates. *Special study options:* academic remediation for entering students, accelerated degree program, adult/continuing education programs, advanced placement credit, cooperative education, distance learning, double majors, English as a second language, honors programs, independent study, internships, part-time degree program, services for LD students, study abroad, summer session for credit. *ROTC:* Army (b). *Unusual degree programs:* accounting.

Computers on Campus Students can access the following: campus intranet, computer help desk, free student e-mail accounts, online (class) grades, online (class) registration, online (class) schedules. Campuswide network is available. Wireless service is available via entire campus.

Student Life *Housing options:* coed, men-only, women-only. Campus housing is university owned. *Activities and organizations:* drama/theater group, student-run newspaper, choral group, national fraternities, national sororities. *Campus security:* 24-hour emergency response devices and patrols, late-night transport/escort service. *Student services:* health clinic, personal/psychological counseling.

Athletics Member NCAA. All Division I. *Intercollegiate sports:* baseball M(s), basketball M(s)/W(s), cross-country running M(s)/W(s), golf M(s)/W(s), tennis M(s)/W(s), track and field M(s)/W(s), volleyball W(s). *Intramural sports:* badminton M/W, basketball M/W, bowling M/W, cheerleading M/W, football M/W, racquetball M/W, soccer M/W, softball M/W, tennis M/W, volleyball M/W.

Standardized Tests *Required:* SAT or ACT (for admission).

Costs (2012–13) *Tuition:* state resident $4168 full-time, $174 per credit hour part-time; nonresident $12,592 full-time, $534 per credit hour part-time. Full-time tuition and fees vary according to course load and degree level. Part-time tuition and fees vary according to course load and degree level. *Required fees:* $997 full-time, $42 per credit hour part-time. *Room and board:* $5656; room only: $3400. Room and board charges vary according to board plan and housing facility. *Payment plan:* installment.

Financial Aid Of all full-time matriculated undergraduates who enrolled in 2011, 10,294 applied for aid, 9,933 were judged to have need, 446 had their need fully met. 829 Federal Work-Study jobs (averaging $2293). 299 state and other part-time jobs (averaging $1960). In 2011, 248 non-need-based awards were made. *Average percent of need met:* 67%. *Average financial aid package:* $9767. *Average need-based loan:* $4786. *Average need-based gift aid:* $10,621. *Average non-need-based aid:* $3082. *Average indebtedness upon graduation:* $15,257.

Applying *Options:* electronic application. *Required:* high school transcript, minimum 2.0 GPA. *Required for some:* interview. *Application deadlines:* 8/11 (freshmen), 8/11 (transfers). *Notification:* continuous (freshmen), continuous (transfers).

Freshman Application Contact Dr. Magdalena Hinojosa, Dean of Admissions and Enrollment Services, The University of Texas–Pan American, Office of Admissions and Records, 1201 West University Drive, Edinburg, TX 78539. *Phone:* 956-665-2999. *Fax:* 956-665-2212. *E-mail:* admissions@utpa.edu. *Website:* http://www.utpa.edu/.

University of the Incarnate Word

San Antonio, Texas

- **Independent Roman Catholic** comprehensive, founded 1881
- **Urban** 200-acre campus with easy access to San Antonio
- **Endowment** $100.0 million
- **Coed** 6,404 undergraduate students, 69% full-time, 62% women, 38% men
- **Moderately difficult** entrance level, 94% of applicants were admitted

Undergraduates 4,388 full-time, 2,016 part-time. Students come from 50 states and territories; 38 other countries; 5% are from out of state; 7% Black or African American, non-Hispanic/Latino; 59% Hispanic/Latino; 2% Asian, non-Hispanic/Latino; 0.2% Native Hawaiian or other Pacific Islander, non-Hispanic/Latino; 0.4% American Indian or Alaska Native, non-Hispanic/Latino; 0.8% Two or more races, non-Hispanic/Latino; 6% Race/ethnicity unknown; 4% international; 13% transferred in; 18% live on campus. *Retention:* 75% of full-time freshmen returned.

Freshmen *Admission:* 3,784 applied, 3,562 admitted, 1,064 enrolled. *Average high school GPA:* 3.47. *Test scores:* SAT critical reading scores over 500: 40%;

SAT math scores over 500: 46%; SAT writing scores over 500: 36%; ACT scores over 18: 77%; SAT critical reading scores over 600: 8%; SAT math scores over 600: 11%; SAT writing scores over 600: 6%; ACT scores over 24: 18%; SAT critical reading scores over 700: 1%; SAT math scores over 700: 1%; SAT writing scores over 700: 1%; ACT scores over 30: 1%.
Faculty *Total:* 533, 53% full-time, 32% with terminal degrees. *Student/faculty ratio:* 14:1.
Academics *Calendar:* semesters. *Degrees:* diplomas, associate, bachelor's, master's, and doctoral. *Special study options:* academic remediation for entering students, accelerated degree program, adult/continuing education programs, advanced placement credit, cooperative education, distance learning, double majors, English as a second language, freshman honors college, honors programs, independent study, internships, off-campus study, part-time degree program, services for LD students, study abroad, summer session for credit. *ROTC:* Army (c), Air Force (c). *Unusual degree programs:* 3-2 business administration; communications and accounting.
Computers on Campus 185 computers/terminals are available on campus for general student use. Students can access the following: computer help desk, free student e-mail accounts, online (class) grades, online (class) registration, online (class) schedules, Ports available in general use area and other locations. Also dedicated computers for graduate/doctoral students. Campuswide network is available. 100% of college-owned or -operated housing units are wired for high-speed Internet access. Wireless service is available in entire campus.
Student Life *Housing options:* coed, men-only, women-only, disabled students. Campus housing is university owned. Freshman campus housing is guaranteed. *Activities and organizations:* drama/theater group, student-run newspaper, radio and television station, choral group, marching band, Society of Leadership and Success, Pre-Pharmacy Association, Alpha Sigma Alpha, Lambda Chi Alpha, Student Government Association House, national fraternities, national sororities. *Campus security:* 24-hour emergency response devices and patrols, late-night transport/escort service, controlled dormitory access. *Student services:* health clinic, personal/psychological counseling.
Athletics Member NCAA. All Division II. *Intercollegiate sports:* baseball M(s), basketball M(s)/W(s), cross-country running M(s)/W(s), football M(s), golf M(s)/W(s), soccer M(s)/W(s), softball W(s), swimming and diving M(s)/W(s), tennis M(s)/W(s), track and field M(s)/W(s), volleyball W(s). *Intramural sports:* basketball M/W, cheerleading M/W, football M/W, racquetball M/W, soccer M/W, softball M/W, tennis M/W, ultimate Frisbee M/W, volleyball M/W, water polo M/W.
Standardized Tests *Required:* SAT or ACT (for admission).
Costs (2012–13) *Comprehensive fee:* $33,784 includes full-time tuition ($22,800), mandatory fees ($890), and room and board ($10,094). Full-time tuition and fees vary according to course load, degree level, location, program, and reciprocity agreements. Part-time tuition: $755 per credit hour. Part-time tuition and fees vary according to course load, degree level, location, program, and reciprocity agreements. *College room only:* $5980. Room and board charges vary according to board plan and housing facility. *Payment plan:* installment. *Waivers:* senior citizens and employees or children of employees.
Financial Aid Of all full-time matriculated undergraduates who enrolled in 2011, 3,375 applied for aid, 3,171 were judged to have need, 847 had their need fully met. In 2011, 194 non-need-based awards were made. *Average percent of need met:* 66%. *Average financial aid package:* $17,809. *Average need-based loan:* $4200. *Average need-based gift aid:* $13,415. *Average non-need-based aid:* $8659.
Applying *Options:* electronic application, deferred entrance. *Application fee:* $20. *Required:* high school transcript. *Required for some:* essay or personal statement, interview. *Recommended:* minimum 2.0 GPA, letter(s) of recommendation recommended for all, required for some. *Application deadlines:* rolling (freshmen), rolling (out-of-state freshmen), rolling (transfers). *Notification:* continuous (freshmen), continuous (out-of-state freshmen), continuous (transfers).
Freshman Application Contact Ms. Heather M. Rodriguez, Director of Undergraduate Admissions, University of the Incarnate Word, 4301 Broadway Avenue, University of the Incarnate Word, San Antonio, TN 78209. *Phone:* 210-829-6005. *Toll-free phone:* 800-749-WORD. *Fax:* 210-829-3921. *E-mail:* hrodrig1@uiwtx.edu.
Website: http://www.uiw.edu/.

Wade College

Dallas, Texas

Freshman Application Contact Wade College, INFOMart, 1950 Stemmons Freeway, Suite 4080, LB 562, Dallas, TX 75207. *Phone:* 214-637-3530. *Toll-free phone:* 800-624-4850.
Website: http://www.wadecollege.edu/.

Wayland Baptist University

Plainview, Texas

- **Independent Baptist** comprehensive, founded 1908
- **Small-town** 80-acre campus
- **Endowment** $68.5 million
- **Coed** 1,385 undergraduate students, 73% full-time, 45% women, 55% men
- **Minimally difficult** entrance level, 97% of applicants were admitted

Undergraduates 1,011 full-time, 374 part-time. Students come from 43 states and territories; 20 other countries; 17% are from out of state; 14% Black or African American, non-Hispanic/Latino; 29% Hispanic/Latino; 0.6% Asian, non-Hispanic/Latino; 0.2% Native Hawaiian or other Pacific Islander, non-Hispanic/Latino; 0.6% American Indian or Alaska Native, non-Hispanic/Latino; 3% Two or more races, non-Hispanic/Latino; 6% Race/ethnicity unknown; 3% international; 7% transferred in; 53% live on campus. *Retention:* 48% of full-time freshmen returned.
Freshmen *Admission:* 556 applied, 537 admitted, 366 enrolled. *Average high school GPA:* 3.23. *Test scores:* SAT critical reading scores over 500: 37%; SAT math scores over 500: 41%; SAT writing scores over 500: 24%; ACT scores over 18: 66%; SAT critical reading scores over 600: 12%; SAT math scores over 600: 15%; SAT writing scores over 600: 7%; ACT scores over 24: 18%; SAT critical reading scores over 700: 2%; SAT writing scores over 700: 1%; ACT scores over 30: 1%.
Faculty *Total:* 153, 66% full-time, 52% with terminal degrees. *Student/faculty ratio:* 10:1.
Academics *Calendar:* semesters. *Degrees:* associate, bachelor's, and master's (branch locations in Anchorage, AK; Amarillo, TX; Luke Air Force Base, AZ; Glorieta, NM; Aiea, HI; Lubbock, TX; San Antonio, TX; Wichita Falls, TX). *Special study options:* academic remediation for entering students, accelerated degree program, adult/continuing education programs, advanced placement credit, distance learning, double majors, external degree program, honors programs, part-time degree program, services for LD students, study abroad, summer session for credit. *ROTC:* Army (c), Air Force (c). *Unusual degree programs:* 3-2 engineering with Texas Tech University.
Computers on Campus 231 computers/terminals are available on campus for general student use. Students can access the following: computer help desk, free student e-mail accounts, online (class) grades, online (class) registration, online (class) schedules. Campuswide network is available. 100% of college-owned or -operated housing units are wired for high-speed Internet access. Wireless service is available via classrooms, computer labs, dorm rooms, libraries, student centers.
Student Life *Housing:* on-campus residence required through junior year. *Options:* men-only, women-only. Campus housing is university owned. Freshman campus housing is guaranteed. *Activities and organizations:* drama/theater group, student-run newspaper, radio and television station, choral group, marching band, student government; national fraternities, national sororities. *Campus security:* 24-hour emergency response devices and patrols, security lighting, campus police department. *Student services:* health clinic, personal/psychological counseling.
Athletics Member NAIA. *Intercollegiate sports:* baseball M(s), basketball M(s)/W(s), cheerleading M(s)/W(s), cross-country running M(s)/W(s), football M(s), golf M(s)/W(s), soccer M(s)/W(s), track and field M(s)/W(s), volleyball W(s), wrestling M(s)/W(s). *Intramural sports:* basketball M/W, football M, soccer M/W, softball M/W, table tennis M/W, volleyball M/W.
Standardized Tests *Required:* SAT or ACT (for admission).
Costs (2012–13) *Comprehensive fee:* $18,787 includes full-time tuition ($13,650), mandatory fees ($980), and room and board ($4157). Full-time tuition and fees vary according to course load and location. Part-time tuition: $455 per credit hour. Part-time tuition and fees vary according to course load and location. *Required fees:* $110 per term part-time. *College room only:* $1368. Room and board charges vary according to board plan and housing facility. *Payment plan:* installment. *Waivers:* employees or children of employees.
Financial Aid Of all full-time matriculated undergraduates who enrolled in 2012, 874 applied for aid, 779 were judged to have need, 76 had their need fully met. 142 Federal Work-Study jobs (averaging $1539). 126 state and other part-time jobs (averaging $1688). In 2012, 153 non-need-based awards were made. *Average percent of need met:* 63%. *Average financial aid package:* $12,153. *Average need-based loan:* $3649. *Average need-based gift aid:* $9176. *Average non-need-based aid:* $8214. *Average indebtedness upon graduation:* $21,981.
Applying *Options:* electronic application. *Application fee:* $35. *Required:* high school transcript. *Required for some:* interview. *Application deadlines:* 8/1 (freshmen), rolling (transfers). *Notification:* continuous (freshmen), continuous (transfers).

Freshman Application Contact Ms. Debbie Stennett, Director of Student Admissions, Wayland Baptist University, 1900 West 7th Street, CMB 1294, Plainview, TX 79072. *Phone:* 806-291-3500. *Toll-free phone:* 800-588-1928. *Fax:* 806-291-1973. *E-mail:* admityou@wbu.edu.
Website: http://www.wbu.edu/.

West Texas A&M University
Canyon, Texas

- **State-supported** comprehensive, founded 1909, part of Texas A&M University System
- **Small-town** 128-acre campus
- **Endowment** $48.4 million
- **Coed** 6,588 undergraduate students, 79% full-time, 55% women, 45% men
- **Moderately difficult** entrance level, 69% of applicants were admitted

Undergraduates 5,226 full-time, 1,362 part-time. Students come from 47 states and territories; 35 other countries; 9% are from out of state; 5% Black or African American, non-Hispanic/Latino; 23% Hispanic/Latino; 1% Asian, non-Hispanic/Latino; 0.1% Native Hawaiian or other Pacific Islander, non-Hispanic/Latino; 0.7% American Indian or Alaska Native, non-Hispanic/Latino; 2% Two or more races, non-Hispanic/Latino; 1% Race/ethnicity unknown; 2% international; 13% transferred in; 26% live on campus. *Retention:* 62% of full-time freshmen returned.
Freshmen *Admission:* 4,109 applied, 2,852 admitted, 1,205 enrolled. *Test scores:* SAT critical reading scores over 500: 39%; SAT math scores over 500: 51%; ACT scores over 18: 84%; SAT critical reading scores over 600: 10%; SAT math scores over 600: 14%; ACT scores over 24: 25%; SAT critical reading scores over 700: 1%; SAT math scores over 700: 1%; ACT scores over 30: 2%.
Faculty *Total:* 384, 69% full-time, 55% with terminal degrees. *Student/faculty ratio:* 20:1.
Academics *Calendar:* semesters. *Degrees:* bachelor's, master's, and doctoral. *Special study options:* academic remediation for entering students, adult/continuing education programs, advanced placement credit, cooperative education, distance learning, double majors, English as a second language, honors programs, independent study, internships, part-time degree program, services for LD students, study abroad, summer session for credit. *Unusual degree programs:* 3-2 engineering with Texas Tech University, Texas A&M University.
Computers on Campus 1,200 computers/terminals and 1,200 ports are available on campus for general student use. Students can access the following: campus intranet, computer help desk, free student e-mail accounts, online (class) grades, online (class) registration, online (class) schedules. Campuswide network is available. 100% of college-owned or -operated housing units are wired for high-speed Internet access. Wireless service is available via entire campus.
Student Life *Housing:* on-campus residence required through sophomore year. *Options:* coed, men-only, women-only, disabled students. Campus housing is university owned. Freshman campus housing is guaranteed. *Activities and organizations:* drama/theater group, student-run newspaper, radio station, choral group, marching band, Residence Hall Association, National Society for Leadership and Success, Student Government, Students in Free Enterprise (SIFE), Baptist Student Ministries, national fraternities, national sororities. *Campus security:* 24-hour emergency response devices and patrols, late-night transport/escort service, controlled dormitory access. *Student services:* health clinic, personal/psychological counseling.
Athletics Member NCAA. All Division II. *Intercollegiate sports:* baseball M(s), basketball M(s)/W(s), bowling M(s)(c)/W(s)(c), cross-country running M(s)/W(s), equestrian sports M(c)/W(s), football M(s), golf M(s)/W(s), soccer M(s)/W(s), softball W(s), track and field M(s)/W(s), volleyball W(s). *Intramural sports:* badminton M/W, basketball M/W, bowling M/W, football M/W, golf M/W, racquetball M/W, soccer M/W, softball M/W, swimming and diving M/W, table tennis M/W, tennis M/W, volleyball M/W, wrestling M.
Standardized Tests *Required:* SAT or ACT (for admission).
Costs (2012–13) *Tuition:* state resident $4730 full-time, $165 per credit hour part-time; nonresident $5630 full-time, $195 per credit hour part-time. Full-time tuition and fees vary according to course load. Part-time tuition and fees vary according to course load. *Required fees:* $2060 full-time, $66 per credit hour part-time, $182 per credit hour part-time. *Room and board:* $5000. Room and board charges vary according to board plan and housing facility. *Payment plan:* installment. *Waivers:* employees or children of employees.
Financial Aid Of all full-time matriculated undergraduates who enrolled in 2011, 3,908 applied for aid, 3,391 were judged to have need, 478 had their need fully met. 152 Federal Work-Study jobs (averaging $1287). 30 state and other part-time jobs (averaging $1148). In 2011, 223 non-need-based awards were made. *Average percent of need met:* 70%. *Average financial aid package:*

$10,451. *Average need-based loan:* $5180. *Average need-based gift aid:* $7857. *Average non-need-based aid:* $3227. *Average indebtedness upon graduation:* $19,774.
Applying *Options:* electronic application, deferred entrance. *Application fee:* $25. *Required:* high school transcript, class rank and Texas high school curriculum or equivalent. *Application deadlines:* rolling (freshmen), rolling (transfers). *Notification:* continuous (freshmen), continuous (transfers).
Freshman Application Contact Mr. Kyle Moore, Director of Admissions, West Texas A&M University, WT Box 60907, Canyon, TX 79016-0001. *Phone:* 806-651-5288. *Toll-free phone:* 800-99-WTAMU. *Fax:* 806-651-5285. *E-mail:* kmoore@mail.wtamu.edu.
Website: http://www.wtamu.edu/.

Wiley College
Marshall, Texas

Director of Admissions Ms. Alvena Jones, Interim Director of Admissions/Recruitment, Wiley College, 711 Wiley Avenue, Marshall, TX 75670-5199. *Phone:* 903-927-3222. *Toll-free phone:* 800-658-6889. *Fax:* 903-923-8878. *E-mail:* ajones@wileyc.edu.
Website: http://www.wileyc.edu/.

UTAH

Argosy University, Salt Lake City
Draper, Utah

Freshman Application Contact Argosy University, Salt Lake City, 121 West Election Road, Suite 300, Draper, UT 84020. *Phone:* 801-601-5000. *Toll-free phone:* 888-639-4756.
Website: http://www.argosy.edu/locations/salt-lake-city/.

The Art Institute of Salt Lake City
Draper, Utah

- **Proprietary** 4-year, part of Education Management Corporation
- **Coed**

Academics *Degrees:* diplomas, associate, and bachelor's.
Freshman Application Contact The Art Institute of Salt Lake City, 121 West Election Road, Suite 100, Draper, UT 84020-9492. *Phone:* 801-601-4700. *Toll-free phone:* 800-978-0096.
Website: http://www.artinstitutes.edu/SaltLakeCity/.

See full-page ad on page 54 and page 1112 for the College Close-Up.

Brigham Young University
Provo, Utah

- **Independent** university, founded 1875, affiliated with The Church of Jesus Christ of Latter-day Saints, part of Church Education System (CES) of The Church of Jesus Christ of Latter-day Saints
- **Suburban** 557-acre campus with easy access to Salt Lake City
- **Coed** 31,060 undergraduate students, 91% full-time, 49% women, 51% men
- **Moderately difficult** entrance level, 55% of applicants were admitted

Undergraduates 28,338 full-time, 2,722 part-time. 63% are from out of state; 0.4% Black or African American, non-Hispanic/Latino; 5% Hispanic/Latino; 2% Asian, non-Hispanic/Latino; 0.6% Native Hawaiian or other Pacific Islander, non-Hispanic/Latino; 0.4% American Indian or Alaska Native, non-Hispanic/Latino; 3% Two or more races, non-Hispanic/Latino; 1% Race/ethnicity unknown; 4% international; 3% transferred in; 19% live on campus. *Retention:* 89% of full-time freshmen returned.
Freshmen *Admission:* 12,557 applied, 6,895 admitted, 5,525 enrolled. *Average high school GPA:* 3.79. *Test scores:* SAT critical reading scores over 500: 94%; SAT math scores over 500: 96%; SAT writing scores over 500: 89%;

ACT scores over 18: 100%; SAT critical reading scores over 600: 66%; SAT math scores over 600: 72%; SAT writing scores over 600: 52%; ACT scores over 24: 92%; SAT critical reading scores over 700: 23%; SAT math scores over 700: 22%; SAT writing scores over 700: 12%; ACT scores over 30: 36%.
Faculty *Total:* 1,739, 71% full-time, 76% with terminal degrees. *Student/faculty ratio:* 23:1.
Academics *Calendar:* semesters. *Degrees:* bachelor's, master's, and doctoral. *Special study options:* adult/continuing education programs, external degree program, off-campus study, part-time degree program. *ROTC:* Army (b), Air Force (b).
Computers on Campus Students can access the following: campus intranet, computer help desk, online (class) grades, online (class) registration, online (class) schedules. Campuswide network is available.
Student Life *Housing options:* men-only, women-only, disabled students. Campus housing is university owned. *Campus security:* 24-hour emergency response devices and patrols, late-night transport/escort service, controlled dormitory access.
Athletics Member NCAA. All Division I except football (Division I-A). *Intercollegiate sports:* baseball M(s), basketball M(s)/W(s), cheerleading M(s)/W(s), cross-country running M(s)/W(s), golf M(s)/W(s), gymnastics W(s), lacrosse M(c), racquetball M/W, rugby M(c), soccer M(c)/W(s), softball W(s), swimming and diving M(s)/W(s), tennis M(s)/W(s), track and field M(s)/W(s), volleyball M(s)/W(s). *Intramural sports:* badminton W, basketball M/W, field hockey M, football M/W, golf M/W, racquetball M/W, soccer M/W, softball M/W, table tennis M/W, tennis M/W, ultimate Frisbee M/W, volleyball M/W, water polo M/W, wrestling M.
Standardized Tests *Required:* SAT or ACT (for admission).
Costs (2013–14) *Comprehensive fee:* $11,910 includes full-time tuition ($4710) and room and board ($7200). Part-time tuition: $242 per credit hour. Part-time tuition and fees vary according to course load. *Room and board:* Room and board charges vary according to board plan, housing facility, and location. *Waivers:* employees or children of employees.
Financial Aid Of all full-time matriculated undergraduates who enrolled in 2011, 14,898 applied for aid, 12,993 were judged to have need, 217 had their need fully met. In 2011, 6645 non-need-based awards were made. *Average percent of need met:* 34%. *Average financial aid package:* $7178. *Average need-based loan:* $4254. *Average need-based gift aid:* $4603. *Average non-need-based aid:* $3649. *Average indebtedness upon graduation:* $14,377.
Applying *Options:* electronic application, early admission, deferred entrance. *Application fee:* $35. *Required:* essay or personal statement, high school transcript, 1 letter of recommendation, interview. *Application deadlines:* 2/1 (freshmen), 3/1 (transfers). *Notification:* continuous (freshmen), continuous (transfers).
Freshman Application Contact Mr. Tom Gourley, Dean of Admissions and Records, Brigham Young University, A-153 Abraham Smoot Building, Provo, UT 84602. *Phone:* 801-422-2507. *Fax:* 801-422-0005. *E-mail:* admissions@byu.edu.
Website: http://www.byu.edu/.

Broadview University–Layton

Layton, Utah

- **Proprietary** 4-year, part of Globe Education Network (GEN) which is composed of Globe University, Minnesota School of Business, Broadview University, The Institute of Production and Recording and Minnesota School of Cosmetology
- **Suburban** campus
- **Coed**

Faculty *Student/faculty ratio:* 20:1.
Academics *Degrees:* diplomas, associate, and bachelor's.
Student Life *Campus security:* 24-hour emergency response devices, late-night transport/escort service.
Standardized Tests *Required:* ACCUPLACER is required of all applicants unless documentation of a minimum ACT composite score of 21 or documentation of a minimum composite score of 1485 on the SAT is presented (for admission).
Costs (2012–13) *Tuition:* $14,400 full-time, $435 per credit part-time. Full-time tuition and fees vary according to course load, degree level, location, and program. Part-time tuition and fees vary according to course load, degree level, location, and program. *Required fees:* $1548 full-time, $43 per credit part-time.
Applying *Options:* electronic application. *Application fee:* $50. *Required:* high school transcript, interview, High school transcript or GED required of all

applicants. *Required for some:* essay or personal statement, 2 letters of recommendation.
Freshman Application Contact Broadview University–Layton, 869 West Hill Field Road, Layton, UT 84041. *Phone:* 801-666-6000. *Toll-free phone:* 866-253-7744.
Website: http://www.broadviewuniversity.edu/.

Broadview University–Orem

Orem, Utah

- **Proprietary** 4-year, part of Globe Education Network (GEN) which is composed of Globe University, Minnesota School of Business, Broadview University, The Institute of Production and Recording and Minnesota School of Cosmetology
- **Small-town** 3-acre campus
- **Coed**

Faculty *Student/faculty ratio:* 17:1.
Academics *Degrees:* diplomas, associate, and bachelor's.
Student Life *Campus security:* 24-hour emergency response devices, late-night transport/escort service.
Standardized Tests *Required:* ACCUPLACER is required of all applicants unless documentation of a minimum ACT composite score of 21 or documentation of a minimum composite score of 1485 on the SAT is presented (for admission).
Costs (2012–13) *Tuition:* $14,400 full-time, $435 per credit part-time. Full-time tuition and fees vary according to course level, course load, degree level, location, and program. Part-time tuition and fees vary according to course level, course load, degree level, location, and program. *Required fees:* $1548 full-time, $43 per credit part-time.
Applying *Options:* electronic application. *Application fee:* $50. *Required:* high school transcript, interview, High school transcript or GED required of all applicants. *Required for some:* essay or personal statement, 2 letters of recommendation.
Freshman Application Contact Broadview University–Orem, 898 North 1200 West, Orem, UT 84057. *Toll-free phone:* 877-822-5838.
Website: http://www.broadviewuniversity.edu/.

Broadview University–Salt Lake City

Salt Lake City, Utah

- **Proprietary** 4-year, part of Globe Education Network (GEN) which is composed of Globe University, Minnesota School of Business, Broadview University, The Institute of Production and Recording and Minnesota School of Cosmetology
- **Urban** 3-acre campus
- **Coed**

Faculty *Student/faculty ratio:* 9:1.
Academics *Degrees:* associate and bachelor's.
Student Life *Campus security:* 24-hour emergency response devices, late-night transport/escort service.
Standardized Tests *Required:* ACCUPLACER is required of all applicants unless documentation of a minimum ACT composite score of 21 or documentation of a minimum composite score of 1485 on the SAT is presented (for admission).
Costs (2012–13) *Tuition:* $14,400 full-time, $460 per credit part-time. Full-time tuition and fees vary according to course level, course load, degree level, location, and program. Part-time tuition and fees vary according to course level, course load, degree level, location, and program. *Required fees:* $1548 full-time, $43 per credit part-time.
Applying *Options:* electronic application. *Application fee:* $50. *Required:* high school transcript, interview. *Required for some:* essay or personal statement, 2 letters of recommendation, GED certificate in lieu of high school transcript.
Freshman Application Contact Broadview University–Salt Lake City, 240 East Morris Avenue, Salt Lake City, UT 84115. *Toll-free phone:* 877-801-8889.
Website: http://www.broadviewuniversity.edu/.

Broadview University–West Jordan

West Jordan, Utah

- **Proprietary** comprehensive, part of Globe Education Network (GEN) which is composed of Globe University, Minnesota School of Business, Broadview University, The Institute of Production and Recording and Minnesota School of Cosmetology
- **Urban** 4-acre campus
- **Coed**

Faculty *Student/faculty ratio:* 15:1.

Academics *Calendar:* quarters. *Degrees:* diplomas, associate, bachelor's, and master's.

Student Life *Campus security:* 24-hour emergency response devices, late-night transport/escort service.

Standardized Tests *Required:* ACCUPLACER is required of all applicants unless documentation of a minimum ACT composite score of 21 or documentation of a minimum composite score of 1485 on the SAT is presented (for admission).

Costs (2012–13) *Tuition:* $14,400 full-time, $460 per credit part-time. Full-time tuition and fees vary according to course level, course load, degree level, location, and program. Part-time tuition and fees vary according to course level, course load, degree level, location, and program. *Required fees:* $1548 full-time, $43 per credit part-time.

Applying *Options:* electronic application. *Application fee:* $50. *Required:* high school transcript, interview, High school transcript or GED required of all applicants. Application fee for Nursing is $100. *Required for some:* essay or personal statement, 2 letters of recommendation.

Freshman Application Contact Broadview University–West Jordan, 1902 West 7800 South, West Jordan, UT 84088. *Phone:* 801-304-4224. *Toll-free phone:* 866-304-4224. *E-mail:* kcooper@utahcollege.edu. *Website:* http://www.broadviewuniversity.edu/.

DeVry University

Sandy, Utah

Freshman Application Contact DeVry University, 9350 South 150 E, Suite 420, Sandy, UT 84070. *Toll-free phone:* 866-338-7941. *Website:* http://www.devry.edu/.

Dixie State College of Utah

St. George, Utah

- **State-supported** 4-year, founded 1911, part of Utah System of Higher Education
- **Small-town** 117-acre campus
- **Endowment** $13.5 million
- **Coed**
- **Noncompetitive** entrance level

Academics *Calendar:* semesters. *Degrees:* certificates, diplomas, associate, and bachelor's.

Student Life *Campus security:* 24-hour emergency response devices and patrols.

Athletics Member NCAA. except baseball (Division II), men's and women's basketball (Division II), men's and women's cross-country running (Division II), football (Division II), golf (Division II), men's and women's soccer (Division II), softball (Division II), tennis (Division II), volleyball (Division II)

Standardized Tests *Recommended:* SAT or ACT (for admission).

Costs (2012–13) *Tuition:* state resident $4089 full-time, $145 per credit hour part-time; nonresident $11,721 full-time, $463 per credit hour part-time. Full-time tuition and fees vary according to course load. Part-time tuition and fees vary according to course load. *Required fees:* $620 full-time, $310 per term part-time. *Room and board:* $4348; room only: $1550. Room and board charges vary according to board plan and housing facility.

Financial Aid *Of all full-time matriculated undergraduates who enrolled in 2011, 4,364 applied for aid, 3,997 were judged to have need, 65 had their need fully met. In 2011, 589 non-need-based awards were made. Average percent of need met:* 35. *Average financial aid package:* $7279. *Average need-based loan:* $3818. *Average need-based gift aid:* $5234. *Average non-need-based aid:* $2206. *Average indebtedness upon graduation:* $22,412. *Financial aid deadline:* 6/30.

Applying *Options:* electronic application, early admission, deferred entrance. *Application fee:* $35. *Required:* high school transcript.

Freshman Application Contact Dixie State College of Utah, 225 South 700 East, St. George, UT 84770-3876. *Phone:* 435-652-7698. *Website:* http://www.dixie.edu/.

Independence University

Salt Lake City, Utah

Freshman Application Contact Ms. Deborah Hopkins, Enrollment Manager, Independence University, 5295 South Commerce Drive, Salt Lake City, UT 84107. *Toll-free phone:* 800-972-5149. *Website:* http://www.independence.edu/.

ITT Technical Institute

Murray, Utah

- **Proprietary** primarily 2-year, founded 1984, part of ITT Educational Services, Inc.
- **Suburban** campus
- **Coed**
- **Minimally difficult** entrance level

Academics *Calendar:* quarters. *Degrees:* associate and bachelor's.

Freshman Application Contact Director of Recruitment, ITT Technical Institute, 920 West Levoy Drive, Murray, UT 84123-2500. *Phone:* 801-263-3313. *Toll-free phone:* 800-365-2136. *Website:* http://www.itt-tech.edu/.

Midwives College of Utah

Salt Lake City, Utah

Freshman Application Contact Kristi Ridd-Young, President, Midwives College of Utah, 1174 East 2700 South, Suite 2, Salt Lake City, UT 84106. *Phone:* 801-649-5230. *Toll-free phone:* 866-680-2756. *Fax:* 866-207-2024. *E-mail:* office@midwifery.edu. *Website:* http://www.midwifery.edu/.

Neumont University

South Jordan, Utah

- **Proprietary** comprehensive, founded 2002
- **Suburban** campus with easy access to Salt Lake City
- **Coed, primarily men** 366 undergraduate students, 100% full-time, 10% women, 90% men
- **Moderately difficult** entrance level, 81% of applicants were admitted

Undergraduates 366 full-time. 80% live on campus. *Retention:* 69% of full-time freshmen returned.

Freshmen *Admission:* 596 applied, 483 admitted, 166 enrolled. *Average high school GPA:* 3.2. *Test scores:* ACT scores over 18: 92%; ACT scores over 24: 50%; ACT scores over 30: 12%.

Faculty *Total:* 26, 50% full-time. *Student/faculty ratio:* 21:1.

Academics *Calendar:* quarters. *Degrees:* bachelor's and master's. *Special study options:* accelerated degree program, services for LD students.

Computers on Campus Students can access the following: campus intranet, computer help desk, free student e-mail accounts, online (class) grades, online (class) registration, online (class) schedules. Campuswide network is available. Wireless service is available via entire campus.

Student Life *Housing options:* men-only, women-only, disabled students. Campus housing is leased by the school and is provided by a third party. Freshman campus housing is guaranteed. *Activities and organizations:* choral group, Neumont Tactical Federation, Epically Good Gamer's Group, Beyond The Screen Order, Rhythm Rockers Gaming Association, Unified Student Government. *Student services:* health clinic, personal/psychological counseling.

Athletics *Intramural sports:* basketball M(c), soccer M(c), table tennis M(c)/W(c).

Standardized Tests *Required:* SAT or ACT (for admission).

Costs (2013–14) *Tuition:* $21,600 full-time, $495 per unit part-time. *Required fees:* $1500 full-time. *Room only:* $4230. *Payment plan:* installment. *Waivers:* employees or children of employees.

Financial Aid *Financial aid deadline:* 7/1.
Applying *Options:* electronic application. *Application fee:* $35. *Required:* essay or personal statement, high school transcript. *Recommended:* 2 letters of recommendation, interview. *Application deadlines:* rolling (freshmen), rolling (transfers).
Freshman Application Contact Karick Heaton, Director of Admissions, Neumont University, 10701 South River Front Parkway, Suite 300, South Jordan, UT 84095. *Phone:* 801-302-2879. *Toll-free phone:* 888-NEUMONT. *Fax:* 801-302-2811. *E-mail:* karick.heaton@neumont.edu. *Website:* http://www.neumont.edu/.

Southern Utah University

Cedar City, Utah

- **State-supported** comprehensive, founded 1897, part of Utah System of Higher Education
- **Small-town** 130-acre campus
- **Endowment** $7.8 million
- **Coed** 7,633 undergraduate students, 73% full-time, 55% women, 45% men
- **Moderately difficult** entrance level, 57% of applicants were admitted

Undergraduates 5,552 full-time, 2,081 part-time. Students come from 48 states and territories; 30 other countries; 16% are from out of state; 1% Black or African American, non-Hispanic/Latino; 5% Hispanic/Latino; 0.8% Asian, non-Hispanic/Latino; 1% Native Hawaiian or other Pacific Islander, non-Hispanic/Latino; 2% American Indian or Alaska Native, non-Hispanic/Latino; 0.8% Two or more races, non-Hispanic/Latino; 2% Race/ethnicity unknown; 4% international; 5% transferred in; 11% live on campus. *Retention:* 66% of full-time freshmen returned.
Freshmen *Admission:* 6,375 applied, 3,655 admitted, 1,264 enrolled. *Average high school GPA:* 3.5. *Test scores:* SAT critical reading scores over 500: 53%; SAT math scores over 500: 60%; ACT scores over 18: 93%; SAT critical reading scores over 600: 16%; SAT math scores over 600: 17%; ACT scores over 24: 42%; SAT critical reading scores over 700: 2%; SAT math scores over 700: 1%; ACT scores over 30: 5%.
Faculty *Total:* 420, 60% full-time, 49% with terminal degrees. *Student/faculty ratio:* 21:1.
Academics *Calendar:* semesters. *Degrees:* certificates, diplomas, associate, bachelor's, and master's. *Special study options:* academic remediation for entering students, adult/continuing education programs, advanced placement credit, cooperative education, distance learning, double majors, English as a second language, honors programs, independent study, internships, part-time degree program, services for LD students, study abroad, summer session for credit. *ROTC:* Army (b).
Computers on Campus 1,040 computers/terminals and 25 ports are available on campus for general student use. Students can access the following: campus intranet, computer help desk, free student e-mail accounts, online (class) grades, online (class) registration, online (class) schedules. Campuswide network is available. 100% of college-owned or -operated housing units are wired for high-speed Internet access. Wireless service is available via entire campus.
Student Life *Housing options:* coed, disabled students. Campus housing is university owned. *Activities and organizations:* drama/theater group, student-run newspaper, radio and television station, choral group, national fraternities, national sororities. *Campus security:* 24-hour emergency response devices, student patrols, late-night transport/escort service, controlled dormitory access. *Student services:* health clinic, personal/psychological counseling, women's center.
Athletics Member NCAA. All Division I. *Intercollegiate sports:* basketball M(s)/W(s), cross-country running M(s)/W(s), football M(s), golf M(s)/W(s), gymnastics W(s), soccer W(s), softball W(s), tennis M(s)/W(s), track and field M(s)/W(s), volleyball W(s). *Intramural sports:* basketball M/W, cheerleading M(c)/W(c), golf M/W, soccer M/W, tennis M/W, volleyball M/W.
Standardized Tests *Required:* SAT or ACT (for admission).
Costs (2012–13) *Tuition:* state resident $4960 full-time, $233 per credit hour part-time; nonresident $16,368 full-time, $773 per credit hour part-time. Full-time tuition and fees vary according to program. Part-time tuition and fees vary according to course load and program. *Required fees:* $616 full-time, $308 per term part-time. *Room only:* $2878. Room and board charges vary according to board plan and housing facility. *Payment plan:* installment. *Waivers:* children of alumni, senior citizens, and employees or children of employees.
Financial Aid Of all full-time matriculated undergraduates who enrolled in 2010, 3,991 applied for aid, 3,582 were judged to have need, 220 had their need fully met. In 2010, 852 non-need-based awards were made. *Average percent of need met:* 55%. *Average financial aid package:* $8831. *Average need-based loan:* $3302. *Average need-based gift aid:* $8717. *Average non-need-based aid:* $4279. *Average indebtedness upon graduation:* $12,632.

Applying *Options:* electronic application, deferred entrance. *Application fee:* $50. *Required:* high school transcript. *Application deadlines:* 5/1 (freshmen), 5/1 (out-of-state freshmen). *Notification:* continuous (freshmen), continuous (out-of-state freshmen).
Freshman Application Contact Southern Utah University, 351 West University Boulevard, Cedar City, UT 84720-2498. *Phone:* 435-586-7740. *Website:* http://www.suu.edu/.

Stevens-Henager College–Ogden/West Haven

Ogden, Utah

Freshman Application Contact Admissions Office, Stevens-Henager College–Ogden/West Haven, 1890 South 1350 West, Ogden, UT 84401. *Phone:* 801-394-7791. *Toll-free phone:* 800-622-2640. *Website:* http://www.stevenshenager.edu/.

Strayer University—Sandy Campus

Sandy, Utah

Freshman Application Contact Strayer University—Sandy Campus, 9815 South Monroe Street, Suite 200, Sandy, UT 84070. *Website:* http://www.strayer.edu/campus/sandy.

University of Phoenix–Utah Campus

Salt Lake City, Utah

Freshman Application Contact Marc Booker, Sr. Director, Office of Admissions and Evaluation, University of Phoenix–Utah Campus, 4615 East Elwood Street, Mail Stop AA-K101, Phoenix, AZ 85040-1958. *Phone:* 602-557-4609. *Toll-free phone:* 866-766-0766. *Fax:* 480-643-1156. *Website:* http://www.phoenix.edu/.

University of Utah

Salt Lake City, Utah

- **State-supported** university, founded 1850, part of Utah System of Higher Education
- **Urban** 1535-acre campus with easy access to Salt Lake City
- **Endowment** $544.0 million
- **Coed** 24,840 undergraduate students, 71% full-time, 44% women, 56% men
- **Moderately difficult** entrance level, 83% of applicants were admitted

Undergraduates 17,518 full-time, 7,322 part-time. Students come from 53 states and territories; 118 other countries; 18% are from out of state; 1% Black or African American, non-Hispanic/Latino; 8% Hispanic/Latino; 5% Asian, non-Hispanic/Latino; 0.7% Native Hawaiian or other Pacific Islander, non-Hispanic/Latino; 0.6% American Indian or Alaska Native, non-Hispanic/Latino; 3% Two or more races, non-Hispanic/Latino; 3% Race/ethnicity unknown; 6% international; 8% transferred in; 14% live on campus. *Retention:* 88% of full-time freshmen returned.
Freshmen *Admission:* 11,118 applied, 9,187 admitted, 3,494 enrolled. *Average high school GPA:* 3.55. *Test scores:* SAT critical reading scores over 500: 79%; SAT math scores over 500: 82%; SAT writing scores over 500: 72%; ACT scores over 18: 95%; SAT critical reading scores over 600: 38%; SAT math scores over 600: 45%; SAT writing scores over 600: 31%; ACT scores over 24: 57%; SAT critical reading scores over 700: 10%; SAT math scores over 700: 11%; SAT writing scores over 700: 5%; ACT scores over 30: 15%.
Faculty *Total:* 2,116, 71% full-time, 66% with terminal degrees. *Student/faculty ratio:* 13:1.
Academics *Calendar:* semesters. *Degrees:* bachelor's, master's, doctoral, post-master's, and postbachelor's certificates. *Special study options:* accelerated degree program, advanced placement credit, cooperative education, distance learning, double majors, English as a second language, freshman honors

college, honors programs, independent study, internships, off-campus study, part-time degree program, services for LD students, student-designed majors, study abroad, summer session for credit. *ROTC:* Army (b), Navy (b), Air Force (b). *Unusual degree programs:* 3-2 engineering; computer science, math, public policy.

Computers on Campus 3,000 computers/terminals are available on campus for general student use. Students can access the following: campus intranet, computer help desk, free student e-mail accounts, online (class) grades, online (class) registration, online (class) schedules, online classes. Campuswide network is available. 100% of college-owned or -operated housing units are wired for high-speed Internet access. Wireless service is available via entire campus.

Student Life *Housing options:* coed, men-only, women-only, disabled students. Campus housing is university owned. *Activities and organizations:* drama/theater group, student-run newspaper, radio and television station, choral group, marching band, Latter-Day Saints Student Association, Lowell Bennion Community Service Center, Newman Center, Center for Ethnic Student Affairs, national fraternities, national sororities. *Campus security:* 24-hour emergency response devices and patrols, student patrols, late-night transport/escort service, controlled dormitory access. *Student services:* health clinic, personal/psychological counseling, women's center, legal services.

Athletics Member NCAA. All Division I. *Intercollegiate sports:* baseball M(s), basketball M(s)/W(s), cheerleading M(s)/W(s), cross-country running W(s), football M(s), golf M(s), gymnastics W(s), lacrosse M(c)/W(c), rugby M(c), skiing (cross-country) M(s)/W(s), skiing (downhill) M(s)/W(s), soccer W(s), softball W(s), swimming and diving M(s)/W(s), table tennis M(c)/W(c), tennis M(s)/W(s), track and field W(s), volleyball W(s), water polo M(c)/W(c). *Intramural sports:* basketball M/W, bowling M/W, fencing M/W, field hockey M/W, football M, ice hockey M, lacrosse M, racquetball M/W, riflery M/W, soccer M/W, softball M/W, squash M/W, tennis M/W, ultimate Frisbee M/W, volleyball M/W.

Standardized Tests *Required:* ACT (for admission), SAT or ACT (for admission).

Costs (2012–13) *Tuition:* state resident $6200 full-time, $174 per credit hour part-time; nonresident $21,704 full-time, $599 per credit hour part-time. Full-time tuition and fees vary according to course level, course load, degree level, program, and student level. Part-time tuition and fees vary according to course level, course load, degree level, program, and student level. *Required fees:* $938 full-time. *Room and board:* $7155; room only: $3719. Room and board charges vary according to board plan, housing facility, and location. *Payment plans:* installment, deferred payment. *Waivers:* senior citizens and employees or children of employees.

Financial Aid Of all full-time matriculated undergraduates who enrolled in 2012, 9,340 applied for aid, 8,049 were judged to have need, 717 had their need fully met. 333 Federal Work-Study jobs (averaging $4880). In 2012, 737 non-need-based awards were made. *Average percent of need met:* 61%. *Average financial aid package:* $15,437. *Average need-based loan:* $4403. *Average need-based gift aid:* $5997. *Average non-need-based aid:* $5652. *Average indebtedness upon graduation:* $20,796.

Applying *Options:* electronic application, early admission, deferred entrance. *Application fee:* $45. *Required:* high school transcript, minimum 2.6 GPA. *Required for some:* essay or personal statement. *Recommended:* minimum 3.0 GPA. *Application deadlines:* 4/1 (freshmen), 4/1 (out-of-state freshmen), 4/1 (transfers). *Notification:* continuous (freshmen), continuous (out-of-state freshmen), continuous (transfers).

Freshman Application Contact Mateo Remsburg, Associate Director, Office of Admissions, University of Utah, 201 S. 1460 E. Rm 250 S, Salt Lake City, UT 84112. *Phone:* 801-581-8761. *Toll-free phone:* 800-685-8856. *Fax:* 801-585-3257. *E-mail:* mremsburg@sa.utah.edu. *Website:* http://www.utah.edu/.

Utah State University

Logan, Utah

- **State-supported** university, founded 1888, part of Utah System of Higher Education
- **Urban** 456-acre campus
- **Endowment** $209.2 million
- **Coed** 25,445 undergraduate students, 61% full-time, 55% women, 45% men
- **Moderately difficult** entrance level, 97% of applicants were admitted

Undergraduates 15,469 full-time, 9,976 part-time. Students come from 53 states and territories; 46 other countries; 23% are from out of state; 1% Black or African American, non-Hispanic/Latino; 5% Hispanic/Latino; 1% Asian, non-Hispanic/Latino; 0.3% Native Hawaiian or other Pacific Islander, non-Hispanic/Latino; 2% American Indian or Alaska Native, non-Hispanic/Latino; 1% Two or more races, non-Hispanic/Latino; 6% Race/ethnicity unknown; 2% international; 7% transferred in. *Retention:* 72% of full-time freshmen returned.

Freshmen *Admission:* 9,052 applied, 8,757 admitted, 3,824 enrolled. *Average high school GPA:* 3.46. *Test scores:* SAT critical reading scores over 500: 71%; SAT math scores over 500: 73%; ACT scores over 18: 93%; SAT critical reading scores over 600: 29%; SAT math scores over 600: 34%; ACT scores over 24: 47%; SAT critical reading scores over 700: 8%; SAT math scores over 700: 9%; ACT scores over 30: 11%.

Faculty *Total:* 1,074, 81% full-time, 69% with terminal degrees. *Student/faculty ratio:* 23:1.

Academics *Calendar:* semesters. *Degrees:* certificates, associate, bachelor's, master's, doctoral, and postbachelor's certificates. *Special study options:* academic remediation for entering students, accelerated degree program, adult/continuing education programs, advanced placement credit, cooperative education, distance learning, double majors, English as a second language, freshman honors college, honors programs, independent study, internships, off-campus study, part-time degree program, services for LD students, student-designed majors, study abroad, summer session for credit. *ROTC:* Army (b), Air Force (b).

Computers on Campus 1,000 computers/terminals are available on campus for general student use. Students can access the following: computer help desk, free student e-mail accounts, online (class) grades, online (class) registration, online (class) schedules. Campuswide network is available. 100% of college-owned or -operated housing units are wired for high-speed Internet access. Wireless service is available via classrooms, computer centers, computer labs, dorm rooms, learning centers, libraries, student centers.

Student Life *Housing options:* coed, men-only, women-only, disabled students. Campus housing is university owned. *Activities and organizations:* drama/theater group, student-run newspaper, radio station, choral group, marching band, Latter-Day Saints Student Association, multicultural clubs, volunteer groups, college councils, national fraternities, national sororities. *Campus security:* 24-hour emergency response devices and patrols, student patrols, late-night transport/escort service, video monitors in pedestrian tunnels. *Student services:* health clinic, personal/psychological counseling, women's center, legal services.

Athletics Member NCAA. All Division I except football (Division I-A). *Intercollegiate sports:* baseball M(c), basketball M(s)/W(s), cross-country running M(s)/W(s), equestrian sports M(c)/W(c), golf M(s), gymnastics W(s), ice hockey M(c), rugby M(c)/W(c), soccer M(c)/W(s), softball W(s), tennis M(s)/W(s), track and field M(s)/W(s), volleyball M(c)/W(s). *Intramural sports:* badminton M/W, basketball M/W, cross-country running M/W, fencing M(c)/W(c), football M/W, golf M/W, ice hockey W(c), lacrosse M(c), racquetball M(c)/W(c), skiing (cross-country) M(c)/W(c), skiing (downhill) M(c)/W(c), soccer M/W, softball M/W, squash M/W, swimming and diving M/W, table tennis M/W, tennis M/W, ultimate Frisbee M(c)/W(c), volleyball M/W, water polo M(c)/W(c).

Standardized Tests *Required:* SAT or ACT (for admission).

Costs (2013–14) *Tuition:* state resident $5273 full-time; nonresident $16,976 full-time. Full-time tuition and fees vary according to course load, location, program, and reciprocity agreements. Part-time tuition and fees vary according to course load, location, program, and reciprocity agreements. *Required fees:* $910 full-time. *Room and board:* $5620; room only: $1920. Room and board charges vary according to board plan and housing facility. *Payment plan:* deferred payment. *Waivers:* minority students, children of alumni, adult students, senior citizens, and employees or children of employees.

Financial Aid Of all full-time matriculated undergraduates who enrolled in 2011, 10,231 applied for aid, 9,024 were judged to have need, 1,345 had their need fully met. 191 Federal Work-Study jobs (averaging $3140). 290 state and other part-time jobs (averaging $3140). In 2011, 1445 non-need-based awards were made. *Average percent of need met:* 60%. *Average financial aid package:* $6970. *Average need-based loan:* $3900. *Average need-based gift aid:* $4300. *Average non-need-based aid:* $2132. *Average indebtedness upon graduation:* $17,200.

Applying *Options:* electronic application, deferred entrance. *Application fee:* $40. *Required:* high school transcript. *Recommended:* minimum 2.8 GPA. *Application deadlines:* rolling (freshmen), rolling (transfers). *Notification:* continuous (freshmen), continuous (transfers).

Freshman Application Contact Mr. Jeff Sorenson, Asst. Director, Admissions Office, Utah State University, 0160 Old Main Hill, Logan, UT 84322-0160. *Phone:* 435-797-1079. *Toll-free phone:* 800-488-8108. *Fax:* 435-797-3708. *E-mail:* admit@usu.edu. *Website:* http://www.usu.edu/.

Utah Valley University

Orem, Utah

- **State-supported** comprehensive, founded 1941, affiliated with Advent Christian Church, part of Utah System of Higher Education
- **Suburban** 422-acre campus with easy access to Salt Lake City
- **Endowment** $11.0 million
- **Coed**
- **Noncompetitive** entrance level

Faculty *Student/faculty ratio:* 25:1.

Academics *Calendar:* semesters. *Degrees:* certificates, diplomas, associate, bachelor's, and master's.

Student Life *Campus security:* 24-hour patrols.

Athletics Member NCAA. All Division I.

Standardized Tests *Required:* SAT or ACT (for admission).

Financial Aid *Of all full-time matriculated undergraduates who enrolled in 2010,* 13,408 applied for aid, 11,327 were judged to have need, 603 had their need fully met. *In 2010,* 1289 non-need-based awards were made. *Average percent of need met:* 55. *Average financial aid package:* $4964. *Average need-based loan:* $2576. *Average need-based gift aid:* $4878. *Average non-need-based aid:* $3780. *Average indebtedness upon graduation:* $13,407. *Financial aid deadline:* 5/1.

Applying *Options:* electronic application, deferred entrance. *Application fee:* $35. *Required:* ACT or SAT, or Accuplacer. *Required for some:* high school transcript.

Freshman Application Contact Mrs. Liz Childs, Senior Director of Admissions, Utah Valley University, 800 West University Parkway, Orem, UT 84058-5999. *Phone:* 801-863-8460. *Fax:* 801-225-4677. *E-mail:* info@uvsc.edu.

Website: http://www.uvu.edu/.

Weber State University

Ogden, Utah

- **State-supported** comprehensive, founded 1889, part of Utah System of Higher Education
- **Urban** 526-acre campus with easy access to Salt Lake City
- **Endowment** $74.9 million
- **Coed** 25,868 undergraduate students, 46% full-time, 53% women, 47% men
- **Noncompetitive** entrance level, 100% of applicants were admitted

Undergraduates 11,784 full-time, 14,084 part-time. Students come from 52 states and territories; 45 other countries; 8% are from out of state; 1% Black or African American, non-Hispanic/Latino; 9% Hispanic/Latino; 1% Asian, non-Hispanic/Latino; 0.3% Native Hawaiian or other Pacific Islander, non-Hispanic/Latino; 0.4% American Indian or Alaska Native, non-Hispanic/Latino; 1% Two or more races, non-Hispanic/Latino; 31% Race/ethnicity unknown; 2% international; 3% transferred in; 3% live on campus. *Retention:* 74% of full-time freshmen returned.

Freshmen *Admission:* 5,561 applied, 5,561 admitted, 2,497 enrolled. *Average high school GPA:* 3.21. *Test scores:* ACT scores over 18: 79%; ACT scores over 24: 29%; ACT scores over 30: 3%.

Faculty *Total:* 976, 45% full-time. *Student/faculty ratio:* 24:1.

Academics *Calendar:* semesters. *Degrees:* certificates, associate, bachelor's, master's, and postbachelor's certificates. *Special study options:* academic remediation for entering students, accelerated degree program, adult/continuing education programs, advanced placement credit, cooperative education, distance learning, double majors, English as a second language, external degree program, freshman honors college, honors programs, independent study, internships, off-campus study, part-time degree program, services for LD students, student-designed majors, study abroad, summer session for credit. *ROTC:* Army (b), Navy (b), Air Force (b).

Computers on Campus 358 computers/terminals are available on campus for general student use. Students can access the following: campus intranet, computer help desk, free student e-mail accounts, online (class) grades, online (class) registration, online (class) schedules. Campuswide network is available. 100% of college-owned or -operated housing units are wired for high-speed Internet access. Wireless service is available via entire campus.

Student Life *Housing options:* men-only, women-only, cooperative, disabled students. Campus housing is university owned and is provided by a third party. *Activities and organizations:* drama/theater group, student-run newspaper, radio and television station, choral group, marching band, LDSSA (Latter-day Saint Student Association), SAA (Student Alumni Association), GSA (Gay-Straight Alliance), Chinese Club, Golden Key Honor Society, national fraterni-

ties, national sororities. *Campus security:* 24-hour emergency response devices and patrols, student patrols, late-night transport/escort service, controlled dormitory access. *Student services:* health clinic, personal/psychological counseling, women's center, legal services.

Athletics Member NCAA. All Division I. *Intercollegiate sports:* archery M(c)/W(c), baseball M(c), basketball M(s)/W(s), bowling M(c)/W(c), cheerleading M(s)/W(s), cross-country running M(s)/W(s), fencing M(c)/W(c), football M(s), golf M(s)/W(s), ice hockey M(c), lacrosse W(c), rock climbing M(c)/W(c), rugby M(c)/W(c), skiing (downhill) M(c)/W(c), soccer M(c)/W(s), softball W(s), tennis M(s)/W(s), track and field M(s)/W(s), volleyball M(c)/W(s), wrestling M(c). *Intramural sports:* basketball M/W, bowling M/W, football M/W, racquetball M/W, soccer M/W, tennis M/W, ultimate Frisbee M/W, volleyball M/W.

Standardized Tests *Required for some:* ACCUPLACER. *Recommended:* SAT or ACT (for admission).

Costs (2012–13) *Tuition:* state resident $3961 full-time, $165 per credit hour part-time; nonresident $12,058 full-time, $502 per credit hour part-time. Full-time tuition and fees vary according to course load and degree level. Part-time tuition and fees vary according to course load and degree level. *Required fees:* $800 full-time, $33 per credit hour part-time. *Room and board:* $5200. Room and board charges vary according to board plan and housing facility. *Payment plan:* installment. *Waivers:* children of alumni, senior citizens, and employees or children of employees.

Financial Aid Of all full-time matriculated undergraduates who enrolled in 2007, 4,981 applied for aid, 4,509 were judged to have need, 174 had their need fully met. In 2007, 1562 non-need-based awards were made. *Average percent of need met:* 50%. *Average financial aid package:* $5878. *Average need-based loan:* $4079. *Average need-based gift aid:* $3622. *Average non-need-based aid:* $2033.

Applying *Options:* electronic application, early admission, deferred entrance. *Application fee:* $30. *Required:* high school transcript. *Application deadlines:* 8/21 (freshmen), rolling (transfers). *Notification:* continuous (freshmen), continuous (transfers).

Freshman Application Contact Laura Albright, Student Recruitment, Weber State University, 1137 University Circle, Ogden, UT 84408-1137. *Phone:* 801-626-6050. *Toll-free phone:* 800-848-7700 (in-state); 800-848-7770 (out-of-state). *Fax:* 801-626-6744. *E-mail:* admissions@weber.edu.

Website: http://www.weber.edu/.

Western Governors University

Salt Lake City, Utah

Freshman Application Contact Western Governors University, 4001 South 700 East, Suite 700, Salt Lake City, UT 84107. *Phone:* 801-274-3280 Ext. 336. *Toll-free phone:* 866-225-5948.

Website: http://www.wgu.edu/.

Westminster College

Salt Lake City, Utah

- **Independent** comprehensive, founded 1875
- **Suburban** 27-acre campus
- **Endowment** $56.7 million
- **Coed** 2,526 undergraduate students, 89% full-time, 54% women, 46% men
- **Moderately difficult** entrance level, 70% of applicants were admitted

Undergraduates 2,260 full-time, 266 part-time. 38% are from out of state; 1% Black or African American, non-Hispanic/Latino; 9% Hispanic/Latino; 3% Asian, non-Hispanic/Latino; 0.5% Native Hawaiian or other Pacific Islander, non-Hispanic/Latino; 1% American Indian or Alaska Native, non-Hispanic/Latino; 2% Two or more races, non-Hispanic/Latino; 8% Race/ethnicity unknown; 5% international; 7% transferred in; 27% live on campus. *Retention:* 78% of full-time freshmen returned.

Freshmen *Admission:* 3,764 applied, 2,616 admitted, 501 enrolled. *Average high school GPA:* 3.5. *Test scores:* SAT critical reading scores over 500: 77%; SAT math scores over 500: 78%; ACT scores over 18: 98%; SAT critical reading scores over 600: 30%; SAT math scores over 600: 34%; ACT scores over 24: 62%; SAT critical reading scores over 700: 6%; SAT math scores over 700: 7%; ACT scores over 30: 7%.

Faculty *Total:* 410, 38% full-time, 55% with terminal degrees. *Student/faculty ratio:* 10:1.

Academics *Calendar:* 4-4-1. *Degrees:* bachelor's, master's, and postbachelor's certificates. *Special study options:* academic remediation for entering students, accelerated degree program, advanced placement credit, cooperative education, distance learning, double majors, English as a second language, external degree program, freshman honors college, honors programs, independent study, internships, off-campus study, part-time degree program, services for LD students, student-designed majors, study abroad, summer session for credit. *ROTC:* Army (c), Navy (c), Air Force (c). *Unusual degree programs:* 3-2 engineering with University of Southern California, Washington University in St. Louis.

Computers on Campus 244 computers/terminals and 457 ports are available on campus for general student use. Students can access the following: campus intranet, computer help desk, free student e-mail accounts, online (class) grades, online (class) registration, online (class) schedules. Campuswide network is available. 100% of college-owned or -operated housing units are wired for high-speed Internet access. Wireless service is available via entire campus.

Student Life *Housing:* on-campus residence required for freshman year. *Options:* coed, disabled students. Campus housing is university owned and leased by the school. Freshman applicants given priority for college housing. *Activities and organizations:* drama/theater group, student-run newspaper, choral group, Associated Students of Westminster College (Student Government), Associated Residents of Westminster College (Residential Government), Westminster Ski and Snowboard Club (WSSC), V-Day, Westminster Entrepreneurship Club. *Campus security:* 24-hour emergency response devices and patrols, student patrols, late-night transport/escort service, controlled dormitory access. *Student services:* health clinic, personal/psychological counseling.

Athletics Member NAIA. *Intercollegiate sports:* basketball M(s)/W(s), cross-country running M(s)/W(s), golf M(s)/W(s), lacrosse M(s)/W, skiing (downhill) M(s)/W(s), soccer M(s)/W(s), track and field M(s)/W(s), volleyball W(s). *Intramural sports:* basketball M/W, skiing (cross-country) M/W, soccer M/W, volleyball M/W.

Standardized Tests *Required:* SAT or ACT (for admission).

Costs (2013–14) *Comprehensive fee:* $36,100 includes full-time tuition ($27,720), mandatory fees ($490), and room and board ($7890). Full-time tuition and fees vary according to course load and program. Part-time tuition: $1155 per credit hour. Part-time tuition and fees vary according to course load and program. *Room and board:* Room and board charges vary according to board plan. *Payment plans:* installment, deferred payment. *Waivers:* employees or children of employees.

Financial Aid Of all full-time matriculated undergraduates who enrolled in 2012, 1,534 applied for aid, 1,335 were judged to have need, 276 had their need fully met. 497 Federal Work-Study jobs (averaging $2452). 217 state and other part-time jobs (averaging $2434). In 2012, 706 non-need-based awards were made. *Average percent of need met:* 76%. *Average financial aid package:* $22,336. *Average need-based loan:* $4736. *Average need-based gift aid:* $17,206. *Average non-need-based aid:* $12,920. *Average indebtedness upon graduation:* $28,323.

Applying *Options:* electronic application, deferred entrance. *Application fee:* $50. *Required:* essay or personal statement, high school transcript, minimum 2.5 GPA, 1 letter of recommendation. *Recommended:* interview. *Application deadlines:* rolling (freshmen), rolling (out-of-state freshmen), rolling (transfers). *Notification:* continuous (freshmen), continuous (out-of-state freshmen), continuous (transfers).

Freshman Application Contact Elizabeth Key, Associate Vice President for Enrollment Management, Westminster College, 1840 South 1300 East, Salt Lake City, UT 84105-3697. *Phone:* 801-832-2200. *Toll-free phone:* 800-748-4753. *Fax:* 801-832-3101. *E-mail:* admission@westminstercollege.edu. *Website:* http://www.westminstercollege.edu/.

VERMONT

Bennington College

Bennington, Vermont

- **Independent** comprehensive, founded 1932
- **Small-town** 440-acre campus with easy access to Albany, NY
- **Endowment** $15.4 million
- **Coed** 688 undergraduate students, 99% full-time, 64% women, 36% men
- **Very difficult** entrance level, 63% of applicants were admitted

Undergraduates 684 full-time, 4 part-time. Students come from 46 states and territories; 36 other countries; 96% are from out of state; 2% Black or African American, non-Hispanic/Latino; 5% Hispanic/Latino; 2% Asian, non-Hispanic/Latino; 3% Two or more races, non-Hispanic/Latino; 4% Race/ethnicity unknown; 7% international; 2% transferred in; 95% live on campus. *Retention:* 83% of full-time freshmen returned.

Freshmen *Admission:* 1,236 applied, 779 admitted, 197 enrolled. *Average high school GPA:* 3.5. *Test scores:* SAT critical reading scores over 500: 100%;

SAT math scores over 500: 99%; SAT writing scores over 500: 99%; ACT scores over 18: 100%; SAT critical reading scores over 600: 87%; SAT math scores over 600: 61%; SAT writing scores over 600: 78%; ACT scores over 24: 95%; SAT critical reading scores over 700: 41%; SAT math scores over 700: 13%; SAT writing scores over 700: 27%; ACT scores over 30: 36%.

Faculty *Total:* 89, 72% full-time, 71% with terminal degrees. *Student/faculty ratio:* 9:1.

Academics *Calendar:* semesters plus winter work term in January and February. *Degrees:* bachelor's, master's, and postbachelor's certificates. *Special study options:* accelerated degree program, double majors, independent study, internships, off-campus study, part-time degree program, services for LD students, student-designed majors, study abroad.

Computers on Campus 100 computers/terminals and 25 ports are available on campus for general student use. Students can access the following: campus intranet, computer help desk, free student e-mail accounts, online (class) schedules. Campuswide network is available. 100% of college-owned or -operated housing units are wired for high-speed Internet access. Wireless service is available via entire campus.

Student Life *Housing:* on-campus residence required through senior year. *Options:* coed, cooperative. Campus housing is university owned. Freshman campus housing is guaranteed. *Activities and organizations:* drama/theater group, student-run newspaper, choral group, Program Activity Council, Bennington Free Press, Student Endowment for the Arts, SILO: Student Journal of Arts and Letters, Bennington Zombie Defense: Humans vs. Zombies Game. *Campus security:* 24-hour emergency response devices and patrols, late-night transport/escort service, prevention/awareness program. *Student services:* health clinic, personal/psychological counseling.

Athletics *Intercollegiate sports:* basketball M(c)/W(c), fencing M(c)/W(c), soccer M(c)/W(c), ultimate Frisbee M(c)/W(c), volleyball M(c)/W(c). *Intramural sports:* archery M/W, badminton M/W, basketball M/W, bowling M/W, cheerleading M/W, cross-country running M/W, equestrian sports M/W, golf M/W, skiing (cross-country) M/W, skiing (downhill) M/W, softball M/W, table tennis M/W, tennis M/W, volleyball M/W, weight lifting M/W.

Costs (2012–13) *Comprehensive fee:* $56,990 includes full-time tuition ($43,070), mandatory fees ($1150), and room and board ($12,770). Part-time tuition: $1440 per credit hour. *College room only:* $6850. *Payment plan:* installment. *Waivers:* employees or children of employees.

Financial Aid Of all full-time matriculated undergraduates who enrolled in 2012, 522 applied for aid, 442 were judged to have need, 52 had their need fully met. 363 Federal Work-Study jobs (averaging $2300). 41 state and other part-time jobs (averaging $2300). In 2012, 178 non-need-based awards were made. *Average percent of need met:* 80%. *Average financial aid package:* $35,822. *Average need-based loan:* $4156. *Average need-based gift aid:* $30,716. *Average non-need-based aid:* $17,121. *Average indebtedness upon graduation:* $25,716. *Financial aid deadline:* 2/15.

Applying *Options:* electronic application, early admission, early decision, early action, deferred entrance. *Application fee:* $60. *Required:* essay or personal statement, high school transcript, 2 letters of recommendation, graded analytic paper. *Recommended:* interview. *Application deadlines:* 1/3 (freshmen), 3/15 (transfers), 12/1 (early action). *Early decision deadline:* 11/15 (for plan 1), 1/3 (for plan 2). *Notification:* 4/1 (freshmen), 5/1 (transfers), 12/20 (early decision plan 1), 2/1 (early decision plan 2), 2/1 (early action).

Freshman Application Contact Ms. Janet Marsden, Vice President for Admissions and Communications, Bennington College, One College Drive, Bennington, VT 05201-6003. *Phone:* 802-440-4312. *Toll-free phone:* 800-833-6845. *Fax:* 802-440-4320. *E-mail:* admissions@bennington.edu. *Website:* http://www.bennington.edu/.

Burlington College

Burlington, Vermont

- **Independent** comprehensive, founded 1972
- **Urban** 32-acre campus with easy access to Montreal
- **Endowment** $100,784
- **Coed**
- **Moderately difficult** entrance level

Faculty *Student/faculty ratio:* 6:1.

Academics *Calendar:* semesters. *Degrees:* certificates, associate, bachelor's, and master's.

Student Life *Campus security:* student patrols.

Costs (2012–13) *Tuition:* $22,410 full-time. Full-time tuition and fees vary according to course load and program. Part-time tuition and fees vary according to course load and program. *Room only:* $6870. Room and board charges vary according to housing facility.

Financial Aid *Of all full-time matriculated undergraduates who enrolled in 2012,* 147 applied for aid, 137 were judged to have need. *In 2012,* 2 non-need-based awards were made. *Average percent of need met:* 47. *Average financial aid package:* $14,460. *Average need-based loan:* $5078. *Average need-based gift aid:* $9164. *Average non-need-based aid:* $5250. *Average indebtedness upon graduation:* $39,107.

Applying *Options:* electronic application, deferred entrance. *Application fee:* $50. *Required:* essay or personal statement, high school transcript, minimum 2.0 GPA, 2 letters of recommendation. *Required for some:* art portfolio required for some. *Recommended:* interview.

Freshman Application Contact Ms. Gillian Homsted, Admissions Director, Burlington College, 351 North Avenue, Burlington, VT 05401-2998. *Phone:* 802-862-9616 Ext. 104. *Toll-free phone:* 800-862-9616. *Fax:* 802-660-4331. *E-mail:* admissions@burlington.edu.
Website: http://www.burlington.edu/.

Castleton State College

Castleton, Vermont

- **State-supported** comprehensive, founded 1787, part of Vermont State Colleges System
- **Rural** 165-acre campus
- **Endowment** $4.9 million
- **Coed** 2,059 undergraduate students, 93% full-time, 52% women, 48% men
- **Moderately difficult** entrance level, 76% of applicants were admitted

Undergraduates 1,906 full-time, 153 part-time. Students come from 26 states and territories; 9 other countries; 30% are from out of state; 1% Black or African American, non-Hispanic/Latino; 2% Hispanic/Latino; 0.8% Asian, non-Hispanic/Latino; 0.6% American Indian or Alaska Native, non-Hispanic/Latino; 0.8% Two or more races, non-Hispanic/Latino; 5% Race/ethnicity unknown; 1% international; 9% transferred in; 54% live on campus. *Retention:* 70% of full-time freshmen returned.

Freshmen *Admission:* 2,737 applied, 2,084 admitted, 470 enrolled. *Average high school GPA:* 2.9. *Test scores:* SAT math scores over 500: 44%; SAT writing scores over 500: 31%; ACT scores over 18: 75%; SAT math scores over 600: 9%; SAT writing scores over 600: 4%; ACT scores over 24: 20%; ACT scores over 30: 2%.

Faculty *Total:* 234, 39% full-time, 53% with terminal degrees. *Student/faculty ratio:* 14:1.

Academics *Calendar:* semesters. *Degrees:* associate, bachelor's, master's, post-master's, and postbachelor's certificates. *Special study options:* academic remediation for entering students, advanced placement credit, cooperative education, double majors, honors programs, independent study, internships, off-campus study, part-time degree program, services for LD students, student-designed majors, study abroad, summer session for credit. *ROTC:* Army (b). *Unusual degree programs:* business administration.

Computers on Campus 250 computers/terminals are available on campus for general student use. Students can access the following: campus intranet, computer help desk, free student e-mail accounts, online (class) grades. Campus-wide network is available. 100% of college-owned or -operated housing units are wired for high-speed Internet access. Wireless service is available via entire campus.

Student Life *Housing:* on-campus residence required for freshman year. *Options:* coed. Campus housing is university owned. Freshman campus housing is guaranteed. *Activities and organizations:* drama/theater group, student-run newspaper, radio station, choral group, marching band, community service, clubs in the academic majors, Women's issues organization, Spanish and International, Skiing/Snowboarding. *Campus security:* 24-hour emergency response devices and patrols, student patrols, late-night transport/escort service, controlled dormitory access. *Student services:* health clinic, personal/psychological counseling.

Athletics Member NCAA. All Division III. *Intercollegiate sports:* baseball M, basketball M/W, cheerleading M(c)/W(c), cross-country running M/W, equestrian sports W(c), field hockey W, football M, golf M, ice hockey M/W, lacrosse M/W, rugby M(c)/W(c), skiing (downhill) M/W, soccer M/W, softball W, tennis M/W, volleyball W. *Intramural sports:* basketball M/W, racquetball M/W, rock climbing M/W, soccer M/W, softball M/W, table tennis M/W, tennis M/W, volleyball M/W, water polo M/W.

Standardized Tests *Required:* SAT or ACT (for admission).

Costs (2013–14) *One-time required fee:* $200. *Tuition:* state resident $9312 full-time, $388 per credit part-time; nonresident $23,040 full-time, $960 per credit part-time. Full-time tuition and fees vary according to program. Part-time tuition and fees vary according to course load and program. *Required fees:* $974 full-time, $40 per credit part-time. *Room and board:* $9138; room only: $5442. Room and board charges vary according to board plan. *Payment plan:* installment. *Waivers:* senior citizens and employees or children of employees.

Financial Aid Of all full-time matriculated undergraduates who enrolled in 2006, 1,471 applied for aid, 1,174 were judged to have need, 371 had their need fully met. 360 Federal Work-Study jobs (averaging $1000). In 2006, 40

MAJORS AND PROGRAMS

Art	Exercise Science	Music	Social Work
Athletic Training	Geology	Nursing	Sociology
Biology	Global Studies	Philosophy	Spanish
Business Administration	Health Education	Physical Education	Sports Administration
Communication	Health Science	Political Science	Theater Arts
Computer Information Systems	History	Psychology	Women's and Gender Studies
Criminal Justice	Literature	Social Sciences	
Environmental Science	Mathematics	Social Studies	

non-need-based awards were made. *Average percent of need met:* 72%. *Average financial aid package:* $9213. *Average need-based loan:* $3715. *Average need-based gift aid:* $4307. *Average non-need-based aid:* $3247. *Average indebtedness upon graduation:* $25,474.

Applying *Options:* electronic application, deferred entrance. *Application fee:* $40. *Required:* essay or personal statement, high school transcript, minimum 2.5 GPA, 2 letters of recommendation. *Recommended:* interview. *Application deadlines:* rolling (freshmen), rolling (out-of-state freshmen), rolling (transfers). *Notification:* continuous (freshmen), continuous (out-of-state freshmen), continuous (transfers).

Freshman Application Contact Mr. Maurice Ouimet, Admissions Director, Castleton State College, Castleton, VT 05735. *Phone:* 802-468-1213. *Toll-free phone:* 800-639-8521. *Fax:* 802-468-1476. *E-mail:* info@castleton.edu. *Website:* http://www.castleton.edu/.

See previous page for display ad and page 1230 for the College Close-Up.

Champlain College

Burlington, Vermont

- **Independent** comprehensive, founded 1878
- **Suburban** 21-acre campus with easy access to Montreal
- **Endowment** $10.2 million
- **Coed** 2,793 undergraduate students, 80% full-time, 40% women, 60% men
- **Moderately difficult** entrance level, 74% of applicants were admitted

Undergraduates 2,236 full-time, 557 part-time. Students come from 53 states and territories; 21 other countries; 67% are from out of state; 2% Black or African American, non-Hispanic/Latino; 3% Hispanic/Latino; 1% Asian, non-Hispanic/Latino; 0.2% Native Hawaiian or other Pacific Islander, non-Hispanic/Latino; 0.4% American Indian or Alaska Native, non-Hispanic/Latino; 2% Two or more races, non-Hispanic/Latino; 20% Race/ethnicity unknown; 0.4% international; 3% transferred in; 49% live on campus. *Retention:* 79% of full-time freshmen returned.

Freshmen *Admission:* 4,444 applied, 3,286 admitted, 601 enrolled. *Average high school GPA:* 3.02. *Test scores:* SAT critical reading scores over 500: 80%; SAT math scores over 500: 78%; SAT writing scores over 500: 72%; ACT scores over 18: 96%; SAT critical reading scores over 600: 35%; SAT math scores over 600: 33%; SAT writing scores over 600: 26%; ACT scores over 24: 55%; SAT critical reading scores over 700: 7%; SAT math scores over 700: 5%; SAT writing scores over 700: 3%; ACT scores over 30: 13%.

Faculty *Total:* 350, 29% full-time, 37% with terminal degrees. *Student/faculty ratio:* 13:1.

Academics *Calendar:* semesters. *Degrees:* certificates, associate, bachelor's, and master's. *Special study options:* adult/continuing education programs, advanced placement credit, cooperative education, distance learning, double majors, independent study, internships, off-campus study, part-time degree program, services for LD students, study abroad, summer session for credit. *ROTC:* Army (c).

Computers on Campus 563 computers/terminals are available on campus for general student use. Students can access the following: campus intranet, computer help desk, free student e-mail accounts, online (class) grades, online (class) registration, online (class) schedules. Campuswide network is available. 100% of college-owned or -operated housing units are wired for high-speed Internet access. Wireless service is available via entire campus.

Student Life *Housing options:* coed. Campus housing is university owned and leased by the school. Freshman campus housing is guaranteed. *Activities and organizations:* drama/theater group, student-run newspaper, choral group, Diversity Champlain, International Club, community service organization, Champlain Players (theater group), Outing Club/Skiing Snowboarding Club. *Campus security:* 24-hour emergency response devices and patrols, late-night transport/escort service, controlled dormitory access. *Student services:* health clinic, personal/psychological counseling.

Athletics *Intramural sports:* basketball M/W, bowling M/W, cross-country running M/W, golf M/W, ice hockey M/W, lacrosse M, sailing M/W, skiing (cross-country) M/W, skiing (downhill) M/W, soccer M/W, ultimate Frisbee M/W, volleyball M/W.

Standardized Tests *Required:* SAT or ACT (for admission). *Required for some:* SAT Subject Tests (for admission).

Costs (2013–14) *Comprehensive fee:* $44,850 includes full-time tuition ($31,250), mandatory fees ($100), and room and board ($13,500). Part-time tuition: $1240 per credit hour. *Payment plan:* installment. *Waivers:* employees or children of employees.

Financial Aid Of all full-time matriculated undergraduates who enrolled in 2011, 1,852 applied for aid, 1,482 were judged to have need, 120 had their need fully met. 694 Federal Work-Study jobs (averaging $2555). In 2011, 263 non-need-based awards were made. *Average percent of need met:* 57%. *Average financial aid package:* $15,953. *Average need-based loan:* $4681. *Average need-based gift aid:* $9479. *Average non-need-based aid:* $5117. *Average indebtedness upon graduation:* $32,102. *Financial aid deadline:* 3/1.

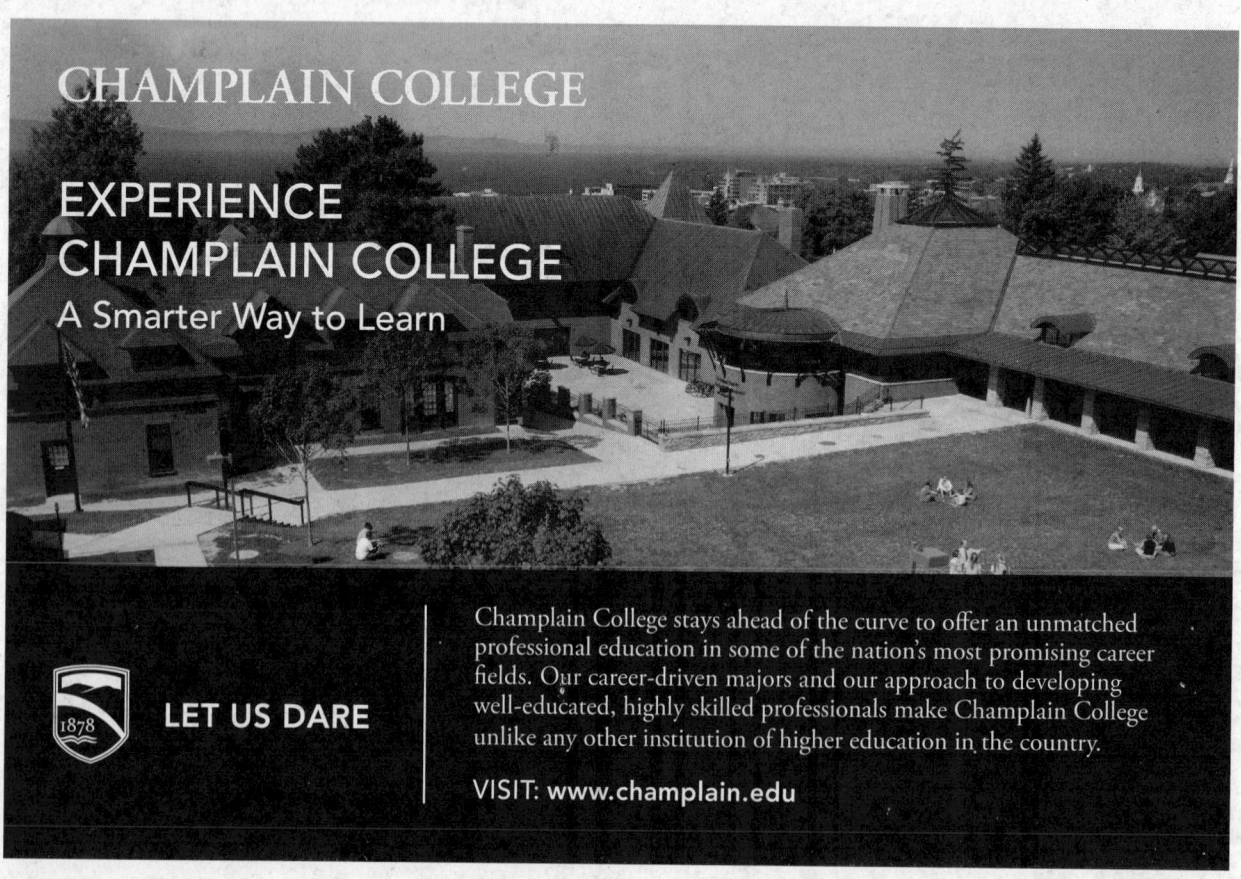

Applying *Options:* electronic application, early decision. *Required:* essay or personal statement, high school transcript. *Recommended:* 1 letter of recommendation, interview. *Application deadlines:* 1/31 (freshmen), rolling (transfers). *Early decision deadline:* 11/15 (for plan 1), 1/15 (for plan 2). *Notification:* 3/25 (freshmen), continuous (transfers), 12/15 (early decision plan 1), 2/15 (early decision plan 2).

Freshman Application Contact Sarah Andriano, Director of Admissions, Champlain College, P.O. Box 670, Burlington, VT 05401. *Phone:* 802-860-2727. *Toll-free phone:* 800-570-5858. *Fax:* 802-860-2767. *E-mail:* admission@champlain.edu.
Website: http://www.champlain.edu/.

See previous page for display ad and page 1234 for the College Close-Up.

College of St. Joseph

Rutland, Vermont

- **Independent Roman Catholic** comprehensive, founded 1950
- **Small-town** 117-acre campus
- **Endowment** $4.5 million
- **Coed**
- **Minimally difficult** entrance level

Faculty *Student/faculty ratio:* 10:1.

Academics *Calendar:* semesters. *Degrees:* associate, bachelor's, master's, and postbachelor's certificates.

Student Life *Campus security:* 24-hour emergency response devices, trained security personnel from 8 pm to 6 am.

Athletics Member USCAA.

Standardized Tests *Required:* SAT or ACT (for admission).

Costs (2012–13) *Comprehensive fee:* $30,000 includes full-time tuition ($20,125), mandatory fees ($475), and room and board ($9400). Full-time tuition and fees vary according to course load, degree level, and program. Part-time tuition: $260 per credit. Part-time tuition and fees vary according to course load, degree level, and program. *Required fees:* $45 per credit part-time. *Room and board:* Room and board charges vary according to housing facility.

Financial Aid *Of all full-time matriculated undergraduates who enrolled in 2011,* 156 applied for aid, 154 were judged to have need, 2 had their need fully met. 42 Federal Work-Study jobs (averaging $1121). 40 state and other part-time jobs (averaging $780). *In 2011,* 2 non-need-based awards were made. *Average percent of need met:* 83. *Average financial aid package:* $21,801. *Average need-based loan:* $7615. *Average need-based gift aid:* $10,928. *Average non-need-based aid:* $978. *Average indebtedness upon graduation:* $42,878.

Applying *Options:* electronic application, early admission, deferred entrance. *Application fee:* $25. *Required:* essay or personal statement, high school transcript, minimum 2.0 GPA, 2 letters of recommendation. *Recommended:* interview.

Freshman Application Contact Mr. Alan Young, Dean of Admissions, College of St. Joseph, 71 Clement Road, Rutland, VT 05701-3899. *Phone:* 802-773-5227. *Toll-free phone:* 877-270-9998. *Fax:* 802-776-5310. *E-mail:* admissions@csj.edu.
Website: http://www.csj.edu/.

Goddard College

Plainfield, Vermont

- **Independent** comprehensive, founded 1938
- **Rural** 200-acre campus
- **Endowment** $932,377
- **Coed** 244 undergraduate students, 100% full-time, 70% women, 30% men
- **Moderately difficult** entrance level, 70% of applicants were admitted

Undergraduates 244 full-time. Students come from 38 states and territories; 3 other countries; 85% are from out of state; 24% transferred in. *Retention:* 63% of full-time freshmen returned.

Freshmen *Admission:* 10 applied, 7 admitted, 7 enrolled.

Faculty *Total:* 104, 13% full-time, 78% with terminal degrees.

Academics *Calendar:* semesters. *Degrees:* bachelor's and master's. *Special study options:* adult/continuing education programs, advanced placement credit, distance learning, double majors, external degree program, independent study, internships, off-campus study, services for LD students, student-designed majors.

Computers on Campus 55 computers/terminals are available on campus for general student use. Students can access the following: campus intranet, com-

puter help desk, free student e-mail accounts, online (class) schedules, library services. Campuswide network is available. 80% of college-owned or -operated housing units are wired for high-speed Internet access. Wireless service is available via entire campus.

Student Life *Housing options:* coed, women-only, disabled students. Campus housing is university owned. *Activities and organizations:* student-run radio station. *Campus security:* 24-hour patrols, patrols by trained security personnel 9 pm to 6 am. *Student services:* personal/psychological counseling.

Costs (2012–13) *Comprehensive fee:* $15,610 includes full-time tuition ($14,036), mandatory fees ($182), and room and board ($1392). Full-time tuition and fees vary according to location, program, and reciprocity agreements. *College room only:* $672. Room and board charges vary according to location. *Payment plan:* installment. *Waivers:* employees or children of employees.

Financial Aid Of all full-time matriculated undergraduates who enrolled in 2010, 315 applied for aid, 273 were judged to have need, 6 had their need fully met. *Average percent of need met:* 41%. *Average financial aid package:* $7824. *Average need-based loan:* $4329. *Average need-based gift aid:* $4539. *Average indebtedness upon graduation:* $23,228.

Applying *Options:* electronic application, deferred entrance. *Application fee:* $20. *Required:* essay or personal statement, high school transcript, 2 letters of recommendation, interview. *Recommended:* four years of English, Mathematics, Social Studies, Natural Sciences; three years of lab science and two years of a foreign language. *Application deadlines:* rolling (freshmen), rolling (out-of-state freshmen), rolling (transfers). *Notification:* continuous (freshmen), continuous (out-of-state freshmen), continuous (transfers).

Freshman Application Contact Jen Morin, Admissions Counselor, Goddard College, 123 Pitkin Road, Plainfield, VT 05667-9432. *Phone:* 800-906-8312 Ext. 262. *Toll-free phone:* 800-906-8312. *Fax:* 802-454-1029. *E-mail:* admissions@goddard.edu.
Website: http://www.goddard.edu/.

Green Mountain College

Poultney, Vermont

Freshman Application Contact Green Mountain College, One Brennan Circle, Poultney, VT 05764. *Phone:* 802-287-8207. *Toll-free phone:* 800-776-6675.
Website: http://www.greenmtn.edu/.

Johnson State College

Johnson, Vermont

- **State-supported** comprehensive, founded 1828, part of Vermont State Colleges System
- **Rural** 350-acre campus with easy access to Montreal
- **Endowment** $2.3 million
- **Coed** 1,647 undergraduate students, 64% full-time, 64% women, 36% men
- **Moderately difficult** entrance level, 86% of applicants were admitted

Undergraduates 1,048 full-time, 599 part-time. Students come from 18 states and territories; 20 other countries; 19% are from out of state; 3% Black or African American, non-Hispanic/Latino; 1% Hispanic/Latino; 1% Asian, non-Hispanic/Latino; 1% American Indian or Alaska Native, non-Hispanic/Latino; 8% Race/ethnicity unknown; 0.1% international; 10% transferred in; 60% live on campus. *Retention:* 64% of full-time freshmen returned.

Freshmen *Admission:* 1,291 applied, 1,107 admitted, 241 enrolled. *Average high school GPA:* 3.32. *Test scores:* SAT critical reading scores over 500: 45%; SAT math scores over 500: 36%; SAT critical reading scores over 600: 11%; SAT math scores over 600: 6%; SAT critical reading scores over 700: 1%.

Faculty *Total:* 137, 36% full-time, 52% with terminal degrees. *Student/faculty ratio:* 16:1.

Academics *Calendar:* semesters. *Degrees:* certificates, associate, bachelor's, master's, and post-master's certificates. *Special study options:* accelerated degree program, advanced placement credit, cooperative education, distance learning, double majors, English as a second language, external degree program, honors programs, independent study, internships, off-campus study, part-time degree program, services for LD students, study abroad, summer session for credit. *ROTC:* Army (c).

Computers on Campus 160 computers/terminals are available on campus for general student use. Students can access the following: campus intranet, computer help desk, free student e-mail accounts, online (class) grades, online (class) registration, online (class) schedules. Campuswide network is available. Wireless service is available via classrooms, libraries, student centers.

Student Life *Housing:* on-campus residence required through sophomore year. *Options:* coed. Campus housing is university owned. Freshman applicants given priority for college housing. *Activities and organizations:* drama/theater group, student-run newspaper, radio station, choral group, SERVE (Break Away), A Global partnership: Students for Children's Right, Ski/Snowboarding Club, Dance Club, Christian Fellowship Club. *Campus security:* 24-hour emergency response devices and patrols, student patrols, late-night transport/escort service, controlled dormitory access. *Student services:* health clinic, personal/psychological counseling, women's center.

Athletics Member NCAA. All Division III. *Intercollegiate sports:* basketball M/W, cross-country running M/W, golf M, lacrosse W, soccer M/W, softball W, tennis M/W, volleyball W. *Intramural sports:* badminton M/W, basketball M/W, cross-country running M/W, golf M(c)/W(c), ice hockey M(c)/W(c), lacrosse M(c)/W, racquetball M/W, rock climbing M(c)/W(c), soccer M/W, softball M/W, swimming and diving M(c)/W(c), table tennis M/W, tennis M/W, volleyball M/W, water polo M/W, weight lifting M/W.

Standardized Tests *Required:* SAT or ACT (for admission).

Costs (2012–13) *Tuition:* state resident $9312 full-time, $372 per credit part-time; nonresident $20,976 full-time, $832 per credit part-time. Full-time tuition and fees vary according to course load. Part-time tuition and fees vary according to course load. *Required fees:* $1231 full-time. *Room and board:* $9138; room only: $5442. Room and board charges vary according to board plan. *Payment plan:* installment. *Waivers:* employees or children of employees.

Financial Aid Of all full-time matriculated undergraduates who enrolled in 2012, 932 applied for aid, 851 were judged to have need, 77 had their need fully met. In 2012, 50 non-need-based awards were made. *Average percent of need met:* 80%. *Average financial aid package:* $15,170. *Average need-based loan:* $8446. *Average need-based gift aid:* $7544. *Average non-need-based aid:* $5788.

Applying *Options:* electronic application, early admission, early action, deferred entrance. *Application fee:* $40. *Required:* essay or personal statement, high school transcript, minimum 2.0 GPA, 1 letter of recommendation. *Recommended:* minimum 2.5 GPA, interview. *Application deadlines:* rolling (freshmen), rolling (out-of-state freshmen), rolling (transfers). *Notification:* continuous (freshmen), continuous (out-of-state freshmen), continuous (transfers).

Freshman Application Contact Bethany Harrington, Admissions Specialist, Johnson State College, 337 College Hill, Johnson, VT 05656. *Phone:* 802-635-1219. *Toll-free phone:* 800-635-2356. *Fax:* 802-635-1230. *E-mail:* jscadmissions@jsc.edu. *Website:* http://www.jsc.edu/.

Lyndon State College

Lyndonville, Vermont

Freshman Application Contact Ms. Cheri Goldrick, Admissions Assistant, Lyndon State College, 1001 College Road, PO Box 919, Lyndonville, VT 05851. *Phone:* 802-626-6451. *Toll-free phone:* 800-225-1998. *Fax:* 802-626-6335. *E-mail:* admissions@lyndonstate.edu. *Website:* http://www.lyndonstate.edu/.

See this page for display ad and page 1372 for the College Close-Up.

Marlboro College

Marlboro, Vermont

- **Independent** comprehensive, founded 1946
- **Rural** 350-acre campus
- **Endowment** $36.8 million
- **Coed**
- **Moderately difficult** entrance level

Faculty *Student/faculty ratio:* 6:1.

Academics *Calendar:* semesters. *Degrees:* bachelor's and master's.

Student Life *Campus security:* 24-hour emergency response devices and patrols.

Costs (2012–13) *Comprehensive fee:* $47,570 includes full-time tuition ($36,300), mandatory fees ($1340), and room and board ($9930). Full-time tuition and fees vary according to program. Part-time tuition: $1210 per credit. Part-time tuition and fees vary according to course load and program. *Required fees:* $210 per year part-time. *College room only:* $5470.

Financial Aid *Of all full-time matriculated undergraduates who enrolled in 2012,* 185 applied for aid, 177 were judged to have need. *In 2012,* 42 non-need-based awards were made. *Average percent of need met:* 75. *Average financial aid package:* $29,090. *Average need-based loan:* $4490. *Average*

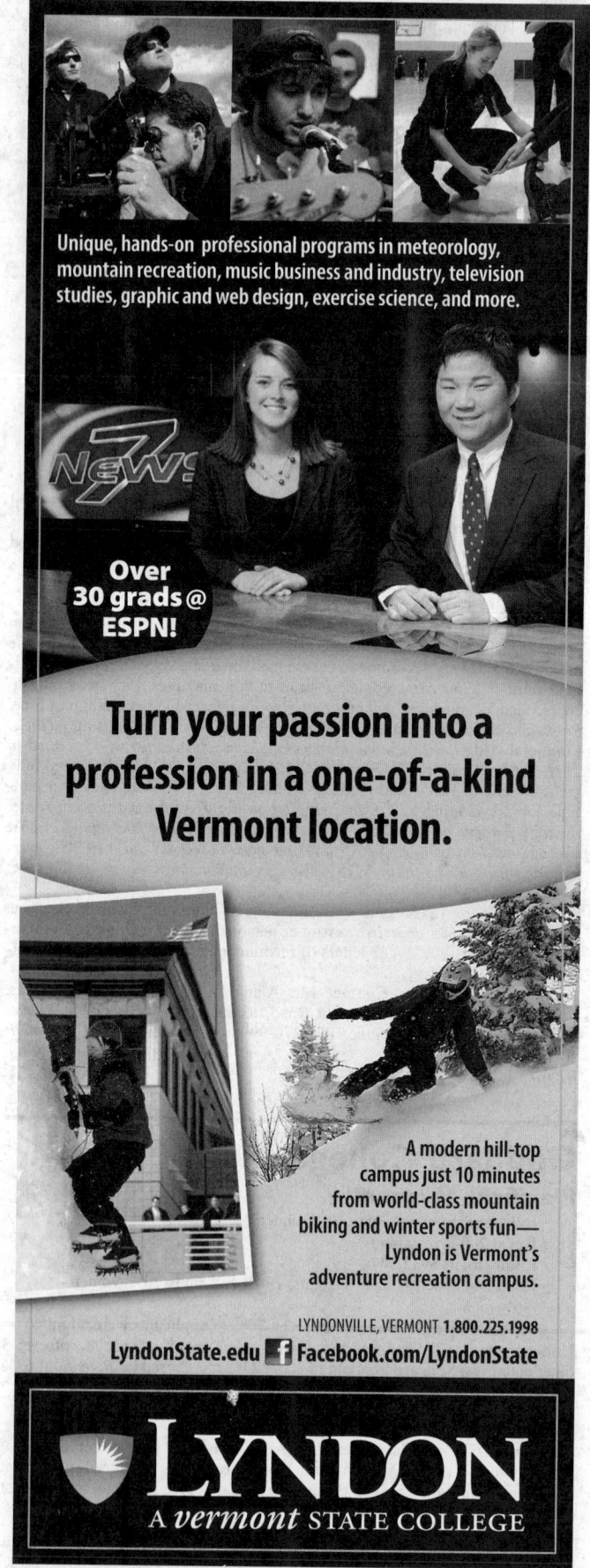

need-based gift aid: $22,908. *Average non-need-based aid:* $11,211. *Average indebtedness upon graduation:* $20,051.

Applying *Options:* electronic application, early admission, early decision, early action, deferred entrance. *Application fee:* $50. *Required:* essay or personal statement, high school transcript, 2 letters of recommendation, analytical essay. *Required for some:* interview. *Recommended:* interview.

Freshman Application Contact Ms. Jessica Nelson, Assistant Director of Admissions, Marlboro College, PO Box A, 2582 South Road, Marlboro, VT 05344-0300. *Phone:* 800-343-0049. *Toll-free phone:* 800-343-0049. *Fax:* 802-451-7555. *E-mail:* admissions@marlboro.edu.
Website: http://www.marlboro.edu/.

Middlebury College

Middlebury, Vermont

- **Independent** comprehensive, founded 1800
- **Small-town** 350-acre campus
- **Coed** 2,516 undergraduate students, 99% full-time, 51% women, 49% men
- **Most difficult** entrance level, 17% of applicants were admitted

Undergraduates 2,493 full-time, 23 part-time. Students come from 55 states and territories; 68 other countries; 94% are from out of state; 2% Black or African American, non-Hispanic/Latino; 7% Hispanic/Latino; 6% Asian, non-Hispanic/Latino; 0.2% American Indian or Alaska Native, non-Hispanic/Latino; 4% Two or more races, non-Hispanic/Latino; 3% Race/ethnicity unknown; 9% international; 0.4% transferred in; 97% live on campus. *Retention:* 97% of full-time freshmen returned.

Freshmen *Admission:* 8,847 applied, 1,518 admitted, 598 enrolled. *Test scores:* SAT critical reading scores over 500: 99%; SAT math scores over 500: 100%; SAT writing scores over 500: 100%; SAT critical reading scores over 600: 87%; SAT math scores over 600: 91%; SAT writing scores over 600: 90%; SAT critical reading scores over 700: 50%; SAT math scores over 700: 50%; SAT writing scores over 700: 57%.

Faculty *Total:* 337, 76% full-time, 90% with terminal degrees. *Student/faculty ratio:* 9:1.

Academics *Calendar:* 4-1-4. *Degrees:* bachelor's, master's, and doctoral. *Special study options:* accelerated degree program, advanced placement credit, double majors, honors programs, independent study, internships, off-campus study, services for LD students, student-designed majors, study abroad, summer session for credit. *ROTC:* Army (c). *Unusual degree programs:* 3-2 engineering with Columbia University, Rensselaer Polytechnic Institute, Dartmouth College.

Computers on Campus 250 computers/terminals are available on campus for general student use. Students can access the following: campus intranet, computer help desk, free student e-mail accounts, online (class) grades, online (class) registration, online (class) schedules, help-line, personal Web pages, file servers. Campuswide network is available. Wireless service is available via entire campus.

Student Life *Housing:* on-campus residence required through junior year. *Options:* coed, disabled students. Campus housing is university owned. Freshman campus housing is guaranteed. *Activities and organizations:* drama/theater group, student-run newspaper, radio station, choral group. *Campus security:* 24-hour patrols, student patrols, late-night transport/escort service, controlled dormitory access. *Student services:* health clinic, personal/psychological counseling, women's center.

Athletics Member NCAA. All Division III except men's and women's skiing (downhill) (Division I). *Intercollegiate sports:* baseball M, basketball M/W, cross-country running M/W, field hockey W, football M, golf M/W, ice hockey M/W, lacrosse M/W, skiing (cross-country) M/W, skiing (downhill) M/W, soccer M/W, softball W, squash W, swimming and diving M/W, tennis M/W, track and field M/W, volleyball W. *Intramural sports:* badminton M/W, basketball M/W, crew M(c)/W(c), cross-country running M/W, equestrian sports M(c)/W(c), football M/W, golf M/W, ice hockey M/W, rock climbing M(c)/W(c), rugby M(c)/W(c), sailing M(c)/W(c), skiing (cross-country) M/W, skiing (downhill) M/W, soccer M/W, softball M/W, squash M(c)/W, swimming and diving M/W, table tennis M/W, tennis M/W, ultimate Frisbee M(c)/W(c), volleyball M/W, water polo M(c)/W(c).

Standardized Tests *Required:* (for admission).

Costs (2013–14) *Comprehensive fee:* $55,570 includes full-time tuition ($43,731) and room and board ($11,839). *Payment plan:* tuition prepayment. *Waivers:* employees or children of employees.

Financial Aid Of all full-time matriculated undergraduates who enrolled in 2012, 1,191 applied for aid, 1,014 were judged to have need, 968 had their need fully met. In 2012, 2 non-need-based awards were made. *Average percent of need met:* 100%. *Average financial aid package:* $39,079. *Average need-based loan:* $3904. *Average need-based gift aid:* $36,245. *Average non-need-*

based aid: $2500. *Average indebtedness upon graduation:* $17,246. *Financial aid deadline:* 2/1.

Applying *Options:* electronic application, early admission, early decision, deferred entrance. *Application fee:* $65. *Required:* essay or personal statement, high school transcript, 3 letters of recommendation. *Recommended:* interview. *Application deadlines:* 1/1 (freshmen), 3/1 (transfers). *Early decision deadline:* 11/10 (for plan 1), 1/1 (for plan 2). *Notification:* 3/31 (freshmen), 4/10 (transfers), 12/15 (early decision plan 1), 2/15 (early decision plan 2).

Freshman Application Contact Mr. Greg Buckles, Dean of Admissions, Middlebury College, Emma Willard House, Middlebury, VT 05753-6002. *Phone:* 802-443-3000. *Fax:* 802-443-2056. *E-mail:* admissions@middlebury.edu.
Website: http://www.middlebury.edu/.

New England Culinary Institute

Montpelier, Vermont

Freshman Application Contact Jan Knutsen, Vice President of Enrollment, New England Culinary Institute, 56 College Street, Montpelier, VT 05602-3115. *Toll-free phone:* 877-223-6324. *Fax:* 802-225-3280. *E-mail:* janknutsen@neci.edu.
Website: http://www.neci.edu/.

Norwich University

Northfield, Vermont

- **Independent** comprehensive, founded 1819
- **Small-town** 1125-acre campus with easy access to Burlington
- **Endowment** $160.1 million
- **Coed, primarily men** 2,321 undergraduate students, 98% full-time, 23% women, 77% men
- **Moderately difficult** entrance level, 65% of applicants were admitted

Undergraduates 2,286 full-time, 35 part-time. Students come from 30 states and territories; 8 other countries; 85% are from out of state; 2% Black or African American, non-Hispanic/Latino; 3% Hispanic/Latino; 2% Asian, non-Hispanic/Latino; 0.2% Native Hawaiian or other Pacific Islander, non-Hispanic/Latino; 0.6% American Indian or Alaska Native, non-Hispanic/Latino; 2% Two or more races, non-Hispanic/Latino; 28% Race/ethnicity unknown; 1% international; 4% transferred in; 82% live on campus. *Retention:* 85% of full-time freshmen returned.

Freshmen *Admission:* 3,135 applied, 2,030 admitted, 712 enrolled. *Average high school GPA:* 3.14. *Test scores:* SAT critical reading scores over 500: 68%; SAT math scores over 500: 77%; ACT scores over 18: 96%; SAT critical reading scores over 600: 21%; SAT math scores over 600: 27%; ACT scores over 24: 50%; SAT critical reading scores over 700: 2%; SAT math scores over 700: 3%; ACT scores over 30: 5%.

Faculty *Total:* 327, 49% full-time. *Student/faculty ratio:* 12:1.

Academics *Calendar:* semesters. *Degrees:* bachelor's, master's, and postbachelor's certificates. *Special study options:* academic remediation for entering students, adult/continuing education programs, advanced placement credit, cooperative education, distance learning, double majors, English as a second language, external degree program, honors programs, independent study, internships, part-time degree program, services for LD students, study abroad, summer session for credit. *ROTC:* Army (b), Navy (b), Air Force (b).

Computers on Campus 200 computers/terminals are available on campus for general student use. Students can access the following: campus intranet, computer help desk, free student e-mail accounts, online (class) grades, online (class) schedules. Campuswide network is available. 100% of college-owned or -operated housing units are wired for high-speed Internet access. Wireless service is available via entire campus.

Student Life *Housing:* on-campus residence required through senior year. *Options:* coed. Campus housing is university owned. Freshman campus housing is guaranteed. *Activities and organizations:* drama/theater group, student-run newspaper, radio station, choral group, marching band, DREAM, NUEMS, IEEE, CJSA, Politeia/Model UN. *Campus security:* 24-hour emergency response devices and patrols, late-night transport/escort service. *Student services:* health clinic, personal/psychological counseling.

Athletics Member NCAA. All Division III. *Intercollegiate sports:* baseball M, basketball M/W, cross-country running M/W, fencing M(c)/W(c), football M, ice hockey M/W(c), lacrosse M, riflery M/W, rugby M(c)/W(c), sailing M(c)/W(c), skiing (cross-country) M(c)/W(c), skiing (downhill) M(c)/W(c), soccer M/W, softball W, swimming and diving M/W, tennis M/W(c), track and field M/W, volleyball M(c)/W(c), weight lifting M(c)/W(c), wrestling M. *Intramural sports:* basketball M/W, cross-country running M/W, football M, golf M/W, ice hockey M/W, lacrosse M/W, racquetball M/W, rugby M/W, soccer M/W, softball W, swimming and diving M/W, tennis M/W, track and field M/W, volleyball M/W, water polo M/W, weight lifting M/W, wrestling M.

Standardized Tests *Required:* SAT or ACT (for admission).

Costs (2012–13) *Comprehensive fee:* $42,758 includes full-time tuition ($30,048), mandatory fees ($1734), and room and board ($10,976). Part-time tuition and fees vary according to course load.

Financial Aid Of all full-time matriculated undergraduates who enrolled in 2012, 1,876 applied for aid, 1,712 were judged to have need, 354 had their need fully met. 760 Federal Work-Study jobs (averaging $1326). In 2012, 451 non-need-based awards were made. *Average percent of need met:* 74%. *Average financial aid package:* $25,644. *Average need-based loan:* $4991. *Average need-based gift aid:* $21,425. *Average non-need-based aid:* $14,104. *Average indebtedness upon graduation:* $35,310.

Applying *Options:* electronic application. *Application fee:* $35. *Required:* essay or personal statement, high school transcript. *Required for some:* portfolio. *Recommended:* minimum 2.0 GPA, 2 letters of recommendation, interview. *Application deadlines:* rolling (freshmen), rolling (transfers). *Notification:* continuous (freshmen), continuous (transfers).

Freshman Application Contact Norwich University, 158 Harmon Drive, Northfield, VT 05663. *Phone:* 802-485-2658. *Toll-free phone:* 800-468-6679. *Website:* http://www.norwich.edu/.

See below for display ad and page 1422 for the College Close-Up.

Saint Michael's College

Colchester, Vermont

- **Independent Roman Catholic** comprehensive, founded 1904
- **Suburban** 440-acre campus with easy access to Montreal
- **Endowment** $69.7 million
- **Coed** 1,971 undergraduate students, 99% full-time, 54% women, 46% men
- **Moderately difficult** entrance level, 78% of applicants were admitted

Undergraduates 1,948 full-time, 23 part-time. Students come from 35 states and territories; 16 other countries; 79% are from out of state; 2% Black or African American, non-Hispanic/Latino; 4% Hispanic/Latino; 2% Asian, non-Hispanic/Latino; 0.2% American Indian or Alaska Native, non-Hispanic/Latino; 1% Two or more races, non-Hispanic/Latino; 0.6% Race/ethnicity unknown;

2% international; 2% transferred in; 96% live on campus. *Retention:* 90% of full-time freshmen returned.

Freshmen *Admission:* 4,578 applied, 3,570 admitted, 544 enrolled. *Average high school GPA:* 3.46. *Test scores:* SAT critical reading scores over 500: 87%; SAT math scores over 500: 85%; SAT writing scores over 500: 85%; ACT scores over 18: 95%; SAT critical reading scores over 600: 44%; SAT math scores over 600: 39%; SAT writing scores over 600: 38%; ACT scores over 24: 71%; SAT critical reading scores over 700: 5%; SAT math scores over 700: 5%; SAT writing scores over 700: 5%; ACT scores over 30: 12%.

Faculty *Total:* 217, 71% full-time, 74% with terminal degrees. *Student/faculty ratio:* 12:1.

Academics *Calendar:* semesters. *Degrees:* bachelor's, master's, post-master's, and postbachelor's certificates. *Special study options:* advanced placement credit, distance learning, double majors, English as a second language, honors programs, independent study, internships, off-campus study, part-time degree program, services for LD students, student-designed majors, study abroad, summer session for credit. *ROTC:* Army (c), Air Force (c). *Unusual degree programs:* 3-2 business administration with Clarkson University; engineering with University of Vermont, and Clarkson University; pre-pharmacy dual degree (BS/D.Pharm) with Albany College of Pharmacy and Health Sciences.

Computers on Campus 490 computers/terminals and 5,000 ports are available on campus for general student use. Students can access the following: computer help desk, free student e-mail accounts, online (class) grades, online (class) registration, online (class) schedules. Campuswide network is available. 100% of college-owned or -operated housing units are wired for high-speed Internet access. Wireless service is available via classrooms, computer centers, computer labs, dorm rooms, libraries, student centers.

Student Life *Housing:* on-campus residence required through senior year. *Options:* coed, men-only, women-only, disabled students. Campus housing is university owned. Freshman campus housing is guaranteed. *Activities and organizations:* drama/theater group, student-run newspaper, radio station, choral group, Student Association (governing board), Mobilization of Volunteer Efforts (MOVE), WWPV-FM (student run radio station), Wilderness Program, student newspaper/online publication (The Defender). *Campus security:* 24-hour emergency response devices and patrols, student patrols, late-night transport/escort service, controlled dormitory access, bicycle patrols; Fire and Rescue Squad serving the surrounding community with professionally trained student volunteers. *Student services:* health clinic, personal/psychological counseling, women's center.

Athletics Member NCAA. All Division II. *Intercollegiate sports:* baseball M, basketball M(s)/W(s), cross-country running M/W, field hockey W, golf M, ice hockey M/W, lacrosse M/W, rugby M(c)/W(c), skiing (cross-country) M/W, skiing (downhill) M/W, soccer M/W, softball W, swimming and diving M/W, tennis M/W, volleyball W. *Intramural sports:* basketball M/W, cross-country running M/W, ice hockey M/W, racquetball M/W, rock climbing M/W, skiing (cross-country) M/W, skiing (downhill) M/W, soccer M/W, softball M/W, table tennis M/W, tennis M/W, track and field M(c)/W(c), ultimate Frisbee M(c)/W(c), volleyball M/W.

Standardized Tests *Recommended:* SAT or ACT (for admission), Saint Michael's is a test-optional institution. Therefore, you do not have to submit standardized test scores (SAT Reasoning Test or ACT with Writing) to be considered for admission.

Costs (2013–14) *Comprehensive fee:* $48,740 includes full-time tuition ($38,690), mandatory fees ($325), and room and board ($9725). Full-time tuition and fees vary according to course load. Part-time tuition: $1290 per credit hour. Part-time tuition and fees vary according to course load. *Room and board:* Room and board charges vary according to board plan and housing facility. *Payment plan:* installment. *Waivers:* employees or children of employees.

Financial Aid Of all full-time matriculated undergraduates who enrolled in 2011, 1,468 applied for aid, 1,270 were judged to have need, 343 had their need fully met. In 2011, 562 non-need-based awards were made. *Average percent of need met:* 76%. *Average financial aid package:* $23,073. *Average need-based loan:* $5212. *Average need-based gift aid:* $18,270. *Average non-need-based aid:* $10,546. *Average indebtedness upon graduation:* $31,736.

Applying *Options:* electronic application, early action, deferred entrance. *Application fee:* $50. *Required:* essay or personal statement, high school transcript. *Recommended:* minimum 3.0 GPA, 3 letters of recommendation, interview. *Application deadlines:* 2/1 (freshmen), 3/15 (transfers), 11/1 (early action). *Notification:* 4/1 (freshmen), 4/15 (transfers), 1/1 (early action).

Freshman Application Contact Ms. Jacqueline Murphy, Director of Admission, Saint Michael's College, One Winooski Park, Colchester, VT 05452. *Phone:* 802-654-3000. *Toll-free phone:* 800-762-8000. *Fax:* 802-654-2906. *E-mail:* admission@smcvt.edu. *Website:* http://www.smcvt.edu/.

See below for display ad and page 1484 for the College Close-Up.

Southern Vermont College

Bennington, Vermont

- **Independent** 4-year, founded 1926
- **Small-town** 371-acre campus with easy access to Albany, NY
- **Endowment** $1.2 million
- **Coed**
- **Minimally difficult** entrance level

Faculty *Student/faculty ratio:* 14:1.

Academics *Calendar:* semesters. *Degrees:* associate and bachelor's.

Student Life *Campus security:* 24-hour patrols, late-night transport/escort service, controlled dormitory access.

Athletics Member NCAA. All Division III.

Standardized Tests *Required:* SAT or ACT (for admission).

Costs (2012–13) *Comprehensive fee:* $31,218 includes full-time tuition ($21,000), mandatory fees ($275), and room and board ($9943). Full-time tuition and fees vary according to program. Part-time tuition: $800 per credit. Part-time tuition and fees vary according to course load and program. *College room only:* $4924. Room and board charges vary according to board plan and housing facility.

Financial Aid *Of all full-time matriculated undergraduates who enrolled in 2011,* 392 applied for aid, 378 were judged to have need. 88 Federal Work-Study jobs (averaging $878). *In 2011,* 23 non-need-based awards were made. *Average percent of need met:* 81. *Average financial aid package:* $13,589. *Average need-based loan:* $3500. *Average need-based gift aid:* $8250. *Average non-need-based aid:* $4865. *Average indebtedness upon graduation:* $24,652.

Applying *Options:* electronic application, early admission, deferred entrance. *Application fee:* $30. *Required:* essay or personal statement, high school transcript, 2 letters of recommendation. *Required for some:* interview, Deans report and college transcripts for transfer students. *Recommended:* minimum 2.0 GPA, interview.

Freshman Application Contact Southern Vermont College, 982 Mansion Drive, Bennington, VT 05201. *Phone:* 802-447-6300. *Fax:* 802-681-2868. *E-mail:* admissions@svc.edu. *Website:* http://www.svc.edu/.

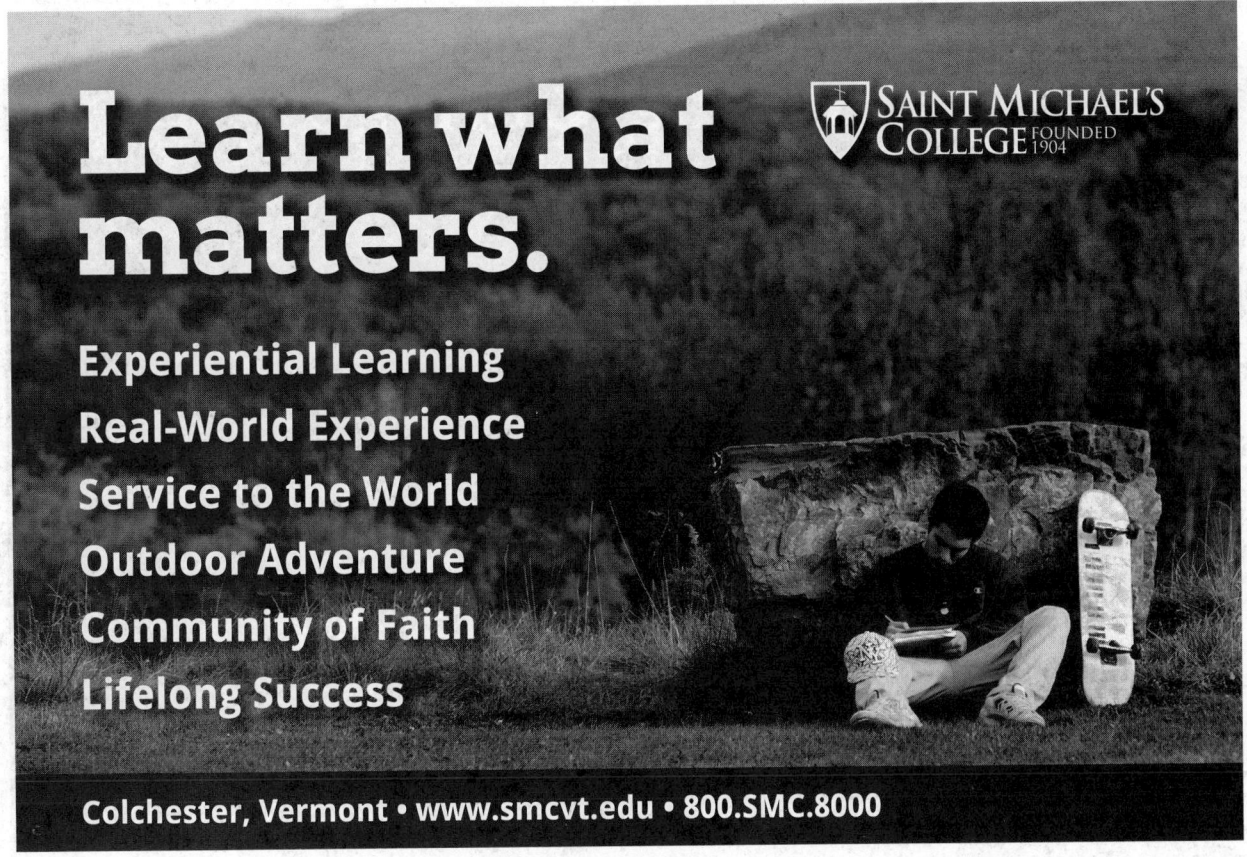

Sterling College

Craftsbury Common, Vermont

- **Independent** 4-year, founded 1958
- **Rural** 430-acre campus
- **Endowment** $876,051
- **Coed** 95 undergraduate students, 86% full-time, 52% women, 48% men
- **Moderately difficult** entrance level, 91% of applicants were admitted

Undergraduates 82 full-time, 13 part-time. 79% are from out of state; 1% Black or African American, non-Hispanic/Latino; 2% Hispanic/Latino; 1% Asian, non-Hispanic/Latino; 5% Two or more races, non-Hispanic/Latino; 14% Race/ethnicity unknown; 17% transferred in; 72% live on campus. *Retention:* 55% of full-time freshmen returned.

Freshmen *Admission:* 53 applied, 48 admitted, 16 enrolled.

Faculty *Total:* 17, 59% full-time, 18% with terminal degrees. *Student/faculty ratio:* 6:1.

Academics *Calendar:* semesters. *Degree:* bachelor's. *Special study options:* advanced placement credit, double majors, independent study, internships, off-campus study, services for LD students, student-designed majors, study abroad, summer session for credit.

Computers on Campus 18 computers/terminals are available on campus for general student use. Students can access the following: campus intranet, computer help desk, free student e-mail accounts. Campuswide network is available. 100% of college-owned or -operated housing units are wired for high-speed Internet access. Wireless service is available via entire campus.

Student Life *Housing options:* coed. Campus housing is university owned. Freshman campus housing is guaranteed. *Activities and organizations:* drama/theater group, choral group, Outing Club, Timbersports Team, Student Union, Art Club, Musical Groups. *Campus security:* 24-hour pager. *Student services:* health clinic, personal/psychological counseling.

Costs (2012–13) *Comprehensive fee:* $37,092 includes full-time tuition ($28,410), mandatory fees ($350), and room and board ($8332). Full-time tuition and fees vary according to course load. Part-time tuition: $900 per credit. Part-time tuition and fees vary according to course load. *Room and board:* Room and board charges vary according to board plan. *Payment plan:* installment. *Waivers:* employees or children of employees.

Financial Aid Of all full-time matriculated undergraduates who enrolled in 2011, 78 applied for aid, 78 were judged to have need, 5 had their need fully met. In 2011, 15 non-need-based awards were made. *Average percent of need met:* 89%. *Average financial aid package:* $30,382. *Average need-based loan:* $5306. *Average need-based gift aid:* $20,832. *Average non-need-based aid:* $4414. *Average indebtedness upon graduation:* $39,724.

Applying *Options:* electronic application, early admission, early action, deferred entrance. *Application fee:* $35. *Required:* essay or personal statement, high school transcript, 2 letters of recommendation. *Recommended:* minimum 2.0 GPA, interview. *Application deadlines:* rolling (freshmen), rolling (transfers), 12/15 (early action). *Notification:* continuous (freshmen), continuous (transfers), 1/15 (early action).

Freshman Application Contact Ms. Lynne A. Birdsall, Director of Admissions, Sterling College, PO Box 72, Craftsbury Common, VT 05827. *Phone:* 802-586-7711 Ext. 135. *Toll-free phone:* 800-648-3591 Ext. 100. *Fax:* 802-586-2596. *E-mail:* lbirdsall@sterlingcollege.edu. *Website:* http://www.sterlingcollege.edu/.

See below for display ad and page 1520 for the College Close-Up.

University of Vermont

Burlington, Vermont

- **State-supported** university, founded 1791
- **Suburban** 459-acre campus
- **Endowment** $299.0 million
- **Coed** 11,211 undergraduate students, 89% full-time, 56% women, 44% men
- **Moderately difficult** entrance level, 77% of applicants were admitted

Undergraduates 9,956 full-time, 1,255 part-time. Students come from 49 states and territories; 30 other countries; 67% are from out of state; 1% Black or African American, non-Hispanic/Latino; 4% Hispanic/Latino; 2% Asian, non-Hispanic/Latino; 0.1% Native Hawaiian or other Pacific Islander, non-Hispanic/Latino; 0.3% American Indian or Alaska Native, non-Hispanic/Latino; 3% Two or more races, non-Hispanic/Latino; 4% Race/ethnicity unknown; 2% international; 4% transferred in; 51% live on campus. *Retention:* 85% of full-time freshmen returned.

Freshmen *Admission:* 21,808 applied, 16,716 admitted, 2,372 enrolled. *Test scores:* SAT critical reading scores over 500: 91%; SAT math scores over 500: 93%; SAT writing scores over 500: 92%; ACT scores over 18: 99%; SAT critical reading scores over 600: 49%; SAT math scores over 600: 53%; SAT writ-

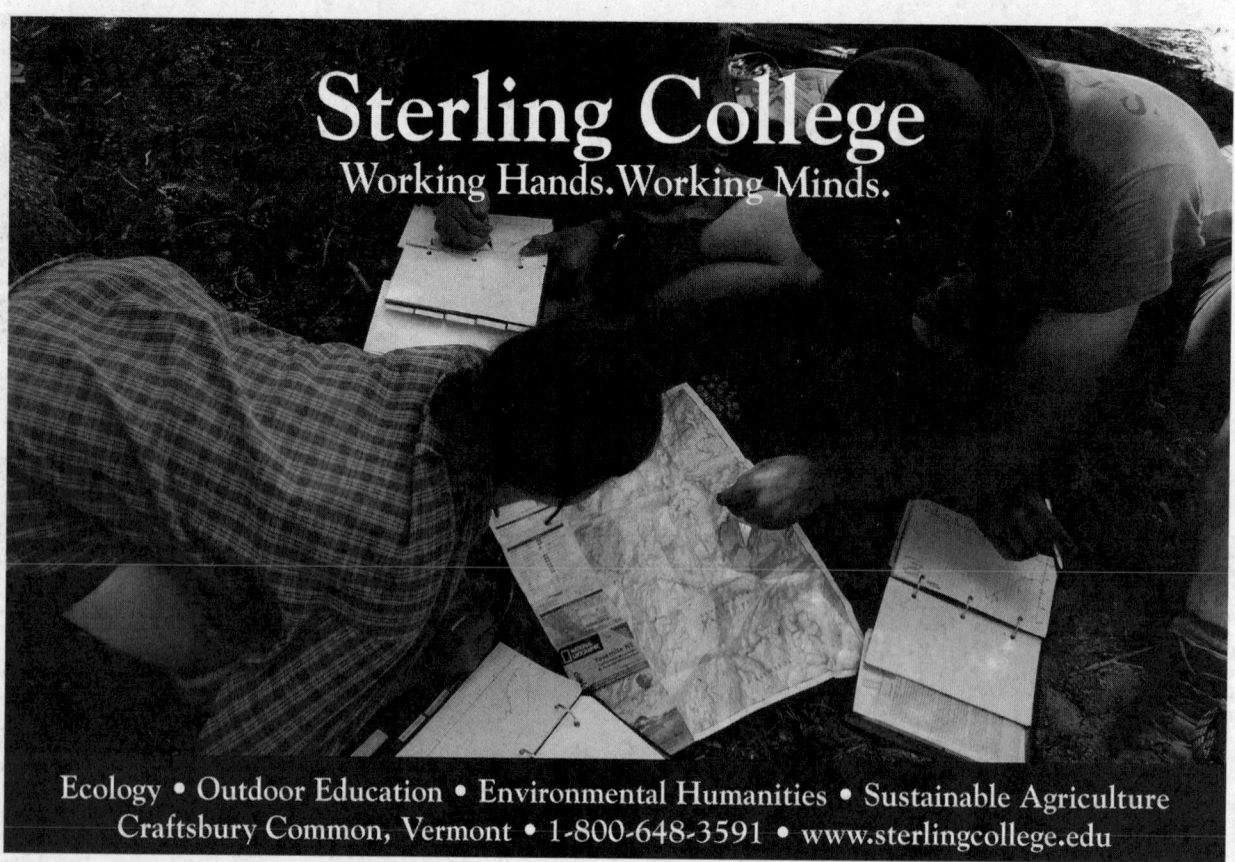

ing scores over 600: 50%; ACT scores over 24: 81%; SAT critical reading scores over 700: 9%; SAT math scores over 700: 9%; SAT writing scores over 700: 8%; ACT scores over 30: 19%.

Faculty *Total:* 755, 80% full-time, 78% with terminal degrees. *Student/faculty ratio:* 17:1.

Academics *Calendar:* semesters. *Degrees:* bachelor's, master's, doctoral, post-master's, and postbachelor's certificates. *Special study options:* adult/continuing education programs, advanced placement credit, cooperative education, distance learning, double majors, freshman honors college, honors programs, independent study, internships, off-campus study, part-time degree program, services for LD students, student-designed majors, study abroad, summer session for credit. *ROTC:* Army (b). *Unusual degree programs:* 3-2 computer science.

Computers on Campus 850 computers/terminals and 299 ports are available on campus for general student use. Students can access the following: campus intranet, computer help desk, free student e-mail accounts, online (class) grades, online (class) registration, online (class) schedules, Web pages, online course support. Campuswide network is available. 100% of college-owned or -operated housing units are wired for high-speed Internet access. Wireless service is available via classrooms, computer centers, computer labs, learning centers, libraries, student centers.

Student Life *Housing:* on-campus residence required through sophomore year. *Options:* coed. Campus housing is university owned. Freshman campus housing is guaranteed. *Activities and organizations:* drama/theater group, student-run newspaper, radio and television station, choral group, Volunteers in Action, Outing Club, Ski and Snowboard Club, national fraternities, national sororities. *Campus security:* 24-hour emergency response devices and patrols, late-night transport/escort service, controlled dormitory access. *Student services:* health clinic, personal/psychological counseling, women's center, legal services.

Athletics Member NCAA. All Division I. *Intercollegiate sports:* basketball M(s)/W(s), cheerleading M(c)/W(c), crew M(c)/W(c), cross-country running M(s)/W(s), equestrian sports M(c)/W(c), fencing M(c)/W(c), field hockey W(s), gymnastics M(c)/W(c), ice hockey M(s)/W(s), lacrosse M(s)/W(s), rugby M(c)/W(c), sailing M(c)/W(c), skiing (cross-country) M(s)/W(s), skiing (downhill) M(s)/W(s), soccer M(s)/W(s), swimming and diving W(s), table tennis M(c)/W(c), track and field M(s)/W(s), ultimate Frisbee M(c)/W(c), volleyball M(c)/W(c), water polo M(c)/W(c). *Intramural sports:* basketball M/W, bowling M/W, football M(c)/W, ice hockey M/W, lacrosse M/W, racquetball M/W, soccer M/W, softball M/W, tennis M/W, volleyball M/W, water polo M/W.

Standardized Tests *Required:* SAT or ACT (for admission).

Costs (2012–13) *Tuition:* state resident $13,344 full-time; nonresident $33,672 full-time. Part-time tuition and fees vary according to course load. *Required fees:* $1910 full-time. *Room and board:* $10,094. Room and board charges vary according to board plan and housing facility. *Waivers:* employees or children of employees.

Financial Aid Of all full-time matriculated undergraduates who enrolled in 2011, 7,204 applied for aid, 6,053 were judged to have need, 654 had their need fully met. 1,392 Federal Work-Study jobs (averaging $1518). In 2011, 2190 non-need-based awards were made. *Average percent of need met:* 65%. *Average financial aid package:* $21,229. *Average need-based loan:* $4555. *Average need-based gift aid:* $14,081. *Average non-need-based aid:* $6643. *Average indebtedness upon graduation:* $27,588.

Applying *Options:* electronic application, early action, deferred entrance. *Application fee:* $55. *Required:* essay or personal statement, high school transcript, 1 letter of recommendation. *Application deadlines:* 1/15 (freshmen), 4/15 (transfers), 11/1 (early action). *Notification:* 3/31 (freshmen), continuous (transfers), 12/15 (early action).

Freshman Application Contact Beth A. Wiser PhD, Director of Admissions, University of Vermont, Office of Admissions, 194 South Prospect Street, Burlington, VT 05401-3596. *Phone:* 802-656-3370. *Fax:* 802-656-8611. *E-mail:* admissions@uvm.edu. *Website:* http://www.uvm.edu/.

Vermont Technical College
Randolph Center, Vermont

- **State-supported** 4-year, founded 1866, part of Vermont State Colleges System
- **Rural** 544-acre campus
- **Coed** 1,645 undergraduate students, 69% full-time, 44% women, 56% men
- **Moderately difficult** entrance level, 63% of applicants were admitted

Undergraduates 1,141 full-time, 504 part-time. 12% are from out of state; 2% Black or African American, non-Hispanic/Latino; 2% Hispanic/Latino; 2% Asian, non-Hispanic/Latino; 0.1% Native Hawaiian or other Pacific Islander, non-Hispanic/Latino; 2% American Indian or Alaska Native, non-Hispanic/

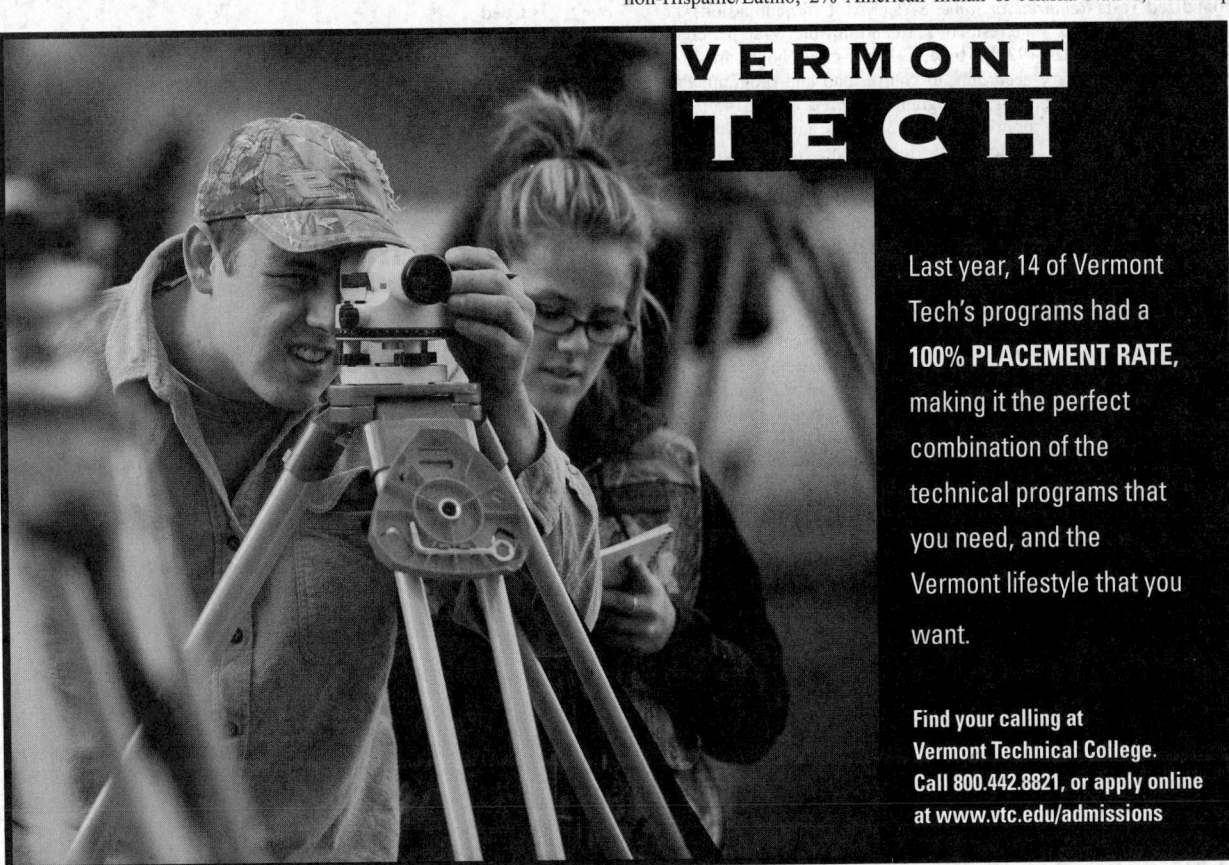

Latino; 0.9% Race/ethnicity unknown; 12% transferred in. *Retention:* 69% of full-time freshmen returned.

Freshmen *Admission:* 825 applied, 518 admitted, 220 enrolled. *Average high school GPA:* 3.01. *Test scores:* SAT critical reading scores over 500: 36%; SAT math scores over 500: 50%; SAT writing scores over 500: 23%; ACT scores over 18: 79%; SAT critical reading scores over 600: 3%; SAT math scores over 600: 11%; SAT writing scores over 600: 2%; ACT scores over 24: 27%; SAT critical reading scores over 700: 1%; SAT math scores over 700: 1%; ACT scores over 30: 3%.

Faculty *Total:* 194, 39% full-time, 14% with terminal degrees. *Student/faculty ratio:* 11:1.

Academics *Calendar:* semesters. *Degrees:* certificates, associate, and bachelor's. *Special study options:* academic remediation for entering students, accelerated degree program, advanced placement credit, cooperative education, distance learning, double majors, English as a second language, honors programs, independent study, internships, part-time degree program, services for LD students, summer session for credit. *ROTC:* Army (c).

Computers on Campus 480 computers/terminals and 600 ports are available on campus for general student use. Students can access the following: campus intranet, computer help desk, free student e-mail accounts, online (class) grades, online (class) registration, online (class) schedules, online (network) file storage, wireless network. Campuswide network is available. 98% of college-owned or -operated housing units are wired for high-speed Internet access. Wireless service is available via entire campus.

Student Life *Housing:* on-campus residence required through sophomore year. *Options:* coed. Campus housing is university owned. *Activities and organizations:* student-run radio and television station, choral group, Student Council (student government), Adventurer's Guild (board and video gaming), WVTC (student radio station), Outing Club, Veterinary Technology Club. *Campus security:* 24-hour emergency response devices and patrols, late-night transport/escort service, controlled dormitory access. *Student services:* health clinic.

Athletics Member USCAA. *Intercollegiate sports:* baseball M, basketball M/W, golf M/W, soccer M/W, softball W. *Intramural sports:* basketball M/W, bowling M(c)/W(c), cross-country running M/W, fencing M(c)/W(c), football M/W, golf M(c)/W(c), ice hockey M(c)/W(c), racquetball M/W, riflery M(c)/W(c), rock climbing M(c)/W(c), rugby M(c), skiing (cross-country) M(c)/W(c), skiing (downhill) M(c)/W(c), soccer M/W, softball M/W, swimming and diving M/W, table tennis M/W, tennis M/W, volleyball M/W, water polo M/W, weight lifting M(c)/W(c).

Standardized Tests *Required for some:* SAT or ACT (for admission).

Costs (2013–14) *Tuition:* state resident $11,088 full-time, $480 per credit hour part-time; nonresident $21,192 full-time, $918 per credit hour part-time. Full-time tuition and fees vary according to course load and program. Part-time tuition and fees vary according to program. *Required fees:* $1456 full-time. *Room and board:* $8786; room only: $5232. Room and board charges vary according to board plan. *Payment plan:* installment. *Waivers:* employees or children of employees.

Financial Aid Of all full-time matriculated undergraduates who enrolled in 2012, 990 applied for aid, 902 were judged to have need, 80 had their need fully met. *Average percent of need met:* 54%. *Average financial aid package:* $11,261. *Average need-based loan:* $3899. *Average need-based gift aid:* $6375. *Average indebtedness upon graduation:* $22,380.

Applying *Options:* electronic application. *Application fee:* $40. *Required:* high school transcript. *Required for some:* essay or personal statement, 2 letters of recommendation, interview. *Recommended:* minimum 3.0 GPA, 2 letters of recommendation, interview. *Application deadlines:* rolling (freshmen), rolling (transfers). *Notification:* continuous (freshmen), continuous (transfers).

Freshman Application Contact Jessica Van Deren, Director of Admissions, Vermont Technical College, PO Box 500, Randolph Center, VT 05061. *Phone:* 802-728-1244. *Toll-free phone:* 800-442-VTC1. *Fax:* 802-728-1390. *E-mail:* admissions@vtc.edu.
Website: http://www.vtc.edu/.

See previous page for display ad and page 1624 for the College Close-Up.

VIRGINIA

Argosy University, Washington DC
Arlington, Virginia

Freshman Application Contact Argosy University, Washington DC, 1550 Wilson Boulevard, Suite 600, Arlington, VA 22209. *Phone:* 703-526-5800. *Toll-free phone:* 866-703-2777.
Website: http://www.argosy.edu/washingtondc/.

The Art Institute of Virginia Beach
Virginia Beach, Virginia
- **Proprietary** 4-year
- **Coed**

Academics *Degrees:* diplomas, associate, and bachelor's.
Freshman Application Contact The Art Institute of Virginia Beach, Two Columbus Center, 4500 Main Street, Suite 100, Virginia Beach, VA 23462. *Phone:* 757-493-6700. *Toll-free phone:* 877-437-4428.
Website: http://www.artinstitutes.edu/virginia-beach/.

See full-page ad on page 54 and page 1124 for the College Close-Up.

The Art Institute of Washington
Arlington, Virginia
- **Proprietary** 4-year, founded 2000, part of Education Management Corporation
- **Urban** campus
- **Coed**

Academics *Calendar:* quarters. *Degrees:* diplomas, associate, and bachelor's.
Freshman Application Contact The Art Institute of Washington, 1820 North Fort Meyer Drive, Arlington, VA 22209. *Phone:* 703-358-9550. *Toll-free phone:* 877-303-3771.
Website: http://www.artinstitutes.edu/arlington/.

See full-page ad on page 54 and page 1126 for the College Close-Up.

The Art Institute of Washington–Dulles
Sterling, Virginia
- **Proprietary** 4-year
- **Coed**

Academics *Degrees:* diplomas, associate, and bachelor's.
Freshman Application Contact The Art Institute of Washington–Dulles, The Corporate Office Park at Dulles Town Center, 21000 Atlantic Boulevard, Suite 100, Sterling, VA 20166. *Phone:* 571-449-4400. *Toll-free phone:* 888-627-5008.
Website: http://www.artinstitutes.edu/washington-dulles/.

See full-page ad on page 54 and page 1128 for the College Close-Up.

Averett University

Danville, Virginia

- **Independent** comprehensive, founded 1859, affiliated with Baptist General Association of Virginia
- **Small-town** 252-acre campus with easy access to Greensboro, Raleigh, Durham, and Cary—NC
- **Endowment** $24.7 million
- **Coed** 892 undergraduate students, 98% full-time, 48% women, 52% men
- **Moderately difficult** entrance level, 58% of applicants were admitted

Undergraduates 870 full-time, 22 part-time. Students come from 23 states and territories; 15 other countries; 30% are from out of state; 27% Black or African American, non-Hispanic/Latino; 3% Hispanic/Latino; 1% Asian, non-Hispanic/Latino; 0.8% American Indian or Alaska Native, non-Hispanic/Latino; 0.4% Race/ethnicity unknown; 9% international; 9% transferred in; 57% live on campus. *Retention:* 62% of full-time freshmen returned.

Freshmen *Admission:* 2,477 applied, 1,430 admitted, 257 enrolled. *Average high school GPA:* 3.23. *Test scores:* SAT critical reading scores over 500: 31%; SAT math scores over 500: 38%; SAT writing scores over 500: 39%; ACT scores over 18: 53%; SAT critical reading scores over 600: 9%; SAT math scores over 600: 10%; SAT writing scores over 600: 9%; ACT scores over 24: 13%; SAT critical reading scores over 700: 2%; SAT math scores over 700: 1%; SAT writing scores over 700: 1%; ACT scores over 30: 4%.

Faculty *Total:* 118, 52% full-time, 39% with terminal degrees. *Student/faculty ratio:* 10:1.

Academics *Calendar:* semesters. *Degrees:* associate, bachelor's, and master's. *Special study options:* academic remediation for entering students, accelerated degree program, adult/continuing education programs, advanced placement credit, cooperative education, distance learning, double majors, external degree program, honors programs, independent study, internships, off-campus study, part-time degree program, services for LD students, student-designed majors, study abroad, summer session for credit.

Computers on Campus 150 computers/terminals are available on campus for general student use. Students can access the following: free student e-mail accounts, online (class) grades, online (class) registration, online (class) schedules. Campuswide network is available. Wireless service is available via entire campus.

Student Life *Housing:* on-campus residence required through junior year. *Options:* coed, men-only, women-only. Campus housing is university owned. Freshman applicants given priority for college housing. *Activities and organizations:* drama/theater group, student-run newspaper, choral group, Student Government Association, Campus Activities Board, Christian Student Union, Averett Gospel Choir, Pi Kappa Phi, national fraternities. *Campus security:* 24-hour emergency response devices and patrols, late-night transport/escort service, controlled dormitory access. *Student services:* personal/psychological counseling.

Athletics Member NCAA. All Division III. *Intercollegiate sports:* baseball M, basketball M/W, cross-country running M/W, equestrian sports M/W, football M, golf M, soccer M/W, softball W, volleyball W. *Intramural sports:* basketball M/W, cheerleading M/W, soccer M/W, softball M/W, table tennis M(c)/W(c), tennis M/W, volleyball M/W.

Standardized Tests *Required:* SAT or ACT (for admission), TOEFL for International students (for admission).

Costs (2012–13) *Comprehensive fee:* $34,320 includes full-time tuition ($25,950) and room and board ($8370). Full-time tuition and fees vary according to course load, degree level, location, and program. Part-time tuition: $1080 per credit hour. Part-time tuition and fees vary according to course load, degree level, location, and program. *College room only:* $5650. Room and board charges vary according to board plan and housing facility. *Payment plan:* installment. *Waivers:* senior citizens and employees or children of employees.

Financial Aid Of all full-time matriculated undergraduates who enrolled in 2012, 786 applied for aid, 736 were judged to have need, 114 had their need fully met. 142 Federal Work-Study jobs (averaging $902). In 2012, 161 non-need-based awards were made. *Average percent of need met:* 74%. *Average financial aid package:* $20,339. *Average need-based loan:* $4654. *Average need-based gift aid:* $16,458. *Average non-need-based aid:* $11,035. *Average indebtedness upon graduation:* $31,373.

Applying *Options:* electronic application. *Required:* high school transcript, minimum 2.5 GPA, High school diploma. *Recommended:* essay or personal statement, 1 letter of recommendation. *Application deadlines:* 8/1 (freshmen), 8/1 (out-of-state freshmen), 8/15 (transfers). *Notification:* continuous (freshmen), continuous (out-of-state freshmen), continuous (transfers).

Freshman Application Contact Mr. Joel Nester, Director of Admissions and International, Averett University, 420 West Main Street, English Hall, Danville, VA 24541. *Phone:* 434-791-5663. *Toll-free phone:* 800-AVERETT. *E-mail:* joel.nester@averett.edu. *Website:* http://www.averett.edu/.

Bethel College

Hampton, Virginia

Admissions Office Contact Bethel College, 1705 Todds Lane, Hampton, VA 23666.
Website: http://bethel-college.com/.

Bluefield College

Bluefield, Virginia

- **Independent Southern Baptist** 4-year, founded 1922
- **Small-town** 82-acre campus
- **Endowment** $5.4 million
- **Coed** 828 undergraduate students, 93% full-time, 53% women, 47% men

Undergraduates 766 full-time, 62 part-time. Students come from 26 states and territories; 4 other countries; 23% are from out of state; 24% Black or African American, non-Hispanic/Latino; 2% Hispanic/Latino; 2% Asian, non-Hispanic/Latino; 0.5% American Indian or Alaska Native, non-Hispanic/Latino; 6% Race/ethnicity unknown; 0.5% international; 7% transferred in; 65% live on campus. *Retention:* 61% of full-time freshmen returned.

Freshmen *Admission:* 144 enrolled. *Average high school GPA:* 3. *Test scores:* SAT critical reading scores over 500: 37%; SAT math scores over 500: 35%; ACT scores over 18: 56%; SAT critical reading scores over 600: 12%; SAT math scores over 600: 7%; ACT scores over 24: 13%; ACT scores over 30: 4%.

Faculty *Total:* 107, 35% full-time, 45% with terminal degrees. *Student/faculty ratio:* 13:1.

Academics *Calendar:* semesters. *Degree:* bachelor's. *Special study options:* academic remediation for entering students, accelerated degree program, adult/continuing education programs, advanced placement credit, cooperative education, distance learning, double majors, honors programs, internships, services for LD students, study abroad, summer session for credit.

Computers on Campus 110 computers/terminals are available on campus for general student use. Students can access the following: campus intranet, free student e-mail accounts, online (class) grades, online (class) registration, online (class) schedules, career assessment tests, library database. Campuswide network is available. 100% of college-owned or -operated housing units are wired for high-speed Internet access. Wireless service is available via entire campus.

Student Life *Housing:* on-campus residence required through junior year. *Options:* men-only, women-only. Campus housing is university owned. Freshman applicants given priority for college housing. *Activities and organizations:* drama/theater group, student-run newspaper, choral group, Baptist Collegiate Ministries, Fellowship of Christian Athletes, Student Union Board, Student Government Association, Arts Club. *Campus security:* controlled dormitory access, night security patrols. *Student services:* personal/psychological counseling.

Athletics Member NAIA, NCCAA. *Intercollegiate sports:* baseball M(s), basketball M(s)/W(s), cross-country running M(s)/W(s), football M(s), golf M(s), soccer M(s)/W(s), softball W(s), tennis M(s)/W(s), volleyball W(s). *Intramural sports:* badminton M/W, baseball M, basketball M/W, football M/W, softball M/W, table tennis M/W, tennis M/W, volleyball M/W.

Standardized Tests *Required:* SAT or ACT (for admission).

Costs (2012–13) *Comprehensive fee:* $28,700 includes full-time tuition ($21,060) and room and board ($7640). Full-time tuition and fees vary according to course load and program. Part-time tuition: $880 per credit. Part-time tuition and fees vary according to course load and program. *College room only:* $2990. Room and board charges vary according to housing facility. *Payment plan:* installment. *Waivers:* senior citizens and employees or children of employees.

Financial Aid Of all full-time matriculated undergraduates who enrolled in 2012, 677 applied for aid, 642 were judged to have need, 87 had their need fully met. 79 Federal Work-Study jobs (averaging $782). In 2012, 58 non-need-based awards were made. *Average percent of need met:* 58%. *Average financial aid package:* $14,060. *Average need-based loan:* $4727. *Average need-based gift aid:* $10,273. *Average non-need-based aid:* $5239. *Average indebtedness upon graduation:* $20,934.

Applying *Required:* high school transcript, minimum 2.0 GPA, SAT/ACT Scores. *Required for some:* essay or personal statement.

Freshman Application Contact Mr. Mark Hipes, Director of Admissions, Bluefield College, 3000 College Drive, Bluefield, VA 24605-1799. *Phone:* 276-326-4340. *Toll-free phone:* 800-872-0175. *Fax:* 276-326-4395. *E-mail:* mhipes@bluefield.edu. *Website:* http://www.bluefield.edu/.

Bon Secours Memorial College of Nursing

Richmond, Virginia

Admissions Office Contact Bon Secours Memorial College of Nursing, 8550 Magellan Parkway, Suite 1100, Richmond, VA 23227-1149. *Toll-free phone:* 866-238-7414.
Website: http://www.bsmcon.edu/.

Bridgewater College

Bridgewater, Virginia

- **Independent** 4-year, founded 1880, affiliated with Church of the Brethren
- **Small-town** 300-acre campus
- **Endowment** $65.4 million
- **Coed** 1,760 undergraduate students, 99% full-time, 56% women, 44% men
- **Moderately difficult** entrance level, 54% of applicants were admitted

Undergraduates 1,748 full-time, 12 part-time. Students come from 28 states and territories; 10 other countries; 22% are from out of state; 8% Black or African American, non-Hispanic/Latino; 3% Hispanic/Latino; 0.9% Asian, non-Hispanic/Latino; 0.1% Native Hawaiian or other Pacific Islander, non-Hispanic/Latino; 0.3% American Indian or Alaska Native, non-Hispanic/Latino; 3% Two or more races, non-Hispanic/Latino; 3% Race/ethnicity unknown; 0.7% international; 4% transferred in; 84% live on campus. *Retention:* 77% of full-time freshmen returned.
Freshmen *Admission:* 6,079 applied, 3,303 admitted, 552 enrolled. *Average high school GPA:* 3.4. *Test scores:* SAT critical reading scores over 500: 59%; SAT math scores over 500: 65%; SAT writing scores over 500: 50%; ACT scores over 18: 92%; SAT critical reading scores over 600: 16%; SAT math scores over 600: 18%; SAT writing scores over 600: 13%; ACT scores over 24: 15%; SAT critical reading scores over 700: 2%; SAT math scores over 700: 2%; SAT writing scores over 700: 1%; ACT scores over 30: 3%.
Faculty *Total:* 138, 77% full-time, 72% with terminal degrees. *Student/faculty ratio:* 15:1.
Academics *Calendar:* 4-1-4. *Degree:* bachelor's. *Special study options:* adult/continuing education programs, advanced placement credit, double majors, honors programs, independent study, internships, off-campus study, part-time degree program, services for LD students, study abroad, summer session for credit. *Unusual degree programs:* 3-2 engineering with George Washington University; Virginia Tech; nursing with Vanderbilt University.
Computers on Campus 203 computers/terminals and 700 ports are available on campus for general student use. Students can access the following: campus intranet, computer help desk, free student e-mail accounts, online (class) grades, online (class) registration, online (class) schedules, Moodle (course management system), campus bulletin board system. Campuswide network is available. 100% of college-owned or -operated housing units are wired for high-speed Internet access. Wireless service is available via entire campus.
Student Life *Housing:* on-campus residence required through senior year. *Options:* coed, men-only, women-only, disabled students. Campus housing is university owned. Freshman campus housing is guaranteed. *Activities and organizations:* drama/theater group, student-run newspaper, radio station, choral group, Equestrian Club, Student Ambassadors, Campus Crusade for Christ (CRU), Eagle Productions (program board), Habitat for Humanity. *Campus security:* 24-hour emergency response devices and patrols, controlled dormitory access, emergency alert system. *Student services:* health clinic, personal/psychological counseling.
Athletics Member NCAA. All Division III. *Intercollegiate sports:* baseball M, basketball M/W, cheerleading M(c)/W(c), cross-country running M/W, equestrian sports M(c)/W(c), field hockey W, football M, golf M/W, lacrosse M/W, soccer M/W, softball W, swimming and diving W, tennis M/W, track and field M/W, volleyball W, wrestling M(c). *Intramural sports:* badminton M/W, basketball M/W, bowling M/W, football M/W, golf M/W, racquetball M/W, soccer M/W, softball M/W, table tennis M/W, tennis M/W, ultimate Frisbee M/W, volleyball M/W.

Standardized Tests *Required:* SAT or ACT (for admission).
Costs (2013–14) *Comprehensive fee:* $39,880 includes full-time tuition ($28,500), mandatory fees ($590), and room and board ($10,790). Part-time tuition: $980 per credit hour. *Required fees:* $40 per term part-time. *College room only:* $5490. Room and board charges vary according to housing facility. *Payment plan:* installment. *Waivers:* senior citizens and employees or children of employees.
Financial Aid Of all full-time matriculated undergraduates who enrolled in 2012, 1,562 applied for aid, 1,449 were judged to have need, 420 had their need fully met. 278 Federal Work-Study jobs (averaging $1174). 157 state and other part-time jobs (averaging $751). In 2012, 293 non-need-based awards were made. *Average percent of need met:* 83%. *Average financial aid package:* $23,927. *Average need-based loan:* $4607. *Average need-based gift aid:* $20,482. *Average non-need-based aid:* $14,907. *Average indebtedness upon graduation:* $31,153.
Applying *Options:* electronic application, deferred entrance. *Application fee:* $30. *Required:* high school transcript, minimum 2.5 GPA, 1 letter of recommendation. *Required for some:* interview. *Recommended:* minimum 2.8 GPA, interview. *Application deadlines:* rolling (freshmen), rolling (out-of-state freshmen), rolling (transfers). *Notification:* continuous (freshmen), continuous (out-of-state freshmen), continuous (transfers).
Freshman Application Contact Mr. Jarret L. Smith, Director of Admissions, Bridgewater College, 402 East College Street, Bridgewater, VA 22812. *Phone:* 540-828-5469. *Toll-free phone:* 800-759-8328. *Fax:* 540-828-5481. *E-mail:* admissions@bridgewater.edu.
Website: http://www.bridgewater.edu/.

Bryant & Stratton College— Richmond Campus

Richmond, Virginia

Freshman Application Contact Mr. David K. Mayle, Director of Admissions, Bryant & Stratton College—Richmond Campus, 8141 Hull Street Road, Richmond, VA 23235-6411. *Phone:* 804-745-2444. *Fax:* 804-745-6884. *E-mail:* tlawson@bryanstratton.edu.
Website: http://www.bryantstratton.edu/.

Bryant & Stratton College— Virginia Beach

Virginia Beach, Virginia

Freshman Application Contact Bryant & Stratton College—Virginia Beach, 301 Centre Pointe Drive, Virginia Beach, VA 23462-4417. *Phone:* 757-499-7900 Ext. 173.
Website: http://www.bryantstratton.edu/.

Centura College

Virginia Beach, Virginia

Freshman Application Contact Admissions Office, Centura College, 2697 Dean Drive, Suite 100, Virginia Beach, VA 23452. *Phone:* 757-340-2121. *Toll-free phone:* 877-575-5627. *Fax:* 757-340-9704.
Website: http://www.centuracollege.edu/.

Chamberlain College of Nursing

Arlington, Virginia

- **Proprietary** 4-year
- **Coed**

Faculty *Student/faculty ratio:* 19:1.
Academics *Calendar:* semesters. *Degree:* bachelor's.
Standardized Tests *Required:* SAT or ACT (for admission).
Costs (2013–14) *Tuition:* $16,360 full-time, $665 per credit hour part-time. Full-time tuition and fees vary according to course load. Part-time tuition and fees vary according to course load. *Required fees:* $600 full-time.

Freshman Application Contact Admissions, Chamberlain College of Nursing, 2450 Crystal Drive, Arlington, VA 22202. *Phone:* 703-416-7300. *Toll-free phone:* 888-556-8CCN.
Website: http://www.chamberlain.edu/.

Christendom College

Front Royal, Virginia
- **Independent Roman Catholic** comprehensive, founded 1977
- **Rural** 100-acre campus with easy access to Washington, DC
- **Endowment** $3.1 million
- **Coed** 388 undergraduate students, 98% full-time, 58% women, 42% men
- **Moderately difficult** entrance level, 83% of applicants were admitted

Undergraduates 381 full-time, 7 part-time. Students come from 45 states and territories; 5 other countries; 75% are from out of state; 2% transferred in; 95% live on campus. *Retention:* 83% of full-time freshmen returned.
Freshmen *Admission:* 254 applied, 211 admitted, 104 enrolled. *Average high school GPA:* 3.7. *Test scores:* SAT critical reading scores over 500: 95%; SAT math scores over 500: 80%; SAT writing scores over 500: 89%; ACT scores over 18: 97%; SAT critical reading scores over 600: 62%; SAT math scores over 600: 34%; SAT writing scores over 600: 65%; ACT scores over 24: 69%; SAT critical reading scores over 700: 29%; SAT math scores over 700: 10%; SAT writing scores over 700: 22%; ACT scores over 30: 7%.
Faculty *Total:* 44, 48% full-time, 59% with terminal degrees. *Student/faculty ratio:* 13:1.
Academics *Calendar:* semesters. *Degrees:* associate, bachelor's, and master's. *Special study options:* academic remediation for entering students, accelerated degree program, advanced placement credit, cooperative education, double majors, independent study, internships, services for LD students, study abroad, summer session for credit.
Computers on Campus 60 computers/terminals are available on campus for general student use. Students can access the following: campus intranet, computer help desk, free student e-mail accounts. Wireless service is available via computer labs, libraries, student centers.
Student Life *Housing:* on-campus residence required through senior year. *Options:* men-only, women-only. Campus housing is university owned. Freshman campus housing is guaranteed. *Activities and organizations:* drama/theater group, student-run newspaper, choral group, drama, choir, Shield of Roses, Legion of Mary, debate team. *Campus security:* 24-hour emergency response devices, late-night transport/escort service, night patrols by trained security personnel. *Student services:* health clinic, personal/psychological counseling.
Athletics Member USCAA. *Intercollegiate sports:* baseball M, basketball M/W, rugby M, soccer M/W, volleyball W. *Intramural sports:* basketball M/W, equestrian sports M/W, fencing M/W, football M/W, racquetball M/W, soccer M/W, table tennis M/W, tennis M/W, volleyball M/W.
Standardized Tests *Required:* SAT or ACT (for admission).
Costs (2013–14) *Comprehensive fee:* $31,000 includes full-time tuition ($22,050), mandatory fees ($670), and room and board ($8280). *Payment plan:* installment. *Waivers:* employees or children of employees.
Financial Aid Of all full-time matriculated undergraduates who enrolled in 2012, 238 applied for aid, 212 were judged to have need, 212 had their need fully met. 145 state and other part-time jobs (averaging $1980). In 2012, 86 non-need-based awards were made. *Average percent of need met:* 90%. *Average financial aid package:* $15,535. *Average need-based loan:* $6550. *Average need-based gift aid:* $7545. *Average non-need-based aid:* $7175. *Average indebtedness upon graduation:* $25,875.
Applying *Options:* electronic application, early admission, early action. *Application fee:* $25. *Required:* essay or personal statement, high school transcript, 2 letters of recommendation. *Recommended:* minimum 3.0 GPA, interview. *Application deadlines:* 3/1 (freshmen), 3/1 (transfers), 12/1 (early action). *Notification:* 4/1 (freshmen), continuous until 4/1 (transfers), 12/15 (early action).
Freshman Application Contact Christendom College, 134 Christendom Drive, Front Royal, VA 22630-5103. *Phone:* 540-636-2900 Ext. 1290. *Toll-free phone:* 800-877-5456.
Website: http://www.christendom.edu/.

Christopher Newport University

Newport News, Virginia
- **State-supported** comprehensive, founded 1960
- **Suburban** 260-acre campus with easy access to Virginia Beach
- **Endowment** $16.3 million
- **Coed** 5,046 undergraduate students, 98% full-time, 57% women, 43% men
- **Very difficult** entrance level, 65% of applicants were admitted

Undergraduates 4,926 full-time, 120 part-time. Students come from 28 states and territories; 35 other countries; 6% are from out of state; 8% Black or African American, non-Hispanic/Latino; 5% Hispanic/Latino; 2% Asian, non-Hispanic/Latino; 0.2% Native Hawaiian or other Pacific Islander, non-Hispanic/Latino; 0.2% American Indian or Alaska Native, non-Hispanic/Latino; 5% Two or more races, non-Hispanic/Latino; 3% Race/ethnicity unknown; 0.2% international; 4% transferred in; 68% live on campus. *Retention:* 85% of full-time freshmen returned.
Freshmen *Admission:* 6,831 applied, 4,412 admitted, 1,376 enrolled. *Average high school GPA:* 3.7. *Test scores:* SAT critical reading scores over 500: 91%; SAT math scores over 500: 91%; ACT scores over 18: 98%; SAT critical reading scores over 600: 44%; SAT math scores over 600: 39%; ACT scores over 24: 53%; SAT critical reading scores over 700: 7%; SAT math scores over 700: 4%; ACT scores over 30: 6%.
Faculty *Total:* 392, 66% full-time, 67% with terminal degrees. *Student/faculty ratio:* 17:1.
Academics *Calendar:* semesters. *Degrees:* bachelor's and master's. *Special study options:* advanced placement credit, double majors, honors programs, independent study, internships, off-campus study, services for LD students, student-designed majors, study abroad, summer session for credit. *ROTC:* Army (b).
Computers on Campus 450 computers/terminals and 1,000 ports are available on campus for general student use. Students can access the following: campus intranet, computer help desk, free student e-mail accounts, online (class) grades, online (class) registration, online (class) schedules, online degree audit. Campuswide network is available. 100% of college-owned or -operated housing units are wired for high-speed Internet access. Wireless service is available via entire campus.
Student Life *Housing:* on-campus residence required through junior year. *Options:* coed, disabled students. Campus housing is university owned. Freshman campus housing is guaranteed. *Activities and organizations:* drama/theater group, student-run newspaper, radio station, choral group, marching band, Intervarsity, Alpha Delta Pi, Alpha Sigma Alpha, Gamma Phi Beta, Phi Mu, national fraternities, national sororities. *Campus security:* 24-hour emergency response devices and patrols, late-night transport/escort service, controlled dormitory access, campus-based University Police; Emergency Notification System; Crime Prevention Programs. *Student services:* health clinic, personal/psychological counseling.
Athletics Member NCAA. All Division III. *Intercollegiate sports:* baseball M, basketball M/W, cheerleading W, cross-country running M/W, field hockey W, football M, golf M, lacrosse M/W, soccer M/W, softball W, tennis M/W, track and field M/W, volleyball W. *Intramural sports:* badminton M/W, basketball M/W, crew M(c)/W(c), equestrian sports M(c)/W(c), field hockey M(c)/W(c), football M/W, ice hockey M(c), lacrosse M(c)/W(c), rock climbing M(c)/W(c), rugby M(c), soccer M/W, softball M/W, swimming and diving M(c)/W(c), table tennis M(c)/W(c), tennis M(c)/W(c), ultimate Frisbee M(c)/W(c), volleyball M(c)/W(c).
Standardized Tests *Required for some:* SAT or ACT (for admission).
Costs (2012–13) *Tuition:* state resident $6210 full-time, $258 per credit hour part-time; nonresident $15,364 full-time, $641 per credit hour part-time. Full-time tuition and fees vary according to course load. Part-time tuition and fees vary according to course load. *Required fees:* $4362 full-time, $181 per credit hour part-time. *Room and board:* $9728; room only: $6358. Room and board charges vary according to board plan and housing facility. *Payment plan:* installment. *Waivers:* senior citizens and employees or children of employees.
Financial Aid Of all full-time matriculated undergraduates who enrolled in 2010, 3,047 applied for aid, 2,160 were judged to have need, 339 had their need fully met. 117 Federal Work-Study jobs (averaging $833). 1,762 state and other part-time jobs (averaging $1177). In 2010, 482 non-need-based awards were made. *Average percent of need met:* 69%. *Average financial aid package:* $8099. *Average need-based loan:* $4033. *Average need-based gift aid:* $5087. *Average non-need-based aid:* $1772. *Average indebtedness upon graduation:* $21,572.
Applying *Options:* electronic application, early admission, early decision, early action, deferred entrance. *Application fee:* $50. *Required:* essay or personal statement, high school transcript, minimum 3.0 GPA. *Required for some:* 2 letters of recommendation, interview. *Application deadlines:* 2/1 (freshmen), 3/1 (transfers), 12/1 (early action). *Early decision deadline:* 11/15. *Notifica-*

tion: 3/15 (freshmen), 5/1 (transfers), 12/15 (early decision), 1/15 (early action).

Freshman Application Contact Mr. Rob Lange, Dean of Admissions, Christopher Newport University, Office of Admissions, 1 Avenue of the Arts, Newport News, VA 23606-3072. *Phone:* 757-594-7015. *Toll-free phone:* 800-333-4268. *Fax:* 757-594-7333. *E-mail:* admit@cnu.edu. *Website:* http://www.cnu.edu/.

The College of William and Mary
Williamsburg, Virginia

- **State-supported** university, founded 1693
- **Small-town** 1200-acre campus with easy access to Richmond
- **Endowment** $644.2 million
- **Coed** 6,171 undergraduate students, 99% full-time, 55% women, 45% men
- **Most difficult** entrance level, 32% of applicants were admitted

Undergraduates 6,097 full-time, 74 part-time. Students come from 55 states and territories; 54 other countries; 32% are from out of state; 7% Black or African American, non-Hispanic/Latino; 9% Hispanic/Latino; 6% Asian, non-Hispanic/Latino; 0.1% Native Hawaiian or other Pacific Islander, non-Hispanic/Latino; 0.3% American Indian or Alaska Native, non-Hispanic/Latino; 4% Two or more races, non-Hispanic/Latino; 10% Race/ethnicity unknown; 4% international; 3% transferred in; 72% live on campus. *Retention:* 96% of full-time freshmen returned.

Freshmen *Admission:* 13,660 applied, 4,394 admitted, 1,467 enrolled. *Average high school GPA:* 4. *Test scores:* SAT critical reading scores over 500: 99%; SAT math scores over 500: 99%; SAT writing scores over 500: 97%; ACT scores over 18: 100%; SAT critical reading scores over 600: 85%; SAT math scores over 600: 85%; SAT writing scores over 600: 84%; ACT scores over 24: 95%; SAT critical reading scores over 700: 46%; SAT math scores over 700: 38%; SAT writing scores over 700: 37%; ACT scores over 30: 61%.

Faculty *Student/faculty ratio:* 12:1.

Academics *Calendar:* semesters. *Degrees:* bachelor's, master's, doctoral, and post-master's certificates. *Special study options:* accelerated degree program, advanced placement credit, double majors, honors programs, independent study, internships, off-campus study, part-time degree program, services for LD students, student-designed majors, study abroad, summer session for credit. *ROTC:* Army (b).

Computers on Campus 300 computers/terminals and 6,500 ports are available on campus for general student use. Students can access the following: campus intranet, computer help desk, free student e-mail accounts, online (class) grades, online (class) registration, online (class) schedules. Campuswide network is available. 100% of college-owned or -operated housing units are wired for high-speed Internet access. Wireless service is available via entire campus.

Student Life *Housing:* on-campus residence required for freshman year. *Options:* coed, disabled students. Campus housing is university owned and leased by the school. Freshman campus housing is guaranteed. *Activities and organizations:* drama/theater group, student-run newspaper, radio and television station, choral group, Alma Mater Productions, Student Assembly, College Partnership for Kids, Residence Hall Association, Alpha Phi Omega, national fraternities, national sororities. *Campus security:* 24-hour emergency response devices and patrols, late-night transport/escort service, controlled dormitory access, The WMPD is a State certified law enforcement agency with 33 employees, providing law enforcement services for the College. *Student services:* health clinic, personal/psychological counseling, legal services.

Athletics Member NCAA. All Division I except football (Division I-AA). *Intercollegiate sports:* baseball M(s), basketball M(s)/W(s), cross-country running M(s)/W(s), field hockey W(s), golf M(s)/W(s), gymnastics M(s)/W(s), lacrosse W(s), soccer M(s)/W(s), swimming and diving M/W, tennis M(s)/W(s), track and field M(s)/W(s), volleyball W(s). *Intramural sports:* badminton M(c)/W(c), baseball M(c), basketball M/W, bowling M/W, crew M(c)/W(c), cross-country running M(c)/W(c), equestrian sports M(c)/W(c), fencing M(c)/W(c), field hockey W(c), football M/W, golf M(c)/W(c), gymnastics M(c)/W(c), ice hockey M(c), lacrosse M(c)/W(c), racquetball M(c)/W(c), rock climbing M(c)/W(c), rugby M(c)/W(c), sailing M(c)/W(c), soccer M/W, softball M/W, squash M(c)/W(c), swimming and diving M(c)/W(c), table tennis M(c)/W(c), tennis M(c)/W(c), ultimate Frisbee M(c)/W(c), volleyball M/W, water polo M(c)/W(c), weight lifting M/W, wrestling M(c).

Standardized Tests *Required:* SAT or ACT (for admission). *Recommended:* SAT Subject Tests (for admission).

Costs (2012–13) *Tuition:* state resident $13,570 full-time; nonresident $37,344 full-time. *Room and board:* $9072; room only: $5790. Room and board charges vary according to board plan and housing facility. *Payment plan:* installment. *Waivers:* senior citizens.

Financial Aid Of all full-time matriculated undergraduates who enrolled in 2011, 3,092 applied for aid, 2,080 were judged to have need, 494 had their need fully met. 144 Federal Work-Study jobs (averaging $1163). In 2011, 291 non-need-based awards were made. *Average percent of need met:* 75%. *Average financial aid package:* $16,407. *Average need-based loan:* $4483. *Average need-based gift aid:* $12,849. *Average non-need-based aid:* $6050. *Average indebtedness upon graduation:* $24,344.

Applying *Options:* electronic application, early admission, early decision, deferred entrance. *Application fee:* $70. *Required:* essay or personal statement, high school transcript, 1 letter of recommendation. *Recommended:* 2 letters of recommendation. *Application deadlines:* 1/1 (freshmen), 3/1 (transfers). *Early decision deadline:* 11/1. *Notification:* 4/1 (freshmen), 5/1 (transfers), 12/1 (early decision).

Freshman Application Contact Timothy Wolfe, Senior Associate Dean of Admission, The College of William and Mary, PO Box 8795, Williamsburg, VA 23187-8795. *Phone:* 757-221-4223. *Fax:* 757-221-1242. *E-mail:* admission@wm.edu. *Website:* http://www.wm.edu/.

Culinary Institute of Virginia
Norfolk, Virginia

Freshman Application Contact Director of Admissions, Culinary Institute of Virginia, 2428 Almeda Avenue, Suite 316, Norfolk, VA 23513. *Phone:* 757-858-2433. *Toll-free phone:* 866-619-CHEF. *E-mail:* hsadmissions@chefva.com. *Website:* http://www.chefva.com/.

DeVry University
Arlington, Virginia

- **Proprietary** comprehensive, founded 2001, part of DeVry University
- **Coed** 542 undergraduate students, 48% full-time, 30% women, 70% men
- **Minimally difficult** entrance level

Undergraduates 258 full-time, 284 part-time. 59% are from out of state; 48% Black or African American, non-Hispanic/Latino; 11% Hispanic/Latino; 4% Asian, non-Hispanic/Latino; 0.6% Native Hawaiian or other Pacific Islander, non-Hispanic/Latino; 0.4% American Indian or Alaska Native, non-Hispanic/Latino; 1% Two or more races, non-Hispanic/Latino; 13% Race/ethnicity unknown; 5% international; 13% transferred in.

Freshmen *Admission:* 37 enrolled.

Faculty *Total:* 181, 8% full-time. *Student/faculty ratio:* 7:1.

Academics *Calendar:* semesters. *Degrees:* associate, bachelor's, master's, and postbachelor's certificates. *Special study options:* adult/continuing education programs, part-time degree program.

Computers on Campus Students can access the following: online (class) registration.

Student Life *Housing:* college housing not available.

Costs (2013–14) *Tuition:* $16,076 full-time, $609 per credit hour part-time. *Required fees:* $80 full-time.

Financial Aid Of all full-time matriculated undergraduates who enrolled in 2007, 175 applied for aid, 164 were judged to have need, 9 had their need fully met. In 2007, 21 non-need-based awards were made. *Average percent of need met:* 38%. *Average financial aid package:* $11,581. *Average need-based loan:* $7979. *Average need-based gift aid:* $5610. *Average non-need-based aid:* $18,172. *Average indebtedness upon graduation:* $12,479.

Applying *Application fee:* $40. *Required:* high school transcript, interview. *Application deadlines:* rolling (freshmen), rolling (transfers). *Notification:* continuous (freshmen), continuous (transfers).

Freshman Application Contact DeVry University, 2450 Crystal Drive, Arlington, VA 22202. *Phone:* 703-414-4000. *Toll-free phone:* 866-338-7941. *Website:* http://www.devry.edu/.

DeVry University
Chesapeake, Virginia

Admissions Office Contact DeVry University, 1317 Executive Boulevard, Suite 100, Chesapeake, VA 23320-3671. *Toll-free phone:* 866-338-7941. *Website:* http://www.devry.edu/.

DeVry University

Manassas, Virginia

Admissions Office Contact DeVry University, 10432 Balls Ford Road, Suite 130, Manassas, VA 20109-3173. *Toll-free phone:* 866-338-7941. *Website:* http://www.devry.edu/.

Eastern Mennonite University

Harrisonburg, Virginia

- **Independent Mennonite** comprehensive, founded 1917
- **Small-town** 93-acre campus
- **Endowment** $19.5 million
- **Coed** 1,124 undergraduate students, 94% full-time, 64% women, 36% men
- **Moderately difficult** entrance level, 70% of applicants were admitted

Undergraduates 1,061 full-time, 63 part-time. Students come from 37 states and territories; 18 other countries; 44% are from out of state; 7% Black or African American, non-Hispanic/Latino; 7% Hispanic/Latino; 2% Asian, non-Hispanic/Latino; 0.2% American Indian or Alaska Native, non-Hispanic/Latino; 1% Two or more races, non-Hispanic/Latino; 3% Race/ethnicity unknown; 3% international; 6% transferred in; 60% live on campus. *Retention:* 81% of full-time freshmen returned.

Freshmen *Admission:* 919 applied, 645 admitted, 217 enrolled. *Average high school GPA:* 3.5. *Test scores:* SAT critical reading scores over 500: 50%; SAT math scores over 500: 52%; SAT writing scores over 500: 43%; ACT scores over 18: 94%; SAT critical reading scores over 600: 25%; SAT math scores over 600: 25%; SAT writing scores over 600: 18%; ACT scores over 24: 57%; SAT critical reading scores over 700: 8%; SAT math scores over 700: 5%; SAT writing scores over 700: 4%; ACT scores over 30: 17%.

Faculty *Total:* 205, 51% full-time. *Student/faculty ratio:* 10:1.

Academics *Calendar:* semesters. *Degrees:* certificates, associate, bachelor's, master's, and postbachelor's certificates. *Special study options:* adult/continuing education programs, advanced placement credit, distance learning, double majors, English as a second language, honors programs, independent study, internships, off-campus study, part-time degree program, services for LD students, study abroad, summer session for credit. *Unusual degree programs:* 3-2 engineering with Catholic University of America.

Computers on Campus 154 computers/terminals are available on campus for general student use. Students can access the following: campus intranet, computer help desk, free student e-mail accounts, online (class) grades, online (class) registration, online (class) schedules. Campuswide network is available. 98% of college-owned or -operated housing units are wired for high-speed Internet access. Wireless service is available via classrooms, dorm rooms, learning centers, libraries, student centers.

Student Life *Housing:* on-campus residence required through junior year. *Options:* coed, cooperative, disabled students. Campus housing is university owned. Freshman campus housing is guaranteed. *Activities and organizations:* drama/theater group, student-run newspaper, choral group, Young People's Christian Association, Student Government Association, Student Education Association, Creation Care Council, Black Student Union. *Campus security:* 24-hour emergency response devices, controlled dormitory access, night watchman. *Student services:* health clinic, personal/psychological counseling.

Athletics Member NCAA. All Division III. *Intercollegiate sports:* baseball M, basketball M/W, cross-country running M/W, field hockey W, golf M/W, soccer M/W, softball W, track and field M/W, volleyball M/W. *Intramural sports:* basketball M/W, football M/W, golf M/W, lacrosse M(c), rock climbing M/W, soccer M/W, softball M/W, table tennis M/W, tennis M/W, volleyball M/W.

Standardized Tests *Required:* SAT or ACT (for admission).

Costs (2013–14) *Comprehensive fee:* $38,770 includes full-time tuition ($28,940), mandatory fees ($140), and room and board ($9690). Part-time tuition and fees vary according to course load. *Room and board:* Room and board charges vary according to board plan and housing facility. *Payment plan:* installment. *Waivers:* employees or children of employees.

Financial Aid Of all full-time matriculated undergraduates who enrolled in 2003, 735 applied for aid, 652 were judged to have need, 246 had their need fully met. 326 Federal Work-Study jobs (averaging $1787). In 2003, 82 non-need-based awards were made. *Average percent of need met:* 87%. *Average financial aid package:* $15,530. *Average need-based loan:* $5665. *Average need-based gift aid:* $5520. *Average non-need-based aid:* $7765. *Average indebtedness upon graduation:* $18,208.

Applying *Options:* electronic application, deferred entrance. *Application fee:* $25. *Required:* high school transcript, minimum 2.2 GPA, Community Lifestyle Commitment. *Required for some:* 2 letters of recommendation. *Recommended:* interview. *Application deadlines:* rolling (freshmen), rolling (transfers). *Notification:* continuous (freshmen), continuous (transfers).

Freshman Application Contact Stephanie C. Shafer, Director of Admissions, Eastern Mennonite University, 1200 Park Road, Harrisonburg, VA 22802. *Phone:* 540-432-4118. *Toll-free phone:* 800-368-2665. *Fax:* 540-432-4444. *E-mail:* admiss@emu.edu. *Website:* http://www.emu.edu/.

ECPI College of Technology

Glen Allen, Virginia

Freshman Application Contact Mr. Jacob Pope, Director, ECPI College of Technology, 4305 Cox Road, Glen Allen, VA 23060. *Phone:* 804-934-0100. *Toll-free phone:* 800-986-1200. *Fax:* 804-934-0054. *E-mail:* jpope@ecpi.edu. *Website:* http://www.ecpi.edu/.

ECPI College of Technology

Manassas, Virginia

Admissions Office Contact ECPI College of Technology, 10021 Balls Ford Road, Manassas, VA 20109. *Toll-free phone:* 866-708-6172. *Website:* http://www.ecpi.edu/.

ECPI College of Technology

Newport News, Virginia

Freshman Application Contact Ms. Cheryl Lokey, Provost, ECPI College of Technology, 1001 Omni Boulevard, #100, Newport News, VA 23606. *Phone:* 757-838-9191. *Toll-free phone:* 866-499-0335. *Fax:* 757-829-5351. *Website:* http://www.ecpi.edu/.

ECPI College of Technology

Richmond, Virginia

Freshman Application Contact Director, ECPI College of Technology, 800 Moorefield Park Drive, Richmond, VA 23236. *Phone:* 804-330-5533. *Toll-free phone:* 800-986-1200. *Fax:* 804-330-5577. *E-mail:* agerard@ecpi.edu. *Website:* http://www.ecpi.edu/.

ECPI College of Technology

Virginia Beach, Virginia

Freshman Application Contact Mrs. Bernadette Rozman Bellas, Vice President, Accreditation and Regulatory Affairs, ECPI College of Technology, 5555 Greenwich Road, Suite 100, Virginia Beach, VA 23462. *Phone:* 757-671-7171. *Toll-free phone:* 866-499-0336. *Fax:* 757-671-8661. *E-mail:* rballance@ecpi.edu. *Website:* http://www.ecpi.edu/.

Emory & Henry College

Emory, Virginia

- **Independent United Methodist** 4-year, founded 1836
- **Rural** 330-acre campus
- **Coed** 897 undergraduate students, 97% full-time, 47% women, 53% men
- 72% of applicants were admitted

Undergraduates 874 full-time, 23 part-time. 36% are from out of state; 10% Black or African American, non-Hispanic/Latino; 2% Hispanic/Latino; 0.4% Asian, non-Hispanic/Latino; 0.4% American Indian or Alaska Native, non-Hispanic/Latino; 2% Two or more races, non-Hispanic/Latino; 4% Race/ethnicity unknown; 0.9% international; 3% transferred in; 77% live on campus. *Retention:* 72% of full-time freshmen returned.

Freshmen *Admission:* 1,217 applied, 878 admitted, 246 enrolled. *Average high school GPA:* 3.5. *Test scores:* SAT critical reading scores over 500: 47%; SAT math scores over 500: 57%; SAT writing scores over 500: 45%; SAT critical reading scores over 600: 13%; SAT math scores over 600: 15%; SAT writing scores over 600: 10%; SAT critical reading scores over 700: 2%; SAT math scores over 700: 1%; SAT writing scores over 700: 1%.

Faculty *Total:* 120, 60% full-time, 57% with terminal degrees. *Student/faculty ratio:* 10:1.

Academics *Calendar:* semesters. *Degrees:* diplomas, bachelor's, and master's. *Special study options:* academic remediation for entering students, advanced placement credit, cooperative education, double majors, external degree program, honors programs, independent study, internships, services for LD students, student-designed majors, study abroad, summer session for credit.

Computers on Campus Students can access the following: campus intranet, computer help desk, free student e-mail accounts, online (class) grades, online (class) registration, online (class) schedules. Campuswide network is available. 100% of college-owned or -operated housing units are wired for high-speed Internet access. Wireless service is available via entire campus.

Student Life *Housing:* on-campus residence required through junior year. *Options:* coed, men-only, women-only. Campus housing is university owned. Freshman campus housing is guaranteed. *Activities and organizations:* drama/theater group, student-run newspaper, radio and television station, choral group. *Campus security:* 24-hour emergency response devices and patrols, late-night transport/escort service, controlled dormitory access. *Student services:* health clinic, personal/psychological counseling.

Athletics Member NCAA. All Division III. *Intercollegiate sports:* baseball M, basketball M/W, cheerleading M(c)/W(c), cross-country running M/W, football M, soccer M/W, softball W, swimming and diving M(c)/W, tennis M/W, volleyball W. *Intramural sports:* basketball M/W, football M/W, racquetball M/W, soccer M/W, table tennis M/W, tennis M/W, ultimate Frisbee M/W, volleyball M/W.

Standardized Tests *Required:* SAT or ACT (for admission).

Costs (2012–13) *Comprehensive fee:* $37,548 includes full-time tuition ($28,122) and room and board ($9426). Full-time tuition and fees vary according to course load, degree level, and location. Part-time tuition: $1125 per credit hour. Part-time tuition and fees vary according to course load, degree level, and location. *College room only:* $4782. Room and board charges vary according to board plan, housing facility, and location. *Payment plans:* installment, deferred payment. *Waivers:* employees or children of employees.

Financial Aid Of all full-time matriculated undergraduates who enrolled in 2012, 789 applied for aid, 733 were judged to have need, 252 had their need fully met. 151 Federal Work-Study jobs (averaging $1119). In 2012, 134 non-need-based awards were made. *Average percent of need met:* 88%. *Average financial aid package:* $25,588. *Average need-based loan:* $4508. *Average need-based gift aid:* $22,596. *Average non-need-based aid:* $14,308. *Average indebtedness upon graduation:* $29,510.

Applying *Options:* electronic application, early action. *Required:* high school transcript. *Recommended:* essay or personal statement, interview. *Application deadlines:* rolling (freshmen), rolling (out-of-state freshmen), rolling (transfers), 12/1 (early action). *Notification:* continuous (freshmen), continuous (out-of-state freshmen), continuous (transfers), 1/1 (early action).

Freshman Application Contact Admissions Office, Emory & Henry College, PO Box 947, Emory, VA 24327-0947. *Phone:* 276-944-4121. *Toll-free phone:* 800-848-5493. *E-mail:* ehadmiss@ehc.edu. *Website:* http://www.ehc.edu/.

Ferrum College

Ferrum, Virginia

- **Independent United Methodist** 4-year, founded 1913
- **Rural** 720-acre campus
- **Endowment** $39.5 million
- **Coed** 1,510 undergraduate students, 98% full-time, 45% women, 55% men
- **Minimally difficult** entrance level, 92% of applicants were admitted

Undergraduates 1,487 full-time, 23 part-time. Students come from 12 states and territories; 7 other countries; 18% are from out of state; 33% Black or African American, non-Hispanic/Latino; 4% Hispanic/Latino; 0.1% Asian, non-Hispanic/Latino; 0.2% Native Hawaiian or other Pacific Islander, non-Hispanic/Latino; 0.5% American Indian or Alaska Native, non-Hispanic/Latino; 5% Two or more races, non-Hispanic/Latino; 5% Race/ethnicity unknown; 0.8% international; 5% transferred in; 90% live on campus. *Retention:* 53% of full-time freshmen returned.

Freshmen *Admission:* 2,589 applied, 2,392 admitted, 550 enrolled. *Average high school GPA:* 2.79. *Test scores:* SAT critical reading scores over 500: 26%; SAT math scores over 500: 24%; SAT writing scores over 500: 15%; SAT critical reading scores over 600: 3%; SAT math scores over 600: 5%; SAT writing scores over 600: 2%.

Faculty *Total:* 125, 63% full-time, 54% with terminal degrees. *Student/faculty ratio:* 16:1.

Academics *Calendar:* semesters. *Degree:* bachelor's. *Special study options:* academic remediation for entering students, adult/continuing education programs, advanced placement credit, double majors, honors programs, internships, services for LD students, student-designed majors, study abroad, summer session for credit. *Unusual degree programs:* 3-2 Sherman College of Straight Chiropractic.

Computers on Campus 89 computers/terminals are available on campus for general student use. Students can access the following: campus intranet, computer help desk, free student e-mail accounts, online (class) grades, online (class) registration, online (class) schedules. Campuswide network is available. 100% of college-owned or -operated housing units are wired for high-speed Internet access. Wireless service is available via entire campus.

Student Life *Housing:* on-campus residence required through senior year. *Options:* coed, women-only, disabled students. Campus housing is university owned. Freshman campus housing is guaranteed. *Activities and organizations:* drama/theater group, student-run newspaper, radio station, choral group, Student Government Association, Agriculture Club, BACCHUS, Panther Productions, African American Student Association, Students in Free Enterprise (SIFE), national sororities. *Campus security:* 24-hour emergency response devices and patrols, student patrols, late-night transport/escort service, controlled dormitory access. *Student services:* health clinic, personal/psychological counseling.

Athletics Member NCAA. All Division III. *Intercollegiate sports:* baseball M, basketball M/W, cheerleading M/W, cross-country running M/W, football M, golf M, lacrosse M/W, soccer M/W, softball W, swimming and diving W, tennis M/W, volleyball W. *Intramural sports:* basketball M/W, football M/W, racquetball M/W, softball M/W, tennis M/W.

Standardized Tests *Required:* SAT or ACT (for admission).

Costs (2013–14) *Comprehensive fee:* $36,555 includes full-time tuition ($27,310), mandatory fees ($115), and room and board ($9130). Part-time tuition: $545 per credit hour.

Financial Aid Of all full-time matriculated undergraduates who enrolled in 2011, 1,452 applied for aid, 1,424 were judged to have need, 358 had their need fully met. 1,021 Federal Work-Study jobs (averaging $2207). In 2011, 44 non-need-based awards were made. *Average percent of need met:* 80%. *Average financial aid package:* $38,937. *Average need-based loan:* $6795. *Average need-based gift aid:* $16,418. *Average non-need-based aid:* $16,287. *Average indebtedness upon graduation:* $24,788.

Applying *Options:* electronic application, early admission, deferred entrance. *Application fee:* $25. *Required:* high school transcript. *Required for some:* interview. *Recommended:* essay or personal statement, minimum 2.0 GPA, 2 letters of recommendation, interview. *Application deadline:* rolling (freshmen). *Notification:* continuous (freshmen).

Freshman Application Contact Ms. Gilda Q. Woods, Associate Vice President for Enrollment Management and Dean of Admissions, Ferrum College, Spilman-Daniel House, PO Box 1000, Ferrum, VA 24088-9001. *Phone:* 540-365-4290. *Toll-free phone:* 800-868-9797. *Fax:* 540-365-4266. *E-mail:* admissions@ferrum.edu. *Website:* http://www.ferrum.edu/.

George Mason University

Fairfax, Virginia

- **State-supported** university, founded 1957
- **Suburban** 817-acre campus with easy access to Washington, DC
- **Endowment** $51.7 million
- **Coed** 20,653 undergraduate students, 79% full-time, 52% women, 48% men
- **Moderately difficult** entrance level, 66% of applicants were admitted

Undergraduates 16,265 full-time, 4,388 part-time. Students come from 50 states and territories; 125 other countries; 11% are from out of state; 9% Black or African American, non-Hispanic/Latino; 11% Hispanic/Latino; 17% Asian, non-Hispanic/Latino; 0.5% Native Hawaiian or other Pacific Islander, non-Hispanic/Latino; 0.2% American Indian or Alaska Native, non-Hispanic/Latino; 5% Two or more races, non-Hispanic/Latino; 8% Race/ethnicity unknown; 4% international; 10% transferred in; 28% live on campus. *Retention:* 86% of full-time freshmen returned.

Freshmen *Admission:* 14,703 applied, 9,667 admitted, 2,694 enrolled. *Average high school GPA:* 3.66. *Test scores:* SAT critical reading scores over 500: 85%; SAT math scores over 500: 89%; ACT scores over 18: 100%; SAT critical reading scores over 600: 37%; SAT math scores over 600: 43%; ACT scores over 24: 70%; SAT critical reading scores over 700: 7%; SAT math scores over 700: 7%; ACT scores over 30: 14%.

Faculty *Total:* 2,379, 51% full-time. *Student/faculty ratio:* 16:1.

Academics *Calendar:* semesters. *Degrees:* bachelor's, master's, doctoral, post-master's, and postbachelor's certificates. *Special study options:* accelerated degree program, adult/continuing education programs, advanced placement credit, cooperative education, distance learning, double majors, English as a second language, freshman honors college, honors programs, independent study, internships, off-campus study, part-time degree program, services for LD students, student-designed majors, study abroad, summer session for credit. *ROTC:* Army (b), Air Force (c). *Unusual degree programs:* 3-2 engineering.

Computers on Campus 629 computers/terminals and 20,000 ports are available on campus for general student use. Students can access the following: campus intranet, computer help desk, free student e-mail accounts, online (class) grades, online (class) registration, online (class) schedules. Campuswide network is available. 100% of college-owned or -operated housing units are wired for high-speed Internet access. Wireless service is available via entire campus.

Student Life *Housing options:* coed, disabled students. Campus housing is university owned and leased by the school. Freshman campus housing is guaranteed. *Activities and organizations:* drama/theater group, student-run newspaper, radio and television station, choral group, Catholic Campus Ministry, Muslim Student Association, National Society of Collegiate Scholars, Campus Crusade for Christ, Institute of Electrical and Electronics Engineers, national fraternities, national sororities. *Campus security:* 24-hour emergency response devices and patrols, student patrols, late-night transport/escort service, controlled dormitory access. *Student services:* health clinic, personal/psychological counseling, women's center.

Athletics Member NCAA. All Division I. *Intercollegiate sports:* baseball M(s), basketball M(s)/W(s), cheerleading M(s)/W(s), crew W(s), cross-country running M(s)/W(s), golf M(s), lacrosse W(s), soccer M(s)/W(s), softball W(s), swimming and diving M(s)/W(s), tennis M(s)/W(s), track and field M(s)/W(s), volleyball M(s)/W(s), wrestling M(s). *Intramural sports:* baseball M(c), basketball M/W, bowling M(c)/W(c), crew M(c), cross-country running M/W, equestrian sports M(c)/W(c), fencing M(c)/W(c), field hockey W(c), football M(c), golf M/W, ice hockey M(c), lacrosse M(c)/W(c), rugby M(c)/W(c), soccer M(c)/W(c), softball M/W, swimming and diving M/W, table tennis M/W, tennis M/W, track and field M/W, ultimate Frisbee M(c)/W(c), volleyball M/W.

Standardized Tests *Required for some:* SAT or ACT (for admission). *Recommended:* SAT and SAT Subject Tests or ACT (for admission).

Costs (2012–13) *One-time required fee:* $180. *Tuition:* state resident $7010 full-time, $292 per credit hour part-time; nonresident $25,154 full-time, $1048 per credit hour part-time. Full-time tuition and fees vary according to course load. Part-time tuition and fees vary according to course load. *Required fees:* $2610 full-time, $109 per credit hour part-time. *Room and board:* $9250; room only: $5510. Room and board charges vary according to board plan and housing facility. *Payment plan:* installment. *Waivers:* senior citizens and employees or children of employees.

Financial Aid Of all full-time matriculated undergraduates who enrolled in 2011, 10,825 applied for aid, 8,558 were judged to have need, 608 had their need fully met. 333 Federal Work-Study jobs (averaging $2284). In 2011, 587 non-need-based awards were made. *Average percent of need met:* 60%. *Average financial aid package:* $11,790. *Average need-based loan:* $4330. *Average need-based gift aid:* $6294. *Average non-need-based aid:* $5407. *Average indebtedness upon graduation:* $25,822.

Applying *Options:* electronic application, early admission, early action, deferred entrance. *Application fee:* $60. *Required:* essay or personal statement, high school transcript, minimum 2.0 GPA. *Required for some:* 3 letters of recommendation, Audition required for School of Dance and School of Music applicants; portfolio required for Art and Visual Technology BFA and Computer Game Design BFA applicants. Interview and audition or portfolio required for School of Theater applicants. *Recommended:* minimum 3.5 GPA. *Application deadlines:* 1/15 (freshmen), 1/15 (out-of-state freshmen), 3/1 (transfers), 11/9 (early action). *Notification:* 4/1 (freshmen), 4/1 (out-of-state freshmen), continuous until 4/1 (transfers), 12/15 (early action).

Freshman Application Contact Sara Dvorak, Associate Director, Admissions, George Mason University, 4400 University Drive, MSN 3A4, Fairfax, VA 22030-4444. *Phone:* 703-993-4450. *Fax:* 703-993-2392. *E-mail:* sdvorak@gmu.edu.
Website: http://www.gmu.edu/.

Hampden-Sydney College
Hampden-Sydney, Virginia

- **Independent** 4-year, founded 1776, affiliated with Presbyterian Church (U.S.A.)
- **Rural** 1340-acre campus with easy access to Richmond
- **Endowment** $129.0 million
- **Men only** 1,080 undergraduate students, 100% full-time
- **Moderately difficult** entrance level, 56% of applicants were admitted

Undergraduates 1,080 full-time. Students come from 33 states and territories; 19 other countries; 29% are from out of state; 9% Black or African American, non-Hispanic/Latino; 2% Hispanic/Latino; 1% Asian, non-Hispanic/Latino; 0.6% American Indian or Alaska Native, non-Hispanic/Latino; 4% Two or more races, non-Hispanic/Latino; 1% Race/ethnicity unknown; 0.8% international; 2% transferred in; 95% live on campus. *Retention:* 78% of full-time freshmen returned.

Freshmen *Admission:* 2,630 applied, 1,463 admitted, 342 enrolled. *Average high school GPA:* 3.4. *Test scores:* SAT critical reading scores over 500: 75%; SAT math scores over 500: 80%; SAT critical reading scores over 600: 34%; SAT math scores over 600: 34%; SAT critical reading scores over 700: 6%; SAT math scores over 700: 4%.

Faculty *Total:* 106, 89% full-time, 92% with terminal degrees. *Student/faculty ratio:* 11:1.

Academics *Calendar:* semesters. *Degree:* bachelor's. *Special study options:* academic remediation for entering students, advanced placement credit, double majors, honors programs, independent study, internships, off-campus study, study abroad, summer session for credit. *ROTC:* Army (c). *Unusual degree programs:* 3-2 engineering with University of Virginia.

Computers on Campus 200 computers/terminals are available on campus for general student use. Students can access the following: campus intranet, computer help desk, free student e-mail accounts, online (class) grades, online (class) registration, online (class) schedules. Campuswide network is available. 100% of college-owned or -operated housing units are wired for high-speed Internet access. Wireless service is available via entire campus.

Student Life *Housing:* on-campus residence required through senior year. *Options:* men-only. Campus housing is university owned. Freshman campus housing is guaranteed. *Activities and organizations:* drama/theater group, student-run newspaper, radio station, choral group, Republican Society, Pre-Health Society, Outdoors Club, Tiger Athletic Club, Pre-Law Society, national fraternities. *Campus security:* 24-hour emergency response devices and patrols. *Student services:* health clinic, personal/psychological counseling.

Athletics Member NCAA. All Division III. *Intercollegiate sports:* baseball M, basketball M, crew M(c), cross-country running M, fencing M(c), football M, golf M, lacrosse M, riflery M(c), rugby M(c), soccer M, swimming and diving M, tennis M, ultimate Frisbee M(c). *Intramural sports:* basketball M, football M, soccer M, softball M, volleyball M.

Standardized Tests *Required:* SAT or ACT (for admission). *Recommended:* SAT Subject Tests (for admission).

Costs (2012–13) *Comprehensive fee:* $46,736 includes full-time tuition ($34,498), mandatory fees ($1072), and room and board ($11,166). *Room and board:* Room and board charges vary according to board plan and housing facility. *Payment plan:* installment. *Waivers:* employees or children of employees.

Financial Aid Of all full-time matriculated undergraduates who enrolled in 2012, 786 applied for aid, 657 were judged to have need, 122 had their need fully met. 255 Federal Work-Study jobs (averaging $1372). In 2012, 409 non-need-based awards were made. *Average percent of need met:* 81%. *Average financial aid package:* $28,572. *Average need-based loan:* $5242. *Average need-based gift aid:* $23,649. *Average non-need-based aid:* $12,527. *Average indebtedness upon graduation:* $30,248.

Applying *Options:* electronic application, early admission, early decision, early action. *Application fee:* $30. *Required:* essay or personal statement, high school transcript, minimum 2.0 GPA, 2 letters of recommendation. *Recommended:* minimum 3.0 GPA, interview. *Application deadlines:* 3/1 (freshmen), 7/1 (transfers), 1/15 (early action). *Early decision deadline:* 11/15. *Notification:* 4/15 (freshmen), 7/31 (transfers), 12/15 (early decision), 2/15 (early action).

Freshman Application Contact Ms. Anita Garland, Dean of Admissions, Hampden-Sydney College, PO Box 667, Hampden-Sydney, VA 23943-0667. *Phone:* 434-223-6120. *Toll-free phone:* 800-755-0733. *Fax:* 434-223-6346. *E-mail:* hsapp@hsc.edu.
Website: http://www.hsc.edu/.

Hampton University

Hampton, Virginia

- **Independent** comprehensive, founded 1868
- **Urban** 314-acre campus with easy access to Norfolk
- **Endowment** $240.0 million
- **Coed** 3,851 undergraduate students, 90% full-time, 64% women, 36% men
- **Moderately difficult** entrance level, 36% of applicants were admitted

Undergraduates 3,464 full-time, 387 part-time. Students come from 45 states and territories; 33 other countries; 51% are from out of state; 94% Black or African American, non-Hispanic/Latino; 0.9% Hispanic/Latino; 0.8% Asian, non-Hispanic/Latino; 0.1% American Indian or Alaska Native, non-Hispanic/Latino; 1% international; 5% transferred in; 53% live on campus. *Retention:* 76% of full-time freshmen returned.

Freshmen *Admission:* 14,503 applied, 5,285 admitted, 866 enrolled. *Average high school GPA:* 3.3. *Test scores:* SAT critical reading scores over 500: 55%; SAT math scores over 500: 57%; ACT scores over 18: 79%; SAT critical reading scores over 600: 12%; SAT math scores over 600: 13%; ACT scores over 24: 21%; SAT critical reading scores over 700: 2%; SAT math scores over 700: 1%; ACT scores over 30: 2%.

Faculty *Total:* 330, 98% full-time. *Student/faculty ratio:* 10:1.

Academics *Calendar:* semesters. *Degrees:* certificates, associate, bachelor's, master's, doctoral, and post-master's certificates. *Special study options:* academic remediation for entering students, accelerated degree program, adult/continuing education programs, advanced placement credit, cooperative education, distance learning, double majors, honors programs, independent study, internships, off-campus study, part-time degree program, services for LD students, study abroad, summer session for credit. *ROTC:* Army (b), Navy (b).

Computers on Campus 1,300 computers/terminals are available on campus for general student use. Students can access the following: campus intranet, computer help desk, free student e-mail accounts, online (class) grades, online (class) registration, online (class) schedules, Banner Systems. Campuswide network is available. Wireless service is available via entire campus.

Student Life *Housing options:* coed, men-only, women-only. Campus housing is university owned. Freshman applicants given priority for college housing. *Activities and organizations:* drama/theater group, student-run newspaper, radio station, choral group, marching band, student government, student leaders, Student Union Board, student recruitment team, resident assistants, national fraternities, national sororities. *Campus security:* 24-hour emergency response devices and patrols, controlled dormitory access, emergency call boxes. *Student services:* health clinic, personal/psychological counseling, women's center.

Athletics Member NCAA. All Division I. *Intercollegiate sports:* basketball M(s)/W(s), bowling W(s), cheerleading W, cross-country running M(s)/W(s), football M(s), golf M(s)/W(s), sailing M(s)/W(s), softball W(s), tennis M(s)/W(s), track and field M(s)/W(s), volleyball W(s). *Intramural sports:* badminton M/W, basketball M/W, bowling W, football M, lacrosse M, sailing M/W, soccer M/W, softball M/W, volleyball W.

Standardized Tests *Required:* SAT or ACT (for admission).

Costs (2013–14) *Comprehensive fee:* $29,954 includes full-time tuition ($18,618), mandatory fees ($2106), and room and board ($9230). Full-time tuition and fees vary according to course load, degree level, location, and program. Part-time tuition: $472 per credit. Part-time tuition and fees vary according to course load and location. *College room only:* $4800. Room and board charges vary according to board plan, housing facility, and location. *Payment plan:* deferred payment. *Waivers:* employees or children of employees.

Financial Aid Of all full-time matriculated undergraduates who enrolled in 2011, 2,176 applied for aid, 1,924 were judged to have need, 1,005 had their need fully met. 196 Federal Work-Study jobs (averaging $704). 14 state and other part-time jobs (averaging $1107). In 2011, 93 non-need-based awards were made. *Average percent of need met:* 54%. *Average financial aid package:* $4982. *Average need-based loan:* $4000. *Average need-based gift aid:* $4587. *Average non-need-based aid:* $12,737. *Average indebtedness upon graduation:* $10,119. *Financial aid deadline:* 4/15.

Applying *Options:* electronic application, early admission, early action, deferred entrance. *Application fee:* $35. *Required:* essay or personal statement, high school transcript, minimum 2.5 GPA, 3 letters of recommendation. *Application deadlines:* 3/1 (freshmen), 11/1 (early action). *Notification:* 12/31 (early action).

Freshman Application Contact Mr. Derrick Boone, Director, Freshman Studies, Hampton University, 204 Student Center, Hampton University, Hampton, VA 23668. *Phone:* 757-727-5901. *Toll-free phone:* 800-624-3328. *Fax:* 757-727-5095. *E-mail:* derrickboone@hamptonu.edu. *Website:* http://www.hamptonu.edu/.

Hollins University

Roanoke, Virginia

- **Independent** comprehensive, founded 1842
- **Suburban** 475-acre campus
- **Endowment** $154.5 million
- **Undergraduate: women only; graduate: coed** 613 undergraduate students, 97% full-time, 100% women
- **Moderately difficult** entrance level, 66% of applicants were admitted

Undergraduates 594 full-time, 19 part-time. Students come from 42 states and territories; 13 other countries; 43% are from out of state; 11% Black or African American, non-Hispanic/Latino; 5% Hispanic/Latino; 2% Asian, non-Hispanic/Latino; 0.3% Native Hawaiian or other Pacific Islander, non-Hispanic/Latino; 0.3% American Indian or Alaska Native, non-Hispanic/Latino; 3% Two or more races, non-Hispanic/Latino; 1% Race/ethnicity unknown; 5% international; 2% transferred in; 77% live on campus. *Retention:* 70% of full-time freshmen returned.

Freshmen *Admission:* 814 applied, 537 admitted, 128 enrolled. *Average high school GPA:* 3.6. *Test scores:* SAT critical reading scores over 500: 81%; SAT math scores over 500: 67%; SAT writing scores over 500: 68%; ACT scores over 18: 92%; SAT critical reading scores over 600: 48%; SAT math scores over 600: 22%; SAT writing scores over 600: 35%; ACT scores over 24: 54%; SAT critical reading scores over 700: 14%; SAT math scores over 700: 2%; SAT writing scores over 700: 10%; ACT scores over 30: 8%.

Faculty *Total:* 105, 68% full-time, 84% with terminal degrees. *Student/faculty ratio:* 9:1.

Academics *Calendar:* 4-1-4. *Degrees:* bachelor's, master's, post-master's, and postbachelor's certificates. *Special study options:* accelerated degree program, adult/continuing education programs, advanced placement credit, double majors, independent study, internships, off-campus study, part-time degree program, services for LD students, student-designed majors, study abroad.

Computers on Campus 100 computers/terminals and 3,000 ports are available on campus for general student use. Students can access the following: campus intranet, computer help desk, free student e-mail accounts, online (class) grades, online (class) registration, online (class) schedules, applications software. Campuswide network is available. 100% of college-owned or -operated housing units are wired for high-speed Internet access. Wireless service is available via entire campus.

Student Life *Housing:* on-campus residence required through senior year. *Options:* women-only, disabled students. Campus housing is university owned. Freshman campus housing is guaranteed. *Activities and organizations:* drama/theater group, student-run newspaper, radio and television station, choral group, Student Government Association, SHARE (volunteer group), Hollins Activity Board, Student Athletic Association, Black Student Alliance. *Campus security:* 24-hour emergency response devices and patrols, late-night transport/escort service, controlled dormitory access, emergency call boxes. *Student services:* health clinic, personal/psychological counseling, women's center.

Athletics Member NCAA. All Division III. *Intercollegiate sports:* basketball W, equestrian sports W, fencing W(c), golf W, lacrosse W, soccer W, swimming and diving W, tennis W, volleyball W.

Standardized Tests *Required:* SAT or ACT (for admission).

Costs (2012–13) *Comprehensive fee:* $43,295 includes full-time tuition ($31,490), mandatory fees ($585), and room and board ($11,220). Part-time tuition: $986 per credit hour. *Required fees:* $149 per term part-time. *College room only:* $6700. *Payment plans:* tuition prepayment, installment. *Waivers:* employees or children of employees.

Financial Aid Of all full-time matriculated undergraduates who enrolled in 2011, 584 applied for aid, 525 were judged to have need, 98 had their need fully met. 132 Federal Work-Study jobs (averaging $1756). 165 state and other part-time jobs (averaging $1725). In 2011, 158 non-need-based awards were made. *Average percent of need met:* 81%. *Average financial aid package:* $25,689. *Average need-based loan:* $4916. *Average need-based gift aid:* $20,643. *Average non-need-based aid:* $17,186. *Average indebtedness upon graduation:* $30,383. *Financial aid deadline:* 2/15.

Applying *Options:* electronic application, early admission, early decision, early action, deferred entrance. *Application fee:* $40. *Required:* essay or personal statement, high school transcript, 2 letters of recommendation. *Recommended:* interview. *Application deadlines:* rolling (freshmen), 12/1 (early action). *Early decision deadline:* 11/1. *Notification:* continuous (freshmen), 11/15 (early decision), 12/15 (early action).

Freshman Application Contact Ms. Nicole Johnson Williams, Associate Dean of Admissions, Hollins University, PO Box 9707, Roanoke, VA 24020-1707. *Phone:* 540-362-6401. *Toll-free phone:* 800-456-9595. *Fax:* 540-362-6218. *E-mail:* huadm@hollins.edu. *Website:* http://www.hollins.edu/.

ITT Technical Institute

Chantilly, Virginia

- **Proprietary** primarily 2-year, founded 2002, part of ITT Educational Services, Inc.
- **Coed**
- **Minimally difficult** entrance level

Academics *Calendar:* quarters. *Degrees:* associate and bachelor's.
Freshman Application Contact Director of Recruitment, ITT Technical Institute, 14420 Abermarle Point Place, Suite 100, Chantilly, VA 20151. *Phone:* 703-263-2541. *Toll-free phone:* 888-895-8324.
Website: http://www.itt-tech.edu/.

ITT Technical Institute

Norfolk, Virginia

- **Proprietary** primarily 2-year, founded 1988, part of ITT Educational Services, Inc.
- **Suburban** campus
- **Coed**
- **Minimally difficult** entrance level

Academics *Calendar:* quarters. *Degrees:* associate and bachelor's.
Financial Aid *Of all full-time matriculated undergraduates who enrolled in 2011,* 3 Federal Work-Study jobs (averaging $5000).
Freshman Application Contact Director of Recruitment, ITT Technical Institute, 863 Glenrock Road, Suite 100, Norfolk, VA 23502-3701. *Phone:* 757-466-1260. *Toll-free phone:* 888-253-8324.
Website: http://www.itt-tech.edu/.

ITT Technical Institute

Richmond, Virginia

- **Proprietary** primarily 2-year, founded 1999, part of ITT Educational Services, Inc.
- **Coed**
- **Minimally difficult** entrance level

Academics *Calendar:* quarters. *Degrees:* associate and bachelor's.
Freshman Application Contact Director of Recruitment, ITT Technical Institute, 300 Gateway Centre Parkway, Richmond, VA 23235. *Phone:* 804-330-4992. *Toll-free phone:* 888-330-4888.
Website: http://www.itt-tech.edu/.

ITT Technical Institute

Salem, Virginia

- **Proprietary** primarily 2-year
- **Coed**
- **Minimally difficult** entrance level

Academics *Degrees:* associate and bachelor's.
Freshman Application Contact Director of Recruitment, ITT Technical Institute, 2159 Apperson Drive, Salem, VA 24153. *Phone:* 540-989-2500. *Toll-free phone:* 877-208-6132.
Website: http://www.itt-tech.edu/.

ITT Technical Institute

Springfield, Virginia

- **Proprietary** primarily 2-year, founded 2002, part of ITT Educational Services, Inc.
- **Coed**
- **Minimally difficult** entrance level

Academics *Calendar:* quarters. *Degrees:* associate and bachelor's.
Freshman Application Contact Director of Recruitment, ITT Technical Institute, 7300 Boston Boulevard, Springfield, VA 22153. *Phone:* 703-440-9535. *Toll-free phone:* 866-817-8324.
Website: http://www.itt-tech.edu/.

James Madison University

Harrisonburg, Virginia

- **State-supported** comprehensive, founded 1908
- **Small-town** 721-acre campus
- **Endowment** $59.6 million
- **Coed** 17,900 undergraduate students, 95% full-time, 59% women, 41% men
- **Very difficult** entrance level, 60% of applicants were admitted

Undergraduates 17,086 full-time, 814 part-time. Students come from 48 states and territories; 60 other countries; 27% are from out of state; 4% Black or African American, non-Hispanic/Latino; 4% Hispanic/Latino; 5% Asian, non-Hispanic/Latino; 0.4% Native Hawaiian or other Pacific Islander, non-Hispanic/Latino; 0.2% American Indian or Alaska Native, non-Hispanic/Latino; 2% Two or more races, non-Hispanic/Latino; 5% Race/ethnicity unknown; 1% international; 4% transferred in; 36% live on campus. *Retention:* 91% of full-time freshmen returned.
Freshmen *Admission:* 22,864 applied, 13,705 admitted, 4,029 enrolled. *Average high school GPA:* 3.83. *Test scores:* SAT critical reading scores over 500: 85%; SAT math scores over 500: 89%; ACT scores over 18: 99%; SAT critical reading scores over 600: 35%; SAT math scores over 600: 40%; ACT scores over 24: 65%; SAT critical reading scores over 700: 5%; SAT math scores over 700: 5%; ACT scores over 30: 6%.
Faculty *Total:* 1,400, 66% full-time, 61% with terminal degrees. *Student/faculty ratio:* 16:1.
Academics *Calendar:* semesters. *Degrees:* bachelor's, master's, doctoral, and post-master's certificates (also offers specialist in education degree). *Special study options:* accelerated degree program, adult/continuing education programs, advanced placement credit, distance learning, double majors, English as a second language, freshman honors college, honors programs, independent study, internships, off-campus study, part-time degree program, services for LD students, student-designed majors, study abroad, summer session for credit. *ROTC:* Army (b), Air Force (c). *Unusual degree programs:* 3-2 forestry with Virginia Polytechnic Institute and State University.
Computers on Campus 600 computers/terminals and 7,000 ports are available on campus for general student use. Students can access the following: campus intranet, computer help desk, free student e-mail accounts, online (class) grades, online (class) registration, online (class) schedules. Campus-wide network is available. 100% of college-owned or -operated housing units are wired for high-speed Internet access. Wireless service is available via classrooms, dorm rooms, learning centers, libraries, student centers.
Student Life *Housing:* on-campus residence required for freshman year. *Options:* coed, disabled students. Campus housing is university owned and leased by the school. Freshman campus housing is guaranteed. *Activities and organizations:* drama/theater group, student-run newspaper, radio station, choral group, marching band, national fraternities, national sororities. *Campus security:* 24-hour emergency response devices and patrols, student patrols, late-night transport/escort service, controlled dormitory access, lighted pathways. *Student services:* health clinic, personal/psychological counseling, women's center.
Athletics Member NCAA. All Division I except football (Division I-AA). *Intercollegiate sports:* baseball M(s), basketball M(s)/W(s), cheerleading M/W, cross-country running W(s), field hockey W(s), golf M(s)/W(s), lacrosse W(s), soccer M(s)/W(s), softball W(s), swimming and diving W(s), tennis M(s)/W(s), track and field W(s), volleyball W(s). *Intramural sports:* archery M(c)/W(c), baseball M(c), basketball M/W, bowling M/W, cheerleading W(c), crew M(c)/W(c), cross-country running M(c)/W(c), equestrian sports M(c)/W(c), fencing M(c)/W(c), field hockey W(c), football M/W, golf M/W, gymnastics M(c)/W(c), ice hockey M(c)/W(c), lacrosse M(c)/W(c), racquetball M/W, rugby M(c)/W(c), skiing (downhill) M(c)/W(c), soccer M/W, softball M/W, squash M(c)/W(c), swimming and diving M(c)/W(c), table tennis M/W, tennis M/W, track and field M(c)/W(c), ultimate Frisbee M(c)/W(c), volleyball M/W, water polo M(c)/W(c), wrestling M(c).
Standardized Tests *Required:* SAT or ACT (for admission).
Costs (2013–14) *Tuition:* $161 per credit hour part-time; state resident $4862 full-time; nonresident $18,850 full-time, $609 per credit hour part-time. *Required fees:* $3946 full-time. *Room and board:* $8630; room only: $4350. Room and board charges vary according to board plan. *Payment plans:* tuition prepayment, installment. *Waivers:* employees or children of employees.
Financial Aid Of all full-time matriculated undergraduates who enrolled in 2012, 10,026 applied for aid, 6,788 were judged to have need, 4,593 had their need fully met. In 2012, 223 non-need-based awards were made. *Average percent of need met:* 46%. *Average financial aid package:* $9240. *Average need-based loan:* $4628. *Average need-based gift aid:* $7405. *Average non-need-based aid:* $3126. *Average indebtedness upon graduation:* $22,792.
Applying *Options:* electronic application, early action, deferred entrance. *Application fee:* $50. *Required:* high school transcript. *Recommended:* mini-

COLLEGES AT-A-GLANCE

mum 3.0 GPA. *Application deadlines:* 1/15 (freshmen), 3/15 (transfers), 11/1 (early action). *Notification:* 4/1 (freshmen), 5/1 (transfers), 1/1 (early action). **Freshman Application Contact** James Madison University, 800 South Main Street, Harrisonburg, VA 22807. *Phone:* 540-568-5681. *Website:* http://www.jmu.edu/.

Jefferson College of Health Sciences

Roanoke, Virginia

Freshman Application Contact Jefferson College of Health Sciences, PO Box 13186, Roanoke, VA 24031-3186. *Phone:* 540-985-9083. *Toll-free phone:* 888-985-8483. *Website:* http://www.jchs.edu/.

Liberty University

Lynchburg, Virginia

- **Independent nondenominational** comprehensive, founded 1971
- **Suburban** 6500-acre campus
- **Coed** 11,581 undergraduate students, 97% full-time, 52% women, 48% men
- **Minimally difficult** entrance level, 23% of applicants were admitted

Undergraduates 11,231 full-time, 350 part-time. Students come from 78 other countries; 58% are from out of state; 7% Black or African American, non-Hispanic/Latino; 3% Hispanic/Latino; 1% Asian, non-Hispanic/Latino; 0.2% Native Hawaiian or other Pacific Islander, non-Hispanic/Latino; 0.4% American Indian or Alaska Native, non-Hispanic/Latino; 2% Two or more races, non-Hispanic/Latino; 10% Race/ethnicity unknown; 6% international; 6% transferred in; 61% live on campus. *Retention:* 81% of full-time freshmen returned.

Freshmen *Admission:* 25,976 applied, 5,907 admitted, 2,629 enrolled. *Average high school GPA:* 3.36. *Test scores:* SAT critical reading scores over 500: 62%; SAT math scores over 500: 57%; SAT writing scores over 500: 57%; ACT scores over 18: 90%; SAT critical reading scores over 600: 21%; SAT

math scores over 600: 18%; SAT writing scores over 600: 17%; ACT scores over 24: 39%; SAT critical reading scores over 700: 3%; SAT math scores over 700: 2%; SAT writing scores over 700: 2%; ACT scores over 30: 7%.

Faculty *Total:* 629, 85% full-time. *Student/faculty ratio:* 23:1.

Academics *Calendar:* semesters. *Degrees:* certificates, associate, bachelor's, master's, doctoral, and post-master's certificates (also offers external degree program with significant enrollment not reflected in profile). *Special study options:* academic remediation for entering students, accelerated degree program, advanced placement credit, cooperative education, distance learning, double majors, English as a second language, external degree program, honors programs, independent study, internships, off-campus study, part-time degree program, services for LD students, student-designed majors, study abroad, summer session for credit. *ROTC:* Army (b), Air Force (c).

Computers on Campus 800 computers/terminals are available on campus for general student use. Students can access the following: computer help desk, free student e-mail accounts, online (class) grades, online (class) registration, online (class) schedules. Campuswide network is available. 100% of college-owned or -operated housing units are wired for high-speed Internet access. Wireless service is available via entire campus.

Student Life *Housing:* on-campus residence required through senior year. *Options:* men-only, women-only, disabled students. Campus housing is university owned. Freshman campus housing is guaranteed. *Activities and organizations:* drama/theater group, student-run newspaper, radio station, choral group, marching band, Campus Serve. *Campus security:* 24-hour patrols, late-night transport/escort service, 24-hour emergency dispatch. *Student services:* health clinic, personal/psychological counseling.

Athletics Member NCAA. All Division I except football (Division I-AA). *Intercollegiate sports:* baseball M(s), basketball M(s)/W(s), cheerleading M(s)/W(s), crew M(c)/W(c), cross-country running M(s)/W(s), equestrian sports W(c), field hockey W(s), golf M(s), ice hockey M(c)/W(c), lacrosse W(s), soccer M(s)/W(s), softball W(s), swimming and diving W(s), tennis M(s)/W(s), track and field M(s)/W(s), volleyball M(c)/W(s). *Intramural sports:* archery M(c)/W(c), basketball M/W, football M/W, lacrosse M(c), racquetball M(c)/W(c), soccer M/W, softball M/W, table tennis M/W, tennis M/W, ultimate Frisbee M(c)/W(c), wrestling M(c).

Standardized Tests *Required:* SAT or ACT (for admission).

Costs (2013–14) *Comprehensive fee:* $28,868 includes full-time tuition ($19,486), mandatory fees ($1406), and room and board ($7976). Full-time tuition and fees vary according to course load. Part-time tuition: $650 per credit hour. Part-time tuition and fees vary according to course load. *Required fees:* $1550 per year part-time. *Room and board:* Room and board charges vary

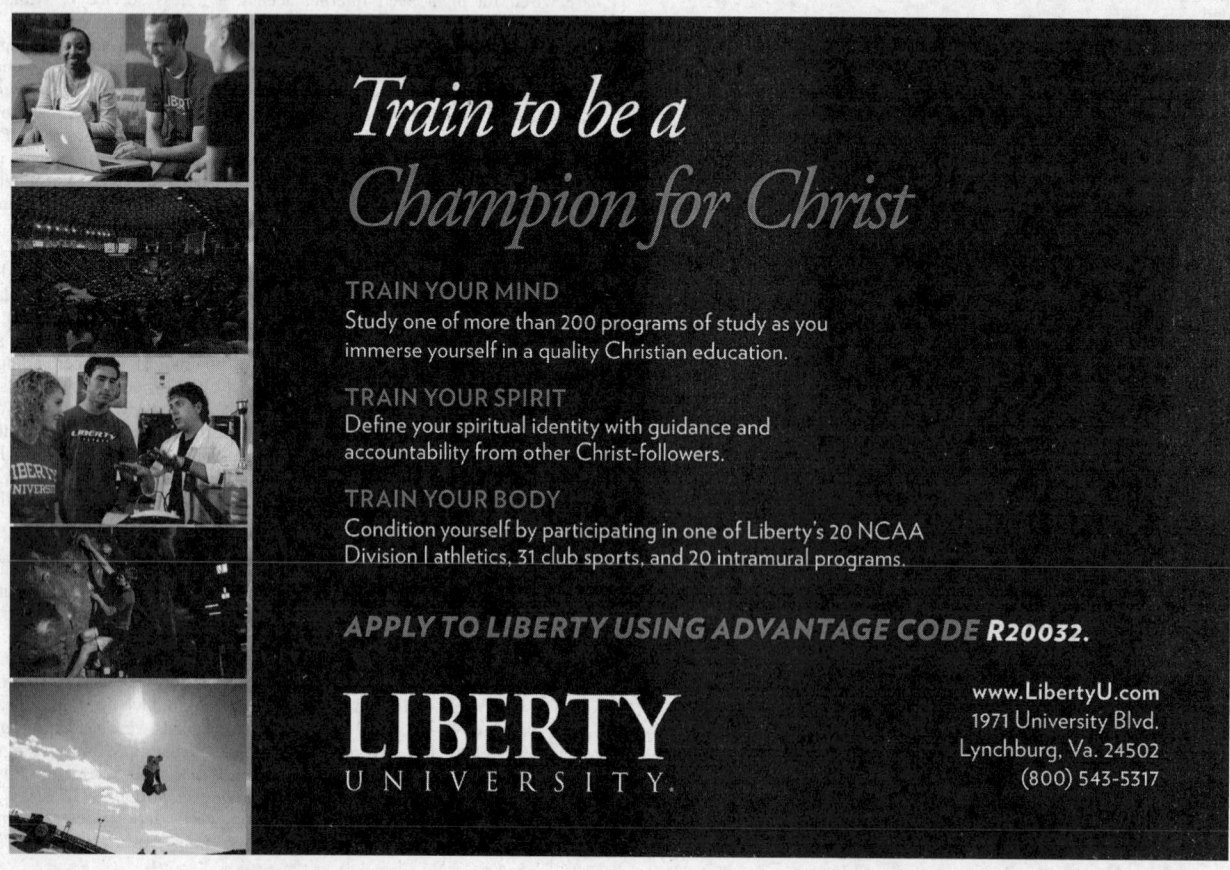

according to housing facility. *Payment plan:* installment. *Waivers:* employees or children of employees.

Financial Aid Of all full-time matriculated undergraduates who enrolled in 2012, 10,198 applied for aid, 8,285 were judged to have need, 909 had their need fully met. In 2012, 741 non-need-based awards were made. *Average percent of need met:* 58%. *Average financial aid package:* $12,985. *Average need-based loan:* $4169. *Average need-based gift aid:* $9065. *Average non-need-based aid:* $7987. *Average indebtedness upon graduation:* $21,830. *Financial aid deadline:* 3/1.

Applying *Options:* electronic application. *Application fee:* $40. *Required:* essay or personal statement, high school transcript, minimum 2.0 GPA. *Recommended:* minimum 2.0 GPA. *Application deadlines:* rolling (freshmen), rolling (out-of-state freshmen), rolling (transfers). *Notification:* continuous (freshmen), continuous (out-of-state freshmen), continuous (transfers).

Freshman Application Contact Dr. Terry Elam, Director of Admissions, Liberty University, 1971 University Boulevard, Lynchburg, VA 24502. *Phone:* 434-592-3966. *Toll-free phone:* 800-543-5317. *Fax:* 800-542-2311. *E-mail:* admissions@liberty.edu. *Website:* http://www.liberty.edu/.

See previous page for display ad and page 1354 for the College Close-Up.

Longwood University

Farmville, Virginia

- **State-supported** comprehensive, founded 1839, part of The State Council of Higher Education for Virginia
- **Small-town** 60-acre campus with easy access to Richmond
- **Endowment** $49.9 million
- **Coed** 4,355 undergraduate students, 91% full-time, 66% women, 34% men
- **Moderately difficult** entrance level, 78% of applicants were admitted

Undergraduates 3,963 full-time, 392 part-time. Students come from 25 states and territories; 15 other countries; 4% are from out of state; 7% Black or African American, non-Hispanic/Latino; 4% Hispanic/Latino; 1% Asian, non-Hispanic/Latino; 0.2% Native Hawaiian or other Pacific Islander, non-Hispanic/Latino; 0.2% American Indian or Alaska Native, non-Hispanic/Latino; 3% Two or more races, non-Hispanic/Latino; 3% Race/ethnicity unknown; 0.8% international; 5% transferred in; 71% live on campus. *Retention:* 79% of full-time freshmen returned.

Freshmen *Admission:* 4,166 applied, 3,234 admitted, 976 enrolled. *Average high school GPA:* 3.39. *Test scores:* SAT critical reading scores over 500: 68%; SAT math scores over 500: 64%; ACT scores over 18: 100%; SAT critical reading scores over 600: 15%; SAT math scores over 600: 11%; ACT scores over 24: 30%; SAT critical reading scores over 700: 1%; SAT math scores over 700: 1%.

Faculty *Total:* 288, 78% full-time, 73% with terminal degrees. *Student/faculty ratio:* 18:1.

Academics *Calendar:* semesters. *Degrees:* bachelor's, master's, post-master's, and postbachelor's certificates. *Special study options:* accelerated degree program, advanced placement credit, distance learning, double majors, English as a second language, honors programs, independent study, internships, off-campus study, part-time degree program, services for LD students, study abroad, summer session for credit. *ROTC:* Army (b). *Unusual degree programs:* 3-2 engineering with University of Virginia, Old Dominion University, Virginia Polytechnic Institute and State University.

Computers on Campus 315 computers/terminals and 650 ports are available on campus for general student use. Students can access the following: campus intranet, computer help desk, free student e-mail accounts, online (class) grades, online (class) registration, online (class) schedules. Campuswide network is available. 100% of college-owned or -operated housing units are wired for high-speed Internet access. Wireless service is available via classrooms, computer centers, computer labs, libraries, student centers.

Student Life *Housing:* on-campus residence required through sophomore year. *Options:* coed, women-only, disabled students. Campus housing is university owned. Freshman campus housing is guaranteed. *Activities and organizations:* drama/theater group, student-run newspaper, radio station, choral group, Student Government Association, Alpha Phi Omega, Inter-Varsity Christian Fellowship, Longwood Ambassadors, Wellness Advocates, national fraternities, national sororities. *Campus security:* 24-hour emergency response devices and patrols, late-night transport/escort service, controlled dormitory access. *Student services:* health clinic, personal/psychological counseling.

Athletics Member NCAA. All Division I. *Intercollegiate sports:* baseball M(s), basketball M(s)/W(s), cross-country running M(s)/W(s), equestrian sports M(c)/W(c), field hockey W(s), football M(c), golf M(s)/W(s), lacrosse M(c)/W(s), rugby M(c)/W(s), soccer M(s)/W(s), softball W(s), swimming and diving M(c)/W(s), tennis M(s)/W(s), volleyball M(c)/W(s), wrestling M(c).

Intramural sports: baseball M(c), basketball M(c)/W(c), bowling M/W, cheerleading M/W, field hockey W(c), football M/W, golf M/W, racquetball M/W, soccer M(c)/W(c), softball M/W, table tennis M/W, tennis M/W, ultimate Frisbee M/W, volleyball M/W.

Standardized Tests *Required:* SAT or ACT (for admission).

Costs (2012–13) *Tuition:* state resident $6120 full-time, $204 per credit hour part-time; nonresident $17,760 full-time, $592 per credit hour part-time. Full-time tuition and fees vary according to course load. Part-time tuition and fees vary according to course load. *Required fees:* $4770 full-time, $159 per credit hour part-time. *Room and board:* $8448; room only: $5524. Room and board charges vary according to board plan, housing facility, and location. *Payment plan:* installment. *Waivers:* senior citizens and employees or children of employees.

Financial Aid Of all full-time matriculated undergraduates who enrolled in 2011, 3,050 applied for aid, 2,244 were judged to have need, 1,102 had their need fully met. 293 Federal Work-Study jobs (averaging $1420). 475 state and other part-time jobs (averaging $1300). In 2011, 167 non-need-based awards were made. *Average percent of need met:* 80%. *Average financial aid package:* $15,866. *Average need-based loan:* $7703. *Average need-based gift aid:* $6311. *Average non-need-based aid:* $4221. *Average indebtedness upon graduation:* $26,439.

Applying *Options:* electronic application, early admission, early action, deferred entrance. *Application fee:* $50. *Required:* essay or personal statement, high school transcript. *Application deadlines:* 3/1 (freshmen), 3/1 (out-of-state freshmen), 3/1 (transfers), 12/1 (early action). *Notification:* 6/1 (freshmen), 6/1 (out-of-state freshmen), continuous until 6/1 (transfers), 1/15 (early action).

Freshman Application Contact Mrs. Sallie McMullin, Dean of Admissions, Longwood University, 201 High Street, Farmville, VA 23909. *Phone:* 434-395-2060. *Toll-free phone:* 800-281-4677. *Fax:* 434-395-2332. *E-mail:* admissions@longwood.edu. *Website:* http://www.longwood.edu/.

Lynchburg College

Lynchburg, Virginia

- **Independent** comprehensive, founded 1903, affiliated with Christian Church (Disciples of Christ)
- **Suburban** 214-acre campus
- **Endowment** $74.6 million
- **Coed** 2,211 undergraduate students, 94% full-time, 59% women, 41% men
- **Moderately difficult** entrance level, 67% of applicants were admitted

Undergraduates 2,088 full-time, 123 part-time. Students come from 33 states and territories; 13 other countries; 33% are from out of state; 10% Black or African American, non-Hispanic/Latino; 3% Hispanic/Latino; 1% Asian, non-Hispanic/Latino; 0.4% American Indian or Alaska Native, non-Hispanic/Latino; 2% Two or more races, non-Hispanic/Latino; 3% Race/ethnicity unknown; 1% international; 4% transferred in; 77% live on campus. *Retention:* 73% of full-time freshmen returned.

Freshmen *Admission:* 4,474 applied, 3,013 admitted, 517 enrolled. *Average high school GPA:* 3.25. *Test scores:* SAT critical reading scores over 500: 51%; SAT math scores over 500: 51%; SAT writing scores over 500: 46%; ACT scores over 18: 84%; SAT critical reading scores over 600: 14%; SAT math scores over 600: 14%; SAT writing scores over 600: 11%; ACT scores over 24: 28%; SAT critical reading scores over 700: 1%; SAT math scores over 700: 1%; SAT writing scores over 700: 1%; ACT scores over 30: 2%.

Faculty *Total:* 297, 63% full-time, 61% with terminal degrees. *Student/faculty ratio:* 11:1.

Academics *Calendar:* semesters. *Degrees:* bachelor's, master's, doctoral, post-master's, and postbachelor's certificates. *Special study options:* accelerated degree program, adult/continuing education programs, advanced placement credit, distance learning, double majors, honors programs, independent study, internships, off-campus study, part-time degree program, services for LD students, study abroad, summer session for credit. *Unusual degree programs:* 3-2 engineering with Old Dominion University, University of Virginia.

Computers on Campus 300 computers/terminals are available on campus for general student use. Students can access the following: campus intranet, computer help desk, free student e-mail accounts, online (class) grades, online (class) registration, online (class) schedules. Campuswide network is available. 100% of college-owned or -operated housing units are wired for high-speed Internet access. Wireless service is available via entire campus.

Student Life *Housing:* on-campus residence required through junior year. *Options:* coed, disabled students. Campus housing is university owned. Freshman campus housing is guaranteed. *Activities and organizations:* drama/theater group, student-run newspaper, choral group, Student Government Association, Student Activities Board, Enrollment Student Ambassadors,

Emergency Services, Greek Life, national fraternities, national sororities. *Campus security:* 24-hour emergency response devices and patrols, late-night transport/escort service, controlled dormitory access. *Student services:* health clinic, personal/psychological counseling.

Athletics Member NCAA. All Division III. *Intercollegiate sports:* baseball M, basketball M/W, cheerleading M/W, cross-country running M/W, equestrian sports M/W, field hockey W, golf M, lacrosse M/W, soccer M/W, softball W, tennis M/W, track and field M/W, volleyball W. *Intramural sports:* basketball M(c)/W(c), equestrian sports M(c)/W(c), field hockey W(c), golf M(c)/W(c), ice hockey M(c), lacrosse M(c)/W(c), rugby M/W, soccer M(c)/W(c), softball W(c), tennis M(c)/W(c), volleyball M/W, wrestling M(c).

Standardized Tests *Required:* SAT or ACT (for admission).

Costs (2012–13) *Comprehensive fee:* $40,685 includes full-time tuition ($31,060), mandatory fees ($945), and room and board ($8680). Part-time tuition: $430 per credit hour. Part-time tuition and fees vary according to course load. *Required fees:* $5 per credit hour part-time. *College room only:* $4360. Room and board charges vary according to board plan and housing facility. *Payment plans:* tuition prepayment, installment. *Waivers:* adult students, senior citizens, and employees or children of employees.

Financial Aid Of all full-time matriculated undergraduates who enrolled in 2011, 1,797 applied for aid, 1,606 were judged to have need, 314 had their need fully met. 295 Federal Work-Study jobs (averaging $1000). 400 state and other part-time jobs (averaging $1400). In 2011, 435 non-need-based awards were made. *Average percent of need met:* 77%. *Average financial aid package:* $21,652. *Average need-based loan:* $3421. *Average need-based gift aid:* $18,151. *Average non-need-based aid:* $11,066. *Average indebtedness upon graduation:* $30,636.

Applying *Options:* electronic application, early admission, early decision, deferred entrance. *Application fee:* $30. *Required:* high school transcript. *Recommended:* essay or personal statement, 2 letters of recommendation, interview. *Application deadlines:* rolling (freshmen), rolling (transfers). *Early decision deadline:* 11/15. *Notification:* continuous (freshmen), continuous (transfers), 12/15 (early decision).

Freshman Application Contact Lynchburg College, 1501 Lakeside Drive, Lynchburg, VA 24501-3199. *Phone:* 434-544-8300. *Toll-free phone:* 800-426-8101.

Website: http://www.lynchburg.edu/.

See below for display ad and page 1370 for the College Close-Up.

Mary Baldwin College
Staunton, Virginia

- **Independent** comprehensive, founded 1842
- **Small-town** 54-acre campus
- **Endowment** $31.9 million
- **Coed, primarily women** 1,526 undergraduate students, 68% full-time, 93% women, 7% men
- **Moderately difficult** entrance level, 54% of applicants were admitted

Undergraduates 1,035 full-time, 491 part-time. Students come from 35 states and territories; 8 other countries; 40% are from out of state; 27% Black or African American, non-Hispanic/Latino; 6% Hispanic/Latino; 2% Asian, non-Hispanic/Latino; 0.1% Native Hawaiian or other Pacific Islander, non-Hispanic/Latino; 0.8% American Indian or Alaska Native, non-Hispanic/Latino; 4% Two or more races, non-Hispanic/Latino; 4% Race/ethnicity unknown; 3% international; 2% transferred in; 48% live on campus. *Retention:* 69% of full-time freshmen returned.

Freshmen *Admission:* 4,909 applied, 2,649 admitted, 245 enrolled. *Average high school GPA:* 3.27. *Test scores:* SAT critical reading scores over 500: 44%; SAT math scores over 500: 30%; SAT writing scores over 500: 36%; ACT scores over 18: 83%; SAT critical reading scores over 600: 18%; SAT math scores over 600: 7%; SAT writing scores over 600: 13%; ACT scores over 24: 35%; SAT critical reading scores over 700: 4%; SAT math scores over 700: 1%; SAT writing scores over 700: 3%; ACT scores over 30: 7%.

Faculty *Total:* 128, 59% full-time, 58% with terminal degrees. *Student/faculty ratio:* 12:1.

Academics *Calendar:* 4-1-4. *Degrees:* certificates, bachelor's, and master's. *Special study options:* academic remediation for entering students, accelerated degree program, adult/continuing education programs, advanced placement credit, double majors, English as a second language, external degree program, freshman honors college, honors programs, independent study, internships, off-campus study, part-time degree program, services for LD students, student-designed majors, study abroad. *ROTC:* Army (b), Navy (c), Air Force (c). *Unusual degree programs:* 3-2 engineering with University of Virginia; nursing with Vanderbilt University.

Computers on Campus 244 computers/terminals are available on campus for general student use. Students can access the following: computer help desk, free student e-mail accounts, online (class) grades, online (class) registration, online (class) schedules, 100% wireless. Campuswide network is available. 100% of college-owned or -operated housing units are wired for high-speed Internet access. Wireless service is available via entire campus.

Student Life *Housing:* on-campus residence required through senior year. *Options:* women-only. Campus housing is university owned. Freshman campus housing is guaranteed. *Activities and organizations:* drama/theater group, student-run newspaper, radio station, choral group, marching band, International Club council, Minority Clubs United, Student Senate, Baldwin Program Board, Resident Hall Association. *Campus security:* 24-hour emergency response devices and patrols, late-night transport/escort service, controlled dormitory access. *Student services:* health clinic, personal/psychological counseling.

Athletics Member NCAA. All Division III. *Intercollegiate sports:* basketball W, cross-country running W, soccer W, softball W, swimming and diving W(c), tennis W, volleyball W. *Intramural sports:* basketball W, fencing W(c), racquetball W, swimming and diving W, volleyball W.

Standardized Tests *Required:* SAT or ACT (for admission).

Costs (2013–14) *One-time required fee:* $100. *Comprehensive fee:* $37,120 includes full-time tuition ($28,360), mandatory fees ($360), and room and board ($8400). Full-time tuition and fees vary according to degree level. Part-time tuition: $427 per semester hour. Part-time tuition and fees vary according to degree level. *Required fees:* $427 per semester hour part-time. *College room only:* $5360. Room and board charges vary according to housing facility. *Payment plan:* installment. *Waivers:* employees or children of employees.

Financial Aid Of all full-time matriculated undergraduates who enrolled in 2012, 944 applied for aid, 877 were judged to have need, 106 had their need fully met. 302 Federal Work-Study jobs (averaging $1255). 79 state and other part-time jobs (averaging $1577). In 2012, 105 non-need-based awards were made. *Average percent of need met:* 69%. *Average financial aid package:* $20,147. *Average need-based loan:* $4352. *Average need-based gift aid:* $15,944. *Average non-need-based aid:* $12,874. *Average indebtedness upon graduation:* $27,642.

Applying *Options:* electronic application, early admission, early decision, deferred entrance. *Application fee:* $35. *Required:* high school transcript, minimum 2.0 GPA, 1 letter of recommendation. *Recommended:* interview. *Application deadlines:* rolling (freshmen), rolling (transfers). *Early decision deadline:* 11/15. *Notification:* continuous (freshmen), continuous (transfers), 12/1 (early decision).

Freshman Application Contact Ms. Roberta Palmer, Director of Admissions, Mary Baldwin College, Frederick and New Streets, Staunton, VA 24401. *Phone:* 540-887-7260. *Toll-free phone:* 800-468-2262. *Fax:* 540-887-7229. *E-mail:* rpalmer@mbc.edu.
Website: http://www.mbc.edu/.

Marymount University

Arlington, Virginia

- **Independent** comprehensive, founded 1950, affiliated with Roman Catholic Church
- **Suburban** 21-acre campus with easy access to Washington, DC
- **Endowment** $23.0 million
- **Coed** 2,470 undergraduate students, 88% full-time, 70% women, 30% men
- **Moderately difficult** entrance level, 80% of applicants were admitted

Undergraduates 2,175 full-time, 295 part-time. Students come from 39 states and territories; 57 other countries; 37% are from out of state; 16% Black or African American, non-Hispanic/Latino; 15% Hispanic/Latino; 8% Asian, non-Hispanic/Latino; 0.5% Native Hawaiian or other Pacific Islander, non-Hispanic/Latino; 0.3% American Indian or Alaska Native, non-Hispanic/Latino; 3% Two or more races, non-Hispanic/Latino; 6% Race/ethnicity unknown; 10% international; 15% transferred in; 34% live on campus. *Retention:* 74% of full-time freshmen returned.

Freshmen *Admission:* 1,945 applied, 1,561 admitted, 375 enrolled. *Average high school GPA:* 3.21. *Test scores:* SAT critical reading scores over 500: 54%; SAT math scores over 500: 48%; SAT writing scores over 500: 49%; ACT scores over 18: 88%; SAT critical reading scores over 600: 11%; SAT math scores over 600: 10%; SAT writing scores over 600: 9%; ACT scores over 24: 25%; SAT critical reading scores over 700: 2%; SAT writing scores over 700: 1%.

Faculty *Total:* 370, 42% full-time, 63% with terminal degrees. *Student/faculty ratio:* 13:1.

Academics *Calendar:* semesters plus 2 summer terms. *Degrees:* certificates, bachelor's, master's, doctoral, post-master's, and postbachelor's certificates. *Special study options:* academic remediation for entering students, accelerated degree program, advanced placement credit, distance learning, double majors, English as a second language, honors programs, independent study, intern-

ships, off-campus study, part-time degree program, services for LD students, student-designed majors, study abroad, summer session for credit. *ROTC:* Army (c).

Computers on Campus 350 computers/terminals are available on campus for general student use. Students can access the following: campus intranet, computer help desk, free student e-mail accounts, online (class) grades, online (class) registration, online (class) schedules, online drive space. Campuswide network is available. 100% of college-owned or -operated housing units are wired for high-speed Internet access. Wireless service is available via entire campus.

Student Life *Housing:* on-campus residence required through sophomore year. *Options:* coed, men-only, women-only. Campus housing is university owned and leased by the school. Freshman applicants given priority for college housing. *Activities and organizations:* drama/theater group, student-run newspaper, choral group, Fashion Club, Student Nurses Association, International Club, Activities Programming Board, Blue Harmony (show choir). *Campus security:* 24-hour emergency response devices and patrols, late-night transport/escort service, controlled dormitory access. *Student services:* health clinic, personal/psychological counseling.

Athletics Member NCAA. All Division III. *Intercollegiate sports:* basketball M/W, cross-country running M/W, golf M, lacrosse M/W, soccer M/W, swimming and diving M/W, volleyball M/W. *Intramural sports:* basketball M/W, cheerleading W, football M/W, soccer M/W, ultimate Frisbee M/W, volleyball M/W, water polo M/W.

Standardized Tests *Required:* SAT or ACT (for admission).

Costs (2013–14) *One-time required fee:* $360. *Comprehensive fee:* $37,980 includes full-time tuition ($26,100), mandatory fees ($330), and room and board ($11,550). Part-time tuition: $850 per credit hour. *Room and board:* Room and board charges vary according to housing facility. *Payment plan:* installment. *Waivers:* senior citizens and employees or children of employees.

Financial Aid Of all full-time matriculated undergraduates who enrolled in 2012, 1,576 applied for aid, 1,387 were judged to have need, 202 had their need fully met. 715 Federal Work-Study jobs (averaging $1873). In 2012, 367 non-need-based awards were made. *Average percent of need met:* 59%. *Average financial aid package:* $16,113. *Average need-based loan:* $4565. *Average need-based gift aid:* $4663. *Average non-need-based aid:* $12,004. *Average indebtedness upon graduation:* $25,598.

Applying *Options:* electronic application, deferred entrance. *Application fee:* $40. *Required:* essay or personal statement, high school transcript, minimum 2.5 GPA, 1 letter of recommendation. *Required for some:* interview. *Recommended:* interview. *Application deadlines:* rolling (freshmen), rolling (transfers). *Notification:* continuous (freshmen), continuous (transfers).

Freshman Application Contact Mr. Mike Canfield, Director of Undergraduate Admissions, Marymount University, 2807 North Glebe Road, Arlington, VA 22207-4299. *Phone:* 703-284-1500. *Toll-free phone:* 800-548-7638. *Fax:* 703-522-0349. *E-mail:* admissions@marymount.edu.
Website: http://www.marymount.edu/.

National College

Danville, Virginia

Freshman Application Contact Admissions Office, National College, 336 Old Riverside Drive, Danville, VA 24541. *Phone:* 434-793-6822. *Toll-free phone:* 888-9-JOBREADY.
Website: http://www.national-college.edu/.

National College

Harrisonburg, Virginia

Director of Admissions Jack Evey, Campus Director, National College, 1515 Country Club Road, Harrisonburg, VA 22802. *Phone:* 540-432-0943. *Toll-free phone:* 888-9-JOBREADY.
Website: http://www.national-college.edu/.

National College

Lynchburg, Virginia

Freshman Application Contact Admissions Representative, National College, 104 Candlewood Court, Lynchburg, VA 24502-2653. *Phone:* 804-239-3500. *Toll-free phone:* 888-9-JOBREADY.
Website: http://www.national-college.edu/.

National College

Salem, Virginia

Freshman Application Contact Director of Admissions, National College, 1813 East Main Street, Salem, VA 24153. *Phone:* 540-986-1800. *Toll-free phone:* 888-9-JOBREADY. *Fax:* 540-444-4198.
Website: http://www.national-college.edu/.

Norfolk State University

Norfolk, Virginia

- **State-supported** comprehensive, founded 1935, part of State Council of Higher Education for Virginia
- **Urban** 134-acre campus
- **Coed** 7,455 undergraduate students, 84% full-time, 64% women, 36% men
- **Moderately difficult** entrance level, 67% of applicants were admitted

Undergraduates 6,263 full-time, 1,192 part-time. 16% are from out of state; 84% Black or African American, non-Hispanic/Latino; 2% Hispanic/Latino; 0.5% Asian, non-Hispanic/Latino; 0.1% Native Hawaiian or other Pacific Islander, non-Hispanic/Latino; 0.2% American Indian or Alaska Native, non-Hispanic/Latino; 2% Two or more races, non-Hispanic/Latino; 5% Race/ethnicity unknown; 0.5% international; 8% transferred in; 38% live on campus. *Retention:* 73% of full-time freshmen returned.
Freshmen *Admission:* 4,226 applied, 2,844 admitted, 1,088 enrolled. *Average high school GPA:* 2.8. *Test scores:* SAT critical reading scores over 500: 84%; SAT math scores over 500: 14%; SAT critical reading scores over 600: 23%; SAT math scores over 600: 1%.
Faculty *Total:* 417, 67% full-time. *Student/faculty ratio:* 19:1.
Academics *Calendar:* semesters. *Degrees:* associate, bachelor's, master's, and doctoral. *ROTC:* Army (b), Navy (b).
Computers on Campus Students can access the following: online (class) registration. Campuswide network is available.
Student Life *Housing options:* men-only, women-only. Campus housing is university owned. *Campus security:* 24-hour emergency response devices and patrols, late-night transport/escort service.
Athletics Member NCAA. All Division I. *Intercollegiate sports:* baseball M(s), basketball M(s)/W(s), bowling W, football M(s), softball W, tennis M(s)/W(s), track and field M(s)/W(s), volleyball W(s).
Standardized Tests *Required:* SAT or ACT (for admission).
Costs (2013–14) *Tuition:* state resident $6860 full-time, $252 per credit hour part-time; nonresident $20,343 full-time, $702 per credit hour part-time. Full-time tuition and fees vary according to course load. Part-time tuition and fees vary according to course load. *Room and board:* $8130. Room and board charges vary according to board plan and housing facility.
Financial Aid *Financial aid deadline:* 5/31.
Applying *Options:* electronic application, deferred entrance. *Required:* high school transcript, minimum 2.3 GPA. *Application deadline:* rolling (transfers).
Freshman Application Contact Mr. Kevin M. Holmes, Director of Recruitment and Admissions, Norfolk State University, 700 Park Avenue, Norfolk, VA 23504. *Phone:* 757-823-9222. *Toll-free phone:* 800-274-1821. *Fax:* 757-823-2078. *E-mail:* admissions@nsu.edu.
Website: http://www.nsu.edu/.

Old Dominion University

Norfolk, Virginia

- **State-supported** university, founded 1930
- **Urban** 251-acre campus with easy access to Virginia Beach
- **Endowment** $168.1 million
- **Coed** 19,612 undergraduate students, 76% full-time, 54% women, 46% men
- **Moderately difficult** entrance level, 72% of applicants were admitted

Undergraduates 14,949 full-time, 4,663 part-time. Students come from 47 states and territories; 69 other countries; 7% are from out of state; 25% Black or African American, non-Hispanic/Latino; 6% Hispanic/Latino; 4% Asian, non-Hispanic/Latino; 0.6% Native Hawaiian or other Pacific Islander, non-Hispanic/Latino; 0.4% American Indian or Alaska Native, non-Hispanic/Latino; 5% Two or more races, non-Hispanic/Latino; 4% Race/ethnicity

unknown; 1% international; 12% transferred in; 24% live on campus. *Retention:* 80% of full-time freshmen returned.
Freshmen *Admission:* 10,656 applied, 7,637 admitted, 2,702 enrolled. *Average high school GPA:* 3.25. *Test scores:* SAT critical reading scores over 500: 51%; SAT math scores over 500: 55%; ACT scores over 18: 81%; SAT critical reading scores over 600: 12%; SAT math scores over 600: 15%; ACT scores over 24: 21%; SAT critical reading scores over 700: 2%; SAT math scores over 700: 2%; ACT scores over 30: 2%.
Faculty *Total:* 1,294, 59% full-time, 57% with terminal degrees. *Student/faculty ratio:* 21:1.
Academics *Calendar:* semesters. *Degrees:* bachelor's, master's, doctoral, and post-master's certificates. *Special study options:* accelerated degree program, adult/continuing education programs, advanced placement credit, cooperative education, distance learning, double majors, English as a second language, freshman honors college, honors programs, independent study, internships, off-campus study, part-time degree program, services for LD students, student-designed majors, study abroad, summer session for credit. *ROTC:* Army (b), Navy (b). *Unusual degree programs:* 3-2 business administration; engineering; nursing; international studies, dental hygiene, communications/humanities, English, English/applied linguistics, history, interdisciplinary studies/humanities, computer science, women's studies/humanities, philosophy/humanities, health science/public health, environmental health/public health.
Computers on Campus 1,130 computers/terminals and 10,000 ports are available on campus for general student use. Students can access the following: campus intranet, computer help desk, free student e-mail accounts, online (class) grades, online (class) registration, online (class) schedules, online courses. Campuswide network is available. 100% of college-owned or -operated housing units are wired for high-speed Internet access. Wireless service is available via classrooms, computer centers, computer labs, dorm rooms, learning centers, libraries, student centers.
Student Life *Housing options:* coed, women-only, disabled students. Campus housing is university owned and leased by the school. Freshman applicants given priority for college housing. *Activities and organizations:* drama/theater group, student-run newspaper, radio station, choral group, marching band, Student Activities Council, F.O.R.E.I.G.N.E.R.S, Veteran Student Association, Anime Club, Ebony Impact Gospel Choir, national fraternities, national sororities. *Campus security:* 24-hour emergency response devices and patrols, student patrols, late-night transport/escort service, controlled dormitory access. *Student services:* health clinic, personal/psychological counseling, women's center.
Athletics Member NCAA. All Division I. *Intercollegiate sports:* baseball M(s), basketball M(s)/W(s), cheerleading W(s), crew M(c)/W(s), fencing M(c)/W(c), field hockey W(s), football M(s), golf M(s)/W(s), ice hockey M(c)/W(c), lacrosse M(c)/W(s), rock climbing M(c)/W(c), rugby M(c)/W(c), sailing M/W, soccer M(s)/W(s), softball W(c), swimming and diving M(s)/W(s), tennis M(s)/W(s), ultimate Frisbee M(c)/W(c), volleyball M(c)/W(c), wrestling M(s). *Intramural sports:* badminton M/W, basketball M/W, cross-country running M/W, golf M/W, racquetball M/W, rock climbing M/W, soccer M/W, softball M/W, table tennis M/W, tennis M/W, ultimate Frisbee M/W, volleyball M/W.
Standardized Tests *Required:* SAT or ACT (for admission).
Costs (2012–13) *Tuition:* state resident $8190 full-time, $273 per credit hour part-time; nonresident $23,070 full-time, $769 per credit hour part-time. *Required fees:* $260 full-time, $59 per term part-time. *Room and board:* $9066; room only: $5210. Room and board charges vary according to board plan and housing facility. *Payment plans:* installment, deferred payment. *Waivers:* senior citizens and employees or children of employees.
Financial Aid Of all full-time matriculated undergraduates who enrolled in 2012, 11,362 applied for aid, 9,217 were judged to have need, 1,248 had their need fully met. 220 Federal Work-Study jobs (averaging $2400). In 2012, 748 non-need-based awards were made. *Average percent of need met:* 49%. *Average financial aid package:* $9551. *Average need-based loan:* $4323. *Average need-based gift aid:* $6418. *Average non-need-based aid:* $3681. *Average indebtedness upon graduation:* $25,585. *Financial aid deadline:* 3/15.
Applying *Options:* electronic application, early admission, early action, deferred entrance. *Application fee:* $50. *Required:* high school transcript, minimum 2.7 GPA, test scores. *Recommended:* essay or personal statement, 1 letter of recommendation. *Application deadlines:* 2/1 (freshmen), 2/1 (out-of-state freshmen), 5/1 (transfers), 12/1 (early action). *Notification:* continuous (freshmen), continuous (out-of-state freshmen), continuous (transfers), 1/15 (early action).
Freshman Application Contact Ms. Shereen Williams, Customer Service Manager, Admissions Office, Old Dominion University, 108 Rollins Hall, 5215 Hampton Boulevard, Norfolk, VA 23529. *Phone:* 757-683-3648. *Toll-free phone:* 800-348-7926. *Fax:* 757-683-3255. *E-mail:* admissions@odu.edu. *Website:* http://www.odu.edu/.

Patrick Henry College

Purcellville, Virginia

- **Independent nondenominational** 4-year, founded 1999
- **Small-town** 106-acre campus with easy access to Washington, DC
- **Coed** 345 undergraduate students, 86% full-time, 47% women, 53% men
- **Very difficult** entrance level, 79% of applicants were admitted

Undergraduates 296 full-time, 49 part-time. Students come from 43 states and territories; 86% are from out of state; 0.6% Black or African American, non-Hispanic/Latino; 2% Hispanic/Latino; 3% Asian, non-Hispanic/Latino; 0.6% Native Hawaiian or other Pacific Islander, non-Hispanic/Latino; 0.3% American Indian or Alaska Native, non-Hispanic/Latino; 12% Race/ethnicity unknown; 3% transferred in; 90% live on campus. *Retention:* 88% of full-time freshmen returned.

Freshmen *Admission:* 239 applied, 190 admitted, 72 enrolled. **Faculty** *Total:* 47, 47% full-time, 64% with terminal degrees. *Student/faculty ratio:* 10:1.

Academics *Calendar:* semesters. *Degree:* bachelor's. *Special study options:* advanced placement credit, independent study, internships, off-campus study, summer session for credit.

Computers on Campus 6 computers/terminals and 100 ports are available on campus for general student use. Students can access the following: campus intranet, computer help desk, free student e-mail accounts, online (class) grades, online (class) registration, online (class) schedules. Campuswide network is available. 100% of college-owned or -operated housing units are wired for high-speed Internet access. Wireless service is available via entire campus.

Student Life *Housing:* on-campus residence required through sophomore year. *Options:* men-only, women-only. Campus housing is university owned. Freshman applicants given priority for college housing. *Activities and organizations:* drama/theater group, student-run newspaper, choral group, Drama Club, Eden Troupe, student government, chorale, College Republicans, Debate/Moot Court. *Campus security:* 24-hour emergency response devices, student patrols, late-night transport/escort service, controlled dormitory access, after hours patrols by trained security personnel.

Athletics *Intercollegiate sports:* basketball M/W, soccer M/W. *Intramural sports:* baseball M, basketball M/W, fencing M(c)/W(c), football M(c), racquetball M(c)/W(c), rugby M(c), table tennis M(c)/W(c), tennis M/W, ultimate Frisbee M/W, volleyball M/W, weight lifting M.

Standardized Tests *Required:* SAT or ACT (for admission).

Costs (2013–14) *Comprehensive fee:* $36,036 includes full-time tuition ($25,570), mandatory fees ($250), and room and board ($10,216). Full-time tuition and fees vary according to course load. Part-time tuition: $1065 per credit hour. Part-time tuition and fees vary according to course level and course load. *Room and board:* Room and board charges vary according to board plan. *Payment plans:* installment, deferred payment. *Waivers:* employees or children of employees.

Financial Aid Of all full-time matriculated undergraduates who enrolled in 2011, 202 applied for aid, 183 were judged to have need. In 2011, 135 non-need-based awards were made. *Average percent of need met:* 50%. *Average financial aid package:* $14,000. *Average need-based gift aid:* $11,000. *Average non-need-based aid:* $8200. *Average indebtedness upon graduation:* $25,500. *Financial aid deadline:* 6/15.

Applying *Options:* electronic application, early action, deferred entrance. *Application fee:* $40. *Required:* essay or personal statement, high school transcript, 2 letters of recommendation, interview, Official transcripts from all colleges attended; Reading List. *Application deadlines:* 6/15 (freshmen), 11/1 (early action). *Notification:* continuous (freshmen).

Freshman Application Contact Patrick Henry College, Ten Patrick Henry Circle, Purcellville, VA 20132. *Phone:* 540-338-1776. *E-mail:* admissions@phc.edu.

Website: http://www.phc.edu/.

Radford University

Radford, Virginia

- **State-supported** comprehensive, founded 1910
- **Small-town** 191-acre campus
- **Endowment** $42.9 million
- **Coed** 8,610 undergraduate students, 96% full-time, 56% women, 44% men
- **Moderately difficult** entrance level, 76% of applicants were admitted

Undergraduates 8,288 full-time, 322 part-time. Students come from 42 states and territories; 59 other countries; 5% are from out of state; 8% Black or African American, non-Hispanic/Latino; 4% Hispanic/Latino; 2% Asian, non-Hispanic/Latino; 0.3% Native Hawaiian or other Pacific Islander, non-Hispanic/Latino; 0.3% American Indian or Alaska Native, non-Hispanic/Latino; 2% Two or more races, non-Hispanic/Latino; 1% Race/ethnicity unknown; 0.6% international; 9% transferred in; 36% live on campus. *Retention:* 74% of full-time freshmen returned.

Freshmen *Admission:* 8,192 applied, 6,256 admitted, 2,053 enrolled. *Average high school GPA:* 3.15. *Test scores:* SAT critical reading scores over 500: 49%; SAT math scores over 500: 54%; SAT writing scores over 500: 41%; ACT scores over 18: 87%; SAT critical reading scores over 600: 8%; SAT math scores over 600: 9%; SAT writing scores over 600: 6%; ACT scores over 24: 21%; SAT critical reading scores over 700: 1%; ACT scores over 30: 1%.

Faculty *Total:* 663, 62% full-time, 61% with terminal degrees. *Student/faculty ratio:* 19:1.

Academics *Calendar:* semesters. *Degrees:* certificates, bachelor's, master's, doctoral, post-master's, and postbachelor's certificates. *Special study options:* accelerated degree program, advanced placement credit, distance learning, double majors, honors programs, independent study, internships, off-campus study, part-time degree program, services for LD students, student-designed majors, study abroad, summer session for credit. *ROTC:* Army (b).

Computers on Campus 772 computers/terminals are available on campus for general student use. Students can access the following: campus intranet, computer help desk, free student e-mail accounts, online (class) grades, online (class) registration, online (class) schedules, online financial aid status and student accounts payable. Campuswide network is available. 100% of college-owned or -operated housing units are wired for high-speed Internet access. Wireless service is available via entire campus.

Student Life *Housing:* on-campus residence required through sophomore year. *Options:* coed, disabled students. Campus housing is university owned and leased by the school. Freshman campus housing is guaranteed. *Activities and organizations:* drama/theater group, student-run newspaper, radio and television station, choral group, Think in Pink, National Society for Collegiate Scholars, Sigma Sigma Sigma (Greek sorority), The American Sign Language Club, Gay-Straight Alliance, national fraternities, national sororities. *Campus security:* 24-hour emergency response devices and patrols, late-night transport/escort service, controlled dormitory access. *Student services:* health clinic, personal/psychological counseling.

Athletics Member NCAA. All Division I. *Intercollegiate sports:* baseball M(s), basketball M(s)/W(s), cross-country running M(s)/W(s), field hockey W(s), golf M(s)/W(s), soccer M(s)/W(s), softball W(s), swimming and diving W(s), tennis M(s)/W(s), track and field M(s)/W(s), volleyball W(s). *Intramural sports:* baseball M(c), basketball M/W, bowling M/W, cross-country running M(c)/W(c), equestrian sports M(c)/W(c), field hockey W(c), football M(c), gymnastics M(c)/W(c), ice hockey M(c), lacrosse M(c)/W(c), riflery M(c)/W(c), rugby M(c), skiing (downhill) M(c)/W(c), soccer M(c)/W(c), softball M/W, swimming and diving M(c)/W(c), table tennis M/W, tennis M/W, ultimate Frisbee M/W, volleyball M/W, weight lifting M/W.

Standardized Tests *Required:* SAT or ACT (for admission).

Costs (2012–13) *Tuition:* state resident $5702 full-time, $238 per credit hour part-time; nonresident $16,826 full-time, $701 per credit hour part-time. Part-time tuition and fees vary according to course load. *Required fees:* $2888 full-time, $121 per credit hour part-time. *Room and board:* $7881; room only: $4307. Room and board charges vary according to board plan and housing facility. *Payment plan:* installment. *Waivers:* senior citizens and employees or children of employees.

Financial Aid Of all full-time matriculated undergraduates who enrolled in 2012, 5,864 applied for aid, 4,397 were judged to have need, 1,241 had their need fully met. 311 Federal Work-Study jobs (averaging $2267). 579 state and other part-time jobs (averaging $1970). In 2012, 288 non-need-based awards were made. *Average percent of need met:* 81%. *Average financial aid package:* $9198. *Average need-based loan:* $4071. *Average need-based gift aid:* $6892. *Average non-need-based aid:* $3371. *Average indebtedness upon graduation:* $25,241.

Applying *Options:* electronic application, early admission, early action, deferred entrance. *Application fee:* $50. *Required:* high school transcript. *Recommended:* essay or personal statement, . *Application deadlines:* 2/1 (freshmen), 6/1 (transfers), 12/1 (early action). *Notification:* 4/1 (freshmen), continuous (transfers), 1/15 (early action).

Freshman Application Contact Mr. James A. Pennix, Dean of Admissions/Interim Vice Provost for Enrollment Management, Radford University, PO Box 6903, Radford, VA 24142. *Phone:* 540-831-5371. *Fax:* 540-831-5038. *E-mail:* admissions@radford.edu.

Website: http://www.radford.edu/.

Randolph College

Lynchburg, Virginia

- **Independent Methodist** comprehensive, founded 1891
- **Suburban** 100-acre campus
- **Coed** 623 undergraduate students, 98% full-time, 63% women, 37% men
- **Moderately difficult** entrance level, 83% of applicants were admitted

Undergraduates 609 full-time, 14 part-time. 59% are from out of state; 9% Black or African American, non-Hispanic/Latino; 6% Hispanic/Latino; 2% Asian, non-Hispanic/Latino; 0.3% American Indian or Alaska Native, non-Hispanic/Latino; 3% Two or more races, non-Hispanic/Latino; 14% international; 5% transferred in; 91% live on campus. *Retention:* 80% of full-time freshmen returned.

Freshmen *Admission:* 892 applied, 742 admitted, 180 enrolled. *Average high school GPA:* 3.49. *Test scores:* SAT critical reading scores over 500: 69%; SAT math scores over 500: 72%; SAT writing scores over 500: 63%; ACT scores over 18: 88%; SAT critical reading scores over 600: 31%; SAT math scores over 600: 30%; SAT writing scores over 600: 24%; ACT scores over 24: 56%; SAT critical reading scores over 700: 10%; SAT math scores over 700: 6%; SAT writing scores over 700: 5%; ACT scores over 30: 17%.

Faculty *Total:* 74, 93% full-time, 88% with terminal degrees. *Student/faculty ratio:* 9:1.

Academics *Calendar:* semesters. *Degrees:* bachelor's and master's. *Special study options:* adult/continuing education programs, part-time degree program.

Computers on Campus Students can access the following: campus intranet, computer help desk, free student e-mail accounts, online (class) grades, online (class) registration, online (class) schedules. Campuswide network is available. 100% of college-owned or -operated housing units are wired for high-speed Internet access. Wireless service is available via entire campus.

Student Life *Housing:* on-campus residence required through senior year. *Options:* coed, women-only. Campus housing is university owned. Freshman campus housing is guaranteed. *Campus security:* 24-hour emergency response devices and patrols, late-night transport/escort service.

Athletics Member NCAA. All Division III. *Intercollegiate sports:* basketball M/W, cross-country running M/W, equestrian sports M/W, lacrosse M/W, soccer M/W, softball W, tennis M/W, volleyball W.

Standardized Tests *Required:* SAT or ACT (for admission).

Costs (2012–13) *Comprehensive fee:* $42,330 includes full-time tuition ($31,030), mandatory fees ($510), and room and board ($10,790). Part-time tuition and fees vary according to course load. *Payment plan:* installment. *Waivers:* adult students and employees or children of employees.

Financial Aid Of all full-time matriculated undergraduates who enrolled in 2011, 442 applied for aid, 390 were judged to have need, 78 had their need fully met. In 2011, 51 non-need-based awards were made. *Average percent of need met:* 77%. *Average financial aid package:* $25,244. *Average need-based loan:* $5706. *Average need-based gift aid:* $19,622. *Average non-need-based aid:* $17,344. *Average indebtedness upon graduation:* $25,321.

Applying *Options:* electronic application, early admission, early action, deferred entrance. *Application fee:* $35. *Required:* essay or personal statement, high school transcript, 2 letters of recommendation. *Recommended:* interview. *Application deadlines:* 3/1 (freshmen), 7/1 (transfers), 12/1 (early action). *Notification:* continuous (freshmen), continuous (transfers), 1/1 (early action).

Freshman Application Contact Ms. Margaret Blount, Director of Admissions, Randolph College, 2500 Rivermont Avenue, Lynchburg, VA 24503-1555. *Phone:* 434-947-8100. *Toll-free phone:* 800-745-7692. *Fax:* 434-947-8996. *E-mail:* admissions@randolphcollege.edu. *Website:* http://www.randolphcollege.edu/.

Randolph-Macon College

Ashland, Virginia

- **Independent United Methodist** 4-year, founded 1830
- **Suburban** 120-acre campus with easy access to Richmond
- **Endowment** $120.8 million
- **Coed** 1,312 undergraduate students, 98% full-time, 52% women, 48% men
- **Moderately difficult** entrance level, 54% of applicants were admitted

Undergraduates 1,286 full-time, 26 part-time. Students come from 31 states and territories; 20 other countries; 26% are from out of state; 12% Black or African American, non-Hispanic/Latino; 4% Hispanic/Latino; 2% Asian, non-Hispanic/Latino; 1% American Indian or Alaska Native, non-Hispanic/Latino; 0.8% Race/ethnicity unknown; 3% international; 3% transferred in; 78% live on campus. *Retention:* 80% of full-time freshmen returned.

Freshmen *Admission:* 4,155 applied, 2,242 admitted, 411 enrolled. *Average high school GPA:* 3.55. *Test scores:* SAT critical reading scores over 500: 77%; SAT math scores over 500: 71%; SAT writing scores over 500: 65%; ACT scores over 18: 98%; SAT critical reading scores over 600: 24%; SAT math scores over 600: 26%; SAT writing scores over 600: 19%; ACT scores over 24: 50%; SAT critical reading scores over 700: 4%; SAT math scores over 700: 3%; SAT writing scores over 700: 1%; ACT scores over 30: 12%.

Faculty *Total:* 148, 63% full-time, 74% with terminal degrees. *Student/faculty ratio:* 12:1.

Academics *Calendar:* 4-1-4. *Degree:* bachelor's. *Special study options:* academic remediation for entering students, accelerated degree program, advanced placement credit, double majors, honors programs, independent study, internships, off-campus study, part-time degree program, services for LD students, study abroad, summer session for credit. *ROTC:* Army (c). *Unusual degree programs:* 3-2 engineering with Columbia University, University of Virginia; forestry with Duke University; accounting with Virginia Commonwealth University.

Computers on Campus 356 computers/terminals and 1,500 ports are available on campus for general student use. Students can access the following: computer help desk, free student e-mail accounts, online (class) registration, online (class) schedules. Campuswide network is available. 100% of college-owned or -operated housing units are wired for high-speed Internet access. Wireless service is available via classrooms, computer labs, dorm rooms, libraries, student centers.

Student Life *Housing:* on-campus residence required through junior year. *Options:* coed, men-only, women-only, disabled students. Campus housing is university owned. Freshman campus housing is guaranteed. *Activities and organizations:* drama/theater group, student-run newspaper, radio and television station, choral group, Residence Hall Association, Campus Activities Board, Student Government Association, Drama Guild, Student Honors Association, national fraternities, national sororities. *Campus security:* 24-hour emergency response devices and patrols, late-night transport/escort service, controlled dormitory access. *Student services:* health clinic, personal/psychological counseling, women's center.

Athletics Member NCAA. All Division III. *Intercollegiate sports:* baseball M, basketball M/W, equestrian sports M(c)/W(c), field hockey W, football M, golf M/W, lacrosse M/W, soccer M/W, softball W, swimming and diving M/W, tennis M/W, volleyball W. *Intramural sports:* badminton M/W, basketball M/W, cheerleading M/W, cross-country running M/W, football M/W, lacrosse M/W, racquetball M/W, rugby M/W, soccer M/W, softball M/W, table tennis M/W, tennis M/W, track and field M/W, ultimate Frisbee M/W, volleyball M/W, water polo M/W.

Standardized Tests *Required:* SAT or ACT (for admission). *Recommended:* SAT Subject Tests (for admission).

Costs (2012–13) *One-time required fee:* $100. *Comprehensive fee:* $43,925 includes full-time tuition ($32,625), mandatory fees ($900), and room and board ($10,400). Full-time tuition and fees vary according to reciprocity agreements. *Part-time tuition:* $3625 per course. *Required fees:* $135 per year part-time. *College room only:* $5755. Room and board charges vary according to board plan and housing facility. *Payment plan:* installment. *Waivers:* employees or children of employees.

Financial Aid Of all full-time matriculated undergraduates who enrolled in 2012, 1,108 applied for aid, 954 were judged to have need, 222 had their need fully met. 194 Federal Work-Study jobs (averaging $1301). In 2012, 320 non-need-based awards were made. *Average percent of need met:* 78%. *Average financial aid package:* $24,819. *Average need-based loan:* $4496. *Average need-based gift aid:* $20,935. *Average non-need-based aid:* $14,834. *Average indebtedness upon graduation:* $31,112.

Applying *Options:* electronic application, early admission, early action, deferred entrance. *Application fee:* $30. *Required:* essay or personal statement, high school transcript, minimum 2.0 GPA, 1 letter of recommendation. *Recommended:* interview. *Application deadlines:* 3/1 (freshmen), 4/1 (transfers), 11/15 (early action). *Notification:* 4/1 (freshmen), 5/1 (transfers), 1/1 (early action).

Freshman Application Contact Anthony Ambrogi, Director of Admissions and Enrollment Research, Randolph-Macon College, PO Box 5005, Ashland, VA 23005-5505. *Phone:* 804-752-7305. *Toll-free phone:* 800-888-1762. *Fax:* 804-752-4707. *E-mail:* admissions@rmc.edu. *Website:* http://www.rmc.edu/.

Regent University

Virginia Beach, Virginia

- **Independent Christian** comprehensive, founded 1977
- **Suburban** 70-acre campus
- **Endowment** $181.0 million
- **Coed** 2,432 undergraduate students, 59% full-time, 63% women, 37% men
- **Minimally difficult** entrance level, 83% of applicants were admitted

Undergraduates 1,442 full-time, 990 part-time. Students come from 50 states and territories; 14 other countries; 52% are from out of state; 19% Black or African American, non-Hispanic/Latino; 5% Hispanic/Latino; 2% Asian, non-Hispanic/Latino; 0.4% American Indian or Alaska Native, non-Hispanic/Latino; 18% Race/ethnicity unknown; 2% international; 18% transferred in; 18% live on campus. *Retention:* 78% of full-time freshmen returned.

Freshmen *Admission:* 1,497 applied, 1,241 admitted, 218 enrolled. *Average high school GPA:* 3.5. *Test scores:* SAT critical reading scores over 500: 65%; SAT math scores over 500: 49%; SAT writing scores over 500: 59%; ACT scores over 18: 91%; SAT critical reading scores over 600: 23%; SAT math scores over 600: 11%; SAT writing scores over 600: 18%; ACT scores over 24: 42%; SAT critical reading scores over 700: 3%; SAT math scores over 700: 1%; SAT writing scores over 700: 3%; ACT scores over 30: 4%.

Faculty *Total:* 569, 30% full-time, 74% with terminal degrees. *Student/faculty ratio:* 16:1.

Academics *Calendar:* trimesters. *Degrees:* associate, bachelor's, master's, doctoral, and post-master's certificates. *Special study options:* academic remediation for entering students, adult/continuing education programs, advanced placement credit, distance learning, double majors, external degree program, internships, off-campus study, part-time degree program, services for LD students, study abroad, summer session for credit. *ROTC:* Army (c), Navy (c).

Computers on Campus 69 computers/terminals and 75 ports are available on campus for general student use. Students can access the following: campus intranet, computer help desk, free student e-mail accounts, online (class) grades, online (class) registration, online (class) schedules. Campuswide network is available. 100% of college-owned or -operated housing units are wired for high-speed Internet access. Wireless service is available via entire campus.

Student Life *Housing:* on-campus residence required for freshman year. *Options:* men-only, women-only, disabled students. Campus housing is university owned. Freshman applicants given priority for college housing. *Activities and organizations:* drama/theater group, student-run newspaper, choral group, Regent Undergraduate Council, Students in Free Enterprise (SIFE), Psychology Club, Student Alumni Ambassadors, Regent Undergraduate Debate Association, national fraternities, national sororities. *Campus security:* 24-hour emergency response devices and patrols, student patrols, late-night transport/escort service, controlled dormitory access. *Student services:* personal/psychological counseling.

Athletics *Intramural sports:* basketball M/W, golf M/W, soccer M/W, tennis M/W, volleyball M/W.

Standardized Tests *Required for some:* SAT or ACT (for admission).

Costs (2013–14) *Comprehensive fee:* $24,390 includes full-time tuition ($15,300), mandatory fees ($660), and room and board ($8430). Full-time tuition and fees vary according to course level, course load, program, and student level. Part-time tuition: $510 per credit hour. Part-time tuition and fees vary according to course level, course load, program, and student level. *Required fees:* $510 per credit hour part-time, $330 per term part-time. *College room only:* $5460. Room and board charges vary according to housing facility. *Payment plan:* installment. *Waivers:* employees or children of employees.

Financial Aid Of all full-time matriculated undergraduates who enrolled in 2012, 1,192 applied for aid, 1,139 were judged to have need, 36 had their need fully met. In 2012, 183 non-need-based awards were made. *Average percent of need met:* 58%. *Average financial aid package:* $11,462. *Average need-based loan:* $4037. *Average need-based gift aid:* $7769. *Average non-need-based aid:* $5571. *Average indebtedness upon graduation:* $45,326.

Applying *Options:* electronic application, deferred entrance. *Application fee:* $50. *Required:* essay or personal statement. *Required for some:* high school transcript, minimum 3.0 GPA. *Application deadlines:* 8/1 (freshmen), 8/1 (out-of-state freshmen), 8/1 (transfers). *Notification:* continuous (freshmen), continuous (out-of-state freshmen), continuous (transfers).

Freshman Application Contact Mr. Ken Baker, Director of Admissions, Regent University, 1000 Regent University Drive, SC 218, Virginia Beach, VA 23464. *Phone:* 757-352-4845. *Toll-free phone:* 800-373-5504. *Fax:* 757-352-4509. *E-mail:* kbaker@regent.edu. *Website:* http://www.regent.edu/.

Roanoke College

Salem, Virginia

- **Independent** 4-year, founded 1842, affiliated with Evangelical Lutheran Church in America
- **Suburban** 80-acre campus
- **Endowment** $116.4 million
- **Coed** 2,060 undergraduate students, 96% full-time, 58% women, 42% men
- **Moderately difficult** entrance level, 69% of applicants were admitted

Undergraduates 1,987 full-time, 73 part-time. Students come from 39 states and territories; 24 other countries; 46% are from out of state; 4% Black or African American, non-Hispanic/Latino; 4% Hispanic/Latino; 1% Asian, non-Hispanic/Latino; 0.3% American Indian or Alaska Native, non-Hispanic/Latino; 3% Two or more races, non-Hispanic/Latino; 2% international; 4% transferred in; 74% live on campus. *Retention:* 81% of full-time freshmen returned.

Freshmen *Admission:* 4,264 applied, 2,957 admitted, 543 enrolled. *Average high school GPA:* 3.44. *Test scores:* SAT critical reading scores over 500: 73%; SAT math scores over 500: 70%; SAT writing scores over 500: 67%; ACT scores over 18: 95%; SAT critical reading scores over 600: 25%; SAT math scores over 600: 25%; SAT writing scores over 600: 21%; ACT scores over 24: 44%; SAT critical reading scores over 700: 3%; SAT math scores over 700: 2%; SAT writing scores over 700: 3%; ACT scores over 30: 3%.

Faculty *Total:* 212, 78% full-time, 70% with terminal degrees. *Student/faculty ratio:* 11:1.

Academics *Calendar:* semesters. *Degree:* bachelor's. *Special study options:* accelerated degree program, adult/continuing education programs, advanced placement credit, double majors, English as a second language, honors programs, independent study, internships, off-campus study, part-time degree program, services for LD students, study abroad, summer session for credit. *Unusual degree programs:* 3-2 engineering with Virginia Polytechnic Institute and State University.

Computers on Campus 207 computers/terminals are available on campus for general student use. Students can access the following: campus intranet, computer help desk, free student e-mail accounts, online (class) grades, online (class) registration, online (class) schedules, discounts on computer hardware and software purchases, free Microsoft Office software, free security software. Campuswide network is available. 100% of college-owned or -operated housing units are wired for high-speed Internet access. Wireless service is available via entire campus.

Student Life *Housing:* on-campus residence required through senior year. *Options:* coed, women-only, disabled students. Campus housing is university owned. Freshman campus housing is guaranteed. *Activities and organizations:* drama/theater group, student-run newspaper, radio station, choral group, Outdoor Adventures, Habitat for Humanity, Honors Association, Campus Activities Board, Inter-Varsity Christian Fellowship, national fraternities, national sororities. *Campus security:* 24-hour emergency response devices and patrols, late-night transport/escort service, controlled dormitory access, Campus emergency phones, Maroon Alert system. *Student services:* health clinic, personal/psychological counseling.

Athletics Member NCAA. All Division III. *Intercollegiate sports:* baseball M, basketball M/W, cross-country running M/W, field hockey W, golf M, lacrosse M/W, soccer M/W, softball W, tennis M/W, track and field M/W, volleyball W. *Intramural sports:* badminton M/W, basketball M/W, cheerleading M/W, equestrian sports M(c)/W(c), football M/W, golf M(c)/W(c), lacrosse M(c), racquetball M/W, rugby M(c), soccer M/W, softball M/W, squash M(c)/W(c), table tennis M/W, tennis M/W, ultimate Frisbee M(c)/W(c), volleyball M/W.

Standardized Tests *Required:* SAT or ACT (for admission).

Costs (2013–14) *One-time required fee:* $125. *Comprehensive fee:* $47,996 includes full-time tuition ($35,108), mandatory fees ($1364), and room and board ($11,524). Full-time tuition and fees vary according to reciprocity agreements. Part-time tuition: $1680 per course. Part-time tuition and fees vary according to course load and reciprocity agreements. *Required fees:* $38 per term part-time. *College room only:* $5310. Room and board charges vary according to board plan and housing facility. *Payment plan:* installment. *Waivers:* senior citizens and employees or children of employees.

Financial Aid Of all full-time matriculated undergraduates who enrolled in 2012, 1,689 applied for aid, 1,503 were judged to have need, 277 had their need fully met. 1,112 Federal Work-Study jobs (averaging $1563). In 2012, 449 non-need-based awards were made. *Average percent of need met:* 77%. *Average financial aid package:* $26,518. *Average need-based loan:* $4784. *Average need-based gift aid:* $21,527. *Average non-need-based aid:* $12,711. *Average indebtedness upon graduation:* $33,004.

Applying *Options:* electronic application, early admission, early decision, deferred entrance. *Application fee:* $30. *Required:* high school transcript. *Recommended:* essay or personal statement, 3 letters of recommendation, interview. *Application deadlines:* 3/15 (freshmen), 8/1 (transfers). *Early decision*

deadline: 11/1. *Notification:* continuous until 4/1 (freshmen), continuous until 8/15 (transfers), 12/1 (early decision), 10/1 (early action).
Freshman Application Contact Admissions Office, Roanoke College, 221 College Lane, Salem, VA 24153. *Phone:* 540-375-2270. *Toll-free phone:* 800-388-2276. *Fax:* 540-375-2267. *E-mail:* admissions@roanoke.edu. *Website:* http://www.roanoke.edu/.

Saint Paul's College

Lawrenceville, Virginia

Freshman Application Contact Saint Paul's College, 115 College Drive, Lawrenceville, VA 23868-1202. *Phone:* 434-848-6493. *Toll-free phone:* 800-678-7071.
Website: http://www.saintpauls.edu/.

Sentara College of Health Sciences

Chesapeake, Virginia

Admissions Office Contact Sentara College of Health Sciences, 1441 Crossways Boulevard, Crossways I, Suite 105, Chesapeake, VA 23320. *Website:* http://www.sentara.edu/.

Shenandoah University

Winchester, Virginia

- **Independent United Methodist** comprehensive, founded 1875
- **Small-town** 125-acre campus with easy access to Baltimore and Washington, D.C.
- **Endowment** $52.7 million
- **Coed** 2,402 undergraduate students, 76% full-time, 63% women, 37% men
- **Moderately difficult** entrance level, 85% of applicants were admitted

Undergraduates 1,837 full-time, 565 part-time. Students come from 35 states and territories; 28 other countries; 36% are from out of state; 12% Black or African American, non-Hispanic/Latino; 3% Hispanic/Latino; 4% Asian, non-Hispanic/Latino; 0.6% Native Hawaiian or other Pacific Islander, non-Hispanic/Latino; 2% American Indian or Alaska Native, non-Hispanic/Latino; 0.9% Two or more races, non-Hispanic/Latino; 5% Race/ethnicity unknown; 3% international; 5% transferred in; 55% live on campus. *Retention:* 80% of full-time freshmen returned.
Freshmen *Admission:* 1,833 applied, 1,550 admitted, 459 enrolled. *Average high school GPA:* 3.36. *Test scores:* SAT critical reading scores over 500: 51%; SAT math scores over 500: 55%; SAT writing scores over 500: 44%; ACT scores over 18: 82%; SAT critical reading scores over 600: 14%; SAT math scores over 600: 18%; SAT writing scores over 600: 11%; ACT scores over 24: 35%; SAT critical reading scores over 700: 2%; SAT math scores over 700: 1%; SAT writing scores over 700: 1%; ACT scores over 30: 4%.
Faculty *Total:* 404, 57% full-time, 65% with terminal degrees. *Student/faculty ratio:* 10:1.
Academics *Calendar:* semesters. *Degrees:* certificates, diplomas, bachelor's, master's, doctoral, post-master's, and postbachelor's certificates. *Special study options:* accelerated degree program, adult/continuing education programs, advanced placement credit, cooperative education, distance learning, double majors, English as a second language, independent study, internships, off-campus study, part-time degree program, services for LD students, student-designed majors, study abroad, summer session for credit. *Unusual degree programs:* 3-2 athletic training.
Computers on Campus 35 computers/terminals and 50 ports are available on campus for general student use. Students can access the following: campus intranet, computer help desk, free student e-mail accounts, online (class) grades, online (class) registration, online (class) schedules, online student account information. Campuswide network is available. 100% of college-owned or -operated housing units are wired for high-speed Internet access. Wireless service is available via entire campus.
Student Life *Housing options:* coed, disabled students. Campus housing is university owned and leased by the school. Freshman campus housing is guaranteed. *Activities and organizations:* drama/theater group, student-run newspa-

per, radio and television station, choral group, Student Government Association, The Graduate Student Association, Campus Activities Network, American Pharmacists Association Academy of Student Pharmacists, Kappa Psi Pharmaceutical Fraternity, Inc. *Campus security:* 24-hour emergency response devices and patrols, late-night transport/escort service, controlled dormitory access, side door alarms. *Student services:* health clinic, personal/psychological counseling, women's center.
Athletics Member NCAA. All Division III. *Intercollegiate sports:* baseball M, basketball M/W, cross-country running M/W, field hockey W, football M, golf M, lacrosse M/W, soccer M/W, softball W, tennis M/W, track and field M/W, volleyball W. *Intramural sports:* basketball M/W, football M/W, soccer M/W, softball M/W, volleyball M/W.
Standardized Tests *Required:* SAT or ACT (for admission).
Costs (2012–13) *Comprehensive fee:* $37,090 includes full-time tuition ($27,550), mandatory fees ($300), and room and board ($9240). Full-time tuition and fees vary according to course load, location, program, and student level. Part-time tuition: $800 per credit hour. Part-time tuition and fees vary according to course load, location, program, and student level. *Room and board:* Room and board charges vary according to board plan and housing facility. *Payment plan:* installment. *Waivers:* employees or children of employees.
Financial Aid Of all full-time matriculated undergraduates who enrolled in 2011, 1,141 applied for aid, 1,073 were judged to have need, 64 had their need fully met. 781 Federal Work-Study jobs (averaging $1941). 396 state and other part-time jobs (averaging $1937). In 2011, 146 non-need-based awards were made. *Average percent of need met:* 71%. *Average financial aid package:* $19,000. *Average need-based loan:* $4500. *Average need-based gift aid:* $8000. *Average non-need-based aid:* $5000. *Average indebtedness upon graduation:* $27,000.
Applying *Options:* electronic application, deferred entrance. *Application fee:* $30. *Required:* high school transcript, 1 letter of recommendation. *Required for some:* essay or personal statement, minimum 3.0 GPA, interview, Applicants are strongly recommended to indicate community and extra-curricular involvement.Conservatory applicants are also required to successfully complete an audition. *Application deadlines:* rolling (freshmen), rolling (transfers). *Notification:* continuous (freshmen), continuous (transfers).
Freshman Application Contact Mr. David Anthony, Dean of Admissions, Shenandoah University, 1460 University Drive, Winchester, VA 22601-5195. *Phone:* 540-665-4581. *Toll-free phone:* 800-432-2266. *Fax:* 540-665-4627. *E-mail:* admit@su.edu.
Website: http://www.su.edu/.

Skyline College

Roanoke, Virginia

Freshman Application Contact Dr. Walter Merchant, Campus Provost (Interim), Skyline College, 5234 Airport Road, Roanoke, VA 24012. *Phone:* 540-563-8080. *Toll-free phone:* 866-708-6178. *Fax:* 540-362-5400. *E-mail:* wmerchant@ecpi.edu.
Website: http://www.skyline.edu/.

Southern Virginia University

Buena Vista, Virginia

Freshman Application Contact Mr. Tony Caputo, Dean of Admissions, Southern Virginia University, One University Hill Drive, Buena Vista, VA 24416. *Phone:* 540-261-2756. *Toll-free phone:* 800-229-8420. *Fax:* 540-261-8559. *E-mail:* admissions@southernvirginia.edu.
Website: http://www.svu.edu/.

South University

Glen Allen, Virginia

- **Proprietary** comprehensive
- **Coed**

Academics *Degrees:* associate, bachelor's, and master's.
Freshman Application Contact South University, 2151 Old Brick Road, Glen Allen, VA 23060. *Phone:* 804-727-6800. *Toll-free phone:* 888-422-5076. *Website:* http://www.southuniversity.edu/richmond.

South University

Virginia Beach, Virginia

- **Proprietary** comprehensive
- **Coed**

Academics *Degrees:* associate, bachelor's, and master's.

Freshman Application Contact South University, 301 Bendix Road, Suite 100, Virginia Beach, VA 23452. *Phone:* 757-493-6900. *Toll-free phone:* 877-206-1845.

Website: http://www.southuniversity.edu/virginia-beach.

Stratford University

Falls Church, Virginia

- **Proprietary** comprehensive, founded 1976
- **Suburban** campus with easy access to Washington, DC
- **Coed** 604 undergraduate students, 23% full-time, 55% women, 45% men
- **Noncompetitive** entrance level, 29% of applicants were admitted

Undergraduates 141 full-time, 463 part-time. 52% are from out of state. *Retention:* 52% of full-time freshmen returned.

Freshmen *Admission:* 218 applied, 64 admitted, 211 enrolled.

Faculty *Total:* 110, 17% full-time, 25% with terminal degrees. *Student/faculty ratio:* 88:1.

Academics *Calendar:* quarters. *Degrees:* certificates, diplomas, associate, bachelor's, and master's. *Special study options:* academic remediation for entering students, accelerated degree program, advanced placement credit, cooperative education, distance learning, English as a second language, internships, part-time degree program, summer session for credit.

Computers on Campus 104 computers/terminals are available on campus for general student use. Students can access the following: campus intranet, computer help desk, free student e-mail accounts, online (class) grades, online (class) registration, online (class) schedules. Campuswide network is available. Wireless service is available via entire campus.

Student Life *Housing:* college housing not available. *Campus security:* 24-hour emergency response devices.

Costs (2013–14) *Tuition:* $370 per quarter hour part-time. *Required fees:* $100 per degree program part-time. *Payment plan:* installment. *Waivers:* employees or children of employees.

Financial Aid Of all full-time matriculated undergraduates who enrolled in 2010, 136 applied for aid, 136 were judged to have need. 11 Federal Work-Study jobs (averaging $3015). *Average need-based loan:* $5660. *Average need-based gift aid:* $1122. *Average indebtedness upon graduation:* $42,981.

Applying *Options:* electronic application, deferred entrance. *Application fee:* $50. *Required:* essay or personal statement, proof of high school graduation or equivalent is required for all students; personal statement, transcript, and letters of recommendation are only required for the Nursing program. *Application deadlines:* rolling (freshmen), rolling (out-of-state freshmen), rolling (transfers). *Notification:* continuous (freshmen), continuous (out-of-state freshmen), continuous (transfers).

Freshman Application Contact Ms. Ann M. Connors, Director of Admissions, Stratford University, 7777 Leesburg Pike, Falls Church, VA 22043. *Phone:* 703-821-8570. *Toll-free phone:* 800-444-0804. *Fax:* 703-734-5339. *E-mail:* jray@stratford.edu.

Website: http://www.stratford.edu/.

Stratford University

Glen Allen, Virginia

- **Proprietary** comprehensive
- **Suburban** campus
- **Coed** 363 undergraduate students, 100% full-time, 65% women, 35% men

Undergraduates 363 full-time. 45% Black or African American, non-Hispanic/Latino; 3% Hispanic/Latino; 21% Asian, non-Hispanic/Latino; 0.2% Native Hawaiian or other Pacific Islander, non-Hispanic/Latino; 0.4% American Indian or Alaska Native, non-Hispanic/Latino; 0.2% Two or more races, non-Hispanic/Latino; 0.4% Race/ethnicity unknown. *Retention:* 63% of full-time freshmen returned.

Freshmen *Admission:* 233 enrolled.

Faculty *Total:* 23, 9% full-time, 48% with terminal degrees. *Student/faculty ratio:* 21:1.

Academics *Degrees:* certificates, diplomas, bachelor's, and master's. *Special study options:* academic remediation for entering students, adult/continuing education programs, cooperative education, external degree program, independent study, internships, part-time degree program.

Freshman Application Contact Stratford University, 11104 W. Broad Street, Glen Allen, VA 23060. *Toll-free phone:* 877-373-5173.

Website: http://www.stratford.edu/.

Stratford University

Newport News, Virginia

- **Proprietary** comprehensive
- **Urban** campus
- **Coed** 152 undergraduate students, 16% full-time, 64% women, 36% men

Undergraduates 24 full-time, 128 part-time. 86% Black or African American, non-Hispanic/Latino; 4% Hispanic/Latino; 4% transferred in. *Retention:* 83% of full-time freshmen returned.

Freshmen *Admission:* 75 enrolled. *Average high school GPA:* 0.

Faculty *Total:* 19, 16% full-time, 11% with terminal degrees. *Student/faculty ratio:* 4:1.

Academics *Degrees:* associate, bachelor's, and master's. *Special study options:* academic remediation for entering students, accelerated degree program, cooperative education, distance learning, external degree program, part-time degree program, services for LD students, summer session for credit.

Computers on Campus 19 computers/terminals and 6 ports are available on campus for general student use. Students can access the following: campus intranet, computer help desk, free student e-mail accounts, online (class) grades, online (class) schedules. Campuswide network is available. Wireless service is available via entire campus.

Student Life *Housing:* college housing not available. *Campus security:* 24-hour emergency response devices, Security officer during evening hours / classes.

Costs (2013–14) *Tuition:* $14,895 full-time, $370 per credit part-time. Full-time tuition and fees vary according to course load and program. Part-time tuition and fees vary according to course load and program. *Required fees:* $100 full-time. *Payment plans:* tuition prepayment, installment. *Waivers:* employees or children of employees.

Applying *Required:* essay or personal statement, high school transcript, interview.

Freshman Application Contact Director of Admissions, Stratford University, 836 J. Clyde Morris Boulevard, Newport News, VA 23601. *Phone:* 757-873.4235. *Toll-free phone:* 855-873-4235.

Website: http://www.stratford.edu/.

Stratford University

Woodbridge, Virginia

- **Proprietary** comprehensive
- **Suburban** campus
- **Coed** 694 undergraduate students, 14% full-time, 73% women, 27% men

Undergraduates 96 full-time, 598 part-time.

Freshmen *Admission:* 132 enrolled.

Faculty *Total:* 51, 29% full-time, 27% with terminal degrees.

Academics *Degrees:* certificates, diplomas, associate, bachelor's, and master's. *Special study options:* academic remediation for entering students, accelerated degree program, adult/continuing education programs, advanced placement credit, cooperative education, distance learning, double majors, independent study, internships, off-campus study, part-time degree program, summer session for credit.

Computers on Campus 100 computers/terminals and 138 ports are available on campus for general student use. Students can access the following: campus intranet, computer help desk, free student e-mail accounts, online (class) grades, online (class) registration, online (class) schedules. Campuswide network is available. Wireless service is available via classrooms, computer centers, computer labs, learning centers, libraries, student centers.

Applying *Options:* electronic application. *Application fee:* $50.

Freshman Application Contact Director of Admissions, Stratford University, 14349 Gideon Drive, Woodbridge, VA 22192. *Phone:* 703-897-1982. *Toll-free phone:* 888-546-1250. *E-mail:* admissions@stratford.edu.

Website: http://www.stratford.edu/.

Strayer University—Alexandria Campus

Alexandria, Virginia

Freshman Application Contact Strayer University—Alexandria Campus, 2730 Eisenhower Avenue, Alexandria, VA 22314. *Website:* http://www.strayer.edu/campus/alexandria.

Strayer University—Arlington Campus

Arlington, Virginia

Freshman Application Contact Strayer University—Arlington Campus, 2121 15th Street North, Arlington, VA 22201. *Website:* http://www.strayer.edu/campus/arlington.

Strayer University—Chesapeake Campus

Chesapeake, Virginia

Freshman Application Contact Strayer University—Chesapeake Campus, 676 Independence Parkway, Suite 300, Chesapeake, VA 23320. *Website:* http://www.strayer.edu/campus/chesapeake/.

Strayer University—Chesterfield Campus

Midlothian, Virginia

Freshman Application Contact Strayer University—Chesterfield Campus, 2820 Waterford Lake Drive, Suite 100, Midlothian, VA 23112. *Website:* http://www.strayer.edu/campus/chesterfield/.

Strayer University— Fredericksburg Campus

Fredericksburg, Virginia

Freshman Application Contact Strayer University—Fredericksburg Campus, 150 Riverside Parkway, Suite 100, Fredericksburg, VA 22406. *Website:* http://www.strayer.edu/campus/fredericksburg.

Strayer University—Henrico Campus

Glen Allen, Virginia

Freshman Application Contact Strayer University—Henrico Campus, 11501 Nuckols Road, Glen Allen, VA 23059. *Website:* http://www.strayer.edu/campus/henrico.

Strayer University—Loudoun Campus

Ashburn, Virginia

Freshman Application Contact Strayer University—Loudoun Campus, 45150 Russell Branch Parkway, Suite 200, Ashburn, VA 20147. *Website:* http://www.strayer.edu/campus/loudoun.

Strayer University—Manassas Campus

Manassas, Virginia

Freshman Application Contact Strayer University—Manassas Campus, 9990 Battleview Parkway, Manassas, VA 20109. *Website:* http://www.strayer.edu/campus/manassas.

Strayer University—Newport News Campus

Newport News, Virginia

Freshman Application Contact Strayer University—Newport News Campus, 99 Old Oyster Point Road, Unit 1, Newport News, VA 23602. *Website:* http://www.strayer.edu/campus/newport-news.

Strayer University—Virginia Beach Campus

Virginia Beach, Virginia

Freshman Application Contact Strayer University—Virginia Beach Campus, 249 Central Park Avenue, Suite 350, Virginia Beach, VA 23462. *Website:* http://www.strayer.edu/campus/virginia-beach.

Strayer University—Woodbridge Campus

Woodbridge, Virginia

Freshman Application Contact Strayer University—Woodbridge Campus, 13385 Minnieville Road, Woodbridge, VA 22192. *Website:* http://www.strayer.edu/campus/woodbridge.

Sweet Briar College

Sweet Briar, Virginia

- **Independent** 4-year, founded 1901
- **Rural** 3250-acre campus
- **Endowment** $84.7 million
- **Women only** 723 undergraduate students, 96% full-time
- **Moderately difficult** entrance level, 79% of applicants were admitted

Undergraduates 695 full-time, 28 part-time. Students come from 43 states and territories; 6 other countries; 50% are from out of state; 9% Black or African American, non-Hispanic/Latino; 6% Hispanic/Latino; 3% Asian, non-Hispanic/Latino; 0.4% Native Hawaiian or other Pacific Islander, non-Hispanic/Latino; 2% American Indian or Alaska Native, non-Hispanic/Latino; 2% Two or more races, non-Hispanic/Latino; 0.9% Race/ethnicity unknown; 1% international; 2% transferred in; 93% live on campus. *Retention:* 74% of full-time freshmen returned.

Freshmen *Admission:* 763 applied, 605 admitted, 176 enrolled. *Average high school GPA:* 3.52. *Test scores:* SAT critical reading scores over 500: 72%; SAT math scores over 500: 58%; SAT writing scores over 500: 61%; ACT scores over 18: 94%; SAT critical reading scores over 600: 30%; SAT math scores over 600: 16%; SAT writing scores over 600: 24%; ACT scores over 24: 62%; SAT critical reading scores over 700: 6%; SAT math scores over 700: 3%; SAT writing scores over 700: 1%; ACT scores over 30: 6%.

Faculty *Total:* 97, 80% full-time, 72% with terminal degrees. *Student/faculty ratio:* 8:1.

Academics *Calendar:* semesters. *Degrees:* bachelor's and master's. *Special study options:* accelerated degree program, adult/continuing education programs, advanced placement credit, cooperative education, double majors, honors programs, independent study, internships, off-campus study, part-time degree program, services for LD students, student-designed majors, study abroad, summer session for credit. *Unusual degree programs:* 3-2 engineering with Virginia Polytechnic Institute and State University, University of Virginia, Columbia University, Washington University in St. Louis.

Computers on Campus 128 computers/terminals and 3,000 ports are available on campus for general student use. Students can access the following: campus intranet, computer help desk, free student e-mail accounts, online (class) grades, online (class) registration, online (class) schedules. Campus-wide network is available. 100% of college-owned or -operated housing units are wired for high-speed Internet access. Wireless service is available via entire campus.

Student Life *Housing:* on-campus residence required through senior year. *Options:* women-only. Campus housing is university owned. Freshman campus housing is guaranteed. *Activities and organizations:* drama/theater group, student-run newspaper, radio and television station, choral group, Student Government Association, Campus Events Organization, Interclub Council, PnP, Environmental Club. *Campus security:* 24-hour emergency response devices and patrols, late-night transport/escort service, controlled dormitory access, front gate security. *Student services:* health clinic, personal/psychological counseling.

Athletics Member NCAA. All Division III. *Intercollegiate sports:* cross-country running W(c), equestrian sports W(c), fencing W(c), field hockey W, lacrosse W, soccer W, softball W, swimming and diving W, tennis W.

Standardized Tests *Required:* SAT or ACT (for admission).

Costs (2012–13) *Comprehensive fee:* $43,765 includes full-time tuition ($31,850), mandatory fees ($475), and room and board ($11,440). Part-time tuition: $885 per credit hour. *Room and board:* Room and board charges vary according to board plan. *Payment plan:* installment. *Waivers:* adult students, senior citizens, and employees or children of employees.

Financial Aid Of all full-time matriculated undergraduates who enrolled in 2011, 501 applied for aid, 427 were judged to have need, 74 had their need fully met. 105 Federal Work-Study jobs (averaging $712). 124 state and other part-time jobs (averaging $934). In 2011, 158 non-need-based awards were made. *Average percent of need met:* 78%. *Average financial aid package:* $25,289. *Average need-based loan:* $4655. *Average need-based gift aid:* $20,738. *Average non-need-based aid:* $11,187. *Average indebtedness upon graduation:* $23,596.

Applying *Options:* electronic application, deferred entrance. *Application fee:* $40. *Required:* essay or personal statement, high school transcript, 2 letters of recommendation. *Required for some:* portfolio with courses taken, list of texts covered, essay about homeschooling, campus visit, interview for home-schooled applicants. *Recommended:* interview. *Application deadlines:* 2/1

(freshmen), 5/1 (transfers). *Notification:* continuous (freshmen), 5/15 (transfers).

Freshman Application Contact Sweet Briar College, PO Box B, Sweet Briar, VA 24595. *Phone:* 434-381-6142. *Toll-free phone:* 800-381-6142. *E-mail:* admissions@sbc.edu.

Website: http://www.sbc.edu/.

See below for display ad and page 1530 for the College Close-Up.

University of Management and Technology

Arlington, Virginia

Freshman Application Contact Vice President, University of Management and Technology, Suite 700, 1901 North Fort Meyers Drive, Arlington, VA 22209. *Phone:* 703-516-0035. *Toll-free phone:* 800-924-4883. *Fax:* 703-516-0985. *E-mail:* admissions@umtweb.edu.

Website: http://www.umtweb.edu/.

University of Mary Washington

Fredericksburg, Virginia

- **State-supported** comprehensive, founded 1908
- **Small-town** 176-acre campus with easy access to Richmond, Washington, DC
- **Endowment** $38.1 million
- **Coed** 4,515 undergraduate students, 86% full-time, 65% women, 35% men
- **Very difficult** entrance level, 77% of applicants were admitted

Undergraduates 3,881 full-time, 634 part-time. Students come from 38 states and territories; 23 other countries; 15% are from out of state; 6% Black or African American, non-Hispanic/Latino; 6% Hispanic/Latino; 5% Asian, non-Hispanic/Latino; 0.2% American Indian or Alaska Native, non-Hispanic/Latino; 4% Two or more races, non-Hispanic/Latino; 14% Race/ethnicity unknown;

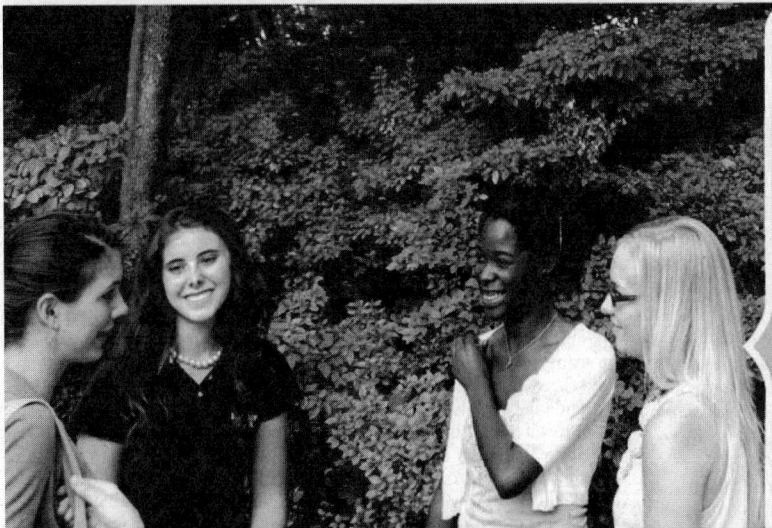

0.8% international; 7% transferred in; 60% live on campus. *Retention:* 83% of full-time freshmen returned.

Freshmen *Admission:* 4,847 applied, 3,724 admitted, 955 enrolled. *Average high school GPA:* 3.48. *Test scores:* SAT critical reading scores over 500: 82%; SAT math scores over 500: 80%; SAT writing scores over 500: 85%; ACT scores over 18: 99%; SAT critical reading scores over 600: 34%; SAT math scores over 600: 32%; SAT writing scores over 600: 35%; ACT scores over 24: 61%; SAT critical reading scores over 700: 5%; SAT math scores over 700: 3%; SAT writing scores over 700: 6%; ACT scores over 30: 10%.

Faculty *Total:* 386, 63% full-time, 70% with terminal degrees. *Student/faculty ratio:* 14:1.

Academics *Calendar:* semesters. *Degrees:* certificates, bachelor's, master's, and postbachelor's certificates. *Special study options:* accelerated degree program, adult/continuing education programs, advanced placement credit, cooperative education, distance learning, double majors, honors programs, independent study, internships, part-time degree program, services for LD students, student-designed majors, study abroad, summer session for credit. *ROTC:* Army (c). *Unusual degree programs:* computer science, elementary education.

Computers on Campus 306 computers/terminals are available on campus for general student use. Students can access the following: campus intranet, computer help desk, free student e-mail accounts, online (class) grades, online (class) registration, online (class) schedules, Library resources, foreign languages resources, course management system. Campuswide network is available. 100% of college-owned or -operated housing units are wired for high-speed Internet access. Wireless service is available via entire campus.

Student Life *Housing:* on-campus residence required through sophomore year. *Options:* coed, men-only, women-only, disabled students. Campus housing is university owned and leased by the school. Freshman campus housing is guaranteed. *Activities and organizations:* drama/theater group, student-run newspaper, radio station, choral group, Students Helping Honduras, Black Student Association, Giant Productions (campus entertainment group), PRISM, Cheap Seats Cinema. *Campus security:* 24-hour emergency response devices and patrols, student patrols, late-night transport/escort service, controlled dormitory access, self-defense and safety classes. *Student services:* health clinic, personal/psychological counseling.

Athletics Member NCAA. All Division III. *Intercollegiate sports:* baseball M, basketball M/W, cheerleading M(c)/W(c), crew M/W, cross-country running M/W, equestrian sports M/W, field hockey W, lacrosse M/W, rugby M(c)/W(c), soccer M/W, softball W, swimming and diving M/W, tennis M/W, track and field M/W, volleyball M(c)/W. *Intramural sports:* badminton M/W, baseball M(c), basketball M/W, bowling M/W, cheerleading M(c)/W(c), fencing M(c)/W(c), field hockey W(c), football M/W, golf M/W, lacrosse M/W(c), skiing (downhill) M(c)/W(c), soccer M/W, softball M/W, swimming and diving M(c)/W(c), tennis M(c)/W(c), ultimate Frisbee M(c)/W(c), volleyball M/W, water polo M/W.

Standardized Tests *Required:* SAT or ACT (for admission). *Recommended:* SAT Subject Tests (for admission).

Costs (2012–13) *One-time required fee:* $60. *Tuition:* state resident $4686 full-time, $200 per credit hour part-time; nonresident $17,000 full-time, $712 per credit hour part-time. Part-time tuition and fees vary according to course load and location. *Required fees:* $4560 full-time, $129 per credit hour part-time, $30 per term part-time. *Room and board:* $10,238; room only: $5384. Room and board charges vary according to board plan and housing facility. *Payment plan:* installment. *Waivers:* senior citizens.

Financial Aid Of all full-time matriculated undergraduates who enrolled in 2010, 2,168 applied for aid, 1,368 were judged to have need, 177 had their need fully met. 31 Federal Work-Study jobs (averaging $1400). 700 state and other part-time jobs (averaging $2200). In 2010, 336 non-need-based awards were made. *Average percent of need met:* 53%. *Average financial aid package:* $8430. *Average need-based loan:* $4280. *Average need-based gift aid:* $6800. *Average non-need-based aid:* $2400. *Average indebtedness upon graduation:* $17,775. *Financial aid deadline:* 5/15.

Applying *Options:* electronic application, early admission, early action, deferred entrance. *Application fee:* $50. *Required:* essay or personal statement, high school transcript. *Application deadlines:* 2/1 (freshmen), 3/1 (transfers), 11/15 (early action). *Notification:* 4/1 (freshmen), 5/15 (transfers), 1/31 (early action).

Freshman Application Contact Ms. Melissa Yakabouski, Acting Associate Dean of Admissions, University of Mary Washington, 1301 College Avenue, Fredericksburg, VA 22401-5358. *Phone:* 540-654-2000. *Toll-free phone:* 800-468-5614. *Fax:* 540-654-1857. *E-mail:* admit@umw.edu. *Website:* http://www.umw.edu/.

University of Phoenix–Northern Virginia Campus
Reston, Virginia

Freshman Application Contact Marc Booker, Sr. Director, Office of Admissions and Evaluation, University of Phoenix–Northern Virginia Campus, 4035 South Riverpoint Parkway, Mail Stop CF-L101, Phoenix, AZ 85040. *Phone:* 602-557-4609. *Toll-free phone:* 866-766-0766. *Fax:* 480-643-1156.
Website: http://www.phoenix.edu/.

University of Phoenix–Richmond Campus
Richmond, Virginia

Freshman Application Contact Marc Booker, Sr. Director, Office of Admissions and Evaluation, University of Phoenix–Richmond Campus, 4035 South Riverpoint Parkway, Mail Stop CF-L101, Phoenix, AZ 85040. *Phone:* 602-557-4609. *Toll-free phone:* 866-766-0766. *Fax:* 480-643-1156.
Website: http://www.phoenix.edu/.

University of Richmond
Richmond, Virginia

- **Independent** comprehensive, founded 1830
- **Suburban** 350-acre campus
- **Endowment** $1.9 billion
- **Coed** 3,074 undergraduate students, 99% full-time, 55% women, 45% men
- **Very difficult** entrance level, 30% of applicants were admitted

Undergraduates 3,031 full-time, 43 part-time. Students come from 48 states and territories; 71 other countries; 79% are from out of state; 8% Black or African American, non-Hispanic/Latino; 6% Hispanic/Latino; 6% Asian, non-Hispanic/Latino; 0.2% American Indian or Alaska Native, non-Hispanic/Latino; 2% Two or more races, non-Hispanic/Latino; 11% Race/ethnicity unknown; 8% international; 2% transferred in; 89% live on campus. *Retention:* 93% of full-time freshmen returned.

Freshmen *Admission:* 10,232 applied, 3,101 admitted, 781 enrolled. *Test scores:* SAT critical reading scores over 500: 96%; SAT math scores over 500: 98%; SAT writing scores over 500: 95%; ACT scores over 18: 100%; SAT critical reading scores over 600: 71%; SAT math scores over 600: 83%; SAT writing scores over 600: 73%; ACT scores over 24: 96%; SAT critical reading scores over 700: 25%; SAT math scores over 700: 36%; SAT writing scores over 700: 24%; ACT scores over 30: 58%.

Faculty *Total:* 427, 75% full-time, 83% with terminal degrees. *Student/faculty ratio:* 9:1.

Academics *Calendar:* semesters. *Degrees:* bachelor's, master's, and doctoral. *Special study options:* advanced placement credit, double majors, English as a second language, honors programs, independent study, internships, off-campus study, part-time degree program, services for LD students, student-designed majors, study abroad, summer session for credit. *ROTC:* Army (b). *Unusual degree programs:* 3-2 engineering with Columbia University School of Engineering & Applied Science.

Computers on Campus 1,018 computers/terminals and 3,300 ports are available on campus for general student use. Students can access the following: campus intranet, computer help desk, free student e-mail accounts, online (class) grades, online (class) registration, online (class) schedules. Campuswide network is available. 100% of college-owned or -operated housing units are wired for high-speed Internet access. Wireless service is available via entire campus.

Student Life *Housing options:* coed, men-only, women-only. Campus housing is university owned. Freshman campus housing is guaranteed. *Activities and organizations:* drama/theater group, student-run newspaper, radio station, choral group, Club Sports, Richmond Rowdies—Facilitates school spirit at athletic events, Alpha Phi Omega Service Fraternity, InterVarsity Christian Fellowship, Student Government Associations, national fraternities, national sororities. *Campus security:* 24-hour emergency response devices and patrols, late-night transport/escort service, controlled dormitory access, campus police. *Student services:* health clinic, personal/psychological counseling, women's center.

Athletics Member NCAA. All Division I except football (Division I-AA). *Intercollegiate sports:* archery M(c)/W(c), badminton M(c)/W(c), baseball M(s), basketball M(s)/W(s), crew M(c)/W(c), cross-country running M(s)/W(s), equestrian sports M(c)/W(c), field hockey W(s), golf M(s)/W(s), ice hockey M(c), lacrosse M(s)/W(s), rugby M(c)/W(c), soccer W(s), squash M(c)/W(c), swimming and diving W(s), tennis M(s)/W(s), track and field W(s), ultimate Frisbee M(c)/W(c), volleyball M(c)/W(c), water polo M(c)/W(c). *Intramural sports:* baseball M(c), basketball M/W, field hockey M(c)/W(c), football M, golf M/W, lacrosse W(c), racquetball M/W, soccer M/W, softball M/W, swimming and diving M/W, table tennis M/W, tennis M/W, volleyball M/W.

Standardized Tests *Required:* SAT or ACT (for admission).

Costs (2013–14) *Comprehensive fee:* $55,590 includes full-time tuition ($45,320) and room and board ($10,270). Full-time tuition and fees vary according to course load. Part-time tuition: $2266 per credit hour. Part-time tuition and fees vary according to course load. *College room only:* $4650. Room and board charges vary according to board plan and housing facility. *Payment plan:* installment. *Waivers:* employees or children of employees.

Financial Aid Of all full-time matriculated undergraduates who enrolled in 2012, 1,771 applied for aid, 1,400 were judged to have need, 1,260 had their need fully met. 519 Federal Work-Study jobs (averaging $1434). In 2012, 478 non-need-based awards were made. *Average percent of need met:* 100%. *Average financial aid package:* $41,836. *Average need-based loan:* $3502. *Average need-based gift aid:* $36,703. *Average non-need-based aid:* $23,005. *Average indebtedness upon graduation:* $21,825. *Financial aid deadline:* 2/15.

Applying *Options:* electronic application, early decision, deferred entrance. *Application fee:* $50. *Required:* essay or personal statement, high school transcript, 1 letter of recommendation. *Application deadlines:* 1/15 (freshmen), 2/15 (transfers). *Early decision deadline:* 11/15 (for plan 1), 1/15 (for plan 2). *Notification:* 4/1 (freshmen), 4/15 (transfers), 12/15 (early decision plan 1), 2/15 (early decision plan 2).

Freshman Application Contact Mr. Gil Villanueva, Dean of Admission, University of Richmond, Brunet Memorial Hall, 28 Westhampton Way, University of Richmond, VA 23173. *Phone:* 804-289-8640. *Toll-free phone:* 800-700-1662. *Fax:* 804-287-6003. *E-mail:* admissions@richmond.edu. *Website:* http://www.richmond.edu/.

University of Virginia

Charlottesville, Virginia

- **State-supported** university, founded 1819
- **Suburban** 1167-acre campus with easy access to Richmond
- **Endowment** $4.7 billion
- **Coed** 15,822 undergraduate students, 94% full-time, 55% women, 45% men
- **Very difficult** entrance level, 30% of applicants were admitted

Undergraduates 14,931 full-time, 891 part-time. Students come from 48 states and territories; 120 other countries; 26% are from out of state; 6% Black or African American, non-Hispanic/Latino; 5% Hispanic/Latino; 11% Asian, non-Hispanic/Latino; 0.1% Native Hawaiian or other Pacific Islander, non-Hispanic/Latino; 0.1% American Indian or Alaska Native, non-Hispanic/Latino; 4% Two or more races, non-Hispanic/Latino; 7% Race/ethnicity unknown; 6% international; 4% transferred in; 41% live on campus. *Retention:* 97% of full-time freshmen returned.

Freshmen *Admission:* 27,193 applied, 8,046 admitted, 3,397 enrolled. *Average high school GPA:* 4.21. *Test scores:* SAT critical reading scores over 500: 97%; SAT math scores over 500: 99%; SAT writing scores over 500: 98%; ACT scores over 18: 99%; SAT critical reading scores over 600: 83%; SAT math scores over 600: 88%; SAT writing scores over 600: 85%; ACT scores over 24: 95%; SAT critical reading scores over 700: 37%; SAT math scores over 700: 48%; SAT writing scores over 700: 42%; ACT scores over 30: 61%.

Faculty *Total:* 1,307, 95% full-time, 90% with terminal degrees. *Student/faculty ratio:* 16:1.

Academics *Calendar:* semesters. *Degrees:* bachelor's, master's, doctoral, and post-master's certificates. *Special study options:* accelerated degree program, adult/continuing education programs, advanced placement credit, cooperative education, double majors, English as a second language, honors programs, independent study, internships, part-time degree program, services for LD students, student-designed majors, study abroad, summer session for credit. *ROTC:* Army (b), Navy (b), Air Force (b). *Unusual degree programs:* 3-2 BA in College of Arts and Sciences/MT in Education.

Computers on Campus 372 computers/terminals are available on campus for general student use. Students can access the following: campus intranet, computer help desk, free student e-mail accounts, online (class) grades, online (class) registration, online (class) schedules, online course management tool. Campuswide network is available. 100% of college-owned or -operated hous-

ing units are wired for high-speed Internet access. Wireless service is available via classrooms, computer centers, computer labs, dorm rooms, learning centers, libraries, student centers.

Student Life *Housing:* on-campus residence required for freshman year. *Options:* coed. Campus housing is university owned. Freshman campus housing is guaranteed. *Activities and organizations:* drama/theater group, student-run newspaper, radio and television station, choral group, marching band, Madison House, student government, university guides, University Union, The Cavalier Daily, national fraternities, national sororities. *Campus security:* 24-hour emergency response devices and patrols, late-night transport/escort service, controlled dormitory access. *Student services:* health clinic, personal/psychological counseling, women's center, legal services.

Athletics Member NCAA. All Division I except football (Division I-A). *Intercollegiate sports:* baseball M(s), basketball M(s)/W(s), crew W(s), cross-country running M(s)/W(s), field hockey W(s), golf M(s)/W(s), lacrosse M(s)/W(s), soccer M(s)/W(s), softball W(s), swimming and diving M(s)/W(s), tennis M(s)/W(s), track and field M(s)/W(s), volleyball W(s), wrestling M(s). *Intramural sports:* archery M(c)/W(c), badminton M(c)/W(c), baseball M(c), basketball M(c)/W(c), cheerleading M(c)/W(c), crew M(c)/W, cross-country running M(c)/W(c), equestrian sports M/W, fencing M(c)/W(c), field hockey W(c), football M, golf M(c)/W(c), gymnastics M(c)/W(c), ice hockey M(c)/W(c), lacrosse M(c)/W(c), racquetball M(c)/W(c), riflery M(c)/W(c), rugby M(c)/W(c), sailing M(c)/W(c), skiing (downhill) M(c)/W(c), soccer M(c)/W(c), softball M/W, squash W(c), swimming and diving M(c)/W(c), table tennis M(c)/W(c), tennis M(c)/W(c), track and field M(c)/W(c), ultimate Frisbee M(c)/W(c), volleyball M(c)/W(c), water polo M(c)/W(c), wrestling M(c)/W(c).

Standardized Tests *Required:* SAT or ACT (for admission). *Recommended:* SAT Subject Tests (for admission), SAT or ACT plus optional ACT writing test (ACT alone does not satisfy requirement). At least two SAT subject tests (student's choice) are recommended.

Costs (2013–14) *Tuition:* state resident $10,016 full-time; nonresident $36,720 full-time. Full-time tuition and fees vary according to program. *Required fees:* $2442 full-time. *Room and board:* $9717; room only: $5337. Room and board charges vary according to board plan and housing facility. *Payment plan:* installment. *Waivers:* senior citizens and employees or children of employees.

Financial Aid Of all full-time matriculated undergraduates who enrolled in 2012, 8,273 applied for aid, 4,595 were judged to have need, 4,367 had their need fully met. In 2012, 1503 non-need-based awards were made. *Average percent of need met:* 98%. *Average financial aid package:* $23,008. *Average need-based loan:* $6131. *Average need-based gift aid:* $18,345. *Average non-need-based aid:* $9863. *Average indebtedness upon graduation:* $21,591.

Applying *Options:* electronic application, early action, deferred entrance. *Application fee:* $60. *Required:* essay or personal statement, high school transcript, 1 letter of recommendation. *Application deadlines:* 1/1 (freshmen), 3/1 (transfers), 11/1 (early action). *Notification:* 4/1 (freshmen), 5/1 (transfers), 1/31 (early action).

Freshman Application Contact Mr. Gregory W. Roberts, Dean of Admission, University of Virginia, PO Box 400160, Charlottesville, VA 22904-4727. *Phone:* 434-982-3200. *Fax:* 434-924-3587. *E-mail:* undergrad-admission@virginia.edu. *Website:* http://www.virginia.edu/.

The University of Virginia's College at Wise

Wise, Virginia

- **State-supported** 4-year, founded 1954, part of University of Virginia
- **Small-town** 396-acre campus
- **Endowment** $50.6 million
- **Coed**
- **Moderately difficult** entrance level

Faculty *Student/faculty ratio:* 15:1.

Academics *Calendar:* semesters. *Degrees:* bachelor's and postbachelor's certificates.

Student Life *Campus security:* 24-hour emergency response devices and patrols, student patrols, late-night transport/escort service, self-defense, informal discussions, pamphlets/posters/films, and crime prevention office.

Athletics Member NAIA.

Standardized Tests *Required:* SAT or ACT (for admission).

Costs (2012–13) *Tuition:* state resident $8107 full-time; nonresident $22,475 full-time. Part-time tuition and fees vary according to course load. *Room and board:* $8876; room only: $5078. Room and board charges vary according to board plan and housing facility. *Payment plans:* installment, deferred payment.

Financial Aid *Of all full-time matriculated undergraduates who enrolled in 2010,* 1,440 applied for aid, 1,231 were judged to have need, 961 had their need fully met. *In 2010,* 77 non-need-based awards were made. *Average percent of need met:* 97. *Average financial aid package:* $9958. *Average need-based loan:* $3462. *Average need-based gift aid:* $5526. *Average non-need-based aid:* $5091. *Average indebtedness upon graduation:* $14,801.

Applying *Options:* early admission, early action. *Application fee:* $25. *Required:* high school transcript, minimum 2.3 GPA. *Recommended:* 2 letters of recommendation.

Freshman Application Contact Mr. Russell D. Necessary, Vice Chancellor for Enrollment Management, The University of Virginia's College at Wise, 1 College Avenue, Wise, VA 24293. *Phone:* 276-328-0322. *Toll-free phone:* 888-282-9324. *Fax:* 276-328-0251. *E-mail:* admissions@uvawise.edu. *Website:* http://www.uvawise.edu/.

Valley Forge Christian College Woodbridge Campus

Woodbridge, Virginia

- **Independent Assemblies of God** 4-year
- **Suburban** campus with easy access to Washington, DC
- **Coed**
- **Minimally difficult** entrance level

Faculty *Student/faculty ratio:* 6:1.

Academics *Degrees:* certificates, associate, and bachelor's.

Student Life *Campus security:* 24-hour emergency response devices.

Costs (2012–13) *Tuition:* $8398 full-time. *Required fees:* $500 full-time. *Payment plans:* installment, deferred payment.

Applying *Application fee:* $75. *Required:* essay or personal statement, high school transcript, minimum 1.5 GPA, interview, Pastor's Recommendation.

Freshman Application Contact Admissions Coordinator, Valley Forge Christian College Woodbridge Campus, 13909 Smoketown Road, Woodbridge, VA 22192. *Phone:* 703-580-4810 Ext. 210. *Toll-free phone:* 800-432-8322. *Website:* http://www.vfcc.edu/woodbridge/.

Virginia Commonwealth University

Richmond, Virginia

- **State-supported** university, founded 1838
- **Urban** 144-acre campus
- **Endowment** $438.1 million
- **Coed** 23,951 undergraduate students, 84% full-time, 56% women, 44% men
- **60%** of applicants were admitted

Undergraduates 20,010 full-time, 3,941 part-time. Students come from 48 states and territories; 109 other countries; 7% are from out of state; 18% Black or African American, non-Hispanic/Latino; 7% Hispanic/Latino; 12% Asian, non-Hispanic/Latino; 0.3% Native Hawaiian or other Pacific Islander, non-Hispanic/Latino; 0.3% American Indian or Alaska Native, non-Hispanic/Latino; 4% Two or more races, non-Hispanic/Latino; 3% Race/ethnicity unknown; 3% international; 8% transferred in; 22% live on campus. *Retention:* 85% of full-time freshmen returned.

Freshmen *Admission:* 15,750 applied, 9,488 admitted, 3,617 enrolled. *Average high school GPA:* 3.6. *Test scores:* SAT critical reading scores over 500: 78%; SAT math scores over 500: 79%; SAT writing scores over 500: 71%; ACT scores over 18: 96%; SAT critical reading scores over 600: 29%; SAT math scores over 600: 29%; SAT writing scores over 600: 24%; ACT scores over 24: 48%; SAT critical reading scores over 700: 6%; SAT math scores over 700: 4%; SAT writing scores over 700: 4%; ACT scores over 30: 7%.

Faculty *Total:* 3,253, 63% full-time. *Student/faculty ratio:* 18:1.

Academics *Calendar:* semesters. *Degrees:* certificates, bachelor's, master's, doctoral, post-master's, and postbachelor's certificates. *Special study options:* academic remediation for entering students, accelerated degree program, adult/continuing education programs, advanced placement credit, cooperative education, distance learning, double majors, English as a second language, freshman honors college, honors programs, independent study, internships, off-campus study, part-time degree program, services for LD students, student-designed majors, study abroad, summer session for credit. *ROTC:* Army (c).

Computers on Campus 1,500 computers/terminals and 81,639 ports are available on campus for general student use. Students can access the following: campus intranet, computer help desk, free student e-mail accounts, online (class) grades, online (class) registration, online (class) schedules. Campus-wide network is available. 100% of college-owned or -operated housing units are wired for high-speed Internet access. Wireless service is available via classrooms, computer centers, computer labs, dorm rooms, learning centers, libraries, student centers.

Student Life *Housing options:* coed. Campus housing is university owned. *Activities and organizations:* drama/theater group, student-run newspaper, radio and television station, choral group, national fraternities, national sororities. *Campus security:* 24-hour emergency response devices and patrols, student patrols, late-night transport/escort service, controlled dormitory access, security personnel in residence halls, RAD classes and special event coverage. *Student services:* health clinic, personal/psychological counseling, women's center.

Athletics Member NCAA. All Division I. *Intercollegiate sports:* baseball M(s), basketball M(s)/W(s), cross-country running M(s)/W(s), field hockey W(s), golf M(s), soccer M(s)/W(s), tennis M(s)/W(s), track and field M(s)/W(s), volleyball W(s). *Intramural sports:* badminton M/W, baseball M(c), basketball M(c)/W, cross-country running M(c)/W(c), equestrian sports M(c)/W(c), field hockey W(c), football M(c), ice hockey M(c), lacrosse M(c), racquetball M/W, rugby M(c)/W(c), skiing (downhill) M(c), soccer M(c)/W(c), softball M/W, swimming and diving M(c)/W(c), table tennis M(c)/W(c), tennis M(c)/W(c), ultimate Frisbee M(c)/W(c), volleyball M/W, weight lifting M(c)/W(c).

Standardized Tests *Required:* SAT or ACT (for admission).

Costs (2012–13) *Tuition:* state resident $7860 full-time, $328 per credit hour part-time; nonresident $21,275 full-time, $886 per credit hour part-time. *Required fees:* $2025 full-time, $78 per credit hour part-time. *Room and board:* $8748. Room and board charges vary according to board plan and housing facility. *Payment plan:* installment. *Waivers:* senior citizens and employees or children of employees.

Financial Aid Of all full-time matriculated undergraduates who enrolled in 2011, 13,931 applied for aid, 11,196 were judged to have need, 867 had their need fully met. 820 Federal Work-Study jobs (averaging $1735). In 2011, 1342 non-need-based awards were made. *Average percent of need met:* 51%. *Average financial aid package:* $9956. *Average need-based loan:* $4340. *Average need-based gift aid:* $5930. *Average non-need-based aid:* $7921. *Average indebtedness upon graduation:* $28,889.

Applying *Options:* electronic application, early admission. *Application fee:* $40. *Required:* high school transcript, SAT or ACT Scores. *Application deadline:* 1/15 (freshmen). *Notification:* 12/1 (freshmen).

Freshman Application Contact Virginia Commonwealth University, 901 West Franklin Street, Richmond, VA 23284-9005. *Phone:* 804-828-6125. *Toll-free phone:* 800-841-3638. *Website:* http://www.vcu.edu/.

Virginia Intermont College

Bristol, Virginia

- **Independent religious** 4-year, founded 1884
- **Small-town** 13-acre campus
- **Endowment** $4.1 million
- **Coed** 496 undergraduate students, 90% full-time, 69% women, 31% men
- **Minimally difficult** entrance level, 99% of applicants were admitted

Undergraduates 447 full-time, 49 part-time. Students come from 34 states and territories; 8 other countries; 44% are from out of state; 8% Black or African American, non-Hispanic/Latino; 2% Hispanic/Latino; 0.4% Asian, non-Hispanic/Latino; 1% American Indian or Alaska Native, non-Hispanic/Latino; 0.4% Two or more races, non-Hispanic/Latino; 5% Race/ethnicity unknown; 2% international; 10% transferred in; 50% live on campus. *Retention:* 61% of full-time freshmen returned.

Freshmen *Admission:* 286 applied, 283 admitted, 82 enrolled. *Average high school GPA:* 3.16. *Test scores:* SAT critical reading scores over 500: 50%; SAT math scores over 500: 41%; SAT writing scores over 500: 39%; ACT scores over 18: 80%; SAT critical reading scores over 600: 15%; SAT math scores over 600: 7%; SAT writing scores over 600: 9%; ACT scores over 24: 23%; SAT critical reading scores over 700: 2%.

Faculty *Total:* 96, 43% full-time, 58% with terminal degrees. *Student/faculty ratio:* 8:1.

Academics *Calendar:* semesters. *Degree:* bachelor's. *Special study options:* academic remediation for entering students, accelerated degree program, adult/continuing education programs, advanced placement credit, double majors, honors programs, independent study, internships, off-campus study, part-time degree program, services for LD students, study abroad, summer session for credit.

Computers on Campus 100 computers/terminals are available on campus for general student use. Students can access the following: campus intranet, computer help desk, free student e-mail accounts, online (class) grades, online (class) registration, online (class) schedules. Campuswide network is available. 100% of college-owned or -operated housing units are wired for high-speed Internet access. Wireless service is available via libraries, student centers.

Student Life *Housing:* on-campus residence required through junior year. *Options:* coed. Campus housing is university owned and leased by the school. Freshman campus housing is guaranteed. *Activities and organizations:* drama/theater group, student-run newspaper, Intermont Green, FCA Fellowship of Christian Athletes, Student Government Association, Sport Management Club, International Issues Club. *Campus security:* 24-hour emergency response devices and patrols, late-night transport/escort service. *Student services:* health clinic, personal/psychological counseling.

Athletics Member NAIA. *Intercollegiate sports:* baseball M(s), basketball M(s)/W(s), equestrian sports M(s)/W(s), golf M(s), soccer M(s)/W(s), softball W(s), volleyball W(s). *Intramural sports:* basketball M/W, bowling M/W, football M/W, golf M/W, soccer M/W, ultimate Frisbee M/W, volleyball M/W.

Standardized Tests *Required:* SAT or ACT (for admission).

Costs (2013–14) *Comprehensive fee:* $32,411 includes full-time tuition ($24,542), mandatory fees ($100), and room and board ($7769). Full-time tuition and fees vary according to course level, course load, program, and reciprocity agreements. Part-time tuition: $491 per credit hour. Part-time tuition and fees vary according to course level, course load, program, and reciprocity agreements. *College room only:* $3760. Room and board charges vary according to board plan and housing facility. *Payment plan:* deferred payment. *Waivers:* senior citizens and employees or children of employees.

Financial Aid Of all full-time matriculated undergraduates who enrolled in 2012, 407 applied for aid, 384 were judged to have need, 37 had their need fully met. In 2012, 44 non-need-based awards were made. *Average percent of need met:* 62%. *Average financial aid package:* $17,904. *Average need-based loan:* $4633. *Average need-based gift aid:* $13,939. *Average non-need-based aid:* $9096. *Average indebtedness upon graduation:* $18,335.

Applying *Options:* electronic application, early admission, early decision, deferred entrance. *Required:* essay or personal statement, high school transcript, minimum 2.5 GPA. *Required for some:* interview, 2 letters of recommendation for students applying to Honors Program. *Application deadlines:* rolling (freshmen), rolling (out-of-state freshmen), rolling (transfers). *Early decision deadline:* 1/1. *Notification:* continuous (freshmen), continuous (out-of-state freshmen), continuous (transfers), 2/15 (early decision).

Freshman Application Contact Geneva Perkins, Virginia Intermont College, 1013 Moore Street, Campus Box D-460, Bristol, VA 24201. *Phone:* 276-466-7892. *Toll-free phone:* 800-451-1842. *Fax:* 276-466-7855. *E-mail:* genevaperkins@vic.edu. *Website:* http://www.vic.edu/.

Virginia International University
Fairfax, Virginia

Freshman Application Contact Admissions Department, Virginia International University, 11200 Waples Mill Road, Fairfax, VA 22030. *Phone:* 703-591-7042 Ext. 313. *Toll-free phone:* 800-514-6848. *Fax:* 703-591-7048. *E-mail:* admissions@viu.edu. *Website:* http://www.viu.edu/.

Virginia Military Institute
Lexington, Virginia

Freshman Application Contact Lt. Col. Tom Mortenson, Associate Director of Admissions, Virginia Military Institute, Admissions Office, Lexington, VA 24450. *Phone:* 540-464-7211. *Toll-free phone:* 800-767-4207. *Fax:* 540-464-7746. *E-mail:* admissions@vmi.edu. *Website:* http://www.vmi.edu/.

Virginia Polytechnic Institute and State University
Blacksburg, Virginia

- **State-supported** university, founded 1872
- **Small-town** 2600-acre campus
- **Endowment** $594.8 million
- **Coed** 23,859 undergraduate students, 98% full-time, 41% women, 59% men
- **Moderately difficult** entrance level, 70% of applicants were admitted

Undergraduates 23,366 full-time, 493 part-time. Students come from 113 other countries; 3% Black or African American, non-Hispanic/Latino; 5% Hispanic/Latino; 8% Asian, non-Hispanic/Latino; 0.1% Native Hawaiian or other Pacific Islander, non-Hispanic/Latino; 0.2% American Indian or Alaska Native, non-Hispanic/Latino; 4% Two or more races, non-Hispanic/Latino; 3% Race/ethnicity unknown; 3% international; 4% transferred in; 36% live on campus. *Retention:* 91% of full-time freshmen returned.

Freshmen *Admission:* 20,191 applied, 14,210 admitted, 5,487 enrolled. *Average high school GPA:* 3.98. *Test scores:* SAT critical reading scores over 500: 76%; SAT math scores over 500: 86%; SAT critical reading scores over 600: 27%; SAT math scores over 600: 46%; SAT critical reading scores over 700: 3%; SAT math scores over 700: 10%.

Faculty *Total:* 1,579, 83% full-time. *Student/faculty ratio:* 16:1.

Academics *Calendar:* semesters. *Degrees:* associate, bachelor's, master's, doctoral, and post-master's certificates. *Special study options:* accelerated degree program, adult/continuing education programs, advanced placement credit, cooperative education, distance learning, double majors, English as a second language, honors programs, independent study, internships, part-time degree program, services for LD students, study abroad, summer session for credit. *ROTC:* Army (b), Navy (b), Air Force (b).

Computers on Campus 8,000 computers/terminals are available on campus for general student use. Students can access the following: campus intranet, computer help desk, free student e-mail accounts, online (class) grades, online (class) registration, online (class) schedules. Campuswide network is available. Wireless service is available via entire campus.

Student Life *Housing:* on-campus residence required for freshman year. *Options:* coed, men-only, women-only. Campus housing is university owned. Freshman campus housing is guaranteed. *Activities and organizations:* drama/theater group, student-run newspaper, radio and television station, choral group, marching band, Virginia Tech Union, Student Government Association, international student organizations, national fraternities, national sororities. *Campus security:* 24-hour emergency response devices and patrols, student patrols, late-night transport/escort service, controlled dormitory access. *Student services:* health clinic, personal/psychological counseling, women's center, legal services.

Athletics Member NCAA. All Division I except football (Division I-A). *Intercollegiate sports:* baseball M, basketball M, cross-country running M/W, golf M(s), lacrosse W(s), soccer M(s)/W(s), swimming and diving M(s)/W(s), tennis M(s)/W(s), track and field M(s)/W(s), ultimate Frisbee M/W, volleyball W. *Intramural sports:* baseball M(c), basketball M, bowling M/W, crew M(c)/W(c), cross-country running M/W, equestrian sports M(c)/W(c), fencing M(c)/W(c), field hockey M(c)/W(c), football M/W, golf M/W, gymnastics M(c)/W(c), ice hockey M/W, lacrosse M(c)/W(c), racquetball M/W, riflery M(c)/W(c), rugby M(c)/W(c), soccer M/W, softball M/W, swimming and diving M/W, table tennis M/W, tennis M/W, volleyball M/W, water polo M/W.

Standardized Tests *Required:* SAT or ACT (for admission). *Required for some:* SAT and SAT Subject Tests or ACT (for admission).

Costs (2012–13) *Tuition:* state resident $9187 full-time; nonresident $23,575 full-time. *Room and board:* $7406; room only: $4190. Room and board charges vary according to board plan. *Payment plan:* installment. *Waivers:* senior citizens and employees or children of employees.

Financial Aid Of all full-time matriculated undergraduates who enrolled in 2011, 15,440 applied for aid, 10,295 were judged to have need, 1,717 had their need fully met. 583 Federal Work-Study jobs (averaging $1122). In 2011, 2697 non-need-based awards were made. *Average percent of need met:* 69%. *Average financial aid package:* $16,279. *Average need-based loan:* $4797. *Average need-based gift aid:* $6594. *Average non-need-based aid:* $4714. *Average indebtedness upon graduation:* $25,759.

Applying *Options:* electronic application, early admission, early decision, deferred entrance. *Application fee:* $60. *Required:* high school transcript. *Recommended:* minimum 3.0 GPA. *Application deadlines:* 1/15 (freshmen), 2/15 (transfers). *Early decision deadline:* 11/1. *Notification:* 4/1 (freshmen), 5/1 (transfers), 12/15 (early decision).

Freshman Application Contact Virginia Polytechnic Institute and State University, Blacksburg, VA 24061. *Phone:* 540-231-6267. *Website:* http://www.vt.edu/.

Virginia State University
Petersburg, Virginia

- **State-supported** comprehensive, founded 1882, part of State Council of Higher Education for Virginia
- **Suburban** 236-acre campus with easy access to Richmond
- **Endowment** $24.0 million
- **Coed** 5,570 undergraduate students, 91% full-time, 60% women, 40% men
- **Minimally difficult** entrance level, 94% of applicants were admitted

Undergraduates 5,082 full-time, 488 part-time. Students come from 39 states and territories; 30% are from out of state; 85% Black or African American, non-Hispanic/Latino; 1% Hispanic/Latino; 0.2% Asian, non-Hispanic/Latino; 0.2% American Indian or Alaska Native, non-Hispanic/Latino; 12% Race/ethnicity unknown; 7% transferred in. *Retention:* 65% of full-time freshmen returned.

Freshmen *Admission:* 5,754 applied, 5,434 admitted, 1,244 enrolled. *Average high school GPA:* 2.8. *Test scores:* SAT critical reading scores over 500: 11%; SAT math scores over 500: 10%; SAT writing scores over 500: 6%; SAT math scores over 600: 1%.

Faculty *Total:* 426, 67% full-time.

Academics *Calendar:* semesters. *Degrees:* associate, bachelor's, master's, doctoral, and postbachelor's certificates. *Special study options:* adult/continuing education programs, advanced placement credit, cooperative education, double majors, honors programs, independent study, internships, off-campus study, part-time degree program, services for LD students, student-designed majors, study abroad, summer session for credit. *ROTC:* Army (b).

Computers on Campus 2,500 computers/terminals are available on campus for general student use. Students can access the following: computer help desk, free student e-mail accounts, online (class) grades, online (class) registration, online (class) schedules. Campuswide network is available. 100% of college-owned or -operated housing units are wired for high-speed Internet access. Wireless service is available via entire campus.

Student Life *Housing:* on-campus residence required for freshman year. *Options:* coed, men-only, women-only. Campus housing is university owned. Freshman applicants given priority for college housing. *Activities and organizations:* drama/theater group, student-run newspaper, choral group, marching band, AbstraKt Entertainment, Golden Key Honor Society, The Betterment of Brothers and Sisters, Diversified Virtue Entertainment, Sankofa, national fraternities, national sororities. *Campus security:* 24-hour emergency response devices and patrols, late-night transport/escort service, controlled dormitory access. *Student services:* health clinic, personal/psychological counseling.

Athletics Member NCAA. All Division II. *Intercollegiate sports:* baseball M(s), basketball M(s)/W(s), bowling W(s), cheerleading M/W, cross-country running M(s)/W(s), football M(s), golf M(s)/W(s), softball W(s), tennis M(s)/W(s), track and field M(s)/W(s), volleyball W(s). *Intramural sports:* basketball M/W, football M, tennis M/W, track and field M/W, volleyball W.

Standardized Tests *Required:* SAT or ACT (for admission).

Costs (2012–13) *Tuition:* state resident $4550 full-time, $311 per credit hour part-time; nonresident $12,988 full-time, $663 per credit hour part-time. Full-time tuition and fees vary according to course load and program. Part-time tuition and fees vary according to course load and program. *Required fees:* $2870 full-time, $10 per credit hour part-time. *Room and board:* $9680; room only: $5816. Room and board charges vary according to board plan and housing facility. *Payment plan:* installment. *Waivers:* senior citizens.

Financial Aid Of all full-time matriculated undergraduates who enrolled in 2012, 5,217 applied for aid, 5,217 were judged to have need, 783 had their need fully met. 300 Federal Work-Study jobs (averaging $2000). In 2012, 574 non-need-based awards were made. *Average percent of need met:* 65%. *Average financial aid package:* $12,401. *Average need-based loan:* $5500. *Average need-based gift aid:* $8196. *Average non-need-based aid:* $1000. *Average indebtedness upon graduation:* $28,250.

Applying *Options:* electronic application. *Application fee:* $25. *Required:* essay or personal statement, high school transcript, minimum 2.2 GPA, 2 letters of recommendation. *Application deadlines:* 5/1 (freshmen), 5/1 (transfers). *Notification:* continuous (freshmen), continuous (transfers).

Freshman Application Contact Mrs. Irene Logan, Director of Admissions, Virginia State University, Office of Admissions, Petersburg, VA 23806-2096. *Phone:* 804-524-5902. *Toll-free phone:* 800-871-7611. *Fax:* 804-524-5055. *E-mail:* ilogan@vsu.edu. *Website:* http://www.vsu.edu/.

Virginia Union University
Richmond, Virginia

- **Independent Baptist** comprehensive, founded 1865
- **Urban** 84-acre campus
- **Endowment** $25.3 million
- **Coed** 1,333 undergraduate students, 97% full-time, 53% women, 47% men
- **Moderately difficult** entrance level, 95% of applicants were admitted

Undergraduates 1,296 full-time, 37 part-time. Students come from 29 states and territories; 50% are from out of state; 97% Black or African American, non-Hispanic/Latino; 0.8% Hispanic/Latino; 0.1% Asian, non-Hispanic/Latino; 0.1% American Indian or Alaska Native, non-Hispanic/Latino; 1% Race/ethnicity unknown; 0.1% international; 4% transferred in. *Retention:* 55% of full-time freshmen returned.

Freshmen *Admission:* 6,910 applied, 6,579 admitted, 418 enrolled. *Average high school GPA:* 2.52.

Faculty *Total:* 114, 68% full-time, 47% with terminal degrees. *Student/faculty ratio:* 15:1.

Academics *Calendar:* semesters. *Degrees:* bachelor's, master's, and doctoral. *Special study options:* academic remediation for entering students, adult/continuing education programs, advanced placement credit, cooperative education, English as a second language, honors programs, internships, off-campus study, summer session for credit. *ROTC:* Army (c). *Unusual degree programs:* 3-2 engineering with Howard University, University of Michigan, University of Iowa, Virginia Commonwealth University.

Computers on Campus 200 computers/terminals are available on campus for general student use. Students can access the following: campus intranet, computer help desk, free student e-mail accounts, online (class) grades, online (class) registration, online (class) schedules, academic research databases. Campuswide network is available. 100% of college-owned or -operated housing units are wired for high-speed Internet access. Wireless service is available via entire campus.

Student Life *Housing options:* coed, men-only, women-only. Campus housing is university owned and leased by the school. Freshman applicants given priority for college housing. *Activities and organizations:* drama/theater group, student-run newspaper, choral group, marching band, Student Government Association, NAACP, NPHC-VUU Chapter (National Pan-Hellenic Council), Mr. and Miss Royal Court, national fraternities, national sororities. *Campus security:* 24-hour emergency response devices and patrols, controlled dormitory access. *Student services:* health clinic, personal/psychological counseling.

Athletics Member NCAA. All Division II. *Intercollegiate sports:* basketball M(s)/W(s), cross-country running M(s)/W(s), football M(s), golf M(s), softball W(s), tennis M(s), track and field M(s)/W(s), volleyball W(s). *Intramural sports:* basketball M, softball W.

Standardized Tests *Required:* SAT or ACT (for admission).

Costs (2012–13) *Comprehensive fee:* $22,302 includes full-time tuition ($13,314), mandatory fees ($1316), and room and board ($7672). Full-time tuition and fees vary according to course level and course load. Part-time tuition: $422 per credit hour. Part-time tuition and fees vary according to course level and course load. *Required fees:* $40 per credit hour part-time. *College room only:* $3600. Room and board charges vary according to housing facility. *Payment plans:* installment, deferred payment. *Waivers:* employees or children of employees.

Financial Aid Of all full-time matriculated undergraduates who enrolled in 2009, 1,163 applied for aid, 1,101 were judged to have need. *Average financial aid package:* $10,921. *Average need-based loan:* $3894. *Average need-based gift aid:* $5371.

Applying *Options:* electronic application, deferred entrance. *Application fee:* $25. *Required:* high school transcript, minimum 2.3 GPA. *Required for some:* interview. *Recommended:* essay or personal statement, minimum 2.5 GPA, 3 letters of recommendation. *Application deadlines:* rolling (freshmen), rolling (transfers). *Notification:* continuous (freshmen), continuous (transfers).

Freshman Application Contact Ms. Sanada Spellman, Assistant Director of Admissions, Virginia Union University, 1500 North Lombardy Street, Richmond, VA 23220-1170. *Phone:* 804-342-3572. *Toll-free phone:* 800-368-3227. *Fax:* 804-342-3511. *E-mail:* slspellman@vuu.edu. *Website:* http://www.vuu.edu/.

Virginia University of Lynchburg
Lynchburg, Virginia

Freshman Application Contact Ms. Cheryl Glass, Director of Admissions, Virginia University of Lynchburg, 2058 Garfield Avenue, Lynchburg, VA

24501. *Phone:* 434-528-5276 Ext. 106. *Fax:* 434-528-4275. *E-mail:* cglass@vul.edu.
Website: http://www.vul.edu/.

Virginia Wesleyan College

Norfolk, Virginia

- **Independent United Methodist** 4-year, founded 1961
- **Urban** 300-acre campus with easy access to Norfolk, Virginia Beach
- **Endowment** $48.6 million
- **Coed** 1,431 undergraduate students, 90% full-time, 63% women, 37% men
- **Moderately difficult** entrance level, 86% of applicants were admitted

Undergraduates 1,288 full-time, 143 part-time. Students come from 32 states and territories; 5 other countries; 25% are from out of state; 23% Black or African American, non-Hispanic/Latino; 7% Hispanic/Latino; 1% Asian, non-Hispanic/Latino; 0.3% Native Hawaiian or other Pacific Islander, non-Hispanic/Latino; 0.5% American Indian or Alaska Native, non-Hispanic/Latino; 5% Two or more races, non-Hispanic/Latino; 4% Race/ethnicity unknown; 0.6% international; 7% transferred in; 61% live on campus. *Retention:* 67% of full-time freshmen returned.
Freshmen *Admission:* 3,890 applied, 3,328 admitted, 435 enrolled. *Average high school GPA:* 3.32. *Test scores:* SAT critical reading scores over 500: 55%; SAT math scores over 500: 50%; SAT writing scores over 500: 44%; ACT scores over 18: 93%; SAT critical reading scores over 600: 17%; SAT math scores over 600: 15%; SAT writing scores over 600: 13%; ACT scores over 24: 32%; SAT critical reading scores over 700: 3%; SAT math scores over 700: 2%; SAT writing scores over 700: 1%; ACT scores over 30: 1%.
Faculty *Total:* 119, 76% full-time. *Student/faculty ratio:* 12:1.
Academics *Calendar:* 4-1-4. *Degree:* bachelor's. *Special study options:* academic remediation for entering students, adult/continuing education programs, advanced placement credit, double majors, freshman honors college, honors programs, independent study, internships, off-campus study, part-time degree program, services for LD students, student-designed majors, study abroad, summer session for credit. *ROTC:* Army (c).
Computers on Campus 130 computers/terminals are available on campus for general student use. Students can access the following: campus intranet, computer help desk, free student e-mail accounts, online (class) grades, online (class) registration, online (class) schedules. Campuswide network is available. 100% of college-owned or -operated housing units are wired for high-speed Internet access. Wireless service is available via entire campus.
Student Life *Housing:* on-campus residence required through senior year. *Options:* coed, women-only, disabled students. Campus housing is university owned. Freshman campus housing is guaranteed. *Activities and organizations:* drama/theater group, student-run newspaper, radio station, choral group, Wesleyan Activities Council, Community service, Student Government Association, student newspaper, Black Student Union, national fraternities, national sororities. *Campus security:* 24-hour emergency response devices and patrols, late-night transport/escort service, controlled dormitory access, well-lit pathways. *Student services:* health clinic, personal/psychological counseling, women's center.
Athletics Member NCAA. All Division III. *Intercollegiate sports:* baseball M, basketball M/W, cheerleading W, cross-country running M/W, field hockey W, golf M, lacrosse M/W, soccer M/W, softball W, tennis M/W, track and field M/W, volleyball W. *Intramural sports:* basketball M/W, crew M(c)/W(c), fencing M(c)/W(c), field hockey W, football M/W, racquetball M/W, soccer M/W, softball M/W, table tennis M/W, ultimate Frisbee M/W, volleyball M/W.
Standardized Tests *Required for some:* SAT or ACT (for admission).
Costs (2013–14) *One-time required fee:* $300. *Comprehensive fee:* $40,690 includes full-time tuition ($31,532), mandatory fees ($650), and room and board ($8508). Full-time tuition and fees vary according to course load. Part-time tuition: $1314 per credit hour. Part-time tuition and fees vary according to course load. *Room and board:* Room and board charges vary according to board plan and housing facility. *Payment plans:* installment, deferred payment. *Waivers:* adult students, senior citizens, and employees or children of employees.
Financial Aid Of all full-time matriculated undergraduates who enrolled in 2011, 1,231 applied for aid, 1,011 were judged to have need, 112 had their need fully met. 182 Federal Work-Study jobs (averaging $911). In 2011, 213 non-need-based awards were made. *Average percent of need met:* 65%. *Average financial aid package:* $20,169. *Average need-based loan:* $7187. *Average need-based gift aid:* $16,700. *Average non-need-based aid:* $15,876. *Average indebtedness upon graduation:* $36,445.
Applying *Options:* electronic application. *Application fee:* $40. *Required:* essay or personal statement, high school transcript, minimum 2.5 GPA.

Required for some: interview. *Application deadlines:* rolling (freshmen), rolling (transfers). *Notification:* continuous (freshmen), continuous (transfers).
Freshman Application Contact Mrs. Kim Harriman, Admissions Receptionist, Virginia Wesleyan College, 1584 Wesleyan Drive, Norfolk, VA 23502-5599. *Phone:* 757-455-3208. *Toll-free phone:* 800-737-8684. *Fax:* 757-461-5238. *E-mail:* admissions@vwc.edu.
Website: http://www.vwc.edu/.

Washington and Lee University

Lexington, Virginia

- **Independent** comprehensive, founded 1749
- **Small-town** 430-acre campus
- **Endowment** $1.3 billion
- **Coed** 1,838 undergraduate students, 100% full-time, 49% women, 51% men
- **Most difficult** entrance level, 19% of applicants were admitted

Undergraduates 1,835 full-time, 3 part-time. Students come from 53 states and territories; 31 other countries; 86% are from out of state; 3% Black or African American, non-Hispanic/Latino; 3% Hispanic/Latino; 3% Asian, non-Hispanic/Latino; 0.2% American Indian or Alaska Native, non-Hispanic/Latino; 2% Two or more races, non-Hispanic/Latino; 2% Race/ethnicity unknown; 4% international; 0.2% transferred in; 59% live on campus. *Retention:* 95% of full-time freshmen returned.
Freshmen *Admission:* 5,972 applied, 1,163 admitted, 479 enrolled. *Test scores:* SAT critical reading scores over 500: 100%; SAT math scores over 500: 100%; SAT writing scores over 500: 100%; ACT scores over 18: 100%; SAT critical reading scores over 600: 96%; SAT math scores over 600: 97%; SAT writing scores over 600: 90%; ACT scores over 24: 100%; SAT critical reading scores over 700: 49%; SAT math scores over 700: 47%; SAT writing scores over 700: 46%; ACT scores over 30: 73%.
Faculty *Total:* 311, 78% full-time, 91% with terminal degrees. *Student/faculty ratio:* 8:1.
Academics *Calendar:* 4-4-2. *Degrees:* bachelor's, master's, and doctoral. *Special study options:* advanced placement credit, double majors, honors programs, independent study, internships, off-campus study, services for LD students, student-designed majors, study abroad. *ROTC:* Army (c).
Computers on Campus 176 computers/terminals and 1,500 ports are available on campus for general student use. Students can access the following: campus intranet, computer help desk, free student e-mail accounts, online (class) grades, online (class) registration, online (class) schedules. Campuswide network is available. 100% of college-owned or -operated housing units are wired for high-speed Internet access. Wireless service is available via entire campus.
Student Life *Housing:* on-campus residence required through sophomore year. *Options:* coed, men-only, women-only, disabled students. Campus housing is university owned. Freshman campus housing is guaranteed. *Activities and organizations:* drama/theater group, student-run newspaper, radio and television station, choral group, Mock Convention, General Activities Board, Nabors Service League, Outing Club, Sports Clubs, national fraternities, national sororities. *Campus security:* 24-hour emergency response devices and patrols, late-night transport/escort service, controlled dormitory access, Emergency Alert System. *Student services:* health clinic, personal/psychological counseling, women's center.
Athletics Member NCAA. All Division III. *Intercollegiate sports:* baseball M, basketball M/W, cheerleading M(c)/W(c), cross-country running M/W, equestrian sports W, fencing M(c)/W(c), field hockey W, football M, golf M/W, ice hockey M(c)/W(c), lacrosse M/W, rugby M(c), skiing (cross-country) M(c)/W(c), soccer M/W, softball W(c), swimming and diving M/W, tennis M/W, track and field M/W, ultimate Frisbee M(c)/W(c), volleyball M(c)/W, wrestling M. *Intramural sports:* badminton M/W, baseball M(c), basketball M/W, equestrian sports W(c), football M/W, golf M/W, lacrosse M(c)/W(c), racquetball M/W, rock climbing M(c), skiing (downhill) M(c)/W(c), soccer M/W, softball M/W, squash M(c)/W(c), swimming and diving M/W, table tennis M/W, tennis M/W, track and field M/W, ultimate Frisbee M/W, volleyball M/W, wrestling M.
Standardized Tests *Required:* SAT or ACT (for admission). *Recommended:* SAT Subject Tests (for admission), 2 unrelated SAT subject tests are recommended, but not required.
Costs (2012–13) *Comprehensive fee:* $52,812 includes full-time tuition ($42,425), mandatory fees ($937), and room and board ($9450). Part-time tuition: $1515 per credit hour. *College room only:* $3840. Room and board charges vary according to board plan and housing facility. *Payment plan:* installment. *Waivers:* employees or children of employees.
Financial Aid Of all full-time matriculated undergraduates who enrolled in 2012, 846 applied for aid, 767 were judged to have need, 767 had their need

fully met. 237 Federal Work-Study jobs (averaging $2000). 381 state and other part-time jobs (averaging $2000). In 2012, 141 non-need-based awards were made. *Average percent of need met:* 100%. *Average financial aid package:* $44,800. *Average need-based loan:* $1180. *Average need-based gift aid:* $38,375. *Average non-need-based aid:* $35,249. *Average indebtedness upon graduation:* $23,409. *Financial aid deadline:* 2/15.

Applying *Options:* electronic application, early decision, deferred entrance. *Application fee:* $50. *Required:* high school transcript, 3 letters of recommendation. *Recommended:* essay or personal statement, interview. *Application deadlines:* 1/1 (freshmen), 4/1 (transfers). *Early decision deadline:* 11/1 (for plan 1), 1/1 (for plan 2). *Notification:* 4/1 (freshmen), continuous (transfers), 12/21 (early decision plan 1), 2/1 (early decision plan 2).

Freshman Application Contact Mr. William M. Hartog, Dean of Admissions and Financial Aid, Washington and Lee University, 204 West Washington Street, Lexington, VA 24450-2116. *Phone:* 540-458-8710. *Fax:* 540-458-8062. *E-mail:* admissions@wlu.edu. *Website:* http://www.wlu.edu/.

Westwood College–Annandale Campus

Annandale, Virginia

Freshman Application Contact Westwood College–Annandale Campus, 7619 Little River Turnpike, 5th Floor, Annandale, VA 22003. *Phone:* 703-642-3633. *Toll-free phone:* 877-305-0049. *Website:* http://www.westwood.edu/.

Westwood College–Arlington Ballston Campus

Arlington, Virginia

Freshman Application Contact Westwood College–Arlington Ballston Campus, 4420 North Fairfax Drive, Arlington, VA 22203. *Phone:* 703-243-1662. *Toll-free phone:* 877-268-5278. *Website:* http://www.westwood.edu/.

World College

Virginia Beach, Virginia

Freshman Application Contact Mrs. Audre Piratzky, Admissions Counselor, World College, 5193 Shore Drive, Suite 105, Virginia Beach, VA 23455. *Phone:* 757-464-4600. *Toll-free phone:* 800-243-6446. *Fax:* 757-464-3687. *E-mail:* instruct@cie-wc.edu. *Website:* http://www.worldcollege.edu/.

WASHINGTON

Antioch University Seattle

Seattle, Washington

Freshman Application Contact Admissions Office, Antioch University Seattle, 2326 Sixth Avenue, Seattle, WA 98121-1814. *Phone:* 206-268-4202. *Toll-free phone:* 888-268-4477. *E-mail:* admissions@antiochseattle.edu. *Website:* http://www.antiochsea.edu/.

Argosy University, Seattle

Seattle, Washington

Freshman Application Contact Argosy University, Seattle, 2601-A Elliott Avenue, Seattle, WA 98121. *Phone:* 206-283-4500. *Toll-free phone:* 866-283-2777. *Website:* http://www.argosy.edu/seattle/.

The Art Institute of Seattle

Seattle, Washington

- **Proprietary** primarily 2-year, founded 1982, part of Education Management Corporation
- **Urban** campus
- **Coed**

Academics *Calendar:* quarters. *Degrees:* diplomas, associate, and bachelor's.

Freshman Application Contact The Art Institute of Seattle, 2323 Elliott Avenue, Seattle, WA 98121-1642. *Phone:* 206-448-6600. *Toll-free phone:* 800-275-2471. *Website:* http://www.artinstitutes.edu/seattle/.

See full-page ad on page 54 and page 1116 for the College Close-Up.

Bastyr University

Kenmore, Washington

- **Independent** upper-level, founded 1978
- **Suburban** 51-acre campus with easy access to Seattle
- **Coed** 221 undergraduate students, 85% full-time, 82% women, 18% men

Undergraduates 187 full-time, 34 part-time. Students come from 24 states and territories; 7 other countries; 25% are from out of state; 3% Black or African American, non-Hispanic/Latino; 5% Hispanic/Latino; 9% Asian, non-Hispanic/Latino; 0.5% Native Hawaiian or other Pacific Islander, non-Hispanic/Latino; 1% American Indian or Alaska Native, non-Hispanic/Latino; 5% Two or more races, non-Hispanic/Latino; 5% Race/ethnicity unknown; 7% international; 44% transferred in; 10% live on campus.

Faculty *Total:* 160, 41% full-time.

Academics *Calendar:* quarters. *Degrees:* certificates, bachelor's, master's, doctoral, and post-master's certificates. *Special study options:* cooperative education, double majors, independent study, internships, part-time degree program, summer session for credit.

Computers on Campus 71 computers/terminals and 20 ports are available on campus for general student use. Students can access the following: campus intranet, computer help desk, free student e-mail accounts, online (class) grades, online (class) schedules. Campuswide network is available. 100% of college-owned or -operated housing units are wired for high-speed Internet access. Wireless service is available via entire campus.

Student Life *Housing options:* coed, disabled students. Campus housing is university owned. *Activities and organizations:* Naturopaths Without Borders, Nature Club, Multicultural Student Association of Natural Medicine, Environmental Action Team, Venture Grant. *Campus security:* student patrols, late-night transport/escort service, controlled dormitory access. *Student services:* health clinic, personal/psychological counseling.

Athletics *Intramural sports:* basketball M, soccer M/W, ultimate Frisbee M/W, volleyball M/W.

Costs (2012–13) *Tuition:* $21,090 full-time, $590 per credit hour part-time. Full-time tuition and fees vary according to course load and program. Part-time tuition and fees vary according to course load and program. *Required fees:* $900 full-time. *Room only:* $7050. Room and board charges vary according to housing facility. *Waivers:* employees or children of employees.

Financial Aid Of all full-time matriculated undergraduates who enrolled in 2011, 186 applied for aid, 184 were judged to have need. 109 Federal Work-Study jobs (averaging $1500). 38 state and other part-time jobs (averaging $1500). *Average percent of need met:* 42%. *Average financial aid package:* $17,052. *Average need-based loan:* $8569. *Average need-based gift aid:* $11,425.

Applying *Options:* electronic application, deferred entrance. *Application fee:* $60. *Application deadline:* 3/15 (transfers).

Application Contact Ms. Lauren Marani, Assistant Director of Admissions, Bastyr University, 14500 Juanita Drive NE, Kenmore, WA 98028-4966. *Phone:* 425-602-1300. *Fax:* 425-602-3090. *E-mail:* admissions@bastyr.edu. *Website:* http://www.bastyr.edu/.

Bellevue College

Bellevue, Washington

Freshman Application Contact Morenika Jacobs, Associate Dean of Enrollment Services, Bellevue College, 3000 Landerholm Circle, SE, Bellevue, WA 98007-6484. *Phone:* 425-564-2205. *Fax:* 425-564-4065. *Website:* http://www.bcc.ctc.edu/.

Central Washington University

Ellensburg, Washington

- **State-supported** comprehensive, founded 1891
- **Small-town** 380-acre campus
- **Coed**
- **Moderately difficult** entrance level

Faculty *Student/faculty ratio:* 21:1.

Academics *Calendar:* quarters. *Degrees:* bachelor's, master's, and postbachelor's certificates.

Student Life *Campus security:* 24-hour emergency response devices and patrols, late-night transport/escort service, controlled dormitory access.

Athletics Member NCAA. All Division II.

Standardized Tests *Required:* SAT or ACT (for admission).

Costs (2012–13) *Tuition:* state resident $7962 full-time, $242 per credit hour part-time; nonresident $18,607 full-time, $596 per credit hour part-time. Part-time tuition and fees vary according to course load. *Required fees:* $984 full-time. *Room and board:* $9240. Room and board charges vary according to board plan and housing facility.

Financial Aid *Of all full-time matriculated undergraduates who enrolled in 2010,* 7,365 applied for aid, 7,195 were judged to have need, 2,328 had their need fully met. *In 2010,* 1 non-need-based awards were made. *Average percent of need met:* 75. *Average financial aid package:* $11,752. *Average need-based loan:* $4102. *Average need-based gift aid:* $7526. *Average non-need-based aid:* $1782. *Average indebtedness upon graduation:* $18,539.

Applying *Options:* electronic application. *Application fee:* $50. *Required:* high school transcript, minimum 2.0 GPA. *Required for some:* essay or personal statement, interview.

Freshman Application Contact Ms. Lisa Garcia-Hanson, Director of Admissions, Central Washington University, 400 East University Way, Ellensburg, WA 98926-7463. *Phone:* 509-963-1211. *Toll-free phone:* 866-298-4968. *Fax:* 509-963-3022. *E-mail:* cwuadmis@cwu.edu. *Website:* http://www.cwu.edu/.

City University of Seattle

Bellevue, Washington

- **Independent** comprehensive, founded 1973
- **Urban** 1-acre campus with easy access to Seattle
- **Coed** 1,035 undergraduate students, 51% full-time, 55% women, 45% men
- **Noncompetitive** entrance level, 100% of applicants were admitted

Undergraduates 532 full-time, 503 part-time. Students come from 45 states and territories; 24 other countries; 6% Black or African American, non-Hispanic/Latino; 6% Hispanic/Latino; 4% Asian, non-Hispanic/Latino; 0.6% Native Hawaiian or other Pacific Islander, non-Hispanic/Latino; 9% American Indian or Alaska Native, non-Hispanic/Latino; 0.5% Two or more races, non-Hispanic/Latino; 27% Race/ethnicity unknown; 10% international; 13% transferred in.

Freshmen *Admission:* 86 applied, 86 admitted, 86 enrolled.

Faculty *Total:* 332, 14% full-time, 23% with terminal degrees. *Student/faculty ratio:* 15:1.

Academics *Calendar:* quarters. *Degrees:* certificates, diplomas, associate, bachelor's, master's, doctoral, post-master's, and postbachelor's certificates. *Special study options:* accelerated degree program, adult/continuing education programs, advanced placement credit, distance learning, double majors, English as a second language, independent study, internships, part-time degree program, services for LD students, student-designed majors, study abroad, summer session for credit.

Computers on Campus 148 computers/terminals are available on campus for general student use. Students can access the following: campus intranet, computer help desk, free student e-mail accounts, online (class) grades, online (class) registration, online (class) schedules. Campuswide network is available. Wireless service is available via classrooms, computer centers, computer labs, libraries.

Student Life *Housing:* college housing not available. *Campus security:* 24-hour emergency response devices. *Student services:* personal/psychological counseling.

Costs (2012–13) *Tuition:* $15,600 full-time, $368 per credit hour part-time. Full-time tuition and fees vary according to course level, course load, degree level, location, program, and reciprocity agreements. Part-time tuition and fees vary according to course level, course load, degree level, location, program, and reciprocity agreements. *Payment plan:* installment. *Waivers:* employees or children of employees.

Financial Aid Of all full-time matriculated undergraduates who enrolled in 2003, 824 applied for aid, 721 were judged to have need. 1 Federal Work-Study job (averaging $1300). In 2003, 18 non-need-based awards were made. *Average percent of need met:* 15%. *Average financial aid package:* $4943. *Average need-based loan:* $4353. *Average need-based gift aid:* $2344. *Average non-need-based aid:* $3738. *Average indebtedness upon graduation:* $16,369.

Applying *Options:* electronic application, deferred entrance. *Application fee:* $50. *Recommended:* high school transcript. *Application deadlines:* rolling (freshmen), rolling (out-of-state freshmen), rolling (transfers). *Notification:* continuous (freshmen), continuous (out-of-state freshmen), continuous (transfers).

Freshman Application Contact Student Services Center, City University of Seattle, 11900 NE First Street, Bellevue, WA 98005. *Phone:* 888-422-4898. *Toll-free phone:* 888-42-CITYU. *E-mail:* info@cityu.edu. *Website:* http://www.cityu.edu/.

Cornish College of the Arts

Seattle, Washington

- **Independent** 4-year, founded 1914
- **Urban** 4-acre campus
- **Endowment** $6.6 million
- **Coed**
- **Moderately difficult** entrance level

Faculty *Student/faculty ratio:* 6:1.

Academics *Calendar:* semesters. *Degree:* bachelor's.

Student Life *Campus security:* 24-hour emergency response devices and patrols, late-night transport/escort service, controlled dormitory access.

Standardized Tests *Recommended:* SAT or ACT (for admission).

Financial Aid *Of all full-time matriculated undergraduates who enrolled in 2010,* 736 applied for aid, 654 were judged to have need, 60 had their need fully met. *In 2010,* 111 non-need-based awards were made. *Average percent of need met:* 52. *Average financial aid package:* $16,134. *Average need-based loan:* $4494. *Average need-based gift aid:* $10,296. *Average non-need-based aid:* $4736. *Average indebtedness upon graduation:* $36,567.

Applying *Options:* electronic application, deferred entrance. *Application fee:* $40. *Required:* essay or personal statement, high school transcript, minimum 2.5 GPA, portfolio or audition. *Required for some:* 2 letters of recommendation. *Recommended:* 2 letters of recommendation, interview.

Freshman Application Contact Ms. Sharron Starling, Director of Admissions, Cornish College of the Arts, 1000 Lenora Street, Seattle, WA 98121. *Phone:* 206-726-5017. *Toll-free phone:* 800-726-ARTS. *Fax:* 206-720-1011. *E-mail:* admissions@cornish.edu. *Website:* http://www.cornish.edu/.

DeVry University

Bellevue, Washington

Admissions Office Contact DeVry University, 600 108th Avenue NE, Suite 230, Bellevue, WA 98004-5110. *Toll-free phone:* 866-338-7941. *Website:* http://www.devry.edu/.

DeVry University

Federal Way, Washington

- **Proprietary** comprehensive, founded 2001, part of DeVry University
- **Suburban** campus
- **Coed** 502 undergraduate students, 50% full-time, 30% women, 70% men
- **Minimally difficult** entrance level

Undergraduates 250 full-time, 252 part-time. 12% are from out of state; 13% Black or African American, non-Hispanic/Latino; 9% Hispanic/Latino; 6% Asian, non-Hispanic/Latino; 2% Native Hawaiian or other Pacific Islander, non-Hispanic/Latino; 0.8% American Indian or Alaska Native, non-Hispanic/Latino; 3% Two or more races, non-Hispanic/Latino; 9% Race/ethnicity unknown; 0.4% international; 18% transferred in.

Freshmen *Admission:* 21 enrolled.

Faculty *Total:* 89, 16% full-time. *Student/faculty ratio:* 10:1.

Academics *Calendar:* semesters. *Degrees:* associate, bachelor's, master's, and postbachelor's certificates. *Special study options:* adult/continuing education programs, part-time degree program.

Student Life *Housing:* college housing not available.
Costs (2013–14) *Tuition:* $16,076 full-time, $609 per credit hour part-time. *Required fees:* $80 full-time.
Financial Aid Of all full-time matriculated undergraduates who enrolled in 2007, 259 applied for aid, 250 were judged to have need, 8 had their need fully met. In 2007, 15 non-need-based awards were made. *Average percent of need met:* 34%. *Average financial aid package:* $10,833. *Average need-based loan:* $6622. *Average need-based gift aid:* $5975. *Average non-need-based aid:* $20,202. *Average indebtedness upon graduation:* $50,600.
Applying *Options:* electronic application. *Application fee:* $40. *Required:* high school transcript, interview. *Application deadlines:* rolling (freshmen), rolling (transfers). *Notification:* continuous (freshmen), continuous (transfers).
Freshman Application Contact DeVry University, 3600 South 344th Way, Federal Way, WA 98001. *Phone:* 253-943-2800. *Toll-free phone:* 866-338-7941.
Website: http://www.devry.edu/.

DigiPen Institute of Technology
Redmond, Washington

- **Proprietary** comprehensive, founded 1988
- **Suburban** 3-acre campus with easy access to Seattle
- **Coed** 884 undergraduate students
- **Minimally difficult** entrance level, 44% of applicants were admitted

Undergraduates Students come from 22 other countries; 47% are from out of state; 0.6% Black or African American, non-Hispanic/Latino; 5% Hispanic/Latino; 6% Asian, non-Hispanic/Latino; 0.2% Native Hawaiian or other Pacific Islander, non-Hispanic/Latino; 0.2% American Indian or Alaska Native, non-Hispanic/Latino; 5% Two or more races, non-Hispanic/Latino; 17% Race/ethnicity unknown; 17% international. *Retention:* 72% of full-time freshmen returned.
Freshmen *Admission:* 468 applied, 205 admitted.
Faculty *Total:* 95, 49% full-time, 33% with terminal degrees. *Student/faculty ratio:* 15:1.
Academics *Calendar:* semesters. *Degrees:* bachelor's and master's. *Special study options:* academic remediation for entering students, accelerated degree program, advanced placement credit, double majors, English as a second language, independent study, internships, services for LD students, study abroad, summer session for credit.
Computers on Campus 1,200 computers/terminals and 500 ports are available on campus for general student use. Students can access the following: campus intranet, computer help desk, free student e-mail accounts, online (class) grades, online (class) registration, online (class) schedules. Campuswide network is available. Wireless service is available via entire campus.
Student Life *Housing options:* coed. Campus housing is leased by the school and is provided by a third party. Freshman applicants given priority for college housing. *Activities and organizations:* Game Testing Club, Guilty Gear Club, Student Association, Audio Freaks, Game Design Club. *Campus security:* late-night transport/escort service, controlled dormitory access, on-site security during campus hours. *Student services:* personal/psychological counseling.
Standardized Tests *Required for some:* SAT or ACT (for admission).
Costs (2013–14) *One-time required fee:* $150. *Comprehensive fee:* $37,001 includes full-time tuition ($26,400), mandatory fees ($160), and room and board ($10,441). Full-time tuition and fees vary according to course load and program. Part-time tuition: $15,460 per year. Part-time tuition and fees vary according to course load and program. *Room and board:* Room and board charges vary according to board plan and housing facility. *Payment plan:* installment. *Waivers:* employees or children of employees.
Financial Aid Of all full-time matriculated undergraduates who enrolled in 2011, 11 applied for aid, 10 were judged to have need. In 2011, 58 non-need-based awards were made. *Average financial aid package:* $7000. *Average need-based loan:* $3981. *Average need-based gift aid:* $3345. *Average non-need-based aid:* $2050. *Average indebtedness upon graduation:* $47,500.
Applying *Options:* electronic application, deferred entrance. *Application fee:* $35. *Required:* essay or personal statement, high school transcript, minimum 2.5 GPA. *Required for some:* art portfolio for BFA in Digital Art and Animation applicants; specific essay requirements for Game Design applicants; audition portfolio for BA in Music and Sound Design applicants. *Recommended:* 2 letters of recommendation. *Application deadlines:* rolling (freshmen), rolling (out-of-state freshmen), rolling (transfers). *Notification:* continuous (freshmen), continuous (out-of-state freshmen), continuous (transfers).
Freshman Application Contact Ms. Danial Powers, Assistant Director of Admissions, DigiPen Institute of Technology, 9931 Willows Road NE, Redmond, WA 98052. *Phone:* 425-558-0299. *Fax:* 425-558-0378. *E-mail:* admissions@digipen.edu.
Website: http://www.digipen.edu/.

Eastern Washington University
Cheney, Washington

- **State-supported** comprehensive, founded 1882
- **Suburban** 335-acre campus with easy access to Spokane
- **Endowment** $21.0 million
- **Coed** 11,360 undergraduate students, 84% full-time, 55% women, 45% men

Undergraduates 9,557 full-time, 1,803 part-time. Students come from 46 states and territories; 20 other countries; 6% are from out of state; 4% Black or African American, non-Hispanic/Latino; 11% Hispanic/Latino; 3% Asian, non-Hispanic/Latino; 0.4% Native Hawaiian or other Pacific Islander, non-Hispanic/Latino; 1% American Indian or Alaska Native, non-Hispanic/Latino; 4% Two or more races, non-Hispanic/Latino; 8% Race/ethnicity unknown; 3% international; 12% transferred in; 20% live on campus. *Retention:* 76% of full-time freshmen returned.
Freshmen *Admission:* 1,572 enrolled. *Average high school GPA:* 3.22. *Test scores:* SAT critical reading scores over 500: 41%; SAT math scores over 500: 49%; SAT writing scores over 500: 35%; ACT scores over 18: 75%; SAT critical reading scores over 600: 9%; SAT math scores over 600: 13%; SAT writing scores over 600: 6%; ACT scores over 24: 25%; SAT critical reading scores over 700: 1%; ACT scores over 30: 2%.
Faculty *Total:* 649, 64% full-time, 62% with terminal degrees. *Student/faculty ratio:* 23:1.
Academics *Calendar:* quarters. *Degrees:* certificates, bachelor's, master's, doctoral, post-master's, and postbachelor's certificates. *Special study options:* academic remediation for entering students, accelerated degree program, advanced placement credit, cooperative education, distance learning, double majors, English as a second language, honors programs, independent study, internships, off-campus study, part-time degree program, services for LD students, student-designed majors, study abroad, summer session for credit. *ROTC:* Army (b). *Unusual degree programs:* 3-2 Master of Occupational Therapy with undergraduate exercise science, therapeutic recreation or interdisciplinary studies.
Computers on Campus 1,012 computers/terminals and 250 ports are available on campus for general student use. Students can access the following: computer help desk, free student e-mail accounts, online (class) grades, online (class) registration, online (class) schedules, 15 gb network disk storage per student; discounted Microsoft and Adobe software; laptops, still and video cameras, projectors for checkout; print credit; black white laser, color laser, and color photo options, large format print service. Campuswide network is available. 100% of college-owned or -operated housing units are wired for high-speed Internet access. Wireless service is available via classrooms, computer centers, computer labs, dorm rooms, learning centers, libraries, student centers.
Student Life *Housing options:* coed, disabled students. Campus housing is university owned. Freshman applicants given priority for college housing. *Activities and organizations:* drama/theater group, student-run newspaper, radio station, choral group, marching band, Circle K International, Saudi Club, Gamers Club, Hui O Hawaii, Sportsman's Club, national fraternities, national sororities. *Campus security:* 24-hour emergency response devices and patrols, student patrols, late-night transport/escort service, controlled dormitory access, emergency call boxes. *Student services:* health clinic, personal/psychological counseling, women's center.
Athletics Member NCAA. All Division I except football (Division I-AA). *Intercollegiate sports:* archery M(c)/W(c), baseball M(c), basketball M(s)/W(s), cheerleading W(c), cross-country running M(s)/W(s), equestrian sports M(c)/W(c), fencing M(c)/W(c), golf W(s), ice hockey M(c)/W(c), rugby M(c)/W(c), soccer M(c)/W(s), softball W(c), tennis M(s)/W(s), track and field M(s)/W(s), volleyball W(s). *Intramural sports:* baseball M/W, basketball M/W, bowling M/W, cross-country running M/W, football M, golf W, racquetball M/W, soccer M/W, softball M/W, tennis M/W, track and field M/W, ultimate Frisbee M(c)/W(c), volleyball M/W, wrestling M(c)/W(c).
Standardized Tests *Required:* SAT or ACT (for admission).
Costs (2012–13) *Tuition:* state resident $7425 full-time, $248 per credit part-time; nonresident $18,168 full-time, $606 per credit part-time. Full-time tuition and fees vary according to program and reciprocity agreements. Part-time tuition and fees vary according to program and reciprocity agreements. *Required fees:* $551 full-time, $551 per year part-time. *Room and board:* $8412; room only: $4500. Room and board charges vary according to board plan and housing facility. *Payment plan:* installment.
Financial Aid Of all full-time matriculated undergraduates who enrolled in 2011, 7,397 applied for aid, 6,201 were judged to have need, 1,459 had their need fully met. 162 Federal Work-Study jobs (averaging $2042). 277 state and other part-time jobs (averaging $2151). In 2011, 433 non-need-based awards were made. *Average percent of need met:* 63%. *Average financial aid package:* $13,333. *Average need-based loan:* $4162. *Average need-based gift aid:*

$7345. *Average non-need-based aid:* $3528. *Average indebtedness upon graduation:* $23,604.

Applying *Required:* high school transcript, minimum 2.0 GPA. *Required for some:* essay or personal statement. *Recommended:* minimum 3.0 GPA.

Freshman Application Contact Ms. Shannon Carr, Director of Admissions, Eastern Washington University, Eastern Washington University, 101 Sutton Hall, Cheney, WA 99004-2447. *Phone:* 509-359-6582. *Fax:* 509-359-6692. *E-mail:* admissions@ewu.edu.
Website: http://www.ewu.edu/.

The Evergreen State College

Olympia, Washington

- **State-supported** comprehensive, founded 1967, part of Washington State Public Baccalaureate Institution
- **Rural** 1000-acre campus with easy access to Seattle
- **Endowment** $7.4 million
- **Coed** 4,193 undergraduate students, 92% full-time, 53% women, 47% men
- **Moderately difficult** entrance level, 98% of applicants were admitted

Undergraduates 3,872 full-time, 321 part-time. Students come from 49 states and territories; 26 other countries; 25% are from out of state; 5% Black or African American, non-Hispanic/Latino; 7% Hispanic/Latino; 3% Asian, non-Hispanic/Latino; 0.5% Native Hawaiian or other Pacific Islander, non-Hispanic/Latino; 2% American Indian or Alaska Native, non-Hispanic/Latino; 6% Two or more races, non-Hispanic/Latino; 9% Race/ethnicity unknown; 0.6% international; 18% transferred in; 20% live on campus. *Retention:* 72% of full-time freshmen returned.

Freshmen *Admission:* 1,650 applied, 1,624 admitted, 534 enrolled. *Average high school GPA:* 3.02. *Test scores:* SAT critical reading scores over 500: 80%; SAT math scores over 500: 63%; SAT writing scores over 500: 66%; ACT scores over 18: 93%; SAT critical reading scores over 600: 43%; SAT math scores over 600: 24%; SAT writing scores over 600: 27%; ACT scores over 24: 56%; SAT critical reading scores over 700: 11%; SAT math scores over 700: 3%; SAT writing scores over 700: 3%; ACT scores over 30: 10%.

Faculty *Total:* 240, 73% full-time, 78% with terminal degrees. *Student/faculty ratio:* 21:1.

Academics *Calendar:* quarters. *Degrees:* bachelor's and master's. *Special study options:* accelerated degree program, advanced placement credit, double majors, independent study, internships, off-campus study, part-time degree program, services for LD students, student-designed majors, study abroad, summer session for credit.

Computers on Campus 470 computers/terminals are available on campus for general student use. Students can access the following: campus intranet, computer help desk, free student e-mail accounts, online (class) grades, online (class) registration, online (class) schedules, Online payment, student accounts history, financial aid records, academic history, housing application, evaluations. Campuswide network is available. 100% of college-owned or -operated housing units are wired for high-speed Internet access. Wireless service is available via entire campus.

Student Life *Housing options:* coed, disabled students. Campus housing is university owned. Freshman campus housing is guaranteed. *Activities and organizations:* drama/theater group, student-run newspaper, radio and television station, choral group, Bike Shop, Women's Resource Center, Asian Pacific Islander Coalition, Freedom First Dance Collective, Community Gardens. *Campus security:* 24-hour emergency response devices and patrols, student patrols, late-night transport/escort service, controlled dormitory access. *Student services:* health clinic, personal/psychological counseling, women's center.

Athletics Member NAIA. *Intercollegiate sports:* basketball M(s)/W(s), crew M(c)/W(c), cross-country running M(s)/W(s), rugby M(c)/W(c), soccer M(s)/W(s), track and field M(s)/W(s), volleyball W(s). *Intramural sports:* archery M(c)/W(c), basketball M/W, fencing M(c)/W(c), soccer M(c)/W(c), tennis M(c)/W(c), ultimate Frisbee M(c)/W(c), volleyball M(c)/W(c), wrestling M(c)/W(c).

Standardized Tests *Required:* SAT or ACT (for admission).

Costs (2012–13) *Tuition:* state resident $7812 full-time, $260 per credit hour part-time; nonresident $18,978 full-time, $633 per credit hour part-time. Full-time tuition and fees vary according to course load, location, and program. Part-time tuition and fees vary according to course load, location, and program. *Required fees:* $583 full-time, $8 per credit hour part-time, $3 per term part-time. *Room and board:* $9240; room only: $6150. Room and board charges vary according to board plan, housing facility, location, and student level. *Waivers:* senior citizens and employees or children of employees.

Financial Aid Of all full-time matriculated undergraduates who enrolled in 2010, 2,953 applied for aid, 2,612 were judged to have need, 282 had their

need fully met. In 2010, 5 non-need-based awards were made. *Average percent of need met:* 70%. *Average financial aid package:* $8600. *Average need-based loan:* $4129. *Average need-based gift aid:* $8564. *Average non-need-based aid:* $6108. *Average indebtedness upon graduation:* $17,545.

Applying *Options:* electronic application, deferred entrance. *Application fee:* $50. *Required:* high school transcript, minimum 2.0 GPA. *Required for some:* essay or personal statement. *Recommended:* essay or personal statement. *Application deadlines:* 2/1 (freshmen), 2/1 (transfers). *Notification:* continuous until 11/1 (freshmen), continuous until 11/1 (transfers).

Freshman Application Contact The Evergreen State College, 2700 Evergreen Parkway, NW, Olympia, WA 98505. *Phone:* 360-867-6170. *Website:* http://www.evergreen.edu/.

Gonzaga University

Spokane, Washington

- **Independent Roman Catholic** comprehensive, founded 1887
- **Urban** 130-acre campus
- **Endowment** $148.3 million
- **Coed** 4,906 undergraduate students, 98% full-time, 54% women, 46% men
- **Moderately difficult** entrance level, 67% of applicants were admitted

Undergraduates 4,805 full-time, 101 part-time. Students come from 46 states and territories; 19 other countries; 51% are from out of state; 1% Black or African American, non-Hispanic/Latino; 8% Hispanic/Latino; 4% Asian, non-Hispanic/Latino; 0.5% Native Hawaiian or other Pacific Islander, non-Hispanic/Latino; 0.6% American Indian or Alaska Native, non-Hispanic/Latino; 5% Two or more races, non-Hispanic/Latino; 6% Race/ethnicity unknown; 2% international; 3% transferred in; 58% live on campus. *Retention:* 94% of full-time freshmen returned.

Freshmen *Admission:* 6,991 applied, 4,650 admitted, 1,096 enrolled. *Average high school GPA:* 3.71. *Test scores:* SAT critical reading scores over 500: 91%; SAT math scores over 500: 95%; ACT scores over 18: 100%; SAT critical reading scores over 600: 43%; SAT math scores over 600: 55%; ACT scores over 24: 85%; SAT critical reading scores over 700: 7%; SAT math scores over 700: 10%; ACT scores over 30: 21%.

Faculty *Total:* 784, 52% full-time, 47% with terminal degrees. *Student/faculty ratio:* 11:1.

Academics *Calendar:* semesters. *Degrees:* bachelor's, master's, doctoral, post-master's, and postbachelor's certificates. *Special study options:* accelerated degree program, adult/continuing education programs, advanced placement credit, double majors, English as a second language, honors programs, independent study, internships, off-campus study, part-time degree program, services for LD students, study abroad, summer session for credit. *ROTC:* Army (b). *Unusual degree programs:* 3-2 nursing.

Computers on Campus 400 computers/terminals and 900 ports are available on campus for general student use. Students can access the following: computer help desk, free student e-mail accounts, online (class) grades, online (class) registration, online (class) schedules. Campuswide network is available. 100% of college-owned or -operated housing units are wired for high-speed Internet access. Wireless service is available via entire campus.

Student Life *Housing:* on-campus residence required through sophomore year. *Options:* coed, men-only, women-only, disabled students. Campus housing is university owned and leased by the school. Freshman campus housing is guaranteed. *Activities and organizations:* drama/theater group, student-run newspaper, radio and television station, choral group, Student Body Association, Search, Circle K, Encore, Knights and Setons. *Campus security:* 24-hour emergency response devices and patrols, late-night transport/escort service, controlled dormitory access. *Student services:* health clinic, personal/psychological counseling.

Athletics Member NCAA. All Division I. *Intercollegiate sports:* baseball M(s), basketball M(s)/W(s), crew M/W(s), cross-country running M(s)/W(s), golf M/W, ice hockey M(c), lacrosse M(c)/W(c), rugby M(c)/W(c), skiing (downhill) M(c)/W(c), soccer M(s)/W(s), tennis M(s)/W(s), track and field M(s)/W(s), ultimate Frisbee M(c)/W(c), volleyball M(c)/W(c). *Intramural sports:* badminton M/W, basketball M/W, football M/W, racquetball M/W, soccer M(c)/W(c), softball M/W, swimming and diving M(c)/W(c), ultimate Frisbee M/W, volleyball M/W.

Standardized Tests *Required:* SAT or ACT (for admission).

Costs (2012–13) *Comprehensive fee:* $42,382 includes full-time tuition ($33,160), mandatory fees ($492), and room and board ($8730). Full-time tuition and fees vary according to course load, location, program, reciprocity agreements, and student level. Part-time tuition: $885 per credit hour. Part-time tuition and fees vary according to course load, location, program, reciprocity agreements, and student level. *College room only:* $4580. Room and board charges vary according to board plan and housing facility. *Payment plans:* installment, deferred payment. *Waivers:* employees or children of employees.

Financial Aid Of all full-time matriculated undergraduates who enrolled in 2011, 3,488 applied for aid, 2,740 were judged to have need, 684 had their need fully met. 411 Federal Work-Study jobs (averaging $2978). 476 state and other part-time jobs (averaging $3807). In 2011, 1747 non-need-based awards were made. *Average percent of need met:* 79%. *Average financial aid package:* $23,564. *Average need-based loan:* $5313. *Average need-based gift aid:* $17,704. *Average non-need-based aid:* $11,412. *Average indebtedness upon graduation:* $23,522.

Applying *Options:* electronic application, early action, deferred entrance. *Application fee:* $50. *Required:* essay or personal statement, high school transcript, minimum 3.0 GPA, 1 letter of recommendation. *Recommended:* interview. *Application deadlines:* 2/1 (freshmen), 6/1 (transfers), 11/15 (early action). *Notification:* 3/15 (freshmen), continuous (transfers), 1/15 (early action).

Freshman Application Contact Ms. Julie McCulloh, Dean of Admission, Gonzaga University, 502 East Boone Avenue, Spokane, WA 99258-0102. *Phone:* 800-322-2584. *Toll-free phone:* 800-322-2584 Ext. 6572. *Fax:* 509-313-6572. *E-mail:* admissions@gonzaga.edu. *Website:* http://www.gonzaga.edu/.

Heritage University

Toppenish, Washington

Freshman Application Contact Miguel Puente, Director of Admissions and Recruitment, Heritage University, 3240 Fort Road, Toppenish, WA 98948-9599. *Phone:* 509-865-8508. *Toll-free phone:* 888-272-6190. *Fax:* 509-865-4469. *E-mail:* admissions@heritage.edu. *Website:* http://www.heritage.edu/.

ITT Technical Institute

Everett, Washington

- **Proprietary** primarily 2-year, part of ITT Educational Services, Inc.
- **Coed**
- **Minimally difficult** entrance level

Academics *Degrees:* associate and bachelor's.

Freshman Application Contact Director of Recruitment, ITT Technical Institute, 1615 75th Street SW, Everett, WA 98203. *Phone:* 425-583-0200. *Toll-free phone:* 800-272-3791. *Website:* http://www.itt-tech.edu/.

ITT Technical Institute

Seattle, Washington

- **Proprietary** primarily 2-year, founded 1932, part of ITT Educational Services, Inc.
- **Urban** campus
- **Coed**
- **Minimally difficult** entrance level

Academics *Calendar:* quarters. *Degrees:* associate and bachelor's.

Freshman Application Contact Director of Recruitment, ITT Technical Institute, 12720 Gateway Drive, Suite 100, Seattle, WA 98168-3333. *Phone:* 206-244-3300. *Toll-free phone:* 800-422-2029. *Website:* http://www.itt-tech.edu/.

ITT Technical Institute

Spokane Valley, Washington

- **Proprietary** primarily 2-year, founded 1985, part of ITT Educational Services, Inc.
- **Suburban** campus
- **Coed**
- **Minimally difficult** entrance level

Academics *Calendar:* quarters. *Degrees:* associate and bachelor's.

Freshman Application Contact Director of Recruitment, ITT Technical Institute, 13518 East Indiana Avenue, Spokane Valley, WA 99216. *Phone:* 509-926-2900. *Toll-free phone:* 800-777-8324. *Website:* http://www.itt-tech.edu/.

Northwest College of Art & Design

Poulsbo, Washington

Freshman Application Contact Mr. Mark Stoddard, Admissions, Northwest College of Art & Design, 16301 Creative Drive, NE, Poulsbo, WA 98370. *Phone:* 360-779-9993. *Toll-free phone:* 800-769-ARTS. *E-mail:* mstoddard@nca.edu. *Website:* http://www.ncad.edu/.

Northwest Indian College

Bellingham, Washington

Freshman Application Contact Office of Admissions, Northwest Indian College, 2522 Kwina Road, Bellingham, WA 98226. *Phone:* 360-676-2772. *Toll-free phone:* 866-676-2772. *Fax:* 360-392-4333. *E-mail:* admissions@nwic.edu. *Website:* http://www.nwic.edu/.

Northwest University

Kirkland, Washington

- **Independent** comprehensive, founded 1934, affiliated with Assemblies of God
- **Suburban** 56-acre campus with easy access to Seattle
- **Endowment** $9.3 million
- **Coed** 1,355 undergraduate students, 86% full-time, 59% women, 41% men
- **Moderately difficult** entrance level, 64% of applicants were admitted

Undergraduates 1,163 full-time, 192 part-time. Students come from 29 states and territories; 16 other countries; 6% are from out of state; 4% Black or African American, non-Hispanic/Latino; 8% Hispanic/Latino; 5% Asian, non-Hispanic/Latino; 1% Native Hawaiian or other Pacific Islander, non-Hispanic/Latino; 1% American Indian or Alaska Native, non-Hispanic/Latino; 2% Two or more races, non-Hispanic/Latino; 2% Race/ethnicity unknown; 2% international; 15% transferred in; 55% live on campus. *Retention:* 86% of full-time freshmen returned.

Freshmen *Admission:* 749 applied, 476 admitted, 215 enrolled. *Average high school GPA:* 3.34. *Test scores:* SAT critical reading scores over 500: 118%; SAT math scores over 500: 122%; SAT writing scores over 500: 111%; ACT scores over 18: 74%; SAT critical reading scores over 600: 43%; SAT math scores over 600: 41%; SAT writing scores over 600: 31%; ACT scores over 24: 29%; SAT critical reading scores over 700: 7%; SAT math scores over 700: 3%; SAT writing scores over 700: 1%.

Faculty *Total:* 206, 28% full-time, 19% with terminal degrees. *Student/faculty ratio:* 13:1.

Academics *Calendar:* semesters. *Degrees:* certificates, diplomas, associate, bachelor's, master's, and doctoral. *Special study options:* academic remediation for entering students, accelerated degree program, adult/continuing education programs, advanced placement credit, cooperative education, double majors, English as a second language, independent study, internships, part-time degree program, study abroad, summer session for credit. *ROTC:* Army (c), Air Force (c).

Computers on Campus 134 computers/terminals are available on campus for general student use. Students can access the following: campus intranet, computer help desk, free student e-mail accounts, online (class) grades, online (class) registration, online (class) schedules, online classes. Campuswide network is available. 100% of college-owned or -operated housing units are wired for high-speed Internet access. Wireless service is available via entire campus.

Student Life *Housing:* on-campus residence required through sophomore year. *Options:* men-only, women-only. Campus housing is university owned. Freshman campus housing is guaranteed. *Activities and organizations:* drama/theater group, student-run newspaper, radio station, choral group, Student Ministries, Pursuit (worship service), Northwest University Business Club, Environmental Stewardship Club. *Campus security:* 24-hour emergency response devices and patrols, late-night transport/escort service, controlled dormitory access. *Student services:* health clinic, personal/psychological counseling.

Athletics Member NAIA. *Intercollegiate sports:* basketball M(s)/W(s), cross-country running M(s)/W(s), soccer M(s)/W(s), track and field M(s)/W(s), volleyball W(s).

Standardized Tests *Required:* SAT or ACT (for admission).

Financial Aid Of all full-time matriculated undergraduates who enrolled in 2012, 1,080 applied for aid, 975 were judged to have need, 144 had their need fully met. 72 Federal Work-Study jobs (averaging $3066). 13 state and other part-time jobs (averaging $4107). In 2012, 151 non-need-based awards were made. *Average percent of need met:* 68%. *Average financial aid package:* $17,722. *Average need-based loan:* $3930. *Average need-based gift aid:* $13,790. *Average non-need-based aid:* $7772. *Average indebtedness upon graduation:* $31,691. *Financial aid deadline:* 8/1.

Applying *Options:* electronic application, early action, deferred entrance. *Application fee:* $30. *Required:* essay or personal statement, high school transcript, minimum 2.3 GPA, 2 letters of recommendation. *Required for some:* interview. *Application deadlines:* 8/1 (freshmen), 8/1 (transfers), 1/15 (early action). *Notification:* continuous (freshmen), continuous (transfers), 2/15 (early action).

Freshman Application Contact Ms. Jessica Pillay, Director of Admissions, Northwest University, PO Box 579, Kirkland, WA 98083-0579. *Phone:* 425-889-5212. *Toll-free phone:* 800-669-3781. *Fax:* 425-889-5224. *E-mail:* admissions@northwestu.edu.
Website: http://www.northwestu.edu/.

Olympic College

Bremerton, Washington

- **State-supported** primarily 2-year, founded 1946, part of Washington State Board for Community and Technical Colleges
- **Suburban** 33-acre campus with easy access to Seattle
- **Coed** 8,260 undergraduate students
- **Noncompetitive** entrance level, 100% of applicants were admitted

Undergraduates 5% Black or African American, non-Hispanic/Latino; 6% Hispanic/Latino; 8% Asian, non-Hispanic/Latino; 2% American Indian or Alaska Native, non-Hispanic/Latino; 1% international.

Freshmen *Admission:* 3,126 applied, 3,126 admitted.

Faculty *Total:* 472, 26% full-time.

Academics *Calendar:* quarters. *Degrees:* certificates, diplomas, associate, and bachelor's. *Special study options:* academic remediation for entering students, adult/continuing education programs, advanced placement credit, cooperative education, distance learning, English as a second language, honors programs, independent study, internships, off-campus study, part-time degree program, services for LD students, summer session for credit.

Computers on Campus 1,300 computers/terminals are available on campus for general student use. Students can access the following: campus intranet, computer help desk, free student e-mail accounts, online (class) grades, online (class) registration, online (class) schedules. Campuswide network is available. Wireless service is available via entire campus.

Student Life *Housing:* college housing not available. *Activities and organizations:* drama/theater group, student-run newspaper, Phi Theta Kappa, International Student Club, MESA/STEM club, Armed Services, ASL. *Campus security:* 24-hour emergency response devices and patrols, student patrols, late-night transport/escort service. *Student services:* personal/psychological counseling.

Athletics *Intercollegiate sports:* baseball M(s), basketball M(s)/W(s), cross-country running M/W, golf M/W, soccer M(s)/W(s), softball W(s), track and field M/W, volleyball W(s). *Intramural sports:* basketball M/W, table tennis M/W, volleyball M/W, weight lifting M/W.

Costs (2012–13) *Tuition:* state resident $3523 full-time, $107 per credit hour part-time; nonresident $3943 full-time, $120 per credit hour part-time. Full-time tuition and fees vary according to course load and degree level. Part-time tuition and fees vary according to course load and degree level. *Required fees:* $195 full-time. *Payment plan:* installment. *Waivers:* senior citizens.

Financial Aid Of all full-time matriculated undergraduates who enrolled in 2011, 105 Federal Work-Study jobs (averaging $2380). 31 state and other part-time jobs (averaging $2880).

Applying *Options:* electronic application. *Required for some:* high school transcript. *Application deadlines:* rolling (freshmen), rolling (out-of-state freshmen), rolling (transfers).

Freshman Application Contact Ms. Jennifer Fyllingness, Director of Admissions, Outreach and International Student Programs, Olympic College, 1600 Chester Avenue, Bremerton, WA 98337-1699. *Phone:* 360-475-7128.

Toll-free phone: 800-259-6718. *Fax:* 360-475-7202. *E-mail:* jfyllingness@olympic.edu.
Website: http://www.olympic.edu/.

Pacific Lutheran University

Tacoma, Washington

- **Independent** comprehensive, founded 1890, affiliated with Evangelical Lutheran Church in America
- **Suburban** 156-acre campus with easy access to Seattle
- **Endowment** $73.2 million
- **Coed** 3,166 undergraduate students, 96% full-time, 62% women, 38% men
- **Moderately difficult** entrance level, 74% of applicants were admitted

Undergraduates 3,028 full-time, 138 part-time. Students come from 44 states and territories; 24 other countries; 23% are from out of state; 3% Black or African American, non-Hispanic/Latino; 7% Hispanic/Latino; 6% Asian, non-Hispanic/Latino; 0.5% Native Hawaiian or other Pacific Islander, non-Hispanic/Latino; 0.8% American Indian or Alaska Native, non-Hispanic/Latino; 7% Two or more races, non-Hispanic/Latino; 1% Race/ethnicity unknown; 4% international; 7% transferred in; 49% live on campus. *Retention:* 83% of full-time freshmen returned.

Freshmen *Admission:* 3,550 applied, 2,613 admitted, 633 enrolled. *Average high school GPA:* 3.62. *Test scores:* SAT critical reading scores over 500: 71%; SAT math scores over 500: 73%; SAT writing scores over 500: 68%; ACT scores over 18: 97%; SAT critical reading scores over 600: 31%; SAT math scores over 600: 32%; SAT writing scores over 600: 23%; ACT scores over 24: 56%; SAT critical reading scores over 700: 6%; SAT math scores over 700: 3%; SAT writing scores over 700: 3%; ACT scores over 30: 9%.

Faculty *Total:* 254, 80% full-time, 80% with terminal degrees. *Student/faculty ratio:* 15:1.

Academics *Calendar:* 4-1-4. *Degrees:* bachelor's, master's, and postbachelor's certificates. *Special study options:* advanced placement credit, cooperative education, double majors, honors programs, independent study, internships, part-time degree program, services for LD students, student-designed majors, study abroad, summer session for credit. *ROTC:* Army (b). *Unusual degree programs:* 3-2 engineering with Columbia University in New York and Washington University in Missouri.

Computers on Campus 435 computers/terminals and 1,200 ports are available on campus for general student use. Students can access the following: campus intranet, computer help desk, free student e-mail accounts, online (class) grades, online (class) registration, online (class) schedules. Campus-wide network is available. 100% of college-owned or -operated housing units are wired for high-speed Internet access. Wireless service is available via entire campus.

Student Life *Housing:* on-campus residence required through sophomore year. *Options:* coed, women-only. Campus housing is university owned. Freshman campus housing is guaranteed. *Activities and organizations:* drama/theater group, student-run newspaper, radio and television station, choral group, Ignite, Circle K, Adult Students Club, Residence Hall Government, Inter-Varsity Fellowship. *Campus security:* 24-hour emergency response devices and patrols, student patrols, late-night transport/escort service, controlled dormitory access. *Student services:* health clinic, personal/psychological counseling, women's center.

Athletics Member NCAA. All Division III. *Intercollegiate sports:* baseball M, basketball M/W, crew M/W, cross-country running M/W, football M, golf M/W, lacrosse M(c)/W(c), soccer M/W, softball W, swimming and diving M/W, tennis M/W, track and field M/W, ultimate Frisbee M(c)/W(c), volleyball M(c)/W. *Intramural sports:* basketball M/W, football M/W, soccer M/W, softball M/W, volleyball M/W.

Standardized Tests *Required:* SAT or ACT (for admission).

Costs (2013–14) *Comprehensive fee:* $44,840 includes full-time tuition ($34,440), mandatory fees ($300), and room and board ($10,100). Full-time tuition and fees vary according to course load. Part-time tuition and fees vary according to course load. *Required fees:* $1030 per semester hour part-time. *College room only:* $4870. Room and board charges vary according to board plan and housing facility. *Payment plan:* installment. *Waivers:* children of alumni and employees or children of employees.

Financial Aid Of all full-time matriculated undergraduates who enrolled in 2011, 2,576 applied for aid, 2,278 were judged to have need, 515 had their need fully met. 652 Federal Work-Study jobs (averaging $2874). 982 state and other part-time jobs (averaging $3015). In 2011, 670 non-need-based awards were made. *Average percent of need met:* 86%. *Average financial aid package:* $29,814. *Average need-based loan:* $8856. *Average need-based gift aid:* $17,506. *Average non-need-based aid:* $13,580. *Average indebtedness upon graduation:* $29,774.

Applying *Options:* electronic application, early admission, deferred entrance. *Application fee:* $40. *Required:* essay or personal statement, high school transcript, 1 letter of recommendation. *Required for some:* interview. *Recommended:* minimum 2.5 GPA. *Application deadlines:* rolling (freshmen), rolling (transfers). *Notification:* continuous (freshmen), continuous (transfers).

Freshman Application Contact Mr. David E Gunovich, Dean of Admission, Pacific Lutheran University, Tacoma, WA 98447. *Phone:* 253-535-7151. *Toll-free phone:* 800-274-6758. *Fax:* 253-536-5136. *E-mail:* admission@plu.edu. *Website:* http://www.plu.edu/.

Peninsula College

Port Angeles, Washington

- **State-supported** primarily 2-year, founded 1961, part of Washington State Community and Technical Colleges
- **Small-town** 75-acre campus
- **Coed**
- **Noncompetitive** entrance level

Faculty *Student/faculty ratio:* 21:1.

Academics *Calendar:* quarters. *Degrees:* certificates, associate, and bachelor's.

Student Life *Campus security:* 8-hour patrols by trained security personnel.

Financial Aid *Of all full-time matriculated undergraduates who enrolled in 2011,* 30 Federal Work-Study jobs (averaging $3600). 25 state and other part-time jobs (averaging $3600).

Applying *Required for some:* high school transcript.

Freshman Application Contact Ms. Pauline Marvin, Peninsula College, 1502 East Lauridsen Boulevard, Port Angeles, WA 98362. *Phone:* 360-417-6596. *Toll-free phone:* 877-452-9277. *Fax:* 360-457-8100. *E-mail:* admissions@pencol.edu.

Website: http://www.pc.ctc.edu/.

Pima Medical Institute

Seattle, Washington

Freshman Application Contact Admissions Office, Pima Medical Institute, 9709 Third Avenue NE, Suite 400, Seattle, WA 98115. *Phone:* 206-322-6100. *Toll-free phone:* 800-477-PIMA (in-state); 888-477-PIMA (out-of-state). *Website:* http://www.pmi.edu/.

Saint Martin's University

Lacey, Washington

- **Independent Roman Catholic** comprehensive, founded 1895
- **Suburban** 380-acre campus with easy access to Seattle
- **Endowment** $16.4 million
- **Coed** 1,479 undergraduate students, 77% full-time, 50% women, 50% men
- **Moderately difficult** entrance level, 82% of applicants were admitted

Undergraduates 1,143 full-time, 336 part-time. Students come from 29 states and territories; 7 other countries; 25% are from out of state; 8% Black or African American, non-Hispanic/Latino; 11% Hispanic/Latino; 5% Asian, non-Hispanic/Latino; 2% Native Hawaiian or other Pacific Islander, non-Hispanic/Latino; 1% American Indian or Alaska Native, non-Hispanic/Latino; 6% Two or more races, non-Hispanic/Latino; 4% Race/ethnicity unknown; 6% international; 12% transferred in; 33% live on campus. *Retention:* 74% of full-time freshmen returned.

Freshmen *Admission:* 808 applied, 665 admitted, 228 enrolled. *Average high school GPA:* 3.38. *Test scores:* SAT critical reading scores over 500: 61%; SAT math scores over 500: 65%; SAT writing scores over 500: 55%; ACT scores over 18: 82%; SAT critical reading scores over 600: 20%; SAT math scores over 600: 23%; SAT writing scores over 600: 11%; ACT scores over 24: 43%; SAT critical reading scores over 700: 4%; SAT math scores over 700: 2%; ACT scores over 30: 3%.

Faculty *Total:* 218, 33% full-time, 43% with terminal degrees. *Student/faculty ratio:* 12:1.

Academics *Calendar:* semesters. *Degrees:* bachelor's, master's, post-master's, and postbachelor's certificates. *Special study options:* academic remediation for entering students, accelerated degree program, adult/continuing education programs, advanced placement credit, cooperative education, distance learning, double majors, English as a second language, independent study, intern-

ships, off-campus study, part-time degree program, services for LD students, study abroad, summer session for credit. *ROTC:* Army (c), Air Force (c).

Computers on Campus 80 computers/terminals and 130 ports are available on campus for general student use. Students can access the following: campus intranet, computer help desk, free student e-mail accounts, online (class) grades, online (class) registration, online (class) schedules. Campuswide network is available. 100% of college-owned or -operated housing units are wired for high-speed Internet access. Wireless service is available via entire campus.

Student Life *Housing:* on-campus residence required through sophomore year. *Options:* coed. Campus housing is university owned. Freshman campus housing is guaranteed. *Activities and organizations:* drama/theater group, student-run newspaper, choral group, International Club, Minorities in Action, Hui O Hawaii, American Society of Civil Engineers, Chemistry. *Campus security:* 24-hour emergency response devices and patrols, student patrols, late-night transport/escort service, controlled dormitory access. *Student services:* health clinic, personal/psychological counseling.

Athletics Member NCAA. All Division II. *Intercollegiate sports:* baseball M(s), basketball M(s)/W(s), cross-country running M(s)/W(s), golf M(s)/W(s), soccer M/W(s), softball W(s), track and field M(s)/W(s), volleyball W(s). *Intramural sports:* basketball M/W, bowling M/W, golf M/W, soccer M/W, softball M/W, table tennis M/W, tennis M/W, ultimate Frisbee M/W, volleyball M/W.

Standardized Tests *Required:* SAT or ACT (for admission).

Costs (2013–14) *Comprehensive fee:* $39,494 includes full-time tuition ($29,500), mandatory fees ($334), and room and board ($9660). Full-time tuition and fees vary according to degree level, location, and program. Part-time tuition: $990 per credit. Part-time tuition and fees vary according to course load, degree level, location, and program. *College room only:* $4820. Room and board charges vary according to board plan. *Payment plan:* installment. *Waivers:* children of alumni and employees or children of employees.

Financial Aid Of all full-time matriculated undergraduates who enrolled in 2011, 1,045 applied for aid, 965 were judged to have need, 166 had their need fully met. 194 Federal Work-Study jobs (averaging $1935). 58 state and other part-time jobs (averaging $4854). In 2011, 84 non-need-based awards were made. *Average percent of need met:* 70%. *Average financial aid package:* $19,370. *Average need-based loan:* $4145. *Average need-based gift aid:* $15,291. *Average non-need-based aid:* $9420. *Average indebtedness upon graduation:* $34,235.

Applying *Options:* electronic application. *Required:* essay or personal statement, high school transcript, minimum 2.5 GPA, 1 letter of recommendation. *Required for some:* interview. *Application deadline:* 8/1 (transfers). *Notification:* 8/15 (freshmen), continuous until 8/15 (transfers).

Freshman Application Contact Ms. Emilie Schnabel, Admissions Counselor, Saint Martin's University, 5000 Abbey Way SE, Lacey, WA 98503-7500. *Phone:* 360-438-4596. *Toll-free phone:* 800-368-8803. *Fax:* 360-412-6189. *E-mail:* admissions@stmartin.edu. *Website:* http://www.stmartin.edu/.

Seattle Pacific University

Seattle, Washington

- **Independent Free Methodist** comprehensive, founded 1891
- **Urban** 35-acre campus
- **Coed** 3,249 undergraduate students, 96% full-time, 67% women, 33% men
- **Moderately difficult** entrance level, 17% of applicants were admitted

Undergraduates 3,108 full-time, 142 part-time. Students come from 43 states and territories; 36 other countries; 37% are from out of state; 4% Black or African American, non-Hispanic/Latino; 8% Hispanic/Latino; 10% Asian, non-Hispanic/Latino; 0.4% American Indian or Alaska Native, non-Hispanic/Latino; 7% Two or more races, non-Hispanic/Latino; 3% Race/ethnicity unknown; 1% international; 7% transferred in; 54% live on campus. *Retention:* 84% of full-time freshmen returned.

Freshmen *Admission:* 4,559 applied, 784 admitted, 784 enrolled. *Average high school GPA:* 3.54. *Test scores:* SAT critical reading scores over 500: 77%; SAT math scores over 500: 77%; SAT writing scores over 500: 75%; ACT scores over 18: 97%; SAT critical reading scores over 600: 34%; SAT math scores over 600: 32%; SAT writing scores over 600: 28%; ACT scores over 24: 61%; SAT critical reading scores over 700: 5%; SAT math scores over 700: 3%; SAT writing scores over 700: 5%; ACT scores over 30: 11%.

Faculty *Total:* 348, 58% full-time, 55% with terminal degrees. *Student/faculty ratio:* 15:1.

Academics *Calendar:* quarters. *Degrees:* bachelor's, master's, doctoral, and post-master's certificates. *Special study options:* academic remediation for entering students, adult/continuing education programs, advanced placement credit, distance learning, double majors, external degree program, honors programs, independent study, internships, off-campus study, part-time degree program, services for LD students, student-designed majors, study abroad, summer session for credit. *ROTC:* Army (c), Navy (c), Air Force (c).

Computers on Campus 150 computers/terminals are available on campus for general student use. Students can access the following: campus intranet, computer help desk, free student e-mail accounts, online (class) grades, online (class) registration, online (class) schedules. Campuswide network is available. Wireless service is available via entire campus.

Student Life *Housing:* on-campus residence required through sophomore year. *Options:* coed, disabled students. Campus housing is university owned. Freshman campus housing is guaranteed. *Activities and organizations:* drama/theater group, student-run newspaper, radio station, choral group, Centurions, Falconettes, forensics organization, Amnesty International, University Players. *Campus security:* 24-hour emergency response devices and patrols, student patrols, late-night transport/escort service, closed-circuit TV monitors. *Student services:* health clinic, personal/psychological counseling.

Athletics Member NCAA. All Division II. *Intercollegiate sports:* basketball M(s)/W(s), crew M/W(s), cross-country running M(s)/W(s), gymnastics W(s), soccer M(s)/W(s), track and field M(s)/W(s), volleyball W(s). *Intramural sports:* archery M/W, basketball M/W, bowling M/W, cross-country running M/W, football M/W, soccer M/W(c), softball M/W, tennis M/W, volleyball M(c)/W(c), weight lifting M/W.

Standardized Tests *Required:* SAT or ACT (for admission). *Required for some:* SAT and SAT Subject Tests or ACT (for admission), SAT Subject Tests (for admission).

Costs (2012–13) *Comprehensive fee:* $41,559 includes full-time tuition ($31,701), mandatory fees ($366), and room and board ($9492). Part-time tuition: $881 per credit hour. Part-time tuition and fees vary according to course load. *Required fees:* $122 per term part-time. *College room only:* $5190. Room and board charges vary according to board plan and housing facility. *Payment plans:* installment, deferred payment. *Waivers:* senior citizens and employees or children of employees.

Financial Aid Of all full-time matriculated undergraduates who enrolled in 2012, 2,572 applied for aid, 2,249 were judged to have need, 116 had their need fully met. 381 Federal Work-Study jobs (averaging $1419). 190 state and other part-time jobs (averaging $1780). In 2012, 611 non-need-based awards were made. *Average percent of need met:* 77%. *Average financial aid package:* $27,783. *Average need-based loan:* $5145. *Average need-based gift aid:* $22,786. *Average non-need-based aid:* $16,655. *Average indebtedness upon graduation:* $28,263.

Applying *Options:* electronic application, early admission, early action. *Application fee:* $50. *Required:* essay or personal statement, high school transcript, minimum 2.5 GPA, 2 letters of recommendation. *Recommended:* interview. *Application deadlines:* 2/1 (freshmen), 8/1 (transfers), 11/15 (early action). *Notification:* 3/1 (freshmen), continuous (transfers), 1/5 (early action).

Freshman Application Contact Mr. Jobe Korb-Nice, Director of Admissions, Seattle Pacific University, 3307 3rd Avenue, West, Seattle, WA 98119-1997. *Phone:* 206-281-2021. *Toll-free phone:* 800-366-3344. *Fax:* 206-281-2669. *E-mail:* admissions@spu.edu. *Website:* http://www.spu.edu/.

Seattle University
Seattle, Washington

- **Independent Roman Catholic** comprehensive, founded 1891
- **Urban** 50-acre campus with easy access to Seattle
- **Coed** 4,589 undergraduate students, 95% full-time, 59% women, 41% men
- **Moderately difficult** entrance level, 71% of applicants were admitted

Undergraduates 4,364 full-time, 225 part-time. Students come from 48 states and territories; 48 other countries; 44% are from out of state; 4% Black or African American, non-Hispanic/Latino; 9% Hispanic/Latino; 16% Asian, non-Hispanic/Latino; 0.9% Native Hawaiian or other Pacific Islander, non-Hispanic/Latino; 0.6% American Indian or Alaska Native, non-Hispanic/Latino; 5% Two or more races, non-Hispanic/Latino; 6% Race/ethnicity unknown; 10% international; 10% transferred in; 41% live on campus. *Retention:* 87% of full-time freshmen returned.

Freshmen *Admission:* 6,862 applied, 4,904 admitted, 903 enrolled. *Average high school GPA:* 3.58. *Test scores:* SAT critical reading scores over 500: 87%; SAT math scores over 500: 90%; SAT writing scores over 500: 87%; ACT scores over 18: 100%; SAT critical reading scores over 600: 42%; SAT math scores over 600: 49%; SAT writing scores over 600: 45%; ACT scores over 24: 76%; SAT critical reading scores over 700: 9%; SAT math scores over 700: 7%; SAT writing scores over 700: 7%; ACT scores over 30: 16%.

Faculty *Total:* 739, 68% full-time, 54% with terminal degrees. *Student/faculty ratio:* 12:1.

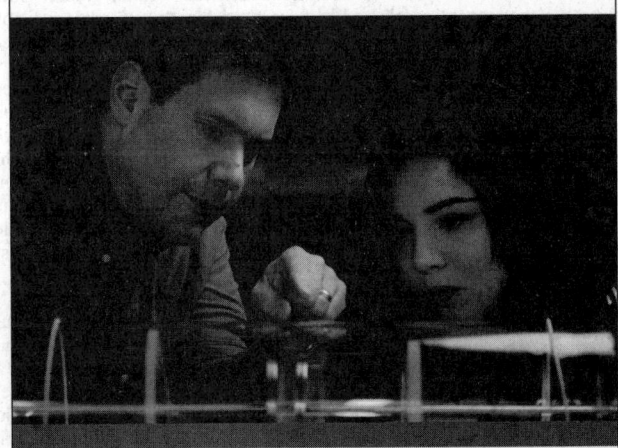

Achieve Excellence.

At Seattle University, you learn by doing with professors who are personally engaged in helping you grow in your field of study. Professional internships, real-world projects and career development are important aspects of SU's commitment to academic excellence. Public service is a big draw for graduates, who often compete for and receive prestigious fellowships such as the Truman Scholarship and the Fulbright. As a nationally-ranked university with prestigious programs in Law, Business, Nursing, Science, and Criminal Justice, Seattle University is the premier independent university of the Northwest.

SEATTLE UNIVERSITY

www.seattleu.edu

Academics *Calendar:* quarters. *Degrees:* bachelor's, master's, doctoral, post-master's, and postbachelor's certificates. *Special study options:* accelerated degree program, adult/continuing education programs, advanced placement credit, double majors, English as a second language, freshman honors college, honors programs, independent study, internships, off-campus study, part-time degree program, services for LD students, student-designed majors, study abroad, summer session for credit. *ROTC:* Army (b), Navy (c), Air Force (c).
Computers on Campus 467 computers/terminals are available on campus for general student use. Students can access the following: campus intranet, computer help desk, free student e-mail accounts, online (class) grades, online (class) registration, online (class) schedules. Campuswide network is available. 100% of college-owned or -operated housing units are wired for high-speed Internet access. Wireless service is available via entire campus.
Student Life *Housing:* on-campus residence required through sophomore year. *Options:* coed, disabled students. Campus housing is university owned and leased by the school. Freshman campus housing is guaranteed. *Activities and organizations:* drama/theater group, student-run newspaper, radio station, choral group, Student Government, Center for Service, Hawaiian Club, International Student Club, Dance Marathon. *Campus security:* 24-hour emergency response devices and patrols, late-night transport/escort service, controlled dormitory access, bicycle patrols. *Student services:* health clinic, personal/psychological counseling, women's center.
Athletics Member NCAA. All Division I. *Intercollegiate sports:* baseball M, basketball M(s)/W(s), cheerleading M(c)/W(c), crew W(c), cross-country running M(s)/W(s), golf M(s)/W(s), soccer M(s)/W(s), softball W(s), swimming and diving M(s)/W(s), tennis M/W, track and field M(s)/W(s), volleyball W(s). *Intramural sports:* archery M(c)/W(c), basketball M/W, crew M(c)/W(c), field hockey M/W, football M/W, riflery M(c)/W(c), rock climbing M/W, skiing (downhill) M(c)/W(c), soccer M/W, softball M/W, tennis M/W, ultimate Frisbee M/W, volleyball M/W, water polo M/W.
Standardized Tests *Required:* SAT or ACT (for admission).
Costs (2012–13) *Comprehensive fee:* $45,096 includes full-time tuition ($34,200), mandatory fees ($600), and room and board ($10,296). Full-time tuition and fees vary according to course load. Part-time tuition: $760 per credit hour. Part-time tuition and fees vary according to course load. *Room and board:* Room and board charges vary according to board plan and housing facility. *Payment plans:* installment, deferred payment. *Waivers:* employees or children of employees.
Financial Aid Of all full-time matriculated undergraduates who enrolled in 2011, 3,348 applied for aid, 2,792 were judged to have need, 264 had their need fully met. In 2011, 244 non-need-based awards were made. *Average percent of need met:* 65%. *Average financial aid package:* $27,519. *Average need-based loan:* $4847. *Average need-based gift aid:* $14,722. *Average non-need-based aid:* $9025. *Average indebtedness upon graduation:* $27,741.
Applying *Options:* electronic application, early action, deferred entrance. *Application fee:* $50. *Required:* essay or personal statement, high school transcript, minimum 2.5 GPA, 2 letters of recommendation. *Application deadlines:* rolling (freshmen), 3/1 (transfers), 11/15 (early action). *Notification:* continuous until 3/1 (freshmen), continuous (transfers), 12/23 (early action).
Freshman Application Contact Melore Nielsen, Acting Dean of Admissions, Seattle University, 901 12th Avenue, PO Box 222000, Seattle, WA 98122-1090. *Phone:* 206-296-2000. *Toll-free phone:* 800-542-0833 (in-state); 800-426-7123 (out-of-state). *Fax:* 206-296-5656. *E-mail:* admissions@seattleu.edu.
Website: http://www.seattleu.edu/.

See previous page for display ad and page 1494 for the College Close-Up.

Trinity Lutheran College

Issaquah, Washington

- **Independent Lutheran** 4-year, founded 1944
- **Urban** 1-acre campus with easy access to Seattle
- **Coed**
- **Minimally difficult** entrance level

Faculty *Student/faculty ratio:* 7:1.
Academics *Calendar:* quarters. *Degrees:* certificates, associate, bachelor's, and postbachelor's certificates.
Student Life *Campus security:* 24-hour emergency response devices, student patrols, controlled dormitory access.
Athletics Member NCCAA.
Standardized Tests *Required:* SAT or ACT (for admission).
Costs (2012–13) *Comprehensive fee:* $30,616 includes full-time tuition ($23,283), mandatory fees ($500), and room and board ($6833). Part-time tuition: $910 per credit hour. Part-time tuition and fees vary according to course load and program. *Required fees:* $910 per credit hour part-time, $150

per year part-time. *College room only:* $5833. Room and board charges vary according to board plan and housing facility.
Applying *Options:* electronic application, early admission, deferred entrance. *Application fee:* $30. *Required:* essay or personal statement, high school transcript, minimum 2.0 GPA, 1 letter of recommendation. *Required for some:* interview.
Freshman Application Contact Ms. Tracy Sisk, Admissions Counselor, Trinity Lutheran College, 2802 Wetmore AVE, Everett, WA 98201. *Phone:* 425-249-4755. *Toll-free phone:* 800-843-5659. *Fax:* 425-249-4801. *E-mail:* tracy.sisk@tlc.edu.
Website: http://www.tlc.edu/.

University of Phoenix–Eastern Washington Campus

Spokane, Washington

Freshman Application Contact Marc Booker, Sr. Director, Office of Admissions and Evaluation, University of Phoenix–Eastern Washington Campus, 4035 South Riverpoint Parkway, Mail Stop CF-L101, Phoenix, AZ 85040. *Phone:* 602-557-4609. *Toll-free phone:* 866-766-0766. *Fax:* 480-643-1156.
Website: http://www.phoenix.edu/.

University of Phoenix–Washington Campus

Tukwila, Washington

Freshman Application Contact Marc Booker, Sr. Director, Office of Admissions and Evaluation, University of Phoenix–Washington Campus, 4615 East Elwood Street, Mail Stop AA-K101, Phoenix, AZ 85040-1958. *Phone:* 602-557-4609. *Toll-free phone:* 866-766-0766. *Fax:* 480-643-1156.
Website: http://www.phoenix.edu/.

University of Puget Sound

Tacoma, Washington

- **Independent** comprehensive, founded 1888
- **Urban** 97-acre campus with easy access to Seattle
- **Endowment** $250.5 million
- **Coed** 2,578 undergraduate students, 99% full-time, 57% women, 43% men
- **Moderately difficult** entrance level, 82% of applicants were admitted

Undergraduates 2,555 full-time, 23 part-time. Students come from 45 states and territories; 15 other countries; 76% are from out of state; 2% Black or African American, non-Hispanic/Latino; 7% Hispanic/Latino; 7% Asian, non-Hispanic/Latino; 0.1% Native Hawaiian or other Pacific Islander, non-Hispanic/Latino; 0.6% American Indian or Alaska Native, non-Hispanic/Latino; 7% Two or more races, non-Hispanic/Latino; 2% Race/ethnicity unknown; 0.7% international; 2% transferred in; 57% live on campus. *Retention:* 86% of full-time freshmen returned.
Freshmen *Admission:* 4,470 applied, 3,673 admitted, 631 enrolled. *Test scores:* SAT critical reading scores over 500: 98%; SAT math scores over 500: 96%; SAT writing scores over 500: 94%; ACT scores over 18: 100%; SAT critical reading scores over 600: 67%; SAT math scores over 600: 67%; SAT writing scores over 600: 60%; ACT scores over 24: 91%; SAT critical reading scores over 700: 21%; SAT math scores over 700: 13%; SAT writing scores over 700: 14%; ACT scores over 30: 31%.
Faculty *Total:* 281, 81% full-time, 78% with terminal degrees. *Student/faculty ratio:* 12:1.
Academics *Calendar:* semesters. *Degrees:* bachelor's, master's, and doctoral. *Special study options:* advanced placement credit, cooperative education, double majors, honors programs, independent study, internships, part-time degree program, services for LD students, student-designed majors, study abroad, summer session for credit. *ROTC:* Army (c). *Unusual degree programs:* 3-2 engineering with Washington University in St. Louis, Columbia University, and University of Southern California.
Computers on Campus 320 computers/terminals and 6,500 ports are available on campus for general student use. Students can access the following: campus intranet, computer help desk, free student e-mail accounts, online

(class) grades, online (class) registration, online (class) schedules, financial aid, admission, student employment. Campuswide network is available. 100% of college-owned or -operated housing units are wired for high-speed Internet access. Wireless service is available via entire campus.

Student Life *Housing:* on-campus residence required through sophomore year. *Options:* coed, disabled students. Campus housing is university owned. Freshman campus housing is guaranteed. *Activities and organizations:* drama/theater group, student-run newspaper, radio station, choral group, Puget Sound Outdoors, Repertory Dance Group, Hui-O-Hawaii, Student Theatre Productions, Relay for Life, national fraternities, national sororities. *Campus security:* 24-hour emergency response devices and patrols, student patrols, late-night transport/escort service, controlled dormitory access, 24-hour locked residence hall entrances, surveillance cameras, and emergency telephone towers. *Student services:* health clinic, personal/psychological counseling.

Athletics Member NCAA. All Division III. *Intercollegiate sports:* baseball M, basketball M/W, cheerleading M/W, crew M/W, cross-country running M/W, fencing M(c)/W(c), football M, golf M/W, lacrosse M(c)/W, rugby M(c)/W(c), sailing M(c)/W(c), skiing (downhill) M(c)/W(c), soccer M/W, softball W, swimming and diving M/W, tennis M/W, track and field M/W, ultimate Frisbee M(c)/W(c), volleyball W, water polo M(c)/W(c). *Intramural sports:* basketball M/W, football M/W, soccer M/W, softball M/W, tennis M/W, volleyball M/W.

Standardized Tests *Required:* SAT or ACT (for admission).

Costs (2013–14) *Comprehensive fee:* $52,648 includes full-time tuition ($41,640), mandatory fees ($228), and room and board ($10,780). Full-time tuition and fees vary according to course load. Part-time tuition: $5250 per unit. Part-time tuition and fees vary according to course load. *College room only:* $5940. Room and board charges vary according to board plan and housing facility. *Payment plans:* installment, deferred payment. *Waivers:* employees or children of employees.

Financial Aid Of all full-time matriculated undergraduates who enrolled in 2012, 1,857 applied for aid, 1,625 were judged to have need, 275 had their need fully met. 535 Federal Work-Study jobs (averaging $2923). 814 state and other part-time jobs (averaging $2724). In 2012, 755 non-need-based awards were made. *Average percent of need met:* 78%. *Average financial aid package:* $30,235. *Average need-based loan:* $6165. *Average need-based gift aid:* $24,447. *Average non-need-based aid:* $12,924. *Average indebtedness upon graduation:* $28,923.

Applying *Options:* electronic application, early admission, early decision, deferred entrance. *Application fee:* $50. *Required:* essay or personal statement, high school transcript, 2 letters of recommendation. *Recommended:* minimum 3.0 GPA, interview. *Application deadlines:* 1/15 (freshmen), 3/1 (transfers).

Early decision deadline: 11/1 (for plan 1), 1/2 (for plan 2). *Notification:* 4/1 (freshmen), continuous (transfers), 12/15 (early decision plan 1), 2/15 (early decision plan 2).

Freshman Application Contact Dr. Jenny Rickard, Vice President for Enrollment, University of Puget Sound, 1500 North Warner Street, CMB 1062, Tacoma, WA 98416. *Phone:* 253-879-3211. *Toll-free phone:* 800-396-7191. *Fax:* 253-879-3993. *E-mail:* admission@pugetsound.edu. *Website:* http://www.pugetsound.edu/.

See below for display ad and page 1594 for the College Close-Up.

University of Washington
Seattle, Washington

- **State-supported** university, founded 1861
- **Urban** 703-acre campus
- **Coed**
- **Moderately difficult** entrance level

Faculty *Student/faculty ratio:* 13:1.

Academics *Calendar:* quarters. *Degrees:* bachelor's, master's, doctoral, and post-master's certificates.

Student Life *Campus security:* 24-hour emergency response devices and patrols, late-night transport/escort service, controlled dormitory access.

Athletics Member NCAA. All Division I except football (Division I-A).

Standardized Tests *Required:* SAT or ACT (for admission).

Costs (2012–13) *Tuition:* state resident $11,305 full-time; nonresident $28,860 full-time. Full-time tuition and fees vary according to course load. Part-time tuition and fees vary according to course load. *Room and board:* Room and board charges vary according to board plan and housing facility.

Financial Aid *Of all full-time matriculated undergraduates who enrolled in 2012,* 14,900 applied for aid, 11,300 were judged to have need, 2,700 had their need fully met. *In 2012,* 805 non-need-based awards were made. *Average percent of need met:* 82. *Average financial aid package:* $18,600. *Average need-based loan:* $7000. *Average need-based gift aid:* $14,000. *Average non-need-based aid:* $6200. *Average indebtedness upon graduation:* $20,800.

Applying *Options:* electronic application, early admission. *Application fee:* $60. *Required:* essay or personal statement, minimum 2.0 GPA. *Required for some:* high school transcript.

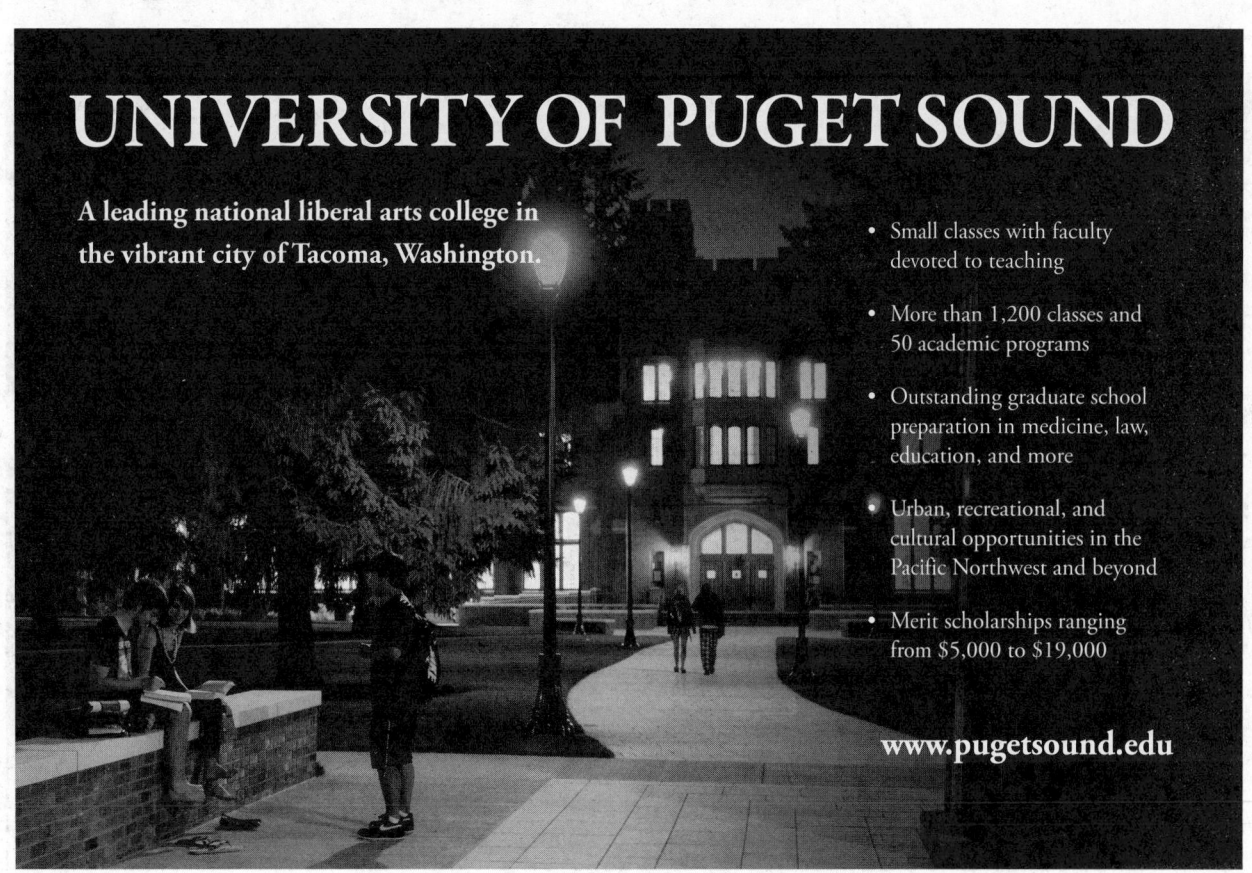

Freshman Application Contact Emily Leggio, Senior Associate Director of Admissions, University of Washington, Seattle, WA 98195. *Phone:* 206-543-9686. *Fax:* 206-685-3655.
Website: http://www.washington.edu/.

University of Washington, Bothell

Bothell, Washington

- **State-supported** comprehensive, founded 1990, part of University of Washington
- **Suburban** 128-acre campus with easy access to Seattle
- **Endowment** $2.8 million
- **Coed** 3,637 undergraduate students, 83% full-time, 50% women, 50% men
- **Moderately difficult** entrance level, 72% of applicants were admitted

Undergraduates 3,030 full-time, 607 part-time. Students come from 19 states and territories; 27 other countries; 2% are from out of state; 4% Black or African American, non-Hispanic/Latino; 6% Hispanic/Latino; 22% Asian, non-Hispanic/Latino; 0.5% Native Hawaiian or other Pacific Islander, non-Hispanic/Latino; 0.9% American Indian or Alaska Native, non-Hispanic/Latino; 4% Two or more races, non-Hispanic/Latino; 4% Race/ethnicity unknown; 5% international; 17% transferred in; 7% live on campus. *Retention:* 78% of full-time freshmen returned.

Freshmen *Admission:* 2,419 applied, 1,732 admitted, 546 enrolled. *Average high school GPA:* 3.3. *Test scores:* SAT critical reading scores over 500: 54%; SAT math scores over 500: 63%; SAT writing scores over 500: 45%; ACT scores over 18: 77%; SAT critical reading scores over 600: 17%; SAT math scores over 600: 23%; SAT writing scores over 600: 10%; ACT scores over 24: 30%; SAT critical reading scores over 700: 2%; SAT math scores over 700: 5%; SAT writing scores over 700: 1%; ACT scores over 30: 7%.

Faculty *Total:* 219, 67% full-time, 73% with terminal degrees. *Student/faculty ratio:* 21:1.

Academics *Degrees:* bachelor's, master's, and postbachelor's certificates. *Special study options:* adult/continuing education programs, advanced placement credit, cooperative education, double majors, honors programs, independent study, internships, off-campus study, part-time degree program, services for LD students, student-designed majors, study abroad, summer session for credit. *ROTC:* Army (c), Navy (c), Air Force (c).

Computers on Campus 400 computers/terminals and 1,100 ports are available on campus for general student use. Students can access the following: computer help desk, free student e-mail accounts, online (class) grades, online (class) registration, online (class) schedules, online course management system. Campuswide network is available. 100% of college-owned or -operated housing units are wired for high-speed Internet access. Wireless service is available via entire campus.

Student Life *Housing options:* coed, disabled students. Campus housing is university owned. Freshman applicants given priority for college housing. *Activities and organizations:* student-run newspaper, Campus Events Board, Collegiate DECA, Associated Students of University of Washington Bothell (ASUWB), Recreation Programs, Diversity Programs. *Campus security:* 24-hour emergency response devices and patrols, late-night transport/escort service. *Student services:* personal/psychological counseling.

Athletics *Intramural sports:* basketball M/W, golf M/W, rock climbing M/W, skiing (downhill) M/W, soccer M/W, softball M/W, table tennis M/W, ultimate Frisbee M/W, volleyball M/W.

Standardized Tests *Required:* SAT or ACT (for admission).

Financial Aid Of all full-time matriculated undergraduates who enrolled in 2011, 2,017 applied for aid, 1,740 were judged to have need, 219 had their need fully met. In 2011, 17 non-need-based awards were made. *Average percent of need met:* 74%. *Average financial aid package:* $15,700. *Average need-based loan:* $6500. *Average need-based gift aid:* $11,500. *Average non-need-based aid:* $4200. *Average indebtedness upon graduation:* $18,559.

Applying *Options:* electronic application, early admission, deferred entrance. *Application fee:* $60. *Required:* essay or personal statement, high school transcript, minimum 2.0 GPA. *Application deadlines:* 1/15 (freshmen), 1/15 (transfers). *Notification:* continuous (freshmen), continuous (transfers).

Freshman Application Contact Molly Ormsby, Associate Director of Admissions, University of Washington, Bothell, 18115 Campus Way NE, Box 358500, Bothell, WA 98011-8246. *Phone:* 425-352-5244. *Fax:* 425-352-5455. *E-mail:* freshmen@uwb.edu.
Website: http://www.uwb.edu/.

See below for display ad and page 1614 for the College Close-Up.

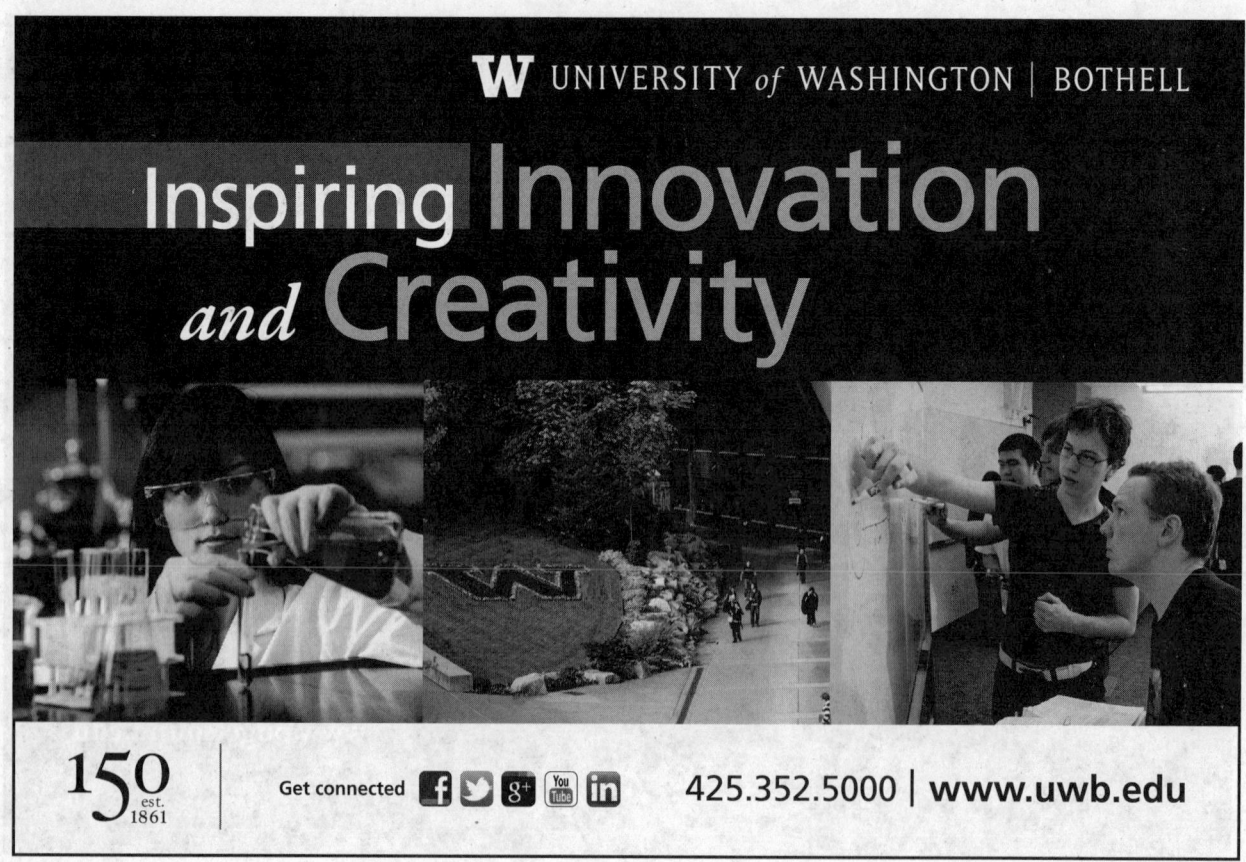

University of Washington, Tacoma

Tacoma, Washington

- **State-supported** comprehensive, founded 1990, part of University of Washington
- **Urban** 46-acre campus with easy access to Seattle
- **Coed** 3,361 undergraduate students, 84% full-time, 54% women, 46% men
- **Minimally difficult** entrance level, 82% of applicants were admitted

Undergraduates 2,825 full-time, 536 part-time. 2% are from out of state; 7% Black or African American, non-Hispanic/Latino; 8% Hispanic/Latino; 15% Asian, non-Hispanic/Latino; 1% Native Hawaiian or other Pacific Islander, non-Hispanic/Latino; 1% American Indian or Alaska Native, non-Hispanic/Latino; 6% Two or more races, non-Hispanic/Latino; 10% Race/ethnicity unknown; 3% international; 24% transferred in. *Retention:* 73% of full-time freshmen returned.

Freshmen *Admission:* 1,166 applied, 960 admitted, 341 enrolled. *Average high school GPA:* 3.23. *Test scores:* SAT critical reading scores over 500: 43%; SAT math scores over 500: 56%; SAT writing scores over 500: 35%; ACT scores over 18: 72%; SAT critical reading scores over 600: 12%; SAT math scores over 600: 14%; SAT writing scores over 600: 7%; ACT scores over 24: 11%; SAT critical reading scores over 700: 1%; SAT math scores over 700: 1%; SAT writing scores over 700: 1%; ACT scores over 30: 2%.

Faculty *Total:* 232, 64% full-time, 61% with terminal degrees. *Student/faculty ratio:* 19:1.

Academics *Calendar:* quarters. *Degrees:* bachelor's, master's, doctoral, post-master's, and postbachelor's certificates. *Special study options:* academic remediation for entering students, accelerated degree program, advanced placement credit, cooperative education, distance learning, double majors, English as a second language, honors programs, independent study, internships, part-time degree program, services for LD students, student-designed majors, study abroad, summer session for credit. *ROTC:* Army (c), Navy (c), Air Force (c).

Computers on Campus Students can access the following: campus intranet, computer help desk, free student e-mail accounts, online (class) grades, online (class) registration, online (class) schedules, online courseware-Blackboard, Canvas & Catalyst proprietary CMS. Campuswide network is available. 100% of college-owned or -operated housing units are wired for high-speed Internet access. Wireless service is available via entire campus.

Student Life *Housing options:* coed, disabled students. Campus housing is provided by a third party. *Activities and organizations:* student-run newspaper, choral group, Accounting Student Association, International Student Association, Partners in Action to Transform Healthcare (PATH), Asian Pacific Islander Student Union (APISU)I, TacPack. *Campus security:* 24-hour emergency response devices and patrols, late-night transport/escort service, key card access to buildings after hours. *Student services:* health clinic, personal/psychological counseling.

Athletics *Intramural sports:* softball M(c).

Standardized Tests *Required:* SAT or ACT (for admission).

Costs (2013–14) *Tuition:* area resident $11,305 full-time, $376 part-time; nonresident $28,860 full-time, $962 part-time. *Required fees:* $597 full-time.

Financial Aid Of all full-time matriculated undergraduates who enrolled in 2012, 2,690 applied for aid, 2,500 were judged to have need, 800 had their need fully met. 100 Federal Work-Study jobs (averaging $2600). 30 state and other part-time jobs (averaging $3000). In 2012, 100 non-need-based awards were made. *Average percent of need met:* 78%. *Average financial aid package:* $17,800. *Average need-based loan:* $6500. *Average need-based gift aid:* $13,600. *Average non-need-based aid:* $1500. *Average indebtedness upon graduation:* $20,700.

Applying *Options:* electronic application, early decision, deferred entrance. *Application fee:* $60. *Required:* essay or personal statement, minimum 2.0 GPA. *Required for some:* high school transcript. *Application deadlines:* 6/1 (freshmen), 4/15 (transfers). *Notification:* continuous (freshmen), continuous (transfers).

Freshman Application Contact Ms. Megan Beresford, Associate Director of University Recruitment, University of Washington, Tacoma, 1900 Commerce Street, Tacoma, WA 98402-3100. *Phone:* 253-692-4742. *Toll-free phone:* 800-736-7750. *Fax:* 253-692-4738. *E-mail:* megan61@u.washington.edu. *Website:* http://www.tacoma.washington.edu/.

Walla Walla University

College Place, Washington

- **Independent Seventh-day Adventist** comprehensive, founded 1892
- **Small-town** 77-acre campus
- **Coed** 1,710 undergraduate students, 93% full-time, 50% women, 50% men
- **Moderately difficult** entrance level, 89% of applicants were admitted

Undergraduates 1,583 full-time, 127 part-time. 62% are from out of state; 2% Black or African American, non-Hispanic/Latino; 11% Hispanic/Latino; 4% Asian, non-Hispanic/Latino; 0.4% Native Hawaiian or other Pacific Islander, non-Hispanic/Latino; 1% American Indian or Alaska Native, non-Hispanic/Latino; 0.1% Two or more races, non-Hispanic/Latino; 3% Race/ethnicity unknown; 6% international; 7% transferred in; 64% live on campus. *Retention:* 83% of full-time freshmen returned.

Freshmen *Admission:* 626 applied, 557 admitted, 396 enrolled. *Average high school GPA:* 3.49. *Test scores:* SAT critical reading scores over 500: 65%; SAT math scores over 500: 60%; SAT writing scores over 500: 61%; ACT scores over 18: 93%; SAT critical reading scores over 600: 27%; SAT math scores over 600: 22%; SAT writing scores over 600: 19%; ACT scores over 24: 50%; SAT critical reading scores over 700: 6%; SAT math scores over 700: 4%; SAT writing scores over 700: 2%; ACT scores over 30: 9%.

Faculty *Total:* 202, 57% full-time, 47% with terminal degrees. *Student/faculty ratio:* 13:1.

Academics *Calendar:* quarters. *Degrees:* diplomas, associate, bachelor's, and master's. *Special study options:* academic remediation for entering students, advanced placement credit, cooperative education, distance learning, double majors, freshman honors college, honors programs, independent study, internships, off-campus study, part-time degree program, services for LD students, study abroad, summer session for credit.

Computers on Campus Students can access the following: campus intranet, computer help desk, free student e-mail accounts, online (class) grades, online (class) registration, online (class) schedules, online forum, online classifieds, online student directory. Campuswide network is available. 100% of college-owned or -operated housing units are wired for high-speed Internet access. Wireless service is available via entire campus.

Student Life *Housing:* on-campus residence required through junior year. *Options:* men-only, women-only, disabled students. Campus housing is university owned and leased by the school. Freshman campus housing is guaranteed. *Activities and organizations:* drama/theater group, student-run newspaper, radio and television station, choral group, Associated Students of Walla Walla University, Campus Ministries, Village Club, OPS Club (Men's residence hall club), AGA Club (women's residence hall club). *Campus security:* 24-hour emergency response devices and patrols, student patrols, late-night transport/escort service, controlled dormitory access. *Student services:* health clinic, personal/psychological counseling.

Athletics Member NAIA. *Intercollegiate sports:* basketball M/W, soccer M, softball W, volleyball W. *Intramural sports:* basketball M/W, football M/W, ice hockey M, softball W, table tennis M/W, volleyball M/W.

Standardized Tests *Required:* SAT or ACT (for admission). *Recommended:* ACT (for admission).

Costs (2013–14) *Comprehensive fee:* $31,347 includes full-time tuition ($24,822), mandatory fees ($555), and room and board ($5970). *College room only:* $3360. Room and board charges vary according to board plan and housing facility.

Financial Aid Of all full-time matriculated undergraduates who enrolled in 2010, 1,269 applied for aid, 972 were judged to have need, 361 had their need fully met. In 2010, 256 non-need-based awards were made. *Average percent of need met:* 90%. *Average financial aid package:* $22,111. *Average need-based loan:* $7475. *Average need-based gift aid:* $8796. *Average non-need-based aid:* $4643. *Average indebtedness upon graduation:* $34,818.

Applying *Options:* electronic application, early decision, deferred entrance. *Application fee:* $40. *Required:* high school transcript, minimum 2.5 GPA. *Application deadlines:* rolling (freshmen), rolling (transfers). *Notification:* continuous (freshmen), continuous (transfers).

Freshman Application Contact Mr. Dallas Weis, Director of Admissions, Walla Walla University, Marketing and Enrollment Services, 204 S. College Avenue, College Place, WA 99324. *Phone:* 509-527-2327. *Toll-free phone:* 800-541-8900. *Fax:* 509-527-2397. *Website:* http://www.wallawalla.edu/.

Washington State University

Pullman, Washington

- **State-supported** university, founded 1890
- **Small-town** 620-acre campus with easy access to Spokane
- **Endowment** $638.4 million
- **Coed** 23,135 undergraduate students, 87% full-time, 50% women, 50% men
- **Moderately difficult** entrance level, 76% of applicants were admitted

Undergraduates 20,082 full-time, 3,053 part-time. 7% are from out of state; 3% Black or African American, non-Hispanic/Latino; 9% Hispanic/Latino; 5% Asian, non-Hispanic/Latino; 0.4% Native Hawaiian or other Pacific Islander, non-Hispanic/Latino; 0.7% American Indian or Alaska Native, non-Hispanic/Latino; 6% Two or more races, non-Hispanic/Latino; 3% Race/ethnicity unknown; 4% international; 10% transferred in; 26% live on campus. *Retention:* 82% of full-time freshmen returned.

Freshmen *Admission:* 14,825 applied, 11,268 admitted, 4,388 enrolled. *Average high school GPA:* 3.3. *Test scores:* SAT critical reading scores over 500: 59%; SAT math scores over 500: 67%; SAT writing scores over 500: 52%; ACT scores over 18: 90%; SAT critical reading scores over 600: 19%; SAT math scores over 600: 25%; SAT writing scores over 600: 13%; ACT scores over 24: 42%; SAT critical reading scores over 700: 3%; SAT math scores over 700: 3%; SAT writing scores over 700: 1%; ACT scores over 30: 7%.

Faculty *Total:* 1,701, 72% full-time, 78% with terminal degrees. *Student/faculty ratio:* 15:1.

Academics *Calendar:* semesters. *Degrees:* certificates, bachelor's, master's, doctoral, post-master's, and postbachelor's certificates. *Special study options:* accelerated degree program, adult/continuing education programs, advanced placement credit, cooperative education, distance learning, double majors, English as a second language, external degree program, honors programs, independent study, internships, off-campus study, part-time degree program, services for LD students, student-designed majors, study abroad, summer session for credit. *ROTC:* Army (b), Navy (c), Air Force (b).

Computers on Campus 2,500 computers/terminals and 2,500 ports are available on campus for general student use. Students can access the following: campus intranet, computer help desk, free student e-mail accounts, online (class) grades, online (class) registration, online (class) schedules. Campuswide network is available. 100% of college-owned or -operated housing units are wired for high-speed Internet access. Wireless service is available via classrooms, computer centers, computer labs, dorm rooms, learning centers, libraries, student centers.

Student Life *Housing:* on-campus residence required for freshman year. *Options:* coed, men-only, women-only, cooperative, disabled students. Campus housing is university owned. Freshman campus housing is guaranteed. *Activities and organizations:* drama/theater group, student-run newspaper, radio and television station, choral group, marching band, Panhellenic Association—Sororities, Interfraternity Council—Fraternities, Student Entertainment Board, International Students Council, ChiLaStAl (Chicana/o Latina/o Student Alliance, national fraternities, national sororities. *Campus security:* 24-hour emergency response devices and patrols, student patrols, late-night transport/escort service, controlled dormitory access. *Student services:* health clinic, personal/psychological counseling, women's center, legal services.

Athletics Member NCAA. All Division I except football (Division I-A). *Intercollegiate sports:* baseball M(s), basketball M(s)/W(s), bowling M(c)/W(c), cheerleading M/W, crew M(c)/W(s), cross-country running M(s)/W(s), fencing M/W(c), golf M(s)/W(s), ice hockey M(c), lacrosse M(c)/W(c), rugby M(c)/W(c), sailing M(c)/W(c), skiing (cross-country) M(c)/W(c), skiing (downhill) M(c)/W(c), soccer M(c)/W(s), softball W(c), swimming and diving W(s), tennis M(c)/W(s), track and field M(s)/W(s), ultimate Frisbee M(c)/W(c), volleyball M(c)/W(s), water polo M(c)/W(c). *Intramural sports:* badminton M/W, basketball M/W, football M/W, golf M/W, racquetball M/W, rock climbing M/W, soccer M/W, softball M/W, table tennis M/W, tennis M/W, ultimate Frisbee M/W, volleyball M/W.

Standardized Tests *Required:* SAT or ACT (for admission).

Costs (2012–13) *Tuition:* state resident $10,874 full-time, $569 per credit hour part-time; nonresident $23,956 full-time, $1141 per credit hour part-time. Full-time tuition and fees vary according to location and reciprocity agreements. Part-time tuition and fees vary according to course load, location, and reciprocity agreements. *Required fees:* $1426 full-time. *Room and board:* $10,524; room only: $6626. Room and board charges vary according to board plan, housing facility, and location. *Waivers:* senior citizens and employees or children of employees.

Financial Aid Of all full-time matriculated undergraduates who enrolled in 2011, 14,442 applied for aid, 11,683 were judged to have need, 4,102 had their need fully met. In 2011, 2211 non-need-based awards were made. *Average percent of need met:* 91%. *Average financial aid package:* $16,761. *Average need-*

based loan: $4442. *Average need-based gift aid:* $9339. *Average non-need-based aid:* $4173. *Average indebtedness upon graduation:* $23,433.

Applying *Options:* electronic application. *Application fee:* $50. *Required:* high school transcript, minimum 2.0 GPA. *Recommended:* essay or personal statement. *Application deadlines:* 1/31 (freshmen), 1/7 (out-of-state freshmen), 1/31 (transfers). *Notification:* continuous until 11/1 (freshmen), continuous until 11/1 (out-of-state freshmen), continuous until 11/1 (transfers).

Freshman Application Contact Ms. Wendy Peterson, Director of Admissions, Washington State University, PO Box 641067, Pullman, WA 99164-1067. *Phone:* 888-468-6978. *Toll-free phone:* 888-468-6978. *Fax:* 509-335-4902. *E-mail:* admissions@wsu.edu.
Website: http://www.wsu.edu/.

Washington State University Spokane

Spokane, Washington

Admissions Office Contact Washington State University Spokane, 412 East Spokane Falls Boulevard, PO Box 1495, Spokane, WA 99210-1495.
Website: http://www.spokane.wsu.edu/.

Washington State University Tri-Cities

Richland, Washington

Admissions Office Contact Washington State University Tri-Cities, 2710 University Drive, Richland, WA 99352-1671.
Website: http://www.tricity.wsu.edu/.

Washington State University Vancouver

Vancouver, Washington

Admissions Office Contact Washington State University Vancouver, 14204 Northeast Salmon Creek Avenue, Vancouver, WA 98686.
Website: http://www.vancouver.wsu.edu/.

Western Washington University

Bellingham, Washington

- **State-supported** comprehensive, founded 1893
- **Small-town** 223-acre campus with easy access to Seattle, Vancouver
- **Coed** 13,902 undergraduate students, 93% full-time, 55% women, 45% men
- **Moderately difficult** entrance level, 80% of applicants were admitted

Undergraduates 12,860 full-time, 1,042 part-time. Students come from 48 states and territories; 36 other countries; 9% are from out of state; 2% Black or African American, non-Hispanic/Latino; 6% Hispanic/Latino; 6% Asian, non-Hispanic/Latino; 0.2% Native Hawaiian or other Pacific Islander, non-Hispanic/Latino; 0.8% American Indian or Alaska Native, non-Hispanic/Latino; 7% Two or more races, non-Hispanic/Latino; 1% Race/ethnicity unknown; 0.9% international; 7% transferred in; 32% live on campus. *Retention:* 85% of full-time freshmen returned.

Freshmen *Admission:* 9,785 applied, 7,799 admitted, 2,688 enrolled. *Average high school GPA:* 3.45. *Test scores:* SAT critical reading scores over 500: 80%; SAT math scores over 500: 81%; ACT scores over 18: 98%; SAT critical reading scores over 600: 35%; SAT math scores over 600: 33%; ACT scores over 24: 61%; SAT critical reading scores over 700: 7%; SAT math scores over 700: 4%; ACT scores over 30: 13%.

Faculty *Total:* 783, 66% full-time, 77% with terminal degrees. *Student/faculty ratio:* 21:1.

Academics *Calendar:* quarters. *Degrees:* certificates, bachelor's, master's, post-master's, and postbachelor's certificates. *Special study options:* accelerated degree program, advanced placement credit, cooperative education, distance learning, double majors, English as a second language, honors programs, independent study, internships, off-campus study, services for LD students, student-designed majors, study abroad, summer session for credit.

Computers on Campus 2,408 computers/terminals are available on campus for general student use. Students can access the following: online (class) registration. Campuswide network is available. 99% of college-owned or -operated housing units are wired for high-speed Internet access. Wireless service is available via classrooms, computer centers, computer labs, dorm rooms, learning centers, libraries, student centers.

Student Life *Housing options:* coed, disabled students. Campus housing is university owned and leased by the school. Freshman campus housing is guaranteed. *Activities and organizations:* drama/theater group, student-run newspaper, radio and television station, choral group, intramurals, Residence Hall Association, Associated Students, Outdoor Center, Ethnic Student Center. *Campus security:* 24-hour emergency response devices and patrols, student patrols, late-night transport/escort service, controlled dormitory access. *Student services:* health clinic, personal/psychological counseling, women's center, legal services.

Athletics Member NCAA. All Division II. *Intercollegiate sports:* basketball M(s)/W(s), cheerleading M/W, crew M(s)/W(s), cross-country running M(s)/W(s), golf M(s)/W(s), soccer M(s)/W(s), softball W(s), track and field M(s)/W(s), volleyball W(s). *Intramural sports:* badminton M/W, baseball M, basketball M/W, ice hockey M, lacrosse M/W, racquetball M/W, rock climbing M/W, sailing M/W, skiing (downhill) M/W, soccer M/W, softball M/W, swimming and diving M/W, table tennis M/W, tennis M/W, volleyball M/W, water polo M/W, wrestling M.

Standardized Tests *Required:* SAT or ACT (for admission).

Costs (2012–13) *Tuition:* state resident $8022 full-time, $267 per credit hour part-time; nonresident $18,369 full-time, $612 per credit hour part-time. Full-time tuition and fees vary according to course load, location, and reciprocity agreements. Part-time tuition and fees vary according to course load, location, and reciprocity agreements. *Required fees:* $783 full-time, $26 per credit hour part-time. *Room and board:* $9372. Room and board charges vary according to board plan, housing facility, and location. *Payment plan:* installment. *Waivers:* minority students and employees or children of employees.

Financial Aid Of all full-time matriculated undergraduates who enrolled in 2012, 8,581 applied for aid, 6,417 were judged to have need, 1,027 had their need fully met. 207 Federal Work-Study jobs (averaging $3181). 488 state and other part-time jobs (averaging $3235). In 2012, 250 non-need-based awards were made. *Average percent of need met:* 85%. *Average financial aid package:* $13,469. *Average need-based loan:* $4457. *Average need-based gift aid:*

$8831. *Average non-need-based aid:* $1907. *Average indebtedness upon graduation:* $20,473.

Applying *Options:* electronic application, deferred entrance. *Application fee:* $55. *Required:* high school transcript. *Recommended:* essay or personal statement. *Application deadlines:* 3/1 (freshmen), 4/1 (transfers). *Notification:* 4/15 (freshmen), continuous until 6/1 (transfers).

Freshman Application Contact Ms. Clara Capron, Director of Admissions, Western Washington University, 516 High Street, Bellingham, WA 98225-9009. *Phone:* 360-650-2422. *Fax:* 360-650-7369. *E-mail:* admit@wwu.edu. *Website:* http://www.wwu.edu/.

Whitman College

Walla Walla, Washington

- **Independent** 4-year, founded 1859
- **Small-town** 117-acre campus
- **Endowment** $401.0 million
- **Coed** 1,539 undergraduate students, 98% full-time, 57% women, 43% men
- **Very difficult** entrance level, 49% of applicants were admitted

Undergraduates 1,508 full-time, 31 part-time. Students come from 48 states and territories; 23 other countries; 66% are from out of state; 1% Black or African American, non-Hispanic/Latino; 6% Hispanic/Latino; 8% Asian, non-Hispanic/Latino; 0.2% Native Hawaiian or other Pacific Islander, non-Hispanic/Latino; 1% American Indian or Alaska Native, non-Hispanic/Latino; 3% Two or more races, non-Hispanic/Latino; 6% Race/ethnicity unknown; 3% international; 1% transferred in; 67% live on campus. *Retention:* 94% of full-time freshmen returned.

Freshmen *Admission:* 2,854 applied, 1,388 admitted, 381 enrolled. *Average high school GPA:* 3.76. *Test scores:* SAT critical reading scores over 500: 98%; SAT math scores over 500: 98%; SAT writing scores over 500: 98%; ACT scores over 18: 100%; SAT critical reading scores over 600: 83%; SAT math scores over 600: 83%; SAT writing scores over 600: 84%; ACT scores over 24: 98%; SAT critical reading scores over 700: 40%; SAT math scores over 700: 31%; SAT writing scores over 700: 33%; ACT scores over 30: 68%.

Faculty *Total:* 205, 71% full-time, 86% with terminal degrees. *Student/faculty ratio:* 9:1.

Academics *Calendar:* semesters. *Degree:* bachelor's. *Special study options:* accelerated degree program, advanced placement credit, cooperative education, double majors, honors programs, independent study, off-campus study, services for LD students, student-designed majors, study abroad. *Unusual degree programs:* 3-2 engineering with California Institute of Technology, Columbia University, Duke University, University of Washington, Washington University in St. Louis; forestry with Duke University; international studies with Monterey Institute of International Studies; oceanography with University of Washington; teacher education with Bank Street College of Education; law with Columbia University.

Computers on Campus 397 computers/terminals are available on campus for general student use. Students can access the following: computer help desk, free student e-mail accounts, online (class) grades, online (class) registration, online (class) schedules, course registration information. Campuswide network is available. 100% of college-owned or -operated housing units are wired for high-speed Internet access. Wireless service is available via classrooms, computer centers, computer labs, dorm rooms, learning centers, libraries, student centers.

Student Life *Housing:* on-campus residence required through sophomore year. *Options:* coed, women-only. Campus housing is university owned. Freshman campus housing is guaranteed. *Activities and organizations:* drama/theater group, student-run newspaper, radio station, choral group, Associated Students, Outdoor Program, Center for Community Service, national fraternities, national sororities. *Campus security:* 24-hour emergency response devices and patrols, student patrols, late-night transport/escort service, controlled dormitory access. *Student services:* health clinic, personal/psychological counseling, women's center.

Athletics Member NCAA. All Division III. *Intercollegiate sports:* baseball M, basketball M/W, cross-country running M/W, fencing M(c)/W(c), golf M/W, ice hockey M(c), lacrosse M(c)/W(c), rugby M(c)/W(c), skiing (cross-country) M(c)/W(c), skiing (downhill) M(c)/W(c), soccer M/W, softball W(c), swimming and diving M/W, tennis M/W, track and field M(c)/W(c), ultimate Frisbee M(c)/W(c), volleyball M(c)/W. *Intramural sports:* basketball M/W, bowling M/W, football M/W, soccer M/W, softball M/W, tennis M/W, ultimate Frisbee M/W, volleyball M/W.

Standardized Tests *Required:* SAT or ACT (for admission).

Costs (2012–13) *Comprehensive fee:* $52,666 includes full-time tuition ($41,790), mandatory fees ($316), and room and board ($10,560). Part-time tuition: $1741 per credit. *College room only:* $4880. Room and board charges vary according to board plan and housing facility. *Payment plan:* deferred payment. *Waivers:* employees or children of employees.

Financial Aid Of all full-time matriculated undergraduates who enrolled in 2012, 871 applied for aid, 727 were judged to have need, 386 had their need fully met. 480 Federal Work-Study jobs (averaging $1891). 162 state and other part-time jobs (averaging $1600). In 2012, 455 non-need-based awards were made. *Average percent of need met:* 97%. *Average financial aid package:* $32,267. *Average need-based loan:* $5025. *Average need-based gift aid:* $26,076. *Average non-need-based aid:* $8745. *Average indebtedness upon graduation:* $16,797. *Financial aid deadline:* 2/1.

Applying *Options:* electronic application, early decision, deferred entrance. *Application fee:* $50. *Required:* essay or personal statement, high school transcript, 1 letter of recommendation. *Recommended:* interview. *Application deadlines:* 1/15 (freshmen), 3/1 (transfers). *Early decision deadline:* 11/15. *Notification:* 4/1 (freshmen), 4/20 (transfers), 12/18 (early decision).

Freshman Application Contact Mr. Tony Cabasco, Dean of Admission and Financial Aid, Whitman College, 515 Boyer Avenue, Walla Walla, WA 99362-2083. *Phone:* 509-527-5176. *Toll-free phone:* 877-462-9448. *Fax:* 509-527-4967. *E-mail:* admission@whitman.edu. *Website:* http://www.whitman.edu/.

See previous page for display ad and page 1648 for the College Close-Up.

Whitworth University

Spokane, Washington

- **Independent Presbyterian** comprehensive, founded 1890
- **Suburban** 200-acre campus
- **Endowment** $98.9 million
- **Coed** 2,348 undergraduate students, 98% full-time, 59% women, 41% men
- **Moderately difficult** entrance level, 52% of applicants were admitted

Undergraduates 2,300 full-time, 48 part-time. Students come from 34 states and territories; 27 other countries; 43% are from out of state; 1% Black or African American, non-Hispanic/Latino; 7% Hispanic/Latino; 3% Asian, non-Hispanic/Latino; 0.2% Native Hawaiian or other Pacific Islander, non-Hispanic/Latino; 0.5% American Indian or Alaska Native, non-Hispanic/Latino; 5% Two or more races, non-Hispanic/Latino; 2% Race/ethnicity unknown; 2% international; 4% transferred in. *Retention:* 85% of full-time freshmen returned.

Freshmen *Admission:* 6,932 applied, 3,624 admitted, 631 enrolled. *Average high school GPA:* 3.77. *Test scores:* SAT critical reading scores over 500: 90%; SAT math scores over 500: 92%; SAT writing scores over 500: 88%; ACT scores over 18: 99%; SAT critical reading scores over 600: 49%; SAT math scores over 600: 58%; SAT writing scores over 600: 45%; ACT scores over 24: 79%; SAT critical reading scores over 700: 12%; SAT math scores over 700: 10%; SAT writing scores over 700: 10%; ACT scores over 30: 24%.

Faculty *Total:* 331, 51% full-time. *Student/faculty ratio:* 11:1.

Academics *Calendar:* 4-1-4. *Degrees:* bachelor's, master's, post-master's, and postbachelor's certificates. *Special study options:* adult/continuing education programs, advanced placement credit, cooperative education, double majors, English as a second language, honors programs, independent study, internships, off-campus study, part-time degree program, services for LD students, student-designed majors, study abroad, summer session for credit. *ROTC:* Army (c). *Unusual degree programs:* 3-2 engineering with Seattle Pacific University, University of Southern California, Washington University in St. Louis, Columbia University; nursing with Washington State University/College of Nursing (WSU/CON).

Computers on Campus 280 computers/terminals and 200 ports are available on campus for general student use. Students can access the following: campus intranet, computer help desk, free student e-mail accounts, online (class) grades, online (class) registration, online (class) schedules. Campuswide network is available. 100% of college-owned or -operated housing units are wired for high-speed Internet access. Wireless service is available via classrooms, computer centers, computer labs, dorm rooms, libraries, student centers.

Student Life *Housing:* on-campus residence required through sophomore year. *Options:* coed, men-only, women-only. Campus housing is university owned. Freshman campus housing is guaranteed. *Activities and organizations:* drama/theater group, student-run newspaper, radio station, choral group, International Club, Young Life, En Christo, Hawaiian Club, intramural sports. *Campus security:* 24-hour emergency response devices and patrols, late-night transport/escort service, controlled dormitory access. *Student services:* health clinic, personal/psychological counseling.

Athletics Member NCAA. All Division III. *Intercollegiate sports:* baseball M, basketball M/W, cross-country running M/W, football M, golf M/W, soccer M/W, softball W, swimming and diving M/W, tennis M/W, track and field M/W, volleyball W. *Intramural sports:* basketball M/W, football M/W, soccer M/W, ultimate Frisbee M/W, volleyball M/W.

Standardized Tests *Required for some:* SAT (for admission), ACT (for admission), SAT or ACT (for admission), SAT and SAT Subject Tests or ACT (for admission), SAT Subject Tests (for admission).

Costs (2012–13) *Comprehensive fee:* $43,710 includes full-time tuition ($33,676), mandatory fees ($670), and room and board ($9364). Part-time tuition: $1403 per credit. *College room only:* $5076. Room and board charges vary according to board plan and housing facility. *Payment plan:* installment. *Waivers:* senior citizens and employees or children of employees.

Financial Aid Of all full-time matriculated undergraduates who enrolled in 2012, 1,797 applied for aid, 1,596 were judged to have need, 303 had their need fully met. 749 Federal Work-Study jobs (averaging $2318). 89 state and other part-time jobs (averaging $2953). In 2012, 565 non-need-based awards were made. *Average percent of need met:* 81%. *Average financial aid package:* $27,969. *Average need-based loan:* $4836. *Average need-based gift aid:* $19,928. *Average non-need-based aid:* $13,715. *Average indebtedness upon graduation:* $23,636.

Applying *Options:* electronic application, early admission, early action, deferred entrance. *Required:* essay or personal statement, high school transcript. *Required for some:* interview. *Application deadlines:* 3/1 (freshmen), 7/1 (transfers), 12/1 (early action). *Notification:* 12/20 (early action).

Freshman Application Contact Ms. Marianne Hansen, Director of Admission, Whitworth University, 300 West, Hawthorne Road, Spokane, WA 99251. *Phone:* 509-777-4348. *Toll-free phone:* 800-533-4668. *Fax:* 509-777-3758. *E-mail:* admission@whitworth.edu. *Website:* http://www.whitworth.edu/.

WEST VIRGINIA

Box 2003, Philippi, WV 26416. *Phone:* 304-457-1700. *Toll-free phone:* 800-263-1549. *Fax:* 304-457-6239. *E-mail:* admissions@ab.edu. *Website:* http://www.ab.edu/.

Alderson-Broaddus College

Philippi, West Virginia

- **Independent** comprehensive, founded 1871, affiliated with American Baptist Churches in the U.S.A.
- **Rural** 170-acre campus
- **Endowment** $18.2 million
- **Coed** 826 undergraduate students, 94% full-time, 49% women, 51% men
- **Moderately difficult** entrance level, 41% of applicants were admitted

Undergraduates 777 full-time, 49 part-time. Students come from 28 states and territories; 8 other countries; 47% are from out of state; 16% Black or African American, non-Hispanic/Latino; 2% Hispanic/Latino; 2% Asian, non-Hispanic/Latino; 0.2% American Indian or Alaska Native, non-Hispanic/Latino; 0.4% Two or more races, non-Hispanic/Latino; 0.5% Race/ethnicity unknown; 2% international; 6% transferred in; 76% live on campus. *Retention:* 66% of full-time freshmen returned.

Freshmen *Admission:* 3,726 applied, 1,514 admitted, 394 enrolled. *Average high school GPA:* 3. *Test scores:* SAT critical reading scores over 500: 33%; SAT math scores over 500: 42%; SAT writing scores over 500: 17%; ACT scores over 18: 91%; SAT critical reading scores over 600: 4%; SAT math scores over 600: 11%; SAT writing scores over 600: 3%; ACT scores over 24: 26%; SAT math scores over 700: 1%; ACT scores over 30: 1%.

Faculty *Total:* 97, 67% full-time, 37% with terminal degrees. *Student/faculty ratio:* 12:1.

Academics *Calendar:* semesters. *Degrees:* certificates, associate, bachelor's, and master's. *Special study options:* advanced placement credit, double majors, honors programs, independent study, internships, part-time degree program, services for LD students, study abroad, summer session for credit.

Computers on Campus 100 computers/terminals and 750 ports are available on campus for general student use. Students can access the following: campus intranet, computer help desk, free student e-mail accounts, online (class) grades, online (class) schedules, course materials, student record information. Campuswide network is available. 100% of college-owned or -operated housing units are wired for high-speed Internet access. Wireless service is available via entire campus.

Student Life *Housing:* on-campus residence required through senior year. *Options:* coed, women-only, disabled students. Campus housing is university owned. Freshman campus housing is guaranteed. *Activities and organizations:* drama/theater group, student-run newspaper, radio and television station, choral group, marching band, AAPA/Hu C. Myers Society, Alpha Beta Nu, Student Athletic Advisory Committee, Sigma Alpha Iota, Kappa Xi Omega. *Campus security:* 24-hour patrols, controlled dormitory access, emergency notification system, lighted pathways and sidewalks. *Student services:* health clinic, personal/psychological counseling.

Athletics Member NCAA. All Division II. *Intercollegiate sports:* baseball M(s), basketball M(s)/W(s), cheerleading M(s)/W(s), cross-country running M(s)/W(s), football M(s), golf M(s)/W(s), gymnastics W(s), lacrosse M(s)/W(s), soccer M(s)/W(s), softball W(s), swimming and diving M(s)/W(s), tennis W(s), track and field M(s)/W(s), volleyball M(s)/W(s), wrestling M(s)/W(s). *Intramural sports:* basketball M/W, bowling M/W, football M/W, golf M/W, racquetball M/W, soccer M/W, softball W, tennis M/W, ultimate Frisbee M/W, volleyball M/W, water polo M/W.

Standardized Tests *Required:* SAT and SAT Subject Tests or ACT (for admission).

Costs (2013–14) *Comprehensive fee:* $29,976 includes full-time tuition ($22,530), mandatory fees ($210), and room and board ($7236). Part-time tuition: $751 per credit. *Room and board:* Room and board charges vary according to housing facility. *Payment plan:* installment. *Waivers:* employees or children of employees.

Financial Aid Of all full-time matriculated undergraduates who enrolled in 2010, 520 applied for aid, 495 were judged to have need, 131 had their need fully met. 189 Federal Work-Study jobs (averaging $1390). 90 state and other part-time jobs (averaging $2198). In 2010, 33 non-need-based awards were made. *Average percent of need met:* 81%. *Average financial aid package:* $21,596. *Average need-based loan:* $4838. *Average need-based gift aid:* $17,655. *Average non-need-based aid:* $8942. *Average indebtedness upon graduation:* $31,751.

Applying *Options:* electronic application, deferred entrance. *Required:* high school transcript, minimum 2.0 GPA. *Required for some:* 3 letters of recommendation, interview. *Application deadlines:* rolling (freshmen), rolling (transfers). *Notification:* 8/31 (freshmen), continuous until 8/31 (transfers).

Freshman Application Contact Mr. Zachary A Ward, Director of Admissions, Alderson-Broaddus College, 101 College Hill Drive, Campus

American Public University System

Charles Town, West Virginia

- **Proprietary** comprehensive, founded 1991
- **Rural** campus with easy access to Washington, DC
- **Coed** 45,772 undergraduate students, 7% full-time, 38% women, 62% men
- **Noncompetitive** entrance level

Undergraduates 3,287 full-time, 42,485 part-time. Students come from 58 states and territories; 77 other countries; 22% Black or African American, non-Hispanic/Latino; 11% Hispanic/Latino; 2% Asian, non-Hispanic/Latino; 1% Native Hawaiian or other Pacific Islander, non-Hispanic/Latino; 0.6% American Indian or Alaska Native, non-Hispanic/Latino; 3% Two or more races, non-Hispanic/Latino; 4% Race/ethnicity unknown; 0.8% international; 12% transferred in.

Freshmen *Admission:* 6,359 enrolled.

Academics *Calendar:* courses start on the first Monday of each month. *Degrees:* certificates, associate, bachelor's, master's, and postbachelor's certificates (profile includes American Public University, American Military University and American Community College). *Special study options:* advanced placement credit, distance learning, external degree program, independent study, internships, part-time degree program, services for LD students, summer session for credit.

Computers on Campus Students can access the following: free student e-mail accounts, online (class) grades, online (class) registration, online (class) schedules.

Student Life *Housing:* college housing not available.

Costs (2013–14) *Tuition:* $6000 full-time, $250 per credit hour part-time. *Required fees:* $400 full-time, $50 per course part-time. *Payment plan:* installment. *Waivers:* employees or children of employees.

Applying *Options:* electronic application, deferred entrance. *Required:* high school transcript, orientation (no-fee). *Application deadlines:* rolling (freshmen), rolling (out-of-state freshmen), rolling (transfers).

Freshman Application Contact Ms. Terry Grant, Associate Vice President, Enrollment Management, American Public University System, 111 West Congress Street, Charles Town, WV 25414. *Phone:* 877-468-6268. *Toll-free phone:* 877-755-2787. *Fax:* 304-724-3788. *E-mail:* info@apus.edu. *Website:* http://www.apus.edu/.

Appalachian Bible College

Bradley, West Virginia

- **Independent nondenominational** comprehensive, founded 1950
- **Small-town** 110-acre campus
- **Endowment** $316,677
- **Coed** 286 undergraduate students, 73% full-time, 48% women, 52% men
- **Noncompetitive** entrance level, 56% of applicants were admitted

Undergraduates 209 full-time, 77 part-time. Students come from 25 states and territories; 6 other countries; 75% are from out of state; 1% Black or African American, non-Hispanic/Latino; 2% Hispanic/Latino; 0.3% Asian, non-Hispanic/Latino; 1% American Indian or Alaska Native, non-Hispanic/Latino; 1% international; 9% transferred in; 95% live on campus. *Retention:* 74% of full-time freshmen returned.

Freshmen *Admission:* 133 applied, 74 admitted, 73 enrolled. *Test scores:* SAT critical reading scores over 500: 63%; SAT math scores over 500: 46%; ACT scores over 18: 86%; SAT critical reading scores over 600: 25%; SAT math scores over 600: 21%; ACT scores over 24: 40%; SAT critical reading scores over 700: 8%; ACT scores over 30: 21%.

Faculty *Total:* 18, 61% full-time, 28% with terminal degrees. *Student/faculty ratio:* 17:1.

Academics *Calendar:* semesters. *Degrees:* certificates, diplomas, associate, bachelor's, master's, and postbachelor's certificates. *Special study options:* academic remediation for entering students, adult/continuing education programs, advanced placement credit, distance learning, double majors, honors programs, independent study, internships, part-time degree program, student-designed majors, summer session for credit.

Computers on Campus 30 computers/terminals are available on campus for general student use. Students can access the following: campus intranet, com-

puter help desk, free student e-mail accounts. Campuswide network is available. 100% of college-owned or -operated housing units are wired for high-speed Internet access. Wireless service is available via computer labs, libraries, student centers.

Student Life *Housing:* on-campus residence required through senior year. *Options:* men-only, women-only. Campus housing is university owned. Freshman campus housing is guaranteed. *Activities and organizations:* drama/theater group, choral group. *Campus security:* 24-hour emergency response devices, patrols by trained security personnel. *Student services:* health clinic, personal/psychological counseling.

Athletics Member NCCAA. *Intercollegiate sports:* basketball M/W, soccer M, volleyball W.

Standardized Tests *Required:* SAT or ACT (for admission).

Costs (2012–13) *Comprehensive fee:* $18,310 includes full-time tuition ($10,800), mandatory fees ($940), and room and board ($6570). Full-time tuition and fees vary according to course load and program. Part-time tuition: $340 per credit hour. Part-time tuition and fees vary according to program. *Required fees:* $34 per credit hour part-time, $365 per term part-time. *Room and board:* Room and board charges vary according to housing facility. *Payment plans:* tuition prepayment, installment. *Waivers:* children of alumni, adult students, senior citizens, and employees or children of employees.

Financial Aid Of all full-time matriculated undergraduates who enrolled in 2011, 188 applied for aid, 176 were judged to have need, 10 had their need fully met. 26 Federal Work-Study jobs (averaging $630). In 2011, 12 non-need-based awards were made. *Average percent of need met:* 56%. *Average financial aid package:* $9337. *Average need-based loan:* $2910. *Average need-based gift aid:* $7851. *Average non-need-based aid:* $1709. *Average indebtedness upon graduation:* $8618. *Financial aid deadline:* 6/15.

Applying *Options:* electronic application, early admission. *Application fee:* $20. *Required:* essay or personal statement, high school transcript, 3 letters of recommendation, interview. *Required for some:* interview. *Recommended:* minimum 2.5 GPA. *Application deadlines:* rolling (freshmen), rolling (transfers).

Freshman Application Contact Miss Rachel Delevan, Admissions Assistant, Appalachian Bible College, 161 College Drive, Bradley, WV 25818. *Phone:* 304-877-6428 Ext. 3213. *Toll-free phone:* 800-678-9ABC. *Fax:* 304-877-5082. *E-mail:* admissions2@abc.edu.
Website: http://www.abc.edu/.

Bethany College

Bethany, West Virginia

- **Independent** comprehensive, founded 1840, affiliated with Christian Church (Disciples of Christ)
- **Rural** 1300-acre campus with easy access to Pittsburgh
- **Coed** 812 undergraduate students, 100% full-time, 40% women, 60% men
- **Moderately difficult** entrance level, 43% of applicants were admitted

Undergraduates 809 full-time, 3 part-time. Students come from 29 states and territories; 4 other countries; 79% are from out of state; 20% Black or African American, non-Hispanic/Latino; 2% Hispanic/Latino; 0.4% Asian, non-Hispanic/Latino; 1% Two or more races, non-Hispanic/Latino; 15% Race/ethnicity unknown; 0.9% international; 4% transferred in; 94% live on campus. *Retention:* 63% of full-time freshmen returned.
Freshmen *Admission:* 1,523 applied, 655 admitted, 265 enrolled. *Average high school GPA:* 2.8. *Test scores:* SAT critical reading scores over 500: 22%; SAT math scores over 500: 32%; SAT writing scores over 500: 61%; ACT scores over 18: 61%; SAT critical reading scores over 600: 4%; SAT math scores over 600: 6%; SAT writing scores over 600: 18%; ACT scores over 24: 19%; SAT math scores over 700: 1%; SAT writing scores over 700: 5%.
Faculty *Total:* 78, 60% full-time, 55% with terminal degrees. *Student/faculty ratio:* 14:1.
Academics *Calendar:* 4-1-4. *Degrees:* bachelor's and master's. *Special study options:* academic remediation for entering students, accelerated degree program, advanced placement credit, distance learning, double majors, English as a second language, independent study, internships, off-campus study, part-time degree program, services for LD students, student-designed majors, study abroad, summer session for credit. *Unusual degree programs:* 3-2 engineering with Columbia University, Case Western Reserve University; Duquesne University, Carnegie Mellon University.
Computers on Campus 145 computers/terminals are available on campus for general student use. Students can access the following: computer help desk, free student e-mail accounts, online (class) grades, online (class) registration, online (class) schedules. Campuswide network is available. 100% of college-owned or -operated housing units are wired for high-speed Internet access. Wireless service is available via entire campus.

Student Life *Housing:* on-campus residence required through senior year. *Options:* coed, men-only, women-only, disabled students. Campus housing is university owned. Freshman campus housing is guaranteed. *Activities and organizations:* drama/theater group, student-run newspaper, radio and television station, choral group, marching band, Student Board of Governors, Outdoor Club, Model United Nations, Public Relations Society, International Student Association, national fraternities, national sororities. *Campus security:* 24-hour emergency response devices and patrols, late-night transport/escort service, controlled dormitory access. *Student services:* health clinic, personal/psychological counseling.

Athletics Member NCAA. All Division III. *Intercollegiate sports:* baseball M, basketball M/W, cross-country running M/W, football M, golf M/W, lacrosse M, soccer M/W, softball W, swimming and diving M/W, tennis M/W, track and field M/W, volleyball W.

Standardized Tests *Required:* SAT or ACT (for admission).

Costs (2012–13) *Comprehensive fee:* $34,326 includes full-time tuition ($23,880), mandatory fees ($900), and room and board ($9546). Part-time tuition: $675 per credit hour. *Required fees:* $113 per term part-time. *College room only:* $5000. Room and board charges vary according to board plan and housing facility. *Payment plan:* installment. *Waivers:* children of alumni and employees or children of employees.

Financial Aid Of all full-time matriculated undergraduates who enrolled in 2009, 777 applied for aid, 699 were judged to have need. In 2009, 60 non-need-based awards were made. *Average percent of need met:* 49%. *Average need-based loan:* $7258. *Average need-based gift aid:* $9824. *Average non-need-based aid:* $7189.

Applying *Options:* electronic application, deferred entrance. *Required:* essay or personal statement, high school transcript, minimum 2.0 GPA, 1 letter of recommendation, documentation of student involvement. *Required for some:* interview. *Recommended:* interview. *Application deadlines:* rolling (freshmen), rolling (out-of-state freshmen), rolling (transfers). *Notification:* 8/15 (freshmen), 8/15 (out-of-state freshmen), continuous until 8/15 (transfers).

Freshman Application Contact R.J. Zitzelsberger, Director of Admission, Bethany College, Office of Admission, Bethany, WV 26032. *Phone:* 304-829-7611. *Toll-free phone:* 800-922-7611. *Fax:* 304-829-7142. *E-mail:* admission@bethanywv.edu.
Website: http://www.bethanywv.edu/.

Bluefield State College

Bluefield, West Virginia

- **State-supported** 4-year, founded 1895, part of West Virginia Higher Education Policy Commission
- **Small-town** 45-acre campus
- **Coed** 1,935 undergraduate students, 82% full-time, 64% women, 36% men
- **Noncompetitive** entrance level, 47% of applicants were admitted

Undergraduates 1,583 full-time, 352 part-time. 3% are from out of state; 10% Black or African American, non-Hispanic/Latino; 0.9% Hispanic/Latino; 0.2% Asian, non-Hispanic/Latino; 0.1% American Indian or Alaska Native, non-Hispanic/Latino; 0.3% Two or more races, non-Hispanic/Latino; 3% international; 12% transferred in. *Retention:* 53% of full-time freshmen returned.
Freshmen *Admission:* 1,026 applied, 480 admitted, 307 enrolled. *Average high school GPA:* 3.25. *Test scores:* SAT critical reading scores over 500: 33%; SAT math scores over 500: 47%; SAT writing scores over 500: 32%; ACT scores over 18: 68%; SAT critical reading scores over 600: 8%; SAT math scores over 600: 6%; SAT writing scores over 600: 4%; ACT scores over 24: 13%; SAT math scores over 700: 2%; ACT scores over 30: 1%.
Faculty *Total:* 140, 53% full-time, 26% with terminal degrees. *Student/faculty ratio:* 17:1.
Academics *Calendar:* semesters. *Degrees:* associate and bachelor's. *Special study options:* adult/continuing education programs, part-time degree program.
Computers on Campus Students can access the following: computer help desk, free student e-mail accounts, online (class) grades, online (class) registration. Campuswide network is available. Wireless service is available via entire campus.

Student Life *Housing:* college housing not available. *Activities and organizations:* drama/theater group, student-run newspaper, radio station, choral group, national fraternities, national sororities. *Campus security:* 24-hour emergency response devices and patrols, student patrols. *Student services:* health clinic, personal/psychological counseling.

Athletics Member NCAA. All Division II. *Intercollegiate sports:* baseball M(s), basketball M(s)/W(s), cheerleading W, cross-country running M(s)/W(s), golf M(s), softball W(s), tennis M(s)/W(s). *Intramural sports:* badminton M/W, basketball M/W, football M, soccer M, swimming and diving M/W, table tennis M/W, volleyball M/W, water polo M/W.

Standardized Tests *Required:* SAT or ACT (for admission).
Costs (2013–14) *Tuition:* $217 per credit hour part-time; state resident $314 per credit hour part-time; nonresident $414 per credit hour part-time. *Payment plan:* installment. *Waivers:* adult students and senior citizens.
Financial Aid Of all full-time matriculated undergraduates who enrolled in 2010, 1,310 applied for aid, 1,120 were judged to have need, 440 had their need fully met. 50 Federal Work-Study jobs. In 2010, 400 non-need-based awards were made. *Average percent of need met:* 70%. *Average financial aid package:* $6800. *Average need-based loan:* $3600. *Average need-based gift aid:* $3500. *Average non-need-based aid:* $1500. *Average indebtedness upon graduation:* $22,000.
Applying *Options:* early admission, deferred entrance. *Required:* high school transcript, minimum 2.0 GPA. *Application deadlines:* rolling (freshmen), rolling (transfers). *Notification:* continuous (freshmen), continuous (transfers).
Freshman Application Contact Bluefield State College, 219 Rock Street, Bluefield, WV 24701-2198. *Phone:* 304-327-4067. *Toll-free phone:* 800-344-8892 Ext. 4065 (in-state); 800-654-7798 Ext. 4065 (out-of-state).
Website: http://www.bluefieldstate.edu/.

Concord University

Athens, West Virginia

- **State-supported** comprehensive, founded 1872, part of State College System of West Virginia
- **Rural** 100-acre campus
- **Endowment** $22.2 million
- **Coed** 2,652 undergraduate students, 90% full-time, 58% women, 42% men
- **Minimally difficult** entrance level, 49% of applicants were admitted

Undergraduates 2,377 full-time, 275 part-time. Students come from 29 states and territories; 22 other countries; 20% are from out of state; 6% Black or African American, non-Hispanic/Latino; 0.9% Hispanic/Latino; 0.7% Asian, non-Hispanic/Latino; 0.2% American Indian or Alaska Native, non-Hispanic/Latino; 3% international; 10% transferred in; 32% live on campus. *Retention:* 62% of full-time freshmen returned.
Freshmen *Admission:* 2,495 applied, 1,224 admitted, 573 enrolled. *Average high school GPA:* 3.23. *Test scores:* SAT critical reading scores over 500: 42%; SAT math scores over 500: 42%; ACT scores over 18: 83%; SAT critical reading scores over 600: 10%; SAT math scores over 600: 8%; ACT scores over 24: 25%; SAT math scores over 700: 1%; ACT scores over 30: 2%.
Faculty *Total:* 216, 58% full-time, 49% with terminal degrees. *Student/faculty ratio:* 16:1.
Academics *Calendar:* semesters. *Degrees:* associate, bachelor's, and master's. *Special study options:* academic remediation for entering students, accelerated degree program, adult/continuing education programs, advanced placement credit, cooperative education, distance learning, double majors, English as a second language, external degree program, honors programs, independent study, internships, off-campus study, part-time degree program, services for LD students, student-designed majors, study abroad, summer session for credit.
Computers on Campus 350 computers/terminals and 1,100 ports are available on campus for general student use. Students can access the following: campus intranet, computer help desk, free student e-mail accounts, online (class) grades, online (class) registration, online (class) schedules. Campuswide network is available. 100% of college-owned or -operated housing units are wired for high-speed Internet access. Wireless service is available via classrooms, computer centers, computer labs, libraries, student centers.
Student Life *Housing:* on-campus residence required through senior year. *Options:* coed, men-only, women-only. Campus housing is university owned. Freshman campus housing is guaranteed. *Activities and organizations:* drama/theater group, student-run newspaper, radio and television station, choral group, marching band, Service Groups, student government, student-run publications, Intramurals, Student Activities Committee, national fraternities, national sororities. *Campus security:* 24-hour emergency response devices and patrols, student patrols, late-night transport/escort service, controlled dormitory access. *Student services:* health clinic, personal/psychological counseling.
Athletics Member NCAA. All Division II. *Intercollegiate sports:* baseball M(s), basketball M(s)/W(s), cheerleading M/W, cross-country running M(s)/W(s), football M(s), golf M(s)/W(s), soccer M(s)/W(s), softball W(s), tennis M(s)/W(s), track and field M(s)/W(s), volleyball W(s). *Intramural sports:* basketball M/W, football M, soccer M/W, tennis M/W, volleyball M/W.
Standardized Tests *Required:* SAT or ACT (for admission).
Costs (2013–14) *Tuition:* state resident $5716 full-time, $238 per credit part-time; nonresident $12,698 full-time, $529 per credit part-time. Full-time tuition and fees vary according to course load. Part-time tuition and fees vary according to course load. *Room and board:* $7386; room only: $3762. Room

and board charges vary according to housing facility. *Payment plan:* installment. *Waivers:* adult students, senior citizens, and employees or children of employees.
Financial Aid Of all full-time matriculated undergraduates who enrolled in 2011, 2,113 applied for aid, 1,774 were judged to have need, 585 had their need fully met. 209 Federal Work-Study jobs (averaging $1428). In 2011, 173 non-need-based awards were made. *Average percent of need met:* 87%. *Average financial aid package:* $17,863. *Average need-based loan:* $3123. *Average need-based gift aid:* $3074. *Average non-need-based aid:* $956. *Average indebtedness upon graduation:* $20,170. *Financial aid deadline:* 4/15.
Applying *Options:* electronic application, early admission, early decision. *Required:* high school transcript, minimum 2.0 GPA. *Required for some:* essay or personal statement, interview. *Recommended:* interview. *Application deadlines:* rolling (freshmen), 1/15 (out-of-state freshmen), rolling (transfers). *Notification:* continuous (freshmen), continuous (transfers).
Freshman Application Contact Mr. Kent Gamble, Director of Enrollment, Concord University, 1000 Vermillion Street, Athens, WV 24712. *Phone:* 304-384-5316. *Toll-free phone:* 888-384-5249. *Fax:* 304-384-9044. *E-mail:* admissions@concord.edu.
Website: http://www.concord.edu/.

Davis & Elkins College

Elkins, West Virginia

Freshman Application Contact Ms. Rene Heckel, Director of Enrollment Management, Davis & Elkins College, 100 Campus Drive, Elkins, WV 26241. *Phone:* 304-637-1974. *Toll-free phone:* 800-624-3157. *Fax:* 304-637-1800. *E-mail:* admiss@davisandelkins.edu.
Website: http://www.dewv.edu/.

Fairmont State University

Fairmont, West Virginia

- **State-supported** comprehensive, founded 1865, part of State College System of West Virginia
- **Small-town** 120-acre campus
- **Endowment** $16.8 million
- **Coed** 4,112 undergraduate students, 87% full-time, 57% women, 43% men
- **Minimally difficult** entrance level, 66% of applicants were admitted

Undergraduates 3,573 full-time, 539 part-time. Students come from 27 states and territories; 25 other countries; 7% are from out of state; 5% Black or African American, non-Hispanic/Latino; 2% Hispanic/Latino; 0.4% Asian, non-Hispanic/Latino; 0.1% Native Hawaiian or other Pacific Islander, non-Hispanic/Latino; 0.2% American Indian or Alaska Native, non-Hispanic/Latino; 2% Two or more races, non-Hispanic/Latino; 1% Race/ethnicity unknown; 2% international; 9% transferred in; 18% live on campus. *Retention:* 64% of full-time freshmen returned.
Freshmen *Admission:* 2,326 applied, 1,527 admitted, 739 enrolled. *Average high school GPA:* 3.17. *Test scores:* SAT critical reading scores over 500: 39%; SAT math scores over 500: 40%; ACT scores over 18: 80%; SAT critical reading scores over 600: 12%; SAT math scores over 600: 8%; ACT scores over 24: 20%; SAT math scores over 700: 2%; ACT scores over 30: 1%.
Faculty *Total:* 326, 52% full-time, 38% with terminal degrees. *Student/faculty ratio:* 17:1.
Academics *Calendar:* semesters. *Degrees:* certificates, associate, bachelor's, and master's. *Special study options:* academic remediation for entering students, accelerated degree program, adult/continuing education programs, advanced placement credit, cooperative education, distance learning, double majors, English as a second language, honors programs, independent study, internships, off-campus study, part-time degree program, services for LD students, study abroad, summer session for credit. *ROTC:* Army (b), Air Force (c).
Computers on Campus 1,350 computers/terminals are available on campus for general student use. Students can access the following: campus intranet, computer help desk, free student e-mail accounts, online (class) grades, online (class) registration, online (class) schedules. Campuswide network is available. Wireless service is available via entire campus.
Student Life *Housing:* on-campus residence required through sophomore year. *Options:* coed, men-only, women-only. Campus housing is university owned. Freshman campus housing is guaranteed. *Activities and organizations:* drama/theater group, student-run newspaper, choral group, marching band, Alpha Phi Omega, Circle K, Society for Non-traditional Students, Criminal Justice Club, Honors Association, national fraternities, national sororities. *Campus security:*

24-hour emergency response devices and patrols, student patrols, controlled dormitory access. *Student services:* health clinic, personal/psychological counseling, legal services.

Athletics Member NCAA. All Division II. *Intercollegiate sports:* baseball M(s), basketball M(s)/W(s), cheerleading W, cross-country running M(s)/W(s), football M(s), golf M(s)/W(s), softball W(s), swimming and diving M(s)/W(s), tennis M(s)/W(s), volleyball W(s). *Intramural sports:* badminton M/W, basketball M/W, bowling M/W, football M, golf M/W, softball M/W, table tennis M/W, tennis M/W, volleyball M/W.

Standardized Tests *Required:* SAT or ACT (for admission).

Costs (2013–14) *Tuition:* state resident $5804 full-time, $243 per credit hour part-time; nonresident $12,240 full-time, $510 per credit hour part-time. Full-time tuition and fees vary according to location. Part-time tuition and fees vary according to course load and location. *Room and board:* $7686; room only: $4186. Room and board charges vary according to board plan and housing facility. *Payment plan:* installment. *Waivers:* employees or children of employees.

Financial Aid Of all full-time matriculated undergraduates who enrolled in 2011, 3,309 applied for aid, 2,796 were judged to have need, 163 had their need fully met. 119 Federal Work-Study jobs (averaging $1687). 275 state and other part-time jobs (averaging $2011). In 2011, 272 non-need-based awards were made. *Average percent of need met:* 65%. *Average financial aid package:* $3115. *Average need-based loan:* $3812. *Average need-based gift aid:* $5750. *Average non-need-based aid:* $5264. *Average indebtedness upon graduation:* $24,060.

Applying *Options:* electronic application. *Required:* high school transcript. *Recommended:* minimum 2.0 GPA. *Application deadlines:* rolling (freshmen), rolling (transfers). *Notification:* continuous (freshmen), continuous (transfers).

Freshman Application Contact Mrs. Lori Schoonmaker, Director of Admissions and Recruiting (Interim Associate), Fairmont State University, 1201 Locust Avenue, Fairmont, WV 26554. *Phone:* 304-367-4892. *Toll-free phone:* 800-641-5678. *Fax:* 304-367-4938. *E-mail:* admit@fairmontstate.edu. *Website:* http://www.fairmontstate.edu/.

Glenville State College

Glenville, West Virginia

- **State-supported** 4-year, founded 1872, part of West Virginia Higher Education Policy Commission
- **Rural** 331-acre campus
- **Endowment** $13.4 million
- **Coed**
- **Noncompetitive** entrance level

Faculty *Student/faculty ratio:* 19:1.

Academics *Calendar:* semesters. *Degrees:* associate and bachelor's.

Student Life *Campus security:* 24-hour emergency response devices and patrols, student patrols, late-night transport/escort service, controlled dormitory access.

Athletics Member NCAA. All Division II.

Standardized Tests *Required:* SAT or ACT (for admission).

Costs (2012–13) *Tuition:* state resident $5860 full-time, $244 per credit hour part-time; nonresident $13,824 full-time, $576 per credit hour part-time. Full-time tuition and fees vary according to course load. *Required fees:* $244 per credit hour part-time. *Room and board:* $8400; room only: $4830. Room and board charges vary according to board plan and housing facility.

Financial Aid *Of all full-time matriculated undergraduates who enrolled in 2012,* 1,117 applied for aid, 1,003 were judged to have need, 184 had their need fully met. 131 Federal Work-Study jobs (averaging $1046). 308 state and other part-time jobs (averaging $2004). *In 2012,* 61 non-need-based awards were made. *Average percent of need met:* 74. *Average financial aid package:* $13,117. *Average need-based loan:* $3928. *Average need-based gift aid:* $5632. *Average non-need-based aid:* $2349. *Average indebtedness upon graduation:* $30,299.

Applying *Options:* electronic application, deferred entrance. *Application fee:* $20. *Required:* high school transcript, minimum 3.0 GPA, college preparatory program. *Required for some:* interview.

Freshman Application Contact Ms. Ashley Weir, Admission Counselor, Glenville State College, 200 High Street, Glenville, WV 26351-1200. *Phone:* 304-462-4128 Ext. 6133. *Toll-free phone:* 800-924-2010. *Fax:* 304-462-8619. *E-mail:* ashley.weir@glenville.edu. *Website:* http://www.glenville.edu/.

Marshall University

Huntington, West Virginia

- **State-supported** university, founded 1837, part of University System of West Virginia
- **Urban** 100-acre campus
- **Coed** 9,885 undergraduate students, 87% full-time, 56% women, 44% men
- **Moderately difficult** entrance level, 80% of applicants were admitted

Undergraduates 8,561 full-time, 1,324 part-time. Students come from 45 states and territories; 35 other countries; 24% are from out of state; 6% Black or African American, non-Hispanic/Latino; 2% Hispanic/Latino; 0.8% Asian, non-Hispanic/Latino; 0.1% Native Hawaiian or other Pacific Islander, non-Hispanic/Latino; 0.3% American Indian or Alaska Native, non-Hispanic/Latino; 2% Two or more races, non-Hispanic/Latino; 3% Race/ethnicity unknown; 1% international; 7% transferred in; 24% live on campus. *Retention:* 71% of full-time freshmen returned.

Freshmen *Admission:* 2,889 applied, 2,306 admitted, 1,908 enrolled. *Average high school GPA:* 3.33. *Test scores:* SAT critical reading scores over 500: 48%; SAT math scores over 500: 56%; ACT scores over 18: 89%; SAT critical reading scores over 600: 14%; SAT math scores over 600: 12%; ACT scores over 24: 33%; SAT critical reading scores over 700: 2%; SAT math scores over 700: 1%; ACT scores over 30: 3%.

Faculty *Total:* 768, 68% full-time, 57% with terminal degrees. *Student/faculty ratio:* 19:1.

Academics *Calendar:* semesters. *Degrees:* associate, bachelor's, master's, doctoral, post-master's, and postbachelor's certificates. *Special study options:* academic remediation for entering students, accelerated degree program, adult/continuing education programs, advanced placement credit, cooperative education, distance learning, double majors, English as a second language, honors programs, independent study, internships, off-campus study, part-time degree program, services for LD students, study abroad, summer session for credit. *ROTC:* Army (b). *Unusual degree programs:* 3-2 forestry with Duke University.

Computers on Campus 1,461 computers/terminals and 2,900 ports are available on campus for general student use. Students can access the following: campus intranet, computer help desk, free student e-mail accounts, online (class) grades, online (class) registration, online (class) schedules, Virtual Computer Lab—MU Remote and Web Conferencing. Campuswide network is available. 100% of college-owned or -operated housing units are wired for high-speed Internet access. Wireless service is available via classrooms, computer centers, computer labs, dorm rooms, learning centers, libraries, student centers.

Student Life *Housing:* on-campus residence required through sophomore year. *Options:* coed, women-only, disabled students. Campus housing is university owned and is provided by a third party. Freshman campus housing is guaranteed. *Activities and organizations:* drama/theater group, student-run newspaper, radio and television station, choral group, marching band, Campus Crusade for Christ, Gamma Beta Phi, The International Students' Organization, Newman Association, Phi Alpha Theta, national fraternities, national sororities. *Campus security:* 24-hour emergency response devices and patrols, student patrols, late-night transport/escort service, controlled dormitory access. *Student services:* health clinic, personal/psychological counseling, women's center, legal services.

Athletics Member NCAA. All Division I except football (Division I-A). *Intercollegiate sports:* baseball M(s), basketball M(s)/W(s), cross-country running M(s)/W(s), golf M(s)/W(s), lacrosse M(c), rugby M(c)/W(c), soccer M(s)/W(s), softball W(s), swimming and diving W(s), tennis W(s), track and field M(s)/W(s), volleyball W(s). *Intramural sports:* basketball M/W, bowling M/W, football M/W, golf M/W, racquetball M/W, soccer M/W, softball M/W, swimming and diving M/W, tennis M/W, track and field M/W, volleyball M/W.

Standardized Tests *Required:* SAT or ACT (for admission).

Costs (2012–13) *Tuition:* state resident $4860 full-time, $203 per credit hour part-time; nonresident $12,860 full-time, $536 per credit hour part-time. Full-time tuition and fees vary according to degree level, location, program, and reciprocity agreements. Part-time tuition and fees vary according to course load, degree level, location, program, and reciprocity agreements. *Required fees:* $1070 full-time. *Room and board:* $8988; room only: $5570. Room and board charges vary according to board plan and housing facility. *Payment plan:* installment. *Waivers:* senior citizens and employees or children of employees.

Financial Aid Of all full-time matriculated undergraduates who enrolled in 2012, 7,485 applied for aid, 5,967 were judged to have need, 1,765 had their need fully met. In 2012, 1138 non-need-based awards were made. *Average percent of need met:* 51%. *Average financial aid package:* $9438. *Average need-based loan:* $7109. *Average need-based gift aid:* $5635. *Average non-need-based aid:* $6406. *Average indebtedness upon graduation:* $26,727.

Applying *Options:* electronic application, deferred entrance. *Application fee:* $30. *Required for some:* high school transcript. *Application deadlines:* rolling (freshmen), rolling (transfers). *Notification:* continuous (freshmen), continuous (transfers).

Freshman Application Contact Dr. Tammy Johnson, Director of Admissions, Marshall University, 1 John Marshall Drive, Huntington, WV 25755. *Phone:* 800-642-3499. *Toll-free phone:* 800-642-3499. *Fax:* 304-696-3135. *E-mail:* admissions@marshall.edu.
Website: http://www.marshall.edu/.

Ohio Valley University

Vienna, West Virginia

- **Independent** comprehensive, founded 1960, affiliated with Church of Christ
- **Small-town** 299-acre campus
- **Endowment** $1.3 million
- **Coed** 436 undergraduate students, 89% full-time, 46% women, 54% men
- **Minimally difficult** entrance level, 42% of applicants were admitted

Undergraduates 386 full-time, 50 part-time. Students come from 31 states and territories; 11 other countries; 59% are from out of state; 7% Black or African American, non-Hispanic/Latino; 3% Hispanic/Latino; 0.2% Asian, non-Hispanic/Latino; 0.2% American Indian or Alaska Native, non-Hispanic/Latino; 1% Two or more races, non-Hispanic/Latino; 4% Race/ethnicity unknown; 8% international; 10% transferred in; 53% live on campus. *Retention:* 46% of full-time freshmen returned.

Freshmen *Admission:* 751 applied, 312 admitted, 100 enrolled. *Average high school GPA:* 3.13. *Test scores:* SAT critical reading scores over 500: 37%; SAT math scores over 500: 58%; SAT writing scores over 500: 26%; ACT scores over 18: 86%; SAT critical reading scores over 600: 16%; SAT math scores over 600: 16%; SAT writing scores over 600: 11%; ACT scores over 24: 33%; ACT scores over 30: 5%.

Faculty *Total:* 83, 27% full-time, 31% with terminal degrees. *Student/faculty ratio:* 10:1.

Academics *Calendar:* semesters. *Degrees:* associate, bachelor's, master's, and postbachelor's certificates. *Special study options:* academic remediation for entering students, adult/continuing education programs, advanced placement credit, cooperative education, distance learning, double majors, English as a second language, honors programs, independent study, internships, part-time degree program, services for LD students, student-designed majors, study abroad, summer session for credit.

Computers on Campus 45 computers/terminals and 45 ports are available on campus for general student use. Students can access the following: campus intranet, computer help desk, free student e-mail accounts, online (class) grades, online (class) registration, online (class) schedules. Campuswide network is available. 100% of college-owned or -operated housing units are wired for high-speed Internet access. Wireless service is available via entire campus.

Student Life *Housing:* on-campus residence required through sophomore year. *Options:* men-only, women-only, disabled students. Campus housing is university owned. Freshman campus housing is guaranteed. *Activities and organizations:* drama/theater group, student-run newspaper, choral group, Social Clubs, Intramural Sports, Theatre Production, Acappella Choir, Ambassadors. *Campus security:* 24-hour emergency response devices and patrols, controlled dormitory access.

Athletics Member NCAA. All Division II. *Intercollegiate sports:* baseball M(s), basketball M(s)/W(s), cross-country running M(s)/W(s), golf M(s)/W(s), lacrosse M(s), soccer M(s)/W(s), softball W(s), volleyball W(s), wrestling M(s). *Intramural sports:* basketball M/W, bowling M/W, football M/W, golf M/W, soccer M/W, softball M/W, volleyball M/W.

Standardized Tests *Required:* SAT or ACT (for admission), SAT and SAT Subject Tests or ACT (for admission).

Costs (2013–14) *Comprehensive fee:* $25,650 includes full-time tuition ($17,000), mandatory fees ($1750), and room and board ($6900). Full-time tuition and fees vary according to course load. Part-time tuition: $475 per credit. Part-time tuition and fees vary according to course load. *Required fees:* $75 per credit part-time. *College room only:* $3500. Room and board charges vary according to board plan and housing facility. *Payment plan:* installment. *Waivers:* employees or children of employees.

Financial Aid Of all full-time matriculated undergraduates who enrolled in 2010, 376 applied for aid, 340 were judged to have need, 61 had their need fully met. In 2010, 48 non-need-based awards were made. *Average percent of need met:* 69%. *Average financial aid package:* $13,166. *Average need-based*

loan: $3979. *Average need-based gift aid:* $9925. *Average non-need-based aid:* $6141. *Average indebtedness upon graduation:* $22,174.

Applying *Options:* electronic application, early admission, early action, deferred entrance. *Required:* high school transcript. *Required for some:* essay or personal statement, interview. *Application deadlines:* 8/30 (freshmen), rolling (transfers). *Notification:* continuous (freshmen), continuous (transfers).

Freshman Application Contact Mrs. Valerie Wright, Admissions Office Manager, Ohio Valley University, 1 Campus View Drive, Vienna, WV 26105. *Phone:* 304-865-6200. *Toll-free phone:* 877-446-8668. *Fax:* 304-865-6001. *E-mail:* admissions@ovu.edu.
Website: http://www.ovu.edu/.

Potomac State College of West Virginia University

Keyser, West Virginia

- **State-supported** primarily 2-year, founded 1901, part of West Virginia Higher Education Policy Commission
- **Small-town** 18-acre campus
- **Coed** 1,781 undergraduate students, 81% full-time, 53% women, 47% men
- **Noncompetitive** entrance level

Undergraduates 1,436 full-time, 345 part-time. Students come from 19 states and territories; 2 other countries; 31% are from out of state; 17% Black or African American, non-Hispanic/Latino; 2% Hispanic/Latino; 0.3% Asian, non-Hispanic/Latino; 0.1% Native Hawaiian or other Pacific Islander, non-Hispanic/Latino; 1% American Indian or Alaska Native, non-Hispanic/Latino; 0.3% Two or more races, non-Hispanic/Latino; 0.7% Race/ethnicity unknown; 0.2% international; 3% transferred in; 28% live on campus. *Retention:* 46% of full-time freshmen returned.

Freshmen *Admission:* 1,006 admitted, 729 enrolled. *Average high school GPA:* 2.82. *Test scores:* SAT critical reading scores over 500: 15%; SAT math scores over 500: 21%; ACT scores over 18: 62%; SAT critical reading scores over 600: 3%; SAT math scores over 600: 2%; ACT scores over 24: 15%; ACT scores over 30: 1%.

Faculty *Total:* 95, 44% full-time, 14% with terminal degrees. *Student/faculty ratio:* 25:1.

Academics *Calendar:* semesters. *Degrees:* associate and bachelor's. *Special study options:* academic remediation for entering students, adult/continuing education programs, advanced placement credit, distance learning, double majors, honors programs, independent study, internships, part-time degree program, services for LD students, study abroad, summer session for credit.

Computers on Campus 35 computers/terminals are available on campus for general student use. Students can access the following: campus intranet, computer help desk, free student e-mail accounts, online (class) grades, online (class) registration, online (class) schedules. Campuswide network is available. 100% of college-owned or -operated housing units are wired for high-speed Internet access. Wireless service is available via classrooms, computer labs, libraries, student centers.

Student Life *Housing:* on-campus residence required through sophomore year. *Options:* coed. Campus housing is university owned. Freshman applicants given priority for college housing. *Activities and organizations:* drama/theater group, student-run newspaper, choral group, Community Chorus, Circle K, Agriculture and Forestry Club, Catamounts Against Cancer, Intramural Program. *Campus security:* 24-hour patrols, late-night transport/escort service, controlled dormitory access. *Student services:* health clinic, personal/psychological counseling.

Athletics Member NJCAA. *Intercollegiate sports:* baseball M(s), basketball M(s)/W(s), soccer M/W, softball W(s), volleyball W(s). *Intramural sports:* basketball M/W, football M/W, volleyball M/W.

Standardized Tests *Recommended:* SAT or ACT (for admission).

Financial Aid Of all full-time matriculated undergraduates who enrolled in 2011, 70 Federal Work-Study jobs (averaging $1300).

Applying *Options:* electronic application. *Required:* high school transcript. *Application deadlines:* rolling (freshmen), rolling (transfers).

Freshman Application Contact Ms. Beth Little, Director of Enrollment Services, Potomac State College of West Virginia University, 75 Arnold Street, Keyser, WV 26726. *Phone:* 304-788-6820. *Toll-free phone:* 800-262-7332 Ext. 6820. *Fax:* 304-788-6939. *E-mail:* go2psc@mail.wvu.edu.
Website: http://www.potomacstatecollege.edu/.

Salem International University

Salem, West Virginia

- **Independent** comprehensive, founded 1888
- **Rural** 300-acre campus
- **Coed** 631 undergraduate students, 100% full-time, 62% women, 38% men

Undergraduates 631 full-time. Students come from 13 states and territories; 13 other countries; 59% are from out of state; 23% Black or African American, non-Hispanic/Latino; 5% Hispanic/Latino; 0.5% Asian, non-Hispanic/Latino; 0.2% Native Hawaiian or other Pacific Islander, non-Hispanic/Latino; 0.6% American Indian or Alaska Native, non-Hispanic/Latino; 0.5% Two or more races, non-Hispanic/Latino; 23% Race/ethnicity unknown; 5% international; 32% live on campus. *Retention:* 43% of full-time freshmen returned.

Freshmen *Admission:* 210 enrolled.

Faculty *Total:* 60, 43% full-time, 18% with terminal degrees. *Student/faculty ratio:* 18:1.

Academics *Calendar:* modular. *Degrees:* certificates, associate, bachelor's, master's, and post-master's certificates. *Special study options:* academic remediation for entering students, accelerated degree program, advanced placement credit, distance learning, double majors, English as a second language, independent study, internships, off-campus study, part-time degree program, services for LD students, study abroad, summer session for credit.

Computers on Campus 104 computers/terminals are available on campus for general student use. Students can access the following: campus intranet, computer help desk, free student e-mail accounts, online (class) grades, online (class) registration, online (class) schedules. Campuswide network is available. 100% of college-owned or -operated housing units are wired for high-speed Internet access. Wireless service is available via entire campus.

Student Life *Housing:* on-campus residence required for freshman year. *Options:* coed, men-only, women-only. Campus housing is university owned. Freshman campus housing is guaranteed. *Activities and organizations:* student government, Alpha Phi Omega, Gamma Beta Phi, national fraternities, national sororities. *Campus security:* 24-hour emergency response devices and patrols. *Student services:* personal/psychological counseling.

Athletics Member NCAA. All Division II. *Intercollegiate sports:* baseball M(s), basketball M(s)/W(s), cheerleading M/W, soccer M(s)/W(s), softball W(s), swimming and diving M(s)/W(s), volleyball W(s), water polo M(s)/W(s). *Intramural sports:* badminton M/W, basketball M/W, racquetball M/W, skiing (downhill) M/W, soccer M/W, softball W, swimming and diving M/W, table tennis M/W, water polo M/W, weight lifting M/W.

Standardized Tests *Required for some:* SAT or ACT (for admission).

Costs (2013–14) *Comprehensive fee:* $21,100 includes full-time tuition ($13,050), mandatory fees ($1650), and room and board ($6400). Full-time tuition and fees vary according to degree level and program. Part-time tuition: $435 per credit. Part-time tuition and fees vary according to degree level and program. *Required fees:* $55 per credit part-time. *College room only:* $2400. *Payment plan:* installment.

Financial Aid Of all full-time matriculated undergraduates who enrolled in 2006, 230 applied for aid, 200 were judged to have need, 120 had their need fully met. 106 Federal Work-Study jobs (averaging $650). 25 state and other part-time jobs (averaging $911). *Average percent of need met:* 100%. *Average financial aid package:* $18,110. *Average need-based loan:* $5500. *Average need-based gift aid:* $5400. *Average non-need-based aid:* $7860. *Average indebtedness upon graduation:* $15,794.

Applying *Required:* high school transcript, minimum 2.0 GPA. *Required for some:* interview. *Recommended:* essay or personal statement, interview.

Freshman Application Contact Mrs. Brenda Davis, Admissions Representative, Salem International University, PO Box 500, Salem, WV 26426-0500. *Phone:* 304-326-1359. *Toll-free phone:* 888-235-5024. *Fax:* 304-326-1592. *E-mail:* admissions@salemiu.edu.
Website: http://www.salemu.edu/.

Shepherd University

Shepherdstown, West Virginia

- **State-supported** comprehensive, founded 1871, part of West Virginia Higher Education Policy Commission
- **Small-town** 320-acre campus with easy access to Washington, DC
- **Endowment** $25.4 million
- **Coed** 4,170 undergraduate students, 84% full-time, 58% women, 42% men
- **Moderately difficult** entrance level, 81% of applicants were admitted

Undergraduates 3,484 full-time, 686 part-time. Students come from 48 states and territories; 16 other countries; 37% are from out of state; 7% Black or African American, non-Hispanic/Latino; 3% Hispanic/Latino; 2% Asian, non-Hispanic/Latino; 0.1% Native Hawaiian or other Pacific Islander, non-Hispanic/Latino; 0.6% American Indian or Alaska Native, non-Hispanic/Latino; 0.2% Two or more races, non-Hispanic/Latino; 5% Race/ethnicity unknown; 0.4% international; 11% transferred in; 34% live on campus. *Retention:* 63% of full-time freshmen returned.

Freshmen *Admission:* 2,023 applied, 1,639 admitted, 756 enrolled. *Average high school GPA:* 3.24. *Test scores:* SAT critical reading scores over 500: 58%; SAT math scores over 500: 49%; ACT scores over 18: 95%; SAT critical reading scores over 600: 13%; SAT math scores over 600: 11%; ACT scores over 24: 31%; SAT critical reading scores over 700: 1%; SAT math scores over 700: 1%; ACT scores over 30: 2%.

Faculty *Total:* 367, 39% full-time, 48% with terminal degrees. *Student/faculty ratio:* 18:1.

Academics *Calendar:* semesters. *Degrees:* bachelor's and master's. *Special study options:* academic remediation for entering students, adult/continuing education programs, advanced placement credit, cooperative education, distance learning, double majors, honors programs, independent study, internships, part-time degree program, services for LD students, study abroad, summer session for credit. *ROTC:* Air Force (c).

Computers on Campus 451 computers/terminals and 150 ports are available on campus for general student use. Students can access the following: campus intranet, computer help desk, free student e-mail accounts, online (class) grades, online (class) registration, online (class) schedules, personal Web pages. Campuswide network is available. 100% of college-owned or -operated housing units are wired for high-speed Internet access. Wireless service is available via classrooms, computer labs, libraries, student centers.

Student Life *Housing:* on-campus residence required through senior year. *Options:* coed. Campus housing is university owned. Freshman applicants given priority for college housing. *Activities and organizations:* drama/theater group, student-run newspaper, radio station, choral group, marching band, Relay for Life, Sigma Sigma Sigma, Ram Marching Band, Student Government Association, Delta Zeta, national fraternities, national sororities. *Campus security:* 24-hour emergency response devices and patrols, late-night transport/escort service, controlled dormitory access, student security in academic buildings, RAVE emergency alert system. *Student services:* health clinic, personal/psychological counseling.

Athletics Member NCAA. All Division II. *Intercollegiate sports:* baseball M(s), basketball M(s)/W(s), football M(s), golf M(s), lacrosse W(s), soccer M(s)/W(s), softball W(s), tennis M(s)/W(s), volleyball W(s). *Intramural sports:* basketball M/W, bowling M/W, football M/W, racquetball M/W, soccer M/W, softball M/W, swimming and diving M/W, table tennis M/W, tennis M/W, ultimate Frisbee M/W, volleyball M/W, water polo M/W, weight lifting M/W, wrestling M/W.

Standardized Tests *Required:* SAT or ACT (for admission).

Costs (2012–13) *Tuition:* state resident $5834 full-time, $237 per credit hour part-time; nonresident $15,136 full-time, $625 per credit hour part-time. Full-time tuition and fees vary according to program and reciprocity agreements. Part-time tuition and fees vary according to program. *Room and board:* $8424. Room and board charges vary according to board plan and housing facility. *Payment plan:* installment. *Waivers:* minority students, senior citizens, and employees or children of employees.

Financial Aid Of all full-time matriculated undergraduates who enrolled in 2012, 3,181 applied for aid, 2,167 were judged to have need, 496 had their need fully met. 112 Federal Work-Study jobs (averaging $1340). 484 state and other part-time jobs (averaging $2258). In 2012, 681 non-need-based awards were made. *Average percent of need met:* 74%. *Average financial aid package:* $11,671. *Average need-based loan:* $4035. *Average need-based gift aid:* $4984. *Average non-need-based aid:* $9946. *Average indebtedness upon graduation:* $23,940.

Applying *Options:* electronic application, early admission, early action, deferred entrance. *Application fee:* $45. *Required:* high school transcript, minimum 2.0 GPA. *Recommended:* essay or personal statement, minimum 3.0 GPA, 3 letters of recommendation. *Application deadlines:* rolling (freshmen), rolling (out-of-state freshmen), rolling (transfers), 11/15 (early action). *Notification:* continuous until 8/15 (freshmen), continuous until 8/15 (out-of-state freshmen), continuous until 8/15 (transfers), 12/15 (early action).

Freshman Application Contact Ms. Kimberly Scranage, Vice President for Enrollment Management, Shepherd University, PO Box 5000, Shepherdstown, WV 25443-5000. *Phone:* 304-876-5212. *Toll-free phone:* 800-344-5231. *Fax:* 304-876-5165. *E-mail:* admissions@shepherd.edu.
Website: http://www.shepherd.edu/.

Strayer University—Teays Valley Campus

Scott Depot, West Virginia

Freshman Application Contact Strayer University—Teays Valley Campus, 100 Corporate Center Drive, Scott Depot, WV 25560. *Website:* http://www.strayer.edu/campus/teays-valley.

University of Charleston

Charleston, West Virginia

- **Independent** comprehensive, founded 1888
- **Urban** 40-acre campus
- **Coed** 1,026 undergraduate students, 97% full-time, 60% women, 40% men
- **Moderately difficult** entrance level, 56% of applicants were admitted

Undergraduates 993 full-time, 33 part-time. Students come from 35 states and territories; 32 other countries; 37% are from out of state; 12% Black or African American, non-Hispanic/Latino; 3% Hispanic/Latino; 1% Asian, non-Hispanic/Latino; 0.4% American Indian or Alaska Native, non-Hispanic/Latino; 1% Two or more races, non-Hispanic/Latino; 7% Race/ethnicity unknown; 10% international; 14% transferred in; 61% live on campus. *Retention:* 70% of full-time freshmen returned.

Freshmen *Admission:* 1,641 applied, 919 admitted, 241 enrolled. *Average high school GPA:* 3.3. *Test scores:* SAT critical reading scores over 500: 38%; SAT math scores over 500: 45%; ACT scores over 18: 89%; SAT critical reading scores over 600: 7%; SAT math scores over 600: 11%; ACT scores over 24: 36%; SAT math scores over 700: 3%; ACT scores over 30: 4%.

Faculty *Total:* 126, 66% full-time. *Student/faculty ratio:* 15:1.

Academics *Calendar:* semesters. *Degrees:* associate, bachelor's, master's, and doctoral. *Special study options:* academic remediation for entering students, accelerated degree program, adult/continuing education programs, advanced placement credit, cooperative education, distance learning, double majors, English as a second language, independent study, internships, part-time degree program, services for LD students, student-designed majors, study abroad, summer session for credit. *ROTC:* Army (b). *Unusual degree programs:* 3-2 business administration.

Computers on Campus 200 computers/terminals are available on campus for general student use. Students can access the following: campus intranet, computer help desk, free student e-mail accounts, online (class) grades, online (class) registration, online (class) schedules. Campuswide network is available. 100% of college-owned or -operated housing units are wired for high-speed Internet access. Wireless service is available via entire campus.

Student Life *Housing:* on-campus residence required through sophomore year. *Options:* coed, disabled students. Campus housing is university owned. Freshman campus housing is guaranteed. *Activities and organizations:* student-run newspaper, choral group, Student Activities Board, American Society of Interior Designers, Student Government Association, Capito Association of Nursing Students, International Student Organization, national fraternities, national sororities. *Campus security:* 24-hour emergency response devices and patrols, student patrols, late-night transport/escort service, controlled dormitory access, radio connection to city police and ambulance. *Student services:* health clinic, personal/psychological counseling.

Athletics Member NCAA. All Division II. *Intercollegiate sports:* baseball M(s), basketball M(s)/W(s), cheerleading W(s), crew W(s), cross-country running W(s), football M(s), golf M(s)/W(s), soccer M(s)/W(s), softball W(s), swimming and diving M(s)/W(s), tennis M(s)/W(s), track and field M(s)/W(s), volleyball W(s). *Intramural sports:* basketball M/W, bowling M/W, football M/W, tennis M/W, volleyball M/W, water polo M/W.

Standardized Tests *Required:* SAT or ACT (for admission).

Costs (2012–13) *Comprehensive fee:* $34,700 includes full-time tuition ($25,500), mandatory fees ($200), and room and board ($9000). Full-time tuition and fees vary according to location and student level. Part-time tuition: $900 per credit hour. Part-time tuition and fees vary according to course load, location, and program. *College room only:* $4900. Room and board charges vary according to board plan, housing facility, and location. *Payment plan:* installment. *Waivers:* children of alumni, senior citizens, and employees or children of employees.

Financial Aid Of all full-time matriculated undergraduates who enrolled in 2011, 971 applied for aid, 971 were judged to have need, 87 had their need fully met. 219 Federal Work-Study jobs (averaging $1200). *Average percent of need met:* 69%. *Average financial aid package:* $21,814. *Average need-based loan:* $4604. *Average need-based gift aid:* $12,787. *Financial aid deadline:* 8/15.

Applying *Options:* electronic application, early admission, deferred entrance. *Application fee:* $25. *Required:* high school transcript, minimum 2.3 GPA. *Required for some:* interview. *Recommended:* essay or personal statement. *Application deadlines:* rolling (freshmen), rolling (out-of-state freshmen), rolling (transfers). *Notification:* continuous (freshmen), continuous (out-of-state freshmen), continuous (transfers).

Freshman Application Contact Sandy Dolin, Application Coordinator, University of Charleston, 2300 MacCorkle Avenue, SE, Charleston, WV 25304. *Phone:* 304-357-4752. *Toll-free phone:* 800-995-GOUC. *E-mail:* admissions@ucwv.edu.
Website: http://www.ucwv.edu/.

West Liberty University

West Liberty, West Virginia

- **State-supported** comprehensive, founded 1837, part of West Virginia Higher Education Policy Commission
- **Rural** campus
- **Coed** 2,718 undergraduate students, 86% full-time, 58% women, 42% men
- **Minimally difficult** entrance level, 28% of applicants were admitted

Undergraduates 2,331 full-time, 387 part-time. Students come from 26 states and territories; 38 other countries; 28% are from out of state; 4% Black or African American, non-Hispanic/Latino; 1% Hispanic/Latino; 0.8% Asian, non-Hispanic/Latino; 0.1% American Indian or Alaska Native, non-Hispanic/Latino; 0.6% Two or more races, non-Hispanic/Latino; 1% Race/ethnicity unknown; 2% international; 9% transferred in; 47% live on campus. *Retention:* 71% of full-time freshmen returned.

Freshmen *Admission:* 1,860 applied, 526 admitted, 526 enrolled. *Average high school GPA:* 3.3. *Test scores:* SAT critical reading scores over 500: 21%; SAT math scores over 500: 25%; ACT scores over 18: 83%; SAT math scores over 600: 2%; ACT scores over 24: 19%; ACT scores over 30: 1%.

Faculty *Total:* 240, 60% full-time, 39% with terminal degrees. *Student/faculty ratio:* 14:1.

Academics *Calendar:* semesters. *Degrees:* associate, bachelor's, and master's. *Special study options:* academic remediation for entering students, accelerated degree program, adult/continuing education programs, advanced placement credit, cooperative education, distance learning, double majors, external degree program, honors programs, independent study, internships, off-campus study, part-time degree program, services for LD students, student-designed majors, study abroad, summer session for credit.

Computers on Campus Students can access the following: campus intranet, computer help desk, free student e-mail accounts, online (class) grades, online (class) registration, online (class) schedules. Campuswide network is available. 100% of college-owned or -operated housing units are wired for high-speed Internet access. Wireless service is available via classrooms, computer labs, dorm rooms, learning centers, libraries, student centers.

Student Life *Housing options:* coed, men-only, women-only, disabled students. Campus housing is university owned. *Campus security:* 24-hour emergency response devices and patrols, controlled dormitory access.

Athletics Member NCAA. All Division II. *Intercollegiate sports:* baseball M(s), basketball M(s)/W(s), cross-country running M(s)/W(s), football M(s), golf M(s)/W(s), softball W(s), tennis M(s)/W(s), track and field M(s)/W(s), volleyball W(s), wrestling M(s). *Intramural sports:* basketball M/W, golf M/W, racquetball M/W, softball M/W, table tennis M/W, tennis M/W, volleyball M/W.

Standardized Tests *Required:* SAT or ACT (for admission).

Costs (2012–13) *Tuition:* state resident $5530 full-time, $230 per credit hour part-time; nonresident $13,140 full-time, $548 per credit hour part-time. Full-time tuition and fees vary according to course load, degree level, and program. Part-time tuition and fees vary according to course load, degree level, and program. *Required fees:* $275 full-time. *Room and board:* $8200; room only: $4720. Room and board charges vary according to board plan and housing facility. *Payment plans:* installment, deferred payment. *Waivers:* senior citizens and employees or children of employees.

Financial Aid Of all full-time matriculated undergraduates who enrolled in 2010, 2,138 applied for aid, 1,799 were judged to have need, 391 had their need fully met. In 2010, 43 non-need-based awards were made. *Average percent of need met:* 70%. *Average financial aid package:* $7990. *Average need-based loan:* $3974. *Average need-based gift aid:* $5196. *Average non-need-based aid:* $1507. *Average indebtedness upon graduation:* $25,000.

Applying *Options:* electronic application. *Required:* high school transcript, minimum 2.0 GPA. *Recommended:* interview. *Application deadlines:* rolling (freshmen), 8/1 (transfers). *Notification:* continuous (freshmen), continuous (transfers).

Freshman Application Contact Ms. Stephanie North, Admissions Counselor, West Liberty University, 208 University Drive, West Liberty, WV 26074. *Phone:* 304-336-8078. *Toll-free phone:* 800-732-6204 (in-state); 866-WESTLIB (out-of-state). *Fax:* 304-336-8403. *E-mail:* wladmsn1@westliberty.edu.
Website: http://www.westliberty.edu/.

West Virginia State University

Institute, West Virginia

- **State-supported** comprehensive, founded 1891, part of State College System of West Virginia
- **Suburban** 98-acre campus
- **Coed** 2,561 undergraduate students, 72% full-time, 56% women, 44% men
- **Minimally difficult** entrance level, 84% of applicants were admitted

Undergraduates 1,848 full-time, 713 part-time. Students come from 22 states and territories; 4 other countries; 8% are from out of state; 7% live on campus. *Retention:* 54% of full-time freshmen returned.
Freshmen *Admission:* 798 applied, 669 admitted. *Average high school GPA:* 3.03.
Faculty *Total:* 179, 66% full-time, 49% with terminal degrees. *Student/faculty ratio:* 15:1.
Academics *Calendar:* semesters. *Degrees:* bachelor's and master's. *Special study options:* academic remediation for entering students, accelerated degree program, adult/continuing education programs, advanced placement credit, cooperative education, external degree program, internships, part-time degree program, services for LD students, summer session for credit. *ROTC:* Army (b).
Computers on Campus Campuswide network is available.
Student Life *Housing:* on-campus residence required for freshman year. *Options:* men-only, women-only. Campus housing is university owned. *Activities and organizations:* student-run newspaper, choral group, marching band, national fraternities, national sororities. *Campus security:* 24-hour emergency response devices and patrols, late-night transport/escort service. *Student services:* health clinic, personal/psychological counseling.
Athletics Member NCAA. All Division II. *Intercollegiate sports:* baseball M, basketball M(s)/W(s), cross-country running M/W, football M(s), golf W, softball W(s), tennis M/W, track and field M/W, volleyball W. *Intramural sports:* baseball M, basketball M/W, bowling M/W, cheerleading W, cross-country running M/W, football M, golf W, softball W, tennis M/W, track and field M/W, volleyball W.
Standardized Tests *Required for some:* SAT or ACT (for admission). *Recommended:* SAT (for admission).
Costs (2012–13) *Tuition:* state resident $5442 full-time, $222 per credit hour part-time; nonresident $12,720 full-time, $525 per credit hour part-time. Full-time tuition and fees vary according to course load and program. Part-time tuition and fees vary according to course load and program. *Room and board:* $6698; room only: $3382. Room and board charges vary according to board plan and housing facility. *Payment plan:* installment.
Financial Aid *Financial aid deadline:* 6/15.
Applying *Options:* electronic application, early admission. *Required:* high school transcript. *Application deadlines:* 8/11 (freshmen), 8/11 (transfers). *Notification:* continuous (freshmen), continuous (transfers).
Freshman Application Contact Ms. Amanda Anderson, Interim Director of Admissions, West Virginia State University, Campus Box 197, PO Box 1000, Ferrell Hall, Room 106, Institute, WV 25112-1000. *Phone:* 304-766-3033. *Toll-free phone:* 800-987-2112. *Fax:* 304-766-5182.
Website: http://www.wvstateu.edu/.

West Virginia University

Morgantown, West Virginia

- **State-supported** university, founded 1867, part of West Virginia Higher Education Policy Commission
- **Small-town** 1400-acre campus with easy access to Pittsburgh
- **Endowment** $403.6 million
- **Coed** 22,827 undergraduate students, 93% full-time, 46% women, 54% men
- **Moderately difficult** entrance level, 85% of applicants were admitted

Undergraduates 21,118 full-time, 1,709 part-time. Students come from 52 states and territories; 71 other countries; 47% are from out of state; 4% Black or African American, non-Hispanic/Latino; 3% Hispanic/Latino; 2% Asian, non-Hispanic/Latino; 0.1% Native Hawaiian or other Pacific Islander, non-Hispanic/Latino; 0.2% American Indian or Alaska Native, non-Hispanic/Latino; 3% Two or more races, non-Hispanic/Latino; 0.4% Race/ethnicity unknown; 3% international; 5% transferred in; 24% live on campus. *Retention:* 77% of full-time freshmen returned.
Freshmen *Admission:* 16,521 applied, 14,060 admitted, 5,135 enrolled. *Average high school GPA:* 3.36. *Test scores:* SAT critical reading scores over 500: 58%; SAT math scores over 500: 67%; ACT scores over 18: 95%; SAT critical reading scores over 600: 13%; SAT math scores over 600: 22%; ACT scores over 24: 46%; SAT critical reading scores over 700: 2%; SAT math scores over 700: 3%; ACT scores over 30: 7%.
Faculty *Total:* 1,360, 74% full-time, 71% with terminal degrees. *Student/faculty ratio:* 23:1.
Academics *Calendar:* semesters. *Degrees:* bachelor's, master's, and doctoral. *Special study options:* academic remediation for entering students, accelerated degree program, adult/continuing education programs, advanced placement credit, distance learning, double majors, English as a second language, external degree program, honors programs, independent study, internships, off-campus study, part-time degree program, services for LD students, student-designed majors, study abroad, summer session for credit. *ROTC:* Army (b), Air Force (b). *Unusual degree programs:* 3-2 education, business/foreign language, occupational therapy, physical therapy, social work.
Computers on Campus 2,500 computers/terminals and 2,500 ports are available on campus for general student use. Students can access the following: campus intranet, computer help desk, free student e-mail accounts, online (class) grades, online (class) registration, online (class) schedules. Campuswide network is available. 100% of college-owned or -operated housing units are wired for high-speed Internet access. Wireless service is available via entire campus.
Student Life *Housing:* on-campus residence required for freshman year. *Options:* coed, men-only, women-only, cooperative, disabled students. Campus housing is university owned and leased by the school. Freshman campus housing is guaranteed. *Activities and organizations:* drama/theater group, student-run newspaper, radio station, choral group, marching band, Residential Hall Association, Alpha Phi Omega, WVU Greek System, Mountaineer Maniacs, Campus Crusade for Christ, national fraternities, national sororities. *Campus security:* 24-hour emergency response devices and patrols, student patrols, late-night transport/escort service, controlled dormitory access, patrol officers just for housing. *Student services:* health clinic, personal/psychological counseling, women's center, legal services.
Athletics Member NCAA. All Division I except football (Division I-A). *Intercollegiate sports:* baseball M(s), basketball M(s)/W(s), crew W(s), cross-country running W(s), gymnastics W(s), riflery M(s)/W(s), soccer M(s)/W(s), swimming and diving M(s)/W(s), tennis W(s), track and field W(s), volleyball W(s), wrestling M(s). *Intramural sports:* archery M(c)/W(c), baseball M(c), basketball M(c)/W(c), bowling M(c)/W(c), cheerleading M(c)/W(c), crew M(c)/W(c), equestrian sports M(c)/W(c), fencing M(c)/W(c), field hockey M(c)/W(c), football M, golf M(c)/W(c), ice hockey M(c), lacrosse M(c)/W(c), racquetball M(c)/W(c), riflery M(c)/W(c), rock climbing M(c)/W(c), rugby M(c)/W(c), skiing (cross-country) M(c)/W(c), skiing (downhill) M(c)/W(c), soccer M(c)/W(c), softball W(c), swimming and diving M(c)/W(c), tennis M(c)/W(c), track and field M(c)/W(c), ultimate Frisbee M(c)/W(c), volleyball M(c)/W(c), wrestling M(c).
Standardized Tests *Required:* SAT or ACT (for admission).
Costs (2012–13) *Tuition:* state resident $6090 full-time, $254 per credit hour part-time; nonresident $18,868 full-time, $786 per credit hour part-time. Full-time tuition and fees vary according to location, program, and reciprocity agreements. Part-time tuition and fees vary according to course load, location, program, and reciprocity agreements. *Room and board:* $8782. Room and board charges vary according to board plan, housing facility, and location. *Payment plan:* installment. *Waivers:* senior citizens and employees or children of employees.
Financial Aid Of all full-time matriculated undergraduates who enrolled in 2012, 19,743 applied for aid, 16,782 were judged to have need, 4,250 had their need fully met. 876 Federal Work-Study jobs (averaging $1974). 1,155 state and other part-time jobs (averaging $2449). In 2012, 5033 non-need-based awards were made. *Average percent of need met:* 75%. *Average financial aid package:* $6270. *Average need-based loan:* $4375. *Average need-based gift aid:* $4748. *Average non-need-based aid:* $2418. *Average indebtedness upon graduation:* $27,511. *Financial aid deadline:* 3/1.
Applying *Application fee:* $45. *Required:* high school transcript, minimum 2.0 GPA. *Required for some:* essay or personal statement, minimum 2.3 GPA. *Application deadlines:* 8/1 (freshmen), 8/1 (transfers). *Notification:* continuous (transfers).
Freshman Application Contact Ms. Marilyn Potts, Director of Admissions, West Virginia University, PO Box 6009, Morgantown, WV 26506-6009.

Phone: 304-293-2124. *Toll-free phone:* 800-344-9881. *Fax:* 304-293-3080. *E-mail:* marilyn.potts@mail.wvu.edu. *Website:* http://www.wvu.edu/.

West Virginia University at Parkersburg

Parkersburg, West Virginia

Freshman Application Contact Christine Post, Associate Dean of Enrollment Management, West Virginia University at Parkersburg, 300 Campus Drive, Parkersburg, WV 26104. *Phone:* 304-424-8223 Ext. 223. *Toll-free phone:* 800-WVA-WVUP. *Fax:* 304-424-8332. *E-mail:* christine.post@mail.wvu.edu. *Website:* http://www.wvup.edu/.

West Virginia University Institute of Technology

Montgomery, West Virginia

- **State-supported** comprehensive, founded 1895
- **Small-town** 200-acre campus
- **Endowment** $1.9 million
- **Coed** 1,107 undergraduate students, 76% full-time, 39% women, 61% men
- **Minimally difficult** entrance level, 51% of applicants were admitted

Undergraduates 840 full-time, 267 part-time. Students come from 29 states and territories; 20 other countries; 17% are from out of state; 6% Black or African American, non-Hispanic/Latino; 2% Hispanic/Latino; 2% Asian, non-Hispanic/Latino; 0.1% Native Hawaiian or other Pacific Islander, non-Hispanic/Latino; 0.5% American Indian or Alaska Native, non-Hispanic/Latino; 0.9% Two or more races, non-Hispanic/Latino; 2% Race/ethnicity unknown; 3% international; 10% transferred in; 28% live on campus. *Retention:* 45% of full-time freshmen returned.

Freshmen *Admission:* 1,033 applied, 530 admitted, 199 enrolled. *Average high school GPA:* 3.27. *Test scores:* ACT scores over 18: 80%; ACT scores over 24: 26%; ACT scores over 30: 3%.

Faculty *Total:* 99, 79% full-time. *Student/faculty ratio:* 11:1.

Academics *Calendar:* semesters. *Degrees:* bachelor's and postbachelor's certificates. *Special study options:* academic remediation for entering students, advanced placement credit, cooperative education, distance learning, double majors, independent study, internships, part-time degree program, services for LD students, student-designed majors, study abroad, summer session for credit. *ROTC:* Army (b). *Unusual degree programs:* 3-2 teacher education with West Virginia University.

Computers on Campus 200 computers/terminals are available on campus for general student use. Students can access the following: computer help desk, free student e-mail accounts, online (class) grades, online (class) registration, online (class) schedules, electronic course materials through eCampus. Campuswide network is available. 100% of college-owned or -operated housing units are wired for high-speed Internet access. Wireless service is available via classrooms, computer centers, computer labs, dorm rooms, learning centers, libraries, student centers.

Student Life *Housing:* on-campus residence required through sophomore year. *Options:* coed. Campus housing is university owned. Freshman campus housing is guaranteed. *Activities and organizations:* drama/theater group, student-run newspaper, Christian Student Union, Student Activities Board, Alpha Phi Omega, Student Government Association, American Society of Mechanical Engineers, national fraternities, national sororities. *Campus security:* 24-hour emergency response devices and patrols. *Student services:* health clinic, personal/psychological counseling.

Athletics Member NAIA, USCAA. *Intercollegiate sports:* baseball M(s), basketball M(s)/W(s), cheerleading M(s)/W(s), cross-country running M(s)/W(s), golf M(s), soccer M(s)/W(s), softball W(s), swimming and diving M(s)/W, volleyball W(s), wrestling M(s).

Standardized Tests *Required:* SAT or ACT (for admission). *Required for some:* TOEFL or IELTS.

Costs (2012–13) *Tuition:* state resident $5558 full-time; nonresident $13,980 full-time. Full-time tuition and fees vary according to program. Part-time tuition and fees vary according to course load and program. *Room and board:* $8414; room only: $4968. Room and board charges vary according to board plan and housing facility. *Payment plan:* installment. *Waivers:* senior citizens.

Financial Aid Of all full-time matriculated undergraduates who enrolled in 2011, 883 applied for aid, 751 were judged to have need, 305 had their need fully met. 28 Federal Work-Study jobs (averaging $4127). 60 state and other part-time jobs. *Average percent of need met:* 42%. *Average financial aid package:* $9125. *Average need-based loan:* $3407. *Average need-based gift aid:* $4974. *Average indebtedness upon graduation:* $19,024.

Applying *Options:* electronic application, early admission. *Required:* high school transcript, minimum 2.0 GPA. *Application deadlines:* rolling (freshmen), rolling (out-of-state freshmen), rolling (transfers). *Notification:* continuous until 8/15 (freshmen), continuous (out-of-state freshmen), continuous until 8/15 (transfers).

Freshman Application Contact West Virginia University Institute of Technology, 405 Fayette Pike, Montgomery, WV 25136. *Phone:* 304-442-3146. *Toll-free phone:* 888-554-8324. *Website:* http://www.wvutech.edu/.

West Virginia Wesleyan College

Buckhannon, West Virginia

- **Independent** comprehensive, founded 1890, affiliated with United Methodist Church
- **Small-town** 180-acre campus
- **Endowment** $34.0 million
- **Coed** 1,315 undergraduate students, 98% full-time, 54% women, 46% men
- **Moderately difficult** entrance level, 78% of applicants were admitted

Undergraduates 1,289 full-time, 26 part-time. Students come from 34 states and territories; 17 other countries; 41% are from out of state; 11% Black or African American, non-Hispanic/Latino; 2% Hispanic/Latino; 0.2% Asian, non-Hispanic/Latino; 0.3% Native Hawaiian or other Pacific Islander, non-Hispanic/Latino; 0.2% American Indian or Alaska Native, non-Hispanic/Latino; 2% Two or more races, non-Hispanic/Latino; 1% Race/ethnicity unknown; 4% international; 5% transferred in; 76% live on campus. *Retention:* 64% of full-time freshmen returned.

Freshmen *Admission:* 2,008 applied, 1,557 admitted, 405 enrolled. *Average high school GPA:* 3.37. *Test scores:* SAT critical reading scores over 500: 46%; SAT math scores over 500: 47%; SAT writing scores over 500: 44%; ACT scores over 18: 86%; SAT critical reading scores over 600: 10%; SAT math scores over 600: 14%; SAT writing scores over 600: 6%; ACT scores over 24: 36%; SAT critical reading scores over 700: 1%; SAT math scores over 700: 1%; ACT scores over 30: 3%.

Faculty *Total:* 156, 57% full-time, 52% with terminal degrees. *Student/faculty ratio:* 12:1.

Academics *Calendar:* semesters. *Degrees:* bachelor's and master's. *Special study options:* academic remediation for entering students, advanced placement credit, double majors, English as a second language, honors programs, independent study, internships, off-campus study, part-time degree program, services for LD students, student-designed majors, study abroad, summer session for credit. *Unusual degree programs:* 3-2 engineering with University of Virginia, West Virginia University, Virginia Polytechnic Institute and State University.

Computers on Campus Students can access the following: campus intranet, computer help desk, free student e-mail accounts, online (class) grades, online (class) registration, online (class) schedules. Campuswide network is available. 100% of college-owned or -operated housing units are wired for high-speed Internet access. Wireless service is available via entire campus.

Student Life *Housing:* on-campus residence required through senior year. *Options:* coed, men-only, women-only, disabled students. Campus housing is university owned. Freshman campus housing is guaranteed. *Activities and organizations:* drama/theater group, student-run newspaper, radio station, choral group, Campus Activities Board, Green Club, Students in Free Enterprise (SIFE), Wesleyan Ambassadors, national fraternities, national sororities. *Campus security:* 24-hour emergency response devices and patrols, student patrols, late-night transport/escort service, controlled dormitory access. *Student services:* health clinic, personal/psychological counseling.

Athletics Member NCAA. All Division II. *Intercollegiate sports:* baseball M(s), basketball M(s)/W(s), cheerleading M/W, cross-country running M(s)/W(s), football M(s), golf M(s)/W(s), lacrosse M(c)/W(s), skiing (downhill) M(c)/W(c), soccer M(s)/W(s), softball W(s), swimming and diving M(s)/W(s), tennis M(s)/W(s), track and field M(s)/W(s), volleyball W(s). *Intramural sports:* basketball M/W, bowling M/W, football M/W, golf M/W, racquetball M/W, soccer M/W, softball M/W, table tennis M/W, volleyball M/W, water polo M/W.

Standardized Tests *Required:* SAT or ACT (for admission). *Required for some:* SAT Subject Tests (for admission).

Costs (2013–14) *Comprehensive fee:* $34,534 includes full-time tuition ($25,650), mandatory fees ($1144), and room and board ($7740). Full-time tuition and fees vary according to course load. Part-time tuition and fees vary according to course load. *Room and board:* Room and board charges vary according to board plan and housing facility. *Payment plan:* installment. *Waivers:* employees or children of employees.

Financial Aid Of all full-time matriculated undergraduates who enrolled in 2011, 1,164 applied for aid, 1,050 were judged to have need, 316 had their need fully met. In 2011, 285 non-need-based awards were made. *Average percent of need met:* 82%. *Average financial aid package:* $24,124. *Average need-based loan:* $3960. *Average need-based gift aid:* $20,770. *Average non-need-based aid:* $11,935. *Average indebtedness upon graduation:* $24,155.

Applying *Options:* electronic application, deferred entrance. *Application fee:* $35. *Required:* high school transcript. *Recommended:* essay or personal statement, interview. *Notification:* continuous (freshmen), continuous (transfers).

Freshman Application Contact John Waltz, Director of Admission, West Virginia Wesleyan College, 59 College Avenue, Buckhannon, WV 26201. *Phone:* 304-473-8510. *Toll-free phone:* 800-722-9933. *Fax:* 304-473-8108. *E-mail:* admission@wvwc.edu.
Website: http://www.wvwc.edu/.

See below for display ad and page 1644 for the College Close-Up.

Wheeling Jesuit University

Wheeling, West Virginia

- **Independent Roman Catholic (Jesuit)** comprehensive, founded 1954
- **Suburban** 65-acre campus with easy access to Pittsburgh
- **Endowment** $19.2 million
- **Coed** 1,173 undergraduate students, 79% full-time, 58% women, 42% men
- **Moderately difficult** entrance level, 63% of applicants were admitted

Undergraduates 929 full-time, 244 part-time. Students come from 28 states and territories; 16 other countries; 68% are from out of state; 4% Black or African American, non-Hispanic/Latino; 2% Hispanic/Latino; 2% Asian, non-Hispanic/Latino; 0.4% Native Hawaiian or other Pacific Islander, non-Hispanic/Latino; 0.3% Two or more races, non-Hispanic/Latino; 22% Race/ethnicity unknown; 3% international; 4% transferred in; 84% live on campus. *Retention:* 72% of full-time freshmen returned.

Freshmen *Admission:* 1,401 applied, 880 admitted, 268 enrolled. *Average high school GPA:* 3.42. *Test scores:* SAT critical reading scores over 500: 59%; SAT math scores over 500: 64%; SAT writing scores over 500: 43%; ACT

scores over 18: 96%; SAT critical reading scores over 600: 13%; SAT math scores over 600: 12%; SAT writing scores over 600: 5%; ACT scores over 24: 39%; SAT math scores over 700: 2%; ACT scores over 30: 5%.

Faculty *Total:* 156, 58% full-time, 56% with terminal degrees. *Student/faculty ratio:* 11:1.

Academics *Calendar:* semesters. *Degrees:* bachelor's, master's, doctoral, post-master's, and postbachelor's certificates. *Special study options:* academic remediation for entering students, accelerated degree program, adult/continuing education programs, advanced placement credit, distance learning, double majors, English as a second language, external degree program, honors programs, independent study, internships, off-campus study, part-time degree program, services for LD students, student-designed majors, study abroad, summer session for credit. *Unusual degree programs:* 3-2 engineering with Case Western Reserve University, West Virginia University.

Computers on Campus 215 computers/terminals are available on campus for general student use. Students can access the following: campus intranet, computer help desk, free student e-mail accounts, online (class) grades, online (class) registration, online (class) schedules. Campuswide network is available. 100% of college-owned or -operated housing units are wired for high-speed Internet access. Wireless service is available via entire campus.

Student Life *Housing:* on-campus residence required through senior year. *Options:* coed, men-only, women-only, cooperative, disabled students. Campus housing is university owned. Freshman campus housing is guaranteed. *Activities and organizations:* drama/theater group, student-run newspaper, radio station, choral group, Campus Activity Board (CAB), Theater Guild, Student Senate, International Student Club, Campus Ministry. *Campus security:* 24-hour emergency response devices and patrols, student patrols, late-night transport/escort service, controlled dormitory access. *Student services:* health clinic, personal/psychological counseling.

Athletics Member NCAA. All Division II. *Intercollegiate sports:* baseball M(s), basketball M(s)/W(s), cheerleading M(c)/W(c), cross-country running M(s)/W(s), golf M(s)/W(s), lacrosse M(s)/W(s), rugby M(s)(c), soccer M(s)/W(s), softball W(s), swimming and diving M(s)/W(s), track and field M(s)/W(s), volleyball W(s), wrestling M(s). *Intramural sports:* basketball M/W, cross-country running M/W, football M, racquetball M/W, soccer M/W, softball M/W, tennis M/W, ultimate Frisbee M/W, volleyball M/W.

Standardized Tests *Required:* SAT or ACT (for admission).

Costs (2012–13) *Comprehensive fee:* $30,640 includes full-time tuition ($24,650), mandatory fees ($990), and room and board ($5000). Part-time tuition: $675 per credit hour. *Room and board:* Room and board charges vary

Just you, front and center.
West Virginia **Wesleyan**

Come check out the Wesleyan experience and see first-hand why *you* should be here. **Call the Office of Admission at 800.722.9933** for an appointment, or go to **www.wvwc.edu** for information on upcoming campus visit days.

according to board plan and housing facility. *Payment plan:* installment. *Waivers:* employees or children of employees.

Financial Aid Of all full-time matriculated undergraduates who enrolled in 2012, 766 applied for aid, 682 were judged to have need, 236 had their need fully met. 148 Federal Work-Study jobs (averaging $2200). 159 state and other part-time jobs (averaging $2200). In 2012, 184 non-need-based awards were made. *Average percent of need met:* 95%. *Average financial aid package:* $22,696. *Average need-based loan:* $4818. *Average need-based gift aid:* $6017. *Average non-need-based aid:* $12,197. *Average indebtedness upon graduation:* $30,516.

Applying *Options:* electronic application, deferred entrance. *Application fee:* $25. *Required:* high school transcript. *Required for some:* interview. *Recommended:* essay or personal statement, minimum 3.0 GPA, 2 letters of recommendation, interview. *Application deadlines:* rolling (freshmen), rolling (transfers). *Notification:* continuous (freshmen), continuous (transfers).

Freshman Application Contact Ms. Kimberly Klaus, Director of Undergraduate Enrollment, Wheeling Jesuit University, 316 Washington Avenue, Wheeling, WV 26003. *Phone:* 304-243-4376. *Toll-free phone:* 800-624-6992 Ext. 2359. *Fax:* 304-243-2397. *E-mail:* bloy@wju.edu. *Website:* http://www.wju.edu/.

WISCONSIN

Alverno College

Milwaukee, Wisconsin

- **Independent Roman Catholic** comprehensive, founded 1887
- **Urban** 46-acre campus
- **Endowment** $19.8 million
- **Undergraduate: women only; graduate: coed** 1,932 undergraduate students, 73% full-time, 100% women
- **Moderately difficult** entrance level, 65% of applicants were admitted

Undergraduates 1,412 full-time, 520 part-time. Students come from 11 states and territories; 12 other countries; 4% are from out of state; 18% Black or African American, non-Hispanic/Latino; 17% Hispanic/Latino; 5% Asian, non-Hispanic/Latino; 0.2% Native Hawaiian or other Pacific Islander, non-Hispanic/Latino; 1% American Indian or Alaska Native, non-Hispanic/Latino; 3% Two or more races, non-Hispanic/Latino; 0.5% international; 10% transferred in; 11% live on campus. *Retention:* 72% of full-time freshmen returned.

Freshmen *Admission:* 643 applied, 418 admitted, 199 enrolled. *Average high school GPA:* 2.83. *Test scores:* ACT scores over 18: 67%; ACT scores over 24: 13%; ACT scores over 30: 2%.

Faculty *Total:* 269, 44% full-time, 74% with terminal degrees. *Student/faculty ratio:* 10:1.

Academics *Calendar:* semesters. *Degrees:* associate, bachelor's, master's, post-master's, and postbachelor's certificates (also offers weekend program with significant enrollment not reflected in profile). *Special study options:* academic remediation for entering students, adult/continuing education programs, advanced placement credit, double majors, independent study, internships, part-time degree program, services for LD students, student-designed majors, study abroad, summer session for credit. *ROTC:* Army (c), Air Force (c).

Computers on Campus 624 computers/terminals are available on campus for general student use. Students can access the following: campus intranet, computer help desk, free student e-mail accounts, online (class) registration, online (class) schedules. Campuswide network is available. 100% of college-owned or -operated housing units are wired for high-speed Internet access. Wireless service is available via classrooms, computer centers, computer labs, dorm rooms, libraries.

Student Life *Housing options:* women-only. Campus housing is university owned. Freshman campus housing is guaranteed. *Activities and organizations:* drama/theater group, student-run newspaper, radio station, choral group, Student Nurses Association, Team Green, Alverno Student Wisconsin Education Association, Circle K, Gay-Straight Alliance. *Campus security:* 24-hour emergency response devices and patrols, late-night transport/escort service, controlled dormitory access, well-lit parking lots and pathways, emergency first-aid and CPR, crisis intervention team and plan in place. *Student services:* health clinic, personal/psychological counseling.

Athletics Member NCAA. All Division III. *Intercollegiate sports:* basketball W, cross-country running W, soccer W, softball W, tennis W, volleyball W.

Standardized Tests *Required:* SAT or ACT (for admission).

Costs (2012–13) *Comprehensive fee:* $29,176 includes full-time tuition ($21,576), mandatory fees ($550), and room and board ($7050). Full-time tuition and fees vary according to program. Part-time tuition: $899 per credit

hour. Part-time tuition and fees vary according to program. *Room and board:* Room and board charges vary according to board plan and housing facility. *Payment plans:* installment, deferred payment. *Waivers:* employees or children of employees.

Financial Aid Of all full-time matriculated undergraduates who enrolled in 2012, 1,338 applied for aid, 1,292 were judged to have need. 99 Federal Work-Study jobs (averaging $2310). In 2012, 81 non-need-based awards were made. *Average financial aid package:* $15,791. *Average need-based loan:* $4206. *Average need-based gift aid:* $12,014. *Average non-need-based aid:* $6168. *Average indebtedness upon graduation:* $41,405.

Applying *Options:* electronic application, deferred entrance. *Application fee:* $20. *Required:* essay or personal statement, high school transcript, 2.0 on any college work, ACT or SAT. *Recommended:* minimum 2.0 GPA, interview. *Application deadlines:* rolling (freshmen), rolling (transfers). *Notification:* continuous (freshmen), continuous (transfers).

Freshman Application Contact Ms. Kristy Moeller, Assistant Director of Undergraduate Admissions, Alverno College, 3400 South 43 Street, PO Box 343922, Milwaukee, WI 53234-3922. *Phone:* 414-382-6111. *Toll-free phone:* 800-933-3401. *Fax:* 414-382-6055. *E-mail:* admissions@alverno.edu. *Website:* http://www.alverno.edu/.

The Art Institute of Wisconsin

Milwaukee, Wisconsin

- **Proprietary** 4-year, part of Education Management Corporation
- **Coed**

Academics *Degrees:* associate and bachelor's.

Freshman Application Contact The Art Institute of Wisconsin, 320 East Buffalo Street, Suite 600, Milwaukee, WI 53202. *Phone:* 414-978-5000. *Toll-free phone:* 877-285-4234. *Website:* http://www.artinstitutes.edu/milwaukee.

See full-page ad on page 54 and page 1130 for the College Close-Up.

Bellin College

Green Bay, Wisconsin

Freshman Application Contact Dr. Penny Croghan, Admissions Director, Bellin College, 3201 Eaton Road, Green Bay, WI 54305. *Phone:* 920-433-5803. *Toll-free phone:* 800-236-8707. *Fax:* 920-433-7416. *E-mail:* admissio@bcon.edu. *Website:* http://www.bellincollege.edu/.

Beloit College

Beloit, Wisconsin

- **Independent** 4-year, founded 1846
- **Small-town** 65-acre campus with easy access to Chicago, Milwaukee
- **Endowment** $113.7 million
- **Coed**
- **Very difficult** entrance level

Faculty *Student/faculty ratio:* 12:1.

Academics *Calendar:* semesters. *Degree:* bachelor's.

Student Life *Campus security:* 24-hour emergency response devices and patrols, late-night transport/escort service, controlled dormitory access.

Athletics Member NCAA. All Division III.

Standardized Tests *Required:* SAT or ACT (for admission).

Costs (2012–13) *Comprehensive fee:* $46,336 includes full-time tuition ($38,194), mandatory fees ($280), and room and board ($7862). Part-time tuition: $4774 per course. *College room only:* $3854. Room and board charges vary according to board plan.

Financial Aid Of all full-time matriculated undergraduates who enrolled in 2011, 1,001 applied for aid, 858 were judged to have need, 427 had their need fully met. *Average percent of need met:* 93. *Average financial aid package:* $32,110.

Applying *Options:* electronic application, early admission, early action, deferred entrance. *Application fee:* $35. *Required:* essay or personal statement, high school transcript, 1 letter of recommendation. *Required for some:* interview. *Recommended:* interview.

Freshman Application Contact Mr. James S. Zielinski, Director of Admissions, Beloit College, 700 College Street, Beloit, WI 53511-5596.

Phone: 608-363-2500. *Toll-free phone:* 800-9-BELOIT. *Fax:* 608-363-2075. *E-mail:* admiss@beloit.edu.
Website: http://www.beloit.edu/.

See below for display ad and page 1154 for the College Close-Up.

Bryant & Stratton College—Milwaukee Campus

Milwaukee, Wisconsin

Freshman Application Contact Mr. Dan Basile, Director of Admissions, Bryant & Stratton College—Milwaukee Campus, 310 West Wisconsin Avenue, Suite 500 East, Milwaukee, WI 53203-2214. *Phone:* 414-276-5200. *Website:* http://www.bryantstratton.edu/.

Bryant & Stratton College—Wauwatosa Campus

Wauwatosa, Wisconsin

Freshman Application Contact Bryant & Stratton College—Wauwatosa Campus, 10950 W. Potter Road, Wauwatosa, WI 53226. *Phone:* 414-302-7000 Ext. 502.
Website: http://www.bryantstratton.edu/.

Cardinal Stritch University

Milwaukee, Wisconsin

- **Independent Roman Catholic** comprehensive, founded 1937
- **Suburban** 40-acre campus with easy access to Milwaukee
- **Endowment** $21.1 million
- **Coed** 2,799 undergraduate students, 84% full-time, 65% women, 35% men
- **Moderately difficult** entrance level, 48% of applicants were admitted

Undergraduates 2,352 full-time, 447 part-time. Students come from 21 states and territories; 2 other countries; 13% are from out of state; 24% Black or African American, non-Hispanic/Latino; 6% Hispanic/Latino; 2% Asian, non-Hispanic/Latino; 0.1% Native Hawaiian or other Pacific Islander, non-Hispanic/Latino; 0.4% American Indian or Alaska Native, non-Hispanic/Latino; 1% Two or more races, non-Hispanic/Latino; 3% Race/ethnicity unknown; 2% international; 5% transferred in; 5% live on campus.
Freshmen *Admission:* 955 applied, 455 admitted, 161 enrolled.
Faculty *Total:* 431, 24% full-time.
Academics *Calendar:* semesters. *Degrees:* certificates, associate, bachelor's, master's, doctoral, post-master's, and postbachelor's certificates. *Special study options:* academic remediation for entering students, accelerated degree program, adult/continuing education programs, advanced placement credit, cooperative education, distance learning, double majors, English as a second language, external degree program, honors programs, independent study, internships, off-campus study, part-time degree program, services for LD students, student-designed majors, summer session for credit.
Computers on Campus 549 computers/terminals and 1,251 ports are available on campus for general student use. Students can access the following: free student e-mail accounts, online (class) grades, online (class) registration, online (class) schedules. Campuswide network is available. Wireless service is available via entire campus.
Student Life *Housing options:* coed. Campus housing is university owned and leased by the school. *Activities and organizations:* drama/theater group, student-run newspaper, radio station, choral group, Residence Hall Association, Student Government Association, Student Activities Board. *Campus security:* 24-hour emergency response devices and patrols, late-night transport/escort service. *Student services:* health clinic, personal/psychological counseling.

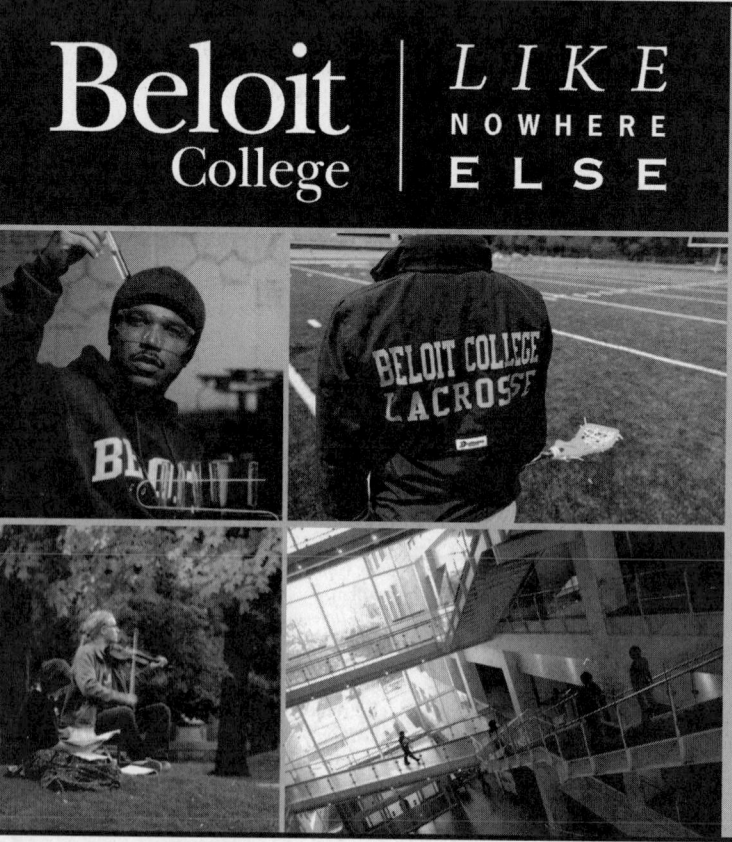

Athletics Member NAIA. *Intercollegiate sports:* baseball M, basketball M/W, cross-country running M/W, soccer M/W, softball W, volleyball M/W. *Intramural sports:* basketball M/W, volleyball M/W.

Standardized Tests *Required:* SAT or ACT (for admission).

Costs (2012–13) *Comprehensive fee:* $31,360 includes full-time tuition ($23,680), mandatory fees ($650), and room and board ($7030). Full-time tuition and fees vary according to degree level and program. Part-time tuition: $740 per credit hour. Part-time tuition and fees vary according to course load, degree level, and program. *Required fees:* $460 per year part-time. *College room only:* $1900. Room and board charges vary according to board plan. *Payment plans:* installment, deferred payment. *Waivers:* employees or children of employees.

Financial Aid Of all full-time matriculated undergraduates who enrolled in 2012, 2,184 applied for aid, 1,896 were judged to have need, 99 had their need fully met. In 2012, 119 non-need-based awards were made. *Average percent of need met:* 42%. *Average financial aid package:* $11,172. *Average need-based loan:* $3954. *Average need-based gift aid:* $8754. *Average non-need-based aid:* $10,971. *Average indebtedness upon graduation:* $27,292.

Applying *Options:* electronic application, deferred entrance. *Required:* essay or personal statement, high school transcript, minimum 2.0 GPA. *Recommended:* interview. *Application deadlines:* 8/1 (freshmen), rolling (transfers). *Notification:* continuous (freshmen).

Freshman Application Contact Ms. Sarah C. Blake, Associate Director of Admissions, Cardinal Stritch University, 6801 N. Yates Road, Milwaukee, WI 53217. *Phone:* 414-410-4052. *Toll-free phone:* 800-347-8822 Ext. 4040. *Fax:* 414-410-4058. *E-mail:* admityou@stritch.edu.

Website: http://www.stritch.edu/.

Carroll University

Waukesha, Wisconsin

Freshman Application Contact Mr. James Wiseman, Vice President of Enrollment, Carroll University, 100 North East Avenue, Waukesha, WI 53186-5593. *Phone:* 262-524-7221. *Toll-free phone:* 800-CARROLL. *Fax:* 262-524-7139. *E-mail:* info@carrollu.edu.

Website: http://www.carrollu.edu/.

Carthage College

Kenosha, Wisconsin

Freshman Application Contact Carthage College, 2001 Alford Park Drive, Kenosha, WI 53140. *Phone:* 262-551-6000. *Toll-free phone:* 800-351-4058.

Website: http://www.carthage.edu/.

Columbia College of Nursing

Milwaukee, Wisconsin

Freshman Application Contact Columbia College of Nursing, 4425 N. Port Washington Road, Milwaukee, WI 53212. *Phone:* 414-326-2336.

Website: http://www.ccon.edu/.

Concordia University Wisconsin

Mequon, Wisconsin

- **Independent** comprehensive, founded 1881, affiliated with Lutheran Church–Missouri Synod, part of Concordia University System
- **Suburban** 192-acre campus with easy access to Milwaukee
- **Coed** 4,419 undergraduate students, 65% full-time, 65% women, 35% men
- **Moderately difficult** entrance level, 70% of applicants were admitted

Undergraduates 2,876 full-time, 1,543 part-time. 20% are from out of state; 18% Black or African American, non-Hispanic/Latino; 2% Hispanic/Latino; 2% Asian, non-Hispanic/Latino; 0.1% Native Hawaiian or other Pacific Islander, non-Hispanic/Latino; 1% American Indian or Alaska Native, non-Hispanic/Latino; 2% Two or more races, non-Hispanic/Latino; 7% Race/ethnicity unknown; 1% international; 4% transferred in; 41% live on campus. *Retention:* 74% of full-time freshmen returned.

Freshmen *Admission:* 2,517 applied, 1,767 admitted, 610 enrolled. *Average high school GPA:* 3.34. *Test scores:* ACT scores over 18: 95%; ACT scores over 24: 41%; ACT scores over 30: 6%.

Faculty *Total:* 382, 42% full-time, 40% with terminal degrees. *Student/faculty ratio:* 14:1.

Academics *Calendar:* 4-1-4. *Degrees:* certificates, associate, bachelor's, master's, doctoral, and post-master's certificates. *Special study options:* academic remediation for entering students, accelerated degree program, adult/continuing education programs, advanced placement credit, distance learning, double majors, English as a second language, independent study, internships, off-campus study, part-time degree program, services for LD students, student-designed majors, study abroad, summer session for credit.

Computers on Campus 225 computers/terminals are available on campus for general student use. Students can access the following: computer help desk, free student e-mail accounts. Campuswide network is available.

Student Life *Housing options:* men-only, women-only. Campus housing is university owned. Freshman applicants given priority for college housing. *Activities and organizations:* drama/theater group, student-run newspaper, radio station, choral group. *Campus security:* 24-hour patrols, student patrols, late-night transport/escort service, controlled dormitory access. *Student services:* health clinic, personal/psychological counseling.

Athletics Member NCAA. All Division III. *Intercollegiate sports:* baseball M, basketball M/W, cross-country running M/W, football M, golf M/W, ice hockey M/W, soccer M/W, softball W, tennis M/W, track and field M/W, volleyball W, wrestling M. *Intramural sports:* basketball M/W, softball M/W, volleyball M/W.

Standardized Tests *Required:* ACT (for admission).

Costs (2012–13) *Comprehensive fee:* $33,020 includes full-time tuition ($23,970) and room and board ($9050). Full-time tuition and fees vary according to program. Part-time tuition and fees vary according to program. *Room and board:* Room and board charges vary according to board plan.

Financial Aid Of all full-time matriculated undergraduates who enrolled in 2012, 2,486 applied for aid, 2,257 were judged to have need, 467 had their need fully met. 261 Federal Work-Study jobs (averaging $1703). In 2012, 305 non-need-based awards were made. *Average percent of need met:* 68%. *Average financial aid package:* $17,777. *Average need-based loan:* $6031. *Average need-based gift aid:* $11,787. *Average non-need-based aid:* $9561. *Average indebtedness upon graduation:* $31,897.

Applying *Application fee:* $35. *Required:* high school transcript, minimum 2.0 GPA. *Required for some:* essay or personal statement, minimum 3.0 GPA, 3 letters of recommendation. *Recommended:* interview. *Application deadlines:* 8/15 (freshmen), rolling (transfers). *Notification:* continuous (freshmen), continuous (transfers).

Freshman Application Contact Ms. Julie Schroeder, Concordia University Wisconsin, Admissions Office, 12800 North Lake Drive, Mequon, WI 53097. *Phone:* 262-243-4305 Ext. 4305. *Toll-free phone:* 888-628-9472. *E-mail:* admission@cuw.edu.

Website: http://www.cuw.edu/.

DeVry University

Milwaukee, Wisconsin

Freshman Application Contact DeVry University, 411 East Wisconsin Avenue, Suite 300, Milwaukee, WI 53202. *Toll-free phone:* 866-338-7941. *Website:* http://www.devry.edu/.

DeVry University

Waukesha, Wisconsin

Admissions Office Contact DeVry University, N14 W23833 Stone Ridge Drive, Suite 450, Waukesha, WI 53188-1157. *Toll-free phone:* 866-338-7941. *Website:* http://www.devry.edu/.

Edgewood College

Madison, Wisconsin

- **Independent Roman Catholic** comprehensive, founded 1927
- **Urban** 55-acre campus
- **Endowment** $17.5 million
- **Coed, primarily women** 2,028 undergraduate students, 82% full-time, 70% women, 30% men
- **Moderately difficult** entrance level, 73% of applicants were admitted

Undergraduates 1,671 full-time, 357 part-time. Students come from 17 states and territories; 38 other countries; 6% are from out of state; 3% Black or African American, non-Hispanic/Latino; 5% Hispanic/Latino; 2% Asian, non-Hispanic/Latino; 0.1% Native Hawaiian or other Pacific Islander, non-Hispanic/Latino; 0.3% American Indian or Alaska Native, non-Hispanic/Latino; 3% Two or more races, non-Hispanic/Latino; 1% Race/ethnicity unknown; 3% international; 10% transferred in; 27% live on campus. *Retention:* 79% of full-time freshmen returned.

Freshmen *Admission:* 1,382 applied, 1,012 admitted, 342 enrolled. *Average high school GPA:* 3.39. *Test scores:* SAT critical reading scores over 500: 88%; ACT scores over 18: 95%; SAT critical reading scores over 600: 25%; ACT scores over 24: 39%; SAT critical reading scores over 700: 13%; ACT scores over 30: 3%.

Faculty *Total:* 319, 48% full-time, 54% with terminal degrees. *Student/faculty ratio:* 11:1.

Academics *Calendar:* semesters. *Degrees:* bachelor's, master's, and doctoral. *Special study options:* academic remediation for entering students, accelerated degree program, adult/continuing education programs, advanced placement credit, cooperative education, distance learning, double majors, honors programs, independent study, internships, off-campus study, part-time degree program, services for LD students, student-designed majors, study abroad, summer session for credit. *ROTC:* Army (c), Navy (c), Air Force (c). *Unusual degree programs:* 3-2 business administration with Accountancy.

Computers on Campus 100 computers/terminals and 200 ports are available on campus for general student use. Students can access the following: campus intranet, computer help desk, free student e-mail accounts, online (class) grades, online (class) registration, online (class) schedules, Online library. Campuswide network is available. 100% of college-owned or -operated housing units are wired for high-speed Internet access. Wireless service is available via entire campus.

Student Life *Housing:* on-campus residence required through sophomore year. *Options:* coed, women-only, disabled students. Campus housing is university owned. Freshman campus housing is guaranteed. *Activities and organizations:* drama/theater group, student-run newspaper, choral group, Circle K, Student Education Association, Student Government Association, Rotaract, Ambassadors. *Campus security:* 24-hour emergency response devices and patrols, student patrols, late-night transport/escort service, controlled dormitory access, Lighted pathways/sidewalks. *Student services:* health clinic, personal/psychological counseling.

Athletics Member NCAA. All Division III. *Intercollegiate sports:* baseball M, basketball M/W, cross-country running M/W, golf M/W, soccer M/W, softball W, tennis M/W, track and field M/W, volleyball W. *Intramural sports:* basketball M/W, soccer M/W, swimming and diving M/W, volleyball M/W.

Standardized Tests *Required:* SAT or ACT (for admission).

Costs (2012–13) *Comprehensive fee:* $32,216 includes full-time tuition ($23,740) and room and board ($8476). Full-time tuition and fees vary according to degree level. Part-time tuition: $747 per credit. Part-time tuition and fees vary according to course load and degree level. *Room and board:* Room and board charges vary according to housing facility. *Payment plan:* installment. *Waivers:* employees or children of employees.

Financial Aid Of all full-time matriculated undergraduates who enrolled in 2011, 1,454 applied for aid, 1,331 were judged to have need, 120 had their need fully met. 433 Federal Work-Study jobs (averaging $2027). 737 state and other part-time jobs (averaging $1961). In 2011, 235 non-need-based awards were made. *Average percent of need met:* 71%. *Average financial aid package:* $17,858. *Average need-based loan:* $5328. *Average need-based gift aid:* $12,225. *Average non-need-based aid:* $4790. *Average indebtedness upon graduation:* $23,464.

Applying *Options:* electronic application, deferred entrance. *Application fee:* $25. *Required:* high school transcript, minimum 2.5 GPA, Students must meet two of the following three requirements. Students must present a cumulative high school GPA of 2.5 on a 4.0 scale, a rank in the top 50% of their high school graduating class and/or a composite score of 18 on the ACT or an equivalent SAT score. *Required for some:* essay or personal statement, 2 letters of recommendation, interview. *Application deadlines:* 8/14 (freshmen), 8/14 (transfers). *Notification:* continuous (freshmen), continuous (transfers).

Freshman Application Contact Ms. Christine Benedict, Director of Undergraduate Admissions, Edgewood College, 1000 Edgewood College Drive, Madison, WI 53711-1997. *Phone:* 608-663-2294. *Toll-free phone:* 800-444-4861 Ext. 2294. *Fax:* 608-663-2214. *E-mail:* admissions@edgewood.edu. *Website:* http://www.edgewood.edu/.

Globe University–Appleton

Grand Chute, Wisconsin

- **Proprietary** 4-year, part of Globe Education Network (GEN) which is composed of Globe University, Minnesota School of Business, Broadview University, The Institute of Production and Recording and Minnesota School of Cosmetology
- **Small-town** 4-acre campus
- **Coed**

Faculty *Student/faculty ratio:* 9:1.

Academics *Degrees:* diplomas, associate, and bachelor's.

Student Life *Campus security:* 24-hour emergency response devices, late-night transport/escort service.

Standardized Tests *Required:* ACCUPLACER is required of all applicants unless documentation of a minimum ACT composite score of 21 or documentation of a minimum composite score of 1485 on the SAT is presented (for admission).

Costs (2012–13) *Tuition:* $15,300 full-time, $460 per credit part-time. Full-time tuition and fees vary according to course load, degree level, location, and program. Part-time tuition and fees vary according to course load, degree level, location, and program. *Required fees:* $1548 full-time, $43 per credit part-time.

Applying *Options:* electronic application. *Application fee:* $50. *Required:* high school transcript, interview, High school transcript or GED required of all applicants. *Required for some:* essay or personal statement, 2 letters of recommendation.

Freshman Application Contact Globe University–Appleton, 5045 West Grande Market Drive, Grand Chute, WI 54913. *Phone:* 920-364-1100. *Website:* http://www.globeuniversity.edu/.

Globe University–Eau Claire

Eau Claire, Wisconsin

- **Proprietary** 4-year, part of Globe Education Network (GEN) which is composed of Globe University, Minnesota School of Business, Broadview University, The Institute of Production and Recording and Minnesota School of Cosmetology
- **Small-town** 5-acre campus with easy access to Minneapolis-St. Paul
- **Coed**

Faculty *Student/faculty ratio:* 19:1.

Academics *Degrees:* diplomas, associate, and bachelor's.

Student Life *Campus security:* 24-hour emergency response devices, late-night transport/escort service.

Standardized Tests *Required:* ACCUPLACER is required of all applicants unless documentation of a minimum ACT composite score of 21 or documentation of a minimum composite score of 1485 on the SAT is presented (for admission).

Costs (2012–13) *Tuition:* $15,300 full-time, $460 per credit part-time. Full-time tuition and fees vary according to course load, degree level, location, and program. Part-time tuition and fees vary according to course load, degree level, location, and program. *Required fees:* $1548 full-time, $43 per credit part-time.

Applying *Options:* electronic application. *Application fee:* $50. *Required:* high school transcript, interview. *Required for some:* essay or personal statement, 2 letters of recommendation, GED certificate in lieu of high school transcript.

Freshman Application Contact Globe University–Eau Claire, 4955 Bullis Farm Road, Eau Claire, WI 54701-5168. *Phone:* 715-855-6600. *Toll-free phone:* 877-303-6060 (in-state); 377-303-6060 (out-of-state). *Website:* http://www.globeuniversity.edu/.

Globe University–Green Bay

Bellevue, Wisconsin

- **Proprietary** 4-year, part of Globe Education Network (GEN) which is composed of Globe University, Minnesota School of Business, Broadview University, The Institute of Production and Recording and Minnesota School of Cosmetology
- **Urban** 5-acre campus
- **Coed**

Faculty *Student/faculty ratio:* 8:1.

Academics *Degrees:* diplomas, associate, and bachelor's.

Student Life *Campus security:* 24-hour emergency response devices, late-night transport/escort service.

Costs (2012–13) *Tuition:* $15,300 full-time, $460 per credit part-time. Full-time tuition and fees vary according to course load, degree level, location, and program. Part-time tuition and fees vary according to course load, degree level, location, and program. *Required fees:* $1548 full-time.

Applying *Options:* electronic application. *Application fee:* $50. *Required:* high school transcript, interview. *Required for some:* essay or personal statement, 2 letters of recommendation, GED certificate in lieu of high school transcript.
Freshman Application Contact Globe University–Green Bay, 2620 Development Drive, Bellevue, WI 54311. *Phone:* 920-264-1600.
Website: http://www.globeuniversity.edu/.

Globe University–La Crosse

Onalaska, Wisconsin

- **Proprietary** 4-year, part of Globe Education Network (GEN) which is composed of Globe University, Minnesota School of Business, Broadview University, The Institute of Production and Recording and Minnesota School of Cosmetology
- **Small-town** campus
- **Coed**

Faculty *Student/faculty ratio:* 9:1.
Academics *Degrees:* diplomas, associate, and bachelor's.
Student Life *Campus security:* 24-hour emergency response devices, late-night transport/escort service.
Standardized Tests *Required:* ACCUPLACER is required of all applicants unless documentation of a minimum ACT composite score of 21 or documentation of a minimum composite score of 1485 on the SAT is presented (for admission).
Costs (2012–13) *Tuition:* $15,300 full-time, $460 per credit part-time. Full-time tuition and fees vary according to course load, degree level, location, and program. Part-time tuition and fees vary according to course load, degree level, location, and program. *Required fees:* $1548 full-time, $43 per credit part-time.
Applying *Options:* electronic application. *Application fee:* $50. *Required:* high school transcript, interview. *Required for some:* essay or personal statement, 2 letters of recommendation, GED certificate in lieu of high school transcript.
Freshman Application Contact Globe University–La Crosse, 2651 Midwest Drive, Onalaska, WI 54650. *Phone:* 608-779-2600.
Website: http://www.globeuniversity.edu/.

Globe University–Madison East

Madison, Wisconsin

- **Proprietary** 4-year, part of Globe Education Network (GEN) which is composed of Globe University, Minnesota School of Business, Broadview University, The Institute of Production and Recording and Minnesota School of Cosmetology
- **Urban** 7-acre campus
- **Coed**

Faculty *Student/faculty ratio:* 10:1.
Academics *Degrees:* diplomas, associate, and bachelor's.
Student Life *Campus security:* 24-hour emergency response devices, late-night transport/escort service.
Standardized Tests *Required:* ACCUPLACER is required of all applicants unless documentation of a minimum ACT composite score of 21 or documentation of a minimum composite score of 1485 on the SAT is presented (for admission).
Costs (2012–13) *Tuition:* $15,300 full-time, $460 per credit part-time. Full-time tuition and fees vary according to course load, degree level, location, and program. Part-time tuition and fees vary according to course load, degree level, location, and program. *Required fees:* $1548 full-time, $43 per credit part-time.
Applying *Options:* electronic application. *Application fee:* $50. *Required:* high school transcript, interview, High school transcript or GED required of all applicants. *Required for some:* essay or personal statement, 2 letters of recommendation.
Freshman Application Contact Globe University–Madison East, 4901 Eastpark Boulevard, Madison, WI 53718. *Phone:* 608-216-9400.
Website: http://www.globeuniversity.edu/.

Globe University–Madison West

Middleton, Wisconsin

- **Proprietary** 4-year, part of Globe Education Network (GEN) which is composed of Globe University, Minnesota School of Business, Broadview University, The Institute of Production and Recording and Minnesota School of Cosmetology
- **Small-town** campus
- **Coed**

Faculty *Student/faculty ratio:* 12:1.
Academics *Degrees:* diplomas, associate, and bachelor's.
Student Life *Campus security:* 24-hour emergency response devices, late-night transport/escort service.
Standardized Tests *Required:* ACCUPLACER is required of all applicants unless documentation of a minimum ACT composite score of 21 or documentation of a minimum composite score of 1485 on the SAT is presented (for admission).
Costs (2012–13) *Tuition:* $15,300 full-time, $460 per credit part-time. Full-time tuition and fees vary according to course load, degree level, location, and program. Part-time tuition and fees vary according to course load, degree level, location, and program. *Required fees:* $1548 full-time.
Applying *Options:* electronic application. *Application fee:* $50. *Required:* high school transcript, interview. *Required for some:* essay or personal statement, 2 letters of recommendation, GED certificate in lieu of high school transcript.
Freshman Application Contact Globe University–Madison West, 1345 Deming Way, Middleton, WI 53562. *Phone:* 608-830-6900.
Website: http://www.globeuniversity.edu/.

Globe University–Wausau

Rothschild, Wisconsin

- **Proprietary** 4-year, part of Globe Education Network (GEN) which is composed of Globe University, Minnesota School of Business, Broadview University, The Institute of Production and Recording and Minnesota School of Cosmetology
- **Small-town** 5-acre campus
- **Coed**

Faculty *Student/faculty ratio:* 11:1.
Academics *Degrees:* diplomas, associate, and bachelor's.
Student Life *Campus security:* 24-hour emergency response devices, late-night transport/escort service.
Standardized Tests *Required:* ACCUPLACER is required of all applicants unless documentation of a minimum ACT composite score of 21 or documentation of a minimum composite score of 1485 on the SAT is presented (for admission).
Costs (2012–13) *Tuition:* $15,300 full-time, $460 per credit part-time. Full-time tuition and fees vary according to course load, degree level, location, and program. Part-time tuition and fees vary according to course load, degree level, location, and program. *Required fees:* $1548 full-time, $43 per credit part-time.
Applying *Options:* electronic application. *Application fee:* $50. *Required:* high school transcript, interview, High school transcript or GED required of all applicants. *Required for some:* essay or personal statement, 2 letters of recommendation.
Freshman Application Contact Globe University–Wausau, 1480 Country Road XX, Rothschild, WI 54474. *Phone:* 715-301-1300.
Website: http://www.globeuniversity.edu/.

Herzing University

Brookfield, Wisconsin

Admissions Office Contact Herzing University, 555 South Executive Drive, Brookfield, WI 53005. *Toll-free phone:* 800-596-0724.
Website: http://www.herzing.edu/brookfield.

Herzing University

Kenosha, Wisconsin

Admissions Office Contact Herzing University, 4006 Washington Road, Kenosha, WI 53144. *Toll-free phone:* 800-596-0724. *Website:* http://www.herzing.edu/kenosha.

Herzing University

Madison, Wisconsin

- **Proprietary** comprehensive, founded 1948, part of Herzing Institutes, Inc.
- **Suburban** campus with easy access to Madison, Milwaukee
- **Coed**

Academics *Calendar:* semesters. *Degrees:* certificates, diplomas, associate, bachelor's, and master's.
Student Life *Campus security:* 24-hour emergency response devices.
Costs (2012–13) *Tuition:* $11,400 full-time, $5760 per year part-time. Full-time tuition and fees vary according to course load, location, and program. Part-time tuition and fees vary according to course load, location, and program.
Financial Aid *Financial aid deadline:* 6/30.
Applying *Required:* high school transcript, interview.
Freshman Application Contact Mr. Tom Beatty, Associate Director of Admissions, Herzing University, 5218 East Terrace Drive, Madison, WI 53718. *Phone:* 608-395-3441. *Toll-free phone:* 800-596-0724. *Fax:* 608-249-8593. *E-mail:* info@msn.herzing.edu.
Website: http://www.herzing.edu/madison/.

Herzing University Online

Milwaukee, Wisconsin

Admissions Office Contact Herzing University Online, 525 North 6th Street, Milwaukee, WI 53203. *Toll-free phone:* 866-508-0748. *Website:* http://www.herzingonline.edu/.

ITT Technical Institute

Germantown, Wisconsin

- **Proprietary** 4-year
- **Coed**
- **Minimally difficult** entrance level

Academics *Degrees:* associate and bachelor's.
Freshman Application Contact Director of Recruiting, ITT Technical Institute, W177 N9886 Rivercrest Drive, Suite 200, Germantown, WI 53022. *Phone:* 262-257-7100. *Toll-free phone:* 877-213-8538. *Website:* http://www.itt-tech.edu/.

ITT Technical Institute

Green Bay, Wisconsin

- **Proprietary** primarily 2-year, founded 2000, part of ITT Educational Services, Inc.
- **Coed**
- **Minimally difficult** entrance level

Academics *Calendar:* quarters. *Degrees:* associate and bachelor's.
Freshman Application Contact Director of Recruitment, ITT Technical Institute, 470 Security Boulevard, Green Bay, WI 54313. *Phone:* 920-662-9000. *Toll-free phone:* 888-884-3626. *Fax:* 920-662-9384.
Website: http://www.itt-tech.edu/.

ITT Technical Institute

Greenfield, Wisconsin

- **Proprietary** primarily 2-year, founded 1968, part of ITT Educational Services, Inc.
- **Suburban** campus
- **Coed**
- **Minimally difficult** entrance level

Academics *Calendar:* quarters. *Degrees:* associate and bachelor's.
Freshman Application Contact Director of Recruitment, ITT Technical Institute, 6300 West Layton Avenue, Greenfield, WI 53220-4612. *Phone:* 414-282-9494.
Website: http://www.itt-tech.edu/.

ITT Technical Institute

Madison, Wisconsin

- **Proprietary** primarily 2-year, part of ITT Educational Services, Inc.
- **Coed**
- **Minimally difficult** entrance level

Academics *Degrees:* associate and bachelor's.
Freshman Application Contact Director of Recruitment, ITT Technical Institute, 2450 Rimrock Road, Suite 100, Madison, WI 53713. *Phone:* 608-288-6301. *Toll-free phone:* 877-628-5960.
Website: http://www.itt-tech.edu/.

Lakeland College

Sheboygan, Wisconsin

- **Independent** comprehensive, founded 1862, affiliated with United Church of Christ
- **Rural** 240-acre campus with easy access to Milwaukee
- **Endowment** $12.1 million
- **Coed** 2,964 undergraduate students, 34% full-time, 56% women, 44% men
- **Minimally difficult** entrance level, 77% of applicants were admitted

Undergraduates 995 full-time, 1,969 part-time. Students come from 30 states and territories; 16 other countries; 17% are from out of state; 6% Black or African American, non-Hispanic/Latino; 5% Hispanic/Latino; 2% Asian, non-Hispanic/Latino; 0.1% Native Hawaiian or other Pacific Islander, non-Hispanic/Latino; 1% American Indian or Alaska Native, non-Hispanic/Latino; 0.9% Two or more races, non-Hispanic/Latino; 0.5% Race/ethnicity unknown; 3% international; 6% transferred in; 67% live on campus. *Retention:* 81% of full-time freshmen returned.
Freshmen *Admission:* 687 applied, 528 admitted, 216 enrolled. *Average high school GPA:* 3. *Test scores:* ACT scores over 18: 86%; ACT scores over 24: 23%; ACT scores over 30: 3%.
Faculty *Total:* 71, 80% full-time, 69% with terminal degrees. *Student/faculty ratio:* 15:1.
Academics *Calendar:* 4-4-1. *Degrees:* bachelor's and master's. *Special study options:* academic remediation for entering students, adult/continuing education programs, advanced placement credit, distance learning, double majors, English as a second language, honors programs, independent study, internships, off-campus study, part-time degree program, services for LD students, study abroad, summer session for credit. *Unusual degree programs:* 3-2 engineering with University of Wisconsin–Madison.
Computers on Campus 157 computers/terminals are available on campus for general student use. Students can access the following: campus intranet, computer help desk, free student e-mail accounts, online (class) grades, online (class) registration, online (class) schedules. Campuswide network is available. 100% of college-owned or -operated housing units are wired for high-speed Internet access. Wireless service is available via entire campus.
Student Life *Housing:* on-campus residence required through senior year. *Options:* coed, men-only, women-only. Campus housing is university owned. Freshman campus housing is guaranteed. *Activities and organizations:* drama/theater group, student-run newspaper, choral group, Lakeland College Campus Activities Board, Student Association, Black Student Union, Mortar Board, Global Students Association. *Campus security:* 24-hour emergency response devices, student patrols, late-night transport/escort service, controlled dormitory access. *Student services:* health clinic, personal/psychological counseling.

Athletics Member NCAA. All Division III. *Intercollegiate sports:* baseball M, basketball M/W, cross-country running M/W, football M, golf M/W, soccer M/W, softball W, tennis M/W, track and field M/W, volleyball M/W, wrestling M.
Standardized Tests *Required:* SAT or ACT (for admission).
Costs (2012–13) *Comprehensive fee:* $28,582 includes full-time tuition ($21,242) and room and board ($7340). Full-time tuition and fees vary according to degree level. Part-time tuition and fees vary according to class time, course load, degree level, and location. No tuition increase for student's term of enrollment. *Room and board:* Room and board charges vary according to board plan and housing facility. *Payment plans:* tuition prepayment, installment, deferred payment. *Waivers:* senior citizens and employees or children of employees.
Financial Aid Of all full-time matriculated undergraduates who enrolled in 2009, 1,372 applied for aid, 1,232 were judged to have need, 114 had their need fully met. 262 Federal Work-Study jobs (averaging $2500). 150 state and other part-time jobs (averaging $2500). In 2009, 189 non-need-based awards were made. *Average percent of need met:* 65%. *Average financial aid package:* $11,992. *Average need-based loan:* $4441. *Average need-based gift aid:* $8840. *Average non-need-based aid:* $8075. *Financial aid deadline:* 7/1.
Applying *Options:* electronic application, deferred entrance. *Required:* essay or personal statement, high school transcript, minimum 2.0 GPA. *Required for some:* interview. *Application deadlines:* rolling (freshmen), rolling (transfers). *Notification:* continuous until 9/1 (freshmen), continuous (transfers).
Freshman Application Contact Mr. Nick Spaeth, Director of Admissions, Lakeland College, PO Box 359, Nash Visitors Center, Sheboygan, WI 53082-0359. *Phone:* 920-565-1007. *Toll-free phone:* 800-569-2166. *Fax:* 920-565-1215. *E-mail:* admissions@lakeland.edu.
Website: http://www.lakeland.edu/.

Lawrence University

Appleton, Wisconsin

- **Independent** 4-year, founded 1847
- **Small-town** 84-acre campus
- **Coed** 1,525 undergraduate students, 97% full-time, 54% women, 46% men
- **Very difficult** entrance level, 76% of applicants were admitted

Undergraduates 1,473 full-time, 52 part-time. 63% are from out of state; 3% Black or African American, non-Hispanic/Latino; 4% Hispanic/Latino; 3% Asian, non-Hispanic/Latino; 0.1% Native Hawaiian or other Pacific Islander, non-Hispanic/Latino; 0.7% American Indian or Alaska Native, non-Hispanic/Latino; 3% Two or more races, non-Hispanic/Latino; 1% Race/ethnicity unknown; 9% international; 2% transferred in; 98% live on campus. *Retention:* 90% of full-time freshmen returned.
Freshmen *Admission:* 2,599 applied, 1,980 admitted, 412 enrolled. *Average high school GPA:* 3.63. *Test scores:* SAT critical reading scores over 500: 93%; SAT math scores over 500: 93%; SAT writing scores over 500: 95%; ACT scores over 18: 99%; SAT critical reading scores over 600: 69%; SAT math scores over 600: 72%; SAT writing scores over 600: 70%; ACT scores over 24: 81%; SAT critical reading scores over 700: 29%; SAT math scores over 700: 29%; SAT writing scores over 700: 23%; ACT scores over 30: 36%.
Faculty *Total:* 196, 82% full-time, 84% with terminal degrees. *Student/faculty ratio:* 9:1.
Academics *Calendar:* trimesters. *Degree:* bachelor's. *Special study options:* advanced placement credit, double majors, independent study, internships, off-campus study, part-time degree program, services for LD students, student-designed majors, study abroad. *Unusual degree programs:* 3-2 engineering with Columbia University in New York, New York, Rensselaer Polytechnic Institute in Troy, New York, Washington University in St. Louis, Missouri; forestry with Duke University; occupational therapy with Washington University in St. Louis.
Computers on Campus Students can access the following: campus intranet, computer help desk, free student e-mail accounts, online (class) grades, online (class) registration, online (class) schedules, online transcripts, financial aid, financial account information. Campuswide network is available. 100% of college-owned or -operated housing units are wired for high-speed Internet access. Wireless service is available via classrooms, computer centers, computer labs, dorm rooms, learning centers, libraries, student centers.
Student Life *Housing:* on-campus residence required through senior year. *Options:* coed, men-only, women-only, cooperative, disabled students. Campus housing is university owned. Freshman campus housing is guaranteed. *Activities and organizations:* drama/theater group, student-run newspaper, radio station, choral group, Lawrence Swing Dancers, Lawrence International, Outdoor Recreation Club, Sustainable Lawrence University Gardens (SLUG), Greenfire, national fraternities, national sororities. *Campus security:* 24-hour emergency response devices and patrols, student patrols, late-night transport/

escort service, controlled dormitory access, evening patrols by trained security personnel. *Student services:* health clinic, personal/psychological counseling.
Athletics Member NCAA. All Division III. *Intercollegiate sports:* baseball M, basketball M/W, crew M(c)/W(c), cross-country running M/W, fencing M/W, football M, golf M, ice hockey M/W(c), soccer M/W, softball W, swimming and diving M/W, tennis M/W, track and field M/W, ultimate Frisbee M(c)/W(c), volleyball M(c)/W. *Intramural sports:* badminton M/W, basketball M/W, fencing M/W, racquetball M/W, skiing (downhill) M/W, soccer M/W, softball M/W, table tennis M/W, tennis M/W, volleyball M/W, water polo M/W.
Costs (2012–13) *Comprehensive fee:* $48,270 includes full-time tuition ($39,732), mandatory fees ($291), and room and board ($8247). *College room only:* $3858. Room and board charges vary according to board plan. *Payment plans:* tuition prepayment, installment. *Waivers:* employees or children of employees.
Financial Aid Of all full-time matriculated undergraduates who enrolled in 2012, 1,060 applied for aid, 910 were judged to have need, 303 had their need fully met. 639 Federal Work-Study jobs (averaging $2347). 255 state and other part-time jobs (averaging $2134). In 2012, 459 non-need-based awards were made. *Average percent of need met:* 88%. *Average financial aid package:* $31,400. *Average need-based loan:* $5476. *Average need-based gift aid:* $24,461. *Average non-need-based aid:* $13,829. *Average indebtedness upon graduation:* $30,724.
Applying *Options:* electronic application, early admission, early decision, early action, deferred entrance. *Application fee:* $40. *Required:* essay or personal statement, high school transcript, 1 letter of recommendation, audition for music program. *Recommended:* minimum 3.0 GPA, interview. *Application deadlines:* 1/15 (freshmen), 4/1 (transfers), 12/1 (early action). *Early decision deadline:* 11/15. *Notification:* 4/1 (freshmen), 5/15 (transfers), 12/1 (early decision), 1/30 (early action).
Freshman Application Contact Mr. Ken Anselment, Dean of Admissions and Financial Aid, Lawrence University, 711 East Boldt Way SPC 29, Appleton, WI 54911-5699. *Phone:* 920-832-6500. *Toll-free phone:* 800-227-0982. *Fax:* 920-832-6782. *E-mail:* excel@lawrence.edu.
Website: http://www.lawrence.edu/.

Maranatha Baptist Bible College

Watertown, Wisconsin

- **Independent Baptist** comprehensive, founded 1968
- **Small-town** 60-acre campus with easy access to Milwaukee
- **Endowment** $206,798
- **Coed** 887 undergraduate students, 78% full-time, 54% women, 46% men
- **Noncompetitive** entrance level, 74% of applicants were admitted

Undergraduates 690 full-time, 197 part-time. Students come from 47 states and territories; 8 other countries; 82% are from out of state; 0.1% Black or African American, non-Hispanic/Latino; 0.9% Hispanic/Latino; 0.8% Asian, non-Hispanic/Latino; 0.1% American Indian or Alaska Native, non-Hispanic/Latino; 2% Two or more races, non-Hispanic/Latino; 39% Race/ethnicity unknown; 0.3% international; 4% transferred in; 71% live on campus. *Retention:* 67% of full-time freshmen returned.
Freshmen *Admission:* 398 applied, 294 admitted, 188 enrolled. *Test scores:* SAT critical reading scores over 500: 71%; SAT math scores over 500: 55%; ACT scores over 18: 90%; SAT critical reading scores over 600: 35%; SAT math scores over 600: 6%; ACT scores over 24: 34%; SAT critical reading scores over 700: 6%; ACT scores over 30: 4%.
Faculty *Total:* 76, 58% full-time, 24% with terminal degrees. *Student/faculty ratio:* 15:1.
Academics *Calendar:* semesters. *Degrees:* certificates, associate, bachelor's, and master's. *Special study options:* academic remediation for entering students, advanced placement credit, distance learning, double majors, independent study, internships, off-campus study, part-time degree program, study abroad, summer session for credit. *ROTC:* Army (b), Air Force (c).
Computers on Campus 120 computers/terminals are available on campus for general student use. Students can access the following: campus intranet, computer help desk, free student e-mail accounts, online (class) grades, online (class) registration, online (class) schedules. Campuswide network is available. 100% of college-owned or -operated housing units are wired for high-speed Internet access. Wireless service is available via entire campus.
Student Life *Housing:* on-campus residence required through senior year. *Options:* men-only, women-only. Campus housing is university owned. Freshman campus housing is guaranteed. *Activities and organizations:* drama/theater group, choral group. *Campus security:* student patrols, late-night transport/escort service, controlled dormitory access. *Student services:* health clinic, personal/psychological counseling.
Athletics Member NCAA, NCCAA. All NCAA Division III. *Intercollegiate sports:* baseball M, basketball M/W, cross-country running M/W, football M,

soccer M/W, softball W, volleyball W, wrestling M. *Intramural sports:* basketball M/W.

Standardized Tests *Required:* SAT or ACT (for admission).

Costs (2013–14) *Comprehensive fee:* $19,340 includes full-time tuition ($11,720), mandatory fees ($1140), and room and board ($6480). Full-time tuition and fees vary according to course load. Part-time tuition: $500 per credit hour. Part-time tuition and fees vary according to course load. *Required fees:* $48 per credit hour part-time. *Payment plan:* installment. *Waivers:* employees or children of employees.

Financial Aid Of all full-time matriculated undergraduates who enrolled in 2011, 692 applied for aid, 637 were judged to have need, 67 had their need fully met. In 2011, 26 non-need-based awards were made. *Average percent of need met:* 49%. *Average financial aid package:* $8896. *Average need-based loan:* $4294. *Average need-based gift aid:* $5663. *Average non-need-based aid:* $2218. *Average indebtedness upon graduation:* $19,470.

Applying *Options:* electronic application. *Application fee:* $50. *Required:* essay or personal statement, high school transcript, 4 letters of recommendation. *Application deadlines:* rolling (freshmen), rolling (transfers). *Notification:* continuous (freshmen), continuous (transfers).

Freshman Application Contact Dr. James Harrison, Director of Admissions, Maranatha Baptist Bible College, 745 West Main Street, Watertown, WI 53094. *Phone:* 920-206-2327. *Toll-free phone:* 800-622-2947. *Fax:* 920-261-9109. *E-mail:* admissions@mbbc.edu. *Website:* http://www.mbbc.edu/.

Marian University

Fond du Lac, Wisconsin

- **Independent Roman Catholic** comprehensive, founded 1936
- **Small-town** 78-acre campus with easy access to Milwaukee
- **Endowment** $7.2 million
- **Coed** 1,798 undergraduate students, 78% full-time, 71% women, 29% men
- **Moderately difficult** entrance level, 77% of applicants were admitted

Undergraduates 1,405 full-time, 393 part-time. Students come from 15 states and territories; 8 other countries; 8% are from out of state; 7% Black or African American, non-Hispanic/Latino; 5% Hispanic/Latino; 2% Asian, non-Hispanic/Latino; 0.1% Native Hawaiian or other Pacific Islander, non-Hispanic/Latino; 0.7% American Indian or Alaska Native, non-Hispanic/Latino; 0.2% Two or more races, non-Hispanic/Latino; 2% Race/ethnicity unknown; 1% international; 8% transferred in; 34% live on campus. *Retention:* 70% of full-time freshmen returned.

Freshmen *Admission:* 1,031 applied, 794 admitted, 283 enrolled. *Average high school GPA:* 3.06. *Test scores:* ACT scores over 18: 75%; ACT scores over 24: 20%; ACT scores over 30: 3%.

Faculty *Total:* 257, 37% full-time, 28% with terminal degrees. *Student/faculty ratio:* 12:1.

Academics *Calendar:* semesters. *Degrees:* certificates, bachelor's, master's, doctoral, and postbachelor's certificates. *Special study options:* academic remediation for entering students, accelerated degree program, advanced placement credit, cooperative education, distance learning, double majors, English as a second language, honors programs, independent study, internships, part-time degree program, services for LD students, student-designed majors, study abroad, summer session for credit. *ROTC:* Army (b).

Computers on Campus 500 computers/terminals are available on campus for general student use. Students can access the following: campus intranet, computer help desk, free student e-mail accounts, online (class) grades, online (class) registration, online (class) schedules. Campuswide network is available. 100% of college-owned or -operated housing units are wired for high-speed Internet access. Wireless service is available via entire campus.

Student Life *Housing:* on-campus residence required through sophomore year. *Options:* coed, disabled students. Campus housing is university owned. Freshman campus housing is guaranteed. *Activities and organizations:* student-run newspaper, choral group, Student Senate, Student Nurses Association, Student Education Association, Science and Math Association, Business Club, national fraternities, national sororities. *Campus security:* 24-hour emergency response devices and patrols, student patrols, late-night transport/escort service, controlled dormitory access. *Student services:* health clinic, personal/psychological counseling.

Athletics Member NCAA. All Division III. *Intercollegiate sports:* baseball M, basketball M/W, cross-country running M/W, golf M/W, ice hockey M/W, soccer M/W, softball W, tennis M/W, volleyball W. *Intramural sports:* badminton M/W, basketball M/W, bowling M/W, football M, skiing (downhill) M/W, softball M, tennis M/W, volleyball M/W.

Standardized Tests *Required:* SAT or ACT (for admission).

Costs (2012–13) *One-time required fee:* $100. *Comprehensive fee:* $29,580 includes full-time tuition ($23,090), mandatory fees ($350), and room and board ($6140). Full-time tuition and fees vary according to course load and program. Part-time tuition: $350 per credit hour. Part-time tuition and fees vary according to course load and program. *College room only:* $3690. Room and board charges vary according to board plan. *Payment plan:* installment. *Waivers:* senior citizens and employees or children of employees.

Financial Aid Of all full-time matriculated undergraduates who enrolled in 2011, 1,436 applied for aid, 1,315 were judged to have need, 138 had their need fully met. 173 Federal Work-Study jobs (averaging $540). 387 state and other part-time jobs (averaging $1611). In 2011, 114 non-need-based awards were made. *Average percent of need met:* 71%. *Average financial aid package:* $16,013. *Average need-based loan:* $6610. *Average need-based gift aid:* $11,754. *Average non-need-based aid:* $4990. *Average indebtedness upon graduation:* $27,000.

Applying *Options:* electronic application, deferred entrance. *Application fee:* $20. *Required:* high school transcript. *Required for some:* interview. *Recommended:* minimum 2.0 GPA, interview. *Application deadlines:* rolling (freshmen), rolling (transfers). *Notification:* 8/15 (freshmen), continuous until 8/15 (transfers).

Freshman Application Contact Shannon LaLuzerne, Senior Director of Admissions, Marian University, 45 South National Avenue, Fond du Lac, WI 54935-4699. *Phone:* 800-262-7426. *Toll-free phone:* 800-2-MARIAN. *Fax:* 920-923-8755. *E-mail:* admit@marianuniversity.edu. *Website:* http://www.marianuniversity.edu/.

Marquette University

Milwaukee, Wisconsin

- **Independent Roman Catholic (Jesuit)** university, founded 1881
- **Urban** 98-acre campus with easy access to Milwaukee
- **Endowment** $407.0 million
- **Coed** 8,293 undergraduate students, 96% full-time, 52% women, 48% men
- **Moderately difficult** entrance level, 55% of applicants were admitted

Undergraduates 7,969 full-time, 324 part-time. Students come from 51 states and territories; 48 other countries; 64% are from out of state; 5% Black or African American, non-Hispanic/Latino; 9% Hispanic/Latino; 5% Asian, non-Hispanic/Latino; 0.2% Native Hawaiian or other Pacific Islander, non-Hispanic/Latino; 0.2% American Indian or Alaska Native, non-Hispanic/Latino; 2% Two or more races, non-Hispanic/Latino; 0.5% Race/ethnicity unknown; 3% international; 2% transferred in; 54% live on campus. *Retention:* 88% of full-time freshmen returned.

Freshmen *Admission:* 22,900 applied, 12,644 admitted, 1,928 enrolled. *Test scores:* SAT critical reading scores over 500: 86%; SAT math scores over 500: 91%; SAT writing scores over 500: 85%; ACT scores over 18: 100%; SAT critical reading scores over 600: 41%; SAT math scores over 600: 55%; SAT writing scores over 600: 41%; ACT scores over 24: 83%; SAT critical reading scores over 700: 9%; SAT math scores over 700: 11%; SAT writing scores over 700: 7%; ACT scores over 30: 24%.

Faculty *Total:* 1,161, 55% full-time, 72% with terminal degrees. *Student/faculty ratio:* 15:1.

Academics *Calendar:* semesters. *Degrees:* bachelor's, master's, doctoral, post-master's, and postbachelor's certificates. *Special study options:* accelerated degree program, adult/continuing education programs, advanced placement credit, cooperative education, distance learning, double majors, English as a second language, honors programs, independent study, internships, off-campus study, part-time degree program, services for LD students, student-designed majors, study abroad, summer session for credit. *ROTC:* Army (b), Navy (b), Air Force (b). *Unusual degree programs:* 3-2 business administration; engineering with Biomedical Engineering, Civil Engineering, Electrical and Computer Engineering, Mechanical Engineering are administered through the Marquette University Graduate School; exercise science/clinical and translational rehabilitation health sciences, speech and language pathology, international affairs, and physical therapy programs are administered through the Graduate School; physical therapy is administered through the College of Health Sciences.

Computers on Campus 1,132 computers/terminals and 550 ports are available on campus for general student use. Students can access the following: campus intranet, computer help desk, free student e-mail accounts, online (class) grades, online (class) registration, online (class) schedules, AV Software, MATLAB. Campuswide network is available. 100% of college-owned or -operated housing units are wired for high-speed Internet access. Wireless service is available via classrooms, computer centers, computer labs, dorm rooms, learning centers, libraries, student centers.

Student Life *Housing:* on-campus residence required through sophomore year. *Options:* coed, men-only, women-only, disabled students. Campus housing is university owned. Freshman campus housing is guaranteed. *Activities and organizations:* drama/theater group, student-run newspaper, radio and television station, choral group, student government, club sports, community service organizations, band/jazz/orchestra, Residence Hall Association, national fraternities, national sororities. *Campus security:* 24-hour emergency response devices and patrols, student patrols, late-night transport/escort service, 24-hour desk attendants in residence halls. *Student services:* health clinic, personal/psychological counseling.

Athletics Member NCAA. All Division I. *Intercollegiate sports:* baseball M(c), basketball M(s)/W(s), cheerleading M/W, crew M(c)/W(c), cross-country running M(s)/W(s), golf M(s), ice hockey M(c), lacrosse M(s)/W(s), rugby M(c)/W(c), sailing M(c)/W(c), skiing (downhill) M(c)/W(c), soccer M(s)/W(s), softball W(c), swimming and diving M(c)/W(c), table tennis M(c)/W(c), tennis M(s)/W(s), track and field M(s)/W(s), ultimate Frisbee M(c)/W(c), volleyball M(c)/W(s), water polo M(c)/W(c). *Intramural sports:* badminton M/W, basketball M/W, equestrian sports M(c)/W(c), fencing M(c)/W(c), football M(c)/W(c), lacrosse M(c)/W(c), soccer M/W, softball M/W, tennis M/W, volleyball M/W, water polo M/W, wrestling M(c).

Standardized Tests *Required:* SAT or ACT (for admission).

Costs (2013–14) *Comprehensive fee:* $45,370 includes full-time tuition ($34,200), mandatory fees ($440), and room and board ($10,730). Full-time tuition and fees vary according to course load and program. Part-time tuition: $995 per credit. Part-time tuition and fees vary according to program. *College room only:* $6900. Room and board charges vary according to housing facility. *Payment plan:* installment. *Waivers:* senior citizens and employees or children of employees.

Financial Aid Of all full-time matriculated undergraduates who enrolled in 2012, 5,912 applied for aid, 4,811 were judged to have need, 1,124 had their need fully met. In 2012, 2832 non-need-based awards were made. *Average percent of need met:* 74%. *Average financial aid package:* $22,236. *Average need-based loan:* $5363. *Average need-based gift aid:* $15,934. *Average non-need-based aid:* $9306. *Average indebtedness upon graduation:* $34,602.

Applying *Options:* electronic application, deferred entrance. *Application fee:* $30. *Required:* essay or personal statement, high school transcript, minimum 2.5 GPA. *Recommended:* minimum 3.4 GPA. *Application deadlines:* 12/1 (freshmen), 6/1 (transfers). *Notification:* 1/31 (freshmen), continuous (transfers).

Freshman Application Contact Mr. Robert Blust, Dean of Admissions and Enrollment Planning, Marquette University, PO Box 1881, Milwaukee, WI 53201-1881. *Phone:* 414-288-7004. *Toll-free phone:* 800-222-6544. *Fax:* 414-288-3764. *E-mail:* admissions@marquette.edu.
Website: http://www.marquette.edu/.

Milwaukee Institute of Art and Design

Milwaukee, Wisconsin

Freshman Application Contact Stacey Steinberg, Director of Admissions, Milwaukee Institute of Art and Design, 273 East Erie Street, Milwaukee, WI 53202. *Phone:* 414-847-3200. *Toll-free phone:* 888-749-MIAD. *Fax:* 414-291-8077. *E-mail:* admissions@miad.edu.
Website: http://www.miad.edu/.

Milwaukee School of Engineering

Milwaukee, Wisconsin

- **Independent** comprehensive, founded 1903
- **Urban** 15-acre campus
- **Endowment** $40.6 million
- **Coed, primarily men** 2,378 undergraduate students, 92% full-time, 22% women, 78% men
- **Moderately difficult** entrance level, 57% of applicants were admitted

Undergraduates 2,193 full-time, 185 part-time. Students come from 33 states and territories; 26 other countries; 31% are from out of state; 2% Black or African American, non-Hispanic/Latino; 4% Hispanic/Latino; 3% Asian, non-Hispanic/Latino; 0.6% Native Hawaiian or other Pacific Islander, non-Hispanic/Latino; 0.5% American Indian or Alaska Native, non-Hispanic/Latino; 1% Two or more races, non-Hispanic/Latino; 5% Race/ethnicity unknown; 6% international; 8% transferred in; 37% live on campus. *Retention:* 81% of full-time freshmen returned.

Freshmen *Admission:* 2,014 applied, 1,147 admitted, 490 enrolled. *Average high school GPA:* 3.64. *Test scores:* SAT critical reading scores over 500: 83%; SAT math scores over 500: 92%; ACT scores over 18: 100%; SAT critical reading scores over 600: 30%; SAT math scores over 600: 73%; ACT scores over 24: 84%; SAT critical reading scores over 700: 11%; SAT math scores over 700: 15%; ACT scores over 30: 25%.

Faculty *Total:* 231, 57% full-time, 56% with terminal degrees. *Student/faculty ratio:* 14:1.

Academics *Calendar:* quarters. *Degrees:* bachelor's and master's. *Special study options:* academic remediation for entering students, adult/continuing education programs, advanced placement credit, double majors, English as a second language, independent study, internships, part-time degree program, services for LD students, study abroad, summer session for credit. *ROTC:* Army (c), Navy (c), Air Force (c).

Computers on Campus 125 computers/terminals and 2,000 ports are available on campus for general student use. Students can access the following: campus intranet, computer help desk, free student e-mail accounts, online (class) grades, online (class) registration, online (class) schedules. Campuswide network is available. 100% of college-owned or -operated housing units are wired for high-speed Internet access. Wireless service is available via entire campus.

Student Life *Housing:* on-campus residence required through sophomore year. *Options:* coed, disabled students. Campus housing is university owned. Freshman campus housing is guaranteed. *Activities and organizations:* drama/theater group, student-run radio station, choral group, Architectural Engineering and Construction Management Societies, Student Athletic Advisory Committee, MAGE, Student Government Association, Student Union Board, national fraternities, national sororities. *Campus security:* 24-hour emergency response devices and patrols, late-night transport/escort service, controlled dormitory access. *Student services:* health clinic, personal/psychological counseling, women's center.

Athletics Member NCAA. All Division III. *Intercollegiate sports:* baseball M, basketball M/W, cheerleading M/W, crew M/W, cross-country running M/W, golf M/W, ice hockey M, lacrosse M, soccer M/W, softball W, tennis M/W, track and field M/W, volleyball M/W, wrestling M. *Intramural sports:* badminton M(c)/W(c), basketball M/W, bowling M(c)/W(c), fencing M(c)/W(c), football M/W, rugby M(c), soccer M/W, softball M/W, swimming and diving M(c)/W(c), ultimate Frisbee M(c)/W(c), volleyball M/W, weight lifting M(c)/W(c).

Standardized Tests *Required:* SAT or ACT (for admission).

Costs (2013–14) *Comprehensive fee:* $42,741 includes full-time tuition ($32,880), mandatory fees ($1590), and room and board ($8271). Full-time tuition and fees vary according to course load. Part-time tuition: $570 per credit. Part-time tuition and fees vary according to course load. *College room only:* $5280. Room and board charges vary according to board plan and housing facility. *Payment plan:* installment. *Waivers:* employees or children of employees.

Financial Aid Of all full-time matriculated undergraduates who enrolled in 2011, 1,946 applied for aid, 1,825 were judged to have need, 244 had their need fully met. 269 Federal Work-Study jobs (averaging $1313). In 2011, 282 non-need-based awards were made. *Average percent of need met:* 68%. *Average financial aid package:* $21,818. *Average need-based loan:* $3608. *Average need-based gift aid:* $18,545. *Average non-need-based aid:* $11,256. *Average indebtedness upon graduation:* $38,038.

Applying *Options:* electronic application, deferred entrance. *Required:* high school transcript, minimum 2.5 GPA. *Required for some:* essay or personal statement, interview. *Application deadlines:* 1/1 (freshmen), 1/1 (transfers). *Notification:* continuous until 10/1 (freshmen), continuous until 10/1 (transfers).

Freshman Application Contact Dana-Marie Grennier, Director of Admissions, Milwaukee School of Engineering, 1025 North Broadway, Milwaukee, WI 53202-3109. *Phone:* 414-277-6761. *Toll-free phone:* 800-332-6763. *Fax:* 414-277-7475. *E-mail:* grennier@msoe.edu.
Website: http://www.msoe.edu/.

Mount Mary College

Milwaukee, Wisconsin

- **Independent Roman Catholic** comprehensive, founded 1913
- **Urban** 80-acre campus
- **Endowment** $10.7 million
- **Undergraduate:** women only; **graduate:** coed 1,054 undergraduate students, 69% full-time, 98% women, 2% men
- **Moderately difficult** entrance level, 49% of applicants were admitted

Undergraduates 727 full-time, 327 part-time. Students come from 6 states and territories; 18 other countries; 4% are from out of state; 24% Black or African American, non-Hispanic/Latino; 13% Hispanic/Latino; 6% Asian, non-

Hispanic/Latino; 0.4% American Indian or Alaska Native, non-Hispanic/Latino; 3% Two or more races, non-Hispanic/Latino; 0.4% Race/ethnicity unknown; 0.8% international; 8% transferred in; 16% live on campus. *Retention:* 67% of full-time freshmen returned.

Freshmen *Admission:* 420 applied, 205 admitted, 95 enrolled. *Average high school GPA:* 3.15. *Test scores:* ACT scores over 18: 69%; ACT scores over 24: 19%; ACT scores over 30: 1%.

Faculty *Total:* 206, 31% full-time, 33% with terminal degrees. *Student/faculty ratio:* 12:1.

Academics *Calendar:* semesters. *Degrees:* bachelor's, master's, doctoral, post-master's, and postbachelor's certificates. *Special study options:* academic remediation for entering students, accelerated degree program, adult/continuing education programs, advanced placement credit, distance learning, double majors, honors programs, independent study, internships, part-time degree program, services for LD students, student-designed majors, study abroad, summer session for credit. *ROTC:* Army (c), Navy (c), . *Unusual degree programs:* 3-2 Occupational Therapy, Public Health.

Computers on Campus 210 computers/terminals and 10 ports are available on campus for general student use. Students can access the following: campus intranet, computer help desk, free student e-mail accounts, online (class) grades, online (class) registration, online (class) schedules. Campuswide network is available. 100% of college-owned or -operated housing units are wired for high-speed Internet access. Wireless service is available via classrooms, computer centers, computer labs, dorm rooms, learning centers, libraries, student centers.

Student Life *Housing options:* women-only. Campus housing is university owned. *Activities and organizations:* student-run newspaper, choral group, Department-affiliated clubs, Campus Ministry, International Club, Student Government, Caroline Hall Council. *Campus security:* 24-hour patrols, late-night transport/escort service, controlled dormitory access. *Student services:* personal/psychological counseling.

Athletics Member NCAA. All Division III. *Intercollegiate sports:* basketball W, cross-country running W, soccer W, softball W, tennis W, volleyball W. *Intramural sports:* swimming and diving W.

Standardized Tests *Required:* SAT or ACT (for admission).

Costs (2013–14) *Comprehensive fee:* $32,836 includes full-time tuition ($24,598), mandatory fees ($500), and room and board ($7738). Full-time tuition and fees vary according to program. Part-time tuition: $746 per credit. Part-time tuition and fees vary according to course load and program. *Required fees:* $310 per year part-time. *Room and board:* Room and board charges vary according to board plan. *Payment plan:* installment. *Waivers:* senior citizens and employees or children of employees.

Financial Aid Of all full-time matriculated undergraduates who enrolled in 2012, 690 applied for aid, 660 were judged to have need, 49 had their need fully met. 115 Federal Work-Study jobs (averaging $1261). 72 state and other part-time jobs (averaging $1985). In 2012, 72 non-need-based awards were made. *Average percent of need met:* 68%. *Average financial aid package:* $19,595. *Average need-based loan:* $4620. *Average need-based gift aid:* $14,767. *Average non-need-based aid:* $8053. *Average indebtedness upon graduation:* $29,618.

Applying *Options:* electronic application, deferred entrance. *Required:* high school transcript. *Required for some:* essay or personal statement, 1 letter of recommendation, interview. *Recommended:* minimum 2.5 GPA. *Application deadlines:* rolling (freshmen), rolling (transfers). *Notification:* continuous (freshmen), continuous (transfers).

Freshman Application Contact Mary Ellen Strieter, Admission Counselor Assistant/Receptionist, Mount Mary College, 2900 North Menomonee River Parkway, Milwaukee, WI 53222. *Phone:* 414-258-4810 Ext. 219. *Toll-free phone:* 800-321-6265. *Fax:* 414-256-0180. *E-mail:* admiss@mtmary.edu. *Website:* http://www.mtmary.edu/.

Northland College

Ashland, Wisconsin

- **Independent** 4-year, founded 1892, affiliated with United Church of Christ
- **Small-town** 130-acre campus
- **Endowment** $18.1 million
- **Coed** 590 undergraduate students, 96% full-time, 55% women, 45% men
- **Moderately difficult** entrance level, 66% of applicants were admitted

Undergraduates 567 full-time, 23 part-time. Students come from 32 states and territories; 6 other countries; 51% are from out of state; 0.9% Black or African American, non-Hispanic/Latino; 5% Hispanic/Latino; 0.7% Asian, non-Hispanic/Latino; 0.2% Native Hawaiian or other Pacific Islander, non-Hispanic/Latino; 2% American Indian or Alaska Native, non-Hispanic/Latino;

2% Two or more races, non-Hispanic/Latino; 10% Race/ethnicity unknown; 2% international; 7% transferred in; 78% live on campus. *Retention:* 78% of full-time freshmen returned.

Freshmen *Admission:* 946 applied, 627 admitted, 183 enrolled. *Average high school GPA:* 3.3. *Test scores:* SAT critical reading scores over 500: 63%; SAT math scores over 500: 68%; SAT writing scores over 500: 63%; ACT scores over 18: 95%; SAT critical reading scores over 600: 47%; SAT math scores over 600: 26%; SAT writing scores over 600: 32%; ACT scores over 24: 51%; SAT critical reading scores over 700: 21%; SAT math scores over 700: 5%; SAT writing scores over 700: 11%; ACT scores over 30: 7%.

Faculty *Total:* 61, 79% full-time, 77% with terminal degrees. *Student/faculty ratio:* 11:1.

Academics *Calendar:* 4-4-1. *Degree:* bachelor's. *Special study options:* advanced placement credit, cooperative education, double majors, honors programs, independent study, internships, off-campus study, part-time degree program, services for LD students, student-designed majors, study abroad, summer session for credit. *Unusual degree programs:* 3-2 engineering with Michigan Technological University, Washington University in St. Louis.

Computers on Campus 125 computers/terminals are available on campus for general student use. Students can access the following: campus intranet, computer help desk, free student e-mail accounts, online (class) grades, online (class) registration, online (class) schedules. Campuswide network is available. 100% of college-owned or -operated housing units are wired for high-speed Internet access. Wireless service is available via classrooms, computer centers, computer labs, learning centers, libraries, student centers.

Student Life *Housing:* on-campus residence required through sophomore year. *Options:* coed, women-only, cooperative. Campus housing is university owned. Freshman campus housing is guaranteed. *Activities and organizations:* drama/theater group, student-run newspaper, radio station, choral group, Northland Volunteer Program, Northland College Student Association, Native American Student Association, Environmental Council, N Club. *Campus security:* 24-hour emergency response devices and patrols, late-night transport/escort service, controlled dormitory access. *Student services:* health clinic, personal/psychological counseling.

Athletics Member NCAA. All Division III. *Intercollegiate sports:* baseball M, basketball M/W, cross-country running M/W, golf M/W, ice hockey M, skiing (cross-country) M(c)/W(c), soccer M/W, softball W, volleyball W. *Intramural sports:* basketball M/W, football M/W, soccer M/W, softball M/W, table tennis M/W, ultimate Frisbee M/W, volleyball M/W.

Standardized Tests *Required:* SAT or ACT (for admission).

Costs (2013–14) *Comprehensive fee:* $37,500 includes full-time tuition ($29,000), mandatory fees ($990), and room and board ($7510). Full-time tuition and fees vary according to course load. Part-time tuition: $600 per credit hour. Part-time tuition and fees vary according to course load. *College room only:* $3220. Room and board charges vary according to board plan and housing facility. *Payment plan:* installment. *Waivers:* employees or children of employees.

Financial Aid Of all full-time matriculated undergraduates who enrolled in 2012, 537 applied for aid, 501 were judged to have need, 82 had their need fully met. 311 Federal Work-Study jobs (averaging $1734). 241 state and other part-time jobs (averaging $1709). In 2012, 55 non-need-based awards were made. *Average percent of need met:* 80%. *Average financial aid package:* $32,660. *Average need-based loan:* $4710. *Average need-based gift aid:* $19,286. *Average non-need-based aid:* $14,097. *Average indebtedness upon graduation:* $24,374.

Applying *Options:* electronic application, deferred entrance. *Required:* high school transcript. *Recommended:* minimum 2.0 GPA. *Application deadlines:* rolling (freshmen), rolling (out-of-state freshmen), rolling (transfers). *Notification:* continuous (freshmen), continuous (out-of-state freshmen), continuous (transfers).

Freshman Application Contact Whitney Menebroeker, Associate Director of Admissions, Northland College, 1411 Ellis Avenue, Ashland, WI 54806. *Phone:* 715-682-1224. *Toll-free phone:* 800-753-1840 (in-state); 800-753-1040 (out-of-state). *Fax:* 715-682-1258. *E-mail:* admit@northland.edu. *Website:* http://www.northland.edu/.

Northland International University

Dunbar, Wisconsin

Admissions Office Contact Northland International University, W10085 Pike Plains Road, Dunbar, WI 54119.
Website: http://www.ni.edu/.

Rasmussen College Appleton

Appleton, Wisconsin

- **Proprietary** 4-year, part of Rasmussen College System
- **Suburban** campus
- **Coed** 328 undergraduate students
- **Minimally difficult** entrance level

Faculty *Student/faculty ratio:* 22:1.

Academics *Degrees:* certificates, diplomas, associate, and bachelor's. *Special study options:* academic remediation for entering students, accelerated degree program, adult/continuing education programs, distance learning, double majors, internships, part-time degree program, summer session for credit.

Computers on Campus 76 computers/terminals are available on campus for general student use. Students can access the following: computer help desk, free student e-mail accounts, online (class) grades, online (class) schedules. Campuswide network is available. Wireless service is available via entire campus.

Student Life *Housing:* college housing not available.

Standardized Tests *Required:* Internal Exam (for admission).

Costs (2013–14) *Tuition:* $12,600 full-time. Full-time tuition and fees vary according to course level, course load, degree level, location, and program. Part-time tuition and fees vary according to course level, course load, degree level, location, and program. *Required fees:* $1800 full-time. *Payment plans:* installment, deferred payment. *Waivers:* employees or children of employees.

Applying *Options:* electronic application, early admission, deferred entrance. *Required:* high school transcript, minimum 2.0 GPA. *Required for some:* interview. *Application deadlines:* rolling (freshmen), rolling (transfers).

Freshman Application Contact Susan Hammerstrom, Director of Admissions, Rasmussen College Appleton, 3500 E. Destination Drive, Appleton, WI 54915. *Phone:* 920-750-5900. *Toll-free phone:* 888-549-6755. *E-mail:* susan.hammerstrom@rasmussen.edu.
Website: http://www.rasmussen.edu/.

Rasmussen College Green Bay

Green Bay, Wisconsin

- **Proprietary** primarily 2-year, part of Rasmussen College System
- **Suburban** campus
- **Coed** 582 undergraduate students
- **Minimally difficult** entrance level

Faculty *Student/faculty ratio:* 22:1.

Academics *Degrees:* certificates, diplomas, associate, and bachelor's. *Special study options:* academic remediation for entering students, accelerated degree program, adult/continuing education programs, distance learning, double majors, internships, part-time degree program, summer session for credit.

Computers on Campus 137 computers/terminals are available on campus for general student use. Students can access the following: computer help desk, free student e-mail accounts, online (class) grades, online (class) schedules. Campuswide network is available. Wireless service is available via entire campus.

Student Life *Housing:* college housing not available.

Standardized Tests *Required:* Internal Exam (for admission).

Costs (2013–14) *Tuition:* $12,600 full-time. Full-time tuition and fees vary according to course level, course load, degree level, location, and program. Part-time tuition and fees vary according to course level, course load, degree level, location, and program. *Required fees:* $1800 full-time. *Payment plans:* installment, deferred payment. *Waivers:* employees or children of employees.

Applying *Options:* electronic application, early admission, deferred entrance. *Required:* high school transcript, minimum 2.0 GPA. *Required for some:* interview. *Application deadlines:* rolling (freshmen), rolling (transfers).

Freshman Application Contact Susan Hammerstrom, Director of Admissions, Rasmussen College Green Bay, 940 South Taylor Street, Suite 100, Green Bay, WI 54303. *Phone:* 920-593-8400. *Toll-free phone:* 888-549-6755. *E-mail:* susan.hammerstrom@rasmussen.edu.
Website: http://www.rasmussen.edu/.

Rasmussen College Wausau

Wausau, Wisconsin

- **Proprietary** 4-year, part of Rasmussen College System
- **Suburban** campus
- **Coed** 580 undergraduate students
- **Minimally difficult** entrance level

Faculty *Student/faculty ratio:* 22:1.

Academics *Degrees:* certificates, diplomas, associate, and bachelor's. *Special study options:* academic remediation for entering students, accelerated degree program, adult/continuing education programs, distance learning, double majors, internships, part-time degree program, summer session for credit.

Computers on Campus 74 computers/terminals are available on campus for general student use. Students can access the following: computer help desk, free student e-mail accounts, online (class) grades, online (class) schedules. Campuswide network is available. Wireless service is available via entire campus.

Student Life *Housing:* college housing not available.

Standardized Tests *Required:* Internal Exam (for admission).

Costs (2013–14) *Tuition:* $12,600 full-time. Full-time tuition and fees vary according to course level, course load, degree level, location, and program. Part-time tuition and fees vary according to course level, course load, degree level, location, and program. *Required fees:* $1800 full-time. *Payment plans:* installment, deferred payment. *Waivers:* employees or children of employees.

Applying *Options:* electronic application, early admission, deferred entrance. *Required:* high school transcript, minimum 2.0 GPA. *Required for some:* interview. *Application deadlines:* rolling (freshmen), rolling (transfers).

Freshman Application Contact Susan Hammerstrom, Director of Admissions, Rasmussen College Wausau, 1101 Westwood Drive, Wausau, WI 54401. *Phone:* 715-841-8000. *Toll-free phone:* 888-549-6755. *E-mail:* susan.hammerstrom@rasmussen.edu.
Website: http://www.rasmussen.edu/.

Ripon College

Ripon, Wisconsin

- **Independent** 4-year, founded 1851
- **Small-town** 250-acre campus with easy access to Milwaukee
- **Endowment** $6.2 million
- **Coed** 931 undergraduate students, 99% full-time, 53% women, 47% men
- **Moderately difficult** entrance level, 78% of applicants were admitted

Undergraduates 921 full-time, 10 part-time. Students come from 31 states and territories; 12 other countries; 25% are from out of state; 2% Black or African American, non-Hispanic/Latino; 5% Hispanic/Latino; 1% Asian, non-Hispanic/Latino; 0.6% American Indian or Alaska Native, non-Hispanic/Latino; 1% Two or more races, non-Hispanic/Latino; 2% Race/ethnicity unknown; 3% international; 2% transferred in; 86% live on campus. *Retention:* 86% of full-time freshmen returned.

Freshmen *Admission:* 1,046 applied, 811 admitted, 205 enrolled. *Average high school GPA:* 3.41. *Test scores:* SAT critical reading scores over 500: 78%; SAT math scores over 500: 75%; ACT scores over 18: 98%; SAT critical reading scores over 600: 36%; SAT math scores over 600: 52%; ACT scores over 24: 56%; SAT critical reading scores over 700: 10%; SAT math scores over 700: 23%; ACT scores over 30: 14%.

Faculty *Total:* 104, 66% full-time, 81% with terminal degrees. *Student/faculty ratio:* 11:1.

Academics *Calendar:* semesters. *Degree:* bachelor's. *Special study options:* accelerated degree program, advanced placement credit, double majors, internships, off-campus study, part-time degree program, services for LD students, student-designed majors, study abroad. *ROTC:* Army (b). *Unusual degree programs:* 3-2 engineering with Rensselaer Polytechnic Institute, Washington University in St. Louis, University of Wisconsin–Madison; forestry with Duke University; nursing with Rush University; environmental studies with Duke University.

Computers on Campus 150 computers/terminals are available on campus for general student use. Students can access the following: campus intranet, computer help desk, free student e-mail accounts, online (class) grades, online (class) schedules. Campuswide network is available. 100% of college-owned or -operated housing units are wired for high-speed Internet access. Wireless service is available via classrooms, libraries, student centers.

Student Life *Housing:* on-campus residence required through senior year. *Options:* coed, men-only, women-only. Campus housing is university owned. Freshman campus housing is guaranteed. *Activities and organizations:* drama/theater group, student-run newspaper, radio station, choral group, Environmental Group, Student Senate, Community Service Coalition, SMAC (Student Media and Activities Committee), national fraternities, national sororities. *Campus security:* 24-hour emergency response devices and patrols, student patrols, late-night transport/escort service, controlled dormitory access. *Student services:* health clinic, personal/psychological counseling.

Athletics Member NCAA. All Division III. *Intercollegiate sports:* baseball M, basketball M/W, cheerleading M(c)/W, cross-country running M/W, football M, golf M/W, rugby M(c)/W(c), soccer M/W, softball W, swimming and diving M/W, tennis M/W, track and field M/W, volleyball W. *Intramural sports:* basketball M/W, bowling M/W, equestrian sports M(c)/W(c), fencing M/W, football M/W, golf M/W, racquetball M/W, soccer M/W, softball M/W, table tennis M/W, tennis M/W, ultimate Frisbee M/W, volleyball M/W.

Standardized Tests *Required:* SAT or ACT (for admission).

Costs (2013–14) *Comprehensive fee:* $40,417 includes full-time tuition ($31,327), mandatory fees ($275), and room and board ($8815). *College room only:* $4665. *Payment plan:* installment. *Waivers:* employees or children of employees.

Financial Aid Of all full-time matriculated undergraduates who enrolled in 2012, 840 applied for aid, 760 were judged to have need, 135 had their need fully met. 437 Federal Work-Study jobs (averaging $1777). 326 state and other part-time jobs (averaging $1727). In 2012, 124 non-need-based awards were made. *Average percent of need met:* 84%. *Average financial aid package:* $25,418. *Average need-based loan:* $5329. *Average need-based gift aid:* $19,763. *Average non-need-based aid:* $10,803. *Average indebtedness upon graduation:* $31,216.

Applying *Options:* electronic application, deferred entrance. *Application fee:* $30. *Required:* essay or personal statement, high school transcript, minimum 2.0 GPA, 1 letter of recommendation. *Required for some:* interview. *Recommended:* interview. *Application deadlines:* rolling (freshmen), rolling (transfers). *Notification:* continuous (freshmen), continuous (transfers).

Freshman Application Contact Office of Admission, Ripon College, 300 Seward Street, PO Box 248, Ripon, WI 54971. *Phone:* 920-748-8337. *Toll-free phone:* 800-947-4766. *Fax:* 920-748-8335. *E-mail:* adminfo@ripon.edu. *Website:* http://www.ripon.edu/.

See below for display ad and page 1454 for the College Close-Up.

St. Norbert College
De Pere, Wisconsin

- **Independent Roman Catholic** comprehensive, founded 1898
- **Suburban** 93-acre campus
- **Endowment** $73.0 million
- **Coed** 2,229 undergraduate students, 97% full-time, 58% women, 42% men
- **Moderately difficult** entrance level, 80% of applicants were admitted

Undergraduates 2,171 full-time; 58 part-time. Students come from 34 states and territories; 32 other countries; 25% are from out of state; 0.8% Black or African American, non-Hispanic/Latino; 2% Hispanic/Latino; 0.9% Asian, non-Hispanic/Latino; 0.5% American Indian or Alaska Native, non-Hispanic/Latino; 2% Two or more races, non-Hispanic/Latino; 4% international; 2% transferred in; 75% live on campus. *Retention:* 84% of full-time freshmen returned.

Freshmen *Admission:* 2,377 applied, 1,910 admitted, 601 enrolled. *Average high school GPA:* 3.48. *Test scores:* ACT scores over 18: 100%; ACT scores over 24: 58%; ACT scores over 30: 9%.

Faculty *Total:* 201, 69% full-time, 71% with terminal degrees. *Student/faculty ratio:* 14:1.

Academics *Calendar:* semesters. *Degrees:* bachelor's and master's. *Special study options:* academic remediation for entering students, advanced placement credit, distance learning, double majors, English as a second language, honors programs, independent study, internships, off-campus study, part-time degree program, services for LD students, student-designed majors, study abroad, summer session for credit. *ROTC:* Army (b).

Computers on Campus 247 computers/terminals are available on campus for general student use. Students can access the following: campus intranet, computer help desk, free student e-mail accounts, online (class) grades, online (class) registration, online (class) schedules. Campuswide network is available. 100% of college-owned or -operated housing units are wired for high-speed Internet access. Wireless service is available via classrooms, computer centers, computer labs, dorm rooms, learning centers, libraries, student centers.

Student Life *Housing:* on-campus residence required through senior year. *Options:* coed, women-only, disabled students. Campus housing is university owned. Freshman campus housing is guaranteed. *Activities and organizations:* drama/theater group, student-run newspaper, radio and television station, cho-

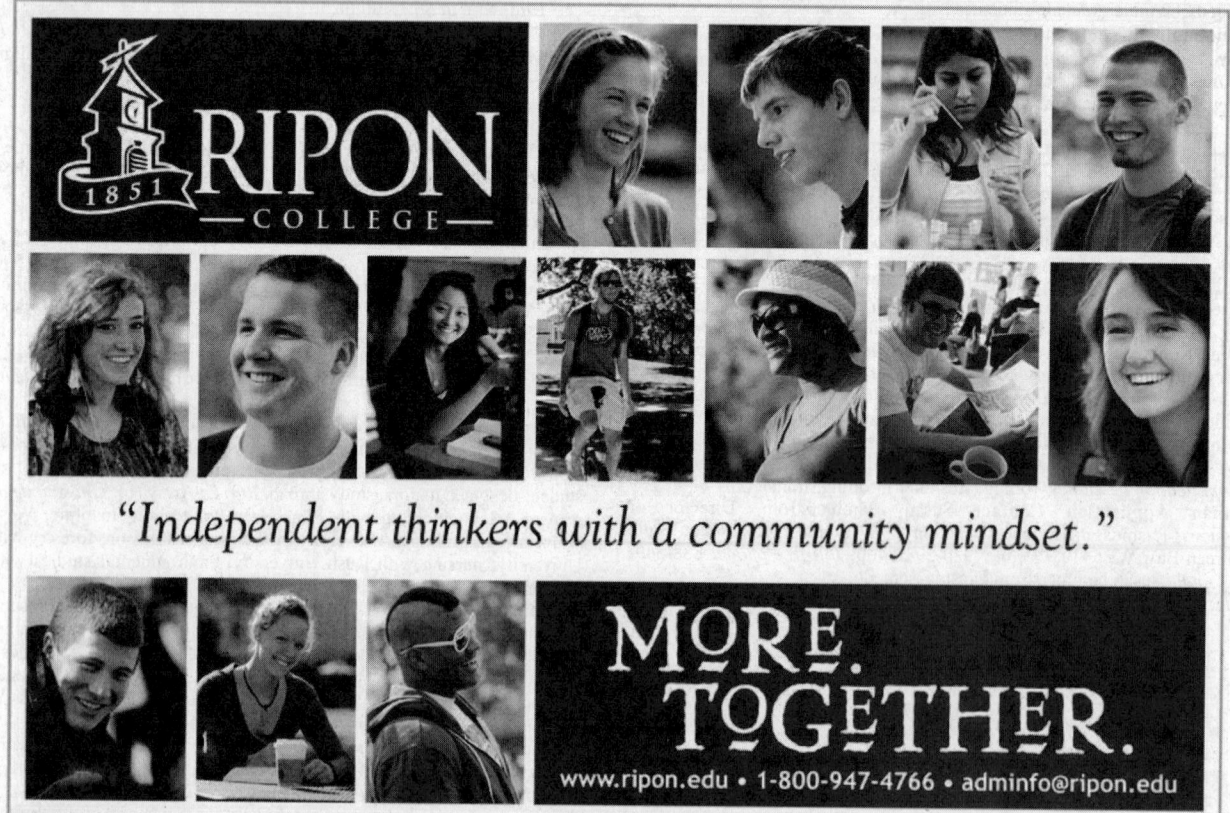

ral group, Wisconsin Student Education Association, Pre-Health Sciences Club, Knight Theatre, Ballroom Club, Circle K, national fraternities, national sororities. *Campus security:* 24-hour emergency response devices and patrols, student patrols, late-night transport/escort service, controlled dormitory access, crime prevention programs. *Student services:* health clinic, personal/psychological counseling, women's center.

Athletics Member NCAA. All Division III. *Intercollegiate sports:* baseball M, basketball M/W, cross-country running M/W, football M, golf M/W, ice hockey M/W, soccer M/W, softball W, tennis M/W, track and field M/W, volleyball W. *Intramural sports:* badminton M/W, basketball M/W, cheerleading M/W, crew M(c)/W(c), football M/W, lacrosse M(c), skiing (downhill) M(c)/W(c), soccer M/W, volleyball M/W.

Standardized Tests *Required:* SAT or ACT (for admission).

Costs (2012–13) *Comprehensive fee:* $38,488 includes full-time tuition ($30,165), mandatory fees ($510), and room and board ($7813). Full-time tuition and fees vary according to course load. Part-time tuition: $943 per credit. Part-time tuition and fees vary according to course load. *College room only:* $4170. Room and board charges vary according to board plan, housing facility, and student level. *Payment plans:* installment, deferred payment. *Waivers:* employees or children of employees.

Financial Aid Of all full-time matriculated undergraduates who enrolled in 2011, 1,696 applied for aid, 1,455 were judged to have need, 430 had their need fully met. 282 Federal Work-Study jobs (averaging $1272). 725 state and other part-time jobs (averaging $1253). In 2011, 553 non-need-based awards were made. *Average percent of need met:* 100%. *Average financial aid package:* $25,822. *Average need-based loan:* $4633. *Average need-based gift aid:* $20,688. *Average non-need-based aid:* $10,440. *Average indebtedness upon graduation:* $31,331.

Applying *Options:* electronic application, deferred entrance. *Application fee:* $25. *Required:* high school transcript, 1 letter of recommendation. *Required for some:* interview. *Recommended:* essay or personal statement. *Application deadlines:* rolling (freshmen), rolling (out-of-state freshmen), rolling (transfers). *Notification:* continuous (freshmen), continuous (out-of-state freshmen), continuous (transfers).

Freshman Application Contact Mr. Edward Lamm, Associate Vice President of Graduate and Undergraduate Enrollment, St. Norbert College, 100 Grant Street, De Pere, WI 54115-2099. *Phone:* 920-403-3005. *Toll-free phone:* 800-236-4878. *Fax:* 920-403-4072. *E-mail:* admit@snc.edu. *Website:* http://www.snc.edu/.

See below for display ad and page 1486 for the College Close-Up.

Silver Lake College of the Holy Family

Manitowoc, Wisconsin

Freshman Application Contact Dan Connolly, Admissions Counselor, Silver Lake College of the Holy Family, 2406 South Alverno Road, Manitowoc, WI 54220. *Phone:* 920-686-6186. *Toll-free phone:* 800-236-4752 Ext. 175. *Fax:* 920-686-6322. *E-mail:* admslc@silver.sl.edu. *Website:* http://www.sl.edu/.

Strayer University—Milwaukee Campus

Milwaukee, Wisconsin

Freshman Application Contact Strayer University—Milwaukee Campus, 9000 West Chester Street, Suite 300, Milwaukee, WI 53214. *Website:* http://www.strayer.edu/campus/milwaukee.

University of Phoenix–Madison Campus

Madison, Wisconsin

Admissions Office Contact University of Phoenix–Madison Campus, 2310 Crossroads Drive, Suite 3000, Madison, WI 53718-2416. *Toll-free phone:* 866-766-0766. *Website:* http://www.phoenix.edu/.

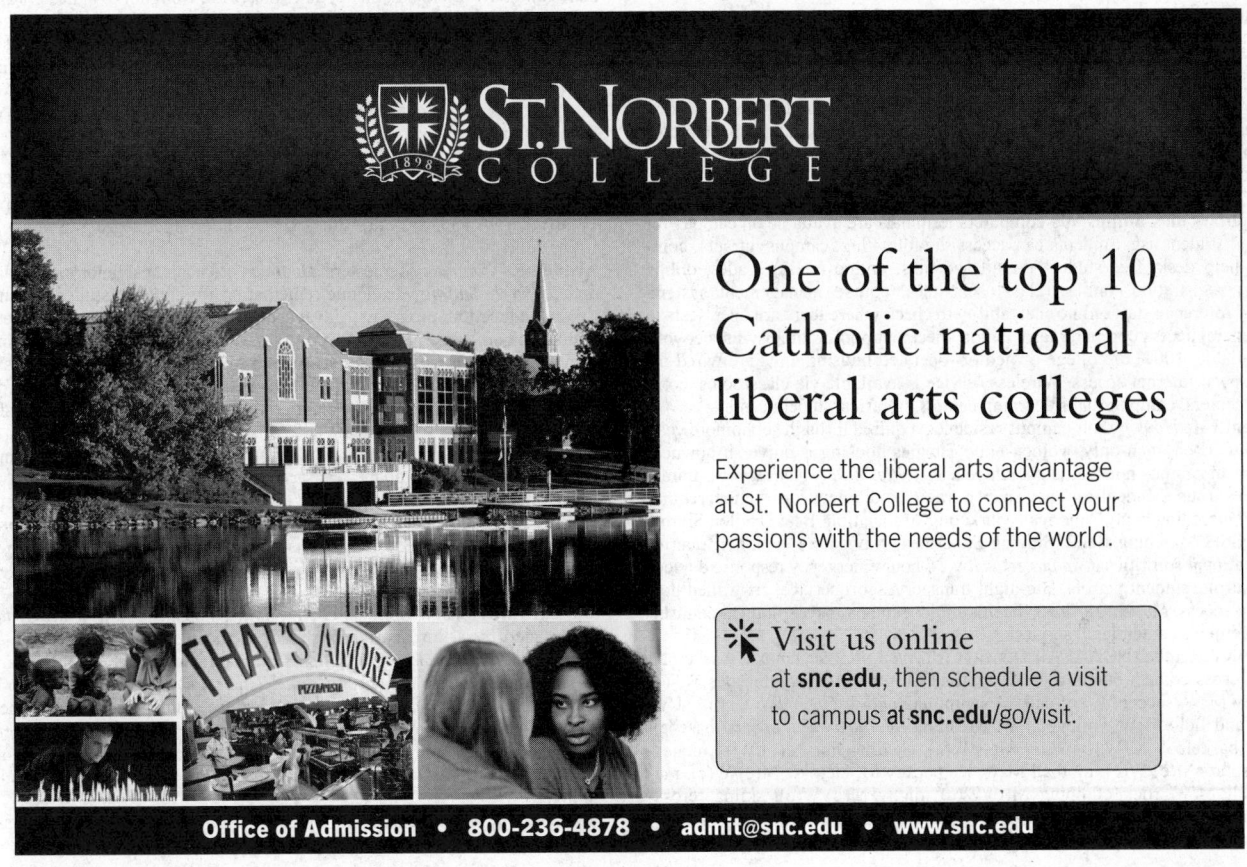

ST. NORBERT COLLEGE

One of the top 10 Catholic national liberal arts colleges

Experience the liberal arts advantage at St. Norbert College to connect your passions with the needs of the world.

✴ Visit us online
at **snc.edu**, then schedule a visit
to campus at **snc.edu**/go/visit.

Office of Admission • 800-236-4878 • admit@snc.edu • www.snc.edu

University of Phoenix–Milwaukee Campus

Milwaukee, Wisconsin

Admissions Office Contact University of Phoenix–Milwaukee Campus, 20075 Watertower Boulevard, Milwaukee, WI 53045. *Toll-free phone:* 866-766-0766.
Website: http://www.phoenix.edu/.

University of Wisconsin–Eau Claire

Eau Claire, Wisconsin

- **State-supported** comprehensive, founded 1916, part of University of Wisconsin System
- **Small-town** 337-acre campus with easy access to Minneapolis-St. Paul
- **Endowment** $44.0 million
- **Coed** 10,499 undergraduate students, 91% full-time, 58% women, 42% men
- **Moderately difficult** entrance level, 76% of applicants were admitted

Undergraduates 9,605 full-time, 894 part-time. Students come from 37 states and territories; 39 other countries; 23% are from out of state; 0.7% Black or African American, non-Hispanic/Latino; 2% Hispanic/Latino; 3% Asian, non-Hispanic/Latino; 0.4% American Indian or Alaska Native, non-Hispanic/Latino; 2% Two or more races, non-Hispanic/Latino; 0.5% Race/ethnicity unknown; 2% international; 6% transferred in; 38% live on campus. *Retention:* 83% of full-time freshmen returned.

Freshmen *Admission:* 6,625 applied, 5,054 admitted, 2,073 enrolled. *Test scores:* SAT critical reading scores over 500: 88%; SAT math scores over 500: 78%; ACT scores over 18: 99%; SAT critical reading scores over 600: 44%; SAT math scores over 600: 44%; ACT scores over 24: 59%; SAT critical reading scores over 700: 19%; SAT math scores over 700: 3%; ACT scores over 30: 6%.

Faculty *Total:* 583, 74% full-time, 71% with terminal degrees. *Student/faculty ratio:* 21:1.

Academics *Calendar:* semesters. *Degrees:* certificates, associate, bachelor's, master's, doctoral, post-master's, and postbachelor's certificates. *Special study options:* academic remediation for entering students, accelerated degree program, adult/continuing education programs, advanced placement credit, cooperative education, distance learning, double majors, English as a second language, external degree program, honors programs, independent study, internships, off-campus study, part-time degree program, services for LD students, student-designed majors, study abroad, summer session for credit. *ROTC:* Army (b).

Computers on Campus 900 computers/terminals are available on campus for general student use. Students can access the following: campus intranet, computer help desk, free student e-mail accounts, online (class) grades, online (class) registration, online (class) schedules, course management system, library reference staff online chat, ability to check where there are open seats in the general access computer labs, laptop check out pool. Campuswide network is available. 100% of college-owned or -operated housing units are wired for high-speed Internet access. Wireless service is available via classrooms, computer centers, computer labs, learning centers, libraries, student centers.

Student Life *Housing:* on-campus residence required through sophomore year. *Options:* coed, men-only, women-only. Campus housing is university owned. Freshman campus housing is guaranteed. *Activities and organizations:* drama/theater group, student-run newspaper, radio and television station, choral group, marching band, American Marketing Association, Beta Upsilon Sigma, Blue Gold Marching Band, Singing Statesmen, Navigators, national fraternities, national sororities. *Campus security:* 24-hour emergency response devices and patrols, student patrols, late-night transport/escort service, controlled dormitory access. *Student services:* health clinic, personal/psychological counseling, women's center, legal services.

Athletics Member NCAA. All Division III. *Intercollegiate sports:* basketball M/W, cross-country running M/W, football M, golf M/W, gymnastics W, ice hockey M/W, soccer W, softball W, swimming and diving M/W, tennis M/W, track and field M/W, volleyball W, wrestling M. *Intramural sports:* baseball M(c), basketball M/W, bowling M(c)/W(c), cheerleading M(c)/W(c), equestrian sports M(c)/W(c), football M/W, ice hockey M, lacrosse M(c)/W(c), racquetball M/W, rock climbing M(c)/W(c), rugby M(c)/W(c), skiing (cross-country) M(c)/W(c), skiing (downhill) M(c)/W(c), soccer M/W, softball M/W, table tennis M(c)/W(c), tennis M/W, ultimate Frisbee M/W, volleyball M/W.

Standardized Tests *Required:* SAT or ACT (for admission).

Costs (2012–13) *Tuition:* state resident $7361 full-time, $307 per credit part-time; nonresident $14,934 full-time, $622 per credit part-time. Full-time tuition and fees vary according to reciprocity agreements. Part-time tuition and fees vary according to reciprocity agreements. *Required fees:* $1330 full-time, $55 per credit part-time, $3 per term part-time. *Room and board:* $6300; room only: $3192. Room and board charges vary according to board plan and housing facility. *Payment plan:* installment. *Waivers:* minority students.

Financial Aid Of all full-time matriculated undergraduates who enrolled in 2011, 7,269 applied for aid, 5,239 were judged to have need, 1,688 had their need fully met. 3,677 Federal Work-Study jobs (averaging $1666). In 2011, 458 non-need-based awards were made. *Average percent of need met:* 89%. *Average financial aid package:* $9224. *Average need-based loan:* $4370. *Average need-based gift aid:* $5640. *Average non-need-based aid:* $1817. *Average indebtedness upon graduation:* $23,825.

Applying *Options:* electronic application, early admission. *Application fee:* $44. *Required:* high school transcript. *Recommended:* essay or personal statement. *Application deadlines:* rolling (freshmen), rolling (transfers). *Notification:* continuous (freshmen), continuous (transfers).

Freshman Application Contact Ms. Kristina Anderson, Executive Director of Enrollment Management and Director of Admissions, University of Wisconsin–Eau Claire, PO Box 4004, Eau Claire, WI 54702-4004. *Phone:* 715-836-5415. *Fax:* 715-836-2409. *E-mail:* admissions@uwec.edu. *Website:* http://www.uwec.edu/.

University of Wisconsin–Green Bay

Green Bay, Wisconsin

- **State-supported** comprehensive, founded 1968, part of University of Wisconsin System
- **Suburban** 700-acre campus with easy access to Milwaukee
- **Endowment** $18.4 million
- **Coed** 6,611 undergraduate students, 70% full-time, 65% women, 35% men
- **Moderately difficult** entrance level, 64% of applicants were admitted

Undergraduates 4,616 full-time, 1,995 part-time. Students come from 39 states and territories; 28 other countries; 7% are from out of state; 1% Black or African American, non-Hispanic/Latino; 3% Hispanic/Latino; 3% Asian, non-Hispanic/Latino; 0.0% Native Hawaiian or other Pacific Islander, non-Hispanic/Latino; 1% American Indian or Alaska Native, non-Hispanic/Latino; 2% Two or more races, non-Hispanic/Latino; 0.4% Race/ethnicity unknown; 1% international; 13% transferred in; 33% live on campus. *Retention:* 74% of full-time freshmen returned.

Freshmen *Admission:* 3,298 applied, 2,111 admitted, 921 enrolled. *Average high school GPA:* 3.34. *Test scores:* ACT scores over 18: 97%; ACT scores over 24: 38%; ACT scores over 30: 2%.

Faculty *Total:* 335, 56% full-time, 55% with terminal degrees. *Student/faculty ratio:* 23:1.

Academics *Calendar:* semesters. *Degrees:* associate, bachelor's, and master's. *Special study options:* academic remediation for entering students, adult/continuing education programs, advanced placement credit, distance learning, double majors, external degree program, independent study, internships, off-campus study, part-time degree program, services for LD students, student-designed majors, study abroad, summer session for credit. *ROTC:* Army (c). *Unusual degree programs:* 3-2 engineering with University of Wisconsin-Milwaukee.

Computers on Campus 550 computers/terminals are available on campus for general student use. Students can access the following: computer help desk, free student e-mail accounts, online (class) grades, online (class) registration, online (class) schedules, online degree progress, online financial records and bill paying. Campuswide network is available. 100% of college-owned or -operated housing units are wired for high-speed Internet access. Wireless service is available via entire campus.

Student Life *Housing options:* coed. Campus housing is university owned and is provided by a third party. Freshman applicants given priority for college housing. *Activities and organizations:* drama/theater group, student-run newspaper, radio station, choral group, Good Times, Psychology and Human Development Club, Student Ambassadors, Residence Hall Apartment Association, Student Government Association. *Campus security:* 24-hour emergency response devices and patrols, late-night transport/escort service, controlled dormitory access. *Student services:* health clinic, personal/psychological counseling.

Athletics Member NCAA. All Division I. *Intercollegiate sports:* basketball M(s)/W(s), cross-country running M(s)/W(s), golf M(s)/W(s), skiing (cross-country) M(s)/W(s), soccer M(s)/W(s), softball W(s), swimming and diving M(s)/W(s), tennis M(s)/W(s), volleyball W(s). *Intramural sports:* basketball M/W, bowling M/W, cheerleading M/W, football M/W, golf M/W, racquetball M/W, sailing M/W, skiing (cross-country) M/W, soccer M/W, softball M/W, swimming and diving M/W, tennis M/W, ultimate Frisbee M/W, volleyball M/W, weight lifting M/W.

Standardized Tests *Required:* SAT or ACT (for admission).

Costs (2012–13) *One-time required fee:* $200. *Tuition:* state resident $6298 full-time, $262 per credit hour part-time; nonresident $13,871 full-time, $578 per credit hour part-time. Full-time tuition and fees vary according to course load and reciprocity agreements. Part-time tuition and fees vary according to reciprocity agreements. *Required fees:* $1350 full-time, $57 per credit hour part-time. *Room and board:* $7076; room only: $4032. Room and board charges vary according to board plan and housing facility. *Payment plan:* installment. *Waivers:* senior citizens.

Financial Aid Of all full-time matriculated undergraduates who enrolled in 2012, 3,997 applied for aid, 3,348 were judged to have need, 1,097 had their need fully met. 200 Federal Work-Study jobs (averaging $2000). In 2012, 174 non-need-based awards were made. *Average percent of need met:* 64%. *Average financial aid package:* $8919. *Average need-based loan:* $7114. *Average need-based gift aid:* $6620. *Average non-need-based aid:* $2776. *Average indebtedness upon graduation:* $23,650.

Applying *Options:* electronic application, deferred entrance. *Application fee:* $44. *Required:* essay or personal statement, high school transcript. *Required for some:* interview. *Application deadlines:* rolling (freshmen), rolling (out-of-state freshmen), rolling (transfers). *Notification:* continuous (freshmen), continuous (out-of-state freshmen), continuous (transfers).

Freshman Application Contact Ms. Pam Harvey-Jacobs, Director of Admissions, University of Wisconsin–Green Bay, 2420 Nicolet Drive, Green Bay, WI 54311-7001. *Phone:* 920-465-2111. *Fax:* 920-465-5754. *E-mail:* uwgb@uwgb.edu.

Website: http://www.uwgb.edu/.

University of Wisconsin–La Crosse

La Crosse, Wisconsin

- **State-supported** comprehensive, founded 1909, part of University of Wisconsin System
- **Suburban** 121-acre campus
- **Endowment** $16.1 million
- **Coed** 9,441 undergraduate students, 95% full-time, 58% women, 42% men
- **Moderately difficult** entrance level, 71% of applicants were admitted

Undergraduates 8,958 full-time, 483 part-time. Students come from 33 states and territories; 29 other countries; 16% are from out of state; 0.7% Black or African American, non-Hispanic/Latino; 3% Hispanic/Latino; 2% Asian, non-Hispanic/Latino; 0.1% Native Hawaiian or other Pacific Islander, non-Hispanic/Latino; 0.3% American Indian or Alaska Native, non-Hispanic/Latino; 3% Two or more races, non-Hispanic/Latino; 0.3% Race/ethnicity unknown; 2% international; 5% transferred in; 37% live on campus. *Retention:* 86% of full-time freshmen returned.

Freshmen *Admission:* 6,908 applied, 4,904 admitted, 1,888 enrolled. *Test scores:* SAT math scores over 500: 77%; SAT writing scores over 500: 65%; ACT scores over 18: 100%; SAT math scores over 600: 50%; SAT writing scores over 600: 23%; ACT scores over 24: 64%; SAT math scores over 700: 12%; ACT scores over 30: 6%.

Faculty *Total:* 572, 80% full-time, 67% with terminal degrees. *Student/faculty ratio:* 20:1.

Academics *Calendar:* semesters. *Degrees:* certificates, associate, bachelor's, master's, doctoral, and postbachelor's certificates. *Special study options:* academic remediation for entering students, adult/continuing education programs, advanced placement credit, cooperative education, distance learning, double majors, English as a second language, independent study, internships, off-campus study, part-time degree program, services for LD students, study abroad, summer session for credit. *ROTC:* Army (b). *Unusual degree programs:* 3-2 engineering with University of Wisconsin-Madison, University of Wisconsin-Milwaukee, University of Wisconsin- Platteville, University of Minnesota; physical therapy and physics, physical therapy and biology, occupational therapy and psychology.

Computers on Campus 200 computers/terminals are available on campus for general student use. Students can access the following: campus intranet, computer help desk, free student e-mail accounts, online (class) grades, online (class) registration, online (class) schedules. Campuswide network is available. 100% of college-owned or -operated housing units are wired for high-speed

Internet access. Wireless service is available via classrooms, computer centers, computer labs, dorm rooms, learning centers, libraries, student centers.

Student Life *Housing:* on-campus residence required for freshman year. *Options:* coed, disabled students. Campus housing is university owned. Freshman applicants given priority for college housing. *Activities and organizations:* drama/theater group, student-run newspaper, radio and television station, choral group, marching band, Sports and Activities Club, Residential Hall Council, religious/spiritual organizations, Human Diversity Organizations, departmental/professional, national fraternities, national sororities. *Campus security:* 24-hour emergency response devices and patrols, late-night transport/escort service, controlled dormitory access. *Student services:* health clinic, personal/psychological counseling, women's center, legal services.

Athletics Member NCAA. All Division III. *Intercollegiate sports:* baseball M, basketball M/W, cross-country running M/W, football M, gymnastics W, soccer W, softball W, swimming and diving M/W, tennis M/W, track and field M/W, volleyball W, wrestling M. *Intramural sports:* archery M(c)/W(c), badminton M/W, basketball M/W, cheerleading M/W, equestrian sports M(c)/W(c), football M/W, golf M/W, ice hockey W(c), lacrosse M(c)/W(c), racquetball M/W, rugby M(c)/W(c), skiing (downhill) M(c)/W(c), soccer M(c)/W(c), softball M/W, table tennis M/W, tennis M/W, ultimate Frisbee M(c)/W(c), volleyball M(c)/W(c), weight lifting M/W.

Standardized Tests *Required:* SAT or ACT (for admission).

Costs (2012–13) *Tuition:* state resident $8754 full-time; nonresident $16,327 full-time. Full-time tuition and fees vary according to program and reciprocity agreements. Part-time tuition and fees vary according to course load, program, and reciprocity agreements. *Room and board:* $6000; room only: $3500. Room and board charges vary according to board plan and housing facility. *Payment plan:* installment. *Waivers:* minority students.

Financial Aid Of all full-time matriculated undergraduates who enrolled in 2011, 6,342 applied for aid, 4,423 were judged to have need, 745 had their need fully met. In 2011, 316 non-need-based awards were made. *Average percent of need met:* 69%. *Average financial aid package:* $7128. *Average need-based loan:* $4105. *Average need-based gift aid:* $5185. *Average non-need-based aid:* $1085. *Average indebtedness upon graduation:* $24,863.

Applying *Options:* electronic application. *Application fee:* $44. *Required:* essay or personal statement, high school transcript. *Required for some:* interview. *Application deadlines:* rolling (freshmen), rolling (out-of-state freshmen), rolling (transfers). *Notification:* continuous (freshmen), continuous (out-of-state freshmen), continuous (transfers).

Freshman Application Contact Mr. Corey Sjoquist, Director of Admissions, University of Wisconsin–La Crosse, 1725 State Street, La Crosse, WI 54601. *Phone:* 608-785-8939. *Fax:* 608-785-8940. *E-mail:* admissions@uwlax.edu. *Website:* http://www.uwlax.edu/.

University of Wisconsin–Madison

Madison, Wisconsin

- **State-supported** university, founded 1848, part of University of Wisconsin System
- **Urban** 936-acre campus with easy access to Milwaukee
- **Endowment** $1.8 billion
- **Coed** 30,863 undergraduate students, 91% full-time, 52% women, 48% men
- **Very difficult** entrance level, 55% of applicants were admitted

Undergraduates 28,188 full-time, 2,675 part-time. Students come from 52 states and territories; 130 other countries; 34% are from out of state; 2% Black or African American, non-Hispanic/Latino; 4% Hispanic/Latino; 5% Asian, non-Hispanic/Latino; 0.1% Native Hawaiian or other Pacific Islander, non-Hispanic/Latino; 0.2% American Indian or Alaska Native, non-Hispanic/Latino; 2% Two or more races, non-Hispanic/Latino; 0.8% Race/ethnicity unknown; 7% international; 4% transferred in; 25% live on campus. *Retention:* 95% of full-time freshmen returned.

Freshmen *Admission:* 29,034 applied, 15,841 admitted, 6,279 enrolled. *Average high school GPA:* 3.84. *Test scores:* SAT critical reading scores over 500: 89%; SAT math scores over 500: 98%; SAT writing scores over 500: 97%; ACT scores over 18: 100%; SAT critical reading scores over 600: 48%; SAT math scores over 600: 87%; SAT writing scores over 600: 69%; ACT scores over 24: 95%; SAT critical reading scores over 700: 13%; SAT math scores over 700: 50%; SAT writing scores over 700: 15%; ACT scores over 30: 35%.

Faculty *Total:* 2,925, 82% full-time, 86% with terminal degrees. *Student/faculty ratio:* 17:1.

Academics *Calendar:* semesters. *Degrees:* bachelor's, master's, doctoral, and post-master's certificates. *Special study options:* accelerated degree program, adult/continuing education programs, advanced placement credit, cooperative education, distance learning, double majors, English as a second language, honors programs, independent study, internships, part-time degree program, services for LD students, student-designed majors, study abroad, summer session for credit. *ROTC:* Army (b), Navy (b), Air Force (b). *Unusual degree programs:* 3-2 BS/MS, BBA/MACC.

Computers on Campus 1,000 computers/terminals are available on campus for general student use. Students can access the following: computer help desk, free student e-mail accounts, online (class) grades, online (class) registration, online (class) schedules. Campuswide network is available. 100% of college-owned or -operated housing units are wired for high-speed Internet access. Wireless service is available via entire campus.

Student Life *Housing options:* coed, men-only, women-only, cooperative. Campus housing is university owned. Freshman applicants given priority for college housing. *Activities and organizations:* drama/theater group, student-run newspaper, radio station, choral group, marching band, national fraternities, national sororities. *Campus security:* 24-hour emergency response devices and patrols, late-night transport/escort service, controlled dormitory access. *Student services:* health clinic, personal/psychological counseling, women's center.

Athletics Member NCAA. All Division I except football (Division I-A). *Intercollegiate sports:* basketball M(s)/W(s), cheerleading M/W, crew M/W, cross-country running M(s)/W(s), fencing M(c)/W(c), golf M(s)/W(s), ice hockey M(s)/W(s), lacrosse M(c)/W(c), racquetball M(c)/W(c), rugby M(c)/W(c), sailing M(c)/W(c), soccer M(s)/W(s), softball W(s), swimming and diving M(s)/W(s), tennis M(s)/W(s), track and field M(s)/W(s), ultimate Frisbee M(c)/W(c), volleyball M(c)/W(s), water polo M(c)/W(c), wrestling M(s). *Intramural sports:* badminton M(c)/W(c), basketball M/W, fencing M(c)/W(c), racquetball M/W, softball M/W, tennis M/W, ultimate Frisbee M/W, volleyball M/W.

Standardized Tests *Required:* SAT or ACT (for admission).

Costs (2012–13) *Tuition:* state resident $9273 full-time, $386 per credit hour part-time; nonresident $25,523 full-time, $1063 per credit hour part-time. Full-time tuition and fees vary according to program and reciprocity agreements. Part-time tuition and fees vary according to course load, program, and reciprocity agreements. *Required fees:* $1111 full-time, $49 per credit hour part-time. *Room and board:* $8080. Room and board charges vary according to board plan and housing facility.

Financial Aid Of all full-time matriculated undergraduates who enrolled in 2012, 15,592 applied for aid, 11,345 were judged to have need, 3,064 had their need fully met. In 2012, 1923 non-need-based awards were made. *Average percent of need met:* 73%. *Average financial aid package:* $12,862. *Average need-based loan:* $5492. *Average need-based gift aid:* $7321. *Average non-need-based aid:* $3260. *Average indebtedness upon graduation:* $24,700.

Applying *Options:* electronic application, deferred entrance. *Application fee:* $44. *Required:* essay or personal statement, high school transcript. *Recommended:* 2 letters of recommendation. *Application deadlines:* 2/1 (freshmen), 2/1 (transfers). *Notification:* continuous (freshmen), continuous (transfers).

Freshman Application Contact Office of Admissions and Recruitment, University of Wisconsin–Madison, 702 West Johnson Street, Suite 101, Madison, WI 53706-1481. *Phone:* 608-262-3961. *Fax:* 608-262-7706. *E-mail:* onwisconsin@admissions.wisc.edu. *Website:* http://www.wisc.edu/.

University of Wisconsin–Milwaukee

Milwaukee, Wisconsin

- **State-supported** university, founded 1956, part of University of Wisconsin System
- **Urban** 104-acre campus
- **Coed** 24,175 undergraduate students, 82% full-time, 51% women, 49% men
- **Moderately difficult** entrance level, 71% of applicants were admitted

Undergraduates 19,721 full-time, 4,454 part-time. Students come from 49 states and territories; 52 other countries; 6% are from out of state; 8% Black or African American, non-Hispanic/Latino; 7% Hispanic/Latino; 6% Asian, non-Hispanic/Latino; 0.1% Native Hawaiian or other Pacific Islander, non-Hispanic/Latino; 0.5% American Indian or Alaska Native, non-Hispanic/Latino; 3% Two or more races, non-Hispanic/Latino; 0.2% Race/ethnicity unknown; 2% international; 7% transferred in; 16% live on campus. *Retention:* 69% of full-time freshmen returned.

Freshmen *Admission:* 10,667 applied, 7,612 admitted, 3,492 enrolled. *Average high school GPA:* 3.09. *Test scores:* ACT scores over 18: 90%; ACT scores over 24: 34%; ACT scores over 30: 3%.

Faculty *Total:* 1,626, 66% full-time, 48% with terminal degrees. *Student/faculty ratio:* 20:1.

Academics *Calendar:* semesters. *Degrees:* certificates, bachelor's, master's, doctoral, post-master's, and postbachelor's certificates. *Special study options:* academic remediation for entering students, accelerated degree program, adult/continuing education programs, advanced placement credit, cooperative education, distance learning, double majors, English as a second language, honors programs, independent study, internships, off-campus study, part-time degree program, services for LD students, student-designed majors, study abroad, summer session for credit. *ROTC:* Army (c), Navy (c), Air Force (c).

Computers on Campus 532 computers/terminals are available on campus for general student use. Students can access the following: campus intranet, computer help desk, free student e-mail accounts, online (class) grades, online (class) registration, online (class) schedules. Campuswide network is available. 100% of college-owned or -operated housing units are wired for high-speed Internet access. Wireless service is available via entire campus.

Student Life *Housing:* on-campus residence required for freshman year. *Options:* coed, disabled students. Campus housing is university owned. Freshman applicants given priority for college housing. *Activities and organizations:* drama/theater group, student-run newspaper, choral group, national fraternities, national sororities. *Campus security:* 24-hour emergency response devices and patrols, student patrols, late-night transport/escort service, controlled dormitory access. *Student services:* health clinic, personal/psychological counseling, women's center, legal services.

Athletics Member NCAA. All Division I. *Intercollegiate sports:* baseball M(s), basketball M(s)/W(s), bowling M(c)/W(c), cross-country running M(s)/W(s), equestrian sports M(c)/W(c), football M(c)/W(c), ice hockey M(c)/W(c), lacrosse M(c)/W(c), rugby M(c)/W(c), sailing M(c)/W(c), soccer M(s)/W(s), swimming and diving M(s)/W(s), tennis W(s), track and field M(s)/W(s), ultimate Frisbee M(c)/W(c), volleyball M(c)/W(s). *Intramural sports:* badminton M/W, baseball M(c)/W(c), basketball M/W, cross-country running M(c)/W(c), racquetball M/W, skiing (downhill) M(c)/W(c), soccer M/W, swimming and diving M/W, tennis M(c)/W(c), track and field M(c)/W(c), volleyball M/W.

Standardized Tests *Required:* SAT or ACT (for admission). *Required for some:* Students whose native language is not English and who were not educated in an entirely English-speaking country will likely need to submit results from the Test of English as a Foreign Language (TOEFL).

Costs (2012–13) *Tuition:* state resident $8091 full-time, $337 per credit part-time; nonresident $17,819 full-time, $742 per credit part-time. Full-time tuition and fees vary according to course load, degree level, location, program, and reciprocity agreements. Part-time tuition and fees vary according to course load, degree level, location, program, and reciprocity agreements. *Required fees:* $1096 full-time. *Room and board:* $7945; room only: $4983. Room and board charges vary according to board plan, housing facility, and location. *Payment plan:* installment. *Waivers:* senior citizens.

Financial Aid Of all full-time matriculated undergraduates who enrolled in 2012, 17,408 applied for aid, 15,532 were judged to have need, 2,091 had their need fully met. In 2012, 54 non-need-based awards were made. *Average percent of need met:* 43%. *Average financial aid package:* $7939. *Average need-based loan:* $4413. *Average need-based gift aid:* $5811. *Average non-need-based aid:* $2803. *Average indebtedness upon graduation:* $32,371.

Applying *Options:* electronic application, deferred entrance. *Application fee:* $44. *Required:* high school transcript. *Recommended:* essay or personal statement. *Application deadlines:* 7/16 (freshmen), 7/16 (transfers). *Notification:* continuous (freshmen), continuous (transfers).

Freshman Application Contact Janis Ford, Director, Admissions and Recruitment, University of Wisconsin–Milwaukee, PO Box 413, Milwaukee, WI 53201-0413. *Phone:* 414-229-3800. *E-mail:* uwmlook@uwm.edu. *Website:* http://www.uwm.edu/.

University of Wisconsin–Oshkosh

Oshkosh, Wisconsin

Freshman Application Contact Mr. Richard Hillman, Associate Director of Admissions, University of Wisconsin–Oshkosh, 800 Algoma Boulevard, Oshkosh, WI 54901. *Phone:* 920-424-0202. *E-mail:* oshadmuw@uwosh.edu. *Website:* http://www.uwosh.edu/.

University of Wisconsin–Parkside

Kenosha, Wisconsin

- **State-supported** comprehensive, founded 1968, part of University of Wisconsin System
- **Suburban** 700-acre campus with easy access to Chicago, Milwaukee
- **Endowment** $2.0 million
- **Coed** 4,601 undergraduate students, 71% full-time, 52% women, 48% men
- **Moderately difficult** entrance level, 57% of applicants were admitted

Undergraduates 3,252 full-time, 1,349 part-time. 11% are from out of state; 10% Black or African American, non-Hispanic/Latino; 10% Hispanic/Latino; 2% Asian, non-Hispanic/Latino; 0.1% Native Hawaiian or other Pacific Islander, non-Hispanic/Latino; 0.2% American Indian or Alaska Native, non-Hispanic/Latino; 3% Two or more races, non-Hispanic/Latino; 0.8% Race/ethnicity unknown; 2% international; 12% transferred in; 16% live on campus. *Retention:* 62% of full-time freshmen returned.

Freshmen *Admission:* 1,883 applied, 1,075 admitted, 712 enrolled. *Average high school GPA:* 2.98. *Test scores:* ACT scores over 18: 87%; ACT scores over 24: 24%; ACT scores over 30: 1%.

Faculty *Total:* 259, 70% full-time, 62% with terminal degrees. *Student/faculty ratio:* 18:1.

Academics *Calendar:* semesters. *Degrees:* certificates, bachelor's, and master's. *Special study options:* academic remediation for entering students, advanced placement credit, distance learning, double majors, external degree program, honors programs, independent study, internships, off-campus study, part-time degree program, services for LD students, study abroad, summer session for credit. *ROTC:* Army (c). *Unusual degree programs:* 3-2 molecular biology.

Computers on Campus 84 computers/terminals are available on campus for general student use. Students can access the following: campus intranet, computer help desk, free student e-mail accounts, online (class) grades, online (class) registration, online (class) schedules. Campuswide network is available. 100% of college-owned or -operated housing units are wired for high-speed Internet access. Wireless service is available via entire campus.

Student Life *Housing:* on-campus residence required through sophomore year. *Options:* coed, disabled students. Campus housing is university owned. *Activities and organizations:* drama/theater group, student-run newspaper, radio station, choral group, Black Student Union, Parkside Asian Organization, Parkside Activities Board, Latinos Unidos, Men's Rugby Club, national fraternities, national sororities. *Campus security:* 24-hour emergency response devices and patrols, late-night transport/escort service, controlled dormitory access. *Student services:* health clinic, personal/psychological counseling, women's center.

Athletics Member NCAA. All Division II. *Intercollegiate sports:* baseball M(s), basketball M(s)/W(s), cross-country running M(s)/W(s), golf M(s), soccer M(s)/W(s), softball W(s), track and field M(s)/W(s), volleyball W(s), wrestling M(s). *Intramural sports:* basketball M/W, cheerleading M(c)/W(c), football M(c), racquetball M/W, rugby M(c)/W(c), soccer M/W, softball M/W, table tennis M/W, tennis M/W, volleyball M/W.

Standardized Tests *Required for some:* SAT or ACT (for admission).

Costs (2013–14) *Tuition:* state resident $6298 full-time, $262 per credit part-time; nonresident $13,871 full-time, $578 per credit part-time. *Required fees:* $989 full-time. *Room and board:* $7082; room only: $4152. Room and board charges vary according to board plan.

Financial Aid Of all full-time matriculated undergraduates who enrolled in 2011, 2,601 applied for aid, 2,210 were judged to have need. *Average need-based gift aid:* $6411.

Applying *Options:* electronic application. *Application fee:* $44. *Required:* high school transcript, minimum of 17 high school units distribution. *Application deadlines:* 8/1 (freshmen), 7/15 (transfers). *Notification:* continuous (freshmen), continuous (transfers).

Freshman Application Contact Mrs. DeAnn Possehl, Director, Enrollment Management, University of Wisconsin–Parkside, PO Box 2000, 900 Wood Road, Kenosha, WI 53141-2000. *Phone:* 262-595-2454. *E-mail:* possehl@uwp.edu.

Website: http://www.uwp.edu/.

University of Wisconsin–Platteville

Platteville, Wisconsin

- **State-supported** comprehensive, founded 1866, part of University of Wisconsin System
- **Small-town** 820-acre campus
- **Coed** 7,648 undergraduate students, 92% full-time, 34% women, 66% men

Undergraduates 7,025 full-time, 623 part-time. 23% are from out of state; 2% Black or African American, non-Hispanic/Latino; 2% Hispanic/Latino; 1% Asian, non-Hispanic/Latino; 0.1% Native Hawaiian or other Pacific Islander, non-Hispanic/Latino; 0.8% American Indian or Alaska Native, non-Hispanic/Latino; 0.5% Race/ethnicity unknown; 0.9% international; 6% transferred in; 43% live on campus. *Retention:* 77% of full-time freshmen returned.

Freshmen *Admission:* 1,639 enrolled. *Test scores:* ACT scores over 18: 94%; ACT scores over 24: 41%; ACT scores over 30: 4%.

Faculty *Total:* 417, 58% full-time, 64% with terminal degrees. *Student/faculty ratio:* 25:1.

Academics *Calendar:* semesters. *Degrees:* certificates, associate, bachelor's, master's, and postbachelor's certificates. *Special study options:* academic remediation for entering students, adult/continuing education programs, advanced placement credit, cooperative education, distance learning, double majors, external degree program, honors programs, independent study, internships, off-campus study, part-time degree program, services for LD students, student-designed majors, study abroad, summer session for credit. *ROTC:* Army (c).

Computers on Campus Students can access the following: campus intranet, computer help desk, free student e-mail accounts, online (class) grades, online (class) registration, online (class) schedules. Campuswide network is available. 100% of college-owned or -operated housing units are wired for high-speed Internet access. Wireless service is available via classrooms, libraries, student centers.

Student Life *Housing:* on-campus residence required through sophomore year. *Options:* coed, men-only, women-only, disabled students. Campus housing is university owned. Freshman campus housing is guaranteed. *Activities and organizations:* drama/theater group, student-run newspaper, radio and television station, choral group, marching band, Criminal Justice Association, Platteville Gaming Association, Dodgeball, American Society of Mechanical Engineers, Outdoor Adventure Club, national fraternities, national sororities. *Campus security:* 24-hour emergency response devices and patrols, student patrols, late-night transport/escort service. *Student services:* health clinic, personal/psychological counseling, women's center.

Athletics Member NCAA. All Division III. *Intercollegiate sports:* baseball M, basketball M/W, bowling M(c)/W(c), cheerleading M/W, cross-country running M/W, football M, golf W, ice hockey M(c)/W(c), lacrosse M(c)/W(c), rugby M(c)/W(c), soccer M/W, softball W, track and field M/W, ultimate Frisbee M(c)/W(c), volleyball M(c)/W, wrestling M. *Intramural sports:* badminton M/W, basketball M/W, bowling M(c)/W(c), cheerleading M(c)/W(c), football M/W, racquetball M/W, soccer M/W, softball M/W, tennis M/W, ultimate Frisbee M/W, volleyball M/W, water polo M/W.

Standardized Tests *Required:* SAT or ACT (for admission). *Recommended:* ACT (for admission).

Costs (2013–14) *Tuition:* state resident $6298 full-time, $262 per credit hour part-time; nonresident $15,036 full-time, $578 per credit hour part-time. *Required fees:* $1165 full-time. *Room and board:* $6464; room only: $3520. Room and board charges vary according to board plan and housing facility. *Payment plan:* installment. *Waivers:* senior citizens.

Financial Aid Of all full-time matriculated undergraduates who enrolled in 2002, 3,289 applied for aid, 2,468 were judged to have need. 382 Federal Work-Study jobs (averaging $1392). In 2002, 652 non-need-based awards were made. *Average financial aid package:* $6161. *Average need-based loan:* $3499. *Average need-based gift aid:* $3599. *Average non-need-based aid:* $1427. *Average indebtedness upon graduation:* $15,785.

Applying *Required:* high school transcript. *Recommended:* essay or personal statement.

Freshman Application Contact Mrs. Angela Udelhofen, Director of Admissions and Enrollment Management, University of Wisconsin–Platteville, 1 University Plaza, 1300 Ullsvik Hall, Platteville, WI 53818-3099. *Phone:* 608-342-1125. *Toll-free phone:* 800-362-5515. *Fax:* 608-342-1122. *E-mail:* rulea@uwplatt.edu.

Website: http://www.uwplatt.edu/.

University of Wisconsin–River Falls

River Falls, Wisconsin

- **State-supported** comprehensive, founded 1874, part of University of Wisconsin System
- **Suburban** 225-acre campus with easy access to Minneapolis-St. Paul
- **Coed**
- **Moderately difficult** entrance level

Faculty *Student/faculty ratio:* 22:1.

Academics *Calendar:* semesters. *Degrees:* certificates, bachelor's, master's, post-master's, and postbachelor's certificates.

Student Life *Campus security:* 24-hour emergency response devices and patrols, student patrols, late-night transport/escort service, controlled dormitory access.

Athletics Member NCAA. All Division III.

Standardized Tests *Required:* SAT or ACT (for admission). *Recommended:* ACT (for admission).

Costs (2012–13) *Tuition:* state resident $6428 full-time, $262 per credit part-time; nonresident $14,001 full-time, $578 per credit part-time. Full-time tuition and fees vary according to course load, degree level, and reciprocity agreements. Part-time tuition and fees vary according to course load, degree level, and reciprocity agreements. *Required fees:* $1272 full-time. *Room and board:* $6902. Room and board charges vary according to board plan and housing facility.

Financial Aid *Of all full-time matriculated undergraduates who enrolled in 2012,* 4,921 applied for aid, 3,829 were judged to have need, 55 had their need fully met. 404 Federal Work-Study jobs (averaging $677). *In 2012,* 85 non-need-based awards were made. *Average percent of need met:* 58. *Average financial aid package:* $6929. *Average need-based loan:* $6406. *Average need-based gift aid:* $4805. *Average non-need-based aid:* $1386. *Average indebtedness upon graduation:* $25,557.

Applying *Options:* electronic application, deferred entrance. *Application fee:* $44. *Required:* essay or personal statement, high school transcript. *Recommended:* Rank in upper 40% of high school class.

Freshman Application Contact University of Wisconsin–River Falls, 410 South Third Street, River Falls, WI 54022. *Phone:* 715-425-3500. *Website:* http://www.uwrf.edu/.

University of Wisconsin–Stevens Point

Stevens Point, Wisconsin

- **State-supported** comprehensive, founded 1894, part of University of Wisconsin System
- **Small-town** 400-acre campus
- **Endowment** $13.9 million
- **Coed** 9,296 undergraduate students, 93% full-time, 52% women, 48% men
- **Moderately difficult** entrance level, 75% of applicants were admitted

Undergraduates 8,644 full-time, 652 part-time. Students come from 36 states and territories; 29 other countries; 9% are from out of state; 1% Black or African American, non-Hispanic/Latino; 2% Hispanic/Latino; 2% Asian, non-Hispanic/Latino; 0.5% American Indian or Alaska Native, non-Hispanic/Latino; 2% Two or more races, non-Hispanic/Latino; 0.5% Race/ethnicity unknown; 2% international; 8% transferred in; 38% live on campus. *Retention:* 82% of full-time freshmen returned.

Freshmen *Admission:* 4,915 applied, 3,672 admitted, 1,637 enrolled. *Average high school GPA:* 3.42. *Test scores:* SAT critical reading scores over 500: 77%; SAT math scores over 500: 68%; SAT writing scores over 500: 55%; ACT scores over 18: 99%; SAT critical reading scores over 600: 23%; SAT math scores over 600: 27%; SAT writing scores over 600: 23%; ACT scores over 24: 42%; SAT critical reading scores over 700: 9%; SAT math scores over 700: 5%; ACT scores over 30: 4%.

Faculty *Total:* 481, 86% full-time, 77% with terminal degrees. *Student/faculty ratio:* 20:1.

Academics *Calendar:* semesters. *Degrees:* associate, bachelor's, master's, and doctoral. *Special study options:* academic remediation for entering students, accelerated degree program, advanced placement credit, cooperative education, distance learning, double majors, English as a second language, independent study, internships, off-campus study, part-time degree program, services

for LD students, student-designed majors, study abroad, summer session for credit. *ROTC:* Army (b).

Computers on Campus 1,233 computers/terminals and 3,963 ports are available on campus for general student use. Students can access the following: computer help desk, free student e-mail accounts, online (class) grades, online (class) registration, online (class) schedules. Campuswide network is available. 100% of college-owned or -operated housing units are wired for high-speed Internet access. Wireless service is available via entire campus.

Student Life *Housing:* on-campus residence required through sophomore year. *Options:* coed, men-only, women-only. Campus housing is university owned. Freshman applicants given priority for college housing. *Activities and organizations:* drama/theater group, student-run newspaper, radio and television station, choral group, The Wildlife Society, Student Impact, WWSP 90-FM radio station, Gender and Sexuality Alliance, Student Wisconsin Education Association, national fraternities, national sororities. *Campus security:* 24-hour emergency response devices and patrols, student patrols, late-night transport/escort service, controlled dormitory access. *Student services:* health clinic, personal/psychological counseling, women's center.

Athletics Member NCAA. All Division III. *Intercollegiate sports:* baseball M, basketball M/W, cross-country running M/W, football M, golf W, ice hockey M/W, soccer W, softball W, swimming and diving M/W, tennis W, track and field M/W, volleyball W, wrestling M. *Intramural sports:* archery M(c)/W(c), badminton M/W, basketball M/W, football M, golf M/W, ice hockey M/W, lacrosse M(c), racquetball M/W, rugby M(c)/W(c), skiing (downhill) M(c)/W(c), soccer M/W, softball M/W, table tennis M/W, tennis M/W, ultimate Frisbee M/W, volleyball M/W.

Standardized Tests *Required:* SAT or ACT (for admission).

Costs (2013–14) *Tuition:* state resident $6298 full-time; nonresident $13,871 full-time. Full-time tuition and fees vary according to course load, program, and reciprocity agreements. Part-time tuition and fees vary according to course load, program, and reciprocity agreements. *Required fees:* $1207 full-time. *Room and board:* $6538; room only: $3788. Room and board charges vary according to board plan and housing facility.

Financial Aid Of all full-time matriculated undergraduates who enrolled in 2011, 7,159 applied for aid, 5,524 were judged to have need, 3,311 had their need fully met. In 2011, 489 non-need-based awards were made. *Average percent of need met:* 69%. *Average financial aid package:* $8213. *Average need-based loan:* $5251. *Average need-based gift aid:* $5727. *Average non-need-based aid:* $2152. *Average indebtedness upon graduation:* $24,054. *Financial aid deadline:* 5/1.

Applying *Options:* electronic application, deferred entrance. *Application fee:* $44. *Required:* high school transcript. *Recommended:* essay or personal statement, 3 letters of recommendation. *Application deadlines:* rolling (freshmen), rolling (transfers). *Notification:* continuous (freshmen), continuous (transfers).

Freshman Application Contact Ms. Terri Crumley, Director of Admissions, University of Wisconsin–Stevens Point, 102 Student Services Center, University of Wisconsin-Stevens Point, Stevens Point, WI 54481. *Phone:* 715-346-2441. *Fax:* 715-346-3296. *E-mail:* tcrumley@uwsp.edu. *Website:* http://www.uwsp.edu/.

University of Wisconsin–Stout

Menomonie, Wisconsin

- **State-supported** comprehensive, founded 1891, part of University of Wisconsin System
- **Small-town** 120-acre campus with easy access to Minneapolis-St. Paul
- **Coed** 8,270 undergraduate students, 83% full-time, 48% women, 52% men
- **Moderately difficult** entrance level, 80% of applicants were admitted

Undergraduates 6,873 full-time, 1,397 part-time. 32% are from out of state; 1% Black or African American, non-Hispanic/Latino; 0.7% Hispanic/Latino; 0.1% Asian, non-Hispanic/Latino; 89% Native Hawaiian or other Pacific Islander, non-Hispanic/Latino; 3% American Indian or Alaska Native, non-Hispanic/Latino; 3% Two or more races, non-Hispanic/Latino; 1% Race/ethnicity unknown; 2% international; 9% transferred in; 40% live on campus. *Retention:* 70% of full-time freshmen returned.

Freshmen *Admission:* 3,388 applied, 2,719 admitted, 1,473 enrolled. *Average high school GPA:* 3.1. *Test scores:* ACT scores over 18: 94%; ACT scores over 24: 31%; ACT scores over 30: 3%.

Faculty *Total:* 472, 85% full-time, 69% with terminal degrees. *Student/faculty ratio:* 19:1.

Academics *Calendar:* 4-1-4. *Degrees:* certificates, bachelor's, master's, post-master's, and postbachelor's certificates. *Special study options:* accelerated degree program, adult/continuing education programs, cooperative education, distance learning, double majors, external degree program, honors programs, independent study, internships, off-campus study, part-time degree program, services for LD students, study abroad, summer session for credit. *ROTC:* Army (b), Air Force (c).

Computers on Campus Students can access the following: computer help desk, free student e-mail accounts, online (class) grades, online (class) registration, online (class) schedules, all undergraduates receive a laptop computer and have unlimited access to Internet. Campuswide network is available. 100% of college-owned or -operated housing units are wired for high-speed Internet access. Wireless service is available via entire campus.

Student Life *Housing:* on-campus residence required through sophomore year. *Options:* coed, disabled students. Campus housing is university owned. Freshman campus housing is guaranteed. *Activities and organizations:* drama/theater group, student-run newspaper, radio and television station, choral group, marching band, national fraternities, national sororities. *Campus security:* 24-hour emergency response devices and patrols, student patrols, controlled dormitory access. *Student services:* health clinic, personal/psychological counseling, legal services.

Athletics Member NCAA. All Division III. *Intercollegiate sports:* baseball M, basketball M/W, cross-country running M/W, football M, gymnastics W, ice hockey M/W(c), soccer M(c)/W, softball W, tennis W, track and field M/W, volleyball M(c)/W. *Intramural sports:* baseball M, basketball M/W, bowling M(c)/W(c), football M/W, golf M/W, ice hockey M/W, racquetball M/W, rugby M(c)/W(c), skiing (cross-country) M(c)/W(c), skiing (downhill) M(c)/W(c), softball M/W, ultimate Frisbee M/W, volleyball M/W.

Standardized Tests *Required:* SAT or ACT (for admission).

Costs (2013–14) *Tuition:* state resident $7014 full-time, $234 per credit hour part-time; nonresident $14,760 full-time, $492 per credit hour part-time. Full-time tuition and fees vary according to degree level and reciprocity agreements. Part-time tuition and fees vary according to degree level and reciprocity agreements. *Required fees:* $1930 full-time. *Room and board:* $6054; room only: $3600. Room and board charges vary according to board plan and housing facility.

Financial Aid Of all full-time matriculated undergraduates who enrolled in 2012, 5,483 applied for aid, 4,232 were judged to have need, 1,752 had their need fully met. 1,627 Federal Work-Study jobs (averaging $1441). In 2012, 70 non-need-based awards were made. *Average percent of need met:* 83%. *Average financial aid package:* $10,590. *Average need-based loan:* $4450. *Average need-based gift aid:* $2465. *Average non-need-based aid:* $2334. *Average indebtedness upon graduation:* $29,879.

Applying *Options:* electronic application. *Application fee:* $44. *Required:* high school transcript. *Required for some:* minimum 2.8 GPA. *Recommended:* minimum 2.5 GPA. *Application deadlines:* rolling (freshmen), rolling (out-of-state freshmen), rolling (transfers). *Notification:* continuous (freshmen), continuous (out-of-state freshmen), continuous (transfers).

Freshman Application Contact Dr. Pamela Holsinger-Fuchs, Executive Director of Enrollment Services, University of Wisconsin–Stout, Admissions, Bowman Hall, Menomonie, WI 54751. *Phone:* 715-232-2639. *Toll-free phone:* 800-HI-STOUT. *Fax:* 715-232-1667. *E-mail:* admissions@uwstout.edu. *Website:* http://www.uwstout.edu/.

University of Wisconsin–Superior

Superior, Wisconsin

- **State-supported** comprehensive, founded 1893, part of University of Wisconsin System
- **Suburban** 230-acre campus
- **Endowment** $2.2 million
- **Coed** 2,550 undergraduate students, 79% full-time, 57% women, 43% men
- **Moderately difficult** entrance level, 76% of applicants were admitted

Undergraduates 2,024 full-time, 526 part-time. Students come from 33 states and territories; 37 other countries; 46% are from out of state; 2% Black or African American, non-Hispanic/Latino; 2% Hispanic/Latino; 1% Asian, non-Hispanic/Latino; 0.2% Native Hawaiian or other Pacific Islander, non-Hispanic/Latino; 2% American Indian or Alaska Native, non-Hispanic/Latino; 2% Two or more races, non-Hispanic/Latino; 0.4% Race/ethnicity unknown; 6% international; 12% transferred in; 28% live on campus. *Retention:* 72% of full-time freshmen returned.

Freshmen *Admission:* 1,001 applied, 761 admitted, 366 enrolled. *Test scores:* ACT scores over 18: 89%; ACT scores over 24: 29%; ACT scores over 30: 2%.

Faculty *Total:* 219, 62% full-time, 47% with terminal degrees. *Student/faculty ratio:* 14:1.

Academics *Calendar:* semesters. *Degrees:* certificates, associate, bachelor's, master's, and post-master's certificates. *Special study options:* academic remediation for entering students, adult/continuing education programs, advanced placement credit, cooperative education, distance learning, double majors,

English as a second language, external degree program, freshman honors college, independent study, internships, off-campus study, part-time degree program, services for LD students, student-designed majors, study abroad, summer session for credit. *ROTC:* Air Force (c). *Unusual degree programs:* 3-2 engineering with Michigan Technological University, University of Wisconsin-Madison; forestry with Michigan Technological University.

Computers on Campus 343 computers/terminals are available on campus for general student use. Students can access the following: campus intranet, computer help desk, free student e-mail accounts, online (class) grades, online (class) registration, online (class) schedules. Campuswide network is available. 100% of college-owned or -operated housing units are wired for high-speed Internet access. Wireless service is available via entire campus.

Student Life *Housing:* on-campus residence required through sophomore year. *Options:* coed, women-only, disabled students. Campus housing is university owned. Freshman campus housing is guaranteed. *Activities and organizations:* drama/theater group, student-run newspaper, radio station, choral group, Student Senate, Student Activities Board, Residence Hall Association, Inter-Varsity Christian Fellowship, World Student Association, national sororities. *Campus security:* 24-hour emergency response devices and patrols, student patrols, late-night transport/escort service, controlled dormitory access. *Student services:* health clinic, personal/psychological counseling, women's center.

Athletics Member NCAA. All Division III. *Intercollegiate sports:* baseball M, basketball M/W, cross-country running M/W, ice hockey M/W, soccer M/W, softball W, track and field M/W, volleyball W. *Intramural sports:* baseball M/W, basketball M/W, football M/W, ice hockey M(c)/W(c), racquetball M/W, riflery M/W, rock climbing M/W, soccer M/W, softball M/W, table tennis M/W, tennis M(c)/W(c), ultimate Frisbee M(c)/W(c), volleyball M(c)/W(c).

Standardized Tests *Required:* SAT or ACT (for admission).

Costs (2012–13) *Tuition:* state resident $6535 full-time, $472 per credit hour part-time; nonresident $14,108 full-time, $776 per credit hour part-time. Full-time tuition and fees vary according to course load and reciprocity agreements. Part-time tuition and fees vary according to course load and reciprocity agreements. *Required fees:* $1369 full-time. *Room and board:* $5992; room only: $3232. Room and board charges vary according to board plan, housing facility, and student level. *Payment plan:* installment.

Financial Aid Of all full-time matriculated undergraduates who enrolled in 2012, 1,646 applied for aid, 1,423 were judged to have need, 262 had their need fully met. In 2012, 24 non-need-based awards were made. *Average financial aid package:* $17,266. *Average need-based loan:* $4039. *Average need-based gift aid:* $4817. *Average non-need-based aid:* $1060. *Average indebtedness upon graduation:* $26,486.

Applying *Options:* electronic application, early admission, deferred entrance. *Application fee:* $44. *Required:* high school transcript. *Required for some:* essay or personal statement, 1 letter of recommendation. *Recommended:* interview. *Application deadlines:* rolling (freshmen), rolling (transfers). *Notification:* continuous (freshmen), continuous (out-of-state freshmen), continuous (transfers).

Freshman Application Contact Tonya Roth, Director of Admissions, University of Wisconsin–Superior, Belknap and Catlin, PO Box 2000, Superior, WI 54880-4500. *Phone:* 715-394-8264. *Fax:* 715-394-8407. *E-mail:* admissions@uwsuper.edu. *Website:* http://www.uwsuper.edu/.

University of Wisconsin–Whitewater

Whitewater, Wisconsin

- **State-supported** comprehensive, founded 1868, part of University of Wisconsin System
- **Small-town** 385-acre campus with easy access to Milwaukee
- **Endowment** $13.0 million
- **Coed**
- **Moderately difficult** entrance level

Faculty *Student/faculty ratio:* 23:1.

Academics *Calendar:* semesters. *Degrees:* associate, bachelor's, and master's.

Student Life *Campus security:* 24-hour emergency response devices, late-night transport/escort service, controlled dormitory access.

Athletics Member NCAA. All Division III.

Standardized Tests *Required for some:* ACT (for admission). *Recommended:* SAT or ACT (for admission).

Costs (2012–13) *Tuition:* state resident $6519 full-time, $272 per credit hour part-time; nonresident $14,092 full-time, $587 per credit hour part-time. Full-time tuition and fees vary according to degree level and reciprocity agreements. *Required fees:* $1009 full-time. *Room and board:* $5736. Room and board charges vary according to board plan.

Financial Aid *Of all full-time matriculated undergraduates who enrolled in 2012,* 7,715 applied for aid, 6,177 were judged to have need, 3,448 had their need fully met. 702 Federal Work-Study jobs (averaging $870). 1,989 state and other part-time jobs (averaging $2011). *In 2012,* 382 non-need-based awards were made. *Average percent of need met:* 63. *Average financial aid package:* $7884. *Average need-based loan:* $4252. *Average need-based gift aid:* $5253. *Average non-need-based aid:* $1854. *Average indebtedness upon graduation:* $25,147.

Applying *Options:* electronic application, deferred entrance. *Application fee:* $44. *Required:* high school transcript.

Freshman Application Contact Mrs. Jodi Hare, Interim Director of Admissions, University of Wisconsin–Whitewater, 800 West Main Street, Whitewater, WI 53190-1790. *Phone:* 262-472-1440 Ext. 1512. *Fax:* 262-472-1515. *E-mail:* uwwadmit@uww.edu.
Website: http://www.uww.edu/.

Viterbo University

La Crosse, Wisconsin

- **Independent Roman Catholic** comprehensive, founded 1890
- **Suburban** 72-acre campus
- **Coed** 2,105 undergraduate students, 75% full-time, 73% women, 27% men
- **Moderately difficult** entrance level, 69% of applicants were admitted

Undergraduates 1,569 full-time, 536 part-time. 23% are from out of state; 2% Black or African American, non-Hispanic/Latino; 2% Hispanic/Latino; 2% Asian, non-Hispanic/Latino; 0.9% American Indian or Alaska Native, non-Hispanic/Latino; 0.3% Race/ethnicity unknown; 0.9% international; 14% transferred in; 33% live on campus. *Retention:* 76% of full-time freshmen returned.

Freshmen *Admission:* 1,655 applied, 1,145 admitted, 306 enrolled. *Average high school GPA:* 3.48. *Test scores:* ACT scores over 18: 96%; ACT scores over 24: 42%; ACT scores over 30: 2%.

Faculty *Total:* 415, 28% full-time, 30% with terminal degrees. *Student/faculty ratio:* 12:1.

Academics *Calendar:* semesters. *Degrees:* certificates, associate, bachelor's, master's, post-master's, and postbachelor's certificates. *Special study options:* accelerated degree program, adult/continuing education programs, distance learning, double majors, English as a second language, honors programs, independent study, internships, part-time degree program, student-designed majors, study abroad. *ROTC:* Army (c).

Computers on Campus Students can access the following: campus intranet, computer help desk, free student e-mail accounts, online (class) grades, online (class) registration, online (class) schedules, Blackboard courses. Campuswide network is available. 100% of college-owned or -operated housing units are wired for high-speed Internet access. Wireless service is available via entire campus.

Student Life *Housing:* on-campus residence required through sophomore year. *Options:* coed, men-only, women-only. Campus housing is university owned. Freshman campus housing is guaranteed. *Activities and organizations:* drama/theater group, student-run newspaper, choral group, Student Activities Board (SAB), Viterbo Student nurses Association (VSNA), Education Club, Colleges Against Cancer (CAL), Residence Hall Council (RHC). *Campus security:* 24-hour emergency response devices, late-night transport/escort service, controlled dormitory access, security officers on campus 5:00 pm to 7:00 am, lighted pathways, emergency evacuation plan, self-defense education programs. *Student services:* health clinic, personal/psychological counseling.

Athletics Member NAIA. *Intercollegiate sports:* baseball M(s), basketball M(s)/W(s), bowling M(s)/W(s), cross-country running M(s)/W(s), golf M(s)/W(s), soccer M(s)/W(s), softball W(s), volleyball W(s). *Intramural sports:* badminton M/W, basketball M/W, bowling M/W, cross-country running M/W, golf M/W, racquetball M/W, rugby M/W, skiing (cross-country) M/W, skiing (downhill) M/W, soccer M/W, softball M/W, swimming and diving M/W, table tennis M/W, tennis M/W, ultimate Frisbee M/W, volleyball M/W.

Standardized Tests *Required:* SAT or ACT (for admission).

Costs (2012–13) *Comprehensive fee:* $30,070 includes full-time tuition ($22,080), mandatory fees ($590), and room and board ($7400). Full-time tuition and fees vary according to program. Part-time tuition and fees vary according to program. *College room only:* $3310. Room and board charges vary according to board plan and housing facility.

Financial Aid Of all full-time matriculated undergraduates who enrolled in 2003, 1,311 applied for aid, 1,208 were judged to have need, 309 had their need fully met. 387 Federal Work-Study jobs (averaging $1680). 19 state and other part-time jobs (averaging $1615). In 2003, 223 non-need-based awards

were made. *Average percent of need met:* 71%. *Average financial aid package:* $13,534. *Average need-based loan:* $4317. *Average need-based gift aid:* $8859. *Average non-need-based aid:* $5629. *Average indebtedness upon graduation:* $16,619.

Applying *Options:* electronic application, deferred entrance. *Application fee:* $25. *Required:* high school transcript, minimum 2.0 GPA. *Required for some:* essay or personal statement, interview, audition for theater and music, portfolio for art. *Application deadlines:* 8/15 (freshmen), 8/1 (transfers). *Notification:* continuous (freshmen), continuous (transfers).

Freshman Application Contact Mrs. Caryn L. Witt, Admissions Assistant, Viterbo University, 900 Viterbo Drive, La Crosse, WI 54601. *Phone:* 608-796-3010. *Toll-free phone:* 800-VITERBO. *Fax:* 608-796-3020. *E-mail:* admission@viterbo.edu.
Website: http://www.viterbo.edu/.

Wisconsin Lutheran College

Milwaukee, Wisconsin

Freshman Application Contact Ms. Meghan Wieselmann, Admissions Office Manager, Wisconsin Lutheran College, 8800 West Bluemound Road, Milwaukee, WI 53226-9942. *Phone:* 414-443-8718. *Fax:* 414-443-8547. *E-mail:* meg.wieselmann@wlc.edu.
Website: http://www.wlc.edu/.

WYOMING

University of Phoenix–Cheyenne Campus

Cheyenne, Wyoming

Admissions Office Contact University of Phoenix–Cheyenne Campus, 6900 Yellowstone Road, Cheyenne, WY 82009. *Toll-free phone:* 866-766-0766. *Website:* http://www.phoenix.edu/.

University of Wyoming

Laramie, Wyoming

- **State-supported** university, founded 1886
- **Small-town** 785-acre campus
- **Endowment** $358.5 million
- **Coed** 10,194 undergraduate students, 82% full-time, 52% women, 48% men
- **Moderately difficult** entrance level, 96% of applicants were admitted

Undergraduates 8,311 full-time, 1,883 part-time. Students come from 50 states and territories; 69 other countries; 30% are from out of state; 1% Black or African American, non-Hispanic/Latino; 5% Hispanic/Latino; 1% Asian, non-Hispanic/Latino; 0.2% Native Hawaiian or other Pacific Islander, non-Hispanic/Latino; 0.7% American Indian or Alaska Native, non-Hispanic/Latino; 2% Two or more races, non-Hispanic/Latino; 5% Race/ethnicity unknown; 4% international; 11% transferred in; 23% live on campus. *Retention:* 76% of full-time freshmen returned.

Freshmen *Admission:* 4,181 applied, 4,001 admitted, 1,584 enrolled. *Average high school GPA:* 3.48. *Test scores:* SAT critical reading scores over 500: 67%; SAT math scores over 500: 76%; ACT scores over 18: 96%; SAT critical reading scores over 600: 29%; SAT math scores over 600: 36%; ACT scores over 24: 56%; SAT critical reading scores over 700: 4%; SAT math scores over 700: 6%; ACT scores over 30: 11%.

Faculty *Total:* 837, 92% full-time, 80% with terminal degrees. *Student/faculty ratio:* 14:1.

Academics *Calendar:* semesters. *Degrees:* certificates, bachelor's, master's, doctoral, post-master's, and postbachelor's certificates. *Special study options:* accelerated degree program, advanced placement credit, distance learning, double majors, external degree program, honors programs, independent study, internships, off-campus study, part-time degree program, services for LD students, student-designed majors, study abroad, summer session for credit. *ROTC:* Army (b), Air Force (b).

Computers on Campus 1,536 computers/terminals are available on campus for general student use. Students can access the following: campus intranet, computer help desk, free student e-mail accounts, online (class) grades, online (class) registration, online (class) schedules. Campuswide network is available. 100% of college-owned or -operated housing units are wired for high-speed Internet access. Wireless service is available via classrooms, computer centers, computer labs, dorm rooms, learning centers, libraries, student centers.

Student Life *Housing:* on-campus residence required for freshman year. *Options:* coed, men-only, women-only, disabled students. Campus housing is university owned. Freshman campus housing is guaranteed. *Activities and organizations:* drama/theater group, student-run newspaper, television station, choral group, marching band, national fraternities, national sororities. *Campus security:* 24-hour emergency response devices and patrols, student patrols, late-night transport/escort service, controlled dormitory access, 24-hour front desk coverage at campus housing and at campus police. *Student services:* health clinic, personal/psychological counseling, women's center, legal services.

Athletics Member NCAA. All Division I except football (Division I-A). *Intercollegiate sports:* badminton M(c)/W(c), baseball M(c), basketball M(s)/W(s), cheerleading M(s)/W(s), cross-country running M(s)/W(s), equestrian sports M(c)/W(c), fencing M(c)/W(c), golf M(s)/W(s), ice hockey M(c)/W(c), lacrosse M(c)/W(c), racquetball M(c)/W(c), riflery M(c)/W(c), rugby M(c)/W(c), skiing (cross-country) M(c)/W(c), skiing (downhill) M(c)/W(c), soccer M(c)/W(s), softball W(c), swimming and diving M(s)/W(s), tennis M(c)/W(s), track and field M(s)/W(s), ultimate Frisbee M(c)/W(c), volleyball W(s), water polo M(c), wrestling M(s). *Intramural sports:* badminton M/W, basketball M/W, bowling M/W, football M/W, golf M/W, racquetball M/W, rock climbing M/W, soccer M/W, softball M/W, swimming and diving M/W, table tennis M/W, tennis M/W, track and field M/W, ultimate Frisbee M/W, volleyball M/W, water polo M/W, weight lifting M/W, wrestling M/W.

Standardized Tests *Required:* SAT or ACT (for admission).

Costs (2012–13) *One-time required fee:* $40. *Tuition:* state resident $3180 full-time, $106 per credit hour part-time; nonresident $12,330 full-time, $411 per credit hour part-time. Full-time tuition and fees vary according to course load, location, and reciprocity agreements. Part-time tuition and fees vary according to course load, location, and reciprocity agreements. *Required fees:* $1098 full-time, $262 per term part-time. *Room and board:* $9084; room only: $3901. Room and board charges vary according to board plan and housing facility. *Payment plan:* installment. *Waivers:* children of alumni, senior citizens, and employees or children of employees.

Financial Aid Of all full-time matriculated undergraduates who enrolled in 2011, 5,537 applied for aid, 4,011 were judged to have need, 683 had their need fully met. In 2011, 872 non-need-based awards were made. *Average percent of need met:* 62%. *Average financial aid package:* $9117. *Average need-based loan:* $4173. *Average need-based gift aid:* $4743. *Average non-need-based aid:* $2827. *Average indebtedness upon graduation:* $21,241.

Applying *Options:* electronic application, deferred entrance. *Application fee:* $40. *Required:* high school transcript, minimum 3.0 GPA, pre-college curriculum; minimum ACT composite of 21 or SAT of 980. *Application deadlines:* 8/10 (freshmen), 8/10 (out-of-state freshmen), 8/10 (transfers). *Notification:* continuous (freshmen), continuous (out-of-state freshmen), continuous (transfers).

Freshman Application Contact Mary Aguayo, Assistant Director of Admissions, University of Wyoming, 1000 E. University Avenue, Dept 3435, Laramie, WY 82071. *Phone:* 307-766-4075. *Toll-free phone:* 800-342-5996. *Fax:* 307-766-4042. *E-mail:* admissions@uwyo.edu. *Website:* http://www.uwyo.edu/.

See below for display ad and page 1616 for the College Close-Up.

GUAM

Pacific Islands University
Mangilao, Guam

Freshman Application Contact Ethel Laco, Admissions Office, Pacific Islands University, 172 Kinney's Road, Mangilao, GU 96913. *Phone:* 671-734-1812. *Fax:* 671-734-1813. *E-mail:* guamcampus@pibc.edu. *Website:* http://www.piu.edu/.

University of Guam
Mangilao, Guam

- **Territory-supported** comprehensive, founded 1952
- **Suburban** 100-acre campus
- **Endowment** $16.4 million
- **Coed** 3,411 undergraduate students, 75% full-time, 59% women, 41% men
- **Noncompetitive** entrance level, 94% of applicants were admitted

Undergraduates 2,551 full-time, 860 part-time. Students come from 36 states and territories; 24 other countries; 1% are from out of state; 0.3% Black or African American, non-Hispanic/Latino; 0.6% Hispanic/Latino; 41% Asian,

non-Hispanic/Latino; 51% Native Hawaiian or other Pacific Islander, non-Hispanic/Latino; 0.1% American Indian or Alaska Native, non-Hispanic/Latino; 2% Race/ethnicity unknown; 1% international; 4% transferred in; 5% live on campus. *Retention:* 76% of full-time freshmen returned.
Freshmen *Admission:* 725 applied, 684 admitted, 597 enrolled. *Average high school GPA:* 3.14.
Faculty *Total:* 258, 71% full-time. *Student/faculty ratio:* 13:1.
Academics *Calendar:* semesters. *Degrees:* certificates, associate, bachelor's, master's, and postbachelor's certificates. *Special study options:* academic remediation for entering students, accelerated degree program, advanced placement credit, cooperative education, distance learning, double majors, English as a second language, honors programs, independent study, internships, off-campus study, part-time degree program, services for LD students, study abroad, summer session for credit. *ROTC:* Army (b).
Computers on Campus 545 computers/terminals and 600 ports are available on campus for general student use. Students can access the following: campus intranet, computer help desk, free student e-mail accounts, online (class) grades, online (class) registration, online (class) schedules, wireless internet access. Campuswide network is available. 100% of college-owned or -operated housing units are wired for high-speed Internet access. Wireless service is available via entire campus.
Student Life *Housing options:* coed. Campus housing is university owned. *Activities and organizations:* drama/theater group, student-run newspaper, choral group, American Marketing Association, Student Nurses Association of Guam, Social Work Student Alliance, GO CNMI, Association of Early Childhood Education International. *Campus security:* 24-hour emergency response devices and patrols, late-night transport/escort service. *Student services:* health clinic, personal/psychological counseling.
Athletics *Intramural sports:* basketball M/W, crew M(c)/W(c), football M, softball M/W, table tennis M/W, volleyball M/W.
Costs (2013–14) *Tuition:* territory resident $4560 full-time, $190 per credit part-time; nonresident $13,560 full-time, $565 per credit part-time. Part-time tuition and fees vary according to course load. *Required fees:* $538 full-time, $269 per term part-time. *Room only:* $1880. Room and board charges vary according to housing facility. *Payment plan:* installment. *Waivers:* senior citizens and employees or children of employees.
Applying *Options:* electronic application, deferred entrance. *Application fee:* $49. *Required:* high school transcript. *Application deadlines:* 6/1 (freshmen), 6/1 (out-of-state freshmen), 6/1 (transfers). *Notification:* continuous (freshmen), continuous (transfers).
Freshman Application Contact Ms. Angelica Anthonio, Admissions Supervisor, University of Guam, Admissions and Records Office, UOG Station, Mangilao, GU 96923. *Phone:* 671-735-2201. *Fax:* 671-735-2203. *E-mail:* admitme@uguam.uog.edu.
Website: http://www.uog.edu/.

NORTHERN MARIANA ISLANDS

Northern Marianas College
Saipan, Northern Mariana Islands

Freshman Application Contact Ms. Leilani M. Basa-Alam, Admission Specialist, Northern Marianas College, PO Box 501250, Saipan, MP 96950-1250. *Phone:* 670-234-3690 Ext. 1539. *Fax:* 670-235-4967. *E-mail:* leilanib@nmcnet.edu.
Website: http://www.nmcnet.edu/.

PUERTO RICO

American University of Puerto Rico
Bayamón, Puerto Rico

- **Independent** comprehensive, founded 1963
- **Urban** 21-acre campus with easy access to San Juan
- **Coed** 2,324 undergraduate students, 91% full-time, 54% women, 46% men
- **Noncompetitive** entrance level, 83% of applicants were admitted

Undergraduates 2,123 full-time, 201 part-time. 100% Hispanic/Latino. *Retention:* 80% of full-time freshmen returned.
Freshmen *Admission:* 325 applied, 271 admitted, 351 enrolled.
Faculty *Total:* 162, 25% full-time, 10% with terminal degrees.
Academics *Calendar:* semesters. *Degrees:* associate, bachelor's, and master's. *Special study options:* adult/continuing education programs, advanced placement credit, cooperative education, distance learning, double majors, English as a second language, freshman honors college, honors programs, independent study, internships, part-time degree program, services for LD students, summer session for credit. *ROTC:* Army (c).
Computers on Campus 359 computers/terminals are available on campus for general student use. Students can access the following: free student e-mail accounts, online (class) grades, online (class) schedules, 8 Wifi access points. Campuswide network is available. Wireless service is available via computer centers, libraries, student centers.
Student Life *Housing:* college housing not available. *Activities and organizations:* drama/theater group, Business Student Association, Information Systems Student Association, Accounting Student Association, Library Club, Office Systems Student Association. *Campus security:* 24-hour patrols. *Student services:* health clinic.
Athletics *Intercollegiate sports:* basketball M/W, swimming and diving M/W, track and field M/W, volleyball M/W.
Standardized Tests *Recommended:* SAT (for admission), SAT and SAT Subject Tests or ACT (for admission), SAT Subject Tests (for admission).
Costs (2013–14) *Tuition:* $4272 full-time, $178 per credit hour part-time. Full-time tuition and fees vary according to class time and course load. Part-time tuition and fees vary according to class time and course load. *Required fees:* $1075 full-time, $175 part-time. *Payment plan:* installment. *Waivers:* employees or children of employees.
Financial Aid Of all full-time matriculated undergraduates who enrolled in 2004, 2,800 applied for aid, 2,780 were judged to have need. *Average percent of need met:* 45%. *Average financial aid package:* $5280. *Average need-based loan:* $30. *Average need-based gift aid:* $5. *Average indebtedness upon graduation:* $7000. *Financial aid deadline:* 5/30.
Applying *Options:* electronic application, deferred entrance. *Application fee:* $25. *Required:* high school transcript. *Notification:* continuous (freshmen), continuous (transfers).
Freshman Application Contact Ms. Keren Llanos Figueroa, Director of Admissions, American University of Puerto Rico, P O Box 2037, Bayamón, PR 00960-2037. *Phone:* 787-620-2040 Ext. 2020. *Fax:* 787-785-7377. *E-mail:* kllanos@aupr.edu.
Website: http://www.aupr.edu/.

Atlantic University College
Guaynabo, Puerto Rico

Director of Admissions Ms. Zaida Perez, Admission's Officer, Atlantic University College, PO Box 3918, Guaynabo, PR 00970. *Phone:* 787-720-1022 Ext. 13. *E-mail:* admisiones@atlanticcollege.edu.
Website: http://www.atlanticu.edu/.

Bayamón Central University
Bayamón, Puerto Rico

- **Independent Roman Catholic** comprehensive, founded 1970
- **Suburban** 55-acre campus with easy access to San Juan
- **Endowment** $1.4 million
- **Coed**
- **Moderately difficult** entrance level

Academics *Calendar:* semesters for undergraduate programs, trimesters for graduate programs. *Degrees:* certificates, associate, bachelor's, and master's.
Student Life *Campus security:* 24-hour patrols.
Standardized Tests *Required:* College Examination Entrance Board Test (for admission).
Costs (2012–13) *Tuition:* $7490 full-time, $165 per credit part-time. Full-time tuition and fees vary according to course level, degree level, and program. Part-time tuition and fees vary according to course level, degree level, and program. *Required fees:* $710 full-time, $165 per credit part-time, $350 per credit part-time.
Applying *Application fee:* $25. *Required:* high school transcript, medical history. *Required for some:* interview. *Recommended:* minimum 2.0 GPA.
Freshman Application Contact Bayamón Central University, PO Box 1725, Bayamón, PR 00960-1725. *Phone:* 787-786-3030 Ext. 2102.
Website: http://www.ucb.edu.pr/.

Caribbean University

Bayamón, Puerto Rico

- **Independent** comprehensive, founded 1969
- **Urban** 16-acre campus with easy access to San Juan
- **Endowment** $321,559
- **Coed** 4,745 undergraduate students, 75% full-time, 59% women, 41% men
- **Minimally difficult** entrance level, 80% of applicants were admitted

Undergraduates 3,572 full-time, 1,173 part-time. Students come from 4 states and territories; 100% Hispanic/Latino.

Freshmen *Admission:* 987 applied, 789 admitted, 1,369 enrolled. *Average high school GPA:* 2.67.

Faculty *Total:* 424, 18% full-time, 20% with terminal degrees. *Student/faculty ratio:* 20:1.

Academics *Calendar:* trimesters. *Degrees:* certificates, associate, bachelor's, and master's. *Special study options:* academic remediation for entering students, accelerated degree program, adult/continuing education programs, English as a second language, part-time degree program, services for LD students, summer session for credit. *ROTC:* Army (c).

Student Life *Activities and organizations:* drama/theater group, choral group, Engineering Student Association, Nursing, Social Work, Speech Therapy, Physical Education. *Campus security:* 24-hour patrols. *Student services:* health clinic, personal/psychological counseling.

Athletics *Intercollegiate sports:* baseball M, basketball M/W, bowling M/W, cheerleading M/W, cross-country running M/W, softball W, table tennis M/W, track and field M/W, volleyball M/W, weight lifting M/W, wrestling M/W. *Intramural sports:* basketball M, cross-country running M/W, gymnastics M/W, table tennis M/W, tennis M/W, track and field M/W, volleyball M/W, weight lifting M.

Standardized Tests *Required for some:* Only for the engineering applicants, we request test for verbal and math attitude offer by the College Board.

Costs (2013–14) *Comprehensive fee:* $13,465 includes full-time tuition ($4080), mandatory fees ($385), and room and board ($9000). Full-time tuition and fees vary according to program. Part-time tuition: $170 per credit hour. Part-time tuition and fees vary according to program. *Required fees:* $225 per term part-time. *College room only:* $5000. *Payment plan:* installment. *Waivers:* employees or children of employees.

Applying *Options:* deferred entrance. *Application fee:* $30. *Required:* high school transcript. *Required for some:* 1 letter of recommendation, interview. *Application deadline:* rolling (freshmen).

Freshman Application Contact Caribbean University, Box 493, Bayamón, PR 00960-0493. *Phone:* 787-780-0070 Ext. 226.

Website: http://www.caribbean.edu/.

Carlos Albizu University

San Juan, Puerto Rico

- **Independent** university, founded 1966
- **Urban** campus
- **Endowment** $732,270
- **Coed, primarily women** 162 undergraduate students, 52% full-time, 86% women, 14% men
- **Noncompetitive** entrance level, 88% of applicants were admitted

Undergraduates 84 full-time, 78 part-time. 1% are from out of state; 62% Hispanic/Latino; 0.6% Race/ethnicity unknown; 65% transferred in.

Freshmen *Admission:* 40 applied, 35 admitted.

Faculty *Total:* 21, 10% full-time, 100% with terminal degrees. *Student/faculty ratio:* 8:1.

Academics *Calendar:* semesters. *Degrees:* bachelor's, master's, and doctoral. *Special study options:* cooperative education, independent study, part-time degree program.

Computers on Campus 55 computers/terminals are available on campus for general student use. Students can access the following: free student e-mail accounts, online (class) grades, online (class) schedules. Campuswide network is available. Wireless service is available via entire campus.

Student Life *Housing:* college housing not available. *Activities and organizations:* Student Council, Community Services, Gender and Sexual Diversity Organization. *Campus security:* 24-hour emergency response devices, late-night transport/escort service, security cameras.

Standardized Tests *Required:* CEEB or SAT (for admission).

Costs (2013–14) *Tuition:* $5940 full-time, $165 per credit part-time. *Required fees:* $979 full-time, $333 per term part-time. *Payment plan:* deferred payment. *Waivers:* employees or children of employees.

Financial Aid Of all full-time matriculated undergraduates who enrolled in 2012, 54 applied for aid, 54 were judged to have need. 6 Federal Work-Study jobs (averaging $1397). *Average percent of need met:* 48%. *Average financial*

aid package: $5204. *Average need-based loan:* $4890. *Average need-based gift aid:* $2388.

Applying *Options:* early admission, deferred entrance. *Required:* minimum 2.0 GPA, 1 letter of recommendation. *Required for some:* health certificate, Good Conduct Crete, official university transcript. *Application deadlines:* 7/16 (freshmen), 7/17 (transfers). *Notification:* continuous (freshmen), continuous (transfers).

Freshman Application Contact Carlos Albizu University, 151 Tanca Street, San Juan, PR 00901. *Phone:* 787-725-6500 Ext. 1521.

Website: http://www.albizu.edu/.

Colegio Universitario de San Juan

San Juan, Puerto Rico

Freshman Application Contact Colegio Universitario de San Juan, Jose R. Oliver Street, Hato Rey, PR 00918. *Phone:* 787-250-7111 Ext. 2227.

Website: http://www.cunisanjuan.edu/.

Columbia Centro Universitario

Caguas, Puerto Rico

- **Proprietary** comprehensive, founded 1966
- **Urban** 6-acre campus with easy access to San Juan
- **Coed** 1,616 undergraduate students, 41% full-time, 69% women, 31% men
- **Noncompetitive** entrance level, 73% of applicants were admitted

Undergraduates 668 full-time, 948 part-time. *Retention:* 57% of full-time freshmen returned.

Freshmen *Admission:* 740 applied, 539 admitted, 263 enrolled.

Faculty *Total:* 127, 18% full-time, 13% with terminal degrees. *Student/faculty ratio:* 25:1.

Academics *Calendar:* semesters. *Degrees:* certificates, associate, bachelor's, and master's. *Special study options:* accelerated degree program, part-time degree program.

Computers on Campus 136 computers/terminals are available on campus for general student use. Students can access the following: campus intranet, free student e-mail accounts, online (class) grades, online (class) registration, online (class) schedules. Campuswide network is available. Wireless service is available via entire campus.

Student Life *Housing:* college housing not available. *Campus security:* 24-hour patrols. *Student services:* personal/psychological counseling.

Costs (2013–14) *Tuition:* $9435 full-time, $1575 per semester hour part-time. Full-time tuition and fees vary according to class time, degree level, and program. Part-time tuition and fees vary according to class time, degree level, and program. *Required fees:* $262 per credit hour part-time. *Payment plan:* installment. *Waivers:* employees or children of employees.

Financial Aid Of all full-time matriculated undergraduates who enrolled in 2008, 974 applied for aid, 818 were judged to have need. 61 Federal Work-Study jobs (averaging $982). *Average percent of need met:* 11%. *Average financial aid package:* $4035.

Applying *Options:* electronic application. *Application fee:* $50. *Required:* high school transcript. *Required for some:* essay or personal statement, minimum 2.0 GPA, 3 letters of recommendation, interview. *Application deadline:* rolling (freshmen). *Notification:* continuous (freshmen).

Freshman Application Contact Mrs. Xiomara Sanchez, Admission Coordinator, Columbia Centro Universitario, PO Box 8517, Caguas, PR 00726. *Phone:* 787-743-4041 Ext. 239. *Fax:* 787-744-7031. *E-mail:* xsanchez@columbianco.edu.

Website: http://www.columbiaco.edu/.

Columbia Centro Universitario

Yauco, Puerto Rico

- **Proprietary** 4-year, founded 1976
- **Urban** campus
- **Coed** 363 undergraduate students, 50% full-time, 77% women, 23% men
- **Minimally difficult** entrance level

Undergraduates 181 full-time, 182 part-time. Students come from 1 other state; 100% Hispanic/Latino.

Freshmen *Admission:* 85 admitted, 62 enrolled. *Average high school GPA:* 2.5.

Faculty *Total:* 39, 23% full-time, 15% with terminal degrees. *Student/faculty ratio:* 13:1.

Academics *Calendar:* trimesters. *Degrees:* certificates, associate, and bachelor's. *Special study options:* cooperative education, distance learning, independent study, part-time degree program.

Computers on Campus 14 computers/terminals are available on campus for general student use. Students can access the following: computer help desk. Wireless service is available via entire campus.

Student Life *Housing:* college housing not available. *Activities and organizations:* Nursing Group, Librarian Group. *Campus security:* 24-hour patrols. *Student services:* personal/psychological counseling.

Costs (2013–14) *Tuition:* $9435 full-time, $1575 per semester hour part-time. Full-time tuition and fees vary according to course load and program. Part-time tuition and fees vary according to course load and program. *Required fees:* $100 full-time, $262 part-time. *Payment plan:* installment.

Applying *Options:* electronic application. *Application fee:* $50. *Required:* high school transcript, minimum 2.0 GPA. *Required for some:* interview. *Application deadlines:* rolling (freshmen), rolling (transfers). *Notification:* continuous (freshmen), continuous (transfers).

Freshman Application Contact Mrs. Carmen Ivette Pabon MSC, Admissions Coordinator, Columbia Centro Universitario, P.O. Box 3062, Yauco, PR 00698. *Phone:* 787-856-0845 Ext. 118. *Fax:* 787-267-0994. *E-mail:* cipabon@columbiaco.edu.
Website: http://www.columbiaco.edu/.

Conservatorio de Musica
San Juan, Puerto Rico

- **Public** comprehensive
- **Urban** 4-acre campus with easy access to Old San Juan
- **Endowment** $901,073
- **Coed**
- **Moderately difficult** entrance level

Faculty *Student/faculty ratio:* 7:1.

Academics *Degrees:* bachelor's, master's, and postbachelor's certificates.

Student Life *Campus security:* 24-hour patrols.

Costs (2012–13) *Tuition:* commonwealth resident $1920 full-time, $80 per credit part-time; nonresident $1920 full-time, $80 per credit part-time. Full-time tuition and fees vary according to course load and degree level. Part-time tuition and fees vary according to course load and degree level. *Required fees:* $850 full-time, $425 per term part-time. *Room and board:* $10,000; room only: $4600.

Applying *Application fee:* $75. *Required:* high school transcript, minimum 2.0 GPA, instrument audition; ear training test. *Required for some:* essay or personal statement, minimum 2.5 GPA. *Recommended:* interview.

Freshman Application Contact Mrs. Ilsamar Hernandez, Admission Director, Conservatorio de Musica, 951 Ponce de Leon Ave., San Juan, PR 00907-3373. *Phone:* 787-751-0160 Ext. 275. *Fax:* 787-764-3581. *E-mail:* ihernandez@cmpr.gobierno.pr.
Website: http://www.cmpr.edu/.

Conservatory of Music of Puerto Rico
San Juan, Puerto Rico

Freshman Application Contact Conservatory of Music of Puerto Rico, 350 Rafael Lamar St at FDR Ave, San Juan, PR 00918. *Phone:* 787-751-0160 Ext. 275.
Website: http://www.cmpr.edu/.

EDP College of Puerto Rico, Inc.
Hato Rey, Puerto Rico

- **Proprietary** comprehensive, founded 1968
- **Urban** 1-acre campus with easy access to San Juan
- **Coed** 1,141 undergraduate students, 63% full-time, 65% women, 35% men
- **Minimally difficult** entrance level, 66% of applicants were admitted

Undergraduates 724 full-time, 417 part-time. Students come from 5 states and territories; 11% are from out of state; 18% transferred in. *Retention:* 89% of full-time freshmen returned.

Freshmen *Admission:* 211 applied, 139 admitted, 107 enrolled. *Average high school GPA:* 2.78.

Faculty *Total:* 93, 30% full-time, 12% with terminal degrees. *Student/faculty ratio:* 15:1.

Academics *Calendar:* semesters. *Degrees:* associate, bachelor's, master's, and postbachelor's certificates. *Special study options:* academic remediation for entering students, accelerated degree program, adult/continuing education programs, advanced placement credit, cooperative education, distance learning, English as a second language, independent study, internships, part-time degree program, services for LD students, summer session for credit.

Computers on Campus 239 computers/terminals and 4 ports are available on campus for general student use. Students can access the following: campus intranet, computer help desk, free student e-mail accounts, online (class) grades, online (class) registration, online (class) schedules. Campuswide network is available. Wireless service is available via entire campus.

Student Life *Housing:* college housing not available. *Activities and organizations:* Student Council, Graduate Student Association, JCI San Juan, Dance Group. *Campus security:* 24-hour emergency response devices, student patrols, late-night transport/escort service, security and emergency telephones in working hours. *Student services:* personal/psychological counseling.

Standardized Tests *Required:* College Entrance Examination Board (CEEB) Test, Institutional Admission Exam (for admission).

Costs (2013–14) *Tuition:* $5400 full-time, $170 per credit hour part-time. Full-time tuition and fees vary according to course load and program. Part-time tuition and fees vary according to course load and program. *Required fees:* $840 full-time, $170 per credit hour part-time, $420 per credit hour part-time. *Payment plan:* installment. *Waivers:* employees or children of employees.

Financial Aid *Of all full-time matriculated undergraduates who enrolled in 2011, 1,028 applied for aid, 1,028 were judged to have need. 35 Federal Work-Study jobs (averaging $1972). Average percent of need met:* 90%. *Average financial aid package:* $5587. *Average need-based loan:* $3137. *Average need-based gift aid:* $5416. *Average indebtedness upon graduation:* $4256.

Applying *Options:* electronic application, early admission, early decision, early action, deferred entrance. *Application fee:* $15. *Required:* high school transcript, minimum 1.6 GPA, placement test or College Board test, vaccination certificate, social security number. *Required for some:* essay or personal statement, minimum 2.5 GPA, 7 letters of recommendation, interview, placement test or College Board test, vaccination certificate, social security number. *Recommended:* minimum 2.0 GPA. *Application deadlines:* rolling (freshmen), rolling (out-of-state freshmen), rolling (transfers).

Freshman Application Contact Ms. Enid Cartagena, Student Affairs Dean, EDP College of Puerto Rico, Inc., Avenue Ponce de Leon, #560, Hato Rey, PR 00918, Puerto Rico. *Phone:* 787-765-3560 Ext. 272. *Fax:* 787-777-0024. *E-mail:* ecartagena@edpuniversity.edu.
Website: http://www.edpcollege.edu/.

EDP College of Puerto Rico–San Sebastian
San Sebastian, Puerto Rico

- **Proprietary** 4-year, founded 1976
- **Rural** campus
- **Coed**
- **Minimally difficult** entrance level

Faculty *Student/faculty ratio:* 17:1.

Academics *Calendar:* semesters. *Degrees:* associate and bachelor's.

Standardized Tests *Required:* College Board or institutional entrance test (for admission).

Costs (2012–13) *Tuition:* $5400 full-time, $156 per credit hour part-time. Full-time tuition and fees vary according to course load and program. Part-time tuition and fees vary according to course load and program. *Required fees:* $720 full-time, $156 per credit hour part-time, $360 per term part-time.

Financial Aid *Of all full-time matriculated undergraduates who enrolled in 2011, 1,019 applied for aid, 1,019 were judged to have need. 43 Federal Work-Study jobs (averaging $1382). Average percent of need met:* 95. *Average financial aid package:* $6052. *Average need-based loan:* $3607. *Average need-based gift aid:* $5299. *Average indebtedness upon graduation:* $4729.

Applying *Application fee:* $15. *Required:* high school transcript, minimum 2.0 GPA. *Required for some:* minimum 2.5 GPA, interview.

Freshman Application Contact Ms. Pilar Cordero, Student Affairs Dean, EDP College of Puerto Rico–San Sebastian, Avenue Betances #49, San Sebastian, PR 00685. *Phone:* 787-896-2252 Ext. 303. *Fax:* 787-896-0066. *E-mail:* pcordero@edpcollege.edu.
Website: http://www.edpcollege.edu/.

Escuela de Artes Plasticas de Puerto Rico
San Juan, Puerto Rico

- **Commonwealth-supported** 4-year, founded 1966
- **Urban** campus
- **Endowment** $1.3 million
- **Coed**
- **Moderately difficult** entrance level

Faculty *Student/faculty ratio:* 13:1.

Academics *Calendar:* 3 semesters each calendar year; participant in Year Round Pell. *Degree:* bachelor's.

Student Life *Campus security:* 24-hour emergency response devices and patrols, security cameras and institutional police of privacy.

Standardized Tests *Recommended:* SAT (for admission).

Financial Aid *Of all full-time matriculated undergraduates who enrolled in 2007,* 276 applied for aid, 276 were judged to have need. 10 Federal Work-Study jobs (averaging $1850). *Average percent of need met:* 82. *Financial aid deadline:* 5/25.

Applying *Application fee:* $25. *Required:* essay or personal statement, high school transcript, minimum 2.0 GPA, interview, The applicants must approve an evaluation regarding artistic skills through a portfolio or seminar and complete the security seminar. *Recommended:* 1 letter of recommendation.

Freshman Application Contact Mrs. Nitza Meléndez, Officer of Admissions, Escuela de Artes Plasticas de Puerto Rico, PO Box 902112, San Juan, PR 00902-1112. *Phone:* 787-725-8120 Ext. 333. *Fax:* 787-721-3798. *E-mail:* nmelendez@eap.edu.

Website: http://www.eap.edu/.

Inter American University of Puerto Rico, Aguadilla Campus

Aguadilla, Puerto Rico

- **Independent** comprehensive, founded 1957, part of Inter American University of Puerto Rico
- **Small-town** 50-acre campus
- **Endowment** $151.5 million
- **Coed** 4,327 undergraduate students, 83% full-time, 53% women, 47% men
- **Moderately difficult** entrance level, 67% of applicants were admitted

Undergraduates 3,612 full-time, 715 part-time. Students come from 28 states and territories; 2% are from out of state; 99% Hispanic/Latino; 1% Two or more races, non-Hispanic/Latino; 3% transferred in. *Retention:* 55% of full-time freshmen returned.

Freshmen *Admission:* 1,266 applied, 847 admitted, 824 enrolled. *Average high school GPA:* 2.9.

Faculty *Total:* 264, 30% full-time, 100% with terminal degrees. *Student/faculty ratio:* 29:1.

Academics *Calendar:* semesters. *Degrees:* certificates, associate, bachelor's, and master's. *Special study options:* academic remediation for entering students, adult/continuing education programs, advanced placement credit, cooperative education, distance learning, double majors, external degree program, honors programs, independent study, internships, part-time degree program, services for LD students, summer session for credit. *ROTC:* Army (b), Air Force (b).

Computers on Campus 716 computers/terminals are available on campus for general student use. Students can access the following: campus intranet, free student e-mail accounts, online (class) grades, online (class) registration, online (class) schedules. Campuswide network is available. Wireless service is available via entire campus.

Student Life *Housing:* college housing not available. *Activities and organizations:* drama/theater group, student-run newspaper, choral group, Criminal Justice Association, Social Workers Association, Nursing Association, Microbiot Science Association, Hotel and Management Association. *Campus security:* 24-hour emergency response devices and patrols. *Student services:* health clinic, personal/psychological counseling, women's center.

Athletics *Intercollegiate sports:* baseball M(s), basketball M(s)/W(s), cheerleading M(s)/W(s), cross-country running M(s)/W(s), soccer M(s)/W(s), softball M(s)/W(s), table tennis M(s)/W(s), tennis M(s)/W(s), track and field M(s)/W(s), volleyball M(s)/W(s), weight lifting M(s)/W(s). *Intramural sports:* basketball M/W, cheerleading M/W, cross-country running M/W, soccer M/W, softball M/W, swimming and diving M/W, table tennis M/W, tennis M/W, track and field M/W, volleyball M/W, weight lifting M/W.

Standardized Tests *Required:* SAT or ACT (for admission), PAA (for admission).

Costs (2013–14) *Tuition:* $5100 full-time. *Required fees:* $514 full-time.

Applying *Options:* electronic application. *Required:* high school transcript, minimum 2.0 GPA. *Application deadlines:* rolling (freshmen), rolling (transfers).

Freshman Application Contact Mrs. Doris Perez, Admissions Director, Inter American University of Puerto Rico, Aguadilla Campus, PO Box 20,000, Road 459 Intersection 463, Aguadilla, PR 00605. *Phone:* 787-891-0925 Ext. 2101. *Fax:* 787-882-3020.

Website: http://www.aguadilla.inter.edu/.

Inter American University of Puerto Rico, Arecibo Campus

Arecibo, Puerto Rico

Freshman Application Contact Ms. Provi Montalvo, Admission Director, Inter American University of Puerto Rico, Arecibo Campus, PO Box 4050, Arecibo, PR 00614-4050. *Phone:* 787-878-5475. *Fax:* 787-880-1624. *E-mail:* pmontalvo@arecibo.inter.edu.

Website: http://www.arecibo.inter.edu/.

Inter American University of Puerto Rico, Barranquitas Campus

Barranquitas, Puerto Rico

Freshman Application Contact Mrs. Aramilda Cartagena, Dean of Students, Inter American University of Puerto Rico, Barranquitas Campus, PO Box 517, Barranquitas, PR 00794. *Phone:* 787-857-3600 Ext. 2009. *Fax:* 787-857-2125. *E-mail:* acartagena@br.inter.edu.

Website: http://www.br.inter.edu/.

Inter American University of Puerto Rico, Bayamón Campus

Bayamón, Puerto Rico

- **Independent** comprehensive, founded 1912, part of Inter American University of Puerto Rico
- **Urban** 51-acre campus with easy access to San Juan
- **Endowment** $151.5 million
- **Coed** 4,802 undergraduate students, 86% full-time, 45% women, 55% men
- 36% of applicants were admitted

Undergraduates 4,129 full-time, 653 part-time. 94% Hispanic/Latino; 6% Two or more races, non-Hispanic/Latino; 3% transferred in. *Retention:* 68% of full-time freshmen returned.

Freshmen *Admission:* 2,463 applied, 882 admitted, 943 enrolled. *Average high school GPA:* 3.

Faculty *Total:* 329, 31% full-time, 23% with terminal degrees. *Student/faculty ratio:* 24:1.

Academics *Calendar:* semesters. *Degrees:* certificates, associate, bachelor's, and master's. *Special study options:* accelerated degree program, adult/continuing education programs, advanced placement credit, cooperative education, distance learning, external degree program, honors programs, independent study, internships, part-time degree program, services for LD students, summer session for credit. *ROTC:* Army (c).

Computers on Campus 610 computers/terminals are available on campus for general student use. Students can access the following: computer help desk, free student e-mail accounts, online (class) grades, online (class) registration. Campuswide network is available.

Student Life *Housing options:* Campus housing is university owned. *Activities and organizations:* student-run newspaper, choral group, Asociacion de Estudiantes de Administracion de Empresas, Estudiantes Unidos por la Ciencia, Asociacion Estudiantes de Aviacion, Consejo de Estudiante, Asociacion Estudiantes de Ingenieria. *Campus security:* 24-hour patrols. *Student services:* health clinic, personal/psychological counseling.

Athletics *Intercollegiate sports:* baseball M(s), basketball M(s)/W(s), cross-country running M(s)/W(s), softball M(s)/W(s), swimming and diving M(s)/W(s), table tennis M(s)/W(s), track and field M(s)/W(s), volleyball M(s)/W(s), weight lifting M(s). *Intramural sports:* basketball M/W, cross-country running M/W, softball M/W, swimming and diving M/W, table tennis M/W, tennis M/W, track and field M/W, volleyball M/W, weight lifting M.

Standardized Tests *Required:* CEEB (for admission). *Required for some:* SAT (for admission).

Costs (2013–14) *Tuition:* $5100 full-time, $260 per semester hour part-time. Full-time tuition and fees vary according to course load and program. Part-time tuition and fees vary according to course load and program. *Required fees:* $520 full-time. *Payment plan:* deferred payment.

Financial Aid *Of all full-time matriculated undergraduates who enrolled in 2011,* 2,858 applied for aid, 2,784 were judged to have need, 7 had their need fully met. *Average percent of need met:* 7%. *Average financial aid package:* $935. *Average need-based loan:* $1446. *Average need-based gift aid:* $345.

Applying *Options:* electronic application. *Required:* high school transcript, minimum 2.0 GPA, 2.5 GPA for engineering programs. *Application deadline:* 7/30 (freshmen). *Notification:* continuous (freshmen), continuous (transfers).

Freshman Application Contact Inter American University of Puerto Rico, Bayamón Campus, 500 Road 830, Bayamón, PR 00957. *Phone:* 787-279-1912 Ext. 2017.
Website: http://www.bc.inter.edu/.

Inter American University of Puerto Rico, Fajardo Campus
Fajardo, Puerto Rico

- **Independent** 4-year, founded 1965, part of Inter American University of Puerto Rico
- **Small-town** 11-acre campus with easy access to San Juan
- **Coed** 2,170 undergraduate students, 75% full-time, 74% women, 26% men
- **Moderately difficult** entrance level, 51% of applicants were admitted

Undergraduates 1,626 full-time, 544 part-time. Students come from 3 states and territories. *Retention:* 67% of full-time freshmen returned.
Freshmen *Admission:* 909 applied, 463 admitted, 467 enrolled. *Average high school GPA:* 2.
Faculty *Total:* 120, 33% full-time, 10% with terminal degrees. *Student/faculty ratio:* 11:1.
Academics *Calendar:* semesters. *Degrees:* certificates, associate, bachelor's, and master's. *Special study options:* academic remediation for entering students, adult/continuing education programs, advanced placement credit, cooperative education, distance learning, English as a second language, external degree program, honors programs, independent study, internships, off-campus study, part-time degree program, services for LD students, summer session for credit. *ROTC:* Army (c).
Computers on Campus 280 computers/terminals are available on campus for general student use. Students can access the following: free student e-mail accounts, online (class) grades, online (class) registration, online (class) schedules. Campuswide network is available. Wireless service is available via entire campus.
Student Life *Housing:* college housing not available. *Activities and organizations:* drama/theater group, Future Teachers Association, Criminal Justice Student Association, Honor Program Association, Computer Science Association, Social Work Association. *Campus security:* 24-hour patrols. *Student services:* personal/psychological counseling.
Athletics *Intercollegiate sports:* baseball M, basketball M(s)/W, bowling M, cheerleading W, softball W, table tennis M/W, tennis M/W, track and field M(s)/W(s), volleyball M/W.
Standardized Tests *Required:* College Board (for admission).
Costs (2013–14) *Tuition:* $4080 full-time, $170 per credit part-time. Full-time tuition and fees vary according to degree level. Part-time tuition and fees vary according to degree level. *Required fees:* $258 full-time. *Payment plans:* installment, deferred payment. *Waivers:* adult students and employees or children of employees.
Applying *Options:* electronic application, early admission, deferred entrance. *Required:* high school transcript. *Required for some:* interview. *Application deadlines:* 5/15 (freshmen), rolling (transfers).
Freshman Application Contact Ms. Ghisita M. Garcia, Administrative Assistant II, Inter American University of Puerto Rico, Fajardo Campus, Call Box 70003, Fajardo, PR 00738-7003. *Phone:* 787-863-2390 Ext. 2210. *Fax:* 787-860-3470. *E-mail:* ghisita.garcia@fajardo.inter.edu. *Website:* http://www.fajardo.inter.edu/.

Inter American University of Puerto Rico, Guayama Campus
Guayama, Puerto Rico

Freshman Application Contact Inter American University of Puerto Rico, Guayama Campus, Call Box 10004, Guayama, PR 00785. *Phone:* 787-864-2222 Ext. 220.
Website: http://www.guayama.inter.edu/.

Inter American University of Puerto Rico, Metropolitan Campus
San Juan, Puerto Rico

Freshman Application Contact Ms. Ida G. Betancourt, Official Admission, Inter American University of Puerto Rico, Metropolitan Campus, PO Box 191293, San Juan, PR 00919-1293. *Phone:* 787-250-1912 Ext. 2188. *Fax:* 787-250-1025. *E-mail:* jbetancourt@metro.inter.edu.
Website: http://metro.inter.edu/.

Inter American University of Puerto Rico, Ponce Campus
Mercedita, Puerto Rico

- **Independent** comprehensive, founded 1962, part of Inter American University of Puerto Rico
- **Urban** 50-acre campus with easy access to San Juan
- **Endowment** $151.5 million
- **Coed** 5,575 undergraduate students, 84% full-time, 59% women, 41% men
- **Moderately difficult** entrance level, 40% of applicants were admitted

Undergraduates 4,697 full-time, 878 part-time. Students come from 39 states and territories; 3 other countries; 9% are from out of state; 98% Hispanic/Latino; 0.1% American Indian or Alaska Native, non-Hispanic/Latino; 2% Two or more races, non-Hispanic/Latino; 2% transferred in. *Retention:* 71% of full-time freshmen returned.
Freshmen *Admission:* 2,464 applied, 990 admitted, 950 enrolled. *Average high school GPA:* 2.93.
Faculty *Total:* 294, 33% full-time, 23% with terminal degrees. *Student/faculty ratio:* 31:1.
Academics *Calendar:* semesters. *Degrees:* associate, bachelor's, and master's. *Special study options:* academic remediation for entering students, adult/continuing education programs, cooperative education, distance learning, English as a second language, honors programs, independent study, internships, off-campus study, part-time degree program, services for LD students, study abroad, summer session for credit.
Computers on Campus 467 computers/terminals and 517 ports are available on campus for general student use. Students can access the following: free student e-mail accounts, online (class) grades, online (class) registration. Campuswide network is available. 100% of college-owned or -operated housing units are wired for high-speed Internet access. Wireless service is available via entire campus.
Student Life *Housing:* college housing not available. *Activities and organizations:* drama/theater group, choral group, marching band, Association of Future Teachers of Special Education, Accounting Students Association, Hotel Management Association, Office Systems Administration Association, Criminal Justice Association. *Campus security:* 24-hour emergency response devices and patrols. *Student services:* health clinic, personal/psychological counseling.
Athletics *Intercollegiate sports:* basketball M(s)/W(s), cross-country running M(s)/W(s), soccer M(s)/W(s), softball M(s)/W(s), table tennis M(s)/W(s), track and field M(s)/W(s), volleyball M(s)/W(s), weight lifting M(s), wrestling M(s)/W(s). *Intramural sports:* basketball M/W, cross-country running M/W, soccer M/W, softball M/W, table tennis M/W, tennis M/W, track and field M/W, volleyball M/W, weight lifting M/W.
Standardized Tests *Required:* CEEB (for admission). *Required for some:* SAT (for admission).
Costs (2013–14) *Tuition:* $4080 full-time, $170 per credit part-time. Full-time tuition and fees vary according to course load and program. Part-time tuition and fees vary according to course load and program. *Required fees:* $426 per semester hour part-time. *Payment plan:* deferred payment.
Applying *Options:* deferred entrance. *Required:* high school transcript, minimum 2.0 GPA. *Application deadlines:* 5/15 (freshmen), 5/15 (transfers).
Freshman Application Contact Mr. Franco Diaz, Admissions Officer, Inter American University of Puerto Rico, Ponce Campus, 104 Turpo Industrial Park, Road #1, Mercedita, PR 00715-1602. *Phone:* 787-284-1912 Ext. 2025. *Fax:* 787-841-0103. *E-mail:* fidiaz@ponce.inter.edu.
Website: http://www.ponce.inter.edu/.

Inter American University of Puerto Rico, San Germán Campus
San Germán, Puerto Rico

- **Independent** university, founded 1912, part of Inter American University of Puerto Rico
- **Small-town** 260-acre campus with easy access to Ponce, Aguadilla, Mayaguez
- **Endowment** $151.5 million
- **Coed** 4,572 undergraduate students, 88% full-time, 53% women, 47% men
- **Moderately difficult** entrance level, 84% of applicants were admitted

Undergraduates 4,044 full-time, 528 part-time. Students come from 11 states and territories; 3 other countries; 0.4% are from out of state; 99% Hispanic/Latino; 1% Two or more races, non-Hispanic/Latino; 2% transferred in; 10% live on campus. *Retention:* 70% of full-time freshmen returned.

Freshmen *Admission:* 1,268 applied, 1,060 admitted, 870 enrolled. *Average high school GPA:* 2.98.

Faculty *Total:* 316, 38% full-time, 36% with terminal degrees. *Student/faculty ratio:* 26:1.

Academics *Calendar:* semesters. *Degrees:* certificates, associate, bachelor's, master's, doctoral, and postbachelor's certificates. *Special study options:* academic remediation for entering students, accelerated degree program, adult/continuing education programs, advanced placement credit, cooperative education, distance learning, double majors, English as a second language, external degree program, honors programs, independent study, internships, off-campus study, part-time degree program, services for LD students, summer session for credit. *ROTC:* Army (c), Navy (c), Air Force (c).

Computers on Campus 930 computers/terminals are available on campus for general student use. Students can access the following: computer help desk, free student e-mail accounts, online (class) grades, online (class) registration, online (class) schedules. Campuswide network is available. Wireless service is available via computer centers, computer labs, dorm rooms, learning centers, libraries, student centers.

Student Life *Housing options:* men-only, women-only. Campus housing is university owned. *Activities and organizations:* drama/theater group, student-run newspaper, choral group, Asociacion de Pre-Medica-Caduceus, Futuros Maestros, Asociacion de Estudiantes De Psicologia (AEPSI), Asociacion de Estudiantes de Contabilidad, Asociacion de Estudiantes del Programa de Honor. *Campus security:* 24-hour emergency response devices and patrols. *Student services:* personal/psychological counseling.

Athletics *Intercollegiate sports:* baseball M(s), basketball M(s)/W(s), cross-country running M(s)/W(s), soccer M(s), softball M/W, swimming and diving M/W, table tennis M(s)/W(s), tennis M(s)/W(s), track and field M(s)/W(s), volleyball M(s)/W(s), weight lifting M(s). *Intramural sports:* badminton M/W, basketball M/W, cross-country running M/W, softball M/W, table tennis M/W, tennis M/W, track and field M/W, volleyball M/W.

Standardized Tests *Required:* CEEB (for admission). *Required for some:* SAT or ACT (for admission).

Costs (2013–14) *Comprehensive fee:* $8320 includes full-time tuition ($5100), mandatory fees ($520), and room and board ($2700). Part-time tuition: $170 per credit. *Required fees:* $170 per credit part-time, $213 per term part-time. *College room only:* $1200. Room and board charges vary according to board plan and housing facility. *Payment plan:* installment. *Waivers:* employees or children of employees.

Financial Aid Of all full-time matriculated undergraduates who enrolled in 2009, 2,797 applied for aid, 2,755 were judged to have need, 4 had their need fully met. *Average percent of need met:* 12%. *Average financial aid package:* $2009. *Average need-based loan:* $3080. *Average need-based gift aid:* $642.

Applying *Options:* electronic application, early admission. *Required:* high school transcript, medical history, vaccination. *Required for some:* 1 letter of recommendation, interview. *Recommended:* essay or personal statement, minimum 2.0 GPA. *Application deadlines:* 5/15 (freshmen), 5/15 (transfers). *Notification:* continuous (freshmen), continuous (transfers).

Freshman Application Contact Prof. Mildred Camacho, Director of Admissions, Inter American University of Puerto Rico, San Germán Campus, PO Box 5100, San German, PR 00683-5008. *Phone:* 787-264-1912 Ext. 7283. *Fax:* 787-892-7020. *E-mail:* milcama@sg.inter.edu. *Website:* http://www.sg.inter.edu/.

National University College
Bayamón, Puerto Rico

Freshman Application Contact Admissions, National University College, PO Box 2036, National College Plaza Building, Bayamón, PR 00960. *Phone:* 787-780-5134. *Toll-free phone:* 800-780-5134. *Fax:* 787-779-4909. *E-mail:* infobayamon@nuc.edu. *Website:* http://www.nuc.edu/.

National University College
Ponce, Puerto Rico

Admissions Office Contact National University College, PO Box 801243, Ponce, PR 00716. *Website:* http://www.nuc.edu/.

National University College
Rio Grande, Puerto Rico

Admissions Office Contact National University College, Carretera #3 Km. 22.1, Bo. Ci?ga Baja, Rio Grande, PR 00745. *Toll-free phone:* 800-981-0812. *Website:* http://www.nuc.edu/.

Polytechnic University of Puerto Rico
Hato Rey, Puerto Rico

- **Independent** comprehensive, founded 1966
- **Urban** 10-acre campus with easy access to San Juan
- **Endowment** $10.7 million
- **Coed, primarily men** 4,031 undergraduate students, 48% full-time, 21% women, 79% men
- **Minimally difficult** entrance level, 95% of applicants were admitted

Undergraduates 1,918 full-time, 2,113 part-time. Students come from 2 states and territories; 12 other countries; 100% Hispanic/Latino. *Retention:* 73% of full-time freshmen returned.

Freshmen *Admission:* 737 applied, 697 admitted, 408 enrolled. *Average high school GPA:* 2.45.

Faculty *Total:* 248, 60% full-time, 30% with terminal degrees. *Student/faculty ratio:* 19:1.

Academics *Calendar:* trimesters. *Degrees:* bachelor's and master's. *Special study options:* academic remediation for entering students, distance learning, English as a second language, independent study, part-time degree program, student-designed majors, summer session for credit. *ROTC:* Army (c).

Computers on Campus 375 computers/terminals and 500 ports are available on campus for general student use. Students can access the following: campus intranet, free student e-mail accounts, online (class) grades, online (class) registration, online (class) schedules. Campuswide network is available. Wireless service is available via entire campus.

Student Life *Housing:* college housing not available. *Activities and organizations:* choral group, ASCE (American Society of Civil Engineering), PRWEA (Puerto Rico Water and Environment Association), ACI (American Concrete Institute), SAE PUPR AERO DESIGN TEAM, SHPE (Society of Hispanic Professional Engineers). *Campus security:* 24-hour patrols. *Student services:* personal/psychological counseling.

Athletics *Intercollegiate sports:* basketball M(s), cross-country running M(s)/W(s), soccer M, table tennis M(s), tennis M(s)/W(s), track and field M(s)/W(s), volleyball M(s)/W(s), wrestling M(s). *Intramural sports:* basketball M.

Standardized Tests *Required for some:* SAT (for admission).

Costs (2013–14) *Tuition:* $6768 full-time, $188 per credit part-time. Full-time tuition and fees vary according to course level, course load, degree level, and program. Part-time tuition and fees vary according to course level, course load, degree level, and program. *Required fees:* $780 full-time, $260 per term part-time. *Payment plan:* deferred payment. *Waivers:* employees or children of employees.

Financial Aid Of all full-time matriculated undergraduates who enrolled in 2008, 2,749 applied for aid, 2,679 were judged to have need, 25 had their need fully met. 121 Federal Work-Study jobs (averaging $1733). *Average percent of need met:* 63%. *Average financial aid package:* $5350. *Average need-based loan:* $4550. *Average need-based gift aid:* $4454. *Financial aid deadline:* 5/15.

Applying *Options:* electronic application, early admission, deferred entrance. *Application fee:* $30. *Required:* high school transcript. *Application deadline:* 8/15 (freshmen).

Freshman Application Contact Ms. Teresa Cardona, Director of Admissions, Polytechnic University of Puerto Rico, PO Box 192017, San Juan, PR 00919-2017. *Phone:* 787-754-8000 Ext. 240. *Fax:* 787-764-8712. *E-mail:* tcardona@pupr.edu. *Website:* http://www.pupr.edu/.

Pontifical Catholic University of Puerto Rico
Ponce, Puerto Rico

Freshman Application Contact Sra. Ana O. Bonilla, Director of Admissions, Pontifical Catholic University of Puerto Rico, 2250 Avenida Las Americas Avenue, Suite 584, Ponce, PR 00717-9777. *Phone:* 787-841-2000 Ext. 1004. *Toll-free phone:* 800-961-7696. *Fax:* 787-840-4295. *E-mail:* admissions@email.pucpr.edu. *Website:* http://www.pucpr.edu/.

Universidad Adventista de las Antillas
Mayagüez, Puerto Rico

- **Independent Seventh-day Adventist** comprehensive, founded 1957
- **Rural** 284-acre campus
- **Endowment** $134,104
- **Coed** 1,241 undergraduate students, 92% full-time, 59% women, 41% men
- **Minimally difficult** entrance level, 87% of applicants were admitted

Undergraduates 1,142 full-time, 99 part-time. Students come from 54 states and territories; 27 other countries; 13% are from out of state; 2% Black or African American, non-Hispanic/Latino; 95% Hispanic/Latino; 0.2% Asian, non-Hispanic/Latino; 2% international; 8% transferred in; 5% live on campus. *Retention:* 68% of full-time freshmen returned.

Freshmen *Admission:* 630 applied, 546 admitted, 238 enrolled.

Faculty *Total:* 95, 46% full-time, 22% with terminal degrees. *Student/faculty ratio:* 18:1.

Academics *Calendar:* semesters. *Degrees:* associate, bachelor's, and master's. *Special study options:* academic remediation for entering students, advanced placement credit, cooperative education, double majors, English as a second language, internships, part-time degree program, services for LD students, summer session for credit.

Computers on Campus 50 computers/terminals are available on campus for general student use. Students can access the following: campus intranet, computer help desk, free student e-mail accounts, online (class) grades, online (class) registration, online (class) schedules. Campuswide network is available. Wireless service is available via classrooms, computer centers, computer labs, dorm rooms, libraries.

Student Life *Housing:* on-campus residence required for freshman year. *Options:* men-only, women-only. Campus housing is university owned. Freshman applicants given priority for college housing. *Activities and organizations:* student-run newspaper, choral group, Score Group, Gymnastic Club, Student Council, Green Movement, 3AM. *Campus security:* 24-hour emergency response devices and patrols, student patrols, controlled dormitory access. *Student services:* health clinic, personal/psychological counseling.

Athletics *Intramural sports:* basketball M/W, soccer M, volleyball M/W.

Standardized Tests *Recommended:* SAT or ACT (for admission), CEEB.

Costs (2013–14) *One-time required fee:* $20. *Comprehensive fee:* $8450 includes full-time tuition ($4950), mandatory fees ($600), and room and board ($2900). Full-time tuition and fees vary according to course load and program. Part-time tuition: $165 per credit hour. Part-time tuition and fees vary according to course load and program. *Required fees:* $235 per term part-time. *College room only:* $1100. Room and board charges vary according to board plan and housing facility. *Payment plan:* installment. *Waivers:* employees or children of employees.

Financial Aid Of all full-time matriculated undergraduates who enrolled in 2011, 1,167 applied for aid, 969 were judged to have need. 164 Federal Work-Study jobs (averaging $826). 236 state and other part-time jobs (averaging $970). *Average percent of need met:* 80%. *Average financial aid package:* $2709. *Average need-based loan:* $2500. *Average need-based gift aid:* $2000. *Average indebtedness upon graduation:* $2355.

Applying *Options:* electronic application, early admission. *Application fee:* $20. *Required:* high school transcript, minimum 2.0 GPA, letters of recommendation. *Required for some:* essay or personal statement, interview. *Application deadlines:* 7/15 (freshmen), 7/15 (transfers).

Freshman Application Contact Mrs. Yolanda Ferrer, Director of Admissions, Universidad Adventista de las Antillas, Oficina de Admisiones, PO Box 118, Mayaguez, PR 00681-0118. *Phone:* 787-834-9595 Ext. 2208. *Fax:* 787-834-9597. *E-mail:* admissions@uaa.edu.
Website: http://www.uaa.edu/.

Universidad Central del Caribe

Bayamón, Puerto Rico

Director of Admissions Admissions Department, Universidad Central del Caribe, PO Box 60-327, Bayamón, PR 00960-6032. *Phone:* 787-740-1611.
Website: http://www.uccaribe.edu/.

Universidad del Este

Carolina, Puerto Rico

Freshman Application Contact Universidad del Este, PO Box 2010, Carolina, PR 00984. *Phone:* 787-257-7373 Ext. 3401.
Website: http://www.suagm.edu/une/.

Universidad del Turabo

Gurabo, Puerto Rico

- **Independent** university, founded 1972, part of Ana G. Méndez University System
- **Urban** 140-acre campus with easy access to San Juan
- **Coed**
- **Minimally difficult** entrance level

Faculty *Student/faculty ratio:* 38:1.

Academics *Calendar:* semesters. *Degrees:* certificates, associate, bachelor's, master's, doctoral, and postbachelor's certificates.

Student Life *Campus security:* 24-hour patrols.

Standardized Tests *Recommended:* SAT (for admission).

Costs (2012–13) *Comprehensive fee:* $26,574 includes full-time tuition ($19,512) and room and board ($7062). Full-time tuition and fees vary according to course level, course load, and program.

Financial Aid *Of all full-time matriculated undergraduates who enrolled in 2012,* 10,000 applied for aid, 10,000 were judged to have need. *Financial aid deadline:* 6/30.

Applying *Options:* electronic application. *Application fee:* $15. *Required:* high school transcript.

Freshman Application Contact Universidad del Turabo, PO Box 3030, Gurabo, PR 00778-3030. *Phone:* 787-743-7979 Ext. 4453.
Website: http://www.suagm.edu/ut/.

Universidad Metropolitana

San Juan, Puerto Rico

Freshman Application Contact Mr. Julio Rodriguez Soiza, Director of Admissions, Universidad Metropolitana, Box 21150, San Juan, PR 00928-1150. *Phone:* 787-766-1717 Ext. 6587. *Toll-free phone:* 800-747-8362. *Fax:* 787-751-0992. *E-mail:* um_frivera@suagm1.suagm.edu.
Website: http://www.suagm.edu/umet/.

Universidad Pentecostal Mizpa

San Juan, Puerto Rico

Director of Admissions Omar Alicea, Recruitment, Universidad Pentecostal Mizpa, Bo Caimito Road 199, Apartado 20966, San Juan, PR 00928-0966. *Phone:* 787-720-4476. *Fax:* 787-720-2012.
Website: http://www.mizpa.edu/.

Universidad Teológica del Caribe

St. Just, Puerto Rico

- **Independent Pentecostal** 4-year, founded 1956
- **Suburban** 4-acre campus with easy access to San Juan
- **Endowment** $1.0 million
- **Coed** 172 undergraduate students, 56% full-time, 36% women, 64% men

Undergraduates 96 full-time, 76 part-time. Students come from 1 other state; 5 other countries; 1% are from out of state; 100% Hispanic/Latino; 9% transferred in. *Retention:* 73% of full-time freshmen returned.

Freshmen *Admission:* 22 admitted, 7 enrolled.

Faculty *Total:* 24, 29% full-time, 25% with terminal degrees. *Student/faculty ratio:* 7:1.

Academics *Calendar:* semesters. *Degree:* certificates, diplomas, and bachelor's. *Special study options:* honors programs, independent study, internships, off-campus study, part-time degree program, services for LD students, summer session for credit.

Computers on Campus 8 computers/terminals and 8 ports are available on campus for general student use. Students can access the following: free student e-mail accounts, online (class) grades, online (class) registration, online (class) schedules. 90% of college-owned or -operated housing units are wired for high-speed Internet access. Wireless service is available via classrooms, computer labs, dorm rooms, libraries, student centers.

Student Life *Housing options:* coed. Campus housing is university owned. *Activities and organizations:* Student Council, Missionary Evangelistic Association, Ministerial Association, FESI. *Campus security:* Private Security Personnel during Special Time. *Student services:* personal/psychological counseling.

Costs (2013–14) *One-time required fee:* $13. *Comprehensive fee:* $6848 includes full-time tuition ($3784), mandatory fees ($664), and room and board ($2400). Full-time tuition and fees vary according to course load. Part-time tuition: $18 per credit. Part-time tuition and fees vary according to course load. *Required fees:* $130 per credit part-time, $3004 per term part-time. *College room only:* $1200. Room and board charges vary according to board plan. *Payment plan:* deferred payment. *Waivers:* employees or children of employees.

Financial Aid Of all full-time matriculated undergraduates who enrolled in 2012, 164 applied for aid, 164 were judged to have need. *Financial aid deadline:* 6/30.

Applying *Options:* early admission. *Application fee:* $25. *Required:* 3 letters of recommendation, interview, Medical Certificate, Certificate of Immunization, 1 photo 2x2 and Bible Content Exam. *Required for some:* high school transcript.

Freshman Application Contact Brenellys Flores, Recruitment Officer, Universidad Teológica del Caribe, PO Box 901, Saint Just, PR 00978-901. *Phone:* 787-761-0640 Ext. 246. *Fax:* 787-748-9220. *E-mail:* promocion@utcpr.edu.
Website: http://www.utcpr.edu/.

University of Phoenix–Puerto Rico Campus

Guaynabo, Puerto Rico

Freshman Application Contact Marc Booker, Sr. Director, Office of Admissions and Evaluation, University of Phoenix–Puerto Rico Campus, 4035 South Riverpoint Parkway, Mail Stop CF-L101, Phoenix, AZ 85040. *Phone:* 602-557-4609. *Toll-free phone:* 866-766-0766. *Fax:* 480-643-1156. *Website:* http://www.phoenix.edu/.

University of Puerto Rico, Aguadilla University College

Aguadilla, Puerto Rico

Director of Admissions Ms. Melba Serrano Lugo, Admissions Officer, University of Puerto Rico, Aguadilla University College, PO Box 6150, Aguadilla, PR 00604. *Phone:* 787-890-2681 Ext. 280. *Website:* http://www.uprag.edu/.

University of Puerto Rico at Arecibo

Arecibo, Puerto Rico

Freshman Application Contact University of Puerto Rico at Arecibo, PO Box 4010, Arecibo, PR 00613. *Phone:* 787-878-2830 Ext. 4101. *Website:* http://www.upra.edu/.

University of Puerto Rico at Bayamón

Bayamón, Puerto Rico

- **Commonwealth-supported** 4-year, founded 1971, part of University of Puerto Rico System
- **Urban** 78-acre campus with easy access to San Juan
- **Coed** 5,051 undergraduate students, 87% full-time, 51% women, 49% men
- **Very difficult** entrance level, 28% of applicants were admitted

Undergraduates 4,406 full-time, 645 part-time. 1% are from out of state; 100% Hispanic/Latino; 11% transferred in. *Retention:* 82% of full-time freshmen returned.
Freshmen *Admission:* 5,147 applied, 1,433 admitted, 1,288 enrolled. *Average high school GPA:* 3.55.
Faculty *Total:* 261, 75% full-time, 43% with terminal degrees. *Student/faculty ratio:* 21:1.
Academics *Calendar:* semesters. *Degrees:* associate and bachelor's. *Special study options:* academic remediation for entering students, adult/continuing education programs, advanced placement credit, cooperative education, honors programs, independent study, internships, part-time degree program, services for LD students, summer session for credit. *ROTC:* Army (b), Air Force (c).
Computers on Campus 760 computers/terminals are available on campus for general student use. Students can access the following: campus intranet, free student e-mail accounts, online (class) grades, online (class) registration, online (class) schedules. Campuswide network is available. Wireless service is available via entire campus.
Student Life *Activities and organizations:* drama/theater group, choral group, American Marketing Association, Collegiate International Secretaries, Electronic Association, Materials Management Association, Society for Human Resources Management. *Campus security:* 24-hour patrols. *Student services:* health clinic, personal/psychological counseling.
Athletics Member NCAA. *Intercollegiate sports:* baseball M(s), basketball M(s)/W(s), cheerleading M(s)/W(s), cross-country running M(s)/W(s), softball M(s)/W(s), table tennis M(s)/W(s), tennis M(s)/W(s), track and field M(s)/W(s), volleyball M(s)/W(s), weight lifting M(s)/W(s), wrestling M(s). *Intramural sports:* table tennis M/W, volleyball M/W.
Standardized Tests *Required:* College Board (for admission).
Costs (2013–14) *Tuition:* commonwealth resident $1870 full-time, $55 per credit part-time; nonresident $3910 full-time, $115 per credit part-time. Full-time tuition and fees vary according to class time, course load, program, and student level. Part-time tuition and fees vary according to class time, course load, program, and student level. No tuition increase for student's term of enrollment. *Required fees:* $342 full-time. *Payment plan:* deferred payment. *Waivers:* employees or children of employees.
Financial Aid Of all full-time matriculated undergraduates who enrolled in 2011, 292 Federal Work-Study jobs (averaging $891).
Applying *Options:* electronic application. *Application fee:* $25. *Required:* high school transcript. *Application deadlines:* 12/15 (freshmen), 2/15 (transfers). *Notification:* 5/1 (freshmen), continuous until 7/1 (transfers).

Freshman Application Contact Ms. Carmen I. Montes, Admissions Director, University of Puerto Rico at Bayamón, OPEI Office, Street 174 #170 Minillas Industrial Park, Bayamon, PR 00959. *Phone:* 787-993-8952 Ext. 4015. *Fax:* 787-993-8929. *E-mail:* carmen.montes@upr.edu. *Website:* http://www.uprb.edu/.

University of Puerto Rico at Carolina

Carolina, Puerto Rico

Director of Admissions Ms. Celia Mendez, Admissions Officer, University of Puerto Rico at Carolina, PO Box 4800, Carolina, PR 00984-4800. *Phone:* 787-757-1485. *Website:* http://uprc.edu/.

University of Puerto Rico at Humacao

Humacao, Puerto Rico

- **Commonwealth-supported** 4-year, founded 1962, part of University of Puerto Rico System
- **Suburban** 62-acre campus with easy access to San Juan
- **Coed**
- **Moderately difficult** entrance level

Faculty *Student/faculty ratio:* 16:1.
Academics *Calendar:* semesters. *Degrees:* associate and bachelor's.
Student Life *Campus security:* 24-hour patrols, 24-hour gate security.
Standardized Tests *Required:* Pruebas de Evaluacion y Admision Universitaria (PEAU) (for admission). *Required for some:* SAT or ACT (for admission), SAT Subject Tests (for admission).
Costs (2012–13) *Tuition:* commonwealth resident $1870 full-time, $55 per credit hour part-time; nonresident $3892 full-time, $114 per credit hour part-time. Full-time tuition and fees vary according to class time, course load, and student level. Part-time tuition and fees vary according to class time, course load, and student level. No tuition increase for student's term of enrollment. *Required fees:* $1142 full-time. *Room and board:* $8280; room only: $3000.
Financial Aid *Of all full-time matriculated undergraduates who enrolled in 2001,* 3,515 applied for aid, 2,883 were judged to have need, 7 had their need fully met. 278 Federal Work-Study jobs (averaging $1318). *Average percent of need met:* 50. *Average financial aid package:* $3929. *Average need-based loan:* $3295. *Average need-based gift aid:* $3664. *Average indebtedness upon graduation:* $2749. *Financial aid deadline:* 6/30.
Applying *Options:* deferred entrance. *Application fee:* $20. *Required:* high school transcript. *Required for some:* interview.
Freshman Application Contact Mrs. Elizabeth Gerena, Director of Admissions, University of Puerto Rico at Humacao, Call Box 860, Humacao, PR 00792. *Phone:* 787-850-9301. *Fax:* 787-850-9428. *E-mail:* elizabeth.gerena@upr.edu. *Website:* http://www.uprh.edu/.

University of Puerto Rico at Ponce

Ponce, Puerto Rico

- **Commonwealth-supported** 4-year, founded 1970, part of University of Puerto Rico System
- **Urban** 86-acre campus with easy access to San Juan
- **Coed** 3,089 undergraduate students, 94% full-time, 58% women, 42% men
- **Moderately difficult** entrance level, 82% of applicants were admitted

Undergraduates 2,900 full-time, 189 part-time. Students come from 1 other state; 100% Hispanic/Latino; 12% transferred in. *Retention:* 81% of full-time freshmen returned.
Freshmen *Admission:* 1,205 applied, 991 admitted, 768 enrolled. *Average high school GPA:* 3.64.
Faculty *Total:* 193, 74% full-time, 27% with terminal degrees. *Student/faculty ratio:* 16:1.
Academics *Calendar:* semesters. *Degrees:* associate and bachelor's. *Special study options:* academic remediation for entering students, accelerated degree program, advanced placement credit, English as a second language, freshman honors college, honors programs, internships, part-time degree program, summer session for credit. *ROTC:* Army (b).
Computers on Campus 81 computers/terminals and 132 ports are available on campus for general student use. Students can access the following: campus intranet, free student e-mail accounts, online (class) registration, online (class) schedules. Campuswide network is available. Wireless service is available via computer centers, computer labs, learning centers, libraries, student centers.
Student Life *Activities and organizations:* drama/theater group, choral group. *Campus security:* 24-hour patrols. *Student services:* health clinic.

Athletics *Intercollegiate sports:* baseball M, basketball M(s)/W(s), cross-country running M(s)/W(s), table tennis M/W, tennis M(s), track and field M(s)/W(s), volleyball M(s)/W(s), weight lifting M(s)/W(s). *Intramural sports:* basketball M/W, cross-country running M/W, racquetball M/W, softball M/W, table tennis M/W, tennis M/W, track and field M/W, volleyball M/W, weight lifting M/W.

Standardized Tests *Required:* SAT and SAT Subject Tests or ACT (for admission).

Costs (2012–13) *Tuition:* commonwealth resident $1870 full-time; nonresident $3824 full-time. Full-time tuition and fees vary according to student level. Part-time tuition and fees vary according to student level. No tuition increase for student's term of enrollment. *Required fees:* $949 full-time. *Room and board:* $8280. *Waivers:* employees or children of employees.

Financial Aid Of all full-time matriculated undergraduates who enrolled in 1998, 3,461 applied for aid, 3,133 were judged to have need. *Average percent of need met:* 40%. *Financial aid deadline:* 6/30.

Applying *Options:* early admission. *Application fee:* $20. *Required:* high school transcript. *Application deadlines:* 11/15 (freshmen), 2/23 (transfers). *Notification:* 3/4 (freshmen), continuous until 5/15 (transfers).

Freshman Application Contact University of Puerto Rico at Ponce, PO Box 7186, Ponce, PR 00732-7186. *Phone:* 787-844-8181 Ext. 2533. *Website:* http://upr-ponce.upr.edu/.

University of Puerto Rico at Utuado

Utuado, Puerto Rico

Freshman Application Contact Mrs. Maria Robles Serrano, Admissions Officer, University of Puerto Rico at Utuado, PO Box 2500, Utuado, PR 00641-2500. *Phone:* 787-894-2828 Ext. 2240. *Website:* http://www.uprutuado.edu/.

University of Puerto Rico, Cayey University College

Cayey, Puerto Rico

Freshman Application Contact University of Puerto Rico, Cayey University College, 205 Avenue Antonio R. Barcelo, Cayey, PR 00736. *Phone:* 787-738-2161 Ext. 2233. *Website:* http://www.cayey.upr.edu/.

University of Puerto Rico, Mayagüez Campus

Mayagüez, Puerto Rico

Freshman Application Contact Ms. Sheila Marty-Rodriquez, Director, Admissions Office, University of Puerto Rico, Mayagüez Campus, PO Box 9000, Mayagüez, PR 00681-9000. *Phone:* 787-265-5465. *Fax:* 787-265-5465. *E-mail:* smarty@uprm.edu. *Website:* http://www.uprm.edu/.

University of Puerto Rico, Medical Sciences Campus

San Juan, Puerto Rico

Freshman Application Contact University of Puerto Rico, Medical Sciences Campus, PO Box 365067, San Juan, PR 00936-5067. *Phone:* 787-758-2525 Ext. 5214. *Website:* http://www.rcm.upr.edu/.

University of Puerto Rico, Río Piedras

San Juan, Puerto Rico

Freshman Application Contact University of Puerto Rico, Río Piedras, PO Box 23300, San Juan, PR 00931-3300. *Phone:* 787-764-0000 Ext. 85700. *Website:* http://www.uprrp.edu/.

University of the Sacred Heart

San Juan, Puerto Rico

Director of Admissions Mr. Luis Heviquez, Director of Admissions, University of the Sacred Heart, PO Box 12383, San Juan, PR 00914-0383. *Phone:* 787-728-1515 Ext. 3237. *Website:* http://www.sagrado.edu/.

VIRGIN ISLANDS

University of the Virgin Islands
Saint Thomas, Virgin Islands

- **Territory-supported** comprehensive, founded 1962
- **Small-town** 518-acre campus
- **Endowment** $26.4 million
- **Coed** 2,240 undergraduate students, 63% full-time, 70% women, 30% men
- **Minimally difficult** entrance level, 96% of applicants were admitted

Undergraduates 1,421 full-time, 819 part-time. Students come from 28 states and territories; 16 other countries; 3% are from out of state; 78% Black or African American, non-Hispanic/Latino; 6% Hispanic/Latino; 0.3% Asian, non-Hispanic/Latino; 6% Race/ethnicity unknown; 6% international; 4% transferred in; 14% live on campus. *Retention:* 70% of full-time freshmen returned.

Freshmen *Admission:* 704 applied, 675 admitted, 399 enrolled. *Average high school GPA:* 2.67. *Test scores:* SAT critical reading scores over 500: 10%; SAT math scores over 500: 10%; SAT writing scores over 500: 10%; ACT scores over 18: 25%; SAT critical reading scores over 600: 1%; SAT math scores over 600: 1%; SAT writing scores over 600: 1%; ACT scores over 24: 2%.

Faculty *Total:* 254, 43% full-time, 43% with terminal degrees. *Student/faculty ratio:* 12:1.

Academics *Calendar:* semesters. *Degrees:* associate, bachelor's, master's, and post-master's certificates. *Special study options:* academic remediation for entering students, adult/continuing education programs, advanced placement credit, distance learning, double majors, external degree program, honors programs, independent study, internships, off-campus study, part-time degree program, services for LD students, study abroad, summer session for credit. *ROTC:* Army (b). *Unusual degree programs:* 3-2 engineering with Columbia University, University of Florida, University of South Carolina.

Computers on Campus 500 computers/terminals are available on campus for general student use. Students can access the following: campus intranet, computer help desk, free student e-mail accounts, online (class) grades, online (class) registration, online (class) schedules. Campuswide network is available. 100% of college-owned or -operated housing units are wired for high-speed Internet access. Wireless service is available via entire campus.

Student Life *Housing options:* coed, men-only, women-only. Campus housing is university owned. *Activities and organizations:* drama/theater group, student-run newspaper, radio station, choral group, The Squad, Predators, Golden Key Honor Society, National Student Exchange Club, St. Kitts and Nevis, national sororities. *Campus security:* 24-hour patrols. *Student services:* health clinic, personal/psychological counseling.

Athletics Member NCAA. *Intercollegiate sports:* basketball M/W, cheerleading W, cross-country running M/W, soccer M, swimming and diving M/W, table tennis M/W, track and field M/W, volleyball M. *Intramural sports:* basketball M/W, sailing M/W, table tennis M/W, tennis M/W, volleyball M/W.

Standardized Tests *Required:* SAT or ACT (for admission).

Costs (2012–13) *Tuition:* territory resident $3990 full-time; nonresident $11,970 full-time. Full-time tuition and fees vary according to reciprocity agreements. Part-time tuition and fees vary according to course load and reciprocity agreements. *Required fees:* $604 full-time. *Room and board:* $9900; room only: $4120. Room and board charges vary according to board plan and housing facility. *Payment plan:* installment. *Waivers:* senior citizens and employees or children of employees.

Financial Aid Of all full-time matriculated undergraduates who enrolled in 2007, 1,202 applied for aid, 1,118 were judged to have need, 10 had their need fully met. 39 Federal Work-Study jobs (averaging $2130). 28 state and other part-time jobs (averaging $1900). In 2007, 5 non-need-based awards were made. *Average financial aid package:* $4450. *Average need-based loan:* $3240. *Average need-based gift aid:* $3440. *Average non-need-based aid:* $8500. *Average indebtedness upon graduation:* $9480.

Applying *Options:* electronic application, early admission, deferred entrance. *Application fee:* $25. *Recommended:* high school transcript, minimum 2.0 GPA. *Application deadlines:* 4/30 (freshmen), 4/30 (transfers). *Notification:* continuous (freshmen), 6/15 (transfers).

Freshman Application Contact Dr. Xuri Maurice Allen, Director of Admissions/Recruitment, University of the Virgin Islands, University of the Virgin Islands, #2 John Brewers Bay, St. Thomas, VI 00802. *Phone:* 340-693-1224. *Fax:* 340-693-1167. *E-mail:* xallen@uvi.edu. *Website:* http://www.uvi.edu/.

Acadia University
Wolfville, Nova Scotia, Canada

- **Province-supported** comprehensive, founded 1838
- **Small-town** 250-acre campus
- **Coed** 3,458 undergraduate students, 96% full-time, 57% women, 43% men
- **Moderately difficult** entrance level, 34% of applicants were admitted

Undergraduates 3,320 full-time, 138 part-time. Students come from 13 provinces and territories; 51 other countries; 46% are from out of state; 6% transferred in; 45% live on campus. *Retention:* 79% of full-time freshmen returned. **Freshmen** *Admission:* 3,759 applied, 1,263 admitted, 868 enrolled. **Faculty** *Total:* 243, 83% with terminal degrees. *Student/faculty ratio:* 15:1.

Academics *Calendar:* Canadian standard year. *Degrees:* bachelor's and master's. *Special study options:* academic remediation for entering students, advanced placement credit, cooperative education, distance learning, double majors, English as a second language, honors programs, internships, off-campus study, part-time degree program, study abroad, summer session for credit.

Computers on Campus 7,000 ports are available on campus for general student use. Students can access the following: campus intranet, computer help desk, free student e-mail accounts, online (class) grades, online (class) registration, online (class) schedules. Campuswide network is available. 100% of college-owned or -operated housing units are wired for high-speed Internet access. Wireless service is available via learning centers, libraries, student centers.

Student Life *Housing options:* coed, women-only. Campus housing is university owned. Freshman campus housing is guaranteed. *Activities and organizations:* drama/theater group, student-run newspaper, radio station, choral group, Dance Acadia, Power Cheerleading, Water Watch Canada, LINC, Biology. *Campus security:* 24-hour emergency response devices and patrols, student patrols, late-night transport/escort service, controlled dormitory access, video surveillance, emergency response, emergency notification, emergency management planning. *Student services:* health clinic, personal/psychological counseling, women's center, legal services.

Athletics Member CIS. *Intercollegiate sports:* basketball M(s)/W(s), cross-country running W, football M(s), ice hockey M(s), rugby W(s), soccer M(s)/W(s), swimming and diving M(s)/W(s), track and field W, volleyball W.

Costs (2012–13) *Tuition:* province resident $6590 Canadian dollars full-time, $817 Canadian dollars per course part-time; nonresident $7612 Canadian dollars full-time, $919 Canadian dollars per course part-time; International tuition $14,808 Canadian dollars full-time. Full-time tuition and fees vary according to course level, course load, degree level, and program. Part-time tuition and fees vary according to course level, course load, degree level, and program. *Required fees:* $249 Canadian dollars full-time, $10 Canadian dollars per course part-time. *Room and board:* $8866 Canadian dollars; room only: $4935 Canadian dollars. Room and board charges vary according to board plan and housing facility. *Payment plan:* installment. *Waivers:* senior citizens and employees or children of employees.

Applying *Options:* electronic application, deferred entrance. *Application fee:* $25 Canadian dollars. *Required:* high school transcript, minimum 2.5 GPA. *Required for some:* essay or personal statement, 1 letter of recommendation, interview. *Application deadlines:* 7/1 (freshmen), 7/1 (out-of-state freshmen), 7/1 (transfers). *Notification:* continuous (freshmen), continuous (out-of-state freshmen), continuous (transfers).

Freshman Application Contact Ms. Anne Scott, Manager of Admissions, Acadia University, Wolfville, NS B4P 2R6, Canada. *Phone:* 902-585-1016. *Toll-free phone:* 877-585-1121. *Fax:* 902-585-1092. *E-mail:* admissions@acadiau.ca. *Website:* http://www.acadiau.ca/.

Alberta Bible College
Calgary, Alberta, Canada

Director of Admissions Brad Olorenshaw, Recruitment Officer, Alberta Bible College, 635 Northmount Drive, NW, Calgary, AB T2K 3J6, Canada. *Phone:* 403-282-2994 Ext. 225. *Toll-free phone:* 877-542-9492. *E-mail:* admissions@abccampus.ca. *Website:* http://www.abccampus.ca/.

Alberta College of Art & Design
Calgary, Alberta, Canada

- **Province-supported** 4-year, founded 1926
- **Urban** 1-acre campus
- **Endowment** $5.1 million
- **Coed** 1,155 undergraduate students, 90% full-time, 72% women, 28% men
- **Moderately difficult** entrance level, 64% of applicants were admitted

Undergraduates 1,042 full-time, 113 part-time. Students come from 9 provinces and territories; 22 other countries; 11% are from out of state; 87% Race/ethnicity unknown; 5% international; 3% transferred in; 9% live on campus. *Retention:* 64% of full-time freshmen returned. **Freshmen** *Admission:* 365 applied, 232 admitted, 284 enrolled. **Faculty** *Total:* 135, 34% full-time, 33% with terminal degrees. *Student/faculty ratio:* 15:1.

Academics *Calendar:* semesters. *Degree:* bachelor's. *Special study options:* academic remediation for entering students, adult/continuing education programs, advanced placement credit, independent study, internships, part-time degree program, services for LD students, study abroad, summer session for credit.

Computers on Campus 103 computers/terminals are available on campus for general student use. Students can access the following: campus intranet, computer help desk, free student e-mail accounts, online (class) grades, online (class) registration, online (class) schedules. Campuswide network is available. 100% of college-owned or -operated housing units are wired for high-speed Internet access. Wireless service is available via entire campus.

Student Life *Housing options:* coed, disabled students. Campus housing is provided by a third party. *Activities and organizations:* The Rendez-Vous Collective, Conceptual Arts Club, Arts Mob, Anime and Gaming Club, ACAD Glass. *Campus security:* 24-hour emergency response devices and patrols, late-night transport/escort service, controlled dormitory access. *Student services:* health clinic, personal/psychological counseling.

Athletics *Intercollegiate sports:* basketball M/W, cross-country running M/W, ice hockey M/W, soccer M/W, volleyball M/W. *Intramural sports:* basketball M/W, bowling M/W, ice hockey M/W, soccer M/W.

Costs (2013–14) *Tuition:* province resident $4435 Canadian dollars full-time, $147 Canadian dollars per credit part-time; nonresident $466 Canadian dollars per credit part-time; International tuition $13,996 Canadian dollars full-time. Full-time tuition and fees vary according to course load, program, and student level. Part-time tuition and fees vary according to course load, program, and student level. *Required fees:* $831 Canadian dollars full-time, $196 Canadian dollars per term part-time. *Room only:* $5904 Canadian dollars. Room and board charges vary according to housing facility. *Waivers:* senior citizens.

Applying *Options:* electronic application, early decision. *Application fee:* $85 Canadian dollars. *Required:* essay or personal statement, high school transcript, minimum 2.0 GPA, portfolio of artwork. *Application deadlines:* 2/1 (freshmen), 2/1 (out-of-state freshmen), 3/1 (transfers). *Notification:* 3/15 (freshmen), 3/15 (out-of-state freshmen), 4/15 (transfers).

Freshman Application Contact Ms. Katie Potapoff, Admissions Officer, Alberta College of Art & Design, 1407-14 Avenue NW, Calgary, AB T2N 4R3, Canada. *Phone:* 403-284-7617. *Toll-free phone:* 800-251-8290. *Fax:* 403-284-7644. *E-mail:* admissions@acad.ca. *Website:* http://www.acad.ca/.

Ambrose University College
Calgary, Alberta, Canada

Director of Admissions Admissions Officer, Ambrose University College, 630, 833 4th Avenue, SW, Calgary, AB T2P 3T5, Canada. *Toll-free phone:* 800-461-1222. *E-mail:* enrolment@ambrose.edu. *Website:* http://www.ambrose.edu/.

Athabasca University
Athabasca, Alberta, Canada

- **Province-supported** comprehensive, founded 1970
- **Small-town** 480-acre campus
- **Endowment** $1.0 million
- **Coed** 35,071 undergraduate students, 68% women, 32% men
- **Noncompetitive** entrance level

Undergraduates 35,071 part-time. Students come from 33 provinces and territories; 87 other countries; 63% are from out of state. **Faculty** *Total:* 384.

Academics *Calendar:* continuous. *Degrees:* certificates, diplomas, bachelor's, master's, doctoral, post-master's, and postbachelor's certificates (offers only external degree programs). *Special study options:* academic remediation for entering students, accelerated degree program, adult/continuing education programs, advanced placement credit, distance learning, double majors, English as a second language, external degree program, independent study, off-campus study, part-time degree program, services for LD students, student-designed majors, study abroad, summer session for credit.

Computers on Campus 28 computers/terminals are available on campus for general student use. Students can access the following: online (class) registration. Campuswide network is available.

Student Life *Housing:* college housing not available. *Activities and organizations:* student-run newspaper. *Campus security:* 24-hour emergency response devices.

Applying *Options:* electronic application. *Application fee:* $60 Canadian dollars. *Application deadlines:* rolling (freshmen), rolling (transfers). *Notification:* continuous (freshmen), continuous (transfers).

Freshman Application Contact Information Centre, Athabasca University, 1 University Drive, Athabasca, AB T9S 3A3, Canada. *Phone:* 800-788-9041. *Toll-free phone:* 800-788-9041. *Fax:* 780-675-6437. *Website:* http://www.athabascau.ca/.

Bishop's University
Sherbrooke, Quebec, Canada

- **Province-supported** comprehensive, founded 1843, part of Association of Universities and Colleges of Canada (AUCC)
- **Small-town** 500-acre campus
- **Coed**
- **Moderately difficult** entrance level

Faculty *Student/faculty ratio:* 15:1.

Academics *Calendar:* semesters most students study from September to late April. Spring semester is May-June. *Degrees:* certificates, bachelor's, and master's.

Student Life *Campus security:* 24-hour emergency response devices and patrols, student patrols, late-night transport/escort service, controlled dormitory access.

Athletics Member CIS.

Standardized Tests *Required:* SAT or ACT (for admission).

Applying *Options:* electronic application, early admission, deferred entrance. *Application fee:* $60 Canadian dollars. *Required:* high school transcript, minimum 3.0 GPA, birth certificate, copy of student visa. *Required for some:* essay or personal statement. *Recommended:* essay or personal statement.

Freshman Application Contact Mrs. Jacqueline Belleau, Coordinator of Student Recruitment, Bishop's University, 2600 College Street, Sherbrooke, QC J1M 0C8, Canada. *Phone:* 819-822-9600 Ext. 2691. *Toll-free phone:* 877-822-8200. *Fax:* 819-822-9661. *E-mail:* recruitment@ubishops.ca. *Website:* http://www.ubishops.ca/.

Booth University College
Winnipeg, Manitoba, Canada

Director of Admissions Chantel Burt, Director of Admission, Booth University College, 447 Webb Place, Winnipeg, MB R3B 2P2, Canada. *Phone:* 204-924-4867. *Toll-free phone:* 877-942-6684. *E-mail:* cburt@boothcollege.ca. *Website:* http://www.boothuc.ca/.

Brandon University
Brandon, Manitoba, Canada

Freshman Application Contact Murray Kerr, Director of Admissions, Brandon University, 270 18th Street, Brandon, MB R7A 6A9, Canada. *Phone:* 204-727-7352. *Toll-free phone:* 800-644-7644. *Fax:* 204-728-3221. *E-mail:* kerr@brandonu.ca. *Website:* http://www.brandonu.ca/.

Briercrest College
Caronport, Saskatchewan, Canada

- **Independent interdenominational** 4-year, founded 1935, part of Briercrest College and Seminary
- **Rural** 300-acre campus
- **Endowment** $1.4 million
- **Coed** 152 undergraduate students, 93% full-time, 44% women, 56% men
- **Noncompetitive** entrance level, 57% of applicants were admitted

Undergraduates 141 full-time, 11 part-time. Students come from 4 provinces and territories; 3 other countries; 0.1% are from out of state; 25% transferred in; 15% live on campus. *Retention:* 42% of full-time freshmen returned.

Freshmen *Admission:* 416 applied, 239 admitted, 152 enrolled.

Academics *Calendar:* semesters. *Degrees:* certificates, diplomas, associate, and bachelor's. *Special study options:* academic remediation for entering students, adult/continuing education programs, distance learning, double majors, external degree program, independent study, internships, off-campus study, part-time degree program, study abroad, summer session for credit. *Unusual degree programs:* 3-2 business administration; social work with Minot State University; education, addictions studies, and communication disorders with Minot State University.

Computers on Campus 21 computers/terminals are available on campus for general student use. Students can access the following: online (class) grades, online (class) registration, online (class) schedules. Campuswide network is available. Wireless service is available via classrooms, computer centers, computer labs, dorm rooms, learning centers, libraries, student centers.

Student Life *Housing:* on-campus residence required through junior year. *Options:* men-only, women-only. Campus housing is university owned. Freshman campus housing is guaranteed. *Activities and organizations:* drama/theater group, choral group. *Campus security:* 24-hour patrols, controlled dormitory access. *Student services:* health clinic, personal/psychological counseling, legal services.

Athletics *Intercollegiate sports:* basketball M/W, ice hockey M, volleyball M/W. *Intramural sports:* basketball M/W, ice hockey M/W, soccer M/W, volleyball M/W.

Standardized Tests *Required for some:* SAT or ACT (for admission).

Costs (2012–13) *Comprehensive fee:* $14,064 Canadian dollars includes full-time tuition ($8310 Canadian dollars), mandatory fees ($150 Canadian dollars), and room and board ($5604 Canadian dollars). Full-time tuition and fees vary according to course load. Part-time tuition: $277 Canadian dollars per credit. Part-time tuition and fees vary according to course load. *Required fees:* $277 Canadian dollars per term part-time. *College room only:* $3488 Canadian dollars. Room and board charges vary according to board plan, housing facility, and location. *Payment plan:* installment.

Applying *Options:* electronic application, deferred entrance. *Application fee:* $50 Canadian dollars. *Required:* essay or personal statement, high school transcript, 1 letter of recommendation, statement of faith. *Required for some:* interview. *Application deadlines:* 8/15 (freshmen), 8/15 (transfers). *Notification:* continuous until 9/1 (freshmen), continuous until 9/1 (transfers).

Freshman Application Contact Mr. Ralph Troshke, Director of Enrolment, Briercrest College, 510 College Drive, Caronport, SK S0H 0S0, Canada. *Phone:* 306-756.3200. *Toll-free phone:* 800-667-5199. *Fax:* 800-667.5199. *E-mail:* admissions@briercrest.ca. *Website:* http://www.briercrest.ca/.

British Columbia Institute of Technology
Burnaby, British Columbia, Canada

Freshman Application Contact Ms. Anna Dosen, Supervisor of Admissions, British Columbia Institute of Technology, 3700 Willingdon Avenue, Burnaby, BC V5G 3H2, Canada. *Phone:* 604-432-8496. *Toll-free phone:* 866-434-1610. *Fax:* 604-431-6917. *Website:* http://www.bcit.ca/.

Brock University
St. Catharines, Ontario, Canada

- **Province-supported** university, founded 1964
- **Urban** 540-acre campus with easy access to Toronto, ON and Buffalo, NY
- **Coed** 16,341 undergraduate students, 100% full-time, 58% women, 42% men

Undergraduates 16,341 full-time. Students come from 70 other countries; 14% live on campus. *Retention:* 86% of full-time freshmen returned.

Freshmen *Admission:* 19,885 applied. *Average high school GPA:* 3.

Faculty *Total:* 578, 100% full-time. *Student/faculty ratio:* 30:1.

Academics *Calendar:* Canadian standard year. *Degrees:* certificates, bachelor's, master's, and doctoral. *Special study options:* academic remediation for entering students, accelerated degree program, adult/continuing education programs, advanced placement credit, cooperative education, double majors, English as a second language, honors programs, internships, part-time degree program, services for LD students, student-designed majors, study abroad, summer session for credit.

Computers on Campus 429 computers/terminals are available on campus for general student use. Students can access the following: computer help desk,

free student e-mail accounts, online (class) grades, online (class) registration, online (class) schedules. Campuswide network is available. 100% of college-owned or -operated housing units are wired for high-speed Internet access. Wireless service is available via classrooms, computer centers, computer labs, learning centers, libraries, student centers.
Student Life *Housing options:* coed, disabled students. Campus housing is university owned and leased by the school. Freshman campus housing is guaranteed. *Activities and organizations:* drama/theater group, student-run newspaper, radio and television station, choral group, International Students Association, Brock University Student Association, Business Administration Association, Brock Christian Fellowship, Ace Brock. *Campus security:* 24-hour emergency response devices and patrols, student patrols, late-night transport/escort service, controlled dormitory access. *Student services:* health clinic, personal/psychological counseling, women's center.
Athletics Member CIS. *Intercollegiate sports:* baseball M, basketball M(s)/W(s), cheerleading M/W, crew M(s)/W(s), cross-country running M/W, fencing M/W, field hockey W(c), ice hockey M(s)/W(s), lacrosse M, rugby M/W, soccer M(s)/W(s), swimming and diving M/W, volleyball W, wrestling M(s)/W(s). *Intramural sports:* badminton M/W, basketball M/W, football M/W, ice hockey M/W, skiing (downhill) M/W, soccer M/W, softball M/W, swimming and diving M/W, ultimate Frisbee M/W, volleyball M/W, water polo M/W.
Standardized Tests *Required:* SAT or ACT (for admission).
Applying *Options:* electronic application. *Required:* high school transcript. *Required for some:* essay or personal statement, interview, audition for Dramatic Arts and Music programs, profile questionnaire for Concurrent Education programs. *Recommended:* minimum 3.0 GPA.
Freshman Application Contact Mrs. Lynn Thompson-Dovi, International Admissions Officer, Brock University, 500 Glenridge Avenue, L2S 3A1, Canada. *Phone:* 905-688-5550 Ext. 3431. *Fax:* 905-688-5488. *E-mail:* admissns@brocku.ca.
Website: http://www.brocku.ca/.

Canadian Mennonite University
Winnipeg, Manitoba, Canada
Freshman Application Contact Mr. Abe Bergen, Director of Enrollment Services, Canadian Mennonite University, 500 Shaftesbury Boulevard, Winnipeg, MB R3P 2N2, Canada. *Phone:* 204-487-3300 Ext. 652. *Toll-free phone:* 877-231-4570. *Fax:* 204-487-3858. *E-mail:* cu@cmu.ca.
Website: http://www.cmu.ca/.

Cape Breton University
Sydney, Nova Scotia, Canada
- **Province-supported** comprehensive, founded 1974
- **Urban** campus
- **Coed**
- **Moderately difficult** entrance level

Academics *Calendar:* semesters. *Degrees:* certificates, diplomas, bachelor's, and master's.
Student Life *Campus security:* 24-hour emergency response devices and patrols, student patrols, late-night transport/escort service, controlled dormitory access.
Athletics Member CIS.
Applying *Options:* early admission, deferred entrance. *Application fee:* $35 Canadian dollars. *Required:* high school transcript. *Required for some:* essay or personal statement, 3 letters of recommendation, interview.
Freshman Application Contact Cape Breton University, Box 5300, 1250 Grand Lake Road, Sydney, NS B1P 6L2, Canada. *Phone:* 902-563-1117. *Toll-free phone:* 888-959-9995.
Website: http://www.cbu.ca/.

Carleton University
Ottawa, Ontario, Canada
Freshman Application Contact Ms. Jean Mullan, Director, Undergraduate Recruitment Office, Carleton University, 1125 Colonel By Drive, Ottawa, ON K1S 5B6, Canada. *Phone:* 613-520-3663. *Toll-free phone:* 888-354-4414. *E-mail:* liaison@admissions.carleton.ca.
Website: http://www.carleton.ca/.

Centennial College
Scarborough, Ontario, Canada
- **Province-supported** 4-year, part of Ontario College Application System
- **Urban** campus with easy access to Greater Toronto Area
- **Coed**

Academics *Degree:* certificates, diplomas, and bachelor's. *Special study options:* cooperative education, distance learning, English as a second language, services for LD students, study abroad.
Computers on Campus Students can access the following: campus intranet, computer help desk, free student e-mail accounts, online (class) grades, online (class) registration, online (class) schedules. Campuswide network is available. Wireless service is available via entire campus.
Student Life *Housing options:* Campus housing is university owned. Freshman applicants given priority for college housing. *Campus security:* 24-hour emergency response devices and patrols. *Student services:* personal/psychological counseling.
Applying *Options:* electronic application. *Application fee:* $95 Canadian dollars. *Required:* high school transcript.
Freshman Application Contact Enrolment Services, Centennial College, PO Box 631, Station 'A', Scarborough, ON M1K 5E9, Canada. *Phone:* 416-289-5325. *Toll-free phone:* 800-268-4419. *E-mail:* success@centennialcollege.ca.
Website: http://www.centennialcollege.ca/.

Collège Dominicain de Philosophie et de Théologie
Ottawa, Ontario, Canada
Freshman Application Contact Fr. Herve Tremblay OP, Registrar, Collège Dominicain de Philosophie et de Théologie, 96 Empress Avenue, Ottawa, ON K1R 7G3, Canada. *Phone:* 613-233-5696 Ext. 308. *Fax:* 613-233-6064. *E-mail:* registraire@collegedominicain.ca.
Website: http://www.collegedominicain.ca/.

Collège universitaire de Saint-Boniface
Saint-Boniface, Manitoba, Canada
Admissions Office Contact Collège universitaire de Saint-Boniface, 200 avenue de la Cathèdrale, Saint-Boniface, MB R2H 0H7, Canada.
Website: http://www.ustboniface.mb.ca/.

Columbia Bible College
Abbotsford, British Columbia, Canada
- **Independent Mennonite Brethren** 4-year, founded 1936
- **Urban** 9-acre campus with easy access to Vancouver
- **Endowment** $758,680
- **Coed** 416 undergraduate students
- **Noncompetitive** entrance level, 75% of applicants were admitted

Undergraduates Students come from 8 provinces and territories; 5 other countries; 19% are from out of state; 35% live on campus. *Retention:* 75% of full-time freshmen returned.
Freshmen *Admission:* 294 applied, 220 admitted.
Faculty *Total:* 37, 32% full-time, 14% with terminal degrees. *Student/faculty ratio:* 18:1.
Academics *Calendar:* semesters. *Degree:* certificates, diplomas, and bachelor's. *Special study options:* academic remediation for entering students, advanced placement credit, distance learning, independent study, internships, off-campus study, part-time degree program, services for LD students, study abroad.
Computers on Campus 30 computers/terminals are available on campus for general student use. Students can access the following: campus intranet, online (class) grades, online (class) schedules. Campuswide network is available. 85% of college-owned or -operated housing units are wired for high-speed Internet access. Wireless service is available via classrooms, computer labs, dorm rooms, libraries, student centers.
Student Life *Housing:* on-campus residence required through sophomore year. *Options:* men-only, women-only. Campus housing is university owned. Freshman applicants given priority for college housing. *Activities and organizations:* choral group. *Campus security:* late-night transport/escort service, controlled dormitory access, night watchman 11 pm to 6 am. *Student services:* personal/psychological counseling.
Athletics *Intercollegiate sports:* basketball M/W, soccer M/W, volleyball M/W.
Costs (2013–14) *Comprehensive fee:* $14,480 Canadian dollars includes full-time tuition ($9270 Canadian dollars) and room and board ($5210 Canadian dollars). Full-time tuition and fees vary according to course load. Part-time tuition: $309 Canadian dollars per credit. Part-time tuition and fees vary according to course load. *Room and board:* Room and board charges vary according to board plan. *Payment plans:* installment, deferred payment. *Waivers:* senior citizens and employees or children of employees.

Financial Aid *Financial aid deadline:* 5/15.
Applying *Options:* electronic application, early admission, early decision, deferred entrance. *Application fee:* $50. *Required:* essay or personal statement, high school transcript, minimum 2.0 GPA, 2 letters of recommendation, must be Christian. *Application deadlines:* 8/15 (freshmen), 8/15 (out-of-state freshmen), 8/15 (transfers). *Early decision deadline:* 5/1. *Notification:* continuous (freshmen), continuous (out-of-state freshmen), continuous (transfers).
Freshman Application Contact Candice Green, Director of Admissions, Columbia Bible College, 2940 Clearbrook Road, Abbotsford, BC V2T 2Z8, Canada. *Phone:* 604-853-3358 Ext. 309. *Toll-free phone:* 800-283-0881. *Fax:* 604-853-3063. *E-mail:* candice.green@columbiabc.edu.
Website: http://www.columbiabc.edu/.

Concordia University
Montréal, Quebec, Canada

- **Province-supported** university, founded 1974, part of Quebec University Network
- **Urban** 52-acre campus with easy access to Montreal
- **Endowment** $77.5 million
- **Coed** 30,446 undergraduate students, 66% full-time, 52% women, 48% men
- **Moderately difficult** entrance level, 67% of applicants were admitted

Undergraduates 20,107 full-time, 10,339 part-time. Students come from 13 provinces and territories; 147 other countries; 10% are from out of state; 2% live on campus. *Retention:* 84% of full-time freshmen returned.
Freshmen *Admission:* 15,347 applied, 10,260 admitted, 5,428 enrolled.
Faculty *Total:* 1,565, 59% full-time. *Student/faculty ratio:* 25:1.
Academics *Calendar:* semesters. *Degrees:* certificates, diplomas, bachelor's, master's, doctoral, and postbachelor's certificates. *Special study options:* academic remediation for entering students, accelerated degree program, adult/continuing education programs, advanced placement credit, cooperative education, distance learning, double majors, English as a second language, honors programs, independent study, internships, off-campus study, part-time degree program, services for LD students, student-designed majors, study abroad, summer session for credit.
Computers on Campus 350 computers/terminals and 3,000 ports are available on campus for general student use. Students can access the following: campus intranet, computer help desk, free student e-mail accounts, online (class) grades, online (class) registration, online (class) schedules, specialized software applications. Campuswide network is available. 67% of college-owned or -operated housing units are wired for high-speed Internet access. Wireless service is available via classrooms, computer centers, computer labs, learning centers, libraries, student centers.
Student Life *Housing options:* coed, men-only, women-only, disabled students. Campus housing is university owned. Freshman applicants given priority for college housing. *Activities and organizations:* drama/theater group, student-run newspaper, radio and television station, choral group, undergraduate student union, departmental clubs, religious clubs, ethnic clubs, social action groups, national fraternities, national sororities. *Campus security:* 24-hour emergency response devices and patrols, student patrols, late-night transport/escort service, controlled dormitory access. *Student services:* health clinic, personal/psychological counseling, women's center.
Athletics Member CIS. *Intercollegiate sports:* baseball M, basketball M(s)/W(s), cross-country running M(c)/W(c), football M(s), golf M(c)/W(c), ice hockey M(s)/W(s), rugby M(s)/W(s), skiing (downhill) M(c)/W(c), soccer M(s)/W(s), wrestling M(s)/W(s). *Intramural sports:* basketball M/W, cross-country running M/W, ice hockey M/W, soccer M/W, ultimate Frisbee M/W, volleyball M/W.
Costs (2012–13) *Tuition:* province resident $2422 Canadian dollars full-time, $81 Canadian dollars per credit part-time; nonresident $6112 Canadian dollars full-time, $205 Canadian dollars per credit part-time; International tuition $16,513 Canadian dollars full-time. Full-time tuition and fees vary according to course load. Part-time tuition and fees vary according to course load. *Required fees:* $1410 Canadian dollars full-time, $47 Canadian dollars per credit part-time. *Room and board:* $7262 Canadian dollars. Room and board charges vary according to board plan, housing facility, and location. *Payment plan:* installment. *Waivers:* senior citizens and employees or children of employees.
Financial Aid Of all full-time matriculated undergraduates who enrolled in 2011, 349 state and other part-time jobs (averaging $1286). *Financial aid deadline:* 3/31.
Applying *Options:* electronic application, deferred entrance. *Application fee:* $100 Canadian dollars. *Required:* high school transcript, minimum 2.5 GPA. *Required for some:* essay or personal statement, minimum 2.9 GPA, 2 letters of recommendation, interview, portfolio/auditions required for Performing and Visual Arts, Communications and Journalism require interview/essay/portfo-

lio. *Application deadlines:* 3/1 (freshmen), 3/1 (out-of-state freshmen), 3/1 (transfers). *Notification:* continuous (freshmen), continuous (transfers).
Freshman Application Contact Ms. Ilze Kraulis, Associate Registrar, Concordia University, 1455 de Maisonneuve Boulevard West, Building LB-719-2, Montreal, QC H3G 1M8, Canada. *Phone:* 514-848-2424 Ext. 2628. *Fax:* 514-848-2621. *E-mail:* ijkrau@alcor.concordia.ca.
Website: http://www.concordia.ca/.

Concordia University College of Alberta
Edmonton, Alberta, Canada

Freshman Application Contact Student and Enrollment Services, Concordia University College of Alberta, 7128 Ada Boulevard, Edmonton, AB T5B 4E4, Canada. *Phone:* 780-479-9220. *Toll-free phone:* 866-479-5200. *Fax:* 780-378-8460. *E-mail:* admits@concordia.ab.ca.
Website: http://www.concordia.ab.ca/.

Crandall University
Moncton, New Brunswick, Canada

- **Independent Baptist** 4-year, founded 1949
- **Urban** 220-acre campus
- **Coed**
- **Minimally difficult** entrance level

Faculty *Student/faculty ratio:* 17:1.
Academics *Calendar:* semesters. *Degrees:* certificates, bachelor's, post-master's, and postbachelor's certificates.
Student Life *Campus security:* 24-hour emergency response devices, student patrols, controlled dormitory access.
Costs (2012–13) *Comprehensive fee:* $14,296 Canadian dollars includes full-time tuition ($7395 Canadian dollars), mandatory fees ($775 Canadian dollars), and room and board ($6126 Canadian dollars). Part-time tuition: $775 Canadian dollars per course. *College room only:* $2686 Canadian dollars. Room and board charges vary according to board plan and housing facility.
Financial Aid *Financial aid deadline:* 5/15.
Applying *Options:* electronic application, early admission, early decision, deferred entrance. *Application fee:* $35 Canadian dollars. *Required:* high school transcript, minimum 2.7 GPA, 3 letters of recommendation. *Required for some:* essay or personal statement, interview.
Freshman Application Contact Mrs. Laura Lutes, Administrative Officer-Admissions and Recruitment, Crandall University, Box 6004, Moncton, NB E1C 9L7, Canada. *Phone:* 506-858-8970 Ext. 6433. *Toll-free phone:* 888-YOU-N-ABU. *Fax:* 506-858-9694. *E-mail:* Laura.lutes@crandallu.ca.
Website: http://www.crandallu.ca/.

Dalhousie University
Halifax, Nova Scotia, Canada

- **Province-supported** university, founded 1818
- **Urban** 80-acre campus
- **Coed** 14,840 undergraduate students, 90% full-time, 56% women, 44% men
- **Moderately difficult** entrance level, 60% of applicants were admitted

Undergraduates 13,360 full-time, 1,480 part-time. Students come from 13 provinces and territories; 97 other countries.
Freshmen *Admission:* 15,702 applied, 9,357 admitted.
Faculty *Student/faculty ratio:* 14:1.
Academics *Calendar:* semesters. *Degrees:* diplomas, bachelor's, master's, doctoral, and postbachelor's certificates. *Special study options:* academic remediation for entering students, accelerated degree program, advanced placement credit, cooperative education, distance learning, double majors, English as a second language, honors programs, internships, off-campus study, part-time degree program, services for LD students, study abroad, summer session for credit.
Computers on Campus 710 computers/terminals are available on campus for general student use. Students can access the following: campus intranet, computer help desk, free student e-mail accounts, online (class) grades, online (class) registration, online (class) schedules. Campuswide network is available. 100% of college-owned or -operated housing units are wired for high-speed Internet access. Wireless service is available via entire campus.
Student Life *Housing options:* coed, women-only, disabled students. Campus housing is university owned. Freshman applicants given priority for college housing. *Activities and organizations:* drama/theater group, student-run newspaper, radio station, choral group, International Students Association, Arts Society, Science Society, Commerce Society, Dalhousie Outdoors Club, national fraternities, national sororities. *Campus security:* 24-hour emergency

response devices and patrols, student patrols, late-night transport/escort service, controlled dormitory access. *Student services:* health clinic, personal/psychological counseling, women's center, legal services.

Athletics Member CIS. *Intercollegiate sports:* basketball M/W, cross-country running M/W, field hockey W(c), ice hockey M/W, soccer M/W, swimming and diving M/W, track and field M/W, volleyball M/W. *Intramural sports:* badminton M(c)/W(c), baseball M(c), basketball M/W, crew M(c)/W(c), cross-country running M/W, fencing M(c)/W(c), field hockey W, football M/W, golf M/W, gymnastics M/W, ice hockey M, lacrosse M, racquetball M/W, rugby M(c)/W(c), sailing M(c)/W(c), skiing (cross-country) M/W, skiing (downhill) M/W, soccer M/W, softball M/W, squash M(c)/W(c), swimming and diving M(c)/W(c), tennis M/W, track and field M/W, ultimate Frisbee M/W, volleyball M/W, water polo M/W, weight lifting M/W, wrestling M(c)/W(c).

Standardized Tests *Required:* SAT or ACT (for admission).

Costs (2012–13) *Tuition:* province resident $7100 Canadian dollars full-time; nonresident $7100 Canadian dollars full-time; International tuition $15,090 Canadian dollars full-time. Full-time tuition and fees vary according to course load, degree level, and program. Part-time tuition and fees vary according to course load, degree level, and program. *Room and board:* $8900 Canadian dollars. Room and board charges vary according to board plan, housing facility, and location. *Waivers:* minority students, senior citizens, and employees or children of employees.

Applying *Options:* electronic application, early admission, deferred entrance. *Application fee:* $65 Canadian dollars. *Required:* high school transcript, minimum 3.0 GPA. *Required for some:* essay or personal statement, 1 letter of recommendation, interview. *Application deadlines:* 6/1 (freshmen), 6/1 (transfers). *Early decision deadline:* 3/15. *Notification:* continuous (freshmen), continuous (transfers), rolling (early decision).

Freshman Application Contact Mairead Barry, Associate Registrar and Director of Admissions, Dalhousie University, Office of the Registrar, Halifax, NS B3H 4H6, Canada. *Phone:* 902-494-2148. *Fax:* 902-494-1630. *E-mail:* admissions@dal.ca.
Website: http://www.dal.ca/.

École Polytechnique de Montréal
Montréal, Quebec, Canada

Admissions Office Contact École Polytechnique de Montréal, CP 6079, Succursale Centre-Ville, Montréal, QC H3C 3A7, Canada.
Website: http://www.polymtl.ca/.

Emily Carr University of Art + Design
Vancouver, British Columbia, Canada

- **Province-supported** comprehensive, founded 1925
- **Urban** campus
- **Coed**
- **Moderately difficult** entrance level

Faculty *Student/faculty ratio:* 18:1.
Academics *Degrees:* bachelor's and master's.
Student Life *Campus security:* 24-hour emergency response devices and patrols.
Costs (2012–13) *Tuition:* province resident $3642 Canadian dollars full-time, $121 Canadian dollars per credit part-time; International tuition $12,500 Canadian dollars full-time. Full-time tuition and fees vary according to course load. Part-time tuition and fees vary according to course load. *Required fees:* $232 Canadian dollars full-time.
Applying *Options:* electronic application. *Application fee:* $40 Canadian dollars. *Required:* essay or personal statement, high school transcript, minimum 2.5 GPA, portfolio and questionnaire.
Freshman Application Contact Admissions, Emily Carr University of Art + Design, 1399 Johnston Street, Vancouver, BC V6H 3R9, Canada. *Phone:* 604-844-3800. *Toll-free phone:* 800-832-7788. *Fax:* 604-844-3801. *E-mail:* admissions@ecuad.ca.
Website: http://www.ecuad.ca/.

Emmanuel Bible College
Kitchener, Ontario, Canada

Freshman Application Contact Emmanuel Bible College, 100 Fergus Avenue, Kitchener, ON N2A 2H2, Canada. *Phone:* 519-894-8900 Ext. 224.
Website: http://www.emmanuelbiblecollege.ca/.

Eston College
Eston, Saskatchewan, Canada

Freshman Application Contact Admissions, Eston College, 730 1st Street E., Box 579, Eston, SK S0L 1A0, Canada. *Phone:* 306-962-3621. *Toll-free phone:* 888-440-3424. *Fax:* 306-962-3810. *E-mail:* admissions@estoncollege.ca.
Website: http://www.estoncollege.ca/.

HEC Montreal
Montréal, Quebec, Canada

- **Province-supported** comprehensive, founded 1910, part of Universite de Montreal
- **Urban** 9-acre campus
- **Coed** 9,581 undergraduate students, 51% full-time, 50% women, 50% men
- **Moderately difficult** entrance level, 57% of applicants were admitted

Undergraduates 4,865 full-time, 4,716 part-time. Students come from 4 provinces and territories; 37 other countries; 0.3% are from out of state. *Retention:* 91% of full-time freshmen returned.
Freshmen *Admission:* 3,045 applied, 1,735 admitted, 990 enrolled.
Faculty *Total:* 669, 42% full-time, 37% with terminal degrees. *Student/faculty ratio:* 21:1.
Academics *Calendar:* trimesters. *Degrees:* certificates, bachelor's, master's, doctoral, and postbachelor's certificates. *Special study options:* academic remediation for entering students, adult/continuing education programs, English as a second language, honors programs, independent study, off-campus study, student-designed majors, study abroad, summer session for credit.
Computers on Campus 211 computers/terminals and 11,000 ports are available on campus for general student use. Students can access the following: campus intranet, computer help desk, free student e-mail accounts, online (class) grades, online (class) registration, online (class) schedules, Complete Learning Management System, corporate calendar and web sites for all the resources available for classes. Campuswide network is available. 100% of college-owned or -operated housing units are wired for high-speed Internet access. Wireless service is available via entire campus.
Student Life *Housing options:* Campus housing is provided by a third party. *Activities and organizations:* student-run newspaper, radio station, choral group, AEMBA (MBA Students' Association), AEMD (MSc and PhD Students' Association), AEDES (Post-Bachelor's Certificate Students' Association), AEHEC (BBA Students' Association), AEPC (Certificate Students' Association). *Campus security:* 24-hour emergency response devices and patrols. *Student services:* health clinic, personal/psychological counseling.
Costs (2012–13) *Tuition:* province resident $2422 Canadian dollars full-time, $81 Canadian dollars per credit part-time; nonresident $6155 Canadian dollars full-time, $205 Canadian dollars per credit part-time; International tuition $17,566 Canadian dollars full-time. Full-time tuition and fees vary according to program. Part-time tuition and fees vary according to program. *Required fees:* $1110 Canadian dollars full-time, $33 Canadian dollars per credit part-time, $72 Canadian dollars per term part-time. *Room and board:* $3640 Canadian dollars. Room and board charges vary according to board plan and housing facility. *Waivers:* employees or children of employees.
Financial Aid Of all full-time matriculated undergraduates who enrolled in 2011, 2,400 applied for aid, 2,000 were judged to have need. 12 state and other part-time jobs (averaging $2700). *Average financial aid package:* $7500. *Average need-based loan:* $3200. *Average need-based gift aid:* $5400. *Average indebtedness upon graduation:* $3200..
Applying *Options:* electronic application, deferred entrance. *Application fee:* $82 Canadian dollars. *Required:* high school transcript. *Required for some:* cote de rendement collegial. *Application deadlines:* 3/1 (freshmen), 2/1 (out-of-state freshmen). *Notification:* continuous (freshmen), continuous (out-of-state freshmen).
Freshman Application Contact Mrs. Yolaine Martineau, Head Admissions Officer, HEC Montreal, 3000 Chemin de la Cote-Sainte-Catherine, Montreal, QC H3T 2A7, Canada. *Phone:* 514-340-6151. *Fax:* 514-340-5640. *E-mail:* admission.info@hec.ca.
Website: http://www.hec.ca/.

Heritage Baptist College and Heritage Theological Seminary
Cambridge, Ontario, Canada

Freshman Application Contact Mr. Mark Walther, Assistant Dean of Students, Heritage Baptist College and Heritage Theological Seminary, New York, NY 10023-6588. *Phone:* 519-651-2869 Ext. 251. *Toll-free phone:* 800-465-1961. *Fax:* 519-651-2870. *E-mail:* mwalther@heritagecollege.net.
Website: http://www.heritage-theo.edu/.

Horizon College & Seminary

Saskatoon, Saskatchewan, Canada

Freshman Application Contact Mrs. Shannon Olson, Assistant Registrar, Horizon College & Seminary, 1303 Jackson Avenue, Saskatoon, SK S7H 2M9, Canada. *Phone:* 306-374-6655. *Toll-free phone:* 877-374-6655. *Fax:* 306-373-6968. *E-mail:* admissions@horizon.edu. *Website:* http://www.horizon.edu/.

The King's University College

Edmonton, Alberta, Canada

- **Independent interdenominational** 4-year, founded 1979
- **Suburban** 20-acre campus
- **Endowment** $1.9 million
- **Coed** 587 undergraduate students, 95% full-time, 56% women, 44% men
- **Moderately difficult** entrance level, 73% of applicants were admitted

Undergraduates 555 full-time, 32 part-time. Students come from 5 provinces and territories; 16 other countries; 14% are from out of state; 20% transferred in; 31% live on campus. *Retention:* 66% of full-time freshmen returned. **Freshmen** *Admission:* 348 applied, 255 admitted, 154 enrolled. *Average high school GPA:* 3.3. **Faculty** *Total:* 111, 45% full-time, 79% with terminal degrees. *Student/faculty ratio:* 9:1. **Academics** *Calendar:* Canadian standard year. *Degrees:* certificates, diplomas, bachelor's, and postbachelor's certificates. *Special study options:* adult/continuing education programs, advanced placement credit, double majors, English as a second language, independent study, internships, off-campus study, part-time degree program, services for LD students, study abroad, summer session for credit. *Unusual degree programs:* 3-2 elementary education, secondary education. **Computers on Campus** 70 computers/terminals are available on campus for general student use. Students can access the following: campus intranet, computer help desk, free student e-mail accounts, online (class) grades, online (class) registration, online (class) schedules. Campuswide network is available. 100% of college-owned or -operated housing units are wired for high-speed Internet access. Wireless service is available via entire campus. **Student Life** *Housing options:* coed, women-only. Campus housing is university owned. Freshman applicants given priority for college housing. *Activities and organizations:* drama/theater group, student-run newspaper, choral group, Micah Action and Awareness, The King's Players (drama club), Chamber and Concert Choirs, King's Science Society, The King's Commerce Association. *Campus security:* 24-hour emergency response devices, student patrols, controlled dormitory access. *Student services:* personal/psychological counseling. **Athletics** *Intercollegiate sports:* basketball M(s)/W(s), soccer M(s)/W(s), volleyball M(s)/W(s). *Intramural sports:* basketball M/W, ice hockey M, soccer M/W, ultimate Frisbee M/W, volleyball M/W. **Costs (2013–14)** *Comprehensive fee:* $17,135 Canadian dollars includes full-time tuition ($10,540 Canadian dollars), mandatory fees ($625 Canadian dollars), and room and board ($5970 Canadian dollars). Full-time tuition and fees vary according to course load. Part-time tuition: $340 Canadian dollars per credit. Part-time tuition and fees vary according to course load. *Required fees:* $156 Canadian dollars per term part-time. *College room only:* $3200 Canadian dollars. Room and board charges vary according to board plan and housing facility. *Payment plan:* installment. *Waivers:* employees or children of employees. **Financial Aid** *Financial aid deadline:* 3/31. **Applying** *Options:* electronic application. *Application fee:* $70 Canadian dollars. *Required:* high school transcript, minimum 2.0 GPA, 1 letter of recommendation. *Required for some:* essay or personal statement, interview. *Application deadlines:* rolling (freshmen), rolling (transfers). *Notification:* 8/15 (freshmen), 8/15 (transfers). **Freshman Application Contact** Mr. Glenn Keeler, Registrar/Director of Admissions, The King's University College, 9125-50 Street, Edmonton, AB T6B 2H3, Canada. *Phone:* 780-465-3500 Ext. 8035. *Toll-free phone:* 800-661-8582. *Fax:* 780-465-3534. *E-mail:* admissions@kingsu.ca. *Website:* http://www.kingsu.ca/.

Kingswood University

Sussex, New Brunswick, Canada

- **Independent** 4-year, founded 1945, affiliated with Wesleyan Church
- **Small-town** 57-acre campus
- **Endowment** $298,761
- **Coed** 212 undergraduate students, 91% full-time, 53% women, 47% men
- **Moderately difficult** entrance level, 42% of applicants were admitted

Undergraduates 193 full-time, 19 part-time. Students come from 5 provinces and territories; 5 other countries; 50% are from out of state; 4% transferred in; 76% live on campus. *Retention:* 71% of full-time freshmen returned. **Freshmen** *Admission:* 171 applied, 71 admitted, 46 enrolled. **Faculty** *Total:* 29, 31% full-time, 34% with terminal degrees. *Student/faculty ratio:* 17:1. **Academics** *Calendar:* semesters. *Degrees:* certificates, associate, and bachelor's. *Special study options:* academic remediation for entering students, advanced placement credit, double majors, internships, part-time degree program, summer session for credit. **Computers on Campus** 20 computers/terminals are available on campus for general student use. Students can access the following: campus intranet, free student e-mail accounts, online (class) grades, online (class) schedules. Campuswide network is available. 100% of college-owned or -operated housing units are wired for high-speed Internet access. Wireless service is available via entire campus. **Student Life** *Housing:* on-campus residence required through junior year. *Options:* men-only, women-only. Campus housing is university owned. Freshman campus housing is guaranteed. *Activities and organizations:* drama/theater group, choral group, Outreach Association, Athletic Association, Student Global Impact, Social Committee, Chorale. *Campus security:* student patrols, controlled dormitory access. *Student services:* personal/psychological counseling. **Athletics** *Intercollegiate sports:* basketball M/W. *Intramural sports:* basketball M/W, ice hockey M/W, soccer M/W, softball M/W, table tennis M/W, volleyball M/W. **Standardized Tests** *Required for some:* SAT or ACT (for admission). **Costs (2013–14)** *Comprehensive fee:* $15,750 Canadian dollars includes full-time tuition ($9450 Canadian dollars), mandatory fees ($600 Canadian dollars), and room and board ($5700 Canadian dollars). Full-time tuition and fees vary according to degree level. Part-time tuition: $315 Canadian dollars per credit hour. Part-time tuition and fees vary according to degree level. *College room only:* $2450 Canadian dollars. Room and board charges vary according to board plan and housing facility. *Payment plan:* installment. *Waivers:* senior citizens and employees or children of employees. **Financial Aid** *Financial aid deadline:* 7/15. **Applying** *Options:* electronic application, early admission. *Application fee:* $20 Canadian dollars. *Required:* essay or personal statement, high school transcript, 2 letters of recommendation. *Recommended:* interview. *Application deadlines:* rolling (freshmen), rolling (transfers). **Freshman Application Contact** Mrs. Shelley Vail, Associate Director for Admissions and Financial Aid, Kingswood University, Kingswood University, PO Box 5125, Sussex, NB E4E 5L2, Canada. *Phone:* 506-432.4422. *Toll-free phone:* 888-432-4422. *Fax:* 506-432.4442. *E-mail:* vails@kingswood.edu. *Website:* http://www.kingswood.edu/.

Lakehead University

Thunder Bay, Ontario, Canada

- **Province-supported** comprehensive, founded 1965
- **Suburban** 345-acre campus
- **Endowment** $37.0 million
- **Coed**
- **Moderately difficult** entrance level

Academics *Calendar:* Canadian standard year. *Degrees:* certificates, diplomas, bachelor's, master's, doctoral, and postbachelor's certificates. **Student Life** *Campus security:* 24-hour emergency response devices and patrols, student patrols, late-night transport/escort service, controlled dormitory access. **Athletics** Member CIS. **Standardized Tests** *Required:* SAT or ACT (for admission). **Financial Aid** *Financial aid deadline:* 6/30. **Applying** *Options:* electronic application, early admission, deferred entrance. *Application fee:* $125 Canadian dollars. *Required:* portfolio for visual arts program, audition for music program, portfolio for media studies. *Required for some:* essay or personal statement, high school transcript. *Recommended:* minimum 3.0 GPA. **Freshman Application Contact** Mr. Nicholas Chamut, Manager of Undergraduate Admissions, Lakehead University, 955 Oliver Road, Thunder Bay, ON P7B 5E1, Canada. *Phone:* 807-343-8676. *Toll-free phone:* 800-465-3959. *Fax:* 807-766-7209. *E-mail:* admissions@lakeheadu.ca. *Website:* http://www.lakeheadu.ca/.

Lakehead University–Orillia
Orillia, Ontario, Canada

Admissions Office Contact Lakehead University–Orillia, 500 University Avenue, Orillia, ON L3V 0B9, Canada. *Website:* http://orillia.lakeheadu.ca/.

Laurentian University
Sudbury, Ontario, Canada

Freshman Application Contact Laurentian University, Ramsey Lake Road, P3E 2C6, Canada. *Phone:* 705-675-1151. *Toll-free phone:* 800-263-4188. *Fax:* 705-675-4891. *E-mail:* admissions@laurentian.ca. *Website:* http://www.laurentian.ca/.

Master's College and Seminary
Peterborough, Ontario, Canada

- **Independent Pentecostal** 4-year, founded 1939
- **Suburban** campus with easy access to Toronto
- **Endowment** $718,092
- **Coed** 294 undergraduate students
- **Noncompetitive** entrance level, 94% of applicants were admitted

Undergraduates Students come from 7 provinces and territories; 2 other countries; 12% are from out of state; 65% live on campus. *Retention:* 81% of full-time freshmen returned. **Freshmen** *Admission:* 137 applied, 129 admitted. **Faculty** *Total:* 31, 16% full-time, 23% with terminal degrees. *Student/faculty ratio:* 8:1. **Academics** *Calendar:* semesters. *Degree:* certificates, diplomas, and bachelor's. *Special study options:* academic remediation for entering students, distance learning, independent study, internships, off-campus study, part-time degree program, services for LD students, summer session for credit. **Computers on Campus** 6 computers/terminals are available on campus for general student use. Students can access the following: computer help desk, free student e-mail accounts, online (class) registration, online (class) schedules. Campuswide network is available. Wireless service is available via entire campus. **Student Life** *Housing:* on-campus residence required for freshman year. *Options:* men-only, women-only. Campus housing is leased by the school. Freshman campus housing is guaranteed. *Campus security:* 24-hour emergency response devices, student patrols, controlled dormitory access. **Costs (2013–14)** *Comprehensive fee:* $12,672 Canadian dollars includes full-time tuition ($6358 Canadian dollars), mandatory fees ($714 Canadian dollars), and room and board ($5600 Canadian dollars). *Payment plan:* installment. *Waivers:* adult students, senior citizens, and employees or children of employees. **Applying** *Options:* deferred entrance. *Application fee:* $75 Canadian dollars. *Required:* essay or personal statement, high school transcript, 3 letters of recommendation, Christian commitment. *Required for some:* interview. *Recommended:* minimum 2.0 GPA. *Application deadlines:* 8/31 (freshmen), 8/31 (transfers). **Freshman Application Contact** Ms. Flora Anthony, Admissions, Master's College and Seminary, 780 Argyle Street, Peterborough, ON K9H 5T2, Canada. *Phone:* 800-295-6368. *Toll-free phone:* 800-295-6368. *Fax:* 705-749-0417. *E-mail:* flora.anthony@mcs.edu. *Website:* http://www.mcs.edu/.

McGill University
Montréal, Quebec, Canada

Freshman Application Contact Enrollment Services, McGill University, 845 Sherbrooke Street West, James Administration Building, Room 205, Montreal, QC H3A 2T5, Canada. *Phone:* 514-398-3910. *Fax:* 514-398-4193. *E-mail:* admissions@mcgill.ca. *Website:* http://www.mcgill.ca/.

McMaster University
Hamilton, Ontario, Canada

Freshman Application Contact Olivia Demerling, Admissions Officer, McMaster University, 1280 Main Street West, Hamilton, ON L8S 4M2, Canada. *Phone:* 905-525-4600. *Fax:* 905-527-1105. *E-mail:* admitmac@mcmaster.ca. *Website:* http://www.mcmaster.ca/.

Memorial University of Newfoundland
St. John's, Newfoundland and Labrador, Canada

Freshman Application Contact Ms. Marian Abbott, Admissions Office, Memorial University of Newfoundland, Elizabeth Avenue, St. John's, NL A1C 5S7, Canada. *Phone:* 709-737-3705. *E-mail:* sturecru@morgan.ucs.mun.ca. *Website:* http://www.mun.ca/.

Mount Allison University
Sackville, New Brunswick, Canada

- **Province-supported** comprehensive, founded 1839
- **Small-town** 50-acre campus
- **Endowment** $65.0 million
- **Coed** 2,675 undergraduate students, 96% full-time, 60% women, 40% men
- **Moderately difficult** entrance level, 74% of applicants were admitted

Undergraduates 2,569 full-time, 106 part-time. Students come from 22 provinces and territories; 45 other countries; 60% are from out of state; 4% transferred in; 50% live on campus. *Retention:* 80% of full-time freshmen returned. **Freshmen** *Admission:* 2,110 applied, 1,551 admitted, 717 enrolled. *Average high school GPA:* 3.31. **Faculty** *Total:* 187, 71% full-time, 88% with terminal degrees. *Student/faculty ratio:* 16:1. **Academics** *Calendar:* Canadian standard year. *Degrees:* certificates, bachelor's, and master's. *Special study options:* academic remediation for entering students, adult/continuing education programs, advanced placement credit, distance learning, double majors, honors programs, independent study, internships, off-campus study, part-time degree program, services for LD students, student-designed majors, study abroad, summer session for credit. **Computers on Campus** 100 computers/terminals and 240 ports are available on campus for general student use. Students can access the following: computer help desk, free student e-mail accounts, online (class) grades, online (class) registration, online (class) schedules, online student account/Websis. Campuswide network is available. 100% of college-owned or -operated housing units are wired for high-speed Internet access. Wireless service is available via entire campus. **Student Life** *Housing options:* coed, women-only, cooperative. Campus housing is university owned. Freshman campus housing is guaranteed. *Activities and organizations:* drama/theater group, student-run newspaper, radio station, choral group, Commerce Society, Windsor Theatre, President's Leadership Development Certificate, Leadership Mount Allison, Garnet and Gold Society. *Campus security:* 24-hour emergency response devices, late-night transport/escort service. *Student services:* health clinic, personal/psychological counseling. **Athletics** Member CIS. *Intercollegiate sports:* basketball M/W, football M, ice hockey W, rugby M/W, soccer M/W, swimming and diving M/W. *Intramural sports:* badminton M/W, baseball M/W, basketball M/W, football M/W, golf M/W, ice hockey M/W, rugby M/W, skiing (cross-country) M/W, skiing (downhill) M/W, soccer M/W, softball M/W, tennis M/W, ultimate Frisbee M/W, volleyball M/W, weight lifting M/W. **Applying** *Options:* electronic application, deferred entrance. *Application fee:* $50 Canadian dollars. *Required:* high school transcript, minimum 2.5 GPA. *Required for some:* essay or personal statement, interview. *Recommended:* 2 letters of recommendation. *Application deadlines:* rolling (freshmen), rolling (transfers). *Notification:* continuous (freshmen), continuous (transfers). **Freshman Application Contact** Mr. Joceylyn Ollerhead, Manager of Admissions, Mount Allison University, 65 York Street, Sackville, NB E4L 1E4, Canada. *Phone:* 506-364-3294. *Fax:* 506-364-2272. *E-mail:* admissions@mta.ca. *Website:* http://www.mta.ca/.

Mount Royal University
Calgary, Alberta, Canada

Freshman Application Contact Admissions Office, Mount Royal University, 4825 Mount Royal Gate SW, Calgary, AB T3E 6K6, Canada. *Phone:* 403-440-5000. *Toll-free phone:* 877-440-5001. *Website:* http://www.mtroyal.ca/.

Mount Saint Vincent University
Halifax, Nova Scotia, Canada

Freshman Application Contact Ms. Heidi Tattrie, Assistant Registrar/Admissions, Mount Saint Vincent University, 166 Bedford Highway, Halifax,

NS B3M2J6, Canada. *Phone:* 902-457-6117. *Toll-free phone:* 877-733-6788. *Fax:* 902-457-6498. *E-mail:* admissions@msvu.ca. *Website:* http://www.msvu.ca/.

Ner Israel Yeshiva College of Toronto
Thornhill, Ontario, Canada

Director of Admissions Rabbi Y. Kravetz, Director of Admissions, Ner Israel Yeshiva College of Toronto, 8950 Bathurst Street, Thornhill, ON L4J 8A7, Canada. *Phone:* 905-731-1224.

Nipissing University
North Bay, Ontario, Canada

Freshman Application Contact Ms. Lori-Ann Beckford, Assistant Registrar, Liaison, Nipissing University, 100 College Drive, Box 5002, North Bay, ON P1B 8L7, Canada. *Phone:* 705-474-3461 Ext. 4518. *Fax:* 705-474-1947. *E-mail:* liaison@nipissingu.ca. *Website:* http://www.nipissingu.ca/.

NSCAD University
Halifax, Nova Scotia, Canada

Freshman Application Contact Mr. Terry Bailey, Director of Admissions and Enrollment Services, NSCAD University, 5163 Duke Street, Halifax, NS B3J 3J6, Canada. *Phone:* 902-494-8129. *Toll-free phone:* 888-444-5989. *Fax:* 902-425-2987. *E-mail:* admissions@nscad.ca. *Website:* http://www.nscad.ca/.

Okanagan College
Kelowna, British Columbia, Canada

- **Province-supported** 4-year, founded 2005, part of Ministry of Advanced Education, Industry Training Authority
- **Urban** 13-acre campus
- **Coed** 3,363 undergraduate students, 63% full-time, 56% women, 44% men

Undergraduates 2,122 full-time, 1,241 part-time. Students come from 10 provinces and territories; 46 other countries; 4% are from out of state; 2% transferred in. *Retention:* 57% of full-time freshmen returned.
Freshmen *Admission:* 923 enrolled.
Faculty *Total:* 241, 72% full-time, 25% with terminal degrees. *Student/faculty ratio:* 14:1.
Academics *Degrees:* certificates, diplomas, associate, and bachelor's. *Special study options:* academic remediation for entering students, adult/continuing education programs, advanced placement credit, cooperative education, distance learning, English as a second language, external degree program, honors programs, internships, off-campus study, part-time degree program, services for LD students, study abroad, summer session for credit.
Computers on Campus 1,050 computers/terminals are available on campus for general student use. Students can access the following: campus intranet, computer help desk, free student e-mail accounts, online (class) grades, online (class) registration, online (class) schedules. Campuswide network is available. 100% of college-owned or -operated housing units are wired for high-speed Internet access. Wireless service is available via entire campus.
Student Life *Housing options:* coed. Campus housing is university owned. *Activities and organizations:* student-run newspaper, choral group. *Campus security:* 24-hour emergency response devices and patrols, late-night transport/escort service, controlled dormitory access. *Student services:* personal/psychological counseling.
Athletics *Intercollegiate sports:* baseball M. *Intramural sports:* volleyball M/W.
Costs (2013–14) *Tuition:* province resident $3140 Canadian dollars full-time, $101 Canadian dollars per credit part-time; nonresident $3140 Canadian dollars full-time, $101 Canadian dollars per credit part-time; International tuition $11,000 Canadian dollars full-time. Full-time tuition and fees vary according to course level, course load, location, and program. Part-time tuition and fees vary according to course level, course load, location, and program. *Required fees:* $714 Canadian dollars full-time, $9 Canadian dollars per credit part-time, $94 Canadian dollars per term part-time. *Room and board:* Room and board charges vary according to housing facility. *Waivers:* senior citizens and employees or children of employees.
Applying *Required for some:* essay or personal statement, high school transcript, minimum 2.0 GPA, interview.
Freshman Application Contact Mr. Paul Campo, Associate Registrar Systems, Okanagan College, 1000 K.L.O. Rd., Kelowna, BC V1Y 4X8,

Canada. *Phone:* 250-762-5445 Ext. 4332. *Toll-free phone:* 877-755-2266. *E-mail:* pgcampo@okanagan.bc.ca. *Website:* http://www.okanagan.bc.ca/.

Prairie Bible Institute
Three Hills, Alberta, Canada

Director of Admissions Mr. Kevin Kirk, Vice President, Marketing and Enrollment Management, Prairie Bible Institute, 330 Sixth Avenue North, PO Box 4000, Three Hills, AB T0M 2N0, Canada. *Phone:* 403-443-5511 Ext. 3007. *Toll-free phone:* 800-661-2425. *E-mail:* admissions@prairie.edu. *Website:* http://www.prairie.edu/.

Providence University College & Theological Seminary
Otterburne, Manitoba, Canada

Freshman Application Contact Mr. Adrian Enns, Director of College Enrollment, Providence University College & Theological Seminary, 10 College Crescent, Otterburne, MB R0A 1G0, Canada. *Phone:* 204-433-7488. *Toll-free phone:* 800-668-7768. *Fax:* 204-433-7158. *E-mail:* info@prov.ca. *Website:* http://www.providenceuc.ca/.

Queen's University at Kingston
Kingston, Ontario, Canada

- **Province-supported** university, founded 1841
- **Urban** 160-acre campus
- **Endowment** $601.9 million
- **Coed**
- **Most difficult** entrance level

Faculty *Student/faculty ratio:* 15:1.
Academics *Calendar:* Canadian standard year. *Degrees:* certificates, bachelor's, master's, and doctoral.
Student Life *Campus security:* 24-hour emergency response devices and patrols, student patrols, late-night transport/escort service, controlled dormitory access.
Athletics Member CIS.
Standardized Tests *Required:* SAT or ACT (for admission).
Financial Aid *Of all full-time matriculated undergraduates who enrolled in 2011,* 442 state and other part-time jobs (averaging $1215). *Average financial aid package:* $9055.
Applying *Options:* deferred entrance. *Application fee:* $180 Canadian dollars. *Required:* essay or personal statement, high school transcript, minimum 2.7 GPA. *Required for some:* 1 letter of recommendation.
Freshman Application Contact Ms. Iveta Reinikovaite, Admission Coordinator, Queen's University at Kingston, Undergraduate Admissions, Gordon Hall, 74 Union Street, Kingston, ON K7L 3N6, Canada. *Phone:* 613-533-2218. *Fax:* 613-533-6810. *E-mail:* admission@queensu.ca. *Website:* http://www.queensu.ca/.

Redeemer University College
Ancaster, Ontario, Canada

Freshman Application Contact Recruitment, Redeemer University College, 777 Garner Road East, Ancaster, ON L9K 1J4, Canada. *Phone:* 905-648-2139 Ext. 4280. *Toll-free phone:* 800-263-6467. *Fax:* 905-648-9545. *E-mail:* recruitment@redeemer.ca. *Website:* http://www.redeemer.ca/.

Rocky Mountain College
Calgary, Alberta, Canada

- **Independent** 4-year, founded 1992, affiliated with Missionary Church
- **Urban** 1-acre campus with easy access to Calgary, Alberta, Canada
- **Endowment** $343,200
- **Coed**
- **Noncompetitive** entrance level

Academics *Calendar:* semesters. *Degree:* certificates, diplomas, and bachelor's. *Special study options:* academic remediation for entering students, adult/continuing education programs, advanced placement credit, distance learning, double majors, internships, part-time degree program, summer session for credit.
Computers on Campus 12 computers/terminals are available on campus for general student use. Students can access the following: campus intranet, computer help desk, free student e-mail accounts, online (class) grades, online

(class) registration, online (class) schedules. Campuswide network is available. 100% of college-owned or -operated housing units are wired for high-speed Internet access. Wireless service is available via entire campus.
Student Life *Activities and organizations:* drama/theater group, choral group. *Campus security:* 24-hour emergency response devices. *Student services:* personal/psychological counseling.
Costs (2013–14) *Tuition:* $310 Canadian dollars per credit part-time.
Applying *Options:* electronic application, deferred entrance. *Application fee:* $50 Canadian dollars. *Required:* essay or personal statement, high school transcript, 2 letters of recommendation. *Required for some:* interview. *Application deadlines:* rolling (freshmen), rolling (transfers).
Freshman Application Contact Rocky Mountain College, 4039 Brentwood Road, NW, Calgary, AB T2L 1L1, Canada. *Phone:* 403-284-5100. *Toll-free phone:* 877-YOUnRMC.
Website: http://www.rockymountaincollege.ca/.

Royal Military College of Canada
Kingston, Ontario, Canada

Freshman Application Contact Royal Military College of Canada, PO Box 17000, Station Forces, Kingston, ON K7K 7B4, Canada. *Phone:* 613-541-6000 Ext. 6579.
Website: http://www.rmc.ca/.

Royal Roads University
Victoria, British Columbia, Canada

Application Contact Royal Roads University, 2005 Sooke Road, Victoria, BC V9B 5Y2, Canada. *Phone:* 250-391-2511. *Toll-free phone:* 800-788-8028.
Website: http://www.royalroads.ca/.

Ryerson University
Toronto, Ontario, Canada

- **Province-supported** comprehensive, founded 1948
- **Urban** 20-acre campus
- **Coed**
- **Moderately difficult** entrance level

Academics *Calendar:* Canadian standard year or semesters depending on program. *Degrees:* certificates, bachelor's, and master's.
Student Life *Campus security:* 24-hour emergency response devices and patrols, late-night transport/escort service, controlled dormitory access, staffed access control is in place 24 hours a day, with ID checks of all persons attempting to enter.
Athletics Member CIS.
Financial Aid *Financial aid deadline:* 1/15.
Applying *Options:* electronic application. *Application fee:* $80 Canadian dollars. *Required:* high school transcript. *Required for some:* essay or personal statement, interview, portfolio, audition, entrance examination.
Freshman Application Contact Michelle Beaton, Manager of International Student Recruitment, Ryerson University, 350 Victoria Street, Toronto, ON M5B 2K3, Canada. *Phone:* 416-979-5080. *Fax:* 416-979-5067. *E-mail:* inquire@ryerson.ca.
Website: http://www.ryerson.ca/.

St. Francis Xavier University
Antigonish, Nova Scotia, Canada

Freshman Application Contact Ms. Sarah Murray, Admissions Officer, St. Francis Xavier University, PO Box 5000, Antigonish, NS B2G 2W5, Canada. *Phone:* 902-867-2219. *Toll-free phone:* 877-867-7839 (in-state); 877-867-STFX (out-of-state). *Fax:* 902-867-2329. *E-mail:* mbarry@stfx.ca.
Website: http://www.stfx.ca/.

Saint Mary's University
Halifax, Nova Scotia, Canada

Director of Admissions Mr. Greg Ferguson, Director of Admissions, Saint Mary's University, Halifax, NS B3H 3C3, Canada. *Phone:* 902-420-5415. *Fax:* 902-496-8100. *E-mail:* greg.ferguson@smu.ca.
Website: http://www.smu.ca/.

Saint Paul University
Ottawa, Ontario, Canada

Director of Admissions Admission and Recruitment Office, Saint Paul University, 223 Main Street, Ottawa, ON K1S 1C4, Canada. *Phone:* 613-236-1393 Ext. 8990. *Toll-free phone:* 800-637-6859. *Fax:* 613-782-3014. *E-mail:* admission@ustpaul.ca.
Website: http://www.ustpaul.ca/.

St. Thomas University
Fredericton, New Brunswick, Canada

- **Independent Roman Catholic** 4-year, founded 1910
- **Small-town** 16-acre campus
- **Endowment** $26.6 million
- **Coed** 2,332 undergraduate students, 94% full-time, 67% women, 33% men
- **Moderately difficult** entrance level, 87% of applicants were admitted

Undergraduates 2,182 full-time, 150 part-time. Students come from 9 provinces and territories; 36 other countries; 21% are from out of state; 96% Race/ethnicity unknown; 4% international; 5% transferred in; 30% live on campus. *Retention:* 70% of full-time freshmen returned.
Freshmen *Admission:* 1,265 applied, 1,105 admitted, 609 enrolled. *Average high school GPA:* 3.4.
Faculty *Total:* 180, 59% full-time, 71% with terminal degrees. *Student/faculty ratio:* 19:1.
Academics *Calendar:* semesters. *Degrees:* certificates, bachelor's, and post-bachelor's certificates. *Special study options:* academic remediation for entering students, accelerated degree program, advanced placement credit, double majors, English as a second language, honors programs, independent study, internships, off-campus study, part-time degree program, services for LD students, student-designed majors, study abroad, summer session for credit.
Computers on Campus 94 computers/terminals are available on campus for general student use. Students can access the following: computer help desk, free student e-mail accounts, online (class) grades, online (class) registration, online (class) schedules, Moodle. Campuswide network is available. 100% of college-owned or -operated housing units are wired for high-speed Internet access. Wireless service is available via entire campus.
Student Life *Housing options:* coed, women-only, disabled students. Campus housing is university owned. Freshman campus housing is guaranteed. *Activities and organizations:* drama/theater group, student-run newspaper, radio station, choral group, Theatre St. Thomas, St. Thomas Student Union, Criminology Society, Model UN, International Students' Association. *Campus security:* 24-hour emergency response devices and patrols, student patrols, late-night transport/escort service, controlled dormitory access. *Student services:* health clinic, personal/psychological counseling, women's center.
Athletics Member CIS. *Intercollegiate sports:* basketball M/W, cross-country running M/W, golf M/W, ice hockey M(s)/W(s), soccer M/W, volleyball M/W. *Intramural sports:* badminton M/W, basketball M/W, cross-country running M/W, fencing M/W, football M, ice hockey M/W, rock climbing M/W, soccer M/W, softball M/W, squash M/W, swimming and diving M/W, table tennis M/W, track and field M/W, ultimate Frisbee M/W, volleyball M/W, water polo M/W.
Standardized Tests *Recommended:* SAT (for admission).
Costs (2012–13) *Comprehensive fee:* $13,096 Canadian dollars includes full-time tuition ($4945 Canadian dollars), mandatory fees ($371 Canadian dollars), and room and board ($7780 Canadian dollars). Full-time tuition and fees vary according to course load, degree level, and program. Part-time tuition: $549 Canadian dollars per course. Part-time tuition and fees vary according to course load. International tuition: $12,855 Canadian dollars full-time. *Required fees:* $31 Canadian dollars per course part-time. *Room and board:* Room and board charges vary according to board plan, housing facility, and location. *Payment plans:* installment, deferred payment. *Waivers:* senior citizens and employees or children of employees.
Financial Aid *Financial aid deadline:* 3/1.
Applying *Options:* electronic application, early action. *Application fee:* $35 Canadian dollars. *Required:* high school transcript, minimum 3.0 GPA. *Required for some:* essay or personal statement, interview. *Application deadlines:* 8/31 (freshmen), 8/31 (transfers), 12/7 (early action). *Notification:* continuous (freshmen), continuous (transfers).
Freshman Application Contact Ms. Kathryn Monti, Director of Admissions, St. Thomas University, Admissions and Welcome Building, Fredericton, NB E3B 5G3, Canada. *Phone:* 506-452-0532. *Fax:* 506-452-0617. *E-mail:* admissions@stu.ca.
Website: http://www.stu.ca/.

Simon Fraser University
Burnaby, British Columbia, Canada

- **Province-supported** university, founded 1965
- **Suburban** campus with easy access to Vancouver
- **Endowment** $176.9 million
- **Coed** 27,123 undergraduate students, 49% full-time, 54% women, 46% men
- **Moderately difficult** entrance level, 52% of applicants were admitted

Undergraduates 13,352 full-time, 13,771 part-time. Students come from 11 provinces and territories; 84 other countries; 9% are from out of state; 5% transferred in; 9% live on campus. *Retention:* 88% of full-time freshmen returned.

Freshmen *Admission:* 14,618 applied, 7,667 admitted, 3,137 enrolled. *Average high school GPA:* 3.35.

Faculty *Total:* 948, 99% full-time, 89% with terminal degrees. *Student/faculty ratio:* 23:1.

Academics *Calendar:* trimesters. *Degrees:* certificates, diplomas, bachelor's, master's, doctoral, post-master's, and postbachelor's certificates. *Special study options:* academic remediation for entering students, adult/continuing education programs, advanced placement credit, cooperative education, distance learning, double majors, English as a second language, honors programs, independent study, internships, off-campus study, part-time degree program, services for LD students, study abroad, summer session for credit.

Computers on Campus 900 computers/terminals are available on campus for general student use. Students can access the following: free student e-mail accounts, online (class) grades, online (class) registration, online (class) schedules. Campuswide network is available. 100% of college-owned or -operated housing units are wired for high-speed Internet access. Wireless service is available via entire campus.

Student Life *Housing options:* coed, women-only, disabled students. Campus housing is university owned. Freshman applicants given priority for college housing. *Activities and organizations:* drama/theater group, student-run newspaper, radio station, The Peak Newspaper, orientation leaders, Crisis line, Women's Centre, Simon Fraser Public Interest Research Group. *Campus security:* 24-hour emergency response devices and patrols, student patrols, late-night transport/escort service, controlled dormitory access, safe-walk stations, 24-hour safe study area. *Student services:* health clinic, personal/psychological counseling, women's center.

Athletics Member NCAA. All Division II. *Intercollegiate sports:* basketball M(s)/W(s), cross-country running M(s)/W(s), football M(s), golf M(s)/W, gymnastics M, soccer M(s)/W(s), softball W(s), swimming and diving M(s)/W(s), track and field M(s)/W(s), volleyball W(s), wrestling M(s)/W(s). *Intramural sports:* archery M(c)/W(c), badminton M(c)/W(c), basketball M/W, cheerleading M(c)/W(c), crew M(c)/W(c), fencing M(c)/W(c), field hockey W(c), football M/W, golf W(c), gymnastics W(c), ice hockey M(c)/W(c), lacrosse M(c), rugby M(c)/W(c), soccer M/W, softball M/W, squash M(c)/W(c), table tennis M(c)/W(c), tennis M/W, ultimate Frisbee M(c)/W(c), volleyball M(c)/W(c), water polo M(c)/W(c).

Standardized Tests *Required for some:* SAT or ACT (for admission).

Financial Aid *Financial aid deadline:* 11/15.

Applying *Options:* electronic application, early admission, deferred entrance. *Application fee:* $75 Canadian dollars. *Required:* high school transcript, minimum 3.0 GPA. *Required for some:* essay or personal statement, interview. *Application deadlines:* 4/30 (freshmen), rolling (transfers). *Notification:* continuous until 6/30 (freshmen), continuous (transfers).

Freshman Application Contact Ms. Louise Legris, Director of Admissions, Simon Fraser University, 8888 University Drive, Burnaby, BC V5A 1S6, Canada. *Phone:* 778-782-3498. *Fax:* 778-782-4969. *E-mail:* undergraduate-admissions@sfu.ca.
Website: http://www.sfu.ca/.

Southern Alberta Institute of Technology
Calgary, Alberta, Canada

Freshman Application Contact Southern Alberta Institute of Technology, 1301 16th Avenue NW, Calgary, AB T2M 0L4, Canada. *Phone:* 403-284-8857. *Toll-free phone:* 877-284-SAIT.
Website: http://www.sait.ca/.

Steinbach Bible College
Steinbach, Manitoba, Canada

Freshman Application Contact Mrs. Kaylene Buhler, Admissions Counselor, Steinbach Bible College, 50 PTH 12 North, Steinbach, MB R5G 1T4, Canada.

Phone: 204-326-6451 Ext. 232. *Toll-free phone:* 800-230-8478. *Fax:* 204-326-6908. *E-mail:* info@sbcollege.ca.
Website: http://www.sbcollege.ca/.

Summit Pacific College
Abbotsford, British Columbia, Canada

Director of Admissions Ms. Melody Deeley, Admissions and Registration, Summit Pacific College, Box 1700, Abbotsford, BC V2S 7E7, Canada. *Phone:* 604-851-7225. *Toll-free phone:* 800-976-8388. *E-mail:* registrar@summitpacific.ca.
Website: http://www.summitpacific.ca/.

Télé-université
Québec, Quebec, Canada

Freshman Application Contact Ms. Louise Bertrand, Registraire, Télé-université, 455, rue de l'Église, C.P. 4800, succ. Terminus, Québec, QC G1K 9H5, Canada. *Phone:* 418-657-2262 Ext. 5307. *Toll-free phone:* 888-843-4333.
Website: http://www.teluq.uquebec.ca/.

Thompson Rivers University
Kamloops, British Columbia, Canada

- **Province-supported** comprehensive, founded 1970, part of Ministry of Advanced Education, Province of British Columbia
- **Small-town** 100-acre campus
- **Endowment** $16.1 million
- **Coed** 7,151 undergraduate students, 89% full-time, 53% women, 47% men
- **82%** of applicants were admitted

Undergraduates 6,360 full-time, 791 part-time. Students come from 11 provinces and territories; 78 other countries; 9% are from out of state; 14% live on campus. *Retention:* 71% of full-time freshmen returned.

Freshmen *Admission:* 2,986 applied, 2,438 admitted.

Faculty *Total:* 457.

Academics *Calendar:* semesters. *Degrees:* certificates, diplomas, associate, bachelor's, master's, and postbachelor's certificates. *Special study options:* academic remediation for entering students, accelerated degree program, adult/continuing education programs, advanced placement credit, cooperative education, distance learning, double majors, English as a second language, external degree program, honors programs, independent study, internships, off-campus study, part-time degree program, services for LD students, study abroad, summer session for credit.

Computers on Campus 1,200 computers/terminals are available on campus for general student use. Students can access the following: campus intranet, computer help desk, free student e-mail accounts, online (class) grades, online (class) registration, online (class) schedules, Learning Management systems including Moodle and Blackboard, Network drive space (250mb), Wireless access, Remote access to their network drive, student elections, Online payments, financial forms/info, updating personal contact information. Campuswide network is available. 100% of college-owned or -operated housing units are wired for high-speed Internet access. Wireless service is available via entire campus.

Student Life *Housing options:* coed. Campus housing is university owned and is provided by a third party. *Activities and organizations:* drama/theater group, student-run newspaper, radio station, choral group, national fraternities, national sororities. *Campus security:* 24-hour emergency response devices and patrols, student patrols, late-night transport/escort service, controlled dormitory access. *Student services:* health clinic, personal/psychological counseling.

Athletics Member CIS. *Intercollegiate sports:* badminton M(s)/W(s), baseball M, basketball M(s)/W(s), cross-country running M/W, golf M, ice hockey M, soccer M(s)/W(s), volleyball M(s)/W(s). *Intramural sports:* crew M/W, football M, ice hockey M, racquetball M/W, rugby M, skiing (cross-country) M/W, skiing (downhill) M/W, softball M/W, squash M/W, swimming and diving M/W, table tennis M/W, track and field M/W.

Costs (2012–13) *Tuition:* province resident $3755 Canadian dollars full-time, $125 Canadian dollars per credit part-time; nonresident $3755 Canadian dollars full-time, $125 Canadian dollars per credit part-time; International tuition $13,800 Canadian dollars full-time. *Required fees:* $635 Canadian dollars full-time, $21 Canadian dollars per credit part-time. *Room only:* $6240 Canadian dollars. Room and board charges vary according to housing facility. *Payment plan:* installment. *Waivers:* senior citizens.

Financial Aid Of all full-time matriculated undergraduates who enrolled in 2009, 85 state and other part-time jobs (averaging $2400). *Financial aid deadline:* 3/1.

Applying *Options:* electronic application, early admission, early decision, deferred entrance. *Application fee:* $26 Canadian dollars. *Required:* high school transcript. *Required for some:* essay or personal statement, interview. *Application deadlines:* 4/30 (freshmen), 4/30 (out-of-state freshmen), 4/30 (transfers). *Early decision deadline:* 3/1 (for plan 1), 3/1 (for plan 2). *Notification:* continuous until 4/30 (freshmen), continuous until 4/30 (out-of-state freshmen), continuous until 4/30 (transfers), 3/1 (early decision plan 1), 3/1 (early decision plan 2).
Freshman Application Contact Mr. Josh Keller, Director, Student Recruitment and Liaison, Thompson Rivers University, 900 McGill Road, Kamloops, BC V2C 0C8, Canada. *Phone:* 250-828-5008. *Fax:* 250-828-5159. *E-mail:* jkeller@tru.ca.
Website: http://www.tru.ca/.

Trent University
Peterborough, Ontario, Canada
- **Province-supported** university, founded 1963
- **Suburban** 1400-acre campus with easy access to Toronto
- **Coed** 7,574 undergraduate students, 85% full-time, 65% women, 35% men
- **Moderately difficult** entrance level, 18% of applicants were admitted

Undergraduates 6,409 full-time, 1,165 part-time. Students come from 12 provinces and territories; 78 other countries; 2% are from out of state; 7% transferred in; 17% live on campus. *Retention:* 84% of full-time freshmen returned.
Freshmen *Admission:* 9,300 applied, 1,700 admitted, 1,502 enrolled.
Faculty *Total:* 500, 60% full-time. *Student/faculty ratio:* 18:1.
Academics *Calendar:* Canadian standard year. *Degrees:* diplomas, bachelor's, master's, and doctoral. *Special study options:* academic remediation for entering students, accelerated degree program, advanced placement credit, cooperative education, distance learning, double majors, English as a second language, honors programs, independent study, internships, off-campus study, part-time degree program, services for LD students, student-designed majors, study abroad, summer session for credit.
Computers on Campus Students can access the following: campus intranet, computer help desk, free student e-mail accounts, online (class) grades, online (class) registration, online (class) schedules, online tuition payment. Campuswide network is available. 100% of college-owned or -operated housing units are wired for high-speed Internet access. Wireless service is available via entire campus.
Student Life *Housing options:* coed, women-only. Campus housing is university owned. Freshman applicants given priority for college housing. *Activities and organizations:* drama/theater group, student-run newspaper, radio station, choral group, Trent Radio, Trent International Program, Trent Central Student Association, Arthur (student newspaper), Excalibur (yearbook). *Campus security:* 24-hour emergency response devices and patrols, student patrols, late-night transport/escort service, controlled dormitory access. *Student services:* health clinic, personal/psychological counseling, women's center.
Athletics Member CIS. *Intercollegiate sports:* crew M/W, cross-country running M/W, fencing M/W, golf M, lacrosse M, rugby M/W, soccer M/W, swimming and diving M/W, track and field M/W, volleyball M/W. *Intramural sports:* badminton M/W, baseball M/W, basketball M/W, cross-country running M/W, football M/W, ice hockey M/W, soccer M/W, softball M/W, squash M/W, swimming and diving M/W, tennis M/W, track and field M/W, ultimate Frisbee M/W, volleyball M/W, water polo M/W.
Costs (2012–13) *Tuition:* province resident $5693 Canadian dollars full-time, $1139 Canadian dollars per course part-time; nonresident $3209 Canadian dollars per course part-time; International tuition $16,045 Canadian dollars full-time. Full-time tuition and fees vary according to location, program, and student level. Part-time tuition and fees vary according to course load, location, program, and student level. *Required fees:* $1389 Canadian dollars full-time, $110 Canadian dollars per credit part-time. *Room and board:* $10,300 Canadian dollars. Room and board charges vary according to board plan, housing facility, and location. *Payment plans:* installment, deferred payment. *Waivers:* employees or children of employees.
Applying *Options:* electronic application, deferred entrance. *Application fee:* $135 Canadian dollars. *Required:* high school transcript, minimum 2.8 GPA. *Required for some:* essay or personal statement, interview. *Application deadlines:* 6/1 (freshmen), 6/1 (transfers). *Notification:* continuous (freshmen), continuous (transfers).
Freshman Application Contact Mr. Kevin Whitmore, Manager, Admissions, Trent University, 1600 West Bank Drive, Peterborough, ON K9J 7B8, Canada. *Phone:* 705-748-1011 Ext. 7748. *Fax:* 705-748-1629. *E-mail:* admissions@trentu.ca.
Website: http://www.trentu.ca/.

Trinity Western University
Langley, British Columbia, Canada
Director of Admissions Director of Admissions, Trinity Western University, 7600 Glover Road, Langley, BC V2Y 1Y1, Canada. *Phone:* 604-888-7511 Ext. 3005. *Toll-free phone:* 888-468-6898. *E-mail:* admissions@twu.ca. *Website:* http://www.twu.ca/.

Tyndale University College & Seminary
Toronto, Ontario, Canada
Freshman Application Contact Tricia McKenley, Admissions Office Coordinator, Tyndale University College & Seminary, 25 Ballyconnor Court, Toronto, ON M2M 4B3, Canada. *Phone:* 416-218-6757 Ext. 6738. *Toll-free phone:* 877-896-3253. *E-mail:* admissions@tydale.ca.
Website: http://www.tyndale.ca/.

Université de Moncton
Moncton, New Brunswick, Canada
Freshman Application Contact Miss Nicole Savois, Chief Admission Officer, Université de Moncton, Moncton, NB E1A 3E9, Canada. *Phone:* 506-858-4115. *Toll-free phone:* 800-363-8336. *E-mail:* gallanrm@umoncton.ca.
Website: http://www.umoncton.ca/.

Université de Montréal
Montréal, Quebec, Canada
Freshman Application Contact Mr. Pierre Chenard, Registrar, Université de Montréal, CP 6128, Succursale Centre-ville, Montréal, QC H3C 3J7, Canada. *Phone:* 514-343-2214. *Fax:* 514-343-2097. *E-mail:* pierre.chenard@umontreal.ca.
Website: http://www.umontreal.ca/.

Université de Sherbrooke
Sherbrooke, Quebec, Canada
- **Independent** university, founded 1954
- **Urban** 800-acre campus with easy access to Montreal
- **Coed** 13,983 undergraduate students, 78% full-time, 55% women, 45% men
- **Moderately difficult** entrance level, 56% of applicants were admitted

Undergraduates 10,842 full-time, 3,141 part-time. Students come from 3 provinces and territories; 30 other countries; 1% are from out of state.
Freshmen *Admission:* 17,302 applied, 9,756 admitted, 2,989 enrolled.
Faculty *Total:* 3,073, 35% full-time.
Academics *Calendar:* Canadian standard year. *Degrees:* certificates, diplomas, bachelor's, master's, and doctoral. *Special study options:* accelerated degree program, adult/continuing education programs, cooperative education, English as a second language, internships, off-campus study, part-time degree program, services for LD students, student-designed majors, study abroad, summer session for credit.
Computers on Campus 300 computers/terminals are available on campus for general student use. Students can access the following: computer help desk, free student e-mail accounts, online (class) registration, online (class) schedules. Campuswide network is available. Wireless service is available via classrooms, computer centers, computer labs, learning centers, libraries.
Student Life *Housing options:* coed. Campus housing is university owned. *Activities and organizations:* drama/theater group, student-run newspaper, radio station. *Campus security:* 24-hour emergency response devices and patrols. *Student services:* health clinic, personal/psychological counseling, legal services.
Athletics Member CIS. *Intercollegiate sports:* badminton M/W, cheerleading M/W, golf M/W, rugby M/W. *Intramural sports:* badminton M/W, basketball M/W, field hockey M/W, ice hockey M, racquetball M/W, soccer M/W, squash M/W, track and field M/W, ultimate Frisbee M/W, volleyball M/W, water polo M/W.
Costs (2013–14) *Tuition:* province resident $2168 Canadian dollars full-time, $72 Canadian dollars per credit part-time; nonresident $5858 Canadian dollars full-time, $195 Canadian dollars per credit part-time; International tuition $16,260 Canadian dollars full-time. Full-time tuition and fees vary according to course load and location. Part-time tuition and fees vary according to course load and location. *Required fees:* $542 Canadian dollars full-time, $13 Canadian dollars per credit part-time, $72 Canadian dollars per term part-time.

Room only: $3360 Canadian dollars. *Waivers:* employees or children of employees.
Financial Aid *Financial aid deadline:* 3/31.
Applying *Options:* electronic application, early admission. *Application fee:* $70 Canadian dollars. *Required:* high school transcript. *Required for some:* interview. *Application deadline:* 3/1 (freshmen). *Notification:* continuous until 5/15 (freshmen).
Freshman Application Contact Ms. Lisa Bedard, Admissions Officer, Université de Sherbrooke, 2500, Boulevard de l'Universite, Sherbrooke, QC J1K 2R1, Canada. *Phone:* 819-821-7687. *Toll-free phone:* 800-267-UDES. *Website:* http://www.usherbrooke.ca/.

Université du Québec à Chicoutimi
Chicoutimi, Quebec, Canada

Freshman Application Contact Mr. Claudio Zoccastello, Admissions Officer, Université du Québec à Chicoutimi, 555, boulevard de L'Université, Chicoutimi, QC G7H 2B1, Canada. *Phone:* 418-545-5005. *E-mail:* czoccast@ uqac.uquebec.ca.
Website: http://www.uqac.ca/.

Université du Québec à Montréal
Montréal, Quebec, Canada

Freshman Application Contact Ms. Lucille Boisselle-Roy, Admissions Officer, Université du Québec à Montréal, CP 8888, Succursale Centreville, Montréal, QC H2L 4S8, Canada. *Phone:* 514-987-3132. *E-mail:* admission@ uqam.ca.
Website: http://www.uqam.ca/.

Université du Québec à Rimouski
Rimouski, Quebec, Canada

Freshman Application Contact Ms. Marie Saint-Laurent, Admissions Officer, Université du Québec à Rimouski, 300 Allee des Ursulines, CP3300, Rimouski QC G5L 3A1, Canada. *Phone:* 418-724-1433. *E-mail:* philippe_horth@uqar.uquebec.ca.
Website: http://www.uqar.ca/.

Université du Québec à Trois-Rivières
Trois-Rivières, Quebec, Canada

Freshman Application Contact Ms. Jean Bois, Admissions Officer, Université du Québec à Trois-Rivières, 3351 blvd des Forges, Case post 500, Trois-Rivières, QC G9A 5H7, Canada. *Phone:* 819-376-5011. *Toll-free phone:* 800-365-0922. *Fax:* 819-376-5232. *E-mail:* registraire@uqtr.ca.
Website: http://www.uqtr.ca/.

Université du Québec, École de technologie supérieure
Montréal, Quebec, Canada

Director of Admissions Mme. Francine Gamache, Registraire, Université du Québec, École de technologie supérieure, 1100, rue Notre Dame Ouest, Montréal, QC H3C 1K3, Canada. *Phone:* 514-396-8885. *E-mail:* admission@ ets.mtl.ca.
Website: http://www.etsmtl.ca/.

Université du Québec en Abitibi-Témiscamingue
Rouyn-Noranda, Quebec, Canada

Freshman Application Contact Mrs. Monique Fay, Admissions Officer, Université du Québec en Abitibi-Témiscamingue, 445 boulevard de l'Université, Rouyn-Noranda, QC J9X 5E4, Canada. *Phone:* 819-762-0971. *E-mail:* micheline.chevalier@uqat.uquebec.ca.
Website: http://www.uqat.ca/.

Université du Québec en Outaouais
Gatineau, Quebec, Canada

- **Province-supported** university, founded 1981, part of Universite du Quebec
- **Small-town** campus with easy access to Ottawa
- **Coed** 5,302 undergraduate students
- **Noncompetitive** entrance level

Undergraduates Students come from 34 other countries.
Academics *Calendar:* trimesters. *Degrees:* certificates, bachelor's, master's, doctoral, post-master's, and postbachelor's certificates. *Special study options:* accelerated degree program, adult/continuing education programs, cooperative education, independent study, internships, off-campus study, part-time degree program, services for LD students, study abroad, summer session for credit.
Computers on Campus 500 computers/terminals are available on campus for general student use. Students can access the following: computer help desk, free student e-mail accounts, online (class) registration, online (class) schedules, pay tuition fees online. Campuswide network is available. Wireless service is available via entire campus.
Student Life *Housing options:* coed. Campus housing is university owned. *Activities and organizations:* student-run newspaper, radio station, AGE (Association Generale des Etudiants), AIESEC (Association Internationale des Etudiants en Sciences Economiques et Commerciales), AEME (Association for Events Management Education), REMAA (Regroupement des Etudiants du Monde de l'Administration des Affaires. *Campus security:* 24-hour emergency response devices and patrols. *Student services:* personal/psychological counseling.
Athletics *Intercollegiate sports:* cheerleading M/W, golf M/W, soccer M/W, swimming and diving M/W, volleyball W. *Intramural sports:* badminton M/W, basketball M/W, ice hockey M, rock climbing M/W, soccer M/W, swimming and diving M/W, table tennis M/W, volleyball M/W, water polo M/W, weight lifting M/W.
Applying *Options:* electronic application. *Application fee:* $60 Canadian dollars. *Required:* high school transcript, birth certificate. *Required for some:* essay or personal statement, 3 letters of recommendation, interview.
Freshman Application Contact Registrar Office, Université du Québec en Outaouais, CP 1250, Succursale Hull, 101 Saint-Jean-Bosco, 101 rue Saint-Jean-Bosco, Gatineau, QC J8X 3X7, Canada. *Phone:* 819-595-3900 Ext. 1850. *Toll-free phone:* 800-567-1283. *Fax:* 819-773-1835. *E-mail:* registraire@ uqo.ca.
Website: http://www.uqo.ca/.

Université Laval
Québec, Quebec, Canada

Freshman Application Contact Promotion and Recruitment Division, Université Laval, Quebec, QC G1K 7P4, Canada. *Phone:* 418-656-2764. *Toll-free phone:* 877-785-2825. *Fax:* 418-656-5216. *E-mail:* info@dap.ulaval.ca.
Website: http://www.ulaval.ca/.

Université Sainte-Anne
Church Point, Nova Scotia, Canada

- **Province-supported** comprehensive, founded 1890
- **Rural** 115-acre campus
- **Endowment** $1.4 million
- **Coed** 498 undergraduate students, 83% full-time, 72% women, 28% men

Undergraduates 413 full-time, 85 part-time. Students come from 9 provinces and territories; 4 other countries; 12% are from out of state; 60% live on campus.
Freshmen *Admission:* 99 enrolled.
Faculty *Total:* 41, 80% full-time.
Academics *Calendar:* semesters. *Degrees:* certificates, diplomas, bachelor's, and master's. *Special study options:* academic remediation for entering students, adult/continuing education programs, cooperative education, distance learning, double majors, English as a second language, off-campus study, part-time degree program, services for LD students, study abroad. *Unusual degree programs:* 3-2 education.
Computers on Campus 30 computers/terminals are available on campus for general student use. Students can access the following: campus intranet, free student e-mail accounts, online (class) grades, online (class) registration, online (class) schedules. Campuswide network is available. 100% of college-owned or -operated housing units are wired for high-speed Internet access. Wireless service is available via entire campus.
Student Life *Housing options:* coed. Campus housing is university owned. *Activities and organizations:* drama/theater group, Student Organization, Amnesty International, Club de Plein Air, Education Committee, Commerce Committee. *Campus security:* student patrols, late-night transport/escort ser-

vice, 14-hour patrols by trained security personnel. *Student services:* health clinic, personal/psychological counseling.

Athletics *Intercollegiate sports:* badminton M/W, volleyball M(c)/W(c). *Intramural sports:* badminton M/W, basketball M/W, ice hockey M/W, skiing (cross-country) M/W, soccer M, swimming and diving M/W, table tennis M/W, tennis M/W, volleyball M/W, weight lifting M/W.

Financial Aid Of all full-time matriculated undergraduates who enrolled in 2011, 50 state and other part-time jobs (averaging $2800).

Applying *Required:* high school transcript. *Required for some:* essay or personal statement, 3 letters of recommendation.

Freshman Application Contact Mrs. Blanche Theriault, Admissions Officer, Université Sainte-Anne, Church Point, NS B0W 1M0, Canada. *Phone:* 902-769-2114 Ext. 116. *E-mail:* admission@usainteanne.ca. *Website:* http://www.usainteanne.ca/.

University of Alberta
Edmonton, Alberta, Canada

- **Province-supported** university, founded 1906
- **Urban** 1200-acre campus
- **Endowment** $767.2 million
- **Coed**
- **Moderately difficult** entrance level

Faculty *Student/faculty ratio:* 20:1.

Academics *Calendar:* Canadian standard year. *Degrees:* certificates, diplomas, bachelor's, master's, doctoral, and postbachelor's certificates.

Student Life *Campus security:* 24-hour emergency response devices and patrols, student patrols, late-night transport/escort service, controlled dormitory access.

Athletics Member CIS.

Standardized Tests *Recommended:* SAT (for admission), ACT (for admission), SAT or ACT (for admission), SAT and SAT Subject Tests or ACT (for admission), SAT Subject Tests (for admission).

Applying *Options:* electronic application, early admission, early decision, early action. *Application fee:* $115 Canadian dollars. *Required for some:* essay or personal statement, high school transcript, interview, portfolios/ auditions required for some programs. *Recommended:* minimum 2.0 GPA.

Freshman Application Contact Ms. Patricia Dalton, Associate Registrar/ Director of Enrollment Management, University of Alberta, 105 Administration Building, Edmonton, AB T6G 2M7, Canada. *Phone:* 780-492-3113. *Fax:* 780-492-4380. *E-mail:* registrar@ualberta.ca. *Website:* http://www.ualberta.ca/.

The University of British Columbia
Vancouver, British Columbia, Canada

- **Province-supported** university, founded 1915
- **Urban** 1000-acre campus with easy access to Vancouver
- **Endowment** $958.1 million
- **Coed** 33,397 undergraduate students, 70% full-time, 54% women, 46% men
- **Very difficult** entrance level, 46% of applicants were admitted

Undergraduates 23,221 full-time, 10,176 part-time. Students come from 39 provinces and territories; 150 other countries; 6% transferred in; 25% live on campus. *Retention:* 92% of full-time freshmen returned.

Freshmen *Admission:* 33,731 applied, 15,601 admitted, 5,639 enrolled.

Faculty *Total:* 2,779, 98% full-time. *Student/faculty ratio:* 15:1.

Academics *Calendar:* Canadian standard year. *Degrees:* certificates, diplomas, bachelor's, master's, doctoral, and postbachelor's certificates. *Special study options:* academic remediation for entering students, adult/continuing education programs, advanced placement credit, cooperative education, distance learning, double majors, English as a second language, freshman honors college, honors programs, internships, off-campus study, part-time degree program, services for LD students, student-designed majors, study abroad, summer session for credit.

Computers on Campus Students can access the following: free student e-mail accounts, online (class) grades, online (class) registration, online (class) schedules. Campuswide network is available. 100% of college-owned or -operated housing units are wired for high-speed Internet access. Wireless service is available via entire campus.

Student Life *Housing options:* coed, men-only, women-only, disabled students. Campus housing is university owned. Freshman applicants given priority for college housing. *Activities and organizations:* drama/theater group, student-run newspaper, radio station, choral group, Ski and Board Club, Dance Club, AIESEC (international leadership organization), UBC Film Society, Varsity Outdoors Club, national fraternities, national sororities. *Campus security:* 24-hour emergency response devices and patrols, student patrols, late-night transport/escort service, 24-hour desk attendants in residence halls. *Student*

services: health clinic, personal/psychological counseling, women's center, legal services.

Athletics Member NAIA, CIS. *Intercollegiate sports:* baseball M(s), basketball M(s)/W(s), cheerleading W(c), crew M(s)/W(s), cross-country running M(s)/W(s), equestrian sports M/W, field hockey M(s)/W(s), football M(s), golf M(s)/W(s), ice hockey M(s)/W(s), rugby M(s)/W(s), skiing (downhill) M/W, soccer M(s)/W(s), softball M/W, swimming and diving M(s)/W(s), track and field M(s)/W(s), volleyball M(s)/W(s). *Intramural sports:* badminton M/W, basketball M/W, cross-country running M/W, fencing M/W, football M/W, gymnastics M/W, ice hockey M/W, racquetball M/W, rock climbing M/W, rugby M/W, sailing M/W, skiing (cross-country) M/W, skiing (downhill) M/W, soccer M/W, softball M/W, squash M/W, swimming and diving M/W, table tennis M/W, tennis M/W, ultimate Frisbee M/W, volleyball M/W, water polo M/W, weight lifting M/W, wrestling M/W.

Standardized Tests *Required for some:* SAT or ACT plus Writing required of applicants following US curriculum.

Costs (2013–14) *Tuition:* province resident $4795 Canadian dollars full-time; nonresident $4795 Canadian dollars full-time; International tuition $23,300 Canadian dollars full-time. Full-time tuition and fees vary according to course load. Part-time tuition and fees vary according to course load. *Required fees:* $721 Canadian dollars full-time. *Room and board:* $8018 Canadian dollars. Room and board charges vary according to board plan, housing facility, and location.

Financial Aid Of all full-time matriculated undergraduates who enrolled in 2011, 13,140 were judged to have need. 1,736 state and other part-time jobs (averaging $1907). In 2011, 6283 non-need-based awards were made. *Average financial aid package:* $11,056. *Average need-based loan:* $9134. *Average need-based gift aid:* $2762. *Average non-need-based aid:* $2067. *Financial aid deadline:* 9/15.

Applying *Options:* electronic application, deferred entrance. *Application fee:* $102 Canadian dollars. *Required:* essay or personal statement, high school transcript, minimum 2.6 GPA, English Language Admission Standard. *Application deadlines:* 1/31 (freshmen), 1/31 (out-of-state freshmen), 1/31 (transfers). *Notification:* continuous (freshmen), continuous (out-of-state freshmen), continuous (transfers).

Freshman Application Contact The University of British Columbia, V6T 1Z1, Canada. *Phone:* 604-822-3014. *Website:* http://www.ubc.ca/.

The University of British Columbia–Okanagan
Kelowna, British Columbia, Canada

- **Province-supported** university, founded 2005, part of Okanagan campus is an integral part of the University of British Columbia, which comprises two campuses and two additional sites
- **Urban** 500-acre campus with easy access to Kelowna
- **Endowment** $952.7 million
- **Coed** 7,507 undergraduate students, 78% full-time, 55% women, 45% men
- **Moderately difficult** entrance level, 50% of applicants were admitted

Undergraduates 5,824 full-time, 1,683 part-time. Students come from 16 provinces and territories; 76 other countries; 40% live on campus. *Retention:* 76% of full-time freshmen returned.

Freshmen *Admission:* 5,387 applied, 2,683 admitted, 1,708 enrolled.

Faculty *Total:* 416, 89% full-time. *Student/faculty ratio:* 15:1.

Academics *Degrees:* certificates, diplomas, bachelor's, master's, doctoral, and postbachelor's certificates. *Special study options:* academic remediation for entering students, advanced placement credit, cooperative education, distance learning, double majors, English as a second language, freshman honors college, honors programs, internships, off-campus study, part-time degree program, services for LD students, student-designed majors, study abroad, summer session for credit.

Computers on Campus Students can access the following: campus intranet, computer help desk, free student e-mail accounts, online (class) grades, online (class) registration, online (class) schedules. Campuswide network is available. 100% of college-owned or -operated housing units are wired for high-speed Internet access. Wireless service is available via entire campus.

Student Life *Housing options:* coed, men-only, women-only. Campus housing is university owned. Freshman campus housing is guaranteed. *Activities and organizations:* drama/theater group, student-run newspaper, radio station, choral group, Save the World, Student Leadership, UBCSUO Mountain Riders Ski and Snowboard Club, Model United Nations, UBCSUO Asian Students' Association, national fraternities, national sororities. *Campus security:* 24-hour emergency response devices and patrols, controlled dormitory access, 24-hour desk attendants in residence halls. *Student services:* health clinic, personal/psychological counseling, women's center, legal services.

Athletics Member CIS. *Intercollegiate sports:* basketball M(s)/W(s), cross-country running M/W, golf M(s)/W(s), rugby M(s)/W(s), soccer M(s)/W(s), volleyball M(s)/W(s). *Intramural sports:* badminton M/W, basketball M/W, cross-country running M/W, field hockey M/W, golf M/W, gymnastics M/W, ice hockey M/W, soccer M/W, tennis M/W, volleyball M/W.

Standardized Tests *Required for some:* SAT or ACT (for admission).

Costs (2013–14) *Tuition:* province resident $4794 Canadian dollars full-time; nonresident $4794 Canadian dollars full-time; International tuition $23,300 Canadian dollars full-time. Full-time tuition and fees vary according to course load. Part-time tuition and fees vary according to course load. *Required fees:* $665 Canadian dollars full-time. *Room and board:* $8641 Canadian dollars. Room and board charges vary according to board plan and housing facility. *Waivers:* senior citizens.

Financial Aid *Financial aid deadline:* 1/31.

Applying *Options:* electronic application, deferred entrance. *Application fee:* $102 Canadian dollars. *Required:* essay or personal statement, high school transcript, minimum 2.6 GPA. *Application deadlines:* 1/31 (freshmen), 1/31 (out-of-state freshmen), 1/31 (transfers). *Notification:* continuous (freshmen), continuous (out-of-state freshmen), continuous (transfers).

Freshman Application Contact International Student Recruitment, The University of British Columbia–Okanagan, UC222 University Centre, 3333 University Way, Kelowna, BC V1V 1V7, Canada. *Phone:* 604-822-3014. *Fax:* 604-822-3599.

Website: http://www.ubc.ca/okanagan/welcome.html.

University of Calgary
Calgary, Alberta, Canada

Freshman Application Contact Kim Vandam, Associate Director of Admissions, University of Calgary, 2500 University Drive NW, Calgary, AB T2N 1N4, Canada. *Phone:* 403-220-3825. *E-mail:* vandam@ucalgary.ca. *Website:* http://www.ucalgary.ca/.

University of Guelph
Guelph, Ontario, Canada

- **Province-supported** university, founded 1964
- **Urban** 1017-acre campus with easy access to Toronto
- **Coed** 18,316 undergraduate students
- **Moderately difficult** entrance level, 64% of applicants were admitted

Undergraduates Students come from 100 other countries; 28% live on campus. *Retention:* 92% of full-time freshmen returned.

Freshmen *Admission:* 22,584 applied, 14,519 admitted. *Average high school GPA:* 3.5.

Faculty *Total:* 860. *Student/faculty ratio:* 22:1.

Academics *Calendar:* trimesters. *Degrees:* certificates, diplomas, associate, bachelor's, master's, and doctoral. *Special study options:* academic remediation for entering students, accelerated degree program, advanced placement credit, cooperative education, distance learning, double majors, English as a second language, freshman honors college, honors programs, independent study, internships, off-campus study, part-time degree program, services for LD students, student-designed majors, study abroad, summer session for credit.

Computers on Campus 1,500 computers/terminals and 16,000 ports are available on campus for general student use. Students can access the following: campus intranet, computer help desk, free student e-mail accounts, online (class) grades, online (class) registration, online (class) schedules. Campus-wide network is available. 100% of college-owned or -operated housing units are wired for high-speed Internet access. Wireless service is available via entire campus.

Student Life *Housing options:* coed, women-only, cooperative, disabled students. Campus housing is university owned and is provided by a third party. Freshman campus housing is guaranteed. *Activities and organizations:* drama/theater group, student-run newspaper, radio station, choral group, Guelph Gryphon Athletics, Habitat for Humanity, Curtain Call Productions, West Indian Students Association, OXFAM-Guelph Chapter. *Campus security:* 24-hour emergency response devices and patrols, student patrols, late-night transport/escort service, controlled dormitory access, video camera surveillance in parking lots, alarms in women's locker room. *Student services:* health clinic, personal/psychological counseling, women's center, legal services.

Athletics Member CIS. *Intercollegiate sports:* baseball M, basketball M/W, crew M/W, cross-country running M/W, field hockey W, football M, golf M/W, ice hockey M/W, lacrosse M/W, rugby M/W, skiing (cross-country) M/W, soccer M/W, swimming and diving M/W, track and field M/W, volleyball M/W, wrestling M/W. *Intramural sports:* archery M(c)/W(c), badminton M/W, basketball M/W, cheerleading M(c)/W(c), fencing M(c)/W(c), football M/W, ice hockey M/W, lacrosse M(c)/W(c), rock climbing M(c)/W(c), soccer M/W, softball M/W, squash M(c)/W(c), tennis M/W, ultimate Frisbee M/W, volleyball M/W, water polo M(c)/W(c).

Standardized Tests *Required:* SAT or ACT (for admission).

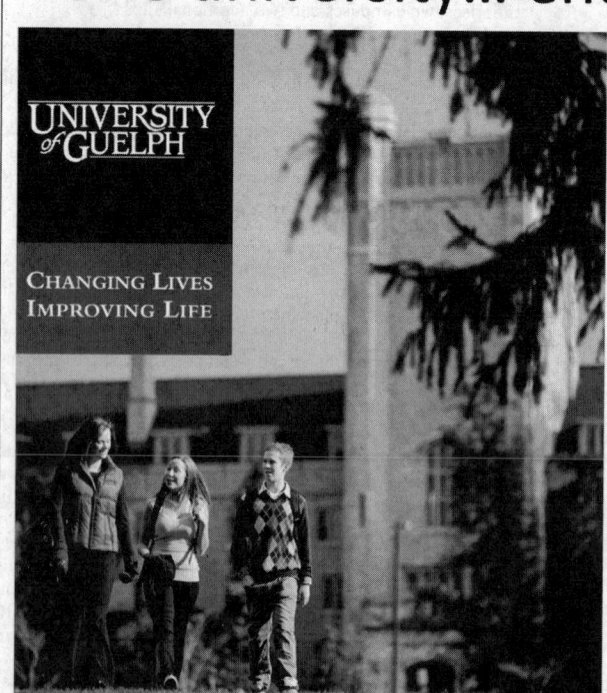

Costs (2012–13) *Tuition:* province resident $5692 Canadian dollars full-time, $1137 Canadian dollars per credit part-time; International tuition $17,430 Canadian dollars full-time. Full-time tuition and fees vary according to course level, degree level, location, program, and reciprocity agreements. Part-time tuition and fees vary according to course level, course load, degree level, location, program, and reciprocity agreements. No tuition increase for student's term of enrollment. *Required fees:* $1180 Canadian dollars full-time, $480 Canadian dollars per credit part-time. *Room and board:* $9764 Canadian dollars; room only: $5364 Canadian dollars. Room and board charges vary according to board plan, housing facility, and location. *Payment plan:* installment. *Waivers:* senior citizens and employees or children of employees.
Applying *Options:* electronic application, early admission, deferred entrance. *Application fee:* $135 Canadian dollars. *Required:* high school transcript, minimum 3.0 GPA. *Required for some:* essay or personal statement. *Application deadlines:* 3/1 (freshmen), 5/1 (transfers). *Notification:* continuous (freshmen), continuous (transfers).
Freshman Application Contact Ms. Janette Hogan, Assistant Registrar, Admissions, University of Guelph, L-3 University Centre, Guelph, ON N1G 2W1, Canada. *Phone:* 519-824-4120 Ext. 58529. *Fax:* 519-766-9481. *E-mail:* jhogan@registrar.uoguelph.ca.
Website: http://www.uoguelph.ca/.

See previous page for display ad and page 1564 for the College Close-Up.

University of King's College
Halifax, Nova Scotia, Canada
Freshman Application Contact Ms. Jill MacBeath, Admissions and Recruitment Coordinator, University of King's College, Registrar's Office, Halifax, NS B3H 3A1, Canada. *Phone:* 902-422-1271. *Fax:* 902-425-8183. *E-mail:* admissions@ukings.ns.ca.
Website: http://www.ukings.ca/.

University of Lethbridge
Lethbridge, Alberta, Canada
- **Province-supported** university, founded 1967
- **Urban** 576-acre campus
- **Endowment** $37.5 million
- **Coed**
- **Moderately difficult** entrance level
Faculty *Student/faculty ratio:* 12:1.
Academics *Calendar:* semesters. *Degrees:* certificates, diplomas, bachelor's, master's, doctoral, post-master's, and postbachelor's certificates.
Student Life *Campus security:* 24-hour emergency response devices and patrols, student patrols, late-night transport/escort service, controlled dormitory access, video camera monitored entrances, hallways.
Athletics Member CIS.
Costs (2012–13) *Tuition:* province resident $4925 Canadian dollars full-time, $493 Canadian dollars per course part-time; nonresident $4925 Canadian dollars full-time, $493 Canadian dollars per course part-time; International tuition $11,150 Canadian dollars full-time. Full-time tuition and fees vary according to course load. Part-time tuition and fees vary according to course load. *Required fees:* $692 Canadian dollars full-time, $118 Canadian dollars per term part-time. *Room and board:* $7932 Canadian dollars; room only: $4608 Canadian dollars. Room and board charges vary according to board plan and housing facility.
Applying *Options:* electronic application, deferred entrance. *Application fee:* $75 Canadian dollars. *Required:* high school transcript, minimum 2.0 GPA. *Required for some:* minimum 3.0 GPA, interview.
Freshman Application Contact Ms. Alice Miller, Assistant Registrar, University of Lethbridge, 4401 University Drive, Lethbridge, AB T1K 3M4, Canada. *Phone:* 403-320-5700. *Fax:* 403-329-5159. *E-mail:* inquiries@uleth.ca.
Website: http://www.uleth.ca/.

University of Manitoba
Winnipeg, Manitoba, Canada
Freshman Application Contact Mr. Peter Dueck, Director of Enrollment Services, University of Manitoba, Winnipeg, MB R3T 2N2, Canada. *Phone:* 204-474-6382.
Website: http://www.umanitoba.ca/.

University of New Brunswick Fredericton
Fredericton, New Brunswick, Canada
- **Province-supported** university, founded 1785, part of Province of NB
- **Urban** 7100-acre campus
- **Endowment** $173.6 million
- **Coed** 9,018 undergraduate students, 89% full-time, 52% women, 48% men
- **Moderately difficult** entrance level, 79% of applicants were admitted
Undergraduates 8,025 full-time, 993 part-time. 20% live on campus.
Freshmen *Admission:* 3,695 applied, 2,907 admitted.
Faculty *Total:* 1,002, 59% full-time. *Student/faculty ratio:* 11:1.
Academics *Calendar:* Canadian standard year. *Degrees:* bachelor's, master's, and doctoral. *Special study options:* accelerated degree program, adult/continuing education programs, advanced placement credit, cooperative education, distance learning, double majors, English as a second language, external degree program, honors programs, independent study, internships, off-campus study, part-time degree program, services for LD students, student-designed majors, study abroad, summer session for credit.
Computers on Campus 1,400 computers/terminals are available on campus for general student use. Students can access the following: campus intranet, computer help desk, free student e-mail accounts, online (class) grades, online (class) registration, online (class) schedules. Campuswide network is available. 100% of college-owned or -operated housing units are wired for high-speed Internet access. Wireless service is available via classrooms, computer centers, computer labs, learning centers, libraries, student centers.
Student Life *Housing options:* coed, men-only, women-only, disabled students. Campus housing is university owned. Freshman campus housing is guaranteed. *Activities and organizations:* drama/theater group, student-run newspaper, radio station, choral group. *Campus security:* 24-hour emergency response devices and patrols, student patrols, late-night transport/escort service, controlled dormitory access. *Student services:* health clinic, personal/psychological counseling, women's center, legal services.
Athletics Member CIS. *Intercollegiate sports:* basketball M/W, cross-country running M/W, ice hockey M, soccer M/W, swimming and diving M/W, track and field M/W, volleyball M/W, wrestling M/W. *Intramural sports:* badminton M/W, baseball M/W, basketball M/W, cheerleading M/W, crew M/W, fencing M/W, field hockey W, ice hockey M/W, rock climbing M/W, rugby M/W, soccer M/W, swimming and diving M/W, volleyball M/W.
Standardized Tests *Required for some:* SAT (for admission).
Financial Aid Of all full-time matriculated undergraduates who enrolled in 2007, 123 state and other part-time jobs (averaging $1264). *Financial aid deadline:* 5/15.
Applying *Options:* electronic application, early admission, deferred entrance. *Application fee:* $45 Canadian dollars. *Required:* high school transcript. *Required for some:* essay or personal statement, 1 letter of recommendation, interview. *Application deadlines:* 3/31 (freshmen), 3/31 (transfers). *Notification:* continuous until 8/31 (freshmen), continuous until 8/31 (transfers).
Freshman Application Contact University of New Brunswick Fredericton, PO Box 4400, Fredericton, NB E3B 5A3, Canada. *Phone:* 506-453-4865.
Website: http://www.unb.ca/.

University of New Brunswick Saint John
Saint John, New Brunswick, Canada
- **Province-supported** comprehensive, founded 1964
- **Urban** 250-acre campus
- **Coed**
- **Moderately difficult** entrance level
Undergraduates 5% live on campus.
Academics *Calendar:* Canadian standard year. *Degrees:* certificates, diplomas, bachelor's, master's, doctoral, and postbachelor's certificates. *Special study options:* academic remediation for entering students, accelerated degree program, adult/continuing education programs, advanced placement credit, cooperative education, distance learning, double majors, English as a second language, honors programs, independent study, internships, off-campus study, part-time degree program, services for LD students, student-designed majors, study abroad, summer session for credit.
Computers on Campus 100 computers/terminals are available on campus for general student use. Students can access the following: campus intranet, computer help desk, free student e-mail accounts, online (class) grades, online (class) registration, online (class) schedules. Campuswide network is available.
Student Life *Housing options:* coed. Campus housing is university owned. *Activities and organizations:* drama/theater group, student-run newspaper,

radio station, choral group, Business Administration Society, OPTAMUS, International Student Association, Chinese Cultural Association, Muslim Student Association. *Campus security:* 24-hour emergency response devices and patrols, student patrols, late-night transport/escort service, controlled dormitory access. *Student services:* personal/psychological counseling, women's center.

Athletics *Intercollegiate sports:* badminton M/W, basketball M/W, crew M/W, cross-country running M/W, fencing M/W, ice hockey M/W, rugby M/W, soccer M/W, volleyball M/W. *Intramural sports:* badminton M/W, basketball M/W, fencing M/W, golf M/W, soccer M/W, table tennis M/W, tennis M/W, volleyball M/W.

Standardized Tests *Required:* SAT (for admission).

Financial Aid Of all full-time matriculated undergraduates who enrolled in 2011, 140 state and other part-time jobs (averaging $500).

Applying *Options:* electronic application, early admission, deferred entrance. *Application fee:* $45 Canadian dollars. *Required:* high school transcript. *Application deadlines:* rolling (freshmen), 3/31 (out-of-state freshmen), rolling (transfers). *Notification:* continuous until 8/31 (freshmen), continuous (out-of-state freshmen), continuous until 8/31 (transfers).

Freshman Application Contact University of New Brunswick Saint John, PO Box 5050, Saint John, NB E2L 4L5, Canada. *Website:* http://www.unb.ca/.

University of Northern British Columbia
Prince George, British Columbia, Canada

Freshman Application Contact Mr. Grant Kerr, Assistant Registrar, Admissions, University of Northern British Columbia, Office of the Registrar, 3333 University Way, Prince George, BC V2N 4Z9, Canada. *Phone:* 250-960-6347. *Fax:* 250-960-6330. *E-mail:* registrar-info@unbc.ca. *Website:* http://www.unbc.ca/.

University of Ottawa
Ottawa, Ontario, Canada

- **Province-supported** university, founded 1848
- **Urban** 43-hectare campus with easy access to Ottawa-Gatineau
- **Endowment** $183.9 million
- **Coed** 35,700 undergraduate students, 84% full-time, 60% women, 40% men
- **Moderately difficult** entrance level, 58% of applicants were admitted

Undergraduates 29,818 full-time, 5,882 part-time. Students come from 13 provinces and territories; 134 other countries; 21% are from out of state; 9% live on campus. *Retention:* 86% of full-time freshmen returned.

Freshmen *Admission:* 41,600 applied, 24,200 admitted. *Average high school GPA:* 3.32.

Faculty *Total:* 2,239, 57% full-time. *Student/faculty ratio:* 25:1.

Academics *Calendar:* semesters. *Degrees:* certificates, diplomas, bachelor's, master's, doctoral, and postbachelor's certificates. *Special study options:* academic remediation for entering students, advanced placement credit, cooperative education, distance learning, double majors, English as a second language, honors programs, internships, off-campus study, part-time degree program, services for LD students, study abroad, summer session for credit. *Unusual degree programs:* 3-2 law, education.

Computers on Campus 1,540 computers/terminals are available on campus for general student use. Students can access the following: computer help desk, free student e-mail accounts, online (class) grades, online (class) registration, online (class) schedules, wireless connection available on campus. Campus-wide network is available. 100% of college-owned or -operated housing units are wired for high-speed Internet access. Wireless service is available via entire campus.

Student Life *Housing options:* coed, disabled students. Campus housing is university owned. Freshman campus housing is guaranteed. *Activities and organizations:* drama/theater group, student-run newspaper, radio station, choral group, Student Federation of the University of Ottawa, Graduate Students Association, national fraternities, national sororities. *Campus security:* 24-hour emergency response devices and patrols, student patrols, late-night transport/escort service, controlled dormitory access. *Student services:* health clinic, personal/psychological counseling, women's center, legal services.

Athletics Member CIS. *Intercollegiate sports:* badminton M(c)/W(c), baseball M(c)/W(c), basketball M(s)/W(s), cheerleading M(c)/W(c), crew M(c)/W(c), cross-country running M(s)/W(s), equestrian sports M(c)/W(c), fencing M(c)/W(c), football M(s), golf M(c)/W(c), ice hockey M(s)/W(s), rugby W(s), soccer M(s)(c)/W(s), swimming and diving M(s)/W(s), track and field M(s)/W(s), ultimate Frisbee M(c)/W(c), volleyball M(c)/W(s), water polo M(c)/W(c).

Intramural sports: basketball M/W, football M, ice hockey M/W, soccer M/W, ultimate Frisbee M/W, volleyball M/W.

Standardized Tests *Required for some:* SAT or ACT required for American citizens.

Costs (2012–13) *One-time required fee:* $360 Canadian dollars. *Tuition:* province resident $5665 Canadian dollars full-time, $225 Canadian dollars per credit part-time; nonresident $715 Canadian dollars per credit part-time; International tuition $18,446 Canadian dollars full-time. Full-time tuition and fees vary according to course load, degree level, program, and student level. Part-time tuition and fees vary according to course load, degree level, program, and student level. *Required fees:* $640 Canadian dollars full-time, $120 Canadian dollars per term part-time. *Room and board:* $6722 Canadian dollars; room only: $4622 Canadian dollars. Room and board charges vary according to board plan and housing facility. *Waivers:* employees or children of employees.

Financial Aid *Financial aid deadline:* 1/31.

Applying *Options:* electronic application, early admission, deferred entrance. *Application fee:* $167 Canadian dollars. *Required:* high school transcript, minimum 3.0 GPA. *Required for some:* interview. *Application deadline:* 6/1 (freshmen). *Notification:* continuous until 8/30 (freshmen).

Freshman Application Contact Ms. Emilie Bertrand, University of Ottawa, 550 Cumberland Street, PO Box 450, Station A, Ottawa, ON K1N 6N5, Canada. *Phone:* 613-562-5800 Ext. 1593. *Fax:* 613-562-5790. *E-mail:* cpharand@uottawa.ca. *Website:* http://www.uottawa.ca/.

University of Prince Edward Island
Charlottetown, Prince Edward Island, Canada

Freshman Application Contact University of Prince Edward Island, 550 University Avenue, Charlottetown, PE C1A 4P3, Canada. *Phone:* 902-566-0634. *Website:* http://www.upei.ca/.

University of Regina
Regina, Saskatchewan, Canada

- **Province-supported** university, founded 1974
- **Urban** 76-hectare campus
- **Endowment** $29.1 million
- **Coed** 11,526 undergraduate students, 81% full-time, 62% women, 38% men
- **Minimally difficult** entrance level, 66% of applicants were admitted

Undergraduates 9,361 full-time, 2,165 part-time. Students come from 13 provinces and territories; 88 other countries; 14% are from out of state; 4% transferred in; 10% live on campus. *Retention:* 81% of full-time freshmen returned.

Freshmen *Admission:* 3,842 applied, 2,545 admitted, 1,668 enrolled. *Average high school GPA:* 3.7.

Faculty *Total:* 484, 100% full-time, 80% with terminal degrees. *Student/faculty ratio:* 23:1.

Academics *Calendar:* semesters. *Degrees:* certificates, diplomas, bachelor's, master's, doctoral, and postbachelor's certificates. *Special study options:* academic remediation for entering students, adult/continuing education programs, advanced placement credit, cooperative education, distance learning, double majors, English as a second language, honors programs, independent study, internships, off-campus study, part-time degree program, services for LD students, student-designed majors, study abroad, summer session for credit.

Computers on Campus 312 computers/terminals and 1,250 ports are available on campus for general student use. Students can access the following: campus intranet, computer help desk, free student e-mail accounts, online (class) grades, online (class) registration, online (class) schedules. Campus-wide network is available. 100% of college-owned or -operated housing units are wired for high-speed Internet access. Wireless service is available via entire campus.

Student Life *Housing options:* disabled students. Campus housing is university owned. Freshman campus housing is guaranteed. *Activities and organizations:* drama/theater group, student-run newspaper, television station, choral group. *Campus security:* 24-hour emergency response devices and patrols, late-night transport/escort service, controlled dormitory access, crime prevention assistance, CCTV, card access and some alarm monitoring. *Student services:* health clinic, personal/psychological counseling, women's center.

Athletics Member CIS. *Intercollegiate sports:* basketball M(s)/W(s), cross-country running M(s)/W(s), football M(s), ice hockey M(s)/W(s), soccer W(s), swimming and diving M(s)/W(s), track and field M(s)/W(s), volleyball M(s)/W(s), wrestling M(s)/W(s). *Intramural sports:* badminton M/W, basketball M/W, cheerleading M(c)/W(c), football M, soccer M/W, softball M/W(c), tennis M/W, ultimate Frisbee M/W, volleyball M/W.

Standardized Tests *Required for some:* SAT or ACT (for admission), SAT Subject Tests (for admission).

Costs (2012–13) *Tuition:* province resident $5756 Canadian dollars full-time, $164 Canadian dollars per credit hour part-time; nonresident $164 Canadian dollars per credit hour part-time; International tuition $20,077 Canadian dollars full-time. Full-time tuition and fees vary according to course load and program. Part-time tuition and fees vary according to course load and program. *Required fees:* $351 Canadian dollars full-time, $95 Canadian dollars per term part-time. *Room and board:* $8835 Canadian dollars; room only: $6160 Canadian dollars. Room and board charges vary according to board plan and housing facility. *Waivers:* senior citizens and employees or children of employees.

Applying *Options:* electronic application, early admission, early action, deferred entrance. *Application fee:* $100 Canadian dollars. *Required:* high school transcript, minimum 2.3 GPA. *Required for some:* essay or personal statement, 2 letters of recommendation, interview, portfolio, audition, some programs require a higher than 2.3 minimum GPA for admission. *Application deadlines:* 8/1 (freshmen), 8/1 (transfers), 3/15 (early action).

Freshman Application Contact University of Regina, 3737 Wascana Parkway, Regina, SK S4S 0A2, Canada. *Phone:* 306-585-4591. *Toll-free phone:* 800-664-4756.

Website: http://www.uregina.ca/.

University of Saskatchewan
Saskatoon, Saskatchewan, Canada

Freshman Application Contact University of Saskatchewan, 105 Administration Place, Saskatoon, SK S7N 5A2, Canada. *Phone:* 306-966-5788.

Website: http://www.usask.ca/.

University of the Fraser Valley
Abbotsford, British Columbia, Canada

Freshman Application Contact Ms. Robin Smith, Admissions Coordinator, University of the Fraser Valley, 33844 King Road, Abbotsford, BC V2S 7M8, Canada. *Phone:* 604-504-7441 Ext. 4540. *Toll-free phone:* 888-823-8734. *Fax:* 604-853-0138. *E-mail:* reginfo@ucfv.ca.

Website: http://www.ufv.ca/.

University of Toronto
Toronto, Ontario, Canada

- **Province-supported** university, founded 1827
- **Urban** 714-hectare campus
- **Endowment** $1.5 billion
- **Coed**
- **Very difficult** entrance level

Faculty *Student/faculty ratio:* 24:1.

Academics *Calendar:* Canadian standard year. *Degrees:* certificates, diplomas, bachelor's, master's, and doctoral.

Student Life *Campus security:* 24-hour emergency response devices and patrols, student patrols, late-night transport/escort service.

Athletics Member CIS.

Standardized Tests *Required:* SAT and SAT Subject Tests or ACT (for admission).

Costs (2012–13) *Tuition:* province resident $5695 Canadian dollars full-time; nonresident $5695 Canadian dollars full-time; International tuition $28,409 Canadian dollars full-time. Full-time tuition and fees vary according to course level, course load, and program. Part-time tuition and fees vary according to course load. *Required fees:* $1300 Canadian dollars full-time. *Room and board:* $13,000 Canadian dollars; room only: $8000 Canadian dollars. Room and board charges vary according to board plan, housing facility, and location.

Applying *Options:* deferred entrance. *Application fee:* $115 Canadian dollars. *Required:* high school transcript. *Required for some:* interview.

Freshman Application Contact University of Toronto, Toronto, ON M5S 1A1, Canada. *Phone:* 416-978-2190. *Fax:* 416-978-7022. *E-mail:* admissions.help@utoronto.ca.

Website: http://www.utoronto.ca/uoft.html.

University of Victoria
Victoria, British Columbia, Canada

Freshman Application Contact Mr. Bruno Rocca, Student Recruitment Director, University of Victoria, PO Box 1700, STN CSC, Victoria, BC V8W 2Y2, Canada. *Phone:* 250-721-8121 Ext. 8109. *Fax:* 250-721-6225. *E-mail:* admit@uvic.ca.

Website: http://www.uvic.ca/.

University of Waterloo
Waterloo, Ontario, Canada

- **Province-supported** university, founded 1957
- **Suburban** 1000-acre campus with easy access to Toronto
- **Coed** 27,862 undergraduate students, 96% full-time, 44% women, 56% men
- **Moderately difficult** entrance level, 53% of applicants were admitted

Undergraduates 26,884 full-time, 978 part-time. Students come from 115 other countries; 23% live on campus. *Retention:* 90% of full-time freshmen returned.

Freshmen *Admission:* 43,347 applied, 23,089 admitted.

Faculty *Total:* 1,093. *Student/faculty ratio:* 30:1.

Academics *Calendar:* trimesters. *Degrees:* certificates, diplomas, bachelor's, master's, doctoral, and postbachelor's certificates. *Special study options:* academic remediation for entering students, accelerated degree program, advanced placement credit, cooperative education, distance learning, double majors, English as a second language, honors programs, independent study, internships, off-campus study, part-time degree program, services for LD students, student-designed majors, study abroad, summer session for credit.

Computers on Campus 6,000 computers/terminals are available on campus for general student use. Students can access the following: computer help desk, free student e-mail accounts, online (class) grades, online (class) registration, online (class) schedules. Campuswide network is available. 100% of college-owned or -operated housing units are wired for high-speed Internet access. Wireless service is available via entire campus.

Student Life *Housing options:* coed, men-only, women-only. Campus housing is university owned. Freshman campus housing is guaranteed. *Activities and organizations:* drama/theater group, student-run newspaper, radio station, choral group, marching band, national fraternities, national sororities. *Campus security:* 24-hour emergency response devices and patrols, student patrols, late-night transport/escort service. *Student services:* health clinic, personal/psychological counseling, women's center, legal services.

Athletics Member CIS. *Intercollegiate sports:* badminton M/W, baseball M, basketball M/W, cheerleading M/W, cross-country running M/W, field hockey M, football M, golf M/W, ice hockey M/W, rugby M/W, skiing (cross-country) M/W, soccer M/W, squash M, swimming and diving M/W, tennis M/W, track and field M/W, volleyball M/W. *Intramural sports:* archery M(c)/W(c), badminton M(c)/W(c), baseball M/W, basketball M/W, crew M(c)/W(c), equestrian sports M(c)/W(c), fencing M(c)/W(c), golf M(c)/W(c), ice hockey M/W, racquetball M(c)/W(c), rock climbing M(c)/W(c), skiing (cross-country) M(c)/W(c), skiing (downhill) M(c)/W(c), soccer M(c)/W(c), squash M(c)/W(c), swimming and diving M(c)/W(c), table tennis M(c)/W(c), tennis M/W, ultimate Frisbee M(c)/W(c), volleyball M/W, water polo M(c)/W(c), weight lifting M(c)/W(c).

Standardized Tests *Required for some:* SAT or ACT (for admission), SAT Subject Tests (for admission).

Applying *Options:* electronic application, early admission, deferred entrance. *Application fee:* $110 Canadian dollars. *Required:* high school transcript. *Required for some:* essay or personal statement, minimum 3.0 GPA, interview. *Application deadline:* 3/28 (freshmen). *Notification:* 5/24 (freshmen), continuous (transfers).

Freshman Application Contact University of Waterloo, 200 University Avenue West, Waterloo, ON N2L 3G1, Canada. *Phone:* 519-888-4567 Ext. 32265.

Website: http://www.uwaterloo.ca/.

The University of Western Ontario
London, Ontario, Canada

- **Province-supported** university, founded 1878
- **Suburban** 499-hectare campus
- **Coed** 31,659 undergraduate students, 91% full-time, 56% women, 44% men
- **Very difficult** entrance level, 52% of applicants were admitted

Undergraduates 28,660 full-time, 2,999 part-time. Students come from 13 provinces and territories; 100 other countries; 6% are from out of state; 21% live on campus. *Retention:* 94% of full-time freshmen returned.

Freshmen *Admission:* 33,270 applied, 17,164 admitted. *Average high school GPA:* 3.9.

Faculty *Total:* 1,408, 100% full-time. *Student/faculty ratio:* 20:1.

Academics *Calendar:* Canadian standard year. *Degrees:* certificates, diplomas, bachelor's, master's, doctoral, and postbachelor's certificates. *Special study options:* academic remediation for entering students, accelerated degree program, adult/continuing education programs, advanced placement credit, cooperative education, distance learning, double majors, English as a second language, honors programs, independent study, internships, off-campus study, part-time degree program, services for LD students, student-designed majors, study abroad, summer session for credit.

Computers on Campus 414 computers/terminals are available on campus for general student use. Students can access the following: campus intranet, computer help desk, free student e-mail accounts, online (class) grades, online (class) registration, online (class) schedules. Campuswide network is available. 100% of college-owned or -operated housing units are wired for high-speed Internet access. Wireless service is available via classrooms, computer centers, computer labs, learning centers, libraries, student centers.

Student Life *Housing options:* coed, disabled students. Campus housing is university owned. Freshman campus housing is guaranteed. *Activities and organizations:* drama/theater group, student-run newspaper, radio and television station, choral group, marching band, Western Investment Club, Pre-Medical Society, Purple Spur Society, Canadian Asian International Students' Association (CAISA), Pre-Law Society, national fraternities, national sororities. *Campus security:* 24-hour emergency response devices and patrols, student patrols, late-night transport/escort service, controlled dormitory access, Campus Community Police, SERT: Student Emergency Response Team, Western Foot Patrol. *Student services:* health clinic, personal/psychological counseling, legal services.

Athletics Member CIS. *Intercollegiate sports:* badminton M/W, baseball M, basketball M/W, cheerleading M/W, crew M/W, cross-country running M/W, equestrian sports W, fencing M/W, field hockey W, football M, golf M/W, ice hockey M/W, lacrosse M/W, rugby M/W, soccer M/W, softball W, squash M/W, swimming and diving M/W, table tennis M/W, tennis M/W, track and field M/W, volleyball M/W, water polo M, wrestling M/W. *Intramural sports:* badminton M/W, basketball M/W, fencing M(c)/W(c), ice hockey M/W, skiing (downhill) M(c)/W(c), soccer M/W, softball M/W, squash M(c)/W(c), swimming and diving M/W, table tennis M(c)/W(c), tennis M/W(c), ultimate Frisbee M/W, volleyball M/W, water polo M/W.

Standardized Tests *Required:* SAT or ACT (for admission).

Costs (2012–13) *Tuition:* province resident $5633 Canadian dollars full-time, $1127 Canadian dollars per course part-time; nonresident $3623 Canadian dollars per course part-time; International tuition $18,113 Canadian dollars full-time. Full-time tuition and fees vary according to program and student level. Part-time tuition and fees vary according to course load, location, program, and student level. *Required fees:* $1249 Canadian dollars full-time, $156 Canadian dollars per course part-time. *Room and board:* $9920 Canadian dollars; room only: $6725 Canadian dollars. Room and board charges vary according to board plan, housing facility, and location. *Payment plans:* installment, deferred payment. *Waivers:* senior citizens and employees or children of employees.

Financial Aid Of all full-time matriculated undergraduates who enrolled in 2011, 1,544 state and other part-time jobs (averaging $1831).

Applying *Options:* electronic application, deferred entrance. *Application fee:* $130 Canadian dollars. *Required:* high school transcript, minimum 3.5 GPA. *Application deadlines:* 6/1 (freshmen), 5/15 (out-of-state freshmen), 6/1 (transfers). *Notification:* continuous (freshmen), continuous (out-of-state freshmen).

Freshman Application Contact Undergraduate Recruitment and Admissions, The University of Western Ontario, The University of Western Ontario, Western Student Services Building, Room 3140, London, ON N6A 3K7, Canada. *Phone:* 519-661-2100. *Fax:* 519-661-3710. *E-mail:* reg-admissions@uwo.ca.
Website: http://www.uwo.ca/.

University of Windsor
Windsor, Ontario, Canada

- **Province-supported** university, founded 1857
- **Urban** 125-acre campus with easy access to Detroit, Michigan, USA
- **Endowment** $56.0 million
- **Coed** 13,620 undergraduate students, 78% full-time, 55% women, 45% men
- **Moderately difficult** entrance level, 78% of applicants were admitted

Undergraduates 10,560 full-time, 3,060 part-time. Students come from 16 provinces and territories; 91 other countries; 5% transferred in; 13% live on campus. *Retention:* 82% of full-time freshmen returned.

Freshmen *Admission:* 12,180 applied, 9,469 admitted, 2,998 enrolled.

Faculty *Total:* 871, 60% full-time, 53% with terminal degrees. *Student/faculty ratio:* 21:1.

Academics *Calendar:* semesters. *Degrees:* certificates, bachelor's, master's, doctoral, and postbachelor's certificates. *Special study options:* academic remediation for entering students, accelerated degree program, adult/continuing education programs, advanced placement credit, cooperative education, distance learning, double majors, external degree program, honors programs, internships, off-campus study, part-time degree program, services for LD students, student-designed majors, study abroad, summer session for credit. *Unusual degree programs:* 3-2 business administration; engineering; social work; computer science.

Computers on Campus 1,225 computers/terminals are available on campus for general student use. Students can access the following: campus intranet, computer help desk, free student e-mail accounts, online (class) grades, online (class) registration, online transcripts, degree audits, grades, bursaries, grants, online applications for graduation. Campuswide network is available. 100% of college-owned or -operated housing units are wired for high-speed Internet access. Wireless service is available via entire campus.

Student Life *Housing options:* coed, men-only, women-only, disabled students. Campus housing is university owned. Freshman campus housing is guaranteed. *Activities and organizations:* drama/theater group, student-run newspaper, radio station, choral group, University of Windsor Student Alliance, Environmental Awareness Association, Social Science Society, Commerce Society, Science Society, national fraternities, national sororities. *Campus security:* 24-hour emergency response devices and patrols, student patrols, late-night transport/escort service, controlled dormitory access. *Student services:* health clinic, personal/psychological counseling, women's center, legal services.

Athletics Member NAIA, CIS. *Intercollegiate sports:* basketball M(s)/W(s), cheerleading M/W, cross-country running M(s)/W(s), football M(s), golf M/W, ice hockey M(s)/W(s), rugby M/W, soccer M(s)/W(s), softball W, track and field M(s)/W(s), volleyball M(s)/W(s). *Intramural sports:* badminton M/W, basketball M/W, bowling M/W, football M/W, golf M/W, ice hockey M/W, rugby M/W, soccer M/W, softball M/W, swimming and diving M/W, table tennis M/W, ultimate Frisbee M/W, volleyball M/W, water polo M/W.

Standardized Tests *Required for some:* SAT or ACT (for admission), SAT and SAT Subject Tests or ACT (for admission), SAT Subject Tests (for admission).

Costs (2013–14) *Tuition:* province resident $5558 Canadian dollars full-time, $860 Canadian dollars per course part-time. Full-time tuition and fees vary according to course load, degree level, location, and program. Part-time tuition and fees vary according to course load, degree level, location, and program. *Required fees:* $591 Canadian dollars full-time. *Room and board:* Room and board charges vary according to board plan and housing facility. *Payment plan:* installment. *Waivers:* senior citizens and employees or children of employees.

Financial Aid Of all full-time matriculated undergraduates who enrolled in 2010, 450 state and other part-time jobs (averaging $1166). *Financial aid deadline:* 6/15.

Applying *Options:* electronic application, early admission. *Application fee:* $60 Canadian dollars. *Required:* high school transcript, minimum 3.0 GPA. *Required for some:* essay or personal statement, minimum 3.3 GPA, 1 letter of recommendation, interview. *Application deadlines:* rolling (freshmen), 7/1 (out-of-state freshmen), rolling (transfers). *Notification:* continuous until 8/30 (freshmen), continuous until 8/30 (transfers).

Freshman Application Contact Ms. Charlene Yates, Manager of Undergraduate Admissions, University of Windsor, Office of the Registrar, 401 Sunset Avenue, Windsor, ON N9B 3P4, Canada. *Phone:* 519-253-3000 Ext. 3332. *Toll-free phone:* 800-864-2860. *Fax:* 519-971-3653. *E-mail:* registrar@uwindsor.ca.
Website: http://www.uwindsor.ca/.

The University of Winnipeg
Winnipeg, Manitoba, Canada

Director of Admissions Mr. Colin Russell, Registrar, The University of Winnipeg, 515 Portage Avenue, Winnipeg, MB R3B 2E9, Canada. *Phone:* 204-786-9776. *Fax:* 204-786-8656. *E-mail:* admissions@uwinnipeg.ca. *Website:* http://www.uwinnipeg.ca/.

Vancouver Island University
Nanaimo, British Columbia, Canada

Freshman Application Contact Ms. Leslie Peterson, Admissions Manager, Vancouver Island University, 900 Fifth Street, Nanaimo, BC V9R 5S5, Canada. *Phone:* 250-740-6355. *Fax:* 250-740-6479. *Website:* http://www.viu.ca/.

Vanguard College
Edmonton, Alberta, Canada

- **Independent** 4-year, founded 1946, affiliated with Pentecostal Assemblies of Canada
- **Urban** 1-hectare campus
- **Coed**

Faculty *Student/faculty ratio:* 11:1.

Academics *Calendar:* semesters. *Degree:* certificates, diplomas, and bachelor's.

Costs (2012–13) *Tuition:* $6435 Canadian dollars full-time, $195 Canadian dollars per credit hour part-time. Full-time tuition and fees vary according to course load and program. Part-time tuition and fees vary according to course load and program. *Required fees:* $1000 Canadian dollars full-time, $12 Canadian dollars per credit hour part-time, $55 Canadian dollars per term part-time. *Room only:* $3600 Canadian dollars. Room and board charges vary according to housing facility.

Applying *Options:* electronic application, early decision. *Application fee:* $75 Canadian dollars. *Required:* essay or personal statement, high school transcript, 2 letters of recommendation.

Freshman Application Contact Vanguard College, 11617 106 Avenue, NW, Edmonton, AB T5H 0S1, Canada. *Phone:* 780-452-0808 Ext. 231. *Toll-free phone:* 866-222-0808. *E-mail:* admissions@vanguardcollege.com. *Website:* http://www.vanguardcollege.com/.

Wilfrid Laurier University
Waterloo, Ontario, Canada

Freshman Application Contact Wilfrid Laurier University, 75 University Avenue West, Waterloo, ON N2L 3C5, Canada. *Phone:* 519-884-0710 Ext. 6099.
Website: http://www.wlu.ca/.

INTERNATIONAL

BULGARIA

American University in Bulgaria
Blagoevgrad, Bulgaria

- **Independent** comprehensive, founded 1991
- **Small-town** 12-acre campus with easy access to Sofia
- **Endowment** $20.0 million
- **Coed** 1,022 undergraduate students, 100% full-time, 51% women, 49% men
- **Very difficult** entrance level, 64% of applicants were admitted

Undergraduates 1,022 full-time. Students come from 40 other countries; 100% Race/ethnicity unknown; 0.2% transferred in; 16% live on campus.
Freshmen *Admission:* 755 applied, 485 admitted, 229 enrolled. *Test scores:* SAT critical reading scores over 500: 71%; SAT math scores over 500: 97%; SAT critical reading scores over 600: 24%; SAT math scores over 600: 68%; SAT critical reading scores over 700: 3%; SAT math scores over 700: 20%.
Faculty *Total:* 78, 65% full-time, 68% with terminal degrees. *Student/faculty ratio:* 17:1.
Academics *Calendar:* semesters. *Degrees:* bachelor's and master's. *Special study options:* advanced placement credit, double majors, honors programs, independent study, internships, services for LD students, study abroad.
Computers on Campus 304 computers/terminals are available on campus for general student use. Students can access the following: computer help desk, free student e-mail accounts, online (class) grades, online (class) registration, online (class) schedules. Campuswide network is available. 100% of college-owned or -operated housing units are wired for high-speed Internet access. Wireless service is available via entire campus.
Student Life *Housing:* on-campus residence required through senior year. *Options:* coed, disabled students. Campus housing is university owned. Freshman campus housing is guaranteed. *Activities and organizations:* drama/theater group, student-run newspaper, radio station, choral group, Computer Science Student Union, Debate Club, Better Community Club, AUBG Broadway Performance Club, Business Club. *Campus security:* 24-hour patrols. *Student services:* health clinic, personal/psychological counseling.
Athletics *Intramural sports:* basketball M/W, cheerleading W(c), equestrian sports M(c)/W(c), football M(c), gymnastics W, soccer M(c), softball M/W, volleyball M/W.
Standardized Tests *Required:* SAT or ACT (for admission). *Required for some:* TOEFL, IELTS, or ESOL for students whose primary language is not English.
Costs (2013–14) *Comprehensive fee:* $11,720 includes full-time tuition ($10,300) and room and board ($1420). Part-time tuition: $429 per credit hour. *College room only:* $1320. Room and board charges vary according to board plan and housing facility. *Waivers:* employees or children of employees.
Applying *Options:* electronic application, early admission, deferred entrance. *Application fee:* $25. *Required:* essay or personal statement, high school transcript, minimum 3.0 GPA, 3 letters of recommendation. *Application deadlines:* 6/1 (freshmen), 6/1 (transfers).
Freshman Application Contact Ms. Boriana Shalyavska, Director of Admissions, American University in Bulgaria, 1 Izmirliev Square 1st floor, Blagoevgrad 2700, Bulgaria. *Phone:* 359-73 888 235. *Fax:* 359-73 883 227. *E-mail:* admissions@aubg.bg. *Website:* http://www.aubg.bg/.

CAYMAN ISLANDS

International College of the Cayman Islands
Newlands, Cayman Islands

Freshman Application Contact International College of the Cayman Islands, PO Box 136, Savannah Post Office, Newlands, Grand Cayman, Cayman Islands. *Phone:* 345-325-6454.
Website: http://www.icci.edu.ky/.

EGYPT

The American University in Cairo
Cairo, Egypt

- **Independent** comprehensive, founded 1919
- **Urban** 260-acre campus
- **Coed** 5,554 undergraduate students, 91% full-time, 52% women, 48% men
- **Very difficult** entrance level, 47% of applicants were admitted

Undergraduates 5,073 full-time, 481 part-time. 0.3% transferred in; 8% live on campus. *Retention:* 91% of full-time freshmen returned.
Freshmen *Admission:* 2,774 applied, 1,295 admitted, 965 enrolled. *Test scores:* SAT critical reading scores over 500: 44%; SAT math scores over 500: 89%; SAT writing scores over 500: 86%; SAT critical reading scores over 600: 9%; SAT math scores over 600: 50%; SAT writing scores over 600: 32%; SAT critical reading scores over 700: 1%; SAT math scores over 700: 12%; SAT writing scores over 700: 5%.
Faculty *Total:* 803, 57% full-time, 69% with terminal degrees. *Student/faculty ratio:* 12:1.
Academics *Calendar:* semesters. *Degrees:* diplomas, bachelor's, master's, and doctoral (majority of students are Egyptians; enrollment open to all nationalities). *Special study options:* academic remediation for entering students, adult/continuing education programs, double majors, English as a second language, independent study, internships, services for LD students, study abroad, summer session for credit.
Computers on Campus 240 computers/terminals are available on campus for general student use. Students can access the following: campus intranet, computer help desk, free student e-mail accounts, online (class) grades, online (class) registration, online (class) schedules, Blackboard, online unofficial transcripts. Campuswide network is available. 100% of college-owned or -operated housing units are wired for high-speed Internet access. Wireless service is available via entire campus.
Student Life *Housing options:* men-only, women-only, disabled students. Campus housing is university owned and leased by the school. Freshman applicants given priority for college housing. *Activities and organizations:* drama/theater group, student-run newspaper, radio station, choral group. *Campus security:* 24-hour emergency response devices and patrols, controlled dormitory access. *Student services:* health clinic, personal/psychological counseling.
Athletics *Intercollegiate sports:* archery M, badminton M/W, basketball M/W, crew M/W, fencing M/W, gymnastics M/W, soccer M/W, squash M/W, swimming and diving M/W, table tennis M/W, tennis M/W, track and field M/W, volleyball M/W, water polo M. *Intramural sports:* basketball M/W, soccer M/

W, squash M/W, table tennis M/W, tennis M/W, volleyball M/W, weight lifting M.

Standardized Tests *Required for some:* SAT or ACT (for admission), SAT Subject Tests (for admission).

Financial Aid Of all full-time matriculated undergraduates who enrolled in 2011, 2,386 applied for aid, 2,149 were judged to have need. *Average financial aid package:* $1590. *Financial aid deadline:* 9/16.

Applying *Options:* electronic application. *Application fee:* $50. *Required:* essay or personal statement, high school transcript, minimum 2.0 GPA. *Application deadlines:* 5/15 (freshmen), 5/15 (transfers). *Notification:* continuous until 7/20 (freshmen), 3/31 (transfers).

Freshman Application Contact Ms. Randa Kamel, Executive Director of Enrollment, The American University in Cairo, AUC Avenue, P.O.Box 74 New Cairo 11835, Cairo, Egypt. *Phone:* 202-26154601. *E-mail:* randakamel@aucegypt.edu.

Website: http://www.aucegypt.edu/.

FRANCE

The American University of Paris
Paris, France

- **Independent** comprehensive, founded 1962
- **Urban** campus
- **Endowment** $968,307
- **Coed** 797 undergraduate students, 90% full-time, 70% women, 30% men
- **Moderately difficult** entrance level, 42% of applicants were admitted

Undergraduates 716 full-time, 81 part-time. Students come from 42 states and territories; 96 other countries; 89% are from out of state; 0.8% transferred in. *Retention:* 69% of full-time freshmen returned.

Freshmen *Admission:* 2,627 applied, 1,113 admitted, 188 enrolled.

Faculty *Total:* 119, 47% full-time, 61% with terminal degrees. *Student/faculty ratio:* 15:1.

Academics *Calendar:* semesters. *Degrees:* bachelor's and master's. *Special study options:* advanced placement credit, cooperative education, double majors, English as a second language, honors programs, independent study, internships, off-campus study, part-time degree program, student-designed majors, study abroad, summer session for credit.

Computers on Campus 150 computers/terminals are available on campus for general student use. Students can access the following: campus intranet, computer help desk, free student e-mail accounts, online (class) grades, online (class) registration, online (class) schedules. Campuswide network is available. Wireless service is available via entire campus.

Student Life *Housing:* college housing not available. *Options:* Campus housing is provided by a third party. *Activities and organizations:* drama/theater group, student-run newspaper, radio and television station, choral group, AUP Student Media (ASM)—Print, Video, Audio, White Mask (Theatre), Student Senate, Student Government Association, Sports Association. *Campus security:* 24-hour emergency response devices. *Student services:* personal/psychological counseling.

Athletics *Intramural sports:* basketball M/W, equestrian sports M/W, football M, golf M/W, racquetball M/W, soccer M/W, squash M/W, tennis M/W, volleyball M/W.

Standardized Tests *Required for some:* SAT or ACT (for admission), TOEFL, TOEIC or IELTS for students whose primary language is not English.

Costs (2013–14) *Comprehensive fee:* 62,567 euros includes full-time tuition (25,890 euros), mandatory fees (27,077 euros), and room and board (9600 euros). Full-time tuition and fees vary according to course load and program. Part-time tuition: 812 euros per credit hour. Part-time tuition and fees vary according to course load and program. *Room and board:* Room and board charges vary according to board plan and housing facility. *Payment plan:* installment. *Waivers:* children of alumni and employees or children of employees.

Financial Aid Of all full-time matriculated undergraduates who enrolled in 2012, 260 applied for aid, 254 were judged to have need. In 2012, 60 non-need-based awards were made. *Average percent of need met:* 41%. *Average financial aid package:* $10,626. *Average need-based loan:* $2350. *Average need-based gift aid:* $9800. *Average non-need-based aid:* $1480.

Applying *Options:* electronic application, deferred entrance. *Application fee:* $65. *Required:* essay or personal statement, high school transcript, 2 letters of recommendation. *Recommended:* minimum 3.0 GPA, interview. *Application deadlines:* 3/15 (freshmen), 3/15 (transfers). *Notification:* continuous (freshmen), continuous (transfers).

Freshman Application Contact International Admissions Office Counselors, The American University of Paris, 6 rue du Colonel Combes, Paris 75007, France. *Phone:* +33 1 40 62 07 20. *Fax:* +33 1 47 05 34 32. *E-mail:* admissions@aup.edu.

Website: http://www.aup.edu/.

Paris College of Art
Paris, France

Freshman Application Contact Sara Krauskopf, Paris College of Art, 14 rue Letellier, F-75015 Paris, France. *Phone:* -331 4577 40 17. *Fax:* 331 4577 44 12. *E-mail:* sara.krauskopf@parsons-paris.com.

Website: http://www.paris.edu/.

Schiller International University
Paris, France

Freshman Application Contact Ms. Kamala Dontamsetti, Associate Director of Admissions, Schiller International University, 300 East Bay Drive, Largo, FL 33770. *Phone:* 727-736-5082 Ext. 234. *Toll-free phone:* 800-261-9571 (in-state); 800-261-9751 (out-of-state). *Fax:* 727-734-0347. *E-mail:* admissions@schiller.edu.

Website: http://www.schiller.edu/.

GERMANY

Schiller International University
Heidelberg, Germany

Freshman Application Contact Ms. Kamala Dontamsetti, Associate Director of Admissions, Schiller International University, 300 East Bay Drive, Largo, FL 33770. *Phone:* 727-736-5082 Ext. 234. *Toll-free phone:* 800-261-9571 (in-state); 800-261-9751 (out-of-state). *Fax:* 727-734-0359. *E-mail:* kamala_dontamsetti@schiller.edu.

Website: http://www.schiller.edu/.

GREECE

American College of Thessaloniki
Pylea, Greece

- **Independent** comprehensive, founded 1886
- **Suburban** 40-acre campus with easy access to Thessaloniki
- **Endowment** $4.3 million
- **Coed** 376 undergraduate students, 84% full-time, 47% women, 53% men
- **Minimally difficult** entrance level, 89% of applicants were admitted

Undergraduates 314 full-time, 62 part-time. Students come from 14 other countries; 40% live on campus. *Retention:* 77% of full-time freshmen returned.

Freshmen *Admission:* 75 applied, 67 admitted, 55 enrolled. *Average high school GPA:* 3.

Faculty *Total:* 41, 37% full-time, 61% with terminal degrees. *Student/faculty ratio:* 15:1.

Academics *Calendar:* semesters. *Degrees:* certificates, bachelor's, and master's. *Special study options:* academic remediation for entering students, accelerated degree program, advanced placement credit, double majors, English as a second language, honors programs, independent study, internships, part-time degree program, services for LD students, study abroad, summer session for credit.

Computers on Campus 155 computers/terminals and 20 ports are available on campus for general student use. Students can access the following: campus intranet, computer help desk, free student e-mail accounts, online (class) grades, online (class) schedules, Remote access to library resources. Campuswide network is available. 100% of college-owned or -operated housing units are wired for high-speed Internet access. Wireless service is available via classrooms, computer centers, learning centers, libraries, student centers.

Student Life *Housing options:* coed. Campus housing is university owned and leased by the school. Freshman applicants given priority for college housing. *Activities and organizations:* Cinema Club, Field Trip Club, ACT Diplomat's Society, Scuba diving, Modern Dance. *Campus security:* 24-hour emergency response devices and patrols. *Student services:* personal/psychological counseling.

Athletics *Intercollegiate sports:* soccer M, table tennis M/W, tennis M/W, volleyball M/W. *Intramural sports:* basketball M/W, football M/W, sailing M/W, table tennis M/W, tennis M/W, volleyball M/W.

Standardized Tests *Recommended:* SAT (for admission).
Costs (2012–13) *Tuition:* $8250 full-time, $275 per credit hour part-time. Part-time tuition and fees vary according to course load. *Required fees:* $100 full-time. *Room only:* $5280. Room and board charges vary according to housing facility. *Waivers:* employees or children of employees.
Applying *Options:* electronic application, deferred entrance. *Application fee:* 95 euros. *Required:* high school transcript, proficiency in English, CV. *Required for some:* essay or personal statement, interview. *Recommended:* minimum 2.0 GPA. *Application deadlines:* rolling (freshmen), rolling (transfers). *Notification:* continuous (freshmen), continuous (transfers).
Freshman Application Contact Mrs. Roula Lebetli, Director of Admissions, American College of Thessaloniki, PO Box 21021, Pylea, Thessaloniki 55510, Greece. *Phone:* +30-2310-398239. *Fax:* +30- 2310-398389. *E-mail:* admissions@act.edu.
Website: http://www.act.edu/.

The American University of Athens
Athens, Greece
Director of Admissions Ms. Thalia Poulos, Director of Admissions, The American University of Athens, 4 Sohou Street and Kifissias Avenue, Neo Psychiko, GR-115 25 Athens, Greece. *Phone:* -30 210-725-9301. *E-mail:* admissions@aua.edu.
Website: http://www.aua.edu/.

DEREE—The American College of Greece
Athens, Greece
- **Independent** 4-year, founded 1875
- **Suburban** 64-acre campus with easy access to Athens
- **Coed** 2,480 undergraduate students, 42% full-time, 50% women, 50% men
- **Moderately difficult** entrance level, 77% of applicants were admitted

Undergraduates 1,040 full-time, 1,440 part-time. Students come from 49 other countries; 2% live on campus. *Retention:* 87% of full-time freshmen returned.
Freshmen *Admission:* 791 applied, 612 admitted. *Average high school GPA:* 2.9. *Test scores:* SAT critical reading scores over 500: 61%; SAT math scores over 500: 63%; SAT critical reading scores over 600: 6%; SAT math scores over 600: 8%.
Faculty *Total:* 189, 72% full-time, 47% with terminal degrees. *Student/faculty ratio:* 13:1.
Academics *Calendar:* 4-1-4. *Degrees:* bachelor's, master's, and postbachelor's certificates. *Special study options:* academic remediation for entering students, accelerated degree program, adult/continuing education programs, advanced placement credit, double majors, English as a second language, honors programs, independent study, internships, part-time degree program, services for LD students, student-designed majors, study abroad, summer session for credit.
Computers on Campus 292 computers/terminals are available on campus for general student use. Students can access the following: computer help desk, free student e-mail accounts, online (class) grades, online (class) registration, online (class) schedules. 100% of college-owned or -operated housing units are wired for high-speed Internet access. Wireless service is available via computer labs, dorm rooms, libraries.
Student Life *Housing options:* coed, disabled students. Campus housing is university owned. *Activities and organizations:* drama/theater group, student-run newspaper, DEREE SAB (Students Activity Board), DEREE Orientation Leaders, DEREE Ambassadors, A.F.C.E.A., DEREE S.E.R.F. *Campus security:* 24-hour emergency response devices and patrols. *Student services:* health clinic, personal/psychological counseling.
Athletics *Intercollegiate sports:* basketball M/W(s), soccer M/W, volleyball W(s), water polo M. *Intramural sports:* basketball M/W, rock climbing M/W, skiing (downhill) M/W, soccer M/W, swimming and diving M/W, table tennis M/W, tennis M/W, track and field M/W, volleyball M/W, water polo M.
Standardized Tests *Recommended:* SAT or ACT (for admission), Not required, optional for US Students.
Costs (2012–13) *One-time required fee:* $140. *Tuition:* $9000 full-time, $315 per credit hour part-time. Full-time tuition and fees vary according to course load. Part-time tuition and fees vary according to course load. *Room only:* Room and board charges vary according to housing facility. *Payment plan:* installment. *Waivers:* employees or children of employees.
Financial Aid *Financial aid deadline:* 9/1.
Applying *Options:* electronic application, deferred entrance. *Required:* essay or personal statement, high school transcript, minimum 2.7 GPA, 1 letter of

recommendation, interview. *Application deadlines:* rolling (freshmen), rolling (transfers). *Notification:* 7/25 (freshmen), 7/25 (transfers).
Freshman Application Contact Ms. Loukia Kanatsouli, Dean of Enrollment and International Students, DEREE—The American College of Greece, 6 Gravias Street, Aghia Paraskevi, Athens 15342, Greece. *Phone:* -30 210-600-9800 Ext. 1474. *E-mail:* lkanatsouli@acg.edu.
Website: http://www.acg.edu/.

IRELAND

Institute of Public Administration
Dublin, Ireland
Director of Admissions Dr. Denis O'Brien, Registrar, Institute of Public Administration, 57-61 Lansdowne Road, Dublin 4, Ireland. *Phone:* 353-1-240-3600. *Fax:* 353-1-668-9135. *E-mail:* undergrad@ipa.ie.
Website: http://www.ipa.ie/.

ITALY

The American University of Rome
Rome, Italy
- **Independent** 4-year, founded 1969
- **Urban** 1-acre campus
- **Endowment** $1.1 million
- **Coed** 364 undergraduate students, 100% full-time, 63% women, 37% men
- **Moderately difficult** entrance level, 54% of applicants were admitted

Undergraduates 364 full-time. Students come from 22 states and territories; 40 other countries; 4% transferred in; 65% live on campus. *Retention:* 79% of full-time freshmen returned.
Freshmen *Admission:* 465 applied, 252 admitted, 41 enrolled. *Average high school GPA:* 3. *Test scores:* SAT writing scores over 500: 81%; ACT scores over 18: 100%; SAT writing scores over 600: 28%; ACT scores over 24: 100%.
Faculty *Total:* 68, 16% full-time, 44% with terminal degrees. *Student/faculty ratio:* 16:1.
Academics *Calendar:* semesters. *Degrees:* associate and bachelor's. *Special study options:* academic remediation for entering students, advanced placement credit, double majors, English as a second language, independent study, internships, off-campus study, part-time degree program, services for LD students, student-designed majors, study abroad, summer session for credit.
Computers on Campus 68 computers/terminals and 80 ports are available on campus for general student use. Students can access the following: campus intranet, computer help desk, free student e-mail accounts, online (class) grades, online (class) registration, online (class) schedules, Learning Management System. Campuswide network is available. 100% of college-owned or -operated housing units are wired for high-speed Internet access. Wireless service is available via computer labs, dorm rooms, libraries, student centers.
Student Life *Housing options:* men-only, women-only. Campus housing is provided by a third party. Freshman applicants given priority for college housing. *Activities and organizations:* drama/theater group, student-run newspaper, Student Government, Community Services, Men and Female soccer teams, Business Club, International Relations Club. *Campus security:* 24-hour emergency response devices, security guards during opening hours and 24-hour surveillance cameras. *Student services:* health clinic, personal/psychological counseling.
Athletics *Intercollegiate sports:* soccer M/W. *Intramural sports:* cross-country running M/W, gymnastics M/W, volleyball M/W.
Standardized Tests *Required for some:* SAT or ACT (for admission).
Costs (2012–13) *One-time required fee:* $190. *Comprehensive fee:* $23,644 includes full-time tuition ($13,940), mandatory fees ($144), and room and board ($9560). Full-time tuition and fees vary according to course load. Part-time tuition: $1745 per course. Part-time tuition and fees vary according to course load. *College room only:* $7600. Room and board charges vary according to housing facility. *Payment plan:* installment. *Waivers:* employees or children of employees.
Applying *Options:* electronic application, deferred entrance. *Application fee:* $75. *Required:* essay or personal statement, high school transcript, minimum 2.5 GPA, 1 letter of recommendation, interview, TOEFL OR IELTS FOR NON-ENGLISH HIGH SCHOOL STUDENTS. *Application deadlines:* rolling

(freshmen), rolling (transfers). *Notification:* continuous (freshmen), continuous (transfers).

Freshman Application Contact Miss Melissa Abraham, Admissions Counselor, The American University of Rome, Via Pietro Roselli 4, Rome 00153, Italy. *Phone:* +39 0658330919. *Toll-free phone:* 877-592-1287. *Fax:* +39 0658330992. *E-mail:* admissions@aur.edu.
Website: http://www.aur.edu/.

See below for display ad and page 1040 for the College Close-Up.

John Cabot University
Rome, Italy

- **Independent** 4-year, founded 1972
- **Urban** campus with easy access to Rome
- **Coed** 1,000 undergraduate students, 100% full-time, 50% women, 50% men

Undergraduates 1,000 full-time. Students come from 66 other countries. *Retention:* 87% of full-time freshmen returned.
Freshmen *Admission:* 100 enrolled. *Average high school GPA:* 3.
Faculty *Total:* 105, 19% full-time, 71% with terminal degrees. *Student/faculty ratio:* 15:1.
Academics *Calendar:* semesters. *Degrees:* associate and bachelor's. *Special study options:* advanced placement credit, cooperative education, double majors, English as a second language, freshman honors college, honors programs, independent study, internships, part-time degree program, study abroad, summer session for credit.
Computers on Campus 80 computers/terminals are available on campus for general student use. Students can access the following: free student e-mail accounts, wireless connection on the campus. Campuswide network is available.
Student Life *Housing options:* coed, men-only, women-only. Campus housing is leased by the school. Freshman campus housing is guaranteed. *Activities and organizations:* drama/theater group, student-run newspaper, Business Club, Model United Nations, Student Government, Universities Fighting World Hunger, Stand. *Campus security:* 24-hour emergency response devices. *Student services:* health clinic, personal/psychological counseling.
Athletics *Intramural sports:* basketball M/W, cross-country running M/W, sailing M/W, skiing (downhill) M/W, soccer M/W, tennis M/W, volleyball M/W.
Standardized Tests *Required for some:* SAT or ACT (for admission).

Costs (2013–14) *Comprehensive fee:* $22,700 includes full-time tuition ($21,500) and room and board ($1200). Full-time tuition and fees vary according to course load, degree level, location, and reciprocity agreements. Part-time tuition and fees vary according to course load, degree level, location, and reciprocity agreements. *College room only:* $12,000. Room and board charges vary according to board plan, housing facility, and location. *Payment plan:* installment. *Waivers:* employees or children of employees.
Applying *Required:* essay or personal statement, high school transcript, 2 letters of recommendation. *Recommended:* minimum 2.7 GPA, interview.
Freshman Application Contact Nadia Spagnoli, Associate Coordinator of Admissions, John Cabot University, Via della Lungara 233, Roma 00165, Italy. *Phone:* 1-866-JCU-Roma. *Toll-free phone:* 866-457-6160. *Fax:* 39 06 589 7429. *E-mail:* admissions@johncabot.edu.
Website: http://www.johncabot.edu/.

KENYA

United States International University
Nairobi, Kenya

- **Independent** comprehensive, founded 1977, part of Alliant International University
- **Urban** 120-acre campus
- **Coed**
- **Moderately difficult** entrance level

Faculty *Student/faculty ratio:* 30:1.
Academics *Calendar:* trimesters. *Degrees:* bachelor's and master's.
Student Life *Campus security:* 24-hour emergency response devices and patrols, 24-hour Hostel reception security desk.
Standardized Tests *Required for some:* TOEFL for students whose high school language of instruction was not English.
Costs (2012–13) *One-time required fee:* 3000 Kenyan shillings. *Comprehensive fee:* 483,510 Kenyan shillings includes full-time tuition (244,800 Kenyan shillings), mandatory fees (21,150 Kenyan shillings), and room and board (217,560 Kenyan shillings). Full-time tuition and fees vary according to course load, degree level, program, and reciprocity agreements. Part-time tuition: 6800 Kenyan shillings per unit. Part-time tuition and fees vary according to

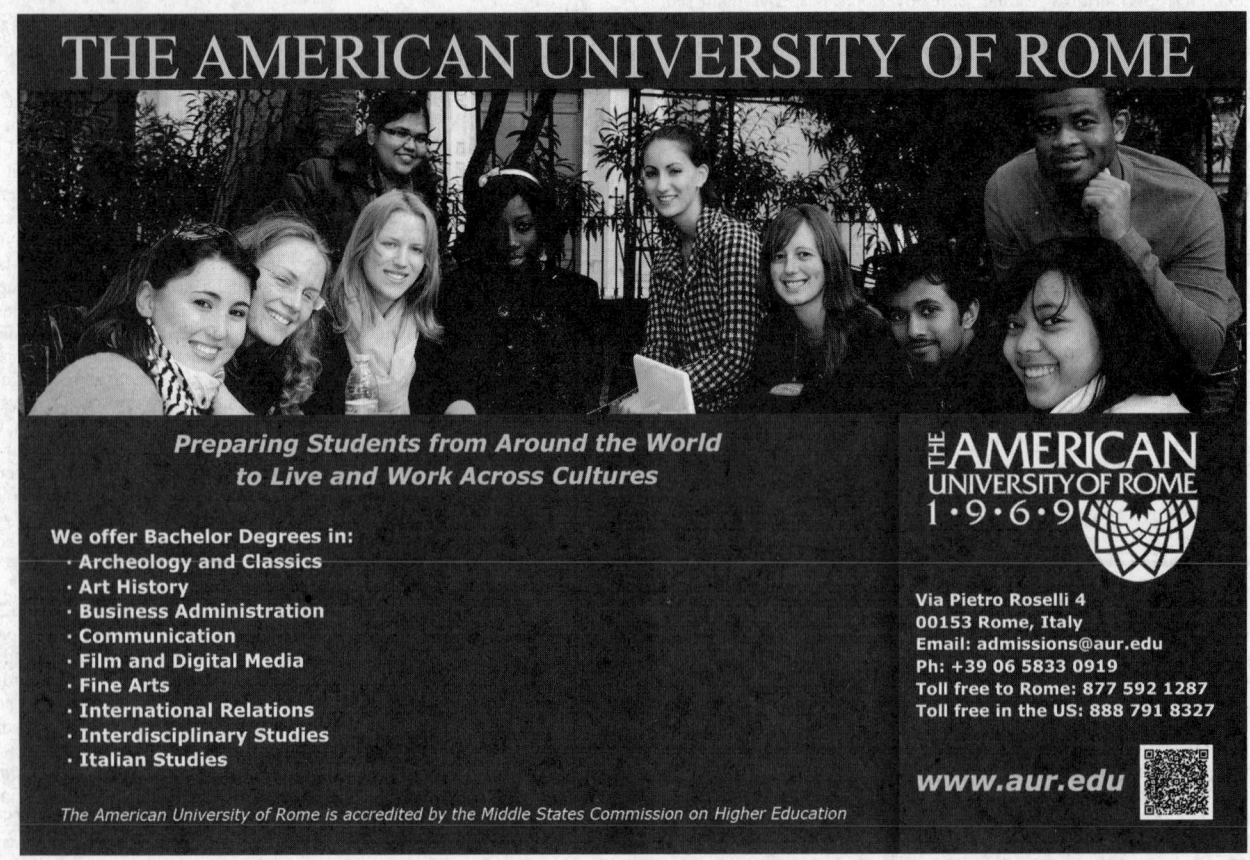

course load, degree level, program, and reciprocity agreements. *Required fees:* 7050 Kenyan shillings per term part-time. *College room only:* 79,380 Kenyan shillings. Room and board charges vary according to board plan.

Applying *Options:* deferred entrance. *Application fee:* 50 Kenyan shillings. *Required:* high school transcript, minimum 2.5 GPA. *Required for some:* interview.

Freshman Application Contact United States International University, PO Box 14634, Thika Road Kasarani, Nairobi 00800, Kenya. *Phone:* 254-02-3606563.

Website: http://www.usiu.ac.ke/.

LEBANON

American University of Beirut

Beirut, Lebanon

- **Independent** university, founded 1866
- **Urban** 61-acre campus with easy access to Beirut
- **Endowment** $498,982
- **Coed** 6,572 undergraduate students, 94% full-time, 50% women, 50% men
- 64% of applicants were admitted

Undergraduates 6,202 full-time, 370 part-time. Students come from 71 other countries; 0.7% transferred in; 16% live on campus. *Retention:* 93% of full-time freshmen returned.

Freshmen *Admission:* 5,093 applied, 3,241 admitted, 1,837 enrolled. *Average high school GPA:* 2.85. *Test scores:* SAT critical reading scores over 500: 50%; SAT math scores over 500: 96%; SAT writing scores over 500: 62%; SAT critical reading scores over 600: 10%; SAT math scores over 600: 73%; SAT writing scores over 600: 15%; SAT critical reading scores over 700: 1%; SAT math scores over 700: 27%; SAT writing scores over 700: 1%.

Faculty *Total:* 833, 67% full-time, 58% with terminal degrees. *Student/faculty ratio:* 11:1.

Academics *Calendar:* semesters. *Degrees:* certificates, diplomas, bachelor's, master's, and doctoral. *Special study options:* academic remediation for entering students, advanced placement credit, double majors, English as a second language, honors programs, independent study, internships, services for LD students, study abroad, summer session for credit.

Computers on Campus 1,437 computers/terminals and 1,500 ports are available on campus for general student use. Students can access the following: campus intranet, computer help desk, free student e-mail accounts, online (class) grades, online (class) registration, online (class) schedules. Campuswide network is available. 100% of college-owned or -operated housing units are wired for high-speed Internet access. Wireless service is available via entire campus.

Student Life *Housing:* on-campus residence required for freshman year. *Options:* men-only, women-only. Campus housing is university owned. Freshman campus housing is guaranteed. *Activities and organizations:* drama/theater group, student-run newspaper, choral group, Red Cross Club, Biology Society, Business Society, Music Club, Palestinian Cultural Club. *Campus security:* 24-hour emergency response devices and patrols, late-night transport/escort service, staff monitors entrance 24/7. *Student services:* health clinic, personal/psychological counseling, legal services.

Athletics *Intercollegiate sports:* basketball M/W, cross-country running M/W, football M, gymnastics M, rugby M, skiing (downhill) M/W, soccer M/W, squash M/W, swimming and diving M/W, table tennis M/W, tennis M/W, track and field M/W, volleyball M/W, water polo M. *Intramural sports:* basketball M/W, cross-country running M/W, gymnastics M, lacrosse M/W, racquetball M/W, soccer M/W, squash M/W, swimming and diving M/W, table tennis M/W, tennis M/W, volleyball M/W, weight lifting M/W.

Standardized Tests *Required:* SAT (for admission). *Required for some:* SAT Subject Tests (for admission).

Costs (2012–13) *Tuition:* $17,700 full-time, $590 per credit part-time. Full-time tuition and fees vary according to course load, degree level, program, and student level. Part-time tuition and fees vary according to course load, degree level, program, and student level. *Required fees:* $563 full-time. *Room only:* $2576. Room and board charges vary according to housing facility and location. *Payment plan:* deferred payment. *Waivers:* employees or children of employees.

Financial Aid Of all full-time matriculated undergraduates who enrolled in 2011, 3,379 applied for aid, 2,739 were judged to have need. 42 state and other part-time jobs (averaging $1348). In 2011, 38 non-need-based awards were made. *Average financial aid package:* $5508. *Average need-based loan:* $4804. *Average need-based gift aid:* $5373. *Average non-need-based aid:* $15,294. *Financial aid deadline:* 2/2.

Applying *Options:* electronic application, early admission, early action, deferred entrance. *Application fee:* $50. *Required:* high school transcript. *Required for some:* 2 letters of recommendation, interview, TOEFL for international applicants. *Recommended:* essay or personal statement. *Application deadlines:* 2/1 (freshmen), 4/30 (transfers), 11/30 (early action). *Notification:* 4/30 (freshmen), continuous until 6/30 (transfers), 1/31 (early action).

Freshman Application Contact Dr. Salim Kanaan, Director of Admissions Office, American University of Beirut, PO Box 11-0236, Riad El-Solh, 1107 2020, Lebanon. *Phone:* -961 1-374 374 Ext. 2592. *Fax:* 961 1-750 775. *E-mail:* admissions@aub.edu.lb.

Website: http://www.aub.edu.lb/.

Lebanese American University

Beirut, Lebanon

- **Private** comprehensive, founded 1835
- **Urban** 58-acre campus with easy access to Beirut Campus: Beirut/Byblos Campus:Byblos,Tripoli
- **Endowment** $298.5 million
- **Coed** 7,457 undergraduate students, 93% full-time, 48% women, 52% men
- **Moderately difficult** entrance level, 78% of applicants were admitted

Undergraduates 6,900 full-time, 557 part-time. Students come from 78 other countries; 21% are from out of state; 1% transferred in; 4% live on campus. *Retention:* 93% of full-time freshmen returned.

Freshmen *Admission:* 3,892 applied, 3,031 admitted, 1,535 enrolled. *Average high school GPA:* 2.8. *Test scores:* SAT critical reading scores over 500: 17%; SAT math scores over 500: 80%; SAT writing scores over 500: 30%; SAT critical reading scores over 600: 2%; SAT math scores over 600: 40%; SAT writing scores over 600: 5%; SAT math scores over 700: 7%.

Faculty *Total:* 697, 40% full-time, 43% with terminal degrees. *Student/faculty ratio:* 18:1.

Academics *Degrees:* bachelor's, master's, doctoral, and postbachelor's certificates. *Special study options:* academic remediation for entering students, double majors, internships, part-time degree program, services for LD students, study abroad, summer session for credit.

Computers on Campus 912 computers/terminals and 2,200 ports are available on campus for general student use. Students can access the following: campus intranet, computer help desk, free student e-mail accounts, online (class) grades, online (class) registration, online (class) schedules, online library book reservation; online forms requests (grades, diplomas, etc.); Online course management system (Blackboard). Campuswide network is available. 100% of college-owned or -operated housing units are wired for high-speed Internet access. Wireless service is available via entire campus.

Student Life *Housing options:* men-only, women-only, disabled students. Campus housing is university owned. *Activities and organizations:* drama/theater group, student-run newspaper, choral group, Model United Nations, Event Organization Club, Red Cross Club, Rotaract Club, Campus Life Club. *Campus security:* 24-hour emergency response devices and patrols, 24/7 security at Residence Halls. *Student services:* health clinic, personal/psychological counseling, women's center.

Athletics *Intercollegiate sports:* badminton M/W, basketball M(s)/W(s), rugby M, soccer M(s)/W(s), swimming and diving M(s)/W(s), table tennis M(s)/W(s), tennis M/W(s), track and field M/W(s), volleyball M(s)/W. *Intramural sports:* basketball M/W, skiing (downhill) M/W, soccer M/W, swimming and diving M/W, table tennis M/W, tennis M/W.

Standardized Tests *Required:* SAT (for admission), Institutional English Test (English Entrance Exam EEE) or International TOFEL (for admission). *Required for some:* SAT Subject Tests (for admission).

Costs (2012–13) *Tuition:* $13,976 full-time. Full-time tuition and fees vary according to course load, degree level, and program. Part-time tuition and fees vary according to course load, degree level, and program. *Required fees:* $469 full-time, $583 per credit part-time. *Room only:* $5304. Room and board charges vary according to housing facility and location. *Payment plan:* deferred payment. *Waivers:* employees or children of employees.

Applying *Options:* electronic application, early admission, early action, deferred entrance. *Application fee:* $50. *Required:* high school transcript, minimum 2.0 GPA, Official high school diploma, SAT I, Institutional English Test (English Entrance Exam EEE) or International TOFEL or SAT Writing. *Application deadlines:* 7/31 (freshmen), 7/31 (out-of-state freshmen), 7/31 (transfers), 1/31 (early action). *Notification:* continuous until 3/15 (freshmen), continuous until 3/15 (out-of-state freshmen), continuous until 3/15 (transfers), 3/15 (early action).

Freshman Application Contact Lebanese American University, PO Box 13-5053, Beirut, Lebanon. *Phone:* 961-9547254 Ext. 2191.

Website: http://www.lau.edu.lb/.

MEXICO

Alliant International University–México City

Mexico City, Mexico

- **Independent** comprehensive, founded 1970, part of Alliant International University
- **Urban** campus with easy access to Mexico City
- **Coed** 290 undergraduate students, 5% full-time, 51% women, 49% men
- **Moderately difficult** entrance level

Undergraduates 15 full-time, 275 part-time. Students come from 4 states and territories; 5 other countries; 0.5% Black or African American, non-Hispanic/Latino; 4% Hispanic/Latino; 2% Race/ethnicity unknown; 93% international. *Retention:* 66% of full-time freshmen returned.
Faculty *Total:* 24, 33% full-time, 54% with terminal degrees. *Student/faculty ratio:* 12:1.
Academics *Calendar:* semesters. *Degrees:* bachelor's and master's. *Special study options:* accelerated degree program, advanced placement credit, English as a second language, internships, summer session for credit.
Computers on Campus 15 computers/terminals are available on campus for general student use. Students can access the following: free student e-mail accounts, online (class) grades, online (class) registration, online (class) schedules. Wireless service is available via entire campus.
Student Life *Housing:* college housing not available. *Activities and organizations:* student-run newspaper, International Business Club, German Club, Student Council.
Standardized Tests *Recommended:* SAT or ACT (for admission).
Costs (2012–13) *Tuition:* $8520 full-time, $355 per unit part-time. Full-time tuition and fees vary according to course load and location. Part-time tuition and fees vary according to course load and location.
Applying *Options:* electronic application, deferred entrance. *Application fee:* 500 Mexican pesos. *Required:* essay or personal statement, high school transcript, minimum 2.0 GPA, 1 letter of recommendation. *Required for some:* interview. *Recommended:* minimum 3.0 GPA. *Application deadlines:* rolling (freshmen), rolling (transfers).
Freshman Application Contact Alliant International University–México City, Hamburgo #115, Col. Juarez, Mexico D.F. 06600, Mexico. *Phone:* -52 5555257651. *E-mail:* mexicoadmissions@alliant.edu.
Website: http://www.alliantmexico.com/.

Instituto Tecnológico y de Estudios Superiores de Monterrey, Campus Central de Veracruz

Córdoba, Mexico

Director of Admissions Ing. Luis Pablo Villareal, Registrar, Instituto Tecnológico y de Estudios Superiores de Monterrey, Campus Central de Veracruz, Avenida Eugenio Garza Sada 1, Apartado Postal 314, 94500 Córdoba, Veracruz, Mexico. *Phone:* -27-13-23-40 Ext. 123.
Website: http://www.ver.itesm.mx/.

Instituto Tecnológico y de Estudios Superiores de Monterrey, Campus Chiapas

Tuxtla Gutiérrez, Mexico

Director of Admissions Lic. Luis Enrique Cancino, Registrar, Instituto Tecnológico y de Estudios Superiores de Monterrey, Campus Chiapas, Carretera a Tapanatepec Km 149&746, Apartado Postal 312, 29000 Tuxtla Gutiérrez, Chiapas, Mexico. *Phone:* -96-15-1723.
Website: http://www.chs.itesm.mx/.

Instituto Tecnológico y de Estudios Superiores de Monterrey, Campus Chihuahua

Chihuahua, Mexico

Director of Admissions Ing. Juan Manuel Fernandez, Registrar, Instituto Tecnológico y de Estudios Superiores de Monterrey, Campus Chihuahua,

Colegio Militar 4700, Colonia Nombre de Dios, Apartado Postal 728, 31300 Chihuahua, Chihuahua, Mexico. *Phone:* -14-17-48-58 Ext. 117.
Website: http://www.chi.itesm.mx/.

Instituto Tecnológico y de Estudios Superiores de Monterrey, Campus Ciudad de México

Ciudad de Mexico, Mexico

Freshman Application Contact Admissions Office, Instituto Tecnológico y de Estudios Superiores de Monterrey, Campus Ciudad de México, Calle del Puente #222 esquina con Periférico, 14380 Colonia Huipulco, Tlalpan, MDF, Mexico. *Phone:* -5-673-6488.
Website: http://www.ccm.itesm.mx/.

Instituto Tecnológico y de Estudios Superiores de Monterrey, Campus Ciudad Juárez

Ciudad Juárez, Mexico

Director of Admissions Lic. Alberto Trejo, Registrar, Instituto Tecnológico y de Estudios Superiores de Monterrey, Campus Ciudad Juárez, Boulevard Tomas Fernandez y Avenida A J Bermudez, Apartado Postal 3105-J, 32320 Ciudad Juárez, Chihuahua, Mexico. *Phone:* -16-17-88-07 Ext. 113.
Website: http://www.cdj.itesm.mx/.

Instituto Tecnológico y de Estudios Superiores de Monterrey, Campus Ciudad Obregón

Ciudad Obregón, Mexico

Director of Admissions Lic. Judith Almeida, Registrar, Instituto Tecnológico y de Estudios Superiores de Monterrey, Campus Ciudad Obregón, Dr Norman E Borlaug Km 14, Apartado Postal 662, 85000 Ciudad Obregón, Sonora, Mexico. *Phone:* -64-15-03-12.
Website: http://www.cob.itesm.mx/.

Instituto Tecnológico y de Estudios Superiores de Monterrey, Campus Colima

Colima, Mexico

Director of Admissions Lic. Manuel Perez Rivera, Registrar, Instituto Tecnológico y de Estudios Superiores de Monterrey, Campus Colima, Prolongacion Ignacio Sandoval s/n, Fraccionamiento Jardines de Vista Hermosa, Apartado Postal 190, 28010 Colima, Colima, Mexico. *Phone:* -33-12-53-39.
Website: http://www.itesm.edu/wps/wcm/connect/Campus/COL/colima/.

Instituto Tecnológico y de Estudios Superiores de Monterrey, Campus Cuernavaca

Temixco, Mexico

Director of Admissions Lic. Miguel Angel Machua, Registrar, Instituto Tecnológico y de Estudios Superiores de Monterrey, Campus Cuernavaca, Paseo de la Reforma 182-A, Colonia Lomas de Cuernavaca, 62000 Temixco, Morelos, Mexico. *Phone:* -73 18-49-57.
Website: http://www.cva.itesm.mx/.

Instituto Tecnológico y de Estudios Superiores de Monterrey, Campus Estado de México

Estado de Mexico, Mexico

Director of Admissions Prof. Jose de Jesus Molina, Registrar, Instituto Tecnológico y de Estudios Superiores de Monterrey, Campus Estado de

México, Carretera Lago de Guadalupe Km. 3.5, Atizapan de Zaragoza, Estado de Mexico 52926, Mexico. *Phone:* -5-873-3600.
Website: http://www.cem.itesm.mx/.

Instituto Tecnológico y de Estudios Superiores de Monterrey, Campus Guadalajara

Zapopan, Mexico

Director of Admissions Ms. Janet Martell Sotomayor, Registration Director, Instituto Tecnológico y de Estudios Superiores de Monterrey, Campus Guadalajara, Avenida General Ramón Corona 2514, Colonia Nuevo Mexico, 45140 Zapopan, Jalisco, Mexico. *Phone:* -3-669-3006.
Website: http://www.gda.itesm.mx/.

Instituto Tecnológico y de Estudios Superiores de Monterrey, Campus Hidalgo

Pachuca, Mexico

Director of Admissions Lic. Lizbet Melo, Registrar, Instituto Tecnológico y de Estudios Superiores de Monterrey, Campus Hidalgo, Boulevard Felipe Angeles s/n al lado de la Unidad Deportiva, Apartado Postal 337, 42090 Pachuca, Hidalgo, Mexico. *Phone:* -714-25-00 Ext. 128.
Website: http://www.hgo.itesm.mx/.

Instituto Tecnológico y de Estudios Superiores de Monterrey, Campus Irapuato

Irapuato, Mexico

Director of Admissions Ing. Marcela Beltrán, Registrar, Instituto Tecnológico y de Estudios Superiores de Monterrey, Campus Irapuato, Paseo Mirador del Valle No. 445, Col. Villas de Irapuato, Apartado Postal 568, 36660 Irapuato, Guanajuato, Mexico. *Phone:* -46-230342.
Website: http://www.ira.itesm.mx/.

Instituto Tecnológico y de Estudios Superiores de Monterrey, Campus Laguna

Torreón, Mexico

Director of Admissions Ing. Aroldo Camargo Soto, Registrar, Instituto Tecnológico y de Estudios Superiores de Monterrey, Campus Laguna, Paseo del Tecnologico s/n Ampliacion La Rosita, Apartado Postal 506, 27250 Torreón, Coahuila, Mexico. *Phone:* -17-20-66-61 Ext. 23.
Website: http://www.lag.itesm.mx/.

Instituto Tecnológico y de Estudios Superiores de Monterrey, Campus León

León, Mexico

Director of Admissions Lic. Eddie Villegas, Registrar, Instituto Tecnológico y de Estudios Superiores de Monterrey, Campus León, Avenida Eugenio Garza Sada s/n Colonia Cerro Gordo, Apartado Postal 872, 37120 León, Guanajuato, Mexico. *Phone:* -47-17-10-00 Ext. 131.
Website: http://www.leo.itesm.mx/.

Instituto Tecnológico y de Estudios Superiores de Monterrey, Campus Mazatlán

Mazatlán, Mexico

Director of Admissions Ing. Martin Ley Urias, Registrar, Instituto Tecnológico y de Estudios Superiores de Monterrey, Campus Mazatlán, Carretera Mazatlan-Higueras, Km 3, Camino al Conchi, Apartado Postal 799, 82000 Mazatlán, Sinaloa, Mexico. *Phone:* -69-80-1143.

Instituto Tecnológico y de Estudios Superiores de Monterrey, Campus Monterrey

Monterrey, Mexico

Director of Admissions Lic. Carlos Ordoñez, International Student Advisor, Instituto Tecnológico y de Estudios Superiores de Monterrey, Campus Monterrey, Avenida Eugenio Garza Sada 2501 Sur Colonia Tecnnologico, Sucursal de Correos J, 64849 Monterrey, Nuevo León, Mexico. *Phone:* -52 81 8328 4065 Ext. 3942.
Website: http://www.mty.itesm.mx/.

Instituto Tecnológico y de Estudios Superiores de Monterrey, Campus Querétaro

Santiago de Querétaro, Mexico

Director of Admissions Lic. Marco Vinicio Lopez, Registrar, Instituto Tecnológico y de Estudios Superiores de Monterrey, Campus Querétaro, Avenida Epigmenio González #500, Apartado Postal 37, 76130 Querétaro, Querétaro, Mexico. *Phone:* -42-17-38-25 Ext. 156.
Website: http://www.qro.itesm.mx/.

Instituto Tecnológico y de Estudios Superiores de Monterrey, Campus Saltillo

Saltillo, Mexico

Director of Admissions Lic. Esteban Ramos, Registrar, Instituto Tecnológico y de Estudios Superiores de Monterrey, Campus Saltillo, Prolongacion Juan de la Barrera 1241 Ote, Apartado Postal 539, 25270 Saltillo, Coahuila, Mexico. *Phone:* -84-15-06-90 Ext. 12.
Website: http://www.sal.itesm.mx/.

Instituto Tecnológico y de Estudios Superiores de Monterrey, Campus San Luis Potosí

San Luis Potosí, Mexico

Director of Admissions Ing. Consuelo Gonzalez, Registrar, Instituto Tecnológico y de Estudios Superiores de Monterrey, Campus San Luis Potosí, Avenida Robles 600, Colonia Jacarandas, Apartado Postal 1473 Suc E, 78140 San Luis Potosí, SLP, Mexico. *Phone:* -48 13-3441 Ext. 14.
Website: http://www.slp.itesm.mx/.

Instituto Tecnológico y de Estudios Superiores de Monterrey, Campus Sinaloa

Culiacán, Mexico

Director of Admissions Lic. Hugo Guerrero, Registrar, Instituto Tecnológico y de Estudios Superiores de Monterrey, Campus Sinaloa, Boulevard Culiacán 3773, Apartado Postal 69-F, 80800 Culiacán, Sinaloa, Mexico. *Phone:* -67-14-03-69.
Website: http://www.sin.itesm.mx/.

Instituto Tecnológico y de Estudios Superiores de Monterrey, Campus Sonora Norte

Hermosillo, Mexico

Director of Admissions Ing. Victor Eduardo Perez Orozco, Library and Admissions/Registration Director, Instituto Tecnológico y de Estudios Superiores de Monterrey, Campus Sonora Norte, Carretera Hermosillo-Nogales Km 9, Apartado Postal 216, 83000 Hermosillo, Sonora, Mexico. *Phone:* -62-15-52-05 Ext. 131.
Website: http://www.her.itesm.mx/.

Instituto Tecnológico y de Estudios Superiores de Monterrey, Campus Tampico

Altimira, Mexico

Director of Admissions Ing. Javier Ponce, Registrar, Instituto Tecnológico y de Estudios Superiores de Monterrey, Campus Tampico, Boulevard Petrocel Km 1.3, Corredor Industrial, Carretera Tampico-Mante, 89120 Altimira, Tamaulipas, Mexico. *Phone:* -126-4-19-79.
Website: http://www.itesm.edu/wps/portal?WCM_GLOBAL_CONTEXT=/migration/TAM2/Tampico.

Instituto Tecnológico y de Estudios Superiores de Monterrey, Campus Toluca

Toluca, Mexico

Director of Admissions Ing. Victor M. Martinez Orta, Registrar, Instituto Tecnológico y de Estudios Superiores de Monterrey, Campus Toluca, Ex-hacienda La Pila, 100 metros al norte de San Antonio Buenavista, 50252 Toluca, Estado de Mexico, Mexico. *Phone:* -72-74-11-92.
Website: http://www.tol.itesm.mx/.

Instituto Tecnológico y de Estudios Superiores de Monterrey, Campus Zacatecas

Zacatecas, Mexico

Director of Admissions Lic. de Lourdes Zorrilla, Business Affairs Director and Registrar, Instituto Tecnológico y de Estudios Superiores de Monterrey, Campus Zacatecas, Calzada Pedro Coronel #16, Frente al Club Bernades, Municipio de Guadalupe, 98000 Zacatecas, Zacatecas, Mexico. *Phone:* -49 23-00-40.
Website: http://www.zac.itesm.mx/.

Universidad de las Americas, A.C.

Mexico City, Mexico

Admissions Office Contact Universidad de las Americas, A.C., Calle de Puebla 223, Col. Roma, 06700 Mexico City, Mexico.
Website: http://www.udla.mx/.

Universidad de las Américas Puebla

Puebla, Mexico

Freshman Application Contact Miss Madet Ruisenor-Quintero, Director of Student Enrollment Office, Universidad de las Américas Puebla, Ex-Hacienda Santa Catarina Martir S/N, Cholula, Puebla 72820, Mexico. *Phone:* -52 229-2024.
Website: http://www.udlap.mx/.

Universidad de Monterrey

San Pedro Garza Garcia, Mexico

Admissions Office Contact Universidad de Monterrey, Av. Ignacio Morones Prieto 4500 Pte, 66238 San Pedro Garza Garca, NL, Mexico. *Toll-free phone:* 800-801-UDEM.
Website: http://www.udem.edu.mx/.

MONACO

The International University of Monaco

Monte Carlo, Monaco

Freshman Application Contact Dr. Gisele Dudognon, Director of Admissions, The International University of Monaco, 2, Avenue Albert II, MC-98000 Principality of Monaco, Monaco. *Phone:* -377 97986 994. *Fax:* 377 92052 830. *E-mail:* gdudognon@monaco.edu.
Website: http://www.monaco.edu/.

NICARAGUA

Ave Maria University–Latin American Campus

San Marcos, Nicaragua

Director of Admissions Mr. Patrick Clark, Director of Admissions, Ave Maria University–Latin American Campus, San Marcos, Carazo, Nicaragua. *Phone:* -43 22314-138. *Toll-free phone:* 800-969-1685. *E-mail:* patrick.clark@avemaria.edu.ni.
Website: http://www.avemaria.edu.ni/.

SOUTH AFRICA

University of South Africa

Pretoria, South Africa

Freshman Application Contact Contact Centre, University of South Africa, PO Box 392, Pretoria 0003, South Africa. *Phone:* 27-11 670-9000. *Fax:* 012 429 4150. *E-mail:* study-info@unisa.ac.za.
Website: http://www.unisa.ac.za/.

SPAIN

Saint Louis University–Madrid Campus

Madrid, Spain

Freshman Application Contact Ms. Maria-Jose Morell, Director of Enrollment Management, Saint Louis University–Madrid Campus, Avenida del Valle, 34, Madrid 28003, Spain. *Phone:* -34 91-554-5858. *Fax:* 34 91-554-6202. *E-mail:* mmorell@slu.edu.
Website: http://spain.slu.edu/.

Schiller International University

Madrid, Spain

Freshman Application Contact Ms. Kamala Dontamsetti, Associate Director of Admissions, Schiller International University, 300 East Bay Drive, Largo, FL 33700. *Phone:* 727-736-5082 Ext. 234. *Toll-free phone:* 800-261-9571 (in-state); 800-261-9751 (out-of-state). *Fax:* 727-734-0359. *E-mail:* admissions@schiller.edu.
Website: http://www.schiller.edu/.

SWITZERLAND

Ecole Hôtelière de Lausanne

Lausanne, Switzerland

Freshman Application Contact Ecole Hôtelière de Lausanne, Le Chalet-a-Gobet, CH-1000 Lausanne 25, Switzerland. *Phone:* -41 21 785 1111.
Website: http://www.ehl.ch/.

Franklin College Switzerland

Sorengo, Switzerland

- **Independent** comprehensive, founded 1969
- **Suburban** 7-acre campus with easy access to Milan, Italy
- **Endowment** $2.9 million
- **Coed** 414 undergraduate students, 99% full-time, 67% women, 33% men
- **Moderately difficult** entrance level, 59% of applicants were admitted

Undergraduates 409 full-time, 5 part-time. Students come from 29 states and territories; 60 other countries; 100% are from out of state; 1% transferred in; 89% live on campus. *Retention:* 72% of full-time freshmen returned.

Freshmen *Admission:* 749 applied, 441 admitted, 122 enrolled. *Average high school GPA:* 3.3. *Test scores:* SAT critical reading scores over 500: 94%; SAT math scores over 500: 88%; SAT writing scores over 500: 91%; ACT scores over 18: 100%; SAT critical reading scores over 600: 66%; SAT math scores over 600: 52%; SAT writing scores over 600: 63%; ACT scores over 24: 74%; SAT critical reading scores over 700: 18%; SAT math scores over 700: 6%; SAT writing scores over 700: 21%; ACT scores over 30: 9%.

Faculty *Total:* 54, 48% full-time, 76% with terminal degrees. *Student/faculty ratio:* 10:1.

Academics *Calendar:* semesters. *Degrees:* associate, bachelor's, and master's. *Special study options:* accelerated degree program, advanced placement credit, double majors, English as a second language, honors programs, independent study, internships, part-time degree program, study abroad, summer session for credit.

Computers on Campus 140 computers/terminals and 20 ports are available on campus for general student use. Students can access the following: campus intranet, computer help desk, free student e-mail accounts, online (class) grades, online (class) registration, online (class) schedules, Live@EDU sky-drive, Moodle, office on-line collaboration tools, LAN Storage space, student access to academic/financial records and portal available in student lounge and libraries. Campuswide network is available. 100% of college-owned or -operated housing units are wired for high-speed Internet access. Wireless service is available via entire campus.

Student Life *Housing:* on-campus residence required through sophomore year. *Options:* coed, women-only. Campus housing is university owned and leased by the school. Freshman campus housing is guaranteed. *Activities and organizations:* drama/theater group, student-run newspaper, Student Government Association, Newspaper, Literary Society, Drama Club, Peer Educators Program. *Campus security:* 24-hour emergency response devices, student patrols, late-night transport/escort service, controlled dormitory access, late night patrols by professional security service personnel. *Student services:* health clinic, personal/psychological counseling.

Athletics *Intramural sports:* basketball M(c)/W(c), ice hockey M(c), skiing (downhill) M(c)/W(c), soccer M(c)/W(c), swimming and diving M(c), tennis M(c)/W(c), volleyball M(c)/W(c), water polo M(c).

Standardized Tests *Required:* SAT or ACT (for admission). *Recommended:* SAT Subject Tests (for admission).

Financial Aid Of all full-time matriculated undergraduates who enrolled in 2011, 192 applied for aid, 186 were judged to have need, 6 had their need fully met. In 2011, 91 non-need-based awards were made. *Average percent of need met:* 39%. *Average financial aid package:* $21,653. *Average need-based loan:* $4125. *Average need-based gift aid:* $17,653. *Average non-need-based aid:* $9494. *Financial aid deadline:* 3/15.

Applying *Options:* electronic application, early action, deferred entrance. *Application fee:* $90. *Required:* essay or personal statement, high school transcript, minimum 2.0 GPA, 3 letters of recommendation. *Recommended:* interview. *Application deadlines:* 3/15 (freshmen), 6/15 (transfers), 12/1 (early action). *Notification:* continuous (freshmen), continuous (transfers), 1/15 (early action).

Freshman Application Contact Peter Dorthe, Director of Admissions, Franklin College Switzerland, Franklin College, US Office, The Graybar Building, Suite 2746, 420 Lexington Avenue, New York, NY 10170. *Phone:* 212-922-9650. *Fax:* 212-922-9870. *E-mail:* Info@fc.edu. *Website:* http://www.fc.edu/.

See this page for display ad and page 1302 for the College Close-Up.

Glion Institute of Higher Education

Glion-sur-Montreux, Switzerland

Freshman Application Contact Admissions, Glion Institute of Higher Education, Route de Glion 111, CH-1823 Glion-sur-Montreux, Switzerland. *Phone:* 41-0 21 989 26 77. *Fax:* 41-0 21 989 26 78. *E-mail:* info@glion.edu. *Website:* http://www.glion.edu/.

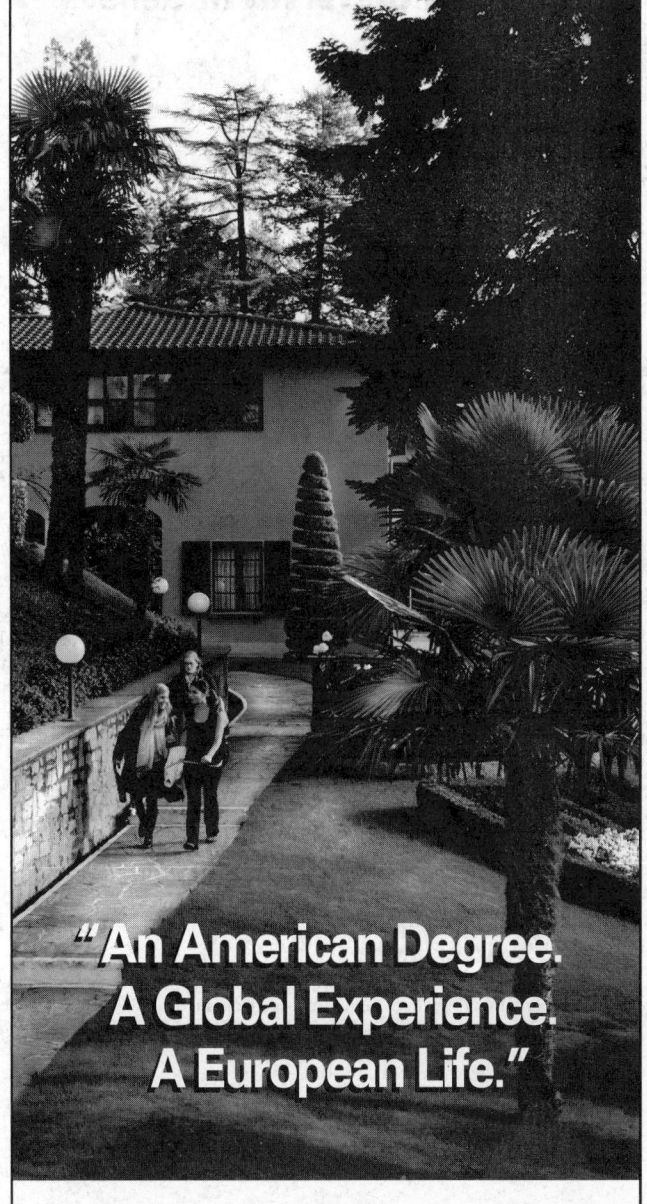

"*An American Degree. A Global Experience. A European Life.*"

Franklin College Switzerland is located on a hillside overlooking Lugano, the principal city of Switzerland's southernmost Italian-speaking canton of Ticino.

The College awards the Bachelor of Arts degree in a number of academic areas, and is fully accredited in the United States by the Commission on Higher Education of the Middle States Association of Colleges and Schools and in Switzerland by the Swiss University Conference.

FRANKLIN
COLLEGE SWITZERLAND

www.fc.edu

International University in Geneva

Geneva, Switzerland

- **Private** comprehensive
- **Urban** campus
- **Coed** 112 undergraduate students, 100% full-time, 47% women, 53% men
- **Moderately difficult** entrance level

Undergraduates 112 full-time. Students come from 62 other countries; 6% transferred in. *Retention:* 94% of full-time freshmen returned.

Freshmen *Admission:* 29 enrolled. *Average high school GPA:* 2.5.

Faculty *Total:* 44, 18% full-time, 36% with terminal degrees. *Student/faculty ratio:* 7:1.

Academics *Calendar:* trimesters. *Degrees:* bachelor's and master's. *Special study options:* academic remediation for entering students, accelerated degree program, advanced placement credit, double majors, English as a second language, independent study, part-time degree program, study abroad, summer session for credit.

Computers on Campus 30 computers/terminals are available on campus for general student use. Students can access the following: campus intranet, computer help desk, free student e-mail accounts, online (class) schedules. Campuswide network is available. Wireless service is available via classrooms, student centers.

Student Life *Housing:* college housing not available. *Activities and organizations:* student-run newspaper, UNICEF, United Nations Women Bazaar. *Student services:* personal/psychological counseling.

Athletics *Intercollegiate sports:* basketball M, tennis M/W, volleyball W.

Applying *Options:* electronic application, early decision, early action, deferred entrance. *Application fee:* $150. *Required:* essay or personal statement, high school transcript, minimum 2.0 GPA. *Required for some:* interview. *Application deadlines:* rolling (freshmen), rolling (transfers). *Notification:* continuous (freshmen), continuous (transfers).

Freshman Application Contact Ms. Sanela Pavlovic, Admissions Officer, International University in Geneva, Geneva 1215, Switzerland. *Phone:* -41 22710-7110. *Toll-free phone:* -01141227107110. *Fax:* 41 22710-7111. *E-mail:* admissions@iun.ch.
Website: http://www.iun.ch/.

Les Roches International School of Hotel Management

Bluche, Switzerland

Freshman Application Contact Enrollment Management Department, Les Roches International School of Hotel Management, CH-3975 Bluche, Switzerland. *Phone:* 41-021 989 26 44. *Fax:* 41-021 989 26 45. *E-mail:* info@lesroches.edu.
Website: http://www.lesroches.cc/.

TAIWAN

Christ's College

Taipei, Taiwan

Freshman Application Contact Lucy Li, Recruiter, Christ's College, No. 51, Ziqiang Road, Tamsui District, New Taipei City 251, Taiwan. *Phone:* +886-2-2809-7661. *Fax:* +886-2-8809-1084. *E-mail:* lucyli@christs-college.org. *Website:* http://www.christc.org.tw/.

UNITED ARAB EMIRATES

The American University in Dubai

Dubai, United Arab Emirates

- **Proprietary** comprehensive, founded 1995
- **Urban** campus
- **Coed**
- 88% of applicants were admitted

Academics *Calendar:* semesters. *Degrees:* certificates, bachelor's, and master's.

Student Life *Campus security:* 24-hour patrols.

Standardized Tests *Required for some:* SAT or ACT (for admission), SAT Subject Tests (for admission).

Applying *Options:* early admission. *Application fee:* 55 United Arab Emirates dirhams. *Required:* high school transcript, minimum 2.0 GPA, 2 letters of recommendation. *Recommended:* essay or personal statement.

Freshman Application Contact Ms. Tala Makhlouf, Associate Director of Admissions, The American University in Dubai, PO Box 28282, Dubai, United Arab Emirates. *Phone:* -971 4 399 9000 Ext. 170. *Fax:* 971 4 399 8899. *E-mail:* admissions@aud.edu.
Website: http://www.aud.edu/.

American University of Sharjah

Sharjah, United Arab Emirates

Director of Admissions Ali Shuhaimy, Vice Chancellor of Enrollment Management, American University of Sharjah, PO Box 26666, Sharjah, United Arab Emirates. *Phone:* -971 6 515-5555. *E-mail:* ashuhaimy@aus.edu.
Website: http://www.aus.edu/.

UNITED KINGDOM

American InterContinental University London
London, United Kingdom

Freshman Application Contact American InterContinental University London, 110 Marylebone High Street, London W1U 4RY, United Kingdom. *Phone:* 877-564-6248. *Toll-free phone:* 888-567-5888. *Fax:* 877-564-6248. *Website:* http://www.aiuniv.edu/.

Hult International Business School
London, United Kingdom

Freshman Application Contact Mrs. Anna Frolander, Executive Director of Undergraduate Admissions, Hult International Business School, 46-47 Russell Square, London WC1B 4JP, United Kingdom. *Phone:* -44 207 341 8555. *E-mail:* anna.frolander@hult.edu. *Website:* http://www.hult.edu/.

Regent's American College London
London, United Kingdom

Director of Admissions Admissions Director, Regent's American College London, Regent's College, Inner Circle, Regent's Park, London NW1 4NS, United Kingdom. *Phone:* 44-0 207 487 7505. *Fax:* 44-0 207 487 7425. *E-mail:* bacl@regents.ac.uk. *Website:* http://www.bacl.ac.uk/.

Richmond, The American International University in London
Richmond, United Kingdom

Freshman Application Contact Mr. Nick Atkinson, Director of United States Admissions, Richmond, The American International University in London, 343 Congress Street, Suite 3100, Boston, MA 02210-1214. *Phone:* 617-450-5617. *Fax:* 617-450-5601. *E-mail:* us_admissions@richmond.ac.uk. *Website:* http://www.richmond.ac.uk/.

See below for display ad and page 1452 for the College Close-Up.

College Close-Ups

ACADEMY OF ART UNIVERSITY
SAN FRANCISCO, CALIFORNIA

The University

In 1929, Academy of Art University founder Richard S. Stephens, who was the advertising creative director of *Sunset* magazine, acted on his belief that "aspiring artists and designers, given proper instruction, hard work, and dedication, can learn the skills needed to become successful professionals." His new school of advertising art consisted of 46 students meeting in one room on San Francisco's Kearny Street.

The instructors, who are professional artists, bring real-world problems, situations, solutions, and practical experience to the students. Thus was born the school's philosophy by the founder: Hire today's best practicing professionals to teach the art and design professionals of tomorrow. At that time, advertising consisted primarily of illustrations, photos, and copy. Consequently, it became necessary to teach beginning students the fundamentals of drawing, painting, color, light, and photography as well as layout and typography.

When Richard A. Stephens succeeded his father as president in 1951, the Foundations Department was added, ensuring all students comprehended the basic principles of traditional art and design. Illustration soon expanded to include fine arts (drawing, painting, sculpture, and printmaking), and advertising design spawned the School of Graphic Design. Fashion (design, textiles, and merchandising) and Interior Design Schools were also added. In 1966, the Academy officially became a college, and in a decade, the Master of Fine Arts degree was offered. Five more buildings were purchased, and by 1992, there were more than 2,500 students.

The leadership of the Academy was then turned over to the third generation, Elisa Stephens, granddaughter of the school's founder. She quickly determined that the school's small School of Computer Arts: New Media had enormous potential to prepare students for multimedia careers when allied with such companies as Silicon Graphics, Pixar, Adobe, and Walt Disney Productions. It is now one of the largest departments at the Academy.

Today, Academy of Art University is the largest private accredited art and design school in the nation with an enrollment of more than 18,000. More than one fifth of the student body is made up of international students. The Academy has over thirty facilities that house classrooms, studios, galleries, and residence halls. The students, who are admitted through an open-enrollment policy, aspire to earn A.A., B.A., B.F.A., M.A., M.F.A., or M. Arch. degrees in twenty-one majors. Students can study in San Francisco or through the Academy's flexible online programs.

The school maintains a fleet of buses to connect the different points of the campus, all of which are located within the city limits of San Francisco, one of the world's most vibrant and beautiful cities. The instructors, who are 80 percent part-time and made up of working art and design professionals, are recruited from all across the nation, and are drawn to the creative and intellectual center that is the Bay Area. Extensive senior-year internship programs allow students to gain valuable experience and develop strong portfolios in their chosen field before graduation.

The Academy is one of the few art and design schools that believe in nurturing the whole artist; this includes developing athletic talents along with artistic ones. Students can participate in intercollegiate, intramural and club sports.

Academy of Art University is an accredited member of the Western Association of Schools and Colleges (WASC), National Association of Schools of Art and Design (NASAD), Council for Interior Design (CIDA) for IAD BFA and IAD MFA, and National Architectural Accrediting Board (NAAB) for M.Arch.

Location

The city of San Francisco is one of the great cultural centers of the world; a melting pot of diversity, ethnicity, and creativity that has spawned major museums and galleries, world-class opera and theaters, dance companies, film production and recording studios,

technological innovation, performing artists ranging from classical to popular music, and numerous other cultural opportunities. The city's status as a tourist mecca located on the Pacific Rim ensures that one encounters people from all corners of the world.

The climate is moderate and offers kaleidoscopic blends of sunshine and fog nine months of the year. The Northpoint campus is located at world-famous Pier 39; one can view Alcatraz Island from classroom windows. Four other buildings are two blocks from historic Union Square in the commercial heart of the city. Three other buildings are located near the Financial District. The city offers myriad locations for field trips and studio visits. World-renowned artists display their creations in the Academy's three nonprofit art galleries, which are open to the public. The University is an urban institution that both draws upon and contributes to the cultural wealth of the community in which it resides.

Majors and Degrees

Academy of Art University offers A.A., B.A., B.F.A., M.A., M.F.A., and M.Arch. degrees and certificates in the following majors: acting (speech, improv, physical acting), advertising (account planning, art direction, copywriting, television commercials), animation/visual effects (background painting/layout design, character development, game design, storyboard art, VFX/compositing, visual development, 3-D modeling), architecture (residential, commercial, green architecture), art education (art studio and design, art history, art for educators, developmental psychology), art history (history of design, studio art and design, philosophy), fashion (fashion design, fashion illustration, knitwear, merchandising, textiles), fine art (ceramics, metal arts, painting/drawing, printmaking, sculpture), game design (prototyping, game art, level design, 3-D modeling) graphic design (corporate and brand identity, motion graphics, multimedia, package design, print and collateral, website design), illustration (cartooning, children's books, editorial, feature film animation, 2-D animation), industrial design (furniture, product, toy, transportation), interior architecture and design (commercial, furniture, residential), landscape architecture (plant design, elements in landscape, grading and drainage, urban open spaces), motion pictures and television (acting, advertising/director–camera, cinematography, directing, editing, producing, production design, screenwriting, special effects), multimedia communications (podcasting, broadcasting, multimedia journalism), music production and sound design for digital media (harmony, music production techniques, scoring for film, music for games), photography (advertising, digital photography, documentary, fine art, photo illustration, photojournalism), and Web design and new media (computer graphics, digital imaging, Web design, information architecture, interactive information graphics, interactive modeling). The Academy's two newest programs are jewelry and metal arts, teaching students elements of fashion jewelry, enameling, stone setting, and casting, and visual development, instilling in students principles of drawing for film, digital painting, and character and scene design.

Academic Programs

A total of 132 credit units are required to earn a Bachelor of Fine Arts degree, consisting of 18 units of foundations courses, 60 units in the major, 9 units of art electives, and 45 units of liberal arts courses. Fundamental courses are related specifically to students' majors to prepare them to begin intense focus courses in their field by the sophomore year. All major courses of study are structured so the student builds upon skills learned the previous semester and advances to the next level of technical or creative proficiency. Some related major courses may be taken concurrently. Each course is worth 3 credits.

Liberal arts courses teach practical applications for forging a professional career in art and design. International students who come from countries where English is not the primary language may take additional ESL classes, as determined by English language proficiency testing. Students are advised to meet with departmental directors at least once during the academic year to have their progress assessed. Portfolios are reviewed before the junior year to determine whether or not a student has progressed sufficiently to continue study at the Academy.

Academic Facilities

The Academy's facilities reflect its commitment to training students for careers in art and design; not only do students have access to some of the most advanced facilities in the nation, but the Academy continually invests in new equipment to ensure that it remains on the cutting edge of technology. By learning on industry-standard equipment, students gain valuable professional skills that make them highly employable.

The School of Photography occupies two buildings, which house individual studios and a wide range of equipment, including full-length shooting studios; Hasselblad, Mamyia, Canon, and Sinar cameras; Broncolor, Norman, and Speedotron strobe systems; black-and-white darkrooms; a color lab facility with single-print stations; and the latest technology for digital imaging and output. In addition, the Academy's modern, professional studio is one of the largest of any photography school in the nation and is ideal for shooting automobiles, motorcycles, and large sets.

The Academy's Fine Art Sculpture Center houses state-of-the-art studios for figure, ceramic, neon/illumination, bronze, metal fabrication, and mold-making sculpture. Students also have use of an off-site bronze-casting facility and foundry. When students graduate from the Academy, they have the opportunity to exhibit in one of the three nonprofit galleries located in the heart of downtown San Francisco's premier gallery district. These street-level facilities are an excellent way for students to promote and sell their work and to gain networking experience.

Multimedia Communications and Graphic Design are housed in the Academy's main building in the heart of San Francisco. Multimedia Communications students have access to a professional studio on the building's first floor. At the School of Industrial Design, students draw inspiration from the Academy's Automotive Museum.

The Library houses more than 30,000 books and magazines, as well as 375 CD titles, 150,000 slides, and 2,000 videos. Computers with Internet access are available to students, as well as an online catalog, color scanners, and color and black-and-white copiers. Workshops and electronic study guides are also available. The Academy Resource Center offers all students free learning support services that include study hall, tutoring, mentoring, mid-point review and study-skills workshops, a writing lab, a state-of-the-art multimedia language lab, an English for Art Program, and a Conversation Partner Program.

Costs

Tuition is $785 per credit unit for undergraduates. Full-time students carry either 12 or 15 units per semester. There is a nonrefundable $120 registration fee—$100 is applicable toward tuition. Lab fees run from $25 to $400 per semester, depending on the class. Tuition and fees are subject to change at any time. Art supplies can run from $250 to $900 per semester, depending on the major. The Academy has most of the expensive technical equipment available for students to borrow or use in a lab.

Academy of Art University operates seventeen residence halls within the city. Several housing options are offered, and costs vary from $7,200 to $14,180 per academic year (fall and spring semesters). For further information, students may contact the Academy Housing Office directly at housing@academyart.edu or 800-544-2787 (toll-free, U.S. only).

Financial Aid

The Academy offers financial aid packages consisting of grants, loans, and work-study to eligible students with a demonstrated need. Low-interest loans are available to all eligible students, regardless of need. As financial aid programs, procedures, and eligibility requirements change frequently, applicants should contact the Financial Aid Office at financialaid@academyart.edu or 800-544-2787 (toll-free, U.S. only).

Faculty

The Academy averages 950 instructors in fall/spring semester, most of whom are full-time art and design professionals and part-time teachers. The student-teacher ratio for undergraduate classes averages 18:1.

Student Government

Although there is no formal student government, each department has between 2 and 3 student representatives who meet with the president as needed throughout the semester to discuss any student issues.

Admission Requirements

Applicants for the A.A., B.A., and B.F.A. programs must have a high school diploma or GED equivalent. There is no portfolio requirement. M.A. and M.F.A. applicants must have a bachelor's degree and submit a portfolio and statement of intent. International students take written and speech tests to determine which ESL classes may have to be completed. Most ESL classes can be taken in conjunction with art and design classes. All foundations classes offer specialized ESL sections with instructors trained for language assistance. The application fee is $100 for undergraduates. A $500 tuition deposit applies to international applicants.

Application and Information

Students may apply to enter the Academy at the beginning of the spring, fall, or summer semesters. Information in this profile is subject to change. Students should contact Academy of Art University for current information or visit www.academyart.edu to learn about total costs, median student loan debt, potential occupations, and other information.

Academy of Art University
79 New Montgomery Street
San Francisco, California 94105
Phone: 415-274-2200
          800-544-2787 (U.S only)
Fax: 415-618-6287
E-mail: info@academyart.edu
Website: http://academyart.edu

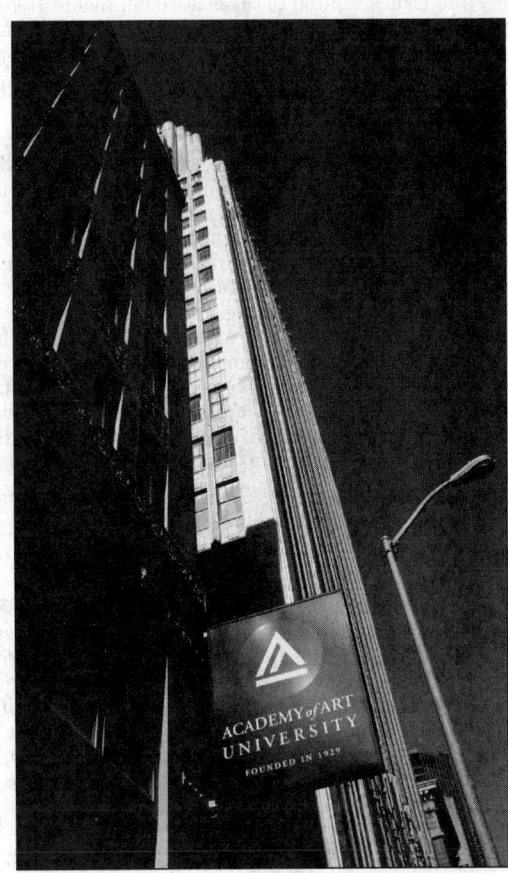

Academy of Art University's downtown campus.

ADELPHI UNIVERSITY
GARDEN CITY, NEW YORK

The University

Adelphi University, founded in 1896, is Long Island's first private coeducational institution of higher learning. A nonsectarian, independent university, Adelphi welcomes men and women of all backgrounds who display intellectual inquisitiveness, academic commitment, and a desire for achievement and purpose in life. The University enrolls 5,103 undergraduates and 2,756 graduate students. Forty-three states and forty-five countries are represented in its diverse student body. The campus is located on 75 landscaped acres in Garden City, New York, 20 miles east of New York City and easily accessible by public transportation. The University also has three off-campus centers: the Manhattan Center in New York City, the Hauppauge Education and Conference Center on Long Island, and the Hudson Valley Center in Poughkeepsie, New York.

Adelphi's schools and programs include the College of Arts and Sciences; the Honors College; the Schools of Nursing and Social Work; the Robert B. Willumstad School of Business; the Ruth S. Ammon School of Education; the Gordon F. Derner Institute of Advanced Psychological Studies; and adult academic programs in University College.

The University's seven residence halls provide all the comforts of home and include a Green Community and honors housing. The residential life staff at Adelphi is committed to bringing education to the residence halls. A lecture and discussion series brings faculty members together with students to examine events of the day and issues related to the classroom. In addition, about 200 seminars, workshops, and events are offered each year. Faculty and guest lecturers lead discussions on such topics as American and global politics, ethnic diversity, legal affairs, job interviewing, sexual conduct, and AIDS.

Opportunities for enhancing life beyond the classroom abound at Adelphi. Students participate in intramural and intercollegiate athletics (including nationally ranked men's and women's soccer, softball, and baseball and men's basketball and lacrosse), drama productions, and more than eighty student clubs, community-service groups, and organizations. Students take advantage of thriving cultural arts programs, including plays, art exhibits, concerts, and lectures; the comprehensive sports and fitness services; and the breathtaking campus. Physical education facilities include a swimming pool; basketball courts; weight-training and exercise rooms; a large indoor running track; and fields for baseball, lacrosse, soccer, and softball. In addition, a vast array of activities such as movies, exhibits, cabarets, symposia, and field trips are scheduled every semester.

The Adelphi student newspaper (The Delphian) and the yearbook (Oracle) welcome writers and photographers.

In the Ruth S. Harley University Center (UC)—a central meeting place on campus—Adelphi students can browse the full-service bookstore, refresh themselves and relax in one of the center's lounges (commuter students have a special lounge equipped with lockers), eat in the UC Café, and enjoy a vast array of activities, including movies, comedy shows, lectures, dance parties, and musical events. Cultural trips are also offered. The UC also houses Adelphi's numerous student organizations including academic clubs, community service and social action clubs, honor societies, and religious and special-interest organizations.

Location

Adelphi's main campus is located in Garden City, New York, a village of stately homes, historic buildings, and parks. The cultural and commercial resources of New York City and the recreation and entertainment of Long Island are only a short distance away by public or private transit.

Majors and Degrees

Undergraduate studies leading to the degrees of Bachelor of Arts (B.A.), Bachelor of Business Administration (B.B.A.), Bachelor of Fine Arts (B.F.A.), Bachelor of Science (B.S.), and Bachelor of Social Work (B.S.W.) are offered at Adelphi. Programs of study at Adelphi include: accounting; African, Black, and Caribbean studies; anthropology/forensic anthropology; art, with specializations in art history, fine arts and studio art* (ceramics, painting, photography, printmaking, sculpture) and graphic design*; art education; biochemistry; biology; business; chemistry; communications (journalism, media studies, moving image production); communication sciences and disorders; computer and management information systems; computer science (game development and information security); criminal justice; dance; economics; education studies, with programs of study in childhood education and adolescent education through the University's Scholar Teacher Education Program (S.T.E.P.); English (literature, creative writing); environmental studies; exercise science; finance; French; history; interdisciplinary studies; languages and international studies (political science, environmental studies, business); Latin American studies; management; marketing; mathematics; music**; music education; nursing; philosophy; physical education; physical education/health education; physics; political science; psychology; social work; sociology; Spanish; sport management; and theatre arts** (acting and design technology). * An art portfolio is required.

** An audition is required.

Five-year bachelor's/master's programs are offered in social work and business, as well as S.T.E.P. in childhood education and adolescent education.

Opportunities for pre-professional studies are available in pre-dental, pre-engineering, pre–environmental studies, pre-law, pre-medicine, pre-optometry, pre-pharmacy, pre–physical therapy/allied health, pre-podiatry, and pre–veterinary medicine.

Academic Programs

The goal of the academic programs at Adelphi is to provide higher education that fosters critical thinking and prepares students for the future. Consistent with the University's approach to liberal arts learning, students take part in the University's general education distribution requirements.

A minimum of 120 credits is required for a baccalaureate degree, with a specified number in the chosen major. Double majors and various minors may be elected. Seniors of superior academic ability may be admitted to graduate courses in their major field.

Off-Campus Programs

Adelphi University offers study-abroad programs that can last several weeks or span an academic year. Students can participate in Adelphi-run programs in such locations as Australia, Costa Rica, Florence, India, and Peru, or join programs run by other educational institutions. Adelphi offers students the opportunity to participate in internship programs that provide access to a variety of industries and locations—in the local Long Island community, the surrounding New York City area, and beyond. Students can also take part in the Community Fellows Program, which pairs students with nonprofit organizations across Long Island and New York City, for 10-week, paid summer internships.

Academic Facilities

The University Libraries include the Swirbul Library, the Archives and Special Collections on the Garden City campus, and the libraries at the Manhattan Center, Hauppauge Education and Conference Center, and the Hudson Valley Center. These libraries contain 600,000 volumes, 806,000 items in microformat, 33,000 audiovisual materials, and access to more than 61,000 electronic journal titles. The University Libraries are fully automated with holdings accessible through the Adelphi Libraries Catalog online (ALICAT). As an enhancement of the traditional reference services, online access is provided to 221 research databases.

The Swirbul Library is also the center of information technology on campus. Its amenities include more than 100 computer workstations that are fully networked for student use and a faculty development lab. Adelphi's technology infrastructure reaches into every classroom and every part of the curriculum to provide web-based learning and other applications of communication and information media.

The 18,000-square-foot Adele and Herbert J. Klapper Center for Fine Arts has greatly expanded Adelphi's art studio and classroom space and offers greater opportunity for nonmajors to take art courses. This is in addition to the current state-of-the-art digital graphics design studio and faculty offices and the expansion of drawing studios in Blodgett Hall.

The Adelphi University Performing Arts Center (AUPAC) showcases prestigious programs in acting, design/technical theater, and music and dance together under one roof. The center features a 500-seat concert hall, dance and recital rooms, music practice rooms, temperature-controlled instrument storage rooms, and a black box theater.

The Center for Recreation and Sports is the home of Adelphi's successful athletics programs. The center's three-story, three-court gym—that converts into a 2,200-seat arena for basketball games and other events—accommodates recreational and intercollegiate athletes and health and physical education students, and can host NCAA tournaments and championships.

Costs

The 2012–13 tuition and fees for full-time undergraduates totalled $29,320. For students living on campus, additional costs included room ($8,420 for a typical double room without air conditioning) and board ($3,500 for a basic meal plan).

Financial Aid

The Office of Student Financial Services administers federal and New York State programs that provide funds to assist students in pursuing their academic goals. In addition to grants based on need, Adelphi annually offers almost 1,000 of its own scholarships based on merit, talent, and extracurricular excellence. Ninety-nine percent of Adelphi freshmen receive some form of financial aid each year. The average financial aid package award for a full-time undergraduate is approximately $19,150.

Faculty

At Adelphi, the quality of education is entrusted to its distinguished faculty members, who are noted for their serious commitment to students as well as for their research and professional contributions. Undergraduate courses are taught by professors, not graduate assistants, and students learn in small, intimate environments.

Student Government

The Student Government Association is the elected student group that represents the opinions of the full-time undergraduate body to the administration and other groups. The Student Government Association hosts speakers, sponsors awareness days, and serves as a voice for student concerns and interests.

Admission Requirements

Recommended admission qualifications include graduation from a four-year public or private high school or equivalent credentials, four years of English, three years of science, three years of mathematics, two to three years of a foreign language or languages, and 4 additional units chosen from the fields mentioned or from history and social studies. Official test results from the SAT or ACT with writing are required.

Personal interviews and campus tours are strongly recommended for all applicants. Arrangements can be made by contacting the Office of Admissions at 516-877-3050.

Application and Information

The following admission credentials should be submitted by applicants: a completed application for admission, the $40 nonrefundable application fee, an official secondary school transcript or GED certificate, official results of the SAT or ACT, and letters of recommendation. Transfer students must submit official transcripts from all colleges previously attended.

Adelphi accepts applications on a rolling basis, with admission twice each year for the semesters beginning in September and January. Freshmen filing dates are December 1 for early action, February 1 for priority consideration for joint-degree programs, March 1 for regular admission to the fall semester (applications received later are reviewed on a rolling basis), and November 1 for regular admission for the spring semester (applications received later are reviewed on a rolling basis). The nonbinding early action plan is available only for the September term. An early action decision means that applicants who submit their completed applications by December 1 receive an admissions decision by December 31 and that they are considered for scholarships and financial aid.

For more information, students should contact:

Office of University Admissions
Adelphi University
One South Avenue
Garden City, New York 11530
Phone: 516-877-3050
        800-ADELPHI (toll-free)
E-mail: admissions@adelphi.edu
Website: adelphi.edu

Adelphi University is a hub for intellectual, cultural, and creative activity with unique learning opportunities both in and outside the classroom.

ALVERNIA UNIVERSITY
READING, PENNSYLVANIA

The University

Located in Berks County, Pennsylvania, Alvernia University offers all the best features of an outstanding university—specialized professional programs, experiential learning, internships, and a variety of leadership opportunities—in the personal setting of a college environment. A private Franciscan institution rooted in the Catholic and liberal arts tradition, the core institutional values—service, humility, peacemaking, contemplation, and collegiality—are as relevant today as they were in 1958 when the school was founded. Students appreciate the small class sizes and breadth of academic programs offered, all taught by faculty who are experts in their fields and equally committed to their students' success. Graduates are prepared to achieve their personal dreams and professional success, and to be engaged citizens and lifelong learners. Alvernia has been honored by the Templeton Foundation as one of the top 100 character-building colleges in the nation and a model of excellence in education. Alvernia was also named a Military Friendly School for 2013 by *G.I. Jobs* magazine. In addition, the University is regularly named to the President's Higher Education Community Service Honor Roll for its commitment to and achievement in community service.

The University's 3,000 total students (1,500 traditional undergraduates) can choose from more than 600 courses and 50 majors and minors in the College of Arts and Sciences and College of Professional Programs. Programs are geared toward real-world learning and preparing students for a rewarding career. Study abroad, internships, and international service trips make learning come alive and allow students to develop practical, valuable skills.

Master's degrees are awarded in occupational therapy, business administration, nursing, community counseling, education, and liberal studies. A Ph.D. program in leadership is also available.

Location

Situated on a scenic 121-acre suburban campus, Alvernia is bordered by a park that features hiking trails, a picnic grove, and a nine-hole disk-golf course. When students want to explore big city life, Philadelphia (60 miles), New York, Baltimore, and Washington, D.C. are all just a short drive away.

Majors and Degrees

Alvernia offers a breadth of academic programs with a boundary-free learning approach. Bachelor's degrees are awarded in the following majors: accounting, athletic training, behavioral health, biochemistry, biology, biology–medical technology, chemistry, chemistry–medical technology, communication, criminal justice administration, education (concentrations in early childhood, early childhood and special, middle school, and secondary), English, forensic science, general science, healthcare science, history, human resource management, liberal studies, marketing, management, mathematics, nursing, occupational therapy, philosophy, political science, psychology, social work, sport management, theater, and theology. Pre-professional programs are available in dentistry, law, medicine, and veterinary studies. Alvernia also offers minors and certificate programs.

Since 1967, the Middle States Association of Colleges and Schools has granted Alvernia accreditation. The education program curriculum is approved by the Pennsylvania State Department of Education. The occupational therapy program is fully accredited by the American Occupational Therapy Association. The Bachelor of Science in Nursing has approval by the Pennsylvania State Board of Nursing and is accredited by the Commission on Collegiate Nursing Education. The athletic training program is accredited by the Commission on Accreditation of Athletic Training Education. The social work program is accredited by the Council on Social Work Education.

The behavioral health program is certified by the Pennsylvania Certification Board. The business department is accredited by the Accreditation Council for Business Schools and Programs.

Academic Programs

Alvernia offers a range of academic programs with a learning approach grounded in the real world. With a foundation in the liberal arts tradition, the curriculum and instruction is designed to help students develop critical thinking skills and explore their own ideas. This approach produces well-rounded individuals who are ready to succeed no matter what path they choose.

Qualified students may participate in the Honors Program, which assists students of outstanding intellectual promise and high motivation that seek a more challenging program and are interested in pursuing future graduate or professional studies. The program encourages students to achieve, often letting them work at their own pace. It facilitates a stimulating exchange of ideas and information between students' varied interests and different disciplines.

In order to earn a bachelor's degree from Alvernia, students must complete a minimum of 123 credits, with 54 credits in the liberal arts. Additional requirements vary by major.

Off-Campus Programs

The Washington Center experience is a popular way for students to expand their education beyond the classroom. Earning college credit while spending a semester in Washington D.C., students serve as interns in a congressional office, government agency, major corporation, newspaper, news network, or nonprofit groups, or an agency devoted to legal affairs, international relations, or business and economics.

Study abroad has become increasingly popular. In recent years, Alvernia students have studied in Great Britain, Germany, Italy, Spain, and in the Semester-at-Sea program.

Campus Facilities

Alvernia has recently invested in several additions to campus including a new laser laboratory to support science programs, state-of-the-art learning suites developed for the criminal justice and counseling programs, an educational technology center that supports all majors, and a new theater and recital hall.

On-campus housing includes traditional residence halls, apartments, suites, and town houses. All residential facilities are clean, spacious and equipped with laundry, cable TV, and phones with voice mail.

The recently completed Campus Commons houses a fitness center; dance/aerobics studio; and a campus "living room," complete with a fireplace, for leisure activities, study, and programs.

Alvernia's campus is fully networked. Students have access to the academic information network and the Internet from their residence hall rooms, as well as from other campus locations including classrooms, the library, and labs. All students may connect personal computers through the University's secure system. Network access and Alvernia email accounts are available to all students.

Costs

For the 2013–14 academic year tuition is $28,500, and room and board is $10,190 (an approximate cost based on Veronica Hall residence and an all-you-can-eat meal plan).

Financial Aid

Ninety-nine percent of students receive some form of financial aid. Financial aid is offered to students whose personal and family resources are insufficient to meet the full cost of an education. Aid usually comes in the form of scholarships, grants, loans, and work-study arrangements. Depending upon their academic record, incoming first-year students may be eligible for one of three merit-based scholarships: the Presidential

Scholarship ($14,000), the Trustee's Scholarship ($12,000), and the Veronica Founder's Scholarship ($10,000). Applicants interested in financial aid should submit the FAFSA as soon as possible after January 1.

Faculty

The dedicated faculty members are accomplished scholars who bring real-world experience into the classroom and are as diversified as the fields of interest that they represent. Faculty members publish in professional journals and other media; present papers and moderate conferences in the region and as far away as India, Italy, Mexico, and South Africa; and serve on boards and committees of professional associations and corporate and community boards.

Student Government and Activities

Alvernia encourages students to take advantage of learning opportunities outside the classroom by participating in any of the more than fifty-five groups including intramural and intercollegiate sports, academic clubs, honor societies, student government, and faith-based environmental and service clubs. Campus organizations offer opportunities to suit the interests of all students, to meet new people, to learn various skills, and to develop leadership abilities.

Athletics are a proud and integral part of the educational mission. Students may participate in intercollegiate, intramural, and club-level programs. Intercollegiate teams compete at the NCAA Division III level. Alvernia is part of the highly competitive Middle Atlantic States Athletic Conference (MAC), and is also a member of the Eastern Collegiate Athletic Conference.

The Office of Student Activities works with the many student organizations to provide a calendar of social, cultural, and other cocurricular activities. The Student Government Association provides an opportunity for leadership through the exercise of personal and group responsibility. All students complete approved community service hours as part of Alvernia's commitment to peace, justice, and the dignity of life. This helps foster devotion to service of others, especially the materially and spiritually disadvantaged of the local and global community.

Admission Requirements

Admission requirements normally include a high school diploma with 16 Carnegie units in the following subjects: English, 4 units; mathematics, 2 units; science, 2 units; social studies, 2 units; and modern languages, 2 units. The remaining units may be made up of academic electives. The University is willing to consider good students whose preparation does not include all of these subjects. Nursing students must fulfill the admission requirements established by the Pennsylvania State Board of Nurse Examiners. The State High School Equivalency Diploma is generally recognized as fulfilling the minimum entrance requirements. Applicants are required to take the SAT; the ACT is also acceptable. Outstanding candidates are considered for entrance to Alvernia at the end of their junior year of high school on the basis of requests made by the candidate and the school. With the approval of their school officials, students may also be admitted to certain courses during their senior year, simultaneously earning credit toward their high school diploma and a college degree.

Application and Information

Many factors are considered for admission, including academic performance, standardized test scores, class rank, extracurricular activities, and community involvement. Application and admission notification is on a rolling basis; however, applicants are encouraged to submit the admission application as early as possible. In addition to their transcripts and SAT or ACT scores, nursing applicants must also submit two letters of recommendation.

Alvernia accepts and/or offers special programs for accelerated high school students, nontraditional students (older than 24), transfer students, students with disabilities, veterans, and international students.

Applicants should submit an application for admission and enclose a nonrefundable $25 processing fee. The application form may be obtained from the Office of Admissions or the University's website at www.alvernia.edu/admissions/undergraduate/apply.html. Applicants should have an official copy of their high school record sent to the Office of Admissions, along with the official results of the SAT or ACT.

Because Alvernia has a rolling admission policy, the Director of Admissions notifies an applicant of acceptance shortly after the necessary credentials are on file and have been reviewed, generally within one month. To reserve a place in the freshman class, all students must make a $300 deposit by May 1. This deposit is credited to the student's account for the first semester but is not refunded if the student fails to attend. Transfer students should have a grade point average of 2.0 or higher on a 4.0 scale and should be aware that only grades of C or better are eligible for credit transfer. Alvernia accepts a maximum of 75 transfer credits; at least 45 credits that are required for graduation must be earned at Alvernia and must satisfy all graduation requirements. A detailed analysis of credits to be transferred is done only after the University has accepted students.

The best way to get to know Alvernia is through a campus visit and tour. Applicants and those considering the school are strongly encouraged to come for an individual campus visit, which will be personalized to match each student's unique interests. Alvernia also hosts information sessions and open houses throughout the year that allow prospective freshmen or transfers to meet current students, talk to admissions and financial aid counselors, and meet faculty and coaches. Overnight and shadow visits are also available.

For more information or to schedule a visit, students should contact:

Director of Admissions
Alvernia University
Reading, Pennsylvania 19607
Phone: 888-ALVERNIA (258-3764, toll-free)
Fax: 610-790-2873
E-mail: admissions@alvernia.edu
Website: http://www.alvernia.edu
http://on.fb.me/Alvernia_University (Facebook)
http://twitter.com/alverniauniv (Twitter)

With a 14:1 student-to-faculty ratio and an average class size of fewer than 20, Alvernia is the perfect size for students to develop and thrive. The Student Center, shown here, is the hub for campus activity.

THE AMERICAN UNIVERSITY OF ROME
ROME, ITALY

The University

Preparing students from around the world to live and work across cultures, The American University of Rome (AUR) blends the best of two worlds, combining the academic attributes of higher education in the United States—American practical know-how, technological capability, and career preparation—with the European and Italian classical tradition education in the humanities and liberal arts. Students leave AUR trained in the fundamental portable skills of language, communication, and critical thinking that allow them to continue to learn and thrive in a complex and interconnected world. For many, the time spent in the uniquely energizing city of Rome is a life-transforming experience.

Founded in 1969, The American University of Rome is the oldest, private independent American institution of higher education in Rome, offering undergraduate degrees in nine disciplines to a student body of around 500 students each semester. It is also a destination for study-abroad students from American colleges and universities for year-long, semester, and summer programs.

AUR's robust academic program is complemented by a rich variety of extracurricular activities including clubs, performing groups, local events, and athletics. Highlights include competitive men's and women's soccer leagues, a coed running club, a yoga club, a men's basketball club, martial arts training, and even a rowing club that allows students to enjoy Rome from a unique and privileged perspective. Studying at AUR also gives students ample opportunities to travel across Italy and Europe.

AUR meets student health needs by offering services of a doctor on campus three to four days a week for primary care at no charge. In addition, a certified professional provides students with free, private psychological counseling.

Students may elect for AUR to arrange housing on their behalf or may choose to make their own housing arrangements. University-facilitated housing consists of furnished apartments in well-established neighborhoods surrounding the university campus. This housing is well suited for students looking for a full-immersion experience in Italian culture.

The American University of Rome is fully accredited by the Middle States Commission on Higher Education and is licensed by the State of Delaware Department of Education to award associate and bachelor's degrees. AUR is incorporated in the District of Columbia as a not-for-profit institution.

Location

Overlooking the historical center, the University is located in the prestigious area of the Janiculum, Rome's highest hill, just a few minutes' walk from the historic Trastevere district and the heart of Rome. With its own gardens of Roman pines, it offers a spectacular view of Rome. The campus is close to two city parks, Villa Sciarra and Villa Pamphili. The area also hosts diplomatic residences and international academies. The neighborhood offers a full range of amenities, including restaurants, shops, cafés, and outdoor markets.

Majors and Degrees

The American University of Rome offers a strong undergraduate curriculum with an international perspective. The Bachelor of Arts degree is awarded in Archeology and Classics, Art History, Communication, Film and Digital Media, Fine Arts, Interdisciplinary Studies, International Relations and Global Politics, and Italian Studies. A Bachelor of Science degree is awarded in Business Administration. The Associate of Arts degree is offered in International Business and Liberal Studies. All courses (except for Italian, Latin, and Greek language courses) are taught in English.

Academic Program

Consistent with the mission of the University, the objectives of The American University of Rome's academic program are: to develop and strengthen basic skills that can prepare graduates for a modern working environment and that will be adaptable to a rapidly evolving economy; to cultivate an awareness of, and sensitivity to, cultural, ethnic, and social diversity and its importance in personal and professional decision making; and to enable students to discover the real-life application of their knowledge.

At a minimum, 1 semester credit hour equals 15 classroom-contact hours of lectures, 30 hours of laboratory or 45 hours of practicum; a total of 120 credits is required to earn a bachelor degree. At least 45 of the last 60 credit hours must be completed in residence at The American University of Rome, and the final semester must be completed in residence. The Associate of Arts and the Associate of Applied Arts degrees each require completion of at least 60 credit hours of coursework. All core courses in the major must be completed with a C grade (2.0) or better. A minimum cumulative or Career Total Grade Point Average (CGPA) of 2.0 is required for completion of all degrees. The majority of courses listed in AUR's catalog carry 3 semester credit hours. Intensive courses worth 4 to 6 credits and 1-credit courses are also available. Internships carry 3 semester credits and require 135 hours of work experience.

AUR follows a semester calendar (fall and spring) and also offers two short summer sessions (June and July).

Academic Facilities

AUR is an urban campus of around 30,000 square feet that provides study space, equipment, and an environment conducive to study and learning. Administrative and academic offices, computer labs, and a student lounge are housed in a four-story villa. Adjacent to the villa, a five-story building offers faculty offices, classrooms, a science lab, a computer classroom, art studios, and tutoring centers. Its terraces at the fourth and fifth floors feature breathtaking views of Rome. Other campus facilities include an auditorium and a multimedia lab, available to communication students enrolled in select film-related courses and equipped with Apple Pro computers and field software. Another two-story liberty villa, Evans' Hall, is AUR's library. It offers a book collection of 12,000 volumes and DVDs, as well as a wealth of electronic resources tailored to the requirements of the degree programs pursued at the University and carefully developed in collaboration with the faculty. The AUR library also participates in interlibrary loan programs throughout Italy.

All AUR classrooms are smart and wireless services are available from locations on and around the campus, such as the gardens and terraces of University buildings as well as a café and the park near the campus. The library and the main computer lab are open long hours and on weekends.

AUR recognizes the importance of supporting an efficient technological infrastructure; provision and enhancement of technology on campus is continuously and updated.

Costs

The estimated cost of attending The American University of Rome for the 2013–14 academic year for full-time undergraduates is €14,600. A nonrefundable tuition deposit of €500 is required from all new students, payable by the deadline indicated on the acceptance letter. The tuition deposit is deducted from the final tuition payment. Some courses require travel or attendance at cultural events, as indicated by the course instructor. The cost of these events and travel is not included in the tuition and must be borne by the student.

The estimated cost of attendance for academic year 2013–14 includes the following: full-time tuition, €14,600; housing, €7600; board, €1600; transportation, €2250; personal expenses, €2240; books, €300; permit to stay fee, €195; health insurance, €192; and new student fees, €200.

Financial Aid

The American University of Rome is committed to assisting students whose financial need and academic merit warrant support. The University aims to give every student the opportunity to take advantage of a high-quality education and, therefore, offers several scholarships. Funds awarded must be applied to tuition expenses. All scholarships offered by AUR are renewable annually, until degree requirements are met for a maximum of four years (depending which comes first).

The American University of Rome is authorized by the U.S. Department of Education to participate in Title IV student financial assistance programs. Eligible students may apply to participate in the Direct Loan Federal Family Education Loan (FFEL) program (subsidized and unsubsidized Federal Stafford Student Loans and Federal PLUS loans). The American University of Rome is considered a foreign school and is not authorized to award federal or state grants.

The American University of Rome offers degree programs that are listed as approved training for eligible U.S. citizens at the Department of Veterans Affairs Post 9/11 G.I. Bill, facility code 21100084.

Faculty

The American University of Rome has an international, culturally diverse faculty. Nearly 75 percent of the full-time faculty members have received doctoral degrees, and all professors either work professionally in their field or are active in scholarly research. The majority is bilingual, and all faculty members act as teachers as well as advisers. The University also invites visiting professors from other universities for short-term residencies.

Student Government

Students are encouraged to take an active role in the student government as a way of contributing to the continued growth and development of the University. Elected officers of the student government meet regularly with the University administration to discuss matters of administrative and academic relevance. They also take responsibility for directing a variety of student social activities, athletic tournaments, club activities, and cultural events. The student government maintains funds for these activities, and the student officers enjoy a wide degree of autonomy in managing these financial resources.

Admission Requirements

Admission to The American University of Rome is highly selective. Candidates for admission to the University are reviewed by the Admissions Committee. Students are selected without regard to age, race, sex, creed, national or ethnic origin, or handicap. Requests for financial aid do not affect decisions on admission.

Candidates for admission must show evidence that they have completed or anticipate completing a level of education equivalent to four years of high school. Applicants for admission from high school or a secondary school are required to submit a completed application form, accompanied by a nonrefundable application fee; an official transcript of high school work; one academic recommendation from a principal, guidance counselor, teacher, or professor; a 500-word personal statement indicating how a study experience in Rome could help further the student's career and life goals; and a 250-word essay of one of the three topics indicated on the application form. Results of the SAT or ACT are required for students graduating from a U.S. high school system, whether in the United States or abroad. Face-to-face or phone interviews are required of all applicants.

Each applicant is reviewed individually. Leadership, motivation, academic improvement, the level of difficulty of the high school program, involvement in activities, and potential for growth are important considerations in the application review process. Applicants whose native language is not English are required to submit scores from the TOEFL or another English language proficiency exam. The English language proficiency exam requirement may be waived for applicants who complete high school at English-speaking institutions. The American University of Rome TOEFL institutional code for reporting purposes is 0579.

Students whose English language skills need development may apply for the Intensive Academic English Language Course in order to benefit from the full academic curriculum at The American University of Rome. Through this program students will develop speaking, listening, reading, and writing skills in English while attending selected credit-based general education courses at AUR.

Advanced standing may be granted for academic credits earned at institutions outside the university system of the United States. Candidates who have credentials from European lyceums, such as the Italian maturità, the International Baccalaureate, the British GCSE A-levels, and other equivalent programs, are evaluated, and advanced credits may be granted on the basis of that evaluation. In most instances, the first year of college (equivalent to 30 semester hours) may be granted. Students applying for advanced standing must submit official records of the last year of lyceum and a copy of the diploma, if granted. If the records are not written in either English or Italian, the admissions office requires a certified translation into English.

The American University of Rome welcomes transfer students. Upon submission of complete official transcripts of all colleges and universities previously attended, the University evaluates the number of transfer credits to be accepted toward fulfilling the requirements for a degree at AUR. Credit is granted only for courses completed with a grade of C or above. Transfer credits may be applied to no more than 50 percent of a student's major degree requirements. Students must earn at least 30 credits at The American University of Rome for an associate degree and at least 45 credits at The American University of Rome for a bachelor's degree.

Application and Information

Applicants are notified of the admission decision two to four weeks after the application, supporting credentials, recommendation letter, and application fee are received.

Prospective students are encouraged to visit the campus. Further information may be obtained via the University's website at www.aur.edu and by contacting the University directly.

The American University of Rome
Via Pietro Roselli, 4
00153 Rome, Italy
Phone: +39-0658330919 (direct dial from U.S.)
      877-592-1287 (toll-free to Rome from U.S.)
      888-791-8327 (toll-free in the U.S.)
Fax: +39-0658330992 (direct fax from U.S.)
      866-287-2025 (toll-free in the U.S.)
Skype: AURomeadmissions or 415-992-5213
E-mail: admissions@aur.edu
Website: http://www.aur.edu
      http://www.facebook.com/TheAmericanUniversityofRome
      https://twitter.com/Life_at_AUR

The University is located in the prestigious area of the Janiculum, Rome's highest hill, just a short walk from the historic Trastevere district and the heart of Rome.

AMRIDGE UNIVERSITY
MONTGOMERY, ALABAMA

The University

Founded in 1967, Amridge University is an independent, coeducational institution dedicated to the spirit of its ideals and Christian heritage. All Amridge University programs are taught from a Christian perspective. Amridge University is one of the nation's leading universities offering distance learning programs and services to adults nationally since 1993. Adding to the prestige of the University is its selection in 1999 by the U.S. Department of Education as one of fifteen initial participants in the Distance Education Demonstration Program. Amridge University worked with the U.S. Department of Education to develop a national model to help chart the future of distance learning.

Accredited by the Southern Association of Colleges and Schools, Amridge University grants associate, bachelor's, master's, and doctoral degrees, all available via a distance learning format. Graduate degrees are awarded in counseling/family therapy, organizational leadership, and religious studies. These degrees foster leadership, counseling and family therapy skills, knowledge, and biblical and Christian ministry skills. The counseling degrees are designed to help prepare students for licensure. Doctoral degrees include Doctor of Ministry and Doctor of Philosophy degrees. These are advanced professional degrees for community organization and church-related vocations, with a concentration designed to prepare participants to counsel families and individuals.

The policy of Amridge University is to provide reasonable accommodation for persons who are handicapped or disabled as designated in Section 504 of the Rehabilitation Act of 1973 and the Americans with Disabilities Act of 1990. Although the Morgan W. Brown building is not equipped with an elevator, the needs of the physically challenged can be met from the first floor. These include registration, counseling, library facilities, classroom facilities, rest rooms, break room facilities, and others. Ample parking is provided.

Location

Amridge University is located in Montgomery, Alabama, the capital city of the state. Strategically located in the central part of the state between Huntsville and Mobile and Atlanta, Georgia, Montgomery is one of the fastest-growing cities in the state and the region. The city is clean and modern, with beautiful residential areas, parks and playgrounds, and fine schools and universities. Students and families can also enjoy its museums, zoo, and facilities of the capitol building.

Montgomery has two major U.S. Air Force installations: Maxwell Air Force Base and Gunter Annex. Maxwell is where the Air War College is located and is a strategic center for education.

The metropolitan area has a population of more than 350,000 citizens. There are many churches and educational institutions. The city has an abundance of good housing in addition to other advantages.

Majors and Degrees

Undergraduate degrees are awarded in Biblical studies, business, homeland security, human development, human resource management, liberal studies, management communication, and public safety and criminal justice. These degrees promote biblical and Christian ministry skills, human development skills, knowledge in the arts, and management communication skills. Amridge University students are fully matriculated students of Amridge University with full student privileges, rights, and responsibilities.

Academic Programs

Amridge University is primarily a distance learning institution, although there are many classes offered on campus. The academic year consists of three semesters: fall, spring, and summer.

A student must fulfill the required semester hours in a major as well as the basic requirements of the core curriculum. All core and major requirements can be received from the University. Amridge University programs have a traditional structure.

Distance education is approved by the Southern Association of Colleges and Schools and the U.S. Department of Education, ensuring that distance education students receive the same high-quality education as on-campus students. Faculty and student services for students on campus are available to distance learners. Amridge University ensures that students have regular contact with faculty and staff members via e-mail and telephone. No residency is required for undergraduates.

In addition to offering distance learning to a diverse array of individuals, Amridge University is a participating member of the GoArmyEd project. This is an online, streamlined process giving soldiers easy access to obtaining funding for their educations.

Academic Facilities

Amridge University sits stately on a 9-acre campus adjoining Interstate 85. A beautiful building houses the administration offices, classrooms, and Library Resource Center.

Costs

Undergraduate tuition per semester hour is $365. First-time full-time students receive a reduced rate of $250 per semester hour. This rate is guaranteed through summer 2015, as long as students maintain continuous full-time enrollment and are in good academic standing.

Financial Aid

Aid from institutionally generated funds is provided on the basis of academic merit, financial need, and other criteria. A limited number of scholarships is available. Priority is given to early applicants.

Federal funding available for undergraduates includes Federal Pell Grant, Federal Supplemental Educational Opportunity Grants (FSEOG), and direct subsidized and unsubsidized loans. Eighty percent of students receive financial aid.

Faculty

The instructional faculty members total approximately 100. Approximately 65 percent of the full-time faculty members hold doctoral degrees, 100 percent hold master's degrees, and 100 percent hold terminal degrees. Faculty members specialize in their areas and have exceptional training in distance learning delivery.

Student Government

Student volunteers serve as members of the Student Advisory Committee. Volunteers are appointed by the Student Services Team, with recommendations from the deans. The committee meets on a regular basis and is reorganized on an annual basis. Concerns, recommendations, and requests are presented directly from the committee to the appropriate University area.

Admission Requirements

Amridge University is open to all persons who are of good character and who are academically qualified. The University has a streamlined admissions process to help potential students complete the process in a timely manner so they can begin their studies. As new technologies and processes become available, Amridge University makes every effort to adopt and use the latest technologies to help the admissions process. Transfer students in good academic standing are invited to apply to Amridge University. Prospective students must submit a $50 nonrefundable fee along with the completed application for admission.

Application and Information

For further information, students may contact:
Carl Byrd
Amridge University
1200 Taylor Road
Montgomery, Alabama 36117
Phone: 334-387-7569
        800-351-4040 Ext. 7569 (toll-free)
Fax: 334-387-3878
E-mail: carlbyrd@amridgeuniversity.edu
Website: http://www.amridgeuniversity.edu

ANNA MARIA COLLEGE
PAXTON, MASSACHUSETTS

The College

Anna Maria College (AMC), a private, four-year, Catholic coeducational college, was founded in 1946 by the Sisters of Saint Anne in Marlboro, Massachusetts. In 1952, AMC moved to its current 192-acre campus in Paxton, Massachusetts. Originally a women's college, AMC has been coeducational since 1973. The College has grown exponentially over the last sixty-five years with a total enrollment of 1,500.

Anna Maria College is a close-knit community. Small class sizes allow for mentor relationships to develop between faculty members and students. Freshman and sophomore classes generally have between 15 and 20 students; some upper-level classes have as few as 10 students. Faculty members teach and advise students based on their knowledge of each person as an individual; classes are never taught by graduate assistants.

As part of its five year strategic plan—Vision 2015—the College has undergone significant change and enhanced its offerings, including a revision of its core curriculum and strengthened extracurricular opportunities, to ensure that students have access to the programs and services that will help develop their mind, body, and spirit so they can become strong leaders in their communities. An honors program with unique study-abroad options has been added, as well as a B.S.N. and paramedic science program. The College has undergone a major reorganization of its academic programs, moving from a divisional structure to organizing the nearly forty different majors into six different schools. As part of the master plan, AMC has already added an all-purpose athletic field and stadium; three new residence halls, one of which offers suite-style housing; a new fitness center; and a new athletic field facility. The College has also invested in new technologies and the entire campus is wireless.

Anna Maria College is accredited by the New England Association of Schools and Colleges, the Council on Social Work Education, the American Music Therapy Association, and the National League for Nursing Accrediting Commission. AMC is approved by the Board of Registration in Nursing in Massachusetts and the Massachusetts Department of Education.

Approximately 70 percent of Anna Maria College's undergraduates reside on campus in the residence halls. Students enjoy a full social life both on campus and within the college-city atmosphere of nearby Worcester.

Anna Maria College's NCAA Division III athletic program offers intercollegiate competition for men (baseball, basketball, cross-country, football, golf, lacrosse, soccer, and tennis) and women (basketball, field hockey, golf, lacrosse, soccer, softball, tennis, and volleyball). Intramural athletics are also available to students who do not wish to participate on competitive sports teams.

Anna Maria College provides a wireless campus. More than 500 computer hookups link classrooms, offices, the Academic Computing Center, computer labs, the library, and all residence hall rooms. In addition to College-owned computers, students have the opportunity to access the College network to gain access to the Internet from any location on campus via the College wireless network and their own computers.

Location

Anna Maria College is located on a 192-acre campus in Paxton, Massachusetts, 8 miles from Worcester's vibrant downtown. The city offers numerous professional, cultural, and entertainment opportunities, and Boston, Providence, and Hartford are only an hour away.

Local attractions include big-name entertainment and minor league sports teams at the DCU Center; art, history, and science museums; classical music performances at Mechanics Hall; theater; and day and night skiing at Wachusett Mountain.

Majors and Degrees

Anna Maria College offers a four-year curriculum of undergraduate instruction leading to bachelor's degrees in the following areas: art, art and business, art therapy, business administration, business administration/MIS, criminal justice, early childhood education, elementary education, English, environmental science, fire science, graphic design, health science, history, human development/human services, humanities (interdisciplinary program), legal studies, liberal arts/general studies, media communications, modern languages, music, music education, music performance, music therapy, nursing, paralegal studies, paramedic science, political science, psychology, public policy, social science, social work, sociology, sport management, studio art, teacher preparation/licensure, teacher of visual art, and theology. Associate degrees are available in business administration and paralegal studies.

Art and music therapy, business, criminal justice, fire science, education, nursing, social work, and psychology are the most popular majors. The Fifth Year Option allows undergraduate students in good academic standing a unique opportunity to earn both their undergraduate and graduate degrees in five years. Fifth-year master's options are available in business administration, counseling psychology, criminal justice, education, emergency management, fire science, pastoral studies/counseling, and visual art.

Academic Programs

When the Sisters of St. Anne founded Anna Maria College in 1946, their mission was to increase access to high-quality education, educational innovation, and respect for service to others through the development of the total human being. That mission has not changed in more than fifty years. As a Catholic college, the relationship between faith and reason is looked at closely. An AMC education is distinct because of its integration of rich tradition, diversity of knowledge, and the understanding of human history, institutions, and societies with Catholic teachings and traditions. The cornerstone of AMC's academic programs is the core curriculum, which integrates the Catholic character with a commitment to liberal arts education.

Students are encouraged to travel beyond their immediate interests to disciplines that may be connected by similar methods, history, theory, or application. The end result is a strong liberal arts foundation with a focused knowledge and professional preparation in a chosen area of concentration. AMC also encourages students to explore their own areas of interest and design their own majors.

While at AMC, students can gain practical experience and explore career options through internship programs, fieldwork, academic seminars, and summer programs. They also learn through required practicums, part-time work, and community service.

Off-Campus Programs

Anna Maria College is a member of the Colleges of Worcester Consortium, a group of twelve area colleges (Anna Maria College, Assumption College, Becker College, Clark University, College of the Holy Cross, Massachusetts College of Pharmacy and Allied Health, Nichols College, Quinsigamond Community College, Tufts University School of Veterinary Medicine, University of Massachusetts Medical School, Worcester Polytechnic Institute, and Worcester State College). Students may enroll in nonmajor courses at any of the member institutions and have credits transferred at no additional cost.

AMC offers several off-campus opportunities for which academic credits are awarded. There are opportunities for study abroad, as well as an Urban Seminar course with travel to various locations worldwide. Students are also eligible to apply for Army and Air Force ROTC programs, available through the Colleges of Worcester Consortium. A Washington, D.C. internship is offered for students in all majors, and a Disney internship is also available.

Academic Facilities

The Mondor-Eagan Library houses Anna Maria College's volumes, stacks, periodicals, study rooms, computer center, resource centers, and language laboratory. The library also houses the main computer terminal, which links the combined material resources of central and western Massachusetts libraries, making more than 4 million books and periodicals accessible to students. Classrooms are located in Trinity Hall, Cardinal Cushing Hall, and Foundress Hall, which also houses the Zecco Performing Arts Center. Trinity Hall also houses the learning center. Other facilities include Madore Chapel, St. Joseph's Hall for sciences, and Miriam Hall for music, performance, and art. The College's master plan also calls for a new academic facility, which will allow AMC to expand both its academic offerings and student population while maintaining small class sizes.

Costs

Tuition and fees for the 2012–13 academic year included tuition, $30,168; fees, $1,996; and room and board, $12,012. Tuition is slightly higher for music majors.

Financial Aid

Ninety-seven percent of the most recent freshman class received financial aid in the form of scholarships, grants, loans, and work-study program awards. Some available sources of funds are the Federal Pell Grant, Federal Supplemental Educational Opportunity Grant, and Federal Perkins Loan programs. To apply for aid, students should submit the Free Application for Federal Student Aid (FAFSA), which can be found at http://www.fafsa.ed.gov. Aid is awarded on the basis of need. Non-need-based scholarships are also available. For further information, students should call 508-849-3366.

Faculty

Anna Maria College has 150 full- and part-time faculty members. Faculty members have a deep respect for scholarship and research and are dedicated to teaching and to the success of the student. The Center for Teaching Excellence provides opportunities for faculty to hone new skills and pursue their research.

Student Government

The Student Government Association (SGA) is the official representative of the student body, serving as the link between students and the administration. There are more than twenty clubs and organizations under the SGA, offering many activities and opportunities to participate in the extracurricular life of AMC.

Admission Requirements

At Anna Maria College, every application is considered individually and weighed on its own merits. Emphasis is placed on the applicant's transcript and recommendations. SAT and ACT scores are optional. Extracurricular activities and leadership positions are also important. Successful completion of a four-year college-preparatory program is required. Application for admission to AMC is encouraged for all academically qualified candidates regardless of race, religion, age, gender, or creed.

Application and Information

To apply, students should submit a completed application form (AMC is a member of the Common Application). An official high school transcript should be sent to the Office of Admission along with an essay and letter of recommendation. Prospective students can schedule a campus visit via the AMC website (www.annamaria.edu) or by calling 508-849-3360. AMC is on rolling admissions, however, the application priority deadline for financial aid is March 1. Students who apply after March 1 do not receive priority for financial aid. Transfer students must submit official transcripts of all postsecondary courses.

Anna Maria College invites students to learn more about AMC's community by visiting the campus. Students should call the Undergraduate Office of Admission to schedule an appointment. For detailed information about Anna Maria College's distinctive programs and campus community, prospective students should contact:

Peter Miller
Dean of Admission and Financial Aid
Anna Maria College
50 Sunset Lane
Paxton, Massachusetts 01612-1198
Phone: 508-849-3360
      800-344-4586 Ext. 360 (toll-free)
Fax: 508-849-3362
E-mail: admission@annamaria.edu
Website: http://www.annamaria.edu

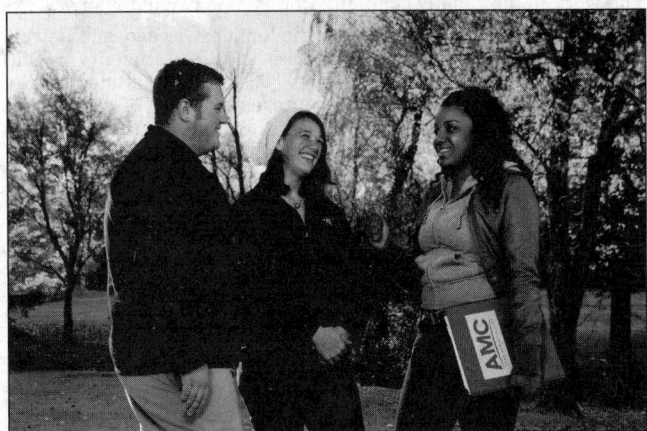

AMC students enjoy the beautiful New England Campus at Anna Maria College.

AQUINAS COLLEGE
GRAND RAPIDS, MICHIGAN

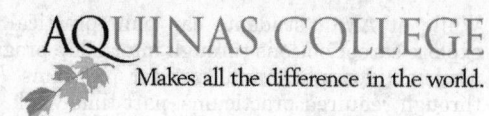

AQUINAS COLLEGE
Makes all the difference in the world.

The College

Located on the eastern edge of the city of Grand Rapids, Aquinas enjoys all of the advantages of Michigan's second-largest city and is just a 3-hour drive from Detroit or Chicago. The Aquinas College campus is an interesting blend of early-nineteenth century architecture coupled with modern-day structures. The campus abounds with natural beauty; it has been called the most beautiful small campus in Michigan. Its ninety species of trees, winding woodland paths, and inviting creeks and ponds create a peaceful 107-acre environment that students of all ages find welcoming.

Founded by the Dominican Sisters of Grand Rapids in 1886, Aquinas has a Catholic heritage and a Christian tradition. For over 125 years, Aquinas College has inspired students to transform the world by providing a liberal arts education infused with the Catholic Dominican values of prayer, study, service, and community. It is lived out by Aquinas students who volunteer their time and talents in the Grand Rapids community and by those who travel to places such as the Dominican Republic; Appalachia, Kentucky; or any of a dozen other service-learning project sites. An ability to see the world from different perspectives is the hallmark of an Aquinas-educated student.

An Aquinas education makes graduates more employable. Each year, hundreds of Aquinas students find businesses, government agencies, and other organizations eager to offer field experience and internship opportunities. Students can find employment and internships with organizations such as the United States Senate, American Cancer Society, Detroit Red Wings, Disney World, Meijer, Grand Rapids Art Museum, Spartan Stores, Steelcase, and the Van Andel Institute, to name a few. Seven out of 10 applicants recommended by the Aquinas premedical advisory committee are admitted to medical school, and 19 of 20 are accepted into other graduate programs. In all, nearly 90 percent of Aquinas seniors find jobs or enroll in graduate school within six months after graduation.

Aquinas sees a liberal arts education as career preparation. The Aquinas general education plan exposes students to the necessary skills that enable them to become critical thinkers, articulate speakers, strong writers, and effective problem solvers. Aquinas faculty members insist that students carry values as well as skills into the workplace. The College's curriculum, with its more than sixty majors, is designed to provide students with both breadth and depth and to foster a thirst for knowledge and truth and a spirit of intellectual dialogue and inquiry. Coupled with nationally recognized internship programs, it prepares students to both live and work in the rapidly changing world of today and tomorrow.

Arriving from places as near as Grand Rapids, Chicago, and Detroit and as far as China and South America, the 2,300 students include 1,600 full-time, 400 part-time, and 300 graduate students. The Insignis program at Aquinas encourages students of exceptional academic ability to participate in social and intellectual activities such as lectures and receptions for visiting scholars and trips to places of cultural interest. Aquinas offers more than sixty student organizations, ranging from intramural teams and departmental clubs to a wide variety of musical groups, student publications, and service organizations.

In addition to its undergraduate degrees, Aquinas also offers Master in the Art of Teaching, Master in Education, Master in Science Education, Master of Management, and Master of Sustainable Business degrees.

Location

Aquinas' location in Grand Rapids allows students to reap the benefits of west Michigan's economic, educational, and cultural center. The city is one of the fastest-growing areas in the Great Lakes region. Grand Rapids combines big-city excitement and small-town charm. There are cosmopolitan amenities ranging from four-star hotels and restaurants to top-notch cultural facilities and entertainment venues. Established attractions include ArtPrize,

Laughfest, the Gerald R. Ford Presidential Museum, the Van Andel Public Museum, the 10,000-seat Fifth Third Park for Whitecaps minor-league baseball, the 70-acre Fredrik Meijer Gardens, and the 12,000-seat Van Andel Arena, home to the Grand Rapids Griffins AHL hockey team and a venue for nationally known music concerts and performances. These major facilities add to the list of popular points of interest, festivals, and special events. With nearly half a million residents, there are abundant recreation, arts, and cultural opportunities available.

Majors and Degrees

Aquinas College offers the following undergraduate degree programs: Bachelor of Arts, Bachelor of Fine Arts, Bachelor of Arts in general education, Bachelor of Music Education, Bachelor of Science, Bachelor of Science in Business Administration, Bachelor of Science in sustainable business, and Bachelor of Science in international business. A Bachelor of Science in Nursing degree program is offered in collaboration with the University of Detroit Mercy and St. Mary's Health Care. Majors and programs of study are offered in accounting, accounting/business administration, art, art/business administration, art history, biology, business administration, business administration/chemistry, business administration/communication, business administration/music, business administration/sport management, chemical physics, chemistry, communication, community leadership, computer information systems, conductive education, drawing, economics, education, English, environmental science, environmental studies, French, geography, German, health, history, international studies, Japanese, journalism/publications, learning disabilities, management information systems, mathematics, music, not-for-profit management, organizational communication, painting, philosophy, photography, physical education and recreation, physics, political science, pre-engineering, printmaking, psychology, sculpture, social science, sociology, Spanish, studio art, sustainable business, theater, theology, urban studies, visual arts administration, and women's studies. Pre-professional programs include dentistry, law, medicine, occupational therapy, physical therapy, and veterinary science.

Associate degrees are also available, including the Associate of Arts and the Associate of Science.

Academic Programs

In addition to their major and minor fields of study, students take an integrated skills course called Inquiry and Expression. This course spans the first semester of the freshman year and has an emphasis on writing integrated with reading critically, oral communication skills, critical thinking, library/electronic research methods, computer utilization, and basic quantitative reasoning. The thematic content is American Pluralism: The Individual in a Diverse America. Sophomores take a yearlong course in the humanities. As juniors, they are required to take 3 hours in Theological Foundation. Students are also required to be proficient in a second language through the 102 level. There also is a distribution plan in the general education plan covering social science, history/philosophy, natural world, artistic and creative studies, technology, and health, physical education, and recreation. A career/professional development component begins in summer orientation and offers career planning courses and activities over four years; topics include assessment of students' strengths, skills, and interests; development of goals, a learning plan, and setting a direction; focus on the individual—wellness, personal finances, and leadership/team skills; awareness of careers, professions, and graduate study; information on making and maintaining a professional portfolio and resume; participating in a professional/career mentor program; career fairs and networking; and experiential learning (choices include internship, service learning, service trips, and study abroad). The College follows a two-semester calendar with a summer session. Aquinas also accepts credit through CLEP, Advanced Placement, and International Baccalaureate.

Off-Campus Programs

Students have the option of participating in the Dominican College Campus Interchange Program. Cooperating colleges are Barry University in Miami, Florida; Dominican College in San Rafael, California; and St. Thomas Aquinas College in Sparkill, New York. Students can increase their foreign language skills through cultural-immersion programs in Costa Rica, France, Italy, Japan, Spain, or Germany. Two Aquinas faculty members accompany 30 students to Aquinas' study center in Tully Cross, Ireland. Students have the opportunity to earn a full semester of credit, travel abroad, and live in a rural Irish community. The curriculum is centered on several aspects of Irish studies.

Academic Facilities

The Grace Hauenstein Library is a $6-million facility with resources that include a public access catalog, audiovisual materials, circulation and course reserve materials, reference services, and interlibrary loan services (free access to more than 60 million books and documents from libraries across the country). Albertus Magnus Hall of Science features the handicapped-accessible Baldwin Observatory and a greenhouse. Other facilities include the Cook Carriage House, a student center, and the Art and Music Center, featuring a darkroom, a 200-seat recital hall, an art gallery, and a sculpture studio. Four new apartment buildings have opened, providing more housing options. The Aquinas Performing Arts Center is a $7-million facility providing a state-of-the-art theater venue.

AQnet allows residents and commuters to wirelessly connect their personal computers or other devices to the Internet while on campus. Students will find centrally located kiosks and computer labs on campus in classrooms, residence halls, the Grace Hauenstein Library, and common areas. E-mail is powered by Google, and over 100 discipline-specific software applications are available as well as high-quality laser printing and access to multimedia technology.

Costs

For 2013–14, tuition is $26,280 and room and board are $8,186 for a total of $34,466. Other expenses, including books, travel, and personal supplies, average $2,000.

Financial Aid

Aquinas College awards both merit-based financial assistance and traditional need-based assistance to qualified students. The Spectrum Scholarship Program was developed to recognize students' achievements in academics, leadership, and service. More than 90 percent of entering freshmen receive some form of financial assistance. The College administers the traditional grant and loan programs, including Ford Federal Direct Loans and Federal PLUS loans. Athletic grants are also available. The College participates in an automatic payment program. This plan assists students in paying costs over a period of time. To apply for financial assistance, students must complete the Free Application for Federal Student Aid (FAFSA).

Faculty

Aquinas faculty members are teachers first: while research plays an important part in the Aquinas faculty's development, teaching remains the number-one priority. In addition to teaching, faculty members serve as academic advisers, mentors, and advisers to various clubs and organizations on campus. With a student-professor ratio of 13:1, faculty members give individual attention and assistance to students. All classes and labs are taught by faculty members, not graduate assistants. Approximately 90 percent of Aquinas faculty members have doctoral or terminal degrees.

Student Government

The Student Senate is the governing body of Aquinas students. Senators are chosen by securing twenty-five signatures of students in support of their involvement. These students have both voice and vote on issues facing the College's Academic Assembly. The senate is responsible for many of the academic, social, recreational, and cultural activities on the campus.

Admission Requirements

Freshman and transfer applications are received on a rolling basis. A candidate for admission to Aquinas is considered on the basis of academic preparation, scholarship, and character. Admission depends on a number of factors, including high school academic record and ACT or SAT test scores. Transfer students must present a minimum 2.0 grade point average on a 4.0 scale. Paper and online applications do not require an application fee. The admissions office reserves the right to review applications on a case-by-case basis. Curriculum, extracurricular activities, and any extenuating circumstances are considered in the decision. Letters of recommendation are encouraged but not required.

Application and Information

Prospective students may submit a free online application for admission at www.aquinas.edu/undergraduate.

For further information, interested students should contact:

Tom Mikowski
Dean of Admissions
Aquinas College
1607 Robinson Road, SE
Grand Rapids, Michigan 49506
Phone: 616-632-2900
        800-678-9593 (toll-free)
E-mail: admissions@aquinas.edu
Website: http://www.aquinas.edu

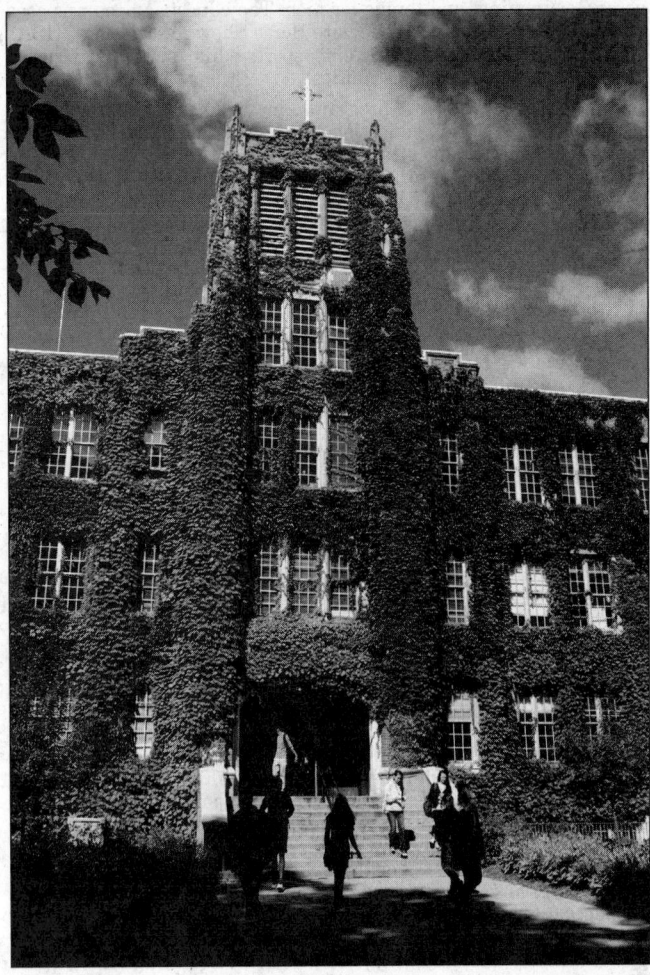

Aquinas College Academic Building.

ARCADIA UNIVERSITY
GLENSIDE, PENNSYLVANIA

The University

Arcadia is a top-ranked private university offering bachelor's, master's, and doctoral degrees. More than 4,000 students choose from among eighty fields of study. *U.S. News & World Report* ranks Arcadia University among the top 30 universities in the North and a top school for the percentage of undergraduate students studying abroad in the 2012 *Open Doors* report. Arcadia's diverse student population represents a cross section of cultural and socioeconomic backgrounds. Enrollment includes over 2,300 undergraduate and 1,600 graduate students. At present, Arcadia students come from forty-six states and twenty-one other countries, and 77 percent of the full-time undergraduate population resides on campus.

Campus life, which includes more than ninety clubs and organizations, athletics, and cultural and social events, is rich and varied. Community service is an integral part of the Arcadia University experience. Students volunteer on neighborhood improvement projects, work at literacy or gerontology centers, and assist disadvantaged or disabled children. NCAA Division III intercollegiate competition is offered in basketball, field hockey, lacrosse, soccer, softball, swimming, tennis, and volleyball for women and baseball, basketball, golf, lacrosse, soccer, swimming, and tennis for men. The equestrian team is coed and competes in the Intercollegiate Horse Show Association (IHSA). Cheerleading is offered as a club sport, while intramural sports provide other athletic opportunities.

Arcadia offers master's programs in business administration, counseling psychology, education, English, forensic science, genetic counseling, health education, humanities, international peace and conflict resolution, international public relations, international relations and diplomacy, physician assistant studies, and public health. A Doctor of Physical Therapy (D.P.T.) and Doctor of Education (Ed.D.) programs in special education and educational leadership are also offered.

Location

Arcadia, located in metropolitan Philadelphia, features a beautiful rolling campus built around the historic landmark Grey Towers Castle. The University is 12 miles from Center City Philadelphia and only 90 minutes from the Jersey shore and Pennsylvania's Pocono Mountains. Students have access to dozens of museums, galleries, performing arts centers, and nightspots; and historic, government, and commercial sites in the metropolitan area.

Majors and Degrees

Arcadia offers Bachelor of Arts degrees in accounting, anthropology, art and design (B.A. or B.F.A.) (art education, art history, ceramics, graphic design, interior design, metals and jewelry, painting, photography, pre–art therapy, printmaking, studio art), biology (allied health, biological basis of behavior, biomedical, conservation, forensics, molecular), business (economics, international economics, international finance, international human resources, international marketing, marketing), chemistry (biochemistry, chemical professions, forensics, health professions), communications (cinema studies, corporate, international cinema, print, video), computer science, computing technology (design, technical), criminal justice, education (art education, elementary and early childhood, middle level, secondary, special education), engineering, English (creative writing, professional writing), environmental studies, fashion studies, forensic science, French studies, global legal studies, global media (cultural studies, digital gaming systems, digital media, fashion studies, film production, media industries, media production, new media journalism, sound and music, visual cultures, visual journalism, world cinema), global security and emergency management, health administration, history, interdisciplinary science, international business and culture, international peace and conflict resolution, international studies (global public health; globalization, development, and human rights; modern Mediterranean world), Italian studies, liberal studies (applied social science for the global citizen, individualized), mathematics (actuarial science), modern languages, optometry, philosophy, physical therapy, physician assistant studies, political science (international politics, prelaw and political theory, U.S. politics and policy), pre-dentistry, pre-medicine, pre-nursing, pre–veterinary medicine, psychology (pre–art therapy, human resources), scientific illustration, sociology (human services), Spanish, Spanish cultural studies, special education, sport psychology, sports management, and theater arts and English. A five-year program combines the B.A. in education with a Master of Education in special education.

Bachelor of Science degrees are offered in accounting, business administration, chemistry, chemistry and business, computer science, international finance, marketing, and mathematics.

Bachelor of Fine Arts degrees are awarded to students majoring in acting or studio arts with concentrations in ceramics, graphic design, interior design, metals and jewelry, painting, photography, and printmaking. Preparation for certification in art education is offered in conjunction with the B.F.A. program, as is preparation for graduate study in art therapy.

Arcadia's physician assistant studies 4+2 program provides a four-year undergraduate degree in a related field, followed by two years of study in Arcadia's Master of Medical Science: Physician Assistant Program. Arcadia undergraduates who satisfy the prerequisites are assured admission to the program. Arcadia also offers a combined undergraduate and graduate (4+2.5) program leading to the Doctor of Physical Therapy, with assured admission for undergrads who meet established criteria. An accelerated 3+3 program also is offered, combining a bachelor's degree in biology with a doctorate in physical therapy. The International Peace and Conflict Resolution 4+2 Program is a four-year undergraduate degree followed by two years of study in the M.A. degree program; an accelerated 3+2 option is also offered. The forensic science program provides a four-year undergraduate program in a related field followed by two years in the Master of Science in Forensic Science (M.S.F.S.) program. A 3+2 Accelerated Forensic Science Program also is offered, allowing academically talented students to earn a B.A. or B.S. in biology/chemistry and an M.S. in forensic science.

Arcadia also offers accelerated three-year bachelor's degrees in business administration, communications, international business and culture, international studies, and psychology. The format can include one summer of service learning and one summer internship at an international or U.S. location.

Arcadia offers several five-year combined programs in education including master's degrees in special education, environmental education, literacy education/reading, literacy education/ESL, technology education, and library science.

A dual-degree (3+2) program in engineering is offered in conjunction with Columbia University. An accelerated (3+4) program with Salus University leads to B.A. and Doctor of Optometry degrees. The 3+2 Environmental Studies program leads to a B.A. in biology and an M.A. in education, with certification in environmental education. A 3+3 pre-law program leads to a B.A. from Arcadia University and a J.D. from Drexel University.

Academic Programs

Arcadia's undergraduate curriculum provides a distinctively global, integrative, and personal learning experience that prepares students to contribute and prosper in a diverse and dynamic world. Students are encouraged to design their own path, explore the globe, make intellectual connections, and develop an area of expertise. There are opportunities to study around the world and make connections across disciplines and cultures. Every student pursues a major, participates in cultural experiences, explores areas of inquiry, and develops intellectual practices.

Highly qualified students may enhance their education through the Honors Program, which merges the best of Arcadia's academic traditions with innovative honors courses and features unique leadership and study-abroad opportunities.

Credit toward graduation is granted for scores of 3 or better on AP exams or earned through the College-Level Examination Program

(CLEP) and locally administered examinations at the discretion of the department.

Arcadia's academic year is divided into two semesters. Three summer sessions are offered, beginning in May and continuing through early August. Most full-time students carry four academic courses in each regular semester; 128 semester hours are required for graduation.

Off-Campus Programs

Arcadia is top-ranked in the nation by *U.S. News & World Report* for international study. With more than 100 programs around the world, the College of Global Studies supports and implements the University's commitment to international education. Students can spend a semester or full year abroad for approximately the same cost as remaining on campus. Many shorter-term options are also available.

Arcadia offers two distinct opportunities for students to study abroad during their first year. The University's Preview program enables first-year students in good academic standing to earn 2 credits while spending their spring break in England, Ireland, Mexico, Scotland, Spain, or other countries. The First Year Study Abroad Experience (FYSAE) gives select incoming students the chance to spend their first or second semester in London, England, or Stirling, Scotland. Arcadia's FYSAE and Preview programs have been recognized as among the most innovative international programs in the country by the American Council on Education, *U.S. News & World Report,* and the Princeton Review.

Arcadia also offers seven Majors Abroad Programs (MAPs). Students in these majors spend a year (two semesters) abroad, taking general courses as well as major-related courses at an overseas institution.

Off-campus study in the Philadelphia area includes internships and fieldwork in most majors. The University requires students to partake in a global connections experience, which may occur overseas, through a domestic study-away program, or locally.

Academic Facilities

The campus includes historical buildings as well as extensive modern facilities. A prime academic resource on Arcadia's campus is Landman Library, which offers students increased technology and access to resources both on campus and around the globe.

Arcadia's newly renovated Kuch Athletic and Recreation Center features the Alumni Gymnasium, which seats 1,500, and the Lenox Pool, with adjacent Jacuzzi. The Kuch Center also includes an indoor track that overlooks the gym, an aerobics/dance studio, a fitness center, locker rooms, saunas, and first aid/training rooms. The Commons student center opened in spring 2012 and features a game room, fireplace lounge, dining area, flexible meeting rooms, an art exhibit space, and more.

Wireless Internet access is available everywhere on campus and extends to every room in the residence halls. Computer labs—including a Mac lab—are available for student use.

Costs

For 2013–14, undergraduate tuition is $36,150. Room and board charges are $12,560 per year and annual student fees are $660.

Financial Aid

On average, 98 percent of full-time undergraduates receive financial aid, and 98 percent receive grants and scholarships. Every effort is made to see that students requiring financial assistance are able to attend Arcadia. Aid is awarded on the basis of need, as determined by the Free Application for Federal Student Aid (FAFSA) and the Arcadia University Financial Aid Application, and is available in the form of grants, loans, and part-time campus employment or some combination of the three. Scholarships are presented annually to entering first-year and transfer students who have achieved academic distinction or have been recognized for outstanding extracurricular accomplishments. Distinguished Scholarships, ranging from $52,000 to $84,000 over four years, and Achievement Awards, ranging from $4,000 to $48,000 over four years, recognize academic excellence, leadership, and extracurricular accomplishments. A limited number of full-tuition scholarships are available to the top entering first-year undergraduates. To receive full consideration, students should complete their applications and submit the FAFSA and Arcadia's Financial Aid Application by March 1.

Faculty

Arcadia University has a faculty with a primary commitment to teaching. The average class size is 15 students, and the student-faculty ratio is 14:1. This fosters an environment in which students and faculty members collaborate on research and writing and engage in informal discussions, field trips, and other activities outside the classroom. Eighty-nine percent of Arcadia faculty members hold terminal degrees, and all courses are taught by faculty members, not graduate assistants.

Student Government

Student life is largely self-regulated by the Student Government Organization (SGO) through the Student Senate. Students serve on most major faculty committees, and student leaders attend Board of Trustees meetings.

Admission Requirements

Students are selected on the basis of educational preparation, intellectual promise, and potential. Emphasis is placed on the candidate's academic record, including the type of program followed and the grades and class rank earned. Standardized test scores also carry significant weight. Counselor and teacher recommendations, participation in school and community activities, and other supporting credentials also are strongly considered.

Freshman applicants must submit an official high school transcript, standardized test scores (SAT or ACT), and counselor and teacher recommendations. Students are encouraged to visit the campus for a student-guided tour and an information session or one-on-one meeting with an admissions counselor.

Transfer applicants may apply for the fall term or at midyear and must submit official college transcripts. In some cases, transfer applicants are required to submit high school transcripts and SAT or ACT scores.

Application and Information

Students are encouraged to submit their applications as early as possible in the senior year. Admission decisions are made on a rolling basis, and applicants are usually notified within four to six weeks of the date of submission of the completed application. For freshman applicants, the priority admissions application deadline for Distinguished Scholarship consideration—as well as consideration for the honors p,rogram, First Year Study Abroad Experience, and accelerated degree programs—is January 15. The priority admissions application deadline for Achievement Award consideration is March 1. The admissions application deadline is also March 1. The transfer student deadline for portfolio review, Honors Program, Distinguished Scholarship consideration, and priority admissions is June 15 for fall-term admission.

Requests for further information should be directed to:

Office of Enrollment Management
Arcadia University
450 South Easton Road
Glenside, Pennsylvania 19038-3295
Phone: 215-572-2910
      877-ARCADIA (877-272-2342, toll-free)
E-mail: admiss@arcadia.edu
Website: http://www.arcadia.edu/pet.asp
      http://www.arcadia.edu/socialmedia

Arcadia University, Grey Towers Castle, Glenside, Pennsylvania.

THE ART INSTITUTE OF ATLANTA
ATLANTA, GEORGIA

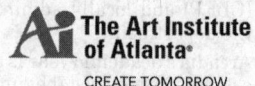

The Art Institute of Atlanta is one of The Art Institutes, a system of over fifty schools throughout North America dedicated to providing hands-on education in the creative and applied arts. The Art Institute of Atlanta offers bachelor's and associate degree programs as well as non-degree programs for students interested in pursuing career opportunities from among tomorrow's 15 million jobs in creative fields like design, fashion, media arts, and culinary (based on information from the U.S. Bureau of Labor Statistics for job growth between 2012 and 2022).

A focused education from The Art Institute of Atlanta can help students turn their creative energy into a powerful tool that can make a difference in the world. Students are part of a collaborative and supportive community, where experienced instructors provide the guidance and skills needed to pursue a career in the creative economy.

The Art Institute of Atlanta is also an important resource for creative industry leaders who value the opportunity provided students to learn by using professional-grade technology to build a portfolio of work to show potential employers after graduation.

Accreditation

The Art Institute of Atlanta, including its branch campuses, The Art Institute of Atlanta-Decatur, The Art Institute of Charleston, The Art Institute of Tennessee—Nashville, The Art Institute of Virginia Beach, The Art Institute of Washington, and The Art Institute of Washington—Dulles, is accredited by the Southern Association of Colleges and Schools Commission on Colleges to award associate and baccalaureate degrees. Contact the Commission on Colleges at 1866 Southern Lane, Decatur, Georgia 30033-4097 or call 404-679-4500 for questions about the accreditation of The Art Institute of Atlanta.

The diploma in baking & pastry, diploma in culinary arts, Associate in Arts degree in culinary arts, Associate in Arts degree in culinary arts with a concentration in baking & pastry, Bachelor of Science degree in food & beverage management, and the Bachelor of Science degree in culinary arts management programs are accredited by the Accrediting Commission of the American Culinary Federation Education Foundation.

The interior design program leading to the Bachelor of Fine Arts degree is accredited by the Council for Interior Design Accreditation, 206 Grandville Avenue, Suite 350, Grand Rapids, Michigan 49503; www.accredit-id.org.

The Art Institute of Atlanta meets the criteria for an exemption from the Georgia Nonpublic Postsecondary Education Commission's (NPEC) regulations as outlined in O.C.G.A.§20-3-250.3(a)(15). The Art Institute of Atlanta is licensed by the Alabama Department of Postsecondary Education, 401 Adams Avenue, Montgomery, Alabama, 36104-4340 and is approved for recruiting purposes only by the Alabama Commission on Higher Education, 100 North Union Street, Montgomery, Alabama 36104-3758.

Location

Atlanta has so much to offer, it's difficult to mention it all here. But the word that best summarizes Atlanta is "energy"—the energy of the people, the vitality of the business community and professional opportunities, and the vibe of the arts and the nightlife. Atlanta's energy pulses through the streets, carries to every neighborhood, and helps to fuel creativity and imaginations.

Atlanta is known as the capital of the New South, and noted as the birthplace of Martin Luther King, Jr. and the host city of the 1996 Summer Olympics. For all intents and purposes, Atlanta started in the 1830s as a transportation hub. The city's story could have ended during the Civil War, but instead it rose from the ashes to become a center of commerce and one of the nation's economic and commercial powerhouses.

Today, Atlanta is a forward-looking city of industrious, innovative and creative people, a vibrant, exciting city where tree-lined neighborhoods are just minutes away from high-rise condos and skyscrapers housing Fortune 500 companies. Atlanta's thriving business environment includes high-tech companies, such as Earthlink, as well as corporate giants like Coca-Cola, CNN-Time Warner, Delta Air Lines, AT&T, and Georgia Pacific.

The city's performing arts district is located in the midtown area at the Woodruff Arts Center. Students can explore some of the country's most important art museums and institutions, including the renowned High Museum of Art, one of the most visited of its kind anywhere in the world. The Museum of Design Atlanta (MODA) is the only design museum in the southeast, and there are also contemporary art museums like the Atlanta Contemporary Art Center and the Museum of Contemporary Art of Georgia.

At The Art Institute of Atlanta, students have access to a wide range of professional sports. Those who are into baseball can take in a Braves game at Turner Field. Football? The NFL's Falcons play at the Georgia Dome. For basketball fans, the Hawks of the NBA and the Dream of the WNBA both play hoops at Philips Arena.

Programs of Study and Degrees

Creativity is all around, and with millions of tomorrow's jobs in creative fields, the world needs more creative professionals. No matter which course of study a student chooses, the instructors at The Art Institutes will guide, support, and help students fine-tune their visual thinking and problem solving, so they can take advantage of the world's growing creative opportunities and put their passion to work. Programs are offered in the areas of design, which focuses on communicating conceptually and helping people connect in living and work spaces; media arts, which centers on utilizing technology to deliver information and entertainment; fashion, where students learn anything from designing clothes for the runway to running a retail shop; and culinary, which exposes learners to international cuisines as well as restaurant management techniques.

Bachelor's degree programs are offered in the areas of advertising, audio production, culinary arts management, designing for tablets: digital publishing, digital filmmaking & video production, digital photography, fashion & retail management, food & beverage management, game art & design, graphic & web design, illustration, interior design, media arts & animation, visual & game programming, and visual effects & motion graphics.

Associate degree programs are offered in the areas of baking & pastry, culinary arts, digital photography, graphic & web design, video production, and wine, spirits, & beverage management (participation in this program for those under 21 years of age will be conducted in accord with state law regarding the possession and consumption of alcoholic beverages).

Diploma programs are offered in advertising design, baking & pastry, commercial photography, culinary arts, digital design, digital image management, fashion retailing, residential interiors, video skills, web design & development, and web design & interactive communications.

The Associate in Arts in culinary arts, the Bachelor of Science in culinary arts management, the Bachelor of Science in food & beverage management, and the Bachelor of Fine Arts in interior design are available in evening and weekend formats.

Program availability and degree offerings are subject to change.

Academic Facilities

The Art Institute of Atlanta provides a learning environment with professional-grade technology applicable to each student's course of study. Students have the opportunity to build a portfolio of work that shows potential employers that they are trained to use the software, hardware, or equipment utilized within the industry. Depending upon the course of study, students are immersed in a creative environment—from classrooms to computer labs to studios—focused on relevant, hands-on education designed to prepare students for the real world.

Costs

Actual tuition and housing costs will vary depending on the program, number of credits enrolled, and actual living arrangements. Please contact a Student Financial Services professional at the school for details.

Financial Aid

Financial aid is available for those who qualify. Students who require financial assistance should first complete and submit a Free Application for Federal Student Aid (FAFSA) online at www.fafsa.ed.gov and meet with a financial aid officer. Students may also apply for a number of scholarships focusing on their specific areas of career interest.

Faculty

Faculty members are hands-on creative professionals with proven experience as business leaders and innovators, hosting a learning environment similar to the career world students will face after graduation. Part instructor, part mentor, their mission is to help develop and transform creative potential into high-demand marketable skills.

Admission Requirements

Prospective students should refer to the current academic catalog for full details regarding admission requirements and process.

Application and Information

To obtain an application, make arrangements for an interview, or tour the school, prospective students should contact:

The Art Institute of Atlanta
6600 Peachtree Dunwoody Road, N.E.
100 Embassy Row
Atlanta, Georgia 30328-1649
Phone: 770-394-8300
        800-275-4242 (toll-free)
Fax: 770-394-0008
Website: http://www.artinstitutes.edu/atlanta

THE ART INSTITUTE OF ATLANTA—DECATUR

DECATUR, GEORGIA

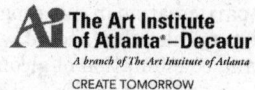

The Art Institute of Atlanta—Decatur, a branch of The Art Institute of Atlanta, is one of The Art Institutes, a system of over fifty schools throughout North America dedicated to providing hands-on education in the creative and applied arts. The Art Institute of Atlanta—Decatur offers bachelor's and associate degree programs as well as non-degree programs for students interested in pursuing career opportunities from among tomorrow's 15 million jobs in creative fields like design, fashion, media arts, and culinary (based on information from the U.S. Bureau of Labor Statistics for job growth between 2012 and 2022).

A focused education from The Art Institute of Atlanta—Decatur can help students turn their creative energy into a powerful tool that can make a difference in the world. Students are part of a collaborative and supportive community, where experienced instructors provide the guidance and skills needed to pursue a career in the creative economy.

The Art Institute of Atlanta—Decatur is also an important resource for creative industry leaders who value the opportunity provided students to learn by using professional-grade technology to build a portfolio of work to show potential employers after graduation.

Accreditation

The Art Institute of Atlanta—Decatur is a branch campus of The Art Institute of Atlanta. The Art Institute of Atlanta is accredited by the Southern Association of Colleges and Schools Commission on Colleges to award associate and baccalaureate degrees. Questions about the accreditation of The Art Institute of Atlanta can be directed to the Commission on Colleges at 1866 Southern Lane, Decatur, Georgia 30033-4097; phone: 404-679-4500.

The Art Institute of Atlanta—Decatur meets the criteria for an exemption from the Georgia Nonpublic Postsecondary Education Commission's (NPEC) regulations as outlined in O.C.G.A.§20-3-250.3(a)(15). The Art Institute of Atlanta—Decatur is licensed by the Alabama Department of Postsecondary Education, 401 Adams Avenue, Montgomery, Alabama, 36104-4340 and is approved for recruiting purposes only by the Alabama Commission on Higher Education, 100 North Union Street, Montgomery, Alabama 36104-3758.

Location

The Art Institute of Atlanta—Decatur is located on the eastern side of the greater Atlanta area. A short drive or MARTA ride from downtown, Decatur is where traditional small-town atmosphere meets the college-town sophistication and excitement—along with all the benefits of being right in the center of a major metropolis.

Decatur has many unique shops, fashion boutiques, theaters, galleries, and businesses focused on creative industries, and restaurants that range from casual to gourmet dining. Most are within walking distance of campus, as are the annual Decatur Arts Festival and the Decatur Book Festival.

Of course, nearby Atlanta has its own attractions. Known as the capital of the New South, it's the birthplace of Martin Luther King, Jr., a major force in the civil rights movement of the 1960s, host city of a Summer Olympics, and a forward-looking city of industrious, innovative, and creative people. This is a vibrant, exciting city where tree-lined neighborhoods are just minutes away from high-rise condos and skyscrapers housing Fortune 500 companies.

Atlanta's thriving business environment includes high-tech companies, such as Earthlink, as well as corporate giants like Coca-Cola, CNN-Time Warner, Delta Air Lines, AT&T, and Georgia Pacific.

Atlanta's performing arts district is located in the midtown area at the Woodruff Arts Center. The city is home to some of the country's most important art museums and institutions, including the renowned High Museum of Art, one of the most-visited of its kind anywhere in the world, and the Museum of Design Atlanta (MODA), the only design museum in the southeast. Students can explore contemporary art museums like the Atlanta Contemporary Art Center and the Museum of Contemporary Art of Georgia.

Students also have access to a wide range of professional sports. Those who are into baseball can take in a Braves game at Turner Field. Football? The NFL's Falcons play at the Georgia Dome. For basketball fans, the Hawks of the NBA and the Dream of the WNBA both play hoops at Philips Arena.

Programs of Study and Degrees

Creativity is all around, and with millions of tomorrow's jobs in creative fields, the world needs more creative professionals. No matter which course of study a student chooses, the instructors at The Art Institutes will guide, support, and help students fine-tine their visual thinking and problem solving, so that they can take advantage of the world's growing creative opportunities and put their passion to work. Programs are offered in the areas of design, which focuses on communicating conceptually and helping people connect in living and work spaces; media arts, which centers on utilizing technology to deliver information and entertainment; and fashion, where students learn anything from designing clothes for the runway to running a retail shop.

Bachelor's degree programs are offered in the areas of advertising, designing for tablets: digital publishing, digital photography, fashion & retail management, fashion design, game art & design, graphic & web design, interior design, and media arts & animation.

Associate degree programs are offered in graphic & web design and digital photography.

Diploma programs are offered in advertising design, digital design, digital image management, fashion retailing, residential interiors, web design & development, and web design & interactive communications.

Program availability and degree offerings are subject to change.

Academic Facilities

The Art Institute of Atlanta—Decatur provides a learning environment with professional-grade technology applicable to each student's course of study. Students have the opportunity to build a portfolio of work that shows potential employers that

they are trained to use the software, hardware, or equipment utilized within the industry. Depending upon the course of study, students are immersed in a creative environment—from classrooms to computer labs to studios—focused on relevant, hands-on education designed to prepare them for the real world.

Costs

Actual tuition and housing costs will vary depending on program, number of credits enrolled, and living arrangements. Prospective students should contact a Student Financial Services professional at the school for details.

Financial Aid

Financial aid is available for those who qualify. Students who require financial assistance should first complete and submit the Free Application for Federal Student Aid (FAFSA) online at www.fafsa.ed.gov and meet with a financial aid officer. Students may also apply for a number of scholarships focusing on their specific areas of career interest.

Faculty

Faculty members are hands-on creative professionals with proven experience as business leaders and innovators, hosting a learning environment similar to the career world students will face after graduation. Part instructor, part mentor, their mission is to help develop and transform creative potential into high-demand marketable skills.

Admission Requirements

Prospective students should refer to the current academic catalog for full details regarding admission requirements and process.

Application and Information

To obtain an application, make arrangements for an interview, or tour the school, prospective students should contact:

The Art Institute of Atlanta—Decatur, a branch of The Art Institute of Atlanta
One West Court Square, Suite 110
Decatur, Georgia 30030
Phone: 404-942-1800
 866-856-6203 (toll-free)
Fax: 404-942-1818
Website: http://www.artinstitutes.edu/decatur

COLLEGE CLOSE-UPS

THE ART INSTITUTE OF AUSTIN
AUSTIN, TEXAS

The Art Institute of Austin, a branch of The Art Institute of Houston, is one of The Art Institutes, a system of over fifty schools throughout North America dedicated to providing hands-on education in the creative and applied arts. The Art Institute of Austin offers bachelor's and associate degree programs as well as non-degree programs for students interested in pursuing career opportunities from among tomorrow's 15 million jobs in creative fields like design, fashion, media arts, and culinary (based on information from the U.S. Bureau of Labor Statistics for job growth between 2012 and 2022).

A focused education from The Art Institute of Austin can help students turn their creative energy into a powerful tool that can make a difference in the world. Students are part of a collaborative and supportive community, where experienced instructors provide the guidance and skills needed to pursue a career in the creative economy.

The Art Institute of Austin is also an important resource for creative industry leaders who value the opportunity provided students to learn by using professional-grade technology to build a portfolio of work to show potential employers after graduation.

Accreditation

The Art Institute of Austin is a branch campus of The Art Institute of Houston. The Art Institute of Houston is accredited by the Southern Association of Colleges and Schools Commission on Colleges to award associate and baccalaureate degrees. Questions about the accreditation of The Art Institute of Houston can be directed to the Commission on Colleges at 1866 Southern Lane, Decatur, Georgia 30033-4097; phone: 404-679-4500.

The Art Institute of Austin holds a Certificate of Authorization acknowledging exemption from Texas Higher Education Coordinating Board regulations.

Location

The Art Institute of Austin is located in a city that's been voted the number-one college town in America by the Travel Channel and the second-best big city by *Money* magazine. *Bicycling* magazine has placed Austin among the 20 most bike-friendly cities. But Austin has even more to offer.

Known for its creativity and originality, Austin is the perfect city to develop one's own creativity. It's a vibrant city that celebrates being both cosmopolitan and unpretentious, high-tech and low-key, and big-city and college-town. The city's unofficial local slogan—"Keep Austin Weird"—refers to the spirit of the city.

Known as the Live Music Capital of the World, Austin has a rich live music scene—the most music venues per capita of any city in the United States. The evidence is everywhere—from the numerous clubs to the annual film/music/interactive festival called South by Southwest to the longest-running concert music show on American TV, "Austin City Limits." Austin is also home to a wonderful ballet, world-class museums, one-of-a-kind shopping, and beautiful outdoor spaces.

In Austin, the work of designers, painters, sculptors, writers, photographers, filmmakers, dancers, and musicians can be found any time of year, any day of the week, in a variety of venues. Check out the art on display through the East or West Austin Studio Tours. Take in a festival or street fair. Head to Arthouse at the Jones Center for the work of new and established artists; the Mexic-Arte Museum and the Carver Museum, which celebrate the area's diversity; the Bob Bullock Museum for a bit of Texas history; and for something a little offbeat, don't miss the Cathedral of Junk, the Austin Art Car Parade, and other eccentric exhibits around town.

And if the free-spirited nature of the city isn't enough for students, the weather certainly is. Austin boasts 300 days of sunshine each year and offers plenty of outdoor activities to take advantage of those days.

Programs of Study and Degrees

Creativity is all around, and with millions of tomorrow's jobs in creative fields, the world needs more creative professionals. No matter which course of study a student chooses, the instructors at The Art Institutes will guide, support, and help students fine-tine their visual thinking and problem solving, so that they can take advantage of the world's growing creative opportunities and put their passion to work. Programs are offered in the areas of design, which focuses on communicating conceptually and helping people connect in living and work spaces; media arts, that centers on utilizing technology to deliver information and entertainment; fashion, where students learn anything from designing clothes for the runway to running a retail shop; and culinary, which exposes learners to international cuisines as well as restaurant management techniques.

Bachelor's degree programs are offered in the areas of advertising design, audio production, culinary management, design & technical graphics, digital filmmaking & video production, fashion & retail management, food & beverage management, game art & design, graphic & web design, hospitality management, interior design, media arts & animation, photography, and visual effects & motion graphics

Associate degree programs are offered in the areas of baking & pastry, culinary arts, graphic design, restaurant & catering management, and web design & interactive media.

Diploma programs are offered in baking & pastry, culinary arts, digital image management, fashion retailing, web design & development, and web design & interactive communications.

Program availability and degree offerings are subject to change.

Academic Facilities

The Art Institute of Austin provides a learning environment with professional-grade technology applicable to each student's course of study. Students have the opportunity to build a portfolio of work that shows potential employers that they are trained to use the software, hardware, and equipment utilized within the industry. Depending upon the course of study, students are immersed in a creative environment—from classrooms to computer labs to studios—focused on relevant, hands-on education designed to prepare them for the real world.

Costs

Actual tuition and housing costs will vary depending on program, number of credits enrolled, and your actual living arrangements. Prospective students should contact a Student Financial Services professional at the school for details.

Financial Aid

Financial aid is available for those who qualify. Students who require financial assistance should first complete and submit the Free Application for Federal Student Aid (FAFSA) online at www.fafsa.ed.gov and meet with a financial aid officer. Students may also apply for a number of scholarships focusing on their specific areas of career interest.

Faculty

Faculty members are hands-on creative professionals with proven experience as business leaders and innovators, hosting a learning environment similar to the career world students will face after graduation. Part instructor, part mentor, their mission is to help develop and transform creative potential into high-demand marketable skills.

Admission Requirements

Prospective students should refer to the current academic catalog for full details regarding admission requirements and process.

Application and Information

To obtain an application, make arrangements for an interview, or tour the school, prospective students should contact:

The Art Institute of Austin, a branch of The Art Institute of
    Houston
101 West Louis Henna Boulevard
Suite 100
Austin, Texas 78728
Phone: 512-691-1707
        866-583-7952 (toll-free)
Fax: 512-691-1790
Website: http://www.artinstitutes.edu/austin

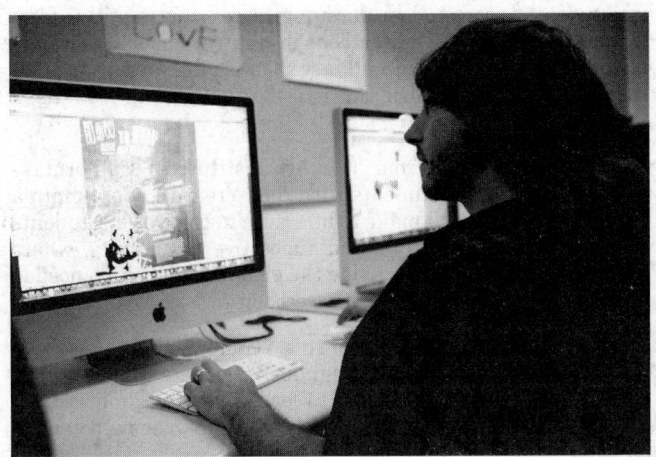

THE ART INSTITUTE OF CALIFORNIA— HOLLYWOOD, A CAMPUS OF ARGOSY UNIVERSITY

NORTH HOLLYWOOD, CALIFORNIA

The Art Institute of California—Hollywood, a campus of Argosy University, is one of The Art Institutes, a system of over fifty schools throughout North America dedicated to providing hands-on education in the creative and applied arts. The Art Institute of California—Hollywood offers bachelor's and associate degree programs as well as non-degree programs for students interested in pursuing career opportunities from among tomorrow's 15 million jobs in creative fields like design, fashion, media arts, and culinary (based on information from the U.S. Bureau of Labor Statistics for job growth from 2012 to 2022).

A focused education from The Art Institute of California— Hollywood can help students turn their creative energy into a powerful tool that can make a difference in the world. Students are part of a collaborative and supportive community, where experienced instructors provide the guidance and skills needed to pursue a career in the creative economy.

The Art Institute of California—Hollywood is also an important resource for creative industry leaders who value the opportunity provided students to learn by using professional-grade technology to build a portfolio of work to show potential employers after graduation.

Accreditation

The Art Institute of California—Hollywood is a campus of Argosy University. Argosy University is accredited by the Accrediting Commission for Senior Colleges and Universities of the Western Association of Schools and Colleges (985 Atlantic Avenue, Suite 100, Alameda, California, 94501; http://www.wascsenior.org).

Location

The Art Institute of California—Hollywood is located in North Hollywood's NoHo Arts District. This is a pedestrian-friendly urban village with direct access to L.A.'s subway system. Students can find a full array of amenities, including contemporary theaters, art galleries, parks, cafés and shops— it's a great environment to pursue a creative education.

The district features the largest concentration of music recording venues west of the Mississippi. The theater district has thirty-one theaters, including two new large venues that expand upon existing theaters, the NoHo Arts Center and the historic El Portal.

L.A. has more museums per capita than any other city in the world. The Los Angeles County Museum of Art is the biggest of its kind in the western U.S. There's also Getty Center, the Museum of Contemporary Art, the Santa Monica Museum of Art at Bergamot Station, and the art galleries lining Gallery Row.

Students can visit many iconic sites and attractions nearby. Cruise Sunset Boulevard and the Sunset Strip, stopping at well-known locations like the Comedy Store, the House of Blues, and Whisky A Go-Go, or drive through Beverly Hills, Pacific Palisades, and Malibu. They can take a visit to Grauman's Chinese Theater and walk the Hollywood Walk of Fame looking for the names of their favorite stars, stroll the paved paths of Venice Beach and meet some colorful characters, take a studio tour, or walk the Santa Monica Pier.

Live sports events are also abundant—the L.A. Dodgers play at beautiful Chavez Ravine, and the Angels play at Angel Stadium of Anaheim. Likewise, there are two local NHL teams—the L.A. Kings play at Staples Center while the Anaheim Ducks call Honda Center home. And both the Clippers and Lakers of the NBA play at Staples Center.

Since L.A. is home to industry giants such as Disney/Capital Cities, ABC, CBS Television City, Paramount, Columbia, and Universal Studios, it's not surprising that the majority of projected new jobs in the city are in the technological and creative areas of the entertainment field.

Programs of Study and Degrees

Creativity is all around, and with millions of tomorrow's jobs in creative fields, the world needs more creative professionals. No matter which course of study a student chooses, the instructors at The Art Institutes will guide, support, and help students fine-tune their visual thinking and problem solving, so that they can take advantage of the world's growing creative opportunities and put their passion to work. Programs are offered in the areas of design, which focuses on communicating conceptually and helping people connect in living and work spaces; media arts, that centers on utilizing technology to deliver information and entertainment; fashion, where students learn anything from designing clothes for the runway to running a retail shop; and culinary, which exposes learners to international cuisines as well as restaurant management techniques.

Bachelor's degree programs are offered in the areas of advertising, audio production, culinary management, design & technical graphics, designing for tablets: digital publishing, digital cinema & video production, digital photography, fashion design, fashion marketing & management, food & beverage management, game art & design, graphic & web design, hospitality food & beverage management, industrial design, interior design, media arts & animation, set & exhibit design, visual & game programming, and visual effects & motion graphics.

Associate degree programs are offered in the areas of audio production, baking & pastry, culinary arts, digital photography, fashion design, fashion marketing, graphic design, and web design & interactive media.

Diploma programs are offered in art of cooking, baking & pastry, fashion retailing, and web design & interactive communications.

The Bachelor of Fine Arts in interior design is available in evening and weekend formats.

Program availability and degree offerings are subject to change.

Academic Facilities

The Art Institute of California—Hollywood provides a learning environment with professional-grade technology applicable to each student's course of study. Students have the opportunity to build a portfolio of work that shows potential employers that they are trained to use the software, hardware, or equipment

utilized within the industry. Depending upon the course of study, students are immersed in a creative environment—from classrooms to computer labs to studios—focused on relevant, hands-on education designed to prepare them for the real world.

Costs

Actual tuition and housing costs will vary depending on program, number of credits enrolled, and living arrangements. Prospective students should contact a Student Financial Services professional at the school for details.

Financial Aid

Financial aid is available for those who qualify. Students who require financial assistance should first complete and submit the Free Application for Federal Student Aid (FAFSA) online at www.fafsa.ed.gov and meet with a financial aid officer. Students may also apply for a number of scholarships focusing on their specific areas of career interest.

Faculty

Faculty members are hands-on creative professionals with proven experience as business leaders and innovators, hosting a learning environment similar to the career world students will face after graduation. Part instructor, part mentor, their mission is to help develop and transform creative potential into high-demand marketable skills.

Admission Requirements

Prospective students should refer to the current academic catalog for full details regarding admission requirements and process

Application and Information

To obtain an application, make arrangements for an interview, or tour the school, prospective students should contact:

The Art Institute of California—Hollywood, a campus of
    Argosy University
5250 Lankershim Boulevard
North Hollywood, California 91601
Phone: 818-299-5100
        877-468-6232 (toll-free)
Fax: 818-299-5150
Website: http://www.artinstitutes.edu/hollywood

THE ART INSTITUTE OF CALIFORNIA— INLAND EMPIRE, A CAMPUS OF ARGOSY UNIVERSITY

SAN BERNARDINO, CALIFORNIA

The Art Institute of California—Inland Empire, a campus of Argosy University, is one of The Art Institutes, a system of over fifty schools throughout North America dedicated to providing hands-on education in the creative and applied arts. The Art Institute of California—Inland Empire offers bachelor's and associate degree programs as well as non-degree programs for students interested in pursuing career opportunities from among tomorrow's 15 million jobs in creative fields like design, fashion, media arts, and culinary (based on information from the U.S. Bureau of Labor Statistics for job growth between 2012 and 2022).

A focused education from The Art Institute of California— Inland Empire can help students turn their creative energy into a powerful tool that can make a difference in the world. Students are part of a collaborative and supportive community, where experienced instructors provide the guidance and skills needed to pursue a career in the creative economy.

The Art Institute of California—Inland Empire is also an important resource for creative industry leaders who value the opportunity provided students to learn by using professional-grade technology to build a portfolio of work to show potential employers after graduation.

Accreditation

The Art Institute of California—Inland Empire is a campus of Argosy University. Argosy University is accredited by the Accrediting Commission for Senior Colleges and Universities of the Western Association of Schools and Colleges (985 Atlantic Avenue, Suite 100, Alameda, California, 94501; http://www.wascsenior.org).

Location

The Art Institute of California—Inland Empire is located in San Bernardino, where students find all the advantages of a major city—culture, shopping, entertainment, creative energy, and opportunity—along with the pace and friendliness, safety, sense of community, and recreational opportunities of a smaller city. It's easy to navigate, fun to explore, and just a short drive from all the excitement and attractions of Los Angeles.

The Art Institute of California—Inland Empire is a great place to get a creative education. The campus setting in this fast-growing city puts students in the middle of a dynamic area where the economy—and the creative community—are thriving.

As the largest city in the county, San Bernardino is the perfect location for aspiring creative artists who seek a metropolitan lifestyle, consistently pleasant weather, and an abundance of outdoor activities. Surfing, water sports, tennis, golf, jogging, mountain biking, and many other outdoor activities are readily available. Mountains, deserts, and the attractions in L.A. are just an hour or two away.

San Bernardino is also close enough to Los Angeles to put the arts and entertainment capital of the world within easy reach for students. L.A. is home to a myriad of museums and galleries, including The Los Angeles County Museum of Art, The Museum of Contemporary Art, The J. Paul Getty Museum, and The Norton Simon Museum. Students can enjoy music and theater under the stars at the Hollywood Bowl or the Greek Theatre, or inside at the Music Center or Dorothy Chandler Pavilion.

L.A.'s iconic sights are all close at hand. Students can drive Sunset Boulevard and the Sunset Strip; visit the Comedy Store, the House of Blues, or Whisky A Go-Go; cruise through Beverly Hills, Pacific Palisades, and Malibu; stop at Grauman's Chinese Theater and walk the Hollywood Walk of Fame; take a studio tour; stroll the paved paths of Venice Beach; or walk the Santa Monica Pier.

L.A. continues to be an economic powerhouse. The city continues to grow; the County of Los Angeles leads the nation in manufacturing. Since L.A. is home to industry giants such as Disney/Capital Cities, ABC, CBS Television City, Paramount, Columbia, and Universal Studios, it's not surprising that the majority of projected new jobs in the city are in the technological and creative areas of the entertainment field.

The best of both worlds—a small-city lifestyle just a short excursion from L.A.—that's what's available for students at The Art Institute of California—Inland Empire.

Programs of Study and Degrees

Creativity is all around, and with millions of tomorrow's jobs in creative fields, the world needs more creative professionals. No matter which course of study a student chooses, the instructors at The Art Institutes will guide, support, and help students fine-tune their visual thinking and problem solving, so that they can take advantage of the world's growing creative opportunities and put their passion to work. Programs are offered in the areas of design, which focuses on communicating conceptually and helping people connect in living and work spaces; media arts, that centers on utilizing technology to deliver information and entertainment; fashion, where students learn anything from designing clothes for the runway to running a retail shop; and culinary, which exposes learners to international cuisines as well as restaurant management techniques.

Bachelor's degree programs are offered in the areas of advertising, audio production, culinary management, design & technical graphics, designing for tablets: digital publishing, digital filmmaking & video production, digital photography, fashion & retail management, fashion design, game art & design, graphic & web design, hospitality food & beverage management, interior design, and media arts & animation.

Associate degree programs are offered in the areas of audio production, baking & pastry, culinary arts, digital photography, and graphic design.

Diploma programs are offered in art of cooking, baking & pastry, fashion retailing, and web design & interactive communications.

The Associate of Science in culinary arts and the Bachelor of Science in interior design are available in evening and weekend format.

Program availability and degree offerings are subject to change.

Academic Facilities

The Art Institute of California—Inland Empire provides a learning environment with professional-grade technology applicable to each student's course of study. Students have the opportunity to build a portfolio of work that shows potential employers that they are trained to use the software, hardware, or equipment utilized within the industry. Depending upon the course of study, students are immersed in a creative environment—from classrooms to computer labs to studios—focused on relevant, hands-on education designed to prepare them for the real world.

Costs

Actual tuition and housing costs will vary depending on program, number of credits enrolled, and living arrangements. Prospective students should contact a Student Financial Services professional at the school for details.

Financial Aid

Financial aid is available for those who qualify. Students who require financial assistance should first complete and submit the Free Application for Federal Student Aid (FAFSA) online at www.fafsa.ed.gov and meet with a financial aid officer. Students may also apply for a number of scholarships focusing on their specific areas of career interest.

Faculty

Faculty members are hands-on creative professionals with proven experience as business leaders and innovators, hosting a learning environment similar to the career world students will face after graduation. Part instructor, part mentor, their mission is to help develop and transform creative potential into high-demand marketable skills.

Admission Requirements

Prospective students should refer to the current academic catalog for full details regarding admission requirements and process.

Application and Information

To obtain an application, make arrangements for an interview, or tour the school, prospective students should contact:

The Art Institute of California—Inland Empire, a campus of Argosy University
674 East Brier Drive
San Bernardino, California 92408-2800
Phone: 909-915-2100
      800-353-0812 (toll-free)
Fax: 909-915-2130
Website: http://www.artinstitutes.edu/inlandempire

THE ART INSTITUTE OF CALIFORNIA— LOS ANGELES, A CAMPUS OF ARGOSY UNIVERSITY

SANTA MONICA, CALIFORNIA

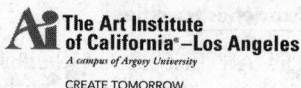

The Art Institute of California—Los Angeles, a campus of Argosy University, is one of The Art Institutes, a system of over fifty schools throughout North America dedicated to providing hands-on education in the creative and applied arts. The Art Institute of California—Los Angeles offers bachelor's and associate degree programs as well as non-degree programs for students interested in pursuing career opportunities from among tomorrow's 15 million jobs in creative fields like design, fashion, media arts, and culinary (based on information from the U.S. Bureau of Labor Statistics for job growth from 2012 to 2022).

A focused education from The Art Institute of California—Los Angeles can help students turn their creative energy into a powerful tool that can make a difference in the world. Students are part of a collaborative and supportive community, where experienced instructors provide the guidance and skills needed to pursue a career in the creative economy.

The Art Institute of California—Los Angeles is also an important resource for creative industry leaders who value the opportunity provided students to learn by using professional-grade technology to build a portfolio of work to show potential employers after graduation.

Accreditation

The Art Institute of California—Los Angeles is a campus of Argosy University. Argosy University is accredited by the Accrediting Commission for Senior Colleges and Universities of the Western Association of Schools and Colleges (985 Atlantic Avenue, Suite 100, Alameda, California, 94501; http://www.wascsenior.org).

The interior design program leading to the Bachelor of Science degree is accredited by the Council for Interior Design Accreditation, www.accredit-id.org, 206 Grandville Avenue, Suite 350, Grand Rapids, Michigan 49503.

The Bachelor of Science degree in culinary management, the Associate of Science degree in culinary arts, the Associate of Science degree in baking & pastry, and diploma programs in art of cooking and baking & pastry are accredited by The Accrediting Commission of the American Culinary Federation Education Foundation.

Location

Los Angeles, the arts and entertainment capital of the world, is the second largest city in the United States. Business, industry, culture, activity, and an enviable climate make this an excellent environment for students pursuing an education in the creative arts.

Immigrants have brought a rich diversity of food, fashion, architecture, entertainment, languages, religions, and world-views, and that are showcased in the largest number of community and ethnic festivals in the nation. L.A. is also home to a myriad of museums and galleries, including the Los Angeles County Museum of Art, the Museum of Contemporary Art, the J. Paul Getty Museum, and the Norton Simon Museum. Students can enjoy music and theater under the stars at the Hollywood Bowl or the Greek Theatre, or inside at the Music Center or Dorothy Chandler Pavilion.

L.A. continues to be an economic powerhouse. The Port of Los Angeles has the highest volume in the country, contributing to the city's status as the largest trade center in the United States and the fifteenth largest economy in the world. The city continues to grow; the County of Los Angeles leads the nation in manufacturing.

Since L.A. is home to industry giants such as Disney/Capital Cities, ABC, CBS Television City, Paramount, Columbia and Universal Studios, it's not surprising that the majority of projected new jobs in the city are in the technological and creative areas of the entertainment field.

L.A. is full of iconic sights and attractions. Students can cruise Sunset Boulevard and the Sunset Strip; stop at the Comedy Store, the House of Blues, or Whisky A Go-Go; drive through Beverly Hills, Pacific Palisades, and Malibu; visit Grauman's Chinese Theater and walk the Hollywood Walk of Fame to see the names of their favorite stars; take a studio tour; stroll the paved paths of Venice Beach; or walk the Santa Monica Pier.

Opportunities to view professional sports abound. There's almost always a baseball game in town during the season—the L.A. Dodgers play at beautiful Chavez Ravine and the Angels play at Angel Stadium of Anaheim. Likewise, there are two local NHL teams—the L.A. Kings play at Staples Center while the Anaheim Ducks call Honda Center home. And both the Clippers and Lakers of the NBA play at Staples Center.

Programs of Study and Degrees

Creativity is all around, and with millions of tomorrow's jobs in creative fields, the world needs more creative professionals. No matter which course of study a student chooses, the instructors at The Art Institutes will guide, support, and help students fine-tune their visual thinking and problem solving, so that they can take advantage of the world's growing creative opportunities and put their passion to work. Programs are offered in the areas of design, which focuses on communicating conceptually and helping people connect in living and work spaces; media arts, that centers on utilizing technology to deliver information and entertainment; fashion, where students learn anything from designing clothes for the runway to running a retail shop; and culinary, which exposes learners to international cuisines as well as restaurant management techniques.

Bachelor's degree programs are offered in the areas of advertising, audio production, culinary management, designing for tablets: digital publishing, digital cinema & video production, digital photography, fashion design, fashion marketing & management, game art & design, game programming, graphic & web design, hospitality food & beverage management, interior design, media arts & animation, and visual effects & motion graphics.

Associate degree programs are offered in the areas of audio production, baking & pastry, culinary arts, digital photography, graphic design, video production, and web design & interactive media.

Diploma programs are offered in art of cooking, baking & pastry, fashion retailing, and web design & interactive communications.

The Associate in Arts in culinary arts, the Bachelor of Science in culinary management, and the Bachelor of Science in interior design are available in evening and weekend formats.

Program availability and degree offerings are subject to change.

Academic Facilities

The Art Institute of California—Los Angeles provides a learning environment with professional-grade technology applicable to each student's course of study. Students have the opportunity to build a portfolio of work that shows potential employers that they are trained to use the software, hardware, or equipment utilized within the industry. Depending upon the course of study, students are immersed in a creative environment—from classrooms to computer labs to studios—focused on relevant, hands-on education designed to prepare them for the real world.

Costs

Actual tuition and housing costs will vary depending on program, number of credits enrolled, and living arrangements. Prospective students should contact a Student Financial Services professional at the school for details.

Financial Aid

Financial aid is available for those who qualify. Students who require financial assistance should first complete and submit the Free Application for Federal Student Aid (FAFSA) online at www.fafsa.ed.gov and meet with a financial aid officer. Students may also apply for a number of scholarships focusing on their specific areas of career interest.

Faculty

Faculty members are hands-on creative professionals with proven experience as business leaders and innovators, hosting a learning environment similar to the career world students will face after graduation. Part instructor, part mentor, their mission is to help develop and transform creative potential into high-demand marketable skills.

Admission Requirements

Prospective students should refer to the current academic catalog for full details regarding admission requirements and process.

Application and Information

To obtain an application, make arrangements for an interview, or tour the school, prospective students should contact:

The Art Institute of California—Los Angeles, a campus of
   Argosy University
2900 31st Street
Santa Monica, California 90405-3035
Phone: 310-752-4700
      888-646-4610 (toll-free)
Fax: 310-752-4708
Website: http://www.artinstitutes.edu/losangeles

THE ART INSTITUTE OF CALIFORNIA—ORANGE COUNTY, A CAMPUS OF ARGOSY UNIVERSITY

The Art Institute of California—Orange County
A campus of Argosy University
CREATE TOMORROW

SANTA ANA, CALIFORNIA

The Art Institute of California—Orange County, a campus of Argosy University, is one of The Art Institutes, a system of over fifty schools throughout North America dedicated to providing hands-on education in the creative and applied arts. The Art Institute of California—Orange County offers bachelor's and associate degree programs as well as non-degree programs for students interested in pursuing career opportunities from among tomorrow's 15 million jobs in creative fields like design, fashion, media arts, and culinary (based on information from the U.S. Bureau of Labor Statistics for job growth from 2012 to 2022).

A focused education from The Art Institute of California—Orange County can help students turn their creative energy into a powerful tool that can make a difference in the world. Students are part of a collaborative and supportive community, where experienced instructors provide the guidance and skills needed to pursue a career in the creative economy.

The Art Institute of California—Orange County is also an important resource for creative industry leaders who value the opportunity provided students to learn by using professional-grade technology to build a portfolio of work to show potential employers after graduation.

Accreditation

The Art Institute of California—Orange County is a campus of Argosy University. Argosy University is accredited by the Accrediting Commission for Senior Colleges and Universities of the Western Association of Schools and Colleges (985 Atlantic Avenue, Suite 100, Alameda, California, 94501; http://www.wascsenior.org).

The interior design program leading to the Bachelor of Science degree is accredited by the Council for Interior Design Accreditation, www.accredit-id.org, 206 Grandville Avenue, Suite 350, Grand Rapids, Michigan 49503.

Location

Welcome aspiring designers, animators, gamers, and chefs—with a thriving metropolis, coastal living, and a creative energy second to none, Orange County is a great place to live, work, and learn.

The Art Institute of California—Orange County sits in a strategic location at the heart of the booming Southern California region that includes the counties of Orange, Los Angeles, San Diego, and Ventura, with a combined population of over 18 million. Southern California is a central hub to the entertainment, advertising, design, aerospace, and culinary industries.

Orange County offers 42 miles of beautiful, sandy, Pacific coastline. Laguna Beach, San Juan Capistrano, and Newport Beach are known the world over, and Huntington Beach is famous as Surf City USA. Wilderness and mountain parks are minutes away for camping, hiking, and biking. Orange County also boasts famous attractions like Disneyland and Knott's Berry Farm, along with events like the annual Laguna Beach Festival of Arts/Pageant of the Masters, and Broadway-quality entertainment at the Orange County Performing Arts Center. Add to this one of the best climates in the world, with more than 250 sunny days a year, and it's no wonder more than 35 million people visit Orange County annually.

The Art Institute of California—Orange County is located in the heart of the county's South Coast Metro region. The new, modern facility is ideally situated in proximity to Orange County's thriving business community, cultural attractions, shopping, entertainment, and famous beaches. Many students commute from the county's more than thirty towns and communities, while others choose apartment living in school-sponsored housing just 2 miles from campus. And it's close enough to Los Angeles to put the arts and entertainment capital of the world within easy reach.

L.A. has a myriad of museums and galleries, including the Los Angeles County Museum of Art, the Museum of Contemporary Art, the J. Paul Getty Museum, and the Norton Simon Museum. Students can enjoy music and theater under the stars at the Hollywood Bowl or the Greek Theatre, or inside at the Music Center or Dorothy Chandler Pavilion.

Since L.A. is home to industry giants such as Disney/Capital Cities, ABC, CBS Television City, Paramount, Columbia, and Universal Studios, it's not surprising that the majority of projected new jobs in the city are in the technological and creative areas of the entertainment field.

The best of both worlds—a small-city lifestyle just a short excursion from L.A.—that's what's available to students at The Art Institute of California—Orange County.

Programs of Study and Degrees

Creativity is all around, and with millions of tomorrow's jobs in creative fields, the world needs more creative professionals. No matter which course of study a student chooses, the instructors at The Art Institutes will guide, support, and help students fine-tune their visual thinking and problem solving, so that they can take advantage of the world's growing creative opportunities and put their passion to work. Programs are offered in the areas of design, which focuses on communicating conceptually and helping people connect in living and work spaces; media arts, that centers on utilizing technology to deliver information and entertainment; fashion, where students learn anything from designing clothes for the runway to running a retail shop; and culinary, which exposes learners to international cuisines as well as restaurant management techniques.

Bachelor's degree programs are offered in the areas of advertising, culinary management, designing for tablets: digital publishing, digital filmmaking & video production, digital photography, fashion design, fashion marketing & management, game art & design, graphic & web design, hospitality food & beverage management, industrial design, interior design, media arts & animation, visual & game programming, and visual effects & motion graphics.

Associate degree programs are offered in the areas of baking & pastry, culinary arts, digital photography, graphic design, and web design & interactive media.

Diploma programs are offered in art of cooking, baking & pastry, fashion retailing, and web design & interactive communications.

The Associate of Science in culinary arts, the Bachelor of Science in culinary management, and the Bachelor of Fine Arts in interior design are available in evening and weekend formats.

Program availability and degree offerings are subject to change.

Academic Facilities

The Art Institute of California—Orange County provides a learning environment with professional-grade technology applicable to each student's course of study. Students have the opportunity to build a portfolio of work that shows potential employers that they are trained to use the software, hardware, or equipment utilized within the industry. Depending upon the course of study, students are immersed in a creative environment—from classrooms to computer labs to studios—focused on relevant, hands-on education designed to prepare them for the real world.

Costs

Actual tuition and housing costs will vary depending on program, number of credits enrolled, and living arrangements. Prospective students should contact a Student Financial Services professional at the school for details.

Financial Aid

Financial aid is available for those who qualify. Students who require financial assistance should first complete and submit the Free Application for Federal Student Aid (FAFSA) online at www.fafsa.ed.gov and meet with a financial aid officer. Students may also apply for a number of scholarships focusing on their specific areas of career interest.

Faculty

Faculty members are hands-on creative professionals with proven experience as business leaders and innovators, hosting a learning environment similar to the career world students will face after graduation. Part instructor, part mentor, their mission is to help develop and transform creative potential into high-demand marketable skills.

Admission Requirements

Prospective students should refer to the current academic catalog for full details regarding admission requirements and process.

Application and Information

To obtain an application, make arrangements for an interview, or tour the school, prospective students should contact:

The Art Institute of California—Orange County, a campus of Argosy University
3601 West Sunflower Avenue
Santa Ana, California 92704-7931
Phone: 714-830-0200
      888-549-3055 (toll-free)
Fax: 714-556-1923
Website: http://www.artinstitutes.edu/orangecounty

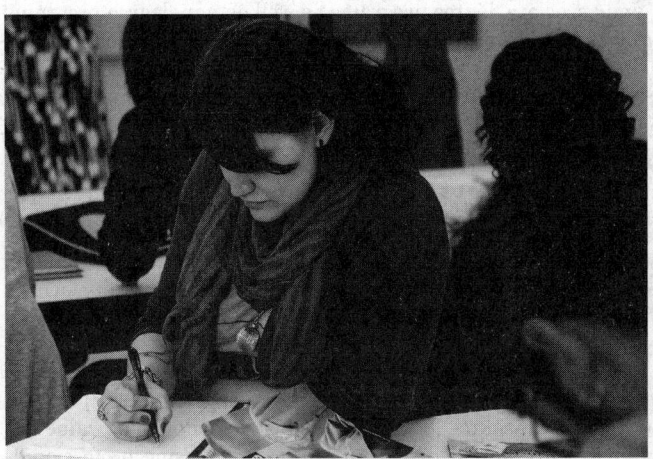

COLLEGE CLOSE-UPS

THE ART INSTITUTE OF CALIFORNIA— SACRAMENTO, A CAMPUS OF ARGOSY UNIVERSITY

SACRAMENTO, CALIFORNIA

The Art Institute of California—Sacramento, a campus of Argosy University, is one of The Art Institutes, a system of over fifty schools throughout North America dedicated to providing hands-on education in the creative and applied arts. The Art Institute of California—Sacramento offers bachelor's and associate degree programs as well as non-degree programs for students interested in pursuing career opportunities from among tomorrow's 15 million jobs in creative fields like design, fashion, media arts, and culinary (based on information from the U.S. Bureau of Labor Statistics for job growth from 2012 to 2022).

A focused education from The Art Institute of California—Sacramento can help students turn their creative energy into a powerful tool that can make a difference in the world. Students are part of a collaborative and supportive community, where experienced instructors provide the guidance and skills needed to pursue a career in the creative economy.

The Art Institute of California—Sacramento is also an important resource for creative industry leaders who value the opportunity provided students to learn by using professional-grade technology to build a portfolio of work to show potential employers after graduation.

Accreditation

The Art Institute of California—Sacramento is a campus of Argosy University. Argosy University is accredited by the Accrediting Commission for Senior Colleges and Universities of the Western Association of Schools and Colleges (985 Atlantic Avenue, Suite 100, Alameda, California, 94501; http://www.wascsenior.org).

Location

When it comes to deciding where to pursue a creative education, location matters. And location is what makes The Art Institute of California—Sacramento an appealing choice. The weather, the recreation, and quality of life make Sacramento a great place to live, study, and work.

Greater Sacramento has been cited as one of the five most livable regions in America. A former gold rush town, Sacramento is now the fourth largest city in California. In addition to state government, the city is a major transportation and commerce hub linking the East with California's coastal cities. It is also a major cultural center, with playhouses, ballet, concert venues, and two professional basketball teams.

The Sacramento Second Saturday Art Walk provides a unique opportunity to view original art and meet the artists who create it. Among the city's museums, the most notable might be the Crocker Art Museum, the oldest public art museum west of the Mississippi.

In addition, Sacramento isn't far from some of the most beautiful parks and other natural resources in the world, including Yosemite National Park and Lake Tahoe.

It's also close enough to San Francisco, one of the most cosmopolitan cities in the world, where cable cars, incredible cuisine, an array of museums, and world-famous attractions like the Golden Gate Bridge and Chinatown await. The city offers a seemingly endless list of attractions: the Golden Gate Bridge, Chinatown, Alcatraz, Fisherman's Wharf, Pier 39, Ghirardelli Square, Coit Tower, Telegraph Hill, Haight-Ashbury, and more.

The Bay Area also offers a wealth of sports action. The San Francisco Giants play baseball at AT&T Park, and the NFL's 49ers play at Candlestick Park. Across the bay there's the Oakland A's, the Raiders, and the Golden State Warriors. Hockey can be found in San Jose with the NHL's Sharks. And the NBA's Sacramento Kings play basketball at the Sleep Train Arena.

Students at The Art Institute of California—Sacramento can work toward a creative career while being within easy reach of some of the world's most popular attractions.

Programs of Study and Degrees

Creativity is all around, and with millions of tomorrow's jobs in creative fields, the world needs more creative professionals. No matter which course of study a student chooses, the instructors at The Art Institutes will guide, support, and help students fine-tune their visual thinking and problem solving, so that they can take advantage of the world's growing creative opportunities and put their passion to work. Programs are offered in the areas of design, which focuses on communicating conceptually and helping people connect in living and work spaces; media arts, that centers on utilizing technology to deliver information and entertainment; fashion, where students learn anything from designing clothes for the runway to running a retail shop; and culinary, which exposes learners to international cuisines as well as restaurant management techniques.

Bachelor's degree programs are offered in the areas of advertising, culinary management, designing for tablets: digital publishing, digital filmmaking & video production, game art & design, graphic & web design, hospitality food & beverage management, interior design, and media arts & animation.

Associate degree programs are offered in the areas of baking & pastry, culinary arts, graphic design, and web design & interactive media.

Diploma programs are offered in art of cooking, baking & pastry, fashion retailing, and web design & interactive communications.

Program availability and degree offerings are subject to change.

Academic Facilities

The Art Institute of California—Sacramento provides a learning environment with professional-grade technology applicable to each student's course of study. Students have the opportunity to build a portfolio of work that shows potential employers that

they are trained to use the software, hardware, or equipment utilized within the industry. Depending upon the course of study, students are immersed in a creative environment—from classrooms to computer labs to studios—focused on relevant, hands-on education designed to prepare them for the real world.

Costs

Actual tuition and housing costs will vary depending on program, number of credits enrolled, and living arrangements. Prospective students should contact a Student Financial Services professional at the school for details.

Financial Aid

Financial aid is available for those who qualify. Students who require financial assistance should first complete and submit the Free Application for Federal Student Aid (FAFSA) online at www.fafsa.ed.gov and meet with a financial aid officer. Students may also apply for a number of scholarships focusing on their specific areas of career interest.

Faculty

Faculty members are hands-on creative professionals with proven experience as business leaders and innovators, hosting a learning environment similar to the career world students will face after graduation. Part instructor, part mentor, their mission is to help develop and transform creative potential into high-demand marketable skills.

Admission Requirements

Prospective students should refer to the current academic catalog for full details regarding admission requirements and process.

Application and Information

To obtain an application, make arrangements for an interview, or tour the school, prospective students should contact:

The Art Institute of California—Sacramento, a campus of
  Argosy University
2850 Gateway Oaks Drive
Suite #100
Sacramento, California 95833
Phone: 916-830-6320
        800-477-1957 (toll-free)
Fax: 916-830-6344
Website: http://www.artinstitutes.edu/sacramento

THE ART INSTITUTE OF CALIFORNIA— SAN DIEGO, A CAMPUS OF ARGOSY UNIVERSITY

SAN DIEGO, CALIFORNIA

The Art Institute of California—San Diego, a campus of Argosy University, is one of The Art Institutes, a system of over fifty schools throughout North America dedicated to providing hands-on education in the creative and applied arts. The Art Institute of California—San Diego offers bachelor's and associate degree programs as well as non-degree programs for students interested in pursuing career opportunities from among tomorrow's 15 million jobs in creative fields like design, fashion, media arts, and culinary (based on information from the U.S. Bureau of Labor Statistics for job growth from 2012 to 2022).

A focused education from The Art Institute of California—San Diego can help students turn their creative energy into a powerful tool that can make a difference in the world. Students are part of a collaborative and supportive community, where experienced instructors provide the guidance and skills needed to pursue a career in the creative economy.

The Art Institute of California—San Diego is also an important resource for creative industry leaders who value the opportunity provided students to learn by using professional-grade technology to build a portfolio of work to show potential employers after graduation.

Accreditation

The Art Institute of California—San Diego is a campus of Argosy University. Argosy University is accredited by the Accrediting Commission for Senior Colleges and Universities of the Western Association of Schools and Colleges (985 Atlantic Avenue, Suite 100, Alameda, California, 94501; http://www.wascsenior.org).

The Associate of Science degree in culinary arts and baking & pastry and Bachelor of Science degree in culinary management are accredited by The Accrediting Commission of the American Culinary Federation Education Foundation.

The interior design program leading to the Bachelor of Science degree is accredited by the Council for Interior Design Accreditation, www.accredit-id.org; 206 Grandville Avenue, Suite 350, Grand Rapids, Michigan 49503.

Location

Located in the heart of San Diego's Mission Valley, The Art Institute of California—San Diego is ideally situated in close proximity to the area's thriving business community, cultural attractions, shopping, entertainment and, of course, its famous beaches.

Travel and Leisure magazine readers rank San Diego as their favorite year-round vacation spot in the entire country. As California's second-largest city, it's the perfect location for aspiring creative professionals who are looking for a metropolitan lifestyle, consistently great weather, and an abundance of outdoor activities.

The city's winning combination of atmosphere and energy attracts leaders from industries that demand a constant supply of creative talent to fuel their success. Likewise, San Diego's international influences and ever-growing tourism provide a world of opportunities for inspiration and for establishing a

career. *Forbes* magazine has named San Diego "Best Place in America for Business and Careers."

Drive just an hour or two from the school, and students can enjoy just about any terrain, scenery, or activity imaginable— mountains, deserts, coastal canyons, forests, or ocean, providing opportunities for surfing, swimming, boating, hiking, tennis, golf, jogging, biking, and more. Los Angeles, the media and entertainment capital of the world, is to the north, while Mexico is to the south.

San Diego offers many regional shopping centers, a wide range of eateries, and destination spots such as the world-class San Diego Zoo. Numerous attractions help spur creativity: Opera, the symphony, a live theater district, and concerts are all readily available. The city's museums include the San Diego Museum of Art, the San Diego Natural History Museum, the San Diego Museum of Man, the Museum of Photographic Arts, the San Diego Maritime Museum, and the San Diego Aircraft Carrier Museum. The Museum of Contemporary Art San Diego (MCASD) is located in nearby La Jolla, with a branch at the Santa Fe Depot downtown.

There are many professional sports teams in San Diego, most notably the Padres, who play baseball at Petco Park, and the NFL's Chargers, who call Qualcomm Stadium home. And San Diego's climate has been rated as one of the ten best by the *Farmer's Almanac,* and as one of the two best summer climates by The Weather Channel.

Programs of Study and Degrees

Creativity is all around, and with millions of tomorrow's jobs in creative fields, the world needs more creative professionals. No matter which course of study a student chooses, the instructors at The Art Institutes will guide, support, and help students fine-tune their visual thinking and problem solving, so that they can take advantage of the world's growing creative opportunities and put their passion to work. Programs are offered in the areas of design, which focuses on communicating conceptually and helping people connect in living and work spaces; media arts, that centers on utilizing technology to deliver information and entertainment; fashion, where students learn anything from designing clothes for the runway to running a retail shop; and culinary, which exposes learners to international cuisines as well as restaurant management techniques.

Bachelor's degree programs are offered in the areas of advertising, audio production, culinary management, design & technical graphics, designing for tablets: digital publishing, digital photography, fashion design, fashion marketing & management, game art & design, graphic & web design, hospitality food & beverage management, interior design, media arts & animation, and visual & game programming.

Associate degree programs are offered in the areas of advertising, audio production, baking & pastry, culinary arts, digital photography, and graphic design.

Diploma programs are offered in art of cooking, baking & pastry, fashion retailing, and web design & interactive communications.

The Bachelor of Fine Arts in interior design is available in evening and weekend formats.

Program availability and degree offerings are subject to change.

Academic Facilities

The Art Institute of California—San Diego provides a learning environment with professional-grade technology applicable to each student's course of study. Students have the opportunity to build a portfolio of work that shows potential employers that they are trained to use the software, hardware, or equipment utilized within the industry. Depending upon the course of study, students are immersed in a creative environment—from classrooms to computer labs to studios—focused on relevant, hands-on education designed to prepare them for the real world.

Costs

Actual tuition and housing costs will vary depending on program, number of credits enrolled, and living arrangements. Prospective students should contact a Student Financial Services professional at the school for details.

Financial Aid

Financial aid is available for those who qualify. Students who require financial assistance should first complete and submit the Free Application for Federal Student Aid (FAFSA) online at www.fafsa.ed.gov and meet with a financial aid officer. Students may also apply for a number of scholarships focusing on their specific areas of career interest.

Faculty

Faculty members are hands-on creative professionals with proven experience as business leaders and innovators, hosting a learning environment similar to the career world students will face after graduation. Part instructor, part mentor, their mission is to help develop and transform creative potential into high-demand marketable skills.

Admission Requirements

Prospective students should refer to the current academic catalog for full details regarding admission requirements and process.

Application and Information

To obtain an application, make arrangements for an interview, or tour the school, prospective students should contact:

The Art Institute of California—San Diego, a campus of
  Argosy University
7650 Mission Valley Road
San Diego, California 92108-4423
Phone: 858-598-1200
      866-275-2422 (toll-free)
Fax: 619-291-3206
Website: http://www.artinstitutes.edu/sandiego

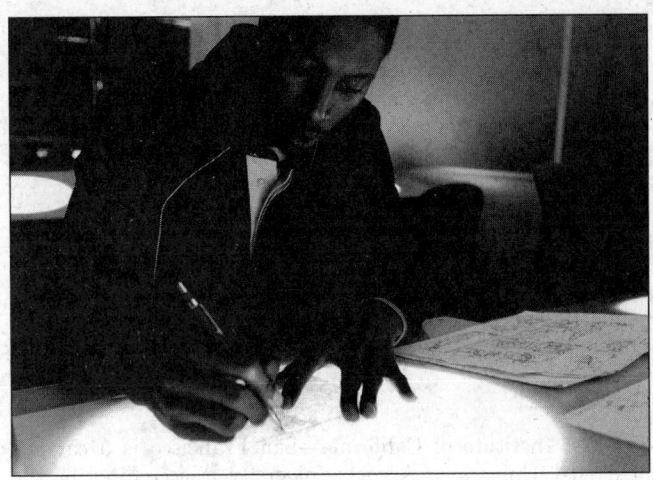

THE ART INSTITUTE OF CALIFORNIA— SAN FRANCISCO, A CAMPUS OF ARGOSY UNIVERSITY

SAN FRANCISCO, CALIFORNIA

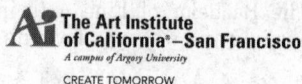

The Art Institute of California—San Francisco, a campus of Argosy University, is one of The Art Institutes, a system of over fifty schools throughout North America dedicated to providing hands-on education in the creative and applied arts. The Art Institute of California—San Francisco offers master's, bachelor's, and associate degree programs as well as non-degree programs for students interested in pursuing career opportunities from among tomorrow's 15 million jobs in creative fields like design, fashion, media arts, and culinary (based on information from the U.S. Bureau of Labor Statistics for job growth from 2012 to 2022).

A focused education from The Art Institute of California—San Francisco can help students turn their creative energy into a powerful tool that can make a difference in the world. Students are part of a collaborative and supportive community, where experienced instructors provide the guidance and skills needed to pursue a career in the creative economy.

The Art Institute of California—San Francisco is also an important resource for creative industry leaders who value the opportunity provided students to learn by using professional-grade technology to build a portfolio of work to show potential employers after graduation.

Accreditation

The Art Institute of California—San Francisco is a campus of Argosy University. Argosy University is accredited by the Accrediting Commission for Senior Colleges and Universities of the Western Association of Schools and Colleges (985 Atlantic Avenue, Suite 100, Alameda, California, 94501; http://www.wascsenior.org).

Location

San Francisco has much to offer: diverse neighborhoods, world-class landmarks, unparalleled cuisine, and a cutting-edge arts community. Add quality educational programs to the mix and you'll find another reason to come to The Art Institute of California—San Francisco.

Attending school here means that students will have the benefits of a world-class city right at hand. The campus is located in the heart of San Francisco, in the vibrant Civic Center, just steps from all forms of public transportation and a weekly farmer's market and an art and craft market. It's just minutes from shopping, dining, museums, and galleries.

Creativity can be fueled at any one of the city's many museums, such as the Exploratorium in the Palace of Fine Arts—one of the first modern science museums and still among the best. The California Palace of the Legion of Honor boasts a collection of works by Monet, Picasso, and Rodin.

Then there are all the sights and sounds that make San Francisco one of the top destinations in the country. Cable cars, the city's moving landmarks; Alcatraz Island; the world-famous Golden Gate Bridge; Chinatown; Lombard Street, billed as the world's crookedest street; Golden Gate Park, which is even larger than Central Park; Fisherman's Wharf, Pier 39, and Ghirardelli Square for the food, clam chowder, street performers, and sea lions; Coit Tower on Telegraph Hill; Haight-Ashbury; and many more.

The Bay Area is also a sports fan's paradise. The San Francisco Giants play baseball at AT&T Park and the NFL's 49ers at Candlestick Park. Across the bay, the Oakland A's and Raiders play at Oakland-Alameda County Coliseum, and the Golden State Warriors of the NBA play at Oracle Arena. To the south are the NHL's San Jose Sharks.

It's easy to get to and from the campus of The Art Institute of California—San Francisco. The school is located at a public transportation hub in the Civic Center that links all major public transportation systems. BART (Bay Area Rapid Transit) arrives from the East Bay and Daly City. Students who live in the city can easily get to the school via MUNI.

Programs of Study and Degrees

Creativity is all around, and with millions of tomorrow's jobs in creative fields, the world needs more creative professionals. No matter which course of study a student chooses, the instructors at The Art Institutes will guide, support, and help students fine-tune their visual thinking and problem solving, so that they can take advantage of the world's growing creative opportunities and put their passion to work. Programs are offered in the areas of design, which focuses on communicating conceptually and helping people connect in living and work spaces; media arts, that centers on utilizing technology to deliver information and entertainment; fashion, where students learn anything from designing clothes for the runway to running a retail shop; and culinary, which exposes learners to international cuisines as well as restaurant management techniques.

A Master of Fine Arts degree program is offered in computer animation.

Bachelor's degree programs are offered in the areas of advertising, audio production, culinary management, designing for tablets: digital publishing, digital filmmaking & video production, digital photography, fashion design, fashion marketing & management, game art & design, graphic & web design, interior design, media arts & animation, visual & game programming, and visual effects & motion graphics.

Associate degree programs are offered in the areas of baking & pastry, culinary arts, digital photography, fashion design, fashion marketing, graphic design, and web design & interactive media.

Diploma programs are offered in art of cooking, baking & pastry, fashion retailing, and web design & interactive communications.

Program availability and degree offerings are subject to change.

COLLEGE CLOSE-UPS

Academic Facilities

The Art Institute of California—San Francisco provides a learning environment with professional-grade technology applicable to each student's course of study. Students have the opportunity to build a portfolio of work that shows potential employers that they are trained to use the software, hardware, or equipment utilized within the industry. Depending upon the course of study, students are immersed in a creative environment—from classrooms to computer labs to studios—focused on relevant, hands-on education designed to prepare them for the real world.

Costs

Actual tuition and housing costs will vary depending on program, number of credits enrolled, and living arrangements. Prospective students should contact a Student Financial Services professional at the school for details.

Financial Aid

Financial aid is available for those who qualify. Students who require financial assistance should first complete and submit the Free Application for Federal Student Aid (FAFSA) online at www.fafsa.ed.gov and meet with a financial aid officer. Students may also apply for a number of scholarships focusing on their specific areas of career interest.

Faculty

Faculty members are hands-on creative professionals with proven experience as business leaders and innovators, hosting a learning environment similar to the career world students will face after graduation. Part instructor, part mentor, their mission is to help develop and transform creative potential into high-demand marketable skills.

Admission Requirements

Prospective students should refer to the current academic catalog for full details regarding admission requirements and process.

Application and Information

To obtain an application, make arrangements for an interview, or tour the school, prospective students should contact:

The Art Institute of California—San Francisco, a campus of
   Argosy University
1170 Market Street
San Francisco, California 94102-4928
Phone: 415-865-0198
        888-493-3261 (toll-free)
Fax: 415-863-6344
Website: http://www.artinstitutes.edu/sanfrancisco

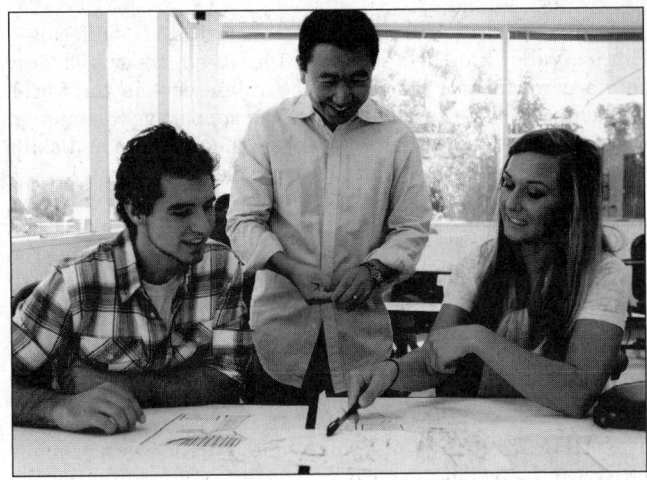

THE ART INSTITUTE OF CALIFORNIA— SILICON VALLEY, A CAMPUS OF ARGOSY UNIVERSITY

SUNNYVALE, CALIFORNIA

The Art Institute of California—Silicon Valley, a campus of Argosy University, is one of The Art Institutes, a system of over fifty schools throughout North America dedicated to providing hands-on education in the creative and applied arts. The Art Institute of California—Silicon Valley offers bachelor's and associate degree programs as well as non-degree programs for students interested in pursuing career opportunities from among tomorrow's 15 million jobs in creative fields like design, fashion, media arts, and culinary (based on information from the U.S. Bureau of Labor Statistics for job growth from 2012 to 2022).

A focused education from The Art Institute of California— Silicon Valley can help students turn their creative energy into a powerful tool that can make a difference in the world. Students are part of a collaborative and supportive community, where experienced instructors provide the guidance and skills needed to pursue a career in the creative economy.

The Art Institute of California—Silicon Valley is also an important resource for creative industry leaders who value the opportunity provided students to learn by using professional-grade technology to build a portfolio of work to show potential employers after graduation.

Accreditation

The Art Institute of California—Silicon Valley is a campus of Argosy University. Argosy University is accredited by the Accrediting Commission for Senior Colleges and Universities of the Western Association of Schools and Colleges (985 Atlantic Avenue, Suite 100, Alameda, California, 94501; http://www.wascsenior.org).

Location

Steve Jobs, Bill Gates, Mark Zuckerberg—the giants of high-tech and social media. Their names are synonymous with the Silicon Valley, the southern part of the San Francisco Bay Area. Putting aside the fact that it's not really a valley, the term "Silicon Valley" originally referred to the region's many silicon chip innovators and manufacturers, but now it refers to all the high-tech businesses in the area—and in the larger sense, the high-tech sector of the U.S. economy. But for an aspiring student looking to prepare for a creative career, it should also refer to The Art Institute of California—Silicon Valley.

The Bay Area is one of the most beautiful places in the United States. The Northern California climate, clean air, gorgeous public parks, pristine beaches, and stunning mountain ranges lining the Pacific coast offer a year-round outdoor lifestyle. Located 45 minutes from San Francisco Bay and 25 miles from the Pacific Ocean, this cosmopolitan area is also known for its premier cultural events—performing arts, outdoor concerts series, and international festivals. It's also headquarters to Fortune 500 companies like Yahoo!, NetApp, and Advanced Micro Devices, as well as aerospace companies Lockheed Martin and Northrup Grumman.

San Francisco is filled with sites to stimulate the creative mind. The Exploratorium in the Palace of Fine Arts is one of the first modern science museums and still among the best. The California Palace of the Legion of Honor offers a collection of works by Monet, Picasso, and Rodin. The city also boasts dining, shopping, and a long list of well-known attractions: cable cars, the Golden Gate Bridge, Chinatown, Lombard Street, Fisherman's Wharf, Pier 39 and Ghirardelli Square, Alcatraz, and more.

For sports fans, the Bay Area has it all. The San Francisco Giants play baseball at AT&T Park, and the NFL's 49ers play at Candlestick Park. Across the Bay, it's the Oakland A's and Raiders at Oakland-Alameda County Coliseum, or the NBA's Golden State Warriors at Oracle Arena. In addition, the NHL's San Jose Sharks play at San Jose's HP Pavilion.

Programs of Study and Degrees

Creativity is all around, and with millions of tomorrow's jobs in creative fields, the world needs more creative professionals. No matter which course of study a student chooses, the instructors at The Art Institutes will guide, support, and help students fine-tune their visual thinking and problem solving, so that they can take advantage of the world's growing creative opportunities and put their passion to work. Programs are offered in the areas of design, which focuses on communicating conceptually and helping people connect in living and work spaces; media arts, that centers on utilizing technology to deliver information and entertainment; fashion, where students learn anything from designing clothes for the runway to running a retail shop; and culinary, which exposes learners to international cuisines as well as restaurant management techniques.

Bachelor's degree programs are offered in the areas of advertising, culinary management, design & technical graphics, designing for tablets: digital publishing, digital filmmaking & video production, digital photography, fashion marketing & management, game art & design, graphic & web design, hospitality food & beverage management, interior design, media arts & animation, and visual effects & motion graphics.

Associate degree programs are offered in the areas of baking & pastry, culinary arts, digital photography, graphic design, and web design & interactive media.

Diploma programs are offered in art of cooking, baking & pastry, fashion retailing, and web design & interactive communications.

Program availability and degree offerings are subject to change.

Academic Facilities

The Art Institute of California—Silicon Valley provides a learning environment with professional-grade technology applicable to each student's course of study. Students have the opportunity to build a portfolio of work that shows potential employers that they are trained to use the software, hardware, or equipment utilized within the industry. Depending upon the course of study, students are immersed in a creative environment—from classrooms to computer labs to studios—focused on relevant, hands-on education designed to prepare them for the real world.

Costs

Actual tuition and housing costs will vary depending on program, number of credits enrolled, and living arrangements. Prospective students should contact a Student Financial Services professional at the school for details.

Financial Aid

Financial aid is available for those who qualify. Students who require financial assistance should first complete and submit the Free Application for Federal Student Aid (FAFSA) online at www.fafsa.ed.gov and meet with a financial aid officer. Students may also apply for a number of scholarships focusing on their specific areas of career interest.

Faculty

Faculty members are hands-on creative professionals with proven experience as business leaders and innovators, hosting a learning environment similar to the career world students will face after graduation. Part instructor, part mentor, their mission is to help develop and transform creative potential into high-demand marketable skills.

Admission Requirements

Prospective students should refer to the current academic catalog for full details regarding admission requirements and process.

Application and Information

To obtain an application, make arrangements for an interview, or tour the school, prospective students should contact:

The Art Institute of California—Silicon Valley, a campus of
    Argosy University
1120 Kifer Road
Sunnyvale, California 94086
Phone: 408-962-6400
        866-583-7961 (toll-free)
Fax: 408-962-6498
Website: http://www.artinstitutes.edu/sunnyvale

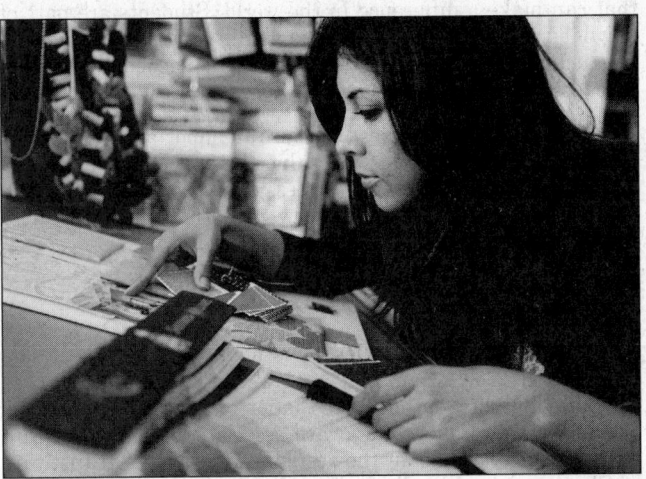

THE ART INSTITUTE OF CHARLESTON
CHARLESTON, SOUTH CAROLINA

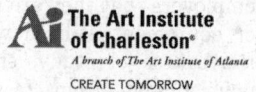

The Art Institute of Charleston, a branch of The Art Institute of Atlanta, is one of The Art Institutes, a system of over fifty schools throughout North America dedicated to providing hands-on education in the creative and applied arts. The Art Institute of Charleston offers bachelor's and associate degree programs as well as non-degree programs for students interested in pursuing career opportunities from among tomorrow's 15 million jobs in creative fields like design, fashion, media arts, and culinary (Based on information from the U.S. Bureau of Labor Statistics for job growth from 2012 to 2022).

A focused education from The Art Institute of Charleston can help students turn their creative energy into a powerful tool that can make a difference in the world. Students are part of a collaborative and supportive community, where experienced instructors provide the guidance and skills needed to pursue a career in the creative economy.

The Art Institute of Charleston is also an important resource for creative industry leaders who value the opportunity provided students to learn by using professional-grade technology to build a portfolio of work to show potential employers after graduation.

Accreditation

The Art Institute of Charleston is a branch campus of The Art Institute of Atlanta. The Art Institute of Atlanta is accredited by the Southern Association of Colleges and Schools Commission on Colleges to award associate and baccalaureate degrees. Questions about the accreditation of The Art Institute of Charleston can be directed to the Commission on Colleges at 1866 Southern Lane, Decatur, Georgia 30033-4097; phone: 404-679-4500.

The Art Institute of Charleston is licensed by the South Carolina Commission on Higher Education, 1122 Lady Street, Suite 300, Columbia, South Carolina 29201; phone: 803-737-2260. Licensure indicates only that minimum standards have been met, it is not equal to or synonymous with accreditation by an accrediting agency recognized by the U.S. Department of Education.

Location

The historic harbor town of Charleston may be small, but it has a little of just about everything for the creative person—a thriving arts community, culturally important architecture and atmosphere, a sense of history, and a quiet but steady creative energy that inspires the imagination.

The campus of The Art Institute of Charleston is located in the middle of this beautiful city, surrounded by opportunities for students to discover exciting new things as they grow personally, academically, and professionally. Charleston, famous as a culinary destination, is also brimming with festivals and events celebrating the visual and performing arts, museums and entertainment, and is considered a new source for many up-and-coming fashion designers.

Charleston is big on creativity, and that gives students the opportunity to make a real impact on—and a significant contribution to—the local design, culinary, fashion, and media scene. They can also gain the kind of real-world experience that can pay off big in the future.

The city streets of coastal Charleston offer a fascinating mix of history, architecture, and culture with a modern sense of style.

King Street is Charleston's main thoroughfare, a shopping mecca that boasts an antiques district, a high-end fashion district, small specialty boutiques, and several art galleries. Perpendicular to King Street is Market Street, featuring the work of local artisans whose talents attract both residents and tourists.

Within a short walk of the school's campus, there is an amazing array of award-winning, legendary restaurants offering regional, classic, and international cuisine—a world of educational opportunities for culinary students and a whole lot of great dining for those with other career interests.

Charleston offers the amenities of a bigger city in a relaxed, friendly, easy-to-navigate community. It's a perfect blend of cosmopolitan culture and small-town charm. And it's a great place for a creative person to learn.

Programs of Study and Degrees

Creativity is all around, and with millions of tomorrow's jobs in creative fields, the world needs more creative professionals. No matter which course of study a student chooses, the instructors at The Art Institutes will guide, support, and help students fine-tune their visual thinking and problem solving, so that they can take advantage of the world's growing creative opportunities and put their passion to work. Programs are offered in the areas of design, which focuses on communicating conceptually and helping people connect in living and work spaces; media arts, that centers on utilizing technology to deliver information and entertainment; fashion, where students learn anything from designing clothes for the runway to running a retail shop; and culinary, which exposes learners to international cuisines as well as restaurant management techniques.

Bachelor's degree programs are offered in the areas of culinary arts management, designing for tablets: digital publishing, digital photography, digital filmmaking & video production, fashion & retail management, fashion design, graphic & web design, and interior design.

Associate degree programs are offered in the areas of culinary arts, culinary arts with a concentration in baking & pastry, graphic & web design, and wine, spirits & beverage management (participation in this program for those under 21 years of age will be conducted in accord with state law regarding the possession and consumption of alcoholic beverages).

Certificate programs are offered in baking & pastry, culinary arts, digital image management, fashion retailing, web design & development, and web design & interactive communications.

Program availability and degree offerings are subject to change.

Academic Facilities

The Art Institute of Charleston provides a learning environment with professional-grade technology applicable to each student's course of study. Students have the opportunity to build a portfolio of work that shows potential employers that they are trained to use the software, hardware, or equipment utilized within the industry. Depending upon the course of study, students are immersed in a creative environment—from classrooms to computer labs to studios—focused on relevant, hands-on education designed to prepare them for the real world.

Costs

Actual tuition and housing costs will vary depending on program, number of credits enrolled, and living arrangements. Prospective students should contact a Student Financial Services professional at the school for details.

Financial Aid

Financial aid is available for those who qualify. Students who require financial assistance should first complete and submit the Free Application for Federal Student Aid (FAFSA) online at www.fafsa.ed.gov and meet with a financial aid officer. Students may also apply for a number of scholarships focusing on their specific areas of career interest.

Faculty

Faculty members are hands-on creative professionals with proven experience as business leaders and innovators, hosting a learning environment similar to the career world students will face after graduation. Part instructor, part mentor, their mission is to help develop and transform creative potential into high-demand marketable skills.

Admission Requirements

Prospective students should refer to the current academic catalog for full details regarding admission requirements and process.

Application and Information

To obtain an application, make arrangements for an interview, or tour the school, prospective students should contact:

The Art Institute of Charleston, a branch of The Art Institute of Atlanta
24 North Market Street
Charleston, South Carolina 29401-2623
Phone: 843-727-3500
866-211-0107 (toll-free)
Fax: 843-727-3440
Website: http://www.artinstitutes.edu/charleston

THE ART INSTITUTE OF CHARLOTTE
CHARLOTTE, NORTH CAROLINA

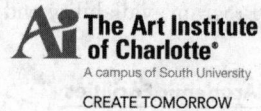

The Art Institute of Charlotte, a campus of South University, is one of The Art Institutes, a system of over fifty schools throughout North America dedicated to providing hands-on education in the creative and applied arts. The Art Institute of Charlotte offers bachelor's and associate degree programs as well as non-degree programs for students interested in pursuing career opportunities from among tomorrow's 15 million jobs in creative fields like design, fashion, media arts, and culinary (based on information from the U.S. Bureau of Labor Statistics for job growth from 2012 to 2022).

A focused education from The Art Institute of Charlotte can help students turn their creative energy into a powerful tool that can make a difference in the world. Students are part of a collaborative and supportive community, where experienced instructors provide the guidance and skills needed to pursue a career in the creative economy.

The Art Institute of Charlotte is also an important resource for creative industry leaders who value the opportunity provided students to learn by using professional-grade technology to build a portfolio of work to show potential employers after graduation.

Accreditation

The Art Institute of Charlotte is a campus of South University. South University is accredited by the Southern Association of Colleges and Schools Commission on Colleges to award certificates, associate degrees, and baccalaureate degrees. Questions about the accreditation of South University can be directed to the Commission on Colleges at 1866 Southern Lane, Decatur, Georgia 30033-4097; phone: 404-679-4500.

The Associate of Science degree in culinary arts is accredited by The Accrediting Commission of the American Culinary Federation Education Foundation.

The Art Institute of Charlotte is licensed to award certificates by the North Carolina State Board of Community Colleges and licensed to award associate and bachelor degrees by the Board of Governors of the University of North Carolina.

Location

If there's one word that best describes Charlotte, it might be "opportunity." Especially for students who want to get started in a creative field. Just being in the middle of a young, dynamic, fresh, and energetic city is a great opportunity to explore exciting new things and grow personally, academically, and professionally.

Students here enjoy everything a major metropolitan area can offer, from dance clubs and concerts to galleries and amusement parks, from the NFL's Carolina Panthers to the high-powered excitement of NASCAR. The Mint Museum of Art and the McColl Center for Visual Art are great resources for anyone studying the applied arts, as are the Mint Museum of Craft + Design, Discovery Place, ImaginOn, and the city's dozens of art galleries.

Charlotte offers music, movies, and a world of places to eat. Students get discounts at the Blumenthal Center for Performing Arts. And the First Friday Night Gallery Crawls are popular in both historic, high-tech SouthEnd and in the funky NoDa area.

Charlotte's thriving business environment includes high-tech companies as well as corporate giants. More than 300 of the Fortune 500 companies have offices here, and Charlotte is second only to New York City as a banking center. The Queen City's high quality of life, reasonable cost of living, friendly people, arts and sports, as well as career opportunities, attract talented people from all over the world.

Programs of Study and Degrees

Creativity is all around, and with millions of tomorrow's jobs in creative fields, the world needs more creative professionals. No matter which course of study a student chooses, the instructors at The Art Institutes will guide, support, and help students fine-tune their visual thinking and problem solving, so that they can take advantage of the world's growing creative opportunities and put their passion to work. Programs are offered in the areas of design, which focuses on communicating conceptually and helping people connect in living and work spaces; media arts, that centers on utilizing technology to deliver information and entertainment; fashion, where students learn anything from designing clothes for the runway to running a retail shop; and culinary, which exposes learners to international cuisines as well as restaurant management techniques.

Bachelor's degree programs are offered in the areas of culinary management, digital filmmaking & video production, fashion & retail management, graphic design, interior design, media arts & animation, photography, and web design & interactive media.

Associate degree programs are offered in the areas of culinary arts, fashion & retail management, fashion design, graphic design, interior design, photography, restaurant & catering management, video production, and web design & interactive media.

Certificate programs are offered in art of cooking, baking & pastry, digital design, digital image management, fashion retailing, residential design, web design, web design & development, and web design & interactive communications.

Program availability and degree offerings are subject to change.

Academic Facilities

The Art Institute of Charlotte provides a learning environment with professional-grade technology applicable to each student's course of study. Students have the opportunity to build a portfolio of work that shows potential employers that they are trained to use the software, hardware, or equipment utilized within the industry. Depending upon the course of study, students are immersed in a creative environment—from classrooms to computer labs to studios—focused on relevant, hands-on education designed to prepare them for the real world.

Costs

Actual tuition and housing costs will vary depending on program, number of credits enrolled, and living arrangements. Prospective students should contact a Student Financial Services professional at the school for details.

Financial Aid

Financial aid is available for those who qualify. Students who require financial assistance should first complete and submit the Free Application for Federal Student Aid (FAFSA) online at www.fafsa.ed.gov and meet with a financial aid officer. Students may also apply for a number of scholarships focusing on their specific areas of career interest.

Faculty

Faculty members are hands-on creative professionals with proven experience as business leaders and innovators, hosting a learning environment similar to the career world students will face after graduation. Part instructor, part mentor, their mission is to help develop and transform creative potential into high-demand marketable skills.

Admission Requirements

Prospective students should refer to the current academic catalog for full details regarding admission requirements and process.

Application and Information

To obtain an application, make arrangements for an interview, or tour the school, prospective students should contact:

The Art Institute of Charlotte, a campus of South University
Three Lake Pointe Plaza
2110 Water Ridge Parkway
Charlotte, North Carolina 28217-4536
Phone: 704-357-8020
        800-872-4417 (toll-free)
Fax: 704-357-1133
Website: http://www.artinstitutes.edu/charlotte

THE ART INSTITUTE OF COLORADO

DENVER, COLORADO

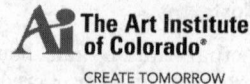

The Art Institute of Colorado is one of The Art Institutes, a system of over fifty schools throughout North America dedicated to providing hands-on education in the creative and applied arts. The Art Institute of Colorado offers bachelor's and associate degree programs as well as non-degree programs for students interested in pursuing career opportunities from among tomorrow's 15 million jobs in creative fields like design, fashion, media arts, and culinary (based on information from the U.S. Bureau of Labor Statistics for job growth from 2012 to 2022).

A focused education from The Art Institute of Colorado can help students turn their creative energy into a powerful tool that can make a difference in the world. Students are part of a collaborative and supportive community, where experienced instructors provide the guidance and skills needed to pursue a career in the creative economy.

The Art Institute of Colorado is also an important resource for creative industry leaders who value the opportunity provided students to learn by using professional-grade technology to build a portfolio of work to show potential employers after graduation.

Accreditation

The Art Institute of Colorado is accredited by the Higher Learning Commission and is a member of the North Central Association (NCA); 30 South LaSalle Street, Suite 7-500, Chicago, Illinois 60604-1413; phone: 800-621-7440; website: www.ncahlc.org.

The Associate of Applied Science in culinary arts degree program is accredited by The Accrediting Commission of the American Culinary Federation Education Foundation.

The interior design program leading to the Bachelor of Arts degree is accredited by the Council for Interior Design Accreditation, 206 Grandville Avenue, Suite 350, Grand Rapids, Michigan 49503; www.accredit-id.org.

The Associate of Applied Science in kitchen & bath design degree program is accredited by the National Kitchen & Bath Association (NKBA). NKBA can be contacted at 687 Willow Grove Street, Hackettstown, New Jersey 07840; phone: 800-843-6522; www.nkba.org.

The Art Institute of Colorado is authorized to award diplomas, Associate of Applied Science degrees, and Bachelor of Arts degrees by the Colorado Department of Higher Education, Commission on Higher Education, 1380 Lawrence Street, Suite 1200, Denver, Colorado 80202.

Location

Denver is located a mile above sea level, between the majestic Rocky Mountains to the west and the High Plains to the east. The Art Institute of Colorado sits in the city's artsy Golden Triangle Museum District that hosts Denver's most prominent cultural attractions in the Civic Center Cultural Complex: the Denver Art Museum, the Michael Graves-designed Central Denver Public Library, Colorado History Museum, Denver Mint, Byers-Evans House and Civic Center Park, and Acoma Street.

Denver, a former gold-rush town, is home to hundreds of restaurants, a restored historic district filled with boutiques and eateries, a collection of museums, a variety of galleries and shopping, the second-largest performing arts center in the nation, three college campuses, and even a unique downtown amusement park, Elitch Gardens. LoDo, the downtown's hip historic district, offers more than ninety brewpubs, sports bars, and music clubs. The 16th Street Mall is a mile-long pedestrian promenade lined with outdoor cafes, restaurants, and shops. Downtown also hosts three beautiful, fan-friendly sports venues: Coors Field for baseball's aptly-named Rockies; the Pepsi Center, where the NBA's Nuggets and the NHL's Avalanche play; and Sports Authority Field at Mile High, home to the NFL's Broncos.

This energetic, young "Mile High" city offers 300 days of sunshine a year, with brilliant blue skies, and stunning mountain scenery. Denver is a clean and green city with more than 200 parks and dozens of tree-lined boulevards. World-class skiing and water sports are just an hour away, amid the breathtaking Rocky Mountain scenery. In the mountains and the city, there are numerous opportunities for biking, hiking, rollerblading, and other individual sports.

Denver has long been a hub of business for the western U.S., with thriving professional organizations, major corporations, high-tech companies, top-notch retail fashion stores, hotels, restaurants, design firms, and many other creative organizations.

Programs of Study and Degrees

Creativity is all around, and with millions of tomorrow's jobs in creative fields, the world needs more creative professionals. No matter which course of study a student chooses, the instructors at The Art Institutes will guide, support, and help students fine-tune their visual thinking and problem solving, so that they can take advantage of the world's growing creative opportunities and put their passion to work. Programs are offered in the areas of design, which focuses on communicating conceptually and helping people connect in living and work spaces; media arts, that centers on utilizing technology to deliver information and entertainment; fashion, where students learn anything from designing clothes for the runway to running a retail shop; and culinary, which exposes learners to international cuisines as well as restaurant management techniques.

Bachelor's degree programs are offered in the areas of audio production, culinary management, design & technical graphics, design management, digital filmmaking & video production, fashion design, fashion retail management, food & beverage management, game art & design, graphic design, graphic & web design, hospitality management, interior design, media arts & animation, photography, visual effects & motion graphics, and web design & interactive media.

Associate degree programs are offered in the areas of baking & pastry, culinary arts, graphic & web design, photography, and video production.

Diploma programs are offered in baking & pastry, culinary arts, digital image management, fashion retailing, web design & development, and web design & interactive communications.

The Associate of Applied Science in culinary arts, the Bachelor of Arts in fashion retail management, the Bachelor of Arts in Interior design, and the Associate of Applied Science in Photography are available in evening and weekend formats.

Program availability and degree offerings are subject to change.

Academic Facilities

The Art Institute of Colorado provides a learning environment with professional-grade technology applicable to each student's course of study. Students have the opportunity to build a portfolio of work that shows potential employers that they are trained to use the software, hardware, or equipment utilized within the industry. Depending upon the course of study, students are immersed in a creative environment—from classrooms to computer labs to studios—focused on relevant, hands-on education designed to prepare them for the real world.

Costs

Actual tuition and housing costs will vary depending on program, number of credits enrolled, and living arrangements. Prospective students should contact a Student Financial Services professional at the school for details.

Financial Aid

Financial aid is available for those who qualify. Students who require financial assistance should first complete and submit the Free Application for Federal Student Aid (FAFSA) online at www.fafsa.ed.gov and meet with a financial aid officer. Students may also apply for a number of scholarships focusing on their specific areas of career interest.

Faculty

Faculty members are hands-on creative professionals with proven experience as business leaders and innovators, hosting a learning environment similar to the career world students will face after graduation. Part instructor, part mentor, their mission is to help develop and transform creative potential into high-demand marketable skills

Admission Requirements

Prospective students should refer to the current academic catalog for full details regarding admission requirements and process.

Application and Information

To obtain an application, make arrangements for an interview, or tour the school, prospective students should contact:

The Art Institute of Colorado
1200 Lincoln Street
Denver, Colorado 80203-2172
Phone: 303-837-0825
      800-275-2420 (toll-free)
Fax: 303-860-8520
Website: http://www.artinstitutes.edu/denver

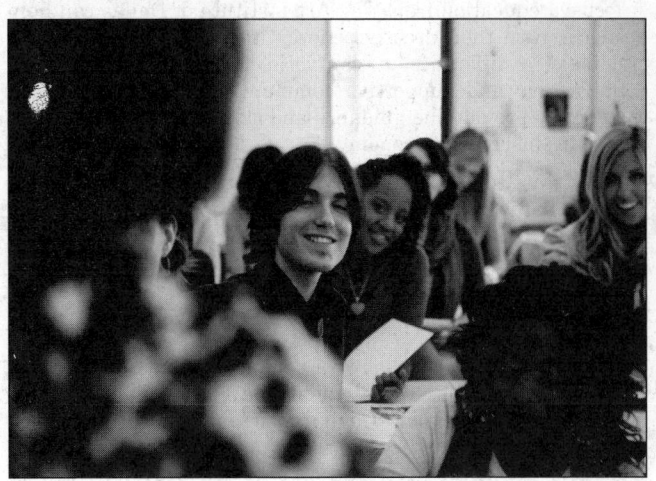

THE ART INSTITUTE OF DALLAS

DALLAS, TEXAS

The Art Institute
of Dallas®
A campus of South University

CREATE TOMORROW

The Art Institute of Dallas, a campus of South University, is one of The Art Institutes, a system of over fifty schools throughout North America dedicated to providing hands-on education in the creative and applied arts. The Art Institute of Dallas offers master's, bachelor's, and associate degree programs as well as non-degree programs for students interested in pursuing career opportunities from among tomorrow's 15 million jobs in creative fields like design, fashion, media arts, and culinary (based on information from the U.S. Bureau of Labor Statistics for job growth from 2012 to 2022).

A focused education from The Art Institute of Dallas can help students turn their creative energy into a powerful tool that can make a difference in the world. Students are part of a collaborative and supportive community, where experienced instructors provide the guidance and skills needed to pursue a career in the creative economy.

The Art Institute of Dallas is also an important resource for creative industry leaders who value the opportunity provided students to learn by using professional-grade technology to build a portfolio of work to show potential employers after graduation.

Accreditation

The Art Institute of Dallas is a campus of South University. South University is accredited by the Southern Association of Colleges and Schools Commission on Colleges to award associate, baccalaureate, masters, and doctorate degrees. Questions about the accreditation of South University can be directed to the Commission on Colleges at 1866 Southern Lane, Decatur, Georgia 30033-4097; phone: 404-679-4500.

The Certificate in the art of cooking and the Associate of Applied Science degree in culinary arts programs are accredited by The Accrediting Commission of the American Culinary Federation Education Foundation.

The interior design program leading to the Bachelor of Fine Arts degree is accredited by the Council for Interior Design Accreditation, 206 Grandville Avenue, Suite 350, Grand Rapids, Michigan 49503; www.accredit-id.org.

The Art Institute of Dallas holds a Certificate of Authorization acknowledging exemption from Texas Higher Education Coordinating Board regulations.

The Art Institute of Dallas is licensed by the Arkansas State Board of Private Career Education.

The Art Institute of Dallas is licensed by the Oklahoma Board of Private Vocational Schools, 3700 North Classen Boulevard, Suite 250, Oklahoma City, Oklahoma 73118; phone: 405-528-3370.

Location

From its origins as a major player in the oil and cotton industries, Dallas—and the entire Dallas-Arlington-Fort Worth Metroplex—has grown to become a truly global center of business and culture. The city's unique blend of southern hospitality and worldly sophistication offers a wonderful environment for students pursing a creative education.

Not only is the Metroplex home to Fortune 500 corporations due to the dynamic business climate, but students find respected museums, symphonies, fabulous shopping, more restaurants per capita than any other city in the nation, and multiple transportation centers such as DFW International Airport, the world's second busiest airport. And there's a wide assortment of world-class cuisine—including barbecue, authentic Mexican, and Tex-Mex.

Deep Ellum, just east of Downtown, was the South's hotbed of jazz as blues in the 1920s and '30s. Today, hundreds of artists operate studios throughout the district alongside bars, pubs, and concert venues. Many public spaces—sides of buildings, sidewalks, streets, and tunnels—are canvases that local artists have turned into murals. There are similar scenes south of the Trinity River, where the Bishop Arts District in Oak Cliff is home to studio artists living in converted warehouses. South of Downtown, the Cedars neighborhood has its own population of artists, along with a growing array of entertainment venues. Southside on Lamar, once a Sears warehouse has been converted into lofts, studios, and shops. The Sculpture Garden at the base of the statuesque Trammell Crow Center in Downtown offers more than twenty statues from the French masters, including Rodin, in a peaceful setting with cascading waters and beautiful gardens.

As for pro sports, Dallas is home to the Cowboys of the NFL, the Stars of the NHL, and the NBA's Mavericks. Arlington, a short drive away, is home to both the Texas Rangers baseball team and Six Flags Over Texas. There's also NASCAR racing at the Texas Motor Speedway, championship rodeo, and horseracing at Lone Star Park.

Dallas also offers an abundance of year-round outdoor activities like tennis, biking, hiking, sailing, ballooning, and just about anything else, thanks to an average of 288 days of sunshine a year.

Programs of Study and Degrees

Creativity is all around, and with millions of tomorrow's jobs in creative fields, the world needs more creative professionals. No matter which course of study a student chooses, the instructors at The Art Institutes will guide, support, and help students fine-tune their visual thinking and problem solving, so that they can take advantage of the world's growing creative opportunities and put their passion to work. Programs are offered in the areas of design, which focuses on communicating conceptually and helping people connect in living and work spaces; media arts, that centers on utilizing technology to deliver information and entertainment; fashion, where students learn anything from designing clothes for the runway to running a retail shop; and culinary, which exposes learners to international cuisines as well as restaurant management techniques.

Bachelor's degree programs are offered in the areas of advertising design, audio production, culinary management, digital filmmaking & video production, fashion & retail management, fashion design, game art & design, graphic design, interior design, media arts & animation, photography, visual effects & motion graphics, and web design & interactive media.

Associate degree programs are offered in the areas of baking & pastry, culinary arts, fashion design, graphic design, photography, restaurant & catering management, and video production.

Certificate programs are offered in baking & pastry, culinary arts, digital image management, fashion retailing, web design & development I, and web design & development II.

The Associate of Applied Science in culinary arts, the Bachelor of Fine Arts in fashion design, the Bachelor of Fine Arts and Associate of Applied Arts in graphic design, and the Bachelor of Fine Arts in interior design are available in evening and weekend formats.

A Master of Arts degree program is offered in design & media management.

Program availability and degree offerings are subject to change.

Academic Facilities

The Art Institute of Dallas provides a learning environment with professional-grade technology applicable to each student's course of study. Students have the opportunity to build a portfolio of work that shows potential employers that they are trained to use the software, hardware, or equipment utilized within the industry. Depending upon the course of study, students are immersed in a creative environment—from classrooms to computer labs to studios—focused on relevant, hands-on education designed to prepare them for the real world.

Costs

Actual tuition and housing costs will vary depending on program, number of credits enrolled, and living arrangements. Prospective students should contact a Student Financial Services professional at the school for details.

Financial Aid

Financial aid is available for those who qualify. Students who require financial assistance should first complete and submit the Free Application for Federal Student Aid (FAFSA) online at www.fafsa.ed.gov and meet with a financial aid officer. Students may also apply for a number of scholarships focusing on their specific areas of career interest.

Faculty

Faculty members are hands-on creative professionals with proven experience as business leaders and innovators, hosting a learning environment similar to the career world students will face after graduation. Part instructor, part mentor, their mission is to help develop and transform creative potential into high-demand marketable skills

Admission Requirements

Prospective students should refer to the current academic catalog for full details regarding admission requirements and process.

Application and Information

To obtain an application, make arrangements for an interview, or tour the school, prospective students should contact:

The Art Institute of Dallas, a campus of South University
8080 Park Lane, Suite 100
Dallas, Texas 75231-5993
Phone: 214-692-8080
           800-275-4243 (toll-free)
Fax: 214-750-9460
Website: http://www.artinstitutes.edu/dallas

COLLEGE CLOSE-UPS

THE ART INSTITUTE OF FORT LAUDERDALE

FORT LAUDERDALE, FLORIDA

The Art Institute of Fort Lauderdale is one of The Art Institutes, a system of over fifty schools throughout North America dedicated to providing hands-on education in the creative and applied arts. The Art Institute of Fort Lauderdale offers bachelor's and associate degree programs as well as non-degree programs for students interested in pursuing career opportunities from among tomorrow's 15 million jobs in creative fields like design, fashion, media arts, and culinary (based on information from the U.S. Bureau of Labor Statistics for job growth from 2012 to 2022).

A focused education from The Art Institute of Fort Lauderdale can help students turn their creative energy into a powerful tool that can make a difference in the world. Students are part of a collaborative and supportive community, where experienced instructors provide the guidance and skills needed to pursue a career in the creative economy.

The Art Institute of Fort Lauderdale is also an important resource for creative industry leaders who value the opportunity provided students to learn by using professional-grade technology to build a portfolio of work to show potential employers after graduation.

Accreditation

The Art Institute of Fort Lauderdale is accredited by the Accrediting Council for Independent Colleges and Schools to award diplomas, associate degrees, and bachelor's degrees. The Accrediting Council for Independent Colleges and Schools is listed as a nationally recognized accrediting agency by the United States Department of Education and is recognized by the Council for Higher Education Accreditation. ACICS can be contacted at 750 First Street NE, Suite 980, Washington, D.C. 20002; phone: 202-336-6780.

The Associate of Science degree in culinary arts and the Bachelor of Science degree in culinary management are accredited by The Accrediting Commission of the American Culinary Federation Education Foundation.

The interior design program leading to the Bachelor of Science degree is accredited by the Council for Interior Design Accreditation, 206 Grandville Avenue, Suite 350, Grand Rapids, Michigan 49503; www.accredit-id.org.

The Art Institute of Fort Lauderdale is licensed by the Commission for Independent Education, Florida Department of Education. Additional information regarding this institution may be obtained by contacting the Commission at 325 West Gaines Street, Suite 1414, Tallahassee, Florida 32399-0400; toll-free number: 888-224-6684.

Location

Known as the "Venice of America" because of its vast system of canals and waterways, the city of Fort Lauderdale draws not only throngs of tourists, but a diverse range of people who live, work, play, and yes, study in its beautiful climate and friendly, small-town atmosphere.

There's more to Fort Lauderdale than amazing beaches and abundant sunshine. The city offers museums, art, festivals, concerts, sports and recreation, unique shops and chic boutiques,

a world of cuisines in a range of settings, and a community that's vibrant and inviting.

The Riverwalk Arts & Entertainment District, Fort Lauderdale's arts and entertainment center, runs along Las Olas Boulevard from the beach to the heart of downtown. The district is anchored in the West by the Broward Center for the Performing Arts. For students looking for a short excursion and a bit of a diversion, there are always the beaches, nightlife, and exotic atmosphere of Miami and South Beach, just a short drive down the coast.

The 180-acre Hugh Taylor Birch State Park sits along the beach and offers nature trails, camping and picnicking areas, and canoeing. The Fort Lauderdale Swap Shop, a huge indoor/outdoor flea market, is the world's largest drive-in movie theater, with a total of 13 screens. And there's an International Swimming Hall of Fame—naturally, right on Fort Lauderdale Beach.

Fort Lauderdale is home to a surprising assortment of corporations, including AutoNation, Citrix Systems, DHL Express, Spirit Airlines, and National Beverage Corporation. The boating industry is also big in Fort Lauderdale, which is a major yacht production center. The city is also home port for over 40,000 boats, and more than 100 marinas and boat yards.

Programs of Study and Degrees

Creativity is all around, and with millions of tomorrow's jobs in creative fields, the world needs more creative professionals. No matter which course of study a student chooses, the instructors at The Art Institutes will guide, support, and help students fine-tune their visual thinking and problem solving, so that they can take advantage of the world's growing creative opportunities and put their passion to work. Programs are offered in the areas of design, which focuses on communicating conceptually and helping people connect in living and work spaces; media arts, that centers on utilizing technology to deliver information and entertainment; fashion, where students learn anything from designing clothes for the runway to running a retail shop; and culinary, which exposes learners to international cuisines as well as restaurant management techniques.

Bachelor's degree programs are offered in the areas of advertising, culinary management, digital filmmaking & video production, fashion design, fashion merchandising, game art & design, graphic design, illustration, industrial design, interior design, media arts & animation, photography, visual effects & motion graphics, and web design & interactive media.

Associate degree programs are offered in the areas of baking & pastry, culinary arts, fashion design, graphic design, interior design, photography, video production, and web design & interactive media.

Diploma programs are offered in baking & pastry, culinary arts, digital image management, fashion retailing, residential design, web design & development, and web design & interactive communications.

Program availability and degree offerings are subject to change.

Academic Facilities

The Art Institute of Fort Lauderdale provides a learning environment with professional-grade technology applicable to each student's course of study. Students have the opportunity to build a portfolio of work that shows potential employers that they are trained to use the software, hardware, or equipment utilized within the industry. Depending upon the course of study, students are immersed in a creative environment—from classrooms to computer labs to studios—focused on relevant, hands-on education designed to prepare them for the real world.

Costs

Actual tuition and housing costs will vary depending on program, number of credits enrolled, and living arrangements. Prospective students can contact a Student Financial Services professional at the school for details.

Financial Aid

Financial aid is available for those who qualify. Students who require financial assistance should first complete and submit the Free Application for Federal Student Aid (FAFSA) online at www.fafsa.ed.gov and meet with a financial aid officer. Students may also apply for a number of scholarships focusing on their specific areas of career interest.

Faculty

Faculty members are hands-on creative professionals with proven experience as business leaders and innovators, hosting a learning environment similar to the career world students will face after graduation. Part instructor, part mentor, their mission is to help develop and transform creative potential into high-demand marketable skills.

Admission Requirements

Prospective students should refer to the current academic catalog for full details regarding admission requirements and process.

Application and Information

To obtain an application, make arrangements for an interview, or tour the school, prospective students should contact:

The Art Institute of Fort Lauderdale
1799 S.E. 17th Street
Fort Lauderdale, Florida 33316-3013
Phone: 954-463-3000
      800-275-7603 (toll-free)
Fax: 954-728-8637
Website: http://www.artinstitutes.edu/fortlauderdale

THE ART INSTITUTE OF FORT WORTH
FORT WORTH, TEXAS

The Art Institute of Fort Worth, a campus of South University, is one of The Art Institutes, a system of over fifty schools throughout North America dedicated to providing hands-on education in the creative and applied arts. The Art Institute of Fort Worth offers bachelor's and associate degree programs as well as non-degree programs for students interested in pursuing career opportunities from among tomorrow's 15 million jobs in creative fields like design, fashion, and media arts (based on information from the U.S. Bureau of Labor Statistics for job growth from 2012 to 2022).

A focused education from The Art Institute of Fort Worth can help students turn their creative energy into a powerful tool that can make a difference in the world. Students are part of a collaborative and supportive community, where experienced instructors provide the guidance and skills needed to pursue a career in the creative economy.

The Art Institute of Fort Worth is also an important resource for creative industry leaders who value the opportunity provided students to learn by using professional-grade technology to build a portfolio of work to show potential employers after graduation.

Accreditation

The Art Institute of Fort Worth is a campus of South University. South University is accredited by the Southern Association of Colleges and Schools Commission on Colleges to award associate, baccalaureate, masters, and doctorate degrees. Questions about the accreditation of South University can be directed to the Commission on Colleges at 1866 Southern Lane, Decatur, Georgia 30033-4097; phone: 404-679-4500.

The Art Institute of Fort Worth holds a Certificate of Authorization acknowledging exemption from Texas Higher Education Coordinating Board regulations.

Location

Fort Worth has historic stockyards, remarkable museums, a thriving and exciting downtown area, the Texas Motor Speedway, and spectacular annual events. It's also a stimulating environment for students to begin their creative careers at The Art Institute of Fort Worth.

Fort Worth began in 1849 as a lonely Army outpost on a bluff overlooking the Trinity River. Today Fort Worth still embraces its proud western heritage and traditional architecture and design.

The city is home to many multinational corporations including Bell Helicopter, Lockheed Martin, Pier 1 Imports, RadioShack, and FUNimation Entertainment, among others.

Downtown Fort Worth is known mainly for its Art Deco and Beaux Arts-style buildings. A popular place for nightlife and entertainment, the Sundance Square area of downtown offers many restaurants, shops, museums, bars, clubs, movie theaters, performing arts, concerts, and festivals all year round. Most of the buildings there retain their early twentieth-century façades.

Fort Worth is home to several visit-worthy museums. The Kimbell Art Museum not only features an outstanding collection of works, the building itself is considered to be among the world's foremost examples of modern architecture. The Museum of Modern Art and the Amon Carter Museum offer some of the most extensive collections of American art anywhere in the world.

The Fort Worth Zoo, with more than 5,000 animals, has been ranked in the top 10 zoos in the United States. For hiking or canoeing enthusiasts, the Fort Worth Nature Center & Refuge in northwest Fort Worth has nearly 4,000 acres of natural area and is one of the largest urban parks of its type in the country.

As for pro sports, the Metroplex is home to the Dallas Stars of the NHL and the NBA's Dallas Mavericks, while Cowboys Stadium houses the Dallas Cowboys of the NFL. The ballpark for a Texas Rangers game is just a short drive to Arlington, where Six Flags Over Texas is also located. In addition, NASCAR racing at the Texas Motor Speedway, championship rodeo, and horseracing are available at Lone Star Park.

Programs of Study and Degrees

Creativity is all around, and with millions of tomorrow's jobs in creative fields, the world needs more creative professionals. No matter which course of study a student chooses, the instructors at The Art Institutes will guide, support, and help students fine-tune their visual thinking and problem solving, so that they can take advantage of the world's growing creative opportunities and put their passion to work. Programs are offered in the areas of design, which focuses on communicating conceptually and helping people connect in living and work spaces; media arts, that centers on utilizing technology to deliver information and entertainment; and fashion, where students learn anything from designing clothes for the runway to running a retail shop.

Bachelor's degree programs are offered in the areas of advertising design, fashion & retail management, graphic design, interior design, media arts & animation, photography, and web design & interactive media.

Associate's degree programs are offered in the areas of graphic design, photography, and web design & interactive media.

Certificate programs are offered in digital image management, fashion retailing, web design & development I, and web design & development II.

Program availability and degree offerings are subject to change.

Academic Facilities

The Art Institute of Fort Worth provides a learning environment with professional-grade technology applicable to each student's course of study. Students have the opportunity to build a portfolio of work that shows potential employers that they are trained to use the software, hardware, or equipment utilized within the industry. Depending upon the course of study, students are immersed in a creative environment—from classrooms to computer labs to studios—focused on relevant, hands-on education designed to prepare them for the real world.

Costs

Actual tuition and housing costs will vary depending on program, number of credits enrolled, and living arrangements. Prospective students can contact a Student Financial Services professional at the school for details.

Financial Aid

Financial aid is available for those who qualify. Students who require financial assistance should first complete and submit the Free Application for Federal Student Aid (FAFSA) online at www.fafsa.ed.gov and meet with a financial aid officer. Students may also apply for a number of scholarships focusing on their specific areas of career interest.

Faculty

Faculty members are hands-on creative professionals with proven experience as business leaders and innovators, hosting a learning environment similar to the career world students will face after graduation. Part instructor, part mentor, their mission is to help develop and transform creative potential into high-demand marketable skills.

Admission Requirements

Prospective students should refer to the current academic catalog for full details regarding admission requirements and process.

Application and Information

To obtain an application, make arrangements for an interview, or tour the school, prospective students should contact:

The Art Institute of Forth Worth, a campus of South University
7000 Calmont Avenue, Suite 150
Fort Worth, Texas 76116
Phone: 817-210-0808
      888-422-9686 (toll-free)
Fax: 817-210-0901
Website: http://www.artinstitutes.edu/fort-worth

THE ART INSTITUTE OF HOUSTON
HOUSTON, TEXAS

The Art Institute of Houston is one of The Art Institutes, a system of over 50 schools throughout North America dedicated to providing hands-on education in the creative and applied arts. The Art Institute of Houston offers bachelor's and associate degree programs as well as non-degree programs for students interested in pursuing career opportunities from among tomorrow's 15 million jobs in creative fields like design, fashion, media arts, and culinary (based on information from the U.S. Bureau of Labor Statistics for job growth from 2012 to 2022).

A focused education from The Art Institute of Houston can help students turn their creative energy into a powerful tool that can make a difference in the world. Students are part of a collaborative and supportive community, where experienced instructors provide the guidance and skills needed to pursue a career in the creative economy.

The Art Institute of Houston is also an important resource for creative industry leaders who value the opportunity provided students to learn by using professional-grade technology to build a portfolio of work to show potential employers after graduation.

Accreditation

The Art Institute of Houston, including its branch campuses, The Art Institute of Houston—North, The Art Institute of Austin, and The Art Institute of San Antonio, is accredited by the Southern Association of Colleges and Schools Commission on Colleges to award associate and baccalaureate degrees. Questions about the accreditation of The Art Institute of Houston can be directed to the Commission on Colleges at 1866 Southern Lane, Decatur, Georgia 30033-4097; phone: 404-679-4500.

The diploma in culinary arts, Associate of Applied Science degree in baking & pastry, Associate of Applied Science degree in culinary arts, and the Bachelor of Science degree in culinary management programs are accredited by The Accrediting Commission of the American Culinary Federation Education Foundation.

The interior design program leading to the Bachelor of Fine Arts degree is accredited by the Council for Interior Design Accreditation, 206 Grandville Avenue, Suite 350, Grand Rapids, Michigan 49503; www.accredit-id.org.

The Art Institute of Houston holds a Certificate of Authorization acknowledging exemption from Texas Higher Education Coordinating Board regulations.

Location

From its abundance of world-class restaurants to its diverse blend of international cultures to its rich world of art exhibits and museums, Houston is a great place to find inspiration. The country's fourth-largest city is all about energy, entertainment, and endless possibilities.

Houston boasts a mild, semi-tropical climate with sunny beaches nearby. A fine arts mecca, Houston is home to several major art museums, a premiere opera, ballet and symphony,

and live theater companies. Culturally diverse, there are several international ethnic communities.

A 17-block area in the middle of downtown composes the Theater District, with the Bayou Place entertainment complex, restaurants, movie theaters, live music venues, plazas, and parks. The Houston Verizon Wireless Theater offers live concerts, stage plays, and stand-up comedy.

Space Center Houston is the official visitors' center of NASA's Lyndon B. Johnson Space Center, which offers interactive exhibits including moon rocks and a shuttle simulator. The Galleria is the biggest shopping mall in Texas and is located in the Uptown District.

Other popular venues include Old Market Square, the Downtown Aquarium, and Sam Houston Race Park. The city's cultural diversity is evident in Chinatown and the Mahatma Gandhi District.

Houston has over 300 parks; one of them, Hermann Park, includes the Houston Zoo and the Houston Museum of Natural Science. Of America's 10 biggest cities, Houston is number one in terms of space set aside for parks and green space. And a recent study of the 50 largest U.S. cities by Walk Score ranked Houston the twenty-third most walkable.

As for ballparks, the Houston Astros play baseball at Minute Maid Park, the NFL's Texans take on the competition at Reliant Stadium, and the Rockets of the NBA play basketball at Toyota Center.

Programs of Study and Degrees

Creativity is all around, and with millions of tomorrow's jobs in creative fields, the world needs more creative professionals. No matter which course of study a student chooses, the instructors at The Art Institutes will guide, support, and help students fine-tune their visual thinking and problem solving, so that they can take advantage of the world's growing creative opportunities and put their passion to work. Programs are offered in the areas of design, which focuses on communicating conceptually and helping people connect in living and work spaces; media arts, that centers on utilizing technology to deliver information and entertainment; fashion, where students learn anything from designing clothes for the runway to running a retail shop; and culinary, which exposes learners to international cuisines as well as restaurant management techniques.

Bachelor's degree programs are offered in the areas of advertising design, audio production, culinary management, design & technical graphics, digital filmmaking & video production, fashion & retail management, fashion design, food & beverage management, game art & design, graphic & web design, hospitality management, interior design, media arts & animation, photography, and visual effects & motion graphics.

Associate degree programs are offered in the areas of baking & pastry, culinary arts, graphic design, restaurant & catering management, and web design & interactive media.

Diploma programs are offered in baking & pastry, culinary arts, digital image management, fashion retailing, web design & development, and web design & interactive communications.

The Associate in Applied Science in culinary arts, the Bachelor of Science in culinary management, the Bachelor of Fine Arts in interior design, and the Bachelor of Fine Arts in web design & interactive media are available in evening and weekend format.

Program availability and degree offerings are subject to change.

Academic Facilities

The Art Institute of Houston provides a learning environment with professional-grade technology applicable to each student's course of study. Students have the opportunity to build a portfolio of work that shows potential employers that they are trained to use the software, hardware, or equipment utilized within the industry. Depending upon the course of study, students are immersed in a creative environment—from classrooms to computer labs to studios—focused on relevant, hands-on education designed to prepare them for the real world.

Costs

Actual tuition and housing costs will vary depending on program, number of credits enrolled, and living arrangements. Prospective students can contact a Student Financial Services professional at the school for details.

Financial Aid

Financial aid is available for those who qualify. Students who require financial assistance should first complete and submit the Free Application for Federal Student Aid (FAFSA) online at www.fafsa.ed.gov and meet with a financial aid officer. Students may also apply for a number of scholarships focusing on their specific areas of career interest.

Faculty

Faculty members are hands-on creative professionals with proven experience as business leaders and innovators, hosting a learning environment similar to the career world students will face after graduation. Part instructor, part mentor, their mission is to help develop and transform creative potential into high-demand marketable skills.

Admission Requirements

Prospective students should refer to the current academic catalog for full details regarding admission requirements and process.

Application and Information

To obtain an application, make arrangements for an interview, or tour the school, prospective students should contact:

The Art Institute of Houston
4140 Southwest Freeway
Houston, Texas 77027
Phone: 713-623-2040
       800-275-4244 (toll-free)
Fax: 713-966-2797
Website: http://www.artinstitutes.edu/houston

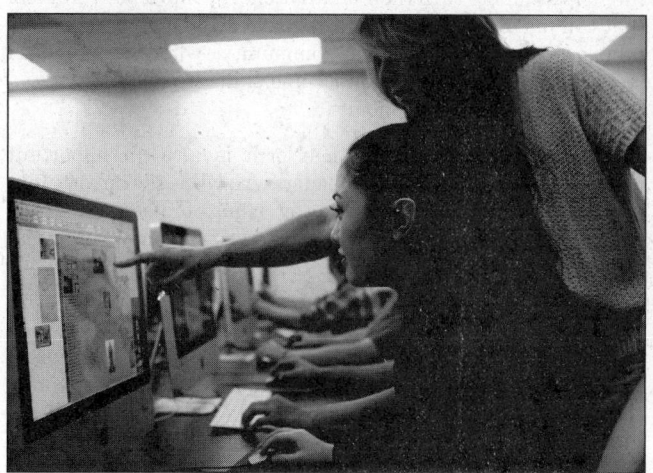

Since The Art Institutes system of schools is comprised of several institutions, see aiprograms.info for program duration, tuition, fees, and other costs, median debt, federal salary data, alumni success, and other important info. The Art Institutes is a system of over 50 schools throughout North America. Programs, credential levels, technology, and scheduling options vary by school, and employment opportunities are not guaranteed. Financial aid is available to those who qualify. Several institutions included in The Art Institutes system are campuses of South University or Argosy University. OH Registration #04-01-1698B, AC0165, AC0080, Licensed by the Florida Commission for Independent Education, License No. 1287, 3427, 3110, 2581. Certified by SCHEV to operate in Virginia. Administrative office: 210 Sixth Avenue, 33rd Floor, Pittsburgh, PA 15222. ©2013 The Art Institutes International LLC.

THE ART INSTITUTE OF HOUSTON—NORTH
HOUSTON, TEXAS

The Art Institute of Houston—North, a branch of The Art Institute of Houston, is one of The Art Institutes, a system of over fifty schools throughout North America dedicated to providing hands-on education in the creative and applied arts. The Art Institute of Houston—North offers bachelor's and associate degree programs as well as non-degree programs for students interested in pursuing career opportunities from among tomorrow's 15 million jobs in creative fields like design, fashion, and media arts (based on information from the U.S. Bureau of Labor Statistics for job growth from 2012 to 2022).

A focused education from The Art Institute of Houston—North can help students turn their creative energy into a powerful tool that can make a difference in the world. Students are part of a collaborative and supportive community, where experienced instructors provide the guidance and skills needed to pursue a career in the creative economy.

The Art Institute of Houston—North is also an important resource for creative industry leaders who value the opportunity provided to students to learn by using professional-grade technology to build a portfolio of work to show potential employers after graduation.

Accreditation

The Art Institute of Houston—North is a branch campus of The Art Institute of Houston. The Art Institute of Houston is accredited by the Southern Association of Colleges and Schools Commission on Colleges to award associate and baccalaureate degrees. Questions about the accreditation of The Art Institute of Houston can be directed to the Commission on Colleges at 1866 Southern Lane, Decatur, Georgia 30033-4097; phone: 404-679-4500.

The Art Institute of Houston—North holds a Certificate of Authorization acknowledging exemption from Texas Higher Education Coordinating Board regulations.

Location

A growing and exciting "edge city," northwest Houston is coming into its own as a center for the visual and performing arts, education, shopping, and recreation. At The Art Institute of Houston—North, students are just minutes from the heart of downtown Houston yet close to lakes and streams, forested parks, quiet neighborhoods, and people who value quality of life and community.

The area boasts a mild, semi-tropical climate with sunny beaches nearby. A fine arts mecca, Houston is home to several major art museums, a premiere opera, ballet and symphony, and live theater companies. Culturally diverse, there are several international ethnic communities. There are great restaurants, an eclectic nightlife, and everything else one would expect from one of the most talked-about cities in the nation and the world.

A 17-block area in the middle of downtown composes the Theater District, with the Bayou Place entertainment complex, along with restaurants, movie theaters, live music venues, plazas, and parks. The Houston Verizon Wireless Theater offers live concerts, stage plays, and stand-up comedy.

Space Center Houston is the official visitors' center of NASA's Lyndon B. Johnson Space Center, which offers interactive exhibits including moon rocks and a shuttle simulator. The Galleria is the biggest shopping mall in Texas and is located in the Uptown District. Other attractions in Houston include Old Market Square, the Downtown Aquarium, and Sam Houston Race Park. The city's cultural diversity is evident in Chinatown and the Mahatma Gandhi District.

Houston has over 300 parks; one of them, Hermann Park, includes the Houston Zoo and the Houston Museum of Natural Science. Of America's 10 biggest cities, Houston is number one in terms of space set aside for parks and green space. And a recent study of the fifty largest U.S. cities by Walk Score ranked Houston the 23rd most walkable

As for ballparks, the Houston Astros play baseball at Minute Maid Park, the NFL's Texans take on the competition at Reliant Stadium, and the Rockets of the NBA play basketball at Toyota Center.

Programs of Study and Degrees

Creativity is all around, and with millions of tomorrow's jobs in creative fields, the world needs more creative professionals. No matter which course of study a student chooses, the instructors at The Art Institutes will guide, support, and help students fine-tune their visual thinking and problem solving, so that they can take advantage of the world's growing creative opportunities and put their passion to work. Programs are offered in the areas of design, which focuses on communicating conceptually and helping people connect in living and work spaces; media arts, that centers on utilizing technology to deliver information and entertainment; and fashion, where students learn anything from designing clothes for the runway to running a retail shop.

Bachelor's degree programs are offered in the areas of advertising design, design & technical graphics, fashion & retail management, game art & design, interior design, media arts & animation, photography, visual effects & motion graphics, and web design & interactive media.

Associate's degree programs are offered in the areas of graphic design and web design & interactive media.

Diploma programs are offered in digital image management, fashion retailing, web design & development, and web design & interactive communications.

Program availability and degree offerings are subject to change.

Academic Facilities

The Art Institute of Houston—North provides a learning environment with professional-grade technology applicable to each student's course of study. Students have the opportunity to build a portfolio of work that shows potential employers that they are trained to use the software, hardware, or equipment

utilized within the industry. Depending upon the course of study, students are immersed in a creative environment—from classrooms to computer labs to studios—focused on relevant, hands-on education designed to prepare them for the real world.

Costs

Actual tuition and housing costs will vary depending on program, number of credits enrolled, and living arrangements. Prospective students should contact a Student Financial Services professional at the school for details.

Financial Aid

Financial aid is available for those who qualify. Students who require financial assistance should first complete and submit the Free Application for Federal Student Aid (FAFSA) online at www.fafsa.ed.gov and meet with a financial aid officer. Students may also apply for a number of scholarships focusing on their specific areas of career interest.

Faculty

Faculty members are hands-on creative professionals with proven experience as business leaders and innovators, hosting a learning environment similar to the career world students will face after graduation. Part instructor, part mentor, their mission is to help develop and transform creative potential into high-demand marketable skills.

Admission Requirements

Prospective students can refer to the current academic catalog for full details regarding admission requirements and process.

Application and Information

To obtain an application, make arrangements for an interview, or tour the school, prospective students should contact:

The Art Institute of Houston—North, a branch of The Art
  Institute of Houston
10740 North Gessner Drive, Suite 190
Houston, Texas 77064
Phone: 281-671-3381
       866-830-4450 (toll-free)
Fax: 281-671-3550
Website: http://www.artinstitutes.edu/houston-north

COLLEGE CLOSE-UPS

THE ART INSTITUTE OF INDIANAPOLIS
INDIANAPOLIS, INDIANA

The Art Institute of Indianapolis is one of The Art Institutes, a system of over fifty schools throughout North America dedicated to providing hands-on education in the creative and applied arts. The Art Institute of Indianapolis offers bachelor's and associate's degree programs as well as non-degree programs for students interested in pursuing career opportunities from among tomorrow's 15 million jobs in creative fields like design, fashion, media arts, and culinary (based on information from the U.S. Bureau of Labor Statistics for job growth from 2012 to 2022).

A focused education from The Art Institute of Indianapolis can help students turn their creative energy into a powerful tool that can make a difference in the world. Students are part of a collaborative and supportive community, where experienced instructors provide the guidance and skills needed to pursue a career in the creative economy.

The Art Institute of Indianapolis is also an important resource for creative industry leaders who value the opportunity provided students to learn by using professional-grade technology to build a portfolio of work to show potential employers after graduation.

Accreditation

The Art Institute of Indianapolis is accredited by the Accrediting Council for Independent Colleges and Schools to award certificates, associate degrees, and bachelor's degrees. The Accrediting Council for Independent Colleges and Schools is listed as a nationally recognized accrediting agency by the United States Department of Education and is recognized by the Council for Higher Education Accreditation. ACICS can be contacted at 750 First Street NE, Suite 980, Washington, D.C. 20002; phone: 202-336-6780.

The Art Institute of Indianapolis is a branch of The Art Institute of Phoenix located in Phoenix, Arizona, and is accredited by the Accrediting Council for Independent Colleges and Schools.

The Art Institute of Indianapolis is regulated by the Board for Proprietary Education, Indiana Commission for Higher Education, 101 West Ohio Street, Suite 670, Indianapolis, Indiana 46204; phone: 317-464-4400.

Location

From the Indy 500 to Fortune 500 companies, Indianapolis is a city of positive energy. It's an energy that flows through the streets, carries to every neighborhood, and fuels the creativity and imaginations of students at The Art Institute of Indianapolis from the first day of classes till they take all that they've learned and step out into the real world.

The campus is located in the northwestern section of the city and housed in The Pyramids, a unique local landmark. The buildings are famous for their abstract, sculptural design: Their opaque concrete walls face the nearby highway, while their glass curtain walls look out onto landscaped grounds.

The city offers friendly people, a vibrant business community with a world of professional opportunities, a wide range of cultural attractions, and a lively nightlife. The twelfth-largest city in the United States, Indianapolis is one of the nation's fastest-growing metropolitan areas. The city's downtown is ranked as one of the best in the United States by both *Forbes* and Livability.com.

There are six cultural districts: Broad Ripple Village, Massachusetts Avenue, Fountain Square, The Wholesale District, Canal and White River State Park, and Indiana Avenue. Harrison Center for the Arts features monthly shows in its galleries, as well as numerous artists' studios. The beautiful Depew Memorial Fountain has been described as a museum without walls. Indianapolis has a wide variety of other museums as well, focused on art, automobiles, sports, history, and science and technology.

The Indianapolis Cultural Trail is an urban bike and pedestrian path connecting the downtown cultural districts, neighborhoods, and entertainment venues. There are benches, bike racks, lighting, signage and bike rentals/drop-offs, along with an interesting assortment of local artwork along the trail. Indianapolis also offers nearly 200 municipal parks, including Eagle Creek Park, one of the biggest urban parks in the country.

Indianapolis is world-famous for the Indianapolis 500, the premier open-wheel car event for over 100 years. The enormous Indianapolis Motor Speedway is also home to the Brickyard 400 and the Red Bull Indianapolis Grand Prix. Other professional sports include Colts football at the enclosed Lucas Oil Stadium and Indiana Pacers basketball at Bankers Life Fieldhouse.

Programs of Study and Degrees

Creativity is all around, and with millions of tomorrow's jobs in creative fields, the world needs more creative professionals. No matter which course of study a student chooses, the instructors at The Art Institutes will guide, support, and help students fine-tune their visual thinking and problem solving, so that they can take advantage of the world's growing creative opportunities and put their passion to work. Programs are offered in the areas of design, which focuses on communicating conceptually and helping people connect in living and work spaces; media arts, that centers on utilizing technology to deliver information and entertainment; fashion, where students learn anything from designing clothes for the runway to running a retail shop; and culinary, which exposes learners to international cuisines as well as restaurant management techniques.

Bachelor's degree programs are offered in the areas of culinary management, digital photography, fashion & retail management, fashion design, graphic & web design, interior design, media arts & animation, and web design & interactive media.

Associate degree programs are offered in baking & pastry, culinary arts, digital photography, and graphic design.

Certificate programs are offered in baking & pastry, culinary arts, and digital design.

Program availability and degree offerings are subject to change.

Academic Facilities

The Art Institute of Indianapolis provides a learning environment with professional-grade technology applicable to each student's course of study. Students have the opportunity to build a portfolio of work that shows potential employers that they are trained to use the software, hardware, or equipment utilized within the industry. Depending upon the course of study, students are immersed in a creative environment—from classrooms to computer labs to studios—focused on relevant, hands-on education designed to prepare them for the real world.

Costs

Actual tuition and housing costs will vary depending on program, number of credits enrolled, and living arrangements. Prospective students can contact a Student Financial Services professional at the school for details.

Financial Aid

Financial aid is available for those who qualify. Students who require financial assistance should first complete and submit the Free Application for Federal Student Aid (FAFSA) online at www.fafsa.ed.gov and meet with a financial aid officer. Students may also apply for a number of scholarships focusing on their specific areas of career interest.

Faculty

Faculty members are hands-on creative professionals with proven experience as business leaders and innovators, hosting a learning environment similar to the career world students will face after graduation. Part instructor, part mentor, their mission is to help develop and transform creative potential into high-demand marketable skills.

Admission Requirements

Please refer to the current academic catalog for full details regarding admission requirements and process.

Application and Information

To obtain an application, make arrangements for an interview, or tour the school, prospective students should contact:

The Art Institute of Indianapolis
3500 Depauw Boulevard, Suite 1010
Indianapolis, Indiana 46268-6124
Phone: 317-613-4800
      866-441-9031 (toll-free)
Fax: 317-613-4808
Website: http://www.artinstitutes.edu/indianapolis

THE ART INSTITUTE OF JACKSONVILLE
JACKSONVILLE, FLORIDA

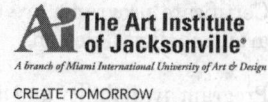

The Art Institute of Jacksonville
A branch of Miami International University of Art & Design

CREATE TOMORROW

The Art Institute of Jacksonville, a branch of Miami International University of Art & Design, is one of The Art Institutes, a system of over fifty schools throughout North America dedicated to providing hands-on education in the creative and applied arts. The Art Institute of Jacksonville offers master's, bachelor's, and associate degree programs as well as non-degree programs for students interested in pursuing career opportunities from among tomorrow's 15 million jobs in creative fields like design, fashion, media arts, and culinary (based on information from the U.S. Bureau of Labor Statistics for job growth from 2012 to 2022).

A focused education from The Art Institute of Jacksonville can help students turn their creative energy into a powerful tool that can make a difference in the world. Students are part of a collaborative and supportive community, where experienced instructors provide the guidance and skills needed to pursue a career in the creative economy.

The Art Institute of Jacksonville is also an important resource for creative industry leaders who value the opportunity provided students to learn by using professional-grade technology to build a portfolio of work to show potential employers after graduation.

Accreditation

The Art Institute of Jacksonville is a branch of Miami International University of Art & Design. Miami International University of Art & Design is accredited by the Southern Association of Colleges and Schools Commission on Colleges to award associate, baccalaureate, and master's degrees. Questions about the accreditation of Miami International University of Art & Design and its branches can be directed to the Commission on Colleges at 1866 Southern Lane, Decatur, Georgia 30033-4097; phone: 404-679-4500.

The Art Institute of Jacksonville is licensed by the Commission for Independent Education, Florida Department of Education. Additional information regarding this institution may be obtained by contacting the Commission at 325 West Gaines Street, Suite 1414, Tallahassee, Florida 32399-0400; phone: 888-224-6684 (toll-free).

Location

Jacksonville is big. Not just in Florida, where it's the most populous city, but in the whole United States, where it occupies the most real estate of any city—enough to encompass more than 500 distinct neighborhoods. It's also a city big enough to offer just about anything for students pursuing a creative education, from music to museums, art to architecture, and shops to shorelines. The Art Institute of Jacksonville puts it all within easy reach.

The downtown Jacksonville Jazz Festival is the second-biggest jazz festival in the United States; Springing the Blues is one of the oldest and largest blues festivals; the World of Nations features events, cuisines, and souvenirs from around the globe; and the Jacksonville Film Festival serves up a wide range of independent films, documentaries, and shorts.

Jacksonville Landing, a popular riverfront dining and shopping area, and the Jacksonville Riverwalks are in the center of the city. The Museum of Contemporary Art Jacksonville features eclectic exhibits along with a collection of over 700 works.

In addition to places to shop and places to eat, Jacksonville is big on undeveloped green spaces. There are miles of white sandy beaches to explore, and places for hiking, camping, sports, and recreation. The city boasts the largest urban park system in the U.S.—over 80,000 acres spread across more than 337 locations, including the Jacksonville-Baldwin Rail Trail, a long narrow park that travels nearly 15 miles. St. Johns River Park, also known as Friendship Park, is the site of Friendship Fountain, one of the most famous spots in Jacksonville and, at the time it was built, the world's tallest and largest fountain. There are plentiful sites to boat, swim, fish, sail, jet ski, surf, or water ski.

The annual Gate River Run is the largest 15k race in the country, drawing over 13,000 runners, spectators, and volunteers. College football's Gator Bowl is held in the city every New Year's Day. And there's pro football too—the Jacksonville Jaguars play at EverBank Field.

Among the major corporations that call Jacksonville home are four Fortune 500 companies: CSX Corporation, Fidelity National Financial, Fidelity National Information Services, and Winn—Dixie Stores, Inc.

Programs of Study and Degrees

Creativity is all around, and with millions of tomorrow's jobs in creative fields, the world needs more creative professionals. No matter which course of study a student chooses, the instructors at The Art Institutes will guide, support, and help students fine-tune their visual thinking and problem solving, so that they can take advantage of the world's growing creative opportunities and put their passion to work. Programs are offered in the areas of design, which focuses on communicating conceptually and helping people connect in living and work spaces; media arts, that centers on utilizing technology to deliver information and entertainment; fashion, where students learn anything from designing clothes for the runway to running a retail shop; and culinary, which exposes learners to international cuisines as well as restaurant management techniques.

Bachelor's degree programs are offered in the areas of culinary management, digital filmmaking & video production, digital photography, fashion & retail management, graphic design, interior design, media arts & animation, and web design & interactive media.

Associate degree programs are offered in the areas of culinary arts, graphic design, and web design & interactive media.

Diploma programs are offered in baking & pastry, culinary arts, digital image management, fashion retailing, web design & development I, and web design & development II.

A Master of Arts degree program is offered in design & media management.

Miami International University of Art & Design is one of the degree-granting institutions for The Design & Media Management degree program. This school's program will also be offered in a synchronous and asynchronous format at its branch campuses, The Art Institute of Tampa and The Art Institute of Jacksonville.

Program availability and degree offerings are subject to change.

Academic Facilities

The Art Institute of Jacksonville provides a learning environment with professional-grade technology applicable to each student's course of study. Students have the opportunity to build a portfolio of work that shows potential employers that they are trained to use the software, hardware, or equipment utilized within the industry. Depending upon the course of study, students are immersed in a creative environment—from classrooms to computer labs to studios—focused on relevant, hands-on education designed to prepare them for the real world.

Costs

Actual tuition and housing costs will vary depending on program, number of credits enrolled, and living arrangements. Prospective students can contact a Student Financial Services professional at the school for details.

Financial Aid

Financial aid is available for those who qualify. Students who require financial assistance should first complete and submit the Free Application for Federal Student Aid (FAFSA) online at www.fafsa.ed.gov and meet with a financial aid officer. Students may also apply for a number of scholarships focusing on their specific areas of career interest.

Faculty

Faculty members are hands-on creative professionals with proven experience as business leaders and innovators, hosting a learning environment similar to the career world students will face after graduation. Part instructor, part mentor, their mission is to help develop and transform creative potential into high-demand marketable skills.

Admission Requirements

Please refer to the current academic catalog for full details regarding admission requirements and process.

Application and Information

To obtain an application, make arrangements for an interview, or tour the school, prospective students should contact:

The Art Institute of Jacksonville, a branch of Miami
    International University of Art & Design
8775 Baypine Road
Jacksonville, Florida 32256-8528
Phone: 904-486-3000
        800-924-1589 (toll-free)
Fax: 904-732-9423
Website: http://www.artinstitutes.edu/jacksonville

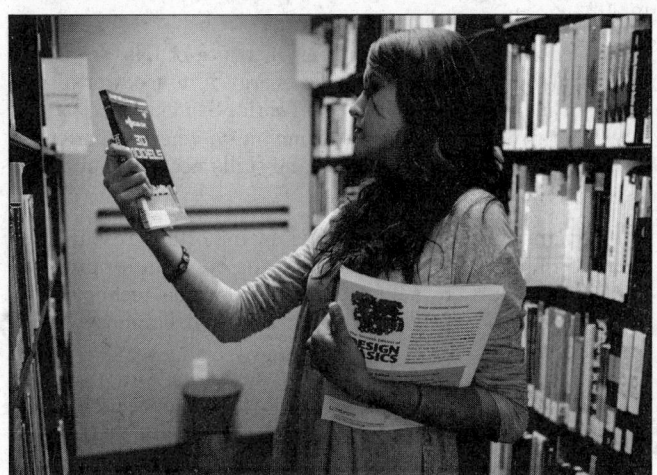

COLLEGE CLOSE-UPS

THE ART INSTITUTE OF LAS VEGAS
HENDERSON, NEVADA

The Art Institute of Las Vegas is one of The Art Institutes, a system of over fifty schools throughout North America dedicated to providing hands-on education in the creative and applied arts. The Art Institute of Las Vegas offers bachelor's and associate degree programs as well as non-degree programs for students interested in pursuing career opportunities from among tomorrow's 15 million jobs in creative fields like design, fashion, media arts, and culinary (based on information from the U.S. Bureau of Labor Statistics for job growth from 2012 to 2022).

A focused education from The Art Institute of Las Vegas can help students turn their creative energy into a powerful tool that can make a difference in the world. Students are part of a collaborative and supportive community, where experienced instructors provide the guidance and skills needed to pursue a career in the creative economy.

The Art Institute of Las Vegas is an important resource for creative industry leaders who value the opportunity provided students to learn by using professional-grade technology to build a portfolio of work to show potential employers after graduation.

Accreditation

The Art Institute of Las Vegas is a branch of The Art Institute of Phoenix located in Phoenix, Arizona. The Art Institute of Las Vegas is accredited by the Accrediting Council for Independent Colleges and Schools to award diplomas, associate degrees, and bachelor's degrees. The Accrediting Council for Independent Colleges and Schools is listed as a nationally recognized accrediting agency by the United States Department of Education and is recognized by the Council for Higher Education Accreditation. ACICS can be contacted at 750 First Street NE, Suite 980, Washington, D.C. 20002; phone: 202-336-6780.

The Bachelor of Arts in interior design degree program is accredited by the National Kitchen & Bath Association (NKBA). NKBA can be contacted at 687 Willow Grove Street, Hackettstown, New Jersey 07840; phone: 800-THE-NKBA; www.nkba.org.

The interior design program leading to the Bachelor of Arts degree is accredited by the Council for Interior Design Accreditation, www.accredit-id.org, 206 Grandville Avenue, Suite 350, Grand Rapids, Michigan 49503.

The Associate of Science in baking & pastry, Associate of Science in culinary arts, and Bachelor of Arts in culinary management programs are accredited by the Accrediting Commission of the American Culinary Federation Education Foundation.

The Art Institute of Las Vegas is licensed to operate by the Commission on Postsecondary Education; 3663 East Sunset Road, Suite 202, Las Vegas, Nevada 89120; phone: 702-486-7330.

Location

Las Vegas is more than just casinos and nightclubs, bright lights, and stage shows. Las Vegas is one of the fastest growing cities in the country, an economic powerhouse, and an outdoor enthusiast's dream. It's also home to The Art Institute of Las Vegas. That may not be glamorous or glitzy, but for students who plan to enter a creative profession, it's very important.

Las Vegas may be known as the entertainment capital of the world—after all, where else can someone see a pyramid, a Roman palace, the canals of Venice, the Eiffel Tower, and the tallest free-standing building west of the Mississippi, all in a quick spin around town? It's quite different from the view of the early Spanish colonials who used the place as just another watering post on a trail from Santa Fe to Los Angeles.

This unique city offers an eclectic array of museums, including the Neon Museum, a museum devoted to organized crime and law enforcement, the National Atomic Testing Museum, and the natural history museum.

For those who love the great outdoors, Las Vegas offers the kind of mild desert weather that makes it even more enjoyable to hike Red Rock Canyon or the Valley of Fire, explore the nearby Grand Canyon or Hoover Dam, or go boating on Lake Mead, the largest man-made lake in the whole country.

Programs of Study and Degrees

Creativity is all around, and with millions of tomorrow's jobs in creative fields, the world needs more creative professionals. No matter which course of study a student chooses, the instructors at The Art Institutes will guide, support, and help students fine-tune their visual thinking and problem solving, so that they can take advantage of the world's growing creative opportunities and put their passion to work. Programs are offered in the areas of design, which focuses on communicating conceptually and helping people connect in living and work spaces; media arts, that centers on utilizing technology to deliver information and entertainment; fashion, where students learn anything from designing clothes for the runway to running a retail shop; and culinary, which exposes learners to international cuisines as well as restaurant management techniques.

Bachelor's degree programs are offered in the areas of advertising, audio production, culinary management, digital filmmaking & video production, digital photography, fashion & retail management, food & beverage management, game art & design, graphic design, interior design, media arts & animation, visual effects & motion graphics, and web design & interactive media.

Associate degree programs are offered in the areas of baking & pastry, culinary arts, digital photography, and drafting technology & design.

Diploma programs are offered in baking & pastry, culinary arts, digital image management, fashion retailing, web design & development, and web design & interactive communications.

Program availability and degree offerings are subject to change.

Academic Facilities

The Art Institute of Las Vegas provides a learning environment with professional-grade technology applicable to each student's course of study. Students have the opportunity to build a portfolio of work that shows potential employers that they are trained to use the software, hardware, or equipment utilized within the industry. Depending upon the course of study, students are immersed in a creative environment—from classrooms to computer labs to studios—focused on relevant, hands-on education designed to prepare them for the real world.

Costs

Actual tuition and housing costs will vary depending on program, number of credits enrolled, and living arrangements. Prospective students should contact a Student Financial Services professional at the school for details.

Financial Aid

Financial aid is available for those who qualify. Students who require financial assistance should first complete and submit the Free Application for Federal Student Aid (FAFSA) online at www.fafsa.ed.gov and meet with a financial aid officer. Students may also apply for a number of scholarships focusing on their specific areas of career interest.

Faculty

Faculty members are hands-on creative professionals with proven experience as business leaders and innovators, hosting a learning environment similar to the career world students will face after graduation. Part instructor, part mentor, their mission is to help develop and transform creative potential into high-demand marketable skills.

Admission Requirements

Prospective students should refer to the current academic catalog for full details regarding admission requirements and process.

Application and Information

To obtain an application, make arrangements for an interview, or tour the school, prospective students should contact:

The Art Institute of Las Vegas
2350 Corporate Circle
Henderson, Nevada 89074-7737
Phone: 702-369-9944
      800-833-2678 (toll-free)
Fax: 702-992-8458
Website: http://www.artinstitutes.edu/lasvegas

THE ART INSTITUTE OF MICHIGAN
NOVI, MICHIGAN

The Art Institute of Michigan is one of The Art Institutes, a system of over fifty schools throughout North America dedicated to providing hands-on education in the creative and applied arts. The Art Institute of Michigan offer bachelor's and associate's degree programs as well as non-degree programs for students interested in pursuing career opportunities from among tomorrow's 15 million jobs in creative fields like design, fashion, media arts, and culinary (based on information from the U.S. Bureau of Labor Statistics for job growth from 2012 to 2022).

A focused education from The Art Institute of Michigan can help students turn their creative energy into a powerful tool that can make a difference in the world. Students are part of a collaborative and supportive community, where experienced instructors provide the guidance and skills needed to pursue a career in the creative economy.

The Art Institute of Michigan is also an important resource for creative industry leaders who value the opportunity provided students to learn by using professional-grade technology to build a portfolio of work to show potential employers after graduation.

Accreditation

The Art Institute of Michigan, as a branch of the Illinois Institute of Art, is accredited by the Higher Learning Commission and is a member of the North Central Association (NCA), 230 S. LaSalle Street, Suite 7-500, Chicago, Illinois 60604-1413; phone: 800-621-7440; www.ncahlc.org.

The Diploma in baking & pastry and Associate of Applied Science in culinary arts programs are accredited by the Accrediting Commission of the American Culinary Federation Education Foundation.

The Art Institute of Michigan is licensed under the laws of the Michigan Department of Labor and Economic Growth.

Location

Novi is one of Michigan's fastest-growing cities. The area offers plenty of opportunities for recreation with its lakes and rolling hills, shopping at its malls, and entertainment at its many nightspots. Novi also has a quaint, walkable downtown area. Novi is also just 25 miles from Detroit, offering students at The Art Institute of Michigan the best of both worlds—small-city convenience and big-city excitement.

Detroit brings to mind cars and music. The center of America's auto industry for a century, the city has seen its share of economic ups and downs, but it continues to reinvent itself and reinvigorate its manufacturing base. A number of local companies are working on emerging technologies such as biotechnology, nanotechnology, information technology, and hydrogen fuel cell development.

For all its industry, Detroit is a very cosmopolitan city. Many of the area's prominent museums are located in the thriving, historic cultural district. Other cultural highlights include the Motown Historical Museum, the Tuskegee Airmen Museum,

the Museum of Contemporary Art Detroit, the Contemporary Art Institute of Detroit, and the Belle Isle Conservatory.

Live music has been a big part of Detroit's nightlife since the late 1940s, and the area has many nationally prominent music venues. Important music events include the Detroit International Jazz Festival, the Detroit Electronic Music Festival, the Motor City Music Conference, the Urban Organic Music Conference, the Concert of Colors, and the hip-hop Summer Jamz Festival.

Detroit has a proud heritage of professional sports—it's one of the few cities that offers all four major pro sports. Baseball's Tigers play at Comerica Park; the Pistons play basketball in suburban Auburn Hills at The Palace of Auburn Hills; the Lions play football at Ford Field; and the Red Wings play hockey at Joe Louis Arena.

Programs of Study and Degrees

Creativity is all around, and with millions of tomorrow's jobs in creative fields, the world needs more creative professionals. No matter which course of study a student chooses, the instructors at The Art Institutes will guide, support, and help students fine-tune their visual thinking and problem solving, so that they can take advantage of the world's growing creative opportunities and put their passion to work. Programs are offered in the areas of design, which focuses on communicating conceptually and helping people connect in living and work spaces; media arts, that centers on utilizing technology to deliver information and entertainment; fashion, where students learn anything from designing clothes for the runway to running a retail shop; and culinary, which exposes learners to international cuisines as well as restaurant management techniques.

Bachelor's degree programs are offered in the areas of audio production, culinary management, digital photography, fashion & marketing management, graphic design, interior design, media arts & animation, and web design & interactive media.

Associate degree programs are offered in the areas of culinary arts, fashion merchandising, graphic design, interior design, and web design & interactive media.

Diploma programs are offered in baking & pastry, culinary arts, digital image management, fashion retailing, web design & development, and web design & interactive communications.

Program availability and degree offerings are subject to change.

Academic Facilities

The Art Institute of Michigan provides a learning environment with professional-grade technology applicable to each student's course of study. Students have the opportunity to build a portfolio of work that shows potential employers that they are trained to use the software, hardware, or equipment utilized within the industry. Depending upon the course of study, students are immersed in a creative environment—from classrooms to computer labs to studios—focused on relevant, hands-on education designed to prepare them for the real world.

Costs

Actual tuition and housing costs will vary depending on program, number of credits enrolled, and actual living arrangements. Prospective students should contact a Student Financial Services professional at the school for details.

Financial Aid

Financial aid is available for those who qualify. Students who require financial assistance should first complete and submit the Free Application for Federal Student Aid (FAFSA) online at www.fafsa.ed.gov and meet with a financial aid officer. Students may also apply for a number of scholarships focusing on their specific areas of career interest.

Faculty

Faculty members are hands-on creative professionals with proven experience as business leaders and innovators, hosting a learning environment similar to the career world students will face after graduation. Part instructor, part mentor, their mission is to help develop and transform creative potential into high-demand marketable skills.

Admission Requirements

Prospective students should refer to the current academic catalog for full details regarding admission requirements and process.

Application and Information

To obtain an application, make arrangements for an interview, or tour the school, students should contact:
The Art Institute of Michigan
28125 Cabot Drive, Suite 120
Novi, Michigan 48377
Phone: 248-675-3800
           800-479-0087 (toll-free)
Fax: 248-675-3830
Website: http://www.artinstitutes.edu/detroit

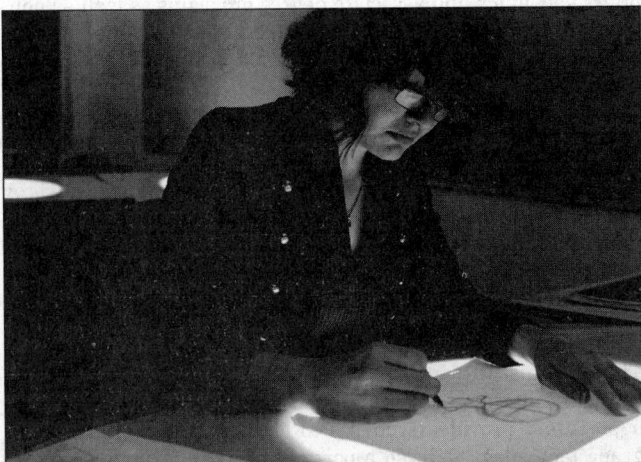

Since The Art Institutes system of schools is comprised of several institutions, see aiprograms.info for program duration, tuition, fees, and other costs, median debt, federal salary data, alumni success, and other important info. The Art Institutes is a system of over 50 schools throughout North America. Programs, credential levels, technology, and scheduling options vary by school, and employment opportunities are not guaranteed. Financial aid is available to those who qualify. Several institutions included in The Art Institutes system are campuses of South University or Argosy University. OH Registration #04-01-1698B, AC0165, AC0080, Licensed by the Florida Commission for Independent Education, License No. 1287, 3427, 3110, 2581. Certified by SCHEV to operate in Virginia. Administrative office: 210 Sixth Avenue, 33rd Floor, Pittsburgh, PA 15222. ©2013 The Art Institutes International LLC

THE ART INSTITUTE OF MICHIGAN—TROY

TROY, MICHIGAN

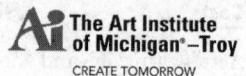

The Art Institute of Michigan—Troy is one of The Art Institutes, a system of over fifty schools throughout North America dedicated to providing hands-on education in the creative and applied arts. The Art Institute of Michigan—Troy offers bachelor's and associate degree programs as well as non-degree programs for students interested in pursuing career opportunities from among tomorrow's 15 million jobs in creative fields like design, fashion, and media arts (based on information from the U.S. Bureau of Labor Statistics for job growth from 2012 to 2022).

A focused education from The Art Institute of Michigan—Troy can help students turn their creative energy into a powerful tool that can make a difference in the world. Students are part of a collaborative and supportive community, where experienced instructors provide the guidance and skills needed to pursue a career in the creative economy.

The Art Institute of Michigan—Troy is also an important resource for creative industry leaders who value the opportunity provided students to learn by using professional-grade technology to build a portfolio of work to show potential employers after graduation.

Accreditation

The Art Institute of Michigan—Troy is an additional location of The Illinois Institute of Art—Chicago, which is accredited by the Higher Learning Commission and a member of the North Central Association, 230 S. LaSalle Street, Suite 7-500, Chicago, Illinois 60604-1413; phone: 800-621-7440; www.ncahlc.org.

The Art Institute of Michigan—Troy is licensed under the laws of the Michigan Department of Labor and Economic Growth.

Location

A northern suburb of Detroit, the city of Troy is a bustling center of business and technology. The city, rated as one of the safest in the nation, is known for its hometown charm, community spirit, and quality of life. Troy offers a variety of entertainment options ranging from museums and theaters to summer jazz concerts and the Troy Daze Festival, which draws 100,000 people every year.

Students at The Art Institute of Michigan—Troy have access to public transportation to get around Troy and to access attractions in nearby Detroit.

The city of Detroit has been undergoing a transformation recently, with a goal of redeveloping the city and restoring it to world-class status. Detroit is diversifying its economy, with a number of local companies working on emerging technologies such as biotechnology, nanotechnology, information technology, and hydrogen fuel cell development.

For all its industry, Detroit is a very cosmopolitan city. Many of the Detroit area's prominent museums are located in the thriving, historic cultural district. Other cultural highlights include the Motown Historical Museum, the Tuskegee Airmen Museum, the Museum of Contemporary Art Detroit, the Contemporary Art Institute of Detroit, and the Belle Isle Conservatory.

Live music has been a big part of Detroit's nightlife since the late 1940s, and the area has many nationally prominent music venues. Live Nation hosts concerts throughout the area, and other concerts are held at DTE Energy Music Theatre and the Palace of Auburn Hills. Important music events include the Detroit International Jazz Festival, the Detroit Electronic Music Festival, the Motor City Music Conference, the Urban Organic Music Conference, the Concert of Colors, and the hip-hop Summer Jamz Festival.

Detroit is one of the few cities where you can watch all four major pro sports. Baseball's Tigers play at Comerica Park; the Pistons play basketball in suburban Auburn Hills at The Palace of Auburn Hills; the Lions play football at Ford Field; and the Red Wings play hockey at Joe Louis Arena.

Programs of Study and Degrees

Creativity is all around, and with millions of tomorrow's jobs in creative fields, the world needs more creative professionals. No matter which course of study a student chooses, the instructors at The Art Institutes will guide, support, and help students fine-tune their visual thinking and problem solving, so that they can take advantage of the world's growing creative opportunities and put their passion to work. Programs are offered in the areas of design, which focuses on communicating conceptually and helping people connect in living and work spaces; media arts, that centers on utilizing technology to deliver information and entertainment; and fashion, where students learn anything from designing clothes for the runway to running a retail shop.

Bachelor's degree programs are offered in the areas of digital photography, fashion marketing & management, graphic design, interior design, media arts & animation, and web design & interactive media.

Associate degree programs are offered in the areas of fashion merchandising and graphic design.

Diploma programs are offered in digital image management, fashion retailing, web design & development, and web design & interactive communications.

Program availability and degree offerings are subject to change.

Academic Facilities

The Art Institute of Michigan—Troy provides a learning environment with professional-grade technology applicable to each student's course of study. Students have the opportunity to build a portfolio of work that shows potential employers that they are trained to use the software, hardware, or equipment utilized within the industry. Depending upon the course of study, students are immersed in a creative environment—from classrooms to computer labs to studios—focused on relevant, hands-on education designed to prepare them for the real world.

Costs

Actual tuition and housing costs will vary depending on program, number of credits enrolled, and living arrangements. Prospective students should contact a Student Financial Services professional at the school for details.

Financial Aid

Financial aid is available for those who qualify. Students who require financial assistance should first complete and submit the Free Application for Federal Student Aid (FAFSA) online at www.fafsa.ed.gov and meet with a financial aid officer. Students may also apply for a number of scholarships focusing on their specific areas of career interest.

Faculty

Faculty members are hands-on creative professionals with proven experience as business leaders and innovators, hosting a learning environment similar to the career world students will face after graduation. Part instructor, part mentor, their mission is to help develop and transform creative potential into high-demand marketable skills.

Admission Requirements

Prospective students should refer to the current academic catalog for full details regarding admission requirements and process.

Application and Information

To obtain an application, make arrangements for an interview, or tour the school, prospective students should contact:

The Art Institute of Michigan—Troy
1414 East Maple Road, Suite 150
Troy, Michigan 48083
Phone: 248-837-3200
      877-320-3275 (toll-free)
Fax: 248-837-3300
Website: http://www.artinstitutes.edu/troy

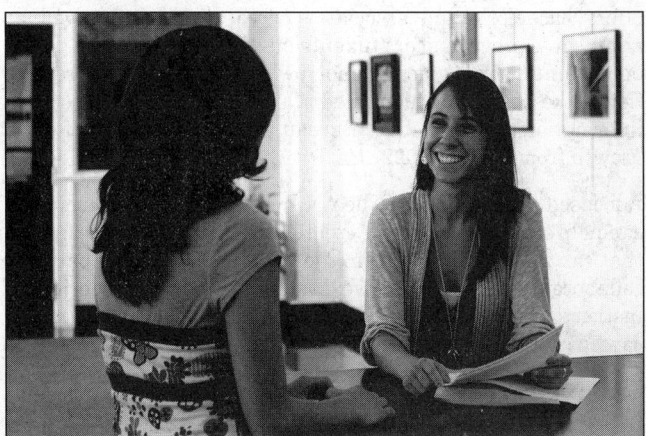

THE ART INSTITUTE OF OHIO—CINCINNATI

CINCINNATI, OHIO

The Art Institute of Ohio—Cincinnati is one of The Art Institutes, a system of over fifty schools throughout North America dedicated to providing hands-on education in the creative and applied arts. The Art Institute of Ohio—Cincinnati offers bachelor's and associate degree programs as well as non-degree programs for students interested in pursuing career opportunities from among tomorrow's 15 million jobs in creative fields like design, fashion, media arts, and culinary (based on information from the U.S. Bureau of Labor Statistics for job growth from 2012 to 2022).

A focused education from The Art Institute of Ohio—Cincinnati can help students turn their creative energy into a powerful tool that can make a difference in the world. Students are part of a collaborative and supportive community, where experienced instructors provide the guidance and skills needed to pursue a career in the creative economy.

The Art Institute of Ohio—Cincinnati is also an important resource for creative industry leaders who value the opportunity provided students to learn by using professional-grade technology to build a portfolio of work to show potential employers after graduation.

Accreditation

The Art Institute of Ohio—Cincinnati, as a branch of The Illinois Institute of Art, is accredited by the Higher Learning Commission and is a member of the North Central Association (NCA), 230 S. LaSalle Street, Suite 7-500, Chicago, Illinois 60604-1413; phone: 800-621-7440; www.ncahlc.org.

The Associate of Applied Science in culinary arts degree program is accredited by The Accrediting Commission of the American Culinary Federation Education Foundation.

The Art Institute of Ohio—Cincinnati holds a provisional Certificate of Authorization for its academic programs by The Ohio Board of Regents, 30 East Broad Street, Columbus, Ohio 43215; phone: 614-466-6000.

The Art Institute of Ohio—Cincinnati is licensed by the Ohio State Board of Career Colleges & Schools, 30 East Broad Street, 24th Floor, Suite 2481, Columbus, Ohio 43215-3138; phone: 614-466-2752.

The Art Institute of Ohio—Cincinnati is regulated by the Board for Proprietary Education, Indiana Commission for Higher Education, W462 Indiana Government Center South, 402 West Washington Street, Indianapolis, Indiana 46204; phone: 317-232-1324 or 317-232-6716; AC0165.

Location

Thanks to its location in the heart of the city, The Art Institute of Ohio—Cincinnati makes it easy for students to enjoy all the culture and excitement a large city has to offer. The city is home to major league sporting events, major concerts, symphony, theater, Kings Island amusement park, award-winning restaurants, and downtown entertainment districts with exciting nightspots.

In the early 1800s, Cincinnati went from a river outpost to perhaps the first middle-American boomtown to rival the bigger coastal cities in size and wealth. Today, Cincinnati is known for its great beauty with steep hills, wooded suburbs, a picturesque downtown riverfront, and four definite seasons. It's a very affordable city with friendly neighbors, great job opportunities, excellent schools, diverse religions, shopping, safety, and lots of things to do.

Cincinnati is famous for its historic architecture. The Over-the-Rhine district features one of the world's largest collections of Italianate architecture. There is a river ferry and many bridges from the city to northern Kentucky, on the other side of the Ohio River. The Roebling Suspension Bridge is the work of John Roebling, who later modeled his much more famous Brooklyn Bridge after this one.

Cincinnati holds many annual festivals and events: Oktoberfest, which celebrates the city's German heritage; Taste of Cincinnati; the Ohio Valley Jazz Festival; the Banbury Music Festival; and the Cincinnati Fringe Festival, Ohio's biggest performing arts festival with twelve days of film, visual art, and music.

There's also plenty of big-league sports. The Cincinnati Reds play baseball at Great American Ballpark, while the Bengals play football at Paul Brown Stadium. Other sports include pro hockey and soccer along with a full slate of college sports.

Programs of Study and Degrees

Creativity is all around, and with millions of tomorrow's jobs in creative fields, the world needs more creative professionals. No matter which course of study a student chooses, the instructors at The Art Institutes will guide, support, and help students fine-tune their visual thinking and problem solving, so that they can take advantage of the world's growing creative opportunities and put their passion to work. Programs are offered in the areas of design, which focuses on communicating conceptually and helping people connect in living and work spaces; media arts, that centers on utilizing technology to deliver information and entertainment; fashion, where students learn anything from designing clothes for the runway to running a retail shop; and culinary, which exposes learners to international cuisines as well as restaurant management techniques.

Bachelor's degree programs are offered in the areas of advertising, culinary management, digital filmmaking & video production, digital photography, fashion marketing & management, graphic design, hospitality management, interior design, media arts & animation, and web design & interactive media.

Associate degree programs are offered in the areas of culinary arts, fashion merchandising, graphic design, hospitality management, interior design, video production, and web design & interactive media.

Diploma programs are offered in baking & pastry, culinary arts, digital image management, fashion retailing, web design & development, and web design & interactive communications.

The Associate in Arts in culinary arts, the Bachelor of Science in culinary arts management, the Bachelor of Science in food & beverage management, and the Bachelor of Fine Arts in interior design are available in evening and weekend formats.

Program availability and degree offerings are subject to change.

Academic Facilities

The Art Institute of Ohio—Cincinnati provides a learning environment with professional-grade technology applicable to each student's course of study. Students have the opportunity to build a portfolio of work that shows potential employers that they are trained to use the software, hardware, or equipment utilized within the industry. Depending upon the course of study, students are immersed in a creative environment—from classrooms to computer labs to studios—focused on relevant, hands-on education designed to prepare them for the real world.

Costs

Actual tuition and housing costs will vary depending on program, number of credits enrolled, and living arrangements. Prospective students should contact a Student Financial Services professional at the school for details.

Financial Aid

Financial aid is available for those who qualify. Students who require financial assistance should first complete and submit the Free Application for Federal Student Aid (FAFSA) online at www.fafsa.ed.gov and meet with a financial aid officer. Students may also apply for a number of scholarships focusing on their specific areas of career interest.

Faculty

Faculty members are hands-on creative professionals with proven experience as business leaders and innovators, hosting a learning environment similar to the career world students will face after graduation. Part instructor, part mentor, their mission is to help develop and transform creative potential into high-demand marketable skills.

Admission Requirements

Prospective students should refer to the current academic catalog for full details regarding admission requirements and process.

Application and Information

To obtain an application, make arrangements for an interview, or tour the school, prospective students should contact:

The Art Institute of Ohio—Cincinnati
8845 Governors Hill Drive, Suite 100
Cincinnati, Ohio 45249-3317
Phone: 513-833-2400
       866-613-5184 (toll-free)
Fax: 877-477-8486
Website: http://www.artinstitutes.edu/cincinnati

THE ART INSTITUTE OF PHILADELPHIA
PHILADELPHIA, PENNSYLVANIA

The Art Institute of Philadelphia is one of The Art Institutes, a system of over fifty schools throughout North America dedicated to providing hands-on education in the creative and applied arts. The Art Institute of Philadelphia offers bachelor's and associate degree programs as well as non-degree programs for students interested in pursuing career opportunities from among tomorrow's 15 million jobs in creative fields like design, fashion, media arts, and culinary (based on information from the U.S. Bureau of Labor Statistics for job growth from 2012 to 2022).

A focused education from The Art Institute of Philadelphia can help students turn their creative energy into a powerful tool that can make a difference in the world. Students are part of a collaborative and supportive community, where experienced instructors provide the guidance and skills needed to pursue a career in the creative economy.

The Art Institute of Philadelphia is also an important resource for creative industry leaders who value the opportunity provided students to learn by using professional-grade technology to build a portfolio of work to show potential employers after graduation.

Accreditation

The Art Institute of Philadelphia is accredited by the Middle States Commission on Higher Education, 3624 Market Street, Philadelphia, Pennsylvania 19104; phone: 267-284-5000.

The Middle States Commission on Higher Education is an institutional accrediting agency recognized by the U.S. Secretary of Education and the Council for Higher Education Accreditation.

The Associate of Science in culinary arts degree program is accredited by The Accrediting Commission of the American Culinary Federation Education Foundation.

The Bachelor of Science in interior design degree program is accredited by the National Kitchen & Bath Association (NKBA). NKBA can be contacted at 687 Willow Grove Street, Hackettstown, New Jersey 07840; phone: 800-THE-NKBA; www.nkba.org.

The interior design program leading to the Bachelor of Science degree is accredited by the Council for Interior Design Accreditation; 206 Grandville Avenue, Suite 350, Grand Rapids, Michigan 49503; www.accredit-id.org.

The Art Institute of Philadelphia is authorized by the Pennsylvania Department of Education to confer the Bachelor of Science degrees, Associate of Science degrees, and diplomas. The Department of Education can be reached by writing to the Commonwealth of Pennsylvania, department of Education Office of Postsecondary and Higher Education, 333 Market Street, Harrisburg, Pennsylvania 17126; phone: 717-783-6788.

Location

Philadelphia is where the United States was born—everywhere in this bustling city are the unmistakable signs of rebirth and revolution. And a student's journey toward creative rebirth and revolution can start at The Art Institute of Philadelphia, conveniently located in the city's downtown.

One of the largest college and university towns in the nation, the Philadelphia area's influx of young people is responsible for much of the vitality of the arts, culture, and design scene. It's evident in everything from North Philadelphia factories that have been given new life as innovative art galleries, to fashion-forward independent boutiques that are opening in nineteenth-century storefronts.

Philadelphia is a big city with a small-town heart. There's an abundance of neighborhoods, ranging from charming to funky. There are iconic symbols of America's history: the Liberty Bell, Constitution Hall, and Independence Hall. The Italian Market is the oldest working outdoor food market in the country, and more than 200 new sidewalk cafes bring the city streets alive at night. And the area's art, design, and fashion businesses and galleries make "Old City" a vibrant and culturally diverse neighborhood with an old world–European feel.

Funk, jazz, hip-hop, world music, punk or alternative rock are all available at local clubs, while classical musicians perform under the soaring dome of the new Kimmel Center. There's Phillies baseball at Citizens Bank Park, Flyers hockey or 76ers basketball at the Wells Fargo Center, and Eagles football at Lincoln Financial Field.

Students seeking relief from the urban scene can hike, bike, run, picnic, or just relax in the over 9,000 acres of green space that make up the city's parks. For cycling enthusiasts, Philadelphia is consistently rated among the top five large cities for that activity, offering more bike lanes than any other city and a network of top-rated off-road trails.

Programs of Study and Degrees

Creativity is all around, and with millions of tomorrow's jobs in creative fields, the world needs more creative professionals. No matter which course of study a student chooses, the instructors at The Art Institutes will guide, support, and help students fine-tune their visual thinking and problem solving, so that they can take advantage of the world's growing creative opportunities and put their passion to work. Programs are offered in the areas of design, which focuses on communicating conceptually and helping people connect in living and work spaces; media arts, that centers on utilizing technology to deliver information and entertainment; fashion, where students learn anything from designing clothes for the runway to running a retail shop; and culinary, which exposes learners to international cuisines as well as restaurant management techniques.

Bachelor's degree programs are offered in the areas of advertising, audio production, culinary management, digital filmmaking & video production, fashion design, fashion marketing, game art & design, graphic design, interior design, media arts & animation, photography, visual effects & motion graphics, and web design & interactive media.

Associate degree programs are offered in the areas of culinary arts, digital filmmaking & video production, fashion design, fashion marketing, graphic design, interior design, photography, visual merchandising, and web design & interactive media.

Diploma programs are offered in baking & pastry, culinary arts, fashion retailing, and web design & development.

The diploma in baking & pastry and the Associate of Science in culinary arts are available in evening and weekend formats.

Program availability and degree offerings are subject to change.

Academic Facilities

The Art Institute of Philadelphia provides a learning environment with professional-grade technology applicable to each student's course of study. Students have the opportunity to build a portfolio of work that shows potential employers that they are trained to use the software, hardware, or equipment utilized within the industry. Depending upon the course of study, students are immersed in a creative environment—from classrooms to computer labs to studios—focused on relevant, hands-on education designed to prepare them for the real world.

Costs

Actual tuition and housing costs will vary depending on program, number of credits enrolled, and living arrangements. Prospective students should contact a Student Financial Services professional at the school for details.

Financial Aid

Financial aid is available for those who qualify. Students who require financial assistance should first complete and submit the Free Application for Federal Student Aid (FAFSA) online at www.fafsa.ed.gov and meet with a financial aid officer. Students may also apply for a number of scholarships focusing on their specific areas of career interest.

Faculty

Faculty members are hands-on creative professionals with proven experience as business leaders and innovators, hosting a learning environment similar to the career world students will face after graduation. Part instructor, part mentor, their mission is to help develop and transform creative potential into high-demand marketable skills.

Admission Requirements

Prospective students should refer to the current academic catalog for full details regarding admission requirements and process.

Application and Information To obtain an application, make arrangements for an interview, or tour the school, prospective students should contact:

The Art Institute of Philadelphia
1622 Chestnut Street
Philadelphia, Pennsylvania 19103-5119
Phone: 215-567-7080
        800-275-2474 (toll-free)
Fax: 215-405-6399
Website: http://www.artinstitutes.edu/philadelphia

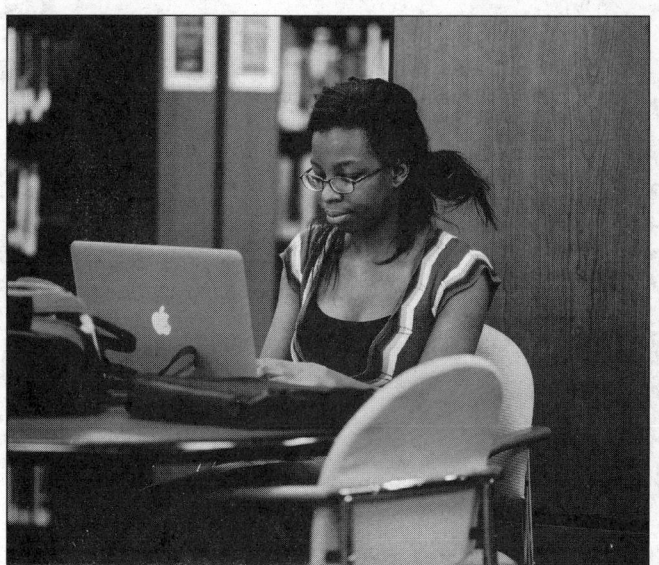

COLLEGE CLOSE-UPS

THE ART INSTITUTE OF PHOENIX
PHOENIX, ARIZONA

The Art Institute of Phoenix is one of The Art Institutes, a system of over fifty schools throughout North America dedicated to providing hands-on education in the creative and applied arts. The Art Institute of Phoenix offers bachelor's and associate degree programs as well as non-degree programs for students interested in pursuing career opportunities from among tomorrow's 15 million jobs in creative fields like design, fashion, media arts, and culinary (based on information from the U.S. Bureau of Labor Statistics for job growth from 2012 to 2022).

A focused education from The Art Institute of Phoenix can help students turn their creative energy into a powerful tool that can make a difference in the world. Students are part of a collaborative and supportive community, where experienced instructors provide the guidance and skills needed to pursue a career in the creative economy.

The Art Institute of Phoenix is also an important resource for creative industry leaders who value the opportunity provided students to learn by using professional-grade technology to build a portfolio of work to show potential employers after graduation.

Accreditation

The Art Institute of Phoenix is accredited by the Accrediting Council for Independent Colleges and Schools to award diplomas, associate degrees, and bachelor's degrees. The Accrediting Council for Independent Colleges and Schools is listed as a nationally recognized accrediting agency by the United States Department of Education and is recognized by the Council for Higher Education Accreditation. ACICS can be contacted at 750 First Street NE, Suite 980, Washington, D.C. 20002; phone: 202-336-6780.

The Associate of Applied Science in culinary arts, the Associate of Applied Science in baking & pastry, and the Bachelor of Arts in culinary management degree programs are accredited by The Accrediting Commission of the American Culinary Federation Education Foundation.

The interior design program leading to the Bachelor of Arts degree is accredited by the Council for Interior Design Accreditation, 206 Grandville Avenue, Suite 350, Grand Rapids, Michigan 49503; www.accredit-id.org.

The Art Institute of Phoenix is authorized by the Arizona State Board for Private Post-secondary Education, 1400 West Washington Street, Room 2560, Phoenix, Arizona 85007; phone: 602-542-5709; http://azppse.state.az.us.

Location

With its sunny days, low humidity, and an average yearly temperature of 72 degrees, it's easy to see why Phoenix is one of the fastest growing cities in the nation. Located in the middle of the state and in the heart of the beautiful Sonoran Desert,

Phoenix is the gateway to cool pine forests, the red rock towers of Sedona, and nature's greatest wonder, the Grand Canyon.

Phoenix is the hub of the Southwest—a high-tech and manufacturing center, surrounded by majestic mountain ranges. It's also an opportune location for students seeking to start their creative careers at The Art Institute of Phoenix.

Home to more than a million people, Phoenix offers sun-filled days and a nightlife that ranges from top comedy and music clubs to cultural icons such as the Phoenix Art Museum, the Phoenix Symphony Orchestra Hall, and many Arizona theater companies.

Phoenix offers professional sports teams as well. The Arizona Diamondbacks play their baseball at Chase Field, the Phoenix Suns play basketball at US Airways Center, and the NFL's Arizona Cardinals play football at the University of Phoenix Stadium.

Programs of Study and Degrees

Creativity is all around, and with millions of tomorrow's jobs in creative fields, the world needs more creative professionals. No matter which course of study a student chooses, the instructors at The Art Institutes will guide, support, and help students fine-tune their visual thinking and problem solving, so that they can take advantage of the world's growing creative opportunities and put their passion to work. Programs are offered in the areas of design, which focuses on communicating conceptually and helping people connect in living and work spaces; media arts, that centers on utilizing technology to deliver information and entertainment; fashion, where students learn anything from designing clothes for the runway to running a retail shop; and culinary, which exposes learners to international cuisines as well as restaurant management techniques.

Bachelor's degree programs are offered in the areas of advertising, culinary management, digital filmmaking & video production, digital photography, fashion design, fashion marketing, game art & design, graphic & web design, hospitality food & beverage management, interior design, media arts & animation, visual & game programming, and visual effects & motion graphics.

Associate degree programs are offered in the areas of baking & pastry, culinary arts, and graphic design.

Diploma programs are offered in baking & pastry, culinary arts, digital image management, fashion retailing, web design & development, and web design & interactive communications.

The Associate of Applied Science in culinary arts, the Bachelor of Arts in culinary management, and the Associate of Applied Science in graphic design are available in evening and weekend formats.

Program availability and degree offerings are subject to change.

Academic Facilities

The Art Institute of Phoenix provides a learning environment with professional-grade technology applicable to each student's course of study. Students have the opportunity to build a portfolio of work that shows potential employers that they are trained to use the software, hardware, or equipment utilized within the industry. Depending upon the course of study, students are immersed in a creative environment—from classrooms to computer labs to studios—focused on relevant, hands-on education designed to prepare them for the real world.

Costs

Actual tuition and housing costs will vary depending on program, number of credits enrolled, and living arrangements. Prospective students should contact a Student Financial Services professional at the school for details.

Financial Aid

Financial aid is available for those who qualify. Students who require financial assistance should first complete and submit the Free Application for Federal Student Aid (FAFSA) online at www.fafsa.ed.gov and meet with a financial aid officer. Students may also apply for a number of scholarships focusing on their specific areas of career interest.

Faculty

Faculty members are hands-on creative professionals with proven experience as business leaders and innovators, hosting a learning environment similar to the career world students will face after graduation. Part instructor, part mentor, their mission is to help develop and transform creative potential into high-demand marketable skills.

Admission Requirements

Prospective students should refer to the current academic catalog for full details regarding admission requirements and process.

Application and Information

To obtain an application, make arrangements for an interview, or tour the school, prospective students should contact:

The Art Institute of Phoenix
2233 West Dunlap Avenue
Phoenix, Arizona 85021-2859
Phone: 602-331-7500
      800-474-2479 (toll-free)
Fax: 602-331-5301
Website: http://www.artinstitutes.edu/phoenix

THE ART INSTITUTE OF PITTSBURGH
PITTSBURGH, PENNSYLVANIA

The Art Institute of Pittsburgh is one of The Art Institutes, a system of over 50 schools throughout North America dedicated to providing hands-on education in the creative and applied arts. The Art Institute of Pittsburgh offers bachelor's and associate degree programs as well as non-degree programs for students interested in pursuing career opportunities from among tomorrow's 15 million jobs in creative fields like design, fashion, media arts, and culinary (based on information from the U.S. Bureau of Labor Statistics for job growth from 2012 to 2022).

A focused education from The Art Institute of Pittsburgh can help students turn their creative energy into a powerful tool that can make a difference in the world. Students are part of a collaborative and supportive community, where experienced instructors provide the guidance and skills needed to pursue a career in the creative economy.

The Art Institute of Pittsburgh is also an important resource for creative industry leaders who value the opportunity provided students to learn by using professional-grade technology to build a portfolio of work to show potential employers after graduation.

Accreditation

The Art Institute of Pittsburgh is accredited by the Middle States Commission on Higher Education, 3624 Market Street, Philadelphia, Pennsylvania 19104; phone: 267-284-5000.

The Middle States Commission on Higher Education is an institutional accrediting agency recognized by the U.S. Secretary of Education and the Council for Higher Education Accreditation.

The Associate of Science degree in culinary arts and the Bachelor of Science in culinary management are accredited by The Accrediting Commission of the American Culinary Federation Education Foundation.

The interior design program leading to the Bachelor of Science degree is accredited by the Council for Interior Design Accreditation, 206 Grandville Avenue, Suite 350, Grand Rapids, Michigan 49503; www.accredit-id.org.

The Art Institute of Pittsburgh is authorized by the Pennsylvania Department of Education to confer Bachelor of Science degrees, Associate of Science degrees, and diplomas. The Department of Education can be reached by writing to the Commonwealth of Pennsylvania, Department of Education Office of Postsecondary and Higher Education, 333 Market Street, Harrisburg, Pennsylvania 17126; phone: 717-783-6788.

The Art Institute of Pittsburgh is registered as a private institution with the Minnesota Office of Higher Education pursuant to Minnesota Statutes, sections 136A.61 to 136A.71. Registration is not an endorsement of the institution. Credits earned at the institution may not transfer to all other institutions.

Location

The Art Institute of Pittsburgh is nestled in the heart of downtown Pittsburgh's Golden Triangle, formed by a confluence of rivers that once marked the fringe of the American frontier. Today, Pittsburgh has emerged as one of America's most livable cities—a renowned leader in health care, technology, education, robotics, the arts, and career opportunities.

Pittsburgh offers a patchwork of diverse styles and nationalities, sprung from the roots of a steel town where people came from around the world to build better lives. Distinctive neighborhood enclaves like Deutschtown and Polish Hill present a sense of both old-world charm and budding potential—especially for creative professionals eager to make their mark in a unique landscape primed for change.

Downtown is a jigsaw puzzle of old and new architecture, ready to be captured by sketch pad or camera. On the fringe is the legendary Strip District, home to a wealth of ethnic grocers and street-side cafés. Each year the city's Oakland, Squirrel Hill, and Shadyside neighborhoods swell with thousands of students drawn to the colleges and universities that make Pittsburgh a top destination for higher learning.

Pittsburgh is home to many classic movie houses, featuring the latest blockbusters as well as the best independent and foreign films. It also has a rich history as host to an ever-growing number of Hollywood productions.

Of course, Pittsburgh is synonymous with the Steelers, Pirates, and Penguins with their exciting home stadiums, but home also to the Andy Warhol Museum and the Carnegie Science Center.

Programs of Study and Degrees

Creativity is all around, and with millions of tomorrow's jobs in creative fields, the world needs more creative professionals. No matter which course of study a student chooses, the instructors at The Art Institutes will guide, support, and help students fine-tune their visual thinking and problem solving, so that they can take advantage of the world's growing creative opportunities and put their passion to work. Programs are offered in the areas of design, which focuses on communicating conceptually and helping people connect in living and work spaces; media arts, that centers on utilizing technology to deliver information and entertainment; fashion, where students learn anything from designing clothes for the runway to running a retail shop; and culinary, which exposes learners to international cuisine as well as restaurant management techniques.

Bachelor's degree programs are offered in the areas of advertising, culinary management, digital filmmaking & video production, entertainment design, fashion & retail management, fashion design, game art & design, graphic design, hotel & restaurant management, industrial design, interior design, media arts & animation, photography, visual effects & motion graphics, and web design & interactive media.

Associate degree programs are offered in the areas of baking & pastry, culinary arts, digital filmmaking & video production, graphic design, industrial design, photography, and web design & interactive media.

Certificate programs are offered in 2D animation, 3D animation, 3D modeling for games, character animation for games, digital workflow, event management, food & beverage operations, internet marketing, portrait photography, and studio photography.

Diploma programs are offered in art of cooking, baking & pastry, digital design, residential planning, and web design.

Program availability and degree offerings are subject to change.

Academic Facilities

The Art Institute of Pittsburgh provides a learning environment with professional-grade technology applicable to each student's course of study. Students have the opportunity to build a portfolio of work that shows potential employers that they are trained to use the software, hardware, or equipment utilized within the industry. Depending upon the course of study, students are immersed in a creative environment—from classrooms to computer labs to studios—focused on relevant, hands-on education designed to prepare them for the real world.

Costs

Actual tuition and housing costs will vary depending on program, number of credits enrolled, and living arrangements. Prospective students should contact a Student Financial Services professional at the school for details.

Financial Aid

Financial aid is available for those who qualify. Students who require financial assistance should first complete and submit the Free Application for Federal Student Aid (FAFSA) online at www.fafsa.ed.gov and meet with a financial aid officer. Students may also apply for a number of scholarships focusing on their specific areas of career interest.

Faculty

Faculty members are hands-on creative professionals with proven experience as business leaders and innovators, hosting a learning environment similar to the career world students will face after graduation. Part instructor, part mentor, their mission is to help develop and transform creative potential into high-demand marketable skills.

Admission Requirements

Prospective students should refer to the current academic catalog for full details regarding admission requirements and process.

Application and Information

To obtain an application, make arrangements for an interview, or tour the school, prospective students should contact:

The Art Institute of Pittsburgh
420 Boulevard of the Allies
Pittsburgh, Pennsylvania 15219-1301
Phone: 412-263-6600
        800-275-2470 (toll-free)
Fax: 412-263-6667
Website: http://www.artinstitutes.edu/pittsburgh

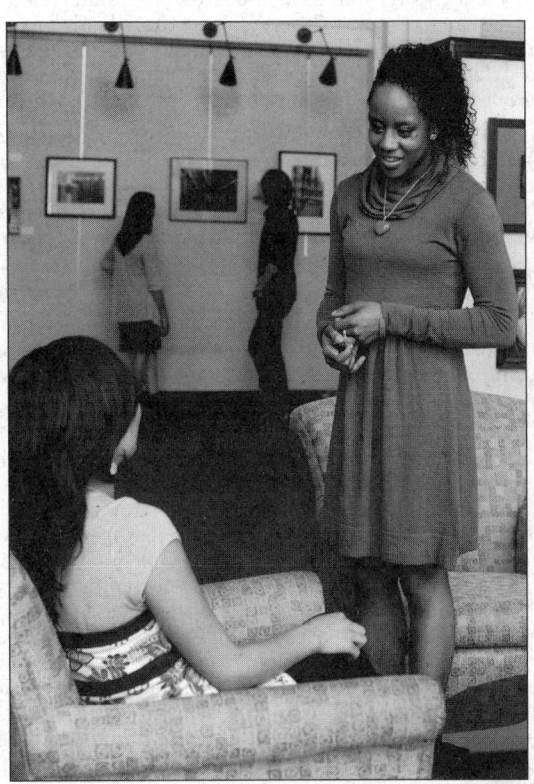

COLLEGE CLOSE-UPS

THE ART INSTITUTE OF PORTLAND
PORTLAND, OREGON

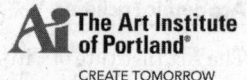

The Art Institute of Portland is one of The Art Institutes, a system of over fifty schools throughout North America dedicated to providing hands-on education in the creative and applied arts. The Art Institute of Portland offers bachelor's and associate's degree programs as well as non-degree programs for students interested in pursuing career opportunities from among tomorrow's 15 million jobs in creative fields like design, fashion, media arts, and culinary (based on information from the U.S. Bureau of Labor Statistics for job growth from 2012 to 2022).

A focused education from The Art Institute of Portland can help students turn their creative energy into a powerful tool that can make a difference in the world. Students are part of a collaborative and supportive community, where experienced instructors provide the guidance and skills needed to pursue a career in the creative economy.

The Art Institute of Portland also an important resource for creative industry leaders who value the opportunity provided students to learn by using professional-grade technology to build a portfolio of work to show potential employers after graduation.

Accreditation

The Art Institute of Portland is accredited by the Northwest Commission on Colleges and Universities. Accreditation of an institution of higher education by the Northwest Commission on Colleges and Universities indicates that it meets or exceeds criteria for the assessment of institutional quality evaluated through a peer review process. An accredited college or university is one which has available the necessary resources to achieve its stated purposes through appropriate educational programs, is substantially doing so, and gives reasonable evidence that it will continue to do so in the foreseeable future. Institutional integrity is also addressed through accreditation. Accreditation by the Northwest Commission on Colleges and Universities is not partial but applies to the institution as a whole. As such, it is not a guarantee of every course or program offered, or the competence of individual graduates. Rather, it provides reasonable assurance about the quality of opportunities available to students who attend the institution.

Inquiries regarding an institution's accredited status by the Northwest Commission on Colleges and Universities should be directed to the administrative staff of the institution. Individuals may also contact: Northwest Commission on Colleges and Universities 8060 165th Avenue N.E., Suite 100, Redmond, Washington 98052; phone: 425-558-4224; www.nwccu.org.

The Interior Design program leading to the Bachelor of Fine Arts degree is accredited by the Council for Interior Design Accreditation, 206 Grandville Avenue, Suite 350, Grand Rapids, Michigan 49503; www.accredit-id.org.

Location

Visual arts, a vibrant music scene, endless outdoor recreation opportunities, cool restaurants, retail stores, and hangouts: Portland, Oregon, is a thriving metropolis that keeps the creative spirit alive. This is a city where art, music, fashion, film, and food are just as hip as the lifestyles of the creative individuals that make their home here.

The surrounding area, including the Willamette River, Columbia River Gorge, and the snow-capped peak of Mount Hood—home of America's longest ski season—is a mecca for bicyclists, wind surfers, snow boarders, skiers, ice climbers, and hikers. Forest Park covers more than 5,000 acres. Washington Park is home to the Oregon Zoo. And Tom McCall Waterfront Park runs the length of downtown along the west bank of the Willamette River.

Portland is well-known for its forward-thinking urban planning and use of land. Due largely to the city's investment in light rail, Portland has been called one of the greenest cities in the world. The city is also referred to as "City of Roses" because its climate is perfect for growing that particular flower and "City of Bridges" because of the many spans that carry its streets across its rivers.

Students find the city's largest art collection at the Portland Art Museum, which recently added a Modern and Contemporary Art wing. There are many more art galleries downtown and in neighborhoods throughout the city. The Oregon Museum of Science and Industry (OMSI) sits on the eastern bank of the Willamette, across from downtown.

Portland boasts a wide array of dining options, indoors and out, to suit every budget and every taste—even if it's just a hot dog while watching the NBA's Portland Trail Blazers play basketball at the Rose Garden.

Programs of Study and Degree Offerings

Creativity is all around, and with millions of tomorrow's jobs in creative fields, the world needs more creative professionals. No matter which course of study a student chooses, the instructors at The Art Institutes will guide, support, and help students fine-tune their visual thinking and problem solving, so that they can take advantage of the world's growing creative opportunities and put their passion to work. Programs are offered in the areas of design, which focuses on communicating conceptually and helping people connect in living and work spaces; media arts, that centers on utilizing technology to deliver information and entertainment; fashion, where students anything from designing clothes for the runway to running a retail shop; and culinary, which exposes learners to international cuisines as well as restaurant management techniques.

Bachelor's degree programs are offered in the areas of advertising, apparel accessory design, apparel design, culinary management, design management, design research, design visualization, digital film & video, fashion marketing, game art & design, graphic & web design, industrial design, interior design, media arts and animation, photography & design, visual & game programming, and visual effects & motion graphics.

Associate degree programs are offered in the areas of apparel accessory design, apparel design, culinary arts, and graphic design.

Diploma programs are offered in art of cooking, baking & pastry, and fashion retailing.

The Associate in Arts in culinary arts, the Bachelor of Science in culinary arts management, the Bachelor of Science in food & beverage management, and the Bachelor of Fine Arts in interior design are available in evening and weekend formats.

Minor(s) are available in sustainability in apparel accessory design, apparel design, design management, design research, fashion marketing, industrial design, and interior design.

Concentration(s) are available in sustainability in culinary management.

Program availability and degree offerings are subject to change.

Academic Facilities

The Art Institute of Portland provides a learning environment with professional-grade technology applicable to each student's course of study. Students have the opportunity to build a portfolio of work that shows potential employers that they are trained to use the software, hardware, or equipment utilized within the industry. Depending upon the course of study, students are immersed in a creative environment—from classrooms to computer labs to studios—focused on relevant, hands-on education designed to prepare them for the real world.

Costs

Actual tuition and housing costs will vary depending on program, number of credits enrolled, and living arrangements. Prospective students should contact a Student Financial Services professional at the school for details.

Financial Aid

Financial aid is available for those who qualify. Students who require financial assistance should first complete and submit the Free Application for Federal Student Aid (FAFSA) online at www.fafsa.ed.gov and meet with a financial aid officer. Students may also apply for a number of scholarships focusing on their specific areas of career interest.

Faculty

Faculty members are hands-on creative professionals with proven experience as business leaders and innovators, hosting a learning environment similar to the career world students will face after graduation. Part instructor, part mentor, their mission is to help develop and transform creative potential into high-demand marketable skills.

Admission Requirements

Prospective students should refer to the current academic catalog for full details regarding admission requirements and process.

Application and Information

To obtain an application, make arrangements for an interview, or tour the school, prospective students should contact:

The Art Institute of Portland
1122 N.W. Davis Street
Portland, Oregon 97209-2911
Phone: 503-228-6528
       888-228-6528 (toll-free)
Fax: 503-227-1945
Website: http://www.artinstitutes.edu/portland

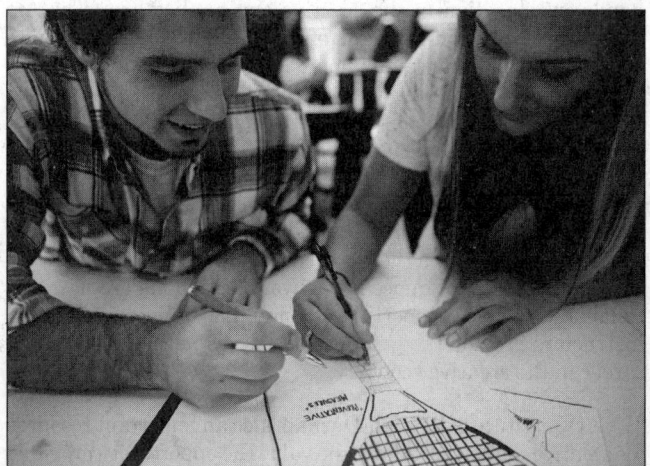

THE ART INSTITUTE OF RALEIGH-DURHAM
DURHAM, NORTH CAROLINA

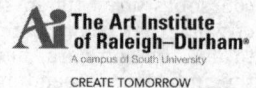

The Art Institute of Raleigh-Durham, a campus of South University, is one of The Art Institutes, a system of over fifty schools throughout North America dedicated to providing hands-on education in the creative and applied arts. The Art Institute of Raleigh-Durham offers bachelor's and associate degree programs as well as non-degree programs for students interested in pursuing career opportunities from among tomorrow's 15 million jobs in creative fields like design, fashion, media arts, and culinary (based on information from the U.S. Bureau of Labor Statistics for job growth from 2012 to 2022).

A focused education from The Art Institute of Raleigh-Durham can help students turn their creative energy into a powerful tool that can make a difference in the world. Students are part of a collaborative and supportive community, where experienced instructors provide the guidance and skills needed to pursue a career in the creative economy.

The Art Institute of Raleigh-Durham also an important resource for creative industry leaders who value the opportunity provided students to learn by using professional-grade technology to build a portfolio of work to show potential employers after graduation.

Accreditation

The Art Institute of Raleigh-Durham is a campus of South University. South University is accredited by the Southern Association of Colleges and Schools Commission on Colleges to award certificates, associate degrees, and baccalaureate degrees. Contact the Commission on Colleges at 1866 Southern Lane, Decatur, Georgia 30033-4097 or call 404-679-4500 for questions about the accreditation of South University.

The Art Institute of Raleigh–Durham is licensed by The Board of Governors of the University of North Carolina to confer Associate of Applied Science and Bachelor of Art degrees.

Location

The Art Institute of Raleigh-Durham is located in the heart of the downtown Durham historical and entertainment district. Events include jazz festivals, blues festivals, symphony concerts, art exhibitions, and all kinds of cultural happenings, such as the American Dance Festival and the Full Frame Documentary Film Festival. The Carolina Theater offers live performances and independent films. The Nasher Museum of Art is nationally known for its traveling exhibitions of contemporary global art. The city's Ninth Street, Brightleaf, and University Drive areas are great places to find something delicious to eat.

The Art Institute of Raleigh-Durham is just 2 hours from the beaches of the Atlantic Ocean; 4 hours from the beautiful Great Smoky Mountains; and not far at all from Charlotte, North Carolina; Richmond, Virginia; and Washington, D.C.

It's also just a stone's throw from Raleigh, where there's a wide assortment of things to see and do. The North Carolina

Museum of Art houses one of the finest collections of American, European, and ancient art in the region. There are also numerous art galleries. The city features over 8,000 acres of green space, more than 100 tennis courts, and five public lakes. Most public buses have bicycle racks, and some roads have dedicated bicycle-only lanes. Raleigh has been designated a Bicycle Friendly Community by the League of American Bicyclists, and the Walk Score ranks Raleigh among the most walkable U.S. cities.

For the Carolina Hurricanes of the NHL, home ice is PNC Arena in Raleigh. Baseball fans enjoy watching the Durham Bulls, the minor-league baseball team made famous by the film "Bull Durham," play in Durham Bulls Athletic Park, where they draw major crowds.

Programs of Study and Degree Offerings

Creativity is all around, and with millions of tomorrow's jobs in creative fields, the world needs more creative professionals. No matter which course of study a student chooses, the instructors at The Art Institutes will guide, support, and help students fine-tune their visual thinking and problem solving, so that they can take advantage of the world's growing creative opportunities and put their passion to work. Programs are offered in the areas of design, which focuses on communicating conceptually and helping people connect in living and work spaces; media arts, that centers on utilizing technology to deliver information and entertainment; fashion, where students learn anything from designing clothes for the runway to running a retail shop; and culinary, which exposes learners to international cuisines as well as restaurant management techniques.

Bachelor's degree programs are offered in the areas of culinary arts management, fashion marketing & management, game art & design, graphic design, interior design, photography, and web design & interactive media.

Associate degree programs are offered in the areas of culinary arts, fashion marketing, graphic design, and web design & interactive media.

Certificate programs are offered in art of cooking, digital image management, fashion retailing, web design & development, and web design & development II.

Program availability and degree offerings are subject to change.

Academic Facilities

The Art Institute of Raleigh-Durham provides a learning environment with professional-grade technology applicable to each student's course of study. Students have the opportunity to build a portfolio of work that shows potential employers that they are trained to use the software, hardware, or equipment utilized within the industry. Depending upon the course of study, students are immersed in a creative environment—from classrooms to computer labs to studios—focused on relevant, hands-on education designed to prepare them for the real world.

Costs

Actual tuition and housing costs will vary depending on program, number of credits enrolled, and living arrangements. Prospective students should contact a Student Financial Services professional at the school for details.

Financial Aid

Financial aid is available for those who qualify. Students who require financial assistance should first complete and submit the Free Application for Federal Student Aid (FAFSA) online at www.fafsa.ed.gov and meet with a financial aid officer. Students may also apply for a number of scholarships focusing on their specific areas of career interest.

Faculty

Faculty members are hands-on creative professionals with proven experience as business leaders and innovators, hosting a learning environment similar to the career world students will face after graduation. Part instructor, part mentor, their mission is to help develop and transform creative potential into high-demand marketable skills.

Admission Requirements

Prospective students should refer to the current academic catalog for full details regarding admission requirements and process.

Application and Information

To obtain an application, make arrangements for an interview, or tour the school, students should contact:

The Art Institute of Raleigh-Durham, a campus of South University
410 Blackwell Street, Suite 200
Durham, North Carolina 27701
Phone: 919-317-3050
        888-245-9593 (toll-free)
Fax: 919-317-3231/919-317-3230
Website: http://www.artinstitutes.edu/raleighdurham

COLLEGE CLOSE-UPS

ART INSTITUTE OF SAINT LOUIS
ST. CHARLES, MISOURI

The Art Institute of St. Louis®
CREATE TOMORROW

The Art Institute of St. Louis is one of The Art Institutes, a system of over 50 schools throughout North America dedicated to providing hands-on education in the creative and applied arts. The Art Institute of St. Louis offers bachelor's and associate degree programs for students interested in pursuing career opportunities from among tomorrow's 15 million jobs in creative fields like design, fashion, media arts, and culinary (based on information from the U.S. Bureau of Labor Statistics for job growth from 2012 to 2022).

A focused education from The Art Institute of St. Louis can help students turn their creative energy into a powerful tool that can make a difference in the world. Students are part of a collaborative and supportive community, where experienced instructors provide the guidance and skills needed to pursue a career in the creative economy.

The Art Institute of St. Louis is also an important resource for creative industry leaders who value the opportunity provided students to learn by using professional-grade technology to build a portfolio of work to show potential employers after graduation.

Accreditation

The Art Institute of St. Louis is accredited by the Accrediting Council for Independent Colleges and Schools (ACICS) to award associate and bachelor degrees. The Accrediting Council for Independent Colleges and Schools is listed as a nationally recognized accrediting agency by the United States Department of Education and is recognized by the Council for Higher Education Accreditation (CHEA). ACICS can be contacted at 750 First Street NE, Suite 980, Washington, D.C., 20002-4241; phone: 202-336-6780.

The Art Institute of St. Louis is approved to operate by the Missouri Department of Higher Education, 205 Jefferson Street, P.O. Box 1469, Jefferson City, Missouri 65102-1469; phone: 573-751-2361 or 800-473-6757 (toll-free); fax: 573-751-6635; E-mail: info@dhe.mo.gov.

Location

The Art Institute of St. Louis is located in the historic city of Saint Charles, just northwest of St. Louis on the banks of the Missouri River. It's the third-oldest city west of the Mississippi—its history is evident along Main Street and the Riverfront, with their various restaurants, shops, and businesses. The city also boasts a casino, an art center, and several popular minor-league sports teams.

Saint Charles offers small-town charm yet is close to the big-city amenities and attractions of St. Louis, a city that's rich in culture with well-known attractions, museums and galleries, music, and performing arts venues.

The St. Louis area offers a fascinating mix of the traditional and contemporary, from one of the top-rated zoos to cultural attractions that rank among the finest in the United States. Destinations include the 630-foot-tall Gateway Arch, the famous monument to America's westward expansion, and the Delmar Loop, one of the city's entertainment, cultural, and restaurant districts, which has been named "One of the Ten Great Streets in America."

There's an abundance of great restaurants, hot nightclubs, and unique shops. Musically, there's everything from rock to jazz to hip-hop, and of course blues, the genre most closely associated with the city.

St. Louis offers plenty of opportunities to get out and enjoy nature, with more than 100 city parks, including Forest Park, one of the largest urban parks in the entire country. Another noteworthy park is the Missouri Botanical Garden, a private garden and botanical research facility and home to the Climatron.

St. Louis is a serious sports town. Busch Stadium is full of fans whenever the Cardinals are in town. The same goes for the Edward Jones Dome when the Rams play football, or the Scottrade Center for Blues hockey.

Considering the advantages of being able to enjoy small-city friendliness and historic charm while being within easy reach of a major U.S. city and all its sophistication and excitement, it's hard to come up with a better all-around spot to pursue one's creative education than at The Art Institute of St. Louis.

Programs of Study and Degree Offerings

Creativity is all around, and with millions of tomorrow's jobs in creative fields, the world needs more creative professionals. No matter which course of study a student chooses, the instructors at The Art Institutes will guide, support, and help students fine-tune their visual thinking and problem solving, so that they can take advantage of the world's growing creative opportunities and put their passion to work. Programs are offered in the areas of design, which focuses on communicating conceptually and helping people connect in living and work spaces; media arts, that centers on utilizing technology to deliver information and entertainment; fashion, where students anything from designing clothes for the runway to running a retail shop; and culinary, which exposes learners to international cuisines as well as restaurant management techniques.

Bachelor's degree programs are offered in the areas of culinary management, digital filmmaking & video production, digital photography, fashion marketing, graphic & web design, and interior design.

Associate degree programs are offered in the areas of culinary arts and graphic & web design (Concentrations available in graphic-design specific and web-design specific).

Program availability and degree offerings are subject to change.

Academic Facilities

The Art Institute of St. Louis provides a learning environment with professional-grade technology applicable to each student's course of study. Students have the opportunity to build a portfolio of work that shows potential employers that they are trained to use the software, hardware, or equipment utilized within the industry. Depending upon the course of study, students are immersed in a creative environment—from classrooms to computer labs to studios—focused on relevant, hands-on education designed to prepare them for the real world.

Costs

Actual tuition and housing costs will vary depending on program, number of credits enrolled, and living arrangements. Prospective students should contact a Student Financial Services professional at the school for details.

Financial Aid

Financial aid is available for those who qualify. Students who require financial assistance should first complete and submit the Free Application for Federal Student Aid (FAFSA) online at www.fafsa.ed.gov and meet with a financial aid officer. Students may also apply for a number of scholarships focusing on their specific areas of career interest.

Faculty

Faculty members are hands-on creative professionals with proven experience as business leaders and innovators, hosting a learning environment similar to the career world students will face after graduation. Part instructor, part mentor, their mission is to help develop and transform creative potential into high-demand marketable skills.

Admission Requirements

Prospective students should refer to the current academic catalog for full details regarding admission requirements and process.

Application and Information

To obtain an application, make arrangements for an interview, or tour the school, prospective students should contact:

The Art Institute of St. Louis
1520 South Fifth Street, Suite 107
St. Charles, Missouri 63303
Phone: 636-688-3010
      855-398-9281 (toll-free)
Fax: 636-688-3012
Website: http://www.artinstitutes.edu/st-louis

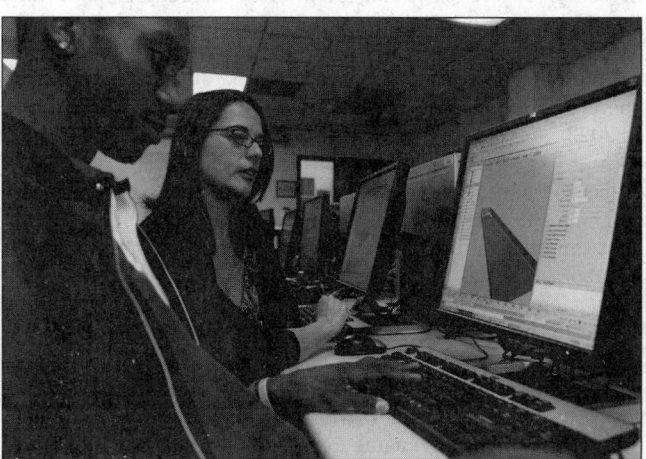

COLLEGE CLOSE-UPS

THE ART INSTITUTE OF SALT LAKE CITY

DRAPER, UTAH

The Art Institute of Salt Lake City is one of The Art Institutes, a system of over 50 schools throughout North America dedicated to providing hands-on education in the creative and applied arts. The Art Institute of Salt Lake City offers bachelor's and associate degree programs as well as non-degree programs for students interested in pursuing career opportunities from among tomorrow's 15 million jobs in creative fields like design, fashion, media arts, and culinary (based on information from the U.S. Bureau of Labor Statistics for job growth from 2012 to 2022).

A focused education from The Art Institute of Salt Lake City can help students turn their creative energy into a powerful tool that can make a difference in the world. Students are part of a collaborative and supportive community, where experienced instructors provide the guidance and skills needed to pursue a career in the creative economy.

The Art Institute of Salt Lake City is also an important resource for creative industry leaders who value the opportunity provided students to learn by using professional-grade technology to build a portfolio of work to show potential employers after graduation.

Accreditation

The Art Institute of Salt Lake City is accredited by the Accrediting Council for Independent Colleges and Schools to award diplomas, associate degrees, and bachelor's degrees. The Accrediting Council for Independent Colleges and Schools is listed as a nationally recognized accrediting agency by the United States Department of Education and is recognized by the Council for Higher Education Accreditation. ACICS can be contacted at 750 First Street NE, Suite 980, Washington, D.C. 20002; phone: 202-336-6780.

The Art Institute of Salt Lake City is a branch of The Art Institute of Phoenix located in Phoenix, Arizona.

The Art Institute of Salt Lake City is exempt from registration pursuant to the Utah Postsecondary Proprietary School Act. Any questions should be directed to the Utah Division of Consumer Protection (UDCP), 160 East 300 South, Second Floor, Salt Lake City, Utah 84114; phone: 801-530-6601.

Location

Known as "Crossroads of the West" for its central position in the western portion of the United States, as well as the fact that the first intercontinental railroad went through the Salt Lake Valley, Salt Lake City is the state's political, economic, and cultural center. The city is internationally recognized as the location of the 2002 Winter Olympics and is known for its namesake, the Great Salt Lake.

Salt Lake City's economy is service-oriented. Major industries include government, trade, transportation, tourism, utilities, and professional and business services. In recent years, the city has developed a strong recreation industry and has become the nation's industrial banking center.

Salt Lake City has four distinct seasons, with long summers and winters; spring and fall serve as brief, comfortable transitions. The area offers a full range of outdoor recreational opportunities. The beauties of the mountain ranges surrounding the Great Salt Lake Valley are there to explore year-round. In the winter, students join local residents and visitors from around the globe who enjoy the slopes of the many nearby ski resorts. In other seasons, climbing, hiking, and biking are popular activities in the picturesque mountains.

The annual Utah Arts Festival draws 80,000 people to its more than 100 artist booths and five musical performance venues. Salt Lake City hosts parts of the famous Sundance Film Festival, the largest independent film festival in the United States. The city also hosts the international Salt Lake City Marathon.

Programs of Study and Degree Offerings

Creativity is all around, and with millions of tomorrow's jobs in creative fields, the world needs more creative professionals. No matter which course of study a student chooses, the instructors at The Art Institutes will guide, support, and help students fine-tune their visual thinking and problem solving, so that they can take advantage of the world's growing creative opportunities and put their passion to work. Programs are offered in the areas of design, which focuses on communicating conceptually and helping people connect in living and work spaces; media arts, that centers on utilizing technology to deliver information and entertainment; fashion, where students learn anything from designing clothes for the runway to running a retail shop; and culinary, which exposes learners to international cuisines as well as restaurant management techniques.

Bachelor's degree programs are offered in the areas of culinary management, digital filmmaking & video production, digital photography, fashion & retail management, game art & design, graphic design, interior design, media arts & animation, and web design & interactive media.

Associate degree programs are offered in the areas of baking & pastry, culinary arts, and graphic design.

Diploma programs are offered in baking & pastry, culinary arts, digital image management, fashion retailing, web design & development, and web design & interactive communications.

Program availability and degree offerings are subject to change.

Academic Facilities

The Art Institute of Salt Lake City provides a learning environment with professional-grade technology applicable to each student's course of study. Students have the opportunity to build a portfolio of work that shows potential employers that they are trained to use the software, hardware, or equipment

utilized within the industry. Depending upon the course of study, students are immersed in a creative environment—from classrooms to computer labs to studios—focused on relevant, hands-on education designed to prepare them for the real world.

Costs

Actual tuition and housing costs will vary depending on program, number of credits enrolled, and living arrangements. Prospective students should contact a Student Financial Services professional at the school for details.

Financial Aid

Financial aid is available for those who qualify. Students who require financial assistance should first complete and submit the Free Application for Federal Student Aid (FAFSA) online at www.fafsa.ed.gov and meet with a financial aid officer. Students may also apply for a number of scholarships focusing on their specific areas of career interest.

Faculty

Faculty members are hands-on creative professionals with proven experience as business leaders and innovators, hosting a learning environment similar to the career world students will face after graduation. Part instructor, part mentor, their mission is to help develop and transform creative potential into high-demand marketable skills.

Admission Requirements

Prospective students should refer to the current academic catalog for full details regarding admission requirements and process.

Application and Information

To obtain an application, make arrangements for an interview, or tour the school, prospective students should contact:

The Art Institute of Salt Lake City
121 West Election Road, Suite 100
Draper, Utah 84020-9492
Phone: 801-601-4700
      800-978-0096 (toll-free)
Fax: 801-601-4724
Website: http://www.artinstitutes.edu/saltlakecity

COLLEGE CLOSE-UPS

THE ART INSTITUTE OF SAN ANTONIO
SAN ANTONIO, TEXAS

The Art Institute of San Antonio, a branch of The Art Institute of Houston, is one of The Art Institutes, a system of over fifty schools throughout North America dedicated to providing hands-on education in the creative and applied arts. The Art Institute of San Antonio offer bachelor's and associate degree programs as well as non-degree programs for students interested in pursuing career opportunities from among tomorrow's 15 million jobs in creative fields like design, fashion, media arts, and culinary (based on information from the U.S. Bureau of Labor Statistics for job growth from 2012 to 2022).

A focused education from The Art Institute of San Antonio can help students turn their creative energy into a powerful tool that can make a difference in the world. Students are part of a collaborative and supportive community, where experienced instructors provide the guidance and skills needed to pursue a career in the creative economy.

The Art Institute of San Antonio is also an important resource for creative industry leaders who value the opportunity provided students to learn by using professional-grade technology to build a portfolio of work to show potential employers after graduation.

Accreditation

The Art Institute of San Antonio is a branch of The Art Institute of Houston. The Art Institute of Houston is accredited by the Southern Association of Colleges and Schools Commission on Colleges to award associate and baccalaureate degrees. Questions about the accreditation of The Art Institute of Houston can be directed to the Commission on Colleges, 1866 Southern Lane, Decatur, Georgia 30033-4097; phone: 404-679-4500.

The Art Institute of San Antonio, a branch of The Art Institute of Houston, holds a Certificate of Authorization acknowledging exemption from Texas Higher Education Coordinating Board regulations.

Location

Deep in the heart of Texas, there's a city that blends many cultures, is rich in history, and is pointed in one direction: up. San Antonio, one of the ten largest cities in the United States, is located in the south-central part of the state. Famous for its Spanish missions, the Alamo, the River Walk, and the Tower of the Americas, San Antonio has more than 25 million visitors each year.

San Antonio is also home to three Air Force bases as well as several museums, parks, Fortune 500 companies, universities, and colleges. Southwest American history, culture, the arts, and a lively nightlife are all part of the experience for students at The Art Institute of San Antonio, which is located just to the north of the city's downtown area.

The city's arts communities, such as Blue Star in Southtown, offer many galleries along with live music, and the Guadalupe Cultural Art Center, on the city's west side is a vibrant area that offers a true San Antonio experience. In addition, there are great collections of authentic folk art, artifacts, and handmade creations. Students can visit Market Square during Fiesta and feast on tacos and gorditas.

The San Antonio area offers the opportunity to enjoy the thrills at any of five theme parks, explore subterranean caves, visit a dude ranch, stroll the cobblestone paths of the River Walk, dine al fresco at the bistros and cafes that line the river, or explore the city's spacious urban park system that 68 miles of trails stretching across 11,000 acres. The city's annual San Antonio Stock Show & Rodeo is one of the largest events of its kind in the country.

For those interested in professional sports, the NBA's San Antonio Spurs play their home games at the AT&T Center.

Programs of Study and Degree Offerings

Creativity is all around, and with millions of tomorrow's jobs in creative fields, the world needs more creative professionals. No matter which course of study a student chooses, the instructors at The Art Institutes will guide, support, and help students fine-tune their visual thinking and problem solving, so that they can take advantage of the world's growing creative opportunities and put their passion to work. Programs are offered in the areas of design, which focuses on communicating conceptually and helping people connect in living and work spaces; media arts, that centers on utilizing technology to deliver information and entertainment; fashion, where students learn anything from designing clothes for the runway to running a retail shop; and culinary, which exposes learners to international cuisines as well as restaurant management techniques.

Bachelor's degree programs are offered in the areas of advertising design, culinary management, design & technical graphics, digital filmmaking & video production, fashion & retail management, fashion design, food & beverage management, game art & design, graphic & web design, hospitality management, interior design, media arts & animation, photography, and visual effects & motion graphics.

Associate degree programs are offered in the areas of baking & pastry, culinary arts, graphic design, restaurant & catering management, and web design & interactive media.

Diploma programs are offered in baking & pastry, culinary arts, digital image management, fashion retailing, web design & development, and web design & interactive communications.

Program availability and degree offerings are subject to change.

Academic Facilities

The Art Institute of San Antonio provides a learning environment with professional-grade technology applicable to each student's course of study. Students have the opportunity to build a portfolio of work that shows potential employers that they are trained to use the software, hardware, or equipment utilized within the industry. Depending upon the course of study, students are immersed in a creative environment—from classrooms to computer labs to studios—focused on relevant, hands-on education designed to prepare them for the real world.

Costs

Actual tuition and housing costs will vary depending on program, number of credits enrolled, and living arrangements. Prospective students should contact a Student Financial Services professional at the school for details.

Financial Aid

Financial aid is available for those who qualify. Students who require financial assistance should first complete and submit the Free Application for Federal Student Aid (FAFSA) online at www.fafsa.ed.gov and meet with a financial aid officer. Students may also apply for a number of scholarships focusing on their specific areas of career interest.

Faculty

Faculty members are hands-on creative professionals with proven experience as business leaders and innovators, hosting a learning environment similar to the career world students will face after graduation. Part instructor, part mentor, their mission is to help develop and transform creative potential into high-demand marketable skills.

Admission Requirements

Prospective students should refer to the current academic catalog for full details regarding admission requirements and process.

Application and Information

To obtain an application, make arrangements for an interview, or tour the school, prospective students should contact:

The Art Institute of San Antonio, a branch of The Art Institute of Houston
10000 IH-10 West, Suite 200
San Antonio, Texas 78230
Phone: 210-338-7320
       888-222-0040 (toll-free)
Fax: 210-338-7321
Website: http://www.artinstitutes.edu/san-antonio

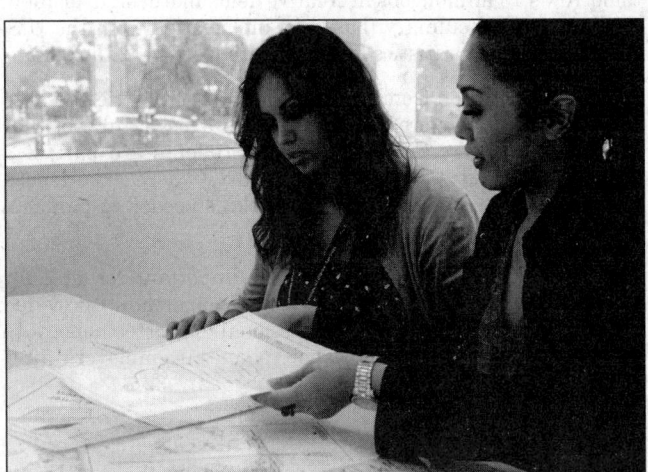

THE ART INSTITUTE OF SEATTLE
SEATTLE, WASHINGTON

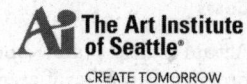

The Art Institute of Seattle is one of The Art Institutes, a system of over 50 schools throughout North America dedicated to providing hands-on education in the creative and applied arts. The Art Institute of Seattle offers bachelor's and associate degree programs as well as non-degree programs for students interested in pursuing career opportunities from among tomorrow's 15 million jobs in creative fields like design, fashion, media arts, and culinary (based on information from the U.S. Bureau of Labor Statistics for job growth from 2012 to 2022).

A focused education from The Art Institute of Seattle can help students turn their creative energy into a powerful tool that can make a difference in the world. Students are part of a collaborative and supportive community, where experienced instructors provide the guidance and skills needed to pursue a career in the creative economy.

The Art Institute of Seattle is also an important resource for creative industry leaders who value the opportunity provided students to learn by using professional-grade technology to build a portfolio of work to show potential employers after graduation.

Accreditation

The Art Institute of Seattle is accredited by the Northwest Commission on Colleges and Universities. Accreditation of an institution of higher education by the Northwest Commission on Colleges and Universities indicates that it meets or exceeds criteria for the assessment of institutional quality evaluated through a peer review process. An accredited college or university is one which has available the necessary resources to achieve its stated purposes through appropriate educational programs, is substantially doing so, and gives reasonable evidence that it will continue to do so in the foreseeable future. Institutional integrity is also addressed through accreditation. Accreditation by the Northwest Commission on Colleges and Universities is not partial but applies to the institution as a whole. As such, it is not a guarantee of every course or program offered, or the competence of individual graduates. Rather, it provides reasonable assurance about the quality of opportunities available to students who attend the institution.

Inquiries regarding an institution's accredited status by the Northwest Commission on Colleges and Universities should be directed to the administrative staff of the institution. Individuals may also contact: Northwest Commission on Colleges and Universities 8060 165th Avenue N.E., Suite 100, Redmond, WA 98052; phone: 425-558-4224; www.nwccu.org.

The Associate of Applied Arts in culinary arts degree program is accredited by The Accrediting Commission of the American Culinary Federation Education Foundation.

The interior design program leading to the Bachelor of Fine Arts degree is accredited by the Council for Interior Design Accreditation, 206 Grandville Avenue, Suite 350, Grand Rapids, Michigan 49503; www.accredit-id.org.

The Art Institute of Seattle is licensed under Chapter 28c.10RCW; inquiries or complaints regarding this or any other private vocational school may be made to the Workforce Training and Education Coordinating Board, 128 10th Avenue SW, P.O. Box 43105, Olympia, Washington 98504-3105; phone: 360-753-5662.

Location

Water, mountains, culture, music, commerce—and of course, coffee and computers. Seattle, a thriving, forward-thinking, sophisticated city in the shadow of majestic Mount Rainier, is an international port on beautiful Puget Sound that offers the finest in arts and entertainment.

The Art Institute of Seattle is situated on the city's Elliott Bay waterfront, just a few blocks from the Belltown neighborhood and its vibrant restaurants and nightlife, and not far from the famous Pike Place Market, the Olympic Sculpture Park, and other interesting attractions.

Seattle boasts a calendar full of cultural events. From the 24-day Seattle International Film Festival to Hempfest, to book fairs, concerts featuring a diverse range of alternative music, performance poetry, and an abundance of art galleries and artists' studios that are open to the public, there's a wide variety of things to see and do in this city.

As for professional sports, Seattle has them covered with baseball's Mariners and the NFL's Seahawks, along with soccer, ice hockey, and women's basketball teams.

In addition, there are museums, covering everything from Asian culture to maritime history to rock 'n roll. The iconic Seattle Space Needle adds a unique feature to the city skyline. Along with the abundance and variety of fresh seafood and local produce, Seattle has earned a spot as one of the country's true culinary capitals.

The Seattle area is home to an array of globally recognized companies. While Starbucks and Microsoft call Seattle home, the city's other corporate residents include the headquarters of Amazon, Expedia, RealNetworks, Getty Images, Corbis, Nintendo of America, REI, Eddie Bauer, Nordstrom, Brooks Running, Fantagraphics Books, Costco, and Weyerhauser, as well as the offices of Adobe, Facebook, and Google.

Programs of Study and Degrees

Creativity is all around, and with millions of tomorrow's jobs in creative fields, the world needs more creative professionals. No matter which course of study a student chooses, the instructors at The Art Institutes will guide, support, and help students fine-tune their visual thinking and problem solving, so that they can take advantage of the world's growing creative opportunities and put their passion to work. Programs are offered in the areas of design, which focuses on communicating conceptually and helping people connect in living and work spaces; media arts, that centers on utilizing technology to deliver information and entertainment; fashion, where students learn anything from designing clothes for the runway to running a retail shop; and culinary, which exposes learners to international cuisines as well as restaurant management techniques.

Bachelor's degree programs are offered in the areas of advertising, audio design technology, culinary arts management, digital filmmaking & video production, fashion design, fashion marketing & management, game art & design, graphic & web design, hospitality food & beverage management, industrial design, interior design, media arts & animation, photography, and visual effects & motion graphics.

Associate degree programs are offered in the areas of audio production, baking & pastry, culinary arts, fashion design, fashion marketing, graphic design, industrial design technology, interior design, photography, video production, and web design & interactive media.

Diploma programs are offered in art of cooking, baking & pastry, digital design, digital image management, fashion retailing, residential design, web design & development, and web design & interactive communications.

Program availability and degree offerings are subject to change.

Academic Facilities

The Art Institute of Seattle provides a learning environment with professional-grade technology applicable to each student's course of study. Students have the opportunity to build a portfolio of work that shows potential employers that they are trained to use the software, hardware, or equipment utilized within the industry. Depending upon the course of study, students are immersed in a creative environment—from classrooms to computer labs to studios—focused on relevant, hands-on education designed to prepare them for the real world.

Costs

Actual tuition and housing costs will vary depending on program, number of credits enrolled, and living arrangements. Prospective students should contact a Student Financial Services professional at the school for details.

Financial Aid

Financial aid is available for those who qualify. Students who require financial assistance should first complete and submit the Free Application for Federal Student Aid (FAFSA) online at www.fafsa.ed.gov and meet with a financial aid officer. Students may also apply for a number of scholarships focusing on their specific areas of career interest.

Faculty

Faculty members are hands-on creative professionals with proven experience as business leaders and innovators, hosting a learning environment similar to the career world students will face after graduation. Part instructor, part mentor, their mission is to help develop and transform creative potential into high-demand marketable skills.

Admission Requirements

Prospective students should refer to the current academic catalog for full details regarding admission requirements and process.

Application and Information

To obtain an application, make arrangements for an interview, or tour the school, prospective students should contact:

The Art Institute of Seattle
2323 Elliott Avenue
Seattle, Washington 98121-1642
Phone: 206-448-6600
　　　　 800-275-2471 (toll-free)
Fax: 206-269-0275
Website: http://www.artinstitutes.edu/seattle

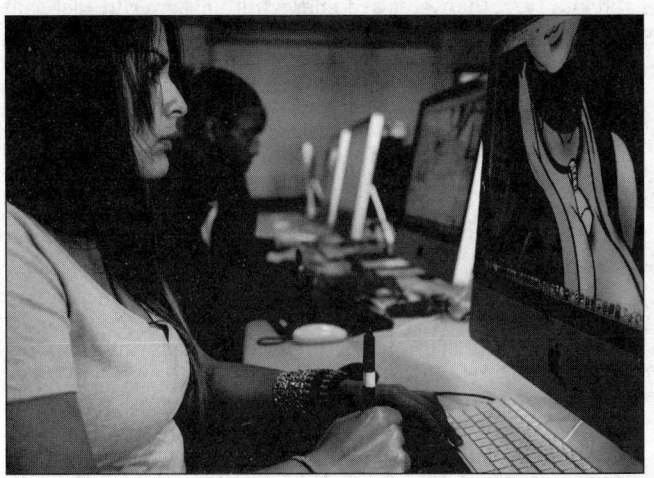

COLLEGE CLOSE-UPS

THE ART INSTITUTE OF TAMPA
TAMPA, FLORIDA

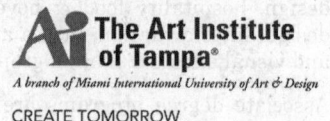

Ai The Art Institute of Tampa®

A branch of Miami International University of Art & Design

CREATE TOMORROW

The Art Institute of Tampa, a branch of Miami International University of Art & Design, is one of The Art Institutes, a system of over fifty schools throughout North America dedicated to providing hands-on education in the creative and applied arts. The Art Institute of Tampa offers master's, bachelor's, and associate degree programs as well as non-degree programs for students interested in pursuing career opportunities from among tomorrow's 15 million jobs in creative fields like design, fashion, media arts, and culinary (based on information from the U.S. Bureau of Labor Statistics for job growth from 2012 to 2022).

A focused education from The Art Institute of Tampa can help students turn their creative energy into a powerful tool that can make a difference in the world. Students are part of a collaborative and supportive community, where experienced instructors provide the guidance and skills needed to pursue a career in the creative economy.

The Art Institute of Tampa also an important resource for creative industry leaders who value the opportunity provided students to learn by using professional-grade technology to build a portfolio of work to show potential employers after graduation.

Accreditation

The Art Institute of Tampa is a branch of Miami International University of Art & Design. Miami International University of Art & Design is accredited by the Southern Association of Colleges and Schools Commission on Colleges to award associate, baccalaureate, and master's degrees. Contact the Commission on Colleges at 1866 Southern Lane, Decatur, Georgia 30033-4097 or call 404-679-4500 for questions about the accreditation of Miami International University of Art & Design and its branches.

The Associate of Arts in baking & pastry, Associate of Arts in culinary arts and the Bachelor of Arts in culinary management programs are accredited by The Accrediting Commission of the American Culinary Federation Education Foundation.

The Art Institute of Tampa is licensed by the Commission for Independent Education, Florida Department of Education. Additional information regarding this institution may be obtained by contacting the Commission at 325 West Gaines Street, Suite 1414, Tallahassee, Florida 32399-0400; phone: 888-224-6684 (toll-free).

Location

The Tampa-St. Petersburg area is Florida's second-largest metropolitan area, with miles of waterfront, sandy beaches, cultural attractions and amusements. Tampa isn't just a city; it's a lifestyle. Whether relaxing and people-watching on Treasure Island Beach, paddling the scenic Hillsborough River, or snorkeling, diving, sailing, fresh and saltwater fishing, kayaking, or just catching some rays, the weather's just right just about every day of the year

Tampa has a growing economy and serves as a major port. Among the major corporations that are headquartered in Tampa are Raymond James, Home Shopping Network, Outback Steakhouse, and a major portion of Citigroup.

The arts are a vital part of the vibrant local community. An abundance of theater groups, orchestras, world-class performance halls, museums, and galleries offer inspiring performances, enriching youth education programs, and exhibits that showcase the world's most talented artists, actors, and musicians. Popular nightspots include Channelside, Bay Street at International Plaza, and Ybor City, the center of Tampa's bustling music scene.

In addition, Tampa offers many theaters, symphony and dance performances, museums, and a diverse range of art galleries that showcase some of the world's most talented artists, actors, and musicians. Highlights include the Tampa Museum of Art, the Museum of Science and Industry, the St. Petersburg Museum of History, the Florida International Museum, and Great Explorations: The Hands-On Museum. One of the city's most popular destinations is the Salvador Dali Museum, home to the world's most comprehensive collection of works by the famed Spanish surrealist.

Whether relaxing at an outdoor café, strolling along the Riverwalk, or unwinding at Curtis Hixon Waterfront Park, it's easy to see why Tampa ranks as one of America's best outdoor cities. Nearby attractions include Busch Gardens, the Florida Aquarium, and Lowry Park Zoo. Professional sports teams include football's Tampa Bay Buccaneers who play at Raymond James Stadium, hockey's Lightning who play at Tampa Bay Times Forum, and the Rays who play just a quick hop across the bay in St. Petersburg.

Programs of Study and Degree Offerings

Creativity is all around, and with millions of tomorrow's jobs in creative fields, the world needs more creative professionals. No matter which course of study a student chooses, the instructors at The Art Institutes will guide, support, and help students fine-tune their visual thinking and problem solving, so that they can take advantage of the world's growing creative opportunities and put their passion to work. Programs are offered in the areas of design, which focuses on communicating conceptually and helping people connect in living and work spaces; media arts, that centers on utilizing technology to deliver information and entertainment; fashion, where students learn anything from designing clothes for the runway to running a retail shop; and culinary, which exposes learners to international cuisines as well as restaurant management techniques.

Bachelor's degree programs are offered in the areas of culinary management, digital filmmaking & video production, digital photography, fashion & retail management, game art & design, graphic design, interior design, media arts & animation, visual effects & motion graphics, and web design & interactive media.

Associate degree programs are offered in the areas of baking & pastry, culinary arts, and graphic design.

Diploma programs are offered in baking & pastry, culinary arts, digital image management, fashion retailing, web design & development I, and web design & development II.

The Master of Arts degree is offered in design & media management.

Program availability and degree offerings are subject to change.

Miami International University of Art & Design is one of the degree-granting institutions for the design & media management degree program. This school's program will also be offered in a synchronous and asynchronous format at its branch campuses, The Art Institute of Tampa and The Art Institute of Jacksonville.

Academic Facilities

The Art Institute of Tampa provides a learning environment with professional-grade technology applicable to each student's course of study. Students have the opportunity to build a portfolio of work that shows potential employers that they are trained to use the software, hardware, or equipment utilized within the industry. Depending upon the course of study, students are immersed in a creative environment—from classrooms to computer labs to studios—focused on relevant, hands-on education designed to prepare them for the real world.

Costs

Actual tuition and housing costs will vary depending on program, number of credits enrolled, and living arrangements. Prospective students should contact a Student Financial Services professional at the school for details.

Financial Aid

Financial aid is available for those who qualify. Students who require financial assistance should first complete and submit the Free Application for Federal Student Aid (FAFSA) online at www.fafsa.ed.gov and meet with a financial aid officer. Students may also apply for a number of scholarships focusing on their specific areas of career interest.

Faculty

Faculty members are hands-on creative professionals with proven experience as business leaders and innovators, hosting a learning environment similar to the career world students will face after graduation. Part instructor, part mentor, their mission is to help develop and transform creative potential into high-demand marketable skills.

Admission Requirements

Prospective students should refer to the current academic catalog for full details regarding admission requirements and process.

Application and Information

To obtain an application, make arrangements for an interview, or tour the school, prospective students should contact:

The Art Institute of Tampa, a branch of Miami International
    University of Art & Design
Parkside at Tampa Bay Park
4401 North Himes Avenue, Suite 150
Tampa, Florida 33614-7086
Phone: 813-873-2112
        866-703-3277 (toll-free)
Fax: 813-873-2171
Website: http://www.artinstitutes.edu/tampa

THE ART INSTITUTE OF TENNESSEE—NASHVILLE

NASHVILLE, TENNESSEE

The Art Institute of Tennessee—Nashville, a branch of The Art Institute of Atlanta, is one of The Art Institutes, a system of over 50 schools throughout North America dedicated to providing hands-on education in the creative and applied arts. The Art Institute of Tennessee—Nashville offers bachelor's and associate degree programs as well as non-degree programs for students interested in pursuing career opportunities from among tomorrow's 15 million jobs in creative fields like design, fashion, media arts, and culinary (based on information from the U.S. Bureau of Labor Statistics for job growth from 2012 to 2022).

A focused education from The Art Institute of Tennessee—Nashville can help students turn their creative energy into a powerful tool that can make a difference in the world. Students are part of a collaborative and supportive community, where experienced instructors provide the guidance and skills needed to pursue a career in the creative economy.

The Art Institute of Tennessee—Nashville is also an important resource for creative industry leaders who value the opportunity provided students to learn by using professional-grade technology to build a portfolio of work to show potential employers after graduation.

Accreditation

The Art Institute of Tennessee—Nashville is a branch campus of The Art Institute of Atlanta. The Art Institute of Atlanta is accredited by the Southern Association of Colleges and Schools Commission on Colleges to award associate and baccalaureate degrees. Contact the Commission on Colleges at 1866 Southern Lane, Decatur, Georgia 30033-4097 or call 404-679-4500 for questions about the accreditation of The Art Institute of Atlanta.

The Art Institute of Tennessee—Nashville is authorized for operation by the Tennessee Higher Education Commission: http://www.state.tn.us/thec/.

Location

Known as Music City USA, Nashville is the capital of Tennessee and is a major center of the music industry—not just of the United States, but the entire world. Located on the Cumberland River, the city is a virtual crossroads of American culture and one of the region's fastest-growing metro areas. Nashville is also an important hub of the health care, publishing, and transportation industries.

Named for Revolutionary War hero Francis Nash, the city took advantage of its strategic location and its accessibility as a river port major railroad hub. The booming post-Civil War economy left Nashville with a legacy of classical-style, iconic buildings—not the least of which is the Parthenon, built in 1897 as a full-scale replica of the ancient structure in Athens, Greece. Today Nashville's Parthenon serves as an art museum featuring everything from classical exhibits to the work of modern artists such as Andy Warhol. It also is responsible for Nashville's other, although lesser-known nickname: the Athens of the South.

The Tennessee Performing Arts Center is the home of the Tennessee Repertory Theatre, Nashville Children's Theatre, the Nashville Opera, and the Nashville Ballet. The Nashville Symphony Orchestra performs regularly at The Schermerhorn Symphony Center. The city's museums and galleries include the renowned Frist Center for the Visual Arts. The Nashville Film Festival is one of the biggest film festivals in the Southern United States. It runs for a week in April and features hundreds of independent films. The Country Music Marathon, which also runs every April, typically draws 25,000 participants from around the world.

The home of the world-famous Grand Ole Opry since 1925, Nashville also hosts a number of professional sports teams, including the NFL's Tennessee Titans and the Nashville Predators of the National Hockey League.

Programs of Study and Degrees

Creativity is all around, and with millions of tomorrow's jobs in creative fields, the world needs more creative professionals. No matter which course of study a student chooses, the instructors at The Art Institutes will guide, support, and help students fine-tune their visual thinking and problem solving, so that they can take advantage of the world's growing creative opportunities and put their passion to work. Programs are offered in the areas of design, which focuses on communicating conceptually and helping people connect in living and work spaces; media arts, that centers on utilizing technology to deliver information and entertainment; fashion, where students learn anything from designing clothes for the runway to running a retail shop; and culinary, which exposes learners to international cuisines as well as restaurant management techniques.

Bachelor's degree programs are offered in the areas of advertising, audio production, culinary arts management, designing for tablets: digital publishing, digital filmmaking & video production, fashion & retail management, graphic & web design, interior design, media arts & animation, and digital photography.

Associate degree programs are offered in the areas of baking & pastry, culinary arts, graphic & web design, and video production.

Diploma programs are offered in baking & pastry, culinary arts, digital image management, fashion retailing, web design & development, and web design & interactive communications.

Program availability and degree offerings are subject to change.

Academic Facilities

The Art Institute of Tennessee—Nashville provides a learning environment with professional-grade technology applicable to each student's course of study. Students have the opportunity to build a portfolio of work that shows potential employers that they are trained to use the software, hardware, or equipment utilized within the industry. Depending upon the course of study, students are immersed in a creative environment—from classrooms to computer labs to studios—focused on relevant, hands-on education designed to prepare them for the real world.

Costs

Actual tuition and housing costs will vary depending on program, number of credits enrolled, and living arrangements. Prospective students should contact a Student Financial Services professional at the school for details.

Financial Aid

Financial aid is available for those who qualify. Students who require financial assistance should first complete and submit the Free Application for Federal Student Aid (FAFSA) online at www.fafsa.ed.gov and meet with a financial aid officer. Students may also apply for a number of scholarships focusing on their specific areas of career interest.

Faculty

Faculty members are hands-on creative professionals with proven experience as business leaders and innovators, hosting a learning environment similar to the career world students will face after graduation. Part instructor, part mentor, their mission is to help develop and transform creative potential into high-demand marketable skills.

Admission Requirements

Prospective students should refer to the current academic catalog for full details regarding admission requirements and process.

Application and Information

To obtain an application, make arrangements for an interview, or tour the school, prospective students should contact:

The Art Institute of Tennessee—Nashville, a branch of The
   Art Institute of Atlanta
100 Centerview Drive, Suite 250
Nashville, Tennessee 37214-3439
Phone: 615-874-1067
      866-747-5770 (toll-free)
Fax: 615-874-3530
Web site: http://www.artinstitutes.edu/nashville

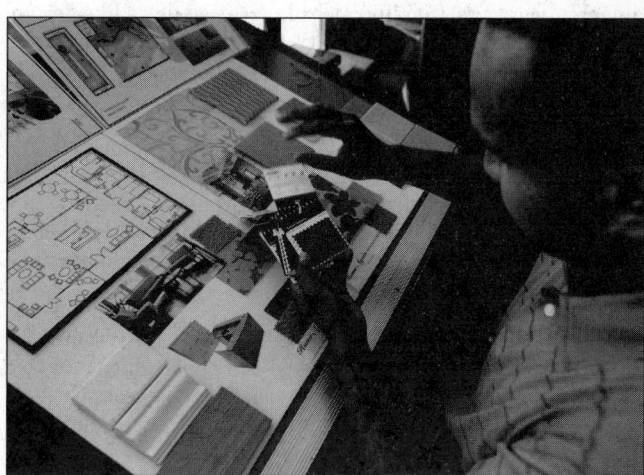

COLLEGE CLOSE-UPS

THE ART INSTITUTE OF TUCSON
TUCSON, ARIZONA

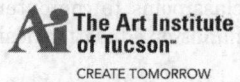

The Art Institute of Tucson is one of The Art Institutes, a system of over fifty schools throughout North America dedicated to providing hands-on education in the creative and applied arts. The Art Institute of Tucson offers bachelor's and associate degree programs as well as non-degree programs for students interested in pursuing career opportunities from among tomorrow's 15 million jobs in creative fields like design, fashion, media arts, and culinary (based on information from the U.S. Bureau of Labor Statistics for job growth from 2012 to 2022).

A focused education from The Art Institute of Tucson can help students turn their creative energy into a powerful tool that can make a difference in the world. Students are part of a collaborative and supportive community, where experienced instructors provide the guidance and skills needed to pursue a career in the creative economy.

The Art Institute of Tucson is also an important resource for creative industry leaders who value the opportunity provided students to learn by using professional-grade technology to build a portfolio of work to show potential employers after graduation.

Accreditation

The Art Institute of Tucson is accredited by the Accrediting Council for Independent Colleges and Schools to award associate and bachelor's degrees. The Accrediting Council for Independent Colleges and Schools is listed as a nationally recognized accrediting agency by the United States Department of Education and is recognized by the Council for Higher Education Accreditation. ACICS can be contacted at 750 First Street NE, Suite 980, Washington, D.C. 20002; phone: 202-336-6780.

The Art Institute of Tucson is authorized by the Arizona State Board for Private Post-secondary Education, 1400 West Washington Street, Room 2560, Phoenix, Arizona 85007; phone: 602-542-5709; http://azppse.state.az.us.

Location

The Art Institute of Tucson is located in a fast-growing, progressive metropolitan area that's also one of the most beautiful places in the United States. Tucson sits on a plain located in the Sonoran Desert, surrounded by five major mountain ranges. Here, students study among postcard images of deserts and mountains. They also explore historic neighborhoods, sample eclectic art, enjoy live music, enjoy the benefits of a bike-friendly city, and generally have a great time.

Tucson's small but vibrant independent music scene is concentrated in the city's downtown area. Among the prominent artists who are based here are Bob Log III, Hipster Daddy-O and the HandGrenades, Giant Sand, The Bled, God of the Sea, Linda Ronstadt, Overcast Off, Calexico, Flagrante Delicto, and local legend Ted Ramirez.

The Tucson Folk Festival takes place downtown the first Saturday and Sunday of May. Along with nationally known headline acts each evening, it showcases over 100 local and regional musicians on five stages, making it is one of the largest free festivals in the nation.

The Center for Creative Photography is a popular Tucson museum that features many works by artists such as Ansel Adams and Edward Weston. The Arizona-Sonora Desert Museum combines a zoo, a botanical garden, and a museum, all dedicated to indigenous plants and animals. Trail Dust Town is an open-air cluster of shops and restaurants that sprang up from the ruins of a long-ago western movie set.

The League of American Bicyclists has awarded Tucson a gold rating for bicycle friendliness. Tucson holds the largest annual perimeter cycling event in the nation, called El Tour de Tucson. The city is known for its winter cycling, and both road and mountain biking are popular in nearby trail areas.

Programs of Study and Degree Offerings

Creativity is all around, and with millions of tomorrow's jobs in creative fields, the world needs more creative professionals. No matter which course of study a student chooses, the instructors at The Art Institutes will guide, support, and help students fine-tune their visual thinking and problem solving, so that they can take advantage of the world's growing creative opportunities and put their passion to work. Programs are offered in the areas of design, which focuses on communicating conceptually and helping people connect in living and work spaces; media arts, that centers on utilizing technology to deliver information and entertainment; fashion, where students learn anything from designing clothes for the runway to running a retail shop; and culinary, which exposes learners to international cuisines as well as restaurant management techniques.

Bachelor's degree programs are offered in the area of advertising, culinary arts, digital filmmaking & video production, digital photography, fashion design, fashion marketing, game art & design, graphic & web design, interior design, media arts & animation, and visual effects & motion graphics.

Associate degree programs are offered in the areas of baking & pastry, culinary arts, and graphic design.

Diploma programs are offered in baking & pastry, culinary arts, digital image management, fashion retailing, web design & development, and web design & interactive communications.

Program availability and degree offerings are subject to change.

Academic Facilities

The Art Institute of Tucson provides a learning environment with professional-grade technology applicable to each student's course of study. Students have the opportunity to build a portfolio of work that shows potential employers that they are trained to use the software, hardware, or equipment utilized within the industry. Depending upon the course of study, students are immersed in a creative environment—from classrooms to computer labs to studios—focused on relevant, hands-on education designed to prepare them for the real world.

Costs

Actual tuition and housing costs will vary depending on program, number of credits enrolled, and living arrangements. Prospective students should contact a Student Financial Services professional at the school for details.

Financial Aid

Financial aid is available for those who qualify. Students who require financial assistance should first complete and submit the Free Application for Federal Student Aid (FAFSA) online at www.fafsa.ed.gov and meet with a financial aid officer. Students may also apply for a number of scholarships focusing on their specific areas of career interest.

Faculty

Faculty members are hands-on creative professionals with proven experience as business leaders and innovators, hosting a learning environment similar to the career world students will face after graduation. Part instructor, part mentor, their mission is to help develop and transform creative potential into high-demand marketable skills.

Admission Requirements

Prospective students should refer to the current academic catalog for full details regarding admission requirements and process.

Application and Information

To obtain an application, make arrangements for an interview, or tour the school, students should contact:

The Art Institute of Tucson
5099 East Grant Road
Suite 100
Tucson, Arizona 85712
Phone: 520-318-2700
       866-690-8850 (toll-free)
Fax: 520-881-4794
Website: http://www.artinstitutes.edu/tucson

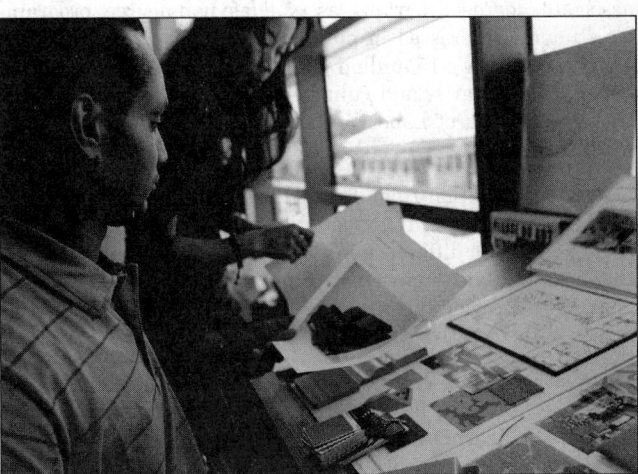

COLLEGE CLOSE-UPS

THE ART INSTITUTE OF VIRGINIA BEACH
VIRGINIA BEACH, VIRGINIA

The Art Institute of Virginia Beach, a branch of The Art Institute of Atlanta, is one of The Art Institutes, a system of over fifty schools throughout North America dedicated to providing hands-on education in the creative and applied arts. The Art Institute of Virginia Beach offers bachelor's and associate degree programs as well as non-degree programs for students interested in pursuing career opportunities from among tomorrow's 15 million jobs in creative fields like design, fashion, media arts, and culinary (based on information from the U.S. Bureau of Labor Statistics for job growth from 2012 to 2022).

A focused education from The Art Institute of Virginia Beach can help students turn their creative energy into a powerful tool that can make a difference in the world. Students are part of a collaborative and supportive community, where experienced instructors provide the guidance and skills needed to pursue a career in the creative economy.

The Art Institute of Virginia Beach is also an important resource for creative industry leaders who value the opportunity provided students to learn by using professional-grade technology to build a portfolio of work to show potential employers after graduation.

Accreditation

The Art Institute of Virginia Beach is a branch campus of The Art Institute of Atlanta. The Art Institute of Atlanta is accredited by the Southern Association of Colleges and Schools Commission on Colleges to award associate and baccalaureate degrees. Contact the Commission on Colleges at 1866 Southern Lane, Decatur, Georgia 30033-4097 or call 404-679-4500 for questions about the accreditation of The Art Institute of Atlanta.

The Art Institute of Virginia Beach, a branch of The Art Institute of Atlanta, is certified to operate in Virginia by The State Council of Higher Education for Virginia, James Monroe Building, 101 North Fourteenth Street, Richmond, Virginia 23219; phone: 804-225-2600.

Location

The Art Institute of Virginia Beach is located in the South Hampton Roads area of southeastern Virginia, near the beautiful sands that line the Atlantic Ocean at the mouth of Chesapeake Bay. Considered the birthplace of America, the Hampton Roads area is home to home to Jamestown, the first permanent English settlement in North America, as well as Colonial Williamsburg. Rich history and beautiful waterfront combine to create a fun and welcoming place for visitors of all ages.

The Virginia Air & Space Center, the Riverside IMAX Theater, Hampton History Museum, and historical Fort Monroe are all located in Hampton. Walk along the Downtown Hampton Public Piers and stop in at the Maritime Center. Relax at Buckroe Beach. Catch a NASCAR race at Langley Speedway. Indulge in some cuisine and shopping at Peninsula Town Center. And head to Hampton Coliseum for events like the annual Hampton Jazz Festival. Colonial Williamsburg and Busch Gardens are located not far to the north.

Virginia Beach offers 28 miles of public beaches, a 3-mile paved boardwalk, and all kinds of events, including the Boardwalk Art Show, the Neptune Festival, the East Coast Surfing Championship, and the Rock 'n Roll Half Marathon. The Virginia Aquarium & Marine Science Center, the Cape Henry Lighthouse, and the Ocean Breeze Waterpark are also in Virginia Beach. Activities include sport fishing, scuba and snorkeling, surfing, sailing, biking, hiking, and just relaxing.

In nearby Norfolk, there are numerous shopping, cultural, and entertainment options. Downtown Norfolk is home to Chrysler Museum of Art, and the USS Wisconsin, the largest battleship in the world can be found at Nauticus, the National Maritime Center. In addition, the AAA Tidewater Tides play baseball at Harbor Park Stadium. Finally, the Norfolk Navy Base, the main port of the U.S. Navy's Atlantic Fleet and the largest naval facility in the world, is located in Portsmouth, near the mouth of Hampton Roads.

The 23-mile-long Chesapeake Bay Bridge-Tunnel spans the mouth of the Chesapeake Bay to connect Virginia Beach with the Delmarva (Delaware, Maryland, and Virginia) Peninsula.

Programs of Study and Degree Offerings

Creativity is all around, and with millions of tomorrow's jobs in creative fields, the world needs more creative professionals. No matter which course of study a student chooses, the instructors at The Art Institutes will guide, support, and help students fine-tune their visual thinking and problem solving, so that they can take advantage of the world's growing creative opportunities and put their passion to work. Programs are offered in the areas of design, which focuses on communicating conceptually and helping people connect in living and work spaces; media arts, that centers on utilizing technology to deliver information and entertainment; fashion, where students learn anything from designing clothes for the runway to running a retail shop; and culinary, which exposes learners to international cuisines as well as restaurant management techniques.

Bachelor's degree programs are offered in the areas of advertising, culinary arts management, designing for tablets: digital publishing, digital photography, fashion & retail management, graphic & web design, interior design, and media arts & animation.

Associate degree programs are offered in the areas of culinary arts and graphic & web design.

Diploma programs are offered in baking & pastry, culinary arts, digital image management, fashion retailing, web design & development, and web design & interactive communications.

Program availability and degree offerings are subject to change.

Academic Facilities

The Art Institute of Virginia Beach provides a learning environment with professional-grade technology applicable to each student's course of study. Students have the opportunity to build a portfolio of work that shows potential employers that they are trained to use the software, hardware, or equipment utilized within the industry. Depending upon the course of study, students are immersed in a creative environment—from classrooms to computer labs to studios—focused on relevant, hands-on education designed to prepare them for the real world.

Costs

Actual tuition and housing costs will vary depending on program, number of credits enrolled, and living arrangements. Prospective students should contact a Student Financial Services professional at the school for details.

Financial Aid

Financial aid is available for those who qualify. Students who require financial assistance should first complete and submit the Free Application for Federal Student Aid (FAFSA) online at www.fafsa.ed.gov and meet with a financial aid officer. Students may also apply for a number of scholarships focusing on their specific areas of career interest.

Faculty

Faculty members are hands-on creative professionals with proven experience as business leaders and innovators, hosting a learning environment similar to the career world students will face after graduation. Part instructor, part mentor, their mission is to help develop and transform creative potential into high-demand marketable skills.

Admission Requirements

Prospective students should refer to the current academic catalog for full details regarding admission requirements and process.

Application and Information

To obtain an application, make arrangements for an interview, or tour the school, prospective students should contact:

The Art Institute of Virginia Beach, a campus of The Art
   Institute of Atlanta
Two Columbus Center
4500 Main Street, Suite 100
Virginia Beach, Virginia 23462
Phone: 757-493-6700
      877-437-4428 (toll-free)
Fax: 757-493-6800
Website: http://www.artinstitutes.edu/virginia-beach

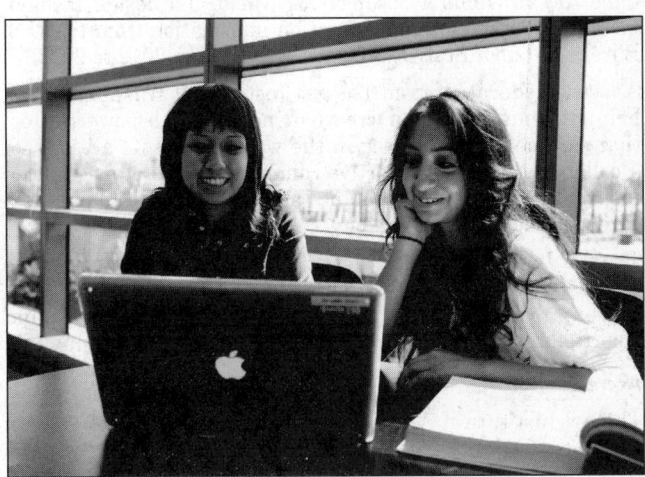

THE ART INSTITUTE OF WASHINGTON
ARLINGTON, VIRGINIA

The Art Institute of Washington (in Arlington, Virginia), a branch of The Art Institute of Atlanta, is one of The Art Institutes, a system of over fifty schools throughout North America dedicated to providing hands-on education in the creative and applied arts. The Art Institute of Washington offers bachelor's and associate degree programs as well as non-degree programs for students interested in pursuing career opportunities from among tomorrow's 15 million jobs in creative fields like design, fashion, media arts, and culinary (based on information from the U.S. Bureau of Labor Statistics for job growth from 2012 to 2022).

A focused education from The Art Institute of Washington can help students turn their creative energy into a powerful tool that can make a difference in the world. Students are part of a collaborative and supportive community, where experienced instructors provide the guidance and skills needed to pursue a career in the creative economy.

The Art Institute of Washington is also an important resource for creative industry leaders who value the opportunity provided students to learn by using professional-grade technology to build a portfolio of work to show potential employers after graduation.

Accreditation

The Art Institute of Washington is a branch campus of The Art Institute of Atlanta. The Art Institute of Atlanta is accredited by the Southern Association of Colleges and Schools Commission on Colleges to award associate and baccalaureate degrees. Questions about the accreditation of The Art Institute of Atlanta can be directed to the Commission on Colleges at 1866 Southern Lane, Decatur, Georgia 30033-4097; phone: 404-679-4500.

The Associate in Arts in culinary arts degree program is accredited by The Accrediting Commission of the American Culinary Federation Education Foundation.

The interior design program leading to the Bachelor of Fine Arts degree is accredited by the Council for Interior Design Accreditation, 206 Grandville Avenue, Suite 350, Grand Rapids, Michigan 49503; www.accredit-id.org.

The Art Institute of Washington, a branch of The Art Institute of Atlanta, is certified to operate in Virginia by The State Council of Higher Education for Virginia, James Monroe Building, 101 North Fourteenth Street, Richmond, Virginia 23219; phone: 804-225-2600.

Location

The Art Institute of Washington is located in the Rosslyn section of Arlington, Virginia, directly across the Potomac River from Georgetown and Washington, D.C., just a short drive or Metro ride away. Originally part of the area surveyed for the nation's capital, Arlington's history is as long as that of Washington itself.

The DC metropolitan area has been nicknamed the melting pot for the extent of ethnic diversity it boasts. With such a mixture of government, culture, history, and symbolism, this city is one of the premier places to visit, live in, and pursue an education.

Today, Arlington is perhaps best known as the home of the Pentagon and the Arlington National Cemetery. But northern Virginia is also home to corporations like Hilton Worldwide and Gannett/USA Today. Fortune 500 companies and other nationally known employers headquartered here include the AES Corporation and Alliant Techsystems. Arlington also boasts a culturally and ethnically diverse population that offers great variety in cuisine, cultural events, and shopping. There's also an extensive county park system with over 80 miles of bicycle and jogging trails.

Arlington's proximity to Washington, D.C. means easy access to the nation's prestigious monuments and museums, including the White House and Capitol Hill, as well as myriad national monuments like the Lincoln and Jefferson Memorials, and such world-class venues as The John F. Kennedy Center for the Performing Arts. The Smithsonian Institution includes numerous museums from the National Portrait Gallery to the National Museum of African Art.

In addition to the many tourist attractions, Washington offers first-rate theatrical and musical entertainment, beautiful parks, and cultural events. Washington, D.C. is also one of the few cities that fields professional teams in each of the major sports: baseball's Nationals play at Nationals Park, the NFL's Redskins call FedEx Field home, and the Capitals of the NHL play hockey at Verizon Center—at least when the NBA Wizards aren't playing basketball there.

From world-class restaurants to national media firms, students at The Art Institute of Washington find many avenues to expand their learning and apply their skills in their chosen field. It's an atmosphere that exudes energy and fuels creativity.

Programs of Study and Degree Offerings

Creativity is all around, and with millions of tomorrow's jobs in creative fields, the world needs more creative professionals. No matter which course of study a student chooses, the instructors at The Art Institutes will guide, support, and help students fine-tune their visual thinking and problem solving, so that they can take advantage of the world's growing creative opportunities and put their passion to work. Programs are offered in the areas of design, which focuses on communicating conceptually and helping people connect in living and work spaces; media arts, that centers on utilizing technology to deliver information and entertainment; fashion, where students learn anything from designing clothes for the runway to running a retail shop; and culinary, which exposes learners to international cuisines as well as restaurant management techniques.

Bachelor's degree programs are offered in the areas of advertising, audio production, culinary arts management, digital filmmaking & video production, designing for tablets: digital publishing, fashion & retail management, food & beverage management, game art & design, graphic & web design, interior design, media arts & animation, digital photography, visual & game programming, and visual effects & motion graphics.

Associate degree programs are offered in the areas of baking & pastry, culinary arts, graphic & web design, digital photography, and video production.

Diploma programs are offered in advertising design, baking & pastry, commercial photography, culinary arts, digital design, digital image management, fashion retailing, video skills, web design & development, and web design & interactive communications.

The Associate in Arts in culinary arts is available in evening and weekend formats.

Program availability and degree offerings are subject to change.

Academic Facilities

The Art Institute of Washington provides a learning environment with professional-grade technology applicable to each student's course of study. Students have the opportunity to build a portfolio of work that shows potential employers that they are trained to use the software, hardware, or equipment utilized within the industry. Depending upon the course of study, students are immersed in a creative environment—from classrooms to computer labs to studios—focused on relevant, hands-on education designed to prepare them for the real world.

Costs

Actual tuition and housing costs will vary depending on program, number of credits enrolled, and living arrangements. Prospective students should contact a Student Financial Services professional at the school for details.

Financial Aid

Financial aid is available for those who qualify. Students who require financial assistance should first complete and submit the Free Application for Federal Student Aid (FAFSA) online at www.fafsa.ed.gov and meet with a financial aid officer. Students may also apply for a number of scholarships focusing on their specific areas of career interest.

Faculty

Faculty members are hands-on creative professionals with proven experience as business leaders and innovators, hosting a learning environment similar to the career world students will face after graduation. Part instructor, part mentor, their mission is to help develop and transform creative potential into high-demand marketable skills.

Admission Requirements

Prospective students should refer to the current academic catalog for full details regarding admission requirements and process.

Application and Information

To obtain an application, make arrangements for an interview, or tour the school, prospective students should contact:

The Art Institute of Washington, a campus of The Art
    Institute of Atlanta
1820 North Fort Myer Drive
Arlington, Virginia 22209-1802
Phone: 703-358-9550
       877-303-3771 (toll-free)
Fax: 703-358-9759
Website: http://www.artinstitutes.edu/arlington

THE ART INSTITUTE OF WASHINGTON—DULLES

DULLES, VIRGINIA

The Art Institute of Washington—Dulles, a branch of The Art Institute of Atlanta, is one of The Art Institutes, a system of over fifty schools throughout North America dedicated to providing hands-on education in the creative and applied arts. The Art Institute of Washington—Dulles offers bachelor's and associate degree programs as well as non-degree programs for students interested in pursuing career opportunities from among tomorrow's 15 million jobs in creative fields like design, fashion, and media arts (based on information from the U.S. Bureau of Labor Statistics for job growth from 2012 to 2022).

A focused education from The Art Institute of Washington—Dulles can help students turn their creative energy into a powerful tool that can make a difference in the world. Students are part of a collaborative and supportive community, where experienced instructors provide the guidance and skills needed to pursue a career in the creative economy.

The Art Institute of Washington—Dulles is also an important resource for creative industry leaders who value the opportunity we provide students to learn by using professional-grade technology to build a portfolio of work to show potential employers after graduation.

Accreditation

The Art Institute of Washington—Dulles is a branch campus of The Art Institute of Atlanta. The Art Institute of Atlanta is accredited by the Southern Association of Colleges and Schools Commission on Colleges to award associate and baccalaureate degrees. Questions about the accreditation of The Art Institute of Atlanta can be directed to the Commission on Colleges at 1866 Southern Lane, Decatur, Georgia 30033-4097; phone: 404-679-4500.

The Art Institute of Washington—Dulles, a branch of The Art Institute of Atlanta, is certified to operate in Virginia by The State Council for Higher Education in Virginia, James Monroe Building, 101 North Fourteenth Street, Richmond, VA 23219; phone: 804-225-2600.

Location

Dulles, Virginia isn't just the home of a sprawling international airport. It's also the home of The Art Institute of Washington—Dulles. Situated in the northeast corner of Loudoun County, Dulles is as rich in historical value as it is in real estate value. A popular suburb for commuters who work in Washington, D.C., the area offers a fascinating mix of the contemporary and traditional in a creative environment that offers inspiring experiences.

The DC metropolitan area has been nicknamed the melting pot for the extent of ethnic diversity it boasts. With such a mixture of government, culture, history, and symbolism, this city is one of the premier places to visit, live in, and pursue an education.

Dulles' proximity to Washington, D.C. means easy access to the nation's prestigious monuments and museums, including the White House and Capitol Hill, as well as myriad national monuments like the Lincoln and Jefferson Memorials, and such world-class venues as The John F. Kennedy Center for the Performing Arts. The Smithsonian Institution includes numerous museums from the National Portrait Gallery to the National Museum of African Art.

In addition to the many tourist attractions, Washington offers first-rate theatrical and musical entertainment, beautiful parks, and cultural events. Washington, D.C. is also one of the few cities that fields professional teams in each of the major sports: baseball's Nationals play at Nationals Park, the NFL's Redskins call FedEx Field home, and the Capitals of the NHL play hockey at Verizon Center—at least when the NBA Wizards aren't playing basketball there.

From world-class restaurants to national media firms, students at The Art Institute of Washington—Dulles find many avenues to expand their learning and apply their skills in their chosen field. It's an atmosphere that exudes energy and fuels creativity.

Programs of Study and Degree Offerings

Creativity is all around, and with millions of tomorrow's jobs in creative fields, the world needs more creative professionals. No matter which course of study a student chooses, the instructors at The Art Institutes will guide, support, and help students fine-tune their visual thinking and problem solving, so that they can take advantage of the world's growing creative opportunities and put their passion to work. Programs are offered in the areas of design, which focuses on communicating conceptually and helping people connect in living and work spaces; media arts, that centers on utilizing technology to deliver information and entertainment; and fashion, where students learn anything from clothes for the runway to running a retail shop.

Bachelor's degree programs are offered in the areas of advertising, designing for tablets: digital publishing, fashion & retail management, game art & design, graphic & web design, interior design, media arts & animation, and photographic imaging.

An Associate of Arts degree is offered in graphic & web design.

Diploma programs are offered in digital image management, fashion retailing, web design & development, and web design & interactive communications.

Program availability and degree offerings are subject to change.

Academic Facilities

The Art Institute of Washington—Dulles provides a learning environment with professional-grade technology applicable to each student's course of study. Students have the opportunity to build a portfolio of work that shows potential employers that they are trained to use the software, hardware, or equipment utilized within the industry. Depending upon the course of study, students are immersed in a creative environment—from classrooms to computer labs to studios—focused on relevant, hands-on education designed to prepare them for the real world.

Costs

Actual tuition and housing costs will vary depending on program, number of credits enrolled, and living arrangements. Prospective students should contact a Student Financial Services professional at the school for details.

Financial Aid

Financial aid is available for those who qualify. Students who require financial assistance should first complete and submit the Free Application for Federal Student Aid (FAFSA) online at www.fafsa.ed.gov and meet with a financial aid officer. Students may also apply for a number of scholarships focusing on their specific areas of career interest.

Faculty

Faculty members are hands-on creative professionals with proven experience as business leaders and innovators, hosting a learning environment similar to the career world students will face after graduation. Part instructor, part mentor, their mission is to help develop and transform creative potential into high-demand marketable skills.

Admission Requirements

Prospective students should refer to the current academic catalog for full details regarding admission requirements and process.

Application and Information

To obtain an application, make arrangements for an interview, or tour the school, prospective students should contact:

The Art Institute of Washington—Dulles, a campus of The Art Institute of Atlanta
The Corporate Office Park at Dulles Town Center
21000 Atlantic Blvd., Suite 100
Dulles, Virginia 20166
Phone: 571-449-4400
        888-627-5008 (toll-free)
Fax: 571-449-4500
Website: http://www.artinstitutes.edu/dulles

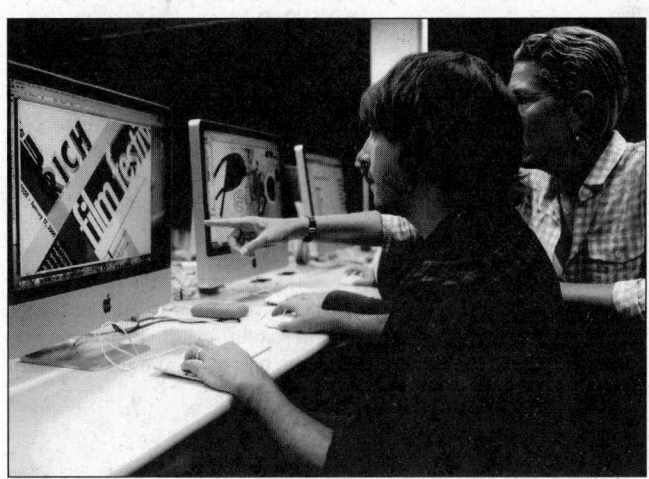

THE ART INSTITUTE OF WISCONSIN

MILWAUKEE, WISCONSIN

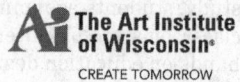

The Art Institute of Wisconsin is one of The Art Institutes, a system of over fifty schools throughout North America dedicated to providing hands-on education in the creative and applied arts. The Art Institute of Wisconsin offers bachelor's and associate degree programs for students interested in pursuing career opportunities from among tomorrow's 15 million jobs in creative fields like design, fashion, media arts, and culinary (based on information from the U.S. Bureau of Labor Statistics for job growth from 2012 to 2022).

A focused education from The Art Institute of Wisconsin can help students turn their creative energy into a powerful tool that can make a difference in the world. Students are part of a collaborative and supportive community, where experienced instructors provide the guidance and skills needed to pursue a career in the creative economy.

The Art Institute of Wisconsin is also an important resource for creative industry leaders who value the opportunity provided students to learn by using professional-grade technology to build a portfolio of work to show potential employers after graduation.

Accreditation

The Art Institute of Wisconsin is accredited by the Accrediting Council for Independent Colleges and Schools to award bachelor's and associate degrees. The Accrediting Council for Independent Colleges and Schools is listed as a nationally recognized accrediting agency by the United States Department of Education and is recognized by the Council for Higher Education Accreditation. ACICS can be contacted at 750 First Street NE, Suite 980, Washington, D.C. 20002; phone: 202-336-6780.

The Art Institute of Wisconsin is authorized by the Wisconsin Educational Approval Board, 201 W. Washington Avenue, 3rd Floor, P.O. Box 8696, Madison, Wisconsin 53708-8696; http://eab.state.wi.us/default.asp.

Location

The Art Institute of Wisconsin is located in the center of Milwaukee, the largest city in the state. Milwaukee is known for its large German population, its many breweries, and its neighborhood brewpubs. But Milwaukee is also home to a large number of cultural, art, music, and food festivals, along with a wide range of museums, performing arts venues, gardens, and parks. Summerfest, an event that's held every late June through early July in Milwaukee, is one of the world's largest music festivals.

Milwaukee serves as the corporate headquarters for more than a dozen Fortune 1000 companies. Recently, five companies in the area were selected as leaders in their respective fields as part of *Fortune* magazine's "World's Most Admired Companies." Milwaukee was also recently ranked by *Forbes* as

the fourth-best city in America for commuters. Also known as the setting for the television shows "Happy Days" and "Laverne and Shirley" in the 1970s and 1980s, Milwaukee is a fascinating mix of the traditional and contemporary for students who are looking an education in the creative and applied arts.

The city also offers the Milwaukee Art Museum, the Haggerty Museum of Art, the Villa Terrace Decorative Arts Museum, the Charles Allis Art Museum, the William F. Eisner Museum of Advertising & Design—and even a museum dedicated to Harley Davidson motorcycles. Milwaukee also has one of the highest per-capita student populations in all of North America.

In Milwaukee, there are plenty of opportunities to cheer on local teams. Baseball's Milwaukee Brewers play under the retractable roof of Miller Park, the NBA's Milwaukee Bucks at Bradley Center, and the legendary Green Bay Packers' stadium, Lambeau Field, is just a few hours' drive north. Milwaukee is a genuine American city that offers a little bit of everything—and a lot of what many students are seeking.

Programs of Study and Degree Offerings

Creativity is all around, and with millions of tomorrow's jobs in creative fields, the world needs more creative professionals. No matter which course of study a student chooses, the instructors at The Art Institutes will guide, support, and help students fine-tune their visual thinking and problem solving, so that they can take advantage of the world's growing creative opportunities and put their passion to work. Programs are offered in the areas of design, which focuses on communicating conceptually and helping people connect in living and work spaces; media arts, that centers on utilizing technology to deliver information and entertainment; fashion, where students learn anything from designing clothes for the runway or run a retail shop; and culinary, which exposes learners to international cuisines as well as restaurant management techniques.

Bachelor's degree programs are offered in the areas of advertising, culinary management, digital filmmaking & video production, fashion design, fashion marketing, game art & design, graphic design, interior design, media arts & animation, visual effects & motion graphics, and web design & interactive media.

Associate degree programs are offered in the areas of baking & pastry, culinary arts, and graphic design.

Program availability and degree offerings are subject to change.

Academic Facilities

The Art Institute of Wisconsin provides a learning environment with professional-grade technology applicable to each student's course of study. Students have the opportunity to build a portfolio of work that shows potential employers that they are trained to use the software, hardware, or equipment

utilized within the industry. Depending upon the course of study, students are immersed in a creative environment—from classrooms to computer labs to studios—focused on relevant, hands-on education designed to prepare them for the real world.

Costs

Actual tuition and housing costs will vary depending on program, number of credits enrolled, and living arrangements. Prospective students should contact a Student Financial Services professional at the school for details.

Financial Aid

Financial aid is available for those who qualify. Students who require financial assistance should first complete and submit the Free Application for Federal Student Aid (FAFSA) online at www.fafsa.ed.gov and meet with a financial aid officer. Students may also apply for a number of scholarships focusing on their specific areas of career interest.

Faculty

Faculty members are hands-on creative professionals with proven experience as business leaders and innovators, hosting a learning environment similar to the career world students will face after graduation. Part instructor, part mentor, their mission is to help develop and transform creative potential into high-demand marketable skills.

Admission Requirements

Prospective students should refer to the current academic catalog for full details regarding admission requirements and process.

Application and Information

To obtain an application, make arrangements for an interview, or tour the school, prospective students should contact:

The Art Institute of Wisconsin
320 East Buffalo Street, Suite 100
Milwaukee, Wisconsin 53202
Phone: 414-978-5000
      877-285-4234 (toll-free)
Fax: 414-978-5182
Website: http://www.artinstitutes.edu/milwaukee

THE ART INSTITUTE OF YORK— PENNSYLVANIA
YORK, PENNSYLVANIA

The Art Institute of York—Pennsylvania is one of The Art Institutes, a system of over fifty schools throughout North America dedicated to providing hands-on education in the creative and applied arts. The Art Institute of York— Pennsylvania offers bachelor's and associate degree programs as well as non-degree programs for students interested in pursuing career opportunities from among tomorrow's 15 million jobs in creative fields like design, fashion, and media arts (based on information from the U.S. Bureau of Labor Statistics for job growth from 2012 to 2022).

A focused education from The Art Institute of York— Pennsylvania can help students turn their creative energy into a powerful tool that can make a difference in the world. Students are part of a collaborative and supportive community, where experienced instructors provide the guidance and skills needed to pursue a career in the creative economy.

The Art Institute of York—Pennsylvania is also an important resource for creative industry leaders who value the opportunity provided students to learn by using professional-grade technology to build a portfolio of work to show potential employers after graduation.

Accreditation

The Art Institute of York—Pennsylvania is accredited by the Accrediting Council for Independent Colleges and Schools to award associate and bachelor's degrees. The Accrediting Council for Independent Colleges and Schools is listed as a nationally recognized accrediting agency by the United Stated Department of Education and is recognized by the Council for Higher Education Accreditation. ACICS can be contacted at 750 First Street NE, Suite 980, Washington, D.C. 20002; phone: 202-336-6780.

The Art Institute of York—Pennsylvania is authorized by the Pennsylvania Department of Education to confer the Bachelor of Science degrees and Associate of Science degrees. The Department of Education can be reached by writing to the Commonwealth of Pennsylvania, Department of Education Office of Postsecondary and Higher Education, 333 Market Street, Harrisburg, Pennsylvania 17126; phone: 717-783-6788.

Location

The Art Institute of York—Pennsylvania is nestled in a community that's steeped in American history, is close to some of America's great cities, and offers a great blend of small-town charm, convenience, and laid-back lifestyle.

Depending on historic lore, York is either the nation's first capital...or the fourth, after Philadelphia; Baltimore, Maryland; and Lancaster, Pennsylvania. It was on the York County Colonial Court House where the words "The United States of America" were first formally proclaimed—and where the first Constitution was adopted.

A leisurely stroll through downtown York offers a taste of the lives of immigrant pioneers, Revolutionary War soldiers, 19th-century farmers, and the craftspeople of today. This is a town that blends the stories of military heroes, business tycoons, and factory workers.

The city has been referred to as an architectural museum, because the downtown features an assortment of well-preserved historic buildings, including the Golden Plough Tavern, which dates back to 1741; the General Horatio Gates House from 1751; the 1766 York Meetinghouse; the 1863 Billmeyer House; the 1888 York Central Market; and the 1907 Moorish Revival Temple Beth Israel. York boasts not just one, but four national historic districts: the Fairmount Historic District, the Northwest York Historic District, the Springdale Historic District, and the York Historic District.

The York County area features several major shopping malls and many outlet shopping centers. With its strong manufacturing and industrial base, the area consistently has one of the lowest unemployment rates in the Commonwealth of Pennsylvania. Students can enjoy a meal, from casual to elegant, at one of the many eateries and restaurants in the downtown area and surrounding the city. York also features two farmers markets, offering fresh fruits, vegetables, homemade baked goods, and more.

The beautiful seaport city of Baltimore is just 45 minutes away, and Harrisburg and Lancaster are just a half-hour drive from The Art Institute of York—Pennsylvania.

Programs of Study and Degree Offerings

Creativity is all around, and with millions of tomorrow's jobs in creative fields, the world needs more creative professionals. No matter which course of study a student chooses, the instructors at The Art Institutes will guide, support, and help students fine-tune their visual thinking and problem solving, so that they can take advantage of the world's growing creative opportunities and put their passion to work. Programs are offered in the areas of design, which focuses on communicating conceptually and helping people connect in living and work spaces; media arts, that centers on utilizing technology to deliver information and entertainment; and fashion, where students learn anything from designing clothes for the runway to running a retail shop.

Bachelor's degree programs are offered in the areas of fashion & retail management, graphic design, interior design, media arts & animation, and web design & interactive media.

The Associate of Science degree is offered in graphic design.

Diploma programs are offered in fashion retailing, web design & development, and web design & interactive communications.

Program availability and degree offerings are subject to change.

Academic Facilities

The Art Institute of York—Pennsylvania provides a learning environment with professional-grade technology applicable to each student's course of study. Students have the opportunity to build a portfolio of work that shows potential employers that they are trained to use the software, hardware, or equipment utilized within the industry. Depending upon the course of study, students are immersed in a creative environment—from classrooms to computer labs to studios—focused on relevant, hands-on education designed to prepare them for the real world.

Costs

Actual tuition and housing costs will vary depending on program, number of credits enrolled, and living arrangements. Prospective students should contact a Student Financial Services professional at the school for details.

Financial Aid

Financial aid is available for those who qualify. Students who require financial assistance should first complete and submit the Free Application for Federal Student Aid (FAFSA) online at www.fafsa.ed.gov and meet with a financial aid officer. Students may also apply for a number of scholarships focusing on their specific areas of career interest.

Faculty

Faculty members are hands-on creative professionals with proven experience as business leaders and innovators, hosting a learning environment similar to the career world students will face after graduation. Part instructor, part mentor, their mission is to help develop and transform creative potential into high-demand marketable skills.

Admission Requirements

Prospective students should refer to the current academic catalog for full details regarding admission requirements and process.

Application and Information

To obtain an application, make arrangements for an interview, or tour the school, students should contact:

The Art Institute of York—Pennsylvania
1409 Williams Road
York, Pennsylvania 17402-9012
Phone: 717-755-2300
      800-864-7725 (toll-free)
Fax: 717-840-1951
Website: http://www.artinstitutes.edu/york

COLLEGE CLOSE-UPS

THE ART INSTITUTES INTERNATIONAL—KANSAS CITY

LENEXA, KANSAS

The Art Institutes International—Kansas City is one of The Art Institutes, a system of over fifty schools throughout North America dedicated to providing hands-on education in the creative and applied arts. The Art Institutes International—Kansas City offers bachelor's and associate degree programs as well as non-degree programs for students interested in pursuing career opportunities from among tomorrow's 15 million jobs in creative fields like design, fashion, media arts, and culinary (based on information from the U.S. Bureau of Labor Statistics for job growth from 2012 to 2022).

A focused education from The Art Institutes International—Kansas City can help students turn their creative energy into a powerful tool that can make a difference in the world. Students are part of a collaborative and supportive community, where experienced instructors provide the guidance and skills needed to pursue a career in the creative economy.

The Art Institutes International—Kansas City is also an important resource for creative industry leaders who value the opportunity provides students to learn by using professional-grade technology to build a portfolio of work to show potential employers after graduation.

Accreditation

The Art Institutes International—Kansas City is accredited by the Accrediting Council for Independent Colleges and Schools to award associate and bachelor's degrees. The Accrediting Council for Independent Colleges and Schools is listed as a nationally recognized accrediting agency by the United States Department of Education and is recognized by the Council for Higher Education Accreditation. ACICS can be contacted at 750 First Street NE, Suite 980, Washington, D.C. 20002; phone: 202-336-6780.

The Kansas Board of Regents has approved The Art Institutes International—Kansas City to operate in the State of Kansas. The Kansas Board of Regents may be contacted at the following address: Kansas Board of Regents, Private Postsecondary Education Division, 1000 SW Jackson Street, Suite 520, Topeka, Kansas 66612-1368; phone: 785-296-0911; fax: 785-296-4526.

Location

The Art Institutes International—Kansas City is located in the heart of a city whose nickname is City of Fountains, which makes sense, considering the fact that there are over 200 fountains there—more than any other city outside Rome.

Kansas City also has more boulevards—132 miles of them—than any city except Paris, leading to another moniker, Paris of the Plains. And because K.C. is at both the population and geographic center of the country, it's also known as the Heart of America.

But no matter what nickname is used, Kansas City is a dynamic city that features a vibrant arts scene, world-class attractions, and an eclectic mix of shops and boutiques. It's well known for barbecue—K.C. has more barbecue restaurants per capita than any other city in the country—and jazz. In fact, that particular music genre has been big in this town since the 1920s, having launched the careers of artists like Count Basie, Bennie Moten, and Charlie "Bird" Parker.

The city's commitment to its parks and landmarks is well known throughout the country, making it one of the most beautiful cities in America. Kansas City has over 200 urban parks, more than 100 tennis courts, and 30 public swimming pools as well as world-class museums, a vibrant arts scene, and superb shopping.

Since it first opened in 1857, the City Market has been one of the biggest public farmers' markets in the entire Midwest, connecting farmers and small businesses to Kansas City's communities. More than thirty merchants are open year-round, offering everything from specialty foods to seafood, from restaurants and cafes to home accessories.

In the world of sports, Kansas City has teams in every professional sport from soccer to roller derby. Baseball's Kansas City Royals play their home games at Kauffman Stadium, and the NFL's Kansas City Chiefs operate right next door at Arrowhead Stadium—the first stadium ever to show instant replay on its scoreboard.

Programs of Study and Degree Offerings

Creativity is all around, and with millions of tomorrow's jobs in creative fields, the world needs more creative professionals. No matter which course of study a student chooses, the instructors at The Art Institutes will guide, support, and help students fine-tune their visual thinking and problem solving, so that they can take advantage of the world's growing creative opportunities and put their passion to work. Programs are offered in the areas of design, which focuses on communicating conceptually and helping people connect in living and work spaces; media arts, that centers on utilizing technology to deliver information and entertainment; fashion, where students learn anything from designing clothes for the runway to running a retail shop; and culinary, which exposes learners to international cuisines as well as restaurant management techniques.

Bachelor's degree programs are offered in the areas of advertising, culinary management, digital filmmaking & video production, fashion marketing, game art & design, graphic design, graphic & web design, interior design, media arts & animation, digital photography, visual effects & motion graphics, and web design & interactive media.

Associate degree programs are offered in the areas of baking & pastry arts, culinary arts, and graphic design.

Diploma programs are offered in baking & pastry, culinary arts, digital image management, fashion retailing, web design & development, and web design & interactive communications.

Program availability and degree offerings are subject to change.

Academic Facilities

The Art Institutes International—Kansas City provides a learning environment with professional-grade technology applicable to each student's course of study. Students have the opportunity to build a portfolio of work that shows potential employers that they are trained to use the software, hardware, or equipment utilized within the industry. Depending upon the course of study, students are immersed in a creative environment—from classrooms to computer labs to studios—focused on relevant, hands-on education designed to prepare them for the real world.

Costs

Actual tuition and housing costs will vary depending on program, number of credits enrolled, and actual living arrangements. Prospective students should contact a Student Financial Services professional at the school for details.

Financial Aid

Financial aid is available for those who qualify. Students who require financial assistance should first complete and submit the Free Application for Federal Student Aid (FAFSA) online at www.fafsa.ed.gov and meet with a financial aid officer. Students may also apply for a number of scholarships focusing on their specific areas of career interest.

Faculty

Faculty members are hands-on creative professionals with proven experience as business leaders and innovators, hosting a learning environment similar to the career world students will face after graduation. Part instructor, part mentor, their mission is to help develop and transform creative potential into high-demand marketable skills.

Admission Requirements

Prospective students should refer to the current academic catalog for full details regarding admission requirements and process.

Application and Information

To obtain an application, make arrangements for an interview, or tour the school, prospective students should contact:

The Art Institutes International—Kansas City
8208 Melrose Drive
Lenexa, Kansas 66214
Phone: 913-217-4600
        866-530-8508 (toll-free)
Fax: 913-217-4690
Website: http://www.artinstitutes.edu/kansascity

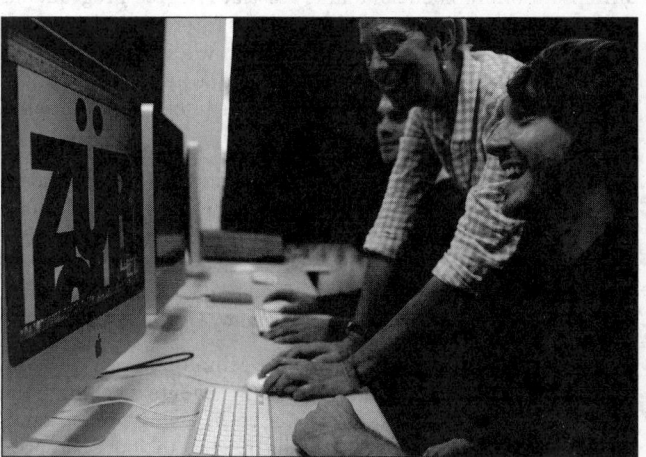

THE ART INSTITUTES INTERNATIONAL MINNESOTA

MINNEAPOLIS, MINNESOTA

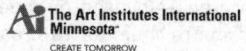

The Art Institutes International Minnesota is one of The Art Institutes, a system of over fifty schools throughout North America dedicated to providing hands-on education in the creative and applied arts. The Art Institutes International Minnesota offers bachelor's and associate degree programs as well as non-degree programs for students interested in pursuing career opportunities from among tomorrow's 15 million jobs in creative fields like design, fashion, media arts, and culinary (based on information from the U.S. Bureau of Labor Statistics for job growth from 2012 to 2022).

A focused education from The Art Institutes International Minnesota can help students turn their creative energy into a powerful tool that can make a difference in the world. Students are part of a collaborative and supportive community, where experienced instructors provide the guidance and skills needed to pursue a career in the creative economy.

The Art Institutes International Minnesota is also an important resource for creative industry leaders who value the opportunity provided students to learn by using professional-grade technology to build a portfolio of work to show potential employers after graduation.

Accreditation

The Art Institutes International Minnesota is accredited by the Accrediting Council for Independent Colleges and Schools to award certificates and associate and bachelor's degrees. The Accrediting Council for Independent Colleges and Schools (ACICS) is listed as a nationally recognized accrediting agency by the United States Department of Education and is recognized by the Council for Higher Education Accreditation. ACICS can be contacted at 750 First Street NE, Suite 980, Washington, D.C. 20002; phone: 202-336-6780.

The Associate in Applied Science in culinary arts degree program is accredited by The Accrediting Commission of the American Culinary Federation Education Foundation.

The Art Institutes International Minnesota is registered as a private institution with the Minnesota Office of Higher Education, 1450 Energy Park Drive, Suite 350, St. Paul, Minnesota 55108; phone: 651-642-0567; www.ohe.state.mn.us; pursuant to sections 136A.61 to 136A.71. Registration is not an endorsement of the institution. Credits earned at the institution may not transfer to all other institutions.

Location

Minneapolis and St. Paul are the famous Twin Cities of Minnesota. A study in contrasts, the cities offer the natural beauty of parks and lakes, yet form a modern metropolis that supports both a vibrant artistic community and bustling business center.

The Twin Cities is an amazing place to experience and create art. Four major art museums, two orchestras, and regional theater offer plenty of creative inspiration. Stroll through the Sculpture Garden at the Walker Art Center. Marvel at the Aquatennial, Winter Carnival, and Renaissance Festival. Wonder at the Minneapolis Museum of Arts. The pop, jazz, and rock scene here earned the Twin Cities the nickname "The Land of 10,000 Bands."

An economically thriving area, Minneapolis is ranked as one of the nation's healthiest business centers, where corporate giants such as 3M, General Mills, Land O' Lakes, and Pillsbury make their homes. Getting around is easy, with a network of mass transit routes, shuttles, and a skyway that connects more than fifty city blocks.

There are 150 city parks for hiking, biking, and skating. In warmer months, spend a sunny afternoon on the beaches of Lake Calhoun. In winter, enjoy ice skating, ice fishing, snowmobiling, and skiing. Four major league sports teams all play right in downtown Minneapolis. Fans cheer on the NFL's Minnesota Vikings at the Metrodome, baseball's Twins at Target Field, the NBA's Timberwolves at Target Center, and the NHL's Wild at the Xcel Energy Center.

Programs of Study and Degree Offerings

Creativity is all around, and with millions of tomorrow's jobs in creative fields, the world needs more creative professionals. No matter which course of study a student chooses, the instructors at The Art Institutes will guide, support, and help students fine-tune their visual thinking and problem solving, so that they can take advantage of the world's growing creative opportunities and put their passion to work. Programs are offered in the areas of design, which focuses on communicating conceptually and helping people connect in living and work spaces; media arts, that centers on utilizing technology to deliver information and entertainment; fashion, where students learn anything from designing clothes for the runway to running a retail shop; and culinary, which exposes learners to international cuisines as well as restaurant management techniques.

Bachelor's degree programs are offered in the areas of advertising, audio production, culinary management, design management, digital film & video production, fashion & retail management, fashion design, graphic design, hospitality management, interior design, media arts & animation, photography, visual effects & motion graphics, and web design & interactive media.

Associate degree programs are offered in the areas of baking & pastry, culinary arts, graphic design, interior design, interior planning with AutoCAD, and web design & interactive media.

Diploma programs are offered in art of cooking, baking & pastry, digital image management, fashion retailing, web design & development, and web design & interactive communications.

Program availability and degree offerings are subject to change.

Academic Facilities

The Art Institutes International Minnesota provides a learning environment with professional-grade technology applicable to each student's course of study. Students have the opportunity to build a portfolio of work that shows potential employers that

they are trained to use the software, hardware, or equipment utilized within the industry. Depending upon the course of study, students are immersed in a creative environment—from classrooms to computer labs to studios—focused on relevant, hands-on education designed to prepare them for the real world.

Costs

Actual tuition and housing costs will vary depending on program, number of credits enrolled, and living arrangements. Prospective students should contact a Student Financial Services professional at the school for details.

Financial Aid

Financial aid is available for those who qualify. Students who require financial assistance should first complete and submit the Free Application for Federal Student Aid (FAFSA) online at www.fafsa.ed.gov and meet with a financial aid officer. Students may also apply for a number of scholarships focusing on their specific areas of career interest.

Faculty

Faculty members are hands-on creative professionals with proven experience as business leaders and innovators, hosting a learning environment similar to the career world students will face after graduation. Part instructor, part mentor, their mission is to help develop and transform creative potential into high-demand marketable skills.

Admission Requirements

Prospective students should refer to the current academic catalog for full details regarding admission requirements and process.

Application and Information

To obtain an application, arrange for an interview, or tour the school, prospective students should contact:

The Art Institutes International Minnesota
15 South 9th Street
Minneapolis, Minnesota 55402-3105
Phone: 612-332-3361
      800-777-3643 (toll-free)
Fax: 612-332-3934
Website: http://www.artinstitutes.edu/minneapolis

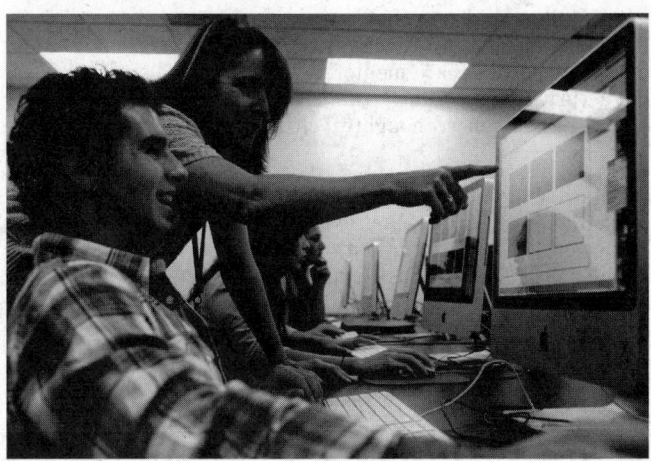

Since The Art Institutes system of schools is comprised of several institutions, see aiprograms.info for program duration, tuition, fees, and other costs, median debt, federal salary data, alumni success, and other important info. The Art Institutes is a system of over 50 schools throughout North America. Programs, credential levels, technology, and scheduling options vary by school, and employment opportunities are not guaranteed. Financial aid is available to those who qualify. Several institutions included in The Art Institutes system are campuses of South University or Argosy University. OH Registration #04-01-1698B, AC0165, AC0080, Licensed by the Florida Commission for Independent Education, License No. 1287, 3427, 3110, 2581. Certified by SCHEV to operate in Virginia. Administrative office: 210 Sixth Avenue, 33rd Floor, Pittsburgh, PA 15222. ©2013 The Art Institutes International LLC.

ASSUMPTION COLLEGE
WORCESTER, MASSACHUSETTS

The College

Assumption College, established in 1904 by the Augustinians of the Assumption, is a coeducational institution known for its classic liberal arts curriculum and strong academic programs in business and professional studies. The College's 2,050 undergraduates choose among 40 majors and 45 minors, gaining a depth and breadth of knowledge that is the foundation of lifelong success. Their educational experience is grounded in the rich Catholic intellectual tradition, which cultivates both the intellect and personal values students need to meet the demands of a constantly changing world. Undergraduates and graduate students are mentored by faculty and staff members in a thriving community that develops graduates known for critical intelligence, thoughtful citizenship, and compassionate service.

The academic atmosphere is marked by individual attention and the quest for personal excellence. With a student-faculty ratio of just 12:1, Assumption's professors serve as mentors who challenge students to ask questions, find their own answers, and grow—intellectually, socially, and spiritually. Students are encouraged to gain hands-on experience at internships and to participate in individual research projects. The result is that 95 percent of the graduates who responded to a survey six months after graduation are either employed or in graduate school.

At Assumption, 90 percent of the undergraduates live on campus and housing is guaranteed for all four years. The campus is lively seven days a week with academic programming, activities sponsored by student clubs and organizations, community service opportunities, campus ministry programs, and intercollegiate, intramural, and club sports. The College's state-of-the-art recreation center supports the well-being of all students.

Location

The College's 185-acre campus is situated in a beautiful, residential neighborhood just minutes from downtown Worcester, Massachusetts. Worcester, the second-largest city in New England, is a vibrant college town, home to 30,000 students. The city offers extensive opportunities for internships in virtually every field, as well as numerous entertainment and community service options. Great restaurants, cultural venues and programs, retail shops, and professional sports teams provide students with many off-campus activities. Worcester is also centrally located, with Boston, Providence, Rhode Island, and Hartford, Connecticut, each an hour's drive away. There are numerous daily commuter trains to Boston.

Majors and Degrees

The College offers Bachelor of Arts degrees. The most popular majors include English (concentrations in literature or writing and mass communications), history, political science, psychology, the natural sciences (biology, biotechnology and molecular biology, chemistry, and environmental science), education, human services and rehabilitation studies, and business disciplines such as accounting, international business, management, marketing, and organizational communication. Minors are offered in forty-five areas. Preprofessional programs are available for medicine, law, and dentistry.

The College has also developed partnerships with a number of highly regarded institutions to provide students with additional options. There is engineering with the University of Notre Dame, environment science with Duke University, and law (3+3 programs with Duquesne, Vermont, and Western New England Law Schools). There are agreements for numerous medical professions, and joint seven-year programs are also available for those interested in podiatry or optometry.

Assumption College offers graduate degrees in business, special education, school counseling, counseling psychology, and rehabilitation counseling.

Academic Programs

The College's classic liberal arts curriculum promotes the lively discussion of the books, ideas, people, and events that have shaped civilization. Faculty members and students explore the rich Catholic intellectual tradition as they seek truth and the nature of the world.

Assumption also offers academic programs and courses that help students achieve their full potential. The College's first-year program, the Tagaste Project, links courses from two disciplines and offers activities that complement classroom experiences. The same 20 students take courses in the fall and spring semesters, enabling them to make important intellectual connections, while getting to know other students. The honors program and the Fortin and Gonthier Foundations of Western Civilization Program encourage students to challenge themselves intellectually. Air Force and Army ROTC are also available.

Assumption College follows a traditional two-semester calendar, from late August to mid-May, as well as an optional January intersession. The Graduate Studies programs and the Center for Continuing and Career Education also offer two summer sessions for students.

Undergraduates complete a core curriculum that provides a strong foundation in the liberal arts. Students must complete 120 credit hours in all the academic programs to earn a degree.

Off-Campus Programs

The College and eleven other institutions of higher learning created the Colleges of Worcester Consortium to offer the 30,000 college students in the area even greater academic and social opportunities. Assumption students may cross-register for academic credit at any of the participating colleges and enjoy their social and cultural events. Free transportation to other participating institutions is available.

Eligible students may choose to spend a semester or a year abroad. Assumption opened a campus in Rome in February, 2013, which is specifically geared toward sophomores. The College's students have studied abroad in Australia, Austria, Chile, China, Costa Rica, the Czech Republic, England, France, Germany, Greece, Ireland, Italy, Japan, the Netherlands, Spain, and other locations. There are also numerous one- and two-week international experiences led by Assumption faculty.

Nearly 60 percent of Assumption students have had at least one internship. They explore their professional choices and broaden their workplace skills at local, regional, national, and international sites. In recent years, they have interned at PBS, the U.S. House of Representatives, Ralph Lauren, the Hungarian Embassy, Smith Barney, Fidelity, *The Daily Show with Jon Stewart*, ABC News, PricewaterhouseCoopers, AT&T, and Sony Japan.

Academic Facilities

The College has invested more than $80 million to enhance the campus facilities. The entire campus is wireless.

The Testa Science Center houses the Department of Natural Sciences and features multiuse classrooms with state-of-the-art technology, ten teaching laboratories, seven laboratories dedicated for faculty and student research, a working greenhouse, and student lounge areas.

The Information Technology Center houses computer labs, technology-rich classrooms, and experienced support staff. Students can learn Web authoring, graphics and animation, digital video, and multimedia production. The digital audio studio is available for all students and faculty members.

Assumption offers a variety of housing options to accommodate the 90 percent of students who live on campus. There are traditional residence halls, suites, a living and learning residence, and apartments with full kitchens. All resident students have individual hard-wired and wireless Internet access in their rooms. The outstanding stadium and athletic facilities support the College's 23 NCAA Division II intercollegiate teams, many recreational programs, and the physical well-being of the entire campus community.

Costs

For 2013–14, tuition is $34,475, room and board are $10,746, and student fees are $500. The board plan is required for all first-year students.

Financial Aid

The College offers financial aid based on demonstrated need and scholastic achievement. The College requires that students submit the Free Application for Federal Student Aid (FAFSA), which is available on January 1. This form should be filed by February 15, so that the College can consider the information as it makes financial aid awards.

All applicants for admission are considered for merit awards up to $22,000 per year. Funds awarded through this program reflect the College's commitment to academic excellence and student leadership.

Faculty

More than 90 percent of the Assumption College faculty members hold the doctoral or highest degree in their field. They are active scholars presenting their ideas and research at professional conferences, writing books and articles, and publishing in journals. With a student-to-faculty ratio of 12:1, professors get to know the students—to mentor, encourage, and help students succeed. Professors work closely with students and challenge them to explore new paths of knowledge and make their own discoveries. All of Assumption's academic advisors are full-time faculty members.

Student Government

There are more than 60 clubs and organizations on campus, offering students opportunities in community service, sports, academics, leadership, and special interests. The Student Government Association (SGA), the elected representatives of the student body, coordinates official communication between the student community and the College administration and officially recognizes student clubs and activities.

Admission Requirements

All applicants must graduate from an accredited secondary school with a minimum of 18 academic units. These units should include 4 years of English, 3 years of mathematics, 2 years of a foreign language, 2 years of history, 2 years of science, and 5 additional academic units.

Admission to Assumption is test-score optional. When submitting an application an essay and recommendations are required. Interviews are recommended, but not required.

The number of solid academic courses, including the number of honors-level or Advanced Placement–level courses, is considered during the application review process.

The Admissions Committee understands that grading standards vary from school to school or from one course to another. Class rank provides some context within which to place the grades of students applying from a given school. Some schools also provide grade distribution charts. The Committee also considers whether the applicant's grade point average or rank in class is weighted or unweighted.

Application and Information

Campus visits are strongly recommended. Appointments can be scheduled Monday through Friday. Group Information Sessions are held most Saturdays in the fall.

Applicants must submit a completed application, a $50 application fee, official transcripts, a recommendation, and an essay. Applications for early action must be received by November 1. There is a second early action deadline of December 15. The deadline for regular admission is February 15. Students may complete the Common Application and Supplement at www.commonapp.org.

For more information, students should contact:

Office of Admissions
Assumption College
500 Salisbury Street
P.O. Box 15005
Worcester, Massachusetts 01609-1296
Phone: 508-767-7285
      866-477-7776 (toll-free)
E-mail: admissions@assumption.edu
Web site: www.assumption.edu

BABSON COLLEGE
WELLESLEY, MASSACHUSETTS

The College

Babson College is the educator, convener, and thought leader for Entrepreneurship of All Kinds™. As the only school to teach Entrepreneurial Thought and Action®, Babson shapes the leaders the world needs: those with strong functional knowledge and the skills and vision to navigate change, accommodate ambiguity, surmount complexity, and motivate teams in a common purpose. Every day, Babson students, faculty, alumni, and staff members address real-world business and societal problems, creating sustainable economic and social value in today's fast-paced global economy. The 2012–13 undergraduate enrollment was 892 women and 1,123 men. Babson is accredited by the International Association for Management Education, AACSB International–The Association to Advance Collegiate Schools of Business, the New England Association of Schools and Colleges, and the European Quality Improvement System (EQUIS).

Babson is a residential college and is a fast-paced community alive with intellectual, cultural, athletic, and social activities. Approximately 85 percent of the undergraduate student body lives on campus all four years in fourteen residence halls. Housing options include fraternity and sorority housing, and entrepreneurial, service-oriented, and other specialty-themed housing.

Babson College is an NCAA Division III school. Most of the College's intercollegiate teams compete in the New England Women's and Men's Athletic Conference (NEWMAC). There are twenty-two men's and women's varsity sports teams, with additional club and intramural sports available to all students. More information is available at www.babsonathletics.com.

The Webster Center features an indoor, 200-meter, six-lane track; a field house; a gymnasium with three basketball courts; a racquetball court; a 25-yard, six-lane pool with 1- and 3-meter diving boards; a fitness center; squash courts; and a dance/aerobics studio. The Babson Skating Center features a 600-seat skating arena. Outdoor facilities include eight tennis courts, an AstroTurf field, a game field, a renovated softball diamond, a baseball field, two sand-based varsity fields, and a club rugby field.

Location

Babson's beautiful 370-acre campus is in Wellesley, Massachusetts, 14 miles west of Boston, a city renowned for its cultural and recreational opportunities. More than sixty colleges and universities bring more than 250,000 college students to the Boston area, making it one of the world's best college towns for cultural exchange and research.

Majors and Degrees

Babson offers a Bachelor of Science degree, a Master of Business Administration degree, three Master of Science degree programs, and executive education programs for business professionals.

Academic Programs

Babson students earn a highly respected Bachelor of Science degree, recognized around the world by employers who appreciate the powerful combination of deep functional knowledge and the entrepreneurial mindset of Babson graduates.

First-year courses at Babson lay the groundwork for students' future courses—and careers—starting with the Foundations of Management and Entrepreneurship (FME) course, a yearlong immersion into the business world. A team of 10–15 students will develop and manage an actual business or service organization, studying organizational behavior, marketing, entrepreneurship, and operations, while emphasizing the integrated role these functions have in a business. Students will have the chance to dabble in all areas of the organization, testing what disciplines and possible careers they would like to pursue further.

Students will also take integrated liberal arts foundation courses providing them with valuable analytic and communication skills and an appreciation for the arts and humanities. Throughout the year, students will develop a deeper understanding (and appreciation) of themselves and their goals, as they continue to prepare to excel in business and in life.

A weekly First-Year Seminar will ease each student's transition to college life by improving teamwork, community living, and communication and study skills. Members of the Babson community—including alumni, faculty, staff members, and peer mentors—provide personal and professional support throughout all four years.

Second-year students take an integrated series of courses in finance, economics, marketing, information technology, management accounting, and operations management. These courses offer functional knowledge of each discipline, but because they are thematically linked, they also provide the broad perspective of a CEO.

Students look at actual business problems via case studies and get real-world experience by studying, touring, interacting with, and presenting to local companies. Pursuing topics more intensively, allows students to focus on certain areas of concentration and begin to formulate ideas on what to pursue in life after college.

Throughout the third and fourth years at Babson, students begin to think about issues with increased confidence, independence, and creativity. There's flexibility to reflect on career options and to pursue courses that align with personal and professional goals. Babson offers a number of concentrations to focus each student's studies. In addition to management and liberal arts electives, students gain field experience via internships or consulting programs. Students may also opt to their education abroad and apply it to real-life situations in countries around the world.

Babson offers twenty-seven optional concentrations in both business and liberal arts disciplines; descriptions can be found at www.babson.edu/concentrations. Students may further plan their own course of study by focusing on certain areas of interest while continuing to benefit from Babson's interdisciplinary approach to learning. Special programs, such as the Weissman program, the Honors Program, the Women's Leadership Program, the Management Consulting Field Experience, the Babson College Fund (student-managed endowment), Master of Science in Accounting (M.S.A.), and independent research allow students to take advantage of customized learning opportunities at Babson.

Entering students may be granted credit or advanced course placement for successful scores on Advanced Placement (AP) examinations administered by the College Board as well as some courses in the International Baccalaureate (I.B.) curriculum.

Babson operates on a two-semester academic calendar. Semesters run from September to December and from late

January through May. An optional credit-bearing three-week winter session is offered in January, and two summer sessions are offered—one from late May to early July and one from mid-July to mid-August.

Off-Campus Programs

Babson has a partnership with Wellesley College and the Franklin W. Olin College of Engineering, an independent institution that opened in 2001, and is located on a 70-acre site adjacent to Babson. Babson, Olin, and Wellesley are collaborating inside and outside the classroom in order to provide extraordinary opportunities in all aspects of the student experience, including joint academic and research programming, student life programming, and lecture series.

Babson's vibrant education abroad programs enable students to spend a summer, semester, or school break abroad. Currently, eighty-three programs are offered in thirty-four countries, and full academic credit is given for approved management and liberal arts courses.

Academic Facilities

Horn Library houses an extensive business collection of print, media, and computerized information resources. Students have campus-wide access to library resources. Horn Computer Center is equipped with a lab that remains open 24 hours a day. Wireless access is available throughout the campus. Every incoming Babson undergraduate student receives a leased laptop computer, which is replaced after the sophomore year.

Other facilities are the Donald W. Reynolds Campus Center, the Richard W. Sorenson Family Visual Arts Center, the Stephen D. Cutler Center for Investments and Finance, the Glavin Family Chapel, and the Arthur M. Blank Center for Entrepreneurship.

Costs

For 2013–14, tuition is $43,520. The total estimated cost for books is $1,020 and other expenses (i.e. transportation and personal) is $1,750.

Financial Aid

Babson is committed to educating students from diverse backgrounds. Applying for financial aid does not affect a student's chances of being admitted to Babson College. Financial assistance is awarded on merit and demonstrated financial need. Assistance for students begins with consideration for student loans and work-study. Those with need beyond the loan and work-study amounts are also considered for Babson grants.

Nearly half of Babson students receive some form of financial assistance. Students should note that need-based financial assistance is available to U.S. citizens and permanent residents of the United States. Babson's merit scholarships include Weissman Scholarships, Presidential Scholarships, the Women's Leadership Awards, and the Diversity Leadership Awards. Application for aid is made by submitting the Free Application for Federal Student Aid (FAFSA) and the Financial Aid PROFILE of the College Scholarship Service. The application deadline for first-year undergraduate students is February 15. For transfer students and September enrollment, the deadline is April 10, and November 15 for January enrollment.

Faculty

Because of Babson's close-knit community, students are able to form close relationships with the faculty. Of the 261 faculty members, 163 are full-time, and 87 percent of the full-time faculty members hold a doctoral degree or its equivalent. Faculty members are accomplished entrepreneurs, executives, scholars, authors, researchers, poets, and artists who bring an intellectual diversity that adds depth to Babson's educational programs and offers students a rich, challenging experience.

Babson's student-faculty ratio is 15:1 and faculty members teach 100 percent of the courses. More information can be found at www.babson.edu/ugradfaculty.

Student Government

Students are encouraged to take an active role in campus activities and student government. The Student Government Association promotes students' interests; allocates funds to campus organizations for academic, social, and recreational activities; licenses student-run businesses; and helps formulate and maintain student regulations. There are over ninety-five student clubs and organizations currently on campus.

Admission Requirements

In selecting new students, the admission office considers each candidate based on academic factors such as high school record, recommendations, standardized test scores, and essays. Nonacademic factors are also considered, including extracurricular activities, demonstrated leadership abilities, character/personal qualities, volunteer work, work experience, creativity and enthusiasm, and a willingness to contribute to the Babson community in meaningful ways. Evaluation is based upon comparisons of the qualifications of those who apply. The degree of competition is set by the caliber of the applicants themselves. Consideration is given to the depth and rigor of each candidate's academic program, academic motivation and achievement, and progress from one year to the next. Prospective students are strongly encouraged to have completed or be currently enrolled in a pre-calculus math class.

Babson College offers three application plans: regular decision, early decision, and early action. For more information about these plans and their deadlines, prospective students should visit Babson's website at www.babson.edu/ugrad. Campus visits and group information sessions with an admission counselor are strongly recommended.

Application and Information

For further information or application forms, students should contact:

Lunder Undergraduate Admission Center
Babson College
Babson Park, Massachusetts 02457-0310
Phone: 781-239-5522
      800-488-3696 (toll-free)
Fax: 781-239-4006
E-mail: ugradadmission@babson.edu
Website: www.babson.edu/ugrad
      www.facebook.com/babsonadmission
      www.twitter.com/BabsonAdmission

Tomasso Hall

BALDWIN WALLACE UNIVERSITY
BEREA, OHIO

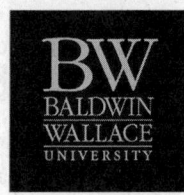

The University

Founded in 1845, Baldwin Wallace University (BW) in Berea, Ohio, is an accredited institution affiliated with the United Methodist Church that blends the hallmarks of a traditional liberal arts education with an emphasis on professional preparation. Baldwin Wallace has a long history of diversity, as it was one of the first institutions of higher learning in Ohio to admit students without regard to race or gender. That spirit of inclusiveness has flourished and evolved into a personalized approach to education, one that stresses individual growth as students learn to learn, respond to new ideas, adapt to new situations, and prepare for the certainty of change.

With an enrollment of approximately 3,100 full-time undergraduate students, BW offers unique opportunities for engaged, transformative learning. The student profile shows that 20 percent of incoming first-year students come from the top 10 percent of their high school classes, with more than 50 percent in the top quarter. In addition to the traditional-aged college student, Baldwin Wallace has helped adult learners for more than fifty years to develop skills, redirect careers, and enhance lives. Today, 500 adult learners of all ages participate in evening and weekend classes in a variety of programs that are designed to accommodate the varying learning styles and schedules of busy adult learners. Another 700 students are enrolled in part-time graduate programs in education and business administration.

Experiential learning is key to a Baldwin Wallace education and is a requirement for all undergraduates. A proven commitment to the liberal arts and sciences—characterized by excellence in teaching and learning—provides a strong foundation for internships, faculty-directed research, performance, and service-learning programs. Students work with faculty and staff to combine these opportunities in a way that prepares graduates for success after college.

In a postgraduation alumni survey, more than 90 percent of respondents found rewarding jobs or entered the graduate or professional school of their choice within nine months of graduation. Some programs—including athletic training, communication disorders, and neuroscience—have close to 100 percent acceptance rates. Several distinguished academic programs are offered. The international Society for Neuroscience (SfN) has named Baldwin Wallace University's neuroscience program the International Undergraduate Program of the Year.

Baldwin Wallace is also home to a world-renowned Conservatory of Music. The undergraduate-only nature of the conservatory offers collaborative mentoring opportunities with a faculty of accomplished artists and extraordinary opportunities for performance in a variety of ensembles. The University hosts the country's oldest collegiate Bach Festival.

BW embraces practices and principles that demonstrate its commitment to the environment. An undergraduate major in sustainability—the first of its kind in Ohio—offers students the opportunity to lead in the twenty-first century. The campus community continues to reduce its environmental footprint through significant recycling efforts, the addition of a wind turbine and food composter, and the use of geothermal heating and cooling systems in three green campus complexes. In addition, BW opened a residence hall dedicated to sustainable living in fall 2012.

Location

BW students enjoy the best of both worlds. Berea, Ohio, with its tree-lined streets, picturesque homes, and population of 19,000, is an ideal college town. At the same time, students are only 20 minutes from the heart of Cleveland, which is home to Fortune 500 companies as well as unique recreational and cultural opportunities. Cleveland offers outstanding museums and galleries, professional sporting events, a world-class orchestra, exciting nightlife, and an extensive park system.

Approximately 1,900 BW students live on campus in a variety of settings, ranging from residential learning communities to University-owned apartments for upperclassmen. A newly renovated residential complex for first-year students is scheduled to open in fall 2013. All full-time students are required to live on campus during their first and second years at Baldwin Wallace, with residency exemptions available for commuting students who live with their families. Residence halls provide students with social and educational programming, a diverse living environment, and leadership opportunities.

Majors and Degrees

Baldwin Wallace offers the Bachelor of Arts (B.A.), Bachelor of Science (B.S.), Bachelor of Science in Education (B.S.E.), Bachelor of Music (B.M.), and Bachelor of Music in Education (B.M.E.) degrees. Majors and programs include accounting, art history, art studio, arts management, athletic training, biology, broadcasting and mass communication, business, chemistry, communication disorders, communication studies, computer information systems, computer science, criminal justice, digital media and design, economics, education, English, exercise science, film studies, finance, French, German, health-care management, health promotion and education, history, human resource management, international business, international studies, management, marketing, mathematical economics, mathematics, medical technology, neuroscience, philosophy, physical education, physics, political science, pre-engineering, pre-pharmacy, pre–physical therapy, psychology, public health, public relations, religion, sociology, software engineering, Spanish, sport management, sustainability, and theater. The Conservatory of Music offers majors in music composition, music education, music history and literature, music in the liberal arts, music management, music performance, music theater, music theory, and music therapy. A Bachelor of Science in Nursing (B.S.N.) degree is offered in an accelerated format to students who have previously completed a bachelor's degree.

Academic Programs

More than sixty majors and several 3-2 cooperative and preprofessional programs are available to traditional BW undergraduates. Evening and weekend programs include sixteen majors and four certificate programs.

Off-Campus Programs

Baldwin Wallace University has institutional partnerships with several other universities around the globe, some of which include Kingston University (England), University of the Sunshine Coast (Australia), Ewha University (Korea), Universidad del Azuay (Ecuador), University of Osnabrück (Germany), Kansai Gaidai University (Japan), Hong Kong Baptist University (China), University of Hull (England), University College Dublin (Ireland), American Business School in Paris, Institute Franklin Universidad Alcala (Spain), York St. John University (England), Washington Center, New York Media Institute at Marist College, Christ College (India), and American University (Washington, D.C.).

In addition to traditional study-abroad programs, with students studying and living on a particular campus for the semester, BW features a series of focused-study tours that are led by BW faculty and staff members and examine specific topics or geographic regions. Some programs involve homestays, while others use hostels and hotels. Quite literally, students learn while on the road. Study tours are offered in alternating academic years.

BW often sponsors faculty-led two- to three-week seminars for credit in May, which are perfect for students who seek an international experience but do not want to be away for extended periods. Destinations have included Vienna, Prague, and Budapest. Recent spring trips have included India and China, and there was a seminar in Europe as well as an environmental excursion to Ecuador. Most locations for study-abroad programs offered during the academic year—such as Australia, China, England, Korea, and Spain—are also offered during the summer term. The Semester at Sea program sends students to ten different countries—such as Brazil, Egypt, India, Japan, and Vietnam—aboard a 23,000-ton ship with 600 other undergraduates.

Academic Facilities

Baldwin Wallace continues to invest in facilities for student learning. In August 2010, the University completed the $29-million renovation and expansion of the Thomas Family Center for Science and Innovation, a facility featuring a combined 100,000 square feet of comprehensive laboratory, research, and study space. This new complex includes the Center for Innovation and Growth, a facility that reflects the synergy of BW's cross-curricular academic offerings through entrepreneurial study and innovation.

In addition, BW opened renovated and expanded facilities for its Conservatory of Music in August 2011. This provides students with additional and improved rehearsal and performing spaces, while remaining home to the Jones Music Library and the Riemenschneider Bach Institute, where priceless Bach-related manuscripts and first editions are stored.

These new facilities complement the extensive offerings already available to students, including twenty campus computer labs; a 4,000-watt campus radio station; recently renovated recreation facilities; an on-campus gallery showcasing the work of student, faculty, and area artists; and the Burrell Memorial Observatory. A new campus master plan, already being implemented, will enhance facilities to support the University mission and create a pedestrian-friendly, environmentally responsible campus with inviting green spaces.

Costs

Baldwin Wallace's tuition ranks among the lowest and most affordable of private colleges in Ohio. In 2013–14, full-time (12–18 credit hours) liberal arts students will pay $36,980 per academic year in tuition, room, board, and fees. Conservatory students will pay $39,300 per academic year. These amounts also include a fully refundable board plan, as well as the cost of a student's books.

Baldwin-Wallace offers a four-year graduation guarantee—a promise that academically prepared students who follow predetermined benchmarks during their study at BW will earn their bachelor's degrees in four years or fewer. If a student who follows the agreement does not graduate in four years, BW will pay up to one year's additional tuition for the additional course work needed to graduate.

Financial Aid

To help students and their families meet the cost of a high-quality education, BW awards more than $50 million annually to students in the form of scholarships, grants, loans, and work-study opportunities. BW is committed to working with students and their families to offer financial support. Nearly all Baldwin Wallace students receive some sort of financial assistance.

Renewable merit scholarships ranging from $1000 to $13,000 are awarded to academically exceptional incoming freshmen. The University also offers special and competitive awards, ranging from $1,000 to $4,000, as well as scholarships for transfer students.

Faculty

Close relationships are at the heart of the BW experience. Most classes average only 19 students, and the student-faculty ratio is 15:1. Professors share their wisdom and experience on a one-to-one basis, helping students choose classes or assisting students in their search for the perfect internship. From corporate executives and lifelong educators to environmentalists and practicing professionals, BW's more than 300 full-time and part-time faculty members bring impressive credentials from their fields. Nearly 80 percent have earned the highest degree in their field. They are dedicated and talented teachers who want to provide an educational experience that goes well beyond the textbook.

Student Government

Student Government consists of three branches—the legislative, the executive, and the judicial. The Student Senate is the official representative body of the students of Baldwin Wallace University. All meetings are open, and all students are welcome to participate. The president and vice president of the student body lead the executive branch and work closely with the Senate to express student body views to the University faculty and administration. The judicial branch of Student Government consists of the supreme court of the student body, which hears cases pertaining to Student Government and the clubs it funds. Elections for student body government occur each February.

Admission Requirements

Applicants must submit the completed application (electronic or paper), a high school transcript, a teacher recommendation, the Secondary School Record Request Form, and the $25 application fee (waived if applying online). SAT and ACT results are optional. (In lieu of standardized test results, students must submit a graded writing sample.) Transfer applicants also must submit college or university transcripts. Candidates applying to the Conservatory of Music also must complete the Conservatory Audition Portfolio.

Application and Information

The deadline for undergraduate admission is May 1. The priority admission deadline is March 1. Applicants are notified, beginning November 1, on a rolling basis within four to six weeks of receipt of a completed application.

Office of Admission
Baldwin-Wallace University
275 Eastland Road
Berea, Ohio 44017-2088
Phone: 440-826-2222
      877-BW-APPLY (toll-free)
Fax: 440-826-3830
E-mail: admission@bw.edu
Website: http://www.bw.edu/admission

The student union building on the campus of Baldwin Wallace University.

BALL STATE UNIVERSITY
MUNCIE, INDIANA

The University

Founded in 1918, Ball State is a selective, residential, state-assisted university. Classified by the Carnegie Foundation for the Advancement of Teaching as a research university, high research activity (RU/H), it provides a broad liberal arts–based education. Offerings include more than 180 undergraduate and 120 graduate programs.

The University enrolls about 21,000 students (approximately 17,800 on campus); about 16,600 are undergraduates and 4,400 are graduate students. Ball State has students enrolled from forty-eight states, two territories, approximately sixty countries, and every county in Indiana. Approximately 700 international students are currently enrolled.

Immersive learning—the hallmark of a Ball State education—pulls together interdisciplinary student teams guided by expert faculty to create unique, high-impact learning experiences that result in real-world situations. Between 2007 and 2012, about 16,400 students completed more than 1,000 immersive learning experiences throughout Indiana and as far away as Hong Kong, Venice, and Malawi. Representative projects include transforming hospital gowns into cozy, dignified apparel for patients with cancer; converting complex statistics into dynamic, informational graphics about water scarcity; and bringing history to life through educational programs for elementary schools.

In addition to undergraduate degrees Ball State University also offers master's, doctoral, and specialist degrees.

Ball State's beautiful, tree-lined campus features 731 acres with more than 100 buildings, including eleven residence hall complexes and two apartment communities. The University also has more than 400 additional acres of research property.

Location

Ball State is located in Muncie, Indiana (population 70,000), which has been named among the most affordable college towns in the United States. Indianapolis, the state capital, is only 1 hour away by car, and Chicago, the third largest U.S. city, is only 4 hours away.

Majors and Degrees

Bachelor's degrees: accounting*; acting; actuarial science; advertising; animation–art; anthropology (general, applied cultural anthropology, archaeology)*; apparel design; applied mathematics; aquatic biology and fisheries; aquatics; archaeology–anthropology; architecture; art; art education (visual arts); art history; athletic training; biochemistry; biology; botany–field; business; business administration*; business education; career and technical education; cellular and molecular biology; ceramics–art; chemistry; chemistry education; child development; child life specialist studies; classical culture; classical languages (Greek and Latin); communication studies (interpersonal, organizational, public)*; computer science; computer technology; construction management; criminal justice and criminology*; dance; dietetics/pre-dietetics; drawing–art; early childhood education; early childhood special education; earth science; earth/space science education; ecology; economics (business*, financial analyst*, liberal arts); elementary education; elementary education–special education, exceptional needs: mild interventions (early and middle childhood); English (creative writing, English studies, literature, rhetoric and writing); English/language arts education (English, communication studies); entrepreneurial management*; environmental management; exercise science; family studies; family and consumer sciences (general, education); fashion merchandising; film and television studies–telecommunications; finance (business finance, financial planning and investments, financial analysis)*; French; French education; general studies; genetics; geography; geology; German; German education; geographic information science–geography; glass–art; graphic arts management; graphic design (visual communication)–art; health science; hearing impaired/deaf education; history*; hospitality and food management; human resource management*; industrial technology; industry and technology information systems–business*; integrated studies; interior design; international business*; Japanese; Japanese education; journalism (graphics, magazine, news, photo); journalism education; landscape architecture; Latin education; legal studies

(business, public law); life science education; marketing*; mathematical economics; mathematical sciences; mathematics education; medical technology; metals–art; meteorology and climatology (general, professional)–geography; microbiology; music; music composition; music education (instrumental/vocal); music media production; music performance (guitar, organ, piano, symphonic instruments, voice); musical theatre; natural resources; news–journalism; news–telecommunications; nursing*; operations and supply chain management–business*; painting–art; philosophy*; photography and intermedia arts –art; physical education (teaching); physical science education; physics (applied, general); physics education; political science (economics, international studies, political science)*; printmaking–art; professional selling; psychological science*; public relations; religious studies*; residential property management; respiratory therapy; risk management and insurance*; sales (professional selling); school health education; science education; sculpture–art; social studies education (economics, geography, government, historical perspectives, psychology, sociology); social work*; sociology*; Spanish; Spanish education; special education (exceptional needs: early childhood, hearing impaired/deaf, mild interventions, severe interventions); speech-language pathology; sport administration; studio art; technology education; telecommunications (film and television studies, news, digital production, sales and promotion); theatre, theatre design and technology; theatre education; theatre production; theatrical studies; travel and tourism–geography; urban planning and development; visual arts education; visual communication (graphic design)–art; wildlife biology and conservation; women's and gender studies; and zoology.

Pre-professional programs: pre-audiology, pre-chiropractic, pre-dental hygiene, pre-dental preparation*, pre-engineering (general, chemical, metallurgical), pre-law, pre-medical preparation*, pre-optometry, pre-pharmacy, pre-physical therapy, pre-physician's assistant studies, and pre-veterinary studies.

*These majors are available in the University's "Degree in 3" program, which allows students to earn a bachelor's degree in three years. Additional information about this program can be found online at www.bsu.edu/degreein3.

Academic Programs

Undergraduate programs combine general studies with majors and minors. Most degrees require 120 semester hours, at least a 2.0 cumulative grade point average, and the last year attending classes on campus. The academic calendar consists of a fall, spring, and summer semester.

The highly selective Honors College enrolls about 1,200 undergraduate students and is Indiana's most comprehensive honors program.

The Learning Center provides free peer tutoring, small-group study sessions, and academic workshops to all Ball State students. Each year, thousands of undergraduate and graduate students use its services. These students earn higher grade point averages and report being highly satisfied with the assistance they receive.

Ball State recognizes that that there are other ways to obtain college credit beside regular enrollment in class. The University grants credit through successful scores on Advanced Placement (AP) tests, International Baccalaureate (IB) exams, College-Level Examination Program (CLEP) tests, military service, departmental examination, and departmental authorization.

Off-Campus Programs

Study-abroad programs—open to all Ball State students—provide a myriad of opportunities to explore intercultural issues outside the classroom and around the world. Programs vary in length, location, and cost. Credit is offered for most programs, so participants aren't required to delay graduation. Some programs may also have work and internship opportunities while studying abroad.

Summer programs are a popular option for students seeking short-term international experiences. Ball State works in coordination with its various colleges to develop discipline-specific field studies and special tours that appeal to students in all majors. Students receive course credit for most programs, and financial aid is applicable. Past programs have ranged in focus from ethnographic studies in British Columbia, student teaching in England, and architecture and urban planning in Germany and Italy.

Academic Facilities

Bracken Library, one of the largest libraries in the state, provides access to about 2.3 million books, periodicals, microforms, maps, government publications, databases, and other media. The facility offers a digital newsstand, enabled to receive television broadcasts from around the world.

Facilities on campus also include an art museum, an observatory and planetarium, outdoor teaching laboratories, a human performance laboratory, greenhouse, and music laboratories. Information Technology Services (ITS) provides vital behind-the-scenes support of applications; computing; conferencing services; development; e-mail; networking; operations; and video and voice services for students, staff, and faculty.

A high-speed wireless network covers all academic and administrative buildings, residence halls, athletic facilities, and popular outdoor campus gathering places. Fiber-optic voice, data, and visual networks also link classrooms, laboratories, and residence halls. Nearly 99 percent of all students have their own computers.

Costs

For full-time undergraduate students in the 2012–13 academic year, tuition and fees (12–18 credit hours per semester) were $8,318 for Indiana residents and $22,988 for out-of-state residents. Room and board started at $7,768. The University technology fee was $336; the Recreation and Wellness Center fee was $174; the Health Center fee was $152; and the residence hall technology fee was $120.

Additional estimated expenses include books and supplies, $1,000, and personal expenses and transportation, $2,800 to $3,200. For more detailed cost information, prospective students should visit the bursar's office website at www.bsu.edu/bursar. A preliminary estimate of a student's final costs after financial aid is available through Ball State's Net Price Calculator at www.bsu.edu/finaid/calculator.

Financial Aid

The Office of Scholarships and Financial Aid is committed to providing exceptional service to students and their families who apply for financial assistance. More than 75 percent of Ball State students receive some kind of financial aid. The Free Application for Federal Student Aid (FAFSA), obtainable from a high school guidance counselor or online, should be filed no later than March 10 of each calendar year.

Faculty

Ball State has nearly 950 full-time faculty members. About 90 percent of all tenured and tenure-track faculty hold the highest degrees in their disciplines, and many have years of professional experience in their areas. The student-faculty ratio is 18 to 1. About 97 percent of classes are taught by faculty, not graduate students, and senior faculty members teach many freshman courses. The average class size is 31 students.

Student Government

The Student Government Association (SGA) is a student-run and operated organization that serves as the voice of Ball State students by advocating student concerns to faculty, administration, and the community, as well as to other students. SGA also serves to appoint students to various University Senate committees dealing with almost all aspects of decision-making at Ball State such as public safety, event programming and scheduling, student rights, ethics and standards, and teaching evaluations. In addition, one student is appointed to serve on Ball State's Board of Trustees.

Admission Requirements

Students who have graduated from an accredited high school or have earned a GED diploma, may apply for admission to Ball State.

Ball State practices rolling admission. This means all applications will be reviewed and an admission decision made after all of an applicant's credentials are received. Ball State's enrollment is limited; admission to a particular semester may depend on space available and the date of the application

Admission Criteria

Prospective students are evaluated on the strength of high school curriculum (including senior year); successful completion of 4 years of English, 3 years of college preparatory mathematics (algebra I, algebra II, and geometry), 3 years of science (2 with lab), and 3 years of social studies (foreign language study is strongly recommended but not required); performance as measured by grades in the above courses or by GED scores (Ball State uses an academic GPA on a 4.0 scale based only on college prep and academic course work completed); curricular patterns or grade trends in academic courses; SAT or ACT scores; and participation in extracurricular activities such as sports, performing groups, student government, student publications, civic, and charitable organizations, etc.

International students can apply for admission through the Rinker Center for International Programs. The Rinker Center is the first contact for international students and assists with admissions applications, immigration and visa issues and overall counseling. More information is available at www.bsu.edu/admissions/international.

Application and Information

Enrollment at Ball State and individual programs is limited, so students are encouraged to apply early to ensure consideration for their preferred entry semester and program. Applications submitted after the priority deadlines will be considered on a space-available basis. When enrollment goals are met for each term, admission will close. Please note that some academic programs have their own applications and priority deadlines as well. The priority application deadlines are as follows: May 1 for the fall semester, January 1 for the spring semester, and May 1 for the summer semester.

Requests for visits and information should be addressed to:

Office of Admissions
Ball State University
Muncie, Indiana 47306
Phone: 765-285-8300
800-482-4BSU (toll-free)
E-mail: askus@bsu.edu
Website: www.bsu.edu/admissions
www.bsu.edu/admissions/international (international students)

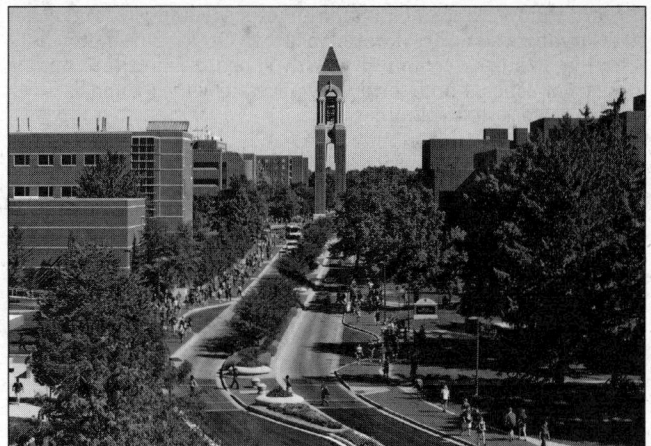

The crowning glory of Ball State's campus, Shafer Tower rises 150 feet in the air and houses forty-eight custom-made carillon bells covering four octaves.

BARD COLLEGE AT SIMON'S ROCK
GREAT BARRINGTON, MASSACHUSETTS

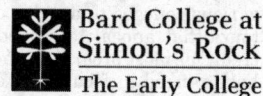

The College

Simon's Rock is the United States' only four-year residential college of the liberal arts and sciences specifically designed to provide bright, highly motivated students with the opportunity to begin college after the tenth or eleventh grade. Students can earn an Associate of Arts (A.A.) degree after two years of study and a Bachelor of Arts (B.A.) degree after four. Merit scholarships and need-based aid are available. The average age of entering students is 16.

Founded in 1964 by Elizabeth Blodgett Hall, in 1979 Simon's Rock became a part of Bard College, located 50 miles away at Annandale-on-Hudson, New York.

Simon's Rock has served as a model for the growing U.S. early college movement. For forty-five years, Simon's Rock has demonstrated that highly motivated high school–age students are fully capable of college work; that they thrive intellectually and socially in a small-college environment; that serving these students well requires a faculty committed to distinction in teaching and scholarship, as well as active participation in the students' social and personal development; and that a coherent general education in the liberal arts and sciences should be the foundation for early college students.

Location

The College is located in Great Barrington, Massachusetts (population 8,500), named the Best Small Town in America in 2012 by *Smithsonian* magazine. Built on 275 rolling and wooded acres in the Berkshire Hills of western Massachusetts, Simon's Rock is just 2½ hours from Boston and New York City. The Berkshires' natural beauty and variety of cultural attractions make the area an unusually appealing place in which to live. The terrain is excellent for hiking, bicycling, cross-country and Alpine skiing, canoeing, and climbing. The Tanglewood Music Festival, Jacob's Pillow Dance Festival, Shakespeare and Co., and other arts organizations are located nearby. Great Barrington is a thriving business community with shops, restaurants, and a variety of schools and service agencies in which Simon's Rock students work and volunteer.

Majors and Degrees

Simon's Rock offers programs leading to the A.A. and B.A. degrees in the liberal arts and sciences. Students may complete their B.A. studies in one of forty-one different concentrations reflecting most traditional disciplines, choose one of several interdisciplinary concentrations, and/or design their own second concentration. Most Simon's Rock B.A. students study more than one discipline.

Academic Programs

The academic program at Simon's Rock combines a core curriculum in the liberal arts and sciences with extensive opportunities for students to pursue their own interests through electives, tutorials, independent studies, internships, and study abroad.

Because students begin college without completing high school, the College works to ensure that all students develop strong analytical abilities, skills in written and verbal expression, and knowledge across disciplines. The core curriculum comprises approximately half of students' total course load during their first two years. Requirements include a writing and thinking workshop, held the week before the regular semester begins; first-year, sophomore, and cultural perspectives seminars; and courses in the arts, mathematics, natural science, and foreign language. The College also requires that students participate in the campus Active Community Engagement program, involving athletics, health and wellness programming, and community service opportunities on and off campus.

All new students are assigned a faculty adviser, who meets with them weekly during their first semester and regularly throughout the rest of their career at Simon's Rock. Classes are small, faculty members are accessible, and opportunities to pursue individual interests are extensive.

After earning the A.A., about 50 percent of students stay to complete their B.A. in one of forty-one concentrations. About 50 percent transfer, usually to highly competitive colleges and universities in the U.S. and abroad. Through the sophomore planning process, students receive individualized guidance from advisers and faculty as they explore options for their last two years of undergraduate study.

Students who stay for a B.A. apply for admission to a concentration through a process called Moderation. Students meet with a group of faculty in their area(s) of interest to review their accomplishments and plan their further education at Simon's Rock. Options include advanced course work at Simon's Rock, junior year study-away programs, independent study, involvement in faculty research projects, specialized tutorials, internships, and courses at Bard College's main campus, which offers more than 800 courses each year. Students may take classes, draw on the expertise of Bard faculty in the Moderation and Thesis processes, or arrange to spend a semester in residence at Bard.

The senior thesis is the focus of each B.A. student's final year. Drawing on the skills in analysis and synthesis acquired during the previous three years, students devote themselves wholeheartedly to the project, which is defined and developed under the guidance of 2 or more faculty members. Recent theses have taken many forms: critical studies in literature, psychological research, musical compositions, creative fiction, translations, scientific experiments, mathematical problem solving, artistic exhibitions and performances, and various combinations of these forms.

The regular academic program is supplemented by a number of signature programs. The Simon's Rock/Columbia University Engineering Program offers three years at Simon's Rock and two years at Columbia's School of Engineering and Applied Science, after which students receive both a B.A. from Simon's Rock and a B.S. from Columbia University. A similar arrangement exists with the engineering school at Dartmouth University.

Through Simon's Rock Scholars at Oxford, a select group of students is admitted to spend their junior year at Lincoln College or St. Catherine's College of the University of Oxford in England each year.

Simon's Rock has a half- or full-year program in creative writing at the Centre for New Writing at the University of Manchester in the UK. The College also has a relationship with Qingdao University in China, where students pursue Chinese language immersion study. Students interested in theater can spend a year at London Dramatic Academy; those interested in photography can study at the International Center of Photography in New York City.

Off-Campus Programs

Students work with the Win Resource Commons and Career Center to find study-abroad opportunities suited to their goals and interests. Established independent programs (the School for

Field Studies, SEA Semester, Global Routes), programs through other schools (Oxford University, the Sorbonne), and special Simon's Rock programs (fieldwork in geography in China) provide immersive in-depth learning. Students have recently taken intensive math instruction at Central European University in Budapest, Hungary; helped build a school in a remote village in northern Thailand; and served as apprentices to dancers, drummers, mask carvers, and batik artists in Bali. Students can also take advantage of Bard's study-abroad and international programs, including special arrangements with universities in Germany, Russia, and South Africa, and intensive language immersion programs in China, France, Germany, Italy, Japan, Morocco, Mexico, and Russia. Programs can last for a semester, a full academic year, or shorter periods during breaks.

Academic Facilities

The Fisher Science and Academic Center houses the College's biology, chemistry, ecology, and physics laboratories; research labs for faculty members and students; classrooms and tutorial rooms; a sixty-seat lecture center; and faculty offices. The Daniel Arts Center incorporates a 350-seat theater and concert hall, a black box theater, and a dance studio and rehearsal facilities; painting, drawing, photography, ceramics, metalworking, printmaking, 3-D, video production, and digital arts studios; exhibition areas; and spaces for large-scale art and set construction. A music hall, a recording studio, and music practice rooms are also available to students in the arts. The campus library houses 104,020 volumes and collections of recordings and periodicals, a listening room, and a language laboratory. Simon's Rock students also have access to the Bard College library. An interlibrary loan system provides access to other college and university collections. The Kilpatrick Athletic Center includes squash courts, a basketball court, an elevated track, a swimming pool, a rock-climbing wall, and a full-service fitness center. The Liebowitz International Center, which opened in 2011, houses faculty and programs focused on global issues, as well as two state-of-the-art classrooms.

Costs

For 2012–13, tuition and fees were $44,075, and room and board were $12,260. There is also a $600 orientation fee for first-year students.

Financial Aid

Simon's Rock is committed to making an early college education available to a diverse group of highly motivated, academically qualified students. U.S. citizens and permanent residents are eligible to apply for federal and state financial assistance programs as well as institutional scholarships and grants. International students are eligible to receive Simon's Rock scholarships and grants. Approximately 85 percent of students receive some form of financial aid. Applicants wishing to be considered for a merit scholarship must submit their applications by February 1.

Faculty

The College has approximately 40 full-time faculty members, all of whom hold either a doctorate or an equivalent degree in their field. Simon's Rock supplements this full-time faculty with visiting scholars, regular adjunct faculty members in music and studio arts, and part-time faculty members in other areas as needed. Faculty members are distinguished not only by their excellence in teaching and advising but also by their sensitivity to the particular developmental needs of the College's younger students.

Student Government

Students at Simon's Rock participate in the governance of the community through elected and appointed positions on College committees that oversee academic and social life. The campus is characterized by respect for individual rights and a strong sense of community.

Admission Requirements

Simon's Rock seeks students who are smart, independent-minded, self-directed, creative, and passionate about learning. The admission staff works closely with prospective students and their parents to ensure that the decision to enter Simon's Rock is the right one. The College understands that students are not defined solely by grades and scores. For this reason, essay responses and a personal interview are required of each applicant. The application also requires an official high school transcript, three letters of recommendation, and a parent's statement. Standardized test scores are optional for most applicants; international students for whom English is not a first language, or who have not studied for at least two years in a school in which English is the primary language of instruction, must submit TOEFL scores.

Application and Information

Candidates should submit their materials by May 31 for fall admission. Applications are reviewed on a rolling basis year-round. Early application is strongly encouraged. The Admission Committee generally notifies applicants of their decision within several weeks of receiving a completed application. The application fee is $50.

Bard College at Simon's Rock is on Facebook (http://www.facebook.com/simonsrock) and Twitter (http://twitter.com/SimonsRock).

To schedule an interview or request further information, students should contact:

Office of Admission
Bard College at Simon's Rock
84 Alford Road
Great Barrington, Massachusetts 01230-1978
Phone: 800-235-7186 (toll-free)
Fax: 413-541-0081
E-mail: startnow@simons-rock.edu
Website: simons-rock.edu

"Everybody wants to learn. Everybody has a touch of something very unique about them." Bethany, entering class of '10.

BARNARD COLLEGE
NEW YORK, NEW YORK

The College

Barnard College was among the pioneers in the late nineteenth-century crusade that sought to make higher education available to young women. Founded in 1889 and formally partnered with Columbia University since 1900, today Barnard serves nearly 2,400 students from almost every state and more than fifty countries. It remains a partner of Columbia, and students at both schools regularly cross-register for courses at either institution. Barnard students have access to the University's resources and graduates receive their degree from Columbia. Despite this close connection, Barnard College remains a small, independent liberal arts college, devoted solely to the undergraduate education of women. The College maintains its own Board of Trustees, faculty, and administrative staff; its own endowment; an independent admissions process; and sole ownership of its property and physical plant. It offers the intimacy of a small college with the added advantages of a university.

The self-contained Barnard campus occupies 4 acres of urban property along Broadway between 116th and 120th streets and serves as an oasis from the hustle and bustle of New York City. An amalgam of styles comprise Barnard's architectural influences, the result is a blending of classic and modern. Barnard Hall, home of the Ethel S. LeFrak '41 and Samuel J. LeFrak Gymnasium, the Barnard Center for Research on Women, the Athena Center for Leadership Studies, and the Julius S. Held Lecture Hall, stands opposite the main gates of the College. The south end of the campus, referred to as the Quad, contains the Brooks, Reid, Hewitt, and Sulzberger residence halls; first-year students are housed in three of the four buildings in the Quad. Additional housing provides those entering as first-years guaranteed housing for four years of continuous enrollment at Barnard. The latest campus addition, the Diana Center, a 70,000-square-foot student center, added a new element of design in 2010. Its seven-story glass structure stretches across campus, linking the historic gates of the entrance, at the south end of campus, to one of the original campus buildings, Milbank Hall, to the north.

Location

Barnard is located on the upper west side of Manhattan, in the safe and student-friendly Morningside Heights neighborhood, directly across from Columbia University, with four other educational institutions as neighbors. Abounding with cultural, educational, internship, and professional opportunities and more than 500,000 college students, New York is Barnard's laboratory.

Majors and Degrees

Students can earn a Bachelor of Arts in the following subjects: Africana studies; American studies; ancient studies; anthropology; architecture; art history; Asian and Middle Eastern cultures; astronomy; biochemistry; biological sciences; chemistry; classics (Greek and Latin); comparative literature; computer science; dance; economics; education; English; environmental biology science or studies; European studies; film studies; French; German; history; human rights; Italian; Jewish studies; mathematics and applied mathematics; medieval and Renaissance studies; music; neuroscience; philosophy; physics; political science; psychology; religion; Russian and Slavic studies; sociology; Spanish and Latin American cultures; statistics; theater; urban studies; and women's, gender, and sexuality studies. The College provides an excellent education program, leading to teaching certification, and prepares students for programs in health and medicine, law, and business.

Barnard College also offers double- and joint-degree programs in cooperation with other schools within the Columbia community. These include a five-year M.P.A./M.I.A. (3-2) program offered in conjunction with the School of International and Public Affairs. In cooperation with the School of Law, Barnard offers an accelerated program in interdisciplinary legal education, where select students can begin their legal studies after three years. Through the School of Engineering and Applied Science, Barnard students can pursue a five-year (3-2) program in all branches of engineering, leading to both an A.B. and a B.S. degree. In cooperation with the School of Dentistry, a limited number of students may enter the Columbia School of Dental and Oral Surgery after three years of undergraduate work. Outside the university, students may earn both an A.B. degree and a Master of Music (M.M.) in a five-year (3-2) program with the Juilliard School. Through an agreement with List College of the Jewish Theological Seminary, students can earn an A.B. degree from Barnard and a B.A. in Hebrew literature.

Academic Programs

Two required courses, First-Year Seminar and First-Year English, set the foundation for a Barnard education with small seminar classes, limited to 16 and 12 students, respectfully. General education requirements are organized around the Nine Ways of Knowing, focusing on topics which reflect the breadth and depth of a true liberal arts education. The Ways of Knowing offer a flexible structure and a wide array of courses in ethics and values, social analysis, cultures in comparison, language, laboratory science, quantitative and deductive reasoning, historical studies, literature, and visual and performing arts.

Advanced placement and I.B. credit are available. Barnard operates on a two-semester calendar, with classes beginning in early September. The fall semester ends in mid-December; classes resume for the spring semester in mid-January and end in mid-May.

Off-Campus Programs

As an independent partner of Columbia University, Barnard offers students open access to courses, libraries, and other facilities of the University. With special permission, students may also register for selected classes in Columbia's graduate and professional schools. In addition, two highly selective lesson exchange programs with the Juilliard School and the nearby Manhattan School of Music allow qualified Barnard students to take music lessons in a conservatory setting.

Barnard has a rich history and tradition of study abroad dating back to the 1930s. Today, qualified students are eligible to study in nearly 100 programs in more than fifty countries worldwide and nearly forty percent of Barnard students spend a semester or year abroad. Students are currently studying in Argentina, Australia, Austria, Bolivia, Brazil, British West Indies, Chile, China, Costa Rica, Czech Republic, Denmark, Ecuador, England, France, Germany, Greece, Hungary, Ireland, Israel, Italy, Japan, Jordan, Kenya, Madagascar, Netherlands, New Zealand, Panama, Peru, Russia, Scotland, Senegal, South Africa, Spain, Switzerland, and other locations. Students may also participate in a domestic exchange with Spelman College in Atlanta or Howard University in Washington, D.C.

Barnard's location offers its students a variety of work experiences through more than 2,500 internships. More than two thirds of Barnard students participate in internships throughout the academic year and summer.

Academic Facilities

Historic Milbank Hall anchors the north end of campus, topped by the 2,500-square-foot Arthur Ross Greenhouse, and housing administrative and faculty offices in addition to the Minor Latham Playhouse. Sulzberger Tower and the residential quadrangle secure the south end of campus where most Barnard students reside.

There are over 300,000 volumes in the library in Lehman Hall (and nearly 12 million in the University library system) with a zine collection written by women (cisgender and transgender) with an emphasis on zines by women of color; dance studios and classrooms in Barnard Hall and its Annex; state-of-the-art science labs in the fourteen-story Altschul Hall; and architecture classrooms with a view in the multipurpose Diana Center, with its terra-cotta glass façade, black box theatre, and art gallery, among other remarkable features. At the heart of it all is the welcoming beauty of Barnard's beloved Lehman Lawn.

Costs

Tuition and fees for 2013–14 are $44,790. Room and board costs are an additional $14,210.

Financial Aid

Financial aid at Barnard is awarded based upon demonstrated need. Federal funds and institutional grants are administered as determined by federal and institutional methodology, assuming College aid is supplementary to family resources. Barnard gives no merit or athletic scholarships. Once need has been established, Barnard covers 100 percent of demonstrated need with a combination of grants, loans, and work-study or student employment. Approximately 50 percent of the students at Barnard receive some form of financial aid.

Barnard College has a need-blind admission policy in which all applications from first-years who are U.S. citizens and permanent residents are judged solely on merit without reference to financial circumstances. International and transfer students are considered for need-based aid from a limited pool of funding.

Faculty

Barnard College employs more than 350 teaching faculty members with a student-faculty ratio is 7:1 (9:1 FTE). Barnard's faculty includes editors of leading scholarly journals, prize-winning novelists and translators, and frequent winners of awards from respected foundations, corporations, and government agencies. They are actively engaged in research and publication in their respective fields, but they regard teaching as their primary commitment. From the start of their time at the College, all students have faculty advisers who assist them in selecting courses and designing individual academic programs, in addition to a vast network of decanal, staff, and peer advising.

Student Government

Barnard women have access to more than eighty clubs and organizations on the College campus alone. Add to this list the hundreds of additional dually recognized clubs with members from both Barnard and Columbia provided for through Barnard's long-standing partnership with the University, and strong friendships develop among students on either side of Broadway. Student groups include performance groups, academic and pre-professional, ethnic and cultural, language, community service, and writing staffs. Social interaction and cooperation between Barnard and Columbia groups is virtually seamless, with Barnard women regularly joining and leading a variety of Columbia organizations. Students, faculty members, and administrators also serve on tripartite committees and share responsibility for policy on curriculum, housing, financial aid, orientation, and the library.

Admission Requirements

The Committee on Admissions selects young women of proven academic strength who exhibit the potential for further intellectual growth. Careful consideration is given to candidates' high school records, recommendations, writing skills, standardized test scores, special abilities and interests, and personal and educational context.

Admission to Barnard is highly selective and candidates for admission to the first-year class are expected to have taken a very rigorous college-preparatory program. Barnard also requires candidates to submit scores from the SAT Reasoning Test, along with two SAT Subject Tests. Alternatively, students may submit scores from the ACT with writing in place of the SAT and subject tests. Students educated in a non-English-speaking setting or who have studied in English for less than five years must also take the TOEFL or IELTS exam. An interview is recommended for first-year students, but is not required

Application and Information

Applicants for first-year admission should apply in the fall of their senior year of high school. Applications must be received by January 1 and must include the nonrefundable application fee. Students are notified in late March. Well-qualified high school seniors who have selected Barnard as their first-choice college may instead apply under the binding early decision plan. Early decision applications must be submitted by November 1. Barnard accepts sophomore and junior transfer students. Transfer applications must be submitted by March 15 for consideration for September and by November 1 for consideration for January.

For more information about Barnard College, students should contact:

Jennifer Fondiller
Dean of Enrollment Management
Barnard College, Office of Admissions
3009 Broadway
New York, New York 10027
Phone: 212-854-2014
Fax: 212-854-6220
E-mail: admissions@barnard.edu
Website: http://www.barnard.edu/admissions

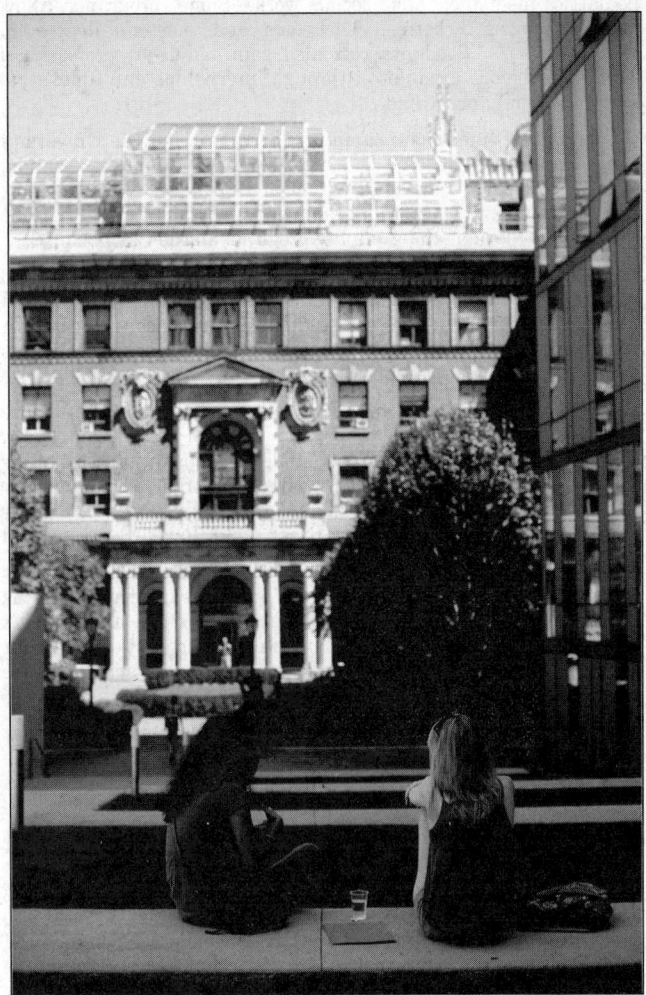

A view of Milbank Hall from the Diana, Barnard's multipurpose student center.

BARRY UNIVERSITY
MIAMI SHORES, FLORIDA

The University

Recognized by *Forbes* magazine as one of America's best colleges, Barry University in Miami Shores, Florida, offers a vibrant university community that empowers students to develop as professionals and well-rounded citizens. Classes are small, so students receive personal attention from distinguished faculty members and advisers. Barry students also join a multicultural student body, with peers from nearly all fifty states and 110 countries. Of the approximately 9,000 students enrolled, almost half are undergraduates.

Barry offers more than 100 bachelor's, master's, and doctoral degree programs in the arts and sciences, business, education, health sciences, human performance and leisure sciences, law, podiatric medicine, and social work. Some programs allow students to earn both a bachelor's and master's degree in just five years. Students can also gain hands-on professional experience before graduation through internships and innovative service-learning programs.

The palm-tree lined main campus is in Miami, but the University also includes the Dwayne O. Andreas School of Law in Orlando; College of Health Sciences location in Hollywood, Florida; adult and continuing education programs at twenty additional locations throughout Florida; and graduate programs in the Caribbean.

Barry's main campus has ten residence halls and two apartment buildings. Each room includes cable television and high-speed Internet access. All students may keep cars on campus. The University's Office of Commuter Student Resources assists students who live off campus.

Barry holds membership in twenty honor societies and hosts more than sixty student organizations, including the dance team, choir, Campus Activities Board, WBRY student radio station, as well as active fraternities and sororities. Barry also promotes community service through organizations including Best Buddies, Habitat for Humanity, Alternative Spring Break, and Pals-4-Paws animal rescue.

At the R. Kirk Landon Student Union, students have access to the bookstore, main dining hall, snack bar, game room, and more. A fully equipped fitness center features weight and cardio equipment and offers a variety of free fitness classes. Intramural sports include basketball, flag football, soccer, softball, and table tennis.

The University fields twelve intercollegiate athletic teams that participate in the NCAA Division II and the Sunshine State Conference. Over the years, the Buccaneers have won nine NCAA championships and have had 243 All-Americans, 272 Scholar All-Americans, and seven NCAA Women of the Year finalists, the most of any Division II school and third overall in the NCAA.

The University is accredited by the Southern Association of Colleges and Schools Commission on Colleges to award bachelor's, master's, specialist, and doctoral degrees. Barry also holds a number of accreditations from professional organizations for specific degree programs.

Location

Barry University is located in sunny Miami Shores, Florida, just a short distance from the beach and part of the exciting, international Miami metroplex. Miami is a center for business, tourism, and entertainment, providing a wide range of internship options and a vibrant cultural scene. Highlights include the world-famous Art Basel Miami Beach contemporary art festival; Calle Ocho, the largest Hispanic street festival in the nation; the Miami International Book Fair; and the Miami International Film Festival. The New World Symphony and the Miami City Ballet provide a full season of performances, while the nearby Wynwood Arts District hosts a free art walk every second Saturday of the month. South Florida is also home to the Miami Heat basketball team, Miami Dolphins football team, the Miami Marlins baseball team, and the Florida Panthers hockey team. The hospitable climate allows for swimming, sailing, scuba diving, golf, tennis, soccer, and other outdoor activities year-round, while the natural beauty of the Florida Keys, Everglades, and coral reefs are just a few hours away. Barry University's Center for Student Involvement regularly coordinates trips to help students experience the best that South Florida has to offer.

Majors and Degrees

Barry University offers the Bachelor of Arts degree in advertising, art (art history, ceramics, graphic design, and painting and/or drawing), broadcast and emerging media, communication studies, English (literature and professional writing), general studies, history, international studies, music, philosophy, photography (biomedical/forensic), prelaw, public relations, Spanish (language and literature and translation and interpretation), theater (acting, dance theater, technical theater, theater publicity), and theology.

The Bachelor of Science degree is offered in accounting, athletic training (five-year seamless B.S. to M.S.), biology (marine, preprofessional), cardiovascular perfusion, clinical biology (histotechnology, medical technology, nuclear medicine technology), chemistry (biochemistry, environmental chemistry, preprofessional), computer information sciences, computer science, criminology, education (B.S. to M.S. option, infancy through early-childhood education, early- and middle-childhood education, special education, ESOL, and reading endorsements), exercise physiology (five-year seamless B.S. to M.S.), finance, international business, management, marketing, mathematical sciences (computational, general, and statistics/actuarial science), physical education and coaching, political science, psychology (forensic, industrial/organizational), sociology, and sport management (diving industry, five-year seamless B.S. to M.S.).

The University also offers the Bachelor of Science in Nursing, the Bachelor of Fine Arts (art and photography), the Bachelor of Music (instrumental performance; music education; sacred music; and voice, opera, and musical theater), and the Bachelor of Social Work.

Minor concentrations are available in specific subject areas as well as in the interdisciplinary areas of Africana studies, film studies, journalism, peace studies, social sciences, and women's studies. Certificates are also offered in Africana studies, photography, Spanish translation and interpretation, and women's studies.

Accelerated undergraduate degree programs are offered for working adults through Barry's evening and weekend programs.

Academic Programs

Barry University is the second-largest private Catholic university in the southeastern United States. Founded in 1940 by the Dominican Sisters of Adrian, Michigan, the University operates on a semester plan. The first semester extends from the end of August to mid-December, and the second semester extends from mid-January to early May. Two 6-week sessions are offered during the summer. Students must maintain a minimum cumulative grade point average of 2.0 (or C) and earn a minimum of 120 credits for a degree. Of these 120 credits, 9 must be in philosophy and theology, 9 in communication—oral and written, 9 in humanities and arts, 9 in physical or natural sciences and mathematics, and 9 in social and behavioral sciences. The traditional full-time academic load is 12 to 18 credits each semester and 6 credits each summer term. Candidates for degree programs may elect a major and area of specialization and must satisfy all requirements of the program that they choose to follow, including all professional preparation requirements. Internships are required for many majors.

An ELS Language Centers program is available to international students who need to increase language proficiency. The Center for Advanced Learning offers a program designed to assist students with learning disabilities who have the intellectual potential and motivation to complete a four-year degree.

The Honors Program offers an active, interdisciplinary honors curriculum designed to add breadth and depth to the educational experience.

Off-Campus Programs

With the assistance of Barry's Career Services staff, students can gain hands-on experience before graduation in Miami's dynamic arts, entertainment, business, education, health care, nonprofit, and professional sports industries.

Honoring the University's commitment to social justice, students also learn by sharing their talents and giving back to the community. In addition to internships, they participate in service learning, which integrates their coursework with community needs. For example, psychology students developed a workshop for first-time home buyers and evaluated a South Florida employment program, while sociology students evaluated HIV/AIDS-related outreach services provided by a local church. Business students have worked with community organizations to analyze development opportunities in the Miami Modern Historic District and teach financial literacy at local schools. These student projects can lead to real-world results.

Barry University also offers summer programs abroad in places such as Europe and China. Barry is also a member of the College Consortium for International Studies, enabling students to participate in programs offered by member colleges and universities in nearly thirty countries. Barry University students may enroll in Air Force ROTC courses through cross-registration at a nearby university.

Academic Facilities

At Barry, students find the resources they need to support their education. Academic facilities include computer labs, multimedia classrooms, the Monsignor William Barry Memorial Library, the Glenn Hubert Learning Center, a performing arts center, a full-service digital television production studio, art studios, photography and digital imaging labs, a human performance lab, an athletic training room, a biomechanics lab, a nursing lab and resource center, and several other labs dedicated to Barry's health, science, and education programs.

Costs

For 2013–14, tuition for full-time undergraduate students for the academic year is $28,160. Student services fees are included in tuition. Room and board costs average $9,440, based on a double-occupancy room. Expenses such as books, supplies, laboratory fees, and transportation are not included in these costs.

Financial Aid

Nearly 90 percent of all undergraduate students at Barry University receive some form of financial aid. Barry participates in the full array of federal and state of Florida financial aid programs. Barry also offers an excellent scholarship program, awarding aid each year to students who demonstrate promise of academic success. Some scholarships may be renewed for up to four years as long as the student meets the renewal criteria. Athletic scholarships are also available.

To be considered for financial assistance, applicants must submit the Free Application for Federal Student Aid (FAFSA). Additional information may be obtained at www.barry.edu/finaid or by contacting the Office of Financial Aid at 800-695-2279 (toll-free) or finaid@barry.edu.

Faculty

Faculty members are easily accessible to students and are committed to providing personal attention. More than 80 percent of faculty members hold a Ph.D. or terminal degree in their field of study. The student-faculty ratio is 14:1.

Student Government

The Student Government Association serves as a liaison between the student body and the administration and faculty. Each year, undergraduate students elect a 4-member Executive Board and a 7-member Senate. Unless otherwise specified, weekly Senate meetings are open, and students are encouraged to participate.

Admission Requirements

In reviewing the credentials of students seeking admission, Barry University considers an applicant's composite efforts. Candidates must provide the following materials: the completed application form, official high school or college transcripts, and the results of the SAT or ACT.

Application and Information

The University has a rolling admissions policy and reviews applications as they are completed. Students are notified of their acceptance once the admissions staff has reviewed all required documents. Prospective students are advised to apply early and may submit their application any time after completion of their junior year in high school. The student's completed application form and supporting credentials should be sent to the Office of Admissions. Students may also apply online at http://www.barry.edu/myBarry.

Barry University
Division of Enrollment Services
11300 Northeast Second Avenue
Miami Shores, Florida 33161-6695
Phone: 305-899-3100
          800-695-2279 (toll-free)
Fax: 305-899-2971
E-mail: admissions@barry.edu
Website: http://www.barry.edu
          http://facebook.com/BarryUniversity (Facebook)
          http://twitter.com/BarryUniversity (Twitter)

Barry's palm-tree lined main campus is in Miami Shores, Florida, just a few miles from the beach and part of the international city of Miami.

BAY STATE COLLEGE
BOSTON, MASSACHUSETTS

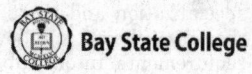
Bay State College

The College

Founded in 1946, Bay State College is a private, independent coeducational institution located in Boston's historic Back Bay. Since its founding, Bay State College has been preparing graduates for outstanding careers and continued education.

The College offers both associate degrees and bachelor's degrees. The educational experience offered through the variety of associate and bachelor's degree programs prepares students to excel in the career of their choice. The College gives students constant access to the people, places, and knowledge they need to succeed. Through the transformative power of its core values of quality, respect, and support, Bay State College has been able to assist students with setting and achieving goals that prepare them for careers and continued education. In fact, with its First-Year Experience, a 1-credit course all students must complete, Bay State College students are exposed to the concept of "action planning." The Bay State College action plan is designed to help students identify their goals and set about a course of action to achieve those goals. Students review their action plan each semester with their academic adviser and evaluate how they are progressing on their plan. This is just one method Bay State College graduates apply to their lives beyond college. The ability to identify, set, and achieve goals is a trait all people aspire to master.

Recognizing that one of the most important aspects of college is life outside the classroom, the Office of Student Affairs seeks to provide services to Bay State College students from orientation through graduation and beyond. There are many clubs and organizations on campus, such as the Criminal Justice Society, the Early Childhood Education Club, the Student Government Association, and the Entertainment Management Association. Bay State College students enjoy the opportunity to create clubs and organizations that meet their interests. Special events throughout the year include a fashion show and a host of events produced by the Entertainment Management Association. Students also enjoy professional sports teams such as the Boston Celtics and the Boston Red Sox.

One of the unique aspects of living at Bay State College is the residence halls. With their location in the historic Back Bay, the buildings are original Victorian town houses and brownstones. Each building has its own character and charm, making living on campus a distinctive experience. Each building has a computer lab with free Internet access, coin-operated laundry, vending machines, a house phone with free local calling, and a social lounge that includes cable television and a microwave oven. Each student room has basic cable service and wireless Internet access.

The Career Services office offers lifetime career assistance to both current students and alumni, continuing to provide assistance and support to them throughout their careers, with career-management counseling, workshops, career panels, guest speakers, resume and cover letter reviews, interview preparation, and job listings.

Bay State College is accredited by the New England Association of Schools and Colleges; is authorized to award the Associate in Science, Associate in Applied Science, and three Bachelor of Science degrees by the commonwealth of Massachusetts; and is a member of several professional educational associations. The College's medical assisting program is accredited by the Accrediting Bureau of Health Education Schools (ABHES). The College's nursing program is accredited by the National League for Nursing Accrediting Commission. The physical therapist assistant studies program is accredited by the Commission on Accreditation in Physical Therapy Education (CAPTE) of the American Physical Therapy Association (APTA).

Location

Located in the historic city of Boston, Massachusetts, and surrounded by dozens of colleges and universities, Bay State College is an ideal setting in which to pursue a college degree. Tree-lined streets around the school are mirrored in the skyscrapers of the Back Bay. The College is located within walking distance of several major-league sports franchises, concert halls, museums, the Freedom Trail, Boston Symphony Hall, the Boston Public Library, and the Boston Public Garden. World-class shopping and major cultural and sporting events help make college life an experience that students will always remember. The College is accessible by the MBTA, commuter rail, and bus and is near Boston Logan International Airport.

Majors and Degrees

Bay State College is continually reviewing, enhancing, and adding new programs to help graduates remain industry-current in their respective fields.

Bachelor's degrees are offered in criminal justice, entertainment management, fashion merchandising, nursing, and management.

Associate degrees are offered in business administration, criminal justice, early childhood education, entertainment management (with a concentration in audio production), fashion design, fashion merchandising, health studies, medical assisting, nursing, physical therapist assistant studies, retail business management, and hospitality management.

Academic Programs

Bay State College operates on a semester calendar. The fall semester runs from early September to late December. The spring semester runs from late January to mid-May. A satellite campus is located in Middleborough, Massachusetts.

Bay State College also offers courses on-ground and online to working adults in its Evening and Online Division. The courses, offered in eight-week sessions, allow more flexibility for students who must balance work and family commitments while pursuing their education.

Off-Campus Programs

The internship program, available in all major areas of study, provides students with practical field experience, enabling them to hone their skills and gain insight into the various technologies employed in their respective fields. Fieldwork is a requirement for many majors and is a great opportunity for students to build resumes, apply what they have learned in the classroom, and gain a competitive advantage in the job market.

Students from Bay State College are among the 250 students participating in the Walt Disney World College Program. During their stay at Walt Disney World, students receive on-the-job training and classroom experience. This is just one of the many internship possibilities for students each year at Bay State College.

Academic Facilities

The library has a combined book collection of approximately 5,300 books. In addition, Bay State College has 100 periodicals and 200 audiovisual titles. The College's sixty computers have access to the Internet and several databases for magazine and journal articles, including ProQuest Academic, LexisNexis Academic, JSTOR, Infotrac, Newsbank, EBSCO, the Internet Public Library, and the Library of Congress Research Tools. The library also participates in an interlibrary-loan program with the Boston Regional Library System.

Costs

Tuition for 2012–13 for full-time students was $22,040 per year (some costs vary by program). Room and board for 2012–13 were $11,800 per year; student services fee, $400; and student activity fee, $50. The cost of books and additional fees varies by major. A residence hall security deposit of $300 and a technology fee of $250 are required of all resident students.

Financial Aid

Financial aid is available to those who qualify. The College's financial aid staff works one-on-one with every student to help them find what is best for their specific situation: scholarships, grants, loans, payment plans, or a combination of those. The College also offers numerous part-time employment and work-study opportunities during the academic year.

Faculty

There are 99 faculty members, with the majority holding advanced degrees. The student-faculty ratio is 15:1.

Student Government

The Student Association serves as the voice of the Bay State College student body. It consists of a group of elected student representatives from the various academic programs. Roles and responsibilities of Student Association members include providing input on College policies and procedures, assuming leadership roles on campus, acting as a voice of the student body, and planning activities and events.

Elections are held every fall, and all students are encouraged to vote. The group comprises representatives from each College department, club, and organization, and membership spans all four class years.

Admission Requirements

An applicant to Bay State College must be a high school graduate, a current high school student working toward graduation, or a recipient of a GED certificate. The Office of Admissions recommends that applicants to the associate degree programs have a minimum 2.0 GPA on a 4.0 scale; if available, applicants may submit SAT or ACT scores. Applicants must receive the recommendation of a Bay State College admissions officer. Applicants to the bachelor's degree programs must have a minimum 2.3 GPA on a 4.0 scale and must also submit SAT or ACT scores. A personal interview is highly recommended for

all students, and parents are encouraged to attend. Students are responsible for arranging for their official high school transcripts, test scores, and letters of recommendation to be submitted to Bay State College. International applicants must also submit high school transcripts translated into English with an explanation of the grading system, a TOEFL score of at least 500 on the paper-based exam or 173 on the computer-based exam if English is not the native language, and financial documentation. The nursing, physical therapist assistant studies program, and Evening and Online Divisions have different or additional admission requirements. For more information about these programs, students should visit the website at http://www.baystate.edu.

The Bay State College Admissions Office notifies applicants of a decision within three weeks of receipt of the transcript and other required documents. When a student is accepted to Bay State College, there is a $100 nonrefundable tuition deposit required to ensure a place in the class, which is credited toward the tuition fee. Deposits are due within thirty days of acceptance. Once a student is accepted, a Bay State College representative creates a personalized financial plan that provides payment options for a Bay State College education.

Application and Information

Applications are accepted on a rolling basis. The fall tuition payment due date is July 1; the spring tuition payment due date is December 1.

Applications should be submitted to:

Admissions Office
Bay State College
122 Commonwealth Avenue
Boston, Massachusetts 02116
Phone: 800-81-LEARN (toll-free)
Fax: 617-249-0400
E-mail: admissions@baystate.edu
Website: http://www.baystate.edu
　　　　http://www.facebook.com/baystatecollege
　　　　http://twitter.com/baystatecollege

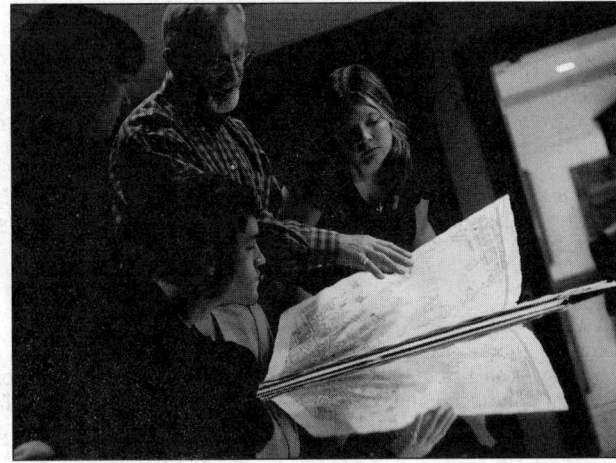

Giving students access is an essential part of a Bay State College education. Students have access to a community of support, experiential learning, faculty with real-world experience, and a dynamic location in the heart of the city.

BELOIT COLLEGE
BELOIT, WISCONSIN

The College

Beloit College is an independent, residential college that engages its students' curiosity and intelligence by putting the liberal arts into practice. Beloit's focus is on teaching and on the close collaboration that takes place among students and faculty members in small classroom and lab settings. Undergraduates learn to approach problems ethically and thoughtfully in an academic community that values international and interdisciplinary perspectives. Active learning is key to the college's educational experience; students conduct research and publish papers with faculty mentors, present the results of their work at Student Symposium and International Symposium, and take advantage of entrepreneurial Venture Grants that send them around the world.

Beloit is Wisconsin's first college, founded by New Englanders on the Midwestern frontier in 1846. Today, a geographically diverse population of 1,300 students is drawn to Beloit's residential campus from forty-nine states and thirty-nine countries. Ten percent come from countries outside the United States, 17 percent of U.S. students are non-Caucasian, and many religious orientations and socioeconomic backgrounds are represented on campus. Beloit students are equally diverse in their academic choices; no more than 10 percent of the seniors are represented in any one of more than fifty majors available.

Seventy percent of Beloit's students participate in some form of athletics—club, intramural, or varsity. Those who live on campus (95 percent) may choose to live on quiet or substance-free floors, in one of three fraternity houses or three sorority houses, or in one of the special-interest houses. Two town-house complexes have been constructed in the past ten years, offering roomy, apartment-style living for juniors and seniors. Meals, served in two campus locations by premier food service provider Bon Appetit, include fresh, locally sourced, organic, vegetarian, and vegan meal options.

New students quickly become part of this active and diverse environment through the Beloit Initiatives program, which provides the framework for a Beloit education through two years of faculty advising, designed to help students transition to Beloit and develop skills and perspectives that will help create their educational trajectory while working one-on-one with a faculty mentor. Initiatives seminars begin the day students arrive on campus and provide an academic grounding and a social network, starting with new student interdisciplinary seminars taught by experienced professors and staff members.

Location

Beloit's 40-acre campus is located on the border between Wisconsin and Illinois, 90 miles northwest of Chicago, 50 miles south of Madison, and 70 miles southwest of Milwaukee, in a small, diverse city of 36,000. Students may take advantage of the resources of the three major metropolitan areas, and Beloit's businesses and civic and service organizations provide numerous internship, job shadowing, and community outreach opportunities. Beloit's academic buildings are clustered around lawns dotted with ancient North American Indian mounds, while residence halls on the other side of campus provide the base of the College's social scene. Karris Track & Field at Strong Memorial Stadium features a new turf field and track. It is located a few blocks east of campus, where men's and women's varsity lacrosse teams played their first games in 2013.

Majors and Degrees

Beloit awards Bachelor of Arts and Bachelor of Science degrees in nineteen departments and more than fifty fields of study. In natural sciences and mathematics, students may choose majors from the departments of biology, biochemistry, chemistry, computer science, environmental studies, geology, health and society, mathematics, and physics. In social sciences, students may choose majors from the departments of anthropology, economics, education and youth studies, international relations, political science, psychology, and sociology. In arts and humanities, majors are offered in the departments of art and art history, classics, English, history, modern languages and literatures, music, philosophy and religious studies, theater/dance/media studies, and women's and gender studies. Students often create a unique interdisciplinary major or minor. The College offers an array of departmental minors. Permanent interdisciplinary minors include African studies, American studies, ancient Mediterranean studies, Asian studies, computational visualization and modeling, environmental studies, European studies, health and society, interdisciplinary studies, journalism, Latin American and Caribbean studies, legal studies, medieval studies, museum studies, performing arts, Russian studies, and women's and gender studies.

Beloit offers 3-2 cooperative programs in engineering and environmental management and forestry, and preprofessional programs in dentistry, law, medicine, and nursing. These programs, which have strong advisory and internship components, complement a major in an appropriate discipline. Beloit students may also earn teaching certification.

Academic Programs

Beloit's academic calendar consists of two 14-week semesters with one-week midterm breaks. At the end of the sophomore year, students are required to declare a major and may add a second major, a minor, or teaching certification. Advising Practicum, a full-day series of workshops and discussions held every semester before advising week, is designed to help students reflect on Beloit's educational opportunities and develop an academic plan tailored to individual interests and goals. Beloit requires students to complete five breadth requirements, a senior-year capstone experience, an experience outside the classroom that puts the liberal arts into practice, three writing-intensive courses, and have significant contact with a culture different from their own. Thirty-one units are required for graduation, each unit representing the equivalent of a course of study involving 4 hours of class time a week per semester.

Off-Campus Programs

Beloit has a century-old tradition of domestic and international off-campus study opportunities, and more than half of new Beloit graduates will have studied and/or conducted research in such a program. Internships, field terms in the humanities and sciences, and summer employment opportunities are arranged through the Liberal Arts in Practice Center.

At Beloit College, study abroad is more an expectation than a luxury. Whether through Beloit's own extensive programs or the Associated Colleges of the Midwest (ACM) and independent programs, Beloit students have studied in more than forty countries worldwide, from Australia to Zimbabwe.

Academic Facilities

Beloit's historic brick and stone buildings coexist with innovative contemporary structures such as the Center for the

Sciences. Completed in 2008, the 117,000-square-foot center is LEED-certified Platinum and includes a vegetated roof, high recycled/reused content, water management systems, and other sustainable features. The College's newest facility, the Hendricks Center for the Arts, opened in the fall of 2010 in downtown Beloit, in a historic building that formerly housed the city's public library. The 48,000-square-foot center provides a centralized home to the College's dance and music programs, and features four studio classrooms, a state-of-the-art film classroom, faculty offices, rehearsal rooms, and design and staging labs. The Logan Museum of Anthropology and the Wright Museum of Art are highly regarded teaching museums that offer students excellent resources for research and work experience. The Neese Performing Arts Theatre complex features a large thrust stage theater, a black-box theater, a scenic design studio, and a complete costume shop. The World Affairs Center is the hub of language and literature study. Nearly 250 student-accessible computer workstations are located throughout campus, with a combination of wireless and wired Internet access in academic buildings. Beloit's library collection is in excess of half a million holdings and provides individual and group study areas, computer labs, and extensive listening and viewing areas for the use of audiovisual materials. A 6,000-square-foot center for entrepreneurship in downtown Beloit provides physical space, office resources, and a recording studio where students can put venture plans of their own design into action.

Costs

Tuition for the 2013–14 academic year is $40,970, fees are $280, a room is $4,256, and board (twenty-meal plan) is $3,000—for a total comprehensive fee of $48,506. While the cost of books and incidental expenses varies, it averages about $1,900.

Financial Aid

Beloit College is committed to making the Beloit experience affordable to all qualified students. The financial aid program recognizes two criteria—scholastic ability and financial need—that may qualify students for awards. During the 2012–13 academic year, more than 90 percent of first-year students received financial assistance through grants, loans, or work-study.

In 2012, new students from families with incomes below $50,000 received an average grant of $31,958; qualifying students from families with incomes above $100,000 received an average grant of $18,140. Beloit's attention to providing students high value has won the College recognition in the Princeton Review's guides, the *Fiske Guide to Colleges,* and *U.S. News & World Report* as among the nation's best buys in top colleges.

Faculty

The focus of Beloit's faculty is great teaching. Beloit professors are innovators who are committed to an educational environment that emphasizes collaborative, hands-on learning in small classes. Of the 114 full-time faculty members, 96 percent hold the highest academic degree in their field. All classes are taught by professors. In classrooms, it is easy for students and faculty members to become immersed in their work, since the student-faculty ratio is 10:1 and the average class size is 15 students. All Beloit professors are also academic advisers who are involved in students' academic concerns as well as their adjustment to life at the College. Discussions begun in the classroom are often continued in an informal setting, such as at a basketball game or over dinner at a professor's house.

Admission Requirements

Admission to Beloit is selective. Beloit seeks applicants with special qualities and talents, as well as those from diverse ethnic, geographic, and economic backgrounds. When reviewing applications, the transcript is the most important element. Beloit has no absolute secondary school requirements but recommends a rigorous college-preparatory program. This includes 4 years of English, 3 years of college-preparatory mathematics, 3 years of laboratory science, 3 years of history or social science, and at least 2 years of a foreign language. Applicants planning to major in the natural sciences should complete 4 years of high school mathematics and be prepared to begin calculus during their first year in college. Seventh-semester grades may be required. A counselor recommendation is a required part of the application. One teacher recommendation is also required. The essay component of Beloit's application is critical. There is no required topic, so students should write about a topic they believe will represent them well. Either SAT or ACT test scores are required, but they are the least important part of the application (TOEFL or IELTS scores are required for international students). Beloit does not consider the SAT or ACT writing exam for purposes of admission. Interviews are not required for admission but are encouraged. Off-campus alumni interviews can be arranged if a student would like to interview but cannot travel to the campus. Transfer applications are considered for August or January entrance. Applicants must hold at least a B average at an accredited college or university.

Application and Information

Beloit offers a binding early decision plan with a deadline of November 1 and notification on or before December 10. In addition, there are two nonbinding early action plans with deadlines of either November 1 or December 1; notification is December 15 and January 15, respectively. The regular decision priority application deadline is January 15, with notification beginning in March. Applications received after January 15 will be given full consideration as space remains available. Beloit does not require an application fee. Admitted students have until May 1 to reply to Beloit.

Review of transfer applications for the fall term begins March 15 and continues through the spring; the deadline for the spring term is November 1. Notification for transfer applications is rolling.

For more information, students should contact:

Admissions Office
Beloit College
700 College Street
Beloit, Wisconsin 53511
Phone: 608-363-2500
    800-9-BELOIT (toll-free)
Fax: 608-363-2075
E-mail: admiss@beloit.edu
Website: http://www.beloit.edu
    http://www.facebook.com/BeloitCollege
    http://twitter.com/beloit_college

A Chaucer and His Contemporaries course takes place in Beloit's Poetry Garden.

BENTLEY UNIVERSITY
WALTHAM, MASSACHUSETTS

The University

Bentley University is an internationally recognized business university, dedicated to preparing the next generation of smart, nimble, and compassionate leaders. Located on a classic New England campus minutes from Boston, Bentley combines an advanced business curriculum with the best of the arts and sciences, taught using the latest technology by a faculty that collaborates across disciplines. Bentley offers a wide variety of majors and minors, as well as optional liberal studies and business studies majors designed to create a modern intersection of the arts and sciences and business that's unique in higher education. Bentley students are highly sought after by today's leading organizations because of their professionalism, exposure to state-of-the-art research tools, and diverse, real-world experience.

In 2012, Bentley was ranked 16th in the nation by the Princeton Review for best career services. The Miller Center for Career Services offers resources including an on-campus recruiting program involving 1,000 national and international companies; an online job and internship database; career fairs; workshops on topics such as interviewing and networking; and a newly developed Career Development Seminar (CDI 1901) for first-year students.

In addition, students can develop a customized four-year development plan, which contributes to the university's outstanding placement rates. In 2012, more than 95 percent of students found employment or enrolled in graduate school within six months of graduation. Their median annual salary was $50,000.

Approximately 98 percent of freshmen live on campus. Twenty-three residence halls provide a range of housing options: dorms, suites, and apartments. Housing is provided for all four years; all residence halls are air-conditioned and typically include study lounges, exercise facilities, TV lounges, and game rooms. In 2010, the Princeton Review ranked Bentley 18th on its list of Dorms Like Palaces.

Students live and learn in a multicultural environment that prepares them to thrive in today's diverse world. International students representing nearly 100 countries make up a large percentage of the student body and bring valuable perspectives to the Bentley community.

Supporting Bentley's commitment to diversity are offices such as the Multicultural Center, Spiritual Life Center, Center for International Students and Scholars, Center for Women in Business, and the Women's Center.

The Student Center is the hub of campus activity and is home to Seasons Dining Room and more than 100 student organizations. These groups represent academics, the arts, media, fraternity and sorority life, and cultural interests.

Athletic programs are a Bentley hallmark and include intramurals, recreational sports, and more than twenty varsity teams in NCAA Divisions I and II. The Dana Athletic Center houses a weight and fitness complex, food court, locker rooms, a gym, a basketball court, volleyball and racquetball courts, a competition-size pool with a diving tank, and saunas. Outdoor facilities include soccer and baseball fields, a track, and tennis courts.

Location

Bentley's location in Waltham, Massachusetts—just minutes west of Boston—puts the city within easy reach. As the country's ultimate university town, Boston's options range from theater to art exhibits, dance clubs to concerts, and championship sports to world-class shopping. Bentley's free shuttle makes regular trips to Harvard Square in Cambridge, just a subway ride from Boston. Boston also offers many opportunities for internships and jobs after graduation.

Majors and Degrees

Bentley's curriculum, focusing on business, technology, and the arts and sciences, provides students with options for shaping an academic program that fits their skills, interests, and career goals.

Bachelor of Science (B.S.) degree programs enable students to gain in-depth knowledge and skills in specific business disciplines: accountancy, actuarial science, computer information systems, corporate finance and accounting, economics–finance, finance, information design and corporate communication, information systems audit and control, management, managerial economics, marketing, and mathematical sciences.

Bentley also offers Bachelor of Arts (B.A.) degree programs with majors in global studies, health sciences, history, liberal arts, media and culture, philosophy, public policy, Spanish studies, and sustainable science. All Bachelor of Arts students gain business experience through either the Business Studies major (BSM) or minor. All students can also choose from minors such as entrepreneurial studies, law, and sports management.

The Liberal Studies major (LSM), an optional double major, can be combined with any business program. It provides students with a competitive edge by building meaningful connections across and within disciplines. To complete the LSM, students do not need to take any extra courses beyond those normally required. It allows students to add another credential to their degree, helping them stand out to employers. LSM concentrations include American studies; earth, environment, and global sustainability; ethics and social responsibility; global perspectives; health and industry; media arts and society; and quantitative perspectives.

Academic Programs

The Bentley curriculum is an integration of business and the liberal arts. The university's 4,200 undergraduates benefit from a breadth of programs and the ability to combine subjects to best fit their interests.

A Bentley education also focuses on gaining hands-on experience in the classroom. Students benefit from classes where they partner with outside companies to solve current business problems and present their solutions directly to company executives. Bentley also offers top applicants a chance to enroll in the Honors Program. Participants select honors-level courses each semester that offer extra intellectual challenge in a seminar atmosphere.

The Master's Candidate program enables students to earn a Bachelor of Business Administration degree and either an Emerging Leaders M.B.A. or Master of Science (M.S.) degree.

Off-Campus Programs

Hands-on experience is emphasized across the curriculum. Internships, study abroad, service-learning, and other opportunities allow students to apply classroom theory in the community.

Each year, more than 90 percent of students complete at least one internship, building valuable work experience and networking connections. Some of the top internship employers include Fidelity Investments, the TJX Companies, Liberty Mutual, Bain & Company, and all of the Big Four accounting firms.

Bentley students can gain insight into different cultures by studying abroad. Programs take place in more than twenty-five countries and vary in length from one week to a full academic year.

Through Bentley's Service-Learning Center, students build skills in business, communication, and teamwork while assisting nonprofit and community-based organizations both locally and internationally.

Academic Facilities

Concepts taught in the classroom are put to use in several high-tech learning laboratories.

Bentley's financial Trading Room combines state-of-the-art technology and real-time data to offer first-hand exposure to financial concepts in simulated trading sessions. Resources include Bloomberg, Capital IQ, Datastream, FactSet, Thomson One Analytics, Portfolio Analysis, MATLAB, S&P Compustat, and Worldscope.

The Center for Marketing Technology plays an integral role in marketing programs. Students gain a full grasp of software options, familiarity with research tools and techniques, and knowledge of new digital marketing frameworks.

The Accounting Center for Electronic Learning and Business Management (ACELAB) introduces cutting-edge technologies that are reshaping the accounting profession. Students have access to auditing and tax preparation software as well as other professional applications from industry leaders such as SAP and Oracle.

The Center for Languages and International Collaboration (CLIC) is a key resource for language courses, international studies majors, and students with an interest in global issues. The center promotes collaboration among Bentley students and their counterparts overseas.

The Media and Culture Labs and Studio feature resources for video production and editing as well as digital photography. The lab provides students with industry-standard software programs for screenwriting, sound mixing, graphic design, and DVD authoring.

The Design and Usability Center (DUC) features labs ideal for usability testing. Students use the applications employed by technical communicators, Web developers, user-interface designers, and usability specialists.

The brand-new CIS Learning and Technology Sandbox is a collaborative space for learning new technologies. Its resources include Google TVs, Xbox 360 with Kinect, study spaces, large-screen TVs, a smart board, specialized networking equipment, and tools such as Windows 8, Linux, and Android development software.

The Bentley Library is outfitted with computer workstations, group study rooms, and wireless network access. It also has an exceptional number of online database resources. In 2010, Bentley was ranked 14th on the Princeton Review's list of best college libraries.

Costs

Tuition for resident and nonresident students during the 2013–14 academic year is $39,600. Room and board (double room, meal plan) costs are $13,445. Additional expenses include books, supplies, technology fee, and personal and travel expenses.

Financial Aid

Bentley's financial aid program includes both scholarships based on academic achievement, which are awarded through the admission process, as well as grants based on financial need. Bentley administered over $96 million in aid to undergraduate students last year. Well over half of that amount came in the form of grants and scholarships directly from Bentley. Significant institutional resources are committed each year so that all academically qualified students have access to a Bentley education regardless of their financial resources. Currently, more than 70 percent of undergraduates receive some type of financial assistance—either grants, scholarships, loans, and/or work study.

Faculty

Bentley faculty members are teacher-scholars known for their classroom skills and cutting-edge research. They bring practical, real-world experience to the classroom, based on years of professional involvement in their fields. Faculty research focuses on issues of prime importance to current business practice. Much of the research is conducted in partnership with leading organizations. A student-faculty ratio of 14:1 and average class size of 24 ensure a personal experience for students. All courses are taught by professors; there are no teaching assistants. Students often note that professors are accessible to them outside of the classroom.

Student Government

Bentley has a number of student governing groups, including the Student Government Association, Residence Hall Association, and the Graduate Student Association.

Admission Requirements

Applicants are encouraged to complete a competitive university preparatory program. Recommendations include 4 years of English, 4 years of mathematics (preferably algebra I and II, geometry, and precalculus or its equivalent), and 3 to 4 years each of history, laboratory science, and a foreign language.

Along with the application, students must submit a secondary school transcript, letters of recommendation from a teacher and a counselor, and official scores of either the SAT or ACT, including the ACT writing test. Bentley has special applications for international students and transfer students. Applicants who are nonnative speakers of English must also supply official scores of the Test of English as a Foreign Language (TOEFL).

Application and Information

Bentley University accepts the Common Application. The application deadline for students enrolling in September is January 15. For students planning to enroll in January, the deadline is November 1. Candidates for the fall semester are notified by April 1; spring semester candidates are notified on a rolling basis.

Prospective students can visit http://www.bentley.edu/undergraduate/applying for application information and deadlines.

For more information, students should contact:

Office of Undergraduate Admission
Bentley University
175 Forest Street
Waltham, Massachusetts 02452-4705
Phone: 781-891-2244
       800-523-2354 (toll-free)
Fax: 781-891-3414
E-mail: ugadmission@bentley.edu
Website: www.bentley.edu
     www.facebook.com/bentleyadmission
     twitter.com/bentleyu

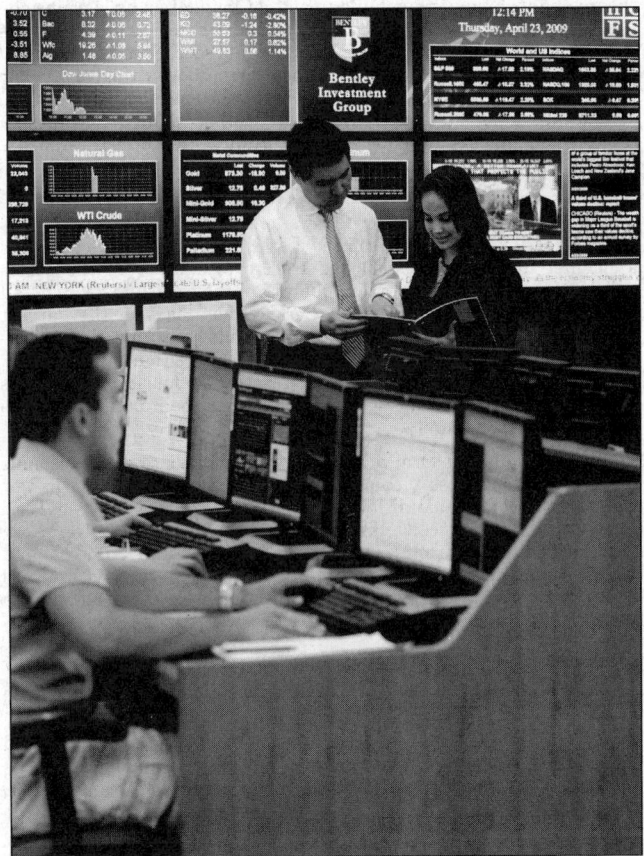

Bentley students have access to professional research tools, cutting-edge software, and other valuable resources in seven high-tech learning labs and state-of-the-art library.

BERKLEE COLLEGE OF MUSIC
BOSTON, MASSACHUSETTS

The College

Berklee College of Music was founded on the revolutionary principle that the best way to prepare students for careers in music is through the study and practice of contemporary music. For more than half a century, the college has evolved to reflect the state of the art of music and the music business, leading the way with the world's first baccalaureate studies in jazz, rock, electric guitar, film scoring, songwriting, turntables, electronic production, and more than a dozen other genres and fields of study. Berklee serves distance learners worldwide through its award-winning online extension school, Berkleemusic.com. The college's national after-school music program for underserved teens, the Berklee City Music Network, is in thirty cities and counting. A new campus in Spain, Berklee in Valencia, hosts the college's first graduate programs in contemporary performance; global entertainment and music business; scoring for film, television, and video games; and music technology innovation. With a diverse and talented student body representing more than eighty countries, and alumni who have collectively won more than 250 Grammys and Latin Grammys, Berklee is the world's premier learning lab for the music of today—and tomorrow.

Berklee has proven its commitment to this approach by wholeheartedly embracing change. The musical landscape looks nothing like it did when Berklee was founded in 1945, but the college has remained current by supplementing its core curriculum with studies in emerging musical genres and indispensable new technology. Berklee also has responded to important developments in music education and music therapy, making good on its promise to improve society through music.

At Berklee, students acquire a strong foundation of contemporary music theory and technique, then build upon that foundation by learning the practical, professional skills needed to sustain a career in music. Majors such as music production and engineering, film scoring, music business/management, electronic production and design, songwriting, and music therapy, as well as traditional mainstays of performance and composition, lead toward either a fully accredited four-year baccalaureate degree or a professional diploma. Perhaps more importantly, they prepare students for employment in the music industry.

Berklee attracts a diverse range of students who reflect the multiplicity of influences in today's music, be it jazz, rock, hip-hop, country, gospel, electronica, Latin, or funk. The college is a magnet for aspiring musicians from every corner of the earth, which gives the school a uniquely international flavor. Of all U.S. colleges and universities, Berklee has one of the largest percentages of undergraduates from outside the United States—more than 25 percent. Reflecting the interplay between music and culture, Berklee creates an environment where aspiring music professionals learn how to integrate new ideas and showcase their distinctive skills in an evolving community.

The college's alumni form a wide network of industry professionals who use their openness, virtuosity, and versatility to take music in new directions. Notable alumni include Jeff Bhasker, Gary Burton, Terri Lyne Carrington, Bruce Cockburn, Juan Luis Guerra, Roy Hargrove, Amy Heidemann (Karmin), Quincy Jones, Diana Krall, Aimee Mann, Arif Mardin, Branford Marsalis, Danilo Pérez, John Scofield, Howard Shore, Alan Silvestri, Esperanza Spalding, Susan Tedeschi, and Gillian Welch.

Location

Berklee College of Music is located in Boston's Fenway Cultural District. An international hub of intellectual and creative exploration, the neighborhood includes many of the world's other great colleges and universities, treasure-filled museums and galleries and world-class performing arts centers such as Symphony Hall and the Wang Center. Great performers appear at the Berklee Performance Center, and the college's all-ages venue Cafe 939 highlights up-and-coming international performers in all genres. In addition to the music made at Berklee, there is a lively club and concert scene in the area with coffee houses featuring folk and bluegrass music; neighborhood clubs offering jazz, reggae, and world music; and clubs specializing in rock, blues, dance, urban, and country music.

Berklee students participate in intramural sports and fitness programs at Berklee and at other ProArts Consortium member institutions; enjoy professional sporting events like baseball with the Boston Red Sox at Fenway Park, hockey with the Boston Bruins, basketball with the Boston Celtics, and football with the New England Patriots; attend theater, club, and concert hall events year-round throughout the city; and walk and bike through the city's many parks and public gardens. The college is on Boston's public transportation system, allowing students to take advantage of all that Boston has to offer.

As of summer 2011, Berklee launched an international campus offering master's of music and art degrees in Valencia, Spain, in the heart of the City of Arts and Sciences complex in the Palau de les Arts. Valencia boasts the highest number of musicians per capita, and thousands of Valencians of all ages are involved in musical activities. With more than 500 symphonic bands throughout the region and representing countless music styles, including classical, rock, pop, and jazz, the Berklee campus in Valencia aims to be a main hub for the study, evolution, and global proliferation of many musical genres, including flamenco, in Europe, Latin America, the Middle East, and all over the world.

Majors and Degrees

Berklee offers a Bachelor of Music (B.M.) degree program and a four-year program leading to a professional diploma. Students may choose to major in composition, contemporary writing and production, electronic production and design, film scoring, jazz composition, music business/management, music education, music production and engineering, music therapy, performance, professional music, and songwriting. In addition, students may choose from nine minors: acoustics, conducting, drama, English, Latin music performance, music and society, psychology, video game scoring, and visual culture/new media studies. The college also offers a five-year, dual-major option in which students graduate with an even more marketable education that expands their career options in the music industry.

Academic Programs

The Bachelor of Music program offers a complete music curriculum combined with liberal arts courses such as English, history, languages, mathematics, philosophy, and physical or social science. Intensive concentration in music subjects provides students with the necessary tools for developing their musical talents to the fullest and preparing for the multifaceted and ever-changing demands of today's professional music. The degree program is especially appropriate for students who wish to earn a formal degree; are interested in pursuing a career in music education, music therapy, or music business/management; or want to continue their studies at the graduate level.

The diploma is designed for students who want to focus exclusively on contemporary music studies and still get the benefits of a Berklee experience, as well as students who have already earned a bachelor's degree at another institution.

All students must complete the core music curriculum, which consists of harmony, arranging, ear training, and introduction to music technology; instrumental studies; ensembles and instrumental labs; and the concentrate courses designated for each major. All degree candidates must complete the general education curriculum and traditional music studies courses.

Off-Campus Programs

Through the Professional Arts Consortium (ProArts), an association of six area institutions dedicated to the performing and visual arts, Berklee students can take courses at leading Boston area arts institutions in communications, modern dance, visual arts, ballet, architectural and graphic design, theater arts, and liberal arts. The other members of the consortium are Boston Architectural Center, the Boston Conservatory, Emerson College, Massachusetts College of Art, and the School of the Museum of Fine Arts.

Students who major in music business/management may be eligible to receive credit for their Berklee course work toward an M.B.A. from Suffolk University.

The Berklee International Network is a shared endeavor designed to promote the effectiveness of contemporary music education among members and to advance the value of contemporary music education internationally. Berklee faculty and staff members visit network member schools annually to conduct workshops and clinics and to audition students for scholarships for full-time study at Berklee. There are currently thirteen members of the network in Brazil, Ecuador, Finland, France, Germany, Greece, Ireland, Israel, Japan, Korea, Malaysia, and Spain.

The college has a robust internship program, with students learning in music companies in Los Angeles, New York, Nashville, London, and beyond, as well as a semester-long global studies program at Berklee's campus in Valencia, Spain.

Academic Facilities

Berklee students have the opportunity to work in the college's state-of-the-art music technology facilities, using some of the most sophisticated recording and synthesis equipment currently available, in addition to facilities specifically designed for the areas of composition, arranging, and film scoring. The facilities at Berklee are furnished with the instruments and equipment that are being used in the world beyond the classroom. Berklee's performance facilities include the Berklee Performance Center, a 1,200-seat concert hall hosting more than 300 student, faculty, and other concerts each year; Cafe 939, a state-of-the-art, all-ages, student-run music venue and coffee house; four recital halls equipped with a variety of sound reinforcement systems; more than forty ensemble rooms; over eighty private instruction studios; about 300 private practice rooms; and an outdoor concert pavilion.

Technological facilities include the Recording Studio Complex, consisting of thirteen studio facilities that offer multitrack digital and analog recording capability, automated mix-down, digital audio editing, video postproduction, 5.1 multichannel surround mixing, and comprehensive signal processing equipment; electronic production and design labs, with nine facilities featuring hundreds of synthesizers, standard and alternate controllers, effects processors, recorders, mixers, computers, and software representing many of the industry's most progressive manufacturers; the Learning Center, a networked, computer-based training facility; the Professional Writing Division MIDI Lab and advanced classroom, with twenty-eight digital audio/MIDI workstations; and film-scoring classroom, labs, and scoring studio complex, offering students the opportunity for hands-on study in the areas of film music composition, conducting, MIDI sequencing, and digital music editing.

Costs

Information on costs is available online at http://berklee.edu/cost.

Financial Aid

A very large percentage of the student body receives some form of financial aid, so no student should allow financial barriers to stop him or her from applying to the college. Funds are available from many different sources, including Berklee and federal and state programs. Students are eligible for merit-based scholarships and, in cases of demonstrated need, federal assistance is provided. Subsidized loans, a tuition-installment plan, and campus employment are also available. Financial aid counselors are available to students and their families to discuss the various options available to them. Students should be aware that there are specific deadlines for federal and state fund applications and for scholarships. Berklee awards more than $30 million in scholarships each year to students from all over the world who demonstrate the potential to succeed in today's music industry.

Berklee's Office of Scholarships and Student Employment provides extensive opportunities for both domestic and international students to apply for merit-based scholarships via audition (entering students) or submission of an achievement portfolio (continuing and returning students who have successfully completed a minimum of two semesters).

Faculty

The personal attention students receive from teachers at Berklee guides them beyond the theoretical so that they can apply what they've learned in their next ensemble rehearsal, evening jam session, or gig. All instruction is administered by Berklee's more than 500 faculty members. Teachers are talented artists who demonstrate their commitment to music education in the classroom and beyond. Most faculty members also write and arrange music, perform in concert halls and clubs, make recordings, or perform on television and radio, and some do it all. All faculty members bring to the classroom knowledge of music and the wisdom that comes from professional music experience.

Student Government

Berklee's broad-based system of governance relies on participation from all areas of the college community. The Council of Students represents the voice and perspectives of students regarding all of the issues reviewed by the college. Students are also asked to serve on a wide variety of college committees that advise administrators on such topics as the college's master plan, honorary degree recipients, Web site, and academic and student policies. And many of Berklee's student leaders have the opportunity to meet with the president, vice presidents, and trustees during the academic year to discuss current issues, concerns, and institutional activities.

Admission Requirements

Berklee's board of admissions seeks students who show high potential—who are creative, collaborative, and who have something extra that sets them apart. The college considers every aspect of an applicant's strengths and looks for candidates who reflect the rich diversity of Berklee's curriculum, with high musical aptitude as players or writers; or in business, production, music therapy, or music education.

The college takes academics into consideration as well as musical aptitude. Berklee does not have specific GPA or test score requirements, nor does it have specific class rank requirements. The audition and interview process, along with a comprehensive and holistic evaluation of each applicant, provides a wealth of information to assess students' ability to succeed at Berklee.

Application and Information

Berklee uses fixed application deadlines for each semester of entry. Applying to the college is a three-step process. All applicants must submit an online application, participate in a live audition and interview, and mail in the appropriate transcripts to be considered for full-time enrollment at the college.

The online application asks that students provide their personal contact information, including whether they are a vocalist or instrumentalist; and their preferred audition and interview location. A live audition and interview is required as part of the application. A complete listing of audition dates, deadlines, and locations throughout the world is available on Berklee's website.

The college also asks that students provide information about their musical and academic background. All supporting materials must be postmarked by the posted deadline date. To learn more about how to apply to the college, and information about the audition and interview experience, students should visit http://www.berklee.edu/admissions.

For further information, students should contact:

Office of Admissions
Berklee College of Music
1140 Boylston Street
Boston, Massachusetts 02215
Phone: 617-266-2222 (worldwide)
      800-BERKLEE (toll-free in the U.S. and Canada)
Fax: 617-747-2047
E-mail: admissions@berklee.edu
Website: http://www.berklee.edu
         http://www.facebook.com/berkleecollege
         http://twitter.com/BerkleeCollege
         http://www.youtube.com/berkleecollege

Berklee College of Music students using state-of-the-art music technology.

BOSTON COLLEGE
CHESTNUT HILL, MASSACHUSETTS

The University

Boston College (BC) was founded in 1863 by the Jesuits to serve the sons of Boston's Irish immigrants. Today a coeducational university on more than 227 acres in Chestnut Hill, BC may seem a world apart from the small school in the crowded heart of Boston that was its first home. Through more than fifteen decades of growth and change, however, BC has held fast to the Jesuit ideals that inspired its founders. A Jesuit education today, as a century ago, is grounded in the liberal arts and in a commitment to the service of others.

Undergraduates may enroll in the College of Arts and Sciences, the Wallace E. Carroll School of Management, the Connell School of Nursing, or the Lynch School of Education.

BC's approximately 9,000 undergraduates come from many backgrounds. The university draws from nearly all fifty states and more than fifty-five countries. Students' religious and cultural backgrounds are similarly diverse. Today, the university's AHANA (African American, Hispanic, Asian, and Native American) and international students make up 29 percent of the undergraduate student body.

In today's complex and increasingly diverse world, the university believes that the best education is one that broadens a student's capacity to reason, think, and make critical judgments in a wide range of areas. Thus, each BC student fulfills a core of liberal arts courses from which he or she can pursue degrees in more than fifty areas of study and choose from more than 1,400 course offerings throughout the university.

According to several recent national publications, BC is in the top tier of the nation's colleges and universities. The foundation for that achievement is the university's scholars and researchers—752 full-time professionals who make up the faculty. The kinship between teachers and students is one of the hallmarks of a BC education; that relationship is nurtured by a student-teacher ratio of 14:1. The median class size at the university is 20 students.

At BC, learning continues beyond the classroom in more than 225 student-run organizations. These include student government, honor societies, language and cultural organizations, performance ensembles, political groups, preprofessional clubs, publications, and service organizations. BC also sponsors thirteen varsity teams for men and sixteen for women, all of which compete at the NCAA Division I level. The College also supports over sixty club and intramural sports.

Boston College's public affairs office maintains university profiles on two social networking sites. Prospective students can become a fan of BC on Facebook (http://www.facebook.com/BostonCollege) or follow BC on Twitter (http://twitter.com/BostonCollege).

Location

Located in the Chestnut Hill section of Newton, BC sits on the doorstep of one of America's great cities, a center of culture and education for more than three centuries. It is an energetic, cosmopolitan city that draws life and enthusiasm from the more than 200,000 college students in residence during the academic year. Located just 6 miles from downtown Boston and with easy access to the city via the trolley system that stops at the foot of the campus, BC offers the best of both worlds: a scenic suburban setting neighboring an exciting metropolitan center.

Majors and Degrees

The College of Arts and Sciences (A&S) is the oldest and largest of the four undergraduate schools at BC. A&S students must complete thirty-eight 1-semester courses, thirty-two of which are in A&S departments. The normal course load is five courses per semester for the first three years and four courses per semester during the senior year. The undergraduate curriculum includes the university core curriculum and ten to twelve courses in the major field, with the remainder of courses chosen as electives. A&S offers degrees in the following areas: art history, biochemistry, biology, chemistry,

classical studies, communication, computer science, economics, English, environmental geosciences, film studies, French, geology, geological studies, geophysics, German studies, Hispanic studies, history, independent major, international studies, Islamic civilizations and societies, Italian, linguistics, mathematics, music, philosophy, physics, political science, psychology, Russian, Slavic studies, sociology, studio art, theater, and theology. Preprofessional advisement is also available in medical, dental, veterinary, and legal programs. Students can also select from twenty-one departmental minors, or seventeen interdisciplinary minors.

The Carroll School of Management educates students to be leaders in business and industry and in public agencies, educational institutions, and service organizations. The Carroll School offers concentrations in accounting, accounting information systems, computer science, corporate reporting and analysis, economics, finance, general management, human resource management, information systems, management and leadership, marketing, and operations and strategic management.

The Lynch School of Education prepares students for education and human services professions. Programs provide a general education, professional preparation, and specialized education in the major field. Fieldwork in area schools is closely linked to course work in each specialization. The Lynch School awards degrees upon completion of thirty-eight courses, including the university core curriculum, a major field of study in education, and a second major in a subject field or an interdisciplinary area in A&S that complements the student's program. Areas of specialization include early childhood education, elementary education, human development, and secondary education. The Lynch School also offers interdisciplinary majors in American heritages, general science, mathematics/computer science, and perspectives on Spanish America.

The Connell School of Nursing offers a four-year program of study leading to a Bachelor of Science degree. The three major components to the curriculum are nursing major courses, electives, and the required university core curriculum. In all courses, principles of wellness, illness, rehabilitation, and health maintenance serve as a theoretical basis in preparing students for professional nursing practice. Nursing courses include traditional classes, simulated and audiovisual laboratory activities on campus, and clinical learning activities in health-care settings.

Academic Programs

Every BC education is centered on a core curriculum—a set of required courses. BC offers a core curriculum because it believes in the unity of knowledge. While the core, which is continually reviewed by a committee of faculty members, varies somewhat by school, its common elements include literature, natural science, writing, philosophy, theology, social science, modern European history, mathematics, fine arts, and the study of a non-European culture.

There are a wide variety of extraordinary academic programs available to BC students to enhance their educational experience. They include, among others, honors programs within each of the university's four undergraduate schools, Undergraduate Faculty Research Fellows, the Scholar of the College, PULSE, and Perspectives on Western Culture.

Off-Campus Programs

BC encourages all students to take part in internship programs. More than half of BC undergraduates participate in at least one internship or prepracticum placement during their college years. Internships can be paid or unpaid and may take place during the academic year or the summer; some carry academic credit.

BC students may take on the challenge of international study in more than sixty programs administered by BC at universities in more than forty countries. BC students who study abroad typically do so in their junior year, but there is also a range of full-year and summer-abroad opportunities. The Office of International Programs helps students with program selection and applications and maintains a library of reference books and professional evaluations of international study programs.

Academic Facilities

BC's eight libraries contain more than 2.8 million printed volumes, over 4.2 million items in microform, 436,597 e-books, 229,424 government documents, 36,940 serial subscriptions, and a wide collection of films and archival items. The resources of the library system range from some of Europe's earliest printed books to hundreds of computerized databases. Students with personal computers have dorm-room access to these databases as well as to Quest and other library information sources through Agora, the campus information network. BC also offers a 24/7 "Ask a Librarian" e-mail service and the capability to text questions to a librarian. In addition, all of BC's libraries and classrooms offer a wireless network that provides access to these resources and the Internet.

Research laboratories in the state-of-the-art science facilities have been specially designed to accommodate the advanced instrumentation required for modern science and to provide flexibility for accommodating new equipment. The $85-million expansion to the Higgins Biology and Physics Center was carefully designed to place classrooms, laboratories, computer facilities, and office space in proximity and to facilitate interaction among faculty members, researchers, and students. In addition to the Center's seventeen new teaching laboratories, special working labs are designed and outfitted for research and teaching in the fields of biology and physics.

Boston College opened Stokes Hall in January 2013. This new $78-million facility was strategically designed to foster interdisciplinary collaboration among BC's humanities departments and enhanced student-faculty interaction, with thirty-six new state-of-the-art classrooms and 200 faculty offices for the Classical Studies, English, History, Philosophy, and Theology departments. Stokes Hall also houses the Academic Advising Center, College of Arts and Sciences Honors Department, and Office of First Year Experience, as well as common areas, conference rooms, a coffee shop, and an outdoor garden and plaza that provide multiple meeting spaces to connect students and faculty.

Costs

Tuition for the 2012–13 academic year was $43,140, which included a student activity fee and campus health fee. The total for room and board was $12,608, which included the board plan. Freshman mandatory fees include a one-time required charge of $458 for first-year orientation and student identification.

Financial Aid

BC maintains a financial aid program to assist deserving and qualified students who might otherwise not be able to attend the university. Boston College is committed to providing funds to meet the full demonstrated need of every admitted student who applies for financial aid. Overall, 68 percent of students receive some form of financial aid. Assistance for freshmen alone included more than $19 million in need-based grants. The university offers financial aid to students based on need as demonstrated by completion of the College Scholarship Service's Financial Aid PROFILE and the Free Application for Federal Student Aid (FAFSA). All requirements and deadlines and complete instructions are available in BC admission literature. An application for financial aid in no way affects a decision on admission.

Each year, BC chooses 15 incoming freshmen as Presidential Scholars to receive merit-based, full-tuition scholarships. Students are selected from all candidates who apply through the early action program.

Faculty

BC has 752 full-time faculty members. Of these faculty members, 98 percent hold doctoral degrees. Approximately 100 Jesuits live on BC-owned property and make up one of the largest Apostolic Jesuit communities in the world. Nearly half of these members are active in the College's administration and teaching.

Student Government

The Undergraduate Government of Boston College (UGBC), formed in 1968, is led by the president and vice president, who are elected in the spring of each year by the entire student body. UGBC's goal is to serve the students by providing services and opportunities and by representing them in the best manner possible to the university community. To accomplish this goal, UGBC provides many educational, social, and cultural programs, such as concerts, lectures, roundtables, and more.

Admission Requirements

The undergraduate admission staff pays particular attention to students who have done well in a demanding college-preparatory curriculum, including Advanced Placement (AP) and honors courses when available. For the class of 2015, there were 34,061 applications for 2,405 places. The majority of incoming freshmen ranked comfortably in the top 10 percent of their high school class. The SAT scores of the middle half of admitted freshmen were 1900–2180. On the ACT, scores of the middle half were between 29 and 32.

Application and Information

Students applying to Boston College for a place in the freshman class must complete both the Common Application and the Boston College Supplemental Application. All applicants should submit the BC Supplemental Application as soon as they have decided to apply to Boston College. Students are encouraged to review the electronic application instructions on BC's website at http://www.bc.edu/applications and then apply at http://www.commonapp.org.

Students applying through the regular admission program must submit the Common Application and all other required forms, along with the $70 application fee, by January 1. Candidates are notified of action taken on their application in early April. Admitted students intending to matriculate are required to forward a confirmation fee to the Admission Office postmarked by May 1.

Students with superior academic credentials who view Boston College as a top choice may apply through the nonbinding early action program. These applicants must submit both application forms, along with the $70 application fee, by November 1. Candidates learn of their admission decision before December 25 but have the standard deadline (May 1) to reserve their places as freshmen. Boston College does permit students to apply under early action if they have applied to an early decision college.

BC accepts approximately 125 transfer students each year. Transfer candidates should request applications for transfer admission from the Office of Undergraduate Admission or via the website at http://www.bc.edu/transfer. In addition to high school records and standardized test results, transfer applicants must furnish transcripts from all postsecondary institutions they have attended.

For more information, students should contact:

Office of Undergraduate Admission
Devlin Hall 208
Boston College
Chestnut Hill, Massachusetts 02467
Phone: 617-552-3100
       800-360-2522 (toll-free)
Fax: 617-552-0798
Website: http://www.bc.edu

BOSTON UNIVERSITY
BOSTON, MASSACHUSETTS

The University

Boston University (BU) is a private teaching and research university ranked in the top 4 percent of universities in the nation by *U.S. News & World Report*. Students study with world-renowned faculty, including Fulbright Scholars, Pulitzer Prize winners, MacArthur Fellows, Nobel Prize winners, and former Poets Laureate. With an average class size of 28 and a 13:1 student-to-faculty ratio, these amazing professors become more than just a face students see in class. There are hundreds of research projects that allow undergraduates to work directly with faculty as early as freshman year through the Undergraduate Research Opportunities Program (UROP). With nine undergraduate schools and colleges, over 250 majors and minors, in-depth global courses, and one of the top 20 study-abroad programs in the country, the challenges at BU are vast and varied.

Among the academic opportunities at BU are several top-ranked programs such as biomedical engineering, occupational therapy, archaeology, business, and deaf studies. High-achieving students can also pursue dual degrees, combined B.A./M.A. programs, or be admitted to the prestigious Arvind and Chandan Nandlal Kilachand Honors College. BU students come from all fifty states and more than 100 countries; they are bright, driven, and inquisitive.

Located in the heart of Boston, students experience the city as an extension of the campus for study, internships, employment, and cultural and recreational activities. With four years of guaranteed campus housing, and 80 percent of undergraduates living on campus all four years, the campus feels like a true residential community in the heart of Boston.

Location

Boston provides an environment rich in intellectual and cultural stimuli; no other city in the world can compete with Boston's remarkable concentration of higher education institutions, world-renowned medical centers, and historic and cultural attractions. Students make up 20 percent of Boston's population during the academic year, enhancing the atmosphere of learning and excitement. The city provides many opportunities for impressive internship and research positions and is a world-class center for attractions including the Museum of Fine Arts, Fenway Park, the Boston Symphony Orchestra, and a thriving theater district.

Majors and Degrees

Boston University grants the B.A., B.S., B.S.B.A., B.L.S., Mus.B., and B.F.A. degrees. Of the University's sixteen schools and colleges, nine offer opportunities for undergraduate study.

As BU's largest academic division, the College of Arts and Sciences (CAS) offers a diverse learning community with world-class research faculty. Students may major in American studies; ancient Greek; ancient Greek and Latin; anthropology; anthropology and religion; archaeology; architectural studies; astronomy; astronomy and physics; biochemistry and molecular biology; biology; biology with a specialization in behavioral biology; biology with a specialization in cell biology, molecular biology, and genetics; biology with a specialization in ecology and conservation biology; biology with a specialization in neurobiology; biology with a specialization in quantitative biology; chemistry; chemistry with specialization in biochemistry; chemistry with specialization in teaching; Chinese language and literature; classical civilization; classics and philosophy; classics and religion; comparative literature; computer science; earth sciences; East Asian studies; economics; economics and mathematics; English; environmental analysis and policy; environmental science; European studies; French and linguistics; French studies; geography with a specialization in human geography; geography with a specialization in physical geography; geophysics and planetary sciences; German language and literature; Hispanic language and literature; history; history of art and architecture; international relations; Italian studies; Japanese and linguistics; Japanese language and literature; Latin; Latin American studies; linguistics; linguistics and philosophy; marine science; mathematics (includes statistics); mathematics and computer science; mathematics and mathematics education; mathematics and philosophy; music (nonperformance);

neuroscience; philosophy; philosophy and physics; philosophy and political science; philosophy and psychology; philosophy and religion; physics; political science; pre-dentistry; pre-law; pre-medicine; pre–veterinary medicine; psychology; religion; Russian language and literature; sociology; and Spanish and linguistics. Special curricula include seven-year accelerated programs in liberal arts medicine or liberal arts dentistry; the Modular Medical Integrated Curriculum (MMEDIC); the BU dual-degree program; the CFA/CAS double-degree program; the SED/CAS double-degree program; and various combined B.A./M.A. degree programs.

The College of Fine Arts (CFA) offers programs in the School of Music (composition and theory, music education, music-nonperformance, musicology, and performance), the School of Theatre (acting, design, stage management, production, and theater arts/performing), and the School of Visual Arts (art education, graphic design, painting, and sculpture). There is also a double-degree program that allows students to earn two bachelor's degrees simultaneously in the CFA and the CAS.

The College of General Studies (CGS) offers a demanding, two-year program in the liberal arts and sciences that features an integrated core curriculum. It stresses an interdisciplinary approach to teaching. After two years, students continue into one of BU's degree-granting schools or colleges to complete their studies.

Located in one of the largest media markets in the nation, the College of Communication (COM) offers majors in communication (advertising, public relations, communication); film and television (production, writing, management); and journalism (with specialization available in broadcast, magazine, news-editorial, online, and photojournalism).

Majors in the College of Engineering (ENG) include biomedical engineering (a program ranked eighth in the country by *U.S. News & World Report*), computer engineering, electrical engineering, mechanical engineering, mechanical engineering with specialization in aerospace, and mechanical engineering with specialization in manufacturing.

The College of Health and Rehabilitation Sciences: Sargent College (SAR) is one of the oldest and top-ranked health sciences schools in the country. It offers programs in athletic training; behavior and health; health science; human physiology; nutrition; and speech, language, and hearing sciences. Also offered are a six-year B.S./D.P.T. program and a six-year program resulting in a B.S. in athletic training/D.P.T.

Areas of concentration in the School of Education (SED) include bilingual education, deaf studies, early childhood education, elementary education, English education, Latin and classical studies education, mathematics education, modern foreign language education, science education, social studies education, and special education. The SED/CAS double-degree program is also offered.

Located in one of the hospitality and tourism capitals of the world, the School of Hospitality Administration (SHA) offers a rigorous program in the management of hotels, restaurants, food and beverage service, travel and tourism, and entertainment.

With a unique global curriculum, the School of Management (SMG) offers majors in accounting, entrepreneurship, finance, general management (business), international management, law, management information systems, marketing, operations and technology management, and organizational behavior.

Academic Programs

A Boston University education combines the elements of a traditional liberal arts education with training for the professions. There are 250 programs of study to choose from, including BU's top-ranked biomedical engineering, occupational therapy, deaf studies, economics, international relations, management information systems, journalism, theatre, and archeology programs. Highly qualified freshmen may also be invited to participate in the prestigious Arvind and Chandan Nandlal Kilachand Honors College.

Boston University has more than ninety study-abroad opportunities that take students around the world for courses, internships, and fieldwork. Opportunities are offered on six continents, in over thirty countries, and in cities such as Auckland, Beijing, Dresden, London, Los Angeles, Madrid, Paris, Sydney, and Washington, D.C. Programs offered include studies in art/architecture, business/economics, engineering, health and human services, journalism/communications, visual/performing arts, and many more. Fieldwork programs may be found in locations that include Ecuador and Spain, with study-abroad options that include programs in Grenoble, Padova, Quito, and Venice. Summer study programs are available in Argentina, Australia, China, England, France, Ireland, Italy, Peru, Spain, and the United States.

BU's Center for Career Development provides students the resources they need to select a major or get internships or part-time jobs in any number of fields.

Boston University operates on a calendar of two semesters and two summer terms. Students generally take four courses each semester; thirty-two courses are required for graduation. Most degree programs are built around a core of humanities and social and natural sciences. Concentrations require eight to thirteen courses. Electives generally total 30–40 percent of the courses taken, allowing for interdisciplinary study.

Academic Facilities

The new Center for Student Services is home to BU's Center for Career Development, Educational Resource Center, Pre-professional Advising Center with pre-med and pre-law advising services, and the two-story Marciano Commons dining hall. West campus now features the modern Student Village, including Agganis Arena; the Fitness and Recreation Center, complete with a 35-foot rock-climbing wall; and high-rise, apartment-style dorms. BU also has a life science and engineering facility with 187,000-square-feet of laboratory and research space for the biology, bioinformatics, chemistry, and bioengineering departments. The state-of-the-art Photonics Center features classroom and laboratory space for the College of Engineering as well as labs designed to support industry partners who seek to develop new photonics-based products. The School of Management building also offers technologically advanced educational facilities, with a dedicated career center and management library.

Through Boston University Information Services and Technology, students have access to public computing facilities equipped with workstations, terminals, and laser printers as well as a high-speed campus network. An 890-seat proscenium theater, studio space for visual arts students, practice rooms for music, and a 575-seat music performance center are indicative of BU's support for the arts. More than 2.8 million library volumes and over 4.7 million microform units are contained in Mugar Memorial Library, where the Twentieth-Century Archives are held, including the papers of Dr. Martin Luther King, Jr., Theodore Roosevelt, Robert Frost, and Bette Davis.

Costs

Tuition for 2013–14 is $43,970, estimated room and board costs are $13,620, and University and college fees are $940. These costs are exclusive of books, supplies, transportation, and personal expenses.

Financial Assistance

Boston University helps students realize their dreams with several different kinds of financial aid: BU scholarships, federal and state grants, federal loans, federal work-study awards, and financing and payment plan options. Financial aid is offered on the basis of calculated financial eligibility, and two or more types of aid are often combined in award packages. Approximately 78 percent of students who apply for aid and enroll at BU receive assistance. Students must submit the FAFSA and the CSS PROFILE by established deadlines to be considered. In addition, the Trustee Scholarship (full tuition) and the Presidential Scholarship ($20,000) are offered to the highest achieving students who apply for admission.

The University makes every effort to assist students with calculated financial eligibility, however funds are limited. All applicants who anticipate the need for financial aid are encouraged to apply.

Faculty

Seventy-eight percent of BU faculty members have a Ph.D. or equivalent and include Nobel Prize winners, Guggenheim scholars, Emmy Award winners, and Sloan Research Fellows. In addition to fulfilling their classroom responsibilities, faculty members are accessible as academic and career advisers who assist students in obtaining internships as well research opportunities.

Admission Requirements

The Board of Admissions considers each candidate individually. Primary emphasis is placed on the strength of the secondary school record, but required test scores, character, breadth of interest, school recommendations, and other personal qualifications are also carefully evaluated. Students are required to submit the SAT or the ACT (with writing). SAT Subject Tests are recommended, but not required, for students submitting the SAT. A full listing of the standardized testing requirements can be found in the requirements and standards chart at http://www.bu.edu/admissions/apply/freshman/program-requirements. Secondary school graduation or an equivalency diploma is required of all candidates; for the College of Fine Arts a prescreening, audition, or a portfolio may be required, depending on the program of interest. For certain programs, interviews and SAT Subject Test scores are required. Boston University offers programs of early decision (binding agreement), early admission, and deferred admission.

Transfer applicants are considered for September or January admission. Transfer students are not eligible for admission to the accelerated liberal arts medical or dental programs or the six-year, combined Bachelor of Science in Health Studies/Doctor of Physical Therapy and Bachelor of Science in Athletic Training/Doctor in Physical Therapy programs. January admission to the College of Fine Arts School of Theatre is also not available to transfer students.

Boston University admits qualified students to all its programs and activities regardless of their race, color, national origin, religion, sex, age, or disability.

Application and Information

Boston University requires the Common Application and the Boston University Supplement. Information on applying is available online at http://www.bu.edu/admissions/apply. The deadline for regular decision applications is January 1. Applicants for early decision must apply by November 1. Accelerated medical and dental program applications are due November 15. The deadline for the Trustee Scholarship (full tuition) and the Presidential Scholarship ($20,000) is December 1. Students must submit the College Scholarship Service (CSS) Financial Aid PROFILE and the Free Application for Federal Student Aid (FAFSA) by February 15.

Transfer students applying for September admission should submit their applications, CSS PROFILE and FAFSA forms by March 1 or by November 1 for January admission.

Boston University Admissions
121 Bay State Road
Boston, Massachusetts 02215
Phone: 617-353-2300
E-mail: admissions@bu.edu
Website: http://www.bu.edu/admissions
http://www.facebook.com/BUadmissions
https://twitter.com/ApplyToBU

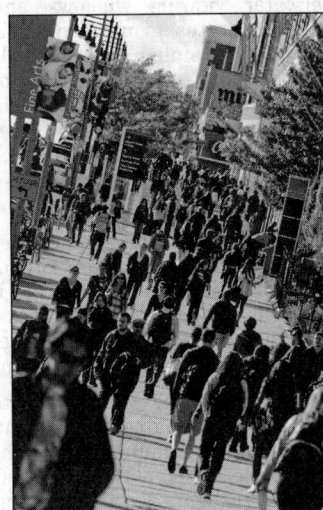

Students at Boston University find that nothing separates them from Boston's world-class museums, vibrant culture, legendary sports teams, rich history, or world-renowned scientific and medical communities.

BOWIE STATE UNIVERSITY
BOWIE, MARYLAND

The University

Bowie State University began as a normal school in the city of Baltimore in 1865, and it has evolved over the years into a four-year, coeducational, liberal arts institution. It is currently situated on a beautiful 500-acre campus in Prince Georges County, Maryland, and offers both graduate and undergraduate programs of study. Teacher education programs were established in 1925; in 1935, with state authorization, a four-year program for the training of elementary school teachers was begun and the school became the Maryland State Teachers College at Bowie. In 1951, with the approval of the State Board of Education, its governing body at the time, the college established a teacher-preparation curriculum for the training of teachers for the core program in the junior high schools. Ten years later, permission was granted to institute a teacher-training program for secondary education. A liberal arts program was established in 1963, and the institution's name was changed to Bowie State College. In 1988, Bowie State achieved university status and joined the University System of Maryland (USM).

Bowie State University's physical plant is valued at more than $225 million, and its current enrollment is 5,608 students, 909 of whom are in the Graduate School. The University has twenty-two buildings on campus with the addition of the $21-million state-of-the-art Center for Learning and Technology that opened in 2000, the $11.8-million Computer Science Center that opened in 2002, and the $19-million Center for Business and Graduate Studies opened in 2007. Two of the buildings, the Communication Arts Center and the physical education complex, were completed in 1973, and an administration building opened in 1977. Seven residence halls, including Goodloe Hall and Alex Haley Hall, a state-of-the-art residence hall that houses honors students, house approximately 850 students. In addition, a 460-bed apartment-style residence hall, Christa McAuliffe, was completed in 2004. The $2.6-million physical education complex houses a 3,000-seat basketball arena, an Olympic-size swimming pool with underwater viewing windows and facilities for 200 spectators, an apparatus gymnasium, a dance studio, a wrestling room, a weight-training room, eight handball/squash courts, a therapy room, and offices for instructors and coaches. The $5.5-million University Activities Center includes a cafeteria. Bowie State has now opened a new $79-million Fine and Performing Arts Center. The 123,000-square-foot building includes a 400-seat main theater, a 200-seat black box theater, a 200-seat recital hall, an art gallery, classrooms, labs, and offices.

Bowie State University considers the student activities program a vital part of the total educational program. Students have access to more than forty different activities. These include student government, the student union, intercollegiate athletics, eight fraternities and sororities, numerous departmental clubs and preprofessional organizations, and music and drama organizations.

The Graduate School grants the Master of Arts in counseling psychology, English, human resource development, mental health counseling, organizational communications, school psychology, and teaching (M.A.T.); the Master of Business Administration; the Master of Education in elementary education, reading education, school administration and supervision, school counseling, secondary education, and special education; the Master of Public Administration; and the Master of Science in applied computational mathematics, computer science, management information systems, and nursing. The Doctor of Education is granted in educational leadership and the Applied Doctor of Science is granted in computer science. The Adler-Dreikurs Institute of Human Relations at Bowie State University is the first fully accredited master's-degree-granting Adlerian institute in the United States.

Bowie State University admits students without regard to sex, religion, or nationality, and the University does not discriminate on the basis of race, creed, color, national or ethnic origin, age, sex, or handicap. The University is accredited by the Middle States Association of Colleges and Schools and approved by the Maryland State Department of Education. Its programs in teacher education, social work education, nursing, business, and computer science are accredited by the National Council for Accreditation of Teacher Education, the National Council on Social Work Education, the National League for Nursing Accrediting Commission, the Maryland Board of Nursing, the Association of Collegiate Business Schools and Programs, and the Computer Science Accreditation Commission of the Computing Sciences Accreditation Board, respectively.

Location

Bowie, Maryland, is in a triangle formed by Annapolis (20 miles east), Baltimore (25 miles north), and Washington, D.C. (17 miles southwest). The suburban setting provides an ideal, safe environment for students and scholars, with access to all of the important cultural, governmental, and business activities in any of the three metropolitan areas.

Majors and Degrees

Bowie State University offers the Bachelor of Arts or Bachelor of Science degree with majors in bioinformatics, biology, business administration, communications media, computer science, computer technology, criminal justice, digital media arts, early childhood education, elementary education, English, English education, fine art, government, history, mathematics, nursing, child and adolescent studies, psychology, science education, social work, sport management, sociology, and technology. A dual-degree program is offered in engineering.

Academic Programs

The University operates on a semester calendar. Academic offerings are housed under four schools (School of Arts and Sciences, School of Education, School of Professional Studies, and the new School of Business) and can be divided into four main areas: humanities, science and mathematics, social sciences, and education. To receive a bachelor's degree, a student must earn a minimum of 120 semester hours with a cumulative grade point average of 2.0 or better. Students are provided the opportunity to complete the General Education Program, acquire lifelong learning skills for a competitive world, and make a successful transition into their junior year. General studies requirements include communication skills, 9 hours; humanities, 9 hours; social sciences, 18 hours; science and mathematics, 9 hours; and physical education, 2 hours. The remaining credit hours can be electives or from major and minor areas of interest. Students must also pass the test of Proficiency in the English Language and must take the national standardized test in their major area.

The Honors Program is designed for students with outstanding academic records and potential and provides a special educational opportunity for young adults with exceptional talent. The program is comprehensive and multidisciplinary in structure and interdisciplinary in application. It has been designed to provide a creative approach to the teaching/learning process and to present activities that encourage the shaping of students' own experiences.

The Special Services Project is a federally funded program designed to retain and graduate first-generation, low-income, and disabled students who have been admitted to Bowie State

University. The purpose of the project is to help students overcome academic and nonacademic barriers to academic success, through participation in specially designed activities, including counseling, tutoring, and workshops on test taking and study skills.

Through the Cooperative Education Program, a student may choose either the alternate or parallel programs of study and work in business, industry, government, or a social-service agency. This program is open to Bowie State students who have completed at least one academic year with a minimum cumulative grade point average of 2.0.

The University participates in the College-Level Examination Program (CLEP), administered by the Educational Testing Service for the College Board, and in the Defense Activity for Non-Traditional Education Support (DANTES) program. The University also has a program for awarding students credit for learning acquired through life and work experience. Under this program, students document their backgrounds in a portfolio, which is reviewed by the faculty. Through all of these programs, qualified students may receive up to 30 credit hours toward their degree. In addition, the University offers an Army ROTC program. Two-year and three-year scholarships are available.

Academic Facilities

The Communication Arts Center, a $6.5-million building that houses the humanities division, contains classrooms, offices, conference rooms, and studio-laboratories and seats approximately 1,000 patrons. The $8.8-million, 345,514-volume Thurgood Marshall Library is centrally located on campus and provides excellent equipment and reference departments for the student body. The microfilm file contains 474,196 items; periodicals number 767. Campus research facilities include science laboratories, television and radio studios, language laboratories, and the Adler-Dreikurs Institute. Access to the library collection is provided through Victor Web, the electronic catalog that also links users to millions of USM volumes. The new Center for Learning and Technology, the main classroom building, features a new supercomputer (one of the fastest computers in the world), fourteen electronic classrooms, two interactive lecture halls, three computer labs, one speech lab, and a 300-seat auditorium and conference center. In addition, the new Computer Science Center has five classrooms and thirteen labs. Finally, the Center for Business and Graduate Studies, which opened in 2007, provides modern classrooms, labs, study space, offices, and administrative support space for the School of Business and the Division of Graduate Studies.

Costs

In 2012–13, the annual cost of tuition, fees, board, and room for a freshman who is a Maryland resident averaged $16,640; for a non-Maryland resident, the cost averaged $26,000. The annual cost for a commuting student who is a Maryland resident was about $7,000; the cost for a commuting student who is not a Maryland resident was about $17,160.

Financial Aid

Federal Pell Grants, Supplemental Grants, Work-Study, Perkins Loans, and Direct Loans are available. University scholarships, tuition waivers, and diversity grants are awarded. Most awards are based on need. Academic scholarships could be offered to students with cumulative weighted grade point averages of at least 3.3 and minimum SAT (reading and math) scores of 1100. In addition, merit awards are given for athletics, music and fine arts, and ROTC. More than 77 percent of all undergraduate students receive some form of financial aid. Deadlines are March 1 for the fall semester and November 15 for the spring semester.

Faculty

More than 60 percent of the 160 full-time faculty members have earned doctoral degrees. The faculty-student ratio is 1:16.

Student Government

All students are members of the Student Government Association, which, in cooperation with the administration, sets the standards for student life. Students are encouraged to assume leadership roles and to participate in the various programs and activities of the University. The Residence Hall Council provides opportunities for students to participate in the administration of residence life and in the cultural growth of the campus community.

Admission Requirements

Maryland residents applying for admission should have a minimum cumulative grade point average in their core high school courses of 2.0 (on a 4.0 scale) and a minimum SAT (reading and math only) score of 900 (or a minimum ACT score of 19). A sliding scale is used for students who have higher grade point averages or SAT scores. Conditional admission may be offered to students with a minimum cumulative grade point average of 2.0 and minimum SAT (reading and math only) scores of 830 to 899 (or a minimum ACT score of 17). Applicants must have earned a high school diploma or a GED certificate. The following courses are required: English, 4 credits; social science/history, 3 credits; mathematics (algebra I, algebra II, and geometry), 3 credits; laboratory sciences, 2 credits; foreign language, 2 credits; and electives, 6 credits. A $40 application fee is charged, and a health certificate must be submitted before entering the University.

Transfer students must have a minimum 2.0 cumulative grade point average for a minimum of 24 transferable credits, or SAT scores are required. International students and mature adults are encouraged to apply.

Application and Information

The application deadline is February 15 for the fall semester and November 1 for spring. Students should apply online at http://www.bowiestate.edu/apply.

Admissions Office
Bowie State University
Bowie, Maryland 20715-9465
Phone: 301-860-3415
      410-880-4100 Ext. 3415 (from the
        Baltimore-Columbia area)
      877-77-BOWIE (toll-free)
Fax: 301-860-3518
E-mail: undergradadmissions@bowiestate.edu
Website: http://www.bowiestate.edu
      http://www.facebook.com/bowiestate
      http://twitter.com/bowiestate

Bowie State students often gather at the "Torch of Truth" near the center of campus.

BRIAR CLIFF UNIVERSITY
SIOUX CITY, IOWA

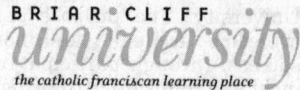

The University

Nurturing personal growth and professional promise—that's the goal of Briar Cliff University. Perched on a hilltop in Northwest Iowa, Briar Cliff University (BCU) is a private institution rooted firmly in the liberal arts and sciences. This Catholic Franciscan institution welcomes students of all faiths. In addition to offering top-quality academics, the University believes the best education shapes more than a student's résumé; it also shapes a student's character.

Briar Cliff University's passion is an authentic interest in each person. Part of the University's mission as the Catholic Franciscan learning place is to provide a values-based experience that teaches students about personal integrity, service, and social responsibility. BCU's core values are integrated in its culture and will make a difference in a student's life at Briar Cliff and beyond. Students exceed their own expectations, becoming leaders and doers. Young men and women of diverse talents and interests share a commitment to serving those in need and caring for the environment.

Briar Cliff University is ranked among the 2013 America's Best Regional Colleges by *U.S. News & World Report*. Home to more than 1,100 students from 31 states and 11 countries, BCU provides a powerful sense of community, where the dignity of every individual is recognized. The focus of the entire faculty and staff is on the students—even the University's president knows students by name. Briar Cliff freshmen have access to Peer Advising Leaders, qualified student leaders who assist new students as they adjust to campus life. This exceptional student service sets Briar Cliff University and its graduates apart.

BCU's Apple iPad program provides incoming Briar Cliff University freshmen with their own Apple iPad tablets to use anywhere on BCU's wireless campus. The ever-expanding library of electronic books, textbooks, and iTunes University (iTunes U) materials available via iPad technology ensures academic agility and cost savings. The iPad technology makes studying more productive and enjoyable, allowing BCU students to be more efficient and engaged. For instance, Briar Cliff theater students use a free application to construct potential theater sets and stage designs for productions. Science majors view internal structures of cells in 3-D with a free cell simulation app. With this technology, students have a wide variety of learning enhancement tools necessary for music, education, criminal justice, science, and other majors.

The University is always looking for innovative techniques to enhance the learning experience. Professors explore new ways to use technology in their courses with multimedia curricula, giving students complete access to all course content. The faculty and the use of technology foster social collaboration through interactive mediums, further improving peer-learning experiences.

A Briar Cliff University education prepares students for the global future. The majority of all Briar Cliff graduates are accepted at first-rate graduate schools or have jobs in their fields upon graduation.

Location

When students select a college, they're choosing a second home. A dynamic metropolitan area of over 120,000 residents, Sioux City is a great place to call home. Sioux City is a larger community with a small-town atmosphere. Students also appreciate the city's low crime rate, moderate cost of living, and the region's Midwestern hospitality and weather. Briar Cliff's hilltop campus is beautiful in all four seasons.

Majors and Degrees

Briar Cliff University offers programs that lead to Bachelor of Arts and Bachelor of Science degrees.

The academic majors offered at BCU include accounting, art, biology, business administration, biochemistry/molecular biology, chemistry, computer science, criminal justice, elementary and secondary education, English, environmental science, graphic design, health, physical education and recreation, history, human resource management, journalism and mass communication, management information systems, marketing, mathematics, medical laboratory science, music, nursing, operations management, political science, professional studies, psychology, radiologic technology, sociology, social work, Spanish, sports management, sports science, theater, theology, and writing.

Briar Cliff University offers pre-professional programs in chiropractic, church ministry, dentistry, engineering, law, medicine, occupational therapy, pharmacy, physical therapy, physician's assistant, and veterinary medicine.

Graduate programs at BCU offer master's degrees for aspiring nurse educators, family nurse practitioners, health care administrators, business leaders, education administrators, and applied behavior analysts.

Academic Programs

With over 40 areas of study, Briar Cliff provides a challenging academic environment. Students receive a broad intellectual background with career development and a hands-on approach to career preparation. Internships, field studies, and research are learning tools used in Briar Cliff curricula. Briar Cliff's new Center for Justice and Center for Health Care Initiatives offers innovative solutions to health care access and justice-related issues in the region. These centers also provide undergraduate and graduate students with real-life experience in their career preparation.

Off-Campus Programs and Internships

Through internships, Briar Cliff students apply classroom learning to real-work situations. The region offers a wealth of internships and employment opportunities with nature centers, insurance companies, semi-pro sports teams, the court system, law enforcement agencies, forensics, social service agencies, news media, and the YMCA. Many students also have internships in their hometowns.

Academic Facilities

Briar Cliff's main academic facility, Heelan Hall, was recently renovated; a three-story, 16,650-square-foot wing was added. The redesign includes state-of-the-art science laboratories, lab prep rooms, classrooms, a business case room, and the project's signature piece—a four-story, 8,150-square-foot atrium with top-floor clerestory windows for natural light. With several new labs, Briar Cliff's biology and chemistry departments offer abundant opportunities for research and experimentation. The Heelan Hall addition also expanded the nursing simulation labs and classrooms for enhanced learning. Briar Cliff's cadaver lab has doubled in size, allowing more students to take part in this valuable learning experience.

The project also included renovations to Heelan Hall's original structure, the historic jewel of the BCU campus, such as upgrades to various classrooms and labs.

The Bishop Mueller Library offers access to over 100,000 print and electronic resources which are accessible both on and off campus. The library is designed with a variety of spaces, including computer labs, study rooms, project collaboration spaces, and comfortable casual seating where students and faculty members may work individually or collaboratively in small groups. Wireless network access is available throughout the facility. The library also offers notebook computers, iPad tablets, and digital media for check out by anyone with a University ID.

Costs

Briar Cliff's tuition for the 2013–14 academic year is $25,464.

Financial Aid

Briar Cliff is very affordable, with numerous scholarships and other forms of financial aid to help students pay their college tuition. Nearly all BCU students receive scholarships, grants, and other forms of financial assistance. The University understands the financial needs of families and works with them to provide generous scholarships to provide generous financial assistance with college tuition, including the following: Presidential Scholarships (full tuition), Academic Achievement Scholarships, Talent Scholarships, Athletic Scholarships, Transfer Scholarships, Connection Scholarships, Alumni Scholarships, Iowa Tuition Grants, Federal Pell Grants, Federal Perkins Loans, Federal SEOG Grants, Federal Direct Loans, Federal Work-Study awards, Federal PLUS Loans, and need-based grants.

Additional information regarding scholarship awards and other financial aid is available online at www.briarcliff.edu.

Faculty

Classes at Briar Cliff are small, averaging about 20 students. With a student-to-faculty ratio of 15:1, BCU students enjoy individualized attention from professors. Briar Cliff professors are well-known for their dedication to student success. Experts in their fields, Briar Cliff professors conduct research, publish articles, maintain strong professional networks, and hold degrees from the nation's finest institutions.

Student Activities

Campus life is rich with a wide variety of competitive sports, social activities, cultural events, international travel, spiritual growth, service-learning, and mission experiences.

At Briar Cliff, a majority of full-time students participate in at least one cocurricular activity. BCU has several nationally recognized intercollegiate athletic teams with a strong history of excellence in intercollegiate sports. Varsity student-athletes enjoy NAIA action in the highly competitive Great Plains Athletic Conference (GPAC).

The Briar Cliff University choirs have been lauded at performances in regional, national, and international venues, performing a wide variety of choral literature that embraces all genres. Briar Cliff students are on the staff for BCU's award-winning literary magazine, *The Briar Cliff Review,* widely acclaimed for its literary and artistic content. *The Briar Cliff Review* has published the works of more than 1,170 writers and artists from the United States and around the world.

Admission Requirements

Students applying to Briar Cliff University should have graduated from an accredited high school with 16 units of high school work, including English, natural sciences, foreign language, social studies, mathematics, and 2 years of high school foreign language. The requirements are flexible and can be found in the course catalog under Academics at www.briarcliff.edu.

Applicants also should have satisfactory scores on the American College Test (ACT) or Scholastic Aptitude Test (SAT). This requirement is waived if the student has been out of high school for five years or more. Full-time students whose test scores or GPA are below standard requirements may request a review. These students may be asked to submit letters of recommendation.

Information for international students is available at www.briarcliff.edu under Admissions.

Application and Information

Briar Cliff University's application and additional information about degree programs, scholarships, and student life are available at www.briarcliff.edu.

For additional information, students should contact:

Office of Admissions
Briar Cliff University
3303 Rebecca Street
Sioux City, Iowa 51104
Phone: 712-279-5200
      800-662-3303 (toll-free)
Fax: 712-279-1632
E-mail: admissions@briarcliff.edu
Website: http://www.briarcliff.edu

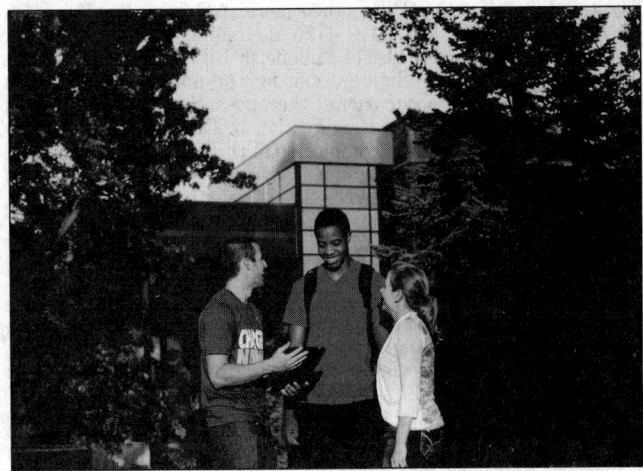

Considering each student's personal or professional goals, a Briar Cliff University education prepares them for the global future. A majority of Briar Cliff graduates are accepted at first-rate graduate schools or have jobs in their fields upon graduation.

BROWN MACKIE COLLEGE — AKRON
AKRON, OHIO

The College

Brown Mackie College — Akron (Brown Mackie College) is one of over twenty-five locations in the Brown Mackie College system of schools (www.brownmackie.edu), which is dedicated to providing educational programs that prepare students to pursue entry-level positions in a competitive, rapidly changing workplace. Brown Mackie College schools offer bachelor's degree, associate degree, diploma, and certificate programs in health sciences, business, information technology, legal studies, and design to more than 20,000 students in the Midwest, Southeast, Southwest, and Western United States.

Brown Mackie College was founded in Cincinnati, Ohio, in February 1927, as a traditional business college. In March 1980, the college added a branch campus in Akron, Ohio. The college outgrew this space and relocated to its current address in January 2007.

Brown Mackie College — Akron is accredited by the Accrediting Council for Independent Colleges and Schools to award bachelor's degrees, associate degrees, and diplomas. The Accrediting Council for Independent Colleges and Schools is listed as a nationally recognized accrediting agency by the United States Department of Education and is recognized by the Council for Higher Education Accreditation. ACICS can be contacted at 750 First Street NE, Suite 980, Washington, D.C. 20002; phone: 202-336-6780.

Brown Mackie College — Akron is licensed by the Ohio State Board of Career Colleges and Schools, 30 East Broad Street, 24th Floor, Suite 2481, Columbus, Ohio 43215-3138; phone: 614-466-2752. Ohio registration # 03-09-1685T.

The Associate of Applied Science in surgical technology program is accredited by the Commission on Accreditation of Allied Health Education Programs (www.caahep.org) upon the recommendation of the Accreditation Review Council on Education in Surgical Technology and Surgical Assisting (ARC/STSA). The Commission on Accreditation of Allied Health Education Programs is located at 1361 Park Street, Clearwater, Florida 33756; phone: 727-210-2350; www.caahep.org.

The Associate of Applied Science in occupational therapy assistant program is accredited by the Accreditation Council for Occupational Therapy Education (ACOTE) of the American Occupational Therapy Association (AOTA), located at 4720 Montgomery Lane, Suite 200, Bethesda, Maryland 20814-3449; phone: 301-652-AOTA. Graduates of the program will be eligible to sit for the national certification examination for the occupational therapy assistant administered by the National Board for Certification in Occupational Therapy (NBCOT). After successful completion of this exam, the individual will be a Certified Occupational Therapy Assistant (COTA). In addition, most states require licensure in order to practice; however, state licenses are usually based on the results of the NBCOT Certification Examination. Note that a felony conviction may affect a graduate's ability to sit for the NBCOT certification examination or attain state licensure.

The Associate of Applied Science in veterinary technology program has provisional programmatic accreditation granted by the American Veterinary Medical Association (AVMA) through the Committee on Veterinary Technician Education and Activities (CVTEA).

The Associate of Applied Science in medical assisting program is accredited by the Commission of Accreditation of Allied Health Education Programs (www.caahep.org) upon the recommendation of the Curriculum Review Board of the Medical Assisting Education Review Board (MAERB). Commission on Accreditation of Allied Health Education Programs can be contacted at 1361 Park Street Clearwater, Florida 33756; 727-210-2350.

Location

Brown Mackie College — Akron is located at 755 White Pond Drive in Akron, Ohio.

Programs of Study and Degree Offerings

Brown Mackie College — Akron provides higher education to traditional and nontraditional students through bachelor's and associate degree and diploma programs that can assist them in enhancing their career opportunities, broadening their perspectives through appropriate general education courses, thinking independently and critically, and improving problem-solving abilities.

The Bachelor of Science degree is awarded in business administration, criminal justice, and health care management.

The Associate of Applied Business degree is awarded in accounting technology, business management, criminal justice, office management, and paralegal.

The Associate of Applied Science degree is awarded in computer networking and applications, database technology, early childhood education, health care administration, information technology, medical assisting, occupational therapy assistant, pharmacy technology, surgical technology, and veterinary technology.

Brown Mackie College offers diploma programs in bookkeeping specialist, criminal justice specialist, general business, medical assistant, medical coding and billing, paralegal assistant, and practical nursing.

The American Medical Technologists (AMT), which offers the certification for Registered Medical Assistant (RMA), accepts the accreditation of Brown Mackie College — Akron. Students will qualify to take the Registered Medical Assistant certification examination upon graduating the Brown Mackie College — Akron medical assistant programs. Graduates of the 48-credit-hour medical assistant program are not qualified to take the AMT/RMA exam.

Brown Mackie College does not guarantee third-party certification/licensing exams. Outside agencies control the requirements for certification/licensing and are subject to change without notification to the College.

Program availability and degree offerings are subject to change.

Academic Programs

Each college quarter comprises twelve weeks. Bachelor's degree programs require a minimum of fifteen quarters to complete. Associate degree programs require a minimum of eight quarters to complete. Programs are offered on a year-round basis, providing students with the ability to work uninterrupted toward their degree. Brown Mackie College offers all programs in a unique One-Course-a-Month format. This schedule allows students to focus studies on only one course for four weeks and has proven convenient for students with multiple obligations, such as jobs and family.

Academic Facilities

Brown Mackie College provides media presentation rooms for special instructional needs, a library that provides instructional resources and academic support for both faculty members and students, and qualified and experienced faculty members who are committed to the academic and technical preparation of their students. Brown Mackie College is nonresidential; students who are unable to commute daily from their homes may request assistance from the Office of Admissions in locating off-campus housing. The college is accessible by public transportation and provides ample parking, available at no charge.

Brown Mackie College — Akron is fully committed to using eTextbooks and computer tablets in the classroom. Utilizing these tablets to access expanded course material, students are able to increase their acumen for using this technology and further enhance their educational experience. Students have the ability to directly download their eTextbooks to their tablet, eliminating the need to carry heavy, physical textbooks and reducing the overall cost of supplies.

Costs

Tuition for the 2012–13 academic year was $314 per credit hour and $20 per credit hour for general fees. Tuition for the practical nursing program was $381 per credit hour and $30 per credit hour for general fees. Tuition for the occupational therapy assistant program was $381 per credit hour and $20 per credit hour for general fees. Tuition for the surgical technology program was $360 per credit hour and $20 per credit hour for general fees. The cost of textbooks, if applicable, and other instructional materials varies by program.

Financial Aid

Financial aid is available to those who qualify. The college maintains a full-time staff of Student Financial Services Advisors to assist qualified students in obtaining financial assistance. The college participates in several student aid programs. Forms of financial aid available through federal resources include the Federal Pell Grant Program, Federal Supplemental Educational Opportunity Grant (FSEOG) Program, Federal Work-Study Program, Federal Stafford Student Loan Program (subsidized and unsubsidized), and the Federal PLUS Loan Program. Eligible students may also apply for veterans' educational benefits. Students with physical or mental disabilities that are a handicap to employment may be eligible for training services through the state Agency for Vocational Rehabilitation. For further information, students should contact the Student Financial Services Office.

Each year, the college makes available President's Scholarships of $1,000 each to qualifying seniors from area high schools. In order to qualify, a senior must be graduating from a participating high school, must have maintained a cumulative grade point average of at least 2.0, and must have submitted a brief essay. The student's extracurricular activities and community service are also considered. These scholarships are available only to students enrolling in one of the college's degree programs. Students awarded the scholarship must enroll at Brown Mackie College between June and September immediately following their high school graduation. Applications for these scholarships can be obtained from the guidance departments of participating high schools and must be completed and returned to Brown Mackie College by March 31.

The Education Foundation was established in 2000 to offer scholarship support to students interested in continuing their education at one of the postsecondary, career-focused schools in the EDMC system. The number and amount of the awards can vary, depending on the funds available. Scholarship applications are considered every quarter. At Brown Mackie College applicants must be currently enrolled in an associate or bachelor's degree program and in their fourth quarter or higher (but no further than their second-to-last quarter) at the time of application. Awards are made based on academic performance and potential, as well as financial need. Interested students should contact the college's Student Financial Service Department for additional information.

Faculty

There are 20 full-time and 39 part-time faculty members. The student-faculty ratio is 17:1.

Admission Requirements

Each applicant for admission is assigned an Assistant Director of Admissions who directs the applicant through the steps of the admissions process, providing information on curriculum, policies, procedures, and services and assisting the applicant in setting up necessary appointments and interviews.

To qualify for admission, each applicant must provide documentation of graduation from an accredited high school or from a state-approved secondary education curriculum or official documentation of high school graduation equivalency. All transcripts become the property of Brown Mackie College. Admission to Brown Mackie College is based upon the applicant meeting the stated requirements, a review of the applicant's previous education records, and a review of the applicant's career interests. If previous academic records indicate that the Brown Mackie College education and training programs would not benefit the applicant, the college reserves the right to advise the applicant not to enroll. Special requirements for enrollment into certain programs are discussed in the descriptions of those programs.

For the most recent information regarding admission requirements, please refer to the current academic catalog.

Application and Information

Applicants must complete and submit an application form along with documentation of graduation from an accredited high school or state-approved secondary education curriculum or official documentation of high school graduation equivalency.

See BMCprograms.info for program duration, tuition, fees and other costs, median debt, federal salary data, alumni success, programmatic accreditation, and other important info.

Brown Mackie College is a system of over twenty-five schools located throughout North America. Programs, credential levels, technology, and scheduling options vary by school, and employment opportunities are not guaranteed. Financial aid is available for those who qualify. Administrative offices are located at 625 Eden Park Drive, Suite 1100; Cincinnati, Ohio 45202; phone: 513.830.2000. ©2013 Brown Mackie College. OH Registration # 03-09-1685T; # 03-09-1686T; # 03-09-1687T; # 03-09-1688T; # 06-03-1781T; AC0150, AC0109, AC0078, AC0045, AC0138, AC0110; Licensed by the Florida Commission for Independent Education, License No. 3206.

For additional information, prospective students should contact:

Senior Director of Admissions
Brown Mackie College — Akron
755 White Pond Drive, Suite 101
Akron, Ohio 44320
United States
Phone: 330-869-3600
Fax: 330-869-3650
E-mail: bmcakadm@brownmackie.edu
Website: http://www.brownmackie.edu/Akron

BROWN MACKIE COLLEGE — ALBUQUERQUE

ALBUQUERQUE, NEW MEXICO

BROWN MACKIE COLLEGE ALBUQUERQUE™

The College

Brown Mackie College — Albuquerque (Brown Mackie College) is one of over twenty-five locations in the Brown Mackie College system of schools (www.brownmackie.edu), which is dedicated to providing educational programs that prepare students to pursue entry-level positions in a competitive, rapidly changing workplace. Brown Mackie College schools offer bachelor's degree, associate degree, diploma, and certificate programs in health sciences, business, information technology, legal studies, and design to over 20,000 students in the Midwest, Southeast, Southwest, and Western United States.

Brown Mackie College was originally founded and approved by the Board of Trustees of Kansas Wesleyan College in Salina, Kansas on July 30, 1892. In 1938, the college was incorporated as the Brown Mackie School of Business under the ownership of Perry E. Brown and A.B. Mackie, former instructors at Kansas Wesleyan University in Salina, Kansas. Their last names formed the name of Brown Mackie. By January 1975, with improvements in curricula and higher degree-granting status, the Brown Mackie School of Business became Brown Mackie College.

Brown Mackie College — Albuquerque is accredited by the Accrediting Council for Independent Colleges and Schools to award bachelor's degrees, associate degrees, and diplomas. The Accrediting Council for Independent Colleges and Schools is listed as a nationally recognized accrediting agency by the United States Department of Education and is recognized by the Council for Higher Education Accreditation. ACICS can be contacted at 750 First Street NE, Suite 980, Washington, D.C. 20002; phone: 202-336-6780.

Brown Mackie College — Albuquerque is licensed by the New Mexico Higher Education Department, 2048 Galisteo Street, Santa Fe, New Mexico 87505-2100; phone: 505-476-8400.

The occupational therapy assistant program is accredited by the Accreditation Council for Occupational Therapy Education (ACOTE) of the American Occupational Therapy Association (AOTA), located at 4720 Montgomery Lane, Suite 200, Bethesda, Maryland 20814-3449; phone: 301-652-AOTA. Graduates of the program will be eligible to sit for the national certification examination for the occupational therapy assistant administered by the National Board for Certification in Occupational Therapy (NBCOT). After successful completion of this exam, the individual will be a Certified Occupational Therapy Assistant (COTA). In addition, most states require licensure in order to practice; however, state licenses are usually based on the results of the NBCOT Certification Examination. Note that a felony conviction may affect a graduate's ability to sit for the NBCOT certification examination or attain state licensure.

The Associate of Applied Science in surgical technology program is accredited by the Accrediting Bureau of Health Education Schools.

The Associate of Applied Science in veterinary technology program has provisional programmatic accreditation granted by the American Veterinary Medical Association (AVMA) through the Committee on Veterinary Technician Education and Activities (CVTEA).

Location

Brown Mackie College — Albuquerque is conveniently located at 10500 Copper Avenue NE, in Albuquerque, New Mexico. The college has a generous parking area and is easily accessible by public transportation.

Programs of Study and Degree Offerings

Brown Mackie College — Albuquerque provides higher education to traditional and nontraditional students through bachelor's degree, associate degree, and diploma programs that assist in enhancing their career opportunities, broadening their perspectives through appropriate general education courses, thinking independently and critically, and improving problem-solving abilities. The college strives to develop within its students the desire for lifelong and continued education.

The Bachelor of Science degree is awarded in business administration, criminal justice, and health care management.

The Associate of Applied Science degree is awarded in accounting technology, architectural design and drafting technology, business management, criminal justice, health care administration, information technology, medical assisting, nursing, occupational therapy assistant, paralegal, pharmacy technology, surgical technology, and veterinary technology.

Brown Mackie College — Albuquerque offers diploma programs in accounting, business, criminal justice, medical assistant, and paralegal assistant.

The American Medical Technologists (AMT), which offers the certification for Registered Medical Assistant (RMA), accepts the accreditation of Brown Mackie College — Albuquerque. Students will qualify to take the Registered Medical Assistant certification examination upon graduating the Brown Mackie College — Albuquerque medical assisting and medical assistant programs. Graduates of the 48-credit-hour Medical Assistant program are not qualified to take the AMT/RMA exam.

Brown Mackie College does not guarantee third-party certification/licensing exams. Outside agencies control the requirements for certification/licensing and are subject to change without notification to the College.

Program availability and degree offerings are subject to change.

Academic Programs

Each college quarter comprises twelve weeks. Bachelor's degree programs require a minimum of sixteen quarters to complete. Associate degree programs require a minimum of eight quarters to complete. Programs are offered on a year-round basis, providing students with the ability to work uninterrupted toward completion of their programs. The college offers all programs in a unique One-Course-a-Month format. This allows students to focus studies on only one course for four weeks. This schedule has proven convenient for students with multiple obligations such as jobs and family.

Academic Facilities

A modern facility, Brown Mackie College — Albuquerque comprises more than 35,000 square feet. The college is equipped with multiple computer labs, housing over 100 computers. High-speed access to the Internet and other online resources are available to students and faculty. Multimedia classrooms are outfitted with overhead projectors, VCR/DVD players, and computers.

Brown Mackie College — Albuquerque is fully committed to using eTextbooks and computer tablets in the classroom. Utilizing these tablets to access expanded course material, students are able to increase their acumen for using this technology and further enhance their educational experience. Students have the ability to directly download their eTextbooks to their tablet, eliminating the need to carry heavy, physical textbooks and reducing the overall cost of supplies.

Brown Mackie College is nonresidential; public transportation and ample parking at no cost are available. The campus is a smoke-free facility.

Costs

Tuition in the 2012–13 academic year for all bachelor's and associate degrees and certificates was $324 per credit hour; fees were $25 per credit hour. Tuition for the occupational therapy assistant program was $355 per credit hour; fees were $25 per credit hour. Tuition for the surgical technology program was $339 per credit hour; fees were $25 per credit hour. Tuition for the nursing program was $390 per credit hour; fees were $30 per credit hour. The cost of textbooks, if applicable, and other instructional materials varies by program.

Financial Aid

Financial aid is available for those who qualify. Brown Mackie College maintains a full-time staff of Student Financial Services Advisors to assist qualified students in obtaining the financial assistance they require to meet their educational expenses. Available resources include federal and state aid, student loans from private lenders, and Federal Work-Study opportunities, both on and off college premises.

Each year, the college makes available President's Scholarships of $1,000 each to qualifying seniors from area high schools. In order to qualify, a senior must have graduated from a participating high school, must have maintained a cumulative grade point average of at least 2.0, and must have submitted a brief essay. The student's extracurricular activities and community service are also considered. These scholarships are available only to students enrolling in one of the college's degree programs. Students awarded the scholarship must enroll at Brown Mackie College — Albuquerque between June and September immediately following their high school graduation. Applications for these scholarships can be obtained from the guidance departments of participating high schools. These applications must be completed and returned to Brown Mackie College by March 31.

The Education Foundation was established in 2000 to offer scholarship support to students interested in continuing their education at one of the postsecondary, career-focused schools in the EDMC system. The number and amount of the awards can vary, depending on the funds available. Scholarship applications are considered every quarter. At Brown Mackie College, applicants must be currently enrolled in an associate or bachelor's degree program and in their fourth quarter or higher (but no further than their second-to-last quarter) at the time of application. Awards are made based on academic performance and potential, as well as financial need. Interested students should contact the college's Student Financial Service Department for additional information.

Faculty

Experienced faculty members provide academic support and are committed to the academic and technical preparation of their students. The college has both full-time and part-time instructors, with a student-faculty ratio of 15:1.

Admission Requirements

Each applicant for admission is assigned an Assistant Director of Admissions who directs the applicant through the steps of the admissions process. Assistant Directors provide information on curriculum, policies, procedures, and services and assist the applicant in setting up necessary appointments and interviews.

To qualify for admission, each applicant must provide documentation of graduation from an accredited high school or from a state-approved secondary education curriculum or provide official documentation of high school graduation equivalency. All transcripts become the property of the college. Admission to the college is based on the applicant meeting the stated requirements, a review of the applicant's previous educational records, and a review of the applicant's career interests. If previous academic records indicate the college's education and training programs would not benefit the applicant, the college reserves the right to advise the applicant not to enroll. Special requirements for enrollment into certain programs are discussed in the descriptions of those programs.

For the most recent information regarding admission requirements, prospective students should refer to the current academic catalog.

Application and Information

Applicants must complete and submit an application form, along with documentation of graduation from an accredited high school or state-approved secondary education curriculum or official documentation of high school graduation equivalency.

See BMCprograms.info for program duration, tuition, fees and other costs, median debt, federal salary data, alumni success, programmatic accreditation and other important info.

Brown Mackie College is a system of over twenty-five schools located throughout North America. Programs, credential levels, technology, and scheduling options vary by school, and employment opportunities are not guaranteed. Financial aid is available for those who qualify. Administrative offices are located at: 625 Eden Park Drive, Suite 1100; Cincinnati, Ohio 45202; phone: 513-830-2000. ©2013 Brown Mackie College. OH Registration # 03-09-1685T; # 03-09-1686T; # 03-09-1687T; # 03-09- 1688T; # 06-03-1781T; AC0150, AC0109, AC0078, AC0045, AC0138, AC0110; Licensed by the Florida Commission for Independent Education, License No. 3206.

For additional information, prospective students should contact:

Director of Admissions
Brown Mackie College — Albuquerque
10500 Copper Avenue, NE
Albuquerque, New Mexico 87123
United States
Phone: 505-559-5200
     877-271-3488 (toll-free)
Fax: 505-559-5222
E-mail: bmcalbadm@brownmackie.edu
Website: http://www.brownmackie.edu/Albuquerque

BROWN MACKIE COLLEGE — BIRMINGHAM
BIRMINGHAM, ALABAMA

The College

Brown Mackie College — Birmingham (Brown Mackie College) is one of over twenty-five locations in the Brown Mackie College system of schools (www.brownmackie.edu), which is dedicated to providing educational programs that prepare students to pursue entry-level positions in a competitive, rapidly changing workplace. Brown Mackie College schools offer bachelor's degree, associate degree, diploma, and certificate programs in health sciences, business, information technology, legal studies, and design to over 20,000 students in the Midwest, Southeast, Southwest, and Western United States.

Brown Mackie College was originally founded and approved by the Board of Trustees of Kansas Wesleyan College in Salina, Kansas on July 30, 1892. In 1938, the College was incorporated as the Brown Mackie School of Business under the ownership of Perry E. Brown and A.B. Mackie, former instructors at Kansas Wesleyan University in Salina, Kansas. Their last names formed the name of Brown Mackie. By January 1975, with improvements in curricula and higher degree-granting status, the Brown Mackie School of Business became Brown Mackie College.

Brown Mackie College — Birmingham is accredited by the Accrediting Council for Independent Colleges and Schools to award bachelor's degrees, associate degrees, and diplomas. The Accrediting Council for Independent Colleges and Schools is listed as a nationally recognized accrediting agency by the United States Department of Education and is recognized by the Council for Higher Education Accreditation. ACICS can be contacted at 750 First Street NE, Suite 980, Washington, D.C. 20002; phone: 202-336-6780.

The occupational therapy assistant program has applied for accreditation to the Accreditation Council for Occupational Therapy Education (ACOTE) of the American Occupational Therapy Association (AOTA), located at 4720 Montgomery Lane, Suite 200, Bethesda, Maryland 20814-3449; phone: 301-652-AOTA. Graduates of the program will be eligible to sit for the national certification examination for the occupational therapy assistant administered by the National Board for Certification in Occupational Therapy (NBCOT). After successful completion of this exam, the individual will be a Certified Occupational Therapy Assistant (COTA). In addition, most states require licensure in order to practice; however, state licenses are usually based on the results of the NBCOT Certification Examination. Note that a felony conviction may affect a graduate's ability to sit for the NBCOT certification examination or attain state licensure.

Location

Brown Mackie College — Birmingham is conveniently located at 105 Vulcan Road, in Birmingham, Alabama. The college has a generous parking area and is easily accessible by public transportation.

Programs of Study and Degree Offerings

Brown Mackie College — Birmingham provides higher education to traditional and nontraditional students through bachelor's degree, associate degree, and diploma programs that assist in enhancing their career opportunities, broadening their perspectives through appropriate general education courses, thinking independently and critically, and improving problem-solving abilities. The college strives to develop within its students the desire for lifelong and continued education.

The Bachelor of Science degree is awarded in business administration, health care management, and legal studies.

The Associate of Science degree is awarded in architectural design and drafting technology, biomedical equipment technology, business management, graphic design, health care administration, information technology, medical assisting, paralegal, and surgical technology.

The Associate of Applied Science degree is awarded in occupational therapy assistant.

The college offers diploma programs in bookkeeping specialist, dental assistant, general business, medical insurance specialist, medical assistant, and paralegal assistant.

The American Medical Technologists (AMT), which offers the certification for Registered Medical Assistant (RMA), accepts the accreditation of Brown Mackie College — Birmingham. Students will qualify to take the Registered Medical Assistant certification examination upon graduating the Brown Mackie College–Birmingham medical assisting and medical assistant programs. Graduates of the 48-credit-hour Medical Assistant program are not qualified to take the AMT/RMA exam.

Brown Mackie College does not guarantee third-party certification/licensing exams. Outside agencies control the requirements for certification/licensing and are subject to change without notification to the college.

Program availability and degree offerings are subject to change.

Academic Programs

Each college quarter comprises twelve weeks. Bachelor's degree programs require a minimum of sixteen quarters to complete. Associate degree programs require a minimum of eight quarters to complete. Programs are offered on a year-round basis, providing students with the ability to work uninterrupted toward completion of their programs. The college offers all programs in a unique One-Course-a-Month format. This allows students to focus studies on only one course for four weeks. This schedule has proven convenient for students with multiple obligations, such as jobs and family.

Academic Facilities

A modern facility, Brown Mackie College offers approximately 35,000 square feet of classroom, computer and allied health labs, library, and office space. The college is equipped with multiple computer labs, housing over 100 computers. High-speed access to the Internet and other online resources are available to students and faculty. Multimedia classrooms are outfitted with overhead projectors, VCR/DVD players, and computers.

An expansion of the facility to 44,000 square feet was completed in May of 2013, providing ten new classrooms, five of which are computer labs, as well as additional administrative space.

Brown Mackie College — Birmingham is fully committed to using eTextbooks and computer tablets in the classroom. Utilizing these tablets to access expanded course material, students are able to increase their acumen for using this technology and further enhance their educational experience. Students have the ability to directly download their eTextbooks to their tablet, eliminating the need to carry heavy, physical textbooks and reducing the overall cost of supplies.

Brown Mackie College is nonresidential; public transportation and ample parking at no cost are available. The campus is a smoke-free facility.

Costs

Tuition in the 2012–13 academic year for most bachelor's and associate degrees and certificates was $315 per credit hour; fees were $20 per credit hour. Tuition for the surgical technology program was $350 per credit hour; fees were $20 per credit hour. Tuition for the occupational therapy assistant program was $381 per credit hour; fees were $20 per credit hour. The cost of textbooks, if applicable, and other instructional materials varies by program.

Financial Aid

Financial aid is available for those who qualify. Brown Mackie College maintains a full-time staff of Student Financial Services Advisors to assist qualified students in obtaining the financial assistance they require to meet their educational expenses. Available resources include federal and state aid, student loans from private lenders, and Federal Work-Study opportunities, both on and off college premises.

Each year, the college makes available President's Scholarships of $1,000 each to qualifying seniors from area high schools. In order to qualify, a senior must have graduated from a participating high school, must have maintained a cumulative grade point average of at least 2.0, and must have submitted a brief essay. The student's extracurricular activities and community service are also considered. These scholarships are available only to students enrolling in one of the college's degree programs. Students awarded the scholarship must enroll at Brown Mackie College — Birmingham between June and September immediately following their high school graduation. Applications for these scholarships can be obtained from the guidance departments of participating high schools. These applications must be completed and returned to Brown Mackie College by March 31.

The Education Foundation was established in 2000 to offer scholarship support to students interested in continuing their education at one of the postsecondary, career-focused schools in the EDMC system. The number and amount of the awards can vary, depending on the funds available. Scholarship applications are considered every quarter. At Brown Mackie College, applicants must be currently enrolled in an associate or bachelor's degree program and in their fourth quarter or higher (but no further than their second-to-last quarter) at the time of application. Awards are made based on academic performance and potential, as well as financial need. Interested students should contact the college's Student Financial Service Department for additional information.

Faculty

Experienced faculty members provide academic support and are committed to the academic and technical preparation of their students. The college has both full-time and part-time instructors, with a student-faculty ratio of 15:1.

Admission Requirements

Each applicant for admission is assigned an Assistant Director of Admissions who directs the applicant through the steps of the admissions process. Assistant Directors provide information on curriculum, policies, procedures, and services and assist the applicant in setting up necessary appointments and interviews. To qualify for admission, each applicant must provide documentation of graduation from an accredited high school or from a state-approved secondary education curriculum or provide official documentation of high school graduation equivalency. All transcripts become the property of the college. Admission to the college is based on the applicant meeting the stated requirements, a review of the applicant's previous educational records, and a review of the applicant's career interests. If previous academic records indicate the college's education and training programs would not benefit the applicant, the college reserves the right to advise the applicant not to enroll. Special requirements for enrollment into certain programs are discussed in the descriptions of those programs.

For the most recent information regarding admission requirements, prospective students should refer to the current academic catalog.

Application and Information

Applicants must complete and submit an application form, along with documentation of graduation from an accredited high school or state-approved secondary education curriculum or official documentation of high school graduation equivalency.

See BMCprograms.info for program duration, tuition, fees and other costs, median debt, federal salary data, alumni success, programmatic accreditation, and other important info.

Brown Mackie College is a system of over twenty-five schools located throughout North America. Programs, credential levels, technology, and scheduling options vary by school, and employment opportunities are not guaranteed. Financial aid is available for those who qualify. Administrative offices are located at 625 Eden Park Drive, Suite 1100; Cincinnati, Ohio 45202; phone: 513.830.2000. ©2013 Brown Mackie College. OH Registration # 03-09-1685T; # 03-09-1686T; # 03-09-1687T; # 03-09-1688T; # 06-03-1781T; AC0150, AC0109, AC0078, AC0045, AC0138, AC0110; Licensed by the Florida Commission for Independent Education, License No. 3206.

For additional information, prospective students should contact:

Director of Admissions
Brown Mackie College — Birmingham
105 Vulcan Road
Suite 100
Birmingham, Alabama 35209
United States
Phone: 205-909-1500
    888-299-4699 (toll free)
Fax: 205-909-1588
E-mail: bmbirmadm@brownmackie.edu
Website: http://www.brownmackie.edu/Birmingham

BROWN MACKIE COLLEGE — BOISE

BOISE, IDAHO

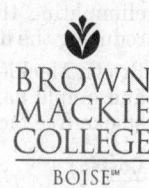

The College

Brown Mackie College — Boise (Brown Mackie College) is one of over twenty-five locations in the Brown Mackie College system of schools (www.brownmackie.edu), which is dedicated to providing educational programs that prepare students to pursue entry-level positions in a competitive, rapidly changing workplace. Brown Mackie College schools offer bachelor's degree, associate degree, diploma, and certificate programs in health sciences, business, information technology, legal studies, and design to over 20,000 students in the Midwest, Southeast, Southwest, and Western United States.

Brown Mackie College — Boise is accredited by the Accrediting Council for Independent Colleges and Schools to award bachelor's degrees, associate degrees, and diplomas. The Accrediting Council for Independent Colleges and Schools is listed as a nationally recognized accrediting agency by the United States Department of Education and is recognized by the Council for Higher Education Accreditation. ACICS can be contacted at 750 First Street NE, Suite 980, Washington, D.C. 20002; phone: 202-336-6780.

Brown Mackie College — Boise is registered with the State Board of Education in accordance with Section 33-2403, Idaho Code.

The occupational therapy assistant program is accredited by the Accreditation Council for Occupational Therapy Education (ACOTE) of the American Occupational Therapy Association (AOTA), located at 4720 Montgomery Lane, Suite 200, Bethesda, Maryland 20814-3449; phone: 301-652-AOTA. Graduates of the program will be eligible to sit for the national certification examination for the occupational therapy assistant administered by the National Board for Certification in Occupational Therapy (NBCOT). After successful completion of this exam, the individual will be a Certified Occupational Therapy Assistant (COTA). In addition, most states require licensure in order to practice; however, state licenses are usually based on the results of the NBCOT Certification Examination. Note that a felony conviction may affect a graduate's ability to sit for the NBCOT certification examination or attain state licensure.

The surgical technology program is accredited by the Accrediting Bureau of Health Education Schools, ABHES.

The veterinary technology program has provisional programmatic accreditation granted by the American Veterinary Medical Association (AVMA) through the Committee on Veterinary Technician Education and Activities (CVTEA).

Location

Brown Mackie College — Boise is conveniently located at 9050 West Overland Road in Boise, Idaho. The college has a generous parking area and is easily accessible by public transportation.

Programs of Study and Degree Offerings

Brown Mackie College — Boise provides higher education to traditional and nontraditional students through bachelor's degree, associate degree, and diploma programs that assist in enhancing their career opportunities, broadening their perspectives through appropriate general education courses, thinking independently and critically, and improving problem-solving abilities.

The Bachelor of Science degree is awarded in business administration, criminal justice, health care management, and legal studies.

The Associate of Science degree is awarded in accounting technology, architectural design and drafting technology, bioscience laboratory technology, business management, criminal justice, health care administration, information technology, paralegal, surgical technology, and veterinary technology.

The Associate of Applied Science degree is awarded in occupational therapy assistant.

Diploma programs are offered in accounting, business, criminal justice, medical assistant, and paralegal assistant.

The American Medical Technologists (AMT), which offers the certification for Registered Medical Assistant (RMA), accepts the accreditation of Brown Mackie College — Boise. Students will qualify to take the Registered Medical Assistant certification examination upon graduating the Brown Mackie College — Boise and medical assistant program. Graduates of the 48-credit-hour medical assistant program are not qualified to take the AMT/RMA exam.

Brown Mackie College does not guarantee third-party certification/licensing exams. Outside agencies control the requirements for certification/licensing and are subject to change without notification to the College.

Program availability and degree offerings are subject to change.

Academic Programs

Each college quarter comprises twelve weeks. Bachelor's degree programs require a minimum of sixteen quarters to complete. Associate degree programs require a minimum of eight quarters to complete. Programs are offered on a year-round basis, providing students with the opportunity to work uninterrupted toward completion of their programs. The college offers all programs in a unique One-Course-a-Month format. This allows students to focus studies on only one course for four weeks. This schedule has proven convenient for students with multiple obligations, such as jobs and family.

Academic Facilities

Opened in 2008, this modern facility offers more than 40,000 square feet of tastefully decorated classrooms, laboratories, and office space designed to specifications of the Brown Mackie College for its business, medical, and technical programs. Instructional equipment is comparable to current technology used in business and industry. Modern classrooms for special instructional needs offer multimedia capabilities with surround sound and overhead projectors accessible through computer or DVD. Internet access and instructional resources are available at the college's library. Experienced faculty members provide academic support and are committed to the academic and technical preparation of their students.

Brown Mackie College — Boise is fully committed to using eTextbooks and computer tablets in the classroom. Utilizing these tablets to access expanded course material, students are able to increase their acumen for using this technology and further enhance their educational experience. Students have the ability to directly download their eTextbooks to their tablet, eliminating the need to carry heavy, physical textbooks and reducing the overall cost of supplies.

The campus is nonresidential; public transportation and ample parking at no cost are available.

Costs

Tuition for programs in the 2012–13 academic year was $324 per credit hour, with a general fee of $20 per credit hour applied to instructional costs for activities and services. Tuition for the occupational therapy assistant courses was $381 per credit hour with a $20 per credit fee applied to instructional costs for activities and services. Tuition for the surgical technology courses was $360 per credit hour with a $20 per credit fee applied to instructional costs for activities and services. The cost of textbooks and other instructional materials varies by program.

Financial Aid

Financial aid is available for those who qualify. The college maintains a full-time staff of Student Financial Services Advisors to assist qualified students in obtaining financial assistance. The college participates in several student aid programs. Forms of financial aid available through federal resources include the Federal Pell Grant Program, Federal Supplemental Educational Opportunity Grant (FSEOG) Program, Federal Work-Study Program, Federal Perkins Loan Program, Federal Stafford Student Loan Program (subsidized and unsubsidized), and the Federal PLUS Loan Program.

Each year, the college makes available President's Scholarships of $1,000 each to qualifying seniors from area high schools. In order to qualify, a senior must be graduating from a participating high school, must be maintaining a cumulative grade point average of at least 2.0, and must submit a brief essay. The student's extracurricular activities and community service are also considered. The President's Scholarship is available only to students enrolling in one of the college's degree programs. Students awarded the scholarship must enroll at Brown Mackie College — Boise between June and September immediately following their high school graduation. Applications for these scholarships can be obtained from the guidance departments of participating high schools. These applications must be completed and returned to Brown Mackie College by March 31.

The Education Foundation was established in 2000 to offer scholarship support to students interested in continuing their education at one of the postsecondary, career-focused schools in the EDMC system. The number and amount of the awards can vary, depending on the funds available. Scholarship applications are considered every quarter. At Brown Mackie College, applicants must be currently enrolled in an associate or bachelor's degree program and in their fourth quarter or higher (but no further than their second-to-last quarter) at the time of application. Awards are made based on academic performance and potential, as well as financial need. Interested students should contact the college's Student Financial Service Department for additional information.

Faculty

There are 14 full-time and 34 part-time faculty members at the college. The average student-faculty ratio is 15:1. Each student is assigned a program department chair as an adviser.

Admission Requirements

Each applicant for admission is assigned an Assistant Director of Admissions who directs the applicant through the steps of the admissions process. Assistant Directors provide information on curriculum, policies, procedures, and services and assist the applicant in setting up necessary appointments and interviews. To qualify for admission, each applicant must provide documentation of graduation from an accredited high school or from a state-approved secondary education curriculum or provide official documentation of high school graduation equivalency. All transcripts become the property of the college.

As part of the admission process, students are given an assessment of academic skills. Although the results of this assessment do not determine eligibility for admission, they provide the college with a means of determining the need for academic support as well as a means by which the college can evaluate the effectiveness of its educational programs. All new students are required to complete this assessment, which is readministered at the end of the student's program, so results may be compared with those of the initial administration.

In addition to the college's general admission requirements, applicants enrolling in the occupational therapy assistant program must document one of the following: a high school cumulative grade point average of at least 2.5, a score on the GED examination of at least 57 (557 if taken on or after January 15, 2002), or completion of 12 quarter-credit hours or 8 semester-credit hours of collegiate course work with a grade point average of at least 2.5. Credit hours may not include Professional Development (CF 1100), the Brown Mackie College–Boise course. Students entering the program must also have completed a biology course with a grade of at least a C (or an average of at least 2.0 on a 4.0 scale).

For the most recent information regarding admission requirements, prospective students should refer to the current academic catalog.

Application and Information

Applicants must complete and submit an application form, along with documentation of graduation from an accredited high school or state-approved secondary education curriculum or official documentation of high school graduation equivalency.

See BMCprograms.info for program duration, tuition, fees and other costs, median debt, federal salary data, alumni success, programmatic accreditation, and other important info.

Brown Mackie College is a system of over twenty-five schools located throughout North America. Programs, credential levels, technology, and scheduling options vary by school, and employment opportunities are not guaranteed. Financial aid is available for those who qualify. Administrative offices are located at 625 Eden Park Drive, Suite 1100; Cincinnati, Ohio 45202; phone: 513-830-2000. ©2013 Brown Mackie College. OH Registration # 03-09-1685T; # 03-09-1686T; # 03-09-1687T; # 03-09- 1688T; # 06-03-1781T; AC0150, AC0109, AC0078, AC0045, AC0138, AC0110; Licensed by the Florida Commission for Independent Education, License No. 3206.

For additional information, prospective students should contact:

Director of Admissions
Brown Mackie College — Boise
9050 W. Overland Road, Suite 100
Boise, Idaho 83709
United States
Phone: 208-321-8800
    888-810-9286 (toll-free)
Fax: 208-375-3249
E-mail: bmcboiadm@brownmackie.edu
Website: http://www.brownmackie.edu/Boise

BROWN MACKIE COLLEGE — CINCINNATI
CINCINNATI, OHIO

The College

Brown Mackie College — Cincinnati (Brown Mackie College) is one of over twenty-five locations in the Brown Mackie College system of schools (www.brownmackie.edu), which is dedicated to providing educational programs that prepare students to pursue entry-level positions in a competitive, rapidly changing workplace. Brown Mackie College schools offer bachelor's degree, associate degree, diploma, and certificate programs in health sciences, business, information technology, legal studies, and design to more than 20,000 students in the Midwest, Southeast, Southwest, and Western United States.

Brown Mackie College — Cincinnati was founded in February 1927 as Southern Ohio Business College. In 1978, the college's main location was relocated from downtown Cincinnati to the Bond Hill–Roselawn area and in 1995 to its current location at 1011 Glendale-Milford Road in the community of Woodlawn.

Brown Mackie College — Cincinnati is accredited by the Accrediting Council for Independent Colleges and Schools to award bachelor's degrees, associate degrees, diplomas, and certificates. The Accrediting Council for Independent Colleges and Schools is listed as a nationally recognized accrediting agency by the United States Department of Education and is recognized by the Council for Higher Education Accreditation. ACICS can be contacted at 750 First Street NE, Suite 980, Washington, D.C. 20002; phone: 202-336-6780.

The Brown Mackie College — Cincinnati Associate of Applied Science degree in surgical technology is accredited by the Commission on Accreditation of Allied Health Education Programs (www.caahep.org), upon the recommendation of the Accreditation Review Committee on Education in Surgical Technology. The Commission on Accreditation of Allied Health Education Programs is located at 1361 Park Street, Clearwater, Florida 33756; phone: 727-210-2350.

The veterinary technology program has provisional programmatic accreditation granted by the American Veterinary Medical Association (AVMA) through the Committee on Veterinary Technician Education and Activities (CVTEA).

The practical nursing diploma program complies with the Ohio Board of Nursing guidelines as set forth in the Ohio Administrative Code, Chapter 4723-5. The program is administered at the following locations: Brown Mackie College — Cincinnati, Brown Mackie College — Findlay, Brown Mackie College — Akron, and Brown Mackie College — North Canton, and all operate under the same approval. The Ohio Board of Nursing is located at 17 South High Street, Suite 400, Columbus, Ohio 43215-3413; phone: 614-466-3947.

The Associate of Applied Science in medical assisting program is accredited by the Commission on Accreditation of Allied Health Education Programs (www.caahep.org) upon the recommendation of the Curriculum Review Board of the Medical Assisting Education Review Board (MAERB). The Commission on Accreditation of Allied Health Education Programs is located at 1361 Park Street Clearwater, Florida 33756; phone: 727-210-2350.

Brown Mackie College — Cincinnati is licensed by the Ohio State Board of Career Colleges and Schools, 30 East Broad Street, 24th Floor, Suite 2481, Columbus, Ohio 43215-3138; phone: 614-466-2752. Ohio registration #03-09-1686T.

Brown Mackie College — Cincinnati is regulated by the Board for Proprietary Education Indiana Commission for Higher Education, 101 West Ohio Street, Suite 670, Indianapolis, Indiana 46204; phone: 317-464-4400. Indiana advertising code: AC0150.

Location

Brown Mackie College — Cincinnati is located in the Woodlawn section of Cincinnati, Ohio. The college is accessible by public transportation and provides parking at no cost.

Programs of Study and Degree Offerings

Brown Mackie College — Cincinnati provides higher education to traditional and nontraditional students through bachelor's degrees, associate degrees, diploma, and certificate programs that can assist them in enhancing their career opportunities, broadening their perspectives through appropriate general education courses, thinking independently and critically, and improving problem-solving abilities. The College strives to develop within its students the desire for lifelong and continued education.

The Bachelor of Science degree is awarded in business administration, criminal justice, health care management, and legal studies.

The Associate of Applied Business degree is awarded in accounting technology, business management, computer networking and applications, criminal justice, information technology, and paralegal.

The Associate of Applied Science degree is awarded in architectural design and drafting technology, audio/video production, biomedical equipment technology, early childhood education, health care administration, pharmacy technology, surgical technology, and veterinary technology.

Diploma programs are offered in audio/video technician, bookkeeping specialist, criminal justice specialist, general business, medical assistant, paralegal assistant, and practical nursing.

The College offers a certificate program in computer networking.

The American Medical Technologists (AMT), which offers the certification for Registered Medical Assistant (RMA), accepts the accreditation of Brown Mackie College — Cincinnati. Students will qualify to take the Registered Medical Assistant certification examination upon graduating the Brown Mackie College—Cincinnati medical assistant program. Graduates of the 48-credit-hour medical assistant program are not qualified to take the AMT/RMA exam.

Brown Mackie College does not guarantee third-party certification/licensing exams. Outside agencies control the requirements for certification/licensing and are subject to change without notification to the College.

Program availability and degree offerings are subject to change.

Academic Programs

Each college quarter comprises twelve weeks. Bachelor's degree programs require a minimum of sixteen quarters to complete. Associate degree programs require a minimum of eight quarters to complete. Programs are offered on a year-round basis, providing students with the ability to work uninterrupted toward their degrees. The College offers all programs in a unique One-Course-a-Month format. This schedule allows students to focus studies on only one course for four weeks and has proven convenient for students with multiple obligations, such as jobs and family.

Academic Facilities

Brown Mackie College — Cincinnati consists of more than 57,000 square feet of classroom, laboratory, and office space at the main campus and more than 28,000 square feet at the learning site. Both sites are designed to specifications of Brown Mackie College for its business, computer, medical, and creative programs.

Brown Mackie College — Cincinnati is fully committed to using eTextbooks and computer tablets in the classroom. Utilizing these tablets to access expanded course material, students are able to increase their acumen for using this technology and further enhance their educational experience. Students have the ability to directly download their eTextbooks to their tablet, eliminating the need to carry heavy, physical textbooks and reducing the overall cost of supplies.

Costs

Tuition for the 2012–13 academic year was $314 per credit hour and $20 per credit hour for general fees. Tuition for the practical nursing program was $381 per credit hour and $30 per credit hour for general fees. Tuition for the surgical technology program was $360 per credit hour and $20 per credit hour for general fees. Tuition for the computer networking and computer networking and applications program was $314 per credit hour and $25 per credit hour for general fees. The cost of textbooks, if applicable, and other instructional materials varies by program.

Financial Aid

Financial aid is available to those who qualify. Brown Mackie College maintains a full-time staff of Student Financial Services Advisers to assist qualified students in obtaining financial assistance. The college participates in several student aid programs. Forms of financial aid available to qualified students through federal resources include the Federal Pell Grant Program, Federal Supplemental Educational Opportunity Grant (FSEOG) Program, Federal Work-Study Program, Federal Perkins Loan Program, Federal Stafford Student Loan Program (subsidized and unsubsidized), and the Federal PLUS Loan Program. Eligible students may apply for state awards, such as veterans' educational benefits. Students with physical or mental disabilities that are a handicap to employment may be eligible for training services through the state Agency for Vocational Rehabilitation. For further information, students should contact the Student Financial Services Office.

Each year, the college makes available President's Scholarships of $1,000 each to qualifying seniors from area high schools. In order to qualify, a senior must be graduating from a participating high school, must have maintained a cumulative grade point average of at least 2.0, and must have submitted a brief essay. The student's extracurricular activities and community service are also considered. The President's Scholarship is available only to students enrolling in one of the college's degree programs. Students awarded the scholarship must enroll at Brown Mackie College — Cincinnati between June and September immediately following their high school graduation. Applications for these scholarships can be obtained from the guidance departments of participating high schools. These applications must be completed and returned to Brown Mackie College by March 31.

The Education Foundation was established in 2000 to offer scholarship support to students interested in continuing their education at one of the postsecondary, career-focused schools in the EDMC system. The number and amount of the awards can vary, depending on the funds available. Scholarship applications are considered every quarter. At Brown Mackie College — Cincinnati, applicants must be currently enrolled in an associate degree program and in their fourth quarter or higher (but no further than their second-to-last quarter) at the time of application. Awards are made based on academic performance and potential, as well as financial need. Interested students should contact the college's Student Financial Services department for additional information.

Faculty

There are 20 full-time and 90 part-time faculty members. The average student-faculty ratio is 20:1. Each student has a faculty and student adviser.

Admission Requirements

Each applicant for admission is assigned an Assistant Director of Admissions, who directs the applicant through the steps of the admissions process, providing information on curriculum, policies, procedures, and services and assisting the applicant in setting up necessary appointments and interviews.

To qualify for admission, each applicant must provide documentation of graduation from an accredited high school or from a state-approved secondary education curriculum or provide official documentation of high school graduation equivalency. All transcripts become the property of the college. Admission to the college is based on the applicant meeting the stated requirements, a review of the applicant's previous educational records, and a review of the applicant's career interests. If previous academic records indicate that the college's education and training programs would not benefit the applicant, the college reserves the right to advise the applicant not to enroll. Special requirements for enrollment into certain programs are discussed in the descriptions of those programs.

For the most recent information regarding admission requirements, please refer to the current academic catalog.

Application and Information

Applicants must complete and submit an application form, along with documentation of graduation from an accredited high school or state-approved secondary education curriculum or official documentation of high school graduation equivalency.

See BMCprograms.info for program duration, tuition, fees and other costs, median debt, federal salary data, alumni success, programmatic accreditation, and other important info.

Brown Mackie College is a system of over twenty-five schools located throughout North America. Programs, credential levels, technology, and scheduling options vary by school, and employment opportunities are not guaranteed. Financial aid is available for those who qualify. Administrative offices are located at 625 Eden Park Drive, Suite 1100; Cincinnati, Ohio 45202; phone: 513-830-2000. ©2013 Brown Mackie College. OH Registration # 03-09-1685T; # 03-09-1686T; # 03-09-1687T; # 03-09- 1688T; # 06-03-1781T; AC0150, AC0109, AC0078, AC0045, AC0138, AC0110; Licensed by the Florida Commission for Independent Education, License No. 3206.

For additional information, prospective students should contact:

Senior Director of Admissions
Brown Mackie College — Cincinnati
1011 Glendale-Milford Road
Cincinnati, Ohio 45215
United States
Phone: 513-771-2424
       800-888-1445 (toll-free)
Fax: 513-771-3413
E-mail: bmcciadm@brownmackie.edu
Website: http://www.brownmackie.edu/Cincinnati

BROWN MACKIE COLLEGE — DALLAS/FORT WORTH
BEDFORD, TEXAS

BROWN
MACKIE
COLLEGE
DALLAS
FT. WORTH℠

The College

Brown Mackie College — Dallas/Fort Worth (Brown Mackie College) is one of over twenty-five locations in the Brown Mackie College system of schools (www.brownmackie.edu), which is dedicated to providing educational programs that prepare students to pursue entry-level positions in a competitive, rapidly changing workplace. Brown Mackie College schools offer bachelor's degree, associate degree, diploma, and certificate programs in health sciences, business, information technology, legal studies, and design to more than 20,000 students in the Midwest, Southeast, Southwest, and Western United States.

Brown Mackie College — Dallas/Fort Worth is accredited by the Accrediting Council for Independent Colleges and Schools to award bachelor's degrees, associate degrees, and diplomas. The Accrediting Council for Independent Colleges and Schools is listed as a nationally recognized accrediting agency by the United States Department of Education and is recognized by the Council for Higher Education Accreditation. ACICS can be contacted at 750 First Street NE, Suite 980, Washington, D.C. 20002; phone: 202-336-6780.

Brown Mackie College — Dallas/Fort Worth is approved and regulated by the Texas Workforce Commission, Career Schools and Colleges, Austin, Texas.

Brown Mackie College — Dallas/Fort Worth holds a Certificate of Authorization acknowledging exemption from the Texas Higher Education Coordinating Board Regulations.

Location

Brown Mackie College — Dallas/Fort Worth is conveniently located at 2200 North Highway 121, Suite 250, Bedford, Texas 76021. A spacious parking lot provides ample parking at no additional charge.

Programs of Study and Degree Offerings

Brown Mackie College — Dallas/Fort Worth provides higher education to traditional and nontraditional students through bachelor's degree, associate degree, and diploma programs that assist them in enhancing their career opportunities, broadening their perspectives through appropriate general education courses, thinking independently and critically, and improving problem-solving abilities. The college strives to develop within its students the desire for lifelong and continued education.

The Bachelor of Science degree is awarded in accounting, business administration, criminal justice, health care management, and information technology.

The Associate of Science degree is awarded in accounting technology, architectural design and drafting technology, biomedical equipment technology, business management, computer networking, graphic design, health care administration, information technology, and surgical technology.

Brown Mackie College offers a medical assistant diploma program.

The American Medical Technologists (AMT), which offers the certification for Registered Medical Assistant (RMA), accepts the accreditation of Brown Mackie College — Dallas/Fort Worth. Students will qualify to take the Registered Medical Assistant certification examination upon graduating the Brown Mackie College — Dallas/Fort Worth medical assistant program. Graduates of the 48-credit-hour medical assistant program are not qualified to take the AMT/RMA exam.

Brown Mackie College does not guarantee third-party certification/licensing exams. Outside agencies control the requirements for certification/licensing and are subject to change without notification to the College.

Program availability and degree offerings are subject to change.

Academic Programs

Each college quarter comprises twelve weeks. Bachelor's degree programs require a minimum of fifteen quarters to complete. Diplomat programs require a minimum of five quarters to complete. Associate degree programs require a minimum of eight quarters to complete. Programs are offered on a year-round basis, providing students with the ability to work uninterrupted toward their degrees. The college offers all programs in a unique One-Course-a-Month format. This allows students to focus studies on only one course for four weeks. This schedule has proven convenient for students with multiple obligations, such as jobs and family.

Academic Facilities

Brown Mackie College — Dallas/Fort Worth offers media presentation rooms for special instructional needs and a library that provides instructional resources and academic support for both faculty members and students.

Brown Mackie College — Dallas/Fort Worth is fully committed to using eTextbooks and computer tablets in the classroom. Utilizing these tablets to access expanded course material, students are able to increase their acumen for using this technology and further enhance their educational experience. Students have the ability to directly download their eTextbooks to their tablet, eliminating the need to carry heavy, physical textbooks and reducing the overall cost of supplies

Brown Mackie College — Dallas/Fort Worth is nonresidential; ample parking is available at no cost. The campus is a smoke-free facility.

Costs

Tuition for the 2012–13 academic year was $324 per credit hour and general fees were $20 per credit hour, with some exceptions. The surgical technology tuition was $371 per credit hour and general fees were $20 per credit hour. The cost of textbooks, if applicable, and other instructional materials varies by program.

Financial Aid

Financial aid is available to those who qualify. The college maintains a full-time staff of Student Financial Services Advisors to assist qualified students in obtaining financial assistance. The college participates in several student aid programs. Forms of financial aid available through federal resources include Federal Pell Grants, Federal Supplemental Educational Opportunity Grants (FSEOG), Federal Work-Study Program awards, Federal Perkins Loans, Federal Stafford Student Loans (subsidized and unsubsidized), and Federal PLUS loans. Eligible students may apply for veterans' educational benefits. Students with physical or mental disabilities that are a handicap to employment may be eligible for training services through the state Vocational Rehabilitation Agency. For further information, students should contact the college Student Financial Services Office.

Each year, the college makes available President's Scholarships of $1,000 each to qualifying seniors from area high schools. In order to qualify, a senior must have graduated from a participating high school, must have maintained a cumulative grade point average of at least 2.0, and must have submitted a brief essay. The student's extracurricular activities and community service are also considered. The President's Scholarship is available only to students enrolling in one of the college's degree programs. Students who receive the scholarship must enroll at Brown Mackie College — Dallas/Fort Worth between June and September immediately following their high school graduation. Applications for these scholarships can be obtained from the guidance departments of participating high schools. These applications must be completed and returned to Brown Mackie College by March 31.

The Education Foundation was established in 2000 to offer scholarship support to students interested in continuing their education at one of the postsecondary, career-focused schools in the EDMC system. The number and amount of the awards can vary, depending on the funds available. Scholarship applications are considered every quarter. At Brown Mackie College applicants must be currently enrolled in an associate or bachelor's degree program and in their fourth quarter or higher (but no further than their second-to-last quarter) at the time of application. Awards are made based on academic performance and potential, as well as financial need. Interested students should contact the college's Student Financial Service Department for additional information.

Faculty

Classes at Brown Mackie College — Dallas/Fort Worth began July 2, 2012. There are 3 full-time and 14 part-time adjunct instructors at the college. The average student-faculty ratio is 14:1. Each student is able to meet and speak with the Director of their program.

Admission Requirements

Each applicant for admission is assigned an Assistant Director of Admissions, who directs the applicant through the steps of the admissions process, providing information on curriculum, policies, procedures, and services and assisting the applicant in setting up necessary appointments and interviews. To qualify for admission, each applicant must provide documentation of graduation from an accredited high school or from a state-approved secondary education curriculum or provide official documentation of high school graduation equivalency. All transcripts become the property of the college. Admission to the college is based upon the applicant meeting the stated requirements, a review of the applicant's previous education records, and a review of the applicant's career interests. If previous academic records indicate the college's education and training programs would not benefit the applicant, the college reserves the right to advise the applicant not to enroll. Special requirements for enrollment into certain programs are discussed in the descriptions of those programs.

For the most recent information regarding admission requirements, prospective students should refer to the current academic catalog.

Application and Information

Applicants must complete and submit an application form, along with documentation of graduation from an accredited high school or state-approved secondary education curriculum or official documentation of high school graduation equivalency.

See BMCprograms.info for program duration, tuition, fees and other costs, median debt, federal salary data, alumni success, programmatic accreditation, and other important info.

Brown Mackie College is a system of over twenty-five schools located throughout North America. Programs, credential levels, technology, and scheduling options vary by school, and employment opportunities are not guaranteed. Financial aid is available for those who qualify. Administrative offices are located at 625 Eden Park Drive, Suite 1100; Cincinnati, Ohio 45202; phone: 513.830.2000. ©2013 Brown Mackie College. OH Registration # 03-09-1685T; # 03-09-1686T; # 03-09-1687T; # 03-09- 1688T; # 06-03-1781T; AC0150, AC0109, AC0078, AC0045, AC0138, AC0110; Licensed by the Florida Commission for Independent Education, License No. 3206.

For additional information, prospective students should contact:
Director of Admissions
Brown Mackie College — Dallas/Fort Worth
2200 North Highway 121, Suite 250
Bedford, Texas 76021
United States
Phone: 817-799-0500
888-299-4799 (toll-free)
Fax: 817-7990515
E-mail: bmcdaladm@brownmackie.edu
Website: http://www.brownmackie.edu/Dallas

BROWN MACKIE COLLEGE — FINDLAY
FINDLAY, OHIO

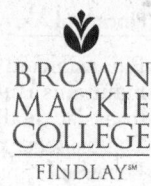

BROWN
MACKIE
COLLEGE
FINDLAY℠

The College

Brown Mackie — Findlay (Brown Mackie College) is one of over twenty-five locations in the Brown Mackie College system of schools (www.brownmackie.edu), which is dedicated to providing educational programs that prepare students to pursue entry-level positions in a competitive, rapidly changing workplace. Brown Mackie College schools offer bachelor's degree, associate degree, diploma, and certificate programs in health sciences, business, information technology, legal studies, and design to more than 20,000 students in the Midwest, Southeast, Southwest, and Western United States.

Brown Mackie College — Findlay was founded in 1926 by William H. Stautzenberger to provide solid business education at a reasonable cost. In 1960, the College was acquired by George R. Hawes, who served as its president until 1969. The college changed its name from Southern Ohio College–Findlay in 2001 to AEC Southern Ohio College; it was changed again to Brown Mackie College — Findlay in November 2004.

Brown Mackie College — Findlay is accredited by the Accrediting Council for Independent Colleges and Schools to award bachelor's degrees, associate degrees, and diplomas. The Accrediting Council for Independent Colleges and Schools is listed as a nationally recognized accrediting agency by the United States Department of Education and is recognized by the Council for Higher Education Accreditation. ACICS can be contacted at 750 First Street NE, Suite 980, Washington, D.C. 20002; phone: 202-336-6780.

The occupational therapy assistant program is accredited by the Accreditation Council for Occupational Therapy Education (ACOTE) of the American Occupational Therapy Association (AOTA), located at 4720 Montgomery Lane, Suite 200, Bethesda, Maryland 20814-3449; phone: 301-652-AOTA. Graduates of the program will be eligible to sit for the national certification examination for the occupational therapy assistant administered by the National Board for Certification in Occupational Therapy (NBCOT). After successful completion of this exam, the individual will be a Certified Occupational Therapy Assistant (COTA). In addition, most states require licensure in order to practice; however, state licenses are usually based on the results of the NBCOT Certification Examination. Note that a felony conviction may affect a graduate's ability to sit for the NBCOT certification examination or attain state licensure.

The Associate of Science in surgical technology program is accredited by the Commission on Accreditation of Allied Health Education Programs (www.caahep.org) upon the recommendation of the Accreditation Review Committee on Education in Surgical Technology.

The Associate of Applied Science in veterinary technology program has provisional programmatic accreditation granted by the American Veterinary Medical Association (AVMA) through the Committee on Veterinary Technician Education and Activities (CVTEA).

Brown Mackie College — Findlay is licensed by the Ohio State Board of Career Colleges and Schools, 30 East Broad Street, 24th Floor, Suite 2481, Columbus, Ohio 43215-3138; phone: 614-466-2752. Ohio registration # 03-09-1687T.

Location

Located at 1700 Fostoria Avenue, Suite 100, in Findlay, Ohio, the college is easily accessible from Interstate 75.

Programs of Study and Degree Offerings

Brown Mackie College — Findlay provides higher education to traditional and nontraditional students through bachelor's degree, associate degree, and diploma programs that can assist them in enhancing their career opportunities, broadening their perspectives through appropriate general education courses, thinking independently and critically, and improving problem-solving abilities. The college strives to develop within its students the desire for lifelong and continued education.

The Bachelor of Science degree is awarded in business administration, criminal justice, and health care management.

The Associate of Applied Business degree is awarded in business management, criminal justice, and paralegal.

The Associate of Applied Science degree is awarded in occupational therapy assistant, pharmacy technology, surgical technology, and veterinary technology.

In addition to the bachelor's and associate degree programs, the college offers diploma programs in criminal justice specialist, dental assistant, general business, medical assistant, paralegal assistant, and practical nursing.

The American Medical Technologists (AMT), which offers the certification for Registered Medical Assistant (RMA), accepts the accreditation of Brown Mackie College — Findlay. Students will qualify to take the Registered Medical Assistant certification examination upon graduating the Brown Mackie College — Findlay medical assistant program. Graduates of the 48-credit-hour medical assistant program are not qualified to take the AMT/RMA exam.

Brown Mackie College does not guarantee third-party certification/licensing exams. Outside agencies control the requirements for certification/licensing and are subject to change without notification to the college.

Program availability and degree offerings are subject to change.

Academic Programs

Each college quarter comprises twelve weeks. Bachelor's degree programs require a minimum of sixteen quarters to complete. Associate degree programs require a minimum of eight quarters to complete. Programs are offered on a year-round basis, providing students with the ability to work uninterrupted toward completion of their programs. The college offers all programs in a unique One-Course-a-Month format. This schedule allows students to focus studies on only one course for four weeks and has proven convenient for students with multiple obligations, such as jobs and family.

Academic Facilities

Brown Mackie College — Findlay is a nonresidential, smoke-free institution. Although the College does not offer residential housing, students who are unable to commute daily from their homes may request assistance from the Admissions Office in locating housing. Ample parking is available at no additional cost.

Brown Mackie College — Findlay is fully committed to using eTextbooks and computer tablets in the classroom. Utilizing these tablets to access expanded course material, students are able to increase their acumen for using this technology and further enhance their educational experience. Students have the ability to directly download their eTextbooks to their tablet, eliminating the need to carry heavy, physical textbooks and reducing the overall cost of supplies.

Costs

Tuition for programs in the 2012–13 academic year was $314 per credit hour, with a general fee of $20 per credit hour. Tuition for the practical nursing diploma program was $381 per credit hour, with a general fee of $30 per credit hour. Tuition for the occupational therapy assistant program was $381 per credit hour, with a general fee of $20 per credit hour. Tuition for the surgical technology program was $360 per credit hour, with a general fee of $20 per credit hour. The length of the program determines total cost. The cost of textbooks, if applicable, and other instructional materials varies by program.

Financial Aid

Financial aid is available to those who qualify. The college maintains a full-time staff of Student Financial Services Advisors to assist qualified students in obtaining financial assistance. The college participates in several student aid programs. Forms of financial aid available through federal resources include the Federal DIRECT Pell Grant Program, Federal Supplemental Educational Opportunity Grant (FSEOG) Program, Federal Work-Study Program, Federal DIRECT Stafford Student Loan Program (subsidized and unsubsidized), the Federal DIRECT PLUS Loan Program, the Ohio College Opportunity Grant (OHCOG), and the Smart Grant. Eligible students may apply for state awards, such as the veterans' educational benefits. Students with physical or mental disabilities that are a handicap to employment may be eligible for training services through the state Agency for Vocational Rehabilitation. For further information, students should contact the college's Student Financial Services Office.

Each year, the college makes available President's Scholarships of $1,000 each to qualifying seniors from area high schools. In order to qualify, a senior must be graduating from a participating high school, must have maintained a cumulative grade point average of at least 2.0, and must have submitted a brief essay. The student's extracurricular activities and community service are also considered. The President's Scholarship is available only to students enrolling in one of the college's degree programs. Students awarded the scholarship must enroll at Brown Mackie College — Findlay between June and September immediately following their high school graduation. Applications for these scholarships can be obtained from the guidance departments of participating high schools. These applications must be completed and returned to Brown Mackie College by March 31.

The Education Foundation was established in 2000 to offer scholarship support to students interested in continuing their education at one of the postsecondary, career-focused schools in the EDMC system. The number and amount of the awards can vary, depending on the funds available. Scholarship applications are considered every quarter. At Brown Mackie College, applicants must be currently enrolled in an associate or bachelor's degree program and in their fourth quarter or higher (but no further than their second-to-last quarter) at the time of application. Awards are made based on academic performance and potential, as well as financial need. Interested students should contact the college's Student Financial Service Department for additional information.

Faculty

There are 27 full-time and 90 part-time adjunct instructors at the college. The average student-faculty ratio is 14:1. Each student is assigned a faculty adviser.

Admission Requirements

Each applicant for admission is assigned an Assistant Director of Admissions, who directs the applicant through the steps of the admissions process, providing information on curriculum, policies, procedures, and services and assisting the applicant in setting up necessary appointments and interviews.

To qualify for admission, each applicant must provide documentation of graduation from an accredited high school or from a state-approved secondary education curriculum or provide official documentation of high school graduation equivalency. All transcripts become the property of the college. Admission to the college is based upon the applicant meeting the stated requirements, a review of the applicant's previous educational records, and a review of the applicant's career interests. If previous academic records indicate that the college's education and training programs would not benefit the applicant, the college reserves the right to advise the applicant not to enroll. Special requirements for enrollment into certain programs are discussed in the descriptions of those programs.

For the most recent information regarding admission requirements, please refer to the current academic catalog.

Application and Information

Applicants must complete and submit an application form, along with documentation of graduation from an accredited high school or state-approved secondary education curriculum or official documentation of high school graduation equivalency.

See BMCprograms.info for program duration, tuition, fees and other costs, median debt, federal salary data, alumni success, programmatic accreditation, and other important info.

Brown Mackie College is a system of over twenty-five schools located throughout North America. Programs, credential levels, technology, and scheduling options vary by school, and employment opportunities are not guaranteed. Financial aid is available for those who qualify. Administrative offices are located at 625 Eden Park Drive, Suite 1100; Cincinnati, Ohio 45202; phone: 513.830.2000. ©2013 Brown Mackie College. OH Registration # 03-09-1685T; # 03-09-1686T; # 03-09-1687T; # 03-09- 1688T; # 06-03-1781T; AC0150, AC0109, AC0078, AC0045, AC0138, AC0110; Licensed by the Florida Commission for Independent Education, License No. 3206.

For additional information, prospective students should contact:

Director of Admissions
Brown Mackie College — Findlay
1700 Fostoria Avenue, Suite 100
Findlay, Ohio 45840
United States
Phone: 419-423-2211
800-842-3687 (toll-free)
Fax: 419-423-0725
E-mail: bmcfiadm@brownmackie.edu
Website: http://www.brownmackie.edu/Findlay

BROWN MACKIE COLLEGE — FORT WAYNE

FORT WAYNE, INDIANA

The College

Brown Mackie College — Fort Wayne (Brown Mackie College) is one of over twenty-five locations in the Brown Mackie College system of schools (www.brownmackie.edu), which is dedicated to providing educational programs that prepare students to pursue entry-level positions in a competitive, rapidly changing workplace. Brown Mackie College schools offer bachelor's degree, associate degree, diploma, and certificate programs in health sciences, business, information technology, legal studies, and design to over 20,000 students in the Midwest, Southeast, Southwest, and Western United States.

Brown Mackie College — Fort Wayne is one of the oldest institutions of its kind in the country and the oldest in the state of Indiana. Established in 1882 as the South Bend Commercial College, the school later changed its name to Michiana College. In 1930, the college was incorporated under the laws of the state of Indiana and was authorized to confer associate degrees and certificates in business. In 1992, the College in South Bend added a branch location in Fort Wayne, Indiana. In 2004, Michiana College changed its name to Brown Mackie College — Fort Wayne.

Brown Mackie College — Fort Wayne is accredited by the Accrediting Council for Independent Colleges and Schools to award bachelor's degrees, associate degrees, diplomas, and certificates. The Accrediting Council for Independent Colleges and Schools is listed as a nationally recognized accrediting agency by the United States Department of Education and is recognized by the Council for Higher Education Accreditation. ACICS can be contacted at 750 First Street NE, Suite 980, Washington, D.C. 20002; phone: 202-336-6780.

The Associate of Science in surgical technology program is accredited by the Accrediting Bureau of Health Education Schools and by the Commission on Accreditation of Allied Health Education Programs (www.caahep.org) upon the recommendation of the Accreditation Review Council on Education in Surgical Technology and Surgical Assisting (ARC/STSA). The Commission on Accreditation of Allied Health Education Programs is located at 1361 Park Street, Clearwater, Florida 33756; phone: 727-210-2350; www.caahep.org.

The Associate of Applied Science in occupational therapy assistant program is accredited by the Accreditation Council for Occupational Therapy Education (ACOTE) of the American Occupational Therapy Association (AOTA), located at 4720 Montgomery Lane, Suite 200, Bethesda, Maryland 20814-3449; phone: 301-652-AOTA. Graduates of the program will be eligible to sit for the national certification examination for the occupational therapy assistant administered by the National Board for Certification in Occupational Therapy (NBCOT). After successful completion of this exam, the individual will be a Certified Occupational Therapy Assistant (COTA). In addition, most states require licensure in order to practice; however, state licenses are usually based on the results of the NBCOT Certification Examination. Note that a felony conviction may affect a graduate's ability to sit for the NBCOT certification examination or attain state licensure.

The Associate of Applied Science in physical therapist assistant program at Brown Mackie College — Fort Wayne is accredited by the Commission on Accreditation in Physical Therapy Education (CAPTE), located at 1111 North Fairfax Street, Alexandria, Virginia 22314; phone: 703-706-3245; e-mail: accreditation@apta.org; www.capteonline.org.

The Associate of Applied Science in veterinary technology program has provisional programmatic accreditation granted by the American Veterinary Medical Association (AVMA) through the Committee on Veterinary Technician Education and Activities (CVTEA).

Brown Mackie College — Fort Wayne is regulated by the Board for Proprietary Education Indiana Commission for Higher Education, 101 West Ohio Street, Suite 670, Indianapolis, Indiana 46204; phone: 317-464-4400. Indiana advertising code: AC-0109.

Location

Brown Mackie College — Fort Wayne is located at 3000 East Coliseum Boulevard in Fort Wayne, Indiana. The college facility is accessible by public transportation. Ample parking is provided at no additional charge. For added convenience, the College also operates a learning site at 2135 South Hannah Drive in Fort Wayne.

Programs of Study and Degree Offerings

Brown Mackie College — Fort Wayne provides higher education to traditional and nontraditional students through bachelor's degree, associate degree, and certificate programs that assist them in enhancing their career opportunities, broadening their perspectives through appropriate general education courses, thinking independently and critically, and improving problem-solving abilities. The college strives to develop within its students the desire for lifelong and continued education.

The Bachelor of Science degree is awarded in business administration, criminal justice, and health care management.

The Associate of Science degree is awarded in accounting technology, business management, criminal justice, health care administration, office management, paralegal, and surgical technology.

The Associate of Applied Science degree is awarded in biomedical equipment technology, health and fitness training, nursing, occupational therapy assistant, physical therapist assistant, and veterinary technology.

Brown Mackie College — Fort Wayne offers certificate programs in bookkeeping specialist, criminal justice, fitness trainer, general business, medical assistant, and paralegal assistant.

The American Medical Technologists (AMT), which offers the certification for Registered Medical Assistant (RMA), accepts the accreditation of Brown Mackie College — Fort Wayne. Students will qualify to take the Registered Medical Assistant certification examination upon graduating the Brown Mackie College — Fort Wayne medical assistant programs. Graduates of the 48-credit-hour medical assistant program are not qualified to take the AMT/RMA exam.

Brown Mackie College does not guarantee third-party certification/licensing exams. Outside agencies control the requirements for certification/licensing and are subject to change without notification to the college.

Program availability and degree offerings are subject to change.

Academic Programs

Each college quarter comprises twelve weeks. Bachelor's degree programs require a minimum of sixteen quarters to complete. Associate degree programs require a minimum of eight quarters to complete. Programs are offered on a year-round basis, providing students with the ability to work uninterrupted toward their degrees. The college offers all programs in a unique One-Course-a-Month format. This allows students to focus studies on only one course for four weeks. This schedule has proven convenient for students with multiple obligations, such as jobs and family.

Academic Facilities

In 2005, the campus relocated to a 75,000-square-foot facility at 3000 East Coliseum Boulevard. Record enrollment allowed the institution to triple in size in less than one year. The three-story building offers a modern, professional environment for study. Ten classrooms are outfitted as "classrooms of the future," with an instructor workstation, full multimedia capabilities, a surround sound system, and projection screen that can be accessed by computer, DVD, or VHS equipment. The Brown Mackie College — Fort Wayne facility includes a criminal justice lab, surgical technology labs, medical labs, computer labs, and occupational and physical therapy labs, as well as a library and bookstore. The labs provide students with hands-on opportunities to apply knowledge and skills learned in the classroom. Students are welcome to use the labs when those facilities are not in use for scheduled classes.

Brown Mackie College — Fort Wayne is fully committed to using eTextbooks and computer tablets in the classroom. Utilizing these tablets to access expanded course material, students are able to increase their acumen for using this technology and further enhance their educational experience. Students have the ability to directly download their eTextbooks to their tablet, eliminating the need to carry heavy, physical textbooks and reducing the overall cost of supplies.

The college is nonresidential; public transportation and ample parking at no cost are available. The campus is a smoke-free facility.

Costs

Tuition in the 2012–13 academic year was $314 per credit hour with fees of $20 per credit hour for all programs except nursing, surgical technology, personal fitness training, occupational therapy assistant studies, and physical therapist assistant studies. Costs for textbooks, if applicable, and other instructional materials vary by program. For the nursing program, tuition was $410 per credit hour; fees were $30 per credit hour. For the surgical technology program, tuition was $360 per credit hour; fees were $20. Tuition for the personal fitness training programs was $324 per credit hour; fees were $30 per credit hour. Textbook expenses are estimated at $400 for the first term, $600 for the second term, and $100 for the third, fourth, and fifth terms. For certain courses in the occupational therapy assistant studies and physical therapist assistant studies programs, tuition was $381 per credit hour; fees were $20 per credit hour.

Financial Aid

The college maintains a full-time staff of Student Financial Services Advisors to assist qualified students in obtaining financial assistance. The college participates in several student aid programs. Forms of financial aid available through federal resources include the Federal Pell Grant Program, Federal Supplemental Educational Opportunity Grant (FSEOG) Program, Federal Work-Study Program, Federal Perkins Loan Program, Federal Stafford Student Loan Program (subsidized and unsubsidized), and the Federal PLUS Loan Program. Eligible students may apply for Indiana state awards, such as the Frank O'Bannon Grant Program (formerly the Indiana State Grant Program), the Higher Education Award, and Twenty-First Century Scholarships for high school students; for the Core 40 awards; and for veterans' educational benefits. For further information, students should contact the Student Financial Services Office.

Each year, the college makes available President's Scholarships of $1,000 each to qualifying seniors from area high schools. In order to qualify, a senior must have graduated from a participating high school, must have maintained a cumulative grade point average of at least 2.0, and must have submitted a brief essay. The student's extracurricular activities and community service are also considered. The President's Scholarship is available only to students enrolling in one of the college's degree programs. Students awarded the scholarship must enroll at Brown Mackie College — Fort Wayne between June and September immediately following their high school graduation. Applications for these scholarships can be obtained from the guidance departments of participating high schools. These applications must be completed and returned to Brown Mackie College by March 31.

The Education Foundation was established in 2000 to offer scholarship support to students interested in continuing their education at one of the postsecondary, career-focused schools in the EDMC system. The number and amount of the awards can vary, depending on the funds available. Scholarship applications are considered every quarter. At Brown Mackie College, applicants must be currently enrolled in an associate or bachelor's degree program and in their fourth quarter or higher (but no further than their second-to-last quarter) at the time of application. Awards are made based on academic performance and potential, as well as financial need. Interested students should contact the college's Student Financial Service Department for additional information.

Faculty

The college has 45 full-time and 80 part-time instructors, with a student-faculty ratio of 15:1. Each student is assigned a faculty adviser.

Admission Requirements

Each applicant for admission is assigned an Assistant Director of Admissions, who directs the applicant through the steps of the admissions process, providing information on curriculum, policies, procedures, and services and assisting the applicant in setting up necessary appointments and interviews. To qualify for admission, each applicant must provide documentation of graduation from an accredited high school or from a state-approved secondary education curriculum or provide official documentation of high school graduation equivalency. All transcripts become the property of the college. Admission to the college is based on the applicant meeting the stated requirements, a review of the applicant's previous educational records, and a review of the applicant's career interests. If previous academic records indicate the college's education and training programs would not benefit the applicant, the college reserves the right to advise the applicant not to enroll. Special requirements for enrollment into certain programs are discussed in the descriptions of those programs.

Application and Information

Applicants must complete and submit an application form, along with documentation of graduation from an accredited high school or state-approved secondary education curriculum or official documentation of high school graduation equivalency.

See BMCprograms.info for program duration, tuition, fees and other costs, median debt, federal salary data, alumni success, programmatic accreditation, and other important info.

Brown Mackie College is a system of over twenty-five schools located throughout North America. Programs, credential levels, technology, and scheduling options vary by school, and employment opportunities are not guaranteed. Financial aid is available for those who qualify. Administrative offices are located at 625 Eden Park Drive, Suite 1100; Cincinnati, Ohio 45202; phone: 513-830-2000. ©2013 Brown Mackie College. OH Registration # 03-09-1685T; # 03-09-1686T; # 03-09-1687T; # 03-09- 1688T; # 06-03-1781T; AC0150, AC0109, AC0078, AC0045, AC0138, AC0110; Licensed by the Florida Commission for Independent Education, License No. 3206.

For additional information, prospective students should contact:

Director of Admissions
Brown Mackie College — Fort Wayne
3000 East Coliseum Boulevard
Fort Wayne, Indiana 46805
United States
Phone: 260-484-4400
          866-433-2289 (toll-free)
Fax: 260-484-2678
E-mail: bmcfwaadm@brownmackie.edu
Website: http://www.brownmackie.edu/FortWayne

BROWN MACKIE COLLEGE — GREENVILLE
GREENVILLE, SOUTH CAROLINA

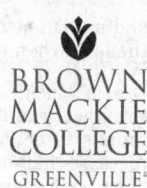

BROWN
MACKIE
COLLEGE
GREENVILLE℠

The College

Brown Mackie College — Greenville (Brown Mackie College) is one of over twenty-five locations in the Brown Mackie College system of schools (www.brownmackie.edu), which is dedicated to providing educational programs that prepare students to pursue entry-level positions in a competitive, rapidly changing workplace. Brown Mackie College schools offer bachelor's degree, associate degree, diploma, and certificate programs in health sciences, business, information technology, and legal studies to over 20,000 students in the Midwest, Southeast, Southwest, and Western United States.

Brown Mackie College was originally founded and approved by the Board of Trustees of Kansas Wesleyan College in Salina, Kansas on July 30, 1892. In 1938, the College was incorporated as The Brown Mackie School of Business under the ownership of Perry E. Brown and A.B. Mackie, former instructors at Kansas Wesleyan University in Salina, Kansas. Their last names formed the name of Brown Mackie. By January 1975, with improvements in curricula and higher-degree-granting status, The Brown Mackie School of Business became Brown Mackie College.

Brown Mackie College — Greenville is accredited by the Accrediting Council for Independent Colleges and Schools to award bachelor's degrees, associate degrees, and certificates. The Accrediting Council for Independent Colleges and Schools is listed as a nationally recognized accrediting agency by the United States Department of Education and is recognized by the Council for Higher Education Accreditation. ACICS can be contacted at 750 First Street NE, Suite 980, Washington, D.C. 20002; phone: 202-336-6780.

Brown Mackie College — Greenville is licensed by the South Carolina Commission on Higher Education, 1122 Lady Street, Suite 300, Columbia, South Carolina 29201; phone: 803-737-2260. Licensure indicates only that minimum standards have been met; it is not equal to or synonymous with accreditation by an accrediting agency recognized by the U.S. Department of Education.

The occupational therapy assistant program is accredited by the Accreditation Council for Occupational Therapy Education (ACOTE) of the American Occupational Therapy Association (AOTA), located at 4720 Montgomery Lane, Suite 200, Bethesda, Maryland 20814-3449; phone: 301-652-AOTA. Graduates of the program will be eligible to sit for the national certification examination for the occupational therapy assistant administered by the National Board for Certification in Occupational Therapy (NBCOT). After successful completion of this exam, the individual will be a Certified Occupational Therapy Assistant (COTA). In addition, most states require licensure in order to practice; however, state licenses are usually based on the results of the NBCOT Certification Examination. Note that a felony conviction may affect a graduate's ability to sit for the NBCOT certification examination or attain state licensure.

Location

Brown Mackie College — Greenville is conveniently located at Two Liberty Square, 75 Beattie Place, Suite 100, in Greenville, South Carolina. The college has a generous parking area and is easily accessible by public transportation.

Programs of Study and Degree Offerings

Brown Mackie College — Greenville provides higher education to traditional and nontraditional students through bachelor's

degree, associate degree, and certificate programs that assist in enhancing their career opportunities, broadening their perspectives through appropriate general education courses, thinking independently and critically, and improving problem-solving abilities. The college strives to develop within its students the desire for lifelong and continued education.

The Bachelor of Science degree is awarded in business administration, criminal justice, health care management, and legal studies.

The Associate of Applied Science degree is awarded in accounting technology, business management, criminal justice, health care administration, information technology, medical assisting, nursing, occupational therapy assistant, office management, paralegal, and surgical technology.

The certificate is awarded in accounting, business, criminal justice, medical assistant, and paralegal assistant.

The American Medical Technologists (AMT), which offers the certification for Registered Medical Assistant (RMA), accepts the accreditation of Brown Mackie College — Greenville. Students will qualify to take the Registered Medical Assistant certification examination upon graduating the Brown Mackie College — Greenville medical assisting and medical assistant programs. Graduates of the 48-credit-hour medical assistant program are not qualified to take the AMT/RMA exam.

Brown Mackie College does not guarantee third-party certification/licensing exams. Outside agencies control the requirements for certification/licensing and are subject to change without notification to the college.

Program availability and degree offerings are subject to change.

Academic Programs

Each college quarter comprises twelve weeks. Bachelor's degree programs require a minimum of sixteen quarters to complete. Associate degree programs require a minimum of eight quarters to complete. Programs are offered on a year-round basis, providing students with the ability to work uninterrupted toward completion of their degrees. The college offers all programs in a unique One-Course-a-Month format. This allows students to focus their studies on only one course for four weeks. This schedule has proven convenient for students with multiple obligations, such as jobs and family.

Academic Facilities

A modern facility, Brown Mackie College — Greenville offers nearly 50,000 square feet. The college is equipped with multiple computer labs housing over one hundred computers. High-speed access to the Internet and other online resources are available for students and faculty. Multimedia classrooms are outfitted with overhead projectors, VCR/DVD players, and computers.

Brown Mackie College — Greenville is fully committed to using eTextbooks and computer tablets in the classroom. Utilizing these tablets to access expanded course material, students are able to increase their acumen for using this technology and further enhance their educational experience. Students have the ability to directly download their eTextbooks to their tablet, eliminating the need to carry heavy, physical textbooks and reducing the overall cost of supplies.

Brown Mackie College is nonresidential; public transportation and ample parking at no cost are available. The college is a smoke-free facility.

Costs

Tuition in the 2012–13 academic year for most bachelor's and associate degrees and certificates was $314 per credit hour; fees were $20 per credit hour. Tuition for the nursing program was $410 per credit hour; fees were $30 per credit hour. Tuition for the occupational therapy assistant program was $381 per credit hour; fees were $20 per credit hour. Tuition for the surgical technology program was $360 per credit hour; fees were $20 per credit hour. The cost of textbooks, if applicable, and other instructional expenses vary by program.

Financial Aid

Financial aid is available for those who qualify. The college maintains a full-time staff of Student Financial Services Advisors to assist qualified students in obtaining the financial assistance they require to meet their educational expenses. Available resources include federal and state aid, student loans from private lenders, and Federal Work-Study opportunities, both on and off college premises.

Each year, the college makes available President's Scholarships of $1,000 each to qualifying seniors from area high schools. In order to qualify, a senior must have graduated from a participating high school, must have maintained a cumulative grade point average of at least 2.0, and must have submitted a brief essay. The student's extracurricular activities and community service are also considered. The President's Scholarship is available only to students enrolling in one of Brown Mackie College's degree programs. Students awarded the scholarship must enroll at Brown Mackie College — Greenville between June and September immediately following their high school graduation. Applications for these scholarships can be obtained from the guidance departments of participating high schools. These applications must be completed and returned to Brown Mackie College by March 31.

The Education Foundation was established in 2000 to offer scholarship support to students interested in continuing their education at one of the postsecondary, career-focused schools in the EDMC system. The number and amount of the awards can vary, depending on the funds available. Scholarship applications are considered every quarter. At Brown Mackie College applicants must be currently enrolled in an associate or bachelor's degree program and in their fourth quarter or higher (but no further than their second-to-last quarter) at the time of application. Awards are made based on academic performance and potential, as well as financial need. Interested students should contact the college's Student Financial Service Department for additional information.

Faculty

Experienced faculty members provide academic support and are committed to the academic and technical preparation of their students. The college has 9 full-time and 30 part-time instructors, with a student-faculty ratio of 24:1. Each student is assigned a faculty adviser.

Admission Requirements

Each applicant for admission is assigned an Assistant Director of Admissions who directs the applicant through the steps of the admissions process. Assistant Directors provide information on curriculum, policies, procedures, and services and assist the applicant in setting up necessary appointments and interviews. To qualify for admission, each applicant must provide documentation of graduation from an accredited high school or from a state-approved secondary education curriculum or provide official documentation of high school graduation equivalency. All transcripts become the property of the college. Admission to the college is based on the applicant meeting the stated requirements, a review of the applicant's previous educational records, and a review of the applicant's career interests. If previous academic records indicate the college's education and training programs would not benefit the applicant, the college reserves the right to advise the applicant not to enroll. Special requirements for enrollment into certain programs are discussed in the descriptions of those programs.

For the most recent information regarding admission requirements, prospective students should refer to the current academic catalog.

Application and Information

Applicants must complete and submit an application form along with documentation of graduation from an accredited high school or state-approved secondary education curriculum or official documentation of high school graduation equivalency.

Brown Mackie College is a system of over twenty-five schools located throughout North America. Programs, credential levels, technology, and scheduling options vary by school, and employment opportunities are not guaranteed. Financial aid is available for those who qualify. Administrative offices are located at 625 Eden Park Drive, Suite 1100; Cincinnati, Ohio 45202; phone: 513.830.2000. ©2013 Brown Mackie College. OH Registration # 03-09-1685T; # 03-09-1686T; # 03-09-1687T; # 03-09-1688T; # 06-03-1781T; AC0150, AC0109, AC0078, AC0045, AC0138, AC0110; Licensed by the Florida Commission for Independent Education, License No. 3206.

See BMCprograms.info for program duration, tuition, fees and other costs, median debt, federal salary data, alumni success, programmatic accreditation, and other important info.

For additional information, prospective students should contact:

Director of Admissions
Brown Mackie College — Greenville
Two Liberty Square
75 Beattie Place, Suite 100
Greenville, South Carolina 29601
United States
Phone: 864-239-5300
         877-479-8465 (toll-free)
Fax: 864-232-4094
E-mail: bmcgrweb@brownmackie.edu
Website: http://www.brownmackie.edu/greenville

BROWN MACKIE COLLEGE — INDIANAPOLIS
INDIANAPOLIS, INDIANA

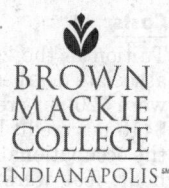

The College

Brown Mackie College—Indianapolis (Brown Mackie College) is one of over twenty-five locations in the Brown Mackie College system of schools (http://www.brownmackie.edu), which is dedicated to providing educational programs that prepare students to pursue entry-level positions in a competitive, rapidly changing workplace. Brown Mackie College schools offer bachelor's degree, associate degree, diploma, and certificate programs in health sciences, business, information technology, legal studies, and design to thousands of students in the Midwest, Southeast, Southwest, and Western United States.

Brown Mackie College — Indianapolis was founded in 2007 as a branch of Brown Mackie College — Findlay, Ohio.

Brown Mackie College — Indianapolis is accredited by the Accrediting Council for Independent Colleges and Schools to award bachelor's degrees, associate degrees, diplomas, and certificates. The Accrediting Council for Independent Colleges and Schools is listed as a nationally recognized accrediting agency by the United States Department of Education and is recognized by the Council for Higher Education Accreditation. ACICS can be contacted at 750 First Street NE, Suite 980, Washington, D.C. 20002; phone: 202-336-6780.

The occupational therapy assistant program is accredited by the Accreditation Council for Occupational Therapy Education (ACOTE) of the American Occupational Therapy Association (AOTA), located at 4720 Montgomery Lane, Suite 200, Bethesda, Maryland 20814-3449; phone: 301-652-AOTA. Graduates of the program will be eligible to sit for the national certification examination for the occupational therapy assistant administered by the National Board for Certification in Occupational Therapy (NBCOT). After successful completion of this exam, the individual will be a Certified Occupational Therapy Assistant (COTA). In addition, most states require licensure in order to practice; however, state licenses are usually based on the results of the NBCOT Certification Examination. Note that a felony conviction may affect a graduate's ability to sit for the NBCOT certification examination or attain state licensure.

The Brown Mackie College—Indianapolis practical nursing diploma program is approved by the Indiana State Board of Nursing, 402 West Washington Street, Room W066, Indianapolis, Indiana 46204; phone: 317-234-2043.

Brown Mackie College — Indianapolis is regulated by the Board for Proprietary Education Indiana Commission for Higher Education, 101 West Ohio Street, Suite 670, Indianapolis, Indiana 46204; phone: 317-464-4400. Indiana advertising code: AC0078.

Location

Brown Mackie College — Indianapolis is conveniently located at 1200 North Meridian Street in Indianapolis, Indiana. The college has a generous parking area and is easily accessible by public transportation.

In November 2011, the college opened an innovative branch learning site on Level 4 of Circle Centre Mall located at 49 West Maryland Street in the heart of downtown Indianapolis. Daily shuttle service is provided to and from the main college.

Programs of Study and Degree Offerings

Brown Mackie College — Indianapolis provides higher education to traditional and nontraditional students through bachelor's degree, associate degree, diploma, and certificate programs that assist them in enhancing their career opportunities, broadening their perspectives through appropriate general education courses, thinking independently and critically, and improving problem-solving abilities. The college strives to develop within its students the desire for lifelong and continued education.

The Bachelor of Science degree is awarded in business administration, criminal justice, and legal studies.

The Associate of Science degree is awarded in business management, criminal justice, health care administration, medical assisting, and paralegal.

The Associate of Applied Science degree is awarded in occupational therapy assistant.

A diploma program in practical nursing is offered.

Brown Mackie College — Indianapolis offers bookkeeping specialist, general business, medical assistant, and medical insurance specialist certificate programs.

The American Medical Technologists (AMT), which offers the certification for Registered Medical Assistant (RMA), accepts the accreditation of Brown Mackie College — Indianapolis. Students will qualify to take the Registered Medical Assistant certification examination upon graduating the Brown Mackie College — Indianapolis medical assisting and medical assistant programs. Graduates of the 48-credit-hour medical assistant program are not qualified to take the AMT/RMA exam.

Brown Mackie College does not guarantee third-party certification/licensing exams. Outside agencies control the requirements for certification/licensing and are subject to change without notification to the college.

Program availability and degree offerings are subject to change.

Academic Programs

Each college quarter comprises twelve weeks. Bachelor's degree programs require a minimum of sixteen quarters to complete. Associate degree programs require a minimum of eight quarters to complete. Programs are offered on a year-round basis, providing students with the ability to work uninterrupted toward their degrees. The college offers all programs in a unique One-Course-a-Month format. This allows students to focus studies on only one course for four weeks. This schedule has proven convenient for students with multiple obligations such as jobs and family. Day and evening classes are available for added flexibility.

Academic Facilities

Opened in January 2008, this modern facility offers more than 22,000 square feet of tastefully decorated classrooms, laboratories, and office space designed to the specifications of the college for its business, healthcare, and technical programs. The Circle Centre Mall branch learning site boasts 25,000 square feet with 20 lecture rooms, computer labs, two medical labs, college store, and more. Instructional equipment is comparable to current technology used in business and industry today. Modern classrooms for special instructional needs offer multimedia capabilities with surround sound and overhead projectors accessible through computer, DVD, or VHS. Internet access and instructional resources are available at the college's library. Experienced faculty members provide academic support and are committed to the academic and technical preparation of their students.

Brown Mackie College — Indianapolis is fully committed to using eTextbooks and computer tablets in the classroom. Utilizing these tablets to access expanded course material, students are able to increase their acumen for using this technology and further enhance their educational experience. Students have the ability to directly download their eTextbooks to their tablet, eliminating the need to carry heavy, physical textbooks and reducing the overall cost of supplies.

Brown Mackie College — Indianapolis is nonresidential; public transportation and ample parking are available at no additional cost.

Costs

Tuition for most programs in the 2012–13 academic year was $332 per credit hour with a general fee of $20 per credit hour. Tuition for the practical nursing diploma program was $381 per credit hour with a general fee of $30 per credit hour applied to instructional costs for activities and services. For the occupational therapy assistant program, the tuition was $381 per credit hour with a general fee of $20 per credit hour.

Financial Aid

Financial aid is available to those who qualify. The college maintains a full-time staff of Student Financial Services Advisors to assist qualified students in obtaining the financial assistance they require to meet their educational expenses. Available resources include federal and state aid, student loans from private lenders, and federal work-study opportunities, both on and off college premises.

Each year, the college makes available President's Scholarships of $1,000 each to qualifying seniors from area high schools. In order to qualify, a senior must be graduating from a participating high school, must be maintaining a cumulative grade point average of at least 2.0, and must submit a brief essay. The student's extracurricular activities and community service are also considered. These scholarships are available only to students enrolling in one of the college's degree programs. Students awarded the scholarship must enroll at Brown Mackie College — Indianapolis between June and September immediately following their high school graduation. Applications for these scholarships can be obtained from the guidance departments of participating high schools. These applications must be completed and returned to Brown Mackie College by March 31.

The Education Foundation was established in 2000 to offer scholarship support to students interested in continuing their education at one of the postsecondary, career-focused schools in the EDMC system. The number and amount of the awards can vary, depending on the funds available. Scholarship applications are considered every quarter. At Brown Mackie College applicants must be currently enrolled in an associate or bachelor's degree program and in their fourth quarter or higher (but no further than their second-to-last quarter) at the time of application. Awards are made based on academic performance and potential, as well as financial need. Interested students should contact the college's Student Financial Service Department for additional information.

Faculty

The college has 24 full-time instructors, 77 adjunct instructors, and 16 lab assistants, with a student-faculty ratio of 12:1. Faculty members provide tutoring and additional academic services to students as needed.

Admission Requirements

Each applicant for admission is assigned an Assistant Director of Admissions, who directs the applicant through the steps of the admissions process, providing information on curriculum, policies, procedures, and services and assisting the applicant in setting up necessary appointments and interviews. To qualify for admission, each applicant must provide documentation of graduation from an accredited high school or from a state-approved secondary education curriculum or provide official documentation of high school graduation equivalency. All transcripts become the property of the college. Admission to the college is based on the applicant meeting the stated requirements, a review of the applicant's previous educational records, and a review of the applicant's career interests. If previous academic records indicate the college's education and training programs would not benefit the applicant, the college reserves the right to advise the applicant not to enroll. Special requirements for enrollment into certain programs are discussed in the descriptions of those programs.

In addition to the college's general admission requirements, applicants enrolling in the practical nursing program must document the following: fulfillment of Brown Mackie College — Indianapolis general requirements; complete physical (must be current to within six months of admission); two-step Mantoux TB skin test (must be current throughout schooling); hepatitis B vaccination or signed refusal; up-to-date immunizations, including tetanus and rubella; record of current CPR certification (certification must be current throughout the clinical experience through healthcare provider certification or the American Heart Association); and hospitalization insurance or a signed waiver.

For the most recent information regarding admission requirements, please refer to the current academic catalog.

Application and Information

Applicants must complete and submit an application form, along with documentation of graduation from an accredited high school or state-approved secondary education curriculum or official documentation of high school graduation equivalency.

Brown Mackie College is a system of over twenty-five schools located throughout North America. Programs, credential levels, technology, and scheduling options vary by school, and employment opportunities are not guaranteed. Financial aid is available for those who qualify. Administrative offices are located at 625 Eden Park Drive, Suite 1100; Cincinnati, Ohio 45202; phone: 513.830.2000. ©2013 Brown Mackie College. OH Registration # 03-09-1685T; # 03-09-1686T; # 03-09-1687T; # 03-09-1688T; # 06-03-1781T; AC0150, AC0109, AC0078, AC0045, AC0138, AC0110; Licensed by the Florida Commission for Independent Education, License No. 3206.

See BMCprograms.info for program duration, tuition, fees and other costs, median debt, federal salary data, alumni success, programmatic accreditation, and other important info.

For additional information, prospective students should contact:

Senior Director of Admissions
Brown Mackie College — Indianapolis
1200 North Meridian Street, Suite 100
Indianapolis, Indiana 46204
United States
Phone: 317-554-8300
       866-255-0279 (toll-free)
Fax: 317-632-4557
E-mail: bmcindadm@brownmackie.edu
Web site: http://www.brownmackie.edu/Indianapolis

BROWN MACKIE COLLEGE — KANSAS CITY

KANSAS CITY, MISSOURI

The College

Brown Mackie College — Kansas City (Brown Mackie College) is one of over twenty-five locations in the Brown Mackie College system of schools (www.brownmackie.edu), which is dedicated to providing educational programs that prepare students to pursue entry-level positions in a competitive, rapidly changing workplace. Brown Mackie College schools offer bachelor's degree, associate degree, certificate, and diploma programs in health sciences, business, information technology, legal studies, and design to over 20,000 students in the Midwest, Southeast, Southwest, and Western United States.

The college was founded in Salina, Kansas, in July 1892 as the Kansas Wesleyan School of Business. In 1938, the college was incorporated as the Brown Mackie School of Business under the ownership of former Kansas Wesleyan instructors Perry E. Brown and A. B. Mackie. It became Brown Mackie College in January 1975.

Brown Mackie College in Lenexa, Kansas is a branch of Brown Mackie College in Salina, Kansas which accredited by the Higher Learning Commission and is a member of the North Central Association (NCA), 230 South LaSalle Street, Suite 7-500, Chicago, Illinois 60604-1413; phone: 800-621-7440 (toll free); www.ncahlc.org.

Brown Mackie College in Lenexa, Kansas is approved and authorized to grant the Associate of Applied Science (A.A.S.) degree and the Bachelor of Science (B.S.) degree by the Kansas Board of Regents, 1000 Southwest Jackson Street, Suite 520, Topeka, Kansas 66612-1368.

The occupational therapy assistant program is accredited by the Accreditation Council for Occupational Therapy Education (ACOTE) of the American Occupational Therapy Association (AOTA), 4720 Montgomery Lane, Suite 200, Bethesda, Maryland 20814-3449; phone: 301-652-AOTA. Graduates of the program will be eligible to sit for the national certification examination for the occupational therapy assistant administered by the National Board for Certification in Occupational Therapy (NBCOT). After successful completion of this exam, the individual will be a Certified Occupational Therapy Assistant (COTA). In addition, most states require licensure in order to practice; however, state licenses are usually based on the results of the NBCOT Certification Examination. Note that a felony conviction may affect a graduate's ability to sit for the NBCOT certification examination or attain state licensure.

The veterinary technology program has provisional programmatic accreditation granted by the American Veterinary Medical Association (AVMA) through the Committee on Veterinary Technician Education and Activities (CVTEA).

Brown Mackie College — Kansas City is nonresidential, smoke free, and provides ample parking at no additional cost.

Location

Brown Mackie College — Kansas City is located at 9705 Lenexa Drive in Lenexa, Kansas, just off Interstate 35 at 95th Street in Johnson County. The Olathe course site is located at 450 North Rogers Road, Suite 175, in Olathe, Kansas, just off Interstate 35 and Santa Fe Street in Johnson County.

Programs of Study and Degree Offerings

Brown Mackie College — Kansas City provides higher education to traditional and nontraditional students through bachelor's degree, associate degree, diploma, and certificate programs that can assist them in enhancing their career opportunities, broadening their perspectives through appropriate general education courses, thinking independently and critically, and improving problem-solving abilities. Brown Mackie College strives to develop within its students the desire for lifelong and continued education.

In most programs, students can participate in day or evening classes, which begin every month. Programs are offered on a year-round basis, providing students with the ability to work uninterrupted toward completion of their programs. Brown Mackie College offers all programs in a unique One Course a Month format. This schedule allows students to focus studies on only one course for four weeks and has proven convenient for students with multiple obligations such as jobs and family.

The Bachelor of Science degree is awarded in business administration and health care management.

The Associate of Applied Science degree is awarded in architectural design and drafting technology, business management, computer software applications, criminal justice, fitness trainer, health care administration, medical assisting, nursing, occupational therapy assistant, and veterinary technology.

Brown Mackie College — Kansas City also offers diploma programs in architectural drafting specialist, criminal justice specialist, general business, medical assistant, and medical insurance specialist.

A certificate program is offered in practical nursing.

The American Medical Technologists (AMT), which offers the certification for Registered Medical Assistant (RMA), accepts the accreditation of Brown Mackie College — Kansas City. Students will qualify to take the Registered Medical Assistant certification examination upon graduating the Brown Mackie College — Kansas City medical assisting and medical assistant programs. Graduates of the 48 credit-hour medical assistant program are not qualified to take the AMT/RMA exam.

Brown Mackie College does not guarantee third-party certification/licensing exams. Outside agencies control the requirements for certification/licensing and are subject to change without notification to the college.

Program availability and degree offerings are subject to change.

Academic Programs

Each college quarter comprises twelve weeks. Bachelor's degree programs require a minimum of sixteen quarters to complete. Associate degree programs require a minimum of eight quarters to complete. Programs are offered on a year-round basis, providing students with the ability to work uninterrupted toward their degrees. The college offers all programs in a unique One-Course-a-Month format. This allows students to focus studies on only one course for four weeks. This schedule has proven convenient for students with multiple obligations such as jobs and family.

Academic Facilities

In addition to classrooms and computer labs, Brown Mackie College — Kansas City maintains a library of curriculum-related resources, technical and general education materials, academic and professional periodicals, and audiovisual resources. Internet access also is available for research. The college has a bookstore that stocks texts, courseware, and other educational supplies required for courses and a variety of personal, recreational, and gift items, including apparel, supplies, and general merchandise incorporating the Brown Mackie College logo. Hours are posted at the bookstore entrance.

Brown Mackie College — Kansas City is fully committed to using eTextbooks and computer tablets in the classroom. Utilizing these tablets to access expanded course material, students are able to increase their acumen for using this technology and further enhance their educational experience. Students have the ability to directly download their eTextbooks to their tablet, eliminating the need to carry heavy, physical textbooks and reducing the overall cost of supplies.

Costs

Tuition for most programs in the 2012–13 academic year was $314 per credit hour and $20 per credit hour for general fees. Tuition for nursing programs was $381 per credit hour with general fees of $30 per credit hour. Tuition for the occupational therapy assistant program was $381 per credit hour with fees of $20 per credit hour. The cost of textbooks, if applicable, and other instructional materials varies by program.

Financial Aid

Financial aid is available to those who qualify. Brown Mackie College — Kansas City maintains a full-time staff of financial aid professionals to assist qualified students in obtaining financial assistance. The college participates in several student aid programs. Forms of financial aid available to qualified students through federal resources include Federal Pell Grants, Federal Supplemental Educational Opportunity Grants (FSEOG), Academic Competitiveness Grant, Federal Work-Study Program, Federal Perkins Loans, Federal Stafford Student Loans (subsidized and unsubsidized), Federal Direct Loans (subsidized and unsubsidized), and the Federal PLUS Program. Eligible students may apply for veterans' educational benefits. Students with physical or mental disabilities that are a handicap to employment may be eligible for training services through the state Vocational Rehabilitation Agency. For further information, students should contact the Brown Mackie College — Kansas City Student Financial Services Office.

Each year, the college makes available President's Scholarships of $1,000 each to qualifying seniors from area high schools. In order to qualify, a senior must be graduating from a participating high school, have maintained a cumulative grade point average of at least 2.0, and submitted a brief essay. The student's extracurricular activities and community service are also considered. The President's Scholarship is available only to students enrolling in one of the college's degree programs. Students awarded the scholarship must enroll at Brown Mackie College — Kansas City between June and September immediately following their high school graduation. Applications for these scholarships can be obtained from the guidance departments of participating high schools. These applications must be completed and returned to the college by March 31.

The Education Foundation was established in 2000 to offer scholarship support to students interested in continuing their education at one of the postsecondary, career-focused schools in the EDMC system. The number and amount of the awards can vary, depending on the funds available. Scholarship applications are considered every quarter. At Brown Mackie College, applicants must be currently enrolled in an associate or bachelor's degree program and in their fourth quarter or higher (but no further than their second-to-last quarter) at the time of application. Awards are made based on academic performance and potential, as well as financial need. Interested students should contact the college's Student Financial Service Department for additional information.

Faculty

There are 23 full-time faculty members and 25 adjunct faculty members. The average class student-instructor ratio is 14:1.

Admission Requirements

Each applicant for admission is assigned an Assistant Director of Admissions, who directs the applicant through the steps of the admissions process, providing information on curriculum, policies, procedures, and services and assisting the applicant in setting necessary appointments and interviews.

To qualify for admission, each applicant must provide documentation of graduation from an accredited high school or from a state-approved secondary education curriculum or provide official documentation of high school graduation equivalency. All transcripts become the property of Brown Mackie College — Kansas City. Admission to the college is based upon the applicant meeting the stated requirements, a review of the applicant's previous education records, and a review of the applicant's career interests. If previous academic records indicate that the Brown Mackie College education and training programs would not benefit the applicant, the college reserves the right to advise the applicant not to enroll. Special requirements for enrollment into certain programs are discussed in the descriptions of those programs.

For the most recent information regarding admission requirements, prospective students should refer to the current academic catalog.

Application and Information

Applicants must complete and submit an application form, along with documentation of graduation from an accredited high school or state-approved secondary education curriculum or official documentation of high school graduation equivalency.

See BMCprograms.info for program duration, tuition, fees and other costs, median debt, federal salary data, alumni success, programmatic accreditation, and other important info.

Brown Mackie College is a system of over twenty-five schools located throughout North America. Programs, credential levels, technology, and scheduling options vary by school, and employment opportunities are not guaranteed. Financial aid is available for those who qualify. Administrative offices are located at 625 Eden Park Drive, Suite 1100; Cincinnati, Ohio 45202; phone: 513.830.2000. ©2013 Brown Mackie College. OH Registration # 03-09-1685T; # 03-09-1686T; # 03-09-1687T; # 03-09-1688T; # 06-03-1781T; AC0150, AC0109, AC0078, AC0045, AC0138, AC0110; Licensed by the Florida Commission for Independent Education, License No. 3206.

For additional information, prospective students should contact:

Director of Admissions
Brown Mackie College — Kansas City
9705 Lenexa Drive
Lenexa, Kansas 66215
United States
Phone: 913-768-1900
800-635-9101 (toll-free)
Fax: 913-495-9555
E-mail: bmckcadm@brownmackie.edu
Web site: http://www.brownmackie.edu/KansasCity

BROWN MACKIE COLLEGE — LOUISVILLE

LOUISVILLE, KENTUCKY

The College

Brown Mackie College — Louisville (Brown Mackie College) is one of over twenty-five locations in the Brown Mackie College system of schools (www.brownmackie.edu), which is dedicated to providing educational programs that prepare students to pursue entry-level positions in a competitive, rapidly changing workplace. Brown Mackie College schools offer bachelor's degree, associate degree, diploma, and certificate programs in health sciences, business, information technology, legal studies, and design to over 20,000 students in the Midwest, Southeast, Southwest, and Western United States.

Brown Mackie College — Louisville opened in 1972 as RETS Institute of Technology. The first RETS school was founded in 1935 in Detroit in response to the rapid growth of radio broadcasting and the need for qualified radio technicians. The RETS Institute changed its name to Brown Mackie College — Louisville in 2004.

Brown Mackie College — Louisville is accredited by the Accrediting Council for Independent Colleges and Schools to award bachelor's degrees, associate degrees, diplomas, and certificates. The Accrediting Council for Independent Colleges and Schools is listed as a nationally recognized accrediting agency by the United States Department of Education. Its accreditation of degree-granting institutions is recognized by the Council for Higher Education Accreditation. ACICS can be contacted at 750 First Street NE, Suite 980, Washington, D.C. 20002; phone: 202-336-6780.

Brown Mackie College — Louisville is licensed by the Kentucky Council on Postsecondary Education, located at 1024 Capital Center Drive, Suite 320, Frankfort, Kentucky 40601.

Brown Mackie College — Louisville is regulated by the Board for Proprietary Education Indiana Commission for Higher Education, 101 West Ohio Street, Suite 670, Indianapolis, Indiana 46204; 317-464-4400. Indiana advertising code: AC0045.

The Associate of Applied Science in veterinary technology program has probationary accreditation by the American Veterinary Medical Association (AVMA) through the Committee on Veterinary Technician Education and Activities (CVTEA). The American Veterinary Medical Association can be contacted at 1931 North Meacham Road, Suite 100, Schaumburg, Illinois, 60173-4360; phone: 800-248-2862.

The Associate of Applied Science in occupational therapy assistant program is accredited by the Accreditation Council for Occupational Therapy Education (ACOTE) of the American Occupational Therapy Association (AOTA), located at 4720 Montgomery Lane, Suite 200, Bethesda, Maryland 20814-3449; phone: 301-652-AOTA. Graduates of the program will be eligible to sit for the national certification examination for the occupational therapy assistant administered by the National Board for Certification in Occupational Therapy (NBCOT). After successful completion of this exam, the individual will be a Certified Occupational Therapy Assistant (COTA). In addition, most states require licensure in order to practice; however, state licenses are usually based on the results of the NBCOT Certification Examination. Note that a felony conviction may affect a graduate's ability to sit for the NBCOT certification examination or attain state licensure

The Associate of Applied Science in Surgical Technology is accredited by the Accrediting Bureau of Health Education Schools (www.abhes.org). The Accrediting Bureau of Health Education Schools can be contacted at 7777 Leesburg Pike, Suite 314 N. Falls Church, Virginia 22043; 703-917-9503.

The Associate of Science in Surgical Technology program is accredited by the Commission on Accreditation of Allied Health Education Programs (www.caahep.org), upon the recommendation of the Accreditation Review Council on Education in Surgical Technology and Surgical Assisting (ARC/STSA). Commission on Accreditation of Allied Health Education Programs, 1361 Park Street, Clearwater, Florida 33756; 727-210-2350.

Location

Brown Mackie College — Louisville is conveniently located at 3605 Fern Valley Road in Louisville, Kentucky. The college has a generous parking area and is easily accessible by public transportation.

Programs of Study and Degree Offerings

Brown Mackie College — Louisville provides higher education to traditional and nontraditional students through bachelor's degree, associate degree, and diploma programs that assist in enhancing their career opportunities, broadening their perspectives through appropriate general education courses, thinking independently and critically, and improving problem-solving abilities.

The Bachelor of Science degree is awarded in business administration, criminal justice, health care management, and legal studies.

The Associate of Applied Business degree is awarded in accounting technology, business management, computer networking, criminal justice, and paralegal.

The Associate of Applied Science degree is awarded in biomedical equipment technology, electronics, graphic design, health care administration, medical assisting, occupational therapy assistant, pharmacy technology, surgical technology, and veterinary technology.

The college offers a diploma program in practical nursing.

The college offers a certificate program in computer networking.

The American Medical Technologists (AMT), which offers the certification for Registered Medical Assistant (RMA), accepts the accreditation of Brown Mackie College — Louisville. Students will qualify to take the Registered Medical Assistant certification examination upon graduating the Brown Mackie College — Louisville medical assisting program.

Brown Mackie College does not guarantee third-party certification/licensing exams. Outside agencies control the requirements for certification/licensing and are subject to change without notification to the college.

Program availability and degree offerings are subject to change.

Academic Programs

Each college quarter comprises twelve weeks. Bachelor's degree programs require a minimum of sixteen quarters to complete. Associate degree programs require a minimum of eight quarters to complete. Programs are offered on a year-round basis, providing students with the ability to work uninterrupted toward completion of their programs. The college offers all programs in a unique One-Course-a-Month format. This allows students to focus studies on only one course for four weeks. This schedule has proven convenient for students with multiple obligations, such as jobs and family.

Academic Facilities

Brown Mackie College — Louisville has more than 69,000 square feet of multipurpose classrooms, including networked computer laboratories, electronics laboratories, veterinary technology labs, medical labs, nursing labs, a resource center, and offices for administrative personnel as well as for student services such as admissions, student financial services, and career-services assistance. In 2009, 6,000 square feet were added to the Louisville location. Included in this build-out are an occupational therapy lab, a criminal justice lab, additional classrooms, and faculty space. In 2010, an additional 25,000 square feet opened at this location. This build-out included a biomedical equipment lab, additional classrooms, a career services center, and additional faculty/administration space.

Brown Mackie College — Louisville is fully committed to using eTextbooks and computer tablets in the classroom. Utilizing these tablets to access expanded course material, students are able to increase their acumen for using this technology and further enhance their educational experience. Students have the ability to directly download their eTextbooks to their tablet, eliminating the need to carry heavy, physical textbooks and reducing the overall cost of supplies.

Brown Mackie College — Louisville is nonresidential; ample parking at no cost is available. Brown Mackie College is a smoke-free facility.

Costs

Tuition for most programs in the 2012–13 academic year was $314 per credit hour, and the general fees were $20 per credit hour. The practical nursing diploma program was $381 per credit hour, and the general fees were $30 per credit hour. The surgical technology program was $360 per credit hour, and the general fees were $20 per credit hour. The occupational therapy program was $381 per credit hour, and the general fees were $20 per credit hour. The computer networking certificate program was $314 per credit hour, and the general fees were $25 per credit hour. The length of the program determines total cost. The cost of textbooks, if applicable, and other instructional materials varies by program.

Financial Aid

Financial aid is available for those who qualify. The college maintains a full-time staff of Student Financial Services Advisors to assist qualified students in obtaining financial assistance. The college participates in several student aid programs. Forms of financial aid available through federal resources include the Federal Pell Grant Program, Federal Supplemental Educational Opportunity Grant (FSEOG) Program, Federal Work-Study Program, Federal Perkins Loan Program, Federal Stafford Student Loan Program (subsidized and unsubsidized), and the Federal PLUS Loan Program.

Each year, the college makes available President's Scholarships of $1,000 each to qualifying seniors from area high schools. In order to qualify, a senior must have graduated from a participating high school, must have maintained a cumulative grade point average of at least 2.0, and must have submitted a brief essay. The student's extracurricular activities and community service are also considered. The President's Scholarship is available only to students enrolling in one of the college's degree programs. Students awarded the scholarship must enroll at Brown Mackie College — Louisville between June and September immediately following their high school graduation. Applications for these scholarships can be obtained from the guidance departments of participating high schools and must be completed and returned to Brown Mackie College by March 31.

The Education Foundation was established in 2000 to offer scholarship support to students interested in continuing their education at one of the postsecondary, career-focused schools in the EDMC system. The number and amount of the awards can vary, depending on the funds available. Scholarship applications are considered every quarter. At Brown Mackie College, applicants must be currently enrolled in an associate or bachelor's degree program and in their fourth quarter or higher (but no further than their second-to-last quarter) at the time of application. Awards are made based on academic performance and potential, as well as financial need. Interested students should contact the college's Student Financial Service Department for additional information.

Faculty

There are 32 full-time and over 100 part-time faculty members at the college. The average student-faculty ratio is 20:1.

Admission Requirements

Each applicant for admission is assigned an Assistant Director of Admissions, who directs the applicant through the steps of the admissions process, providing information on curriculum, policies, procedures, and services and assisting the applicant in setting up necessary appointments and interviews.

To qualify for admission, each applicant must provide documentation of graduation from an accredited high school or from a state-approved secondary education curriculum or official documentation of high school graduation equivalency. All transcripts become the property of the college. Admission to the college is based on the applicant meeting the stated requirements, a review of the applicant's previous educational records, and a review of the applicant's career interests. If previous academic records indicate the college's education and training programs would not benefit the applicant, the college reserves the right to advise the applicant not to enroll. Special requirements for enrollment into certain programs are discussed in the descriptions of those programs.

In addition to the college's general admission requirements, applicants enrolling in either the occupational therapy assistant program or the surgical technology program must document one of the following: a high school cumulative grade point average of at least

2.5, a score on the GED examination of at least 57 (557 if taken on or after January 15, 2002), or completion of 12 quarter-credit hours or 8 semester-credit hours of collegiate course work with a grade point average of at least 2.5. Credit hours may not include Professional Development (CF 1100), the Brown Mackie College — Louisville course. Students entering the program must also have completed a biology course with a grade of at least a C (or an average of at least 2.0 on a 4.0 scale).

In addition to the college's general admission requirements, applicants enrolling in the practical nursing program must complete several documents, listed below. A record of proof must appear in the student's file prior to the start of the nursing fundamentals course. No student will be admitted to a clinical agency unless all paperwork is completed. The paperwork is a requirement of all contracted agencies. This paperwork includes records of (1) a complete physical, current to within six months of admission; (2) a two-step Mantoux test that is kept current throughout schooling; (3) a hepatitis B vaccination or signed refusal; (4) up-to-date immunizations, including tetanus and rubella; (5) a record of current CPR certification that is maintained throughout the student's clinical experience; and (6) hospitalization insurance or a signed waiver.

For the most recent information regarding admission requirements, prospective students should refer to the current academic catalog.

Application and Information

Applicants must complete and submit an application form along with documentation of graduation from an accredited high school or completion of state-approved secondary education curriculum or official documentation of high school graduation equivalency.

See BMCprograms.info for program duration, tuition, fees and other costs, median debt, federal salary data, alumni success, programmatic accreditation, and other important info.

Brown Mackie College is a system of over twenty-five schools located throughout North America. Programs, credential levels, technology, and scheduling options vary by school, and employment opportunities are not guaranteed. Financial aid is available for those who qualify. Administrative offices are located at 625 Eden Park Drive, Suite 1100; Cincinnati, Ohio 45202; phone: 513.830.2000. ©2013 Brown Mackie College. OH Registration # 03-09-1685T; # 03-09-1686T; # 03-09-1687T; # 03-09-1688T; # 06-03-1781T; AC0150, AC0109, AC0078, AC0045, AC0138, AC0110; Licensed by the Florida Commission for Independent Education, License No. 3206.

For additional information, prospective students should contact:

Brown Mackie College — Louisville
3605 Fern Valley Road
Louisville, Kentucky 40219
United States
Phone: 502-968-7191
      800-999-7387 (toll-free)
Fax: 502-357-9956
E-mail: bmcloadm@brownmackie.edu
Website: http://www.brownmackie.edu/Louisville

BROWN MACKIE COLLEGE — MERRILLVILLE
MERRILLVILLE, INDIANA

The College

Brown Mackie College — Merrillville (Brown Mackie College) is one of over twenty-five locations in the Brown Mackie College system of schools (www.brownmackie.edu), which is dedicated to providing educational programs that prepare students to pursue entry-level positions in a competitive, rapidly changing workplace. Brown Mackie College schools offer bachelor's degree, associate degree, diploma, and certificate programs in health sciences, business, information technology, legal studies, and design to over 20,000 students in the Midwest, Southeast, Southwest, and Western United States.

Founded in 1890 by A. N. Hirons as LaPorte Business College in LaPorte, Indiana, the institution later became known as Commonwealth Business College. In 1919, ownership was transferred to Grace and J. J. Moore, who successfully operated the College under the name of Reese School of Business for several decades. In 1975, the College came under the ownership of Steven C. Smith as Commonwealth Business College. A second location, now known as Brown Mackie College — Merrillville, was opened in 1984 in Merrillville, Indiana.

Brown Mackie College — Merrillville is accredited by the Accrediting Council for Independent Colleges and Schools to award bachelor's degrees, associate degrees, diplomas, and certificates. The Accrediting Council for Independent Colleges and Schools is listed as a nationally recognized accrediting agency by the United States Department of Education and is recognized by the Council for Higher Education Accreditation. ACICS can be contacted at 750 First Street NE, Suite 980, Washington, D.C. 20002; phone: 202-336-6780.

Brown Mackie College — Merrillville is regulated by the Board for Proprietary Education Indiana Commission for Higher Education, 101 West Ohio Street, Suite 670, Indianapolis, Indiana 46204; phone: 317-464-4400. Indiana advertising code: AC0138.

The Brown Mackie College — Merrillville Associate of Science in Medical Assisting is accredited by the Accrediting Bureau of Health Education Schools (www.abhes.org). The Accrediting Bureau of Health Education Schools can be contacted at 7777 Leesburg Pike, Suite 314 N. Falls Church, Virginia 22043; 703-917-9503.

Brown Mackie College — Merrillville Associate of Science in surgical technology program is accredited by the Commission on Accreditation of Allied Health Education Programs (www.caahep.og) upon the recommendation of the Accreditation Review Committee on Education in Surgical Technology and Surgical Assisting (ARC/STSA). The Commission on Accreditation of Allied Health Education Programs can be contacted at 1361 Park Street, Clearwater, Florida 33756; 727-210-2350.

The Associate of Applied Science in occupational therapy assistant program is accredited by the Accreditation Council for Occupational Therapy Education (ACOTE) of the American Occupational Therapy Association (AOTA), 4720 Montgomery Lane, Suite 200, Bethesda, Maryland 20814-3449; phone: 301-652-AOTA. Graduates of the program will be eligible to sit for the national certification examination for the occupational therapy assistant administered by the National Board for Certification in Occupational Therapy (NBCOT). After successful completion of this exam, the individual will be a Certified Occupational Therapy Assistant (COTA). In addition, most states require licensure in order to practice; however, state licenses are usually based on the results of the NBCOT Certification Examination. Note that a felony conviction may affect a graduate's ability to sit for the NBCOT certification examination or attain state licensure.

Location

Brown Mackie College — Merrillville is conveniently located in northwest Indiana at 1000 East 80th Place, Merrillville, in the Twin Towers business complex just west of the intersection of U.S. Route 30 and Interstate 65. A spacious parking lot provides ample parking at no additional charge.

The college is a nonresidential, smoke-free institution.

Programs of Study and Degree Offerings

Brown Mackie College — Merrillville provides higher education to traditional and nontraditional students through bachelor's degree, associate degree, diploma, and certificate programs that assist in enhancing their career opportunities, broadening their perspectives through appropriate general education courses, thinking independently and critically, and improving problem-solving abilities. The college strives to develop within its students the desire for lifelong and continued education.

The Bachelor of Science degree is awarded in business administration and criminal justice.

The Associate of Science degree is awarded in accounting technology, biomedical equipment technician, business management, criminal justice, health care management, legal studies, medical office management, paralegal, and surgical technology.

The Associate of Applied Science degree is awarded in occupational therapy assistant.

The college offers certificate programs in bookkeeping specialist, criminal justice specialist, general business, graphic design assistant, medical assistant, medical billing and coding, medical insurance specialist, and paralegal assistant.

The American Medical Technologists (AMT), which offers the certification for Registered Medical Assistant (RMA), accepts the accreditation of Brown Mackie College — Merrillville. Students will qualify to take the Registered Medical Assistant certification examination upon graduating the Brown Mackie College — Merrillville medical assistant program. Graduates of the 48-credit-hour medical assistant program are not qualified to take the AMT/RMA exam.

Brown Mackie College does not guarantee third-party certification/licensing exams. Outside agencies control the requirements for certification/licensing and are subject to change without notification to the college.

Program availability and degree offerings are subject to change.

Academic Programs

Each college quarter comprises ten to twelve weeks. Bachelor's degree programs require a minimum of sixteen quarters to complete. Associate degree programs require a minimum of eight quarters to complete. Programs are offered on a year-round basis, providing students with the ability to work uninterrupted toward completion of their programs. The college offers all programs in a unique One-Course-a-Month format. This allows students to focus on only one course for four weeks. This schedule has proven convenient for students with multiple obligations, such as jobs and family.

Academic Facilities

Occupying 26,000 square feet, Brown Mackie College — Merrillville was opened to students in October 1998 in the Twin Towers complex of Merrillville and comprises several instructional rooms, including five computer labs with networked computers and four medical laboratories. The administrative offices, college library, and student lounge are all easily accessible to students. The college bookstore stocks texts, courseware, and other educational supplies required for courses at the college. Students also find a variety of personal, recreational, and gift items, including apparel, supplies, and general merchandise incorporating the college logo. Hours are posted at the bookstore entrance.

Brown Mackie College — Merrillville is fully committed to using eTextbooks and computer tablets in the classroom. Utilizing these tablets to access expanded course material, students are able to increase their acumen for using this technology and further enhance their educational experience. Students have the ability to directly download their eTextbooks to their tablet, eliminating the need to carry heavy, physical textbooks and reducing the overall cost of supplies.

Costs

Tuition for most programs in the 2012–13 academic year was $314 per credit hour and fees were $20 per credit hour, with some exceptions. For the surgical technology program, tuition was $360 per credit hour and fees were $20 per credit hour. For the occupational therapy assistant program, tuition was $381 per credit hour and fees were $20 per credit hour. The length of the program determines total cost. Textbook fees, if applicable, vary according to program.

Financial Aid

Financial aid is available to those who qualify. The college maintains a full-time staff of Student Financial Services Advisors to assist qualified students in obtaining financial assistance. The college participates in several student aid programs. Forms of financial aid available through federal resources include the Federal Pell Grant Program, Federal Supplemental Educational Opportunity Grant (FSEOG) Program, Federal Work-Study Program, Federal Perkins Loan Program, Federal Stafford Student Loan Program (subsidized and unsubsidized), and the Federal PLUS Loan Program. Eligible students may apply for Indiana state awards, such as the Higher Education Award and Twenty-First Century Scholarships for high school students, the Core 40 awards, and veterans' educational benefits. Students with physical or mental disabilities that are a handicap to employment may be eligible for training services through the state's Bureau of Vocational Rehabilitation. For further information, students should contact the college's Student Financial Services Office.

Each year, the college makes available President's Scholarships of $1,000 each to qualifying seniors from area high schools. In order to qualify, a senior must be graduating from a participating high school, must be maintaining a cumulative grade point average of at least 2.0, and must submit a brief essay. The student's extracurricular activities and community service are also considered. These scholarships are available only to students enrolling in one of the college's degree programs. Students awarded the scholarship must enroll at Brown Mackie College — Merrillville between June and September immediately following their high school graduation. Applications for these scholarships can be obtained from the guidance departments of participating high schools and must be completed and returned to Brown Mackie College by March 31.

The Education Foundation was established in 2000 to offer scholarship support to students interested in continuing their education at one of the postsecondary, career-focused schools in the EDMC system. The number and amount of the awards can vary, depending on the funds available. Scholarship applications are considered every quarter. At Brown Mackie College, applicants must be currently enrolled in an associate or bachelor's degree program and in their fourth quarter or higher (but no further than their second-to-last quarter) at the time of application. Awards are made based on academic performance and potential, as well as financial need. Interested students should contact the college's Student Financial Service Department for additional information.

Faculty

There are approximately 60 full-time and 25 part-time faculty members at the college, practitioners in their fields of expertise. The average student-faculty ratio is 17:1.

Admission Requirements

Each applicant for admission is assigned an Assistant Director of Admissions who directs the applicant through the steps of the admissions process, providing information on curriculum, policies, procedures, and services and assisting the applicant in setting up necessary appointments and interviews. To qualify for admission, each applicant must provide documentation of graduation from an accredited high school or completion of a state-approved secondary education curriculum or official documentation of high school graduation equivalency. All transcripts become the property of the college.

As part of the admission process, students are given an assessment of academic skills. Although the results of this assessment do not determine eligibility for admission, they provide the college with a means of determining the need for academic support as well as a means by which the college can evaluate the effectiveness of its educational programs. All new students are required to complete this assessment, which is readministered at the end of the student's program, so results may be compared with those of the initial administration.

In addition to the college's general admission requirements, applicants enrolling in the practical nursing program must complete several documents, listed below. A record of proof must appear in the student's file prior to the start of the nursing fundamentals course. No student will be admitted to a clinical agency unless all paperwork is completed. The paperwork is a requirement of all contracted agencies. This paperwork includes records of (1) a complete physical, current to within six months of admission; (2) a two-step Mantoux test that is kept current throughout schooling; (3) a hepatitis B vaccination or signed refusal; (4) up-to-date immunizations, including tetanus and rubella; (5) a record of current CPR certification that is maintained throughout the student's clinical experience; and (6) hospitalization insurance or a signed waiver.

For the most recent information regarding admission requirements, prospective students should refer to the current academic catalog.

Application and Information

Applicants must complete and submit an application form along with documentation of graduation from an accredited high school or completion of state-approved secondary education curriculum or provide official documentation of high school graduation equivalency.

See BMCprograms.info for program duration, tuition, fees and other costs, median debt, federal salary data, alumni success, programmatic accreditation, and other important info.

Brown Mackie College is a system of over twenty-five schools located throughout North America. Programs, credential levels, technology, and scheduling options vary by school, and employment opportunities are not guaranteed. Financial aid is available for those who qualify. Administrative offices are located at 625 Eden Park Drive, Suite 1100; Cincinnati, Ohio 45202; phone: 513.830.2000. ©2013 Brown Mackie College. OH Registration # 03-09-1685T; # 03-09-1686T; # 03-09-1687T; # 03-09-1688T; # 06-03-1781T; AC0150, AC0109, AC0078, AC0045, AC0138, AC0110; Licensed by the Florida Commission for Independent Education, License No. 3206.

For additional information, prospective students should contact:

Brown Mackie College — Merrillville
1000 East 80th Place, Suite 205M
Merrillville, Indiana 46410
United States
Phone: 219-769-3321
        800-258-3321 (toll-free)
Fax: 219-738-1076
E-mail: bmcmeadm@brownmackie.edu
Website: http://www.brownmackie.edu/Merrillville

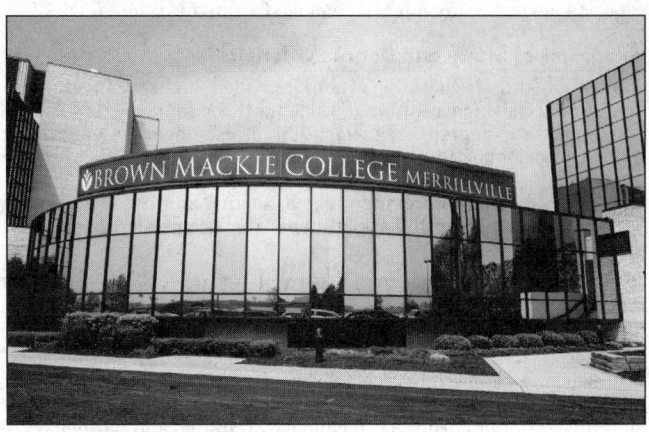

BROWN MACKIE COLLEGE — MIAMI
MIRAMAR, FLORIDA

The College

Brown Mackie College — Miami (Brown Mackie College) is one of over twenty-five locations in the Brown Mackie College system of schools (www.brownmackie.edu), which is dedicated to providing educational programs that prepare students to pursue entry-level positions in a competitive, rapidly changing workplace. Brown Mackie College schools offer bachelor's degree, associate degree, diploma, and certificate programs in health sciences, business, information technology, legal studies, criminal justice, early childhood education, and design to over 20,000 students in the Midwest, Southeast, Southwest, and Western United States.

Brown Mackie College — Miami is accredited by the Accrediting Council for Independent Colleges and Schools to award bachelor's degrees, associate degrees, and diplomas. The Accrediting Council for Independent Colleges and Schools is listed as a nationally recognized accrediting agency by the United States Department of Education and is recognized by the Council for Higher Education Accreditation. ACICS can be contacted at 750 First Street NE, Suite 980, Washington, D.C. 20002; phone: 202-336-6780.

Brown Mackie College — Miami is licensed by the Commission for Independent Education, Florida Department of Education. Additional information regarding this institution may be obtained by contacting the Commission at 325 West Gaines Street, Suite 1414; Tallahassee, Florida 32399-0400; phone: 888-224-6684 (toll-free). Licensed by the Commission for Independent Education, License No. 3206.

The Brown Mackie College – Miami location is approved by the Florida Board of Nursing to offer the Associate in Science in Nursing; 4052 Bald Cypress Way, Bin C-02; Tallahassee, Florida 32399-3252; 850-488-0595; http://www.doh.state.fl.us/mqa/nursing/index.html.

Location

Brown Mackie College — Miami recent moved its main campus to Miramar, Florida in Broward County. Here, the college occupies space on the first, second, and third floors within the newly renovated Space Coast Building. Brown Mackie College — Miami maintains a presence in the downtown Miami, Florida area through an additional location on the fifth and sixth floors of the Bayfront Building at 100 South Biscayne Boulevard, Miami, Florida 33131. Both locations provide access to several transportation options including private shuttle, Metro Mover and City Bus Metro Rail, and Florida's regional Tri-Rail system. Ample parking is also available at no cost to students.

The college is a nonresidential, smoke-free institution.

Programs of Study and Degree Offerings

Brown Mackie College — Miami provides higher education to traditional and nontraditional students through bachelor's degree and associate degree programs that assist them in enhancing their career opportunities, broadening their perspectives through appropriate general education courses, thinking independently and critically, and improving problem-solving abilities. The college strives to develop within its students the desire for lifelong and continued education.

The Bachelor of Science degree is awarded in business administration, criminal justice, health care management, and information technology.

The Associate of Science degree is awarded in accounting technology, biomedical equipment technology, business management, computer networking, criminal justice, early childhood education, health care administration, information technology, nursing, and paralegal.

The college offers diploma programs in criminal justice specialist, medical assistant, medical insurance specialist, and paralegal assistant.

Brown Mackie College does not guarantee third-party certification/licensing exams. Outside agencies control the requirements for certification/licensing and are subject to change without notification to the college.

Program availability and degree offerings are subject to change.

Academic Programs

Each college quarter comprises twelve weeks. Bachelor's degree programs require a minimum of sixteen quarters to complete. Associate degree programs require a minimum of eight quarters to complete. Programs are offered on a year-round basis, providing students with the ability to work uninterrupted toward their degrees. The college offers all programs in a unique One-Course-a-Month format. This allows students to focus studies on only one course for four weeks. This schedule has proven convenient for students with multiple obligations, such as jobs and family.

Academic Facilities

Brown Mackie College — Miami main campus is conveniently located at 3700 Lakeside Drive, Miramar, Florida 33027. The college occupies more than 40,000 square feet on the first, second and third floors of the Space Coast building, which is located in central Miramar.

The two nursing labs, as well as multiple computer classrooms, offer students a modern and professional environment for study. A medical assisting lab is used to instruct clinical medical skills. The college offers a computer networking lab as well as biomedical equipment technology lab for hands-on use and repair of equipment. The facility offers an equipped criminal justice lab including a crime scene and computers with facial recognition software. Each student has access to the technology, tools, and facilities needed to complete projects in each subject area. Students are welcome to use the labs when they are not being used for scheduled classes.

The college features a comfortable student lounge as well as a college store offering retail items including iPad accessories, kits specific to programs of study, and college apparel. The onsite library offers multimedia resources including laptop and iPad stations, power towers for convenient connectivity, books, and electronic resources specific to all academic programs offered.

The college offers an additional academic location in downtown Miami on the fifth and sixth floors of the Bayfront Plaza building. This location offers a number of computer classrooms as well as a criminal justice lab with a crime scene and facial recognition software. The downtown location also has an onsite library including laptop and iPad stations, books, and a wealth of electronic resources specific to all academic programs offered. Course delivery at both Brown Mackie College – Miami locations includes on-ground as well as blended courses.

Brown Mackie College — Miami is fully committed to using eTextbooks and computer tablets in the classroom. Utilizing these tablets to access expanded course material, students are able to increase their acumen for using this technology and further enhance their educational experience. Students have the ability to directly download their eTextbooks to their tablet, eliminating the need to carry heavy, physical textbooks and reducing the overall cost of supplies.

Costs

Tuition in the 2012–13 academic year for most programs was $391 per credit hour; fees were $20 per credit hour. For the nursing program, tuition was $410 per credit hour; fees were $30 per credit hour. Textbooks, if applicable, and other instructional materials vary by program.

Financial Aid

Financial aid is available for those who qualify. The college maintains a full-time staff of Student Financial Services Advisors to assist qualified students in obtaining financial assistance. The college participates in several student aid programs. Forms of financial aid available to qualified students through federal resources include the Federal Pell Grant Program, Federal Supplemental Educational Opportunity Grant (FSEOG) Program, Federal Work-Study Program, Federal Perkins Loan Program, Federal Stafford Student Loan Program (subsidized and unsubsidized), Federal PLUS loan program, and Florida State grant program. Eligible students may apply for veterans' educational benefits. Students with physical or mental disabilities that are a handicap to employment may be eligible for training services through the state Agency for Vocational Rehabilitation. For further information, students should contact the Student Financial Services Office.

Each year, the college makes available President's Scholarships of $1,000 each to qualifying seniors from area high schools. In order to qualify, a senior must be graduating from a participating high school, must be maintaining a cumulative grade point average of at least 2.0, and must submit a brief essay. The student's extracurricular activities and community service are also considered. The President's Scholarship is available only to students enrolling in one of the college's degree programs. Students awarded the scholarship must enroll at Brown Mackie College — Miami between June and September immediately following their high school graduation. Applications for these scholarships can be obtained from the guidance departments of participating high schools and must be completed and returned to Brown Mackie College by March 31. Those awarded scholarships will be notified by April 30. A list of participating high schools may be obtained from the campus Admissions Office.

The Education Foundation was established in 2000 to offer scholarship support to students interested in continuing their education at one of the postsecondary, career-focused schools in the EDMC system. The number and amount of the awards can vary, depending on the funds available. Scholarship applications are considered every quarter. At Brown Mackie College, applicants must be currently enrolled in an associate or bachelor's degree program and in their fourth quarter or higher (but no further than their second-to-last quarter) at the time of application. Awards are made based on academic performance and potential, as well as financial need. Interested students should contact the college's Student Financial Service Department for additional information.

Faculty

There are 15 full-time and more than 70 adjunct faculty members at the college. The average student-faculty ratio is 15:1.

Admission Requirements

Each applicant for admission is assigned an Assistant Director of Admissions who directs the applicant through the steps of the admissions process, providing information on curriculum, policies, procedures, and services, and assisting the applicant in setting up necessary appointments and interviews. To qualify for admission, applicants must be graduates of a public or private high school or education center that is accredited by an agency that is recognized by the U.S. Department of Education or the State of Florida's Department of Education or any of its approved agents or must provide official documentation of high school graduation equivalency. As part of the admissions process, applicants must sign a document attesting to graduation or completion and containing the information to obtain verification of such. Official high school transcripts or official documentation of high school graduation equivalency must be obtained within the first term (90 days) or the student will be withdrawn from the institution following established guidelines for withdrawn students noted in the catalog. Title IV aid will not be dispersed until verification of graduation or completion has been received by the College.

Students seeking entry into the college with a high school diploma completed in a foreign country must provide an original U.S.-equivalency evaluation from an evaluating agency that is a member of the National Association of Credential Evaluation Services (NACES) (http://www.naces.org/) or the Association of International

Credential Evaluators, Inc. (AICES) (http://www.aice-eval.org/). The cost of evaluating the foreign transcript is borne by the college. Brown Mackie College — Miami is authorized under Federal law to enroll nonimmigrant students. Applicants seeking entry into the college with a high school diploma completed in a foreign country must provide an original U. S. equivalency evaluation from a recognized evaluating agency. The cost of evaluating the foreign transcript is borne by the applicant.

For the most recent information regarding admission requirements, prospective students should refer to the current academic catalog.

Application and Information

Applicants must complete and submit an application form, along with documentation of graduation from an accredited high school or state-approved secondary education curriculum or official documentation of high school graduation equivalency.

Specific details regarding program duration, tuition, fees and other costs, median debt, federal salary data, alumni success, programmatic accreditation, and other important information is available online at BMCprograms.info.

Brown Mackie College is a system of over twenty-five schools located throughout North America. Programs, credential levels, technology, and scheduling options vary by school, and employment opportunities are not guaranteed. Financial aid is available for those who qualify. Administrative offices are located at 625 Eden Park Drive, Suite 1100; Cincinnati, Ohio 45202; phone: 513.830.2000. ©2013 Brown Mackie College. OH Registration # 03-09-1685T; # 03-09-1686T; # 03-09-1687T; # 03-09-1688T; # 06-03-1781T; AC0150, AC0109, AC0078, AC0045, AC0138, AC0110; Licensed by the Florida Commission for Independent Education, License No. 3206.

For additional information, prospective students should contact:

Director of Admissions
Brown Mackie College — Miami
3700 Lakeside Drive
Miramar, Florida 33027-3264
United States
Phone: 305-341-6600
        866-505-0335 (toll-free)
Fax: 305-373-8814
E-mail: bmmiaadm@brownmackie.edu
Website: http://www.brownmackie.edu/Miami

BROWN MACKIE COLLEGE — MICHIGAN CITY

MICHIGAN CITY, INDIANA

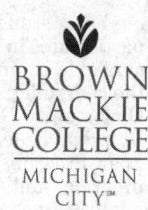
BROWN
MACKIE
COLLEGE
MICHIGAN
CITY™

The College

Brown Mackie College — Michigan City (Brown Mackie College) is one of over twenty-five locations in the Brown Mackie College system of schools (www.brownmackie.edu), which is dedicated to providing educational programs that prepare students to pursue entry-level positions in a competitive, rapidly changing workplace. Brown Mackie College schools offer bachelor's degree, associate degree, diploma, and certificate programs in health sciences, business, information technology, legal studies, and design to over 20,000 students in the Midwest, Southeast, Southwest, and Western United States.

Founded in 1890 by A. N. Hirons as LaPorte Business College in LaPorte, Indiana, the institution later became known as Commonwealth Business College. In 1919, ownership was transferred to Grace and J. J. Moore, who successfully operated the college under the name of Reese School of Business for several decades. In 1975, the college came under the ownership of Steven C. Smith as Commonwealth Business College. In 1997, the college relocated to its present site in Michigan City, Indiana. The College was acquired by Education Management Corporation (EDMC) on September 2, 2003, and changed its name to Brown Mackie College — Michigan City in November 2003.

Brown Mackie College — Michigan City is accredited by the Accrediting Council for Independent Colleges and Schools to award bachelor's degrees, associate degrees, and certificates. The Accrediting Council for Independent Colleges and Schools is listed as a nationally recognized accrediting agency by the United States Department of Education and is recognized by the Council for Higher Education Accreditation. ACICS can be contacted at 750 First Street NE, Suite 980, Washington, D.C. 20002; phone: 202-336-6780.

Brown Mackie College — Michigan City is regulated by the Board for Proprietary Education Indiana Commission for Higher Education, W462 Indiana Government Center South, 402 West Washington Street, Indianapolis, Indiana 46204, 317-232-1324 or 317-232-6716. Indiana Advertising Code: AC0138.

The Associate of Science in veterinary technology program has provisional programmatic accreditation granted by the American Veterinary Medical Association (AVMA) through the Committee on Veterinary Technician Education and Activities (CVTEA) 1931 N. Meachum Road, Suite 100, Schaumburg, Illinois 60173. AVMA's telephone number is 800-248-2862.

The Associate of Science in medical assisting program is accredited by the Accrediting Bureau of Health Education Schools.

Location

Brown Mackie College — Michigan City is conveniently located in northwest Indiana, at 1001 East U.S. Highway 20, Michigan City, 1 mile north of Interstate 94, 2 miles east of the intersection of routes 20 and 421.

The college is a nonresidential, smoke-free institution.

Programs of Study and Degree Offerings

Brown Mackie College — Michigan City provides higher education to traditional and nontraditional students through bachelor's degree, associate degree, and certificate programs that assist in enhancing their career opportunities, broadening their perspectives through appropriate general education courses, thinking independently and critically, and improving problem-solving abilities. Brown Mackie College strives to develop within its students the desire for lifelong and continued education.

The Bachelor of Science degree is awarded in business administration, and criminal justice.

The Associate of Science degree is awarded in accounting technology, business management, criminal justice, and veterinary technology.

The college offers certificate programs in criminal justice specialist, general business, and medical assistant.

The American Medical Technologists (AMT), which offers the certification for Registered Medical Assistant (RMA), accepts the accreditation of Brown Mackie College — Michigan City. Students will qualify to take the Registered Medical Assistant certification examination upon graduating the Brown Mackie College — Michigan City medical assistant program.

Brown Mackie College does not guarantee third-party certification/licensing exams. Outside agencies control the requirements for certification/licensing and are subject to change without notification to the college.

The degree and certificate programs described in this catalog are approved for veteran's training by the Indiana State Approving Agency for Veterans Training.

Program availability and degree offerings are subject to change.

Academic Programs

Each college quarter comprises twelve weeks. Bachelor's degree programs require a minimum of fifteen quarters to complete. Associate degree programs require a minimum of eight quarters to complete. Programs are offered on a year-round basis, providing students with the ability to work uninterrupted toward their degrees. The college offers all programs in a unique One-Course-a-Month format. This allows students to focus studies on only one course for four weeks. This schedule has proven convenient for students with multiple obligations such as jobs and family.

Academic Facilities

In November 2012, the campus relocated to a 29,000-square-foot facility at 1001 East U.S. Highway 20. The new space offers a modern, professional environment for study with a floor plan that features 20 new classrooms with new computers, furniture, audio/visual equipment, and networking equipment for podium additions. The Brown Mackie College — Michigan City facility includes six computer labs, two medical assisting labs, a criminal justice lab, and a veterinary technology lab. The labs provide students with hands-on opportunities to apply knowledge and skills learned in the classroom. Students are welcome to use the labs when those facilities are not in use for scheduled classes. There is a student lounge, a bookstore, and new digital signage in the reception area as well as directional signage throughout the space.

Brown Mackie College — Michigan City is fully committed to using eTextbooks and computer tablets in the classroom. Utilizing these tablets to access expanded course material, students are able to increase their acumen for using this technology and further enhance their educational experience. Students have the ability to directly download their eTextbooks to their tablet, eliminating the need to carry heavy, physical textbooks and reducing the overall cost of supplies.

Costs

Tuition in the 2012–13 academic year was $314 per credit hour and fees were $20 per credit hour. Textbook fees, if applicable, vary according to the program.

Financial Aid

The college maintains a full-time staff of Student Financial Services Advisors to assist qualified students in obtaining financial assistance. The college participates in several student aid programs. Forms of financial aid available to qualified students through federal resources include the Federal Pell Grant Program, Federal Supplemental Educational Opportunity Grant (FSEOG) Program, Federal Work-Study Program, Federal Stafford Student Loan Program (subsidized and unsubsidized), and Federal PLUS loan program.

Eligible students may apply for Indiana state awards, such as the Frank O'Bannon Grant Program (formerly the Higher Education Award) and Twenty-First Century Scholarships for high school students, the Core 40 awards, and veterans' educational benefits. Students with physical or mental disabilities that are a handicap to employment may be eligible for training services through the state's Bureau of Vocational Rehabilitation. For further information, students should contact the college's Student Financial Services Office.

Brown Mackie College — Michigan City is eligible for, and participates in, certain Title IV financial aid programs, state grant programs, and vocational education contracts with private vocational institutions. The college is authorized to enroll students as Vocational Rehabilitation program participants and as Social Security beneficiaries. The college does not participate in the Department of Education's Leave of Absence Program.

Each year, the college makes available President's Scholarships of $1,000 each to qualifying seniors from area high schools. In order to qualify, a senior must be graduating from a participating high school, must be maintaining a cumulative grade point average of at least 2.0, and must submit a brief essay. The student's extracurricular activities and community service are also considered. These scholarships are available only to students enrolling in one of the college's degree programs. Students awarded the scholarship must enroll at Brown Mackie College — Michigan City between June and September immediately following their high school graduation. Applications for these scholarships can be obtained from the guidance departments of participating high schools. These applications must be completed and returned to Brown Mackie College by March 31.

The Education Foundation was established in 2000 to offer scholarship support to students interested in continuing their education at one of the postsecondary, career-focused schools in the EDMC system. The number and amount of the awards can vary, depending on the funds available. Scholarship applications are considered every quarter. At Brown Mackie College, applicants must be currently enrolled in an associate or bachelor's degree program and in their fourth quarter or higher (but no further than their second-to-last quarter) at the time of application. Awards are made based on academic performance and potential, as well as financial need. Interested students should contact the college's Student Financial Service Department for additional information.

Faculty

There are 9 full-time and 31 part-time faculty members at the college. The average student-faculty ratio is 13:1. Each student is assigned a department chair.

Admission Requirements

Each applicant for admission is assigned an Assistant Director of Admissions, who directs the applicant through the steps of the admissions process, providing information on curriculum, policies, procedures, and services and assisting the applicant in setting up necessary appointments and interviews. To be considered for admission to Brown Mackie College — Michigan City, each applicant must provide documentation of graduation from an accredited high school or completion of a state-approved secondary education curriculum or official documentation of high school graduation equivalency. All transcripts become the property of Brown Mackie College.

As part of the admission process, students are given an assessment of academic skills. Although the results of this assessment do not determine eligibility for admission, they provide the college with a means of determining the need for academic support, as well as a means by which the college can evaluate the effectiveness of its educational programs. All new students are required to complete this assessment.

For the most recent information regarding admission requirements, prospective students should refer to the current academic catalog.

Application and Information

Applicants must complete and submit an application form along with documentation of graduation from an accredited high school or completion of a state-approved secondary education curriculum or provide official documentation of high school graduation equivalency.

Specific details regarding program duration, tuition, fees and other costs, median debt, federal salary data, alumni success, programmatic accreditation, and other important information is available online at BMCprograms.info.

Brown Mackie College is a system of over twenty-five schools located throughout North America. Programs, credential levels, technology, and scheduling options vary by school, and employment opportunities are not guaranteed. Financial aid is available for those who qualify. Administrative offices are located at 625 Eden Park Drive, Suite 1100; Cincinnati, Ohio 45202; phone: 513.830.2000. ©2013 Brown Mackie College. OH Registration # 03-09-1685T; # 03-09-1686T; # 03-09-1687T; # 03-09-1688T; # 06-03-1781T; AC0150, AC0109, AC0078, AC0045, AC0138, AC0110; Licensed by the Florida Commission for Independent Education, License No. 3206.

For additional information, prospective students should contact:

Senior Director of Admissions
Brown Mackie College — Michigan City
1001 East U.S. Highway 20
Michigan City, Indiana 46360
United States
Phone: 219-877-3100
     800-519-2416 (toll-free)
Fax: 219-877-3110
E-mail: bmcmcadm@brownmackie.edu
Website: http://www.brownmackie.edu/MichiganCity

BROWN MACKIE COLLEGE — NORTH CANTON

NORTH CANTON, OHIO

The College

Brown Mackie College — North Canton (Brown Mackie College) is one of over twenty-five locations in the Brown Mackie College system of schools (www.brownmackie.edu), which is dedicated to providing educational programs that prepare students to pursue entry-level positions in a competitive, rapidly changing workplace. Brown Mackie College schools offer bachelor's degree, associate degree, diploma, and certificate programs in health sciences, business, information technology, legal studies, and design to more than 20,000 students in the Midwest, Southeast, Southwest, and Western United States.

The college opened in the 1980s as the National Electronics Institute. In 2002, the Southern Ohio College took ownership. The following year, it became part of the Brown Mackie College family of schools.

Brown Mackie College — North Canton is accredited by the Accrediting Council for Independent Colleges and Schools to award bachelor's degrees, associate degrees, and diplomas. The Accrediting Council for Independent Colleges and Schools is listed as a nationally recognized accrediting agency by the United States Department of Education and is recognized by the Council for Higher Education Accreditation. ACICS can be contacted at 750 First Street NE, Suite 980, Washington, D.C. 20002; phone: 202-336-6780.

Brown Mackie College — North Canton is licensed by the Ohio State Board of Career Colleges and Schools, located at 30 East Broad Street, 24th Floor, Suite 2481, Columbus, Ohio 43215-3138; phone: 614-466-2752. Ohio registration # 03-09-1688T.

The Associate of Science in surgical technology program is accredited by the Accrediting Bureau of Health Education Schools. (ABHES). The Accrediting Bureau of Health Education Schools may be contacted at 7777 Leesburg Pike, Suite 314, N. Falls Church, Virginia 22043; 703-917-9503.

The Associate of Science in veterinary technology program has provisional programmatic accreditation granted by the American Veterinary Medical Association (AVMA) through the Committee on Veterinary Technician Education and Activities (CVTEA).

Location

Brown Mackie College — North Canton is located at 4300 Munson Street, NW in Canton, Ohio. The school is easily accessible from I-77 and Route 687 and by the SARTA bus line.

Programs of Study and Degree Offerings

Brown Mackie College — North Canton provides higher education to traditional and nontraditional students through associate degree, bachelor's degree, and diploma programs that can assist students in enhancing their career opportunities, broadening their perspectives through appropriate general education courses, thinking independently and critically, and improving problem-solving abilities. The college strives to develop within its students the desire for lifelong and continued education.

The Bachelor of Science degree is awarded in business administration, criminal justice, health care management, and legal studies.

The Associate of Applied Business degree is awarded in accounting technology, business management, criminal justice, and paralegal.

The Associate of Applied Science degree is awarded in computer networking and applications, health care administration, medical assisting, pharmacy technology, surgical technology, and veterinary technology.

The college also offers diploma programs in bookkeeping specialist, computer aided design & drafting technician, criminal justice specialist, general business, medical assistant, paralegal assistant, and practical nursing.

The American Medical Technologists (AMT), which offers the certification for Registered Medical Assistant (RMA), accepts the accreditation of Brown Mackie College — North Canton. Students will qualify to take the Registered Medical Assistant certification examination upon graduating the Brown Mackie College — North Canton medical assistant program. Graduates of the 48-credit-hour medical assistant program are not qualified to take the AMT/RMA exam.

Brown Mackie College does not guarantee third-party certification/licensing exams. Outside agencies control the requirements for certification/licensing and are subject to change without notification to the college.

Program availability and degree offerings are subject to change.

Academic Programs

Each college quarter comprises twelve weeks. Bachelor's degree programs require a minimum of sixteen quarters to complete. Associate degree programs require a minimum of eight quarters to complete. Programs are offered on a year-round basis, providing students with the ability to work uninterrupted toward their degrees. The college offers all programs in a unique One-Course-a-Month format. This schedule allows students to focus studies on only one course for four weeks and has proven convenient for students with multiple obligations, such as jobs and family.

Academic Facilities

The college comprises administrative offices, faculty and student lounges, a reception area, and spacious classrooms and laboratories. Instructional equipment includes personal computers, LANs, printers, and LCD projectors. The library provides support for the academic programs through volumes covering a broad range of subjects, as well as through Internet access. Vehicle parking is provided for both students and staff members.

Brown Mackie College — North Canton is fully committed to using eTextbooks and computer tablets in the classroom. Utilizing these tablets to access expanded course material, students are able to increase their acumen for using this technology and further enhance their educational experience. Students have the ability to directly download their eTextbooks to their tablet, eliminating the need to carry heavy, physical textbooks and reducing the overall cost of supplies.

Costs

Tuition for the 2012–13 academic year was $314 per credit hour and $20 per credit hour for general fees. The tuition for the surgical technology program was $360 per credit hour and $20 per credit hour for general fees. The tuition for the practical nursing program was $381 per credit hour and $30 per credit hour for general fees. The cost of textbooks, if applicable, and other instructional materials varies by program.

Financial Aid

Financial aid is available to those who qualify. The college maintains a full-time staff of Student Financial Services Advisors to assist qualified students in obtaining financial assistance. The college participates in several student aid programs. Forms of financial aid available through federal resources include the Federal Pell Grant Program, Federal Supplemental Educational Opportunity Grant (FSEOG) Program, Federal Work-Study Program, Federal Perkins Loan Program, Federal Stafford Student Loan Program (subsidized and unsubsidized), and the Federal PLUS Loan Program. Eligible students may also apply for state awards and veterans' educational benefits. Students with physical or mental disabilities that are a handicap to employment may be eligible for training services through the state Agency for Vocational Rehabilitation. For further information, students should contact the college's Student Financial Services Office.

Each year, the college makes available President's Scholarships of $1,000 each to qualifying seniors from area high schools. In order to qualify, a senior must be graduating from a participating high school, must be maintaining a cumulative grade point average of at least 2.0, and must submit a brief essay. The student's extracurricular activities and community service are also considered. The President's Scholarship is available only to students enrolling in one of the college's degree programs. Students awarded the scholarship must enroll at Brown Mackie College — North Canton between June and September immediately following their high school graduation. Applications for these scholarships can be obtained from the guidance departments of participating high schools. These applications must be completed and returned to Brown Mackie College by March 31.

The Education Foundation was established in 2000 to offer scholarship support to students interested in continuing their education at one of the postsecondary, career-focused schools in the EDMC system. The number and amount of the awards can vary, depending on the funds available. Scholarship applications are considered every quarter. At Brown Mackie College, applicants must be currently enrolled in an associate or bachelor's degree program and in their fourth quarter or higher (but no further than their second-to-last quarter) at the time of application. Awards are made based on academic performance and potential, as well as financial need. Interested students should contact the college's Student Financial Service Department for additional information.

Faculty

There are approximately 20 full-time and approximately 35 part-time faculty members. The average student-faculty ratio is approximately 19:1. Each student has a faculty and student adviser.

Admission Requirements

Each applicant for admission is assigned an Assistant Director of Admissions, who directs the applicant through the steps of the admissions process, providing information on curriculum, policies, procedures, and services and assisting the applicant in setting up necessary appointments and interviews. To qualify for admission, each applicant must provide documentation of graduation from an accredited high school or from a state-approved secondary education curriculum or official documentation of high school graduation equivalency. All transcripts become the property of the college. Admission to the college is based upon the applicant meeting the stated requirements, a review of the applicant's previous education records, and a review of the applicant's career interests. If previous academic records indicate that the college's education and training programs would not benefit the applicant, the college reserves the right to advise the applicant not to enroll. Special requirements for enrollment into certain programs are discussed in the descriptions of those programs.

For the most recent information regarding admission requirements, prospective students should refer to the current academic catalog.

Application and Information

Applicants must complete and submit an application form, along with documentation of graduation from an accredited high school or state-approved secondary education curriculum or official documentation of high school graduation equivalency.

Specific details regarding program duration, tuition, fees and other costs, median debt, federal salary data, alumni success, programmatic accreditation, and other important information is available online at BMCprograms.info.

Brown Mackie College is a system of over twenty-five schools located throughout North America. Programs, credential levels, technology, and scheduling options vary by school, and employment opportunities are not guaranteed. Financial aid is available for those who qualify. Administrative offices are located at 625 Eden Park Drive, Suite 1100; Cincinnati, Ohio 45202; phone: 513.830.2000. ©2013 Brown Mackie College. OH Registration # 03-09-1685T; # 03-09-1686T; # 03-09-1687T; # 03-09-1688T; # 06-03-1781T; AC0150, AC0109, AC0078, AC0045, AC0138, AC0110; Licensed by the Florida Commission for Independent Education, License No. 3206.

For additional information, prospective students should contact:

Director of Admissions
Brown Mackie College — North Canton
4300 Munson Street NW
Canton, Ohio 44718-3674
United States
Phone: 330-494-1214
Fax: 330-494-8112
E-mail: bmcncweb@brownmackie.edu
Website: http://www.brownmackie.edu/North-Canton

BROWN MACKIE COLLEGE —
NORTHERN KENTUCKY

FORT MITCHELL, KENTUCKY

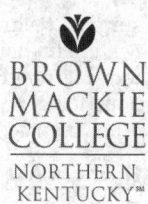

The College

Brown Mackie College — Northern Kentucky (Brown Mackie College) is one of over twenty-five locations in the Brown Mackie College system of schools (www.brownmackie.edu), which is dedicated to providing educational programs that prepare students to pursue entry-level positions in a competitive, rapidly changing workplace. Brown Mackie College schools offer bachelor's degree, associate degree, diploma, and certificate programs in health sciences, business, information technology, legal studies, and design to more than 20,000 students in the Midwest, Southeast, Southwest, and Western United States.

The college was founded in Cincinnati, Ohio, in February 1927 as a traditional business college. In May 1981, the college opened a branch location in northern Kentucky, which in 1986 moved to its current location in Fort Mitchell.

Brown Mackie College — Northern Kentucky is accredited by the Accrediting Council for Independent Colleges and Schools to award bachelor's degrees, associate degrees, and diplomas. The Accrediting Council for Independent Colleges and Schools is listed as a nationally recognized accrediting agency by the United States Department of Education and is recognized by the Council for Higher Education Accreditation. ACICS can be contacted at 750 First Street NE, Suite 980, Washington, D.C. 20002; phone: 202-336-6780.

Brown Mackie College — Northern Kentucky is regulated by the Board for Proprietary Education Indiana Commission for Higher Education, 101 West Ohio Street, Suite 670, Indianapolis, Indiana 46204; 317-464-4400. IN Advertising Code: AC0150.

Brown Mackie College — Northern Kentucky is licensed by the Kentucky Council on Postsecondary Education, located at 1024 Capital Center Drive, Suite 320, Frankfort, Kentucky 40601.

Brown Mackie College — Northern Kentucky is licensed by the Ohio State Board of Career Colleges and Schools, located at 30 East Broad Street, 24th Floor, Suite 2481, Columbus, Ohio 43215-3138; phone: 614-466-2752. Ohio registration # 06-03-1781T.

Brown Mackie College — Northern Kentucky is licensed by the Kentucky Council on Postsecondary Education, located at 1024 Capital Center Drive, Suite 320, Frankfort, Kentucky 40601.

The occupational therapy assistant program is accredited by the Accreditation Council for Occupational Therapy Education (ACOTE) of the American Occupational Therapy Association (AOTA), located at 4720 Montgomery Lane, Suite 200, Bethesda, Maryland 20814-3449; phone: 301-652-AOTA. Graduates of the program will be eligible to sit for the national certification examination for the occupational therapy assistant administered by the National Board for Certification in Occupational Therapy (NBCOT). After successful completion of this exam, the individual will be a Certified Occupational Therapy Assistant (COTA). In addition, most states require licensure in order to practice; however, state licenses are usually based on the results of the NBCOT Certification Examination. Note that a felony conviction may affect a graduate's ability to sit for the NBCOT certification examination or attain state licensure.

The Associate of Applied Science in surgical technology program is accredited by the Commission on Accreditation of Allied Health Education Programs (http://www.caahep.org) upon the recommendation of the Accreditation Review Council on Education in Surgical Technology and Surgical Assisting (ARC/STSA).

The Kentucky Board of Nursing has granted conditional approval status for the prelicensure of the practical nursing diploma program at Brown Mackie College — Northern Kentucky. A factor in the decision was based on the graduates' first-time NCLEX pass rate of 75 percent.

Location

Brown Mackie College — Northern Kentucky is conveniently located at 309 Buttermilk Pike in Fort Mitchell, Kentucky. A spacious parking lot provides ample parking at no additional charge.

Programs of Study and Degree Offerings

Brown Mackie College — Northern Kentucky provides higher education to traditional and nontraditional students through bachelor's degree, associate degree, and diploma programs that assist them in enhancing their career opportunities, broadening their perspectives through appropriate general education courses, thinking independently and critically, and improving problem-solving abilities. The college strives to develop within its students the desire for lifelong and continued education.

The Bachelor of Science degree is awarded in business administration, criminal justice, health care management, and legal studies.

The Associate of Applied Business degree is awarded in accounting technology, business management, computer software technology, criminal justice, information technology, and paralegal.

The Associate of Applied Science degree is awarded in computer aided design & drafting, health care administration, medical assisting, occupational therapy assistant, pharmacy technology, and surgical technology.

Brown Mackie College — Northern Kentucky offers a diploma program in accounting, business, computer software applications, medical assistant, and practical nursing.

The American Medical Technologists (AMT), which offers the certification for Registered Medical Assistant (RMA), accepts the accreditation of Brown Mackie College — Northern Kentucky. Students will qualify to take the Registered Medical Assistant certification examination upon graduating the Brown Mackie College — Northern Kentucky medical assistant program. Graduates of the 48-credit-hour medical assistant program are not qualified to take the AMT/RMA exam.

Brown Mackie College does not guarantee third-party certification/licensing exams. Outside agencies control the requirements for certification/licensing and are subject to change without notification to the college.

Program availability and degree offerings are subject to change.

Academic Programs

Each college quarter comprises ten to twelve weeks. Bachelor's degree programs require a minimum of sixteen quarters to complete. Associate degree programs require a minimum of eight quarters to complete. Programs are offered on a year-round basis, providing students with the ability to work uninterrupted toward their degrees. The college offers all programs in a unique One-Course-a-Month format. This allows students to focus studies on only one course for four weeks. This schedule has proven convenient for students with multiple obligations, such as jobs and family.

Academic Facilities

Brown Mackie College offers media presentation rooms for special instructional needs and a library that provides instructional resources and academic support for both faculty members and students.

Brown Mackie College — Northern Kentucky is fully committed to using eTextbooks and computer tablets in the classroom. Utilizing these tablets to access expanded course material, students are able to increase their acumen for using this technology and further enhance their educational experience. Students have the ability to directly download their eTextbooks to their tablet, eliminating the need to carry heavy, physical textbooks and reducing the overall cost of supplies.

The college is nonresidential; public transportation and ample parking at no cost are available. The school is a smoke-free facility.

Costs

Tuition for the 2012–13 academic year was $314 per credit hour and general fees were $20 per credit hour, with some exceptions. The practical nursing program tuition was $381 per credit hour and general fees were $30 per credit hour. The surgical technology tuition was $360 per credit hour and general fees were $20 per credit hour. Tuition for the occupational therapy assistant program was $381 per credit hour and general fees were $20 per credit hour. The cost of textbooks, if applicable, and other instructional materials varies by program.

Financial Aid

Financial aid is available to those who qualify. The college maintains a full-time staff of Student Financial Services Advisors to assist qualified students in obtaining financial assistance. The college participates in several student aid programs. Forms of financial aid available through federal resources include Federal Pell Grants, Federal Supplemental Educational Opportunity Grants (FSEOG), Federal Work-Study Program awards, Federal Stafford Student Loans (subsidized and unsubsidized), and Federal PLUS loans. Eligible students may apply for veterans' educational benefits. Students with physical or mental disabilities that are a handicap to employment may be eligible for training services through the state Vocational Rehabilitation Agency. For further information, students should contact the Student Financial Services Office.

Each year, the college makes available President's Scholarships of $1,000 each to qualifying seniors from area high schools. In order to qualify, a senior must have graduated from a participating high school, must have maintained a cumulative grade point average of at least 2.0, and must have submitted a brief essay. The student's extracurricular activities and community service are also considered. The President's Scholarship is available only to students enrolling in one of the college's degree programs. Students who receive the scholarship must enroll at Brown Mackie College — Northern Kentucky between June and September immediately following their high school graduation. Applications for these scholarships can be obtained from the guidance departments of participating high schools. These applications must be completed and returned to Brown Mackie College by March 31.

The Education Foundation was established in 2000 to offer scholarship support to students interested in continuing their education at one of the postsecondary, career-focused schools in the EDMC system. The number and amount of the awards can vary, depending on the funds available. Scholarship applications are considered every quarter. At Brown Mackie College, applicants must be currently enrolled in an associate or bachelor's degree program and in their fourth quarter or higher (but no further than their second-to-last quarter) at the time of application. Awards are made based on academic performance and potential, as well as financial need. Interested students should contact the college's Student Financial Service Department for additional information.

Faculty

There are 12 full-time and 30 adjunct faculty members. The student-faculty ratio is 12:1.

Admission Requirements

Each applicant for admission is assigned an Assistant Director of Admissions, who directs the applicant through the steps of the admissions process, providing information on curriculum, policies, procedures, and services and assisting the applicant in setting up necessary appointments and interviews. To qualify for admission, each applicant must provide documentation of graduation from an accredited high school or from a state-approved secondary education curriculum or provide official documentation of high school graduation equivalency. All transcripts become the property of the college. Admission to the college is based upon the applicant meeting the stated requirements, a review of the applicant's previous education records, and a review of the applicant's career interests. If previous academic records indicate the college's education and training programs would not benefit the applicant, the college reserves the right to advise the applicant not to enroll. Special requirements for enrollment into certain programs are discussed in the descriptions of those programs.

In addition to the college's general admission requirements, applicants enrolling in the practical nursing program must complete several documents, listed below. A record of proof must appear in the student's file prior to the start of the nursing fundamentals course. No student will be admitted to a clinical agency unless all paperwork is completed. The paperwork is a requirement of all contracted agencies. This paperwork includes records of (1) a complete physical, current to within six months of admission; (2) a two-step Mantoux test that is kept current throughout schooling; (3) a hepatitis B vaccination or signed refusal; (4) up-to-date immunizations, including tetanus and rubella; (5) a record of current CPR certification that is maintained throughout the student's clinical experience; and (6) hospitalization insurance or a signed waiver.

For the most recent information regarding admission requirements, prospective students should refer to the current academic catalog.

Application and Information

Applicants must complete and submit an application form, along with documentation of graduation from an accredited high school or state-approved secondary education curriculum or official documentation of high school graduation equivalency.

Specific details regarding program duration, tuition, fees and other costs, median debt, federal salary data, alumni success, programmatic accreditation, and other important information is available online at BMCprograms.info.

Brown Mackie College is a system of over twenty-five schools located throughout North America. Programs, credential levels, technology, and scheduling options vary by school, and employment opportunities are not guaranteed. Financial aid is available for those who qualify. Administrative offices are located at 625 Eden Park Drive, Suite 1100; Cincinnati, Ohio 45202; phone: 513.830.2000. ©2013 Brown Mackie College. OH Registration # 03-09-1685T; # 03-09-1686T; # 03-09-1687T; # 03-09-1688T; # 06-03-1781T; AC0150, AC0109, AC0078, AC0045, AC0138, AC0110; Licensed by the Florida Commission for Independent Education, License No. 3206.

For additional information, prospective students should contact:

Director of Admissions
Brown Mackie College — Northern Kentucky
309 Buttermilk Pike
Fort Mitchell, Kentucky 41017
United States
Phone: 859-341-5627
         800-888-1445 (toll-free)
Fax: 859-341-6483
E-mail: bmcnkadm@brownmackie.edu
Web site: http://www.brownmackie.edu/NorthernKentucky

BROWN MACKIE COLLEGE — OKLAHOMA CITY

OKLAHOMA CITY, OKLAHOMA

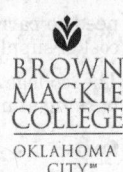

The College

Brown Mackie College — Oklahoma City (Brown Mackie College) is one of over twenty-five locations in the Brown Mackie College system of schools (www.brownmackie.edu), which is dedicated to providing educational programs that prepare students to pursue entry-level positions in a competitive, rapidly changing workplace. Brown Mackie College schools offer bachelor's degree, associate degree, certificate, and diploma programs in health sciences, business, information technology, legal studies, and design to over 20,000 students in the Midwest, Southeast, Southwest, and Western United States.

Brown Mackie College — Oklahoma City is a branch campus of Brown Mackie College — Salina which is accredited by the Higher Learning Commission and a member of the North Central Association, 230 South LaSalle Street, Suite 7-500, Chicago, Illinois 60604-1413; phone: 800-621-7440 (toll-free); www.ncahlc.org.

This institution has been granted authority to operate in Oklahoma by the Oklahoma State Regents for Higher Education (OSRHE), 655 Research Parkway, Suite 200, Oklahoma City, Oklahoma 73101; phone: 405-225-9100.

The Associate of Applied Science in occupational therapy assistant program has applied for accreditation to the Accreditation Council for Occupational Therapy Education (ACOTE) of the American Occupational Therapy Association (AOTA), located at 4720 Montgomery Lane, Suite 200, Bethesda, Maryland 20814-3449; phone: 301-652-AOTA. Graduates of the program will be eligible to sit for the national certification examination for the occupational therapy assistant administered by the National Board for Certification in Occupational Therapy (NBCOT). After successful completion of this exam, the individual will be a Certified Occupational Therapy Assistant (COTA). In addition, most states require licensure in order to practice; however, state licenses are usually based on the results of the NBCOT Certification Examination. Note that a felony conviction may affect a graduate's ability to sit for the NBCOT certification examination or attain state licensure.

Location

Brown Mackie College — Oklahoma City is located at 7101 Northwest Expressway, Suite 800, in Oklahoma City, Oklahoma.

Programs of Study and Degree Offerings

Brown Mackie College — Oklahoma City provides higher education to traditional and nontraditional students through associate degree programs that can assist students in enhancing their career opportunities, broadening their perspectives through appropriate general education courses, thinking independently and critically, and improving problem-solving abilities. Brown Mackie College strives to develop within its students the desire for lifelong and continued education.

The Bachelor of Science degree is awarded in business administration and health care management.

The Associate of Applied Science degree is awarded in accounting technology, business management, health care administration, medical assisting, occupational therapy assistant, and paralegal.

The American Medical Technologists (AMT), which offers the certification for Registered Medical Assistant (RMA), accepts the accreditation of Brown Mackie College — Oklahoma City. Students will qualify to take the Registered Medical Assistant certification examination upon graduating the Brown Mackie College — Oklahoma City medical assisting program.

Brown Mackie College does not guarantee third-party certification/licensing exams. Outside agencies control the requirements for certification/licensing and are subject to change without notification to the college.

Program availability and degree offerings are subject to change.

Academic Programs

Each college quarter comprises twelve weeks. Associate degree programs require a minimum of eight quarters to complete. Programs are offered on a year-round basis, providing students with the ability to work uninterrupted toward their degrees. Brown Mackie College offers all programs in a unique One Course a Month format. This schedule allows students to focus studies on only one course for four weeks and has proven convenient for students with multiple obligations such as jobs and family.

Academic Facilities

Brown Mackie College — Oklahoma City comprises administrative offices, faculty and student lounges, a reception area, and spacious classrooms and laboratories. Instructional equipment includes personal computers, LANs, printers, and transcribers. The library provides support for the academic programs through volumes covering a broad range of subjects, as well as through Internet access. Vehicle parking is provided for both students and staff members.

Brown Mackie College — Oklahoma City is fully committed to using eTextbooks and computer tablets in the classroom. Utilizing these tablets to access expanded course material, students are able to increase their acumen for using this technology and further enhance their educational experience. Students have the ability to directly download their eTextbooks to their tablet, eliminating the need to carry heavy, physical textbooks and reducing the overall cost of supplies.

The college is nonresidential; public transportation and ample parking at no cost are available. The school is a smoke-free facility.

Costs

Tuition for the 20112–13 academic year was $314 per credit hour, and $20 per credit hour for general fees. Tuition for the occupational therapy assistant program was $381 per credit hour, and $20 per credit hour for general fees. The cost of textbooks, if applicable, and other instructional materials varies by program.

Financial Aid

Financial aid is available to those who qualify. Brown Mackie College — Oklahoma City maintains a full-time staff of financial aid professionals to assist qualified students in obtaining financial assistance. The college participates in several student aid programs. Forms of financial aid available through federal resources include the Federal Pell Grant Program, Federal Supplemental Educational Opportunity Grant (FSEOG) Program, Federal Work-Study Program, Federal Perkins Loan Program, Federal Stafford Student Loan Program (subsidized and unsubsidized), and the Federal PLUS Loan Program. Eligible students may also apply for state awards and veterans' educational benefits. Students with physical or mental disabilities that are a handicap to employment may be eligible for training services through the state Agency for Vocational Rehabilitation. For further information, students should contact the Brown Mackie College — Oklahoma City Student Financial Services Office.

Each year, the college makes available President's Scholarships of $1,000 each to qualifying seniors from area high schools. In order to qualify, a senior must be graduating from a participating high school, have maintained a cumulative grade point average of at least 2.0, and submitted a brief essay. The student's extracurricular activities and community service are also considered. The President's Scholarship is available only to students enrolling in one of the college's degree programs. Students awarded the scholarship must enroll at Brown Mackie College — Oklahoma City between June and September immediately following their high school graduation. Applications for these scholarships can be obtained from the guidance departments of participating high schools. These applications must be completed and returned to the college by March 31.

The Education Foundation was established in 2000 to offer scholarship support to students interested in continuing their education at one of the postsecondary, career-focused schools in the EDMC system. The number and amount of the awards can vary, depending on the funds available. Scholarship applications are considered every quarter. At Brown Mackie College, applicants must be currently enrolled in an associate or bachelor's degree program and in their fourth quarter or higher (but no further than their second-to-last quarter) at the time of application. Awards are made based on academic performance and potential, as well as financial need. Interested students should contact the college's Student Financial Service Department for additional information.

Faculty

There are 11 full-time and 30 adjunct faculty members. The student-faculty ratio is 15:1.

Admission Requirements

Each applicant for admission is assigned an Assistant Director of Admissions who directs the applicant through the steps of the admissions process, providing information on curriculum, policies, procedures, and services and assisting the applicant in setting necessary appointments and interviews.

To qualify for admission, each applicant must provide documentation of graduation from an accredited high school or from a state-approved secondary education curriculum or provide official documentation of high school graduation equivalency. All transcripts become the property of Brown Mackie College — Oklahoma City. Admission to the college is based upon the applicant meeting the stated requirements, a review of the applicant's previous education records, and a review of the applicant's career interests. If previous academic records indicate that the Brown Mackie College education and training programs would not benefit the applicant, the college reserves the right to advise the applicant not to enroll. Special requirements for enrollment into certain programs are discussed in the descriptions of those programs.

For the most recent information regarding admission requirements, prospective students should refer to the current academic catalog.

Application and Information

Applicants must complete and submit an application form along with documentation of graduation from an accredited high school or state-approved secondary education curriculum, or applicants must provide official documentation of high school graduation equivalency.

Specific details regarding program duration, tuition, fees and other costs, median debt, federal salary data, alumni success, programmatic accreditation, and other important information is available at BMCprograms.info.

Brown Mackie College is a system of over twenty-five schools located throughout North America. Programs, credential levels, technology, and scheduling options vary by school, and employment opportunities are not guaranteed. Financial aid is available for those who qualify. Administrative offices are located at 625 Eden Park Drive, Suite 1100; Cincinnati, Ohio 45202; phone: 513.830.2000. ©2013 Brown Mackie College. OH Registration # 03-09-1685T; # 03-09-1686T; # 03-09-1687T; # 03-09-1688T; # 06-03-1781T; AC0150, AC0109, AC0078, AC0045, AC0138, AC0110; Licensed by the Florida Commission for Independent Education, License No. 3206.

For additional information, prospective students should contact:

Director of Admissions
Brown Mackie College — Oklahoma City
7101 Northwest Expressway, Suite 800
Oklahoma City, Oklahoma 73132
Phone: 405-621-8000
        888-229-3280 (toll-free)
Fax: 405-621-8055
E-mail: bmcokcadm@brownmackie.edu
Website: http://www.brownmackie.edu/Oklahoma-City

BROWN MACKIE COLLEGE — ST. LOUIS
FENTON, MISSOURI

The College

Brown Mackie College — St. Louis (Brown Mackie College) is one of over twenty-five locations in the Brown Mackie College system of schools (www.brownmackie.edu), which is dedicated to providing educational programs that prepare students to pursue entry-level positions in a competitive, rapidly changing workplace. Brown Mackie College schools offer bachelor's degree, associate degree, diploma, and certificate programs in health sciences, business, information technology, legal studies, and design to over 20,000 students in the Midwest, Southeast, Southwest, and Western United States.

Brown Mackie College was originally founded and approved by the Board of Trustees of Kansas Wesleyan College in Salina, Kansas on July 30, 1892. In 1938, the College was incorporated as The Brown Mackie School of Business under the ownership of Perry E. Brown and A.B. Mackie, former instructors at Kansas Wesleyan University in Salina, Kansas. Their last names formed the name of Brown Mackie. By January 1975, with improvements in curricula and higher-degree-granting status, The Brown Mackie School of Business became Brown Mackie College.

Brown Mackie College — St. Louis is accredited by the Accrediting Council for Independent Colleges and Schools to award bachelor's degrees, associate degrees, and certificates. The Accrediting Council for Independent Colleges and Schools is listed as a nationally recognized accrediting agency by the United States Department of Education and is recognized by the Council for Higher Education Accreditation. ACICS can be contacted at 750 First Street NE, Suite 980, Washington, D.C. 20002; phone: 202-336-6780.

The Associate of Applied Science in occupational therapy assistant program is accredited by the Accreditation Council for Occupational Therapy Education (ACOTE) of the American Occupational Therapy Association (AOTA), located at 4720 Montgomery Lane, Suite 200, Bethesda, Maryland 20814-3449; phone: 301-652-AOTA. Graduates of the program will be eligible to sit for the national certification examination for the occupational therapy assistant administered by the National Board for Certification in Occupational Therapy (NBCOT). After successful completion of this exam, the individual will be a Certified Occupational Therapy Assistant (COTA). In addition, most states require licensure in order to practice; however, state licenses are usually based on the results of the NBCOT Certification Examination. Note that a felony conviction may affect a graduate's ability to sit for the NBCOT certification examination or attain state licensure.

The Associate of Science in surgical technology program is accredited by the Accrediting Bureau of Health Education Schools (ABHES).

The Associate of Applied Science in veterinary technology program has provisional programmatic accreditation granted by the American Veterinary Medical Association (AVMA) through the Committee on Veterinary Technician Education and Activities (CVTEA).

Location

Brown Mackie College — St. Louis is conveniently located at #2 Soccer Park Road in Fenton, Missouri. The college has a generous parking area available to students and staff.

Programs of Study and Degree Offerings

Brown Mackie College — St. Louis provides higher education to traditional and nontraditional students through bachelor's and associate degree programs that assist in enhancing their career opportunities, broadening their perspectives through appropriate general education courses, thinking independently and critically, and improving problem-solving abilities. The college strives to develop within its students the desire for lifelong and continued education.

The Bachelor of Science degree is awarded in business administration, criminal justice, health care management, and legal studies.

The Associate of Applied Science degree is awarded in accounting technology, biomedical equipment technology, business management, criminal justice, health care administration, information technology, nursing, occupational therapy assistant, paralegal, surgical technology, and veterinary technology.

The college offers certificate programs in accounting, biomedical equipment technician, business, criminal justice, medical assistant, and paralegal assistant.

The American Medical Technologists (AMT), which offers the certification for Registered Medical Assistant (RMA), accepts the accreditation of Brown Mackie College — St. Louis. Students will qualify to take the Registered Medical Assistant certification examination upon graduating the Brown Mackie College — St. Louis medical assistant program. Graduates of the 48-credit-hour medical assistant program are not qualified to take the AMT/RMA exam.

Brown Mackie College does not guarantee third-party certification/licensing exams. Outside agencies control the requirements for certification/licensing and are subject to change without notification to the college.

Program availability and degree offerings are subject to change.

Academic Programs

Each college quarter comprises twelve weeks. Bachelor degree programs require a minimum of sixteen quarters to complete. Associate degree programs require a minimum of eight quarters to complete. Programs are offered on a year-round basis, providing students with the ability to work uninterrupted toward completion of their programs. The college offers all programs in a unique One-Course-a-Month format. This allows students to focus studies on only one course for four weeks. This schedule has proven convenient for students with multiple obligations, such as jobs and family.

Academic Facilities

A modern facility, Brown Mackie College — St. Louis offers more than 30,000 square feet. The college is equipped with multiple computer labs, housing over 100 computers. High-speed access to the Internet and other online resources are available for students and faculty. Multimedia classrooms are outfitted with overhead projectors, VCR/DVD players, and computers.

Brown Mackie College — St. Louis is fully committed to using eTextbooks and computer tablets in the classroom. Utilizing these tablets to access expanded course material, students are able to increase their acumen for using this technology and further enhance their educational experience. Students have the ability to directly download their eTextbooks to their tablet, eliminating the need to carry heavy, physical textbooks and reducing the overall cost of supplies.

Brown Mackie College — St. Louis is nonresidential and is a smoke-free facility.

Costs

Tuition in the 2012–13 academic year for most bachelor's and associate degrees and diploma programs was $288 per credit hour; fees were $20 per credit hour. Tuition for the surgical technology program was $339 per credit hour; fees were $20 per credit hour. Tuition for the nursing program was $410 per credit hour; fees were $30 per credit hour. Tuition for the occupational therapy assistant program was $355 per credit hour; fees were $20 per credit hour. The cost of textbooks, if applicable, and other instructional materials varies by program.

Financial Aid

Financial aid is available for those who qualify. The college maintains a full-time staff of Student Financial Services Advisors to assist qualified students in obtaining the financial assistance they require to meet their educational expenses. Available resources include federal and state aid, student loans from private lenders, and Federal Work-Study opportunities, both on and off college premises.

Each year, the college makes available President's Scholarships of $1,000 each to qualifying seniors from area high schools. In order to qualify, a senior must have graduated from a participating high school, must have maintained a cumulative grade point average of at least 2.0, and must have submitted a brief essay. The student's extracurricular activities and community service are also considered. These scholarships are available only to students enrolling in one of the college's degree programs. Students awarded the scholarship must enroll at Brown Mackie College — St. Louis between June and September immediately following their high school graduation. Applications for these scholarships can be obtained from the guidance departments of participating high schools. These applications must be completed and returned to Brown Mackie College by March 31.

The Education Foundation was established in 2000 to offer scholarship support to students interested in continuing their education at one of the postsecondary, career-focused schools in the EDMC system. The number and amount of the awards can vary, depending on the funds available. Scholarship applications are considered every quarter. At Brown Mackie College, applicants must be currently enrolled in an associate or bachelor's degree program and in their fourth quarter or higher (but no further than their second-to-last quarter) at the time of application. Awards are made based on academic performance and potential, as well as financial need. Interested students should contact the college's Student Financial Service Department for additional information.

Faculty

Experienced faculty members provide academic support and are committed to the academic and technical preparation of their students. The college has 12 full-time and 23 part-time instructors, with a student-faculty ratio of 20:1.

Admission Requirements

Each applicant for admission is assigned an Assistant Director of Admissions who directs the applicant through the steps of the admissions process. Assistant Directors provide information on curriculum, policies, procedures, and services and assist the applicant in setting up necessary appointments and interviews. To qualify for admission, each applicant must provide documentation of graduation from an accredited high school or from a state-approved secondary education curriculum or official documentation of high school graduation equivalency. All transcripts become the property of the college. Admission to the college is based on the applicant meeting the stated requirements, a review of the applicant's previous educational records, and a review of the applicant's career interests. If previous academic records indicate the college's education and training programs would not benefit the applicant, the college reserves the right to advise the applicant not to enroll. Special requirements for enrollment into certain programs are discussed in the descriptions of those programs.

For the most recent information regarding admission requirements, prospective students should refer to the current academic catalog.

Application and Information

Applicants must complete and submit an application form, along with documentation of graduation from an accredited high school or state-approved secondary education curriculum or official documentation of high school graduation equivalency.

Specific details regarding program duration, tuition, fees and other costs, median debt, federal salary data, alumni success, programmatic accreditation, and other important information are available online at BMCprograms.info.

Brown Mackie College is a system of over twenty-five schools located throughout North America. Programs, credential levels, technology, and scheduling options vary by school, and employment opportunities are not guaranteed. Financial aid is available for those who qualify. Administrative offices are located at 625 Eden Park Drive, Suite 1100; Cincinnati, Ohio 45202; phone: 513.830.2000. ©2013 Brown Mackie College. OH Registration # 03-09-1685T; # 03-09-1686T; # 03-09-1687T; # 03-09- 1688T; # 06-03-1781T; AC0150, AC0109, AC0078, AC0045, AC0138, AC0110; Licensed by the Florida Commission for Independent Education, License No. 3206.

For additional information, prospective students should contact:

Director of Admissions
Brown Mackie College — St. Louis
#2 Soccer Park Road
Fenton, Missouri 63026
United States
Phone: 636-651-3290
      888-874-4375 (toll-free)
Fax: 636-651-3349
E-mail: bmcstladm@brownmackie.edu
Website: http://www.brownmackie.edu/StLouis

BROWN MACKIE COLLEGE — SALINA
SALINA, KANSAS

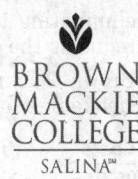

The College

Brown Mackie College — Salina (Brown Mackie College) is one of over twenty-five locations in the Brown Mackie College system of schools (www.brownmackie.edu), which is dedicated to providing educational programs that prepare students to pursue entry-level positions in a competitive, rapidly changing workplace. Brown Mackie College schools offer bachelor's degree, associate degree, certificate, and diploma programs in health sciences, business, information technology, legal studies, and design to over 20,000 students in the Midwest, Southeast, Southwest, and Western United States.

The college was originally founded in July 1892 as the Kansas Wesleyan School of Business. In 1938, the college was incorporated as the Brown Mackie School of Business under the ownership of former Kansas Wesleyan instructors Perry E. Brown and A. B. Mackie; it became Brown Mackie College in January 1975.

Brown Mackie College — Salina is accredited by the Higher Learning Commission and is a member of the North Central Association (NCA), 230 South LaSalle Street, Suite 7-500, Chicago, Illinois 60604-1413; phone: 800-621-7440 (toll-free); www.ncahlc.org.

Brown Mackie College — Salina is approved and authorized to grant the Associate of Applied Science (A.A.S.) degree, Associate of General Studies (A.G.S.) degree and the Bachelor of Science (B.S.) degree by the Kansas Board of Regents, 1000 SW Jackson Street, Suite 520, Topeka, Kansas 66612-1368.

The Associate of Applied Science in occupational therapy assistant program is accredited by the Accreditation Council for Occupational Therapy Education (ACOTE) of the American Occupational Therapy Association (AOTA), located at 4720 Montgomery Lane, Suite 200, Bethesda, Maryland 20814-3449; phone: 301-652-AOTA. Graduates of the program will be eligible to sit for the national certification examination for the occupational therapy assistant administered by the National Board for Certification in Occupational Therapy (NBCOT). After successful completion of this exam, the individual will be a Certified Occupational Therapy Assistant (COTA). In addition, most states require licensure in order to practice; however, state licenses are usually based on the results of the NBCOT Certification Examination. Note that a felony conviction may affect a graduate's ability to sit for the NBCOT certification examination or attain state licensure.

The Associate of Applied Science in veterinary technology program has provisional programmatic accreditation granted by the American Veterinary Medical Association (AVMA) through the Committee on Veterinary Technician Education and Activities (CVTEA).

Location

Brown Mackie College — Salina is located at 2106 South Ninth Street in Salina, Kansas.

Programs of Study and Degree Offerings

Brown Mackie College — Salina provides higher education to traditional and nontraditional students through bachelor's degree, associate degree, diploma, and certificate programs that can assist them in enhancing their career opportunities, broadening their perspectives through appropriate general education courses, thinking independently and critically, and improving problem-solving abilities. The college strives to develop within its students the desire for lifelong and continued education.

In most programs, students can participate in day or evening classes, which begin every month. Programs are offered on a year-round basis, providing students with the ability to work uninterrupted toward completion of their programs. Brown Mackie College offers all programs in a unique One Course a Month format. This schedule allows students to focus studies on only one course for four weeks and has proven convenient for students with multiple obligations such as jobs and family.

The Bachelor of Science degree is awarded in business administration and health care management.

The Associate of Applied Science degree is awarded in accounting technology, business management, computer aided design and drafting technology, computer networking & applications, criminal justice, health and fitness training, health care administration, medical assisting, nursing, occupational therapy assistant, paralegal, and veterinary technology.

An associate degree in general studies is also offered to create a greater level of flexibility for students who may be unsure of their career choice, who want a more generalized education, or who want to transfer to a baccalaureate program.

The college also offers diploma programs in bookkeeping specialist, computer aided designer/drafter, criminal justice specialist, fitness trainer, general business, medical assistant, medical insurance specialist, and networking specialist.

Certificate programs are offered in network engineer specialist and practical nursing.

The American Medical Technologists (AMT), which offers the certification for Registered Medical Assistant (RMA), accepts the accreditation of Brown Mackie College — Salina. Students will qualify to take the RMA certification examination upon graduating the Brown Mackie College — Salina medical assisting and medical assistant programs. Graduates of the 48 credit-hour medical assistant program are not qualified to take the AMT/RMA exam.

Brown Mackie College does not guarantee third-party certification/licensing exams. Outside agencies control the requirements for certification/licensing and are subject to change without notification to the college.

Program availability and degree offerings are subject to change.

Academic Programs

Each college quarter comprises twelve weeks. Bachelor's degree programs require a minimum of sixteen quarters to complete. Associate degree programs require a minimum of eight quarters to complete. Programs are offered on a year-round basis, providing students with the ability to work uninterrupted toward completion of their programs. The college offers all programs in a unique One-Course-a-Month format. This allows students to focus studies on only one course for four weeks. This schedule has proven convenient for students with multiple obligations, such as jobs and family.

Academic Facilities

In addition to classrooms and computer labs, Brown Mackie College — Salina maintains a library of curriculum-related resources, technical and general education materials, academic and professional periodicals, and audiovisual resources. Internet access is also available for research. The college has a bookstore that stocks texts, courseware, and other educational supplies that are required for courses and a variety of personal, recreational, and gift items, including apparel, supplies, and general merchandise incorporating the Brown Mackie College logo. Hours are posted at the bookstore entrance.

Brown Mackie College — Salina is fully committed to using eTextbooks and computer tablets in the classroom. Utilizing these tablets to access expanded course material, students are able to increase their acumen for using this technology and further enhance their educational experience. Students have the ability to directly download their eTextbooks to their tablet, eliminating the need to carry heavy, physical textbooks and reducing the overall cost of supplies.

Costs

Tuition for the 2012–13 academic year was $314 per credit hour and general fees were $20 per credit hour. Tuition for computer networking was $314 per credit hour and general fees were $25 per credit hour. Tuition for the fitness programs was $324 per credit hour and general fees were $30 per credit hour. Tuition for the nursing programs was $381 per credit hour and general fees were $30 per credit hour. Tuition for the occupational therapy assistant program was $381 per credit hour and general fees were $20 per credit hour. The cost of textbooks, if applicable, and other instructional materials varies by program.

Financial Aid

Financial aid is available to those who qualify. Brown Mackie College — Salina maintains a full-time staff of financial aid professionals to assist qualified students in obtaining financial assistance. The college participates in several student aid programs. Forms of financial aid that are available through federal resources include Federal Pell Grants, Federal Supplemental Educational Opportunity Grants (FSEOG), Academic Competitiveness Grant, Federal Work-Study Program awards, Federal Perkins Loans, Federal Stafford Student Loans (subsidized and unsubsidized), and Federal PLUS loans. Eligible students may apply for veterans' educational benefits. Students with physical or mental disabilities that are a handicap to employment may be eligible for training services through the state Vocational Rehabilitation Agency. For further information, students should contact the Brown Mackie College — Salina Student Financial Services Office.

Each year, the college makes available President's Scholarships of $1,000 each to qualifying seniors from area high schools. In order to qualify, a senior must be graduating from a participating high school, have maintained a cumulative grade point average of at least 2.0, and submitted a brief essay. The student's extracurricular activities and community service are also considered. The President's Scholarship is available only to students enrolling in one of the college's degree programs. Students awarded the scholarship must enroll at Brown Mackie College — Salina between June and September immediately following their high school graduation. Applications for these scholarships can be obtained from the guidance departments of participating high schools. These applications must be completed and returned to the college by March 31.

The Education Foundation was established in 2000 to offer scholarship support to students interested in continuing their education at one of the postsecondary, career-focused schools in the EDMC system. The number and amount of the awards can vary, depending on the funds available. Scholarship applications are considered every quarter. At Brown Mackie College, applicants must be currently enrolled in an associate or bachelor's degree program and in their fourth quarter or higher (but no further than their second-to-last quarter) at the time of application. Awards are made based on academic performance and potential, as well as financial need. Interested students should contact the college's Student Financial Service Department for additional information.

The Merit Scholarship is a college-sponsored scholarship that may be awarded to students who demonstrate exceptional academic ability. To qualify for a Merit Scholarship, an applicant or student must have scored 21 or higher on the ACT or 900 or higher on the SAT. The maximum amount awarded by this scholarship to any student is $500.

Athletic scholarships may be awarded to students who participate in athletic programs that are sponsored by Brown Mackie College — Salina. Current sports are men's baseball, men's and women's basketball, and women's fast-pitch softball. Maximum awards for any applicant or student are determined by the college president. Further information is available from the Athletic Office. Recipients of athletic scholarships must achieve a cumulative grade point average of at least 2.0 by their graduation. Recipients who fail to maintain full-time status or the required grade point average forfeit their awards.

Faculty

There are 21 full-time and 19 adjunct faculty members. The average student-instructor ratio is 15:1.

Admission Requirements

Each applicant for admission is assigned to an Assistant Director of Admissions, who directs the applicant through the steps of the admissions process, providing information on curriculum, policies, procedures, and services and assisting the applicant in setting necessary appointments and interviews.

To qualify for admission, each applicant must provide documentation of graduation from an accredited high school or from a state-approved secondary education curriculum or provide official documentation of high school graduation equivalency. All transcripts become the property of Brown Mackie College. Admission to the college is based upon the applicant meeting the above requirements, a review of the applicant's previous education records, and a review of the applicant's career interests. If previous academic records indicate that the Brown Mackie College education and training programs would not benefit the applicant, the college reserves the right to advise the applicant not to enroll. Special requirements for enrollment into certain programs are discussed in the descriptions of those programs.

For the most recent information regarding admissions requirements, prospective students should refer to the most current academic catalog.

Application and Information

Applicants must complete and submit an application form, along with documentation of graduation from an accredited high school or state-approved secondary education curriculum or official documentation of high school graduation equivalency.

Specific details regarding program duration, tuition, fees and other costs, median debt, federal salary data, alumni success, programmatic accreditation, and other important information is available online at BMCprograms.info.

Brown Mackie College is a system of over twenty-five schools located throughout North America. Programs, credential levels, technology, and scheduling options vary by school, and employment opportunities are not guaranteed. Financial aid is available for those who qualify. Administrative offices are located at 625 Eden Park Drive, Suite 1100; Cincinnati, Ohio 45202; phone: 513.830.2000. ©2013 Brown Mackie College. OH Registration # 03-09-1685T; # 03-09-1686T; # 03-09-1687T; # 03-09-1688T; # 06-03-1781T; AC0150, AC0109, AC0078, AC0045, AC0138, AC0110; Licensed by the Florida Commission for Independent Education, License No. 3206.

For additional information, prospective students should contact:

Director of Admissions
Brown Mackie College — Salina
2106 South Ninth Street
Salina, Kansas 67401
Phone: 785-825-5422
        800-365-0433 (toll-free)
Fax: 785-827-7623
E-mail: bmcsaadm@brownmackie.edu
Website: http://www.brownmackie.edu/Salina

BROWN MACKIE COLLEGE —
SAN ANTONIO
SAN ANTONIO, TEXAS

The College

Brown Mackie College — San Antonio (Brown Mackie College) is one of over twenty-five locations in the Brown Mackie College system of schools (www.brownmackie.edu), which is dedicated to providing educational programs that prepare students to pursue entry-level positions in a competitive, rapidly changing workplace. Brown Mackie College schools offer bachelor's degree, associate degree, diploma, and certificate programs in health sciences, business, information technology, legal studies, and design to over 20,000 students in the Midwest, Southeast, Southwest, and Western United States.

Brown Mackie College was originally founded and approved by the Board of Trustees of Kansas Wesleyan College in Salina, Kansas on July 30, 1892. In 1938, the College was incorporated as the Brown Mackie School of Business under the ownership of Perry E. Brown and A. B. Mackie, former instructors at Kansas Wesleyan University in Salina, Kansas. Their last names formed the name of Brown Mackie. By January 1975, with improvements in curricula and higher-degree-granting status, the Brown Mackie School of Business became Brown Mackie College.

Brown Mackie College — San Antonio is accredited by the Accrediting Council for Independent Colleges and Schools to award bachelor's degrees and associate degrees. The Accrediting Council for Independent Colleges and Schools is listed as a nationally recognized accrediting agency by the United States Department of Education and is recognized by the Council for Higher Education Accreditation. ACICS can be contacted at 750 First Street NE, Suite 980, Washington, D.C. 20002; phone: 202-336-6780.

Brown Mackie College — San Antonio is approved and regulated by the Texas Workforce Commission, Career School and Colleges, Austin, Texas.

Brown Mackie College — San Antonio holds a Certificate of Authorization acknowledging exemption from Texas Higher Education Coordinating Board regulations.

Location

Brown Mackie College — San Antonio is conveniently located at 4715 Fredericksburg Road in San Antonio, Texas. The college has a generous parking area and is easily accessible by public transportation.

Programs of Study and Degree Offerings

Brown Mackie College — San Antonio provides higher education to traditional and nontraditional students through bachelor's degree and associate degree programs that assist in enhancing their career opportunities, broadening their perspectives through appropriate general education courses, thinking independently and critically, and improving problem-solving abilities. The college strives to develop within its students the desire for lifelong and continued education.

The Bachelor of Science degree is awarded in business administration, criminal justice, health care management, and legal studies.

The Associate of Science degree is awarded in accounting technology, architectural design and drafting technology, business management, criminal justice, health care administration, information technology, medical assisting, paralegal, pharmacy technology, and surgical technology.

Brown Mackie College — San Antonio offers a diploma program in medical assistant.

The American Medical Technologists (AMT), which offers the certification for Registered Medical Assistant (RMA), accepts the accreditation of Brown Mackie College — San Antonio. Students will qualify to take the Registered Medical Assistant certification examination upon graduating the Brown Mackie College — San Antonio medical assisting and medical assistant programs.

Brown Mackie College does not guarantee third-party certification/licensing exams. Outside agencies control the requirements for certification/licensing and are subject to change without notification to the college.

Program availability and degree offerings are subject to change.

Academic Programs

Each college quarter comprises twelve weeks. Bachelor's degree programs require a minimum of sixteen quarters to complete. Associate degree programs require a minimum of eight quarters to complete. Programs are offered on a year-round basis, providing students with the ability to work uninterrupted toward completion of their programs. The college offers all programs in a unique One-Course-a-Month format. This allows students to focus studies on only one course for four weeks. This schedule has proven convenient for students with multiple obligations, such as jobs and family.

Academic Facilities

A modern facility, Brown Mackie College — San Antonio offers more than 35,000 square feet. The college is equipped with multiple computer labs, housing over 100 computers. High-speed access to the Internet and other online resources are available to students and faculty. Multimedia classrooms are outfitted with overhead projectors, VCR/DVD players, and computers.

Brown Mackie College — San Antonio is fully committed to using eTextbooks and computer tablets in the classroom. Utilizing these tablets to access expanded course material, students are able to increase their acumen for using this technology and further enhance their educational experience. Students have the ability to directly download their eTextbooks to their tablet, eliminating the need to carry heavy, physical textbooks and reducing the overall cost of supplies.

The college is nonresidential; public transportation and ample parking at no cost are available. The campus is a smoke-free facility.

Costs

Tuition in the 2012–13 academic year for most of the bachelor's and associate degrees was $324 per credit hour; fees were $20 per credit hour. Tuition for the surgical technology program was $360 per credit hour; fees were $20 per credit hour. The cost of textbooks, if applicable, and other instructional materials varies by program.

Financial Aid

Financial aid is available for those who qualify. The college maintains a full-time staff of Student Financial Services Advisors to assist qualified students in obtaining the financial assistance they require to meet their educational expenses. Available resources include federal and state aid, student loans from private lenders, and Federal Work-Study opportunities, both on and off college premises.

Each year, the college makes available President's Scholarships of $1,000 each to qualifying seniors from area high schools. In order to qualify, a senior must have graduated from a participating high school, must have maintained a cumulative grade point average of at least 2.0, and must have submitted a brief essay. The student's extracurricular activities and community service are also considered. These scholarships are available only to students enrolling in one of the college's degree programs. Students awarded the scholarship must enroll at Brown Mackie College — San Antonio between June and September immediately following their high school graduation. Applications for these scholarships can be obtained from the guidance departments of participating high schools. These applications must be completed and returned to Brown Mackie College by March 31.

The Education Foundation was established in 2000 to offer scholarship support to students interested in continuing their education at one of the postsecondary, career-focused schools in the EDMC system. The number and amount of the awards can vary, depending on the funds available. Scholarship applications are considered every quarter. At Brown Mackie College, applicants must be currently enrolled in an associate or bachelor's degree program and in their fourth quarter or higher (but no further than their second-to-last quarter) at the time of application. Awards are made based on academic performance and potential, as well as financial need. Interested students should contact the college's Student Financial Service Department for additional information.

Faculty

Experienced faculty members provide academic support and are committed to the academic and technical preparation of their students. The college has both full-time and part-time instructors, with a student-faculty ratio of 15:1.

Admission Requirements

Each applicant for admission is assigned an Assistant Director of Admissions who directs the applicant through the steps of the admissions process. Assistant Directors provide information on curriculum, policies, procedures, and services and assist the applicant in setting up necessary appointments and interviews. To qualify for admission, each applicant must provide documentation of graduation from an accredited high school or from a state-approved secondary education curriculum or official documentation of high school graduation equivalency. All transcripts become the property of the college. Admission to the college is based on the applicant meeting the stated requirements, a review of the applicant's previous educational records, and a review of the applicant's career interests. If previous academic records indicate the college's education and training programs would not benefit the applicant, the college reserves the right to advise the applicant not to enroll. Special requirements for enrollment into certain programs are discussed in the descriptions of those programs.

For the most recent information regarding admission requirements, prospective students should refer to the current academic catalog.

Application and Information

Applicants must complete and submit an application form, along with documentation of graduation from an accredited high school or state-approved secondary education curriculum or official documentation of high school graduation equivalency.

Specific details regarding program duration, tuition, fees and other costs, median debt, federal salary data, alumni success, programmatic accreditation, and other important information is available online at BMCprograms.info.

Brown Mackie College is a system of over twenty-five schools located throughout North America. Programs, credential levels, technology, and scheduling options vary by school, and employment opportunities are not guaranteed. Financial aid is available for those who qualify. Administrative offices are located at 625 Eden Park Drive, Suite 1100; Cincinnati, Ohio 45202; phone: 513.830.2000. ©2013 Brown Mackie College. OH Registration # 03-09-1685T; # 03-09-1686T; # 03-09-1687T; # 03-09-1688T; # 06-03-1781T; AC0150, AC0109, AC0078, AC0045, AC0138, AC0110; Licensed by the Florida Commission for Independent Education, License No. 3206.

For additional information, prospective students should contact:

Director of Admissions
Brown Mackie College — San Antonio
4715 Fredericksburg Road, Suite 100
San Antonio, Texas 78229
United States
Phone: 210-428-2210
      877-460-1714 (toll-free)
Fax: 210-428-2265
E-mail: bmsanadm@brownmackie.edu
Website: http://www.brownmackie.edu/SanAntonio

BROWN MACKIE COLLEGE — SOUTH BEND
SOUTH BEND, INDIANA

The College

Brown Mackie College — South Bend (Brown Mackie College) is one of over twenty-five locations in the Brown Mackie College system of schools (www.brownmackie.edu), which is dedicated to providing educational programs that prepare students to pursue entry-level positions in a competitive, rapidly changing workplace. Brown Mackie College schools offer bachelor's degree, associate degree, diploma, and certificate programs in health sciences, business, information technology, legal studies, and design to over 20,000 students in the Midwest, Southeast, Southwest, and Western United States.

Brown Mackie College — South Bend is one of the oldest institutions of its kind in the country and the oldest in the state of Indiana. Established in 1882 as the South Bend Commercial College, the school later changed its name to Michiana College. In 1930, the school was incorporated under the laws of the state of Indiana and was authorized to confer associate degrees and certificates in business. The college relocated to East Jefferson Boulevard in 1987. In September 2009, Brown Mackie College — South Bend officially opened a new 46,000-square-foot facility at 3454 Douglas Road in South Bend, Indiana.

Brown Mackie College — South Bend is accredited by the Accrediting Council for Independent Colleges and Schools to award bachelor's degrees, associate degrees, diplomas, and certificates. The Accrediting Council for Independent Colleges and Schools is listed as a nationally recognized accrediting agency by the United States Department of Education and is recognized by the Council for Higher Education Accreditation. ACICS can be contacted at 750 First Street NE, Suite 980, Washington, D.C. 20002; phone: 202-336-6780.

Brown Mackie College — South Bend is regulated by the Board for Proprietary Education Indiana Commission for Higher Education, 101 West Ohio Street, Suite 550, Indianapolis, Indiana 46204; phone: 317-464-4400. Indiana advertising code: AC-0110.

The practical nursing diploma program is accredited by the Indiana State Board of Nursing, located at 402 West Washington Street, Room W066, Indianapolis, Indiana 46204; phone: 317-234-2043.

The Associate of Science in medical assisting is accredited by the Commission on Accreditation of Allied Health Education Program (www.caahep.org) upon the recommendation of the Curriculum Review Board of the American Association of Medical Assistants Endowment (AAMAE). The Commission on Accreditation of Allied Health Education Programs is located at 1361 Park Street, Clearwater, Florida 33756; phone: 727-210-2350.

The Associate of Applied Science in occupational therapy assistant program is accredited by the Accreditation Council for Occupational Therapy Education (ACOTE) of the American Occupational Therapy Association (AOTA), located at 4720 Montgomery Lane, Suite 200, Bethesda, Maryland 20814-3449; phone: 301-652-AOTA. Graduates of the program will be eligible to sit for the national certification examination for the occupational therapy assistant administered by the National Board for Certification in Occupational Therapy (NBCOT). After successful completion of this exam, the individual will be a Certified Occupational Therapy Assistant (COTA). In addition, most states require licensure in order to practice; however, state licenses are usually based on the results of the NBCOT Certification Examination. Note that a felony conviction may affect a graduate's ability to sit for the NBCOT certification examination or attain state licensure.

The Physical Therapist Assistant program has been granted Probationary Accreditation by the Commission on Accreditation in Physical Therapy Education (CAPTE) of the American Physical Therapy Association (APTA), 1111 North Fairfax Street, Alexandria, Virginia 22314; 703-706-3241.

The Associate of Science in veterinary technology program has provisional programmatic accreditation granted by the American Veterinary Medical Association (AVMA) through the Committee on Veterinary Technician Education and Activities (CVTEA).

Location

Brown Mackie College — South Bend is conveniently located at 3454 Douglas Road in South Bend, Indiana. The college has a generous parking area and is also easily accessible by public transportation.

The college is a nonresidential, smoke-free institution.

Programs of Study and Degree Offerings

Brown Mackie College — South Bend provides higher education to traditional and nontraditional students through bachelor's degrees, associate degrees, diploma, and certificate programs that assist in enhancing their career opportunities, broadening their perspectives through appropriate general education courses, thinking independently and critically, and improving problem-solving abilities.

The Bachelor of Science degree is awarded in business administration, criminal justice, health care management, and legal studies.

The Associate of Science degree is awarded in accounting technology, business management, computer software technology, criminal justice, health care administration, information technology, paralegal, and veterinary technology.

The Associate of Applied Science degree is awarded in occupational therapy assistant and physical therapist assistant.

Brown Mackie College — South Bend offers a diploma program in practical nursing.

The college offers the following certificate programs: bookkeeping specialist, criminal justice specialist, general business, medical assistant, medical coding and billing, and paralegal assistant.

The American Medical Technologists (AMT), which offers the certification for Registered Medical Assistant (RMA), accepts the accreditation of Brown Mackie College — South Bend. Students will qualify to take the Registered Medical Assistant certification examination upon graduating the Brown Mackie College — South Bend medical assistant certificate program. Graduates of the 48-credit-hour medical assistant certificate program are not qualified to take the AMT/RMA exam.

Brown Mackie College does not guarantee third-party certification/licensing exams. Outside agencies control the requirements for certification/licensing and are subject to change without notification to the college.

Program availability and degree offerings are subject to change.

Academic Programs

Each college quarter comprises twelve weeks. Bachelor's degree programs require a minimum of sixteen quarters to complete. Associate degree programs require a minimum of eight quarters to complete. Programs are offered on a year-round basis, providing students with the ability to work uninterrupted toward completion of their programs. The college offers all programs in a unique One-Course-a-Month format. This allows students to focus studies on only one course for four weeks. This schedule has proven convenient for students with multiple obligations, such as jobs and family.

Academic Facilities

Brown Mackie College — South Bend's new location has a generous parking area and is easily accessible by public transportation. The college's smoke-free, three-story 46,000-square-foot building offers a modern, professional environment for study. The facility offers "classrooms of the future," with instructor workstations and full multimedia capabilities that include surround sound and projection screens that can be accessed by computer, DVD, and VHS. The new facility includes medical, computer, and occupational and physical therapy labs, as well as a library and bookstore. The labs provide students with hands-on opportunities to apply knowledge and skills learned in the classroom. The veterinary technology lab is 2,600 square feet and includes surgery areas, treatment areas, and kennels.

Brown Mackie College — South Bend is fully committed to using eTextbooks and computer tablets in the classroom. Utilizing these tablets to access expanded course material, students are able to increase their acumen for using this technology and further enhance their educational experience. Students have the ability to directly download their eTextbooks to their tablet, eliminating the need to carry heavy, physical textbooks and reducing the overall cost of supplies.

Costs

Tuition for programs in the 2012–13 academic year was $314 per credit hour, with a general fee of $20 per credit hour applied to instructional costs for activities and services. Tuition for the practical nursing program was $381 per credit hour, with a general fee of $30 per credit hour applied to instructional costs for activities and services. Tuition for the physical therapist assistant program was $381 per credit hour with a general fee of $20 per credit hour. Tuition for the occupational therapy assistant program was $381 per credit hour with a general fee of $20 per credit hour. Textbooks, if applicable, and other instructional materials vary by program.

Financial Aid

Financial aid is available for those who qualify. The college maintains a full-time staff of Student Financial Services Advisors to assist qualified students in obtaining financial assistance. The college participates in several student aid programs. Forms of financial aid available through federal resources include the Federal Pell Grant Program, Federal Supplemental Educational Opportunity Grant (FSEOG) Program, Federal Work-Study Program, Federal Perkins Loan Program, Federal Stafford Student Loan Program (subsidized and unsubsidized), and the Federal PLUS Loan Program.

Eligible students may apply for Indiana state awards, such as the Frank O'Bannon Grant Program (formerly the Indiana Higher Education Grant) and Twenty-First Century Scholars Program for high school students, for the Core 40 awards, and for veterans' educational benefits. Students with physical or mental disabilities that are a handicap may be eligible for training services through the state's Bureau of Vocational Rehabilitation. For further information, students should contact the Student Financial Services Office.

Each year, the college makes available President's Scholarships of $1,000 each to qualifying seniors from area high schools. In order to qualify, a senior must be graduating from a participating high school, must be maintaining a cumulative grade point average of at least 2.0, and must submit a brief essay. The student's extracurricular activities and community service are also considered. The President's Scholarship is available only to students enrolling in one of the college's degree programs. Students awarded the scholarship must enroll at Brown Mackie College — South Bend between June and September immediately following their high school graduation. Applications for these scholarships can be obtained from the guidance departments of participating high schools. These applications must be completed and returned to Brown Mackie College by March 31.

The Education Foundation was established in 2000 to offer scholarship support to students interested in continuing their education at one of the postsecondary, career-focused schools in the EDMC system. The number and amount of the awards can vary, depending on the funds available. Scholarship applications are considered every quarter. At Brown Mackie College, applicants must be currently enrolled in an associate or bachelor's degree program and in their fourth quarter or higher (but no further than their second-to-last quarter) at the time of application. Awards are made based on academic performance and potential, as well as financial need. Interested students should contact the college's Student Financial Service Department for additional information.

Faculty

There are 24 full-time and 36 part-time faculty members at the college. The average student-faculty ratio is 11:1. Each student is assigned a program director as an adviser.

Admission Requirements

Each applicant for admission is assigned an Assistant Director of Admissions, who directs the applicant through the steps of the admissions process, providing information on curriculum, policies, procedures, and services and assisting the applicant in setting up necessary appointments and interviews. To qualify for admission, each applicant must provide documentation of graduation from an accredited high school or from a state-approved secondary education curriculum or official documentation of high school graduation equivalency. All transcripts become the property of the college.

Admission to the college is based on the applicant meeting the stated requirements, a review of the applicant's previous educational records, and a review of the applicant's career interests. If previous academic records indicate the college's education and training programs would not benefit the applicant, the college reserves the right to advise the applicant not to enroll. Special requirements for enrollment into certain programs are discussed in the descriptions of those programs.

In addition to the college's general admission requirements, applicants enrolling in the occupational therapy assistant (OTA) program must meet some additional requirements. They must complete the COMPASS assessment before the first course is scheduled to determine if transitional courses are needed (minimal scores: reading 75, writing 60, math 51). If minimum scores or better are attained on all three sections, the student is scheduled in CF1000–Professional Development. If the student's scores are below the minimum on any of the sections, the student is advised of placement in transitional course(s). After successful completion of all the required transitional courses, the student will have one opportunity to retake the COMPASS assessment and achieve the minimum score(s). If the student does not successfully obtain the minimum scores in all three sections on the second attempt, the student will not be allowed to continue in the OTA program, but can be considered for another program at Brown Mackie College.

In addition to the college's general admission requirements, applicants enrolling in the physical therapist assistant program must document the following: a minimum high school cumulative grade point average of 3.0 on a 4.0 scale or a minimum score of 600 on the GED examination (if taken on or after January 15, 2002) or 60 (if taken before January 15, 2002); a minimum of 12 quarter-credit hours or 9 semester-credit hours of consecutive collegiate coursework with a minimum GPA of 3.0 on a 4.0 scale (may be completed at Brown Mackie College); a biology course in high school or college with a minimum grade of a B (3.0 on a 4.0 scale); and 20 hours (total) of documented observation, volunteer, or employment hours in at least two different physical therapy settings with no less than 8 hours in one setting completed within the past three years.

In addition to the college's general admission requirements, applicants enrolling in the practical nursing program must document the following: fulfillment of Brown Mackie College—South Bend general requirements; complete physical (must be current to within six months of admission); two-step Mantoux TB skin test (must be current throughout schooling); hepatitis B vaccination or signed refusal; up-to-date immunizations, including tetanus and rubella; record of current CPR certification (certification must be current throughout the clinical experience through healthcare provider certification or the American Heart Association); and hospitalization insurance or a signed waiver.

For the most recent administration regarding admission requirements, prospective students should refer to the current academic catalog.

Application and Information

Applicants must complete and submit an application form, along with documentation of graduation from an accredited high school or state-approved secondary education curriculum or official documentation of high school graduation equivalency.

Specific details regarding program duration, tuition, fees and other costs, median debt, federal salary data, alumni success, programmatic accreditation, and other important information are available at BMCprograms.info.

Brown Mackie College is a system of over twenty-five schools located throughout North America. Programs, credential levels, technology, and scheduling options vary by school, and employment opportunities are not guaranteed. Financial aid is available for those who qualify. Administrative offices are located at 625 Eden Park Drive, Suite 1100; Cincinnati, Ohio 45202; phone: 513.830.2000. ©2013 Brown Mackie College. OH Registration # 03-09-1685T; # 03-09-1686T; # 03-09-1687T; # 03-09- 1688T; # 06-03-1781T; AC0150, AC0109, AC0078, AC0045, AC0138, AC0110; Licensed by the Florida Commission for Independent Education, License No. 3206.

For additional information, prospective students should contact:

Director of Admissions
Brown Mackie College — South Bend
3454 Douglas Road
South Bend, Indiana 46635
United States
Phone: 574-237-0774
        800-743-2447(toll-free)
Fax: 574-237-3585
E-mail: bmcsbadm@brownmackie.edu
Web site: http://www.brownmackie.edu/SouthBend

BROWN MACKIE COLLEGE — TUCSON
TUCSON, ARIZONA

BROWN
MACKIE
COLLEGE
TUCSON℠

The College

Brown Mackie College — Tucson (Brown Mackie College) is one of over twenty-five locations in the Brown Mackie College system of schools (www.brownmackie.edu), which is dedicated to providing educational programs that prepare students to pursue entry-level positions in a competitive, rapidly changing workplace. Brown Mackie College schools offer bachelor's degree, associate degree, diploma, and certificate programs in health sciences, business, information technology, legal studies, and design to over 20,000 students in the Midwest, Southeast, Southwest, and Western United States.

Brown Mackie College was originally founded and approved by the Board of Trustees of Kansas Wesleyan College in Salina, Kansas on July 30, 1892. In 1938, the college was incorporated as The Brown Mackie School of Business under the ownership of Perry E. Brown and A. B. Mackie, former instructors at Kansas Wesleyan University in Salina, Kansas. Their last names formed the name of Brown Mackie. By January 1975, with improvements in curricula and higher-degree-granting status, The Brown Mackie School of Business became Brown Mackie College.

Brown Mackie College entered the Arizona market in 2007 when it purchased a school that had been previously established in the Tucson area. That school had an established history in the community and was converted into what is now known as Brown Mackie College — Tucson. The historical timeline of Brown Mackie College — Tucson started in 1972 when Rockland West Corporation first formed a partnership with Lamson Business College. At that time, the school was a career college that offered only short-term programs focusing on computer training and secretarial skills. In 1994, the college became accredited as a junior college and began offering associate degrees in academic subjects. The mission was then modified to include the goal of instilling in graduates an appreciation for lifelong learning through the general education courses that became a part of every program.

In 1996, the college applied for and received status as a senior college by the Accrediting Commission of Independent Colleges and Schools. This gave the school the ability to offer course work leading to a Bachelor of Science degree in business administration. Since then, the program offerings for bachelor's and associate degrees have expanded.

In 1986, the college moved from 5001 East Speedway to the 4585 East Speedway location where it remains today. In 2008, two of the college's three buildings were remodeled, which resulted in updated classrooms; networked computer laboratories; new medical, surgical technology, and forensics laboratories; a larger library and offices for student services such as academics, admissions, and student financial services; and a full-service college store. In 2009, the third building was remodeled and now provides newer classrooms and a new career services department.

Brown Mackie College — Tucson is accredited by the Accrediting Council for Independent Colleges and Schools to award bachelor's degrees, associate degrees, and diplomas. The Accrediting Council for Independent Colleges and Schools is listed as a nationally recognized accrediting agency by the United States Department of Education and is recognized by the Council for Higher Education Accreditation. ACICS can be contacted at 750 First Street NE, Suite 980, Washington, D.C. 20002; phone: 202-336-6780.

Brown Mackie College — Tucson is authorized by the Arizona State Board for Private Post-secondary Education, located at 1400 West Washington Street, Room 2560, Phoenix, Arizona 85007; phone: 602-542-5709; http://azppse.state.az.us.

The Associate of Science in surgical technology program is accredited by the Accrediting Bureau of Health Education Schools.

The Associate of Applied Science in occupational therapy assistant program is accredited by the Accreditation Council for Occupational Therapy Education (ACOTE) of the American Occupational Therapy Association (AOTA), located at 4720 Montgomery Lane, Suite 200, Bethesda, Maryland 20814-3449; phone: 301-652-AOTA. Graduates of the program will be eligible to sit for the national certification examination for the occupational therapy assistant administered by the National Board for Certification in Occupational Therapy (NBCOT). After successful completion of this exam, the individual will be a Certified Occupational Therapy Assistant (COTA). In addition, most states require licensure in order to practice; however, state licenses are usually based on the results of the NBCOT Certification Examination. Note that a felony conviction may affect a graduate's ability to sit for the NBCOT certification examination or attain state licensure.

Location

Brown Mackie College — Tucson is conveniently located at 4585 East Speedway Boulevard in Tucson, Arizona. The College has a generous parking area and is also easily accessible by public transportation.

Programs of Study and Degree Offerings

Brown Mackie College — Tucson provides higher education to traditional and nontraditional students through bachelor's degree, associate degree, and diploma programs that assist in enhancing their career opportunities, broadening their perspectives through appropriate general education courses, thinking independently and critically, and improving problem-solving abilities. The college strives to develop within its students the desire for lifelong and continued education.

The Bachelor of Science degree is awarded in accounting, business administration, criminal justice, health care management, and information technology.

The Associate of Science degree is awarded in accounting technology, business management, computer networking and security, criminal justice, graphic design, health care administration, medical assisting, and surgical technology.

The Associate of Applied Science degree is awarded in biomedical equipment technology and occupational therapy assistant.

A diploma is awarded in graphic design assistant, medical assistant, and practical nursing.

The American Medical Technologists (AMT), which offers the certification for Registered Medical Assistant (RMA), accepts the accreditation of Brown Mackie College — Tucson. Students will qualify to take the Registered Medical Assistant certification examination upon graduating the Brown Mackie College — Tucson medical assisting and medical assistant programs. Graduates of the 48-credit-hour medical assistant program are not qualified to take the AMT/RMA exam.

Brown Mackie College does not guarantee third-party certification/licensing exams. Outside agencies control the requirements for certification/licensing and are subject to change without notification to the college.

Program availability and degree offerings are subject to change.

Academic Programs

Each college quarter comprises twelve weeks. Bachelor's degree programs require a minimum of sixteen quarters to complete. Associate degree programs require a minimum of eight quarters to complete. Programs are offered on a year-round basis, providing students with the ability to work uninterrupted toward their degrees. The college offers all programs in a unique One-Course-a-Month format. This allows students to focus studies on only one course for four weeks. This schedule has proven convenient for students with multiple obligations, such as jobs and family.

Academic Facilities

A modern facility, Brown Mackie College — Tucson offers more than 31,000 square feet. The college is equipped with multiple computer labs housing over 200 computers. High-speed access to the Internet and other online resources are available for students and faculty. Multimedia classrooms are outfitted with overhead projectors, VCR/DVD players, and computers. The college is nonresidential; public transportation and parking at no cost are available.

Brown Mackie College — Tucson is fully committed to using eTextbooks and computer tablets in the classroom. Utilizing these tablets to access expanded course material, students are able to increase their acumen for using this technology and further enhance their educational experience. Students have the ability to directly download their eTextbooks to their tablet, eliminating the need to carry heavy, physical textbooks and reducing the overall cost of supplies.

Costs

Tuition in the 2012–13 academic year for most bachelor's, associate, and diploma programs was $344 per credit hour; fees were $20 per credit hour. Tuition for the fitness training programs was $344 per credit hour; fees were $30 per credit hour. Tuition for the surgical technology program was $360 per credit hour; fees were $20 per credit hour. Tuition for the occupational therapy assistant program was $381 per credit hour; fees were $20 per credit hour. Tuition for the practical nursing program was $381 per credit hour; fees were $30 per credit hour. Textbooks, if applicable, and other instructional expenses vary by program.

Financial Aid

Financial aid is available for those who qualify. The college maintains a full-time staff of Student Financial Services Advisors to assist qualified students in obtaining the financial assistance they require to meet their educational expenses. Available resources include federal and state aid, student loans from private lenders, and Federal Work-Study opportunities, both on and off college premises.

Each year, the college makes available President's Scholarships of $1,000 each to qualifying seniors from area high schools. In order to qualify, a senior must be graduating from a participating high school, must be maintaining a cumulative grade point average of at least 2.0, and must submit a brief essay. The student's extracurricular activities and community service are also considered. These scholarships are available only to students enrolling in one of the college's degree programs. Students awarded the scholarship must enroll at Brown Mackie College — Tucson between June and September immediately following their high school graduation. Applications for these scholarships can be obtained from the guidance departments of participating high schools. These applications must be completed and returned to Brown Mackie College by March 31.

The Education Foundation was established in 2000 to offer scholarship support to students interested in continuing their education at one of the postsecondary, career-focused schools in the EDMC system. The number and amount of the awards can vary, depending on the funds available. Scholarship applications are considered every quarter. At Brown Mackie College, applicants must be currently enrolled in an associate or bachelor's degree program and in their fourth quarter or higher (but no further than their second-to-last quarter) at the time of application. Awards are made based on academic performance and potential, as well as financial need. Interested students should contact the college's Student Financial Service Department for additional information.

Faculty

Experienced faculty members provide academic support and are committed to the academic and technical preparation of their students. The college has 15 full-time and 35 part-time instructors, with a student-faculty ratio of 12:1. Each student is assigned a faculty adviser.

Admission Requirements

Each applicant for admission is assigned an Assistant Director of Admissions who directs the applicant through the steps of the admissions process. Assistant Directors provide information on curriculum, policies, procedures, and services and assist the applicant in setting up necessary appointments and interviews. To qualify for admission, each applicant must provide documentation of graduation from an accredited high school or from a state-approved secondary education curriculum or official documentation of high school graduation equivalency. All transcripts become the property of the college. Admission to the college is based on the applicant meeting the stated requirements, a review of the applicant's previous educational records, and a review of the applicant's career interests. If previous academic records indicate the college's education and training programs would not benefit the applicant, the college reserves the right to advise the applicant not to enroll. Special requirements for enrollment into certain programs are discussed in the descriptions of those programs.

For the most recent information regarding admission requirements, prospective students should refer to the current academic catalog.

Application and Information

Applicants must complete and submit an application form, along with documentation of graduation from an accredited high school or state-approved secondary education curriculum or official documentation of high school graduation equivalency.

Specific details regarding program duration, tuition, fees and other costs, median debt, federal salary data, alumni success, programmatic accreditation, and other important information are available at BMCprograms.info.

Brown Mackie College is a system of over twenty-five schools located throughout North America. Programs, credential levels, technology, and scheduling options vary by school, and employment opportunities are not guaranteed. Financial aid is available for those who qualify. Administrative offices are located at 625 Eden Park Drive, Suite 1100; Cincinnati, Ohio 45202; phone: 513.830.2000. ©2013 Brown Mackie College. OH Registration # 03-09-1685T; # 03-09-1686T; # 03-09-1687T; # 03-09- 1688T; # 06-03-1781T; AC0150, AC0109, AC0078, AC0045, AC0138, AC0110; Licensed by the Florida Commission for Independent Education, License No. 3206.

For additional information, prospective students should contact:

Senior Director of Admissions
Brown Mackie College — Tucson
4585 East Speedway Boulevard, Suite 204
Tucson, Arizona 85712
United States
Phone: 520-319-3300
Fax: 520-319-3495
E-mail: bmctuadm@brownmackie.edu
Web site: http://www.brownmackie.edu/Tucson

BROWN MACKIE COLLEGE — TULSA
TULSA, OKLAHOMA

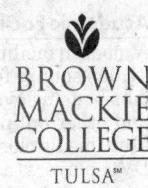

BROWN
MACKIE
COLLEGE
TULSA℠

The College

Brown Mackie College — Tulsa (Brown Mackie College) is one of over twenty-five locations in the Brown Mackie College system of schools (www.brownmackie.edu), which is dedicated to providing educational programs that prepare students to pursue entry-level positions in a competitive, rapidly changing workplace. Brown Mackie College schools offer bachelor's degree, associate degree, diploma, and certificate programs in health sciences, business, information technology, legal studies, and design to over 20,000 students in the Midwest, Southeast, Southwest, and Western United States.

Brown Mackie College — Tulsa was founded in 2008 as a branch of Brown Mackie College — South Bend, Indiana.

Brown Mackie College — Tulsa is accredited by the Accrediting Council for Independent Colleges and Schools to award bachelor's degrees, associate degrees, and diplomas. The Accrediting Council for Independent Colleges and Schools is listed as a nationally recognized accrediting agency by the United States Department of Education and is recognized by the Council for Higher Education Accreditation. ACICS can be contacted at 750 First Street NE, Suite 980, Washington, D.C. 20002; phone: 202-336-6780.

This institution is licensed by the Oklahoma Board of Private Vocational Schools (OBPVS), 3700 North Classen Boulevard, Suite 250, Oklahoma City, Oklahoma 73118; phone: 405-528-3370.

This institution has been granted authority to operate in Oklahoma by the Oklahoma State Regents for Higher Education (OSRHE), 655 Research Parkway, Suite 200, Oklahoma City, Oklahoma 73101; phone: 405-225-9100; www.okhighered.org.

The occupational therapy assistant program is accredited by the Accreditation Council for Occupational Therapy Education (ACOTE) of the American Occupational Therapy Association (AOTA), located at 4720 Montgomery Lane, Suite 200, Bethesda, Maryland 20814-3449; phone: 301-652-AOTA. Graduates of the program will be eligible to sit for the national certification examination for the occupational therapy assistant administered by the National Board for Certification in Occupational Therapy (NBCOT). After successful completion of this exam, the individual will be a Certified Occupational Therapy Assistant (COTA). In addition, most states require licensure in order to practice; however, state licenses are usually based on the results of the NBCOT Certification Examination. Note that a felony conviction may affect a graduate's ability to sit for the NBCOT certification examination or attain state licensure.

Location

Brown Mackie College — Tulsa is conveniently located at 4608 South Garnett Road, Suite 110 in Tulsa, Oklahoma. The College has a generous parking area and is easily accessible by public transportation.

Programs of Study and Degree Offerings

Brown Mackie College — Tulsa provides higher education to traditional and nontraditional students through bachelor's degree, associate degree, and diploma programs that assist in enhancing their career opportunities, broadening their perspectives through appropriate general education courses, thinking independently and critically, and improving problem-solving abilities. The college strives to develop within its students the desire for lifelong and continued education.

The Bachelor of Science degree is awarded in business administration, criminal justice, and health care management.

The Associate of Applied Science degree is awarded in accounting technology, business management, criminal justice, health care administration, information technology, medical assisting, nursing, occupational therapy assistant, paralegal, and surgical technology.

Diploma programs are offered in accounting, business, criminal justice, medical assistant, and paralegal assistant.

The American Medical Technologists (AMT), which offers the certification for Registered Medical Assistant (RMA), accepts the accreditation of Brown Mackie College — Tulsa. Students will qualify to take the Registered Medical Assistant certification examination upon graduating the Brown Mackie College — Tulsa medical assisting and medical assistant programs. Graduates of the 48-credit-hour medical assistant program are not qualified to take the AMT/RMA exam.

Brown Mackie College does not guarantee third-party certification/licensing exams. Outside agencies control the requirements for certification/licensing and are subject to change without notification to the college.

Program availability and degree offerings are subject to change.

Academic Programs

Each college quarter comprises twelve weeks. Bachelor's degree programs require a minimum of fifteen quarters to complete. Associate degree programs require a minimum of eight quarters to complete. Programs are offered on a year-round basis, providing students with the ability to work uninterrupted toward completion of their programs. The college offers all programs in a unique One-Course-a-Month format. This allows students to focus on only one course for four weeks. This schedule has proven convenient for students with multiple obligations, such as jobs and family.

Academic Facilities

Opened in 2008, this modern facility offers more than 25,000 square feet of tastefully decorated classrooms, laboratories, and office space designed to specifications of Brown Mackie College for its business, medical, and technical programs. Instructional equipment is comparable to current technology used in business and industry today. Modern classrooms for special instructional needs offer multimedia capabilities with surround sound and overhead projectors accessible through computer, DVD, or VHS. Internet access and instructional resources are available at the college's library. Experienced faculty members provide academic support and are committed to the academic and technical preparation of their students.

Brown Mackie College — Tulsa is fully committed to using eTextbooks and computer tablets in the classroom. Utilizing these tablets to access expanded course material, students are able to increase their acumen for using this technology and further enhance their educational experience. Students have the ability to directly download their eTextbooks to their tablet, eliminating the need to carry heavy, physical textbooks and reducing the overall cost of supplies.

The college is nonresidential; public transportation and ample parking at no cost are available.

Costs

Tuition for programs in the 2012–13 academic year was $314 per credit hour, with a general fee of $20 per credit hour applied to instructional costs for activities and services. Tuition for the occupational therapy program was $381 per credit hour with a general fee of $20 per credit hour applied to instructional costs for activities. Tuition for the surgical technology program was $360 per credit hour with a general fee of $20 per credit hour applied to instructional costs for activities. Tuition for the nursing program was $410 per credit hour with a general fee of $30 per credit hour applied to instructional costs for activities. Textbooks, if applicable, and other instructional materials vary by program.

Financial Aid

Financial aid is available for those who qualify. The college maintains a full-time staff of Student Financial Services Advisors to assist qualified students in obtaining financial assistance. The college participates in several student aid programs. Forms of financial aid available through federal resources include the Federal Pell Grant Program, Federal Supplemental Educational Opportunity Grant (FSEOG) Program, Federal Work-Study Program, Federal Perkins Loan Program, Federal Stafford Student Loan Program (subsidized and unsubsidized), and the Federal PLUS Loan Program.

Admission Requirements

Each applicant for admission is assigned an Assistant Director of Admissions, who directs the applicant through the steps of the admissions process, providing information on curriculum, policies, procedures, and services and assisting the applicant in setting up necessary appointments and interviews. To qualify for admission, applicants must be a graduate of a public or private high school or a correspondence school or education center that is accredited by an agency that is recognized by the U.S. or State of Oklahoma Department of Education or any of its approved agents. As part of the admissions process, applicants must sign a document attesting to graduation or completion and containing the information to obtain verification of such. Verification must be obtained within the first term (90 days) or the student will be withdrawn from the institution following established guidelines for withdrawn students noted in the catalog. Title IV aid will not be dispersed until verification of graduation or completion has been received by the college. All transcripts become the property of the college.

Students are given an assessment of academic skills. Although the results of this assessment do not determine eligibility for admission, they provide the college with a means of determining the need for academic support.

For the most recent information regarding admission requirements, prospective students should refer to the current academic catalog.

Application and Information

Applicants must complete and submit an application form, along with documentation of graduation from an accredited high school or state-approved secondary education curriculum or official documentation of high school graduation equivalency.

Specific details regarding program duration, tuition, fees and other costs, median debt, federal salary data, alumni success, programmatic accreditation, and other important information are available at BMCprograms.info.

Brown Mackie College is a system of over twenty-five schools located throughout North America. Programs, credential levels, technology, and scheduling options vary by school, and employment opportunities are not guaranteed. Financial aid is available for those who qualify. Administrative offices are located at 625 Eden Park Drive, Suite 1100; Cincinnati, Ohio 45202; phone: 513.830.2000. ©2013 Brown Mackie College. OH Registration # 03-09-1685T; # 03-09-1686T; # 03-09-1687T; # 03-09- 1688T; # 06-03-1781T; AC0150, AC0109, AC0078, AC0045, AC0138, AC0110; Licensed by the Florida Commission for Independent Education, License No. 3206.

For additional information, prospective students should contact:

Senior Director of Admissions
Brown Mackie College–Tulsa
4608 South Garnett Road, Suite 110
Tulsa, Oklahoma 74146
United States
Phone: 918-628-3700
         888-794-8411 (toll-free)
Fax: 918-828-9083
E-mail: bmctuladm@brownmackie.edu
Website: http://www.brownmackie.edu/Tulsa

BUCKNELL UNIVERSITY
LEWISBURG, PENNSYLVANIA

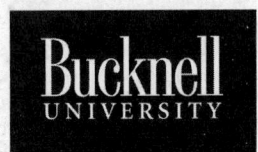

The University

Bucknell University is a highly selective private liberal arts university with academic programs in the arts, engineering, humanities, management, and social and natural sciences, and broad opportunities beyond the classroom. The University's 3,500 undergraduates can choose from more than fifty majors and sixty-five minors. Student satisfaction at the University is extremely high: 95 percent of first-year students entering in the Class of 2015 returned for their sophomore year. Likewise, students consistently graduate on time, with Bucknell having an 85 percent four-year graduation rate for the class of 2012—a rate among the highest of all four-year colleges. According to the 2012–13 PayScale College Salary Survey, Bucknell ranks thirty-seventh among private colleges and universities and tenth among liberal arts institutions for alumni mid-career salary. Each entering class consists of about 925 students.

The faculty at Bucknell creates an environment of free-flowing ideas and engaging discussions. Professors teach every class, getting to know students personally and encouraging them to create their own challenges. Bucknell professors are also dedicated and passionate scholars who frequently receive awards and grants for their work. Often, they involve students in hands-on research and creative projects outside of class.

Students participate in many activities in addition to their academic endeavors. Bucknell offers Division I athletics along with intramural and club sports, Greek life, and about 150 student-run clubs and organizations. These organizations focus on diverse topics from social and environmental causes to cultural awareness, poetry slams, volunteering and service, and politics. Students can also enrich their religious and spiritual lives through multiple University and student-led faith organizations.

The University is a close-knit community with nearly all of its undergraduates living on campus. Visiting scholars and speakers come to Bucknell nearly every week, often focusing on cultures, societies, and economies around the globe. Learning happens off campus, too. Students frequently perform service work both locally and as far away as Nicaragua and Uganda. They secure summer internships with nonprofit organizations and corporations. They study abroad through one of University's own programs or through 130 other approved programs in Africa, Asia, Europe, and South America. And after they graduate, they live, work, volunteer, and study all over the world.

Alumni of Bucknell succeed in their careers because they possess a combination of skills, knowledge, and flexibility of mind that employers seek. To prepare students, the University offers career services including advising, networking, mock interviews, internship and externship support, and employer fairs The placement rate is consistently high: 94.5 percent of the class of 2011 was employed, in graduate school, both employed or in graduate school, or volunteering within nine months of graduation.

Location

With its green spaces, red brick buildings, striking vistas, and academic quadrangles, Bucknell's campus is a quintessential college environment in the heart of scenic central Pennsylvania. The shops and restaurants of historic downtown Lewisburg, including the Barnes & Noble at Bucknell University bookstore and the historic Campus Theatre, lie within walking distance of campus. Lewisburg also hosts a variety of fun and unique community events throughout the year including the Victorian Parade, an ice festival in the winter, and an arts festival in the spring. The University is located within a 3- to 4-hour drive of most of the major Eastern cities, including New York City; Washington, D.C.; Philadelphia; and Pittsburgh.

Majors and Degrees

Bucknell provides students with a choice of more than fifty majors in a variety of liberal arts and professional fields. Bachelor of Arts degrees are available in animal behavior, anthropology, art, art history, biology, chemistry, classics (Greek or Latin concentrations), comparative humanities, computer science, East Asian studies (China or Japan concentrations), economics, education, English (creative writing or film/media studies concentrations), environmental geology, environmental studies, French, geography, geology, German, history, international relations (Africa, Europe, East Asia, Latin America, Middle East, North America, or Russia concentrations), Italian studies, Latin American studies, linguistics, mathematics (general, pure mathematics, or statistics concentrations), music, philosophy, physics, political science, psychology, religion, Russian, sociology (general, human services, or legal studies concentrations), Spanish, theater, and women's and gender studies.

The music program offers a Bachelor of Music degree with majors in music composition, music education, music history, and performance.

Bachelor of Science degrees are available in animal behavior, biology, cell biology and biochemistry, chemistry, computer science, engineering (in the disciplines of biomedical, chemical, civil, computer, electrical, environmental, and mechanical engineering as well as a degree in computer science and engineering), environmental geology, environmental studies, geology, interdisciplinary studies in economics and mathematics, mathematics (general, pure mathematics, or statistics concentrations), neuroscience, and physics.

Bachelor of Science in Business Administration degrees are available in four majors: accounting and financial management; global management; managing for sustainability; and markets, innovation, and design.

Bachelor of Science in Education degrees are available in early childhood development and elementary education.

In consultation with an academic adviser, students also may design their own major based around their individualized educational goals. Select engineering students also have the option of completing one of two five-year interdisciplinary programs; these programs lead to a B.S. in an engineering field and either a B.A. in another discipline or a specially designed Bachelor of Management for Engineers degree.

Academic Programs

Requirements for each degree program vary, but all students are required to complete three writing courses. Special programs are offered to encourage each student's personal and intellectual development. Examples include the first-year foundation seminars, an introductory engineering course open to students in the College of Arts and Sciences, and Bucknell's Residential Colleges program. These living-learning communities are theme-based options for first-year students that combine classroom and out-of-class activities in themed housing. Current themes are the arts, discovery (science), environmental issues, global affairs, humanities, languages and cultures, social justice, and society and technology.

Off-Campus Programs

Bucknell University's Office of International Education offers one of the largest study-abroad programs available at an undergraduate liberal arts institution. More than 45 percent of Bucknell's students study abroad for a year, a semester, and/or a summer. Bucknell sponsors semester-long "Bucknell in" programs in London, France, and Spain. During the summer, the University offers programs in Denmark, Northern Ireland, Nicaragua, South Africa, and the Virgin Islands. Through Engineering 290, engineering majors can spend three weeks abroad studying engineering and its impact on society. Destinations have included China, Argentina, and Costa Rica.

In addition to "Bucknell in" programs, the University is affiliated with 130 other programs worldwide. Shorter-term service and learning programs are also available in places such as New Orleans and the Dominican Republic, along with internship programs in

Philadelphia or Washington, D.C. Financial aid, grants, and scholarships apply toward study abroad.

Academic Facilities

Bucknell's 450-acre campus includes facilities for art, engineering, music, the sciences, theater, and dance and a 1,200-seat performance hall. Bertrand Library holds 833,000 volumes, provides access to more than 35,000 periodicals, and offers thousands of audiovisual materials. Computer labs are available across campus, and most of campus is wireless-accessible. All student residences are connected to the residential network, featuring a high-speed data connection for each student. Science and engineering programs have professional-grade instrumentation available for student use.

Costs

The comprehensive fee for 2013–14 is $58,160, including $46,902 for tuition and fees and $11,258 for standard room and board.

Financial Aid

About 50 percent of students receive financial aid from the University, and 62 percent receive financial aid of some form, including need-based scholarships, loans, work-study, and a limited amount of merit scholarships. In 2012–13, Bucknell budgeted over $46 million toward scholarship aid for undergraduates. Another $18 million was awarded in student loans, $2.5 million in work-study, and $2.5 million in federal and state grants. The average total financial aid package in the fall of 2012 for first-year students with financial need was about $28,000. The average student loan debt upon graduation is about $21,000.

Arts merit scholarships are available in the areas of art and art history, dance, English (creative writing, literature, film/media studies), music, and theater (design and technology, performance).

If prospective students and their families believe they will need financial aid, they must file the Financial Aid CSS PROFILE with the College Scholarship Service before January 15.

Faculty

Bucknell has more than 350 full-time, tenure-line faculty members; 97 percent of them hold doctorates or appropriate terminal degrees. The student-faculty ratio is 10:1.

Bucknell professors uphold the teacher-scholar ideal. They are committed to providing an excellent undergraduate education and also actively pursuing their scholarly work. Many students collaborate with faculty members in research, and these projects regularly lead to joint publications and poster presentations at professional conferences.

Student Government

The Bucknell Student Government serves as the official voice of Bucknell students. It distributes funds for most student clubs and organizations, and its representatives serve on standing committees of the Board of Trustees and other University governance groups.

Admission Requirements

Admission decisions focus on intellectual ability; quality of preparation as demonstrated by achievement in rigorous high school courses and SAT or ACT scores; special talent; significant contribution to school or community; evidence of strong character and integrity; and excellent writing skills. The University seeks qualified students from all backgrounds throughout the United States and abroad.

Application and Information

Regular decision applications should be filed before January 15 of the senior year in high school for notification by April 1. SAT and/or ACT results must be submitted before March 1. Early decision candidates may apply for early decision–round one consideration by November 15 or early decision–round two consideration by January 15. Applications for transfer students should be submitted by March 15 for studies beginning the following fall and by November 1 for the spring semester.

Robert G. Springall
Dean of Admissions
Bucknell University
Lewisburg, Pennsylvania 17837
United States
Phone: 570-577-3000
Fax: 570-577-3538
E-mail: admissions@bucknell.edu
Website: http://www.bucknell.edu
  www.facebook.com/BucknellU
  Twitter @BucknellU

Bertrand Library, Bucknell University, Lewisburg, Pennsylvania.

CALIFORNIA COLLEGE OF THE ARTS
SAN FRANCISCO AND OAKLAND, CALIFORNIA

The College

California College of the Arts (CCA) (www.cca.edu), founded in 1907, offers studies in twenty-one undergraduate and eleven graduate majors in the areas of fine art, architecture, design, and writing. It has two campuses, in San Francisco and Oakland, which both provide an intimate, private-college environment. Students and faculty members create a supportive community of friends, colleagues, and mentors. Students discover their creative passions and develop their individual points of view, and they are particularly encouraged to experiment across disciplines. CCA welcomes students who want to make art that matters.

Whether a student's dream involves making a film, designing sustainable products or buildings, painting outside the lines, or working within their community, CCA offers an excellent environment to pursue those dreams. Students develop skills that will serve them well, both during their college years and after graduation. Innovative courses with real-world applications include ENGAGE at CCA, a family of courses embedded throughout the curriculum in which students work with outside experts to find solutions to community issues. The IMPACT Social Entrepreneurship awards give multiple $10,000 awards each year to interdisciplinary teams of students, enabling them to undertake a major project over the summer, anywhere in the world.

CCA alumni have been successful in a vast range of creative endeavors. In the past year, Anthropologie released a new clothing collection based on artwork by Mia Christopher (Painting/Drawing 2012). Ashley Eva Brock (Fashion Design 2012) was awarded the *Surface* magazine Emerging Talent Award, which includes an internship with the New York fashion designer Rubin Singer. Steve Purcell (Interdisciplinary Fine Arts 1982) codirected Disney • Pixar's new movie *Brave*. Erik Adigard (Graphic Design 1987) received a Rome Prize for design. And Patrick Coyne (Graphic Design 1983), editor and designer of *Communication Arts*, was awarded the prestigious AIGA Fellow Award.

BusinessWeek magazine has named CCA one of the world's best design schools, and the *Princeton Review* cites it as one of the greenest colleges in the U.S. CCA is accredited by the Western Association of Schools and Colleges, the National Association of Schools of Art and Design, the National Architectural Accrediting Board, and the Council for Interior Design Accreditation.

CCA has approximately 1,450 undergraduate and 470 graduate students. The average class size is 18. Among the undergraduates, 61 percent are women, 39 percent are men, 18 percent are from underrepresented populations, and 18 percent are international students. Of the entering class, 59 percent are first-time freshmen and 41 percent are transfer and second-degree students. About 28 percent come from out of state.

About 77 percent of first-year students live on campus. Throughout the year, the residential-life staff hosts social and educational programs ranging from movie nights to museum trips and lectures by outside professionals.

Students are encouraged to join existing clubs and organizations or to form new ones. They are active in preprofessional groups, including the American Institute of Architecture Students (AIAS), American Institute of Graphic Arts (AIGA), Industrial Designers Society of America (IDSA), and International Interior Design Association (IIDA).

Location

The San Francisco Bay Area is known for creative and technological innovation, environmental leadership, and thriving art and design communities. It is home to world-class museums and alternative galleries as well as active endeavors in theater, music, dance, film, and literature. Beaches, hiking and biking trails, the Napa Valley, Monterey, Lake Tahoe, the Sierra Nevada mountains, and Yosemite National Park are all nearby.

CCA's San Francisco campus occupies several buildings in the Potrero Hill neighborhood, along what the city has newly dubbed the Innovation Corridor. The Oakland campus occupies 4 acres in the Rockridge neighborhood, 3 miles from the University of California, Berkeley. A free shuttle connects the campuses and residence halls. Both campuses are easily accessible via public transportation.

Majors and Degrees

CCA offers the Bachelor of Fine Arts (B.F.A.) degree in animation, ceramics, community arts, fashion design, film, furniture, glass, graphic design, illustration, industrial design, interaction design, interior design, jewelry/metal arts, painting/drawing, photography, printmaking, sculpture, and textiles. The College offers the Bachelor of Arts (B.A.) degree in visual studies and writing and literature. CCA also offers a bachelor of architecture (B.Arch.) degree, a five-year program. More information is available at http://www.cca.edu/academics.

CCA offers the M.F.A. in comics, design, film, fine arts, and writing; the M.A. in curatorial practice and visual and critical studies; the M.Arch., M.A.A.D, and M.A.U.D.L. in architecture; and the M.B.A. in design strategy. Graduate fine arts concentrations include ceramics, film, furniture, glass, jewelry/metal arts, painting/drawing, photography, printmaking, sculpture, textiles, and social practice.

Academic Programs

The B.F.A. requires the completion of 126 semester units (75 in studio work and 51 in humanities and sciences). The B.A. requires 126 semester units (51 in humanities and sciences, 36 in the major, and 39 in studio work). The B.Arch. requires 165 semester units, including the core program and a 9-semester major program. For details, prospective students can visit http://www.cca.edu/academics.

Undergraduates begin with a core curriculum, which covers a variety of artistic media, principles, and processes as well as writing, literature, art history, and critical theory.

CCA operates on a two-semester academic calendar with a six-week summer session. Summer programs include the Pre-College Program for high school students (participants earn college credit).

Off-Campus Programs

Qualified upper-division students may spend a semester at one of thirty-two other U.S. art schools through the Association of Independent Colleges of Art and Design (AICAD). Students may cross-register at Mills College or Holy Names University, both in Oakland.

Through the International Exchange Program, students may spend a semester at one of more than thirty colleges around the world. CCA also offers summer study-abroad courses.

Academic Facilities

The Oakland campus is home to the First Year Program and the programs in animation, ceramics, community arts, glass, jewelry/metal arts, photography, printmaking, sculpture, textiles, visual studies, and writing and literature. Painting and drawing courses are held on both campuses. Animation students have dedicated studios and equipment for digital video, film, and sound production. The ceramics facilities include numerous gas and electric kilns. Sculpture facilities include a bronze foundry, a wax-working area, a plaster and mold-making room, a metal fabrication studio, and a woodshop. Textiles facilities include a computerized weaving lab, a digital Jacquard TC-1 loom, and a fiber sculpture studio. For printmaking there are lithography presses, a 40x60 American French Tool etching press, a silkscreening and papermaking complex, and a letterpress lab. The two-floor photography center includes a new digital classroom.

The San Francisco campus houses the programs in architecture, fashion design, film, furniture, graphic design, illustration, industrial design, interaction design, interior design, and painting/drawing as well as all of the graduate programs. There is a state-of-the-art digital production facility and stage. The studio and shop facilities include a furniture studio, a model-making studio, an alternative materials studio, a rapid-prototyping studio, a hybrid lab for interactive technology, a welding studio, a plaster room, a sanding room, and a spray booth. The MFA Program in writing has its own building. A brand-new Campus Center has a student lounge downstairs and student exhibition space upstairs. The Wattis Institute for Contemporary Arts makes international artists and their work accessible to students through exhibitions, the Capp Street Project residency program, lectures, symposia, and publications.

CCA's fourteen dedicated computer labs are available to all students 16 to 24 hours daily, whenever they are not being used for classes. The labs have Intel-based Macintosh computers and a complete range of software. There is a rapid prototyping studio for 3-D printing.

CCA's libraries (one on each campus) specialize in art and design. On the San Francisco campus there is also a materials library (one of very few such libraries at an educational institution) that contains thousands of material samples.

The College has several dedicated on-campus spaces for the exhibition of student work, and individual departments and courses frequently present off-campus shows of student work. Many of these exhibitions are organized by students, which gives them valuable hands-on gallery experience.

Costs

Tuition for the 2012–13 academic year was $38,448 for full-time undergraduates and $1,602 per unit for part-time students. Tuition is the same for California and out-of-state residents. Campus housing cost an additional $7,700. Total costs for 2012–13 were $54,298, which included $38,7989 in tuition and fees, $10,550 for room and board, $1,500 for books and supplies, and $3,450 for miscellaneous expenses.

Additional information is available at http://www.cca.edu/students/handbook/tuition_fees.

Financial Aid

Last year 87 percent of CCA students received financial aid from some source. Approximately 76 percent received CCA scholarships. The college offers financial aid in the form of scholarships, grants, loans, and work-study programs. There are both need- and merit-based awards. An estimate of potential scholarship and financial aid can be generated with the net cost calculator at http://www.cca.edu/financialaid.

Students seeking merit scholarships must submit their admissions application by February 1. Students applying for financial assistance should submit the FAFSA by March 1. CCA continues to award aid after March 1 as funding permits.

Students can apply for grants and loans throughout the year. CCA is approved for veterans who wish to attend under the Veterans Administration Educational Benefits Program. CCA offers an interest-free payment plan.

Faculty

CCA's faculty includes 500 artists, architects, designers, writers, and scholars, most of whom combine teaching with professional work in their respective fields. Faculty members serve as advisers to first-year students. Additional details are available at http://www.cca.edu/academics/faculty.

Student Government

The Student Council includes students from all areas of CCA and sponsors extracurricular activities, including films, receptions, and gallery excursions.

Admission Requirements

Admitted undergraduates must have a high school diploma or equivalent. Applications are reviewed on an individualized basis, taking into account academic achievements, creative abilities, individual achievements and activities, a personal essay, recommendations, and a portfolio. Prospective students can find more information at http://www.cca.edu/admissions.

Application and Information

For undergraduates, there are two priority deadlines for fall admission: February 1 and March 1. Those interested in applying for merit scholarships should submit their applications by February 1. The priority deadline for spring undergraduate applicants is October 1. Students who meet the admissions priority deadlines receive first consideration for housing, financial aid, and course selection. Applications are reviewed in the order they are received. There is a nonrefundable application fee of $60. It is possible to register for courses as a nondegree student (on a space-available basis).

Students may schedule a campus visit, request information, and apply online at http://www.cca.edu/admissions. For additional information, please contact:

Office of Enrollment Services
California College of the Arts
1111 Eighth Street
San Francisco, California 94107-2247
Phone: 800-447-1ART (toll-free)
Fax: 415-703-9539
Website: http://www.cca.edu
　　　　　http://www.facebook.com/CaliforniaCollegeoftheArts
　　　　　http://twitter.com/CACollegeofArts
　　　　　http://www.youtube.com/user/CCAart

A painting class meets on the San Francisco campus of California College of the Arts.

CALIFORNIA INSTITUTE OF THE ARTS   CalARTS

VALENCIA, CALIFORNIA

The Institute

CalArts educates professional artists in a unique learning environment founded on the principles of art-making excellence, experimentation, critical reflection, and independent inquiry. Throughout its history, CalArts has sought to advance the practice of art and promote its understanding in a broad social, cultural, and historical context. CalArts offers students the knowledge and expertise of leading professional artists and scholars and a full complement of art-making tools. In return, it asks for the highest artistic and academic achievement. Reflecting its longstanding commitment to new forms and expressions in art, CalArts invites creative risk-taking and urges active collaboration and exchange among artists, artistic disciplines, and cultural traditions.

CalArts is the first higher educational institution in the United States to offer undergraduate and graduate degrees in both visual and performing arts. It was established in 1961 by Walt and Roy Disney through the merger of two professional schools, the Los Angeles Conservatory of Music and the Chouinard Art Institute.

Since its founding, CalArts has been recognized internationally as a leader in every discipline in which it provides instruction. Its artists and alumni have defined, and continue to extend, the very forefront of creative practice as we know it today.

At the graduate level, the Institute grants the Master of Fine Arts (M.F.A.) degree in art, dance, film/video, theater, and creative writing and the Master of Arts (M.A.) degree in aesthetics and politics, and a Doctor of Musical Arts (D.M.A.) degree in performer-composer. Graduate programs take one, two, or three years to complete, depending on the individual program. Certificates and advanced certificates are also offered.

The total enrollment of the Institute is approximately 1,441 men and women, of whom 938 are undergraduates. The student body is gender balanced and geographically diverse, with students hailing from fifty states and thirty-one different countries.

Location

Thirty miles north of downtown Los Angeles, CalArts occupies 60 acres on hills overlooking the incorporated city of Santa Clarita. Rapid development in this peaceful suburban area has resulted in new residential communities and an ever-increasing population of more than 150,000. Los Angeles, the second-largest city in the United States and an important international hub for the arts, offers a vast array of professional and cultural resources.

Majors and Degrees

California Institute of the Arts grants the Bachelor of Fine Arts (B.F.A.) degree in art, dance, film/video, music, and theater; the Master of Fine Arts (M.F.A.) degree in art, dance, film/video, theater, and writing; the Master of Arts (M.A.) degree in aesthetics and politics; and the Doctor of Musical Arts (D.M.A.) degree in performer-composer.

Academic Programs

Students must apply to and enroll in a specific program within a particular school. A modified, nontraditional grading system is utilized, with each school's curriculum being determined by the special demands of the discipline. Instruction proceeds according to the student's preparation and need, with the student receiving guidance from a faculty mentor.

Undergraduate programs take four years or eight semesters and a minimum of 120 semester units to complete. All undergraduate students must fulfill the Critical Studies Requirements (40 percent of the total curriculum), which include courses in the humanities, social sciences, cultural studies, and natural sciences. These courses are intended to inform and influence each student's artistic practice.

Academic Facilities

Open 24 hours a day, the campus houses classrooms, art studios, animation studios, rehearsal rooms, and dance studios; galleries; theaters for drama, dance, and film; a music performance hall; costume, scenery, and machine shops; photo labs; computer and media labs; editing suites for film and video; and digital recording studios.

CalArts students also take advantage of a variety of special initiatives designed to respond to the realities of the social and cultural world today. These range from the Community Arts Partnership (CAP), which offers students a chance to teach in community and public school settings to the Cotsen Center for Puppetry and the Arts, which allows students to explore the potential of puppetry in their art-making and from the groundbreaking Center for New Performance, the professional wing of CalArts' Schools of Performance where students and faculty members collaborate on professionally presented performances, to the Institute's contemporary art journal Afterall, copublished with London's Central Saint Martins College of Art and Design, and the literary magazine Black Clock, published in association with CalArts' M.F.A. Writing Program.

The most momentous of these initiatives is the Roy and Edna Disney/CalArts Theater, or REDCAT, part of the Walt Disney Concert Hall complex in downtown Los Angeles. Designed by Frank Gehry, REDCAT includes a state-of-the-art, flexible performance space, a 3,000-square-foot gallery, and a café. REDCAT plays host to the most interesting new experimental theater, dance, music, art, film and video, and literature from Southern California, the nation, and the world. In the process, CalArts brings new resources to its students' education through performances, master classes, and residencies by visiting artists and helps its students make a seamless transition into the local, national, and international arts communities.

The library contains a collection designed especially for the visual and performing arts. In addition to holding more than 95,000 volumes, the library includes musical scores, sound recordings, films, videotapes, and slides that enable students to progress on their own in obtaining knowledge relevant to their specific studies.

Costs

Tuition for 2013–14 is $39,976 for the academic year. Room charges range from $4264 to $7970 per year, and board costs between $3710 and $4265. The cost of books and supplies varies according to major.

Financial Aid

The Financial Aid Office at CalArts is dedicated to helping students meet the cost of attendance at the Institute. Funds made available through the Financial Aid Office are awarded on a combination of need and artistic merit. Need is determined by completing and submitting the FAFSA (Free Application for Federal Student Aid). CalArts offers a limited number of merit-only awards; however, to be considered for these awards, students must have completed the FAFSA.

CalArts offers the following financial aid programs: Institute scholarships and grants, Federal Pell Grants, Federal Supplemental Educational Opportunity Grants, Federal Work-Study Program awards, Federal Perkins Loans, Federal Stafford Loans, and Cal Grants. Details of these financial aid programs are available from the Financial Aid Office.

Faculty

The faculty numbers approximately 300, including both full- and part-time members. The student-faculty ratio is approximately 8:1. Faculty members maintain active, often prolific, careers in their respective disciplines. Their approach to teaching combines rigorous instruction with careful guidance and individualized attention, a process that empowers students to define their own artistic objectives. Every student works closely with an assigned faculty mentor.

Student Government

Student government is conducted through the Student Council, whose members are elected by the student body. In addition, students are active participants in a variety of Institute-wide standing committees, the composition of which also includes a Board of Trustees, faculty members, and staff members.

Admission Requirements

CalArts welcomes application for admission from any individual engaged in the visual and performing arts. The main criterion for admission is artistic merit, as assessed by the faculty of the individual programs. An artist statement, letters of recommendation, and school transcripts are also required.

Application and Information

For application forms and additional information, prospective students should visit http://calarts.edu/admissions/apply or contact:

Office of Admissions
California Institute of the Arts
24700 McBean Parkway
Valencia, California 91355
Phone: 661-255-1050
E-mail: admissions@calarts.edu
Web site: http://www.calarts.edu

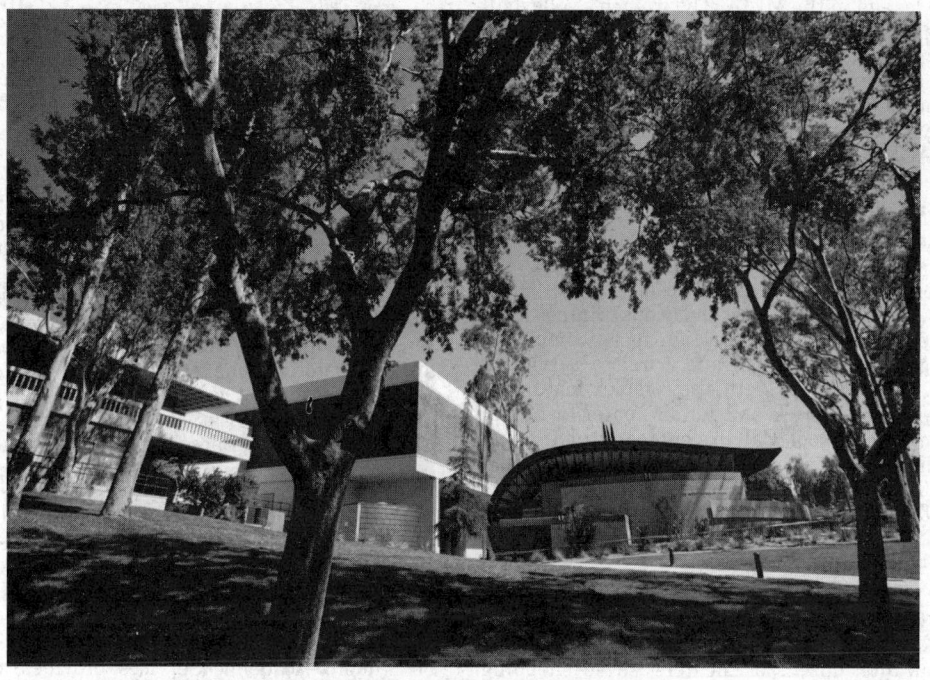

The 60-acre campus of CalArts. 30 miles north of Los Angeles, overlooks the city of Santa Clarita.

CALVIN COLLEGE
GRAND RAPIDS, MICHIGAN

The College

Calvin College is best known for the integration of intellect and Christian faith. In every aspect of college life—teaching and learning, athletics and the arts, campus life and community activities—the Calvin community aims to live *coram Deo*, before the face of God.

Calvin is one of the nation's largest and most respected Christian colleges, bringing together 4,008 students and 305 full-time faculty members in a collaborative learning experience. Founded in 1876 and named for John Calvin, the sixteenth-century Protestant reformer, the College's commitment to students has not changed, teaching them to think courageously, connect globally, live faithfully, and become world-ready learners.

Calvin students come from nearly every state and forty-eight countries, and they study in more than 100 academic options. Most students are between 18 and 23 years old. Calvin maintains a strong affiliation with the Christian Reformed Church, yet students from more than fifty church denominations choose Calvin for its intentional blend of faith and learning.

A Calvin education helps students develop the faith, knowledge, and skills they need to walk confidently into life. In a survey of the class of 2011, 75 percent of the respondents were professionally employed, and 23 percent were pursuing graduate study. The Career Development Office equips students for internships, job interviews, and the search for full-time employment after graduation. Calvin students also receive practical experience; more than 80 percent of recent graduates reported having at least one internship while at Calvin.

Calvin is an NCAA Division III school and participates in the Michigan Intercollegiate Athletic Association. Calvin ranks eighth among all NCAA schools in the number of Academic All-American student-athletes since 2000. Calvin's twenty-one teams regularly earn national rankings in Division III athletics and frequently lead the league in the MIAA. The women's volleyball team won the national championship in 2010; the men's basketball team won the national championship in 1992 and 2000; and the women's cross-country team captured the national championship in 1998 and 1999. In 2000, 2003, 2004, and 2006, the men's cross-country team won national championships. The men's ice-hockey club won the 2004 ACHA DIII national championship. Fourteen teams have finished as national runners-up. The most recent addition to Calvin athletics is lacrosse.

Designed by a student of Frank Lloyd Wright, Calvin's 400-acre wooded campus connects green spaces with modern architecture and remarkable resources. Fifteen residence halls, eleven apartment buildings, and two spacious dining halls accommodate 2,600 resident students. High-speed computing is available throughout the campus, and wireless service is offered in many locations. Calvin's athletic complex features a 5,000-seat arena, an indoor track and tennis center, a health center, and an Olympic-size pool. Calvin's outdoor athletic sites include baseball and softball diamonds, a premier soccer field with seating for 1,500 and two practice fields, an eight-lane track, a six-court tennis facility, a paved jogging path, and two sand volleyball courts.

Location

Calvin is located in Grand Rapids, Michigan, a metropolitan area of more than 600,000 people which offers every urban amenity. Hundreds of restaurants, dozens of theaters, seven shopping malls, and a fine selection of museums and parks are within a short drive. Premed and nursing students take advantage of the Medical Mile, a street that is flanked with new medical and scientific research facilities. Lake Michigan beaches, ski areas, parks, and trails are within a 40-minute drive.

Majors and Degrees

The Bachelor of Arts and Bachelor of Science degrees are offered, with major concentrations in accounting, art, art history, Asian studies, biochemistry, biology, biotechnology, business, chemistry, Chinese, classical studies, communication arts and sciences, computer science, digital communications, Dutch, early childhood education, economics, elementary and secondary education, engineering, English, environmental science, environmental studies, exercise science, film studies, French, geography, geology, German, Greek, history, information systems, international development studies, international relations, Japanese, Latin, linguistics, literature, mathematics and statistics, media production, media studies, music, nursing, philosophy, physical education, physics/astronomy, political science, psychology, public health, recreation, religion, social work, sociology, Spanish, special education, speech pathology and audiology, sport management, theater, and writing.

Professional programs include engineering (chemical, civil/environmental, electrical/computer, mechanical); natural resources; architecture (minor); predentistry; prelaw; premedicine; prepharmacy; pre–physical therapy; pre–seminary studies; social work; and elementary, early childhood, secondary, and special education. Minor concentrations are available in African and African diaspora studies, archaeology, astronomy, coaching, dance, ESL, gender studies, health education, journalism, medieval studies, ministry studies, missions, urban studies, and youth ministry leadership. Calvin also offers a Master of Education (M.Ed.) degree and a Master of Speech-Language Pathology degree (MA-SP) program.

Academic Programs

Calvin's multifaceted liberal arts curriculum helps students connect the way they think with the way they live. Calvin's core curriculum begins with a first-year gateway course, *Developing a Christian Mind,* and ends with a capstone course in the senior year.

The College follows a 4-1-4 academic calendar, consisting of two 4-month semesters with a three-week January interim term.

Core curriculum requirements include foreign language, history, literature and arts, mathematics, natural sciences, philosophy, physical education, religion, social sciences, and written and spoken rhetoric. Some requirements can be satisfied by advanced high school work, by completing college-level work in high school, or by examination. Satisfactory scores on Advanced Placement (AP), International Baccalaureate (I.B.), and/or CLEP exams are also accepted. Incoming students with an ACT composite of at least 29 who are interested in nursing and meet other admissions requirements will receive automatic admission to Calvin's nursing program. The Calvin Honors Program offers highly motivated students a greater depth of learning and advanced course work. The John M. Perkins Leadership Fellows Program offers select first- and second-year students opportunities to advance their skills while exploring real-life issues. The Office of Student Academic Services provides academic counseling, tutoring, training in study skills, and review courses in key subjects for all students.

Off-Campus Programs

Calvin offers semester-long study-abroad programs in Britain, China, France, Ghana, Honduras, Hungary, the Netherlands, Peru, and Spain; there are U.S.-based programs in New Mexico and Washington, D.C. Calvin offers many other programs in cooperation with other colleges, including programs of the Council for Christian Colleges and Universities in Central America, Hollywood, Egypt, and Moscow. Some students may fulfill their foreign language requirement through study-abroad programs. Many courses offered during the January interim are also taught abroad.

Academic Facilities

The four-floor Science Complex features extensive laboratories, an atom trapper, and an observatory. The Engineering Building provides space for engineering students to do research, design, and project construction. The DeVries Hall of Science includes medical research laboratories and classrooms. The Spoelhof College Center houses administrative offices, a social research center, six art studios, and a 340-seat auditorium. The Covenant Fine Arts Center features a 1,100-seat auditorium, the Center Art Gallery, a 240-seat recital hall, classrooms, and music suites.

The Hekman Library includes a five-level, computerized library containing more than 800,000 bound volumes, 2,750 periodicals, an extensive collection of microfiche, records and tapes, and government publications; more than 1,500 students can be comfortably seated at study carrels and tables. The complex also houses the Information Technology Center, the Calvin Center for Christian Scholarship, the Meeter Center for Calvinism Studies, a distance-learning classroom, a graphics production lab, and a curriculum center for teacher education students. The DeVos Communications Center is home to a 150-seat video theater, a television studio, an audio studio, digital audio and video editing labs, and a speech pathology and audiology clinic. The Prince Conference Center houses seminars, meetings, retreats, and hotel rooms.

Costs

Tuition and fees for 2012–13 are $26,705. Room and board charges are $9,110 for resident students with a twenty-one-meal-per-week plan (ten- and fifteen-meal-per-week plans are also available). About $1,000 is needed for textbooks.

Financial Aid

Over 75 percent of first-year students are awarded an academic scholarship in amounts ranging from $1,000 to $15,000. Sixty percent of Calvin students receive need-based financial aid; demonstrated need is the most important criterion in determining eligibility. Students wishing to be considered for financial aid must be admitted to the College and must submit the Free Application for Federal Student Aid (FAFSA) and Calvin's Supplemental Application for Financial Aid. February 15 is the filing deadline for maximum consideration. Financial awards to eligible applicants consist of state and federal grants, loans, Federal Work-Study Program funds, and institutional grants and scholarships. More than 1,800 jobs are available on campus, and placement preference is given to students with financial need. Calvin's Student Employment Office also helps students find off-campus employment.

Faculty

Calvin's outstanding faculty members have distinguished themselves through publication and research, yet each is available 10–15 hours per week outside of class. More than 82 percent have earned the highest academic degree in their field. Each faculty member is a professing Christian, committed to the integration of his or her personal faith and discipline. There are over 305 full-time and 77 part-time faculty members; the faculty-student ratio is 1:11.

Student Government

Calvin encourages student development and responsible action by clearly expressing its expectations and de-emphasizing regulations. Campus rules are designed to build a Christian academic community. The 27-member Student Senate oversees the budgets for student publications, homecoming, the film arts, and supervises most student activities. Student members serve on most faculty committees governing the College. Each residence hall has its own governing council and judiciary committee.

Admission Requirements

Applicants should be graduates of an accredited high school program and should have completed satisfactorily at least 15 units of college-preparatory work, including 3 in English and 3 in algebra and geometry. Applicants with high school averages of C+ (2.5) or higher who score above 20 on the ACT composite or above 470 on both the math and critical reading sections of the SAT are typically given regular admission. Applicants with lower grades and scores, or those with deficiencies in their high school preparation, may be admitted under special conditions. International students should refer to http://www.calvin.edu/international for application procedures. Students who come from a non-English-speaking culture must submit results of the TOEFL or IELTS or provide other documentation of English-language proficiency.

Application and Information

Applicants must submit a completed application form, a high school or college transcript, results of the ACT or SAT, and an educational recommendation completed by a teacher or counselor. Admission decisions are made on a rolling basis beginning in mid-October. Applicants for fall admission are urged to complete their file before February 1 in order to receive maximum consideration for scholarships; the deadline for admission is August 15 for U.S. and Canadian applicants and April 1 for international applicants, as long as space is available. Prospective students and parents are warmly invited to visit the campus to experience life at Calvin firsthand.

For more information, prospective students should contact:
Office of Admissions and Financial Aid
Calvin College
3201 Burton Street, SE
Grand Rapids, Michigan 49546
Phone: 616-526-6106 (admissions)
       616-526-6134 (financial aid)
       616-526-8480 (TTY)
       800-688-0122 (toll-free in North America)
Fax: 616-526-6777
E-mail: admissions@calvin.edu
      finaid@calvin.edu
Website: http://www.calvin.edu
       http://www.facebook.com/calvinadmissions
       http://twitter.com/calvincollege

Recognized as one of the finest research libraries in western Michigan, the Hekman Library is a hub of student and faculty activity on the Calvin College campus.

CARLOW UNIVERSITY
PITTSBURGH, PENNSYLVANIA

The University

Carlow University was founded in 1929 in response to a local need for a Catholic women's college. The mission of the University is to involve people, primarily women, in a process of self-directed lifelong learning that frees them to think clearly and creatively, to discover and to challenge or affirm cultural and aesthetic values, to respond reverently to God and others, and to render competent and compassionate service in personal and professional life. Although Carlow makes explicit its strong continuing commitment to the education of women, it welcomes men. The University's mission has been confirmed over the years by the growing number of students who come seeking a solid liberal arts education as well as strong career preparation. In addition to its undergraduate programs, the University offers an M.B.A., an M.F.A., a Master of Science in fraud and forensics, and other graduate degrees.

Current enrollment exceeds 2,300 students. Carlow's students have various backgrounds and come mainly from the Middle Atlantic states; the majority are from western Pennsylvania.

Placement and career counseling, free professional and peer tutorial services, the Center for Academic Achievement, the Disabilities Service Office, student health, personal counseling programs, and campus ministry are support services available to students.

Cocurricular organizations include the Student Government Association, the Commuter Student Association, the International Student Association, the Purple Menace newspaper, and United Black Students, among many others.

The University has a large group of students involved in community service and volunteerism. Spring break service projects have taken students to Jamaica, the Virgin Islands, Arizona, Arkansas, Texas, Ireland, and many other locations. Academic- or career-oriented organizations include Alpha Phi Omega (national service/honor society), American Chemical Society, Beta Beta Beta (biology club), Business Leaders of Carlow, the Council for Exceptional Children, Kappa Delta Epsilon (for education majors), Social Work Organization, Student Nurses Association of Pennsylvania, Phi Chi Theta (business fraternity), and the Psychology Club. Special-interest groups include Blessed, the Gospel choir; the Environmental Clean-up Organization; Pep Band; Spirit; Student Athlete Association; Theater Group; and Women in Communication (WIC).

The athletic program includes women's intercollegiate basketball, soccer, softball, tennis, and volleyball as well as a selection of physical education courses, including aerobics, fitness and weight control, martial arts/self-defense, modern dance, water aerobics, weight training, and yoga. Wellness and fitness services include individual health assessment, fitness programming, and nutrition counseling.

Popular campus events include entertainment, film series, carnivals, Homecoming, Mercy Founders Week, a St. Patrick's Day celebration and parade, the International Festival, Black History Month events, Women's History Month events, and theater productions.

The University's central location gives students opportunities for internships in various businesses and agencies. Students in health-related fields complete their clinical experiences in the many fine teaching hospitals and private health-care facilities in the city of Pittsburgh. City buses stop in front of the campus, and campus parking is available for commuting students.

Location

Carlow University is located on a 15-acre campus in the heart of Oakland, one of the nation's biggest college towns and the educational, cultural, and medical center of Pittsburgh. Nine other colleges and universities at which students can cross-register are within walking distance or just minutes away by bus. Schenley Park, Carnegie Library and Museums, Phipps Conservatory, Carnegie Music and Lecture Halls, and the Oakland shopping district are all a short walk from the campus. Downtown Pittsburgh is only a 10-minute bus ride away. Greater Pittsburgh International Airport is a 30-minute drive from the Carlow campus.

Majors and Degrees

Carlow University grants the undergraduate degrees of Bachelor of Arts, Bachelor of Science, Bachelor of Science in Nursing, and Bachelor of Social Work. Programs include accounting, art, art/art education, art/art history, art/ceramics, art/graphic design, art/interactive media design, art/painting and drawing, art/photography, art with a certificate in art therapy preparation, biology (with concentrations in forensic medical and legal investigations/autopsy specialization, human biology, molecular cell and biotechnology, and organismal/ecological biology), business management, business management/communication, chemistry, communication studies, creative writing, early childhood education, elementary education, English, forensic accounting, health science (available to students who have previously earned an associate degree), history, human resource management and technology, information systems management, liberal studies, marketing, mathematics, nursing, philosophy, political science, professional writing, professional writing/business, psychology, public policy and leadership, scientific/medical marketing, social work, sociology, sociology/criminal justice, Spanish, special education, and theology. An independent major, designed by the student, may also be arranged.

Certification programs are offered in forensic accounting, perfusion technology (biology majors only) and secondary education (biology, chemistry, English, general science, mathematics, and social studies).

The University offers 3-2 programs in engineering in three areas: biology/environmental engineering, chemistry/chemical engineering, and mathematics/engineering. In addition, there is a 3-2 program in environmental science.

Academic Programs

Carlow's primary concern is the development of the student as a lifelong learner. To this end, members of the Carlow community—students, faculty, and staff—recognize the integrity and value of each person in the daily life and work of the University. The academic programs are broad and flexible, including opportunities for double majors, single majors with certification in education, minors, certificate programs, and changes of major. Transfer students are warmly welcomed.

The University operates on the two-semester system, August to December and January to May. Summer sessions, a variable number of weeks in length, are offered every year. Most courses carry 3 credits (laboratory courses, among others, carry 4 credits). Students normally take five courses each semester. Each student must demonstrate basic competence in English composition, speech and interpersonal communication, reading comprehension, and mathematics. Required of all students is one course each in a lab science, history, literature, mathematics, social/behavioral science (such as psychology or sociology), theology, fine arts, philosophy, women's studies, and political science or economics, as well as one global perspective course. Students are also required to take an interdisciplinary course, which is selected from a variety of subject areas. Students in nursing, education, social work, psychology, management, and perfusion technology are required to do fieldwork as part of their program. Field placements and internships are guaranteed and encouraged in all areas of study. An honors program is open to eligible students. After the first semester of the first year, one course per semester (outside of the major) may be taken on a pass-fail basis. Some courses may be challenged, for credit or exemption, by passing an examination. CLEP general exam credits may be used for this purpose as well.

The University gives women and men the opportunity to return to the classroom at various stages of their lives. Adult learners may enroll in full-time and part-time degree programs, noncredit enrichment courses, seminars, and workshops. Scheduling options include day, evening, accelerated, weekend, and online courses.

Academic Facilities

Grace Library, a five-level multipurpose learning center in the heart of the campus, currently contains more than 100,000 books, subscribes to over 350 print journals, and offers access to more than 4,500 online journals. The library houses the offices of the President and Provost. The Center for Academic Achievement, the mailroom, the bookstore, Academic Affairs, the Center for Career Enrichment, Printing Services, the International Poetry Forum, University Archives, and computer laboratories are also located here. Kresge Theatre, a 300-seat auditorium, is located on the fifth level as well.

Curran Hall houses the School of Nursing and includes a state-of-the-art nursing skills lab and conference and seminar rooms. Frances Warde Hall is a residence hall that also houses the School of Education, art labs, student affairs offices, and the campus café. Antonian Hall houses the 1,000-seat Sister Rosemary Heyl Theatre, the School for Social Change, the fine arts department, and classrooms as well as administrative offices for admissions, financial aid, advising, the registrar, and student accounts.

The cafeteria and the Campus School of Carlow University (kindergarten through grade 8) are located in Tiernan Hall. St. Joseph Hall contains the gymnasium, fitness center, and swimming pool, and Aquinas Hall houses classrooms, the humanities division, the International Student Center, and faculty and staff offices.

Carlow's A. J. Palumbo Hall of Science and Technology houses state-of-the-art teaching/research laboratories in physics, organic and advanced chemistry, genetics, cell biology, and gross anatomy; a herbarium to store dry plant specimens; a greenhouse; an amphitheater for scientific presentations; and the Bayer Children's Science Learning Laboratory.

Carlow University's campus computer network features Internet accounts and e-mail, network and Internet access from any location on campus. There is one network port per pillow in the residence halls.

Costs

Tuition for 2012–13 was $24,438 for full-time students. Room and board charges for the year were $9,630 for double occupancy.

Financial Aid

Financial aid in the form of grants, scholarships, loans, and student employment is available to eligible applicants. More than 90 percent of all full-time students receive some type of financial assistance. The University expects that most aid recipients assume a portion of their expenses through loans and/or part-time employment. Job opportunities are available on campus in a wide variety of positions, and students are placed, whenever possible, in positions that coincide with their skills and interests. Basketball, soccer, softball, tennis, and volleyball scholarships are also available.

Faculty

Carlow's student-faculty ratio is 12:1, and faculty members are readily available to help plan individualized programs of study, to provide assistance relating to field placements and internships, and to assist in career preparation. The student's major adviser is normally a faculty member in the department.

Student Government

All registered students are members of the Student Government Association (SGA). Through the SGA, students act as equal participants with the administration, faculty, and staff in general governance. The SGA promotes the general welfare of the students and is the advocate to ensure that the academic, social, and spiritual needs of students are met. SGA is empowered to charter all student organizations.

Admission Requirements

Applicants are evaluated on the basis of their secondary school record, class rank, and scores on the SAT or ACT. The Committee on Admissions recognizes that school curricula vary greatly and always gives careful consideration to the application of an able student whose course work or grading scale is more challenging or whose preparation differs from the traditional program. A personal interview is strongly recommended but not required. Overnight visits, a day of classes, campus tours, and meals are available and are strongly encouraged. Throughout the year, the University sponsors programs that give candidates the opportunity to tour the campus and meet faculty and staff members and Carlow students.

Application and Information

Although Carlow subscribes to the rolling admission plan, high school students are encouraged to submit an application early in the first semester of the senior year. Students interested in early notification should apply by September 30. The University's priority admission and scholarship deadline is February 15.

Students may apply online or request an application form by contacting:

Office of Admissions
Carlow University
3333 Fifth Avenue
Pittsburgh, Pennsylvania 15213
Phone: 412-578-6059
800-333-2275 (toll-free)
E-mail: admissions@carlow.edu
Website: http://www.carlow.edu

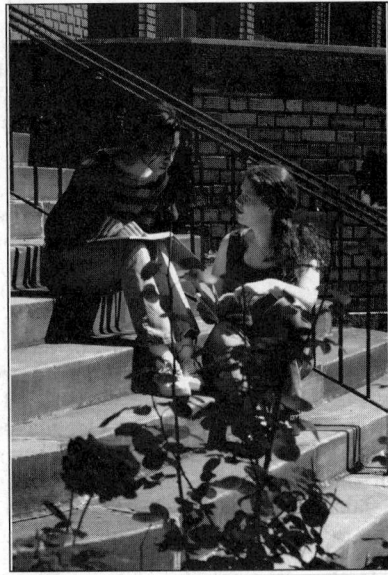

Two students take advantage of a sunny spring day to study outside at Carlow University.

CARSON-NEWMAN UNIVERSITY
JEFFERSON CITY, TENNESSEE

The University

Founded in 1851 by Tennessee Baptists, Carson-Newman University (C-N) is a private, coeducational, Christian liberal arts university. C-N has an enrollment of 1,967 students, of which some 297 are graduate students. The average class size is 16 students, and the student to faculty ratio is 12:1. Each fall, Carson-Newman enrolls approximately 450 freshmen. While most states are represented, students come primarily from the Southeastern United States, with Tennessee accounting for 77 percent of C-N students.

In addition to its outstanding academics, the University also provides many opportunities for student involvement in various clubs and organizations, nationally recognized varsity athletics, intramural athletics, music and drama groups, an award-winning forensics team, and many other extracurricular activities. The majority of C-N students live on campus in one of the five residence halls or two apartment complexes.

Carson-Newman also offers seventeen graduate programs including master's degrees in education and teaching (educational leadership, education/curriculum and instruction, teaching/curriculum and instruction, English as a second language), counseling (counseling, school counseling, spiritual guidance and care), business (business administration), nursing (RN to M.S.N., family nurse practitioner, nurse educator), religion (applied theology), and applied social justice.

Location

C-N is conveniently located in eastern Tennessee, just 30 miles from Knoxville and 45 miles from Gatlinburg, the gateway to the Great Smoky Mountains. Students appreciate the diverse opportunities available in the city and in the outdoor areas. Shopping, dining, and entertainment opportunities are available near the campus.

Majors and Degrees

The University awards Bachelor of Arts, Bachelor of Music, Bachelor of Science, and Bachelor of Science in Nursing degrees. In addition, an Associate of Arts in Christian ministries degree is also offered.

Majors are available in art (art, photography), business (accounting, business administration, finance economics, management, marketing), communication studies and theater (advertising/public relations, media studies, film, speech), education (athletic coaching, elementary education, physical education/health, secondary certification, special education), English (creative writing, literature), exercise science, family and consumer sciences (child and family studies, consumer services, [fashion design and merchandising], foods and nutrition, interior design, retail), early childhood education, exercise science, foreign language (biblical languages, Spanish), general studies, history, human services, mathematics, music (church music, music composition, music education, music theory, music with an outside field, piano and organ performance, vocal performance), natural and physical science (biochemistry, biology, chemistry, physics), nursing, philosophy (philosophy, philosophy/religion), political science, psychology (applied psychology, general psychology, social entrepreneurship), religion, and sociology.

Carson-Newman offers extremely strong curricula in preparation for professional and health professions. Preparatory programs are offered in dentistry, law, medicine, and physical therapy. In cooperation with several other institutions, C-N offers binary programs in pharmacy.

Academic Programs

Carson-Newman University operates on a traditional semester system. May term is a three-week intensive period of study giving students the opportunity to earn 3 credit hours. Summer terms are also offered.

All baccalaureate degrees require completion of 128 semester hours. Students must complete the C-N liberal arts core requirements and a total of 36 semester hours at the junior/senior level. Specific course requirements vary depending on major and degree program. Honors courses, independent study, and internships are available to students who qualify. Advanced credit is available for students who achieve required scores on AP exams, CLEP tests, and C-N departmental examinations.

New students are assigned a faculty adviser, who assists with course selection and student concerns. Career planning and tutoring services are also available through the Life Directions Center. Carson-Newman's exceptionally high placement rate in professional programs in medicine, law, business, and theological study is a testimony to the excellence of its rigorous academic program.

Off-Campus Programs

Students have the opportunity to spend an entire semester abroad by participating in the London Semester and other study-abroad opportunities. Carson-Newman, along with International Enrichment, Inc., provides all academic and nonacademic support services.

The Washington Semester is available as an internship program primarily for political science and prelaw majors. Through the program, students earn credit for work in the nation's capital. Art and foreign language majors may earn credit while studying and traveling throughout Europe during the three-week May term.

Carson-Newman's film program offers students the opportunity to earn college credit while participating in internships with regional filmmakers. Through a partnership with the Los Angeles Film Studies Center, accepted students also have an opportunity to live in L.A. and participate in a program that offers the chance to work and study with Hollywood filmmakers.

Academic Facilities

Carson-Newman offers the facilities and resources necessary for the enrichment of each student's education. Facilities include numerous computer labs; a campus-wide computer network; a media service center; a Digital Café; two theaters for drama production; Thomas Recital Hall, two art galleries and twenty-three individual art studios; the Stephens-Burnette Library; and the Maddox Student Activities Center. Recent construction projects have added two academic buildings to campus. These include Blye-Poteat Hall, home to the Department of Family and Consumer Sciences and Ted Russell Hall, which houses the Department of Business.

Costs

The annual cost at Carson-Newman, including room, board, and tuition, is well below the national average for four-year private colleges. Tuition for 2012–13 was $21,660, room averaged $2,566, board averaged $3,840, the student activity fee was approximately $490, and the technology fee was approximately $490. Students should allow about per year $1,400 for books.

Financial Aid

Carson-Newman allocates thousands of dollars each year to help supplement the resources of families. Financial aid awards are tailored to assist in meeting students' economic needs. Carson-Newman participates in all state and federal aid programs and awards aid based on demonstrated need as documented by a need analysis form, such as the Free Application for Federal Student Aid (FAFSA). Carson-Newman also awards merit academic scholarships based on achievement. The priority deadline for filing financial assistance forms is February 1. Additional information is available at http://www.cn.edu/administration/financial-assistance.

Faculty

Carson-Newman faculty members are known for their interaction with students both inside and outside of classes. The student-faculty ratio at C-N is 12:1, so students are sure to receive individual attention. Faculty members are involved in scholarly pursuits such as authoring books, leading national scholastic organizations, and research, but their primary focus is teaching.

Student Government

The Student Government Association (SGA) represents the entire student body by voicing student concerns in campus affairs. The purpose of SGA is to promote the welfare of every student through justice, to protect individual rights and freedoms, to encourage high standards of conduct, and to train students in the general principles of self-government.

Admission Requirements

Carson-Newman University seeks applicants who demonstrate academic preparation and who possess an appreciation of and sensitivity to a Christian education and a liberal arts curriculum. Carson-Newman accepts applications for freshman and transfer admission for each term of enrollment (fall, spring, and summer). Prospective students can obtain additional admissions information at www.cn.edu/admissions.

Application and Information

Applicants must submit all required application materials (application, official transcripts, and test scores) in order to be considered for admission. Admission decisions are made on a rolling basis, and students are notified within two weeks of receipt of all required documents.

For more information, prospective students should contact the Office of Undergraduate Admissions at 865-471-3223, admitme@cn.edu or visit www.cn.edu.

Students may also follow C-N admissions on Facebook (www.facebook.com/Carson.Newman) or Twitter (twitter.com/cnadmissions).

For additional information, contact:

Office of Undergraduate Admissions
Carson-Newman University
Jefferson City, Tennessee 37760
Phone: 865-471-3223
      800-678-9061 (toll-free)
E-mail: admitme@cn.edu
Website: http://www.cn.edu
      http://www.facebook.com/Carson.Newman
      http://twitter.com/cnadmissions

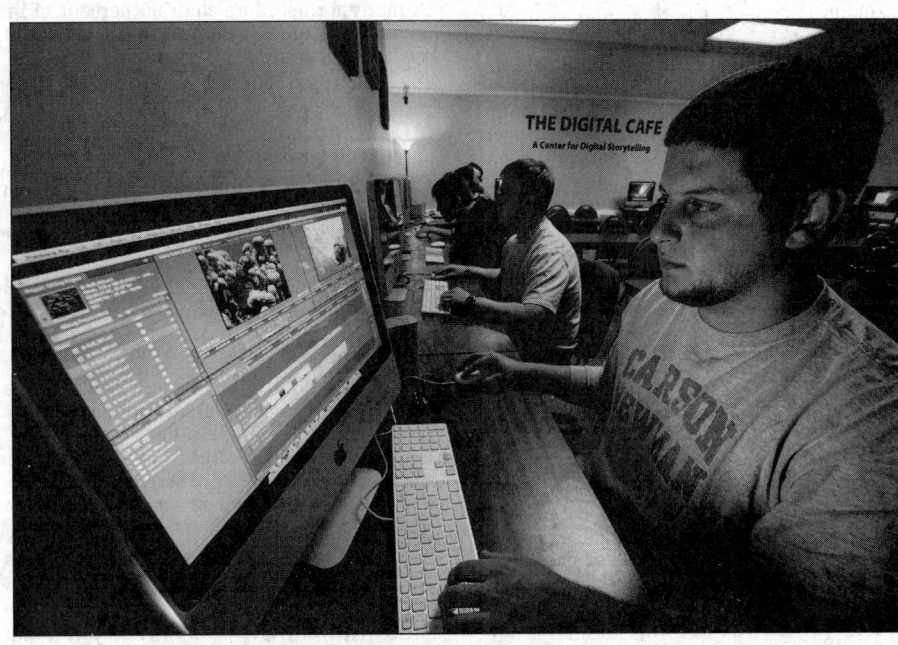

Operated through Carson-Newman's Communication Department, the Digital Café serves as a student development center for digital storytelling. Students are encouraged to explore innovative ways to tell multimedia stories.

CASE WESTERN RESERVE UNIVERSITY
CLEVELAND, OHIO

The University

Ranking consistently among the top private universities in the United States, Case Western Reserve University (CWRU) offers unlimited opportunities for motivated students. Its faculty members challenge and support students to help them flourish, and its partnerships with world-class cultural, educational, and scientific institutions ensure that undergraduate education extends beyond the classroom.

Challenging and innovative academic programs and experiential learning opportunities are at the core of the undergraduate experience. More than 4,200 undergraduates are enrolled in the University's programs in the arts, engineering, humanities, management, natural sciences, nursing, and social and behavioral sciences. Students access CWRU's graduate and professional schools in these areas as well as dental medicine, law, medicine, and social work.

Students are involved in more than 160 student organizations, including athletic, performance, religious, cultural, media, and community-service organizations. Greek life consists of fifteen fraternities and eight sororities, with approximately 35 percent of undergraduate students participating. Residence halls are coeducational, and more than 80 percent of students reside on campus.

A charter member of the University Athletic Association, an NCAA Division III conference, CWRU has won championships in cross-country, football, softball, track and field, and wrestling. Twenty percent of undergraduates wear the blue-and-white Spartans uniform, and 70 percent join an intramural team. Club sports include fencing, golf, ice hockey, skiing, and Ultimate (Frisbee).

Location

CWRU is located in Cleveland's University Circle, a unique cultural district comprising 550 acres of parks, gardens, museums, schools, hospitals, religious institutions, and human-service organizations. The Cleveland Museum of Art, the Cleveland Museum of Natural History, the Museum of Contemporary Art, and Severance Hall, home of the Cleveland Orchestra, are within walking distance; downtown Cleveland is 10 minutes away by car or public transportation. Partnerships in education and research among University Circle institutions enable students to make full use of resources beyond those of the University itself, and students receive free access to these and other local institutions, including the Rock and Roll Hall of Fame and Museum in downtown Cleveland.

Majors and Degrees

CWRU has a single-door admission policy—once students are admitted, they can pursue any major(s) they wish. Programs of study leading to the Bachelor of Arts degree include anthropology, art history, Asian studies, astronomy, biochemistry, biology, chemistry, classics, cognitive science, communication sciences, computer science, dance, economics, English, environmental geology, environmental studies, French, French and Francophone studies, geological sciences, German, German studies, history, history and philosophy of science, international studies, Japanese studies, mathematics, music, nutrition, nutritional biochemistry and metabolism, philosophy, physics, political science, psychology, religious studies, sociology, Spanish, statistics, theater, women's and gender studies, and world literature. The following B.A. programs are available as a second major: American studies, environmental studies, evolutionary biology, gerontological studies, natural sciences, pre-architecture, and teacher education.

Bachelor of Science degrees are offered in the following fields: accountancy, aerospace engineering, applied mathematics, art education, astronomy, biochemistry, biology, biomedical engineering, chemical engineering, chemistry, civil engineering, computer engineering, computer science, electrical engineering, engineering physics, geological sciences, management (business), materials science and engineering, mathematics, mathematics and physics, mechanical engineering, music education, nursing, nutrition, nutritional biochemistry and metabolism, physics, polymer science and engineering, statistics, systems and control engineering, systems biology, and an undesignated engineering major.

Minor areas of concentration are offered in most areas of major study, as well as art studio, artificial intelligence, banking and finance, childhood studies, Chinese, computer gaming, electronics, entrepreneurial studies, ethnic studies, film, health communication, Italian, Japanese, Judaic studies, marketing, mechanical design and manufacturing, public policy, Russian, and sports medicine.

Students may work toward a combined B.A./B.S. degree or integrate undergraduate and graduate studies to complete both the bachelor's and master's degrees in five years or less. Students who are interested in both the liberal arts and engineering can benefit from the 3–2 Binary Program. Students spend three years at one of forty participating liberal arts colleges and then spend two years at CWRU studying engineering or a related field. Graduates of this program receive both a B.A. and a B.S. degree.

Academic Programs

Students in all majors participate in SAGES, the Seminar Approach to General Education and Scholarship program. SAGES consists of four engaging seminars that emphasize written and verbal communication skills and concludes with a senior capstone project. Through a combination of core curricula, major requirements, and minors or approved course sequences, all undergraduates receive a broad educational base as well as specialized knowledge in their chosen fields.

At Case Western Reserve University, hands-on learning comes in many forms. More than 95 percent of graduates say they took advantage of at least one of the many hands-on learning opportunities available, including:

Co-op: CWRU has one of only eleven co-op programs in the U.S. recognized by the Accreditation Council for Cooperative Education (ACCE). Students studying engineering, science, management, and accounting are eligible.

Clinicals: CWRU nursing students begin clinical placements during their first semester on campus. Upon graduation, students accrue more than 1,600 clinical hours—nearly double the national average.

Internships: Many students utilize the resources of the Career Center to help them find internships in their field of study. On-campus job fairs and employer visits also help students network and find opportunities.

Research: CWRU is among the country's leading independent research universities, ranking among the top 15 private universities receiving federal funding for research. The SOURCE (Support of Undergraduate Research and Creative Endeavors) office allows students to engage in research relevant to their academic study and provides guidance on acquiring research funding.

Service Learning: CWRU offers numerous volunteer opportunities connected to a student's academic interests. The Center for Civic Engagement and Learning connects students with community partners.

Study Abroad: CWRU offers many different types of study-abroad programs. Students have the opportunity to spend a full year or a semester in a traditional immersion arrangement or can choose from shorter-term programs.

Off-Campus Programs

More than one third of CWRU undergraduates take advantage of opportunities to have an educational experience abroad. The University offers short-term programs during winter, spring, and summer breaks, as well as more traditional semester-long study-abroad programs in several countries. Some students also choose to complete internships, research and co-ops abroad.

Academic Facilities

The Kelvin Smith Library is home to more than 1.7 million items and located in the heart of campus. Through reciprocal borrowing arrangements, CWRU students have access to the holdings of the Cleveland Public Library as well as the libraries of five University Circle institutions; the members of OhioLINK, a network that includes state colleges and universities; and the State Library of Ohio; and several private institutions. CWRU is classified by the Carnegie Foundation as a university with very high research activity (RU/VH), and its lab facilities are state of the art. The University operates two astronomical observatories, a biological field station, a $6-million undergraduate engineering lab, and nearly 100 other designated research centers and laboratories, including think[box], the University invention center. The University's high-speed communications network links every residence hall room with computing centers, libraries, and databases on and off campus. CWRU's wireless network is one of the largest in the country. Other computer facilities on campus offer various models of computers and a wide variety of software programs, available free of charge to CWRU students.

The University Farm, located in nearby Hunting Valley, Ohio, offers educational opportunities in natural settings. Its 389 acres encompass a variety of deciduous forests, ravines, waterfalls, meadows, ponds, and a self-contained natural watershed.

Costs

For 2012–13, tuition totalled $40,120. Room and board cost an average of $12,436. Other required fees totalled $835.

Financial Aid

Financial aid consisting of grants, loans, and work assistance is awarded on the basis of a student's need. Applicants are required to file the Free Application for Federal Student Aid (FAFSA) and the CSS/Financial Aid PROFILE. Students are automatically considered for merit-based scholarships when they apply to the University; these awards typically range from $10,000 to $30,000. Students also are encouraged to apply separately for a select number of scholarships that require applicants to audition, provide additional information, or respond to an essay prompt.

Faculty

The undergraduate student-faculty ratio at CWRU is 9:1. Ninety-five percent of credit hours are taught by faculty members, not graduate students. Each school and the College of Arts and Sciences provides advisers who are available for both academic and personal advice. Once a student has chosen a major, a member of the department in which the student is majoring acts as his or her academic adviser. Undergraduate students have several opportunities to partner with faculty members on research or special projects, allowing for valuable learning opportunities, mentoring, networking, and personal development.

Student Government

CWRU's Undergraduate Student Government represents all undergraduate students. The assembly acts as a liaison between undergraduate students and the faculty, administration, and other groups; grants recognition to undergraduate organizations; and has the responsibility and authority to allocate funds from student activity fees to student organizations. The Residence Hall Association is a governing body for on-campus living; the University Program Board plans special events; and the Interfraternity Congress and Panhellenic Council govern the Greek community.

Admission Requirements

Case Western Reserve University reviews each application for admission carefully, taking into consideration academic background, life experiences, and interests. There is no minimum test score or GPA range used to gauge a student's potential for admission. In terms of meeting academic requirements for admission, CWRU looks for students who have been successful in a variety of challenging classes. The admission staff understands that every school is different, so staff evaluates student transcripts specifically against their high school's curriculum.

Prior to high school graduation, it is recommended that students pursue 4 units of English, 3 units of math, 3 units of science (2 of which must be laboratory science), 3 units of social studies, and 2 units of foreign language. The University recommends that applicants interested in engineering and the sciences have an additional unit of math and laboratory science. For students interested in the liberal arts, it is recommended that students take an additional unit of social studies and foreign language.

The University requires an essay. The essay is a writing requirement with no word minimum or maximum, and the content is chosen by the applicant. An interview is not a required part of the admission process, but it is strongly recommended. To receive full consideration for admission and scholarships, students must take the SAT or ACT prior to their selected application deadline.

Application and Information

Nonbinding early action applications are due November 1, and students are notified by December 15. January 15 is the deadline for regular decision applications, and students are notified by March 20. Application deadlines for transfer students are May 1 for fall admission and October 1 for spring admission. The application deadline for the Pre-professional Scholars Program (medicine, dentistry, law, or social work) is December 1. Students can apply to CWRU via the online Common Application. The fall semester begins in late August.

Interviews with admission professionals, campus visits, group information sessions, and other resources are available to all prospective students.

For more information, students should contact:

Office of Enrollment Management
Case Western Reserve University
10900 Euclid Avenue
Cleveland, Ohio 44106-7055
Phone: 216-368-4450
E-mail: admission@case.edu
Website: http://admission.case.edu
    http://facebook.com/cwruadmission
    http://twitter.com/cwruadmission

Aerial view of Case Western Reserve University's campus and its surroundings in Cleveland's University Circle.

CASTLETON STATE COLLEGE
CASTLETON, VERMONT

The College

Castleton State College was founded in 1787; it was the first institution of higher learning in Vermont and the eighteenth in the United States. The 165-acre campus is located in Castleton, a historic Vermont village. Sixty-five percent of the 1,900 full-time undergraduate students at the College are Vermonters; the balance of the student population comes from New England and the Middle Atlantic states.

Castleton is committed to providing an undergraduate education in which the liberal arts and career preparation complement each other. Through an innovative program called Soundings, freshmen earn academic credit by attending a series of special events that include theater, music, dance, film, debate, and opinion from influential people. New students also participate in the First-Year Seminar, giving them the opportunity to develop the skills of a successful college student. First-year students may apply for the College's honors program. Community service and internships play an important role in a Castleton education.

There are eleven major residence halls. Together, the residences accommodate nearly 1,100 students. Each residence hall room is equipped with at least two Internet hookups and wireless access, which give each student the opportunity to access the Web and e-mail using their own personal computer. There is no additional charge for this service. Each room is also equipped with cable TV connections. Off-campus housing is available in the Castleton, Fair Haven, and Rutland areas. Students who live on campus eat in Huden Dining Hall. All students are allowed to have automobiles on campus.

More than forty clubs and organizations provide a wide variety of student activities that include club sports, an FM radio station, the student newspaper, and an active outing club. Other clubs relate to college majors and future careers; still others serve the College or local community. Castleton is a member of the North Atlantic Conference of NCAA Division III. Castleton offers twenty intercollegiate sports. Men compete in baseball, basketball, cross-country running, football, golf, ice hockey, lacrosse, skiing, soccer, and tennis. Women compete in basketball, cross-country running, field hockey, ice hockey, lacrosse, skiing, soccer, softball, tennis, and volleyball. A majority of Castleton's students are involved in the intramural and recreational sports program.

Castleton recently completed a $25.7-million project that included renovation and expansion of the Campus Center and the gymnasium, construction of a stadium, and improvements to the athletic fields. In 2012, Castleton completed a new 162-bed residence hall overlooking the athletic fields.

Location

The campus is 12 miles west of Rutland, one of Vermont's largest cities. Montreal, Boston, Hartford, Albany, and New York City are all within easy driving distance. Amtrak passenger trains to and from New York City stop in the village of Castleton. Killington and Pico ski areas, Lake Bomoseen, and the Green Mountains provide excellent recreational opportunities and an exceptional living and learning environment.

Majors and Degrees

Castleton State College offers B.A. or B.S. degrees in more than thirty areas of study: accounting, American literature, art, athletic training, biology, children's literature, computer information systems, communication, criminal justice, digital media, elementary education, environmental science, exercise science, forensic psychology, geology, health education, health science, history, journalism, management, marketing, mass media, mathematics, music, music education, nursing, physical education, psychology, public relations, secondary education, social work, sociology, Spanish, special education, sports administration, theater arts, and world literature. Associate degrees can be earned in business, communication, computer programming, criminal justice, general studies, or nursing.

Academic Programs

The Castleton curriculum is designed to provide the student with a strong liberal arts background plus the opportunity for career preparation in a specific area. All four-year students are required to complete a core of general education requirements during the four-year degree program. The first year of study can be used by the undecided student to explore various areas of interest. The student with a specific career interest may begin study in the major field as a freshman, although four-year students are not required to formally declare their major until the end of the sophomore year.

Castleton students typically enroll in five courses each semester. The academic calendar consists of two 15-week semesters and three 4-week summer sessions. Grading is traditional, and a pass/no-pass option is available. Internships and field experiences complement many of the academic programs at Castleton and are required in the communication, criminal justice, social work, and education programs.

Students may transfer internally from two-year to four-year programs in business, communication, computer information systems, criminal justice, and general studies. Students who transfer to Castleton after graduating from an accredited two-year college are granted full transfer credit for all academic work up to 64 credits or the number required for the associate degree.

Freshman students achieving at least a 3.5 grade point average in their first year at Castleton are recognized by the Castleton Chapter of Phi Eta Sigma, a national honor society that recognizes freshman scholastic achievement in colleges throughout the country. Outstanding junior and senior scholars are recognized by the Castleton Chapter of Alpha Chi. Pinnacle, the honor society for nontraditional students, honors qualified candidates. There are honor societies in business administration, women's studies, history, science and mathematics, theater arts, education, psychology, and Spanish. Students who have achieved a 4.0 grade point average are named to the President's List of Outstanding Students and those with a 3.5 grade point average or better to the Dean's List.

Academic Facilities

The Calvin Coolidge Library houses a collection of more than 500,000 books, periodicals, microforms, and nonprint media. Access to Castleton's library resources and outside scholarly sources is made possible through numerous online and CD databases; a sophisticated, networked electronic library system; the Internet; and strong consortial relationships within the state of Vermont. An audiovisual media facility provides a wide range of audiovisual equipment, including digital video editing, digital cameras, and presentation equipment.

Castleton's Stafford Academic Center houses the Computing Center, a high-tech multimedia lecture hall, distance learning classrooms, and the departments of education, mathematics, and nursing.

The Spartan Athletic Complex houses Glenbrook Gymnasium, the athletic training rooms, a swimming pool, two racquetball courts, two fitness centers, and a large indoor activity area.

Spartan Arena, the home of the men's and women's ice hockey teams, is a short drive away.

The Fine Arts Center contains a 500-seat auditorium; facilities for art, drama, dance, and music. A new television studio opened in 2010 as part of an addition to Leavenworth Hall.

The Jeffords Center houses science classrooms and laboratories, a state-of-the-art auditorium, laboratories for faculty and student research projects, and a greenhouse. An astronomical observatory is a short walk away.

There are more than 225 personal computers designated for student use located in labs across the campus.

Costs

Costs for 2012–13 were as follows: tuition for Vermont residents, $8,928, and for nonresidents, $21,528. Room and board expenses totalled $8,786. Annual fees were $936. The orientation and registration for new students was $200.

Financial Aid

Eighty percent of Castleton's full-time undergraduate students receive financial assistance from federal, state, College, or other sources. Grants, loans, and work-study jobs are available for qualified students. Applicants for financial aid should file the Free Application for Federal Student Aid (FAFSA) form by April 1 of the senior year in high school. All financial aid awards are based on need.

Most Castleton scholarships are awarded as part of the College's honors scholarship program. Amounts range from $1000 to $10,000 per year. First-year students who have a combined critical reading and math SAT score of at least 1100 and have a GPA of at least 3.3 on a 4.0 scale are eligible for one of these scholarships. Additional scholarships are available to new students based on certain academic credentials, service to their community, and financial need. There are also special scholarships for students wishing to study music or Spanish.

Faculty

The full-time faculty at Castleton consists of 92 men and women, 96 percent of whom hold terminal degrees in their field. Adjunct faculty members, many of them local businesspeople and members of the professions, complement the efforts of the full-time faculty. The student-faculty ratio is 14:1. Each student has a faculty member as an adviser.

Student Government

The Student Association is the chief vehicle of student government. All students who are registered for 8 or more credit hours are members. Elected representatives hold membership on most College committees, including the Curriculum and Cultural Affairs Committees. Students are also able to develop leadership qualities by participating in the various clubs and other organizations on campus.

Admission Requirements

Applicants are evaluated on the basis of their secondary school records, standardized test scores, and recommendations. Admission is granted to those applicants who have demonstrated their ability and potential to meet the challenges of a postsecondary learning experience.

Application and Information

Students may apply for admission through the Common Application. Under Castleton's rolling admission policy, applications are processed throughout the year, and candidates are notified of the admission decision as soon as their folders are complete. Students are admitted in the fall and spring semesters.

For more information about Castleton State College or to arrange a campus visit, students should contact:

Office of Admissions
Castleton State College
Castleton, Vermont 05735
Phone: 802-468-1213
        800-639-8521 (toll-free)
Fax: 802-468-1476
E-mail: info@castleton.edu
Website: http://www.castleton.edu
        http://tiny.cc/nhamg (Facebook)

The village of Castleton, in Vermont's scenic Lakes Region, is 12 miles west of Rutland, the state's second largest city. Beyond Rutland are the Green Mountains and the best skiing and snowboarding in New England.

CEDAR CREST COLLEGE
ALLENTOWN, PENNSYLVANIA

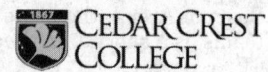

The College

Cedar Crest College was founded in 1867 and for more than 145 years has taken a bold approach to education by providing women with the competitive edge needed to succeed. A liberal arts college by design, Cedar Crest prepares women to lead in a global society. Approximately 1,600 students attend the College annually, representing twenty-seven states and twenty countries. Current students, alumnae, and future students maintain an active presence on the Cedar Crest Twitter and Facebook pages.

Cedar Crest College has more than thirty academic programs and faculty members who put a unique spin on traditional majors such as business and marketing, communication, English, and performing arts. In addition, Cedar Crest College has renowned programs in forensic science (one of fourteen accredited programs in the country and the only one affiliated with a women's college), social work (the only accredited program in the Lehigh Valley), and genetic engineering (one of the oldest programs in the country).

The College's health and wellness program has received a gold award for student health, wellness, and counseling from the National Association of Student Personnel Administrators. Their health and wellness initiative includes personal sports training; nutrition counseling; and a full schedule of dance, yoga, and aerobics classes. The Rodale Aquatic Center for Civic Health, a state-of-the-art, two-pool complex, offers health and fitness opportunities for the entire campus community. The campus also has tennis courts; regulation fields for field hockey, lacrosse, soccer, and softball; and a fitness center.

Cedar Crest students participate in nine NCAA Division III intercollegiate sports: basketball, cross-country, field hockey, lacrosse, soccer, softball, swimming, tennis, and volleyball. The College athletic department also supports club sports including equestrian, and cheerleading. The Falcons belong to the Colonial States Athletic Conference (CSAC) and compete against institutions in Pennsylvania, New Jersey, and Delaware. Cedar Crest student-athletes are held to high academic standards and have proven that it's possible to succeed both on the court and in the classroom. The CSAC recently awarded Cedar Crest student-athletes the first institutional achievement award for earning the highest grade point average in the Conference, and Cedar Crest teams have won several national academic awards. In 2011, basketball center Lizzy Sunderhause was recognized with the Jostens Trophy, awarded for excellence on the court and in the classroom and community.

Cedar Crest students hold leadership positions in more than forty clubs and organizations on campus. Student clubs range from the Student Government Association and Student Activities Board to the Literary Club and Biology Club. The College prepares women to lead in their future careers, community, and in life. Leadership retreats and community service opportunities are held throughout the year. The campus completes more than 20,000 hours in community service annually. Service opportunities are available throughout the Lehigh Valley at schools, hospitals, animal shelters, and Habitat for Humanity. At Cedar Crest, students serve early and often.

Cedar Crest upperclass students have the opportunity to live and learn together in the College's living-learning communities. These communities focus on a variety of relevant and timely topics such as global social justice, environmental ethics, entrepreneurship, and the arts. They bring together students who share a common interest, regardless of major or career focus. Sharing perspectives and lifestyles in this group setting enhances the students' educational journey as they gain intellectual appreciation and global awareness, apply and hone leadership skills, and make a difference locally and globally. These communities are the epitome of the seamless college experience as students live together, take a house class together, travel together, and develop close relationships with a faculty member affiliated with the community.

Through the Career Planning Office, students are placed in competitive internships near the campus and in major cities.

Cedar Crest's academic programs are fully accredited by the Middle States Association of Colleges and Schools and, where appropriate, by the American Academy of Forensic Science, American Medical Association, American Dietetic Association, American Bar Association, National League for Nursing Accrediting Commission, National Council on Social Work Education, and the Departments of Education of New York, New Jersey, and Pennsylvania. The College offers master's degrees in three fields: education, forensic science, and nursing.

Location

Students enjoy Cedar Crest's park-like campus, nestled in the heart of the Lehigh Valley in the West End of Allentown, Pennsylvania. The campus is a beautiful 84-acre nationally registered arboretum with more than 130 species of trees. The College is within easy distance of the extensive Allentown park system, high-end retail shopping, well-known restaurants, cultural activities, and the Pocono ski and outdoor resorts.

Cedar Crest is located in College Valley, home to more than 32,000 students at eight colleges within 20 minutes of campus. Students can participate in student- and faculty-led trips to nearby Philadelphia (less than 1 hour from campus) and New York City (less than 2 hours away). Students can explore the metropolitan areas of the East Coast, including Washington, D.C., Baltimore, and Boston, while enjoying the benefits of a small, suburban campus.

Majors and Degrees

Cedar Crest offers more than thirty fields of study in the arts, humanities, social sciences, business, and sciences. The combination of majors and course offerings provides students with a strong liberal arts background. The College also offers preprofessional programs in dentistry, law, medicine, and veterinary medicine. These well-respected academic programs provide individual support for students as they create an academic experience that is both personal and practical. Students are expected to be involved in planning their academic pathway from the very beginning.

Academic Programs

Self-designed majors, double majors, minors, and individual and group research projects are available and reflect the academic emphasis at the undergraduate level. Students may begin conducting research as early as their first year on campus. Students can also begin writing for the campus newspaper or hosting their own radio shows early in their college career.

The honors program at Cedar Crest is cross-disciplinary and designed for women who have demonstrated a record of high academic achievement. The honors program offers students a unique opportunity for growth and enrichment. Honors courses are marked by their engaging classroom environment, diverse and challenging coursework, and graduate-level research experiences.

Through a consortium with the Lehigh Valley Association of Independent Colleges, Cedar Crest upperclass students may cross-register and take courses at Lehigh and DeSales Universities and Lafayette, Moravian, and Muhlenberg Colleges at no additional cost.

Off-Campus Programs

Cedar Crest students are encouraged to pursue internships in their area of study. Internships enable students to gain practical experience at major corporations, small businesses, national nonprofit organizations, and top health-care facilities. Cedar Crest students have served internships with CNN, as a foreign correspondent with the United Nations, and with the FBI, working on a database for DNA fingerprinting.

The College stresses the importance of global awareness and encourages students to take advantage of study-abroad opportunities. Cedar Crest also offers courses with a short trip-abroad component lasting one to two weeks.

Academic Facilities

Learning spaces include hospital simulation labs, a ceramic studio, a state-of-the art nutrition laboratory, music practice rooms, *The Crestiad* newsroom, dance and art studios and workshops, theaters, genetic engineering laboratories, forensic science laboratories, a papermaking studio, media convergence lab, and a greenhouse.

Cedar Crest students socialize and dine in the Tompkins College Center, the hub of student activity. The center is home to Samuels Theatre, club meeting rooms, the dining hall, and the Falcon's Nest café.

Costs

For 2012–13, tuition was $31,196; room and board were $9,990.

Financial Aid

Student applications are reviewed for scholarship eligibility at the time of acceptance. The College's scholarships are awarded based on high school merit, leadership, and service. The College also holds an annual scholarship competition that awards one high-achieving student a full tuition scholarship for four years.

The financial aid program at Cedar Crest is based on financial need and includes grants, loans, and employment. Students applying for need-based financial aid should file the Free Application for Federal Student Aid (FAFSA).

Students are encouraged to use Cedar Crest's student aid calculator to receive a fast, accurate estimate of their financial aid package, including scholarships, grants, and loans. This calculator is available at http://www.cedarcrest.edu/calculator.

Faculty

Cedar Crest faculty members demand excellence, creating a challenging and supportive environment that allows students to grow and thrive. Faculty members are working artists, published writers, accomplished actors, international business professionals, and scientists making discoveries that will impact us all. They strive to ensure that student learning extends beyond the classroom.

Cedar Crest students meet one-on-one with a faculty mentor to build course schedules and discuss future plans. Students also work closely with faculty on groundbreaking research in all disciplines. This research can lead to national presentations and professional publications.

Admission Requirements

Cedar Crest welcomes applications from first-year students entering after high school and those seeking to transfer from another college or university. The admissions process looks at the entire student, from academic course work and standardized test scores to leadership potential, volunteer service, employment, and special talents.

Application and Information

Students are encouraged to visit the campus as they begin the application process, and can register for a visit at unleashed.cedarcrest.edu/visit. Applications are reviewed on a rolling basis, so they are processed and evaluated as soon as all materials have been received. Applicants are notified of their admissions decision beginning September 15 for the following fall semester. The priority deadline to apply for scholarship review is February 15.

Students can apply online at unleashed.cedarcrest.edu/apply-now or through the Common Application at https://www.commonapp.org.

Vice President for Enrollment Management
Cedar Crest College
100 College Drive
Allentown, Pennsylvania 18104-6196
Phone: 800-360-1222 (toll-free)
Fax: 610-606-4647
E-mail: admissions@cedarcrest.edu
Website: unleashed.cedarcrest.edu
　　　　www.facebook.com/CedarCrestCollege
　　　　twitter.com/cedarcrestcolle

Cedar Crest College is a great place to live and learn! The campus community comprises smart, creative women who will shape the world.

CHAMPLAIN COLLEGE
BURLINGTON, VERMONT

The College

Champlain College is a coeducational, private, nonprofit college founded in 1878. Career-minded students have been the focus of Champlain College since it was founded. Today, that long-standing tradition continues with outstanding undergraduate and online undergraduate courses, along with robust online certificate and degree programs, and nine master's degree programs.

Its 22-acre campus, home to 2,000 full-time students, is nestled among the stately maple trees of Burlington's historic Hill Section, overlooking Lake Champlain and the Adirondacks of New York to the west. Many of the College's buildings are restored Victorian-era private homes, which give students a unique atmosphere in which to learn and live.

The spirit of innovation and relevance are highlighted in the majors, minors, and specializations offered in the areas of business, communications, creative media, education, social services, computer innovation, and information technology. Undergraduates find Champlain's "upside-down curriculum" puts them into essential courses with award-winning professors from day one, right through to graduation.

Students take advantage of offerings from the Bring Your Own Business (BYOBiz) program, Life Experience and Action Dimension (LEAD), the Emergent Media Center, Leahy Center for Digital Investigation, Champlain College Publishing Initiative and the Center for Service and Civic Engagement. There are also more than fifty student clubs and organizations offering a full range of activities and community service opportunities.

Champlain is striving to build a diverse community. Students from thirty-seven states and eighteen countries attend Champlain. Classes are small (about 17 students), with the overall student to faculty ratio at 13:1. Nearly half of Champlain students elect to study abroad at Champlain campuses in Montreal, Canada or Dublin, Ireland; with Champlain-sponsored immersive programs in China or Morocco; or other third-party programs.

Champlain is committed to sustainable practices and its Perry Hall Welcome Center is Platinum LEED-certified Platinum—the highest ranking—by the U.S. Green Building Council for use of geothermal and other energy efficient practices. It was included in the 2012 Princeton Review's *Guide to 322 Green Colleges*.

Champlain was ranked in the top 15 North Regional Colleges in *U.S. News & World Report's* 2013 *Best Colleges*, and was included in the Princeton Review's 2013 *The Best 377 Colleges*.

Champlain College is accredited by the New England Association of Schools and Colleges, Inc. through its Commission on Institutions of Higher Education.

Location

Burlington is a small New England city of 43,000 (in a metro area of 211,000) and a classic college town of nearly 15,000 students located on the eastern shore of Lake Champlain in northern Vermont. The Green Mountains form the eastern horizon and the Adirondack Mountains of New York frame the western horizon. Montreal, Quebec, is 94 miles to the north, Boston is 220 miles to the southeast, and New York city is 285 miles to the south.

Burlington is one of the nation's most progressive cities, and it is the cultural center of Vermont. The Arts and Entertainment Channel (A&E) ranked Burlington as the nation's "Best Place to Live" and Businessinsider.com names it one of the "15 Hottest American Cities of the Future." It consistently ranks as one of the best college towns in the country.

Five colleges are located in the area, along with one of the leading medical centers on the East Coast. There is an international airport; an Amtrak passenger train route with connections to Montreal, New York City, and Washington, D.C.; and a long-distance bus service to Boston, Hartford, and New York City.

The Church Street Marketplace, located just a few blocks from the campus, attracts both locals and tourists to its numerous shops, coffee bars, and restaurants. Three television stations, fifteen radio stations, and daily and weekly newspapers serve the area.

Majors and Degrees

Champlain College offers Bachelor of Science, Fine Arts, Social Work, and Business Administration degrees, with majors in accounting, business administration, international business, management & innovation, management of creative media, marketing, broadcasting & streaming media, communication, creative media, filmmaking, game art & animation, game design, graphic design & digital media, professional writing, public relations, computer & digital forensics, computer information technology, computer networking & cyberSecurity, computer science & innovation, game programming, criminal justice, education (certification for grades K–6, 5–9, and 7–12), environmental policy, legal studies, psychology, radiography, and social work. Students may also enter as an undeclared/undecided major.

Academic Programs

The mission of Champlain College is to provide motivated students with the opportunity, environment, and tools to achieve their goals for professional success and meaningful involvement in their community.

The upside-down curriculum format offers students the ability to concentrate on courses in their major in their first two years of their four-year college experience. Internships are offered in many of the majors, often within the first two years of study, and a majority of students go directly into their chosen career field upon graduation. Some 90 percent of the Class of 2011 that responded to a survey secured employment relevant to their field of study within twelve months of graduating.

The Princeton Review's 2012 *Best Colleges* ranked Champlain in the top 20 for "Classroom Discussions Encouraged" (#3) and "Best Classroom Experience" (#17).

Champlain is also affiliated with New York University and Thunderbird School of Global Management for postgraduate studies and degrees. The Stiller School of Business offers majors the opportunity to pursue advanced international business studies. An Army ROTC program is offered in conjunction with the nearby University of Vermont.

Off-Campus Programs

The Office of International Education ensures that students graduate prepared to be globally engaged citizens with international experience and global perspective. Champlain integrates international education into all aspects of the student experience through the curriculum, study-abroad opportunities, foreign language, campus and community programming, internships, and service learning. Champlain College has campuses in Montreal and Dublin, and provides opportunities for students to study abroad through approved third-party providers at other locations.

The criminal justice major offers two options for the second semester of the fourth year. Students may apply to spend the term at the Vermont Police Academy or at the Federal Law Enforcement Training Center in Georgia.

Academic Facilities

Champlain's technical facilities are impressive and continue to expand and evolve each year to incorporate the latest equipment and software and to match the nature and requirements of the College's cutting-edge majors. All buildings offer wireless connection to the Internet.

The Holly D. and Robert E. Miller Information Commons received the 2012 Excellence in Academic Libraries Award from the Association of College and Research Libraries (ACRL). It incorporates the features of a traditional library but showcases advanced technologies such as multimedia laboratories, integrated wireless computer networks, specialized electronic classrooms, and online distance learning systems to enhance a student's ability to conduct research, as well as the accounting and math lab, writing center, and the center for instructional practice.

The William R. Hauke Family Campus Center houses the lab for oral communication, multimedia labs, telecommunications facilities, and classrooms. Freeman Hall includes science labs, a student-teaching classroom for education majors, and faculty offices. A digital filmmaking sound stage is located at the Miller Center at Lakeside Campus.

Joyce Learning Center has multiuse classrooms, and a lab for education majors. Foster Hall includes the Mac lab for multimedia/graphic design majors and two other computer labs. The Perry Hall Barn also includes a full Mac lab. The radiography simulator is located in the Gallery.

The IDX Student Life Center features the student dining complex, student lounge, recreation areas, the gymnasium, locker rooms, dance studio, and exercise facility.

Costs

Tuition for 2012–13 was $29,765; room and board were $13,195. Total tuition, fees, and room and board totalled $42,960.

Financial Aid

Champlain assists over 85 percent of its students with grants and scholarships directly from the College, and awards the funds based on both merit and financial need. The financial aid program at Champlain consists of grants and scholarships from the College, federal and state governments and outside sources, federal work-study, loans from the federal government and private lenders, and the Yellow Ribbon program for veterans and their families.

Champlain provides financial and scholarship support for top students with a variety of backgrounds. Special effort is made to include opportunities for new Americans, U.S. veterans, single parents, and Vermont students who are first in their family to attend college.

Students interested in receiving financial aid must complete the Free Application for Federal Student Aid (FAFSA).

Faculty

Champlain's faculty members bring the requisite academic credentials to the classroom, but have also built their careers in the workplace, bringing practical professional experience to the educational experience. In addition to more than 100 full-time professors, the College employs nearly 250 adjunct professors who bring their professional expertise and academic training to the classroom. Champlain faculty members are noted for their accessibility and willingness to act as mentors for their students. Six of Champlain's professors were included in the Princeton Review's *The Best 300 Professors* in 2012.

Admission Requirements

The College requires an official high school transcript, SAT or ACT scores, two letters of recommendation, and a completed application form in order to be considered for admission. Graduation from a recognized secondary school is required (or an equivalency certificate/GED) as a condition of acceptance. Personal interviews are highly recommended for all candidates and may be required of applicants to certain majors. Students applying to major in game design, game art & animation, graphic design & digital media, digital

filmmaking, creative media, and professional writing must submit a portfolio. Students may earn advanced standing by submitting appropriate scores on Advanced Placement and International Baccalaureate exams.

Students can apply through the early or regular decision programs. Early decision is a binding agreement, and students are encouraged to apply through this program only if Champlain College is their first choice. Deadlines are November 15 for early decision I (with notification by December 15) and January 15 for early decision II (with notification around February 15). Regular decision applications are due on February 1 (with decisions sent out around March 15).

Candidates for transfer admission are required to submit an official high school transcript with SAT or ACT scores, official college transcript(s), and a completed application form in order to be considered for admission with advanced standing. Transfer credit is given for academic courses from an accredited college completed with a grade of C or better.

Champlain College admits students without regard to race, creed, color, national and ethnic origin, religion, age, gender, sexual orientation, or qualified disability, and does not discriminate in the administration of its educational and admission policies, scholarships and loan programs, or other College-administered programs. Champlain College makes reasonable accommodations to the disabilities of otherwise-qualified students, applicants or employees.

Application Information

Champlain College uses the Common Application as well as the Champlain College application. Links to both can be found at www.champlain.edu/apply.

Director of Admissions
Champlain College
163 South Willard Street
P.O. Box 670
Burlington, Vermont 05402-0670
Phone: 802-860-2727
            800-570-5858 (toll-free)
Fax: 802-860-2767
E-mail: admission@champlain.edu
Website: http://www.champlain.edu

The Champlain College campus offers wonderful views of beautiful Lake Champlain just down the hill from campus. Champlain's commitment to sustainability has resulted in Aiken Hall and Perry Hall Welcome Center receiving LEED certification from the U.S. Green Building Council for energy-efficient features.

CHAPMAN UNIVERSITY
ORANGE, CALIFORNIA

The University

During its 151-year history, Chapman University has evolved from a small, traditional liberal arts college into a comprehensive university distinguished for its extraordinary blend of liberal arts, science, and professional programs. Film and television production, business and economics, theatre, dance, music, education, and the natural and applied sciences—Chapman boasts a breadth of fields usually only found at larger institutions. Chapman University's mission is to develop global citizen-leaders who are distinctively prepared to improve their community and their world.

With beautiful grounds and stately buildings, Chapman is one of the oldest schools on the West Coast, yet its park-like campus is also one of the most modern. More than a dozen buildings have been built or renovated in just the last two decades, with four more on the drawing board. Architecturally impressive residence halls and apartment buildings offer students exciting lifestyle amenities within a vibrant Southern California setting.

Chapman University's academic structure includes the Wilkinson College of Humanities and Social Sciences; the Dodge College of Film and Media Arts; the AACSB International–accredited Argyros School of Business and Economics; the CTC-approved College of Educational Studies; the ABA-accredited School of Law; the Schmid College of Science and Technology; and the College of Performing Arts, which includes the NASM-accredited Hall-Musco Conservatory of Music, the NAST-accredited Department of Theatre, and the NASD-accredited Department of Dance.

With its central Orange County, California, location and more than 7,000 undergraduate, graduate, and professional school students, the University environment is alive with activity. In addition to the temperate climate, Chapman students enjoy a dynamic, eclectic, and outdoor-oriented lifestyle, both on campus and off. Students come from all walks of life; from across the country and from all over the world, each student brings his or her own unique view of what makes a true global citizen. Over the past five years, Chapman students have been named Truman, Fulbright, Soros, and Rotary scholars; *USA Today* All-USA College Academic Team members; NCAA All-Americans; and NCAA Academic All-Americans.

Chapman's long and distinguished heritage in intercollegiate athletics includes five NCAA national championships in baseball, tennis, and softball. The Panthers compete in the NCAA Division III Southern California Intercollegiate Athletic Conference (SCIAC) and field teams in baseball, basketball, cross-country, football, golf, lacrosse, soccer, softball, swimming, tennis, track and field, volleyball, and water polo. Approximately 20 percent of Chapman's student body participates in intercollegiate athletics.

More than 100 clubs and organizations are recognized on campus, many with commitments to a wide range of community service efforts. Chapman's Greek system includes nine nationally chartered fraternities for men and eight nationally chartered sororities for women. Intramural sports, on-campus intercollegiate athletic events, as well as music, art, and theatre productions provide students with plenty to do outside of class. And that's just on campus—with San Diego to the south and Los Angeles to the north, the only hard thing is deciding what to do.

Prominent Chapman alumni include the Honorable Loretta Sanchez '88, member of Congress; the Honorable David Bonior '72, member of Congress; CNBC World anchorwoman, Bettina Chua '88; television and film producers John Copeland '73, Jon Garcia '93, and John David Currey '98; cinematographer Gene Jackson '70; Miss California 2011, Noelle Freeman '11; St. John's University basketball coach Steve Lavin '88; Major League Baseball executive, Gordon Blakely '76; Major League Baseball Cy Young Award winner Randy Jones '72; Tony Award nominee and star of Broadway's *Showboat,* Michel Bell '68; resident tenor at the Staatsoper-Vienna John Nuzzo '91; and former U.S. Ambassador to Spain and philanthropist George L. Argyros '65.

Location

Orange County, California, has been rated by *Places Rated Almanac* as "the number one place to live in North America," citing superior climate and cultural, recreational, educational, and career-entree opportunities. Orange County's central location between two major cities means there is never a lack of entertainment choices. It is, in fact, home to the happiest place on Earth—Disneyland is literally minutes from campus.

The Segerstrom Center for the Arts, Major League Baseball's Los Angeles Angels of Anaheim, and the National Hockey League's Anaheim Ducks are all nearby Chapman's campus in Old Towne Orange. Pristine West Coast beaches are less than 10 miles from the campus, and seasonal snow skiing is 90 minutes away. The average year-round temperature on campus is 71°F, and the daily sea breeze from the nearby Pacific Ocean keeps the air cool, clean, and smog free.

Majors and Degrees

Chapman awards the Bachelor of Arts degree in the fields of accounting, art, art history, athletic training, biochemistry, biological sciences, business administration, chemistry, communication studies, computer information systems, computer science, creative producing, creative writing, dance, digital arts, economics, education, English, environmental science and policy, film production, film studies, French, graphic design, health sciences, history, integrated educational studies, mathematics, mathematics and civil engineering, music, music composition, music education, music performance, peace studies, philosophy, physics and computational science, political science, psychology, public relations and advertising, religious studies, screen acting, screenwriting, sociology, Spanish, studio art, television and broadcast journalism, and theatre. Programs are offered in pre-law and pre-health, while graduate degrees are offered in business (M.B.A.); law (J.D.); education (M.A., Ph.D.); English (M.A., M.F.A.); international studies, (M.A.); computational sciences (M.S., Ph.D.); food sciences (M.S., M.S./M.B.A.); film (M.A., M.F.A., M.F.A./M.B.A., M.F.A./J.D.); economic systems design (M.S.); health and strategic communication (M.S.); physical therapy (D.P.T.); hazards, global, and environmental change (M.S.); and marriage and family therapy (M.A.).

Academic Programs

For many, college is a time of uncertainty. The Academic Advising Center is a place students can come for information, resources, and referrals. Chapman's Academic Advising Center offers personalized services for all students, supporting and helping to shape their educational goals. Students are encouraged to develop individualized plans for realizing the goals they set. The center is responsible for advising in all majors and serves all undeclared students. General academic counseling is offered, plus placement testing services. Individual appointments are available, though students can stop by any time, or access many of the center's resources online. Advising workshops are regularly available. The Tutoring, Learning, and Testing Center also offers students peer tutoring, study technique development, and advocacy services.

A wide variety of study and research opportunities are available through Chapman's academic and research centers. These include the Anderson Center for Economic Research; the Schweitzer Institute; the Rodgers Center for Holocaust Education; the Center for Educational and Social Equity; the Fowles Center for Creative Writing; the Leatherby Center for Entrepreneurship and Business Ethics; the Schmid Center for International Business; the Hoag Center for Real Estate and Finance; the Institute for the Study of Religion, Economics, and Society; the Economic Science Institute; and the Institute for Quantum Studies.

Requirements for graduation are commensurate with the philosophy of education fostered at Chapman. The program of studies is designed to ensure a breadth of selection in the liberal arts, as well as depth of preparation in the student's major field. The minimum graduation requirements include successful completion (C average) of 124 semester credits, of which 36 must be earned in the upper division. Competence in reading, written communication, oral communication, computation, and library usage is required of all students. Chapman's general education sequence provides a broad introduction to the humanities, social sciences, and natural sciences. Students select general education classes with the guidance of their faculty adviser. A maximum of 32 semester credits may be gained through Advanced Placement (AP), College-Level Examination Program (CLEP), and departmental examinations.

Chapman's academic year operates on a 4-1-4 modified semester system. January is reserved for an optional four-week interterm during which students can take a traditional course in an accelerated time frame or take more experiential courses, such as travel-study or travel abroad opportunities. Ample opportunities are available for alternative learning experiences. Internships and cooperative education programs are recommended. Students may also undertake in-depth individual study or research in their major field in conjunction with a faculty member.

Academic Facilities

Chapman's stunning campus continues to grow by leaps and bounds. Major additions to the campus over the past few years include the 100,000-square-foot Leatherby Libraries complex, housing eight discipline-specific individual libraries, a cyber courtyard, and a 24-hour study commons and coffee bar. The Oliphant Hall addition to the Conservatory of Music is a 24,000-square-foot space featuring fourteen teaching studios, a 60-seat lecture hall, music therapy laboratory, and orchestra hall. In addition to the Conservatory of Music's Bertea and Oliphant Halls, the College of Performing Arts facilities include the Moulton Fine Arts Complex featuring the 250-seat repertory-style Waltmar Theatre, a black box theatre, the Guggenheim Art Gallery, and the Partridge Dance Center. The Fish Interfaith Center features the 12,500-square-foot Wallace All-Faiths Chapel, recognized by *Architectural Digest* for innovation in design. The 200,000-square-foot Sandhu Residence and Conference center houses the primary on-campus dining facility for resident students, as well as a conference center and residence hall. The 90,000-square-foot Argyros Forum includes the newly expanded student union with additional campus dining options, as well as conference and classroom facilities. The 800-seat Memorial Auditorium is the primary performance and assembly venue on campus and is listed on the National Register of Historic Places. Athletic facilities include the 2,500-seat Hutton Sports Center; the 2,000-seat Ernie Chapman Stadium for football, lacrosse, and soccer; and the 500-seat Allred Aquatics Center swim stadium/Olympic pool complex. Beckman Hall is the center for business and information technology—the newly opened Janes Financial Center with its twelve Bloomberg terminals is housed here. The Hashinger Science Center features laboratories for nuclear science, radiation, crystallography, genetics, food science, physics, and computational sciences.

Costs

For the 2012–13 academic year, full-time tuition and fees (including accident and health services fee and associated student membership fee) were $41,040. Annual room and board costs averaged $13,000, while the estimated yearly cost for books was $1,000.

Financial Aid

More than 85 percent of Chapman students benefit from some form of financial aid or scholarship assistance. Need-based financial awards include a combination of grants, scholarships, loans, and work-study jobs on campus. Awards are renewable, assuming that students complete the annual application process on time. By using a combination of Chapman's internal resources and federal and state funding, an individual financial aid package can be tailored in an effort to meet the student's financial need. Merit and talent scholarship awards, regardless of financial need, round out the impressive financial assistance that Chapman offers.

Faculty

The University's faculty is composed of some 430 individuals, more than 80 percent of whom hold doctoral or other terminal degrees. Their primary commitment is to undergraduate teaching, although most are also actively involved in scholarly research and publication. Teaching assistants or graduate assistants are typically not used for the instruction of undergraduate classes, a fact upon which Chapman prides itself. Chapman's enviable student-faculty ratio of 14:1 allows extensive interaction between the faculty members and students.

Student Government

Chapman has an annually elected associated student government that actively participates in the administration of the University.

Admission Requirements

Admission to Chapman is selective. In 2012, admission was granted to 41 percent of the applicant pool. The University is interested in admitting students whose prior records indicate that they will be successful in a competitive collegiate environment. Freshman applicants are considered for admission based primarily on the nature and sequence of their high school course work, grade point average achieved, their results on either the SAT or ACT examination, co-curricular involvements, and personal characteristics. Transfer candidates are considered for admission on the basis of their course work and cumulative grade point average earned at other regionally accredited postsecondary institutions, their co-curricular involvements, and personal characteristics.

Application and Information

Chapman University exclusively uses the Common Application (http://www.commonapp.org), as well as a Chapman-specific supplement to the Common Application and departmental applications for those applying to the art, dance, film, music, or theatre programs. Candidates are strongly encouraged to visit and tour the campus and participate in an information session led by an admission officer. Arrangements for a group information session and campus tour can be made through the Office of Admission.

Freshman applicants can choose either a nonbinding November 15 early action application deadline or the January 15 regular application deadline. Transfer applicants must apply before the March 15 transfer deadline. Freshman candidates who apply after January 15 and transfer candidates who apply after March 15 are considered on a space-available basis.

For further information, students should contact:

Office of Admission
Chapman University
One University Drive
Orange, California 92866
Phone: 714-997-6711
      888-CUAPPLY (toll-free)
Fax: 714-997-6713
E-mail: admit@chapman.edu
Website: http://www.chapman.edu
      http://www.facebook.com/ChapmanUniversity

Located in Southern California, Chapman University is a private university providing students with a unique blend of hands-on learning and professional programs to prepare graduates for an ever-changing global landscape.

CHESTNUT HILL COLLEGE
PHILADELPHIA, PENNSYLVANIA

The College

Chestnut Hill College is a four-year, coeducational, Catholic liberal arts college. Founded in 1924 by the Sisters of St. Joseph, the mission of the college centers on the growth of the whole student, academically and personally.

Located in Philadelphia, the campus is situated on 75 acres overlooking the Wissahickon Creek. Students have the dual benefit of an idyllic campus and access to a cultural metropolis.

Enrolling more than 2,000 students, Chestnut Hill College is a diverse community of learners. Traditional students comprise the School of Undergraduate Studies. Working adults are enrolled in the School of Continuing and Professional Studies which offers accelerated undergraduate programs. Chestnut Hill awards the M.Ed., M.A., and M.S. in the School of Graduate Studies, and the college also awards a doctoral degree in clinical psychology (Psy.D.).

When it comes to activities, students enthusiastically engage in the many clubs, organizations, and programming available. From community service to theater, special interest clubs, and most notably Quidditch, Chestnut Hill College offers a unique social outlet for everyone.

The college is a member of NCAA Division II and competes in baseball (men), basketball (men and women), cross-country (men and women), golf (men and women), indoor track (men and women), lacrosse (men and women), outdoor track (men and women), soccer (men and women), softball (women), tennis (men and women), and volleyball (women). A swimming pool, a gymnasium, a state-of-the-art fitness center, as well as outdoor basketball and tennis courts, provide excellent athletic facilities for Chestnut Hill's students.

Location

Chestnut Hill College is located in the northwest corner of Philadelphia—where city meets suburbs.

The college is bordered by the wooded hills of Fairmount Park, yet only a 20-minute ride by train or car to Center City Philadelphia where students can enjoy a wide variety of dining, cultural, and sporting events. Among the many attractions are the museums that grace Philadelphia, from its landmark Museum of Art to the Rodin Museum, the Living History Museum, the Franklin Institute, and numerous others. The city's history is reflected throughout, but is most prominent in the areas surrounding Independence Hall, Society Hill, and Penn's Landing. The greater Philadelphia area is also home to more than seventy colleges and universities, which offer further opportunities for socialization and an extensive range of activities.

The heart of the Philadelphia neighborhood, Chestnut Hill, is just one mile beyond the college campus.

An official historic district reminiscent of a colonial village, this section of Philadelphia provides convenient opportunities for shopping, dining, and transportation to downtown Philadelphia. Chestnut Hill College is a school in a suburban setting with all the advantages of a cosmopolitan experience.

Majors and Degrees

Bachelor of Arts, Bachelor of Science, and Bachelor of Music degrees are offered with majors in accounting; biochemistry; biology; business administration, chemistry; communications; communications and technology; computer and information science; computer and information technology; criminal justice; early childhood education: PreK –4 (with an option of Montessori certification); middle level education: 4–8; secondary education: 7–12 (with a co-major in a specific content area); English literature; English literature and communications; environmental science; forensic biology; forensic chemistry; French; history; human services; international business, language, and culture; marketing; mathematics; mathematical and computer science; molecular biology; music; music education; political science; psychology; sociology; and Spanish.

Combined bachelor's/master's programs are offered in education; administration of human services; psychology; instructional technology; and international business, language, and cultures.

Dual-degree programs in radiological sciences, bioscience technologies, and physician assistant studies are offered in partnership with Thomas Jefferson University and Arcadia University.

Academic Programs

The academic year consists of two 15-week semesters. There are also two 6-week summer sessions.

As a liberal arts college, Chestnut Hill offers courses of study that provide the student with a broad background in the fine arts and humanities, a knowledge of science, and a keen awareness of the social problems of the day, as well as intensive, in-depth study in a major field.

Chestnut Hill College confers a B.S., B.M., or B.A. degree to students who earn 120 semester hours of credit and satisfy specific requirements set by the faculty. A student with the ability and proper motivation may be permitted to major in two departments. It is understood that the student will satisfy the requirements of both departments. A student may also choose to create an individualized major to fit the needs of distinctive academic pursuits.

Each year, select students are invited into an interdisciplinary honors program that challenges intellectual initiative and provides the opportunity for independent study and seminar discussion. Students may apply for admission prior to first year enrollment or before the start of sophomore year. Sophomores of high scholastic standing are invited by their major departments to engage in a program of independent study during their junior and senior years. This opportunity for independent study and original research culminates in an honors thesis, which is a prerequisite for the conferring of honors at graduation.

Off-Campus Programs

At Chestnut Hill College, students have many opportunities and options for when and where to study abroad. Whether for a year, a semester, a summer session, or spring break, there is a program to fit the needs of each student.

With the assistance of advisors and professors, students can use their imagination and interests to develop an off-campus program.

Chestnut Hill College participates in a consortium arrangement with seven colleges throughout the nation, founded by the Sisters of St. Joseph. As participants, students can study at any other member institution for a semester or a year, while maintaining status as full-time Chestnut Hill students.

In recent years, Chestnut Hill College students have enrolled in institutions in London, Madrid, Rome, Salzburg, Vienna, and other European centers. Chestnut Hill College maintains agreements with Regent's College London, the Sorbonne and the American Business School in Paris, the Centre d'Etudes

Franco-Americain de Management in Lyons, and Seisen University in Japan for study abroad.

The growing interest of students in acquiring on-the-job experience while still in college has prompted the development of many departmental internship programs, which provide students with the opportunity to gain professional experience in their major while earning academic credit. Chestnut Hill also has an office of career development, through which professionals assist students in finding jobs that correspond to their career interests and academic pursuits.

Academic Facilities

The Logue Library houses approximately 140,000 volumes and thousands more e-books and periodicals. It is also home to a rare book room that contains first editions and special editions, the Gruber Theater, the fine Curriculum Library for elementary education, and an Irish literature collection.

Well-equipped science laboratories, a math center, a multimedia technology center, a writing enrichment center, individual practice rooms for music students, a spacious art studio, a planetarium, and an observatory are among the many other outstanding facilities on campus.

Martino Hall, which opened in 2000 and was designed to maintain the architectural history of the college, provides room for a performance center, gymnasium, or convocation center. The second and third floors house "smart" classrooms. Fitzsimmons Hall opened its doors in fall 2006 offering resident students suite-style living accommodations.

The college recently acquired the neighboring 35-acre Sugarloaf Mansion estate and has renovated the existing buildings. This new facility offers additional resident housing, classrooms, a second student dining facility, office space, and conferencing capability.

Costs

General expenses for 2012–13 were tuition $31,000; and room and board approximately $9,340.

Financial Aid

Financial aid is available in the form of academic scholarships, loans, work-study grants, state grants, federal grants and loans, and Chestnut Hill College grants. Merit-based scholarships and awards are granted for academic achievement. All other types of aid are based on financial need and are awarded in financial aid packages that combine various forms of aid and are tailored to each student's need. More than 75 percent of Chestnut Hill College students receive financial aid to meet college costs. All applicants for aid should file the Free Application for Federal Student Aid (FAFSA). Merit-based scholarships and awards are granted for academic achievement.

Faculty

Evidence of Chestnut Hill's vitality can be seen in its faculty. While their primary interest is teaching, faculty members are also engaged in research, publication, travel, and other professional activities. More than 82 percent of the faculty members hold terminal degrees. The men and women who make up this group are deeply interested in both their subject and their students. Their qualifications include international degrees from Bangalore University (India), the University of London, and the University of Paris, and domestic degrees from Boston College, Bryn Mawr College, Catholic University of America, Columbia University, Creighton University, Duke University, Fordham University, Harvard University, Middlebury College, the New School for Social Research, New York University, Purdue University, Saint Louis University, Temple University, and the Universities of Arizona, Delaware,

Massachusetts, Minnesota, Montana, New Mexico, North Carolina, Notre Dame, and Pennsylvania. Chestnut Hill College's faculty-student ratio is 1:11.

Student Government

A student at Chestnut Hill College has the opportunity to think independently and approach decisions creatively. Students, in conjunction with members of the faculty and administration, make judgments concerning all collegiate affairs. Several organizations provide structure for the decision-making process. Students join members of the faculty and administration on the Curriculum Committee and the College Council. The Academic, Social-Cultural, and Student Affairs Committees of the Student Organization identify, represent, and meet campus needs.

Admission Requirements

Chestnut Hill College welcomes students whose aptitudes and academic records show a desire to accept a challenge. Applications are judged by the Admissions Committee on the basis of intellectual ability, academic achievement (class rank and performance in high school, including completion of 16 academic units), and SAT or ACT results.

Students should submit a completed application, application fee, SAT or ACT scores, and a high school transcript. Letters of recommendation, a personal statement, and other supporting documentation are strongly encouraged. An interview is recommended and may be required. A student wishing to transfer to Chestnut Hill College is asked to submit a transcript from all colleges previously attended.

Application and Information

Applications are processed on a rolling admission system. To arrange an interview or to obtain more detailed information about the academic program, students should contact:

Office of Admissions
School of Undergraduate Studies
Chestnut Hill College
9601 Germantown Avenue
Philadelphia, Pennsylvania 19118
Phone: 215-248-7001
      800-248-0052 (toll-free)
E-mail: admissions@chc.edu
Website: http://www.chc.edu

Chestnut Hill College offers 75 acres of scenic beauty while still being minutes away from Philadelphia.

CHEYNEY UNIVERSITY OF PENNSYLVANIA
CHEYNEY, PENNSYLVANIA

The University

Founded in 1837, Cheyney University of Pennsylvania is America's oldest historically black institution of higher education and today, it leverages its rich history of providing access to a quality liberal arts education for all students in order to produce visionary leaders and responsible citizens. Cheyney University is a Wi-Fi campus and home to solid undergraduate programs in biology and chemistry; the Keystone Honors Academy; the Call Me MISTER teaching program; the accredited hotel, restaurant, and tourism management program; the Ed Bradley Broadcast Center (television); and the Aquaculture Research and Teaching Laboratory. Cheyney University offers baccalaureate and master's degree programs at two locations, Cheyney and Philadelphia Multi-University Center. Cheyney University recently celebrated its 175th Anniversary. The Princeton Review has announced that Cheyney University will be included in the 2013 edition of the *Guide to 322 Green Colleges*.

The University has a proud legacy of educating some of the finest teachers in the country along with elected and appointed government officials, scientists, community leaders, lawyers, physicians, entrepreneurs, corporate and business leaders, and communication professionals. Alumni include the late Ed Bradley (*60 Minutes* journalist), Jim Vance (longtime Washington D.C. news anchor), Gladys Styles Johnston (former chancellor, University of Nebraska at Kearney), The Honorable Thaddeus Kirkland (PA-159th District), and Robert W. Bogle (President/CEO Philadelphia Tribune), to name just a few.

Cheyney University is in the business of developing human potential and talent and does so through an intellectually challenging environment and personal attention to every student—a hallmark of the Cheyney experience. Prospective students are encouraged to get to know the vibrant Cheyney University community. Cheyney provides living and learning opportunities to help students realize their full potential and acquire academic achievements, all in a friendly, caring, and nurturing environment.

The University sits on a 275-acre campus of rolling hillsides in southeastern Pennsylvania. The heart of the campus is its historic quadrangle, with renovated buildings dating back to the early 1900s. Cheyney University's historic campus is located in one of the most scenic and developing suburban areas in Pennsylvania. The pride of the Cheyney University community is evident in its faculty, its staff members, its students, and its alumni.

The campus offers five residence halls, including a brand-new $40 million 400-bed LEED-certified suite-style residence hall. The University is complemented by a library; a state-of-the art graphic design lab; two theaters for the performing arts, Dudley Theatre and the recently renovated Marian Anderson Music Center; a dining hall; a student union with a snack bar and a fitness center; and athletic facilities.

Over 1,200 students choose from more than thirty undergraduate and graduate degree programs and participate in more than forty clubs, societies, and student organizations. The University is an NCAA Division-II institution, with twelve intercollegiate sports teams. Cheyney's student-athletes are viewed as students first. Academic achievements in the classroom, together with the development of character; individual and team skills; the will to win; and a sense of fair play and sportsmanship in athletic competition create the distinction in the University's intercollegiate athletics programs. Cheyney University was known as a basketball powerhouse for both men's (1978 NCAA National Champions) and women (1982 NCAA Final Four).

Cheyney University is part of the Pennsylvania State System of Higher Education and is regionally accredited by the Middle States Commission on Higher Education as well as the Accreditation Commission for Programs in Hospitality Administration and the Pennsylvania Department of Education.

Location

Cheyney University's main campus is 25 miles west of Philadelphia, Pennsylvania. SEPTA bus service is available between the campus, Philadelphia, Chester, and several sites in Delaware County. Wilmington, Delaware, is only 15 miles south of Cheyney; New York City and Washington, D.C. are just 2 hours away. The campus is easily accessible via the Pennsylvania Turnpike and Interstate 95.

Cheyney University—Philadelphia Multi-University Center City is located at 701 Market Street (7th and Market Street) in Center City, Philadelphia.

Majors and Degrees

Undergraduate degrees are the Bachelor of Fine Arts, Bachelor of Arts, Bachelor of Science, and Associate of Science in Nanotechnology. Graduate degrees are the Master of Education and Master of Public Administration. A complete list of academic majors is available on the University's website at www.cheyney.edu.

Academic Programs

The completion of 120 semester hours is required for a bachelor's degree. Of the 120 hours, 40 percent are in general education and 60 percent are in the humanities, social sciences, natural sciences, mathematics, health and physical education, and electives. Cheyney University accepts transfer credits from community colleges and other universities. Cheyney University has become a school of choice for those science, technology, engineering and mathematics (STEM) students seeking the unique opportunities and nurturing environment that one finds in the intimate academic environment of a smaller university. Currently, 106 students are enrolled as STEM majors.

In 2010 and 2011, the University's hotel, tourism, and restaurant management program was recognized by Diverse Issues in Higher Education as a top degree producer.

Cheyney's Keystone Honors Academy is a learning community of high-achieving students. The Academy consists of 130 students, and the average cumulative GPA is 3.7. Some of these students are recipients of full scholarships. The Academy offers its members study-abroad opportunities, internship experiences, professional development, and graduate school preparation. Members of the Academy spend time in the Keystone Living Learning Center, which boast two smart classrooms, a library, a cyber café, and residence for honors students. There are more than 500 Keystone Honors Academy alumni. Alumni often earn spots in prestigious graduate programs across the U.S. as well as internationally and/or work at prominent corporations and national laboratories.

The University College Model is a unique student-focused program that helps freshmen and sophomore students transition into college academically and socially. The University College combines targeted advising, mentoring, counseling, and career services to ensure student development and progress toward graduation. The Academic Success Center provides support services through tutors and counselors for students who need additional academic support.

Academic Facilities

In keeping with the University's vision to prepare more students in STEM, a new $22-million science center is under construction. The 40,000-square-foot facility will include standard and advanced chemistry labs; biology labs; mathematics and computer science classrooms; physics classrooms; seminar rooms; a computer laboratory; faculty offices; and a conference room. A special feature—a planetarium—will be located adjacent to the main lobby. A freestanding greenhouse will also accompany the new building. The science center is targeted to achieve the U.S. Green Building Council's LEED Silver Certification.

Cheyney University's location in Philadelphia, the Philadelphia Multi-University Center, is located at 701 Market Street. This newly-renovated high-tech space houses the University's graduate degree programs (Master of Education and Master of Public Administration) and accelerated undergraduate degree-completion programs. This location is also available for commuter students who wish to pursue their undergraduate degrees in a shorter period of time.

The Leslie Pinckney Hill Library offers access to library networks and research resources. It houses approximately 200,000 books plus a periodical collection of more than 23,000 bound volumes and 1,100 current subscriptions. Audiovisual media and CD-ROM full-text/image databases as well as Internet access are also available. The library also houses the famed Schomburg Collection of African American History and Culture on microfilm.

The Vaux-Logan Auditorium supports academics and features newly enhanced lighting, sound and projection technology, upgraded seating, and new stage flooring.

The Aquaculture Research and Teaching Laboratory is a 12,000-square-foot learning lab for biology and aquaculture students. The Center also serves as a commercial production facility for wholesale basil production and tilapia fish sales, which benefit the University. The Cheyney University name appears on Herban Farms packages of basil sold in ACME, Giant, and Wegmans stores.

Costs

For the 2012–13 academic year, tuition and fees for Pennsylvania residents was $8,602 for full-time students (12–18 credits). For students from other states and international students, full-time tuition and fees total $12,966. For current tuition and fees information, prospective students should visit the website at www.cheyney.edu.

Financial Aid

The University makes every possible effort to enable interested and qualified students to take advantage of its educational opportunities. Financial assistance may be available in the form of academic scholarships, grants, loans, and the Federal Work-Study Program. Financial aid packages are developed for qualified students based on individual student need. Students wishing to apply for financial aid must complete the Free Application for Federal Student Aid (FAFSA). Students should pay strict attention to all state and federal application deadlines.

Faculty

Cheyney University has over 145 full-time and part-time faculty members. The student-to-faculty ratio is approximately 15:1, and each student has a faculty adviser.

Student Government

All students are members of the Student Government Cooperative Association (SGCA), which sponsors many cultural, educational, and social events and brings speakers and performers to the campus. SGCA and other student representatives sit on all University committees. A student representative is also selected to serve on the University's Council of Trustees.

Admission Requirements

Applicants to Cheyney University are evaluated on the following criteria: GPA, SAT or ACT scores, class rank, and academic curriculum. Letters of recommendation and an essay are encouraged. Admission requirements include graduation from an approved secondary school or a General Education Development (GED) certificate from an approved agency. Students are encouraged to visit the campus and have an admission interview. Transfer students in good standing, with at least a 2.0 grade point average, are welcomed to apply for admission.

Application and Information

Students are admitted for the fall or spring semester and can apply online. Along with a completed application, the University must receive an official, final copy of the high school transcript, SAT or ACT scores, and a nonrefundable application fee. Transfer students are required to submit official transcripts from all colleges or universities previously attended.

For additional information contact:

Office of Admissions
Cheyney University of Pennsylvania
1837 University Circle
P.O. Box 149
Cheyney, Pennsylvania 19319-0149
Phone: 610-399-2275
      800-CHEYNEY (toll-free)
E-mail: admissions@cheyney.edu
Website: http://www.cheyney.edu

Cheyney's newest 400-bed residence hall opened in August 2012.

CLEMSON UNIVERSITY
CLEMSON, SOUTH CAROLINA

The University

One of the country's most selective public research universities, Clemson was founded in 1889 with a mission to be a "high seminary of learning" dedicated to teaching, research, and service. Today, these three concepts remain at the heart of the University and provide the framework for an exceptional educational experience.

At Clemson University, professors take the time to get to know students and explore innovative ways of teaching. Exceptional teaching is one reason Clemson's retention and graduation rates rank among the highest in the country for public universities.

Exceptional teaching is also why Clemson continues to attract an increasingly talented student body. In 2012, more than half of the entering freshmen were ranked in the top 10 percent of their high school classes, and the freshman class averaged 1246 on the critical reading and math sections of the SAT.

Clemson is committed to world-class research, with externally funded research expenditures totaling $101.5 million in 2011–12. New awards to Clemson totaled more than $99 million in 2011–12.

The University is also invested in the success of its students. In the 2011–12 academic year, Clemson's student retention rate was more than 91 percent. Much of this is due to the Academic Success Center (ASC). Established in 2001, the ASC has been recognized nationally and internationally by organizations related to tutoring, supplemental instruction, and collegiate learning. The ASC moved into a new facility in 2012 where it offers free one-on-one tutoring services for more than 80 courses and provides tutoring for additional courses as the need arises. Supplemental instruction, academic skills workshops, and academic counseling are also available—free to all Clemson students. It is estimated that more than 50 percent of freshmen use ASC services during their first semester.

Clemson has also received national recognition for its innovative Communication Across the Curriculum (CAC) program, ranking ninth on the *U.S. News & World Report* list of public colleges and universities identified as making writing across all curriculums a priority. At Clemson, CAC has become a standard teaching method used in nearly every department. Professors use CAC to focus on providing real-life challenges that require students to think and communicate effectively.

From cheering the Tigers at a football game to socializing at the Hendrix Student Center, Clemson students can participate in a wide variety of activities outside the classroom. The more than 400 campus clubs and organizations include fraternities and sororities, as well as honorary, international, military, performing arts, political, professional, religious, service, social interest, special interest, sports and fitness, and student media programs and activities.

With seventeen intercollegiate sports, Clemson offers exciting spectator sports year-round. Clemson is a charter member of the Atlantic Coast Conference and is an NCAA Division I school. Admission to regular-season home events is included in University fees for full-time students.

Clemson University is accredited by the Commission on Colleges of the Southern Association of Colleges and Schools to award bachelor's, master's, specialist, and doctoral degrees. Questions about the accreditation of Clemson University can be directed to the Commission on Colleges at 1866 Southern Lane, Decatur, Georgia 30033-4097; phone: 404-679-4500.

Location

Approximately midway between Charlotte, North Carolina, and Atlanta, Georgia, Clemson University is located on 1,400 acres in the foothills of the Blue Ridge Mountains and along the shores of Hartwell Lake. Great weather and proximity to natural wonders and large cities offer year-round recreational opportunities.

The University's enrollment of more than 20,000 undergraduate and graduate students makes it a defining presence in Clemson, South Carolina, a town of about 14,000. Students may live on campus in one of the twenty-one residence halls and four apartment complexes, most of which are within a 10-minute walk to class or downtown.

Majors and Degrees

Clemson offers approximately 80 undergraduate and 110 graduate degree programs through five academic colleges: Agriculture, Forestry, and Life Sciences; Architecture, Arts, and Humanities; Business and Behavioral Science; Engineering and Science; and Health, Education, and Human Development. Undergraduate students can earn B.A., B.S., or preprofessional degrees in accounting; agricultural education; agricultural mechanization and business; animal and veterinary sciences; anthropology; applied economics and statistics; architecture; art; biochemistry; biological sciences; biosystems engineering; chemical engineering; chemistry; civil engineering; communication studies; computer engineering; computer information systems; computer science; construction science and management; early childhood education; economics; electrical engineering; elementary education; English; environmental and natural resources; environmental engineering; financial management; food science; forest resource management; genetics; geology; graphic communications; health science; history; horticulture; industrial engineering; landscape architecture; language and international health; language and international trade; management; marketing; materials science and engineering; mathematical sciences; mathematics teaching; mechanical engineering; microbiology; modern languages; nursing; packaging science; parks, recreation, and tourism management; philosophy; physics; political science; prepharmacy; preprofessional heath studies; pre–rehabilitation sciences; pre–veterinary medicine; production studies in performing arts; psychology; science teaching; secondary education; sociology; soils and sustainable crop systems; special education; turfgrass; and wildlife and fisheries biology.

Academic Programs

Clemson's academic year is divided into two semesters. The fall semester begins in mid-August and the spring semester starts in early January. Three summer sessions and four mini-semesters are also available. Students average 16 credit hours per semester, and Clemson requires all students to complete some general education classes specified by the University before graduation. The number of completed credit hours required for graduation varies, depending on the major.

Calhoun Honors College is a University-wide program that combines the strengths of a public, land-grant university with those of a highly selective small college. Calhoun Scholars may choose to pursue departmental honors within their specific academic discipline. In addition, EUREKA! (Experiences in Undergraduate Research, Exploration, and Knowledge Advancement) is a unique and exciting program that enables honors students to pursue research and scholarly activities with faculty members across all disciplines. The advantages of membership in the Honors College include priority registration, extended library loan privileges, honors research grants, and a special living-learning community.

The National Scholars Program is a highly selective program for exceptional students who strive to meet their highest intellectual potential. One of its goals is to develop the interests and talents students need to compete for Rhodes, Marshall, and Truman scholarships; Fulbright Grants; National Science Foundation Graduate Fellowships; and other prestigious international fellowships. In 2012, 11 Clemson students received National Science Foundation Graduate Fellowships and 6 others received honorable mentions. Four recent Clemson graduates received Fulbright grants to conduct research or teach abroad.

Clemson's Creative Inquiry (CI) program allows undergraduate students to engage in research about problems that spring from their own curiosity, from a professor's challenge, or from the pressing needs of the world around them. Team-based investigations are led by a faculty mentor and typically span two to four semesters. Students take ownership of their projects and take the risks necessary to solve problems and get answers. This invaluable experience produces exceptional graduates, capable of thinking critically, solving problems as a team, and communicating and presenting their ideas to others.

Clemson's nationally recognized Programs for Educational Enrichment and Retention (PEER) is committed to improving the academic performance of underrepresented students in engineering and science. According to a 2012 survey by the magazine *Diverse: Issues In Higher*

Education, Clemson ranks eighth among the nation's universities in graduating African-American students in engineering.

Off-Campus Programs

Clemson's students are strongly encouraged to incorporate a study-abroad experience in their overall Clemson journey. Programs are available on six continents for all disciplines and interests. These include faculty-led programs, exchange programs, and programs available through Clemson's partnerships with study-abroad providers and institutions.

Students in a variety of majors also have opportunities at other Clemson campuses around the world, including the Archbold Center in Dominica; the Daniel Center in Genoa, Italy; and the Clemson University Brussels Center in Belgium. There are other campuses around South Carolina, including Greenville and Charleston.

The Cooperative Education program provides an opportunity for students to alternate periods of academic study with semesters of paid, career-related, engaged-learning experiences to bridge the gap between academic study and its application in professional practice. Clemson's Michelin® Career Center helps to pair students with companies seeking interns or co-op students. Clemson is ranked in the top 10 for universities that produced the largest percentage of interns among the class of 2011, according to *U.S. News & World Report*'s "The Short List."

And because co-op experiences have been proven to enhance academic performance and provide a competitive edge when seeking full-time employment, Clemson students can now add on-campus internship experiences to their resumes. Students can work part- or full-time, with many in full-time positions having the option of earning credit. The University has made an investment to fund a portion of these experiences, so these on-campus jobs are paid positions.

Academic Facilities

The Clemson campus is a blend of historic buildings and advanced research facilities surrounded by stately trees and lush greenery.

Clemson's main library, the Robert M. Cooper Library, is located at the center of campus and provides a variety of services and up-to-date collections. The University's wireless networking capability lets students communicate with professors and classmates, read online course materials, check e-mail, and conduct research—all from their own laptops. Students are required to complete an electronic portfolio prior to graduation, allowing them the opportunity to present themselves through a creative venue to prospective employers and graduate schools.

The campus offers an array of facilities and programs designed to enhance a student's entire educational experience. These include the Pearce Center for Professional Communication, Class of 1941 Studio for Student Communication, Rutland Center for Ethics, and the Academic Success Center.

Clemson real estate holdings also include more than 32,000 acres of forestry and agricultural lands throughout the state, the majority of which are dedicated to the University's research and service missions.

Costs

For the 2012–13 academic year, undergraduate tuition and fees were $13,076 for South Carolina residents and $30,004 for out-of-state residents. Room and board costs were approximately $7,914, and books and supplies were around $1,098. Estimated personal and transportation expenses were $3,698, and the one-time laptop computer cost was about $1,700.

Financial Aid

Financial aid is usually awarded on the basis of need to supplement the amount students and their parents can contribute to college expenses. The University also awards some scholarships based entirely on academic merit. Clemson offers financial aid in the form of grants, scholarships, loans, and part-time employment.

Entering freshmen are evaluated on a competitive basis for scholarships using the admission application. There is no separate scholarship application. For academic recruiting scholarships, selection of domestic students is based on test scores, high school class rank, and other academic factors. Stipends for in-state residents range from $500 per year to the full cost of attendance. Merit scholarships for out-of-state students range from $5,000 per year to the full cost of attendance. Academic recruiting scholarships are available only to entering freshmen and are renewable for three additional years provided that the minimum standards are maintained. The application for admission is the first step for prospective freshmen to be considered for merit awards.

General scholarships are awarded to both entering freshmen and upperclassmen. These may have special criteria set up by the donor, such as a certain residency, major, or career interest. Because of the restrictions on many of these scholarships, it is impossible to predict the recipients. The scholarship selection process is very competitive. Stipends range from $250 to $7,500.

Faculty

Clemson has more than 1,100 full-time faculty members, with around 88 percent holding a Ph.D. or terminal degree in their fields. In addition, the University has more than 195 part-time faculty members. Faculty honors include the Fulbright Scholarship, Guggenheim Fellowship, National Science Foundation CAREER Award, National Institutes of Health Senior Scientist Award, and membership in the American Academy of Arts and Sciences. The average class size is 31, and the student-to-faculty ratio is 18:1.

Admission Requirements

In 2012, the University received about 18,500 applications for a fall freshman class of more than 3,400. Transfer applications were received from about 2,300 students, 1,160 of whom enrolled. Undergraduate applications are available online at clemson.edu/prospectivestudents.

For freshman applicants, the following factors are considered: class standing, standardized test scores (SAT or ACT), high school curriculum, grades, and choice of major. All entering freshmen must have completed 4 credits of English, 3 credits of mathematics, 3 credits of laboratory science, 3 credits of a foreign language (in the same language), 3 credits of social sciences, 1 credit of U.S. history, 1 credit of physical education or ROTC, and 1 credit of fine arts.

To be considered for transfer admission, candidates must have completed a full year of college study (a minimum of 30 semester hours or 45 quarter hours of transferable work), earned a cumulative GPA of at least 2.5 on a 4.0 scale (3.0 preferred), and completed freshman-level courses in English, science, and mathematics for their intended major at Clemson. Students may also transfer into Clemson after successful completion of their freshman year through the Bridge program, a collaborative first-year academic and residential life partnership between Clemson University and Tri-County Technical College. Bridge is available by invitation only to qualified Clemson freshman applicants who have the potential to be successful at Clemson but, due to its competitive admissions landscape, could not be admitted directly into the University for their freshman year.

Application and Information

Application deadlines for freshman admissions are December 1 (priority date for fall semester), May 1 (fall semester), and December 15 (spring semester). For transfer admissions, the application deadlines are July 1 (fall semester) and December 15 (spring semester).

Office of Admissions
Clemson University
105 Sikes Hall, Box 345124
Clemson, South Carolina 29634-5124
Phone: 864-656-2287
Fax: 864-656-2464
E-mail: cuadmissions@clemson.edu
Website: http://www.clemson.edu/prospectivestudents

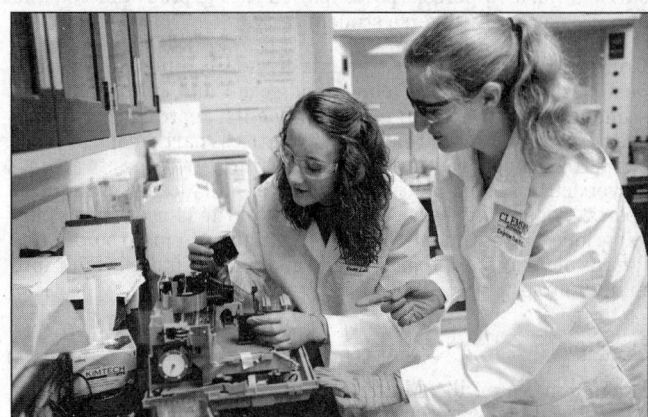

Undergraduate students at Clemson University have many chances to engage in research and work alongside faculty mentors.

COLBY COLLEGE
WATERVILLE, MAINE

The College

Colby, founded in 1813 and one of America's best liberal arts colleges, combines a challenging academic program, an emphasis on undergraduate research, and an active community life—all on one of the nation's most beautiful campuses. Colby's reach is global—in its recruitment of a diverse student body and faculty, in the scope of its curriculum, and in the number of undergraduates who study abroad.

The College is guided by the belief that the best preparation for life is a broad acquaintance with human knowledge. Liberal arts students graduate with the competence and flexibility to thrive in an increasingly complex world. Colby has a superior record of placing students who seek postgraduate study, and career opportunities for graduates are virtually unlimited. As of July 2012, 82 percent of the Class of 2012 was employed, was admitted to graduate school, or had received full-time fellowships.

Research across the curriculum: Colby is a national leader at incorporating research into the curriculum in all disciplines. This approach to learning fosters strong critical-thinking skills, a lively imagination, and a capacity for independent work. It also contributes to faculty members' strong and supportive relationships with students.

Green Colby: Colby achieved carbon neutrality in April 2013—two years ahead of schedule—and is one of the first colleges in the country to have reached this milestone. The College has also been recognized by the Environmental Protection Agency and Maine's governors for its commitment to environmental stewardship in academic programs and in campus operations. Notable initiatives include a new biomass-fueled heating plant and eight LEED-certified buildings on campus, more than any other institution in Maine. New campus facilities and major renovations are built to LEED silver certification standards. In addition, Colby's environmental studies program is one of the oldest and finest in the nation.

Internationalization: In 2005 Colby became one of the first ten colleges or universities in the U.S. to win the Senator Paul Simon Award for Campus Internationalization. The award recognized Colby's commitment to international content in the curriculum, a 70-percent participation rate in study abroad, and an internationally diverse student body.

Community: Almost all students live on campus, and with a host of clubs, activities, teams, and social and cultural events, students are busy. Colby's 1,800 students, representing nearly every state and more than sixty countries, participate in more than 100 student-run organizations, thirty-two varsity teams, eleven club sports, and more than a half dozen intramural sports. Community service is also part of the fabric of the Colby experience. The student-run Colby Volunteer Center coordinates dozens of volunteer programs, and civic engagement is built into many courses.

Location

Located in Waterville, Maine, Colby is 20 minutes from the state capital and about an hour from Portland, Maine's largest city. Maine's western mountains, including the Sugarloaf ski area, are just over an hour to the north, and the Atlantic Coast is less than an hour to the east. Acadia National Park and Mt. Katahdin are both accessible as day trips. The 714-acre campus includes Johnson Pond and a 128-acre arboretum and bird sanctuary.

Majors and Degrees

Colby awards the Bachelor of Arts degree, with majors in African-American studies; American studies; anthropology; art; art–art history; art–studio art; biology; biology–cell and molecular biology/biochemistry; biology–ecology and evolution; biology–interdisciplinary computation; biology–neuroscience; chemistry; chemistry–biochemistry; chemistry–cell and molecular biology/biochemistry; chemistry–environmental science; classical civilization; classical civilization–anthropology; classical civilization–English; classics; classics–English; computer science; East Asian studies; economics; economics–mathematics; economics–financial markets; English; English–creative writing; environmental studies–policy; environmental studies–science; environmental studies–interdisciplinary computation; French studies; geology; geoscience; German studies; global studies: government; history; Latin American studies; mathematics; mathematical sciences; mathematical sciences–statistics; music; philosophy; physics; psychology; psychology–neuroscience; religious studies; Russian language and culture; science, technology, and society; sociology; Spanish; theater and dance; theater and dance–interdisciplinary computation; and women's, gender, and sexuality studies.

Minors are available in thirty-one fields of study, including administrative science, African studies, Chinese, cinema studies, creative writing, education, environmental studies, German, human development, indigenous peoples of the Americas, Italian studies, Japanese, and Jewish studies.

Academic Programs

Colby's liberal arts program offers a broad educational foundation. In-depth study in a major provides a detailed understanding of at least one discipline's methods and perspectives. In addition to their major, students may complete one or two minors, a second major, a combined major, or an interdisciplinary major. A self-designed independent major may also be approved for students. Secondary school teacher certification may be obtained, and dual-degree engineering programs are offered with Dartmouth College and Columbia University.

Colby's 4-1-4 academic calendar includes an exploratory term in January known as Jan Plan. During the month of January, students can choose from a variety of academic pursuits including classes in subjects such as blacksmithing or fly fishing, internships at top firms around the globe, language immersion experiences, or classes that will fulfill a distribution requirement. Though Colby requires students to complete three Jan Plan terms, 90 percent of students elect to do four.

The Goldfarb Center for Public Affairs and Civic Engagement was formed in 2003 to connect teaching and research with contemporary political, economic, and social issues. The Goldfarb Center provides a venue in which students and faculty members can think and work across disciplinary boundaries to develop creative approaches to complex local, national, and global challenges.

Off-Campus Programs

More than two thirds of Colby students take advantage of international or off-campus domestic study opportunities. Many participate in Colby's own programs in France, Spain, and Russia. Other students select approved non-Colby programs in countries throughout the world. Domestic off-campus programs include the Washington Semester and Colby at Bigelow Laboratory in East Boothbay, Maine, as well as exchange programs with Howard University in Washington, D.C., the Claremont Colleges in California, and Clark Atlanta University in Georgia. Colby's financial aid may be applied to any approved off-campus study.

Academic Facilities

After opening several new buildings within the last decade, Colby continues to add academic facilities—most recently a 26,000-square-foot expansion to the Colby College Museum of Art and a new science building. The museum's new pavilion opens in July 2013, and will feature a photography lab and additional studio space for students. Colby's museum is the largest art museum in Maine. The 36,000-square-foot science building is scheduled to open in fall 2014 with classrooms and laboratories for computer science, psychology, and mathematics.

In 2007 Colby opened two new buildings: the Pulver Pavilion, part of a completely overhauled student center, and the Diamond Building, home to social science departments, interdisciplinary programs, and the Goldfarb Center.

The Bixler Art and Music Center includes an art and music library, music practice rooms, and a 300-seat auditorium. The Runnals Building contains the 274-seat Strider Theater, a dance studio, and the Cellar Theater for improvisational workshops and small productions.

Current science facilities include teaching and research laboratories, animal rooms, research greenhouses, exhibit space, and a science library. In addition, the Collins Observatory features a 14-inch telescope equipped with a high-quality CCD camera and other research-grade equipment. A wide range of sophisticated science equipment is accessible to students beginning in their first year.

Colby has three libraries on campus with access to almost 1 million books, microtexts, and other items, most of which are found in open stacks. The library catalog is online, many resources are available through the library's website, and partnerships with other libraries provide easy access to millions of other resources.

Computers are available for student use in clusters and teaching labs, and Wi-Fi is available across campus. The Information Technology Services staff runs a help desk and an extensive software library is available to students. There are no fees for any of these services.

The Alfond Athletic Center, one of the largest indoor athletic and fitness facilities in northern New England, features an indoor track, swimming pool, ice arena, gymnasium, fitness center, aerobics studio, squash courts, tennis courts, and climbing wall. Outdoor facilities include two synthetic turf fields, 50 acres of playing fields, cross-country skiing and running trails, tennis courts, and an all-weather track.

Costs

For the 2013–14 academic year, the comprehensive fee is $57,510. Personal expenses, books, and supplies average $1,600 annually.

Financial Aid

The College is committed to making a Colby education affordable to all qualified students and has a number of policies in place to achieve that goal. Student financial aid packages meet 100 percent of determined need for every admitted student, and they do not include loans. Grants, drawn from College funds, federal, and state programs, and outside scholarship agencies, as well as student employment compose the financial aid package. In addition, the College waives the application fee for online applicants; provides services to the families of all entering students regardless of income levels; and offers information on payment plans, additional financing options, and campus jobs.

Faculty

Colby has 174 full-time faculty members. The student-faculty ratio is 10:1, and the median class size is 16. Ninety-eight percent of full-time faculty members hold doctorates or final degrees in their fields, and many have national or international reputations. A faculty-in-residence program provides housing for about a dozen faculty families in campus residence halls, and a faculty-associates program fosters further faculty involvement in campus life.

Student Government

Colby students govern many aspects of campus life through the Student Government Association (SGA). Students also serve on most College boards and committees, including the Board of Trustees. The SGA deals with academic, cultural, and residential affairs and supports more than 100 clubs and organizations.

Admission Requirements

Admission is highly selective. Evaluations are made on the basis of academic achievement and ability, interest and excitement in learning, character, and maturity. The quality of a candidate's preparation is judged by his or her academic record, references from school authorities, and standardized test scores. Colby seeks applicants from diverse geographical, racial, and economic backgrounds who have special qualities or talents to contribute to the College. A minimum of 16 academic preparatory credits is recommended, including four years of English, at least three years of a foreign language, three years of college-preparatory mathematics, two years of a laboratory science, two years of history or social science, and two academic electives.

Colby offers early entrance and early decision options. Advanced standing may be established by examination, taken either through the department or through the Advanced Placement Program, the International Baccalaureate, or other standard tests. Some transfer students are considered for admission each year.

Applicants are encouraged to visit the campus for interviews, tours, classes, and meals.

Application and Information

Applications for regular admission must be submitted by January 1. Those wishing to be considered for early decision may choose either the fall or winter option. Fall option applicants must complete the application process by November 15 and winter option applicants by January 1.

For admissions information, students should contact:

Office of Admissions and Financial Aid
Colby College
4800 Mayflower Hill
Waterville, Maine 04901-8848
Phone: 800-723-3032 (toll-free)
E-mail: admissions@colby.edu
Website: http://www.colby.edu

Students enjoy a sunny afternoon on Miller Quad.

THE COLLEGE OF NEW JERSEY
EWING TOWNSHIP, NEW JERSEY

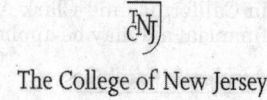

The College

The College of New Jersey (TCNJ) welcomes students who have the talent and motivation to succeed in a highly rigorous academic environment. A public institution founded in 1855, the College enrolls about 6,500 full-time undergraduates, two thirds of whom reside on campus. Today it is heralded by *U.S. News & World Report* as well as *Barron's* as one of the most competitive schools in the nation, public or private. TCNJ serves a diverse student body, preparing graduates to be leaders in their chosen fields.

TCNJ has set the standard for public higher education. Students report they find TCNJ large enough to provide a full range of academic and extracurricular choices, yet small enough to be a genuine residential community of friends and fellow learners. With professors easily available in and out of class and facilities of enviable quality, TCNJ represents an exceptional value in higher education.

The College of New Jersey's academic approach combines those of both traditional liberal arts schools and professional schools. A liberal learning curriculum ensures that all students are grounded in the beliefs and values of civic responsibility and intellectual and scholarly growth and that they receive a well-rounded education in the liberal arts. Interdisciplinary studies, internships, research, and faculty mentoring all are part of an educational approach designed to produce successful leaders. While a very high percentage of graduates find immediate employment related to their fields of study, more than 20 percent go directly into graduate schools across the country.

All first- and second-year students are guaranteed on-campus housing, and most juniors and seniors continue to live on campus. Rooming arrangements are quite flexible, from doubles in freshman residence halls to suites and single rooms in campus town houses or apartments for upperclass students. A nationally recognized residence life program and more than 200 student organizations offer numerous opportunities for friendship, personal growth, and leadership. An exceptional 96 percent of first-year students return for their sophomore year.

The arts flourish in two theaters, a recital hall, an art gallery, and numerous other campus venues. Student performances, professional groups on tour, and a large variety of films, lectures, local bands, and solo entertainers fill the academic year with cultural options—many of them free, the rest at low cost.

Student wellness has a high priority, with many facilities for recreation and physical conditioning. In Packer Hall, the campus has access to a larger fitness center, a 25-meter swimming and diving pool, and a basketball court. The Student Recreation Center offers racquetball courts, four tennis courts that are convertible to basketball or volleyball use, a weight room, and an indoor track. Other facilities include a lighted field with an artificial surface, eight lighted outdoor tennis courts, an outdoor beach volleyball court, and numerous athletic fields.

As a Division III member of the National Collegiate Athletic Association, TCNJ offers twenty sports: ten for men and ten for women. Since 1979, TCNJ student-athletes have amassed thirty-nine national championships and thirty-one runner-up awards, giving the College an aggregate of seventy-one first- and second-place finishes. That figure tops the nation's 400-plus Division III colleges and universities during the past thirty years. TCNJ has produced 44 individual national champions and 58 CoSIDA Academic All-Americans. Over the past seventeen years, TCNJ has finished in the top ten of the Learfield Sports Director's Cup races sixteen times. The ranking is based on the cumulative performance of each sport of all competing NCAA Division III institutions.

In addition to its NCAA athletics, TCNJ offers a wide variety of recreation programs for intramural competition and self-governing sports clubs. More than 3,500 students play with these less demanding, but spirited and competitive teams, each year, some of which have intercollegiate schedules.

The College's undergraduate programs are accredited by the Middle States Association of Colleges and Schools and by professional associations in business, chemistry, computer science, education, education of the deaf, engineering, music, and nursing.

Location

The College of New Jersey is set on 289 acres in suburban Ewing Township, approximately 15 minutes from downtown Princeton; 10 minutes from Bucks County, Pennsylvania; and 5 miles from the state capital of Trenton. Woodlands and lakes surround the thirty-nine major academic and residential buildings. The campus is 30 miles from the theaters and museums of Philadelphia and 60 miles from those in New York City. In 2013, TCNJ is slated to break ground on Campus Town, a series of residential and commercial establishments along the edge of the campus.

Majors and Degrees

The College of New Jersey offers programs leading to the Bachelor of Arts, Bachelor of Fine Arts, Bachelor of Music, Bachelor of Science, Bachelor of Science in Engineering, and Bachelor of Science in Nursing degrees.

The B.A. is awarded in art education; art history; communication studies; economics; English, including journalism and professional writing options; history; interactive multimedia; international studies; mathematics and statistics; philosophy; political science; psychology; sociology; Spanish; and women's and gender studies. The B.F.A. is awarded in digital arts, and fine art and graphic design. The B.M. is awarded in music (performance and education). The B.S. is granted in accountancy, biology, biomedical engineering, business administration (finance, general business, information systems management, international business, management, and marketing), chemistry, computer engineering, computer science, early childhood education, economics, electrical engineering, elementary education, engineering science, health and physical education, law and justice, mechanical engineering, physics, and technology education. Teacher preparation is available in many arts and science majors.

TCNJ offers three five-year combined Master of Arts in Teaching degrees with dual certification in elementary education, and either special education, urban education, or deaf and hard-of-hearing education. Students may also enroll in a seven-year B.S./M.D. degree program with UMDNJ—New Jersey Medical School (Newark) or a seven-year B.S./O.D. degree program with the State University of New York College of Optometry. The College also offers a Medical Careers Advisory Committee for premed students and a Pre-Law Advisement Committee for students planning a career in law.

Academic Programs

All academic courses contain a significant out-of-class requirement and provide for even more student-faculty interaction. All baccalaureate degrees require at least thirty-two courses, including a core curriculum in the traditional arts and sciences.

The thirty-week year is divided into fall and spring semesters; a summer session offers courses in two 5-week sessions and one 6-week session. Winter Session guarantees all of the benefits of a full-time TCNJ course in a more compact time frame, in addition to study-abroad opportunities. For those students who find that they cannot fit study abroad into their standard semester, Winter Session offers courses everywhere from New Orleans to London. The average class size for freshman-level lectures is 24 students and for upper-division lectures, 22 students.

All first-year students participate in a First Seminar Program that links residential learning with small classes taught by full-time faculty members. Seminars, independent studies, and capstone courses give many students the opportunity for challenging advanced study in close collaboration with faculty members. TCNJ students publish the results of these endeavors or present them at national and regional conferences.

The honors program offers students the particularly challenging academic experiences that allow normal progress toward the degree. Whenever possible, honors courses have an interdisciplinary perspective and curriculum, concentrating on central themes within significant periods in the cultural development of civilization. Honors courses in the major consist of either specially designated sections or independent study. All honors classes are small, personal, and stimulating.

Off-Campus Programs

TCNJ offers students a variety of full-year and one-semester programs of study abroad as well as study at other state colleges and universities within the United States. Exchange programs are available in 80 cities in Australia, Austria, Canada, Denmark, France, Germany, Greece, Israel, Japan, Mexico, the United Kingdom, and numerous other countries. National exchanges are available at more than 130 participating institutions in the United States, the U.S. Virgin Islands, Puerto Rico, and Guam. The College of New Jersey hosts the New Jersey State Consortium for International Studies.

Academic Facilities

TCNJ has been nationally recognized as one of the most beautiful campuses in the nation. Within the past several years, TCNJ has built and opened a Science Complex, Biology Building, Social Science Building, College Spiritual Center, Art and Interactive Media Building, Education Building, student apartments, and a state-of-the-art library, which serves as the intellectual and social hub of the campus. Campuswide networking provides full Internet accessibility from all residence hall rooms and more than twenty student computing laboratories.

Costs

For up-to-date information on in-state and out-of state tuition and fees costs, as well as room and board figures, prospective students should go online to http://www.tcnj.edu/~sfs/tuition/index.html.

Financial Aid

Approximately 80 percent of full-time undergraduates receive some form of financial aid, such as federal, state, and institutional grants; merit scholarships; student employment; and loan assistance. The Free Application for Federal Student Aid (FAFSA) or Renewal FAFSA is used to apply for all types of aid.

Scholarships and grants include The College of New Jersey Merit Scholars Program, Bonner Scholars, Chairman of the Board Merit Scholars, the New Jersey Tuition Aid Grant, Federal Pell Grants, Federal Supplemental Educational Opportunity Grants (FSEOG), Educational Opportunity Fund (EOF) Promise Award, and Army and Air Force ROTC Scholarships, as well as other institutional scholarships. Loans include the Federal Subsidized and Unsubsidized Stafford Loans, the Federal Perkins Loan, the Federal Parent Loan for Undergraduate Students (PLUS), the New Jersey CLASS Loan, private/alternative loans, nursing loans, and short-term emergency loan funds. Student employment options include the need-based Federal Work-Study Program (on- and off-campus positions) as well as institutionally supported campus jobs.

Faculty

The approximately 335 full-time members of the College of New Jersey faculty are teachers and scholars. While teaching is their primary commitment, they are also active researchers, authors, artists, performers, and regular contributors in their academic disciplines. No classes are taught by graduate assistants. The student-faculty ratio is 12:1. From their first day, students study with faculty members who may be researching new ways to use solar energy; writing a new text, play, or novel; or investigating the life cycle of desert ferns. Members of the faculty have attracted many significant grants, fellowships, and awards, including the Bancroft Prize in history, Fulbright Scholarships, and grants from the National Science Foundation, the National Institute for Advanced Study, the Guggenheim Foundation, and the National Endowment for the Humanities. Faculty members mentor their students, preparing them for careers, graduate and professional schools, and prestigious fellowships such as the Fulbright, Truman, and Marshall Fellowships recently awarded to TCNJ students.

Student Governance and Programming

The Student Government Association, comprising all undergraduate students at the College, is governed by elected representatives. The Residence Hall Association provides the mechanism for student input into campus housing policies, and members of the Student Finance Board oversee and administer approximately $500,000 in student funds. The College Union Board sponsors a wide range of special events, including recent visits by Seth Meyer, Cornel West, Nev Schulman, and John Oliver.

Admission Requirements

The College of New Jersey seeks students who can succeed in a highly selective academic program and who show intellectual curiosity, academic talent, and the potential to contribute to the life of the College. The College is committed to attracting students from diverse economic, racial, social, and geographic backgrounds. A high school record of at least 16 college-preparatory credits, high school class rank, SAT scores, and special interests, skills, and qualities of all kinds can be influential. Certain departments, such as art and music, use additional criteria to evaluate candidates seeking admission into their programs. The College of New Jersey reviews candidates holistically and takes into consideration the variations in high schools and communities in which the applicants reside.

Application and Information

The College of New Jersey is a member of the Common Application. The deadline for applications for Spring admission is November 1 and for Fall admission, January 15. There is a $75 application fee. Candidates who apply only to the College of New Jersey under the early decision plan may apply before November 15 and will be notified on or before December 15. Students applying in to the seven-year medical program must apply by December 1. For Fall admission, the College subscribes to the candidates' reply date of May 1 for payment of $600.

For more information, students should contact:

Director of Admissions
The College of New Jersey
P.O. Box 7718
Ewing, New Jersey 08628-0718
Phone: 609-771-2131
Website: http://www.tcnj.edu

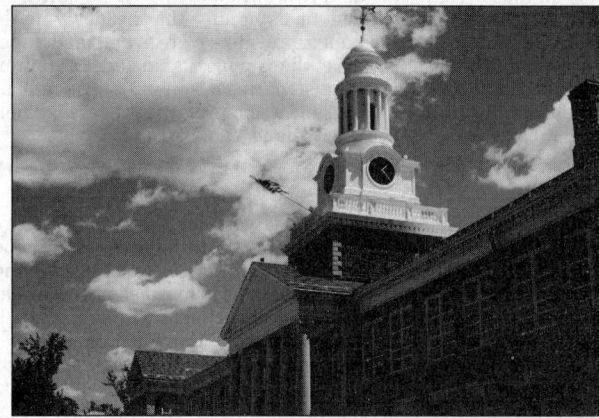

The campus of The College of New Jersey, recognized as one of the most beautiful campuses in the United States.

COLLEGE OF STATEN ISLAND OF THE CITY UNIVERSITY OF NEW YORK

STATEN ISLAND, NEW YORK

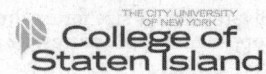

The College and the University

Founded in 1976 from the merger of two existing colleges, the College of Staten Island (CSI) is a four-year senior college within the City University of New York (CUNY) and is Staten Island's only public institution of higher learning. CSI is dedicated to access and excellence and currently serves over 14,300 students.

The College of Staten Island was established through the union of Staten Island Community College (CUNY's first community college, founded in 1955) and Richmond College (CUNY's first upper-division college, founded in 1965).

Offering over eighty programs and areas of study, the College ensures that students receive a thorough liberal arts education through core requirements that include classes in the arts and humanities, mathematics, science, and social sciences.

In addition to the exciting array of undergraduate degrees and majors available, CSI also awards the Master of Arts degree in Cinema and Media Studies, English, Environmental Science, History, and Liberal Studies; the Master of Science degree in Accounting, Biology, Business Management, Computer Science, Mental Health Counseling, Neuroscience, Mental Retardation and Developmental Disabilities, and Nursing: Adult Health and Gerontological; and the Master of Science in Education degree in Childhood Education, Adolescence, and Special Education in a selection of concentrations. Post-master's advanced certificates are offered in Leadership in Education, Nursing: Nursing Education, and Nursing: Cultural Competence.

The graduate teacher education program prepares students to teach at the early childhood, elementary, and secondary levels. The academic work and field experience meet the requirements for the certification and licensing examinations given by the state and city of New York.

Further, CSI offers doctoral programs jointly with the CUNY Graduate School in Biochemistry, Biology, Polymer Chemistry, Computer Science, Physical Therapy, and Physics.

CSI offers students an opportunity to live on campus in luxury apartment-style housing. Located in two brand-new buildings, Dolphin Cove North and South contain 133 furnished apartments housing 454 residents. The buildings offer both private and semi-private bedroom accommodations with semi-private bathrooms and full kitchens for residents. Other amenities include a study lounge, fitness center, and convenient parking. Housing is filled on a first-come, first-served basis.

CSI's Sports and Recreation Center is a 77,000-square-foot multipurpose facility providing basketball, handball/paddleball, racquetball, and volleyball courts; locker rooms; a gym; instructional areas; an indoor eight-lane 25-meter swimming pool; and offices for faculty members. Recreational fields occupy the meadows in the northwest quadrant of the campus, providing a green and landscaped open area at the main approach to the campus that includes a running track, indoor and outdoor tennis courts, a soccer field, handball/paddleball courts, softball fields, and a semiprofessional baseball field (original home field to the Staten Island Yankees).

Location

CSI is located on a sprawling 204-acre campus located in the heart of Staten Island. The campus is the largest single site for a college, public or private, within New York City. With its scenic landscape, the grounds and facilities create a rural oasis in an urban setting. Classrooms and academic offices are located in fourteen neo-Georgian buildings that form two quadrangles connected by the campus walk, which extends between the Library and the Campus Center. Seven well-built and equipped buildings—the Library, Dolphin Cove North and South, the Campus Center, the Biological Sciences/Chemical Sciences building, the Center for the Arts, and the Sports and Recreation Center—provide outstanding facilities for scholastic and community activities.

CSI's location offers students the better of two worlds, with Staten Island providing a suburban environment with some of the most interesting landscapes in the metropolitan area; and Manhattan, the

center of cultural and social life of the city, being only 25 minutes from the island by ferry. The Verrazano-Narrows Bridge provides direct access between Staten Island and Brooklyn.

Majors and Degrees

CSI offers an Associate in Arts and an Associate in Science degree. The Associate in Applied Science degree is offered in Business, Computer Technology, and Nursing.

The Bachelor of Arts degree is conferred in African American Studies; American Studies; Art, Art with a Studio Art or Art History concentration, Cinema Studies; Economics; English; English with a Writing, Linguistics, Literature, or Dramatic Literature concentration; History; International Studies; Italian Studies; Modern Languages; Music; Philosophy; Political Science; Psychology; Science, Letters, and Society; Sociology-Anthropology; Social Work; Spanish; and Women's, Gender, and Sexuality Studies.

The Bachelor of Science degree is offered in Accounting; Art with a Photography concentration; Biochemistry; Bioinformatics; Biology; Business; Business with a Finance, International Business, Management, or Marketing concentration; Chemistry; Communications with a Journalism, Media Studies, Design and Digital Media, or Corporate Communications concentration; Computer Science, Computer Science/Mathematics; Dramatic Arts; Economics; Economics with a Business or Finance specialization; Engineering Science with a Computer/Electrical/Mechanical specialization; Mathematics; Medical Technology; Music; Music with an Electronics concentration; Nursing (upper-division program); Pre-Professional studies in Dentistry, Medicine, Optometry, Podiatry, and Law; and Physics.

Academic Programs

CSI offers two-year programs in career areas and in liberal arts and sciences and four-year programs with majors in the traditional fields of study. General education requirements have been established for all degrees. The associate degree programs require 60–64 credits, depending on the field; the bachelor's degree programs generally require 120 credits. Credit may be awarded for internships and independent study, and credit may also be earned by examination (CLEP) and for experiential learning. Depending on the field of study, minors are an additional 12–30 credits, and double majors are an additional 60 credits. Students may graduate with honors in most bachelor's degree majors.

The College follows a two-semester calendar, with classes scheduled during both day and evening. The Office of Weekend and Evening Services offers a variety of course combinations leading to associate and bachelor's degrees, providing opportunities for nontraditional students with weekday career commitments to pursue a college education at more convenient times. Intensive summer and winter sessions are also offered to students who would like to accelerate their degrees.

Selective Programs: The College of Staten Island offers a number of selective academic programs, learning communities, and undergraduate research opportunities. Programs include Macaulay Honors College at CSI (MHC), a full scholarship program that provides high achieving students with a special honors curriculum of innovative and challenging courses during the first and second years of study; the Verrazano School, a local honors program designed to offer students a unique undergraduate education through academically motivated learning communities; Teacher Education Honors Academy at CSI (TEHA), a scholarship program designed to highly train select students majoring in mathematics, biology, chemistry, or physics to teach in DOE middle and high schools.

Off-Campus Programs

The College gives a number of courses for credit at off-campus locations throughout the city through internships at major corporations and other fieldwork. Exceptional study-abroad opportunities are available through CSI's Center for International Service, which offers students the option of earning academic credit for study in Belgium, China, Denmark, Ecuador, England, Greece, Italy, Japan, or Spain.

Academic Facilities

The academic buildings are designed to house approximately 300 state-of-the-art laboratories and classrooms, each with its own computer lab, study lounge for students, departmental program, and faculty offices. Academic and research programs are served by a computer network that allows students and faculty full access to specialized software, the Internet, online library resources, and e-mail within a wireless environment.

The Campus Center incorporates co-curricular activities for a complete personal growth experience. The two-story rotunda at the heart of the structure contains the main dining facilities, the College's health services, a bookstore, offices for student organizations, study lounges, a small performance/café space, game rooms with the latest game consoles, and the state-of-the-art studios of WSIA, the student-operated FM radio station.

The Center for the Arts complex provides facilities for teaching in the instructional wing and areas of public assembly in the public wing. The complex of public facilities includes a 911-seat auditorium, a 442-seat fully equipped theater, a 156-seat recital hall, a 142-seat lecture hall, an experimental black box theater, art galleries, and a conference center. Classrooms, lecture halls, studios, screening rooms, and offices for faculty members are located in the instructional wing.

The CSI Library is staffed with 12 full-time librarians and 10 adjunct librarians who also hold faculty status and rank. In addition, the library has 40 support staff members. The library's total collection consists of approximately 250,000 books, 150,000 eBooks, 215 print journal subscriptions, 53,000 electronic journals, 190 electronic resources, 3,500 films and videos, and more than 5,000 sound recordings. The library's online catalog, CUNY+Plus, provides complete access to the collections, including access to holdings of other CUNY libraries. Students also have electronic access to database and research tools 24 hours a day via the Internet. In addition, the library maintains a collection of current textbooks donated by the CSI Student Government. These and other course materials are available at the Reserve Desk. Wireless laptops are loaned to students for use throughout the library. The library building also houses the Office of Academic Support and the Cybercafé, which offers Starbucks® coffee.

The laboratory science building provides facilities for teaching and for two research centers: the Center for Environmental Science and the Center for Developmental Neuroscience and Developmental Disabilities. It consists of a research wing and an instructional wing. State-of-the-art laboratories serve students and faculty members in their teaching and research.

The CSI Astrophysical Observatory is a world-class resource that has been recognized by the International Astronomical Union as an official asteroid-tracking station.

CSI is dedicated to keeping its campus up-to-date during these technology-centric times. Planned updates include the highly innovative Interdisciplinary High-Performance Computational Center and expansions to the Library and Campus Center.

Costs

For 2013–14, undergraduate tuition for New York State residents (NYS) is $230 per credit for resident part-time matriculated students, $2,715 per semester for resident full-time matriculated students, and $340 per credit for resident non-degree students. Nonresident full- and part-time students are charged $485 per credit, and nonresident non-degree students are charged $720 per credit. Graduate NYS resident tuition is $4,345 per semester for students attending the College full-time and $365 per credit for resident part-time students. Nonresidents are charged $675 per credit for full- and part-time attendance.

Financial Aid

Financial aid is available through state and federal programs and includes the New York State Tuition Assistance Program (TAP) awards, Federal Pell Grants, Federal Supplemental Educational Opportunity Grants (FSEOG), Search for Elevation and Education through Knowledge (SEEK) awards, Federal Work-Study Program awards, and student loan programs. Information about programs, application procedures, and deadlines is available from the Financial Aid Office.

CSI Presidential Scholarships are awarded annually to full-time students based on academic merit and service. In addition, endowments have been established for merit-based scholarships in a number of fields. Further information about scholarships is available from the Career and Scholarship Center.

Faculty

The College has a full-time faculty of 319, of whom approximately 92 percent hold a doctoral degree or the equivalent. These faculty members have made significant contributions in many areas of scholarship, creativity, and public service. Numerous faculty members have received prestigious grants and awards, and more than 30 serve as members of CUNY's doctoral faculty.

Student Government

A single body, the Senate, is composed of 25 elected students and represents the interests of the College's students, serving as liaison to faculty and administrators. The Senate derives funding from the Student Activity Fee, and through its various commissions and committees, it sponsors many academic and nonacademic programs.

Admission Requirements

A freshman applicant seeking admission to a bachelor's degree program must pass the CUNY Assessment Tests (CATs) in reading, writing, and mathematics unless he or she qualifies for exemption based on their SAT, ACT, or Regents Examination scores. Admission to a bachelor's degree program is determined by a profile based on the applicant's high school courses, academic average, and the combined verbal and mathematics SAT scores. An applicant whose score reaches or exceeds the College's minimum index number is admitted to a bachelor's degree program. A faculty admissions committee may consider the admission of applicants whose scores approach the College's minimum index number. Students transferring to baccalaureate programs who have fewer than 30 credits must have a GPA of at least 2.00 and must meet freshman entrance criteria. Students must pass the CATs prior to enrolling in a bachelor degree program or if they are transferring from another college in CUNY.

Entering first-year students may be admitted to associate-level programs if they have graduated from an accredited high school or have earned an equivalency diploma (GED) with a satisfactory score.

As a general rule, the College requires a grade point average equivalent of 2.00 for transfer as a matriculated student into a two-year degree program.

Application and Information

Requests for further information and application materials should be directed to:

College of Staten Island
The City University of New York
Office of Recruitment and Admissions, Building 2A, Room 103
Staten Island, New York 10314
Phone: 718-982-2010
E-mail: admissions@csi.cuny.edu
Website: www.csi.cuny.edu

The CSI Library offers electronic access to database and research tools 24 hours a day via the Internet, in addition to maintaining a collection of current textbooks donated by the CSI Student Government.

THE COLLEGE OF WOOSTER

WOOSTER, OHIO

The College

The College of Wooster is America's premier college for mentored undergraduate research. The academic program built around those research experiences helps every student develop abilities prized by employers and graduate schools alike: independent judgment, analytical ability, creativity, project- and time-management skills, self confidence, and strong written and oral communication skills.

Founded as a Presbyterian college in 1866, Wooster has been an independent, residential college of the liberal arts and sciences since 1969. With small classes (61 percent have fewer than 20 students) and an 11:1 student-faculty ratio, students receive close attention both in and out of the classroom. More information can be found at http://www.wooster.edu/about.

Wooster's 2,000 students come from forty-seven states and forty-one countries, from all backgrounds and life experiences. Wooster's distinctive sense of spirit is evident to visitors on campus.

Ninety-six percent of Wooster students live on campus. First-year students live together in various residence halls, and roommate matches are made using the Myers Briggs Personality test. After the first year, the options multiply. Wooster's program houses allow students to live with a group of 7 to 14 others and work on a service project in the community throughout the year.

One third of Wooster students follow their passion for making music through three choirs, a symphony orchestra, symphonic and marching bands, a jazz ensemble, four a cappella groups, and other ensembles. Another third participate in intercollegiate athletics. Wooster has produced 45 All Americans in eleven sports in the past six years and has won seventy-five NCAC championships since 1985.

From the improv group *Don't Throw Shoes,* to the student-run investment club (managing a $2.7-million portfolio for the College's endowment), and the cricket team to the radio station, there is something for just about every interest.

Location

The College is located in Wooster, Ohio, a vibrant city of 26,000 with a strong, diversified economy; a downtown full of great restaurants and shops; national chains like Starbucks, Chipotle, Panera, and Kohl's; and easy access to outdoor recreation opportunities. Wooster's business community is strong and growing, and provides opportunities for Wooster students both before and after graduation. Wooster is 55 miles southwest of Cleveland and 30 miles southwest of Akron.

Majors and Degrees

The College of Wooster offers the degrees of Bachelor of Arts, Bachelor of Music, and Bachelor of Music Education. A student may choose from more than fifty-five majors and programs of study, including Africana studies; anthropology; ancient Mediterranean studies; archaeology; art history; art–studio; biochemistry and molecular biology; biology; business economics; chemical physics; chemistry; Chinese studies; classical studies (Greek, Latin, classical civilization); communication sciences and disorders; communication studies; comparative literature; computer science; East Asian Studies; economics; English; French; geology; German studies; history; international relations; mathematics; music; music education; music history and literature; music performance; music theory–composition; music therapy; neuroscience; philosophy; physics; political science; psychology; religious studies; Russian studies; sociology; Spanish; student-designed major (e.g., journalism, sports medicine); theater and dance; urban studies; and women's, gender, and sexuality studies. In addition, minors are available in most areas as well as education (with licensure in elementary or secondary teaching), environmental studies, film studies, international business, Latin American studies, physical education, and South Asian Studies.

Wooster offers dual-degree programs in cooperation with other institutions that lead to either two bachelor's degrees (one from each

institution) or a bachelor's degree from Wooster and a master's from the cooperating institution. The dual-degree programs are in the areas of architecture, dentistry, engineering, forestry and environmental studies, nursing, polymer science, and social work.

The College's preprofessional advising programs provide students with advice on the development of an appropriate academic program, cocurricular and volunteer experiences, guidance on summer research opportunities, lectures by leaders in the various professions, and information about the process of selecting and applying to graduate and professional schools. Wooster's preprofessional programs are in the areas of architecture, business, engineering, forestry and environmental studies, heath professions, law, seminary studies, and social work.

Academic Programs

Students begin their academic journey with First-Year Seminar, a writing-intensive course that exercises their intellect and sharpens their critical faculties (http://www.wooster.edu/Academics). In a class of no more than 15, with a professor who is also their academic adviser, students approach a wide range of texts, questioning and analyzing them to tease out meaning and then formulating arguments through extensive writing and discussion.

To ensure that they are conversant with forms of inquiry and discourse in a range of disciplines, students select courses in each of three areas: arts and humanities, history and social sciences, and mathematical and natural sciences. They also gain insight into other cultures through a course in global and cultural perspectives and another in religious perspectives.

Once a major is selected, students engage with the scholarship of that field, master its particular methodologies, and have numerous opportunities to work with faculty members on research projects (as early as the second semester of the first year), participate in internships, or study abroad.

It all culminates in the senior Independent Study (I.S.) project. Working one-on-one with a faculty adviser over the course of a year, students conduct research, create art, or shape a performance that demonstrates their understanding of a discipline and their ability to communicate that knowledge to others. Although called Independent Study, it is a deeply collaborative journey that the student and the faculty adviser take together. In effect, students are guaranteed a 1:1 student-faculty ratio for one class each semester of their senior year. In weekly one-on-one meetings, the adviser helps refine and focus the topic, suggests areas for exploration, asks questions that provoke thought and creativity, and evaluates progress. Students, in turn, review and synthesize literature related to the subject, plan and conduct research in the lab, or work to realize a creative vision in the studio, recital hall, or theater. Students present drafts of their work to their advisers, who offer feedback as close collaborators.

If the I.S. project requires travel or special equipment or supplies, the College's Henry J. Copeland Fund for Independent Study can help. In a typical year, the fund disburses almost $100,000 to support a diverse array of student projects, from studying the lives of West African immigrants in Paris or producing a documentary on survivors of Hiroshima to researching ways to purify methane gas to permit its use as a renewable energy source. When the I.S. is complete, students may find themselves presenting the results at a national conference in their discipline or coauthoring papers with their advisers. (Geology professor Mark Wilson has published articles with more than 40 student coauthors.)

Throughout the I.S. project, students learn how to analyze a problem, gather and evaluate information, propose a solution, test its validity, and communicate the results clearly and persuasively. The completed I.S. gives employers tangible proof of resourcefulness, creativity, and communication skills. It also marks the student as an independent scholar who is ready to take on graduate-level research wherever his or her interests lead, which is why Wooster ranks twenty-eighth overall among all liberal arts colleges for graduates who have gone on to earn a Ph.D., seventh in the physical sciences, twentieth in geology, thirty-seventh in math and computer science, and forty-first in life sciences.

Off-Campus Programs

Students who wish to enrich their undergraduate experience by off-campus study may choose from a variety of fully accredited programs. Wooster sponsors a number of its own off-campus programs in the United States and abroad, and through its membership in the Great Lakes Colleges Association and its affiliations, offers off-campus study opportunities in more than fifty countries spanning the globe.

A variety of off-campus opportunities within the United States provide both academic and internship experiences. The Washington Semester and the Semester at the United Nations offer extensive possibilities in national and international government. There is also a fine-arts semester in New York City. Other internship possibilities exist in business, the humanities, the natural sciences, and psychology.

Academic Facilities

The College libraries consist of the Andrews Library, the adjacent Flo K. Gault Library for Independent Study, and the nearby Timken Science Library in Frick Hall. Together, they contain more than 1 million books, periodicals, microforms, electronic journals, videotapes, and audio recordings. As a member of CONSORT and OhioLINK, the libraries can provide almost any book from Ohio's academic libraries within two to three days. The libraries subscribe to a wide variety of electronic databases and to some 5,000 periodicals in electronic form, all available campuswide via the computing network. The libraries house more than 300 study carrels, each of which is equipped with electrical and data connections.

The Collaborative Research Environment, or CoRE, is a new addition to Andrews Library: a place for students to brainstorm ideas, work together on projects using digital and traditional media, or present their work to others.

In addition, Andrews Library houses APEX, Wooster's new center for academic, internship, leadership, and career advising.

All academic buildings and residence hall rooms are connected to the campus network, and secure wireless service is available throughout campus.

The College's science facilities contain the most up-to-date laboratory equipment, libraries, technology, and instrumentation, including ultraviolet, visible, fluorescence, and infrared spectrometers; a scanning electron microscope; an atomic force microscope; a nuclear magnetic resonance spectrometer; a mass spectrometer; an X-ray diffractometer; and various chromatographs.

Wooster's Learning Center provides academic support for students, and priority is given to students with identified learning disabilities. Professional staff members work with individual students on time management, organization skills, and effective study strategies. The Writing Center provides writing assistance through one-to-one tutorial sessions and group workshops.

The Freedlander Theatre complex contains excellent technical equipment and a separate theater for students' experimental productions. The speech facility houses a radio station and a speech and hearing clinic that also serves the community.

The Scheide Music Center, a 35,000-square-foot complex, contains five classrooms, eleven teaching studios, twenty-three soundproof practice rooms, a music library, and a listening lab. The Timken Rehearsal Hall and the acoustically balanced Gault Recital Hall are "tunable" so that the halls can be rendered "live" to greater or lesser degrees.

The Ebert Art Center has space for studio art and art history. The building includes classrooms, individual studios for senior studio art majors, and the Sussel and Burton D. Morgan Art Galleries.

Costs

The comprehensive fee (room, board, tuition, and fees) for 2013–14 is $51,600.

Financial Aid

Financial assistance is awarded on merit and/or need. Need-based aid is determined by the Free Application for Federal Student Aid (FAFSA). Applications for need-based aid should be submitted by February 15.

The College of Wooster believes in recognizing individual talent and hard work. Thus, Wooster offers merit-based scholarships up to $20,000 in a number of academic, performance, and leadership areas. All scholarship awards are applicable only toward tuition and are renewable for four years.

Faculty

Faculty members, 96 percent of whom hold a doctoral degree or terminal degree in their field, are dedicated to meeting the educational needs of individual students; they strive to help them realize their inherent potential.

Student Government

The Campus Council, which consists of representatives from the student body, faculty, and administration, is the main legislative body in the areas of student life and cocurricular affairs. The Student Government Association, the Black Students Association, and the International Student Association also contribute to policymaking at Wooster. Students may attend open meetings of the faculty and are represented on several faculty committees.

Admission Requirements

A list of admissions requirements and the steps in the application process can be found online at www.wooster.edu/apply.

The deadline for Regular Admission is February 15, with admissions notifications sent by April 1 and a reply deadline of May 1. Wooster offers two Early Decision deadlines: EDI deadline is November 1, notification is November 15, and reply deadline is December 1; EDII deadline is January 15, notification is February 1, and reply deadline is February 15. Early Action candidates must apply by November 15 and are notified by December 31. Students are encouraged to visit the campus and have a personal interview.

The College of Wooster does not discriminate on the basis of age, sex, race, creed, national origin, handicap, sexual orientation, political affiliation, or veteran or military status in the admission of students or in their participation in College educational programs, activities, financial aid, or employment.

Application and Information

Office of Admissions
The College of Wooster
Wooster, Ohio 44691
Phone: 330-263-2000 Ext. 2270 or 2322
        800-877-9905
Fax: 330-263-2621
E-mail: admissions@wooster.edu
Web site: www.wooster.edu
      www.facebook.com/CollegeofWooster
      http://twitter.com/woosteredu

The academic quad at The College of Wooster.

COLUMBIA COLLEGE CHICAGO
CHICAGO, ILLINOIS

The College

Columbia College Chicago is the largest, most diverse private nonprofit arts and media college in the nation. The College offers a four-year liberal arts education specifically tailored for a community of gifted, highly motivated students who want to turn their creative talents into rewarding careers. The student body is comprised of approximately 11,200 students who come from all 50 states and 40+ countries. When considering applicants the College performs a holistic review of the student—not just test scores or class rank—and then provides the rigorous academics and unparalleled resources necessary to prepare students for success in a highly competitive twenty-first century marketplace.

Columbia offers bachelor's degrees in more than 120 programs of study in the arts, media, and communications. The curriculum is designed to provide students with a practical, real-world understanding of their chosen field and prepare them to meet professional expectations. Columbia's faculty members are industry insiders (artists, designers, writers, filmmakers, executives, journalists, musicians, entrepreneurs, dancers) with national reputations who share their first-hand experience with students both in and out of the classroom. This interaction with a faculty of gifted, award-winning professionals provides students with access to valuable expertise, insight, viewpoints, and industry-current aesthetics.

The College hosts about 700 on-campus events each year, including film screenings, student-produced television shows, dance concerts, readings, plays, concerts, gallery openings, the annual Mary Blood Ball, and the 24-Hour Night celebration.

When students aren't showing at campus galleries, writing for the student magazine and award-winning newspaper, performing on stage, attending screenings, freestyling at open-mic events, reading at poetry slams, producing shows for television and radio stations, or taking an active role in the College's 85+ social and academic clubs and organizations, they are interacting with the larger Chicago community around them. The presence of Columbia's students can be felt in theaters, bookstores, nightclubs, concert venues, museums, businesses, and media outlets throughout the city.

Location

Columbia is located in an eclectic, urban area of Chicago's historic South Loop neighborhood. Close by are several other colleges and universities, Navy Pier, the Adler Planetarium, the Art Institute, the Field Museum, the Chicago Symphony, the Museum of Contemporary Art, the Harold Washington Library, Lake Michigan, and the Theatre District. Convenient public transportation allows Columbia's students to utilize the whole city as a social, cultural, educational, and professional resource, effectively turning the entire city into their campus.

Majors and Degrees

Columbia awards the Bachelor of Arts (B.A.), Bachelor of Fine Arts (B.F.A.), Bachelor of Science (B.S.), and Bachelor of Music (B.M.) degrees.

The School of Fine and Performing Arts offers majors in art and design (advertising art direction, art and design, art history, fine arts, graphic design, illustration, interior architecture, and product design); arts, entertainment, and media management (advanced management, live and performing arts management, media management, music business management, sports management, and visual arts management); dance (pedagogy, dancemaking); fashion studies (fashion design, fashion business); fiction writing (fiction writing, playwriting); music (composition; contemporary, urban, and popular music; instrumental performance; instrumental jazz; vocal performance); photography (commercial, fine art, photojournalism); and theatre (acting, comedy writing and performance, directing, musical theatre, technical theatre, and theatre design).

The School of Media Arts offers majors in acoustics; audio arts and acoustics (audio for visual media, design and production, live and installed sound); film and video (animation, cinema studies, cinematography, directing, documentary, post-production, producing, screenwriting, sound for cinema,); game design (game art, game development, sound design); game programming; interactive arts and media; journalism (broadcast journalism, magazine writing/editing, news reporting and writing, and science journalism); marketing communication (advertising, marketing, and public relations); mobile media programming; radio; television (Internet and mobile media, post-production/effects, production/directing, writing/producing).

The School of Liberal Arts and Sciences offers majors in American Sign Language–English interpretation; humanities, history, and social sciences (cultural studies); education (early childhood education, teacher certification); English (creative writing–poetry, creative writing–nonfiction); and science and mathematics (art and materials conservation).

Academic Programs

Degree requirements are as follows: B.A. degree, 120 credits, 42 in the liberal arts and sciences (LAS) core curriculum; B.F.A. degree, 128 credits as designated by department, 36 in the LAS core; B.Mus. degree, 128 credits, 84 in music, 36 in LAS core; B.S. degree, 128 credits as designated by department, 36 in LAS core.

At the graduate level, Columbia College Chicago awards the Master of Arts (M.A.) in dance/movement therapy and counseling, interdisciplinary arts, and journalism; the Master of Fine Arts (M.F.A.) in creative writing–fiction, creative writing–poetry, creative writing—nonfiction, film and video—creative producing, film and video—cinema directing, interdisciplinary arts and media, interdisciplinary book and paper arts, music composition for the screen, and photography; the Master of Arts in Teaching (M.A.T.) in art education and elementary education; and the Master of Arts Management (M.A.M.) in arts, entertainment, and media management. Columbia also offers three certificate programs in the field of dance/movement therapy: the graduate Laban certificate in movement analysis, the alternate route certificate, and the movement pattern analysis consultant certificate.

Columbia also has an extensive internship program that offers its students access to some of the most renowned corporations and institutions in the world. The College believes that exposing students to real-world working environments is an invaluable element of their education and provides them with the necessary experience they will need upon graduation.

Columbia College Chicago's Portfolio Center is uniquely geared to assist students with professional-grade portfolio development. The Portfolio Center links industry professionals and alumni with current students through workshops, portfolio sessions, and networking events. The Portfolio Center also maintains Talent Pool, a unique "3-D" portfolio tool that allows students to show off their work while simultaneously connecting with both their peers and industry professionals. Students are expected to graduate with a body of work suitable for professional presentation.

Open to all students, Columbia's Learning Studio is an academic support center designed to help students navigate Columbia's rigorous and creative curriculum by providing a comfortable space where they can find support for their individual learning needs and styles. Services include tutoring in math, science, and writing; peer study groups; and services for students with disabilities.

Off-Campus Programs

Columbia College offers several study-abroad opportunities through both student exchange and individual departmental programs. Among the countries in which students may have the opportunity to study are Austria, China, the Czech Republic, England, France, Germany, Ireland, Italy, Mexico, and South Korea.

Columbia also offers domestic off-campus training programs. Comedy Studies is a full semester's worth of immersive study in comedic literature, history, writing, and performance with the comedic experts at Chicago's famed Second City. Semester in Los Angeles is an immersion program open to all students who wish to gain invaluable real-world experience working in the entertainment industry. The Semester in L.A. program is based out of Raleigh Studios in Hollywood, California.

Academic Facilities

The Columbia College campus occupies 23 campus buildings that house advanced facilities for radio, television, art, computer graphics, photography, interactive arts and media, fashion design, and film. These facilities are state-of-the-art and include professionally equipped color and black-and-white darkrooms, digital imaging resources, photography and film stages, film and video editing suites, and studios for painting, drawing, and 3-D design. Other on-campus resources include the Museum of Contemporary Photography (one of only two such facilities in the country), and the Audio Technology Center (a recording production and research facility). The Media Production Center is a unique multimedia education and production complex that houses two soundstages, digital classrooms, labs, and a motion-capture studio. The dance, music, and theatre departments each have separate centers designed for their program's individual rehearsal and performance needs. In addition, Columbia has extensive computer facilities for use by students, as well as dedicated computer resources geared for specific departmental needs.

The College's library contains 307,000 titles; 47,000 e-books; 19,000 films and videos; and unique collections of film and television scripts, fashion samples, international photography periodicals, and music scores. The library also subscribes to more than 1,000 journals and magazines and over 100 electronic databases. As a member of a statewide online computer catalog and resource-sharing network, the library provides students with access to the resources of seventy-six academic institutions and millions of books.

Costs

For the 2012–13 academic year, full tuition (12 to 16 credit hours) was $10,600 for each fifteen-week semester, or $21,200 per year. Part-time tuition (up to 11 credit hours) was $732 per credit hour. Summer school tuition was $586 per credit hour. Some courses require additional service or laboratory fees.

To enroll, applicants are required to confirm their decision by submitting a $250 tuition deposit (nonrefundable after May 1). Required nonrefundable fees that are charged each semester include the registration fee, $50; the student activity fee, $85 ($45 for part-time students); the U-Pass, $100 (for unlimited access to the public transportation system); and a health center fee, $40 ($25 for part-time students). There is also a one-time $30 library deposit that is refunded when the student leaves the College.

Financial Aid

Columbia makes every effort to help students obtain financial assistance, including grants, scholarships, on-campus work, and loans. The Office of Student Financial Services administers federal and state grant and loan programs. The College also provides information for students seeking part-time employment both on and off campus. On-campus jobs are available in technical, clerical, secretarial, and food service areas.

Columbia College Chicago offers a variety of scholarships for incoming and continuing students. Scholarships are offered based on one or more of the following criteria: financial need, academic merit, creative accomplishments, and area of study. Information about scholarships is available through the Office of Undergraduate Admissions.

Admission Requirements

Columbia College invites applications from all students interested in studying the arts, media, and communication disciplines. Columbia does not require portfolios or previous experience in any discipline to be considered for admission. To apply for admission, all students must submit high school transcripts, a letter of recommendation, a personal essay, and a $35 application fee. ACT or SAT scores are not required but are strongly encouraged. Graduation from high school or an earned GED certificate is a requirement for admission consideration. Transfer students must also submit transcripts from all other colleges and universities attended.

Application and Information

Students are strongly advised to apply early. The priority date is May 1 for the fall semester, November 15 for the spring semester, and April 15 for the summer term. Applicants are notified of their admission decision within three to four weeks after the College receives all the required information and documents. Students who want to live in on-campus housing are strongly advised to apply early. Housing assignments are offered on a first-come, first-served basis until full occupancy is achieved.

All students are strongly encouraged to tour the College. To arrange for a tour, students should call the Office of Undergraduate Admissions or sign up online.

For more information, students should contact:

Office of Undergraduate Admissions
Columbia College Chicago
600 South Michigan Avenue
Chicago, Illinois 60605
Phone: 312-369-7130
Fax: 312-369-8024
E-mail: admissions@colum.edu
Website: http://www.colum.edu

Columbia College Chicago © Andreas Larsson

COLUMBIA UNIVERSITY
Columbia College/The Fu Foundation School of
Engineering and Applied Science
NEW YORK, NEW YORK

The University

Columbia College and The Fu Foundation School of Engineering and Applied Science (Columbia Engineering) offer their students unique advantages; they are at the same time small, selective colleges and integral components of a major research university. Students benefit from over 250 years of rich history and distinction, easy access to the immense resources of New York City and a dynamic residential community where "Columbia blue" is worn with pride at events ranging from Lions' basketball games to the World Leaders Forum, from Glass House Rocks to late-night study sessions in the dorms.

The Columbia College student body is approximately 4,500 students; the Columbia Engineering student body is roughly 1,500. Students come from all fifty states and over ninety countries. They represent a dazzling array of ethnic, social, economic, cultural, religious, and geographic backgrounds. The diversity of Columbia's student body reflects the diversity of New York City, the world's most international city.

Columbia guarantees four years of on-campus housing to all entering first-year students. Nearly all undergraduates remain in University residence halls for all four years.

Columbia students take part in extracurricular groups of all kinds: artistic (theater, musical, and dance), athletic (thirty-one Division I varsity sports and dozens of club and intramural sports), communications (the *Columbia Daily Spectator,* the *Columbia Journal of Literary Criticism,* WKCR-FM, a campus television station, and many others), community service (Amnesty International, Big Brother/Big Sister programs, after-hours tutoring programs, a volunteer ambulance squad, and partnerships with dozens of hospitals, soup kitchens, and homeless shelters), and preprofessional (the Charles Drew Pre-Medical Society, the National Society of Black Engineers, and more). Other groups represent students' ethnic, religious, political, and gender identities. There are twenty-eight fraternities and sororities. Alfred Lerner Hall houses office and meeting space for student organizations, a black box theater, a cinema, the Center for Student Advising, and many dining options.

Location

Columbia shares its Morningside Heights neighborhood with a number of other famous institutions: Barnard College, the Cathedral of St. John the Divine, Union Theological Seminary, Jewish Theological Seminary, and the Manhattan School of Music, to name a few. Many faculty members from Columbia and the other surrounding schools make their homes in the neighborhood. Morningside Heights is an area known for bookstores, wonderfully varied restaurants, and merchants that cater to student tastes, student budgets, and student hours.

Students are encouraged to and assisted in making full use of New York's breathtaking variety of cultural, recreational, and professional resources. Through the Columbia University Arts Initiative, students can receive discounted tickets to Broadway shows, film screenings, art galleries, and a multitude of cultural events in New York City. Passport to NYC offers students free access to over thirty museums throughout the city. Columbia students can be found any day of the week exploring the Metropolitan Museum of Art, the Museum of Modern Art, the Guggenheim Museum, the Museum of African Art, the Museo del Barrio, the Asia Society, or any other of the city's hundreds of museums and galleries. Any evening, they might be discovering the theatrical offerings on, off, or "off-off" Broadway (or on campus); attending the opera, ballet, or symphony at Lincoln Center; enjoying jazz in Greenwich Village or blues at the Apollo; sampling *pai gwat* in Chinatown; or biking or boating in Central Park. Columbia's internship programs offer students opportunities to explore career pathways in depth; nowhere else in the world does the concentration of industries allow such a range of possibilities. New York's public transportation system puts the entire city within easy reach of Columbia students; the campus is directly served by a subway line and five bus routes.

Majors and Degrees

Columbia College grants the B.A. degree in more than eighty programs of study in the humanities, social sciences, and pure sciences, including many interdisciplinary majors. Columbia Engineering grants the B.S. degree in sixteen engineering fields. A five-year program that begins in either school allows students to receive both a B.A. from Columbia College and a B.S. from Columbia Engineering.

Joint degree programs offer selected students the opportunity to combine their undergraduate work with study in Columbia University's schools of law and international affairs and with the Juilliard School.

Academic Programs

Columbia College is known for its Core Curriculum, a set of common courses required of all undergraduates and considered the necessary general education for students, irrespective of their choice in major. The communal learning—with all students encountering the same texts and issues at the same time—and the critical dialogue experienced in small seminars are the distinctive features of the Core. Begun in the early part of the twentieth century, the Core Curriculum is one of the founding experiments in liberal higher education in the United States and it remains vibrant as it enters its tenth decade. One of the two oldest courses in the Core is Contemporary Civilization, a year-long historical survey of Western civilization's religious, political, and moral philosophies; the second is Literature Humanities, a year-long introduction to Western culture's most seminal and meaningful literary works. A second year of humanities offers a semester each of music and art appreciation, encouraging students to experience the cultural treasures of New York City. The Global Core requirement enlarges the scope of inquiry beyond the Western focus in order to promote learning and thought about the variety of cultures and the diversity of traditions that interact in the United States and the world today. The Frontiers of Science course outlines the approaches that scientists take to answer interesting problems in the natural world and introduces students to scientific research methods. The Core Curriculum exposes Columbia's multicultural student body to a variety of disciplines, preparing them for the complex questions and issues of modern society.

The strength of Columbia's Engineering's education is in its uniquely broad curriculum, preparing students not only to be world-class engineers, but also to be global leaders across industries. In addition to taking rigorous math and science courses typically offered at top undergraduate programs, Columbia Engineering students are also required to take courses in the liberal arts alongside their College counterparts, providing them with interdisciplinary tools for real-world problem solving. This type of broad academic exposure is what alumni often cite as the foundation of their later academic and professional success. Another hallmark of the Columbia Engineering education is The Art of Engineering, where students are introduced to the field through interactive lectures, group projects, and guest speakers. A key component of the course is a semester-long, hands-on group project. Past examples of projects include mathematically modeling the U.S. elections, designing vital signs monitors, and modifying a laser pointer by adding a microprocessor to enable it to transmit analog music to a wireless speaker and digital data over long distances. In addition to the technical issues discussed in the course, other key issues of importance in professional engineering such as ethics, project management, and societal impact are addressed.

Off-Campus Programs

Columbia students, with the help of an adviser from the Office of Global Programs, may choose among nearly 200 study-abroad programs on nearly every continent, many of which are Columbia-specific programs and exchanges.

Columbia maintains a network of global centers, developing opportunities for research, scholarship, teaching, and service across borders. With eight international locations ranging from Turkey to Chile and Kenya to China, undergraduate options include summer Arabic language programs in Amman, Jordan or a semester-long French literature program in Paris at Columbia's Reid Hall. Columbia also has direct enrollment agreements with many partner institutions abroad, as well as a growing number of exchange programs with universities abroad.

Columbia was the first U.S. college to offer an integrated year-abroad program with the Universities of Oxford and Cambridge. Other programs allow students to work at the University of Kyoto in Japan or at the Free University of Berlin in Germany.

Academic Facilities

Columbia has the fifth-largest research library system in the world, consisting of 10 million volumes and 26 million manuscripts within 3,000 collections. Included in the twenty-two libraries are collections of particular significance, such as those of the Avery Architectural and Fine Arts Library, the Starr East Asian Library, the Rare Book and Manuscript Library, and the Burke Library of Union Theological Seminary. All divisions are open to Columbia undergraduates. The majority of campus has wireless access including most residence halls. The new Northwest Corner Building houses cutting-edge labs that bring together researchers in biology, chemistry, physics, and engineering, as well as a science library, lecture hall, and café. Students may also make use of an electronic music lab, a cyclotron, an oral history collection, the facilities and programs of the Lamont-Doherty Earth Observatory, and oceanographic research ships.

Costs

Tuition for the 2012–13 academic year was $45,028. Room and board for all first-year students were $11,496. With typical fees, books, and supplies, the total cost of a year at Columbia was approximately $62,163.

Financial Aid

All first-year candidates who are U.S. citizens or have U.S. permanent resident or political refugee status, are considered for admission without regard to their financial need. International students who do not fit into the above categories should be aware that their admissions process is not need-blind; their financial need is taken into account at the time of admission. Regardless of citizenship, Columbia meets the full demonstrated need of every student admitted as a first-year for all four years of study. Columbia has eliminated loans for all students receiving financial aid and replaced them with University grant money. Parental contributions have also been significantly reduced for a large portion of students receiving financial aid. Prospective students should go to http://www.studentaffairs.columbia.edu/finaid/ for information on specific requirements and deadlines. All financial aid at Columbia is based on need; no aid is given in the form of academic, athletic, artistic, or other merit awards. The Office of Financial Aid and Educational Financing believes that cost should not be a barrier to students pursuing their educational dreams.

Faculty

The student-to-faculty ratio is 6:1. Core Curriculum classes are capped at 22 students, and almost 80 percent of classes have 20 students or less. The Columbia faculty is committed to both teaching and research, and all faculty members teach undergraduates, even the president of the University. All faculty members maintain office hours, and each student receives a faculty adviser from the department that he or she chooses as a major.

Admission Requirements

The Columbia first-year class of 1,400 students is selected from a much larger pool of applicants through a holistic, committee-based review process. Candidates for admission are expected to demonstrate the necessary ability and interest to do successful college work in a variety of disciplines as required for the Columbia degree. The following secondary school preparation is recommended: 4 years of English, including meaningful work in literature and writing; 3 (preferably 4) years of mathematics, including precalculus and calculus where offered; 3 (preferably 4) years of history and social studies; 3 or more years of the same foreign language; and 3 (preferably 4) years of laboratory science (including chemistry and physics where available). The Admissions Committee recognizes that secondary schools vary in offerings and standards; consideration is given to applicants whose preparations differ from the recommended course of study but have taken advantage of what their schools offer.

Standardized tests are required for admission, according to the following guidelines. Students may take the SAT with Writing, and students who take the test more than once are evaluated on the highest score they receive in any individual section. Applicants may alternately take the ACT with Writing, which is graded on a 36-point scale. Students taking the test more than once are evaluated on the highest composite score they receive. The writing component of the ACT is mandatory for candidates for Columbia.

In addition to either the SAT or ACT, students must also take two SAT Subject Tests. For Columbia College, they may take any two tests; for The Fu Foundation School of Engineering and Applied Science, they must take any mathematics test and either the physics or the chemistry test.

Students who attend a school that does not give conventional grades or who are homeschooled must take two additional SAT Subject Tests in addition to all requirements outlined above for Columbia College or The Fu Foundation School of Engineering and Applied Science.

It is absolutely imperative that applicants to either Columbia College or The Fu Foundation School of Engineering Applied Science have the testing service report their standardized test scores directly to the Office of Admissions (SAT code 2116, ACT code 2717).

Transfer students may enter Columbia in September only.

The College has a Visiting Students Program, which allows students to attend for one or both semesters of their sophomore, junior, or senior year.

Application and Information

Columbia utilizes the Common Application and requires the Columbia University Supplement. Candidates for whom Columbia is their definite first choice may apply under the Early Decision plan; the deadline is November 1 for all application material, and a decision is rendered by December 15. The deadline for Regular Decision applications is January 1. Candidates are notified of the Admissions Committee's decisions on or about April 1. Admitted candidates must respond to Columbia's offer of admission by May 1. Candidates admitted to Columbia under Early Decision are required to withdraw their applications to other colleges. The application fee is $80. The fee may be waived if a candidate provides documentation that it would cause financial hardship.

For further information, interested students should contact:

Office of Undergraduate Admissions
Columbia University
1130 Amsterdam Avenue, MC2807
New York, New York 10027
Phone: 212-854-2522
Fax: 212-854-1209
E-mail: ugrad-ask@columbia.edu
Website: http://www.studentaffairs.columbia.edu/admissions
　　　　http://www.facebook.com/columbiaadmissions

COLUMBIA UNIVERSITY
SCHOOL OF GENERAL STUDIES
NEW YORK, NEW YORK

The University and The School

The School of General Studies (GS) of Columbia University is one of the finest liberal arts colleges in the United States created specifically for returning and nontraditional students seeking a rigorous, traditional, Ivy League undergraduate education full or part time. Most students at GS have, for personal or professional reasons, interrupted their educations, never attended college, or are only able to attend part time. GS is unique among colleges of its type, because its students are fully integrated into the Columbia undergraduate curriculum: they take the same courses with the same faculty members and earn the same degree as all other Columbia undergraduates.

GS students come from varied backgrounds and all walks of life. Many students work full time while pursuing a degree, and many have family responsibilities; others attend classes full time and experience Columbia's more traditional college life. In the classroom, the diversity and varied personal experience of the student body promote discussion and debate, fostering an environment of academic rigor and intellectual development. GS has approximately 1,600 undergraduate degree candidates and more than 500 Postbac Premed students. The average age of the GS student body is 29. More than 60 percent of GS students attend classes full time.

In addition to its bachelor's degree program, GS offers combined undergraduate/graduate degree programs with Columbia's Schools of Social Work, International and Public Affairs, Law, Business, Dental Medicine, Teachers College, and the College of Physicians and Surgeons. More than 70 percent of the students go on to earn advanced degrees after graduation.

Location

Columbia University is located in Morningside Heights, on the Upper West Side of Manhattan. The University's neighbors include the Union Theological Seminary, the Jewish Theological Seminary, the Manhattan School of Music, St. Luke's Hospital, Riverside Church, and the Cathedral of St. John the Divine. The diversity of intellectual and social activities offered by these institutions is one of Columbia's great assets as a university; another is New York City itself, which offers Columbia students a rich and almost boundless variety of social, cultural, and recreational opportunities that are themselves an education.

Majors and Degrees

The School of General Studies grants the B.A. and B.S. degrees and offers more than seventy majors and concentrations, which include: African studies; African American studies; American studies; ancient studies; anthropology; applied mathematics; archaeology; architecture; architecture, history and theory; art history; art history–visual arts; astronomy; astrophysics; biochemistry; biology; biophysics; chemical physics; chemistry; classical studies; classics; comparative literature and society; computer science; computer science–mathematics; creative writing; dance; drama and theater arts; earth science; East Asian studies; East Central European studies; economics; economics–mathematics; economics–operations research; economics–philosophy; economics–political science; economics–statistics; English and comparative literature; environmental biology; environmental chemistry; environmental science; ethnicity and race studies; evolutionary biology of the human species; film studies; financial economics; French; French and Francophone studies; German literature and cultural history; Hispanic studies; history; human rights; information science, Italian cultural studies; Italian language and literature; Latin American and Caribbean studies; mathematics; mathematics–statistics; Middle Eastern, South Asian, and African studies; music; neuroscience and behavior; philosophy; physics; political science; political science–statistics; psychology; regional studies; religion; Russian language and culture; Russian literature and culture; Slavic studies; sociology; statistics; sustainable development; urban studies; visual arts; women's and gender studies; and Yiddish studies. Individually designed majors are also available.

GS is home to the oldest and largest postbaccalaureate premedical program in the United States, as well as dual-degree programs with the French university Sciences Po, Hong Kong's City University, and the Jewish Theological Seminary. Students enrolled in these interdisciplinary programs can earn two bachelor's degrees from two schools over four years.

The Dual BA Program between Columbia University and Sciences Po is an intensive, transatlantic course of study in which undergraduate students earn bachelor's degrees from both Sciences Po and Columbia University in four years. Students spend two years at one of three Sciences Po campuses, each of which is devoted to a particular region of the world and offers a heavy linguistic and cultural focus. After completing Sciences Po's interdisciplinary social sciences curriculum, Dual BA students matriculate at GS to complete the requirements for a major, as well as fulfill core distribution requirements in a variety of disciplines, including literature, art, music, science, and the humanities. Upon graduation, Dual BA Program students are eligible for guaranteed admission to a graduate program at Sciences Po. Admission to the program is highly competitive, and high school seniors are eligible to apply.

Academic Programs

The School of General Studies offers a traditional liberal arts education designed to provide students with the broad knowledge and intellectual skills that foster continued education and growth in the years after college as well as providing a sound foundation for positions of responsibility in the professional world.

Requirements for the bachelor's degree comprise three elements: (1) core requirements, intended to develop in students the ability to write and communicate clearly; to understand the modes of thought that characterize the humanities, social sciences, and sciences; to gain familiarity with central cultural ideas through literature, fine arts, and music; and to acquire a working proficiency in a foreign language; (2) major requirements, designed to give students sustained and coherent exposure to a particular discipline in an area of strong intellectual interest; and (3) elective courses, in which students pursue particular interests and skills for their own personal growth or for their relationship to future professional or personal objectives. Students are required to complete a minimum of 124 credits for the bachelor's degree; 60 of these may be in transfer credit, but at least 64 credits (including the last 30 credits) must be completed at Columbia. In addition to the usual graduation honors (cum laude, magna cum laude, and summa cum laude), honors programs for superior students are available in a majority of the University's departments.

Off-Campus Programs

Columbia students may enhance their academic experiences through various study abroad programs around the world. For example, students may spend a term at the Reid Hall Program in the Montparnasse district of Paris, the Berlin Consortium for German Studies, the Kyoto Consortium for Japanese Studies, or the Language Program in Beijing, China. In addition, students may apply to participate in one of the dozens of Columbia-approved study abroad programs located in countries around the world.

Academic Facilities

The Columbia University Libraries constitute the nation's sixth-largest academic library system, with a collection of more than 10.4 million volumes, more than 6 million microform pieces, 26 million manuscript items, and 900,000 rare books. Of the twenty-two libraries in the system, five are designated Distinctive Collections because of their unusual depth and nationally recognized excellence. All library divisions are available to GS students. The

University's Computer Center is one of the largest and most powerful university installations in the world and has remote units and terminals in several parts of the campus to enhance its accessibility. The Fairchild Life Sciences Building houses research facilities, laboratories, electron microscopes, and a vast amount of biochemical equipment used for teaching and research. The University's physics building has been the scene of many important developments in the recent history of physics, including the invention of the laser and the first U.S. demonstration of nuclear fission.

Costs

For the 2012–13 academic year, tuition was $1,454 per credit, and annual living (room and board) and personal expenses (books, local commuting costs, and miscellaneous expenses) were $22,045.

Financial Aid

The School of General Studies awards financial aid based upon need and academic ability. Approximately 70 percent of GS degree candidates receive some form of financial aid, including Federal Pell Grants, New York State TAP Grants, Federal Stafford and unsubsidized Stafford Loans, Federal Perkins Loans, General Studies Scholarships, and Federal Work-Study Program awards. Priority application deadlines for new students are March 1 (early action) and June 1 (regular decision) for the fall semester and October 1 (early action) and November 1 (regular decision) for the spring semester. The average scholarship award ranges from $7,500 to $9,000 for first-year students.

Faculty

Students in the School of General Studies take courses with professors who are members of the Columbia University Faculty of Arts and Sciences. These distinguished scholars in virtually every discipline also teach in Columbia College, the Graduate School of Arts and Sciences, and the School of International and Public Affairs. Full-time and part-time students have many opportunities to work closely with faculty members, both in small classes and in research projects. Faculty members also serve as advisers to students majoring in their area of study and maintain regular office hours to see students.

Student Government

One student of the School represents GS students in the University Senate, a decision-making body comprising students, faculty members, and administrative staff members from each division of the University. In addition, 2 GS students sit as voting members on the Committee on Instruction, which oversees the curriculum of the School. The General Studies Student Council elects officers each year and sponsors activities for students. The Premedical Association (PMA) sponsors events related to the medical school admissions process.

Admission Requirements

The GS admission policy is geared to the maturity and varied backgrounds of its students. Aptitude and motivation are considered along with past academic performance, standardized test scores, and employment history. The School's admission decisions are based on a careful review of each application and reflect the Admissions Committee's considered judgment of the applicant's maturity, academic potential, and present ability to undertake course work at Columbia.

Admission requirements include a completed application form; a 1,500- to 2,000-word autobiographical statement describing the applicant's past educational history and work experience, present situation, and future plans; two letters of recommendation from academic or professional evaluators; an official high school transcript; official transcripts from all colleges and universities attended; official SAT or ACT scores (applicants may take the General Studies Admissions Examination); and a nonrefundable application fee of $80.

Students from outside the United States may apply to the School of General Studies to start or complete a baccalaureate degree. In addition to the materials described above, international applicants must submit official TOEFL scores or take the Columbia University American Language Program Essay Exam.

Application and Information

Application deadlines are March 1 for early action (nonbinding), and June 1 for the fall semester, October 1 for early action (nonbinding), and November 1 for the spring semester, and April 1 for the summer semester. Applicants from countries outside the U.S. are urged to apply by August 15 for the spring semester and April 1 for the fall semester. Applications are reviewed as they are completed, and applicants are notified of decisions shortly thereafter.

For more information, students should contact:

Curtis M. Rodgers, Dean of Enrollment Management
Office of Admissions and Financial Aid
School of General Studies
408 Lewisohn Hall
2970 Broadway
Columbia University, Mail Code 4101
New York, New York 10027
Phone: 212-854-2772
E-mail: gsdegree@columbia.edu
Website: http://www.gs.columbia.edu
http://facebook.com/ColumbiaGS
http://www.twitter.com/ColumbiaGS
http://www.youtube.com/GSColumbia

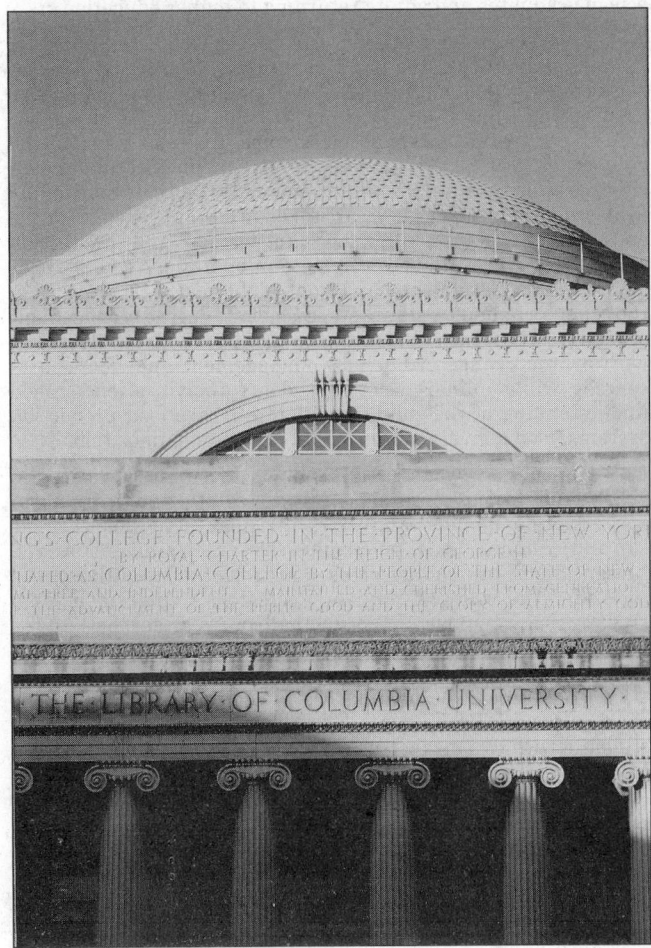

Columbia University, Low Memorial Library.

THE CULINARY INSTITUTE OF AMERICA
HYDE PARK, NEW YORK

THE WORLD'S PREMIER
CULINARY COLLEGE

The Institute

The Culinary Institute of America (CIA) is a private, not-for-profit college dedicated to providing the world's best undergraduate education, with bachelor's and associate degrees as well as majors in culinary arts, baking and pastry arts, and culinary science. Guided by its core values of excellence, leadership, professionalism, ethics, and respect for diversity, the CIA strives to foster an atmosphere where students can develop both professionally and personally. At the CIA, aspiring culinarians gain the general knowledge and specific skills they need to grow into positions of leadership in the foodservice and hospitality industry, the largest private employer in the United States.

Founded in 1946, The Culinary Institute of America today enrolls more than 2,800 students from virtually every state and thirty countries around the world, all united by their shared passion for food. The CIA student body has a balance of recent high school graduates and adults returning to higher education.

As the world's premier culinary college, the CIA is renowned for its gold-standard degree programs, expert faculty, and world-class educational facilities. All CIA degree programs emphasize professional, hands-on learning in the college's kitchens, bakeshops, restaurants, and classrooms. CIA classes span the culinary globe, exploring great cultures, cooking techniques, and cuisines to prepare students for the diversity and creativity of the foodservice industry. Classes are taken in a progressive sequence optimized to build skills, food knowledge, and production experience. These studies culminate in operations courses that give students both kitchen and front-of-the-house experiences in the college's famous restaurants. Bachelor's degree management students also focus on foodservice management development, with a broad range of business management and liberal arts courses, while culinary science students apply a science-based understanding of the culinary arts to improve food production systems, food delivery systems, and customer satisfaction.

CIA students enjoy an active campus life, with a variety of year-round fitness programs, intercollegiate and intramural sports, student clubs, and extracurricular activities such as ski and camping trips, on-campus live entertainment events, presentations by leading chefs and industry executives, and cook-offs. The college's Student Recreation Center includes a six-lane pool, a gymnasium, racquetball courts, an aerobics studio, a fitness center and free-weight room, a game room, outdoor tennis courts, and the Courtside Café. Four coed residence halls, six lodges, and three townhouses provide on-campus housing for more than 1,700 students. The college's dining plan provides students with two meals per instructional day.

The Culinary Institute of America is accredited by the Middle States Commission on Higher Education, 3624 Market Street, Philadelphia, Pennsylvania 19104 (telephone: 215-662-5000). The Middle States Commission on Higher Education is an institutional accrediting agency recognized by the U.S. Secretary of Education and the Council for Higher Education Accreditation.

Location

The CIA's scenic 170-acre campus is set along the east bank of the Hudson River in Hyde Park, New York, conveniently located 1½–2 hours from New York City and Albany.

The Mid-Hudson region's attractions and recreational opportunities offer something for everyone in both rural and urban settings. There are a number of state parks and historic sites throughout the area. Students can taste wines at local vineyards, visit farmer's markets, and pick apples at nearby orchards. To the west lie the Catskill and Shawangunk Mountains, with many opportunities for hiking, skiing, rock climbing, mountain biking, and sightseeing. Concerts, plays, films, and other cultural and special events are offered regularly at the many colleges, theaters, and community facilities throughout the Hudson Valley and Catskill regions. In addition, students can take advantage of the campus's proximity to New York City to experience the culture, arts, and nightlife of this exciting city and food mecca.

Majors and Degrees

At its New York campus, The Culinary Institute of America awards the degree of Bachelor of Professional Studies (BPS) in baking and pastry arts management, culinary arts management, and culinary science, as well as the degree of Associate in Occupational Studies (AOS) in baking and pastry arts and in culinary arts.

Academic Programs

At the core of The Culinary Institute of America's curriculum lies more than 1,300 hours of hands-on instruction in its kitchens and bakeshops as well as classes developing the managerial skills and creative thinking that today's culinary professional requires. Students learn about foods, cooking and baking techniques, cuisines, and business fundamentals while advancing through skills and production kitchens. They also gain invaluable experience in a paid externship program and by cooking and serving in the college's bakery café or in some of the four fine-dining public restaurants on campus. Bachelor's degree management students also take courses in marketing, communications, psychology, foreign languages and cultures, accounting and the use of computers in the food business, and financial and human resources management. Students in the culinary science bachelor's program compare traditional techniques of food production and food delivery systems with new methods using modern equipment technologies, and broaden their knowledge and skills in science-related classes.

Students must earn 132 total credits in culinary arts management, baking and pastry arts management, or culinary science to graduate with a bachelor's degree. Students must earn 69 total credits in culinary arts or in baking and pastry arts to graduate with an associate degree. Students who earn their associate degrees at the CIA's California or Texas campuses can transfer to the New York campus to complete the bachelor's degree program.

Off-Campus Programs

All students work in externships for a minimum of 18 weeks (600 hours). These externships provide students with valuable on-the-job experience at one of more than 1,200 top foodservice and hospitality properties—such as hotels, restaurants, and resorts—around the world. Bachelor's degree students also participate in a travel experience to one of a number of exciting destination choices, such as Spain, Italy, China, and France, and can choose to focus their education track in concentrations such as American Food Studies: Farm-to-Table Cooking and Advanced Wine, Beverage, and Hospitality that include a semester at the CIA's California campus in the world-renowned Napa Valley.

Academic Facilities

CIA students learn the fundamentals of the culinary and baking and pastry arts in the college's forty-one professionally equipped production kitchens and bakeshops and five student-staffed public restaurants on campus—American Bounty Restaurant, The Bocuse Restaurant, Ristorante Caterina de' Medici, St. Andrew's Café, and Apple Pie Bakery Café. Classes are centered in the college's main building, Roth Hall, as well as in the Shunsuke Takaki School of Baking and Pastry, General Foods Nutrition Center, and Colavita Center for Italian Food and Wine. The CIA regularly hosts world-renowned chefs for lectures, cooking demonstrations, and discussions with students in its Danny Kaye Theatre, Anheuser-Busch Theatre, and Ecolab Theatre.

Other valuable academic resources include the 86,000-volume Conrad N. Hilton Library, which contains the largest culinary collection of any culinary school; audiovisual programs to supplement course work; computer labs and workstations; and a wireless network that allows students to access online resources from almost anywhere on campus.

Costs

Freshman tuition for academic year 2013–14 is $26,460. Board is $1,365 per semester, which includes two meals per instructional day. Housing costs range from $3,050 to $3,890 per semester, depending on the room to which the student is assigned.

Additional required fees for the freshman year include a confirmation fee of $100, equipment fees of $1,000 for culinary supplies or $1,790 for baking and pastry supplies, and a general fee of $630 per semester, which includes student activity and exam fees, as well as secondary student accident insurance. The CIA offers students a tuition installment plan. Details are available from the college's Bursar's Office.

Financial Aid

Approximately 90 percent of the CIA's students receive financial aid in the form of scholarships, grants, loans, and work-study. Federal programs offered at the college include the Federal Pell Grant, Federal Supplemental Educational Opportunity Grant (SEOG), Federal Direct Loans (Subsidized and Unsubsidized), Federal Perkins Loan, Federal Work-Study Program (which provides a variety of on-campus and community service jobs to eligible students), Federal PLUS, and veterans' benefits. Students should also investigate their own state's programs and apply if those grants or scholarships can be used in New York State.

Students who have applied for admission or who are currently enrolled at the CIA may apply for scholarships offered by various organizations in the foodservice industry. A list of these scholarships, which are administered by the college, is available from the Financial Aid Office.

Faculty

The college's faculty is composed of more than 150 chefs and instructors from sixteen countries whose credentials and industry experience are unmatched in culinary education. The 17:1 student-faculty ratio in hands-on classes provides student support and mentoring, while giving students the opportunity to work in an environment closely representative of the foodservice industry.

Student Government

All students in good standing are members of the Student Government Association (SGA). The association's Executive Board acts as a liaison between students and the administration. The SGA helps support student activities and funds all student clubs and committees.

Admission Requirements

The Admissions Committee seeks candidates who have demonstrated a commitment to a culinary career and who have the personal initiative, confidence, and motivation to succeed. The basic requirements are successful completion of a secondary school education or its equivalent and some experience in the foodservice and hospitality industry. The applicant's educational record is evaluated on the basis of overall performance and the type of program taken. Academics and leadership ability are key

requirements for the bachelor's degree program. SATs or ACTs are strongly recommended but not required.

Preference is given to candidates who have worked in foodservice, particularly in a kitchen that offers a varied menu. Before entering the program, students are required to have had six months work in either the front-of-house or back-of-house at a non–fast-food establishment with a professional kitchen. Students can also gain the required experience through 1 year in a high school culinary program active in SkillsUSA, FCCLA, or ProStart, or through a semester of college-level work in hands-on cooking or baking classes. Candidates do not need this experience to apply for admission—the requirement must be met before they enter the CIA.

Applicants must submit a formal application for admission, a nonrefundable $50 application fee, an official secondary school transcript (not a student copy), responses to three essay questions from the college, and an official college transcript, if applicable. Students applying directly from high school may include an optional secondary school report. In addition, associate degree candidates must provide one recommendation, and bachelor's applicants must provide two.

Application and Information

Students may apply for admission to the CIA year-round, as the college offers multiple enrollment seasons from which to choose. Applicants should submit their materials according to the enrollment schedule (available at the website listed below) that corresponds to the season they are interested in beginning the degree program. Students are notified of an admission decision according to that schedule.

For information, to schedule a tour, or to participate in an Admissions Information Session, students should contact:

Admissions Office
The Culinary Institute of America
1946 Campus Drive
Hyde Park, New York 12538-1499
Phone: 1-800-CULINARY (toll-free)
E-mail: admissions@culinary.edu
Website: http://www.ciachef.edu/admissions

Set along the banks of the Hudson River, The Culinary Institute of America's New York campus lies on 170 scenic acres in historic Hyde Park.

CURRY COLLEGE
MILTON, MASSACHUSETTS

The College

Curry College is a private institution that offers academic majors in liberal arts disciplines and professional fields. The College's curriculum and programs focus on the two hallmarks of a Curry education: a high respect for the individuality of every student and a developmental approach to learning that maximizes opportunities for achievement.

Students are attracted to Curry's friendly and caring academic community. One-on-one faculty-student relationships provide many opportunities for personalized instruction and close interaction. The average class size is 20 students, and the student-faculty ratio is 10:1. The student body consists of approximately 2,000 traditional undergraduate students. Approximately 1,450 students reside on the Curry campus.

Curry students have access to a wide range of cocurricular and extracurricular activities, including participation in the student newspaper and other campus media; performing arts programs, including theater and dance; and intramural sports or one of fourteen NCAA Division III athletic teams. Varsity sports for men are baseball, basketball, football, ice hockey, lacrosse, soccer, and tennis; women's varsity sports are basketball, cross-country, lacrosse, soccer, softball, tennis, and volleyball.

Curry College is accredited by the New England Association of Schools and Colleges; its nursing programs are accredited by the Commission on Collegiate Nursing Education (CCNE).

The College was founded in Boston in 1879 and moved to its present campus in Milton in 1952. The internationally acclaimed Program for Advancement of Learning (PAL) was established in 1970 as the nation's first college-level program for students with language-based learning differences. In 1974, the College absorbed the Perry Normal School, which prepared teachers for careers, and in 1977 it entered into a collaborative relationship with Children's Hospital Medical Center, which resulted in the establishment of Curry's Division of Nursing Studies.

Curry offers four master's degree programs, including a Master of Education (M.Ed.) established in 1981; a Master of Arts (M.A.) in criminal justice established in 1998; a Master of Business Administration (M.B.A.) established in 2005; and a Master of Science in Nursing (M.S.N) established in 2008.

As at its founding, Curry remains a dynamic and forward-looking institution committed to providing a highly individualized educational experience.

Location

Curry is located in Milton, Massachusetts, a residential suburb near the exceptional resources of Boston. Students enjoy the benefits of a traditional, 135-acre, wooded New England campus that also offers access to the amenities of a large city. The greater Boston area provides students with a diversity of cultural, educational, recreational, and sports activities. A wide variety of corporations, hospitals, agencies, broadcasting stations, and schools offer excellent internship and job opportunities for Curry students. The College operates a shuttle bus to the MBTA trains that run into Boston.

Majors and Degrees

Curry College awards the following Bachelor of Arts (B.A.) degrees: biology; child, youth, and community education; communication (with concentrations in corporate communication, film, multimedia journalism, public relations, radio broadcasting/audio production, relational communication, television/digital video, and theater); criminal justice; early childhood education; elementary education; English (with concentrations in American studies, creative writing, literary genre and movements, traditional literary heritage, journalism, professional writing, and women in literature); environmental science; graphic design; information technology; integrated liberal studies; management (with concentrations in accounting, entrepreneurship, finance, human resources, marketing, residential property management, and sports management); philosophy; politics and history; psychology (with concentrations in counseling, developmental psychology, gerontology, health, and substance-abuse counseling); sociology (with concentrations in ethnic and gender studies and service in the community); special education; and visual arts (with a concentration in studio arts).

Curry College awards the following Bachelor of Science (B.S.) degrees: community health and wellness, and nursing.

Special minors are available in numerous areas, including dance, music, religion, Spanish, women's studies, and writing. For students with design majors, provision is made in the areas in which they have a special interest.

Academic Programs

A central liberal arts curriculum, which is required for all students, incorporates a variety of academic disciplines into every student's plan of study. Curry's programs integrate theoretical classroom learning with a wide variety of field internships.

Curry College operates on a two-semester calendar with a summer session. To graduate, students must complete at least 120 credit hours for a B.A. or B.S. degree. In both cases, a minimum 2.0 cumulative average must be achieved.

Many academic programs enrich and facilitate a Curry education. The First-Year Seminar, the Honors Program, the Women's Studies Program, and the Internship Program are representative of that focus on special interests and diverse learning needs.

The Program for Advancement of Learning (PAL) is a credited program designed to help intelligent, motivated, language-based learning-disabled students to achieve at the college level. PAL provides individual or small-group instruction, textbooks on tape, and untimed examinations, as well as a variety of other applied technologies. Students must apply to the PAL program in order to take advantage of PAL's services. Students receive credit for enrollment in the program for the first year and are able to continue in the program as long as needed.

Off-Campus Programs

Curry students may earn up to 30 credit hours for field internships. In consultation with faculty members, students develop learning contracts that articulate their educational and personal goals and establish criteria for the evaluation of their field experience. Students may also arrange to study abroad or at another institution within the United States while enrolled at Curry.

Academic Facilities

The Levin Memorial Library houses tens of thousands of print volumes, electronic books, electronic journals, and other serial subscriptions. Levin Library is equipped with three computer labs containing PCs and Macintosh computers, laser printers, color printers, and state-of-the-art optical scanning equipment. The library houses the Academic Enrichment Center, where students may secure assistance in reading, writing, mathematics, and the development of study skills and is also home to the Educational

Technology Center full of resources and materials for education students.

The Science Building includes five laboratories. The Kennedy Academic Center houses a simulated hospital room for use as a nursing laboratory; the Nursing Resource Center, which is equipped with an interactive video lab; and a laboratory for experimental psychology equipped with biofeedback, computer control, and animal and human learning facilities. The Webb Learning Center, with its own computer lab, maintains a complete tape library of all textbooks used at the College. The Hafer Academic Center features the Hirsh Communication Center and its state-of-the-art television studio. Curry students operate WMLN-FM, the College's award-winning, 172-watt radio station. WMLN-FM also streams online at http://streaming.curry.edu/wmln-online.

The Academic and Performance Center features a 250-seat multipurpose auditorium, classrooms equipped with wireless laptop connectivity and SMART Board technology, breakout conference rooms, a stock-trading classroom, and a café-style food court.

The new Student Center is an 84,000-square-foot facility that includes state-of-the-art areas for studying, co-curricular and extracurricular activities, dining, and athletics.

Costs

Tuition for the 2012–13 academic year was $31,900. Room and board were $12,760 (based on a fourteen-meal-per week plan). The cost of the Program for Advancement of Learning (PAL) was $6,550. The cost of books, supplies, and personal expenses varies from $900 to $2,000.

Financial Aid

Curry provides financial assistance for students who need funding in order to attend college. The financial aid program consists of federal, state, and Curry College scholarships, grants, work-study awards, student assistant jobs, and loans. Approximately 70 percent of the student body receives financial aid. All students applying for financial aid must submit the Free Application for Federal Student Aid (FAFSA) by March 1. Students applying for financial aid should contact the Financial Aid Office.

Faculty

There are 122 full-time faculty members at Curry, 73 percent of whom hold terminal degrees in their fields. In addition, each year the College hires highly qualified part-time faculty members and visiting lecturers to augment its teaching staff. Although primarily a teaching faculty, Curry's faculty members are also engaged in writing, research, and consulting.

Student Government

The purpose of the Student Government Association (SGA) is the advancement of the College community and the promotion of the general welfare of students. SGA seeks to increase student involvement in the formulation of College policies, communicate effectively with all constituencies of the College, and promote student participation within the institution. Members of SGA host an annual campus meeting with the College President and the senior management of the College.

Admission Requirements

Curry College accepts students who have the necessary preparation and educational background to meet the requirements of the College, regardless of race, religion, national or ethnic origin, age, sex, sexual orientation, or physical handicap. Freshman students are selected on the basis of a combination of the following: secondary school record, scores on the SAT or ACT, recommendation of the secondary school, and the candidate's readiness for college. To be considered for admission, students must generally present at least 16 units of high school work, preferably at the college-preparatory level, from an approved secondary school. A recommended program of studies includes the following: 4 years of English, at least 3 years of mathematics, 2 years of a foreign language, 2 years of science (including at least 1 year of a laboratory science), and 2 years of social studies. Applicants should contact the Admission Office to discuss any possible exceptions to these requirements. A GED certificate is acceptable in lieu of a high school diploma. Curry College seeks well-rounded students who can contribute to the Curry community in athletic, artistic, and social endeavors, as well as in the academic sphere.

Application and Information

Curry's recommended application deadline is April 1; however, Curry operates on a rolling admission basis. Students may apply for September or January entrance. Applicants for the nursing program may only apply for the fall semester. Applicants must submit an application and fee, an official high school transcript, scores from the SAT or ACT, and a counselor's recommendation. Transfer students must also submit official college transcripts, along with a College Official's Report form. If English is not the primary language of the applicant, then results of the Test of English as a Foreign Language (TOEFL) must be submitted. An interview is optional, but not required. The Admission Committee evaluates each application as soon as all required credentials are received, beginning in October. The College is a member of the Common Application.

Applicants to the Program for Advancement of Learning (PAL) must submit a completed application by March 1. PAL applicants must also submit the results of a recently administered Wechsler Adult Intelligence Scale (WAIS-R) test. Achievement testing in reading comprehension, written language, and math must also be submitted. The SAT or ACT requirement is waived for PAL applicants. Final decisions on admission to the program are made once all credentials are complete.

For more information about Curry College, students should contact:

Jane Patricia Fidler
Dean of Admission
Curry College
Milton, Massachusetts 02186
Phone: 617-333-2210
        800-669-0686 (toll-free)
Fax: 617-333-2114
E-mail: curryadm@curry.edu
Website: http://www.curry.edu
         http://on.fb.me/CurryColl_adm
         http://twitter.com/CurryAdmission

The suburban campus of Curry College is just minutes away from the city of Boston.

DAEMEN COLLEGE
AMHERST, NEW YORK

DAEMEN
COLLEGE
A World of Opportunity

The College

Founded in 1947, Daemen College is a private, independent, coeducational college located in suburban Amherst, New York. Attributes at the heart of a Daemen education include: courage, curiosity, creativity, critical thinking, imagination, knowledge, innovation, professionalism, and success.

Daemen College prepares students for twenty-first century careers and service to the local and global community. The College offers rigorous academic programs that are aligned with current market demands that develop the liberal arts–based skills and competencies necessary for professional excellence. Daemen strengthens career readiness through professional development initiatives. It fosters the global competency of its students and faculty by increasing global content in the curriculum, increasing participation in experiential learning opportunities, and continuing to grow its population of students and faculty from international and other diverse backgrounds.

Daemen has approximately 2,000 undergraduate and 1,000 graduate students. Students come from all over New York and the United States, as well as from fifty other countries. Modern apartment-style residence halls provide separate housing for male and female students, in addition to a five-story traditional residence hall. All residence halls have kitchens, laundry facilities, and lounges. More than fifty student organizations, themed dinners, movie nights, internationally famous speakers, and more contribute to a dynamic campus life.

The Center for Veterans and Veteran Family Services at Daemen provides a comprehensive support system for the admissions process, financial information, academic support, career preparation, and physical and social needs. Daemen has been designated a Military Friendly School.

The Wildcats are a member of the United States Collegiate Athletic Association (USCAA) and have entered Candidacy Year 1 of the NCAA Division II membership process. Daemen offers men's and women's basketball, cross-country, soccer, tennis, and track and field (indoor/outdoor), as well as men's golf and women's volleyball.

Location

Daemen's beautiful suburban 39-acre campus is located in Amherst, New York, just minutes away from the city of Buffalo. Renowned for the arts, Buffalo offers exceptional theater, music, art, restaurants, and major league sports; it is also very close to scenic Niagara Falls and Canada. The campus is easily accessible by the major rail, plane, and motor routes that serve Buffalo.

Majors and Degrees

Daemen's Division of Arts and Sciences is just the place for students interested in becoming anything from a novelist to an occupational psychologist. Its programs allow students to unleash the full range of their sensibilities—right brain, left brain, or both. In the visual and performing arts programs, art is seen as both a lifestyle and a life-work; art and design students are challenged to find creative solutions. Students interested in foreign languages can receive personalized instruction and become fluent in French, Spanish, or Chinese. History and government majors examine everything from ancient history to the politics of globalization, leading to careers in public affairs, foreign correspondence, law, and more. English majors become acquainted with everything from syntax to Shakespeare, and move on to professions such as magazine journalist and high school teacher. A math degree can lead to careers in teaching, research, architecture, meteorology, and banking,

among others. Those studying natural sciences can major in biochemistry, biology, and natural science; a chemistry minor is also available. Biology students can specialize in environmental studies, while other specialties include health sciences, forensic science, and individual studies. Career opportunities range from wildlife biology to medicine and dentistry. Students can explore Christianity, Buddhism, Islam, Judaism, and more in the philosophy and religious studies program, perhaps leading to work ranging from library research to interfaith advisement. Psychology majors have the opportunity to study topics ranging from neuropsychology to human sexuality, in preparation for careers in family therapy, school counseling, law enforcement, and other challenging areas. Interdisciplinary programs include global and local sustainability.

The Division of Health and Human Services offers career paths that lead to many destinations for students, from special education teachers to athletic trainers, and tax accountants to parole officers. Accounting majors crunch numbers, but they also consider global issues to become financial analysts, company comptrollers, tax accountants, and more. Athletic training lets students assume responsibility for overseeing an athlete's total health care—through a five-year B.S./M.S. program. Business administration majors focus on economics, accounting, and marketing, but also on diversity and global management. Graduates work as market research analysts, HR managers, and more. Future teachers in the education program study childhood/early childhood and special education and visual arts education, with certification opportunities in several areas. Health-care studies covers all aspects of practical health-care delivery. Students can choose from one of three concentrations and leverage exceptional service-learning opportunities and professional internships. The nursing partner program allows future nurses to earn both their associate and bachelor's degrees in four years. Physical therapy offers a doctorate after six years. Studies span orthopedics, pediatrics, geriatrics, tissue mechanics, sports medicine, wound healing, and more. Daemen's physical therapy students have a first-time pass rate on the National Exam that exceeds both New York State and national averages, with a current three-year weighted average ultimate pass rate of 100 percent. The physician assistant program prepares students to become licensed to practice medicine with physician supervision. Service-learning opportunities include an annual trip to the Dominican Republic. The rigor of Daemen's program is evident in the 95–100 percent first attempt pass rate on the NCCPA Certification Exam (the national average is 92–94 percent). Students interested in shaping communities can choose Daemen's social work program, with an abundance of practical service learning opportunities. Graduates enjoy careers as counselors, therapists, probation/parole officers, school social workers, and in other human service areas.

Majors at Daemen include: accounting (B.S./M.S.); animation; art, with an emphasis in applied theatre, drawing, graphic design, illustration, painting/sculpture, or visual arts education K–12; arts administration, with an emphasis in comprehensive arts, fine arts, or theater; athletic training (B.S./M.S.); biology, with an emphasis available in adolescence education 7–12 or environmental studies; biochemistry, with several pre-professional programs available; business administration, with an emphasis available in human resource management, international business, marketing, or sport management; education, with an emphasis in childhood education 1–6, childhood education/special education 1–6, or early childhood education/special education B–2; English, with an emphasis available in adolescence education 7–12 or communication/public relations; French, with an emphasis available in adolescence education 7–12; health-care studies, with an emphasis available in community health, complementary and alternative health-care practices, or health and fitness training; history; history and government, with an emphasis available in adolescence education 7–12 or environmental studies; mathematics, with an emphasis available in adolescence education 7–12; natural sciences, with an emphasis available in environmental studies, forensic science, health science; nursing (partner program); paralegal studies; physical therapy (B.S.N.S./D.P.T.); physician assistant studies (B.S./M.S.); political science; psychology; religious studies; social work; and Spanish, with an emphasis available in adolescence education 7–12; and sustainability (global and local).

Academic Programs

Daemen has been named a College of Distinction for its exemplary commitment to engaged students, great teaching, vibrant communities, and successful outcomes.

Daemen College recognizes that education needs to prepare students for professional, intellectual, and civic leadership. The key to fostering the development of these skills is the core curriculum—a common educational experience for all students, regardless of major. The core is designed to strengthen students' abilities to become intellectually curious, acquire professional rewards, become responsible citizens, and deal with change. The seven core competencies are introduced at the freshman level, and are emphasized across the entire curriculum so that students develop a greater understanding of, appreciation for, and practice of these important life skills through their academic work. Research is carried out on a host of different fronts, from an innovative student/faculty think tank, to a high-profile wound therapy initiative. General research projects that include an enormous diversity of interests are showcased annually in the College's increasingly popular Academic Festival, held each spring. The honors program meets the intellectual needs of the best students, ensuring that the Daemen experience challenges their minds and fosters their potential to contribute both to the community and to society at large.

Off-Campus Programs

Career Services helps students to find an internship or co-op position to gain real-world experience in their area of interest. Daemen students say this chance to gain more insight into their fields prepares them better for employment after graduation. Internships are available in a wide range of fields, including business, sports, the arts, industry, government, health-related entities, nonprofit organizations, educational institutions, and cultural organizations. These can be local, national, or international and include excellent opportunities with the Washington Internship Institute.

Daemen's Office of Global Programs coordinates distinctive international programs. In today's global economy, it is vital that students learn about different cultures, political systems, and histories. International study is a staple of the Daemen experience. Students choose from semesters abroad, summer programs, and accelerated January term trips.

Daemen believes strongly in learning through service. All undergraduate students at Daemen engage in various service learning activities. Students participate as individuals or groups in short- and long-term projects or assignments that benefit the local, national, or global communities. Daemen founded and operates the Center for Sustainable Communities and Civic Engagement and is founder and headquarters for the Western New York Service Learning Coalition.

Academic Facilities

The Research and Information Commons, a green building, is a technological showcase—a hub of academic research, as well as the academic and social heart of the campus.

The Center for Visual & Performing Arts is a dramatic new space which features a spacious gallery, studios, a performance/lecture space, production area, computer labs, and an outdoor classroom.

The International Center for Excellence in Animation is located off campus. The 17,000-square-foot center is equipped with five studios, three editing rooms, a library/video library, and screening room.

Costs

For the 2012–13 academic year, tuition and fees were $23,130, and room and board were $10,700.

Financial Aid

Daemen creates individualized financial aid packages. Generous scholarships make attending the College very affordable. Over 92 percent of full-time undergraduates received some kind of financial assistance. Daemen awards merit scholarships based on academic and leadership achievement.

Faculty

Daemen has approximately 297 faculty members (full- and part-time). Small class sizes and a 15:1 student-faculty ratio ensure that students will have an engaging and interactive classroom experience.

Admission Requirements

Daemen offers a rolling admissions policy. The average student enrolled has a 91 GPA and 1060 SAT. Daemen has a test-optional policy which provides students with a choice regarding the submission of standardized test scores.

The admissions staff helps guide students through the process from start to finish. Students can create a personalized Daemen Connection web page at daemen.edu/admissions.

Application and Information

Prospective students can apply for free online at daemen.edu/apply or commonapp.org.
Daemen College
4380 Main Street
Amherst, New York 14226
Phone: 716-839-8225
         800-462-7652 (toll-free)
         716-218-8830 (text)
E-mail: admissions@daemen.edu
Website: daemen.edu

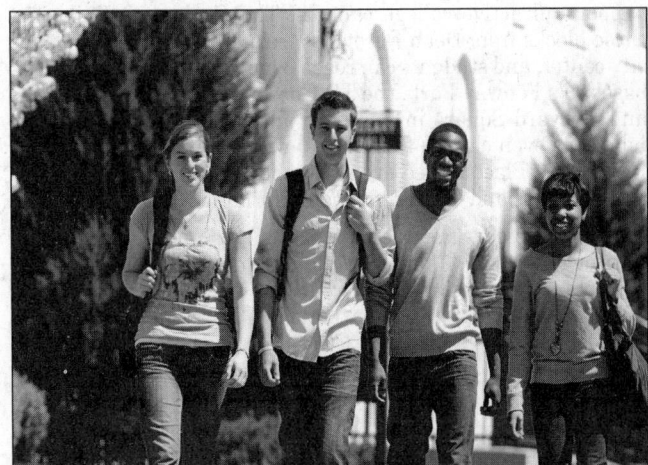

Visit Daemen—that's the best way to really get a feel for what the College has to offer.

DEAN COLLEGE
FRANKLIN, MASSACHUSETTS

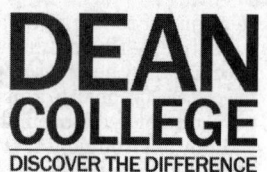

The College

Founded in 1865, Dean is a unique New England college awarding both four-year baccalaureate and two-year associate degrees. Students may choose from nearly two-dozen academic programs supported by state-of-the-art facilities, a dedicated teaching faculty, and professional advising known for exceptional personalized academic support.

Located 45-minutes outside Boston in the town of Franklin, Massachusetts, Dean's attractive 100-acre campus is home to WGAO-FM, the Joan Phelps Palladino School of Dance, and several buildings listed on the National Register of Historic Places. There are two fitness centers, a gymnasium, athletic fields, and indoor pool as well as a library learning commons, an advising center, a 214-seat theater, and dance studios.

Nearly all of Dean's 1,100 full-time students live on campus, and housing is available for all four years. The student body is impressively diverse with more than 30 states and 25 countries represented (and an additional 500 part-time students). The College sponsors 10 championship-caliber athletic teams, an Honors Program, internship and study abroad opportunities, an executive lecture series, and dozens of clubs, performance groups, and student organizations.

Dean College graduates are very successful. Of those receiving a bachelor's degree last year, 85 percent were employed or attending graduate school within 3 months—95 percent within six months. Among associate degree graduates, 98 percent were accepted as transfers to highly selective universities across the United States or had plans to continue their bachelor's degree at Dean.

Location

Dean's home town, Franklin, is a charming, historic Massachusetts community. The suburban setting is safe and convenient to downtown Boston with sufficient stores and restaurants to support an active college campus. The Commuter Rail—just three blocks from Dean—provides frequent train service to the city center, and students can reach popular destinations such as baseball's Fenway Park, the TD Garden, Museum of Fine Arts, and Harvard Square in less than an hour. Providence, Rhode Island, is even closer (40 minutes) where students can shop at Providence Place or see events at the Dunkin' Donuts Center and Rhode Island Center for the Performing Arts.

The area's biggest attractions are only minutes from Dean: Patriot Place and Gillette Stadium (home of the New England Patriots), the fashionable Wrentham Outlets, and Comcast Center outdoor amphitheater. For day trips, students can easily get to the beaches on Cape Cod, see Newport's mansions, or reach the mountains in nearby New Hampshire and Vermont.

Majors and Degrees

Dean College provides a wide range of programs across four academic schools: the School of Liberal Arts & Sciences, School of the Arts, School of Business, and the Joan Phelps Palladino School of Dance.

Bachelor's degrees are available in arts and entertainment management (with concentrations in dance, media studies, and theatre), business (with concentrations in management,

sport management, human resource management, and public relations), dance (with concentrations in performance/ choreography, dance education, and studio management), liberal arts and studies (including English, history, psychology, sociology, and individually designed), and theatre (with concentrations in acting, technical theatre, and musical theatre).

Dean also offers associate degree programs in business, criminal justice, dance, early childhood education, English, general studies, health sciences (including pre-nursing), history, mathematics, media studies and communications, psychology, science, sociology, sport fitness studies (with concentrations in athletic training, exercise science, physical education, and sports management), and theatre/musical theatre.

Academic Programs

Dean is accredited by the New England Association of Schools and Colleges. Graduation requirements include a 2.0 cumulative grade point average (GPA) and demonstrate competency in reading/writing, mathematics, and computers. Bachelor's degree candidates must complete a required internship or other experiential learning opportunity related to their major.

Unique to Dean is a special first semester course entitled Dean 100-Dean Foundations. Designed to assist new students with the academic and personal transition to college, this course covers a variety of learning and study strategies essential for collegiate success. Students apply these strategies to their daily experience as a college student and develop an individual plan that promotes a successful student transition.

The Honors Program at Dean offers academically talented students an opportunity to engage in stimulating and challenging courses, seminars, and colloquia. Students who meet the honors entrance criteria enroll in special course sections reserved for honors students or may enhance non-honors courses with additional intensive readings and analysis approved by the instructors. The Honors Program also offers exciting academic and cultural activities outside the traditional classroom environment.

Study-abroad and study-away opportunities are increasingly popular at Dean. Students may choose programs across the globe through cooperative arrangements facilitated by the College or take advantage of Dean's relationship with the Washington Center Program for study and internships in Washington, D.C.

The Dean Leadership Institute sponsors an Executive Lecture Series that brings leaders in business, media, and the arts to campus. Featured speakers share their insights into post-graduate opportunities and help build each student's career network. Recent guests include Bert Jacobs (Life is Good), Bob Kraft (Kraft Group/New England Patriots), Anne Finucane (Bank of America), and James Roosevelt (Tufts Health Plan).

The Arch Learning Community provides comprehensive support for students with diagnosed learning differences. Arch students receive dedicated academic advising and a cohort educational model specially designed to help LD students maximize their academic and personal potential and find success within the rigors of a traditional college curriculum.

Academic Facilities

Students have access to a wide range of facilities, including the newly renovated Green Family Library-Learning Commons and E. Ross Anderson Library, Berenson Writing Center, and Morton Family Learning Center—all housed under one roof. Together, these form the hub of Dean's academic support efforts. There are print and online resources for class projects, academic coaches to provide professional one-on-one mentoring, peer tutoring services, the Technology Service Center, and space for weekly faculty drop-in sessions where students can participate in group or individual advising.

Other academic facilities include the A.W. Pierce Technology and Science Center, which houses science and computer labs as well as the Alden Center high-tech master classroom; the Dean College Children's Center, an on-campus pre-school, which doubles as a learning laboratory for student teachers; and Campus Center, where students can find the Advising Center, Main Stage Theater, Guidrey Center multipurpose room, student activities office, and newly renovated classrooms featuring SmartBoard technology.

Costs

The basic costs related to attending Dean College for 2012–13 were $33,230 for tuition and fees and $14,260 for room and board.

Financial Aid

Last year, the College provided more than $17 million of merit-based financial aid, with the average Dean award ranging from $10,000 to $20,000. These awards are based solely on the information students provide in their application for admission—not financial need—and help to reduce the average cost of attendance by more than 30 percent.

Approximately 90 percent of all full-time students receive academic grants not based on demonstrated financial need. Since the mission of Dean College is to nurture the potential within its students, these scholarships focus on current performance as well as future potential. They are based on academic or athletic performance, performing arts talent, place of residence, and academic promise. In addition, most students apply for—and receive—federal and state financial aid, which is separate from (and can be added to) Dean's scholarship awards.

Student financial aid packages are generally a combination of grants, loans, and work-study, contingent upon demonstrated financial need and the availability of funds. The College participates in all Federal Title IV and Federal Family Education Loan Programs. Students must submit the Free Application for Federal Student Aid (FAFSA) in order to be considered for need-based aid. Upon receipt of a valid FAFSA, full-time students are considered for all of the financial aid programs that Dean administers. Residents of Massachusetts and other reciprocal states may also be eligible for state scholarships, grants, or loans.

Faculty

Dean's dedicated faculty members, advisers, and educational specialists—some of the best in their respective fields—offer direct, personal involvement to help students obtain the full value of their college experience. The student-faculty ratio is 17:1.

Student Government

The Student Government Association serves as a liaison between the student body and Dean College administration. It disseminates information about College policies, seeks out student opinion, allocates funds collected from the activities fee to clubs and organizations through a budget request process, and coordinates the activities of various clubs, groups, and organizations campus wide.

Admission Requirements

Every application to Dean is carefully reviewed by the Admission Committee. In addition to the application form, students must submit an official high school transcript, a letter of recommendation from a guidance counselor or teacher, a personal statement or essay, and SAT or ACT scores. Interviews are not required but are strongly recommended. Students applying for the dance and theatre programs must audition.

Application and Information

Students who identify Dean as a top choice may choose to apply under the early action plan, with an application deadline of December 1. The College accepts applications on a rolling basis thereafter, though it is recommended that applications be submitted by March 15 to ensure access to the highest level of financial aid and priority in housing and class registration. Once an application is complete, an admissions decision is typically made within two weeks.

For more information, contact:

Office of Admissions
Dean College
99 Main Street
Franklin, Massachusetts 02038
Phone: 508-541-1508
        877-TRY-DEAN (toll-free)
E-mail: admissions@dean.edu
Website: http://www.dean.edu

Dean Hall, built in 1865 when Dean College was established.

DELAWARE VALLEY COLLEGE
DOYLESTOWN, PENNSYLVANIA

The College

Founded in 1896, Delaware Valley College (DelVal) is a private, coeducational four-year college enrolling approximately 1,700 full-time undergraduate students. The College concentrates on producing graduates who can fill employers' needs. DelVal is known for its experiential learning philosophy which combines theory with practice. The College is growing and continuing to expand opportunities for experience-based, cross-disciplinary learning.

DelVal tends to attract pre–veterinary science students; some of its most popular majors are small animal science, equine science, and conservation and wildlife management. Other science offerings include chemistry, environmental design, food science, microbiology and biotechnology, and zoology. The College also offers strong programs in business, criminal justice, counseling psychology, and media and communications. DelVal offers master's programs and extensive course offerings in continuing education, including a curriculum that provides adult learners with teacher certification.

Students attend Delaware Valley College, first and foremost, to prepare to enter professional careers. DelVal has an excellent record when it comes to job placement, proving that the time-honored educational philosophy of "scholarship with applied experience" is successful. A high percentage of graduates find employment in their field of study or enter graduate school within six months of graduation.

In addition to its academic programs, the College offers a wide range of extracurricular activities and events. DelVal has more than seventy clubs and organizations, many of which are linked with a specific major. Student publications include the weekly *RamPages* (newspaper), the *Cornucopia* (yearbook), and the *The Gleaner* (literary magazine). The College band and chorale give students the chance to demonstrate their musical talents. There are active minority and international clubs on campus. DelVal students are connected to the community in a variety of ways that are relevant to their majors. A-Day, the student-run campuswide fair, annually attracts 50,000 visitors who enjoy the festival, the entertainment, and the academically oriented projects.

Approximately 60 percent of students live on campus in ten residence halls. A full range of intercollegiate and intramural athletics programs (NCAA Division III, ECAC, and MAC) for both women and men is offered. All elements of the College's educational and recreational programs are in place to develop students as open-minded professionals who are capable of expanding their horizons in a future of unlimited possibilities.

DelVal offers graduate programs in general business, educational leadership, food and agribusiness, and accounting. The College also offers an online master's program in global leadership.

DelVal is officially recognized by the Middle States Commission on Higher Education.

Location

The College is located in historic Bucks County, Pennsylvania, approximately 30 miles north of Philadelphia and 70 miles southwest of New York City. Bucks County is one of the fastest-growing areas in the United States, yet it maintains its rich historical and agricultural heritage. The Doylestown area, where DelVal's main campus is located is rich in educational and cultural resources, including museums, a county courthouse, and a library which further enhance the educational opportunities available to students.

The Pennsylvania and New Jersey Turnpikes provide quick access to the College. A commuter railway system links the College with Philadelphia, providing daily scheduled arrivals and departures, right on campus. The College enjoys a relationship with its surrounding community that is mutually beneficial. Many students find convenient employment opportunities with local businesses, and the community benefits from the many events and activities that are held on campus.

Majors and Degrees

Delaware Valley College offers a variety of strong programs and is particularly strong in the life sciences. The College offers more than twenty-seven majors and specializations including biology (with programs in botany, environmental biology, microbiology/biotechnology, pre-professional biology, and zoology); business administration (with programs in accounting, financial services, general business administration, entrepreneurship, management, marketing, and sports management); chemistry and biochemistry; counseling psychology; English; media and communication; secondary education (with programs in agriculture, biology, business, chemistry, English, general science, and social studies); agribusiness; animal biotechnology (with programs in conservation and wildlife management, small animal science, and zoo science); animal science (with programs in equine science and management, livestock science and management, and science); dairy science; equine studies (with programs in equibusiness and equine training); food science, nutrition, and management (with programs in food science, food technology, nutrition science and restaurant and food service management); agronomy and environmental science (with programs in crop science, environmental science, and turf management); horticulture (with programs in commercial crop production and marketing/plant health management, hydroponic crop science, and plant sciences and biotechnology); and ornamental horticulture (with programs in environmental design, floriculture and nursery production and marketing, and landscape contracting and management).

The College also offers pre-professional preparation in dentistry, law, medicine, optometry, and veterinary medicine.

For students interested in applying to veterinary school in their third year, Delaware Valley College offers the 3+1 Program, where a contract is completed prior to May of the sophomore year. The program allows the student to enter veterinary school after three years (96 credits). After acceptance and verified completion of the first full academic year at a nationally accredited professional school, DelVal will confer the Bachelor of Science degree to the student.

Academic Programs

All courses are taught from a liberal arts perspective, which broadens the students' appreciation of cultural heritage. The College is committed to producing graduates who are both highly competent in their areas of study and skilled in more general areas such as communication, mathematics, and technology. Academic programs at DelVal combine theory with practice and students leave with valuable work experience. The College stresses a practical, hands-on approach to learning. Delaware Valley College's Experiential Learning Program (ExLP) provides active, hands-on applied experiences tied to specific academic objectives and outcomes as a requirement for graduation. It provides students the opportunity to participate in real-world activities as a basis for learning and to develop specific career goals and aspirations.

The academic calendar consists of two 15-week semesters, with an optional January term, and two optional summer sessions.

Off-Campus Programs

Students can earn credit by studying abroad. DelVal has programs that take students to the Hartpury College in the United Kingdom and the University of Podlasie in Poland. The Polish exchange program is free for students and is funded by the Copernicus Society of America.

Academic Facilities

Many of the courses taught at Delaware Valley College are laboratory or field oriented. The 571-acre main campus includes classrooms, modern laboratories, greenhouses, an arboretum, a library, livestock and dairy farms, an equestrian center, 400 acres of agricultural land, and 60 acres of horticultural land. Approximately 225 acres are dedicated to field crops for dairy and livestock operations, which include beef and dairy cattle, sheep, swine and standard-bred horses. Approximately 60 acres are used for horticulture (including plantings of apples, peaches and various fruits, vegetables, and nuts). DelVal also maintains an apiary for beekeeping programs.

These facilities serve just one purpose: to support the education and experience students need to succeed. Two additional campuses provide extensive opportunities for students. The Roth Living Farm Museum, in Montgomery County, is dedicated to providing historical information on farming practices. The Gemmel Campus, located 8 miles from main campus in Jamison, Pennsylvania, is a pristine, 398-acre farm. It houses an 18-acre apple orchard and students enjoy soils and other environmental science classes there. The DelVal philosophy is that students learn best when classroom learning and hands-on experience are combined. The facilities are designed with that goal in mind, and the faculty and staff utilize every building on campus in pursuit of the mission of preparing students for careers and future studies.

DelVal students benefit from the low student-laboratory ratio. This enables ready access to equipment, which is imperative to learning. Specifically, the College utilizes biology, chemistry, physics, plant science, and animal science laboratories. Facilities include a tissue culture laboratory, a food processing plant, a greenhouse-laboratory complex, a dairy, a small-animal science center, equine breeding barns, and an indoor equestrian center. The campus is itself a recognized arboretum that is managed by students and faculty members. These facilities are all supported by the Krauskopf Memorial Library, which houses some 80,000 publications.

Costs

Estimated costs for the 2011–12 academic year were: tuition and fees $30,946, room $4,916, residential meal plan $5,926, and books and supplies $1,000 (if purchasing new books). However, DelVal offers a textbook rental program which allows students to rent textbooks for one semester for 35 percent of the cost of a new book. To keep a book for two semesters students pay 54 percent of the cost of a new book. This program significantly reduces student costs. A student who would spend $1,000 annually purchasing new books at another institution would spend just $350 annually if they rented all of their books at DelVal.

Financial Aid

The College is committed to providing financial assistance so that every student is able to meet the costs of obtaining a college education. Approximately 98 percent of full-time undergraduates receive some type of financial aid. The College offers merit scholarships and grants for students with exceptional academic promise and participates in federal government programs such as Federal Pell Grants, Federal Supplemental Educational Opportunity Grants, Federal Perkins Loans, Federal Work-Study, Federal Academic Competitiveness grants, Federal SMART grants, and Federal TEACH grants. Students can borrow under the Federal Direct Loan program, and parents can borrow under the Federal Parent Direct Loan program. Residents of Pennsylvania can also apply for state grants through PHEAA.

Faculty

All courses at DelVal are taught by faculty members, not graduate students. The College's faculty is made up of dedicated professors who combine professional experience with deep theoretical knowledge. The faculty includes 82 full-time members as well as additional part-time instructors, who are friendly and accessible and always ready to help individual students make the most of the educational opportunities offered by the College. Approximately 60 percent of DelVal professors hold the highest degree available in their fields. The student-faculty ratio is 15:1.

Student Government

Students are encouraged to make the most of extracurricular activities to ensure that their education includes as many different experiences as possible. The student government acts to coordinate the activities of all organizations on campus and sponsors a variety of mixers, movies, concerts, and speakers.

Admission Requirements

The College seeks to recruit a diverse population of talented, motivated, and promising students, and draws them from across the nation. Criteria for admission include the application, academic transcripts, class rank, SAT or ACT scores, letters of recommendation, and a personal interview (recommended). While DelVal has a rolling admission period, applications should be submitted as early as possible in the senior year of high school, preferably by the end of the first marking period.

Application and Information

For more information about Delaware Valley College and its academic, athletic, and financial aid programs, students should contact:

Office of Admissions
Delaware Valley College
700 East Butler Avenue
Doylestown, Pennsylvania 18901-2697
Phone: 215-489-2211
       800-2DELVAL (toll-free)
Fax: 215-230-2968
E-mail: admitme@delval.edu
Website: http://www.delval.edu
       http://www.facebook.com/delval
       http://twitter.com/delvalcollege

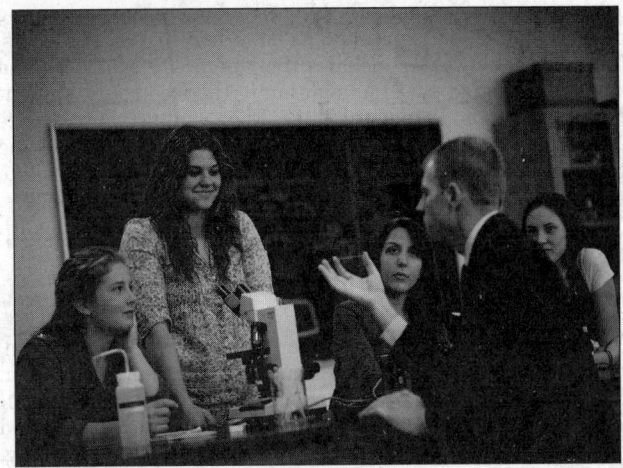

Delaware Valley College students are doing incredible things, from working on research projects in the labs to building rooftop gardens across the globe. Students at DelVal get the opportunity to find their passions and discover who they will become.

DeSALES UNIVERSITY
CENTER VALLEY, PENNSYLVANIA

The University

DeSales University is a private, four-year Catholic university for men and women that is administered by the Oblates of St. Francis de Sales. Its mission is to provide high-quality higher education according to the philosophy of Christian humanism. The University imparts knowledge about, and develops talents for, personal, familial, and societal living, enriching the human community and enhancing the dignity of the individual through its educational endeavors. The University is accredited by the Middle States Association of Colleges and Schools.

In 1961, Joseph McShea was appointed Bishop of the new Allentown Diocese. At the time, the Diocese did not include a Catholic college for men. At the request of Bishop McShea, the Oblates of St. Francis de Sales agreed to assume responsibility for establishing a liberal arts college to serve this need. Allentown College of St. Francis de Sales received a charter to grant bachelor's degrees in 1964, and the first classes began in 1965. The College became coeducational in 1970; throughout the 1980s and 1990s, it began to offer graduate and cooperative education programs. These changes led to the college attaining university status, and it was renamed DeSales University in 2001.

Today, DeSales is home to more than 3,000 undergraduate and graduate students. Life on campus best illustrates DeSales' identity as a Christian humanist institution. Approximately 70 percent of the University's 1,600 undergraduate students live on campus and take full advantage of the rich opportunities provided. Students participate in more than forty clubs and organizations that encompass art, politics, and intramural sports; sixteen athletic teams competing in the NCAA Division III, including basketball, soccer, field hockey, and lacrosse; social outreach; student activities; and a Campus Ministry that enables students to participate in retreats and social justice groups. Billera Hall houses facilities for intercollegiate and intramural sports and fitness activities. The McShea Student Union contains health services and counseling offices. The Labuda Center for the Performing Arts houses the performing arts division, and it is proud of its forty-year history of success. The University Center includes the University bookstore and expanded meeting space in addition to the food court, student dining facility, and student lounge. Eight suite-style residence halls offer a range of living options, including living-learning communities, which allows students with common interests to live together. The Gambet Center for Business and Healthcare, a building dedicated to the University's business and health care programs, opened in spring 2013.

Location

The Lehigh Valley contains three cities, including Allentown, the third-largest city in Pennsylvania; Bethlehem; and Easton. The region offers a wide range of year-round recreational activities, from skiing and skating in the winter to golf and swimming in the summer, and theater, dance, fine dining, shopping, and music year-round.

The Lehigh Valley has a wide variety of museums, art galleries, and concert venues for every taste and age group, while farmers' markets are a common sight throughout the region.

Amusement parks like Dorney Park and Wildwater Kingdom and the Crayola Factory are nearby, as are Kutztown Festival and other annual celebrations. The Promenade Shops at Saucon Valley offer more than sixty-five stores and restaurants and a state-of-the-art movie theater. For those wanting to travel beyond the region, the Lehigh Valley is less than 2 hours from New York City and 1 hour from Philadelphia.

Majors and Degrees

The University offers undergraduate degrees in more than thirty programs, including accounting, biochemistry-molecular biology, biology, business, chemistry, communications, computer science, criminal justice, dance, digital art, early childhood education, English, finance, history, international business, law and society, liberal studies, management, management of information technology, marketing, marriage and family studies, mathematics, media studies, nursing, pharmaceutical marketing, philosophy, physician assistant studies, political science, pre-medicine, psychology, Spanish, sport and exercise science, sport management, television and film, theater, and theology.

Academic Programs

Students must complete forty courses with a minimum GPA of 2.0 to earn a bachelor's degree. Each degree program has three components. The General Education Core requires completion of sixteen courses, including two courses in English; three physical education courses; two courses in a foreign language or world cultures; two courses in history or political science; one course in art or music; one course in literature; five courses in modes of thinking, concentrating on literature, mathematics, natural science, philosophy, and social science; and three courses in theology. The major provides a thorough and systematic study of one subject area. The major requires completion of sixteen courses. As an alternative, a student may choose to enroll in a special degree program, which may extend the number of required courses. Electives comprise the remaining eight course requirements. Electives provide opportunities for learning in areas of special interest outside the student's major. Some students may want to consider a dual major, in which case the student must complete the requirements of both fields of study. Students who wish to complete a minor must take six courses within that field of study.

Off-Campus Programs

DeSales encourages qualified students to study abroad during the summer and/or the academic year. The University offers qualified students in a number of disciplines the opportunity to spend a semester in England, Greece, Italy, Ireland, Switzerland, France, and Monte Carlo. More importantly, DeSales is employing a new model of intensive hands-on engagement through short-stay co-curricular trips of students, faculty, and staff. Trips to Ireland, Germany, Peru, and South Africa for short-stay intensive travel have been combined with academic courses, the activities of student organizations, or out-of-season competition for the University's athletic teams

Academic Facilities

The campus contains twenty-four buildings. A state-of-the-art 37,000-square-foot Science Center houses classrooms and laboratories for the natural sciences. Trexler Library contains more than 550,000 items, including 132,000 volumes and 40,000 electronic books, more than 12,000 electronic journals and newspapers, and 400,000 microfiche items. The periodical collection includes 550 paper and microform subscriptions. Collections of the other five independent colleges of the Lehigh Valley, totaling more than 1 million volumes, are available through an interlibrary loan system. The University maintains ten computing laboratories or classrooms.

The University recently opened a 77,000-square-foot academic building that houses the school's business division and health care majors. The Gambet Center for Business and Healthcare features a simulated trading room for business and finance majors, standardized patient areas, and a gross anatomy lab.

Costs

In 2012–13, full-time tuition was $29,000 per academic year. Other annual fees included a Student Center fee and a technology fee totaling $1,150. For students living on campus, room and board cost $10,970 per year.

Financial Aid

Nearly 90 percent of incoming students receive some form of financial aid. Students must complete the Free Application for Federal Student Aid and mail it to the processing center indicated on the form with DeSales University's Title IV code number, which is 003986, after January 1 of the student's senior year. The Office of Financial Aid processes requests for assistance on both a date priority and a financial need basis. The types and amounts of assistance a student will receive are specified in an award letter. The package also provides students and parents with a payment options letter, which outlines the three ways a student can finance the remaining cost of education. Parents may apply for a Federal Parent Loan for Undergraduate Students, students may apply for an alternative loan, or they may take advantage of a monthly billing plan.

All applicants are automatically considered for merit scholarships, which are awarded to incoming first-year students based upon academic achievement. Priority consideration is given to students who apply by December 1 of their senior year. Scholarships include Presidential Scholarships, which can award up to full tuition to students who earn a combined SAT score (math and critical reasoning sections) of at least 1350 (29 ACT) and rank in the top 5 percent of their high school class; Trustee Scholarships of $7,000 to $10,000 for students who achieve a combined SAT score (math and critical reasoning sections) of at least 1200 (27 ACT) and rank in the top 15 percent of their high school class; and DeSales Scholarships of $5,000 for students who achieve a combined SAT score (math and critical reasoning sections) of at least 1100 (24 ACT) and rank in the top 25 percent of their high school class. Department scholarships are awarded to students who attend scholarship day and demonstrate excellence in their field of study.

Faculty

There are 103 full-time faculty members teaching at the University. Eighty-five percent of the professors have a doctorate or the highest degree in their specialty. The average class size is 18 students, and the student-faculty ratio is 15:1. Students are assigned a faculty member from their chosen field of study to serve as an academic adviser; undeclared students are assigned to a faculty member who assists them in planning courses, deciding upon a major, and moving toward declaring a major.

Student Government

The Student Government Association is the liaison between the students and the administration. The Executive Board and each of the four undergraduate classes elect a president, vice president, secretary, and treasurer, for a total of 20 officers.

Admission Requirements

Admission is based on past academic achievement, particularly within a college-preparatory course of study, as well as the student's potential for future growth. Preferably, this includes four years of English; three to four years of college-preparatory mathematics; two years of modern, foreign, or classical language; and at least two laboratory science courses. Quality of academic performance is the single most important factor in the decision-making process.

Application and Information

DeSales University is a Common Application school and it uses a rolling admissions process; the University notifies applicants of their admission status within four weeks of receiving all application materials. To apply, students must submit a completed application, official high school or home school transcripts, official SAT or ACT scores, two letters of recommendation, and the $30 application fee. An on-campus interview is recommended but not required. For maximum consideration for scholarships, students are encouraged to apply by December 1.

Prospective students may direct their applications or requests for additional information to:

Admissions Office
DeSales University
2755 Station Avenue
Center Valley, Pennsylvania 18034-9568
Phone: 610-282-1100
E-mail: admiss@desales.edu
Website: http://www.desales.edu

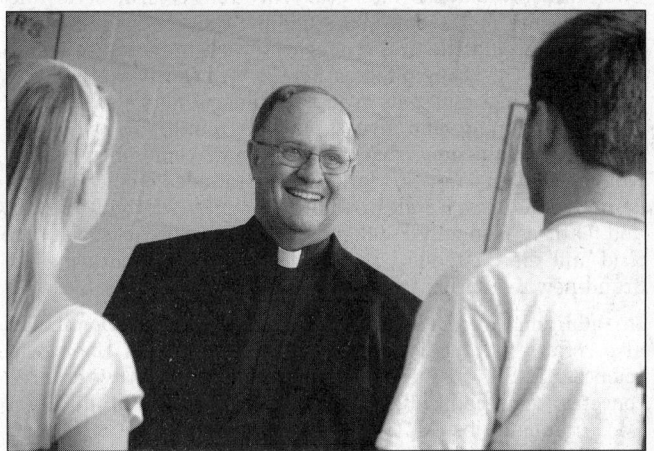

Fr. Bernard O'Connor, O.S.F.S., president of DeSales University, teaches a philosophy class every fall semester. Here, he mingles with students.

DOMINICAN UNIVERSITY OF CALIFORNIA
SAN RAFAEL, CALIFORNIA

DOMINICAN
UNIVERSITY
of CALIFORNIA
1890

The University

Dominican University of California is an independent, coeducational university of Catholic heritage in San Rafael, California, with an intimate 11:1 student-faculty ratio, more than 2,200 students (1,600 undergraduate and 600 graduate students), and over 357 full- and part-time faculty members. Dominican was founded in 1890 by the Dominican Sisters of San Rafael. The University enjoys a century-long reputation for excellence in scholarship, research, and community outreach. A central focus at Dominican is for undergraduate students and faculty members to actively connect with the community at large and develop the whole person bound in the spirit. Dominican helps to support the spiritual nature of all people on campus through its ministry. Several different religious faiths are represented at Dominican.

Dominican supports twelve intercollegiate teams that compete in the NCAA's Pacific Western Conference: men's and women's basketball, golf, cross-country, and soccer; men's lacrosse; and women's softball, tennis, and volleyball. In addition to being fierce competitors, Dominican's Penguins are dedicated student athletes. The school's teams have earned the Pacific West Conference Academic Achievement Award in each of the last three years.

In addition to academics, a large part of the college experience is the social aspect. Students at Dominican make their student life experiences ones to remember. Students can get involved in Student Government (ASDU), Campus Ministry, or other clubs and organizations on campus. After a fun activity, students head to their residence halls for some rest, the dining hall for a quick snack, the Conlan Recreation Center for a workout, or attend one of the many lectures Dominican hosts featuring prominent speakers.

Dominican's residence halls vary in architectural style and accommodate more than 600 students; there is a dining hall for resident students and others who wish to purchase meals on campus. The Conlan Recreation Center hosts basketball and volleyball games and seats over 1,000 fans. Conlan also features a weight-training and fitness room, a multipurpose room, lockers, athletic department offices, and conference rooms. Outside Conlan there is a lane pool surrounded by picturesque gardens. The John F. Allen Athletics Complex was built in 2012 and features Kennelly Field, a new multipurpose artificial turf field and the Castellucci Family Tennis Center, featuring six brand-new regulation tennis courts.

In addition to its undergraduate programs, Dominican also offers the following graduate programs: biological sciences (M.S.), business administration (M.B.A.) with three concentrations, counseling psychology (M.S., M.F.T.), education (M.S.), humanities (M.A.), clinical nurse leader (M.S.N.), and occupational therapy (M.S.O.T.).

Location

San Francisco, the mountains, the ocean—everything is within reach. Located in San Rafael, California, 12 miles north of the Golden Gate Bridge, Dominican's proximity to San Francisco offers students immediate access to a wide range of internship, service, employment, cultural, and recreational opportunities. In addition, Dominican's campus, located at the base of a mountain and a 10-minute drive to the beach, is a nature lover's dream.

Majors and Degrees

Dominican offers students twenty-four majors and twenty-three minors. There are four schools within the University: the School of Arts, Humanities, and Social Sciences; the School of Business and Leadership; the School of Education and Counseling Psychology; and the School of Health and Natural Sciences.

Undergraduate degrees (B.A., B.S., B.S.N., and B.F.A.) are awarded and every student has the opportunity to graduate in four academic years. There are several specialty degree programs offered at Dominican, as well as multiple academic honors societies and honors programs. Some of these include the B.F.A. in dance, a direct-entry nursing program, a five-year program leading to the Bachelor of Science in health science and the Master of Science in occupational therapy, the 4+1 M.B.A. program, and the Dual Degree/Dual Credential Program.

Academic Programs

The General Education Program offers exposure to the major areas of knowledge in the humanities, arts, and natural and social sciences. It is designed to provide a sequence of courses with a thematic focus that integrates the wisdom and perspectives of several disciplines. The focus assists students in discovering relationships between areas of knowledge, beliefs, cultures, and peoples that differ globally and historically, as well as in acquiring an awareness of tradition, a love of discovery, a respect for the diversity of the human condition, and a realization of human interdependence. Courses within the General Education Program also expose students to a variety of learning experiences, including discussion, lectures, seminars, simulations, practicums, and quiet reflection.

Dominican University of California's incoming first-year students spend their first year exploring the origins and evolution of the universe in an interactive, multidisciplinary course based on Big History. Throughout the year, students gain a greater understanding of today's issues by studying the many links between nature and humankind. Big History is an emerging academic discipline that provides a unifying overview of the 14-billion-year history of the universe, from the big bang to the present day. Big History synthesizes history, astronomy, chemistry, biology, geology, sociology, and other fields to provide a cohesive picture, to scale, of the history of the human race and its relationship to the planet.

Opportunities to Engage the World

Japan, Australia, Spain, Sweden, Indonesia, South Africa—the world is at Dominican students' fingertips. Fostering an appreciation of cultural diversity and global interdependence is a fundamental part of a Dominican education. The University encourages students to develop a rich understanding of different cultural perspectives and experiences, and there is no better way to do that than by spending time living, learning, and working in another country.

Dominican encourages students to study abroad for two reasons: personal growth and professional development. There is a growing demand, across industries and geographic locations, for professionals who are multilingual and multicultural. Studying abroad and learning a new language can give students the competitive edge that they will need once they graduate.

A hallmark of a Dominican education is the belief that the most important aspect of a quality education is the personal interaction between professor and student. A program of engaged learning builds on this premise, incorporating active, collaborative learning in the classroom with enriching educational experiences beyond the physical classroom. These high-impact practices actively engage students in the learning process, enhancing their experience with the content, making the interaction personal and memorable.

Engaged learning at Dominican includes study abroad, internships, leadership, undergraduate research programs, and service learning initiatives. These experiences are interwoven with Dominican's distinctive programs, offering students a multitude of outlets to better understand themselves and the world around them.

Costs

Undergraduate full-time tuition (12–17 units per semester) is $40,150 per year for the 2013–14 year. Fees are $450; room and board (a fourteen-meal-per-week plan) costs are approximately $13,000 for the year.

Financial Aid

Financial aid is awarded on the basis of need and merit. Merit awards are available for both first-year and transfer students based on academic achievement. Dominican participates in various federal and state need-based financial aid programs and also has its own financial aid funds available, donated by generous alumni and friends, to help meet University costs.

Need-based financial aid comes in the form of scholarships, grants, part-time employment, and loans. The federal and state financial aid programs are the Federal Supplemental Educational Opportunity Grant, Teacher Education Assistance for College and Higher Education (TEACH) Grant, Federal Pell Grant, Federal Work-Study Program, Federal Direct Stafford Student Loans, Federal Direct PLUS loans, and Cal Grants A and B. Eligibility for need-based aid is determined after the student, who must be a citizen or permanent resident of the United States, files the Free Application for Federal Student Aid (FAFSA). The need-based financial aid deadline for first-priority consideration is March 2, although late applications are accepted.

Faculty

Students find themselves intellectually challenged by the faculty members who hold degrees from colleges and universities throughout the world. The faculty is committed to individualized teaching and careful supervision of students' development. Seventy-three percent of Dominican's full-time faculty members hold doctorates or other terminal degrees. The student-faculty ratio is 11:1, ensuring students receive a highly personal education.

Student Government

The primary group that helps students plan and provide campus activities, distributes activity funds, initiates changes in policy, and represents themselves to the University's administration and the broader community is ASDU. This group of elected student representatives serves both as the student activities association and the student government board. The members of the ASDU Senate are representatives from all four class levels of regular day-program students.

Admission Requirements

Dominican University of California welcomes applications from prospective students of all ages, religions, races, and national origins. The University believes that academic potential is measured by more than grades alone. Each candidate for admission is given individual consideration and is evaluated by the Office of Admissions on the basis of the student's past scholastic record, present motivation, and potential intellectual development, as indicated by all of the admission materials submitted.

The application materials for first-year students include the following: a completed application; an official high school transcript to date; one letter of recommendation from a teacher, administrator, or counselor; scores from either the SAT or ACT; and a personal essay, as described in the application. Transfer students must submit a completed application and their high school transcript and official test scores if they have fewer than 24 transfer units. In addition, they must send official college transcripts to date; a personal essay as described in the application; proof of high school graduation; and one academic letter of recommendation or one professional letter of reference. Applications for admission are reviewed on a rolling basis; the sooner the student completes the application, the sooner the student will receive an admission decision. The priority deadline for the fall semester is February 1, and for the spring semester the deadline is November 1.

Application and Information

Students may apply online at the University's website (www.dominican.edu), or by using the Common Application. Students may also obtain admissions information by contacting:

Dominican University of California
Office of Admissions
50 Acacia Avenue
San Rafael, California 94901-2298
Phone: 415-485-3204
　　　　888-323-6763 (toll-free)
Fax: 415-485-3214
E-mail: enroll@dominican.edu
Website: dominican.edu

Students have described Dominican as "zen-like" and "gorgeous." Come see what they mean.

DOWLING COLLEGE
OAKDALE, NEW YORK

The College

Dowling College, on the South Shore of Long Island, is an independent, comprehensive institution in the liberal arts tradition that specializes in truly personalized education: small classes, teachers who focus on one-on-one and collaborative work with their students, hands-on learning, and career-oriented programs in the arts and sciences, aviation, business, and education. With nearly fifty years of experience, Dowling offers both residential and commuter students the opportunity to join a welcoming family of learners and to forge a pathway to future success.

Dowling believes that education is personal and that personal attention from committed, full-time faculty is the key to academic success. There are no lecture halls, and no classroom holds more than 35 students; average class size is 15, even for introductory classes. Every student has a full-time faculty adviser, and students and professors get to know each other personally. While all faculty members engage in research, Dowling's primary focus is on teaching and learning.

Learning, however, doesn't only take place in the classroom. Dowling's programs emphasize hands-on experience through internships, collaborative learning, and service programs with internship opportunities in companies throughout the New York metropolitan area. In addition, academic programs stress hands-on learning. Students majoring in earth sciences have travelled to Iceland to study volcanoes and glaciers, and have researched horseshoe crabs through CEECOM (The Center for Estuarine, Environmental and Coastal Oceans Monitoring). Students in communication arts write copy for TV channels that include Nickelodeon and others, and sport management students become marketing interns with local sports teams such as the New York Mets and the New York Islanders.

Location

Located on the beautiful South Shore of Long Island (just 50 minutes from Manhattan and minutes from ocean beaches), Dowling's main campus sits on the banks of the Connetquot River, which is on the lush grounds of the former summer mansion of William K. Vanderbilt. A spacious 105-acre second campus—with classrooms, residential dorms, aviation facilities, and athletic fields—is located 15 miles east of the main campus in Shirley, adjacent to Brookhaven Airport. Dowling offers free shuttle bus service between the campuses.

Majors and Degrees

Dowling offers forty undergraduate career-oriented degree programs in arts and sciences, aviation, business, and education, as well as twelve graduate degree programs (six M.B.A. programs, five M.S. programs in education and sport management, and a new M.S. in environmental microbiology), and two Ed.D. degrees in educational administration. In addition, the College offers advanced certificates (both in-class and online), for educators and business executives who want to expand their training.

Dowling is working to develop new, career-oriented majors and programs. New programs include the B.S. in criminal justice management, the B.A. in gerontology, and the B.S. in TESOL (teaching English to speakers of other languages). Future programs being considered include a B.S. in wine industry, to be created in cooperation with the Long Island Vineyards.

Dowling's School of Arts and Sciences offers majors in the arts and humanities, math and science, and social sciences. Dowling's vibrant creative writing program boasts its own student art/literary magazine, *Riverrun*, as well as writing and spoken word clubs, and a yearly writers' conference. Cutting-edge programs in graphic design and digital arts and communication arts offer internship components. Psychology, one of the College's most popular majors, offers fascinating courses that range from "Psychological Science Fiction in Film" to "Forensic Psychology and Law." In the STEM field, Dowling College prepares students for growing career sectors, as evidenced by the hands-on B.A. in earth science, the newly revised programs in math and computer science, a five-year joint B.A./M.B.A in chemistry and general management/leadership, and a new graduate degree in environmental microbiology.

Dowling College's School of Education is one of the largest teacher and administration preparation programs in New York, with more than 5,000 teachers working on Long Island having received their education degrees from Dowling College. Students interested in becoming teachers can obtain teaching certification in areas such as special education, literacy education, or early childhood education. For those seeking a career in sports or sports management, Dowling offers a popular B.S. in physical education and sport management.

Students enrolled in the Townsend School of Business develop the skills necessary to prepare them for the challenges in today's competitive marketplace. Dowling tailors its program to accommodate the working population, offering a completely online B.B.A. in management and leadership and M.B.A. degrees, both online and on weekends. *U.S. News and World Report* lists Dowling's online graduate business degree as one of the top online programs in the nation. Dowling's graduates become motivated entrepreneurs and executives, taking full advantage of the business opportunities and trends in today's business world.

The School of Aviation trains students for careers in air traffic control, aviation management, and commercial piloting. Dowling graduates are recruited by employers who know that the students have received a balanced liberal arts background, as well as experience with the industry's most advanced equipment. Situated at Brookhaven Airport, the School of Aviation offers extensive flying opportunities with close proximity to some of the world's most varied and demanding airspace.

Academic Programs

Dowling has recently revised its core curriculum to allow for enhanced student flexibility, moving toward a system of distribution requirements that allows major and minor courses to count toward the core, giving students many ways to broaden their academic horizons. Students choose a First Year Experience Seminar and a capstone Senior Seminar in subjects ranging from earthquakes to sport in world culture to veterans affairs, as well as courses that stress fundamental skills in writing and math. These classes ensure that students graduate with a solid grounding in the liberal arts, along with the skills that are essential for success.

Dowling also has a thriving honors program, with designated honors scholarships, for exceptional students who take special honors courses and perform community service.

Academic Facilities

With over $50 million invested in the campus infrastructure since 2000, Dowling's facilities are designed to enhance every student's learning experience.

One thing students will not find on campus is a single lecture hall; this helps create a more personal learning environment. Smart classrooms bring the curriculum to life with Internet access, digital projectors, and the Blackboard Learning System, which enables students to access and share documents from anywhere in the world. A new science laboratory, flight and air traffic control simulators, new classrooms, a newly converted Music House, and a newly redesigned library are just some of the exciting improvements around the Dowling College campus.

On-campus amenities include the Lion's Den student lounge, a convenient fitness center, and two cafeterias—with the Oakdale cafeteria overlooking the scenic Connetquot River.

Costs

Full-time undergraduate tuition is $25,324 for 24–34 credits, with fees of approximately $950. Graduate tuition is $980 per credit hour.

Housing costs range from $9,930 to $10,790 per year for dormitories in Oakdale or Brookhaven. Tuition for the distance-learning M.B.A. is $796 per credit hour. Doctoral program tuition is $52,000 for the full program. Tuition for the Saturday M.B.A. is $38,500 for the full program.

Financial Aid

There are numerous sources of financial aid available to help students achieve their goal of earning a degree from Dowling College. More than 75 percent of Dowling students receive some sort of financial aid to cover all or part of their educational costs. Numerous designated or endowed scholarships are available, including the Honors Scholarship, the Dowling College Faculty Scholarship, the Myrka Gonzalez and David Ochoa Latino Student Endowed Scholarship, and Presidential Endowed Scholarships. Dowling's goal is to bring its high-quality education within the financial reach of all its students.

Faculty

Dowling prides itself on the quality of its faculty and the personal one-on-one relationship between faculty and students. Over 95 percent of full-time faculty members hold a Ph.D. or the highest degree in their field. All classes at Dowling are taught by dedicated full-time faculty or exceptionally qualified adjunct faculty—not teaching assistants. Every faculty member serves as both instructor and mentor to his/her students, with all faculty serving as advisers, and many working one-on-one with their students.

Student Government and Organizations

Through the elected Student Government Association (SGA), students participate in self-government and promote student-run activities. With more than forty clubs and organizations, as well as frequent events and outings, Dowling offers a vibrant community for students. Fifteen highly competitive varsity teams compete in NCAA Division II at the beautiful state-of-the-art fields at the Brookhaven campus. Dowling's men's lacrosse team won the 2012 national championship and in 2012, the women's basketball team made it to the NCAA finals. In recent years, the Golden Lions have compiled an overall record of 178–98–6 in ECC-sponsored sports, earning regular season championships in volleyball, women's basketball, and women's lacrosse. Varsity teams include men's and women's basketball, cross-country, lacrosse, rowing, soccer, and tennis; men's baseball and golf; and women's volleyball and softball. Club sports include cheerleading, equestrian, and dance team.

There's always something happening at Dowling. Students can paddle one of the campus kayaks in front of historic Fortunoff Hall, take part in an intramural sport, or check out art exhibits at Dowling's Anthony Giordano Gallery.

Admission Requirements

Prospective students or applicants must provide evidence of a strong high school academic performance; SAT or ACT scores; and one or more letter(s) of recommendation from a high school or college guidance counselor, teacher, or school-based administrator. Dowling also accepts transfer students from both community and four-year colleges, allowing the transfer of up to 75 credits from a two-year college and up to 90 from a four-year college.

Application and Information

Dowling accepts students on a rolling basis but encourages early application (by March 1 for the fall semester and by December 15 for the spring semester). To ensure consideration for a wide range of scholarships, Dowling also encourages students to consider applying under its early action application program by submitting materials by December 31 (with a decision guaranteed by January 31).

The best way to discover Dowling is to experience it first-hand. Prospective students can meet with an enrollment counselor, sit in on a class, talk with a full-time faculty member in their proposed field of study, or schedule a tour of the College's historic Vanderbilt mansion at the Rudolph-Oakdale campus, or at the airport runways and athletic fields of the 105-acre Brookhaven Campus. Prospective students can call 631-244-1390 for application information or to schedule a visit. They are also invited to visit the College's website at www.dowling.edu, and to follow Dowling via Twitter or Facebook.

Office of Admission
Dowling College
150 Idle Hour Boulevard
Fortunoff Hall, Room 225
Oakdale, New York 11769
Phone: 631-244-3141
        800-369-5464 (toll-free)
Fax: 631-244-1078
E-mail: admissions@dowling.edu
Website: http://www.dowling.edu

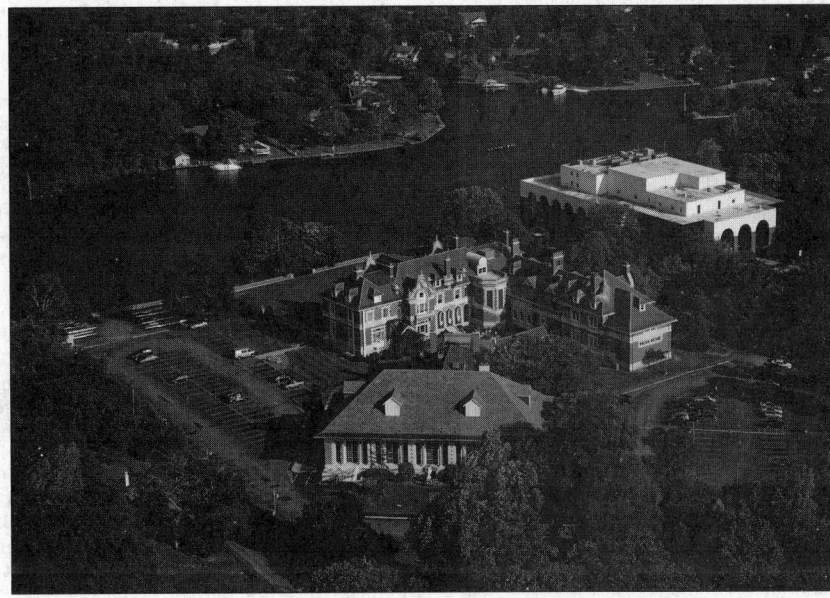

Aerial shot of Dowling College's Oakdale Campus.

DREXEL UNIVERSITY
PHILADELPHIA, PENNSYLVANIA

The University

Drexel University is a private, nonsectarian, coeducational university that has maintained a reputation for academic excellence since its founding in 1891. The University's technologically focused approach to learning prepares undergraduates for a variety of careers and graduate school. Full-time work experience through the cooperative education program is a vital part of a Drexel education. Students gain professional experience in jobs related to their career interests by alternating classroom study with periods of full-time employment. Last year's undergraduate enrollment numbered 12,750 full-time students representing forty-eight states and 116 other countries. International students compose about 13 percent of the undergraduate population. Drexel University grants associate, bachelor's, master's, and doctoral degrees and certificates in a variety of programs.

Nine residential halls house almost 4,000 students on campus. Both the Campus Activities Board (CAB) and Drexel's nearly thirty active fraternities and sororities sponsor events such as dances, lectures, excursions, community service projects, and free movie screenings. Students can also take part in a variety of extracurricular activities and over 300 student organizations, including musical groups, MAD Dragon Records, a radio station, a filmmaking society, dance troupes, theatrical productions, a cable TV station, a student-run newspaper, and communities of faith. Drexel offers eighteen Division I varsity athletic programs and competes in the Colonial Athletic Association Conference. The University also sponsors intramural and club sports.

Drexel is committed to expanding its already vast educational opportunities. In 2006, Drexel opened the Earle Mack School of Law, which earned full accreditation from the American Bar Association in 2011. In January 2009, Drexel opened Drexel University Sacramento, which offers a bachelor's completion program in Business Administration and graduate degrees in both online and traditional classroom formats. In addition, through a partnership with Burlington County College (BCC) in Mount Laurel, New Jersey, Drexel at BCC offers a satellite campus where transfer students from southern New Jersey can earn a bachelor's degree in certain programs.

Location

Drexel is located in the heart of Philadelphia, the nation's fifth-largest metropolitan area, and shares its University City neighborhood with the University of Pennsylvania and the University of the Sciences. With thousands of student residents, University City is a great place for students to spend their college years in an urban campus setting, surrounded by the amenities of the city and the diversity of their peers. Philadelphia is home to some of the nation's best historical and cultural attractions and offers the vibrant nightlife, choice restaurants, dynamic arts, and major league athletics of a first-class city. Drexel's location offers easy access to public transportation. The Drexel shuttle provides convenient, free transportation between campuses. Adjacent to Drexel's University City Campus, Amtrak's 30th Street Station is a hub for trains and buses to the Philadelphia suburbs, New York City, Washington, D.C., and beyond.

Majors and Degrees

Whatever their interests, students at Drexel are at the forefront of their fields. Drexel comprises thirteen colleges and schools that offer more than seventy undergraduate majors and over fifteen accelerated degree programs. Academic majors include accounting, animation and visual effects, anthropology, architectural engineering, architecture, behavioral health counseling, biological sciences, biomedical engineering, business and engineering, business for Still-Deciding Students®, chemical engineering, chemistry, civil engineering, communication, computer engineering, computer science, construction management, criminal justice, culinary arts, culinary science, custom-designed major, dance, design and merchandising, economics, electrical engineering, elementary education, engineering, engineering for Still-Deciding Students®, engineering technology, English, entertainment and arts management, entrepreneurship, environmental engineering, environmental science, environmental

studies, fashion design, film and video, finance, game art and production, general business, general humanities and social sciences for Still-Deciding Students®, graphic design, health services administration, history, hospitality management, information systems, information technology, interactive digital media, interior design, international area studies, international business, invasive cardiovascular technology, legal studies, management information systems, marketing, materials science and engineering, mathematics, mechanical engineering, media arts and design for Still-Deciding Students®, music industry, nursing, nutrition and foods, operations and supply chain management, pathway to health professions, philosophy, photography, physics, political science, product design, property management, psychology, radiologic technology, science for Still-Deciding Students®, screenwriting and playwriting, secondary education, sociology, software engineering, sport management, and television production and media management.

Drexel applicants can pursue an accelerated degree program, which allows students to earn more than one degree in a shortened period of time. Accelerated degree options include the B.A./B.S./J.D. in law; B.A./B.S./M.D. in medicine; B.S./D.P.T. in physical therapy; B.S./M.H.S. in physician assistant studies; B.S./M.P.H. in public health; B.S./M.B.A. programs in business, culinary arts, culinary science, design and merchandising, entertainment and arts management, hospitality management, information systems, information technology, and music industry; B.S./M.S. programs in accounting, biomedical engineering, communication, education, engineering, psychology, and majors within the iSchool; and B.A./B.S. in history/M.S. in library and information sciences.

Academic Programs

Qualified students can apply to the Pennoni Honors College, which is open to students in every academic discipline. The honors program offers special living communities designed for the exceptional student and opportunities for social activities, traveling, and independent projects. Specific classes for honors students and honors sections of general and required courses are available. Students who satisfy the program requirements qualify for Graduation with Distinction.

Drexel students have opportunities to conduct research. The STAR (Students Tackling Advanced Research) Scholars program invites qualified students to participate in faculty-mentored research projects in their chosen fields as early as the freshman year. Students who take part in research may be eligible for stipends or academic credit.

Off-Campus Programs

Classroom study is essential, but experience makes all the difference. Through Drexel Co-op, students have the opportunity to test-drive their degree in a professional setting by alternating periods of full-time work experience with periods of classroom study. Students can earn up to eighteen months of workplace experience before graduation in paid full-time positions with employers such as Fortune 500 companies, major pharmaceutical companies, and top design firms, as well as nonprofit agencies and government organizations. More than 1,200 employers in thirty-five states and thirty-five international locations participate in the Drexel Co-op program. The average six-month co-op salary is $16,063.

Drexel has an active study-abroad program in more than two dozen countries around the world that allows students from all majors to spend a term or several terms studying abroad, earning credit toward their degrees and gaining valuable international experience. Freshman Frontiers: First Term in Dublin, Drexel's newest option for studying abroad, is a selective program that enables students in qualifying majors to study at the Dublin Business School and School of Arts for the first term of their freshman year. With any Drexel-sponsored program, students pay Drexel tuition rates and receive financial aid while abroad.

Academic Facilities

Drexel has five campus locations: University City Campus, Center City Campus, Queen Lane Campus, Drexel University Sacramento, and Drexel at BCC. The University's library system comprises the W. W. Hagerty Library, the Library Learning Terrace, the Legal Research Center, and three health sciences libraries. The W. W. Hagerty Library, the University's central library located on the University City campus, maintains subscriptions to nearly 12,000 electronic journals, which are accessed via the library website, along with academic journals and 200 databases. Students may borrow laptops for use in the library. The Library Learning Terrace, a 3,000-square-foot flexible learning space located in a residence hall and staffed by librarians, enables students to learn and research collaboratively through a variety of technologies. The Legal Research Center on the third floor of the law school shares University databases while continuing to acquire new material. The additional libraries on the health sciences campuses provide study space, 75,000 books, and network access to the same set of online journals and databases.

The University is expanding through the addition of several new, state-of-the-art buildings. Opened in fall 2012, the URBN Center houses the Westphal College of Media Arts & Design and provides space for exhibitions, labs, studios, and a black box theater. The Papadakis Integrated Sciences Building, featuring North America's largest biowall, opened in 2011. This five-story, 130,000-square-foot building contains thirty-nine research and teaching laboratories used by the biological sciences. Millennium Hall is a seventeen-story, green-certified residence hall that opened in 2010 and serves as home to students in the Pennoni Honors College. The twelve-story, 177,500-square-foot LeBow College of Business building and the Chestnut Square complex, featuring mixed-use housing and retail, are currently under construction.

Costs

Cost of attendance at Drexel is determined by the co-op plan. Depending on the academic course of study, students can select the Three Co-op Option or the One Co-op Option. The Three Co-op Option includes three six-month periods of full-time employment and takes five years to complete. The One Co-op Option includes just one six-month period of full-time employment and takes four years to complete. The full-time undergraduate tuition for the 2012–13 academic year was $33,800 for the Three Co-op Option and $41,500 for the One Co-op Option. Costs for on-campus housing and the campus meal plan average around $14,000 per year. Fees are approximately $2,300 per year, depending on the degree program.

Financial Aid

Nearly 80 percent of freshmen applied for financial aid in the 2012–13 academic year. The average financial assistance package, including academic, athletic, or performing arts scholarships; grants; loans; part-time work-study employment; and federal programs, was $23,000. All incoming students are encouraged to submit the Free Application for Federal Student Aid (FAFSA) by February 15. Notification to students begins mid-March. Drexel offers an achievement-based award with an annual value of up to $27,000 to qualified incoming freshmen and transfer students. Criteria include a strong academic record and involvement in extracurricular and community service activities. The Drexel Liberty Scholarship also provides fifty full-tuition scholarships to low-income students who are Philadelphia residents and who attend Philadelphia high schools.

Faculty

Approximately 95 percent of Drexel's full-time faculty members hold a Ph.D. or the highest degree in their field. The University requires faculty members engaged in research and graduate-level teaching to also teach at the undergraduate level, allowing the undergraduate student to benefit from the research activities of the faculty. Specially selected faculty members serve as advisers for freshmen. The student-faculty ratio is 10:1.

Admission Requirements

All colleges within the University require completion of a college-preparatory program in high school that includes at least 3 years of mathematics and 1 year of laboratory science. Students applying to major in the sciences or business and engineering are required to take 4 years of mathematics (through trigonometry) and 2 years of laboratory science. Engineering requires 4 years of mathematics (through trigonometry and precalculus), chemistry, and physics. The quality of academic performance is more important than merely meeting minimum requirements. The strength of preparation is judged primarily by rank in class or relative grade point average, by

the degree of improvement in the quality of the academic record, and by the comments and recommendations from principals, guidance counselors, or teachers. Freshman applicants are required to take the SAT or the ACT. Students who were accepted and enrolled in the fall of 2012 had an average unweighted GPA of 3.6 on a 4.0 scale and an average SAT of 1226 out of 1600, including the math and critical reading sections. An essay or personal statement is required, the subject of which is dependent on the major and program. Transfer applicants must have a minimum 2.5 cumulative average (2.75 for biomedical engineering, business and engineering, engineering, information systems, and information technology; 2.8 for health sciences; 3.0 for nursing and biological sciences; and 3.2 for physics) for consideration and generally are expected to complete at least 24 credits at a regionally accredited four-year college or two-year community college in a program of study comparable to the one being sought at Drexel.

Application and Information

Applications are available online (http://www.drexel.edu/ugapp) or from the address listed below. The Common Application is accepted as well. Applications must be accompanied by a nonrefundable application fee of $75; however, the fee is waived for online applications or applications submitted during a campus visit. Students who are certain Drexel is their first-choice college may apply through the early decision process. Early decision applications are due November 15 and decisions are rendered by December 15. Students applying to the B.A./B.S./M.D or B.S./M.S. in psychology accelerated degree programs are not eligible to apply early decision. Early decision is binding; students admitted through the early decision process are required to confirm their intention to enroll by January 15. Applications for the B.A./B.S./M.D. accelerated degree program are also due November 15. Applications for regular full-time undergraduate status are due January 15, with admissions decisions rendered no later than April 1. Drexel subscribes to the College Board Candidates Reply Date of May 1. Transfer students should apply at least three months before the beginning of the term in which they wish to enroll.

Undergraduate Admissions
Drexel University
3141 Chestnut Street
Philadelphia, Pennsylvania 19104-2876
Phone: 215-895-2400
       800-2-DREXEL (toll-free)
Website: http://www.drexel.edu/admissions (admissions)
          http://www.drexel.edu/ugapp (application)
          http://www.facebook.com/drexeladmission (Facebook)
          http://twitter.com/DrexelAdmission (Twitter)

Ms. Joan McDonald
Senior Vice President of Enrollment Management
Drexel University
Phone: 800-2-DREXEL (toll-free)
Fax: 215-895-1285
E-mail: enroll@drexel.edu

Drexel's mascot, Mario the Dragon, facing Market Street and the Recreation Center.

D'YOUVILLE COLLEGE
BUFFALO, NEW YORK

The College

D'Youville College is a leading institution of higher learning for traditional and nontraditional undergraduate, master's, and doctoral level students from around the world. A significant number of the students come from Western New York and Canada. Students receive a well-rounded general education and specific training and experiences to improve the quality of life across the globe. D'Youville is a nurturing community that seeks to ensure the success of each student in diverse fields such as health care, education, and business. D'Youville offers the diversity and academic excellence of a large school, and the attention and sincerity of a small one.

D'Youville is a private, coeducational, liberal arts and professional college that has offered students an education of high quality since 1908. The College was the first in western New York to offer baccalaureate degrees to women. Its current enrollment is 3,200 men and women. Students may choose from thirty undergraduate and graduate degree programs that are enhanced by a 14:1 student-faculty ratio. The College is committed to helping its students to grow not only in academics but also in the social and personal areas of their college experience.

Students residing in Marguerite Hall or the new student apartment complex have a scenic view of the Niagara River and Lake Erie, which separate the U.S. and Canadian shorelines. The Koessler Administration Building, which once housed the entire college, now contains administrative offices, the chapel, Kavinoky Theatre, and the Learning Center. The Student Center, the focal point of leisure and extracurricular activities, has a new gymnasium, a swimming pool, fitness and wellness area, a training room, a dance studio, a general recreation center, and the main dining facilities. Student organizations and regularly scheduled activities, including intramural sports, NCAA Division III intercollegiate sports (baseball, basketball, crew, volleyball, golf, cross-country, soccer, and softball), a club hockey team, a ski club, the College newspaper, the yearbook, and social organizations, as well as academic programs, all help to make up an active campus life.

Location

D'Youville is situated on Buffalo's residential west side. The College is within minutes of many local attractions, including the downtown shopping center, the Kleinhans Music Hall, the Albright-Knox Art Gallery, two museums, and several theaters that offer stage productions. Seasonal changes in the area offer a variety of recreational opportunities. Buffalo is only 90 miles from Toronto and 25 minutes from Niagara Falls, making it a gateway to recreation areas in western New York and Ontario. Holiday Valley, a skier's paradise, is an hour's drive away. The city is served by the New York State Thruway, Amtrak, Greyhound and Trailways bus lines, and most major airlines.

D'Youville enjoys a diversified interchange with the community due to its affiliations with schools, hospitals, and social agencies in the area. College students in the Buffalo area number more than 60,000.

Majors and Degrees

D'Youville offers the degrees of Bachelor of Arts (B.A.), Bachelor of Science (B.S.), and Bachelor of Science in Nursing (B.S.N.). Majors include accounting, biology, business management, chemistry, chiropractic, dietetics, education (elementary, secondary, and special), English, exercise and sports studies, global studies, health services management, history, international business, liberal studies for education, mathematics, nursing, occupational therapy, pharmacy, philosophy, physical therapy, physician assistant studies, preprofessional studies (dental, law, medicine, and veterinary studies), psychology, and sociology. Five-year combined bachelor's/master's (B.S./M.S.) programs are offered in accounting (B.S)/international business (M.S.), dietetics, education, international business, occupational therapy, and physician assistant studies. A six-year B.S./D.P.T. program is offered in physical therapy. A seven-year B.S./D.C. program is offered in chiropractic studies. The Doctor of Pharmacy program began in 2010 with an early assurance program for prepharmacy students.

Academic Programs

The area of concentration recognizes individual differences and varying interests but still provides sufficient specialization in one discipline to form a foundation for graduate studies and professional careers. Students attending D'Youville are expected to complete the requirements of their chosen concentration while earning a minimum of 120 credit hours. Core requirements include humanities, 24 hours; social science, 12 hours; science, 7 hours; mathematics/computer science, 6 hours; and electives, 9 hours. A cumulative average of at least 2.0 must be maintained to meet graduation requirements. Sixteen credit hours, or five or six courses per semester, are considered a normal workload. Internships to meet specific career goals may be arranged in any major.

The College offers a Career Discovery Program that was purposely designed for the undecided student. This program, which can last for two years, offers credit courses and internships meeting two years of study in any major.

The academic year is composed of two semesters, each lasting approximately fifteen weeks. The first semester, including final examinations, ends before the Christmas holidays. During the eight-week summer sessions, programs of selected courses are given at all levels on a daily basis.

Off-Campus Programs

The baccalaureate program in nursing is affiliated with thirteen area hospitals and public health agencies. The education program is affiliated with local elementary, junior high, and secondary schools and with special education centers in the area for purposes of student teaching. The chiropractic, occupational therapy, physical therapy, and physician assistant programs are affiliated with appropriate clinical settings throughout the United States.

Academic Facilities

D'Youville's modern Montante Family Library offers state-of-the-art computer reference capabilities for both in-house and off-site users, including access to over seventy online databases. The multimillion-dollar Alt Health Science Building houses laboratories, including those for anatomy, organic chemistry, and gross anatomy; activity and daily living labs for the health professions; and additional laboratories for physics, chemistry, quantitative analysis, and computer science. It also houses classrooms, faculty member offices, and development centers, including one for career development. This is augmented by the modern Bauer Family Academic Center, which provides state-of-the-art classrooms, laboratories, and faculty offices.

Costs

For 2013–14, tuition is $11,480 per semester, and room and board cost $5,260 per semester. A general college fee of $230 is required and is based on credit hours taken; a Student Association fee of $40 per semester is applied toward concerts, yearbooks, activities, and guest lectures. A $100 deposit ($150 for dietetics, physician assistant studies, occupational therapy, and physical therapy programs), credited toward tuition, must be submitted by all candidates who accept an offer of admission.

Financial Aid

D'Youville attempts to provide financial aid for students who would not otherwise be able to attend. Determination of aid is based on the Free Application for Federal Student Aid. Aid is available in the form of grants, loans, and employment on campus. D'Youville automatically offers scholarships for academic achievement to all eligible incoming students.

All students may qualify for D'Youville's Academic Scholarship Program, which offers scholarships with total values up to $67,500. Students who apply, are accepted, and meet the criteria instantly qualify for one of these scholarships, all of which are renewable annually. These scholarships are not based on need. The three scholarship programs are the Honors Scholarship, the Academic Distinction Scholarship, and the Achievement Scholarship. The Honors Scholarship requires an 87 academic average, a minimum SAT score of 1100 (math and critical reading) or an ACT score of at least 24, and awards 50 percent of tuition and 25 percent of room and board costs. The Academic Distinction Scholarship requires SAT scores of at least 1000 (math and critical reading) or ACT scores of 21 to 23 and an academic average of at least 85. It awards 25 percent of tuition and 50 percent of room and board costs. The Achievement Scholarship criteria include SAT scores of 900 to 1090 (math and critical reading) or ACT scores of 19 to 23 and an academic average of 80 to 84. This scholarship awards $1,000–$5,000. The Transfer Honors Scholarship is based on a starting GPA of 2.75. This scholarship's award ranges from $1,000 to $5,000.

Faculty

The ratio of faculty members to students is 1:14. All members of the full-time instructional staff hold a doctorate or another advanced degree. Faculty members act as advisers and are available for consultation with students.

Student Government

The Student Association (SA), a representative form of student self-government, seeks to inspire in its members dedication to the intellectual, social, and moral ideals of the College and works closely with the administration and faculty. All students of D'Youville are considered members of the SA and may be elected to the executive council and the student senate. There are seventeen academic and social clubs affiliated with the SA.

Admission Requirements

An applicant must be a high school graduate or have a high school equivalency diploma before matriculating. The applicant should have a college-preparatory background, including required English and history courses and a sequence in either mathematics or science. Scores on the SAT or the ACT are also required for admission. High school advanced placement credit is acceptable and transferable. The admission decision is based on high school grade point average, rank in class, and scores on the SAT or ACT. Students who have difficulty meeting normal admission standards may be admitted with a reduced academic load.

The College Learning Center offers academic assistance to students whose education has been interrupted or has not prepared them adequately for college courses. The Tutor Bank, a system of peer tutoring, offers the assistance of qualified students to those who need help in specific academic disciplines.

Application and Information

D'Youville admits students on a rolling admission basis; therefore, applications are reviewed as they are received by the admissions office. Transfer students who have a quality point average of at least 2.0 are encouraged to apply by December 1 for the spring semester and by July 1 for the fall semester. A brochure listing course offerings and giving details about costs and room and board is available upon request.

Steve Smith
Director of Admissions
D'Youville College
One D'Youville Square
320 Porter Avenue
Buffalo, New York 14201-1084
Phone: 716-829-7600
      800-777-3921 (toll-free)
Fax: 716-829-7900
E-mail: admissions@dyc.edu
Website: http://www.dyc.edu
      http://www.dyc.edu/facebook
      http://www.dyc.edu/twitter

ELIZABETHTOWN COLLEGE
ELIZABETHTOWN, PENNSYLVANIA

The College

Founded in 1899, Elizabethtown College is a selective, private institution committed to the liberal arts and sciences and professional studies, with a motto of "Educate for service." Elizabethtown prepares its students for rich lives of purpose and meaning, while advancing independent thought, personal integrity, and social justice. Ninety-five percent of the members of the class of 2011 were employed or enrolled in graduate school within eight months of graduation.

The College is home to more than 1,900 traditional students from twenty-seven states and twenty-three countries. Eighty-eight percent of students live on the 200-acre campus in residence halls, senior town houses and apartments, and college-owned houses called student-directed learning communities. Wireless access is available in all campus buildings.

In addition to an active intramural and club sports program, Blue Jay Athletics fields ten NCAA Division III teams for men (baseball, basketball, cross-country, golf, lacrosse, soccer, swimming, tennis, track and field, and wrestling) and ten for women (basketball, cross-country, field hockey, lacrosse, soccer, softball, swimming, tennis, track and field, and volleyball).

The Center for Student Success offers academic advising, personal counseling, and health and wellness programming. Career Services provides students of all class years with professional and career development services. The Center for Student Involvement houses the following offices: Student Activities (OSA), International Student Services, Diversity, and Chaplain/Religious Life.

The campus offers four dining venues: a traditional dining space, a deli/quick-serve/convenience store, a coffee shop, and a late-night food truck. Recreational spaces and offerings include The Body Shop, Thompson Gymnasium, fitness classes, an outdoor track, a pool, and lots of paths and green space. Koon's Activity Venue is a multipurpose entertainment and educational space. Leffler Chapel and Performance Center features an 840-seat auditorium. The campus events calendar boasts more than 125 arts and cultural happenings each academic year, not including student-run programming from OSA and the 80+ campus clubs.

Elizabethtown holds accreditations from the Middle States Commission for Higher Education, American Chemical Society for Clinical Lab Services, National Association of Schools of Music, National Council on Social Work Education, Accreditation Council for Occupational Therapy Education, Association of Collegiate Business Schools and Programs, and the Accreditation Board for Engineering and Technology Inc.

In addition to its traditional undergraduate programs, Elizabethtown also offers a Master of Science degree in occupational therapy and, through its School of Continuing and Professional Studies, a Master of Business Administration.

Location

Elizabethtown borough is a community of 20,000 people located in historic Lancaster County in south-central Pennsylvania, within 20 minutes of Harrisburg (the state capital), Hershey, and Lancaster; 90 minutes from Philadelphia and Baltimore; and a few hours from New York and Washington, D.C. Elizabethtown is easily accessible by Amtrak train service from New York, Philadelphia, and Pittsburgh, and the Harrisburg International Airport is 15 minutes away.

Majors and Degrees

Bachelor of Arts degrees are awarded in communications, criminal justice, economics, engineering, English, fine arts, French, German, history, international business, Japanese, music, philosophy, political philosophy and legal studies, political science, psychology, religious studies, secondary education, social work, sociology-anthropology, Spanish, and theatre.

Bachelor of Science degrees are offered in accounting, actuarial science, biochemistry, biology, biotechnology, business administration, chemistry, computer engineering, computer science, elementary education, engineering, environmental science, forestry and environmental management, general science education, health and occupation, industrial engineering management, information systems, mathematics, physics, secondary education, social sciences, and social studies.

Bachelor of Music degrees are offered in music education and music therapy.

Elizabeth College offers more than ninety minors and concentrations, including Asian studies, as well as seven secondary education certification programs.

The College offers a variety of cooperative programs that allow qualified students to combine undergraduate studies with direct admission into graduate school. These include the Doctor of Physical Therapy programs at Thomas Jefferson University and Widener University, the Doctor of Osteopathic Medicine program at Philadelphia College of Osteopathic Medicine, Temple University's School of Dentistry, and the Master of Molecular Medicine program with Drexel University College of Medicine.

The Primary Care Pre-Admissions Program through the Pennsylvania State University College of Medicine at the Milton S. Hershey Medical Center provides options for Elizabethtown students who are Pennsylvania residents and are pursuing careers in internal medicine, family practice, and pediatrics.

The College also offers a Law Early Admissions program (LEAP) with Drexel University's Earle Mack School of Law and Widener University School of Law.

Academic Programs

An interdisciplinary first-year seminar and a strong core curriculum create a solid foundation for a student's chosen area of study. The core develops critical analysis and communication skills that ensure adaptability in the ever-changing global job market. Independent and directed studies, undergraduate research, and internships are available.

The Elizabethtown College Honors Program offers top students a highly selective program of study with the opportunity for a stipend to fund professional development, research, or travel-related study.

Called to Lead is a leadership-building program that helps students aspire to lead a purposeful life. Scholarship and Creative Arts Day, held each spring, gives students of all majors and class years the chance to showcase their research or creative works. The Center for Global Understanding and Peacemaking, Bowers Writers House, and The Young Center for Anabaptist and Pietist Studies offer various academic programming. The Momentum program, a pre-orientation program helps first-generation college students prepare for the academic expectations of Elizabethtown.

The College operates on a semester calendar. First-year students arrive in the last week of August, and examinations are given prior to the winter break. The spring semester begins in the middle of January and runs through early May. Students may earn credit toward graduation through Advanced Placement examinations, College-Level Examination Program tests, or tests administered by the individual departments.

Off-Campus Programs

Elizabethtown offers its students high-impact, real-world learning experiences, and guarantees the opportunity to pursue at least two of the following: undergraduate research, study abroad, community-based learning, and internships/fieldwork.

Students may study abroad for a semester in twenty-six different locations on six continents through the College's affiliate programs. Short-term academic study tours or service-learning trips are also available. The Center for Community and Civic Engagement offers numerous community-based learning experiences locally and beyond.

Academic Facilities

The High Library's four stories contain more than 250,000 volumes and an extensive collection of journals and other research materials, plus Wi-Fi; computers and printers; conference rooms; and private, individual, and group study areas. Librarians help students with research projects and teach classes in using library resources effectively.

The campus features numerous academic buildings, including the James B. Hoover Center for Business and The Masters Center for Science, Mathematics, and Engineering. The student center, Brossman Commons, is home to the Tempest Theatre and a dance studio, and Zug Memorial Hall houses a recital hall and private and group practice rooms. Steinman Center for Communications and Arts features a television studio and radio station. The College houses three art galleries and the Masters Mineral Gallery.

Elizabethtown is home to The Young Center for Anabaptist and Pietist Studies, a world-renowned research center focusing on the Amish and other similar religions. The S. Dale High Center for Family Business, a local research and resource center for family-owned businesses, often partners with academic departments for events and programs.

Costs

For 2013–14, tuition is $38,200 and room and board are $9,400, for a total comprehensive fee of $47,600. Students should also plan on an additional cost of about $2,000 for books, transportation, and personal expenses, for a total cost of $49,600. Financial aid is based on this figure.

Financial Aid

Elizabethtown College works with students and their families to make education affordable. Ninety-three percent of students receive some form of aid; packages are typically a combination of scholarships, grants, loans, and student employment. More than half of Elizabethtown's first-year students with the strongest academic credentials receive renewable merit-based scholarships, which are awarded on a competitive basis and without regard to need.

To apply for aid, students must file the Free Application for Federal Student Aid (FAFSA) and the Elizabethtown College need-based financial aid application. Students are assigned a personal financial aid counselor to help them throughout their years at the College. Elizabethtown's deadline for financial consideration is March 15.

Faculty

Elizabethtown has a teaching faculty of 131 full-time professors. The student-faculty ratio is 12:1. More than 90 percent of the full-time faculty members hold a Ph.D. or the highest earned degree in their field. In addition to being assigned a faculty adviser through the First-Year Seminar program, when students declare a major, they are also assigned a new faculty adviser within that department.

Student Government

Students play an active role in campus governance through the Student Senate, the Campus Residence Association, and other organizations. Members of the Student Senate are elected from each class to advocate for students, coordinate special events, and allocate funds for student activities and more than ninety student-run clubs and organizations. Students Working to Entertain E-town (S.W.E.E.T.) allocates funding for weekend programs, campus social activities, and entertainment for the College community.

Admission Requirements

Elizabethtown considers the right fit to be more than SAT scores and GPA; other factors considered at the College are academic fit, co-curricular fit, and social fit. Admissions decisions are made without regard to sex, sexual orientation, race, religion, physical handicap, or place of residence. On average, 60 percent of all applicants are accepted. The middle 50 percent of enrolled students scored between 1040 and 1240 on the critical reading and mathematics sections of the SAT, and 36 percent were in the top 10 percent of their high school class.

The College seeks diversity and students who display leadership abilities or special talents are considered highly desirable. Campus interviews are highly recommended but not required for most students, although the College reserves the right to require interviews in special cases. Applicants to the Honors Program and occupational therapy program are required to interview. Auditions are required for music students.

Early admission is available for highly qualified high school juniors.

Application and Information

The College operates on a rolling admission basis—applications are processed as they are received—and the application deadline is March 1. Students can apply using the Common Application or online at the College's website. Applicants must submit a high school transcript, first-quarter grades, SAT or ACT scores, two letters of recommendation, and a personal statement, essay, or graded paper. Early application is strongly recommended. Accepted students should notify the College of their decision to attend by May 1; matriculation after that date is on a space-available basis. Students who are interested in the Elizabethtown College Honors Program must submit a completed application by January 15.

For more information, students should contact:

Debra Murray
Director of Admissions
Elizabethtown College
One Alpha Drive
Elizabethtown, Pennsylvania 17022-2298
Phone: 717-361-1400
Fax: 717-361-1365
E-mail: admissions@etown.edu
Website: http://www.etown.edu

Elizabethtown College, home to about 1,900 students, offers more than fifty majors and more than ninety minors and concentrations.

ELMIRA COLLEGE
ELMIRA, NEW YORK

The College

Elmira College is a small, private, coeducational college that is recognized for its emphasis on education of high quality in the liberal arts and preprofessional programs. One of the oldest colleges in the United States, Elmira was founded in 1855. The College has always produced graduates interested in both community service and successful careers. Friendliness, personal attention, strong college spirit, and support for learning beyond the classroom help to make Elmira a unique community. Elmira College is one of only 270 colleges in the nation to be granted a chapter of the prestigious Phi Beta Kappa honor society.

The full-time undergraduate enrollment is about 1,200 men and women. The students at Elmira represent more than thirty-five states, primarily those in the Northeast, with the highest representation coming from New York, New Jersey, Massachusetts, Connecticut, Maine, and Pennsylvania. International students from thirty-one countries were enrolled in 2012. Ninety-seven percent of the full-time undergraduates live in College residence halls, and dormitory rooms are equipped to provide direct access to the Internet. Wireless access is also available in classrooms and common areas, as well as other hot spots campuswide.

The intercollegiate sports program includes men's and women's basketball, golf, ice hockey, lacrosse, soccer, and tennis and women's cheerleading, field hockey, softball, and volleyball. Baseball and women's cross-country will be added in the Fall of 2014. Intramural programs are also available. Emerson Hall houses the student fitness center, a pool, and a gym capable of seating 1,000, as well as the Gibson Theatre, which has a state-of-the-art sound and lighting system. Professional societies; clubs; music, dance, and drama groups; a student-operated FM radio station; and the student newspaper, yearbook, and literary magazine also provide numerous opportunities for extracurricular activity.

Location

Elmira College is located in the city of Elmira, which has a population of 35,000, in the Finger Lakes region of New York. The campus is a 10-minute walk from downtown Elmira. The relationship between the College and the local community is excellent, and numerous community activities and facilities are open to students, including the Elmira Symphony and Choral Society, the Elmira Little Theatre, clubs and civic groups, museums, movies, and a performing arts center. Excellent recreational areas are available in upstate New York and nearby Pennsylvania.

Majors and Degrees

Elmira College offers programs leading to the bachelor's degree in more than thirty-five majors, including accounting, American studies, art, art education, biology, biology-chemistry, business administration, chemistry, classical studies, clinical laboratory science, criminal justice, economics, childhood and adolescent education, English literature, environmental studies, French, history, human services, individualized studies, international business, international studies, mathematics, music, nursing, philosophy and religion, political science, psychology, public affairs, social studies, sociology and anthropology, Spanish, speech and hearing, and theater. Secondary teaching certification is offered in several areas. 4-1 M.B.A. programs are available at Alfred University, Clarkson University, Rochester Institute of Technology, and Union College. Army and Air Force ROTC are available through respective units at Cornell University.

Preprofessional preparation is offered in education, medical technology, nursing, and speech pathology and audiology. Faculty advisers assist those who seek preparation for graduate study in dentistry, law, or medicine in choosing appropriate course work. Nearly 50 percent of Elmira graduates pursue graduate study.

Academic Programs

The College's calendar is composed of two 12-week terms followed by a six-week term in the spring. Students enroll for four subjects during the twelve-week terms, completing the first term by mid-December and the second during the first week of April. Term III, the six-week term, running from mid-April through May, may be devoted to a particular project involving travel, internship, research, or independent study. Students are required to participate in internships in order to gain practical and meaningful experience related to their program of study. Credit is awarded for these experiences. Forty percent of Elmira College students study abroad at least once during their four years of study.

Special opportunities for outstanding students include participation in thirteen national honorary societies on campus and a chance to assist faculty members in research. The College also offers an accelerated three-year graduation option for outstanding students, and an Advanced Placement Program is available.

Army ROTC and Air Force ROTC are available.

Off-Campus Programs

Through the study-abroad programs, students may study in the United Kingdom, France, Spain, and Japan, as well as in other countries throughout Europe and Asia. Students from Elmira may spend Term III studying marine and island ecology or doing sociological research on the island of San Salvador in the Bahamas. The six-week Term III permits students in any major to study abroad, and students are able to participate in this program starting in their freshman year. Students have the opportunity to spend their junior year abroad studying for either one term or three years in any foreign country.

Academic Facilities

The Elmira campus offers exceptional academic facilities in a beautiful setting. The modern Gannett-Tripp Library houses more than 391,000 volumes, receives 2,500 periodicals, and includes a special Mark Twain collection room and photography and audiovisual facilities.

The College Computer Center offers four PC and Apple Macintosh microcomputer labs for student use.

A Center for Mark Twain Studies has been established at Quarry Farm, the author's summer home, which is located only a few miles from campus. The College also operates a Speech and Hearing Clinic on campus, which serves the public and provides valuable clinical experience for undergraduate students. Excellent facilities for drama and music are available.

Costs

Tuition for 2013–14 is $36,600, room is $6,300, board is $5,500, and fees are $1,550.

Financial Aid

Financial aid is available for both freshmen and transfer students. Awards are based upon the Free Application for Federal Student Aid (FAFSA) as well as the student's past academic performance. Types of aid include grants, scholarships, loans, and work opportunities. Sources of aid include college, federal, state, and private dollars. In addition, superior students may qualify for non-need-based Elmira College Honors Scholarships, which are available to both freshmen and transfer students and range from $13,000 to $26,000, with full-tuition scholarships available to Valedictorians and Salutatorians of graduating high school classes. Scholarships are renewable throughout 4 years of study at EC. About 97 percent of students receive merit or need-based financial aid from the College.

Faculty

Members of the faculty are chosen for their ability in and dedication to teaching. All full-time faculty members serve as advisers. Currently, the full-time faculty consists of 10 full professors, 28 associate professors, 30 assistant professors, and 12 instructors. One hundred percent of the full-time faculty hold the Ph.D. or highest degree necessary to teach undergraduate students in their field.

Student Government

Student government, an important part of the educational system at Elmira College, prepares students for active and responsible citizenship in society. Student government organizations include the Student Senate, the Judicial Board, and the Student Activities Board.

Admission Requirements

The Office of Admissions at Elmira College uses a rolling admission system. Each applicant is evaluated individually on the basis of his or her total application, including academic record, rank in class, SAT or ACT scores, essay, activities, letters of recommendation, and goals. The College strongly advises a personal interview. The recommendations of teachers and guidance counselors are also important. Special consideration is given to applicants from distant states and other countries, applicants with special skills, and applicants who are prepared to become actively involved in the campus community.

Elmira has two early decision programs available to students.

Application and Information

For further information, applicants should contact:

Director of Admissions
Elmira College
Elmira, New York 14901
United States
Phone: 800-935-6472 (toll-free)
E-mail: admissions@elmira.edu
Web site: http://www.elmira.edu.

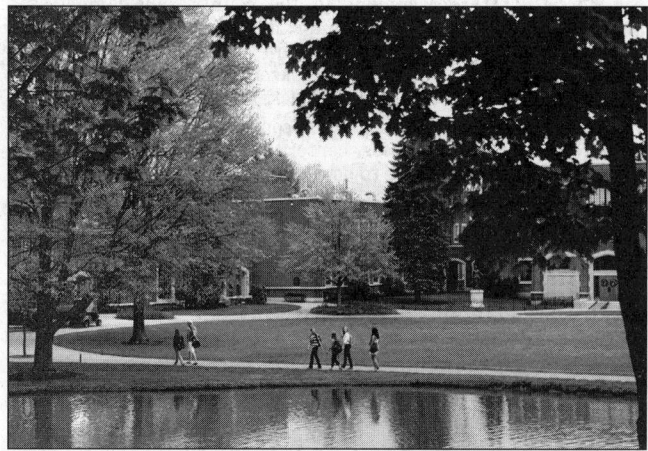

Elmira College: share in a tradition that changes lives.

EMBRY-RIDDLE AERONAUTICAL UNIVERSITY

DAYTONA BEACH, FLORIDA

The University

Embry-Riddle Aeronautical University's reputation as the leader in aviation and aerospace education is recognized worldwide. The University's history and legacy date back almost to the time of the Wright brothers, and in 2009 the University introduced the nation's first and only Ph.D. program in aviation. Embry-Riddle is an independent, nonsectarian, not-for-profit, coeducational university serving culturally diverse students seeking careers in aviation, aerospace, engineering, business, and related fields. Residential campuses in Daytona Beach, Florida, and Prescott, Arizona, provide education in a traditional setting, while the worldwide campus provides instruction through more than 150 centers in the United States, Europe, Canada, and the Middle East and through online learning.

Approximately 4,500 undergraduate students and 500 graduate students are currently enrolled at the 185-acre Daytona Beach residential campus. Students come from all fifty states, and nearly 100 countries are represented, making Embry-Riddle a truly international university.

Currently twenty-five undergraduate degree programs, nine graduate programs, and three doctoral programs are offered at the Daytona Beach campus. Embry-Riddle's premier aeronautical science (professional pilot) program and award-winning aerospace engineering program are the largest on campus and among the largest of their type in the nation.

Embry-Riddle conducts applied research and is leading the development of the Next Generation Air Transportation System along with the Federal Aviation Administration, Lockheed Martin, Boeing, and other high-tech organizations. Student research projects include development of green technologies like Embry-Riddle's EcoCar and the world's first-of-its-kind hybrid aircraft. Alumni are leaders in every facet of the aviation and aerospace industries and serve as a strong network and resource for students.

Students at the Daytona Beach campus enjoy a wide array of activities and clubs, many focused on aviation and aerospace, as well as fraternities, sororities, and recreational opportunities. Forty-three percent of students live on campus.

Embry-Riddle's award-winning precision flight demonstration teams offer students the opportunity to compete nationally in air and ground events. Embry-Riddle also has the largest all-volunteer Air Force ROTC detachment in the country and among the fastest-growing Navy ROTC units and Army ROTC battalions. Embry-Riddle athletes compete in the NAIA as well as intramural sports, including baseball, basketball, crew, cross-country, golf, soccer, tennis, track, volleyball, and ice hockey. The 68,000-square-foot ICI Center contains two full-size NCAA basketball courts, a fitness center, and a weight room. The ICI Center provides a place to host sporting events and assemblies. The University sports complex also includes a two soccer fields, the Sliwa Stadium ballpark, the Ambassador William Crotty Tennis Center, and the Track and Field Complex. The Tine Davis Fitness Center is adjacent to the pool and features comprehensive fitness services and wellness programs. Recent expansions to athletic facilities include a softball complex for the newest athletic offering in women's fast-pitch softball, as well as two artificial turf fields for intramural competition.

The 5,300-square-foot interfaith chapel accommodates the variety of faiths represented by the student body of Embry-Riddle. It consists of a 140-seat nondenominational worship area and four prayer rooms (Catholic, Jewish, Muslim, and Protestant).

Location

The year-round clear flying weather and the resort communities surrounding Embry-Riddle's residential campus in Daytona Beach, Florida, offer students an excellent environment in which to study, fly, and enjoy recreational activities. The campus, which is located adjacent to the Daytona Beach International Airport, is only 3 miles from what is called the world's most famous beach. The high-technology industries located in nearby Orlando provide the University with an outstanding support base. In addition, the Kennedy Space Center is less than a 2-hour drive from campus.

Majors and Degrees

The Daytona Beach campus of Embry-Riddle awards undergraduate degrees at the baccalaureate and associate level. Bachelor of Science degrees are offered in a variety of areas, each with a focus on the aviation and aerospace industries. The newest major in unmanned aircraft systems science (open only to U.S. citizens) combines Embry-Riddle's expertise in flight, air traffic management, safety and engineering. The College of Engineering offers majors in aerospace engineering, civil engineering, computer engineering, electrical engineering, mechanical engineering, and software engineering. All engineering programs, including Engineering Physics, are ABET accredited. Students who are interested in business administration may elect to major in management or air transportation. The College of Aviation awards degrees in aeronautical science (professional piloting), air traffic management, applied meteorology, aviation maintenance science, and safety science. Other majors include interdisciplinary studies (design your own major), communication, computational mathematics, homeland security, human factors psychology, and space physics. Students entering Embry-Riddle with an undecided major have the opportunity to explore a variety of academic pursuits before making a commitment to a specific track.

Academic Programs

Even a field as specialized as aviation requires a broad educational background. General education courses required of all students who are pursuing a baccalaureate program include communication skills, such as English composition, literature, and technical report writing; humanities; social sciences; mathematics; physical science; economics; and computer science. To ensure academic success, Embry-Riddle provides free tutorial services.

The academic year is divided into two semesters of fifteen weeks each, with the summer session divided into two terms. The average course load for each fall or spring semester is 15 credit hours.

Study abroad offers students the opportunity to better understand the global nature of the aviation and aerospace industries. Cooperative education adds value to the educational experience and allows students to gain real-world career skills.

Academic Facilities

The College of Aviation building at the Daytona Beach campus provides an unsurpassed environment for aviation education and research. The multimillion-dollar simulation laboratories duplicate the components and functions in the national airspace system, including capabilities to replicate actual weather reporting, airports, airways, air traffic control, flow control, and pilot and aircraft performance as found in the national air transportation system. Flight instruction is provided in the Embry-Riddle fleet of sixty-plus aircraft and a wide array of flight training devices. Aircraft are equipped with Automatic Dependent Surveillance-Broadcast (ADS-B) technology that decreases hazards associated with traffic, weather, and terrain. The High-Altitude Normobaric Lab allows students to experience the symptoms of high-altitude hypoxia to better enable them to recognize and recover from this threat. Embry-Riddle is the first university in the nation to acquire this technology.

The Advanced Flight Simulation Center gives Embry-Riddle students the opportunity to train in world-class simulators. The center, with more than 20,000 square feet of space and four high bays, currently houses two advanced aviation training devices (AATDs), eight Cessna 172S NAVIIIs (Skyhawk), two Diamond DA42 TAE Twin Stars, two Diamond DA42 L360s, and one Canadair Regional Jet (CRJ-200). These devices duplicate the actual cockpit, adverse weather conditions, a full range of emergency situations, and virtually any flight pattern and complement flight training done in actual aircraft. Flight simulation enables students to learn aircraft performance, experience aerodynamic effects, and perform flight maneuvers immediately and without risk. Qualified to Level 6, the University's devices faithfully reproduce Embry-Riddle's fleet of single-engine and multiengine aircraft and are equipped with 220-degree panoramic visual theaters. In addition, the Aviation Building houses air traffic control and tower simulators, one motion-based disorientation trainer, and six basic aviation training devices (BATDs).

The James Hagedorn Aviation Complex, completed in the fall of 2011, includes 96,000 square feet in a three-building facility and is home to flight training operations, aircraft maintenance training, and a fleet maintenance hangar. The Emil Buehler Aviation Maintenance Science building's cutting-edge labs dedicated to aircraft systems, turbine engines, metallic and composite materials, and avionics electronics prepare students to become maintenance professionals. The facility includes classrooms, a licensed engine-repair station, a machine shop, offices, and a third-floor observation deck overlooking the flight line and Daytona Beach International Airport runways.

The facilities in the Lehman Engineering and Technology Center serve academic departments including Human Factors and Systems, Engineering Physics and Space Physics, Mathematics and Computer Science, and all the engineering disciplines. Labs include the atmospheric physics research lab, flight dynamics and simulation lab, materials testing lab, structures lab, aerospace composites lab, real time lab, aerospace engineering and design lab, wind tunnels, airport noise abatement lab, electronic communications and microwave lab, microcomputer and digital lab, circuits and power lab, electricity and magnetism thermo lab, human factors research lab, and many more. Students use the labs to work in teams to develop hands-on projects. Research is conducted by faculty members and graduate and undergraduate students.

The 18,500-square-foot Capt. Willie Miller Instructional Center, a lecture auditorium and classroom complex, provides space for large audience events, including presentations by distinguished lecturers and speakers.

The College of Business academic building features the aviation operations simulation lab, which is used to develop and evaluate aviation/airline operational strategies and processes. In addition, the College's Teaching Airport, a partnership between Embry-Riddle and Daytona Beach International Airport, is focused on teaching, research, and public outreach.

The Jack R. Hunt Memorial Library is a 49,000-square-foot facility with a seating capacity of 800. The library houses more than 230,000 volumes and book titles, and more than 340,000 items of microfiche, periodicals, documents, newspapers, and media programs. Among the library's resources is a historical aviation collection donated by the Manufacturers Aircraft Association (MAA) in 1976. This collection includes a continuous run of *Aviation Week & Space Technology* dating from 1916 to the present and a complete set of *Jane's All the World's Aircraft* dating from 1909 to the present. The library provides rapid interlibrary loan service and wireless access points as well as computer terminals for research.

Costs

For the 2012–13 academic year, tuition and fees were $15,360 per semester. Flight fees are charged in addition to tuition. On-campus room and board costs were approximately $4,700 per semester. Personal expenses, books, and fees are in addition to the above. Costs are subject to change.

Financial Aid

Applicants for financial aid are required to complete the Department of Education's Free Application for Federal Student Aid (FAFSA) and any other documents requested by the University. Students are encouraged to apply early if they wish to be considered for all types of programs. Florida residents may also apply for several additional programs that are available through the state. All applicants are automatically reviewed for merit scholarship eligibility.

Faculty

The faculty members provide an excellent balance of professional experience and academic achievement. There is also a healthy balance between maturity and youth among the faculty. Faculty members who teach in the specialized and major programs have had professional experience in their areas of instruction. The student-faculty ratio is 16:1, and the average class size is 25. The primary concern of each faculty member is personalized teaching in classrooms and laboratories, on the flight line, and in student advising.

Student Government

The University places great emphasis on student self-government. The Student Government Association supports publication of the weekly newspaper and oversees the Touch 'n Go Office that organizes campus entertainment and broadcast of the student radio station, Eagles FM. In addition, the president of the Student Government Association is a voting member of the University's Board of Trustees.

Admission Requirements

Admission is open to any qualified applicant, regardless of creed, sex, race, national origin, handicap, or geographical location. Admission decisions are based on high school grades and course load, college courses attempted, SAT or ACT scores, and letters of recommendation. Embry-Riddle encourages every student to visit the campus before making the decision to attend the University.

Transfer students are required to submit transcripts from all colleges and universities attended. High school transcripts are not required if the student has earned 30 college credits or more.

Application and Information

Embry-Riddle requires each applicant to submit an application form and fee, SAT or ACT scores, two letters of recommendation, and an official high school/college transcript. Flight students must provide an FAA Class I or Class II medical certificate. When a student is accepted for admission, tuition and housing deposits are required by May 1. Embry-Riddle operates on a rolling admissions basis and admission decisions are rendered throughout the year.

University Admissions
Embry-Riddle Aeronautical University
P.O. Box 11767
Daytona Beach, Florida 32120-1767
Phone: 386-226-6100
      800-862-2416 (toll-free nationwide)
E-mail: dbadmit@erau.edu
Website: http://www.erau.edu/db
      http://twitter.com/ERAUniv
      http://www.youtube.com/EmbryRiddleUniv

Embry-Riddle Aeronautical University's Daytona Beach, Florida, campus.

EMERSON COLLEGE
BOSTON, MASSACHUSETTS

1 8 8 0

The College

Founded in 1880, Emerson is one of the premier colleges in the United States for the study of communication and the arts. Students may choose from more than two-dozen undergraduate and graduate programs supported by state-of-the-art facilities and a nationally renowned faculty. The campus is home to WERS-FM, the oldest noncommercial radio station in Boston; the historic 1,200-seat Cutler Majestic Theatre; and *Ploughshares,* the award-winning literary journal for new writing.

A pioneer in the fields of communication and performing arts, Emerson was one of the first colleges in the nation to establish a program in children's theater (1919), an undergraduate program in broadcasting (1937), professional-level training in speech pathology and audiology (1935), educational FM radio (1949), closed-circuit television (1955), and a B.F.A. degree program in film as early as 1972. In 1980, the College created the country's first graduate program in professional writing and publishing.

Today, Emerson's more than 3,400 undergraduate and 800 graduate students come from across the United States and more than forty countries. Approximately 1,900 students live on campus, some in special learning communities, such as the Writers' Block and Digital Culture Floor. All of the College's residence halls are air conditioned with cable television and Internet access. Wireless service is available in several campus locations. There is a fitness center, athletic field, and a brand-new facility that houses two theaters, multiple rehearsal spaces, a professional sound stage, and a fully functional scene shop.

Emerson College is fully accredited by the New England Association of Schools and Colleges.

In addition to its undergraduate programs, Emerson College offers ten master's degree programs for its graduate students.

Location

With dozens of institutions of higher learning, Boston is considered one of the country's best-known college towns. The city contains a wealth of diversions ranging from scenic harbor cruises and Boston Pops concerts to baseball's Fenway Park and the legendary Boston Marathon. Emerson's campus is located on Boston Common in the heart of the city's Theater District—within sight of the Massachusetts State House and walking distance from the historic Freedom Trail, Boston Public Garden, Chinatown, Financial District, and numerous restaurants and museums. Boston is also an international city with more than thirty foreign consulates, a busy international airport, and several multinational corporations.

Majors and Degrees

Emerson confers Bachelor of Arts, Bachelor of Fine Arts, and Bachelor of Science degrees. Students can major in acting; communication disorders; communication studies; marketing communications; media production (animation and motion media, digital postproduction, film, interactive media, sound design, studio television production, writing for film and television); media studies; musical theater; political communication: leadership, politics, and social advocacy; journalism; stage and production management; theater design/technology; theater education; theater studies; and writing, literature, and publishing. Popular minors include business studies and entrepreneurship. Interdisciplinary and self-designed majors, as well as an honors program, are available through the College's Institute for Liberal Arts and Interdisciplinary Studies.

Academic Programs

Emerson's academic calendar consists of two fifteen-week semesters, plus two six-week sessions during the summer months. The requirements for graduation combine general education and liberal arts courses with advanced, specialized classes that are specific to individual departments and majors. Internships for academic credit are available in almost every major and the Institute for Liberal Arts and Interdisciplinary Studies offers exciting first-year seminars, independent study options, and innovative courses that cut across academic disciplines.

Off-Campus Programs

Internships are popular with Emerson students. Hundreds of placements exist throughout Boston and in major cities across the country, including the College's Los Angeles Center—a residential study and internship program in the heart of the world's entertainment capital.

Emerson also sponsors a semester-long study program in Washington, D.C., the Netherlands, and China. In addition, there is a summer film program in Prague and course cross-registration with the six-member Boston ProArts Consortium, whose members include the Berklee College of Music, the Boston Conservatory, Boston Architectural Center, Emerson, the School of the Museum of Fine Arts, and Massachusetts College of Art.

Academic Facilities

Emerson possesses the highest quality visual and media arts equipment, including sound-treated television studios, digital editing labs, audio postproduction suites with analog and digital peripherals, industry-standard software, and a professional marketing-research suite/focus room. In fact, more than half of Emerson's campus has been built new or completely refurbished since 2002. There are two radio stations, an on-campus clinic to observe speech and hearing therapy, and an integrated digital newsroom for aspiring journalists. The eleven-story Tufte Performance and Production Center houses expanded performance and rehearsal space, a theater design/technology center, makeup lab, and costume shop.

Emerson's Iwasaki Library houses more than 175,000 volumes and serial subscriptions, 11,000 microforms, 9,000 audio/visual materials, and 30,000 e-books. The library's Web pages are designed to serve as a gateway for research and can be accessed from the library's workstations, computers located throughout the campus, and dormitory rooms or off-campus apartments, using a student account. Emerson students can also access the resources of a dozen cooperating libraries through the College's membership in the Fenway Library Consortium.

Costs

The basic direct expenses related to attending Emerson College for the 2013–14 academic year are $35,072 for tuition and fees, and $14,516 for double room and board. Approximately $3,700 should be allotted for books and supplies, health insurance, and personal expenses, including travel.

Financial Aid

Each year, more than two thirds of Emerson's student body receives some form of financial assistance, packaged in awards that typically combine grant and scholarship, loan, and College work-study. Academic scholarships ranging from $10,000 to half-tuition are awarded on a limited basis to students who meet high academic standards. Special performance-based scholarships are available up to $14,000 to exceptional students in the performing arts.

In order to apply for financial assistance, students must complete the Free Application for Federal Student Assistance (FAFSA) and CSS PROFILE form. Deadlines are March 1 for September admission or November 15 for January admission. More information about financial assistance at Emerson can be found online at http://www.emerson.edu/financial-aid or by contacting the Student Service Center at 617-824-8655 or finaid@emerson.edu.

Faculty

With a student-teacher ratio of 13:1, students at Emerson develop close relationships with remarkably talented and active instructors. Faculty members are nationally recognized and award-winning authors, directors, producers, consultants, playwrights, and editors. The vast majority of the faculty members have earned doctorates or the highest degree obtainable in their field.

Student Government

Emerson has more than eighty student organizations and performance groups, fourteen NCAA intercollegiate teams, and several student publications and honor societies. The Student Government Association, in cooperation with the Office of Student Affairs staff, plans and executes student activities, allocates and supervises funding for clubs, and serves as a liaison between the student body and the College administration.

Admission Requirements

Emerson accepts the Common Application and Application Supplement. Students whose interests and abilities are compatible with the College's specialty in communication and the arts are welcome to apply. Admission is competitive. Each year, more than 8,000 applications are received for a class of around 850. Selection is based on academic promise as indicated by secondary school performance, recommendations, writing competency, and SAT or ACT scores (or TOEFL if English is not the first language). The College also considers personal qualities as seen in extracurricular activities, community involvement, and demonstrated leadership.

The academic preparation for successful candidates should include 4 years of English and 3 years each of mathematics, science, social science, and a single foreign language. Candidates for programs offered by the Department of Performing Arts are asked to fulfill additional requirements (a theatrical resume and one of the following: audition, interview, portfolio, or essay) found on a dedicated website, http://stagedoor.emerson.edu. Applicants for the film program must submit a sample of creative work: either a five-to-ten page script or 5–7 minute video.

Application and Information

First-year candidates for September admission should file their application by January 5. Early action applications are due November 1. The regular admission deadline for January admission is November 1.

Transfer students should submit their applications and supporting credentials by March 15 for September admission or November 1 for January admission.

Office of Undergraduate Admission
Emerson College
120 Boylston Street
Boston, Massachusetts 02116-4624
Phone: 617-824-8600
Fax: 617-824-8609
E-mail: admission@emerson.edu
Website: http://www.emerson.edu
http://www.facebook.com/emersoncollege
http://www.twitter.com/emersoncollege

Emerson College: Bringing innovation to communication and the arts.

EVANGEL UNIVERSITY
SPRINGFIELD, MISSOURI

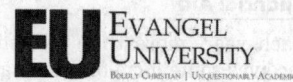

The University

Boldly Christian • Unquestionably Academic

Evangel University is one of the top Christian universities in the country. With ten academic departments, the University offers more than 100 undergraduate academic programs and nine master's degree programs. Evangel is a residential university, drawing more than 2,100 students from all fifty states and many foreign countries.

Through Evangel's Adult Studies Program, accelerated degree-completion programs are available for working adults. In addition, master's degrees are offered in education, counseling, psychology, music, and organizational leadership.

As the national university of arts, sciences, and professions of the Assemblies of God, Evangel trains young people for leadership positions in business, government, church, and home.

The Evangel campus is more than just buildings. It is a network of classmates who become lifelong friends as well as staff and faculty members who become mentors. The Activities Board, made up of members of the student body, presents activities throughout the year to create lifelong memories. Highlights include Harvest Fest, Spring Fling, homecoming events, and end-of-the-year banquets. Intramural athletic teams are a great outlet for stress relief after class and provide a chance to meet people from across campus. Residence halls encourage healthy relationships by providing hall-wide and individual floor activities. Roommates and hall mates become more than friends; they become family.

Evangel students may choose to be members of the marching band, a rare opportunity for a Christian college campus. Opportunities also abound for involvement in campus theatrical productions and musicals.

Evangel is part of the Heart of America Athletic Conference and has intercollegiate sports teams for men in football, basketball, baseball, track and field, cross-country, and golf. There is also club-level soccer for men. Women can participate in volleyball, basketball, softball, track and field, cross-country, and tennis.

Crusader athletes are also actively involved in outreach through the athletic ministries program. Formed in 2009, T.E.A.M. (The Evangel Athletics Ministry) gives athletes the opportunity to serve local agencies and experience short-term international ministry trips. T.E.A.M. gives student athletes the chance to blend a passion for their sports with a passion for serving others.

Athletes plan and organize the T.E.A.M. trips with their teams and coaches. Trips often include competitions against local teams, educational experiences, service projects, team-building activities, and exciting cultural excursions. Students often return from their trips with renewed focus on their relationships with God and with others. They have a deeper appreciation for their experiences in the United States and are more aware of the depth and meaning of their calling and their Evangel academic and athletic career.

At Evangel, students' spiritual growth is encouraged through chapel services, biblical teaching, and a wide range of service opportunities on campus and in the community. Residence hall directors, the campus pastor, professors, and staff members are all available to lend a listening ear or provide direction as students progress through the formative years of young adulthood. Friends are there to encourage and inspire one another. Doctrine is not dictated, but one's beliefs are strengthened, supported, and clarified through the community of faith at Evangel.

Evangel graduates enjoy great acceptance in the marketplace and graduate schools throughout the United States and abroad. Recent graduates have secured positions in all areas of the workforce—from classrooms to Top 5 accounting firms. Some have made the choice to matriculate at prestigious universities, from Cambridge to Yale to the Washington University School of Medicine.

The value of a Christian college education is evidenced in the lives of more than 24,000 alumni who are serving around the world. These alumni include such prominent people as renowned cardiothoracic surgeon and artificial heart pioneer Dr. James Long; acclaimed singer/songwriter and author Sara Groves; *New York Times* best-selling author Beverly Lewis; the Honorable Sam Der-Yeghiayan, U.S. federal judge for the Northern District of Illinois; Bob Ferguson, Vice President, Global Cadillac at General Motors; Steve Poppen, Vice President of Finance of the NFL's Minnesota Vikings; Don Zimmerman, Senior Vice President/Chief Information Officer, Wendy's/Arby's Group, Inc.; Phil Stanton, founding member of "Blue Man Group;" Dr. Barry Corey, President of Biola University in La Mirada, California; and Darin Stahl, Special Agent, U.S. Secret Service.

Location

Evangel is located at the heart of one of the fastest-growing—yet safest and cleanest—cities in the nation. Rated one of the Top 10 Places to Live and Work by *Employment Review* magazine and "Missouri's #1 Sports town" by *Sports Illustrated,* Springfield is a medium-sized city with abundant job opportunities, as well as hotels, shopping, coffeehouses, restaurants, and many churches. It is also only an hour away from the lakes and entertainment of Branson, Missouri.

Majors and Degrees

There are more than 100 academic programs available at Evangel University through ten academic departments. They offer Bachelor of Arts (B.A.), Bachelor of Fine Arts (B.F.A.), Bachelor of Business Administration (B.B.A.), Bachelor of Music (B.M.), Bachelor of Science (B.S.), and Bachelor of Social Work (B.S.W.) degrees.

The **Behavioral Sciences Department** offers majors in criminal justice, psychology (5-year B.S./M.S.), psychology (traditional), and social work.

The **Business Department** offers majors in accounting, business education, finance, management, marketing, and nonprofit business and social enterprise.

The **Communication Department** offers majors in advertising and public relations, broadcasting, communication studies, digital arts, film, journalism, and political communication.

The **Education Department** offers majors in art education (K–12), biology education, business education, chemistry education, early childhood education, elementary education, English education, mathematics education, middle school education, music education, physical education, Spanish education, and theatre/speech education.

The **Humanities Department** offers majors in art (graphic design), art (studio track), art education (K–12), English, English education, Spanish, Spanish education (K–12), theatre, theatre/music, and theatre/speech education.

The **Kinesiology Department** offers majors in athletic training, exercise science, physical education (K–12), and recreation and sport management.

The **Music Department** offers majors in music (B.A.), music industry (recording technology or music business), music (worship leadership), music education (K–12), and music performance.

The **Science and Technology Department** offers majors in biological chemistry, biology, biology education, chemistry, chemistry education, computer information systems, computer science, environmental science, health-care/nursing, mathematics, mathematics education, and medical technology. Pre-professional programs (taken as a biology, chemistry, biological chemistry, or mathematics major) are available in chiropractic studies, dentistry, engineering, medicine, occupational therapy, optometry, pharmacy, physical therapy, physician assistant, and veterinary science.

The **Social Sciences Department** offers majors in government (political science), history, international studies, public administration, social science, and social studies education. A pre-professional program in legal studies (pre-law and paralegal) is available for government majors.

The **Theology Department** offers majors in biblical languages, biblical studies, and intercultural studies (missions).

For further details, visit www.evangel.edu/academics/undergraduate/programs-list/.

Accreditation

The University holds accreditation, not only with the Higher Learning Commission (North Central Association of Colleges and Schools), but also with the National Council for Accreditation of Teacher Education, National Association of Schools of Music, and the Council on Social Work Education. Evangel also is in candidacy status for accreditation with the Accreditation Council for Business Schools and Programs (ACBSP).

Off-Campus Programs

Learning at Evangel is not limited to the classroom. Each year, hundreds of students travel throughout the United States and abroad with music groups, service teams, or study-abroad programs. During the past 28 years, the concert choir and concert orchestra have both toured in the 48 contiguous states, Canada, the Bahamas, and 15 countries in Europe. In addition, the concert choir has performed for 2 U.S. presidents and has been honored with four solo performances at Carnegie Hall.

Academic Facilities

The University recently completed an extensive campus development program, with nine major construction projects since 1997, including two 3-story academic buildings, a student fitness center, the state-of-the-art Barnett Fine Arts Center, and Riggs Hall, the new administration building.

When Evangel University was founded, its leaders demonstrated their commitment to academic achievement by building the Klaude Kendrick Library as the first permanent structure on campus. The building was completed in 1963. This commitment to research and scholarship has remained a priority as the University continually seeks to improve library services and adopt electronic and technological resources. Evangel students have access to a wide variety of innovative library and media services, as well as assistance from a committed staff of trained library professionals who are committed to students' academic success.

Faculty

Professors are committed to teaching from a biblical worldview. The integration of faith, learning, and life has been the focus of the institution since its formation in 1955. The student-teacher ratio is 15:1, which allows for individualized attention for students and provides for a rich, academic experience where faculty members often serve as mentors and form lifelong bonds with their students.

Costs

As one of the most affordable Christian universities in the nation, Evangel is committed to providing the best possible academic experience at a reasonable cost. For the 2013–14 academic year, the estimated cost per semester is $13,415. This includes tuition (12–18 credits), $9,460; room and board (double-room occupancy and 19-meal plan), $3,455; and additional fees.

Financial Aid

Evangel University not only strives for academic excellence, but it also strives to keep costs low. In addition, approximately 90 percent of Evangel students receive financial aid. The University offers a wide variety of scholarships and grants designed to help students finance their education at EU. For more information, students should visit www.evangel.edu/financial/scholarships/.

Admissions Requirements

As a committed Christian campus devoted to the highest standard of academic excellence, Evangel University is guided by a set of admissions requirements meant to provide the best spiritual and academic environment for its students. General requirements include the following:

- **Faith**—As a boldly Christian university, all students must make a profession of faith in Jesus Christ as their personal Lord and Savior.
- **Diploma**—Graduation from high school, or having the equivalent of a high school diploma such as the General Education Development (GED) examination
- **Core Subjects**—A minimum 2.0 GPA in core college-prep classes (English, math, social sciences and science with a lab)
- **Grade Average**—A minimum "C" average (Students with a weak academic record may be considered; however to remain at Evangel, students must meet academic standards.)
- **Standardized Tests**—ACT or SAT test scores should be reported to the University.

For more information, prospective students should go online to www.evangel.edu/admissions/requirements/.

Application Information

Evangel does everything it can to make a prospective student's admissions process a fun and exciting experience. EU Visits are premier visit opportunities that occur almost every Friday, offering tracks for both parents and prospective students. To schedule a visit to EU's campus, visit www.evangel.edu/admissions/campus-visits/.

Applications are available online at www.evangel.edu/admissions/apply-online/.

Evangel University has a rolling deadline. The application process opens September 1 for the following academic year, and the application fee is waived online from September 1 to November 15.

For more information, prospective students should contact:

Office of Enrollment Management
Riggs Hall, Suite 203
Evangel University
1111 N. Glenstone Avenue
Springfield, Missouri 65802
Phone: 417-865- 2811 Ext. 7346
E-mail: admissions@evangel.edu
Website: www.evangel.edu

Evangel University is a private, Christian university of arts, sciences, and professions. With an enrollment of more than 2,000 students from all 50 states and abroad, Evangel offers more than 100 undergraduate academic programs and nine master's degree programs.

FASHION INSTITUTE OF TECHNOLOGY
State University of New York
NEW YORK, NEW YORK

Fashion Institute of Technology
State University of New York

The College

The Fashion Institute of Technology (FIT) is New York City's celebrated urban college for creative and business talent. A State University of New York (SUNY) college of art and design, business, and technology, FIT is a dynamic mix of innovative achievers, original thinkers, and industry pioneers, with over forty programs of study leading to the Associate of Arts (A.A.S.), Bachelor of Fine Arts (B.F.A.), and Bachelor of Science (B.S.) degrees. The School of Graduate Studies offers seven programs leading to a Master of Arts (M.A.), Master of Fine Arts (M.F.A.), or Master of Professional Studies (M.P.S.) degree. FIT is accredited by the Middle States Association of Colleges and Schools, National Association of Schools of Art and Design, and Council for Interior Design Accreditation. FIT serves approximately 10,000 students from the greater metropolitan area, New York State, across the country, and around the world, offering full- and part-time study options, evening/weekend degree programs, and online studies.

The college provides a singular approach to higher education—blending a real-world-based curriculum and hands-on instruction with a rigorous liberal arts foundation, marrying design and business, supporting individual creativity in a collaborative environment, and encouraging faculty members to match teaching expertise with professional experience. FIT's mission is to produce well-rounded graduates prepared for career success: doers and thinkers who become the next generation of business pacesetters and creative icons. It offers a complete college experience with a vibrant student and residential life.

FIT's four residence halls house 2,300 students in fully furnished traditional and suite-style accommodations with a full meal plan option. Residential counselors and student staff members live in the residence halls, helping students adjust to college life and New York City.

The college is home to more than seventy student organizations, including academic societies, athletic teams, major-related organizations, and special-interest clubs. Student-run publications include a campus newspaper, a literary and art magazine, and the FIT yearbook.

FIT has intercollegiate teams in cross-country, half marathon, track and field, table tennis, tennis, soccer, swimming and diving, and volleyball. Athletics and Recreation offers students a full array of group fitness classes, including aerobics, dance, spin, and yoga at no extra cost. Students can also work out on their own in a 5,000-square-foot fitness center. Open gym activities allow students to participate in both team and individual sports.

The David Dubinsky Student Center houses student lounges, a game room, a full-service dining hall and café, a student radio station, a student-run boutique, student government and club offices, health services, gyms, a dance studio, a fitness center, a counseling center, disability services, studios, and laboratories.

Location

Occupying an entire block in Manhattan's Chelsea neighborhood, FIT's campus places students at the heart of the fashion, advertising, visual arts, design, business, and communications industries. Students gain unparalleled exposure to their field through internships, field trips, and professional connections. A wide range of cultural and entertainment options—from dining to galleries to theater—are available within walking distance of the campus, which also offers convenient access to subway and bus lines and major rail and bus transportation hubs.

Majors and Degrees

FIT offers sixteen Associate in Applied Science (A.A.S.) and twenty-five baccalaureate programs. All first-time students complete a two-year A.A.S. program in their major area of study and then typically continue in a related, two-year Bachelor of Fine Arts (B.F.A.) or Bachelor of Science (B.S.) program. Some students choose to begin their careers after earning the A.A.S., which qualifies them for entry-level positions in their chosen field. All programs include a required liberal arts component. In addition, FIT has a variety of liberal arts minors that students may elect to complete.

The School of Art and Design offers eleven A.A.S. and thirteen B.F.A. programs, the Jay and Patty Baker School of Business and Technology offers four A.A.S. and ten B.S. programs, and the School of Liberal Arts offers one A.A.S. and two B.S. programs and sixteen minors.

The sixteen A.A.S. programs, all of which provide the foundation for one or more corresponding baccalaureate-level programs, are accessories design*, advertising and marketing communications*, communication design foundation*, fashion design*, fashion merchandising management* (with an online option), filmmaking, fine arts, illustration, interior design, jewelry design*, menswear, photography, production management: fashion and related industries, textile development and marketing*, textile/surface design*, and visual presentation and exhibition design. Programs with an * are also available as a one-year option for students with acceptable transferable credits, and the one-year fashion merchandising management A.A.S. program is offered fully online.

The thirteen B.F.A. programs are accessories design, advertising design, computer animation and interactive media, fabric styling, fashion design (specializations in children's wear, intimate apparel, knitwear, special occasion, and sportswear), fine arts, graphic design, illustration, interior design, packaging design, photography and the digital image, textile/surface design, and toy design.

The twelve B.S. programs are advertising and marketing communications, art history and museum professions, cosmetics and fragrance marketing, direct and interactive marketing, entrepreneurship for the fashion and design industries, fashion merchandising management, film and media, home products development, international trade and marketing for the fashion industries, production management: fashion and related industries, technical design, and textile development and marketing.

FIT offers nine degree programs available through evening/weekend study that include advertising and marketing communications (A.A.S. and B.S.), communication design foundation (A.A.S.), fashion design (A.A.S.), fashion merchandising management (A.A.S. and B.S.), graphic design (B.F.A.), illustration (B.F.A.), and international trade and marketing for the fashion industries (B.S.). The international trade and marketing degree (B.S.) is also available fully online.

Academic Programs

Each undergraduate program includes a core of traditional liberal arts courses. The School of Liberal Arts offers FIT students the opportunity to minor in a variety of liberal arts areas in two forms: traditional subject-based minors and interdisciplinary minors unique to the FIT liberal arts curriculum. Selected minors include film and media, economics, English literature, international politics, psychology, Latin American studies, and sustainability.

The Career and Internship Center offers lifetime placement services to graduates. Internships are a required element of most programs and are available to all students. Nearly one third of FIT student interns are offered employment on completion of their internships.

The Presidential Scholars honors program, available to academically exceptional students in all disciplines, offers special liberal arts courses, projects, colloquiums, extracurricular activities, and off-campus visits designed to broaden horizons and stimulate discourse. Presidential Scholars are also awarded priority course registration and an annual merit stipend.

Precollege programs (Saturday Live, Sunday Live, and Summer Live) are available to middle and high school students during the fall, spring, and summer. More than 100 courses provide the chance to learn in an innovative environment, to develop art and design portfolios, to explore the business and technological sides of a wide range of creative careers, and to discover natural talents and abilities.

The School of Continuing Education and Professional Studies provides evening and weekend credit and noncredit classes to students and working professionals who want to pursue a degree or certificate or further their knowledge and in a particular area, as well as a wide range of classes for high school students on weekends and in the summer.

Off-Campus Programs

FIT has two campuses in Italy—one in Milan, one in Florence—where students study fashion design or fashion merchandising management and gain firsthand experience in the dynamics of European fashion. The study-abroad experience allows students to immerse themselves in diverse cultures and prepares them to live and work in a global community. Australia, China, England, France, and Mexico are some of the other countries where FIT offers study-abroad courses. Students can study abroad during the winter or summer sessions, or for a semester or a full academic year.

Academic Facilities

FIT provides its students with an urban campus of classrooms, laboratories, and studios that reflect the most advanced educational and professional practices. The Fred P. Pomerantz Art and Design Center houses studios, a printmaking room, display and exhibit design rooms, a model-making workshop, and a graphics printing service bureau. The Peter G. Scotese Computer-Aided Design and Communications Facility allows students to explore the latest advancements in technology and their integration in design, photography, and computer graphics and animation. The fragrance studio, a professionally equipped fragrance development laboratory, is the only one of its kind on a U.S. college campus. Cutting and sewing laboratories offer the most advanced design and cutting machinery among educational facilities in the United States. The lighting laboratory, an educational and professional development facility, features more than 400 commercially available lighting fixtures. Other college facilities include a broadcasting studio, knitting and weaving labs, a multimedia foreign language laboratory, forty-six computer labs containing nearly 1,200 Mac and PC workstations, and several additional labs with computers reserved for students in specific programs.

The Museum at FIT is New York City's only museum dedicated to fashion. Students, designers, and historians use it for research and inspiration. The museum, which is accredited by the American Alliance of Museums, operates year-round, and its exhibitions are free and open to the public. The Gladys Marcus Library provides more than 300,000 volumes of print, nonprint, and electronic materials. The newspaper and periodicals collection includes 500 current subscriptions. Online resources include more than 90 searchable databases. The library also offers specialized resources, such as clipping files, fashion and trend forecasting services, and sketch collections.

Also on campus are three multimedia venues—the Katie Murphy Amphitheatre, the Morris W. and Fannie B. Haft Auditorium, and the John E. Reeves Great Hall—used for student presentations, industry panels, conferences, and special events.

Costs

For 2012–13, the associate-level tuition per semester was $2,100 for in-state residents and $6,300 for nonresidents. Baccalaureate-level tuition per semester was $2,884 for in-state residents and $7,715 for nonresidents. Housing costs ranged from $6,119 to $6,299 per semester for traditional residence hall accommodations with mandatory meal plan and from $5,241 to $9,521 for apartment-style accommodations. Meal plans varied from $1,643 to $2,105 per semester. Textbook costs and other nominal fees, such as locker rental or laboratory use, vary per program. Costs are subject to change.

Financial Aid

FIT attempts to remove financial barriers to college entrance by providing scholarships, grants, loans, and work-study employment for students in financial need. Over two-thirds of full-time, matriculated students who complete the federal financial aid application process receive some type of assistance through loans and/or grants. The college directly administers its own institutional grants and scholarships, which are provided by the FIT Foundation.

College-administered federal funding includes Federal Pell Grants, Federal Perkins Loans, Federal Supplemental Educational Opportunity Grants, Federal Work-Study, and Federal Family Educational Loans, which include student and parent loans. New York State residents who meet state guidelines for eligibility may also receive Tuition Assistance Program (TAP) and/or Educational Opportunity Program (EOP) grants. Financial aid applicants must file the Free Application for Federal Student Aid (FAFSA), through which they apply for the Federal Pell Grant. Students are also encouraged to apply for all available outside sources of aid. Additional documentation may be requested by the Financial Aid Office. Applications for financial aid should be completed prior to February 15 for fall admission or prior to November 1 for spring admission.

Faculty

FIT's faculty is drawn from top professionals who bring their experience to the classroom and introduce students to the real-world opportunities and challenges of their disciplines through field trips, guest lectures, and sponsored competitions. Academic departments consult with industry advisory boards in their fields, ensuring that the curriculum and classroom technology reflect evolving industry practice. Student-instructor interaction is encouraged, with a maximum class size of 25, and courses are structured to foster participation, independent thinking, and self-expression.

Student Government

The Student Council, the governing body of the FIT Student Association, gives all students the privileges and responsibilities of citizens in a self-governing college community. Many faculty committees include student representatives, and the president of the student government sits on FIT's Board of Trustees.

Admission Requirements

Applicants for admission must be either candidates for or recipients of a high school diploma or a General Educational Development (GED) certificate. Admission is based on strength and performance in college-preparatory course work and the student essay. A portfolio evaluation is required for art and design majors. Specific portfolio requirements are explained on FIT's website. SAT and ACT scores are required for placement in math and English classes and for students applying to the Presidential Scholars honors program. International applicants whose native language is not English must submit scores from TOEFL or IELTS examinations.

Transfer students must submit official transcripts for admission and credit evaluation. Students may qualify for the one-year A.A.S. option if they hold a baccalaureate degree from an accredited college or if they have a minimum of 30 transferable credits from an accredited college, including 24 credits that are equivalent to FIT's liberal arts requirements, and at least one semester of physical education.

Students seeking admission to a B.F.A. or B.S. program must hold an A.A.S. degree from FIT or an equivalent degree from an accredited and approved college. They must also meet the appropriate prerequisites for the specific major and must have completed FIT's liberal arts requirements. Further requirements may include an individual interview with a department committee, review of academic standing, and a portfolio review (for applicants to B.F.A. programs). Any student who applies for transfer to FIT from a four-year program must have completed a minimum of 60 credits, including the requisite art or technical courses and the liberal arts requirements.

Application and Information

Students wishing to visit FIT are encouraged to attend a group information session and take a tour of FIT's campus. The visit schedule is available online at fitnyc.edu/visitfit. A virtual tour of the campus can be found online at fitnyc.edu/virtualtour. Interested candidates may apply online at fitnyc.edu/admissions.

For more information, students should contact:

Admissions
Fashion Institute of Technology
227 West 27th Street, Room C139
New York, NY 10001-5992
Phone: 212-217-3760
      800-GO-TO-FIT (toll-free)
E-mail: fitinfo@fitnyc.edu
Website: http://www.fitnyc.edu
      http://www.facebook.com/FashionInstituteofTechnology

FIDM/FASHION INSTITUTE OF DESIGN & MERCHANDISING
LOS ANGELES, CALIFORNIA

The Institute

FIDM/Fashion Institute of Design & Merchandising provides a dynamic and exciting community of learning in the fashion, interior design, digital arts, and entertainment industries. Students can launch into one of thousands of exciting careers in as little as two years. FIDM offers two-year and four-year degree programs— Bachelor of Science, Associate of Arts (A.A.), A.A. Professional Designation, and A.A. Advanced Study.

FIDM offers a highly focused education that prepares students for the professional world. Students can choose from twenty-two specialized creative business and design majors.

Established in 1969, FIDM is a private college that is proud to enroll more than 7,500 students a year and has graduated nearly 50,000 students. Graduates are automatically granted a free membership in the Alumni Association, which keeps them well connected while providing up-to-the-minute alumni news and information. FIDM alumni chapters can be found in thirty-five locations around the United States, Europe, and Asia.

Career planning and job placement are among the most important services offered by the college. Career assistance includes job search techniques, preparation for employment interviews, resume preparation, virtual portfolios, and job adjustment assistance. FIDM's full-time Career Center department and advisors partner one-on-one with current students and graduates to help them move forward on their career path, within their chosen major. Employers post over 19,000 jobs a year on FIDM's alumni job search site, which is available 24/7 exclusively to FIDM students and graduates. FIDM Career Advisors connect students to internships and directly to people in the industry. FIDM also offers Job Fairs, Open Portfolio Days, and networking days to allow students to meet alumni and industry leaders face-to-face. Because of the college's long-standing industry relationships, many firms come to FIDM first to recruit its students. Over 90 percent of FIDM Graduates in all majors are successfully employed in their field of study within six months of graduation. Some of FIDM's successful graduates include celebrity designers Nick Verreos, Monique Lhuillier, and the co-founder of Juicy Couture, as well as Hollywood costume designer Marlene Stewart.

FIDM's ethnically and culturally diverse student body is one of the factors that attracts students. The current population includes students from more than thirty different countries. The Student Activities Department plans and coordinates social activities, cultural events, and community projects. Student organizations include the ASID Student Chapter, Cross-Cultural Student Alliance, American Association of Textile Chemists and Colorists Phi Theta Kappa Honor Society, and the Alumni Association. The students also produce *FIDM MODE,* the student magazine that promotes awareness about the design industry, current events, and FIDM student life.

FIDM is accredited by the Accrediting Commission for Community and Junior and Senior Colleges of the Western Association of Schools and Colleges (WASC) and the National Association of Schools of Art and Design (NASAD).

Location

FIDM's main campus is in the heart of downtown Los Angeles near the famed California Market Center and Fashion District. There are additional California campuses in San Francisco, San Diego, and Orange County. A virtual tour of the campuses and their locations is available at http://fidm.edu/visit-fidm/virtual-tour/.

FIDM Los Angeles is nestled at the center of an incredibly vibrant apparel and entertainment hub, surrounded by the fashion, entertainment, jewelry, and financial districts. It is situated next to beautiful Grand Hope Park, a tree-filled oasis amid the hustle and bustle of downtown Los Angeles. Newly renovated by acclaimed architect Clive Wilkinson, **FIDM San Francisco** stands in the heart of historic Union Square. The country's third-largest shopping area and stimulating atmosphere combined with the industry-based staff and faculty make this campus as incredible as the city in which it is located. The **FIDM Orange County** campus is a dynamic visual experience with ultra-modern lofts, an indoor/outdoor student lounge, eye-popping colors, and a one-of-a-kind audio-visual igloo. Also designed by world-renowned architect Clive Wilkinson, this campus has received several prestigious architectural awards and has been featured in numerous national magazines. **FIDM San Diego's** gorgeous campus overlooks PETCO Park and is near the historic Gaslamp district and the San Diego harbor. FIDM's newest campus is sophisticated, stylish, and tech savvy, reflecting the importance of California's fastest-growing city and its appeal to the global industry.

Majors and Degrees

The Bachelor of Science (B.S.) in Business Management program offers students the opportunity to develop the additional necessary skills and knowledge to run a business or even launch their own. In the program, students learn business strategy, entrepreneurial creativity, and management skills for success in business. Graduates of this program are prepared to enter the global industries of fashion, interior design, and entertainment, and are ready to compete when entering the corporate world or undertaking an entrepreneurial venture.

Many FIDM A.A. graduates take their skills to the next level through FIDM's B.S. in Business Management program. Only FIDM Graduates from A.A majors are eligible to apply to the Bachelors program, which is offered at the Los Angeles and San Francisco campuses and available online. Students from all FIDM majors study and collaborate on business projects and take courses in accounting, human resource management, international finance, ethics, leadership, and more, giving them extensive knowledge of managing a business and the creative edge that is a growing necessity in the corporate world. FIDM's unique industry partnerships offer exciting opportunities for students through internships, events, and guest speakers, with companies such as Forever 21, JCPenney, Mattel, NBC Universal, Oakley, Smashbox, and Stila.

FIDM offers Associate of Arts degrees and Advanced Study programs that are available to students who have previously completed an A.A. degree at FIDM, and Professional Designation degree programs for students who want to enhance their previous education from another college or are interested in transferring to FIDM.

FIDM offers Associate of Arts degrees in Apparel Industry Management, Beauty Industry Merchandising & Marketing, Digital Media, Fashion Design, Fashion Knitwear Design, Graphic Design, Interior Design, Jewelry Design, Merchandise Marketing (Fashion Merchandising or Product Development), Textile Design, and Visual Communications. All of these programs offer the highly specialized curriculum of a specific major combined with a core general education/liberal arts foundation.

Students from other regionally accredited college programs have the opportunity to complement their previous college education by enrolling in FIDM's Professional Designation programs. Students can determine which credits will transfer and receive a personalized schedule toward completion of their Professional Designation program by consulting with FIDM Admissions Advisors. FIDM offers Professional Designation programs in Apparel Industry Management, Fashion Design, Beauty Industry Management, Digital Media, Graphic Design, Interior Design, Jewelry Design, Merchandising and Marketing (or Product Development), Textile Design, Fashion Knitwear Design, and Visual Communications.

For more information about FIDM transfer programs, students should visit http://fidm.edu/go/admissionstransfer.

Academic Programs

FIDM operates on a four-quarter academic calendar. Students can choose from twenty-two specialized creative business and design majors. New students may begin their studies at the start of any quarter throughout the year. Detailed information about FIDM majors is also available online at http://fidm.edu/en/Majors/.

Department chairs and trained advisers assist students in selecting the correct sequence of courses to complete degree requirements. The counseling department provides personal guidance and referral to outside counseling services and matches peer tutors to specific students' needs. Individual Development and Education Assistance (IDEA) Centers at each campus provide students with additional educational assistance in the areas of writing, mathematics, computer competency, study skills, research skills, and reading comprehension.

FIDM's eLearning program, which includes the B.S. in Business Management and some classes in other majors, ensures that a student's educational experience can take place anywhere. The online courses are designed to replicate the experience of classes on campus. Students in the eLearning program are granted the same high-quality education as students on campus and have immediate access to valuable campus resources, including the FIDM Library, Career Advisors, and instructors.

Off-Campus Programs

Internships are available within each major. Paid and volunteer positions provide work experience for students to gain practical application of classroom skills.

FIDM provides the opportunity for students to participate in academic study tours in Europe, Asia, and New York. These tours are specifically designed to broaden and enhance the specialized education offered at FIDM. Participants may earn academic credit under faculty-supervised directed studies. Exchange programs are also available with Esmod, Paris; Instituto Artictico dell' Abbigliamento Marangoni, Milan; Accademia Internazionale d'Alta Mode e d'Arte del Costume Koefia, Rome; St. Martins School of Art, London; College of Distributive Trades, London; and Janette Klein Design School, Mexico City.

Academic Facilities

FIDM's award-winning campuses feature design studios with computer labs and innovative study spaces, spacious classrooms, imaginative common areas, and state-of-the-industry technology. Computer labs support and enhance the educational programs of the Institute. Specialized labs offer computerized cutting and marking; graphic, interior, and textile design; word processing; and database management.

The FIDM Library goes beyond traditional sources of information. It houses a print and electronic collection of over 2.5 million titles that encompass all subject areas, with an emphasis on fashion, interior design, retailing, and costume. The library subscribes to over 160 international and national periodicals, offering the latest information on art, design, graphics, fashion, beauty, business, and current trends. The FIDM Library also features an international video library, subscriptions to major predictive services, interior design workrooms, textile samples, a trimmings/findings collection, and access to the Internet. The FIDM Museum & Galleries Permanent and Study Collections contain more than 12,000 garments from the eighteenth century to present day, including film and theater costumes. One of the largest collections in the United States, it features top designer holdings including Chanel, Yves Saint Laurent, Dior, and Lacroix. The collection also includes items from the California Historical Society (First Families), the Hollywood Collection, and the Rudi Gernreich Collection.

Costs

For the 2012–13 academic year, tuition, fees, books, and most supplies started at $27,910, depending on the selected major.

First-year application fees range from $225 for California residents to $525 for international students.

Financial Aid

There are several sources of financial funding available to the student, including federal financial aid and education loan programs, California state aid programs, institutional loan programs, and FIDM awards and scholarships. The FIDM Student Financial Services Office and FIDM Admissions Advisors work one-on-one with students and parents to help them find funding for their FIDM education. More information on FIDM scholarships and financial aid can be found at http://fidm.edu/go/fidmscholarships.

Faculty

FIDM faculty members are selected as specialists in their fields, working professionals with impressive resumes and invaluable industry connections. They bring daily exposure from their industry into the classroom for the benefit of the students. In pursuit of the best faculty members, consideration is given to both academic excellence and practical experience.

Admission Requirements

Students are accepted into one of FIDM's specialized Associate of Arts degree programs packed with 16–25 challenging courses per major. Associate of Arts programs are designed for high school graduates or applicants with strong GED scores. They offer the highly specialized curriculum of a specific major, as well as a traditional liberal arts/general studies foundation. Official transcripts from high school/secondary schools and all colleges/universities attended are needed to apply. International students must send transcripts accompanied by official English translations. Three recommendations from teachers, counselors, or employers are also required for admission. FIDM provides a reference request form on its website on the Admissions section under "How To Apply." All references must be sealed and mailed to the school when applying. An admissions essay portion and portfolio/entrance project requirement, which is specific to the student's selected major, are also available on the website's Admissions section under "How To Apply." For more information on the application process, prospective students can go to www.fidm.edu.

Application and Information

Applications are accepted on an ongoing basis. All prospective students should contact:

FIDM/Fashion Institute of Design & Merchandising
919 South Grand Avenue
Los Angeles, California 90015
Phone: 800-624-1200 (toll-free)
      213-624-1201 (outside the United States)
Fax: 213-624-4799
Website: http://www.fidm.edu
      http://www.facebook.com/home.php/#!/FIDMCollege
      http://twitter.com/#!/FIDM

FIDM Los Angeles Campus Exterior.

FITCHBURG STATE UNIVERSITY
FITCHBURG, MASSACHUSETTS

The University

Fitchburg State University is a public, liberal arts center of learning, dedicated to teaching, with thriving career-oriented and professional education programs. The University prepares its graduates for jobs in their fields and continues to place more than 70 percent of its graduates in their chosen professions within six months of graduation.

Fitchburg State's excellent academic reputation and graduate placement can be attributed to a nationally recognized faculty and a strong commitment to teaching. The University enrolls approximately 3,500 undergraduate students in its day and evening divisions and another 3,500 students in its graduate and continuing education programs. The average undergraduate class size is 21, and the overall student-teacher ratio remains low at 17:1. Each student is assigned to an academic adviser to assist with planning an individualized program of study. In addition, each department has access to state-of-the-art equipment and there is an extensive internship network that spreads throughout New England and across the country.

Student life at Fitchburg State is active and fun. There are numerous and varied opportunities for student leadership and involvement. More than sixty student-run clubs and organizations are on campus, including academic, cultural, and ethnic; profession-oriented; performance; sports and fitness; social and volunteer; fraternities and sororities; student government; and academic honor societies. Hundreds of popular and well-attended activities take place during the year, including films, lectures, concerts, seminars, coffeehouses, pub entertainment, recreational tournaments, a performing arts series, and visual arts exhibits, to name just a few. The University's students participate in exciting Division III athletics, offering sixteen intercollegiate varsity sports teams for both men and women, and there is a variety of intramural sports for all students. The beautiful, well-equipped Recreation Center has all the equipment and activities students need to stay healthy and have fun.

In addition to Bachelor of Arts and Bachelor of Science degrees, Fitchburg State confers the Master of Arts; the Master of Arts in Teaching (M.A.T.); the Master in Business Administration (M.B.A.); the Master of Education (M.Ed.) in several disciplines; and the Master of Science (M.S.) in applied communication, computer science, mental health and school counseling, and forensic nursing. Several Certificate of Advanced Graduate Studies (C.A.G.S.) and other graduate-level certificate programs are available as well.

Location

The University is located in a residential area near the center of Fitchburg, a city with a population of 43,000, which serves as the hub of the commercial and industrial life of north-central Massachusetts. Fitchburg State owns the Wallace Civic Center which is home to the University's ice hockey team and provides many activities each year, such as exhibits, fairs, performances, free public ice skating, local hockey events, and lectures. The City of Fitchburg offers many opportunities for study and practical experience in the areas of sociology, psychology, health, computer technology, business, industry, political organization, and community service. Outdoor activities, including skiing, camping, hiking, canoeing, and fishing, are just minutes from the campus.

The historic and literary centers of Lexington and Concord and the city of Boston are only about an hour from the University. It's very easy to get to Boston—the commuter rail station is right on the edge of campus. The city of Worcester, the third largest in New England, is only one-half hour to the south. Fitchburg offers students the convenience of a residential campus with easy access to all the amenities that the surrounding area offers.

Majors and Degrees

Fitchburg State University offers the Bachelor of Arts, Bachelor of Science, and Bachelor of Science in Education degrees and offers the following undergraduate programs: accounting; architectural technology; biology; biotechnology; business administration; clinical exercise physiology; cognitive science; communications media studies; computer information systems; computer science; construction technology; criminal justice; developmental psychology; earth systems science; economics; education, with teacher education programs available in early childhood education, elementary education, middle school education, secondary education (with emphases in biology, English, history, and mathematics), special education with emphases in severe disabilities (all levels) and moderate disabilities (pre-K–8), and technology education; electronics engineering technology; English studies; environmental biology; exercise and sports science; energy management; film/video production; fitness management; game design; geography; geo/physical sciences; graphic design; health sciences; history; human services; industrial and organizational psychology; interactive media; humanities–interdisciplinary studies; industrial technology; international business and economics; literature; management; manufacturing engineering technology; marketing; mathematics; nursing; photography; political science; professional communication; professional writing; psychology; sociology; technical theater arts; theater; undeclared/pre-major; and the following pre-professional programs: dentistry, law, medicine, and veterinary medicine.

Academic Programs

The University operates on a two-semester calendar. The first semester begins in early September and ends in mid-December, and the second semester begins in mid-January and ends in mid-May.

The curriculum has a strong liberal arts and sciences requirement, which provides a solid foundation for either further academic study or a career. Students obtain practical experience through numerous internships in social agencies, government offices, hospitals, and corporations related to their interests. Some major programs require an extensive supervised practicum to complete degree requirements. For education and nursing majors, a broad spectrum of student teaching and clinical experience is incorporated into their respective programs of study. The University's four-year honors program culminates in a senior thesis or project.

Off-Campus Programs

Fitchburg State is one of nine state universities under the jurisdiction of the Massachusetts Department of Higher Education. Through this affiliation, students may participate in the College Academic Program Sharing program, which allows study for a semester or a year at another university. For a rewarding cultural exchange experience, the Office of International Education provides undergraduate students the opportunity to study abroad at a variety of colleges and universities all over the world. Programs vary in length from a few weeks to as long as a semester or a year. Some of the locations in the exchange program include Australia, Canada, China, England, France, Ireland, Italy, Japan, New Zealand, Russia, Scotland, Spain, and Sweden.

Academic Facilities

The University has a number of special facilities. A well-equipped Academic Success Center includes offices for academic advising, career services, disability services, math and writing centers, multicultural student services, and peer tutoring. The McKay Campus School is a pre-K through fourth grade elementary school located on the campus, which gives education majors direct experience in a fully operational school. The Instructional Media Center has extensive, modern, well-equipped facilities which support the industrial education and industrial technology programs. The nursing program utilizes an on-campus clinical lab that simulates a hospital setting with several computerized training models: SimMan, SimBaby, and SimNewB. The communications media program possesses a full range of the latest equipment, such as media/film composers, digital audio workstations, a full-color dye-sublimation printer, CD recording and slide-scanning equipment, multiple editing rooms, a production studio, darkrooms, and graphic design computer labs. Communication students at Fitchburg State have access to many of the labs and facilities as early as their freshman year.

Costs

Fitchburg State University seeks to provide a very affordable education. Annual tuition for residents of Massachusetts was $970 per year in 2012–13; out-of-state tuition was $7,050. Required annual fees in 2012–13 totaled $7,740. The estimated annual total for a full-time, on-campus student from Massachusetts was $17,312 and for an out-of-state student, it was $23,392. Fees are subject to change.

Financial Aid

Many sources of financial aid are available to Fitchburg State students. The University participates in federal and state programs. Packages consisting of grants, loans, work-study awards, and scholarships are given to students demonstrating financial need and academic merit. All students who submit a completed application for admission by February 1 will automatically be considered for all available merit scholarships for the fall semester. Financial aid applications (including the FAFSA) for the fall semester must be completed by the preceding March 1 to be given priority consideration. Over $27 million in financial aid is granted annually to approximately 80 percent of Fitchburg State students making a quality education affordable for many deserving students.

Faculty

More than 92 percent of Fitchburg State's 192 full-time faculty members hold earned doctoral or other terminal degrees. Full professors teach freshman classes as well as advanced courses and serve as academic advisers to students majoring in their respective programs. Faculty members are accessible, engaging, and available to teach and advise students throughout their four years at the University.

Student Government

All full-time undergraduate students are members of the Student Government Association (SGA). The purpose of the SGA is to encourage responsibility and cooperation in democratic self-government; to form an official body for expressing the judgments of students and fostering activities and matters of general student interest; and to promote full understanding and cooperation among the students, the faculty members, and the administration in order to further the welfare of the University.

The governing body of the SGA consists of 6 SGA officers and a General Council, which includes these officers and 55 elected representatives of classes and residence halls, as well as the commuter student population. The SGA operates through a number of standing and ad hoc committees; membership is open to all students.

A 14-member All-University Committee, representing students, the faculty, and the administration, makes recommendations to the president of the University concerning matters of campus-wide policy.

Admission Requirements

As part of the Massachusetts State University system, Fitchburg State evaluates each applicant from any state, based on standards set by the Massachusetts Department of Higher Education and the University. The University considers high school curriculum, grade point average, SAT and/or ACT scores, school and community service, recommendations, application essay, life experience, special talents, and learning styles. The state admissions standards place significant attention on the student's high school record and SAT or ACT scores. The record of achievement in high school is the single most important item in the applicant's academic credentials. Freshman applicants should have completed a college-preparatory program that includes 16 college-preparatory units, with 4 units in English, 2 units in the same foreign language, 2 units in social studies, 3 units in mathematics (algebra I and II and geometry), 3 units in the natural sciences (2 of which must be laboratory courses), and 2 college-preparatory electives.

An essay is required; however, interviews are not required. Applicants who have questions about the programs and admission procedures at the University are encouraged to contact the Admissions Office to speak with a counselor.

The University encourages applications from transfer students and enrolls about 400 each year. An official transcript from each college previously attended must be submitted along with the application for admission.

International students are also encouraged to apply. Scores on the Test of English as a Foreign Language (TOEFL), evaluations of all international transcripts, and translations of international transcripts must be submitted in addition to the application for admission. Additional information for international students is available on the University's website.

Application and Information

Fitchburg State University reviews applications on a rolling basis, sending its first set of admission decisions for the fall semester by mid-December. The priority deadline for applications is March 1. Applicants to the communications media and nursing programs are reviewed against a higher set of admissions standards and are strongly encouraged to submit their applications by the January 1 priority deadline. In addition, applicants who wish to be considered for merit scholarships and the honors program must complete their admission and financial aid application process (i.e., submit all required materials) by February 1.

Transfer applicants are encouraged to apply by April 15 for the fall and by November 1 for the spring semester. International applicants applying for the fall semester must complete the application process by March 15 if they require on-campus housing and by July 15 if they are not in need of campus housing. Applicants for the spring semester must file their application for admission by December 1.

For further information, students should contact:

Admissions Office
Fitchburg State University
160 Pearl Street
Fitchburg, Massachusetts 01420
Phone: 800-705-9692 (toll-free)
Fax: 978-665-4540
E-mail: admissions@fitchburgstate.edu
Website: www.fitchburgstate.edu
 www.facebook.com/FitchburgStateAdmissions
 twitter.com/FITCHBURG_STATE

Built in 1910 as the Edgerly School, the current Edgerly Hall was one of the first junior high schools in the United States.

FIVE TOWNS COLLEGE
DIX HILLS, NEW YORK

MUSIC • BUSINESS • EDUCATION
MEDIA • PERFORMING ARTS

The College

Located on Long Island's North Shore, Five Towns College offers students the opportunity to study in a suburban environment that is close to New York City. Founded in 1972, Five Towns College is an independent, nonsectarian, coeducational institution that places its emphasis on the student as an individual. Many students are drawn to the College because of its strong reputation in music, media, education, and the performing arts. The College offers associate and bachelor's degrees. The College also offers programs leading to the Master of Music (M.M.) degree in jazz/commercial music and in music education as well as a Master of Science in Education (M.S.Ed.) and a Doctor of Musical Arts (D.M.A.).

From as far away as England and South Korea and from as close as Long Island and New York City, the 1,000 undergraduate and graduate students reflect a rich cultural diversity. The College's enrollment is 55 percent men and 45 percent women, with a minority population of approximately 30 percent. The College's music programs are contemporary jazz in nature, although classical musicians are also part of this creative community. The most popular programs are audio recording technology, broadcasting, journalism, music performance, music business, music and elementary teacher education, theater, and film/video production.

Coeducational living accommodations are available on campus. The Five Towns College Living/Learning Center is a modern complex containing four residence life halls. Each residence hall contains single- and double-occupancy rooms equipped with private bathrooms, broadband Internet access, cable television, and other amenities.

Location

The College's beautiful 35-acre campus, located in the wooded countryside of Dix Hills, New York, provides students with a quiet college setting to pursue their studies. Just off campus is Long Island's bustling Route 110 corridor, home to numerous national and multinational corporations. New York City, with everything from Lincoln Center to Broadway, is just a train ride away and provides students with some of the best cultural advantages in the world.

Closer to the campus, the many communities of Long Island abound with cultural and recreational opportunities. The College is located within the historic town of Huntington, which is home to the Cinema Arts Center, Hecksher Museum, Vanderbilt Museum, and numerous restaurants, coffeehouses, and quaint shops. The nearby shores of Jones Beach State Park and the Fire Island National Seashore are world renowned for their white, sandy beaches.

Majors and Degrees

Five Towns College offers the Associate in Arts (A.A.) degree in liberal arts, the Associate in Science (A.S.) degree in business administration; and the Associate in Applied Science (A.A.S.) degree in business management and in jazz commercial music, with concentrations in audio recording technology and music business.

The College offers the Bachelor of Music (Mus.B.) degree in music education and in jazz/commercial music, with concentrations in audio recording technology, composition/songwriting, music business, musical theater, and performance; the Bachelor of Fine Arts (B.F.A.) degree in theater or film/video arts; the Bachelor of Professional Studies (B.P.S.) degree in business management, with concentrations in audio recording technology and music

business; the Bachelor of Science (B.S.) degree in childhood education; and the B.S. in mass communication, which features broadcasting and journalism concentrations.

Academic Programs

The following describes some of the more popular programs at Five Towns College. For a complete description of the College's academic program, students should visit the Five Towns College website at http://www.ftc.edu.

The music education program is designed for students interested in a career as a teacher of music in a public or private school. The undergraduate program leads to New York State provisional certification. The course work provides professional training and includes a student-teaching experience. The audio recording technology concentration is designed to provide students with the tools needed to succeed as professional studio engineers and producers in the music industry. The music business concentration is designed for students interested in a career in entertainment-related business fields. The course work includes the technical, legal, production, management, and merchandising aspects of the music business. The composition/songwriting concentration provides intensive instruction in a core of technical studies in harmony, orchestration, counterpoint, MIDI, songwriting, form and analysis, arranging, and composition for those who intend to pursue careers as composers, arrangers, and songwriters. The performance concentration includes a common core of technical studies and a foundation of specialized courses, such as music history, harmony, counterpoint, improvisation, ensemble performance, and private instruction. The theater arts program is designed for students interested in careers as actors, entertainers, scenic designers, directors, stage managers, and lighting or sound directors. The film/video program includes extensive technical preparation in videography, filmmaking, linear and nonlinear editing, storyboarding, scriptwriting, producing, and directing for filmmakers and videographers. Elementary education students are prepared as teachers for grades 1–6, while those interested in journalism and broadcasting are prepared for careers in radio, television, newspaper, or editorial writing.

To earn a bachelor's degree, students must accumulate between 122 and 130 credits, depending on the program of study, with a proper distribution of courses and a GPA of a minimum of 2.0. To earn an associate degree, students must accumulate between 62 and 66 credits.

Internships

Off-campus internship opportunities are available to Five Towns College students who have fulfilled the necessary prerequisites, including a cumulative grade point average of at least 2.5, with a 3.0 in their major. In recent semesters, students have interned for major corporations such as MTV, Atlantic Records, Polygram Records, CBS, ABC, EMI Records, MCA Records, Sony Records, The Power Station, Universal Mastering Studios, Channel 12 News, and many others.

Academic Facilities

Five Towns College occupies a multi-winged facility that comprises approximately 120,000 square feet and includes a 500-seat auditorium, production studios, athletic and dining facilities, classrooms, PC and iMac computer labs with a student center. T-3 lines connect the College's completely fiber-optic computer network to the Internet. All students have access to this network and are provided with an e-mail account.

The Five Towns College Library has more than 50,000 print and nonprint materials. These include nearly 32,000 books and print items, 450 periodical titles, and approximately 5,000 records, 2,600 DVDs, and more than 4,300 CDs. Through its membership in the Long Island Library Resource Council (LILRC), students have access to other academic and public libraries.

The John Lennon Center for Music and Technology at Five Towns College houses state-of-the-art audio recording studios and a fully loaded electronic music/MIDI computer lab. The studios and lab feature industry-standard recording equipment and software programs that rival major recording facilities around the world, such as a 72-channel SSL 9000J and Neve Genesys mixing console; Telefunken, Neumann, AKG, Royer, Blue, and other microphones; outboard gear such as Manley, API, Chandler Limited, Lexicon, Universal Audio, and Apogee; and the latest versions of Pro Tools, Logic, Reason, and Sibelius. The film/video division uses Sony PMW-EX3 XD cameras with SxS cards, Canon 5D Mark II cameras, and Arriflex Super 16-mm film cameras. Editing suites offer Final Cut Pro and Adobe CS4 Creative Suite on iMac computers. Students utilize these facilities to develop their skills while creating professional-quality productions, both in the studio and on location under the supervision of industry professionals. Student productions include short films, music videos, documentaries, public service announcements, commercials, and live events, among many others.

The Dix Hills Center for Performing Arts at Five Towns College is an acoustically "perfect" venue, with digital lighting systems, digital sound reinforcement for concert production, and a Barco 6300 digital projection system for multimedia productions. The professional stage is 60 feet wide, with a proscenium opening of 16 feet and 32 feet of fly space. Students utilize this facility to produce live concerts, plays, musicals, and other performances or special presentations.

Costs

The tuition for 2013–14 is $20,400 per year. Miscellaneous fees total approximately $400, and books cost about $500. Private instruction fees for performing music students are $800 per semester.

Financial Aid

The annual tuition at Five Towns College is among the lowest of all the private colleges in the region. Nevertheless, approximately 82 percent of all students receive some form of financial assistance. Need-based and/or merit-based grants, scholarships, loans, and work-study programs are available to qualified recipients, including transfer students. Prospective students are urged to contact the Financial Aid Office as early as possible.

Faculty

The College's growing faculty consists of 120 full- and part-time members. The student-faculty ratio is 14:1. While the faculty is more strongly committed to teaching than to research, many members continue to be active in their respective areas of expertise.

Student Government

Student Government Association (SGA) serves as a voice of the students to the faculty and administration. Students can get involved through organizations and committees. All recognized organizations and committees fall under the jurisdiction of the SGA. The SGA is the elected representative student body of the campus and is responsible for creating many of the policy-making decisions that affect organizations and student life.

There are several media clubs and organizations for students. They include *Keynotes* (the College yearbook), *The Record* (the student newspaper), and WFTU (the College radio station).

Admission Requirements

The College encourages applications from students who will engage themselves in its creative community. Students applying to the College should have attained a minimum high school average grade of 78 percent. The SAT or ACT exam is required for all freshmen. Transfer students must also submit official transcripts of all college-level work as well as their high school transcripts. International students from non-English-speaking countries must submit a TOEFL Internet score of at least 78 or its equivalent. The College does not accept students on an early admissions basis, although early decision is available. Candidates for admission must submit a completed Application for Undergraduate Admission, official high school transcripts, at least two letters of recommendation, and a personal statement. International students must submit their TOEFL scores, financial documentation and sponsor information.

Application and Information

Admission into any music program is contingent upon passing an audition demonstrating skill in performance on a major instrument or vocally. Admission into the theater program is also contingent upon passing an audition. In some cases, the Admissions Committee may request an on-campus interview with an applicant. Music, theater, and film/video students are encouraged to submit an electronic portfolio or DVD, if they are unable to audition in person. An online application is available on the College website at www.ftc.edu. Students can apply either electronically or by mail.

Except for applicants applying on an early decision basis, new students are accepted on a rolling basis, with decisions for the fall and spring semesters mailed starting February 15 and December 1, respectively. There is an application fee of $35.

For further information, students should contact the Admissions Office at 631-656-2110 or admissions@ftc.edu.

Director of Admissions
Five Towns College
305 North Service Road
Dix Hills, New York 11746-5871
Phone: 631-656-2110
Fax: 631-656-2172
E-mail: admissions@ftc.edu
Website: http://www.ftc.edu

A student mixes on the SSL 9000J 72-channel console in one of the College's four state-of-the art recording studios.

FLORIDA ATLANTIC UNIVERSITY
BOCA RATON, FLORIDA

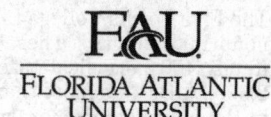

The University

Florida Atlantic University (FAU) offers students a world-class education in a beautiful subtropical setting in Boca Raton, Florida. A comprehensive public university that is fully accredited by the Southern Association of Colleges and Schools, FAU is currently serving over 30,000 students at sites throughout its six-county service region in southeast Florida, with state-of-the-art student housing available on the Boca Raton and Jupiter campuses.

Student life as an FAU Owl has never been better. From a football team playing in the on-campus stadium to over 300 organizations that serve every academic and leisure-time interest, there's something for everyone at FAU. The University has an outstanding faculty of more than 1,000 accomplished scholars and researchers who are known for their excellence in teaching and mentoring. Enrichment opportunities abound, including honors education, internships, hands-on research, and study-abroad experiences. FAU offers 19 varsity sport teams plus cheer and dance. Students learn in beautiful campus environments, and the beach is never far away.

The **Boca Raton campus** is FAU's first and largest campus. It occupies more than 850 acres just east of I-95, only 3 miles from the Atlantic Ocean. The campus features state-of-the-art labs and classrooms, suite-style student housing, and vibrant campus life. FAU's recreation and fitness center includes an aquatic center, three indoor basketball/volleyball courts, and a cardio/free-weight area. The recreation and wellness complex includes tennis courts, a track, and a variety of fields for club and intramural sports competition. It is home to the Florida Atlantic Research and Development Park and the nation's largest Lifelong Learning Society.

FAU's second-largest campus, the **Davie campus,** offers a wide variety of 2+2 programs in partnership with Broward College. The campus is also the base of operations for FAU's Everglades research and restoration efforts.

FAU Jupiter is home to the John D. MacArthur campus, which offers a wide range of upper division and graduate programs. The Harriet L. Wilkes Honors College, the Center for Environmental Studies, the Hibel Museum of Art, the new research facility for Scripps Florida, and the Max Planck Florida Institute are all located on the Jupiter campus.

FAU Harbor Branch Oceanographic Institution's 600-acre campus is located in Fort Pierce. The institute features a 40,000-square-foot Marine Sciences Building, which houses specially equipped labs and classrooms. It provides an ideal setting for marine science research and teaching.

FAU Fort Lauderdale is home to a mix of professional and design-oriented programs.

The University's Charles E. Schmidt College of Medicine enrolled its first medical school class in Fall 2011. The College of Medicine is partnering with FAU's Wilkes Honors College to offer select students early provisional admission to medical school, making it possible to receive both a bachelor's degree and an M.D. from FAU in only seven or eight years. Incoming freshmen who are accepted into the Wilkes Medical Scholars Program will begin their undergraduate programs already assured of a spot in FAU's new medical school, provided they complete all program requirements.

FAU enhances the economic, human, and cultural development of the surrounding communities and beyond through its partnerships with other educational institutions, local businesses, industries, and civic and cultural organizations.

Florida Atlantic University is accredited by the Commission on Colleges of the Southern Association of Colleges and Schools to award associate, bachelor's, master's, and doctoral degrees. In addition, it is accredited by 14 professional agencies. FAU is also a member of the National Association of State Universities and Land-Grant Colleges and the Council of Graduate Schools in the United States.

Location

All of Florida Atlantic University's campuses are located in South Florida.

South Florida's climate is subtropical, with an average year-round temperature of 75 degrees. FAU's campuses are within easy driving distance of major airports, restaurants, shopping, cultural activities, and some of the most beautiful beaches and recreational facilities to be found anywhere.

Majors and Degrees

FAU offers programs leading to the Bachelor of Arts (B.A.), Bachelor of Science (B.S.), and specialized bachelor's degrees. A minimum of 120 credit hours is required for a bachelor's degree.

The College for Design and Social Inquiry offers majors in architecture, criminal justice, public management, public safety administration, social work, and urban and regional planning.

The Dorothy F. Schmidt College of Arts and Letters offers majors in anthropology, arts and humanities, Caribbean and Latin American studies, communication and multimedia studies, English, history, Jewish studies, languages and linguistics, music, philosophy, political science, social science, sociology, theater, and visual arts and art history.

The College of Business offers majors in accounting, economics, finance, health administration, hospitality management, international business and trade, management leadership and entrepreneurship, management information systems, and marketing.

The Harriet L. Wilkes Honors College in Jupiter offers a liberal arts and sciences education in a highly selective environment. Concentrations include American studies, anthropology, biological sciences/pre-med, chemistry, economics, English literature, environmental studies, history, international studies, Latin American studies, law and society, marine biology, math and science, mathematics, philosophy, physics, political science, psychology, Spanish, and women's studies.

The University Honors Program at the Boca Raton campus provides exceptional and rewarding learning opportunities through special honors seminars. The goal of the program is to give students a learning experience that will prepare them to continue their education throughout their lives.

The College of Education offers majors in early care and education, elementary education, exceptional student education, exercise science and health promotion, and secondary education.

The College of Engineering and Computer Science offers majors in computer science as well as civil, computer, electrical, environmental, geomatics, mechanical, ocean engineering, and information engineering technology. FAU established the nation's first ocean engineering degree program in 1965 and now conducts millions of dollars in research annually.

The Christine E. Lynn College of Nursing offers a B.S. in Nursing degree and is nationally and internationally known for developing innovative approaches to nursing education within a caring philosophy.

The Charles E. Schmidt College of Science has majors in biological science, chemistry, geography, geology, mathematics, neuroscience, physics, and psychology. The Charles E. Schmidt College of Science also offers a pre-health professions certificate for any students interested in pursuing careers in dentistry, general medicine, optometry, pharmacy, physical therapy, and veterinary medicine.

Academic Programs

The University offers more than 180 undergraduate and graduate degree programs in fields that span the arts and humanities, the sciences, medicine, nursing, accounting, business, education, public administration, social work, architecture, engineering, computer science, and more. Academically accomplished students can take advantage of honors programs offered on the Boca Raton and Jupiter campuses. Florida Atlantic University is developing academic programming and research initiatives that align with its three signature strategic themes: marine and coastal issues, biotechnology, and contemporary societal challenges.

Off-Campus Programs

While there is no substitute for the dynamic synergy created in the classroom, FAU faculty and students seek out real-world experiences that enhance the classroom experience, such as internships, hands-on research, and study-abroad opportunities. FAU has exchange agreements with international schools in locations such as France, Germany, Japan, Sweden, Brazil, Finland, Ireland, Spain, Portugal, South Korea, Thailand, and many other locations.

Academic Facilities

The Boca Raton campus features 10 colleges with a multitude of academic resources. The Dorothy F. Schmidt College of Arts and Letters features a 75,000-square-foot, three-building complex comprising a performance arts center, an art gallery, a theater, a visual arts center, lecture halls, classrooms, and offices. The College of Business occupies a four-story building including wireless classrooms with a simulated trading room floor. The College of Education's four-story, 90,000-square-foot facility houses its academic departments and offers a teaching gymnasium, an early childhood center, and the A. D. Henderson University School operated by the College of Education. There is also a marine sciences center, Gumbo Limbo, located between the Intracoastal Waterway and the Atlantic Ocean; it provides teaching and research facilities. The Christine E. Lynn College of Nursing is housed in a state-of-the-art building, which is LEED-certified Gold. The five-story S. E. Wimberly Library houses a large collection of monographs, serials, and other academic resources. Computer labs, study lounges, a media center and tutoring services also provide valuable academic support for students.

FAU continues to enhance the campus environment with the addition of many new facilities including the Marleen and Harold Forkas Alumni Center; the College of Engineering and Computer Science facility, which has received LEED Platinum certification; and the new Culture and Society building, which includes the Living Room Theaters, a 200-seat digital movie complex.

Costs

For the 2012–13 academic year, in-state tuition was $199.54 per credit hour and out-of-state tuition was $718.09 per credit hour. Average on-campus room and board costs are $11,556. Approximate expenses are $1,220 for books, $2,217 for personal items, and $3,167 for transportation for off-campus students. Fees are subject to change.

Financial Aid

Approximately $186 million in financial aid is awarded each year. A comprehensive program of student financial aid includes scholarships, grants, loans, and work-study that may provide assistance from initial enrollment through graduate study. As a member of the College Scholarship Service of the College Board, the University is guided by the principles and policies of that organization. Students who are interested in applying for need-based aid must complete the Free Application for Federal Student Aid (FAFSA), which is available online at http://www.fau.edu/finaid. Students are strongly encouraged to complete the FAFSA in January for fall admission. The process of applying for aid normally takes six to eight weeks. The priority deadline is March 1.

There are a variety of scholarships for academic, athletic, or artistic talent. Students should visit the Admissions website at http://www.fau.edu/admissions for more information on academic scholarships and should check with individual departments for information on athletic or artistic scholarships.

Faculty

Recognizing that the excellence of its faculty is the true measure of the worth of a university, FAU has brought together a distinguished group of scholars who hold a balanced dedication to both teaching and research. Faculty members come from more than thirty states and several countries. The majority hold a doctorate or professional degree. They all represent a high level of professional experience and academic attainment and are committed to the development of a vigorous educational program of the highest caliber.

Student Government

FAU gives students an active role on virtually all University and faculty committees, including the Curriculum Committee, the Board of Trustees, college advisory councils, the Student Government Association, and Residence Hall Councils, as well as the interclub, interfraternity, and Panhellenic groups. Students also serve on the University Senate along with faculty and staff members.

Admission Requirements

Admission to the University is selective and limited to applicants who have graduated from regionally accredited high schools or who have achieved a certain level on the GED certificate exam. Evaluation is based on the academic course grade point average and rigor of curriculum combined with acceptable results on the SAT or ACT. Candidates for admission should have the 18 required academic high school units. An application, a nonrefundable $30 application fee, official transcripts, and the official results of the SAT or ACT are required to be considered for admission.

For detailed additional requirements and additional information, students should visit http://www.fau.edu/admissions.

Application and Information

Office of Undergraduate Admissions
Florida Atlantic University
777 Glades Road
Boca Raton, Florida 33431
Phone: 561-297-3040
E-mail: admissions@fau.edu
Website: http://www.fau.edu

FLORIDA SOUTHERN COLLEGE
LAKELAND, FLORIDA

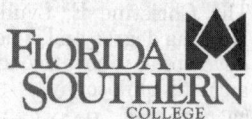

The College

The oldest private college in the state, Florida Southern College (FSC) was chartered in 1883 and settled on the shores of spectacular Lake Hollingsworth in Lakeland in 1922.

Today, Florida Southern is a nationally ranked, residential, coeducational, and comprehensive college recognized for its commitment to providing engaged learning experiences to its students. Florida Southern's 2,185 students represent forty-five states and forty-two foreign countries. Students choose Florida Southern because of its national reputation for dynamic, hands-on learning in an atmosphere that is friendly and personal.

Experiencing the world beyond the classroom is an essential part of a Florida Southern education. Along with providing ample opportunities to conduct lab and field research, become involved in community service, and perform, Florida Southern guarantees each student an internship and study-abroad experience. Florida Southern also guarantees its students will graduate in four years.

Members of the community take great pride in the beautiful campus, a historic landmark and home to the world's largest single-site collection of buildings designed by renowned architect Frank Lloyd Wright.

As a residential community, Florida Southern provides its students with a wide range of housing options, including all-female and all-male halls, coed halls, suite-style living arrangements, and two-bedroom apartments. The College also dedicates spaces to various majors, honors students, and fraternity and sorority life. Accommodations are well equipped and feature stunning views of the lake, contemporary student lounges, modern kitchens and bathrooms, and wireless Internet access.

Athletic facilities are first rate. The newly renovated George Jenkins Field House includes a three-court gymnasium, a weight room, and an athletic training room. The popular Nina B. Hollis Wellness Center, the hub of student life, offers a fully equipped fitness center, an aerobics/dance studio, an intramural gymnasium, racquetball courts, and a competition-size swimming pool. Directly across from the Wellness Center is Lake Hollingsworth, which offers kayaks, paddleboats, and waterskiing.

The student body is extremely involved. With more than eighty clubs, Florida Southern offers countless ways for students to pursue their interests while making lasting connections. FSC is home to fourteen national Greek fraternities and sororities. Popular student activities include intercollegiate and intramural sports; drama and music groups; publications; and organizations related to academic, political, religious, and social interests. A high percentage of students are involved in volunteer programs in the community, state, and internationally.

Location

Florida Southern's campus consists of approximately 110 acres on the shore of Lake Hollingsworth in Lakeland, Florida, a dynamic suburban community of about 120,000 residents in the heart of Florida's high-tech corridor. The campus is within walking distance of Lakeland's historic downtown, and Lakeland is just 45 minutes from Tampa and an hour from Orlando. Within an hour's drive of the state's major recreational attractions, including Walt Disney World and award-winning beaches, the College is ideally situated for internships and job opportunities with leading corporations that tap into one of the largest markets in the United States. Students enjoy Festival of Fine Arts series performances in music, dance, and drama; distinguished speakers; and business symposiums. The local Lakeland Center also offers many cultural and entertainment opportunities.

Majors and Degrees

Florida Southern College offers Bachelor of Arts, Bachelor of Fine Arts, Bachelor of Music, Bachelor of Music Education, Bachelor of Science, and Bachelor of Science in Nursing degrees in more than fifty majors including accounting, art (art education, art history, graphic design, and studio art), athletic training, biochemistry and molecular biology, biology, business administration (career tracks in finance, international business, management, marketing, and sport management), chemistry, citrus, communication (advertising and public relations; broadcast, print, and online media; interpersonal communication; and political communication), criminology, economics, education (elementary, music, physical, and secondary), English, history, health science, horticultural science (including recreational turf-grass management and landscape design), human movement and performance, marine biology, mathematics, mathematics/computer science, music (music education, music management, and music performance), nursing, philosophy, political science, psychology, religion, sociology, Spanish, theater arts (musical theater and technical theater/design), and youth ministry. Divisional majors are available in humanities and social science.

Outstanding preprofessional programs are offered in dentistry, engineering, law, medicine, pharmacy, physical therapy, theology, and veterinary medicine. Florida Southern's premed program boasts a 100 percent placement rate into medical school.

An honors program provides special opportunities for a select group of entering first-year students to explore topics of common interest in an integrated and interdisciplinary fashion.

Academic Programs

All degree programs require the satisfactory completion of a minimum of 128 semester hours with a minimum grade point average of 2.0. Students and professors work together in discussion-based classes featuring debate, collaborative projects, and other forms of engaged learning. The College operates on the semester system, with two 15-week semesters, and summer sessions. The average course load is 16 hours per semester. Students are required to complete a general education curriculum designed to help develop knowledge, skills, and attitudes for lifelong success, in addition to their major course work. Credit by examination is awarded on the basis of successful scores on Advanced Placement tests, the International Baccalaureate (I.B.), and College-Level Examination Program (CLEP) tests.

The FSC experience is career focused from day one. The College's career counselors help students explore their strengths and provide continual evaluation of career options with personalized guidance on resume building, interviewing, and landing the ideal first postcollege job.

Approximately 20 percent of Florida Southern graduates opt to continue their studies in graduate school.

Off-campus Programs

Entering first-year students are guaranteed a travel-study opportunity during their junior or senior year at Florida Southern. Students have traveled to Africa, the Caribbean, China, Costa Rica, England, France, Italy, Mexico, Washington, D.C., and other exciting destinations.

Florida Southern College is also affiliated with The Washington Center (TWC), a highly regarded, nonpartisan internship provider with international scope. As the only private institution of higher education in the state to affiliate with TWC, FSC students have access to prestigious and valuable field experiences. Programs range from tailored internships that are academic and work-experience based for governmental, international, corporate, and nonprofit organizations, to intensive-learning academic seminars focused on timely topics.

Academic Facilities

Situated in an orange grove overlooking scenic Lake Hollingsworth, the FSC campus combines beautiful landscape with modern buildings designed by world-famous architects.

The campus's newest academic buildings, the Joe K. and Alberta Blanton Nursing Building, home to the College's growing School of Nursing, features patient simulators in the state-of-the art treatment simulation laboratory. The Dr. Marcene H. and Robert E. Christoverson Humanities Building comprises contemporary classrooms along with language labs, the film studies center, and a gallery. Recently renovated, Frank Lloyd Wright's Polk Science Building is home to FSC's natural science and premedical programs and is outfitted with a wide range of cutting-edge instrumentation, such as a nuclear magnetic resonance spectrometer, the preeminent device in determining the structure of chemical compounds. The building also features the world's only Wright-designed planetarium.

The Marshall and Vera Lea Rinker Technology Center is the nucleus for learning on campus. It houses the College's main computer lab, classrooms, and small group study areas and provides students with the latest technologies. Most recently, Florida Southern broke ground on the 40,000-square-foot Becker Business Building. The facility, slated to open in 2015, is designed by renowned architect Robert A. M. Stern. This premiere business education center will not only feature high-tech classrooms equipped with the latest educational technology, it will also house a simulated trading floor that will function as a laboratory in which students can learn firsthand about investment analysis and trading strategies.

An integral part of the intellectual life of the College, FSC's E. T. Roux Library provides access to a rich collection of materials, including print and digital books; periodicals; electronic databases; a media collection that includes CDs, DVDs, and CD-ROMs; a substantial microforms collection; and seating for more than 350 students. Adjacent is the Sarah D. and L. Kirk McKay, Jr., Archives Center which houses the archival materials of the Florida Conference of the United Methodist Church, the Center for Florida History collection, the Florida Citrus Archives, along with the College's collection of Frank Lloyd Wright memorabilia.

The campus also boasts a fine arts complex which includes Branscomb Memorial Auditorium (which seats 1,800 and is nationally known for its perfect acoustics), the Marjorie M. McKinley Music Building, the Melvin Art Gallery, and the Loca Lee Buckner Theater.

Florida Southern is also home to the Roberts Academy, the first transitional school for children with dyslexia in the state of Florida, and a preschool lab, each providing an opportunity for students majoring in elementary education to observe and teach.

Costs

The comprehensive cost for 2013–14 is $38,090 per year ($27,930 for tuition and standard fees and $9,510 for room and board). FSC estimates that $1,150 is adequate for books and supplies, and $1,500 should cover personal expenses, exclusive of travel to and from home.

Financial Aid

Consistently rated as a best value, ninety-six percent of all FSC students receive financial assistance. Each year, Florida Southern offers more than $20 million in college aid on the basis of academic merit; talent in athletics (baseball, basketball, cross-country, golf, soccer, softball, swimming, tennis, volleyball, or lacrosse), fine arts, theater, leadership, or community service; student need, and other factors. To demonstrate need, an applicant is required to file the Free Application for Federal Student Aid (FAFSA).

The Office of Financial Aid understands that everyone's financial situation is different and offers students assistance in meeting their educational expenses through scholarships, grants, loans, and campus employment. Applicants for aid must reapply each year. Florida Southern participates in the Federal Perkins Loan, Federal Supplemental Educational Opportunity Grant, and Federal Work-Study college-based programs. All applicants are expected to apply for any entitlement grant for which they are eligible, such as a Federal Pell Grant and, for Florida residents, the Florida Student Assistance Grant. The Federal Stafford Direct Student Loan Program is also available. The completed FAFSA and the College's financial aid application must be filed with the Financial Aid Office by April 1. Early application is encouraged for students seeking academic scholarships.

Faculty

FSC faculty members are more than professors—they function as advisers, mentors, and a true partner in a student's learning. The student-faculty ratio is 13:1 and 90 percent of Florida Southern's faculty members have doctoral or other terminal degrees. Not only are they top scholars in their fields, they are devoted to providing students with personalized attention and a truly outstanding education. Faculty members are selected not only for their teaching abilities but for their ability to relate to the needs and concerns of their students.

Admission Requirements

Florida Southern looks for two things in applicants: performance and promise. The majority of students who have been accepted have had a grade of B or better in college-preparatory courses (including four courses in English, three in mathematics, and the balance divided among science, foreign language, and social science); and have earned minimum scores of 500 on each of the verbal and math portions of the SAT or a composite score of at least 23 on the ACT. The Admissions Office is committed to reviewing individual applicants on their own merits, based on the level of challenge attempted, patterns of grades over time, recommendations from references, and an applicant's own assessment of the learning environment best suited to his or her needs. Evidence of leadership and community service also are typical attributes of a successful applicant.

Applicants must graduate from an accredited high school with a minimum of 19 credits, 16 of which must be academic. Qualified high school juniors may apply for early admission if they have the recommendation of their secondary school and have had a personal interview with the Director of Admissions. Applications from transfers are welcome, as are those from students resuming their education and from older students who have delayed their entrance into college. Transfer applicants should have a minimum 2.5 grade point average and be graduates of or be eligible to return to their former institutions. Transfer students with fewer than 25 semester hours must submit high school transcripts and standardized test scores. Applicants who hold Associate of Arts degrees from regionally accredited two-year institutions are typically granted junior standing. All applicants are encouraged to interview; an interview may be required for some candidates.

Application and Information

An application is considered by the Admissions Committee when it has been received with required test scores and references, and transcripts from each school attended. Because all students are required to live on campus unless they are seniors, married, or living with their parents, early application is desirable to ensure that housing is available. The freshman application priority date is March 1. The deadline for early decision applicants is December 1.

For more information about Florida Southern College, prospective students should contact:

Office of Admissions
Florida Southern College
111 Lake Hollingsworth Drive
Lakeland, Florida 33801-5698
Phone: 800-274-4131 (toll-free)
E-mail: fscadm@flsouthern.edu
Website: http://www.flsouthern.edu

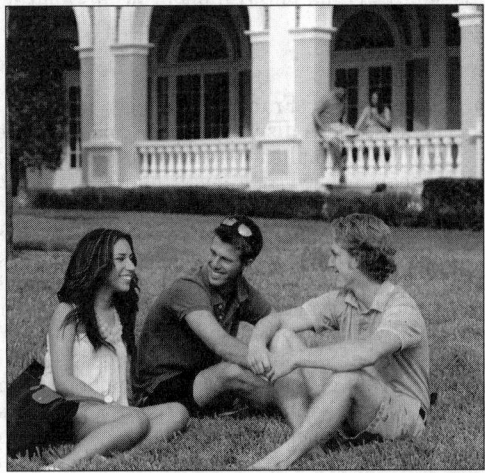

Students enjoying the Florida sun in front of the classic Joseph-Reynolds Residence Hall, constructed in 1922.

FRANKLIN COLLEGE
FRANKLIN, INDIANA

The College

As an innovative scientist, diplomat, thinker, writer, and leader, Benjamin Franklin's remarkable life and accomplishments left a mark on not only a young nation, but also the world. Named in the spirit of this extraordinary American icon, Franklin College continues his legacy of exploration and knowledge.

Since its founding in 1834, Franklin College has a long history of preparing students for lives committed to excellence, leadership, and service. With a comprehensive liberal arts curriculum combined with a leading-edge professional development program, Franklin College provides an education that blends thinking with doing, reasoning with acting, and discovering with challenging.

Small classes and dedicated faculty members ensure that students get the attention needed to succeed, and Franklin's career and graduate school admission rates prove this.

Franklin combines liberal arts training with preprofessional development like no other college. Students can develop the competencies and resources necessary to be successful in their personal and professional lives through Franklin's innovative Professional Development Program (PDP). This exciting program gives them the opportunity to dine with corporate executives, network with national and community leaders, learn the finer points of corporate communication, and develop a level of polish and sophistication that sets them apart from other college graduates.

Location

Located in the heart of the Midwest, Franklin College offers students the best of both a small community and a big city's excitement.

Franklin, Indiana, is only 20 miles south of Indianapolis, which is the state's capital city and the thirteenth largest city in the U.S. It offers a wide variety of internship opportunities, as well as athletic, cultural, and entertainment events that appeal to all students.

Majors and Degrees

Flagship programs at Franklin College include athletic training, business, journalism, pre-med, and education. The Pulliam School of Journalism is one of a few comprehensive journalism schools housed at a small liberal arts institution. Student media opportunities include a student-run PR agency, a student newspaper, magazine, and radio show. Franklin's journalism students also have the opportunity to work at the Indiana Statehouse Bureau in downtown Indianapolis. After graduation, education majors are placed at 97 percent or higher in the classroom, while business students repeatedly score in the top 5 percent on the National College Business Examination. One hundred percent of athletic training majors are employed six months after graduation. Preparation for graduate school is exceptional, with 85 percent of students gaining admission to medical school and 90 percent of applicants accepted to law school.

Franklin College confers more than twenty-eight Bachelor of Arts degrees in the following areas: accounting, American studies, art (art history and studio art), biology, business (finance, general, international business, management, and marketing), Canadian studies, chemistry, computer science/computer information systems, economics, education (elementary, middle school, and secondary), English, exercise science, French, history, individualized major, journalism (advertising/public relations, broadcasting, and news-editorial), mathematical science (applied, pure, and quantitative analysis), music (instrumental and vocal), philosophy, physical education, political science, psychology, religious studies, sociology (criminology and social work), Spanish, and theater. Franklin also offers thirty-six different minors, including areas like fine arts, creative writing, leadership, and physics.

Engineering is offered as a 3+2 program. Students earn a Bachelor of Arts degree from Franklin College and a Bachelor of Science degree in one of the engineering disciplines from the Purdue School of Engineering and Technology (IUPUI).

Students considering a career in dentistry, medical technology, medicine, optometry, pharmacy, physical therapy, or veterinary medicine arrange their program with the advice of the pre-professional adviser of the science division. Students seeking a career in law plan their program in consultation with prelaw advisers. Students planning a career in secondary education may elect an academic area of concentration that will satisfy the state requirements for a teaching major. The education department is endorsed and approved by the Indiana Professional Standards Board and the National Council for Accreditation of Teacher Education (NCATE).

Academic Programs

The current academic program is the result of the faculty's plan to meet the express needs of students; the primary emphasis is on the unity of knowledge. Franklin believes in the importance of providing students with a liberal arts background while they develop talents for a particular professional career. Approximately one third of each student's total course work is composed of the prescribed and exploratory courses that make up the general education core curriculum.

All of Franklin's academic departments offer individualized study, allowing a student to pursue his or her field of interest in depth. Students interested in pursuing a major not offered at Franklin may submit a proposal for their individualized major.

Franklin College operates on a 4-1-4 academic calendar, which allows tremendous opportunities for students throughout the academic year. The fall semester begins towards the end of August and ends before Christmas; the spring semester begins in February and ends in the middle of May. The two semesters are broken up by a special four-week Winter Term program during the month of January. Winter Term is designed to allow students to study in areas of particular interest to them, either within or outside their major field of study. Some January classes offer students the opportunity to travel to locations such as Belize, England, France, Italy, and Mexico.

Students can also take advantage of internship opportunities during winter term, offering practical experience under the supervision of a professional. Internships are available during winter term, summer, fall semester, and spring semester. The location of the College in proximity to downtown Indianapolis, allows students to complete internships with nationally known Fortune 500 companies. Ninety-five percent of Franklin College students complete an internship prior to graduation.

Franklin gives credit in seventeen academic areas for successful scores on CLEP subject examinations; credit is also granted for successful scores on the Advanced Placement tests of the College Board. The Running Start Program enables talented high school students to get an early start on their college education.

Study-Away-From-Campus Programs

Franklin College students can participate in a variety of international and domestic study-away from campus opportunities. Students at the College have the opportunity to study away beginning as early as their freshman year. This experience is a key component of a liberal arts education. Not only does it allow students to learn about other cultures and countries of the world, it also helps them develop problem-solving and cross-cultural communication skills. In a global economy, this experience can be invaluable upon graduation.

Franklin College offers many ways for students to broaden their horizons, including a semester or year away, a Winter Term travel course, or a summer away. Options range from two weeks to a full year. Students can take courses for their major, earn credits for electives, complete an internship, or take part in a service-learning experience.

Academic Facilities

Franklin College has two campus buildings listed on the National Historic Register. Old Main, the original home of the College, and Shirk Hall, home of the Pulliam School of Journalism, are footholds of the rich past and recent renovation of the Franklin College campus. Classrooms and administrative, business, and professorial offices, along with computer laboratories, occupy Old Main; Shirk Hall also houses classrooms and the radio station.

A. A. Barnes Science Building houses all physics, biology, and chemistry department classrooms and laboratories. The Spurlock Center gymnasium and fitness center provides workout and weight equipment to students in order to maintain a healthy lifestyle.

The Dietz Center for Professional Development is the home of the Professional Development Program. State-of-the-art conference rooms and computer facilities enhance Franklin's career programming commitment to its students.

The B. F. Hamilton Library, containing more than 117,000 volumes and collections of microfilm, slides, art reproductions, recordings, and periodicals, is a member of P.A.L.N.I. (Private Academic Library Network of Indiana). The library also houses the Academic Resource Center (ARC), where students can receive help with their individual studies. The Johnson Center for Fine Arts provides classrooms and practice and performance accommodations, and it houses the facilities and meeting rooms for the Leadership Program.

Costs

The direct cost for the 2013–14 academic year is $36,235. This amount is derived from tuition, which is $27,510; residence hall, which is $4,860; student fees of $185; and Winter Term meal fees of $350 plus the meal plan, which is $3,330.

Financial Aid

The Franklin College financial aid program assists students who might not otherwise be able to attend college and rewards applicants for excellent academic achievement in high school. Awards are based on scholarship, curricular and extracurricular activities, and financial need. Aid involving financial need includes Franklin College grants, loans, and employment. Franklin participates in the Federal Stafford Student Loan and Federal Work-Study programs. Merit-based scholarships ranging from $2,500 to full tuition are awarded to students based on academic performance, activities, and standardized test scores. Scholarships are renewable for each of the recipient's four academic years at Franklin, provided students maintain specific GPA requirements and advance in class status each year. Franklin College encourages all students and families to file the Free Application for Federal Student Aid (FAFSA) in order to receive additional financial aid.

Faculty

The 12:1 student-faculty ratio allows Franklin faculty members to provide excellent instruction in small classes that promote participatory learning. Nearly 90 percent of current faculty members have obtained the highest degree in their field. Faculty members serve as advisers and provide supplemental attention outside the classroom. While many faculty members carry on research and publish their work, their main emphasis is teaching. No classes are taught by graduate students or teaching assistants.

Student Organizations

Franklin College offers more than sixty clubs and organizations such as Student Congress, Black Student Union, Greek Life, and Student Entertainment Board. These organizations allow students to plan on-campus concerts/events, represent the student body to change campus policies, and volunteer their time with the College's Habitat for Humanity programs from the first year. In addition to the existing organizations, the College allows students to set up new groups of their interests.

Admission Requirements

Applications for admission to Franklin College are evaluated on an individual basis. A student's potential academic and personal contributions to the College, recommendations, school and community activities, academic record, and standardized test scores are taken into consideration by the Admissions Committee. A student should complete a strong college-preparatory program. Candidates for admission are urged to visit the campus in order to experience the College community. The College offers different visit opportunities—from personal visits to open houses, all provide opportunities to meet current students, professors, and coaches, and to take a campus tour.

Application and Information

To be considered for admission, an applicant must submit a completed application (paper or online), a transcript of all secondary school and college work attempted, and either SAT or ACT scores. A decision regarding acceptance is made after the College receives all necessary credentials. Notification is sent immediately after the Enrollment Committee has acted.

Office of Admission
Franklin College
101 Branigin Boulevard
Franklin, Indiana 46131
Phone: 317-738-8075
   888-852-6471 (toll-free)
Fax: 317-738-8274
E-mail: admissions@franklincollege.edu
Website: http://admissions.franklincollege.edu
   http://www.facebook.com/fcadmissions

Old Main is the oldest academic building on the Franklin College campus.

FRANKLIN COLLEGE SWITZERLAND
LUGANO, SWITZERLAND

The College

Franklin College Switzerland, named for the United States' first and most illustrious ambassador to Europe, was founded in 1969 as a nonprofit, independent, postsecondary institution. It takes as its cornerstone Benjamin Franklin's vigorous support of intellectual interchange between nations. An American liberal arts institution in an international environment, Franklin is fully accredited in the United States by the Commission on Higher Education of the Middle States Association of Colleges and Schools and in Switzerland by the Swiss University Conference.

Franklin College places a strong emphasis on cross-cultural perspectives, advocating that international studies should be an integral part of a college education, as a prelude to, and basis for, a student's commitment to a major field of study. Franklin defines higher education from its beginning as the experience of thinking internationally. Its emphasis on global perspectives, both academic and social, is designed to affect the direction and meaning of a student's college experience, life, and career.

The essence of a Franklin College education is the exposure of its students to cultures other than their own, providing them with a better understanding of others, the world, and their place in the world. The College's location in Lugano, a vibrant Swiss city that is part of the cultural milieu of northern Italy, ensures a constant commingling of cultures in a quadrilingual nation. Students and faculty members, many who have a cross-cultural background, come to Franklin College from every corner of the globe, further strengthening international study and experiences.

Approximately 60 percent of the students come from the United States; 40 percent are from Europe, Asia, Africa, South America, and the Middle East. Bringing diverse experiences and perspectives to college life, they live in College residences both on and near the campus. These apartments all have kitchens available, and two campus dining facilities provide regular meal service and a diverse meal plan. Resident Assistants supervise all campus buildings.

Campus activities are varied. Franklin's Student Government Association (SGA) promotes a student newspaper; a literary magazine; a drama society; cultural, language, and sports clubs; and numerous social events that take advantage of southern Switzerland's extensive recreational resources. There are competitive College sports teams in men's and women's soccer, and student-organized games include basketball, soccer, and volleyball. In addition, the Athletic Director connects interested students with a considerable number of local Swiss clubs and teams that welcome newcomers: basketball, ice hockey, soccer, and volleyball teams, as well as crew, fencing, flying, golf, hang gliding, ice skating, judo, parachuting, riding, rock climbing, sailing, swimming, tennis, track, and windsurfing clubs. By joining these local groups, Franklin students become part of the region's local community; they are themselves essential to the cross-cultural learning the College promotes.

Location

Franklin College Switzerland's campus is in the community of Sorengo, a section of the city of Lugano, southern Switzerland's principal business, banking, medical, and cultural center. Easily accessible from the campus either by public transportation or on foot, downtown Lugano and its surrounding lakeside villages are renowned for their scenic beauty and Mediterranean climate. Palm trees line lakefront piazzas, and an outdoor lifestyle is typical of Ticino, the Italian-speaking canton of Switzerland that best exemplifies Swiss versatility in all three of the national languages—Italian, German, and French.

Throughout the year, Lugano features outstanding cultural activities at the world-famous Thyssen art collection, the Swiss-Italian radio station with its own permanent symphony orchestra, and the International Convention Center, which attracts guest performers from around the world. Nine public museums,

many art galleries, several movie houses, and a multitude of restaurants and discotheques make for a range of recreational choices normally found only in a large city. A covered ice rink, swimming pools, and a wide range of other sports facilities are maintained by local sports clubs; Lugano and the southern part of Switzerland offer access to an extraordinary variety of sports activities. In the spring and fall, Ticino's most popular recreation is hiking. In winter, skiing is available in San Bernardino and Andermatt, about an hour from the campus, or in the fabled St. Moritz, Davos, Klosters, and Zermatt.

Majors and Degrees

The Bachelor of Arts program offers majors in art history and visual culture, communication and media studies, comparative literary and cultural studies, environmental studies, French studies, history, international banking and finance, international economics, international management, international relations, Italian studies, literature, and visual and communication arts, with combined and double majors in a number of study areas. The Associate in Arts degree program provides a strong liberal arts foundation for students who usually continue their education in a baccalaureate degree program.

Academic Programs

Franklin's curriculum promotes international awareness and critical thinking, while being interdisciplinary in the highest tradition of a liberal arts education. The courses of study explore the diverse disciplines that enlighten an educated human being. Students must complete at least 125 credit hours to be eligible for the B.A. degree and 64 for the A.A. degree, while maintaining a minimum cumulative grade point average of 2.0 on a 4.0 scale.

As an integral credit-bearing part of the academic program, twice a year (in mid-October and mid-March) students participate in two-week, faculty-led Academic Travel programs to various destinations in Eastern and Western Europe, Africa, Asia, Latin America, and North America.

All degree candidates must demonstrate a foreign language proficiency in a language other than their mother tongue equivalent to three years of university-level instruction in one of the languages taught at Franklin. This requirement is met by successfully completing appropriate courses at Franklin or by passing an equivalency test administered by the language department.

In addition to their major field of study, students may minor in another course of study. The number of credit hours (12 to 15) and the program of courses are subject to departmental approval.

The College operates on a two-semester calendar, with classes starting in late August and mid-January; two 4-week intensive summer sessions are also available. A required orientation program for all new students is held in August and mid-January.

Off-Campus Programs

Franklin's renowned Academic Travel Program is a fully integrated part of the regular curriculum. Each semester, students participate in two weeks of faculty-led academic travel. More than any other program of study, it gives students an opportunity to learn through experience. Travel destinations for 2012–13 included the Baltic States, Belgium, Brazil, Cyprus, Denmark, England, France, Germany, Holland, Iceland, Republic of Ireland and Northern Ireland, Italy, Malawi, Morocco, Mozambique, Poland, Romania, Scotland, Serbia, South Korea, Spain, Switzerland, Turkey, and the United States.

Internships are also available. Students with academic interest in any area may apply for an internship after two semesters of residence at Franklin, either by asking to be considered for one of the internships provided by the College or by arranging for an appointment themselves. The Assistant Dean of Student Life coordinates the internship program; a student may earn a maximum of 3 credit hours in an assignment.

Students in good standing who major in modern languages are eligible for study in a country where the target language is spoken; such study is limited to one semester at an approved institution.

Academic Facilities

The Franklin College Libraries contain over 38,000 volumes in English and six other languages, as well as over 100 print newspapers and journals. In addition to the print and multimedia collections, the libraries subscribe to many online indexes and full-text databases, including ProQuest, EBSCO, LexisNexis University, MarketLine, Columbia International Affairs Online (CIAO), and ARTstor. Public Internet-access computers are available in the libraries and computer lab for student research use.

Costs

The comprehensive fee for the 2012–13 academic year was $47,110. This figure includes the cost of tuition, room and board, academic travel, and student fees. The estimated cost of personal expenses and incidentals, including textbooks, is $6,500 per year. The estimated cost range to fly round-trip from the United States is from $1,100 to $1,400.

Financial Aid

Franklin College Switzerland offers academic merit awards and need-based financial aid to qualified students. U.S. applicants for financial aid must submit the FAFSA for evaluation. Veterans' and Social Security benefits are also available to eligible students. Federal Stafford Student Loans and PLUS loans may be obtained through the Department of Education's Direct Loan Program. International students must submit the International Student Financial Aid Form. Campus scholarships are also available. Students interested in applying for one can do so by requesting information about available Life Long Learning Scholarships through the Office of Student Life at the beginning of each semester.

Faculty

Franklin College Switzerland has 58 full-time and part-time professors, approximately half of whom are American or British; others are of various nationalities. The majority have advanced degrees from prestigious American universities, the others from highly recognized British and Continental universities; most have lived, studied, worked, and taught in a variety of countries. The teaching staff characterizes the cross-cultural essence of the College. Professors are committed to both the European and global arenas of study; are knowledgeable about particular countries enough to organize and lead rewarding academic travels; are competent in more than one language; and are dedicated to the personal, discursive style of teaching required by a small liberal arts college with small classes. The faculty members also advise the various student activities, lead local excursions, and regularly contribute to the College's co-curricular program of lectures. In addition, each faculty member acts as academic counselor to a number of students. The faculty-conducted Academic Travel Program promotes the intellectual friendship between teacher and student essential to a liberal arts education. Franklin's student-faculty ratio is approximately 10:1.

Student Government

The student body elects the members of the Student Government Association (SGA). The SGA sponsors several interest groups including an award-winning Model United Nations team, Business Society, the *Franklin Voice* (student newspaper), Sustainability Club, and AIESEC, as well as several social events. In addition, the SGA collaborates with the local community to host events, such as a biannual blood drive. The SGA is actively involved in campus governance by appointing members to participate in meetings of the Curriculum Committee, Faculty Assembly, and the Appeals Board.

Admission Requirements

Franklin College Switzerland seeks students who are eager to meet the challenge of studying and living in Europe, serious about undertaking college-level learning, and prepared to contribute positively to the intellectual life of the College. To identify such students, and also to ensure a diverse student population, the College Admissions Committee considers both academic and personal facts, including the student's academic record, evaluations by teachers and counselors, standardized test scores, extracurricular interests and talents, and academic distinctions. Admission to the College is limited and therefore competitive. To achieve the best match between the student and Franklin, a personal interview is strongly recommended; one can be arranged by contacting the Admissions Office in Lugano or New York. Applicants to the freshman class must submit a completed application form (using either the Franklin application or the Common Application) with a nonrefundable fee of $90; an essay and personal statement; an official transcript of their secondary school record; SAT or ACT scores, either included on transcripts or forwarded by the testing service to Franklin College (CEEB code number 0922; ACT code number 5223); and three letters of academic evaluation. Applicants whose first language is not English must submit their score on either the SAT or ACT, or Test of English as a Foreign Language (TOEFL)/International English Language Testing System (IELTS). TOEFL scores should be at least 79 (Internet-based test) or 550 (paper-based test). IELTS scores should be above 6.0. Transfer applicants and institute applicants are required to submit a completed application and a nonrefundable application fee of $90, an official transcript of their college record, a dean's report from the dean of students, and one letter of academic recommendation. The application fee is waived for all applicants who apply by January 15. In addition, applicants who submit their application by December 1 qualify for a free round trip ticket from New York to Zurich.

Application Deadlines and Information

The priority application deadline for fall entry is March 15 for applicants to the freshman class and June 15 for transfer and study-abroad applicants. The application deadline for the spring semester is November 15. Admission decisions are made on a rolling basis, allowing consideration for enrollment after the priority deadline. Applicants can usually expect a decision within three weeks from the time their application is completed. All inquiries and applications should be directed to the nearest Admissions Office.

Franklin College Switzerland
U.S. Office, Suite 2746
420 Lexington Avenue
New York, NY 10170
Phone: 212-922-9650
Fax: 212-922-9870
E-mail: info@fc.edu

Peter Dorthe
Director of Admissions
Franklin College Switzerland
Via Ponte Tresa, 29
6924 Sorengo/Lugano
Switzerland
Phone: 41-91-986-3613
Fax: 41-91-993-3906
E-mail: info@fc.edu
Website: www.fc.edu
    www.facebook.com/franklincollegeswitzerland

Franklin students enjoying terrace dining at the Grotto, Franklin College Switzerland's casual dining area.

GANNON UNIVERSITY
ERIE, PENNSYLVANIA

Believe in the possibilities.

The University

Gannon University, which is consistently named one of America's Best Colleges by *U.S. News & World Report,* is dedicated to excellence in holistic education. The oldest part of the University is Villa Maria College, which was founded in 1925 by the Sisters of St. Joseph. In 1933, Archbishop John Mark Gannon established Cathedral College, a two-year institution, which by 1941 had evolved into a four-year college, the Gannon School of Arts and Sciences. The name Gannon College was adopted in 1944, and Gannon achieved university status in 1979. Villa Maria College subsequently merged with Gannon University in 1989.

Gannon's campus is located in the heart of downtown Erie, giving students the benefit of internships with businesses, law and law-enforcement agencies, health-care facilities, industries, and social service organizations. It is within walking distance of stores, shops, restaurants, and theaters. The campus consists of forty-six buildings located within six city blocks. Among these buildings is the Carneval Athletic Pavilion, which has a pool; three gyms; a running track; a weight room; courts for racquetball, handball, volleyball and basketball; and other facilities. Also on campus are three residence halls, nine apartment buildings, classroom and faculty office buildings, an administration building, and a multipurpose chapel building. The Waldron Campus Center is a focal point that gives students the opportunity to meet and socialize between classes with faculty members and other students.

Gannon offers students a broad intramural sports program that runs throughout the entire year. In Division II intercollegiate athletics, Gannon offers men's baseball, basketball, cross-country, football, golf, soccer, swimming and diving, water polo, and wrestling and women's basketball, cross-country, golf, lacrosse, soccer, softball, swimming and diving, volleyball, and water polo. Gannon's athletes utilize the Gannon University Field, a multipurpose athletic facility that is conveniently located on campus.

There are over 4,035 students at Gannon, more than 3,000 of whom are undergraduates. The ratio of commuters to resident students is approximately 1:4. To assist in internship placement, career development and employment, and tutoring services, students will find the Student Success Center a must to visit when on campus.

Location

Erie is Pennsylvania's fourth-largest city and is located in the northwestern corner of the state on the shore of Lake Erie. Erie is approximately 120 miles north of Pittsburgh, Pennsylvania; 90 miles east of Cleveland, Ohio; and 90 miles southwest of Buffalo, New York. The campus is within 5 miles of Interstates 79 and 90 and 5 miles from Erie International Airport. Erie is also serviced by rail and bus transportation.

Majors and Degrees

The College of Humanities, Education, and Social Sciences awards the Bachelor of Arts and Bachelor of Science degrees.

In the College of Humanities, Education and Social Sciences, the areas of study from which students may select a major are communication arts, criminal justice, English (with concentrations in applied communications, literature, and writing), foreign language and international studies, foreign language and literature, history, international studies, journalism communications, leadership studies, legal studies, liberal arts, mortuary science, philosophy, political science, prelaw, a 3+3 prelaw program that includes early admission to

Duquesne University, psychology, social work, theater, theater and communication arts, and theology.

In the School of Education, the areas of study from which students may select a major are early childhood education Pre-K–4, early childhood education PreK–4/special education PreK–8, middle level education 4–8, middle level education 4–8/special education Prek–8, secondary education (in biology, English, mathematics, and social studies).

The Morosky College of Health Professions and Sciences offers degrees in the health professions and sciences. The degrees offered in the health professions include medical technology, nursing, nutrition and human performance, occupational therapy, physical therapy, physician assistant, radiologic sciences, respiratory care, sport and exercise science, and undecided health science.

The School of Sciences offers degrees in bioinformatics, biology, chemistry, environmental science, mathematics, and science. Also offered are preprofessional programs for students who wish to enter medical, dental, or veterinary school, as well as accelerated and cooperative medical programs in allopathy, osteopathy, optometry, podiatry, and pharmacy.

The Morosky College of Health Professions and Sciences is located in the Robert H. Morosky Academic Center. This 99,000-square-foot facility includes classrooms, labs, and faculty offices. It also includes a 5,800-square-foot state-of-the-art Patient Simulation Center.

The College of Engineering and Business offers degrees in a variety of areas. Students may choose from majors in biomedical engineering, chemical engineering (cooperative program), computer science, electrical engineering, electrical engineering (five-year co-op program), environmental engineering, information systems, mechanical engineering, mechanical engineering (five-year co-op program), and software engineering. Business majors include accounting, advertising communications, business administration, entrepreneurship, finance, international business, management, marketing, risk management and insurance, and sports management and marketing. All business students are required to participate in an internship before graduation.

The associate degree program offers Associate of Science and Associate of Arts degrees. Areas of study in which students may major are accounting, business administration, criminal justice, early childhood education, legal studies, radiologic sciences, and respiratory care.

Academic Programs

Each undergraduate program has its own sequence of requirements. Students in all programs must complete credits in liberal studies. A faculty adviser is assigned to each student to assist with academic planning. A department chairperson and faculty adviser also assist each student in selecting courses that fulfill requirements and best meet the student's desired career objectives. The basic graduation requirements for bachelor's degree candidates are 128 credit hours, including completion of requirements for their major and the liberal studies program. To earn an associate degree, students must usually complete 60 to 68 credit hours, depending on the program. Students may receive credit through the Advanced Placement program.

Gannon offers a program for students with learning disabilities (PSLD) and an Army ROTC program that is open to interested students.

Gannon's academic calendar consists of two full semesters, running from August to December and from January to May. There are also optional summer classes.

Academic Facilities

The Nash Library contains over 265,000 books, 4,000 audiovisual items, and 300 periodicals (along with online subscriptions to over 58,000 more). Special collections include University Archives, the curriculum library, and entertainment DVDs (over 1,000 and growing). Interlibrary loan is available for items not owned by Nash. In addition, reference service and information literacy instruction are integral components of the library's educational mission. The library is open 97 hours per week during fall and spring semesters and provides a variety of spaces for study including tables, lounge-type furniture, private study carrels, and group study rooms. There are several computer workstations with Internet and Microsoft Office access, and the entire building is covered by Gannon's wireless network. Laptop computers are available for in-library use.

The A. J. Palumbo Academic Center houses the College of Humanities, Education and Social Sciences. It offers some of the finest laboratories, technology, and classrooms available today. From education to criminal justice and foreign language programs, the faculty members and facilities in Palumbo provide high-quality education. The University's honors program also has a home in the Palumbo Center.

The Zurn Science Center has laboratories for research in biology, anatomy, physics, chemistry, and engineering. The building also houses an open engineering computer lab as well as additional computer labs for student use. There are numerous classrooms and two auditoriums in the building. Among other University facilities are additional classroom buildings, a radio station, and a theater. All academic buildings are wireless.

Costs

For 2013–14, full-time tuition was $13,500 per semester ($14,315 for engineering and health sciences), or $27,000 per academic year ($28,630 for engineering and health sciences). Tuition for part-time students was $650 per credit hour. Room and board were approximately $5,025 per semester. The total cost for the academic year at Gannon was between $27,194 and $28,824 for commuting students and $37,244 and $38,874 for resident students, depending on the program of study.

Financial Aid

In order to bring a Gannon education to qualified students who could not otherwise afford it, the University offers an integrated financial aid program of scholarships, grants, loans, and employment. Gannon's financial aid program is open to all full-time students attending classes during the period from August to May. It is highly recommended that all students seeking financial aid should file the admissions and financial aid applications by the preferred deadline of March 15. Numerous scholarship opportunities are available to qualified students. Each year the University offers its top incoming freshmen the ability to compete for full tuition scholarships. Application deadline for this competition is December 15 with on-campus competition taking place in late January.

Faculty

Gannon's faculty consists of 200 lay and religious men and women, and 72 percent of the full-time faculty members have either doctoral or terminal degrees. The student-faculty ratio is about 14:1, and average class size is approximately 25 students in each class. Most faculty members assist in the faculty adviser program, giving each student individual attention and counseling on academic and personal matters.

Student Government

The Student Government Association (SGA) is composed of students elected by members of their class. Through the SGA, students can play a responsible role in the planning and working of the University. SGA has voting representatives on all of the standing committees of the University. Members of the SGA not only research existing policies and problems, they also look for new ways to improve the academic life of students. The SGA also plans social events for the student body.

Admission Requirements

Gannon University actively recruits students of all races, creeds, and ages from all geographic regions. Transfer and international students are encouraged to seek admission. Applicants are required to submit scores (including senior-year scores) on either the SAT or ACT; an up-to-date transcript of the high school record, showing rank in class (plus a college transcript for transfer applicants); a completed application form; and a nonrefundable $25 fee. Admission decisions are based upon numerous factors, central of which is the strength of the high school record, as demonstrated through grades and relative class standing and SAT and/or ACT scores and other test scores that may be available. Recommendations and personal statements also affect admission decisions. Transfer and international students should check with the admissions office for special application procedures.

Application and Information

Students applying for admission in the fall semester should start the application process at the beginning of their senior year in high school. Gannon operates on a rolling admissions basis, which means that there is no deadline for filing applications, with the exceptions of the LECOM (Lake Erie College of Osteopathic Medicine) and PCOM (Philadelphia College of Osteopathic Medicine) 4+4 Medical Programs and the accelerated pharmacy options, which have a deadline of December 1 for the fall semester. Due to the competitiveness of the program, students who are interested in the physician assistant studies or nursing programs are highly encouraged to file their applications in September. The physician assistant studies program has a November 1 application deadline. Early applications are recommended, as are enrollment deposits.

For further information, students should contact:

Office of Admissions
Gannon University
109 University Square
Erie, Pennsylvania 16541
Phone: 814-871-7240
         800-GANNON-U (426-6668, toll-free)
Fax: 814-871-5803
E-mail: admissions@gannon.edu
Website: http://www.gannon.edu

Gannon University is a caring community of dynamic faculty and staff who educate motivated students in an environment focused on Catholic values.

THE GEORGE WASHINGTON UNIVERSITY

WASHINGTON, D.C.

The University

Located just four blocks from the White House, the George Washington University (GW) is the largest institution of higher education in the nation's capital. Founded in 1821 by an Act of Congress, GW is a private nonsectarian coeducational institution accredited by the Middle States Association of Colleges and Universities. GW prides itself in being at the forefront of major research endeavors, while providing a stimulating intellectual environment where students and faculty members put knowledge into action.

The student population at GW consists of approximately 10,200 undergraduates and 14,800 graduates. Undergraduates hail from all fifty states, the District of Columbia, Puerto Rico, the Virgin Islands, and 120 countries. The undergraduate student population is 10 percent Asian American, 6.6 percent African American, 7.3 percent Hispanic American, and 8.1 percent international.

GW comprises two fully integrated campuses, the Foggy Bottom campus and the Mount Vernon campus. Both campuses are located in historic D.C. neighborhoods that offer vibrant and distinctive residential options to freshmen and continuing students. The Foggy Bottom campus is situated in the center of downtown D.C., neighbored by the Kennedy Center, the Watergate complex, the State Department, and the White House. The 26-acre Mount Vernon campus is home to athletic facilities and is surrounded by embassy and diplomatic residences.

GW guarantees housing for entering freshmen and sophomores and houses more than 75 percent of undergraduates in thirty-seven residence halls. GW offers a number of living arrangements, including apartment-style living for upperclassmen and residential town houses. GW's academic residential communities philosophy guarantees that residence hall life is a valuable extension of the undergraduate academic experience. With nearly 100 percent of the entering class living in university housing, the atmosphere proves to be academically as well as socially stimulating.

GW hosts a strong intercollegiate varsity athletic program with twenty-three teams participating in the NCAA Division I and Atlantic 10 Conference. They include men's baseball, basketball, crew, cross-country, golf, sailing, soccer, swimming, tennis, and water polo, and women's basketball, crew, cross-country, gymnastics, soccer, swimming and diving, tennis, volleyball, and water polo. Students interested in playing sports, but not quite up to the varsity level, may join a number of university-supported club and intramural sports.

There are more than 400 student-created and student-run organizations at GW. These organizations run the spectrum from academic to cultural, spiritual to recreational, and political to artistic. In addition to these special-interest organizations, GW is home to twenty-eight national sororities and fraternities, fifteen multicultural Greek chapters, the Student Association (details in the Student Government section), the Program Board, the *GW Hatchet* (GW's independent newspaper), and WRGW (the campus radio station). The Division of Student Affairs plans hallmark program events for students on campus, ranging from Welcome Week to the Excellence in Student Life Awards.

Location

Many students at GW also choose to immerse themselves in the excitement of Washington D.C., which has been called the most livable city on the East Coast and one of the best college towns in the United States. Washington, D.C., offers an infinite array of internships and cooperative education experiences, allowing GW students to explore their career aspirations outside of the four walls of the classroom. GW students have interned at the White House, the World Bank, IBM, the U.S. House of Representatives and Senate, NASA, the National Zoo, and CNN, among many other world famous organizations.

The 17 million tourists that flock to Washington, D.C., every year experience the vibrant college town and young professional social scene in the nation's capital. There are more than 50,000 college students in the D.C. metropolitan area.

Majors and Degrees

GW offers a wide range of undergraduate programs in six undergraduate schools: the Columbian College of Arts and Sciences, the Elliott School of International Affairs, the School of Business, the School of Engineering and Applied Science, the School of Media and Public Affairs, and the School of Public Health and Health Services.

GW offers more than 3,000 courses in over 70 majors, and yet, the average class size is only 28. Students may earn an undergraduate degree in a single field of study, or they may choose to double major, major in one field and minor in another, participate in an interdisciplinary program, or create their own individualized field of study.

The university awards an array of bachelor's degrees, including Bachelor of Arts (B.A.), Bachelor of Science (B.S.), Bachelor of Accountancy (B.Accy.), and Bachelor of Business Administration (B.B.A.).

A variety of joint-degree programs are available to undergraduates. In addition to a seven-year accelerated B.A./M.D. program, the university offers nearly fifty 5-year bachelor's/master's combined programs, some of which students enter as freshmen.

Academic Programs

Most undergraduate students must complete 120 credit hours to be eligible for graduation, which means that the average student carries 15 credit hours (five courses) per semester. All students at GW are required to participate in the university's writing program. In addition, each school has general curriculum requirements, ranging from 17 to 45 credit hours.

GW is home to nineteen honor societies, including Phi Beta Kappa and Golden Key National Honor Society. GW offers a variety of specialized academic programs. The University Honors Program, which does not replace a regular program of study but rather enhances it with intellectually challenging analysis and discussion, consists of approximately 500 undergraduates.

The seven-year accelerated B.A./M.D. Program is designed for students who wish to obtain a strong foundation in the liberal arts prior to becoming physicians, enabling them to accomplish that goal in a shorter amount of time than a traditional program of study.

Off-Campus Programs

GW students are encouraged to study abroad in order to expand their worldview and their educational opportunities. GW offers study abroad centers in Madrid, Paris, England, and Latin America (Chile, Costa Rica, and Argentina), as well as affiliated and exchange programs. Each year, more than 1,800 GW undergraduates study abroad in nearly seventy countries.

Many GW students also take advantage of cooperative education (co-op), which provides students with an opportunity to gain valuable paid work experiences directly related to their major. The Career Center manages the program, in partnership with area employers, to ensure that co-op experiences are substantive and well-supervised. Similarly, most GW students engage in internships, which serve as a means for students to gain practical, professional experience and to augment their academic knowledge. Internships can be paid or unpaid, offered for academic credit, and can last for as long (or short) as the student and employer choose. The Career Center also acts as a clearinghouse for internship positions.

Academic Facilities

The Gelman Library houses more than 2 million volumes and, as a member of the Washington Research Library Consortium (WRLC), offers GW students access to more than 12 million items at nine area universities. Gelman Library is open 168 hours per week, offering 24-hour study lounges, group discussion rooms, computer labs, walk-up reference consultation, and an interlibrary loan service. GW provides on-site and remote access to ALADIN, the shared online catalogue of WRLC libraries, plus databases indexing periodical articles and some full-text journals. GW is also home to the Eckles Library, the Jacob Burns Law Library, the Himmelfarb Health Sciences Library, and the Virginia Science and Technology Campus Library.

GW is infused with the latest, state-of-the-art facilities enhancing campus life. Completed and planned projects include the Science and Engineering Hall; the School of Public Health and Health Services building; the George Washington University Museum, which will house the Textile Museum; and an 850 bed residence hall with faculty suites, affinity housing, and retail space.

Costs

In response to family concerns about paying for college, GW has instituted a fixed tuition plan. Under this plan, the tuition remains the same each year for students who remain enrolled in full-time status during their undergraduate programs. Therefore, except for marginal increases in housing costs, cost of attendance will not rise. Students who entered in fall 2012 have tuition costs of $45,735 per year for four years. Room and board costs are approximately $10,530.

Financial Aid

The ability to finance a GW education is a priority, so the Office of Student Financial Assistance seeks to assist students and their families in meeting the costs to attend the university. The university budgets more than $160 million for undergraduate financial assistance, which includes scholarships and need-based assistance. In addition, GW offers families the opportunity to participate in a ten-month payment plan.

By applying for admission, students with outstanding academic credentials are automatically considered for Presidential Academic Scholarships. More than 20 percent of GW's freshmen receive merit-based financial assistance. In addition, approximately 50 percent of freshmen receive need-based assistance with an average package of over $35,257.

The Presidential Scholars in the Arts Program awards scholarships to, and encourages the work of, entering freshmen who have shown promise in the fine arts (ceramics, design, drawing, painting, photography, and sculpture), music, theater, technical theater, directing, dance, and choreography.

More information about financial aid at GW can be obtained online at http://www.gwu.edu. Both merit scholarships and a portion of need-based financial aid are guaranteed for all four years for students who remain enrolled in full-time status during their undergraduate program.

Faculty

There is 1 faculty member for every 14 students at GW. Ninety-three percent of GW's full-time faculty members hold a doctoral degree. Part-time and adjunct faculty members are often leaders in their fields of expertise. GW professors are engaging, eminently qualified, and well connected, which allows for a robust intellectual community.

Student Government

The Student Association (SA) is an organization chartered by GW's Board of Trustees to represent students and their concerns. Any person registered for any academic credit at GW is a member of the SA. The SA undertakes initiatives related to academics, community service, neighborhood relations, and student activities.

Admission Requirements

GW receives approximately 22,000 applications for freshman admission and aims to recruit a class of 2,350. Admitted students have strong academic records and the demonstrated ability to achieve success in their college endeavors. To be considered for admission, applicants must submit the following credentials: application and fee, high school transcripts, essays, letters of recommendation from a teacher and a guidance counselor, and either SAT or ACT scores. Details can be obtained online at http://www.gwu.edu. GW also accepts the Common Application, with the GW supplement to the Common Application. Freshman interviews are not required, but may be helpful.

Application and Information

GW has a number of application options: regular decision, early decision I, and early decision II. Prospective students should consult the website (http://www.gwu.edu) for the application and deadlines.

Office of Admissions
The George Washington University
2121 I Street, NW, Suite 201
Washington, D.C. 20052
Phone: 202-994-6040
E-mail: gwadm@gwu.edu
Website: http://www.gwu.edu

Kogan Plaza on the GW campus.

GRAND VIEW UNIVERSITY

DES MOINES, IOWA

The University

Grand View University is a liberal arts institution affiliated with the Evangelical Lutheran Church in America. Founded more than 100 years ago, Grand View offers a high-quality education to a diverse student body in a career-oriented, liberal arts–grounded curriculum at two campus locations in greater Des Moines. Grand View welcomes traditional students, adult learners, and graduate students representing a wide range of religious and cultural backgrounds.

At Grand View, students find a winning combination of high-quality programs, experienced professors, and caring individuals. With 2,300 students and an average class size of 16, students get to know their professors and other students well. They learn independence and seek responsibility in Grand View's educational environment. Learning is an interactive process at Grand View—students engage in lively discussions, work on real-world projects, and participate in career-related work experiences.

Grand View stands out from other universities because of its partnerships with leading businesses and organizations in Des Moines, which has led to challenging internships. Grand View is known for its ability to connect students with exciting and challenging career opportunities. For nearly a decade and a half, nearly 100 percent of students found jobs right after graduation or continued their education.

Students are encouraged to develop leadership and team skills through involvement in campus organizations, which include intercollegiate and intramural athletics, speech and theater groups, major department clubs, student government, and musical ensembles. Active honorary societies include Alpha Chi, Alpha Mu Gamma, Alpha Psi Omega, Alpha Sigma Lambda, Beta Beta Beta, Phi Eta Sigma, Sigma Theta Tau, and Theta Alpha Kappa among others. Grand View's student leadership program provides opportunities for students without leadership experience to seek and develop critical thinking, interpersonal, and networking skills.

Student athletes compete in men's baseball, basketball, bowling, cross-country, football, golf, soccer, tennis, track and field, volleyball, and wrestling, and women's basketball, bowling, competitive cheer, competitive dance, cross-country, golf, soccer, softball, tennis, track and field, and volleyball. Grand View participates in the Midwest Collegiate Conference of the National Association of Intercollegiate Athletics. Athletic scholarships are available.

Two locations offer Grand View students convenient scheduling options for their program of study. Weekend and evening classes are offered at the main campus in Des Moines and at Grand View's campus in Johnston, Iowa. For motivated students seeking to complete their degree quickly, accelerated schedules are offered for several of sixteen evening majors.

Location

Grand View is located in Des Moines, a metropolitan area of more than half a million people in central Iowa. Des Moines is the state capital and serves as the communications hub for Iowa. Nationally recognized organizations that have their corporate offices in Des Moines include Pioneer Hi-Bred International, Inc.; the Principal Financial Group; Meredith Corporation; and the *Des Moines Register*.

In essence, Grand View's campus is the entire city of Des Moines—as part of the Grand View community, students are not limited by the confines of a small school or small town. In a given day, students can catch an Iowa Cubs professional baseball doubleheader, head down to the Court Avenue district for great food and nightlife, or take in a concert at Wells Fargo Arena.

A thriving arts program in Des Moines features the Des Moines Metro Opera, Ballet Iowa, the Des Moines Symphony, the Des Moines Art Center, and the Des Moines Playhouse. The summer Des Moines Arts Festival is ranked third in the nation.

Des Moines features four distinct and beautiful seasons. Except for a month or so of bundle-up, see-your-breath weather, the climate is ideal for outdoor activities. Grand View students can take advantage of terrific recreational opportunities, including several golf courses, Saylorville Lake, and many city parks and state forests.

Easily accessible from Interstates 35 and 80, Grand View is 4 hours from Minneapolis, 6 hours from Chicago, and 3 hours from Kansas City.

Majors and Degrees

Grand View University grants the Bachelor of Arts degree and offers forty majors in areas such as accounting, applied mathematics, art education, biology, biochemistry, biotechnology, business administration (with concentrations in agricultural business, finance, human resource management, management, marketing, and real estate), church music, computer science, criminal justice, digital media production, elementary education, English, general studies–liberal arts, graphic design, graphic journalism, health promotion, history, human services, individualized major, journalism, management information systems, mass communication, music, music education, organizational studies, paralegal studies, physical science, political studies (prelaw or public administration), psychology, religion, secondary education, service management, sociology–liberal arts, Spanish for careers and professionals, theater arts, and studio arts. Grand View also offers a Bachelor of Science degree in nursing, as well as an RN to B.S.N. program. In addition, the University offers certificate programs in art therapy, human resource management, in-house communication, real estate, Spanish essentials, and sport management, as well as a postbaccalaureate certificate in accounting.

The Master of Science in Innovative Leadership program is an interdisciplinary advanced degree with tracks in business, education, and nursing. This cutting-edge, 40-credit-hour program qualifies graduates as organizational leaders, clinical nurse leaders, and teacher leaders.

Academic Programs

Grand View operates on a 4-4-1 academic calendar. The first semester runs from September to December. The second semester begins in early January and ends in late April. Three one-month summer sessions are offered in May, June, and July, as is a summer trimester evening program.

In the fall of 2013, Grand View is slated to launch its new general education core, which takes an innovative, integrated approach to developing essential abilities employers seek in graduates, such as writing, speaking, analysis, problem-solving, and critical thinking. Through their coursework, students can gain the personal and intellectual depth that will help them thrive in today's knowledge-based economy and in their communities.

The Logos Honors Program augments the general education core. By invitation, freshman and sophomore students enrolled in this program complete a series of courses designed to challenge exceptional students.

An active study-abroad program gives students opportunities to learn in an international setting, particularly through a partnership with the Danish Institute for Study Abroad.

The Grand View academic mission is to provide a diverse student body with an academically rigorous education. In order to meet this commitment, Grand View provides a variety of learning environments and teaching techniques. The university's academic support programs and services were lauded as a national model by the examining team from the North Central Association of Colleges and Schools during reaccreditation in 2005, when the University received complete ten-year accreditation with no follow-up required.

Costs

For 2012–13, the comprehensive cost for freshmen living on campus was approximately $29,320, which included tuition, an activity fee, a technology fee, a parking fee, and room and board. Students have several residential and meal plan options that affect cost. Health services and Internet access are also included in the comprehensive fee.

Financial Aid

Typically, most full-time Grand View students received financial assistance. The average freshman full-time award package is usually around $24,500 with about $16,000 in grants and scholarships, and the remainder in work-study and student loans. The amount of aid is determined through a combination of merit and analysis of need as determined through the Free Application for Federal Student Aid. The priority deadline for financial aid is March 1. Students receive notification of financial aid packages following acceptance of admission to the University and receipt of their financial aid analysis of need.

Faculty

There are approximately 90 full-time faculty members and 90 part-time faculty members. More than 70 percent hold terminal degrees. All classes are taught by professors; no graduate or teaching assistants instruct Grand View classes.

Student Government

Students participate in University governance. The Student Activities Council and Viking Council plan student activities that promote educational, social, cultural, and recreational aspects of student life. Students serve as representatives on faculty and staff search committees, programming committees, and student life committees.

Admission Requirements

Applicants' files are reviewed to determine their preparedness for a Grand View education. Official high school transcripts and submission of ACT or SAT scores are required for applicants with less than 24 semester hours of college credit. Applicants transferring from another college are required to submit official transcripts from all colleges previously attended.

Application and Information

For more information about Grand View, students should contact:
Admissions Office
Grand View University
1200 Grandview Avenue
Des Moines, Iowa 50316
Phone: 515-263-2810
        800-444-6083 (toll-free)
Fax: 515-263-2974
E-mail: admissions@grandview.edu
Website: http://www.admissions.grandview.edu
        http://www.facebook.com/pages/Grand-View-
            University/315068091675 (Facebook)

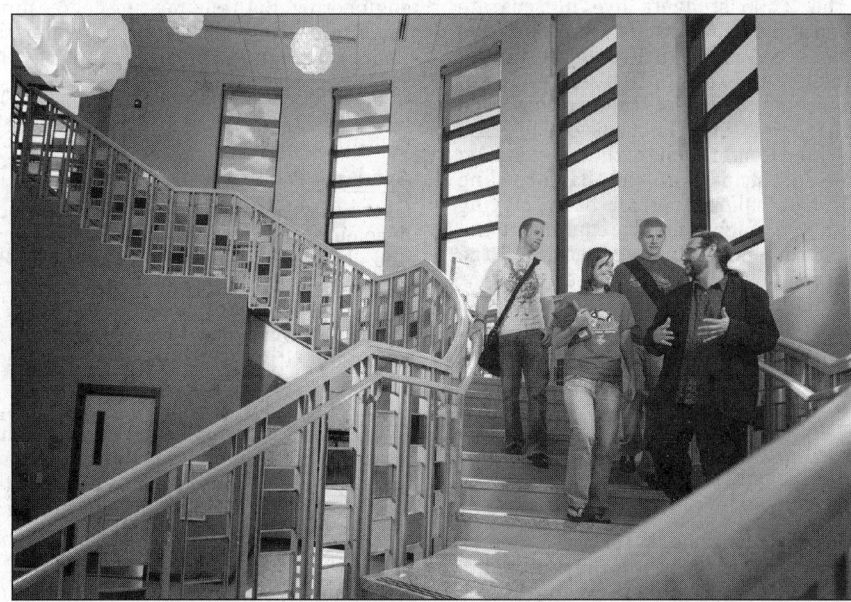

Grand View students chat with a professor on their way to class.

GROVE CITY COLLEGE
GROVE CITY, PENNSYLVANIA

GROVE CITY
COLLEGE

The College

Because Faith and Freedom Matter

The beautifully landscaped campus of Grove City College stretches more than 180 acres and includes nearly thirty neo-Gothic buildings valued at more than $100 million. The campus is considered one of the loveliest in the nation. While the College has changed to meet the needs of the society it serves, its basic philosophy has remained unchanged since its founding in 1876. It is a Christian liberal arts and sciences institution of ideal size and dedicated to the principle of providing the highest-quality education at the lowest possible cost. Wishing to remain truly independent and to retain its distinctive qualities as a private school governed by private citizens (trustees), it is one of the very few colleges in the country that does not accept any federal funding. It is informally affiliated with the Presbyterian Church (U.S.A.) but not narrowly denominational; the College believes that to be well educated a student should be exposed to the central ideas of the Christian faith. A 20-minute chapel program offered Tuesday and Thursday mornings, along with a Sunday evening worship service, challenges students in their faith. Sixteen chapel services per semester are required out of over fifty opportunities. Christian organizations and activities exist to provide fellowship and spiritual growth.

Grove City attracts students from all over the United States. While most come from Pennsylvania, Ohio, New Jersey, Virginia, and New York, forty-five states and eight other countries were represented in 2012–13. In the most recent freshman class (of those submitting a rank), 97 percent of the women and 93 percent of the men ranked in the top fifth of their high school class. Their average SAT combined score was 1227 (combining only the critical reading and math scores); the average ACT composite score was 27.

Ninety-four percent of the 2,506 students live in separate men's and women's residence halls. All others are commuters or participants in a study-abroad program. A full program of cultural, professional, athletic, and social activities is offered. An arena, Crawford Auditorium, and the J. Howard Pew Fine Arts Center are used for athletics, concerts, movies, plays, and lectures. The Physical Learning Center is one of the finest among the nation's small colleges and includes an eight-lane bowling alley, two swimming pools, handball/racquetball courts, playing surfaces, fitness rooms with free weights, aerobic equipment and Cybex machines, an indoor three-lane running track, and the basketball arena. The Breen Student Union provides an eatery; mailroom; bookstore; commuters' lounge; and a commons area for dining, studying, and socializing. The Ketler and South Hall Recreation Lounges are also available for cooking, games, and socializing. There are more than 145 organizations and special interest groups, including local fraternities and sororities. No alcohol or drugs are permitted on campus. The athletic activities include extensive intramural, club, and varsity sports programs that provide nineteen intercollegiate teams that compete at the NCAA Division III level for men and women.

The College's well-established placement services, ranked recently by The Princeton Review as twelfth in the nation, are used constantly by students. A complete file of personal data, scholastic records, and recommendations is prepared for each participant. These files are available to the scores of prospective employers who visit the campus annually to interview the graduating seniors. One of Grove City's strengths is placing students in business, industrial, and teaching positions, as well as in professional institutions such as medical schools.

Prospective students may check out Grove City College's web page at www.gcc.edu.

Location

Grove City, a town of 8,000 people, is 60 miles north of Pittsburgh and is located 4 miles from restaurants, hotels, and a 140-store outlet mall. Convenient to I-79 and I-80, Grove City is only a day's drive from Chicago, New York City, Toronto, and Washington, D.C. The municipal airport has a 4,500-foot runway, and there is bus service to Pittsburgh.

Majors and Degrees

Grove City College offers undergraduate degrees in liberal arts, sciences, engineering, and music. The Bachelor of Arts (B.A.) is offered with majors in Biblical and religious studies, communication studies, economics, English, history, modern language (French and Spanish), philosophy, political science, psychology, secondary education, and sociology. Pre-professional students in law or theology usually earn the B.A. degree. Interdisciplinary major programs are also available for qualified students.

The Bachelor of Science is granted with majors in accounting, applied physics/computer, biochemistry, biology, business management, chemistry, computer information systems, computer science, PreK–4 elementary education, PreK–8 special education, entrepreneurship, exercise science, financial management, industrial management, international business, marketing management, mathematics, middle level education, molecular biology, physics, and psychology. Pre-professional students often select one of these majors for dentistry, medicine, or other health fields.

The Bachelor of Science in Mechanical Engineering degree is also offered. The Bachelor of Science in Electrical Engineering degree provides for concentration areas in either electrical or computer engineering. Both engineering degree programs are accredited by the Engineering Accreditation Commission of the Accreditation Board for Engineering and Technology, Inc. (ABET).

The Bachelor of Music degree is awarded to those who major in music. Programs may also include concentrations in business, education, performing arts, and religion.

Academic Programs

Grove City College's goal is to assist young men and women in developing as complete individuals—academically, spiritually, and physically. The general education requirements provide all students with a high level of cultural literacy and communication skills. They include 46 semester hours of courses with emphases in the humanities, social sciences, and natural sciences; in quantitative and logical reasoning; physical education; and in science, faith, and technology, as well as a language requirement for all majors except engineering and science. Degree candidates must also complete the requirements in their field of concentration and electives. To graduate, a student must have completed a minimum 128 semester hours as well as the chapel attendance requirement. On average, 78 percent of those entering as freshmen stay and receive a diploma in four years and 82 percent in six years.

A distinctive liberal arts–engineering program includes engineering courses plus courses in the humanities to provide students with a well-grounded preparation for entering the engineering field, as well as the civic and cultural life of society. The Austrian economics program exposes students to all economic philosophies, yet strongly advocates economic freedoms and free markets.

Grove City follows the semester calendar plan. Academic credit may be granted to incoming freshmen on the basis of scores on appropriate Advanced Placement tests, International Baccalaureate tests, or College-Level Examination Program tests. Honors courses, independent study, seminars, and the opportunity for students to study abroad for credit are also offered.

Academic Facilities

The Hall of Arts and Letters is a state-of-the-art teaching facility featuring a 200-seat lecture hall, forty classrooms (including multimedia-equipped rooms and tiered "case study" rooms), eighty faculty offices, the Early Education Center, the Curriculum Library, and language, computer, and video production labs.

The College library houses 162,000 books and serial backfiles; 3,500 audio/video tapes, CDs, and DVDs; and 112 current serial subscriptions. In addition, the College has access to 58,885 journal titles through its collection of full-text journal databases.

The College owns an observatory and the remote structure is utilized for astronomy classes as well as faculty and student research. Modern, well-equipped laboratories for biology, chemistry, engineering, and physics are also available, as are facilities for language and piano studies.

The Weir C. Ketler Technological Learning Center consists of computers for walk-up access, a lecture hall, video production lab, the College's FM radio station, and the campus copy center. It also houses the computer help desk and repair center that support the student technology initiative. All freshmen receive their own tablet PC and color printer/scanner/copier.

The J. Howard Pew Fine Arts Center has art, photography, and music studios; a rehearsal hall; a small theater; a museum; an art gallery; music practice rooms; and a 675-seat, acoustically tunable auditorium and stage large enough to accommodate the most elaborate drama productions and concerts. An addition contains additional classrooms, practice rooms, and a 180-seat recital hall.

Costs

As a relatively small, financially sound college, Grove City is able to charge an unusually low tuition in comparison to other independent institutions of similar quality. The 2013–14 annual tuition charge is $14,880 for all degrees. The cost of a tablet PC for all freshmen is included in the tuition fees. There is no comprehensive fee. Part-time tuition is $465 per credit. Room and board are $8,108. Expenses for books, laundry, transportation, and personal needs vary considerably with the lifestyle of the individual.

Financial Aid

Because the College's tuition charges are low, every student, in effect, receives significant financial assistance. Fifty percent of the freshmen receive additional aid from Grove City. Students applying for financial assistance must complete Grove City College's financial aid form. Job opportunities are available both on and off campus.

Faculty

The focus of the Grove City faculty members is on teaching students, although many members are involved with research and writing. Ninety-two percent of the full-time faculty members hold doctorates. Many of the administrative staff members also teach part-time in various departments. The student-faculty ratio is approximately 15:1. Faculty members emphasize teaching and attention to the students' individual needs; they also participate extensively in the College's extracurricular programs.

Student Government

The Student Government Association provides an opportunity for direct student interaction with the faculty members and administration in matters relating to campus activities. Students serve on regular College committees (library, publications, religious activities, and student activities) and also on the Men's and Women's Governing Board and the Discipline Committee.

Admission Requirements

The College seeks academically qualified students without regard to race, color, sex, religion, or national or ethnic origin. An applicant for admission should be a high school graduate with the following recommended units: English, 4; foreign language, 3; mathematics, 3; history, 2; and science, 3. Engineering, science, and mathematics majors should have 4 units each in both mathematics and science. An interview is highly recommended, especially for those who live within a day's drive (400 miles). Auditions are required for music majors.

Transfer students may receive advanced standing if they have maintained good academic standing at their previous institution(s).

Application and Information

A regular admission applicant should take the SAT or ACT by October or November of the senior year in high school. The application should include scores on the SAT (preferred) or the ACT; a high school transcript; two letters of recommendation, one from the student's principal or counselor and the other from a pastor; and a nonrefundable application fee of $50. An application may be submitted after the eleventh grade. An early decision applicant should take the entrance test in the eleventh grade, visit the College for an interview, and submit the application by November 15; notification of the admission decision is mailed on December 15. Approved early decision applicants must accept by January 15 and submit a nonrefundable deposit of $250.

Applicants seeking regular decision must submit the completed application and supporting documents by February 1 of their senior year. Notification of the admission decision is mailed on March 15. Students who are offered admission should reply as soon as possible, but no later than May 1, and include a nonrefundable deposit of $250. Applications received after February 1 are considered as space permits.

Additional information may be obtained from:

Sarah E. Gibbs
Director of Admissions
Grove City College
100 Campus Drive
Grove City, Pennsylvania 16127-2104
Phone: 724-458-2100
Fax: 724-458-3395
E-mail: admissions@gcc.edu
Website: http://www.gcc.edu
www.facebook.com/GCCAdmissions (Facebook)
http://twitter.com/GroveCtyCollege (Twitter)

Chapel is just one aspect of an authentically Christian environment at Grove City College.

GWYNEDD-MERCY COLLEGE
GWYNEDD VALLEY, PENNSYLVANIA

Gwynedd-Mercy
College

The College

Founded by the Sisters of Mercy, Gwynedd-Mercy College (GMC) is a Catholic college offering a strong foundation in the liberal arts. For more than sixty years, Gwynedd-Mercy College has been "Bringing Futures Into Focus" by preparing students to become top professionals in the fields of arts and sciences, business, education, and nursing and health professions. GMC offers more than forty associate, bachelor's, and master's degree programs on a full- and part-time basis. GMC's academic distinction lies in the intersection of excellent programs in health care, education, and business administration, which prepare students to become leaders in the region's powerful and growing life sciences industry.

Located just 30 minutes from Philadelphia and with an enrollment of nearly 2,700 students, Gwynedd-Mercy College is large enough to offer a vibrant campus life but small enough that professors can develop mentoring relationships with students. The College educates students in the Mercy tradition of service to society, preparing graduates who not only are recruited for jobs but also create lives and careers with deep meaning. In the 2013 edition of *U.S. News & World Report*'s "Best Colleges," Gwynedd-Mercy College ranked in the first tier of its category, in part because of its high graduation and retention rates.

Gwynedd-Mercy College has nineteen NCAA Division III athletic teams, including baseball, basketball, cheerleading, cross-country, field hockey, indoor/outdoor track and field, lacrosse, soccer, softball, tennis, and volleyball. The men's baseball and men's and women's basketball teams have won various championships. The College also offers a variety of intramural sports. The field hockey, soccer, lacrosse, and track and field teams compete at the College's new Outdoor Athletic Complex, which offers a turf field and Olympic-size track.

Students are encouraged to participate in activities and student government so that they can socialize with friends, develop talents, and build leadership skills. The College offers more than thirty clubs and organizations, including campus ministry, a nationally renowned choir, the yearbook staff, and social committees. Students can write for the College newspaper, the *Gwynmercian,* which has received a first-place rating with special merit from the American Scholastic Press Association. Through the on-campus chapter of the Mercy Works Program, students can help the poor with fund-raising efforts and adopt-a-family programs at the Thanksgiving and Christmas holidays. Some students decide to give a year of service after graduation to Mercy Volunteer Corps' nationwide outreach program.

On campus, students can choose from four residence halls for rooming and dine at several eateries which offer full meals, sandwiches, pizza, salads, breakfast and coffee. The Late Night Lounge has events every weekend, including movie nights, dances, comedians, rock band competitions, and game parties.

At the graduate level, Gwynedd-Mercy College offers master's degree programs in business (management), education (educational administration, school counseling, special education, and a Master Teacher program), and nursing (nurse educator, nurse practitioner, and clinical nurse specialist).

Location

Gwynedd-Mercy's idyllic 160-acre campus is located in Gwynedd Valley, Pennsylvania, a suburb 20 miles from downtown Philadelphia. Old City, South Street, and sports arenas are a 25- to 30-minute car or train ride from the campus. The College is situated just minutes from several major highways, including the Pennsylvania Turnpike. In addition to the vibrant city life

of Philadelphia, students can travel to the New Jersey beaches or the Pocono Mountains, which are only 2 hours from the campus.

Majors and Degrees

Gwynedd-Mercy offers baccalaureate degrees in accounting, behavioral/social gerontology, biology, communication, computer information science, criminal justice, elementary education, English, finance, history, human resource management, human services, management, marketing, mathematics, medical laboratory science, nursing, philosophy, psychology, radiologic technology, radiation therapy, respiratory care, special education, and sports management.

Associate degrees are awarded in cardiovascular technology, liberal studies, natural science, nursing, and respiratory care.

Academic Programs

The school year is divided into two semesters, and most baccalaureate degree programs require the completion of a minimum of 125 credit hours. GMC maintains a strong liberal arts component in all of its degree programs. Whether the student chooses to major in one of the liberal arts or to pursue a professionally oriented degree, courses are required in language, literature and the fine arts, humanities, and behavioral, social, and natural sciences. Students have access to the Academic Resource Center for free class tutoring and assistance with improving their writing skills.

Individualized internships and work-experience programs are available and recommended in all majors to give students firsthand experience in their chosen major. Nearby Fortune 500 companies offer a variety of experiences to students in business and accounting. TAP, the Teacher Assistant Program, places every education major in the classroom one day a week beginning in the freshman year. All allied health and nursing programs require clinical experience. The 2-2 programs—those with an associate degree to bachelor's degree progression—offer allied health and nursing students the opportunity to gain employment in their field while continuing toward the baccalaureate degree. The School of Business maintains a successful work-experience semester. Through this internship, students earn credit while gaining valuable experience in challenging positions.

Students are encouraged to develop a global perspective through various study-abroad opportunities. In 2010, the College launched a study-abroad program to Brescia, Italy. During the monthlong program, students took courses in Italian language, culture, and philosophy; rode bikes to get around town; and toured Italy on weekends.

Off-Campus Programs

The excellent on-campus laboratory facilities are extended by affiliations with more than 200 hospitals and health-care agencies in Pennsylvania, New Jersey, and Delaware, where students may complete their clinical experience. Merck provides a one-semester industrial laboratory experience for qualified biology majors. Gwynedd-Mercy College maintains a close relationship with nearby companies, including Johnson & Johnson, McNeil, and Sun Company, for work-experience programs.

Academic Facilities

Gwynedd-Mercy has expanded its physical facilities as its student enrollment has increased. The Sister Isabelle Keiss Center for Health and Science houses the Schools of Nursing and Allied Health Professions and the Division of Natural Sciences. The

50,000-square-foot state-of-the-art facility offers laboratories for areas such as nursing skills, respiratory care, cardiovascular technology, radiation therapy, health information technology, organic chemistry, and microbiology. Plans are underway to construct a new academic facility to house both the School of Education and the School of Business. The College's Griffin Complex houses the College's Student Union—which is equipped with a game room, full gymnasium and track, racquetball court, and weight room. The College offers four residence halls that house 40 percent of the school population. Theaters include the Julia Ball Auditorium, a small in-the-round theater, and an upgraded TV production studio. The Student Technology Center is equipped with personal computers and printers and the latest software for student use. The Valie Genuardi Hobbit House, a private school for preschoolers where students in the School of Education are trained, is situated on campus.

Costs

The 2012–13 academic-year tuition (two semesters) for full-time students (12 to 18 credits per semester) was $27,740. The tuition for allied health and nursing students was $29,240. Room and board were, on average, $10,000. Professional liability fees for students enrolled in clinical components and lab fees are extra.

Financial Aid

Gwynedd-Mercy's financial aid program is designed to provide financial assistance to academically qualified students whose resources are inadequate to meet the costs of attending the College. The student Financial Aid Committee endeavors to assist as many students as possible, using Gwynedd-Mercy funds as well as federal, state, and other available funds. Aid is awarded on the basis of demonstrated financial need, academic proficiency, and responsible campus citizenship.

A financial aid packet is sent, with instructions, to those who request it on their application form. High school students should request the Free Application for Federal Student Aid (FAFSA) from their guidance office. In 2012–13, 91 percent of Gwynedd-Mercy College full-time students received some form of financial aid. March 15 is the deadline for freshmen entering in the fall semester. The deadline for Academic Scholarships is February 1.

Faculty

The student-faculty ratio is 13:1, allowing for personal contact, advising, and after-class instruction. This is a widely acknowledged strength of the GMC experience. For nursing students in the clinical setting, there are never more than 8 students to 1 clinical adviser; in the allied health programs, there often is one-to-one instruction. The quality of teaching is enhanced by the diversified interests of the faculty. The 181 faculty members teach both day and evening classes, allowing students the greatest flexibility in scheduling. Free tutoring is available in all disciplines.

Student Government

All students are encouraged to take part in the responsibilities of student government. This student participation and shared responsibility for the welfare of the College are promoted through a framework of committees.

Admission Requirements

Admission to Gwynedd-Mercy College is based on a student's high school record, rank in class, SAT or ACT scores, counselor's recommendation, and choice of major. Entrance requirements vary with the program. The rolling admission policy allows the student to be informed of the admission decision within two to three weeks after submitting their application.

GMC awards College credit for satisfactory completion of Advanced Placement courses. The exam score must be 3 or above.

A minimum 2.0 grade point average (on a 4.0 scale) is generally required to transfer from another college. Gwynedd-Mercy College does, however, retain the right to require a higher GPA for admission to some programs.

Gwynedd-Mercy College does not discriminate on the basis of race, age, national origin, religion, sex, or disability in the administration of its educational, admission, scholarship, or loan policies.

Application and Information

All prospective applicants are urged to visit the campus to meet and talk with an admission counselor, a dean, or a program director. To apply for admission, applicants should complete the online application available at http://www.gmc.edu. First-time freshmen must also submit an official high school transcript or equivalency certificate; a written recommendation from a principal, teacher, guidance counselor, or employer; and results of the SAT or ACT (for recent high school graduates). All applicants should verify that they meet the specific requirements and have the necessary high school prerequisites for admission.

Students who wish to transfer to Gwynedd-Mercy College should submit the same online application, high school and college transcripts, and a letter of recommendation.

For additional information or to schedule campus tours and visits, students are encouraged to contact the Campus Guest Program Office at campusguestprogram@gmc.edu or 215-641-5514.

For more information, contact:
Office of Admissions
Gwynedd-Mercy College
1325 Sumneytown Pike
P.O. Box 901
Gwynedd Valley, Pennsylvania 19437-0901
Phone: 800-DIAL-GMC (toll-free)
E-mail: admissions@gmc.edu
Website: www.gmc.edu/admissions/
      https://twitter.com/GMCin140
      https://www.facebook.com/pages/
        Gwynedd-Mercy-College/115132581899548?sk=wall

Gwynedd-Mercy College students walking on campus during a beautiful spring day.

HARDING UNIVERSITY
SEARCY, ARKANSAS

The University

As an institution rooted in Christian principles and a liberal arts tradition since 1924, Harding University challenges its students to pursue scholarship, service, teamwork, excellence, and commitment. Harding is ranked by *U.S. News and World Report* and Princeton Review as one of the top liberal arts universities in the South and attracts exceptional high school students from almost every U.S. state and more than 53 countries.

The University is accredited by nine organizations, including the Higher Learning Commission of the North Central Association of Colleges and Schools. Housed within nine colleges, including the Honors College and College of Allied Health, students can choose from a wide range of majors: from humanities and theology to business and education to natural and health sciences. In addition to undergraduate work, students may pursue graduate-, specialist-, and doctorate-level degrees in one of the 14 programs offered. With a student-teacher ratio of 17 to 1, strong relationships are built in and out of the classroom.

Students can cultivate friendships and interests with 114 academic and professional organizations and 29 social clubs. Ranging from the arts, music, politics, business, diversity, children, missions, service, and the environment, the clubs on campus offer a variety of interests to explore.

Provided with a Christian perspective through which to appreciate various disciplines, students excel as scholars and develop leadership skills. As a result, Harding alumni display character, conviction, and a competitive edge and are prepared for success at prestigious graduate schools and companies throughout the nation.

Location

Harding is located in Searcy, Arkansas, and offers students a hometown feeling with easy access to major cities. The University is about an hour away from Little Rock, Arkansas, and the Bill and Hillary Clinton National Airport and is about 2 hours away from Memphis, Tennessee.

Majors and Degrees

The University offers more than 100 academic majors, including 14 preprofessional programs, taught by top instructors.

Within the College of Allied Health, students may earn a Bachelor of Arts degree in communication sciences and disorders.

The College of Arts and Humanities offers a wide range of degrees in the humanities, arts, English language and literature, foreign language and international studies, history and social science, mass communication, music, oral communication, and theater.

In the College of Bible and Ministry, there are degrees in Bible and religion, biblical languages, Christian education, missions, preaching, and youth and family ministry.

Students in the Paul R. Carter College of Business Administration may receive degrees in accounting, economics, finance, global economic development, health care management, international business management, management information systems, marketing, and professional sales.

Those interested in teaching may earn degrees in early childhood P–4, middle childhood/early adolescence English/language arts/social science 4–8, middle childhood/early adolescence math/science 4–8, secondary education, and special education endorsement (P–3) in the Cannon-Clary College of Education.

The Carr College of Nursing offers a Bachelor of Science in Nursing.

Lastly, the College of Sciences allows students to study health sciences, behavioral sciences, biology, chemistry, computer science, engineering and physics, exercise and sport sciences, family and consumer sciences, kinesiology, and mathematics.

Academic Programs

For the basic requirements necessary for each degree, prospective students should visit the Harding University online catalog at www.harding.edu/catalog.

Students may apply and participate in the Honors College with acceptance based on acceptance to the University and an ACT score of 27 or higher or an SAT score of 1220 or higher. These students may take honors-level courses and graduate with honors.

In addition, various majors may allow students to receive their teaching licensure in the process.

Off-Campus Programs

Harding offers seven study abroad programs in Australia, Chile, England, France, Greece, Italy, and Zambia that will help expand cultural awareness and understanding. Nearly 50 percent of each graduating class takes advantage of one of these semester-long programs. At each location, students are accompanied and taught by University faculty. Costs are based on 16 tuition hours and include housing and meals.

Academic Facilities

Harding's campus consists of 13 academic buildings, cafeteria, 2 auditoriums, a library, a performing arts center, a student center, student health services, 14 residence halls, and 6 apartment complexes.

Costs

The basic undergraduate, on-campus cost for 2012–13 for 15 hours of enrollment per semester was $7,395 for a semester and $14,790 for the year. Tuition was $493 per course hour. Students paid $450 a year for a required technology fee, $3,094 for a standard dorm, and $3,098 for a standard meal plan of 210 meals plus a $200 declining cash balance. The overall total came to $21,432.

Financial Aid

On average, 94 percent of Harding University undergraduate students receive financial assistance. In 2011–12, Harding awarded students more than $10 million in institutional need-based grants and more than $20 million in institutional scholarships. In addition, students received nearly $10 million in federal, state, and externally funded scholarships and grants.

Admission Requirements

Students wishing to apply to Harding must have a 19 ACT or 900 SAT and 3.0 high school GPA (on a 4.0 scale). In addition, high school graduates should have completed at least 15 units in academic subjects. Specifically, an applicant should have completed 4 units of English, 3 units of mathematics (taken from general math, geometry, algebra, trigonometry, precalculus, or calculus), 3 units of social studies (taken from civics, American history, world history, or geography), and 2 units of natural science (taken from physical science, biology, physics, or chemistry). Students planning to major in any area of health care are strongly encouraged to take one or more chemistry courses while in high school. Although not required for admission, two years of foreign language is recommended. The additional units may come from any academic area.

Application and Information

Prospective students may apply online at www.harding.edu/apply/.

Because Harding receives so many applications, it recommends that students apply before the fall of their senior year of high school—even if they haven't taken the ACT or SAT. Admissions advisers are glad to help students through this process.

For more information, prospective students should contact:
Harding University
Box 12234
Searcy, Arkansas 72143-2234
Phone: 501-279-4000
Website: http://www.harding.edu
http://www.facebook.com/HardingU
http://www.twitter.com/HardingU

Each year Harding University's student population comes from almost all 50 states and more than 50 other nations. With more than 6,800 students, Harding is the largest private college or university in Arkansas.

HAVERFORD COLLEGE
HAVERFORD, PENNSYLVANIA

The College

Founded in 1833 as the first college established by members of the Society of Friends (Quakers), Haverford College has chosen to remain small, undergraduate, and residential in order to offer students remarkable classroom and research opportunities while maintaining a strong sense of community. Haverford's Honor Code, created and implemented by students, is an important part of the College's identity. The Code allows students to directly confront academic and social issues in a spirit of cooperation and mutual respect.

Haverford's 1,198 students represent forty-four states, Puerto Rico, the District of Columbia, and thirty-eight countries. Thirty-two percent of the students are students of color and 9 percent are international students.

Haverford is a residential campus with 98 percent of the students and 61 percent of the faculty living on campus. Housing on Haverford's campus is single-sex or coed, and residence halls vary in accommodations from 4-person apartments to suites and singles. Other choices of residence facilities include the Ira De A. Reid House (Black Cultural Center), La Casa Hispanica, Quaker House, and an environmental house.

Haverford's athletic teams participate in NCAA Division III. Intercollegiate sports include baseball, basketball, cricket, cross-country, fencing, field hockey, lacrosse, soccer, softball, squash, tennis, track and field, and volleyball. Haverford also sponsors several club and intramural sports teams. Athletic facilities include the Douglas B. Gardner Integrated Athletic Center, the Alumni Field House, the John A. Lester Cricket Pavilion, and Swan Field—Haverford's turf field.

Location

The College is located 8 miles (16 kilometers) west of Center City Philadelphia on a wooded campus of 216 acres. Haverford's proximity to the fifth-largest city in the United States allows its students to take advantage of the many social, cultural, and educational resources that this historic area offers. Extensive public transportation allows students easy access to the city and environs.

Majors and Degrees

Majors leading to a B.A. or B.S. degree are offered in thirty departments: anthropology, archaeology, astronomy, biology, chemistry, classics, comparative literature, computer science, East Asian studies (including Chinese and Japanese), economics, English, fine arts, French, geology, German, growth and structure of cities, history, history of art, Italian, mathematics, music, philosophy, physics, political science, psychology, religion, Romance languages, Russian, sociology, and Spanish. Students may minor, arrange an interdepartmental or double major, or design an individual major. Approximately 30 percent of the students major in the sciences or mathematics, 40 percent in the social sciences, and 30 percent in the humanities. Ten percent have double, interdepartmental, or special majors. A 4+1 engineering program with the University of Pennsylvania is available to students who qualify.

Other programs that students may incorporate into their curricula include Africana studies, biochemistry and biophysics,

creative writing, dance, education, environmental studies, gender and sexuality studies, Hebrew and Judaic studies, Hispanic and Hispanic American studies, international economic relations, Latin American and Iberian studies, linguistics, mathematical economics, neural and behavioral science, peace and conflict studies, pre-business, prelaw, pre-medicine, and theater.

Academic Programs

The academic experience at Haverford is centered around a deep commitment to the core values of a liberal arts education and its emphasis on the dual pursuit of a breadth of study and in-depth work. While the College mandates that all students take classes across the academic spectrum, there is no core curriculum of specific required courses. Instead, Haverford's system of distribution requirements ensures that students will take at least three classes in each of the divisions of the College (humanities, natural sciences, and social sciences) while allowing them the flexibility to choose courses they find truly interesting. In addition, students must fulfill requirements in foreign language, writing, and quantitative course work. Majors are selected at the end of the sophomore year.

Haverford's small size and exclusive focus on undergraduate education allow students to count on discussion-based classes and research opportunities that students at most colleges would not be able to experience until graduate school. It is common for Haverford students to pursue independent study and approximately half will study abroad, typically during the junior year.

Haverford's three academic centers—the John B. Hurford Humanities Center, the Marian E. Koshland Integrated Natural Sciences Center, and the Center for Peace and Global Citizenship—provide opportunities for integrated learning, bringing students and faculty in related fields together and promoting conversation and collaboration across disciplines. The centers also help to bring an outward view to students' education by sponsoring speaker series, artists in residence, and colloquia on campus.

One of Haverford's distinctive features is its extensive academic and social cooperation with Bryn Mawr College. Students may take courses or major at either school, live on either campus, and eat on either campus. There are more than 2,000 cross-registrations annually. Both colleges jointly operate a weekly newspaper, a drama club, a radio station, an orchestra, social action groups, and intramural sports. A free bus service between the two campuses, which are a mile apart, facilitates cooperative arrangements. Haverford and Bryn Mawr also share library resources with nearby Swarthmore College. All three college libraries are linked electronically, and students have instant access to library resources through the campus computer network. Combined holdings are in excess of 1.5 million volumes.

Off-Campus Programs

Haverford students may take advantage of course offerings at Swarthmore College and the University of Pennsylvania in addition to courses at Bryn Mawr. Students may also enhance their college experiences by arranging study abroad at one of seventy-six programs overseas or study away at Claremont McKenna, Fisk, Spelman, or Pitzer colleges.

Academic Facilities

Major facilities include the James P. Magill Library (580,000 volumes); computer centers; the Koshland Integrated Natural Sciences Center for the physical sciences, biology, and psychology; the Strawbridge Observatory for astronomy; the Music Center; Gest Center for Cross-Cultural Study of Religion; the Fine Arts Center; Marshall Auditorium; and the Language Learning Center. Academic buildings and dormitories are linked by a campuswide computer network.

Costs

The total approximate costs for 2012–13 were $57,202. This consisted of $43,310 for tuition, $13,290 for room and board, and a student activity fee of $392. New students have a one-time orientation fee of $210.

Financial Aid

Fifty-eight percent of Haverford's students receive financial aid, which is awarded solely based on need. Candidates for Haverford College–funded aid must file the online College Board PROFILE application and the online Free Application for Federal Student Aid (FAFSA), along with other forms. Complete information on forms and deadlines to apply for financial aid at Haverford, including links to the PROFILE and FAFSA, are available at http://www.haverford.edu/financialaid. Early decision applicants must file for financial aid by November 15 and regular decision applicants by January 31. Further details are available on the website. Haverford's PROFILE code is 2289, and the FAFSA code is 003274.

Faculty

The student-faculty ratio is 8:1. The faculty devotes its full teaching time to undergraduates. There are no graduate assistants. The regular faculty is supplemented by 90 to 100 scholars, artists, and public figures who visit the College annually under the auspices of seven specially endowed funds.

Student Government

The Students' Association has responsibility for nearly all aspects of student life. The Haverford Honor Code, established and administered by students, has been in existence since 1897. The Honor Code makes possible a climate of trust, concern, and respect, which produces a campus atmosphere conducive to learning and personal growth. The code provides for students' academic and social freedom within the confines of agreed-upon community standards. Exams are not proctored, and the students schedule their own final exams. The code is administered by an elected Honor Council of 16 students, 4 from each class at the College. Each year, the students meet to discuss resolutions and changes in the Honor Code and to approve its adoption. The students also elect several members of the student body to serve on faculty committees and as nonvoting representatives to the Board of Managers (trustees).

Admission Requirements

Admission to Haverford is highly competitive. Admitted students have strong academic records and represent a diversity of backgrounds and interests. The primary criteria for admission are academic and personal qualities as shown by the school record, standardized test scores, extracurricular achievement, and personal recommendations. A combination of qualities that indicate academic and personal promise and potential for growth at Haverford is more significant than any single factor. Of the most recent first-year class, 92 percent rank in the top 10 percent of their high school class, and their SAT scores range from 500 to 800. The mean SAT ranges are 650–760 critical reasoning, 660–760 math, and 670–760 writing. All candidates are required to take the ACT with writing or the SAT Reasoning Test and two SAT Subject Tests. A visit to campus to meet students, observe classes, and have an interview is recommended. Students who live within 150 miles of the campus are strongly recommended to arrange an on-campus interview. A first-choice early decision plan and a deferred matriculation plan are offered.

Admission of transfer students to Haverford is also highly competitive. A limited number of transfer students are accepted each year. Candidates must have completed one full year of college, with a minimum grade point average of 3.0 (B). Campus visits are strongly recommended for those wishing to transfer. A transfer student must spend a minimum of two years at Haverford in order to receive a degree.

Application and Information

The application deadlines for admission are November 15 for early decision candidates, January 15 for regular decision candidates, and March 31 for transfer candidates. Haverford uses the Common Application, which is available in school guidance offices and online. The admission office is open from 9 a.m. to 5 p.m. on weekdays (8:30 a.m. to 4:30 p.m. from June through August) and, during the fall, from 10 a.m. to 1 p.m. on Saturday.

For more information or to arrange an interview or tour appointment, students should contact:

Office of Admission and Financial Aid
Haverford College
370 Lancaster Avenue
Haverford, Pennsylvania 19041-1392
Phone: 610-896-1350
      610-896-1436 (TTY/TDD)
Fax: 610-896-1338
E-mail: admission@haverford.edu (Admission)
     finaid@haverford.edu (Financial Aid)
Website: http://www.haverford.edu

Haverford is consistently ranked among the top academic institutions in the country. The rigorous academic program focuses on individual growth, intellectual exploration, and pushing the boundaries of each discipline. Most classes are taught seminar style with an emphasis on discussion and debate.

HAWAI'I PACIFIC UNIVERSITY
HONOLULU, HAWAI'I

The University

Hawai'i Pacific University (HPU) is the state's leading private, not-for-profit university with a student population of approximately 7,500. HPU is one of the most culturally diverse universities in America with students from all 50 U.S. states and more than 80 countries. Founded in 1965, HPU prides itself on maintaining strong academic programs, small class sizes, individual attention to students, and a diverse faculty and student population. HPU offers more than 50 acclaimed undergraduate programs and 14 distinguished graduate programs. HPU is recognized in *U.S. News & World Report*'s "Best Colleges" guide, and The Princeton Review recognized HPU in its review of U.S. colleges as a "Best Western" college. In addition, *Barron*'s business magazine recognized HPU as a "Best Buy" in college education and *Bloomberg Businessweek* recognized HPU for having the "Best Undergraduate Return on Investment" among any Hawai'i College or University. HPU is accredited by the Western Association of Schools and Colleges, the National League for Nursing Accrediting Commission, the Commission on Collegiate Nursing Education (CCNE), and the Council on Social Work Education, and it is recognized by the Hawaii Commission on Postsecondary Education.

The diversity of HPU's student body stimulates learning about other cultures firsthand, both inside and outside of the classroom. Students are encouraged to examine the values, customs, traditions, and principles of others to gain a clearer understanding of their own perspectives. HPU students develop friendships with students from throughout the world and form important connections for success in a global economy.

HPU has NCAA Division II intercollegiate sports. Men's athletic programs include baseball, basketball, cross-country, golf, soccer, and tennis. Women's athletics include basketball, cross-country, golf, soccer, softball, tennis, and volleyball. HPU's women's softball team as well as its cheerleading squad and dance team have received numerous national championship titles.

The housing office at HPU offers many services and living options for students. Residence halls with cafeteria service are available on the Hawai'i Loa campus, while off-campus apartments are available in the Honolulu and Waikiki areas for those seeking more independent living arrangements.

Location

Hawai'i Pacific University combines the excitement of an urban downtown campus with the serenity of a residential campus. The urban campus is located in downtown Honolulu, the business and financial center of the Pacific. This campus is composed of eight buildings in the heart of Honolulu's business district, and is home to the College of Business Administration and the College of Humanities and Social Sciences. The campus location makes it easy for students to commute to and also find and maintain internship opportunities at neighboring businesses.

Eight miles away, on the windward side of the island, the 135-acre Hawai'i Loa Campus is set in the lush foothills of the Ko'olau mountains and is home to the College of Nursing and Health Sciences and the College of Natural and Computational Sciences. The Hawai'i Loa Campus has residence halls, dining commons, the Educational Technology Center, a student center, and outdoor recreational facilities, including a soccer field, tennis courts, a softball field, and an exercise room.

HPU is also affiliated with the Oceanic Institute, a 56-acre aquaculture research facility located at Makapu'u Point on the southeastern coast of O'ahu, Hawai'i. At the facility, undergraduate and graduate students are able to get hands-on experience in marine science. All three sites are conveniently linked by a free shuttle.

Majors and Programs

Hawai'i Pacific University offers programs that lead to the undergraduate degrees of Bachelor of Arts (B.A.), Bachelor of Science (B.S.), Bachelor of Science in Business Administration (B.S.B.A.), Bachelor of Science in Nursing (B.S.N.), and Bachelor of Social Work (B.S.W.).

Undergraduate programs include accounting, advertising/public relations, anthropology, Asian studies, biochemistry, biology, business (general), business economics, chemistry, communication, computer information systems, computer science, diplomacy and military studies, economics, secondary education (concurrent program), elementary education, English, entrepreneurial studies, environmental science, environmental studies, finance, health science, history, human resource development, human resource management, humanities, international business, international studies, journalism, justice administration, management, marine biology, marketing, mathematics (concentrations in applied math, engineering (3-2), mathematics education, and pure math), multimedia cinematic production, integrated multimedia, nursing, oceanography, political science, pre-health studies programs, pre–physical therapy, psychology, public administration, social work, sociology, teaching English to speakers of other languages, theatre (individualized), and travel industry management.

In addition to the undergraduate programs, HPU offers fourteen graduate programs. The Master of Arts (M.A.) is offered in clinical mental health counseling, communications, diplomacy and military studies, global leadership and sustainable development, human resource management, organizational change, and teaching English as a second language. The Master of Business Administration (M.B.A.) is available in accounting, e-business, economics, finance, human resource management, information systems, international business, management, marketing, and travel industry management. Other graduate programs include Master of Education in Secondary Education and the Master of Education in Elementary Education (M.Ed.), Master of Science in Information Systems (M.S.I.S.), Master of Science in Marine Science (M.S.M.S.), Master of Science in Nursing (M.S.N.), and Master of Social Work (M.S.W.)

Academic Programs

The baccalaureate student must complete at least 124 semester hours of credit. Of these credits, 45 provide the student with a strong foundation in the liberal arts, while the remaining credits are composed of appropriate upper-division classes in the student's major and related areas. The academic year operates on a semester system, with regular fall and spring semesters as well as shorter sessions, including one winter and three summer sessions. By attending the supplemental summer and winter sessions, a student may complete the baccalaureate degree program in three years. A five-year B.S.B.A./M.B.A. program is also available.

Off-Campus Programs

As part of its emphasis on international education and global citizenship, Hawai'i Pacific University offers study-abroad opportunities that complement and enhance students' academic experience. Study-abroad opportunities are available in nearly seventy different countries with more than 300 approved programs of study. HPU undergraduates and graduates who have completed at least one semester of studies at HPU and intend to complete a degree at HPU are eligible to apply.

The Career Services Center offers a comprehensive education/internship program to further develop students' studies and elevate their career-related position through experience. HPU intertwines academic and cocurricular programs with the world of work so students gain academic credit, work experience, and a salary. HPU students have done co-ops and internships at some of the world's best-known companies and organizations, including American Express Financial Advisors; Deloitte & Touche, LLP; the FBI; Hilton Hotels; Microsoft; Oceanic Institute; Polo Ralph Lauren; and Walt Disney World. The staff at the Career Services Center continues to work with students before and after graduation, assisting with everything from resume writing to job interview preparation.

Academic Facilities

The downtown campus comprises eight buildings in the center of Honolulu's business district. One of these buildings is the HPU Frear Center, which houses state-of-the-art classrooms, a communication lab, and high-tech information systems classrooms. HPU's Meader Library provides a multitude of general and specialized resources, including a business reference collection, a National Endowment for the Humanities (NEH) collection, and many online databases and journals. The circulating book collections support communications, computer studies, education, literature, social sciences, and other curriculum areas. Also available are study areas, group study rooms, computer workstations, and wireless Internet. The Tutoring and Testing Center provides free tutoring in all core subjects. The expanded downtown computer lab includes more than 420 computers for student use.

On the suburban and residential Hawai'i Loa campus, academic life revolves around the Amos N. Starr and Juliette Montague Cooke Academic Center (AC). The AC houses classrooms; organic chemistry, nuclear magnetic resonance, and regular laboratories; faculty and staff offices; a theater; an art gallery; and the Atherton Library, which includes circulating and reference book collections in the areas of art, history, marine science, nursing, and Hawai'i and the Pacific. In addition, the library provides access to electronic books (e-books), databases, study rooms, IBM computers, and wireless Internet. Computers are also available for library research, e-mail, and word processing.

HPU is also affiliated with the Oceanic Institute, a major research center specializing in marine biology, marine aquaculture, biotechnology, and ocean resource management. It is located on a 56-acre site at Makapu'u Point on the windward coast of O'ahu, Hawai'i. Learning, internship, and research opportunities abound in this hands-on learning environment.

Costs

For the 2013–14 academic year, undergraduate tuition is $19,980 for most majors, while books, health insurance, and other expenses cost approximately $3,480. Tuition for junior- or senior-year nursing majors is $25,650. The cost to live in on-campus residence halls or off-campus apartments is comparable; room and board is estimated at $12,550 for a double occupancy room. There is an additional $500 refundable security deposit required for residence halls and off-campus apartments.

Financial Aid

HPU offers most forms of federal financial aid, including student grant and loan programs, as well as loans for parents of dependent students. Over 70 percent of the University's students benefit from federal financial aid programs or a wide range of institutional scholarships. Students should complete the Free Application for Federal Student Aid (FAFSA) to be considered for federal aid programs. While aid can be awarded throughout the academic year, students should complete the application prior to the March 1 priority deadline to be considered for all available funding. Current financial aid and scholarship information is available at www.hpu.edu/financialaid.

Faculty

HPU faculty members are renowned for the personal interest they take in each of their students. HPU is proud to offer more than 600 full- and part-time faculty members with outstanding academic and business credentials from around the world, providing HPU students access to a world's worth of knowledge and experiences. A vast majority of HPU faculty members hold the highest degrees in their fields. The student-faculty ratio is 14:1, and the average class size is less than 20.

Student Government

HPU students can join one of many student clubs and organizations; run for office in Hawai'i Pacific University's Student Government Association, the University's governing body; participate in Army or Air Force ROTC; write for the student newspaper, *Kalamalama;* edit the school's literary journal, *Hawai'i Pacific Review;* or join HPU's stage and pep band or the International Choral and Vocal Ensemble.

A variety of on-campus activities and events are organized for students by the Student Life Office, including Movie on the Mall, Music on the Mall, intramural sports tournaments, and recreational activities. Annual events include Pa'ina at the Pier, Club Carnival, Welcome Week, Da Freakshow, Halloween Hoopla, and Pacific Bowl.

Admission Requirements

Hawai'i Pacific University seeks students who are motivated and show academic promise. The Admissions Office requires that applicants complete and forward the admission application and their high school transcripts. Transfer students should also submit college transcripts. SAT and/or ACT scores should be submitted if these scores are not posted in their transcripts. First-time freshmen are expected to have a minimum GPA of 2.5 (on a 4.0 scale) in college-preparatory courses. HPU recommends that students complete 4 years of English, 4 years of history or social science, 3 years of math, and 2 years of science. Transfer students with 24 or more postsecondary credits are required to have a GPA of 2.0 or above. For students with less than 24 credits, a combination of college and high school GPA is used.

The marine science and environmental science programs require students to maintain a GPA of 3.0 or above and to take 3 years of science, including biology and chemistry (physics is recommended), as well as mathematics through trigonometry (calculus is recommended). Transfer students must demonstrate ability in science and math at the college level. Students not meeting the above criteria are encouraged to enroll at HPU without declaring a major to demonstrate the ability to do college-level work in science and math.

Application and Information

Candidates are notified of admission decisions on a rolling basis (year-round); the University usually responds within two weeks of receipt of application materials. Early entrance and deferred entrance are available.

For further information and for application materials, contact:

Office of Admissions
Hawai'i Pacific University
1164 Bishop Street, Suite 200
Honolulu, Hawai'i 96813
Phone: 808-544-0238
      866-CALL-HPU (toll-free in U.S. and Canada)
Fax: 808-544-1136
E-mail: admissions@hpu.edu
Website: www.hpu.edu/petersons

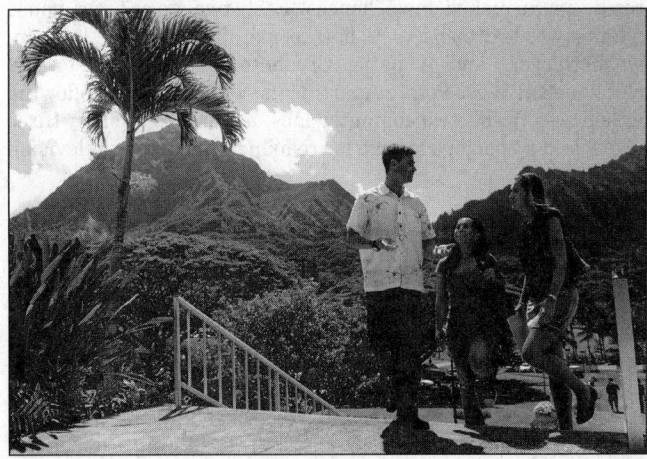

HPU faculty are renowned for the personal interest they take in each and every one of their students. This happens naturally at HPU because of their student-centered approach, small class sizes, low student-to-faculty ratio, and emphasis on one-on-one guidance.

HICKEY COLLEGE
ST. LOUIS, MISSOURI

The College

Founded in 1933 by Dr. Margaret Hickey, Hickey College has grown from a business school to a college offering education and experience in the fields of accounting; administrative support; applied management; computer applications, networking, and programming; culinary arts; graphic design; legal administrative assistant; medical administrative assistant; paralegal studies; and veterinary technology studies.

In keeping with her feeling that "We must identify ourselves with public responsibility," Dr. Hickey developed a unique educational program based on thorough training and personality development combined with careful placement in positions best suited to the students' interests and abilities. While holding to Dr. Hickey's philosophy, the faculty and staff continuously strive to move toward the challenges of the future. The continuing success of Hickey College has been largely due to a highly motivated student population, a staff of dedicated teachers and personnel, and the respect and acceptance of the business community.

Hickey College's graduation rate was 85 percent for the reporting year 2011. This high rate reflects the College's committed faculty, hands-on curriculum, and accelerated programs.

Some students live in the College's student residence facilities, allowing them to make new friends and round out their Hickey College experience. The primary residence facility for students is West Pointe Apartments, located near the main campus. Students choosing to live in the residence facilities reside in furnished town houses. Each two-story town house offers two bedrooms, 1½ bathrooms, living area, kitchen, washer/dryer, and a patio. Students enjoy access to the clubhouse at West Pointe Apartments, which has the following amenities: Wi-Fi, two computer labs, a workout facility, three pools, and a spacious lounge for relaxing or watching television with friends.

Campus activities vary each year, but students may work together on fundraising initiatives, attend field trips related to their programs of study, and participate in holiday celebrations. An admissions representative can provide more specific information about recent activities.

Hickey College is accredited by the Accrediting Council for Independent Colleges and Schools to award diplomas, associate degrees, and bachelor's degrees. The Accrediting Council for Independent Colleges and Schools is listed as a nationally recognized accrediting agency by the United States Department of Education and is recognized by the Council for Higher Education Accreditation: 750 First Street NE, Suite 980, Washington, D.C. 20002; phone: 202-336-6780.

The Veterinary Technology Program is accredited by the Committee on Veterinary Technician Education and Activities (CVTEA) of the American Veterinary Medical Association (AVMA). The Culinary Arts program is accredited by the American Culinary Federation Education Foundation (ACFEF).

Location

Hickey College is located at 940 West Port Plaza Drive, 15 minutes from downtown St. Louis, Missouri. The location offers convenient access to St. Louis' many cultural and recreational facilities. Among these are museums, botanical gardens, planetariums, theaters, cultural exhibitions, sporting events, parks, and public libraries.

Hickey College Veterinary Technician students attend classes at the Vet Tech Institute at Hickey College, 2780 North Lindbergh Boulevard, while the College's culinary arts students attend classes at the Culinary Institute of St. Louis at Hickey College, 2700 North Lindbergh Boulevard, both in St. Louis.

Academic Programs

Hickey College offers a wide choice of programs, each designed to prepare students for a particular career. Relatively short, yet remarkably comprehensive, these programs are carefully planned to provide the best education possible in the field of the student's choice. Hickey College offers seventeen specialized programs during the day. Students may select from nine major areas of study: accounting; administrative assistant; computer specialist, programming, and network management; culinary arts; graphic design; legal administrative assistant; medical administrative assistant; paralegal studies; and veterinary technology studies.

Hickey College's evening education division offers a Bachelor of Applied Management. The program combines the technical and business-related courses completed in a Hickey College diploma or associate degree program.

Off-Campus Programs

Externships are available for students who choose to enroll into the culinary arts associate degree, paralegal studies, or veterinary technology programs. The externship for these programs is part of the curriculum.

Academic Facilities

Hickey College provides a business atmosphere in an educational setting. The facilities are furnished with the latest instructional equipment. The school offers a professional learning and growing environment for today's career-minded students. Hickey College is equipped to accommodate the handicapped.

The general academic space contains a library and classrooms. Six of the classrooms are equipped with microcomputers, and the remainder is furnished as lecture rooms.

The Vet Tech Institute at Hickey College contains a library equipped with microcomputers as well as seven lecture/laboratory classrooms that include space equipped with long tables and rolling chairs, a veterinary technician laboratory, a kennel, a radiography facility, a surgery suite, and a surgery preparation area.

The Culinary Institute of St. Louis at Hickey College building contains a library, five kitchens, five lecture classrooms, and one classroom equipped with microcomputers.

Costs

For calendar year 2013, all programs are $6,900 per semester. The final half-semester of 4½-semester Culinary Arts Associate Degree program is $600. The final half-semester of the 4½-semester Veterinary Technology program is $2,900. Lab fees for Culinary Arts and veterinary technology programs are $230 per semester. Residence facilities fees are $2,920 per semester. Textbook and supplies will vary from semester to semester. These charges will range from $520 to $940 per semester. The actual charges will be disclosed each academic year as the financial plan is completed.

Financial Aid

A variety of financial plans are available to assist qualified students in securing a business education, regardless of financial status or family income level. These plans include a combination of student loans, grants, scholarships, and payment plans. The variety of available plans affords flexibility in choosing the one best suited for a specific need. Hickey College offers individual financial planning sessions for each student and family beginning with the completion of the Free Application for Federal Student Aid. Information about these plans is available from the Admissions or Financial Aid Office.

Faculty

At Hickey College, the majority of classes are taught by faculty members teaching full-time. Having such a high proportion of full-time teachers is unusual and reflects the College's mission to provide a high-quality education. Hickey College's faculty members are committed to the students and the College.

Students are the priority—faculty members take pride in encouraging and challenging students and make it a point to be available for help and direction. Although class size varies, it usually averages 30 students. This enables the faculty members to get to know the interests and goals of each student.

Admission Requirements

The basic requirement for admission to Hickey College is graduation from a valid high school, private school, or equivalent (GED). Applicants are admitted for enrollment on the basis of previous scholastic records as evidenced by a transcript of work completed in high school or college. Previous training in business subjects is generally not required.

Application and Information

Potential students should call or write the Admissions Department to request an application form. To apply for enrollment, the student should complete the application form and submit it with the $50 application fee to the Director of Admissions, Hickey College, 940 West Port Plaza, St. Louis, Missouri 63146. Potential students may also apply online at www.hickeycollege.edu.

For more information, contact:

Director of Admissions
Hickey College
940 West Port Plaza
St. Louis, Missouri 63146
Web site: www.hickeycollege.edu

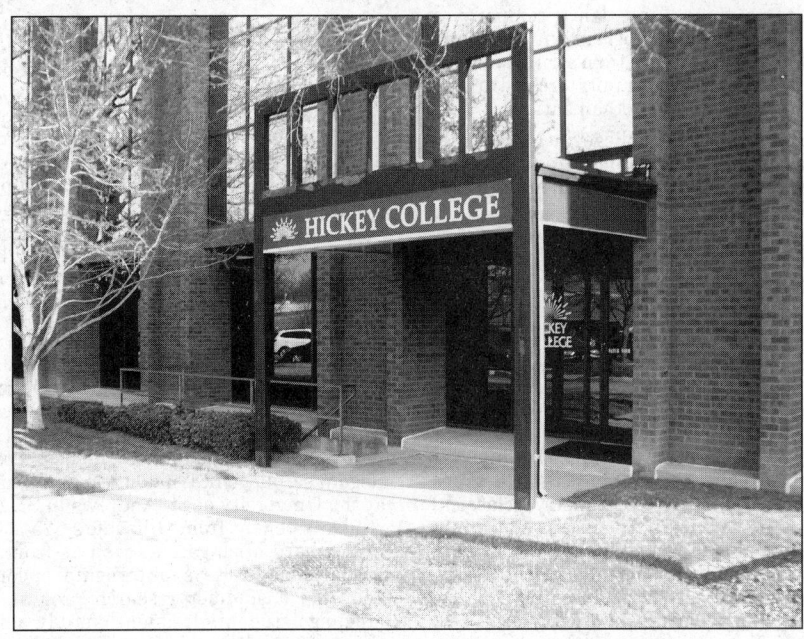

Hickey College offers a unique educational program based on thorough training, personality development, and placement in areas best-suited to each student's interests and abilities.

HILLSDALE COLLEGE
HILLSDALE, MICHIGAN

The College

Hillsdale College is a private, independent, nonsectarian institution of higher learning founded in 1844 by men and women who described themselves as "grateful to God for the inestimable blessings" resulting from civil and religious liberty and as "believing that the diffusion of learning is essential to the perpetuity of those blessings." The College has maintained institutional independence since its founding by refusing to accept aid from or control by federal authorities. Far-reaching private support from a national constituency has enabled Hillsdale to continue its trusteeship of the intellectual and spiritual inheritance derived from the Judeo-Christian faith and Greco-Roman culture.

The undergraduate enrollment for fall 2012 was 1,400, of whom 47 percent were men. The College draws students from forty-eight states and eight other countries. Approximately 40 percent of students are from Michigan. The entering freshman class in 2012 had an average high school grade point average of 3.81 and mean ACT (29) and SAT (1980) scores well above national averages. Hillsdale students are housed in dormitories, fraternity and sorority houses, and various off-campus dwellings. Single and double rooms are available on campus; there are no coed dormitories. Each College-owned residence hall is supervised by a resident director and resident advisers. All freshmen (except commuters) are required to live on campus; upperclass students seeking to live off campus must apply to the dean of men or dean of women for this privilege.

Hillsdale's Charger athletes compete in 12 intercollegiate NCAA Division II varsity sports as part of the Great Lakes Intercollegiate Athletic Conference (GLIAC). Since 1998, the College has produced 94 athletic All-Americans and 28 conference champions, and Hillsdale teams have qualified for national tournaments seventeen times. Thirty-one athletes have earned national academic honors in their respective sports as well. An active intramural program is also available. Four national fraternities, three national sororities, and more than 100 other social, academic, spiritual, and service organizations provide Hillsdale students with a diverse array of cocurricular opportunities. A resident drama troupe and dance company, a concert choir, and chamber chorale, a jazz program with big band and combos, instrumental chamber ensembles from string quartets to percussion ensemble, and a College-community orchestra and band constitute the College's performing arts organizations.

Special student services provided by the College include career planning and placement counseling, academic advising and tutoring, and a health service staffed by a physician and a resident nurse.

Location

Hillsdale College is located amidst the hills, dales, and lakes of south-central Michigan. The Indiana and Ohio turnpikes are each 30 minutes away, and the College is within close reach of such metropolitan areas as Detroit, Chicago, Cleveland, Toledo, Ft. Wayne, and Indianapolis. The town of Hillsdale is a county seat with a population of 10,000. Stores, churches, restaurants, and movie theaters are all within walking distance of the campus.

Majors and Degrees

Hillsdale awards Bachelor of Arts and Bachelor of Science degrees in accounting, art, biochemistry, biology, chemistry, classical studies, computational mathematics, economics, education, English, exercise science, financial management, French, German, Greek, history, Latin, marketing/management, mathematics, music, philosophy, physical education, physics, politics, psychology, religion, Spanish, speech, sport management, sport psychology, and theater. Interdisciplinary majors in American studies, Christian studies, comparative literature, European studies, international studies in business and foreign language, political economy, and sociology and social thought are also available. Preprofessional programs are offered in allied health services (including optometry,

physical therapy, nursing, and medical technology), dentistry, engineering, environmental sciences, forestry, law, medicine, osteopathy, theology, and veterinary medicine.

Academic Programs

Hillsdale operates on a two-semester schedule, with the fall term beginning in late August and ending in mid-December and the spring term beginning in mid-January and ending in mid-May. Two 3-week summer sessions are also offered.

The College believes that a sound classical liberal arts education includes study in the humanities, natural sciences, and social sciences, and each student is required to complete a structured core of courses in these areas. All students declare a major by the end of the sophomore year. To graduate, students must complete a minimum 124 hours of course work and fulfill the requirements of at least one major field. The B.A. program includes a foreign language proficiency requirement. The B.S. program requires additional studies in mathematics and the natural sciences.

The honors program enables exceptionally talented students interested in an interdisciplinary community of learning to develop their intellectual potential through an accelerated college core and honors seminars in the junior and senior years. Discussions, guest lectures, and travel opportunities contribute to the social cohesiveness of the group. All honors students complete a senior thesis on an interdisciplinary topic of their choosing.

The Center for Constructive Alternatives conducts four weeklong symposia during the academic year and is one of the largest college lecture series in America. These programs, with themes ranging from historical to political, business, science, and the arts, bring to the campus distinguished scholars and public figures of national and international renown. All students are required to enroll in two full seminars for credit prior to graduation, one in the first two years and one in the final two years of the curriculum.

Off-Campus Programs

For forty years, the Washington Hillsdale Internship Program (WHIP) has provided students the opportunity to participate in full-time, academically intensive internships in the nation's capital. The program has been significantly bolstered with the 2008 establishment of the Hillsdale College Allan P. Kirby, Jr. Center for Constitutional Studies and Citizenship in Washington, D.C. Past interns and fellows have been placed in locations as challenging and rewarding as the U.S. House of Representatives, the U.S. Senate, the White House, various think tanks including the Heritage Foundation, news and media outlets, national security agencies, lobbying firms, international trade and relations organizations, and private sector companies.

Through the College's affiliations with the Center for Medieval and Renaissance Studies and the Oxford Study Abroad Program, Hillsdale students are able to study abroad for a summer or a year at one of the more than thirty colleges of Oxford University. Hillsdale offers a summer business program in cooperation with Regent's College in London, England, and the opportunity to study at the University of St. Andrews in St. Andrews, Scotland. Science students benefit from Hillsdale's 685-acre field research laboratory in northern Michigan, as well as from a marine biology program in the Florida Keys, internship opportunities with the Omaha Zoo, and a summer research program in South Africa. Foreign language students frequently study abroad in Argentina, France, Germany, and Spain. Qualified individual students who wish to study in another country for a semester or a year are assisted by their faculty adviser and the registrar in planning a program that enables them to gain academic credit as well as take full advantage of their experience.

Academic Facilities

The Hillsdale College Mossey Library is a three-floor facility with a collection of more than 952,000 volumes. In addition to the main study and research collections, the Library also contains a number of rare and special holdings, including the Ludwig von Mises, Russell Kirk, Richardson Heritage, and Richard Weaver collections. Connected to other Michigan libraries through MelCat, and with college libraries nationwide via interlibrary loan, students have access to most any material necessary for on-campus research. Numerous individual study areas and group study rooms are available for students, as well as computer research terminals.

Lane and Kendall Halls at the front of campus serve as the primary academic facilities in the humanities and contain classroom space and faculty offices, as well as a special laboratory for experimental psychology. The Strosacker Science Center houses the departments of biology, chemistry, and physics. The Joseph H. Moss Family Laboratory Wing, completed in 2008, is a 17,000-square-foot addition that includes a microbiology/cell biology lab, anatomy/physiology lab with human cadaver access, conservation genetics lab, water lab, greenhouse, and organic/general chemistry labs. The 32,000-square-foot Herbert Henry Dow Science Building provides additional classrooms, research laboratories, animal rooms, and a computer lab. The Mary Randall Preschool is a circular laboratory school in which nursery school children are taught by students specializing in early childhood education and psychology. Experts in the field have called this building "a model for the nation." The Hillsdale Academy, a K–12 private model school, provides additional opportunities for classroom observation.

The Roche Sports Complex is a facility available to varsity athletes and the general student body alike. The building houses the 60,000-square-foot Jesse Philips Arena, which features a six-lane, 200-meter running track and basketball/volleyball court. The building also houses the John "Jack" McAvoy Natatorium for swimming and diving, an exercise physiology and sports medicine facility, three racquetball courts, extensive locker room space, and a weight/fitness room. Adjacent is the 7,000-seat capacity Frank "Muddy" Waters Stadium, which features an artificial surface football field; all-weather, Olympic-quality eight-lane running track; outdoor tennis courts; and fields for soccer, baseball, and women's softball. The new Margot V. Biermann Athletic Center houses a six-lane track and four tennis courts.

The Sage Center for the Arts is home to the departments of art, theater, and speech. This 47,000-square-foot facility contains studios, classroom space, an exhibition gallery, a prop- and scene-construction shop, a sound studio, graphics lab, black box theatre, and the Markel Auditorium, a 353-seat performance hall (with orchestra pit). Completed in 2003, the 32,809-square-foot Howard Music Hall houses office, studio, classroom, rehearsal, and performance space for the John E. N. and Dede Howard Department of Music. Notable features include the McNamara Rehearsal Hall, Conrad Recital Hall, and studio space for percussion and jazz studies. Lower-level practice rooms are available to students during business hours without reservation.

Dedicated in January 2008, the 53,000-square-foot Grewcock Student Union is the center of student life. The two-story structure houses the cafeteria, bookstore, student mail center, offices for student activities and publications, a lounge with a 100-inch flat screen television, a formal lounge and conference room, AJ's Café, and a game area. The entire building is wireless, and any Hillsdale student can check out a laptop at the main desk.

Costs

Annual tuition for the 2012–13 academic year was $21,390, room was $4,290, board was $4,350, and mandatory fees were $540. Books, supplies, and personal expenses (including travel, recreation, and clothing) are estimated at $3,000 per year.

Financial Aid

Financial aid at Hillsdale is available in many forms. Academic scholarships are awarded on a competitive basis, regardless of financial need, to students who rank in the top 10 percent of their high school class and have standardized test scores in the top 10 percent according to national test norms. The priority deadline for academic scholarship consideration is January 1. The application for admission also serves as the Hillsdale application for merit-based aid. Athletic scholarships are available on a competitive basis in men's baseball and football; men's and women's basketball, track, and cross-country; and women's swimming and volleyball. The departments of art and music also award a select number of scholarships based on strength of portfolio/audition. To apply for aid on the basis of financial need, students are required to file Hillsdale's Confidential Family Financial Statement (CFFS) in January or February of the year of prospective enrollment at Hillsdale. Grants and loans are available from the College.

Faculty

The faculty consists of 117 full-time members. No classes are taught by graduate students. The size and closeness of the College community enable personal attention and faculty mentorship inside the classroom and during office visits after class. Each student has a faculty adviser for core and major coursework who directs the program of study and provides academic and career counseling. Hillsdale's faculty considers teaching their first priority. Many faculty members also engage in research and scholarly writing, supported by summer and sabbatical leaves funded by the College, and are often invited to comment on the national scene in lecture programs and media outlets.

Student Government

Hillsdale's student government and campus organizations offer students special opportunities to develop leadership skills that enrich both their collegiate experience and lives after graduation. The governing organization of the student body is the Student Federation, which is composed of 18 elected representatives. This group funds student organizations, sponsors all-College entertainment, and acts upon matters of concern to the student community.

Admission Requirements

Admission is a privilege extended to students who will benefit from, and contribute to, the academic, social, and spiritual environments of the College. Important determinants for admission are intellectual curiosity, ambition, leadership, and volunteerism. Accordingly, grade point average, test scores, class rank, strength of curriculum, extracurricular activities, interviews, self-evaluations, writing samples in the form of two essays, and recommendations are all reviewed carefully and are important in the evaluation process. An admissions interview is strongly encouraged. Although some factors are necessarily more important than others, seldom is any single criterion, however important, decisive.

Transfer students must submit the standard application, including the high school record, SAT or ACT scores, transcripts from all colleges previously attended, and a transfer form from the dean of students of the most recent college attended. Applications by transfers are evaluated similarly to nontransfers.

Candidates for admission from other countries follow the regular entrance procedures. Students who come from a non-English-speaking country must demonstrate proficiency in English by satisfactory performance on the Test of English as a Foreign Language (TOEFL) or the Michigan Test of English Proficiency or at an ESL Center.

Application and Information

Students may apply to Hillsdale College any time after the completion of the junior year of high school. A formal application includes a completed application form accompanied by a nonrefundable fee of $35 (free if submitted online) and all required credentials. Application plans include early decision (November 15), early action (December 15), and regular decision (February 15). Hillsdale College has been distinguished since its founding in 1844 by voluntarily adhering to a nondiscriminatory policy regarding race, religion, sex, and national or ethnic origin—long before the government began regulating such matters.

All records and forms should be mailed to:

Admissions Office
Hillsdale College
33 East College Street
Hillsdale, Michigan 49242-1298
Phone: 517-607-2327
Fax: 517-607-2223
E-mail: admissions@hillsdale.edu
Website: http://www.hillsdale.edu

HOFSTRA UNIVERSITY
HEMPSTEAD, NEW YORK

The University

Hofstra University is the largest private college on Long Island, New York. Since its founding in 1935, Hofstra has evolved into a nationally and internationally renowned university that continues to achieve recognition as an institution of academic excellence. Hofstra is consistently recognized on the best colleges lists of *U.S. News & World Report,* the Princeton Review, *Fiske, Washington Monthly,* and *Forbes.*

Among other private Long Island colleges, Hofstra is the only university that grants the Phi Beta Kappa distinction, and it has the largest number of students and professionals going on to pursue graduate and postgraduate programs of study.

The Hofstra North Shore-LIJ School of Medicine at Hofstra University welcomed its second class of students in August 2012. Incoming medical school students train as emergency medical technicians by working shifts on North Shore-LIJ Health System ambulances. In addition, Hofstra recently established a School of Engineering and Applied Science with an innovative co-op and cross-disciplinary education program, and a School of Health Sciences and Human Services dedicated to educating students to become effective and compassionate clinicians, evidence-based practitioners, policy makers, managers and advocates who promote health equity.

Hofstra's diverse and driven student body of more than 11,000 can choose from about 140 undergraduate and 150 graduate program options in liberal arts and sciences, business, engineering, communication, teacher education, law, health and human services, and honors studies. Hofstra offers more than 100 dual-degree programs, giving students the opportunity to earn both a graduate and undergraduate degree in less time than if each degree was pursued separately. More information is available at hofstra.edu/academics or hofstra.edu/dualdegree.

Hofstra hosts hundreds of social, academic, and cultural events each year, drawing together scholars, business leaders, authors, celebrities, health care professionals, politicians, and journalists from across the nation and around the world. These events help foster a connection between in-classroom work and extracurricular interests. In addition, Hofstra offers 17 intercollegiate athletic programs that compete at the NCAA Division I level and more than 200 academic, fraternal/sororal, media, multicultural, performance, pre-professional, religious, social, social/political, and sports clubs and organizations.

The David S. Mack Sports and Exhibition Complex, a 93,000-square-foot facility, is home to the Hofstra Pride men's and women's basketball teams and wrestling, and is also the site for events such as commencements, exhibitions, trade shows, televised political events, and concerts. Other on-campus recreational and athletic facilities include an indoor, Olympic-sized swimming pool, and various athletic playing fields.

Each year, the University is visited by more than 400 employers who recognize how much Hofstra students have to offer. In addition to the plentiful networking opportunities on campus, students may choose to do an internship at a top company on Long Island or in New York City, thus gaining critical work experience that will give them an edge in a competitive job market.

At Hofstra, students join a network of more than 124,000 graduates. Outstanding alumni include Academy Award–winning film director and producer Francis Ford Coppola; best-selling author Nelson DeMille; vascular surgeon Dr. Donna Mendes; president of the New York Yankees Randy Levine; from *Everybody Loves Raymond,* creator, executive producer, and writer Philip Rosenthal and actress Monica Horan; president of H. J. Kalikow & Company and former MTA chairman Peter S. Kalikow; actresses Lainie Kazan and Susan Sullivan; and New York State Comptroller Thomas P. DiNapoli.

At Hofstra, it's all about choice. Students may choose to live in one of the 37 residence halls, each with a unique flair and life of its own, including living/learning communities. In addition, Hofstra students can choose from 18 on-campus dining facilities.

Location

Hofstra is located only 25 miles east of New York City—a short train ride is all it takes for students to attend theater performances, concerts, professional sporting events, and museum exhibitions and to pursue the many internship opportunities available in the city. The University, which blends longstanding traditions with twenty-first-century resources, is home to both ivy-covered classrooms buildings and modern, elegant facilities. On the vibrant campus, students will find exceptional and technologically advanced classrooms, six theaters, a state-of-the-art fitness center, an accredited museum, modern athletic facilities, and an impressive 10-floor library that holds more than 1 million print volumes and 24/7 electronic access to more than 125,000 journals and books.

Majors and Degrees

The Bachelor of Arts (B.A.) is awarded in African studies, American studies, anthropology, art history, Asian studies, biology, chemistry, Chinese, Chinese studies, classics, comparative literature and languages, computer science, criminology, dance, drama, early childhood and childhood education (with dual major in another discipline), early childhood education (with dual major in another discipline), economics, elementary education (with dual major in another discipline), engineering science, English, English education, film studies and production, fine arts, foreign language education (French, German, Italian, Russian, Spanish), French, geography, geology, German, global studies, Hebrew, history, Ibero-American studies, Italian, Jewish studies, journalism, labor studies, Latin, Latin American and Caribbean studies, liberal arts, linguistics, mass media studies, math education (with a dual major in another discipline), mathematical economics, mathematics, music, philosophy, physics, political science, pre-health, psychology, public relations, radio production and studies, religion, Russian, science education (biology, chemistry, earth science, physics), social studies education (with a dual major in another discipline), sociology, Spanish, speech communication and rhetorical studies, speech-language-hearing sciences, sustainability studies, urban ecology, video/television, and women's studies.

The Bachelor of Business Administration (B.B.A.) is awarded in accounting, entrepreneurship, finance, information technology, international business, legal studies in business, management, marketing, and supply chain management.

The Bachelor of Science (B.S.) is offered in applied physics, athletic training, biochemistry, biology, business economics, chemistry, community health, computer engineering, computer science, computer science and mathematics (dual major), electrical engineering, environmental resources, exercise science, fine arts, forensic science, geology, health education, health science, industrial engineering, mathematical business economics, mathematics, mechanical engineering, music, physics, pre-medical, sustainability studies, urban ecology, video/television, video/television and business, and video/television and film.

The Bachelor of Science in Education (B.S.Ed.) is offered with specializations in dance, fine arts, music, and physical education.

The Bachelor of Engineering (B.E.) is offered in engineering science with specializations in biomedical engineering and civil engineering.

The Bachelor of Fine Arts (B.F.A.) is awarded in theater arts with specializations in performance and production.

Combined (dual) degrees offered include Bachelor of Arts/Juris Doctor (B.A./J.D.) in collaboration with the Maruice A. Deane School of Law at Hofstra University, B.S./M.S. in physician assistant studies, B.S./M.D. and B.A./M.D., through the Hofstra North Shore–LIJ School of Medicine at Hofstra University, and various majors and concentrations leading to the B.A./M.B.A., B.S./M.B.A., B.A./M.S.Ed., B.A./M.A., B.A./M.S., B.S./M.S., B.B.A./M.S.Ed., B.B.A./M.S., and B.B.A./M.B.A.

Academic Programs

Requirements for graduation vary among schools and majors. A liberal arts core curriculum is an integral part of all areas of concentration. The University calendar is organized on a traditional semester system, and also includes one January session and three summer sessions.

Hofstra offers innovative programs designed to meet the needs of its diverse student body. These include Hofstra University Honors College, Legal Education Accelerated Program (LEAP), Hofstra 4+4 Program, First-Year Connections, and living/learning communities.

Hofstra University Honors College provides a rich academic and extracurricular experience for students who show exceptional potential and desire to excel. Honors students can elect to study in any of the University's undergraduate programs and are involved in all fields of advanced study, including premedical/prehealth professional studies, prelaw, engineering, business, communication and media arts, humanities, and social sciences.

The Legal Education Accelerated Program allows students to earn both a B.A. and a J.D. in just six years.

The Hofstra 4+4 Program allows students to earn both a bachelor's degree (B.A. or B.S.) and M.D. in eight years in collaboration with the Hofstra North Shore-LIJ School of Medicine at Hofstra University.

First-Year Connections, an integrated academic and social program, helps first-year students connect with one another as well as with all the resources and opportunities offered at the University. The program, which offers seminars and course clusters, features small classes taught by distinguished faculty in areas of interest ranging from architecture to writing. These courses introduce students to the intellectual and social life of the University and satisfy the general education requirements for all majors.

Through Hofstra's living/learning communities, learning is not limited to the four walls of the classroom, or even to the borders of the campus. Here, students are exposed to environments that are intellectually stimulating, supportive, and conducive to building lasting friendships and a memorable first-year experience. These living/learning communities are associated with several first-year clusters and seminars, giving students the opportunity to live with many of the same students they are in class with, as well as students who share the same passion for political and civic issues, health sciences, or business and the arts.

Off-Campus Programs

Hofstra extends learning beyond the classroom through varied internship programs and study-abroad opportunities. The internship programs take advantage of Hofstra's proximity to New York City, allowing students to gain on-the-job experience in areas such as finance, business, media, advertising, and entertainment. Through study-abroad programs in Europe, Asia, South America, and other locations, students can explore the world while earning college credits. More information is available at hofstra.edu/studyabroad.

Academic Facilities

Hofstra students live and learn on a campus that is home to state-of-the-art facilities and resources. C. V. Starr Hall, home to the Frank G. Zarb School of Business, features the Martin B. Greenberg Trading Room, which has the largest number of Bloomberg Professional terminals among all academic trading rooms in the United States and around the world. The School of Communication's Dempster Hall contains one of the largest broadcast facilities in the northeastern United States as well as a converged newsroom and multimedia classroom. Plus, Hofstra students benefit from real-world experience at the on-campus radio station, WRHU 88.7 FM (Radio Hofstra University), which has a 35-mile broadcast range and is webcast at wrhu.org. Hagedorn Hall, where the School of Education is located, features a technologically robust learning environment complete with interactive whiteboards, computer-driven instructor stations and wireless communication.

Costs

The 2012–13 annual tuition and fees at Hofstra University for a full-time undergraduate student was $35,950. The cost of housing and dining plan was approximately $12,370. Books and supplies cost approximately $1,000; personal expenses and transportation generally amount to $3,056. For the full tuition and fees schedule, students should visit hofstra.edu/tuition.

Financial Aid

Hofstra University works hard to make a private college education affordable for students and families, and offers several financial aid options for new undergraduates, including interest-free payment plans and a money-saving four-year locked-in rate for tuition and fees (hofstra.edu/lockedintuitionrate) that can help students manage costs from admission through graduation. In fall 2012, Hofstra awarded $22.6 million to first-year students and a total of $71.6 million in institutional gift assistance to all enrolled undergraduates. For detailed information, students should visit hofstra.edu/FinancialAid.

Faculty

Hofstra's hardworking, ambitious students are taught by Guggenheim Fellows and Fulbright scholars; Emmy Award recipients; prize-winning scientists; leaders in business, education and the health sciences; and knowledgeable and insightful thinkers. The 1,135 faculty members, of whom 517 are full-time, are experts in their fields and are dedicated to and focused on providing the foundation and tools students need to succeed. Hofstra's faculty members affirm the value of education—93 percent of full-time faculty members hold the highest degree attainable in their fields. Plus, students at Hofstra learn from faculty members—not graduate students. With an average undergraduate class size of 21 and a student-to-faculty ratio of 14:1, Hofstra students are challenged and encouraged to debate, question, research, discuss, and think critically in an open and broad-minded learning environment.

Student Government

The Student Government Association is a student-run governing body that supervises and coordinates all student activities and serves as a liaison with the faculty and administration. The Student Government Association sends representatives to the committees of the University Senate. A judicial board has responsibility for promoting justice in the conduct of student affairs.

Admission Requirements

Hofstra is a competitive institution that seeks to enroll students who demonstrate academic ability, intellectual curiosity, and the motivation to be successful and contribute to the campus community. Careful consideration is given to a student's high school record, types of courses taken, SAT or ACT scores, letters of recommendation, extracurricular involvement, and the personal essay. The most competitive applicants will have followed a rigorous college preparatory curriculum, and will have taken advantage of honors and advanced placement level courses where appropriate. The Office of Admission prefers to see a high school curriculum that includes 4 years of English, 3 to 4 years of social studies, 2 to 3 years of foreign language, 3 years of mathematics, and 3 years of science. Prospective engineering majors need at least 4 years of mathematics, 1 year of chemistry, and 1 year of physics. Campus visits are strongly recommended. Hofstra accepts applications from first-year, transfer, and international students.

The University offers an early action option for students whose first choice is Hofstra. There are two early action periods: when an application is submitted by November 15, notification is made to the student by December 15; when an application is submitted by December 15, notification is made to the student by January 15. Students applying for regular decision are considered on a rolling basis.

First-year applicants must submit an application, $70 application fee, high school transcript, SAT or ACT scores, essay, and letter of recommendation. Hofstra accepts applications via mail or online and participates in the Common Application; the online application fee is $60.

For more information, students should contact:

Application and Information

Hofstra University
Office of Undergraduate Admission
100 Hofstra University
Hempstead, New York 11549-1000
Phone: 516-463-6700
    800-HOFSTRA (toll-free)
Fax: 516-463-5100
E-mail: admission@hofstra.edu
Website: http://www.hofstra.edu/admission

HOLY FAMILY UNIVERSITY
PHILADELPHIA, PENNSYLVANIA

The University

Holy Family University is a fully accredited, Catholic, private, coeducational, four-year university located in Northeast Philadelphia's residential Torresdale neighborhood. Founded in 1954 by the Sisters of the Holy Family of Nazareth, Holy Family provides liberal arts and professional programs for more than 2,100 undergraduate students through day, evening, and summer sessions.

From the moment students arrive on campus, they are being prepared to make an impact. From classroom immersion and co-op experiences to service opportunities and Division II athletics, students learn and grow in an outcome-oriented environment that offers countless opportunities to get involved and engaged.

Holy Family University works to extend the learning experience beyond the classroom to create a holistic education that fosters a student's personal development. The University provides various residential housing experiences, including a traditional dormitory, apartment-style units, and the state-of-the-art Stevenson Lane Residence, which offers suite-style living with well thought-out design and amenities that reflect contemporary campus housing trends. All of these options are meant to help guide students through their own personal development within a supportive community.

Upon graduating, Holy Family students are ready for the next level of impact. They arrive with bold dreams, and they leave for careers in teaching, nursing, science, law, business, and more. The University offers a highly supportive learning environment that lifts and empowers students and values their aspirations. Holy Family is a place where dreams of every kind are honored, encouraged, and pursued with a passion.

Location

The University is based at its Northeast Philadelphia campus, which serves as home of the traditional undergraduate program. Located less than a mile from Bucks County, Holy Family offers the benefits of a big city in a quiet, park-like, suburban setting. The campus offers student housing for full-time undergraduates. With easy access to regional rail lines, city bus routes, and nearby expressways, students can experience all that Philadelphia has to offer.

Majors and Degrees

Holy Family offers undergraduate courses leading to the Bachelor of Arts (B.A.) and Bachelor of Science (B.S.) degrees. Majors include accounting, art (with tracks in graphic design, pre-art therapy, and studio art), biochemistry, biology, biology-medical technology, communications, computer management information systems, criminal justice, education (early childhood pre K–4; special education PK–8; middle level 4–8 with concentrations in language arts and reading, mathematics, science, and social studies; secondary education with certifications in art, biology, English, history/social studies, and mathematics), English/literature, finance, fire

science and public safety administration (transfers only), health and physical education, history, interdisciplinary humanities, international business, management-marketing, mathematics, nursing, political science, psychobiology, psychology, psychology for business, radiologic science, religious studies, sociology, and sport marketing-management. Preprofessional programs are also available in art therapy, dentistry, law, medicine, optometry, pharmacy, physical therapy, podiatry, physician's assistant studies, and veterinary studies.

Academic Programs

Holy Family's curriculum stands within the mainstream of a 2,000-year-old Christian liberal arts tradition. The core curriculum of religious studies, philosophy, the humanities, and the social and natural sciences implements the objectives of the University in a general way. It also contributes to the formation of liberally educated students who find their education is functional in the twenty-first century. Students are encouraged to seek not merely information but also personal formation and enrichment.

In addition to the core curriculum, students take course work in their division concentrations within the School of Arts and Sciences, the School of Business Administration, the School of Education, the School of Nursing and Allied Health Professions, or the Division of Extended Learning. Interdisciplinary programs, specialized programs of study, and minors are also available.

Off-Campus Programs

Holy Family's cooperative education program is highly successful and nationally recognized. Co-ops and internships are designed to support classroom learning by enabling students to apply the concepts they've studied to actual job situations. These real-world lessons enhance students' skills and understanding and allow them to explore various work settings and careers, all while earning academic credit. Holy Family partners with more than 500 corporations, companies, government agencies, and nonprofit organizations throughout Greater Philadelphia, and the results are impressive. Students in the co-op program enjoy an 85 percent permanent placement rate, while the national average is just 76 percent.

Academic Facilities

The University Library houses 147,800 books, magazines, journals, DVDs, and videos to support the learning, teaching, and informational needs of the Holy Family community. The library offers print and online access to the full text of 10,800 journals and periodicals, and three dozen full-text databases are available on and off campus. In addition, the library has over 14,500 electronic books available from home or campus via NetLibrary and other interfaces.

The library's curriculum section contains elementary and secondary school textbooks, curriculum guides, instruction kits, and hundreds of children's books, both fiction and nonfiction.

It also has a special English as a second language (ESL) collection for those who teach non-native speakers.

Computer laboratories are located in several facilities, including Holy Family Hall, the Education and Technology Center, the Campus Center, and the University Library. Wireless network access is also available throughout the campus buildings and residence halls.

In addition to general classrooms and laboratories, Holy Family has special facilities to enable students in certain majors to learn in environments that mirror those they will encounter in their professional lives. The Education and Technology Center houses five classrooms specially designed to model primary and secondary classroom instruction for the University's education students. These model classrooms allow children with certain disabilities, such as vision or hearing impairment, to be integrated fully into a regular classroom and provide Holy Family's Education graduates with valuable experience using adaptive technology in a classroom environment. The Nurse Education Building includes a nursing simulation and practice laboratory.

Costs

For 2013–14, tuition and fees are $27,100, and room and board are $12,330.

Financial Aid

Holy Family is committed to helping students and their families achieve the goal of a private university education. Holy Family maintains one of the lowest tuition rates among private colleges and universities in the region, and more than 85 percent of its students receive some form of financial aid. The University is committed to providing education to qualified students regardless of means and views financial assistance as a cooperative investment in a student's education.

In addition to state and federal programs, students can take advantage of a variety of Holy Family need- and merit-based scholarships and grants.

Faculty

Classes at Holy Family are usually no larger than 20 students, and many have as few as 7–10 students. A student-to-faculty ratio of 12:1 provides a smaller, more personal learning environment. Students know their professors, and those professors know them as well. Personalized, individual treatment is the norm: students are called on by name, receive answers to their questions, and most importantly, get additional help if they need it. This is not a college where hundreds of students crowd into an auditorium and silently take notes from a distant, faceless instructor. A Holy Family education is designed to be more—more personal, more welcoming, and more attuned to each student's success.

Student Government

Representatives to Holy Family's Student Government Association are elected by the student body for the following academic year and share responsibility for student life and activities. The Vice President for Student Services serves as an adviser to the Student Government Association and as the liaison between the students and the administration.

Admission Requirements

When it comes to potential students, Holy Family University is more interested in a student's quality of work and general promise and seriousness of purpose. While a student's academic record is considered, their interests, personal integrity, and desire to pursue a quality education are also important factors. Holy Family values diversity in all of its manifestations; neither religious affiliation nor ethnic characteristics influence the granting of admission.

Applicants are expected to have graduated from an accredited high school or equivalent; received acceptable scores on the SAT or ACT; and completed 4 units of English, 2 units of history, 3 units of mathematics, 2 units of modern foreign language, 2 units of science, and 3 electives.

Application and Information

For application forms, a catalog, or further information, students should contact:

Undergraduate Admissions Office
Holy Family University
9801 Frankford Avenue
Philadelphia, Pennsylvania 19114
Phone: 215-637-3050
Fax: 215-281-1022
E-mail: admissions@holyfamily.edu
Website: http://www.holyfamily.edu
http://www.facebook.com/HolyFamilyUniversity
http://twitter.com/holyfamilyu

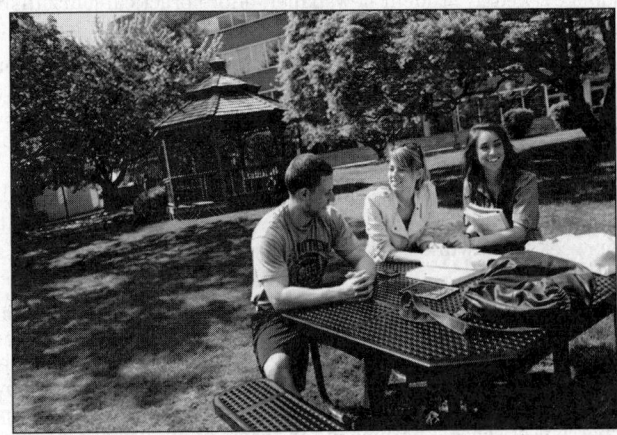

Holy Family's supportive scholarly community studies, works, and plays on a suburban-like campus just minutes from the vibrancy of Center City Philadelphia.

HOUGHTON COLLEGE
HOUGHTON, NEW YORK

The College

Founded in 1883, Houghton College is one of America's most highly regarded Christian liberal arts colleges. Founded by The Wesleyan Church, Houghton attracts students from more than forty denominations. Houghton has an enrollment of 1,100 full-time undergraduate students who represent thirty-five states and thirty countries. Most students live in College housing within the distinctly residential environment, while many faculty members live within walking distance of the campus. Houghton's 1,300 acres in the scenic Genesee Valley of western New York offer students various recreational opportunities. The College operates a 386-acre equestrian center and both downhill and cross-country ski facilities.

Accredited by the Middle States Association of Colleges and Schools and the National Association of Schools of Music, Houghton's selective admission ensures an academically able student body. Most students represent the top 20 percent of their high school's graduating class, possess SAT or ACT scores commensurate with a competitive college, and are active in their churches and communities. Houghton offers more than forty majors and programs. Students benefit from the instruction and guidance of experienced professors beginning with their first year of study.

Extensive cocurricular opportunities at Houghton include a competitive intercollegiate athletic program that fields eighteen teams for men and women, a wide array of intramural leagues, numerous Christian service organizations, student publications, music groups, and student government. The student-guided Campus Activities Board sponsors regular Christian contemporary concerts and other student activities. Student chapel services meet three times per week. *The Star*, the College's weekly student newspaper, offers practical journalism experience.

The residential experience is at the heart of a Houghton education. First-year students and sophomores are required to live in a College residential hall. Juniors and seniors may also choose from town houses and approved community houses for off-campus living.

All resident students are required to participate in the College's board plan. Most students enjoy Houghton's twenty-one-meal-per-week plan, while those living in a town house may opt for a reduced plan.

Year after year, Houghton is commended by numerous national publications. Of all member institutions of the Council for Christian Colleges and Universities, Houghton College is ranked in the top ten in the national liberal arts category by *U.S. News & World Report. Forbes* ranks Houghton in the top 4 percent of schools nationwide in terms of quality of teaching, career prospects for alumni, and graduation rates. The Princeton Review names Houghton a Best College in the Northeast and also lists Houghton in its Green College Guide.

In addition to its undergraduate programs, Houghton College also offers Master of Music and Master of Arts in Music degrees through the Greatbatch School of Music.

Location

Houghton students benefit from the College's location in the rolling hills of western New York. The College's vast property—among the nation's leaders in campus acreage—offers numerous recreational opportunities, while nearby Letchworth State Park is one of the state's natural treasures. The metropolitan cities of Rochester and Buffalo, an hour's drive from Houghton, offer cultural, entertainment, and shopping venues.

Majors and Degrees

Houghton grants Bachelor of Arts, Bachelor of Science, Bachelor of Fine Arts, and Bachelor of Music degrees. Majors and programs are available in accounting, adolescence education (grades 7–12), applied art and design, applied physics, art, art education (PreK–12), Bible, biology, business administration, chemistry, childhood education (grades 1–6), Christian formation, communication, computer science, English, environmental studies, general science, history, humanities, information technology management, intercultural studies, international development, mathematics, medical technology, ministerial studies, music composition, music education, music performance, philosophy, physical education, physical/health education, physics, political science, pre-art therapy, pre-dentistry, pre-law, pre-medicine, pre-optometry, pre-pharmacy, pre–physical therapy, pre-seminary, pre–veterinary science, psychology, recreation, religion, sociology, Spanish, TESOL (grades K–12) and writing.

An adult degree-completion program (B.S. in management), designed for those with two years of college credit, is offered at locations throughout western New York.

Houghton provides accelerated graduate degree programs in conjunction with leading institutions across New York State. A 3-2 engineering program is available through cooperation with Clarkson University. A 3+4 co-operative doctorate program in pharmacy (Pharm.D.) is offered in conjunction with the University of Buffalo. Accelerated 4+1 M.B.A. programs have been arranged through Alfred University, Clarkson University, Niagara University, and Rochester Institute of Technology.

Academic Programs

Most bachelor's degrees at Houghton consist of 124 credit hours. As a traditional liberal arts institution, Houghton requires all students to complete an integrative studies curriculum in addition to courses in their major and minor fields of study. Integrative studies requirements include courses in writing, literature, communication, foreign language, social science, history, mathematics, natural science, Bible, religion/philosophy, and fine arts. Lecture and seminar courses with classes averaging 21 students create a positive learning environment and daily interaction between professors and students.

Houghton offers three interdisciplinary Honors Programs, giving select first-year students a unique opportunity for enhanced study. Contemporary Contexts and East Meets West engage students in the study of significant questions and include a three-week study abroad trip to Europe. Science Honors allows students extensive opportunities for research and discovery within an integrative problem-driven program.

The College follows a 4-4-1 calendar. In addition to the fall and spring semesters, the College offers May Term, a two- to four-week term where students may enroll in one concentrated course. Both on- and off-campus courses are available during May Term.

Houghton accepts credit from the Advanced Placement Program of the College Board. Generally, students must achieve a final exam score of 4 or higher to receive credit from Houghton. CLEP credit may also be accepted for subject exams only. Students may also earn credit through the International Baccalaureate program; credit is awarded for higher-level subjects passed with a 5 or above. Students wishing to challenge the College's foreign language requirement may take a College-administered placement test. A portion or all of the foreign language requirement may be waived, although no credit hours are granted.

Army ROTC is offered through cooperation with nearby St. Bonaventure University.

Off-Campus Programs

Over half of Houghton students study off-campus before they graduate. Houghton operates semester-long programs in Tanzania, the Balkans, and Australia/New Zealand. As a member of the Council for Christian Colleges and Universities, Houghton is able to offer many off-campus opportunities, including the American Studies Program in Washington, D.C.; the Contemporary Music Center in Nashville, Tennessee; the Latin American Studies Program in Costa Rica; the Film Studies Center in Los Angeles, California; the Middle East Studies Program in Cairo, Egypt; the Oxford Summer School Program; and programs in China, India, and Uganda.

Academic Facilities

The recently updated Stephen Paine Science Center contains classrooms, teaching and research laboratories, offices, study areas, an instrument room, a greenhouse, and machine shop.

The Chamberlain Center offers 49,000 square feet of classrooms, learning resource facilities, laboratories, faculty offices, digital media lab, a state-of-the-art business investment center, and the Center for Academic Success and Advisement. Other major facilities include a modern, well-equipped athletic complex; four residence halls and thirty town houses accommodating more than 900 students; the 1,200-seat Wesley Chapel; the Campus Center; the Stevens Arts Studios; a 386-acre equestrian center; and several outdoor athletic and recreational areas. Houghton's Center for the Arts features an acoustically designed recital hall, a music library, numerous practice rooms, spacious teaching studios, an instrumental rehearsal hall, and a professional digital recording studio.

Costs

Houghton's tuition and fees are $27,728 for the 2013–14 academic year. Room and board (twenty-one meals per week) total $8,012. Other indirect expenses, including books, supplies, and travel, average $1,500.

Financial Aid

Houghton administers more than $26 million in aid annually, benefiting 97 percent of the student body. Traditional federal and New York State aid, including Federal Pell Grants, TAP, FSEOG, work-study, and Federal Perkins Loans, is available for students demonstrating need through the Free Application for Federal Student Aid (FAFSA). The priority application deadline for financial aid is March 1. Houghton also offers academic scholarships and Excellence Scholarships for students in various academic areas. The James S. Luckey Scholarship, named for the college's first president, covers 100 percent of tuition costs for 4 students each year.

Faculty

The College's faculty currently totals approximately 125 members, 71 of whom are full-time. More than 80 percent hold the terminal degree in their discipline. All courses are taught by qualified professors, not teaching assistants or graduate students. All full-time students work directly with a faculty adviser in their area of study. The College maintains a student-faculty ratio of 12:1, with classes averaging approximately 21 students.

Student Government

The Houghton Student Government Association consists of elected student representatives. This College-sponsored organization allows students to have a direct impact on their college experience in areas ranging from academics to residence life to cocurricular activities. Most College committees include student representatives.

Admission Requirements

Houghton's competitive admission process seeks applicants who clearly possess the academic and personal qualities necessary for a successful experience at Houghton. Candidates for admission should submit a high school transcript indicating at least 16 units of college-preparatory course work. The academic evaluation of each applicant includes a review of the quality of the high school curriculum, grade point average, rank in class, and scores from the SAT or ACT. Other important application materials include the applicant's character recommendation and an essay regarding the student's interest in attending a Christian institution. Transfer students are evaluated on the basis of the above information in addition to the college-level course work completed to date.

The Office of Admission responds to applications for admission on a rolling basis. Students applying before December 1 will receive priority consideration for scholarships. The College subscribes to and supports the national Candidates Reply Date of May 1.

Application and Information

For application materials, students should contact:
Admission Office
Houghton College
1 Willard Avenue
Houghton, New York 14744
Phone: 585-567-9353
          800-777-2556 (toll-free)
E-mail: admission@houghton.edu
Website: http://www.houghton.edu

A view across the quad at Houghton College.

HUNTER COLLEGE OF
THE CITY UNIVERSITY OF NEW YORK
NEW YORK, NEW YORK

The College

In 1870, Thomas Hunter founded Hunter College to train young women to become school teachers. Their contributions helped make New York City's schools among the most highly regarded public school systems in the world. Today, Hunter College is a coeducational liberal arts college serving 21,000 undergraduate and graduate students of all racial, ethnic, and cultural backgrounds. Wide offerings in the liberal arts and sciences and three professional schools—education, health sciences, and social work—meet the highest academic standards. A distinguished faculty encourages intellectual and personal growth in each student.

Location

Hunter students study in the heart of Manhattan. Many of the world's finest museums, libraries, concert halls, cultural centers, and theaters are just a quick walk away.

Majors and Degrees

Hunter College offers bachelor's and master's degrees in the arts and sciences, education, health professions, nursing, and social work, along with several combined (B.A./M.A. or B.A./M.S.) degrees. The following programs of study are available: accounting, Africana and Puerto Rican/Latino studies, anthropology, archaeology, art history, biological sciences, chemistry, Chinese language and literature, classical studies, community health education, comparative literature, computer science, dance, economics, elementary education, environmental studies, English, English language arts, film, French, geography, German, Greek, Hebrew, history, honors curriculum, Italian, Jewish social studies, Latin, Latin American and Caribbean Studies, Latin and Greek, mathematics, media studies, medical laboratory sciences, music, nursing, nutrition and food science, philosophy, physics, political science, psychology, religion, Romance languages, Russian, secondary education, sociology, Spanish, statistics, studio art, theater, urban studies, and women's studies. Secondary education programs are for grades 7–12 unless otherwise noted and include biology, chemistry, Chinese, dance (pre-K–12), English, French, German, Hebrew, Italian, mathematics, music (pre-K–12, accelerated B.A./M.A. program only), physics, Russian, social studies, and Spanish.

Special programs in anthropology, biological sciences/environmental and occupational health sciences, biopharmacology, biotechnology, economics, English, history, mathematics, music, physics, sociology/social research, and statistics and applied mathematics lead to the combined bachelor's/master's degree, enabling highly qualified students to earn both degrees more quickly.

Hunter College also provides preprofessional advisement and preparation for advanced study in chiropractic, dentistry, engineering, law, medicine, optometry, osteopathy, pharmacy, podiatry, and veterinary medicine.

Academic Programs

Hunter instills a rich and informed sense of the possibilities of humanity in its students and expects them to carry their liberal arts education forward in their careers, their public responsibilities, and their personal lives.

The College trains its students in the sciences, the humanities, and a number of professional fields. As they strive to achieve their career goals, students are expected to perceive their chosen fields of study as only a part of a wider realm of knowledge. Undergraduate programs of study at Hunter consist of four parts, totaling 120 credits: a general education requirement, a pluralism and diversity requirement, a concentration of in-depth study (major), and elective courses.

Undergraduate students at Hunter who exhibit intellectual curiosity and exceptional ability may apply to the Thomas Hunter Scholars Program, an interdisciplinary program that individualizes study according to needs and interests and grants a Bachelor of Arts degree.

Students may earn sophomore standing (up to 30 credits) if they score well on the College-Level Examination Program (CLEP) subject tests, the Advanced Placement examinations of the College Board, and the Regents College Examination (RCE) Program of New York State.

Off-Campus Programs

Hunter College taps Manhattan to allow innumerable internships. Hosts have included Atlantic Records, CNN, the Council on Foreign Relations, DreamWorks SKG, Madison Square Garden, Metropolitan Museum of Art, New York City Council, Simon & Schuster, and many more. Interns perform curatorial and administrative work in museums, research and production work on TV news shows and newspapers, design work in commercial graphics, and booking, managing, and technical work in theaters.

Academic Facilities

The College is made up of five sites in Manhattan. The largest, a modern complex of buildings connected by skywalks at 68th Street and Lexington Avenue, sits above a convenient subway stop. This campus offers programs in the arts and sciences and in teacher education.

Downtown on East 25th Street, the Brookdale Campus houses the Division of the Schools of the Health Professions, which includes the Hunter-Bellevue School of Nursing, one of the nation's largest nursing programs, and the School of Health Sciences.

Uptown on East 119th Street is the Silberman School of Social Work at Hunter College. This campus also encompasses Hunter's programs in public health, nutrition, and community health.

Downtown on Manhattan's West Side, Hunter's brand new Studio Art Building houses a 7,000-square-foot gallery and provides M.F.A. students with individual studios that are among the best in the city.

At East 94th Street, the Campus Schools house an elementary school and a high school for the intellectually gifted that are renowned, as is the College itself, for a long tradition of academic excellence.

All locations are minutes from Grand Central Terminal, Penn Station, and the New York/New Jersey Port Authority Bus

Terminal, making Hunter easily accessible from Connecticut, Westchester, New Jersey, and Long Island.

The collections of the Hunter College libraries are housed in the Jacqueline Grennan Wexler Library and the Art Slide Library (located at the main campus), as well as at the branch libraries at the Brookdale Campus and the School of Social Work. The libraries hold over 800,000 volumes, 3,000 periodicals, a nonprint collection of more than 1 million microforms, and 250,000 art slides in addition to records, tapes, scores, music CDs, and videos. Recently, Hunter installed new computer, multimedia, and Internet labs and its first CD-ROM network. The CD-ROM network provides access to indexes, abstracts, and complete texts and multimedia resources, and Internet labs make the World Wide Web accessible.

Costs

Hunter College is affordable. In fall 2013, New York State residents enrolled as full-time, matriculated students are slated to pay $2,865 per semester ($245 per credit part-time). Nonresidents enrolled as full-time, matriculated students will pay $510 per credit. All students pay a student activity fee ($84.50 per semester for full-time students and $54.45 per semester for part-time students) and a $15-per-semester consolidated fee.

Financial Aid

Hunter College participates in all state and federal financial aid programs. Financial aid is available to matriculated students in the form of grants, loans, and work-study. Grants provide funds that do not have to be repaid. Loans must be repaid in regular installments over a prescribed period of time. Work-study consists of part-time employment, either on campus or in an outside agency. More information is available from the Office of Financial Aid at 212-772-4820.

Entering freshmen whose high school records indicate a high level of academic achievement may apply to the Macaulay Honors College at Hunter College. This prestigious program offers a generous financial aid package, including a full academic scholarship, as well as extensive benefits, including a free room at the Hunter College Residence Hall for two years. In addition, Hunter College offers a wide array of other scholarships.

Faculty

Thanks to its location in the heart of New York City, Hunter College attracts a special kind of faculty member. Some are well-known scholars and researchers in their fields, such as biologists involved in advanced research on genetic structure. Others are professionals with active careers in the city, including well-known painters, sculptors, architects, and urban design experts. Hunter's faculty also includes environmental health scientists who work on occupational health and safety issues, nursing administrators who work in the country's leading hospitals, and film directors, theater critics, and musicians who are engaged in New York City's cultural milieu. Many members of the faculty are nationally renowned; they maintain Hunter's reputation for academic excellence through outstanding teaching and cutting-edge publications and by securing millions of dollars in annual grants for research.

Student Government

Several governing assemblies involve students in Hunter's governance. The College Senate, the legislative body of the College, includes faculty members, students, and administrators. Two student governments (undergraduate and graduate) also play essential roles in the life of the College. Students with voting power sit on faculty and administrative committees.

Admission Requirements

Candidates for freshman admission are considered based on the overall strength of their academic preparation, cumulative high school averages, and SAT or ACT scores. Freshman students who entered in fall 2012 had a high school academic grade point average of 88.7 and an SAT score of 1220 (math and verbal only). The College recommends 4 years of English, 4 years of social studies, 3 years of mathematics, 2 years of a foreign language, 2 years of laboratory sciences, and 1 year of performing or visual arts as the minimum academic preparation for success in college.

Students are considered transfer applicants if they have previously attended any college, university, and/or proprietary school since graduating from high school or secondary school. This applies whether or not the student is seeking transfer credit. Transfer students in fall 2012 had a cumulative grade point average of 3.14 with an average of 75.6 credits attempted. For more information, applicants should visit Hunter College's website.

Application and Information

Applicants are considered for fall (September) and spring (February) admission. Applications for the fall must be filed no later than September 15 and for spring, no later than February 1. All applications must be filed on the CUNY website at http://www.cuny.edu.

Welcome Center
Hunter College
695 Park Avenue, Room 100N
New York, New York 10065
Phone: 212-772-4490
E-mail: WelcomeCenter@hunter.cuny.edu
Website: http://www.hunter.cuny.edu/ugprospects
http://www.facebook.com/groups/263613092099
(Welcome Center)
http://www.flickr.com/photos/welcome_center

Students at Hunter College enjoy the convenience of skywalks that connect all four buildings at the 68th Street campus. Hunter's Upper East Side location provides easy access to some of New York's finest offerings; Central Park and the Metropolitan Museum of Art are just blocks away.

THE ILLINOIS INSTITUTE OF ART—CHICAGO

CHICAGO, ILLINOIS

The Illinois Institute of Art—Chicago is one of The Art Institutes, a system of over fifty schools throughout North America dedicated to providing hands-on education in the creative and applied arts. The Illinois Institute of Art—Chicago offers bachelor's and associate degree programs as well as non-degree programs for students interested in pursuing career opportunities from among tomorrow's 15 million jobs in creative fields like design, fashion, media arts, and culinary (based on information from the U.S. Bureau of Labor Statistics for job growth from 2012 to 2022).

A focused education from The Illinois Institute of Art—Chicago can help students turn their creative energy into a powerful tool that can make a difference in the world. Students are part of a collaborative and supportive community, where experienced instructors provide the guidance and skills needed to pursue a career in the creative economy.

The Illinois Institute of Art—Chicago is also an important resource for creative industry leaders who value the opportunity provided students to learn by using professional-grade technology to build a portfolio of work to show potential employers after graduation.

Accreditation

The Illinois Institute of Art is accredited by the Higher Learning Commission and is a member of the North Central Association (NCA), 230 South LaSalle Street, Suite 7-500, Chicago, Illinois 60604-1413; phone: 800-621-7440 (toll-free); www.ncahlc.org.

The Associate of Applied Science degree program in culinary arts is accredited by The Accrediting Commission of the American Culinary Federation Education Foundation.

The interior design program leading to the Bachelor of Fine Arts degree is accredited by the Council for Interior Design Accreditation, 206 Grandville Avenue, Suite 350, Grand Rapids, Michigan 49503; www.accredit-id.org.

The Illinois Institute of Art—Chicago is authorized by the Illinois Board of Higher Education, Division of Private Business and Vocational Schools, 431 East Adams, Second Floor, Springfield, Illinois 62701; phone: 217-782-2551; www.ibhe.state.il.us/default.htm.

Location

Studying in the heart of the city puts students within easy reach of Chicago's many design, fashion, and advertising resources. The main campus of The Illinois Institute of Art—Chicago is situated in the vast design complex that contains the Apparel Center/Merchandise Mart, a glamorous fashion showcase of the Magnificent Mile, and the impressive Advertising Row of North Michigan Avenue. Many of the city's cultural attractions, as well as the leading fashion stores, are within walking distance of campus. The Culinary facility is located in the heart of The Loop, one block from Chicago's two largest department stores and within the newly revived theater district.

Chicago is a city of extraordinary architecture, 29 miles of lakefront, parks, neighborhood festivals, museums, and cultural attractions. Magnificent harbors, parks, beaches, and a wide variety of restaurants all contribute to the thriving city life. Visitors enjoy the well-known Midwestern hospitality and flock to well-known attractions like the Magnificent Mile, Navy Pier, and Millennium Park.

The city is also well known for its music traditions, from jazz to blues, from soul to gospel, house music to hip-hop.

Chicago is a world center of business, communications, and art and is also the home of some of the world's most passionate sports fans. The Cubs play at legendary Wrigley Field on the city's north side and the White Sox at U.S. Cellular Field on the south side. The Bulls play basketball at United Center, which is also where the NHL's Blackhawks play hockey. And the Chicago Bears make their home at Soldier Field.

Programs of Study and Degree Offerings

Creativity is all around, and with millions of tomorrow's jobs in creative fields, the world needs more creative professionals. No matter which course of study a student chooses, the instructors at The Art Institutes will guide, support, and help students fine-tune their visual thinking and problem solving, so that they can take advantage of the world's growing creative opportunities and put their passion to work. Programs are offered in the areas of design, which focuses on communicating conceptually and helping people connect in living and work spaces; media arts, that centers on utilizing technology to deliver information and entertainment; fashion, where students learn anything from designing clothes for the runway to running a retail shop; and culinary, which exposes learners to international cuisines as well as restaurant management techniques.

Bachelor's degree programs are offered in the areas of advertising, audio production, culinary management, digital filmmaking & video production, digital photography, fashion design, fashion marketing & management, game art & design, graphic design, hospitality management, illustration & design, interior design, and media arts & animation.

Associate degree programs are offered in the areas of culinary arts, fashion merchandising, graphic design, and hospitality management.

Diploma programs are offered in baking & pastry, culinary arts, digital image management, and fashion retailing.

A certificate program is offered in professional baking & pastry.

The Associate of Applied Science in culinary arts, the Bachelor of Applied Science in culinary management, Associate of Applied Science in graphic design, and the Bachelor of Fine Arts in interior design are available in evening and weekend formats.

Program availability and degree offerings are subject to change.

Academic Facilities

The Illinois Institute of Art—Chicago provides a learning environment with professional-grade technology applicable to each student's course of study. Students have the opportunity to build a portfolio of work that shows potential employers that they are trained to use the software, hardware, or equipment utilized within the industry. Depending upon the course of study, students are immersed in a creative environment—from classrooms to computer labs to studios—focused on relevant, hands-on education designed to prepare them for the real world.

Costs

Actual tuition and housing costs will vary depending on program, number of credits enrolled, and living arrangements. Prospective students should contact a Student Financial Services professional at the school for details.

Financial Aid

Financial aid is available for those who qualify. Students who require financial assistance should first complete and submit the Free Application for Federal Student Aid (FAFSA) online at www.fafsa.ed.gov and meet with a financial aid officer. Students may also apply for a number of scholarships focusing on their specific areas of career interest.

Faculty

Faculty members are hands-on creative professionals with proven experience as business leaders and innovators, hosting a learning environment similar to the career world students will face after graduation. Part instructor, part mentor, their mission is to help develop and transform creative potential into high-demand marketable skills.

Admission Requirements

Prospective students should refer to the current academic catalog for full details regarding admission requirements and process.

Application and Information

To obtain an application, make arrangements for an interview, or tour the school, students should contact:

The Illinois Institute of Art—Chicago
350 North Orleans Street, Suite 136-L
Chicago, Illinois 60654-1593
Phone: 312-280-3500
   800-351-3450 (toll-free)
Fax: 312-280-8562
Website: http://www.artinstitutes.edu/chicago

THE ILLINOIS INSTITUTE OF ART—SCHAUMBURG

SCHAUMBURG, ILLINOIS

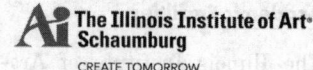

The Illinois Institute of Art—Schaumburg is one of The Art Institutes, a system of over fifty schools throughout North America dedicated to providing hands-on education in the creative and applied arts. The Illinois Institute of Art—Schaumburg offers bachelor's and associate degree programs as well as non-degree programs for students interested in pursuing career opportunities from among tomorrow's 15 million jobs in creative fields like design, fashion, media arts, and culinary (based on information from the U.S. Bureau of Labor Statistics for job growth from 2012 to 2022).

A focused education from The Illinois Institute of Art—Schaumburg can help students turn their creative energy into a powerful tool that can make a difference in the world. Students are part of a collaborative and supportive community, where experienced instructors provide the guidance and skills needed to pursue a career in the creative economy.

The Illinois Institute of Art—Schaumburg is also an important resource for creative industry leaders who value the opportunity provided students to learn by using professional-grade technology to build a portfolio of work to show potential employers after graduation.

Accreditation

The Illinois Institute of Art is accredited by the Higher Learning Commission and is a member of the North Central Association (NCA), 230 South LaSalle Street, Suite 7-500, Chicago, Illinois 60604-1413; phone: 800-621-7440 (toll-free); www.ncahlc.org.

The interior design program leading to the Bachelor of Fine Arts degree is accredited by the Council for Interior Design Accreditation, 206 Grandville Avenue, Suite 350, Grand Rapids, Michigan 49503; www.accredit-id.org.

The Illinois Institute of Art—Schaumburg is authorized by the Illinois Board of Higher Education, Division of Private Business and Vocational Schools, 431 East Adams, Second Floor, Springfield, Illinois 62701; phone: 217-782-2551; www.ibhe.state.il.us/default.htm.

Location

The Village of Schaumburg has emerged as the preeminent community in Chicago's thriving northwest suburbs. Schaumburg is characterized by a mixture of commercial/retail, office, and industrial development. There are 1,100 acres of parks; three outdoor skating rinks; tennis courts; and shopping, dining, and entertainment venues. This thoughtfully planned balance offers the convenience and sophistication of an urban environment along with the peace and tranquility of nearby open spaces. It's a great place to grow as a student and a person.

Just 26 miles to the southeast is Chicago, a world center of business, communications, and art. It is also the home of some of the world's most passionate sports fans. Join them to watch the Cubs play at legendary Wrigley Field on the city's north side or the White Sox at U.S. Cellular Field on the south side. The Bulls play basketball at the United Center, which is also where the NHL's Blackhawks play hockey. And football's Chicago Bears make their home at Soldier Field.

Chicago is a city of extraordinary architecture, 29 miles of lakefront, parks, neighborhood festivals, museums, and cultural attractions. In addition, magnificent harbors, parks, beaches, and a wide variety of restaurants all contribute to the thriving city life. Visitors enjoy the well-known Midwestern hospitality and flock to such popular attractions as the Magnificent Mile, Navy Pier, and Millennium Park.

Chicago is also well known for its music traditions, from jazz to blues, soul to gospel, and house music to hip-hop.

Programs of Study and Degree Offerings

Creativity is all around, and with millions of tomorrow's jobs in creative fields, the world needs more creative professionals. No matter which course of study a student chooses, the instructors at The Art Institutes will guide, support, and help students fine-tune their visual thinking and problem solving, so that they can take advantage of the world's growing creative opportunities and put their passion to work. Programs are offered in the areas of design, which focuses on communicating conceptually and helping people connect in living and work spaces; media arts, that centers on utilizing technology to deliver information and entertainment; fashion, where students learn anything from designing clothes for the runway to running a retail shop; and culinary, which exposes learners to international cuisines as well as restaurant management techniques.

Bachelor's degree programs are offered in the areas of advertising, audio production, digital filmmaking & video production, digital photography, fashion design, fashion marketing & management, game art & design, graphic design, hospitality management, illustration & design, interior design, media arts & animation, visual effects & motion graphics, and web design & interactive media.

Associate degree programs are offered in the areas of fashion merchandising, graphic design, hospitality management, and web design & interactive management.

Diploma programs are offered in digital design, digital image management, fashion retailing, residential planning, web design & development, and web design & interactive communications.

The Diploma in digital design, the Bachelor of Fine Arts in game art & design, Associate of Applied Science and Bachelor of Fine Arts in graphic design, the Bachelor of Fine Arts, in interior design, the Bachelor of Fine Arts in media arts & animation, the Diploma in residential planning, and the Associate of Applied Science and Bachelor of Fine Arts in web design & interactive media are available in evening and weekend formats.

Program availability and degree offerings are subject to change.

Academic Facilities

The Illinois Institute of Art—Schaumburg provides a learning environment with professional-grade technology applicable to each student's course of study. Students have the opportunity to build a portfolio of work that shows potential employers that they are trained to use the software, hardware, or equipment utilized within the industry. Depending upon the course of study, students are immersed in a creative environment—from classrooms to computer labs to studios—focused on relevant, hands-on education designed to prepare them for the real world.

Costs

Actual tuition and housing costs will vary depending on program, number of credits enrolled, and living arrangements. Prospective students should contact a Student Financial Services professional at the school for details.

Financial Aid

Financial aid is available for those who qualify. Students who require financial assistance should first complete and submit the Free Application for Federal Student Aid (FAFSA) online at www.fafsa.ed.gov and meet with a financial aid officer. Students may also apply for a number of scholarships focusing on their specific areas of career interest.

Faculty

Faculty members are hands-on creative professionals with proven experience as business leaders and innovators, hosting a learning environment similar to the career world students will face after graduation. Part instructor, part mentor, their mission is to help develop and transform creative potential into high-demand marketable skills.

Admission Requirements

Prospective students should refer to the current academic catalog for full details regarding admission requirements and process.

Application and Information

To obtain an application, make arrangements for an interview, or tour the school, prospective students should contact:

The Illinois Institute of Art—Schaumburg
1000 North Plaza Drive, Suite 100
Schaumburg, Illinois 60173-4990
Phone: 847-619-3450
       800-314-3450 (toll-free)
Fax: 847-619-3064
Website: http://www.artinstitutes.edu/schaumburg

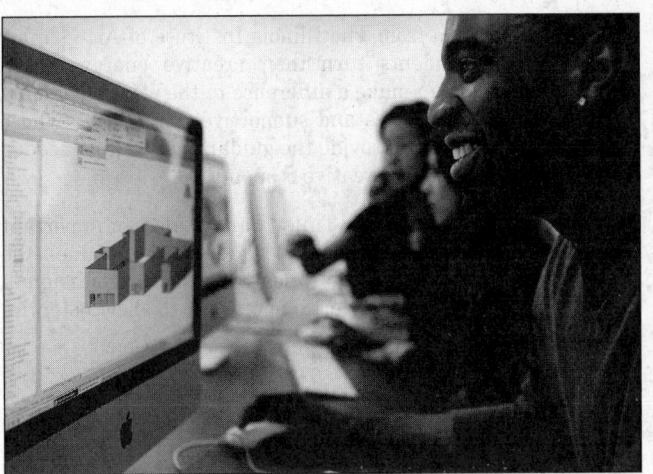

Since The Art Institutes system of schools is comprised of several institutions, see aiprograms.info for program duration, tuition, fees, and other costs, median debt, federal salary data, alumni success, and other important info. The Art Institutes is a system of over 50 schools throughout North America. Programs, credential levels, technology, and scheduling options vary by school, and employment opportunities are not guaranteed. Financial aid is available to those who qualify. Several institutions included in The Art Institutes system are campuses of South University or Argosy University. OH Registration #04-01-1698B, AC0165, AC0080, Licensed by the Florida Commission for Independent Education, License No. 1287, 3427, 3110, 2581. Certified by SCHEV to operate in Virginia. Administrative office: 210 Sixth Avenue, 33rd Floor, Pittsburgh, PA 15222. ©2013 The Art Institutes International LLC.

THE ILLINOIS INSTITUTE OF ART—TINLEY PARK

TINLEY PARK, ILLINOIS

Ai **The Illinois Institute of Art®**
Tinley Park
CREATE TOMORROW

The Illinois Institute of Art—Tinley Park is one of The Art Institutes, a system of over fifty schools throughout North America dedicated to providing hands-on education in the creative and applied arts. The Illinois Institute of Art—Tinley Park offers bachelor's and associate degree programs as well as non-degree programs for students interested in pursuing career opportunities from among tomorrow's 15 million jobs in creative fields like design, fashion, and media arts (based on information from the U.S. Bureau of Labor Statistics for job growth from 2012 to 2022).

A focused education from The Illinois Institute of Art—Tinley Park can help students turn their creative energy into a powerful tool that can make a difference in the world. Students are part of a collaborative and supportive community, where experienced instructors provide the guidance and skills needed to pursue a career in the creative economy.

The Illinois Institute of Art—Tinley Park is also an important resource for creative industry leaders who value the opportunity provided students to learn by using professional-grade technology to build a portfolio of work to show potential employers after graduation.

Accreditation

The Illinois Institute of Art—Tinley Park is an additional location of the Illinois Institute of Art—Chicago, which is accredited by the Higher Learning Commission and is a member of the North Central Association (NCA), 230 South LaSalle Street, Suite 7-500, Chicago, Illinois 60604-1413; phone: 800-621-7440; www.ncahlc.org.

The Illinois Institute of Art—Tinley Park is authorized by the Illinois Board of Higher Education, Division of Private Business and Vocational Schools, 431 East Adams, Second Floor, Springfield, Illinois 62701; 217-782-2551; www.ibhe.state.il.us/default.htm.

Location

The village of Tinley Park, just a short drive or train ride south from Chicago, is one of the most rapidly growing communities in this Midwest metropolitan area. Oak Park Avenue, the village's main thoroughfare, offers restaurants, shops, and businesses that make up the renovated historic district. In the summer, there are concerts in the plaza, drive-in-style movie nights, block parties, flea markets, farmers markets, and festivals.

In addition, there is a water park at the Bettenhausen Recreation Center, ball fields, Freedom Park, concerts at the First Midwest Bank Amphitheatre, and events at the Convention Center.

One of the village's most popular events is the Benches on the Avenue public art project, in which handcrafted wooden seating created by local artists is placed along Oak Park Avenue for the summer. Students are able to take the train to downtown Chicago.

Chicago is a world center of business, communications, and art. It is also the home of some of the world's most passionate sports fans. The Cubs play at legendary Wrigley Field on the city's north side, and the White Sox play at U.S. Cellular Field on the south side. The Bulls play basketball at United Center, which is also where the NHL's Blackhawks play hockey. And football's Chicago Bears make their home at Soldier Field.

Chicago is a city of extraordinary architecture, 29 miles of lakefront, parks, neighborhood festivals, museums, and cultural attractions. Magnificent harbors, parks, beaches, and a wide variety of restaurants all contribute to the thriving city life. Visitors enjoy the well-known Midwestern hospitality and flock to such famous attractions as the Magnificent Mile, Navy Pier, and Millennium Park.

Chicago is also well known for its music traditions—from jazz to blues, from soul to gospel, and from house music to hip-hop.

Programs of Study and Degrees

Creativity is all around, and with millions of tomorrow's jobs in creative fields, the world needs more creative professionals. No matter which course of study a student chooses, the instructors at The Art Institutes will guide, support, and help students fine-tune their visual thinking and problem solving, so that they can take advantage of the world's growing creative opportunities and put their passion to work. Programs are offered in the areas of design, which focuses on communicating conceptually and helping people connect in living and work spaces; media arts, that centers on utilizing technology to deliver information and entertainment; and fashion, where students learn anything from designing clothes for the runway to running a retail shop.

Bachelor's degree programs are offered in the areas of advertising, digital photography, fashion marketing & management, graphic design, interior design, and media arts & animation.

Associate degree programs are offered in the areas of fashion merchandising and graphic design.

Diploma programs are offered in digital image management, fashion retailing, web design & development, and web design & interactive communications.

Program availability and degree offerings are subject to change.

Academic Facilities

The Illinois Institute of Art—Tinley Park provides a learning environment with professional-grade technology applicable to each student's course of study. Students have the opportunity to build a portfolio of work that shows potential employers that they are trained to use the software, hardware, or equipment utilized within the industry. Depending upon the course of study, students are immersed in a creative environment—from classrooms to computer labs to studios—focused on relevant, hands-on education designed to prepare them for the real world.

Costs

Actual tuition and housing costs will vary depending on program, number of credits enrolled, and living arrangements. Prospective students should contact a Student Financial Services professional at the school for details.

Financial Aid

Financial aid is available for those who qualify. Students who require financial assistance should first complete and submit the Free Application for Federal Student Aid (FAFSA) online at www.fafsa.ed.gov and meet with a financial aid officer. Students may also apply for a number of scholarships focusing on their specific areas of career interest.

Faculty

Faculty members are hands-on creative professionals with proven experience as business leaders and innovators, hosting a learning environment similar to the career world students will face after graduation. Part instructor, part mentor, their mission is to help develop and transform creative potential into high-demand marketable skills.

Admission Requirements

Prospective students should refer to the current academic catalog for full details regarding admission requirements and process.

Application and Information

To obtain an application, make arrangements for an interview, or tour the school, prospective students should contact:

The Illinois Institute of Art—Tinley Park
18670 Graphic Drive
Tinley Park, Illinois 60477
Phone: 708-781-4200
       877-342-3298 (toll-free)
Fax: 708-781-4201
Website: http://www.artinstitutes.edu/tinleypark

THE JOHNS HOPKINS UNIVERSITY
Krieger School of Arts and Sciences and Whiting School of Engineering
BALTIMORE, MARYLAND

The University

Privately endowed, the Johns Hopkins University (JHU) was founded in 1876 as the first American university committed to the idea that knowledge should be discovered, rather than merely transmitted. Daniel Coit Gilman, the first president of Johns Hopkins, stated that the object of the University was "not so much to impart knowledge as to whet the appetite, exhibit methods, develop powers, strengthen judgment, and invigorate the intellectual and moral forces." Today, Johns Hopkins continues to stress creative scholarship by providing research-oriented education for undergraduates. Students in all disciplines are encouraged to explore intellectual questions and discover new ideas within a supportive environment.

Johns Hopkins seeks diversity in its students, who come from all fifty states and from seventy-one other countries. Of the total undergraduate enrollment of approximately 5,000 students, about 48 percent are women and 52 percent are men. All out-of-town freshmen and sophomores must live in campus residence halls. In addition, University-owned housing, located directly across from the University on North Charles Street, is available for juniors and seniors. Upperclassmen may also live in private housing or in Greek housing. Johns Hopkins has thirteen fraternities and nine sororities in the Inter-Fraternity Council and the Panhellenic Council.

The Homewood campus is active and lively, with many different events such as films, concerts, seminars, and athletic games being offered each week. The Student Council runs a number of activities, including a popular Spring Fair each year. Men's varsity teams compete in twelve sports. In the fall, men's teams compete in cross-country, football, soccer, and water polo. In the winter, basketball, fencing, swimming, and wrestling are offered. The big sports season at Johns Hopkins is spring, with baseball, lacrosse, tennis, and track and field. The men's and women's lacrosse teams compete at the Division I level, and the men have won forty-four national championships. Women's varsity sports also include basketball, cross-country, fencing, field hockey, soccer, swimming, tennis, track and field, and volleyball. An extensive and popular intramural program is also available. The O'Connor Recreation Center contains basketball and volleyball courts, a running track, racquetball courts, a rock-climbing wall, a weight room, and fitness and aerobic areas. In addition to the athletic programs, there are over 400 student-run clubs that hold events throughout the year. From the performing arts to hobby-centered clubs, there are many options for students of all interests.

Location

Johns Hopkins University's Homewood campus is on 140 acres of lush greenery, bounded on all sides by residential areas. Johns Hopkins offers the best of both worlds—the tranquil seclusion of the campus plus the adjacent urban environment. Two museums are owned by the University: Homewood Museum, on campus, and Evergreen Museum & Library, located nearby on North Charles Street, both of which provide academic opportunities for students. The Baltimore Museum of Art is on the southwest corner of the campus. The Walters Art Museum, a 10-minute drive away, has a collection that spans civilizations from Egypt to the 19th century, and many smaller museums, galleries, and outdoor showings feature local artists. The University is located just three miles from the heart of downtown Baltimore; the theater, symphony, and opera are 10 minutes away, as are Oriole Park at Camden Yards and M&T Bank Stadium. Weekend activities include visiting Baltimore's Inner Harbor, home to the National Aquarium and many other attractions; enjoying an ethnic festival by the water; sailing on the Chesapeake Bay; and hiking around the Maryland countryside. Washington, D.C. is a 50-minute drive by car or a 1-hour train ride. Opportunities abound for on- and off-campus entertainment.

Majors and Degrees

Bachelor of Arts degrees are awarded in Africana studies, anthropology, archaeology, behavioral biology, biology, biophysics, chemistry, classics, cognitive science, earth and planetary sciences, East Asian studies, economics, English, film and media studies, French, German, global environmental change and sustainability, history, history of art, history of science and technology, interdisciplinary studies, international studies, Italian, Latin American studies, mathematics, natural sciences, Near Eastern studies, neuroscience, philosophy, physics, political science, psychology, public health studies, Romance languages, sociology, Spanish, and the Writing Seminars. A Bachelor of Arts degree in engineering is available for students who seek preparation for professional careers (such as law or business) with a technological orientation. The B.A. in engineering is awarded in applied mathematics and statistics, biomedical engineering, computer science, electrical engineering, general engineering, and geography. Bachelor of Science degrees are awarded in applied mathematics and statistics, biomedical engineering, chemical and biomolecular engineering, civil engineering, computer engineering, computer science, electrical engineering, environmental engineering, materials science and engineering, mechanical engineering, molecular and cellular biology, and physics.

Accelerated bachelor's/master's degree programs are offered in biology, biophysics, German, history, international studies, mathematics, neuroscience, policy studies, psychology, public health studies, and Spanish. Accelerated B.S./M.S.E. programs are offered in most engineering departments. A dual-degree program leading to a Bachelor of Arts or Bachelor of Science degree and a Bachelor of Music degree is available in cooperation with the University's Peabody Institute and Conservatory of Music.

Academic Programs

The departments in the Krieger School of Arts and Sciences and the Whiting School of Engineering comprise four general areas for undergraduate programs: engineering, humanities, natural sciences, and social sciences. If a student has special interests that fall outside the bounds of the departmental majors, an individual program can be devised, or a student may study independently with the guidance of a faculty member. Qualified students may complete their degree requirements in fewer than four years.

Johns Hopkins has an extremely flexible program. There are no required freshman courses. All students must fulfill distribution requirements as well as the requirements for their major; the distribution requirements include a writing element. In most majors, 120 credits are required for graduation. Johns Hopkins has a 4-1-4 calendar.

The University offers the Army ROTC program on campus and the Air Force ROTC program in cooperation with the University of Maryland, College Park.

Off-Campus Programs

If qualified, a student may undertake a program for study abroad, normally during the junior year. Programs are offered at Johns Hopkins' international center in Bologna, Italy, as well as in Paris, France; Madrid, Spain; Berlin, Germany; and Latin America and through independent study-abroad programs with Johns Hopkins credit. Currently, there are more than 500 students studying abroad in over thirty countries. The University also participates in a cooperative program with other colleges in the Baltimore area. Undergraduates may take courses at the other divisions of Johns Hopkins University, including the Peabody Conservatory, the School of Nursing, the Bloomberg School of Public Health, the Nitze School of Advanced International Studies, the School of Education, the Carey Business School, and the School of Medicine.

Academic Facilities

The Milton S. Eisenhower Library on the Homewood campus is part of the University's Sheridan Libraries, which comprise the Milton S. Eisenhower Library, the John Work Garrett Library, the Albert D. Hutzler Undergraduate Reading Room, and the George

Peabody Library. Together, these libraries provide one of the most comprehensive learning resources in the world, containing more than 3.7 million books, more than 55,000 print and electronic journals, more than 700,000 electronic books, more than 10,000 videos and DVDs, more than 216,000 maps, and significant rare books, manuscripts, and archival resources.

The Mattin Student Arts Center contains the Swirnow Theater, a dance studio, music practice rooms, film and digital labs, darkrooms, a café, art studios, and spaces for students to gather. Hodson Hall includes classrooms, a meeting room for the Board of Trustees, the archives of the Hodson Trust, and a 500-seat auditorium, in which every seat is wired to the Internet. Clark Hall houses a state-of-the-art research and teaching facility for biomedical engineering. Charles Commons, a 618-person residential complex and dining facility, also houses the University's two-story Barnes and Noble bookstore.

The Brown Foundation Digital Media Center offers an environment where students can bring artistic inspiration to life using digital tools. It features twelve high-end computers that enable digital and audio composition and editing, animation, virtual painting, and 3-D modeling. All campus buildings are networked with each other and the other Johns Hopkins campuses.

Opened in 2012, the Brody Learning Commons is an exciting addition to campus that has already been embraced by the student community as a place to gather, study, and collaborate. The building connects to the Milton S. Eisenhower Library and contains the latest learning technology, including TeamSpot, interactive projectors that allow student to write on walls; Lifecam cameras; and video teleconferencing capabilities, all to support collaborative work. The building, constructed with current student input, features ample natural light and has achieved LEED Silver certification.

Costs

Costs for 2012–13 were $43,930 for tuition and $13,390 for room and board. Travel, books, and personal expenses vary.

Financial Aid

Financial aid is based on demonstrated eligibility, as determined by the Free Application for Federal Student Aid (FAFSA) at the time of acceptance. Approximately 42 percent of students receive financial assistance. Students must reapply for financial aid each year with the FAFSA and the College Scholarship Service (CSS) Financial Aid PROFILE. Johns Hopkins offers several merit-based scholarships, including the Hodson Trust Scholarship. Johns Hopkins also offers Army ROTC scholarships worth up to full tuition. The Baltimore Scholars Program provides full-tuition scholarships to eligible Baltimore City public high school graduates. In addition, several scholarships and grants allow undergraduates to pursue research opportunities, even as freshmen.

Faculty

The University's intellectual reputation is based on the strength of its faculty, of whom 91 percent hold a doctorate. The student-faculty ratio is 13:1. The well-known professors at Johns Hopkins teach both undergraduate and graduate students, which means that students receive a great deal of personal attention both in and out of the classroom. Johns Hopkins has a large number of notable professors, including 50 American Academy of Arts and Sciences fellows, 3 National Medal of Science winners, 2 Presidential Medal of Freedom winners, and 6 MacArthur Fellows. Faculty members are always accessible to advise and assist students and to work with them on research projects.

Student Government

Johns Hopkins students enjoy the benefits of a well-organized and far-reaching student government, which is led by a powerful Student Council. The council is composed of elected class representatives and officers, but it relies on the active participation of many students in its numerous committees, boards, and commissions. Through the Student Activities Commission, the University encourages initiative and independence by giving students full responsibility and control of funds for various clubs and organizations.

Admission Requirements

In choosing from a large number of applicants, the University selects those men and women who will benefit from a Johns Hopkins education, and who will add something to the campus community. A student's intellectual interests and accomplishments are of primary importance, and the Admissions Committee carefully examines each applicant's scholastic record, standardized test results, essays, and recommendations from secondary school officials and other sources about the student's character, intellectual curiosity, seriousness of purpose, and range of extracurricular involvement. The application essays are an important part of how the Admissions Committee learns more about students during the application review process. Two teacher recommendations are required. In addition, the SAT or the ACT with writing test is required. For students submitting SAT scores, Johns Hopkins recommends the submission of SAT Subject Tests, and if submitted, requests results from three tests. Students should consult the website for additional details on test requirements. Every year, the University enrolls a first-year class of approximately 1,300 men and women from all parts of the United States and a number of other countries. In addition, transfer students from other colleges and universities are admitted to the sophomore and junior classes. Advanced-standing credit is granted from college-level work completed at an accredited college or through the Advanced Placement and International Baccalaureate programs.

Application and Information

Johns Hopkins accepts the Common Application and the Universal College Application, both with a Johns Hopkins supplement. The application deadline is January 1. If applicants consider Johns Hopkins to be their first choice, they may apply under the early decision plan. This requires that the application be filed by November 1. Notification is given by April 1 for regular decision students and by December 15 for those applying under the early decision plan. Students wishing to enroll in the biomedical engineering (BME) program must indicate BME as their first choice of major on their application. Freshmen who are BME majors are admitted specifically as such.

Office of Undergraduate Admissions
The Johns Hopkins University
Mason Hall
3400 North Charles Street
Baltimore, Maryland 21218-2683
Phone: 410-516-8171
Fax: 410-516-6025
E-mail: gotojhu@jhu.edu
Website: http://apply.jhu.edu

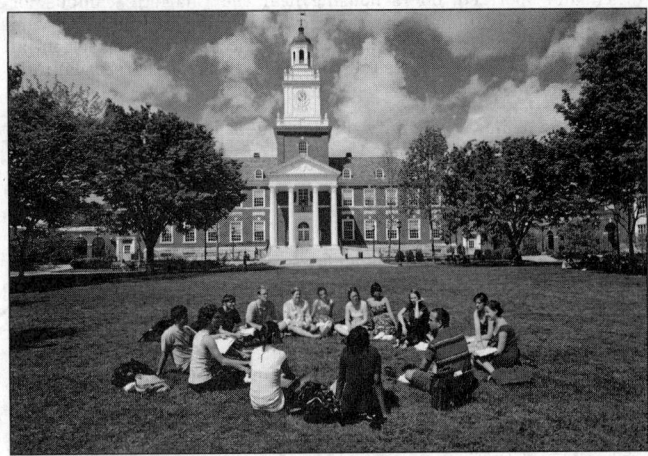

Johns Hopkins students enjoy class in front of Gilman Hall.

JOHNSON & WALES UNIVERSITY
PROVIDENCE, RHODE ISLAND

The University

Johnson & Wales University (JWU), founded in 1914, is a nonprofit, private institution. A recognized leader in experience-based education, the University offers accredited degrees to approximately 17,000 graduate and undergraduate students, representing all fifty states and ninety-seven countries. An innovative educational leader, JWU offers degree programs in arts and sciences, business, culinary arts, education, nutrition, hospitality and technology. Its unique model integrates arts and sciences and industry focused education with work experience and leadership opportunities, inspiring students to achieve professional success and lifelong personal growth. The University has four campuses in Providence, Rhode Island; North Miami, Florida; Denver, Colorado; and Charlotte, North Carolina.

JWU is a professionally-focused institution offering programs in a variety of areas. JWU's educational approach is designed to help students identify a field of interest and acquire the knowledge, skills, and experience to excel in that field. The University's unique education model integrates academics and professional skills, related work experiences, community and leadership opportunities, and career services. Students develop academic schedules and work experience plans relevant to their career goals, starting in their first term. In addition to undergraduate degree programs, JWU offers graduate degree programs, including an M.B.A. program with concentrations in accounting, hospitality, and information technology; an M.Ed. program in teaching and learning; and M.A.T. programs in teaching (with or without certification) including elementary education, elementary special education, and food service education. The University also offers an Ed.D. program in educational leadership.

Students are involved in a variety of extracurricular activities. Many students at the University are members of national student organizations such as Business Professionals of America; DECA (Collegiate DECA), Future Business Leaders of America (Phi Beta Lambda); Family, Career, Community Leaders of America (FCCLA); National FFA; Junior Achievement; SkillsUSA; and Technology Association of America. Sports and fitness programs include aerobics, baseball, basketball, golf, ice hockey, sailing, soccer, tennis, volleyball, and wrestling.

The University maintains twenty-seven residence halls throughout its four campuses. In addition, City View Towers, which is independently owned and operated, offers housing near the Charlotte campus for upperclassmen. Student services include academic counseling and testing, a tutorial center, and health services. JWU's Experiential Education and Career Services office provides extensive career planning and placement services.

Johnson & Wales University is accredited by the New England Association of Schools and Colleges Inc. (NEASC), through its Commission on Institutions of Higher Education.

Location

The location of each of the University's campuses enables students to take advantage of internship and part-time work activities offered by many nearby businesses, community groups, and government agencies. All of Johnson & Wales' city campuses retain a small-town feel and easy accessibility to students. The urban setting of the Providence campus provides students proximity to the city's many cultural and recreational facilities. The North Miami campus is a short trip from the sun and fun of Fort Lauderdale and the culture and diversity of Miami. The Denver campus offers students great opportunities as the nation's sixth-leading tourist destination and *Forbes* magazine's "fifth best place in America for business and careers." The Charlotte campus is located in a vibrant urban setting that combines commercial and residential life. More than 260 Fortune 500 companies have offices in Charlotte, which is known as the second-largest financial center in the U.S.

Majors and Degrees

The degree programs described in this section are for the 2013–14 academic year and are subject to change. Students may pursue concentrations related to their program of study to further tailor their degrees to their specific interests and career goals.

The University's Providence campus offers degree programs in accounting; advertising and marketing communications; baking and pastry arts; baking and pastry arts and food service management; business administration; counseling psychology; communication studies; criminal justice; culinary arts; culinary arts and food service management; culinary nutrition; electronics engineering; engineering design and configuration management; entrepreneurship; equine business management; equine business management/riding; fashion merchandising and retail marketing; finance; food service entrepreneurship; graphic design and digital media; hotel and lodging management; international business; international hotel and tourism management; liberal studies; management; management accounting; marketing; network engineering; restaurant, food, and beverage management; risk management; software engineering; sports/entertainment/event management; and travel, tourism, and hospitality management.

In its adult and continuing education division, Johnson & Wales' Providence campus offers associate and bachelor's degrees in arts and sciences, business, culinary arts, hospitality, and technology.

The North Miami campus offers degree programs in baking and pastry arts; business administration; criminal justice; culinary arts; culinary arts and food service management; fashion merchandising and retail marketing; hotel and lodging management; management; marketing; pastry arts and food service management; restaurant, food, and beverage management; sports/entertainment/event management; and travel, tourism, and hospitality management.

The Denver campus offers degree programs in baking and pastry arts; baking and pastry arts and food service management; business administration; criminal justice; culinary arts; culinary arts and food service management; culinary nutrition; fashion merchandising and retail marketing; hotel and lodging management; restaurant, food, and beverage management; and sports/entertainment/event management. Students can also earn degrees in culinary arts and baking and pastry arts through the adult and continuing education division.

The Charlotte campus offers degree programs in baking and pastry arts; baking and pastry arts and food service management; business administration; culinary arts; culinary arts and food service management; fashion merchandising and retail marketing; hotel and lodging management; management; management accounting; marketing; restaurant, food, and beverage management; and sports/entertainment/event management.

Academic Programs

Johnson & Wales University offers programs in arts and sciences, business, culinary arts, hospitality, and technology within an academic structure of three 11-week terms.

Learning by doing is an important part of experiential education at JWU, and many programs include laboratory studies as well as formal internship requirements. Students get real-life work experience beginning their freshman year. Special advanced-placement programs are featured for high school seniors with exceptional skills in culinary arts or baking and pastry arts. In addition, JWU awards credit for certain courses based on the successful completion of Challenge, CLEP, or Portfolio Assessments. All degree candidates must successfully complete the required number of courses and/or quarter credit hours, as prescribed in the various curricula.

Off-Campus Programs

At Johnson & Wales, students get hands-on learning experiences from the start, inside and outside the classroom. Many of the majors offer internships at University-owned, or at one of our partner, facilities. The hotel-restaurant management program features an internship at the Radisson Hotel Providence Airport or the DoubleTree by Hilton Charlotte Gateway Village; both are full-service hotel complexes that are owned and/or operated by the University (the Radisson and DoubleTree are corporate franchises). For all majors, optional career internships are available with businesses throughout the United States and worldwide, such as Marriott International, Compass Group NAD, Foxwoods Resort and Casino, and Putnam Investments. Most internships are one term in duration and carry 13.5 quarter hours of credit. International exchange and term-abroad programs are also offered.

Academic Facilities

The facilities of the Providence campus are located throughout the intimate state of Rhode Island and in nearby Massachusetts. The Downcity campus in Providence is home to the University's College of Business, The Hospitality College, the School of Arts and Sciences, and the School of Technology. A number of academic and residential facilities are located at this campus, as are several training facilities. The Harborside campus, also in Providence but located a short distance away from the Downcity campus, houses the University's College of Culinary Arts. This campus has five student residence halls as well as specialized classrooms and laboratories, production kitchens, bakeshops, dining rooms, a storeroom, and meat-cutting facilities. This campus is also home to the Alan Shawn Feinstein Graduate School, the School of Education, the University Recreation and Athletic Center, a student activities office, a bookstore, a gymnasium, a dining center, a snack bar, and a Starbucks.

JWU's North Miami campus is located in the heart of North Miami, between Miami and Fort Lauderdale. Facilities include academic classrooms, production/demonstration kitchens, a bakeshop, residence halls, and a specially designed conference center.

The Denver campus, located in the Park Hill neighborhood, combines old-world charm with the latest technological resources, including stately turn-of-the-century buildings and newer student centers in a quiet park landscape. The traditional residential campus is fully wired, with computers in every classroom and laboratory.

The Charlotte campus is located in the heart of Gateway Village in Uptown Charlotte. The academic center is home to a 200-seat auditorium, a production kitchen, state-of-the-art culinary laboratories, classrooms, seminar rooms, and computer labs.

Costs

Tuition at all campuses for 2013–14 is $27,156. Room and board plans range from $8,499 to $12,000. There is also an orientation fee of $300 for new students. Books and supplies are estimated at $800 to $900 per year, depending on the program.

Room and board fees vary at each campus. Students should consult the respective campus catalogs for further details.

Financial Aid

Johnson & Wales students are eligible to apply for a variety of financial aid programs, including the Federal Pell Grant, Federal Supplemental Educational Opportunity Grant, Federal Work-Study, and Federal Perkins Loan programs. They are also eligible for University-based student scholarship programs and state-supported grants and scholarships. In the past, approximately 90 percent of the University's entering students have received some sort of financial assistance. Students must submit the Free Application for Federal Student Aid (FAFSA) to the Federal Student Aid Processor to be considered for financial aid. Early application is strongly suggested for full consideration.

Faculty

The University's 520 full-time and 430 part-time faculty members (all campuses) are oriented toward instruction rather than research. Many are chosen for their professional experience in business, culinary arts, hospitality services, or technology. The student-faculty ratio is 23:1.

Student Government

Student Government Association (SGA) is the voice of students on campus and serves as the governing student organization on campus. Students are elected to major leadership positions in the spring, and senator positions are available to any interested student in the fall. SGA is responsible for allocating student funds, recognizing new organizations, and addressing student concerns on campus.

Admission Requirements

Johnson & Wales seeks students who are professionally focused and have a true desire to succeed. Academic qualifications are important, but an applicant's motivation and interest in doing well are given special consideration. Graduation from high school or the equivalent credentials are required for admission. It is recommended that students applying for admission into the culinary arts and baking and pastry arts programs have some prior education or experience in food service. Although tests are not required for most programs, all applicants are encouraged to submit scores from the SAT or ACT. Students are selected by Admissions to join the Honors program upon entrance to the university. To be eligible, students must have taken a college prep curriculum, maintained an average of B or better, placed in the top 25 percent of the high school graduating class, submitted SAT/ACT scores at or above the national average, and entered JWU in the fall of their first year. High school juniors may apply for early admission under the Early Enrollment Program (EEP). Transfer students are required to submit official high school and college transcripts. Credits to be transferred from other institutions are evaluated on the basis of their equivalent at Johnson & Wales.

Application and Information

Johnson & Wales does not require an application fee. After submitting the application, the student is responsible for requesting that appropriate transcripts be forwarded to JWU's Admissions. While there is no deadline, students are advised to apply as early as possible before the intended date of enrollment to ensure full consideration of their application. Applications are accepted for terms beginning in September, December, and March and for the summer sessions (for most programs).

For more information about JWU, prospective students can visit **www. jwu.edu/hs** or apply online at **www.jwu.edu/apply**.

Inquiries can also be addressed to:

Admissions
Johnson & Wales University
8 Abbott Park Place
Providence, Rhode Island 02903
Phone: 401-598-1000
        800-DIAL-JWU (toll-free)
Fax: 401-598-4901
E-mail: jwu@admissions.jwu.edu
Website: http://www.jwu.edu/hs
        http://www.facebook.com/JohnsonandWales

Johnson & Wales University offers degree programs in arts and sciences, business, culinary arts, hospitality, and technology.

KETTERING UNIVERSITY
FLINT, MICHIGAN

The University

Founded in 1919, Kettering University is a private university specializing in science, technology, engineering, math (STEM), and business degrees. The school enrolls about 1,800 undergraduate students and offers a 13:1 student-faculty ratio. Most classes have fewer than 20 students and are taught by Ph.D.-level professors, not teaching assistants. This combination of small class size and highly qualified teaching staff ensures students a much more personalized learning experience.

Kettering is a highly acclaimed university with the one of the country's most modern cooperative education and experiential learning programs. Whatever major is chosen, students alternate between study terms and full-time work terms. During study terms, students learn material in small, intense classes taught by University professors. During work terms, students work as paid professionals at corporations related to their studies and interests. Kettering students have done everything from testing ballistic systems for the U.S. government to reengineering crowd management at Disney World. Kettering has the only cooperative education and experiential learning program of its kind where students begin working as early as their freshman year. By graduation from Kettering, students have up to 2½ years of professional experience and impressive resumes. Traditionally, nearly all Kettering students graduate with job offers or grad school acceptances in hand.

Kettering University's cooperative education and experiential learning program pairs hands-on education with real-world experience—all undergraduate students alternate between on-campus study terms and full-time terms of employment with one of more than 500 corporate partners. This unique system of education prepares students to be technology innovators—professionals with cutting-edge skills who are ready to compete in tomorrow's business environment.

Kettering University is accredited by the North Central Association of Colleges and Schools, the Accreditation Board for Engineering and Technology (ABET), and the Association of Collegiate Business Schools and Programs (ACBSP). Kettering is also a member of the National Commission of Cooperative Education (NCCE) and the Association of Independent Technological Universities.

Besides being academically ahead of the game, Kettering students bring a wide range of skills and interests with them to campus. To make sure that students get a life along with an education, Kettering offers more than fifty student organizations, including thirteen fraternities and five sororities, an active student government, a state-of-the-art recreation and fitness facility, and very competitive intramural sports. Recreation facilities include athletic fields, tennis courts, and a recreation center with an Olympic-size, six-lane swimming pool; aerobic fitness rooms; a full line of Nautilus equipment; and basketball, tennis, and racquetball courts. A public golf course is adjacent to the campus.

Kettering also offers Master of Science degree programs in engineering, engineering management, operations management, manufacturing operations, lean manufacturing

and an M.B.A. program. Graduate certificates in global leadership, healthcare systems management, green business, supply chain management, and healthcare systems engineering are also available.

Professional counseling, support services, and health-care services are available. To learn more about Kettering, potential students may visit the University's site on Facebook at http://www.facebook.com/KetteringAdmissions or on Twitter at http://www.twitter.com/Ready4Kettering.

Location

Kettering University is located in Flint, Michigan, which is 60 miles west of Lake Huron and 60 miles north of Detroit. Flint has approximately 102,000 residents and a metropolitan area population of 420,000.

Flint is particularly proud of its Cultural Center, which is only 10 minutes from Kettering's campus. Built and endowed entirely by the gifts of private citizens, the Cultural Center includes the Alfred P. Sloan Museum, the Whiting Auditorium (home of the Flint Symphony and host to leading stage shows and entertainers), the Robert T. Longway Planetarium (Michigan's largest and best-equipped sky show facility), the Flint Institute of Arts, the F. A. Bower Theater, the Dort Institute of Music, Mott Community College, and the Flint Public Library. Nearby is the University of Michigan–Flint campus.

The area also offers numerous outdoor and indoor recreational opportunities. Within a few minutes' drive are downhill and cross-country skiing facilities, lakes for the entire range of water sports, a wide selection of good public golf courses, excellent indoor and outdoor skating rinks, and plentiful shopping facilities and restaurants

Majors and Degrees

Kettering University offers a 4½-year, professional cooperative education and experiential learning program with Bachelor of Science degrees in applied biology, applied mathematics, applied physics, biochemistry, bioinformatics, business administration, chemical engineering, chemistry, computer engineering, computer science, electrical engineering, engineering physics, industrial engineering, and mechanical engineering. Kettering also offers a Bachelor of Business Administration degree.

Kettering also offers a variety of dual-degree programs and more than fifty minors, specialties, and concentrations, to ensure that students' degrees are custom-fit to their interests and career goals. Examples include computer gaming, fuel cells and hybrid technology, system and data security, premed, and prelaw.

Academic Programs

Although each program at Kettering University has its own requirements, 160 credit hours are generally required for graduation. The program involves nine academic terms and nine work terms, two of which are focused on the capstone thesis project, which is a major work project assigned by the employer. Students alternate between eleven-week periods of academic study on the campus in Flint and twelve-week periods of related work experience with their corporate employer. The academic year consists of two 3-month academic terms on campus and two 3-month terms of paid work experience.

Academic Facilities

Kettering University offers some of the best facilities, labs, and educational resources in the world, and students start using them as early as their freshman year. The Crash Safety Center, for example, is the only one of its kind in the nation used in an undergraduate program. The University also offers labs in areas such as fuel-cell research, polymer optimization, machining, acoustics, and more.

Kettering is fully networked and allows 24-hour access to computer resources and the Internet from dorms and labs. A 445-student residence hall and an apartment complex are located on the campus for student housing. The library offers more than 100,000 cataloged volumes and 540 periodicals. And through online resources like Kettering Connect and Blackboard, students can always be in touch with professors and University staff members.

Costs

For 2012–13, tuition costs were $33,946 and room and board cost $6,660.

Starting in the 2012–13 academic year, Kettering is offering fixed-rate tuition, becoming the first STEM university in Michigan to do so. For students making normal progress towards their degrees, tuition rates will not change during their course of study, removing some of the guesswork associated with budgeting for college costs.

Financial Aid

Kettering University wants to invest in its students, so it does what it takes to help finance their education through scholarships, loans, and work-study opportunities. More than 92 percent of the students receive some sort of financial aid. Factor in co-op earnings—between $40,000 and $65,000 over the course of the college career—and the new fixed-rate tuition guarantee, and students are looking at one of the best values in education today. In addition, Kettering's Merit Scholarship program awards students with extremely generous scholarship packages.

Students should fill out the Free Application for Federal Student Aid (FAFSA) and request a copy of the analysis to be sent to Kettering University. The University works to create a financial aid package for based on those results.

Faculty

Kettering University's 122 full-time faculty members have teaching as their main responsibility. Most professors have industrial experience in addition to academic credentials and maintain contact with industry through consulting, sponsored research, and advising on student thesis projects. More than 90 percent of faculty members hold a doctorate. Because only half of the students are on campus at any one time, class sizes are small, and opportunities for enrichment and extra help are readily available.

Admission Requirements

Admission to Kettering University is competitive and based on scholastic achievement and extracurricular interests, activities, and achievements. Applicants are required to have earned the following: 3 years of English, 2 years algebra, 1 year of geometry, 1 semester of trigonometry, 2 years of lab science (1 must be physics or chemistry; both are recommended). Applicants must submit results of the SAT or ACT (Kettering's ACT code number is 1998 and the SAT code number is 1246).

Most Kettering University students are in the top 10 percent of their graduating class. Kettering University also welcomes students wishing to transfer from other colleges and universities. The transfer alternative is an excellent way to gain admission for students who do not enroll as freshmen.

Application and Information

Students can apply online at http://www.kettering.edu/apply. Students should call 800-955-4464 ext. 7865 for assistance.

Kettering officials review applications and let students know if they have been accepted. Although Kettering accepts and processes applications throughout the year, it is best to apply as early as possible. Once accepted, students receive information on programs and the professional co-op program, which are only available to admitted students. Students should complete the co-op registration (resume) online and pay a $300 tuition deposit (to be credited to the first-semester tuition). The deposit shows that a student is as serious about Kettering as Kettering is about the student and ensures a place in the entering class and eligibility to begin the co-op employment search process.

Admissions Office
Kettering University
1700 University Avenue
Flint, Michigan 48504
United States
Phone: 810-762-7865
      800-955-4464 Ext. 7865 (toll-free in the United States and Canada)
E-mail: admissions@kettering.edu
Website: http://www.kettering.edu/admissions
      http://www.facebook.com/KetteringAdmissions
      http://www.twitter.com/Ready4Kettering

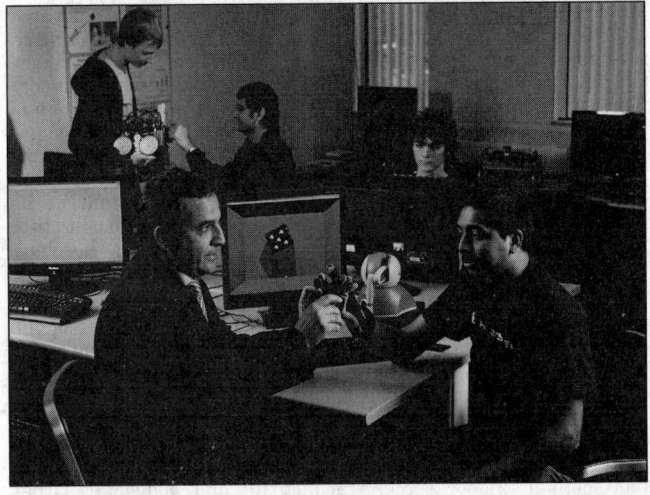

Kettering prepares its students to go farther.

KING'S COLLEGE
WILKES-BARRE, PENNSYLVANIA

The College

King's College is an independent, coed, four-year Catholic college with 2,700 students. Founded in 1946 by the Holy Cross Priests and Brothers from the University of Notre Dame, King's prepares students for a purposeful life, with an education that integrates the human values inherent in a broadly based liberal arts curriculum. The College encourages the religious, moral, personal, and social development of its students.

In addition to the undergraduate degrees, King's College offers a Master of Science (M.S.) degree in health-care administration, a Master of Education (M.Ed.) degree in reading or curriculum and development instruction, and a five-year physician assistant studies program leading to a master's degree.

Academic advising begins before students enroll and continues with an innovative program of career development across the curriculum. King's Academic Skills Center includes a nationally certified tutoring program and a faculty-staffed writing center. More than 70 percent of students who attend King's graduate from the College, which is well above the national average, and 99 percent are employed or attend graduate school within six months of graduation.

The quaint urban campus comprises eight city blocks and features many buildings and centers that house King's numerous academic programs, including the Charles E. and Mary Parente Life Sciences Center, the Mulligan Physical Sciences Center, and the William G. McGowan School of Business. The 15-acre campus also includes Monarch Court; the Sheehy-Farmer Campus Center, which offers an art gallery, an outdoor waterfall and patio, a student restaurant, and marketplace dining; the J. Carroll McCormick Campus Ministry Center; and the William S. Scandlon Physical Education Center, which features a 3,200-seat basketball arena, wrestling facilities, racquetball and handball courts, an Olympic-size swimming pool, a wellness center, and a state-of-the-art sports medicine facility. In addition, an expansion of the Scandlon Center was recently completed, which includes three multipurpose courts as well as new offices, meeting rooms, and additional sports medicine facilities. The student health center is located in André Hall, a newly renovated building which is almost twice the size of the former health center, which now allows a consulting physician to be on call at all times. The six-story administration and science buildings form a unit that houses the College's newly renovated theater, the Susquehanna Room dining hall and coffee bar, administrative offices, science laboratories, and classrooms. Residence halls have cable television, wireless Internet access, and 24-hour computer labs. Many of King's athletic teams train and compete just two miles from campus at the Robert L. Betzler Athletic Complex, a 33.5-acre athletic facility that includes McCarthy Stadium; a field house; and fields for baseball, softball, men's and women's soccer, football, and field hockey.

There are fifty student organizations that provide King's students with the opportunity to explore interests outside of the classroom. King's has 19 NCAA Division III teams including men's baseball, basketball, football, golf, lacrosse, soccer, swimming, tennis, and wrestling; women's basketball, field hockey, lacrosse, soccer, softball, swimming, tennis, and volleyball; and coed cross-country. The College offers cheerleading, ice hockey, and track and field as club sports. Intramural sports include basketball, flag football, indoor soccer, racquetball, and dodgeball. Other cocurricular activities include: academic clubs in almost every department, the King's Players (theater), Cantores Christi Regis (choir), Campus Ministry, the Experiencing the Arts Series, *The Crown* (student newspaper), the *Regis* (yearbook), and the *SCOP* (literary magazine).

Location

The King's campus is located in a residential area near downtown Wilkes-Barre, Pennsylvania, a city of approximately 50,000 on the banks of the Susquehanna River. A growing city, Wilkes-Barre has developed both economically and culturally, yet it has avoided many typical urban problems. Shopping malls, multiplex theaters, a brand new riverfront park, art galleries, and restaurants are nearby. Two blocks from King's is the F. M. Kirby Center, which has hosted national performances, music groups, traveling theater, and more. National recording acts regularly perform in nearby venues.

King's is a short drive from several ski resorts, state parks, and major lakes where students can participate in many seasonal outdoor activities. Students can also enjoy professional sports action including the New York Yankees' AAA baseball team, the Pocono International Raceway which hosts two NASCAR races each season, and the Pittsburgh Penguins' minor-league ice hockey team. The Mohegan Sun Arena is the host to many concerts and events, and is the site of the King's commencement. The campus is close to major metropolitan areas including New York City and Philadelphia (each a 2½-hour drive); Washington, D.C., and the attractions of New England are within a 4-hour drive.

Majors and Degrees

King's awards the Master of Science, Master of Education, Bachelor of Arts, Bachelor of Science, Associate of Arts, and Associate of Science degrees. The College's thirty-seven major programs are offered in the arts and sciences and the William G. McGowan School of Business, which is accredited by AACSB International—The Association to Advance Collegiate Schools of Business.

Arts and sciences include the humanities and social sciences division (computers and information systems, criminal justice, economics, English–literature, English–professional writing, French, history, mass communications, philosophy, political science, psychology, sociology, Spanish, theater, and theology); the education division, which is accredited by NCATE (preschool–grade 4, secondary certification, and special education); the science division (biology, chemistry, computer science, engineering, environmental science, environmental studies, general science, mathematics, neuroscience, and physics); and the allied health division (clinical lab science, physician assistant studies, and athletics training education/sports medicine accredited by CAAHEP). Available majors in the William G. McGowan School of Business are accounting, finance, human resources management, international business, management, and marketing. King's offers pre-professional programs in chiropractic, dentistry, law, medicine, optometry, pharmacy, and veterinary science. The engineering program is a 3+2 dual-degree program with the University of Notre Dame, in which students spend three years at King's and then two years at Notre Dame.

Academic Programs

The general education program at King's is recognized nationwide by its peers. King's is included in *Barron's Best Buys in College Education* and has been honored in eighteen consecutive issues of *U.S. News & World Report's Best Colleges Guide*. The College was also recognized by the John Templeton Foundation Honor Roll for Character-Building Colleges, the Forbes/CCAP list of America's best colleges, and is one of sixteen institutions nationwide named to the Greater Expectations initiative.

The honors program offers highly motivated students the challenge of learning in discussion-centered courses that explore distinctive subject matter with exciting and innovative approaches. Twenty honor societies encourage students to excel in their chosen fields and recognize students for their academic distinction; members are honored each year at the All-College Honors Convocation. Science students receive hands-on lab training much earlier than students at other institutions and work together with faculty members on real-world research projects.

Off-Campus Programs

Experiential learning (via internships) is available in conjunction with almost every major. King's students have interned at CNN, the New York Stock Exchange, PricewaterhouseCoopers, the U.S. House of Representatives, U.S. Senators' offices, the U.S. Department of

Energy, Walt Disney World, and Xerox Corporation, among other places. Every year, students are placed with local, regional, and national companies around the globe.

Through the study-abroad program many of King's students have studied on campuses throughout Europe, Thailand, China, Australia, and various other countries.

Academic Facilities

King's facilities include the 51,000-square-foot, three-story D. Leonard Corgan Library, which contains several study rooms, a 100-seat auditorium, a 160,000-volume collection, and a computerized catalog, which students can access from their home or residence hall. The library provides full-text databases from every computer on campus, and access to college and research libraries throughout the United States. Students and faculty members also have direct access to more than 1 million volumes through the local library cooperative (NEPBC).

King's features computer labs with more than 440 PCs, 24-hour labs in residence halls, e-mail accounts for all students, computerized library databases, multimedia classrooms with a variety of instructional aids, course discussions on Moodle, distance-learning facilities for teleconferencing, and cross-registration with area colleges that enables students to take courses complementary to their majors.

The Charles E. and Mary Parente Life Sciences Center, which contains a molecular biology laboratory and a genomics center, includes computer facilities, instrumentation rooms, a rooftop greenhouse, and environmental chambers. The Mulligan Physical Sciences Center includes modern research laboratories, computer facilities, and state-of-the-art instrumentation used for molecular identification.

Costs

For the 2012–13 academic year, tuition for full-time students was $29,174. Room and board totaled $11,228.

Financial Aid

King's assists all qualified students through its financial aid programs. Currently, more than 97 percent of King's students receive financial aid in the form of scholarships, grants, work-study, or loans. Last year, our average financial aid was $22,303, taking a significant amount of the financial obligation away from the student and their family. The average net cost of tuition, room, and board for 2012–13 was $17,891. Aid is awarded on the basis of demonstrated financial need, the difference between the total cost of education and the expected family contribution.

In addition to financial aid programs, installment payment plans are available, offering students and/or their families the ability to make monthly payments throughout the academic year. Students who wish to be considered for financial aid must fill out the Free Application for Federal Student Aid (FAFSA) and the King's College Financial Aid Application. The preferred filing deadline for new freshmen is February 15. Forms are mailed to students accepted for admission but can be completed prior to acceptance.

Faculty

King's College has 136 full-time and 101 part-time faculty members. Eighty-five percent of the full-time faculty members have a Ph.D. or an equivalent terminal degree. Graduate assistants do not teach courses. The student-faculty ratio is 14:1.

Student Government

The student government coordinates and participates in numerous activities for both the student body and the surrounding community. It regularly holds open forums for students and senior administrators at the College, coordinates informal socials for the students with the College president, and makes presentations at each meeting of the Board of Directors. In addition, the student government sponsors events that foster awareness for social and justice issues and a celebration of cultural diversity.

Admission Requirements

King's encourages applications from qualified high school students and those who wish to transfer from another institution. To be considered for admission, students must be prepared to successfully pursue a program of study at the College, as evidenced by the quality of previous academic and extracurricular performance, the recommendation of school officials and character references, and the student's display of personal promise, maturity, and motivation. King's admits students of any race, sex, color, creed, or national or ethnic origin.

Admission decisions are made for both high school students and transfer students with the understanding that all current courses and examinations will be completed satisfactorily. Candidates should complete 4 years of mathematics (through trigonometry or precalculus). One year each of high school chemistry, biology, and physics is also strongly recommended.

The Office of Admission offers two methods for candidates to apply for admission: the SAT/ACT Traditional Choice and the Standardized Test Option/Essay Choice. Applicants are required to state their preference prior to the application review, and the decision is nonreversible. Students who select the SAT/ACT Traditional Choice must submit a completed application, official high school transcripts, SAT or ACT scores, guidance counselor recommendation, an essay, and the $30 application fee, which is waived if students apply online. Students who choose the Standardized Test Option/Essay Choice must submit a completed application, official high school transcripts, an official graded writing sample from either their junior or senior year—submitted and notarized by the high school guidance office, guidance counselor recommendation, an essay, and the $30 application fee, which is waived if students apply online.

Application and Information

Applicants should forward a completed application and the $30 fee to the Office of Admission or apply online at www.kings.edu in order to waive the application fee. Secondary and postsecondary (if applicable) transcripts must be sent. Admission decisions are not made until all credentials are received. King's subscribes to a rolling admission policy. Decisions are announced within two weeks from the date of application. Upon notification of acceptance, a $200 nonrefundable deposit is requested to reserve a place in the class. The deposit deadline is May 1 but may be extended upon request. To schedule an interview, obtain an application form, or for more information, students should contact:

Office of Admission
King's College
133 North River Street
Wilkes-Barre, Pennsylvania 18711
Phone: 570-208-5858
       888-KINGS-PA (toll-free)
E-mail: admissions@kings.edu
Website: http://www.kings.edu
       http://www.facebook.com/kingscollegepa
       http://twitter.com/KingsCollege_PA

Professor Garrett Barr engages students on a beautiful spring day at King's College.

LAWRENCE TECHNOLOGICAL UNIVERSITY

SOUTHFIELD, MICHIGAN

Lawrence
Technological
University

The University

Lawrence Technological University is a premier private university offering over 100 undergraduate and graduate degrees in architecture and design, arts and sciences, engineering, and management. The University's Leadership Program, integrated into all bachelor's degrees, helps students gain critical thinking, teamwork, and communication skills. An honors program is available to highly qualified students, as well as Quest, which encourages students to explore their interests on a deeper level. Lawrence Tech is known for cutting-edge technology, small class sizes, and a commitment to theory and practice. The 102-acre campus features state-of-the-art learning facilities and many housing, recreation, and meal service options.

The University, including its graduate programs, is accredited by the Higher Learning Commission and is a member of the North Central Association of Colleges and Schools. Appropriate national professional agencies provide additional accreditation to various programs in architecture, interior architecture/design, imaging, administration and management, chemistry, and engineering.

Most Lawrence Tech students are employed within one month of graduation and according to a *Bloomberg Businessweek* survey, the earning power of an LTU bachelor's degree ranks in the top 20 percent of all U.S. university degrees.

Approximately 4,500 students attend Lawrence Tech; more than 500 live in on-campus housing. Women make up 24 percent of the student body, and 31 states and 42 countries are represented on campus.

LTU offers an exciting student life. More than 60 student clubs and organizations, including fraternities, sororities, honor societies, and student chapters of professional groups, sponsor a variety of activities.

A member of the National Association of Intercollegiate Athletics, Lawrence Tech offers Blue Devil varsity sports in men's and women's basketball, soccer, cross-country, and lacrosse; men's bowling; and women's volleyball and dance team. The men's hockey team plays in the American Collegiate Hockey Association (ACHA Division III). Intramural sports leagues and tournaments in badminton, basketball, billiards, dodge ball, flag football, golf, racquetball, soccer, softball, table tennis, tennis, volleyball, and wallyball are active throughout the academic year. Club sports include lacrosse, mixed martial arts, and biking. The Don Ridler Field House is open to all students and features a fitness track, gymnasium, racquetball courts, game room, saunas, and weight and conditioning room.

Location

Southfield is a dynamic suburb in southeastern Michigan that provides a pleasant balance between big-city opportunities and a quiet residential atmosphere. Within a few miles of the campus, students can find many restaurants, parks, shopping areas, and cultural and recreational facilities. Research, manufacturing, scientific, and business enterprises are also nearby and convenient for students in co-op and internship programs as well as those who work full- or part-time while attending classes. More than 200 Fortune 500 companies have headquarters or business operations in the area.

Majors and Degrees

Most LTU programs are available days or evenings; many are offered online and on weekends. Dual majors and customized degree programs are available. Preprofessional programs are offered in dentistry, law, and medicine. A post-baccalaureate certificate in premedical studies is also available.

The College of Architecture and Design offers bachelor's degrees in architecture, game art, graphic design, industrial design, interaction design, interior architecture, and transportation design. A certificate is available in building information modeling and computer visualization. Lawrence Tech enrolls more architectural

students than any other school in Michigan, and is one of the ten largest architecture schools in the nation.

The College of Arts and Sciences awards bachelor's degrees in chemical biology, chemistry, computer science (business software development, game software development, network software development, and scientific software development), English and communication arts, environmental chemistry, humanities, mathematics, mathematics and computer science, media communication, molecular and cell biology, physics, physics and computer science, and psychology (clinical psychology, industrial/organizational psychology, and premedical/biobehavioral psychology). Associate degrees are offered in chemical technology, general studies, and radio and television broadcasting. Minors offered are biology, business management, chemistry, computer science, economics, English, general sciences, history, mathematics, media communication, philosophy, physics, psychology, Spanish, technical and professional communication, and television and video production. Certificates can be earned in computer science, entrepreneurial skills, entrepreneurial strategy, film and production techniques, industrial/organizational psychology, and technical and professional communication.

The College of Engineering offers bachelor's degrees in architectural engineering (combining bachelor's and master's programs), audio engineering technology, biomedical engineering, civil engineering, civil engineering and architecture, computer engineering, construction management, electrical engineering (electrical energy systems and electronics engineering), engineering technology, industrial operations engineering, mechanical engineering (alternative energy, automotive, manufacturing, solid mechanics, and thermo fluids), and robotics engineering. The College offers evening associate programs in communications engineering technology, construction engineering technology, manufacturing engineering technology, and mechanical engineering technology. Also available are minors in aeronautical engineering and energy engineering, and certificates in aeronautical engineering, alternative energy engineering technology, biochemical engineering, bioelectronics, biomechanics, electrical power systems, and embedded systems.

The College of Management awards bachelor's degrees in business administration (general business, information technology, and marketing) and a minor in business.

Academic Programs

Graduation from Lawrence Tech's undergraduate programs requires completion with an overall GPA of at least 2.0. Most disciplines combine a strong concentration in the major with a core curriculum of natural science, social science, humanities, and mathematics requirements. Double majors are possible.

Off-Campus Programs

Lawrence Technological University students have the opportunity to participate in co-op programs, alternating semesters of classes and work. Internships are also available.

The University also offers programs in Detroit, Lansing, Petoskey, and Traverse City, Michigan, and Toronto, Canada. Lawrence Tech partners with universities in China, Europe, India, Mexico, and the Middle East. LTU's study-abroad program is open to all students.

Lawrence Tech's Detroit Studio and Innovation Center gives architecture students the opportunity to explore community-based architectural, urban design, and community development projects. Architecture students also regularly build homes for Habitat for Humanity.

The Global Engineering Program allows the University's engineering students to work and study abroad and brings international engineering students to campus for further study.

Academic Facilities

Lawrence Tech is committed to providing students the tools they need to compete and succeed in a technology-driven world. The University supplies undergrads with high-end, personal computers customized with all the industry-standard software needed for their classes, a unique benefit valued up to $15,000.

The library houses a wide selection of print and electronic materials, including numerous online databases and full-text periodical titles accessible on or off campus.

Students use advanced facilities, including architectural and design studios; a structural testing center; a wind tunnel; wood, metal, and model shops; dedicated labs for constructing Baja- and Formula-style competition vehicles; and labs for alternative energy, robotics, biomedical research, graphics, and much more.

The Center for Innovative Materials Research is a state-of-the-art laboratory for the research, development, and testing of composite materials for defense and infrastructure applications. Students participate in related research projects as part of their academic programs.

The Automotive Engineering Institute provides students opportunities to conduct sponsored research on a unique four-wheel drive vehicle chassis dynamometer, which measures many areas of vehicle performance.

LTU also owns a nearby Frank Lloyd Wright–designed home that is used as a study center.

The A. Alfred Taubman Student Services Center consolidates all student support services—from admissions through career services—into a convenient one-stop center. This innovative 42,000-square-foot building utilizes energy-efficient and environmentally friendly features and technologies, serving as a living laboratory for students to study.

Costs

Tuition for all undergrads includes a laptop or tablet computer. The 2012–13 tuition for students majoring in arts and sciences was $770 per credit hour for basic studies courses and $840 for other arts and sciences and management courses. Sophomores in arts and sciences and management paid $890 per credit hour, while the tuition for juniors and seniors in the two majors was $935 per credit hour. In architecture and design and engineering, tuition for freshmen and sophomores was $930 to $935 per credit hour; for juniors and seniors, it was $955 per credit hour.

A normal course load is 12–17 credit hours per semester. The undergraduate registration fee is $135 each semester. International students on temporary visas must have sufficient funds to pay for an entire year of tuition, room and board, and books at the time of first registration. Additional fees for specific labs and studio courses vary.

Financial Aid

Approximately 75 percent of full-time students receive financial assistance and the University awards over $43 million in scholarships, grants, loans, and work-study funds each academic year. Many privately funded scholarships are awarded to qualified students, based on need and/or scholastic performance. Part-time employment is available at the University for full-time students. Student loans are also available.

Faculty

Approximately 430 full- and part-time faculty members teach at Lawrence Technological University. Many part-time faculty members hold full-time jobs in industry and bring their real-world perspective to the classroom. Nearly 80 percent of the full-time faculty members hold a doctoral or terminal degree in their field. Faculty involvement is extensive in student chapters of professional associations that meet on campus. Many faculty members are active and/or registered professionals in their fields. LTU's student-faculty ratio is 11:1. Most classes average 19 or fewer students, and less than 1 percent of the classes have more than 50.

Student Government

The Student Government sponsors and supports a variety of campus activities. More than fifty student clubs and organizations, including fraternities, sororities, honor societies, and student chapters of professional groups, are also active on campus.

Admission Requirements

Admissions decisions are based on a student's recalculated GPA, ACT/SAT scores, essay, and letters of recommendation. Strong emphasis is placed on grade trends as well as the strength of the curriculum and rigor of a student's senior schedule. A portfolio is required for transportation design, industrial design, and game art majors.

Application and Information

LTU programs start in August and January. An optional summer semester begins in May. Students must submit transcripts from all schools attended, along with a nonrefundable $30 application fee. Applicants may have their application fee waived at www.ltu.edu/applyfree. To view a University catalog and learn more, potential students can visit www.ltu.edu or contact:

Office of Admissions
Lawrence Technological University
21000 West Ten Mile Road
Southfield, Michigan 48075-1058
Phone: 248-204-3160 or 800-225-5588 (toll-free)
Fax: 248-204-2228
E-mail: admissions@ltu.edu
Website: http://www.ltu.edu
http://www.facebook.com/lawrencetech
http://twitter.com/LawrenceTechU

Students on the Lawrence Technological University quad. Three-hundred feet below, 120 geothermal wells heat and cool the sustainable A. Alfred Taubman Student Services Center.

LEBANON VALLEY COLLEGE
ANNVILLE, PENNSYLVANIA

The College

Through innovative academic programs and challenging learning experiences provided in a diverse and supportive campus environment, Lebanon Valley College (LVC) offers each student a transformative educational experience. LVC graduates are accomplished, confident citizens and leaders well prepared to make meaningful contributions to their professions and communities; the current governor of Pennsylvania is an alumni.

Founded in 1866, LVC was the first college east of the Alleghenies to offer higher education to both men and women. Now, 147 years later, the College remains an innovative leader—enjoying the number two ranking on *U.S. News & World Report's* Great Schools, Great Prices list, and ranking among the top baccalaureate colleges in its category for the nineteenth consecutive year. A community-minded student body, an engaging and inclusive faculty, academic programs that stress experience-based education, and a generous merit-based scholarship program distinguish this private liberal arts college. Students who graduate in the top 30 percent of their high school class receive an automatic LVC scholarship of one-quarter to one-half of the cost of tuition.

Lebanon Valley aims to educate its 1,630 students to become people of broad vision, capable of making informed decisions, and prepared for a life of service to others. To that end, the College provides an education that imparts the knowledge, skills, and values necessary to live and work in a changing, diverse, and fragile world. In the process, they develop the desire and ability to think deeply, ask critical questions, solve complex problems, and communicate effectively, preparing themselves to be competitive and flexible in whatever career they pursue or challenge they encounter.

Lebanon Valley College professors strive to continue the College's proud tradition of inspired teaching with the dedication and commitment to community service that has long been an LVC hallmark. A supportive, sophisticated community and a 13:1 student-faculty ratio ensure that students have direct access to the men and women who teach and guide them; relationships beyond the classroom are common.

One of the most significant aspects of teaching and learning at LVC is inclusive research in the sciences and humanities. Each summer, dozens of LVC students work alongside their professors as funded research assistants, contributing to important discoveries while gaining invaluable skills and experiences. Many LVC students coauthor articles in scientific or other academic journals or present their work at professional conferences while they are still in college. This experiential learning supports independent student research, internships, and student-faculty research/scholarly work across all disciplines, and provides opportunities seldom found at the undergraduate level.

LVC's strong advising, straightforward requirements, and outstanding student support services mean that the majority of students are able to graduate in four years. If a student is not able to earn the LVC bachelor's degree in four years because of a course scheduling problem, the College will cover the costs of any additional course work the student needs.

LVC's forty-seven buildings provide for every aspect of college life. The College's twenty-seven student residences include four apartment-style halls. Academic buildings feature enhanced classrooms with the latest technology for teaching and learning. Two student centers, one of which just benefitted from a $13.3-million renovation, support learning and development outside the traditional classroom, group study, and extracurricular interests. Students enjoy a recreational sports center; a varsity gymnasium; a newly completed all-sports turf stadium; soccer, baseball, and softball parks; and a state-of-the-art physical therapy facility. The baseball and soccer fields were each named National Collegiate Athletic Association (NCAA) field of the year in their respective categories, and the softball park has twice been recognized as regional field of the year.

LVC's career services staff helps students research careers and establish contacts with potential employers, and offers seminars on resume writing and interviewing skills. The Career Connections alumni database provides students direct access to successful alumni in their fields—men and women who have volunteered to mentor, advise, or otherwise assist LVC students or recent graduates. In an average year, approximately 76 percent of graduates who respond to an annual survey are employed, and approximately 30 percent are in graduate or professional school within six months of graduation.

Location

Annville is a small town of approximately 5,000 residents located near Pennsylvania Dutch country, just 10 minutes east of Hershey and within a 2- to 3-hour drive of Philadelphia, Baltimore, New York, and Washington, D.C. Nestled in a beautiful valley, the College is located on a 340-acre site. A wide variety of internship opportunities, potential employment options, cultural events, and other activities are available on campus and within the surrounding communities.

Majors and Degrees

The College confers five baccalaureate degrees. The Bachelor of Arts is available in art and art history, criminal justice, economics, English, French, German, historical communications, history, international studies, music, music business, philosophy, political science, religion, sociology, Spanish, and certain self-designed majors.

The Bachelor of Science is available in accounting, actuarial science, biochemistry and molecular biology, biology, business administration, chemistry, computer science, cooperative engineering, digital communications, early childhood education, early childhood/special education, healthcare management, health science, mathematics, music education, physics, psychobiology, psychology, and certain self-designed majors.

The Bachelor of Science in Chemistry, Bachelor of Science in Medical Technology, and Bachelor of Music (with an emphasis in music recording technology) are also available.

Lebanon Valley offers master's degree programs in business, music education, and science education; a doctoral program in physical therapy; and preprofessional programs in dentistry, law, medicine, ministry, pharmacy, and veterinary medicine.

Academic Programs

Lebanon Valley has long been known for the strength of its academic programs and the achievement of its faculty members and alumni. The sciences are a particular strength, with well-equipped and up-to-date laboratories. Over the years, more than half of LVC's graduates in the sciences have earned advanced and Ph.D. degrees. The College has won research grants from the National Science Foundation, National Institutes of Health, Dow, Exxon, and Merck/AAAS.

Other particularly well-known and respected LVC programs include actuarial science (nearly 100 percent of graduates land high-paying jobs), physical therapy (which offers a six-year doctoral program), music (the music recording technology major is especially popular), business (which provides the fundamentals of accounting and business administration within a strong liberal arts context), and education (alumni of which are in high demand throughout the region).

Each student's academic program is complemented by a wide range of extracurricular activities. The College's more than ninety clubs, organizations, and other student-run initiatives mean ample opportunities for leadership. Many students choose to participate in community outreach, often by volunteering in the surrounding communities. More than 25 percent of students play on one or more of LVC's twenty-four Division III athletics teams, and many more play club or intramural sports. All students benefit from extensive campus programming that includes guest lectures, concerts, conferences, symposia, and a variety of cultural activities.

Off-Campus Programs

Students are encouraged to take advantage of numerous off-campus study opportunities offered by the College. Options abroad include programs in Argentina, Australia, China, England, France, Germany, Greece, Italy, the Netherlands, New Zealand, Northern Ireland, and Spain, or several short-term, faculty-led options. Internship-based programs in Washington, D.C., and Philadelphia are also popular options. A student's scholarship funding and financial aid can be transferred to most of the programs, making study abroad available to all students, regardless of their family's financial situation.

Internships are another important aspect of experience-based learning at LVC. With guidance from professors and help from professional counselors, students in every major find internship placements, gain professional experiences, and build confidence, all of which helps when it comes time to apply for a job.

Academic Facilities

Lebanon Valley's tree-lined walkways and beautiful gardens provide the perfect backdrop for academic and social facilities teeming with technology. The Bishop Library contains more than 225,000 books, CDs, and DVDs, as well as more than 3,000 electronic journal subscriptions, 130 online databases, and 31,000 full-text journals and newspapers. The library, residence halls, smart classrooms, and administrative offices are all linked to the campus wireless network, maximizing the effectiveness and mobility of learning. Well-equipped, up-to-date laboratories provide students with the tools and technologies they need to conduct cutting-edge research, independently or in partnership with faculty.

Costs

Annual tuition for the 2012–13 school year was $33,670. Room and board charges were $9,180 and fees were $800.

Financial Aid

Committed to helping all families afford the first-rate education it offers, LVC has received national recognition for its generous and distinctive merit-based scholarship program, which rewards strong high school performance with automatic merit scholarships. Students who graduate in the top 30 percent of their high school class receive an automatic LVC scholarship equivalent to one-quarter to one-half the cost of tuition.

Merit- and need-based financial assistance is also available. In 2012–13, the College committed more than $24 million to merit- and need-based aid. Overall, 95 percent of LVC students receive some form of financial assistance from the College. Students and their families should complete the Free Application for Federal Student Aid (FAFSA) to determine eligibility. The priority deadline for filing for financial aid is March 1.

Faculty

The LVC faculty includes scientists, scholars, artists, and professionals in a wide range of fields, many of whom are respected contributors to their disciplines. LVC professors are dedicated to teaching and are drawn to the College for its close-knit community and for the opportunity to be actively involved in the students' educational growth. Most faculty members are involved in research, scholarship, and professional organizations and play an active role in helping students find internships and getting started with their own research. Of LVC's 103 professors, 90 percent have earned a Ph.D. or equivalent terminal degree. The College is committed to maintaining a low student-teacher ratio of 13:1 (FTE). The average class size is 20, and all courses are taught by professors, not graduate students.

Student Government

Lebanon Valley students participate in the College's governing system through Student Government and the Student Programming Board. Student Government fosters understanding, communication, and cooperation among students, faculty, and administration. Different student groups and students meet regularly with LVC president Lewis Thayne, ensuring that there is a clear line of communication between the student body and the administration. The Student Programming Board organizes off-campus trips and schedules comedians, musicians, and other on-campus entertainment.

Admission Requirements

The LVC admission process is selective, and the applicant's academic record is the most important factor in admission decisions. The College seeks students from a variety of backgrounds as well as those who display leadership abilities, a commitment to community involvement, and special talents or interests that might benefit or enrich the LVC community. Competitive applicants will have pursued a challenging high school course of study that includes at least 4 courses in English, 2 in foreign language, 3 in mathematics, 2 in science, and 1 in social studies. Additional course work in math and science is strongly recommended. More than 70 percent of recent incoming LVC students rank among the top 30 percent of their high school class. Submission of SAT or ACT scores is optional. Advanced standing is offered through CLEP and AP examinations.

Application and Information

To apply, students should submit a completed application, a $30 application fee, and official copies of their high school transcript. Although Lebanon Valley has a rolling admission process, students are encouraged to apply during the fall of their senior year. Personal visits to campus are encouraged.

For more information, applicants should contact:

William J. Brown Jr.
Vice President of Enrollment
Lebanon Valley College
101 North College Avenue
Annville, Pennsylvania 17003-1400
Phone: 866-LVC-4ADM (866-582-4236, toll-free)
Fax: 717-867-6026
E-mail: admission@lvc.edu
Website: www.lvc.edu

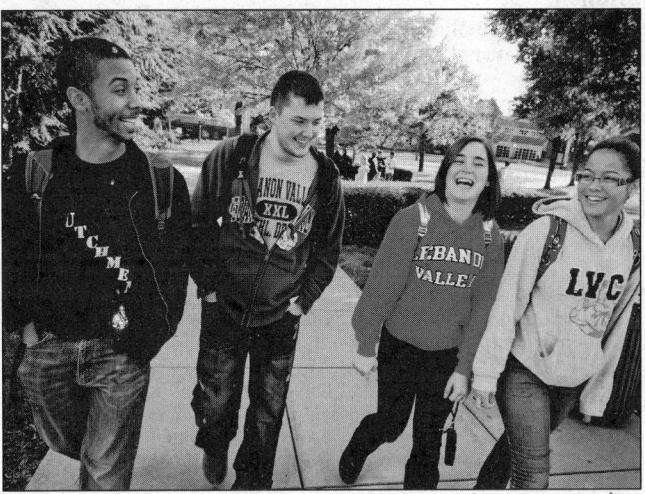

The Lebanon Valley College community is close-knit and welcoming.

LE MOYNE COLLEGE
SYRACUSE, NEW YORK

LE MOYNE
SPIRIT. INQUIRY. LEADERSHIP. *JESUIT*.

The College

Le Moyne College is a four-year, coeducational Jesuit college of approximately 2,500 undergraduate students that uniquely balances a comprehensive liberal arts education with preparation for specific career paths or graduate study. Founded by the Society of Jesus in 1946, Le Moyne is the second youngest of the twenty-eight Jesuit colleges and universities in the United States. Its emphasis is on the education of the whole person and on the search for meaning and value as integral parts of an intellectual life. Le Moyne's personal approach to education is reflected in the quality of contact between students and faculty members.

A wide range of student-directed activities, athletics, clubs, and service organizations complement the academic experience. Intramural sports are very popular with Le Moyne students; nearly 85 percent of the students participate. Le Moyne also has seventeen NCAA intercollegiate teams (eight for men and nine for women). Athletic facilities include a new soccer/lacrosse turf field, softball and baseball fields; basketball, and racquetball courts; a weight-training and fitness center; practice fields; and two gymnasiums. A recreation center houses an Olympic-size indoor swimming pool, jogging track, indoor tennis and volleyball courts, and additional basketball, racquetball, and fitness areas.

Nearly 80 percent of students live in residence halls, apartments, and town houses on campus. The Residence Hall Councils and the Le Moyne Student Programming Board organize a variety of campus activities, including concerts, dances, a weekly film series, student talent programs, and special lectures as well as off-campus trips and skiing excursions. The College recently opened a plaza, which houses its bookstore, a café, and a pizzeria. The new Dolphin Den, which features a food court and a convenience store, has quickly become a popular space for students to meet, have a bite to eat, or just spend a quiet moment relaxing.

Location

Le Moyne's 160-plus acre, tree-lined campus is located in a residential setting 10 minutes from downtown Syracuse, the heart of New York State, whose metropolitan population is about 700,000. Syracuse is convenient to most major cities throughout the Northeast, New England, and Canada and offers a wide array of shopping centers and restaurants, many near Le Moyne. Syracuse offers year-round entertainment in the form of rock concerts at the Landmark Theatre, professional baseball and hockey, Bristol Omnitheatre, Syracuse Stage, Everson Museum of Art, and the Armory Square district downtown, which offers one-of-a-kind eateries, pubs, and coffeehouses in addition to a wide variety of social and cultural events. All are easily accessible via the excellent public transportation service, which schedules regular stops on Le Moyne's campus. Just a few miles outside the city are the rolling hills, picturesque lakes, and miles of open country for which central New York is renowned. An extensive network of state and county parks, recreational areas, and other facilities offer an abundance of recreational opportunities, including swimming, boating, hiking, downhill and cross-country skiing, snowboarding, and golf.

Majors and Degrees

Le Moyne College awards the Bachelor of Arts degree in biological sciences, communication (advertising, filmmaking, journalism, media studies, music and culture, music industry, music journalism, public relations, television/radio), computer science, criminology (human services, international affairs, law enforcement, research), economics, English (creative writing, literature), French, history, mathematics (actuarial science, pure mathematics, statistics), peace and global studies, philosophy, physics, political science, psychology, religious studies, sociology (anthropology, criminology, human services, research and theory), Spanish, and theater arts. The Bachelor of Science degree is awarded in biochemistry, biological sciences

(health professions, molecular biology, neurobiology), chemistry, economics, environmental science systems, environmental studies, general science, physics, and psychology. The Bachelor of Science in business is awarded in accounting, applied management analysis, finance, information systems, management and leadership, and marketing. A Bachelor of Science in nursing is also offered.

Students may minor in arts administration, business administration, Catholic studies, classical humanities, film, gender and women's studies, Irish literature, Italian, Latin, legal studies, health information systems, human resource management, management information systems, medieval studies, music, urban and regional studies, or visual arts as well as most of the major fields of study offered. Preprofessional programs are offered in dentistry, law, medicine, optometry, physical therapy, direct-entry physician assistant studies, podiatry, and veterinary science. Students may prepare for teaching careers through certification programs in adolescent education, dual adolescent/special education, dual childhood/special education, and TESOL.

Le Moyne College and the L. C. Smith College of Engineering and Computer Science at Syracuse University offer a dual-degree program in which students may earn a bachelor's degree from Le Moyne and a master's degree in engineering from Syracuse University in as few as five years. Concentrations include aerospace; chemical, electrical, and mechanical engineering; computer science; and other fields of engineering.

Formal accelerated 3-4 programs are offered in dentistry, optometry, and podiatry in cooperation with the State University of New York at Buffalo School of Dental Medicine, Pennsylvania College of Optometry at Salus University, and the New York College of Podiatric Medicine. Predental students may also participate in an early assurance program with the State University of New York at Buffalo School of Dental Medicine. Cooperative 3-2 dual-degree programs in engineering are available with Clarkson University, Manhattan College, and University of Detroit Mercy.

SUNY Upstate Medical University in Syracuse offers students pursuing careers in the health-related professions an accelerated 3-3 doctoral-level transfer program in physical therapy as well as two-year cooperative transfer programs in medical technology, and respiratory care. Premedical students at Le Moyne are also offered the opportunity to participate in a medical school early assurance program. An early assurance program for premedical students is also available through the State University of New York at Buffalo School of Medicine.

Academic Programs

While each major department has its own sequence requirements for the minimum 120 credit hours needed for the Le Moyne degree, the College is convinced that there is a fundamental intellectual discipline that should characterize the graduate of a superior liberal arts college. Le Moyne's core curriculum provides this foundation by including studies of English language and literature, philosophy, history, religious studies, natural sciences, and social sciences.

For exceptional students, Le Moyne offers an integral honors program that includes an interdisciplinary humanities sequence as well as departmental honors courses. Le Moyne also offers a part-time course of study during evening hours through its Center for Continuing Education.

Le Moyne students may enroll in Army and Air Force ROTC programs in conjunction with Syracuse University.

Off-Campus Programs

The study-abroad program allows qualified students to spend a semester or year in almost any country throughout the world. Le Moyne College has study-abroad programs or affiliations in the Czech Republic, Dominican Republic, England, Germany, Ireland,

Scotland, and Spain. Students can also use partner programs to study in locations such as Australia, Costa Rica, Egypt, France, Italy, Japan, and South Africa. Le Moyne is a participant in the sixty-member New York State Visiting Student Program. As part of the mission of preparing future leaders, Le Moyne College places a strong emphasis on career preparation through internships and other forms of experiential education. Academic departments and the Office of Career Services both provide programs and services for students interested in interning part-time and full-time, both locally and in major cities such as New York and Washington, D.C. The Offices of Service Learning and the Academic Deans are also involved in experiential education to promote learning outside the classroom. In the sciences, students take part in campus research with mentor faculty members. Others receive assistance in pursuing outstanding opportunities off campus in leading research laboratories and health-care settings. The College has maintained a long-standing relationship with the Washington Center internship programs, where students from all majors complete full-time semester-long internships in Washington, D.C., with government, business, or major nonprofit organizations. Faculty members in the Political Science Department assist students interested in opportunities in Albany, New York state's seat of government, with either the New York State Senate or Assembly. Finally, the education programs at Le Moyne put students into school classrooms starting immediately as freshmen and continuing each year until graduation.

Academic Facilities

Le Moyne students benefit from an ongoing commitment to technological excellence. The College's forty-two buildings are equipped with accounting, biology, chemistry, computer science, physics, psychology, and statistics laboratories. The W. Carroll Coyne Center for the Performing Arts houses generous production, performance, and classroom space; the latest light and sound technology; scene and costume shops; an aerobics and dance studio; and rehearsal rooms for instrumental and choral music. Academic facilities also include an extensively renovated color television studio; a radio/recording studio; a receiver-antenna satellite dish; transmission and scanning electron microscopes; a nuclear magnetic resonance spectrometer; a gas chromatograph/mass spectrophotometer; a 240,000-volume, open-stack library; and extensive on-site computer facilities. A fiber-optic network enables students to access the library system, the campus network, and the Internet from several computer labs around the campus or from their personal computers in their rooms. All classrooms are smart classrooms, with multimedia capabilities that expand and enrich the learning process. Le Moyne students have access to other libraries through the Central New York Library Resources Council, and the campus Academic Support Center is available to students for instructional support. In addition, Le Moyne recently opened a 48,000-square-foot addition to its existing science complex.

Costs

For 2013–14, Le Moyne's tuition is $29,470. Room and board charges are $11,740. Additional fees amount to approximately $990, and books and supplies cost approximately $700.

Financial Aid

Financial aid is offered to a large percentage of Le Moyne's students through scholarships, grants, loans, and work-study assignments. Le Moyne offers a generous program of merit-based academic and athletic scholarships as well as financial aid based on a student's need and academic promise. Federal funds are available through the Federal Pell Grant, Federal Work-Study, Federal Supplemental Educational Opportunity Grant, and Federal Perkins Loan programs. A student's eligibility for need-based financial aid is determined from both the Free Application for Federal Student Aid (FAFSA) and the Le Moyne Financial Aid Application Form. It is recommended that these forms be mailed by February 1.

Faculty

The Le Moyne full-time faculty numbers 150 men and women; 94 percent have earned the highest degree in their field. With an average class size of 21, a student-faculty ratio of 13:1, and private offices for all full-time faculty members, the College promotes a personal as well as an academic relationship between students and faculty members. All classroom instruction is done by faculty members, and they are happy to assist and encourage students who wish to pursue undergraduate research through tutorials or senior research projects. These projects are carried out in an atmosphere free of competition from graduate students for books, laboratories, or professors' time. Le Moyne emphasizes advising and academic counseling for students throughout their four years.

Student Government

The College encourages student leadership in all activities. Positions of leadership are open to students in all class years. Students are represented by a Student Senate and have formal representation through the senate on most College-wide committees involved in decision making and policy formation.

Admission Requirements

Le Moyne seeks qualified students who are well prepared for serious academic study. Secondary school preparation must have included at least 17 college-preparatory high school units, 4 of which must be in English, 4 in social studies, 3–4 in mathematics, 3–4 in foreign language, and 3–4 in science. It is also recommended that prospective science and mathematics majors complete 4 units of mathematics and science. Submitting scores from standardized tests is optional for admission to Le Moyne, but scores from the SAT or ACT will be considered if students choose to submit them. However, to be considered for the more prestigious scholarships (Presidential, Dean, Ignatian or Loyola), standardized test scores are required. Campus visits are strongly recommended, as the admission process is a personal one. As bases for selection, academic achievement and secondary school recommendations are of primary importance.

Application and Information

The Admission Committee reviews applications and mails decisions on a rolling admission cycle beginning December 1. The priority deadline for applications is February 1; all students who wish to be considered for academic merit scholarships should have a completed application on file in the Office of Admission before this date. Transfer students are encouraged to apply before June 1 for the fall semester and December 1 for the spring semester. Orientation programs for incoming freshmen and transfer students take place in midsummer.

Dennis J. Nicholson
Dean of Admission
Le Moyne College
Syracuse, New York 13214-1399
Phone: 315-445-4300
      800-333-4733 (toll-free)
E-mail: admission@lemoyne.edu
Website: http://www.lemoyne.edu

Grewen Hall, the College's oldest building, overlooks Le Moyne's beautiful 160-plus acre campus.

LEWIS & CLARK COLLEGE
PORTLAND, OREGON

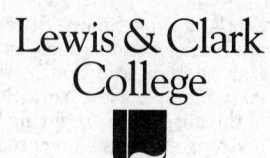

The College

A private college with a public conscience, Lewis & Clark College has a global reach that extends well beyond its location in Portland, Oregon. Located on a 137-acre campus in a wooded residential area 6 miles from downtown, the College is a starting point for students to explore the wider world and their place in it.

The student body is known for its geographic diversity. In fall 2012, of the 2150 undergraduates, 21 percent were from Oregon, and 79 percent came from forty-seven other states plus the District of Columbia and represented seventy-two countries. Approximately 70 percent live in housing on campus, most of which is coed (91 percent). There are no fraternities or sororities.

The College offers numerous co-curricular activities, including twelve music groups; nine media organizations; eleven religious/spiritual life groups; sixteen international, cultural, and diversity clubs; and nearly seventy student organizations. Cultural events such as lectures, student-run symposia, art exhibits, theater productions, concerts, recitals, and dance performances occur on a regular basis. Currently, there are nineteen NCAA Division III varsity athletic teams, eight club teams, and numerous intramural sports. The renowned College Outdoors Program offers adventures such as backpacking, rafting, skiing, snowshoeing, caving, winter camping, sea kayaking, and environmental service projects in Oregon's and Washington's nearby wilderness areas.

Location

Portland has long been known for its livability and its excellent transportation system. Public buses and a free College shuttle run from the Lewis & Clark campus to downtown Portland. The vibrant metropolitan area (population 2 million) offers resources and opportunities for entertainment, study, work, and internships. The city has 10,447 acres of parks, thirty-three music associations, thirty-five theater and dance companies, more than ninety galleries and museums, and more than 1,000 restaurants. Professional sports teams compete in soccer, hockey, and NBA basketball. For those looking for outdoor pursuits, Mount Hood, offering skiing ten months per year, is 50 miles away, and Oregon's rugged coastline lies 90 miles to the west.

Majors and Degrees

Lewis & Clark offers programs leading to the Bachelor of Arts degree. Academic majors include art (art history and studio art), biochemistry and molecular biology, biology, chemistry, computer science, computer science and mathematics, East Asian studies, economics (international, management, public policy, theory), English, environmental studies, foreign languages, French studies, German studies, Hispanic studies, history, international affairs, mathematics, music, philosophy, physics, political science, psychology, rhetoric and media studies, religious studies, sociology/anthropology, and theater. Students may also design a major or pursue a double major and numerous minors. Pre-professional preparation is available in the fields of law, medicine, business, and education.

Dual-degree (3-2 and 4-2) programs in engineering are offered in cooperation with Columbia University, Washington University (St. Louis), the University of Southern California, and Oregon Health and Science University. A 4-2 B.A./M.B.A. program is offered in cooperation with the University of Rochester's Simon Graduate School of Business. A 4-1 B.A./M.A.T. program is offered through Lewis & Clark's Graduate School of Education and Counseling. In addition, there is a guaranteed admission agreement with Lewis & Clark's Law School for students meeting certain criteria.

Academic Programs

The liberal arts curriculum offers sufficient structure to ensure depth and breadth of study, but it also incorporates a high degree of freedom. In the four-year plan of study, approximately one third of a student's time is devoted to general education, one third to a major program, and one third to elective courses. Students are also encouraged to participate in departmental honors programs, undergraduate research, independent study, and internships.

The academic calendar consists of two 15-week semesters. A normal load is four 4 semester-hour academic courses, plus one or more activity courses. The fall semester begins early in September and ends before Christmas, and the spring semester begins in mid-January and ends in early May. A limited number of courses are offered during two summer sessions.

The community of scholars at Lewis & Clark College is dedicated to personal and academic excellence. Joining the Lewis & Clark community obligates each member to observe the principles of mutual respect, academic integrity, civil discourse, and responsible decision-making.

Off-Campus Programs

Lewis & Clark offers nationally recognized international and off-campus study opportunities. Usually, 20 to 24 students plus a faculty leader participate in each program. More than half of the College's graduates have taken advantage of these outstanding programs, often satisfying General Education or major requirements at the same time.

Overseas study may have either a general-culture focus or a specialized academic focus. Sites for overseas study programs from 2013 through 2016 are Australia, Chile, China, Cuba, Dominican Republic, Ecuador, England, France, Germany, Greece, India, Ireland, Italy, Japan, Kenya/Tanzania, Morocco, New Zealand, Russia, Scotland, Senegal, Spain, and Vietnam. Domestic programs are available in the Arizona borderlands, New York, and Washington, D.C.

Academic Facilities

The Aubrey R. Watzek Library is open 24 hours per day when school is in session and offers individualized reference assistance for students. The library houses more than 740,000 items and its website provides access to its catalog as well as to a full range of electronic resources. The library is a member of Summit, a consortium of thirty-six academic libraries that have a unified catalog that enables students to request and receive materials from member libraries within two days.

Music department facilities include a 410-seat recital hall equipped with an orchestra pit and stage elevator; an extensive collection of more than 4,000 records, CDs, and tape recordings; twenty-two practice rooms; forty-three pianos; two harpsichords; a Baroque organ; an electronic music studio; Zimbabwe marimbas; and an Indonesian gamelan orchestra. The 600-seat chapel houses an 85-rank Casavant organ.

The visual arts center is equipped with studio space for painting, drawing, ceramics, sculpture, design, and printmaking as well as a photography lab. The department also has a Visual Resources Collection of 50,000 slides and several thousand digital images representing artwork from a wide range of media, time periods, world regions, and cultures. The humanities and social sciences also enjoy state-of-the-art classrooms and lab facilities.

The natural science buildings are equipped with modern instrumentation to support collaborative student-faculty research. Among the notable facilities are laboratories for the study of astrophysics, the biomechanics of animal locomotion, human-computer interactions, molecular modeling and parallel computing, a scanning electron microscope, a modern greenhouse, and an astronomical observatory with Newtonian and solar telescopes. Ecological investigations and studies of the environmental impacts of human activity are conducted both on the College's heavily wooded campus and at the nearby Tryon Creek State Park.

Computer labs house more than 130 Macintosh and Microsoft Windows computers, along with peripherals such as scanners, printers, and digital video editing equipment. Digital, still and video cameras, digital audio recorders, and more are available for checkout. All residence halls have wireless networks. The institution has an 800 Mbps connection to the Internet.

Costs

Tuition and fees for 2012–13 were $40,330. The room and board charge was $10,268 for fourteen (flex) meals per week; other meal plans are also available. The estimate for books and personal expenses is $2,040.

Financial Aid

In 2011–12, 82 percent of the College's students received some form of financial assistance. Institutional, state, and federal resources, including Federal Pell Grants, Federal Supplemental Educational Opportunity Grants, Federal Perkins Loans, and Federal Work-Study awards, may be part of an aid award. Other options include low-interest Federal Stafford Student Loans and opportunities to work on and off campus. To receive priority consideration for need-based financial aid, students must meet appropriate deadlines for admission and should submit the Free Application for Federal Student Aid (FAFSA) and the CSS/Financial Aid PROFILE application by February 15.

Lewis & Clark offers renewable merit-based scholarships and participation awards to students who demonstrate the qualities of mind, self-discipline, and commitment to learning that characterize the best in Lewis & Clark students. These awards range from $1,000 to full tuition. Many of these scholarships are awarded through the admissions process and don't require a separate application. Others require additional paper work. Full details on merit-based scholarship opportunities can be found at http://www.lclark.edu/offices/financial_aid.

Faculty

The 136 full-time members of the faculty are committed to undergraduate teaching and advising and are also active in research, writing, and publishing. Involving students in the research process is of high priority. Ninety-six percent of the full-time faculty members hold a Ph.D. or the highest advanced degree in their discipline. The student-faculty ratio is 12:1. The average class size is 19, with 88 percent of classes having 29 or fewer students.

Student Government

The Associated Students of Lewis & Clark (ASLC) consists of a Student Senate, governing boards, and appointed students who serve on faculty constitutional, standing, and special committees. The 30 members of the Student Academic Affairs Board (SAAB) are appointed on a departmental basis to support student academic initiatives. One quarter of the total ASLC budget of more than $400,000 is used by SAAB in support of fellow undergraduate students.

Admission Requirements

Lewis & Clark College seeks first-year and transfer applicants who are committed to academic excellence and personal growth. Admission is competitive. Applications are carefully reviewed and examined for degree of academic preparation, ability to express ideas in essay form, participation in activities, citizenship and community service, and support given by the school through recommendations. Campus visits are encouraged. Interviews are available but not required. Recommended high school preparation includes 4 years of English, 3 to 4 years of history or social science, 4 years of mathematics, 3 years of laboratory science, 2 to 3 years of foreign language, and 1 year of fine arts. The SAT or ACT is required, unless the student is applying via the test-optional Portfolio Path.

Application and Information

First-year applicants should submit the Common Application (online or paper); the required Common Application Supplement; a personal essay; an official academic transcript, including senior grades from the first marking period; one recommendation from a counselor; and at least one reference from an academic teacher. The application fee is waived if the applicant uses the online Common Application. Application deadlines for the fall semester are November 1 for nonbinding early action (notification by January 1) and January 15 for regular decision (notification by April 1).

Transfer applicants are evaluated on a rolling basis. To ensure full consideration, the College strongly recommends that transfer students submit all credentials before the end of March.

The application deadline for first-year and transfer students for the spring semester is November 1 (notification within three weeks of file completion). The test-optional Portfolio Path admissions program provides an opportunity for applicants who have shown exceptional academic initiative to demonstrate the full extent of their pursuits by presenting a portfolio of their academic work. Under this plan, SAT or ACT scores are optional. More details about the Portfolio Path can be found online at go.lclark.edu/portfolio_path.

For more information about Lewis & Clark College or to arrange a visit, students should contact:

Office of Admissions
Lewis & Clark College
0615 SW Palatine Hill Road
Portland, Oregon 97219-7899
Phone: 503-768-7040
      800-444-4111 (toll-free)
Fax: 503-768-7055
E-mail: admissions@lclark.edu
Website: www.lclark.edu

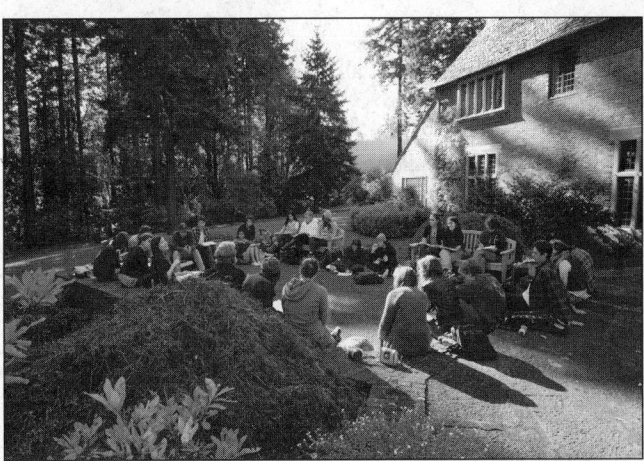

Lewis & Clark students learn through a rigorous curriculum that builds intellectual depth and breadth, creativity, and critical thinking skills in its graduates.

LIBERTY UNIVERSITY
LYNCHBURG, VIRGINIA

The University

Founded in 1971, Liberty University provides a comprehensive Christian environment committed to academic excellence at the undergraduate, graduate, post-master's, and doctorate levels. The university is situated on more than 6,800 acres, complete with state-of-the-art classrooms and exceptional residence, study, leisure, and recreational facilities. Liberty is accredited by the State Council of Higher Education for Virginia and is accredited by the Commission on Colleges of the Southern Association of Colleges and Schools (SACS) to award certificate, associate, bachelor's, master's, and doctoral degrees. More than 12,600 resident undergraduate and graduate students compose the student body, representing all fifty states and more than eighty countries.

Liberty's facilities include the following:

- 19,200-seat Williams Stadium
- 10,000-seat Vines Center
- Hancock Welcome Center
- Matthews-Hopkins Track complex
- Tolsma indoor track
- Tower Theater
- 2,500-seat Liberty baseball stadium
- LaHaye Ice Center
- State-of-the-art, 83,968-square-foot LaHaye Student Center, which includes a lounge, five full-length basketball courts, cardio and weight rooms, a café, multipurpose rooms, an aerobic room, and a 25-yard swimming pool
- Liberty University Equestrian Center
- Liberty Mountain Snowflex Centre, the first snowless ski slope of its kind in North America
- The new Jerry Falwell Library, scheduled to open in spring 2014

Liberty's intercollegiate athletic program includes teams that compete in NCAA Division I. Men compete in baseball, basketball, cross-country, football, golf, indoor and outdoor track and field, soccer, and tennis. Women compete in basketball, cross-country, field hockey, lacrosse, soccer, indoor and outdoor track and field, softball, swimming, tennis, and volleyball. In addition, 31 sports programs are available at the club level, including ice hockey, lacrosse, and volleyball for men, and ice hockey and ice skating for women. Intramural competition is offered for both men and women in 20 sports, including ultimate frisbee and men's and women's flag football.

Residence halls include traditional-style housing, quad-living residences, and new apartment-style living within walking distance of main campus. These new apartments include furnishings, a kitchen, laundry facilities, and the Campus East Clubhouse, which offers billiards, PlayStation, Xbox, satellite TV, a theater, a computer lounge, the Campus East Market, and an outdoor pool. In 2013, construction began on residence hall towers that will house 1,200 students on the main campus.

Liberty offers more than 200 programs of study, with a wide variety of both undergraduate and graduate degrees. Teacher licensure is available at the graduate level in early childhood (K–3), elementary (K–6), and secondary (7–12) education; administration/supervision; gifted education; reading; school counseling; and special education.

Through the Liberty University Baptist Theological Seminary, the university offers both online and resident graduate degrees, including a Master of Arts in Religion, Master of Divinity, Master of Theology, Doctor of Philosophy in Theology and Apologetics, and Doctor of Ministry.

Liberty University's School of Law opened in August 2004 and the first graduating class received degrees in May 2007. The School of Law, which is housed in Green Hall, is accredited by the American Bar Association (ABA). The school is equipped with multimedia technology, two seminar rooms, a mock trial courtroom, the Ehrhorn Law Library, a study center with 24-hour student access, law review offices, seven professional skills rooms, an administrative suite, a faculty suite, and an academic support suite.

For international students, Liberty offers the English Language Institute (ELI). English grammar, comprehension, and reading are taught and an ELI certificate is awarded upon completion of these programs.

Location

The university is located in Lynchburg City (population 75,000), in the heart of Virginia, near the scenic Blue Ridge Mountains. The city is more than 200 years old and is noted for its culture, beauty, and educational advantages. Nearby are historic sites such as Thomas Jefferson's Poplar Forest, Appomattox Court House, Natural Bridge, historic Lexington, Washington, D.C., and many other places of interest.

The city of Lynchburg also offers a wide variety of recreational activities. Excellent sports facilities and programs, cultural events at the Lynchburg Fine Arts Center, beautiful lakes and streams, and many other local attractions enhance the lives of Lynchburg residents. Lynchburg also has more than 2,000 hotel rooms, numerous outlets and malls, and a number of restaurants that serve a wide variety of cuisines. Lynchburg is conveniently accessible by bus, train, and the Lynchburg Regional Airport, serviced by US Airways Express.

Majors and Degrees

Liberty offers more than 300 unique undergraduate and graduate programs of study, in both residential and online formats. Prospective students can visit www.Liberty.edu/Academics to view all of Liberty's programs.

A teacher licensure option is available at the elementary (K–6), middle school (6–8), and secondary (7–12) levels in biology, business, computer science, English, history/social sciences, mathematics, and work and family studies, and at the comprehensive (K–12) level in teaching English as a second language, health/physical education, music (choral or instrumental), and special education.

Academic Programs

In addition to the courses required by each specific major, students must complete general education courses in humanities, natural sciences and mathematics, social sciences, physical education, and religion.

Liberty is on a semester calendar. During the summer, there are several one- and two-week intensive courses offered. Winter courses are also offered between semesters.

The university also offers higher education degrees for the adult learner online. As the world's largest private, nonprofit online educator, Liberty University Online is also accredited by the Commission on Colleges of the Southern Association of Colleges and Schools to award associate, bachelor's, master's, and doctoral degrees. For more information, students should call 877-298-9615 or visit the web page at www.LUOnline.com.

Academic Facilities

Liberty is committed to providing first-class facilities. The Arthur S. DeMoss Learning Center, Liberty's academic hub, is a four-story, 500,000-square-foot Jeffersonian-style building that encompasses most of the university's academic departments. All classrooms contain large computer screens for interactive learning. This impressive facility is one of the largest academic buildings in central Virginia and houses the campus library, which currently contains 283,000 bound or microfilmed volumes. Construction on a new library, named in honor of Liberty's founder and president, the late Dr. Jerry Falwell, Sr., was started in Spring 2012. The Jerry Falwell Library will have a storage and retrieval system, allowing Liberty's collection of electronic and traditional print resources to grow to nearly a half-million items.

Students may find employment or volunteer their services in the university's 50,000-watt FM radio station or student-run radio and TV stations. The Theatre Arts Department's Tower Theater features 640 seats and more than 12,000-square-feet of backstage and technical support space. The Human Performance Laboratory enhances student learning and research capabilities through the use of a Bodpod, Oxycon Mobile, Trackmaster treadmills, altitude chambers, and Concept2 Model E. Rowing Ergometers. In addition, new aviation facilities are located near the Lynchburg Regional Airport.

Costs

Tuition, room, board, and fees for the 2013–14 school year are $28,744 for full-time students. Additional fees, such as lab costs, are required for specific classes and are listed in the course guide. Vehicles are permitted on campus if they are registered with the university.

Financial Aid

Liberty conveniently offers a variety of grants, scholarships, and on-campus jobs. All major, federally funded student financial aid programs are available. Academic, athletic, merit, talent, National Merit, and other Liberty assistance grants are also available for qualified candidates. Students are required to submit a Free Application for Federal Student Aid (FAFSA) to the U.S. Department of Education and include Liberty University's school code (010392) on that application. The FAFSA is available online at www.FAFSA.ed.gov. This form is the student's application for all financial aid, and it is recommended that all families use the IRS Data Retrieval Tool in the FAFSA, if available. Approximately 96 percent of the student body received some type of aid in 2012.

Faculty

The university employs more than 2,000 nontenured full- and part-time faculty members, including respected scholars and professionals with real-world experience.

Student Government

Students elect representatives to serve on the Student Senate. This group provides leadership recommendations and suggestions to the student development staff. Student Senate members organize and direct activities and civic programs.

Admission Requirements

All applicants should be familiar with Liberty's philosophy and expectations before applying. Applicants to the A.A., B.A., and B.S. programs must be high school graduates and must submit an official copy of their high school transcript, indicating graduation date (or GED test scores, if applicable). An essay of 200 to 400 words must be submitted answering the question, 'How will your personal faith and beliefs contribute to Liberty's mission to develop Christ-centered leaders?' (www.Liberty.edu/MissionStatement). Applicants must also submit either ACT or SAT scores, which are used for academic counseling and placement. High school transcripts and SAT/ACT requirements are waived if the student is more than 22 years of age, transfers at least 60 hours or holds an associate degree from an accredited institution. The applicant must also demonstrate the ability to do college-level work. Although interviews are not required, prospective students are encouraged to visit the campus. Four "College For A Weekend" (CFAW) events are scheduled each year, giving prospective students an opportunity to participate in classes, attend social and athletic events, experience residence hall life, and interact with students and faculty members.

Application and Information

Admissions decisions are made on a rolling basis; however January 31 is the priority deadline for fall enrollment. Applicants are encouraged to complete the application process by January 31 to be considered for maximum scholarship opportunities. Applicants for the spring term should complete the process by November 1, although early October is preferred. Late applicants are accepted on a space-available basis.

To learn more about Liberty, students should contact:

Resident Admissions Office
Liberty University
1971 University Boulevard
Lynchburg, Virginia 24502
Phone: 800-543-5317 (toll-free)
Fax: 800-542-2311 (toll-free)
E-mail: admissions@liberty.edu
Website: http://www.LibertyU.com
        http://www.Liberty.edu

Liberty University, the world's largest Christian university, is located on more than 6,800 acres in Lynchburg, Virginia.

LIM COLLEGE
NEW YORK, NEW YORK

LIM COLLEGE

The College

With its flagship location situated in a lovely town house in the center of the fashion capital of the world, LIM College has been a major force in fashion and business education for over seven decades. Its graduates can be found throughout all aspects of the industry, and its high standards of education have earned LIM College accreditation from the Middle States Association of Colleges and Schools.

LIM College is a highly personal school where students learn about the business of fashion, with an emphasis on academic and professional study. Lifelong friends are made at LIM College, as well as lifelong careers. Although most students come to the College directly from high school or transfer from other colleges, there are also those of nontraditional college age who enroll. Students come to LIM College from many parts of the country and the world. The current enrollment is approximately 1,500 undergraduates.

LIM College prides itself on its employment rate. The Department of Experiential Education and Career Management is one of LIM College's chief assets. Each student receives extensive career assistance throughout their time at the College, beginning in the first semester. This counseling helps direct students to positions within their field of study. Students seeking employment from the 2011 graduating class had a 97 percent employment rate within a year of graduation.

The unique nature of LIM College's curriculum provides students with a foundation of core courses in liberal arts and business while offering diverse and intensive hands-on preparation in the fashion industry. This affords graduates the opportunity to accept executive training, merchandising, management, marketing, and communications positions in a wide variety of areas within the fashion and business worlds.

Support services are important at LIM College. In addition to academic and career advising, personal counseling is available. Because of the College's small size and the close relationships between students and staff members, any faculty member or administrator is readily accessible to help and advise all students. LIM College's Advisory Board members, all successful fashion industry executives, may also serve as mentors to students, offering additional guidance and advice.

LIM College has a very dynamic student life. Active clubs include the Fashion Club, Student Life Activities Board, Student Government Association, Dance Team, and many more. There are also student publications including the *LIMLIGHT* yearbook and *Fashion Sense* magazine.

LIM College proudly opened a new residence hall in 2008. Located at 1760 Third Avenue, this state-of-the-art facility boasts a plethora of modern amenities. All rooms have private bathrooms, complementary wireless Internet access, phone service, and over 100 cable channels. Rooms are also equipped with full refrigerators and 25-inch flat-screen televisions. The facility also contains a private gym, game room, computer lab, and three full-service kitchens.

LIM College's Open House program offers students and their families the opportunity to tour the school's campus and learn not only of LIM College's unique academic programs, but also of the vast array of careers found in the fashion industry. The day also includes special presentations on financial aid, study abroad, clubs, and much more. Current LIM College students assist in hosting the event and are available to answer questions. LIM College also offers many other opportunities to visit including weekly information sessions, Transfer Services Days, webinars, mock classes for accepted students, and other periodically scheduled special events.

Location

LIM College is situated in four buildings—on East 53rd, East 54th, and East 45th Streets; and on Fifth Avenue, one of the most fashionable locales in the world. A whole world of fashion is at the College's doorstep and includes such famous stores as Saks Fifth

Avenue, Henri Bendel, Armani, and Ralph Lauren. New York City is the headquarters for the garment, cosmetics, advertising, publishing, and textile industries, all of which are essential to the fashion industry and are visited regularly by LIM College students. The College incorporates all of these resources into the curriculum. For example, the Fashion Magazines course may include trips to photography studios, modeling agencies, or tours of magazine offices and advertising firms. New York City offers LIM College students an unparalleled learning experience.

Majors and Degrees

LIM College offers four-year programs in fashion merchandising, management, marketing, and visual merchandising, leading to a Bachelor of Business Administration (B.B.A.) or a Bachelor of Professional Studies (B.P.S.) degree; also offered is a two-year program in fashion merchandising leading to the Associate in Applied Sciences (A.A.S.) degree. The fashion merchandising program has tracks in either traditional apparel and accessories or a new home fashions track. LIM College also offers two graduate programs: the Master of Business Administration (M.B.A.) in either entrepreneurship or fashion management and the Master of Professional Studies (M.P.S.) in merchandising and retail management. The College also offers a broad variety of concentrations, such as fashion publishing and event planning, which allow students to pursue a focused area of study that complements their major.

Academic Programs

LIM College offers a combination of classroom education and supervised practical fieldwork that has been designed to prepare students for executive training programs and other entry-level executive positions in various areas of the fashion industry.

Experiential learning is an integral part of the LIM College curriculum. The internship program helps students become truly prepared for successful careers within fashion and fashion-related industries. All students are required to take three internships in order to earn their bachelor's degree at LIM College. Each internship has a prerequisite seminar attached to it that includes activities such as field trips, guest speakers, and portfolio-building that help students network with industry professionals and develop into dynamic business leaders. The Industry Exploration internship focuses on understanding the nature of the fashion industry through a retail experience, while the Career Pathing internship allows students to explore potential career fields, such as management, publishing, cosmetics, advertising, public relations, or fashion forecasting. Both of these internships dovetail with academic courses the students have taken during previous semesters. The third and final internship is the semester-long Senior Co-op, which is a required four-day-a-week placement in a field related to the student's chosen area of specialization. Co-ops may lead students to positions at fashion magazines, public relations firms, buying offices, or other essential areas of the fashion industry. The Senior Co-op serves as the ideal culmination of the academic experience and a perfect transition into the business world, preparing undergraduates for the challenge and excitement of their future careers.

To graduate, students must complete 127 credits for the bachelor's degree (130 for visual merchandising). Associate degree candidates must earn 68 credits. All students must maintain a grade point average of at least 2.0, and satisfactorily complete the cooperative work assignments.

LIM College accepts qualified students as transfers throughout the four years. The maximum number of credits that LIM will accept is 65. Transfer students must complete the last consecutive 46 credits at LIM College, including the Senior Co-op semester.

The College calendar runs on a traditional semester format, offering both fall and spring start dates. Also offered are summer and Saturday Fashion Lab programs for high school students. The specially selected courses, such as Fashion Buying and Fashion Magazines, blend academics with hands-on experience and are a great way to explore the fashion industry.

Off-Campus Programs

Study-abroad options are available, including study in locales such as Barcelona, Rome, Melbourne, Paris, London, and China.

Academic Facilities

The 5,000-square-foot Adrian G. Marcuse library contains 98,000 volumes and online books pertaining to fashion, management, marketing, and the liberal arts, as well as 240 professional and academic journals. The library has more than forty computer terminals that connect to the Internet and provide access to online databases through the library's subscriptions. DVDs and VHS cassettes useful for fashion-related studies are also available. Personal computers are available for use in the library, lounges, and classrooms. The student-to-computer ratio is 4:1. The Math Center and Writing Centers offer one-on-one tutoring for all students.

LIM College's facility on Fifth Avenue is equipped with two fashion merchandising studios. There are also two new 1,100-square-foot visual merchandising studios, as well as a state-of-the-art Color and Materials Laboratory at the new location.

Costs

Tuition for the 2013–14 school year is $23,070 with additional mandatory fees of $575. Housing charges for the 2013–14 year are $15,850. Students who commute spend from $1,200 to $2,000 for transportation, depending on distance. The personal expense allowance is $1,500.

Financial Aid

LIM College believes that lack of funds should not keep students from attaining a degree; thus, admissions decisions and financial aid are totally separate, and a request for aid has no effect on admissions. About 81 percent of LIM College's students received some form of financial aid during the 2011–12 school year. Institutional scholarships, Federal Pell Grants, Federal Supplemental Educational Opportunity Grants, and New York State TAP grants are all available for eligible students. In addition, the College participates in the Federal Stafford Loan program for students and Federal PLUS Loan program for parents. The College also works with several private lenders to offer alternative education loans for students to supplement their federal loans. International students are eligible to apply for alternative loans with a credit-worthy U.S.-based co-signer. The Free Application for Federal Student Aid (FAFSA) should be filed by all applicants by March 1 for priority consideration. Aid is granted on the basis of financial need and scholarships are merit based, although some awards take need into consideration. Details of the financial aid programs are available on the LIM College website or are available directly from the Office of Student Financial Services.

LIM College features a Merit Scholarship Program for incoming freshmen and transfer students. These scholarship monies are awarded for academic achievement in high school or college. Students can remain eligible for their scholarship throughout their stay at the College by maintaining a GPA of 3.0 or above. LIM College's Fashion Education Foundation also administers a number of merit scholarships (both need and non-need based) other than direct institutional awards.

Faculty

LIM College prides itself on its faculty members. In the fall 2012 semester, 78 percent of the College's faculty had an advanced degree, including 100 percent of the faculty within the departments of Arts and Communications and Math, Finance, and Technology. All professional subject faculty members have wide business and professional experience and many, through their business contacts, bring guests to class to share in the lectures and discussions. The student-faculty ratio is 8:1, and the average class size is 17.

Each student is assigned an academic adviser. Work-study and career guidance is provided by the Department of Experiential Education and Career Management, with conferences held before, during, and after the cooperative work assignments and prior to placement interviews. Students are always welcome to discuss career options at any other time as well.

Student Government

The Office of Student Life is the center of student activities and clubs at LIM College. This department supports student government, approves other student organizations, and establishes operating budgets. One of LIM College's more popular clubs is the Fashion Club, which plans an annual fashion show that recently hosted over 1,000 people. Another popular activity is the student-run *Fashion Sense* magazine. LIM College's Office of Student Life plans many other activities including diversity programming, philanthropic service, and new student orientation.

Admission Requirements

All undergraduate applicants are required to submit high school transcripts, SAT or ACT scores, two letters of recommendation, an essay, and the completed application with the application fee. Transfer students must also submit all college transcripts. Undergraduate Admissions will waive the standardized test requirement if the student has earned 30 credit hours. International students should review the LIM College website and contact the Office of Admissions for specific requirements. It is also strongly suggested that all applicants create an activity sheet or resume highlighting their experience, with emphasis on business and fashion activities.

Application and Information

LIM College's Admissions Committee recognizes that many intangibles go into the making of a successful student, and it evaluates each applicant individually and holistically. The College uses a rolling admission policy. Applicants are informed of the admission decision within approximately four to six weeks after all admission requirements have been fulfilled. An application may be obtained from the LIM College website or by contacting the Admissions Office.

Kristina Ortiz
Assistant Dean of Admissions
LIM College
12 East 53rd Street
New York, New York 10022-5268
Phone: 212-752-1530
      800-677-1323 (toll-free outside New York City)
Fax: 212-750-3432
E-mail: admissions@limcollege.edu
Website: http://www.limcollege.edu
      http://www.facebook.com/LIMCollege
      http://twitter.com/LIMcollege

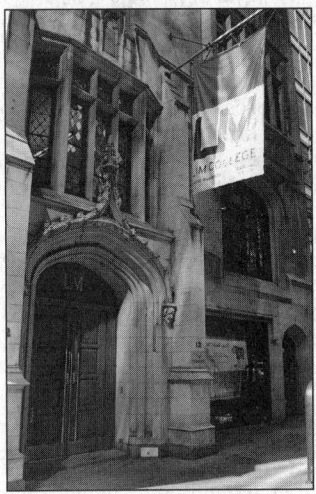

LIM College's flagship location, The Townhouse, is located right off Fifth Avenue in Midtown Manhattan.

LINDENWOOD UNIVERSITY
ST. CHARLES, MISSOURI

The University

An independent teaching university founded in 1827, Lindenwood is the second oldest university west of the Mississippi River. Lindenwood is a dynamic four-year liberal arts institution dedicated to excellence, delivering a high-quality education that leads to the development of the whole person and preparation for life and work after graduation, through more than 130 undergraduate and graduate degree programs.

Lindenwood University is a member of and/or accredited by the Higher Learning Commission of the North Central Association of Colleges and Schools, the Accreditation Council for Business Schools and Programs, the Council on Social Work Education, the Commission on Accreditation of Athletic Training Education, and the Missouri Department of Elementary and Secondary Education, and it is fully endorsed by the Society for Human Resource Management. Lindenwood is a member of the Teacher Education Accreditation Council and the Council for Higher Education Accreditation.

Lindenwood University is authorized to grant associate, bachelor's, master's, Education Specialist, and Doctor of Education degrees. Lindenwood is an independent, public-serving, liberal arts university that has a historical relationship with the Presbyterian Church and is committed to the values inherent in the Judeo-Christian tradition. Lindenwood welcomes students from all religious denominations.

The University's twenty-seven NCAA Division II athletic teams compete in the Mid-America Intercollegiate Athletics Association (MIAA), one of the top conferences in the division. Another twenty Student Life sports and competitive programs compete in an array of college-level organizations specific to the individual programs. Over the last ten years, Lindenwood athletic teams have won more than forty national championships. On-campus athletic facilities consist of the Robert F. Hyland Performance Arena, the Harlen C. Hunter Stadium, the Lou Brock Sports Complex for baseball and softball, and an eight-lane all-weather running track. Students also participate in an assortment of intramural sports at the University's Fitness Center and the Evans Commons.

More than seventy student organizations and clubs, including the Lindenwood Student Government Association and the Student Senate, provide avenues for extended personal growth, leadership, and community service. The University radio station, 50,000-watt KCLC-FM, and LUTV, Lindenwood's HD television station, are staffed by students, as is the *Lindenwood Legacy* student newspaper and LindenLink, an online source of news and feature content.

Students wishing to live on campus may choose from residence halls, houses, and apartment-style living. Eight new residence halls have opened since 2000, and in 2010, Lindenwood acquired the former Days Inn in St. Charles for student housing. Sibley Hall, named in honor of founders Mary Easton and Major George C. Sibley, was built in 1856 to replace the original log cabin that served as the first University building. It is listed on the National Register of Historic Places and is now a women's residence hall. All residential buildings have easy access to University facilities.

Location

The 500-acre campus is located in St. Charles, Missouri, a city of about 55,000 people, situated 20 miles from downtown St. Louis. Resting on the banks of the Missouri River, just south of the Mississippi, St. Charles is the site of Missouri's first state capital. The area offers a wide range of opportunities for all types of interests and is particularly rich in state heritage and attractions associated with the history of America's westward expansion. Lindenwood's proximity to a major city allows students to enjoy theme parks, a delightful zoo, professional sporting events, Broadway plays and theater, performances of a world-renowned symphony orchestra, state parks, and lakes. St. Louis–Lambert International Airport is located just 5 miles from Lindenwood University on Interstate 70.

Majors and Degrees

With a foundation as solid as the campus' century-old linden trees, the academic programs of Lindenwood University have a tradition of excellence and innovation. Lindenwood awards Bachelor of Arts, Bachelor of Fine Arts, and Bachelor of Science degrees with majors in sixty-five subject areas—from accounting to unified sciences.

Preprofessional courses are offered in chiropractic science, dentistry, engineering, health, law, medicine, optometry, nursing, and veterinary science. In addition, programs in engineering are available in conjunction with Washington University in St. Louis, the University of Missouri–Columbia, the University of Missouri—St. Louis, and the Missouri University of Science and Technology in Rolla. In fall 2013, the University is slated to launch a two-year Bachelor of Science in Nursing completion degree program for RNs who already have a two-year associate degree in nursing. Additional health science degrees are planned for the future.

Academic Programs

The emphasis at Lindenwood University is on an individualized liberal arts education with career-oriented preparation. Students fulfill general education requirements, participate in the University's Work and Learn Program when qualified, and acquire an in-depth knowledge of at least one area of study as a major. Lindenwood requires the completion of 128 credit hours to earn a bachelor's degree.

Academic Facilities

The Margaret Leggat Butler Library houses volumes, microfilm items, and a computer lab and subscribes to hundreds of periodicals. Roemer Hall serves as the main administration building and has classrooms and faculty offices on the upper floors. Young Science Hall houses an auditorium, laboratories, and classrooms for natural science, mathematics, and computer science, as well as a theater that is home to the University's film series. Newly renovated and expanded Harmon Hall houses the School of Business and Entrepreneurship with classrooms, offices, and the Dunseth Auditorium. The Lindenwood University Cultural Center provides a 750-seat auditorium, classrooms, meeting rooms, and offices. It is the site of theatrical productions, concerts, convocations, and lectures and is the headquarters of the University's accelerated evening programs. In addition, the Spellmann Campus Center houses a state-of-the-art cafeteria, Macintosh and PC computer labs, classrooms, conference rooms, networking and campus life offices, career planning and placement services, and the studios of KCLC. In August 2011, Lindenwood opened the 119,000-square-foot Evans Common, which houses a variety of amenities for students, including basketball and multipurpose courts, an array of the latest fitness equipment, movie and music rooms, and a new dining hall with a food court configuration, among others. The 132,000-square-foot J. Scheidegger Center for the Arts, completed in 2008, is home to Lindenwood's Theatre, Dance, and Music Departments, as well as the 1,200-seat Bezemes Family Theater, the 250-seat Emerson Black Box Theater, the Boyle Family Gallery, and the Charter Communications LUTV HD Studio.

Costs

For the academic year 2013–14, tuition is $14,875. Students who choose to live on campus pay $7,430 for room and board, plus $360 for communications service and $350 for a health and activity fee. There is a refundable $300 room deposit. Books and other supplies are extra.

Financial Aid

Financial aid is available to all qualified students. A student must submit the Free Application for Federal Student Aid (FAFSA). To qualify for the full amount of financial aid, students must submit their federal financial aid forms before April 1. As determined by the evaluation, a student's financial need may be met with a combination of federal, state, and institutional sources of aid. In addition, institutional awards are available in the areas of academics, leadership, athletics, drama, yearbook/newspaper, and music. Resident students may earn $2,400 toward their expenses by working on campus.

Faculty

Lindenwood has approximately 240 full-time faculty members, who serve as teachers, mentors, and advisers to their students. Faculty members advise students regarding majors and other matters to help them succeed academically.

Student Government

The Lindenwood Student Government Association (LSGA) is made up of representatives elected by the student body. LSGA has the responsibility of providing a balanced program of cultural, social, and recreational events and activities throughout the year. In addition, an elected Student Senate meets periodically with the University president regarding matters of interest to the student body.

Admission Requirements

To apply for admission, a student should submit a completed application form with a nonrefundable $30 application fee, a transcript of high school and/or college work, and ACT or SAT scores.

Applicants are evaluated on an individual basis, and admission is based on an analysis of the student's grade point average, ACT or SAT scores, extracurricular activities, recommendations, and personal qualifications. Students are admitted without regard to race, sex, or national origin.

Application and Information

Admission to Lindenwood is on a rolling basis; students are encouraged to apply by April 15 for the fall semester and by December 1 for the spring semester. Notification of the admission decision is mailed soon after all required materials are received and evaluated by the Office of Undergraduate Day Admissions.

Applications for admission, financial aid, and scholarships and other information about Lindenwood University can be obtained by contacting:

Undergraduate Day Admissions
Lindenwood University
209 South Kingshighway
St. Charles, Missouri 63301-1695
Phone: 636-949-4949
Fax: 636-949-4989
Website: www.lindenwood.edu
www.facebook.com/LUDayAdmissions

Student life at Lindenwood University.

LINFIELD COLLEGE
McMINNVILLE, OREGON

Linfield College

The College

Linfield College (1858) is an independent, coeducational, residential, comprehensive liberal arts and sciences college dedicated to providing an educational environment conducive to learning and participation. There are 1,700 full-time students on the McMinnville campus. These students come primarily from the thirteen Western states (twenty states overall) but also from twenty-four other countries. Students of color make up 23 percent of the student body, and 7 percent of students are international. Most students are between 18 and 22. Linfield is primarily residential, with seventeen residence halls, each accommodating between 10 and 100 residents. Each hall establishes its own calendar of social, educational, and recreational events throughout the year. Students who reside on campus eat their meals in the College dining hall. Houses and apartments are available for upper-division students. Social clubs, professional organizations, four sororities and four fraternities, service clubs, and almost forty other organizations play an important role in the daily life of a Linfield student. Linfield's winning athletics tradition fosters participation at all levels of competition. Women compete in intercollegiate basketball, cross-country, golf, lacrosse, soccer, softball, swimming, tennis, track and field, and volleyball. Men compete in intercollegiate baseball, basketball, cross-country, football, golf, soccer, swimming, tennis, and track and field. Water polo, Ultimate (Frisbee), and men's lacrosse are club sports. Linfield also has an extensive and active year-round intramural program.

Linfield hosts the Oregon Nobel Laureate Symposium, one of five such symposiums worldwide. At each symposium, several Nobel laureates come to share their backgrounds and expertise within the context of a basic theme.

The Linfield–Good Samaritan School of Nursing, an academic unit of the College at its Portland campus, prepares students for careers in nursing. This campus, at the Good Samaritan Hospital and Medical Center, has residence facilities, food service options, and a residence life program. In 2006, the Portland campus programs became open only to transfer admission.

Location

Located in McMinnville, 40 miles southwest of Portland, Linfield College is a leader in the cultural, educational, and recreational events of the fast-growing community of 35,000. Linfield is situated on 193 acres with most classrooms no more than a 10-minute walk from any of the twenty-four on-campus apartment buildings and residence halls. With most students living on campus, Linfield offers a welcoming and lively community.

Coffeehouses, cinemas, boutiques, a community theater, the Evergreen Air and Space Museum (including an IMAX theater and water park), bowling alleys, and a wide variety of restaurants are within walking distance for Linfield students. The central Oregon coast is an hour to the west, and the outdoor activity areas of the Oregon Cascade Range, including year-round skiing at Mount Hood, are two hours to the east. Salem, the state capital of Oregon, is 25 miles to the southeast, and Eugene is 80 miles south. Rainfall in western Oregon averages 42 inches annually and the winter temperature averages 41°F.

Majors and Degrees

Linfield offers the Bachelor of Arts degree in communication arts, creative writing, electronic arts, English, Francophone African Studies, French studies, German, German studies, history, intercultural communication, international relations, Japanese, mass communication, music, philosophy, political science, religious studies, sociology, Spanish, studio art, and theater arts. The Bachelor of Arts or Bachelor of Science degree is offered in accounting, anthropology, applied physics, athletic training, biochemistry and molecular biology, biology, business, chemistry, computing science, economics, elementary education, environmental studies, exercise science, finance, general science, health education, international business, marketing, management, mathematics, physical education, physics, and psychology. A Bachelor of Science in Nursing (B.S.N.) is also available. The College has programs to prepare students for advanced study in any health profession, including medicine, as well as law. The education department offers a strong program of teacher certification at the secondary and elementary levels. A 3-2 engineering program is available in cooperation with Oregon State University, Washington State University, and the University of Southern California.

Academic Programs

The academic year is divided into two 15-week semesters (fall and spring) and an optional four-week winter term in January. The January Term offers regular departmental courses and off-campus and international study. Academic courses are assigned 1–5 semester credit hours each; 125 credits are required for a B.A. or a B.S. degree. Students divide their time equally among required general education courses, a major area of study, and elective subjects. The Linfield Curriculum courses, selected to provide a solid foundation in the liberal arts, require students to take 3 semester hours in each of the six Modes of Inquiry as well as one upper-division course in one of these areas. These Modes of Inquiry are as follows: Vital Past; Ultimate Questions; Individuals, Systems, and Societies; Natural World; Creative Studies; and Quantitative Reasoning. In addition, students are required to take a writing-intensive course, a course addressing global pluralisms, and a course dealing with United States pluralism. Individually designed majors are available with faculty approval. Students majoring in a foreign language spend an academic year in a country in which the language being studied is the native tongue.

The College offers courses in English through the English Language and Culture Program. These courses are designed to help international students whose native language is not English to achieve competence in academic and social English skills, so that they may work effectively in their undergraduate classes at Linfield.

Off-Campus Programs

Off-campus educational experiences include the Semester Abroad program, involving four months of study in Australia, Austria, China, Costa Rica, Ecuador, England, France, Ireland, Japan, New Zealand, Norway, Senegal, South Korea, and Spain. Transportation for the first round-trip is included in the cost of tuition, and most of these study programs cost the same as a semester on campus. January Term study-abroad programs for four weeks are also offered. Recent offerings included Health Care in Kenya; China's Solutions to Energy Issues in the Twenty-first Century; Art and Visual Culture of Catalonia, Spain; and Australia: From Colony to Asian Power.

Academic Facilities

Over the last decade, the College has opened two residence halls, six apartment buildings, the James F. Miller Fine Arts Center, the Marshall Theatre and communication arts facility, the Vivian A. Bull Center for Music, and the Nicholson Library. The library covers 56,000 square feet and combines traditional collections of books and journals with the new and changing digital and electronic technology to provide access to the web and web-based designs. The studio theater has an audience seating capacity of up to 140 and includes space for set construction and design.

In 2011, Linfield reopened the former library to provide new classroom and office space for the departments of business, economics, English, and philosophy. This state-of-the-art facility, T. J. Day Hall, includes the College's writing center and the Linfield Center for the Northwest (LCN). The LCN cultivates regionally relevant partnerships for training, research, service learning, and cultural or artistic exchanges. These opportunities promote student engagement in regional issues and produce real-world change. T. J. Day Hall is Linfield's first LEED-certified Gold building, underscoring the College's commitment to sustainability and conservation.

Murdock and Graf Halls house the biology, chemistry, and physics departments and up-to-date laboratories and equipment. Other facilities include art galleries and studios, a 250-watt FM radio station, an experimental psychology lab, dance and music studios, a preschool, and a 425-seat auditorium that houses a three-manual, 48-rank Casavant pipe organ.

Linfield students benefit from a communications and technology network that includes phone service, voice mail, e-mail, and wireless Internet connections in each residence hall room. In addition, there is wireless access in the library and other academic areas of the campus.

The Health and Physical Education/Recreation Complex houses three gymnasiums; weight rooms; fitness laboratories with a hydrostatic weighing tank, a metabolic and pulmonary measuring system, and an electrocardiovascular exercise ECG system; an eight-lane, 25-yard indoor pool; handball and racquetball courts; classrooms; offices; and a 28,000-square-foot field house.

Costs

For 2012–13, tuition and fees were $34,000 per two-semester year, board was $4,220, and a double room was $5,180. There was a $201 per-credit fee for on-campus January Term classes.

Financial Aid

Eligibility for most of Linfield's assistance programs is based on need as determined by a federally approved needs analysis processor. The only form required for need-based programs is the Free Application for Federal Student Aid (FAFSA). Linfield participates in the federal grant, loan, and work programs, and other forms of financial assistance on the basis of demonstrated need.

The College awards scholarships to full-time students based on scholastic achievement, independent of financial need. These academic scholarships vary from 30 to 60 percent of tuition. A number of criteria are used when determining scholarships, including grade point average, strength of curriculum, and standardized test scores. Linfield sponsors special scholarships for National Merit finalists. The College also sponsors an annual Competitive Scholarship Day in February. Participation is limited to high school seniors who meet particular academic requirements and apply by December 1. Each academic department offers prizes ranging from $12,000 to $20,000, divided over the student's four years at Linfield. Scholarships are also available to students from the departments of music, theater, and communication who demonstrate outstanding leadership and community service. Financial assistance for non–U.S. citizens is limited to partial-tuition scholarships and the opportunity to work part-time on campus.

Faculty

There are 124 faculty members, each of whom is committed to undergraduate teaching and scholarship. Ninety-three percent have doctoral or other terminal degrees within their field. The student-faculty ratio is 12:1, and faculty members serve as academic advisers. There are no teaching assistants.

Student Government

Students have a significant voice in establishing and changing College policies and regulations. The Student Senate, chosen through campus elections, is the focus of student opinion and debate. Students are represented on most College governing councils and committees with faculty members and trustees, and they are encouraged to express and implement their ideas on academic or extracurricular matters.

Admission Requirements

Admission to Linfield College is selective. Admission is granted to students who are likely to grow and succeed in a personal and challenging liberal arts environment. Each applicant is judged on individual merit, based on high school performance, a writing sample, recommendations from teachers and counselors, precollege standardized test results (ACT or SAT), and the depth and quality of an applicant's involvement in community and school activities. Linfield is a member of the Common Application Association.

International students whose education has been in a language other than English must submit certified English translations of their academic work. Proficiency in English is required, as demonstrated by an official TOEFL score report.

Application and Information

The early action deadline is November 15 (with notification by January 15) and the regular decision priority deadline is February 15 (with notification by April 1).

Interviews are not required, but students are encouraged to visit. Appointments should be made in advance and can be requested online at http://www.linfield.edu/stopby. The Linfield website provides students with information on academic programs, student life, and athletics.

Interested students are encouraged to contact:

Office of Admission
Linfield College
900 SE Baker Street
McMinnville, Oregon 97128
Phone: 503-883-2213
     800-640-2287 (toll-free)
Fax: 503-883-2472
E-mail: admission@linfield.edu
Website: http://www.linfield.edu/admission
    http://www.facebook.com/linfieldadmit
    http://twitter.com/linfieldadmit

Linfield College is located 1 hour southwest of Portland, Oregon's largest city, on nearly 200 acres. Nearly sixty buildings, many built in Georgian colonial style, house forty academic departments among a grove of oak trees.

LOYOLA MARYMOUNT UNIVERSITY
LOS ANGELES, CALIFORNIA

The University

Loyola Marymount University (LMU), situated on a picturesque campus, offers competitive students an education of high quality in a dynamic and supportive atmosphere. As successor to the oldest institution of learning in southern California, St. Vincent's College, the University is steeped in a tradition and history of dedication to academic excellence and the total development of its students. Although the emphasis is within the undergraduate program (full-time enrollment is approximately 5,800 and part-time enrollment is approximately 250), approximately 1,950 students pursue master's degrees in the fields of arts, arts in teaching, business administration, education, film, and science (including engineering). The Doctor of Education in educational leadership for social justice is offered by the School of Education. The School of Law, situated at a separate campus, has both day and evening divisions and offers the Juris Doctor degree. Law school enrollment is 1,320.

Fifty-five percent of the undergraduate students (95 percent of freshmen) live on campus and are able to choose accommodations in one of eleven residential halls or six apartment complexes. Students have access to a sports pavilion, one swimming pool, baseball and soccer fields, tennis and volleyball courts, and four indoor racquetball courts. The Fritz B. Burns Recreation Center includes three additional courts and a fitness center. LMU fields teams in twelve Division I intercollegiate sports (baseball, basketball, cheer, crew, cross-country, golf, soccer, softball, swimming, tennis, women's volleyball, and water polo) and has club teams in lacrosse, rugby, men's volleyball, and more. Over 2,000 undergraduate students participate in the active intramural program, which includes coed sports. Student organizations include nine service organizations, the AM/FM radio station (KXLU), Chemistry Society, Black Student Union, Han Tao Chinese Cultural Club, MEChA, Business Law Society, Student-Athlete Advisory Committee, University choruses, fraternities and sororities, and various honor and service groups. LMU's Debate Team and Air Force ROTC detachment have received national recognition in their respective areas.

Location

LMU is ideally located on a 142-acre bluff that overlooks the southwest section of Los Angeles and the Pacific Ocean from Malibu to Santa Monica. The campus is close to the beach, and the University community enjoys a cool, clean coastal climate. LMU is near the metropolitan complex, but it has the benefits of the slower pace of its residential community, Westchester. Los Angeles International Airport is 10 minutes away, and nearby freeways provide easy access to the city and its cultural and recreational activities.

Majors and Degrees

Loyola Marymount University offers the B.A. in the fields of African American studies, animation, art history, Asian Pacific studies, biology, Chicano studies, classical civilizations, classics, communication studies, dance, economics, English, European studies, film and television production, French, Greek, history, humanities, Latin, liberal studies (elementary education), mathematics, music, philosophy, political science, production (film and television), psychology, recording arts, screenwriting, sociology, Spanish, studio arts, theater arts, theological studies, urban studies, and women's studies. The College of Business Administration offers the Bachelor of Science degree in accounting and applied information management systems and the Bachelor of Business Administration degree with majors in entrepreneurship, finance, management, and marketing. The College of Science and Engineering offers bachelor's degrees in applied mathematics, athletic training, biochemistry, biology, chemistry, computer science, engineering (civil, electrical, and mechanical), engineering physics, environmental science, health and human sciences, mathematics, and physics.

Academic Programs

While specific course requirements differ with each area of study, a common core with course work in the fields of American diversity, college writing, creative and critical arts, ethics, history, literature, mathematics/science/technology, philosophy, rhetorical arts, social science, and theology provides the foundation for a well-rounded education for all LMU students. The interdepartmental honors program provides challenges for the exceptional student.

The academic calendar consists of two semesters and two 6-week optional summer sessions. The fall semester begins in late August and ends before Christmas. The spring semester usually begins in mid-January and ends in mid-May. Students may earn credit when receiving scores of 4 or 5 through Advanced Placement (AP) examinations and scores of 5 or above on International Baccalaureate (IB) examinations.

Off-Campus Programs

Students who are interested in studying abroad can apply to LMU summer and semester programs, selected Association of Jesuit Colleges and Universities (AJCU) programs, reciprocal exchanges, and other approved programs in a variety of locations. LMU offers programs in Africa, Argentina, Australia, China, England, France, Germany, Greece, Honduras, Ireland, Italy, Japan, Mexico, New Zealand, the Philippines, South Korea, Spain, and many others. Depending on the program, students may receive credits and/or grades for their participation. Financial aid eligibility for study abroad is determined by program and the type of aid the student receives. Courses may be conducted in English, the language of the host country, or both. In addition, LMU offers internship programs through which students can earn practical training and sometimes even course credit. The programs range from student involvement in political campaigns to the counseling of underrepresented youths to professional work at film/TV studios.

Academic Facilities

The William H. Hannon Library is the newest and most sophisticated library facility in Los Angeles. The new, state-of-the-art 88,000-square-foot library is the cultural and intellectual hub of the Loyola Marymount University campus. Its three above-ground stories and two basement levels have space for more than 1 million volumes, and the more than 100 computer workstations, four classrooms, and dozens of group study rooms will facilitate all forms of learning. The Law School Library, located within the School of Law in downtown Los Angeles, contains more than 560,000 volumes and microforms and is a depository for government documents of the state of California and the United States. It also has complete holdings of all publications relating to California law. The communication arts complex houses the Louis B. Mayer Motion Picture Theatre, a full-size color-television studio, a motion-picture soundstage, and state-of-the-art industry equipment. Strub Theatre offers excellent theatrical facilities for the performing arts of drama and dance.

Costs

Tuition for the 2012–13 academic year was $38,917. The cost of room and board varies with options that students select—for example, a full- or partial-meal plan, an apartment on campus, or a residence hall. However, the average yearly cost is approximately $13,835. Students should expect to spend about $1,656 for books and supplies and $2,277 for additional miscellaneous expenses.

Financial Aid

Approximately 82 percent of the University's undergraduate students receive some type of financial assistance. Students applying for aid must file the Free Application for Federal Student Aid (FAFSA). All students are expected to apply for the Federal Pell Grant, and California residents must apply for the California grants. LMU offers both need-based aid and merit-based awards in amounts up to the full tuition Trustee Scholarship. The priority date for the financial aid application is February 1.

Faculty

LMU's faculty is dedicated to undergraduate teaching and is easily accessible to students. Ninety-nine percent of the faculty members hold a Ph.D. or terminal degree in their area of instruction; the average class size is 21.

Student Government

LMU believes that active student input is an essential part of the undergraduate years. Students sit on every University committee, including the Board of Trustees, with full voting rights. Students operate the campus recreation centers, manage the dormitories as resident advisers, and participate in over 160 clubs and organizations. Student actions have resulted in the development of such things as a campus farmer's market, outdoor concert series, club sports teams, social justice events, and community service programs.

Admission Requirements

Admission to LMU is selective, and a candidate is expected to present a strong record in college-preparatory courses. In determining an applicant's eligibility, the University gives careful consideration to the student's academic preparation, national test scores, letters of recommendation, extracurricular activities, and family relationships to the University. A personal interview is not required for admission. Prospective candidates are encouraged to visit the campus. LMU offers campus tours Monday through Saturday during the academic year and Monday through Friday during the summer.

Application and Information

Applicants must submit official transcripts from the last high school attended and from each college attended, arrange for SAT or ACT scores to be sent to the Office of Admission, submit a recommendation form from an official of the last school attended, and file the Common Application and LMU supplement with the $60 nonrefundable fee. Applications are considered when all necessary documents have been received prior to the deadline of the semester for which application is made. The priority deadline for freshman applicants for the fall semester is November 1 for early action and January 15 for regular decision. Early action applicants receive a decision by December 20. The deadline for transfer applicants for the fall semester is March 15. Fall transfer applicants who apply by February 1 will receive early consideration for fall transfer. The priority deadline for spring semester admission is October 15 for both freshman and transfer applicants.

International students are welcome to apply to LMU and follow the same admission procedures as domestic students. International students must also demonstrate English proficiency by submitting TOEFL results with a minimum score of 80 or an IELTS exam of 6.5 overall bandwidth. LMU also offers conditional admission through ELS language centers. International students must also provide a statement of financial responsibility for all obligations covering the full period of time for which the student is making application. All records of previous academic training must be original or authentic copies with notarization and have notarized English translations.

For more information about Loyola Marymount University, prospective students should contact:

Matthew X. Fissinger
Director of Admission
Loyola Marymount University
1 LMU Drive, Suite 100
Los Angeles, California 90045
Phone: 310-338-2750
  800-LMU-INFO (toll-free)
Fax: 310-338-2797
E-mail: admissions@lmu.edu
Website: http://www.lmu.edu/
   http://www.lmu.edu/mobile
   http://www.facebook.com/lmuadmission
   http://twitter.com/LMUAdmission
   http://www.youtube.com/user/LMUAdmission

Between classes at Loyola Marymount University.

LOYOLA UNIVERSITY MARYLAND
BALTIMORE, MARYLAND

The University

Loyola University Maryland a Jesuit, Catholic comprehensive university committed to the educational and spiritual traditions of the Society of Jesus and the development of the whole person. Accordingly, the University inspires students to learn, lead, and serve in a diverse and changing world.

Loyola's current full-time undergraduate enrollment is 3,917; more than 82 percent of the student body lives on campus. The University encourages co-curricular activities that contribute to the academic, social, and spiritual growth of the student. These include social and cultural organizations, student government activities, an ROTC program, national honor societies, and Division I athletic programs such as basketball, cross-country, golf, lacrosse, soccer, swimming and diving, tennis, track, and volleyball. The majority of the student body participates in the wide variety of club and intramural sports offered.

In recent years, Loyola's campus has undergone significant expansion. Thirteen apartment complexes and four first-year residence halls provide Loyola students with on-campus housing. In 2011, the Donnelly Science Center was expanded, making it the largest academic building on the Evergreen campus. The Andrew White Student Center offers several dining choices, as well as spacious meeting and recreational space. The Student Center also provides facilities for athletics, the Communication Department, and the fine arts, including the McManus Theatre and the 4,000-seat Reitz Arena. The Center also has an art gallery, classrooms, black box theater and music, photography, and studio art labs. Loyola's recreational sports facility is the Fitness and Aquatic Center. This 115,000-square-foot athletic facility provides an indoor pool, basketball courts, squash courts, a climbing wall, fitness equipment, tracks, and outdoor playing fields. The Ridley Athletic Complex, completed in spring 2010, is a 6,000-seat grandstand stadium with locker rooms, a weight-training suite, an expertly staffed first-aid suite, concession areas, and memorabilia for sale on-site.

Location

The Loyola campus is located in a residential area of north Baltimore, 5 miles from the Inner Harbor area. This location offers the student the advantages of quiet residential living with the attractions of city life. The metropolitan area has a wide variety of theaters, museums, professional and intercollegiate sports events, and historical points of interest. Other colleges and universities in the vicinity help to expand the social calendar and academic life.

Majors and Degrees

Loyola offers programs more than 30 majors. The Bachelor of Arts degree is awarded in art history, classical civilization, classics, communication, comparative cultures and literary studies, computer science, economics, elementary education, English, fine arts, French, German, global studies, history, philosophy, political science, psychology, sociology, Spanish, speech pathology/audiology, theology, and writing. The Bachelor of Business Administration degree is awarded in accounting, business economics, finance, general business, information systems, international business, management, and marketing. The Bachelor of Science degree is awarded in biology, chemistry, computer science, engineering science, mathematical science, statistics, and physics.

Academic Programs

The curriculum at Loyola is divided into three parts: the core, the major, and electives. The core contains those courses that Loyola considers essential to the liberal arts curriculum. These courses, which are required of all students regardless of major, are completed throughout the four years. The core consists of a classical or modern language, English literature, writing, mathematics and natural science, social science, fine arts, history, philosophy, ethics, and theology. The major enables students to pursue their specialized area of study in depth. Electives give students the opportunity to broaden their intellectual and cultural background in areas of special interest. To prepare for graduate study, students may enroll in one of four pre-professional programs: dental, law, medical, or veterinary.

An honors program and honors housing are available to outstanding students. The honors program stresses independent work by specially grouping students in many of the core courses. Honors housing provides an environment that is conducive to study and close social interaction.

Off-Campus Programs

Loyola University Maryland participates in a cooperative program with Notre Dame of Maryland University, Johns Hopkins University, Goucher College, Morgan State University, Towson University, the Peabody Conservatory of Music, and the Maryland Institute College of Art. Loyola students may cross-register at any of these area colleges and universities.

Students in good academic standing may pursue studies abroad through Loyola's programs in Accra, Ghana; Copenhagen, Denmark; Glasgow, Scotland; Leuven, Belgium; Bangkok, Thailand; Alcalá, Spain; Melbourne, Australia; Newcastle, England; Auckland, New Zealand; Beijing, China; Cork, Ireland; Rome, Italy; Paris, France; and San Salvador, El Salvador. Loyola also participates in exchange programs with eight other countries and assists students in applying to a variety of non-Loyola affiliated international study programs each year.

Academic Facilities

Loyola celebrated the completion of the Donnelly Science Center expansion in September 2011. The 15,000-square-foot addition provides class laboratory spaces, research laboratories, offices, a conference room for the natural sciences, storage, a vivarium, a microscopy center, and a robotics laboratory. Spacious hallways connecting the building's wings on all levels include spaces for science displays and gathering areas for students and faculty in biology, chemistry, physics, computer science, and engineering.

The Sellinger School of Business and Management is Loyola's AACSB-accredited business school. Highlights of this school include experiential learning requirements, the Sellinger Scholars honors program, many student associations, and the Student Experiential Learning Lab, a state-of-the-art trading room that allows students access to the three most widely used databases in the finance industry—Reuters, Morningstar, and Bloomberg—and features a six-screen video display for breaking news and real-time market updates and a scrolling price ticker.

Costs

For 2013–14, tuition for all undergraduate students is $41,820 per year. Room for first-year students is $9,300. Student fees are estimated at $1,400.

Financial Aid

The University strives to make a Loyola education accessible for qualified students of all socio-economic backgrounds. Financial aid is awarded based on academic ability and financial need. Seventy-two percent of the student body receives financial assistance in the forms of Loyola University Maryland grants and scholarships, state scholarships, Federal Pell Grants, Federal Supplemental Educational Opportunity Grants, Federal Perkins Loans, and Federal Work-Study Program opportunities. To apply for financial assistance, students must submit the Free Application for Federal Student Aid and the Financial Aid PROFILE through the College Scholarship Service in Princeton, New Jersey. The financial aid application deadline is February 15.

Faculty

Loyola intends to maintain its faculty-student ratio of approximately 1:12 and an average class size of 21 students to ensure its continued focus on students as individuals. Of the 350 full-time faculty members, 88 percent have a Ph.D. or terminal degree in their field and 75 percent are tenured or on the tenure track. No classes are taught by graduate students or teaching assistants.

Student Government

The Student Government serves three chief functions, which make its existence not only valuable but also necessary. These functions are to represent the student body outside the University, to provide leadership within the student body, and to perform services, both social and academic, for the students. Responsibility for budgeting activities also rests with the Student Government. The president of the Student Government is a member of the College Academic Council.

Admission Requirements

The admission evaluation at Loyola combines an analysis of academic information submitted along with a review of recommendations, the record of extracurricular involvement and evidence of special talent, leadership, and service. The admission committee does not use a formula or have strict cutoffs. Instead, the admission office's goal is to conduct a balanced and individual review, taking a number of factors into account. Submission of SAT and ACT scores is optional for all first-year applicants, excluding home-school students. Students who choose not to submit standardized test scores must submit an additional letter of recommendation or personal essay. The University welcomes applications from students of character, intelligence, and motivation, without discrimination on the grounds of race or religious belief.

Application and Information

Interested students seeking to enroll at Loyola may apply online using the Loyola Application or the Common Application. Each applicant must submit a school counselor letter of recommendation, a teacher letter of recommendation, and a personal statement. Applicants for all forms of financial aid must submit the Financial Aid PROFILE of the College Scholarship Service (CSS Profile) and the Free Application for Federal Student Aid (FAFSA). A $50 application fee must accompany the application for admission.

For additional information, students are encouraged to contact:
Undergraduate Admission Office
Loyola University Maryland
4501 North Charles Street
Baltimore, Maryland 21210-2699
Phone: 410-617-5012
    800-221-9107 (toll-free)
Web site: http://www.loyola.edu/undergraduate
    http://www.facebook.com/
    LoyolaMarylandAdmission
    https://twitter.com/chooseloyola

Loyola University Maryland is located in residential Baltimore, 6 miles from the Inner Harbor and less than an hour from Washington, D.C., giving students access to an array of cultural events, restaurants, shops, and internship opportunities.

LOYOLA UNIVERSITY NEW ORLEANS
NEW ORLEANS, LOUISIANA

The University

Founded by the Jesuits in 1912, Loyola University's more than 35,000 graduates have excelled in innumerable professional fields for over ninety years. The 3,000 undergraduate students (5,000 students total) enjoy the individual attention of a caring faculty in a university dedicated to creating community and fostering individualism while educating the whole person, not only intellectually, but spiritually, socially, and athletically. Loyola students represent forty-eight states, the District of Columbia, Puerto Rico, the Virgin Islands, and fifty-four countries. This diversity is found in a setting where the average class size is 22 students. Almost 65 percent of the students permanently reside outside Louisiana, and 34 percent belong to minority groups.

Loyola's 20-acre main campus and 4-acre Broadway campus are located in the historic uptown area of New Orleans and are hubs of student activity. The University's residence halls, equipped with computer labs, kitchen, laundry, and study facilities, are home to nearly 80 percent of the freshmen who reside on campus. The Joseph A. Danna Center, the student center, houses six food venues, including the Orleans Room, Flambeaux's, Fresh Market, Smoothie King, and Satchmo's, Loyola's own jazz hall and sushi bar. An art gallery and post office can also be found in the Danna Center. Nationally affiliated fraternities and sororities are among Loyola's more than 120 student organizations. During the fall's Organizational Fair, students can join the Pacemaker Award–winning newspaper, the Loyola University Community Action Program (a volunteer community service organization, the largest organization on campus), the University's award-winning Bateman team, or one of the many special interest groups. Students can also take this opportunity to sign up for one of Loyola's club sports. Every year, approximately one third of the student body participates in club sports, such as cheerleading, crew, cycling, dance, golf, swimming, and volleyball, as well as in men's rugby and soccer. Loyola participates in the National Association of Intercollegiate Athletics (NAIA) men's baseball, basketball, cross-country, golf, tennis, and track and women's basketball, cross-country, golf, tennis, track, and volleyball. The University Sports Complex offers six multipurpose courts, an elevated running track, an Olympic-style swimming pool, weight rooms, and aerobics and combat-sports facilities.

Career development services include individualized consultation and counseling (with personality and career-interest testing), a career exploration course, career-related speakers, and a career information library. Publications include information on a wide range of career choices, graduate school directories, scholarship and financial aid directories, and field-specific directories of employers.

The Joseph A. Butt, S.J., College of Business is fully accredited at both the undergraduate and graduate levels by the Association to Advance Collegiate Schools of Business–AACSB International, and houses the Mildred Soule and Clarence A. Lengendre Chair in Business Ethics. The College of Music and Fine Arts offers students opportunities in music industry studies and music performance areas as well as visual and theater arts. Students in the College of Humanities and Natural Sciences might choose premed preparation, psychology, or areas in the humanities, such as history or modern foreign languages. The College of Social Sciences houses a School of Mass Communication that offers award winning programs in advertising, journalism, and public relations.

Location

Loyola's main campus fronts oak-lined St. Charles Avenue in uptown New Orleans. Its red-brick, Tudor-Gothic buildings overlook Audubon Park, home of the famous Audubon Zoo. The downtown area is a 20-minute streetcar ride away, allowing students to take advantage of the city's broad cultural and artistic environment. Considering that New Orleans enjoys an average temperature of 70 degrees, students can enjoy year-round outdoor activities in a city famous for its food, music, and cultural festivals. Lake Pontchartrain is within the city limits and provides facilities for water sports.

Majors and Degrees

Loyola University grants degrees in four-year undergraduate programs. The College of Humanities and Natural Sciences grants the B.A. degree in classical studies, English literature, English writing, environmental studies, film and digital media, French, history, Latin American studies, philosophy, religious studies (Christianity and world religions), and Spanish. It grants the B.S. in biological sciences (predentistry, premedicine, and pre–veterinary studies), biochemistry (premedicine), chemistry (premedicine, pre-engineering), chemistry/forensic science, computational mathematics, environmental science, mathematics, physics (pre-engineering, premedicine), psychology, and psychology (premedicine). The College of Business awards the B.B.A. degree in economics, finance, international business, management, and marketing, as well as the Bachelor of Accountancy. The College of Music and Fine Arts grants the B.M. in composition, jazz studies, music education, music industry studies, music therapy and performance (instrumental and vocal), and grants the B.S. in music industry studies. The College also grants a B.A. in graphic arts, theater arts, theater arts–communications, theater arts (with a minor in business administration), and studio arts and a B.F.A. in studio arts. The College of Social Sciences offers the B.A. in criminal justice, economics environmental science, mass communication, political science, and sociology. The School of Mass Communication offers concentrations in advertising, journalism, and public relations.

Minors are available in all disciplines offered as majors. African and African-American studies, American studies, Asian studies, Catholic studies, computational science, computer science, environmental studies, film studies, Latin American studies, medieval studies, Middle East peace studies, New Orleans studies, and women's studies are offered as interdisciplinary minors addressing important areas of national and international concern. Loyola also offers secondary education certification.

Academic Programs

Once enrolled at Loyola, students are introduced to the Common Curriculum, designed to give them a well-rounded preparation in their major field of concentration, as well as the ability to understand and reflect on disciplines allied to or outside their major. The curriculum is divided into four categories: major, minor, Common Curriculum, and elective courses. Students must meet the requirements of their degree program as specified by their particular college; the minimum four-year program requires 120 hours. Common Curriculum courses include seven introductory courses in English composition, math, science, philosophy, religion, literature, and history and nine upper-division courses in humanities, social science, and natural science. The College of Business requires that all students with junior or senior standing complete a 3-credit-hour internship prior to graduation. Internships provide professional-level experience in area business firms and not-for-profit organizations, along with college credit for semester-long participation. The College of Humanities and Natural Sciences also requires a minimum of one year of study in a modern foreign language. The honors program and independent studies provide special opportunities for qualified students.

Off-Campus Programs

Through the Center for International Education, more than one third of the student body has an international experience each year. Loyola offers summer programs in Germany, Greece, Ireland, London, and Mexico, as well as opportunities to study in over fifty different countries including Belgium, Morocco, China, and Argentina through various consortium programs. Through consortium arrangements in the city of New Orleans, students may cross-register for courses for credit at Xavier

University and Tulane University and participate with these institutions in joint social-cultural events. In addition, the University offers a rigorous internship program in New Orleans at businesses, institutions, and schools to give students practical experience in their fields, including business, communications, modern foreign languages, music, and writing. Loyola offers a 3-3 program with the Loyola College of Law for students interested in pursuing a prelaw track, an early acceptance program with Tulane University Medical School, and a five-year M.B.A. program through the College of Business.

Academic Facilities

A $13-million Communications/Music Complex includes classrooms, offices, specialized instructional facilities for the College of Music and Fine Arts and the School of Mass Communication, and a 600-seat performance facility for the College of Music and Fine Arts.

Computing is an integral part of campus life at Loyola. The University provides more than 450 computers in seventeen computer labs throughout the campus. These labs consist of Windows- and Macintosh-based computers with a wide variety of application software and access to the Internet. Loyola's high-speed Ethernet network can also be accessed from locations such as residence halls, the library, and other public areas. A noteworthy characteristic of Loyola's computing resources is its student-centered emphasis. For example, specialized computer labs exist in the Writing Across the Curriculum Center, English and Math Basic Skills Labs, Poverty Law Clinic, and Business Solutions Center.

The Broadway campus, two blocks down St. Charles Avenue, houses the Loyola College of Law, the visual arts department, the Division of Institutional Advancement, and a residence hall.

Other facilities on campus include the J. Edgar and Louise S. Monroe Library, the region's most technologically advanced facility and the 2003 recipient of the Association of College and Research Libraries' Excellence in Academic Libraries Award, which contains more than 367,000 volumes and provides access to over 27,000 electronic books and more than 23,000 electronic journals. The Monroe Library also offers more than 660,000 microform units and 2,500 media titles. There are also specialized libraries for music and law. The 150,000-square-foot Monroe Library contains 1,800 computer links, media/instructional technology services, a visual arts center, and the Lindy Boggs National Center for Community Literacy. The library also offers three 24-hour microcomputer labs, two multimedia classrooms, and sixteen group-study rooms.

Costs

For the full-time undergraduate student attending during 2013–14, tuition is $35,504 for the year. The cost of residence halls (double occupancy) and a complete meal plan is $11,862 for the year. This does not include a $1,416 University fee.

Financial Aid

Loyola University's endowment provides money for financial aid in addition to that provided by federal funding. Assistance in the forms of merit- and talent-based scholarships, loans, work-study program awards, and grants is awarded on the basis of academic achievement and need. More than 450 scholarships are awarded annually to students with competitive grades and test scores. Scholarship offers are not made until after admission. Notifications of awards are sent in early February. Awards of need-based financial aid packages are made on a first-come, first-served basis and are announced in mid-March. Eighty-four percent of Loyola students receive some form of financial aid.

Faculty

Behind every program at Loyola is a faculty of Jesuit and lay professors who are especially well qualified in their particular fields. The Jesuit Order, recognized throughout the world for its educational contributions over the centuries, administers the University's faculty of 258 full-time professors, of whom 91 percent hold the terminal degree in their field. Loyola also employs 148 part-time instructors. No graduate assistants teach classes. The student-faculty ratio of 12:1 emphasizes the University's special quality of personal involvement and concern for each student and his or her particular needs.

Student Government

Loyola's Student Government Association consists of representatives elected by the student body from each of the four colleges and the law school. The association conducts general meetings, elections, and student activities. Student representatives sit on nearly all University committees.

Admission Requirements

Prospective students must submit an application, resume, essay, a high school transcript or GED test results, ACT or SAT scores, and one letter of recommendation from a counselor or teacher. Individual attention is given to each application form.

Auditions are required for students applying to performance majors in the College of Music and Fine Arts. An interview and a portfolio are required for final acceptance to the B.S. in Music Industry Studies program.

December 1 is the priority deadline for freshman admission and scholarship consideration. January 15 is the regular deadline for freshman scholarship consideration. February 15 is the regular deadline for freshman admission consideration. Applications will be accepted after February 15 as space allows.

Transfer students are required to submit an official transcript for each institution previously attended along with their transfer application. Transfer scholarships are available to spring applicants as well as fall. Transfer students interested in competing for a scholarship should apply by March 1 if possible, and no later than April 15. For nonscholarship admission consideration, transfer students should apply no later than May 15 for the fall semester and no later than December 1 for the spring semester.

Application and Information

Interested students are encouraged to contact:

Office of Admissions
Loyola University New Orleans
6363 St. Charles Avenue, Box 18
New Orleans, Louisiana 70118
Phone: 504-865-3240
        800-4-LOYOLA (toll-free)
Fax: 504-865-3383
E-mail: admit@loyno.edu
Website: http://www.loyno.edu

Loyola is located on beautiful, oak-lined St. Charles Avenue adjacent to Audubon Park.

LUTHER COLLEGE
DECORAH, IOWA

The College

Luther College, founded in 1861 by Norwegian immigrants, is a four-year residential liberal arts college of the Lutheran church (ELCA). The College is an academic community of faith and learning where students of promise from all beliefs and backgrounds have the freedom to learn, to express themselves, to perform, to compete, and to grow. Located in Decorah, Iowa, the College is home to approximately 2,500 students from thirty-seven states and forty-seven countries. Thirty percent of the students are from Iowa; 85 percent come from the four-state area of Iowa, Minnesota, Wisconsin, and Illinois. In 2012–13, 132 international students choose to study at Luther.

In keeping with its liberal arts tradition, the College requires students to develop a depth of knowledge in their chosen major and a breadth of knowledge through exposure to a wide range of subjects and intellectual approaches (general requirements). Learning at Luther is about engagement: faculty members who are passionate in their teaching and scholarship; students who are bright, active, and involved; and a College community characterized by personal attention, hands-on experiences, academic challenge, and community support. At Luther, all students become immersed in the liberal arts through the College's Paideia program. This program, which is uncommon in its approach, helps train students' minds and develop their research and writing skills as they explore human cultures and history. In addition, Luther offers a Phi Beta Kappa chapter and departmental honor societies, evidence of the quality of teaching and learning on campus.

At Luther, students are encouraged to seek out connections between their lives in the classroom and their lives outside the classroom. The College provides a stimulating cultural and educational atmosphere by bringing distinguished public figures, theater groups, musicians, and educators to the campus. Cocurricular activities are an important part of college life. The College sponsors six choirs, three orchestras, three bands, two jazz bands, and a full theater and dance program. Numerous student organizations and societies provide ample opportunities for student involvement in meaningful activities. As a community of faith, students can participate in chapel, weekly Sunday worship, and outreach teams.

Nineteen intercollegiate sports are offered. Men may participate in ten sports: baseball, basketball, cross-country, football, golf, soccer, swimming, tennis, track and field, and wrestling. Women compete in nine intercollegiate sports: basketball, cross-country, golf, soccer, softball, swimming, tennis, track and field, and volleyball. Club sports include Ultimate (Frisbee), rugby, and women's lacrosse. Seventy percent of the student body is involved in an extensive intramural and recreational sports program. Available for recreational use are twelve outdoor tennis courts, an eight-lane polyurethane 400-meter track, numerous cross-country running and ski trails, and 15 acres of intramural fields. The well-equipped Regents Center houses four hardwood basketball courts, a wrestling complex, three racquetball courts, and a 3,000-seat gymnasium. A sports forum accommodates a six-lane, 200-meter indoor track; six indoor tennis courts; locker rooms; and athletic training facilities. The Legends Fitness for Life Center provides the latest fitness equipment and a 30-foot-high rock-climbing wall. A new aquatic center scheduled to open in 2013 will feature an eight-lane stainless steel pool complete with diving well.

Location

The College is located in Decorah, a city of 8,100 people in the scenic bluff country of northeast Iowa. The Upper Iowa River, which runs through the campus, is designated as a National Scenic and Recreational River. Rich in Scandinavian heritage, Decorah is a popular recreation area, providing opportunities for canoeing, kayaking, fishing, hunting, cross-country skiing, camping, hiking, biking, and spelunking. Three airports are located within a 75-mile radius of Decorah: in Rochester, Minnesota; Waterloo, Iowa; and La Crosse, Wisconsin.

Majors and Degrees

Luther College grants the Bachelor of Arts (B.A.) degree and offers majors in accounting, Africana studies, anthropology, art, athletic training, biology, business (management), chemistry, classics, communication studies, computer science, dance, economics, elementary education, English, environmental studies, exercise science, French, German, health, history, intermedia arts, international studies, management, mathematics, mathematics/statistics, music, nursing, philosophy, physical education, physics, political science, psychology, religion, Russian studies, Scandinavian studies, secondary education, social work, sociology, Spanish, theater, wellness, and women's and gender studies. Preprofessional preparation is offered in dentistry, engineering, law, medicine, optometry, pharmacy, physical therapy, and veterinary medicine.

Academic Programs

Luther operates on a 4-1-4 academic calendar. The first semester runs from September to December, followed by a three-week January Term and the second semester, which runs from February to May. Two four-week summer sessions are offered in June and July. All students must complete at least thirty regular courses and two January-term courses in order to graduate from Luther. Other requirements for graduation include four common foundational courses: Paideia (111 and 112); foreign language (typically one or two courses); religion (two courses, one of which must be in biblical studies); and wellness (two 1-credit courses). In addition to a focused area of study (the major, which usually requires eight to ten courses), Luther requires all students to take courses in three general fields of inquiry: the natural world (two courses); human behavior (two courses); and human expression (two courses). Before graduating, students are required to bring together all they have learned in two culminating experiences: senior project (one course); and Paideia 450. Luther students also develop the perspectives and skills they will utilize in their lives as citizens and professionals equipped for distinguished service. A qualified student may develop an interdisciplinary major with a faculty adviser.

Off-Campus Programs

Luther operates under the belief that the best education connects students with global issues and helps them engage with the larger world. Luther is consistently ranked among the top 10 baccalaureate colleges in the nation for the number of students studying abroad prior to graduation.

Luther's off-campus programs not only span the globe, but also offer in-depth and immersive study in a wide variety of subjects. Students may participate in programs during fall and spring semesters, the January Term, and summer sessions.

Luther's signature off-campus programs include an academic-year program in Nottingham, England; a semester program in Sliema, Malta; a semester program in Münster, Germany; and a semester program in Coldigioco, Italy. In addition, Luther is part of a thirteen-college consortium which runs a successful Washington Semester in Washington, D.C. Students also have options for urban study at several centers in Chicago.

Each January Term, 300–400 Luther students study on twenty to twenty-five faculty-led domestic and international programs. Many students appreciate the flexibility of these shorter off-campus experiences; other students use January Term programs as springboards to longer immersion experiences.

Finally, Luther students have a wide variety of off-campus options through Luther-affiliated programs, such as those sponsored by the Associated Colleges of the Midwest, Institute for Study Abroad–Butler University, the Institute for the International Education of Students (IES), and International Studies Abroad (ISA), among others.

Academic Facilities

The 1,000-acre campus includes the Preus Library, housing 330,000 volumes, 700 print periodicals, 75,000 electronic books, and the College art collection. Two science teaching facilities, Sampson Hoffland Laboratories and Valders Hall of Science, feature modern, well-equipped labs as well as a planetarium, a greenhouse, a herbarium, a live-animal center, a human anatomy laboratory, a natural history museum, and a psychology sleep laboratory. Within easy walking distance of the campus, the field study area offers an ideal setting for studies in aquatic biology, ecology, and field biology. Five ponds, two reestablished prairies, marshes, wooded areas, and agricultural lands are available for classwork and independent study. The College has fiber-based and wireless campus networks connecting a variety of PC and Mac computers (in several environments) to shared computing resources and to the Internet. More than 400 microcomputers and terminals are available for student use throughout the campus.

Luther College maintains radio station KWLC-AM, and the College's affiliate station, KLSE-FM, is part of the Minnesota Public Radio network. Luther is also home to the largest archaeological research center in Iowa. The modern language department maintains a twenty-five-station electronic classroom, and the psychology department houses a twenty-station IBM interactive computer network.

The economics and business, mathematics, and computer science departments are located in the impressive F. W. Olin Building, where students can experience simultaneous decision making via a computer network in the Round Table Room.

The award-winning Jenson-Noble Hall of Music contains 32,000 square feet of classrooms, studios, practice rooms, and rehearsal rooms for keyboard, vocal, and instrumental music. The Center for Faith and Life (CFL) houses a 42-stop/62-rank organ in the 1,600-seat auditorium for the performing arts. A 200-seat recital hall, a 24-hour meditation chapel, and one of four campus art galleries are located in the CFL as well. The Center for the Arts serves as the home for theater, dance, and the arts.

Costs

For 2013–14, the comprehensive fee is $43,940, which includes tuition, facilities fees, room, board, subscription to student publications, and admission to College-supported concerts, lectures, and other events. A room telephone, cable TV, computer access from residence hall rooms, and a health-service program are also included. Private music lessons are $425 per semester. It is estimated that an additional $3,000 is adequate for books, clothing, entertainment, and other personal expenses.

Financial Aid

More than 98 percent of all Luther students receive financial aid in the form of grants, scholarships, low-interest loans, and work-study jobs on campus. Luther awards Founders, President's, and Dean's Scholarships to those demonstrating superior academic achievement. The amount of aid given is determined by an analysis of the Free Application for Federal Student Aid (FAFSA).

Faculty

There are 178 full-time faculty members; 93 percent hold a Ph.D., first professional, or other terminal degree. The student-faculty ratio is 12:1.

Student Government

Students share in the governance of the College and participate in social and cultural programming. They have full membership on most College committees, majority representation in the Community Assembly, and nonvoting representation on the Board of Regents.

Admission Requirements

Admission is selective. An applicant must be a graduate of an accredited high school and have completed at least 4 units of English, 3 units of mathematics, 3 units of social science, and 2 units of natural science. It is strongly recommended that the applicant have at least two years of a foreign language. Sixty-one percent of entering students rank in the top quarter of their high school class.

Transfer students may enroll at the beginning of the fall or spring semester or the January term.

Application and Information

An application, SAT or ACT scores, an educator's reference, and a transcript of previous academic work are required for admission. On-campus interviews are recommended but not required. For more information about Luther, students should contact:

Admissions Office
Luther College
700 College Drive
Decorah, Iowa 52101-1042
Phone: 563-387-1287
      800-458-8437 (toll-free)
Fax: 563-387-2159
E-mail: admissions@luther.edu (admissions)
    finaid@luther.edu (financial aid)
    global@luther.edu (international)
Website: http://admissions.luther.edu
    http://www.facebook.com/luthercollege1861
    http://twitter.com/luthercollege

Luther College students learn in a community that emphasizes rigorous academics, a world-class music program, champion athletics, and opportunities to put their classroom learning to the test through internships, independent research, and study abroad. Typically, 96 percent of Luther graduates are employed, attending graduate school, or engaged in an internship or volunteer work within eight months of graduation.

LYNCHBURG COLLEGE
LYNCHBURG, VIRGINIA

The College

Lynchburg College is a fully accredited, coeducational, liberal arts college affiliated with the Christian Church (Disciples of Christ). It offers undergraduate programs in the liberal arts, sciences, and professional disciplines (including business, communications, education, and nursing) and graduate programs in business, education, and nursing. A Doctor of Physical Therapy program (www.lynchburg.edu/dpt) debuted in 2010 followed by a Doctor of Education in Leadership Studies in 2011. Lynchburg College (LC) is committed to the principle that every individual is of infinite worth, and it endeavors to provide a program of liberal arts education consistent with the needs of contemporary society. It draws its undergraduate and graduate student body of approximately 2,800 men and women from thirty-seven states and nine countries. The College community is largely residential, with approximately 75 percent of the full-time undergraduate student body living on campus. Approximately 35 percent of the undergraduates are from out of state. The 214-acre campus has long been considered one of the most beautiful in the South. Thirty-seven buildings of mostly Georgian Colonial design have the majestic Blue Ridge Mountains as a backdrop.

A wide variety of activities is available in the Lynchburg College community: service and honor organizations, including the national Bonner Leaders Program; more than 100 clubs and organizations; three fraternities; and seven sororities, as well as opportunities to participate in dramatic productions, student publications, religious activities, and musical performances. The Outdoor Leadership Program provides adventure-based leadership and team-building opportunities for individuals and groups. Community service (www.lynchburg.edu/volunteering-and-service) is a distinguishing feature of Lynchburg College students, staff, and faculty, who last year contributed more than 70,000 volunteer hours to the community through such projects as Habitat for Humanity, Camp Jaycees, Special Olympics, and other programs, earning the College a place on the President's Higher Education Community Service Honor Roll.

The varsity athletic program (http://athletics.lynchburg.edu) is diverse and includes twenty-one sports. The College participates in NCAA Division III and is a charter member of the Old Dominion Athletic Conference. In addition, the College supports several club sports for men and women. The Turner Athletic Facility includes exercise and fitness areas, a dance studio, and one of the top exercise physiology labs in Virginia.

Thanks to recent renovations, Shellenberger Field is now a state-of-the-art athletic field sporting new artificial turf, an eight-lane track, night lighting, and a 3,000-spectator capacity stadium with chair and bleacher seating. Men's and women's soccer, lacrosse, track and field, and field hockey are played on Shellenberger Field as well as intramural and club sports. Several upgrades have also been made to Moon Field and include a permanent softball outfield fence and new areas for the track and field events of javelin, hammer, shot put, and discus. Fox Field, the baseball field, was updated recently to include batting cages, a press box, and seating for up to 1,000 fans.

Location

Lynchburg College (www.lynchburg.edu) is located in central Virginia, 100 miles from Richmond, 180 miles southwest of Washington, D.C., and 50 miles east of Roanoke. Greater Lynchburg is a growing business and industrial center with a population of more than 240,000. The city is noted for its climate, culture, and historic landmarks. It is within an easy drive of the Blue Ridge Mountains, where many popular lakes and resorts are located. Air, bus, and railroad transportation place Lynchburg within easy reach of any urban center.

Majors and Degrees

Lynchburg College offers the Bachelor of Arts degree in the following fields: accounting, art (graphic design or studio art), business administration, communication studies (convergent journalism, social influence, electronic media or public relations), economics (financial or general), English (literature or writing), French, history, international relations, management, marketing, music (instrumental or vocal education, instrumental or vocal performance), philosophy,

political science, religious studies, sociology (cultural studies, deviance and crime, human services), Spanish, sports management, and theater. The Bachelor of Science degree is offered in the following fields: athletic training, biology, biomedical science, chemistry, computer science, environmental science, exercise physiology, health promotion, human development and learning (elementary education or special education), mathematics, nursing, physics, and psychology. For more information, prospective students should visit www.lynchburg.edu/majors-and-minors.

Pre-professional and professional courses are available for students who want preparation for careers in art therapy, dentistry, engineering, forestry and wildlife management, law, library science, medicine, ministry and ministry-related occupations, occupational therapy, optometry, pharmacy, physical therapy, and veterinary medicine.

Academic Programs

To be eligible for a degree, a student must complete at least 124 semester hours of college-level academic work. In addition, a degree candidate must have a grade point average of at least 2.0 on all work undertaken, plus an average of at least 2.0 or higher depending on the program on all work undertaken in the major field.

The curriculum at Lynchburg College is divided into two general areas: General Education Requirements (GERs) and the Major. General Education Requirements (GERs) are selected from the broad disciplines of world literature, fine arts, philosophy, religious studies, mathematics, history, social science, laboratory science, foreign languages, and health and movement science. All students are exposed to each of these academic areas. The College offers thirty-nine majors, ranging from education and business to the sciences and the humanities; fifty-two minors; as well as thirteen pre-professional programs. This curriculum offers students breadth (GERs) as well as depth (the major). Additional hours are available for students to explore coursework in free elective hours of their choice. Also students may devote their free elective hours to a minor to enhance their education.

Outstanding students may be selected to participate in the College's Westover Honors Program (www.lynchburg.edu/westoverhonors), the purpose of which is to attract, stimulate, challenge, and fulfill academically gifted students. The program offers a challenging curriculum that promotes intellectual curiosity and independent thinking and places strong emphasis on creative problem solving.

The College operates on an early semester calendar. The first semester begins in late August and ends before Christmas, and the second semester runs from mid-January to early May. An optional winter term abroad is also offered.

Lynchburg College offers twenty-three computer labs on campus, outfitted with both PCs and Macs. New students may bring a computer of their own or utilize one of the many available on campus. All students are assigned an email account and have access to the Internet. All residence hall rooms are wired for network access and the Intranet, which serves the College community. Wireless Internet access is available in most areas of the campus.

Off-Campus Programs

Various agency and intercollegiate exchange programs are available. Students may engage in foreign-study programs and are encouraged to do so. In addition, any student who wishes to study abroad may do so as part of the College's study-abroad program (www.lynchburg.edu/study-abroad).

Internships, organized through the Academic and Career Services Office, are available locally, nationally, and internationally (www.lynchburg.edu/career-services). More than 1,000 internships are already established, and new sites are developed each year. Lynchburg College, Randolph College, and Sweet Briar College, as members of the Tri-College Consortium of Virginia, maintain cooperative relationships for sharing facilities and offerings.

Academic Facilities

The Hobbs Science Center provides an outstanding learning environment for students pursuing studies in biology, chemistry, physics, biomedical sciences, environmental science, psychology, mathematics, and computer science. In addition to state-of-the-art research labs, including a cadaver lab, students studying environmental science can utilize the online weather station, GIS and remote sensing software, and digitizer. This facility is also used during the summer by the Virginia Governor's School for Math and Science to provide programming for selected high school students.

Schewel Hall, a $12-million classroom and laboratory facility, houses the School of Business and Economics, the Communication Studies program, foreign languages, performing arts, and multiple venues for students to congregate and study. This 67,000-square-foot facility includes technology-based classrooms, computer laboratories, and specialized teaching-learning settings, including a model stock exchange room, a digital darkroom, and a multimedia development center with television and recording studios. Sydnor Performance Hall seats 250 people for concerts, lectures, and other programs.

The Daura Art Gallery (www.lynchburg.edu/daura-gallery) is the major repository of more than 1,000 works of Pierre Daura, the Catalan-American artist for whom the Gallery is named. Each year, The Daura Gallery features traveling exhibitions throughout the academic year and is the site for the Senior Art Show in which chosen student works are exhibited.

Lynchburg College's Claytor Nature Study Center provides an outdoor classroom and laboratory for hands-on, field-based environmental study and research. Located at the foot of the Blue Ridge Mountains in Bedford County, the Claytor Center was run as a farm from the late 1700s until the mid-1990s, when it was given to the college by A. Boyd Claytor III, a member of the LC Board of Trustees. The property has two small lakes, woodlands, wetlands, grasslands, rare plants, formal gardens, a primitive campground, and 3 miles of hiking trails. Conference, meeting, and retreat facilities are also available at the Center. The land is now managed for environmental conservation and restoration through agreements with the Virginia Outdoors Foundation and the USDA's Natural Resources Conservation Service.

The A. Boyd Claytor III Education and Research Facility, a 7,700-square-foot multipurpose building, offers LC students and regional K–12 students and teachers an ideal location for learning with seminar, laboratory, classroom, conference, and retreat space.

Also located at the Center is the Belk Astronomical Observatory, a 700-square-foot facility that boasts an RC Optical Systems 20-inch (0.51 meter) Truss Ritchey-Chrétien telescope. The facility also includes a 384-square-foot observation deck equipped with twelve piers for mounting smaller telescopes. An observatory control room is equipped with instrumentation that will allow LC to pursue astronomical research in conjunction with other regional colleges and universities.

Costs

For resident students who entered Lynchburg College in the 2012–13 session, total charges were $39,885; this included $31,060 for tuition, $7,880 for room and board, and $945 for student fees (www.lynchburg.edu/undergraduate-admission/tuition-fees).

Financial Aid

Lynchburg College administers a financial aid program of more than $20 million. These resources are awarded to students for meritorious achievement and/or for demonstrated need. Lynchburg College offers academic scholarships (www.lynchburg.edu/financial-aid/scholarships) that range from $3,000 to $14,000 and are based on performance and accomplishments at the high school or community college level. These awards are renewable each year until the student graduates, as long as the recipient maintains a qualifying minimum academic average each year. Students are identified to receive these scholarships through the admission application; no separate application is necessary. Free early aid estimates are available for students. More than 98 percent of last year's entering class received academic and/or need-based financial aid. The average amount of aid received was $23,500.

To determine eligibility for need-based financial aid, the student should complete the Free Application for Federal Student Aid (FAFSA), which may be obtained at most high schools and at the College. The FAFSA results determine the student's eligibility for federally funded grants and loans and other support such as work-study opportunities. In addition, students from Virginia are eligible to apply for the Virginia Tuition Assistance grant.

Faculty

The Lynchburg College faculty has 185 full-time members, 82 percent of whom hold the doctorate or terminal degree in their field. The student-faculty ratio is 12:1. While many faculty members are involved in research projects, it is a College policy that the faculty's top priorities must be in the classroom.

Admission Requirements

A candidate for admission to Lynchburg College (www.lynchburg.edu/undergraduate-admission) should be a graduate of an approved secondary school with a minimum of 16 academic units or the equivalent, as shown by examination. It is required that the academic work include major emphases in the areas of English, foreign language, social science, natural sciences, and mathematics. An applicant must demonstrate above-average academic ability in all areas of study, as admission is competitive. In support of the record, a student must present satisfactory scores on the ACT or SAT (critical reading and math scores are used to determine admission decisions and merit scholarship awards). It is recommended that all students have a personal interview and visit the campus beginning the spring semester of their junior year or during their senior year. Enrollment Office hours during the academic year are 9 to 5 Monday through Friday and 10 to noon on Saturday during the academic year.

Application and Information

Early decision admission applications must be received by November 15 (www.lynchburg.edu/undergraduate-admission/freshman-application-steps); notification of acceptance is made by December 15. All other applications are processed on a rolling admissions basis. Applicants are notified of the status of their application usually within two to four weeks of the date their application file is completed.

For information, students should contact:

Sharon Walters-Bower, Director of Admissions
Lynchburg College
1501 Lakeside Drive
Lynchburg, Virginia 24501
Phone: 434-544-8300
      800-426-8101 (toll-free)
Fax: 434-544-8653
E-mail: admissions@lynchburg.edu
Website: http://www.lynchburg.edu
      http://www.facebook.com/lynchburgcollege
      http://twitter.com/lynchburg
      http://www.youtube.com/lynchburgcollege
      http://www.flickr.com/photos/lynchburgcollege

Schewel Hall is a popular campus meeting place housing classrooms, meeting and study rooms, and technology studios like the multi-camera television studio and digital control room.

LYNDON STATE COLLEGE
LYNDONVILLE, VERMONT

The College

This small college shines a bright light. For the 1,400 students who come here from Vermont, New England, and around the world, Lyndon State College (LSC) offers a hands-on, experiential education, nationally recognized professional programs, and an incredibly friendly atmosphere—all leading directly to rewarding careers or graduate study. Recent grads enjoy a 93 percent job or graduate school placement rate within six months of graduation.

The hallmark of a Lyndon education is experiential learning, starting as freshmen with the first-year experience; one- or two-day hands-on activities that serve as an introduction to a chosen major. New students can be confident that they are pursuing the right field of study while rubbing shoulders with faculty members and other students in their department.

A Lyndon education can take students anywhere. There are more than 30 LSC alumni at ESPN. Lyndon's meteorology grads are famously found everywhere there's weather; The Weather Channel's Jim Cantore is a graduate and returns to campus every fall to teach the next generation of LSC broadcast meteorologists. Graduates of Lyndon's Mountain Recreation Management program—the first program of its kind in the country—are national leaders in the winter resort and recreation industry. The 2011 U.S. Small Businessperson of the Year graduated from Lyndon in 2006.

This is all a result of the real-world experiences students can immerse themselves in at Lyndon. Music business and industry interns can be found working on concert tours for world-famous musician. Lyndon atmospheric sciences regularly take first place in national forecasting competitions. Electronic journalism arts students routinely win national awards for their daily live news broadcasts—including a coveted Emmy™ award for the nation's best college newscast.

Campus events range from the intellectual to the physical, with abundant opportunities for learning and fun. A rich mix of comedy, music, speakers, theater, performing arts, film, off-campus travel, adventure programming, and community service is offered by the College to enrich life outside the classroom. The College's popular music business and industry program guarantees a lively live music scene. First-run films are shown in the campus theater twice a week. Traditions from far to near—from Guatemala, India, and Russia to Vermont sugar-on-snow parties—are part of Lyndon's diverse campus culture.

There are more than thirty student organizations including the campus radio station (91.5 FM The Impulse); an award-winning student newspaper (The Critic, www.lyndonstatecritic.com); theater group (Twilight Players); and numerous sports, social, service, and academic clubs.

Lyndon competes in NCAA Division III athletics in baseball, basketball, cross-country, lacrosse, soccer, softball, tennis, and volleyball. LSC's cross-country squads are perennial champs. Intercollege club sports include hockey and rugby. The majority of Lyndon's students participate in an intramural sport. More sports information can be found online at http://www.lyndonhornets.com.

Lyndon is Vermont's adventure recreation campus. On campus there's an indoor climbing center, ice climbing on "Fountain Mountain," eighteen holes of disc golf, two ropes courses, a terrain park, biking and hiking trails, and a new skate park. Students canoe, kayak, paddleboard, skate, play hockey, fish, and "spring dip" in and on the College's three ponds. Nearby there's skiing and snowboarding at Burke Mountain and Jay Peak. Kingdom Trails, a 100-mile network consistently rated as

the finest bike trail system in the Eastern United States, is just 10 minutes from campus (and was created by alums of LSC's recreation department).

There are ten residence halls, including a new 132-unit, apartment-style hall for juniors and seniors. Each room is equipped with Internet, cable TV, and telephone. Students who live on campus eat at the Stevens Dining Hall and the Hornet's Nest Snack Bar. All students are allowed to have vehicles on campus.

Location

The modern 174-acre campus is located in Lyndonville, Vermont, high on a hillside overlooking Burke Mountain in the heart of Vermont's scenic Northeast Kingdom, a *National Geographic*–designated geotourism area. It is easily accessible from all points by Interstate 91, a 3-hour drive from Boston and Springfield, Massachusetts, and 2.5 hours from Montreal. Additional information on the area can be found at http://www.nekchamber.com.

Majors and Degrees

Lyndon offers bachelor's degrees in accounting, animation and illustration, applied psychology/human services, atmospheric sciences/meteorology, business administration, cinema/video production, computing, criminal justice, design for print and web, elementary education, electronic journalism arts/television studies, English, environmental science, exercise science, liberal studies, natural science, mathematics, mountain recreation management, music business and industry, philosophy, professional media communications, secondary education (English, mathematics, natural sciences, and social sciences), sports management, sustainability studies, and visual communications.

Associate degrees are offered in applied science, business administration, computing, electronic journalism arts/television studies, general studies, human services, music business and industry, professional media communications, special education, visual arts, and visual communications.

There are graduate programs in education and liberal studies.

Academics

Lyndon was established in 1911 as a one-room teacher-training college with 3 students. Teacher training is still a big part of the picture, but today, LSC is best known for innovative professional programs that combine real-world experience with a traditional education in the liberal arts.

Lyndon operates on a two-semester calendar plus a six-week summer-session. To graduate with a bachelor's degree, students must complete 122 hours of credit and meet College and program requirements. Sixty-two semester hours are required for associate degrees. Incoming students are tested for competence in writing and mathematics; deficiencies must be made up in noncredit classes during the first two semesters.

Lyndon's Academic Support Center, Career Planning and Placement Office, Financial Aid Office, Student Life, and Health Services are just some of the entities that serve the needs and promote the well-being of students. Complete information can be found at www.lyndonstate.edu/degree-programs.

Off-Campus Programs

Off-campus study is part of the curriculum in all majors in the form of paid and unpaid internships, site visits, hands-on projects, research, independent study, and/or field trips.

Lyndon grants credit for study in other countries through an approved program such as the Experiment in International Living or the American Institute for Foreign Study. Lyndon offers faculty- and staff-accompanied trips each semester to places such as Greece, Russia, Ecuador, England, China, Guatemala, Kenya, and many other countries of personal and academic interest.

Academic Facilities

Lyndon State College offers a modern, well-equipped campus. There are smart classrooms, two lecture halls, six computer classrooms, six science labs, and two general computer labs. There is a digital media, graphic design, video editing, and photo lab; a GIS-mapping lab; comprehensive weather center, atmospheric science lab, and observation deck; two exercise science labs; a recording studio/music business and industry lab; an instructional materials center for education majors; a psychology lab and reading lab; and LSC TV's News7 broadcast production studio. The Alexander Twilight Theatre and ASAC 100 Conference Hall provide flexible space for gatherings, activities, and performances of all kinds.

The library maintains a collection of more than 110,000 circulating volumes as well as periodicals, audio and video materials, and microfiche collections.

Costs

The 2013–14 tuition for Vermont residents is $9,312 per year; for nonresidents, it is $19,968. The NEBHE regional program allows for a $6,000 discount for New England students in eligible programs (program eligibility by state can be found at www.lyndonstate. edu/NEBHE); $5,000 discount for eligible New Hampshire and many New York students regardless of program. Room and board (21-meal plan) for one academic year is $9,138. Required College fees, not including health and accident insurance, total $974. Total expenses for a Vermont resident living on campus are $19,724; for a nonresident, $30,380. Miscellaneous expenses were estimated at $1,100. Complete information on costs can be found at www.lyndonstate.edu/tuition.

Financial Aid

Financial aid is available in the form of loans, grants, and campus employment under the Federal Work-Study Program. Approximately 85 percent of the student population receives some type of financial aid from institutional and outside sources. Approximately 35 percent of students are employed by either the Federal Work-Study Program or the Lyndon dining hall.

Applicants for aid are required to complete the Free Application for Federal Student Aid (FAFSA). In addition to filing the FAFSA, transfer students are required to have a financial aid transcript completed by the financial aid officer of each college they attended.

Faculty

Lyndon's faculty consists of 155 members, 95 percent of whom hold the highest degree in their field from research institutions such as Harvard, Columbia, Yale, and USC. Many of Lyndon's professors have come to Lyndon to teach following prestigious careers at corporations and organizations such as CNN, National Public Radio, and Hewlett-Packard. Some are successful entrepreneurs, offering real world expertise to back up their classroom teaching.

Faculty members serve as academic advisers and mentors to students and student organizations. Student evaluation of teaching is a formal process and is used in personnel decisions.

Student Government

Students actively represent Lyndon on the Vermont State Colleges' Board of Trustees, in the Vermont State Colleges' Student Association, and on many campus committees. The Student Senate heads the student organizations.

Admission Requirements

Lyndon emphasizes academic success as reflected on high school or college transcripts, and social and academic potential as reflected in letters of recommendation. Lyndon seeks applicants whose academic record reveals maturity and motivation as well as a sense of responsibility and leadership.

Entrance requirements include 4 years of English and 2 to 3 years each of mathematics, science, and history. Foreign language is desired. International students seeking to attend Lyndon can find detailed information on the College's website. The SAT is required. Complete information about admissions requirements is available at www.LyndonState.edu/apply.

Admission requirements for transfer students are the same as those for freshman applicants, but an official transcript must also be obtained from each college-level institution that the applicant has attended. Transcripts are required even if no credit is being transferred from a particular institution. Transfer credit may be given at Lyndon for all courses completed with the equivalent of a grade of C or higher at accredited or officially approved institutions.

Application and Information

Interested prospective students can apply online at www. LyndonState.edu/apply. A nonrefundable $44 fee must accompany each application. First-year applicants who are unable to afford the application fee should complete the paper application and ask their guidance counselor to sign a College Board fee waiver, or print a copy of the NACAC application fee waiver and ask their counselor to complete it. When these forms are ready, prospective students should mail them to Lyndon, along with their application, all transcripts of academic work completed, and their board scores. Lyndon State College accepts the Common Application.

For further information, students should contact:

Office of Admissions
Lyndon State College
P.O. Box 919
Lyndonville, Vermont 05851
Phone: 800-225-1998 (toll-free)
Fax: 802-626-6335
E-mail: admissions@lyndonstate.edu
Website: http://www.lyndonstate.edu

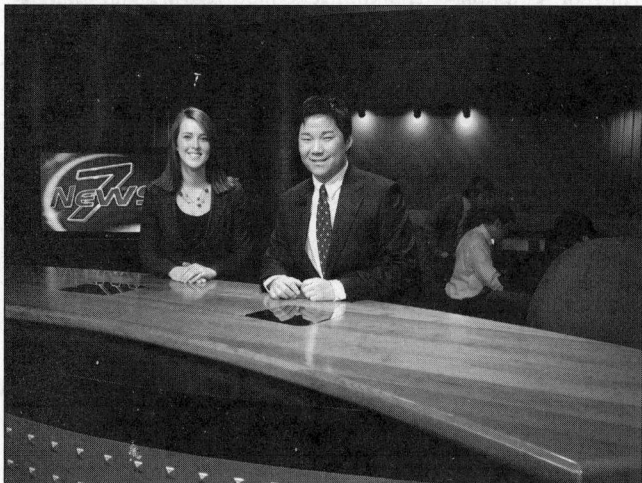

Students on the set of Lyndon's award-winning News 7. Since 2004, the student-produced daily newscasts have garnered forty-four regional and national awards, including an Emmy for the nation's best college newscast.

MANHATTAN COLLEGE
RIVERDALE, NEW YORK

The College

Manhattan College has more than sixty programs that build upon a strong liberal arts foundation and offer professional preparation in arts, business, education, science, and engineering. Learning extends beyond the classroom through internships in New York City and beyond.

The College is one of only a few U.S. colleges to have chapters of all five of these distinguished national honor societies: Phi Beta Kappa, Beta Gamma Sigma, Kappa Delta Pi, Sigma Xi, and Beta Pi.

Manhattan placed nineteenth among 850 U.S. colleges and universities on the Payscale.com 2012 Return on Investment (ROI) Rankings: College Education Value Compared survey, which demonstrates the long-term professional success of Manhattan graduates.

Following in the Lasallian Catholic tradition, many Manhattan College students actively define their commitment to social justice by balancing their traditional lifestyles with immersion and service experiences around the city, country, and world.

Each year, Campus Ministry and Social Action (CMSA) organizes several L.O.V.E. programs (Lasallian Outreach Volunteer Experience), which give students the opportunity to travel to some of the world's poorest areas in New Orleans, Kenya, Ecuador, the Dominican Republic, and West Virginia and volunteer with people of very different socioeconomic backgrounds.

Manhattan College Jaspers do not have to travel far to lend a helping hand. The Lasallian Collegians group volunteers on campus and in New York City by arranging school blood drives, toy drives, soup kitchen trips, and food runs. In addition, the Arches, a new learning-living resident program, offers first-year students the opportunity to live in community, attend two classes together, and experience New York City through service projects in the city.

The tight-knit College community is comprised of 3,500 students. With a 12:1 student-to-faculty ratio, professors know students personally and care about their success. The majority of students live on the traditional collegiate campus, which is just a subway ride from New York City.

Location

Manhattan College's 22-acre campus is located 10 miles north of midtown Manhattan in the suburban Riverdale section of the Bronx, about a mile from Westchester County. The College is located in the world's greatest cultural hub, where renowned museums and landmarks serve as off-campus classrooms. Students have access to internship and job opportunities at some of the country's most prestigious companies.

Majors and Degrees

Arts: The liberal arts curriculum of the School of Arts provides programs that lead to a Bachelor of Arts or Bachelor of Science degree with majors in the humanities and the social sciences, including communication, economics, English, fine arts, French, government, history, labor studies, modern foreign languages, philosophy, psychology, religious studies, and sociology. Interdisciplinary majors include international studies, peace studies, and urban studies.

Science: In the School of Science, programs lead to a Bachelor of Science or Bachelor of Arts degree with majors in biochemistry, biology, chemistry, computer science, mathematics, and physics. Pre-medical, pre-dental, and pre–veterinary studies programs are also available.

Engineering: The School of Engineering has a well-deserved reputation as one of the best college engineering schools in the nation and offers programs leading to a Bachelor of Science degree in chemical, civil, computer, electrical, and mechanical engineering. The program is fully accredited by the Educational Accreditation Commission of ABET. Graduate programs are also available in chemical, civil, computer, electrical, environmental, and mechanical engineering.

Business: The School of Business, accredited by AACSB International, has programs leading to a Bachelor of Science in Business Administration degree with majors in accounting, computer information systems, economics, finance, global business studies, management, and marketing. In addition, Manhattan College also offers the following graduate programs: the Bachelor of Science in Professional Accounting/Master of Business Administration and the Bachelor of Science in Business/Master of Business Administration, which offer students the opportunity to complete a five-year multiple award program.

Education and Health: The School of Education and Health offers a curriculum leading to a Bachelor of Arts degree in childhood education, childhood/special education (dual program), and adolescent education. The physical education curriculum leads to a Bachelor of Science degree in physical education and exercise science. The health curriculum leads to a Bachelor of Science degree in allied health, with a concentration in health-care administration, health counseling, or scientific foundations. Curricula in radiological and health sciences lead to a Bachelor of Science in radiation therapy or nuclear medicine technology. In addition, the School of Education and Health offers the five-year childhood/special education program, which allows the student to receive a bachelor's and master's degree with eligibility to pursue certification for grades 1–6 in regular and special education. The School of Education and Health also offers master's degrees and professional diplomas in school counseling, mental health counseling, special education, and school building leadership. All programs are approved by the New York State Education Department and accredited by the Teacher Education Accreditation Council (TEAC).

Academic Programs

The core curriculum shared by the School of Arts and the School of Science studies some of the vital works of humankind, explores new ideas, examines the meaning of scientific experimentation, and encourages a student to develop his or her thinking and leadership abilities. The major programs offer advanced work in specific humanistic and scientific disciplines and opportunities to work on research projects in collaboration with faculty scholars.

In the School of Engineering, all engineering students follow a common core curriculum during the first two years and choose a major at the beginning of the junior year. Each curriculum includes a generous selection of courses in basic sciences, the engineering sciences, humanistic studies, and mathematics.

The School of Business prepares students for positions of executive responsibility in business, government, and nonprofit organizations. The business curriculum is based on a strong commitment to liberal education and is well balanced between professional business courses, humanities, sciences, and social sciences. This is a reflection of the school's belief that executives should be broadly educated and should involve themselves, as well as their organizations, in efforts to solve social problems.

The School of Education and Health prepares students for teaching, counseling, and health professions. Students complete the College's core curriculum in liberal arts and sciences and then complete a major in various programs in the school's three departments: education, physical education and exercise science, and radiological and health professions. All programs include internships/practicums in schools, hospitals, or other institutions. Graduates of the school's teacher-preparation programs receive New York State provisional teaching certification. The school also offers a five-year B.A./M.S. program in childhood/special education and special education.

Off-Campus Programs

Manhattan College also offers summer study-abroad programs in many countries; arrangements can be made to study in a country of choice. Students in the School of Business may participate in the International Field Studies Seminar. As participants, they spend time in another country studying the effect of that environment on international firms. Career services and co-op education integrate classroom theory with the practical experience of a job in industry, business, the social services, the arts, or government. Portions of the education courses are conducted in New York City schools, so that student teachers may gain experience in urban education at an early stage.

Academic Facilities

There are more than forty scientific and engineering laboratories at Manhattan, including the Research and Learning Center, as well as a modern language laboratory and a computer information systems laboratory. Manhattan's newly built O'Malley Library is a state-of-the-art facility featuring modern accommodations for study and research.

Both commuters and residents can take advantage of the College's fitness center and newly renovated cafeterias. They have a variety of eating options, as well as spaces to relax and enjoy a snack while watching large screen televisions. The Commuter Lounge serves as a crossroads for students between classes while on campus.

Costs

For 2013–14, the tuition for Manhattan College is $33,000 per year plus program fee. Room and board for the year is $13,080.

Financial Aid

Manhattan grants or administers financial assistance in the form of tuition awards to students on the basis of need and/or ability. Need is evaluated by submitting the FAFSA. In addition to a merit scholarship fund, Manhattan offers endowed scholarships, special category scholarships and grants, student athletic grants, Federal Pell Grants, Federal Supplemental Educational Opportunity Grants, student loans, Federal Work-Study Program awards, and New York State financial assistance are also available to students who qualify. More than one-third of all students receive merit aid with 88 percent of the students receiving aid.

Faculty

Manhattan's faculty has 210 full-time faculty members. Ninety-five percent of the faculty members hold doctorates. Faculty members serve on the college senate, the council for faculty affairs, and numerous faculty and campus committees. They are available to students for informal guidance and counseling and also serve as official moderators of many campus organizations.

Admission Requirements

Manhattan has a long-standing policy of nondiscrimination. No applicant is refused admission because of race, color, religion, age, national origin, sex, or disability. All applicants must present an academic diploma from an accredited high school and must offer a minimum of 16 credits in academic subjects. Liberal arts candidates must be proficient in at least one foreign language. At the discretion of the Committee on Admissions,

quantitative requirements may be modified for applicants with especially strong records who show promise of doing well in college. In the selection process, attention is given to scholastic ability, as indicated by grades and rank in class, as well as to standardized test scores and recommendations from teachers and counselors. All candidates must submit either SAT or ACT results. An interview with a member of the admission staff can be arranged but is not required. Applicants may submit scores on the General Educational Development test in lieu of a formal high school diploma; however, all such applicants must submit the results of the appropriate College Board tests. Manhattan College offers early acceptance for high school seniors, admission to advanced standing, advanced placement, and credit by examination. Junior college or other transfer students are welcome. Manhattan College requires applicants whose native language is not English to take the Test of English as a Foreign Language (TOEFL), the SAT, or ACT exam. The average SAT scores of entering freshmen in 2012 were 535 in mathematics and 526 in the verbal portion.

Application and Information

Application forms are furnished by the Admission Office on request and available on the Manhattan College website. The Common Application, which is available in many high school guidance offices and online, may also be used. Students must send the application to the admission office at Manhattan College. The high school report, recommendation letters, and transcript must be submitted by the high school guidance counselor. This should be done after six terms of high school or right after the seventh term. There is a rolling admissions policy and a March 1 deadline for financial aid applications. A nonrefundable application fee of $60 is required.

For more information, contact:

William J. Bisset
Vice President for Enrollment Management
Manhattan College
Riverdale, New York 10471
United States
Phone: 718-862-7200
        800-MC2-XCEL (toll-free)
E-mail: admit@manhattan.edu
Website: http://www.manhattan.edu

Manhattan College centers a great deal of its campus activity around the main quadrangle.

MANHATTANVILLE COLLEGE
PURCHASE, NEW YORK

The College

While the 100 beautiful acres that make up Manhattanville are located in a quiet suburban setting, the culture, entertainment, and excitement of New York City are only 30 miles away. The private coeducational college founded in 1841 draws its 1,700 students from fifty-one countries and thirty-three states. Manhattanville College is ranked in the *Princeton Review* and *Newsweek* as one of the best colleges for undergraduate study. Manhattanville College has created a small global village. This richly diverse community embodies the College's mission: to educate students to be ethical and socially responsible leaders in a global community.

Learning is at the heart of Manhattanville, and the College's proximity to New York City creates a constant flow of opportunity that brings learning to life. Manhattanville students know how to have fun, but they also have a sense of purpose. The College's social conscience is informed by a commitment to serving the community. The Corporation for National and Community Service has named Manhattanville College in the 2013 President's Higher Education Community Service Honor Roll for excellent services. The Duchesne Center serves as the coordinator and catalyst for service learning, community outreach, culture, and leadership across the College campus and around the world. Last year, students participated in 30,000 hours of community service. Manhattanville students actively seek opportunities to serve humanitarian causes in the developing world.

Manhattanville's global perspective is enriched by its role as a Non-Governmental Organization of the United Nations. Select students have an opportunity to intern at the UN and to study with an ambassador.

Location

Manhattanville's campus lies in the heart of Westchester County, bordered on the east by Long Island Sound and on the west by the Hudson River. From the roof of Reid Castle, which serves as the campus's main hall, the skyline of Manhattan is visible. This proximity to the city that calls itself the "Capital of the World" is one of Manhattanville's many assets. The College provides free transportation to the city on Saturdays and to Manhattan-bound commuter trains seven days a week so students can take advantage of all New York City has to offer.

Majors and Degrees

Manhattanville College offers undergraduate degrees in more than fifty academic concentrations in the arts and sciences, including Bachelor of Arts (B.A.), Bachelor of Science (B.S.), Bachelor of Fine Arts (B.F.A.), and Bachelor of Music (B.Mus.) degrees; a self-designed major; a double major with teacher certification; and preparation for professional and graduate study (prelaw, premedical, pre–physical therapy, and pre–speech language pathology).

Students may choose from the following areas of study: African studies, American studies, art history, art (studio), Asian studies, biochemistry, biology, chemistry, classical civilizations, communications studies, computer science, creative writing, dance and theater, dance therapy, economics, education, English, environmental studies, film studies, finance, French, German, history, Holocaust and genocide studies, human resource management, international management, international studies, Irish studies, Italian, Latin American studies, legal studies, management, mathematics, museum studies, music, music education, music management, musical theater, music technology, neuroscience, philosophy, political science, prelaw, premedical, pre–physical therapy, pre–speech language pathology, psychology,

self-designed major, social justice, sociology, Spanish, sport studies, theater education, women's studies, world literature, and world religions.

This listing can be found online at http://www.Manhattanville.edu/AcademicMajors.

Academic Programs

Manhattanville College offers full-time, part-time, and accelerated opportunities for study as well as dual-degree programs. The Manhattanville curriculum nurtures intellectual curiosity and independent thinking. Students and professors form close collaborative relationships beginning with the Preceptorial, an interdisciplinary survey of the liberal arts that is required of all freshmen.

The core of the Manhattanville curriculum is the Portfolio System, which provides for a level of flexibility that is unusual in traditional liberal arts education. Under the guidance of a faculty adviser, the student maps an academic and co-curricular program, establishing a major and minor from different branches of the liberal arts. The student may begin studies in the chosen field as early as the freshman year. Over the course of four years of study, the student assembles a portfolio consisting of study plans, evidence of academic proficiency in written critical analysis and qualitative research, annual evaluations, transcripts, and examples of the student's best work. A College-wide review board evaluates the portfolio. The Portfolio system is used as a teaching and learning tool.

A special option for B.A. candidates is the self-designed major. If a student's interests direct them beyond existing departmental majors, they may propose a program of study to the Board of Academic Standards. Manhattanville students also have the opportunity to earn academic credit for internships in New York City.

Manhattanville College offers college credit for A-level exams, International Baccalaureate, and Advanced Placement examinations.

Off-Campus Programs

Manhattanville offers more than 100 study-abroad opportunities through either direct exchange programs or study-abroad providers at various levels of language proficiency, including Argentina, Belgium (internship at the European Union), Chile, England, France, Germany, Ireland, Italy, Japan, South Africa, Mexico, and Spain, among others. There is also a world of over 450 domestic and international internship possibilities with leading groups such as Apple, Condé Nast, IBM, and MasterCard.

Academic Facilities

The Manhattanville Library capitalizes on the power of the Internet to connect students with information and analysis found in powerful subscription databases, electronic journals, and electronic books. Manhattanville is one of the first colleges in the U.S. to outsource a service that enables students to interact online with experienced reference librarians at any time of the day or night from anywhere in the world. The virtual research service, "Ask a Librarian 24/7," uses co-browsing to connect students with professional librarians who can answer questions about research and help students navigate the College's extensive array of subscription databases and other library resources. Manhattanville's teaching library, which supports the School of Education, ranks among the foremost undergraduate teaching libraries in the country. The Menendez Language Laboratory includes videos and record libraries that provide materials for class instruction and individual practice in

French, Spanish, Russian, Italian, German, Chinese, Japanese, Hindi, Marathi, Modern Hebrew, and English as a second language. The College provides a writing clinic, a reading clinic, audiovisual facilities, and a bibliographic instruction program. The library building is open 24 hours a day, seven days a week through most of the fall and spring semesters, and it has computer labs, quiet study areas, group-study rooms, and a café where students and faculty members can meet informally.

Among the College's other academic facilities and resources are the art studio, science laboratories, the performing arts facilities, and student media facilities.

The College has state-of-the-art computers, computer labs, and campus networking for student use and instruction. In addition, advanced music technology systems offer performing arts students limitless opportunities for creativity.

Costs

For the 2013–14 academic year, tuition is $34,020 and the average room and board costs are $14,524.

Financial Aid

Manhattanville College offers both merit scholarships and need-based financial aid. Nearly 80 percent of students receive financial awards. The Free Application for Federal Student Aid (FAFSA) is required. The types of awards available are honors, merit, arts, and community service scholarships; Manhattanville grants and scholarships; Federal Perkins Loans; Federal Stafford Student Loans; Federal Pell Grants; Federal Supplemental Educational Opportunity Grants; Federal Work-Study Program awards; and Tuition Assistance Program awards.

For scholarship information and advice about financial aid eligibility, prospective students should visit www.manhattanville. edu, click on Undergraduate, and then click on Cost and Aid.

Faculty

Nearly 90 percent of faculty members have Ph.D. or terminal degrees in their fields. Many faculty members live on the campus. The Manhattanville curriculum nurtures intellectual curiosity and independent thinking. The student-faculty ratio of 16:1 promotes close and collaborative relationships between faculty members and students, aided by the structure of the curriculum and the Portfolio System, which fosters collaboration between student and faculty adviser. Faculty members, not teaching assistants, teach all Manhattanville classes, and 84 percent of the classes have 20 or fewer students.

Student Government

Students in large measure shape the quality of life on the Manhattanville campus. Elected representatives of the student body run the student government, which serves as a principal means of communication among the administration, faculty members, and students. Its board of directors is responsible for formulating policy on student life and for implementing this policy through various committees. Student government members also serve on the College's policymaking and ad hoc committees.

Admission Requirements

Manhattanville College admits candidates for undergraduate degrees if their academic records indicate a competence to engage in a challenging liberal arts curriculum. Admission to the College is selective, and the most important consideration is the student's secondary school performance. When weighing this aspect, the admissions committee evaluates the quality of the school, the strength of the student's program, and success in those studies. Next, the committee considers the various recommendations that are submitted on behalf of the student, along with standardized test scores if submitted (Manhattanville is a test-optional institution) and the student's personal statement. A campus interview is strongly recommended. Students who plan to specialize in music or dance and theater should come to Manhattanville for an audition or should secure permission to submit a DVD. Students who plan to apply for the B.F.A. degree program should present portfolios to the art department for evaluation. Students who plan to study in these areas may audition for scholarships.

Application and Information

Applying is straightforward—Manhattanville College is a Common Application exclusive institution: submit the completed application, official high school transcript, letters of recommendation, a personal statement, the Manhattanville Supplement form, and optional SAT or ACT scores. Transfer applicants should submit an official transcript from each school attended. Admission is rolling with a priority deadline of March 1. Early decision deadline is December 1. For details, students should visit http://mville.edu/ UndergraduateAdmissions or contact the College via e-mail at admissions@mville.edu or by phone at 800-328-4553 (toll-free) or 914-323-5464.

The College subscribes to the Candidates Reply Date. Applications should be submitted as early in the senior year as possible. Candidates may apply online at www.manhattanville.edu.

Manhattanville College is committed to equality of educational opportunity, and is an equal opportunity employer. The College does not discriminate against current or prospective students and employees on the basis of race, color, sex, national and ethnic origin, religion, age, disability, or any other legally protected characteristic. This College policy is implemented in educational and admissions policies, scholarship and loan programs, athletic and other school-administered programs, and in employee-related programs.

For further information, students should contact:

Office of Undergraduate Admissions
Manhattanville College
2900 Purchase Street
Purchase, New York 10577
United States
Phone: 914-323-5464
800-32-VILLE (toll-free)
E-mail: admissions@mville.edu
Website: http://www.manhattanville.edu
           http://www.facebook.com/Manhattanville
           http://www.twitter.com/Mville_College

Reid Hall (The Castle) is the centerpiece of the Manhattanville College campus.

MARYMOUNT MANHATTAN COLLEGE
NEW YORK, NEW YORK

MarymountManhattan
a college of the liberal arts

The College

Marymount Manhattan College (MMC) is an urban, independent, coeducational, undergraduate liberal arts college. The mission of the College is to educate a socially and economically diverse population by fostering intellectual achievement and personal growth and by providing opportunities for career development. Inherent in this mission is the intent to develop an awareness of social, political, cultural, and ethical issues in the belief that this awareness will lead to concern for, participation in, and the improvement of society. To accomplish this mission, the College offers a strong program in the arts and sciences to students of all ages, as well as substantial preprofessional preparation. Central to these efforts is the particular attention given to the individual student. Marymount Manhattan College also seeks to be a resource and learning center for the metropolitan community.

The social and extracurricular life of the student body of approximately 2,000 students centers on more than forty clubs and organizations sponsored through the Office of Student Development and Activities, including the Go Green Coalition, Psychology Club, French Club, Philosophy Club, Science Society, Black and Latino Student Organization, the student newspaper and yearbook, WMMC Radio, Student Government Association, intramural sports, and other special interest organizations. Students attend musical events, and MMC's own off-Broadway theater, the only one on the Upper East Side of Manhattan, offers students an opportunity to participate in student productions.

The Office of Residence Life at Marymount Manhattan College is committed to providing residents with numerous opportunities and experiences that foster intellectual achievement and social and personal growth. Students are encouraged to become involved in the many activities that are sponsored by Residence Life and are assisted with assuming responsibility for their own lives and living environment. The College provides housing for approximately 750 students at the 55th Street Residence Hall and at 1760, located on Third Avenue and East 97th Street. The buildings offer suite-style, traditional dormitories, or apartment-style living, with classrooms, lounges, a laundry room, and rehearsal space. Additional off-campus facilities are obtained as needed.

The Office of Career Development and Internships serves the entire College community by providing an integrated program of academic and career counseling. The office helps students by offering internship opportunities and workshops in job placement, resume writing, and graduate school preparation. Other College services include personal and financial aid counseling and campus ministry.

Location

Marymount Manhattan College is centrally located on Manhattan's Upper East Side at 221 East 71st Street between Second and Third avenues. Within walking distance of the campus are the Frick, Metropolitan, Whitney, and Guggenheim museums; the Asian Society, French Institute, and National Audubon Society; Central Park; New York Hospital and Sloan-Kettering Research Center; and public libraries. All forms of public transportation are easily accessible. Within minutes of the College are shops, restaurants, and movie theaters. This location gives students the opportunity to take advantage of New York City's rich culture and to explore a variety of neighborhoods.

Majors and Degrees

Marymount Manhattan College offers programs leading to the Bachelor of Arts (B.A.), Bachelor of Science (B.S.), and Bachelor of Fine Arts (B.F.A.) degrees. Majors are offered in accounting, acting, art (concentrations in art history, graphic design, photography, and studio art), biology, business, business management, communication arts, dance, English and world literatures, history, interdisciplinary studies, international studies, philosophy and religious studies, political science, psychology, sociology, speech-language pathology

and audiology, and theater arts. Minors offered are accounting, art history, arts management, art therapy, Asian studies, biology, business management, chemistry, creative writing, drama therapy, economics, English and world literatures, environmental studies, forensic psychology, French and Francophone studies, gender and sexuality studies, graphic design, Hispanic studies, history, international studies, journalism, justice studies, mathematics, media studies, music, musical theater, neuroscience, philosophy, photography, political economy, political science, promotional and professional communication, psychology, religious studies, sociology, social work, speech-language pathology and audiology, studio art, and theater.

Academic Programs

Marymount Manhattan College has designed its programs to enable students to meet the challenges of contemporary society. MMC is committed to the belief that a liberal arts education provides students with the ability and the flexibility to manage change and with broad understanding and the communication and problem-solving skills that are essential for success in any career and in life. To accomplish its goals, the College offers a liberal arts education, integrated with preprofessional training opportunities and individualized attention. The curricula are organized into five divisions: humanities, fine and performing arts, sciences, social sciences, and business management. Also offered are special-interest sequences that complement the student's major and minor, with added concentration in such areas as art history, creative writing, finance and investments, international business, marketing, photography, pre-dentistry, pre-law, pre-medicine, pre–veterinary science, and social work. The College's small size provides students with an individually planned academic career, reflects students' academic needs and interests, and supports their career goals.

Candidates for the B.A., B.S., and B.F.A. degrees must complete 120 credits. To qualify for a degree, a student must maintain an overall scholastic average of at least 2.0. Requirements for certificate programs vary.

The College recognizes various types of nontraditional credit, including credit for acceptable scores on the Advanced Placement (AP), International Baccalaureate (I.B.), College-Level Examination Program (CLEP), and New York State College Proficiency Examination (CPE) tests and credit for life experience.

MMC encourages its students to participate in internship programs in New York City at hospitals, financial institutions, magazines, publishing houses, media firms, art galleries, museums, and off-Broadway theaters.

Off-Campus Programs

The College's Academic Year Abroad offers an opportunity for students to broaden their educational experience and to gain cultural perspectives through study at other colleges in the Americas and overseas. Students may spend one or both semesters of their junior year in this program. MMC summer sessions and January inter-sessions also offer students opportunities in travel/study-abroad courses in Egypt, France, Great Britain, Greece, Eastern Europe, Ireland, Italy, Russia, Spain, and many others.

Academic Facilities

The Thomas J. Shanahan Library at MMC is a library/learning center. It contains more than 100,000 volumes in open stacks and maintains an extensive periodical collection. The media center, on the main library floor, houses nonprint materials, microfiche, microfilm, filmstrips, slides, tapes, videotapes, DVDs, and records. Through the library's affiliation with the New York Metropolitan Reference and Research Library Agency, MMC faculty members and students have access to the materials of the member libraries. The library also participates in the Online Computer Library Center (OCLC), a computerized database of the holdings of some

4,000 libraries that is currently being used for cataloging and reference purposes.

The modern 250-seat Theresa Lang Theatre has a special acoustical design, a sprung dance floor, a full technical balcony with equipment for lighting and sound, thirty-five counterweighted-line sets in the fly system, dressing rooms, and a scene shop. Students benefit from exposure to the numerous professional dance, opera, and theatrical groups that perform at the College.

Top-notch laboratory facilities strengthen education in two areas in which MMC has always excelled—science and communication arts.

MMC's science facilities in biology, chemistry, and physics underwent a total reconstruction valued at close to $1 million, thanks to the generosity of the Samuel Freeman Charitable Trust and the Ira De Camp Foundation. The Samuel Freeman Science Center opens many new doors of opportunity to students who are biology/pre-medicine majors or who are interested in pursuing careers in other science or health-related fields.

The College's Theresa Lang Center for Producing features the latest in digital computer technology and is one of the most advanced facilities of its kind in New York City. With digital multimedia capability, a decor inspired by top television postproduction houses, and access to the public library's B. Altman Advanced Learning Superblock, the center further enhances students' skills in traditional video and television production and allows them to develop, design, and evaluate cutting-edge multimedia projects. In conjunction with the Communication Arts Department, the College offers students a media library, where many videos, DVDs, and screening computers are available to students.

The Commons is a two-tiered dining facility and student lounge. Students also have an outdoor dining option, since the Commons opens out onto the Lowerre Family Terrace, a 5,000-square-foot rooftop garden, complete with a stone water-wall, a deck, and Wi-Fi service, that connects the two main campus buildings.

Costs

For the 2012–13 academic year, full-time tuition and fees were $25,668. Room and board costs were $14,228 per year. For part-time students, tuition was $816 per credit. Additional fees are applicable for various laboratory and studio classes.

Financial Aid

The College administers a variety of financial aid programs, including scholarships sponsored by the College. Some of the awards are based on academic achievement; others are based on financial need. Students are also eligible for aid through a wide variety of state and federal programs. In addition, a number of jobs are available for students on campus, and the Offices of Financial Aid and Academic and Career Advisement can help students locate part-time off-campus jobs to help finance their education. More than 85 percent of MMC students receive some form of financial assistance. Therefore, limited finances alone need not prevent any student from attending the College. Priority consideration for merit- and need-based financial aid is November 15 for spring admission and March 15 for fall admission.

Faculty

Marymount Manhattan College's student-faculty ratio is 12:1. In addition to the staff of the advisement office, faculty members act as advisers to students. Full-time faculty members teach in all sessions and divisions (days, evenings, and some weekends). Part-time instructors, who are drawn from the wealth of experienced teaching professionals in New York City, supplement the full-time faculty.

Student Government

The Student Government Association responds to three areas of concern at MMC. The association primarily serves the needs of its constituents by managing the student government budget, planning and publicizing events, and establishing organizations that reflect the interests of the students. In addition, the association assists faculty and administrative groups and committees in their policy and procedural tasks and communicates the results of committee work to the student body. Finally, the Student Government Association provides special representatives for students' rights and freedoms through established and clearly defined channels of authority.

Admission Requirements

Marymount Manhattan College seeks candidates with qualities that indicate potential for success in higher education and the ability to contribute to the College community. Admission is based on a combination of factors: the student's academic program, including scholastic average; two recommendations (judicial form required for transfer students in lieu of one recommendation) from teachers, counselors, or employers; an essay; and SAT or ACT scores. TOEFL, IELTS, or PTE scores are required for international student applicants.

Each year the College enrolls an increasing number of transfer students. Transfer students may receive up to 90 credits for course work completed at a regionally accredited postsecondary institution with a grade of C- or better. Transcripts are evaluated on a course-by-course basis.

Application and Information

The admissions application must be received by March 15 (fall entry) and November 15 (spring entry) for priority consideration for MMC scholarships. Students may apply online. For application forms and for more information about Marymount Manhattan College, students should contact:
Office of Admission
Marymount Manhattan College
221 East 71st Street
New York, New York 10021
Phone: 212-517-0430
      800-MARYMOUNT (toll-free)
Fax: 212-517-0448
E-mail: admissions@mmm.edu
Website: http://www.mmm.edu
      https://www.facebook.com/MarymountManhattan (Facebook)
      http://twitter.com/NYCMarymount (Twitter)

Marymount Manhattan College, in the heart of Manhattan.

MARYWOOD UNIVERSITY
SCRANTON, PENNSYLVANIA

The University

Marywood University is coeducational, comprehensive, residential, and Catholic. Founded in 1915 by the Sisters, Servants of the Immaculate Heart of Mary, the University serves men and women from a variety of backgrounds and religions. The University enrolls more than 3,400 students in an array of undergraduate and graduate programs. Motivated by a pioneering, progressive spirit, Marywood provides a framework for educational excellence that enables students to develop fully as persons and to master professional and leadership skills that are necessary for meeting human needs.

Students at Marywood have the opportunity to build on their academic interests and proactively shape their educational experience. Students' energy and intellectual curiosity guides their work, growth, and success. Marywood believes in the power of the individual and in the premise that education is the most empowering tool.

Marywood is fully accredited by the Commission on Higher Education of the Middle States Association of Colleges and Schools. Accreditations/approvals have been granted by Accreditation Review Committee on Education for the Physician Assistant, American Psychological Association, American Art Therapy Association, American Music Therapy Association, Commission on Accreditation for Dietetics Education, American Dietetic Association, Council on Academic Accreditation, American Speech-Language-Hearing Association, Association of Collegiate Business Schools and Programs, Commission on Accreditation of Athletic Training Education, Council for Accreditation of Counseling and Related Educational Programs, Council on Social Work Education, National Association of Schools of Art and Design, National Association of Schools of Music, National Council for Accreditation of Teacher Education, and National League for Nursing Accrediting Commission.

The athletic program for women and men at Marywood provides students with opportunities to play on competitive intercollegiate, club, and intramural teams. Students compete on an intercollegiate basis in baseball, basketball, cross-country, field hockey, lacrosse, soccer, softball, swimming/diving, tennis, and volleyball. Marywood is a member of NCAA Division III, the Colonial States Athletic Conference (CSAC), and the Eastern College Athletic Conference. Marywood's teams have been successful, winning titles in basketball, field hockey, lacrosse, soccer, softball, tennis, and volleyball. In addition, Marywood teams and individuals have participated in tournaments at the national level.

Prospective students can connect with Marywood through social networks including Facebook (http://facebook.com/marywoodu), Twitter (http://twitter.com/marywoodu), and YouTube (http://youtube.com/marywoodu).

Location

Situated on a hilltop, Marywood's scenic 115-acre campus is part of an attractive residential area of the city of Scranton, in northeastern Pennsylvania. With a population of 78,000, Scranton is the fifth-largest city in Pennsylvania and is the county seat of Lackawanna County (the county population is approximately 213,000). Marywood is relatively close to many major cities of the Northeast; traveling by car, it is 1 hour to Binghamton; 2½ hours to New York and Philadelphia; 4 hours to Washington, D.C.; and 5½ hours to Boston. Several airlines serve the Wilkes-Barre/Scranton International Airport, which is 20 minutes from the campus. The Pocono Mountains, offering spectacular scenery and an abundance of outdoor recreational opportunities, including downhill skiing, are a short distance from the campus.

Majors and Degrees

Marywood University offers a variety of majors and minors at the undergraduate level. Individually designed majors, developed with faculty guidance, and double and interdisciplinary majors are also available. Several five-year bachelor's/master's degree programs are offered.

At the undergraduate level, Marywood University awards the Bachelor of Arts (B.A.), Bachelor of Architecture (B.Arch.), Bachelor of Business Administration (B.B.A.), Bachelor of Environmental Design in Architecture (B.E.D.A.), Bachelor of Fine Arts (B.F.A.), Bachelor of Music (B.M.), Bachelor of Science (B.S.), Bachelor of Science in Nursing (B.S.N.), and Bachelor of Social Work (B.S.W.).

Marywood offers majors and minors in the following areas of study: accounting, ad hoc (self-designed), advertising and public relations, architecture and interior architecture/design, art (studio: ceramics, painting, sculpture; design: graphic design, illustration, photography), art education, art therapy, arts administration (art, music, theater), aviation management, biology, biotechnology, communication sciences and disorders (speech-language pathology), comprehensive social sciences (general, history, sociology), computer information and telecommunications systems, computer science (minor), criminal justice, dance/movement (minor), digital media and broadcast production (broadcast, corporate), early childhood education, education (elementary, secondary), English, environmental science, family and consumer sciences education, financial planning, French, general science education, health and physical education (athletic training, education, physical activity), health services administration, history/political science, hospitality management, industrial/organizational psychology, international business, journalism, management, marketing, mathematics, medical technology/clinical laboratory science, multimedia (minor), music, music education, music therapy, nursing, nutrition and dietetics (coordinated program, didactic program), performance, performing arts, philosophy, physician assistant studies, psychology, psychology/clinical practice, public administration, religious studies, retail business management, science, social sciences secondary education, social work, Spanish, special education/elementary education (dual certification), theater, and women's studies (minor).

Preprofessional programs are offered in chiropractic, communication sciences and disorders, dentistry, law, medicine, physician assistant studies, and veterinary medicine. A joint seven-year bachelor's/doctoral program in chiropractic involves three years of study on the Marywood campus and additional work at New York Chiropractic College, which is located in Seneca Falls, New York.

Marywood offers bachelor's to master's degree programs in architecture, biotechnology, communication arts, criminal justice, financial information services, health services administration, physician assistant studies, and speech language pathology.

Academic Programs

Undergraduate degrees are offered in approximately sixty academic programs, including the arts, sciences, music, fine arts, social work, and nursing. All students are required to complete a core curriculum in the liberal arts in addition to the courses in their major. Opportunities for undergraduates abound through double majors, honors and independent-study programs, practicums, internships, and study abroad. Army and Air Force ROTC programs are available.

Off-Campus Programs

Study-abroad opportunities are available in countries such as Australia, Canada, England, France, Mexico, and Spain. Through Studio Art Centers International (SACI), art students may study in Florence, Italy.

Academic Facilities

In recent years, the University has made $100 million in improvements to the campus, including new athletic, residence hall, and dining facilities, and one of the finest studio arts facilities in the northeast. The Insalaco Center for Studio Arts features 60,000 square feet of fully equipped studios, labs, and classroom spaces for a broad variety of artistic disciplines. The Center for Architectural Studies offers students two levels of studio space in a spacious, adaptive re-use of Marywood's former gymnasium and pool space.

Costs

Tuition for full-time students (12–18 credits per semester) for the 2013–14 academic year is a flat fee of $29,340. There is also a general fee of $1,100 for full-time students. Costs for room and board for a full academic year are approximately $13,566, depending on which meal plan is selected and the desired room occupancy. Costs of books and supplies are estimated at $1,000.

Financial Aid

Marywood offers a comprehensive program of financial aid to assist students in meeting educational costs. Eligibility for federal and state programs is based on demonstrated financial need, as determined by a federal eligibility formula that analyzes family income and assets. In addition, approximately $28 million in institutional aid is awarded annually to Marywood students. Applicants to Marywood are considered for all financial assistance programs for which they qualify. Candidates are required to submit the Free Application for Federal Student Aid (FAFSA) and the Marywood application form, preferably by February 15.

Faculty

Among faculty members at Marywood, 165 are full-time, and 90 percent of these hold the Ph.D. or the highest degree in their field. The student-faculty ratio is 13:1. Faculty members are evaluated on their teaching and on their scholarly and artistic activities.

Student Government

All matriculated students in the undergraduate school are members of the Student Government Association (SGA). The SGA operates with a number of committees, including the Student Council, the Resident Committee, and the Commuter Committee. The association plays a key role in establishing a positive campus environment.

Admission Requirements

Candidates for admission should demonstrate reasonable progress toward graduation in an accredited secondary school, have graduated from a secondary school, or offer evidence of an equivalent secondary education. Each candidate should show satisfactory academic preparation in 16 units of subject matter, including 4 units of English, 3 units of social studies, 2 units of mathematics, 1 unit of science with laboratory, and 6 additional units. Either SAT or ACT scores are required for those who wish to enter as freshmen.

In addition to fulfilling general admission requirements, candidates for admission to a degree program in architecture, art, education, music, nursing, pre–physician assistant studies, and speech language pathology must meet special standards established by the department. Prior to enrollment, music, theater, and art candidates are required to audition or to present an art portfolio.

For certain programs, candidates without the recommended distribution of units may be eligible for admission if their course work as a whole and the results of their tests offer evidence of a strong foundation for college work. Candidates who are deficient in required course work may complete the appropriate work during the summer or the first year in college.

A student who demonstrates satisfactory academic performance at another college may apply for admission as a transfer student. Academic courses presented for transfer should be equivalents of courses required by the programs of study at Marywood. Students should have earned a grade of C or higher in their course work; C– will not transfer. A student should expect to earn a minimum of 60 credits at Marywood University; ordinarily, at least one half of the credits required for a major must also be earned at Marywood.

International candidates are required to meet the academic standards for admission, demonstrate proficiency in the use of the English language, and submit documentation of having sufficient funds to cover educational and living expenses for the duration of study. To certify proficiency in the use of English, international applicants whose primary language is not English must submit scores from the Test of English as a Foreign Language (TOEFL) or the IELTS.

Application and Information

Applications for admission are considered on a rolling basis; however, candidates are strongly encouraged to submit applications by March 1. Applications received after March 1 are considered on the basis of available space in particular programs. To be considered for admission, freshman applicants must submit to the Office of Admissions a completed application (paper or online), a nonrefundable $35 application fee (waived if applying online), an official high school transcript with an indication of class rank, an official report of scores from the SAT or ACT, and at least one letter of recommendation. Students can apply online at http://www.marywood.edu/admissions/applying/.

Transfer students must submit a completed application, a nonrefundable $35 application fee (waived if applying online), an official high school transcript, official academic transcript(s) reflecting all college course work for which the candidate has enrolled, and at least one letter of recommendation.

All submitted credentials become the property of Marywood and are not returnable to the applicant. Admission standards and policies are free of discrimination on grounds of race, color, national origin, sex, age, or disability.

For further information, interested students should contact:

Christian DiGregorio, Director
University Admissions
Marywood University
2300 Adams Avenue
Scranton, Pennsylvania 18509
Phone: 570-348-6234
      TO-MARYWOOD (866-279-9663, toll-free)
Fax: 570-961-4763
E-mail: yourfuture@marywood.edu
Website: http://marywood.edu/admissions
      http://www.facebook.com/marywoodu
      http://www.twitter.com/marywoodu
      http://www.youtube.com/marywoodu

The Center for Architectural Studies in Marywood University's School of Architecture.

MENLO COLLEGE
ATHERTON, CALIFORNIA

MENLO COLLEGE
Silicon Valley's Business School

The College

Menlo College, an independent, coeducational, nonsectarian institution, stands out among institutions of higher education in five distinct ways: programs, location, small size, athletics, and alumni. Rather than offer a traditional set of majors as many institutions do, Menlo concentrates on providing excellent programs in business management and psychology with a strong foundation in the liberal arts. Menlo's location in the heart of Silicon Valley allows the College to train tomorrow's leaders in an intimate, student-centered, academically challenging environment. The College is small enough to be a real community but large enough to support a wide array of intercollegiate sports, student organizations, and internship opportunities, giving students the confidence and breadth of experience to flourish after graduation. The College's distinguished alumni provide a strong base of support for graduates, which helps students make the transition from college to career with great success.

A Menlo education is a process that trains and cultivates leaders. This process begins with a broad-based liberal arts foundation in the humanities, mathematics, sciences, and social sciences. At the same time students are challenged to enrich and develop their writing, critical-thinking, and decision-making skills. Next, students enter rich major programs staffed by outstanding faculty who are experts in their fields. The advantage is a cutting-edge curriculum that prepares students to succeed. Menlo's superior business program is renowned throughout the world and has produced generations of dynamic and successful business, industrial, and civic leaders around the globe.

The learning process does not end in the classroom. Students in the management program are required to complete six units of internship as part of their degree program. All students are encouraged to participate in internships and study programs that bridge the gap between theory and practice. These opportunities range from Fortune 500 companies to innovative start-up enterprises, from San Francisco to South America, Asia, and Europe. Not only do participants gain hands-on experience, they also grow personally as they encounter diverse peoples, cultures, and values.

As a whole, College-sponsored activities promote self-exploration and often lead to the discovery of hidden talents. Students can participate in a variety of clubs or organizations, such as the Alpha Chi National Honor Society and the Poetry, Art, and Music Society. They cultivate leadership skills through student government and student life positions and special workshops that tackle pressing contemporary issues.

This commitment to personal and intellectual growth, coupled with Menlo's ideal location in the heart of Silicon Valley, draws students from all across the United States and around the world. The global village is a reality at Menlo, given the broad social, religious, cultural, and national makeup of the student body. The appreciation of different cultures that results becomes a tremendous advantage in the marketplace.

Menlo's warm, friendly atmosphere is enhanced by its residential status. Nearly two-thirds of all students live in one of five residence halls. Nearby off-campus apartments (for students who are older than 21 or married) are also an option.

For accomplished athletes who enjoy the exhilaration of intercollegiate competition, Menlo offers men's baseball, basketball, cross-country, football, golf, soccer, and wrestling and women's basketball, cross-country, golf, soccer, softball, volleyball, and wrestling. In addition, Menlo offers competitive cheerleading as a coeducational sport. The College competes in the NAIA Pacific Conference. Intramural sports are also popular, and altogether almost 50 percent of students participate in sports.

To meet students' health needs, the College provides care via the Menlo Medical Clinic. Counseling services are offered by faculty and residence-life staff members.

Whether in the classroom, in the laboratory, or on the playing field, Menlo College nurtures students by offering programs, activities, and services that foster individual success.

Location

Menlo College is located on the San Francisco peninsula in the town of Atherton, a residential community near the cities of Menlo Park and Palo Alto. The area ranks among the most attractive and exciting in the world, with numerous cultural resources and a temperate climate. San Francisco lies 30 miles to the north. Many other important educational centers are within an hour's drive of Menlo, making the area an exciting place in which to study and live. The campus is in the heart of Silicon Valley, where high-tech companies in the electronics, computer, aerospace, biotechnology, and pharmaceutical industries are literally transforming the world in which we live and work. Surrounding the San Francisco Bay Area is the great natural beauty of northern California, extending from the spectacular California coast to the majestic Sierra Nevada Mountains. Favorite spots such as Big Sur, Monterey Bay, Lake Tahoe, Napa Valley, and Yosemite National Park are just a few hours' drive from Menlo.

Fields of Study

Menlo College offers the following fields of study: accounting, entrepreneurship, finance, human resource management, international management, management, management information systems, marketing, marketing communication, psychology, sports management, real estate, pre-law, and an individually designed major where students can combine existing programs to create their own majors.

Academic Programs

Menlo College operates on a semester calendar. To earn a bachelor's degree, students must complete 124 units of credit and maintain good academic standing.

Menlo's renowned Academic Success Center provides resources for increasing students' academic ability and morale. Included are innovative approaches to counseling and tutoring. The goal is to develop strong self-advocacy and to assist faculty members in meeting the needs of a varied student population using an assortment of individualized, small-group, and computer-based instruction. This method facilitates study and discussion of course material, tutoring, and test preparation.

Off-Campus Programs

The difference between obtaining an exciting professional position with opportunity for advancement and growth and settling for second best often comes down to experience. Internships enable students to apply theory to practice—to take classroom knowledge and test its relevancy. Students spend one or more semesters working on- or off-campus in their fields of study, obtaining academic credit and/or financial compensation and valuable insight.

Academic Facilities

Bowman Library maintains a strong collection of books and periodicals, including electronic journals, books, and AV materials. The Bowman Library's Electronic Information Gateway provides access to general and specialized online research databases, including full-text periodicals and reference resources as well as high-speed access to the Internet and World Wide Web. The Library contains rooms for group study, viewing AV materials, and photocopying. In addition, wireless access to the campus network resources is available through the library's laptop computer checkout program.

The Resource for Online Services and Information Electronically (ROSIE) is Menlo College's electronic information gateway, providing access 24 hours a day, seven days a week through the web from the library, residence halls, and off-campus sites to the online catalog, electronic research databases, and reference assistance. ROSIE also provides access to the online research-skills tutorial required of all students through the Menlo College General Education curriculum.

Menlo College's computer labs provide students with access to state-of-the-art PC and Macintosh hardware, software, and networking capabilities. All computer-lab equipment is connected to the campus network as well as the Internet and World Wide Web. Classroom labs include both individual workstations and presentation facilities. The Open Access Lab is open daily and is staffed by experienced monitors who are familiar with all lab equipment and applications and are able to provide students with the best possible technical and instructional services. With a 3.5:1 student-computer ratio, Menlo College offers students ample access to a wide range of computing resources for both classroom assignments and personal use.

Costs

Tuition and fees for 2013–14 are $36,500. Residence costs, including room and board, are $11,902.

Financial Aid

Menlo is noted for a strong program of merit and need-based aid. Approximately 90 percent of Menlo's students enroll with financial assistance, including Menlo scholarships, achievement awards, and on-campus employment as well as Federal Pell Grants, Federal Stafford Student Loans, Federal PLUS loans, and others. Students transferring to Menlo are fully eligible to be considered for financial aid. Merit scholarships of up to $19,000 per year are available for both domestic and international students.

Faculty

The College faculty is composed of approximately 80 members, both full- and part-time. Guest lecturers from business, industry, and other professions add to the breadth of instruction. Faculty members are readily available to give students personal help and counseling. A student-teacher ratio of 14:1 allows for small classes and individual attention to students' progress.

Student Government

Students elect their own representatives to Student Government, which is responsible for legislative and executive decisions affecting student activities and the coordination of student affairs. At Menlo, students take the lead in shaping their education and the future of their College.

Admission Requirements

The Admission Committee considers each candidate individually through the assessment of academic achievement and personal qualities, talents, and interests. There is an early-action plan for entering freshmen, and transfer students are welcome. Applicants are evaluated on the basis of their academic record, course of study, personal recommendations, school activities, essay, and scores on either the SAT or ACT. A personal visit is strongly recommended but not required. The College looks for freshmen with both breadth and depth of academic background in college preparatory subjects. Transfer students are evaluated on the strength of their college programs. Applicants are considered without regard to age, race, color, creed, gender, sexual orientation, national origin, marital status, disability, or any other characteristic protected by law.

Application and Information

Students may enter Menlo College at the opening of the fall or spring semester. Application deadlines are: early action deadline, December 1; priority deadline for freshmen, February 1 for fall and November 1 for spring; and priority deadline for transfers, April 1.

For further information concerning admission, students should contact:

Office of Admission
Menlo College
1000 El Camino Real
Atherton, California 94027-4301
Phone: 650-543-3753
        800-55-MENLO (toll-free)
Fax: 650-543-4496
E-mail: admissions@menlo.edu
Website: http://www.menlo.edu

Different backgrounds, one Menlo community.

MIAMI INTERNATIONAL UNIVERSITY OF ART & DESIGN

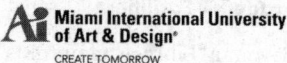

Miami International University of Art & Design is one of The Art Institutes, a system of over fifty schools throughout North America dedicated to providing hands-on education in the creative and applied arts. Miami International University of Art & Design offers master's, bachelor's, and associate degree programs as well as non-degree programs for students interested in pursuing career opportunities from among tomorrow's 15 million jobs in creative fields like design, fashion, and media arts (based on information from the U.S. Bureau of Labor Statistics for job growth from 2012 to 2022).

A focused education from Miami International University of Art & Design can help students turn their creative energy into a powerful tool that can make a difference in the world. Students are part of a collaborative and supportive community, where experienced instructors provide the guidance and skills needed to pursue a career in the creative economy.

Miami International University of Art and Design is also an important resource for creative industry leaders who value the opportunity provided students to learn by using professional-grade technology to build a portfolio of work to show potential employers after graduation.

Accreditation

Miami International University of Art & Design, including its branches The Art Institute of Tampa and The Art Institute of Jacksonville, is accredited by the Southern Association of Colleges and Schools Commission on Colleges to award associate, baccalaureate, and master's degrees. Questions about the accreditation of Miami International University of Art & Design and its branches can be directed to the Commission on Colleges, 1866 Southern Lane, Decatur, Georgia 30033-4097; phone: 404-679-4500.

The interior design program leading to the Bachelor of Fine Arts at Miami International University of Art & Design (Miami Campus) is accredited by the Council for Interior Design Accreditation, 206 Grandville Avenue, Suite 350, Grand Rapids, Michigan 49503; www.accredit-id.org.

Miami International University of Art & Design is licensed by the Commission for Independent Education, Florida Department of Education. Additional information regarding this institution may be obtained by contacting the Commission at 325 West Gaines Street, Suite 1414, Tallahassee, Florida 32399-0400; phone: 888-224-6684 (toll-free).

Location

Situated on the eastern edge of downtown Miami, adjacent to a causeway linking the city to legendary hot spot South Beach, Miami International University of Art & Design is right in the center of one of the world's most fascinating, exciting, and diverse cities.

Miami is earning a name as an international, multicultural city that's a fusion of culture, tradition, and exotic flavors. Its unique connection and proximity to its Latin American neighbors makes Miami a true melting pot of rich cultures, traditions, and festivals.

Thanks to its Latin American and Hispanic connection, Miami has become a base of operations for hundreds of companies seeking to gain an economic foothold in these growing markets. The city continues to develop and grow, along with its economy and its status as an international player.

The arts, fashion, and design also thrive in Miami. Each year, the City of Miami hosts Art Basel, the winter equivalent of the world's largest art show held in Basel, Switzerland. Talented artists, art dealers, galleries, and museums come from all over the world to exhibit throughout the city during Art Basel.

The area is also home to attractions like the historic Art Deco District of South Beach, the Design District, Wynwood Art District, and Coconut Grove. As the focal point of performing arts activity in South Florida, Adrienne Arsht Center for the Performing Arts of Miami-Dade County serves as a showcase for the finest in established and developing cultural programs. And of course, nearby Miami Beach and particularly South Beach offer a wide range of foods, shops, activities, nightlife, and people to explore.

Miami is known for its miles of beautiful beaches and for being the winter home of countless celebrities, as well as the setting for many movies and TV shows such as "CSI Miami." The NFL's Miami Dolphins play in Sun Life Stadium; baseball's Miami Marlins play at Marlins Park; and the Miami Heat of the NBA and the Florida Panthers of the NHL play in BB&T Center.

Vibrant, multicultural, and rapidly growing, Miami is a city like none other. Miami International University of Art & Design and its student body and faculty reflect Miami's diversity, its commitment to the growth of the arts, and its reputation as a center of international commerce and success.

Programs of Study and Degree Offerings

Creativity is all around, and with millions of tomorrow's jobs in creative fields, the world needs more creative professionals. No matter which course of study a student chooses, the instructors at The Art Institutes will guide, support, and help students fine-tune their visual thinking and problem solving, so that they can take advantage of the world's growing creative opportunities and put their passion to work. Programs are offered in the areas of design, which focuses on communicating conceptually and helping people connect in living and work spaces; media arts, that centers on utilizing technology to deliver information and entertainment; and fashion, where students learn anything from designing clothes for the runway to running a retail shop.

Bachelor's degree programs are offered in the areas of advertising, audio production, computer animation, digital filmmaking & video production, fashion design, fashion merchandising, film & digital production, graphic design, interior design, photography, visual arts, visual effects & motion graphics, and web design & interactive media.

Associate degree programs are offered in the areas of accessory design, fashion design, and fashion merchandising.

Diploma programs are offered in digital image management, fashion retailing, web design & development I, and web design & development II.

Master's degree programs are offered in design & media management*, film, graphic design, interior design, and visual arts.

Program availability and degree offerings are subject to change.

*Miami International University of Art & Design is one of the degree-granting institutions for The Design & Media Management degree program. This school's program will also be offered in a synchronous and asynchronous format at its branch campuses, The Art Institute of Tampa and The Art Institute of Jacksonville.

Academic Facilities

Miami International University of Art & Design provides a learning environment with professional-grade technology applicable to each student's course of study. Students have the opportunity to build a portfolio of work that shows potential employers that they are trained to use the software, hardware, or equipment utilized within the industry. Depending upon the course of study, students are immersed in a creative environment—from classrooms to computer labs to studios—focused on relevant, hands-on education designed to prepare them for the real world.

Costs

Actual tuition and housing costs will vary depending on program, number of credits enrolled, and living arrangements. Prospective students should contact a Student Financial Services professional at the school for details.

Financial Aid

Financial aid is available for those who qualify. Students who require financial assistance should first complete and submit the Free Application for Federal Student Aid (FAFSA) online at www.fafsa.ed.gov and meet with a financial aid officer. Students may also apply for a number of scholarships focusing on their specific areas of career interest.

Faculty

Faculty members are hands-on creative professionals with proven experience as business leaders and innovators, hosting a learning environment similar to the career world students will face after graduation. Part instructor, part mentor, their mission is to help develop and transform creative potential into high-demand marketable skills.

Admission Requirements

Prospective students should refer to the current academic catalog for full details regarding admission requirements and process.

Application and Information

To obtain an application, make arrangements for an interview, or tour the school, prospective students should contact:

Miami International University of Art & Design
1501 Biscayne Boulevard, Suite 100
Miami, Florida 33132-1418
Phone: 305-428-5700
      800-225-9023 (toll-free)
Fax: 305-374-5933
Website: http://www.artinstitutes.edu/miami

MICHIGAN TECHNOLOGICAL UNIVERSITY

HOUGHTON, MICHIGAN

The University

Michigan Technological University is a leading public research university developing new technologies and preparing students to create the future for a prosperous and sustainable world through its 130+ undergraduate and graduate degree programs. More than 7,000 students from all fifty states and more than sixty nations enjoy beautiful Upper Michigan. Enrollment of international students is at an all-time high of 14.7 percent. Michigan Tech is rated a Best in the Midwest by the *Princeton Review*.

In addition, *U.S. News & World Report* has ranked Michigan Tech in the top tier of national universities, and fifty-eighth among national public universities. Eight of Tech's graduate engineering programs have also been highly ranked.

Students work together on real-world industry projects as part of the Enterprise program, from virtual reality to forest management and from satellites to hybrid SUVs. Michigan Tech has one of the nation's largest programs in scientific and technical communication and is in the top 15 nationally in degrees awarded in environmental, mechanical, and geological/mining engineering.

New to campus is the Great Lakes Research Center, an innovative, ecofriendly waterfront structure uniting Michigan Tech's strengths in freshwater and Great Lakes research and scholarship in interdisciplinary collaborations.

Degree programs are offered in the College of Engineering, College of Sciences and Arts, School of Business and Economics, School of Technology, and School of Forest Resources and Environmental Science, as well as the Graduate School.

Michigan Tech is accredited by the North Central Association of Colleges and Schools. Engineering programs are accredited by the Engineering Accreditation Commission of the Accreditation Board for Engineering and Technology (ABET), Inc.; technology programs are accredited by the Technology Accreditation Commission of ABET; and the surveying engineering program is accredited by the Related Accreditation Commission of ABET. The forestry program is accredited by the Society of American Foresters, the chemistry program offers American Chemical Society–approved options, and the secondary teacher certification programs are approved by the Michigan Board of Education. The School of Business and Economics is accredited by the Association to Advance Collegiate Schools of Business International, the premier business accrediting organization in the United States. Only about 400 U.S. business programs have earned this distinction.

Residence halls are close to classrooms and well connected. They include ultrafast Ethernet lines, and wireless zones abound all across the campus. Residence halls also feature Finnish saunas, their own cable TV system, lounges, and weight-lifting and laundry facilities. First-year students must live in the residence halls, and they can choose from meal plans and numerous food options. Students can also eat, relax, and study at the Memorial Union, the center of campus life and home to many student organization offices, the bookstore, billiards, and a bowling alley.

In athletics, the hockey Huskies have been national champions three times and compete in the NCAA Division I Western Collegiate Hockey Association. Football, men's and women's basketball, tennis, cross-country, track, and women's soccer and volleyball teams compete in the Division II Great Lakes Intercollegiate Athletic Conference against teams from Michigan, Wisconsin, Ohio, Pennsylvania, Indiana, and Illinois.

Most Michigan Tech students compete in intramural sports, from bowling to wrestling and from dodgeball to swimming. Club sports include lacrosse, women's hockey, and paintball. The biggest game on campus, however, is broomball, where students slide around on ice and hit a rubber ball with a broom. The Student Development Complex includes a health center, swimming and diving pools, gyms (one with a running track), a rifle range, an ice arena, and a weight room. A community health center and child-care center are nearby.

Traditions include K-Day, which is an afternoon to enjoy McLain State Park on the shores of Lake Superior, and the Parade of Nations, a celebration (including food) of the sixty nations of the world that have students and faculty and staff members at Michigan Tech. At Homecoming, students dress in their worst attire and parade through the campus in autos that barely run. The biggest event is Winter Carnival, when students build massive snow statues on campus and around the area. Skits, queen competitions, first-class entertainment, ice hockey, and tourists make this a great experience. Before finals, students take a break on the campus mall for Spring Fling and celebrate with games, food booths, music, and more. Students also staff the weekly newspaper, *The Lode*, and the campus radio station, WMTU.

Location

Michigan Tech is situated on the Keweenaw Waterway in the hills of Houghton in a safe, friendly environment. The area offers abundant opportunities for outdoor recreation, including the University's own ski hill; cross-country skiing, running, and biking trails; and golf course. A waterfront jogging and biking trail cuts through the campus. Houghton is located about a 4 hours' drive from Green Bay, 7 hours from Minneapolis, and 10 hours from Detroit. The Houghton County Memorial Airport has daily flights to Chicago that connect to other major cities; bus service to Houghton is also available.

Majors and Degrees

The School of Technology awards Bachelor of Science degrees in computer network and system administration, construction management, electrical engineering technology, industrial technology, mechanical engineering technology, and surveying engineering.

The College of Engineering offers Bachelor of Science degrees in applied geophysics, biomedical engineering, chemical engineering, civil engineering, computer engineering, electrical engineering, engineering (mechanical design or manufacturing), environmental engineering, geological engineering, geology, materials science and engineering, and mechanical engineering.

The School of Business and Economics awards Bachelor of Science degrees in accounting, economics, finance, management, management information systems, and marketing.

The School of Forest Resources and Environmental Science awards Bachelor of Science degrees in applied ecology and environmental sciences, forestry, and wildlife ecology and management.

The College of Sciences and Arts awards Bachelor of Science degrees in anthropology; applied physics; audio production and technology; biochemistry and molecular biology; bioinformatics; biology, cheminformatics; chemistry; communication, culture, and media; cultural studies; computer science; computer systems science; English; exercise science; mathematics; medical laboratory science; pharmaceutical chemistry; physics;

preprofessional programs (medicine, dentistry, pharmacy, and law); psychology; scientific and technical communication; social sciences; software engineering; sports and fitness management; and theater and entertainment technology. The CSA awards the Bachelor of Arts degree in communication, culture, and media; history; liberal arts; physics; scientific and technical communication; sound design; theater and electronic media performance; and theater and entertainment technology. The College of Sciences and Arts also awards a two-year associate degree in humanities.

The **secondary education program** offers certification in biology, chemistry, computer science, earth science, economics, English, integrated science, mathematics, physics, and social studies.

Michigan Tech offers a number of **certificate programs** to allow students to gain knowledge in interdisciplinary areas.

Academic Program

Michigan Tech operates on a fifteen-week fall and spring semester system, with three options available for summer: two 7-week tracks and one 14-week track. Typically, students must have 130 credits to graduate, but the amount varies by department. Students must also complete the general education requirements, which help students develop strong scholastic habits. Some graduate courses are open to undergraduates with faculty approval. The International Programs and Services Office helps international students adjust to life in Houghton. More than 1,000 students from approximately sixty other nations study at Michigan Tech. Students may also study abroad in one of thirty nations, improving their global perspective.

Off-Campus Programs

The Career Center works with more than 300 industries, businesses, and organizations to help students find cooperative, internship, and summer employment opportunities. Job fairs are held on campus and elsewhere in the region. Michigan Tech students average five job interviews before they graduate.

Academic Facilities

The J. R. Van Pelt and John and Ruanne Opie Library contains more than 526,000 physical volumes, more than 75,000 electronic books, and provides subscription or consortia access to more than 10,000 electronic journals. The library regularly receives approximately 10,000 serials and periodicals. The archives maintain a collection of original materials on the history of the Keweenaw region, including the records of various copper-mining companies. The Rozsa Center for the Performing Arts is within walking distance of all residence halls and features nationally known lecturers, musicians, comedians, and theatrical performers as well as Michigan Tech's own productions. The A. E. Seaman Mineral Museum, the official "Mineralogical Museum of Michigan," houses one of the nation's premier collections of crystals, minerals, and ores.

Costs

Annual tuition is $13,095 for Michigan residents and $27,000 for out-of-state students; room and board is $8,865. Required fees and computer fees total approximately $700, and books and supplies total approximately $1,200.

Financial Aid

Currently, 90 percent of Michigan Tech's students receive financial aid, totaling nearly $110 million annually. Four kinds of assistance are available to Michigan Tech students, including scholarships, grants, student loans, and part-time employment. The financial aid process begins with filing an application for admission. Students should apply for admission by January 15 of the year in which they plan to enroll.

Faculty

Most of the 485 faculty members possess terminal degrees. Ninety-five percent of undergraduate classes are taught by faculty members; the student-faculty ratio is 12:1. Faculty members balance teaching and research and are known for their student support.

Student Government

Undergraduate Student Government and the Graduate Student Government allow students to get involved in University governance. Fraternities and sororities maintain a strong presence on campus, and there are more than 180 student organizations, including academic/professional, ethnic/cultural, service, religious, sporting, governmental, media, and honor societies.

Admission Requirements

Michigan Tech has a selective admissions policy. The University admits only those applicants who give definite evidence that they are qualified through education, academic capability, aptitudes, interests, and character to complete the University's requirements. Once students are accepted for admission, every effort is made by the faculty and staff members to help students realize their potential.

Application and Information

Applications received by January 15 are given priority consideration for admission and merit-based scholarships. Undergraduate and graduate applications are free. First-year applicants are required to submit official ACT or SAT test scores. A high school counselor information page must also be completed by a high school counselor or principal and sent to the Admissions Office with an official high school transcript. Transfer students must have official college transcripts sent directly to Michigan Tech. An official high school transcript and ACT/SAT scores may also be required. International students should contact the International Programs and Services Office. Following acceptance by Michigan Tech, students receive a packet containing information regarding on-campus housing and various University deadlines.

For more information, prospective students should contact:

Admissions Office
Michigan Technological University
1400 Townsend Drive
Houghton, Michigan 49931-1295
Phone: 888-688-1885 (toll-free)
Website: http://admissions.mtu.edu

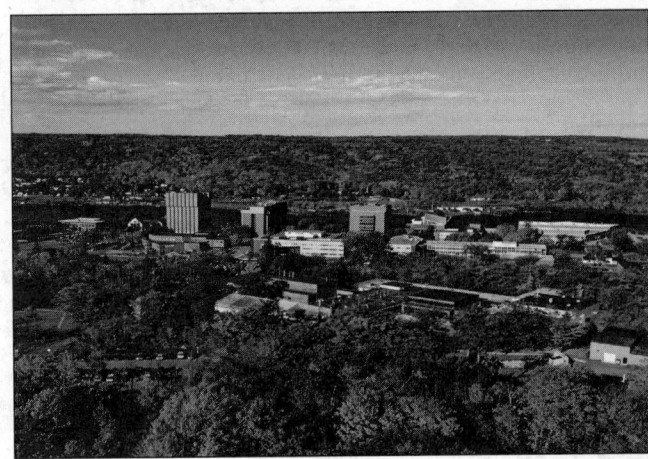

There's a fine line between crazy and smart—and it runs right through the middle of the Michigan Tech campus! Here, students find incredible hands-on research; innovative degree programs; a slew of student organizations; hiking, biking, and ski trails; towering snow statues; and awesome campus celebrations—there isn't a moment to be bored!

MIDAMERICA NAZARENE UNIVERSITY

OLATHE, KANSAS

The University

MidAmerica Nazarene University (MNU) is a comprehensive liberal arts university of approximately 1,350 undergraduate students and 500 graduate students. A faith-based university, MNU welcomes students of all religious backgrounds; approximately 40 percent of the student population is Nazarene.

MNU educates students for a life of purpose. With service-learning woven into course work and University-sponsored opportunities to minister in the local community, students prepare not only for a career, but to make the world a better place. The University's most popular areas of study include business, accounting, nursing, teacher education, forensic chemistry and biology, criminal justice, music, ministry, and multimedia. More information on MNU's academic programs is available online at http://www.mnu.edu/academic.

The average ACT score of incoming freshmen is 22.1; the average GPA is 3.32. Students hail from thirty-six states, five countries, and forty-plus denominations. The student to faculty ratio is 18:1.

MidAmerica Nazarene University offers NAIA Division I baseball, men's and women's basketball, cheerleading, football, men's and women's soccer, softball, and volleyball. Detailed information about MNU's athletic programs can be found at http://www.mnusports.com.

Each residence hall has a lobby or shared lobby where students can meet to study, watch television, or just hang out with friends. Each room is equipped for phone, satellite television, and Internet service. Several of MNU's residence halls offer suite-style living options for up to six students.

Location

MidAmerica Nazarene University is located in Olathe, Kansas, a residential community of approximately 125,000 just 20 minutes from the heart of Kansas City, with all the cultural advantages of a major metropolitan area. Olathe offers a lifestyle of exceptional quality. The city's school district and health care system are routinely recognized among the best in the nation. Outdoor recreation offers a variety of activities, including running, jogging, bicycling, fishing, boating, team sports, and just relaxing. Olathe has two public lakes—Olathe Lake, with 172 acres of water surface, and Cedar Lake, with 45 acres. The proximity to downtown Kansas City provides internship opportunities in the areas of business, technology, the arts, creative services, and health care.

Majors and Degrees

Students can earn an Associate of Arts (A.A.) degree in general business, liberal arts, or music ministry.

The Bachelor of Arts (B.A.) degree is available in accounting, athletic training, the Bible and theology, biology, biology education, business administration, business education, business psychology, chemistry, corporate communication, criminal justice, elementary education, English, English language arts education, forensic biology, forensic chemistry, graphic design, history, history and government education, intercultural studies, kinesiology, marketing, mathematics, mathematics education, middle school mathematics, middle school science, ministry, multimedia, music, organizational leadership, physical education, psychology, sociology, sports management, and youth and family ministry.

MNU also offers the Bachelor of Music Education (B.M.Ed.) degree and the Bachelor of Science in Nursing (B.S.N.) degree.

Academic Programs

MNU students receive direction from advisors in choosing a major, discovering their interests, finding a mentor, and preparation for interviews.

At MNU, hands-on learning and real-world experience are core components of each student's education. For example, criminal justice majors learn in the University's own forensics lab, then intern for local police departments or laboratories. Communications students build public relations skills by helping nonprofit organizations, and nursing majors train on the latest medical technology including state-of-the-art patient simulators.

Off-Campus Programs

MNU Europe is the University's international program. Students travel to, live, and study in Busingen, Germany, a quaint European village with a small college campus. Courses may last a few weeks to an entire semester. Courses are taught by MNU professors and adjuncts in a variety of subjects fulfilling both general education and elective requirements.

As a member of the Council for Christian Colleges and Universities (CCCU), a national association of more than 100 Christian colleges and universities, MNU makes a number of off-campus learning opportunities available. Domestic programs are available in Washington, D.C.; Los Angeles; and Martha's Vineyard, Massachusetts. Students have also studied abroad in China, Costa Rica, Egypt, Germany, Russia, and the United Kingdom through this cooperative program.

Academic Facilities

The 40,000-square-foot Bell Cultural Events Center features state-of-the-art practice, recital, and performance facilities for the fine arts division, as well as a black-box theater and 500-seat performance hall for music and drama productions. Osborne Hall houses the Department of Science and Mathematics, while Lunn Hall houses administrative offices. Dobson Hall contains an art studio and a graphic-design computer lab.

The largest facility on campus, the 70,000-square-foot Cook Center, houses Bell Family Arena, two practice gyms, and the Athletic Training and Athletics department offices. It is also home to MNU's School of Nursing and Health Science. Metz Hall houses the Department of Behavioral Sciences, School of Business Administration, and School of Education and Counseling. One of several on-campus computer labs is also located in this facility.

A virtual tour of the MNU campus is available online at http://www.mnu.edu/campus-virtual-tour.html.

Costs

While fees vary according to course load, costs for a full-time student total around $29,500, which includes tuition ($21,250), mandatory fees ($1,000), and room and board ($7,250). Part-time tuition and fees vary according to course load.

Financial Aid

The perception that a private university isn't affordable is false—the truth is, any higher education requires a significant investment. But about 92 percent of students at MNU receive some form of financial aid. MNU scholarships are available for academics, athletics and fine arts. Information and applications may be obtained from Student Financial Services at 913-971-3298 or https://www.mnu.edu/financial-aid-scholarships.html.

Faculty

MNU students receive personal attention from their instructors. It is not uncommon to find faculty members in residence hall rooms talking with students or even inviting students into their homes for dinner. MNU faculty members have decades of real-world experience in many industries and fields.

Student Government

Associated Student Government (ASG) exists to discover God's agenda as students serve God and the campus community. ASG offers plenty of opportunities for students to get involved through many different campus activities and service-learning opportunities.

Admission Requirements

Prospective students should have graduated from an accredited high school and have completed the ACT or SAT exam. While the University does not require specific subjects for entrance, it does recommend that students complete 3 units of math, 4 units of English, 3 units of science, 3 units of social studies, and 1 unit of foreign language. Students over 18 who have not graduated from high school can submit GED scores.

Application and Information

Students must submit the completed application, official high school transcripts, ACT or SAT scores, and the housing questionnaire, provided by Admissions. International students must also submit TOEFL scores. The deadline for the fall semester is August 1; the spring semester deadline is December 15.

For more information on how to apply to MNU, prospective students should visit www.mnu.edu/incoming-freshmen.html or contact:

MNU Office of Admissions
MidAmerica Nazarene University
2030 East College Way
Olathe, Kansas 66062-1899
United States
Phone: 913-971-3380
       800-800-8887 (toll-free)
E-mail: admissions@mnu.edu
Website: www.mnu.edu
       www.facebook.com/MNUPioneers
       www.vimeo.com/choosemnu

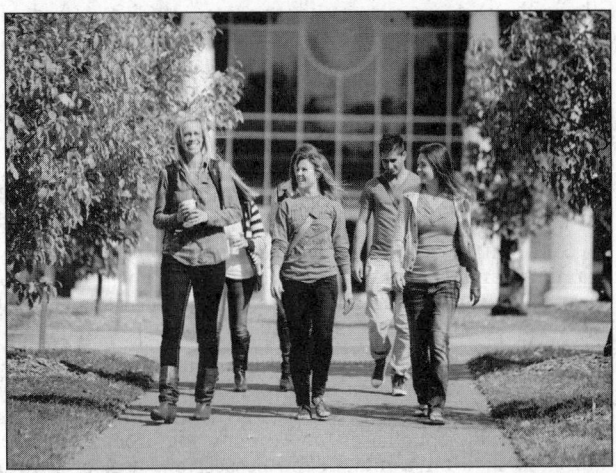

With over 40 majors, MNU students graduate ready to lead and serve, no matter what their field.

MILLERSVILLE UNIVERSITY OF PENNSYLVANIA

MILLERSVILLE, PENNSYLVANIA

Millersville University
SEIZE THE OPPORTUNITY

The University

Millersville University is among the highest ranked public universities in its class in Pennsylvania according to the *U.S. News & World Report*. Millersville University offers a wide range of programs and a commitment to high-quality undergraduate instruction. Millersville's student body of approximately 8,700, including 7,600 undergraduates, is large enough for the University to offer a wide variety of programs. The University is small enough, however, to provide friendly service and individual attention. Students report that the relaxed, friendly campus atmosphere is one of the things they like best. The Millersville campus features a beautiful green and flowered landscape, a lake with resident swans, and clean, well-maintained facilities.

Millersville University was established more than 150 years ago, in 1855, as a normal school, the first one in Pennsylvania. It remained a teachers' college until 1962, when it was authorized to offer liberal arts degrees. It has been Millersville University of Pennsylvania since 1983.

The two reasons students most frequently cite for choosing Millersville are its excellent academic reputation and affordable tuition. The most popular majors are education, business administration, psychology, English, speech communications, and social work. Millersville's undergraduates are diverse; 1 in 9 students attends part-time, 17 percent are members of a racial/ethnic minority group, and 10 percent are more than 25 years old. Thirty-three percent of Millersville undergraduates are from Lancaster County, 63 percent from elsewhere in Pennsylvania, 4 percent from out of state, and 2 percent from other countries.

The University offers a wide range of intercollegiate varsity, intramural, and club sports; special interest clubs; fraternities and sororities; musical organizations; and publications. A broad program of cultural events is offered.

Thirty-one percent of undergraduates live in campus residence halls, with the rest commuting from home or living nearby. Coed dormitories and apartments are available for students. Freshmen and sophomores not commuting from home are required to live on campus. The possession, use, or sale of alcoholic beverages and illegal drugs is prohibited on the University campus. Smoking is prohibited in all academic and residential buildings on campus. Freshmen and sophomores living on campus are not permitted to have motor vehicles.

Special services provided for students include free tutoring, academic advisement, career planning and placement, personal counseling, health services, wellness activities, and special facilities for commuters.

Location

Millersville is 3 miles from Lancaster city, a growing metropolitan area. Lancaster County is an exceptionally friendly and beautiful area with a large number of stores, restaurants, theaters, parks, and tourist attractions. The campus is served by the area bus system, and Lancaster has train and air service.

Lancaster County is one of the fastest-growing counties in Pennsylvania and has one of the lowest unemployment rates in the state. The local economy is unusually sound and diverse. Sixty percent of Millersville graduates settle within the county.

Millersville University is conveniently located to a number of major metropolitan areas in the Northeast. It's just 1½ hours from Philadelphia and Baltimore, 2½ hours from Washington D.C., and 3 hours from New York City.

Majors and Degrees

Millersville offers the Bachelor of Arts degree in anthropology, art, biology, chemistry, earth sciences, economics, English, environmental geology, French, geography, German, government and political affairs, history, international studies, mathematics, music, philosophy, physics, psychology, social work, sociology, and Spanish.

The Bachelor of Science degree is offered in allied health technology; applied engineering, safety and technology; biology; business administration; chemistry; communications and theatre; computer science; geology; mathematics; meteorology; occupational safety and environmental health; ocean sciences and coastal sciences; and physics.

The Bachelor of Science in Education degree with teaching certification is offered in art education, biology, chemistry, earth sciences, Pre-K–4 education, English, French, German, mathematics, middle level education, music education, physics, social studies, Spanish, special education, and technology education.

The University also offers the Bachelor of Fine Arts degree in art; the Bachelor of Science in nursing degree for RNs only; the Associate of Science degree in chemistry; and the Associate of Technology degree in applied engineering, safety and technology.

Most majors offer several options that permit specialization, including accounting, finance, international business, management, and marketing in business. Students should refer to the website for a complete listing. More than sixty-five minors are offered along with 3-2 engineering programs for chemistry majors. Special advisement is available for students interested in premedicine and prelaw.

Academic Programs

Millersville University places a strong emphasis on the liberal arts. Nearly half of the courses required for all its undergraduate degrees, including those with technical or professional majors, are in the liberal arts. This prepares students for a lifetime of learning and gives them a background in writing, speaking, analysis, and critical thinking across a broad range of subjects.

Millersville's baccalaureate degree programs have four common curricular elements: proficiency requirements in English composition and speech; the general education program, which constitutes about half the curriculum; the major field of study; and elective courses, if needed, to meet the minimum of 120 credits required for graduation. Within this framework, students have many choices in developing programs of study.

The general education program has requirements in writing, speaking, humanities, natural sciences and mathematics, social sciences, and interdisciplinary and/or multicultural study. There is also a health and physical education requirement.

Millersville offers a University Honors College, departmental honors programs, independent study, a pass/fail option, remedial courses, and special advisement to students who are undecided about a major.

The University operates on a 4-1-4 academic calendar with summer sessions.

Off-Campus Programs

An exchange agreement with Franklin & Marshall College allows Millersville students to take Franklin & Marshall courses not offered at Millersville. Cooperative education internships are available to students in most majors, and some majors offer or require specialized internships. Millersville has study-abroad programs in Australia, Chile, China, England, France, Germany, Ireland, Japan, Peru, Scotland, South Africa, and Spain. Qualified students who wish to study abroad elsewhere may do so through the University's cooperative arrangements with other colleges and universities.

Academic Facilities

With numerous study areas, classrooms, and even a café, the Dr. Francine G. McNairy Library and Learning Forum is a relaxing and visually pleasing place where students can study and work. Materials from other libraries are available through interlibrary loan.

The University's computing facilities support both PC and Macintosh platforms. There are more than 400 terminals and computers available in multiple computer labs across campus. On-campus access to the Internet is available for all faculty members and students. Wireless access is available in all buildings, residence halls, classrooms, and offices.

Other University facilities include an extensive scientific instrumentation inventory, industry and technology laboratories, a variety of art studios and galleries, two visual and performing arts centers, a state-of-the-art sound studio, three gymnasiums, two swimming pools, radio and television production facilities, soundproof music practice modules, and a language laboratory.

Costs

Annual tuition and fees in 2012–13 were $8,599 for Pennsylvania residents and $18,425 for out-of-state students. Annual room and board charges for 2012–13 were $9,234.

Financial Aid

Approximately 79 percent of Millersville undergraduates receive financial aid through grants, scholarships, employment, and loans. Scholarships are available on the basis of academic performance. Federal Pell and Federal Supplemental Educational Opportunity grants and Pennsylvania Higher Education Assistance Agency (PHEAA) grants are awarded on the basis of need. Students may also qualify for Federal Perkins Loans and Federal Stafford Student Loans. On-campus and off-campus job opportunities are plentiful.

Students applying for a federal or state grant, Federal Work-Study, or a Federal Perkins Loan must complete the Free Application for Federal Student Aid. The forms are available from high school guidance offices, from the Financial Aid Office, or online at http://www.fafsa.ed.gov. Deadlines are given in the forms' instructions.

Faculty

Millersville University faculty members are dedicated to teaching and to offering individual attention. They take a personal interest in their students' lives and careers and are solely responsible for providing academic advisement. The University keeps a relatively low student-faculty ratio of 22:1 and an average class size of approximately 25. No classes are taught by graduate assistants. Ninety-eight percent of the 300 full-time faculty members hold a doctorate or the terminal degree in their field.

Student Government

Millersville University students participate in University governance through the Student Senate, faculty-student committees, and representation on the Faculty Senate, the Council of Trustees, and the Millersville Borough Council. The Student Senate works with faculty members and the administration on major University policies.

Admission Requirements

Millersville University admits approximately half its applicants. More than 80 percent of its full-time freshmen rank in the top 40 percent of their high school class. Academic records are the most important factor in admission decisions. Applicants must have successfully completed at least 4 years of high school English, 3 years of social studies, 3 years of mathematics, and 3 years of science (1 unit must be a lab). In addition, 2 years of foreign language is strongly recommended.

Because an important part of the college experience is meeting people with backgrounds and interests different from one's own, Millersville University is committed to recruiting a diversified student body. SAT or ACT scores are required. Interviews, recommendations, and essays are not required. Out-of-state, international, and transfer applicants are welcome. Exceptional high school students may apply for early admission at the end of their junior year. Admitted applicants may request to defer their admission for one semester. Advanced standing is offered through CLEP and AP examinations.

Application and Information

To apply, students should submit a completed application along with a $50 processing fee and official copies of the high school record and SAT or ACT scores. The online application fee is $35. The University has a rolling admission policy, and students are encouraged to apply early (by mid-November) in their senior year for fall admission. Applicants are usually notified of a decision within a month after a completed application is received.

For application forms and additional information, students should contact:

Office of Admissions
Millersville University of Pennsylvania
P.O. Box 1002
Millersville, Pennsylvania 17551-0302
Phone: 717-872-3371
        800-MU-ADMIT (toll-free)
E-mail: admissions@millersville.edu
Website: http://www.millersville.edu
YouTube: http://www.youtube.com/millersvilleu
Facebook: https://www.facebook.com/villeadmissions
Twitter: @VilleAdmissions
Blog: Millersvilleuniversityadmissions.blogspot.com

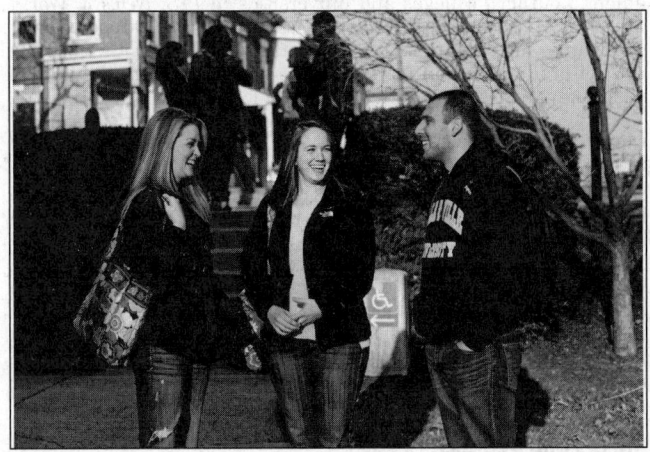

Students on the campus of Millersville University of Pennsylvania.

MILLIGAN COLLEGE
MILLIGAN COLLEGE, TENNESSEE

The College

Milligan College is a four-year private Christian liberal arts college in northeast Tennessee. From its beginning in 1866, Milligan College has integrated academic excellence with a Christian worldview, and its mission is to educate men and women as Christian servant-leaders. A comprehensive humanities program and a core curriculum are complemented by specialized training in thirty majors and several master's degrees. Christian perspectives are integrated throughout the curriculum and student life activities as students are prepared intellectually and spiritually to change lives and shape culture.

Milligan's student body of 1,200 comes from more than thirty states and fourteen nations. Eighty percent of traditional students live on the campus. More than forty clubs and organizations provide opportunities to develop leadership skills. A wide variety of activities and campus events encourage social, cultural, and spiritual growth. Milligan College is affiliated with the Christian Churches/Churches of Christ, but the interdenominational student body is diverse.

All campus facilities are networked and most have wireless access. Every residence hall room and apartment features a high-speed data connection to the campus network and the Internet as well as telephone service, voice mail, and cable TV.

Milligan is well recognized as an NAIA athletic powerhouse with a highly competitive athletic program in twenty-four varsity sports. In the past ten years, Milligan has won more than fifty conference titles and made fifty-eight national tournament appearances. Men's varsity teams include baseball, basketball, cross-country, cycling, golf, soccer, swimming, tennis, volleyball, and indoor and outdoor track and field. Women's varsity teams include basketball, cheerleading, cross-country, cycling, dance, golf, soccer, softball, swimming, tennis, indoor and outdoor track and field, and volleyball.

Milligan is accredited by the Commission on Colleges of the Southern Association of Colleges and Schools to award bachelor's and master's degrees. Questions about the accreditation of Milligan College can be directed to the Commission on Colleges, 1866 Southern Lane, Decatur, Georgia 30033-4097; phone: 404-679-4500.

In addition to thirty undergraduate majors, Milligan offers a Master of Science in Counseling degree, a Master of Education degree, a Master of Science in Occupational Therapy degree, and a Master of Business Administration degree. Milligan continues to be named among Southern colleges and universities in *U.S. News & World Report's* America's Best Colleges issue. Nearly 100 percent of Milligan graduates are employed or in graduate school within one year of graduation and more than 75 percent of premed students who take the MCAT are accepted to medical school

Location

Milligan's picturesque 195-acre campus, which comprises more than twenty buildings of Colonial architecture, is located in the beautiful mountains of northeast Tennessee, just minutes from Johnson City and the dynamic Tri-Cities region. Students enjoy historical locations, theaters, parks, restaurants, and shops; explore the breathtaking Appalachian Mountains by hiking or camping in state parks near the campus; visit local lakes and rivers for outdoor recreation; or ski the nearby North Carolina slopes. Because Milligan believes leadership is about service, students are encouraged to be active in the local community. Many are employed in internships or part-time work in area businesses.

Majors and Degrees

The Bachelor of Science, Bachelor of Arts, and Bachelor of Science in Nursing degrees are offered. Undergraduate majors include accounting, allied health science, applied finance and accounting, Bible (children's ministry, general studies, missions, pastoral ministry, youth ministry), biology, business administration (accounting, economics, general, health care administration, international business, legal studies, management, marketing, sports management), chemistry, child and youth development, child life, communications (digital media studies, film studies, interpersonal and public communication, multimedia journalism, public relations), computer information systems, computer science, education (professional teacher licensure), English, fine arts (art, film studies, music, photography, theater arts), history, human performance and exercise science (exercise science, fitness and wellness, physical education, sports management), humanities, interdisciplinary honors, language arts, mathematics, music (performance, jazz studies), music education (licensure in vocal, instrumental), nursing, political science, psychology (general, preprofessional), public leadership and service, sociology, and worship leadership.

Professional teacher licensure areas include early childhood, elementary education, K–12, middle grades, secondary, and special education. Preprofessional programs are available in dentistry, law, medicine, occupational therapy, optometry, pharmacy, and physical therapy. An accelerated program for adults is available in business administration and early childhood education.

Academic Programs

Milligan College offers students a liberal arts education taught from a perspective of God's activity with humanity. The College's strong core curriculum educates students toward the world in an open and constructive way. The candidate for the bachelor's degree must have completed a major and electives to total a minimum of 128 semester hours of credit, with at least a 2.0 GPA. Core curriculum requirements include courses in humanities, the Bible, social sciences, ethnic studies, laboratory science, speech communication, mathematics, and health/fitness.

Realizing that not all college-level learning occurs in a college classroom, prior learning assessment programs provide a method by which other modes of learning can be evaluated for college credit. The Advanced Placement (AP) program, the College-Level Examination Program (CLEP), Defense Activity for Non-Traditional Educational Support (DANTES) programs, and the International Baccalaureate (I.B.) program are available to all students interested in receiving college credit for studies or work experience already completed.

Milligan College operates on a semester system (semesters begin in August and January) with two 4-week summer sessions in June and July or one 8-week term. Also available are short-term classes during January term (one week before the onset of the spring semester) and May term (the weeks between the spring semester and the summer sessions).

Off-Campus Programs

Students can go beyond geographical and cultural boundaries and earn up to 16 hours of credit with Milligan's Study Abroad Program or with the many off-campus learning opportunities sponsored by the Council for Christian Colleges & Universities. These include an American Studies Program in Washington, D.C.; Australia Studies Centre; China Studies Program; Contemporary Music Center in Nashville; India Studies Program; Latin American Studies Program in Costa Rica; Los Angeles Film Studies Center; Middle East Studies Program in Cairo; Oxford Summer Programme; Russian Studies Program; Scholars' Semester in Oxford; Summer Institute of Journalism in Washington, D.C.; and Uganda Studies Program.

Through an affiliation with the International Business Institute, business majors can earn college credit through an intensive ten-week summer program in Europe. Milligan also offers a three-week summer humanities tour in Europe, during which students explore the origins of Western civilization. In addition, internship opportunities offer students college credit and work experience in their field of interest.

Academic Facilities

Milligan College's library has extensive holdings and online access to other major libraries and databases. Special collections within the library contain materials on the history of the College, the Restoration Movement, and the local area. The library also participates in resource-sharing agreements with Emmanuel Christian Seminary and East Tennessee State University. The Writing and Study Skills Center offers access to resources, instruction, and tutoring for academic success. Television and radio production studios and an FM radio station provide on-site training for communication students. A darkroom and art gallery feature works by fine arts students. Standardized laboratory facilities, including a gross anatomy lab, are available for general and advanced work in the sciences.

A new housing village, slated to open in fall 2013, allows Milligan to keep up with its growth, while preserving a close-knit residential community. Other recent on-campus projects include a new state-of-the-art theater and convocation facility; renovation of the College's main classroom building and several other lecture halls and labs; and the addition of a new education center, a new tennis complex, and a new wellness center.

Costs

Tuition for 2012–13 was $25,735. Room and board were $5,850. Additional fees were approximately $1,025. Typical annual miscellaneous costs (books, supplies, etc.) were approximately $1,000. As a private institution, Milligan supplements student fees with income from endowments and gifts from alumni, friends, and churches in order to keep tuition below the national average of similar four-year private institutions.

Financial Aid

Approximately 98 percent of all students at Milligan College receive federal, state, institutional, and/or outside (such as from a church or private foundation) aid, including both academic scholarships and need-based grants. Milligan has increased its financial aid offerings each year, spending more than $9 million last year to assist in meeting students' financial needs. Financial assistance is allocated on the basis of need demonstrated by information supplied on the Free Application for Federal Student Aid (FAFSA), which should be completed by January 1 for priority consideration. Returning students must complete and submit a Milligan College Financial Aid Scholarship/Renewal Application. The Milligan College Office of Financial Aid begins mailing award letters between March 1 and March 15.

Faculty

Eighty percent of Milligan's faculty members have earned the highest degree in their field from well-respected colleges and universities in the United States and abroad. Professors integrate biblical truths into their classes and are active leaders both on and off the campus. The low student-faculty ratio and small classes put the student at the center of attention and allow faculty members to cultivate special mentoring relationships with students. Professors serve as advisers to students from registration to graduation and are often instrumental in helping students find employment or gain admission to graduate school following graduation. Milligan's faculty members are mature and caring scholars who are committed to world-class scholarship, excellence in teaching, and their students.

Student Government

The Student Government Association (SGA) serves as the official representative voice of Milligan students and promotes academic, social, and spiritual activities for the campus community. SGA operates under a constitution approved and supported by the administration of the College, promotes well-ordered conduct among students, and enforces the regulations of the College. SGA leadership is provided by an executive council and representatives from throughout the campus. As a Christian college, Milligan adopts basic moral and social principles and expects students to serve Christ in an atmosphere of trust, encouragement, and respect for one another.

Admission Requirements

Character, ability, preparation, and seriousness of purpose are the qualities emphasized in considering applicants for acceptance to Milligan College. Overall excellence of performance in high school subjects, as well as evidence of Christian commitment and academic potential, provide the basis for admission to Milligan College. These qualities are evaluated by consideration of each applicant's academic record (based on transcripts), two personal references, ACT or SAT scores, and participation in extracurricular activities. Some majors, such as music and theater, may require auditions and interviews. All applicants should have a high school diploma or the equivalent and have completed a college-preparatory curriculum with course work in English, math, science, history and/or social sciences, foreign language, and some work in speech, music, or art in preparation for study in a liberal arts curriculum. Satisfactory scores on the ACT or SAT are required of all applicants to the freshman class. The average ACT score for the current first-year class is 24. Transfer students should have a grade point average of 2.5 or above and must follow the same application procedures as first-time students, with the addition of providing official transcripts of all previous college work. ACT or SAT scores and high school transcripts are not required for transfer students with at least 24 earned semester hours.

Application and Information

Applications are processed on a rolling basis, and early application is encouraged. Notification is also given on a rolling basis. An application packet, complete with detailed instructions and requirements, can be obtained from the Admissions Office.

For further information, students should contact:

Admissions Office
Milligan College
P.O. Box 210
Milligan College, Tennessee 37682
Phone: 423-461-8730
        800-262-8337 (toll-free)
Fax: 423-461-8982
E-mail: admissions@milligan.edu (general)
        visits@milligan.edu (visits)
Website: http://www.milligan.edu

Milligan College is a Christian liberal arts college that unites humanities, sciences, and fine arts with a Christian worldview.

MILLS COLLEGE
OAKLAND, CALIFORNIA

MILLS

The College

For more than 160 years, Mills College has shaped women's lives. Offering a progressive liberal arts and sciences curriculum taught by nationally renowned faculty, Mills gives students the personal attention that leads to extraordinary learning. At Mills, students gain the ability to make their voices heard, the strength to risk bold visions, an eagerness to experiment, and a desire to change the world.

Nestled on 135 lush acres in the heart of the San Francisco Bay Area, Mills College is a hidden gem. The idyllic setting, combined with the College's community of forward-thinking individuals, makes Mills home to one of the most dynamic, creative liberal arts educations available to women today.

Historically a college for women only, Mills continues that proud tradition today at the undergraduate level. To provide enhanced professional opportunities for all students, Mills also offers renowned graduate programs that are open to both women and men. Ranked one of the top colleges in the West by *U.S. News & World Report*, Mills has also been named one of the greenest colleges in the nation by The Princeton Review.

Mills provides a collaborative, interactive learning environment that encourages intellectual exploration and self-discovery. The faculty of distinguished scholars and artists is dedicated to developing the strengths of every student, preparing them for lifelong intellectual, personal, and professional growth. With an impressive student-teacher ratio of 10:1, Mills women are assured of access to and support from these inspiring professors. The hallmark of a Mills education is the collaboration between students and faculty members that goes beyond the classroom and into innovative research.

Mills students also compete in six intercollegiate sports—cross-country, rowing, soccer, swimming, tennis, and volleyball—as members of the National Collegiate Athletic Association (NCAA) Division III. Students may also participate in recreational activity courses for credit or take advantage of the on-campus fitness facilities and off-campus excursions.

Location

Located in the foothills of Oakland, California, Mills offers students access to the diverse metropolitan centers that make up the greater San Francisco Bay Area. Amid the rolling hills and the century-old eucalyptus trees of the Mills campus, students find a welcoming place to live and learn, with new friends and new ideas at every turn. The campus is heavily accented with Mediterranean-style buildings, many designed by architectural innovator Julia Morgan. Paths and streams wind their way through groves and meadows that pervade the 135-acre wooded campus.

Outside the campus gates, students have access to the dynamic Bay Area, with Berkeley, San Francisco, Napa, and Silicon Valley nearby. The close proximity allows Mills students to connect with centers of learning, business, and technology; pursue research and internship opportunities; and explore the Bay Area's many sources of cultural, social, and recreational enrichment.

Majors and Degrees

With more than forty different majors to choose from at Mills, students find themselves active, engaged participants in their own learning. Students have the chance to work directly with nationally renowned faculty members and get involved in their innovative work and research.

Mills offers the Bachelor of Arts (B.A.) degree in American studies; anthropology; art (history and studio); biochemistry and molecular biology; biology; biopsychology; business economics; chemistry; child development; computer science; dance; economics; English (creative writing and literature); environmental science; environmental studies; ethnic studies; French and Francophone studies; government; history; intermedia arts; international relations; Latin American studies; literary and cultural studies;

mathematics; music; philosophy; political, legal, and economic analysis; psychology; public policy; sociology; Spanish and Spanish American studies; and women's, gender and sexuality studies. The major in child development meets the requirements for a state child development permit for teaching in preschool and day-care centers and provides a strong basis for graduate school and for many other careers. Special pre-law and pre-medical advising is available.

Mills offers the Bachelor of Science (B.S.) degree in biochemistry and molecular biology, biology, biopsychology, chemistry, environmental science, and mathematics. Mills also provides the first two years of courses leading to a Bachelor of Science in Nursing degree from Samuel Merritt University.

Students can also choose to create their own major, working with 3 faculty advisers to plan an individual program that draws courses from across the curriculum and creates an integrated and unique educational experience.

Mills offers six unique programs that enable students with clear career goals in certain fields to earn a bachelor's and a master's degree in five years. These degree programs are the 4+1 B.A./M.B.A. business administration program, the 4+1 B.A./M.A. infant mental health program, the 4+1 B.A./M.A. interdisciplinary computer science program, the 4+1 B.A./M.A. mathematics program, the 4+1 B.A./M.P.P. public policy program, and the 4+1 B.A./M.A./credential program in teacher education. Students must meet specific academic requirements to successfully complete these special programs.

Academic Programs

To earn a Mills bachelor's degree, students complete 34 semester course credits (usually four courses each semester). Grading is traditional, and a pass-fail option is available outside the major.

The innovative General Education Program is guided by a thoughtfully constructed set of learning outcomes, instead of a list of required courses. Each student designs her own program with the guidance of her faculty adviser, tailoring it to the student's specific needs and interests. The program places the work a student does in her major in a larger context and ensures that she explores and appreciates realms of knowledge beyond her field. The general education requirements fall into three outcome categories: skills (written communication, quantitative and computational reasoning, and information literacy/information technology); perspectives (women and gender, and multicultural); and disciplinary experiences (creation and criticism in the arts, historical perspectives, natural sciences, and human institutions and behavior).

Career Services offers a comprehensive career counseling and coaching program to assist students in clarifying their goals. Workshops, individual counseling sessions, an extensive internship program, a strong alumnae network, and special opportunities to meet Bay Area business leaders and top professional women all help students to focus their interests and plan career goals.

Off-Campus Programs

Mills has exchange or visiting programs with eleven American colleges and universities, including American, Barnard, Manhattanville, Mount Holyoke, Simmons, Spelman, Swarthmore, Wellesley, and Wheaton.

With programs in Europe, Africa, South America, Asia, and Australia—in nearly every country in the world—Mills encourages adventurous students with a minimum 3.0 GPA to study abroad. Mills also has exchange programs with universities in Hong Kong and South Korea.

Sophomores, juniors, and seniors may cross-register for one course per semester at the following schools: Berkeley City College; California College of the Arts; California State University, East Bay; Chabot College; City College of San Francisco; College of Alameda; College of Marin; Contra Costa College; Diablo Valley College; Graduate Theological Union; Holy Names University; Laney College; Merritt College; Napa Valley College; Saint Mary's

College of California; Skyline College; Sonoma State University; and University of California, Berkeley.

Academic Facilities

Mills' commitment to providing students with exceptional academic resources is underscored by the two environmentally friendly buildings on campus. The home of the Lorry I. Lokey Graduate School of Business hosts both undergraduate and graduate classes and achieved Leadership in Energy and Environmental Design (LEED) Gold certification. Students enjoy smart classrooms and lecture halls with the latest educational technology and light-filled community areas that encourage student collaboration. The Betty Irene Moore Natural Sciences Building provides students with a state-of-the-art learning environment that is also a model of green construction. The LEED-certified Platinum facility features high-tech classrooms, multiple teaching laboratories, and a research lab.

The Jeannik Méquet Littlefield Concert Hall features an expanded stage area for larger performances and enhanced acoustic features for improved performing and recording quality. Nearby Lisser Hall contains a flexible proscenium stage as well as a small experimental theater.

The open-stack, computerized F. W. Olin Library provides students with access to more than 240,000 volumes in addition to more than 22,000 rare books and manuscripts. A web-based catalog and more than 60 databases, including Academic Search, LexisNexis, PsycINFO, and Britannica Online are available 24 hours a day via the library's website.

The Mills College Art Museum houses the largest permanent collection of any liberal arts college on the West Coast and presents a changing array of innovative exhibitions. The highly regarded Children's School at Mills College provides hands-on experience for students preparing for careers in early childhood education.

Costs

In 2013–14, tuition and fees are $40,210 and room and board are $12,625. Students should calculate the costs of travel, books, and personal expenses on an individual basis.

Financial Aid

Mills College is committed to ensuring that a Mills education is within reach for those who have the desire and the qualifications to attend. Financial aid options at Mills include grants and scholarships, loans, and student employment. Some are funded by Mills directly, and others are state and federal programs.

In fall 2012, more than 80 percent of undergraduates at the College received some type of financial assistance in the form of grants, scholarships, loans, or on-campus employment. Ninety-three percent of Mills students received some portion of their aid directly from Mills. Awards are based on need and academic merit. Mills makes a special effort to provide financial aid to all students who demonstrate need.

All first-year students and transfer candidates must file the Free Application for Federal Student Aid (FAFSA) and the Mills College Financial Aid Form to be considered for government aid and need-based Mills scholarship funds. The FAFSA is required for non-Mills aid, such as the Federal Pell Grant and the Federal Supplemental Educational Opportunity Grant. California residents must also file the Cal Grant GPA Verification Form to be considered for a Cal Grant. More than 50 percent of Mills students have some of their demonstrated need offset by such non-Mills awards.

Faculty

More than 65 percent of the Mills faculty members are women, enabling students to work with professional women mentors in every academic area. Faculty members are selected for their teaching ability and scholarly achievement; 91 percent of full-time faculty members hold the highest degrees in their fields. Nearly 30 percent of the full- and part-time faculty are members of minority groups.

Student Government

An important goal of an education at Mills is to develop leadership skills, and participating in student government can be instrumental in furthering this goal. The Associated Students of Mills College (ASMC) is run by an executive board of 15 elected or appointed positions. Following a student-drafted Constitution, the board supports student organizations, student publications, campus-wide events, and various student initiatives. From academic issues to social events to honor code concerns, the ASMC is the voice of the student body to the College administration.

Admission Requirements

Most first-year students admitted to Mills have a B+ average and have followed a full college-preparatory course in their secondary school, including 4 years of English, 3 to 4 years of mathematics, 2 to 4 years of foreign languages, 2 to 4 years of social sciences, and 2 to 4 years of a laboratory science. Additional course work in fine arts is given positive consideration, as is evidence of special talents or interests. Mills is interested in individuals, not statistical averages, so each application is carefully reviewed. Credit may be awarded for the College Board Advanced Placement tests and the International Baccalaureate program's higher level examinations.

Applications from transfers are welcome, as are those from students resuming their education or women who have delayed their entrance to college or who wish to continue work on their bachelor's degrees. The SAT or ACT requirement is waived if 24 or more transferable semester hours are presented. For international applications, both the SAT and TOEFL are required. Applications should be accompanied by transcripts, letters of recommendation, SAT/ACT scores, and a writing sample. An interview, either on campus or with an alumna representative, is strongly recommended for all applicants.

Application and Information

For first-year students, fall admission application deadlines are November 15 for early action and February 1 for regular decision. All required materials are due by February 1.

For transfer students, fall admission application deadlines are March 1 for priority scholarship consideration and April 1 for regular decision.

The spring admission application deadline for both first-year and transfer students is November 1. Admission decisions are mailed on a rolling basis.

For more information, students should contact:

Office of Undergraduate Admission
Mills College
5000 MacArthur Boulevard
Oakland, California 94613
Phone: 510-430-2135
　　　800-87-MILLS (toll-free)
Fax: 510-430-3298
E-mail: admission@mills.edu
Website: http://www.mills.edu
　　　http://www.facebook.com/millscollege (Facebook)
　　　http://twitter.com/millscollege (Twitter)
　　　http://youtube.com/millscollege (YouTube)

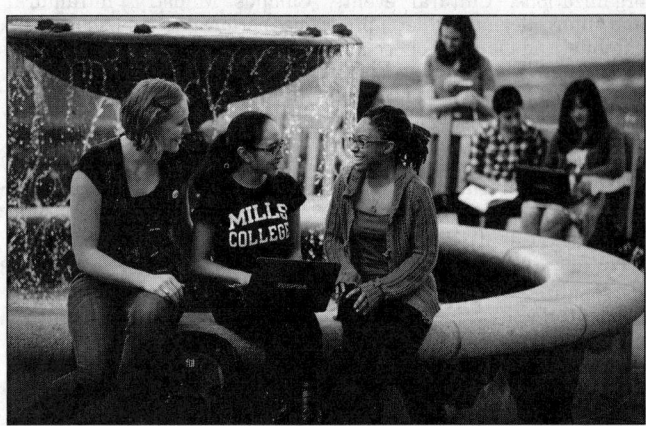

Mills women discover their best selves—and prepare to change the world.

MISERICORDIA UNIVERSITY
DALLAS, PENNSYLVANIA

The University

Misericordia University is a high-quality liberal arts and professional studies institution rooted in service to others and committed to challenging academics and the personal attention students deserve. Founded by the Religious Sisters of Mercy, Misericordia offers undergraduate and graduate programs to resident and commuter students, as well as adult students. Current enrollment is more than 3,000 men and women.

Misericordia provides an atmosphere designed to stimulate critical thinking, independent judgment, and creativity, as well as encourage the development of curiosity, good study habits, and personal values. The University also cultivates a spirit of community service and a lifelong love of learning in its students through extracurricular activities, experiential learning, and challenging academic programs. In the National Survey of Student Engagement, Misericordia students say they are more involved in learning and have better relationships with faculty members and peers than students at other similar institutions. Misericordia is also ranked in the top tier of *U.S. News & World Report's* America's Best Colleges 2012 in the Master's North category.

The University is fully accredited by the Middle States Association of Colleges and Schools. Its programs in nursing, social work, medical imaging, occupational therapy, physical therapy, and speech-language pathology are accredited by the National League for Nursing Accrediting Commission, the Council on Social Work Education, the Joint Review Committee on Education in Radiologic Technology, the American Occupational Therapy Association, the American Physical Therapy Association, and the American Speech-Language and Hearing Association, respectively. A new physician assistant studies program was granted Accreditation–Provisional by ARC-PA and is excited to accept new students.

Misericordia operates five residential facilities and eighteen town house units, with a total capacity of over 1,000 students. This includes the new MacDowell Hall which opened in fall 2012. Three nearby homes are reserved for upper-level students. Residents have a number of options, including single rooms and wellness housing. Each residence hall offers study rooms, laundry facilities, and recreational lounges. The Metz Dining Hall is located in the Banks Student Life Center, which also houses the Cougar's Den coffeehouse and the renovated Student Union, which features flat-screen televisions, pool, and foosball tables.

There are numerous campus activities. Besides Student Government, there are forty-one chartered student clubs and organizations. Cultural events, Campus Ministry, intramural and intercollegiate athletic programs, performing arts shows, art exhibits, and many other social activities complement the academic experience. The new Metz Field House provides enhanced facilities for student athletes. In keeping with the University's tradition of mercy, service, justice, and hospitality, students have opportunities to develop leadership potential through service projects. MU earned a spot on the President's National Community Service Honor Roll for the past several years.

On spring break, students have served the needy in rural Appalachia, the Gulf Coast, Texas, California, and the South Bronx. Students have volunteered abroad in Jamaica and Romania.

Personalized attention is the key to the support available in the Student Success Center. A psychologist, counselors, therapists, and peer counselors conduct workshops each semester on a variety of topics, including test anxiety, stress management, time management, and goal setting. Many services are free of charge to students and contacts are confidential.

First-year students may join the Guaranteed Placement Program (GPP) through the Insalaco Center for Career Development. The GPP program includes academic standards; cocurricular activities, such as leadership and service projects; internships; resume development; and interviewing skills. If a student fulfills the program requirements and is not employed in his or her field or enrolled in graduate or professional school within six months of graduation, a paid internship is assured. The center also co-presents the Choice Program, offering special guidance for students who haven't chosen a major. Opportunities for career exploration, cooperative education, and internships help students to develop the skills they need to enter the working world.

Student Health Services staff members provide first aid, assessment and treatment of common illnesses, and referrals for more serious health conditions. Health center activities are directed by a nurse practitioner. A self-care room offers reference materials and up-to-date information on personal health concerns. All services are confidential.

A rapidly evolving world has increased the number of adults who seek higher education. Misericordia offers bachelor's, master's, and doctoral programs for adults, including Expressway, an accelerated bachelor's degree program; Women with Children, which provides housing and support services for single women with children; and evening, online, and weekend formats for people with families and full-time jobs.

At Misericordia University, students can earn master's and/or doctoral degrees by attending classes online, in the evening, and/or on weekends. The small-class format enhances critical thinking and decision-making skills and draws out a variety of viewpoints that help broaden the perspectives of the student. Master's degrees are available in education, nurse practitioner studies, occupational therapy, physician assistant studies, speech-language pathology, business administration, and organizational management. A doctoral program in physical therapy is available to students entering in a full-time format, and a doctoral program in occupational therapy is available for graduate students via part-time study, including online and in-class components.

Location

Located on a more than 124-acre campus in northeastern Pennsylvania, Misericordia University is the oldest institution of higher education in Luzerne County. Expansive lawns and thick stands of trees dominate the campus. It is 9 miles from the city of Wilkes-Barre. The area offers shopping centers, malls, cinemas, skiing, professional sporting events, and a variety of cultural activities. Pennsylvania's largest natural lake and two state parks are nearby, as are Pocono ski resorts. Metropolitan New York and Philadelphia are each within a 3-hour drive. Public and college-sponsored transportation serves the campus.

Majors and Degrees

Misericordia University awards the Bachelor of Arts (B.A.) degree in English, history, communications, government, liberal studies, and philosophy. The Bachelor of Science (B.S.) degree is awarded in accounting, biochemistry, biology, business administration, chemistry, clinical laboratory science, communications, computer science, diagnostic medical sonography, elementary education, health-care management, information technology, management, marketing, mathematics, math/computer science, medical imaging, medical science, professional studies, psychology, secondary education, special education, and sport management. After completing the medical science bachelor's degree, students can opt for seamless transition into the master's degree in physician assistant studies. A Bachelor of Science in Nursing (B.S.N.) is awarded to nursing majors, and a Bachelor of Science in Social Work (B.S.W.) is awarded to social work majors. Specializations in accounting, early childhood education, prelaw, special education, and preprofessional occupations are also available. Certification programs include addictions counseling, child welfare services, diagnostic medical sonography, geriatric care management, gerontology, health-care informatics, nuclear medicine, and secondary education and may be taken in support of several degrees offered by Misericordia or as stand-alone programs.

The University offers five-year entry-level graduate majors in occupational therapy and speech-language pathology. Students graduate with a master's degree in speech-language pathology or occupational therapy and a bachelor's degree in health sciences. The physical therapy program is a 6½-year doctoral program. Students graduate with a bachelor's degree in one of several areas and a Doctor of Physical Therapy (D.P.T.) degree.

Academic Programs

Candidates for the B.A., B.S., B.S.N., or B.S.W. must fulfill a 48-credit liberal arts core curriculum in addition to the requirements of their chosen major to graduate. They must earn at least 36 credit hours in a chosen field. For regularly enrolled students, the average requirement for a baccalaureate degree is a total of 126 credits. Other options include minors, specializations, certifications, and electives.

Courses are offered on a semester basis, beginning in August and January and ending in December and May. Summer, weekend, and accelerated courses are also available.

Academic Facilities

The chemistry, physics, and biology departments all have fully equipped research laboratories available to students in these fields. State-of-the-art equipment includes high-performance liquid chromatography (HPLC), a rotary evaporator, an infrared spectrophotometer, and gas chromatography. The science building contains a gross anatomy laboratory, a rare asset for a university of this size. The University also houses an energized radiation laboratory for the medical imaging program. The new Passan Hall–College of Health Sciences provides classrooms and high-tech laboratories for the occupational therapy, physical therapy, speech-language pathology, and nursing programs in a facility devoted to these majors.

In addition to the four main computer labs, most other campus buildings and common areas offer wireless Internet access. The University operates e-MU, a secure online portal where students can access e-mail, course schedules, class registration tools, and student account and registration information from a single sign-on.

Mercy Hall, the original administrative building, offers multipurpose academic classrooms and facilities. Many key student service departments, including the registrar, student accounts, and financial aid are centralized in one area in Mercy Hall. Insalaco Hall, a new state-of-the-art classroom and conference building, provides a modern art gallery, café, computer labs, an ensemble room, fine arts classroom, music teaching and practice areas, and the Assistive Technology Research Institute.

The new MacDowell Residence Hall hosts three ultramodern classrooms on the first floor.

The three-story Bevevino Library covers 37,500 square feet and houses stacks for 90,000 volumes. Materials include information and communication technology and a reference section that offers books, serials, and a variety of periodicals as well as reference search tools.

Costs

Full-time undergraduate tuition for 2012–13 was $25,890 per year. The general fee was $1,240. Housing options include traditional rooms, suites, town houses, and wellness housing. The median room cost was $6,620. All resident students must participate in a ten-, fourteen-, or nineteen- meal plan. In addition, town house residents are eligible to choose a five-meal plan. The median board cost is $4,230.

Financial Aid

All students applying for financial aid must complete the Free Application for Federal Student Aid (FAFSA) by May 1. This is used for Federal Pell Grants, Federal Supplemental Educational Opportunity Grants (FSEOG), subsidized and unsubsidized Federal Direct Student Loans, Federal Perkins Loans, nursing loans, and the Federal Work-Study Program. This application is also the basis upon which state and institutional aid is awarded. The University also offers a no-interest monthly payment plan. Many scholarships are available including $10.7 million in presidential scholarships based on academic ability and $2.9 million in McAuley Awards for students who have experience in leadership roles and volunteer service.

Faculty

There are 112 full-time faculty members. A student-faculty ratio of 12:1 results in students receiving a great deal of individual attention from a highly qualified faculty; 87 percent of the faculty members hold doctorates or other terminal degrees. Besides student academic advising, the faculty members also serve as advisers to clubs.

Student Government

An active student government organization serves as a liaison between the students and the faculty and staff members. The administration enables students to become involved by serving as student representatives on various University committees.

Admission Requirements

Misericordia University admits applicants based on their secondary school record, high school recommendation, extracurricular activities, and personal promise. The University requires SAT or ACT scores.

Transfer students with a cumulative average of at least 2.0 (4.0 scale) may be considered for admission and may receive advanced standing. Some majors require a 2.5 or higher cumulative average. Transfer students must submit official high school transcripts and a transcript of work completed at other colleges and universities.

Application and Information

Applicants must submit an official application form (available upon request), transcripts, and SAT or ACT scores. Applicants may also apply through the University's website. There is a nonrefundable application fee of $35, which is waived for students who visit the campus or apply online.

The University considers applications on a rolling basis. Usually, candidates are notified of the admission decision within three weeks of receipt of all required materials.

Office of Admissions
Misericordia University
301 Lake Street
Dallas, Pennsylvania 18612-1090
Phone: 570-674-6461
           866-262-6363 (toll free)
Fax: 570-675-2441
E-mail: admiss@misericordia.edu
Website: http://admissions.misericordia.edu
           www.twitter.com/misericordiau
           www.facebook.com/misericordiauniversity

Misericordia University introduced football in 2012 to round out an already successful athletics program. The new Metz Field House and turf on Mangelsdorf Field provide first-rate facilities for student athletes.

MOLLOY COLLEGE
ROCKVILLE CENTRE, NEW YORK

The College

In 1955, 44 students became part of an exciting new tradition in higher education on Long Island. As the first freshman class of Molloy College, located in Rockville Centre, New York, these young students made a commitment to academic excellence. So did the College, which had a distinguished faculty of 15 and a library containing 5,000 books.

Today, Molloy offers students a rich and multidimensional education experience. The Long Island school encourages critical thinking and creative exploration in a personal community setting. Molloy combines the strengths of academic excellence and leadership with personal, compassionate mentoring to bring out the best in every student.

For over fifty years, Molloy College has evolved to become a dynamic learning institution with outstanding faculty, advanced technology, and a wide range of academic programs. In addition, Molloy has expanded its reach, offering graduate level courses at its Suffolk Center in East Farmingdale, New York, along with a number of on-site opportunities at area hospitals and school districts.

Molloy College students possess the confidence needed to live and work in this fast-paced, ever-changing world. The College has expanded its global learning program, where students travel from Rockville Centre and study abroad in Belgium, India, Italy, France, Spain, Thailand, and Australia. By traveling from Long Island and immersing themselves in cultures in other parts of the world, students gain knowledge while learning acceptance and understanding.

Closer to home, Molloy College students make a difference in Rockville Centre as well as other nearby local communities. For example, as part of Molloy's tradition of service, students become involved in a number of service projects that include BoxTown, a program to raise social consciousness about the issue of homelessness.

Athletics and academics go hand-in-hand at Molloy College, where students are known for both their athletic and scholastic success. The Long Island school has a winning tradition in a number of NCAA Division II athletic programs, and in 2010 the women's softball team became one of only eight teams in the country to qualify for the College World Series.

Campus life in Rockville Centre, New York, is alive and vibrant, with more than forty student clubs and honor societies. In 2011, Molloy opened its first residence hall, which can house more than 150 students. In addition, a new student center (which also opened in the fall of 2011) provides new opportunities for Molloy students to study, interact with their fellow students, or simply relax.

Molloy College has become a focal point for civic discourse with key community forums. Top regional, national, and international leaders (including former Secretary of State Colin Powell and *Newsweek International* editor Fareed Zakaria) have come to Rockville Centre to visit the College and address critical and timely issues.

In recent years Molloy launched two new initiatives to enhance students' experience. The Sustainability Institute at Molloy College is Long Island's first-ever venture combining environmental advocacy and sustainability education within an academic institution, and the new sustainability minor provides students with a solid background in this critical subject. Molloy also started its new Irish Studies Institute recently with a presentation from Bertie Ahern, the former prime minister of Ireland.

Through Molloy College's divers programs, personal attention from faculty, and commitment to improving both Long Island and the world, students develop an "I will" attitude that prepares them to enter the professional world, ready and able to make a difference.

Location

Located on a 30-acre campus in Rockville Centre, Long Island, Molloy College is close to metropolitan New York and all its diverse and rich resources. The College is easily accessible from all parts of Nassau, Suffolk, and Queens counties.

Majors and Degrees

Molloy College offers the A.A. degree in liberal arts; the A.A.S. degree in nuclear medicine technology, respiratory therapy, and cardiovascular technology; and B.A., B.S., B.F.A., or B.S.W. degrees in accounting, art, biology, business management, communications (which just added a new media major), computer information systems, computer science, criminal justice, English, environmental studies, finance, history, interdisciplinary studies, international peace and justice studies, mathematics, modern languages, music, music therapy, nuclear medicine (new in fall 2013), nursing, philosophy, political science, psychology, social work, sociology, speech-language pathology/audiology, and theology. Teacher certification programs are available in childhood (1–6), adolescence (7–12), and special education. Dual certification is available for birth–grade 2/childhood 1–6.

Special advisement is offered for students interested in pre-dental, pre-law, pre-medical, or pre–veterinary science programs.

On the graduate level, Molloy College offers a Master of Science degree as well as post-master's certification in nursing and education. M.B.A. programs are available in business, accounting, and personal financial planning. A Master of Social Work is offered through Molloy's partnership with Fordham University. Molloy also offers graduate degrees in criminal justice, music therapy, and speech pathology. In 2010, the College launched its first doctoral program, a Ph.D. in nursing.

The internship program at the College offers students the opportunity for on-the-job experience along with the classroom exposure so essential to the completely educated person. Internships are available in all areas of study.

Academic Programs

Advanced Placement credit is granted for a score of 3 or better on the AP exam. CLEP and CPE credit is also given. Molloy has a 4-1-4 academic calendar.

Academic Facilities

The Molloy campus has several new additions. The College's first residence hall opened in fall 2011, and there is also a new student center. In late 2011 Molloy also opened a new 550-seat performing arts theater, which will serve the campus as well as the surrounding communities.

The James E. Tobin Library houses a collection of 110,000 volumes, along with hundreds of subscriptions to print journals and periodicals. Students and faculty members have access to the library's databases on campus and off campus as well as through the College's website. The library also houses a library instruction room, where librarians meet with professors and individual classes for instruction on the use of the databases and related research methods. The Tobin Library is a wireless facility. In the Media Center, over 3,000 DVDs and VHS tapes support the curriculum.

Students may use more than 300 computers located in nineteen labs and open space areas. The College has 100 percent wireless coverage for portable devices.

The Wilbur Arts Center features numerous art studios, music studios, a cable television studio, and the Lucille B. Hays Theatre. Molloy's new performing arts center opened in the Public Square student center in fall 2011, providing additional rehearsal and performance space for students, while bringing world-class performers to the College's campus.

Kellenberg Hall houses six science labs, a language lab, and the education resource center. The Casey Center houses two nursing labs, and the behavioral sciences research facility is located in Siena Hall.

Costs

For 2012–13, tuition was $23,410 and required fees were approximately $1,010. Students can expect to spend about $1400 on books and supplies and approximately $2,400 in miscellaneous expenses.

Financial Aid

More than 85 percent of the student body of Molloy College is awarded financial aid in the form of scholarships, grants, loans, and Federal Work-Study Program employment. Financial aid awards are based on academic achievement and financial need. Completion of the Free Application for Federal Student Aid (FAFSA) is required. No-need scholarships and grants are also available.

Students who have attained a 95 percent or better high school average and a minimum combined score of 1280 on the SAT (composite math and verbal scores) are considered for the Molloy Scholars' Program, which awards full-tuition scholarships. Partial scholarships are available under Dominican, Community Service, and Fine Arts Scholarships. The Transfer Scholarship Program grants partial-tuition scholarships to students transferring into Molloy College with at least a 3.0 cumulative average. Athletic grants (Division II only) are awarded to full-time students based on athletic ability in a variety of sports. The Community Service Award is awarded to full-time freshmen demonstrating a commitment to their community and their school.

Faculty

The over 500 full-time and part-time faculty members at Molloy are dedicated as much to the students as to their respective fields. The 10:1 student-faculty ratio allows for small classes where students can receive the individual attention they deserve.

In addition to their teaching responsibilities, faculty members advise students in their fields to help them select courses that both satisfy major course requirements and lead to the attainment of career goals.

Student Government

Every member of the Molloy College student body belongs to the Molloy Student Association, whose elected leaders form the Molloy Student Government. This group of students provides the leadership necessary to keep extracurricular life at Molloy College alive, productive, and practical.

Admission Requirements

Recommended admission qualifications include graduation from a four-year public or private high school or equivalent (GED test) with a minimum of 18.5 units, including 4 in English, 4 in social studies, 3 in a foreign language, 3 in mathematics, and 3 in science. Nursing applicants must have taken courses in biology and chemistry. Mathematics applicants must have taken 4 units of math and 3 of science (including chemistry or physics). Biology applicants must have credits in biology, chemistry, and physics and 4 units of math. A portfolio is required of art applicants, and music students must audition. Social work applicants must file a special application with the director of the social work program.

The admissions committee bases its selection of candidates on the secondary school record, SAT or ACT scores, class rank, and the school's recommendation. A particular talent or ability can be important. Character and personality, extracurricular participation, and alumni relationships are all considered. On-campus interviews are recommended but not required.

The St. Thomas Aquinas Program, which houses both HEOP and the Albertus Magnus Program, may be an option for students not normally eligible for admission.

Molloy College also offers an honors program for a select group of academically gifted students. The program is open to entering freshmen in all majors.

Application and Information

To apply to Molloy College, students should submit the following credentials to the Admissions Office: a completed application for admission, a nonrefundable $30 application fee, an official high school transcript or GED score report, official results of the SAT or ACT, and official college transcripts (transfer students only).

The College uses a rolling admission system. Students are advised of an admission decision within a few weeks after the application filing process is complete.

For further information, prospective students should contact:

Director of Admissions
Molloy College
1000 Hempstead Avenue
P.O. Box 5002
Rockville Centre, New York 11571-5002
Phone: 888-4-MOLLOY (toll-free)
Website: http://www.molloy.edu

Molloy College combines academic excellence and leadership with personal, compassionate mentoring to bring out the best in every student.

MONMOUTH UNIVERSITY
WEST LONG BRANCH, NEW JERSEY

The University

Monmouth University is a dynamic, first-tier, private university that empowers students to reach their full potential as leaders. Through small classes, individual attention, and innovative faculty members, students are afforded a challenging learning environment on one of the most beautiful campuses in New Jersey, which blends classic beauty with the latest technology.

The University has a diverse student body comprised of more than 6,000 undergraduate and graduate students. While many are from the Northeast, students come from all across the United States, as well as nations around the world. For those choosing University housing, Monmouth offers traditional residence halls and garden-style apartments. Some University-sponsored beachfront campus housing is also offered to students who meet certain requirements. Housing is guaranteed for first-year and sophomore students who return their enrollment deposits and contracts by the May 1 deadline.

Students at Monmouth have an assortment of extracurricular activities to choose from, including more than seventy-five student-run clubs and organizations, such as the Student Government Association, the campus newspaper (*The Outlook*), the online news portal (*The Verge*), the FM radio station (WMCX), the television station (Hawk TV), the yearbook (*Shadows*), the literary magazine (*Monmouth Review*), and various sororities and fraternities. Special events are held throughout the year, including art exhibits, concerts, lectures, and sightseeing trips.

In addition, students can cheer on Monmouth's NCAA Division I athletics teams. Monmouth is proud to host a successful inter-collegiate athletics program that fields twenty-one teams for men and women. The University's basketball and track and field teams compete in the 153,200-square-foot Multipurpose Activity Center (MAC), which features a 4,100-seat arena and a 200-meter, six-lane indoor track. All Monmouth students have access to the MAC, which also houses a modern fitness center, locker rooms, conference space, the University Store, and more. Outdoor facilities on campus include tennis courts; an all-weather track; and baseball, football, soccer, and softball fields.

Monmouth is a destination that offers something for everyone, and it strives to ensure that students have the resources and support to pursue their goals. For instance, the Center for Student Success (CSS) assists students through a variety of academic and career counseling services and programs. Furthermore, students who complete their degrees benefit from continued relationships with the Monmouth family. Many graduates return to campus to visit friends, discuss projects with faculty members, and even recruit the next generation of alumni.

Location

Located in the safe, suburban area of West Long Branch, New Jersey, Monmouth is approximately 1 hour from both New York City and Philadelphia, making it easier for students to link classroom academics with real-world experiences. The University is close to many technology firms and financial institutions, which provide both employment possibilities for graduates and opportunities for undergraduates to gain experience through internships and cooperative education.

In addition, Monmouth's 156-acre campus is only 1 mile from the beaches of the Atlantic Ocean. This provides a natural classroom for students, particularly those in the University's marine and environmental biology and policy program. Many restaurants, shops, and theaters are also nearby, allowing students to have a fun, enriching college experience.

Majors and Degrees

Monmouth University offers thirty-four baccalaureate degree programs in six academic schools that share the University's commitment to providing the highest level of education through innovative techniques and personal attention. The **Leon Hess Business School** awards bachelor's degrees in business administration with concentrations in accounting, economics, finance, international business, management, marketing, and real estate. The **School of Education** awards bachelor's degrees that allow students to earn certification as elementary and secondary school teachers; the school also offers various endorsements, such as English as a second language and teacher of students with disabilities. The **Wayne D. McMurray School of Humanities and Social Sciences** awards bachelor's degrees in anthropology, art, communication, criminal justice, English, fine arts, foreign language, history, homeland security, music, political science, psychology, sociology, and theatre arts. A Spanish and international business B.A. degree is awarded jointly through the Leon Hess Business School and the School of Humanities and Social Sciences. The **School of Science** awards bachelor's degrees in biology, chemistry, clinical laboratory sciences, computer science, marine and environmental biology and policy, mathematics, medical laboratory science, and software engineering. The **School of Social Work** awards the Bachelor of Social Work degree. The **Marjorie K. Unterberg School of Nursing and Health Studies** awards bachelor's degrees in health studies and health and physical education, as well as the Bachelor of Science in Nursing (available only to upper-division transfer students). A preprofessional advising program is available for students who intend to pursue careers in medicine, dentistry, or other healthcare fields. Monmouth also offers a number of Five-Year Baccalaureate/Master's programs, which enable qualified students to earn a bachelor's and a master's degree in five years in business, computer science, criminal justice, education (select programs), English, history, political science/public policy, psychology/school counseling, social work, or software engineering.

Academic Programs

The curriculum at Monmouth is focused on creating the next generation of leaders who are attuned to today's globally oriented, technological society and yet are grounded in the liberal arts. The University also emphasizes writing, speaking, and other interpersonal skills that are critical to personal growth and professional success. Monmouth equips every student with technological literacy and experiential education—real-world experience related to the student's academic major.

Experiential education (Ex Ed) is an invaluable part of the curriculum for all Monmouth students, enabling them to gain experience in corporations, local businesses, nonprofits, government, and schools. The Ex Ed requirement at Monmouth can be completed in various ways; for instance, education majors earn Ex Ed credit for completing a semester of student teaching. The University also partners with the Washington Center, allowing students to earn credit for experiential learning gained through internships and symposia in the nation's capital.

Genuine concern for the individual student characterizes the entire educational program at Monmouth. Professors, not teaching assistants, conduct all courses and supervise all laboratories. They also strive to help students develop values, such as citizenship and social responsibility, that enable graduates to make significant contributions to their communities and society.

In addition, the University's Honors School allows qualified students to participate in an educational environment that encourages and supports intellectual and personal excellence. First-year courses are clustered to enhance interactive learning, with professors who develop common themes and assignments. Honors classes are distinguished by in-depth coverage of material through discussion and writing, smaller class sizes, and a heightened student-faculty rapport. In their final year, each Honors School student researches, writes, and publicly presents an honors thesis, guided by a faculty member who serves as their academic mentor.

Academic Facilities

Monmouth's fifty-four buildings provide a synthesis of historical architecture and modern aesthetics. The campus' signature building is Woodrow Wilson Hall, a National Historic Landmark, which houses classrooms and administrative offices and served as Daddy Warbucks' mansion in the film *Annie*. Two other buildings on campus have rich histories: the Monmouth University Library and Lauren K. Woods Theatre. The library, the former mansion of Murry and Leonie Guggenheim, displays many charming architectural features and holds 340,000 print and online monographs, 155 databases (e-journals, videos, and e-books), and over 49,000 electronic and print journal subscriptions. Woods Theatre, once the Guggenheim carriage house, features a variety of performances and lets students experience all phases of the theater arts.

One of Monmouth's most unique buildings is the Jules L. Plangere Jr. Center for Communication, which is home to the Department of Communication and provides state-of-the-art studios and editing facilities. The newest facility on campus is Joan and Robert Rechnitz Hall, which houses the Department of Art and Design, an art gallery, three Mac labs, a reception area, and an animation and editing studio.

All academic programs are amply supported by state-of-the-art computer hardware and software and classroom/laboratory facilities. The major components supporting Monmouth's academic programs include Windows, Mac OS, and Unix systems connected via an expansive wired and wireless network, which spans twenty-three buildings and encompasses more than 2,400 workstations in general and specialty labs and classrooms.

Costs

For 2012–13, tuition and fees were approximately $29,710 per year. Annual room and board costs were approximately $10,802; actual costs are determined by the type of room and meal plan selected. Costs are subject to change for 2013–14.

Financial Aid

Monmouth believes that qualified students should not be denied an educational opportunity due to lack of financial resources. Financial aid staff members counsel students and their families and assist them in obtaining the maximum financial aid possible. In a cooperative effort, the University utilizes institutional, federal, and state resources and expects a reasonable family contribution toward the cost of attendance. In developing each student's award package, all resources available are utilized to address individual circumstances and provide equitable treatment for all applicants.

A wide range of University scholarships and grants are offered to all prospective full-time, first-year, and transfer students on the basis of academic performance and without regard to financial need. Eligibility for University scholarship and grant funding varies according to the quality of the student's previous academic record. Award amounts range from $1,500 to $16,000. Scholarships and grants are renewed at the same amount for each year of the student's undergraduate career, provided the student maintains satisfactory levels of academic performance. Academic excellence scholarship recipients must maintain a minimum 3.0 cumulative GPA; academic grant recipients must maintain a minimum 2.5 cumulative GPA; and incentive grant recipients must maintain a minimum 2.0 cumulative GPA.

The University also participates in all federal and state grant and loan programs. To establish eligibility for these programs and capitalize on available assistance, students should complete the Free Application for Federal Student Aid (FAFSA) as soon after January 1 as possible. Students and their families may call 732-571-3463, e-mail finaid@monmouth.edu, or visit the Financial Aid Office for assistance.

Students interested in attending Monmouth can get an estimate of their eligibility for federal, state, and institutional aid, even before submitting their application. To complete the University's Scholarship Inquiry Form and Net Price Calculator, students should visit www.monmouth.edu/scholarship.

Faculty

The University's professors are leaders in their fields and contribute through research, publishing, and consulting services to their respective academic areas. There are 266 full-time and 364 part-time faculty members. Approximately 83 percent of full-time faculty members have doctorates or terminal degrees in their fields. The average class size is 21, and the student-faculty ratio is 14:1.

Student Government

The Student Government Association (SGA) is an important and necessary voice in the University community; its views are recognized and respected. Monmouth students who wish to get involved with SGA can also do so as general members. This flexible form of involvement does not require a student to run for a position or participate in any one of the elections that are sponsored by SGA. More information is available at www.monmouth.edu/sga.

Admission Requirements

Many factors are considered in an admission application. For first-year applicants, a committee evaluates the required high school transcripts and SAT or ACT scores. Counselor recommendations, a resume of activities including leadership positions held, and other information supporting the application are welcome. Campus tours and information sessions with admission counselors are available. Transfer students must submit official transcripts from all colleges attended. If transfer students have earned fewer than 24 transferable credits, they must fulfill first-year admission requirements as well.

Application and Information

Early action is a nonbinding option for students with a strong desire to enroll at Monmouth. The early action application deadline is December 1, and the admission decision notification date is January 15. The application deadline for regular decision is March 1, with an admission decision notification date prior to April 1. Applications received after March 1 are considered on a space-available basis. First-year housing is guaranteed for students who submit the required enrollment deposit, housing deposit, and housing contract by May 1. Students who submit their deposits and housing contract after May 1 may be placed on a wait list for admission and/or housing.

For further information, students should contact:

Office of Undergraduate Admission
Monmouth University
400 Cedar Avenue
West Long Branch, New Jersey 07764-1898
Phone: 732-571-3456
　　　　800-543-9671 (toll-free)
Fax: 732-263-5166
E-mail: admission@monmouth.edu
Website: http://www.monmouth.edu
　　　　http://www.facebook.com/monmouthuniversity
　　　　http://www.twitter.com/monmouthu
　　　　http://www.youtube.com/monmouthuniversity

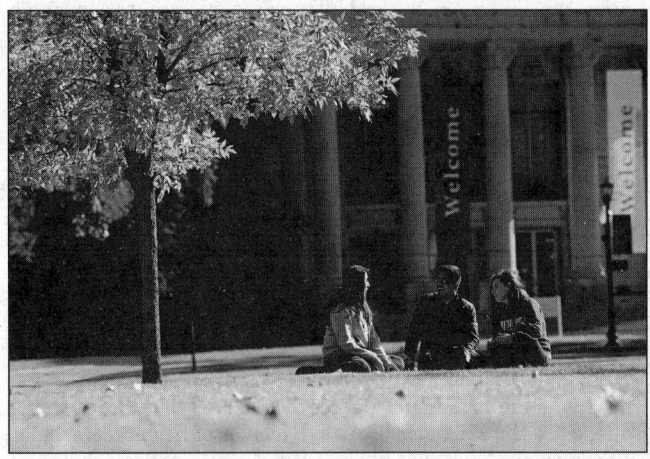

Monmouth students enjoy a challenging learning environment on a campus that offers classical beauty and the latest technology.

MORNINGSIDE COLLEGE
SIOUX CITY, IOWA

MORNINGSIDE COLLEGE

The College

The Morningside College experience cultivates a passion for lifelong learning and a dedication to ethical leadership and civic responsibility. For nearly 120 years, the goal of Morningside College has been to provide students with an education of the highest quality. Morningside is rooted in a strong church-related, liberal arts tradition, and its challenge is to prepare students to be flexible in thought, open in attitude, and confident in themselves.

Founded in 1894, Morningside College is a private, four-year, coeducational, liberal arts institution affiliated with the United Methodist Church. The College seeks both students and faculty members representing diverse social, cultural, ethnic, racial, and national backgrounds.

At the graduate level, Morningside confers a Master of Arts in Teaching, with professional educator or special education tracks.

Morningside College's 1,200 full-time undergraduate students are encouraged to participate in a wide variety of activities, including departmental, professional, and religious organizations; honor societies; and sororities and fraternities. A newspaper, literary magazine, and campus radio station are all student directed. These activities provide students with many opportunities to develop leadership, interpersonal, and social skills. Since nearly all activities on campus are student initiated and student directed, ample opportunities for leadership development exist. Music recitals and concerts, theater productions, and a campus events series are held each semester. Intercollegiate athletics are available for men in baseball, basketball, cross-country, football, golf, soccer, swimming, tennis, track and field, and wrestling and for women in basketball, cross-country, golf, soccer, softball, swimming, tennis, track, and volleyball. Cheer and dance squads are also part of the athletic department. Bowling is slated to become a varsity sport for the 2013–14 season, with competition on the national level. A variety of intramural activities are available.

The Hindman-Hobbs Center includes a pool, saunas, racquetball courts, a weight room, basketball courts, a wrestling room, and a jogging track as well as classroom facilities and offices.

Location

Morningside College is located on a 68-acre campus in Sioux City, the fourth-largest city in Iowa. The campus is based in a residential section of the community, adjacent to a city park, swimming pool, and tennis courts and within 5 minutes of major regional shopping centers. The Sioux City metropolitan area offers a blend of urban shopping, commerce, and recreation in a scenic setting. Students find Morningside's Sioux City location to be advantageous in seeking internship opportunities and full- or part-time employment.

Majors and Degrees

The five undergraduate degrees conferred by Morningside College are the Bachelor of Arts, Bachelor of Science, Bachelor of Science in Nursing, Bachelor of Music, and Bachelor of Music Education. Career programs consist of accounting, advertising, art, biology, business administration, chemistry, computer science, corporate communications, elementary education, engineering physics, English, graphic arts, history, interdisciplinary studies, marketing, mass communications, mathematics, music, nursing, philosophy, photography, political science, psychology, religious studies, Spanish, special education, and theater. Students choosing to teach in secondary school may be certified in most academic majors.

In cooperation with other institutions, Morningside offers preprofessional programs in dentistry, engineering, law, medical technology, medicine, the ministry, optometry, pharmacy, physical therapy, physician assistant studies, and veterinary medicine.

Academic Programs

Morningside operates on a two-semester system; sessions are held from late August to December and from January to early May. Evening classes are offered each semester. A three-week May Term and a six-week summer session are also available.

The Morningside College experience provides an education that develops the whole person through an emphasis on critical thinking, effective communication, cultural understanding, practical wisdom, spiritual discernment, and ethical action. By working with talented faculty members in a large number of majors, caring college staff members who provide numerous opportunities for valuable cocurricular experiences, and other exceptional and interesting students with whom they will form lifelong connections, Morningside students gain the knowledge, skills, and personal dispositions that will ensure their success.

Special opportunities include a voluntary Interdepartmental Honors Program, in which students meet weekly to discuss ideas that have shaped history from the ancient world into the future. Friday Is Writing Day, offered in a weekly discussion format, allows students and faculty members to read aloud and react to one another's writing.

Every entering full-time student is provided with a notebook computer that is used in classroom work. Student technology services include high-speed Internet connection, ports in all residence halls and classrooms, web-accessible personal e-mail accounts, a digital library accessible day and night, specialized computer labs to support academic programs, and wireless network access points across campus.

Off-Campus Programs

Morningside students who qualify have the opportunity to take advantage of special programs for off-campus study. Programs are available for a semester or the entire school year. The College has agreements with schools in Italy, England, Japan, and Northern Ireland.

Students participate in exchange programs with the Consortium Institute of Management and Business Analysis (CIMBA) in Italy; Kansai Gaidai University in Japan; Queen's University, the University of Ulster, Belfast Metropolitan College, Stranmillis University College, and St. Mary's University College in Northern Ireland; and Edge Hill University, the Centre for Medieval and Renaissance Studies, and Regent's American College London in England.

A cooperative program with Central College in Pella, Iowa, allows Morningside students to study abroad in Australia, China, England, France, Mexico, the Netherlands, Spain, and Wales.

In addition, Morningside has opportunities for students to enroll for a semester at American University in Washington, D.C., to study the U.S. government in action. Students may also be nominated for a semester at Drew University in New Jersey to study the United Nations. Students who participate in these programs maintain their enrollment at Morningside College.

Academic Facilities

The Hickman-Johnson-Furrow Learning Center is the home of the library and the Academic Support Services Center. The library has more than 99,000 volumes, nearly 3,000 audio recordings and video materials, and nearly 440 current print periodical subscriptions. Online accessibility includes student/faculty access to more than 18,000 full-text journals. The library's web-based, integrated online system allows seamless access to numerous subscription databases as well as other online catalogs and websites. The library building also houses the Spoonholder Café, classrooms, the Mass Communication Department, and a computer lab.

Charles City College Hall is listed on the National Register of Historic Places and houses classrooms and offices for the History and Political Science, Philosophy, Religious Studies, and Theatre Departments.

The Eugene C. Eppley Fine Arts Building is one of the finest music and art facilities in the Midwest. The auditorium seats 1,400 and is noted for its acoustical qualities and the majestic Sanford Memorial Organ. The MacCollin Classroom Building, adjoining the auditorium, houses offices, art studios, practice rooms, and classrooms for music and art students.

The Helen Levitt Art Gallery adjoins the Eppley Auditorium and is home to the Levitt art collection, which includes work by internationally famous artists.

Lewis Hall, the second-oldest building on campus, is the site of the Education, English, Modern Languages, and Nursing Departments as well as administrative offices.

The Robert M. Lincoln Center houses the College's Division of Business Administration and Economics and contains a library, auditorium, a conference room, several classrooms, and the Center for Entrepreneurship Education.

The James and Sharon Walker Science Center features up-to-date laboratories and classrooms and houses offices for the Natural Sciences and Mathematics Division.

In 2012, Morningside announced plans to construct a new advising center and a new classroom building that will house the Education and Nursing Departments, along with a proposed applied agricultural studies program.

Costs

Tuition and fees for 2012–13 were $25,000, and room and board were $7,620. These figures do not include books and personal expenses.

Financial Aid

In 2011–12, more than $33 million was awarded in financial aid to Morningside students, with an average financial aid package of $24,978 for a full-time student. The financial aid resources of federal, state, and College programs are available to Morningside students through a combination of scholarships, grants, loans, and work-study employment. Financial assistance is offered to 100 percent of full-time students.

Students are encouraged to submit the Free Application for Federal Student Aid (FAFSA) as early as possible. The College's code number is 001879. The annual priority deadline for need-based financial aid is March 1.

Faculty

Nearly 70 percent of Morningside College's 79 full-time faculty members have earned the terminal degree in their chosen field. The College also employs 49 part-time instructors and has a 13:1 student-faculty ratio.

Student Government

Student government is directly responsible for regulation, supervision, and coordination of student campus activities. The president of the student body is a voting member of the Board of Directors, allowing for student input in decisions facing the Board.

Admission Requirements

Morningside College selects students for admission whose scholastic achievement and personal abilities provide a foundation for success at the college level. While the College seeks students who rank in the upper half of their graduating class, each application is considered on an individual basis. The student's academic record, class rank, and test scores are considered. Transfer students must have earned 24 transferable semester hours of a 2.25 or better cumulative GPA on previous college work to qualify for automatic admission. It is the policy and practice of Morningside College to not discriminate against persons on the basis of age, sex, religion, creed, race, color, national or ethnic origin, sexual orientation, or physical or mental disability.

Application and Information

Rolling admission allows for flexibility; however, prospective students are encouraged to apply as early as possible before the semester in which they wish to enroll. Transfer and international students are welcome. Catalogs, application forms, and financial aid forms are available from the Office of Admissions.

For further information, students should contact:

Office of Admissions
Morningside College
1501 Morningside Avenue
Sioux City, Iowa 51106
Phone: 712-274-5111
         800-831-0806 (toll-free)
E-mail: mscadm@morningside.edu
Website: http://www.morningside.edu
         http://www.facebook.com/msideadmissions

Morningside College students enjoy one of the most attractive campuses in the Midwest.

MOUNT ALOYSIUS COLLEGE
CRESSON, PENNSYLVANIA

The College

Mount Aloysius College is a private, accessible, and affordable Catholic liberal arts college sponsored by the Religious Sisters of Mercy. The College welcomes people of all faith traditions. Established in 1853, Mount Aloysius College offers both undergraduate and graduate education. Since the founding of the College, nearly 14,000 students have become proud Mount Aloysius alumni. The College is committed to providing small class sizes, and students benefit from accessible faculty and staff. Mount Aloysius students come mostly from throughout Pennsylvania and the mid-Atlantic Region. There are over 2,500 students enrolled (unduplicated headcount).

Mount Aloysius College is one of 16 Mercy Colleges nationwide. Students are encouraged to synthesize faith with learning, to develop competence with compassion, to apply their talents and gifts to the service of others, and to assume leadership in their community.

Student activities play a distinctive role in personal growth. At Mount Aloysius College, there are approximately 100 organized clubs, groups, honor societies, and an intramural sports program. Activities include a student newspaper, residence hall associations, student government, cheerleading, dance team, scholarship-funded theater and choir programs, and a student activities planning board. Mount Aloysius fun includes social events, intramural sports, athletic events, comedians, live music, theater, educational events, campus forums, and awesome guest lectures.

Mount Aloysius College is a member of NCAA Division III. Athletic programs involve both women and men and include basketball, cross-country, golf, soccer, and tennis. Men's baseball and women's softball and volleyball are also offered. Athletes benefit from the Ray S. and Louise S. Walker Athletic Field Complex, which includes a softball field, one of the finest soccer fields in the area, and the Calandra-Smith baseball complex. Recently the Mountie Stables were opened to the College and to the community. The Stables add dugouts, lockers, showers, storage, and concession facilities to the school's athletic infrastructure.

Construction is underway on a spectacular 90,000-square-foot Athletic Convocation and Wellness Center on the western edge of the beautiful and expansive campus. This facility is scheduled to open in early 2014 and will take Mount Aloysius College athletics to a new level. The facility will also add a welcomed special events venue to the Southern Allegheny Mountains.

The main campus building is a picturesque structure dating to 1897. It houses the admissions, financial aid, security, health, and academic offices, along with the Office of the President, classrooms, the Region's premiere nursing simulation center, and the Wolf-Kuhn Art Gallery. Cosgrave Center is the hub of campus life. The building contains the dining hall, snack bar, bookstore, child-care center (part of the elementary education/early childhood program at the College), lounges, recreational rooms, student affairs offices, and meeting rooms. The College's Health and Physical Fitness Center is currently the main athletic arena. It has seating capacity for 2,000 and serves as home to The Mounties' fans. The facility contains three basketball courts, three volleyball courts, a tennis court, a weight and exercise room equipped with a sauna, two locker rooms, office areas, changing rooms for sports officials, public restrooms, a lobby, and a vestibule. Ihmsen Halls are key housing facilities for residential students. Misciagna Residence is a state-of-the-art residence hall, providing 25 suites and private bathrooms. McAuley Hall features both double and single rooms and a large multipurpose room and study lounges on all three floors. Alumni Hall is a historic, multipurpose facility used for College drama, musicals, lectures, and performing arts events. The College operates 12 months per year and opens its facilities to the Southern Allegheny community.

The College is 100 percent wireless, and smart classrooms are located throughout the campus.

Mount Aloysius is fully accredited by the Middle States Association of Colleges and Schools and approved by the Pennsylvania Department of Education. All nursing and health studies programs are fully accredited by their professional accrediting bodies, including the National League for Nursing Accrediting Commission, the Commission on Accreditation for Programs of Diagnostic Medical Sonography, the Commission on Accreditation in Physical Therapy Education, the American Association of Medical Assistants, and the Joint Commission on Accreditation for Programs of Surgical Technology.

In addition to its undergraduate programs, Mount Aloysius offers master's degrees in business administration, community counseling, and psychology.

Location

Mount Aloysius College is located in the scenic Southern Allegheny Mountains of west-central Pennsylvania, in the town of Cresson. Convenient and accessible from U.S. Route 22, the College's setting is rural but mere minutes from State College, Altoona, and Johnstown, Pennsylvania. The area has warm, beautiful summers; brisk, breathtaking autumns; invigorating winters; and cool, blooming springs. Well-maintained facilities are close and available for biking, golfing, swimming, horseback riding, waterskiing, boating, hiking, spelunking, cross-country and down-hill skiing, picnicking, and amusement and water parks. A well-kept system of State Parks is convenient to the College as are shopping malls, golf courses, and numerous historical sites.

Majors and Degrees

Mount Aloysius College awards bachelor's and associate degrees in the arts, sciences, and health studies fields in both career-oriented and traditional liberal arts programs. Baccalaureate degrees are available in accounting, behavioral and social science, biology and general science, business administration, which includes a fifth-year M.B.A. option, computer science, criminology, elementary/early childhood education and secondary education (with certifications), English, general science, history/political science, humanities, information technology, math/science, medical imaging, nursing (RN-B.S.N. program), nursing (2+2), occupational therapy (3-2), physical therapy (4-2), physician assistant studies (3-2), prelaw, psychology, sign language/interpreter education, and undecided/exploratory. Associate degrees are offered in applied technology, business administration, criminology, early childhood studies, general studies, legal studies, liberal arts, medical assistant studies, nursing, nursing (LPN to RN), physical therapist assistant studies, pre-nursing, radiography/medical imaging, sign language/deaf studies, and surgical technology.

Academic Programs

Whether preparing students for careers upon graduation or for graduate school, Mount Aloysius recognizes the importance of a broad and liberal education. Thus, in addition to receiving solid preparation for a chosen career, every student at the College receives a foundation in the arts, sciences, and humanities through an outstanding core curriculum. Strong emphasis is placed on the specialized courses within each program of study, and many academic programs combine classroom experience with internships and related training at area clinical sites, agencies, and institutions. In addition to its regular academic programs, Mount Aloysius offers independent and directed study with a commitment to service, a central component to a Mercy education. The College has an excellent honors program and academic services area. The academic calendar has two traditional semesters and optional summer sessions.

Off-Campus Programs

An important feature of many academic programs is off-campus training. The majority of the College's programs of study require credit-yielding practicums at partnering hospitals, public and private schools, or health or human service agencies. Students in all health programs benefit from required clinical training during their time at the College.

Academic Facilities

In 1995, Mount Aloysius College opened both a new Library and a new era, signifying greater access to information for the College community. This state-of-the-art Library is the campus hub for technology and study. With a Buhl Electronic Classroom and more than 80,000 print and nonprint titles, the Library is an impressive, 31,000-square-foot facility with ample seating space, four group-study rooms, a reading lounge, a law library and classroom, an unparalleled 18,000-volume Ecumenical Collection donated by Pastor Gerald Myers, and ample room for expansion. This facility is completely automated, with an online catalog and access to remote libraries and the Internet through more than 30 workstations. The Library also houses the Information Technology Center, home to 15 multimedia workstations and the latest educational software.

Pierce Hall serves as the campus science center. A state-of-the-art, 31,000-square-foot facility, it was completed in 1997. Pierce Hall houses all science labs, health science centers, and the offices of science faculty. Academic Hall is home to the College Honors Program. It houses classrooms, labs, seminar rooms, faculty offices, and electronic classrooms. The College is proud of its bridge to the past and its progress in providing twenty-first century learning facilities.

Costs

Annual tuition and fees for the 2012–13 academic year for full-time students were $18,640; room and board were $8,080. Up-to-date cost information is available online at www.mtaloy.edu/tuition_and_aid/tuition_and_fees.

Financial Aid

Mount Aloysius prides itself on affordability. Many MAC students hail from proud families of modest means and many are first-generation students. The College understands the expense involved in acquiring a quality education and encourages all students to apply for all available aid. Through the Office of Financial Aid, the College assists students in applying for state and federal grants, loans, work-study awards, merit scholarships and more. The College awards academic monies based on GPA and SAT or ACT scores. These awards are renewable over a four-year period and range from $1,000 to $10,000 per year. Mount Aloysius College participates in all federal and state programs; fully 94 percent of Mount Aloysius College students receive some form of financial aid. *U.S. News & World Report* has ranked Mount Aloysius College as one of the best-priced private liberal arts colleges in the United States.

Faculty

The Mount Aloysius faculty consists of approximately 175 members, whose primary responsibility is teaching and advising students. Many faculty members hold advanced or terminal degrees and are expected to maintain close instructional ties with students. Many professors hold national, professional certificates in such disciplines as criminology, education, law, and

nursing. The Mount Aloysius student-faculty ratio of 14:1 allows close contact between students and faculty members, providing personal attention in a highly structured environment—a key ingredient in the College's academic philosophy.

Student Government

The Student Government Association (SGA) represents students on all issues that concern the College. The SGA appoints student representatives to all student-oriented College committees. The College encourages student participation in the general governance structure and other matters concerning the development and implementation of policies on residential student life.

Admission Requirements

The College enrolls a freshman class of approximately 350 students. The total class of 550 includes transfer students. Admission is selective, based on academic promise, as indicated by a student's secondary school performance and activities, standardized test scores, and special experience and talents. Applicants are required to have or expected to earn a diploma from an approved secondary school or a GED diploma. Submission of official transcripts and SAT or ACT scores is required. In addition to the general admission requirements, specific admission requirements exist for the health programs.

For further information, students should visit the College's website at http://www.mtaloy.edu. Prospective students are encouraged to visit the scenic 193-acre campus. The College is open Monday to Friday from 8:30 a.m. to 5 p.m. and on select Saturdays.

Application and Information

To apply for admission to Mount Aloysius College, candidates are encouraged to submit their application and $30 application fee to the Office of Undergraduate and Graduate Admissions. In addition, students may apply online.

For further information, students should contact:
Office of Undergraduate and Graduate Admissions
Mount Aloysius College
7373 Admiral Peary Highway
Cresson, Pennsylvania 16630
Phone: 814-886-6383
        888-823-2220 (toll-free)
Fax: 814-886-6441
E-mail: admissions@mtaloy.edu
Website: http://www.mtaloy.edu

The iconic Main Building at Mount Aloysius College, Cresson, Pennsylvania, dates from the late 19th century. Inside Main, and throughout the beautiful 193-acre campus, is laser-new technology, with 100 percent wireless broadband access and an extensive arsenal of educational simulators in the nursing and health sciences.

MUHLENBERG COLLEGE
ALLENTOWN, PENNSYLVANIA

The College

Founded in 1848, Muhlenberg College aims to develop independent critical thinkers who are intellectually agile, characterized by a zeal for reasoned and civil debate, knowledgeable about the achievements and traditions of diverse civilizations and cultures, able to express ideas with clarity and grace, committed to lifelong learning, equipped with ethical values, and prepared for lives of leadership and service.

Muhlenberg students achieve the College's goals by assuming strong individual responsibility for intense involvement in vigorous academic work and for personal involvement within the College community. The more than 100 student organizations provide outlets for the diversified cultural, athletic, religious, social, leadership, and service interests of the students. The campus is primarily residential; more than 90 percent of the 2,200 students live on campus. A close sense of community develops naturally, one in which their diversified academic and personal interests enable students to contribute positively to the intellectual and personal growth of their peers.

Students are aided by an active Career Center in relating academic and personal knowledge and skills to appropriate career goals and in obtaining positions upon graduation. About one third of a typical graduating class proceeds immediately to graduate or professional school.

Location

Muhlenberg College is located on a campus of 86 acres in suburban west Allentown, an area made up primarily of attractive family homes and parks. The downtown area of Allentown, a city of approximately 105,000 people, is a 10-minute ride from the campus. The College is located 90 miles west of New York City and 60 miles north of Philadelphia.

Majors and Degrees

Muhlenberg offers the Bachelor of Arts (A.B.) degree in the following fields: accounting, American studies, anthropology, art, business, dance, economics, English, film studies, finance, French, German, history, history/government, international studies, Jewish studies, media and communication, music, philosophy, philosophy/political thought, political economy, political science, psychology, religious studies, Russian studies, social science, sociology, Spanish, and theater arts. The Bachelor of Science (B.S.) degree is offered in the following fields: biochemistry, biology, chemistry, computer science, environmental science, mathematics, natural sciences, neuroscience, and physics. Students may also design their own major. Minors are offered in most of the major fields, as well as in Africana studies, women's studies, public health, sustainability studies, and Asian traditions.

In addition, students may receive certification to teach at the elementary and secondary levels. Other opportunities include

a 4-4 dual-admission program with Drexel University College of Medicine; a 3-4 dental program with the University of Pennsylvania; a 3-3 B.S./Ph.D. program in physical therapy with Thomas Jefferson University; a 3-2 B.S./M.S. program in occupational therapy with Thomas Jefferson University; a 3-2/4-2 combined program in engineering, offered in cooperation with Columbia University; a 3-2 combined program in forestry, offered in cooperation with Duke University; and a 4-4 dual-admission program with SUNY College of Optometry.

Academic Programs

The A.B. and B.S. programs emphasize breadth of study in the liberal arts as well as in-depth study of a particular academic major. All students must fulfill requirements in the arts, foreign culture, the humanities, social sciences, and natural sciences. Strong achievement on Advanced Placement examinations may enable a student to receive advanced placement, possibly with credit. Scores of 4 or 5 earn automatic credit. Scores of 3 are evaluated by the appropriate department.

Students work closely with academic advisers to formulate programs well suited to their individual interests, abilities, needs, and goals. Generally, students are expected to declare their major at the end of the freshman year; however, many students later change their academic major with no difficulty. A double major is possible, and about a third of Muhlenberg students graduate with a double major. The College also enriches the freshman-year experience through more than thirty special-focus First-Year Seminars. Seniors have the opportunity to synthesize and integrate their academic experience through a Culminating Undergraduate Experience (CUE).

Off-Campus Programs

Study abroad is available through Muhlenberg's Semester-in-London Program, Netherlands semester, Dublin semester, or more than 160 affiliate agreements with international universities all over the world. In addition, the Lehigh Valley Association of Independent Colleges sponsors summer study-abroad options in England, France, Germany, Israel, and Spain. Credit for study-abroad programs sponsored by other institutions or by private agencies may also be transferred to Muhlenberg by special arrangement.

Students may participate in a variety of internships in local businesses, health-care facilities, schools, public agencies, theaters, broadcasting stations, and magazines. Government internships in Harrisburg, Pennsylvania, and Washington, D.C., and an Ethics and Public Affairs semester in Washington, D.C., as well as a New York City semester at Jewish Theological Seminary are also available.

Students may enroll in courses offered at any of the five other member institutions of the Lehigh Valley Association of Independent Colleges: Lafayette College, Lehigh University, Cedar Crest College, DeSales University, and Moravian College.

Academic Facilities

Muhlenberg's library collection contains more than 200,000 volumes as well as numerous government documents, periodicals, and electronic and online resources. The $12-million Harry C. Trexler Library, a state-of-the-art library facility, opened in 1988. Students may also use library materials owned by the other institutions participating in the Lehigh Valley Association of Independent Colleges.

The Baker Center for the Arts was designed for Muhlenberg by the well-known architect Philip Johnson. It houses a modern theater complex, a recital hall, classrooms, art studios, and a fine arts gallery. The Trexler Pavilion for Theater and Dance opened in 2000 and provides dance performance and studio space, a new theater, a Black Box, and additional arts spaces. The College augmented its arts facilities with the Rehearsal House in 2011.

Life science facilities include numerous laboratories, classrooms, two electron microscopes, a DNA sequencer, an isolation room used for growing and studying viruses, and a museum of natural history. Facilities supporting students in the physical sciences include equipment for optics, electronics, and atomic, nuclear, and solid-state physics. A new 40,000-square-foot addition to the science facilities opened in fall 2006. The College uses a UNIX/Windows computer system with Novell software, and supports both Microsoft and Apple applications throughout campus.

Costs

The comprehensive tuition and fees for the 2012–13 academic year was $41,510. The room and board fee averaged $9,835. The total cost for a resident student was approximately $51,345.

Financial Aid

Muhlenberg College endeavors to make its educational opportunities available to all qualified students regardless of their financial circumstances. While most financial aid at Muhlenberg is based on financial need as demonstrated by the College Scholarship Service Financial Aid PROFILE and FAFSA, there is also significant merit aid available. Typically, about 75 percent of Muhlenberg's students qualify for and receive financial aid.

Faculty

The Muhlenberg faculty consists of 168 full-time and 119 part-time members. Ninety percent of full-time faculty members hold doctoral or terminal degrees. While many faculty members are distinguished for their scholarly research, teaching is the main emphasis of their work. Professors at all levels work closely with students both inside and outside of the classroom. Many department heads teach introductory courses.

Student Government

Muhlenberg students are expected to demonstrate a high level of responsibility with regard to their own governance and to participate extensively in internal decision-making and communication processes throughout the campus. These responsibilities are coordinated by the United Student Government, which transacts all business pertaining to the student body. This organization is in charge of a student activities budget of more than $350,000. In addition, 2 students serve as representatives to the Board of Trustees, and students hold full voting privileges on many faculty committees.

Admission Requirements

The College selects students who give evidence of ability and scholastic achievement, seriousness of purpose, and the capacity to make constructive contributions to the College community. Approximately 70 percent of a typical freshman class ranked in the top fifth of their secondary school class. SAT scores for entering freshmen average approximately 610 verbal, 620 math, and 615 writing.

Submission of SAT or ACT scores is optional. An on-campus interview is strongly recommended for all applicants and required for students who choose not to submit standardized test scores.

Application and Information

Students who wish to be considered for admission should submit a completed application form as early as possible during their senior year of secondary school and no later than February 15. Regular decision candidates receive notice of admission decisions in late March. Early decision plans are available, and the College fills approximately half of its freshman class via early decision. Transfer admission is also possible.

For further information, interested students should contact:

Christopher Hooker-Haring
Dean of Admission and Financial Aid
Muhlenberg College
Allentown, Pennsylvania 18104-5586
Phone: 484-664-3200
E-mail: admissions@muhlenberg.edu
Website: http://www.muhlenberg.edu

The Bell Tower of the Haas College Center stands as the focal point of the Muhlenberg College campus.

NEUMANN UNIVERSITY
ASTON, PENNSYLVANIA

The University

Neumann University (http://www.neumann.edu), a Catholic coeducational institution in the Franciscan tradition, recognizes the value of developing intellectual excellence, professional competence, and strong community life. As a university that balances the liberal arts with the professions, Neumann was founded to meet and expand the educational and professional horizons of men and women through instruction that is based on values, ethical behavior, and service to others. With its Living and Learning Center (multimedia-capable residences), Neumann University is able to serve a diverse geographic and demographic population.

Founded and sponsored by the Sisters of St. Francis of Philadelphia, the University is committed to a varied student body and welcomes students of all denominations. Current enrollment is 3,100.

The Life Center houses the Meagher Theatre, the Bruder Athletic Center, and the Crossroads Cafe dining facility. Intercollegiate sports include women's basketball, cross-country, field hockey, ice hockey, indoor track, lacrosse, soccer, softball, tennis, track, and volleyball; and men's baseball, basketball, cross-country, golf, ice hockey, indoor track, lacrosse, soccer, tennis, and track. Neumann University competes as a member of the National Collegiate Athletic Association (NCAA) Division III, the Colonial States Athletic Conference, and the Eastern Collegiate Athletic Conference (ECAC). Intramural sports are available to all members of the campus community.

The Living and Learning Center is designed to provide a state-of-the-art residential experience, with a focus on education within a real-world living environment. Technologically smart, the center connects students to both faculty members and friends via wireless Internet, which is available in every suite and apartment. The system provides full access to campus resources and activities, as well as activities and resources worldwide. The center also houses a separate computer lab, a fitness center, a reflection room, various study rooms with warming kitchens for group study or meetings, and a laundry.

The University provides a full range of services to students, including career placement, career and personal counseling, a tutoring program, and health services.

Neumann students are involved in a wide variety of campus and community activities. Major and special interest clubs are available for student participation. Clubs bring together students who share common interests and help foster new friendships.

At Neumann, the spiritual dimension of one's life is recognized as integral to total human development. The Ministry Team provides a pastoral presence on campus and promotes a sense of community. The entire University community is invited to serve the needs of the poor and neglected in society through various outreach programs, with special attention to the need for peace and justice in the world today.

Neumann is well positioned to respond to the academic and extracurricular needs of students who are of traditional or nontraditional age, commuters or residents, and full-time or part-time.

In addition to undergraduate programs, Neumann confers master's degrees in accounting, education, nursing, organizational and strategic leadership, pastoral counseling, and sport and entertainment management as well as doctoral degrees in education (Ed.D.) and physical therapy (D.P.T.).

Location

Neumann, with a beautiful 68-acre suburban campus in Aston, Delaware County, Pennsylvania, is a short distance from Philadelphia; Wilmington, Delaware; southern New Jersey; and Maryland. It is easily accessible from major arteries such as I-95, Route 476, Route 1, and the Pennsylvania Turnpike.

Majors and Degrees

Neumann offers strong academic majors leading to a Bachelor of Arts degree or a Bachelor of Science degree in accounting, arts production and performance, athletic training, biology, business administration, communication and media arts, computer and information management, criminal justice, education, English, environmental studies, international business, liberal arts, marketing, nursing, political science, psychology, and sport and entertainment management. The education programs lead to teacher certification in early elementary (PK–4), special education (PK–8) or secondary education. Pre-professional programs in law and medicine are also available. An accelerated evening program for adults leads to an Associate of Arts, Bachelor of Arts, or Bachelor of Science degree in liberal studies or professional studies.

Academic Programs

The academic program at Neumann University is composed of a core curriculum (required of all students), a major area of study (chosen by each student), and a wide range of elective offerings. Students may also choose a minor area of study. The University's broad base of liberal arts offerings prepares students for the intellectual and social challenges they will face in the employment marketplace and throughout their lives. The core is intended to provide basic knowledge of the liberal arts and sciences; develop verbal, written, and symbolic communication skills; and stimulate interest in a broad range of topics for the purpose of enhancing the individual's contributions to society, thereby enabling the individual to realize full human potential.

Classroom instruction is supplemented by cooperative education and internships, through which students can earn credit and gain experience by working in a job related to their career interest. Fieldwork and student teaching are required of all education majors. Clinical practice for the nursing major occurs in a variety of health-care facilities in the tri-state area.

The honors program is an opportunity for academically talented students to explore imaginative and innovative perspectives on learning. It is also an opportunity to stimulate and motivate students to expand their knowledge and interest and to strive for greater excellence. Moreover, it is a reward for prior perseverance and dedication as well as an obligation to use skills and abilities in service to others. Admission to the honors program is by invitation.

Neumann University has transfer articulation agreements with numerous schools throughout the area.

Academic Facilities

The Child Development Center is a state-of-the-art, octagonal-shaped building, specifically designed to house an educational program for preschoolers. As a state-licensed day-care facility, it enrolls children of Neumann students, the faculty, and the community. The Child Development Center is part of the Division of Education and Human Services. Students enrolled in education courses use the center for observation, practical experience, and student teaching.

The Academic Computing Center is located on the ground floor of the University. The computers are viewed as tools to support all fields of study and all students and faculty members. Neumann University has installed a wireless Local Area Network (LAN) that connects various computers and provides shared services such as printing, e-mail, and support for the instructional use of computers by providing for the sharing of files. Computers are available to all students, as is software related to various academic disciplines.

The University library contains a balanced collection of more than 55,000 physical volumes and films, 13,000 e-books, and nearly 50,000 electronic journals. E-books and journals can be accessed from anywhere with an Internet connection. Collaboration with faculty and membership in local consortia (TCLC, SEPCHE) ensures access to the most relevant resources for academic success. Professional librarians provide in-person research support seven days a week and also create online Research Guides and video tutorials for around-the-clock assistance. Librarians also provide cutting-edge instruction to help develop essential 21st Century skills like critical thinking, technological literacy, and information management. Quiet study rooms, collaborative group spaces, and an open computer lab and Wi-Fi collectively support student study needs.

Costs

Tuition for full-time students (12 to 19 credits per semester) in 2012–13 was $23,262. Room and board were $11,070 (full meal plan).

Financial Aid

Typically, about 95 percent of Neumann undergraduate students receive some form of financial aid (scholarships, grants, and student loans).

Neumann offers a variety of renewable scholarships each year to entering full-time freshmen and transfer students. Interested applicants should contact the Office of Admissions and Financial Aid as soon as possible to determine eligibility.

In addition to Neumann scholarships, funds are available through the Federal Pell Grant, Federal Supplemental Educational Opportunity Grant, and Federal Work-Study Programs. Many states provide grant money to attend Neumann (non-Pennsylvania residents should check with their state's higher education agency for details). Veterans Administration benefits can be received by qualified veterans or their dependents. Federal Stafford Student Loans and Federal PLUS Program loans are available and can be applied for through Neumann's preferred lender or any participating bank. Neumann also offers institutional need-based grants. All students requesting financial aid must complete the Free Application for Federal Student Aid (FAFSA) each year to determine eligibility. In order to expedite processing, the FAFSA should be submitted by March 15 for the following school year. Financial aid funds are renewable annually based on need, as determined by the FAFSA results.

Faculty

Neumann students describe faculty members as sincere, hard-working, determined, and energetic. Faculty members view themselves, first, as teachers and are proud partners in their students' journeys toward professional careers. Each student has a faculty adviser, who assists in arranging a program designed to meet the student's educational goals. Many faculty members serve as moderators of student clubs. The student-faculty ratio is 13:1.

Student Government

The Student Government Association (SGA) is the representative body for all students. Its function is to implement the aims and purposes of the University, foster cooperation in student relationships, assist the University in being responsive to the needs of the student body, and encourage personal responsibility for an intelligent system of student self-government. Through the Student Activities Board, social functions are planned throughout the year. Students serve on various University committees, including the Student Affairs Committee of the Board, Academic Advising Committee, Honors Program Committee, Registration/Orientation Task Force, and Student Judicial Board. For full-time students, a Student Government Association fee of $80 per semester is required.

Admission Requirements

Neumann has a rolling admission policy and accepts applications throughout the year. Applicants are considered on the basis of high school record, SAT or ACT scores, recommendations, class rank, and other indicators of potential to succeed in university-level studies. Applications for admission are reviewed without regard to sex, race, creed, color, national origin, age, sexual orientation, pregnancy, military status, religion, or disability. Applicants should be graduates of an accredited high school (or present equivalent credentials) and have a recommended curriculum of 16 units of high school course work, distributed as follows: 4 in English, 2 to 3 in science, 2 in mathematics, 2 in social studies, 2 in foreign language, and 4 in electives. Students intending to pursue a major in biology or clinical laboratory science must have at least 1 year of high school biology and chemistry, and high school physics is highly recommended.

Neumann participates in the Advanced Placement (AP) Program and the College-Level Examination Program (CLEP).

An interview and tour of the campus are highly recommended for all prospective students and parents. Visits can be arranged by contacting the Office of Admissions.

Application and Information

Applicants for freshman admission are requested to have SAT or ACT scores and high school transcripts sent to the Office of Admissions. A nonrefundable $35 application fee should accompany the completed application. A free application is available online at http://www.neumann.edu.

Neumann University welcomes applications from students who have attended or are currently attending either two-year or four-year regionally accredited institutions of higher learning.

For further information, students should contact:

Office of Admissions
Neumann University
One Neumann Drive
Aston, Pennsylvania 19014-1298
Phone: 610-558-5616
        800-9NEUMANN (toll-free)
E-mail: neumann@neumann.edu
Website: http://www.neumann.edu

Students love the newest building on campus, the Mirenda Center for Sport, Spirituality, and Character Development.

NEW COLLEGE OF FLORIDA
SARASOTA, FLORIDA

The College

New College of Florida offers serious students the opportunity to pursue rigorous academic study in an environment designed to promote depth in thinking, free exchange of ideas, and highly individualized interaction with faculty members.

Study is focused in the arts and sciences and is highly accelerated and independent. A recent study of the College's graduates found that 80 percent pursue graduate or professional study, gaining admission to Harvard, Yale, MIT, Brown, Georgetown, Berkeley, and other leading graduate programs. New College is competitive with other top schools in the nation when it comes to the percentage of graduates who go on to earn the Ph.D., especially in the sciences.

New College was founded as a private institution in 1960 with a devotion to the values implicit in a liberal arts education and a dedication to creating an innovative academic program where talented students and outstanding faculty members could come together and pursue learning through small classes, seminars, and independent study to pursue advanced undergraduate research. Entry into Florida's public university system in 1975 served to strengthen and perpetuate the idealistic vision and academic mission of the College's founders. These qualities, as well as the College's national reputation, were enhanced further in 2001 when New College was designated as the official Honors College in the liberal arts and sciences for the State University System of Florida. A public-private funding arrangement provides students at New College with a private honors college experience at a public college cost. As a result, the College is regularly featured in guidebooks as being among the nation's leading educational values and as one of the country's top small, public colleges.

New College's student population is 825, of whom approximately 60 percent are women. Approximately 20 percent of students are out-of-state or overseas residents. Through active recruitment of out-of-state students, the College plans to increase its percentage of non-Florida residents in the years ahead. First-year and second-year students must live on campus, but many continuing students choose to live on campus as well. In fact, five new, state-of-the-art residence halls opened at the start of the 2007–08 academic year, allowing New College to house nearly 80 percent of students on campus. The new residence halls include a variety of accommodation options to match student lifestyle interests and incorporate the latest in green building technology. Architecture for the new buildings complements existing campus living communities, such as the College's historic Pei Residence Halls, which were designed by the eminent architect I. M. Pei in the 1960s. The historic, 131-room Pei complex provides rooms with individual entrances, private baths, central air-conditioning, and various combinations of large picture windows, sliding glass doors, and/or balconies. Two other campus residence halls, Dort and Goldstein, provide apartment-style housing with four single rooms, two bathrooms, and a common living room and kitchenette in each unit. Dining facilities on campus include a campus dining hall with full meal plans available for both on- and off-campus students, a snack bar and deli, and the student-owned and -operated Four Winds Café. The College's Counseling and Wellness Center offers basic health care, personal counseling, and a variety of related services.

New College student life is informal. Activities are largely student initiated and include academic, artistic, religious, political, and recreational pursuits. The College's 110-acre bay front location on the Gulf of Mexico includes basketball, racquetball, tennis, and volleyball courts; a multipurpose soccer and athletic field; a running trail; a 25-meter swimming pool; and a comprehensive fitness center. Sailboats, kayaks, and canoes are also available for use by students and faculty members free of charge.

Prospective students can learn more about New College of Florida by visiting its Web site, Facebook, and Twitter pages, and YouTube channel (see Contact Information).

Location

Situated along the coastline of the Gulf of Mexico in southwest Florida, New College serves as the northern gateway to Sarasota, a bustling city with more than 250,000 residents. Located 50 miles south of Tampa,

Sarasota is noted for its recreational, cultural, and artistic attractions, including beautiful white-sand beaches and an abundance of professional theater, art, and music venues. Notably, New College sits adjacent to the world-famous John and Mable Ringling Museum of Art, which offers students free entry to view its Baroque and Renaissance art collections.

The climate is semitropical, consisting of long, warm springs and autumns plus mild winters. Transportation from throughout the nation and within the city is readily accessible. Many major airlines serve Sarasota-Bradenton International Airport, which is adjacent to the College. Within the city, buses link the campus to downtown, shopping malls, parks, and beaches. While mass transit is available, bicycling is the favored means of transportation among students. The College's Office of Student Affairs offers group outings on a regular basis to the downtown Sarasota Farmers Market, grocery stores, and other venues around town.

Majors and Degrees

New College awards the Bachelor of Arts degree in liberal arts and sciences. Each of the College's nearly forty different areas of concentration (majors) is an individualized program of study that students design in consultation with, and with the approval of, faculty members. These include anthropology, applied mathematics, art, art history, biochemistry, biology, chemistry, Chinese language and culture, classics, economics, English, environmental studies, European studies, French language and literature, German language and literature, history, humanities, international and area studies, Latin American studies, literature, marine biology, mathematics, medieval and Renaissance studies, music, natural sciences, neurobiology, philosophy, physics, political science, psychology, public policy, religion, Russian language and literature, social sciences, sociology, Spanish language and culture, Spanish language and literature, and urban studies. Partial areas of concentration include computational science, gender studies, and theater. Students may also pursue self-designed concentrations, with faculty permission. Pre-medical, pre-law, and pre-M.B.A. advising and guidelines are provided by faculty members and by the Center for Career Education and Off-Campus Studies.

Academic Programs

New College of Florida's academic program aims to encourage academic excellence, creativity, and personal initiative and to provide essential tools for lifelong intellectual, personal, and professional growth. The College's distinctive curriculum enables students, in close consultation with faculty members, to develop programs of seminars, tutorials, independent research, and off-campus experiences that meet each student's personal academic interests and goals.

At the end of each semester, rather than grades, students receive detailed narrative evaluations as well as satisfactory/unsatisfactory assessments of their work from individual faculty members. Graduation requirements include satisfactory completion of seven academic contracts (one per semester), three independent-study projects, a senior thesis, and an oral baccalaureate examination. In addition to the requirements for individual majors, students must complete eight courses within the liberal arts curriculum, with at least one course each in the humanities, social sciences, and natural sciences. Students must also meet basic mathematics and computer literacy requirements, and pass or be exempted from Florida's College-Level Academic Skills Test.

The College operates on a 4-1-4 calendar year. The College offers a January interterm when students undertake independent study projects, which they design and complete under faculty sponsorship.

Off-Campus Programs

Internships, fieldwork, and independent research away from the campus offer New College students the opportunity to gain new skills and evaluate career interests. New College believes that off-campus study can make a major contribution to an undergraduate education and facilitates such study through its flexible, individualized curriculum and special support services. New College is a member of the National Student Exchange, which provides access to nearly 200 universities with programs in the U.S. and abroad (many with comparable tuition costs). Students may also participate in programs offered by independent providers, such as the School for International Training and AustraLearn, as well as international programs available through the State University System of Florida and Center for Cross Cultural Studies. With faculty approval, students may pursue off-campus independent study or participate in programs including Living Routes, which offers nontraditional venues for study abroad.

Academic Facilities

New College's wireless-equipped Jane Bancroft Cook Library is befitting of one of the country's leading colleges for the liberal arts and has an open stack arrangement that allows free access to most materials. Administration, trustees, faculty members, and the New College Library Association have implemented an ambitious acquisition program to expand the current holdings of approximately 274,000 volumes. An expansion of the library's visual image collection is also in the works. In total, the library subscribes to more than 900 serial titles, including 700 magazines and journals and many state, national, and international newspapers. In addition, through computer networks and other cooperative programs, New College students and faculty members have access to hundreds of online databases and electronic journals and newspapers, as well as numerous online document delivery services. Through a comprehensive online interlibrary loan system, New College students have convenient access to holdings throughout the State University System of Florida.

The Harry Sudakoff Conference Center on campus hosts visiting lecturers, meetings of campus and community organizations, and a wide range of special events. The Caples Fine Arts Complex includes the 264-seat Mildred Sainer Music and Arts Pavilion, which features student, local, and national performances; the Lota Mundy Music Building, which houses eight music practice rooms, plus the Benjamin and Barbara Slavin Electronic Music Studio; the Christianne Felsmann Fine Arts Building; the Betty Isermann Fine Arts Gallery and Studio; and a sculpture studio. Science facilities include the R. V. Heiser Natural Sciences Complex, which houses laboratories, classrooms, offices, a computer lab, two electron microscopes, and an auditorium, as well as the $2.5-million Rhoda and Jack Pritzker Marine Biology Research Center. The marine center, one of the leading marine research centers in southwest Florida, features state-of-the-art culture rooms, laboratories, and aquariums with water drawn from Sarasota Bay. Saltwater effluent from the tanks is cleaned by means of a wetland constructed in 2001 as part of a New College senior thesis project. The College's 35,000-square-foot Academic Center, which opened in 2011, was awarded LEED Gold certification by the U.S. Green Building Council. It includes a state-of-the-art computer lab, classrooms, faculty offices, and a student lounge. Outside the center is Koski Plaza with the Four Winds sculpture, Koski Bell Tower, built-in benches, and green space.

Costs

For the 2012–13 academic year, in-state tuition and fees at New College of Florida were $6,783 and out-of-state tuition and fees were $29,812. Room and board costs were $8,598.

Financial Aid

The actual cost of providing New College of Florida's highly individualized honors college experience is far greater than the state funding appropriated for support of the College. The New College Foundation secures independent funding to provide for the remaining costs. Part of the foundation's endowment produces income for scholarships.

Approximately 96 percent of New College students receive some form of financial assistance, including academic scholarships and need-based financial aid. To apply for financial aid, students should file the Free Application for Federal Student Aid (FAFSA). February 15 is the priority date for need-based financial aid. All first-time college students who complete applications by February 15 and who are admitted to New College are guaranteed academic scholarship funding. No additional scholarship application is necessary.

Faculty

Of New College's regular, full-time faculty members, 99 percent hold the highest degree awarded in their field of study, which in most cases is the doctorate. They have come to New College from the finest universities nationally and abroad, drawn to an environment that emphasizes excellence in teaching and fosters a close-knit community of scholars. Faculty members sponsor individual students in the formulation of their academic programs, gradually moving toward a form of mentorship through which joint research is sometimes pursued. A 10:1 student-faculty ratio is a key factor in the College's individualized approach to education. At New College, all classes are taught by faculty, not by teaching assistants.

Student Government

Student input is a decisive factor in campus governance. Elected student representatives serve on the Board of Trustees and most major policymaking committees, and are voting participants in divisional and campuswide faculty meetings. The New College Student Alliance, the College's student government, has authority over funding for recreational events, social events, student clubs and organizations on campus, and allocation of the Green Fee for environmentally friendly projects.

Admission Requirements

New College of Florida seeks highly capable students eager to take responsibility for their own education. The admissions staff reviews each candidate individually, assessing his or her potential for success within, and contribution to, the College's unique environment. Course selection, academic record, and writing ability are focal points of the committee's review. The majority of first-year students entering in fall 2012 ranked in the top 20 percent of their high school class. The middle 50 percent of SAT takers had a combined score of 1230–1380 on the critical reading and math sections. The middle 50 percent of ACT takers had a composite score of 26–31.

All prospective students may apply for entrance to either the fall or the spring term. However, the College reserves the right to cancel the spring admission cycle if its enrollment goals have been met. Candidates must submit an admission application, supplement, fee or fee waiver, official transcript(s), SAT or ACT scores, and a letter of recommendation. A campus visit and demonstrated interest are also recommended for all those with serious interest in applying.

Application and Information

Admissions application materials and descriptive literature are available through the New College Office of Admissions and Financial Aid. The College has two application deadlines for the fall class: November 1 (the priority deadline) and April 15. Notification of the admissions decision occurs by April 1 and April 25, respectively. A completed application and all supporting documents must be submitted to the Admissions Office before a candidate is considered for admission.

Inquiries and application requests should be directed to:

Kathleen M. Killion
Dean of Enrollment Services
New College of Florida
5800 Bay Shore Road
Sarasota, Florida 34243-2109
United States
Phone: 941-487-5000
Fax: 941-487-5001
E-mail: admissions@ncf.edu
Web site: http://www.ncf.edu
http://www.facebook.com/newcollegeofflorida
http://twitter.com/NewCollegeofFL
http://www.youtube.com/user/NewCollegeofFL

New College of Florida's historic waterfront campus features spectacular sunsets, wetlands, an intertidal lagoon, and boat access.

THE NEW ENGLAND INSTITUTE OF ART
BROOKLINE, MASSACHUSETTS

The New England Institute of Art is one of The Art Institutes, a system of over fifty schools throughout North America dedicated to providing hands-on education in the creative and applied arts. The New England Institute of Art offers bachelor's and associate degree programs as well as non-degree programs for students interested in pursuing career opportunities from among tomorrow's 15 million jobs in creative fields like design, fashion, and media arts (based on information from the U.S. Bureau of Labor Statistics for job growth from 2012 to 2022).

A focused education from The New England Institute of Art can help students turn their creative energy into a powerful tool that can make a difference in the world. Students are part of a collaborative and supportive community, where experienced instructors provide the guidance and skills needed to pursue a career in the creative economy.

The New England Institute of Art is also an important resource for creative industry leaders who value the opportunity provided students to learn by using professional-grade technology to build a portfolio of work to show potential employers after graduation.

Accreditation

The New England Institute of Art is accredited by the New England Association of Schools and Colleges (NEASC) through its Commission on Institutions of Higher Education (CIHE), 3 Burlington Woods Drive, Suite 100, Burlington, Massachusetts 01803-4531; phone: 781-405-7700.

The New England Institute of Art is authorized to award Associate in Science and Bachelor of Science degrees by the Commonwealth of Massachusetts, Massachusetts Department of Higher Education, One Ashburton Place, Room 1401, Boston, Massachusetts 02108-1696; phone: 617-994-6950.

Location

The New England Institute of Art is located in the Town of Brookline, right on the Boston line, just a short distance from famous Fenway Park and the Museum of Fine Arts. Brookline is a unique blend of busy streets and rolling countryside, upscale shops and small pubs, gracious apartment buildings and large estates. It is also home to many academic and scientific professionals who work at nearby medical centers in Boston and in some of the more than eighty schools and colleges in the area.

Among its many attractions, Brookline features its own working farm, the oldest country club in the nation, a town golf course, the home where President John F. Kennedy was born, a hillside park overlooking Boston with an open-air skating rink, a transportation museum, and many neighborhood parks.

Its major retail centers, such as Coolidge Corner and Brookline Village, are bustling pedestrian areas with antique stores, coffee shops, bookstores, fresh fruit and vegetable markets, delicatessens, and restaurants.

Convenient light rail service can take students from the school into downtown Boston—or any of its many neighborhoods, from the Back Bay to Beacon Hill to Boston Harbor, each with its own unique character, history, and charm. Boston is a relatively compact city that's easy to walk. Follow the red bricks of the Freedom Trail, visit the Museum of Fine Arts, Faneuil Hall, Quincy Market, Boston Common, the USS Constitution, Rowes Wharf, the New England Aquarium, and more.

Besides the Red Sox at Fenway, the NBA's Boston Celtics and the Boston Bruins of the NHL both play at the TD Garden, while the NFL's New England Patriots play football at Gillette Stadium in nearby Foxboro, Massachusetts. And, of course, there's the world-famous Boston Marathon.

Programs of Study and Degree Offerings

Creativity is all around, and with millions of tomorrow's jobs in creative fields, the world needs more creative professionals. No matter which course of study a student chooses, the instructors at The Art Institutes will guide, support, and help students fine-tune their visual thinking and problem solving, so that they can take advantage of the world's growing creative opportunities and put their passion to work. Programs are offered in the areas of design, which focuses on communicating conceptually and helping people connect in living and work spaces; media arts, that centers on utilizing technology to deliver information and entertainment; and fashion, where students learn anything from designing clothes for the runway to running a retail shop.

Bachelor's degree programs are offered in the areas of audio & media technology, digital filmmaking & video production, fashion & retail management, graphic design, interior design, media arts & animation*, photography, sound & motion picture technical arts, and web design & interactive media. (*Concentration[s] available in game art.)

Associate degree programs are offered in the areas of audio production and photography.

Certificate programs are offered in audio production, multimedia & web design I, multimedia & web design II, and photography.

Program availability and degree offerings are subject to change.

Academic Facilities

The New England Institute of Art provides a learning environment with professional-grade technology applicable to each student's course of study. Students have the opportunity to build a portfolio of work that shows potential employers that they are trained to use the software, hardware, or equipment utilized within the industry. Depending upon the course of study, students are immersed in a creative environment—from classrooms to computer labs to studios—focused on relevant, hands-on education designed to prepare them for the real world.

Costs

Actual tuition and housing costs will vary depending on program, number of credits enrolled, and actual living arrangements. Prospective students should contact a Student Financial Services professional at the school for details.

Financial Aid

Financial aid is available for those who qualify. Students who require financial assistance should first complete and submit the Free Application for Federal Student Aid (FAFSA) online at www.fafsa.ed.gov and meet with a financial aid officer. Students may also apply for a number of scholarships focusing on their specific areas of career interest.

Faculty

Faculty members are hands-on creative professionals with proven experience as business leaders and innovators, hosting a learning environment similar to the career world students will face after graduation. Part instructor, part mentor, their mission is to help develop and transform creative potential into high-demand marketable skills.

Admission Requirements

Prospective students should refer to the current academic catalog for full details regarding admission requirements and process.

Application and Information

To obtain an application, make arrangements for an interview, or tour the school, prospective students should contact:

The New England Institute of Art
10 Brookline Place West
Brookline, Massachusetts 02445-7295
Phone: 617-739-1700
 800-903-4425 (toll-free)
Fax: 617-582-4500
Website: http://www.artinstitutes.edu/boston

THE NEW SCHOOL
NEW YORK, NEW YORK

The University

An essential part of New York City's artistic and intellectual life since 1919, The New School is a leading university that offers some of the nation's most respected academic programs in art and design, liberal arts, management and policy, and the performing arts. These programs are closely connected with all that New York City has to offer—its history, its culture, its energy, and its opportunities.

Founded by a group of progressive educators, The New School aspired to be everything the old school was not—open to dissenting opinions and freedom of expression in art and scholarship. Today, New School students continue to create thoughtful and provocative art and collaborate across disciplines to address many of the world's most pressing problems.

For undergraduates, The New School offers five distinctive colleges in the arts and the humanities: Parsons The New School for Design, Eugene Lang College The New School for Liberal Arts, Mannes College The New School for Music, The New School for Jazz and Contemporary Music, and The New School for Drama. In addition, The New School for Public Engagement offers undergraduate programs in liberal arts and psychology, on campus and online, designed specifically for transfer students and working adults. Each of The New School's programs expose students to an exciting and challenging course of study headed by a faculty of artists, scholars, and professionals who practice what they teach.

Location

New York City offers virtually unlimited cultural, artistic, recreational, and intellectual resources that make it one of the world's great cities. New York's Greenwich Village is where most New School students attend class, and the streets themselves become a kind of classroom. Fashion students at Parsons The New School for Design take many of their classes in Midtown New York's Fashion District. Students studying at Mannes College The New School for Music attend school on Manhattan's Upper West Side, a short distance from Lincoln Center, Carnegie Hall, and other major music venues.

Beginning in fall 2013, Parsons is slated to offer bachelor's and master's degree programs in Paris, with courses taught in English. Parsons Paris is located in a newly renovated historic building at 45 rue Saint-Roch, a short walk from the Louvre, the Palais Garnier, Gaîté Lyrique media arts center, and Notre Dame cathedral. Classes will be held there and at locations throughout the city. (The Paris campus is awaiting review by the Middle States Commission on Higher Education.)

Majors and Degrees

Eugene Lang College The New School for Liberal Arts offers the B.A. in the arts (concentrations in arts in context, dance, music, theater, and visual arts), B.A. in culture and media, B.A. in economics, B.A. in education studies, B.A./B.S. in environmental studies, B.A. in global studies, B.A. in history, B.A. in global studies, B.A. in interdisciplinary science (tracks in biology of health, science of the environment, and history and philosophy of science), and B.A. in liberal arts (self-designed program or concentration in social inquiry), B.A. in literary studies (concentrations in literature and writing), B.A. in philosophy, B.A. in politics, B.A. in psychology, B.A. in urban studies, and a B.A.-B.F.A. dual degree with Parsons The New School for Design and The New School for Jazz and Contemporary Music.

Parsons The New School for Design in New York City offers the B.F.A. in architectural design, B.F.A. in communication

design, B.F.A. in design and technology, B.A./B.S. in environmental studies, B.F.A. in fashion design, B.F.A. in fine arts, B.F.A. in illustration, B.F.A. in integrated design, B.F.A. in interior design, B.F.A. in photography, B.F.A. in product design, B.B.A. in strategic design and management, B.S. in urban design, and a B.A.-B.F.A. dual degree with Eugene Lang College. Parsons Paris is scheduled to offer the B.F.A. in art, media, and technology; B.F.A. in fashion design, and B.B.A. in strategic design and management. (The Paris campus is awaiting review by the Middle States Commission on Higher Education).

Mannes College The New School for Music offers the Bachelor of Music, Bachelor of Science, and undergraduate diploma. Areas of study at Mannes are orchestral instruments, piano, harpsichord, orchestral conducting, choral conducting, voice, classical guitar, composition, and theory.

The New School for Jazz and Contemporary Music offers the Bachelor of Fine Arts and a B.A.-B.F.A. dual degree with Eugene Lang College.

The New School for Drama offers the B.F.A. in dramatic arts.

Academic Programs

One of the nation's largest and most prestigious degree-granting colleges of art and design, **Parsons The New School for Design** has been a forerunner in the field since its founding in 1896. Its intensive programs and distinguished faculty embrace innovation, pioneer new uses of technology, and instill in students a global perspective in design. By focusing on the fundamentals of art and design as well as the liberal arts, Parsons leads students to understand the social and economic implications of their work.

Eugene Lang College The New School for Liberal Arts provides the advantages of a small, intimate liberal arts college and the resources of a major university. Lang attracts smart, creative, and independent students who value the opportunity to be challenged in small, seminar-style classes. Committed leaders, scholars, and newsmakers teach these talented young people in an interdisciplinary context.

Lang enables students to accelerate their progress toward a master's degree by combining their undergraduate work with graduate study at one of The New School's graduate programs. Dual bachelor's-master's degree programs offered at Lang include anthropology, economics, environmental policy and sustainability management, historical studies, international affairs, liberal studies, media studies, nonprofit management, organizational change management, philosophy, politics, psychology, sociology, teaching English to speakers of other languages, and urban policy analysis and management.

Mannes College The New School for Music is a preeminent conservatory of classical music for undergraduate and graduate students who are considering a career in music. Mannes College is a community of compassionate musicians who encourage collaboration rather than competition and professional development rather than personal pressure.

The New School for Jazz and Contemporary Music was founded on the principle that working artists should play a role in jazz education. Jazz students' mentors are 75 of the city's leading musicians, and their companions are some of the most promising young players in the country. There are scores of student ensembles and literally hundreds of public performances every year.

In addition to offering the B.F.A. degree, The New School for Jazz and Contemporary Music offers students the opportunity to combine their B.F.A. studies with a certificate program in creative arts therapies.

The four-year B.F.A. program in dramatic arts at **The New School for Drama** prepares students to be twenty-first–century artists and creative thinkers. Professionalism and community are at the core of the program, which provides a rich multidisciplinary, project-based investigation of theater arts and focuses on the development of critical thinking and collaborative skills.

The B.A.-B.F.A. program at The New School is a five-year, dual degree program through which students can earn a Bachelor of Arts degree from Eugene Lang College The New School for Liberal Arts and a Bachelor of Fine Arts degree from either Parsons The New School for Design or The New School for Jazz and Contemporary Music.

Off-Campus Programs

The New School believes that students learn both in and out of the classroom. With access to a wide array of internships, apprenticeships with top designers, and performance opportunities in venues from downtown clubs to Lincoln Center, students can shape their education and take advantage of all the university and the city have to offer.

Students can pursue internships in almost every field in New York City. Recently, New School students have landed internships at the ACLU, Apple, Beth Israel Hospital, *The Cobert Report*, Condé Nast, DKNY, GLAAD, Guggenheim, HBO, Marvel, MTV, NFL, Open Society Institute, Random House, Sesame Workshop, Sony Entertainment, the Village Voice, and WNYC, among many others.

Academic Facilities

In addition having access to the university's three libraries—devoted to social sciences, art and design, and European and American classical music—New School students can use the Research Library Consortium of South Manhattan, one of the largest university library consortiums in the United States. Students have access to state-of-the-art computing and media facilities, including an advanced production facility where portable production equipment is available for student use. The university also provides studios and practice rooms for students of art and design, music, and dance.

Costs

Tuition varies by division and by program. Tuition for full-time undergraduate programs in 2012–13 ranged from $36,660 to $39,280, plus fees. More specific information regarding tuition and fees is available online at www.newschool.edu/tuition. Room and board cost approximately $15,260, depending on the student's choice of meal plan and dormitory accommodations.

Financial Aid

Students are encouraged to apply for aid by filing the Free Application for Federal Student Aid (FAFSA) and requesting that a copy of the need analysis report be sent to The New School (FAFSA code number 002780). Qualified College students are eligible for all federal and state financial aid programs in addition to university gift aid. University aid is awarded on the basis of need and merit and is part of a package consisting of both gift aid (grants and/or scholarships) and a self-help component (loans and Federal Work-Study Program awards). Aid is renewable each year as long as need continues and students maintain satisfactory academic standing at the College. Special attention is given to continuing students who have done exceptionally well.

Faculty

The New School prides itself on its small student-faculty ratio and was ranked first in *U.S. News & Report*'s 2013 edition of Best Colleges for having the highest proportion of classes with fewer than 20 students.

Individual attention is one of the qualities that set New School programs apart. That means students will have the opportunity to work closely with legends of New York's music scene at The New School for Jazz and Contemporary Music, with leaders of New York's art and design world at Parsons, with members of some of New York's most prestigious orchestras, chamber music groups, and opera companies at Mannes College, with professionals from New York's theater community at The New School for Drama, and with exceptional scholars, artists, and professionals at Eugene Lang College and in The New School for Public Engagement's undergraduate programs for transfer students and working adults.

Student Government

The University Student Senate (USS) is the official student government of The New School. Elected from all divisions of the university, student senators present student concerns to administration, maintain a USS website, plan all-campus parties and events, and co-fund events thrown by other people.

Admission Requirements

The New School welcomes admission applications from students of diverse racial, ethnic, religious, and political backgrounds whose past performance and academic and personal promise make them likely to gain from and add to The New School community. The university seeks students who combine inquisitiveness and seriousness of purpose with the ability to engage in a distinctive, rigorous undergraduate program. Specific admission requirements vary by division. To learn about admission requirements for specific programs, prospective students may visit www.newschool.edu/admission.

Application and Information

Freshmen, transfers, and visiting students may apply for either the September (fall) or January (spring) semester for all divisions of The New School except Mannes College and the New School for Drama. Application deadlines for freshman and transfer students vary by division. Details regarding fees, deadlines, and other application information can be found online at www. newschool.edu/admission.

For further information, students should contact:

The New School
Office of Admission
72 Fifth Avenue
New York, New York 10011
Phone: 212-229-5150
      800-292-3040 (toll-free)
E-mail: admission@newschool.edu
Website: www.newschool.edu/admission

New York City is a laboratory that enriches academic study and artistic exploration..

NIAGARA UNIVERSITY
NIAGARA UNIVERSITY, NEW YORK

The University

Niagara University (NU), founded in 1856, is a private, independent university rooted in a Catholic and Vincentian tradition. The suburban campus combines the old and new; both ivy-covered buildings and modern architectural structures are among its thirty-three buildings. The University is easily accessible from every major city in the eastern and midwestern United States via the New York State Thruway, Buffalo International Airport, and rail and bus service.

There are approximately 3,300 undergraduate and 870 graduate students enrolled at Niagara. A large percentage of these students take advantage of the more than 100 extracurricular and cocurricular activities offered. Volunteer work in the community is popular among the students and enhances community relations. Students work with numerous organizations, including Habitat for Humanity, Big Brothers/Big Sisters, and the Skating Association for the Blind and Handicapped.

University teams compete on the Division I level and are members of the NCAA, the Metro Atlantic Athletic Conference and Atlantic Hockey Conference. Intercollegiate sports for men include baseball, basketball, cross-country, golf, ice hockey, soccer, swimming and diving, and tennis. Intercollegiate sports for women include basketball, cross-country, golf, lacrosse, outdoor track and field, soccer, softball, swimming and diving, tennis, and volleyball. Club sports include cheerleading, danceline, hockey, martial arts, rugby, skiing, and wrestling. The Kiernan Center offers a variety of sports and recreational facilities, including a multipurpose gymnasium, a swimming and diving pool, an indoor track, racquetball courts, free-weight and Nautilus rooms, and aerobics rooms. There are several outdoor athletic fields as well as basketball and tennis courts.

Additional student services include the Health Center, which provides inpatient and outpatient care during the day; the Learning Center, which provides free tutoring services; and the Office of Career Services, which offers professional and career counseling. Other services include counseling, orientation, academic planning, career planning, and job placement.

Niagara University's housing accommodations include five residence halls, a grouping of five small cottages, and a student apartment complex.

The University offers graduate studies in business, counseling, criminal justice, educational leadership, interdisciplinary studies, sport management and a Ph.D. in leadership and policy.

Location

Niagara University's picturesque 160-acre campus is located in the town of Lewiston, New York, 2 minutes off I-190 on Route 104. The campus is situated on Monteagle Ridge overlooking the lower Niagara River, which connects the two Great Lakes of Erie and Ontario. The University's suburban campus setting is just a few miles from the world-famous Niagara Falls, 20 minutes from Buffalo, which offers a variety of cultural events, sports, and entertainment opportunities, and just 90 minutes from Rochester and Toronto, Canada's largest metropolitan area. In addition, the University is minutes away from the quaint village of Lewiston, New York, and the city of Niagara Falls, New York.

Majors and Degrees

The College of Arts and Sciences offers the Bachelor of Arts degree in art history with museum studies, chemistry, communication studies, English, French, history, international studies, liberal arts, life sciences, mathematics, philosophy, political science (with a concentration in environmental studies), psychology, religious studies, social sciences, sociology, and Spanish. The Bachelor of Science degree is awarded in biochemistry (with a concentration in bioinformatics), biology (with concentrations in bioinformatics, biotechnology, and environmental studies), chemistry (with a concentration in computational chemistry and environmental

studies), computer and information sciences, criminal justice and criminology, mathematics, nursing, and social work. This division also offers the Bachelor of Fine Arts degree in theater studies (with concentrations in design technology, general theater, and performance). Preprofessional programs are offered in dentistry, law, medicine, pharmacy, veterinary medicine, and Army ROTC. An Associate of Arts degree is available in general studies. Enrichment courses in fine arts and languages are also available. A combination five-year B.S./M.S. program is available to students in the criminal justice administration program, as well as an accelerated nursing program and a R.N. to B.S.N. program for students who already have their R.N.

In addition to the programs listed above NU offers a number of preprofessional partnerships. These include a 3+4 partnership in pharmacy with the State University of New York at Buffalo (SUNY), a 2+3 partnership in pharmacy with Lake Erie College of Osteopathic Medicine (LECOM), a 3+4 partnership in medicine with LECOM, and a 3+4 partnership in dentistry with SUNY at Buffalo. Qualified premedical Niagara students are eligible to apply for the early assurance program sponsored by the SUNY at Buffalo.

Niagara University's College of Business Administration is accredited by AACSB International—The Association to Advance Collegiate Schools of Business and offers a B.B.A. and a combination B.B.A./M.B.A. degree (five-year program) in accounting. This division offers B.S. degrees in economics, finance, management (with concentrations in human resources, international business, and supply chain management), and marketing. In addition, an A.A.S. degree can be earned in business.

Real-world learning occurs through internships, study abroad, and cooperative education programs as well as research being conducted in several business-focused campus centers. These centers include the Family Business Center, the Center for Supply Chain Management, and the Center for International Accounting.

Holding the highest accreditations possible in both the United States and Canada—the United States National Council for Teacher Education (NCATE) and Canada's Ontario College of Teachers—Niagara University's College of Education provides students with an option of earning dual certification to teach in both countries. The College of Education offers bachelor's degree programs leading to New York State initial certification in early childhood (birth–grade 6), childhood (grades 1–6), childhood and middle childhood (grades 1–9), middle childhood and adolescence (grades 5–12), adolescence (grades 7–12), certification for teaching students with disabilities (grades 1–6 childhood and grades 7–12 adolescence), and in Teaching English to Speakers of Other Languages (TESOL). All education majors pursue an academic concentration to establish expertise in one of the following subject areas: biology, business, chemistry, English, French, liberal arts, mathematics, social studies, and Spanish. Business education is offered only at grades 5–12. The academic concentration in liberal arts can only be pursued in the early childhood and childhood (birth–grade 6), and special education and childhood (grades 1–6). Most other states, and Puerto Rico, have reciprocity agreements with New York, so an NU education would qualify education majors to teach in those states as well.

The College of Hospitality and Tourism Management provides a career-oriented curriculum leading to a B.S. degree in three specific areas: hotel and restaurant management (with concentrations in food and beverage management; luxury hospitality operations; and hotel planning, development, and operations), sport management (with concentrations in sport operations and revenue management), and tourism and recreation management (with concentrations in event and meeting management and tourism destination management). The College of Hospitality and Tourism Management offered the world's first bachelor's degree in tourism. NU's hotel and restaurant program, the second oldest in New York State, has the distinction of being the seventh program nationally to be accredited by the Accreditation Commission for Programs in Hospitality

Administration by the Council of Hotel, Restaurant, and Institutional Education. The College introduces students to a comprehensive body of knowledge about the hotel, restaurant, tourism, and recreational areas and applies this knowledge to current industry challenges. The College requires that its students accumulate 800 hours of industry-related experience. These and other practical experiences offer NU students the knowledge necessary to advance in the field. Students work with industry leaders in classroom projects, join academic clubs and professional organizations, and participate in special trips to trade shows and conventions and specially designed study-abroad experiences, making NU a national leader in the area.

For students who are undecided about which major to choose, Niagara University offers an award-winning Academic Exploration Program (AEP). AEP provides a structured opportunity for students to participate in a thorough, organized process of selecting a major that meets their academic talents and career goals.

Academic Programs

Niagara University's curricula enable students to pursue their academic preferences and to complete courses that lead to proficiency in other academic areas. Courses that have been considered upper-division courses are available to all students. This provides students with the opportunity to take more challenging courses early in their collegiate career. The honors program provides special academic opportunities that stimulate, encourage, and challenge participants. In addition, an accelerated three-year degree program is offered to qualified students.

Niagara grants credit for successful scores on the Advanced Placement, College-Level Examination Program, and the International Baccalaureate tests.

Internships, research, independent study, and cooperative education are available in many academic programs. An Army ROTC program is also offered.

The University operates on a two-semester plan (fall and spring). A comprehensive summer session offers a variety of courses.

NU is fully accredited by the Middle States Association of Colleges and Schools. The University's programs in the respective areas are accredited by the National Council for Accreditation of Teacher Education, AACSB International–The Association to Advance Collegiate Schools of Business, and the Council on Social Work Education. The chemistry department has the approval of the American Chemical Society. The travel, hotel, and restaurant administration program is accredited by the Commission for Programs in Hospitality Administration.

Off-Campus Programs

For those students who wish to study abroad, the University offers semester and summer programs in Australia, Chile, China, England, France, Ireland, Italy, Mexico, Spain, Thailand, and many other countries. Students may choose from 150 programs in more than thirty countries available through the University's membership in the American Institute for Foreign Studies, Center for Cross-Cultural Study, College Consortium for International Studies, Global Learning Semesters, and Semester at Sea.

Academic Facilities

The University's open-stack library exceeds 200,000 books and has more than 22,000 periodical titles as well as reference databases accessible through the Internet. The library is housed in a modern facility that includes seating for 500 people, including individual study carrels. The library is affiliated with the Online Computer Library Center (OCLC) network.

The Academic Complex, the home to the College of Education and the College of Business Administration (Bisgrove Hall), is a state-of-the-art learning facility, with a simulated trading floor in the new Glynn Atrium. Dunleavy Hall, outstanding both educationally and architecturally, includes a computerized lecture hall and TV production rooms. The University's facilities also include the Computer Center; St. Vincent's Hall; the Kiernan Center, NU's athletic and recreation center; the Elizabeth Ann Clune Center for Theatre; the Castellani Art Museum; Dwyer Arena, a dual-rink ice hockey complex; and the B. Thomas Golisano Center for Integrated Sciences, scheduled to open in fall 2013.

Costs

Tuition for 2012–13 was $26,100. Room and board (with a choice of meal plans) cost an additional $11,300 per year. Fees were estimated at $1,250 per year. Niagara estimates that an additional $2,500 to $3,050 per year is adequate for books, laundry, and other essentials, such as travel to and from home.

Financial Aid

Ninety-eight percent of the entering freshmen received a financial aid package averaging more than $23,000 per year. They receive assistance in the form of merit scholarships, loans, grants, or campus employment. Students seeking financial aid should file the Free Application for Federal Student Aid (FAFSA). New York State residents should also file a Tuition Assistance Program (TAP) application.

Faculty

Niagara University has a dedicated, accessible faculty that genuinely cares about the academic and personal growth of their students. Their commitment to teaching is their primary concern. A student-faculty ratio of 12:1 and an average class size of approximately 24 allow personal attention and classroom interaction.

Admission Requirements

The University welcomes men and women who have demonstrated aptitude and academic achievement at the high school level. Either SAT or ACT test scores are required. International students are required to submit the results of their TOEFL examination. Interviews are recommended. Transfer students are accepted in any semester. (Transfer credit is evaluated individually by the dean of each division.) Students who complete high school in less than four years are eligible for early admission. Students may also apply under an early action program. Economically and educationally disadvantaged students from New York State are eligible to apply for admission through the Higher Educational Opportunity Program (HEOP).

Application and Information

Niagara operates on a rolling admission basis and adheres to the College Board Candidates Reply Date. A visit to the campus is encouraged, and overnight accommodations in a residence hall are available through the Niagara Nights program.

Information on all aspects of the University can be obtained by contacting the Office of Admissions or by visiting www.niagara.edu.

Mark Wojnowski
Director of Admissions
Niagara University
Niagara University, New York 14109-2011
Phone: 716-286-8700
      800-462-2111 (toll-free)
Fax: 716-286-8710
E-mail: admissions@niagara.edu
Website: http://www.niagara.edu
      http://www.facebook.com/niagarau
      http://twitter.com/niagarauniv

Adjacent to the international border between the United States and Canada, Niagara University's 160-acre campus runs along the top of picturesque Monteagle Ridge, overlooking the Niagara River gorge just 4 miles north of the world-famous waterfalls.

NORTHEASTERN UNIVERSITY
BOSTON, MASSACHUSETTS

 Northeastern University

The University

There is a certain energy about Northeastern. It comes from bright, ambitious students with a sense of purpose. In the classroom, in the workplace, in campus activities, and in the city of Boston—the ultimate college town—Northeastern students stimulate their minds, investigate career options, participate in community affairs, and graduate personally and professionally prepared for their future careers or for graduate school.

Northeastern is a leader in interdisciplinary and translational research; urban engagement; and the integration of classroom learning with real-world experience. Classroom studies are integrated with experiential learning opportunities—anchored by the world's largest, most innovative cooperative education program—to prepare students for a lifetime of achievement. It is the Northeastern difference.

The current undergraduate enrollment of 16,385 is made up of students of all backgrounds, interests, and tastes, giving Northeastern its distinctive, urban style. This diversity shows in the range of available activities. Students can join a cultural club, participate in research, perform with the Silver Masque, go on a ski trip, play basketball, tutor local children, learn to ballroom dance, and much more. Students have many opportunities to make friends, try something new, become a leader, or simply have fun. Students can also find quiet corners of the campus that feel far from city streets where they can read or just relax, sprawled on a wooden bench under a shade tree; sip gourmet coffee from a nearby campus café; or listen to a midday jazz performance behind the Curry Student Center amid the art of Northeastern's sculpture park. The 73-acre campus is dynamic and welcoming, a beautiful stretch of leafy green in the heart of Boston. Its compact size lets students get to class on time or rush back for a forgotten book.

Location

Northeastern's residential campus lies in the heart of Boston, where the distinctive neighborhoods of the Back Bay, the South End, the Fenway, and Roxbury meet. In the past five years, Northeastern has built a host of new on-campus residence halls, more than doubling the amount of housing available to undergraduates. The newest residence halls offer apartment-style living with modern kitchens complete with dishwashers, disposals, and full-sized appliances; cable hookups; and data jacks. Many have amazing views of the Boston skyline.

The Back Bay area, known for its many cultural and educational institutions, is steps from Symphony Hall, the New England Conservatory of Music, the Museum of Fine Arts, and the Isabella Stewart Gardner Museum. The South End is home to elegant Victorian row houses, exciting arts, hidden gardens and some of the finest dining in Boston. The Fenway area, with its beautiful rose garden, bicycle and jogging paths, and Fenway Park (home of the Boston Red Sox), is just a few blocks away.

Majors and Degrees

Northeastern's academic programs are divided among eight colleges: the College of Arts, Media, and Design; the D'Amore-McKim School of Business; the College of Computer and Information Science; the College of Engineering; the Bouvé College of Health Sciences; the College of Professional Studies; the College of Science; and the College of Social Sciences and Humanities. Top-notch faculty members with a variety of research interests personally guide students through their studies.

The College of Arts, Media, and Design awards undergraduate degrees in architecture, art, cinema studies (combined major options only), communication studies, digital art, game design (combined major options only), graphic design, interactive media (combined major options only), landscape architecture, journalism, music (concentrations in music history and analysis, music industry, and music technology), studio art (in collaboration with the School of the Museum of Fine Arts, Boston), and theater (including concentrations in performance and production).

The College of Business Administration offers two tracks: the Bachelor of Science in Business Administration (B.S.B.A.) and the Bachelor of Science in International Business (B.S.I.B.). The B.S.I.B. program includes language instruction and international study and work. The College offers concentrations in accounting, entrepreneurship and innovation, finance and insurance, management, management information systems, marketing, and supply chain management.

The College of Computer and Information Science awards degrees in computer science and information science and also offers combined majors, combining computer science with business, cognitive psychology, game design, mathematics, physics, biology, multimedia arts, music technology, or digital art.

The College of Engineering offers degrees in chemical, civil, computer, electrical, industrial, and mechanical engineering.

The Bouvé College of Health Sciences awards degrees in health sciences, nursing, pharmacy, and speech-language pathology and audiology. The college also offers a six-year Doctor of Pharmacy degree and a six-year program leading to a Master of Science in Physical Therapy.

The College of Professional Studies offers undergraduate and graduate degree programs in a wide range of disciplines, with an emphasis on global options. The college is also home to the School of Education.

The College of Science awards undergraduate degrees in applied physics, behavioral neuroscience, biochemistry, biology, biomedical physics, chemistry, environmental science, environmental studies, linguistics, mathematics, physics, and psychology.

The College of Social Sciences and Humanities awards undergraduate degrees in African American studies, American Sign Language, Asian studies, criminal justice, cultural anthropology, economics, English, history, human services, international affairs, Jewish studies (combined major options only), philosophy, political science, religious studies, sociology, and Spanish.

Academic Programs

At the heart of a Northeastern education lies award-winning professors and faculty mentors, rigorous and innovative curriculum, undergraduate research and global experiences that challenge and transform. Innovative programs encompass a wide range of majors, concentrations, and interdisciplinary studies along with honors, preprofessional, and study-abroad programs.

Northeastern's approach integrates academics with a variety of experiential learning opportunities including research, global experience, service learning, and the University's signature cooperative education program (co-op), enabling students to discover their path before they leave college.

Through the internationally known co-op program, after completing their freshman year, students alternate classroom learning with periods of full-time (usually paid) work or other types of hands-on learning related to their major or interests, earning their bachelor's degree in either four or five years. Graduates accumulate as many as eighteen months of professional experience, professional contacts, and the social confidence that gives them a significant edge in the job market over new graduates without experience. By working in varied jobs and settings, students learn what they like—and do not like—before committing to a permanent position. In fact, some Northeastern graduates may even go to work for a co-op employer after graduation. Northeastern students graduate knowing what they only could have learned on the job: how to conduct themselves, what to wear, how to interpret a company's culture, how to get things done, and how to write a resume and interview successfully.

Co-op employers include some of the country's largest and most reputable companies, such as Pfizer, John Hancock, Fidelity Investments, General Electric, Massachusetts General Hospital, and the *Boston Globe*. Students also enjoy international placements for a semester or a year abroad; co-op employers recruit from Australia, Scotland, Italy, and Spain, among many other countries.

Experiential learning opportunities—including U.S. and international co-op, service-learning, research, and study abroad—are currently available in 92 countries around the world.

The University Honors Program gives students opportunities to participate in enriched educational experiences and offers opportunities that include honors sections of required academic courses, honors seminars, independent research, and study abroad. The University also offers Army, Naval Nursing, and Air Force ROTC. The Disability Resource Center provides many support services that enable students with disabilities to participate fully in the life of the University community.

Academic Facilities

Northeastern is home to thirty-seven research centers, including the Center for Labor Market Studies, the Barnett Institute of Chemical and Biological Analysis, the Center for High-rate Nanomanufacturing, the Institute on Race and Justice, and many others. Students have ample opportunities to work alongside their professors to aid and conduct research on a variety of topics as undergraduates.

The University libraries system comprises Snell Library, a 240,000-square-foot-central library on the Boston Campus, the School of Law Library (also on the Boston Campus) and a small supplemental collection at the Nahant Marine Science Center. Total non-law holdings as of June 30, 2011 include 932,999 print volumes, 206,507 e-books, 1,489,153 microfilms, and 70,225 current serials subscriptions, with access to 59,926 electronic journals. In addition, Snell Library houses 23,437 audio, video, and computer software items, and 5,712 linear feet of archival material. The library is a selective depository of federal government publications and currently holds 143,905 printed government documents.

Northeastern University provides a broad range of academic and administrative computer resources available to students and faculty and staff members. Many computing resources are available, including Internet connections for all offices and University-owned residence halls, technology-assisted classrooms, computer labs, and the myNEU portal, which allows student to access many administrative and academic functions online. There is also extensive wireless network access, found in the library, Student Center, and many dorms.

Costs

For 2012–13, tuition was $39,320, and room and board were $13,140. Whether students choose to earn their undergraduate degree in four or five years (including experiential educational periods), tuition is charged only for the academic experience, not for the experiential educational periods.

Financial Aid

The University operates a substantial aid program designed to make attendance at Northeastern feasible for all qualified students. By coordinating the resources of the University and various public and private scholarship programs, the Office of Student Financial Services was recently able to provide more than $170 million in grant and scholarship assistance. About 85 percent of the freshman class received some form of financial aid. Northeastern participates in all federal aid programs. Financial aid is based on need and academic merit and may consist of grants, loans, work-study employment, or any combination of the three. To apply, students must file a Free Application for Federal Student Aid (FAFSA) and a CSS PROFILE form with the College Scholarship Service by the priority filing date of February 15.

Faculty

The University has more than 1,500 full- and part-time faculty members with a wide variety of research and teaching interests and specialties and a staff of academic counselors in each college who work closely with students to assist them in developing programs suited to their interests and abilities. Each student is assigned both an academic and a co-op adviser. The co-op advisor aids in resume building and interview skills and tactics. In addition, the adviser aids in developing contacts with business and co-op employers as well as networking and eventual job searches.

Admission Requirements

Students may enter the University with advanced credit on the basis of test scores on Advanced Placement (AP) examinations, the College-Level Examination Program (CLEP), the International Baccalaureate (I.B.), or on successful completion of accredited college-level courses before enrollment at Northeastern. In addition to the application for admission, prospective freshmen must submit official high school transcript(s) (or official GED score reports), including their senior-year grades; official transcripts for any college-level course work taken while a secondary-school student; written recommendations from their secondary school guidance counselor and a teacher; and scores on the SAT (Northeastern's College Board code is 3667) or ACT, including the writing section. Please visit the University's website for additional admission details and transfer admissions requirements (www.northeastern.edu/admissions).

Application and Information

Admission to Northeastern is selective and competitive. For the freshman class entering in fall 2013, the University received more than 47,000 applications for 2,800 places in the freshman class. Students who thrive in a challenging academic environment—and outside the classroom in activities like Northeastern's dynamic global experiential learning options—are best suited for a Northeastern education. Experiential learning will expand the student's initiative, adaptability, confidence, poise, and ability to work collaboratively, which are the foundations of leadership.

November 1 is the deadline for the early action admission program. Students who have carefully explored their college options and have decided that Northeastern is where they want to enroll may choose to apply under the early action program. The deadline for the regular admission program is January 15. If accepted for fall admission either through the early action program or the regular admission program, freshmen are required to send a tuition deposit by May 1 to secure a place in the class. For transfer students, the priority deadline for the fall is May 1. Admission decisions for transfer applicants are made on a space-available, rolling basis. November 1 is the deadline for January transfer admission for both freshman and transfer applicants and for international applicants for January admission. Admission decisions for spring applicants are made on a space-available, rolling basis. Northeastern offers a variety of visit options including information sessions and campus tours. For more information, or to register, visit www.northeastern.edu/admissions/visitcampus.

For more information, students should contact:

Office of Undergraduate Admissions
240 West Village F
Northeastern University
360 Huntington Avenue
Boston, Massachusetts 02115
Phone: 617-373-2200
E-mail: admissions@neu.edu
Website: http://www.northeastern.edu/admissions

Students in a West Village residence hall enjoy spectacular Boston vistas as well as interaction with the faculty-in-residence.

NORTHERN KENTUCKY UNIVERSITY
HIGHLAND HEIGHTS, KENTUCKY

The University

Northern Kentucky University (NKU) was founded in 1968 and is the newest of Kentucky's eight state universities. The atmosphere of the campus is futuristic, emphasizing a high-quality education by supporting the liberal arts. Major buildings are of modern, contemporary architectural design and are set on 300 acres of rolling countryside. NKU has an enrollment of approximately 16,000 students from forty-two states and ninety-two countries and is accredited by the Southern Association of Colleges and Schools. The Salmon P. Chase College of Law is accredited by both the American Bar Association and the Association of American Law Schools.

There are more than 200 student organizations. NKU competes in the NCAA Division I Atlantic Sun Conference. Intercollegiate sports are offered for men and women in basketball, cheerleading, cross-country, track, golf, soccer, and tennis; for men in baseball; and for women in fast-pitch softball and volleyball. Intramural activities vary by semester, but include basketball, dodgeball, field hockey, flag football, ice hockey, racquetball, soccer, softball, tae kwan do, volleyball, and many others. A complete listing is available on the University's website at http://www.nku.edu/~camprec/index.htm.

Location

NKU is located in the largest metropolitan area of any state university in Kentucky. It is located at the junction of U.S. Highway 27 and Interstates 275 and 471 in Highland Heights, Kentucky, 8 miles southeast of Cincinnati, Ohio. NKU is only 60 miles from Dayton, 79 miles from Lexington, 93 miles from Louisville, and 114 miles from Indianapolis. While the immediate surroundings are suburban, NKU is part of the metropolitan area of greater Cincinnati.

Majors and Degrees

Northern Kentucky University awards the Bachelor of Arts, Bachelor of Fine Arts, Bachelor of Music, Bachelor of Science, Bachelor of Science in Nursing, and Bachelor of Social Work degrees. NKU also offers preprofessional programs, secondary education teacher certification, certificates, and the Associate of Applied Science degree.

The B.A. and B.S. degrees are offered in accounting, anthropology, athletic training, art (teaching), biological sciences, business administration, business education, business informatics, chemistry, chemistry/biology, computer education technology, computer information technology, computer science, criminal justice, early childhood education, economics, electronic engineering technology, electronic media and broadcasting, elementary education, English, entrepreneurship, environmental science, finance, French, geography, geology, German, graphic design, health science, history, industrial education, human resources, construction management, international studies, journalism, liberal studies, management, mechanical and manufacturing engineering, marketing, mathematics, media informatics, mental health–human services, middle grades education, organizational leadership, organizational systems technology, organizational systems technology management, philosophy, photography, physical education, physical education recreation, physics, political science, psychology, public relations, radio-TV, recreation-fitness, social studies (teaching), sociology, Spanish, special education, speech communication, sports business, and theater.

The B.F.A. degree is granted in art and in theater arts. The B.Mus. degree is offered in music. The B.S.N. degree is offered in the nursing major and the B.S.W. degree in the social work major.

Preprofessional programs are available in dentistry, engineering, forestry, human resources, law, medicine, optometry, pharmacy, physician assistant studies, physical therapy, veterinary medicine, and wildlife management. In addition, the University offers majors, minors, and areas of discipline for secondary education teacher certification.

The University also awards the A.A.S. degree in construction technology, criminal justice, human services, integrative studies, prebusiness studies, radiologic technology, and respiratory care.

Academic Programs

NKU operates on a semester calendar. To receive a bachelor's degree, students must complete a minimum of 120 credit hours. At least 60 credit hours are required for the associate degree.

The University offers a variety of career planning and placement, internship, independent study, work-study, and cooperative-education programs. There is also an advising, counseling, and testing Center available. Other programs include an honors program, a program that allows for the dual enrollment of high school students, a program where students can combine their career interests in the liberal arts and engineering fields, and University 101, an orientation program for freshmen and transfer students.

NKU recognizes credit earned through the Advanced Placement (AP) Program and the general, subject, and institutional tests of specific College-Level Examination Program (CLEP). A maximum of 45 credit hours may be applied toward the bachelor's degree from the AP and CLEP examinations. The International Baccalaureate program allows students to earn credit in science, mathematics, psychology, and languages.

Off-Campus Programs

A variety of study-abroad opportunities are available to NKU students through membership in several consortia, through NKU exchange agreements with international universities, and through independent NKU professor-led trips.

Study in Australia, Belize, England, Ghana, Hong Kong, India, Ireland, Jamaica, and Scotland is possible in a wide range of courses and programs available through NKU's membership in the Cooperative Center for Study Abroad (CCSA).

The Kentucky Institute for International Studies (KIIS) offers students academic language programs in Argentina, Austria, Brazil, China, Costa Rica, Czech Republic, Denmark, Ecuador, France, Germany, Greece, Italy, Japan, Mexico, Poland, Spain, Turkey, and Ukraine.

The NKU Office of International Programs has student and faculty exchanges with universities in Costa Rica, Denmark, France, Germany, Japan, Korea, Mexico, Russia, Scotland, and Spain.

Academic Facilities

Among the academic facilities at NKU are an anthropology museum, a biology museum, and an art gallery with rotating exhibits. NKU also has a new laser projection planetarium. NKU becomes only the seventh institution worldwide to boast such equipment, joining six major planetariums in cities such as Tokyo, Los Angeles, and London. In addition, the University has nursing, respiratory care, and radiologic technology laboratories. In spring of 2008, NKU opened a 9000-seat arena called the Bank of Kentucky Center. NKU's brand-new Student Union, a student-centered facility, and focal point for campus programs and student organizations, was also completed in 2008. In the fall of 2011, NKU's Griffin Hall opened. This building, the new home of the College of Informatics, is designed to help students interested in communication and media, computer science, information technology, or management information systems become the new generation of professionals who will build the region's information economy. The W. Frank Steely Library at NKU contains 311,155 book titles and maintains 1,729 paper periodical subscriptions (additional periodicals are available in electronic format). Computer laboratories offer students opportunities to learn and utilize a variety of software programs. The Computer Science Department and Criminal Justice Department have collaborated to offer students a computer forensics minor to teach students how to handle digital evidence and how to present such evidence in court.

Costs

Tuition and fees for 2012–13 were $7,872 for Kentucky students, $12,552 for metro students and $15,744 for nonresidents. Other costs included $6,500–$8,000 for room and meals, about $850 for books and supplies, and $2,773 for miscellaneous expenses.

Financial Aid

Northern Kentucky University awards more than $2 million in academic scholarships each year to the incoming freshman class. The University awards scholarships to highly motivated students who demonstrate strong academic performance. Students who achieve a 3.0 GPA and a 23 ACT or 1050 SAT are considered for academic awards. The University offers numerous scholarship levels. Each scholarship level has merit guidelines that students must meet to qualify. To be considered to academic scholarships, interested students need to apply for admission by January 15 (based on availability of funds). There is no separate scholarship application for general Northern Kentucky University academic scholarships. Students who qualify for a scholarship receive an award letter upon acceptance to NKU. Prosepctive students can visit scholarships.nku.edu for information on additional scholarships that do require an application, letters of recommendation, or essay. There is no deadline for the University's financial aid application; however, students who wish to receive institutional aid must apply by February 1 for priority consideration. Applicants are notified of acceptance on a rolling basis.

Faculty

More than 82 percent of the faculty members at NKU hold a doctoral degree or the terminal degree in their field. Classes are small, with an average class size of 24 and a student-faculty ratio of 17:1. All classes are taught by faculty members; no classes are taught by graduate assistants.

Student Government

Student Government (SG) is the elected student assembly at Northern Kentucky University. It is the official student voice on campus and represents the student viewpoint on University committees. All SG meetings are open, and students are encouraged to attend.

Admission Requirements

Incoming freshmen must submit an application for admission; arrange for the official ACT, SAT, or COMPASS score report to be sent; and request that the high school send an official transcript. In order to be considered for regular admission, a student must meet precollege curriculum requirements for Kentucky and institutional admission standards. Out-of-state applicants must also meet the Kentucky precollege curriculum requirements.

Based on the review of official test results and the precollege curriculum, students are admitted into one of two categories: regular admission or admission with conditions. Students who have two or more deficiencies are encouraged to retake the ACT or SAT so an additional review can be completed. Students with two or more deficiencies may be asked to submit an essay, letters of recommendation, and an activities portfolio before an admission decision can be rendered. Students with two or more deficiencies who are offered admission will be required to participate in the Pathfinders Program, which is designed to enhance student engagement and provide tools needed for future academic achievement. The program includes: mandatory advising, completion of University 101 (Introduction to College) course, participation in study tables, tutoring, and college success workshops. Some degree programs require that students meet additional criteria; more information is available in the current catalog (http://www.nku.edu).

Application and Information

The $40 paper application fee may be waived for applicants with demonstrated need. The fall semester early action and scholarship deadline is January 15, assured consideration deadline is February 1, enrollment confirmation deadline is May 1, and the final deadline is July 1. The priority application deadline for the nursing program is January 31. The priority application deadline for the respiratory care program is February 15.

For more information, students should contact:
Office of Admissions
Northern Kentucky University
Highland Heights, Kentucky 41099
Phone: 859-572-5220
      800-637-9948 (toll-free)
E-mail: admitnku@nku.edu
Website: http://admissions.nku.edu
      http://www.facebook.com/nkuedu
      http://twitter.com.nkuedu

Northern Kentucky University's modern campus is set in Highland Heights, just minutes from downtown Cincinnati.

NORWICH UNIVERSITY
NORTHFIELD, VERMONT

NORWICH
UNIVERSITY
Expect Challenge. Achieve Distinction.

The University

Norwich University was established in 1819 as the first private military college in America. It was at Norwich that the idea of the citizen-soldier developed and eventually evolved into the Reserve Officer Training Corps (ROTC) program. Norwich was the first private college to offer civil engineering, and many University alumni were involved in the construction of the nation's continental railway system. In 1974, Norwich became one of the first military colleges to admit women into its Corps of Cadets, preceding the federal academies.

Norwich University offers a diverse blend of disciplines, teaching styles, and viewpoints. Students enrolled in the Corps of Cadets have a more disciplined, challenging, and structured path through college, while their civilian student classmates lead a more traditional collegiate lifestyle. However, both groups are coeducational and attend classes and participate in sports and other activities together.

In keeping with its mission, Norwich provides opportunities for all of its students to develop leadership skills with a strong commitment to community service. Both groups gain skills such as leadership, honor, and integrity, which are required to be successful in today's job market. These two diverse groups of students are very different and yet have much in common—they are Norwich.

Norwich University has an enrollment of 2,300 students from more than forty-five states and twenty countries. The University's minority enrollment is consistently higher (by percentage) than that of any other Vermont university or college.

The athletic facilities at Norwich are comparable to the best at any of New England's Division III universities. The main athletic complex, Andrews Hall, features a gymnasium, racquetball courts, a modernized athletic training room, an equipment room, and laundry facilities. Kreitzberg Arena is a multipurpose facility with a seating capacity of 1,500 and a fully equipped weight room. It was here that the University's men's hockey team won the Division III National Championship in 2003. The recently constructed 22,000-square-foot Doyle Hall facility connects the Kreitzberg Arena and Andrews Hall. Doyle Hall features a new Hall of Fame lobby at the main entrance into the athletic complex and includes a grand stairway, ticket booth, concessions area, and restroom facilities. The new facility also provides the athletic department with offices for coaches, team meeting rooms, and locker room facilities.

Plumley Armory has a huge gym as well as an indoor track, weight and aerobics rooms, a wrestling room, and an indoor swimming pool. Shapiro Field House has 50,000 square feet of floor space and includes a 200-meter indoor track, tennis courts, and a climbing wall. The newly developed Shaw Outdoor Center at the base of Paine Mountain offers students a variety of outdoor recreational activities including trails for jogging, cross-country running races, hiking, snowshoeing, cross-country skiing, sledding, and mountain biking. Equipment to participate in these activities is available to students free of charge. The 1,200-acre campus includes numerous playing fields for baseball, football, rugby, soccer, and softball. Norwich also has a paintball course, a rappel tower, and an obstacle and confidence course.

Norwich has the only professional five-year Master of Architecture program in northern New England. The University also offers online graduate degrees in business administration, diplomacy, information assurance, nursing, public administration, business continuity, organizational leadership, civil engineering, history and military history.

Location

Norwich University is located in the heart of the Green Mountains of Vermont, right in the middle of ski country. Some of the nation's most popular resorts, such as Stowe, Sugarbush, and Killington, are located within an hour's drive. Vermont is world renowned as one of America's most beautiful states. Nature's playground is just outside the dorm room—skiing, snowboarding, telemark skiing, cross-country skiing, snowshoeing, rock climbing, hiking, mountain biking, canoeing, kayaking, and more are available.

The University campus is located in the small town of Northfield, Vermont. Northfield is 10 miles south of the state capital of Montpelier and is 50 miles from Burlington, the largest city in Vermont. Both Montpelier and Burlington are cultural centers for the arts. Burlington International Airport is within an hour's drive. In addition, the cities of Boston and Montreal are only a 3-hour drive from the campus.

Majors and Degrees

Norwich offers students more than thirty academic majors from which to choose. The Bachelor of Arts degree is awarded in criminal justice, English, history, international studies, political science, studies in war and peace, psychology, and Spanish. The Bachelor of Science degree is awarded in accounting, architectural studies; biochemistry, biology, chemistry, civil engineering, communications, computer/electrical engineering, computer science, computer security and information assurance, engineering management, environmental science, geology, management, mathematics, mechanical engineering, nursing, physical education, physics, sports medicine, and strategic studies and defense analysis. Teacher licensure, prelaw, premedical, and predental programs are also available.

Academic Programs

Norwich University is dedicated to the discovery, preservation, and dissemination of knowledge and the search for truth. Norwich is distinctive in that it maintains a strong emphasis on the development of leadership in both military and civilian pursuits and in providing for the educational needs of students. The University's mission is to foster in each student the growth of self-discipline, personal integrity, social responsibility, physical fitness, respect for law, and intellectual ability essential for full and effective participation in a free society.

For students enrolling in the Corps of Cadets, six semesters of Reserve Officer Training Corps are required. Norwich is considered the birthplace of ROTC; therefore, all four service branches can be found on campus. Prior to their junior year, cadets may elect to contract with their ROTC program and be considered upon graduation for a commission as officers in the Army, Navy, Air Force, or Marine Corps. Cadets not on an ROTC scholarship are not required to join the military.

Students typically take an average of five classes per semester. Each semester is sixteen weeks long, with holiday breaks at Thanksgiving, Christmas, and New Year's and in March during spring break. The academic year normally begins the last week in August and ends after the first week in May.

Academic Facilities

The academic facilities at Norwich are among the finest in New England. Completed in 1997, the math and science building was designed to keep classes small. Its labs hold no more than 16 students, and all of the classrooms are hardwired to allow for multimedia presentations. Students can find numerous computer labs across the campus, and the Kreitzberg Library offers students plenty of resources, space, and technology. Students may research Norwich's facilities on the University's website.

Costs

For 2013–14, tuition and fees are $16,684 per semester. The cost of room and board is $5,762 per semester. Books and personal expenses average $1,250 per semester. Cadets pay a uniform fee of $815 per semester in each of their first two years.

Financial Aid

Most families assume they cannot afford a private college education and fall victim to sticker shock, but a Norwich education can often be an affordable option for a family. Last year, 97 percent of Norwich students shared in more than $65 million of financial aid from all sources, including ROTC scholarships. This included an aggressive need-based financial aid program that enabled deserving students to secure a private education at Norwich.

Norwich awards many institutional scholarships based on academic merit. A student's high school GPA and ACT or SAT scores determine the level of scholarship. These scholarships may pay from $7,000 to $18,000 of the student's tuition for four years. Students are required to maintain a specified GPA in order to renew the scholarship each year. Norwich also offers scholarships to students who attend the University's Future Leader Camp, participate in National Drill Team competitions, and who are in leadership positions in the Civil Air Patrol. Prospective students should contact an admissions counselor for more details about these scholarships.

Norwich also offers a large number of institutional grants based on financial need. A student must file the Free Application for Federal Student Aid (FAFSA) to be considered for these grants.

Students who bring a three- or four-year ROTC scholarship to Norwich are eligible for the General I. D. White Scholarship, which covers the cost of room and board. Students who are interested in applying for an ROTC scholarship should visit the individual ROTC detachment's web page on the Norwich University website.

Faculty

The student-faculty ratio is 14:1. Faculty members are full-time instructors with advanced degrees; 72 percent hold a doctorate. Small classes help promote a close relationship between faculty members and students. Students are assigned faculty advisers within each academic division.

Student Government

The Norwich University Corps of Cadets is a military organization made up of and led by cadets under the supervision of the Commandant of Cadets. Members of the Corps and student body preside over the University Honor Council. The University's honor code binds all Norwich students. Members of the Corps and student body also participate on the Student Affairs Committee, whose members include the Dean of Students, members of the faculty, and the Senior Vice President and Commandant

of Cadets. This committee serves as the voice of the Norwich community and provides a channel of communication for change.

Admission Requirements

Admission to Norwich is based on a review of the applicant's academic record, personal essay, letters of recommendation, and extracurricular activities. Students at Norwich are heavily involved in community service and leadership development activities. Applicants should be able to demonstrate participation in activities both inside and outside of their high school.

Norwich is looking for students who want to become leaders, serve others, and give back to their communities. While the admissions office uses a rolling admissions system (meaning applications may be submitted at any time), there is a priority deadline of March 1. Students applying for admission or financial aid after March 1 are admitted on a space-available basis.

Application and Information

Students can visit the University's website or contact the University for more information.

Admissions Office
Norwich University
27 I. D. White Avenue
Northfield, Vermont 05663
Phone: 800-468-6679 (toll-free)
Fax: 802-485-2032
E-mail: nuadm@norwich.edu
Website: http://www.norwich.edu
http://www.facebook.com/NorwichUniversity

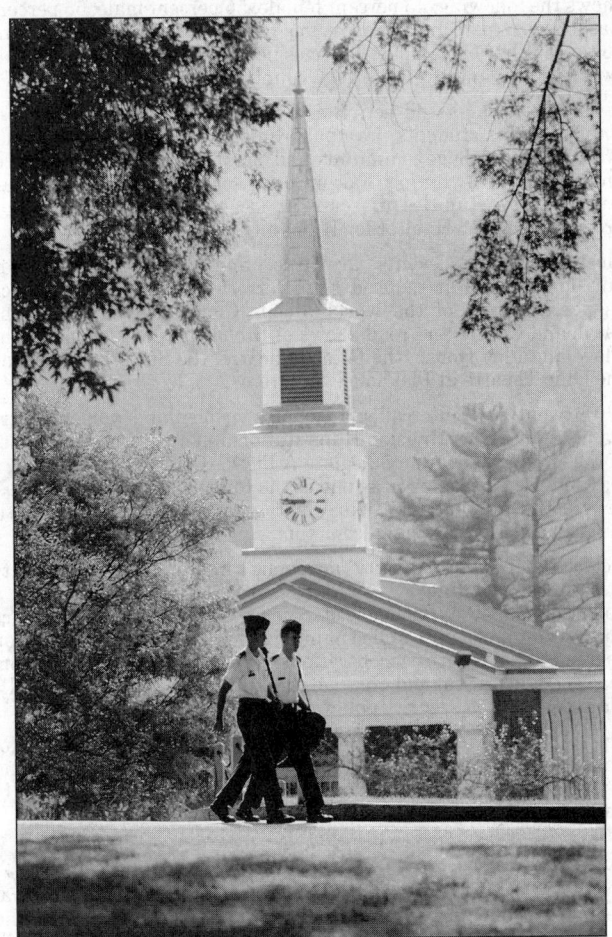

A view of Norwich University's campus.

NOTRE DAME COLLEGE
SOUTH EUCLID, OHIO

The College

Notre Dame College, a Catholic institution in the tradition of the Sisters of Notre Dame, educates a diverse population in the liberal arts for personal, professional, and global responsibility. Notre Dame College offers stimulating academics, personalized attention, small class sizes, Division II intercollegiate athletics, and vibrant student life.

Founded in 1922 by the Sisters of Notre Dame, the College has grown strategically to keep pace with the rapidly changing needs of students and the dramatic changes in higher education. But it has never lost sight of its emphasis on teaching students not only how to make a good living but also how to live a good life. The College believes that truly progressive education selectively blends traditional values with new ideas that represent real growth. Within the scope of a career-oriented liberal arts education, students can grow to meet the challenges of the present and the future.

Under the leadership of President Dr. Andrew P. Roth since 2003, Notre Dame College (NDC) is rapidly becoming one of the finest small, Catholic, residential, liberal arts colleges in the Great Lakes region. Founded as an all-women's school, the College became coeducational in 2001, and total enrollment has since grown from 875 to 2,150, a remarkable 240 percent increase.

A snapshot of the fall 2012 traditional NDC student population shows the following: 45 percent female, 55 percent male; 55 percent Catholic; 28 percent minority; 55 percent student-athletes; and 53 percent live on campus. The mosaic of NDC students represents twenty states and twelve foreign countries.

A variety of clubs and activities enrich the overall experience of the 2,100-plus students. Campus Ministry promotes the spiritual growth of the College community and facilitates community service, and the award-winning FalconCorps service program provides students opportunities to serve at local charities and national programs such as Habitat for Humanity.

Most on-campus events are free, and students often may purchase tickets at reduced rates for off-campus programs such as performances of the world-famous Cleveland Orchestra, the Cleveland Opera, and road shows of Broadway productions at the Cleveland Play House, the Palace Theatre, the State Theatre, and the Ohio Theatre at Playhouse Square.

With twenty-two intercollegiate sports for men and women, Notre Dame is an NCAA Division II institution and an associate member of the Great Lakes Intercollegiate Athletics Conference (GLIAC), a league widely recognized as one of the top Division II conferences. Prospective students can learn more about NDC Falcon athletic programs at NotreDameFalcons.com.

Notre Dame offers quality academic programs in over thirty disciplines including a nationally accredited education major, a business major, a Bachelor of Science in Nursing, intelligence analysis and research, and criminal justice. A Master of Education degree is offered with concentrations available in special education, reading, and critical and creative thinking. The College launched a Master of Arts in security policy studies in fall 2011.

The College is accredited by both the North Central Association of Colleges and Schools and NCATE and is registered for the awarding of state teachers' licenses by the State of Ohio Department of Education.

Location

Located in South Euclid, Ohio, the 53-acre campus is in a residential neighborhood just 25 minutes from downtown Cleveland and all the excitement and cultural wealth of the city, such as the Rock and Roll Hall of Fame and Museum; the Cleveland Metroparks; University Circle; several professional sports teams; and one of the richest cultural, theatrical, entertainment, health-care, and employment regions in the nation. Only five minutes from Legacy Village and Beachwood Place, Cleveland's lifestyle retail centers, the area combines all the opportunities of a major urban and educational center with the relaxed atmosphere of a suburb.

The beautiful campus provides the perfect setting for the Clara Fritzsche Library; the historic Administration Building which houses classrooms, labs, and offices; Regina Hall and Regina Auditorium; Connelly Center, the dining hall and student center; Keller Center, the recreational and fitness facility; Falcon Café; and five residence halls, including two newer apartment-style facilities that house 288 upper-class students.

Majors and Degrees

The College awards the Bachelor of Arts degree in accounting (business administration); biology; chemistry; communication; education, including early childhood (pre-K–3), middle childhood (4–9), and young adult education and mild-moderate intervention specialist studies; English; graphic design; history/political science; information systems; international business; management; marketing; mathematics; psychology; public administration; sports management; studio art; and theology.

The Bachelor of Science is awarded in biology, chemistry, and mathematics. A student can also design his or her own major that leads to a Bachelor of Arts or Bachelor of Science degree by combining two or three academic areas, such as graphic design, human resource management, and public relations. Notre Dame College also offers a Bachelor of Science in Nursing program. An RN to B.S.N. completion program is also available.

Teacher licensure is available in early childhood education, middle childhood education, adolescent/young adult education, and multiage for mild/moderate intervention specialist studies.

The Associate in Arts degree is awarded at the completion of two-year programs in business management and pastoral ministry. The Center for Pastoral Theology and Ministry grants a two-year catechetical diploma and the College awards a Bachelor of Arts degree.

Academic Programs

For the bachelor's degree, students must earn 128 semester hours of credit, with a minimum cumulative grade point average of 2.0. From 36 to 68 semester hours of credit are required in the major field of study.

Through a cooperative education program, students can earn a maximum of 6 credit hours for paid or volunteer work experience related to their academic field of study. All students are required to complete a coop or internship experience.

Advanced Placement credit is awarded to students who have demonstrated the ability to pursue course work beyond the level of entering freshmen, as indicated by their scores on the Advanced Placement (AP) or College-Level Examination Program (CLEP) tests of the College Board. College credit is given on the basis of a decision made jointly by the academic dean and the department involved.

Academic Facilities

The Career Services Center coordinates co-op jobs and internships for students and interacts with faculty to create meaningful programs that link academics to the workplace. It further offers graduate school advising, résumé preparation assistance, interviewing and job search coaching, posting of positions available, and a resource library. On-campus recruiting opportunities attract scores of employers to the College to meet students firsthand.

The Clara Fritzsche Library houses a modern media center and has a capacity for 100,000 volumes. As a member of OhioLINK, the

College also has online access to members throughout the state, with access to more than 31 million library items and more than 90 research databases.

The Dwyer Success Center consists of an electronic classroom, a student computer lab, a writing lab, a test proctoring room and a tutoring room. The writing lab is staffed by English faculty who provide professional writing assistance to students free of charge. The tutoring room is staffed with graduate assistants and upper-class peer tutors for one-on-one study skills and subject specific assistance.

The multimedia lab for graphic design majors offers PC and Macintosh technology for advanced multimedia production capabilities.

The Finn Center for Adult, Graduate, Online, and Professional Programs unifies all aspects of adult education at NDC, providing convenient, flexible programs for educational advancement on days, nights, weekends, and the Web. Housing the Office of Adult and Graduate Admissions and the Office of Professional Development, the Finn Center offers professional development classes, associate degrees, bachelor's degrees, postbaccalaureate programs, and master's degrees.

Students with documented learning differences, such as attention deficit disorder (ADD), attention deficit hyperactivity disorder (ADHD), dyslexia, Asperger's syndrome, and specific learning disabilities (SLD) can enroll in the College's Academic Support Center to receive comprehensive support services. These include tutoring, academic advising, and access to a large array of adaptive equipment. In order to be accepted into the Learning Differences Program, students must meet the admission requirements of Notre Dame College. To participate in the Academic Support Center, students must submit documentation of a learning disability.

Costs

For the 2012–13 academic year tuition and fee charges were $25,514. Room and board costs were $8,296 for double occupancy.

Financial Aid

Notre Dame believes that all qualified students should have the opportunity to attend college, and provides need-, merit-, and athletic-based aid to its students. A comprehensive financial assistance program of more than $25 million assists nearly 93 percent of all full-time students. Students applying for aid must submit the Free Application for Federal Student Aid (FAFSA).

Faculty

The College has 57 full-time faculty members, augmented by highly qualified instructors. Faculty members hold advanced degrees from more than thirty universities in the United States, Canada, and Europe.

Student Government

The Undergraduate Student Government (USG) is the central coordinating group for all student organizations. In addition, students have representation on various College committees.

Admission Requirements

Notre Dame College admits students who demonstrate potential for success in rigorous academic work. In fulfilling its mission, the College seeks to attract students of diverse religious, racial, and economic backgrounds. Candidates for admission as first-time, full-time freshmen are reviewed on an individual basis, and decisions are based on a broad range of criteria. The most important consideration is the candidate's high school performance, as demonstrated by her/his overall grade average, class rank, grade trends, and level of courses completed. Aptitude for verbal and mathematical reasoning, as measured by performance on standardized tests, is also considered. In addition, counselor and teacher recommendations are reviewed.

Notre Dame College recommends that students complete at least 16 units of high school credit in academic subjects as a prerequisite for matriculation in the College. The distribution of these subject areas and the units are as follows: English, 4; mathematics, 3 (to include algebra I, geometry, and algebra II); science, 3 (with laboratory experience); social studies, 3; foreign language, 2 (from the same language); and fine arts, 1. Applicants should generally rank in the upper half of their high school graduating class and have a minimum average of C+. Either ACT or SAT scores are accepted.

The College has a fair and generous policy on the transfer of academic credit earned within the preceding five years at a regionally accredited college or university. Students wishing to transfer from other regionally accredited colleges and universities are admitted to advanced standing upon presentation of satisfactory evidence of scholarship and character.

Special consideration may be granted to an applicant whose academic preparation is not consistent with the requirements stated above.

Notre Dame College strongly recommends that prospective students schedule an appointment to visit the campus and talk with an admissions counselor.

Application and Information

A free application is available online at NotreDameCollege.edu. The College maintains a rolling admission policy. To apply, students should submit the completed application for undergraduate admission, an official transcript of their high school record and results of the ACT or SAT to:

Office of Admissions
Notre Dame College
4545 College Road
South Euclid, Ohio 44121
Phone: 216-373-5355
      877-NDC-OHIO Ext. 5355 (toll-free)
Fax: 216-373-5278
E-mail: admissions@ndc.edu
Website: http://NotreDameCollege.edu
        http://www.facebook.com/NotreDameCollege
        http://twitter.com/NotreDameOhio
        http://www.youtube/notredamecollege

Fall semester is one of the most beautiful times of the year at Notre Dame College in South Euclid, Ohio.

OHIO NORTHERN UNIVERSITY

ADA, OHIO

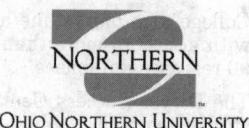

The University

Founded in 1871, Ohio Northern University (ONU) is a private, comprehensive university, comprising five colleges (Arts & Sciences, Business Administration, Engineering, Law, and Pharmacy) that blend liberal and professional education. Talented, motivated students engage in abundant activities in and out of the classroom and graduate with an education that provides one of the highest returns on investment in the nation.

Ohio Northern is a student-centered, service-oriented, values-based institution affiliated with the United Methodist Church and committed to a rigorous pursuit of academic inquiry and achievement. Education is a collaborative process, and students work side-by-side with accomplished faculty in a constant pursuit of new knowledge. The result is serious research, real collaboration, and meaningful learning experiences.

Students can choose from a variety of campus activities including nearly 200 student organizations; four national sororities and five national fraternities; fine arts, music, and theatrical events; and intramural and club sports. Residence hall living is an integral part of the educational program, contributing to a student's personal development. There are nine residence halls on campus as well as eight campus apartment complexes and an Affinity Housing complex.

A member of the NCAA Division III Ohio Athletic Conference, ONU has eleven men's teams (baseball, basketball, cross-country, football, golf, soccer, swimming and diving, tennis, indoor and outdoor track, and wrestling) and ten women's teams (basketball, cross-country, fast-pitch softball, golf, soccer, swimming and diving, tennis, indoor and outdoor track, and volleyball).

Location

Ohio Northern University's campus is situated on 342 beautiful acres in the village of Ada (population 5,500). Located in northwestern Ohio, ONU is easily accessible by major highways and conveniently located near major cities such as Columbus, Dayton, Toledo, and Fort Wayne, Indiana.

Majors and Degrees

Ohio Northern University offers the undergraduate degrees of Bachelor of Arts, Bachelor of Fine Arts, Bachelor of Music, Bachelor of Science, Bachelor of Science in Business Administration, Bachelor of Science in Civil Engineering, Bachelor of Science in Medical Laboratory Science, Bachelor of Science in Computer Engineering, Bachelor of Science in Electrical Engineering, Bachelor of Science in Engineering Education, Bachelor of Science in Mechanical Engineering, and Bachelor of Science in Nursing. In addition, to the undergraduate programs, ONU offers a Master of Professional Practice in Accounting; Juris Doctor; Doctor of Pharmacy (Pharm.D.), which is a 0-6, direct entry program; and the Master of Laws (LL.M.) in Democratic Governance and Rule of Law.

Majors are offered in accounting, advertising design, applied mathematics, art education, athletic training, biochemistry, biology, chemistry, civil engineering, communication studies, computer engineering, computer science, construction management, creative writing, criminal justice, early childhood education, electrical engineering, engineering education, environmental and field biology, exercise physiology, forensic biology, French, German, graphic design, history, language arts education, literature, management, manufacturing technology, marketing, mathematical statistics, mathematics, mechanical engineering, medical laboratory science, middle childhood education, molecular biology, multimedia journalism, music, music education, musical theatre, nursing, performance, pharmaceutical business, pharmacy, philosophy, physics, political science, professional writing, psychology, public relations, religion, social studies, sociology, Spanish, sport management, studio arts, technology education, theatre, theatre production, and youth ministry.

Special preprofessional programs are available in dentistry, law, medicine, occupational therapy, optometry, physical therapy, physician assistant, seminary, and veterinary medicine. Teacher licensure programs are offered at the early childhood, middle childhood, adolescent/young adult, and multiage levels within eighteen programs and two endorsement areas.

Changes in programs of study are updated at www.onu.edu.

Academic Programs

The Getty College of Arts & Sciences creatively combines a traditional liberal arts education with cutting-edge preprofessional studies. The college offers more than fifty majors in seventeen academic departments, and students can earn a Bachelor of Arts, Bachelor of Fine Arts, Bachelor of Music, Bachelor of Science, Bachelor of Science in Medical Laboratory Science, or Bachelor of Science in Nursing degree.

Students in the sciences have been honored by the Barry M. Goldwater Scholarship and Excellence in Education Foundation for nine consecutive years. The college has also been recognized as one of the top 200 programs in the nation for creative students in *Creative Colleges: A Guide for Student Actors, Artists, Dancers, Musicians and Writers*.

Working closely with dedicated faculty members, students complete the general education requirements, delve deeply into advanced courses, and engage in research, internships, practicum experiences, study abroad, and more.

The James F. Dicke College of Business Administration focuses on creating ethical, entrepreneurial, and engaged business and civic leaders. The college offers a rigorous academic curriculum with a signature program in pharmaceutical business. Internships are required by the college and are available year-round. There are international programs, including study abroad, work abroad, and study tours. An office of experiential learning supports students looking for these opportunities. The course of study for the Bachelor of Science in Business Administration includes a four-year business core experience themed around business planning. Personal attention and mentoring from faculty members, small intimate classes, and active student organizations combine with an emphasis on experiential learning, global awareness, and the entrepreneurial spirit. The college is accredited by the AACSB International—The Association to Advance Collegiate Schools of Business. In April 2013, the Dicke College of Business Administration was ranked by *Bloomberg Businessweek* among the top 100 undergraduate business programs in the U.S. and the top private school business program in Ohio.

One of the top 50 undergraduate programs in the nation for the past five years (*U.S. News & World Report*), the T.J. Smull College of Engineering provides a premier undergraduate experience that inspires creativity and supports innovation. The college features five accredited, disciplinary majors in civil, computer, electrical, and mechanical engineering and computer science. The recently added engineering education degree supports the demand for high school math teachers with engineering degrees.

The courses for the first academic year are essentially the same for each degree program, offering students an easy track to move from one program to another if initially uncertain which disciplines they prefer to study.

An optional five-year co-op program is available for students in each program, provided they maintain a minimum 2.5 GPA. There is an emphasis on team projects, and students participate in various design competitions. Many opportunities are available for valuable work experience through the co-op and internship programs, with a historically high job-placement rate for graduates.

For more than 125 years, the Raabe College of Pharmacy has offered distinctive, challenging, and comprehensive training for some of the nation's most talented pharmacists. This University signature program features a six-year Doctor of Pharmacy (Pharm.D.) degree accredited by the American Council on Pharmaceutical Education. This program is direct-entry, admitting students immediately from high school into the college's professional program. This approach enables students to take pharmacy courses from the very first day. A rigorous curriculum utilizes an innovative modular format to organize learning around the human body systems and patient care implementation.

Cutting-edge clinical facilities include the Pharmacy Skills Center, where students access state-of-the-art compounding/counseling pods with portable OTC simulation stations. Students gain considerable experience through a strong undergraduate research program and may pursue minors or dual majors in other areas. Faculty members are teaching-focused but remain current in their research disciplines. Upon graduation, students are well schooled in every aspect of pharmacy and have a high placement rate.

Off-Campus Programs

Many majors may take part in study-abroad programs developed in consultation with faculty members. Field experiences and internships are available to most majors. Externships are required of all pharmacy majors and place students in retail and clinical experiences. Teacher licensure requires one semester of primary or secondary classroom teaching experience under the supervision of practicing teachers. Additional opportunities include computer science and mathematics co-op programs (professional practice), engineering co-op programs (professional practice, domestic and international), and an honors program. All off-campus learning experiences carry credit.

Academic Facilities

Among the nineteen modern academic buildings on campus, the newest is the Mathile Center for the Natural Sciences, which expands the science-learning environment. This 95,145-square-foot student-centered academic research and learning facility blends hands-on teaching excellence with advanced technology in a functional modern environment.

The College of Business Administration's Dicke Hall offers students a modern setting for high-tech classrooms, meeting rooms and a 150-seat lecture forum.

ONU's Heterick Memorial Library and the Taggart Law Library provide information resources and services to support course offerings and foster independent study.

The Freed Center for the Performing Arts houses Communications and Theatre Arts classrooms and features a 550-seat theater/concert hall, a 120-seat studio theater, and television and radio production facilities. WONB-FM is the commercial-free voice of ONU.

Costs

Charges for the 2013–14 year are $47,240 for tuition, fees, room, and board for the Colleges of Arts & Sciences and Business Administration; $49,720 for the College of Engineering; and $51,760 for the College of Pharmacy. These totals are based on tuition, double-occupancy air-conditioned room, and a carte-blanche meal plan.

Financial Aid

Even with one of the highest returns on investment in the nation, ONU invests more than $58 million toward merit-based scholarships and need-based resources. To be considered, the student should submit the FAFSA to the University along with the admission application.

Faculty

More than 220 full-time faculty members bring extensive academic, work, travel, and life experience to their classrooms. Ohio Northern values excellence, innovation, technology, diversity, and its people.

With a 12:1 student-faculty ratio, students get lots of personal attention from professors who are passionate about teaching and mentoring.

Student Government

The Student Senate provides self-government in many areas of student life and seeks to further ideals of character and service to the University. The Student Senate serves as the official representative group of the student body to the University administration and agencies in matters pertaining to the student body.

Admission Requirements

High school students applying for admission to the University should present an official transcript indicating at least 16 total units of study, including work in specific academic areas as indicated by each college. Applicants are also required to submit scores on the ACT and/or SAT. For scholarship purposes, the traditional sections of the ACT and the SAT are considered. An on-campus interview is also recommended.

Application and Information

In the Colleges of Arts & Sciences, Business Administration, and Engineering, a student's file is considered complete when it contains the application, official high school transcript, and ACT and/or SAT scores. The College of Pharmacy requires a personal statement and a recommendation in addition to the previous items.

The College of Pharmacy's application deadline is December 1 for entering freshmen. A campus visit is strongly encouraged for consideration for admittance into this college.

Requests for catalogs or additional information should be directed to:

Office of Admissions
Ohio Northern University
525 South Main Street
Ada, Ohio 45810
Phone: 888-408-4668 (toll-free)
Fax: 419-772-2821
E-mail: admissions-ug@onu.edu
Website: www.onu.edu
      www.facebook.com/ohionorthern
      www.twitter.com/onuadmissions

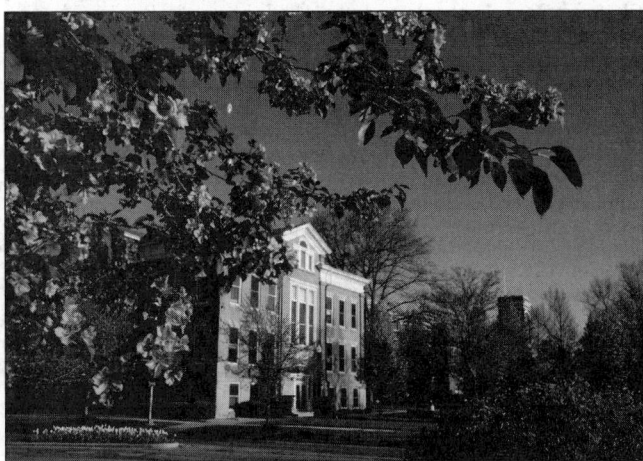

Hill Memorial and its clock tower are mainstays of the front of campus.

OHIO WESLEYAN UNIVERSITY
DELAWARE, OHIO

The University

Ohio Wesleyan is a national liberal arts university with a major international presence. It is remarkable for the depth of its academic and pre-professional programs, the international dimension of its curriculum, its focus on community through leadership and service, and its unwavering commitment to linking theory and practice in a global context and in every field of study.

A selective residential institution, Ohio Wesleyan is home to about 1,850 undergraduates, with a nearly equal number of men and women. Students come from nearly every state and more than forty countries, lending a rich diversity to the campus community; most students live on the attractive 200-acre campus. Housing options include six large residence halls; two residences primarily for seniors; a living-learning residence for students in business disciplines; a residential honors house; several themed houses; and seven fraternity houses. The five sorority houses are nonresidential.

One of the richest of OWU's cocurricular traditions is service. Nearly the entire student body participates in at least one community service or philanthropic project each year. For five consecutive years, the school earned a place on the Presidential Honor Roll for Community Service, with Distinction, and in 2009–10, the University earned the President's Award for Excellence in General Community Service, one of only three colleges and universities in the country to be so honored that year.

Each year, students may enjoy more than 100 concerts, plays, dance programs, films, exhibits, and speakers. The Department of Theatre & Dance stages four major productions each year, while the Department of Music sponsors four large performance groups and a variety of smaller ensembles. Students also publish the nation's oldest independent student newspaper.

OWU is home to twenty-three Division III varsity athletic teams. In 2011, the men's soccer team took the Division III National Championship for the second time, and the coach, Dr. Jay Martin, became the all-time winningest coach in collegiate men's soccer across all NCAA divisions. Intramural and club sports programs are extensive, and off-campus recreation opportunities are abundant.

Location

Delaware combines a small-town pace with easy access to the state capital, Columbus, the sixteenth-largest city in America. Twenty miles south of the campus, Columbus provides many internship opportunities, fine dining and shopping, and cultural events that complement those on campus.

Majors and Degrees

Ohio Wesleyan offers the Bachelor of Arts in accounting; ancient, medieval, and Renaissance studies; astronomy; biological sciences (botany, genetics, microbiology, and zoology); chemistry; classics; computer science; economics (including accounting, finance, economics, international business, and management economics); education (elementary and secondary licensure in seventeen areas); English literature and writing; fine arts; French; geography; geology; German; health and human kinetics; history; humanities; journalism; mathematics; music (applied or history/literature); philosophy; physics; planetary science; politics and government; psychology; religion; sociology/anthropology; Spanish; and theatre and dance. Interdisciplinary majors include ancient, medieval, and Renaissance studies; Black world studies; East Asian studies; environmental studies; international business; international studies; Latin American studies; neuroscience; planetary science; urban studies; and women's and gender studies. Pre-professional studies include pre-law, pre-medicine, pre-engineering, pre-dentistry, pre–veterinary medicine, pre-optometry, pre-theology, and pre–physical therapy. Students also may design majors in topical, period, or regional studies.

Two professional degrees are awarded: the Bachelor of Fine Arts in art history, arts education, and studio art, and the Bachelor of Music

in music education and performance. Combined-degree programs are offered in engineering, optometry, and physical therapy. Ohio Wesleyan is one of only thirteen colleges in the United States that has a 3-2 engineering program with the Caltech.

Academic Programs

Ohio Wesleyan emphasizes theory-to-practice opportunities in a global context. Each year, travel-learning courses invite students to travel internationally with their classmates and professors as part of the course curriculum. Competitive theory-to-practice grants provide University-funded opportunities for students to design their own research projects, complete internships, participate in service, or experience cultural immersion throughout the world. Ohio Wesleyan also provides a robust offering of traditional study-abroad options; formal programs are offered in more than twenty countries. Ohio Wesleyan Course Connections networks provide opportunities for students to study a topic of interest in depth and over a protracted period of time by taking topical courses in a variety of disciplines and departments.

Students must demonstrate competence in English composition and a foreign language (often through placement testing) and to complete distributional study in the natural and social sciences, the humanities, and the arts; some of these requirements may be met in Course Connections classes. Many students double major and self-designed majors are not uncommon. Thirty-four courses are required for graduation.

Advanced placement is available with or without credit. In the four-year honors program, even first-year students have opportunities to work individually with faculty mentors on research, directed readings, or original creative work. Undergraduate students frequently present research to prestigious societies and nationally recognized organizations. Upperclass students also are encouraged to participate in independent study. One of the twenty-six scholastic honorary societies with chapters on campus, Ohio Wesleyan's chapter of Phi Beta Kappa is 106 years old.

Ohio Wesleyan offers the Economics Management Fellows Program for talented first-year students with an interest in business. This program offers special classes and seminars, a generous book allowance, networking opportunities with alumni executives and others, and a spring study trip to meet with business leaders.

Off-Campus Programs

Full-semester internships and apprenticeships, as well as programs of advanced research, are available to students. Many are approved by the Great Lakes Colleges Association, Inc. (GLCA), a highly regarded academic consortium of thirteen independent institutions. Programs are available at the Philadelphia Center, the GLCA New York Arts Program, and the Oak Ridge Science Semester. Other cooperative arrangements include the Newberry Library Program, Wesleyan in Washington, and the Drew University United Nations Semester. Students also conduct research locally at the U.S. Department of Agriculture (USDA) Laboratories in Delaware, the nearby Columbus Zoo, The Wilds, and several other sites. The Summer Science Research Program offers selected students the opportunity for an intensive, ten-week, one-to-one research experience with a faculty mentor. It concludes with a symposium at which research results are presented to the entire campus.

Academic Facilities

The Beeghly Library houses more than 550,000 holdings, one of the largest collections in the country for a private university of Ohio Wesleyan's size. The library's federal documents depository is among the nation's oldest and largest, providing an additional 200,000 reference publications. Beeghly Library also offers the Online Computer Library Center's most advanced cataloging system. The collection is enhanced by OhioLINK and CONSORT membership. An Internet Café within the Beeghly Library provides students with a 24-hour study area. The latest generation of wireless communication allows students to work online anywhere on the campus.

The Schimmel/Conrades Science Center is a 145,000-square-foot, three-level building that houses state-of-the-art instrumentation, including a scanning transmission electron microscope, all for undergraduate use. The Hobson Science Library in the science center consolidates all of OWU's science holdings. The University has a state-of-the-art Geographic Information Systems Computer Laboratory. The R. W. Corns Building houses the Woltemade Center for Economics, Business, and Entrepreneurship; the Department of Economics; the Sagan Academic Resource Center; and Information Systems. Perkins Observatory features a 32-inch reflecting telescope and two smaller instruments; an on-campus student observatory includes a 9.5-inch refracting telescope. Two University wilderness preserves cover a total of 100 acres. Other special facilities include the multistage Chappelear Drama Center; Sanborn Hall, home to the Music Department, Jemison Auditorium, and the Kinnison Music Library; and the 1,100-seat Gray Chapel, which houses the largest of only six Klais concert organs in the nation.

Costs

The general fee for 2012–13 was $51,180. This amount covered tuition and fees ($40,250) and room and board ($10,670). Books and personal expenses average $1,100. Nominal fees are charged for some studio art courses, off-campus study, private music lessons for students who are not majoring in music, and student teaching.

Financial Aid

OWU awards financial assistance to almost every entering freshman who demonstrates need. Aid packages include a combination of grants, loans, and employment. Federal and state aid are often part of an aid package. Nearly 70 percent of all undergraduates receive need-based financial assistance; another 25 percent are granted merit-based aid. More than three-quarters of all aid is awarded in the form of grants and scholarships.

The University awards several merit scholarship programs, ranging from $1,000 to full tuition. The school awarded more than 2,000 scholarships to new and prospective students for 2011–12. Private loan programs and flexible payment plans are available to all students, regardless of demonstrated financial need.

Faculty

The full-time faculty numbers 142, providing a student-faculty ratio of approximately 11:1. One hundred percent of the full-time tenure-track faculty members hold the highest degree in their fields. Although committed first to teaching and advising, most faculty members maintain active research programs and publish important articles and books; others are practicing artists who create and exhibit original works of art and theater.

Student Government

Students have a significant voice in the government of campus life. The Wesleyan Council on Student Affairs formulates basic policy. Students also sit on judicial boards, individual department student boards, and nine faculty committees. They are represented at all meetings of the Board of Trustees.

Admission Requirements

The admission process is competitive. Each student's application is individually reviewed. Although the applicant's academic record and strength of academic program are the most important factors, followed closely by teacher and counselor evaluations and SAT or ACT scores, many other aspects are considered, such as evidence of creativity, community service, and leadership. A minimum sixteen-course preparatory program is required. Four units of English and 3 each of mathematics, social studies, science, and foreign language are recommended, but variations of this program are considered. SAT Subject Tests are not required but may qualify students for advanced placement. Candidates for the Bachelor of Music degree must audition (tapes are accepted). Early action and transfer admission are offered. Campus interviews are strongly recommended but not required. For the 2011–12 school year, approximately 3,835 applications were received; 74 percent of the applicants gained admission.

Application and Information

Students are urged to complete the application as early as possible in the senior year, especially if they are applying for merit- or need-based financial aid. Once complete credentials (application, transcript, recommendations, and SAT or ACT scores) are received, decisions are made on a rolling basis after January 1. The student's response is required by May 1. The deadline for Early Action I application is November 30; the deadline for Early Action II application is January 15. Notification is given within four weeks after application is complete. After April 1, students are admitted on a space-available, rolling admission basis.

For further information, students should contact:

Office of Admission
Ohio Wesleyan University
Delaware, Ohio 43015
Phone: 740-368-3020
800-922-8953 (toll-free)
Fax: 740-368-3314
E-mail: owuadmit@owu.edu
Website: http://choose.owu.edu
http://www.facebook.com/OhioWesleyanUniversity
http://twitter.com/ohiowesleyan

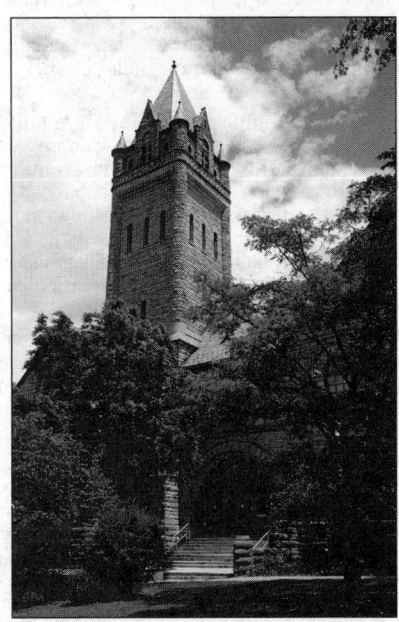

Ohio Wesleyan's historic University Hall, which houses administrative offices and the 1,100-seat Gray Chapel.

OLIVET NAZARENE UNIVERSITY
BOURBONNAIS, ILLINOIS

The University

Olivet Nazarene University (ONU) is a private, Christian liberal arts university with a strong emphasis on both academic excellence and Christ-centered living. Olivet's campus offers world-class facilities for learning and entertainment—some of the finest in the Midwest. The educational atmosphere promotes academic rigor, fun, relationship building, and spiritual growth.

Olivet's high retention, graduation, and employment/placement rates demonstrate the University's commitment to student success. Faculty, staff, and administration are dedicated to teaching, encouraging, and mentoring each student as a whole person—academically, socially, and spiritually.

With 4,500 students (2,500 undergraduates), Olivet offers an ideal student population for a private institution, maintaining diversity without compromising the commitment to personalized attention. Among the student body, more than forty denominations, most U.S. states, and more than twenty countries are represented.

ONU offers a championship-caliber athletics program with twenty intercollegiate men's and women's sports in all, and more than half of the student body participates in a robust intramural sports program. Music and drama groups involve hundreds of students, and many clubs invite students to pursue a wide variety of interests. Olivet students also commit to serving in dozens of ministry groups and volunteer efforts, small-group Bible studies, and weekly student-led worship services.

The University recently completed several large building projects including the Betty and Kenneth Hawkins Centennial Chapel, a 3,046-seat venue for worship, concerts, and events and the new Student Life and Recreation Center, which opened in December 2012. The Center includes an eight-lane Mondo-surface running track, two pools, a four-story rock climbing wall, four basketball courts, additional workout facilities, a game area, a spacious central lounge where students can gather for recreation or study, and several classrooms.

The University is home to the Chicago Bears' summer training camp. The camp draws thousands of fans to campus each year, as well as dozens of national sportscasters and media representatives from Chicago, the nation's second-largest media market.

Olivet is also home of the Shine.FM network, one of the top-rated contemporary Christian radio networks in the country. Shine.FM is a network of five stations impacting Chicagoland, Indianapolis, and Northwest Indiana, as well as the thousands of additional listeners who access Shine.FM online or through mobile apps. Olivet's broadcasting students work alongside seasoned professionals in operating the station. Students also benefit from the outstanding Christian recording artists Shine.FM brings to campus for concerts and appearances each year, such as Switchfoot, NeedtoBreathe, TobyMac, and Newsboys.

In addition to traditional undergraduate programs, Olivet offers eight degree-completion and continuing studies programs, more than twenty master's degree programs, and a Doctor of Education in ethical leadership through the School of Graduate and Continuing Studies (SGCS). Striving to meet the needs of the ever-expanding number of adults returning to school, the SGCS helps working adults complete their degree requirements without interrupting their employment. Courses and programs also provide resources to help enhance their personal and professional lives in a constantly changing world.

The SGCS offers courses on the main campus in Bourbonnais and throughout the Chicago area. Numerous students gather with other working adults for classes in churches, schools, hospitals, and other locations convenient to their homes or workplaces.

Location

The main University campus is located just 50 miles south of Chicago's Loop in the historic village of Bourbonnais, Ill. The area includes malls, restaurants, entertainment, and outdoor recreation centered on the Kankakee River State Park system. Olivet students enjoy many activities nearby and often make the quick trip north for the limitless offerings of Chicago and its surroundings.

Students find numerous opportunities for employment and internships in the area and among the vast professional resources of Chicago. They also find themselves working side-by-side with faculty and staff members in local and regional ministry projects. Olivet students continue to make valuable contributions, both professionally and ministerially, to area businesses, churches, and parachurch and nonprofit organizations.

Majors and Degrees

Olivet confers Bachelor of Arts (B.A.) and/or Bachelor of Science (B.S.) degrees in more than 100 fields of study (majors, minors, and concentrations), including: accounting; actuarial science; art; art (education); athletic training; biblical languages; biblical studies; biochemistry; biology; broadcast journalism; business administration; business information systems; chemistry; child development; Christian education; children's ministry; coaching; commercial graphics/marketing; communication studies; computer science; corporate communication; criminal justice; dietetics; digital media: graphics; digital media: photography; drawing and illustration; early childhood education; earth and space science; economics and finance; elementary education; engineering (electrical, mechanical, computer, geological); English; English as a second language; English education; environmental science; exercise science; family and consumer sciences; family and consumer sciences education; family studies; fashion merchandising; film studies; finance; forensic chemistry; French; general studies; geography; geological sciences; geology; Greek; health education; Hebrew; history; housing and environmental design; hospitality; information systems; information technology; intercultural studies; international business; international marketing; literature; management; marketing; mass communication; mathematics; mathematics education; media production; military affairs; military science; missions/intercultural studies; multimedia studies; music; music composition; music education; music performance; musical theater; not-for-profit management; nursing; painting; pastoral ministry; philosophy; philosophy and religion; physical education/health; physical science; political science; pre-dental; pre-law; pre-medicine; pre-optometry; pre-pharmacy; pre–physician's assistant studies; pre–physical therapy; pre-seminary; pre–veterinary science; print/online journalism; psychology; public policy; public relations; radio broadcasting; recreation and leisure studies; religion; religious studies; science education; secondary education; social science; social science education; social work; sociology; Spanish; Spanish education; sport management; television/video production; theater; writing; youth ministry; and zoology.

Academic Programs

Olivet seeks to offer an "education with a Christian purpose." This commitment to Christ mandates nothing less than the highest-quality academic programs. Olivet's liberal arts curriculum requires that students complete 45 to 58 hours of general-education courses. With the addition of major and minor programs of study, students must complete a minimum of 128 credit hours to obtain a bachelor's degree. Credit may be earned through AP and CLEP tests. Students may also participate in ROTC.

Olivet operates on a two-semester schedule, from August to May. Two summer sessions are also available.

Off-Campus Programs

Olivet students are encouraged to participate in the various off-campus study programs offered each semester. Sponsored programs include: Nazarene International Language Institute; Focus Leadership Institute (Focus on the Family); and Council for Christian Colleges and Universities programs, such as American

Studies Program in Washington, D.C., Australian Studies Centre, China Studies Program, Contemporary Music Center in Nashville, Los Angeles Film Studies Center, Middle East Studies Program, Russian Studies Program, Scholar's Semester in Oxford, Uganda Studies Program, and the Washington Journalism Center.

Other recognized programs include: AuSable Institute, International Business Institute, Romanian Studies Program, and Tokyo Christian University. Costs are usually comparable to a semester at Olivet, and credit is given for these programs. In addition, some sources of financial aid are applicable.

Many Olivet students participate in numerous educational and missions-oriented short-term trips that are available during the Christmas, spring, and summer breaks.

Academic Facilities

Olivet's 250-acre campus offers outstanding academic facilities. These include high-quality performance halls and athletic venues; natural science, engineering, and nursing laboratories with industry standard facilities and equipment; SMART classrooms; and an observatory. Each department uses the most current software in its field. More than a dozen campus computer labs are available for student use, and the campuswide wireless network gives students online access 24 hours a day.

Strickler Planetarium, one of the few all-digital planetaria located on a college campus, was completely renovated in 2008 with the same technology used in Chicago's Adler Planetarium.

Benner Library and Resource Center provides unlimited access to any material a student needs, either on site or through the interlibrary loan system. The library recently passed the 1 million mark in annual electronic resource searches. Links to electronic resources—such as eBooks and websites—in the library's online catalog are at 82,000. Full text downloads from Olivet's new Digital Commons, a virtual collection of scholarship by Olivet faculty and students, topped over 16,000 in just over a year. In 2010–11, library staff processed 36,500 circulation transactions, and gate count (people entering the library on campus) was 304,064.

Costs

Tuition, based on 12 to 18 credit hours, is $29,050 for 2013–14. Room and board, based on double occupancy and a meal plan, are estimated to cost $7,900 for the year. Additional fees will be $840 per year.

Financial Aid

Approximately 99 percent of traditional undergraduates receive a total of $35.4 million in federal and state grants and institutional scholarships annually.

Olivet's cost continues to be competitive for private colleges nationwide. The friendly staff is committed to making an Olivet education affordable for every young person.

The University participates in all federal and state financial aid programs. The priority deadline for filing the Free Application for Federal Student Aid (FAFSA) is March 1. To apply for aid, students must fill out the FAFSA as well as Olivet's application for financial aid. The student must be an accepted applicant before a financial aid package can be created.

Olivet offers a monthly installment plan in addition to the traditional three-payment plan.

Faculty

Teaching is a ministry for Olivet's more than 120 full-time faculty members. These dedicated Christians are the key to excellence in education, both inside and outside the classroom. Olivet's 17:1 student-faculty ratio gives them an opportunity to teach, mentor, and encourage students on a personal level. They are deeply committed and involved in campus life, whether sponsoring social organizations and clubs, participating in talent shows, tutoring students in their offices, or talking over lunch with students in the dining room.

Student Government

The Associated Student Council is the student government organization on campus. The executive council consists of a president, vice president of finance, vice president of spiritual life, vice president of social affairs, vice president of publicity, vice president of women's residential life, vice president of men's residential life, vice president of office management, the *GlimmerGlass* (student newspaper) editor, and the *Aurora* (yearbook) editor. They work alongside the University's administrative team to ensure the health and promotion of campus activities and organizations.

Admission Requirements

Admission to Olivet is moderately difficult. Students are considered for admission on the basis of their high school GPA and ACT or SAT scores. An ACT score is required for placement in courses. For international students, TOEFL results are an additional factor in the admission decision. Students with low test scores and GPAs may be admitted on a provisional basis. A campus visit and interview are strongly recommended for all prospective students.

Application and Information

Admission is on a rolling basis. The application deadline is May 1. An early decision is required for some scholarships. Students may apply online through Olivet's website or in print by mail. The application process includes the written (or electronic) application, high school transcripts, ACT or SAT scores, and a health form. An enrollment deposit is collected to prioritize both student housing and class registration.

For more information or to arrange a campus visit, contact:

Office of Admissions
Olivet Nazarene University
One University Avenue
Bourbonnais, Illinois 60914
Phone: 800-648-1463 (toll-free)
E-mail: admissions@olivet.edu
Website: http://www.olivet.edu
　　　　http://www.youtube.com/olivetnazareneu
　　　　http://on.fb.me/OlivetNazareneUniversityClassof2016
　　　　　(Facebook)
　　　　http://twitter.com/OlivetNazareneU
　　　　http://www.flickr.com/photos/olivet/collections

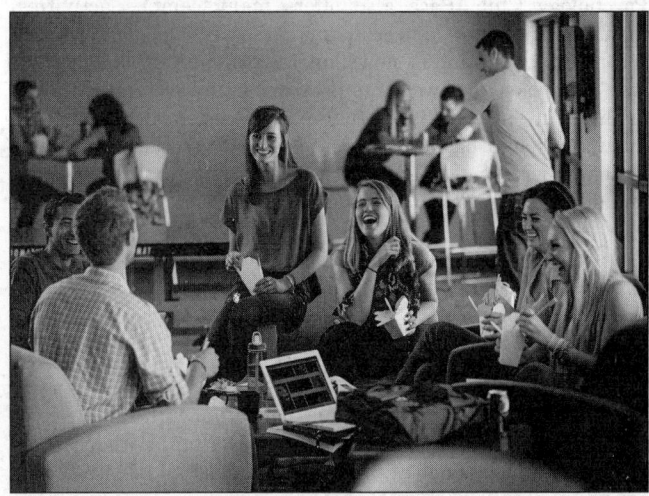

Nestled among the student apartments, steps from the center of campus, The Oaks lounge and game room provides a retreat from studies, with table tennis, pool tables, vending and café, exercise facilities, multiple media outlets, and a movie-viewing room.

PACE UNIVERSITY
NEW YORK CITY AND WESTCHESTER, NEW YORK

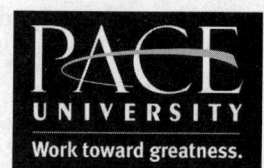

The University

Founded in 1906, Pace University is a leading private metropolitan university that offers an exceptional liberal arts education combined with superior career preparation, two strategic undergraduate New York locations, and robust scholarships and financial aid. The diverse student population of 8,025 undergraduates (5,025 in New York City and 3,000 in Westchester) is enrolled in more than 3,000 courses across 100-plus majors and combined degree programs. These are offered through five undergraduate schools and colleges: the Lubin School of Business, the Dyson College of Arts and Sciences, the Seidenberg School of Computer Science and Information Systems, the School of Education, and the College of Health Professions. Pace University offers career preparation through the largest internship programs in New York. Each year, over 1,200 students intern at more than 500 partner companies throughout metropolitan New York, Westchester County, and southern Connecticut.

Many student-led clubs and organizations are active on the campus, including the Pace Advertising Club, African Students Association, the Pace Association for Collegiate Entrepreneurs, the Student Government Association, and the Collegiate Psychology Club. Pace also offers many campus activities, including student government associations, fraternities, sororities, two campus newspapers, two literary magazines, two yearbooks, and two campus broadcasting systems. Athletic facilities are available for students, and intercollegiate sports include baseball, basketball, cross-country, cheerleading, dance, football, lacrosse, women's soccer, women's softball, swimming and diving, and women's volleyball.

The student body is diverse, representing forty-eight states, five U.S. territories, and more than 100 countries.

Location

Pace University is a multicampus institution with campuses in both New York City and Westchester, New York. Both locations are within reach of cultural, business, and social resources and opportunities. The New York City campus is located in the heart of the Financial District in lower Manhattan, and within a short walking distance of Wall Street and the South Street Seaport. Lincoln Center, Broadway theaters, museums, and many world-famous attractions are minutes away by public transportation. Located 35 miles north of New York City, the Westchester campus offers a traditional college experience: state-of-the-art science and video production labs, competitive athletics, fraternities and sororities, and access to internship opportunities at many Fortune 500 companies. Both campuses are accessible by car and public transportation.

Students can take courses at either campus, and housing is available in both New York City and Westchester. Residence halls are equipped with complimentary cable TV, telephone, and high-speed Internet access.

Majors and Degrees

The following programs are offered at both the New York City and Westchester campuses. The Bachelor of Business Administration (B.B.A.) is offered with majors in accounting–general, accounting–public, finance, general business, information systems, international management, management (with concentrations in business, entrepreneurship, and human resources), and marketing (with concentrations in advertising and integrated marketing communications, and global marketing management). In addition, a five-year combined B.B.A./M.B.A in public accounting is available for qualified students. The Bachelor of Arts (B.A.) degree is granted in American studies, biology, computer science, economics, environmental studies, film and screen studies, history, information systems, liberal studies, mathematics, philosophy and religious studies, political science, and psychology. The Bachelor of Science (B.S.) degree is offered in biochemistry, biology, biology–pre-professional (occupational therapy, optometry, physical therapy, and podiatry), business economics, chemistry, computer science, criminal justice, environmental science, information systems, information technology, mathematics, professional computer studies, and professional studies÷.

Certain programs are available only on one campus. The B.S. program in forensic science; the B.B.A. programs in arts and entertainment management, hospitality and tourism management, and quantitative business analysis; the B.F.A. programs in acting, art, commercial dance, and musical theater; and the B.A. programs in art history; communication science and disorders; communication studies; directing; English language and literature; language, culture, and world trade; Latin American studies; modern languages and culture; sociology-anthropology; Spanish; teaching students with speech and language disabilities; theater arts (acting and design/technical); and women's and gender studies are offered only at the New York City campus. The B.A. programs in applied psychology and human relations, biological psychology, childhood education, communication arts and journalism, communications, adolescent education (biology, chemistry, earth science, English, history/social studies, mathematics), English, English and communications, education, and personality and social psychology, and the B.S. programs in art, nursing, and physics are available at the Westchester campus only.

Pace University offers a five-year engineering programs in cooperation with Manhattan College and Rensselaer Polytechnic Institute. Students attend Pace for three years and either Manhattan College or Rensselaer for two years. Upon successful completion, students receive a B.S. degree in chemistry from Pace and either a Bachelor of Chemical Engineering (B.C.E.) in chemical engineering from Manhattan or a B.S. degree in engineering from Rensselaer.

Academic Programs

At Pace University, an innovative core curriculum allows students to develop critical thinking and communication skills by studying subject areas that are integrated around a theme. Students can choose from civic engagement and public values, critical writing, world traditions and cultures, and public speaking. Students also participate in community-based learning where they are given opportunities to practice their skills in real-life settings. Selective academic programs in the University are preparatory for professional training in dentistry, law, medicine, and veterinary science.

The Pforzheimer Honors College is a highly esteemed opportunity at Pace—a community of talented undergraduate scholars studying under the distinguished faculty of the University's five undergraduate schools and colleges. It is a place to excel and realize potential.

Pace University's internship program is nationally recognized and offers qualified students the opportunity to gain experience in their field of study while earning a four-year degree. Students can choose full-time, part-time, or summer positions working in an area directly related to their major course of study. Pace University ranks fifth in the country and first in the New York Metropolitan Area on *U.S. News & World Report's* 2013 short list for its high percentage of undergraduate with internship experience.

Academic Facilities

The Pace University Library is a comprehensive teaching library and student learning center, a virtual library that combines strong core collections with ubiquitous access to global Internet resources to support broad and diversified curricula. Reciprocal borrowing and access accords, traditional interlibrary loan services, and commercial document delivery options supplement the aggregate library. Pace offers Instructional Services librarians, a state-of-the-art electronic classroom, digital reference services, and multimedia applications. Pace's computer resource centers are linked to high-speed data networks and feature sophisticated hardware and software to facilitate active learning. Pace supports high-speed Internet and Internet2 access on every campus— residence facilities are wired, and most public areas are enabled for wireless connectivity. Full-motion videoconference facilities enable remote delivery of instruction between campus sites for synchronous learning applications.

Costs

For the 2012–13 academic year, undergraduate tuition was $35,320 per year for full-time study. The cost for an on-campus double-occupancy room and board was $12,590–$14,800, with different housing options available.

Financial Aid

Pace University strives to provide opportunities to students of diverse backgrounds and varied circumstances and is committed to offering financial aid to students to the fullest extent of its resources. University-sponsored scholarships are awarded to students on the basis of academic merit, service to the community, and financial need. The goal is to offer every student as much financial assistance as possible, based upon availability and need. Last year, Pace students received more than $289 million in aid. Pace's comprehensive student financial aid assistance program includes scholarships, grants, on-campus employment, student loans (federal and alternative plans), and tuition payment plans. Pace participates in all federal financial aid programs and the New York State Tuition Assistance Program (TAP) and honors awards from other states' incentive grant programs.

Students should submit the Free Application for Federal Student Aid (FAFSA) by February 15 for priority consideration for the fall semester. Pace University's new Net Price Calculator (www.pace.edu/calculator) is an online tool designed to help students and their families estimate their financial aid package. Many find that Pace is actually more affordable than similar public and private colleges due to the scholarship and financial aid awards offered to families.

Faculty

First and foremost, Pace University professors are dedicated teachers. All Pace classes are taught by professors. Students will never take a course taught by a teaching assistant. Faculty members also bring real-world experience and scholarship into the classroom through their work with outside companies and organizations and by leading cutting-edge research projects. Faculty members come from the best graduate and doctoral programs in the country. Professors—four fifths of whom hold Ph.D.'s—have earned degrees from the University of Pennsylvania, Harvard, Brown, Columbia, and Yale. Pace professors work closely with students to not only broaden their academic horizons, but to show how their work in the classroom is applicable to their future careers.

Admission Requirements

A minimum of 16 academic units from an accredited secondary school, or equivalent, are required. Academic subjects in high school should be distributed as follows: 4 years of English, 3–4 years of college-preparatory mathematics, 2 years of foreign language, 3–4 years of history/social science, 2 years of laboratory science, and 2–3 units of academic electives. All domestic applicants are required to take either the SAT or ACT examination and have results forwarded to the University. International students are required to take the TOEFL, IELTS, or PTE.

Application and Information

The freshman application deadline is February 15. Transfer applications are reviewed on a rolling basis. Requests for application forms and information for both the New York City and Westchester campuses should be addressed to:

Enrollment Information Center
Pace University
One Pace Plaza
New York, New York 10038
Phone: 800-874-7223 (toll-free)
E-mail: infoctr@pace.edu
Website: http://www.pace.edu

PACIFIC UNIVERSITY
FOREST GROVE, OREGON

Pacific University Oregon

The University

Pacific University is a private, fully accredited university with more than sixty undergraduate fields of study and fourteen graduate and professional programs. It draws more than 3,400 students to its campuses in Forest Grove, Hillsboro, and Eugene, Oregon.

Students come to Pacific University from all over the United States and abroad, creating a diverse and dynamic student body. Students are taught by the University's full-time faculty members, who are devoted to teaching and to forming close, nurturing relationships with their students.

Pacific particularly draws students to its undergraduate programs in the natural sciences, education, business, the social sciences, and the humanities. It is known for its excellent liberal arts foundation, a welcoming and personal learning environment, and the superior preparation its students receive for the health professions and for medical school.

Most freshmen participate in a semester-long first-year seminar program designed to introduce students to college-level writing and research expectations. The core curriculum emphasizes writing, reasoning, and communication skills, as well as global perspectives and service. Pacific University also offers a senior capstone project, a year-long research project designed and implemented by students and culminating in a presentation to the University community.

Pacific University emphasizes the educational benefits of research projects, internships, study-abroad experiences, and service learning. Pacific offers twenty-six study-abroad programs in eleven countries, as well as short-term travel courses during an optional January term. The University also provides many opportunities for service, both on campus and within the broader community.

Most undergraduates study on the Forest Grove Campus, and freshmen and sophomores under 21 are required to live in one of the University's on-campus residence facilities, which include six residence halls, one of which is an apartment complex. The residential nature of the campus creates a vibrant living environment, where students develop close, lifelong friendships.

Architecture at Pacific is a pleasant blend of the old and new. Old College Hall, the first permanent structure built at Pacific University and one of the oldest educational buildings west of the Mississippi, serves as the University museum. Recent construction includes the new University library, Berglund Hall, Burlingham Hall, and Gilbert Hall, all LEED-certified buildings reflecting the University's commitment to sustainability.

There are more than sixty student interest groups on campus, including student media, academic societies, religious and political organizations, and service clubs. One of the largest student organizations, Na Haumana O Hawaii, unites Pacific's significant population of students from Hawaii and presents an authentic luau each year. Pacific University also is home to an active Greek system.

Pacific University is a member of the NCAA Division III Northwest Conference and offers twenty-three varsity teams for men and women. Men's sports include baseball, basketball, cross-country, football, golf, soccer, swimming, tennis, track and field, and wrestling. Women compete in basketball, cross-country, golf, lacrosse, soccer, softball, swimming, tennis, track and field, volleyball, and wrestling. Students also can take part in several intramural sports teams. The campus athletic center houses a gymnasium, fitness center, state-of-the-art indoor field house featuring FieldTurf, handball/racquetball courts, wrestling room, and a sports medicine training facility. The Lincoln Park Athletic Complex, a partnership with the City of Forest Grove, features an 1,100-seat stadium with a nine-lane, 400-meter track, a FieldTurf soccer and lacrosse field, a Bond baseball field, a varsity softball field, and other park amenities.

The Pacific Outback provides additional outdoor recreation opportunities for students, including training, equipment, and trips for snowboarding and skiing, rock climbing, camping, kayaking, and much more.

Students can rent a bicycle for a semester or for the year through the Outback to get around the bike-able Forest Grove community. The University also offers electrical vehicle charging stations, a car-sharing program, and discounted passes for the Portland area's mass transit system.

Location

Pacific University was founded in Forest Grove, Oregon. The historic college town, population 21,000, today is home to the 55-acre, oak-covered campus situated in Oregon wine country at the foothills of the coastal mountain range. About 25 miles from downtown Portland and just an hour from the beach or from Mount Hood, Forest Grove is the perfect home base from which to explore the Portland metropolitan area or the endless opportunities Oregon offers for hiking, skiing, camping, fishing, beachcombing, and bicycling.

Meanwhile, Pacific University also offers its health professions programs on its growing campus in Hillsboro, Oregon, a major city within the Portland metro area. Located on the regional light-rail line in the Hillsboro Health and Education District, the Health Professions Campus connects students with world-class learning opportunities even as they provide care to underserved populations throughout the region.

A third campus in Eugene, Oregon, serves the College of Education, which offers undergraduate and graduate level programs leading to teacher licensure and advanced professional certifications.

Majors and Degrees

The College of Arts & Sciences offers majors leading to bachelor of arts and bachelor of science degrees in anthropology/sociology, applied science, art, bioinformatics, biology, chemistry, computer science, dance, economics, English, environmental science, exercise science, history, international studies (with emphasis in Asian studies, Latin American studies, Western European studies, American studies, or international policy), mathematics, media arts (with majors in film and video, integrated media, or journalism), modern languages (including Chinese, French, German, Japanese, or Spanish), music (including performance and education), philosophy, physics, politics and government, psychology, public health, social work, sociology, and theatre. The College of Arts & Sciences also offers a Master of Fine Arts in writing through a low-residency program.

The College of Business offers majors in accounting, finance, international business, marketing, and business administration.

The College of Education offers an undergraduate major in education and learning, as well as a minor in communication sciences and disorders. Graduate programs in the College of Education include a fifth-year Master of Arts in Teaching, a Master of Arts in Teaching special education, a Master of Education, and several endorsement options, as well as a master's degree in speech-language pathology.

The College of Health Professions offers an undergraduate degree in dental health science, as well as graduate programs including the Master of Athletic Training, Doctor of Audiology, Master of Healthcare Administration, Doctor of Occupational Therapy, Doctor of Pharmacy, Doctor of Physical Therapy, master's in physician assistant studies, and several master's and doctorate programs in professional psychology. Also available are graduate-level certificate programs in gerontology and healthcare compliance.

The College of Optometry offers a Doctor of Optometry program and a master's degree in vision science.

Undergraduate programs operate on a two-semester program with an optional January term and limited summer courses. Most graduate and professional programs have year-round calendars.

Costs

Tuition and fees for the 2012–13 school year were $35,260. Room and board were $9,992 for a double room and a University meal plan. Pacific has consistently been named one of the best values west of the Mississippi by several national publications, including *U.S. News & World Report*.

Financial Aid

Financial assistance at Pacific is awarded on the basis of demonstrated need, academic merit, and talent. The Free Application for Federal Student Aid (FAFSA) is used in evaluating need. Prospective students are encouraged to apply for financial assistance by submitting the FAFSA to the federal processor as soon after January 1 as possible. Pacific provides financial assistance through grants, scholarships, loans, and part-time employment. Further information is available via e-mail at financialaid@pacificu.edu.

Faculty

Pacific's outstanding faculty members provide the foundation for the University's academic program. A student-faculty ratio of 10:1 and an average class size of 19 students in the College of Arts & Sciences allows for personal attention from the professors. Pacific does not use graduate or teaching assistants; all faculty members teach their own courses.

Admission Requirements

Pacific University is selective in considering new students. Primary consideration is given to a candidate's academic preparation and potential for successful study at the college level, as assessed by evaluating the student's transcripts of college-preparatory work, counselor and teacher recommendations, personal essay, SAT and/or ACT scores, and other student-submitted information. Transfer students must submit high school records and test scores if they have completed less than 30 semester hours, plus official transcripts from any institution previously attended.

Application and Information

Students may apply early and may be notified early through the modified rolling admissions plan. Pacific University is an exclusive member of the Common Application. The regular priority deadline for admission is February 1. For additional information, interested students should contact:

Office of Admissions
Pacific University
2043 College Way
Forest Grove, Oregon 97116
Phone: 503-352-2218
800-677-6712 (toll-free)
E-mail: admissions@pacificu.edu
Website: http://www.pacificu.edu
      http://www.facebook.com/pacificu

Pacific University is home to the unique and legendary Boxer mascot. Based on an ancient Chinese statue, Boxer is a mythical creature that resembles both a dog and a dragon. The original statue has been missing for decades, but the spirit of Boxer—representing pride, honor, and cultural diversity—is very much alive at Pacific University.

PEPPERDINE UNIVERSITY
Seaver College
MALIBU, CALIFORNIA

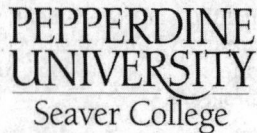

The University and The College

Pepperdine University is a private, faith-based university committed to the highest standards of academic excellence and Christian values, where students are strengthened for lives of purpose, service, and leadership.

Seaver College is the undergraduate liberal arts college of the University and is accredited by the Accrediting Commission for Senior Colleges and Universities of the Western Association of Schools and Colleges. Approximately 53 percent of Seaver's 3,289 students come from California, 36 percent from the other forty-nine states, and 9 percent from other countries. The 2012–13 freshman class had a median high school GPA of 3.56. On-campus housing is available to all students. However, first-year and second-year students are required to live on campus and receive priority housing. Students who live on campus may live in one of the 22 suite-style residence halls, Lovernich Residential Complex, Rockwell Tower Residence Hall, or the University apartments.

A wide range of student organizations and activities are available, including social, honor, service, spiritual, professional, divisional, and special interest clubs. Pepperdine also provides students with opportunities to be involved in the campus radio station, weekly student newspaper, and television broadcast.

Pepperdine participates in intercollegiate sports, including baseball, men's and women's basketball, men's and women's cross-country, men's and women's golf, men's and women's tennis, men's and women's track, men's and women's volleyball, women's sand volleyball, men's water polo, and women's swimming and diving. The University is a member of the West Coast Conference, the National Collegiate Athletic Association, and the Southern California Women's Intercollegiate Athletic Conference. Both men's and women's teams compete in Division I and have been very successful in regional and national competitions. Sports facilities include a 3,500-seat gymnasium, an Olympic-size swimming pool, a tennis pavilion and sixteen additional tennis courts, an intramural field, a baseball diamond, and a 2,000-seat baseball stadium.

The Master of Arts degree is offered at Seaver College in American studies, communication, media production, and religion. The Master of Science degree is offered in the fields of communication and ministry. The Master of Divinity degree is also offered, as well as the Master of Fine Arts in writing for film and television.

The School of Law awards the J.D., Master of Dispute Resolution, and Master of Laws degrees, and the School of Public Policy offers the Master of Public Policy; both schools are located on the Malibu campus. The Graduate School of Education and Psychology and the George L. Graziadio School of Business and Management offer graduate degrees at four locations in the Los Angeles area.

Location

Nestled in the Santa Monica Mountains overlooking the Pacific Ocean but less than an hour from Los Angeles, Seaver's Malibu campus offers both the serenity of a tranquil setting and the advantages of proximity to a major metropolitan area. Malibu has a movie theater, excellent restaurants, and two small shopping centers complete with banking facilities and a variety of shops and services. The winding seashore, the rugged beauty of Malibu Canyon, and the clean air provide an environment conducive to study, while the moderate climate permits year-round outdoor recreation. In addition to making use of the physical education facilities on campus, students can enjoy swimming, surfing, horseback riding, fishing, hiking, boating, and other activities in the vicinity. As an international center for trade, recreation, culture, industry, and education, Los Angeles provides students with a wide range of opportunities.

Majors and Degrees

Seaver College awards the Bachelor of Arts in advertising, art, art history, biology, chemistry, communication, creative writing, economics, English, film studies, French, German, Hispanic studies, history, integrated marketing communication, international studies, Italian, journalism, liberal arts, math education, media production, music, natural science, philosophy, political science, psychology, public relations, religion, sociology, Spanish, sports medicine, theater and music, theater and television, and theater arts.

The Bachelor of Science is awarded in accounting, biology, business administration, chemistry, computer science/mathematics, international business, mathematics, nutritional science, physics, and sports medicine. A teacher education program offers credentials in single or multiple subjects.

Academic Programs

The academic programs at Seaver College provide students with a liberal arts education in a Christian atmosphere and relate it to the dynamic qualities of life in the twenty-first century. Students must complete 128 units for the B.A. or B.S. degree, including 64 units in general education requirements and 40 or more in upper-division studies. Major requirements may be fulfilled through three basic arrangements. Students who specialize in a discipline must complete at least 24 units of upper-division work in their chosen discipline. Students may choose an interdisciplinary major, entailing at least 40 units of upper-division work, with courses ranging broadly across disciplinary lines within a division and on occasion crossing divisional lines, in one of the following fields of study: Communication, English, humanities, international studies, liberal arts, or religion. Alternatively, students may initiate a contract major by presenting an application for specific upper-division courses to the Dean of Seaver College.

Seaver College functions on a semester plan; the regular academic year consists of two semesters from late August to April. In addition to the regular academic year, summer sessions run from late April to early August.

At Seaver, instruction and study are adapted both to students' abilities and to the nature of the course content, instead of utilizing only the traditional lecture method. Programs involve several types of learning experiences: Seminars, integrated lectures, individual study, fieldwork, and laboratories. The Dean's List of undergraduate students in the top 10 percent of the class with a grade point index not lower than 3.5 is published each semester. Other honors include cum laude for students graduating with a scholastic level of at least 3.5, magna cum laude for 3.7, and summa cum laude for 3.9.

Off-Campus Programs

Seaver offers students the opportunity to study abroad in Buenos Aires, Argentina; Florence, Italy; Heidelberg, Germany; Lausanne, Switzerland; London, England; and Shanghai, China. The academic programs emphasize European, Latin American, or Asian history and culture. Seaver also offers summer special interest programs in Fiji, Scotland, and East Africa. Classes are taught by Seaver faculty members. Serious study and the daily experiences of living in another country give students a special depth of understanding of other cultures and a broader world perspective.

The Buenos Aires program accommodates approximately 60 students who live in the homes of carefully selected host families. The Florence program houses approximately 55 students who live in a Florentine villa and residential complex with classrooms, a library, a computer facility, and recreational facilities. The Heidelberg program has space for approximately 50 students at the Moore Haus, located near the city's famous castle. Classes are held in modern facilities in downtown Heidelberg. The Lausanne program accommodates about 70 students. The Pepperdine facility is located in La Croisée near the center of Lausanne, which has a picturesque view of Lake Geneva and the French Alps. The London program has space for approximately 40 students in the Knightsbridge area.

In addition to living quarters, the facility includes classrooms, a library, a computer room, offices, and a student center. The Shanghai program accommodates approximately 40 students who live in the Pepperdine-owned jia, meaning "house," which is located in the French Concession area near the American Consulate. The majority of the international program facilities are University-owned.

Academic Facilities

The Malibu campus is home to academic complexes containing seminar and lecture rooms, art studios, communication facilities, science and computer laboratories, mini-theaters, a recital hall, and administrative offices. The Payson Library is the global gateway to knowledge and provides students access to thousands of online journals, articles, and periodicals through various databases. It houses a collection of approximately 553,420 volumes. Payson Library serves as a sanctuary for study, learning, and research by encouraging discovery, contemplation, social discourse, and creative expression. The 300-seat George Elkins Auditorium is used for public presentations and lectures. The Center for the Arts facility includes the renowned Frederick R. Weisman Museum of Art and the Smothers Theatre, which seats 450 people and is used for dance, music, and theater performances. The Center for Communication and Business building houses a state-of-the-art radio and television production center where students have the opportunity to work on Pepperdine's cable television and radio stations.

Costs

Costs for the 2012–13 academic year were $42,520 for tuition, $12,600 for room and board, and $252 for additional fees.

Financial Aid

Approximately 80 percent of Seaver's students receive some form of financial assistance through scholarships, loans, grants, work-study programs, or jobs within the University. To be eligible for financial assistance from institutional resources, an undergraduate student must be enrolled in at least 12 units. An applicant must be admitted to the University before being awarded assistance, but the financial assistance application may be submitted with an admission application. To ensure full consideration, the Pepperdine financial assistance application should be submitted by February 15 for the fall semester and October 15 for the spring semester. Students are also responsible for applying for the California State Scholarship (California residents only) and Federal Pell Grant by submitting the Free Application for Federal Student Aid (FAFSA) in addition to Pepperdine's one-page financial assistance form.

Faculty

Seaver College's faculty includes men and women of high academic distinction whose primary focus is instruction with a secondary focus on research. 54 percent of faculty members are full-time, and 90 percent of full-time faculty members hold a doctorate or terminal degree in their field. The student-faculty ratio of 13:1, with an average classroom size of 20 students, allows ample individual assistance through classroom instruction and counseling. Upon enrollment, each student is assigned an academic adviser from among the faculty members. A qualified counseling staff is also available to assist with personal, professional, and academic needs.

Student Government

The Student Government Association (SGA) is composed of student leaders dedicated to providing Pepperdine's students with quality representation through innovative advocacy programs. SGA serves as the voice of the students to the Seaver administration and works in coordination with the Campus Life Office in establishing activities and maintaining school policies. SGA coordinates over 150 on-campus events each year including movies, sightseeing trips, guest performances, dances, speakers, and more. Pepperdine has eight nationally recognized sororities and five fraternities and there are over sixty different student organizations on campus that focus on a range interests, including academic, language, art, music, dance, drama, sports, and politics.

Admission Requirements

Applicants are admitted on the basis of their academic record, SAT or ACT scores, and personal information and references. Students who have completed at least 30 transferable semester units with a minimum grade point average of 3.0 are considered for admission as transfer students. Students who apply with fewer than 30 units are classified as first-year students with transfer units. To ensure full consideration for the fall semester, students should apply by the January 5 deadline. October 15 is the regular deadline for the spring semester. Decision letter dates are announced in the current application form.

Seaver College seeks to enroll a diverse student body. As such, Pepperdine University does not unlawfully discriminate on the basis of any status or condition protected by applicable federal or state law in the administration of its educational policies, admission, financial assistance, employment, educational programs, or activities.

Application and Information

To request information, students should contact:
Laura Kalinkewicz, Director of Admission
Seaver College
Pepperdine University
Malibu, California 90263-4392
Phone: 310-506-4392
Fax: 310-506-4861
Website: http://seaver.pepperdine.edu
Facebook: http://on.fb.me/Seaver_Admission
Twitter: http://twitter.com/#!/SeaverAdmission
YouTube: http://bit.ly/YouTube_Pepperdine
Pinterest: http://pinterest.com/seaveradmission/
Flicker: http://www.flickr.com/photos/seaveradmission

The 830-acre Malibu campus of Pepperdine University, Seaver College, overlooks the Pacific Ocean, 35 miles west of Los Angeles, California.

PILLAR COLLEGE
NEWARK AND SOMERSET, NEW JERSEY

The College

Pillar College educates, inspires, and equips students for excellent scholarship, service, and leadership. Rooted in and committed to Christian faith and love, Pillar College fosters intellectual, spiritual, and social development among its diverse student population at various instructional sites. Founded in 1908, Pillar College is New Jersey's only evangelical Christian college, and holds the highest accreditation available to any college or university. The College provides classes in Newark, Somerset, and other instructional sites in New Jersey.

Pillar College offers a unique blend of spiritual enrichment, academic excellence, and social fulfillment. The student body includes a broad spectrum of ages, races, interests, and personalities, reflecting the wide diversity of the metropolitan corridor of the Northeast. Through Godly instructors, rich curricula in career-shaping majors, spiritually enthusiastic students, valuable enriching internships, and global learning experiences, Pillar College offers students what they need to be equipped for their future.

Location

Pillar College is a non-residential college with instructional sites in Newark and Somerset County, New Jersey. Its Newark Campus occupies over 25,000 square feet of classroom, administrative, and conference/community space on the first, seventh and twentieth floors of the Military Park Building in the heart of downtown Newark. Both locations enjoy easy access to public transportation and major state and Interstate highways. Pillar College sites are a short drive from New York City, state parks, historical sites, hiking trails, professional and minor league sports, and New Jersey beaches.

Majors and Degrees

The Bachelor of Arts (B.A.) degree is a four-year, 120 credit-hour course of study. The B.A. is awarded upon successful completion of all requirements, which include a core curriculum consisting of Biblical studies and general education and major requirements. Majors include Biblical studies, Business Administration/Management, and Psychology/Counseling. Areas of concentration include Worship/Music/Media, Youth Ministry, Organizational Leadership, Communication, and Marriage and Family Counseling.

Academic Programs

Committed to providing accredited college degrees for all qualified, motivated students, Pillar College has developed unique and flexible programs of study designed to meet the needs of diverse students in all stages of life. Besides traditional Fall and Spring semester classes, the College also offers courses in condensed nine-week modules in evenings and on Saturdays. Many adult students choose the College's Life Enhancing Accelerated Degree (LEAD) program. Students form small groups, attend class one night per week, and earn college credits for life experiences and competencies.

Pillar College's newest innovation is Programa BLEND (BiLingual Entry Degree) designed for Spanish-speaking students. BLEND enables students to take general education and other core classes taught in Spanish for two years while completing English as a Second Language (ESL). Students can then complete their bachelor's degree in Psychology and Counseling, Business Administration and Management, or Biblical studies in English.

Academic Facilities

The Newark Campus occupies two floors of the Military Park Building, 60 Park Place. Located one block south of the Performing Arts Center (PAC) and four blocks north of the Prudential Center, the Military Park Building is a prestigious high-rise building that hosts an interesting array of professional corporations. Both Pillar locations boast beautiful student lounges and state-of-the-art classroom and media center facilities. The Newark Campus features student service offices, a library, and the College's administrative offices.

Costs

Pillar College is committed to providing an excellent, cost-effective education for its students. Tuition and fee rates, payable each semester, are set annually according to economic conditions within the College and industry standards. Tuition and fees for full-time traditional students are $8,602 per semester.

Financial Aid

Pillar College operates a full student financial aid program, including grants, scholarships, loans, and employment, allowing any student a realistic opportunity to finance their college education. More than 95 percent of all Pillar College students who apply for financial assistance to further their education receive it. The College is aware that each family has a unique financial situation and the financial aid staff is available to work with students to find the resources to fund their education.

Student Government

The Student Government seeks to fairly represent the interests and concerns of each member of the student body. Its purpose is to address student needs efficiently and effectively, uphold the code of conduct of the community, and to initiate positive activities and programs for the benefit of Pillar College students. The Student Government, working in close cooperation with the College's Director of Student Life, brings the students as a community into a closer and more vital relationship with the rest of the College community.

Admission Requirements

Pillar College admits all qualified students of any race, color, disability, national or ethnic origin to all the rights, privileges, programs, and activities available through the College. Pillar College does not discriminate on the basis of gender, race, color, disability, national or ethnic origin in administration of its educational policies, admission policies, financial aid, or other school-administered programs. In addition to enrolling, students enter into a covenant of respect for the Faith Statement and agree to adhere to the Ethos Statement. Prospective students and other persons interested in learning more about the College are cordially invited to arrange for a campus visit. Admissions requirements include an application, two recommendations, a personal statement, and official transcripts from all previous institutions. Pillar College, in compliance with the New Jersey Administrative Code (N.J.A.C. 8:57-6.5-6.9) and Health Department regulations, requires persons born January 1, 1957, or later to show proof of vaccinations for measles, mumps, rubella, and Hepatitis-B prior to arrival at school.

Application and Information

For an application form, catalog, and all forms required for admissions, students can contact:

Pillar College
60 Park Place, Suite 701
Newark, New Jersey 07102
Phone: 800-234-9305 (toll-free)
E-mail: info@pillar.edu
Website: http://www.pillar.edu

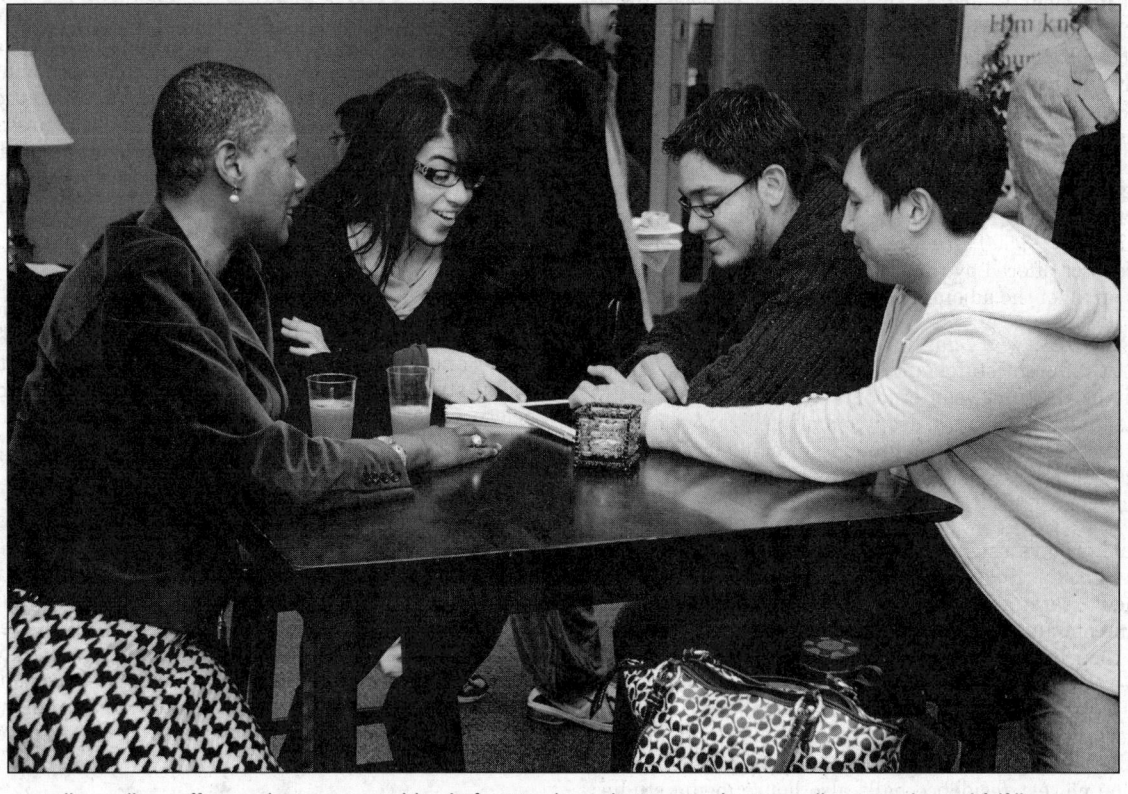

Pillar College offers students a unique blend of spiritual enrichment, academic excellence, and social fulfillment.

PITZER COLLEGE
CLAREMONT, CALIFORNIA

The College

Pitzer is a nationally recognized independent, residential liberal arts college. With a strong emphasis on the five core values of social responsibility, student engagement, environmental sustainability, interdisciplinary studies, and intercultural understanding, Pitzer believes that students should take an active role in their education and their world.

Pitzer was founded in 1963 and today offers forty majors in the arts, humanities, sciences, and social sciences. Majors with the largest enrollments currently include art, biology, English, environmental studies, intercultural and international studies, media studies, organizational studies, political studies, psychology, and sociology. Pitzer students have a great deal of freedom to choose the courses they want to take and even have the opportunity to design their own major.

Pitzer offers the best of both worlds: membership in a small, close-knit academic community and access to the resources of a midsize university through the College's partnership with the Claremont Colleges. The Claremont Colleges are a consortium of five distinct undergraduate colleges (Pitzer, Claremont McKenna, Harvey Mudd, Pomona, and Scripps) and two graduate institutions (Claremont Graduate University and the Keck Institute for Applied Biological Sciences). Each college has its own personality, but all share major facilities such as the library, bookstore, campus security, health services, counseling center, ethnic study centers, queer resource center, and chaplains' offices. The total enrollment of all of the colleges is approximately 6,500 students. Students at Pitzer may enroll in courses offered by the other colleges and consult with professors on all of the adjoining campuses.

In 2012, the first-year class of 256 students represented twenty-eight different states and eight other countries. About 57 percent of the first-year students came from outside of California. Pitzer has had a deep commitment to welcoming members of underrepresented groups since its founding. In 2012, students of color made up approximately 33 percent of the entering class.

Residential life plays a significant role in a student's educational experience. Each of Pitzer's residence halls establishes its own Hall Council to serve as a forum for addressing and meeting the needs of the community. Pitzer students have a long tradition of arranging their living communities based on common interests. All rooms are wired for Internet access, television, and phone service. After opening three new LEED Gold residence halls in 2007, Pitzer proudly opened an additional four LEED Platinum residence halls for sophomores, juniors, and seniors in the fall of 2012. The newest residence halls also house media studies facilities, an art gallery and a demonstration kitchen.

Opportunities for student engagement abound at Pitzer. Students can participate in a wide variety of sports, clubs, community service programs, and social activities. Currently, more than 150 student organizations allow students to get involved in a wide variety of activities. Pitzer partners with Pomona College to offer NCAA Division III teams in baseball, basketball, cross-country, football, golf, soccer, softball, swimming and diving, tennis, track and field, volleyball, and water polo. Club sports include crew, cycling, lacrosse, rugby, Ultimate (Frisbee), and volleyball. Intramural sports include inner tube water polo, squash, chess, flag football, and table tennis.

Location

Pitzer is located in the city of Claremont (population 35,000) at the base of the San Gabriel Mountains, about 35 miles east of Los Angeles and 80 miles west of Palm Springs. The College is just a short drive away from rock climbing at Joshua Tree National Park, ski resorts, the beaches of Southern California, and the Getty, Norton Simon, and other Los Angeles County museums.

Majors and Degrees

Pitzer offers a Bachelor of Arts degree in Africana studies, American studies, anthropology, art, art history, Asian American studies, biochemistry, biology, chemistry, Chicano/Latino studies, classics, dance, economics, English/world literature, environmental analysis, gender and feminist studies, history, human biology, international and intercultural studies, international political economy, linguistics, management engineering, mathematical economics, mathematics, media studies, modern language, literature and cultures: Spanish, molecular biology, music, neuroscience, organismal biology, organizational studies, philosophy, physics, political studies, psychology, religious studies, science and management, science, technology and society, sociology, and theater.

Minors are available in Africana studies, anthropology, art, art history, Asian American studies, biology, classics, dance, economics, English/world literature, environmental analysis, gender and feminist studies, history, linguistics, mathematics, media studies, music, philosophy, science, technology and society, sociology, Spanish, and theater.

Academic Programs

To earn their Bachelor of Arts degree, students are required to complete thirty-two courses with approximately one third of those courses in their major. Students work with faculty advisers to organize a curriculum that meets the educational objectives of the College: breadth of knowledge, understanding in depth, written expression, interdisciplinary and intercultural exploration, and social responsibility and the ethical implications of knowledge and action. Specific course requirements depend on the student's academic interests. Certain concentrations require a senior thesis.

The system of cross-registration at the Claremont Colleges provides Pitzer students with the opportunity to take advantage of the wide range of courses available at each of the other colleges. Students may also enroll in certain courses at Claremont Graduate University with the instructor's approval.

The College observes a semester calendar; classes begin in early September and end in mid-May. There is a study break near the middle of each semester and another break between semesters from mid-December through mid-January.

Off-Campus Programs

Almost 80 percent of Pitzer students participate in study-abroad programs. Pitzer currently approves twelve exchanges with U.S. institutions and over fifty international study options in Argentina, Australia, Botswana, Brazil, Bulgaria, Canada, Chile, China, Costa Rica, Cuba, Denmark, Ecuador, England, France, Germany, Ghana, Hong Kong, Hungary, Iceland, Israel, Italy, Japan, Korea, Mexico, Morocco, Netherlands, Nepal, New Zealand, Singapore, South Africa, Spain, Sweden, Thailand, and Turkey.

Academic Facilities

The central services of the Claremont Colleges include the Honnold-Mudd Library, which houses more than 2 million volumes and more than 6,000 serial subscriptions. Other shared facilities include theaters, music halls, music and dance studios, the W. M. Keck Science Center (shared with Claremont McKenna and Scripps Colleges), and a wellness center that includes counseling and health services.

Specialized facilities at Pitzer include a newly renovated auditorium, a television studio, film editing suites, art galleries, social science laboratories, an arboretum, a reading library, and several computing facilities, including a 24-hour computer center.

Costs

Expenses for 2012–13 were as follows: tuition and fees, $43,402; room and board, $13,864; and books and personal expenses, $2,000. Travel expenses vary. Costs are subject to change for 2013–14.

Financial Aid

Approximately 42 percent of Pitzer's students receive aid in the forms of grants, loans, and work-study. Pitzer's financial aid is primarily need-based and in order to apply for aid, students must complete the Free Application for Federal Student Aid (FAFSA) and the CSS/Financial Aid PROFILE. California residents should also apply for California state grants. Students must reapply for aid each spring. Pitzer is committed to meeting 100 percent of the demonstrated need of all accepted students.

Faculty

One hundred percent of Pitzer's faculty members hold a Ph.D. or the terminal degree in their fields. All courses are taught by faculty members, and the student-faculty ratio is 11:1. Faculty members are readily available for academic advising. In keeping with Pitzer's commitment to interdisciplinary learning, most faculty members are conversant with at least one other field of study in addition to the area of their degrees and may teach in more than one area.

Student Government

Pitzer's governmental structure is distinctive among American colleges. Instead of the traditional college governance style which restricts student participation to limited areas, Pitzer students are represented on all standing committees of the College, including those that deal with the most vital and sensitive issues of the College community. Though this model demands a serious time commitment from those who choose to participate, it offers interested students an active educational experience and the opportunity to make a genuine impact on the life of the College and its students, faculty, and staff.

Admission Requirements

Pitzer has developed a highly personalized admission process. Each applicant is considered on the basis of his or her own strengths. In general, the College seeks students who have performed well in high school, have shown a significant amount of involvement in activities outside of the classroom, are motivated to learn, and are interested in the opportunity to take an active role in planning their education in a liberal arts framework. The selection process is designed to help achieve a diverse and energetic class. Selection is based on high school transcripts, rigor of curriculum, recommendations, essays, extracurricular activities and other special talents. Applicants are encouraged to visit campus and arrange for an interview.

Application and Information

Pitzer College offers both early decision and regular decision for prospective applicants. Students interested in applying early must submit a completed application by November 15 and are notified in late December. Interviews for early decision are required by December 1. Regular decision candidates must submit their applications for admission by January 1 and are notified by April 1. Interviews are not required for regular decision candidates but are highly recommended and should be completed by December 15. All applicants must supply an official transcript of grades, two teacher evaluations, one counselor or school official recommendation, and the application fee of $60 by the necessary deadline. Pitzer accepts the Common Application for first-year students. When submitting the Common Application, students must also complete a supplement, which is available on the Common Application website.

Pitzer's admission process is test optional. Students who have an unweighted GPA of 3.5 or higher or who are in the top 10 percent of their class are exempt from needing to submit any testing. Students who do not fall within one of those ranges have multiple options for the kind of testing they would like to submit. Students can contact the College for further details.

For additional information, students should contact:

Office of Admission
Pitzer College
1050 North Mills Avenue
Claremont, California 91711-6101
Phone: 909-621-8129
Fax: 909-621-8770
E-mail: admission@pitzer.edu
Website: http://www.pitzer.edu
       http://twitter.com/pitzercollege

Pitzer's newest residence halls are LEED-certified Platinum.

PRATT INSTITUTE
BROOKLYN, NEW YORK

The Institute

Industrialist and philanthropist Charles Pratt founded Pratt Institute in 1887 to educate students for various professions on a nondegree level. As the educational preparation necessary for various professions expanded, Pratt Institute moved to offer baccalaureate degrees with its first granted in 1938 and its first graduate degree granted in 1950. Now, with twenty-seven undergraduate majors and concentrations, Pratt offers students a wide variety of programs in which to major or take elective courses.

With all of its undergraduate ranked programs in art, design, and architecture ranked among the top ten in the country, Pratt has been ranked among the top design schools in the United States by *Business Week*. Pratt has continued to add programs at all educational levels, including undergraduate programs in creative writing and critical and visual studies; undergraduate and graduate programs in art history and art and design education (teacher certification); and graduate programs in arts and cultural management, historic preservation, and design management.

In addition to the four-year programs on its Brooklyn campus, Pratt offers students several additional locations to pursue their education: a two-year program in Utica, New York, at PrattMWP; an associate degree program and four-year degree in construction management in Manhattan; and an affiliated campus in Delaware, DCAD.

Although the characteristics and educational requirements of the professions for which Pratt prepares students have changed over the course of a century, the Institute has succeeded in pursuing its abiding purpose—to blend theoretical learning with professional and humanistic development—and has kept its curricula current by hiring practicing professionals to teach. Standards are high, modeled after the professional world. Faculty members connect students with internships and eventually jobs after graduation. Industry projects and internships provide students with real-world experience.

Pratt Institute offers four-year bachelor's, two-year associate, and master's degrees. In educating more than five generations of students to be creative, technically skilled, and adaptable professionals as well as responsible citizens, Pratt has gained a national and international reputation that attracts undergraduate and graduate students from forty-six U.S. states and over seventy-five countries. Most students who choose Pratt are committed to the study of art, design, architecture, or creative writing and to their career objectives.

A short subway or bus ride from the museums, galleries, and design centers of both Manhattan and Brooklyn, Pratt Institute's main campus in Brooklyn, New York features twenty-five buildings of differing architectural styles spread throughout a beautifully landscaped 25-acre campus. The campus was recently ranked by *Architectural Digest* as one of the top ten campuses nationwide with the best architecture. It includes a contemporary sculpture garden (ranked among the top ten campus art collections by *Public Art Review*), an athletic center, residence halls, dining halls, outstanding studio facilities, and historic buildings. Nineteen of the buildings house studios, classrooms, laboratories, administrative offices, auditoria, sports facilities, food services, and student centers. A new, green, LEED-certified Gold building houses student administrative services including admissions, undergraduate and graduate digital arts programs, and various administrative offices, including student financial services and the registrar's offices. Six buildings are student residences, including the Stabile Hall freshman residence,

which provides studio space on each floor. There are adequate parking facilities for residents and commuters. Student services include career planning and placement, health and counseling, and student development. More than sixty student organizations are available including fraternities and sororities, honorary societies, professional societies, and clubs.

Location

Pratt Institute, the country's premier college of art, design, writing, and architecture, has its main campus in the Clinton Hill section of Brooklyn, just minutes from downtown Manhattan. Ninety-two percent of Pratt's freshmen and over half of its undergraduates live on the tree-lined Brooklyn campus. Minutes from the Brooklyn Museum and the Brooklyn Academy of Music, Pratt is ideally located, providing students with a green oasis just minutes from the art capital of the world, Manhattan. The Manhattan campus is located in Chelsea. The Utica campus, home to two-year programs in fine art, communications design, photography, and art and design education (teacher certification), is located in upstate New York. The affiliated Delaware campus, offering a two-year degree in fine art, communications design, photography, animation, and interior design, is located in Wilmington, Delaware.

Majors and Degrees

Pratt Institute offers the Bachelor of Architecture, Bachelor of Fine Arts, Bachelor of Art, Bachelor of Industrial Design, Bachelor of Professional Studies, Bachelor of Science, Associate of Occupational Studies, and Associate of Applied Science degrees.

The Bachelor of Architecture degree program is a five-year, accredited program. For the Bachelor of Fine Arts degree, a candidate may choose to major in art and design education (teacher certification), art history, communications design (advertising art direction, graphic design, illustration), digital arts (traditional and digital animation, interactive arts), fashion design, film/video, fine arts (ceramics, drawing, jewelry, painting, printmaking, sculpture), interior design, photography, or writing. The Bachelor of Arts is offered in critical and visual studies and art history. The Bachelor of Industrial Design is offered for students interested in car, product, and furniture design. In the Bachelor of Professional Studies degree program, the major is in construction management. Students seeking the Bachelor of Science degree can major in construction management.

The two-year Associate of Occupational Studies degree is offered in digital design and interactive media, graphic design, and illustration. The Associate of Applied Science is offered in painting/drawing and graphic design/illustration. The two-year Associate of Applied Science degree is transferable to a four-year program.

Students may also earn combined bachelor's/master's degrees. Programs include the B.F.A./M.S. in art and design education as well as art history.

Academic Programs

Educating artists and creative professionals to be responsible contributors to society has been the mission of Pratt Institute since it assembled its first group of students in 1887. Within the structure of that professional education, Pratt students are encouraged to acquire the diverse knowledge that is necessary for them to succeed in their chosen fields including sustainability. In addition to the professional studies, the curriculum in each of Pratt's schools includes a broad range of liberal arts courses. Students from all schools take these courses together and have the opportunity to examine the interrelationships of art, science, technology, and human need.

At the time of graduation, students in the associate degree programs have completed 67 credit hours of course work. In the bachelor's programs, credit-hour requirements range from 132 to 135 credits, depending on the particular program. For the Bachelor of Architecture degree, 170 credits are required.

Pratt's academic calendar consists of two semesters plus optional summer terms that allow students to choose alternative courses or various options usually not offered during the fall or spring semester. Two summer sessions are offered.

Off-Campus Programs

Pratt Institute offers credit for a wide variety of off-campus study programs. The internship program offers qualified students challenging on-the-job experience related to their major fields of interest; this extension of the classroom and laboratory into the professional world adds a practical dimension to periods of on-campus study.

International programs, available during all academic sessions, have included art and design offerings in the cities of Copenhagen and Rome and in the countries of England, France, Italy, and South Africa. Architecture programs have been held in Italy, Finland, and Japan. New programs are developed regularly in these and other countries. A semester-long program is offered in Rome each year.

Academic Facilities

Founded as the first free library in Brooklyn, the Pratt Institute Library now has more than 176,674 bound volumes, 84,604 art books, 237 print and online art and art history journals, a rare book collection, and subscriptions to journals online through JSTOR, EBSCO, and others. The library also has serial backfiles and other material, including government documents; 251,603 audiovisual materials; and 3,996 microforms and subscribes to 925 periodicals—the largest collection of any independent art school. With their ID cards, Pratt students also have access to numerous college libraries in the metropolitan area. Multi-Media Services has been developed to facilitate and improve the educational communication process by providing materials in multimedia formats to support and enrich the Institute's curricula.

Extensive studio and state-of-the-art computer lab facilities are provided for all Pratt students. In the School of Art and Design, these include studio, shop, and technical facilities for work in all media, from the traditional to the most experimental. Gallery space, both on campus and at Pratt Manhattan, is extensive, showing the work of students, alumni, faculty members, staff members, and other well-known artists, architects, and designers. The Pratt Center for Community Development functions as a laboratory for the study of planning and advocacy issues in real-world situations including sustainable planning.

Costs

Tuition for the 2013–14 academic year is $41,226. Room charges are $6,928 per academic year. A meal plan is available, and costs about $3,780 for the year. The fees are approximately $1,900. The estimated cost of books and supplies is $2,100 per academic year. Students should allow an additional $1,800 for transportation and personal expenses. For an updated list of tuition and fees, prospective students should visit www.pratt.edu/costs_and_budgeting.

Financial Aid

Pratt Institute offers a large number of merit-based scholarships, need-based grants, loans, and awards based on academic achievement, talent, financial need, or all three. More than 75 percent of Pratt students receive financial assistance through one or more of these kinds of aid. Through funds from the federal and state governments, contributions from Pratt alumni, and

industry scholarships, Pratt is able to maintain generous financial aid program in a time of escalating costs.

Faculty

The faculty at Pratt Institute is exceptional in that a large number of practicing professionals augment the regular full-time faculty. There are 138 full-time and 911 part-time faculty members; there are no graduate teaching assistants. In small classes and studios, students have easy access to professors whose natural environment is the design studio, the architectural office, or the industrial research department. Faculty members often connect students with internships and eventually jobs.

Student Government

The Student Government Association (SGA) maintains primary responsibility for all student interests and involvement at Pratt. The SGA structure includes the Executive Committee, Senate, Finance Committee, Buildings and Grounds Committee, Academic and Administrative Affairs Committee, and Program Board. Student representatives serve on the Board of Trustees and on its various committees. All undergraduate students are encouraged to become involved in the SGA, whose main functions are allocating and administering funds collected through the student activities fee, scheduling student activities, and representing the student viewpoint to the rest of the Pratt community.

Admission Requirements

Pratt Institute attracts and enrolls highly motivated and talented students from diverse backgrounds. Applications are welcome from all qualified students, regardless of age, sex, race, color, religion, national origin, or handicap. Admission standards at Pratt are high. One of the major components for admission consideration in art, design, or architecture is the evaluation of a student's art or writing portfolio, which must be submitted along with the other required documents.

All applicants must submit official transcripts and one letter of recommendation from a guidance counselor or teacher. Additional professional requirements are specific to each school or major. Instructions can be found at www.pratt.edu/apply. Prospective students should select their level (freshman or transfer) and international students should also read the international requirements. Most disciplines at Pratt require a portfolio.

The admission committee bases its decisions on careful reviews of all credentials submitted by applicants in relation to the requirements of the program to which students seek admission. The SAT or ACT and a strong college-preparatory background are required of all applicants for four-year programs. International students must submit TOEFL or IELTS scores or SAT scores, but not both. In certain cases, an extraordinary talent may offset a low grade or a test score.

Application and Information

Pratt has two admissions deadlines: November 1 for early action and January 5 for regular admissions. To receive full consideration, students must submit their applications by January 5 for anticipated entrance in the fall semester and by October 1 for anticipated entrance in the spring semester.

For more information about Pratt Institute, students should contact:

Office of Admissions
Pratt Institute
200 Willoughby Avenue
Brooklyn, New York 11205
Phone: 718-636-3514
    800-331-0834 (toll-free)
E-mail: admissions@pratt.edu
Website: http://www.pratt.edu
    http://on.fb.me/pratt_admissions (Facebook)
    http://www.pratt.edu/request (Catalog request)

QUEENS COLLEGE OF THE CITY UNIVERSITY OF NEW YORK

FLUSHING, NEW YORK

The College

Queens College (QC), with more than 12,500 undergraduates, is one of the largest four-year colleges in the City University of New York (CUNY) system. The College opened in 1937 with the goal of offering a first-rate education to talented people of all backgrounds and financial means. It enjoys a national reputation for its liberal arts and sciences and preprofessional programs. Students come from more than 150 nations; the result is an unusually rich education that gives Queens College graduates a competitive edge in today's global society.

The 77-acre campus is lined with trees surrounding grassy open spaces and a traditional quad. Some of the original Spanish-style stucco-and-tile buildings from the early 1900s still stand, including Jefferson Hall, which houses the beautiful Welcome Center. Powdermaker Hall, the major classroom building, has state-of-the-art technology throughout, and the College's science labs recently underwent a $30-million renovation. The entire campus has Wi-Fi capability and students may relax and meet friends in the spacious Student Union and the College's many cafés, lounges, and recreation and dining areas.

With the opening of the College's first residence hall, The Summit, Queens College shed its commuter school identity. It offers students the option of enjoying all the benefits of living on campus. The low-rise facility provides individually climate-controlled single- and double-room accommodations in suites with shared kitchen and lounge areas. It has its own exercise facility and was recently LEED-certified Gold for its green initiatives.

The administration remains dedicated to making its many commuter students feel that QC is their home away from home. The professionally staffed Child Development Center offers inexpensive child-care services to students with children. There are more than 100 clubs on campus, from the Accounting Honors Society and Alliance of Latin American Students to clubs for theater, fencing, environmental science, science fiction, and the fine arts. The only CUNY college that participates in Division II sports, QC sponsors nineteen men's and women's teams and has some of the finest athletics facilities in the metro area. Ongoing cultural events include readings by renowned authors such as Jamaica Kincaid, Edward Albee, and Jonathan Franzen; and concerts, theater, and dance performances by world-famous artists. QC is also home to the Godwin-Ternbach Museum, the only comprehensive museum in the borough of Queens, with art from antiquity to the present.

The College's centers and institutes serve students and the larger urban community by addressing society's most important challenges—such as cancer, pollution, and racism—and exploring the heritages of the borough's many ethnic communities, including Asians, Greeks, Italians, and Jews.

Queens College has had a chapter of Phi Beta Kappa since 1950 (less than 10 percent of U.S. liberal arts colleges are members of Phi Beta Kappa, the nation's oldest and most respected undergraduate honors organization). In 1968, Queens College became a member of Sigma Xi, the national science honor society. The American Association of University Women includes Queens College in its list of approved colleges for membership.

Location

Queens College, located off Exit 24 of the Long Island Expressway, is in a residential area of Flushing and is easily accessible by public transportation. It is only 20 minutes from Manhattan, whose magnificent skyline overlooks the campus quad.

Majors and Degrees

The Bachelor of Arts degree is awarded in accounting, Africana studies, American studies, anthropology, art, art history, biology, Byzantine and modern Greek studies, chemistry, Chinese, communication arts and media, communication sciences and disorders, comparative literature, computer science, drama and theater, East Asian studies, economics, education (early childhood and elementary), English, environmental sciences, environmental studies, film studies, French, geology, German, Greek, Hebrew, history, home economics, Italian, Jewish studies, labor studies, Latin, Latin American area studies, linguistics, mathematics, Middle Eastern studies, music, neuroscience, philosophy, physics, political science and government, psychology, religious studies, Russian, sociology, Spanish, studio art, theater-dance, urban studies, and women's studies.

The Bachelor of Arts program in secondary school teaching includes the following subject areas: Africana studies, anthropology, biology, chemistry, economics, English, French, geology, German, history, Italian, Latin American area studies, mathematics, physics, political science and government, sociology, Spanish, and urban studies.

The College also awards the Bachelor of Arts in interdisciplinary studies; an individualized Bachelor of Arts program; the Bachelor of Business Administration; the Bachelor of Fine Arts in studio art; the Bachelor of Music in instrumental or vocal performance studies; and the Bachelor of Science in applied social science, computer science, environmental sciences, geology, graphic design, nutrition and exercise sciences, physical education, and physics.

The Departments of Chemistry, Computer Science, Philosophy, Physics, and Political Science and the Aaron Copland School of Music offer qualified undergraduates the opportunity to take combined bachelor's and master's degree programs.

Pre-engineering students can take advantage of a 3-2 transfer program through the physics department that offers admission to Columbia University after three years at QC. Following two years at Columbia, students graduate with a B.A. in physics from Queens and an engineering B.A. from Columbia.

Special interdisciplinary programs include Africana studies, American studies, Asian-American community studies, business and liberal arts, business administration, Byzantine and modern Greek studies, Honors in Mathematics and Natural Sciences, Honors in the Humanities, Honors in the Social Sciences, Irish studies, Italian American studies, journalism, Latin American and Latino studies, and religious studies. Special programs and advisement are also available in accounting, pre-engineering, pre-law, and the pre-health professions.

Academic Programs

Queens College awards bachelor's and master's degrees in the arts and humanities, education, mathematics and the natural sciences, and social sciences. Certificate programs provide additional training in specialties in education, library science, and psychology. QC also participates in doctoral programs overseen by CUNY's graduate center; many of these programs involve lab work or clinical studies conducted on the Flushing campus.

Honors programs are central to the College's tradition of value and excellence, enhancing education by providing opportunities for faculty mentorship, advanced research, and other individualized projects. These programs create a community of learners in which students enjoy small classes, while still having access to QC's many resources and diverse student body. The emphasis is on discussion and projects rather than lectures.

Queens College is the only CUNY institution in the borough participating in the Macaulay Honors College, which supports gifted students with full tuition, a free laptop, a $7,500 grant over four years, and other benefits. A flagship program of CUNY, it provides an enhanced undergraduate education to academically gifted students. Since its inauguration in 2001, the Honors College has grown rapidly, drawing on the unique resources of CUNY and New York's cultural, scientific, government, and business communities to provide its students with a broad-based and challenging liberal arts education.

In addition, QC has its own multidisciplinary Freshman Honors Program and divisional honors programs in the humanities, math and natural sciences, and social sciences. Outstanding high school seniors may apply to become Queens College scholars. Prospective math teachers may qualify for scholarships and other incentives through QC's innovative math education program, TIME 2000. Business and Liberal Arts—designed for top-performing underclassmen regardless of their major—familiarizes students with basic business disciplines and offers internships sponsored by participating corporations.

The wide range of majors and interdisciplinary studies, combined with the award-winning Freshman Year Initiative program, encourages students to explore their interests and abilities to the fullest. Most degree programs require the completion of 120 credits.

The Bachelor of Business Administration (B.B.A.) degree provides a solid business education that responds to the demand of employers for specific quantitative and technological skills. Students may choose from three majors: finance, international business, and actuarial studies. The B.B.A. also has an investments/chartered financial analyst track to prepare students for the CFA examination, the only such undergraduate program in New York.

Study-abroad opportunities range from relatively short summer and winter intersession courses to programs that last a semester or two. Exchange programs allow students to study for up to a year in dozens of countries and other parts of the U.S.

The Adult Collegiate Education program, offered to students 25 and older, includes the option of obtaining college credit for life achievement. The Weekend College allows busy students to pursue their degrees by taking classes on Saturdays and Sundays.

Academic Facilities

Among the many centers where research and creativity are joined in the pursuit of knowledge is the Kupferberg Center for the Visual and Performing Arts, which brings together the College's academic departments in the arts (music, drama, theatre, and dance, and media studies), and its museums (the Godwin-Ternbach, the Queens College Art Center, and the Louis Armstrong House Museum). The center's venues include the newly renovated 2,200-seat Colden Auditorium; the Goldstein Theatre, designed especially for the staging of experimental student productions; and the Aaron Copland School of Music facility, which includes thirty-five practice rooms and the 491-seat LeFrak Concert Hall. The College is also home to the Gertz Center, which investigates communication disabilities and provides clinical experience for students of speech and hearing therapy.

Queens College administers the historic Louis Armstrong House Museum in Corona with its vast personal collection of Armstrong photographs, papers, recordings, and memorabilia that draws scholars and jazz fans from around the world. The Benjamin Rosenthal Library, with its soaring, light-filled atrium and art center, has more than 1 million print and electronic volumes.

Costs

For New York State residents, undergraduate tuition is $2,715 per semester. For out-of-state and international students, undergraduate tuition is $485 per credit. There are various expenses each semester, such as student activity and technology fees.

Financial Aid

More than 50 percent of Queens College students receive need-based financial aid, which may include state and federal loans and grants, Tuition Assistance Program awards, Regents Scholarships, Federal Direct Student Loans, Federal Pell Grants, State Aid for Native Americans, and Federal Work-Study awards.

The Queens College Scholars Program offers a variety of merit-based scholarships to full-time freshmen, with awards of $3,000 per year. Selection is competitive, and scholarships are awarded on the basis of the high school record, test scores (SAT and SAT Subject Tests), writing ability, letters of recommendation, and extracurricular activities. Scholarships are renewable with continued high academic achievement. Applicants who rank in or near the top 10 percent of their class and have a rigorous academic program, excellent grades, and minimum combined SAT (critical reading and math) scores of 1250 are encouraged to apply. The deadline is December 1.

Faculty

The Queens College faculty consists of top scholars who are dedicated to teaching and research, and enjoy working in a diverse urban environment. Many are relatively new to campus; half were hired between 2002 and 2008. There are 606 full-time professors, almost 85 percent of whom have the terminal degree in their fields (not all fields offer doctorates); 67 percent have tenure. Many also teach in the doctoral programs at the CUNY Graduate Center. Faculty members have received numerous fellowships, awards, and research grants from such prestigious organizations as the National Science Foundation (including eight Early Career Development grants) and the National Institutes of Health. In recent years, faculty members received two Guggenheim awards and two Fulbright grants. CUNY has recognized the excellence of the faculty by honoring 11 members with the title of Distinguished Professor in fields as diverse as chemistry, economics, English, history, and physics. Among the more widely known faculty members are scientists Nicholas K. Coch and Steven Markowitz, historian Morris Rossabi, sociologists Harry Levine and Stephen Steinberg, and writers Jeffrey Renard Allen, Kimiko Hahn, and John Tytell.

Student Government

Through the Student Association, students at Queens run many services and activities that influence the daily operations of the College. Its elected officers and senators poll students regularly about relevant topics and sponsor such services as free legal advice, apartment and tutor referral, and voter registration. In addition, students constitute one third of the College's Academic Senate.

Admission Requirements

Queens College seeks to admit freshmen who have completed a strong college-preparatory program in high school with at least a B+ average. Admission is based on a variety of factors, including high school grades, academic program, and SAT or ACT scores. Successful candidates have chosen a well-rounded program of study that includes academic course work in English (4 years), foreign language (3 years), math (3 years), lab science (2 years), and social studies (4 years).

The Search for Education, Elevation & Knowledge Program (SEEK) offers academic support, counseling, and financial assistance to motivated students who would not otherwise qualify for admission. The SEEK Program has its own admissions criteria, including financial need.

For earliest consideration, students should apply by January 1 for fall admission and by September 15 for spring admission.

Application and Information

The staff of the Undergraduate Office of Admissions is available to answer questions and give more information. To make an appointment for a tour or to meet with a counselor, students should contact:

Office of Admissions
Jefferson Hall
Queens College of the City University of New York
65-30 Kissena Boulevard
Queens, New York 11367-1597
Phone: 718-997-5600
E-mail: admissions@qc.edu
Website: http://www.qc.cuny.edu
        http://on.fb.me/QueensColl_CUNY (Facebook)
        http://twitter.com/QC_News
        http://bit.ly/YouTube_CUNY-QC (YouTube)
        http://bit.ly/itunes_CUNY-QC (iTunes)

A view of the Queens College quad, part of a 77-acre campus in New York City, where students from more than 150 nations receive a solid education for today's global society.

QUINNIPIAC UNIVERSITY
HAMDEN, CONNECTICUT

The University

Quinnipiac University offers four-year and graduate-level degree programs leading to careers in health sciences, nursing, business, communications, engineering, natural sciences, education, liberal arts, law, and medicine. A curriculum that combines a career focus with a globally oriented liberal arts background prepares graduates for the future, whether they start their careers right after commencement or opt to pursue advanced study. The Frank H. Netter MD School of Medicine welcomes its first class in Fall 2013!

Quinnipiac is coeducational and nonsectarian and currently enrolls 6,231 full-time undergraduates, 1,238 full-time graduate and law students, and 1,145 part-time students in its undergraduate, graduate, and professional programs. Twenty-five percent of the students are residents of Connecticut; the rest represent primarily the northeast corridor, in all a total of 28 states including California and Texas and several countries. Quinnipiac is big enough to sustain a wide variety of people and programs but small enough to keep students from getting lost in the shuffle. Life on campus emphasizes students' personal, as well as academic, growth. The approximately 100 student organizations and extracurricular activities, including intramural and intercollegiate (NCAA Division I) athletics, give students a chance to exercise their talents, muscles, and leadership skills. The University has a student newspaper, TV station, and an FM radio station (WQAQ) and twenty-one intercollegiate teams in men's baseball, basketball, cross-country, ice hockey, lacrosse, soccer, and tennis, and in women's acrobatics and tumbling, basketball, cross-country, field hockey, golf, ice hockey, lacrosse, rugby, soccer, softball, tennis, track (indoor and outdoor), and volleyball. Teams compete in the Northeast Conference (NEC) through Spring 2013, but will join the MAAC conference in the fall of 2013; men's and women's ice hockey teams are members in the ECAC. The men's ice hockey team was ranked #1 in the country for much of 2013 and played in the "Frozen Four" finals, the women's basketball team won the NEC championship, and women's rugby was undefeated in 2013.

The University has three distinct campus settings. The 250-acre Mount Carmel campus has fifty buildings including the Arnold Bernhard Library, academic facilities, an athletic and recreation center, and twenty-five residence halls of different styles, mainly for freshmen and sophomores, with traditional double and quad (4-person) rooms, suites, and multilevel suites and apartments with kitchens. About 95 percent of all freshmen and 75 percent of the total undergraduate population live in Quinnipiac housing. The nearby 250-acre York Hill campus includes the TD Bank Sports Center with twin 3,500-seat arenas for ice hockey and basketball; a suite-style with single and double rooms 1,500-bed residence halls and townhouses for juniors and seniors; "Rocky Top," a lodge-like student center; spectacular views; and a multilevel parking garage for 2,000 vehicles. Seniors may also live in University-owned houses or apartments. A free shuttle takes students between the two campuses. Just 4 miles away is the 104-acre North Haven campus with state-of-the-art facilities for graduate and upper division offerings in several programs in the Schools of Health Sciences, Nursing, Education, and Medicine and will be joined by the School of Law in 2014.

The Athletic and Recreation Center includes a 24,000-square-foot recreation/fitness facility with a large free-weight room; an exercise machine center; aerobics studios; basketball, volleyball, and tennis courts; and a suspended indoor track. There are also lighted tennis courts, playing fields, and miles of scenic routes for running and biking.

Career planning takes place in each of the schools with assistance from the deans' offices. It begins with faculty advisement, along with career exploration, a strong focus on internships and clinical placements, exploration of various major and job fields, and exposure to prospective employers and job preparation. Approximately 30 percent of the undergraduate student population remains at Quinnipiac for their graduate degree in combined or direct entry majors, particularly in education, business, physical and occupational therapy, and physician assistant programs.

Graduate programs lead to the Master of Science (M.S.) degree in accounting, information technology, interactive media, journalism, molecular and cell biology, organizational leadership, public relations,

and teacher leadership; the Master of Health Science in anesthesiologist assistant, medical lab sciences, cardiovascular perfusion, pathologist assistant, and physician assistant; a Master of Science in Nursing plus the Doctor of Nursing Practice in adult and family nursing; the Doctor of Physical Therapy, the Master of Business Administration; the Master of Business Administration in Health Care Management; the Master of Business Administration–Chartered Financial Analyst; and the Master of Arts in Teaching and the Master of Social Work. The Quinnipiac University School of Law offers full-time and part-time programs leading to a J.D. degree or J.D./M.B.A. degree in combination with the School of Business. Several of the graduate degree programs are offered online or in a hybrid format. The School of Medicine focuses on developing doctors as part of a health-care team with a focus on primary medicine.

Location

Situated at the foot of Sleeping Giant Mountain in Hamden, Connecticut, Quinnipiac provides the best of the suburbs and the city. The University is only 8 miles from New Haven, 30 minutes from Hartford (the state capital), and less than 2 hours from New York City and Boston. Bordering the campus is the 1,700-acre Sleeping Giant State Park, for walking and hiking. The free campus shuttle takes students to shopping and restaurants in nearby Hamden and North Haven, plus to New Haven, where they can visit the acclaimed Yale Center for British Art, attend a performance at the Shubert or Long Wharf Theater (which hosts productions by Quinnipiac's Theater Department), find great restaurants, and have easy access to Metro North and Amtrak at the New Haven train station.

Majors and Degrees

The Schools of Health Sciences and Nursing grant bachelor's degrees in athletic training/sports medicine, biomedical science, diagnostic imaging, health and science studies, microbiology/molecular biology, nursing, occupational therapy (5½-year entry-level master's), physical therapy (6- or 7-year entry-level doctorate), and physician assistant studies (6-year freshman entry-level master's). Students who wish to prepare for entry into medical, dental, chiropractic, veterinary, or other medical schools work with a premed adviser and take classes that prepare them to sit for the various entrance exams.

The School of Business and Engineering (accredited by AACSB International and ranked 61 in the top 100 Best Undergraduate Business Schools in 2013 *Bloomberg BusinessWeek*) offers bachelor's degree programs in accounting, advertising, biomedical marketing, economics, entrepreneurship, finance, computer information systems, international business, management, and marketing. The school offers an innovative Business 3+1 BS/MBA program in four years to highly qualified students, also a fast-track, five-year combined-degree program in which students may be awarded the B.S. degree in business and a graduate degree in accounting, business administration, or computer information systems (M.S. or M.B.A.). The Engineering program has majors in mechanical, industrial, civil, and software engineering.

The College of Arts and Sciences offers bachelor's degree programs in behavioral neuroscience, biochemistry, biology, chemistry, computer science, criminal justice, English, gerontology, history, interactive digital design, legal studies (paralegal), liberal studies, mathematics, philosophy, political science, psychology, social services, sociology, Spanish, and theater. Qualified students can go on to the Master of Science in molecular and cell biology program or pursue graduate programs in education, business, law, journalism, interactive media, and social work.

The School of Communications offers undergraduate majors in communications/media studies; film, video, and interactive media; journalism; and public relations, plus a B.F.A. in film and graduate programs in journalism, public relations, and interactive media.

The School of Education's five-year program for undergraduates provides certification for teaching elementary and secondary grades through a B.A./Master of Arts in Teaching (M.A.T.) program (accredited by NCATE).

Academic Programs

All degree programs at Quinnipiac University are offered through one of the five academic schools. The academic year consists of two 15-week fall and spring semesters and two summer sessions. All baccalaureate candidates are required to complete the University Curriculum, which consists of up to 46 of the 120 semester hours of credit generally needed for graduation at the bachelor's degree level. The foundation of the University Curriculum is three university seminars, which focus on the broad theme of community: individual, national, and global in scope. The Writing Across the Curriculum initiative (WAC) stresses the improvement in writing skills in all subject areas. The University honors program addresses the needs and interests of the most academically talented and committed students. Advanced placement, credit, or both are given for appropriate scores on Advanced Placement tests and CLEP general and subject examinations as well as for scores of 4 or higher in the International Baccalaureate higher-level subjects.

Off-Campus Programs

Students can study abroad in a variety of countries. Most students choose a study-abroad option in their sophomore year, many at our affiliated program in Ireland. Students in any of the five under-graduate schools can also get hands-on experience in their field through off-campus internships and clinical placements in the health sciences. Academic credit is available for internships and affiliations, which are often part of degree requirements.

Academic Facilities

Academic life focuses on the Bernhard Library. This attractive facility provides individual carrels and small rooms for group study and is open 24/7 during the fall and spring semesters. A wireless network provides access to automated library systems and extensive Web-based resources.

Quinnipiac University was identified as one of the top ten most-wired campuses in the country by *PC Magazine* in January 2007. All incoming students must bring or purchase a laptop computer for use in classes and in the residence halls. An information technology desk offers tech support as needed.

The multimedia and video laboratories in the Ed McMahon Mass Communications Center each have the latest Mac workstations and software. The computer cluster in the Financial Technology Center at the School of Business is a high-tech, simulated trading floor providing students with the opportunity to access real-time financial data, conduct interactive trading simulations, and develop financial models in preparation for careers in finance.

The Lender School of Business Center has satellite capabilities and the Ed McMahon Mass Communications Center, and contains a state-of-the-art, fully digital, high-definition TV production studio; audio production, print journalism, and desktop publishing laboratories; and a news technology center.

The Graduate and Health Sciences Center on the North Haven campus provides state-of-the-art facilities for the health sciences programs in diagnostic imaging, nursing, occupational therapy, physical therapy, physician assistant, and radiologist assistant. In addition to a breathtaking location and expansive exterior and interior spaces, there are specialized facilities and equipment for the various health sciences disciplines, such as movement study/motion analysis and biomechanics labs; the ergonomics and assistive technology lab; a model adaptive apartment; an orthopedics lab; several rehabilitative sciences labs; CT scan, MRI, radiography, ultrasound, and mammography facilities; and the latest clinical skills simulation labs for adults and pediatric/neonatal patients including an intensive care unit, physical diagnosis lab, physical exam suite, and health assessment labs, which duplicate care in an outpatient primary care setting.

Costs

The 2013–14 cost is $53,380, of which tuition and fees (12–16 credits per semester) are $39,330. Room and board average $14,250. Other expenses, estimated at $2,000 per year, include books, laboratory, and course fees associated with specific courses, and personal travel expenses.

Financial Aid

Quinnipiac designs financial aid packages to include need-based grants and merit-based scholarships that do not have to be repaid, plus self-help financial aid programs such as federal and University-based work study, and loans. Students and families seeking need-based aid will file the College Scholarship Service's Financial Aid PROFILE plus the Free Application for Federal Student Aid (FAFSA) to determine need. Transfer students are eligible for the same need-based financial aid consideration as first-time freshmen.

Faculty

The faculty is characterized by its teaching competence and outstanding academic qualifications. Of the 369 full-time faculty members, 85 percent have earned a Ph.D. or the appropriate terminal degree in their field. The faculty also includes a number of part-time teachers who are practicing professionals and experts in their fields. Classes are taught by these scholars and professionals and not by student instructors, and a low student-faculty ratio promotes close associations among faculty members and students.

Student Government

The Student Government is the student legislative body of Quinnipiac. It represents student opinion, promotes student welfare, supervises student organizations, appropriates funds for student groups, and provides voting student representation on the Board of Trustees.

Admission Requirements

Quinnipiac seeks students from a broad range of backgrounds. On average, freshman students have a 3.4 GPA or better average in college-preparatory courses (transfer students generally have a 2.5 GPA or better), rank in the top 25 percent of their high school class, and have an average combined score of 1120 on the SAT (critical reading plus math). Visits to the campus for an interview, open house, group information session, or a campus tour are strongly encouraged. Transfer students are welcome to make an appointment to discuss requirements and the transfer of credit from previous institutions. Quinnipiac sponsors four open house programs during the year and several Saturday morning information sessions followed by a campus tour.

Application and Information

Quinnipiac generally receives about 20,000 applications for admission and admits about 65 percent, to enroll an incoming class of 1,800 freshmen and 200 transfer students. Quinnipiac has a rolling admission policy for its undergraduate programs and therefore recommends that freshman applicants submit their application materials starting early in the fall of their senior year and well before the deadline of February 1. Students applying to the physical therapy, nursing, and physician assistant studies programs should submit their applications by November 15. An early decision (binding) option is available in all majors with an application deadline of November 1. Applications begin to be reviewed as soon as they are complete, and the University begins notifying students of decisions in December. Quinnipiac is a member of the Common Application and recommends that applications be submitted online. Students placed on a waiting list are notified of any openings by June 1. Quinnipiac subscribes to the May 1 Candidates Reply Date Agreement. For information about full-time undergraduate study, students should contact:

Office of Undergraduate Admissions
Quinnipiac University
Hamden, Connecticut 06518-1940
Phone: 203-582-8600
      800-462-1944 (toll-free)
Fax: 203-582-8906
E-mail: admissions@quinnipiac.edu
Web site: http://www.quinnipiac.edu
    http://www.facebook.com/QuinnipiacUniversity
    http://twitter.com/QU_Admissions
    http://quadmissions.blogspot.com/
    http://www.youtube.com/quinnipiacuniversity
    http://www.quinnipiac.edu/rss.xml

For information regarding transfer and part-time study:

Office of Transfer and Part-time Admissions
Quinnipiac University
Hamden, Connecticut 06518-1940
Phone: 203-582-8612
Fax: 203-582-8906
E-mail: transferadmissions@quinnipiac.edu

REED COLLEGE
PORTLAND, OREGON

The College

For its 1,418 students and 139 faculty members, Reed College is foremost an intellectual community. Since classes began in 1911, Reed has attracted students with a high degree of self-discipline and a genuine enthusiasm for academic work and intellectual challenge. Reed comprises a diverse student body; more than four fifths of Reed's students come from outside the Northwest, with a quarter from the Northeast and 8 percent from outside the United States. Twenty-five percent of Reed's incoming students are members of historically underrepresented ethnic groups. In fall 2008, Reed opened five new residence halls, which enable 75 percent of students to live on campus.

Campus social opportunities are open to all, with no closed clubs or organizations; there are no sororities or fraternities at Reed. Community life is full of activity and variety with more than seventy student organizations. Although there are competitive club sports at Reed, such as rugby, soccer, and Ultimate (Frisbee), there are no varsity athletic teams. Fitness and the development of lifelong skills take precedence over competition.

Location

Reed's 119-acre wooded campus is located in a quiet, residential section of southeast Portland. The nearby ocean and mountains of the Pacific Northwest provide a balance to the social and cultural offerings of the greater Portland metropolitan area. Reed is an hour and a half away from both the coast and the ski slopes on Mount Hood, where Reed owns a ski cabin for use by the Reed community. Portland is a comfortable, welcoming metropolis of 1.5 million people, offering every urban opportunity, crisscrossed by bike paths and excellent public transportation, home to a great local music and theater scene, police on bikes and horses, tranquil Japanese and Chinese gardens, noisy downtown clubs, a floating dance floor, a plethora of bridges, the largest independent bookstore in the world, and 30-pound salmon swimming past the city lights.

Majors and Degrees

Reed College awards the Bachelor of Arts degree in a wide variety of fields, based on work in traditional departments or in interdisciplinary combinations. Students may select from the following majors: American studies, anthropology, art, biochemistry and molecular biology, biology, chemistry, chemistry-physics, Chinese literature, Chinese studies, classics, classics-religion, dance-theater, economics, English literature, environmental studies, French literature, general literature, German literature, history, history-literature, international and comparative policy studies, linguistics, literature-theater, mathematics, mathematics-economics, mathematics-physics, music, philosophy, physics, political science, psychology, religion, Russian literature, sociology, Spanish literature, and theater.

Students may also design additional interdisciplinary majors. The approval of such special programs, which link two or more disciplines, is reviewed by the student's adviser and the departments concerned.

Reed offers several combined 3-2 programs, which allow the student to earn both a bachelor's degree from Reed and a professional degree from the cooperating institution. Science programs and institutions include engineering (California Institute of Technology, Columbia University, and Rensselaer Polytechnic Institute), computer science (University of Washington), and environmental sciences (Duke University). The College also has a combined program in fine arts (Pacific Northwest College of Art).

Academic Programs

Hallmarks of academic life at Reed include the small-group conference method of teaching and its reliance on active student participation, a de-emphasis of grades, a yearlong interdisciplinary humanities program, and an integrated academic program that balances the breadth of traditional course content and distribution requirements with flexibility in designing an in-depth senior thesis. The development of skills in preparation for a life of learning takes precedence over the mere memorization of facts. In addition to fulfilling the requirements for the major, taking the humanities course, and writing the senior thesis, students must satisfy a distributional requirement, consisting of two core classes from each of the following academic groups: literature, philosophy, and the arts; history, social sciences, and psychology; the natural sciences; and math, foreign language, logic, and linguistics. Students must also take two classes from one other department outside their major course of study.

Off-Campus Programs

Reed participates in domestic exchange programs with Howard University in Washington, D.C.; Sarah Lawrence College in New York; and Sea Education Association in Massachusetts. In addition, Reed provides study-abroad opportunities for students in Australia, Argentina, China, Costa Rica, Cuba, Ecuador, Egypt, France, Germany, Greece, Hungary, Ireland, Morocco, Italy, Kenya, Lebanon, Russia, South Africa, Spain, Turks and Caicos, and the United Kingdom. Students may also arrange independent study plans in consultation with appropriate faculty members, the director for off-campus studies, and the registrar.

Academic Facilities

Students have access to Reed's substantial library collection (629,871 volumes, 17,169 periodicals, and 350,209 government documents) by searching the online catalog in the library or from any computer on the campus network. Through its participation in PORTALS (Portland Area Library System) and Summit, a union catalog of Oregon and Washington academic libraries, Reed provides online access to other library catalogs and databases. Students may borrow materials directly from academic libraries in the Portland area, and they have access to collections worldwide through interlibrary loan. In addition, the Reed library accommodates a first-rate art gallery, a language lab, and a music listening facility. The Reed library is open 18 hours most days and 24 hours a day during examinations.

Computer technology is highly developed at Reed and widely used for instruction, research, and communication by all members of the College community. A state-of-the-art campus network links all residence halls, classrooms, laboratories, offices, and the library to one another and to the global Internet. The Educational Technology Center houses more than 100 computers and a variety of other teaching and technology resources that are used by students and faculty and staff members. The science laboratories at Reed are among the best equipped of any undergraduate college in the United States. These include the A. A. Knowlton Laboratory of Physics, the Arthur F. Scott Laboratory of Chemistry, and the L. E. Griffin Memorial Biology Building. Reed's research nuclear reactor (the only such reactor in the country that is staffed primarily by undergraduates) and radiochemistry lab are actively used for student research, instruction, and training. For those interested in the arts, the campus houses studio art facilities that recently saw a $2-million expansion, performing arts facilities, twenty instrumental practice rooms, a computer music laboratory, a recording system, and an 800-seat auditorium. Slated to be complete in time for the fall 2013 semester, Reed's new $28-million Performing Arts Building represents a major step forward in the College's commitment to the important role the arts have played throughout Reed's first 100 years. For the first time in Reed's history, the departments of music, dance, and theatre will be housed in one building that includes rehearsal and performance space, offices, scene and costume studios, collaborative spaces, and a multimedia lab. Other popular facilities include a radio station and a modern sports center.

Costs

Tuition for 2012–13 was $44,200, and room and board was $11,460. The student body fee was $260, bringing the yearly total cost to approximately $55,920. The cost of books and incidental expenses averages $2,000.

Financial Aid

About half of the Reed student body receives financial assistance from the College. A full need-based financial aid program makes Reed accessible to students from a wide range of economic backgrounds. The College guarantees to meet the full demonstrated need of all continuing students in good academic standing who complete their financial aid applications on time. Reed's own funds are the primary source of grants to students. The College budgeted more than $22 million for this purpose in 2012–13. Reed also administers federal and state grants as well as federally subsidized loan programs. Campus employment and work-study programs are available. The size of a financial aid award is based solely upon analysis of the student's need. The average amount awarded to students receiving financial aid in 2012–13 was $39,885, which includes grants, loans, and work opportunities. Reed students' average graduating loan debt for all four years is $19,407, well below the national average.

Faculty

All classes at Reed are taught by professors, about 90 percent of whom hold the highest degree in their field. The average class has 15 students. Reed students point to the opportunity to work closely with faculty members as one of the great benefits of a Reed education. Reed faculty members point to the opportunity to work with students who are serious scholars as one of the great benefits of teaching at Reed. Faculty members commit themselves primarily to teaching, with scholarly and scientific research furthering this primary goal; they view students as partners in learning, often serving as coauthors and coinvestigators on professional papers and research projects. This close association is due, in large part, to a 10:1 student-faculty ratio and the one-on-one relationship between thesis adviser (a professor) and student during the senior year.

Student Government

The Student Senate is the central body in student governance. The Senate consists of the student body president, vice president, and 8 student representatives, all elected by the students. Its two primary functions are to allocate student body funds and to represent student interests and concerns to the faculty, administration, and Board of Trustees. The Senate distributes approximately $40,000 each semester to the many student organizations on campus. As agreed under the community constitution, students participate fully in discussions and decisions on a wide variety of issues. The Student Committee on Academic Policy and Planning participates in debate about the curriculum at Reed; many other committees, from the Library Board to the Reactor Committee, have substantial student input. The Senate and student body president make all student appointments to such committees.

Admission Requirements

Reed welcomes applications from freshman and transfer candidates who are genuinely committed to the pursuit of a liberal arts education and a rigorous academic program. Those applicants are admitted who, in the view of the Admission Committee, are most likely to become successful members of and contribute significantly and honorably to the Reed community. The College is committed to maintaining a student body distinguished by its intellectual passion, yet diversified in its range of backgrounds, interests, and talents.

Admission decisions are based on many integrated factors, but academic accomplishments and talents are given the greatest weight in the selection process. A strong secondary school preparation, including honors and advanced courses where available, improves a student's chances for admission. Such a program usually includes 4 years of English and 3 to 4 years of mathematics (through precalculus), science, foreign language, and history or social studies. Given the wide variation in high school programs and quality, however, there are no fixed requirements for secondary school courses. Applicants are expected to have obtained a secondary school diploma prior to enrollment, although exceptions are occasionally made. There are no cutoff points for high school or college grades or for test scores.

Reed recognizes the qualities of character—in particular, motivation, intellectual curiosity, individual responsibility, and community and social consciousness—as important considerations in the selection process, beyond a demonstrated commitment to academic excellence. Thus, the Admission Committee looks for students whose accomplishments and interests in various fields of endeavor will contribute to the overall liveliness of the Reed community. Personal interviews, either on or off campus, are not a requirement in the admission process but are strongly recommended whenever possible. Applications for early decision should be submitted by November 15 (Option I) or December 20 (Option II), regular freshman admission by January 15, and transfer candidates by March 1.

Application and Information

The Office of Admission is open Monday through Friday from 8:30 a.m. until 5 p.m. (Pacific time) all year, except for major holidays. The Admission Office is also open on select Saturdays in the spring and fall. Students may apply online at http://www.reed.edu/apply/apply_reed.html.

For further information or to arrange a campus tour, overnight stay, information session, or interview, students should contact:

Office of Admission
Reed College
3203 Southeast Woodstock Boulevard
Portland, Oregon 97202-8199
Phone: 503-777-7511
      800-547-4750 (toll-free)
Fax: 503-777-7553
E-mail: admission@reed.edu
Website: http://www.reed.edu

On a warm day at Reed College, it's not uncommon to see some classes meeting on the front lawn. Students have a great appreciation for passionate discussion, intellectual inquiry, and bright and sunny days.

THE RICHARD STOCKTON COLLEGE
OF NEW JERSEY
GALLOWAY, NEW JERSEY

STOCKTON
NEW JERSEY'S
DISTINCTIVE
Public College

The College

Thinking translates into doing at Stockton. Students can get hands-on experience in nursing, public health, or physical therapy at the two hospitals on campus; conduct computational science or IT research in the high-powered computer labs or at nearby technology centers; "live" a hospitality and tourism internship 24/7 at the Seaview, Stockton's world-class resort; study artistic techniques firsthand through a partnership with the nearby Noyes Museum of Art and at the Philadelphia Museum of Art, just an hour away; or bask in the beautiful, 2,000-acre campus in the Pinelands Natural Reserve just minutes from the ocean, natural labs perfect for Stockton's nationally recognized marine science and environmental studies programs.

Most Stockton students engage in independent study with a faculty mentor. Small classes allow for discussion, debate, and discovery—guided by Fulbright scholars, the most-published scientist in the world, and professors who care as much about teaching as research.

Rooted in a deep social and environmental consciousness, Stockton offers extensive service learning and human rights opportunities and has become an international leader in alternative energy research and conservation efforts.

Founded in 1969, the College was named for Richard Stockton, one of the New Jersey signers of the Declaration of Independence. A young institution, Stockton already has a tradition of anticipating and leading changes that other universities and colleges follow. The College offers bachelor's, master's, and doctoral degree programs designed to challenge the brightest students. Stockton offers many of the academic, technological, and cultural advantages of a large university, but with the community spirit typical of smaller colleges.

Stockton enrolls over 8,400 students from New Jersey, the Mid-Atlantic states, and foreign countries, providing distinctive educational programs and experiences that extend learning beyond the classroom. The curriculum develops the students' analytic and creative capabilities and encourages individually planned courses of study.

Over 10,000 events, more than 130 clubs and organizations, Greek life, and academic and honor societies enhance the Stockton experience. Extensive intramural and club sports; NCAA Division III sports teams including men's baseball, basketball, lacrosse, and soccer, women's basketball, crew, field hockey, lacrosse, soccer, softball, tennis, and volleyball, and men's and women's cross-country and track and field; and a multipurpose Sports Center provide exercise for the body as well as the mind. Students who participate in cocurricular activities have their experiences documented through the ULTRA (Undergraduate Learning, Training, and Awareness) program, culminating in a co-curricular transcript.

A new 154,000-square-foot Campus Center provides a focal point for campus and hub for student, staff, and visitor activity. It is a one-stop-shop for conducting College business, bookstore purchases, student organization meetings, and larger all-College events, as well as performances and lectures in the 255-seat theater, a food court, coffee shop, game room, and plenty of space for students to meet and socialize.

The Residential Life Center offers yet another gathering space within two student housing areas. With meeting rooms, convenience store, and computer lab, the center encourages activities for both organized and informal student groups.

Lakeside Lodge has a convenience store, snack bar, outdoor concert area, computer lab, multipurpose room for large programs, smaller meeting room, and a lakefront beach.

Stockton provides on-campus housing for almost 4,000 students in traditional residence halls, apartments, and for select students, at Stockton Seaview. All complexes are furnished and air conditioned, with cable TV, telephone service, and Internet access. Other students choose to live off campus in nearby townhouse and apartment complexes or winter rentals in one of the local seashore towns.

In addition to its undergraduate programs, Stockton offers the following graduate degrees: Doctor of Physical Therapy; Master of Arts in

American studies, criminal justice, Holocaust and genocide studies, education, educational leadership, and instructional technology; Master of Business Administration; Master of Science in communication disorders, computational science, nursing, occupational therapy, and social work; and a Professional Science Master's in environmental science. Certificate and endorsement programs are offered in bilingual/bicultural education, ESL (English as a second language), family nurse practitioner, forensic psychology, health professions prep, homeland security, learning disabilities teacher consultant, middle school endorsement, New Jersey standard supervisor endorsement, preschool–grade 3 endorsement, reading specialist, special education, and student assistance coordinator.

Stockton College is accredited by the Commission on Higher Education of the Middle States Association of Colleges and Schools. In addition, the social work program is accredited by the Council on Social Work Education; teacher education is approved by the New Jersey Department of Education, the National Association of State Directors of Teacher Education and Certification, and the Teacher Education Accreditation Council; nursing is accredited by the New Jersey Board of Nursing and the Commission on Collegiate Nursing Education; chemistry is accredited by the American Chemical Society; physical therapy is accredited by the Commission on Accreditation in Physical Therapy Education (CAPTE) of the American Physical Therapy Association; environmental health/public health is accredited by the National Environmental Health Sciences and Protection Accreditation Council; health administration is accredited by the Association of University Programs in Health Administration; occupational therapy is accredited by the Accreditation Council for Occupational Therapy Education (ACOTE) of the American Occupational Therapy Association (AOTA), and communication disorders (speech pathology/audiology) is accredited by the American Speech-Language-Hearing Association and Council on Academic Accreditation in Audiology and Speech-Language Pathology.

Location

Stockton is located on a stunning 2,000-acre campus in Galloway, New Jersey, nestled in the environmentally protected Pinelands National Reserve, just minutes west of Atlantic City and Jersey Shore beaches; an hour from Philadelphia and 2 hours from New York City. Courses are also offered online, at the Atlantic City campus, and at the Hammonton, Manahawkin, and Woodbine Instructional Sites. The Stockton Seaview Resort and its two championship golf courses in Absecon, allow the College to expand its hospitality and tourism management program, enhance the college experience for students, and preserve an iconic landmark in the region. Collaboration with the Sam Azeez Museum of Woodbine Heritage and the Noyes Museum of Art provides enriching exhibitions and educational programs. Concerts, art exhibitions, lectures, recreation, and sports on campus are complemented by nearby Jersey Shore resort destinations. Within a 15-minute drive, students find shopping, dining, and cultural attractions, as well as the entertainment of Atlantic City.

Majors and Degrees

The Bachelor of Arts, Bachelor of Fine Arts, and Bachelor of Science degrees are offered in studies in the arts (visual and performing), biochemistry/molecular biology, biology, business (accounting, finance, financial planning, management, marketing), chemistry, communications, computational science, computer science and information systems, criminal justice (forensic psychology/investigation, homeland security), economics, education, environmental science, geology, health sciences, historical studies, hospitality and tourism management, languages and culture studies, liberal studies, literature, marine science, mathematics, nursing, philosophy and religion, physics, political science, psychology, public health, sociology and anthropology, social work, and sustainability.

The College also offers preprofessional preparation in dentistry, law, medicine, pharmacy, veterinary medicine, communication disorders (speech therapy), occupational therapy, and physical therapy, with the master's in occupational therapy, communication disorders, and doctorate in physical therapy completed at Stockton. Also, there are accelerated seven-year dual-degree articulation agreements with the University of Medicine and Dentistry of New Jersey (Robert Wood Johnson Medical School, New Jersey Medical School, School of Osteopathic Medicine, New Jersey Dental School), the Pennsylvania College of Podiatric Medicine, and the New York College of Podiatric Medicine. In addition, articulation programs with Cornell University for veterinary medicine and hospitality and tourism management, as well as five-year, dual-degree programs with New Jersey Institute of Technology and Rutgers University for engineering. Additionally, students can graduate from Stockton with a Bachelor of Science degree in biochemistry/molecular biology and finish their Doctor of Pharmacy degree through the Ernest Mario School of Pharmacy at Rutgers University.

Academic Programs

To earn a baccalaureate degree from Stockton, a student must satisfactorily complete a minimum of 128 semester credits. Degree programs include a combination of general studies and program (major) studies. Bachelor of Arts students must earn 64 credits in general studies; Bachelor of Science students must earn 48. General studies courses are cross-disciplinary courses designed to introduce students to all major areas of the curriculum and to the intellectual skills necessary for success in college. Students must select courses from each major curricular area. The only required courses within general studies are basic studies (up to three); students may be exempt from these courses based on testing. Bachelor of Arts students must earn 64 credits in major studies; Bachelor of Science students must earn 80. Requirements are carefully structured and emphasize sequences of specific courses.

Stockton students have the opportunity to influence what and how they learn by participating in the major decisions that shape their academic lives. The preceptorial system enables students to work on a personalized basis with a faculty-staff preceptor in planning and evaluating courses and in exploring various career alternatives.

Off-Campus Programs

Off-campus experiences for credit are a key feature of most programs. Internships, research projects, and field studies extend learning beyond the classroom. Study abroad, Semester at Sea, and an honors program are also available.

The Washington Internship Program provides additional professional work experience opportunities. Stockton sends more students to the program than any other college or university outside the Washington, D.C., area.

Coordination of off-campus internship programs is provided by academic offices as well as the Career Center; coordination of foreign study is provided by the coordinator of international education.

Academic Facilities

Stockton's campus serves as a living-learning center. Academic, recreational, and living spaces are mixed to promote interaction among students, faculty, and staff. The facilities, all constructed since 1971, include several large classroom/office buildings, an extensive library, lecture hall/auditorium, art gallery, performing arts center, and new unified science center.

The library contains 300,000+ volumes, over 2,600 periodical subscriptions, 280,000 government documents, more than 19,000 reels of microfilm, and about 68,000 other units of microtext. Media collections include films, slides, videotapes, audiotapes, CDs, and records. The library also houses a special New Jersey Pine Barrens collection; depository for federal, state, and Atlantic City documents; and the Sara and Sam Schoffer Holocaust Resource Center.

Costs

Costs for the 2012–13 academic year were $12,322 for in-state students and $18,715 for out-of-state students (flat-rate tuition up to 40 credits per year, fees); on-campus housing and board were $10,796 (double-occupancy residence room, Ultimate 19 meal plan). Books, supplies, transportation, and personal items are extra. Costs are subject to change.

Financial Aid

Financial aid is available as scholarships, grants, loans, and work-study. Need-based financial aid is awarded according to student and family need. Students seeking financial aid should file the Free Application for Federal Student Aid (FAFSA) by March 1. Stockton offers aggressive

and generous merit-based aid awards to academically talented freshmen and transfer students based on standardized test scores, grade point average, high school class rank, and college-level performance.

Faculty

Stockton's faculty represent highly diverse academic, training, and social backgrounds, with 95 percent holding terminal degrees in their field. Faculty members work closely with students through small class sizes and individual research opportunities and share with students and staff members the initiative and responsibility for social, recreational, and cultural programs and activities. This arrangement supports the exceptional rapport and learning relationships among students and faculty members.

Student Government

The RSCNJ Student Senate consists of 25 student members. The advisory council is made up of 1 faculty member and 2 staff members. Student senators hold office for one year. The Student Senate reviews and makes recommendations on budgets of funded student organizations and acts as the official representative of the student body.

Admission Requirements

Stockton operates on rolling admission. Fall admission deadline is May 1 for most freshmen. Students should check the website for special program deadlines. Transfer deadline for fall admission is June 1. Spring (January) admission deadline for all students is December 1. Students may apply for admission to the fall or spring term and are notified of the admission decision as soon as their application file has been completed and reviewed. Freshman applicants must submit ACT and/or SAT scores. All students must submit official transcripts from all educational institutions attended. Admission is selective.

Early acceptance may be offered for highly qualified high school students in their junior year. Armed Services veterans and those who have been away from formal education for some time are also invited to apply for admission. Stockton makes no distinction between part- and full-time students in offering admission.

Stockton offers special admission to a limited number of New Jersey students from educationally and financially disadvantaged backgrounds. Students wishing to explore this opportunity should contact the Admissions Office.

Application and Information

For more information, prospective students should contact:

Dean of Enrollment Management
The Richard Stockton College of New Jersey
101 Vera King Farris Drive
Galloway, New Jersey 08205-9441
Phone: 609-652-4261
   866-RSC-2885 (toll-free)
Fax: 609-626-5541
E-mail: admissions@stockton.edu
Website: Stockton.edu/admissions
   Facebook.com/richardstocktoncollege
   Twitter.com/#!/Stockton_edu

Independent thinking is what Stockton is all about. Small classes allow for discussion, debate, discovery, and unbelievable faculty/student interaction—mere minutes from Jersey Shore beaches, an hour from Philadelphia, and 2 hours from New York City!

RICHMOND, THE AMERICAN INTERNATIONAL UNIVERSITY IN LONDON

LONDON, ENGLAND

RICHMOND
THE AMERICAN INTERNATIONAL
UNIVERSITY
IN LONDON

The University

Richmond, The American International University in London, prepares men and women to serve with purpose and generosity in an interdependent and multicultural world. Richmond offers a strong academic program with many choices of fields of study, an exceptional faculty, superb campus life, and fellow students from all over the world. In the United States, Richmond is accredited by the Commission on Higher Education of the Middle States Association of Colleges and Schools, a regional accrediting body recognized by the U.S. Department of Education. Richmond is accredited in the United Kingdom by the Open University and holds related degree validation. The University's undergraduate and graduate degrees are designated by the United Kingdom's Department of Education and Employment. The University is a comprehensive American liberal arts and professional university. In addition to the undergraduate degree programs described below, Richmond offers M.A. and M.Sc. degrees in a range of different subjects.

Freshmen and sophomores study and live at the Richmond campus, 7 miles from central London. Junior and senior years are spent at the Kensington campus in one of London's most beautiful residential and historic districts. As part of their four-year B.A. degree program, students may spend a semester or a year studying at one of the University's two international study centers in Florence and Rome, Italy. Richmond currently enrolls over 1,000 students from more than 100 countries. Approximately 38 percent of the degree students are from Europe and the United Kingdom, 4 percent are from Asia, 6 percent are from the Middle East, 6 percent of the student body represents the continent of Africa, and 1 percent is from South America. The remaining 45 percent of the degree students are from North America. About 350 study-abroad students from various universities are enrolled for a semester or a year at Richmond.

Small classes, averaging 17–20 students, enable students to receive personal attention from professors in a supportive environment. The curriculum and academic advising system are structured to enable students to choose courses that provide broad knowledge, relevant skills, and an understanding of the world's many cultures and nations.

Richmond students supplement academic programs with activities that complement and balance the classroom experience. Many extracurricular and cocurricular programs are available to students, including student government, the Green Project, Model United Nations, Amnesty International, RTV (Richmond Television), Top of the Hill music club, and sports and business clubs.

Location

The Richmond Hill campus in the London suburb of Richmond offers a variety of entertainment, shopping, cultural, and recreational opportunities. Only yards from the University campus is Richmond Park, more than 2,200 acres of rolling hills and lush woodland, where one can ride horses, play tennis, jog, or simply relax. The journey from Richmond into Central London takes approximately 30 minutes using public transportation.

The Kensington campus is located in the heart of London's Borough of Kensington, which has fine museums, libraries, theatres, concert halls, historic buildings, and well-known

cultural and educational resources. The University takes full advantage of London's cultural and social resources through selected academic courses, work experience placements with multinational corporations, and special visits to museums, art galleries, theatres, and concert halls.

Majors and Degrees

Richmond operates its academic program on the American system. The University offers the four-year Bachelor of Arts (B.A.) degree in more than twenty majors, with a further choice of seventeen minors. Majors offered by the University include: art, design, and media; business administration (entrepreneurship, fashion marketing, finance, international business, marketing); communications; development economics, development studies; economics; film studies; financial economics; history; international journalism and media; international relations; performance and theatre arts; political science; and psychology.

Academic Programs

In order to graduate with the dual-validated U.S. and U.K. degree [B.A./B.A. (Honors)], students must earn a minimum of 120 credits. Usually, this means taking a full load for four years, or eight semesters. Within these 120 credits, students must complete all course requirements for their majors. Students must also meet the University's Language Proficiency and General Education requirements. In addition, valuable work experience for credit is offered through the International Internship program. Placements have been at the International Herald Tribune, General Electric, The House of Commons, CNN, the United Nations, Lloyds Bank, the Museum of London, and Sony Music Corporation.

Credit is also awarded for Advanced Placement tests (6 credits for each subject grade of 3, 4, or 5); a grade of A, B, or C on the A Level exams is awarded 9 credits (6 for D or E). Credit is also awarded for the International Baccalaureate, the Baccalauréat de l'Enseignement du Second Degré (France), the Abitur/Reifzeugnis (Germany), the Diploma di Maturità (Italy), and the School Leaving Diploma (Denmark, Finland, Norway, and Sweden).

The fall semester begins in early September and ends in mid-December. The spring semester begins in mid-January and runs through mid-May. A session of summer school runs from mid-May to late June.

Off-Campus Programs

Students may complement their studies in London with a semester, year, or summer at one of two international study centers. The centers are located in Florence and Rome, Italy, and each offer an intensive study of the language and culture of the country. The Florence Study Center emphasizes studio and fine arts. The Rome Study Center offers courses in Italian language and culture, art history, economics, and political science.

Academic Facilities

Information technology is integrated into the curriculum in ways that are natural to the discipline under study. Supporting this are eight student computer laboratories with more than 140 current-specification computers, which connect to the Internet and are networked for student, faculty, and administrative use. Wireless network access is also available on campus.

Richmond's libraries support the courses taught at each campus. Students may use either campus library. The libraries house over 95,000 items including books, DVDs, music CDs, company annual reports, and student theses. In addition, the libraries have subscriptions to a number of journal and magazine titles, along with a variety of national and international newspapers. Richmond students also have access to the many specialized libraries within the London area.

Costs

Tuition for the 2013–14 academic year is $27,000. Room and board is $13,740. Personal expenses, books and supplies, clothing, recreation, and travel costs also need to be factored in as these are not included in tuition and room and board fees.

Financial Aid

Merit-based scholarships are awarded annually to students of high academic ability. Financial aid for U.S. citizens includes Federal Direct Stafford Student Loans and Federal PLUS loans. All U.S. citizens must file the Free Application for Federal Student Aid (FAFSA) to qualify for federal loans. The FAFSA school code for Richmond is G10594. Students should contact the admissions office for details regarding application procedures for scholarships and financial aid.

Faculty

The student-faculty ratio of 11:1 enables optimum interaction and individualized instructional assistance. The 92 faculty members (44 full-time, 48 part-time) have professional degrees from top European and American universities such as Harvard, the University of California (Berkeley), the University of Michigan, Cambridge, Oxford, the London School of Economics, the Royal College of Art, and the University of Bonn.

Student Government

The Richmond Student Union acts as a resource for all students, student organizations, and clubs to voice their opinions and ideas. The Student Union functions as a network between the student body and the administration. Using student ideas, it holds events and seeks to feature student talent while enhancing the overall University experience. The Student Union is ongoing in its development and thus offers possibilities for students to shape and change it. It is an organization directed by students for students and is structured to provide flexibility as well as the opportunity for all students to become involved.

Admission Requirements

Applicants are admitted on the basis of academic performance, references, intended major, and career interests. The required autobiographical essay is of paramount importance. Applicants to Richmond have usually completed a total of twelve years of primary and secondary school with a minimum grade of C+ (2.5 out of 4.0) in the American high school grading system, or its equivalent. British system students should have attained a minimum of three A levels (grades BBC) in acceptable academic subjects, one of which must be mathematics or science. Equivalent qualifications gained under other educational systems are also considered for the purpose of admission.

Students must submit a completed application form and application fee, an essay, transcripts of all secondary and postsecondary school work, and one confidential letter of academic recommendation. SAT or ACT scores are optional. The ATP code for Richmond is 0823L. The ACT code is 5244. Evidence of proficiency in the English language is required from students whose first language is not English or who did not attend English-speaking schools. Standardized test scores, such as the TOEFL or the IELTS are considered in assessing students' language capability.

Richmond admits students on a rolling basis, and applicants are encouraged to submit their application at the earliest opportunity. All documents in languages other than English must be accompanied by official translations. Applicants are usually notified of a decision within three to four weeks.

Application and Information

An application for admission and further information may be submitted online at www.richmond.ac.uk using either the Richmond Direct Application or the Common Application, or UCAS.

Applicants residing in North America should contact:
Director of Admissions for North America
Office of Admissions
Richmond, The American International University in London
343 Congress Street, Suite 3100
Boston, Massachusetts 02210-1214
Phone: 617-450-5617
Fax: 617-450-5601
E-mail: usadmissions@richmond.ac.uk
Website: http://www.richmond.ac.uk

Applicants residing in all other countries outside of North America should contact:
Head of Enquiries and Admissions
UK Office of Admissions
Richmond, The American International University in London
Queens Road, Richmond
Surrey TW10 6JP
England
Phone: 44-20-8332-9000
Fax: 44-20-8332-1596
E-mail: enrol@richmond.ac.uk
Website: http://www.richmond.ac.uk

Students outside Richmond University in London.

RIPON COLLEGE
RIPON, WISCONSIN

The College

Together with the other members of its tightly knit learning community, Ripon students often feel as if they learn more deeply, live more fully, and achieve more success. There are more opportunities to be involved, lead, speak out, make a difference, and explore new interests than at many colleges many times its size. Through collaborative learning, group living, teamwork, and networking, students tap into the power of a community where all work together to ensure their success, at Ripon and beyond. The best residential liberal arts colleges strive to be true learning communities like Ripon. Ripon succeeds better than most, because the enrollment of just under 1,000 students is perfect for fostering connections inside and outside the classroom. Students flourish in this environment of mutual respect, where shared values are elevated and diverse ideas are valued. Students who are seeking academic challenge and want to benefit from an environment of personal attention and support should take a closer look at Ripon. In classes that average 20 students, professors are able to know the students and their strengths and capabilities extraordinarily well. They tailor course work to make sure students are always challenged to perform at the top of their game, yet they are always ready to provide extra support when needed. Faculty members collaborate with students on research projects, suggest independent-study topics, and connect them with internships and other active learning experiences.

A Ripon education can take graduates anywhere. A student could study psychology and play basketball and then become a seven-time Grammy winner like jazz singer Al Jarreau, '62; guide a space shuttle into orbit like Jeff Bantle, '80, a chief flight director with NASA; or become an international opera star like Gail Dobish, '76. A student could set records in medical science like neonatologist Dr. John Muraskas, '78, who is on record for saving the world's smallest premature baby, or a student might end up studying at Oxford University as a Rhodes Scholar like Zach Morris '02, who also found time to play touch football with former President Bill Clinton and spend an evening at Buckingham Palace with the Queen.

The list of student clubs and organizations is ever changing, reflecting students' ever-changing interests. A recent addition is FUERZA Alliance, designed to educate students about Latino cultures and to provide services to the Spanish-speaking community of Ripon.

Every day at Ripon is packed with a host of activities such as concerts (there are eight vocal and instrumental groups that perform regularly on campus, as well as many individual student and faculty recitals). The Caestecker Fine Arts Series and the Chamber Music at Ripon Series annually bring national performers to the campus. The Theatre Department sponsors two major productions annually, plus a series of student-directed one-act plays. The most recent Ripon Film Festival (an annual showcase for independent films from around the country) included the premiere of a feature-length horror film written, directed by, and starring a Ripon student.

Ripon's NCAA Division III intercollegiate teams compete in the Midwest Conference. Men's varsity sports include baseball, basketball, cross-country, cycling, football, golf, indoor and outdoor track and field, soccer, swimming and diving, and tennis. Women's varsity sports include basketball, cross-country, cycling, dance, golf, indoor and outdoor track and field, soccer, softball, swimming and diving, tennis, and volleyball.

Location

Located on 250 tree-lined, rolling acres adjacent to downtown Ripon, the campus looks and feels like a college should. Ripon's twenty-six first-rate buildings are a striking combination of historic (ten campus structures listed on the National Register of Historic Places) and modern architecture.

Majors and Degrees

Majors include anthropology, art, art history, biology, business management, chemistry, chemistry/biology, communication, computer science, economics, educational studies, English, environmental sciences, exercise science, foreign languages, French, German, global studies, history, Latin American area studies, mathematics, music, philosophy, physics, politics and government, psychobiology, psychology, religion, sociology, Spanish, and theater. Programs are also available in dramatic literature, entrepreneurship, leadership studies, museum studies, national security studies, nonprofit management, sports medicine/athletic training, studio art, and women's studies.

Preprofessional programs include dentistry, journalism, law and government, library and information science, medicine, ministry, optometry, physical therapy, and veterinary medicine.

Dual-degree programs include allied health sciences/medical technology, engineering, forestry, and social welfare.

Certification programs include education certification, early childhood, elementary, elementary/middle school, secondary, secondary/middle, music K–12, and physical education K–12.

Academic Programs

Ripon's liberal arts curriculum is designed to introduce students to a wide variety of disciplines. About 40 percent of the students complete double or triple majors, whereas some create special self-designed majors. Excellent communications skills—written and oral—as well as critical-thinking and problem-solving skills are the hallmark of a Ripon education, regardless of major. In addition, the leadership studies program and the newly established ethical leadership program provide a strong foundation for leadership skills. An Army ROTC program is also available.

Off-Campus Programs

Ripon offers more than forty different off-campus programs of varying lengths to choose from, each one officially sanctioned by and affiliated with Ripon. Although most programs are connected with a major or minor program, all are open to every Ripon student, regardless of major.

U.S. programs include Chicago Urban Studies Semester, Fisk University–Ripon Exchange Program, Newberry Seminar in the Humanities, Oak Ridge Science Semester, Washington Semester, and Woods Hole Marine Biology.

International programs include Alicante, Spain; Amman, Jordan; Bonn, Germany Program; Budapest Semester; Cordoba, Argentina; Botswana; Costa Rica; Cross-Cultural Study Center in Seville, Spain; Florence Program; India Studies; Japan Study; London and Florence Program in the Arts; Madrid Program; Montpellier, France; Paris, France; Russia Program; St. Andrews, Scotland; Sea Education Association (marine biology abroad); Sea Semester at Woods Hole; Swansea Program; Tanzania; Toledo, Spain; and University of Wales in Bangor.

Academic Facilities

Constant additions and improvements, such as a recent multimillion-dollar apartment-style residence hall, the renovation and classroom expansion of Todd Wehr Hall, and upgrades to upperclass residence halls, the library, the bookstore, dining facilities, and a coffee shop, maintain Ripon's ability to meet the needs of today and tomorrow. Technology services include high-speed Internet, e-mail, and video communication. Intranet and Internet services are accessible from systems located throughout the College. The campuswide network provides access from every room, and several wireless hot spots in key areas let students access the world without being tied down.

The library staff provides friendly, efficient circulation, reference, instruction, and interlibrary loan services that aid in research. The library also houses the College archives, a computer lab, and more than a dozen online databases. Library holdings include 164,000 volumes, 800 current periodicals, and microfilms.

The C. J. Rodman Center for the Arts is home to a theater with a state-of-the-art computerized lighting system, a recital hall with one of only fifty existing Bedient organs, an art gallery, and a sculpture garden.

The J. M. Storzer Center includes an Olympic-size pool, a first-class gymnasium, tennis and racquetball courts, a dance studio, training facilities, and a weight room. The outdoor playing fields and courts are among the best in their class. In addition, a large, modern exercise facility was recently added in the main student residence area.

Costs

Tuition for 2013–14 is $31,327, room and board are $8,815, and fees are $275, for a total cost of $40,417.

Financial Aid

Ripon has been consistently recognized as a best value by all of the national ranking organizations. More than 90 percent of Ripon students receive some form of merit-based scholarship and/or need-based grants and loans.

Ripon recognizes and rewards students' success in high school with its institutionally funded scholarships, based not only on academic merit but also on special achievements in other areas, such as the creative arts. The scholarships range from $1,000 to full tuition. Ripon participates in all federal and state need-based financial aid programs. The financial aid counselors work individually with students and their families to investigate every possible financial resource for which they are eligible.

Faculty

Ripon has 57 full-time and 25 part-time faculty members. Ninety-seven percent of the full-time faculty members have Ph.D.'s.

Admission Requirements

Ripon enrolls students who are expected to contribute to and benefit from the academic and residential programs provided. Ripon does not discriminate on the basis of gender, sexual orientation, race, color, age, religion, national or ethnic origin, or disability in the administration of its educational policies, admission practices, scholarship and loan programs, and athletic and other College-administered programs.

Application and Information

The faculty committee on academic standards establishes the criteria for admission. The school considers a variety of factors, including secondary school record, standardized test scores (SAT or ACT), recommendations, a written essay, and extracurricular or community service activities. Ripon's admission process reflects the personal attention students can expect to receive during their college careers, and applicants are encouraged to provide any additional information they consider helpful.

For further information, students should contact:

Leigh D. Mlodzik
Dean of Admission
Ripon College
300 Seward Street
P.O. Box 248
Ripon, Wisconsin 54971-0248
Phone: 800-947-4766 (toll-free)
E-mail: adminfo@ripon.edu
Website: http://www.ripon.edu

Ripon College students and their families celebrate commencement on the lawn of Harwood Memorial Union.

RIVIER UNIVERSITY
NASHUA, NEW HAMPSHIRE

The University

Rivier University, a private Catholic university founded in 1933 by the Sisters of the Presentation of Mary, has earned a reputation for academic excellence with both distinguished and distinctive programs. Rivier offers many of the region's leading programs at the undergraduate, graduate, postgraduate, and doctoral levels.

"Nashua is our home and the world is our classroom," is the University's guiding force to providing students a Rivier experience that ensures students develop an awareness and appreciation of diverse cultures in New England and around the world. The Rivier community also offers a dynamic student leadership experience, with service opportunities integrated in the curriculum, in the campus culture, and in the hearts and minds of students as stated in the University's mission.

Rivier's School of Undergraduate Studies enrolls approximately 1,559 students, including more than 850 full-time day students. With a 17:1 student-faculty ratio, day students have plenty of opportunities to connect with faculty and become active members of the academic community.

The majority of undergraduate students enroll from the six New England states. Rivier also attracts students from all over the United States as well as international students representing countries in Africa, Asia, Europe, the Middle East, and South America. Students who live on campus reside in four modern residence halls, some with suite-style options. Rivier also provides substance-free housing and honors housing. The Dion Center houses the University's student center and the dining room, which is scheduled to reopen in fall 2013, following a renovation. The commuter lounge, the mailroom, a campus store, student development offices, and meeting rooms are also available in the Dion Center.

The Office of Student Development, the Student Government Association, and more than 17 student clubs and organizations provide a calendar of social, cultural, and recreational activities, including concerts, live entertainment, films, and sporting events. The University and student organizations frequently organize outings, including trips to locations such as Boston and New York. Students also enjoy a variety of performances by the Rivier Theater Company.

Rivier's orientation for new students introduces them to the University's wide array of services, such as academic advisers, the Writing and Resource Center, and peer tutors. The Health Services Center and Counseling Center ensure students' physical and emotional well-being. A full-time chaplain and Campus Ministry team coordinate spiritual activities and service opportunities, while a comprehensive career development service helps students prepare for employment after graduation.

Rivier is a Division III member of the NCAA and sponsors 13 intercollegiate sports. Rivier Raiders compete in men's and women's soccer, volleyball, cross-country, basketball, and lacrosse; men's baseball; and women's field hockey and softball. The men's volleyball team has been nationally ranked every year since 2001. The Muldoon Health and Fitness Center is home to Rivier's varsity athletics, fitness activities, and recreation programs including volleyball, floor hockey, basketball, weight training, indoor soccer, and more. The campus also has a turf rectangular field and a natural grass softball field, as well as a beach volleyball court and cross-country trail. Student athletes can take advantage of an on-campus athletic training clinic for injury assessment and rehab.

Location

Nashua (population 87,000) is located in southern New Hampshire. The city of Boston lies within easy access 40 miles to the south. Local access to public transportation provides for easy travel to and from the campus. Recreational activities abound year-round at nearby lakes and ski areas, in the White Mountains to the north, and at the seacoast, just an hour's drive to the east. The Manchester airport is a 15-minute drive from campus, convenient for students who must access air travel.

Majors and Degrees

Rivier University awards Bachelor of Arts and Bachelor of Science degrees in the following areas: biology (allied health and environmental science), biology education, business, criminal justice, early childhood education, education and community leadership, elementary education, English, English education, finance, global studies, history, human development, international studies, liberal studies, management, marketing, marketing communications, mathematics, mathematics education, modern languages (modern language education and Spanish), nursing, political science, psychology, social studies education, sociology, special education, and transnational security studies. The University offers preprofessional programs in law, dentistry, medicine, and veterinary medicine. Associate degrees are offered in early childhood education, liberal studies, and nursing.

Academic Programs

Rivier University offers both professional studies and liberal arts programs to prepare students for a fast-changing, highly technological, and global society. The broad-based curriculum focuses on preparing students for challenging and rewarding careers and furthering their personal growth. The University is launching a new core curriculum for fall 2013 offering opportunities for service learning, servant leadership, civic engagement, and community service to support the intellectual growth of students and enhance student leadership. Students will choose from courses in three areas: humanities and social sciences, mathematics and natural sciences, and languages in the core complement. The new core is aligned with the Association of American Colleges and Universities' (AAC&U) essential learning outcomes, which provide Rivier graduates with the strong intellectual and practical skills that are in demand in the workplace. The bachelor's degree requires a minimum of 120 credits with a grade point average of at least 2.0. For the associate degree, the student must complete a minimum of 60 credits with a grade point average of at least 2.0.

All departments encourage qualified students to pursue internships in their field of study during their junior or senior year. Education specialists student teach in local schools. Nursing majors complete clinical rotations in healthcare facilities throughout southern New Hampshire and northern Massachusetts. History, law, and political science majors may work in a law office, business, legal-assistance agency, or government agency, and the University's new global studies program offers students a global perspective and opportunities. Sociology and psychology majors work with local social service agencies. English and marketing communications majors work in public relations, broadcasting, or corporate communications positions. Business majors work in marketing, management, and technology. The new transnational security studies program prepares students for today's changing world by closely examining global security issues, especially emerging transnational threats such as terrorism, weapons of mass destruction, regional and ethnic conflicts, and international crime.

Honors and awards for students include placement on the dean's list, membership in Kappa Gamma Pi, listing in *Who's Who Among Students in American Universities and Colleges*, listing in *The National Dean's List*, and degrees with honors. Academically talented students may also apply to the four-year honors program.

The academic year is divided into two 15-week semesters, with first-semester examinations held before Christmas break. Students usually take five courses each semester. Academic credit may be granted to incoming freshmen on the basis of scores on Advanced

Placement tests and CLEP examinations. Students may also "challenge" courses and receive credit by special examination.

Off-Campus Programs

Through Rivier University's membership in the New Hampshire College and University Council, a sixteen-member consortium of senior and two-year colleges, Rivier students may register for courses at any of the member colleges and receive transfer credits.

Academic Facilities

Academic facilities include Memorial Hall, which houses 14 classrooms, the new Office of Global Engagement, faculty offices, a lecture hall, a behavioral science lab, and Rivier's art gallery. The Academic Computer Center features up to 68 workstations with a full range of cutting-edge software and Internet/e-mail access. Regina Library houses approximately 90,000 print volumes and over 45,000 e-books, and provides access to more than 3 million volumes in 12 area libraries, as well as online access to licensed databases in virtually every academic subject. The Writing and Resource Center offers assistance from professional writing consultants as well as student tutors. Other academic facilities include nursing and science laboratories; a physical assessment lab and nursing skills simulation lab, which provide nursing students with practical experience using blood pressure cuffs, ophthalmoscopes, IV pumps, high-fidelity patient simulators, and more; the McLean Center for Finance and Economics; the BAE Student Research Lab; a clinical psychology lab; electronic classrooms offering multimedia learning tools; and the Benoit Education Center, which houses the eight-classroom Landry Early Childhood Center, observation rooms, and an educational resource center.

Costs

Tuition and fees for the academic year 2013–14 are $27,480; room and board, $10,570; and books and supplies, approximately $1,200. Students should expect to pay a $150 activities fee each semester.

Financial Aid

Financial aid is awarded on the basis of the financial need of the student and family. Approximately 98 percent of Rivier's full-time undergraduate students receive financial aid from the University or from government or private sources. Federal aid includes Federal Pell Grants, Federal Supplemental Educational Opportunity Grants, Federal Perkins Loans, Federal Direct Stafford Student Loans, the Federal Direct PLUS loan program, and the Federal Work-Study Program. To be considered for financial aid, a student must file the Free Application for Federal Student Aid (FAFSA) with the federal government as soon as possible after January 1 for the coming year. FAFSA results should be on file with the University Financial Aid Office prior to March 1 for the following academic year. Each applicant is assessed individually to determine the best combination of grant, work, scholarship, and loan amounts to meet the need of the student. The University awards more than $6 million in merit-based scholarships and grants annually. For more information, students should contact the Office of Financial Aid.

Faculty

The University employs 71 full-time faculty members. The full-time student–faculty ratio is 17:1. Part-time instructors in specialized areas are working professionals who bring current knowledge and expertise in their field to their classes. All classes are taught by faculty members, and department chairs serve as academic advisers to students in their major programs.

Student Government

Every full-time day student automatically becomes a member of the Student Government Association (SGA) upon registration and payment of the student activity fee. The main goals of the SGA are to stimulate active participation in all University functions, to establish and maintain effective channels of communication among members of the University community and the community at large, and to foster a mutual trust, encourage a spirit of cooperation, and initiate new endeavors. The SGA also supervises student clubs and organizations and oversees their finances. The SGA Executive Board serves as the channel of communication through which the views of the students on institutional policies reach the University administration.

Admission Requirements

Applicants for admission should ordinarily have completed, in an accredited high school, a minimum of 16 academic units, including 4 in English, 2 in a modern foreign language, 3 in mathematics, 2 in social science, 2 in science, and 3 in electives. The most successful candidates are in the upper half of their class, with at least a B average. The University requires SAT or ACT scores as part of the student's overall admissions file. Average SAT scores trend around 1340. A personal interview is strongly recommended but not required.

Rivier welcomes applications from qualified transfer candidates from accredited institutions, as well as applications from international students. Transfer students must forward transcripts of all previous college work and a high school transcript. International students must fulfill the requirements for general admission; they may also be required to submit Test of English as a Foreign Language (TOEFL) scores. Deferred admission may be granted to students who wish to postpone entrance for up to one year, provided they have not been enrolled full-time at another postsecondary institution.

Application and Information

Applications must be accompanied by an essay, SAT scores, one letter of recommendation, and a high school transcript. The School of Undergraduate Studies employs a system of rolling admission that allows qualified students to be admitted approximately one month after their application is completed. Transfers should apply by June 1 for fall admission and by December 1 for spring admission. Those applying for financial aid should observe the March 1 deadline. Interviews are arranged through the Admissions Office. Students may apply online at the University's website.

For an application or additional information, please contact:

Office of Undergraduate Admissions
Rivier University
420 South Main Street
Nashua, New Hampshire 03060
Phone: 603-897-8507
    800-44-RIVIER (toll-free)
Fax: 603-891-1799
E-mail: admissions@rivier.edu
Website: http://www.rivier.edu

Students enjoy Rivier's great location in the heart of New England—approximately an hour's drive from Boston, the mountains, and the seacoast.

ROBERT MORRIS UNIVERSITY
MOON TOWNSHIP, PENNSYLVANIA

The University

A private university in Pittsburgh's suburban hills, Robert Morris University (RMU) is set on a 230-acre former estate that is a short drive from the cultural and commercial opportunities of a major city. Founded in 1921, RMU offers more than sixty undergraduate programs and twenty graduate programs, including many online options, providing its 5,000 students academic excellence with a professional focus.

The University built its reputation in the business fields of accounting, finance, marketing, and management. It has grown to include programs in communications, information systems, engineering, mathematics, science, education, social sciences, and nursing. RMU uses a student engagement transcript to document internships, service-learning activities, study abroad, leadership roles, and other learning outside the classroom. This focus on engaged learning contributes to the 95 percent placement rate of graduates in careers or graduate school within a year of graduation.

RMU is a teaching-centered institution featuring small classes taught by professors and a student-faculty ratio of 15:1. The campus is growing, with new buildings for both the School of Business and the School of Communications and Information Systems that have opened since 2011, and a new nursing simulation center in the design stage. New residence halls accommodate a growing student population. More than 80 percent of freshmen live in campus housing.

Visiting international scholars and a variety of opportunities to study abroad—for a semester or just a few weeks—enrich students' global perspectives. Students can participate in any of nearly 100 clubs and organizations. The Student Life Office organizes dances, parties, movie screenings, comedy acts, health and wellness fairs, educational programs, and day trips. Business organizations, professional clubs, and honor societies provide students with career preparation opportunities.

The University's competitive athletics program fields twenty-three NCAA Division I teams, and the Colonials have won numerous titles and championships. The men's basketball team famously upset the reigning NCAA champion Kentucky Wildcats here in the Charles Sewall Center in the first round of the 2013 NIT. Coach John Banaszak, three-time Super Steeler, leads the football team at Joe Walton Stadium. The region's only Division I men's and women's ice hockey teams play at the RMU Island Sports Center, a 32-acre sports and recreation complex with two ice rinks, two multipurpose rinks, an indoor golf driving range, a miniature golf course, a pro shop, and a restaurant and banquet facility. Students can also participate in a number of club and intramural sports on campus.

Location

The 230-acre main campus is located in Moon Township, Pennsylvania, just 15 minutes from Pittsburgh International Airport and 17 miles from downtown Pittsburgh. The RMU Island Sports Center is 15 minutes from campus on Neville Island.

Majors and Degrees

Robert Morris University offers more than sixty undergraduate programs of study: accounting, actuarial science, advertising, biology, biomedical engineering, business, communication, competitive intelligence systems, computer information systems, corporate communications, cyber forensics, economics, elementary education (early childhood, midlevel, and special education concentrations), engineering, English, environmental science, finance, graphic design, health services administration, history and government, hospitality and tourism management, industrial engineering, information sciences, intelligence systems, journalism, management, manufacturing engineering, marketing, mathematics, mechanical engineering, media arts, nuclear medicine technology, nursing, organizational leadership, photography, prelaw, premedicine, predentistry, pre–chiropractic medicine, pre–osteopathic medicine, pre–veterinary medicine, professional communications/information systems, public relations, psychology, secondary education (biology, business/computer/information technology, communication, English, mathematics, and social studies concentrations), social science, sociology, software development, software engineering, special education, sport management, sport psychology, theater, TV/video production, web design, and web development.

Fully online bachelor's degree programs are available in economics, health services administration, hospitality and tourism, organizational leadership, professional and technical writing, and psychology.

The University offers five-year integrated bachelor's/master's degree programs, medical school affiliation, cooperative education programs, and an honors program.

Academic Programs

Robert Morris operates on a two-semester schedule with various summer sessions. A total of 126 credits are required for the bachelor's degree. Internship or co-op credits of 3 to 12 hours may be used toward degree requirements. The University participates in a cross-registration program with nine local colleges through the Pittsburgh Council on Higher Education consortium.

Academic Facilities

Learning resources include a traditional library with more than 137,000 bound volumes, 80 reference databases, and 600 periodical subscriptions.

The Academic Media Center, with full production facilities, provides students with opportunities to collaborate on projects in all areas of media, including television/video production, audio production, and photography.

State-of-the-art laboratory facilities support the engineering, mathematics, science, and nursing programs. The new business school facility features a simulated stock trading floor and videoconferencing center. The nursing school utilizes patient simulators. Students in media arts have new, well-equipped studio and display space.

Costs

Annual tuition for the 2013–14 year is a $24,460 flat rate, based on a 24- to 36-credit, two-semester schedule. Room and board fees were $9,986 based on double occupancy and the Patriot meal plan.

Financial Aid

Eighty-nine percent of RMU undergraduates receive some sort of financial aid, including scholarships, grants, loans, and work-study programs. Both need-based and achievement-based awards are available. All applicants must complete the admissions application, the Free Application for Federal Student Aid, and the grant forms from their own state.

Faculty

The University has more than 450 full- and part-time faculty members; 81 percent of full-time faculty members hold terminal degrees. The student-faculty ratio is 15:1 and the average class size is 24. Students may take advantage of the expertise offered by the faculty in academic advisement and counseling, as well as counseling from the staff at the Center for Student Success.

Student Government

The Student Government Association represents all student organizations, including fraternities and sororities. Members participate in the planning of all social and cultural events on campus.

Admission Requirements

First-time freshmen must submit an application for admission with a $30 application fee (waived for online applicants), official high school transcripts or GED credential, and official SAT or ACT scores. Preference is given to applicants with a minimum 3.0 high school GPA and a combined SAT score of 1000 or a composite ACT score of 22.

Transfer students who have earned credits from another regionally accredited institution must submit transcripts from all postsecondary institutions attended and must have a minimum 2.0 GPA. Students with less than 30 college credits must also submit high school transcripts or GED credential.

Interviews are not required for admission except for students interested in the engineering, elementary education, and nursing programs. Students are encouraged to arrange for a campus visit with an enrollment manager.

Robert Morris University is committed to a policy of nondiscrimination on the basis of race, sex, color, religion, national origin, or handicap.

Application and Information

Students are encouraged to submit applications in the fall of their senior year of high school. Official transcripts and counselor recommendations should accompany the application; there is a $30 application processing fee that is waived for online applicants.

Robert Morris uses a rolling admission system; students are considered for acceptance as soon as all application materials have been received and evaluated.

For additional information and application materials, students should contact:

Kellie Laurenzi
Dean of Admissions
Robert Morris University
6001 University Boulevard
Moon Township, Pennsylvania 15108
Phone: 800-762-0097 (toll-free)
Website: http://www.rmu.edu
　　　　　http://www.facebook.com/RMUpgh
　　　　　http://twitter.com/rmu
　　　　　http://www.youtube.com/RMUNewsTube

Robert Morris University's 230-acre campus in suburban Pittsburgh offers a scenic place to live, learn, and play.

ROBERTS WESLEYAN COLLEGE
ROCHESTER, NEW YORK

The College

Roberts Wesleyan College is characterized by its mission: scholarship, spiritual formation, and service. Roberts was founded in 1866 as the first Free Methodist academic institution in North America. Since then, the institution has continually adapted its programs to meet the current academic, professional, and personal needs of its students. The integration of broad-based intellectual thought with the Judeo-Christian heritage continues to be the motivation for Roberts Wesleyan's existence. The College fosters wholesome principles by setting standards for student life, requiring regular chapel attendance, and maintaining a perspective rich in values within the classroom.

The current enrollment is 1,752: 1,253 women and 499 men. Although students come primarily from New York State, thirty other states and thirty-three other countries are represented. The majority of students are between 18 and 25 years of age, but there is a growing population of married and older students. The traditional undergraduate population is primarily residential, with approximately 65 percent of students living on campus.

Roberts offers a broad selection of student activities. Student leaders work with the Associate Dean for Student Programming to plan numerous events each year, including social, cultural, and religious programs. The College's suburban Rochester location also allows students to take advantage of cultural and academic opportunities in the community. The College's intramural program complements the intercollegiate sports program. There are seven varsity sports for men: basketball, cross-country, golf, lacrosse, soccer, tennis, and track and field, and seven varsity sports for women: basketball, cross-country, lacrosse, soccer, tennis, track and field, and volleyball. Students may take advantage of the newly renovated Voller Athletic Center, which has a pool, four basketball courts, an indoor track, racquetball courts, a weight room, saunas, a student center, BT's Café, and a bookstore. Other College services available to students include the Career Services Office, academic advisement, counseling, and assistance from the Learning Center.

The College is a member of the Middle States Association of Colleges and Schools, the Association of Colleges and Universities of the State of New York, Rochester Area Colleges, the Association of Free Methodist Educational Institutions, the Council of Independent Colleges and Universities, and the Council for Christian Colleges & Universities. The programs in accounting, art, business, education, management, marketing, music, nursing, and social work are professionally accredited. The Department of Visual Arts is accredited by the National Association of Schools of Art and Design. The Department of Music & Performing Arts is accredited by the National Association of Schools of Music. The Department of Nursing is accredited by the Commission on Collegiate Nursing Education. The Department of Social Work is accredited by the Council on Social Work Education. The Department of Business and Management is accredited by the International Assembly for Collegiate Business Education. The Department of Teacher Education is accredited by New York State Regents Accreditation of Teacher Education.

In addition to undergraduate programs, Roberts offers the Master of Education, Master of Science in Health Administration, Master of Science in Health Information Administration, Master of Science in Nursing Education, Master of Science in Nursing Leadership and Administration, Master of Science in School Counseling, Master of Science in School Psychology, Master of Science in Strategic Leadership, Master of Science in Strategic Marketing, and Master of Social Work degree programs. Northeastern Seminary at Roberts Wesleyan College offers the Master of Arts in Theological Studies, Master of Divinity, Master of Divinity/Master of Social Work (with Roberts), and Doctor of Ministry degree programs.

Location

Roberts Wesleyan College is located 8 miles southwest of Rochester, New York, in the suburb of North Chili. Rochester, with a metropolitan-area population of more than 1 million, is a thriving cultural and corporate area. Eastman School of Music, the Rochester Philharmonic Orchestra, and several leading corporations, such as Eastman Kodak, Xerox, Paychex, Bausch & Lomb, and PAETEC are based there.

The College seeks a strong relationship with the community, and the resulting internships and opportunities for practical work are particularly advantageous for Roberts students. Students and graduates benefit from the employment opportunities that result from Rochester's economy. Lake Ontario, Niagara Falls, Watkins Glen, Letchworth Park, and the Finger Lakes are all nearby.

Majors and Degrees

Baccalaureate degrees are offered in accounting and information management, adolescence and special education (biology, chemistry, English, mathematics, physics, social studies, and Spanish), art–graphic design, art—studio art, art—time-based media, biblical studies, biochemistry, biology, biology with concentration in medical technology, business administration, chemistry, childhood and special education (elementary education), communication, comprehensive science, comprehensive social studies, computer science, criminal justice, cross-disciplinary studies, early childhood and special education, economic crime investigation, elementary education (childhood and special education), engineering (with RIT, RPI, or Clarkson), English, forensic science, health administration, history, humanities, information systems management, international business, liberal arts, management and social entrepreneurship, marketing, mathematics, ministry, music, music education, music performance (instrument, piano, and voice), nursing, organizational management, pharmacy (with University at Buffalo), physical education, physics, psychology, religion/philosophy, secondary education (adolescence education), social work, Spanish, and special education and childhood education (elementary education).

A 3-2 program in engineering is offered in cooperation with Clarkson University, Rensselaer Polytechnic Institute (RPI), and Rochester Institute of Technology (RIT). The program leads to a B.S. in mathematics, chemistry, or physics from Roberts Wesleyan College and a B.S. in engineering from Clarkson, RPI, or RIT. A B.S./M.S. program is also available with RIT.

Secondary (grades 5–12) teaching certification may be earned in biology, chemistry, English, mathematics, physics, social studies, and Spanish. Preprofessional programs include dentistry, law, medicine, pharmacy, physical therapy, and veterinary medicine. Other areas of preparation include library science and medical technology.

Academic Programs

Roberts endeavors to involve each student in learning experiences that promote commitment to Christian stewardship and service to society. Approximately 45 semester hours of core courses are required of each baccalaureate degree candidate. These liberal arts survey courses introduce four main fields of knowledge: biological science, physical science, and mathematics; history and the behavioral sciences; language, literature, and the fine arts; and biblical studies and philosophy. A minimum of 124 semester hours is required for graduation with a baccalaureate degree, including a minimum of 30 to 81 semester hours within the student's major discipline.

Many academic programs at Roberts Wesleyan include internships or practical work experiences. Independent study and cross-cultural study opportunities are also available. Students may receive credit through the Advanced Placement Program, the International Baccalaureate Program, or the College-Level Examination Program. The Learning Center provides assistance for students possessing exceptional skills or a deficiency in any area.

The College calendar consists of two 15-week semesters, September to December and January to May, and three sessions in the summer.

Off-Campus Programs

Various off-campus opportunities exist for which credit is awarded. These include the Appalachian Semester in Kentucky, Focus on the Family Institute in Colorado, Spanish language studies at the University of Murcia in Spain or the Instituto Espanol Murallas de Avila, EDUVenture in Irian Jaya, Jamaica Theological Seminary Semester, and a semester or full year of study at Richmond College in London, England. Under the direction of a Roberts professor, students may also participate in a short-term exchange study program with Osaka Christian College and Seminary in Osaka, Japan. There are also opportunities for off-campus experiences through the Council for Christian Colleges & Universities. These include the American Studies Program, Australia Studies Centre, China Studies Program, Contemporary Music Center, India Studies Program, Latin American Studies Program, Los Angeles Film Studies Center, Middle East Studies Program, Oxford Summer Programme, Uganda Studies Program, and Washington Journalism Center. The January Experience Program offers transcultural and enrichment courses in this country or abroad. In addition, through Robert's membership in the Rochester Area Colleges consortium, students may cross-register to take courses at other member institutions.

Academic Facilities

The 43,000-square-foot B. Thomas Golisano Library is a LEED-certified building with a geothermal heating and cooling system. The Golisano Library includes a 24-hour computer lab and study café, two smart classrooms for bibliographic instruction (including forty computer stations), two fireplaces for comfortable study areas, 375 student stations, and a graduate study room. The library holds 132,000 volumes (with room for 300,000), 1,100 periodicals, more than 100 online databases (most with full text, including JSTOR), Internet access, and 171,000 microforms, recordings, and filmstrips. Also included in the library are the Learning Center, the Historical Center, and Archives. Through its participation in the Rochester Regional Research Library Council, the library provides access to extensive interlibrary loan resources.

Well-equipped science laboratories, a lecture auditorium, and computer laboratories connected to the campus network are included in the Merlin G. Smith Science Center. The new Hastings Center for Academics houses the undergraduate departments of business and teacher education. Other facilities include the music studios, practice rooms, and recital auditorium of Cox Hall; the newly renovated Carpenter Hall which includes classrooms, studios and offices for the social science, social work and visual arts departments; the Cultural Life Center, which houses Shewan Recital Hall, Hale Auditorium, and Davison Art Gallery; the Rinker Community Service Center; and the soccer stadium and Mondo track. Wireless Internet access is available throughout campus.

Costs

Tuition for full-time study for the 2013–14 academic year is $26,352 but varies if a student's course load is fewer than 12 or more than 18 credit hours. There are additional fees for music and laboratory courses. Room and board is $9,630; miscellaneous fees are $1,012. Book costs and personal expenses vary with individual needs.

Financial Aid

Roberts Wesleyan College offers a complete financial aid program, consisting of grants, scholarships, loans, and employment. Filing the Free Application for Federal Student Aid (FAFSA) is a prerequisite for determining eligibility for most financial aid programs. Sources of aid include Federal Pell Grants, Federal Supplemental Educational Opportunity Grants, Federal Perkins Loans, and Federal Stafford Student Loans; New York State Tuition Assistance Program awards; and institutional resources. Numerous on-campus employment opportunities are available. Institutional aid is also available in recognition of academic, athletic, artistic, and musical achievement. More than 98 percent of the student body receives financial aid each year. Currently, Roberts is ranked as a 2013 top-tier Northern master's university by *U.S. News & World Report* and listed by the Princeton Review as one of 2013's Best Northern Colleges. Roberts is also on the 2012–13 Christian Colleges of Distinction list.

Faculty

The primary concern of the faculty at Roberts Wesleyan College is to provide a high-quality educational experience. Sixty-six percent of the professors hold the doctoral or terminal degree, and all are well respected within their specific discipline. The 92 full-time and 167 part-time faculty members are committed to Christian higher education and are genuinely interested in each student's development. A 14:1 student-faculty ratio allows for individualized attention, and most professors go beyond teaching and advising to participate in campus activities.

Student Government

All students belong to the Student Association and have the freedom to express their opinions to the staff, faculty, and administration. There are also elected senators and officers, under the direction of the Office of Student Development, who act as liaisons between the student body and administration in areas concerning academics and student activities.

Admission Requirements

Because the type of student a college enrolls significantly determines the personality of the institution, Roberts Wesleyan seeks students whose personal lives are characterized by honesty, integrity, and devotion to high moral and ethical standards. Admission consideration is given to applicants who rank in the upper third of their graduating class and have earned a minimum of 12 academic units of high school credit, with no fewer than 4 units in English, 2 units in algebra (or 1 in algebra and 1 in geometry), and 1 unit in biology, chemistry, or physics. Three years each of social studies, a foreign language, and science are strongly recommended. Further preparation in mathematics and science is required of applicants who wish to enter degree programs in nursing, mathematics, or science. Scores on the SAT or ACT and a formal recommendation are required. Special talents are considered an asset for applicants but are not required. An on-campus admission interview is strongly recommended. In admitting students, the College does not discriminate on the basis of race, age, color, sex, handicap, creed, or national or ethnic origin. Children of alumni and staff members are considered on the same basis as other applicants.

Transfer students have the same admission requirements as first-time students and must also have transcripts forwarded to the College from all institutions they have attended. Credit is usually accepted from regionally accredited institutions for any course in which a grade of C– or above has been earned if the course parallels a course given at Roberts.

Application and Information

Applicants should submit an application form online, a completed recommendation form, SAT or ACT scores, and transcripts from all schools previously attended. Art students should prepare a portfolio for review by the art faculty, and music students should schedule an audition with the Music Department. Students are encouraged to submit an application prior to the February 1 priority deadline. Admission decisions are made on a rolling basis, and students are notified of the admission decision as soon as all of their credentials have been received and evaluated.

For more information, students should contact:

Office of Admissions
Roberts Wesleyan College
2301 Westside Drive
Rochester, New York 14624-1997
United States
Phone: 585-594-6400
      800-777-4RWC (toll-free)
Fax: 585-594-6371
E-mail: admissions@roberts.edu
Website: http://www.roberts.edu

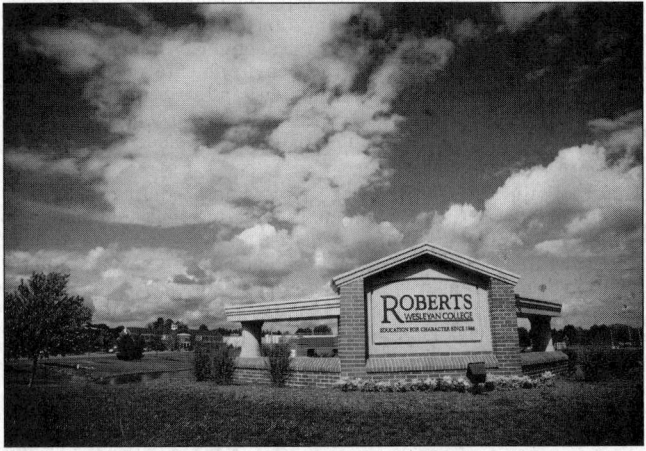

Located just outside of Rochester, New York—considered one of America's most livable cities—Roberts is a vibrant private Christian institution with a tradition of excellence and educating for character since 1966.

ROCHESTER INSTITUTE OF TECHNOLOGY
ROCHESTER, NEW YORK

R·I·T

The Institute

Rochester Institute of Technology (RIT) is one of the world's leading career-oriented, technological universities. RIT offers more than ninety undergraduate programs in areas such as engineering, computing, information technology, engineering technology, business, hospitality, science, art, design, photography, biomedical sciences, game design and development, and the liberal arts including psychology, advertising and public relations, and public policy. Students may choose from more than 100 different minors to develop personal and professional interests that complement their academic program. RIT is a world leader in experiential education, which is integrated into many programs through cooperative education, internships, study abroad, and undergraduate research. As home to the National Technical Institute for the Deaf (NTID), RIT is a leader in providing access services for deaf and hard-of-hearing students. RIT enrolls students from every state and more than 100 countries.

Close to 70 percent of RIT's approximately 12,200 full-time undergraduate students live on the campus in residence halls or campus apartments.

Because RIT's student body is so diverse, there are many different activities, clubs, organizations, and sports in which students participate. Each year, RIT's more than 200 student organizations sponsor over 1,300 on-campus activities. RIT offers twenty-three varsity sports, including Division I men's and women's hockey. Recreational facilities are exceptional and include an ice rink, an aquatics center, a field house with an indoor track, and fitness facilities.

Location

The greater Rochester area has a population of about 800,000. Per-capita income is among the highest in the nation for metropolitan centers. The area's many internationally known industries employ a high proportion of scientists, technologists, and skilled workers. Rochester's industries have always been closely associated with RIT's programs and progress. Rochester is also a hub for higher education with twelve colleges and universities in the area.

Majors and Degrees

The College of Applied Science and Technology offers the Bachelor of Science (B.S.) degree in civil engineering technology, computer engineering technology, electrical engineering technology, electrical/mechanical engineering technology, manufacturing engineering technology, and mechanical engineering technology. It also grants the Bachelor of Science in environmental sustainability, health and safety, international hospitality and service management, and packaging science. An undeclared option allowing freshmen to delay selecting a major for up to a year is available in the School of Engineering Technology.

The E. Philip Saunders College of Business offers the B.S. in accounting, finance, new media marketing, international business, management, management information systems, and marketing. An accelerated B.S./M.B.A. option is available, as are several minors, including entrepreneurship and digital business. An undeclared option allowing freshmen to delay the selection of their major for up to one year is available.

The B. Thomas Golisano College of Computing and Information Sciences offers the B.S. in computer science, game design and development, information technology, information security and forensics, medical informatics, networking and systems administration, new media interactive development, and software engineering. The college also offers a computing exploration option for undeclared freshman students.

The Kate Gleason College of Engineering grants the B.S. in biomedical engineering, chemical engineering, computer engineering, electrical engineering, industrial and systems engineering, mechanical engineering, and microelectronic engineering. Degree options in aerospace, automotive, bioengineering, biomedical, energy and environment, ergonomics, information systems, manufacturing, and software engineering are also offered within the college. Accelerated B.S./M.S. options are available. The Engineering Exploration Program, which allows freshmen to delay the selection of their major for up to one year, is available.

The College of Health Sciences and Technology offers B.S. programs in biomedical sciences, diagnostic medical sonography, nutrition management, and a five-year physician assistant B.S./M.S. program.

The College of Imaging Arts and Sciences offers the Bachelor of Fine Arts in advertising photography; ceramics and ceramic sculpture, digital cinema, film and animation, fine art photography, fine arts studio, glass, graphic design, illustration, industrial design, interior design, medical illustration, metals and jewelry design, new media design and imaging, photojournalism, 3-D digital graphics, visual media, and woodworking. The college also offers B.S. programs in biomedical photographic communications, digital media, graphic media, imaging and photographic technology, and new media/publishing. An undeclared option allowing freshmen to delay the selection of their major for up to one year is available in the School of Art, the School of Design, and the School for American Crafts.

The College of Liberal Arts offers B.S. programs in advertising and public relations, communication, criminal justice, economics, journalism, international and global studies, museum studies, philosophy, psychology, public policy, and sociology and anthropology. The Liberal Arts Exploration Program is designed to help undecided students formulate education and career plans.

The College of Science offers B.S. programs in applied mathematics, applied statistics, biology, biochemistry, bioinformatics, biotechnology and molecular bioscience, chemistry, computational mathematics, environmental science, imaging science, physics, and polymer chemistry. Special options are available in premedical studies (medicine, dentistry, veterinary medicine). Minors are available in astronomy, exercise science, imaging science, mathematics, physics, and statistics. Accelerated B.S./M.S. and B.S./M.B.A. programs are available. General Science Exploration allows freshmen to delay the selection of their major for up to one year.

Home of the National Technical Institute for the Deaf, RIT is a leader in providing educational opportunities and access services for deaf and hard-of-hearing students. NTID awards associate degree programs and offers pre-baccalaureate studies for deaf and hard-of-hearing students. The associate degree programs prepare students for immediate employment after graduation or transfer into one of RIT's bachelor's degree programs. The pre-baccalaureate studies program prepares students, who may not qualify initially, for entry into RIT's bachelor's degree programs. Nearly 500 of the 1,300 deaf and hard-of-hearing students at RIT are enrolled in bachelor's degree programs in the other eight colleges.

Academic Programs

Most students entering as freshmen enroll directly in the college and academic program of their choice. Options for undeclared students are offered by most colleges. A University Studies program is available for entering freshmen who wish to explore programs in two or more colleges. Undergraduates may choose from more than 100 different minors. Double-majors and accelerated dual-degree (combined bachelor's/masters) options are available. The RIT honors program admits approximately 150 freshmen annually. Air Force and Army ROTC programs are available on the campus. A Naval ROTC program is offered jointly with the University of Rochester.

Every academic program at RIT offers some form of experiential education opportunity, including cooperative education, internships, study abroad, undergraduate research, and industry-sponsored projects. Notable among these programs is RIT's world-renowned cooperative education program (co-op). The College of Applied Science and Technology, the E. Philip Saunders College of Business, the B. Thomas Golisano College of Computing and Information

Sciences, and the Kate Gleason College of Engineering all require co-op for undergraduate students. It is available on an optional basis in other RIT colleges. Co-op students alternate periods of full-time study with periods of full-time paid work experience in business and industry directly related to their field of study and career interests. Last year more than 3,500 students completed co-op assignments with nearly 2,000 employers, earning collectively in excess of $33 million.

Off-Campus Programs

RIT has four international branch campuses. The American College of Management and Technology is located in Dubrovnik and Zagreb, Croatia and offers undergraduate degree programs in hospitality and service management, information technology, and international business. The American University of Kosovo in Pristina provides career-oriented programs that foster links between the university, industry, and government in support of workforce development. RIT Dubai offers graduate and undergraduate programs in business, engineering, service leadership, and information sciences. RIT offers a growing study-abroad program.

Academic Facilities

Excellent facilities add to the quality of academic life. Students have access to a laser-optics laboratory, an observatory, more than 100 color and black-and-white photography darkrooms, electronic prepress and publishing equipment, ceramic kilns, glass furnaces, a blacksmithing area, a student-operated restaurant, computer graphics and robotic labs, and some of the most up-to-date microelectronic, telecommunications, and computer engineering facilities in the U.S. RIT's Wallace Library is a true multimedia learning center. Its collections are exceptionally extensive in the areas of art and design, education for the deaf, photography, and printing.

RIT is a leader in academic computing, and students use state-of-the-art computer equipment regardless of their major. Central computer systems can be accessed via a high-speed data network connecting the library, academic facilities, residence hall rooms, and on-campus apartments. There are more than sixty locations campuswide, with wireless networking connectivity utilizing 802.11b technology. The RIT campus network is served by two OC3 connections, each operating at a data rate of 155 Mbps, and one T3 connection operating at 45 Mbps. RIT is among a select group of institutions with access to the Internet2 research network, a collaborative research and development effort led by more than 170 U.S. universities working in partnership with industry and government.

Costs

For 2012–13, undergraduate tuition for the academic year (three academic quarters) was $32,784. Fees, including the activities and health fees, are $474. Room and board (twenty meals per week) cost $10,800.

Financial Aid

Approximately 77 percent of RIT's full-time undergraduates receive some form of financial aid that includes RIT scholarships, alumni or industry-supported scholarships, and state and federal government grants. A variety of loans and part-time work positions are available. The FAFSA must be submitted by March 1. Giving full recognition to scholarship apart from financial need, RIT awards a number of academic scholarships based on grades, test scores, and activities. Freshmen applying by February 1 and transfers applying by April 1 are considered for these scholarships.

Faculty

There are 966 full-time faculty members, 509 part-time faculty members, and an administrative and supporting staff of more than 1,800. Approximately 70 percent of the faculty members have earned a Ph.D. or the terminal degree in their field.

Student Government

The Student Government is the representative body for students. It works with RIT administration, faculty, and staff members to communicate the needs and desires of the student body and to communicate decisions of the administration to students. Fraternity and sorority members, off-campus and hearing-impaired students, and students from minority groups elect special representative bodies. All full-time and part-time undergraduate and graduate students are represented in Student Government.

Admission Requirements

Admission to RIT is competitive and varies from selective to highly selective depending on the desired program of study. The major factors determining freshman admission are strength of academic program, high school performance, and ACT or SAT test results. College performance is the main factor for transfer candidates. Students applying for many programs in art and design must submit a portfolio as part of the application process.

RIT promotes and values diversity and admits qualified men and women of any race, color, national or ethnic origin, religion, sexual orientation, gender identity, gender expression, or marital status. RIT does not discriminate on the basis of handicap in the recruitment or admission of students or in the operation of any of its programs or activities, as specified by federal laws and regulations.

Application and Information

An application, a nonrefundable processing fee of $60, official transcripts of all secondary school or college records, and SAT or ACT scores (for prospective freshmen) should be forwarded to RIT. Freshman applicants who provide all required materials for fall entry by February 1 receive admission notification by March 15. Prospective freshmen who apply after February 1 are considered on a space-available basis; all transfer students are notified of the admission decision on a rolling basis four to six weeks after their applications are complete. A binding early decision plan is offered to prospective freshmen who have completed applications and credentials filed by December 1 to receive notification by January 15.

For application forms, students should contact:

Director of Undergraduate Admissions
Rochester Institute of Technology
60 Lomb Memorial Drive
Rochester, New York 14623-5604
Phone: 585-475-6631
Fax: 585-475-7424
E-mail: admissions@rit.edu
Website: http://www.rit.edu
　　　　http://www.facebook.com/RITfb
　　　　http://twitter.com/RITAdmissions

A view of the campus.

ST. BONAVENTURE UNIVERSITY
ST. BONAVENTURE, NEW YORK

The University

St. Bonaventure University provides a values-based education with individual attention from professors, a beautiful residential setting, and a friendly, close-knit atmosphere. Of the 2,400 students enrolled, 1,900 are undergraduates. More than 74 percent of the undergraduates are full-time residents. Complementing St. Bonaventure's traditions are innovative degree programs, computerized career placement aids, comprehensive student life activities, and modern academic facilities. Among major campus events during the academic year are concerts and coffeehouse acts, indoor and outdoor recreational programs, current and classic film offerings, and dramatic and musical plays. Aspiring writers and broadcasters from all academic majors—Bonaventure has produced 5 Pulitzer Prize winners—find challenging and plentiful opportunities working with one of the four University media: WSBU-88.3 FM-The Buzz, the nationally ranked campus radio station; *The Bona Venture,* the award-winning weekly newspaper; *The Bonadieu,* the yearbook; and *The Laurel,* the nation's oldest student literary publication, which marked its 114th anniversary in 2013. Other organizations on campus include academic fraternities, academic honor societies, a variety of club and intramural sports, and arts organizations that include choral, instrumental, dance, and drama ensembles. The Thomas Merton Ministry Center is open 24 hours a day and aims to foster a community of friendship and mutual service. Many students take the opportunity to serve as Bona Buddies to area children or senior citizens; help with the national award–winning soup kitchen The Warming House; or volunteer in one of many service organizations, including SIFE and BonaResponds, one of the most active collegiate disaster relief organizations in the nation. Volunteer opportunities include immersion experiences and service opportunities with the poor, both in the U.S. and abroad.

St. Bonaventure University students enjoy two athletic facilities: the $6.2-million Richter Center, which is open 24 hours a day, features three basketball courts, a running/walking track, racquetball/squash/wallyball courts, an aerobics room, a recreational area for roller hockey, a weight room, a cardiovascular fitness room, locker rooms, an equipment check-out, a reception area, and a climbing wall; and the Reilly Center, housing a 5,500-seat sports arena, swimming pool, and weight room. Also available are outdoor tennis and basketball courts and a nine-hole golf course. NCAA Division I athletics for men are baseball, basketball, cross-country, golf, soccer, swimming, and tennis. Division I competition for women includes basketball, cross-country, lacrosse, soccer, softball, swimming, and tennis. St. Bonaventure is a member of the Atlantic 10 conference, and both basketball teams made their NCAA tournaments in 2012.

In addition to its undergraduate programs, St. Bonaventure offers the Master of Arts degree in English and in Franciscan studies (summers only). A Master of Science in Education program includes adolescence education, counselor education, differentiated instruction, educational leadership, literacy, school building leader, and school district leader. A Master of Business Administration program in integrated marketing communications and a Master of Arts program in strategic leadership are also offered.

Location

St. Bonaventure is located on Route 417 between Olean, a city of approximately 17,000 residents, and Allegany, a village with about 2,000 residents. Shops, restaurants, and movie theaters are all within walking distance. The campus is spread over 500 acres in a valley surrounded by the Allegheny Mountains.

The free Bona Bus connects the campus with Olean and Allegany, carrying students to and from the area attractions. The region around St. Bonaventure provides a beautiful setting for many outdoor activities. Holiday Valley, a renowned ski resort, is just 20 miles away, and nearby Allegany State Park offers excellent facilities for swimming, boating, and hiking. St. Bonaventure is accessible by car, bus, and commercial air transportation, with Buffalo/Niagara International the nearest major airport.

Majors and Degrees

St. Bonaventure University grants the Bachelor of Arts degree with majors in art, art history, classical languages, English, gerontology, history, interdisciplinary studies, international studies, journalism and mass communication, strategic communication and digital media, modern languages (French and Spanish), music, philosophy, political science, psychology, sociology, theater, theology, and women's studies. The Bachelor of Science is granted with majors in biochemistry, bioinformatics, biology, chemistry, childhood studies, computer science, early childhood education, economics, elementary/special education (dual certification), environmental science, interdisciplinary studies, mathematics, physical education, physics, psychology, and sport studies. The Bachelor of Business Administration is granted with majors in accounting, finance, management sciences, and marketing. St. Bonaventure's dual-admission/combined-degree programs offer unique opportunities for students pursuing careers in medicine, dentistry, pharmacy, and physical therapy.

Academic Programs

Students in all majors begin their intellectual journey in Clare College, St. Bonaventure's nationally acclaimed core curriculum, which offers a values-based education grounded in the vision of St. Francis and St. Bonaventure.

A candidate for a bachelor's degree must complete at least 120 credit hours, with a cumulative index of 2.0 or better in the major field and the overall program. A pass/fail grade option, available to all upperclass students, may be elected for one course per semester, but not for courses in a student's major field.

Advanced credit is granted for grades of C or better on either the College Proficiency Examination or the College-Level Examination Program (CLEP) tests. Advanced placement is granted on the basis of scores obtained on the College Board's Advanced Placement (AP) examinations.

Men and women may also elect to participate in the University's Army ROTC program, MacArthur Award winner as best small unit in the nation in 1998.

Off-Campus Programs

Through St. Bonaventure's membership in the College Consortium for International Studies (CCIS), St. Bonaventure students have access to six continents. More than sixty semester-long international study programs, including St. Bonaventure–sponsored study in Italy, Spain, Ireland, and Australia, are available to students in good academic standing in their junior year. Faculty-directed, short-term opportunities include a three-week intersession in China, the Francis E. Kelly Oxford summer program, and a three-week travel study program to Mexico. For further information, students should contact the Office of International Studies. Fieldwork or internships are available in several major programs.

Academic Facilities

Friedsam Memorial Library houses more than 250,000 volumes and includes a tri-level resource center with a curriculum center, the University archives, and digital media and conferencing centers, as well as world-class special collections. An automated online card catalog greatly improves research capabilities.

The William F. Walsh Science Center opened in 2008 and doubled the space for science studies. It houses state-of-the-art computer science, laboratory and classroom space, biology labs, organic and general chemistry labs, a Natural World lab, a 150-seat indoor amphitheater, and faculty offices integrated with lab space for better student-teacher accessibility. It is attached to historic De La Roche Hall, which received a major face-lift in 2008.

The John J. Murphy Professional Building is home to the Russell J. Jandoli School of Journalism and Mass Communication. The Bob Koop Broadcast Journalism Laboratory features a television studio with an anchor desk, digital and videotape editing bays, while a remote TV production studio allows for live broadcasting of athletic events. A fiberoptic network connects microcomputers in academic and administrative areas. There are seven labs for student use with more than 100 Macintosh systems. St. Bonaventure students also have wireless Internet access across campus. The state-of-the-art Swan Business Center is slated to open in August 2013 and will house the School of Business.

An annex to Plassmann Hall houses computer-adaptable education classrooms, seminar rooms, and offices for the education faculty. An observatory allows students access to three compact telescopes, two 8-inch Celestron telescopes, and one 11-inch Schmidt-Cassegrain telescope, and a heated classroom.

The Regina A. Quick Center for the Arts provides acoustically designed classroom space for music courses and painting and drawing studios. The center also includes a musical instrument digital interface lab, a 325-seat theater, and an atrium that is often used for receptions and impromptu musical performances. The F. Donald Kenney Museum and Art Study Wing includes four climate-controlled galleries offering nationally acclaimed traveling exhibits, works from the University's permanent collections, and student exhibits.

Historic Hickey Dining Hall received a spectacular makeover in 2006, and a 5,500-square-foot coffee café and gourmet deli opened in spring 2007. Some residence halls were overhauled in 2006, while the new science center and a $2.2-million library addition to house the University's rare books collection opened in 2008.

Costs

For 2012–13, the annual costs were $28,727 for tuition and $965 for fees. Room and meal plans averaged $10,104 per year.

Financial Aid

Students who qualify for financial aid normally receive a package consisting of a combination of scholarships, grants, loans, and work-study awards. An average financial aid package for an incoming freshman is more than $21,000. Athletic grants-in-aid are available for men in baseball, basketball, golf, soccer, swimming, and tennis; and for women in basketball, lacrosse, soccer, softball, swimming, and tennis. Music scholarships are also available. Students must file the Free Application for Federal Student Aid (FAFSA) to be considered for financial assistance. For more complete details, a student should contact the director of financial aid at the University.

Faculty

Like the student body, the 155 full-time and 67 part-time faculty members at St. Bonaventure come from a wide range of geographic, ethnic, and religious backgrounds. The student-faculty ratio of 13:1 allows faculty members the time to help each student to understand different modes of thinking, develop as a person, and lay a foundation for lifelong learning. Eighty-four percent of the faculty members hold the terminal degree in their

field. Friars, many of whom teach and live on campus, add to the unique atmosphere of St. Bonaventure.

Student Government

Life at St. Bonaventure is centered on the residence halls, and the foundation of student government begins in the dormitories with the Residence Hall Councils. The elected council members determine the norms by which the residents are guided in their daily lives. The Student Government, whose members are elected from the student body, serves as the general student-governing unit, and its members serve on every major University board and committee.

Admission Requirements

St. Bonaventure University welcomes applications for admission from all serious candidates from a variety of backgrounds. St. Bonaventure University provides equal opportunity without regard to race, creed, color, gender, age, national or ethnic origin, marital status, veteran status, or disability in admission, employment, and in all of its educational programs and activities. Applicants, who are welcome to apply online, must show evidence of academic achievement to be selected for admission. The criteria used in making admission decisions, in order of importance, are quality of the high school curriculum, grade point average in college-preparatory courses, ACT (preferred) or SAT scores, class rank, recommendations from high school teachers and counselors, and extracurricular activities.

Application and Information

For more information about St. Bonaventure University, prospective students should contact:

Office of Admission
St. Bonaventure University
P.O. Box D
St. Bonaventure, New York 14778
Phone: 716-375-2400
      800-462-5050 (toll-free)
E-mail: admissions@sbu.edu
Website: http://www.sbu.edu

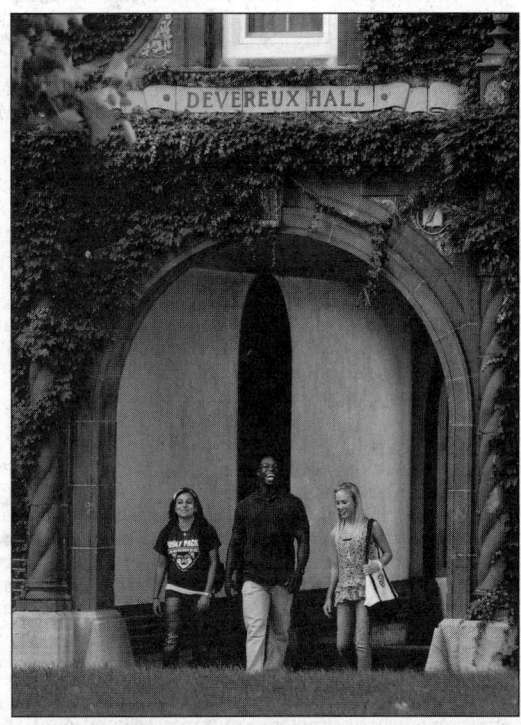

Built in 1928 and renovated in 1999, Devereux Hall is an example of the beautiful Florentine architecture found at St. Bonaventure University.

SAINT FRANCIS UNIVERSITY
LORETTO, PENNSYLVANIA

SAINT FRANCIS
UNIVERSITY
FOUNDED 1847

The University

Saint Francis University is a small, coeducational, liberal arts university. The University was founded in 1847 and conducted under the tradition of the Franciscan Friars of the Third Order Regular. The University is concerned with the development of each student for the world of today. For more than 150 years, the University's philosophy of education and student life has continued to emphasize two values: instruction of high quality and respect for the student as an individual. The University believes that a liberal arts education, encompassing a major field of study, is the soundest kind of preparation a student can have for a productive life. In recent years, Saint Francis University has garnered recognition for advances in study abroad and outreach in health care. In addition, *U.S. News & World Report* has named Saint Francis as a Best Value institution. The University is accredited by the Middle States Association of Colleges and Schools. Departmental accreditations include the Accreditation Review Commission on Education for the Physician Assistant, Inc., Commission on Collegiate Nursing Education, Council on Social Work Education, and others. A complete list of accreditations may be found in the University catalog.

Students at Saint Francis University can find a number of outlets for their talents, interests, and abilities. Departmental clubs; volunteer organizations; social, business, and service fraternities; social sororities; and a service sorority are part of campus life. Athletics have played a major role in the University's history, and the athletics program offers twenty-two NCAA Division I sports for men and women as well as intramural sports. All athletic teams compete in the Northeast Conference. The Student Activities Organization sponsors an impressive program of lectures, films, and concerts. The Southern Alleghenies Museum of Art, separately chartered, is located on the campus as well.

The full-time undergraduate enrollment is 726 men and 916 women; the University as a whole enrolls 2,433 students. Saint Francis University offers Associate of Science degrees in business administration, and religious education. On the graduate level, Saint Francis grants a Master of Arts degree in human resource management and industrial relations. The University also offers the Master of Business Administration, Master of Education, Master of Health Science, Master of Medical Science, Master of Physician Assistant Science, and Master of Science in Occupational Therapy degrees. A doctoral degree in physical therapy is also available.

Location

Saint Francis University is situated on 600 acres in the heart of the Allegheny Mountains. The campus is located in the borough of Loretto, which has a population of approximately 1,400. The campus is 6 miles from the county seat of Ebensburg, which has a population of 4,000. The cities of Johnstown and Altoona are within 25 miles of Loretto and have populations of 35,000 and 55,000, respectively. The University is a 90-minute drive east of Pittsburgh.

Majors and Degrees

Saint Francis University grants the Bachelor of Arts degree and offers majors in American studies, biology, computer science, engineering (3-2 program), English, English/communications, history, mathematics, philosophy, political science, psychology, public administration/government service, religious studies, and sociology. The Bachelor of Science degree is also granted, with majors in accounting, biology, chemistry, computer science, economics and finance, elementary education/special education, environmental engineering, environmental management (3-2 program), environmental studies (interdisciplinary), exercise physiology, management information systems, marketing, mathematics, medical technology, nursing, occupational therapy (five-year master's), pharmacy (2+3 or 2+4), physical therapy (six-year doctoral degree), physician assistant science (five-year master's), podiatric science, psychology, public administration/government service, public health, social work, and sociology.

Areas of pre-professional study include chiropractic studies, dentistry, engineering (3-2 program), law, medicine, optometry, pharmacy, podiatry, and veterinary medicine. Areas of concentration within majors include bioinformatics, computer science, criminal justice, environmental science, forensics, gaming/new media design and production, healthcare management, information technology and security, international studies, marine education, molecular biology, political communications, public management, and public relations. The University also grants secondary education certification in the areas of biology, chemistry, English, general science, history, mathematics, and social studies. A 3-2 cooperative program with Duke University in forestry and environmental management, a 3+4 accelerated program in primary care, a 2+3 accelerated program and a 3+3 program in pharmacy with Lake Erie College of Osteopathic Medicine, and a 3+4 accelerated program leading to the baccalaureate and Doctor of Dental Medicine degrees with Temple University are also offered.

It is possible for students to major in one area and minor in another or to have a double major. A self-designed major program is available as well. The University offers an honors program to challenge intellectually ambitious students from all disciplines. While pursuing their major field of study, students enroll in the full four-year curriculum, which allows in-depth, creative study in a variety of subject areas.

A continuing education program provides credit and noncredit courses on campus, online, and in the communities surrounding Loretto. The Office of Adult Degree and Continuing Studies offers a variety of academic programs ranging from certificate programs to bachelor's degree programs. Areas of study include business, computer systems management, health sciences, and religious studies.

Academic Programs

The program of study leading to a bachelor's degree is usually completed in eight semesters. To qualify for graduation, a student must follow a program of study approved by the Office of the Provost that totals at least 128 credits distributed among liberal arts courses, major requirements, collateral requirements, and general electives. All students, regardless of major, are required to complete the University's general education program of 58 credits.

The academic calendar is divided into two semesters and three summer sessions.

Electronic capabilities at Saint Francis University enable students to access library holdings and communicate with professors, fellow students, and the world through the use of personal computers via e-mail and the Internet. Every classroom and residence hall room is wired for Internet access or can be accessed through the wireless network. The University has several classrooms equipped with state-of-the-art equipment that allows videoconferencing. All students receive a laptop computer as part of their tuition.

Off-Campus Programs

Students at Saint Francis University may, with permission of the University's administration, spend their junior year of study abroad or may earn credit for participation in summer programs conducted in Canada, France, Germany, Spain, and other countries by accredited American colleges and universities.

Students are encouraged to take advantage of the University's study abroad facility in Ambialet, France. The Semester in France program offers study for students within any major for the same tuition costs as studying on campus.

A number of departments offer students the opportunity for off-campus study. For some majors, such as nursing, occupational therapy, physical therapy, physician assistant science, education, medical technology, and social work, off-campus study is required; in all other majors, an internship is available as an elective. Such an internship can be a meaningful experience and can significantly enhance a student's career preparation.

Academic Facilities

In fall 2013 the University's School of Science is slated to begin operations in the new 70,000-square-foot-Science Center. This center, with its state-of-the-art laboratories and research facilities, will be a tremendous complement to Saint Francis' already high-quality instruction and will serve as the campus' flagship facility for science and technology programs. The DiSepio Institute for Rural Health & Wellness, a 30,000-square-foot education and research center, opened its doors in 2009. The facility includes a human performance laboratory, a state-of-the-art fitness facility, and rehabilitation services. The final phase of the campuswide master plan involves the renovation of Sullivan Hall to house modern classroom and lab space, tailored to meet the needs of health science students. An additional project centered on academic facilities includes the renovation of Schwab Hall in order to house the entire School of Business.

The six-story Pasquerilla Library contains more than 150,000 volumes. Other features of the library are general study areas, seminar rooms, reading rooms, several multimedia classrooms, and technologically equipped study rooms.

Costs

For 2013–14, tuition is estimated at $28,942, room and board at $10,208, and the technology program at $1,050, for a total of $40,200. The technology fee provides each student with a Lenovo ThinkPad supported by the on-campus Information Technology staff.

Financial Aid

Approximately 90 percent of the Saint Francis University student body receives financial aid. In addition to participating in federal and state need-based student aid programs, Saint Francis University offers its own substantial grant program and a generous scholarship program that is based on SAT or ACT scores, high school average, and class rank. Academic awards range from $1,000 to $16,500.

Faculty

Faculty members are chosen for their knowledge of subject matter, as well as for their ability to communicate. Of the teaching faculty at Saint Francis University, 80 percent hold a doctorate or the highest degree attainable in their specific field of expertise. No teaching assistants or graduate students teach classes at Saint Francis University.

Student Government

The Student Government Association's Steering Committee involves students who are interested in self-government. Students also serve on a number of committees in the Faculty Senate. The Student Government offices are located in the John F. Kennedy Student Center, which also houses a 600-seat auditorium, a campus bookstore and post office, a study lounge, and a café.

Admission Requirements

The admission committee considers applicants and renders decisions on the basis of the secondary school record, the recommendation of the secondary school principal or counselor, and the results of the SAT or ACT. Applicants to the School of Health Science should be aware of specified application requirements and deadlines. Applicants should have a minimum of 16 academic units and are strongly encouraged to visit the University campus for an admission interview and tour. Interviews and campus tours are available Monday through Friday throughout the year and select Saturday mornings while classes are in session.

Transfer students must submit a formal transfer application and a college clearance form in addition to official transcripts from each high school and college previously attended. Transfer students receive an advanced standing evaluation after an offer of admission has been made.

Saint Francis University, an equal opportunity/affirmative action employer, complies with applicable federal and state laws regarding nondiscrimination and affirmative action, including Title IX of the Educational Amendments of 1972, Titles VI and VII of the Civil Rights Act of 1964, and Section 504 of the Rehabilitation Act of 1973. Saint Francis University is committed to a policy of nondiscrimination and equal opportunity in employment, education programs and activities, and admissions that includes all persons regardless of race, gender, color, religion, national origin or ancestry, age, marital status, disability, or Vietnam-era veteran status. Inquiries or complaints may be addressed to the University's Director of Human Resources/Affirmative Action/Title IX Coordinator, Saint Francis University, Loretto, Pennsylvania 15940; telephone: 814-472-3264. For other University information, students should call 814-472-3000.

Application and Information

The University operates under a rolling admission policy. The application deadline for the physical therapy and occupational therapy programs is January 15. The deadline for the physician assistant science program is December 1. For more information about Saint Francis University, students should contact:

Vice President for Enrollment Management
Saint Francis University
P.O. Box 600
Loretto, Pennsylvania 15940
Phone: 814-472-3100
      866-342-5738 (toll-free)
E-mail: admissions@francis.edu
Website: http://www.francis.edu
    http://www.facebook.com/SaintFrancisUniversity(Facebook)
    http://twitter.com/SaintFrancisPA (Twitter)

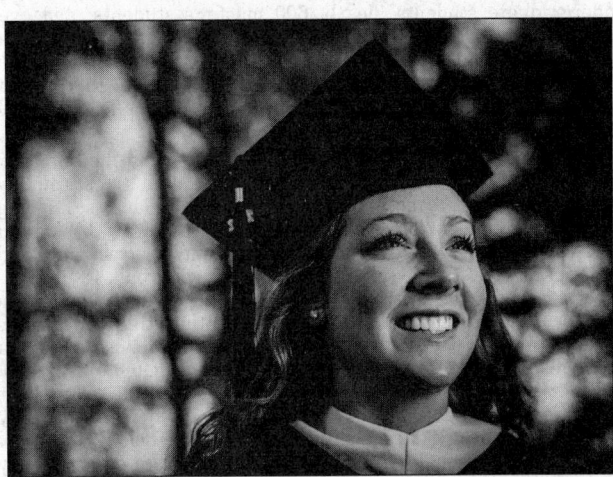

Starting from a great place gets students off to a great start. Just six months after graduation, 97 percent of Saint Francis University grads are either employed or in graduate school.

ST. JOHN FISHER COLLEGE
ROCHESTER, NEW YORK

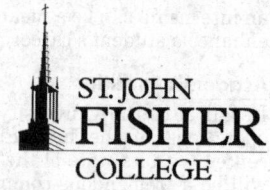

The College

Founded in 1948 by the Basilian fathers, St. John Fisher College is dedicated to serving the individual needs of its students. Originally a Catholic college for men, Fisher is now an independent, coeducational college with 59 percent women and 49 percent resident students. The College offers thirty-two undergraduate programs in business, the humanities, nursing, natural sciences, and social sciences, and is accredited by the Middle States Association of Colleges and Schools. The College also offers ten master's programs and three doctoral programs leading to the Master of Business Administration, the Master of Science, the Master of Science in Education, the Doctor of Education, the Doctor of Nursing Practice, and the Doctor of Pharmacy.

Fisher's unique First-Year Program reaches beyond the transition to college to focus on developing responsible campus citizens with independent learning skills, who fully explore educational and career aspirations. The Learning Community Program gives first-year students the opportunity to take courses in clusters that focus on a central theme. Through this approach to learning, students and faculty members examine a complex topic from multiple perspectives and discover connections among various disciplines. Fisher's Learning Communities also enable students to learn cooperatively and develop close working relationships with other students and faculty members.

All of the residence halls have been renovated, giving all students access to the Internet and cable TV in their rooms. Keough Hall, the College's newest residence, opened in September 2005 and added more than 200 beds.

Fisher offers a full range of extracurricular activities designed to cater to the diverse interests of the 2,700 full-time and 200 part-time undergraduate students, nearly 600 master's students, and over 400 doctoral students. Such activities include a student newspaper, a student TV club, a complete intramural program, and more than seventy student clubs and organizations. In addition, the Student Activities Board sponsors appearances by on-campus lecturers and entertainers.

Fisher is a member of NCAA Division III, ECAC, and the Empire 8. Men's intercollegiate sports are baseball, basketball, cross-country, football, golf, indoor and outdoor track and field, lacrosse, rowing, soccer, and tennis. Women's intercollegiate sports are basketball, cross-country, field hockey, golf, indoor and outdoor track and field, lacrosse, rowing, soccer, softball, tennis, and volleyball. Club sports include ice hockey, volleyball, and men's and women's rugby. The Student Life Center, which is the hub of the athletic activities, includes courts for basketball, racquetball, and volleyball; a sauna; a lounge; and a fitness area. Growney Stadium, complete with 2,100 bleacher seats and a press box, is equipped with an all-weather synthetic playing field to allow for all-season and nighttime play. Other on-campus athletics facilities include a nine-hole golf course, a softball field, a baseball complex, and two grass practice fields. A new track and field complex opened in summer 2011. Each year, Fisher is proud to host the Buffalo Bills summer training camp on campus.

Location

Located on 154 park-like acres, Fisher offers a balance of city activity and suburban tranquility. Just 10 minutes from the Fisher campus, Rochester, New York, the "World's Image Centre," offers many cultural attractions, including the Eastman Theater, the Rochester Philharmonic Orchestra, the International Museum of Photography at George Eastman House, the Rochester Museum and Science Center, the Memorial Art Gallery, and the Strasenburgh Planetarium. Home to a number of Fortune 500 companies, such as Xerox Corporation and Bausch and Lomb, the city of Rochester offers Fisher students opportunities for internships and employment after graduation.

Majors and Degrees

St. John Fisher College offers courses leading to the Bachelor of Arts and Bachelor of Science degrees. Undergraduate majors are offered in accounting, American studies, anthropology, biology, chemistry,

communication/journalism, computer science, digital cultures and technologies, economics, education (inclusive education in childhood and adolescence), English, finance, French, history, human resources management, interdisciplinary studies, international studies, legal studies, management, marketing, mathematics, nursing, philosophy, physics, political science, psychology, religious studies, sociology, Spanish, sport management, and statistics.

Fisher offers an online RN-to-B.S. in nursing degree-completion program and a fast-track B.S.-M.S. in advanced practice nursing. The College also offers a cooperative engineering program with the University of Detroit, Clarkson University, Manhattan College, Columbia University, and the University at Buffalo, the State University of New York.

Academic Programs

The bachelor's degree is conferred upon those who complete a minimum of 120 semester hours of credit with a cumulative GPA of at least 2.0. Thirty hours of credit and half of the requirements for the major must be earned at St. John Fisher College.

Students who complete the M.B.A. with a concentration in accounting will meet the 150-hour education licensing requirements to become a CPA in New York State. Students also may complete the 150-hour education license requirement by completing the B.S. degree and taking specific additional courses at the undergraduate and graduate level.

Off-Campus Programs

Fisher offers a multitude of special programs that are designed to complement its academic programs. Students in many disciplines can take advantage of an internship program, Albany and Washington Semesters, and cross-registration with fourteen member colleges of the Rochester Area College Consortium. Over twenty courses include a service-learning component, which addresses real community needs while enhancing the learning experience within the classroom. Study-abroad opportunities throughout the world are also available to students.

Academic Facilities

Over the last fifteen years, most of the academic and athletic facilities on campus have been upgraded and enhanced. Classrooms have been modernized and outfitted with state-of-the-art media facilities. Laboratory space has been upgraded with state-of-the-market educational technology. The Golisano Academic Gateway, complete with the Frontier Cyber Café and the learning resource center, opened in January 2001. The Ralph C. Wilson, Jr. Building opened in September 2003, expanding classroom capacity by 20 percent and providing additional faculty offices, seminar rooms, and meeting spaces.

The Campus Center opened in fall 2005 and serves as the hub and central gathering place of student activity on campus. This two-story facility supports general student gathering spaces, which include a performance space, recreational area, offices for student clubs and organizations, and the College Store (bookstore), all located on the first floor. The second floor of the Campus Center houses the Offices of the Dean of Students, Residential Life, Campus Life, and Campus Ministry, as well as additional student organization offices and meeting spaces.

The Charles J. Lavery Library meets the information needs of twenty-first-century students. A blend of traditional and electronic resources covering a broad range of subjects is available to the Fisher community. The library's print collection is supplemented by an extensive offering of online scholarly resources. Information resources include 245,000 volumes, 8,000 audiovisual items, and access to approximately 60,000 print and electronic periodical titles.

The Learning Commons supports student learning, research, and use of technology. This state-of-the-art facility enables students to conduct research and produce projects in one location, steps away from a Help Desk staffed by technology students and librarians. The librarians are information specialists committed to the academic success of all students. There is also a 24/7 online-chat reference service. Individual research guidance is available by appointment. Librarians also teach classes in information literacy and subject-specific research to all levels of students.

Lavery Library is a member of the Rochester Regional Library Council, representing a regional collection of more than 3,400,000 titles. Interlibrary loan staff can obtain resources not owned by Lavery Library from regional, national, and international libraries.

Costs

Tuition for 2013–14 is $27,870. Room and board costs are $10,940 with a meal plan and a room in one of Fisher's residence halls, and fees are $560.

Financial Aid

Committed to helping students meet the cost of their education, Fisher works to assess each individual's financial need. Financial aid is provided through scholarships, grants, loans, and work-study arrangements and is awarded by Fisher, the state, and the federal government. In 2012–13, the average financial aid package was $20,000 and 100 percent of incoming full-time freshmen receive a grant or scholarship.

St. John Fisher College offers a generous academic scholarship program that is based on high school average, strength of curriculum, and SAT or ACT scores. Students eligible for academic scholarships are automatically notified by the Office of Freshman Admissions. Merit scholarship award amounts are $10,000 to $14,000 per year. The College also offers an honors program and a science scholars program. The award in each of these programs is $3,000 per year, in addition to any academic scholarships for which the student qualifies.

Seventeen years ago, the College introduced the Service Scholars Program. This program is designed to recognize and reward high school seniors who demonstrate an ongoing interest in serving the needs of others through a commitment to community service. Scholarship awards equal one half of the total yearly cost of tuition, and on-campus room and board for four years. St. John Fisher College was recently named, for the seventh time, to the President's Higher Education Community Service Honor Roll for exemplary service efforts and service to disadvantaged youth.

In 1998, the College announced the creation of the Fannie and Sam Constantino First Generation Scholarship Program, designed to provide financial and academic assistance to high school students whose parents did not graduate from a postsecondary institution—much like the pioneer classes of St. John Fisher College. Recipients receive annual scholarships ranging from $5,000 up to one half of the total cost of Fisher's tuition and on-campus room and board.

Faculty

Fisher's 218 full-time faculty members are dedicated to helping students, both in and out of the classroom, as they strive to achieve their goals. Eighty-eight percent of full-time faculty members hold doctoral or terminal degrees. The student-teacher ratio of 13:1 offers a personal approach to education; 75 percent of all classes have fewer than 30 students. Fisher's Office of Academic Affairs and an outstanding faculty share responsibility for academic advising, helping students to explore the 32 majors that are available to them.

Student Government

Student leadership skills are developed through the Student Government Association, which is responsible for the social, cultural, and judicial areas of student life. Resident students elect a Resident Student Association, while commuting students elect a Commuter Council to represent them in planning special activities. The Student Activities Board is responsible for social activities and cultural events throughout the academic year.

Admission Requirements

Admission to St. John Fisher College is based primarily on the following: grade point average; strength of curriculum; scores on standardized tests (SAT/ACT); a personal statement, essay, or graded paper; extracurricular activities and/or work experience; and the counselor/teacher recommendation.

A candidate for admission to the freshman class must be a graduate of an approved secondary school and present a minimum of 16 units of college-preparatory course work in English, foreign languages, mathematics, and natural and social sciences. An applicant should present a secondary school average of 85 percent or above in these academic subjects.

Fisher welcomes qualified transfer students from two- and four-year colleges for both the fall and spring terms. To be considered for admission, transfer students must have a cumulative grade point average of 2.0 or better. If the student has obtained an A.A., A.S., or A.A.S. degree, 60 to 66 credit hours are transferred. All transfer applicants should consult the Undergraduate Catalog on the College's website for details.

The College has various special admission programs, including early decision, abbreviated procedures for veterans and other military personnel, and admission for part-time study.

The College offers the Arthur O. Eve Higher Education Opportunity Program (HEOP) for students who need special academic and financial assistance. The program provides academic support services, counseling, and financial aid for qualified students to help them achieve academic success.

Fisher grants college credit for satisfactory grades on the Advanced Placement test, the International Baccalaureate (I.B.) program exams, and the College-Level Examination Program (CLEP). Only students who receive a 3 or higher in all AP subjects and a 4 or higher on the AP science and language exams are granted Advanced Placement credit. CLEP and I.B. scoring guidelines are available through the Office of Freshman Admissions. Credit is only granted for subject-specific CLEP exams. In addition, recognizing the college-level course work being completed at the high school level, St. John Fisher College will consider granting credit for any college course work in which a student earns a grade of "C" or better.

Application and Information

Applications are accepted on a rolling basis. Early-decision applications are due December 1. The admissions application deadline for merit scholarship consideration is January 15.

Although a personal interview is not required for admission, all applicants are encouraged to visit the College. Interviews, information sessions, and campus tours are available during the week and on selected Saturdays throughout the year.

For additional information or an application, students should contact:

Office of Freshman Admissions
St. John Fisher College
3690 East Avenue
Rochester, New York 14618
Phone: 585-385-8064
      800-444-4640 (toll-free)
Fax: 585-385-8386
E-mail: admissions@sjfc.edu
Website: http://www.sjfc.edu/admissions/freshman
      http://www.facebook.com/StJohnFisherCollege
      http://twitter.com/FisherNews
      http://www.youtube.com/user/StJohnFisherCollege

Kearney Hall, St. John Fisher College's main administration building.

ST. JOHN'S COLLEGE
ANNAPOLIS, MARYLAND, AND SANTA FE, NEW MEXICO

StJOHN'S
College

ANNAPOLIS · SANTA FE

The College

St. John's College is a community dedicated to liberal education. Such education seeks to free men and women from the tyrannies of unexamined opinions and inherited prejudices. It also endeavors to enable them to make intelligent, free choices concerning the ends and means of both public and private life.

At St. John's, freedom is pursued mainly through thoughtful conversation about great books of the Western tradition. The books that are at the heart of learning at St. John's stand among the original sources of our intellectual tradition. They are timeless and timely; they not only illuminate the persisting questions of human existence, but also have great relevance to contemporary problems.

Location

St. John's College was chartered in Annapolis, Maryland, in 1784, and traces its roots back to 1696. The current academic program was introduced in 1937, transforming an undistinguished liberal arts college into a world leader in education. In 1964, a second campus was opened at the foot of the mountains surrounding Santa Fe, a cultural center and the capital of New Mexico.

The two campuses, which operate as equal partners, are remarkable both in their sameness and their differences. The same singular academic program is pursued in both locations, and both campuses draw remarkable students from all over the world, but it is there where most overt similarity ends. The Annapolis campus is Eastern, about 40 feet above sea level, on a mostly level 36-acre piece of land in the center of the beautiful historic district of the state capital, with green lawns and colonial red brick buildings; the Santa Fe campus is Southwestern, about 7300 feet above sea level, on a mostly hilly 250-acre piece of land several miles from the beautiful historic district of the state capital, with territorial-style buildings and magnificent mountain vistas. Annapolis is in the close-to-everything mid-Atlantic world, with Baltimore and Washington D.C. nearby, bringing big-city benefits to a small town; while Santa Fe offers a world-class music and arts scene in a splendid high-desert environment that calls students outdoor to ski, hike, raft, and breathe some of the sweetest air in the world. Students have the option to transfer between the two campuses from year to year.

Both campuses have the luxury of being small enough that the community on each can function as a community rather than a conglomeration. Fall 2012 enrollment in Annapolis was 447 (244 men and 203 women), and in Santa Fe 345 (198 men, 147 women).

Majors and Degrees

All students at St. John's earn a B.A. in liberal arts. There are no majors: the entire course of study is a required curriculum.

This unusual arrangement allows students to have a coherent and cumulative experience, with all concurrently running classes making sense when taken together, and each year's work forming the foundation for what lies ahead. Without the option of electives, the prescribed curriculum may seem confining, but students experience the opposite effect: within the structure there is a tremendous amount of intellectual freedom.

After all following the same undergraduate course of study, alumni of St. John's pursue the gamut of careers: 20 percent go into business; 19 percent into education; 15 percent into communication and the arts; 10 percent into law; 9 percent

into health; and 8 percent into computer work. The rest become everything from social workers to intelligence agents, from organic farmers to Peace Corps officials.

Academic Programs

The academic program is a unified, cohesive whole; instruction takes the form of annual sequences of related seminars, tutorials, and laboratories, in each of which the books that form the core of the curriculum are the basis of study and discussion. All classes are small discussion groups and range in size from between 12 and 16 students in tutorials to between 18 and 20 in seminars and laboratories.

Seminar (all four years, twice a week in the evening): Seminars, considered the heart of the program, are devoted to reading works of the greatest minds and engaging in thoughtful discussion about them. The first-year seminar focuses on Greek authors; the second on the works of the Roman, medieval, and early Renaissance periods; the third on books of the seventeenth and eighteenth centuries; and the fourth on writings from the nineteenth and twentieth centuries. The seminar consists almost exclusively of student conversation. Everyone's opinion must be heard and must also be supported by argument and evidence. The role of the faculty members is not to give information or to produce the "right" interpretation; it is to guide the discussion, to aid in defining the issues, and to help the students to understand the authors, the issues, and themselves. Reason is the only recognized authority.

Language Tutorial (all four years, three times a week): In the language tutorial, Greek is studied in the first two years and French in the last two. By translating works written in Greek and French into English and comparing those languages with each other as well as with English, the student gains an appreciation of all three and learns something of the nature of language in general.

Mathematics Tutorial (all four years, three times a week): The mathematics tutorial seeks to affect an understanding of the fundamental nature and intention of mathematics. Throughout the four years, the student is in contact not only with the pure science of mathematics but also with the foundations of mathematical physics and astronomy. The blackboard becomes an arena of logical struggle, which brings the imagination constantly into play.

Music Tutorial (twice a week in the sophomore year): The music tutorial aims at understanding music through study of musical theory and analysis of significant works. Students investigate rhythm, the diatonic system, ratios of musical intervals, melody, counterpoint, and harmony.

Laboratory (twice a week in the freshman, junior, and senior years): The laboratory weaves together the main themes of physics, biology, and chemistry with careful scrutiny of the interplay of hypothesis, theory, and observed fact.

Lecture On Friday evenings, the College community assembles for a formal lecture or concert by a tutor or visitor (or a play presented by the student theater group). It is the only time the students are lectured to. The subject of the lecture may sometimes be related to the academic program, but it is not part of the students' classes. No one takes notes: part of the lecture experience is to sharpen the ability to listen thoughtfully and retain well. Afterward, interested students and faculty members engage the speaker or performer in a formal Question

Period, which often takes on the nature of a conversation, and not infrequently lasts into the night.

Summer Program The Summer Academy at St. John's College offers rising high school juniors and seniors a variety of one-week residential programs based on the academic program at the College: reading and discussing great works of Western civilization. The academic program is supplemented by a variety of cultural, social, and athletic activities.

Academic Facilities

The library on each campus—about 100,000 volumes in Annapolis, nearly 60,000 in Santa Fe—emphasizes material appropriate to the nature of the academic program, supplemented by a more general collection and by a variety of special collections. Recordings and representative periodicals and newspapers are included. Academic facilities on each campus also include the resources and equipment necessary for study and experimentation in physics, chemistry, and biology (including a planetarium in Annapolis); for audition and performance of music; for display and studio work in art, photography, and other crafts; and for drama productions.

Costs

For 2013–14, annual tuition and fees total $45,846. Room and board are $10,456–$10,954. Books and supplies range in cost from $450 to $600.

Financial Aid

Both need-based and merit aid are available. The application for financial aid is the CSS PROFILE, supplemented by the Free Application for Federal Student Aid (FAFSA). About 75 percent of all St. John's students receive need-based aid, usually in a combination of grants, loans, and employment, and the College is committed to meeting 100 percent of demonstrated need.

There is no separate merit aid application; all approved applicants are considered for merit awards based on their admissions applications.

Faculty

The faculty-student ratio is 1:8. Faculty members all hold the same rank, and are called Tutors, in recognition of their role as intellectual guides. While most have Ph.D.'s in specific disciplines, they all participate in the wholeness of the curriculum by teaching all classes within their area of academic expertise and beyond it.

Student Life

Students are drawn to St. John's seeking a top-of-the-line liberal education; when they join the campus community they find not only an exceptional academic experience but a rich and coherent campus environment. While the academic program serves to unite the community with a single purpose, life on campus is balanced between study and play, between the social and the solitary, between purpose and leisure, between the mundane and the eternal.

Above all, community life at St. John's is inclusive. Sports teams are open to all who want to play, and it's not uncommon for an experienced player pass the ball to a beginner, even in a game that counts. Students pursue their outside interests—music, theater, publications, religion, politics, government, community service, athletics, dance, art, and more—in a spectrum of clubs and groups.

Admission Requirements

The College accepts the Common Application, using a supplement to ask essential questions about the candidate's intellectual background and interest in St. John's. The application essays are the most important part of the application, but the Admissions Committee also considers the student's preparedness as evidenced in the high school transcript. Standardized test scores are optional for most candidates but may prove helpful. There are no minimums for grades or test scores; both may be made irrelevant by what the candidate writes. The Admissions Committee considers each application as a whole, asking whether the candidate is at a point in his or her education that indicates a readiness to thrive in the academic program at the College. Although interviews are not required except in special cases, they are encouraged. Interested students are urged to visit either campus for a day or overnight visit to sit in on seminars and tutorials, and to talk with students and faculty.

Application and Information

Students may be admitted to either campus for the fall term or, if they are prepared to continue their studies through the following summer, in January on the Santa Fe campus. Application must be made to one campus or the other, not to both. Early action dates are November 15 and January 15; after the early action period the Admissions Committee reviews applications on a rolling basis for as long as space remains in the class.

For information about the academic program and the extracurricular life of the College, students should contact:
Sarah G. Morse
Director of Admissions
St. John's College
Annapolis, Maryland 21404
Phone: 800-727-9238 (toll-free)
E-mail: admissions@sjca.edu
Website: http://www.stjohnscollege.edu

Larry Clendenin
Director of Admissions
St. John's College
Santa Fe, New Mexico 87501
Phone: 800-331-5232 (toll-free)
E-mail: admissions@sjcsf.edu
Website: http://www.stjohnscollege.edu

St. John's College at Annapolis.

ST. JOSEPH'S COLLEGE
BROOKLYN AND PATCHOGUE, NEW YORK

The College

Since 1916, St. Joseph's College has been inspiring students to transform their lives. A private coeducational institution with campuses in Brooklyn and Patchogue, Long Island, the College enrolls nearly 6,000 undergraduates and over 500 graduate students in its School of Arts and Sciences and School of Professional and Graduate Studies. St. Joseph's consistently earns a place among top colleges in the Region, as ranked by *U.S. News & World Report*. In addition, St. Joseph's is the most affordable private college in the New York metropolitan area and Long Island.

St. Joseph's College helps students turn aspirations into accomplishments. In addition to offering a liberal arts education of the highest quality, St. Joseph's offers students an unrivaled degree of personal attention, encouraging them to lead lives characterized by integrity, a commitment to upholding intellectual and spiritual values, social responsibility, and service to others.

St. Joseph's students immerse themselves in learning in ways that go far beyond the classroom, through independent projects, team-building assignments, internships, community service opportunities, and study-abroad programs designed to suit every schedule. Moreover, with just 15 students for every professor on campus, St. Joseph's students easily find mentors to guide them in everything from academics to focusing on future career and life goals.

Although most of St. Joseph's students commute at both campuses, the Brooklyn campus offers student housing through Educational Housing Services at the nearby St. George Residence. Each of the campuses offers a lively atmosphere enriched by social events, athletic competitions, and a Common Hour to encourage students to explore new possibilities for fun, leadership, and connections. On any given day at St. Joseph's, students might come to campus to hear a Pulitzer Prize–winning author, enjoy a jazz concert, join a community service effort, view an art exhibit, attend an athletic event, or engage in a political debate over dinner with other students and professors. Each campus supports over thirty student clubs and activities, including intercollegiate basketball; women's softball, swimming, tennis, and volleyball; men's baseball, tennis, and volleyball; and coed cross-country. The Long Island campus also offers men's soccer, and a coed equestrian team.

For undergraduates, St. Joseph's offers fast tracks to advanced degrees through special affiliated programs in accounting, and podiatry. The School of Professional and Graduate Studies at St. Joseph's College offers a wide range of graduate programs in education, human services, management, and nursing, including the Executive M.B.A., an M.B.A. in accounting, an M.B.A. in health-care management, and the M.S. in nursing, to name a few.

Location

The Brooklyn campus is located in the Clinton Hill Historic District, a neighborhood where so many of New York's wealthiest citizens once lived that it was dubbed Brooklyn's "Gold Coast" in the 1920s. Today this area is home to several prestigious schools, including the Pratt Institute of Art and the Brooklyn Academy of Music, and serves as a hub of cultural and intellectual activity, as well as the newly constructed Barclay's Center, home of the Brooklyn Nets NBA team. This convenient location allows students to enjoy the freedom of a safe, well-landscaped campus and surroundings easily accessible to New York City by car or public transportation.

St. Joseph's Long Island campus is located in the village of Patchogue on Great South Bay, about 50 miles from Manhattan and 60 miles from Montauk Point. Patchogue offers plenty to do, with fine harbors, shops, restaurants, athletic fields, and tennis courts right in the village. There are lovely parks nearby as well as museums, golf courses, hiking and ski trails, and beaches. Patchogue is easily accessible via Long Island Rail Road, bus service, or ferry. A major regional airport, MacArthur Airport, is just minutes away.

Majors and Degrees

Through individual attention, interactive teaching, and intensive advising, St. Joseph's meets students where they are academically, then guides them through the essential next steps to help them stretch intellectually, personally, and professionally. St. Joseph's offers four-year programs leading to B.A. and B.S. degrees at both the Brooklyn and Patchogue campuses, with majors in accounting, business administration, biology, chemistry, child study, computer information systems, criminal justice, English, history, human relations, journalism and new media studies, marketing, mathematics, medical technology, recreation, psychology, social sciences: economics, sociology and political science, Spanish, and speech communications. Among these majors are a variety of minors and certificate programs from which students can choose.

No matter what major students choose, they can also earn additional certificates designed to help them delve deeper into specific interests and give them a head start when entering the workforce. Certificate programs include criminology/criminal justice; gerontology; information technology; leadership and supervision; management, marketing, advertising, and public relations; and religious studies.

For students interested in a fast track to an advanced degree after completing their undergraduate studies, St. Joseph's offers special affiliated programs. The Brooklyn campus also offers an accelerated biomedical program in cooperation with the New York College of Podiatric Medicine. This program allows students to receive a B.S. in biology and a doctorate in podiatric medicine within six years. Students at both the Brooklyn and Patchogue campuses can earn B.S./M.B.A. degrees in accounting within five years or can choose to pursue pre-professional programs in law, teaching, and numerous health fields, including dentistry, medicine, and optometry. In addition, the College has several B.A./M.A. special education degrees, which give students the opportunity to earn a bachelor's and master's degree in just five years.

Those with nontraditional academic backgrounds or with professional training and experience can pursue degrees in community health, general studies, health administration, nursing, and organizational management through St. Joseph's School of Professional and Graduate Studies at either campus.

Academic Programs

The School of Arts and Sciences at each campus operates on the semester system, with additional courses offered in January and during the summer. St. Joseph's students take a core curriculum of 128 credits to graduate; a wide range of choices allows students to tailor their academic programs to their personal and professional needs. The College recognizes the Advanced Placement (AP) Program and offers credit and placement for scores of 3 or above on AP tests. In each case, the score is reviewed by the registrar and/or department chairperson to determine credit and placement.

The School of Professional and Graduate Studies on each campus offers flexible schedules, summer programs, and online courses to meet the needs of working students. Courses may meet for a semester or for six- or twelve-week sessions.

Academic Facilities

The Brooklyn campus is composed of eight buildings, including historic landmark buildings. Students majoring in the widely recognized child-study program use the Dillon Child Study Center, which is a laboratory preschool enrolling approximately 100 hundred students and a teaching and observation resource right on campus. McEntegart Hall, a modern five-level structure, houses the library, audiovisual resource center, curriculum library, archives, and computer labs. Other academic facilities include top-notch biology, chemistry, computer, physics, and psychology research laboratories. A state-of-the-art athletic complex is under construction on school grounds, with a scheduled completion date of 2013.

At the Long Island campus, students enjoy 28 acres of well-landscaped grounds and athletic fields. The main building houses administrative and faculty offices; laboratories for biology, chemistry, physics, and psychology; the computer center; art and music studios; the Local History Center; and the Office of Counseling. The library building houses a curriculum library, seminar rooms, administrative offices, and classrooms. This campus also features the John A. Danzi Recreation/Fitness Center, which includes a competition-sized swimming pool, fitness rooms, and a full-sized gym with an elevated track. The 33,000-square-foot Business and Technology Center allows St. Joseph's students to integrate technology into their studies. The Clare Rose Playhouse serves as a cultural center where students and local communities can explore theater production and performance.

A high-speed fiber-optic network connects all offices, institutional facilities, computer laboratories, and libraries on both the Brooklyn and Long Island campuses. Direct Internet access is available to all students and faculty and staff members through the College's server. The integrated online library system enables students to locate and check out books at either campus and provides links to online databases and other electronic information sources.

Costs

The 2012–13 annual full-time tuition rate for undergraduates was $19,500, or $715 per credit.

Financial Aid

St. Joseph's offers scholarships and grants-in-aid. Students who wish to apply for either form of assistance must file the Free Application for Federal Student Aid (FAFSA) and a state aid form. After a student has been accepted to the College and all financial aid forms are processed, the Financial Aid Office prepares aid packages that usually consist of federal, state, and College funds. St. Joseph's is fully approved for veterans. Campus work-study programs are also available.

Faculty

With nearly 500 faculty members who are widely respected scholars in their fields and a student-faculty ratio of 15:1, St. Joseph's students benefit from close professional and personal working relationships with their professors. Faculty members serve as academic advisers, are active on student affairs committees, and act as moderators in student organizations.

Admission Requirements

St. Joseph's College seeks a diverse student body and welcomes applications from high school students, transfer students, and those students who may have a non-traditional academic background. The College offers programs to serve all of these groups.

Students who wish to enter as freshmen are expected to have completed at least 18 units of college-preparatory work by the end of their senior year. This should include the following distribution: 4 years of English, 2 years of foreign language, 3 years of mathematics, 2 years of science, and 4 years of social studies. Applicants interested in accounting, allied health fields, biology, business administration, chemistry, or mathematics should have more extensive backgrounds in mathematics and science. In addition, the College requires the submission of official results from the critical reading and math sections of the SAT.

St. Joseph's College accepts a block transfer of credits from students holding an A.A. or A.S. degree in certain majors from an accredited junior or community college. All other transfers are considered on an individual basis.

Application and Information

Admission is offered on a rolling basis. Applications and supporting documents should be submitted online or to the appropriate school. The College reviews each application carefully and usually sends a decision one month after receiving all necessary credentials. For more information and an online application, students can access the website at http://www.sjcny.edu.

Brooklyn Campus:

Director of Admissions
St. Joseph's College
245 Clinton Avenue
Brooklyn, New York 11205
Phone: 718-940-5800

Long Island Campus:

Director of Admissions
St. Joseph's College
155 West Roe Boulevard
Patchogue, New York 11772
Phone: 631-687-4500
Website: http://www.sjcny.edu
http://www.facebook.com/SJCNY
http://twitter.com/#!/SJCNY

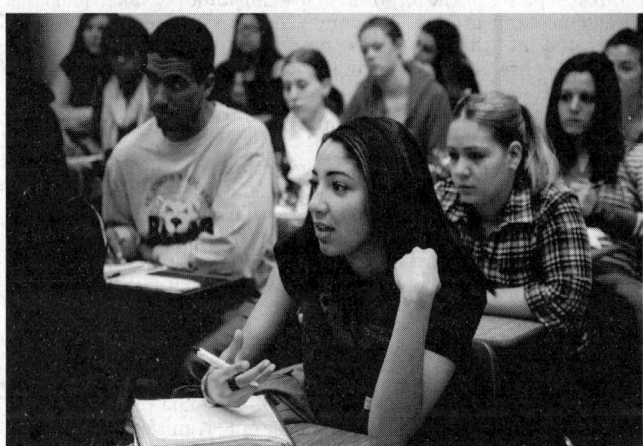

Class sizes at St. Joseph's College are personal, with no more than 15 to 20 students.

SAINT JOSEPH'S UNIVERSITY
PHILADELPHIA, PENNSYLVANIA

The University

Saint Joseph's University is a nationally recognized, Catholic, Jesuit university. For 160 years, Saint Joseph's has advanced the professional and personal ambitions of men and women by providing a rigorous Jesuit education—one that demands high achievement, expands knowledge, deepens understanding, stresses effective reasoning and communication, develops moral and spiritual character, and imparts enduring pride. One of only 152 schools with a Phi Beta Kappa chapter and business school accreditation by AACSB International–The Association to Advance Collegiate Schools of Business, Saint Joseph's is the home to 4,650 traditional undergraduate day students, 700 College of Professional and Liberal Studies adult undergraduate students, and 3,600 graduate and doctoral students.

As a Jesuit university, Saint Joseph's believes each student realizes his or her fullest potential through challenging classroom study, hands-on learning opportunities, and a commitment to excellence in all endeavors. The University also reinforces the individual's lifelong engagement with the greater world. Graduates of Saint Joseph's attain success in their careers with the help of an extensive network of alumni who have become leading figures in business, law, medicine, education, the arts, technology, government, and public service.

A Saint Joseph's education encompasses all aspects of personal growth and development, reflecting the Ignatian credo of *cura personalis*. Guided by a faculty that is committed to both teaching and scholarship, students develop intellectually through an intense Jesuit liberal arts curriculum and advanced study in a chosen discipline. Students mature socially by participating in Saint Joseph's campus life, noted for its rich variety of activities, infectious enthusiasm, and mutual respect. Students grow ethically and spiritually by living their own values in the larger society beyond the campus.

Steeped in the Jesuit, Catholic tradition, Saint Joseph's provides a rigorous, intensive education that both disciplines and expands the mind. Students develop a lifelong desire to learn and grow while also acquiring the skills and knowledge necessary for success in their professional lives. At the core of this education is a general education requirement, which exposes students to primary fields of inquiry and the cultural values that shape their world. A Jesuit emphasis on engaged teaching and mentoring permeates the university. Faculty members at Saint Joseph's, many of whom are leading scholars in their disciplines, expect students to perform at the highest level and set demanding standards in the classroom.

Saint Joseph's is at the forefront of utilizing innovative technologies to enhance and promote learning. These technologies are widely integrated into the educational process both in class and beyond, where they are also used for individual and collaborative research projects. By mastering these tools and achieving technological fluency, Saint Joseph's students gain a valuable edge in their careers.

Saint Joseph's students engage enthusiastically in all facets of campus life—academic, social, athletic, ethical, and spiritual. Their active participation creates a vibrant, dynamic campus community, one that embraces a "not for spectators" attitude. In all their activities, students emphasize personal integrity as well as a respect and concern for others. This produces a mutually supportive, humane, and tolerant environment for individual success and service to others.

Location

Located on the edge of metropolitan Philadelphia, Saint Joseph's provides ready access to the vast career opportunities and cultural resources of America's fifth-largest city, while affording students a cohesive and intimate campus experience.

Because of its location, Saint Joseph's has close ties to the people, professional opportunities, and cultural life of Philadelphia.

Students enjoy direct access to internships, cooperative education programs, and positions in virtually all careers, most of which have a major presence in the Philadelphia area. Saint Joseph's location also offers ample outlets for community involvement and service, and students can easily take advantage of Philadelphia's professional sports, entertainment, and cultural events.

Majors and Degrees

Saint Joseph's offers full-time baccalaureate degree programs in over fifty major fields of study and numerous specialty programs, which are administered by two separate colleges.

The College of Arts and Sciences awards a bachelor's degree in actuarial science, ancient studies, art, art education, Asian studies, biology, chemical biology, chemistry, communication studies, computer science, criminal justice, economics, education (early childhood/elementary PreK–4; early childhood/elementary PreK–4 + special education K–8 (double major), elementary/middle years 4–8), English, environmental science, European studies, French, French studies, German, history, interdisciplinary health services, international relations, Italian, mathematics, music, philosophy, physics, political science, psychology, religious studies, sociology, Spanish, theater and film, and theology.

The Erivan K. Haub School of Business awards a bachelor's degree in accounting; business administration; business intelligence; family business and entrepreneurship; finance; financial planning; food marketing; international business; leadership, ethics, and organizational sustainability; managing human capital; marketing; pharmaceutical and healthcare marketing; risk management and insurance; and sports marketing. A co-op program is available for all business majors.

Five-year B.S./M.S. programs are offered in education, international marketing, psychology, and writing studies. The University also offers special academic programs in aerospace studies (Air Force ROTC), Africana studies, allied health (bioscience technologies, nursing, occupational therapy, physical therapy [D.P.T.], and radiologic sciences), American studies, autism studies, behavioral neuroscience, business ethics, environmental and sustainability studies, faith-justice studies, gender studies, interdisciplinary health care ethics, Latin American studies, linguistics, medieval and renaissance studies, music industry, and teacher certification at the elementary and secondary levels. Preprofessional study is available in most major fields.

Academic Programs

At Saint Joseph's University, the aim of providing the student with the qualities of a liberally educated individual is pursued through a threefold plan encompassing forty courses. The major concentration (ten to sixteen courses) is intended to provide students with depth in a given field in order to prepare them for effective work in that field or graduate study. The general education program (fifteen to eighteen courses) is intended to ensure that students have mastered basic skills necessary for further work, have been exposed to the main divisions of learning, have been introduced to several new fields of study, and have acquired an appreciation for diversity and an ethically-informed perspective. Art and literature, non-native languages, mathematics, natural sciences, history, social sciences, philosophy, and theology are among the areas of study included in the general education program. Free electives (six to fifteen courses) are intended to provide flexibility by encouraging students to pursue studies in areas they have found interesting, to test their interest in an unexplored area, or to deepen their knowledge in the major field.

A competitive honors program is available for qualified students, as are independent and interdisciplinary study options. Claver House provides a place for honors students to have meetings, take classes, study, and conduct research.

Off-Campus Programs

Saint Joseph's offers the opportunity to study abroad and directly sponsors programs each year in Europe, Africa, Asia, Australia, Latin America, and the United Kingdom. International study tours have been made to Africa, Australia, Brazil, Canada, Greece, Ireland, Italy, Japan, Scotland, and Spain.

Students may take advantage of an arrangement with the Washington Center for Internships and Academic Seminars, which allows for a one-semester internship in the nation's capital.

Fieldwork experiences are required in several majors, and the University's location provides for internship opportunities to support virtually all other disciplines. The Career Development Center offers a wide array of services and provides opportunities for on-campus interviews.

Academic Facilities

The facilities at Saint Joseph's are a blend of the old and the new. Barbelin/Lonergan Hall is a fine example of collegiate Gothic architecture. Its spire carillon tower rises above the campus and is easily the most recognizable landmark at Saint Joseph's. Mandeville Hall, a modern international academic center, is the home of the Erivan K. Haub School of Business. Mandeville Hall offers classrooms with state-of-the-art technology, and a Wall Street trading room, with access to electronic sources of financial and investment data. The Francis A. Drexel Library and the Campbell Collection in Food Marketing house a collection of approximately 354,850 volumes, 1,450 print journals, 57,000 full-text electronic journals 4,700 online books, and 863,500 microforms. The new Post Learning Commons has become a hub for students seeking space for both studying and relaxation, with its floor-to-ceiling windows for spectacular views of the campus, expanded and varied study spaces, plush lounges, and a café. Villiger Residence Hall was added to the campus in 2012, and has welcomed its first 400 residents. Villiger and three other on-campus residence halls house the entire freshman class.

Costs

Current tuition for one academic year is $37,670. The average cost for room and board is $12,800. These costs do not include student fees associated with specific majors or residence halls.

Financial Aid

The majority of Saint Joseph's students receive merit and/or federal financial assistance. Approximately 93 percent of the University's student body receives assistance in the form of academic and athletic scholarships, grants, loans, and work-study funds. In 2012 Saint Joseph's awarded more than $50 million in institutional merit- and need-based aid.

Students are automatically considered for merit scholarships upon application to the University. Students who wish to be considered for federal financial assistance should submit the Free Application for Federal Student Aid (FAFSA). Residents from states other than Pennsylvania should file the FAFSA and the proper state grant application from the Education Assistance Agency of their resident state. The preferred deadline is February 15.

Faculty

Saint Joseph's esteemed research faculty is committed to undergraduate teaching. A student-faculty ratio of 13:1 and an average class size of 24 offer excellent opportunities for students and faculty members to interact, both inside and outside the classroom. Approximately 99 percent of the full-time, tenure-track faculty members hold a doctorate or terminal degree in their field.

Student Government

The Office of Student Leadership and Activities is dedicated to enhancing the educational development of students by providing opportunities for involvement in co-curricular programs and services. These include leadership programs, student clubs and organizations, Greek life, event programming and planning, and the University Student Senate. Through innovative programming that complements academic and personal development, the University nurtures the mind, body, and spirit of each individual student while enhancing the Jesuit mission of the University.

The University Student Senate, the governing board for the student body, is dedicated to addressing student issues through advocacy and policy recommendations. The senate consists of an executive board that includes the president, executive vice president, speaker of the senate, vice president for financial affairs, vice president for student life, four elected representatives from each class, and five appointed at-large members. The senate has four standing committees: Academic Affairs, Student Budget Allocations, Campus Life, and Administrative Services. Elections for the senate take place in April. Freshman representatives are elected in September.

The Student Union Board, known as SUB, is a student-run organization that encourages the development of student leadership, responsibility, and social competency by planning and participating in campus programs. These activities are designed to enhance the educational, recreational, cultural, and social aspects of the collegiate experience. All registered undergraduate students are welcome to take part in the activities and to be a part of the standing committees that are responsible for the programming.

Admission Requirements

Candidates for admission to the freshman class must submit evidence of academic achievement in a college-preparatory program, which should emphasize study in English, mathematics, foreign languages (classical or modern), science, history, and social studies. Successful candidates have traditionally completed a secondary school background that included the following: 4 credits of English; 3 credits of mathematics; 3 credits of science; 3 credits of social science; 2 credits of second/foreign language; 1 credit fine or performing arts. Applicants are required to submit SAT or ACT scores.

Application and Information

To apply to St. Joseph's University, a completed application form may be submitted with the $60 application fee. Students are accepted to the University and merit scholarships are awarded within the context of a deadline admissions policy with an early action application deadline of November 15 and a regular decision deadline of February 1. More information is available online at sju.edu/apply.

Office of Undergraduate Admissions
Saint Joseph's University
5600 City Avenue
Philadelphia, Pennsylvania 19131-1395
Phone: 610-660-1300
        1-888-BE-A-HAWK (232-4295) (toll-free)
E-mail: admit@sju.edu
Website: sju.edu/admissions
        facebook.com/sjuadmissions

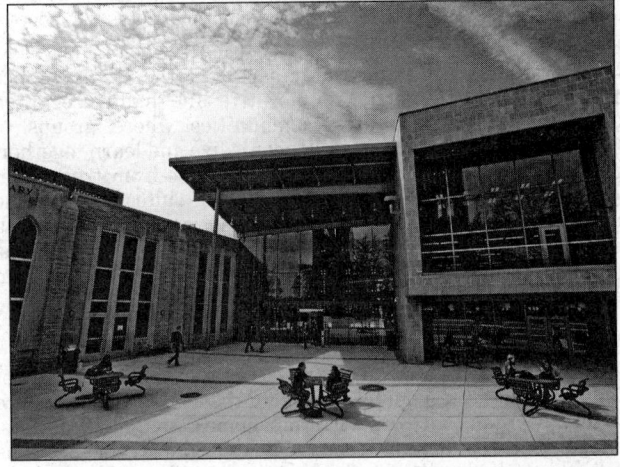

The Post Learning Commons Building at Saint Joseph's University, a new campus addition. (Photo credit: Melissa Kelly)

ST. LAWRENCE UNIVERSITY
CANTON, NEW YORK

The University

St. Lawrence University invites students to learn new ways of seeing the world, voicing ideas, and connecting with others. Graduates have the tools with which to think clearly, express themselves persuasively, and step into the world community with an understanding of their responsibility to all people and to the planet.

Founded in 1856, St. Lawrence is the oldest continuously coeducational degree-granting institution of higher learning in New York State. Initially established as a theology school for the Universalist Church, it quickly evolved into the liberal arts college that it is today. St. Lawrence is a private, nonsectarian university of approximately 2,400 undergraduate men and women, with a small graduate program in education. St. Lawrence is known for its residential/academic First-Year Program, its international study opportunities and area studies programs, its students' strong interest in the environment and the outdoors, and its friendliness.

St. Lawrence students are self-starters. The self-designed major is popular, intramural sports leagues are always full, and more than 100 student organizations serve broad interests, from communication to community service and creativity to social action. The University routinely hosts well-known speakers, and concerts, plays, and films are regulars on the weekly events calendar.

St. Lawrence students have historically placed high value on athletic activity, and a large number participate in varsity, intramural, or club sports. The thirty-two varsity men's and women's teams compete at the Division III level of the NCAA, with the exception of men's and women's ice hockey, which compete in Division I. Recreational facilities include cross-country ski and running trails, indoor and outdoor tennis courts, an athletic complex with a gymnasium, two field houses, a 133-station fitness center, a three-story climbing wall, a pool, an ice rink, an equestrian center, a boathouse, a golf course, a nine-lane all-weather track, an artificial-turf field for lacrosse and field hockey, ten squash courts, and performance fields for soccer, football, baseball, and softball.

Residential life is an important aspect of the St. Lawrence experience. The University's innovative and highly regarded First-Year Program creates communities where groups of approximately 30–35 first-year students live and learn together. In the upperclass years, students can choose from traditional dormitories, Greek chapter houses, and suites and theme cottages that focus on student interests such as low-impact living and community service. Seniors may also choose town houses. St. Lawrence sponsors a full range of student services, from counseling to career planning.

Location

St. Lawrence is situated on a 1,000-acre campus in the village of Canton, New York (population 6,400), the seat of St. Lawrence County. Canton, with its Victorian homes, tree-lined streets, village green, and small shops, is typical of college towns throughout the Northeast. Students and residents often mix in stores, at athletic events, and in community projects. Ottawa, Canada's capital, is 75 minutes to the north, while Lake Placid, one of America's hiking and skiing meccas, is 90 minutes to the southeast.

Majors and Degrees

St. Lawrence offers the Bachelor of Arts and Bachelor of Science degrees; students can choose from thirty-six majors and have the option of picking one of thirty-seven minors. Combined five-year programs with other institutions are in place in engineering and management, and specialized advising is offered in preparation for postgraduate work in dentistry, law, medicine, nursing, physical therapy, and veterinary medicine.

Academic Programs

St. Lawrence's foremost mission is to provide its students with a liberal arts education. Students complete requirements in six areas and concentrated work in a major field as well as demonstrating competence in writing. Close faculty-student interaction is a hallmark of a St. Lawrence education. Every semester, many students engage in independent or honors projects, often working with professors on joint research projects that lead to publication in leading scholarly journals. A senior project is required in most majors.

Off-Campus Programs

St. Lawrence University supports a variety of off-campus programs on six continents that allow students to enrich their majors, expand their world, gain cross-cultural skills, and prepare to be responsible global citizens. More than 50 percent of St. Lawrence students study in one of the University's international programs during their collegiate careers. St. Lawrence operates programs in Australia, Austria, Canada, China, Costa Rica, the Czech Republic, Denmark, England, France, India, Italy, Japan, Kenya, New Zealand, Spain, Thailand, and Trinidad and Tobago. In addition, the University's membership in the International Student Exchange Program permits students to directly enroll in universities in more than thirty-five additional countries. St. Lawrence also operates programs at two other campuses in the United States: Fisk University in Nashville, Tennessee, and American University in Washington, D.C. St. Lawrence also administers its own Adirondack Semester Program and a New York City Semester Program. The Kenya semester program is based out of the University's owned and operated campus, rooted deep in tradition, in the suburbs of Nairobi. The program strives to provide students with a unique study-abroad experience.

Academic Facilities

Owen D. Young Library and Launders Science Library contain more than half a million volumes as well as electronic resources and ample space for reading and research. Griffiths Arts Center is the home of the University's fine arts and performance and communication studies programs as well as two theaters and an art gallery in which selections from St. Lawrence's 7,000-piece collection are frequently shown. The Peterson-Kermani Performance Hall, a 19,000-square-foot space for the performing arts, is part of the campus dedicated to the arts. A unified science complex houses the Departments of Biology, Chemistry, Physics, Psychology, Geology, and Mathematics, Computer Science and Statistics and is connected via a covered hallway to the science library and computing center. The 120,000-square-foot Johnson Hall of Science was the first LEED-certified gold science building in New York State. Richardson Hall, St. Lawrence's oldest building and on the National Register of Historic Places, is home to the English and religious studies departments. Other departments can be found in academic buildings clustered on one part of the campus, so classrooms are not a long walk apart.

Costs

The comprehensive fee for 2012–13 was $55,510, including tuition, fees, and average room and board. Students should allow approximately $1,650 for books and personal expenses.

Financial Aid

St. Lawrence awards both merit scholarships and need-based financial aid. More than 94 percent of the University's students receive some form of financial assistance, including scholarships, grants, student loans, and campus jobs. St. Lawrence is committed to assisting as many students as possible and recognizes academic and personal achievement in making financial aid decisions. To apply for need-based financial aid, students must file the Free Application for Federal Student Aid (FAFSA) and the CSS Profile form between January 1 and February 1 and request that the results be sent directly to St. Lawrence.

Faculty

The 192 members of St. Lawrence's faculty are teachers and scholars. While teaching and advising are their primary responsibilities, they are also active researchers, artists, performers, and regular contributors in their academic disciplines. Faculty members teach all courses at St. Lawrence; no undergraduate courses are taught by graduate students. Active teaching assistants and tutoring programs, involving qualified upperclass students, are closely supervised by faculty members. The student-faculty ratio is about 12:1. Faculty members hold regular office hours, serve as academic advisers to students, and frequently take part in extracurricular activities on campus.

Student Government

The Thelomathesian Society, comprising all students on campus, is governed by a senate of elected representatives. The senate distributes funds in support of student activities and provides 2 student delegates to the University's Board of Trustees.

Admission Requirements

St. Lawrence seeks students who can be successful in a demanding academic program and who can contribute to the quality of life of the community. The University is committed to enrolling students who represent the widest possible diversity of economic, social, ethnic, and geographic backgrounds. Academic preparation and ability are the most important criteria, but demonstrated ability in the creative arts, athletics, or social service is also a measure of a student's potential to benefit the St. Lawrence community. Candidates may choose whether or not they submit standardized test scores (SAT or ACT); University admissions are test-optional. A campus visit is strongly encouraged, and interviews may be scheduled on campus or off campus in certain areas.

Although there is no set distribution of required high school courses, successful applicants typically show strong preparation in the humanities, the social sciences, mathematics, and the natural sciences. Honors, Advanced Placement, and International Baccalaureate courses are opportunities for applicants to demonstrate intellectual maturity and curiosity, qualities highly valued in the admission process.

Application and Information

St. Lawrence uses the Common Application, with the St. Lawrence Supplement, as its sole application form. The application is available on the University's website. The application processing fee is $60. Regular decision applications should be submitted by February 1, with notification in mid-March. Students who decide that St. Lawrence is their first choice may apply early decision. The priority deadline for early decision begins November 1; students may commit to early decision up until February 1. Early decision candidates will generally be notified within two weeks of receipt of a completed application.

Transfer candidates should submit applications no later than November 1 for the spring semester or March 1 for the fall semester.

To request an application or for more information, students should contact:

Office of Admissions and Financial Aid
St. Lawrence University
Canton, New York 13617
Phone: 315-229-5261 (admissions)
       800-285-1856 (admissions, toll-free)
       315-229-5265 (financial aid)
       800-355-0863 (financial aid, toll-free)
E-mail: admissions@stlawu.edu
finaid@stlawu.edu
Website: http://www.stlawu.edu
         http://www.facebook.com/SLU2017
         http://twitter.com/StLawrenceU
         http://www.youtube.com/StLawrenceU

A typical fall classroom at St. Lawrence University.

SAINT LEO UNIVERSITY
SAINT LEO, FLORIDA

The University

Founded in 1889, Saint Leo University is now recognized as one of the nation's leading Catholic teaching universities and a school of international consequence. The University Campus in Saint Leo, Florida, serves the education needs of just under 2,200 traditional-age undergraduate students. The University also offers a variety of dynamic graduate programs, a weekend and evening program for working adults, and both undergraduate and graduate degree programs through eighteen education centers in seven states and through the Center for Online Learning, which houses the University's cutting-edge online degree programs.

The University College student body represents 44 states and territories, as well as 56 countries. International students make up 14 percent of the student population. Minority students represent 38 percent of the University College enrollment. Approximately 62 percent of traditional full-time students live in one of thirteen residence halls, with two more residence halls coming online for 2012–13 and 2014.

Students can participate in the nationally recognized honors program and the more than seventy-five different clubs and organizations on campus, including national fraternities and sororities. The Student Government Union and various campus organizations also sponsor movies, concerts, art exhibits, lectures, dances, and other special events throughout the academic year.

Saint Leo is a member of the Sunshine State Conference and competes in NCAA Division II intercollegiate athletics for men and women. Men's sports include baseball, basketball, cross-country, golf, lacrosse, soccer, swimming, and tennis. Women compete in basketball, cross-country, golf, lacrosse, soccer, softball, swimming, tennis, and volleyball. Students can also participate in a wide variety of intramurals. Campus recreational facilities include lighted racquetball and tennis courts; soccer, baseball, and softball fields; a weight room/fitness center; and a heated outdoor competition-size swimming pool. The campus is bordered by a 154-acre lake and an eighteen-hole golf course.

Saint Leo is committed to giving its students an education that prepares them for the future. The goal of the University is to develop the whole person, both academically and personally, by providing a values-based education in the Benedictine tradition. In a recent satisfaction survey, 97 percent of respondents said they would recommend Saint Leo to a friend.

Saint Leo University is accredited by the Commission on Colleges of the Southern Association of Colleges and Schools to award the associate, bachelor's, and master's degrees. Saint Leo University's degree program in social work is accredited by the Commission on Accreditation of the Council on Social Work Education (B.S.W. level). The Donald R. Tapia School of Business is accredited by the International Assembly for Collegiate Business Education (IACBE). The University's undergraduate sport business program is nationally approved by the Sport Management Program Review Council (SMPRC). Saint Leo University also has Teacher Education Programs approval by the State of Florida Department of Education.

In addition to associate and bachelor's degrees, Saint Leo University offers a Master of Accounting (M.Acc.); Master of Business Administration (M.B.A.) degree; a Master of Education (M.Ed.) degree; Master of Science (M.S.) degrees in criminal justice, criminal justice administration, critical incident management, and instructional design; a Master of Arts (M.A.) degree in theology; a Master of Social Work (M.S.W.); and an education specialist degree. The University will begin offering the Doctor of Business Administration (D.B.A.) degree in 2013.

Location

Saint Leo is located 35 minutes north of Tampa and 90 minutes west of Orlando. The lakeside campus occupies 186 acres of rolling hills and wooded grounds. The rural setting is conducive to academic success, but the University is located near enough to metropolitan areas to give the students the advantage of a wide variety of social and professional opportunities.

Majors and Degrees

Saint Leo University offers more than 50 traditional majors, pre-professional studies, specializations, endorsements, and programs. Undergraduate degrees offered are the Bachelor of Arts, Bachelor of Science, and Bachelor of Social Work.

The Donald R. Tapia School of Business offers degrees in accounting, communication management, computer information systems, computer science, economics, health care management, hospitality management, human resources management, international tourism, management, marketing, multimedia management, and sport business. The School of Arts and Sciences offers majors in biology, English, global studies, history, mathematics, medical technology, political science, psychology, religion, and sociology. The School of Education and Social Services offers majors in criminal justice, elementary education, middle grades education, secondary education, and social work.

Programs for students interested in professional studies in chiropractic, dentistry, law, medicine, occupational therapy, physical therapy, and veterinary science are also offered.

Academic Programs

Saint Leo's new University Explorations general education program ensures that all graduates have a solid grounding in theories, issues, and knowledge to prepare them for successful careers and graduate work. The program develops the skills that are the foundation of a liberal arts education and that today's employers demand. Students learn essential skills in critical thinking and decision making, effective communication, problem solving, analysis, and creativity. Students complete foundation courses in English composition, mathematics, and computer skills. Students then select courses of interest from liberal arts learning clusters including The Human Adventure, The Human Mosaic, Science in a Changing World, The Creative Life, and The Reflective and Spiritual Life.

Saint Leo has an academic skills program to assist first-year students in their adjustment to university life. Included in this program are freshman studies, tutoring, and advising.

Students who demonstrate course mastery for any course listed in the catalog have the opportunity to receive up to 40 hours of credit through examination. Detailed information about credit by examination is available through the Registrar's Office.

Most students at Saint Leo earn the credits needed for their bachelor's degree through a four-year program of study. All major programs require a 2.0 minimum grade point average for graduation.

Off-Campus Programs

Saint Leo University is committed to helping students expand their horizons through study-abroad programs. Students have the opportunity to spend a semester studying in London, Madrid, Paris, Rome, Australia, Ecuador, Germany, Greece, Ireland, Scotland, and various other cities within the United Kingdom. Articulation agreements also afford study opportunities throughout Asia and the Pacific Rim.

Students are also able to work with their professors and academic advisor to identify and pursue a wide variety of internship options, further enhancing the real-world experience component of their education.

Academic Facilities

The Cannon Memorial Library contains 94,146 volumes, and provides access to 235,000 e-books (non-unique e-book titles),

534 print periodical subscriptions, 147,929 unique e-journal titles, and 76 online databases. Also located in the library are the Hugh Culverhouse Computer Instruction Center classrooms, a student computer lab, and two VTT-equipped instruction/conference rooms.

Lab facilities include three teaching labs and one research lab for biology; two teaching labs, one research lab, and an instrumentation room for chemistry; and one physics lab. Labs have undergone comprehensive renovations, the most recent in 2012. The state-of-the-art building housing the Donald R. Tapia School of Business opened in fall 2011 and features SMART board technology, a Mac computer lab, and a broadcast studio.

Students are encouraged to utilize the University's Learning Resource Center (LRC). The LRC is housed in the Student Activities Building and features study and meeting space for small groups as well as such technology as high-speed laser printers. Professional and peer tutoring services are available to students and may be scheduled through the LRC. Central to campus is the Student Community Center, which houses the dining hall, campus bookstore, student lounge, and Lion's Lair snack shop, as well as substantial meeting space for groups of various sizes.

The University's campus is a mostly wireless environment. All students who reside in campus housing receive a state-of-the-art laptop computer or iPad. For students living off campus, laptops are available for use through the library.

Costs

For the 2013–14 school year, tuition is $19,240; freshman room and board costs are $9,680, and mandatory fees are $680. Miscellaneous indirect costs for the year (such as books, personal living expenses, insurance, and travel) are estimated at $4,708.

Financial Aid

Financial aid, both federally funded and awarded by the University, is available in the form of scholarships, grants, and loans. Financial aid is allocated on the basis of academic performance and need, as determined by the federal government from the financial information provided on the Free Application for Federal Student Aid (FAFSA). On-campus jobs are available for students, with priority given to students with demonstrated financial need. Ninety-two percent of students receive some form of financial aid.

Faculty

At Saint Leo University, outstanding teaching and active learning go hand in hand. Caring and capable faculty members provide students with knowledge, guidance, academic support, and a broad range of learning opportunities both in and outside the classroom. Students enjoy small classes (average class size is 18) and develop close relationships with experienced, well-qualified professors. At Saint Leo, 83 percent of full-time instructional faculty members hold the terminal degree in their field.

Student Government

A significant contribution to the University comes from the activities initiated by the Student Government Union (SGU). The SGU is an annually elected body organized and conducted in accordance with democratic procedures. This organization strives to foster leadership and loyalty among the students, to formulate recommendations for student life, and to recognize all extracurricular activities.

Admission Requirements

All candidates for admission should be, or expect to be, graduates of secondary schools accredited by a regional or state accrediting agency. Applicants should show successful progress toward graduation with a minimum of 16 academic units of course work: 4 units of English, 3 units of mathematics (algebra I and II and geometry), 3 units of social studies, 2 units of science, 2 units of a foreign language, and 2 units of electives. All domestic applicants are recommended to take the SAT or the ACT examination, although the University does offer a test-optional policy for admission. A letter of recommendation from the student's guidance counselor is also required. Average SAT score (math and critical reading) for students entering in fall 2012 was 1032; average composite ACT score was 21; average GPA was 3.5. Students may request to be considered for admission under a test-optional policy that requires additional credentials in lieu of standardized test scores. Students who do not meet regular admission criteria are reviewed by the Admissions Committee for the Learning Enhancement for Academic Progress (LEAP) program, a preparatory program that has a summer attendance component.

Once the applicant has submitted the application with the $40 application fee (fee is waived if application is submitted online), high school transcripts, test scores (optional if utilizing test-optional policy), and letter of recommendation, the file is reviewed and a decision is rendered. Notification is on a rolling basis. The priority application deadline is January 15; all applicants are encouraged to apply early.

Transfer and international students are also encouraged to apply. The same general admission procedures are required, along with at least a 2.5 average for all college work (for transfer students) and a score of at least 550 (paper-based test) or 78 (Internet-based test) on the TOEFL (for international students for whom English is not the primary language of instruction).

Campus visits are strongly recommended. The Office of Admissions is open from Monday through Friday from 8 a.m. to 5 p.m. and on select Saturdays during the academic year from 9 a.m. to noon. Appointments are preferred. Campus tours are available Monday through Friday at 10 a.m. and 2 p.m., as well as at 10 a.m. on select Saturdays during the academic year. Summer tours are available Monday through Friday at 10 a.m. and 2 p.m. as well. The Office of Admissions is closed on Sunday.

Application and Information

Additional information and application forms can be obtained by contacting the Office of Admissions. Candidates may apply online at www.saintleo.edu/apply.

Reggie Hill
Director of Admissions
Office of Admissions—MC2008
Saint Leo University
P.O. Box 6665
Saint Leo, Florida 33574-6665
Phone: 352-588-8283
       800-334-5532 (toll-free)
Fax: 352-588-8257
E-mail: admission@saintleo.edu
Website: http://www.saintleo.edu

The Saint Leo University campus.

ST. LOUIS COLLEGE OF PHARMACY

ST. LOUIS, MISSOURI

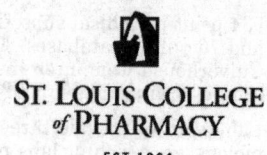

The College

Founded in 1864, St. Louis College of Pharmacy is the fourth oldest and tenth largest college of pharmacy in the nation. Members of the first board of trustees included pharmacists, physicians, and business leaders, such as Henry Shaw, founder of the Missouri Botanical Garden, and John O'Fallon, nephew of explorer William Clark. Approximately 73 percent of St. Louis–area pharmacists are graduates of the College. Its 6,800 alumni practice in forty-nine states and thirteen different countries.

Grounded in rich tradition and history, St. Louis College of Pharmacy faculty, students, alumni, and staff have collaborated to create a strategic plan, STLCOP 20/20, that will not only secure the College's legacy, but will enhance its impact on the practice of pharmacy locally, regionally, and nationally. Over the next decade, the College will strive to diversify academic offerings, advance a community-centered research and scholarship agenda, establish economically sustainable pharmacy practice models, ensure that personal and professional growth is a hallmark of the College community, and reach beyond campus to impact communities in innovative ways.

St. Louis College of Pharmacy is a small, private college that admits students directly from high school and integrates the liberal arts and sciences into a Doctor of Pharmacy program. Students in the most recent freshman class have an average ACT score of 27 and an average high school grade point average of 3.65. More than 1,290 students from thirty states are currently enrolled at the College.

The College offers a curriculum that is focused on math and science and integrates coursework in the liberal arts and professional studies. During the course of the program, students will apply their knowledge and explore pharmacy career options in diverse clinical settings through introductory and advanced pharmacy practice experiences. Students will have opportunities to conduct research, do original work, and present at professional conferences. A St. Louis College of Pharmacy education prepares students to practice in a variety of areas: community or hospital pharmacies, managed care, consultant pharmacies, the pharmaceutical industry, military, academia, or pharmacy associations.

With nearly 50 clubs and organizations on campus, St. Louis College of Pharmacy provides a full college experience, including professional and social fraternities, intramurals, club sports, pharmacy organizations, and special interest groups. The College participates in ten NAIA sports: men's and women's cross-country, men's and women's basketball, women's softball, men's and women's track and field, men's and women's tennis, and women's volleyball. The College's small size offers its residents and commuters opportunities to become an integral part of the campus experience.

Residence Hall is in the center of the 8-acre campus and houses 265 students and 10 resident assistants. Students become part of a supportive environment that emphasizes community and personal development. Residence Life staff organizes social and educational activities designed to provide residents opportunities to both relax and gain skills to help them be successful at St. Louis College of Pharmacy and life beyond the College. All students have use of the cafeteria space, attached to Residence Hall, for 3 meals a day and as a study space late into the night.

All first-year students are given priority for housing, regardless of where they live. First-year students are not allowed to have a vehicle on campus.

St. Louis College of Pharmacy also provides multiple resources and support to help students succeed in class and manage college life. Assistance is offered in many ways, including individual counseling, tutoring, individual coaching, student-to-student mentoring, and disability accommodations.

The St. Louis College of Pharmacy's Doctor of Pharmacy degree is accredited by the Accreditation Council for Pharmacy Education and the North Central Association of Colleges and Schools.

Location

Only a few miles from the Gateway Arch, St. Louis College of Pharmacy is located in one of America's most prestigious biomedical complexes, including Barnes-Jewish Hospital, Washington University School of Medicine, the Siteman Cancer Center, St. Louis Children's Hospital, and the Goldfarb School of Nursing at Barnes-Jewish College. The campus is one block from Forest Park, with its 1,300 acres of green space, tennis courts, ice-skating rink, golf course, and world-class museums, zoo, outdoor opera theater, and science center. Students at the College are near the cultural and entertainment scene of St. Louis on a safe, 8-acre campus within a block of public transportation.

Majors and Degrees

Students at St. Louis College of Pharmacy progress through a curriculum which integrates courses in liberal arts and sciences with a professional program leading to the Doctor of Pharmacy (Pharm.D.) degree.

Academic Programs

The Doctor of Pharmacy program includes intensive courses in biology, chemistry, mathematics, and physics, as well as electives in literature, humanities, and social and behavioral sciences. Introductory practice experiences throughout the curriculum give students the opportunity to apply their education and enable students to develop knowledge, communication skills, and professional values through interaction with other health-care practitioners and patients. During the sixth year of the curriculum, students participate in a series of eight 5-week pharmacy rotations.

Off-Campus Programs

Students have opportunities to participate in advanced practice experiences across the country at more than 600 community and hospital settings. The College's close proximity to Barnes-Jewish Hospital and Washington University School of Medicine also gives students access to nearby research, work-study, and volunteer opportunities.

Academic Facilities

Jones Hall contains the majority of College classrooms, lecture halls, laboratories, and faculty and administrative offices. The College's O. J. Cloughly Alumni Library, located on the first floor of Jones Hall, not only offers many educational resources, including subject databases, print and electronic books and journals, magazines, newspapers, and audiovisual materials but also provides a quiet, comfortable environment where students may read and study. In addition, the online portion of the library gives students, faculty, and staff of the College the opportunity to explore what the library has to offer, with access to databases, e-books, electronic journals, and interlibrary loan requests, all from the comfort of their home or office. Whelpley Hall features a 300-seat auditorium in addition to small- and medium-sized classrooms.

Costs

For the 2013–14 academic year tuition for students in year one is $25,390, in year two is $25,075, and in years three through six is $27,539. A notebook computer (issued to all new students) and lab fees are included in tuition costs. Room and board costs for the academic year are $9,100 for shared units and $8,690 for suites. Additional costs, including books, student activity fees, student health fees, professional program fees, and new student program fees vary each year but average $900 per semester.

Financial Aid

St. Louis College of Pharmacy offers need-based and merit-based financial assistance. The College participates in all applicable federal and state financial aid programs. Scholarships, grants, loans, and student employment are offered to help qualified students pay for college expenses. Financial aid may be funded by the federal or state government, the College, benefactors and friends of the College, or other sponsoring organizations or agencies. Merit-based scholarships are offered to qualified students regardless of need.

Students planning to attend the College in the fall semester should submit the Free Application for Federal Student Aid (FAFSA). The College begins awarding financial aid in February and continues until all funds are exhausted.

Student Government, Clubs, and Organizations

The Student Body Union (SBU) serves as the governing body of students at the College. SBU is responsible for student appointments to administrative and faculty committees. SBU oversees disbursement of student activity funds, which are used to support student publications, social activities, theater and musical productions, and provide support for student organizations.

Some campus organizations include the following: Campus Crusade for Christ (CRU), Catholic Students Organization, ConjuRings (literary magazine), Environmental Action Committee, EUTS Dance Team, Gay/Straight Alliance (GSA), GEARS (Gaming, Electronics, Anime, Rec, Sci-Fi), International Students Organization (ISO), Outdoor Club, Pharmakon (school newspaper), Prescripto (yearbook), Roller Hockey, Royal Chorale, Society of Apothecaries and Dreamers, STLCOP Book Club ("Booksies"), Student Ambassadors, Student Body Union (SBU), Student Organization for Drug and Alcohol Awareness (SODAA), and theater.

Admission Requirements

All students applying for admission to St. Louis College of Pharmacy must present evidence of the satisfactory completion of a four-year course of study in, and graduation from, a high school approved by a recognized accrediting body. The high school course of study should include 4 units of English; 4 units of math, including algebra 1 and 2 and geometry; and at least 3 units of science, including biology/lab and chemistry lab. First-year students must have a high GPA of at least 3.0 (on a 4.0 scale), rank in the upper 50 percent of their graduating class, and have a minimum composite score of 23 on the ACT and/or SAT combined score of 1110. Minimum subscore requirement for math is 24; minimum subscore requirements for English, science, and reading are 21.

Required application materials include the following: completed application and $50 nonrefundable application fee; high school transcripts including cumulative GPA and senior-year class rank; official ACT or SAT results; guidance counselor recommendation; science teacher recommendation; personal essay; declaration of finances form (international students only); English language test results, such as TOEFL (only U.S. and non-U.S. citizens whose native language is not English; a copy of U.S. Citizenship and Immigration Service status (international students only); and test results from the Pharmacy College Admission Test (transfer students only).

Early decision students who wish to accept an offer of admission must confirm their intention to enroll by submitting a $500 tuition deposit within 15 business days of acceptance notification. Regular decision students must submit a $300 deposit within 15 business days of acceptance of notification. The application deadline for transfer students is March 1. However, the PharmCAS deadline for submission of all admission materials is February 1. Transfer students are accepted into the third year of the program.

Application and Information

Application deadlines can be found online at www.stlcop.edu.

For additional information or to apply, students should contact:
Registrar/Director of Admissions
St. Louis College of Pharmacy
4588 Parkview Place
St. Louis, Missouri 63110
Phone: 314-367-8700 Ext. 8313
      800-278-5267 (toll-free)
E-mail: pbryant@stlcop.edu
Website: http://www.stlcop.edu
        http://www.facebook.com/STLCOP
        http://twitter.com/STLCOPedu

Located in the heart of one of the world's finest biomedical research and patient-care centers, St. Louis College of Pharmacy provides innovative education, research, and career opportunities for students.

SAINT MARY'S COLLEGE
NOTRE DAME, INDIANA

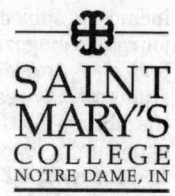

SAINT MARY'S
COLLEGE
NOTRE DAME, IN

The College

Saint Mary's College is an academic community where women discover and develop their talents, explore their passions, and embark on experiences that help them discover who they are meant to be. Student interests are as diverse as the student population, but they learn together with a common goal—to make a difference in the world.

The College's four-year, liberal arts education challenges students to realize their potential. Every area of study emphasizes the exceptional writing and critical thinking skills needed to become a confident leader.

Founded by the Sisters of the Holy Cross in 1844, Saint Mary's is a pioneer in the education of women. Saint Mary's is a Catholic college that empowers women by providing a solid liberal arts foundation, leadership development, and a focus on social responsibility.

With more than 1,400 students from forty-two U.S states and territories and fifteen countries, Saint Mary's brings together women from a wide range of backgrounds and experiences. International and diverse students compose 17 percent of the student body.

Saint Mary's unique relationship with the University of Notre Dame provides students with access to the exciting atmosphere of a large university—just across the street. Students at both schools can take courses at either institution. Saint Mary's students can audition for Notre Dame's legendary marching band; or work for the *Observer*, the daily newspaper published jointly by Notre Dame and Saint Mary's. In addition, students participate in dances, concerts, lectures, and social organizations on both campuses.

Saint Mary's campus life is centered on the women who live and learn there. Women lead and organize more than sixty clubs and organizations, eight varsity athletic teams, service opportunities through the Office for Civic and Social Engagement, and take part in numerous other events and activities.

Saint Mary's residential campus becomes the students' second home. Saint Mary's five residence halls include Opus Hall, which offers apartment-style living for seniors on campus. Residence halls host events such as dances and coffee nights with the College president, and compete with each other in intramural athletics. Each hall and floor forms its own community within a community. All residence halls have chapels, and the Church of Loretto, the main worship space, offers daily Mass.

As an NCAA Division III school and a member of the Michigan Intercollegiate Athletic Association, Saint Mary's sponsors varsity teams in basketball, cross-country, golf, soccer, softball, swimming and diving, tennis, and volleyball. Lacrosse will become a varsity sport in the 2013–14 academic year. Club sports, cosponsored with Notre Dame, include gymnastics and figure skating. In addition, Saint Mary's offers many intramural sports. Angela Athletic Facility has multipurpose courts and a training and fitness center with weight and cardio machines, a rock-climbing wall, and fitness classes for every level.

Location

Saint Mary's beautiful 100-acre campus, set alongside the Saint Joseph River, is across the street from the University of Notre Dame, minutes north of the city of South Bend (population 101,000), and 90 miles from Chicago. Saint Mary's students are integrally involved in the South Bend community, which provides opportunities for internships, field practicums, and volunteer service. Nearly 90 percent of Saint Mary's students engage in service by the time they graduate. The national average is approximately 55 percent.

Majors and Degrees

Saint Mary's College offers five degree programs: Bachelor of Arts, Bachelor of Science, Bachelor of Business Administration, Bachelor of Fine Arts, and Bachelor of Music.

The Bachelor of Arts degree program includes majors in art (concentrations in studio art and art history); biology; chemistry; communication studies; communicative disorders; economics; elementary education; English literature; English writing; English literature and writing; French; global studies; history (including a concentration in women's history); humanistic studies; Italian; mathematics; music; philosophy; political science, psychology, religious studies, social work, sociology, Spanish; statistics and actuarial mathematics; a student-designed major for approved, qualified students; and theater.

Students may obtain a Bachelor of Science degree in biology (concentrations in ecology, evolution, and environmental biology; cellular/molecular biology; and integrative biology), chemistry (including a concentration in biochemistry), computational mathematics, mathematics, nursing, statistics and actuarial mathematics, and a student-designed major for approved, qualified students.

The Bachelor of Business Administration degree program offers majors in accounting, business administration, and management information systems (concentrations include accounting, finance, international business, management, management information systems, and marketing).

Saint Mary's College offers a Bachelor of Fine Arts degree, with specialization in ceramics, fiber, new media art, painting, photo media, printmaking, and sculpture.

The Bachelor of Music degree program offers majors in music and music education. The College is a member of the National Association of Schools of Music.

Superior students who are candidates for either a B.A. or a B.S. degree may, with faculty approval, design a program of study outside the traditional department structure, called a student-designed major.

For students interested in engineering, a five-year, dual-degree program offered in cooperation with the University of Notre Dame leads to a bachelor's degree from Saint Mary's College and a Bachelor of Science in Engineering degree from Notre Dame in aerospace, chemical, civil, computer, electrical, environmental, or mechanical engineering.

Saint Mary's education department, accredited by the National Council for Accreditation of Teacher Education, offers an elementary education major (grades K–6) and a secondary education minor (grades 5–12). With an elementary education major, students can also receive mild intervention licensure (K–6) and an Indiana reading licensure (P–12). Minors in English as a second language and early childhood education are also offered. In addition, the department offers programs for those interested in teaching the visual arts or music. Secondary education requires a major in one of the following: English, modern languages (French, Spanish), mathematics, science (science majors must complete licensing requirements in one of the following areas: chemistry, life science), history (history majors must complete additional course work in political science and one of the following: sociology, psychology, economics), and political science (political science majors must complete additional course work in history and one of the following: sociology, psychology, economics).

The College offers more than forty minors, including American history, anthropology, environmental studies, information science, justice studies, Latin American studies, and women's studies.

Academic Programs

In addition to completing the required credit hours in her major, every student completes a senior comprehensive in her major, which may take the form of a thesis, a research or creative project, or a written or oral examination, depending on the discipline. All students must also complete a writing-intensive "W" course, usually in the first year, and an advanced portfolio of writing in the major discipline, usually in the senior year.

Off-Campus Programs

Intercultural competence is a cornerstone of the liberal arts education. Saint Mary's couples that with travel and adventure through study-abroad experiences in sixteen locations: Argentina, Australia, Austria, China, Ecuador, England, France, Greece, Honduras, Ireland, Italy, Morocco, South Africa, South Korea, Spain, and Uganda. Saint Mary's students may also study in other countries through a cooperative program with the University of Notre Dame. Domestic programs include a semester at American University in Washington, D.C. for political science majors, opportunities for student teachers in Native American communities, and the Catalyst Trip, a journey to sites significant to the history of social justice.

Academic Facilities

Saint Mary's academic buildings support its students' learning through access to technology systems, software, and services. Several buildings have computer labs in addition to computer "collaboratories," where students and faculty members can conduct online research in classroom settings.

The Cushwa-Leighton Library houses a collection of more than 228,000 volumes. Also located in the library are the Trumper Computer Center, the Instructional Technology Resource Center, and a rare book room.

Laboratory facilities are available for biology, chemistry, physics, psychology, and foreign language students. Art studios, music practice rooms, the O'Laughlin Auditorium, and Moreau's Little Theatre provide space for fine arts creation, practice, and performance. The Spes Unica academic building provides students with technology-equipped classrooms, group and individual study spaces, and presentation spaces.

The Early Childhood Development Center provides education and psychology majors with a unique opportunity to work with young children on campus. Other facilities include the Madeleva classroom building, Science Hall, Havican nursing facility, and Moreau Art Galleries.

Costs

Expenses for the 2012–13 academic year included tuition and fees, $33,280; room and board, $10,140 (average); and miscellaneous expenses (books, transportation, and living costs), $2,500.

Financial Aid

The College strives to make a Saint Mary's education available for every admitted student by offering financial aid packages that might include need-based assistance, merit scholarships, outside scholarships, and work-study opportunities. Last year, more than 95 percent of Saint Mary's students received financial aid totaling more than $20 million in College grants and scholarships.

All applicants for financial aid must complete the College Board PROFILE and the Free Application for Federal Student Aid (FAFSA) each year that they desire assistance.

Faculty

Saint Mary's professors are experts in their fields of study and mentors to their students inside and outside the classroom. Of the 130 full-time faculty members, 87 percent hold earned doctorates or other terminal degrees. Saint Mary's also has 76 part-time faculty members.

Student Government

The Student Government Association (SGA) is a dynamic student-led organization that sponsors extracurricular and co-curricular activities including service projects, social events, and learning experiences. It provides student participants with an abundance of leadership opportunities complete with leadership training. SGA has voting representatives on the president's two highest advisory boards, the Student Affairs Council and the Academic Affairs Council. A student is also a voting member of the College's Board of Trustees.

Admission Requirements

Applicants for admission to Saint Mary's College should be graduates of an accredited high school. Home-schooled students are encouraged to apply. All applicants must complete a four-year, college-preparatory curriculum that consists of a minimum of 16 academic (Carnegie) units. One unit represents one full year of study. The minimum requirements are: 4 units of English literature and composition, 2 units of the same foreign language, 3 units of college-preparatory mathematics (beginning with algebra I), 2 units of laboratory science, and 2 units of history or social science. The remaining required units should consist of three additional units in the above listed subjects.

Applications must include an academic transcript showing current rank (if available) and senior-year courses, a counselor/administrator recommendation, SAT or ACT scores, and an essay. There is no application fee, and Saint Mary's is a member of the Common Application.

An interview with an admission officer is recommended. Saint Mary's encourages students to visit the campus for a tour and interview. In addition, the Office of Admission can make arrangements for students who wish to attend classes or stay overnight.

Application and Information

Saint Mary's has two application and notification programs: early decision and modified rolling admission. Highly qualified students who have selected Saint Mary's as their first choice for admission may apply under the early decision program. The application deadline is November 15, and the notification date is December 15. Students who apply for modified rolling admission and whose application files are complete on or before December 1 are notified of the admission decision in mid-January. Applications received after December 1 are reviewed in the order in which they become complete. The priority application deadline for regular admission is February 15. Applications are accepted, however, as long as space is available.

Interested students are encouraged to contact:

Office of Admission
Saint Mary's College
Notre Dame, Indiana 46556-5001
Phone: 574-284-4587
      800-551-7621 (toll-free)
Fax: 574-284-4841
E-mail: admission@saintmarys.edu
Website: www.saintmarys.edu
      facebook.com/saintmaryscollege
      @saintmarys on Twitter

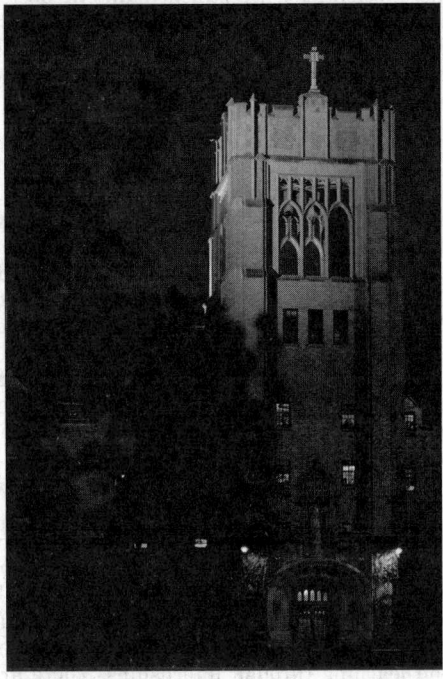

Educating women—mind, body, and spirit—since 1844.

SAINT MICHAEL'S COLLEGE
COLCHESTER, VERMONT

The College

What matters?

Saint Michael's College believes that a college education should prepare students not only for a meaningful career, but also for a meaningful life.

That's why Saint Michael's students start by building a strong liberal studies foundation, then they dive deep into their majors. By the time they graduate, students have developed essential skills and knowledge to help them be successful in any field. And in the meantime, they've also been engaged in service (through the College's popular MOVE program), in the great outdoors (with Saint Michael's ground-breaking Wilderness Program and Smuggs' Ski Pass), and with the close campus community in meaningful ways that educate the body, mind, and spirit.

And happiness matters. At Saint Michael's, prospective students find bright, engaged, friendly, happy students and faculty members. The College's formula for happiness is its close campus community, its perspective-changing exploration of the liberal arts, its legacy of faith and service, and its stunning Vermont location.

All this happiness and engagement underscores Saint Michael's successes: The College is among only 280 colleges and universities nationwide to host a prestigious Phi Beta Kappa chapter on campus. Recent graduates are Rhodes Scholars, Pickering Fellows, medical students, law students, dental students, medical researchers, pharmacists, new media specialists, sports writers, nonprofit directors, and more. Alumni include a U.S. Senator, one of the founders of MTV, noted authors, scientists, investment bankers, doctors, social workers, teachers, professors, and scholars. No matter what career paths they choose, Saint Michael's alumni take with them a solid liberal arts foundation, a strong sense of self, and a desire to give back to their communities.

Students at Saint Michael's are seriously involved with life on campus, taking on leadership roles, rallying support for worthy causes, and generally making things happen. Because everyone lives on campus (student housing is guaranteed for all four years), there's an incredible sense of community, and students always find someone ready for whatever adventures they have in mind—from taking on a research project to rock climbing. Nearly one third of Saint Mike's students study abroad for a semester, an academic year, or a summer. A new Quad Commons and residence hall, scheduled to open in fall 2013, adds more than 50 new rooms and four stories of living space, including a cafe, digital lounge, gym, game room and meditation space.

Location

Saint Michael's beautiful, safe 440-acre campus is just 3 miles from Burlington, which is Vermont's largest city. Burlington is a vibrant college town that is home to 14,000 students who attend five local colleges and universities. Downtown Burlington is a thriving city center of businesses that offer great opportunities for hands-on learning through internships. There are tons of shops, restaurants, and cafés, the Church Street Marketplace, and a lively local music scene as well as tons of places to ski, skate, kayak, and bike. The Smuggs' pass lets students to take advantage of some of the best skiing in the East, and

the renowned Wilderness Program offers dozens of outdoor adventure opportunities. Saint Michael's Cultural Pass gives students deep discounts to fine arts performances at Burlington's famous Flynn Theater.

The Burlington International Airport, Amtrak station and Greyhound bus station are all only a 10-minute drive from the campus.

Majors and Degrees

Saint Michael's College offers bachelor's degrees with a liberal arts foundation. The College offers 34 majors in the following areas: accounting, American studies, art, art education, biochemistry, biology, business administration, chemistry, classics, computer science, economics, elementary and secondary education, engineering, English, environmental studies, French, gender/women's studies, history, information systems, mathematics, media studies/journalism/digital arts, modern languages and literature, music, philosophy, physics, political science, pre-pharmacy, psychology, religious studies, sociology, Spanish, and theater. In addition, advising programs for premedicine, prelaw, predentistry, and pre–veterinary studies are available in addition to 37 minors, including interdisciplinary areas.

Dual-degree programs are available in engineering through Clarkson University (Potsdam, New York) and the University of Vermont (Burlington, Vermont); pharmacy through Albany College of Pharmacy's Burlington campus; and physical therapy through the University of Vermont. A 4+1 M.B.A. program is offered in conjunction with Clarkson University.

Academic Programs

Saint Michael's prepares its students for life after college with a dynamic liberal arts curriculum designed to foster intellectual curiosity and exploration, including a highly competitive honors program and many opportunities for self-directed study. The College's curriculum emphasizes a solid understanding of building blocks of a meaningful life as a well-rounded, thoughtful person: humanities, social sciences, religious studies, philosophy, natural sciences, mathematics, and fine arts. Saint Michael's students develop excellent communication skills through writing intensive courses and foreign language requirements. And the curriculum pays serious attention to questions of ethics and responsible citizenship.

The Saint Michael's academic year consists of two semesters and an optional summer session. The College's focus is on undergraduate instruction, and its small classes support this primary emphasis. Saint Michael's has a strong faculty-student research tradition and provides competitive opportunities for research for academic credit and with faculty during the academic year and over the summer.

Nowhere is Saint Michael's mission more evident than in its service-learning opportunities. Service-learning at Saint Michael's is a credit-bearing, educational experience in which students in an academic course participate in a thoughtfully organized service activity that meets identified community needs. Students reflect on the service activities in ways that develop further understanding of course content, a broader appreciation of the discipline, and an enhanced sense of civic responsibility.

Off-Campus Programs

At Saint Michael's, students can gain hands-on experience with an internship related to their career goals and majors. Internships are available both locally and in other selected areas around the United States and abroad. Sites include scientific research laboratories, brokerage houses, hospitals, schools, newspapers, and accounting firms. Saint Michael's students are given free access to the county's public transportation system which grants them easy access to the city of Burlington.

Nearly a third of Saint Michael's students study abroad for a semester or an academic year. Unique Saint Michael's programs include study-abroad experiences at University of the Americas, Mexico; College of Ripon and York St. John, England; Kansai Gaidai University, Japan; and a Washington, D.C., semester program. In recent years, many students have studied abroad in locations such as Australia, Botswana, China, France, Ghana, Ireland, Italy, Nepal, Samoa, and Spain.

Academic Facilities

Saint Michael's has a Main Campus and a North Campus. Main Campus is home to almost all academic and administrative buildings. The Jeremiah Durick Library holds 227,000 volumes; 110 research databases; access to articles from more than 25,000 online journals; and 10,000 electronic books, maps, videos, and other items. Students have access to more than 120 computers connected to the College's campuswide information technology network. This network provides access to PC applications, including Microsoft Windows 7, the Internet, e-mail, and the College library. Most campus areas have wireless Internet access.

Cheray Science Center has recently renovated facilities for the study of biochemistry, biology, chemistry, environmental science, and physics.

Saint Edmund's Hall, an impressive academic complex, includes media labs, psychology labs, computer facilities, and language labs, in addition to traditional classroom and lecture hall space.

Costs

Tuition and residence fees for the 2013–14 academic year are $48,740. The residence fee includes housing and meals and is based on a standard double room and a standard meal plan. Housing options on campus include traditional residence halls, apartment-style housing, and suite-style housing. Some science, journalism, language, and art courses require laboratory fees. Book, personal, and travel expenses vary according to course selection and individual needs.

Financial Aid

Approximately 90 percent of admitted students receive financial aid in the form of loans, grants, and work-study dollars. Students must file the FAFSA by February 15 for fall-semester enrollment. Saint Michael's students have a 1.1 percent default rate compared to the national average default rate of 9.8 percent.

Faculty

Saint Michael's faculty members are known not only for being experts in their fields but for sharing that expertise effectively with their students. Their doors are always open, too—it's not unusual to join professors for coffee or lunch, or to be invited to their homes for dinner. Students find faculty members at fundraisers and on the sidelines of athletic games. And chances are excellent that they'll know every student's name by the end of the first week of class. Saint Michael's remarkable faculty includes 150 full-time professors, 94 percent of whom have the doctoral or terminal degree in their field. Many have been recipients of grants, awards, and honors in recent years. While undergraduate instruction is the focus of the College, faculty members remain active in their field through research and publication, often facilitated through sabbaticals.

Student Government

The Student Association (SA), an active and important part of campus life, is an elected body of students that authorizes and funds most other student activities and organizations. Representatives from the SA sit on many campuswide committees, including the Curriculum Committee and various committees of the Board of Trustees.

Admission Requirements

Successful applicants to Saint Michael's typically rank in the top 25 percent of their high school class and have a strong college-preparatory background. Students should have completed 16 units of courses in English, foreign language, mathematics, science, and social science. SAT or ACT scores are optional. For reference, of those who opted to submit them, the average SAT score last year ranged between 1600 and 1890, and the average ACT score ranged between 25 and 26. In addition, students should submit a counselor recommendation and any teacher recommendations they choose. Transfer applicants must submit transcripts of all college work in addition to their final high school transcript.

Application and Information

Saint Michael's offers an early action admission program deadline of either November 1 or December 1, as well as a regular action deadline of February 1. The transfer application deadline is March 15. Students should consult the website for application deadlines and information. Candidates for the fall semester are notified of their admission decision on or before April 1. A limited number of students may be admitted to the spring semester and should have their applications in by November 1. The College adheres to the Candidates Reply Date of May 1 for the fall semester.

For further information, students should contact:
Office of Admission
Saint Michael's College
One Winooski Park, Box 7
Colchester, Vermont 05439
Phone: 800-762-8000 (toll-free)
Fax: 802-654-2906
E-mail: admission@smcvt.edu
Website: http://www.smcvt.edu

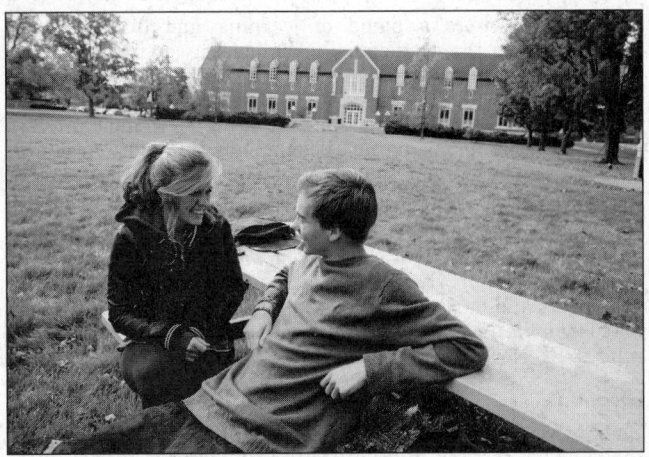

Visitors to Saint Michael's picturesque campus can see why it's been called one of the happiest colleges in the United States.

ST. NORBERT COLLEGE
DE PERE, WISCONSIN

The College

A new state-of-the-art library, new outdoor athletics complex, renovated student services center, new welcome center, new student commons, and construction underway on a nearly $40 million science center—these are just a few of the exciting things happening at St. Norbert College. The riverfront campus is part of the thriving corporate, entertainment, educational, arts, and cultural environment of northeastern Wisconsin. Learning takes place in residence halls and classrooms, in the community, and, literally, around the world.

The St. Norbert learning community helps students become critical thinkers, strong writers, and able communicators, in a setting that encourages student-faculty collaborations. The graduate-level work done by St. Norbert undergraduates, even as first-year students, is notable and puts them ahead of their peers when heading to graduate school or the workforce.

St. Norbert seeks to challenge student viewpoints and encourage exploration of new or different ideas, in an environment where students from around the world come together in exploration of local and global perspectives.

Faculty members at St. Norbert are active researchers and creators who make ongoing contributions to their fields. They're also compassionate individuals who care not only about their students' grades, but also about their growth, making time for one-on-one conversations with students on a daily basis. Student success is their top priority, and they regularly give out their home or cell phone numbers for easy student access.

St. Norbert offers more than forty programs of study, including several pre-professional programs. Students can also design their own major. Opportunities to study abroad abound, with numerous service opportunities for students locally, nationally, and internationally.

Each St. Norbert student is paired with an adviser who helps ensure that the student is on track with classes and will graduate in four years. St. Norbert's innovative career services office provides service throughout college and beyond; the alumni career network helps students find their first job as well as their last one. When students are surveyed nine months after graduation, 94 percent are typically employed or attending graduate school.

Student life offers a blend of learning and fun. Students flourish within the academically challenging environment, but with more than seventy clubs and organizations on campus, there's no shortage of ways to become involved outside the classroom. The twenty Division III athletics teams produce conference champions, national champions, and more Academic All-Americans than any school in the Midwest Conference.

Students frequently comment on the sense of community and worldwide opportunities available at St. Norbert. They talk about the challenges of the classroom and the heartfelt rewards of the service opportunities. Graduates value the friendships with peers and faculty members that started at St. Norbert and may last a lifetime. Some students love the campus so much they refer to St. Norbert as their home.

Location

The St. Norbert campus, approximately 108 acres, is located on the banks of the Fox River in De Pere, Wisconsin, just minutes south of Green Bay, a metropolitan area of about 230,000 people. Rich culture, arts, and entertainment are present in historic De Pere and the greater Green Bay area, recognized as one of the 100 best communities for young people by America's Promise Alliance. The campus is part of a vibrant eighteen-county region of 1.2 million people, with paid internship opportunities at Fortune 500 companies, hospitals, schools, and service organizations.

Majors and Degrees

St. Norbert offers programs leading to the Bachelor of Arts, Bachelor of Science, Bachelor of Music, and Bachelor of Business Administration degrees. Students also have the opportunity of applying their education at St. Norbert toward any of the master's degree programs, highlighted by the Master of Arts in Liberal Studies and Master of Theological Studies.

Programs of study at St. Norbert include: accounting, American studies, anthropology, art–fine arts, art–graphic design, biology–biomedical, biology–organismal, business administration, chemistry, chemistry–biochemistry, classical studies, communication and media studies, computer science, computer science–business information systems, computer science–graphic design and implementation, economics, education, English, English–creative writing, environmental science, French, geography, geology, German, history, human services (social work), international business and language area studies, international studies, Japanese, leadership studies, mathematics, military science/ROTC, music, natural sciences, peace and justice, philosophy, physics, political science, pre-dental, pre-engineering, pre-law, pre-medical, pre-nursing, pre-pharmacy, pre-veterinary, psychology, religious studies, religious studies–youth ministry, sociology, Spanish, teacher education, theater studies, and women's and gender studies.

Academic Programs

As a liberal arts institution, the college prepares students for a lifetime of challenges and opportunities by equipping them with exceptional communication abilities, as well as critical-thinking, problem-solving, and leadership skills. An honors program offers additional challenge in areas of general education to those of superior ability. St. Norbert has the highest four-year graduation rate in Wisconsin, backed by a four-year graduation guarantee.

Several St. Norbert students are recipients of full Army ROTC scholarships each year. Among the college's alumni are an impressive 12 Army generals who completed ROTC at St. Norbert.

Off-Campus Programs

St. Norbert students, regardless of major, can spend a summer, a semester, or a year abroad. In fact, 30 percent of St. Norbert students spend at least one semester abroad during their four years compared to less than 4 percent nationally. The college has more than seventy-five study-abroad program sites in thirty countries on six continents. An international study component is a part of majors in French, Spanish, and German, and both the international business program and the international studies major. All approved international study carries regular academic credit. St. Norbert scholarship assistance and other financial aid carry over to overseas study.

St. Norbert considers international experience vital to today's graduates and it is a key component of the college's educational mission. St. Norbert's international curriculum, taught by a faculty committed to global learning, prepares students to live in a global society. A Washington semester is also available through American University in Washington, D.C.

Additional service-learning opportunities are available throughout the year. Students can participate in the TRIPS (Turning Responsibility into Powerful Service) program in local, national, and international locations, or participate in a variety of other off-campus service opportunities.

Academic Facilities

A new $20-million state-of-the-art library houses more than 250,000 volumes, with more than 3,000 volumes added to the collection each year. The 80,000-square-foot library features enhanced technology, flexible study and classroom spaces, and a 24-hour computer study area.

The F. K. Bemis International Center provides students with opportunities to prepare for careers with greater international emphasis. Students from more than thirty countries attend St. Norbert College annually. The center also serves as a resource for K–12 schools and Wisconsin businesses for language instruction, translation, and interpretation.

The John Minahan Science Hall currently houses the science programs and thirty-eight laboratories. Construction is well underway on renovation and expansion of this building, and the Medical College of Wisconsin has selected St. Norbert for the location of its northeast Wisconsin program.

Thirteen residence halls provide the link between living and learning at St. Norbert. Some residence halls focus on community service or feature campus programs, such as the Women's Center or the honors program. A new apartment-style residence hall offers upperclassmen a transitional experience to living on their own. Many halls have chapels for students.

A new outdoor athletics complex provides the practice and competition venue for football, soccer, and track and field. The newly remodeled Michels Commons is where students eat their meals and gather in Dale's Sports Lounge on evenings and weekends. Chefs prepare meals in front of the students and are able to get immediate feedback on favorite recipes.

Costs

For 2012–13, tuition and required fees for full-time students totaled $30,675 for the year. Room and board costs averaged $7,813 per year.

Financial Aid

Students share in more than $50 million of financial aid each year, including scholarships and grants, campus jobs, and educational loans. More than 95 percent of St. Norbert students receive financial aid, with the average aid amount of more than $24,000 for first-year students. There are both need-based and merit-based awards.

Need-based awards are made on the basis of the Free Application for Federal Student Aid (FAFSA; St. Norbert College's code is 003892) and the St. Norbert College institutional application for financial aid. First-year applicants should submit these forms by March of their senior year of high school.

A multitude of work-study positions exist on campus as well as paid campus internships.

Faculty

The St. Norbert faculty is composed of 201 men and women, with at least 87 percent of the full-time faculty members holding the doctoral or other terminal degree in their field. The student-faculty ratio is 14:1, and student success is a top priority of the faculty. They work closely with students in their major area of study, help students prepare for graduate school, write letters of recommendation, and work with those who seek independent study and research opportunities. Research fellowships and collaborations with faculty members are available to all students, who may ultimately have the opportunity to present their research findings collaboratively with faculty members at national conferences. Faculty members also work with Career Services in its professional practice program.

Student Government

The college's Student Government Association (SGA) is active on campus, with representation extending as far as the college's board of trustees. The president of the college and his cabinet respect the voice of the student body, and openly discuss issues that impact students and the college community.

Admission Requirements

St. Norbert College welcomes enrollment from a diverse group of students who are prepared academically and who will make a contribution to the college's living and learning community. Every completed application is considered carefully, and students who are likely to succeed in this environment are accepted. In 2012, more than 86 percent of the first-year class ranked in the top half of their high school senior class, the average GPA was 3.5, and the average ACT composite score was 25. Students with superior scores and grades are invited to enroll in the honors program.

Application and Information

Because the college gives preference to students according to the date of admission and enrollment deposit, it benefits students to apply as early as possible in their senior year. Notification of the admission decision is made on a rolling basis beginning in late September. A $350 nonrefundable deposit is required to confirm enrollment.

For more information about St. Norbert College, students should contact:

Edward Lamm
Associate Vice President of Undergraduate and Graduate Enrollment
St. Norbert College
100 Grant Street
De Pere, Wisconsin 54115
Phone: 920-403-3005
        800-236-4878 (toll-free)
E-mail: admit@snc.edu
Website: http://www.snc.edu
         http://www.snc.edu/go/socialmedia

With the picturesque St. Norbert campus just across the river, students frequent the Fox River Trail for a ride, a run, or a rest.

ST. THOMAS AQUINAS COLLEGE
SPARKILL, NEW YORK

ŠT. THOMAS AQUINAS COLLEGE

The College

St. Thomas Aquinas College (STAC) was founded in 1952 as a three-year teacher-training college with 30 students. Today, the College offers more than 100 different majors, minors, specializations, and dual degree programs and has a total student body of 2,700 in all programs, on and off campus. Much growth and development has taken place over the College's history. The College offers a Master of Science in Education, with concentrations in literacy education, special education, and educational leadership as well as postgraduate certificate programs in literacy and special education. The College also offers a Master of Business Administration (M.B.A.) program with concentrations in finance, management, and marketing; and an online M.B.A. in general studies. St. Thomas offers a Master of Science in Teaching program for individuals without a background in teacher education who are seeking a career change. Certification is offered in childhood education, grades 1–6; childhood education and special education, grades 1–6; and adolescence education, grades 7–12. The College is home to New York University's Master in Social Work program.

The suburban campus includes two residential complexes: Aquinas Village, which consists of self-contained townhouse units that house 300 students, and the McNelis Commons, which consists of townhouse residential units that house 375 students and a common dining hall and laundry building. Approximately 40 percent of the College's full-time student population resides on campus.

Extracurricular activities are provided through forty different organizations, including the Spartan Volunteers, a community service program; a student-run radio station (WSTK); the Laetare Players dramatic and musical club; and the student-edited campus newspaper and yearbook. The College has excellent sports facilities, and several of its athletic teams have competed in national championships. The College fields NCAA Division II teams in men's and women's cross-country, golf, indoor track and field, and tennis; women's basketball, lacrosse, soccer, and softball; and men's baseball, basketball, and soccer. There are a number of club sports including equestrian, ice hockey, cheerleading and dance, bowling, and ski and snowboarding, as well as intramural athletics.

The College has a campus ministry office, a health office, and residence life, career placement, and counseling services.

Location

The College is located in Sparkill, a hamlet in southern Rockland County, New York, 16 miles north of New York City and adjacent to Bergen County, New Jersey.

Majors and Degrees

St. Thomas Aquinas College's School of Business offers accounting (and accounting as a dual degree with an M.B.A. degree), business administration, finance, marketing, and sports management. Minors are offered in business administration, marketing, economics, human resource management, international business, and management information systems. Specializations are in management relations/industrial and organizational psychology.

The School of Arts & Sciences offers degrees in the humanities, mathematics, natural sciences, and social sciences. Programs are available in art therapy, art and graphic design, communication arts, English, philosophy and religious studies, Romance languages, Spanish, mathematics, computer and information sciences, biology, forensic science, medical technology, natural sciences, criminal justice, psychology, therapeutic recreation,

social science, and history. There are specializations in biology, chemistry, and physics. Minors include art therapy, biology, chemistry, communication arts, computer information science, criminal justice, English, fine arts, graphic design, history, journalism, mathematics, performing arts, physics, public relations, religious studies, Spanish, social media, sociology, therapeutic recreation, and writing. A full listing of all programs can be found online at www.stac.edu.

The School of Education offers programs in grades 1–6 childhood education, the same plus special education, and grades 7–12 adolescence education, the latter offering certification in biology, English, history, mathematics, science and technology, natural science with either biology or chemistry, social sciences, and Spanish. An art education program with certifications in grades K–12 is offered as well as a middle school extension that adds to either the elementary or secondary degree, enabling the student to certify for all middle school grades.

The College offers a five-year dual-degree program in mathematics/engineering with the George Washington University (GWU) or Manhattan College. Students study at St. Thomas for three years. After completion of their final two years at either GWU or Manhattan, they earn a B.S. in mathematics from STAC and a B.S. in engineering from one of the other two institutions. The College also offers several dual-degree options in biology: a dual degree in biology (B.S. from STAC) and biomedical engineering (M.S. from Polytechnic University), a dual degree in biology (B.S. from STAC) and physical therapy (D.P.T. from New York Medical College), a dual degree in biology (B.S. from STAC) and chiropractic (D.C. from New York Chiropractic College), and a dual degree in biology (B.S. from STAC) and podiatry (D.P.M. from New York College of Podiatric Medicine). There are several other strategic alliances, such as preferred admission to St. John's University School of Law in New York and a similar program with Barry University School of Law in Florida that includes scholarship funds. St. Thomas seeks out additional strategic opportunities for its undergraduate and graduate students on a regular basis; students should contact the College for information about new alliances.

Academic Programs

The College strives to develop students who are not only generally educated but also possess advanced knowledge in specialized areas, are prepared for further study, and have the background to undertake fulfilling careers. To earn a bachelor's degree, students must complete a total of 120 semester hours, including a minimum of 51 credits in a core curriculum; complete all requirements for the specific major; and complete the final 30 hours at St. Thomas. The College awards up to 30 credits for life experience and up to 30 credits for achievement on the College-Level Examination Program (CLEP). The College operates on a semester calendar (quarterly on the M.B.A. level). Students may enroll in classes in the fall, winter (a one-month session), spring, and summer (three separate sessions). Classes are scheduled during the day and evening, and students are permitted considerable academic flexibility in planning their programs.

Students can pursue independent study and internships, and many majors require a field practicum. The College maintains an active Center for Academic Excellence as a resource for enhancing academic performance, and students are encouraged to meet regularly with faculty advisers for academic guidance and career direction.

Several programs supplement the traditional academic areas. The College has a widely recognized program for college-age learning-disabled students, called the Pathways Program (at an additional cost). The College also participates in the New York State Higher Education Opportunity Program and provides an honors program for exceptionally qualified students with a limited number of full-tuition-scholarships. The honors program includes summer study at Oxford University.

Off-Campus Programs

The College offers a campus interchange program involving three other fully accredited colleges (Barry University in Miami Shores, Florida; Dominican College of San Rafael in San Rafael, California; and Aquinas College in Grand Rapids, Michigan) through which a student may attend a semester at one of the participating colleges during the junior year. The College also offers a number of study-abroad opportunities for students throughout the entire year with as short a period as one week for a communication arts class in London.

The study-abroad program provides opportunities at colleges and universities in such places as Brazil, Canada, England, France, Hungary, Ireland, Italy, Morocco, and Spain. Several other locations are also available.

The College offers courses for an associate degree program at West Point for eligible students at the United States Military Academy.

Academic Facilities

Borelli Hall features new classrooms with interactive board technologies. Costello Hall houses the science laboratories, technology theaters, and Azarian-McCullough Art Gallery. Spellman Hall houses a multiroom technology corridor, with a state-of-the-art communication studio where students produce their own news show, and technology and language labs. Lougheed Library provides a variety of online research opportunities for students. Aquinas Hall houses athletic facilities and a fitness center. Maguire Hall is home to classrooms, art studios, and the Sullivan Theater. Additional meeting areas are provided in the Romano Student-Alumni Center and in the two residence complexes, McNelis Commons and Aquinas Village. There is an after-hours club in the McNelis Commons dining hall for student activities.

Costs

For 2012–13, the tuition for full-time study (12 to 16 credits per semester) was $24,610. Room and board at the College Commons were $11,000. Certain studio, laboratory, and computer courses carry fees.

Financial Aid

In 2011–12, 80 percent of the student body received financial aid. The College is committed to providing competent but needy students with the resources necessary to continue their education. Students must submit the Free Application for Federal Student Aid each year. The College awards academic and merit scholarships from $5,000 up to full-tuition scholarships and provides need-based aid from the College as well as athletic grants and all federal and New York State aid programs.

St. Thomas strives to partner with the student to make college education affordable. The College has one of the lowest private college tuition rates in New York State, and scholarships make it even more affordable. The College is also a member of the Yellow Ribbon program for veterans enabling a qualified veteran to study with a full tuition scholarship.

Faculty

The faculty has 70 full-time and 55 part-time members; 80 percent have terminal degrees. The student-faculty ratio is 18:1. All faculty members participate in the academic advising of students and serve on College committees. Many serve as advisers to extracurricular activities.

Student Government

The Student Government consists of elected members who officially represent the student body, are responsible for planning and implementing student-originated programs, and coordinate and oversee all extracurricular organizations. Through its various offices, students play a vital part in offering consultation on new policies, planning social and cultural events, managing student funds, and operating the judicial system. In addition, the College Forum, which is composed of elected students, faculty members, alumni, administrators, and trustees, meets regularly to discuss policies, procedures, long-range plans, and any problems affecting the College.

Admission Requirements

All applicants must have successfully completed an approved secondary school program or the equivalent, including 4 years in English, 3 years in mathematics, 3 years in science, 3 years of foreign language, and 4 years of social studies. Applicants whose high school background varies from the recommended pattern are considered. Freshman applicants must submit the application for admission, including an essay, high school transcripts, SAT or ACT scores, and their guidance counselor's recommendation. Transfer students must submit the application and official transcripts of all previous college work. An academic evaluation is prepared for every matriculant.

Application and Information

Candidates should submit completed application forms to the Admissions and Financial Aid Office and must request that their official transcripts be sent to the Admissions Office from their school. Students are notified of the admission decision on a rolling basis upon receipt of all the necessary credentials. The College is a member of the Common Application and students can find the link to apply on its website, http://www.stac.edu.

The College does not discriminate against students, faculty and staff members, and other beneficiaries on the basis of race, color, national origin, gender, age, sexual orientation, disability, marital status, genetic predisposition, carrier status, veteran status, or religious affiliation in admission to or in the provision of its programs and services. The Section 504 Coordinator, the Title IX Coordinator, and the Age Act Coordinator is Marian Hall, Executive Director of Human Resources, 845-398-4038.

For more information or an application, students should contact:

Admissions and Financial Aid Office
St. Thomas Aquinas College
125 Route 340
Sparkill, New York 10976-1050
Phone: 800-999-STAC (toll-free)
Website: http://www.stac.edu

At St. Thomas Aquinas College, student-faculty interaction fosters innovative thinking.

SALISBURY UNIVERSITY
SALISBURY, MARYLAND

The University

A Maryland University of National Distinction, Salisbury University (SU) consistently ranks among the top 10 percent of public and private institutions in national guidebooks and magazines. A member of the University System of Maryland (USM), SU emphasizes undergraduate research, study abroad, professional internships, and community engagement as pillars of its academic programs.

A midsize university of 7,969 undergraduates and 402 full-time faculty members on a 197-acre campus, SU provides a private college feel with the opportunities and affordability of a public institution. This distinct combination is why 98 percent of recent graduates say they would recommend SU. The foundation of SU's success is the relationship between students and professors. Full professors serve as undergraduate advisers, and routinely lead students on trips and retreats, from exploring the Chesapeake Bay to touring Europe. Their professional concern for educating the whole student has had measurable results. According to the latest figures, SU has among the fastest time-to-degree average and the highest four-year graduation rate of all comprehensive institutions in the USM. Students have earned prestigious honors including the Gates Cambridge Scholarship and Fulbright Fellowship. This success has not gone unnoticed. For the sixteenth consecutive year, SU is among *U.S. News & World Report*'s Top Public Universities in the North, one of the highest-placing public master's-level universities in Maryland. For the fourteenth consecutive year, SU is one of *The Princeton Review's* Best Colleges. *Kiplinger's Personal Finance* magazine has named SU among the top 100 best value public colleges in the nation.

Salisbury students come from twenty-eight states, the District of Columbia, and sixty-three other countries. Almost 60 percent are from Maryland's western shore (which contains the Metropolitan Baltimore-Washington corridor). Many of SU's 100-plus student organizations and clubs find a home in the Guerrieri University Center. An NCAA Division III member of intercollegiate athletics, SU has twenty-one varsity sports that compete in the Capital Athletic Conference and in the Empire Eight Athletic Football Conference. Women's sports are basketball, cross-country, field hockey, lacrosse, soccer, softball, swimming, tennis, indoor and outdoor track and field, and volleyball. Men's sports are baseball, basketball, cross-country, football, lacrosse, soccer, swimming, tennis, and indoor and outdoor track and field. The Sea Gulls have won sixteen national championships, ten in men's lacrosse, five in field hockey, and one in women's lacrosse. A leading Division III program, Salisbury athletics are consistently ranked in the top 25 of the national Directors' Cup standings. Nearly half of the student body participates in twenty-two intramural programs and fourteen sports clubs.

The University has three art galleries; supports film and distinguished lecture series and artist-in-residence programs; maintains WSCL/WSDL-FM (national public radio affiliates) and WXSU-FM (a student-run radio station); offers performing arts disciplines in music, theater, and dance; and serves as the home of the Salisbury Symphony Orchestra. Beyond the campus are Maryland's scenic Eastern Shore, the pleasures of Ocean City, Maryland (a nearby popular beach resort), and the activities of an energetic Outdoor Club. Faculty members lead trips abroad during spring break, and winter and summer terms.

Location

With a regional population of roughly 99,000, Salisbury is the cultural and economic hub of Delmarva (containing portions of Delaware, Maryland, and Virginia), a historically and ecologically rich peninsula located between the Atlantic Ocean and Chesapeake Bay. The city is 30 minutes west of the beaches of Assateague and Ocean City, Maryland; about 2 hours from Baltimore, Wilmington, Norfolk, and Washington, D.C.; and 4½ hours from New York City.

Majors and Degrees

Three undergraduate degrees are offered in addition to the Bachelor of Arts and Bachelor of Science: the Bachelor of Arts in Social Work (B.A.S.W.), the Bachelor of Science in Nursing (B.S.N.), and the Bachelor of Fine Arts (B.F.A.) in art. B.A. degrees are awarded in art, communication arts, conflict analysis and dispute resolution, economics, English, English for speakers of other languages, environmental studies, fine arts, French, history, interdisciplinary studies, international studies, music, philosophy, political science, psychology, sociology, Spanish, social work, and theater. B.S. degrees are awarded in accounting, athletic training, biology, business administration, chemistry, clinical laboratory science/medical technology, computer science, early childhood education, earth science, elementary education, exercise science, finance, geography and geosciences, health education, information systems, interdisciplinary studies, management, marketing, mathematics, nursing, physical education, physics, and respiratory therapy.

The University also offers fourteen graduate programs, and a new Doctorate of Nursing Practice.

Academic Programs

At Salisbury University, majors are designed to educate the whole student. While gaining a liberal arts education, for example, students in preprofessional programs prepare for careers in dentistry, law, medicine, optometry, pharmacy, physical therapy, podiatry, and veterinary science. Certification programs train educators for both elementary and secondary teaching. Dual-degree programs with the University of Maryland Eastern Shore (UMES) enable students to earn two bachelor's degrees in four years in biology/environmental marine science and social work/sociology. SU, Old Dominion University, Widener University, and the University of Maryland College Park also collaborate on an engineering degree. New partnerships with two Estonian universities allow students to study cybersecurity internationally. SU supports an Army Reserve Officers' Training Corps (ROTC) program on campus. The business school is accredited by The Association to Advance Collegiate Schools of Business and the Network of International Business Schools. Other national accreditations are in chemistry, education, allied health (respiratory therapy, exercise science, and athletic training programs), social work, clinical laboratory science (medical technology program), music, and nursing and through the Middle States Commission on Higher Education.

SU's fifty-seven academic programs are administered through four schools: the Franklin P. Perdue School of Business, the Samuel W. and Marilyn C. Seidel School of Education and Professional Studies, the Charles R. and Martha N. Fulton School of Liberal Arts, and the Richard A. Henson School of Science and Technology. All four schools are endowed, a rarity among public institutions nationwide. These endowments have enriched the scholastic climate of the campus, providing expanded scholarships, resources, and opportunities.

University planning encourages interdisciplinary study. Students in all majors must take a minimum of nine courses in three disciplines: history, humanities and social sciences, and mathematical and natural sciences. Two courses are required in English composition and literature. One course is required in health fitness. All courses, from science to music to physical education, require written assignments in analysis/criticism, research, or creative writing.

SU's advising system has been praised by students in a Maryland Higher Education Commission survey as one of the best in the state. Orientation programs help freshmen make a successful transition to college. SU's New Student Seminars offer an orientation-in-the-wilderness experience, which won the Maryland Association for Higher Education Distinguished Program Award. Orientation options include cycling in Maine and canoeing in Canada.

Incoming students may earn credit through Advanced Placement and departmental challenge examinations and the College-Level Examination Program (CLEP) for nontraditional educational experiences. Internships have included work abroad, legislative service in Washington, D.C. and Annapolis, and media experience in fields from fine arts to television. Students who relish intellectual challenge are invited to join the honors program housed in the

Thomas E. Bellavance Honors Center. Others present research at national and international conferences. SU is also the only university in Maryland to twice host the National Conference on Undergraduate Research. Study-abroad programs are popular. Education students teach in New Zealand, nursing students provide aid in Africa, and all students may enroll in new Salisbury Abroad programs in Ecuador, Estonia, China, Spain, France, Scotland, and Italy for the same cost as tuition, room, and board in Maryland.

Academic Facilities

The SU campus is in the midst of an extensive transformation with planning under way for a new Academic Commons. Sea Gull Square, a 600-bed residence hall and retail complex, opened in fall 2011, the same time as a state-of-the-art home for the Perdue School of Business. Also ongoing are multimillion-dollar renovations for residence halls. The campus' first parking garage opened in fall 2009. SU is pursuing U.S. Green Building Council LEED Silver or Gold certifications for all current projects. New in 2008 was the University Fitness Center and SU's 165,000-square-foot Teacher Education and Technology Center, lauded as a showcase facility for education in the mid-Atlantic. The building, with its award-winning design, features Smart classrooms and an Integrated Media Center with a 24-track audio recording studio, 15 editing suites, a cutting-edge digital exhibition gallery, a digital photography lab and one of the few campus-based high-definition digital video production studios in the nation.

Henson Science Hall, SU's $42-million science education and research building, is one of the largest in Maryland. Blackwell Library is the main research center on campus, with more than a quarter-million books and bound periodicals and computers with access to databases, such as FirstSearch. Fourteen computer labs are part of the campus network, providing students with various software applications, e-mail, and the Internet. Resident students have network connections in their rooms and all academic and administrative buildings offer wireless Internet access. Fulton Hall is home to the fine and performing arts, and the Center for Conflict Resolution engages students in mediation efforts at home and abroad. The only institution in the USM with an endowed theater program, SU boasts three theaters for performing arts. Off the main campus, the Edward H. Nabb Research Center for Delmarva History and Culture is a treasure trove of information for students and visitors. SU's Ward Museum of Wildfowl Art was named one of the "10 Great Places to See American Folk Art" by *USA Today*.

Costs

Maryland residents paid undergraduate tuition and fees of $7,700 for the 2012–13 academic year. Tuition for out-of-state undergraduates was $16,046. Students living on campus paid about $9,620 for room and board; the figure varies, depending on the residence hall and meal plan.

Financial Aid

Financial assistance is available to students through loans, grants, scholarships, and on- and off-campus employment. The University participates in the Federal Perkins Loan, Federal Pell Grant, Federal Supplemental Educational Opportunity Grant, and Federal Work-Study and Direct Loan Programs. Numerous other forms of financial aid on the state and local levels are based exclusively on demonstrated financial need. All students who wish to apply for financial assistance must complete the Free Application for Federal Student Aid (FAFSA) by February 15. Complete details are available through the University's Admissions and Financial Aid Offices.

The University's Work Experience Program provides on-campus jobs for students. They can work up to 20 hours a week and typically earn $1,500 to $2,000 per semester, in positions related to their academic interest or other areas. Non-need academic scholarships for incoming freshmen are awarded on the basis of high school performance and SAT scores, if provided. Applying for admission is the initial step in applying for these scholarships.

Faculty

Faculty members at Salisbury have won national teaching, research, and leadership awards. Ninety-five percent of the tenure-track faculty members, many of whom are National Endowment for the Humanities and Fulbright professors, have the Ph.D. or other highest degree in their field. Professors not only publish but also donate countless hours to community service, thus teaching by deed as well as word. The student-professor ratio is 17:1; smaller classes are not unusual.

Student Government

Shared governance is a hallmark of campus life, and students are actively involved in all its aspects. The Student Government Association (SGA) serves as a liaison to the faculty and administration. SGA officers serve on many University committees, both administrative and academic, including the President's Advisory Team. The all-student Appropriations Board budgets activity fees to clubs and organizations. Students are encouraged to participate in events, many sponsored by the Student Organization for Activity Planning.

Admission Requirements

The University seeks to admit outstanding students who bring diverse talents, experiences, and points of view to campus. Most successful candidates for admission have earned above-average high school grades in a strong academic program and a score above the national average on the SAT or ACT. The high school record, test scores, essay, and recommendations of the high school principal and guidance counselors are considered. Interviews are not required, but applicants are encouraged to discuss programs and procedures for housing and financial aid with the staff of the Admissions and Financial Aid Offices.

The University has an SAT/ACT optional admissions policy. Applicants who have earned a weighted GPA of 3.5 or higher on a 4.0 scale have the choice of submitting a standardized test score. The SAT or ACT is required for applicants with a weighted GPA below 3.5 or who wish to be considered for University scholarships.

Transfer students must have earned at least 24 semester hours at an accredited community college or four-year college or university and have a minimum 2.0 average (on a 4.0 scale). For transfer students who have attempted fewer than 24 hours at another institution, the University's admission policy for entering freshmen applies.

Application and Information

Applications are accepted beginning August 1 for the spring and fall semesters. Applications received by November 1 for the spring semester and by January 15 for the fall semester are given the fullest attention. The University reserves the right to close admissions when the projected enrollment is met. The application is available online at http://www.salisbury.edu/apply. For further information, students should contact:

Admissions Office
Salisbury University
1200 Camden Avenue
Salisbury, Maryland 21801-6862
Phone: 410-543-6161
      888-543-0148 (toll-free)
Fax: 410-546-6016
E-mail: admissions@salisbury.edu
Website: http://www.salisbury.edu
      http://on.fb.me/SalisburyU (Facebook)
      http://twitter.com/salisburyu

Salisbury University's Perdue Hall, new home of the Franklin P. Perdue School of Business.

SCHOOL OF THE ART INSTITUTE OF CHICAGO
CHICAGO, ILLINOIS

The School

Founded in 1866, the School of the Art Institute of Chicago (SAIC) offers acclaimed liberal arts-based undergraduate degrees with studio practice at their core. The School of the Art Institute of Chicago fosters the conceptual and technical education of artists, designers, and scholars from across the nation and around the world in a highly professional, studio-oriented, and academically rigorous environment, encouraging excellence, critical inquiry, and experimentation. SAIC was recognized as "the most influential art school in the nation" by a poll conducted by Columbia University and a panel of national art critics. *U.S. News and World Report* ranked SAIC's Master of Fine Arts in Studio program as number two among 220 competing programs.

SAIC's 2,400 undergraduate and 665 graduate students and a faculty of artists, designers, and scholars work in an environment that facilitates idea exchange, resource sharing, and critiquing and refining both technical abilities and conceptual concerns. More than ever before, contemporary artists cross media and disciplinary practices and utilize a wide variety of materials and processes to create their work. Through SAIC's unique, interdisciplinary curriculum, emerging artists, designers, and visual scholars are fully prepared for professional practice.

In order to prepare students for what is it like to be a creative professional, for whom the highest value is placed on the relationship between idea and execution, and to allow students to take creative risks, SAIC has a critique-based assessment tool and a credit/no-credit grading system. Students also take 6 credits of off-campus study—including study trips and internships—to allow them to make real-world connections and consider their work in the context of what is happening outside the classroom.

Students may live in one of two distinctive residence facilities, with rooms like loft-style apartments, each with their own bathroom and kitchenette. The residence halls have 24-hour security; controlled access; spacious, well-lit studios with 24-hour access; TV lounges; computer labs; and laundry facilities. Students can immerse themselves in a community of fellow artists, live in the heart of Chicago's loop, and enjoy conveniences unavailable in most student apartments.

Students have access to a wide variety of unique resources, beginning with the premiere collection of SAIC's sister institution, the Art Institute of Chicago, the third largest art museum in the world and the Ryerson & Burnham Libraries, the largest art and architecture research libraries in the country. The Gene Siskel Film Center presents significant programs of world cinema and presentations by an international array of film and video artists. SAIC's Video Data Bank houses more than 1,600 titles and is the leading resource in the United States for videotapes by and about contemporary artists.

The School of the Art Institute of Chicago also offers a broad spectrum of services to accommodate its diverse population, including a Career and Cooperative Internship Center international student office, multicultural affairs office, health and counseling services, Disability and Learning Resource Center, and an extensive program for academic advising.

The School of the Art Institute of Chicago is accredited by the Higher Learning Commission of the North Central Association of Colleges and Schools and by the National Association of Schools of Art and Design.

Location

The School of the Art Institute of Chicago is located in the heart of downtown Chicago, home to the nation's second-largest art scene that includes world-class museums, numerous galleries, alternative spaces, and organizations that support the arts. Chicago is a city of diverse neighborhoods, each with its own atmosphere, customs, and cuisine. Students have a wide variety of cultural and recreational resources from which to choose: ballet, opera, theater, orchestra halls, cinemas, libraries, architecture, blues and jazz clubs, parks,

ethnic restaurants, a variety of world-class sports venues, street and music festivals.

Chicago itself is a vital part of the campus, as a source of social and cultural activities and the stimulus for ideas and attitudes ultimately expressed through art. Peter Frank, art critic and curator says, "Of all American cities, Chicago has contributed the most solid and distinctive artwork and art thinking. The School of the Art Institute of Chicago is at the nucleus of this longstanding distinction."

The School of the Art Institute of Chicago is located across the street from Millennium Park, a twenty-first-century marvel that SAIC faculty members and students played a key role in creating. One of the signature pieces of public art, the Crown Fountain by Spanish artist Jaume Plensa, was created with the assistance of SAIC students and faculty, who collaborated with Plensa in producing the 1,000 video portraits that are screened continuously on the fountain's twin video towers. The park, with its unique mix of art, architecture, and green space, has become SAIC's quad.

Majors and Degrees

SAIC students do not declare majors, and may work in multiple areas of interest or concentrate in a single discipline. Areas of study include: animation, architecture, art and technology, art education, art history, ceramics, designed objects, drawing, fashion design, fiber, filmmaking, interior architecture, new media, painting, performance, photography, print media, sculpture, sound, video, visual communication, visual and critical studies, and writing. Beginning in their first semester, students are assigned an academic adviser who helps mentor and guide them to ensure that they are making the most of the courses and opportunities available to them.

SAIC offers six undergraduate degrees. The Bachelor of Fine Arts (B.F.A.) degree in studio allows students to develop a particularized course of study in the visual arts. The openness of the curriculum allows for creative, idiosyncratic, and tailored programs, thereby emulating the very process of art making. Academic advising, provided by the Office of Student Affairs, helps students in determining their particular path of study. The School of the Art Institute of Chicago offers Illinois teacher certification (K–12) through its B.F.A. with an emphasis in art education, with a goal of graduating artists and teachers who are informed and engaged citizens, creators and critics of visual culture. The Bachelor of Arts (B.A.) in Art History entails substantial course work in art history supported by additional course work in liberal arts and in studio departments. The B.F.A. with an emphasis in writing offers a solid grounding in literary conventions, a practical exposure to form in fiction and poetry, and an enhanced ability to read and critique peers' work, while encouraging students to openly explore what "writing" is.

The Bachelor of Arts in visual and critical studies allows students to pursue in-depth academic study in the creative environment of an art school, sharing classes with students in the B.F.A. programs. Core courses provide students with diverse critical methods for exploring the cultural meanings of visual phenomena as they relate to social, economic, and material circumstances.

The Bachelor of Interior Architecture (B.I.A.) is intended for students interested in interdisciplinary study and a focus in contemporary, professional design practices, such as sustainability, embedded and emerging technologies, and designed objects.

Academic Program

Completion of 132 hours is required for the all degrees with the exception of SAIC's B.F.A. with Emphasis in Art Education, which requires completion of 138 hours and fulfills the requirements for the State of Illinois K–12 Visual Arts Teaching Certificate (Type 10); approximately two thirds is in studio areas and one third is in academic course work. All entering students who have completed fewer than 15 credit hours of college-level studio art must enroll in the courses in the Contemporary Practice department. Students take liberal arts courses in the humanities, natural sciences, mathematics, and social sciences and are required to complete an art history requirement. The B.A. in Art History program consists of 85 percent art history and liberal art credits and 15 percent studio.

Off-Campus Programs

The off-campus study requirement is an opportunity for students to gain practical experience at the same time as they gain a broader sense of society and the world.

Students can choose from a wide variety of off-campus programs. The Mobility program allows students to attend partner schools within the United States and Canada and includes the New York Studio semester. SAIC also maintains semester exchange agreements with a multitude schools in Europe, Asia, and South America. The Off-Campus Programs Office works closely with students to help them develop their individual programs. SAIC faculty members lead study trips during each summer and winter interim session to ever changing destinations such as Cuba, New York, Puerto Rico, Venice, and Vietnam.

SAIC is home to the largest and most successful arts-related cooperative education program in the country, providing employment opportunities throughout Chicago and worldwide with individual artists; museums; galleries; multimedia firms; film, video, and animation production houses; interior architecture firms; fashion designers; and community service organizations.

Academic Facilities

SAIC's campus encompasses six buildings in downtown Chicago. There are fully equipped studios for each area of concentration, and SAIC's policy allows 24-hour access to facilities.

SAIC is committed to new technologies and the integration of computer-based resources throughout the curriculum. Currently, more than sixty digital technology courses are taught each semester in nearly all departmental areas. A laptop program coupled with state-of-the-art facilities and accessible resources provides cutting-edge creative capability to students. Facilities available to all students include general-access computer labs equipped with the latest-model Apple computers and high-end peripherals; a Service Bureau, providing professional digital output, including laser cutting and 3-D printing; Media Centers, offering a wide variety of equipment for student loan; wood and metal shops; and fabrication studios.

The John M. Flaxman Library supports the entire SAIC curriculum in the arts, liberal arts, and sciences. Web-accessible resources include SAIC's own growing digital library, a traditional online library catalog, e-reserves, and a rich assortment of full-text licensed databases. The Joan Flasch Artists' Book Collection contains more than 3,000 artists' books along with a research collection of exhibition catalogs and other related material.

Exhibition spaces include the acclaimed Sullivan Galleries offering 32,000 square feet of exhibition space—the only single contemporary exhibition site of its size in the Chicago Loop, and the Betty Rymer Gallery, which highlights work from departments and presents special exhibitions. In addition, Student Union Galleries, provide exhibition space, including a street-level gallery just off of Michigan Avenue, for currently enrolled students.

Costs

Tuition for the 2013–14 academic year is $39,810 for full-time undergraduate students or $1,327 per credit hour. A double room in student housing is $10,700, and a meal plan costs $1,500 for the academic year.

Financial Aid

The School of the Art Institute of Chicago makes every effort to assist students who need help in financing their education. Through an extensive financial aid program, a substantial amount of gift aid funding from private, institutional, state, and federal sources is distributed annually. In addition to scholarships and grants, SAIC grants merit scholarships and offers an extensive college work-study program. For the 2012–13 academic year, $29,000,000 in aid was awarded to undergraduate students, and 95 percent of the incoming class received some form of financial aid. To apply for financial aid, students should complete the FAFSA. To receive priority consideration, students should submit completed forms to the Financial Aid Office no later than March 1. All awards are made on a first-come, first-served basis to students in good standing who demonstrate need.

Faculty

Faculty members are selected for their skills, insight, and dedication as teachers and for their professional accomplishments as artists, designers, and scholars. There are currently more than 600 full- and part-time faculty members, among them NEA grant recipients, Louis Comfort Tiffany Foundation Fellowship recipients, and Rockefeller Foundation grant recipients. SAIC's faculty members have their work exhibited in museums, galleries, and festivals nationally and internationally. They publish books, plays, poetry, and criticism; organize and curate exhibitions; and design, build, and preserve buildings throughout the world. Each year, 100 or more well-known visiting artists, including poets, political activists, and visual artists, present workshops and provide individual student critiques through the Visiting Artists Program. Notable alumni include Claes Oldenburg, Ivan Albright, Edward Gorey, Georgia O'Keeffe, David Sedaris, Cynthia Rowley, and Vincente Minnelli.

Student Government

Student Government officers are elected each spring, and they promote student interests and concerns to the broader School community by serving on a variety of faculty and administrative staff committees. Student Government also provides funds for the more than forty student groups on campus. All students are encouraged to attend the weekly open Student Government meetings.

Admission Requirements

Applicants are required to submit the Common Application; a nonrefundable application fee of $65 for domestic students ($85 for international students); a portfolio consisting of ten to fifteen examples of recent work, a minimum of 5 minutes of time-based work; a statement of purpose; transcript(s) from high school(s) or an official copy of the high school equivalency certificate; transcripts from any college previously attended; and one letter of recommendation. Domestic applicants must submit either scores from the SAT or the ACT. Any transfer applicant who has successfully completed the School of the Art Institute of Chicago's English requirements and/or other liberal arts course work at another accredited college may be exempt from standardized test requirements for admission. All international undergraduate students who are not U.S. citizens or permanent residents or are nonnative English speakers are required to take either the TOEFL or the IELTS.

Application and Information

Prospective students are required to submit their applications through the Common Application, available online at www.saic.edu/ugapp. The applicant's portfolio and academic credentials are reviewed and evaluated by the Admissions Office. Students applying by the early application deadline of December 1 are eligible for priority scholarship, housing and registration. Priority merit scholarship deadline is February 1 for first-time freshmen and March 1 for transfer students. Students who anticipate a need for financial assistance are urged to complete their applications for admission and financial aid by March 1 for the fall semester and November 15 for the spring semester in order to receive priority consideration.

Admissions Office
School of the Art Institute of Chicago
36 South Wabash, Suite 1201
Chicago, Illinois 60603
Phone: 312-629-6100
     800-232-7242 (toll-free)
Fax: 312-629-6101
Email: ugadmiss@saic.edu
Web site: http://www.saic.edu/ug

SEATTLE UNIVERSITY
SEATTLE, WASHINGTON

The University

Seattle University (SU) provides an ideal environment for motivated students interested in self-reliance, awareness of different cultures, social justice, and the fulfillment that comes from making a difference in the world. Its location in the center of one of the nation's most diverse and progressive cities attracts a varied student body, faculty, and staff. Its urban setting promotes the development of leadership skills and independence and provides a variety of opportunities for students to apply what they learn through internships, clinical experiences, and volunteer work.

As a Jesuit institution, Seattle University is part of a network of twenty-eight colleges and universities and forty-six high schools across the United States noted for both academic strength and a commitment to social justice. Seattle U's core curriculum provides a rigorous liberal arts and sciences foundation designed to develop leadership skills, enhance global awareness, and enable graduates to serve others. In the Jesuit educational tradition, students are taught to understand the world deeply, build strong intellectual skills, and prepare to be thoughtful and empowered leaders for a better world.

Seattle University is noted for its focus on the individual through small, faculty-taught classes and an engaging student life program. The result is graduates who enjoy successful and fulfilling lives. Seattle University is recognized as one of the leading institutions in the Pacific Northwest in producing Truman and Wilson scholars.

Fall quarter 2012 had a freshman class of 916, with 60 percent coming from outside Washington State. The ethnic breakdown for the class was 54 percent white, 21 percent Asian American, and 14 percent African American, Latino, and American Indian. The 4,631 undergraduate students represent fifty-two states and territories and ninety-four nations. International students make up approximately 9 percent of the student body.

Approximately 1,900 students in total and 92 percent of freshmen live on campus in four residence halls and an apartment complex. Students are required to live on campus for both their freshman and sophomore years unless they are able to commute from home.

Seattle University has more than 130 extracurricular clubs and organizations, including the Hui O Nani Hawaiian Club, Engineers Without Borders, Outdoor Adventure and Recreation, Beta Alpha Psi (national accounting honorary), and other professional honoraries and clubs. SU Athletics (http://goseattleu.com/) is an NCAA Division I program and has eight varsity teams for men (baseball, basketball, cross-country, golf, soccer, swimming, tennis, and track) and ten for women (basketball, cross-country, golf, rowing, soccer, softball, swimming, tennis, track, and volleyball).

The Connolly Athletic Center serves as the major facility for varsity and intramural athletics and recreation. The center features two swimming pools, two full-size gymnasiums, and locker room saunas. A 6-acre complex provides fields for outdoor sports. The William F. Eisiminger Fitness Center, which opened in fall 2011, provides 21,000 square feet of fitness and cardio equipment, weights, lockers, and studio and classroom spaces.

Seattle University receives the highest professional accreditation from the Accreditation Board for Engineering and Technology, AACSB International–The Association to Advance Collegiate Schools of Business, American Bar Association, American Chemical Society, Association of Theological Schools, Commission on Accreditation of Allied Health Education Programs, National Association of Schools of Public Affairs and Administration, National Council for Accreditation of Teacher Education, Commission on Collegiate Nursing Education, Council on Social Work Education, and Northwest Commission on Colleges and Universities.

Location

Nestled between two mountain ranges, containing three lakes, and situated along Puget Sound, Seattle is a magnificent setting for a university. The city pulses with music, art, and culture. Seattle is the Pacific Northwest's center for legal, medical, business, and high-tech industries, and Seattle University students supplement their studies through internships, research, volunteer projects, mentorships, and meeting alumni in their fields.

Seattle's residents love the outdoors, and areas for skiing, hiking, backpacking, and climbing are within an hour of campus. Biking, walking, and jogging are also popular, with paths and trails throughout the city.

Seattle's sights and sounds, rich ethnic diversity, celebrated restaurants, eclectic entertainment, major-league athletics, theater, opera, and ballet are within walking distance, and are a central part of the Seattle University experience.

Majors and Degrees

Seattle University offers programs in six major academic units. The Albers School of Business and Economics awards degrees in accounting, business administration, business economics, information systems, economics, finance, international business, international economic development, management, and marketing. The College of Arts and Sciences grants degrees in art history, Asian studies, communication studies, creative writing, criminal justice, cultural anthropology, digital design, environmental studies, English, film studies, fine arts, French, history, international studies, journalism, liberal studies, military science/ROTC, philosophy, photography, political science, psychology, public affairs, social work, sociology, Spanish, sport and exercise science, strategic communication, string performance, theater, theology/religious studies, visual art, and women and gender studies. The College of Nursing offers a Bachelor of Science in Nursing degree. The Matteo Ricci College awards degrees in humanities for leadership and humanities for teaching. The College of Science and Engineering offers degree programs in biochemistry, biology, cell and molecular biology, chemistry, civil engineering, clinical laboratory science, computer engineering, computer science, diagnostic ultrasound, electrical engineering, environmental engineering, environmental science, general science, marine and conservation biology, mathematics, mechanical engineering, and physics. Preprofessional programs include dentistry, law, medicine, optometry, and veterinary medicine.

Academic Programs

The Core Curriculum has several distinguishing characteristics in keeping with the Jesuit educational tradition: it provides an integrated freshman year; gives order and sequence to student learning; provides experience in the methods and content of the range of liberal arts, sciences, philosophy, and theology; calls for active learning in all classes, for practice in writing and thinking, and for an awareness of values; and it fosters a global perspective and a sense of social and personal responsibility.

Seattle University offers two honors program options for students seeking rigorous academic challenge. The University Honors Program is a small, humanities-focused learning community with a curriculum that examines the most significant texts and ideas of Western culture. The Core Honors Program involves seminar sections of nine required courses in English, history, philosophy, social science, and theology/religious studies; this option is particularly suited to students in professional degree programs, for whom participation in University Honors is less feasible due to specific major requirements and scheduling conflicts.

Seattle University operates on a quarter calendar. The fall quarter begins in mid-September; the winter quarter in early January; the spring quarter in late March; and the summer quarter in mid-June. Undergraduates typically take 15 credit hours per quarter for the fall, winter, and spring quarters.

Off-Campus Programs

Seattle University offers a diverse array of short- and long-term international study programs. Some are appropriate for any student interested in study of a particular culture or language, while others are designed to complement specific majors. Short-term programs include opportunities in Brazil, Costa Rica, France, India, Ireland, Italy, Japan, Korea, Mexico, South Africa, and Sweden. Long-term programs, which last an entire academic quarter or more, are available for Austria, Belize, China, Denmark, Ecuador, France, Ghana, Japan, Mexico, and Spain. Students also have the opportunity to intern with non-governmental organizations in Asia, Africa, and Latin America through the unique International Development Internship Program (IDIP), which embodies the Jesuit emphasis on social justice and global awareness. Additional study-abroad programs in other nations, in conjunction with other colleges' overseas programs, are also offered. Arrangements are made through the Education Abroad Office.

Academic Facilities

The Seattle University campus has undergone more than $200 million in recent improvements. Twelve academic buildings house classrooms, thirty-four instructional laboratories, twenty-five specialized laboratories, computer facilities, and other instructional equipment to support state-of-the-art instruction.

The newly renovated Lemieux Library and McGoldrick Learning Commons has nearly 300,000 volumes and 2,700 current serial subscriptions, 1,300 online databases, and microforms periodicals. Study carrels provide quiet study space while lounges accommodate study groups. The library's Media Production Center houses a recording studio, control room, audio/video editing facilities, and a theater-style screening room.

The Albers School of Business and Economics features classrooms designed to enhance student interaction and access to high-tech teaching equipment.

The College of Nursing's 20,000-square-foot clinical performance laboratory is among the most technically advanced clinical laboratories in the country. It joins two clinical practice rooms and a suite of laboratories.

The Lee Center for the Arts is a showcase for theater and musical performances. This modern building seats 135 and includes a prop room, dressing room, costume shop, and professional lighting and sound booths that give students career-building technical skills.

The Chapel of St. Ignatius is Seattle University's spiritual center. This award-winning structure is recognized as a place of beauty, contemplation, and worship.

Costs

For academic year 2012–13, tuition was $34,200; room and meals were $10,296. The estimate for books, fees, and personal expenses is $6,114. Costs are subject to change.

Financial Aid

Seattle University awarded $43.2 million in its own financial aid to fall 2011 freshmen, including merit scholarships ranging from $7,000 to $44,500. The average financial aid package was $27,519. Students are required to apply for financial aid by February 1, as awards are made early each spring for the following fall quarter. Applications received after this deadline are evaluated in order received for any remaining aid. Students must submit the Free Application for Federal Student Aid (FAFSA) and be accepted for admission to be considered for financial assistance. Scholarships are awarded on the basis of academic achievement, extracurricular involvement, and community service.

Faculty

There are 505 full-time faculty members, 76 percent of whom possess doctoral or terminal degrees. All classes are taught by faculty. With an average class size of 20 and a faculty-to-student ratio of 1:13, the primary responsibility of Seattle University professors is the success of their students. Faculty members are available to provide assistance outside of class, to help students with research, and to assist in arranging internships. Faculty advisers provide guidance, direction, and encouragement throughout a student's academic career. New students are assigned faculty advisers prior to registration according to their major.

Student Government

All undergraduates belong to the Student Government of Seattle University (SGSU), the central student organization on campus. SGSU is organized around an elected president, an executive vice president, a vice president of finance, and an activities vice president. A 12-member representative council oversees every facet of the student body and is responsible for policymaking and providing a diverse activities program to meet the needs of Seattle University's student body. In addition, SGSU communicates student needs to the administration and faculty.

Admission Requirements

Freshman applicants are required to have completed a college-preparatory program upon high school graduation, including 4 years of English, 3 years of social studies/history, 3 years of mathematics, 2 years of laboratory science, and 2 years of a foreign language. Applicants to the College of Science and Engineering must complete 4 units of college-preparatory mathematics for admission to any of its specific majors; laboratory chemistry and laboratory physics are prerequisites for engineering program consideration. Applicants to the nursing major must complete laboratory biology and chemistry to be considered for admission.

ACT or SAT scores, an official high school transcript, a counselor recommendation, a teacher recommendation, and an essay are also required for freshman admission consideration. The middle 50 percent of 2011 freshmen had GPAs between 3.3 and 3.9 on a 4.0 scale and ACT scores between 24 and 29 or SAT scores between 530 and 640 (critical reading), 520 and 630 (math), and 520 and 630 (writing). College credit is awarded to those who have successfully completed Advanced Placement or International Baccalaureate examinations. Qualifying scores can be obtained by contacting the Office of the Registrar.

Application and Information

Students can apply directly online at commonapp.org; the forms can also be downloaded from the Seattle University website at http://www.seattleu.edu.

High school students applying for early action consideration must apply by November 15 of their senior year. Those applying for regular admission consideration must apply by January 15. The priority application deadline for fall transfer applicants is March 1.

Campus visits can be scheduled Monday through Friday and many Saturdays. Prospective students should contact Admissions for availability. With two weeks' notice, visitors can be scheduled to attend a class, meet with a faculty adviser, participate in a campus tour, and speak individually with an Admissions representative.

For additional information students should contact:

Admissions Office
Seattle University
901 12th Avenue
Seattle, Washington 98122-1090
Phone: 206-220-8040
      800-426-7123 (toll-free)
E-mail: admissions@seattleu.edu
Website: http://www.seattleu.edu
        http://www.facebook.com/seattleu
        http://twitter.com/seattleu

Seattle U's campus is in the heart of a vibrant, culturally rich city.

SHIPPENSBURG UNIVERSITY OF PENNSYLVANIA
SHIPPENSBURG, PENNSYLVANIA

The University

Located in south-central Pennsylvania, Shippensburg University has offered a quality, affordable education for more than 140 years. The University's goal is to equip students with the degree, knowledge, experiences, and skills to be active community participants. Shippensburg is a public university enrolling 7,800 students; 52 percent are women and 48 percent are men. Classes are small with a student-faculty ratio of 20:1. The University is a member of the Pennsylvania State System of Higher Education and is accredited by the Middle States Association of Colleges and Schools.

Ship, as the students call it, offers more than seventy-five programs of study within three colleges: Arts and Science, Business, and Education and Human Services. There is also an Office of Undeclared Students, a School of Graduate Studies, and an Office of Professional Continuing and Distance Education, which offers online courses and degree completion programs for undergraduates.

Shippensburg prides itself on offering learning opportunities beyond the classroom. Students can participate in research projects with faculty. Most universities reserve this privilege for graduate students. As a result, Ship students develop an edge at both graduate school and in the job market. Many academic programs at Ship have service-learning opportunities where students take what they have learned in the classroom and apply it in the community. Accounting majors assist local low-income families with tax preparation and English students help with literacy programs. Each year students log in more than 20,000 hours of community service. Shippensburg is the only university in Pennsylvania with a public elementary school on campus. The Grace B. Luhrs University Elementary School allows students to interact and observe children in grades K–5. The Family and Child Center is available for toddler and preschool children.

Students have numerous opportunities to step into positions of influence on projects, teams, and in student organization. This helps them develop teamwork, decision-making, and motivational skill, which are important to employers. Ship has more than 200 student clubs and organizations including musical and theatrical performing groups, fraternities and sororities, academic and honorary societies, and more. Student activities are complemented by programs that bring nationally and internationally known speakers and performers to the University's Luhrs Performing Arts Center.

The University's eight traditional residence halls are being replaced with suite-style halls. Three suite facilities opened in 2013, three more will open in 2014, and the remaining are due to be completed by 2015. The traditional residence hall rooms have cable and Internet connections and are double occupancy. The suite unit configurations include 2 persons/one bedroom, 2 persons/two bedrooms, and 4 persons/two bedrooms. Suite units have air conditioning, carpeting, cable and wireless Internet connections, kitchenettes, and furnished living rooms. There are laundry facilities on each floor, common kitchens, and game rooms. Student safety is emphasized through controlled access to the residence halls, trained supervisory personnel, and a keycard entry system. There is also an apartment-style student housing facility and designated Honors housing.

Athletic facilities for both intercollegiate and intramural sports include a 2,768-seat field house, an 8,000-seat stadium, a gymnasium, outdoor tennis courts, indoor and outdoor tracks, an indoor swimming pool, squash and handball courts, a rehabilitation center, and sand volleyball courts. The University is a member of the Pennsylvania State Athletic Conference and NCAA Division II. Intercollegiate sports for men are baseball, basketball, cross-country, football, soccer, swimming, track and field, and wrestling. Women's intercollegiate sports are basketball, cross-country, field hockey, lacrosse, soccer, softball, swimming, tennis, track and field, and volleyball. There are six intramural sports including street hockey, and sixteen club sports including rugby and quidditch.

ShipRec, the student recreation center, includes a cardio/strength area with thirty-nine cardiovascular machines with individual televisions, four multipurpose courts, a group fitness studio, and an elevated running track.

The Etter Health and Wellness Center is open from 7:30 a.m. to 11:30 p.m. and is equipped with modern examination, treatment, and emergency rooms; beds for inpatient care; and a self-care unit for minor health conditions. Chambersburg Hospital is 20 minutes from campus.

Students have access to comprehensive counseling services in academic, career, psychological, social, personal growth, and religious areas. The Career Development Center offers career counseling, workshops in resume preparation, job interview techniques, and job search assistance.

Location

Shippensburg University is situated on 200 rolling acres overlooking its namesake community, a borough of approximately 6,700 people in south-central Pennsylvania. The University is about 40 minutes southwest of Harrisburg, 2 hours from both Baltimore and Washington, D.C., and 2½ hours from Philadelphia. The campus is within easy walking distance of the center of town.

Majors and Degrees

Undergraduate degrees conferred are the Bachelor of Arts (B.A.), Bachelor of Science (B.S.), Bachelor of Science in Business Administration (B.S.B.A.), Bachelor of Science in Education (B.S.Ed.), and Bachelor of Social Work (B.S.W.).

The College of Arts and Sciences awards the B.A. degree in art (computer graphics); communication/journalism (electronic media, print media, public relations); English (writing); French; history (public history); human communication studies; interdisciplinary arts; international studies, political science; psychology; secondary certification (art, English, French, and Spanish); sociology; and Spanish. The B.S. degree is awarded in applied physics (nanofabrication); biology (biotechnology/pre–forensic science, ecology and environment, health professions, medical technology); chemistry (biochemistry, business, computational, environmental, forensics, pre-pharmacy); computer engineering; computer science (computer graphics, embedded programming, related discipline, software engineering); economics (business, mathematics, political science, public administration, social studies); geoenvironmental studies; geography (geographic information systems, human-environmental, land use); healthcare administration; mathematics (applied, statistics); physics (nanofabrication); professional studies (technical leadership and administration); public administration; and secondary education (biology, biology/environmental education, chemistry, mathematics). The B.S.Ed. degree is awarded in earth and space science, physics, social studies/geography, and social studies/history.

The John L. Grove College of Business awards the B.S.B.A. degree in accounting, finance (personal financial planning), information technology for business education, logistics, management (entrepreneurship, human resource, international management), management information systems, marketing, and supply chain management.

The College of Education and Human Services awards the B.S. degree in criminal justice and exercise science; the B.S.W. degree in social work; and the B.S.Ed. degree in early childhood/elementary education PK–4, and elementary/middle-level education 4–8, (language arts, math, science, social studies).

Preprofessional preparation is available for admission to schools of chiropractic, dentistry, engineering, forensic science, law, medicine, optometry, pharmacy, physical therapy, podiatry, and veterinary medicine.

Shippensburg University offers 2+2 transfer programs in the allied health fields of biotechnology, nursing, occupational therapy (2+3), P.A.C.E. Program (2+2, 3+3), and radiologic sciences.

Academic Programs

The University is on the semester system with a fall semester beginning in late August and a spring semester beginning in mid-January. Three terms, one of three weeks and two of five weeks, compose the summer program. Online courses are offered during a four-week winter term.

The general education program, which comprises half of the credits required for graduation, is the core of the undergraduate curriculum. It includes courses to develop competence in writing, speaking, mathematics, and historical perspectives. The program ensures exposure to logic and numbers; linguistic, literary, artistic, and cultural traditions; biological and physical sciences; political, economic, and geographic sciences; and social and behavioral sciences. Ample elective opportunities are available.

The University requires students to take one approved diversity course for a total of 3 credit hours.

Academic options include an honors program, independent study and research, internships, field experience, the Marine Science Consortium Program at Wallops Island, and Army ROTC.

Academic Facilities

The library and multimedia services unit helps students develop skills in information gathering, critical evaluation, and creating media presentations of research findings. It provides assistance in locating and delivering books and articles in the Lehman Library, the Luhrs Library Media Center, online databases, and from other libraries through interlibrary loan services. Students can receive online reference and research support, guidance in citing resources and avoiding plagiarism, and technology support. Digital cameras, digital camcorders, LCD projectors, laptops, and other equipment are available and can be checked out for student use.

Student instruction is supported by multiple computer systems for student e-mail and computer network connections to the Internet. Every student has e-mail, file storage, and home page accounts on the University's servers. Several hundred terminals or personal computers for student use are available in residence halls, the library, academic buildings, microcomputer labs, and the Computing Technologies Center. Students with their own computers also have access to the systems. All students can use the systems 24 hours a day and have unlimited computer time at no additional expense. Most buildings have wireless network capabilities and several have satellite capability for distance education. The University also has its own campuswide information system available on and off campus.

Costs

For Pennsylvania residents, the cost per semester in 2012–13 included tuition of $3,214; room and board, $3,745; educational services fee, $339; technology fee, $179; student activities fee, $240; student union fee, $265; comprehensive health fee, $155; and student recreation fee, $185. Nonresidents paid tuition of $7,232 per semester; high-achieving nonresidents paid $5,625; STEM major nonresidents paid $5,625; and dual-admit nonresidents paid $4,821.

Financial Aid

The University's extensive financial aid program helps students who deserve a college education but who cannot afford to pay the full cost themselves. Shippensburg offers a wide range of aid in the form of grants, scholarships, loans, and campus employment. Most aid is awarded as a package consisting of all types for which the applicant is qualified. Nearly 80 percent of undergraduates receive some form of financial assistance.

Faculty

The University has 447 full- and part-time faculty members. The undergraduate student-faculty ratio is 20:1. Approximately 85 percent of the full-time instructional faculty members hold a doctorate or other terminal degree in their field. Each student has a faculty adviser.

Student Government

Shippensburg's strong student organization, built around a Student Senate, standing committees, and an Activities Program Board, provides a highly diversified program of student activities. Students sit on many policymaking administration-faculty committees and administer their own budget for the Student Services, Inc.

Admission Requirements

A student's potential for success is judged by the high school average, rank in class, aptitude test scores (SAT or ACT), and recommendations. The high school record is generally considered the most important factor. A college-preparatory program, consisting of 4 units of English, at least 3 units of math, 3 units in the sciences, 2 units of social studies, and 2 units in the same foreign language, is strongly recommended. A campus interview and visit are encouraged. Transfer students in good standing are welcome.

Application and Information

To be considered for admission, a student should submit an application with a $40 application fee online at http://www.ship.edu/admissions/apply. The high school transcript, recommendations, and aptitude test results should be sent by the high school. Transfer students must submit college transcripts. The Admissions Office operates on a rolling basis.

For application materials and additional information, students should contact:

Dean of Enrollment Services
Shippensburg University of Pennsylvania
1871 Old Main Drive
Shippensburg, Pennsylvania 17257
Phone: 717-477-1231
Fax: 717-477-4016
E-mail: admiss@ship.edu
Website: http://www.ship.edu
　　　　http://www.facebook.com/SHIPAdmissions

Located in south-central Pennsylvania, Shippensburg University offers daily information sessions and tours for prospective students.

SHORTER UNIVERSITY
ROME, GEORGIA

The University

Shorter University is a Christian university committed to excellence in education. The University offers a welcoming, nurturing environment where students are educated for life and career. Hallmarks of the Shorter experience include superior academic programs; a caring, Christ-centered atmosphere; individualized attention; opportunities for service and leadership; an outstanding program of intercollegiate athletics; a comprehensive study-abroad program; and academic, talent, and need-based financial aid.

The University was founded in 1873 through the generosity of a Baptist layman, Alfred Shorter and the vision of his pastor, Rev. Luther Rice Gwaltney. They led in founding the school, which was named Cherokee Baptist Female College. The name was changed to Shorter College in 1923. The College became coeducational in 1951. On June 1, 2010, the College changed its name to Shorter University.

Shorter's enrollment of 3,000 includes students in traditional and online programs as well as those in accelerated degree programs for working adults. Approximately 1,500 of these students are located on the main campus in Rome. Students come from all parts of the United States and from other countries around the world. Shorter University has an overall graduate school acceptance rate of 80 percent and an impressive 82 percent acceptance rate to medical colleges over the past twenty-one years.

Shorter is committed to providing a high-quality education in an intentionally Christian atmosphere. Each year, the campus is visited by noted Christian leaders, scholars, and outstanding musical performers and the University provides a wide range of spiritual growth opportunities.

The largest religious organization on campus is the Baptist Collegiate Ministries (BCM), which includes Christians of many denominations. Student publications include a newspaper, a yearbook, and a literary magazine. Highly skilled music and drama groups include the Shorter Chorale, the Shorter University Choruses, the Shorter Theater Company, the Opera Workshop, and the Shorter Marching Band.

The University has two fraternities and three sororities as well as chapters of two national music fraternities and honor societies for majors in biology, communication, English, music, religion, and social sciences. Shorter University is transitioning to membership in the Gulf South Conference of NCAA Division II; the University is also a member of the National Christian College Athletic Association. Varsity teams compete in men's baseball, basketball, football, golf, lacrosse, soccer, tennis, track and field, and wrestling and in women's basketball, golf, soccer, softball, tennis, track and field, and volleyball. Shorter also competes in coed and all-girl competitive cheerleading.

Location

The University is situated on a 150-acre campus in Rome, Georgia and is located just 65 miles northwest of Atlanta and 65 miles south of Chattanooga, Tennessee. The University sponsors numerous events, including faculty, alumni, student, and guest musical recitals; guest lectures; recitals; drama and opera productions; art exhibits; and athletic events.

Majors and Degrees

Shorter University offers seven baccalaureate and five master's degrees: the Bachelor of Arts, the Bachelor of Business Administration, the Bachelor of Fine Arts, the Bachelor of Music, the Bachelor of Science, the Bachelor of Science in Education, the Bachelor of Science in Nursing, the Master of Accountancy, the Master of Arts, the Master of Arts in Teaching, the Master of Business Administration, and the Master of Education.

The Bachelor of Arts is offered in Christian studies, communication arts, criminal justice, English, English education, history and political science, international studies, liberal arts, music,

psychology, Spanish, and theatre. The Bachelor of Science is offered in biology, chemistry, Christian studies, computer information systems, communication arts, computer information systems, criminal justice, ecology and field biology, general science education, general studies, history and political science, history education, mathematics, mathematics education, natural science, and psychology. The Bachelor of Business Administration is offered in accounting, economics, general business, management, marketing, management information systems, and sport management. The Bachelor of Science in Education is offered in early childhood education (P–5) and middle grades (4–8). Programs leading to certification in secondary school teaching are available in English, general science, history, and mathematics. Certification is also offered in music for grades K–12. The Bachelor of Fine Arts is offered in art, musical theater, and theater. The Bachelor of Music is offered in church music, music education, piano pedagogy, piano performance, and voice performance. Preprofessional programs are available in allied health, dentistry, law, medicine, pharmacy, physical therapy, physician's assistant studies, and veterinary medicine.

Academic Programs

Shorter is accredited by the Southern Association of Colleges and Schools. The music programs are accredited by the National Association of Schools of Music; teacher education programs are approved by the Georgia Professional Standards Commission; and the baccalaureate program in nursing is accredited by the Commission on Collegiate Nursing Education. Small classes taught by dedicated and highly qualified professors ensure that each student receives an education that is both challenging and personally rewarding. For any degree, a candidate must have earned a minimum of 126 semester hours; some degrees require a greater number of hours.

As part of the orientation program at the beginning of the fall semester, each new student is assigned to one of several small orientation groups that assist the student in adjusting to University life; the student is also assigned to an academic adviser, who assists in the selection and scheduling of courses. Early registration sessions are available in the summer.

The academic calendar is divided into two semesters from August to May, with two mini sessions offered during the summer. On-campus evening classes are available in selected disciplines. Shorter offers an honors program that spans all four years and provides students with learning opportunities that are not generally available to undergraduates.

Off-Campus Programs

Shorter's College of Adult and Professional Programs offers courses specially designed for working adults, on campus and in Gwinnett, Riverdale, and North Atlanta, Georgia. CAPP students study at the associate, bachelor's, and master's degree levels. Majors are business, education, and human services.

Shorter University offers several study-abroad programs immediately following the end of the second semester in May, including MAYTERM (in Europe), the Asia Program, and the Americas Program. Studies in other countries can be arranged on an individual basis through the Office of International Programs.

Academic Facilities

Livingston Library, which was dedicated in 1976, houses more than 213,297 books, 582 periodical subscriptions, 8,099 microform materials, 12,134 audio/video items, 38,312 e-books, and 7,000 e-journals. The library also contains conference rooms (for both individual and group study), projection rooms, a graphics preparation room, computer terminals, typewriters, and music listening facilities for student use. The adjacent Nelson and Trudy Price Learning Center was opened in 2012 and includes 18,000 square feet of space that features a two-story cathedral atrium, a fireplace, study areas, and a coffee shop.

The Alice Allgood Cooper Fine Arts Building and the Randall H. Minor Fine Arts Building are connected to form an outstanding fine arts complex, providing facilities for the departments of music, communication arts, and art. The Cooper Building contains classrooms, music faculty offices, the art department's drawing and painting studio, and Brookes Chapel, the meeting place for convocations, concerts, recitals, and lectures. A renovated home adjacent to the campus houses expanded art facilities. The Minor Building contains classrooms, twenty-five music practice rooms (with a baby grand piano in each), a choral rehearsal room, faculty offices, photography facilities, a theater, a desktop publishing lab, a radio studio, and an art gallery. Rome Hall contains classrooms, science laboratories, faculty offices, lounges, and the Robert T. Connor exhibit of some 150 African and North American animals and skins. Alumni Hall houses the educational materials center and faculty offices. The Winthrop-King Centre houses offices for coaches, a basketball gym, a dance and aerobic studio, two racquetball courts, and an indoor jogging track. The Fitton Student Union contains the campus bookstore, a 24-hour study room, the campus post office, and an indoor swimming pool. Two computer labs are available for general student use. Computer labs for business and communication arts are also available. All residence halls have Internet access. The Robert H. Ledbetter College of Business is located adjacent to the main campus in a facility that offers seven academic classrooms, three computer labs, faculty offices, and student lounges. The College of Nursing is located in the heart of Rome's medical community and provides state-of-the-art lab equipment, simulators, computer labs, and classroom facilities.

Costs

Tuition for the 2013–14 academic year is $19,300 and fees are $430. Room and board charges are $9,400.

Financial Aid

Shorter University offers aid through each of the five federal programs: the Federal Pell Grant, Federal Supplemental Educational Opportunity Grant, Federal Work-Study Program, Federal Perkins Loan, and Federal Stafford Student Loan. Full-time students who are Georgia residents are eligible to receive the Georgia Tuition Equalization Grant and may be eligible to receive the HOPE Scholarship. Scholarships are offered for achievement in academics, music, art, theater, humanities, and athletics. Awards range from $500 to full tuition, room, and board. Academic scholarships are renewable each year, provided the student maintains at least the required grade point average. Special grants and scholarships are available to students who plan to enter church-related vocations or who are dependents of full-time employees of a Georgia Baptist church, institution, or agency. Shorter University offers need-based aid to students with demonstrated financial need as determined by the Free Application for Federal Student Aid (FAFSA).

Faculty

The Shorter faculty is composed of 110 full-time, highly qualified professors. A favorable student-teacher ratio of 13:1 in traditional programs ensures that each student receives individual attention.

Student Government

One of Shorter's truly distinctive features is that students may participate in a wide variety of significant extracurricular activities, each of which affords a chance to develop social and leadership skills that prepare a student to succeed in a competitive world. The Student Government Association (SGA) is the official voice of the students. Through SGA's Executive Council, judicial boards, and special committees, students are directly involved in the life of the University.

Admission Requirements

Students are admitted into the freshman class based on their academic grade point average, and SAT or ACT scores. (A review of the student's goals and their compatibility with the purpose of the University are also determining factors.) The University requires 4 years of English, 4 years of mathematics (including 2 years of algebra), 3 years of history/social science, 3 years of science, and 2 units of foreign language. In addition to the general requirements for admission to the University, students majoring in music must meet the following requirements: each student must perform in an audition of approximately 10 minutes in his or her major medium, and each student must take a series of music placement tests. Students must successfully fulfill these requirements prior to the beginning of classes in August of their freshman year, since the music curriculum requires at least four years for completion. An audition is also required for students majoring in theater, and an art portfolio review is required for students majoring in art. High school students who have completed their junior year, have an outstanding academic record, and have completed the units outlined above may be considered for early admission. High school seniors entering in their senior year may be admitted on a joint-enrollment basis. Such students should have above-average grades and SAT or ACT scores. Transfer and international students are also welcome to apply.

For international students, a minimum paper-based TOEFL score of 500, Internet-based score of 61, or computer-based score of 173 is required. All international students must have their academic credentials evaluated by WES or another transcript evaluation service affiliated with the National Association of Credential Evaluation Services (NACES). For all transfer students, credit for college work below a C may not be transferred. Homeschooled students should contact the Office of Admissions directly for requirements.

Application and Information

Shorter University accepts students on a rolling basis. Campus visits are highly recommended through a personal campus tour or a Saturday at Shorter event.

Director of Admissions
Shorter University
315 Shorter Avenue
Rome, Georgia 30165-4298
Phone: 706-233-7319
　　　800-868-6980 Ext. 7319 (toll-free)
Fax: 706-233-7224
E-mail: admissions@shorter.edu
Website: http://admissions.shorter.edu

Shorter University is located on a 150-acre hilltop campus in Rome, Georgia. The Front Circle, pictured here, is a spot where students enjoy all types of activities including gathering between classes, enjoying movie night, or playing a pick-up game of Frisbee.

SIMMONS COLLEGE
BOSTON, MASSACHUSETTS

The College

Steeped in a tradition of cultivating the intellectual and professional growth of women, Simmons College is a warm and engaging community with a national reputation of academic excellence. Founded in 1899, Simmons was the first college in the United States to offer women a liberal arts education integrated with career preparation. Today, Simmons embraces the opportunity to provide a transformative learning experience for students, fostering intellectual growth alongside their passion to forge a path to a meaningful career. Located in the heart of Boston, Simmons is best known for its small classes, access to faculty, and internship and research opportunities. Students say that Simmons's location offers the best of both worlds—an intimate college experience in the heart of a vibrant and bustling city. Simmons's nearly 2,000 undergraduates appreciate the fact that they can easily access the city's rich social and cultural resources but also come home to a safe, friendly campus. The quintessential New England residential campus features nine brick residence halls and a private, landscaped quad, as well as Bartol Dining Hall, the state-of-the-art Holmes Sports Center, a student-run café, and the campus health center.

Location

Considered by many to be the best college town in the nation, Boston has more than fifty colleges and universities, and approximately 250,000 students. The historic, tree-lined Simmons campus is located in Boston's eclectic Fenway neighborhood, which is alive with music and fine arts, medical care and research, action and activism, and the resounding cheers of baseball fans at legendary Fenway Park. From campus, it's a safe, easy stroll to other colleges and universities as well as shops, cafés, clubs, museums, movie theaters, parks, and public transportation. Students can hop aboard the "T" (Boston's public transportation system) and head to destinations such as the Italian North End, Chinatown, Harvard Square, the boutiques of Newbury Street, the Harbor, and Boston's many other diverse neighborhoods.

Majors and Degrees

Simmons offers more than forty majors and programs. Popular majors include nursing, biology, communications, management, psychology, and physical therapy/exercise science. Faculty advisors help each student create a plan that fulfills requirements and satisfies her personal and professional goals. A number of integrated degrees and accelerated programs allow students to go directly from undergraduate study to earning a graduate degree in less time than traditional programs. Students can accelerate to graduate degrees in areas such as business, education, health care, liberal arts, physical therapy, social work, and science information technology. Simmons also offers individually designed pre-professional programs for dentistry, law, medicine, and veterinary medicine. Simmons students typically declare a major by the end of their sophomore year, and nearly a third choose to double major.

Academic Program

Simmons offers a strong foundation in the liberal arts that helps transform intellectual curiosity into meaningful life's work. Each student explores a variety of subjects while gaining an in-depth theoretical and practical understanding of her major. First-year core courses emphasize critical thinking and writing skills, while integrating two or more subjects, ranging from sustainability and Buddhist studies to social justice and visual communication. To complement the theoretical knowledge learned in the classroom, Simmons offers many experiential opportunities, including an outstanding honors program, an award-winning service-learning center, and an abundance of study-abroad options, from short travel courses to a full year abroad.

The hallmark of a Simmons education is the independent learning requirement, which students fulfill through internships, fieldwork, and research projects. Science students co-publish research with faculty in nationally recognized academic journals as undergraduate students. Most students take advantage of the abundance of competitive internship opportunities available in Boston. In addition, Simmons's Longwood Medical Area partnerships provide outstanding clinical opportunities at Boston's world-renowned hospitals. On campus, students conduct research using state-of-the-art equipment in areas such as materials science, gene splicing, and computer modeling. Yet the most important aspect of Simmons's approach to hands-on learning is that professors frequently invite undergraduates to collaborate on professional research projects, articles, and presentations, as early as their freshman year.

Off-Campus Programs

Simmons is a member of the Colleges of the Fenway consortium, which allows students to participate in social events and cross-register with neighboring colleges, including Emmanuel College, Massachusetts College of Art, Massachusetts College of Pharmacy and Allied Health Sciences, Wentworth Institute of Technology, and Wheelock College.

Simmons encourages students to spend an entire semester or year abroad, and assists them in finding programs and scholarships for international study. For students who are unable to spend this length of time abroad, there are more than twelve short-term travel courses, which take students to another country for three weeks. Short-term international courses provide unique opportunities to study topics such as chemistry in China, sustainability in Iceland, Spanish in Argentina, or history and civilization in Japan.

A domestic exchange program allows qualified juniors to spend a semester at Belmont University, Mills College, Spelman College, or Fisk University. In addition, students, usually junior political science or international relations majors, may also apply for the Washington Semester at American University in Washington, D.C.

Service learning, a teaching method that combines community service with academic instruction, is integral to a Simmons education. More than 20 percent of Simmons students participate in service learning each semester, administered by the award-winning Scott/Ross Center for Community Service. These opportunities range from education initiatives to physical therapy clinics in needy areas of Boston.

Other opportunities include Success Connection, a mentoring program that matches select seniors with highly successful Simmons alumnae, and the Barbara Lee Internship Fellows program, which places students in Massachusetts legislators' offices and policy advocacy groups for one semester.

Academic Facilities

The beautiful Simmons campus offers an attractive, practical mix of historic and modern architecture, including state-of-the-art facilities and conveniences. Wireless Internet service is available throughout the campus, as well as many strategically placed web and print stations where students can check e-mail, print a paper, or surf the Internet. Students can also go to the Pottruck Technology Center, a state-of-the-art computer-learning lab, where staff are available to assist them with new software and general computer skills. In addition, students have access to iMac centers, scanners, printers, digital cameras, video equipment, art studios, and music practice rooms.

Simmons's award-winning radio station streams live every day, and the Trustman Art Gallery hosts seasonal openings featuring student art, as well as community artists. Students can relax, eat, and study at the Fens dining hall; two coffee bars; one of the many quiet spaces located around campus; or at the Student Activities Center, which has vending machines, meeting rooms, print stations, a flat screen TV, and a comfortable lounge area.

The Park Science Center offers technologically advanced learning environments, including faculty and student research facilities, fully equipped science laboratories, state-of-the art nursing simulation labs, environmental rooms, observation rooms for psychological testing, and food science kitchens.

The newly renovated Beatley Library offers a number of student-centered services, including laptop loans, sophisticated online library service, technology-equipped study rooms, and interlibrary loan, which connects students to dozens of libraries throughout Boston. In addition, students can schedule a research appointment with a librarian to help refine search techniques and choose the highest-quality information available.

Costs

Undergraduate tuition and fees for the 2012–13 academic year were $17,175 per semester; room and board charges were $6,570 per semester. Total costs, not including books, supplies, and personal expenses, were $47,490 for the year.

Financial Aid

More than 97 percent of Simmons' first-year students receive some form of financial aid. Scholarships, grants, loans, and federal work-study are determined by the Free Application for Federal Student Aid (FAFSA). Simmons also awards academic merit scholarships, ranging from $2,000 to full-tuition awards, renewable for four years.

Faculty

As a student-focused institution, Simmons offers a learning experience that is highly collaborative and personal. Professors include distinguished researchers, published authors, Fulbright scholars, health professionals, and community leaders. They advise numerous government, nonprofit, and corporate organizations in the United States and around the world, yet they passionately uphold their primary obligation to teach and mentor. Students say the small classes, intellectual focus, and welcoming environment contribute to their confidence and success. Over 70 percent of Simmons's undergraduate professors are women. Nearly all of the liberal arts faculty members hold doctorates in their field. A 13:1 student-teacher ratio ensures that every student receives individual attention and reinforces the strong tie between students and professors.

Student Government

The Student Government Association (SGA) coordinates the policies and activities of various student organizations, allocates the student activities funds, and promotes the interests of the student body by working closely with the Simmons faculty and administration. Simmons fosters a student-centered environment and encourages each individual to actively participate in the College community in a way that is right for her. Simmons has more than fifty student organizations, clubs, and academic liaisons, including honor societies, cultural organizations, volunteer programs, a literary magazine, a campus newspaper, and ten NCAA Division III varsity teams. In addition, every academic department has a student liaison that participates in department evaluations and helps promote educational and social activities for students and faculty and staff members.

Admission Requirements

Admission to Simmons College is highly selective. The admission committee looks for students who have excelled both in and out of the classroom, and evaluates high school performance, SAT or ACT scores, recommendations, and the application essay. If English is not the applicant's first language, the TOEFL, IELTS, or a comparable exam score is required. Typical high school preparation for entrance includes 4 years of English, 4 years of math, 3–4 years of lab sciences, and 3–4 years of a foreign language. Although not required, an interview is strongly recommended.

Simmons welcomes applications from prospective freshmen, transfer students, international students, and students who are over the age of 24.

Application and Information

Students may apply online, using the Common Application, or submit a print application, along with the $55 fee and all supporting credentials. The early action deadline (nonbinding) is December 1. The regular freshman application deadline is February 1. Transfer students are evaluated on a continual basis; the preferred filing date for applications for the fall semester is April 1. All students applying for the spring should submit their application by November 1.

Simmons encourages prospective students and their families to attend an admission event or request an individual visit.

For further information, interested students should contact:

Office of Undergraduate Admission
Simmons College
300 The Fenway
Boston, Massachusetts 02115
Phone: 800-345-8468 (toll-free)
Fax: 617-521-3190
E-mail: ugadm@simmons.edu
Website: www.simmons.edu
    www.facebook.com/SimmonsCollege
    www.twitter.com/SimmonsCollege
    www.youtube.com/SimmonsCollege

Simmons offers an oasis in the heart of Boston, America's number-one college town.

SIMPSON COLLEGE

INDIANOLA, IOWA

SIMPSON COLLEGE

The College

Founded in 1860, Simpson College is a private liberal arts college affiliated with the United Methodist Church. Simpson produces successful students by combining the best of a liberal arts education with outstanding career preparation and extracurricular programs. With 1,500 full-time students and a student to faculty ratio of 14:1, students have the opportunity to work closely with their professors. Simpson's faculty members are as dedicated to their fields of study as they are to teaching—and it shows in the classroom. When this type of dedication and passion is combined with well-prepared and motivated students, the potential for success is unlimited.

The campus is located just minutes from Iowa's capital city, Des Moines, which recently was ranked number one for business and careers. The proximity to Des Moines allows Simpson students to take advantage of an abundance of internship opportunities. Whether working with Fortune 500 companies, spending time in an elementary school, or gaining resume-building experiences in a medical field, students learn to push their own boundaries. Simpson's guaranteed internship program gives students an advantage in today's competitive job market.

Simpson's beautiful, tree-lined campus in Indianola provides small-town friendliness and safety, while the campus facilities are continually enhanced and updated for academic and recreational opportunities. Recent multimillion-dollar projects include the renovation and expansion of Blank Performing Arts Center (2011), renovation of outdoor athletic facilities (2011), and the addition of a stunning new student center (2012). A $6 million expansion and renovation of the Cowles Athletic and Carse Fitness Center is slated to be completed in December 2013.

Simpson's 4-4-1 academic calendar includes a May Term that provides students with unique learning opportunities in the classroom, internship settings, or while studying abroad. Throughout the year, students take advantage of Simpson's innovative Engaged Citizenship Curriculum. The curriculum allows students to gain skills and experiences valued most by employers while choosing classes that interest them. Simpson's "SC in 3" pathway allows high school students entering college with 24 or more college credits to finish a full, high-quality Simpson degree in three years, decreasing the cost of college and increasing their earning potential.

Extracurricular activities at Simpson are designed to supplement and reinforce the academic program and contribute toward a total learning experience. Activities range from an award-winning music program to nationally recognized NCAA Division III athletic teams. Students have the opportunity to participate in student government, campus publications, religious life, music, theater, departmental clubs, and various other organizations. Simpson has seven Greek chapters on campus, including three national fraternities, one local fraternity, and three national sororities; each with their own house. Simpson competes in 19 intercollegiate sports and has an extensive intramural program.

Location

Simpson is located in Indianola, a residential community with a population of 14,400. Indianola is 12 miles south of Des Moines, with easy access to Interstates 35 and 80. The Des Moines International Airport is 20 minutes from campus. Indianola is host to nationally known events including the Des Moines Metropolitan Opera and the National Balloon Classic. The vibrant, small-town community has many choices for entertainment and recreation including Lake Ahquabi State Park, Summerset Trail, and unique restaurants and shops within walking distance of campus on the town square. Indianola's proximity to Des Moines gives students plenty of distinct advantages. Within minutes, students are right in the heart of some of the best entertainment and employment options Iowa and the Midwest have to offer.

Majors and Degrees

Simpson College grants Bachelor of Arts and Bachelor of Music degrees. Majors include accounting, actuarial science, applied philosophy, art, athletic training, biochemistry, biology, chemistry, communication and media studies, computer information systems, computer science, criminal justice, economics, education (elementary and secondary including art), English, environmental science, exercise science, forensic science/biochemistry, French, German, graphic design, history, integrated marketing communication, interdisciplinary studies, international management, international relations, management, marketing, mathematics, music, music education, music performance, neuroscience, philosophy, physical education, physics, political science, psychology, religion, sociology, Spanish, sports administration, studio art, and theater arts.

Simpson also offers pre-professional programs in dentistry, engineering, law, medicine, optometry, pharmacy, physical therapy, theology/ministry, and veterinary medicine. Concentration areas such as early childhood education and ethics are available, as well as many additional minors, including women's studies, social work, human resources management, Latin American studies, and coaching endorsements.

Academic Programs

Simpson College operates on a 4-4-1 academic calendar. The first semester starts in late August and ends in mid-December; the second semester starts in mid-January and ends in late April. A three-week session takes place during the month of May. During this period, students participate in a field experience/internship, study abroad, or take a course on campus with a hands-on focus.

The First Year Program is an extensive program of orientation, team building, mentoring, community service, advising, and course work structured to help new students adapt to their first year of college. The program begins with summer orientation and continues throughout the academic year. The academic component of the First-Year Program is the Simpson Colloquium, a joint classroom and advising concept that is unique among first-year programs. These courses are small in size—no more than 18 first-year students each—and all are taught by each student's faculty adviser.

With Simpson's Engaged Citizenship Curriculum, students delve deeper in their courses and focus more on projects that provide hands-on understanding of the subject matter. These courses allow students to work closely and build strong relationships with faculty members, one of the hallmarks of a Simpson education. The curriculum encourages students to take advantage of Simpson's community partnerships, hold internships, study abroad, or conduct independent research. It was developed in response to research that indicates future employers are looking for effective communicators, innovators, and problem solvers. Simpson is on the forefront of providing the kind of experiential, liberal arts education that college graduates need to succeed in their careers and achieve fulfillment in their lives.

Off-Campus Programs

Simpson provides many opportunities for studying abroad, with the choice of a semester-long program or a three-week May Term. Simpson's semester-long, faculty-led study-abroad programs include London, England; Schorndorf, Germany; Chiang Mai, Thailand; Tahiti, French Polynesia; Adelaide, Australia; and Rosario, Argentina. Students also have the opportunity for semester study-abroad programs in France, Spain, Italy, Australia, and more locations.

In addition, 10 to 15 travel courses are offered each May Term. Recent destinations include Africa, Central America, Great Britain, France, Greece, Ireland, New Zealand, the Galapagos Islands, Brazil, Argentina, and Scandinavia. May Term study abroad courses are led by Simpson faculty members and give students the opportunity to experience a different culture while gaining a stronger global perspective. Simpson has been recognized as one of the top 100 colleges in the nation for the highest percentage of students who study abroad—43 percent of Simpson students will travel abroad by the time they graduate.

The Capitol Hill Internship Program (CHIP) provides students with the opportunity to spend either the fall or spring semester in Washington, D.C. Past participants have had various experiences including interning for members of Congress, the Smithsonian Institution, the Republican National Committee, the Justice Department, CNN, the Australian Embassy, and FOX News.

Academic Facilities

Simpson has a wireless campus network with high-speed Internet access. There are numerous computer labs throughout campus where students can use standard office suite applications or specialized, discipline-specific applications.

The Carver Science Center, named after Simpson's most distinguished alumnus George Washington Carver, provides state-of-the-art research facilities, computer labs, a cadaver lab, and classrooms.

The Henry H. and Thomas H. McNeill Hall houses classrooms for management, accounting, and economics. In addition, the hall houses a seminar room and the Pioneer Hi-Bred International Conference Center.

The Amy Robertson Music Center is home to Simpson's acclaimed music department and contains the Sven and Mildred Lekberg Recital Hall, ten studios, twenty-two practice rooms, a music computer lab, and the band rehearsal room. The Salsbury Wing includes a choral rehearsal room, a classroom, and studios.

Dunn Library, a modern academic learning resource center, contains over 175,000 items including books, periodicals, videos/DVDs, and CDs. Many resources (print and online) can be located from the library website. Additional materials for research can be obtained through a national interlibrary loan network. The Hawley Academic Resource and Advising Center, which provides free academic support services to all students, is located in Dunn Library.

The A. H. and Theo Blank Performing Arts Center underwent a multimillion-dollar expansion and renovation in 2011. The center accommodates Simpson's well-known programs in theater arts and opera. It includes the magnificent 500-seat Pote Theatre, with both proscenium and hydraulically controlled thrust stages, a studio theater, the Barborka Gallery, technical facilities, and shops and classrooms.

Wallace Hall, named to the National Register of Historic Places in 1991, contains facilities for education, sociology, and applied social science.

Mary Berry Hall, renovated during the summer of 2008, houses the psychology department as well as faculty offices, six new labs, a control room for observation and data processing, and an animal care space. In addition, the building is home to humanities classrooms, a language lab, and the Farnham Art Gallery.

The Gaumer Center contains offices for Communication and Media Studies and Art and provides space for *The Simpsonian*, the college newspaper, and radio station KSTM.

Faculty

Simpson offers one professor for every 14 students, and 90 percent of full-time faculty members have earned the highest degree in their fields. Simpson's faculty members serve as academic advisers as well as teachers. Their commitment goes beyond the classroom as they often attend college plays, operas, and athletic events, reinforcing their sincere interest in the lives of the students and their ultimate success.

Costs

Tuition and fees for 2013–14 are $30,999; room charges are $3,860; and board is $4,103. These figures do not include books, music fees, or personal expenses.

Financial Aid

Simpson College is dedicated to making it financially feasible for qualified students to experience the advantages of a Simpson education. In fact, 99 percent of Simpson students receive some form of financial assistance. Generous gifts from alumni, trustees, and friends of the College—in addition to state and federal student aid programs—make this opportunity possible. Simpson offers financial assistance on both a need and non-need basis. Need is determined by filing the Free Application for Federal Student Aid.

Financial assistance granted on a non-need basis includes generous academic scholarships (awarded on the basis of prior academic records) and talent scholarships (available in theater, music, and art). The talent scholarships are determined by audition/portfolio.

Also, specific scholarships such as the John C. Culver Fellowship, the Iowa History Center Scholarship, and the Wesley Service Scholarship can be obtained through application.

Admission Requirements

Admission to Simpson College is competitive. A strong academic record is essential. Applications are acted upon by an admissions committee, which is elected by the faculty and represents the five academic divisions of the College. These faculty members consider the college-preparatory courses taken and the grades received in those courses, rank in class, and standardized test scores (ACT and/or SAT), including test sub scores, as well as a high school report form and guidance counselor recommendation.

Transfer applicants are accepted on the basis of successful completion of academic work at an accredited college or university.

Application and Information

Applications are accepted on a rolling basis beginning in early fall and continuing on a space-available basis. Simpson's rolling admission policy allows flexibility; however, early application is recommended. Applications can be found on the school website.

For additional information or to obtain application materials, students should contact:

Office of Admissions
Simpson College
701 North C Street
Indianola, Iowa 50125
Phone: 515-961-1624
      800-362-2454 Ext. 1624 (toll-free)
E-mail: admiss@simpson.edu
Website: http://www.simpson.edu
      http://www.facebook.com/simpsoncollege
      http://twitter.com/simpsoncollege
      http://www.youtube.com/simpsonweb

Simpson's new $14-million Kent Campus Center opened in fall 2012 and has quickly become the prime meeting place for students.

SKIDMORE COLLEGE
SARATOGA SPRINGS, NEW YORK

The College

Skidmore College is an independent liberal arts college of 2,400 men and women from 50 states and 50 countries that prides itself on its creative approaches to just about everything. Hence, the College's belief that creative thought matters. Founded by Lucy Skidmore Scribner as the Skidmore School of Arts in 1911, it became Skidmore College in 1922. In addition to being accredited by the Middle States Association of Colleges and Schools, the College has a chapter of Phi Beta Kappa and program accreditation with the Council on Social Work Education and the National Association of Schools of Art and Design. Throughout its history, Skidmore has displayed a spirit of innovation and imagination in response to need and opportunity. In the 1960s the College built an entirely new campus; in 1971 it became coeducational; in 1983 it completely revised its curriculum, creating a comprehensive liberal studies program focused on interdisciplinarity (revised again in 2005 with the creation of the First-Year Experience program); and in 1993, it installed the Master of Arts in Liberal Studies program, primarily for adult learners. Skidmore has embraced change, seeing in it the opportunity to serve the needs and aspirations of its students. By expanding and refining its programs, the College has broadened its educational mission to respond to the opportunities and challenges of a global society.

Students enjoy a full schedule of intellectual, cultural, and social activities, such as lectures, visiting scholars in residence, art exhibits, concerts, and dance and theater performances. There are approximately 100 student organizations, including a weekly newspaper, radio and TV stations, numerous ethnic and cultural associations, an art and literary journal, and a student-volunteer network. There are no fraternities or sororities, which helps ensure an inclusive environment. A strong NCAA Division III intercollegiate sports program for men and women—nineteen teams in all—includes baseball, basketball, field hockey, golf, ice hockey, lacrosse, riding, rowing, soccer, softball, swimming and diving, tennis, and volleyball. Skidmore competes in the Liberty League, which also includes Bard, Clarkson, Hobart and William Smith, Rensselaer Polytechnic Institute, Rochester Institute of Technology, St. Lawrence, Union, and Vassar. The College has vigorous intramural; club sport; and health, fitness, and wellness programming.

Skidmore's campus includes more than fifty buildings. The Williamson Sports and Recreation Complex has a pool and diving well, racquet-sport courts, basketball and volleyball courts, several intramural gyms, three dance studios, a weight room, a fitness center, and a human performance laboratory. Adjacent to the complex are Wachenheim Field, a small stadium with an artificial turf field for soccer, lacrosse, and intramurals, and a 400-meter all-weather track; dedicated softball and field hockey turf fields; and the lighted Wenger Tennis Courts. The Frances Young Tang Teaching Museum and Art Gallery, unique in its interdisciplinary approach to exhibits and programming, opened in 2000.

Two major additions were made to the campus in 2006. The "green" Northwoods Apartments opened with 380 single-room units in ten new buildings. A completely renovated dining hall, Murray-Aikins, also opened, offering extensive vegetarian, vegan, and international options, freshly made pasta, locally grown organic items, and a broad array of daily choices. The Arthur Zankel Music Center, an award-winning, state-of-the-art music building with a 600-seat auditorium, opened in 2010. Construction of new 238-bed residence hall facilities, Sussman Village, is well underway, with phase I completed in fall 2012 and phase II slated for completion in late 2013.

Location

Saratoga Springs, 30 miles north of Albany, New York's state capital, is perennially short-listed as one of the most interesting and vibrant small cities in the U.S. Famed for health, history, and horses—its mineral waters, Revolutionary War battlefield, and the nation's oldest thoroughbred racetrack—Saratoga is equally renowned as an arts and cultural destination. The Saratoga Performing Arts

Center is summer home to the New York City Ballet, Philadelphia Orchestra, and Lake George Opera, and is a performing venue for top rock and jazz musicians. The city's downtown is just a 10-minute walk from Skidmore and is brimming with galleries, clubs, shops, coffeehouses, and restaurants. The city's location near the foothills of the Adirondack Mountains puts an abundance of outdoor recreational opportunities—major ski areas, state parks, large lakes, and mountainous regions of eastern New York, Vermont, and western Massachusetts—within an hour's drive. Boston, New York City, and Montreal are each approximately 180 miles from the campus.

In terms of transportation, bus service is available from Saratoga Springs to New York City, Montreal, Boston, and other major cities. There are daily trains to and from New York City and Montreal. Rental cars are available at the Albany International Airport, which is served by major airlines. The College is located near Exit 15 of I-87 (the Northway).

Majors and Degrees

Skidmore College grants degrees in nearly 50 different academic disciplines, including a Bachelor of Arts degree in the following liberal arts subjects: American studies, anthropology, Asian studies, biology, chemistry, classics, computer science, economics, English, environmental studies, foreign languages and literatures (French, German, and Spanish), French area studies, gender studies, geosciences, government, history, history of art, international affairs, mathematics, music, neuroscience, philosophy, physics, psychology, religious studies, and sociology. The Bachelor of Science degree is granted in areas of a more professional nature, including business, dance, education studies, exercise science, social work, studio art, and theater. There are more than 10 interdepartmental majors, economics-sociology and government-Spanish being just two examples. Self-determined majors, double majors, and minors are also available. In keeping with the College's creative spirit and the realities of the marketplace, more than half of Skidmore students choose a second major or minor.

Through partnerships with other institutions, Skidmore offers enhanced program/degree offerings in business, education, engineering, nursing, and physical and occupational therapy. These include 4+1 M.B.A. programs with Clarkson University, Rochester Institute of Technology, and Union Graduate College; the Whitman MBA Advantage program with Syracuse University; 4+1 M.S.A. and M.S.F. programs with Syracuse; a 4+1 M.A.T. program with Union College; 3+2 programs in engineering with Dartmouth College and Clarkson; 4+1/4+2 programs in physical therapy and/or occupational therapy (Sage Graduate School), and a 4+1 nursing program (New York University School of Nursing). Skidmore also has certification programs in teaching and social work and pre-professional programs in law and medicine.

Academic Programs

The Skidmore journey begins with the First-Year Experience which introduces students to the rigorous interdisciplinary academic program and overall approach to learning and connects them with a faculty adviser/mentor. Talented but economically disadvantaged students who have been accepted into the Opportunity Program (Higher Education Opportunity Program or Academic Opportunity Program) participate in a month-long summer program. A small percentage of students opt to apply for entry into Skidmore's Honors Forum on the basis of academic achievement and aspirations, leadership qualities, and civic commitment.

Generally, students choose a major by the end of sophomore year. In the interest of breadth, they are also expected to take one to two courses in both quantitative reasoning and expository writing, and at least one course in each of the following: lab science, social science, arts, humanities, and culture. There is plenty of academic support through Student Academic Services. In addition there are specific programs for prelaw and premed students. In their junior and senior years, students often add value to their courses of study through faculty-student collaborative research, internships, volunteerism, service learning, and off-campus study.

Off-Campus Programs

About 60 percent of Skidmore's students spend a semester or year off campus. In addition to Skidmore programs in China, England, France, and Spain, students can access approximately 140 international programs through the College's Approved Programs structure, including programs in Africa, Asia, Europe, Latin America, and Australia. Students can also study at some 200 other U.S. campuses, thanks to Skidmore's affiliation with National Student Exchange. All academic majors and minors can be accommodated and transfer credits are guaranteed for students studying on an Approved Program. Financial aid is transferable to most off-campus study programs. The College also offers a Washington Semester (internship in conjunction with American University) and a semester at the Marine Biological Laboratory in Woods Hole, Massachusetts.

Arrangements for student internships (for academic credit) are made through Skidmore's academic departments or the Office of Career Development. More than 50 percent of students are involved in volunteer work, much of it local. There are also up to 50 courses each semester with service-learning components.

Academic Facilities

Skidmore's 890-acre campus offers more than 50 buildings, designed and arranged to blend with the natural surroundings and to foster intellectual and social interaction. The newest academic building, the Arthur Zankel Music Center, features a spectacular 600-seat recital hall and a state-of-the-art recording studio. Skidmore's visual and performing arts space includes the Saisselin Art Building, with studios and the Schick Art Gallery; the Janet Kinghorn Bernhard Theater, with a seating capacity of 350, and an experimental black box theater; and the Dance Center. The Tang Museum provides a focal point for cross-disciplinary study through the visual arts. The Dana Science Center offers state-of-the-art teaching and research space, including a center for microscopy imaging. Dana links the College's science departments to the Department of Mathematics and Computer Science in neighboring Harder Hall, which features a Linux lab with more than 20 workstations for advanced computer science projects.

Costs

In 2013–2014, tuition is $44,820, required fees $904, room $7,214, and board $4,988 for a total of $57,926.

Financial Aid

About half of Skidmore's students receive some form of financial assistance. Aid is awarded on the basis of demonstrated financial need and is provided in the form of a student-aid package that usually includes a grant, campus job, and loan. Students interested in applying for admission are encouraged to do so regardless of their intention to seek financial aid. The FAFSA, a copy of the federal income tax form, and the CSS PROFILE must be filed each year. The College hosts an annual Filene Music Scholarship Competition to award four $48,000 ($12,000 per year) scholarships on the basis of musical ability without regard to financial need. Five to seven $15,000 scholarships ($60,000 over four years) in math and science are also awarded annually. Information concerning scholarships, grants, loans, and/or work awards can be obtained through the Office of Financial Aid.

Faculty

Skidmore College has some 250 faculty members and 70 part-time members, 84 percent of whom hold the doctoral degree or the highest degree in their field. The student-to-faculty ratio is about 9:1 and the average class size is 16. Although actively engaged in research and publication in their individual fields, the Skidmore faculty members regard teaching as their primary commitment. All students have faculty advisers who assist them in selecting courses and in designing individual academic programs.

Student Government

Students at Skidmore play an active role in College governance. Through the Student Government Association (SGA) and membership on a number of major College committees, they participate in academic and social life. The SGA operates under the authority granted by the Board of Trustees and is dedicated to democratic self-government and responsible citizenship. Within the association, elected faculty members and student representatives serve on the All-College Council, the Academic Integrity Board, and the Social Integrity Board.

Broad concerns of the SGA include educational policy, elections, social and student events, first-year orientation, student publications, and student clubs and organizations.

Admission Requirements

Those seeking admission to Skidmore's first-year class should complete a secondary school curriculum that includes at least 16 credits in college-preparatory courses. The Admissions Committee is also pleased to consider applications from qualified high school juniors who plan to accelerate and enter college early. Applicants typically have completed 4 years of English, 4 years of a foreign language, 4 years of mathematics, 4 years of social studies, and 3–4 years of laboratory science. Applicants must provide a secondary school transcript, standardized test scores (SAT with writing or ACT with writing), letters of recommendation from two teachers of academic subjects, and a report from their guidance counselor. Skidmore recommends that applicants submit scores for three SAT Subject Tests. A campus visit and interview is also recommended.

Through its participation in the Higher Education Opportunity Program (HEOP) Skidmore enrolls capable, energetic, and ambitious New York state residents who, because of their academic and financial situations, would not otherwise gain admission to the College under traditional requirements.

Application and Information

Applicants for admission must complete the Common Application—preferably online at www.commonapp.org—and submit it with a $65 fee or request a fee waiver from their adviser. All information should be postmarked by January 15. Applications from early decision candidates should be submitted by November 15 for the Round I early decision plan or by January 15 for the Round II early decision plan. Transfer candidates are urged to apply by April 1 for the next fall term and by November 15 for the next spring term. In addition to a high school transcript and standardized test scores, transfer candidates are required to submit, by the appropriate deadlines, an official transcript of all college-level work completed, recommendations from two professors, and a statement regarding personal and academic standing from the dean of students at the current college. International students are given special attention throughout the admissions process. Applicants whose first language is not English are encouraged to submit the results of the Test of English as a Foreign Language (TOEFL). There are a limited number of need-based financial aid awards available for outstanding international students.

Mary Lou W. Bates
Dean of Admissions and Financial Aid
Skidmore College
815 North Broadway
Saratoga Springs, New York 12866
Phone: 518-580-5570
        800-867-6007 (toll-free)
E-mail: admissions@skidmore.edu
Website: http://www.skidmore.edu
        http://www.facebook.com/SkidmoreCollege
        http://twitter.com/skidmorecollege
        http://www.youtube.com/skidmorecollege

SMITH COLLEGE
NORTHAMPTON, MASSACHUSETTS

The College

Smith College was founded in 1871 as a liberal arts college for women and rapidly became one of the first such institutions to match the standards and facilities of the best colleges of the day. Today, with 2,500 undergraduates on campus and 250 studying elsewhere, Smith is the largest privately endowed college for women in the country. Graduate degrees (master's, Ph.D.) are offered in a number of departments and in the Smith College School for Social Work. Currently, fifty states and more than sixty countries are represented in the Smith student body. Over 60 percent of the students in each entering class were in the top 10 percent of their high school class; most chose Smith because of the excellence of its faculty and curriculum. Although most Smith students are between the ages of 18 and 22, Smith's Ada Comstock Scholars Program enables older women whose educations have been interrupted and who meet the College's admission standards to pursue an A.B. degree in part-time or full-time study.

Smith's house system is unusual and highly regarded. Each of the College's thirty-five houses is home to between 12 and 100 women. There are fifteen dining rooms that offer different menus, themes, and types of food. The house system stresses individual freedom, group autonomy, and mutual respect. Other residences, such as a cooperative house, and apartments, are also available. Smith offers a wide variety of extracurricular activities, ranging from service organizations to musical groups and from student publications to thirteen intercollegiate sports teams. The already varied cultural and social opportunities—lectures, workshops, dance and theatrical performances, art exhibits, concerts, and social events—are increased by participation in Five Colleges, Inc., a consortium that opens to Smith students classes and activities at Amherst, Hampshire, and Mount Holyoke colleges and at the University of Massachusetts. Smith's athletic facilities include two gymnasiums, five squash courts, a six-lane swimming pool with 1- and 3-meter diving boards, a human performance laboratory, climbing wall, fitness center, and an indoor track and tennis facility, which houses four tennis courts and a 200-meter track. Outside are 30 acres of athletic fields, a 400-meter track, a 5,000-meter cross-country course, and twelve lighted tennis courts. Smith also has indoor and outdoor Olympic-size riding rings and a forty-two-unit stable.

Location

Northampton, a small cosmopolitan city with a population of more than 30,000, is in the Connecticut River valley of western Massachusetts. It is 93 miles west of Boston and 156 miles northeast of New York City. There are many shops and restaurants within walking distance of the campus and within the service area of a free Five College bus system. Buses run frequently to Boston and New York. Many students are involved in local organizations, and some intern in local city or county offices. Others participate on an extracurricular level in nonprofit agencies.

Majors and Degrees

Smith College awards the Bachelor of Arts (A.B.) degree. Areas of major concentration include Afro-American studies, American studies, anthropology, architecture, art (history and studio), astronomy, biochemistry, biological sciences, chemistry, classical studies, classics, comparative literature, computer science, dance, East Asian languages and cultures, East Asian studies, economics, education and child study, engineering, English language and literature, environmental science and policy, film studies, French studies, geosciences, German studies, government, Greek, history, Italian language and literature, Italian studies, Jewish studies, Latin,

Latin American and Latino/Latina studies, mathematics, medieval studies, music, neuroscience, philosophy, physics, Portuguese-Brazilian studies, psychology, religion, Russian civilization, Russian literature, sociology, Spanish, theater, and women and gender studies. Interdepartmental majors and minors are offered in a variety of fields.

Academic Programs

The academic year is divided into two semesters, the first ending before winter recess. Noncredit Interterm courses are offered during January. Smith believes in the goals of a liberal arts education. With an open curriculum, students have flexibility to choose from more than 1,000 courses. The only requirement outside a student's field of concentration is one writing-intensive course. The normal course load consists of 16 credits in each of eight semesters, to total the 128 credits of academic work that are required. There are no specific distribution requirements, but 64 credits must be taken outside the major field of study. A student may also complete the requirements of two departmental majors or of one departmental major and another departmental minor. Concentrations in archives, biomathematical sciences, book studies, Buddhist studies, community engagement and social change, environmental studies: sustainable foods, global financial institutions, museum studies, poetry, and South Asia studies offer students a way to organize intellectual and practical experiences around a focused area of interest. The Smith Centers for Engagement, Learning, and Leadership—the Global Studies Center; the Center for the Environment, Ecological Design, and Sustainability; the Center for Work and Life; and the Center for Community Collaborations—respond to emerging student and scholarly interests, provide contexts for internships and independent projects, and address real-world challenges.

Through credit earned on Advanced Placement or International Baccalaureate examinations and by summer study, some students may be able to accelerate and complete degree requirements in six or seven semesters. The Departmental Honors Program enables a student with a strong academic background to study a particular topic in depth or undertake research in the field of her major.

Off-Campus Programs

Smith students may take academic courses and participate in social and cultural activities at any of the institutions participating in the Five College consortium, described above. Smith students may also spend a year at another member institution of the Twelve College Exchange Program (Amherst, Bowdoin, Connecticut, Dartmouth, Mount Holyoke, Trinity, Vassar, Wellesley, Wesleyan, and Wheaton) or spend a year at Spelman College or Pomona College. Some students participate in the Jean Picker Semester-in-Washington Program in public policy, a fall internship program in Washington, D.C., sponsored by the College's Department of Government. The American Studies Program offers an internship at the Smithsonian Institution.

Smith offers Junior Year Abroad programs in Florence, Geneva, Hamburg, and Paris. Students may apply to affiliated programs in more than thirty other countries. Students eligible for financial aid are able to take that aid with them to any approved program.

Academic Facilities

The Smith College Libraries comprise the largest undergraduate library system of any liberal arts college in the country. The 1.4 million holdings are housed in the centrally located William Allan Neilson Library and in the libraries of the fine arts, performing arts, and science centers. The Neilson Library also houses a rare book room, the Nonprint Resource Center, the College archives, and the Sophia Smith Collection, a women's history archive. The Clark Science Center is a five-building complex that accommodates the nearly 30 percent of students who major in the sciences. The facilities include general laboratories, a molecular genetics facility, classrooms, a rooftop astronomy observatory, animal care facilities, scanning and transmission electron microscopes, an analytic ultracentrifuge, and a high-field nuclear magnetic resonance spectrometer. Ford Hall houses computer science, chemistry, biochemistry, molecular biology, and the Picker Engineering program. Academic computer facilities include networked Windows and Macintosh computers in public labs, classrooms, the libraries, and the foreign language center. All buildings and student residences are networked, and Internet access is available at no charge. There is wireless access in many buildings. Smith also has a digital design studio and several electronic classrooms. Bass Hall houses the psychology department, the scientific computing center, and Young Library, one of the largest undergraduate science libraries in the country. The Bass laboratories provide numerous facilities for research in neuroscience. The Mendenhall Center for the Performing Arts contains an experimental theater and a traditional theater, dance studios, and television and audio recording rooms. Sage Hall, the music building, includes an electronic music studio, a small recital hall, dozens of practice rooms, and a 750-seat concert hall. The Smith College Museum of Art houses one of the finest teaching collections in the country, and Hillyer Hall contains art studios as well as printmaking, darkroom, and sculpture facilities.

Costs

Tuition for 2013–14 is $42,840. The room and board charge for regular student residences is $14,410. The activity fee is $274.

Financial Aid

More than 70 percent of all Smith students receive some form of financial assistance from grants, loans, and/or campus jobs. Aid is awarded on the basis of need, as determined by the College. Each applicant must submit the Smith Aid Application (available on Smith's website), the Free Application for Federal Student Aid (FAFSA), the PROFILE form from the College Scholarship Service, and a copy of the current federal income tax return. Smith meets full demonstrated need for all admitted students who apply for aid by the published deadlines. The first portion of an aid award is an offer of a loan and campus employment; the remaining need is covered by grants from federal, state, and/or College funds. Merit-based aid is also available on a limited and highly competitive basis.

Faculty

The teaching of undergraduate women is the priority of the Smith faculty. There are approximately 300 faculty members; nearly all have earned doctoral degrees and are well-known in their professional fields. Close ties between undergraduates and their professors are forged through small classes (70 percent have 20 or fewer students) and generous access to faculty members during and outside of regular office hours.

Student Government

Smith students assume much of the responsibility for their personal, social, and academic life at the College through the Student Government Association, which gives students representation on major college-policy committees.

Admission Requirements

Smith seeks students whose motivation, academic preparation, and diversity of interests will enable them to profit from and contribute to the varied possibilities of a liberal arts college. Smith is interested in the woman behind the numbers. As a highly competitive college, Smith gives primary consideration to the academic record of each candidate for admission. Strong high school programs have a basis of 4 years of English, at least 3 years in one foreign language or 2 years in each of two languages, 3 years of mathematics, 3 years of science, and 2 years of history. It is hoped that areas of special interest will have been pursued in depth. SAT or ACT scores are optional for U.S. citizens and U.S. permanent residents. Standardized tests (SAT, ACT, TOEFL or IELTS) are required for international citizens. The SAT or ACT is required for international citizens

being instructed in English. The TOEFL or IELTS is required for international citizens being instructed in a language other than English. International students who are attending high school in the U.S. must submit SAT or ACT scores. SAT Subject Tests are optional for any applicant. An interview is strongly recommended. A first-choice early decision plan is available.

Applications are also welcomed from students who wish to transfer from other college-level institutions or who wish to enter the Visiting Students Program or the Ada Comstock Scholars Program.

Smith College is committed to maintaining a diverse community in an atmosphere of mutual respect and appreciation of differences. Smith College does not discriminate in its educational and employment policies on the bases of race, color, creed, religion, national/ethnic origin, sex, sexual orientation, or age or with regard to the bases outlined in the Veterans Readjustment Act and the Americans with Disabilities Act. Smith's admission policies and practices are guided by the same principle, concerning women applying to the undergraduate program and all applicants to the graduate programs.

Application and Information

A prospective first-year student interested in applying to Smith has three options: fall early decision, winter early decision, or regular decision. The fall early decision deadline is November 15, and applicants receive a decision by mid-December. The deadline for winter early decision is January 1, and students receive a decision in late January. Regular decision applicants must complete the Common Application by January 15; all other parts of the application are due by February 1. These candidates receive their admission decision by April 1. The deadline for January transfer admission is November 15; students receive an admission decision in mid-December. The preferred deadline for September transfer admission is February 1, with notification in late March. Transfer applications are accepted until May 15, and decisions are made by early June. Application deadlines for the Visiting Student Programs are July 1 (for September admission) and December 15 (for January admission). Deadlines for the Ada Comstock Scholars Program are November 15 (for January admission) and February 1 (for September admission).

For more information about Smith College, students should contact:

Dean of Admission
Smith College
Northampton, Massachusetts 01063
Phone: 413-585-2500
　　　　800-383-3232 (toll-free)
Fax: 413-585-2527
E-mail: admission@smith.edu
Website: http://www.smith.edu
　　　　http://www.facebook.com/smithcollege
　　　　http://twitter.com/smithcollege

SOUTHERN CONNECTICUT STATE UNIVERSITY

NEW HAVEN, CONNECTICUT

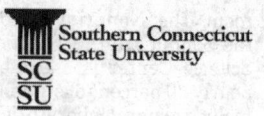

The University

The rich academic and social environment at Southern Connecticut State University encourages students to discover who they are, who they want to be, and how to realize their dreams. A public coeducational university founded in 1893, Southern offers 114 undergraduate and graduate programs. Fascinating internships, unique research opportunities, a challenging faculty, and a dynamic campus enrich every program. Southern is located in New Haven, the heart of "academic Connecticut."

Southern has five academic schools: Arts and Sciences, Business, Education, Health and Human Services, and Graduate Studies. Southern offers several programs, including the Honors College, for high-achieving students. The Honors College is a four-year alternative program featuring team-taught interdisciplinary courses, symposia, and requires students to complete an honors thesis or project in their senior year. The Office of Student Supportive Services offers tutorial support and coordinates special programs for veterans, international students, and students with learning, physical, and emotional disabilities.

The student body represents diverse ethnic and socioeconomic groups. Although most students reside in Connecticut, students from more than twenty states and thirty countries also enroll at Southern. About 11,000 students attend Southern, including 8,700 undergraduates. More than a third of the full-time undergraduates live on campus in ten residence halls and townhouses. Other students commute or reside in off-campus housing in the Southern neighborhood. All on-campus housing includes high-speed Internet service via RESNET. In spring 2013, Southern opened its new 1,200-space Wintergreen parking garage, which includes three charging stations for electric vehicles.

Southern supports more than 100 campus clubs and organizations, ranging from academic and career groups to religious, theatrical, and political clubs.

Competitive athletes and eager amateurs enjoy intramural and intercollegiate sports programs at Southern. Intramural and club sports include coed three-on-three and five-on-five basketball, cheerleading, flag football, coed floor hockey, a golf tournament, ice hockey (men), karate, rugby (men and women), skiing and snowboarding, coed softball, Ultimate (Frisbee), coed soccer, a tennis tournament, Wiffle ball, and coed volleyball. A member of the National Collegiate Athletic Association (NCAA), the Eastern College Athletic Conference, and the Northeast-10 Conference, Southern offers student-athletes competitive opportunities in several intercollegiate sports. A university with a long tradition of athletic excellence, Southern is highly competitive among NCAA Division II colleges and universities, having earned ten NCAA team championships and seventy-two individual championships. Southern offers intercollegiate competition in men's baseball, basketball, cross-country, football, soccer, swimming, and track and field. Southern offers intercollegiate programs for women in basketball, cross-country, field hockey, gymnastics, lacrosse, soccer, softball, swimming, track and field, and volleyball. Outstanding facilities are available to all athletes in Moore Fieldhouse, Pelz Gymnasium, and the Jess Dow Field outdoor sports complex.

Location

New Haven, Connecticut, is a sophisticated city of 130,000 people that abuts picturesque Long Island Sound. Southern is located in the city's Westville section, near historic West Rock Park. Rich in tradition, New Haven is a classic college town; about 35,000 students attend its half-dozen fine universities and colleges. Only 75 miles from New York City and 3 hours from Boston, New Haven is an integral part of the economic, cultural, and social life of the Northeast. Students enjoy easy access to outstanding cultural opportunities, including movies, restaurants, clubs, concerts, seaside activities, sports, museums, and world-famous theater at the Yale Repertory, the Shubert, and Long Wharf.

Majors and Degrees

Southern offers the Bachelor of Arts (B.A.) and the Bachelor of Science (B.S.) degrees. The Bachelor of Arts degree is awarded in anthropology, art (art history and studio art), biology, chemistry (biochemistry), communication (communication disorders and media studies), earth science, economics, English, French, geography, German, history, Italian, journalism, liberal studies, mathematics, media studies, music, philosophy, physics, political science, psychology, sociology, Spanish, and theater.

The Bachelor of Science degree is awarded in anthropology (archeology, cultural, general, linguistics, and physical), art (ceramics, graphic design, jewelry making, painting, photography, printmaking, and sculpture), athletic training, biology, business (accounting, business economics, finance, international business, management, managing information systems, and marketing), chemistry and biochemistry, communication (creative message construction, interpersonal/relational, organizational communication, and video production), computer science (information systems), earth science (environmental, geology, and oceanography), exercise science (human performance and teacher education), geography, information and library science, journalism, mathematics, nursing, physics, political science, psychology (research), public health (environmental and health promotion), recreation and leisure (community, outdoor, and therapeutic), social work, and sociology.

The Bachelor of Science degree with teaching certification is offered in art education, early childhood education, and elementary education.

The Bachelor of Science degree with certification for secondary education is offered in biology, chemistry, earth science, English, exercise science, French, geography, German, history and social science, Italian, mathematics, physics, political science, Spanish, sociology, and special education.

Southern also offers pre-professional study in dentistry, engineering, law, medicine, and veterinary medicine.

Academic Programs

The University operates on a two-semester calendar. The fall semester usually begins the first week in September and ends in mid-December. The spring semester, which includes a one-week spring recess in March, typically begins in mid-January and ends in mid-May. Southern also offers several summer session programs and an intersession program in January.

Southern maintains a strong commitment to the liberal arts and sciences as fundamental elements of a high-quality education. To ensure all students acquire the best education possible, Southern offers a strong yet flexible program that underscores the basics while encouraging individual choice. All baccalaureate degree candidates must complete a minimum of 122 hours of credit. Majors consist of at least 30 prescribed hours of credit in one specific, approved field. Degree candidates also must fulfill the liberal education program requirements. In addition, all bachelor's degree candidates must meet a foreign language requirement. Some professional B.S. degree programs enable students to develop a minor or a concentration in addition to the major with 12 credits in electives.

Off-Campus Programs

Southern's location in the heart of a major urban area enables the University to cultivate a growing list of meaningful regional internships. Aspiring social workers enjoy learning opportunities that extend beyond the classroom into New Haven's dynamic urban environment. Students in the B.S. nursing degree program acquire clinical experience at Yale–New Haven Hospital, the Hospital of Saint Raphael, and other sites that are linked by distance learning programs. Internships also are available for journalism students in city newsrooms and local TV stations. The University also offers internships at Long Wharf Theatre; ESPN Broadcasting; the Circle in the Square Theatre in New York City; MTV; Shearson Lehman Brothers, Inc.; and others.

Academic Facilities

A $260-million building program has transformed Southern campus life. The four-level, 125,000-square-foot Michael J. Adanti Student Center is a hub of campus life and includes a ballroom, movie theater, fitness center, an expansive bookstore, a food court, a TV lounge, and many meeting and conference rooms. A new home for the School of Business opened in summer 2012. Engleman Hall, the University's main academic building, was renovated and expanded to include state-of-the-art classrooms, departmental libraries, and conference rooms. A new wing has been added to the Hilton C. Buley Library. When renovations to the library are completed in 2013, the facility's size will be doubled. In fall 2013, Southern expects to break ground for a new 98,322-square-foot laboratory science building.

Other campus facilities include a satellite-equipped journalism lab; a modern television studio in the Ralph Earl Hall of Fine Arts; the John Lyman Center for the Performing Arts, a 1,650-seat theater for major productions; the Robert Kendall Drama Lab for experimental theater; the Center for the Environment; the Multicultural Center; the Communication Disorders Center; the Adaptive Technology Lab; and the Disability Resources Center.

Costs

Annual tuition and fees for 2013–14 for Connecticut residents are $8,541. Tuition and fees for out-of-state residents are $19,573. On-campus room and board fees for the year are $11,005. Student books, supplies, and personal expenses average about $2,000 per year. All costs are subject to change. Prospective students should contact the Office of Financial Aid and Scholarships for current information.

Financial Aid

The Office of Financial Aid and Scholarships coordinates grants, scholarships, long-term low-interest loans, and part-time student employment for students and families who demonstrate financial need. The University offers the Federal Perkins Loan, the Federal Pell Grant, the Federal Supplemental Educational Opportunity Grant, the Federal Stafford Student Loan, the Federal PLUS loan, and the Federal Work-Study Program. Southern also provides alumni scholarships. Southern's tuition installment plan enables matriculated students to make monthly tuition payments throughout the academic year. More than 60 percent of Southern's undergraduates receive financial aid. Students who seek assistance must complete the Free Application for Federal Student Aid (FAFSA) and send it to the central processor for receipt by March 15. Prospective students can file the FAFSA form on paper or on the web at http://www.fafsa.ed.gov.

Faculty

Like the University's student body, Southern's faculty members represent a broad spectrum of backgrounds, interests, and scholarly achievements. Southern's more than 700 faculty members share a deep commitment to teaching, writing, and research. Of the more than 400 full-time faculty members, about 85 percent hold a Ph.D. or terminal degree from major colleges and universities around the world. Many faculty members serve as academic advisers. In addition, the University offers counseling to help students with academic, personal, and career decisions.

Student Government

The Student Government Association is the voice of the undergraduate student body at Southern. The organization's 24 voting members meet regularly to discuss students' interests in a variety of areas, such as funding and academic policies. Student Government Association members also serve with administrators and faculty members on key University committees. Residential students govern themselves through their respective residence hall councils and the Inter-Residence Council.

Admission Requirements

Southern's selective admission policy considers each student as an individual, with particular consideration given to personal accomplishments and motivation. Southern seeks students with diverse cultural values and backgrounds; no applicant is accepted or rejected because of race, color, gender, sexual orientation, age, disability, religion, or national origin. Candidates must be high school graduates or hold an equivalency diploma. Their secondary school program should include at least 13 academic units of college-preparatory work, including 4 years of English, 3 years of mathematics (algebra 1, geometry, and algebra 2), 2 years of foreign language, 2 years of science (including 1 year of laboratory science), and 2 years of social sciences (including U.S. history). Other factors include the student's high school record, class rank (preferably in the upper 50 percent), and competitive SAT or ACT scores.

Application and Information

Candidates for admission should apply early in the fall of their high school senior year. The Admissions Office mails its first acceptance notice in early December. Early applicants have priority for housing and financial aid. Applicants must submit academic records, including a complete transcript of high school grades and class rank; an online admission application; a $50 nonrefundable fee; a written recommendation from a high school principal, teacher, or school guidance counselor; and a copy of the SAT or ACT score report. For additional information, students should contact the Admissions House, Southern Connecticut State University, 131 Farnham Avenue, New Haven, Connecticut 06515. Students are encouraged to apply online by visiting the University's website and clicking on Admissions. Students can find more information about the University on Facebook and Twitter.

Alexis S. Haakonsen
Director of Undergraduate Admissions
Admissions House
Southern Connecticut State University
131 Farnham Avenue
New Haven, Connecticut 06515-1355
Phone: 203-392-SCSU
    888-500-SCSU (toll-free)
Website: http://www.SouthernCT.edu

Southern's beautiful suburban campus and its cosmopolitan location in New Haven, Connecticut, offer students tremendous opportunities to experience and explore all that New Haven has to offer, including arts, culture, history, and entertainment, as well as student teaching and internship opportunities.

SOUTHERN NEW HAMPSHIRE UNIVERSITY
MANCHESTER, NEW HAMPSHIRE

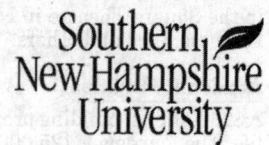

The University

The prevailing wisdom at Southern New Hampshire University (SNHU) has always been that there are no limits to what students can achieve. As an institution, there are seemingly no limits to what SNHU can achieve as well.

In 2012, SNHU was named the twelfth most innovative company in the world by Fast Company, ranking ahead of industry giants like the NFL, Starbucks, and LinkedIn. SNHU was the only educational institution on the list, an impressive achievement for a university that is committed to consistently reinventing the way that education is delivered and received.

Academic programs are created with the real world in mind, so students are prepared to launch successful careers when they graduate. Classes are taught by highly credentialed faculty who have professional experience and remain current in their fields. Academic and personal support is readily available, both inside and outside the classroom. If students need help, faculty and staff will rally around them quickly.

The University operates on the belief that college should change students' lives, not break the bank—a private university education should be affordable. That's why financial aid has been increased. Students with high school GPAs of 2.5 and higher may receive up to $20,000 in grants and scholarships. About 90 percent of the students at SNHU receive some kind of financial aid.

The University has 2,585 traditional, full-time undergraduate day students, with a total enrollment in all divisions (day, evening, weekend, and online undergraduate and graduate students) of 17,534. Programs are offered on campus, on location at the University's centers in New Hampshire and Maine, and online. SNHU offers undergraduate programs in business, culinary arts, education, hospitality, and liberal arts and more than 60 graduate programs.

SNHU is the first carbon-neutral school in New Hampshire. There are several projects under construction that will enhance the student experience. A new 300-bed freshman dormitory is slated to open in fall 2013. This building will feature a sustainable design, high-efficiency lighting systems, and individual temperature controls in the rooms. Construction began in spring 2013 for a new Learning Commons which will house the library, media services, instructional support and the IT help desk. The building is expected to be completed by fall 2014. Additional campus features include a state-of-the-art academic center (built in 2009), a dining hall (built in 2010), updated dorms and apartment buildings, a simulated stock trading room, multimedia classrooms, an auditorium, the museum-quality McIninch Art Gallery, virtual science labs, technology-ready buildings, a library with resources that can be accessed via the Internet, a fitness center that rivals private commercial gyms, athletic fields, cooking labs, a bakery, and the award-winning student-run restaurant, The Quill.

Students can participate in one of the University's more than fifty-five student clubs or start new ones. Intercollegiate teams compete in Division II of the NCAA, and the Northeast-10 Conference. Sports include baseball, men's and women's basketball, cheerleading, men's and women's cross-country, golf, ice hockey, men's and women's lacrosse, men's and women's soccer, softball, men's and women's tennis, and women's volleyball. SNHU recently announced plans to add women's bowling, field hockey, golf, and outdoor track and field. Intramural sports, including basketball, flag football, indoor soccer, and volleyball are also extremely popular. SNHU's powerful athletic teams dominate on the field—and in the classroom. The University's student-athletes earned honors from the NCAA and USA Today for high grades and 100 percent graduation rates.

Athletic facilities include an indoor, 25-meter, competition-size swimming pool; a racquetball court; an aerobic studio; cardiovascular equipment; four outdoor lighted tennis courts; outdoor basketball and beach volleyball courts; a soccer/lacrosse turf field; baseball and softball fields; and two indoor gymnasiums with four basketball courts and areas for indoor soccer, indoor tennis, volleyball, and other activities. The fitness center has 4,000 square feet of strength equipment and a 1,500-square-foot cardio deck.

The Wellness Center provides short-term health care, health education, and counseling services for students, and the buildings and facilities are accessible to people with disabilities. In addition, the Center develops a robust schedule of events around issues ranging from bullying and domestic violence prevention to nutrition and physical fitness.

The Career Development Center provides assistance with resume development, letter writing, company research, networking, and informational interviewing, in addition to facilitating internships and job placement. Lifetime career services and counseling are available to all current students as well as alumni.

Location

The University is ideally located, with easy access to downtown Manchester, New Hampshire's largest city. Manchester has also been named one of the top college towns in the country. Public transportation is available, and students may keep cars on campus. The mountains, beaches, and Boston are only an hour away. CQ Press has repeatedly named New Hampshire one of the nation's most livable states.

Majors and Degrees

The University has three schools: the School of Arts and Sciences, the School of Business, and the School of Education. The University offers associate, bachelor's, master's, and doctoral degrees. Undergraduate programs provide students with a strong general education foundation and the knowledge and skills they need to succeed in their careers.

The School of Arts and Sciences offers degrees in communication, computer information technology (B.A. option), creative writing, English language and literature, environmental management, environmental science, forensic psychology, game design and development (B.A. option), graphic design and media arts, history, justice studies, justice studies/crime & criminology, justice studies/law & legal process, justice studies/policing & law enforcement, justice studies/terrorism & homeland security, liberal arts, mathematics, political science, psychology, psychology/child and adolescent development, psychology/mental health, and sociology.

The School of Business majors include accounting, accounting/finance, accounting/information systems, baking & pastry arts (A.S.), business administration, business studies, computer information technology (B.S. option), culinary arts (A.S.), culinary management (B.S.), fashion merchandising (A.S.), fashion merchandising and management (B.A.), finance/economics, game design and development (B.S. option), hospitality business, hospitality management, international business, marketing, sport management, technical management, and the unique Degree in Three program—offered in business administration, marketing, and sport management. Students are able to earn a Bachelor of Science degree in three years through a blend of traditional and non-classroom experiences in the real world. The overall goal of the program is to foster and enhance effective communications, critical thinking, and teamwork. The program enables students to save up to $40,000 in tuition, room, and board; take a traditional course load of five classes per semester; graduate in six semesters with no night, weekend, or summer courses; secure internships and participate in community events; and pursue interests—graduate school, employment, study abroad, etc.—instead of a fourth year.

The School of Education majors include child development leadership, early childhood education, elementary education, English education, middle school mathematics education, middle school science education, music education, social studies education, and special education.

A University honors program, a prelaw program, and a pre-M.B.A. program are also available for students seeking additional challenges.

Academic Programs

At Southern New Hampshire University, undergraduate students receive a broad education in the liberal arts and intense practice in oral and written communication, coupled with the specific knowledge and skills they need to succeed in their chosen fields.

Recognizing that successful leaders must be able to view problems from a variety of perspectives, the University mandates that all students complete courses in writing, the fine arts, the social sciences, mathematics, science, and public speaking. Students also have the opportunity to take elective courses in whatever areas capture their curiosity and may elect to concentrate their electives to earn a minor. The University curriculum offers both structure and flexibility.

Off-Campus Programs

Southern New Hampshire University is adept at mixing academic theory with practical experience inside and outside the classroom. Undergraduates participate in off-campus cooperative education experiences/internships, earning 3 to 12 academic credits. Such opportunities are based on a student's major and career goals and typically are taken during a student's junior or senior year. Students work with faculty members and the Career Development Office to find appropriate assignments. About 70 percent of those who complete co-ops/internships are offered positions by their employers.

The University has established relationships with a number of respected, high-profile employers who provide internship and job opportunities, including Fidelity Investments, Google, IBM, New York Life, Walt Disney World, LEGO Systems, the Boston Celtics, the Boston Red Sox, and Marriott International.

Students also work with real-world off-campus partners in their courses. For example, marketing students have created media campaigns for area businesses and education students assist local teachers in their classrooms. The University's graduates are in demand because businesses know they have been prepared to contribute both on the job and in their communities.

Opportunities for studying abroad are available at a number of partnering institutions in countries around the world.

Costs

Undergraduate tuition and fees for the 2013–14 academic year are $28,884. Typical room and board charges are an additional $11,132. Students should plan to budget funds for books, supplies, travel, and personal expenses.

All students are required to bring wireless laptop computers. Culinary arts students need to purchase uniforms and knife sets.

Financial Aid

More than 90 percent of the University's students receive some form of financial aid, which may include need-based grants, academic and commuter scholarships, work-study funds, and loans. The average aid package has a value of more than $18,888 and includes a combination of scholarships, grants, loans, and employment sources.

The University participates in the Federal Work-Study Program, the Federal Perkins Loan Program, and the Federal Supplemental Educational Opportunity Grant Program. The school is also eligible under the Federal Stafford Student Loan Program and the Federal Pell Grant Program. Aid applicants must complete the Free Application for Federal Student Aid (FAFSA) by the priority deadline of March 15. The One Stop/Financial Aid Office can provide the appropriate forms, or students can go online to http://www.fafsa.ed.gov. Academic, athletic, and leadership scholarships are available for students who qualify.

Faculty

The University has more than 128 full-time faculty members and more than 200 part-time instructors. The student-faculty ratio is 15:1. Nearly 75 percent of the full-time faculty members hold Ph.D.'s or the equivalent in their areas of expertise.

The instructional programs blend theory with practice to stimulate students' professional development and personal growth. Faculty members bring extensive academic, work, travel, and life experiences to their classrooms. Although their primary goal is teaching, faculty members remain current in their disciplines. Outside the classroom, faculty members are management consultants, CPAs, analysts, small-business owners, economists, accountants, marketing professionals, entrepreneurs, innkeepers, chefs, world travelers, artists, poets, novelists, psychologists, and much more.

Student Government

The Student Government Association is led by 25 students, including 5 officers, who represent all the students at the University. Its primary function is to represent the student body in campus affairs and to dispense student activity funds. One student is appointed to represent the student body on the Board of Trustees. Students are also appointed to most other standing committees, including the Dining Services Committee, Residence Life Committee, Public Safety Committee, the Curriculum Advisory Committee, and the Library Committee.

Admission Requirements

Applicants for admission are evaluated individually on the basis of academic credentials and personal characteristics. When reviewing applicants, primary emphasis is placed on a student's academic record, as demonstrated by the quality and level of college-preparatory course work and achievement attained. Most successful candidates admitted to SNHU present a program of study consisting of 16 college-preparatory courses, including 4 years of English, 3 or more years of mathematics, 2 or more years of science, and 2 or more years of social science. Separate consideration is given to admission decisions for transfer, culinary arts, 3-Year Honors Program, nontraditional, and international applicants. Students may apply online at www.snhu.edu or via the Common Application.

Application and Information

Applicants for undergraduate day programs must submit an application (Common Application or online at www.snhu.edu/apply), college essay, $40 application fee, and the following application materials: official high school transcript, one letter of recommendation from a school counselor or teacher. SNHU is a test-optional institution and SAT/ACT scores are not required.

Freshman applicants can apply before November 15 to be considered for the early action deadline. The University operates on a rolling admission basis, however there is a priority application deadline of March 15. Admission and scholarship decisions are made within 30 days of receiving the required admission materials.

For more information about Southern New Hampshire University, students should contact:

Office of Undergraduate Admission
Southern New Hampshire University
2500 North River Road
Manchester, New Hampshire 03106-1045
Phone: 603-645-9611
      800-642-4968 (toll-free)
Fax: 603-645-9693
Website: http://www.snhu.edu
      http://www.facebook.com/snhuoncampus
      http://www.twitter.com/snhuoncampus

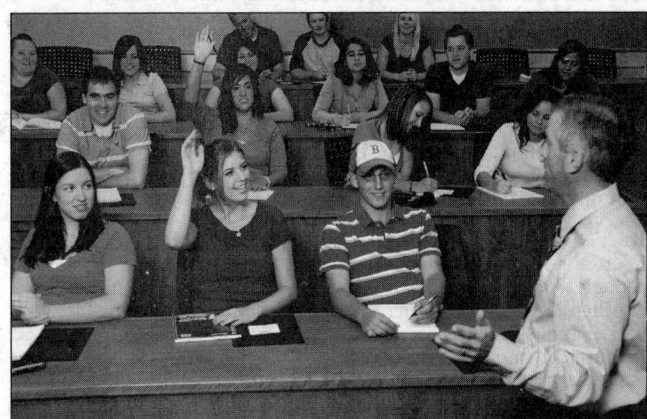

At SNHU, students can study over forty majors in the schools of arts and sciences, business, and education.

SPRINGFIELD COLLEGE
SPRINGFIELD, MASSACHUSETTS

The College

Real-world experience through fieldwork and internships, combined with outstanding academic preparation, gives Springfield College graduates a competitive advantage when they move on to careers or graduate education. Students perform fieldwork, internships, or service learning as early as their first semester, gaining valuable experience while following the College's mission of leadership in service to others.

Internationally renowned for educating leaders in health sciences, human and social services, sports and movement studies, education, business, and the arts and sciences, Springfield College offers bachelor's, master's, and doctorate degree programs, and it is accredited by the New England Association of Schools and Colleges (NEASC).

The Mission: Springfield College is a private, coeducational institution that was founded in 1885 with its own Humanics philosophy: "to educate students, in spirit, mind, and body for leadership in service to others." Humanics has remained the College mission to this day, and students, faculty members, and administration are committed to that mission.

The College has been named to the President's Higher Education Community Service Honor Roll, has received Carnegie Foundation Community Engagement Classification, and has won the Jostens/NADIIIAA Award of Merit for community service by student athletes. The Institute for International Sport named it one of the fifteen most influential educators through sport in America. It is designated by the YMCA of the USA as a premier leadership development center.

Student Population: An ethnically diverse student body of 3,284 undergraduate and graduate students at the main campus comes primarily from the Northeastern United States but also from across the country and around the world.

Cocurricular Activities: Enriching the undergraduate experience is an array of cocurricular activities, health and wellness programs, arts and cultural events; an extensive campus recreation program; and one of the nation's largest athletics programs for a midsized college. There are more than 100 organizations and opportunities for involvement. More than 80 percent of undergraduates participate in some form of athletics, including varsity teams, intramurals, or club sports. There are men's and women's teams in basketball, cross-country, gymnastics, lacrosse, soccer, swimming, diving, tennis, track and volleyball; women's teams in field hockey and softball; and men's teams in baseball, football, golf, and wrestling.

Campus Facilities: Ten campus residence halls provide guaranteed on-campus housing. Options include traditional residence halls and suite-style accommodations with private rooms for 2 to 4 students along with a shared lounge, kitchen, and bathrooms. There are single-gender and coeducational residences. Seniors may choose to live off campus. The main student dining facility features a range of fresh food options. There are snack and other light-fare services around the campus, including a food court with a two-story atrium.

Recreational Facilities: The award-winning Wellness & Recreation Complex facilities represent the best and the latest in collegiate recreational centers. The $22.5-million complex, with another $1.8 million in furnishings and equipment, opened in 2008 and includes the interconnected Wellness Center, Field House, and Athletic Training/Exercise Science Complex with 160,560 square feet of instructional, athletic, and recreational space adjoining the Physical Education Complex and Art Linkletter Natatorium.

The new buildings support the College's degree programs in athletic training, physical education, exercise science, sport management, and related areas. They also contain and support the new center for campus recreation and wellness with its comprehensive programming serving the entire campus community.

Location

Springfield College's picturesque, 150-acre campus includes several new and newly renovated state-of-the-art facilities that blend with traditional campus architecture. On the shores of Lake Massasoit in the Pioneer Valley, Springfield College is located in Springfield, the third-largest city in Massachusetts and fourth-largest in New England (Boston, Worcester, and Providence are larger). A wide range of social, cultural, and athletic activities enhance the valley, as well as twelve other colleges and universities. For example, Springfield Symphony Hall is the site of concerts, plays, musicals, and dance performances; the MassMutual Center in Springfield is home to the American Hockey League's Springfield Falcons; and the Naismith Memorial Basketball Hall of Fame is an international attraction.

Nearby cities and towns offer many additional attractions. Northampton bustles with trendy shops, coffee houses, galleries, theater productions, health food stores, nightclubs, and restaurants. The Berkshire Hills offer hiking, skiing, biking, and other outdoor activities. Boston lies 90 miles to the east, New York City is less than a 3-hour drive away, Vermont is 1 hour away, and Bradley International Airport is 20 miles south.

Majors and Degrees

Springfield College offers Bachelor of Science or Bachelor of Arts degrees in: American studies, applied exercise science, art, art therapy, athletic training/doctor of physical therapy (seven-year dual-degree program), biology, business administration (opportunity for a unique "4 + 1" program culminating in an M.B.A.), communications/sports journalism, communication sciences and disorders, computer and information sciences, computer graphics/digital arts, criminal justice, dance, early childhood education, elementary education, emergency medical services management, English, general studies, health science/general studies, health services administration, health education (health studies), history, mathematics, mathematics and computer technology, nutritional sciences, occupational therapy, physical education (movement and sport studies), physical therapy (entry-level 6½-year program culminating in a doctor of physical therapy degree), physician assistant (entry-level six-year program culminating in a Master of Science degree), psychology, recreation management, rehabilitation and disability studies, secondary education, sociology, sport management, sports biology, youth development, and exploratory studies (undeclared).

Academic Program

Consistent with the Springfield College Humanics philosophy, undergraduate education takes a holistic approach and prepares the student—in spirit, mind, and body—for a life of leadership in fields that help others.

The College has a two-semester academic calendar. To graduate, students must complete 120 credits including required courses for the major field of study, electives, and required courses for all students (writing, computer applications, arts and humanities, analytical and natural sciences, social sciences, international/multicultural studies, social justice, and physical education). Students may also earn credit for successful completion of Advanced Placement (AP) high school courses, and through the DANTES subject standard test and the College-Level Examination Program (CLEP) administered by the College Board.

Springfield College has agreements with several medical schools, which guarantee acceptance of its qualified students. In addition, many Springfield College programs allow undergraduates to take graduate-level courses.

There are campus chapters of the following honor societies: Beta Beta Beta (biology), Kappa Delta Pi (education), Phi Alpha (social work), Phi Epsilon Kappa (health, physical education, recreation or safety), and Psi Chi (psychology).

Off-Campus Programs

For fieldwork, internships, and service learning, the College maintains relationships with businesses, nonprofits, public and private agencies, and schools. Sites have included the Naismith Memorial Basketball Hall of Fame, American Hockey League, *The Boston Globe,* YMCAs, American Heart Association, MassMutual, Children's Hospital, Hilton Head Crowne Plaza, Reebok Health and Fitness Center, Baystate Medical Center, parks and recreation departments, and others.

Extensive study-abroad programs are available. Students may also enroll in courses at some of the other colleges in the Springfield area.

Academic Facilities

Technologically up-to-date, the campus is wireless and has smart classrooms, computer labs, a videoconferencing facility, a conference center, a language laboratory, a television studio, a journalism lab, a radio station, and more.

Science facilities include the recently renovated Schoo-Bemis Science Center with state-of-the-art equipment; the Athletic Training/ Exercise Science Complex, cited as one of the most outstanding in the nation; and the Allied Health Sciences Center, with a human anatomy laboratory and sophisticated equipment for physical testing, analysis, and treatment. Herbert P. Blake Hall contains labs, testing, and treatment facilities, including the medical simulation laboratory, or sim lab, that features high-fidelity 3G adult and baby patient-simulator mannequins that respond like humans, allowing students to experience realistic, hands-on training and complicated medical techniques. Locklin Hall contains a well-equipped rehabilitation assessment and counseling services center.

For arts studies and programs, the newly renovated Fuller Arts Center and Appleton Auditorium is the site of performances, and the Visual Arts Center contains studio workspace and a public exhibition center.

The East Campus comprises a 57-acre forest ecosystem with camping facilities and lake shoreline. It is a training ground for students in several academic programs. The Springfield College Child Development Center is an exceptional fieldwork facility for students of education and psychology.

Babson Library, well known for its resources in physical education, psychology, education, and health and human services, contains a rich collection of full-text print and digital materials. Library staff members assist, and students have access to a full range of information sources.

Costs

For the 2012–13 academic year, tuition and fees were $31,690. Room and board costs were $10,630.

Financial Aid

Students are encouraged to apply for grants, loans, and student employment. Springfield College financial aid is based on need and academic achievement. The College gives full consideration to students who submit the Free Application for Federal Student Aid and the Springfield College Financial Aid Application by March 15 for first-year students and May 1 for transfer students. Students not eligible for financial aid may be considered for campus employment.

Faculty

Most of the 208 faculty members hold doctorates or other terminal degrees. The student-teacher ratio is 13:1.

Student Government

The Student Government Association, managed by elected students, promotes students' interests and welfare. It guides and finances more than thirty student organizations, adopts policies affecting students, and is a liaison between students and the College administration.

Admission Requirements

Springfield College evaluates applicants on the basis of academic and personal factors. Applications for regular admission or early decision must be submitted to the Office of Undergraduate Admissions and include a completed application form, a high school transcript, one personal reference, and SAT or ACT scores. Transfer students must also submit a transcript and a dean's report from each college attended.

Application due dates for the 2014–15 academic year are as follows: undergraduate applicants, April 1; transfer students, August 1; athletic training and physical therapy programs, December 1; and physician assistant and occupational therapy programs, January 15.

Springfield College is interested in meeting each applicant and encourages candidates to visit the College and experience campus life. The College offers personal interviews, campus tours, and open-house programs and also facilitates contact with alumni and current students.

Application and Information

Springfield College's Admissions Committee reviews applications upon receiving them.

Application forms and information may be obtained from:
Office of Admissions
Springfield College
263 Alden Street
Springfield, Massachusetts 01109
Phone: 413-748-3136
    800-343-1257 (toll-free)
E-mail: admissions@springfieldcollege.edu
Website: www.springfieldcollege.edu

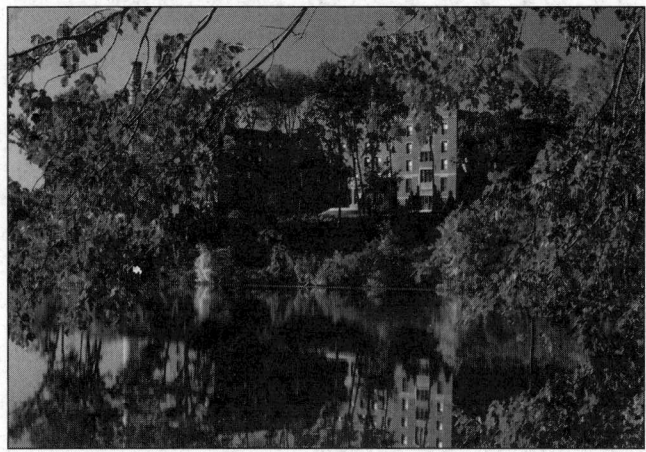

Situated on Lake Massasoit, Alumni Hall was built in 1927 and is the oldest residence hall on the Springfield College campus.

STATE UNIVERSITY OF NEW YORK AT OSWEGO

OSWEGO, NEW YORK

The University

Founded in 1861, SUNY Oswego is now a comprehensive college with an excellent academic reputation and commitment to teaching, learning, research, and service. Total enrollment, including part-time and graduate students, is approximately 8,100 students. Approximately 6,800 students are currently enrolled as full-time undergraduates. More than 110 liberal arts and career-oriented programs are offered through the College of Liberal Arts and Sciences; School of Business; School of Communication, Media, and the Arts; and School of Education. The School of Education is nationally accredited by the National Council for the Accreditation of Teacher Education (NCATE), and the School of Business is internationally accredited by AACSB–The Association to Advance Collegiate Schools of Business. Other individual programs within the College of Liberal Arts and Sciences and the School of Communication, Media, and the Arts are accredited by specific discipline-oriented accrediting organizations.

Located on 696 acres on the southern shore of Lake Ontario, the spacious tree-lined campus consists of fifty-six buildings. Twelve residence halls and The Village townhouse complex, offer a variety of on-campus housing opportunities to all degree-seeking students. More than 170 extracurricular organizations cover a wide range of social, academic, cultural, and intellectual interests. Theater, art, film, music, dance, and discussion events fill the campus cultural calendar. There is a full slate of twenty-four NCAA Division III intercollegiate sports for men and women, along with a full complement of competitive club sports and intramural athletics.

Oswego, a selective college, receives over 13,000 applications for some 2,000 freshman and transfer openings each fall. Accredited by the Middle States Association of Colleges and Schools, it has been recognized by a number of authoritative guides for its outstanding academic opportunities and high academic standards. In recent years, SUNY Oswego has been cited for excellence and selectivity in *U.S. News & World Report's Best Colleges Guide, Colleges of Distinction,* and in both the Princeton Review's *Best Northeastern Colleges* and their *Best Value Colleges* for 2013.

Oswego is undergoing an $800 million comprehensive renewal project; recently completed projects include a $56-million campus and convocation center and a $35-million campus townhouse village for 350 students. The $118-million Richard S. Shineman Center for Science, Engineering, and Innovation; a new Biological Field Station lab facility; and the newly renovated Romney Field House are all slated to open in the fall of 2013. In addition, major renovations and additions to the School of Education's Park and Wilber Halls are due to be completed in 2014.

Location

With a population of nearly 20,000, the city of Oswego is a modest-sized, friendly upstate New York community. It is the country's oldest freshwater port and one of the leading ports on the Great Lakes and St. Lawrence Seaway. The city and its surrounding area are known for summer and winter recreation, including camping, boating, sailing, fishing, tennis, golf, ice skating, alpine and cross-country skiing, snowboarding, and sledding. It is at the heart of the booming sports fishing industry, with a thriving tourism scene. The campus is conveniently located 35 miles northwest of Syracuse and 65 miles east of Rochester. Students traveling by rail or air may utilize bus service to Oswego through the Regional Transportation Center located adjacent to one of the largest malls in the northeast, Destiny USA in Syracuse.

Majors and Degrees

SUNY Oswego awards the Bachelor of Arts (B.A.), Bachelor of Science (B.S.), and Bachelor of Fine Arts (B.F.A.) degrees.

Through the College of Liberal Arts and Sciences, students can earn a baccalaureate degree in American studies, anthropology, applied mathematics, applied mathematical economics, biochemistry, biology, chemistry, cinema and screen studies, cognitive science, computer science, creative writing, economics, electrical and computer engineering, English, French, geochemistry, geology, German, global and international studies, history, human development, information science, language and international trade, linguistics, mathematics, meteorology, philosophy, philosophy-psychology, physics, political science, psychology, public justice, sociology, software engineering, Spanish, women's studies, and zoology.

The School of Business offers B.S. degree programs in accounting, business administration, finance, human resource management, management accounting, marketing, operations management and information systems, and risk management and insurance.

The School of Communication, Media, and the Arts offers baccalaureate degree programs in art, broadcasting and mass communication, communication and social interaction, graphic design, journalism, music, public relations, and theater.

The School of Education offers B.S. degree programs in adolescence education, childhood education, teaching English to speakers of other languages (TESOL), technology education, technology management, vocational-teacher preparation, and wellness management.

In addition, three innovative five-year combined bachelor's and master's programs are available: a bachelor's degree in accounting with a master's in business administration, a bachelor's in psychology with an M.B.A., and a bachelor's in psychology with a master's in human computer interaction.

Cooperative programs include a 3+2 engineering program leading to a bachelor's degree from Oswego in physics and a B.S. in engineering from Case Western Reserve, Clarkson, or SUNY Binghamton; a 2+2 program leading to a B.S. in medical imaging sciences, as well as a 3+3 or 3+4 program leading to a B.S./D.P.T. in physical therapy from SUNY Upstate Medical University; and a 3+4 preoptometry program leading to a bachelor's in chemistry from Oswego and an O.D. in optometry from SUNY College of Optometry.

Academic Programs

Oswego offers students a broad range of courses in the liberal arts and in preprofessional and professional studies. In addition to core courses within a major, all students must satisfy general education requirements designed to strengthen basic writing and analytical proficiency, give students awareness of their cultural heritage, and provide a level of literacy in the social and behavioral sciences, natural sciences, and humanities. By completing these general education requirements during their first two years of study, students are able to select a major with a sense of confidence and purpose. Students who are certain of their academic interest may begin working on their major program in their first year.

Before arriving on campus, students are assigned an adviser from either their major area or the college's Student Advisement Center. Advisers assist students who have not declared a major; help with academic, personal, and career concerns; and collaborate in scheduling courses needed for graduation. In addition, most students are matched with a first-year peer adviser, an older student, to help them face the challenges of their first year. The college has more than 500 undeclared students; many drawn by Oswego's reputation for helping learners find their way in education and life.

Students may consider applying for the college's honors program, which provides a challenging academic experience for high achievers regardless of major. Students also have the option of receiving credit through proficiency CLEP and Advanced Placement examinations while still in high school.

Off-Campus Programs

Opportunities exist for students to broaden their knowledge of other countries by participating in one of eighty different summer or semester overseas academic programs offered. Programs are available throughout the world, and costs are held as close as possible to the cost of an average semester on the Oswego campus. A newer option is short study-abroad quarter courses offering an intensive curriculum followed by a one-to-two-week experience in a foreign country.

Through cooperative arrangements, Oswego also participates in semester programs in Albany and Washington.

Internships and other field experiences are available for students from all disciplines through the Experience-Based Education Office. Each year, more than 1,000 Oswego students participate in internships and career-awareness activities on campus, in the local area, and throughout the Northeast, the country, and the world.

Academic Facilities

Penfield Library is a high-tech information center supporting the curriculum, teaching, and research of SUNY Oswego. The library houses a collection of over 450,000 bound volumes, including partial U.S. and New York State government documents depositories, and provides access to nearly 26,000 print and/or electronic journals, magazines, and newspapers. Through Interlibrary Loan, Penfield can provide additional materials from libraries all over the world. The library's listening area has more than 12,000 recordings, cassettes, and CDs. Additional facilities include the Lake Effect Café, an online catalog, a 24-hour study room with computers, study carrels, wireless Internet access, and computer labs with word processing.

Campuswide computer technology services support students in their classroom, residence, and Internet activities. Students receive an account at the time of enrollment that can be activated online to access e-mail and other web services. High-speed Internet service is available from all residence hall rooms via Ethernet and wireless networks. Wireless access is also available in most locations throughout the campus, including academic buildings, the Campus Center complex, Hewitt Union, Penfield Library, and all resident dining centers. Other services include technology training workshops, Internet troubleshooting via an active helpdesk, web support for student clubs and organizations, free antivirus software and campuswide Gmail. The campus maintains hundreds of Macintosh and Windows-based computers in ten public-access labs. Students also have access to more than 500 computers and numerous Sun workstations in forty specialized departmental labs.

Adjacent to the campus, the college maintains the 330-acre Rice Creek Field Station, with its new $3-million, 7,200-square-foot lab facility scheduled to open in fall 2013. The facility has two lab/classrooms, a lecture room, and exhibit areas with an indoor viewing gallery, providing a unique vista of the creek and pond. College classes and community education programs are regularly held at the field station, which ranks among the five most extensively used facilities of its kind in the country.

Tyler Hall, Oswego's fine arts center, has two art galleries that feature annual traveling exhibitions, locally produced theme exhibitions, and the best work of students and faculty members. Tyler Hall's Waterman Theatre hosts student plays, musical performances, and productions by internationally renowned traveling artists.

The WRVO Stations, the college's 50,000-watt public radio outlet, provides outstanding on-campus internship opportunities. Communication Department facilities also include two new all-digital television studios, a modern radio lab, and two new journalism labs in Lanigan Hall. Student-run TV and radio stations and the college newspaper are located in the new Campus Center facilities.

Costs

Tuition for 2012–13 was $2,785 per semester for New York State residents and $7,410 per semester for nonresidents. Room and board charges were approximately $6,250 per semester for entering students, depending on the meal plan, and additional fees totaled approximately $635 per semester. SUNY Oswego guarantees that a student's initial first-year costs for room and board will be frozen for up to four consecutive years. Although many activities on campus are free of charge, students need to budget for personal expenses.

Financial Aid

Need-based financial assistance consists of grants, loans, and part-time employment. Oswego offers approximately $80 million in aid to its students annually. Students interested in financial aid must file a Free Application for Federal Student Aid (FAFSA). New York State residents also need to file an application for the state's Tuition Assistance Program. Priority is given to applications on file by March 1 for the fall term and November 15 for the spring term.

Oswego offers a very generous merit scholarship program. Students receive over $4 million annually in merit scholarships and approximately 35 percent of the entering freshman class receives one. The average four-year renewable scholarship is more than $2,400 per year. For scholarship qualifications and details, students should visit http://www.oswego.edu/admissions/scholarships.

Faculty

Consisting of more than 300 full-time members, Oswego's faculty is dedicated to undergraduate students. With approximately 88 percent of them holding doctoral or other terminal degrees from many of the finest institutions in the country, students can be assured of the opportunity for an outstanding undergraduate education. The student-faculty ratio is approximately 18:1. While dedicated to teaching first and foremost, Oswego's faculty members are also actively engaged in research—often in partnership with undergraduate students—as well as publications and public service.

Student Government

Students at SUNY Oswego are represented by the Student Association, which has as its aim the efficient and intelligent governance of a democratic student body. The functions of the Student Association are divided among various committees that allocate funds to student organizations, intercollegiate and intramural athletics, the student newspaper, literary magazine, TV studios, and radio station, as well as various social, cultural, and intellectual activities on campus.

Admission Requirements

Admission to Oswego is competitive, with high school average, academic program, and standardized test scores being the most important criteria for applicants. Special talents such as artistic, musical, athletic, and creative writing skills are also considered. The Committee on Admissions accepts results of either the ACT or the SAT. A campus admissions visit is encouraged.

Transfer students in good standing are encouraged to apply for admission. The average GPA for entering transfer students is 3.0.

Application and Information

Oswego accepts both The Common Application and the SUNY Application for admission. Both applications are available online at http://www.oswego.edu/apply. Oswego evaluates applications as they are completed and as space remains available. Applications completed by January 15 for the fall term or October 15 for the spring term are ensured equal consideration. Applications received after those dates are considered as space remains available.

Prospective students and their parents are encouraged to visit the campus to participate in a student-guided tour and speak with an admissions counselor. Visits can be scheduled online at www.oswego.edu/admissions. Interested candidates can also call the Office of Admissions in advance to schedule a visit.

For further information, students should contact:

Office of Admissions
229 Sheldon Hall
SUNY Oswego
Oswego, New York 13126
Phone: 315-312-2250
Fax: 315-312-3260
E-mail: admiss@oswego.edu
Website: http://www.oswego.edu

SUNY Oswego is located on 696 acres on the southern shore of Lake Ontario.

STATE UNIVERSITY OF NEW YORK COLLEGE OF ENVIRONMENTAL SCIENCE AND FORESTRY

SYRACUSE, NEW YORK

The College

The SUNY College of Environmental Science and Forestry (ESF) is one of the nation's largest and most widely recognized environmental colleges. Founded in 1911, the College has grown beyond its original emphasis on forestry to include professional education in environmental science, landscape architecture, environmental studies, and engineering in addition to distinguished programs in the biological and physical sciences. Throughout its history, the College has focused on addressing the environmental issues of the time in its three mission areas—instruction, research, and public service. EFS graduates are well-prepared for environmental careers through specialized academic programs and a holistic approach to solving today's environmental and resource problems.

A leader in its field, ESF is one of the specialized doctoral degree–granting colleges within the State University of New York System. The College currently supports undergraduate and graduate degree programs in more than thirty environmentally-related disciplines. Graduate programs lead to the Master of Science (M.S.), Master of Landscape Architecture (M.L.A.), Master of Professional Studies (M.P.S.), and Doctor of Philosophy (Ph.D.) degrees. ESF's research program is conducted throughout the world and research funding totals more than $15 million per year.

ESF's main campus is located on 12 acres adjacent to Syracuse University and SUNY Upstate Medical University in an urban residential setting. There are 1,600 full-time and 500 part-time undergraduates enrolled (40 percent are women). The College's unique partnership with Syracuse University offers ESF students the opportunity to take additional classes there for academic diversity and depth, and to participate in cultural events, student clubs, fraternities and sororities, and professional organizations.

ESF recently celebrated its centennial anniversary with special activities that included the opening of Centennial Hall, an environmentally friendly residence hall that houses 452 ESF students in a combination of double rooms and student apartments.

The new ESF Gateway Center is scheduled to open in 2013. It will provide a hub for campus events and serve as a showcase for the College's sustainability efforts. The center will feature a wood pellet–fueled heat-and-power plant designed to generate enough energy for five campus buildings.

Location

Syracuse, a metropolitan area of more than 730,000 people, is a leader in the health care and education industries and is recognized as one of the nation's emerging centers for the development of green technologies. It offers many cultural, recreational, and educational opportunities, including museums, live theater, college and professional sports, and historic points of interest. Syracuse is centrally located at the crossing point of two Northeast superhighways. The driving time to Syracuse from New York City, Philadelphia, Boston, Toronto, and Montreal is about 5 hours; from Buffalo and Albany, about 3 hours. The city is served by a modern international airport and major bus and rail lines.

Majors and Degrees

The SUNY College of Environmental Science and Forestry offers three undergraduate degrees: the Bachelor of Science (B.S.), the Bachelor of Landscape Architecture (B.L.A.), and the Associate in Applied Science (A.A.S.). The B.S. degree is awarded in aquatic and fisheries science, bioprocess engineering, biotechnology, chemistry, conservation biology, construction management, environmental biology, environmental resources engineering, environmental science, environmental studies, forest ecosystem science, forest health, forest resources management, natural history and interpretation, natural resources management, paper engineering, paper science, sustainable energy management, and wildlife science. A number of options and concentrations are offered within specific curricula. The B.L.A. degree, which requires a semester of off-campus study, is awarded in landscape architecture. Two-year A.A.S. degrees are awarded in forest technology, land surveying technology, and environmental and natural resources conservation at ESF's Ranger School campus in Wanakena, New York.

Academic Programs

All students at ESF have opportunities for specialized study as well as research and field experience. The Department of Environmental and Forest Biology is the largest department on campus and encompasses seven different majors, including biotechnology, conservation biology, wildlife science, aquatic and fisheries science, forest health, and natural history and interpretation. Biology students are required to complete a four-week period of summer field study, usually at ESF's Cranberry Lake Biological Station, following their sophomore or junior year. Options for specialization within the chemistry program include biochemistry, environmental chemistry, and natural and synthetic polymer chemistry. Biology and chemistry students can also earn their secondary science teacher certification through Syracuse University.

The construction management program teaches management, analysis, and design skills used in today's green construction process, with an emphasis on environmental and engineering issues.

Environmental resources engineering students learn skills in such areas as biological, environmental, and water resources engineering; mapping science; and geographic information systems. The closely related environmental science program also deals with engineering science, along with areas of focus in watershed science, health and the environment, earth and atmospheric systems science, environmental analysis, and renewable energy.

Bioprocess engineering students focus on the engineering, biology, and chemistry of ecologically sound industrial technologies and processes, giving students career opportunities in areas such as chemical engineering and bioengineering, pharmaceuticals, and renewable energy. The forest resources management curriculum offers areas of focus in forest management, measurement, and policy, along with forest ecology and biology. The program includes a minor in management offered in conjunction with Syracuse University. Natural resources management students can concentrate in specialized areas such as recreation or water resources management. Forest and natural resources management students are required to complete a four-week period of summer field study at ESF's Wanakena campus prior to the junior year.

The environmental studies major offers specializations in environmental communication and writing; biological science applications; and environmental policy, planning, and law. The landscape architecture program is a five-year bachelor's degree that is accredited by the ASLA to provide preparation to enter this licensed profession. Students study site design, urban and regional planning, historic preservation, community and environmental design, and computer applications. During the first semester of the fifth year, the landscape architecture curriculum requires participation in off-campus independent study. Paper engineering students can study process and product design and environmental engineering applied to the pulp, paper, and related chemical industries, while paper science students focus on a variety of industry-specific research and management areas. In addition, ESF offers excellent preparation for graduate study in health professions, law, veterinary science, and medicine; the College has a joint admission agreement with the College of Medicine at nearby SUNY Upstate Medical University.

Academic Facilities

Specialized facilities and equipment include electron microscopes, plant-growth chambers, climate-controlled greenhouses, an animal environmental simulation chamber, a bioacoustical laboratory, a radioisotope laboratory, numerous computer labs, nuclear magnetic resonance spectrometers, gas chromatography apparatus, a mass spectrometer, ultracentrifuges, and X-ray and infrared spectrophotometers. The photogrammetric and geodetic facilities of the environmental resources engineering department are among the most extensive available in the United States. The paper science and engineering laboratory has a semi-commercial paper mill with accessory equipment. The sustainable construction management and engineering department has a strength-of-materials laboratory, a pilot-scale plywood laboratory, and a machining laboratory. The landscape architecture faculty has a one-of-a-kind environmental simulation laboratory. The greenhouses and forest insectary in Illick Hall are used to produce plant and insect materials for the classroom and laboratory. Extensive collections are available, including wood samples from all over the world, botanical materials, insects, birds, mammals, and fishes. The Roosevelt Wild Life Collection contains more than 10,000 species of well-preserved vertebrate and invertebrate animals and also recognizes the environmental interests and contributions of U.S. president Theodore Roosevelt.

The F. Franklin Moon Library includes the Academic Success Center for tutorial support in mathematics, writing, and other courses. Moon Library contains more than 100,000 specialized catalog items, including more than 1,800 research journals. The library also provides comprehensive abstract and indexing services relevant to the College's programs. Library facilities and services are supplemented by the collections at Syracuse University and the SUNY Upstate Medical University, both within walking distance.

ESF's regional campuses in Tully, Warrensburg, Cranberry Lake, Newcomb, and Wanakena, New York, offer a great diversity of forest sites that are used as outdoor teaching laboratories and for intensive research. ESF operates numerous field stations and provides students and faculty with access to over 25,000 acres of College-owned forest properties to support its instruction, research, and public service programs. These special properties make ESF one of the largest college campuses in the world.

Costs

Estimated costs for the 2013–14 academic year included resident tuition and fees of $6,547 and out-of-state tuition and fees of $15,797. Room and board expenses were $13,930. Books, personal expenses, and travel were estimated at $2,250.

Financial Aid

A wide variety of financial aid is available for ESF students, and more than 85 percent of the students receive some type of support. The forms of financial aid include merit- and need-based scholarships, grants, low-interest student loans, and student employment programs. All students are encouraged to apply for financial aid by completing the Free Application for Federal Student Aid (FAFSA).

Faculty

Faculty members at ESF are highly trained and dedicated to the College's teaching, research, and public-service missions. There are close to 140 full-time and 46 adjunct faculty members. Many are nationally and internationally recognized for their expertise in specialized fields. Nearly all regular faculty members hold twelve-month appointments. Just over 80 percent are tenured, and more than half are full professors, of whom 93 percent have earned doctorates. There is no distinction between the undergraduate and graduate faculty. Faculty members teach at both levels, and no courses are taught by teaching assistants. Faculty members serve as advisers to students and student groups and encourage excellence in scholarship and research. The student-faculty ratio is about 12:1.

Student Government

The College has a representative Undergraduate Student Association, and student representatives also participate in a counterpart association at Syracuse University. The ESF student government organizes and presents student social activities, and its representatives attend College administrative meetings, communicate students' concerns and ideas to the administration, and serve as a conduit of information back to the student body. ESF students are obligated to abide by Syracuse University's rules and regulations when accessing classes or student services there.

Admission Requirements

Students who are interested in ESF have four enrollment options: early decision, regular freshman admission, guaranteed transfer admission, and regular transfer admission.

Outstanding high school seniors who have selected SUNY-ESF as their top choice may apply for early decision, a binding, first-choice application/early notification program for fall-entry freshmen. Students filing an application for early decision admission must meet the SUNY application filing deadline date of November 15 and provide supporting credentials to SUNY-ESF by December 1. Students applying for early decision are notified by February 1.

Regular freshman admission is a second option for applicants who want to enroll immediately following high school. These candidates should demonstrate strong academic performance in a college-preparatory program, with emphasis on mathematics and science preparation. Students applying for regular freshmen entry are notified by March 1. All freshman candidates apply for admission to their intended programs of study.

Guaranteed transfer admission (GTA) candidates apply to ESF as high school seniors but are offered admission for either their sophomore or junior year. Students who plan to attend another college prior to transferring to ESF select this option to ensure a place at ESF for their chosen entry date. This option may also be offered to students who do not meet the freshman admission criteria. Those who are accepted for guaranteed transfer admission receive a letter of acceptance, contingent upon the successful completion of all the prerequisite courses required for the curriculum they have selected. The prerequisite courses are outlined and described in an enclosure with the student's acceptance letter and can also be found on the College's website at http://www.esf.edu.

Students are considered for admission to ESF on the basis of their previous college course work, overall academic aptitude, and interest in the College's programs. Consideration is given to both the quality and the appropriateness of each student's prior academic experience. The College has developed cooperative transfer programs with two-year colleges in New York, Connecticut, Massachusetts, New Jersey, and Pennsylvania. All admission acceptances are conditional upon satisfactory completion of course work in progress.

Application and Information

Students may apply for fall or spring admission. Admission decisions are made on a rolling basis until the class is filled. ESF accepts either the State University of New York Application form or the Common Application. Links to both applications can be found online at http://www.esf.edu/admissions/freshman/apply.htm. Requests for more information should be directed to:

Office of Undergraduate Admissions
State University of New York College of Environmental Science and Forestry
1 Forestry Drive
Syracuse, New York 13210-2779
Phone: 315-470-6600
Fax: 315-470-6933
E-mail: esfinfo@esf.edu
Website: http://www.esf.edu
http://www.facebook.com/sunyesf
http://twitter.com/sunyesf/
http://www.youtube.com/user/SUNYESFVIDEO

The SUNY College of Environmental Science and Forestry is enhancing the student experience with the addition of a new residence hall, Centennial Hall, and the Gateway Center, which will house an event center and Admissions and Outreach offices.

STATE UNIVERSITY OF NEW YORK INSTITUTE OF TECHNOLOGY

UTICA, NEW YORK

The College

The State University of New York Institute of Technology (SUNYIT) offers undergraduate degree programs in technology and professional studies. SUNYIT's broad curriculum embraces STEM (science, engineering, technology, and mathematics) programs and also offers degree programs in professional studies and the humanities. Students enjoy close contact with faculty members in small classes, many with fewer than 20 students.

Founded in 1966, SUNYIT offers twenty-one bachelor's degree programs for freshmen and undergraduate transfer students and nine graduate degrees, including the Master of Business Administration in technology management.

SUNYIT enrolled 1,900 undergraduate and 600 graduate students on both a full-time and part-time basis in fall 2012. The men-women ratio was approximately 1:1. International students comprise approximately 3 percent of the student body, representing over twenty nations, and 12.5 percent of students were members of minority groups.

SUNYIT students can receive services through the Campus Life, Career Services, Health and Wellness, and Counseling Center offices. Three residence halls provide on-campus housing for more than 800 students. In addition to providing a wide variety of intramural sports for students, SUNYIT has competitive intercollegiate teams in men's and women's basketball, cross-country, lacrosse, soccer, and volleyball; men's baseball; and women's softball.

Location

SUNYIT is located in Marcy, New York, part of the Utica-Rome metropolitan area. With a population of nearly 300,000, Utica-Rome is in the geographic center of New York State, approximately 220 miles from New York City and 190 miles from Buffalo on the New York State Thruway. Utica-Rome has a variety of recreational and educational opportunities; museums, theaters, restaurants, and professional sports events are minutes away from campus by car or bus. The Adirondack Mountains and a variety of recreational opportunities such as hiking, boating, and skiing are an important part of the region's quality of life. Served by bus, Amtrak, and major airlines (airports in Syracuse and Albany), the Utica-Rome area is easily reached from locations throughout the eastern United States.

Majors and Degrees

SUNYIT awards the following baccalaureate degrees: Bachelor of Professional Studies (B.P.S.), Bachelor of Science (B.S.), Bachelor of Arts (B.A.), and Bachelor of Business Administration (B.B.A.). At the graduate level, the Master of Science (M.S.) and Master of Business Administration (M.B.A.) degrees are awarded.

Academic majors available to undergraduate students include accounting, applied mathematics, applied computing, biology, business administration, civil engineering, civil engineering technology, community and behavioral health, communication and information design, computer and information science, computer engineering technology, computer information systems, electrical engineering, electrical engineering technology, health information management, mechanical engineering technology, network and computer security, nursing, psychology, and sociology.

A number of options and concentrations within specific curricula are also available, as are minors in accounting, anthropology, biology, computer and information science, communication and information design, computer information systems, computer

science, entrepreneurship, finance, health information management, human resources management, marketing, mathematics, nanotechnology, network and computer security, physics, psychology, sociology, and technology and culture.

Academic Programs

SUNYIT's academic year is divided into two semesters and runs from September through May. Summer sessions are also available.

Baccalaureate degree requirements vary from program to program but usually consist of a combination of specific major courses and liberal arts studies. Specializations and other options exist within the departments of Business Management; Communication and Humanities; Computer Information Sciences; Engineering, Science, and Mathematics; Engineering Technologies; Nursing and Health Professions; and Social and Behavioral Sciences. Specializations are developed through the use of electives and individual advisement.

Off-Campus Programs

Internship and cooperative education experiences are integral to effective career planning and job search strategies. These experiences can influence career plans by providing an opportunity for occupational exploration, developing marketable career-related skills and characteristics, and establishing a network of contacts that can provide relevant and timely information critical to the career decision-making process. In addition, employers are increasingly using internships and cooperative education programs as training opportunities leading to full-time permanent employment. All students, regardless of major, are encouraged to consider gaining experience in their chosen field that complements classroom learning. For additional information, students should contact the academic department or the Office of Career Services.

Academic Facilities

SUNYIT's academic facilities are located on its large, scenic campus just north of the city of Utica, easily accessible by municipal bus service. The campus consists of six building complexes, a facilities building, and residence halls. Several new buildings have opened, including a $13.8-million student center, a $23-million first-year residence hall, and a $20-million field house that hosts athletic events and large campus functions. Construction has begun on a technology complex that will connect a sophisticated faculty- and student-learning environment with high-tech industry tenants.

The Cayan Library provides traditional and online library services and a learning commons, with individual help provided by learning center staff, as well as group and individual study rooms.

Kunsela Hall contains administrative offices, classrooms, the campus bookstore, and laboratories for many technology programs. Donovan Hall houses classrooms; faculty offices; and laboratory facilities for other programs, including business, mechanical engineering technology, communication and information design, nursing, and the arts and sciences. The Campus Center contains a newly renovated cafeteria for residential students, gymnasium, and recreational facilities.

Costs

Costs for the 2012–13 academic year included state resident tuition and fees of $6,744. Out-of-state tuition and fees were $15,994. Room and board costs were $11,210; personal expenses, books, supplies, and travel cost approximately $3,000. The total expenses were $20,954 for New York State residents and $30,204 for out-of-state students. Costs may be subject to change. Graduate student costs will vary; more information is available on the SUNYIT website.

Financial Aid

A wide variety of financial aid is available to students at SUNYIT. Academic scholarships are awarded for the entering fall class, and are based on merit, personal achievement, and other factors. Additional financial aid is awarded on the basis of need, as determined by an assessment of the Free Application for Federal Student Aid. At present, approximately 85 percent of the students receive financial assistance. The forms of financial aid available include Tuition Assistance Program awards (for New York State residents only), Federal Supplemental Educational Opportunity Grants, Federal Pell Grants, Federal Work-Study Program employment, Federal Perkins Loans, federal Nursing Student Loans, Federal Direct Student Loans, a variety of state-sponsored loans, and a broad range of private scholarships and grants. Students with a cumulative transfer GPA of 3.25 or better or a high school average of 90 are automatically considered for merit scholarships at the time of their application.

Faculty

SUNYIT faculty members come from all over the world and are committed to teaching, research, and service to the community. Among the faculty members are a Distinguished Service Professor, Fulbright Scholars, and numerous recipients of Chancellor's Awards for Excellence. More than 80 percent of SUNYIT's full-time faculty members have doctoral or terminal degrees. The faculty members are fully engaged in academic orientation and advisement, individualized instruction, cooperative faculty-student efforts in research projects, and concern for students as individuals. In the classroom, the average student-faculty ratio is 19:1.

Student Government

All full-time undergraduates are members of the SUNYIT Student Association. Its primary functions are to develop and monitor the student-activity-fee budget, to approve and oversee all student organizations, to debate issues of concern to students and take action as needed, and to develop programs of interest to all students. Student government consists of a 7-person executive committee and 11 senators. Students are encouraged to take an active role in the governance process, and many opportunities for involvement, in addition to those listed above, are available for interested students.

Admission Requirements

Generally, freshman applicants should carry a B/B+ average in a college-preparatory program and have achieved an SAT score in the 1000–1100 range (or approximately 22–24 composite ACT score). Admission is based on high school average, SAT or ACT scores, strength of course work, and other relevant information.

For transfer students, most programs require a minimum GPA of 2.7 for guaranteed admission; some programs require a higher GPA or additional application materials. Transfer students below a 2.7 GPA but who have earned an A.A., A.S., or A.A.S. degree may be admitted under special circumstances. Transfer students are required to furnish an official transcript from all previous colleges they attended.

Students with a cumulative GPA of at least 3.25 are automatically considered for merit scholarships; no separate application is required.

Application and Information

The deadline for all applications is August 1 for fall entry and December 1 for spring entry. Prospective students are encouraged to apply early as programs may close prior to application deadlines.

All applications are reviewed on an individual basis. All EOP applicants are also required to complete a supplemental application and are encouraged to apply for fall semester by December 1. The recommended application deadline for EOP and regular admission is February 15. However, applications received after that date will be considered on a rolling basis. Notification of admissions decisions begins on December 15.

SUNYIT participates in the SUNY early action program. Early action students must submit their application by November 1 and complete their application by November 15; applications are reviewed and students are notified of admission by December 15. Students admitted under early action are required to submit a deposit by May 1.

Students who wish to apply should apply online through the SUNYIT website. A copy of the State University of New York application booklet can also be obtained from a two-year college, a local high school, or the Admissions Office. Application forms for international students may also be obtained through the SUNYIT website or the Admissions Office.

SUNYIT adheres to the principle that all persons should have equal opportunity and access to its educational facilities without regard to race, creed, sex, or national origin.

Official transcripts from all previously attended high schools and colleges should be sent to the Director of Admissions. All communications and requests for additional information should also be directed to:

Director of Admissions
SUNYIT
100 Seymour Road
Utica, New York 13502
Phone: 315-792-7500
        866-2SUNYIT (toll-free)
Fax: 315-792-7837
E-mail: admissions@sunyit.edu
Website: http://www.sunyit.edu

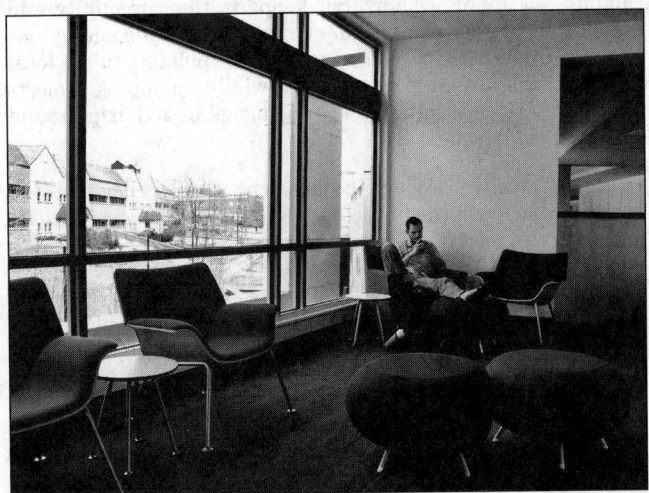

A student relaxes on the second floor of the Student Center, a short walk from the main SUNYIT academic building, Donovan Hall.

STERLING COLLEGE
CRAFTSBURY COMMON, VERMONT

The College

Sterling College is a small and progressive liberal arts college in northern Vermont. The College's small size, environmental focus, and commitment to grassroots sustainability all make it unique.

Sterling College knows that the most rewarding learning is hands-on learning. Whether offered on campus in a laboratory or seminar room, on the side of a mountain, or in a barn or pasture, classes at Sterling are small and foster experiential learning and deep inquiry through close relationships between faculty members and students.

Students gain insight into theory, integrate research into study, and learn how to use tools such as a chainsaw, a compass, and a tractor as part of daily life.

Sterling College removes the barriers between living one's life and learning. It is for the student who wants to commit to becoming an environmental steward and looks forward to the rigor and challenge of working with both hands and mind.

Authentic Sustainability: Sterling was among the very first colleges in the United States to link the liberal arts to ecology, outdoor education, environmental humanities, and sustainable agriculture. Sterling believes that the wellbeing of humanity depends on small, interconnected communities, committed to conscientious practices in agriculture and energy use, and in stewardship of our air, soil, and water.

Sterling College was eating local food and advocating for sustainability in the 1970s, and it continues to do so today. The campus is a living system that supports the community and the educational mission. Students monitor campus energy use and food production, teach classes on sustainability in the local public school system, participate in wildlife mapping projects and citizen science initiatives, and engage in activism around environmental issues.

In 2013, Sterling College became the third college in the United States, and the first college in Vermont, to announce its intention to divest its endowment from fossil fuels.

"I came to Sterling to . . . learn about the people and places of the rural Northeast. My future goal is to do nonprofit community work in rural America by organizing communities that are fighting battles of environmental and social justice, and helping them determine their own destinies. By actually participating in environmental justice with fellow students and faculty while studying environmental law and land use planning in class, I have learned a lot about the political process." —*Ira Powsner '13*

Work: Students are part of the daily work of the college. Regardless of financial need, all students work on campus, whether in the kitchen, on the farm, in the woodshop, or elsewhere. Sterling College is one of only seven colleges recognized by the federal government as a Work College—a college where student work is an integral and mandatory part of the educational process, as opposed to being an appended requirement. Sterling is also the only Work College in the northeast.

Besides working on campus, a highlight of the Sterling education is a ten-week, 6-credit internship anywhere in the world. Internships in agriculture, cross-cultural education, ecotourism, environmental education, hydrology, land and resource management, outdoor education and leadership, and wildlife rehabilitation and research are popular options.

"I was drawn to Sterling because of the work program. I know that at the end of four years I will walk away from Sterling with a resume full of work and life experiences that any employer would find of interest. A college education here trains you to be a leader through engaged practice in community living."— *Allyson Makuch '15*

Community: At Sterling students and faculty not only live together, they work to create community together. Sterling College strives to be an educational community in which people of all backgrounds and identities feel at home, where differences are embraced, and where individuals take responsibility for furthering the dignity of all.

Professors at Sterling are united by an affinity for small-town life, ecological awareness, a strong interest in relating human experience to natural resources, and a determination to work with students as whole people.

Sterling is small and remains so by design. It is the only college in the nation where the entire community of students and faculty sit together each week for community meeting. Everyone is on a first name basis, including the president, deans, and faculty.

Community life is informal. Sterling College students aren't as interested in the kind of structured events and clubs found on most campuses—they're more likely to enjoy a long weekend of hiking, a lively evening of contra dancing, caring for beehives with friends, snowshoeing at the Craftsbury Outdoor Center, or sitting by a bonfire at the College's lean-tos above the Black River.

Location

Sterling's rural location is one of the College's most prized characteristics. The campus boasts 130 acres, with an additional 300 acres of boreal research forest.

Sterling students love living in Craftsbury Common. The focal point of the village is the "Common" and the quintessential New England white clapboard buildings that border it. This area of Vermont is also a place of innovation, and is an important center for a revolution in rural food systems of farms and enterprises such as Pete's Greens, Hill Farmstead Brewery, High Mowing Seeds, Jasper Hill Cheese, and Vermont Soy, just to name a few.

This region of Vermont is known as the "Northeast Kingdom," and is an international destination for outdoor sports and adventure. There are four ski areas within 45 minutes of the college. When city life beckons, however, Burlington is about an hour or so away.

Majors and Degrees

Sterling College offers Bachelor of Arts degrees in ecology, environmental humanities, outdoor education, and sustainable agriculture. Students can also choose to design their own major, and some examples include agroecology, environmental justice, conservation education, and international agriculture and business.

Off-Campus Programs

A Sterling education is both local and global. Through Global Field Studies, students and faculty have the opportunity to travel together to look at issues related to environmental stewardship and to experience rich ecological and cultural diversity. Recent programs have included experiences in the Bahamas, Belize, Canada, Israel, Maine, and the Sierra Nevada.

All new students, accompanied by 5 to 6 faculty members, take part in Winter Expedition, a four-day, three-night trek along the ridge of the nearby Lowell Mountain Range. Winter Expedition is a 47-year tradition at Sterling College.

Academic Facilities

The campus has sixteen residential, administrative, and classroom buildings. Facilities include a woodshop, a darkroom, two computer rooms and an environmental science computer lab, two greenhouses, and the Brown Library.

Outdoor teaching facilities include a challenge course with a climbing wall, a managed wood lot, recreation and nature trails, large organic gardens, and a diverse livestock farm with solar- and wind-powered barns. Students spend about 40 percent of their class time outside the traditional classroom setting.

Costs

Tuition for the 2013–14 academic year is $28,978, room and board are $8,498, and fees are $766.

Financial Aid

College is a big investment, but Sterling College offers robust financial aid packages, and the Office of Admission and Financial Aid works closely with students and families to plan an affordable path to graduation. Sterling College also awards over $1 million each year in need- and merit-based grants and scholarships. All students determined to have financial need receive assistance, and participation in the Work Program earns each student additional funds that help offset the cost of attendance.

Faculty

The typical class size at Sterling is 10, and the student-to-faculty ratio is 7 to 1. Sterling's faculty is composed of 17 full-time members and 17 part-time members. 85 percent of the professors hold an advanced degree. In a continuous attempt to bring learning to life, professors teach in both traditional and experiential ways.

Admission Requirements

Sterling College endeavors to enroll a diverse student population reflecting a broad range of interests and lived experiences. Good students who have demonstrated a commitment to the values that underlie Sterling's mission—a concern for environmental stewardship, social justice, and personal integrity—are strongly encouraged to apply.

Sterling College offers admission to both first-time college applicants and transfer applicants. Application review at Sterling is a highly individualized process, characterized by a personal approach. In arriving at an admission decision, the College looks for evidence of a combination of the following characteristics:

- Academic preparation, intellectual curiosity, and creativity
- Passion for environmental stewardship and social justice
- Enthusiasm for hard work and interest in seeking out challenges
- Interest in experiential education and intrepid outlook on learning
- Desire to be part of a small community in a rural location

Application and Information

High school seniors who wish to receive an early response to their application may apply for Early Action or Early Decision. For Early Decision, a completed application must be on file by November 15 to be notified of a decision on or before December 15. For Early Action, a completed application must be on file on or before December 15 to be notified of a decision on or before January 15. All other applicants are encouraged to submit applications before June 1 for fall enrollment, January 1 for spring enrollment, and April 1 for summer enrollment. Once completed, an application is reviewed for admission within two weeks.

Students should contact:

Tim Patterson, Director of Admission and Financial Aid
Sterling College
P.O. Box 72
Craftsbury Common, Vermont 05827
United States
Phone: 802-586-7711
800-648-3591 (toll-free)
Fax: 802-586-2596
E-mail: admissions@sterlingcollege.edu
Website: http://www.sterlingcollege.edu
    www.facebook.com/SterlingCollegeVT
    www.twitter.com/SterlingCollegeVT

Sterling College combines structured academic study with experiential challenges and work to help students become problem solvers and stewards of the environment.

STEVENSON UNIVERSITY
STEVENSON AND OWINGS MILLS, MARYLAND

The University

Stevenson University (SU), formerly Villa Julie College, is a coeducational, independent institution dedicated to providing its 3,900 undergraduate and graduate students with a career-focused liberal arts education. Individual attention from faculty members, extensive career preparation gained through real-world training, and two ideal locations just north of Baltimore, Maryland, in Stevenson and Owings Mills, make the University truly unique.

At SU, academic quality is viewed as a personalized education that fosters intellectual growth and prepares students to thrive in the working world after graduation. With a student-faculty ratio of 13:1, it is easy to understand why students often cite the congenial rapport with faculty members as one of the University's strong points.

Through Stevenson University's concept of Learning Beyond, students step outside of the classroom to take their learning to the next level. Experiential learning opportunities include study abroad, service learning, field placements, internships, and independent research. In addition, through an approach known as Career Architecture℠, each student develops a professional career plan based on their values, skills, and strengths.

Stevenson's graduates maintain a placement rate that tops 95 percent each year, with students acquiring jobs or going on to further their education within six months of graduation.

At SU, students enjoy more than fifty clubs and organizations, multiple honor societies, and NCAA Division III athletics. The following sports are offered: men's and women's basketball, cross-country, lacrosse, soccer, tennis, track and field, and volleyball; men's baseball, golf, and football; and women's field hockey, ice hockey, and softball. Cheerleading, dance, and intramural sports are also extremely popular.

In addition to its undergraduate programs, the University offers the following master's degree programs: business and technology management, forensic science, cyber forensics, forensic studies, healthcare management, and nursing.

Location

Stevenson University has two beautiful campuses in the heart of Maryland, in Stevenson and Owings Mills. SU students truly appreciate the beauty of a rural campus as well as the convenience and appeal of a more urban setting.

The original 60-acre Greenspring Campus is nestled among the rolling hills in Stevenson, Maryland. The Owings Mills Campus is a thriving center of student activity and offers both academic and residential facilities. Classes are held on both campuses, and the University provides a free shuttle service that runs between these locations.

The Stevenson campus is slated to expand in fall 2013 with the addition of the 28-acre Owings Mills North location (adjacent to the Owings Mills campus), which will house the School of Design and the School of the Sciences.

Majors and Degrees

Stevenson University offers the following bachelor's degree programs: accounting; applied mathematics; biology; biotechnology; business administration; business communication; business information systems; chemistry; computer information systems; criminal justice; early childhood education: liberal arts and technology; elementary education: liberal arts and technology; English language and literature; fashion design; fashion merchandising; film, video, and theater; human services; interdisciplinary studies; medical technology; middle school education; nursing; nursing: RN

to B.S.; paralegal studies; psychology; public history; and visual communication design.

Stevenson's B.S. to M.S. degree programs give students the option of earning both a bachelor's and a master's degree in as few as five years. Graduate study begins in the spring semester of the junior year and runs concurrently with undergraduate work until the end of the spring semester of the senior year. All subsequent course work is at the graduate level.

Academic Programs

At SU, academic quality is regarded as a personalized curriculum that prepares students to enter the working world with the knowledge and skills that employers value. SU infuses the traditional liberal arts education with a distinct career focus. The University's goal is to prepare students for employment, graduate study, and productive involvement in today's world.

Academic Facilities

From recent enhancements to the Greenspring Campus to brand-new facilities at the Owings Mills Campus, the University provides modern facilities that serve the needs of all students.

The University's Greenspring Campus includes a 350-seat theater, multiple computer labs and classrooms, video and graphic studios, science laboratories, a student union, and athletic facilities. Each classroom and laboratory on the campus is capable of multimedia projection and computer-assisted learning.

Also at the Greenspring Campus is the Verizon Center for Excellence in Teaching and Learning. The center comprises classrooms equipped with technology that accommodates distance learning.

The Owings Mills Campus hosts the University's newest facilities, including an expansive student center and dining hall, a 10,000-square-foot community center, an expansive athletic complex with a new gymnasium, multiple classrooms and study spaces, a fitness center, and additional athletic fields. The state-of-the art Mustang Stadium opened in 2011.

The Howard S. Brown School of Business and Leadership offers twelve traditional classrooms and seven seminar halls. The facility also includes two distance-learning labs where students are able to interact with other learners worldwide, six computer labs utilizing the most up-to-date equipment, a student lounge, a law library, and a high-tech digital mock trial courtroom.

The University's library, located on the Greenspring Campus, has an extensive collection of more than 100,000 printed volumes, periodicals, videotapes and audiotapes, CDs, and microfilm and microfiche selections and an interlibrary loan consortium. In addition to the electronic databases it owns, the library has access to thousands of outside databases, such as LexisNexis Academic Universe, WESTLAW, Dialog, and Dow Jones News Retrieval.

Costs

Stevenson is among the most affordable universities in the state of Maryland. For the 2013–14 academic year, tuition and fees for full-time students are $27,082. Room and board for the 2013–14 year are $12,490.

Financial Aid

Stevenson University offers financial assistance to qualified students in the form of grants, scholarships, loans, student employment, and a special payment plan. On average, approximately 90 percent of the University's students receive some form of financial assistance. The University has a generous scholarship program that grants awards based on academic merit. SU participates in all major federal aid programs as well as all Maryland state programs. Applicants are required to file the Free Application for Federal Student Aid (FAFSA). The priority deadline for filing is February 15.

Faculty

The faculty at Stevenson University is primarily a teaching faculty. The University's 13:1 student-teacher ratio demonstrates the institution's dedication to personalized education. A majority of the full-time faculty members have the doctoral or terminal degree offered in their field, and a significant number are widely published. In addition, many are concurrently employed as professional specialists in their fields.

Student Government

The Student Government Association (SGA) facilitates an environment that encourages students to express their thoughts and opinions concerning Stevenson University, its policies, and sponsored activities. The SGA serves as the principal governing body of all campus clubs and activities. In conjunction with the Office of Student Affairs, the SGA organizes an array of campuswide events that promote the social aspects of college life. Each student at Stevenson is welcome and encouraged to participate in all SGA functions.

Admission Requirements

Applications for admission to Stevenson University are reviewed on a rolling basis. In evaluating each applicant, the University considers the applicant's high school academic record, SAT or ACT scores, recommendations, writing sample, and any other special talents or personal interests. Admission to the University is determined without regard for race, color, sex, religion, national or ethnic origin, or handicap. SU complies with all applicable laws and federal regulations regarding discrimination and accessibility on the condition of handicap, age, veteran status, or otherwise.

Application and Information

Applications for admission to undergraduate programs should be received by March 1 for fall-semester entry and October 15 for spring-semester entry. Scholarship consideration adheres to earlier deadlines. Applications received after these dates are reviewed on a space-available basis. Students applying to the University as freshmen must submit official high school transcripts, standardized test scores, the Counselor Recommendation Form, typed responses to the essay questions listed on the application, and a $40 nonrefundable application fee. The application fee is waived for all students who apply online at www.stevenson.edu. Transfer students must submit official transcripts from all colleges or universities they have attended and should contact the Transfer Admissions Counselor to discuss additional credential requirements.

For further information and application forms, students should contact:

Admissions Office
Garrison Hall, Suite 200
Stevenson University
100 Campus Circle
Owings Mills, Maryland 21117-7804
Phone: 410-486-7001
      877-468-6852 (toll-free)
Fax: 443-352-4440
E-mail: admissions@stevenson.edu
Website: http://www.stevenson.edu

The residences at Stevenson University offer spacious apartments and suites with extensive amenities.

STONEHILL COLLEGE
EASTON, MASSACHUSETTS

STONEHILL
COLLEGE

The College

Stonehill College is a selective coed Catholic college with a welcoming, academically challenging community of more than 2,600 students on a beautiful, active campus 22 miles south of Boston. Stonehill offers more than eighty diverse majors and minors in the liberal arts, sciences, and business to prepare students for a life of learning, leadership, and responsible citizenship. More than 80 percent of Stonehill students complete an internship, study abroad, practicum, or field experience by the time they graduate.

More than 80 percent of Stonehill students participate in at least one sport on campus. Stonehill competes in the Northeast-10 Conference, the largest NCAA Division II conference in the country, and offers twenty different varsity sports, including baseball, lacrosse, football, basketball, and soccer. The extensive intramural program offers two different levels of competition in basketball, dodgeball, field hockey, kickball, softball, and more. Club sports such as rugby and volleyball are yet another option, offering a spirited, fun experience without the demands of NCAA conference-sanctioned athletics.

Founded by the Congregation of Holy Cross in 1948, Stonehill's mission is "to educate the whole person so that each graduate thinks, acts, and leads with courage toward the creation of a more just and compassionate world." The idea of making the world a better place is part of the Catholic faith and an intrinsic element of the Stonehill experience. Each year, about 2,000 Stonehill students (about 77 percent of the student body) participate in community service. Last year, Stonehill students provided more than 90,000 hours of service.

Stonehill consistently receives nationwide recognition as one of the country's top colleges. Recently, *U.S. News & World Report*'s "America's Best Colleges" guide singled out Stonehill as a top up-and-coming school. The Princeton Review recently chose Stonehill as one of the best in the nation for career services, most accessible professors, intramural sports, study abroad, and more.

Location

Stonehill is in Easton, Massachusetts, a friendly residential community nestled between New England's largest capital cities. Just 22 miles from Boston, America's number-one college town, and 37 miles from Providence, it is perfectly situated for internships, service opportunities, job prospects, museums, professional sports, cultural events, and more.

Whether the countless trees are in full bloom in the spring or the leaves are bursting into reds and golds in the fall, Stonehill is beautiful every season of the year. Encompassing 384 acres, Stonehill's New England college campus features traditional landscaping, ponds, wooded trails, and Georgian-style architecture.

Majors and Degrees

Students may receive Bachelor of Arts degrees in American studies, art history, arts administration (museum studies and performing arts concentrations), biology, Catholic studies, chemistry, communication (communication studies and mediated communication concentrations), criminology, economics, education (early childhood/elementary and secondary education minor), English, environmental studies, foreign languages, French, gender and sexuality studies, graphic design, healthcare administration, history, interdisciplinary studies, mathematics, philosophy, physics (generalist and astronomy concentrations), political science and international studies (government and politics, international relations, and public administration and

public policy concentrations), psychology, religious studies, sociology, Spanish, studio arts, visual and performing arts (generalist and music concentrations).

Bachelor of Science degrees are offered in biochemistry, biology, chemistry, computer science, mathematics, neuroscience, and physics. Bachelor of Science in Business Administration degrees are offered in accounting, finance, international business, management, and marketing. Stonehill's business department is accredited by the AACSB. In addition, Stonehill College partners with the University of Notre Dame to offer a combination 3+2 program in engineering with concentrations in aerospace, chemical, civil, computer, electrical, environmental engineering, environmental earth sciences, and mechanical engineering.

Pre-professional advising programs are offered in dentistry, education, law, medicine, veterinary science, and medical technology. Students interested in the field of education can receive early childhood, elementary, middle, and secondary school teacher certification. Students may pursue a double major as well as design their own major by combining various departmental courses into a comprehensive multidisciplinary program.

Academic Programs

The core of Stonehill's liberal arts curriculum is the Cornerstone Program, which leads students to examine themselves, society, culture, and the natural world through courses in ethics, sciences, language, and more.

Stonehill's students and alumni succeed because the entire college community collaborates to help them develop the knowledge, skills, and character to meet their professional goals and to live lives of purpose and integrity. Its graduates can be found around the world enrolled in top graduate programs, enjoying meaningful careers, and working to improve their communities.

Within one year of graduation, 98 percent of Stonehill graduates over the last five years were employed, doing service work, or in graduate school. Last year, 53 percent of graduating seniors were employed at organizations such as Goldman Sachs, the New England Patriots, and Brigham and Women's Hospital. Others joined or applied for yearlong volunteer service programs such as the Peace Corps, Teach for America, AmeriCorps, and World Teach.

On average, Stonehill students graduate at a higher rate and in less time than students at many other colleges and universities. About 80 percent of Stonehill students graduate within four years. Stonehill's four-year graduation rate is higher than at public institutions where the national average is five years.

Off-Campus Programs

At Stonehill, students are given experiential learning opportunities that allow them in-depth exploration of what they learn in the classroom and the opportunity to apply it in the real world. The National Survey of Student Engagement ranks Stonehill in the top 10 percent of colleges nationwide for its enriching educational experiences such as competitive internships, nationally ranked study-abroad opportunities, and cocurricular programs.

Students take part in interdisciplinary Learning Communities (LCs), which combine two academic courses from different disciplines with a team-taught seminar that explores an interrelated topic. Some LCs even incorporate travel to places such as Ireland, Italy, the Florida Everglades, and the deserts of the Southwest.

In addition, Stonehill is ranked thirteenth in the nation among baccalaureate institutions for semester-long study abroad programs by the Institute of International Education. About 40 percent of Stonehill students study abroad before graduation in dozens of countries, including Argentina, Australia, China, Greece, Morocco, and South Africa.

Academic Facilities

Stonehill is dedicated to developing programs and projects that will continually improve quality of life for everyone on campus. Its multimillion dollar science center, opened in 2009, provides state-of-the-art labs, observation rooms, research areas, and a café to faculty, staff, and students.

Kaplan's *Insiders Guide to the 320 Most Interesting Colleges* ranked Stonehill among the colleges with the Best Freshman Housing. It's no wonder that more than 90 percent of Stonehill's students live on campus and very few leave on the weekends. In addition, all resident students are guaranteed housing for all four years. Students can choose from a variety of living options, including suites, townhouses, and double- and triple-occupancy rooms, and take advantage of amenities such as communal TV lounges, kitchen and laundry facilities, recreation rooms, pool tables, basketball courts, beach volleyball courts, and outdoor grills for barbeques.

Costs

For the 2012–13 academic year, Stonehill's costs were $35,110 for tuition and $13,310 for room and board.

Financial Aid

Stonehill is committed to helping each qualified student find the resources to make the dream of a Stonehill education become reality. Stonehill offers loans, grants, scholarships, employment programs, and tuition payment plans to help students become a part of the community here. In the 2012–13 academic year, Stonehill distributed $50.5 million in financial aid to a student body of 2,471. This year, 93 percent of full-time students received some form of aid. On average, students received $25,423 each in scholarships, grants, loans, and work-study. A wide range of competitive merit-based scholarships is also available to outstanding students who do not demonstrate a financial need.

To file for Stonehill scholarship and/or financial aid consideration, students should complete the online CSS PROFILE form at https://profileonline.collegeboard.com. Stonehill's CSS PROFILE code is 3770. In addition, students must file the Free Application for Federal Student Aid (FAFSA) online at http://www.fafsa. ed.gov to be considered for government funds. Stonehill's FAFSA code is 002217.

Faculty

With a student-faculty ratio of 13:1 and an average class size of 19, Stonehill sees individual attention as a key component of our academic programs. Stonehill's accomplished faculty champions its students throughout all four years and is dedicated to teaching and conducting publishable research with students to help with their integrated learning process. Students benefit from graduate-level access to high-tech equipment, attend professional academic conferences, and coauthor in-depth papers, while guided by faculty mentors. Stonehill students take advantage of collaborating one-on-one with their professors on a regular basis and they will always be taught by a faculty member, not a teaching assistant or graduate student.

Student Government

From enjoying on-campus activities to just hanging out with friends, students have plenty of opportunities for fun at Stonehill. The Student Government Association (SGA) is one of the country's most active—its programming won an award from the National Association of Campus Activities—so there's always something happening, from concerts and guest speakers to contests and game shows. More than seventy clubs and organizations are available, including the College's arts and entertainment magazine *Rolling Stonehill,* the Ski/Snowboard Club, and the Neuroscience Society.

Stonehill also offers free transportation to Boston's public subway system, allowing easy access to the excitement of the city. And with Stonehill's unique Fun Fund, students can get up to $200 to pay for entertainment with friends, such as a show in New York City, a pottery class, or a Red Sox game.

Admission Requirements

Admission to Stonehill is selective. Last year, Stonehill admitted 815 students into the class of 2016. Stonehill actively seeks an academically strong and geographically, culturally, and ethnically diverse student body. In the admission process, all information on each applicant is carefully considered, but academic performance and high school curriculum are given the greatest weight. The Admission Committee evaluates the depth and strength of each applicant's course selection and the consistency of their grades. Competitive students should have completed a strong academic program from among their high school's most challenging offerings. Stonehill admission is test optional, but students may choose to submit scores from either the SAT or ACT. The Admission Committee also evaluates extracurricular activities, work, volunteer and community activities, recommendations, and writing samples. Stonehill awards credit for strong scores on AP, CLEP, and higher-level International Baccalaureate exams.

Application and Information

Aspirants for Stonehill, as first-year, transfer, or international students may apply online at https://www.commonapp.org. The Common Application is also available in paper form at high school guidance offices.

Stonehill offers three admission plans for first-year candidates: early decision (binding), early action (nonbinding), and regular decision. November 1 is the deadline for early action and January 15 is the deadline for regular decision.

Dean of Admission and Enrollment
Stonehill College
320 Washington Street
Easton, Massachusetts 02357-5610
United States
Phone: 508-565-1373
Fax: 508-565-1545
E-mail: admission@stonehill.edu
Website: http://www.stonehill.edu
　　　　http://stonehillcollegeadmissions.org (Admission)

Stonehill College campus.

STONY BROOK UNIVERSITY, STATE UNIVERSITY OF NEW YORK

STONY BROOK, LONG ISLAND, NEW YORK

The University

An educational and research institution of world renown, Stony Brook is included among the top 1 percent of universities worldwide by the *Times Higher Education World University Rankings* and among the top forty public national universities by *U.S. News & World Report.* Stony Brook is one of just sixty-two research universities that belong to the elite Association of American Universities (AAU), based on the excellence of its research and education programs. Its tuition is one of the lowest among AAU institutions, making a Stony Brook education a smart choice.

Stony Brook offers more than 200 majors, minors, and combined-degree programs of exceptional strength. Major academic units of the University include the College of Arts and Sciences, College of Engineering and Applied Sciences, College of Business, School of Journalism, School of Marine and Atmospheric Sciences, and the five schools of the health sciences: Medicine, Health Technology and Management, Dental Medicine, Nursing, and Social Welfare.

The award-winning Undergraduate Research and Creative Activities (URECA) program involves undergraduates in research in nearly every discipline and has produced Beckman, Goldwater, and Marshall scholars.

Stony Brook enrolls 24,149 full- and part-time students—16,003 undergraduates and 8,146 graduate and professional students. Students hail from nearly all fifty states and 110 countries. Nearly 20,000 students are enrolled full time. Approximately 86 percent of Stony Brook's freshmen live in campus residence halls, which are organized as small residential colleges to foster social, intellectual, and cultural interaction.

The Stony Brook Seawolves' twenty varsity teams compete in NCAA Division I and include men's baseball and football; women's softball and volleyball; and men's and women's basketball, cross-country, lacrosse, soccer, swimming, tennis, and indoor and outdoor track and field. Athletic facilities include Kenneth P. LaValle Stadium, which seats up to 8,300 and Joe Nathan Field, dedicated to alumnus and Major League pitcher Joe Nathan ('97). The complex also features an 8,000-square-foot strength and conditioning center, basketball courts, tennis courts, bicycle and jogging paths, handball courts, and a track. A new Campus Recreation Center opened in 2012 with 85,000 square feet of gymnasiums, fitness studios, an indoor track, workout space, lounges, and classrooms for dance, yoga, and other activities.

Location

Situated on 1,039 wooded acres, Stony Brook is located midway between New York City and the Hamptons on Long Island's East End, a setting rich in both natural and architectural beauty. Students enjoy large wooded areas on and around campus. Sandy beaches, a harbor, and a historic hamlet that was once home to George Washington's Revolutionary War spy ring are all close by, as well as a major indoor mall and multiplex movie theater. A train station on the University's perimeter offers students easy access to New York City.

Majors and Degrees

The University offers sixty-seven undergraduate majors leading to the Bachelor of Arts (B.A.), Bachelor of Science (B.S.), and Bachelor of Engineering (B.E.) degrees in the following: Africana studies; American studies; anthropology; applied mathematics and statistics; art history and criticism; Asian and Asian American studies; astronomy and planetary sciences; athletic training; atmospheric and oceanic sciences; biochemistry; biology; biomedical engineering; business management; chemical and molecular engineering; chemistry; cinema and cultural studies; civil engineering; clinical laboratory sciences; coastal environmental studies; comparative literature; computer engineering; computer science; earth and space sciences; economics; ecosystems and human impact; electrical engineering; electrical engineering online; engineering chemistry; engineering science; English; environmental design, policy, and planning; environmental humanities; environmental studies; European studies; French; geology; German; health science; history; information systems; Italian; journalism; linguistics; marine sciences; marine vertebrate biology; mathematics; mechanical engineering; multidisciplinary studies; music; nursing; pharmacology; philosophy; physics; political science; psychology; religious studies; respiratory care; social work; sociology; Spanish; studio art; sustainability studies; technological systems management; theater arts; and women's and gender studies. The University also offers seventy-nine minors.

Students may earn New York State provisional certification for secondary school teaching in biology, chemistry, Chinese, earth science, English, French, German, Italian, Japanese, mathematics, physics, social studies, Spanish, and K–12 in teaching English as a second language. A combined-degree program is available in which students earn an M.B.A. along with their choice of nearly any undergraduate major. Dual-bachelor's/master's-degree programs are also available in many other disciplines, including an M.P.H. Integrated eight-year bachelor's/M.D. and bachelor's/D.D.S. programs are offered to exceptional high school students, enabling them to participate in medical school and dental school classes and activities as undergraduates.

Academic Programs

All freshmen belong to one of six themed undergraduate colleges that offer a dynamic first-year experience and promote student success. The undergraduate college program at Stony Brook provides students with an intimate college experience through academic and residential advising, one-credit classes in small-group settings, and informal gatherings with faculty members.

Innovative programs include a news literacy course, the first of its kind in the nation, offered through the School of Journalism, the only public undergraduate journalism school in New York. Also noteworthy are the Sustainability Studies program, which offers eleven majors and minors leading to green careers, and the combined-degree, Fast-Track M.B.A. program.

Stony Brook's Honors College has a special curriculum and high-achieving students in the program enjoy small seminar courses and the opportunity to work closely with faculty members. A mentoring program, small study groups, and special classes are highlights of Stony Brook's Women in Science and Engineering (WISE) program, for women talented in math, science, or engineering. There also are Living-Learning Centers, which enable students with common interests to live and learn together.

Stony Brook may accept up to 30 credits by examination toward the bachelor's degree through such means as AP, CLEP, CPE, higher-level International Baccalaureate subjects, and Stony Brook's own Challenge Program. Students need a minimum of 120 credits for the B.A. or B.S. degree and 128 credits for the B.E. degree; 39 of these credits must be earned at the upper-division level. All students must satisfy general education requirements and maintain at least a 2.0 cumulative grade point average. Grading is traditional; a pass/no-credit option is available for some elective courses. Stony Brook's academic year starts in late August and ends in mid-May, with the exception of some health sciences programs that begin in June or July.

Off-Campus Programs

An international academic experience is now a necessity for students who wish to remain competitive for employment or for professional or graduate study. The Office of International Academic Programs provides a variety of study-abroad opportunities ranging in length from a winter or summer session, to a semester, to an academic year.

Opportunities also exist for students to earn academic credit and gain valuable experience while participating in internships and field research. Placements include government agencies and laboratories, including nearby Brookhaven National Laboratory. Other options are the Turkana Basin Institute in Kenya, hospitals and clinics, businesses and industries, and legal and social agencies on Long Island and in New York City, Albany, and Washington, D.C. Stony Brook also participates in the National Student Exchange Program.

Academic Facilities

Stony Brook's major academic facilities include the Frank Melville Jr. Memorial Library, Stony Brook University Hospital, and the five-theater Staller Center for the Arts. Stony Brook is also home to myriad centers, laboratories, and institutes. Some of these include the Simons Center for Geometry and Physics, Center of Excellence in Wireless and Information Technology, Advanced Energy Research and Technology Center, Institute for Theoretical Physics, Institute for Terrestrial and Planetary Atmospheres, Center for High-Pressure Research, Center for Biotechnology, Howard Hughes Medical Institute, Centers for Molecular Medicine and Biology Learning Laboratories, and Center for Regional Policy Studies. Located on Long Island's East End, Stony Brook Southampton is the site of the School of Marine and Atmospheric Sciences Marine Station and graduate arts programs.

Costs

The University's high standards combined with its low tuition make a Stony Brook education an excellent value. For 2012–13, the annual tuition and fees for New York State residents were $7,559. Nonresident tuition and fees were $18,179. Room and board cost $10,998. Books and supplies were estimated at $900.

Financial Aid

The Office of Financial Aid and Scholarship Services administers scholarships and three basic categories of aid: loans, employment opportunities, and grants. To apply for aid, a student must complete the Free Application for Federal Student Aid (FAFSA) as soon after January 1 as possible for the upcoming academic year. Stony Brook University's federal school code is 002838. Upon filing the FAFSA, New York State residents will receive the Express Tuition Assistance Program Application for New York State tuition assistance. The University's commitment to excellence shows in the number and value of merit scholarships offered to high-achieving students. Special scholarships are offered to those admitted to the Honors College and Women in Science and Engineering programs, as well as to Intel Science Talent Research and National Merit Scholarship Competition finalists and semifinalists, valedictorians, and salutatorians. To receive the fullest consideration for merit scholarships, freshman applicants should submit their application by January 15.

Faculty

Stony Brook's more than 2,800 faculty members are tops in their fields and include scholars such as John Milnor, professor of mathematics and winner of the Abel Prize, and winners of four Nobel Prizes, one Pulitzer Prize, five MacArthur Fellowships, and three Grammy Awards. They are also dedicated teachers and include more than 100 recipients of the Chancellor's Awards for Excellence in Teaching. Ninety-eight percent of full-time faculty members have doctorates or terminal degrees in their fields. Faculty members are credited with more than 1,700 inventions and more than 500 patents.

Student Government

Undergraduates are represented by the Undergraduate Student Government (USG), with members elected by the students. Student representatives help shape University policy and advise fellow students as members of the University Senate and other organizations. USG administers an annual budget of $3 million, which it uses to sponsor more than 300 student interest clubs and organizations. Varied student interests are represented by groups as diverse as Alternative Spring Break Outreach; the Belly Dancing Club; the Chess Club; the Commuter Student Association; the Pre-Med Society; the Science Fiction Forum; Stony Brook Pre-Law; several cultural clubs that include the African Students Union, Asian Students Alliance, Caribbean Students Organization, Club India, and Latin American Student Organization; and sports clubs that include the equestrian team, field hockey, ice hockey, quidditch, rugby, and sailing.

Admission Requirements

Stony Brook is a selective institution and evaluates applicants on an individual basis. The Admissions Committee seeks to enroll the strongest and most diverse class possible. Freshman admission is based primarily upon the strength and breadth of the student's academic preparatory program, grade point average, and standardized test scores. Additional criteria include the essay, extracurricular activities, and letters of recommendation. Students who have attended college or university after graduating from high school are eligible to apply as transfers. Transfer applicants are expected to have performed well in a strong academic program. If fewer than 24 college credits were earned, the student's high school record and standardized test scores are also required. Transfer students applying to the upper-division programs in the health sciences must have completed at least 57 credits in liberal arts and sciences and some specific course prerequisites.

Application and Information

Students are encouraged to submit applications for fall admission no later than January 15. Both the SUNY application and the Common Application are accepted. There is a $50 application fee. A supplemental application, which includes an essay and a letter of recommendation, is required for freshmen.

Information sessions with admissions counselors and campus tours with knowledgeable student guides also are available throughout the year; interested students should schedule their visit online.

For more information, contact:

Office of Undergraduate Admissions
Stony Brook University
Stony Brook, New York 11794-1901
Phone: 631-632-6868
        631-632-6859 (TDD)
Fax: 631-632-9898
E-mail: enroll@stonybrook.edu
Website: http://www.stonybrook.edu/admissions

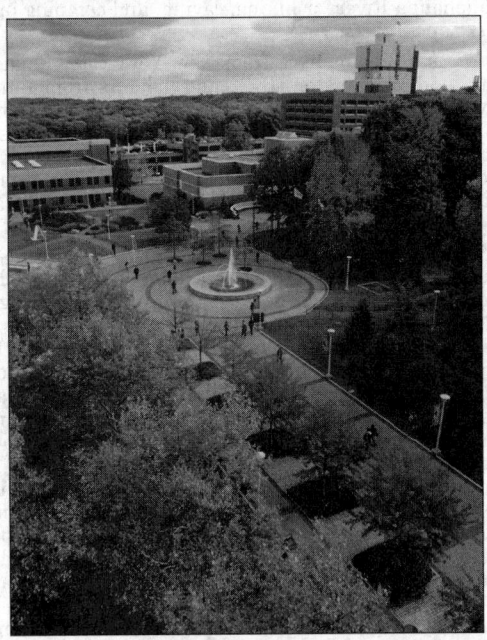

Stony Brook University combines a small-college environment with all the advantages of a major research university for a fraction of the cost of comparable institutions.

SUSQUEHANNA UNIVERSITY
SELINSGROVE, PENNSYLVANIA

The University

By nearly every indicator, Susquehanna University excels at preparing its graduates to achieve, lead, and serve in a diverse and interconnected world. Students benefit from more than 50 majors and minors encompassing a balance of liberal arts and professional studies programs, a highly qualified faculty, and state-of-the-art facilities that support intellectual and personal growth.

The value of experiential learning—study away, internships, and research—is supported by strong extracurriculars. With more than 100 student organizations, 23 NCAA Division III varsity sports, and nationally recognized volunteer programs, students find opportunities to learn and grow well beyond the classroom.

A Susquehanna education is a proven advantage. Graduates consistently say their Susquehanna experiences have given them a competitive edge over other recent graduates entering the workplace. Typically 94 percent of graduates are employed full-time or enrolled in graduate or professional school within six months of graduation—an exceptionally high percentage compared with other institutions. Furthermore, 97 percent of graduates say they would recommend Susquehanna to a high school senior.

Location

Students find themselves at home in the eclectic town of Selinsgrove, Pennsylvania, nestled between the banks of the Susquehanna River and the foothills of the Appalachian Mountains. Favorite activities include checking out the shops on Market Street; enjoying the local flavor of downtown restaurants; kayaking, floating, or tubing down the Susquehanna River; or hiking, caving, and camping in nearby state parks and forests.

Selinsgrove is a 3-hour drive from New York City, Philadelphia, Baltimore, and Washington, D.C., and 4 hours from Pittsburgh. Pennsylvania's capital of Harrisburg is approximately 60 miles from the campus, and the Harrisburg International Airport is served by American, United, Delta, Northwest, and US Airways; several commuter airlines; and major rental-car agencies. The Penn Valley Airport in Selinsgrove has facilities for private and charter aircraft.

Majors and Degrees

Susquehanna students pursue a Bachelor of Arts, Bachelor of Music, or Bachelor of Science degree in the following areas: accounting, anthropology, art history, biochemistry, biology, business administration (emphasis in entrepreneurship, finance, global management, information systems, or marketing), chemistry, communications (emphasis in digital media with tracks in broadcasting and journalism; emphasis in strategic communication with tracks in public relations and corporate communications; and emphasis in communication arts with tracks in speech communications, communications studies, and teacher certification), computer science, creative writing, earth and environmental sciences, ecology, economics (emphasis in financial economics, general economics, global economy, or financial markets), education (certification in early childhood, pre-K through 4, or secondary 7–12 in many areas), English, French, German, graphic design, history, information systems, international studies (emphasis in Asian studies, comparative cultural studies, developing world studies, diplomacy, European studies, international trade and development, or sustainable development), Italian, mathematics, music, music composition, music education, music performance, philosophy, physics, political science, psychology, religion, sociology, Spanish, studio art (emphasis in painting and drawing or photography), and theater (emphasis in performance or production and design).

Preprofessional programs are offered in dentistry, law, medicine, ministry, teaching and veterinary medicine and include one-on-one advising, related internships, and test preparation for the MCAT and LSAT. Cooperative programs in allied health are offered with Thomas Jefferson University in Philadelphia, in dentistry with Temple University School of Dental Medicine in Philadelphia, and in forestry and environmental management with Duke University in Durham, North Carolina.

Minors are available in almost every major area and in the following additional areas: actuarial science, advertising, anthropology, Asian studies, dance, diversity studies, film studies, health care studies, international business and foreign language, international relations, Italian, Jewish studies, legal studies, literature, music technology, music theory, publishing and editing, and women's studies.

Academic Programs

Susquehanna's Central Curriculum is a hybrid model of liberal arts and practical education that emphasizes critical-thinking skills and ethics, and teaches students to put those skills to work in today's world. Throughout their four years at Susquehanna, students develop intellectual skills through courses of their choosing that examine the richness of thought, human interaction, human connections, and the natural world.

Susquehanna's campus community explores a university theme each academic year. The theme is intended to focus classroom discussion, lectures, artistic performances, and student activities around a central idea for in-depth exploration. Past themes include Life on the Fringes, Religion in the Public Square, Sustainability, What Does It Mean to Be Educated?, and Freedom and Responsibility. Reflecting the theme, the Common Reading Program asks Susquehanna faculty, staff, and incoming students to read a related common text every summer.

Susquehanna houses the Arlin M. Adams Center for Law and Society as a complementary program to the Central Curriculum. The Adams Center explores the rich intersections between law and various other disciplines. It provides a forum and research opportunities for examining issues affecting human rights and social responsibility, involving science and technology, and requiring constitutional interpretation. The Adams Center provides several venues for student learning, including internships and field experiences, networking, professional seminars, independent study, research projects, enhanced library resources, symposia, and lectures. Guest speakers for the Adams Center have included nationally known experts and a Supreme Court justice.

Recently founded is the Center for Adolescent Research and Education (CARE) at Susquehanna University which examines factors in teen decision-making. The center operates under the direction of Stephen Wallace, a 1981 graduate of the University who comes back to Susquehanna after 15 years as board chair and CEO of the national SADD (Students Against Destructive Decisions) organization, and with three decades of experience as a school psychologist, adolescent counselor, researcher, author, and motivational speaker. The center seeks to be the preeminent authoritative information source for parents, educators, mentors, coaches, and health professionals concerned with the attitudes and behaviors of adolescents and young adults.

Off-Campus Programs

Susquehanna's Global Opportunities (GO) program, the only one of its kind in the nation, requires every student to have a cross-cultural experience away from campus, either in the United States or abroad. In 2013, the university received the prestigious Andrew Heiskell Award for Internationalizing the Campus from the Institute of International Education, in recognition of the GO program. A student's GO experience might include a traditional semester study-abroad program (GO Long), a short-term faculty or staff-led program (GO Short), a self-designed experience proposed and accepted in advance, or service in a cross-cultural setting.

GO is flexible and affordable. Susquehanna currently offers 75 GO Long programs, most of which cost approximately the same as a semester on campus. GO Short programs are even more affordable, because they involve a shorter stay away from campus. There are currently 26 GO Short programs with more in development. Most forms of financial aid, including scholarships, are available during GO experiences.

About two thirds of Susquehanna's students participate in nationally recognized community service projects, with an annual average of more than 25,000 hours of community service delivered to the Susquehanna Valley and beyond.

Academic Facilities

Susquehanna's facilities include a rich mix of historic and new buildings. Two buildings are on the National Register of Historic Places and others, completed in recent years, have won architectural and design awards.

In fall 2010 the Natural Sciences Center opened, which has transformed teaching and learning for all Susquehanna students. With a prominent spot on the 325-acre campus, the 81,000-square-foot science facility is the school's largest academic building. The facility houses Susquehanna's biology, chemistry, and earth and environmental sciences programs. The new science building demonstrates Susquehanna's strong commitment to sustainability and environmental responsibility. The building earned the U.S. Green Building Council's LEED silver-level certification. The investment benefits all students, because science education is a part of the Central Curriculum. The initiative advances other programs at Susquehanna, with the former science building, Fisher Hall, renovated to accommodate anticipated enrollment gains. That building now houses several academic departments, in addition to the Center for Academic Achievement, the Career Development Center, and the Letterbox editing and publishing suite.

Susquehanna's Natural Sciences Center also complements other, already outstanding academic facilities available to students. Apfelbaum Hall, completed in 1999, is home to the Sigmund Weis School of Business and the Department of Communications. Apfelbaum houses two television studios, multimedia classrooms, a presentation room, and numerous small-group study rooms. Cunningham Center for Music and Art, renovated and expanded in 2002, offers contemporary art and music teaching facilities and flexible practice and performance space, including Stretansky Concert Hall, a 320-seat venue designed to optimize choral and instrumental music. Weber Chapel Auditorium is home to a classic, 1,500-seat theater, with a revolving stage and recording studio for students studying music technology. Additional performance space for theater students is available in the Degenstein Center Theater, which houses a modern 450-seat proscenium teaching theater with a counterweight fly system and an intimate, black-box studio theater. Every student takes full advantage of the Blough-Weis Library. The attractive, technologically advanced library offers online access to thousands of journal articles; more than 330,000 books, DVDs and CDs; and comfortable spaces for group and quiet study. Students and faculty members have online access from any computer connected to the Internet. The library also houses Susquehanna's Media Center.

Costs

Tuition and fees for 2013–14 are $38,780. Room and board costs are $10,390. A student's personal expenses, including books, travel, and other costs, are estimated at $1,600 to $1,900 per year.

Financial Aid

More than 90 percent of Susquehanna students receive some form of financial aid. All students are encouraged to apply for need-based financial aid by filing both the Free Application for Federal Student Aid (FAFSA) and the CSS PROFILE forms. Every applicant for admission to Susquehanna also is considered for merit awards regardless of financial need. Renewable for four years, Susquehanna's merit scholarships are awarded based on academic achievement, talent in a particular area of University interest, or community involvement. Susquehanna is a participant in the Tuition Exchange program for children of employees at participating institutions. The University also participates in the Yellow Ribbon Program for veterans of the wars in Iraq and Afghanistan.

Faculty

Susquehanna's faculty members serve as advisers and creative mentors to their students both in the classroom and beyond. Whether meeting one-on-one with a student for more in-depth instruction after class or making their homes available for barbecues, faculty members make themselves accessible to students in a variety of formal and informal settings. Professors who seek employment at Susquehanna value the opportunity to live and learn alongside their students. By graduation, many Susquehanna students have shared a stage with faculty members, whether through a recital or a national conference presentation.

Of the 141 full-time professors, 92 percent hold a doctorate or terminal degree in their field. The student-faculty ratio is 12:1.

Student Government

Susquehanna's Student Government Association is a self-governing organization providing representation of the student body in University affairs. The main function of the legislative body is the allocation of student activities fees to recognized clubs, student groups, campus projects, and University activities. Senators are elected each year and serve as student representatives to various offices and groups on campus.

Admission Requirements

Susquehanna's average accepted student earns a GPA of 3.39 in a competitive college-prep curriculum. For those students who choose to submit test scores, the midrange SAT score is 1020–1220, and the midrange ACT score is 22–26. Students may choose to apply under the Write Option, which allows two graded, critical writing samples to serve as a substitute for SAT or ACT scores.

Susquehanna looks for exceptional students who are attracted by its academic challenges and extracurricular opportunities. Admission is competitive. The University considers what it can do for students and how students might contribute to Susquehanna. It assesses applications based on course selections, grades, and class rank as well as factors such as motivation, creativity, and leadership. Honors program students typically rank in the top 10 percent.

Susquehanna strongly encourages prospective students to visit the campus and interview with a member of the admissions staff. Counselors are happy to answer questions and explain programs firsthand. Students can see the facilities and meet with faculty members, coaches, and students. Susquehanna can arrange for class visits or overnight stays in residence halls during the academic year.

Application and Information

Susquehanna accepts the Common Application, which is free to file online. Students applying to the Bachelor of Music degree program are required to audition. Students applying to major in graphic design or creative writing are required to submit a portfolio of their work.

Office of Admissions
Susquehanna University
514 University Avenue
Selinsgrove, Pennsylvania 17870-1164
Phone: 570-372-4260
       800-326-9672 (toll-free)
Fax: 570-372-2722
E-mail: suadmiss@susqu.edu
Website: http://www.susqu.edu

Historic Seibert Hall at Susquehanna University.

SWEET BRIAR COLLEGE
SWEET BRIAR, VIRGINIA

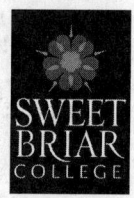

The College

Deeply committed to the education of women since its founding in 1901, Sweet Briar College is consistently ranked as one of the top national liberal arts and sciences colleges in the country. Its excellent academic reputation, beautiful campus, and attention to the individual attract ambitious, intellectually self-confident women who want to excel. Students can expect their Sweet Briar experience to allow them to fulfill their promise as scholars and leaders, while enjoying the close-knit friendships and camaraderie that come with a personal, residential community.

A Sweet Briar education sets in motion the conviction that any goal is achievable. Small classes (averaging 12 students per class) and a student-faculty ratio of 8:1 ensure personal attention and academic interaction. Students work one-on-one with faculty members who are committed to each student's academic success. The College has a wide geographic, ethnic, and socioeconomic representation. About 700 women from more than forty states and nineteen countries are enrolled at Sweet Briar's Virginia campus; another 120 students are enrolled in Sweet Briar's coed Junior Year in France and Junior Year in Spain programs. Any student may have a car.

Students who derive the most from the Sweet Briar experience are those who participate in and contribute to community life, striking a good balance between academic work and the rest of life. They recognize that one of the advantages of the College is the unlimited opportunities for women to participate and assume leadership roles in many types of organizations and activities. About fifty campus organizations are available, including honor societies, a literary journal, community service groups, a multicultural club, political groups, a student newspaper, drama and dance clubs, a radio station, and singing groups. Students plan and participate in an extensive array of concerts, films, and dance and theater productions as well as workshops and master classes by visiting scholars and performers. Visitors have included best-selling novelists Masha Hamilton and Barbara Kingsolver, physicist Brian Greene, food journalist Michael Pollan, environmental attorney Robert F. Kennedy Jr., columnist Christine Brennan, and naturalist E. O. Wilson.

Twenty-one campus buildings, the work of renowned American architect Ralph Adams Cram, are on the National Register of Historic Places. In 2006, Sweet Briar opened a beautiful new studio arts facility. Sweet Briar is the only college in the United States with a residential artists' colony on its campus. Known as the Virginia Center for the Creative Arts, the colony is a working retreat for international writers, visual artists, and composers. In 2009, the College opened a 53,000-square-foot fitness and athletic center addition to the existing gymnasium, and a sixty-bed apartment-style residence facility for upperclass students. The on-campus equestrian center, one of the largest and best college facilities in the country, attracts both competitive and recreational riders. Sweet Briar's equestrian program, both competitive and instructional, consistently garners national recognition. The 100-acre Rogers Riding Center has a 120-foot by 300-foot indoor arena, well-appointed stables for approximately 80 horses, several outdoor rings, numerous paddocks, and miles of hacking trails—all within walking distance of the main campus.

In 2009, Sweet Briar upgraded its computer network to a state-of-the-art wireless platform that allows high-speed Internet access from all academic and administrative buildings, as well as residence hall rooms. Connection to the campus network is also possible from most outdoor, student-used spaces.

In 2004, Sweet Briar launched two graduate degree programs: the Master of Arts in Teaching and the Master of Education. These programs are rooted in the teaching philosophy of differentiated curriculum and instruction. Sweet Briar also established a new degree program in engineering, only the second such undergraduate program at a women's college. The Sweet Briar B.S. in engineering science program is ABET accredited.

Varsity athletes compete in NCAA Division III field hockey, lacrosse, soccer, softball, swimming, and tennis. Club sports include cross-country, fencing, volleyball, and riding.

Location

Sweet Briar's 3,250-acre campus in the foothills of the Blue Ridge Mountains includes hiking, biking, and riding trails and two lakes that provide spectacular venues for outdoor recreational activities. The College is centrally located on the outskirts of Lynchburg, Virginia, southwest of Washington, D.C., and Charlottesville. Students also enjoy activities in nearby Roanoke and Richmond.

Majors and Degrees

Sweet Briar awards the Bachelor of Arts, Bachelor of Science, and Bachelor of Fine Arts degrees. The College offers majors in anthropology, art history, biochemistry and molecular biology, biology, business management, chemistry, classics, dance, economics, education, engineering science, English, English and creative writing, environmental science, French, government, history, international affairs, mathematics, modern languages and literatures, music, musical theater, philosophy, physics, psychology, religion, sociology, Spanish, studio art, and theater.

Additional areas of study, minors, and certificate programs include archeology; arts management; equine studies; engineering (3-2 dual degree); journalism, new media, and communications; Latin American studies; law and society; medieval and Renaissance studies; pre-law; pre-medicine; and pre–veterinary science. Students may design an interdisciplinary major focused on a topic of special interest or may construct personalized majors.

Academic Programs

Sweet Briar's mission is to prepare women to be active, responsible members of a world community. Underscoring every one of the major fields of study is the idea that the best way to learn about the world is to experience it. The curriculum emphasizes hands-on learning, comprehensive understanding, analysis, reflection, creativity, and communication across disciplines. The academic programs are nationally celebrated. To add to this, the College recently adopted a strategic plan that includes emphasis on providing an education that is dynamic, digitally sophisticated, connected, and entrepreneurial. Making the most effective use of Sweet Briar's unique campus as a "landscape for learning," the strategic plan aims at an educational experience that prepares students to engage with today's digital world, be ready to adapt to the dizzying rate of technological change, and encourage entrepreneurial thinking across disciplines.

The general education program has four components—composition and writing, skills requirements, experiences requirements, and knowledge areas requirements—that work together to ensure the development of strong communication and quantitative reasoning skills. Independent studies and seminars are included in most majors, with a culminating senior course or exercise required in most majors. Sweet Briar has a chapter of Phi Beta Kappa and was the first women's college to establish a chapter of the pre-law honorary society Phi Alpha Delta. It also has a four-year honors program that is nationally recognized for its innovative partnering of interdisciplinary academic and co-curricular programs. Honors students may take special tutorials and seminars as well as complete a yearlong research project culminating in an honors thesis on an original topic.

Sweet Briar's two-semester calendar allows students to participate in intensive courses, independent research projects, or internships on campus or throughout the world.

Off-Campus Programs

By the time they graduate, more than a third of Sweet Briar students have studied abroad. The Sweet Briar Junior Year in France was the first program in Paris for American students. Students from colleges and universities across the country have participated in the coed program. The successful Junior Year in Spain is recognized as the premier program in Seville. The College has special relationships with the University of St. Andrews in Scotland, Heidelberg University in Germany, Doshisha Women's College in Japan, and the University of Urbino in Italy. Sweet Briar students have also chosen the following destinations for study abroad: Australia, China, the Czech Republic, Denmark, Greece, Holland, Ireland, Jamaica, Korea, Mongolia, Morocco, New Zealand, Thailand, and Vietnam. Off-campus study may also include an Environmental Junior Year, the Washington Semester at American University, and summer programs at St. Anne's College in Oxford, England. In addition, summer programs are available in Australia; Central America, including Costa Rica; Münster, Germany; Rome and Urbino, Italy; Nepal; and Spain.

Sweet Briar participates in the Tri-College Consortium with Randolph College and Lynchburg College. In addition to taking courses at the other colleges, students can participate in combined social and cultural activities on those campuses.

Academic Facilities

Sweet Briar's library collection of over 300,000 print items, nearly 50,000 journals, and access to millions of items through electronic databases supports high levels of student learning. The collection offers special depth in the areas of art history, the sciences, religion, and music.

Computer labs running Mac and Windows operating systems are open 24 hours a day; there is wireless and wired high-speed Internet access throughout campus. The student-computer ratio is 6:1.

Sweet Briar's engineering department lab includes a 5-Kip-capacity Universal Test Machine; a United Tru-Blue Rockwell hardness tester; a set of gauged beams and test fixtures for mechanics experiments; eight new computers, each with NI ELVIS and Labview with Protoboards; and a well-equipped machine shop. Students studying science use state-of-the-art equipment that enhances faculty-student collaborative research. Biology equipment includes a scanning electron microscope with digital imaging system, equipment for plant and animal tissue culture, and DNA sequencing equipment. Chemistry students have access to two nuclear magnetic resonance spectrometers (NMR; 400 MHz and 60 MHz), an atomic absorption spectrometer (AAS), a diode array UV/Vis spectrometer, a Fourier-transform infrared spectrometer (FT-IR), a modular LASER laboratory, a gas chromatograph/mass spectrograph (GC/MS), a high-pressure liquid chromatograph (HPLC), and a differential scanning calorimeter (DSC). Physics equipment includes a scanning tunneling microscope, an X-ray crystallography system, a 10-inch-diameter reflecting telescope, and holographic instrumentation.

The environmental studies program occupies two sites. A renovated train station provides classroom and laboratory space equipped with a Rigaku Miniflex powder X-ray diffraction system for mineralogical analysis, a Rocklabs bench-top ring mill for grinding rock and soil samples, a drying oven, a high-temperature muffle furnace, and more. An adjacent caboose car provides office space for faculty members. A water treatment plant was also converted to an education/nature center and environmental lab; equipment includes instrumentation for sampling water, soil, wastewater, and sediment, including N-Con composite samplers, macroinvertebrate samplers, and specialized water-collection devices.

The Babcock Fine Arts Center includes individual practice rooms, an electronic piano lab, dance studios, theaters, and Murchison Lane Auditorium for lectures and performing arts. Two former dairy barns were renovated for classroom and office space to house studio arts, including a ceramics and sculpture studio; four large studios for painting, drawing, and printmaking; and a photo studio and darkroom.

The Academic Resource Center (ARC) provides free of charge to all students academic support services that include assistance with papers and study strategies, a personalized time management system, stress management advice, tutoring information, and one-on-one peer mentoring. The ARC also provides support and learning strategies for students with diagnosed learning differences.

Costs

For 2013–14, tuition and fees are $33,605 and room and board total $11,800. Books and supplies are estimated at $1,200 and personal expenses averaged $1,250.

Financial Aid

A family's financial circumstance does not limit a student's choices at Sweet Briar because of the College's generous financial aid program. More than 95 percent of enrolling students receive financial assistance from the College, including merit scholarships, need-based grants, loans, and work-study awards. Scholarships for international students are also available on a competitive basis.

Faculty

Sweet Briar's faculty members have been commended by numerous regional and national educational groups for their excellence in teaching. Faculty members are actively engaged in teaching, research, publishing, and other forms of creative activity. More than 85 percent of full-time faculty members have a doctorate or the highest professional degree in his or her field. All classes are taught by a faculty member. About half of the faculty members are women.

Student Government

The Student Government Association (SGA) is founded upon a highly developed concept of honor and student ownership and involvement. The Honor System applies to all phases of academic and social life. Each entering student becomes a full member of the Student Government Association upon taking the Honor Pledge, which states that Sweet Briar women do not lie, cheat, steal, or violate the rights of others. Students participate in the governance of the College through the many offices and committee positions of the Student Government Association. SGA and its committees are largely responsible for the self-governance of the student body.

Admission Requirements

Sweet Briar seeks talented women who are adventurous, enthusiastic about learning, and want to take an active part in their education. The Admissions Committee looks for qualities such as independent thinking, ethical principles, assertiveness, and an appreciation of diversity. Sweet Briar welcomes students of all economic, ethnic, geographic, religious, and social backgrounds.

Requirements normally include a minimum of 4 units in English, 3 in mathematics, 3 in social studies, 2 sequential years in a foreign language, and 3 units in science, as well as additional units in these subjects to total 16. Most candidates have 20 such academic units. Special attention is given to the difficulty of the applicant's curriculum and her academic achievement in the classroom; scores on the SAT or ACT are required. An interview at the College is strongly encouraged but not required. Candidates who are unable to visit the campus are invited to meet with staff members or talk with alumnae in their hometowns.

Application and Information

Prospective students are encouraged to contact the admissions office for the appropriate application deadlines and options. Sweet Briar will notify each student of acceptance within one month of the date her application becomes complete. A completed application includes a transcript of the candidate's academic work, scores on the required test, recommendations from the guidance counselor and a teacher, and an essay written by the candidate. There is a $40 application fee, which may be waived at the request of the student's guidance counselor if it is deemed to be a financial burden. Sweet Briar also accepts the Common Application (a supplement is required). All materials and requests for information should be sent to the admissions office at the address listed below.

Dean of Admissions
Sweet Briar College
P.O. Box 1052
Sweet Briar, Virginia 24595
Phone: 434-381-6142
      800-381-6142 (toll-free)
Fax: 434-381-6152
E-mail: admissions@sbc.edu
Website: http://www.sbc.edu

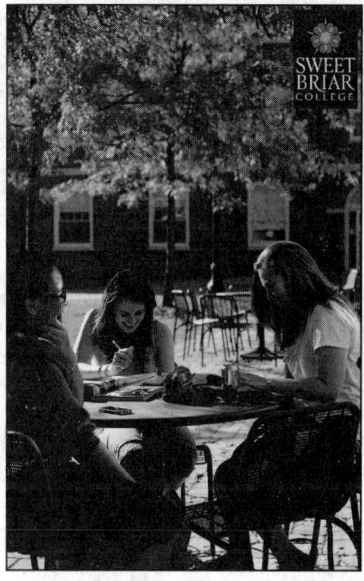

Young women who value a rigorous academic program with supportive and engaging professors will find what they seek at Sweet Briar College.

SYRACUSE UNIVERSITY
SYRACUSE, NEW YORK

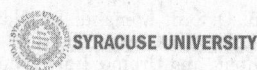

The University

Syracuse University (SU), which was founded in 1870, is an independent, privately endowed university with an international reputation. Students attend from all over the United States and from more than 100 other countries. There are about 17,300 students enrolled; 13,000 are undergraduates. Approximately 70 percent of the students live in University housing, which includes residence halls, apartments, and town houses. The 200-acre campus features a main grassy quadrangle surrounded by academic buildings, with residential facilities nearby. The campus is situated on a hill overlooking the downtown area of Syracuse. Social life is centered on the campus, and there are innumerable recreational, athletic, and academic activities. The 50,000-seat Carrier Dome is the site of concerts, sports events, and commencement. All of campus is connected to the University's wireless networks.

Location

The city of Syracuse (metropolitan-area population of over 650,000 is the business, educational, and cultural hub of central New York. The city offers professional theater and opera, as well as visiting artists and performers. Highlights of the downtown area include the Everson Museum of Art, the Milton J. Rubenstein Museum of Science and Technology (MOST), the impressive Civic Center, Syracuse Stage, and the Armory Square shopping area. Central New York has many lakes, parks, mountains, and outstanding recreational opportunities.

Majors and Degrees

Syracuse University awards the Bachelor of Arts (B.A.), Bachelor of Science (B.S.), Bachelor of Architecture (B.Arch.), Bachelor of Industrial Design (B.I.D.), Bachelor of Music (B.Mus.), and Bachelor of Fine Arts (B.F.A.) degrees.

The School of Architecture offers a five-year baccalaureate program leading to the first professional degree of B.Arch.

Over 50 departmental and interdisciplinary majors are offered in the College of Arts and Sciences including African-American studies, American studies, anthropology, art, art history, biochemistry, biology, biophysical science, chemistry, classical civilization, classics (Greek and Latin), communication sciences and disorders, economics, English and textual studies, European literature, fine arts, French, geography, geology (Earth sciences), German, Greek, history, history of architecture, international relations, Italian, Latin, Latino–Latin American studies, linguistic studies, mathematics, Middle Eastern studies, modern foreign languages, music, music history and cultures, philosophy, physics, policy studies (public affairs), political philosophy, political science, psychology, religion, religion and society, Russian, Russian and Central European studies, sociology, Spanish, women's studies, and writing and rhetoric. Integrated Learning Majors are offered in ethics, forensic science, neuroscience, and energy and its impacts.

The David B. Falk College of Sport and Human Dynamics majors include child and family studies, nutrition/dietetics, nutrition science, public health, social work, and sport management.

The School of Education offers majors in art education, elementary education (inclusive with special education), health and exercise science (including pre–physical therapy and 3+3 D.P.T.), music education, physical education, health and physical education, secondary education, selected studies in education, and special education (inclusive with elementary education and with early childhood education).

The L. C. Smith College of Engineering and Computer Science majors include aerospace, chemical, civil, computer, electrical, environmental, and mechanical engineering; bioengineering; computer science; and systems and information science (dual degree with the School of Information Studies).

The School of Information Studies offers four-year bachelor's degree programs in information management and technology, and systems and information science (dual degree with the College of Engineering and Computer Science).

The Martin J. Whitman School of Management majors include accounting, entrepreneurship and emerging enterprises, finance, management, marketing management, real estate, retail management, and supply chain management.

The S. I. Newhouse School of Public Communications majors are in the following areas: advertising, broadcast and digital journalism, graphic design, magazine, newspaper and online journalism, photography, public relations, and television/radio/film.

The College of Visual and Performing Arts majors are in the following areas: art and design, communication and rhetorical studies, drama, music, and transmedia. Art and design majors offered are ceramics, communications design, (includes advertising design), fashion design, history of art, illustration, industrial and interaction design, environmental and interior design, jewelry and metalsmithing, painting, printmaking, and sculpture. Transmedia majors include art photography, art video, computer art and animation, and film. Drama majors include theater design and technology, acting, musical theater, and stage management. Music majors include music composition, music industry, performance organ, performance percussion, performance piano, performance strings, performance voice, performance wind instruments, and the Bandier Program which leads to a bachelor of science degree in recording and allied entertainment industries. The Department of Communication and Rhetorical Studies offers a Bachelor of Science degree.

Academic Programs

The University operates on a two-semester calendar with two 6-week summer sessions. Students generally take five 3-credit-hour courses each semester. A minimum of 120 credit hours is required for graduation. Special programs include dual and combined enrollment, selected studies, internships, an honors program, ROTC, and preprofessional advising for students going on to study dentistry, law, medicine, or veterinary science.

Off-Campus Programs

The Syracuse University Abroad program operates centers in London, Madrid, Hong Kong, Beijing, Florence, Santiago (Chile), Strasbourg, and Istanbul. SU Abroad also offers opportunities through world partners in over thirty other countries, including Australia, Costa Rica, Ecuador, Egypt, India, Ireland, Japan, Korea, Poland, and Russia. First-year Discovery Programs allow incoming freshmen studying in the liberal arts to complete their fall semester in Florence or Strasbourg.

Academic Facilities

The academic buildings at Syracuse University span the century, with fifteen listed in the National Register of Historic Places and others representative of some of the most modern and technologically sophisticated architecture in the country. The Ernest Stevenson Bird Library houses approximately 3.1 million printed volumes, more than 16,000 online and print journals, and extensive collections of microforms, maps, images, music scores, sound recordings, video, rare books, and manuscripts. The University has computer facilities with laboratories and a data communications network that links computers to hundreds of terminals. The $107-million, 230,000-square-foot Life Sciences Complex combines research and teaching wings for biology, chemistry, and biochemistry. The

Newhouse Communications Center has some of the finest facilities available for journalism and telecommunications. Slocum Hall, home to the School of Architecture, includes a new auditorium, gallery, and space for studio and research. The Center for Science and Technology is a state-of-the-art facility uniting research and academic programs in computer science and technology. It also houses the CASE Center for research in computer applications and software engineering. The new five-story addition to Link Hall, home of the L.C. Smith College of Engineering and Computer Science, features a three-story, high bay lab that houses a crane and space for civil engineering students to build and test structures. The high-tech Melvin A. Eggers Hall offers superior facilities for the University's social science programs. The multimillion-dollar Whitman School of Management building provides students with access to the latest educational technologies and plenty of space for team meetings and work.

Costs

Tuition for 2012–13 was $37,610. The costs for housing and meals averaged $13,692, and fees were $1,394. Books and supplies averaged $1,342; travel expenses, $612; and personal expenses, $950. Therefore, the total cost of attendance was approximately $55,600.

Financial Aid

About 80 percent of all entering first-year and transfer students receive some form of financial aid. By filing the Free Application for Federal Student Aid (FAFSA) and the CSS Financial Aid PROFILE, students are automatically considered for all financial aid programs administered by Syracuse University, including federal financial aid, Syracuse University Grants, and Federal Work-Study Program awards. Merit-based scholarships are available to both first-year and transfer students, based on the information provided in the application for admission. Syracuse University evaluates candidates for admission without respect to financial need. Information on financial aid policies, procedures, and deadlines can be obtained from the Office of Financial Aid and Scholarship Programs.

Faculty

The majority of faculty members hold the highest degree in their professional field. There are over 900 full-time faculty members, including recognized experts in their fields who teach at both the graduate and undergraduate levels.

Student Government

The Syracuse University Student Association works to protect students' rights and offers services through its three branches—the executive, the legislative, and the judicial.

Admission Requirements

Syracuse University seeks a diverse student body from all social, cultural, and educational backgrounds. Each candidate is evaluated individually, based on the requirements of the college of the University to which he or she has applied. Emphasis is placed on students' high school performance, standardized test scores (SAT or ACT), an essay, recommendations, extracurricular activities and community service, and portfolios or auditions, when required. Special admission requirements and deadlines for some programs are described on the University's Web site.

Syracuse University is an Equal Opportunity/Affirmative Action institution and does not discriminate on the basis of race, creed, color, gender, national origin, religion, marital status, age, disability, sexual orientation, or gender identity or expression.

Application and Information

Regular decision applicants for the fall semester should submit their completed application along with transcripts, standardized test scores, the essay, teacher recommendations, and the counselor evaluation by January 1 (submission deadline). Notification begins in mid-March. Completed applications for early decision applicants must be submitted by November 15. Notification begins in mid-December.

Detailed information may be obtained by contacting:

Office of Admissions
100 Crouse-Hinds Hall
900 South Crouse Avenue
Syracuse University
Syracuse, New York 13244-2130
Phone: 315-443-3611
E-mail: orange@syr.edu
Website: http://admissions.syr.edu

The historic buildings that make up the SU campus stand in testimony to the many years of distinction that are at the foundation of Syracuse University.

TEMPLE UNIVERSITY
PHILADELPHIA, PENNSYLVANIA

The University

Students who visit Temple University's Main Campus find they are quite impressed. Cutting-edge facilities and great faculty members create a dynamic academic environment that draws students from around the world. But what can transform a student's life at Temple happens outside the classroom as well. Temple is located in Philadelphia, a dynamic, world-class city with a diverse ethnic mix, a robust economy, and a thriving music and art scene. It is the perfect place to live and study. Two spectacular new academic buildings opened on Main Campus in 2009—the Tyler School of Art and the Fox School of Business and Management's Alter Hall. Tyler's new architecture building opened in fall 2011. The newly renovated Pearson-McGonigle complex opened in 2012, adding additional academic and athletic space to campus. The newest residential facility, Mitchell and Hilarie Morgan Hall is scheduled to welcome students in 2013.

Students who prefer not to attend college in the city should take a look at the Ambler campus, Temple's 187-acre suburban home. Just about all undergraduate programs can be started there, and eighteen can be fully completed there. Ambler's $17-million Learning Center includes smart classrooms; fully integrated technology, including wireless access throughout the building; five computer lab/classrooms; a math, science, and writing center; a video editing lab; a café; and a 300-seat auditorium.

Temple's other local campus is the Health Sciences Center, where the College of Health Professions and Social Work, Temple University Hospital, Temple University School of Medicine, and Temple Dental School are located.

Temple is in the city, but it has a large residential student population—about 12,000 students living on and around Main Campus. The calendar is crammed with theater, dance, and music performances. The Liacouras Center, Temple's 10,200-seat entertainment complex, hosts the University's NCAA Division I basketball games (free tickets for students!) as well as concerts. Great performers like Kanye West, Green Day, Maroon 5, John Mayer, Counting Crows, Rusted Root, Alicia Keys, and Bob Dylan have performed at the Liacouras Center. Temple has every type of student doing every type of activity. Beyond sports, students can join one of 100 or so clubs and organizations and take full advantage of the rich resources and recreation activities offered by Philadelphia and the surrounding area.

Location

Philadelphia has a lot more than juicy sandwiches and cream cheese. With more than 100 museums, 700 Zagat-rated restaurants, and the largest landscaped park in the country—Fairmount Park at 4,180 acres—Philly has a lot to offer. It is a walkable, manageable city that is just 1.5 miles from Temple's Main Campus. Just four stops on a quick subway ride and students are in Center City—or what most would call downtown. Shop, eat, play, or just chill. In addition, students can find a variety of internships in all fields in the Philadelphia area, and Temple has more than 100,000 alumni in the region who love to hire Temple students.

Majors and Degrees

Center for the Arts:

The **Tyler School of Art** offers the Bachelor of Fine Arts with concentrations in ceramics/glass, fibers, graphic and interactive design, metals/jewelry/CAD-CAM, painting, photography, printmaking, and sculpture; the Bachelor of Arts in art history and visual studies; and the Bachelor of Science in art education. Tyler's Architecture Program confers the Bachelor of Science in architecture (preprofessional), architectural preservation, and facilities management.

The **Boyer College of Music and Dance** offers the Bachelor of Music in composition, dance, jazz studies, music education, music history, music therapy, performance (specific instrument or voice), and theory; the Bachelor of Fine Arts is offered in dance.

The **Division of Theater, Film, and Media Arts** offers the Bachelor of Arts in theater and film and media arts.

The **Fox School of Business and Management** offers the Bachelor of Business Administration in accounting, actuarial science, business

management, economics, entrepreneurship, finance, human resource management, international business administration, legal studies, management information systems, marketing, real estate, and risk management and insurance.

The **School of Media and Communication** offers the Bachelor of Arts in advertising, communication studies, journalism, media studies and production, and strategic communication.

The **College of Education** offers the Bachelor of Science in adult and organizational development, career and technical education, early childhood education, middle grades education, and secondary education.

The **College of Engineering** offers the Bachelor of Science in Engineering in civil engineering, electrical engineering, engineering (general program), and mechanical engineering. The Bachelor of Science is offered in bioengineering, construction management technology, and general engineering technology.

The **College of Health Professions and Social Work** offers the Bachelor of Science in athletic training; health information management; kinesiology; linguistics; nursing; public health; speech, language, and hearing; and therapeutic recreation.

The **College of Liberal Arts** offers the Bachelor of Arts in African American studies, American studies, anthropology, Asian studies, classics, criminal justice, economics, English, environmental studies, French, geography and urban studies, German, history, Italian, Jewish studies, Latin American studies, mathematical economics, neuroscience (systems, behavior, and plasticity), philosophy, political science, psychology, religion, sociology, Spanish, and women's studies.

The **College of Science and Technology** offers the Bachelor of Science in applied mathematics, biochemistry, biology, biophysics, chemistry, computer science, environmental science, geology, information science and technology, mathematical economics, mathematics, physics, neuroscience (cell and molecular), and pre-pharmacy.

The **School of Social Work** offers the Bachelor of Social Work degree.

The **School of Tourism and Hospitality Management** offers the Bachelor of Science in sport and recreation management and in tourism and hospitality management.

In addition, the **School of Environmental Design at Ambler** offers Bachelor of Science degree programs in horticulture and landscape architecture and in community and regional planning.

Academic Programs

Temple provides an excellent and affordable education, which not only prepares the student for the specific demands of a career, but also enhances an understanding of the world and the ability to continue learning throughout life.

All students are required to complete the General Education curriculum, a cross-section of courses that form the intellectual foundation of a Temple education, which includes a Philadelphia Experience theme. Many first-year students take advantage of Learning Communities—groups of 20 to 30 participants who pursue common studies under the direction of a faculty team. They spend a semester together, taking a few common courses, participating in faculty-led discussion groups, studying together, and taking field trips related to their studies.

University Studies is a home for the many students who have not declared a major and for students interested in graduate or professional programs in health fields. Academically qualified students may seek extra intellectual challenge through the honors program, taking about a quarter of their course work in the program's smaller, more demanding classes.

After graduation, students are well prepared for the job world. Temple's Career Center arranges cooperative education assignments, schedules on-campus interviews with employers and graduate schools, offers employment skills workshops, provides career and graduate school advisement, and maintains a network of thousands of successful Temple alumni.

Academic Facilities

With more than fifty computer labs and a 90 percent wireless campus, information is more accessible than ever. An exciting new addition to the Main Campus is the Teaching, Education, Collaboration, and Help (TECH) Center. With up to 700 computers (600 fixed workstations and up to 100 laptop loaners), the TECH Center is one of the largest of its kind in the nation; thirteen breakout rooms where students can work on group projects and practice presentations; six specialized labs within the primary center, including video editing, graphic design/CAD, music composition, language/interactive audio, quiet zone, and software development facility; a 24-hour computer help desk for students and faculty and staff members; a 4,260-square-foot Temple Welcome Center (run by the Admissions Office) to host visits to the University by prospective students and their families; and a Starbucks café.

Costs

Tuition and fees for the 2012–13 academic year were $13,596 for Pennsylvania residents and $23,422 for out-of-state residents (tuition rates can vary by major). Room and board for the academic year were about $9,300.

Financial Aid

Scholarships, grants, loans, and work-study programs are available. Four-year academic merit scholarships for talented entering freshmen range from $3,000 to full tuition for Pennsylvania residents and $5,000 to full tuition for nonresidents. Students need only apply for admission to be eligible for these scholarships. Applicants for need-based aid must file the Free Application for Federal Student Aid (FAFSA). Transfer students must file a financial aid transcript, even if they have received no aid from their previous school.

Faculty

At Temple, faculty members are valued not only for their ability to pursue knowledge, but also to share that knowledge with students. Full-time faculty members teach many introductory courses, and often act as academic advisers; from their first semester students can expect to have contact with the people at the forefront of their fields, winners of prestigious teaching and research awards such as the Lindback, the Golden Apple, the Sowell, the Fulbright, the Guggenheim, the Carnegie, and the National Endowment.

Temple recently welcomed the largest group of new tenured and tenure-track faculty members in recent history. Faculty members were hired away from leading universities and research centers, including Princeton University, Brown University, the University of Wisconsin–Madison, the University of Maryland, Wellesley College, and the Cleveland Clinic. Nearly every college at Temple has been joined by at least one new presidential faculty recruit.

In addition to being superlative teachers and researchers, Temple faculty members are also known for their practical experience. For example, a marketing class may be led by a successful entrepreneur, or music lessons given by a member of the Philadelphia Orchestra. Marine biologists, newspaper editors, published authors, practicing architects, and health care professionals all bring their expertise to the classroom to enhance students' education. In 2012, Temple faculty members published or produced 5,700 scholarly and creative works.

Admission Requirements

For freshman admissions, high school grades (quality of courses, grade trends), standardized test scores, and other factors (the required essay, recommendations, extracurricular activities, work or leadership experience, and other personal circumstances) are considered. Temple uses a sliding scale rather than absolute cut-offs for GPA and test scores. SAT subject tests and personal interviews are not required. The deadline for freshman admission is March 1; however, students should apply in the fall of their senior year. Official copies of high school transcripts, recommendation letter (at least one required), and standardized test scores must be sent directly to the admissions office. The deadline for spring admission is November 1.

Temple has rolling admissions and early action decision plans. Those interested in early action must submit a completed application by November 1 and will receive notification by mid-December. Note that Tyler School of Art applicants cannot apply via early action. Freshman decisions begin in early fall, and letters are sent four to six weeks after that point. Temple's admissions process is holistic; every aspect of the student's academic history is considered. Typically, students with a B+ average or better in a strong, college-prep curriculum in grades 9–12 and in the top 30 percent of their graduating classes are accepted. The SAT is required with all three sections considered—admitted students average 500–600 on each section. If students opt to take the ACT, they must also complete the writing section.

Freshman students who apply are automatically considered for merit-based scholarships and honors. Temple requires one recommendation letter—typically from a school/college counselor or academic teacher. The best way to apply is online. The application fee is $55—most students apply online. Students applying in 2014 may also apply via the Common Application.

Temple University welcomes transfer applicants from both two-year and four-year colleges and universities around the country and the world. Transfer students comprise more than half of each entering class and are a vital part of the vibrant campus community. Applicants are considered transfer students if they will have attempted 15 or more college-level credits by the time they apply. If this is not the case, they should apply as freshman students. In making admissions decisions, careful consideration is given to the quality of a student's program and the number of credits earned and the grade point average achieved. The average GPA for new transfer students is a 3.1 (on a 4.0 scale). The following programs have higher minimum grade point average requirements: architecture, nursing, and pharmacy. For most programs, transfer students must complete the application process by June 1 for the fall semester or by November 1 for the spring semester. The fall semester transfer application deadline for music is March 1. The fall priority deadline for nursing is February 15. Transfer applicants must request that all high schools and colleges that they previously attended send official transcripts to the Office of Undergraduate Admissions at Temple University by these deadlines. SAT or ACT scores are not required if an applicant has earned at least 15 college-level credits.

Application and Information

A completed file should contain an application form accompanied by a nonrefundable application fee, a secondary school transcript (sent by the student's school), and SAT or ACT scores. The University has a rolling admission policy; applicants are notified of the admission decision as soon as possible after all credentials have been received and reviewed. Students who select Temple's early action option will be notified no later than mid-December

For additional information, students may contact:

Office of Undergraduate Admissions
Temple University (041-09)
Philadelphia, Pennsylvania 19122-6096
Phone: 215-204-7200
       888-340-2222 (toll-free)
E-mail: askanowl@temple.edu
Website: http://admissions.temple.edu
      http://www.facebook.com/TempleU
      Twitter: @admissionsTU

Liacouras Walk on Main Campus.

THOMAS MORE COLLEGE
CRESTVIEW HILLS, KENTUCKY

The College

Thomas More College features a very strong academic reputation, small class sizes, and an ongoing dedication to scholarly pursuits based on the foundation of a Catholic liberal arts curriculum. Located in Northern Kentucky, just minutes from Cincinnati, Ohio, the College provides vibrant on-campus residential life in close proximity to a major metropolitan area. The result is an outstanding location offering all of the activities and resources of a major city with a suburban setting. With small class sizes and engaged faculty dedicated to teaching, the academic experience is one of personal attention and a hands-on approach to learning that forms the basis of a Thomas More education.

The student population includes 1,900 undergraduates and graduates. There are 960 traditional undergraduates attending classes full-time, of whom 350 are resident students. The student body is drawn primarily from the states of Kentucky, Ohio, and Indiana, but many other states and a number of countries are also represented. In addition to its undergraduate programs, Thomas More College offers graduate programs in business administration (M.B.A.) teaching (M.A.T.) and launched a Master of Education (M.Ed.) program in the fall of 2011. Students who choose to live on campus reside in either a suite-style residence hall or one of three town-house-style residence halls. All residence halls offer comfortable, air-conditioned rooms; Internet and cable TV access; academic tutoring; and free laundry facilities. The 27,000-square-foot Student Center contains a spacious bookstore, computer and study lounges, a game room, campus life offices, a café, and a dance rehearsal studio.

The college experience is enhanced through participation in many academic, social, and sports organizations. Intercollegiate athletics are part of the Presidents' Athletic Conference governed by NCAA Division III. Thomas More College competes in men's baseball, basketball, cross-country, football, golf, soccer, tennis, and track and field, and women's basketball, cross-country, fast-pitch softball, golf, soccer, tennis, track and field, and volleyball. Intramural sports offered include coed flag football, basketball, cornhole, dodgeball, softball, and volleyball. Thomas More College is proud to welcome fans to its athletic facilities, including the Bank of Kentucky Field for football, soccer, and track and field; the Connor Convocation Center which houses basketball and volleyball facilities; and the College's baseball and softball fields. Students can also enjoy beautiful facilities for swimming, tennis, racquetball, and basketball and a complete fitness area at the Five Seasons Sports Club, adjacent to the campus.

Location

Thomas More College is located in northern Kentucky, 10 minutes south of Cincinnati, Ohio. The campus is convenient to major highways, and the Greater Cincinnati/Northern Kentucky International Airport is just 10 minutes from the College. Thomas More's suburban setting provides a safe environment for students and numerous opportunities for employment and internships. All students are permitted to have cars on campus, with no charge for a parking pass.

The College's location offers a wide array of cultural and sporting events. Local attractions include the Broadway Series, the Cincinnati Pops, the Cincinnati Zoo, the Newport Aquarium, the Riverbend Music Center, and the Cincinnati Reds and Bengals. Numerous shopping areas and restaurants are also available, including the Crestview Hills Town Center, located across the street from the College.

Majors and Degrees

Thomas More College offers bachelor's degrees in accounting, art, biology, business administration, chemistry, computer information systems, communications, criminal justice, economics, education, English, environmental science, forensic science, history, humanities, international studies, mathematics, medical laboratory science, nursing, philosophy, physics, political science, psychology, Spanish, sports and entertainment marketing, sociology, speech and theater, and theology. Associate degrees are available in each of these content areas as well as art history, French, gerontology, pre–legal studies, and Web design.

Preprofessional programs are available in dentistry, engineering, law, medicine, occupational therapy, optometry, pharmacy, physical therapy, and veterinary science.

TMC3: The Three-Year Degree Program at Thomas More College is an innovative three-year degree program that enables motivated undergraduate students in pursuit of a bachelor's degree a traditional college experience and an extra year of earning power. Qualified students can save both time and money by completing a traditional four-year bachelor's degree in just three years at a very competitive tuition rate. The three-year degree is completed during the course of eight semesters. While TMC3 compresses the time frame to attain a degree by an entire year, the classes themselves are not accelerated. The structure of TMC3 is year-round, with students generally taking 18 hours in the fall and spring semesters and 12 hours in two summer terms.

Academic Programs

To earn the Bachelor of Arts, Bachelor of Science, or Bachelor of Science in Nursing degree, a student must complete 128 credit hours, including 61 credit hours in liberal arts courses. The Associate of Arts degree requires the completion of 64 credit hours, including a liberal arts component. In addition to the traditional format, the College's TAP program offers associate, bachelor's, and master's degrees in business administration that are provided in an accelerated format for working adults.

The academic calendar for traditional students is composed of a fall and a spring semester and two summer sessions. The accelerated format includes classes year-round.

The Cooperative Education program enables students to gain hands-on professional experience in their field of interest. All students are eligible for this program after the completion of their freshman year. Cooperative Air Force and Army ROTC programs are available in conjunction with nearby universities. The nursing and sociology departments have excellent working relationships with nearby hospitals and social service agencies.

Off-Campus Programs

Nineteen area colleges, including Thomas More College, form the Greater Cincinnati Consortium of Colleges and Universities, through which all students at the local member colleges may take courses not available at their home institution. Thomas

More encourages full-time students to take advantage of this opportunity for curriculum enrichment through cross-registration. In addition, students who wish to study abroad as part of their undergraduate education have a number of possibilities open to them, including exchanges at Lingnan University in Hong Kong, Mary Immaculate College in Ireland, and Eichstaett University in Germany.

Academic Facilities

The recently renovated library has a collection of more than 129,000 volumes of books, periodicals, and audiovisual materials; as a selective depository, it houses more than 8,400 volumes of U.S. government documents. In addition, the library's membership in the Southwest Ohio and Neighboring Libraries gives Thomas More students access to more than 15 million books and more than 75,000 periodicals held by seventy-five other libraries in the region.

Thomas More's computer facilities include computer classrooms and six labs for student use. Student computers are also available in some academic departments and in the library. All PCs are connected to a campuswide Novell network, with wireless access to e-mail, the Internet, and an on-campus Intranet server.

Students in the science programs receive hands-on experience through the use of the newly remodeled classrooms and labs and Biology Field Station, located on the Ohio River. These facilities allow students to participate in undergraduate research programs in such areas as immunology, forestry, environmental studies, astronomy, trace analysis, and synthesis. Research projects have been funded by the National Science Foundation and the National Institutes of Health.

Costs

The 2012–13 annual cost for Thomas More College was $25,750 for tuition and $6,710 for room (double occupancy) and board. There was a differential fee of $30 per semester hour for all nursing courses. The Student Activity fee was $15 per semester and the computer fee was $360 per semester for full-time students. The cost of books was estimated at $800 per year.

Financial Aid

Thomas More College is an excellent educational value offering a wide range of financial aid opportunities, assisting 100 percent of its full-time students in meeting college costs. Awards are determined on a rolling basis, with priority consideration given to applications filed by February 1. Financial aid awards are based on economic need, merit, scholastic achievement, and extracurricular activities. The filing of the Free Application for Federal Student Aid (FAFSA) and the Thomas More College Application for Financial Aid and Scholarship is required before any awards are determined. Other Thomas More College awards may require additional applications.

An extensive Federal Work-Study Program is in place, and there are excellent opportunities for outside employment in the immediate area.

Faculty

The faculty is committed to the ideals of a Catholic liberal arts education, with the main focus on teaching. The faculty has 135 members, including 71 who are full-time; 66 percent hold tenure and 69 percent hold doctoral or other terminal degrees. Faculty members serve as academic advisers to students in their disciplines. The student-faculty ratio is 16:1.

Student Government

The purpose of the Student Government Association is to serve as the official representative organization of the Thomas More College student body; to serve as the liaison between the student body and the faculty, administration, and Board of Trustees; to promote student projects and activities and improve the quality of student life; to assist the Dean of Students in supervising student organizations and student activities on campus; to protect the rights of the individual; and to preserve the general welfare of the student body of Thomas More College.

Admission Requirements

The admission criteria are as follows: an applicant should have a high school grade point average (based on college-preparatory courses) of 85 percent or better (2.5 on 4.0 scale), and a minimum composite score of 20 on the ACT Assessment, with a minimum of 18 in English, or a minimum combined score of 940 on the SAT, with a minimum of 450 on the verbal portion. If the applicant does not meet all the admission criteria, the file is forwarded to the Admissions Committee for individual consideration.

Transfer students with 24 or more semester hours of transferable credit and an overall grade point average of at least 2.0 on a 4.0 scale are automatically accepted. Transfer students with fewer than 24 transferable hours must meet the general admission criteria outlined above.

The applicant must provide a completed application with a nonrefundable $25 fee (waived for online applicants), high school transcripts, college transcripts (if applicable), and ACT or SAT score reports.

Application and Information

Thomas More College operates under a rolling admission policy, with a final application deadline of August 15. Admission decisions are usually made within two weeks of receiving all application materials. Students can apply online at the College's website. The $25 application fee is waived for online applications.

For further information or to schedule a campus visit, students should contact:

Billy Sarge
Associate Director of Admissions and Director of Recruitment
Thomas More College
333 Thomas More Parkway
Crestview Hills, Kentucky 41017-3495
Phone: 859-344-3332
         800-825-4557 (toll-free)
E-mail: admissions@thomasmore.edu
Website: http://www.thomasmore.edu

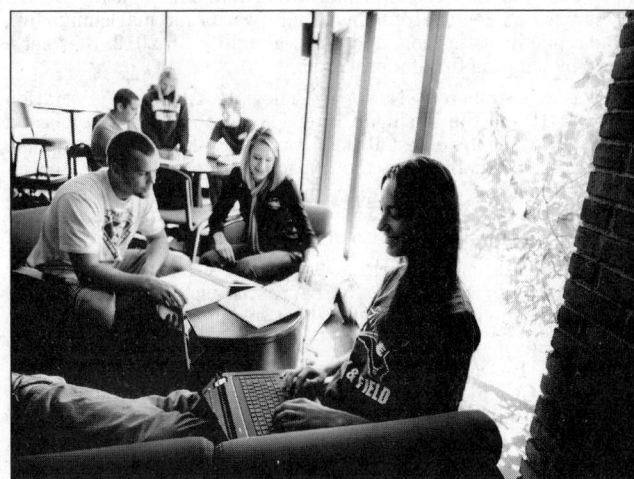

A common sight at TMC: students studying and socializing in the lounge outside of Seiler Commons.

TRINE UNIVERSITY
ANGOLA, INDIANA

The University

Trine University is a private, independent, coeducational institution offering associate, baccalaureate, and graduate degrees to students in more than thirty-five programs, including engineering, mathematics, forensic science, business, education, communication, golf management, exercise science, and criminal justice. Trine also offers a five-year combined Bachelor of Science and Master of Engineering program with majors in civil, mechanical, and biomedical engineering.

Since its founding in 1884, Trine has focused on providing an innovative, quality, career-oriented, project-based education. With a worldwide reputation for being job-ready, Trine graduates are in demand. In 2012, 91 percent of graduates were employed or enrolled in graduate school within six months of commencement.

Trine's current main campus undergraduate enrollment is more than 1,900. More than 1,000 students live on campus in one of sixteen residence halls, private villas, or fully furnished suite-style apartments—some of which overlook Trine's eighteen-hole championship golf course. Trine is one of very few small, private schools in the country to offer this amenity.

The University's 450-acre campus includes the Rick L. and Vicki L. James University Center, which houses a dining hall, campus store, fitness center, 320-seat Fabiani Theatre, mail center, radio station WEAX, and the LINK, a one-stop location that supports learning, and provides access to information, resources, and tools for knowledge discovery.

The University's inviting atmosphere complements the seriousness and determination with which Trine students pursue their academic goals. Students enjoy opportunities to develop friendships and to build leadership and teamwork skills through their participation in more than sixty campus organizations.

Trine has a reputation for academic rigor and success. Chemical engineering seniors have won the American Institute of Chemical Engineers (AIChE) national individual design competition several times in recent years and have produced the safest design for five of the past six years. Mechanical engineering students can study in one of the top cast-metals programs in North America, as determined by the Foundry Educational Foundation. A team of Trine civil engineering students won best design in the annual Plank-A-Palooza competition in Fort Wayne, Indiana. Trine's Tau Alpha Omicron chapter of the American Criminal Association (ACJA) annually wins regional and national awards for marksmanship, crime scene investigation, and physical agility. In 2012, they set a record by winning fifty-four awards.

Trine is a member of National Collegiate Athletic Association Division III and the Michigan Intercollegiate Athletic Association (MIAA), the nation's oldest athletic conference. Men's sports include baseball, basketball, cross-country, football, golf, lacrosse, soccer, tennis, track, and wrestling. Women's sports include basketball, cross-country, golf, lacrosse, soccer, softball, tennis, track, and volleyball. Many students also play on intramural sports teams.

Trine's football team won three consecutive MIAA championships and advanced to round two of NCAA post-season play in both 2009 and 2010. Trine wrestler Elias Larson was named all-American in 2010 and 2011.

The Keith Busse/Steel Dynamics Inc. Athletic and Recreation Center (ARC), which contains a 200-meter indoor track and training and practice facilities for other sports, opened in 2009 to develop Trine's track and field program year-round and to support tennis, additional sports, and intramurals.

The Fred Zollner Athletic Stadium opened in 2010 and serves the football, lacrosse, and soccer programs.

Student organizations include the student senate, honor societies, professional organizations, drama club, music ensembles, pep and marching bands, Habitat for Humanity, and more. In addition, thirteen social fraternities and sororities provide on-campus opportunities for service and camaraderie for upperclassmen.

Trine University is accredited by the Higher Learning Commission and a member of the North Central Association (www.hlcommission.org; phone: 312-263-0456). Trine's programs in chemical engineering, civil engineering, computer engineering, electrical engineering, and mechanical engineering are accredited by the Engineering Accreditation Commission of ABET (111 Market Place, Suite 1050, Baltimore, Maryland, 21202-4012; phone 410-347-7700). All teacher preparation programs are accredited by the National Council for the Accreditation of Teacher Education (www.ncate.org) and the Department of Education/Office of Educator Licensing and Development (www.doe.state.in.us/dps). The Ketner School of Business, Bachelor of Science in business administration program is accredited by the Accreditation Council for Business Schools and Programs (www.acbsp.org). Accredited majors include: accounting, business administration, entrepreneurship, finance, golf management, management, marketing, and sport management. Associate degree programs in accounting and business administration are also accredited.

Location

Trine is in Angola, Indiana, the heart of northeast Indiana's scenic lake resort region, halfway between the metropolitan areas of Chicago and Cleveland. Just a 45-minute drive from Fort Wayne, Indiana, Trine offers the safety and ease of a small-town environment, near some of the nation's most vital cities. Pokagon State Park provides year-round recreational opportunities for the community and is just 5 miles north of Trine's campus.

Majors and Degrees

The Allen School of Engineering and Technology awards Bachelor of Science degrees in chemical and bioprocess, civil, computer, electrical, computer, and mechanical engineering and design engineering technology. Minors are offered in aeronautical, bioprocess, environmental, metallurgical, and structural engineering.

Well-qualified high school graduates may be admitted directly into a five-year combined Bachelor of Science and Masters of Engineering program. Civil, mechanical, and biomedical engineers with the skills necessary to design complex systems are highly sought by industry professionals; therefore, the degree is practice-oriented with a heavy emphasis on design, as opposed to the research emphasis of a traditional Master of Science degree. Upon completion of this program, both the Bachelor of Science in civil, mechanical, or biomedical engineering and the Master of Engineering degree are awarded.

The Ketner School of Business awards Bachelor of Science in Business Administration degrees with majors in accounting, business administration, communication, entrepreneurship, finance, golf management, management, marketing, and sport management.

The Franks School of Education awards Bachelor of Science degrees in elementary, health and physical, mathematics, science, and social studies education.

The Jannen School of Arts and Sciences awards Bachelor of Arts degrees with majors in general studies (pre-legal, self-designated, and social studies), and psychology. The school also awards Bachelor of Science degrees with majors in biology, chemistry, criminal justice, exercise science, forensic science, informatics, and mathematics. A premedical professional track is also available.

Academic Programs

Trine University's engineering programs concentrate on providing a fundamental, application-oriented engineering education which includes extensive laboratory instruction. In addition to concentrated studies in a specialized area, students are required to complete courses in communication skills, socio-humanistic studies, and analysis and design.

The University's business programs include a broad range of practical experience to acquaint the student with the practices, procedures, and problems of the contemporary business professional. Guest lecturers frequently visit campus and students are given many experiential learning opportunities.

Off-Campus Programs

Co-op and internship opportunities are encouraged. Semesters of classroom study are alternated with professional work experience, which can give students a competitive edge in the job market and offset college expenses. The length of a co-op program depends upon the student's class status when entering the program.

Academic Facilities

Fawick Hall of Engineering houses the Chemical and Bioprocess, Civil and Environmental, Electrical and Computer, and Mechanical and Aerospace Engineering departments, as well as the Engineering Technology department. Trine students use sophisticated equipment such as a scanning electron microscope and rapid prototyping machines in their laboratories and design projects. Each computer lab features state-of-the-art software.

The Best Hall of Science contains classrooms and science laboratories; the Fairfield Lecture Room; the Department of Mathematics; the Department of Science; and the Department of Criminal Justice, Psychology, and Social Sciences.

Recent renovations to the Ketner School of Business and Franks School of Education include new infrastructure and technology, including a fiber-optic network, a wireless environment, and shared multimedia access to resources for teaching (SMART) classrooms. The T. Furth Center for Performing Arts is undergoing a $7-million renovation (estimated completion fall 2014) that will provide classrooms for choral and instrumental music and an auditorium for drama and music productions.

The University channeled more than $2 million into campus-wide technology upgrades. The LINK houses a digital classroom, a "my office" area with computers, and a global workspace with videoconferencing stations. In addition, iPads, Kindles, digital camcorders, and other devices are available for checkout from the Tech Bar. More than 200 computers dedicated to student access are available in labs across campus. Every room in student residences is wired to the University network and the Internet, and all academic facilities and residential common areas are fitted with wireless Internet access.

Costs

Tuition for the academic year (two semesters) in 2013–14 is $28,700 ($31,000 for engineering). Room and standard meal plan (nineteen meals per week) for the academic year costs $9,500 (double occupancy).

Financial Aid

Financial aid may be awarded in the form of scholarships, grants, loans, or campus employment. Any of these aids or any combination may supplement family and student resources to meet basic educational expenses. Trine requires the Free Application for Federal Student Aid (FAFSA) and recommends its submission by March 1.

Faculty

Trine has a full-time faculty of 88 members. Most have doctoral degrees and professional experience. The student-faculty ratio is 15:1.

Student Government

The student senate is organized for the purpose of providing funding and formulating policies for campus organizations. Representatives to the senate are elected by each class and from each of four school on main campus.

Admission Requirements

Graduation from an approved high school or equivalent preparation is required for admission. Selection is made without regard to race, religion, or gender. The University requires applicants to take the ACT or SAT prior to approval for admission (writing sections are optional).

Admission requirements for engineering include 4 years of English, 1 year of chemistry, 1 year of physics, 1 year of social studies, 2 years of algebra, 1 year of geometry, and ½ year of trigonometry. All other applicants must have the following high school credits: 4 years of English, 3 years of mathematics, 3 years of science, and 3 years of social studies.

Graduates of pre-professional or college-parallel programs at approved community or junior colleges are eligible for transfer into Trine's baccalaureate programs. Qualified graduates of these programs may be granted junior standing upon transfer. In general, credit may be allowed in subjects that parallel Trine programs, provided the student earned a grade of C or better in the course.

Application and Information

Trine University's online application is available at www.trine.edu; there is no application fee. The University admits applicants on the basis of scholastic achievement and academic potential. Admission decisions are made on a rolling basis. Applicants are notified of their status within two weeks of receipt of their application, high school record, and test scores. Transfer students must also submit an official copy of their college transcript(s).

Interested students and their parents are encouraged to visit the campus. Arrangements can be made by writing or calling the Office of Admission.

For additional information, students should call or write:

Office of Admission
Trine University
One University Avenue
Angola, Indiana 46703-1764
United States
Phone: 260-665-4100
       800-347-4878 (toll-free within continental United States)
E-mail: admit@trine.edu
Website: www.trine.edu
      www.facebook.com/trineadmissions
      www.youtube/trineuniversity

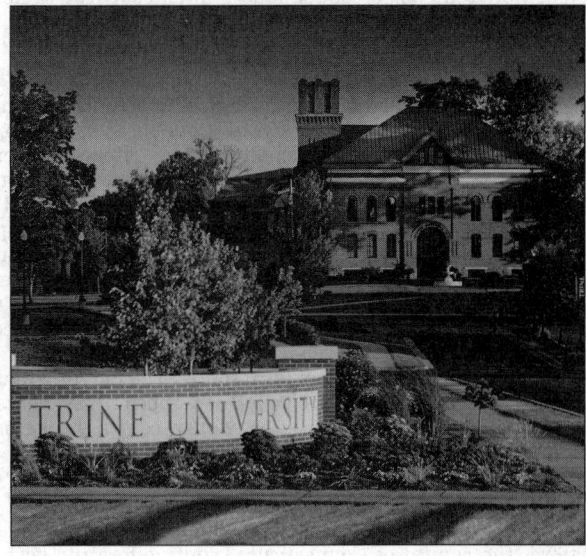

TRINITY COLLEGE
HARTFORD, CONNECTICUT

The College

Since its founding in 1823, Trinity has provided an undergraduate education of uncommon quality. Widely acknowledged as one of the top liberal arts colleges in the country, Trinity has been recognized by a panel of national education editors for its bold and innovative ideas to advance the cause of higher education and ensure greater access.

In its commitment to the rigorous pursuit of the liberal arts and to instruction that is personal and conversational, Trinity is an ideal college. At the same time, Trinity is in close touch with the world beyond its campus. In that respect and in terms of the outstanding opportunities Trinity's capital city location offers students, a Trinity education is indeed a real education.

While remaining faithful to the classic liberal arts tradition, Trinity offers a distinctive educational experience that prepares students for the challenges and opportunities of the twenty-first century. Building on its traditional strengths in the arts and humanities and exceptional offerings in science and engineering, Trinity engages students in a conversation with the world through its Center for Urban and Global Studies, study-abroad programs, interdisciplinary programs, and innovative, rigorous programs that draw on the rich cultural, educational, and professional assets of Hartford. State-of-the-art electronic facilities support Trinity's advanced use of information technology in classrooms. The heart of a Trinity education, however, remains the personal encounter between professor and student, the intellectual partnership that discovers a world of ideas and ignites a passion for learning.

Trinity's students come from forty-seven states and fifty-four countries. The College believes that a diverse community makes learning flourish. Trinity's undergraduate enrollment of more than 2,200 students is about equally comprised of men and women. More than 90 percent of undergraduates live on campus in College housing. Trinity is engaged in continuing campus revitalization programs that preserve its impressive Gothic buildings as it also develops a campus for the twenty-first century.

Trinity offers a rich array of extracurricular activities—films, plays, concerts, musical theater, sports, academic symposia, and visits by nationally and internationally known writers, speakers, and performers. Participation is an important word on campus, and Trinity students have abundant opportunities to lead and to be involved in numerous student clubs; special interest groups; theater, dance, and music groups; debate; academic programs; campus cinema; Trinity's radio station; and many student publications. With 19 acres of playing fields, Trinity also offers an extensive athletic program. About 40 percent of the student body participates on twenty-nine men's and women's varsity teams (Division III) and roster of intramural sports. The Ferris Athletic Center features a swimming pool, a fully equipped fitness center, crew tanks, eight international-size squash courts, basketball courts, and an indoor track.

Location

Situated on a beautiful 100-acre campus in the center of Hartford, the capital of Connecticut, Trinity offers the best of both worlds—a supportive and active campus community located in a city that provides students with myriad opportunities for internships, community service, and cultural exploration. Hartford's businesses, governmental agencies, cultural organizations, and nonprofit institutions offer Trinity students hundreds of opportunities to explore careers through the College's extensive internship program. Hartford has a number of cultural institutions, including the Wadsworth Atheneum (the

oldest public art museum in the nation), Mark Twain House, Harriet Beecher Stowe Center, Hartford Symphony, Hartford Stage, and a number of smaller theaters and clubs that provide a cultural stew of dance, theater, and music. The shopping districts of Hartford and surrounding suburbs are nearby. The impressive Connecticut coast is easily accessible, and Boston and New York are each about 2 hours from campus. Off campus, Trinity students have access to a field station in Ashford, Connecticut, dedicated to research in the natural sciences and a wide range of environmental educational endeavors.

Majors and Degrees

On the undergraduate level, the College offers a Bachelor of Arts degree and a Bachelor of Science degree. Trinity offers thirty-eight majors, including American studies; anthropology; art history; biochemistry; biology; chemistry; classical civilization; classics; computer science; economics; educational studies; engineering; English; environmental science; French; German studies; Hispanic studies; history; interdisciplinary computing; international studies; Italian studies; Jewish studies; language and culture studies (Arabic, Chinese, Hebrew, Japanese); mathematics; music; neuroscience; philosophy; physics; political science; student-designed interdisciplinary major; psychology; public policy and law; religion; Russian; sociology; studio arts; theater and dance; and women, gender, and sexuality. Urban studies is slated to be added as a new major in the fall 2013 semester.

Academic Programs

Featuring approximately 900 courses, Trinity's curriculum provides a framework within which students may explore the many dimensions of an undergraduate education. At the same time, the curriculum offers each student flexibility to experiment, to deepen old interests and develop new ones, and to acquire specialized training in a major field. Students must demonstrate proficiency in writing, mathematics, and a second language, and fulfill a five-part distribution requirement that consists of at least one course in each of the following categories: arts, humanities, natural sciences, numerical and symbolic reasoning, and social sciences. They must complete a writing intensive requirement and a second-language requirement and also take a first-year seminar and at least one course that focuses on global engagement.

Off-Campus Programs

More than 50 percent of Trinity students study abroad for a semester or a year at Trinity's Rome Campus, at one of seven additional Trinity global learning sites, or throughout the globe. Trinity-sponsored global learning sites operate in Argentina, Austria, France, Spain, South Africa, Trinidad, and China. Through the theater and dance department, Trinity offers the Trinity/La MaMa Performing Arts Program in New York City, an extraordinary program that provides intensive study in theater, dance, and performance.

Academic Facilities

The Raether Library and Information Technology Center is home to the Raether and Watkinson Libraries, as well as the Computing Center. It is a place where students and faculty members come together for the serious work of scholarship, where researchers can pore over a book or conduct investigations through a wide selection of online databases. The Raether Library houses over 1 million print books and bound collections, including electronic books, and approximately 90,000 periodical titles received (paper, microfilm, and electronic). In addition, an online catalog linked with Wesleyan University and Connecticut College provides access to more than 2 million titles. The Watkinson Library, with its impressive collection of rare books, manuscripts, and other unique resources, supports a broad range of research interests.

The campus is fully wired, with every student room connected to the College network and the web. Public access computers are also available 24 hours a day in select facilities.

Costs

Costs for the 2012–13 academic year were $43,570 for tuition, $11,800 for room and board, and $2,160 for fees.

Financial Aid

Each student admitted to Trinity who qualifies for aid receives a package that fully meets his or her calculated need. Students must file the Free Application for Federal Student Aid (FAFSA) as well as the Financial Aid PROFILE of the College Scholarship Service. Admissions applications are due by January 1; FAFSA and PROFILE applications are due by February 1. Students are notified of admission and aid decisions by the first week of April. Normally, need is met with a financial aid package that includes grant assistance, work-study, and federal student loans. Federal funds for which accepted students are eligible include Pell Grants, Perkins Loans, Stafford Loans, and PLUS Loans. State scholarships and private grants are also available. The College administers a large student employment program, and most students who demonstrate need are granted an on-campus job as part of their financial aid package. The ratio of grant assistance to loans and work-study aid is sometimes affected by the academic strength of the student's record. Trinity continues to expand its aid budget to keep pace with the College's goal to increase the socioeconomic and ethnic diversity on campus. Forty percent of the students receive financial aid.

Faculty

The distinctive strength of a Trinity education has always been the close interaction between students and a faculty of devoted teacher-scholars. A student-faculty ratio of 10:1 enables supportive yet challenging educational experiences that establish a foundation for lifetime learning and enables students to pursue academic interests with passion. Students have numerous opportunities to collaborate with faculty members in conducting research; many students have made joint presentations at international, national, or local symposia or have published jointly prepared papers. All courses are taught by Trinity faculty members and not by graduate assistants.

Although the first calling of Trinity's professors is teaching, they are also active publishing scholars of national and international distinction. History professor Joan Hedrick, for example, won the Pulitzer Prize for her biography of Harriet Beecher Stowe. Other notable professors include Henry DePhillips, distinguished chemist and researcher on art restoration; Dan Lloyd, acclaimed philosopher and author of *Radiant Cool*; Judy Dworin, accomplished dancer and performance choreographer; Samuel Kassow, distinguished historian; and Joseph Palladino, an authority on biomedical engineering. Trinity professors pride themselves on their accessibility and keen interest in helping students.

Student Government

Trinity fosters the growth of future leaders by providing students with many opportunities to exercise and test their leadership skills. The Student Government Association (SGA), for example, provides students a strong voice in social, cultural, and—through membership on faculty committees—academic matters. Composed of elected class representatives, the SGA constantly seeks the expertise and insights of all interested students, and its committees offer enterprising students many chances to participate and to develop leadership skills.

Admission Requirements

Trinity seeks an ethnically and geographically diverse group of highly motivated students who have completed a rigorous course of study in secondary school and have demonstrated energy, talent, and leadership in a variety of extracurricular activities. Trinity has no specific GPA minimums or test-score cutoffs. The College is highly selective, and its candidates typically have an A– high school average. At least 16 academic units of college-preparatory course work are recommended, including a minimum of 4 years of English, 3 years of foreign language, 2 years of laboratory science, 2 years of algebra, 1 year of geometry, and 2 years of history. Last year, over 7,000 men and women from all over the nation and world applied for admission to the College, which enrolls an entering class of approximately 590 students. Transfer students with a 3.0 GPA in a strong course of study at another accredited college or university are considered for admission to the sophomore or junior classes.

Admissions officers review each application individually; decisions are based on each candidate's academic record (course of study and GPA), recommendations from secondary school teachers and counselors, test scores, personal strengths, talents, activities, and application.

Application and Information

Students must submit completed applications to the Admissions Office. Application deadlines are November 15 for early decision I applicants (with notification by mid-December), January 1 for early decision II applicants (with notification by mid-February), and January 1 for regular decision applicants (with notification by early April). Transfer applicants must submit applications by April 1 for admission in the following fall semester (with notification by mid-June) and by November 15 for admission in the following spring semester (with notification by early January). Prospective students may submit an electronic Common Application at http://www.commonapp.org.

Inquiries should be made to:

Larry Dow
Dean of Admissions and Financial Aid
Admissions Office
Trinity College
Hartford, Connecticut 06106-3100
Phone: 860-297-2180
Fax: 860-297-2287
E-mail: admissions.office@trincoll.edu
Website: http://www.trincoll.edu/admissions
        http://www.facebook.com/trincoll
        http://www.youtube.com/trincoll

The Long Walk at Trinity College. *(Photo by Bob Handelman)*

TRUMAN STATE UNIVERSITY
KIRKSVILLE, MISSOURI

The University

Truman has forged a national reputation for offering an exceptionally high-quality undergraduate education at a competitive price. For the sixteenth consecutive year, *U.S. News & World Report* has ranked Truman as the number one public institution in the Midwest offering bachelor's and master's degrees. In addition, Truman is recognized by *Kiplinger's Personal Finance* as one of the nation's best values in public education.

A commitment to student achievement and learning is at the core of everything Truman does. This commitment is evidenced by faculty and staff members who recognize the importance of providing students with the opportunity to interact with their professors both in and out of the classroom. With class sizes averaging only 24 students and 90 percent having fewer than 40 students, scholars find ample opportunity to ask questions of professors as well as interact with their multitalented peers. Truman's academic environment is enhanced by a student body that achieves at remarkable levels. The 2012 freshman class had an ACT midrange of 25 to 30 and an average GPA of 3.76 on a 4.0 scale. In addition, numerous opportunities exist for students to engage in undergraduate research. Each year, approximately 1,200 students work alongside professors on University research projects, gaining confidence, knowledge, and skill in their chosen disciplines. The University offers these students the opportunity to present the results of their research at the annual Student Research Conference. In addition, selected students travel to the National Undergraduate Research Symposium to present their research findings. Undergraduate research stipends are also available.

Students wishing to attend Truman to become a teacher must first complete a bachelor's degree in an academic discipline and then apply for admission into professional study at the master's level to obtain a Master of Arts in Education (M.A.E). Through this program, certification can be achieved for elementary education, middle school education, secondary education, and special education.

With more than 240 University organizations available to students, encompassing service, Greek, honorary, professional, religious, social, political, and recreational influences, Truman students have tremendous opportunities to become involved while enrolled at the University. Truman's Student Activities Board provides special guests such as Tony La Russa, comic acts such as Donald Glover and Judah Friedlander, and musical artists like B.o.B., Sara Bareilles, and Regina Spektor. In addition, admission to all varsity athletic events, Truman theater productions, and Lyceum Series events is free to Truman students. Recent theater productions have included *Spring Awakening*, *Rebel Voices*, and *Brighton Beach Memoirs*.

Location

Truman is located in Kirksville, a town of approximately 17,000 nestled in the northeast corner of Missouri. The town square, located within walking distance of the Truman campus, provides a connection to Kirksville's past. A multiplex movie theater is located on the town square; local merchants operate specialized gift, book, and clothing stores; and several restaurants offer a wide selection of American and international cuisine.

The Kirksville Aquatic Center is a great place to have fun and get fit. This indoor/outdoor pool complex offers a variety of activities, classes, and programs designed to appeal to people of all ages. The complex includes a six-lane indoor swimming pool, perfect for swimming, relaxing, or playing a game of water-basketball. The outdoor pool is designed with a zero-depth entry, a 1-meter diving board, and four 25-yard outdoor lap lanes as well as a 20-foot water slide.

The northeast region of Missouri is also home to Thousand Hills State Park. A 3,252-acre state park and 573-acre lake for camping, hiking, biking, fishing, swimming, boating, and waterskiing is located within 10 minutes of the Truman campus.

Majors and Degrees

Undergraduate degrees offered by Truman include the Bachelor of Arts (B.A.), Bachelor of Science (B.S.), Bachelor of Music: Performance (B.M.), Bachelor of Fine Arts (B.F.A.), and Bachelor of Science in Nursing (B.S.N.). Truman offers more than forty areas of study in the following disciplines: accounting, agricultural science, athletic training, art, art history, biology, business administration, chemistry, classics, communication, communication disorders, computer science, creative writing, economics, English, exercise science, French, German, health science, history, interdisciplinary studies, justice systems, linguistics, mathematics, music, music: performance, nursing, philosophy and religion, physics, political science, psychology, Romance languages, Russian, sociology/anthropology, Spanish, and theatre.

Professional paths include but are not limited to dentistry, engineering, law, medicine, optometry, pharmacy, physical therapy, and veterinary medicine.

Academic Programs

Truman is Missouri's premier liberal arts and sciences university and the only highly selective public institution in the state. The Liberal Studies Program is the heart of Truman's curriculum and is intended to serve as a foundation for all major programs of study offered by the University. Truman's mission is to offer an exemplary undergraduate education, grounded in the liberal arts and sciences, in the context of a public institution of higher learning. Truman seeks to provide the kind of education in the liberal arts and sciences that has historically been offered only at private colleges. The program is a blend of two intellectual traditions in higher education, one that emphasizes the traditional thought and learning of the culture, as reflected in the classical works produced by it, and the other that emphasizes personal investigation and freedom of discovery. The philosophy behind the Liberal Studies Program is based on a commitment that Truman has made to provide students with essential skills needed for lifelong learning, breadth across the traditional liberal arts and sciences through exposure to various discipline-based modes of inquiry, and interconnecting perspectives that stress interdisciplinary thinking and integration as well as linkage to other cultures and experiences. All students graduating from Truman must complete 63 or more credit hours in liberal arts and sciences courses.

Truman also offers an especially challenging Honors Scholar Program. This program provides students with the opportunity to select the most rigorous honors courses to satisfy the liberal arts component of their respective programs. Students who successfully complete this program benefit from an even richer academic experience and also receive special recognition at graduation and distinction on their academic transcripts. Departmental honors are also available in several disciplines.

Off-Campus Programs

Each year, approximately 400 Truman students participate in enriching and life-changing study-abroad experiences. Truman's own study-abroad programs, combined with programs offered through Truman's membership in the College Consortium for International Studies, International Student Exchange Program, AustraLearn, and the Council on International Educational Exchange, provide students with study-abroad opportunities in more than sixty countries worldwide, including Australia, China, England, Finland, France, Italy, Russia, Spain, and Thailand.

In cooperation with the Washington Center for Internships and Academic Seminars, Truman offers a wide variety of experiential internships in Washington, D.C. Included are work-experience opportunities in such areas as public administration, the fine and performing arts, foreign affairs/diplomacy, government affairs, criminal justice, international relations, health and human services, environmental policy, business administration, and communications as well as other areas. Placement sites include nonprofit groups, media organizations, the State Department, Congress, museums, and much more.

Truman requires internships in education, health science, and exercise science and annually offers internship opportunities with the Missouri State Legislature. In recent years, students have completed internships with United States senators, the governor of Missouri, business and industry managers, zoos, broadcast and print media professionals, accountants, advertising agencies, physical therapists, musicians, artists, and the United States Supreme Court.

Academic Facilities

The Truman campus is beautifully situated on an expanse of 140 acres near downtown Kirksville. Featured among the forty facilities on campus is Pickler Memorial Library. This 460,116-volume facility provides a state-of-the-art library resource for students and faculty members alike. Materials not available in Pickler Memorial Library can be obtained through the Interlibrary Loan Office and MOBIUS.

Recent improvements to campus facilities include the expansion of the Pershing Building with the new health sciences wing, which was completed for the fall 2011 semester. Facility improvements included the new Fontaine C. Piper Movement Analysis Lab, a human performance lab, an expanded clinic for communication disorders, athletic training rooms, and a brand-new nursing simulation center. The renovations to the Student Union Building were completed in 2008 with an expanded Center for Student Involvement, new technology, mural restoration, and a completely renovated university bookstore.

The West Campus Suites opened to students in 2006. Each suite is equipped with a living room, two bedrooms housing 2 students each, closet space, a large bathroom, and central air conditioning. Renovations have been completed on Missouri Hall. Improvements included a 2,500-square-foot addition, laundry facilities on every floor, and individually controlled heating and cooling in each room. Renovations are also complete on Blanton/Nason/Brewer, Dobson Hall, and Ryle Hall, which was finished in 2011.

Additional campus facilities include a student media center with a TV studio, a radio station, print media production facilities, a biofeedback laboratory, an organic chemistry lab, an analytical chemistry lab, an observatory, a greenhouse, a 5,000-seat football stadium, a soccer field, tennis courts, softball and baseball diamonds, a 3,000-seat arena with three basketball courts, an Olympic-size swimming pool, a multicultural affairs center, a writing center, a student success center, and a career center.

Costs

Tuition for Missouri residents for the 2012–13 academic year was $6,978; out-of-state tuition was $12,714. Room and board totals for both Missouri residents and nonresidents start at $7,040. Additional fees included a $315 freshman orientation fee, an annual $84 activities fee, a $54 Student Health Center fee, an annual $100 athletic fee, a $105 parking fee for those with a vehicle, and the costs of books and personal expenses.

Financial Aid

Truman offers automatic scholarships ranging from $500 to $5,000. Competitive scholarship awards vary from $500 up to full tuition, room and board, plus a $4,000 study-abroad stipend. The application for admission also serves as the application for the automatic and competitive scholarship programs.

Several scholarships are awarded to students for excellence in music, theatre, debate/forensics, or art. These scholarships are available for instrumental, strings, or vocal music; acting or dramatic production; speech or debate; and studio art or art history. Of special interest to piano students is the Truman Piano Fellowship Competition.

The National Collegiate Athletic Association and the University authorize a limited number of grants to outstanding athletes. The value of this aid may vary with each individual recipient.

Truman accepts the Free Application for Federal Student Aid (FAFSA) and participates in all Federal Title IV financial aid programs. Financial aid estimates are available upon request.

Faculty

Truman State University is committed to teaching the academically talented undergraduate student. The University has 316 full-time faculty members and 57 part-time faculty members. Of these, 98 percent teach undergraduates and graduate teaching assistants only teach 1 percent of classes. Most major graduate institutions are represented among the Truman faculty, including Harvard, Princeton, Yale, Brown, Cornell, Oxford, and the Sorbonne. The student-faculty ratio at Truman is 16:1.

Student Government

Student Senate is the official elected governing body of the Student Association, representing approximately 5,800 students. Its mission is to represent the views of the Student Association in the formulation of the University policy through legislation and membership on all University committees; to facilitate communication and mutual understanding among the Student Association, faculty and staff members, and administration; to maintain a cohesive vision for the future of the University; and to actively participate in the fulfillment of the University's mission as an exemplary public liberal arts and sciences university.

Admission Requirements

Admission to Truman is competitive. Each applicant is evaluated for admission based upon academic and cocurricular record, ACT or SAT results, and the admission essay. Truman requires the following high school core: 4 units of English, 3 units of mathematics (4 recommended), 3 units of social studies/history, 3 units of natural science, 1 unit of fine arts, and 2 units of the same foreign language.

Application and Information

The priority deadline for admission is December 1. Students who have applied by this date are considered for all applicable competitive scholarships. Applications are processed on a rolling basis. There is no application fee. Students may apply online at the University's website.

For further information or to schedule a campus visit, students should contact:

Admission Office
Ruth W. Towne Museum and Visitors Center
Truman State University
100 East Normal
Kirksville, Missouri 63501
Phone: 660-785-4114
      800-892-7792
Fax: 660-785-7456
E-mail: admissions@truman.edu
Website: http://admissions.truman.edu

Bulldog football takes the field!

UNION COLLEGE
SCHENECTADY, NEW YORK

UNION
COLLEGE

FOUNDED 1795

The College

Chartered by the state of New York in 1795, Union College is one of the nation's oldest and most distinguished liberal arts colleges. A four-year, independent residential college serving approximately 2,200 undergraduate men and women, Union is known for its academic rigor, flexible programs, and close-knit community.

True to its 200-year tradition of innovation, the Union curriculum offers a multitude of academic and intellectual options. There is an increasing emphasis on interdepartmental and interdisciplinary programs that blend liberal arts with science and engineering in a way that encourages students to think creatively, ethically, and entrepreneurially. In 2012, 64 percent of Union students major in the arts, humanities, and social sciences, with 36 percent majoring in the sciences and engineering.

Originally all-male, the College became coeducational in 1970; today approximately half of Union's students are women. In the 2012–13 first-year class, approximately 19 percent of students self-identify as members of a multicultural group; 7 percent are international students. Students come from thirty-seven countries and thirty-seven states and U.S. territories.

The international experience is a hallmark of a Union education, with nearly 60 percent of students pursuing studies, research, internships, and other programs abroad. On campus, opportunities for leadership, discussion, and community abound in the Minerva system, offering residential, academic, and social programs. Every incoming student is assigned to one of seven Minerva Houses, which also involve faculty and staff.

There are more than 100 student organizations, ten residential Greek organizations, and more than a dozen theme houses centered around such common interests as the arts, cooking, language studies, literature, LGBTQ issues, music, and religious diversity. Cultural events include concerts, theater, dance, and film, as well as art exhibits at the Mandeville Gallery, Wikoff Student Gallery, and Burns Arts Atrium. About 89 percent of all students live in residence halls or college-owned houses, including traditional dorms, Minerva Houses, fraternity and sorority houses, townhouses, and College Park Hall. The Kenney Community Center is Union's headquarters for volunteering as well as a hub for activism and leadership. It connects students with organizations such as America Reads, Big Brothers Big Sisters, City Mission, Habitat for Humanity, Hospice, and numerous other tutoring programs, anti-hunger and anti-poverty groups, and civic projects.

Union's comprehensive athletics program offers twenty-six varsity intercollegiate teams; fifty-five men's, women's, and coed intramural and club sports; and other recreational, wellness, and fitness activities. Union is a Division III school with Division I men's and women's ice hockey. It is a member of the NCAA, the Liberty League, and ECAC Hockey.

The Becker Career Center helps students with career planning, internships, and the graduate school and job search. Recent trends show that about a third of graduating seniors go directly to graduate or professional schools, and Union has earned an excellent reputation for placing graduates in medical, law, and business schools. Union's more than 22,000 alumni include U.S. President Chester A. Arthur (Class of 1848); U.S. Secretary of State William Henry Seward (Class of 1820); Nobel Prize, National Book Award, and MacArthur genius award winners; Olympic medalists; and pioneers in business, engineering, entertainment, journalism, law, and medicine.

Location

Union is set on 100 acres in Schenectady, an historic city of 62,000 founded by the Dutch. In 1813, Union became the first unified campus in America with a distinctive design by noted French architect Joseph Jacques Ramée. Its centerpiece is the sixteen-sided Nott Memorial, a National Historic Landmark used for study, symposia, exhibits, and special events.

Schenectady is a small urban environment that is reinventing itself after the decline of traditional industries. It is part of Upstate New York's picturesque Capital-Saratoga Region, with nearly 1 million residents. The region includes the state capital, Albany, and has a rich cultural heritage and a burgeoning high-tech industry. As "Tech Valley," the area is home to GE, with its emphasis on alternative energy and Global Foundries, a fast-growing semiconductor company. Tech Valley offers a variety of opportunities for internships, job placements, and student/faculty research.

A 15-minute drive from Albany International Airport, Union College is 3 hours by car from New York City and Boston, 4 hours from Montreal, and close to East Coast ski slopes and the Adirondack Mountains.

In 2011, Union strengthened its historic relationship with the Adirondacks by purchasing the former home of conservationist Paul Schaefer, located in nearby Niskayuna. Now known as the Kelly Adirondack Center at Union College, it houses the Adirondack Research Library, the largest collection on the Adirondacks outside of the Adirondack Park. The Kelly Center offers many programs and opportunities to advance Union's understanding of the mountains, wilderness and waterways of this tremendous natural resource.

Majors and Degrees

Union offers more than forty majors as well as double majors; combined majors and minors; interdepartmental and multidisciplinary concentrations; and area, ethnic, and cultural studies programs. The self-designed Organizing Theme major is for the student with intellectual curiosity in a particular topic involving multiple disciplines. Most students take three courses in each of the three 10-week terms that comprise Union's trimester system. The average introductory class has 18 students; the average upper-level class, 15.

Most of Union's newest majors, such as bioengineering, neuroscience, and religious studies, and minors, such as computational methods and Jewish studies, encourage learning at the intersection of the liberal arts and sciences. Among the courses that cross traditional disciplinary boundaries are The Illustrated Organism, a class for artists and scientists, and New Wall of China, offered through the departments of Modern Languages and Literatures, and Environmental Science, Policy and Engineering. Union's Internal Education Foundation provides funding for special, innovative projects.

Union offers Bachelor of Arts (B.A.) and Bachelor of Science (B.S.) degrees. Students may declare up to two minors. Union also offers an eight-year leadership in medicine program (LIM) with Albany Medical College and Union Graduate College; a six-year law and public policy program with Albany Law School (B.A. and J.D.); and five-year bachelor's/M.B.A. or bachelor's/M.A.T. programs with Union Graduate College. The fourteen academic honor societies include Phi Beta Kappa, the first chapter established in New York (1817).

Academic Programs

Nearly every academic department requires students to complete some form of research in their subject area, and students have opportunities to work one-on-one with their professors. They often co-author publications and present at conferences, such as the National Conference on Undergraduate Research (NCUR). Many participate in internships at businesses, hospitals, and social service organizations. The Steinmetz Symposium showcases the work of hundreds of student researchers through oral, dance, music, art, and poster sessions each spring.

The Campus Wide Computation Initiative, part of a National Science Foundation grant, helps students integrate computation into various fields of study. Through the Michael Rapaport ('59) Ethics Across the Curriculum initiative, faculty members from different departments offer courses that provide extensive training in everyday ethics. Writing Across the Curriculum requires all students to take five designated courses from at least two divisions and one Senior Writing Experience. The First-Year Preceptorial (FYP), a mandatory interdisciplinary course for first-year students, emphasizes critical reading and thinking skills, writing, speaking, and gender and cultural diversity. The Sophomore Research Seminar (SRS), also required, promotes research and writing skills. The Senior Thesis or Capstone Project encourages students to research, prepare and design their own project around an issue or problem or interest.

Off-Campus Programs

Nearly 60 percent of all Union students go abroad. Most programs are led by Union faculty. Many programs combine elements of entrepreneurship, research, or community service. There are also opportunities for extended terms, formal exchanges, research trips, and independent study. Three-week mini-terms, for 1 credit, are offered during winter and summer in various U.S. cities and countries. Many students get involved in continuing hurricane relief efforts in New Orleans. The Civil Rights Public History Mini-Term explores the American Civil Rights Movement in key cities and states. The newest mini-terms include Bali, Russia, Senegal, Diversity of the Adirondacks, Holocaust History, and Restoring Jewish Cemeteries.

Academic Facilities

Union's nearly 100 buildings include the F.W. Olin Center, which features interactive computerization capabilities that make the building adaptable for use by nearly every academic department. The Science and Engineering Center houses the Center for Bioengineering and Computational Biology. Here, students can use sophisticated research tools such as a nuclear magnetic resonance spectrometer, a Pelletron accelerator, a centrifuge, and a scanning electron microscope. The College's Center for Neuroscience is located in Butterfield Hall. Opened in 2012, it includes five research laboratories, faculty space, and research training areas for this growing interdisciplinary program.

Schaffer Library has 617,945 volumes, 786 current periodicals (paper), and 9,267 electronic subscriptions. There are also 300 databases that provide access to a quarter-million printed books, documents, and scores. Flanking the library are the humanities building and the revamped social sciences building, Lippman Hall. Featuring advanced technology and designed to promote faculty-student interaction, Lippman Hall is home to the departments of economics, history, political science, and sociology, and the religious studies program.

The $22-million Peter Irving Wold Science and Engineering Center, opened in 2011, is a home for interdisciplinary studies across departments. The Wold Center's laboratories are dedicated to energy and environmental engineering, electrical engineering and music research, renewable energy systems, biochemistry, aerogel fabrication, and robotics. In addition, the Kelly Advanced Computing Lab houses the IBM High-Performance Computing Cluster, which offers some of the most advanced computing capabilities among the nation's undergraduate liberal arts schools.

The Arts Building, located in North Colonnade, includes the Burns Atrium, where work by students, faculty, and alumni is exhibited. The Taylor Music Center includes the Fred L. Emerson Auditorium, an all-Steinway performance and teaching space with state-of-the-art recording technology. The Yulman Theater is home to Mountebanks, the country's oldest student performing group. The Henle Dance Pavilion, slated to open in May 2013, overlooks Jackson's Garden and features classrooms, rehearsal and performance spaces, a costume shop, meeting rooms, and a gallery. The newly constructed Wicker Wellness Center, scheduled to open in 2014, will offer a comprehensive array of health, wellness, and counseling services.

Costs

Union's tuition for the 2013–14 academic year is $46,314; room and board are $11,463; and mandatory fees are $471. The estimated cost for books and personal expenses is $1,900.

Financial Aid

Union is committed to admitting an economically diverse student body and to meeting the full demonstrated need of all admitted students. The College offers $38 million annually in aid. The average Union need-based scholarship is $29,000; the average merit award is $10,000. Those families that are unable to pay full tuition and fees are typically covered by a financial aid package consisting of a grant, loan, and work opportunity. About half of all applicants apply for financial aid; more than 60 percent of all students receive financial assistance from the College.

Candidates for aid should complete the Free Application for Federal Student Aid (FAFSA) and the College Scholarship Service's PROFILE form and mail them directly to the appropriate agencies by February 1. For more information, prospective students should visit http://www.union.edu/Admissions/index.php.

Faculty

Close student-faculty interaction and small classes are a hallmark of the Union experience. The close relationship between students and faculty motivates students to learn through inquiry and discourse. Excluding library staff, 98 percent of the faculty members hold a doctorate or terminal degree. Class size is generally small, with a 10:1 student-faculty ratio. Many upper-level courses function as seminars.

Student Government

Students play an integral role in directing the present and future course of Union. With full voting rights on the two councils that recommend changes to educational policy and student life, students are engaged and active leaders on campus. Students also participate in groups that advise the President on matters like budgetary planning and long-range needs. Each year, two students are elected to membership on the College's Board of Trustees. Opportunities for leadership also abound with the Minerva houses, theme houses, Kenney Community Center, and other clubs.

Admission Requirements

Roughly 5,000 applicants seek first-year class positions on an annual basis; approximately 60 percent are in the top 10 percent of their secondary school class. In evaluating each application, admissions counselors look at the prospective student's grades, rigor of courses taken, class rank, teacher recommendations, and extracurricular involvement. Typically, 16 units of secondary school preparation are required for admission. These should include credits in certain fundamental subjects, such as English, a foreign language, mathematics, social studies, and science. It is strongly recommended that students visit Union for an admission interview and a student-guided tour. Alumni interviews may be requested online.

A student can choose not to submit his or her SAT or ACT scores for review, except for accelerated programs. Those interested in accelerated programs must submit the SAT and two SAT Subject Tests.

Application and Information

Early decision candidates have two options. The application deadline (including all supporting credentials) for Option I is November 15, with notification by December 15. Option II has a January 15 deadline (including all supporting credentials) and February 15 notification. Applications for regular decision admission must be filed by January 15, with decisions mailed by April 1.

Applications to the leadership in medicine program are due no later than December 15. Those for the law and public policy program must be filed no later than January 1. Those deferred under early decision and all regular applicants are given a final decision by April 1. Union adheres to the Candidates Reply Date of May 1.

Office of Admissions
Grant Hall
Union College
Schenectady, New York 12308
Phone: 518-388-6112
Fax: 518-388-6986
E-mail: admissions@union.edu
Website: http://www.union.edu

The sixteen-sided Nott Memorial is Union College's centerpiece.

UNION UNIVERSITY
JACKSON, TENNESSEE

The University

Union University is committed to renewing minds and reclaiming the great Christian intellectual tradition. Students benefit from more than 100 programs of study that are academically challenging as well as Christ-centered. This private, four-year, liberal arts–based university was founded in 1823 and is affiliated with the Tennessee Baptist Convention.

Excellence-driven, Christ-centered, people-focused, and future-directed are Union's four core values.

Union has consistently received national recognition for academic excellence, value, and community service. *U.S. News & World Report* again has ranked Union among the top 15 regional universities in the South. Union has been listed among the top-tier schools in the South every year since 1997. Union was listed among only forty-seven schools nationwide "where the faculty has an unusually strong commitment to undergraduate teaching." It was the fourth consecutive year Union appeared on that list. For the fifth straight year, the publication listed Union among forty-six up-and-coming schools in the nation that "have recently made the most promising and innovative changes in the areas of academics, faculty, student life, campus, or facilities." Also for the fifth straight year, Union was selected as an "A-Plus School for B Students" in the South. Union's freshman retention rate of 91 percent was tied for highest among regional universities in the South.

America's 100 Best College Buys ranks Union among the nation's best for combining academic quality and affordable price.

Union has been named to the President's Higher Education Community Service Honor Roll every year since the award was established in 2006.

More than 4,200 undergraduate and graduate students from forty-four states and thirty-three countries are represented in the student body.

Union provides each resident student with a private bedroom within apartment-style complexes, most of which were built in recent years. Four students share an apartment, which has Internet connection, a kitchen, living room, washer/dryer unit, and two bathrooms.

A new student commons building features two fireplaces, TV and multipurpose rooms, piano and band practice rooms, two kitchens, a gymnasium, a walking track, and outdoor grills and patios. The University coffeehouse is another favorite student destination for concerts, conversation, and study.

Union offers more than fifty major student-produced music and theater events each year. The University has sixty campus clubs, societies, fraternities, sororities, and other organizations. Students enjoy varsity and intramural sports and community service activities. In addition, students and faculty set aside at least one day a year to serve the local community though more than fifty different volunteer projects.

Union graduates enjoy a high acceptance rate at top graduate and law schools. Nearly 100 percent of faculty-recommended health science students have been accepted to medical school or professional graduate study. More than 80 percent of all graduates are accepted by graduate schools or employed, some with Fortune 500 companies, within a month of receiving their degrees. Nearly 77 percent of Union seniors plan to complete postgraduate work.

In 2011 the National Collegiate Athletic Association approved Union University's application to begin the transition to NCAA Division II affiliation. Union now competes in the prestigious Gulf South Conference, one of the premier conferences in Division II; it expects to be eligible for postseason play in 2014–15, upon successful completion of the transition process.

Location

Union is located in Jackson, Tennessee, a growing community 80 miles east of Memphis and 120 miles west of Nashville along the I-40 corridor. The Jackson area has a population of about 100,000. Students find convenient access to entertainment, shopping, and other services. Jackson hosts many cultural, recreational, and sporting events. Daily commercial flights are available at airports in Memphis and Nashville; commuter air service is available between those cities and Jackson.

Majors and Degrees

Undergraduate students can choose majors from among the following programs of study: art (ceramics, digital media studies, drawing, graphic design, painting, photography, sculpture); biology (general, cell and molecular biology, zoology, conservation biology); business administration (accounting, actuarial science, business administration, economics, international business, management, management for non-business professionals, marketing); chemistry (biochemistry, chemical physics, chemistry, medical technology); communication arts (advertising, broadcast journalism, digital media studies, film studies, journalism, media communications, photojournalism, public relations, speech, theater and speech, theater); computer science (computer information systems, computer science, digital media studies, information technology); education (elementary education, learning foundations, grades pre K–3, K–6, 4–8, special education modified, comprehensive, teacher licensure K–12 and secondary areas); engineering (electrical, mechanical); English (creative writing, literature); history; honors (general honors, discipline-specific honors); international and intercultural studies (global studies, humanitarian studies, regional studies, study abroad); language (applied linguistics, French, Spanish, teaching English as a second language); mathematics (actuarial science, mathematics); music (church music, Christian studies, communication arts, music management, music marketing, music education, band, choral, music theory, performance, organ, piano, voice); nursing; physical education, wellness and sport (athletic training, athletic coaching, health education, physical education, sport management, communication, marketing, ministry, sports medicine and wellness); physics (engineering physics, physical science, physics); political science; psychology; social work; sociology (family studies, sociology); theology and missions (Biblical studies languages, Christian ministry and missions, Christian studies, Christian thought and tradition, philosophy, sport ministry). Pre-professional programs include chiropractics, cytotechnology, dentistry, dental hygiene, health information management, medicine, occupational therapy, optometry, pharmacy, physical therapy, physician assistant studies, podiatry, and veterinary medicine.

Teacher licensure and discipline-specific honors are available for many of these areas of study.

Academic Programs

A Union University education is widely known for integrating faith and learning. Students are encouraged to move toward a mature reflection of what the truths of Christian faith mean in every field of study. Undergraduates are given research opportunities through the Scholarship Symposium and other programs.

The Honors Community is made up of serious-minded students who are eager to make the most of their college education, and faculty members who know them on a first-name basis. Honors courses are designed to stretch a student as a thinker, a reader, and a writer with the support and guidance of faculty across the disciplines.

Union's acclaimed Keystone Program offers academic support for students who may fall short of some minimum admission requirements. The program provides these students with the necessary tools to progress academically, with many achieving a level of success they may not have thought possible.

Union's academic calendar is divided into fall (August to December) and spring (February to May) semesters, January term, and three summer terms. Evening accelerated courses are available each term.

Off-Campus Programs

Students from a variety of academic areas participate in internships with regional and national companies. Study abroad includes destinations such as Belgium, China, Costa Rica, France, Great Britain, Italy, Jordan, Mexico, Poland, and Spain. Union students also have the opportunity to go on short-term mission Global Outreach trips to locations in Africa, Asia, Central America, Europe, and the United States.

Academic Facilities

Union's wooded campus features about forty academic and residence buildings and excellent athletic facilities. More than $120 million in new campus construction has been completed during the past decade, including several new Georgian-Colonial classroom buildings that support top-level teaching and research facilities. Pharmacy, science, and nursing students benefit from state-of-the-art laboratories and simulation environments. Communication students produce a daily live news program in the University's HD television studio. Other academic amenities include top-quality lecture facilities; fine and performing arts practice rooms and recital halls; theaters; digital media labs; and biology, chemistry, physics, and engineering laboratories.

Plans for construction of a new library building are under way. Adjacent to classroom buildings and residence complexes, the new library is designed to meet the research and technology needs of the twenty-first century scholar. The current library houses open stacks as well as periodicals, microfilm and microfiche, archives, and electronic resources. Students also have easy access to the combined collections of more than 41,000 libraries worldwide. The Stephen Olford Center library and the R. C. Ryan Center for Biblical Studies library house several unique collections and are also available to students.

Union provides three large computer labs on the Jackson campus for student use. Each residential student has a port for the campus network and Internet access. Wireless access is available in many areas. Additional computer labs are specialized for use by various academic programs.

Costs

The annual cost for a full-time student for the 2012–13 academic year was $24,940 for tuition (up to 16 hours per semester) and $8,430 for housing and meals (100 meals per semester). Prices for housing and meals may vary slightly according to a student's preferences.

Financial Aid

More than 90 percent of Union students receive some financial aid based on need or merit. Union awards competitive scholarships and grants to qualified students. The University helps connect students with other financial resources such as loans, student-work programs, privately funded scholarships, and a host of state and federal assistance programs.

Faculty

Union University invests in faculty members who are experts in their fields and committed to excellence in teaching, advising, and mentoring. These faculty members put a priority on classroom teaching, but also join students in the pursuit of significant research, especially at the undergraduate level. Eighty-four percent of the faculty members hold doctorates or the highest degree offered in their field of study. The student-faculty ratio is 11:1, and all classes are taught by faculty members.

Student Government

Union's Student Government Association functions through its executive, legislative, and judicial branches. Its elected officers and representatives serve as the official voice of the students in institutional matters.

Admission Requirements

Applicants must graduate from an accredited high school with at least 20 units in the areas of English, foreign language, mathematics, social and natural sciences, and approved electives. In addition, students who qualify for unconditional admission must meet or exceed two of the following three admissions criteria: a 2.5 core GPA, a composite score of 22 on the ACT or 1020 (math and critical reading combined) on the SAT, and a ranking in the top 50 percent of their high school class. A state high school equivalency diploma is accepted in lieu of a high school diploma. Union also actively seeks to admit home-schooled students.

Transfer students who have completed at least 24 semester hours of transferable credit at an accredited college may also apply. Transfer students with less than 24 semester hours must meet freshman and transfer admission requirements.

Application and Information

Applicants must complete and return the Union University application for undergraduate admission along with the $35 application fee. All official transcripts and results of either the ACT or SAT must be requested and mailed directly to the Office of Undergraduate Admissions. Applications are accepted and decisions rendered on a rolling basis.

For more information or to request an application, students should contact:

Office of Undergraduate Admissions
Union University
1050 Union University Drive
Jackson, Tennessee 38305-3697
Phone: 731-661-5100
    800-33-UNION (toll-free)
E-mail: info@uu.edu
Website: www.uu.edu
    www.uu.edu/apply

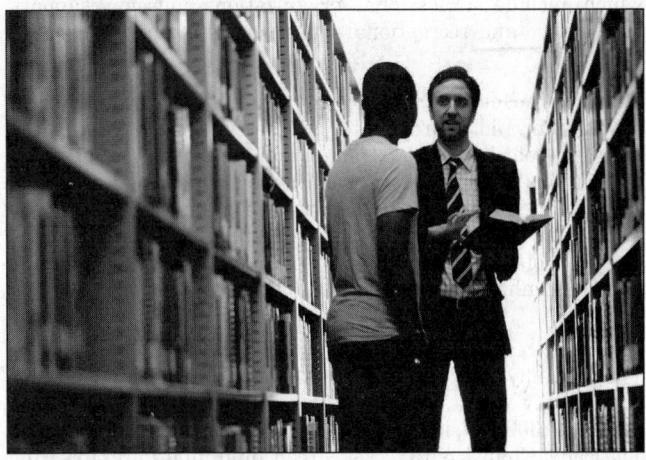

More than 4,200 undergraduate and graduate students come to Union University from 44 states and 33 countries.

UNITED STATES AIR FORCE ACADEMY
COLORADO SPRINGS, COLORADO

U.S. AIR FORCE
ACADEMY

The Academy

Established in 1954, the Air Force Academy prepares and motivates cadets for careers as Air Force officers. The Academy stresses character development, military training, and physical fitness as well as academics, emphasizing leadership in all areas.

The total enrollment is approximately 4,000; nearly 1,000 fourth-class (freshman) students enter each year. The composition of the student body mirrors that of the Air Force officer corps: about 23 percent women and 26 percent minorities. Students come from all 50 states and several other countries. Their common bond is the desire to be military officers. All cadets must live in on-campus dormitories and wear uniforms.

The Academy is accredited by the North Central Association of Colleges and Schools. Its engineering programs are approved by the Engineering Accreditation Commission of the Accreditation Board for Engineering and Technology, and its computer courses are approved by the Computing Sciences Accreditation Board. The chemistry and biochemistry majors fulfill the requirements of the Commission on Professional Training of the American Chemical Society.

All cadets must participate in intramural, club, or intercollegiate athletics every semester. The intramural sports include basketball, boxing (men's), cross-country, flag football, flickerball, rugby (men's and women's), soccer, softball, team handball, tennis, Ultimate (Frisbee), volleyball, and wallyball. The intercollegiate teams compete in Division I of the NCAA regionally and nationally. The men's teams include baseball, basketball, boxing, cheerleading, cross-country, diving, fencing, football, golf, gymnastics, hockey, indoor and outdoor track, lacrosse, rifle, soccer, swimming, tennis, water polo, and wrestling. The women's teams include basketball, cheerleading, cross-country, diving, fencing, gymnastics, indoor and outdoor track, rifle, soccer, swimming, tennis, and volleyball. Cadets may also choose from more than 80 extracurricular activities, which include professional organizations, mission support, competitive and recreational clubs, sports groups, and hobby clubs.

Qualified Academy graduates may enter flight training upon graduation, and approximately 75 percent of the students in each graduating class pursue graduate education at other institutions within 10 years of their graduation. Each year, numerous Academy graduates receive graduate scholarships and fellowships, such as the Marshall, Rhodes, National Science Foundation, National Collegiate Athletic Association, and Guggenheim awards.

Location

The Academy campus sits in the foothills of the Rampart Range of the Rocky Mountains in a setting of natural beauty. Built on a mesa at 7,300 feet, it is one of Colorado's top tourist attractions. The Cadet Chapel, with its seventeen aluminum spires towering 150 feet into the air, highlights the contemporary architecture of the buildings in the cadet area. The space-age effect reflects the Academy's mission of preparing cadets to become officers and leaders in the Air Force of the future. The Academy borders the northern edge of Colorado Springs, which lies at the foot of the famous 14,100-foot Pikes Peak. Colorado Springs has a metropolitan population of more than 500,000. Denver, the state's capital, has a population of almost 2.5 million in its greater metropolitan area and is located 55 miles north of the Academy. In addition to the social, sports, and cultural activities available in these cities, cadets enjoy skiing, hunting, horseback riding, white-water rafting, and other activities in the Colorado Rocky Mountains and nearby resorts.

Majors and Degrees

Graduates of the four-year service academy receive the Bachelor of Science (B.S.) degree and a commission as second lieutenants in the Air Force. The B.S. is granted in aeronautical engineering, astronautical engineering, basic sciences, behavioral sciences, biology, chemistry, civil engineering, computer engineering, computer science, economics, electrical engineering, English, environmental engineering, foreign area studies, general engineering, geospatial science, history, humanities, legal studies, management, mathematical sciences, mechanical engineering, meteorology, military strategic studies, operations research, philosophy, physics, political science, social sciences, space operations, systems engineering, and systems engineering management. The Academy also offers minors in foreign languages, philosophy, and religion studies.

Academic Programs

A class enters the Academy during the last week in June or the first week in July. Incoming cadets undergo a strenuous 38-day summer training program that tests both their mental and physical abilities. Upperclass cadets conduct basic cadet training; commissioned officers serve as advisers. Basic cadets who complete this program are accepted into the Cadet Wing as fourth-class cadets. The academic year starts in early August and continues through May. During the first two years, cadets concentrate on core courses in engineering, humanities, science, and social science. During the last two years, they specialize in an academic major.

The required core courses prepare cadets for a broad scope of activity as Air Force officers. The core curriculum embraces courses in academic subjects, leadership and military training, and physical education and athletics. In addition, cadets complete the requirements for any of the academic majors. To be eligible for graduation, cadets must also demonstrate an aptitude for commissioned service and leadership, demonstrate character consistent with professional military service, maintain a minimum cumulative grade point average and core grade point average of 2.0, and complete a minimum of 141 credit hours. The curriculum includes many elective courses.

All students must begin as freshmen; however, cadets who have taken some of the core course material prior to entry into the Academy may receive transfer or validation credit for this work. They may then substitute other courses for those granted transfer credit. Cadets who maintain the required grade point average may take advanced study classes.

The Academy aviation program familiarizes all cadets with operational activities of the Air Force. Optional courses provide instruction in soaring, parachuting, navigation, and basic flying. Those who take these courses may fulfill the requirements for

Federal Aviation Administration pilot or glider certificates. Cadets who qualify and are selected for pilot or navigator training may enter Air Education and Training Command flight programs following graduation from the Academy. Diversified summer programs in aviation and military training prepare cadets for officer responsibilities in the Air Force. Cadets may select their programs from several optional assignments at the Air Force Academy and other military installations.

Off-Campus Programs

Selected cadets may exchange visits with cadets from the Military Academy, Naval Academy, Coast Guard Academy, or one of several international Air Force academies. The exchange program varies from one to two weeks for most of the international programs to a semester for the other U.S. service academies and the Canadian, Chilean, French, German, and Spanish Air Force academies, to name a few.

Academic Facilities

The Air Force Academy's excellent facilities support the academic, military, and athletics programs. Most classrooms accommodate small class sessions, averaging 17 students. Several classes and assemblies meet in larger lecture halls. Well-equipped laboratories supplement classroom instruction. Cadets conduct experiments using the aeronautics laboratory's wind tunnels, shock tubes, and rocket engines. A local network connects every dorm room, faculty and staff office, classroom, and laboratory at the Academy, and all entering cadets purchase notebook computers for academic and personal use. The Academy library, with more than 1.5 million volumes, supports all educational programs and maintains a collection of historical materials concerning aeronautics.

Costs

There are no tuition charges; the cost, including room, board, and medical and dental care, is borne entirely by the U.S. government in exchange for a commitment to serve. In addition, cadets receive a monthly salary to pay for supplies, clothing, and personal expenses. Careful management of the money covers obligations, with a small amount remaining for personal use.

Financial Aid

All cadets are on full scholarship at the Air Force Academy, as described above.

Faculty

The Academy's faculty is composed of Air Force officers and civilian professors. A few officers from other branches of the U.S. Armed Forces, those from allied nations, and distinguished civilian visiting professors supplement the faculty. There are no graduate student instructors. Faculty members must have a master's degree, and many have earned doctorates. Their educational backgrounds represent many outstanding colleges and universities in the United States, as well as some international institutions of higher education. Faculty members sponsor, coach, and referee extracurricular activities and athletics; adopt squadrons and attend their special events; and provide academic, career, and personal counseling.

Student Government

The Air Force Academy trains cadets for future leadership by allowing them to hold positions of responsibility in the Cadet Wing, the organization to which all cadets are assigned. The wing is under the operational supervision of first-class cadets (seniors). They hold cadet officer rank and command the wing and the subordinate units of groups, squadrons, flights, and elements. Through this organization, upperclass cadets are responsible for military training of the underclasses, the honor education and honor system, character development, and ethics and human relations programs.

Admission Requirements

Each year, young men and women who are U.S. citizens may be appointed from all states and territories of the nation. Citizens of other countries are admitted in limited numbers. Applicants must be at least 17 and not yet 23 years of age on July 1 of the year in which they desire to be admitted, be unmarried, have no dependents, and be of high moral character. They must be in good physical health.

Applicants must receive an official nomination. Members of Congress make the majority of the nominations for residents of their states and districts. Senators and representatives nominate young men and women who have excelled academically in high school, have demonstrated leadership potential through school activities, are physically fit, are respected by associates, and want to pursue military careers. Applicants need not know their member of Congress personally. Students may be eligible in nomination categories other than congressional. Students should ask high school counselors or Air Force Admissions Liaison Officers about other categories and apply for nominations in all categories for which they are eligible.

To enter the Academy upon graduation from high school, students should apply as soon as possible after March 1 of their junior year. If successful in receiving a nomination, they must take a physical fitness test, a medical exam, and either the SAT or the ACT.

Application and Information

High school juniors may obtain the application online at http://www.academyadmissions.com. Applicants should study the instructions and follow the proper application procedures. Air Force Admissions Liaison Officers, located in all states, assist students and counselors with the application and testing requirements.

HQ USAFA/RRS
2304 Cadet Drive, Suite 2400
USAF Academy, Colorado 80840-5025
Phone: 800-443-9266 (toll-free)
Website: http://www.academyadmissions.com

A flyover adds to the celebration as cadets graduate from the United States Air Force Academy.

UNITED STATES MERCHANT MARINE ACADEMY
KINGS POINT, NEW YORK

The Academy

The United States Merchant Marine Academy is a four-year, tuition-free federal service academy that was founded in 1943 to educate and train maritime shipping industry (merchant marine) officers, officers on active duty in the armed forces, and leaders in the maritime and intermodal transportation industry. It is an accredited, degree-granting college whose students are commissioned as ensigns in the Navy Reserve upon graduation. The Academy is one of the world's foremost institutions in the field of maritime education and is operated under the Maritime Administration (MARAD) of the U.S. Department of Transportation.

There are approximately 975 men and women enrolled as midshipmen at the Academy. Their daily routine at Kings Point is very demanding. The academic day begins at 7:30 a.m. and concludes at 4 p.m. After classes, midshipmen are free to participate in recreational activities until dinnertime. After dinner, they are required to devote their time to study and academic preparation.

The extracurricular program is broad and varied. In addition to varsity athletics in twenty-five intercollegiate sports, the Academy has an extensive intramural program that permits all students to enjoy physical activity and competition.

The nonathletic activities are also wide ranging and abundant, falling into as many categories as there are individual interests. Publications and the Drill Team, Glee Club, Regimental Band, Scuba-Diving Club, Eagle Scout Association, International Relations Club, and Fencing Club are but a few of the pursuits available to the midshipmen. Regimental and class dances and informal mixers provide the midshipmen with an interesting social program.

Midshipmen are granted liberty on weekends, leave at Thanksgiving, winter holidays (December), spring trimester break, and annual leave in June–July after graduation and before the next academic term begins. Perhaps the most unusual and exciting part of the Academy curriculum is the Shipboard Training Program (Sea Year). Each midshipman, during three trimesters of the sophomore and junior years, serves 300–360 days at sea aboard commercially operated American-flag merchant ships. This exceptional work-study program takes the midshipmen to many parts of the world and provides them with practical experience on several different types of vessels. It can be said that the world is their campus during their three trimesters of sea service.

Location

The Academy is located on 80.5 acres of land at Kings Point, on the North Shore of Long Island. Kings Point is a suburban residential community only 20 miles east of midtown New York City, close to various cultural and recreational facilities.

Majors and Degrees

A graduate of the U.S. Merchant Marine Academy receives a Bachelor of Science degree, a merchant marine license as a third mate or third assistant engineer, and a commission as an ensign in the U.S. Navy Reserve. Graduates may apply to the Army, Navy, Air Force, Marine Corps, Coast Guard, or National Oceanic and Atmospheric Administration (NOAA) to serve on active duty. Five major programs are offered: marine transportation for the preparation of deck officers; marine engineering for students interested in becoming engineering officers; marine engineering systems, which, in addition to leading to a license as a third

assistant engineer, is accredited by the Accreditation Board for Engineering and Technology (ABET) and includes a curriculum with greater depth in mathematics and a significant component of engineering design, as compared to the marine engineering curriculum; marine engineering and shipyard management, which is also accredited by ABET; and logistics and intermodal transportation, a marine transportation program focusing on logistics and intermodal systems management.

Academic Programs

During the first trimester of the plebe (or freshman) year, all students take a common program of mathematics, science, English, and professional courses. This background enables midshipmen to determine intelligently the area of their special interest. After the first trimester, midshipmen select their major and from then on concentrate on a program aligned with their career choice. The professional majors each consist of required core courses in technical and general education areas as well as selected electives. The option program consists of six courses for marine transportation and marine engineering majors, who have a choice of taking a series of related elective courses in a specific area of concentration or any individual elective course for which they qualify. These courses include such specialized fields as nuclear engineering, management science, computer science, chemistry, and naval architecture. By choosing to take the series of related courses, midshipmen can develop a proficiency in a subspecialty, supplementing their major field of study. Students in the marine engineering systems majors are not offered the choice of electives because of the required course load in their programs. General education courses make up about one third of each of the professional curriculums, and all midshipmen are required to take naval science courses prescribed by the Department of the Navy.

Thus, the Academy provides a balanced program of theoretical and practical study designed to provide the undergraduate with technical competence, leadership skills, and the well-rounded general education so essential for responsible citizenship in contemporary society.

Exemption credit may be awarded for college-level work completed at an accredited college if the course is equivalent to a course offered at the Academy.

Academic Facilities

With the exception of Wiley Hall, the former residence of Walter P. Chrysler and now an administration building, all the buildings of the Academy have been constructed since 1942. The interfaith chapel was dedicated in 1961, a three-story library was completed in 1968, and an indoor swimming pool and an engineering and science wing have been added since 1972. A modernization of all other academic buildings was completed in 1982. The Dean ('45) and Barbara White Admissions Center was dedicated in 2004. Upgrades to the dormitories and other facilities are currently under way, with four of the six company berthing buildings already renovated.

Costs

Tuition, room and board, and medical and dental care are provided by the U.S. government. In addition, the government pays for books and the initial issue of uniforms. Each midshipman also receives $974.40 per month during periods when they are assigned aboard ship for training. Entering plebes are required to pay a little more than $2,500 to cover the initial cost of a laptop computer as well as lab fees, equipment, and service, license, and activity fees. Upperclass members are also charged for service, license, and activity fees for the trimesters they are on campus (when they are not at sea).

Financial Aid

In effect, each midshipman receives a four-year scholarship from the U.S. government. Financial assistance is also available through the Federal Pell Grant Program, the Federal Stafford Student Loan Program, and the Federal PLUS (parent loan) Program. Students may also use outside scholarships to defray their costs.

Faculty

The Academy has 84 full-time faculty members and a student-faculty ratio of approximately 11:1. One third of the faculty members are licensed deck or engineering officers. Most hold advanced degrees in an academic discipline: 90 percent of the total faculty members hold master's degrees or higher; 50 percent have earned doctorates.

Student Government

The student body at the Academy is organized along military lines as a regiment, consisting of two battalions. Regimental life at the Academy is a form of student government and is an important part of the midshipman's total educational and leadership learning experience. The first classmen, or seniors, under the direction of the Commandant of Midshipmen, are responsible for exercising military command of the regiment and for administering the daily routine of the midshipmen. The military program is designed to develop leadership ability, self-discipline, and a sense of responsibility—attributes that are essential for effective citizenship as well as for a successful career as an officer.

Admission Requirements

Candidates for admission must be American citizens, be at least 17 years of age, must not have passed their twenty-fifth birthday by July 1 of the year of entry into the Academy, and be of good moral character. Candidates must be nominated by a U.S. representative or senator and must compete for vacancies allocated to their state in proportion to its representation in Congress. Candidates must achieve qualifying scores on the standard administration (timed) SAT or ACT. Candidates must have successfully completed chemistry or physics (including lab), as well as mathematics up to and including one semester of trigonometry or precalculus. Candidates' competitive standing is determined by their College Board score, their high school academic record and extracurricular participation, and their overall leadership potential. All candidates must meet the physical requirements for appointment as a midshipman in the Navy Reserve. Although not required, all applicants are strongly encouraged to perform a day or overnight visit to learn firsthand about midshipman life and academics. Visits are arranged through the Admissions Office when classes are in session, which is from mid-August to May.

Application and Information

Prospective candidates should write to the Admissions Office. They are sent detailed information on the nomination process, required tests, application procedures, and specific requirements. It is advisable to apply for a nomination during the late spring of the junior year in high school. The deadline for applications is March 1 of the year of desired entry.

Further information may be obtained by contacting:

Director of Admissions
U.S. Merchant Marine Academy
300 Steamboat Road
Kings Point, New York 11024-1699
Phone: 516-726-5640
      866-546-4778 (toll-free)
Fax: 516-773-5390
E-mail: admissions@usmma.edu
Website: http://www.usmma.edu

An aerial view of the 80.5 acre "sea campus" of the U.S. Merchant Marine Academy at Kings Point, Long Island, on the shores of Long Island Sound.

UNIVERSITY OF ALASKA FAIRBANKS
FAIRBANKS, ALASKA

The University

The University of Alaska Fairbanks (UAF) draws students into a welcoming community, offering inspiring and transformational educational challenges—from the personal to the global—in the vast laboratory that is Alaska. Founded in 1917, UAF is Alaska's top teaching and research university. Total enrollment is close to 11,000 students; 84 percent are from Alaska and 16 percent are from the rest of the U.S. and fifty-two other countries.

The 2,250-acre Fairbanks campus, located near the center of Alaska, offers limitless opportunities for activity and recreation. Academic buildings and residences make up the core of campus and just beyond are miles of trails, two lakes, and a boreal forest research and recreational area. Most of the UAF's research institutes, including the Geophysical Institute and the International Arctic Research Center, are clustered on the West Ridge, with incredible views of the Tanana Valley and Alaska Range. The University's Agricultural and Forestry Experiment Station is on campus, as are a Cooperative Fish and Wildlife Research Unit and various state and federal agencies and laboratories. The new Margaret Murie Building, with 100,000 square feet of life science classrooms and laboratories, is scheduled to open its doors to students and researchers in fall 2013. Plans are underway to renovate the existing engineering facility and construct a new six-story building alongside, doubling the space available for College of Engineering and Mines labs, classrooms, and offices.

The Student Recreation Center houses a variety of sports and physical activity facilities, including multipurpose areas for aerobics, badminton, calisthenics, dance, gymnastics, judo, karate, tennis, and volleyball; a rifle and pistol range; courts for handball, racquetball, and squash; an elevated 200-meter, three-lane jogging track; a swimming pool; weight-training and modern fitness equipment areas; an ice arena for recreational skating and hockey; and a three-story climbing wall. There is also an outdoor rock/ice climbing wall and a ski and snowboard terrain park.

The student union, the William Ransom Wood Center , is the focus of numerous activities for students and faculty members. The center houses meeting and exhibit rooms, lounges and television areas, student government offices, campus information, a pub, bowling alley, games room, cafeteria, snack bar, and an espresso bar. Construction on a major expansion to the Wood Center dining facilities is slated to begin in 2013.

Intercollegiate athletics include men's and women's basketball, cross-country running and skiing, men's ice hockey, and women's volleyball and swim teams. The University also has an outstanding rifle team which has produced several Olympic athletes and earned ten NCAA championships.

Location

The campus of the University of Alaska Fairbanks is situated on a ridge overlooking the Tanana River valley and the city of Fairbanks. With a population of more than 99,000 in the metro area, Fairbanks is a major trade center for outlying towns and villages in Interior Alaska. The city is connected to the rest of the state and the lower forty-eight states by air and highway. Municipal bus service is available between downtown Fairbanks, the surrounding area, and campus. A convenient shuttle bus service is available on campus.

Fairbanks offers the sophistication of larger cities while maintaining the atmosphere of a smaller, more personal town. Denali National Park and Preserve and other vast wilderness areas are close at hand, and Anchorage is 350 miles south via the Parks Highway. Members of the Fairbanks and UAF communities unite to perform in the Fairbanks Symphony, Arctic Chamber Orchestra, and in many other musical and theatrical programs.

Majors and Degrees

The University of Alaska Fairbanks awards occupational endorsements, certificates, A.A., A.S., A.A.S., B.A., B.A.S., B.B.A., B.E.M., B.F.A., B.M., B.S., and B.T. degrees in accounting; administrative assistant; airframe studies; Alaska Native studies; anthropology; applied accounting; applied business; applied physics; apprenticeship technology; art; arts and sciences; aviation maintenance technology; automotive technology; aviation technology; biological sciences; bookkeeping technician; business administration; chemistry; child development and family services; civil engineering; communication; community health; computer science; culinary arts; diesel/heavy equipment; dental assisting; drafting technology; early childhood; earth science; economics; electrical engineering; elementary education; emergency services; English; entry-level welder; Eskimo (Inupiaq and Yup'ik); facility maintenance; film; financial services representative; fisheries; food science and nutrition; foreign languages; general science; geography; geological engineering; geology; health care reimbursement; health technology; high latitude range management; history; human services; information technology specialist; instrumentation technology; interdisciplinary studies; Japanese studies; journalism; justice; law enforcement academy; linguistics; mathematics; mechanical engineering; medical assistant; medical office technologies;; mining applications and technologies; mining engineering; music; Native language education; natural resources management (including forestry); Northern studies; nurse aide; paralegal studies; paramedic academy; paramedicine; petroleum engineering; philosophy; phlebotomy; physics; political science; powerplant; power generation; process technology; professional piloting; psychology; renewable resources; rural development; rural human services; rural utilities business management; Russian studies; safety, health, and environmental awareness technology; social work; sociology; sustainable energy; technology; theater; tribal management; veterinary science; welding and materials technology; and wildlife biology and conservation.

Pre-professional opportunities and advising are available in dentistry, law, library science, medicine, pharmacy, physical therapy, physician assistant studies, and veterinary medicine.

Academic Programs

The academic year is divided into two semesters; registration begins in early April for the fall semester and in November for the spring semester. Preregistration is available for returning students. In addition, there are three-week, six-week, and twelve-week summer sessions and between-semester two-week sessions in January and May.

The University is organized into the colleges of Engineering and Mines, Liberal Arts, Natural Science and Mathematics, Rural and Community Development, and the schools of Education, Fisheries and Ocean Sciences, Management, and Natural Resources and Agricultural Sciences. A minimum of 120 credits must be completed for the four-year baccalaureate degree programs.

Students who receive scores of 3 or higher on the College Board's Advanced Placement tests may be awarded credit by the University. Students graduating from any school offering the International Baccalaureate Programme should review a comprehensive list of transfer credits available at www.uaf.edu/catalog/current/admissions/table9.html. Enrolled students may challenge courses for credit by successfully completing College-Level Examination Program examinations or by completing locally prepared examinations. Requests for advanced-placement credit and credit by examination are coordinated through the Office of Admissions and the Registrar.

The Office of Undergraduate Research and Scholarly Activity supports and develops UAF's diverse and robust programs to engage undergraduate students in research and creative scholarship. URSA helps students pursue research from a single credit of first-year seminar to independent scholarly investigations or a senior thesis.

The honors program is designed for highly motivated undergraduate students who wish to acquirean advanced understanding of the natural and social sciences, the arts, and the humanities. Prospective honors students need a minimum ACT plus writing composite score of 27 or a minimum combined SAT score of 1820, with an emphasis placed on high scores in English and mathematics. UAF also has chapters of nationally recognized honor societies such as Golden Key and Phi Kappa Phi.

Off-Campus Programs

The University maintains active exchange programs with universities around the world. Membership in the University of the Arctic's north2north exchange program provides UAF students an extensive array of placement opportunities throughout the circumpolar North. UAF also offers a variety of study-abroad programs, including the Northwest Council on Study Abroad, which provides study opportunities with UAF and other U.S. faculty members worldwide. Additional study programs and internships are available through affiliates maintaining sites in numerous countries. UAF is also a member of the National Student Exchange, participating with more than 180 colleges and universities throughout the United States, in U.S. territories, and at nine locations in Canada.

Academic Facilities

The Fine Arts Complex features a 480-seat theater, a 1,072-seat concert hall, FM public radio (KUAC) and educational-television (PBS) studios, an art gallery, and the Elmer E. Rasmuson Library. The library collection contains more than 1.1 million volumes, including the prestigious Alaska and Polar Regions Collection. Electronic catalogs provide access to collections in 11,000 libraries nationwide.

Students have free use of the University's academic computing facilities, in labs, classrooms, dorm rooms, and other campus locations including wireless access.

The University of Alaska Museum of the North attracts nearly 100,000 visitors each year to Interior Alaska and is located on the Fairbanks campus. The museum collects, preserves, and exhibits materials from Alaska and the North.

Costs

In 2013–14, tuition and fees are $2,520 per semester for full-time (15 credits) students. Nonresident students will pay $9,000 for 15 credits of tuition each semester. Generally, to qualify as a resident, a student must show proof they have been living in Alaska for two years. Residents of Alaska, and of cities having sister-city agreements with any Alaska city, are eligible for resident tuition rates.

The approximate cost per semester for books and supplies is $1,400. A double-occupancy residence hall room on campus cost $1,840 per semester during the 2012–13 academic year. Meal plans cost $1,740–$2,040 per semester. All costs are subject to change.

If the student lives in a Western Undergraduate Exchange state (http://www.uaf.edu/admissions/other/wue), tuition is approximately 1.5 times that of an Alaska resident.

Financial Aid

A large portion of financial aid is derived from the Alaska Supplemental Education Loan Program, which is available to all students attending UAF, regardless of residency. Three kinds of aid are available: grants and scholarships (which need not be repaid), loans, and part-time employment. Inquiries should be sent by e-mail to the Financial Aid Office at financialaid@uaf.edu. Academic Merit and Human Achievement scholarships are one-year scholarships ranging from $2,500–$15,000 that are awarded by the Office of Admissions and the Registrar. To apply, students should submit for review a scholarship application, an application for admission, a high school transcript, and test scores. Questions about this scholarship should be directed to the Office of Admissions and the Registrar. The deadline for University of Alaska and UAF-funded scholarships is February 15. Prospective students should check the financial aid website (www.uaf.edu/finaid) for information about grants, loans, and other aid and applicable due dates.

Faculty

Fifty-nine percent of full-time faculty members and 41 percent of part-time faculty hold doctoral or terminal degrees, and many are engaged in research. In keeping with University policy, faculty members provide academic counseling for students. The combination of a student-faculty ratio of 12:1, and ready access to instructors for help outside of class leads to an excellent educational experience for students.

Admission Requirements

For admission to a baccalaureate program, applicants must be high school graduates with a GPA of at least 2.5 in a high school core curriculum of 16 credits and a cumulative grade point average of at least 3.0, or 2.5 plus an ACT plus writing score of 18 or SAT score of 1290 (including writing skills section). Transfer students must also have a minimum grade point average of 2.0 in all previous college work.

Applicants for a major in a scientific or technical field may be required to present a higher grade point average and to have completed specific background courses before being accepted into the major department.

Application and Information

The application deadlines are May 1 for the summer semester, June 15 for the fall semester, and November 1 for the spring semester. A $50 application fee is required when the application is submitted. Applicants are notified of the admission decision once all application materials have been received.

For more information, applicants should contact:

Office of Admissions and the Registrar
University of Alaska Fairbanks
P.O. Box 757480
Fairbanks, Alaska 99775-7480
Phone: 907-474-7500
      800-478-1823 (toll-free)
E-mail: admissions@uaf.edu
Website: http://www.uaf.edu/admissions
      https://uaonline.alaska.edu (to apply)

Students make their way across campus on a November afternoon.

UNIVERSITY OF CENTRAL FLORIDA
ORLANDO, FLORIDA

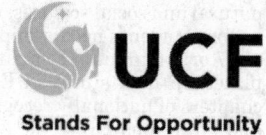

The University

The University of Central Florida (UCF) is a comprehensive research university with approximately 59,500 students. As one of the nation's fastest-growing universities in the South and the second largest in the nation, UCF enrolls an academically talented and diverse student body representing all fifty states and more than 120 countries. The University offers educational and research programs that complement the regional economy, with strong components in aerospace engineering, business, education, film, health, hospitality management, medicine, nursing, and social sciences. UCF's programs in communication and the fine arts help to meet the cultural and recreational needs of a growing metropolitan area. The University also offers many graduate programs leading to master's and doctoral degrees, including a doctorate of physical therapy. The UCF College of Medicine offers the M.D. degree.

UCF is accredited by the Commission on Colleges of the Southern Association of Colleges and Schools. In addition, a number of scientific, professional, and academic bodies confer accreditation in specific disciplines and groups of disciplines.

UCF has established extensive partnerships with businesses and industries in the central Florida area that provide students with research and learning experiences. These partnerships bring practical learning environments to UCF students through co-op, internship programs, and joint curriculum development strategies.

The on-campus and campus-affiliated housing facilities include traditional residence halls, apartment-style options, and Greek housing that accommodate approximately 10,000 students. Several thousand students live in apartments located within walking distance of the campus. Approximately 400 students live in on-campus Greek housing.

Students participate in more than 400 student organizations, including special-interest clubs, multicultural organizations, fraternities and sororities, honor societies, and academic and preprofessional organizations. The Office of Student Involvement schedules a wide array of extracurricular programs, including concerts, movies, and guest speakers.

The University of Central Florida is a member of the NCAA and is slated to join the Big East in fall 2013. All teams compete on the NCAA Division I level. UCF's men's teams compete in intercollegiate baseball, basketball, football, golf, soccer, and tennis. Women's teams compete in basketball, cross-country, golf, rowing, soccer, softball, tennis, track and field, and volleyball. Intercollegiate coed club activities include championship cheerleading, crew, and waterskiing teams. The University intramural sports program offers many options including disc golf, flag football, floor hockey, racquetball, soccer, softball, tennis, and volleyball.

Location

The University of Central Florida is located on 1,415 acres approximately 13 miles east of downtown Orlando. In addition to the academic programs offered on the Orlando campus, upper-division students can work toward a degree at ten locations around the central Florida area.

Majors and Degrees

The University offers the degrees of Bachelor of Applied Science, Bachelor of Arts, Bachelor of Arts in Business Administration, Bachelor of Engineering Technology, Bachelor of Fine Arts, Bachelor of Science, Bachelor of Science in Business Administration, Bachelor of Science in Education, Bachelor of Science in Engineering, Bachelor of Science in Nursing, and Bachelor of Science in Social Sciences. These degrees are available in the colleges listed below, with majors or areas of specialization as indicated.

The College of Arts and Humanities offers degrees in art, architecture, digital media, English, film, French, history, humanities, Latin American studies, music, philosophy, photography, religious studies, Spanish, and theater.

The College of Business Administration offers degrees in accounting, business economics, economics, finance, general business administration, management, marketing, and real estate. The College also offers a minor in international business.

The College of Education offers degrees in art education, early childhood development and education, elementary education, English language arts education, foreign language education, mathematics education, science education, social science education, sports and exercise science, and technical education and industry training.

The College of Engineering and Computer Science offers degrees in aerospace engineering, civil engineering, computer engineering, computer science, construction engineering, electrical engineering, environmental engineering, industrial engineering, information technology, and mechanical engineering.

The College of Health and Public Affairs offers degrees in athletic training, communication sciences and disorders, criminal justice, health informatics and information management, health services administration, health sciences, legal studies, public administration, physical therapy (master's program), and social work.

The College of Medicine and the Burnett School of Biomedical Sciences offers degrees in biomedical sciences, biotechnology, and medical laboratory sciences.

The College of Nursing offers degrees in nursing.

The College of Sciences offers degrees in advertising/public relations, anthropology, biology, chemistry, forensic science, interpersonal and organizational communications, international and global studies, journalism, mathematics, physics, political science, psychology, radio/television, sociology, social sciences, and statistics.

The Rosen College of Hospitality Management offers degrees in event management, hospitality management, and restaurant and foodservice management.

Preprofessional programs are offered in chiropractic, dentistry, medicine, optometry, pharmacy, physical assistant studies, physical therapy, podiatry, and veterinary medicine.

A degree in interdisciplinary studies is available through the Office of Undergraduate Studies.

Academic Programs

UCF provides a total education through a core curriculum of 36 hours of general education courses. In addition to fulfilling the general education requirement, each student must complete the necessary major and/or minor requirements to reach the minimum of 120 semester hours necessary for graduation.

Several special programs help students reach their academic and leadership potential. The Burnett Honors College at UCF encourages students to achieve academic excellence through small classes and interactive symposia. The innovative Leadership Enrichment and Academic Development (LEAD) Scholars Program fosters leadership and service commitment through a comprehensive student development program for freshmen. The Major Exploration Program (MEP) helps entering freshmen define their career goals and develop an academic strategy to reach those goals. The University also offers an increasing number of online courses and degree programs.

UCF offers Air Force and Army ROTC programs.

Off-Campus Programs

Career Services and Experiential Learning offers programs in which students alternate semesters of classroom study with equal periods of paid employment in government, industry, or business. The Department of Modern Languages offers summer study-abroad programs in Canada, Eastern Europe, France, Germany, Italy, Japan, Poland, Spain, Sweden, and Russia. Courses are available in the subject areas of language (all levels), art, and civilization. UCF is also a participant in the National Student Exchange Consortium.

Academic Facilities

In addition to the academic programs offered on the Orlando campus, upper division students can work toward a degree at ten campuses located throughout Central Florida. These regional campuses work cooperatively with local community colleges to provide all four years of course work in many academic areas. The library houses nearly 1.4 million volumes and subscribes to more than 10,000 periodicals and journals. In addition, students have access to an online computer catalog that provides information on the collections of the State University System libraries. An extensive online network of more than 500 computer terminals and a network of nearly 1,000 IBM PCs cover the campus. The Institute for Simulation and Training gives students the opportunity to pursue undergraduate research. The College of Optics and Photonics allows faculty members and students to work directly with industry personnel in conducting basic and applied research at the regional and national levels. The Central Florida Research Park, adjacent to the UCF campus, houses more than ninety important high-technology firms and agencies. This proximity fosters relationships between industry and the University, which strengthens the academic programs at UCF.

Costs

For Florida residents, the cost of tuition and fees in 2012–13, based on a full-time course load, was $6,246 for the year; for out-of-state residents, the cost was $22,345. Room and board were approximately $9,020 per year, books and supplies cost approximately $800.

Financial Aid

Financial aid is awarded according to each student's demonstrated financial need in relation to college costs and may include grants, loans, scholarships, and part-time employment. Programs based upon need include the Federal Perkins Loan, Federal Pell Grant, Florida Student Assistance Grant, Federal Work-Study, Florida College Career Work-Study Program, and Federal Stafford Student Loan. To qualify for these programs, students must complete the Free Application for Federal Student Aid (FAFSA). The priority application deadline is March 1. Sixty-seven percent of UCF students receive some form of financial assistance.

Faculty

The University's teaching faculty consists of 1,959 full-time members and adjunct members. Seventy-five percent of the full-time faculty members hold a doctoral degree. Undergraduate instruction is given primarily by the full-time and adjunct faculty members; graduate students play a very minor role in undergraduate instruction. Students are assigned to a faculty adviser in their area of specialization for assistance in academic matters. The student-faculty ratio is 31:1.

Student Government

UCF's Student Government Association provides an opportunity for students to become involved at UCF. Every UCF student is encouraged to voice his or her opinion through senate representatives. Student Government is divided into three branches—the student-elected executive branch, the student-elected legislative branch, and the appointed judicial branch. Student Government is responsible for the allocation of all activity and service fees paid by students as a part of their tuition. This money goes toward student services, including the online Macintosh lab, homecoming activities, campus activities board, legal services, and funding for clubs and organizations. Admission is free to all events directly sponsored by the Student Government.

Admission Requirements

A freshman applicant is a student with fewer than 12 hours of college course work after high school graduation. The most important criteria in the admission decision for these applicants are the high school academic record, quality and level of difficulty of courses, grade point average, grade trends, and SAT or ACT test scores. UCF operates on a rolling admission basis. Students are generally notified of their initial admission decision within two to three weeks after receipt of the application and all official supporting documents. If the number of qualified applicants exceeds the number that the University is permitted to enroll, a waiting list is established.

All applicants must have earned a minimum of 18 high school academic units (yearlong courses that are not remedial in nature).

These include 4 units of English (3 must include substantial writing), 4 units of mathematics at or above algebra I, 3 units of natural science (2 must include a laboratory), 3 units of social science, 2 units of one foreign language, and 2 units of academic electives. Grades in honors, International Baccalaureate, Advanced Placement, AICE, dual-enrollment, pre-AP, pre-IB, and pre-AICE courses are given additional weight in the GPA computation. Students must meet the Florida Department of Education minimum eligibility to be considered for admission. Applicants should understand that the satisfaction of minimum requirements does not guarantee admission to UCF.

Transfer applicants with fewer than 60 semester hours of college course work must submit official high school transcripts, SAT or ACT test scores, and all official college transcripts. Transfer students with more than 60 semester hours or who have earned an Associate in Arts degree or a statewide articulated Associate in Science degree from a Florida public community or state college need only submit all official college transcripts. A transfer credit summary evaluation is provided to students once they are offered admission to UCF.

Application and Information

Students are encouraged to apply several months in advance and can apply online at http://admissions.ucf.edu. It is recommended that freshman students apply early during the fall semester of their senior year. Applications are accepted up to one year prior to the start of the term for which enrollment is desired. Priority application deadlines are May 1 for the fall term (July 1 for transfers), November 1 for the spring term, and March 1 for the summer term.

The Campus Visit Experience, which includes an information session and a campus tour, is offered Monday through Friday at 10 and 2 (except holidays). Students can sign up for a campus visit online at http://admissions.ucf.edu.

For more information, contact:

Office of Undergraduate Admissions
University of Central Florida
P.O. Box 160111
Orlando, Florida 32816-0111
Phone: 407-823-3000
E-mail: admission@.ucf.edu
Website: http://www.ucf.edu

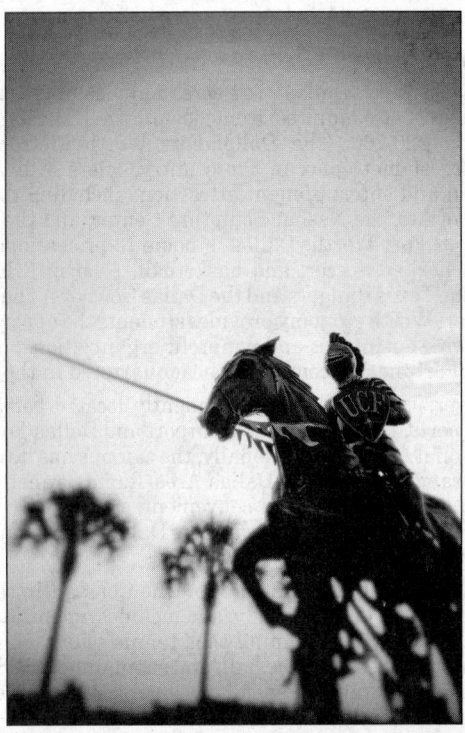

The Charging Knight symbolizes UCF's excellence in academics, partnerships, and athletics.

UNIVERSITY OF DALLAS
IRVING, TEXAS, AND ROME, ITALY

The University

The University of Dallas is a private, Catholic coeducational liberal arts university dedicated to the pursuit of wisdom, truth, and virtue as the proper and primary goals of education. Approximately 1,350 undergraduate students from fifty states and fifteen countries make up the student body, and more than half of the undergraduate student body comes from outside the state of Texas. In addition, 82 percent of the current undergraduate student body is Catholic.

The University of Dallas (UD) is a center of learning, and the experience on campus is intensive and highly directed. Students choose to come to the University because they are serious students. While they engage in a full complement of extracurricular activities and independent study, it is the act of learning in association with professors that shapes their college years. Because the undergraduate college is small and largely residential, it forms a close-knit community.

Spiritual life on the University of Dallas campus is an important aspect of the undergraduate experience. The University's core values include embracing the Catholic intellection tradition and maintaining a dialogue between faith and reason; these values continually have an important role both inside and outside of the classroom. The main church on campus, Church of the Incarnation, offers daily Mass as well as reconciliation. Holy Trinity Seminary, Albert the Great Priory, and Cistercian Abbey are also available for students to participate in Mass and other spiritual growth activities, and Campus Ministry offers a wide variety of spiritual and service opportunities for students of all faiths and backgrounds, such as lectures and alternative spring break.

Location

The University of Dallas' 744-acre main campus is located approximately 15 minutes from downtown Dallas in Irving, population 220,700. The Dallas-Fort Worth Metroplex, the fourth-largest metroplex in the country, offers a diverse mix of cultural and entertainment attractions including the Dallas Museum of Art, the Nasher Sculpture Center, and the Kimball Museum in Fort Worth. Dallas is home to professional sports teams in hockey, soccer, and basketball. Nearby Arlington is home to the Texas Rangers and the Dallas Cowboys. The thriving Dallas-Fort Worth economy provides students the opportunity to connect with businesses and nonprofit organizations, including eighteen Fortune 500 companies headquartered in the area.

The University of Dallas is conveniently located between two major airports, Dallas Love Field Airport and Dallas/Fort Worth International Airport. Additionally, the campus has its own stop on the Orange Line of the Dallas Area Rapid Transit (DART) light rail system, providing convenient access to Irving, the Trinity Railway Express, downtown Dallas, and major DFW attractions.

The University of Dallas' 12-acre Eugene Constantin campus is located just south of Rome, Italy, and includes amenities such as a working vineyard, swimming pool, tennis courts, classrooms, library, suite-style residence hall, and cappuccino bar. Students have the opportunity to spend an entire semester studying abroad on the Rome campus.

Majors and Degrees

Choosing a specific major affords students the opportunity to further their curiosity in a particular area of study. The University of Dallas offers twenty-seven majors, which can be combined in double majors to match each student's interest. Thirty-two concentrations (minors) are available to broaden academic expertise. In addition, cooperative degree programs in nursing and engineering allow students to earn dual degrees from the University of Dallas and its partnering local universities. Pre-professional programs in architecture, dentistry, engineering, law, medicine, ministerial programs, and physical therapy are also available to prepare students academically for rigorous graduate programs and demanding professions. Undergraduate and post-baccalaureate certification is available to students interested in teaching at the elementary, middle, or secondary school level.

Regardless of major, all University of Dallas students are required to complete a major-specific project to culminate their undergraduate career. Whether completing their own research, writing an extensive thesis, taking comprehensive exams, or completing an intensive practicum, students find that they are well-prepared to succeed upon graduation.

Academic Programs

University of Dallas students thrive on a rigorous academic program distinguished by UD's nationally recognized Core curriculum. Based on the belief that truth and virtue exist and are the proper objects of search in an education, the Core curriculum is a two-year course of study through which every UD student directly encounters Western civilization's greatest authors, leaders, and artists by reading classic, original works. Every student becomes familiar with the same works of literature and the same great books and concepts, fostering a natural understanding and exchange of ideas. The Core curriculum is comprehensive, encompassing English, philosophy, mathematics, fine arts, science, classics, modern languages, American civilization, Western civilization, politics, economics, and theology.

Off-Campus Programs

The academic experience is heightened and enriched by spending a semester abroad on the Eugene Constantin campus in Italy. Because of the accessibility and affordability of the Rome program, all students are encouraged to participate and the majority chooses to, usually during their sophomore year. The Rome curriculum builds on the Core and is a coherent and integral part of the undergraduate education. The courses, such as Art and Architecture and Western Theological Tradition, are selected from the Core curriculum and deepen students' understanding and appreciation of Western civilization by allowing them to experience history and culture firsthand.

Students are also encouraged to become involved in the Irving community and to take advantage of the arts and entertainment offerings in the area. Community service opportunities such as spending time at local nursing homes, repairing homes for underprivileged families, and tutoring local students are available on a weekly basis. In addition, through a program called Dallas Year, students have access to highly-discounted tickets to area events such as the State Fair of Texas or a Dallas Cowboys football game, and transportation is provided to and from the event.

Academic Facilities

The Science Center houses some of the most advanced tools for scientific research available, including a working observatory. The Haggerty Arts Village has established the University as a leading center for ceramics and fine arts in the Southwest. Drama productions are staged in the Margaret Jonsson Theater. Blakely Library holds more than 300,000 volumes, including the personal library of the late political philosopher Wilmoore Kendall.

Costs

Annual tuition and fees for the 2013–14 academic year are $33,110. Room and board costs are approximately $10,400. Costs are the same for both in-state and out-of-state students.

Financial Aid

Approximately 80 percent of University of Dallas students receive some type of merit- or need-based aid to help offset the cost of attendance. The application for admission serves as the application for institutional scholarships which range from $5,000 up to full tuition and are based on GPA and test scores (ACT or SAT). Academic merit scholarships are renewable for four years, providing eligibility requirements set forth in the scholarship letter are met.

A limited number of other scholarships are available to students who excel in a particular area of study or have achieved superior academic achievement such as National Merit Finalists, National Achievement Scholars, National Hispanic Scholars, and Phi Theta Kappa members.

All students who submit a Free Application for Federal Student Aid (FAFSA) are considered for financial assistance based on their family's finances. These forms of assistance include federal, state, or institutional grants; low-interest student loans; and work-study programs. Priority is given to applicants whose FAFSA is received by the University of Dallas on or before March 1.

Faculty

The University of Dallas has 127 full-time faculty members, 90 percent of whom hold a doctorate or equivalent highest academic degree in their discipline. As top scholars in their field, professors value the academic freedom the University offers, allowing them to unreservedly explore intellectual inquiries both within and outside their disciplines. University of Dallas students benefit from a 12:1 student to faculty ratio and an average class size of 17 students, providing each and every student with the individual attention and mentoring they deserve.

Student Government, Clubs, and Organizations

Through the elected Student Governing Board, students are responsible for all nonacademic matters that affect their life at the University of Dallas. Guided by the mission of the University and in accordance with the teachings and principles of the Catholic Church, the representatives in student government are dedicated to enhancing the quality of student life by promoting both the academic and social traditions of the University.

The University of Dallas also offers over forty clubs and organizations that allow students to become involved in areas of extracurricular or academic interest, as well as develop vital leadership skills. From Best Buddies to the Pre-Health Society to Crusaders for Life, students can choose to get involved in many different ways. In addition, if several students have a shared interest that is not represented by current clubs and organizations, they are encouraged to start a new club.

Furthermore, the University of Dallas competes in NCAA Division III athletics and is a member of the Southern Collegiate Athletic Conference. Sports include baseball (M), basketball (M, W), cross country (M, W), golf (M), lacrosse (M, W), soccer (M, W), softball (W), track and field (M, W), and volleyball (W). Intramural sports are also offered to all students.

Admission Requirements

The University of Dallas performs a holistic review of applications, so no rigid cutoff for test scores or GPA is adhered to in the admission process. For the fall 2012 incoming freshman class, the average SAT score was approximately 1200 (on a 1600 scale), and the average ACT score was 26. The average GPA was 3.65 on a 4.0 scale.

The University seeks students who are not only academically well-prepared to succeed, but who will also contribute to the University of Dallas community. Letters of recommendation, the essay, and the supplement answers are all considered in determining a student's overall fit for the University. Interviews are not required, but students are highly encouraged to schedule a campus visit and meet with an admission counselor to discuss the admission process as well as any opportunities for scholarship or financial aid.

Application and Information

Applicants are required to submit the following items: application (Common Application or Apply Texas), UD supplement, the $40 application fee or fee waiver, essay, teacher recommendation, counselor recommendation, official high school transcript, and official test scores (ACT or SAT). The Early Action I deadline is November 1; the Early Action II deadline is December 1. The Freshman Priority Scholarship deadline is January 15, and the regular admission deadline is March 1. Rolling admission is March 2–August 1.

Students interested in transferring to the University of Dallas must submit transcripts from all colleges previously attended. Transfer students should apply by December 1 for spring entry or July 1 for fall entry.

For more information, students should contact:

Office of Undergraduate Admission and Financial Aid
University of Dallas
1845 East Northgate Drive
Irving, Texas 75062
Phone: 972-721-5266
        800-628-6999 (toll-free)
Website: http://www.udallas.edu/admissions

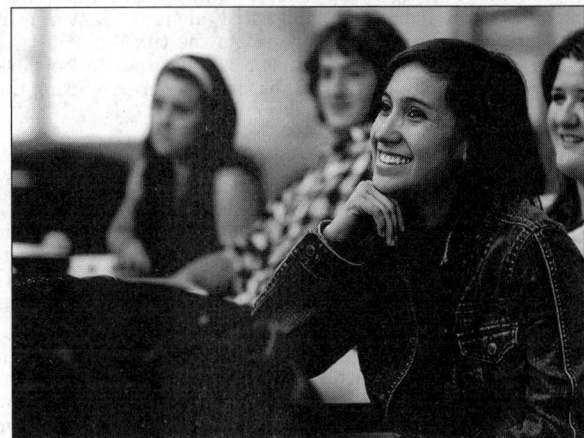

The University's Core curriculum allows students to explore many fields of study and come to understand the interconnected nature of all knowledge.

UNIVERSITY OF DENVER
DENVER, COLORADO

The University

Since its founding in 1864, the University of Denver (DU) has grown into one of the West's premier private universities, blending the friendliness and personal attention of a small college with the resources and intellectual diversity of an advanced research institution. As the oldest private university in the Rocky Mountain region, the University is home not only to a top-ranked undergraduate program but also to a number of world-renowned research centers and professional programs, including the Josef Korbel School of International Studies, the Sturm College of Law, and the Daniels College of Business.

The 125-acre campus brings together 5,029 traditional undergraduate students and 6,347 graduate students from fifty states and over eighty countries. In an environment that prizes innovation, cross-disciplinary exploration, and adventurous learning partnerships between students and faculty, students embark on a personalized educational journey inspired and framed by a spirit of exploration and openness.

Whatever their backgrounds and majors, DU students are engaged and active, taking advantage of the region's many recreation and cultural opportunities—everything from world-class skiing and white-water rafting to award-winning professional theater and alternative music. On campus, students attend performances at the three-venue Newman Center for the Performing Arts and cheer for the seventeen varsity teams that compete in NCAA Division I Athletics at the Ritchie Center for Sports & Wellness.

The University of Denver is accredited by the North Central Association of Colleges and Schools. The Carnegie Foundation classifies the University of Denver as a Doctoral/Research University–Extensive.

Location

Located just 8 miles from bustling downtown Denver and mere minutes from the Rocky Mountain foothills, the University of Denver's tree-shaded campus is surrounded by pleasant urban neighborhoods offering coffee shops, retail stores, and diverse restaurants. The institution is located along a light-rail line and major bus lines, providing access to the city's arts districts, shopping centers, sports arenas, and an extensive network of parks. DU students can ride all public transportation for free, using their University-supplied Smart Cards.

Majors and Degrees

The University of Denver offers twelve bachelor's degrees in over 100 programs of study, including the arts, business, computer science, engineering, humanities, international studies, mathematics, natural sciences, and social sciences. Students who are interested in pre-professional programs can choose from law, medical, dental, and veterinary programs that prepare them for professional study beyond their undergraduate degree.

In addition, the University offers 4+1 and 3+2 dual-degree programs that allow students to complete both a bachelor's and master's degree in five years or less. These dual-degree programs are currently offered in business, education, social work, engineering, art history, international studies, public policy, and natural sciences.

Academic Programs

Undergraduate programs at the University—which operates on the quarter system—emphasize experiential, dynamic, and cross-disciplinary learning.

First-year students enroll in a first-year seminar. Generally limited to 20 students, these seminars focus on a topic that reflects the professor's research interests. This professor, who serves as a mentor throughout the student's first year, introduces the class to university-level work and inquiry, while also advising students on everything from time management to University procedures. The seminar is complemented by a two-quarter writing sequence that trains students to conduct research, construct arguments, and write persuasively for the academic setting. The University's emphasis on writing continues throughout the next three years, with upper-division writing-intensive classes across the disciplines. By the time they graduate, DU students have developed the communication skills that are essential for career success.

Undergraduate students also complete foundations courses in mathematics and computer science, the arts and humanities, natural sciences, and social sciences. DU's common curriculum ensures that students have a wide base of knowledge upon graduation.

Because the University believes in the value of hands-on learning, students are encouraged to collaborate with faculty members and peers on research projects and creative endeavors. Through the Partners in Scholarship (PinS) program, the University sponsors student work through grants that fund field studies, research trips, and special materials. At year's end, students share their research and findings at a special symposium for their peers.

Thanks to opportunities like these, the University's academic programs earn high marks from students. In the 2012 National Survey of Student Engagement (NSSE), first-year students and seniors at 546 participating U.S. colleges and universities reported their satisfaction with their own campus. National results revealed that DU students reported significantly higher levels of satisfaction than the average of students at all other participating doctoral-extensive schools for level of academic challenge, involvement in active and collaborative learning, interaction with faculty members, and enriched educational experiences.

Off-Campus Programs

To groom students for the challenges of global citizenship, the University of Denver sponsors Cherrington Global Scholars, a for-credit program that aims to send every eligible junior and senior abroad for at least a quarter of study. The University believes so strongly in this opportunity to expand understanding and foster connections that it ensures qualifying students pay no more for the experience than for a quarter spent on campus. The University budgets about $10 million each year in support of this outstanding program. Nearly 70 percent of all DU students participate in study-abroad programs, the sixth-highest percentage in the nation.

Academic Facilities

In the last decade, the University has invested nearly $500 million in new buildings and learning centers to ensure that students can prepare for the challenges awaiting them after graduation. These include the Robert and Judi Newman Center for the Performing Arts, home to the University's celebrated Lamont School of Music and host to a performing arts series known for its adventurous offerings; the Daniels College of Business, which houses eleven case-style meeting rooms, nine seminar classrooms, and an Advanced Technology Center; the Knoebel School of Hospitality Management, home to a full-production kitchen, a beverage-management center, a 120-person dining hall, a student-run coffee shop, and a student-faculty-staff commons; F. W. Olin Hall, which houses ten teaching labs and a greenhouse; and the Anderson Academic Commons, which serves as the new library and hub of the University with a central campus location, multimedia software support services, and a full complement of individual and group study areas and rooms.

Other facilities support the University's commitment to community living and wellness, such as the Nelson Residence Hall which features suites, common kitchens on each floor, a central courtyard, a grand dining hall, and an outdoor dining patio. The Ritchie Center for Sports and Wellness brings students and members of the Denver community together to work out, try new sports, and watch the Pioneer athletic teams. With a state-of-the-art fitness center, a natatorium, a field house, two ice arenas, a gymnastics venue, a lacrosse stadium, a newly remodeled soccer stadium, and a tennis pavilion, the Ritchie Center complex supports the active lifestyle that DU students value.

Nagel Residence Hall serves as a campus gathering place, welcoming students and faculty at its food court, providing numerous locations for group study sessions, and offering studio space for students wanting to explore their artistic side. In keeping with the University's far-reaching sustainability initiative, the green building is LEED certified, meaning it uses key resources more efficiently than conventional buildings.

In recent years the University also completed construction on a spectacular new home for both the Morgridge College of Education and the Marsico Institute for Early Learning and Literacy. The influential institute serves as a regional and national nucleus for research and policy analysis on issues related to improving learning environments for young children.

Costs

For the 2012–13 academic year, tuition was $38,232, fees were estimated at $945, and on-campus room and board costs were $10,818—for a total cost of $49,995. Because the University of Denver is a private institution, costs are the same for in-state and out-of-state students.

Financial Aid

The University of Denver offers two types of financial assistance to students: need-based aid, which includes scholarships, grants, loans, and work-study based on financial need; and merit-based awards, which include scholarships based on merit or special talent. Each year, the Financial Aid office awards over $100 million in need- and merit-based assistance to undergraduate students. About 49 percent of full-time DU undergraduates demonstrate financial need and receive some form of need-based assistance.

To recognize achievement in the classroom, the sports arena, leadership, and in music, theater, and art, the University sponsors a number of merit-based scholarships. Although the requirements vary from scholarship to scholarship, most are renewable each year if the student maintains a specified minimum GPA. A complete listing of scholarships is posted at http://www.du.edu/financialaid.

Need-based financial aid is computed using a number of factors, including family income, assets, size, and the number of family members attending college at the same time. DU utilizes both the CSS PROFILE and the Free Application for Federal Student Aid (FAFSA) to determine need-based aid. Need-based awards generally combine scholarships, grants, loans, and work-study opportunities from a variety of federal, state, and institutional sources. The financial aid offer may also include any competitive scholarships the student has been awarded at the point of admission. To help determine how much need- and merit-based aid might be available to a prospective student and his or her family, DU offers access to a comprehensive net price calculator, found at www.du.edu/estimator.

The priority deadline for applying for financial aid is February 15. Because financial aid funds are limited, students who complete their financial aid applications in a timely manner are more likely to maximize financial aid resources. Funding for certain awards may not be available as time passes. The student's financial aid package cannot be determined until he or she is officially admitted to DU. More information on applying for financial aid at DU is available at http://www.du.edu/financialaid.

Faculty

DU professors teach 99 percent of undergraduate courses, ensuring students work closely with faculty members and the intensity of the learning environment is maximized. The average class size is 21 students; 82 percent of undergraduate classes have fewer than 30 students and 95 percent of classes have fewer than 50 students.

Committed teachers, innovative researchers, and prolific publishers, University of Denver professors often include undergraduate students in their research projects and fieldwork. It is not uncommon for an undergraduate student to share publication credit with a professor or to participate in groundbreaking research with tangible, transformational benefits for humankind.

Student Government

At the University of Denver, the student population is represented by the Undergraduate Student Government (USG), whose elected representatives participate in the University's legislative process and communicate student issues to the administration. In addition, the USG oversees the allocation of the student activities fee and the licensing of DU's 100-plus student organizations. In the past few years this group has worked extensively on issues ranging from sustainability to diversity and academic affairs to spirit on campus.

The USG includes senators from each major, each geographic area (on-campus, off-campus), and each class (senior, junior, etc.). The USG Executive Board includes an adviser, graduate adviser, president, vice president, and a cabinet of members.

Admission Requirements

Admission to the University of Denver is selective. Students are evaluated individually on the basis of their academic record, test scores, essay, and recommendations. In making its admission decisions, the University seeks to foster an academic community of geographically, ethnically, and economically diverse learners. The admission committee seeks students who are committed to integrity, innovation, inclusiveness, leadership, academic excellence, and community engagement.

Applicants are required to submit either the Common Application or the DU Pioneer Application—both are posted on the DU website. In addition, applicants are required to submit their high school transcripts, scores from either the SAT or ACT (DU uses the superscore system), an essay, and a high school counselor recommendation. Students may also submit a teacher recommendation, although it is not required.

Application and Information

The University of Denver offers two application programs for first-year domestic students seeking fall-quarter admission. Early action (deadline of November 1) is a nonbinding program leading to an admission decision in late December. Regular decision (deadline of January 15), also nonbinding, is the final admission deadline for fall-quarter consideration. Regular decision applicants receive their admission decision in mid-March.

To learn more about the University of Denver, students should contact:

University of Denver
Undergraduate Admission
2197 South University Boulevard
Denver, Colorado, 80208-9401
United States
Phone: 303-871-2036
   800-525-9495 (toll-free)
E-mail: admission@du.edu
Website: http://www.du.edu/admission
   http://www.youtube.com/uofdenver
   http://www.facebook.com/uofdenveradmission
   http://twitter.com/uofdenver

University of Denver

UNIVERSITY OF DUBUQUE
DUBUQUE, IOWA

UNIVERSITY *of*
DUBUQUE

The University

The University of Dubuque (UD) is a private, Presbyterian, professional university with a focus in the liberal arts, as well as a theological seminary located in Iowa's first city—Dubuque. The Key City is on the Mississippi River at the point where the borders of Wisconsin, Illinois, and Iowa meet. Founded in 1852, the University offers programs in the undergraduate and graduate college and in the graduate theological seminary. The University's mission of encouraging intellectual, moral, and spiritual development dates back to its founding.

Throughout its history, the University has been known as a place of educational opportunity. Even today, a large portion of its students are from first-generation or underrepresented populations. The University of Dubuque's welcoming interfaith community of approximately 2,000 students comes from across the country and around the globe.

Because students from many nations attend the University of Dubuque, UD offers students a cosmopolitan atmosphere. The school is convinced that students living in today's world are better prepared for life if they have a global perspective. American and international student interaction on campus, as well as the movement of faculty members and students across international boundaries, is essential for a meaningful education, human enrichment, and intercultural global awareness.

Location

The University of Dubuque's scenic 77-acre campus, located in eastern Iowa, is in the heart of the Midwest. Dubuque is a city for all seasons. From bluffs blazing with autumn oranges and reds to the river sparkling with summer's blues and greens, the area scenery is spectacular year-round. Dubuque, the oldest city in Iowa, is a dynamic community built along the majestic Mississippi River and surrounded by dramatic bluffs. The setting is ideal for outdoor enthusiasts, with four seasons of ample outlets for recreation, including hiking, biking, boating, skiing, camping, golfing, climbing, and caving.

Dubuque offers the amenities of a larger city with the security and comfort of a smaller town. A lively cultural scene includes the Grand Opera House, the Dubuque Symphony Orchestra, and the Dubuque Museum of Art. The National Mississippi River Museum and Aquarium and the National Farm Toy Museum provide glimpses of the area's past. The city's theater productions, boutiques, and restaurants are wonderful ways to take a study break.

Nearby are some of the Midwest's most interesting cities, an easy drive for a weekend road trip. Historic Galena offers quaint shops and period architecture, while vibrant Chicago is famous for its museums and nightlife. Madison, Milwaukee, and Minneapolis–St. Paul are only hours away.

Majors and Degrees

With twenty-four undergraduate majors, the University prepares students for careers in a variety of fields. From future teachers to corporate leaders to aspiring pilots, the University of Dubuque helps students achieve their career goals.

The University's business and education departments have the most majors. The education department's future teachers graduate with twice as many field-experience hours as required by the state of Iowa.

The University's nursing program was reinstated in the fall 2004 semester. The program offers a Bachelor of Science in Nursing (B.S.N.) degree. Nursing began at University of Dubuque in 1976 and, until 1997, the program offered fully accredited RN-to-B.S.N., B.S.N., and M.S.N. nursing preparation. The University is accredited by the American Association of Colleges of Nursing.

Academic departments encourage internships as an experiential component to complement classroom learning. For example, environmental science majors take advantage of the natural classroom of the Mississippi River, where students study the interaction between people and the environment. Aviation majors complete internships at the Dubuque Regional Airport or major airlines in addition to flying state-of-the-art equipment from UD's Garlick Flight Operations Center.

Academic Programs

The University of Dubuque education aims at helping students develop patterns of scholarship that make them effective learners throughout life. UD students are nurtured in the virtues of scholarship: the desire for understanding different peoples and cultures, an interest in learning, the skills to use multiple resources to explore ideas and find answers for life's questions, an understanding of conceptual connections, and the ability to reason and communicate effectively. Each graduate develops depth of knowledge in a particular field of study based on an integration of this field, the liberal arts, and his or her values.

University of Dubuque students begin to understand their chosen field of study by experiencing how it relates to other areas of knowledge. The process of exploring a variety of interests and possibilities in course work and in University activities results in the choice of a major. Current trends indicate that today's graduates change jobs and/or careers several times during their lifetimes. Therefore, professional preparation is more than a narrow, vocationally oriented process through which students prepare for one specific job. Rather, it is the development of transferable skills and attributes that allow students to succeed in a changing job market.

In the University of Dubuque community, the arts foster intellectual, emotional, and spiritual development. In literature, the visual arts, dance, drama, and music, students not only find aesthetic pleasure but also learn about other people's ideas, beliefs, and experiences and come to deeper understandings of their own.

Because of the University's location near the Mississippi—one of the world's great river systems—students have an appreciation of environmental issues. Through academic endeavors involving formal and experiential learning, students develop an understanding of the basic processes that underpin various ecological communities and of the complex interaction of human activities on the environment. The University of Dubuque encourages individuals to integrate their knowledge of the environment into personal, ethical, and spiritual guidelines, which can be used to improve their lives, their communities, and society.

The Lester G. and Michael Lester Wendt Character Initiative, supported by a substantial endowment, integrates virtues and values such as truthfulness, honesty, fairness, and the Golden Rule across the curriculum and throughout the University.

The University's Learning Institute for Fulfillment and Engagement (LIFE) offers an accelerated baccalaureate degree program for adult learners. Geared to adult learners age 23 and over, the UD LIFE program is designed to offer a flexible format, allowing students to earn a bachelor's degree in as few as three years and a master's degree in as few as eighteen months. Offering classes on weekday evenings as well as online, the program helps adults balance their studies, career, and family life.

Off-Campus Programs

As a member of the Dubuque Tri-College Cooperative Effort, the University of Dubuque offers its students the opportunity to attend and receive credit for courses at Clarke College and Loras College, also in the city, thus providing access to the many different faculty members, professional societies, educational opportunities, and social activities of combined campuses of more than 4,500 students.

The University of Dubuque affirms the value of an international/intercultural experience and considers it to be an important component of any student's education. Overseas travel, exchanges, and study programs are available to help increase the global perspective of the students and to promote cross-cultural education.

Academic Facilities

Heritage Center, an 80,000-square-foot performing arts and campus center, opened in May 2013. The new facility is central to the University of Dubuque campus, and provides a multitude of venues to serve students, faculty, staff, and the public. "Art by osmosis" is the overarching theme of the new building, inviting people of all walks to happen upon art in its myriad forms, intentionally and accidentally, as they visit Heritage Center for their work, study, recreation, and entertainment. The primary functions of the building can be categorized as a casual student campus center and formal public areas, with overlapping meant to encourage interaction and interest. The student areas are designed to provide educational spaces, group and individual study settings, student services, offices, and hospitality; the public areas provide performance venues, associated gathering spaces, gallery space, heritage display, offices, and hospitality.

The Chlapaty Recreation and Wellness Center, which opened in October 2008, is an 87,000-square-foot facility enveloping the existing football stadium as well as additional construction to the west. Features include a 6,900-square-foot, two-level fitness center, including areas for cardiovascular workouts and free weights/machines, as well as a room for activities such as Pilates and yoga; a 200-meter, six-lane indoor track with synthetic flooring for fitness walking and performance; four multiuse courts nested in the center of the track for intramurals and indoor practices; a training room and examination rooms; home, visitor, officials, and faculty/staff locker rooms; a juice bar and lounge area; a 3,000-seat football stadium, including east side visitor seating for 1,000 and an expanded concessions area; and a lighted field, synthetic field turf surface, and new eight-lane outdoor track.

The expanded and renovated University Science Center opened for classes in January 2007. With an additional 21,000 square feet of space, the University can devote the proper resources to its growing science programs. The new facility accommodates efficient laboratories, including state-of-the-art equipment and safety measures, bringing the science programs to the forefront of current teaching methods. Laboratory spaces include geology, zoology, general biology, cell/microbiology, science education, nursing, general chemistry, organic chemistry, geographic information systems (GIS), and five research labs to accommodate student-faculty collaborative research projects.

Costs

Tuition costs for the 2013–14 academic year are $24,360. Average room and board costs are $8,140. These costs do not include books, supplies, personal expenses, and travel.

Financial Aid

Ninety-six percent of the University of Dubuque's students receive financial assistance through scholarships, awards and grants, loans, or work-study programs. The average financial assistance package for 2012–13 was $19,950. All levels of household incomes receive financial assistance.

To apply for financial assistance, applicants must submit a completed application package for admission to the University of Dubuque, file a FAFSA after January 1 and before April 1 (the priority deadline), and send or fax a copy of the completed FAFSA to the University of Dubuque Office of Student Financial Planning. Institutional, federal, state, and alternative loan programs are all available as forms of financial assistance.

Faculty

Seventy percent of University of Dubuque faculty members have earned a Ph.D. or other terminal degree. The student-faculty ratio is 15:1.

Student Government

The Student Government Association (SGA) represents the student body through general election of individual student representatives. The SGA sponsors four campus organizations, the University Program Council (UPC), the Spartan Spirit Club, Under The Bell Tower (student newspaper), and The Key (student yearbook). SGA provides student representatives for a number of key administrative committees.

Admission Requirements

An applicant for admission to the University of Dubuque undergraduate program is a graduate of a high school or equivalent (GED) and presents a minimum of 15 high school units, of which 10 are from academic fields (English, social studies, natural science, mathematics, foreign language). Either ACT or SAT scores are required. The Admission Committee looks at the application and transcript for indications of school achievement as well as aspiration, creativity, and adventurousness. Applicants to the University are usually active in cocurricular activities and these, as well as leadership qualities and character, are considered. An on-campus visit is encouraged. Two recommendations and an essay are requested and read with care.

Application and Information

First-year students are admitted to the University on a rolling basis. When the application and all supporting materials (e.g., transcripts and teacher and counselor recommendations) have been received, admission decisions are made by the Admission Committee and students are advised of the University's decision.

Transfer students who are enrolled or who were previously enrolled at another college or university may apply for transfer to the University of Dubuque. The University considers transfer applications for fall and spring semesters.

In addition to completing the application materials required for first-year applicants, transfer applicants must submit a complete official transcript for all college courses taken and grades received and a complete official transcript for all secondary school courses taken and grades received.

For further information, students should contact:

Office of Admission
University of Dubuque
2000 University Avenue
Dubuque, Iowa 52001
Phone: 563-589-3000
        800-722-5583 (toll-free)
E-mail: admssns@dbq.edu
Website: http://www.dbq.edu

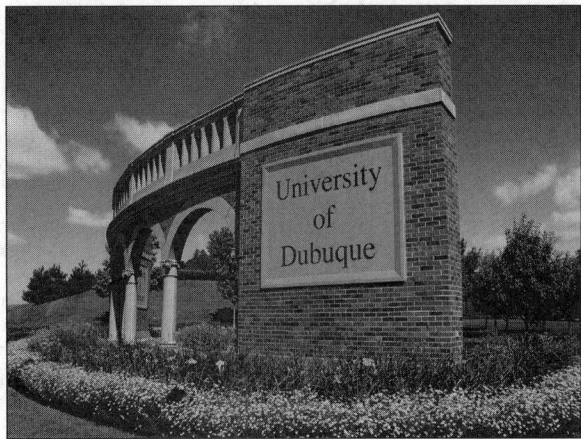

Marking the entrance to South Campus is a colonnade reminiscent of the Steffens Colonnade that is a familiar Dubuque landmark along the North Campus entrance on University Avenue.

THE UNIVERSITY OF FINDLAY
FINDLAY, OHIO

The University

The University of Findlay (UF) is a midsized private university with more than 3,600 students. Founded in 1882 by the Churches of God, General Conference, and the citizens of Findlay, it is a flexible, forward-looking university that is constantly seeking ways to serve students and the community. Service is a priority at Findlay, with new students spending a half-day volunteering in the community before they even begin classes. In 2010, the University was named to the President's Higher Education Community Service Honor Roll for exemplary service efforts to America's communities for the second consecutive year.

The University of Findlay offers nearly sixty bachelor's degree programs and nine master's degree programs, including athletic training; business administration; education; health informatics, environmental, safety, and health management; occupational therapy; physician assistant studies; rhetoric and writing; and teaching English to speakers of other languages (TESOL) and bilingual education. UF also offers two first-professional doctoral degree programs including the Doctor of Pharmacy (Pharm.D.) and Doctor of Physical Therapy. Findlay also has a robust online university that includes a business degree completion program and M.B.A. program.

The largest programs at Findlay are animal science/pre–veterinary medicine, equestrian studies, pharmacy, business administration, and education. Majors in the sciences and health professions include athletic training, chemistry, computer science, equestrian studies (English, western, and equine business management), nuclear medicine, occupational therapy, physical therapy, and animal science/pre–veterinary medicine. Business degrees are founded in a comprehensive core program with eleven different majors.

The University of Findlay's academic programs emphasize experiential learning in every major, including opportunities for internships, undergraduate research, and work-related experiences.

Most of Findlay's students come from Ohio and the surrounding states of Michigan, Indiana, and Pennsylvania. More than thirty other states are also represented. UF also has a strong international student population, with more than 300 international students from twenty-seven countries and territories.

Resident students live in eight modern residence halls and several town-house-style apartments. Social life at Findlay centers on student organizations, intramural sports, and Greek life. Organizations include department and special interest clubs, the newspaper, musical groups, a radio station, Circle K, and Aristos Eklektos (honors).

Athletic programs are affiliated with NCAA Division II and the Great Lakes Intercollegiate Athletic Conference, with the exception of the equestrian teams, which have won national championships in the Intercollegiate Horse Show Association. Findlay offers ten intercollegiate sports for men: baseball, basketball, cross-country, football, golf, indoor and outdoor track and field, soccer, swimming and diving, tennis, and wrestling. It has eleven varsity sports for women: basketball, cheerleading, cross-country, golf, indoor and outdoor track and field, lacrosse, soccer, softball, swimming and diving, tennis, and volleyball. UF also has two mixed sports, western and English equestrian riding. Athletic scholarships are available.

The Croy Physical Education Center has a 25-meter swimming pool, a gymnasium, offices, and classrooms. The 130,000-square-foot Koehler Recreation and Fitness Complex contains a six-lane, NCAA-regulation track; sand pits for long jump; state-of-the-art timing system; wrestling room; four multipurpose courts; locker rooms; and offices for the athletic department. Also under the same roof is a general student recreation center, which includes a cardio center; basketball, volleyball, and tennis courts; a rock-climbing wall; a game room; and more.

Student services include career and placement counseling, the Cosiano Health Center, the Oiler Success Center, academic tutoring and personal counseling, and study skills assistance through the Academic Support Center.

Location

Findlay was voted the most livable micropolitan city in Ohio and scored among the top twelve 12 in the United States. It is within easy driving distance of Toledo, Columbus, Detroit, and Fort Wayne. Interstate 75 and the Ohio Turnpike (Interstates 80 and 90) are major highways serving the area. Airports in Toledo, Columbus, and Detroit are convenient. The town of Findlay has nearly 39,000 residents and is home to Marathon Oil Corporation and Cooper Tire and Rubber Company. The Findlay campus consists of more than 388 acres on several sites. A 152-acre campus-owned farm houses the pre-veterinary medicine and western equestrian studies programs, including a 31,000-square-foot animal science center with two 50-seat classrooms, a laboratory, a pharmacy, a student lounge, locker rooms, offices, instructional demonstration areas, holding pens, and other animal servicing areas. A second 32-acre facility houses the English riding program. Approximately 450 horses are stabled and trained at the equestrian facilities, which offer barns and indoor and outdoor riding arenas.

Many opportunities exist for students who want business-related and social service agency experience. The University has established strong relationships with the community, which supports athletic and cultural events on the campus. Besides the full program of on-campus activities, off-campus trips to cultural and entertainment events are scheduled. The city of Findlay, which has an excellent business climate, offers part-time job opportunities, volunteer service organizations, and the chance to be involved with the larger civic community. Findlay's campus is attractive, safe, comfortable, and friendly.

Majors and Degrees

The Bachelor of Arts (B.A.) degree is awarded in the following majors: adolescent/young adult/integrated English/language arts, adolescent/young adult/integrated social studies, art, art management, children's book illustration, criminal justice, English, English as an international language, graphic design, history, Japanese, journalism, law and the liberal arts, middle childhood/language arts/social studies, multiage/drama/theater, multiage/Japanese, multiage/Spanish, multiage/visual arts, philosophy/applied philosophy, political science, psychology, public relations, religious studies, social work, sociology, Spanish, studio art, teaching English to speakers of other languages, and theater. Minors are offered in numerous areas.

The Bachelor of Science (B.S.) degree is granted in accounting; adolescent/young adult/earth science; adolescent/young adult/integrated mathematics; adolescent/young adult/life science; animal science; biology (recommended for those interested in physician assistant or medical studies); business administration; business management; chemistry (recommended for those interested in medical studies); computer science; early childhood; economics; entrepreneurship; environmental, safety, and occupational health management; equestrian studies (English and Western emphases); equine business management; finance; forensic science; health education; health science (in preparation for occupational therapy or physical therapy); health studies; hospitality management; human resource management; international business; intervention specialist/mild to moderate disabilities; marketing; mathematics; medical laboratory science; middle childhood/language arts/math; middle childhood/language arts/science; middle childhood/math/science; middle childhood/math/social studies; middle childhood/science/social studies; multiage/health education; multiage/physical education; nuclear medicine technology; operations and logistics; physical education; positron emission tomography/computer technology; sport and event management and strength and conditioning.

The Associate of Arts degree is available in accounting, computer science, criminal justice administration (corrections or law enforcement emphases), English as an international language, equestrian studies (English and western riding), financial management, human resource management, management information systems, nuclear medicine technology, personal training, positron emission tomography/computed tomography (PET/CT), sales/retail management, and small business/entrepreneurship. Certificate programs are available in a variety of areas.

Academic Programs

Findlay operates on the semester system. Students must complete at least 124 semester hours with a minimum overall grade point average of 2.0 to earn a bachelor's degree. General education requirements and competency requirements in English, computer literacy, and speech must be fulfilled. The Gateway Program offers students the chance to develop those skills in writing, reading, and thinking needed for their success as college students. Study skills, time management, and academic advising are included. Students are selected for this program at the time of admission. The honors program provides additional challenge to those students who qualify on the basis of academic credentials. Study- and travel-abroad programs are offered by various departments. Credit and/or placement can be earned through Advanced Placement (AP) exams.

The equestrian program is a well-recognized program of its kind and serves approximately 280 students from throughout the United States and abroad. Majors in equine business management and in English and western riding are offered. The instruction, both in the classroom and on horseback, makes use of the expertise of recognized national equestrian champions.

The pre–veterinary medicine program, using the farm facilities, offers the advantages of hands-on experience with livestock and an internship program in a distinctive curriculum. Graduates of the pre-veterinary program have been accepted to all twenty-eight veterinary schools in the United States, and several internationally.

The Nuclear Medicine Institute provides the training necessary to qualify students for careers in nuclear medicine technology, a growing health-related career field.

Academic Facilities

The focal point of the Findlay campus is Old Main, which houses classrooms, faculty and administrative offices, the computer center, facilities for various student activities, the Oiler Success Center, and the Ritz Auditorium. Shafer Library is a member of a consortium that provides extensive resources to students. The Virginia B. Gardner Fine Arts Pavilion houses the Mazza Museum of International Art from Children's Books, the first and largest teaching museum in the world dedicated to literacy and children's book art. The Davis Building serves as home to the College of Education, the College of Pharmacy, and numerous science research labs. In 2006, the University acquired and renovated a building at 300 Davis Street, with its 62,000 square feet comprising the largest addition of academic space since the construction of Old Main. Other academic buildings include the Frost Science Center and the Egner Center for the Performing Arts, which houses a 200-seat theater.

Costs

Tuition for the 2013–14 academic year is $28,894 for most programs. Room and board costs $9,258. There are additional tuition charges for equestrian studies and pre–veterinary medicine.

Financial Aid

Assistance is based on need as well as scholastic achievement. In 2011–12, 85 percent of UF students received institutional financial aid from the University. The average need-based financial aid package for freshmen was more than $20,000 in fall 2012. Merit scholarships at UF range from $10,000 to $16,000 a year. Notification of aid awards is made on a rolling basis. Work-study jobs are available. Scholarships for high-achieving students and student athletes are offered.

Faculty

The 15:1 student-faculty ratio results in small classes, with an average class size of 20 students. Professors know their students, and every student has a faculty adviser.

Student Government

The Student Government Association (SGA) and the Campus Program Board are involved in planning and implementing student activities. SGA provides leadership experience for students and enhances cooperation among faculty members, the administration, and students. A representative from SGA sits on the Board of Trustees. The Campus Program Board plans activities for recreation and cultural enrichment.

Admission Requirements

The University of Findlay considers each applicant on an individualized basis. The University accepts applications on a rolling basis, but it encourages students to complete applications by January 15, as the class fills rapidly. Application deadlines are August 1 for the fall semester and December 15 for the spring semester. Major factors associated with rendering a decision include GPA, standardized test scores, and strength of curriculum. Although it is not required, a campus admission visit is encouraged. Applicants to Findlay should have a college-preparatory high school background, including 4 years of English, 3 to 4 years of mathematics, 2 to 3 years of social studies, and 2 years of science. A foreign language is recommended but not required. Results of the ACT or SAT should be submitted with the application for admission. Transfer students must be eligible to return to the institution last attended and must submit transcripts of all college work. For students not meeting regular minimum admission requirements, Findlay has a Gateway Program, which provides skill building and academic support during the first semester of the freshman year. Findlay is an equal opportunity institution in admission and employment.

Application and Information

For application forms and other information, students may contact:

Office of Admissions
The University of Findlay
1000 North Main Street
Findlay, Ohio 45840
Phone: 419-434-4732
    800-548-0932 (toll-free)
E-mail: admissions@findlay.edu
Website: http://www.findlay.edu
    http://on.fb.me/UFindlay (Facebook)

The University of Findlay's Old Main is an original building on campus and houses the College of Business and many student support services.

UNIVERSITY OF GUELPH
GUELPH, ONTARIO, CANADA

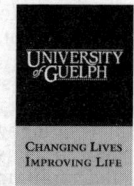

The University

The University of Guelph is ranked within Times Higher Education's Top 100 under 50 and is consistently recognized as one of Canada's top Comprehensive Universities. It is a high-quality, student-focused, residential university that is committed to innovative programs and research, dynamic student-faculty interaction, and an integration of learning and research. It offers a wide range of undergraduate and graduate programs in the arts, humanities, social sciences, engineering, and natural sciences. Building on these core disciplines, Guelph also has a strong commitment to interdisciplinary programs, to a selected range of professional and applied programs, and to agriculture and veterinary medicine as areas of special responsibility.

Established in 1964 when three century-old founding colleges joined with a new college of arts and science, the University of Guelph is a vital community of more than 22,000 students on a campus of historical and modern buildings connected by redbrick walkways. By Canadian standards, Guelph is of medium size, offering a wide range of academic programs while providing a safe, accommodating environment. On-campus living is available for more than 5,000 students, with new first-semester students guaranteed on-campus housing if they apply and submit a deposit before the deadline.

Guelph features state-of-the-art athletic facilities that include a double arena with an Olympic-size ice surface, two pools, a field house and indoor track, aerobic and weight-training gymnasiums, six squash courts, and a climbing wall. Guelph offers thirty varsity sports teams and in recent years has fielded national and provincial championship football, hockey, track and field, and rugby teams.

Guelph ensures a personal approach to learning with a 1:20 faculty-student ratio in 63 percent of its classes. The success of the Center for New Students, which assists students with the transition from secondary school to university, is reflected in Guelph's 91.6 percent student retention rate and a 94.2 percent graduate employment rate, both well above the Canadian national average.

For graduate students, the University of Guelph offers a Doctor of Veterinary Medicine degree as well as several graduate diploma programs and more than eighty master's and doctoral degree programs. The graduate calendar is available on the Web at http://www.uoguelph.ca/GraduateStudies.

Location

The University of Guelph's main campus is located in the southwestern Ontario region the New York Times calls Canada's Technology Triangle, a locale known for its high-caliber educational institutions and innovative companies. This city of more than 122,000 features internationally recognized folk, jazz, and writers' festivals as well as a multipurpose performing arts center and a sports and entertainment center. Positioned within an hour's drive of Toronto, Canada's largest city, Guelph offers the comfort of small-community living with the excitement of an international metropolis at its doorstep. In addition to the main campus, the University of Guelph offers many dynamic degrees in Toronto at the University of Guelph–Humber and regional campuses throughout Ontario in Alfred, Kemptville, and Ridgetown.

Majors and Degrees

The University of Guelph offers a number of undergraduate degree programs. Programs followed by an asterisk (*) indicate degrees that students can pursue in a traditional four-year or in a five-year co-op format. Co-ops offer students the opportunity to work in three to five different companies in paid work placements that result in one year of full-time work as a part of the degree experience.

The University of Guelph offers Bachelor of Arts degrees in anthropology; art history; classical studies; criminal justice and public policy; economics*; English; environmental governance; European studies; French studies; food, agriculture, and resource economics; geography; Hispanic studies; history; information systems and human behavior; international development; major to be determined; mathematical economics*;

mathematics; music; philosophy; political science; psychology*; sociology; studio art; and theater studies. In addition, a Bachelor of Arts and Sciences degree is available to students who excel in both arts/social sciences and sciences.

Bachelor of Applied Science degrees are available in applied human nutrition; child, youth, and family*; and adult development*.

Bachelor of Commerce degrees are available in accounting*, food and agricultural business*, hotel and food administration*, leadership and organizational management, management economics and finance*, marketing management*, public management*, real estate and housing*, tourism management, and undeclared (first year only).

Bachelor of Bio-Resource Management degrees are available in environmental management and equine management. Students in these programs begin their studies in the regional campuses and finish the final two years in Guelph.

The Bachelor of Computing degrees are available in computer science* and software engineering*.

Bachelor of Engineering degrees are available in biological engineering*, biomedical engineering*, computer engineering*, environmental engineering*, engineering systems and computing*, mechanical engineering*, water resources engineering*, and undeclared (first year only).

Bachelor of Science degrees are available in animal biology, applied mathematics and statistics* (co-op only), biological and pharmaceutical chemistry*, bio-medical science, biochemistry*, biodiversity, biological science, biological and medical physics*, chemical physics*, chemistry*, environmental biology, environmental geoscience and geomatics, food science*, human kinetics, marine and freshwater biology, mathematics, microbiology*, molecular biology and genetics, nanoscience*, nutritional and nutraceutical sciences, physical science, physics*, plant science, psychology (brain and cognition), theoretical physics, toxicology*, wildlife biology and conservation, and zoology.

Bachelor of Science in Agriculture degrees are available in animal science; crop, horticulture, and turfgrass sciences; honors agriculture; and organic agriculture.

Bachelor of Science in Environmental Sciences degrees are available in ecology*, environmental economics and policy*, environment and resource management*, and environmental sciences*.

The University of Guelph also offers a Bachelor of Landscape Architecture degree, a Doctor of Veterinary Medicine degree, and associate diplomas.

University of Guelph–Humber programs include honors degrees in business administration (accounting, finance, international business, marketing, and small business management and entrepreneurship); applied science (early childhood services, family and community social services, justice studies, kinesiology, or psychology); and applied arts in media studies (journalism, public relations, digital communications, and image arts).

Academic Programs

The academic year is divided into three semesters: fall (September through December), winter (January through April), and summer (May through August), with the majority of students in attendance during the fall and winter semesters. Fall is the normal entry point for all semester one students. However, transfer students who apply by deadlines are considered for many programs at all entry points.

Four-year honors degrees require the completion of eight semesters. Three-year general degrees require the completion of six semesters. A typical full-time semester totals 2.5 credits.

Off-Campus Programs

An important part of Guelph's mission is to attract students from around the world and develop a global perspective in its students. The campus attracts more than 800 international students from over 100 countries, maintains fifty-six exchange programs with thirty countries, and offers six semester-abroad options. In addition, approximately 500 Guelph students study, research, or work each year in Africa, Australia, Europe, and South and Central America.

Nearly 2,000 students participate in co-op work semesters, making the co-op program at the University of Guelph one of the highest in co-op student enrollments among Ontario universities. Guelph also offers more than 100 distance degree credit courses to nearly 8,000 Open Learning course registrants.

Academic Facilities

Guelph's two libraries are linked with libraries at two other universities in the region, providing students with access to 7.5 million items through a state-of-the-art automated library system. Guelph's library holdings include Canada's largest collection of theater archives, extensive Scottish study materials, and one of the best collections of postcolonial African literature in Canada.

A 30-acre research park adjacent to the campus is home to a growing number of research-intensive industries. Industry and government trust Guelph's faculty members to meet their research needs, offering approximately Can$157.9 million annually for research that ranges from workplace efficiency to developing better approaches to food packaging and marketing to ensuring the availability of clean water.

All students receive free central computing accounts, which allow access to the University's integrated electronic services from on or off campus. Services include e-mail, access to the Internet, computer-assisted instruction, conferencing, course selection, and high-quality laser printing. Student residences are directly connected to the Internet via the campus high-speed network. Off-campus students have access to chargeable high-speed Internet providers.

The campus also features two art galleries; a sculpture park; two performance stages; a covered field house; a Can$144-million Science Complex; a Can$44.6-million engineering facility expansion; the Guelph Institute for the Environment; the Bio-diversity Institute of Ontario, which is the world's first center for high-volume DNA barcoding; and the Can$70-million pathobiology/animal health laboratory. The 408-acre arboretum on the west side of the campus has nearly 5 miles of jogging trails and nature paths.

Costs

Full-time tuition for the 2012–13 academic year ranged from Can$2846 to Can$4940 per semester for Canadian residents and from Can$8715 to Can$11,406 per semester for international students. Mandatory fees totaled approximately Can$530 per semester, with slight variations according to each college. International students must purchase health-care coverage through the University. The cost for international students to attend Guelph for two semesters, including tuition and academic fees, health coverage, housing, clothing, food, and books, totaled between Can$30,432 and Can$35,816.

Financial Aid

The University of Guelph is committed to ensuring that a university education remains an attainable goal. In total, Can$22.6 million in annual student financial aid is given in the form of scholarships, awards, bursaries, and work-study opportunities. There are scholarships (ranging from Can$500 to Can$6000) and bursaries specifically designed for international students who are allowed to work on and off campus.

Faculty

The percentage of Guelph's 860 full-time professors who hold the Ph.D. degree or its equivalent is 99 percent, and all strive to bring the excitement and process of research into the learning environment. More than 100 professors have been recognized for excellence in teaching by external agencies, their peers, and students. No comparably sized university in the country has more 3M awards, Canada's most prestigious university teaching honor. Guelph has 19 Fellows of the Royal Society of Canada among its researchers.

Student Government

Students are involved at all levels of University government, from the residence council to the Senate and the Board of Governors. The Central Student Association (CSA), which represents all undergraduate students, oversees more than fifty student clubs that range from political to recreational. In addition, there are more than fifty academic and other student-government organizations located on campus. Students also have access to a number of service groups on campus, which range

from the Ontario Public Interest Research Group to a community radio station to Engineers without Borders and Habitat for Humanity.

Admission Requirements

Ontario applicants must present the Ontario Secondary School Diploma (OSSD), with a minimum of six 4U or 4M courses and specific subject requirements for the degree program desired. English 4U is required for all degree programs. For those outside Ontario, the secondary graduation certificate that would admit a student to a university in his or her home country is normally acceptable. Applicants must also satisfy the specific subject requirements for the program desired. Applicants who have completed the International Baccalaureate (I.B.) are granted credit for higher-level courses with grades of 5 or better to a maximum of 2.0 credits. Applicants who have completed Advanced Placement (AP) exams with a minimum grade of 4 are eligible to receive University credit to a maximum of 2.0 credits, which is subject to the discretion of the appropriate faculty. United States applicants are required to have a minimum unweighted cumulative grade point average of 3.0 and a combined SAT score of at least 1100 (critical reading and math components) or an ACT score of at least 24. Applicants should include specific subject requirements at the highest secondary school level offered.

Interested students should call Admission Services or refer to its website at http://admission.uoguelph.ca for application and deadline dates, detailed admission information, and downloadable application forms. Students interested in University of Guelph–Humber programs should contact Admission Services at http://www.guelphhumber.ca.

Application and Information

For additional information about admissions, academic programs, or University visits and tours, students should contact:

Admission Services
Office of Registrarial Services
Third Floor, University Centre
University of Guelph
Guelph, Ontario N1G 2W1
Canada
Phone: 519-821-2130 or 519-824-4120 Ext. 58721
Fax: 519-766-9481
E-mail: internat@uoguelph.ca (International inquiries)
　　　　usa@uoguelph.ca (U.S. inquiries)
　　　　admission@registrar.uoguelph.ca (Canadian inquiries)
Website: http://admission.uoguelph.ca
　　　　　http://www.guelphhumber.ca

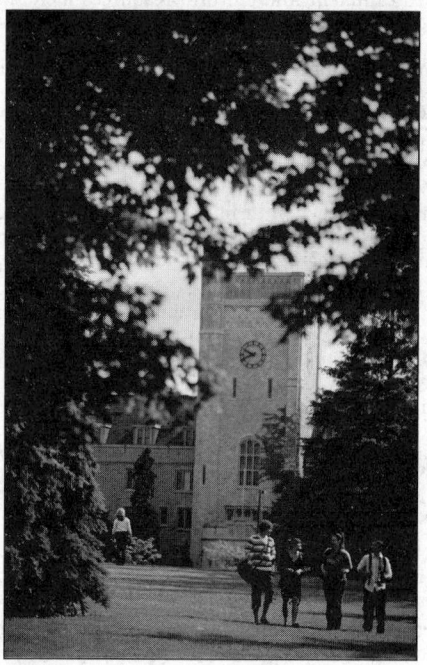

Students on the campus of the University of Guelph.

UNIVERSITY OF HARTFORD
WEST HARTFORD, CONNECTICUT

The University

The University of Hartford is a fully accredited, independent, nonsectarian institution. The University is composed of seven degree-granting schools and colleges: the College of Arts and Sciences; College of Engineering, Technology, and Architecture; College of Education, Nursing, and Health Professions; Hillyer College; the Barney School of Business; the Hartford Art School; and The Hartt School.

The current full-time undergraduate enrollment is approximately 4,600 men and women. A wide range of interests, goals, and backgrounds is found among the students, who represent fifty states and forty countries. There are about 100 organized student groups, including clubs devoted to special interests or to political, professional, religious, or civic activities as well as service learning and community service activities and groups. Intercollegiate (NCAA Division I) and intramural athletics, student publications, and AM and FM radio stations provide further opportunities for extracurricular involvement. In addition, The Hartt School, the Hartford Art School, and the University Players present a variety of concerts, exhibitions, and theatrical productions each year. Recreational and fitness needs of the University community as well as intramural and intercollegiate sports are served by a well-equipped 130,000-square-foot sports center and outdoor athletic facilities.

More than 66 percent of all full-time undergraduates reside on campus. The University offers a wide array of residence halls, from traditional dormitory-style to fully equipped town house–style apartments.

Location

The University is located in the residential suburb of West Hartford. Whether it's to eat at the Cheesecake Factory and catch a movie at Criterion Cinemas, or shop at Ann Taylor or REI, West Hartford is a great place to visit. The Hartford area also boasts an impressive array of entertainment and cultural resources including the New England Dodge Music Center and the Bushnell Performing Arts Center. The campus is easily accessible by both train and bus and is located about 25 minutes from Bradley International Airport.

Majors and Degrees

The College of Arts and Sciences offers majors in art history, biology, chemistry, chemistry-biology, cinema, communication, computer science, criminal justice, economics, English, foreign languages and cultures, history, international studies, Judaic studies, mathematics, philosophy, physics, political economy, politics and government, psychology, rhetoric and professional writing, and sociology.

Within the College of Education, Nursing, and Health Professions, there are majors in early childhood education, elementary education, integrated special education/elementary education, secondary education with a concentration in English or mathematics, health sciences, nursing (for registered nurses only), radiologic technology, respiratory therapy, a combined B.S. in health science, and doctorate in physical therapy (B.S./D.P.T.) program, as well as a combined B.S. in health science and a Master of Science in Prosthetics and Orthotics (B.S./M.S.P.O.) program.

The Hartford Art School offers Bachelor of Fine Arts degrees in ceramics, design, drawing, illustration, media arts, painting, photography, printmaking, sculpture, and visual communication.

At the Hartt School, students can major in actor training, applied music (guitar, orchestral instrument, organ, piano, pre–cantorial studies, and voice), composition, dance (ballet pedagogy or performance emphases), jazz studies, music, music education, music history, music management, music production and technology, music theater, music theory, and performing arts management (interdisciplinary program offered in conjunction with the Barney School of Business). There are also five-year double majors offered within the Hartt School.

Majors for the Bachelor of Science in Business Administration (B.S.B.A.) degree in the Barney School of Business are accounting, economics and finance, entrepreneurial studies, finance and insurance, management, and marketing.

Additional B.S. programs, offered by the College of Engineering, Technology, and Architecture include ABET-accredited programs in electrical, mechanical, civil, computer, and biomedical engineering as well as interdisciplinary B.S.E. options. The newest offering in the mechanical engineering department is a concentration in energy engineering and sustainable design. The most popular B.S.E. options are acoustical engineering and music (interdisciplinary program in conjunction with the Hartt School), biomedical engineering, and environmental engineering. Technology programs include the Bachelor of Science in architectural engineering technology, audio engineering technology, computer engineering technology, electronic engineering technology, and mechanical engineering technology as well as the Associate in Applied Science in electronic engineering technology (A.S.) and the Associate in Applied Science in computer engineering technology (A.S.).

Hillyer College offers the Associate of Arts and provides the general education course work required to complete most of the University's baccalaureate programs. Particular emphasis is placed on the development of academic skills through small classes and close faculty-student interaction.

University Studies offers the Bachelor of University Studies, a B.A. degree program created for the part-time adult student who typically has previous college experience and seeks to complete a baccalaureate degree. Also offered is a B.A. degree program in multimedia website design and development for full-time undergraduates. Created for students who want to learn how to use and develop multimedia technologies that fit into today's wired world, this program combines courses across several disciplines where students create and use technology with user interaction in mind.

Academic Programs

The University of Hartford enjoys a national reputation for the breadth and depth of its academic programs. As highlighted above, eighty-four undergraduate majors are offered through seven schools and colleges. Students are encouraged to sample a variety of academic areas. Those who have special interests can develop interdisciplinary majors that combine courses from the different schools within the University. Academic advisers are assigned to all students to help guide them in curriculum choices, career exploration, and the transition to University life. The University also has a special program to assist students who may be undecided about a major. A reading and writing center provides individual support to help students increase their proficiency in writing, research, reading comprehension, and speed as well as study and test-taking skills. Further help in math is given through the Math Tutoring Lab, which is staffed by full-time faculty members and math majors. Career Services provides vocational counseling and information on occupations, employers, testing, and graduate schools; serves as a reference and credential source; and provides an on-campus recruiting program for graduating students. University College addresses the needs of the part-time adult learner through courses, programs, and educational counseling. A trained counseling staff is available to assist part-time students in planning their education and resolving their special concerns and needs. Selected students are encouraged to participate in the honors program. Honors students have the opportunity to graduate with an honors degree.

Off-Campus Programs

Intercampus registration through the Hartford Consortium for Higher Education permits University of Hartford students to take certain courses at the School of the Hartford Ballet, Saint Joseph

College, and Trinity College. Teaching majors in the College of Education, Nursing, and Health Professions have opportunities for field and/or clinical experiences where applicable. A central internship and cooperative education office is available to custom-tailor work experiences within many of the University's programs.

Academic Facilities

Seven schools and colleges are housed on the main campus. The Harry Jack Gray Center houses the William H. Mortensen Library; the Mildred P. Allen Memorial Library; the Museum of American Political Life; the Harry J. Gray Conference Center; the Joseloff Gallery; the University Bookstore; studios for architecture, art, radio, and television; and the communication department. The library has approximately 583,000 items, including books, musical scores, recordings, periodicals, journals, and microfilm units as well as high-speed and wireless Internet access. Extensive resources are also available through the Hartford Consortium for Higher Education, the Hartford Library, and the Interlibrary Loan systems.

The new state-of-the-art Mort and Irma Handel Performing Arts Center, located 5 minutes from the main campus, is a 55,000-square-foot facility that houses five dance studios, four theater rehearsal studios, two black box theaters, a small dining facility, and faculty and staff offices. The Handel Performing Arts Center provides a rehearsal and performance environment for the Hartt School's dancers.

The University of Hartford Computer Center houses the central computer systems and operates a high-performance campus-wide network, which connects all student residential housing, all academic buildings on campus, and the University's remote locations. The University's network is connected via a high-speed telecommunication link to the Internet. The residential network gives each student resident his or her own high-speed Ethernet connection to the campus network and the Internet. All of the University network resources may be accessed on campus in any University facility and off campus by using computers with network connectivity.

Public access computing labs, used by all students of the University, are provided at various locations around the campus. In addition, college-specific labs are available to students. All labs are equipped with microcomputers (both PCs and Macs) and are connected to the campus network and the Internet. Typical microcomputer software includes word processing, spreadsheet, database management, and graphics programs; programming languages; and web browsers for accessing the Internet. Help is available from on-duty lab assistants. In addition to these computer labs, there are specialized computer facilities for instruction and learning. Wireless Internet access is available in all academic buildings, libraries, and dining facilities.

Costs

Tuition for incoming students was $30,618 for the 2012–13 academic year; fees, $1,554; on-campus room costs, $7,328; and board, $4,776. A variety of on-campus housing accommodates the University's residential student population.

Financial Aid

Financial aid for University of Hartford students totals approximately $98 million annually, including student loans. Scholarships, grants, loans, and work-study opportunities are provided through the federal government, private agencies, interested individuals, and University funds. University funds are disbursed based on the college or school in which the student is enrolled, availability of funds, applicant pool, and competition for funds. More than 93 percent of new full-time undergraduate students receive some type of University assistance;

the average out-of-pocket expense is $17,999 (estimate) per year. Partial-tuition scholarships are awarded to entering students who have demonstrated outstanding academic achievement or talent.

Faculty

There are 848 full-time and adjunct faculty members. The undergraduate and graduate faculties are essentially the same group, and 86 percent of the members hold the terminal degree in their field. Academic and personal advisory service is readily available. Each new student is assigned to a faculty adviser during summer orientation.

Student Government

The student governing body that represents all full-time students is the Student Government Association, through which students and faculty join in developing and coordinating the co-curricular activities of the University. Students are also represented on all major administrative committees, including the Board of Regents.

Admission Requirements

The Office of Admission considers the quality of the secondary school curriculum, academic performance in secondary school, ACT or SAT results, evidence of a desire to succeed, and leadership qualities shown by academic and extracurricular activities. Auditions, portfolios, and other tests are required of music and art applicants.

Application and Information

The University employs a rolling admission policy. For further information, students should visit the University on the Internet at http://admission.hartford.edu or contact:

Office of Admission
University of Hartford
West Hartford, Connecticut 06117
Phone: 860-768-4296
      800-947-4303 (toll-free)
Fax: 860-768-4961
E-mail: admission@hartford.edu
Website: http://admission.hartford.edu

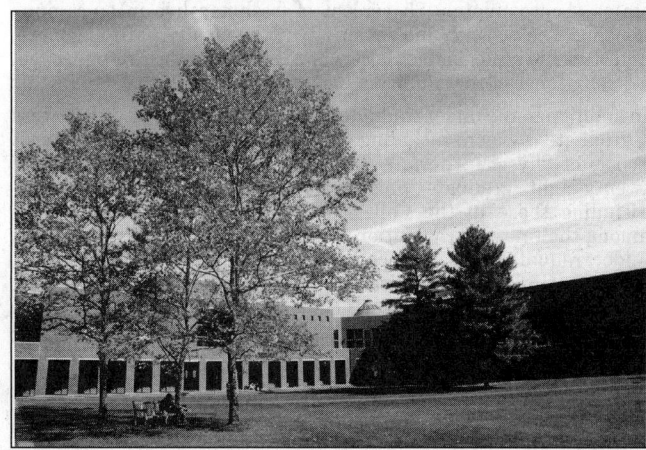

The University of Hartford is a suburban campus conveniently located between New York and Boston and only minutes away from downtown Hartford, Connecticut. Students can focus on studies while still being able to enjoy all that the nearby cities have to offer.

UNIVERSITY OF INDIANAPOLIS
INDIANAPOLIS, INDIANA

The University

The University of Indianapolis (UIndy) seeks to inspire excellence with a personal approach to education and a commitment to academic quality. Outstanding faculty members inspire students in small class sizes that allow individual attention and students are encouraged to apply their knowledge to real-world situations through internships, active learning in the classroom, and community service. A private, residential, comprehensive university founded in 1902 and affiliated with the United Methodist Church, the University of Indianapolis welcomes students of many nations and faiths from around the world. Every year, more than 5,000 full-time and part-time students, both undergraduate and graduate, benefit from the University's commitment to offering outstanding academic programs in more than eighty major fields of study. The University of Indianapolis accepts qualified applicants for admission without regard to race, color, sex, sexual orientation, age, religion, creed, marital status, and ethnic or national origin.

Students indicate that they chose UIndy because of its challenging yet supportive atmosphere, relatively small size, and the advantages of its location in the distinctive southside area of a thriving state capital city. As a result, there is a great sense of community and pride on campus. The University helps students to determine and achieve their individual academic goals. UIndy has experienced much growth and has instituted many enhancements recently, including Roberts Hall, the newest upperclassmen residence hall; the expansion of the Schwitzer Student Center; and the addition of the Athletics and Recreation Center.

More than 3,000 full-time undergraduate students are enrolled. There are students from more than sixty countries and thirty-five states. Approximately 85 percent of freshmen live in on-campus housing. The warmth and sensitivity of the faculty, staff members, and students alike enable those who are a part of the campus to feel a strong sense of community.

In addition to the undergraduate division, the University also offers a graduate division, including the nationally recognized Krannert School of Physical Therapy. The University of Indianapolis offers twenty-eight graduate programs and five doctoral programs, including those in the College of Health Sciences, which rank among the finest in the nation. The most popular programs in the undergraduate division include pre–physical therapy, business, athletic training, communication, nursing, education, pre-medical studies, psychology, and music.

Social life is organized through the numerous social, common-interest clubs available for students who wish to become involved in extracurricular activities. There are seven residence halls: six house both men and women, and one is only for women. Two-bedroom, one-bathroom apartments are also available to upperclassmen. Students must be admitted on a full-time basis in order to be assigned housing. NCAA Division II sports for men include baseball, basketball, cross-country, football, golf, soccer, swimming and diving, tennis, track and field (indoor and outdoor), and wrestling. NCAA Division II sports for women include basketball, cross-country, golf, soccer, softball, swimming and diving, tennis, track and field (indoor and outdoor), and volleyball. Intramural sports are also offered for men and women in flag football, basketball, softball, soccer, volleyball, indoor soccer, Ultimate (Frisbee), and wiffleball.

Location

The University is located in the University Heights neighborhood on the south side of Indianapolis, which is the nation's second-largest capital city. Indianapolis and the surrounding area constitute a metropolis of nearly 2-million people. The city offers numerous valuable internship and service-learning experiences as well as recreational and cultural opportunities for students. The campus is extremely accessible, just a few blocks from two major interstate highways (I-65 and I-465). IndyGo bus service is the city's public transportation system. Nonlocal options include Greyhound Bus Lines, Amtrak trains, and Megabus that arrive daily in downtown Indianapolis just 10 minutes from the campus. The Indianapolis International Airport is about 20 minutes away.

Majors and Degrees

The undergraduate programs are offered through the College of Arts and Sciences, College of Health Sciences, School of Business, School of Education, School of Nursing, and School of Psychological Sciences. The degrees awarded are the Associate in Arts, Associate in Science, Associate in Science in Nursing, Bachelor of Arts, Bachelor of Fine Arts, Bachelor of Music, Bachelor of Science, Bachelor of Science in Nursing, and Bachelor of Social Work.

Baccalaureate and pre-professional fields of study include accounting (CPA/non-CPA), actuarial science, anthropology, archeology, art, athletic training, biology, business administration, chemistry, communication, community health education, computer engineering (dual degree), computer science, criminal justice, earth-space sciences, economics, electrical engineering (dual degree), elementary education, English, entrepreneurship, environmental science, environmental sustainability, exercise science, experimental studies, finance, French, German, global leadership, history, human biology, human resource management, international business, international relations, management, management information systems, marketing, mathematics, mechanical engineering (dual degree), medical technology, music, music performance, nursing, philosophy, physics, political science, pre–art therapy, pre-dental, pre-optometry, pre-pharmacy, pre-law, pre-medical studies, pre–occupational therapy, pre-pharmacy, pre–physical therapy, pre-theology, pre–veterinary science, psychology, religion, respiratory therapy, secondary education, social work, sociology, Spanish, sports management, sports information, sports marketing, studio art, theater, youth ministry, and visual communication design.

Teaching majors are offered in business education (all grades), chemistry, earth-space science, English, French, life science, mathematics, music (all grades), physical education (all grades), physics, social studies, Spanish, speech communication, theater, and visual arts (grades 5–12).

Associate degrees are awarded in business administration, chemistry, information systems, liberal arts, nursing, and physical therapist assistant studies.

The University also offers the Healthy Diploma that provides students with the skills, knowledge, and motivation to achieve and/or maintain healthy a lifestyle as students and employees.

Academic Programs

The University of Indianapolis provides a top-notch education that combines a liberal arts and career-oriented curriculum that graduates describe as life changing. Students find a powerful combination of features designed to inspire them to excellence. Faculty and staff members take a personal interest in students and encourage them to explore their interests and apply what they learn, so they can excel when it comes time to make their place in the world.

Students can choose from more than eighty undergraduate academic programs. The goal of the liberal arts core classes is to provide learning above and beyond the student's major field, therefore students study topics and cultures that pique their interest in unexpected ways.

Students appreciate the curriculum because they don't have to wait to apply what they learn. University of Indianapolis students have time—before they graduate—to practice what they learn. Most majors offer practical experiences, which give students an edge in the job market. The Indianapolis location is an excellent resource when it comes to finding internships, field experiences, service-learning opportunities, or part-time employment. Internships let students sample their future careers and gain some of the knowledge and experience they admire in their professors. The University offers a host of possibilities for virtually any major. The Office of Career Services helps students identify an appropriate major and arranges off-campus internships related to their field of study.

Off-Campus Programs

The University operates a fully owned branch campus in Athens, Greece, that offers students a unique exchange program. Located within walking distance of the storied Acropolis, the Plaka, Constitution Square, and other historic landmarks, the University of Indianapolis–Athens offers students the opportunity to explore and experience Greece both inside and outside the classroom. Currently, the Athens campus offers twenty-nine undergraduate programs in the arts and sciences, business, and psychology. Short-term study trips, as well as full-semester study-abroad programs, are available to students through the Odyssey program. In addition, students at the main campus have many opportunities to travel to Athens on shorter trips during vacations or during the Spring Term in May. Other partnerships and extension sites for direct credit include Israel, Belize, and the People's Republic of China. Other off-campus study opportunities take place during the Spring Term, including assorted overseas travel options.

Academic Facilities

Krannert Memorial Library, which operates an online card catalog, houses more than 175,000 volumes, more than 1,000 periodicals, more than 19,000 microfilm/microform/microfiche records, and the Indianapolis Mayoral Archives. The library is home to a full media center. The communication department, with new state-of-the-art equipment for its radio station and television studio, is located in Esch Hall. Martin Hall contains outstanding resources for the Schools of Nursing, Physical Therapy, and Occupational Therapy and is connected to Lilly Science Hall, which recently underwent a major upgrade to all its science labs. Access to computers is available in all of the academic buildings. Students have access to the campus-wide information system from their rooms in the residence halls, and the entire campus is wireless. Ransburg Auditorium, with seating for nearly 800, is the setting for concerts, recitals, and theatrical productions. The Christel DeHaan Fine Arts Center features state-of-the-art music and art facilities; an art gallery; and a 502-seat, Viennese-style concert hall.

Costs

Direct costs for the 2013–14 academic year are $24,420 for tuition and $8,790 for room and board. Indirect costs are estimated at $1,094 for books and supplies, an average of $1,116 for transportation, and $2,188 to $4,222 for miscellaneous and personal expenses.

Financial Aid

All applicants for admission are eligible to apply for financial aid. Indiana residents should file the Free Application for Federal Student Aid (FAFSA) by March 10 to qualify for State of Indiana financial aid programs. All students should file the FAFSA along with the University of Indianapolis Application for Financial Aid by March 10 for priority consideration. For the 2012–13 academic year, about 88 percent of the enrolled full-time students received financial aid with an average financial aid package of $15,132 for entering students.

Faculty

UIndy's student-faculty ratio is 13:1 and the average class size is 18. Graduate students do not teach any undergraduate classes, instead the classes are taught by faculty members.

Student Government

The Indianapolis Student Government (ISG) consists of students elected to leadership positions plus student representatives from each class, chosen for a one-year term in an annual student body election. ISG's main focus is to pass resolutions regarding student concerns.

Admission Requirements

Applicants for admission must be high school graduates or have a GED certificate and are expected to have taken a college-preparatory curriculum in high school. Applicants for regular admission should have completed a minimum of 4 years of English, 3 years of mathematics, 3 years of laboratory science, 2 years of social science (U.S. history and government,), and 2 years of any foreign language. In addition, applicants for full-time admission without restrictions should rank in the upper half of their class and have average to above-average SAT or ACT scores. Essays are not required for admission. For immediate consideration, transfer applicants must have achieved a good overall record and have earned at least a C average in previous college or university work. An on-campus visit is recommended any time after the junior year of high school. To apply for admission, the Application for Admission, official high school transcript, official college transcript (if applicable), and official SAT or ACT scores should be forwarded to the Office of Admissions.

Application and Information

All applications are reviewed on a rolling basis—an admission decision is made as soon as all documents are received, and notifications are mailed immediately thereafter. There is no deadline for applications, but high school seniors are encouraged to apply during the fall semester of their senior year. Scholarships are also awarded on a rolling basis. Admitted students are notified of scholarships they have been awarded shortly after they have been accepted.

Requests for appointments and information about the University should be directed to:

University of Indianapolis
1400 East Hanna Avenue
Indianapolis, Indiana 46227-3697
United States
Phone: 866-421-7173 (toll-free)
      317-788-3216
Fax: 317-788-3300
E-mail: admissions@uindy.edu
Website: uindy.edu
    facebook.com/uindy
    twitter.com/uindy
    youtube.com/uindytv

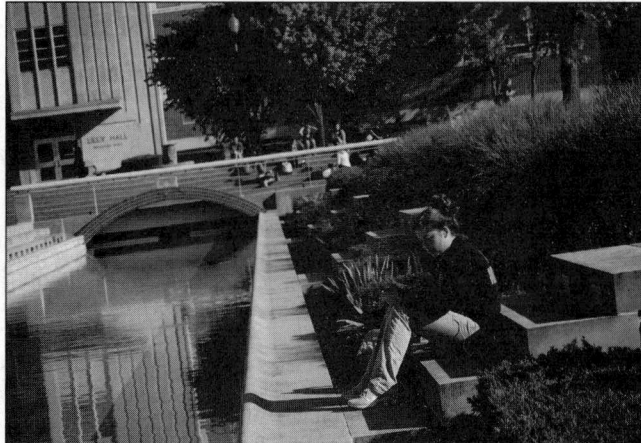

Smith Mall, the centerpiece of the University of Indianapolis campus, features a beautifully landscaped water garden canal.

UNIVERSITY OF MAINE
ORONO, MAINE

The University

The University of Maine (UMaine) offers the extensive academic opportunities expected from a major research university, with the close-knit feel of a small college. As Maine's flagship university, UMaine offers the state's most comprehensive academic experience, with more than 90 undergraduate majors and academic programs, 75 master's degree programs, and 30 doctoral programs. All majors benefit from a firm foundation in the liberal arts. Top students are invited to join UMaine's Honors College, one of the country's oldest and most prestigious.

The University of Maine is one of the National Science Foundation's top 100 research universities, and its facilities and faculty have an international reputation for excellence.

UMaine students have extraordinary opportunities to gain real-world experience through research and experiential learning. SPIFFY, the student investment club, manages a $1.8-million real-money portfolio. Wildlife ecology majors learn about bear behavior by going out and tagging cubs. Engineering majors secure co-ops and internships that often lead to employment after graduation. Education majors take advantage of urban, rural, and international student-teaching opportunities.

Location

There's no place like Maine, and UMaine students explore the great outdoors whenever they can. There are 15 miles of walking, biking, and cross-country skiing trails on campus. Some of the best skiing in the East is located within easy driving distance of campus, as are Bar Harbor, Acadia National Park, and Baxter State Park, the northern terminus of the Appalachian Trail.

Orono is a classic college town, bounded by the Stillwater and Penobscot Rivers, located in the heart of Maine. The University of Maine is 10 minutes from the state's third-largest city, Bangor, and its international airport.

UMaine's 660-acre campus was designed by legendary landscape architect Frederick Law Olmsted, who also designed Central Park in New York City and the U.S. Capitol grounds in Washington, D.C. It is a traditional New England campus, with ivy-covered brick buildings, towering pines, and incredible fall foliage.

Majors and Degrees

UMaine offers more than 90 majors and programs across five colleges—the College of Education and Human Development; the College of Engineering; the College of Liberal Arts and Sciences; the College of Natural Sciences, Forestry, and Agriculture; and the Honors College—as well as the Maine Business School. In addition, the Explorations program is designed to help undecided students identify a major from across UMaine's colleges while making progress toward their degree. The Division of Lifelong Learning offers online classes and distance-learning opportunities for students who need a flexible class schedule.

Academic Programs

UMaine provides a comprehensive academic and student experience, yielding graduates who are well educated, well adjusted, and well prepared to assume leadership roles in society. The university seeks to foster excellence and innovation through inspired, dedicated teaching and the discovery of new knowledge.

Students at the University of Maine benefit from a solid liberal arts foundation. They develop and refine the qualities they need to more fully engage with the world around them—critical thinking, curiosity, a sense of discovery, and a broader perspective—no matter what discipline they choose.

UMaine's Honors College provides an in-depth, academically challenging curriculum for qualified students in any major.

Undergraduate research is a priority and a point of pride. UMaine is the state's largest research university and graduate degree-granting institution, providing rich and varied opportunities for undergraduates to participate in research. Students publish, travel, and work alongside UMaine's world-class scholars and scientists. The Center for Undergraduate Research was established in 2008 to connect students with faculty projects that suit their interests. For many, research provides an opportunity for a mentor-mentee relationship different from—and often richer than—that of teacher-student. Skills developed through research and scholarship make students more competitive in the workplace and graduate school.

Off-Campus Programs

When UMaine students travel, they don't just go to Boston for the weekend. They go global, through study abroad, international volunteerism, and the worldwide research opportunities available to undergraduates. In recent semesters, UMaine students have traveled to China to learn more about the country's emerging financial markets, to Italy to explore Renaissance art history at the source, to Turkey to study film, and to Brazil to learn about a sensitive and diverse ecosystem from one of the world's leading conservation biologists (who also happens to be a UMaine professor and alumnus).

Academic Facilities

UMaine is home to state-of-the-art research facilities, classrooms, and teaching laboratories. Among the highlights are the Climate Change Institute, which has been featured on *60 Minutes*; the Laboratory for Surface Science and Technology, which is a hub for cutting-edge sensor and nanotechnology research; and the Advanced Structures and Composites Center, which is leading the nation in deepwater offshore wind energy development.

Fogler Library, the state's largest library, houses approximately 1 million volumes, subscribes to more than 4,000 periodicals and serial titles, and serves as a depository for more than 2.2 million government documents. In addition, Fogler provides access to countless online documents.

The University of Maine is also a cultural hub. It is home to the region's premier performing arts center, the Collins Center for the Arts, as well as several museums and galleries.

Costs

The University of Maine System Board of Trustees adjusts costs annually. For the 2013–14 academic year, tuition is estimated at $279 per credit hour for undergraduate state residents and $841 per credit hour for nonresident students. The average credit load for full-time students is 15 credit hours per semester or 30 credit hours for the academic year. Canadian and nonresident students who qualify for the New England Regional Program will pay an estimated $419 per credit hour. Required university fees (about $2,224 per year for a full-time student) include the Unified Fee, which provides a variety of health-care services and admission to cultural, recreational, and athletic events. Books and supplies average about $1,000 for the academic year. Room and board charges for the academic year are about $9,148. These costs are subject to change.

Financial Aid

UMaine requires all financial aid applicants to file the Free Application for Federal Student Aid (FAFSA). The priority deadline to apply for aid is March 1. Awards usually consist of a combination of several types of aid, ranging from grants and scholarships to work-study jobs and student loans. In addition, students who apply through the early action admissions program (complete application submitted by December 15) will be considered for UMaine merit scholarships based on high school achievement, as demonstrated by high school rank, grade point average, and standardized test results (SAT and ACT).

Faculty

There's a common misconception that if students choose a university rather than a small college, they'll get lost in the shuffle. They'll never see a professor—only teaching assistants—until they're in grad school. But at the University of Maine, the majority of undergraduate classes are taught by professors, and many of those faculty members go on to become friends and mentors to their students. UMaine's professors are known for having an open-door policy. Students have opportunities to work alongside some of the most renowned scholars and scientists in the world, whether they're talking civil engineering over dinner at Pat's Pizza or traversing an Antarctic ice sheet with researchers from UMaine's Climate Change Institute.

Student Government

Student Government, Inc. is the independent, representative body for UMaine's undergraduate students. An elected president, vice president, and vice president of financial affairs direct and coordinate Student Government programs at the University of Maine. Student Government works closely with the Office of the Vice President for Student Affairs and appoints 200 student representatives to various university committees involved with the planning and implementation of residence hall programs, student discipline, athletics, and cultural activities on campus.

Admission Requirements

Admission to the University of Maine is a selective process. Successful applicants are those whose scholastic achievement, intellectual curiosity, and established study habits promise success in a comprehensive university environment. Strength of the high school curriculum, grades received, class rank, counselor recommendation, and either SAT or ACT scores are the primary criteria for admission. Essays and information regarding school and community activities provide additional information that may help the admissions committee evaluate potential for success.

UMaine recognizes advanced work completed in secondary schools by means of Advanced Placement tests. In addition, students who demonstrate advanced knowledge may be exempted from certain courses and requirements if they pass examinations specially developed by the university's academic departments.

Application and Information

Applicants may submit electronic or paper versions of the Common Application or the University of Maine System application and may also apply via the Common Application. UMaine requires a supplement for the Common Application. Additional required documents for all applicants include official high school transcripts and counselor recommendations. Traditional-age applicants are required to submit scores from either the SAT or ACT.

The University of Maine has an early action deadline of December 15. Students whose complete applications are postmarked by December 15 are reviewed by the end of January. Early action candidates are given first consideration for the Honors College and merit scholarships awarded by the Admissions Office.

All other applicants are encouraged to submit their applications and all supporting documents by February 1 and are notified by rolling admission.

Students applying for the spring semester are encouraged to submit applications by December 1. Applications after these dates are processed on a space-available basis. Applications and all supporting documents should be sent to UMS Processing, P.O. Box 412, Bangor, Maine 04402-0412.

Office of Admissions
5713 Chadbourne Hall
University of Maine
Orono, Maine 04469-5713
Phone: 207-581-1561
      877-486-2364 (toll-free)
Fax: 207-581-1213
E-mail: um-admit@maine.edu
Website: go.umaine.edu
      facebook.com/UMaineAdmissions
      twitter.com/GoUMaine

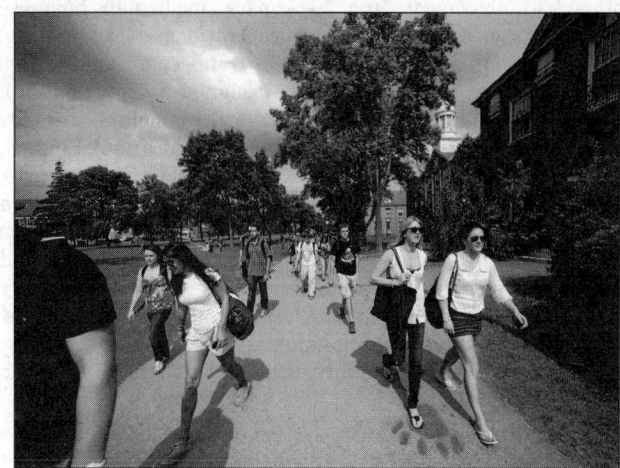

The Mall is the heart of the University of Maine campus.

UNIVERSITY OF MAINE AT MACHIAS
MACHIAS, MAINE

The University

Located on the spectacular Bold Coast of Maine, the University of Maine at Machias (UMM) is New England's only public environmental liberal arts college. The college was incorporated in 1909 and is a member of the University of Maine system. Small classes (the average is 17 students) and a faculty-student ratio of 1:13 contribute to an academic atmosphere that is intimate and intense and where independent thinking is encouraged.

Although many UMM students are from the state of Maine, the University's environmental emphasis, distinctive programs, and location attract many others from the New England, mid-Atlantic, and Midwest regions of the country.

Location

Machias, Maine, is a classic small New England town located on the tidal Machias River, with a town center that includes a number of retail stores, restaurants (including fast food), a supermarket, a natural foods store, and churches of various denominations. The greater Machias–area population is 5,000. The region is a popular outdoor recreation destination, with ocean beaches, inland lakes and streams, and miles of mountains, forests, and trails.

Downeast Maine has been a source of inspiration for generations of artists, outdoorsmen, mariners, and environmentalists. UMM's coastal location provides a unique learning environment, with excellent opportunities for fieldwork, hands-on learning, and cooperative education and internship experiences.

Majors and Degrees

UMM awards Bachelor of Arts and Bachelor of Science degrees in biology (concentrations in fisheries biology; wildlife biology; and pre-professional preparation in dentistry, medicine, optometry, pharmacy, and veterinary medicine); business and entrepreneurial studies (concentrations in accounting, business sustainability, management, and sport and fitness management); college studies (self-designed program option); education (elementary education, environmental literacy education, secondary education, and special education); English, creative writing, and book arts (concentrations in book arts, creative writing, and literary studies); environmental recreation and tourism management (areas of specialization in leisure programming, recreation and natural resources, and sport and fitness management); environmental studies; interdisciplinary fine arts (concentrations in book arts, creative writing, music, and visual arts); interdisciplinary studies; marine biology; and psychology and community studies (disabilities in youth concentration).

Academic Programs

Bachelor's degree candidates must complete at least 120 credit hours with a minimum cumulative grade point average of 2.0

and must also complete the core requirements in business studies, fine arts, humanities, physical education, science/mathematics, and social sciences.

Academic Facilities

All of the University's academic buildings are of modern construction and include a well-equipped science building with laboratories, a greenhouse, marine science aquariums, and a marine teaching and research laboratory. A Geographic Information Systems Laboratory and Service Center is located in Torrey Hall. Computer labs, some of which are open 24 hours a day, seven days a week for student use, house the latest in technology hardware and software. Located off-campus, UMM has an ongoing partnership with the Downeast Institute for Applied Marine Research and Education, where students conduct shellfish and finfish research.

Merrill Library provides a 24-hour study center with computer workstations for students, houses a collection of more than 100,000 volumes, and is linked to other libraries and educational resources throughout the state. A computer center with cross-campus networking and multiple computer labs enhances all of UMM's programs and provides access to the Internet and the web. Individual computer access is also available in every residence hall room. The University of Maine at Machias Student Support Center provides faculty, peer, and professional assistance as well as computer and audiovisual aids for all students. A residence facility with contemporary suites and single rooms was completed in 2003.

The Reynolds Athletic Center includes a large gymnasium, an aquatics center with a competition-size pool, a state-of-the-art fitness center, racquetball/handball courts, and a recreational equipment center, in which students may check out canoes, kayaks, snowshoes, cross-country skis, bicycles, and camping equipment. The Flaherty Early Care and Education Center provides child-care facilities for the community and the University; it also provides an on-campus site for UMM elementary teacher education students to participate in field studies.

A wide variety of student activities, from meetings to coffeehouses and other social events, are accommodated in the Student Center. Located in the same building, the campus radio station, WUMM, is run entirely by students. The Performing Arts Center, a 358-seat amphitheater auditorium, is host to numerous campus and community meetings, seminars, festivals, and performing arts and theatrical presentations.

Costs

The basic expenses for the 2012–13 academic year (based on a 15-credit-hour load per semester) were $6,660 per year for in-state tuition and $18,480 per year for out-of-state tuition. The University of Maine at Machias participates in the New England Board of Higher Education Regional Student program, which allows reduced tuition ($9,990 per year) for students from the other New England states who are enrolled in specific academic programs.

Financial Aid

The University of Maine at Machias administers scholarships, loans, grants, and work-study awards. The Acada Scholarship in the amount of $7,500 is awarded to first-year out-of-state students who have a 3.60 GPA, or a score of 1100 on the SAT (critical reading and math parts combined) or a 23 composite score on the ACT. The Sunrise Scholarship in the amount of $6,500 is awarded to first-year out-of-state students who have a 3.0 GPA, or a score of 950 on the SAT (critical reading and math parts combined) or a 20 composite score on the ACT. The Bold Coast Award, in the amount of $1,000 for in-state students and $2,500 for out-of-state students, is awarded to first-year students with 2.40 GPA, or a score of 880 on the SAT (critical reading and math parts combined) or an 18 composite score on the ACT. The Presidential Scholarship in the amount of $2,000 is awarded to first-year in-state students who have a 3.0 GPA, or a score of 1000 on the SAT (critical reading and math parts combined), or a 22 composite score on the ACT. Out-of-state transfer students receive a $5,500 Presidential Scholarship if they have a 2.75 GPA. In-state transfer students receive a $2,000 Presidential Scholarship if they have a 2.75 GPA. Financial aid awards are made on the basis of need, and students must submit the Free Application for Federal Student Aid (FAFSA) to the College Scholarship Service. March 15 is the University's financial aid priority deadline.

Faculty

Nearly all University of Maine at Machias faculty members hold the highest degree in their professional field. The faculty-student ratio is 1:13. All faculty members work as advisers and mentors to students within their areas of academic expertise. Usually on a first-name basis, faculty members develop a close relationship with students during their years of study at UMM and beyond.

Student Government

The University of Maine at Machias is a member of the University of Maine Organization of Student Governments and operates its own Student Senate. Students are encouraged to become involved and participate.

Admission Requirements

Graduation from secondary school or a high school equivalency diploma is the basic requirement for admission. Applicants to the University should have followed a college-preparatory high school program with 4 years of English, 3 years of math, 3 lab sciences, 2 social sciences, a foreign language, and computer utilization. If a student is entering one of the business programs, consideration is given to business courses taken in high school. However, college-preparatory English, math, science, and social science courses are still necessary. Scores from the SAT or ACT are also required. Applicants should rank in the top half of their high school class and have an overall grade average of B or better.

The University of Maine at Machias does not discriminate on the basis of race, creed, color, sex, or national origin and is an Equal Opportunity/Affirmative Action Employer.

Application and Information

The University of Maine at Machias operates on a rolling admission system. Candidates should complete their applications as early as possible. Students may apply for early admission, through which they may be admitted directly into the University after completing three years of secondary school. Candidates for this program must have recommendations of support from their guidance counselor, principal, superintendent, and/or school board. Their high school grades should place them in the top 15 percent of their class. UMM accepts applications from transfer students. Transfer applicants should complete their applications by June 1 for the fall term or by December 1 for the spring term.

Application materials and additional information may be obtained by contacting:

Director of Admissions
University of Maine at Machias
116 O'Brien Avenue
Machias, Maine 04654
Phone: 207-255-1318
        888-468-6866 (toll-free)
Fax: 207-255-1363
E-mail: ummadmissions@maine.edu
Website: http://www.machias.edu

Students at the University of Maine at Machias engaged in experiential learning on the coast of Maine.

UNIVERSITY OF MASSACHUSETTS BOSTON
BOSTON, MASSACHUSETTS

The University

Since 1964 the University of Massachusetts Boston (UMass Boston) has provided access to superior public education at a modest cost, in the state's capital city of Boston. With nearly 16,000 commuting students in its undergraduate, graduate, and advancing education programs, UMass Boston is the second-largest campus in the University of Massachusetts system, comprised of scholars who take pride in academic excellence, diversity, research, and service. The school's academic research and scholarship are tightly woven into the public and community service needs of Boston and modern metropolitan life.

UMass Boston's students represent an extraordinary range of economic, political, spiritual, and ethnic backgrounds, talents, and interests. Many come straight from high school. Others transfer from two- and four-year colleges. And while most come from within the Commonwealth of Massachusetts, many grew up in other states and countries.

UMass Boston has a vibrant student life. No matter what a student's social and intellectual interests, he or she can find engaging activities. From student government to student literary endeavors; from a champion chess team to working with inner-city youth; from academically affiliated clubs and athletic opportunities to a unique course-credit-based leadership-development program, students are sure to find just the right activity to complement their own classroom experiences.

The University's student body shares a strong motivation to succeed academically and to relate their classroom pursuits to career aspirations. The University Advising Center helps by providing comprehensive academic support, planning, and career advising services. A team of professional counselors provides personalized assistance for students to design their course of study, utilize tutorial and mentoring services, choose a major and career path, and develop interviewing, resume-writing, and job-search skills.

Location

From its beautifully landscaped peninsula on Boston Harbor, just south of downtown Boston, the University overlooks Dorchester Bay and the harbor islands. Its neighbors are the John F. Kennedy Presidential Library and the Massachusetts State Archives and Commonwealth Museum, and soon it will also share the site with the Edward M. Kennedy Institute for the United States Senate.

With its entrance along a bayside promenade drive just half a mile off Interstate Route 93, the campus is easily accessed by both public transportation and automobile. The Office of Undergraduate Admissions provides a number of free parking spaces in its Campus Center garage. A free shuttle bus runs every few minutes between the Massachusetts Bay Transit Authority's (MBTA) JFK/UMass Red Line "T" stop and the front door of the school's Campus Center. Student MBTA discount passes are available for frequent users.

Many students commute from home, while others utilize the Office of Student Housing for help finding a rental property and/or roommates. The University wants all its students to be at home at UMass Boston.

Boston itself, with its worldwide standing as a cultural center and well-earned reputation as America's favorite college town, offers UMass Boston students a wealth of resources for exploration and entertainment. Everything, from Fenway Park and TD Garden to Symphony Hall and the Museum of Fine Arts, is easily accessible from UMass Boston.

Majors and Degrees

Five undergraduate colleges award bachelor's degrees: the College of Liberal Arts and the College of Science and Mathematics (with thirty-eight majors, twenty-six minors and programs of study, and seven certificate programs between them), the College of Management (with two majors and eleven concentrations), the College of Nursing and Health Sciences (with a B.S.N., an online RN-to-B.S.N., and an accelerated B.S.N. program, as well as the B.S. program in exercise and health sciences), and the College of Public and Community Service (with two majors and two certificate programs). In addition, the College of Education and Human Development offers a non-licensure bachelor's degree in early education and care in inclusive settings (EECIS), as well as a program of study for those interested in earning teacher licensure during their undergraduate years. Also offered are premed and prelaw programs, programs for honors study, credit by examination, and advanced placement.

A joint arts or science bachelor's/master's degree program in business is available for high academic achievers, as is a bachelor's degree in liberal arts or science with a minor in management.

Academic Programs

The academic calendar runs from early September through the end of May. There is also an optional, month-long winter session in January, and summer school sessions are available beginning in May, June, and July. Matriculating students may choose to attend full- or part-time and may adjust their schedules from semester to semester. A minimum of 30 credits must be earned at UMass Boston as a residency requirement for graduation.

The College of Liberal Arts and the College of Science and Mathematics each require 120 credits to graduate. The general education curriculum comprises three elements: the distribution requirement, the core curriculum requirement, and the writing requirement. In addition, the requirements of the major must be fulfilled. Both colleges offer an honors program and an individual major option.

In the College of Management, the 120-credit undergraduate program leads to a B.S. degree in management or information technology. By fulfilling the general education, management, and elective course work requirements, students build a liberal arts foundation and receive the theoretical, technical, and functional training needed to succeed in the business world. An honors program is also offered.

The College of Nursing and Health Science's traditional B.S. program in nursing requires 123 credits for graduation, including general education courses and 63 credits of intensive study in the principles and practices of nursing. The exercise and health sciences B.S. program prepares students for the technical aspects of a professional discipline and gives them a solid foundation in the liberal arts. Students may also elect to enter the honors program in nursing.

The College of Public and Community Service (CPCS) offers an online degree-completion program in community studies, as well as a B.A. program in human services. Students may draw upon a variety of supplemental learning options in pursuit of their degree, including classroom study, self-directed study, and project-based learning. The honors program is also open to CPCS students.

Off-Campus Programs

The National Student Exchange Program offers UMass Boston students the opportunity to study at one of more than seventy participating colleges and universities in forty states at a cost comparable to the cost of attending UMass Boston. The study-abroad program is available for students with a 3.0 GPA or better who seek international travel and academic experiences, and it offers summer and winter session programs in other countries as well. UMass Boston participates in the New England Regional Student Program and the Boston Five-College Exchange Program.

Cooperative education and internship programs place students in work assignments related directly to their fields of study so that they may apply what they learn in the classroom to practical work settings. Under the co-op program, students are placed in full-time, paid positions for six-month work periods. Under the internship program, students are placed on a part-time basis, usually 15 to 20 hours per week, during a semester or over the summer months. Some are paid internships; others are volunteer opportunities.

Both co-op and internship placements combine relevant practical learning, valuable work experience, career awareness, resume enhancement, personal and professional growth, and, in many instances, opportunities for academic credit, good pay, and a permanent job after graduation.

Academic Facilities

The Joseph P. Healey Library holds a collection of more than 600,000 volumes, 85,000 electronic and print journals and newspapers, 60,000 electronic books, 100 databases, and 5,000 academic videos, DVDs, and films related to the campus's academic studies. The library's electronic resources are available on and off campus, 24/7 using a library barcode. UMass Boston is an active member of the Boston Library Consortium, and is also a partner in nationwide resource-sharing networks of scholarly and study resources. These offer access to a total of nearly 30 million volumes, via point-and-click. Students may obtain a library consortium card to check out books from any of the consortia libraries.

The Information Technology Services Division (ITSD) provides seven-day-a-week access to general-use computer labs, including the Adaptive Computing Lab, Graduate Research Center, media and language labs, and a media viewing center, all located within the Healey Library Information Commons, which also houses the IT Service Desk. The campus has many technology-enhanced classrooms and auditoria equipped with state-of-the-art audiovisual equipment and network connections. ITSD provides wireless access in most public spaces, ensuring that a wide variety of information technology and data communications resources is available to students. The Kennedy Presidential Library is linked to the University by a variety of educational programs, enabling students to conduct research utilizing the extensive resources of that library's archives. Next door, the Archives of the Commonwealth of Massachusetts are also a rich informational depository, covering more than 5½ centuries of Massachusetts history. The new Edward M. Kennedy Institute for the United States Senate, scheduled to open in 2013, will provide further academic research opportunities.

The state-of-the-art Campus Center provides easy access to student services, dining services, and spectacular meeting spaces, along with computer terminals and wireless Internet access. The new integrated science complex has been designed to provide enhanced academic opportunities for scientific study, research, and development for UMass Boston students and faculty. And ground has been broken for a new academic building to house additional classroom, office, meeting, dining, conference and performance spaces, providing room for further program and study growth.

Costs

Tuition and fees for the spring 2013 semester were $5,997 for Massachusetts residents studying full-time (12 or more credits) or $13,089 for out-of-state students. Students enrolling part-time were charged tuition according to the number of credits taken, with Massachusetts residents paying tuition at $71.50 per credit and out-of-state residents paying $406.50 per credit. Annual mandatory fees for in-state residents ranged up to $10,280 and up to $16,420 for out-of-state students.

Financial Aid

Financial aid is based on need and/or merit. Applicants must complete the Free Application for Federal Student Aid (FAFSA), keeping in mind a priority deadline of March 1 for fall semester and November 1 for spring semester. Need-based aid is awarded to students who demonstrate financial need, as determined by federal methodology. Aid consists of grants, waivers, and merit scholarships as well as self-help in the form of loans and work-study employment. An on-time applicant is automatically considered for all financial aid programs administered by the Office of Financial Aid Services.

Faculty

UMass Boston is proud of its 1,083 distinguished faculty members, some 93 percent of whom have terminal degrees in their field. UMass Boston has a student-faculty ratio of about 16:1 and a small class size that averages but 28 students. The faculty's top priority is teaching and advising students, although they also conduct research, publish materials, and participate in grant activities and professional organizations. Faculty members maintain office hours for students and make themselves accessible as mentors. Faculty and academic issues are governed by the Faculty Council.

Student Government

The undergraduate Student Senate consists of elected members from the undergraduate colleges and programs, and it participates fully in matters related to the quality of student life and the allocation of the student activities trust fund. Students are represented on numerous University- and college-based committees and councils that initiate major policy and procedural recommendations, forwarding those recommendations to governance bodies and the administration for enactment.

Admission Requirements

A freshman candidate for admission to the University should have earned a minimum of 16 academic units in high school that include 4 years of English, 3 years of mathematics, 3 years of science (including 2 with laboratory requirements), 2 years of social science (including 1 of U.S. history), 2 years of a single foreign language, and 2 years of electives in the arts or computer science (excluding vocational training). The student must also present satisfactory scores on either the SAT or ACT. The University looks for students with a strong academic background, as determined by a recalculated grade point average, and each candidate's academic program choices, motivation, achievement, and annual progress are closely scrutinized.

UMass Boston encourages qualified international students to apply for admission. Submission of a separate Declaration of Finances (DCF) form is required, along with supporting documents. Test of English as a Foreign Language (TOEFL) scores are required of all students educated in a non-English language educational system.

Transfer students are considered based on a review of all college academic credentials. Several academic majors and programs have specific higher requirements for transfer students, but, in general, a minimum 2.5 GPA is required.

Participation in a campus tour and group information session with an admissions counselor is strongly encouraged.

Application and Information

For information about the application process, deadlines, and informational materials, students should contact

Enrollment Information Services
University of Massachusetts Boston
100 Morrissey Boulevard
Boston, Massachusetts 02125-3393
Phone: 617-287-6000
      617-287-6010 (TTY/TDD)
Fax: 617-287-5999
E-mail: enrollment.info@umb.edu
Website: http://www.umb.edu
      http://on.fb.me/UMassBoston (Facebook)
      http://twitter.com/umassboston (Twitter)

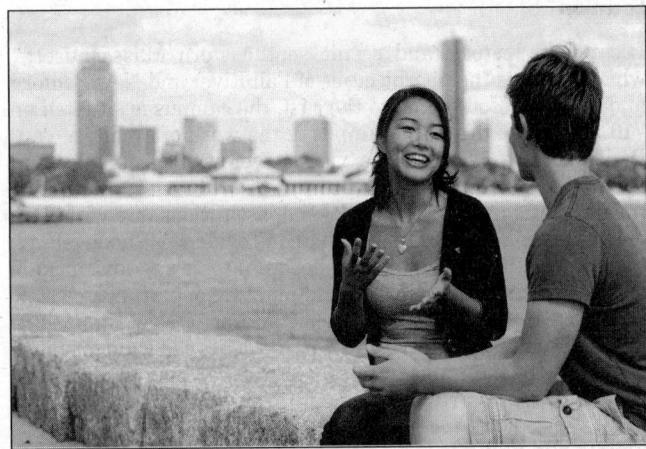

UMass Boston is situated on a scenic peninsula just south of downtown Boston.

UNIVERSITY OF MASSACHUSETTS DARTMOUTH
NORTH DARTMOUTH, MASSACHUSETTS

The University

The University of Massachusetts Dartmouth traces its roots to 1895 when the Massachusetts legislature chartered the New Bedford Textile School and the Bradford Durfee Textile School in Fall River. As the region's economic base shifted from textiles to more diverse manufacturing and service industries, the program of the colleges changed. Courses were developed to respond to the needs of new generations of students, stimulated by the clear economic and social advantages of a well-educated citizenry. In 1962, Southeastern Massachusetts Technological Institute (SMTI) was created, and in 1969, out of a need and a clear demand for a comprehensive public university, SMTI became Southeastern Massachusetts University. Then, in 1988, the Swain School of Design merged with the University's College of Visual and Performing Arts.

In 1991, a new University of Massachusetts system was created, which combined the Amherst and Boston campuses with the University of Lowell, Southeastern Massachusetts University, and the Medical Center in Worcester. Today, UMass Dartmouth provides educational programs, research, extension, and continuing education and cybereducation in the liberal and creative arts and sciences and in the professions. A broad range of bachelor's, master's, and doctoral degrees are offered. Graduate programs lead to the Master of Arts, Master of Business Administration, Master of Arts in Teaching, Master of Fine Arts, Master of Art Education, and Master of Science. A Ph.D. is offered in electrical engineering, chemical engineering, biomedical engineering, marine science, and physics.

UMass Dartmouth enrolls approximately 9,300 students; 90 percent are from Massachusetts, with a growing number from other states and countries outside the United States. A residential campus with a variety of student organizations, athletic programs, cultural opportunities, and interest groups, the University fosters personal development, diversity, and responsible citizenship.

Location

Located in historic and scenic southeastern Massachusetts, which includes the nearby cities of Fall River and New Bedford and the Cape Cod region to the east, the campus is situated on 710 acres. The dramatic campus is the work of architect Paul Rudolph, former dean of the Yale University School of Art and Architecture. Metropolitan areas, with libraries, museums, theaters, and numerous educational institutions, are within an hour's drive: Boston to the north and Providence, Rhode Island, to the west. Recreational sites are minutes away and include beaches, hiking, and cultural and nightlife opportunities. New York City is 4 hours by car; the mountains of New Hampshire and Vermont are 3 to 4 hours away. Students can walk to homes and shops in the immediate area of the campus, while public transportation is available to nearby communities.

Majors and Degrees

There are five colleges within the University: College of Arts and Sciences (twenty majors); Charlton College of Business (seven majors); Engineering (eight majors); Nursing (one major); and Visual and Performing Arts (twelve majors). In addition, honors programs, interdisciplinary studies, prelaw, premedical

advising, and a number of different minors and options are available within various departments. The University offers Bachelor of Arts, Bachelor of Fine Arts, Bachelor of Science, and Bachelor of Science in Nursing degrees at the undergraduate level. A complete list of majors is available online at www.umassd.edu/undergraduate/fieldsofstudy.

Academic Programs

The University operates on a two-semester calendar, with the fall semester beginning the first week of September and concluding in mid-December and the spring semester beginning in late January and concluding in late May. A three-week intersession is offered between semesters. Summer-term courses are offered in June, July, and early August. Undergraduate students usually enroll in four or five courses each semester, and a typical course earns 3 credits. An undergraduate degree requires a minimum of 120 credits (there are a few majors that require 135 credits); a student can complete degree requirements for a specified major within a department or an approved interdepartmental major (30 credits). Students must also complete requirements according to the degree being sought.

Other learning opportunities include independent study, contract learning, and directed study; study abroad; study at a nearby university through cross-registration; and credit by examination. UMass Dartmouth is a member of SACHEM (Southeastern Association for Cooperation in Higher Education in Massachusetts), allowing for cross-registration at Bridgewater State University, Bristol Community College, Cape Cod Community College, Dean College, Massachusetts Maritime Academy, Massasoit Community College, Stonehill College, and Wheaton College. Students can take advantage of exchange agreements with partner institutions in a number of countries including Australia, Belgium, China, Egypt, England, France, Germany, Ireland, Italy, Portugal, and Spain. Students may also take initiative in finding other programs in addition to the exchange-agreement institutions.

The College of Engineering and the Charlton College of Business provide students an opportunity to gain work experience through cooperative education.

Academic Facilities

Students are benefitting from a campuswide $175-million building and renovation program to upgrade and improve academic facilities, including a $45-million renovation to the library, which has created a state-of-the-art, LEED-certified space to serve as both the intellectual and social heart of campus. Access to technology is an integral part of the curriculum. All academic buildings, including student residences, are connected to a campuswide network through both intranet and a WiMAX wireless network. UMass Dartmouth is only the second campus in the country to implement a WiMAX system. Computing clusters, located in the library and in most classroom buildings, support the classwork of students. Multiple computer labs (Apple and PC) are readily available throughout campus. The University library supports all programs of instruction and research with 460,000 volumes, 46,000 e-journals, and 1,900 periodicals. A large interlibrary loan network and delivery system makes millions of volumes available to the students.

Each of the five colleges within the University is housed in academic facilities designed for its purposes with classrooms, laboratories, study spaces, galleries, faculty offices, and lounges.

Costs

In-state tuition and fees for 2012–13 were $11,681; non-Massachusetts resident tuition and fees were $23,028. Room and board expenses were $10,574 (based on a nineteen-meal plan and a double room for a year). Books and supplies cost approximately $1,200 a year depending on a student's courses. Specific fees may be assessed, depending on a student's course of study.

Financial Aid

Nearly all students are eligible for some type of financial aid. UMass Dartmouth awards financial aid based on federal, state, and institutional guidelines; students must submit the Free Application for Federal Student Aid (FAFSA). In determining need, the Financial Aid Services Office considers the total costs of attending the University (tuition, fees, books, room and board, the cost of commuting, and an allowance for living and personal expenses). The difference between total University cost and the estimate of expected family contribution is the amount that the financial aid staff considers to be financial need. Typically, UMass Dartmouth financial aid awards at least 86 percent of a student's demonstrated need. Students are encouraged to submit their FAFSA by March 1 for priority consideration in the awarding process. More information about UMass Dartmouth financial aid and scholarships is available online at www.umassd.edu/financialaid.

Faculty

The faculty, numbering 375 full-time members, is distributed over twenty-nine departments in the five colleges. Ninety-six percent of the faculty members hold the terminal degree in their chosen discipline (e.g., business, fine arts, education). A student-faculty ratio of 18:1 ensures that classes are reasonably sized, with an average class size of 29 students. Faculty members are actively engaged in advising students, providing guidance throughout a student's academic career.

Student Government

The Student Senate is the governing body offering a forum for debate on matters of importance to the student body. The Student Judiciary, a system of courts or judicial agencies, provides students and organizations with the protection of due process in all disciplinary matters. A student is also elected to the University of Massachusetts Board of Trustees. Students serve on the Board of Governors, policy makers for the Campus Center; the Resident Hall Congress; and the Student Activities Board. Students are active, voting participants on policymaking committees that regulate both academic and social aspects of the University.

Admission Requirements

Admission is selective. Applicants are evaluated both by the general standards of the University and by the special standards of the academic areas that they request. In addition, the Board of Higher Education sets guidelines governing admission standards for the University. Admission to some colleges or majors may be limited by spaces available. Students are admitted on a rolling basis with no set deadline. Qualified candidates are accepted until the capacity has been reached in the program of choice. Each applicant's record is assessed on the basis of the depth and rigor of the secondary school program, rank in class and grade point average, SAT or ACT results, college-level records for transfer applicants, and other appropriate measures.

The University realizes its commitment to equal access through standard, as well as alternative, admission programs. For College Now, the alternative program, applicants must meet at least one of three eligibility criteria: low-income status, limited English background, or first generation in the family to attend college.

All applicants for freshman admission to the University are required to submit an application form with the $60 application fee, a transcript of the secondary school record, SAT or ACT results, and any other information that candidates consider important for the admissions committee to review. Transfer students, who compose approximately one quarter of the new student population every year, are required to submit records for all college-level work completed in addition to the application form. The admission process is virtually the same for transfer candidates, with primary emphasis on the student's previous college/university record. UMass Dartmouth participates in the Mass Transfer program for students from Massachusetts who are transferring from a public two-year institution, as well as several joint admission partnerships with regional two-year colleges. More information can be found online at www.umassd.edu/transferexperience.

Application and Information

Students are invited to visit the University for a campus tour and an information session with an admissions officer. Some majors, such as nursing, may close early due to enrollment capacity. Nursing applicants are encouraged to apply by February 1 for priority consideration. UMass Dartmouth practices rolling admission and most decisions are made within three weeks of the completion of an application. Application forms and related information is available at www.umassd.edu/apply.

For more information, contact:

Office of Admissions
UMass Dartmouth
285 Old Westport Road
North Dartmouth, Massachusetts 02747-2300
Phone: 508-999-8605
Fax: 508-999-8755
E-mail: admissions@umassd.edu
Website: www.umassd.edu/admissions/

UMass Dartmouth: World Class. Within Reach.

UNIVERSITY OF MASSACHUSETTS LOWELL

LOWELL, MASSACHUSETTS

The University

The University of Massachusetts (UMass) Lowell is a nationally recognized doctoral-level research university. It is ranked in the top tier of *U.S. News & World Report's* national universities. Founded in 1894, the University has built a tradition of innovation, entrepreneurship, and partnerships with industry and the community to advance research, provide public service, and enrich the student educational experience. Its graduates are ready to contribute meaningfully in the work place, to build lives around the principles and passions they develop at UMass, and to make a difference in communities anywhere in the world.

The University is part of the five-campus University of Massachusetts system and comprises six colleges: the College of Fine Arts, Humanities and Social Sciences; the College of Sciences; the Francis College of Engineering; the School of Health and Environment; the Manning School of Business; and the Graduate School of Education. Together, the colleges offer more than 120 programs to UMass Lowell's 9,500 undergraduate students. The Graduate School enrolls nearly 4,000 students in thirty-six master's degree and twenty-three doctoral programs. The UMass Lowell education focuses on putting the lessons of the classroom into practice. Students have multiple opportunities for co-ops, internships, service-learning activities, and undergraduate research, all of which give them relevant hands-on experience in their fields. A real-world focus is reflected in the interdisciplinary nature of many academic initiatives. These include grant-funded projects such as Artbotics and Sound Thinking, which combine the arts and computer science, and interdisciplinary minors such as energy engineering; Asian studies; and technology, society, and human values. All programs are accredited at the highest levels.

UMass Lowell offers dozens of programs that allow students to stay as little as one extra year to earn both a bachelor's and a master's degree, giving them a competitive advantage as they enter the workplace. The undergraduate experience is enhanced by the diverse and international campus community and extensive opportunities for studying abroad. The University has developed nearly 100 partnerships with prestigious institutions in sixty countries that reflect the diversity its own community and contemporary geopolitics. UMass Lowell offers a robust honors program for those students who want to achieve at the highest level as well as programs and resources designed to help students succeed. Academic and residential learning communities help first-year students make the transition to college by fostering connections among small groups with similar academic interests. The Centers for Learning offers a range of tutoring and other support programs and the Center for Career Services and Cooperative Education helps students transition to the working world. The University maintains a student-faculty ratio of 14:1.

The University community is ethnically, culturally, and economically diverse. Nearly half of all students, and 83 percent of incoming freshmen, choose to live in University housing, which ranges from traditional residence halls to apartments and suite-style housing scheduled to open fall 2013. Students are active in a wide variety of community service activities and in more than 120 campus organizations that range from academic and athletic to recreational and special interest groups. Examples include a marching band, a weekly student newspaper, an FM radio station, and the Off-Broadway Players. A vibrant campus life includes rallying for the nationally ranked River Hawks men's ice hockey team which competes in Hockey East. As of fall 2013, all seventeen varsity teams for men and women are slated to compete in Division I.

Location

The University is located in Lowell, a city of 110,000 that has gained national attention by successfully leveraging its history, ethnic diversity, and entrepreneurial spirit to create a vital urban center. The site of a unique, urban National Historical Park that honors the city as the birthplace of the industrial revolution, Lowell is also home to an acclaimed professional theater company, literary and folk festivals, and museums that include the Museum of American Textile History and the Whistler House Museum. Located 25 miles from the cultural and educational riches of Boston and Cambridge, Lowell is situated within the region's major business corridors, which provide internship and co-op opportunities for students. It is also within an hour of ocean beaches and the lakes and mountains of New Hampshire via major highways and regional train and bus service.

Majors and Degrees

Dual majors are permitted. Dual B.A./B.S. and an array of bachelor's-to-master's degree programs are available in all fields. Pre-dental and pre-medical programs are also available.

The College of Fine Arts, Humanities and Social Sciences offers baccalaureate programs in American studies, art, criminal justice, design, economics, English, environmental studies, history, liberal arts, modern languages, music business, music performance, music studies, peace and conflict studies, philosophy, political science, psychology, sociology, and sound recording technology.

The College of Sciences offers baccalaureate programs in biological sciences; chemistry with an option in forensics science; computer science; environmental, earth, and atmospheric sciences (meteorology); mathematics; and physics.

The James B. Francis College of Engineering offers baccalaureate day programs in chemical, civil and environmental, electrical and computer, mechanical, and plastics engineering. Engineering programs are accredited by the Accreditation Board for Engineering and Technology, Inc. (ABET).

The School of Health and Environment offers baccalaureate day programs in clinical sciences, which is accredited by the National Accrediting Agency for Clinical Laboratory Sciences (NAACLS); community health education; environmental health; exercise physiology; medical technology; nursing, which is accredited by the National League for Nursing Accrediting Commission (NLNAC); and nutritional science.

The Manning School of Business offers baccalaureate day programs, all of which are accredited by AACSB International—The Association to Advance Collegiate Schools of Business—in business administration (B.S.B.A.), with concentrations in accounting, entrepreneurship, finance, international business, management, management information systems, marketing, and supply chain and operations management.

The University's Graduate School of Education offers widely respected master's and doctoral programs, as well as a range of initial certification courses.

The University's Division of Continuing Studies and Corporate Education offers a wide range of evening programs through all six colleges, delivered online and on campus.

Academic Programs

The University operates on a calendar of two semesters, a three-week intersession in January, and a summer term with two sessions. Full-time undergraduates generally take five courses each semester. A minimum of 120 credits is required for baccalaureate degrees; the minimum credits required for professional degree programs are generally higher. A University general education requirement is imposed for all baccalaureate programs. Majors require 30–60 credits. Elective course options vary widely according to the degree program and major area. Professional degree program options and requirements follow specific accreditation guidelines. Maximum curricular freedom is permitted in B.A. programs. The academic climate is serious and competitive and requires self-motivation.

Academic Facilities

The campus is in the midst of a bold expansion. The Emerging Technologies and Innovation Center, a state-of-the-art facility focused on applications of nanotechnology in manufacturing, defense, and medicine, opened fall 2012 and will be followed by a Health and Social Sciences building, two new suite-style residence halls, a student center, and business school building. The Campus Recreation Center provides additional spaces for recreation and fitness instruction. Recent renovations to both libraries have created new learning commons equipped with learning technologies and areas for quiet and group study. State-of-the-art facilities include six sound recording technology studios, a nursing simulation lab, and a manufacturing lab where engineering and management students team up to produce microelectronic components.

Costs

The annual costs for 2012–13 for full-time undergraduate residents of Massachusetts were $11,847 per year; for nonresidents of Massachusetts, they were $24,896 per year. Room and board charges were $10,282 per year. Accident insurance is covered by fees; major medical insurance is optional. Books and supplies are estimated at $400 to $600, depending on the program. Quoted rates are subject to change.

Financial Aid

The University is committed to making higher education accessible to all qualified students. The University participates in federal and state programs, assisting students through grants-in-aid, loans, employment opportunities, and scholarships. The amount of a financial aid award is determined by need, as indicated by the Free Application for Federal Student Aid (FAFSA), which should be filed by March 1. The University awards a growing number of merit-based scholarships. In fiscal 2012, the campus awarded $120 million in financial aid and met approximately 92 percent of need.

Faculty

Faculty members are respected researchers who value their commitment to teaching and extend the learning experience beyond the classroom. The full-time resident faculty members number 556. The part-time day faculty members number approximately 150. In addition, approximately 175 part-time faculty members are employed in continuing education programs. Most faculty members teach and conduct research in their disciplines. Graduate teaching assistants also hold part-time instructional positions, particularly as discussion section leaders and laboratory teaching assistants.

Student Government

The Student Government Association and the Residence Hall Association provide opportunities in student government at the all-campus level. Leadership opportunities are provided in residence halls and student organizations. Students also participate in the disciplinary system and in most University committees.

Admission Requirements

All undergraduate day applicants must have a high school diploma or a general equivalency diploma and satisfactory SAT scores. The incoming freshman class for fall 2012 had an average GPA of 3.26 and the average SAT score (combined reading and math) was 1127. Students whose high school average is below the required minimum may be considered for admission if they present SAT verbal and mathematics scores that are higher than those specified for the admission of degree candidates by the college or program to which they wish to apply.

Transfer students are considered for fall- or spring-semester admissions. Transcripts of completed work must be on file prior to acceptance. Depending on the number of transfer credits and college GPA, transfer students who seek admission as matriculating day students may be asked to provide a high school record and SAT scores.

Application and Information

For day programs, the University admits students through early action, regular admission, and transfer admission. Entering freshmen are admitted for the fall or spring semester. The early action deadline for freshman applications is December 1; the preferred deadline for regular admission is February 15. Applicants to the nursing program are encouraged to apply by the early action deadline. The preferred deadline for transfer applications is August 15 for the fall semester and January 7 for the spring semester.

For application forms and further information, students should contact:
Office of Undergraduate Admissions
University of Massachusetts Lowell
883 Broadway Street
Suite 110
Lowell, Massachusetts 01854-5104
Phone: 978-934-3931
Website: http://www.uml.edu
http://www.facebook.com/umlowell
http://www.twitter.com/umasslowell
http://www.youtube.com/user/umasslowell

UMass Lowell graduates are ready for work, life, and all that the world has to offer.

UNIVERSITY OF MEMPHIS
MEMPHIS, TENNESSEE

The University

Located on a beautifully landscaped campus in the heart of one of the South's largest and most progressive cities, the University of Memphis (U of M) is the flagship institution of the Tennessee Board of Regents System. Since its beginning in 1912, the University has matured into a major public, metropolitan university recognized regionally and nationally for its academic, research, and athletic programs. The U of M offers more than 254 areas of study from which to choose.

The University campus comprises 1,607 acres at nine sites, including the Lambuth Campus in Jackson, Tennessee. In addition to the main campus, the Park Avenue campus contains spacious living accommodations for married students, a research park, and outstanding varsity athletic training facilities. U of M also owns the Meeman Biological Field Station, a 623-acre tract used for biological and ecological studies.

The University of Memphis is an Equal Opportunity/Affirmative Action institution committed to the education of a diverse student body. It has a total enrollment of 22,365 students, including 17,795 undergraduates from almost every state and many other countries. Approximately 54 percent of University of Memphis students are between the ages of 18 and 22, and members of minority groups account for 35 percent of the enrollment.

Location

The greater Memphis area has a population of approximately 1.3 million, which makes the city the twentieth largest in the country. Centrally located on the Mississippi River, Memphis is an active hub for business, agriculture, and the transportation industry. The city has the Mid-South's largest medical center and offers many cultural and entertainment opportunities. Major museum exhibits, sporting events, concerts, art shows, lectures, and even barbecue contests take place throughout the year. The AAA baseball team, the Redbirds, and the NBA team, the Grizzlies, both make their homes in Memphis. With its many businesses, industries, and schools, Memphis provides students with employment opportunities in a variety of fields during and after their college careers.

Majors and Degrees

The College of Arts and Sciences offers undergraduate majors organized into three concentration groups: the humanities, the natural and mathematical sciences, and the social sciences. Three degree programs are offered: the Bachelor of Arts, the Bachelor of Science, and the Bachelor of Science in Chemistry. Majors include African and African-American studies, anthropology, biology, chemistry, computer science, criminology and criminal justice, earth sciences, economics, English, foreign languages and literatures, history, international studies, mathematical sciences, philosophy, physics, political science, psychology, social work, and sociology. Minors are available in each of those areas, as well as interdisciplinary minors in aerospace studies, Asian studies, emergency management, environmental studies, Judaic studies, legal thought and liberal arts, military science, naval science, nonprofit management studies, public administration, religious studies, and women's studies.

The Fogelman College of Business and Economics offers programs of study leading to the Bachelor of Business Administration degree. Majors include accounting, business economics, finance, hospitality and resort management, international business, management, management information systems, marketing management, and supply chain management. The programs of the College of Business and Economics are fully accredited by AACSB International—The Association to Advance Collegiate Schools of Business.

The College of Communication and Fine Arts is made up of the Departments of Architecture, Art, Communication, Journalism, Theatre and Dance, and the Rudi E. Scheidt School of Music. Majors include architecture, art, art history, communication,

interior design, journalism, music, music industry, and theater. The college offers three undergraduate degrees: the Bachelor of Arts, the Bachelor of Fine Arts, and the Bachelor of Music.

The College of Education, Health and Human Sciences (CEHHS) at the University of Memphis is among a select few institutions nationwide to meet, without a weakness, National Council for the Accreditation of Teacher Education standards. It is home to more nationally recognized educator programs than any other public university in Tennessee. In addition to teacher education, the college offers accredited degree programs in counseling, health and sport sciences, and leadership. CEHHS takes pride in being home to twenty-one research centers and/or institutes that are as diverse in their focus as the faculty and departments in the College, and in building partnerships with the dynamic communities that it serves.

The Herff College of Engineering offers undergraduate programs in biomedical, civil, computer, electrical, and mechanical engineering and engineering technology. High-ability students have the opportunity to work with faculty members on world-class research for global companies such as FedEx, for governmental organizations such as the U.S. Army Corps of Engineers, or for other premier organizations such as St. Jude Children's Research Hospital.

The University College offers two nontraditional degrees, the Bachelor of Liberal Studies and the Bachelor of Professional Studies, for students with experience, talents, and interests served through personally designed or multidisciplinary programs.

The University of Memphis also offers specialized degree programs. The Loewenberg School of Nursing offers a Bachelor of Science in Nursing degree. The program is accredited by the National League for Nursing Accrediting Commission and the Commission on Collegiate Education in Nursing. Students benefit from exceptional learning opportunities at healthcare agencies in the Memphis area, including ten major hospitals.

Preprofessional training is offered for students who intend to enter law school or a college of dentistry, medicine, nursing, optometry, pharmacy, physical therapy, or veterinary medicine. The University also offers Air Force, Army, and Navy ROTC programs.

The University of Memphis has joined forty-five Tennessee Board of Regents institutions in offering Regents Online Degree Programs. The U of M offers four degree programs: the Bachelor of Liberal Studies in interdisciplinary studies, the Bachelor of Professional Studies in information technology, the Bachelor of Professional Studies in organizational leadership, and the Bachelor of Professional Studies in international organizational leadership. These degree programs are entirely online and are transferable among the participating institutions.

Academic Programs

Freshmen who have not declared a major are advised through the Academic Counseling Center in preparation for formal enrollment in one of the degree-granting colleges. Those freshmen who have chosen a major are assigned to their degree-granting college immediately for academic advising. Each student initially selects courses from the General Education Program, which offers classes ensuring the acquisition of breadth as well as depth of knowledge in various fields. In addition to meeting the requirements of the General Education Program, all students must meet the requirements for their specific degree. The Helen Hardin Honors Program, designed for academically ambitious and talented students, is the largest in the state. There is also an active Emerging Leaders program.

The academic year begins in late August and is divided into two semesters and a summer session. The fall semester ends in mid-December, and the spring semester begins in mid-January. There are also courses offered during shorter sessions within the semesters.

Off-Campus Programs

Students at the University of Memphis have the opportunity to participate in study-abroad programs and the National Student Exchange program. These programs allow students to study in more than fifty other countries as well as in other locations within the continental United States. The University also offers credit and noncredit courses at various locations throughout west Tennessee.

Academic Facilities

The University Libraries of the University of Memphis comprise the Ned R. McWherter Library and four branch libraries: Communications Sciences, Mathematics, Music, and the Lambuth Campus in Jackson, Tennessee. The University Libraries' collections include more than 1.3 million bound volumes, 9.9 million manuscripts, 70,921 electronic books, 3.75 million microfilms and microfiches, 614,167 government documents, and 14,705 CDs. Patrons also have access to more than 150 electronic indexes/full-text resources. The libraries also serve the general public and maintain a strong user-instruction program. The learning commons extends throughout the McWherter Library, with a commons room on the first floor where the Research and Information Services desk is located. The McWherter Library has wireless capabilities supporting the 168 public-use computers that give users access to all University-provided software applications. Laptop computers are available for loan to students. The University Libraries house the Regional Federal Depository Library for the State of Tennessee and receive all publications, maps, and electronic data distributed by the U.S. Government Printing Office. The Libraries' Preservation and Special Collections Department has holdings on the history and culture of the South, the lower Mississippi River Valley, the Mid-South, Tennessee, the Civil War, and African-American history, including the Civil Rights Movement.

The Department of Theatre and Dance and the Rudi E. Scheidt School of Music, in their adjoining facilities, make an appreciable contribution to campus activities with live drama and concert series, films, and programming over WUMR, the student-staffed campus radio station. Included among the many research facilities at the University of Memphis are the Benjamin L. Hooks Institute for Social Change, the Integrated Microscopy Center, the FedEx Center for Supply Chain Management, the Institute for Artificial Intelligence, the Ground Water Institute, and the Barbara K. Lipman Early Childhood School and Research Institute.

The state of Tennessee has designated five Centers of Excellence at the University: the Center for Applied Psychological Research, the Center for Research Initiatives and Strategies for the Communicatively Impaired, the Center for Research in Educational Policy, the Institute of Egyptian Art and Archaeology, and the Center for Earthquake Research and Information.

Costs

In 2012–13, in-state students paid a maintenance fee of $277 per hour for part-time study until they reached 12 hours ($3,324), when the maintenance fee was lowered to $55 per hour for additional hours over 12. Out-of-state students paid a maintenance fee of $890 per hour for part-time study until they reached 12 hours ($10,680), when the maintenance fee rate was reduced to $178 per hour for additional hours over 12. On-campus residence hall rates ranged from $3,580 to $6,640 for an academic year. All part-time students paid an additional program service fee of $82.50 per hour for part-time study until they reached six hours, when the program service fee was highest at $628.

Financial Aid

Financial assistance is provided through four basic sources: scholarships, grants, loans, and employment. Scholarships are offered through the Scholarship Office as well as through various academic, performance, and athletic departments. Residents of Tennessee may be eligible for the state's HOPE Scholarship. An application for admission is required to be considered for general and distinguished academic scholarship programs. Applicants for financial aid must submit the completed Free Application for Federal Student Aid (FAFSA) to the Financial Aid Office, which places the student under consideration for all financial aid programs. The priority deadline for filing the FAFSA is February 1. More than $200 million is awarded annually. The University operates two programs of student employment: the Federal Work-Study Program and a regular work program.

Faculty

The University of Memphis has 935 full-time faculty members. In addition, many adjunct professors are hired from the community to teach in their fields of expertise.

Student Government

The Student Government Association consists of officers, a senate, a cabinet, and a judiciary elected annually by the student body. Its goals are to present the opinions of the student body to the administration, to enact legislation beneficial to the students, and to promote a broad range of student activities.

Admission Requirements

The admission of entering freshmen is based on the transcript of a four-year course of study at an approved or accredited high school that includes prescribed units of English, mathematics, natural/physical sciences, U.S. history, social studies, foreign language, and visual/performing arts. The General Educational Development test and high school equivalency diploma are accepted when applicable. The admissions process is a competitive one and is based on a student's cumulative high school grade point average and ACT or SAT scores. The average ACT for the fall 2012 freshman class was 22.57, and the average GPA was 3.38. The admission of transfer students is based on the applicant's grade point average, academic standing at a former institution, and scores on the approved admission tests. Transfer students will often be required to provide a high school transcript.

Application and Information

Inquiries about admission and requests for information about any undergraduate college of the University should be addressed to the Office of Admissions. Applications and supporting credentials must be submitted to the Office of Admissions before the beginning of the intended term of entry. While the established application deadlines are July 1 for the fall semester, December 1 for the spring semester, and May 1 for the summer session, early application is strongly encouraged so applicants can be considered for scholarship opportunities and take advantage of early registration. A student must apply and be accepted by February 1 to be considered for academic merit scholarships. Additional scholarships may have earlier deadlines. Prospective students are encouraged to visit the University for a campus tour, which can be set up at http://www.memphis.edu/admissions/visitcampus.php or by contacting the Office of Admissions.

For more information, contact:

Office of Admissions, Recruitment and Orientation Services
University of Memphis
101 John Wilder Tower
Memphis, Tennessee 38152-3520
Phone: 901-678-2169
      800-669-2678 (toll-free)
Website: http://www.memphis.edu
      http://on.fb.me/UofMemphis (Facebook)
      http://www.twitter.com/uofmemphis

The beautiful University of Memphis campus.

UNIVERSITY OF NEVADA, LAS VEGAS
LAS VEGAS, NEVADA

The University

The University of Nevada, Las Vegas (UNLV), is recognized nationally as a comprehensive teaching and research university that provides students with an excellent education at a reasonable cost. UNLV has established itself as a premier metropolitan research university. All UNLV programs are accredited by the Northwest Association of Schools and Colleges. Individual programs have further accreditation from professional accrediting organizations.

Since its founding in 1957, UNLV has seen dramatic growth in both its academic programs and its facilities. There are 220 undergraduate, master's, and doctoral degree programs offered to more than 28,000 students. Of UNLV's students, 82 percent are undergraduates, 82 percent are Nevada residents, 49 percent are members of minority groups, and 4 percent are international students. The average class size is 30.

The University is located on a beautifully landscaped 350-acre campus. Classes are held in comfortable, well-equipped buildings that are showcases of modern architecture.

UNLV's residential life program provides students with a secure, convenient place to live on the University campus. The modern residence halls are organized into suites of two rooms joined by a bathroom. Four students share a suite, with 2 per room. UNLV's dining facilities are excellent, providing students with quality, quantity, and choice.

More than 300 groups offer students an active social life, including intramural sports, Greek organizations, ethnic and religious clubs, a student newspaper, and campus radio and television stations. UNLV's Division of Student Life provides an array of advising, tutorial, and counseling services. The Disability Resource Center provides textbooks on tape, interpreters for the deaf, lab assistants, and other services to students with disabilities.

Numerous concerts are performed throughout the year by UNLV's student music groups, choirs, dance companies, and ensembles. The Department of Theatre Arts also offers an excellent season of comedies, dramas, and musicals performed by students and community members, as well as performances by national professional touring companies. The student government sponsors lectures, films, concerts, and entertainment throughout the year.

Location

Las Vegas, touted by historian Hal Rothman as the First City of the Twenty-First Century, is located at the southern tip of Nevada in a desert valley surrounded by mountains. The Las Vegas metropolitan area is a rapidly growing community of more than 2 million residents with a strong sense of family and community pride. The surrounding area is one of the Southwest's most picturesque, offering residents outdoor recreation year-round. Within a 50-mile radius lie the shores of Lake Mead, Hoover Dam, and the Colorado River recreation area; the snow-skiing and hiking trails of 12,000-foot Mount Charleston; and a panoramic view of rugged rock mountains. Las Vegas has an average of 320 days of sunshine per year. The average daytime winter temperature is 60 degrees Fahrenheit. Summer daytime temperatures are usually more than 100 degrees Fahrenheit.

Majors and Degrees

Undergraduate programs are offered by the Colleges of Education, Fine Arts, Health Sciences, Honors, Liberal Arts, and Sciences; the School of Nursing, Health and Human Sciences, Lee Business School, and the Greenspun College of Urban Affairs; the Howard R. Hughes College of Engineering; and the William F. Harrah College of Hotel Administration.

Majors include accounting, Afro-American studies, anthropology, architecture, art, art history, athletic training, biochemistry, biological sciences (including pre-professional), chemistry, civil and environmental engineering, communications studies, comprehensive medical imaging, computer engineering, computer science, construction management, criminal justice, dance,

early childhood education, earth and environmental science, economics, electrical engineering, elementary education, English, entertainment engineering and design, entrepreneurship, film, finance, French, gaming management, geology, German, health-care administration, health physics, history, hospitality management, human services, interior architecture and design, international business, journalism and media studies, kinesiology, landscape architecture, management, management information systems, marketing, mathematical sciences, mechanical engineering, meeting and event management, multidisciplinary studies, music, nuclear medicine, nursing, nutritional sciences, philosophy, physics, political science, professional golf management, psychology, public administration, public health, real estate and urban economics, restaurant management, Romance languages, secondary education, social work, sociology, Spanish, special education, theatre, women's studies, and undeclared.

Academic Programs

The UNLV General Education Core requirement, which must be completed by all baccalaureate degree candidates, consists of courses in English composition and literature, international and multicultural studies, logic, mathematics, computer science or statistics, U.S. and Nevada constitutions, social sciences, natural sciences, fine arts, and humanities. The balance of baccalaureate degree programs consists of college and departmental requirements. The number of credit hours required for baccalaureate degrees varies between 124 and 136, depending on the program of study. Numerous special academic opportunities are available, such as dual majors, dual baccalaureates, approved minors, internships, international studies, interdisciplinary programs, honors programs, and nontraditional credit (military credits, Advanced Placement Program, College-Level Examination Program, and correspondence credits).

The UNLV Honors College is a selective undergraduate college that offers a unique liberal arts and sciences experience for high-achieving and highly motivated students in any major.

The UNLV academic calendar has two semesters (fall and spring), each lasting approximately sixteen weeks. Three summer sessions are held from mid-May through August.

Off-Campus Programs

International study-abroad programs are available throughout the year, with opportunities to spend one semester, one academic year, or a summer abroad. Academic credits earned in UNLV study-abroad programs are part of regular authorized course offerings. Students can make normal progress toward their UNLV degree while utilizing international resources and experiencing a different culture.

Academic Facilities

The campus has an excellent Curriculum Materials Library, which is used extensively by local school teachers and University students. The National Supercomputing Center for Energy and the Environment facilitates study of the engineering, socioeconomic, transportation, and social impacts of energy and hazardous waste management along with other appropriate studies. The center includes a Cray YMP 2/215 supercomputer and a Sun 4/490 front-end computer, ten color graphics workstations, and a Silicon Graphics workstation. There are many public computer labs on the UNLV campus with easy access for student use.

Costs

For the 2013–14 academic year, average room and board costs are under $10,000 per year. Nonresident tuition and fees are $19,278 per year (12 credits per semester), and in-state tuition and fees are $5,368 per year (12 credits per semester). Residents of fourteen states (Alaska, Arizona, California, Colorado, Hawaii, Idaho, Montana, New Mexico, North Dakota, Oregon, South Dakota,

Utah, Washington, and Wyoming) may also qualify (based on GPA) for reduced tuition rates through the Western Undergraduate Exchange (WUE) Scholarship Program.

Financial Aid

UNLV provides a variety of financial assistance to qualified students. Loans, grants, scholarships, and employment are all awarded to help students meet their educational expenses while attending UNLV. All students should explore every possible resource. A student's eligibility may be determined by financial need, scholastic achievement, special skills, or service. Prospective students may complete a scholarship application prior to or at the same time as the application for admission. The deadline to apply for scholarships is February 1. It is recommended that the Free Application for Federal Student Aid (FAFSA) is submitted by the February 1 priority deadline. Additional information can be found at finaid.unlv.edu.

Faculty

More than 850 full-time instructional faculty members are involved in teaching, research, and community service. The scholars and scientists at UNLV are warm, caring people committed as much to excellence in teaching as they are to their research. Academic advising is available to every degree-seeking student at UNLV. Graduate assistants have limited teaching and laboratory assignments.

Student Government

All undergraduate students are automatically members of the Consolidated Students of the University of Nevada, Las Vegas (CSUN). CSUN is a self-governing body and is recognized by UNLV's faculty and the Nevada System of Higher Education. All officers are elected by the student body. CSUN has many boards and committees in which students are encouraged to get involved. CSUN provides students an opportunity to practice their communication skills and enrich their education both socially and academically.

Admission Requirements

Standard admission to UNLV is based on a student's academic record and placement examination scores. Incoming freshman students must earn a minimum 3.0 weighted grade point average (GPA) in the academic core in order to be considered for admission. The academic core consist of 4 years of English; 3 years of algebra or higher-level mathematics, such as algebra II, geometry, precalculus, or calculus; 3 years of natural science, with at least 2 years in a lab science; and 3 years of social studies. A minimum composite score of 22 on the ACT or a score of at least 1040 (critical reading and math) on the SAT can be used to waive the GPA requirement, however all students must meet the core course requirement. Official ACT or SAT test scores are also required for admission, scholarship consideration, and English and math placement.

Transfer students who have 24 or more transferable college credits with at least a 2.50 GPA are eligible to transfer to UNLV. Transfer course work must have been completed at regionally accredited colleges or universities. Students must also be in good standing and eligible to return to the university or college last attended (i.e., an applicant cannot be on academic or behavioral suspension). Transfer students who have earned fewer than 24 cumulative transferable college credits must fulfill the freshman admission requirements and have a 2.5 overall GPA in their college credits.

Students who do not meet the minimum requirements may be eligible to appeal through the Faculty Senate Admissions Committee.

Application and Information

Priority consideration is given to students who apply by February 1 for the fall and summer semester and October 1 for the spring semester. The nonrefundable application fee of $60 for domestic students and $95 for international students cannot be waived.

Prospective students may access the UNLV applications and catalog at unlv.edu.

For further assistance, students may contact:

Office of Admissions
University of Nevada, Las Vegas
Box 451021
4505 S Maryland Parkway
Las Vegas, Nevada 89154-1021
Phone: 702-774-UNLV (8658) (office of admissions)
702-895-3011 (main university number)
702-895-3424 (financial aid)
Fax: 702-774-8008
Website: http://www.unlv.edu

UNLV, located in one of the most exciting cities in the world, was recently ranked the eighth most diverse and the twelfth most popular university by *U.S. News & World Report*.

UNIVERSITY OF NEW ENGLAND
BIDDEFORD AND PORTLAND, MAINE

The University

The University of New England (UNE) is a top-ranked, independent, coeducational university committed to academic excellence and the enhancement of the quality of life for the people, organizations, and communities it serves. UNE is an innovative health sciences university grounded in the liberal arts. The University fosters critical inquiry through a student-centered academic environment rich in research, scholarship, creative activity, and service while providing opportunities for acquiring and applying knowledge in selected clinical, professional, and community settings.

UNE's student body of 5,587 includes 2,790 undergraduates, 967 doctor's degree–professional practice students, and 1,830 graduate students. UNE's total twelve-month student enrollment for the 2011–12 academic year was 8,085, which included all degree- and non–degree-seeking, full-and part-time, and online students. There were 4,753 undergraduate students; 2,346 graduate students; and 986 professional students. Students enroll in a wide variety of academic programs in UNE's six colleges: the College of Arts and Sciences, the College of Graduate Studies, the College of Osteopathic Medicine (housing Maine's only medical school), the College of Pharmacy, the Westbrook College of Health Professions, and the College of Dental Medicine. At the undergraduate level students represent thirty-five different states and several other countries in over forty undergraduate degree programs.

The University of New England's philosophy of education and student life places emphasis on the quality of instruction and the practical application of academic material. Each program includes the opportunity for learning in a community-based setting. Internships, co-ops, clinicals, and student teaching provide the practical experiences that allow students at UNE to apply the skills learned in the classroom to real job situations.

UNE traces its history to 1831 with the founding of Westbrook College, one of Maine's oldest institutions of learning. Today's University represents a union of three unique higher education institutions through the combining of St. Francis College and the New England College of Osteopathic Medicine in 1978 and Westbrook College in 1996. The University now has two campuses in southern Maine, offering students close proximity to all the academic and support resources UNE has to offer.

UNE's Student Academic Success Center provides a wide range of services to assist with student health, academic support, educational and career planning, and equal opportunities during their academic experience. The Office of Career Services provides academic and career exploration assistance, assistance in applying to graduate schools, self-assessment and personal interest exploration.

The University offers a variety of cultural and social events and encourages students to become involved in activities, clubs, and sports. Popular interests include scuba diving, skiing, hiking, biking, varsity and intramural sports, swimming, surfing, music, theater, and community service programs. Opportunities for such activities are available at on-campus facilities such as the Harold Alfond Forum, a 106,000-square-foot facility featuring an ice hockey rink, basketball court, classroom and lab space, fitness center, and multipurpose courts.

The UNE Department of Athletics operates an NCAA Division III varsity athletics program. Varsity sports for men are basketball, cross-country, golf, lacrosse, soccer, and ice hockey. Varsity sports for women are basketball, cross-country, field hockey, golf, ice hockey, lacrosse, soccer, softball, swimming, and volleyball.

Location

The University of New England currently has two campuses. The oceanside Biddeford Campus is located on a beautiful site in Biddeford, Maine, where the Saco River flows into the Atlantic Ocean. With more than 4,000 feet of water frontage, enjoying the ocean comes naturally to students. The 540-acre Biddeford Campus is home to the College of Arts and Sciences, the College of Osteopathic Medicine, the Harold Alfond Center for Health Sciences, and the Marine Science Education and Research Center, which houses the Marine Animal Rehabilitation Center.

Twenty miles to the north is UNE's Portland Campus, a 41-acre quintessential historic New England campus in Portland, Maine. The campus is home to the Westbrook College of Health Professions, the College of Graduate Studies, the College of Pharmacy, and the College of Dental Medicine. The UNE Art Gallery, the Maine Women Writers Collection, and the Dental Hygiene Clinic are also on the Portland Campus.

Students at both campuses can enjoy the vibrant social life offered in Portland, a city regularly recognized as one of the nation's most livable small cities, and the dynamic outdoor recreational activities that have made Maine a prime tourist destination. Southern Maine is conveniently serviced by a number of airlines at the Portland International Jetport as well as by bus and train.

UNE is slated to open a third campus in Tangier, Morocco in 2014. At no additional cost, UNE students may choose to spend a semester or a year at UNE's Tangier campus learning about the culture and languages while taking their college courses in English.

Majors and Degrees

UNE offers highly competitive undergraduate and graduate programs in a variety of areas. On the undergraduate level, the University confers Bachelor of Arts and Bachelor of Science degrees. Qualified undergraduate students also have the opportunity to move directly into a master's level or doctoral program through the Graduate Pathways to Success (GPS) program.

Bachelor's degrees are offered in animal behavior, applied exercise science, aquaculture and aquarium science, art education, athletic training, biochemistry, biological sciences, business administration, chemistry, communications, dental hygiene, elementary education, English, environmental science, environmental studies, health, wellness and occupational studies, history, laboratory science, liberal studies (including pre-law), marine sciences, mathematics, medical biology (pre-dental, pre-medicine, pre-optometry, pre–physical therapy, and pre–veterinary studies), neuroscience, nursing, political science, psychology, psychology and social relations, secondary education, sociology, and sport management.

Master's degrees are offered in biological sciences, education, marine sciences, medical education leadership, nurse anesthesia studies, occupational therapy, physician assistant studies, public health, and social work.

Doctoral degrees offered include dental medicine (D.M.D.), education leadership (Ed.D.), osteopathic medicine (D.O.), pharmacy (Pharm.D.), and physical therapy (D.P.T.).

Academic Programs

UNE's academic programs ensure that students have plenty of opportunities for extensive fieldwork, clinical experiences, research, internships, and global experiences at both the undergraduate and graduate levels. All undergraduate programs at UNE have a core curriculum as a common thread. Designed to provide a foundation in the liberal arts, the core reflects the values of the college and is designed to prepare students for living informed, thoughtful, and active lives in a complex and changing society.

Off-Campus Programs

UNE is committed to supplementing the traditional learning process with practical applications. All students are encouraged to participate in cooperative education programs, field placements, and practicums. These experiences provide valuable learning situations and increase a student's exposure to job-related opportunities, and they are required for graduation by most majors. Students also have the opportunity to arrange a study-abroad experience.

Academic Facilities

On the Biddeford Campus, classroom and office spaces are housed in several facilities across campus, including the Jack S. Ketchum Library. The Department of Creative and Fine Arts offers a dedicated building that provides faculty offices and studio space for drawing, painting, printmaking, sculpting, and photography. Several research facilities are on campus, including the Marine Science Education and Research Center, which includes the Marine Animal Rehabilitation Center; the Harold Alfond Center for Health Sciences, with biology and chemistry labs as well as lecture halls, classrooms, a gross anatomy lab, and UNE's medical school facilities; the Pickus Center for Biomedical Research; and the Peter and Cécile Morgane Hall, a science center providing additional classrooms and an undergraduate teaching laboratory.

On the University's Portland Campus, Ludcke Auditorium is used for a variety of academic programs. Coleman Dental Hygiene Building houses classroom, clinic, and faculty space. The Blewett Science Center, home to UNE's nursing program, consists of science labs, classrooms, and the Clinical Simulation Program (CSP), which provides customized training and education for students and health professionals. Proctor Hall is also a classroom building and is home to the Proctor Learning and Career Center. The Josephine S. Abplanalp Library houses study space and a computer lab, as well as the Maine Women Writers Collection. The College of Pharmacy is a LEED-certified academic and research facility with teaching and research laboratories and a lecture hall. The College of Dental Medicine has its administration offices in historic Goddard Hall, and the new Patient Care Center will be its clinical and academic home.

Costs

The costs per academic year for 2012–13 were: tuition, $30,750; room and board, $12,500; and fees, $1,120.

Financial Aid

In 2011–12, approximately 98 percent of all full-time students received some form of financial assistance. The average package was $26,000 including scholarships, grants, loans, and employment. The University of New England has an extensive academic scholarship program. Merit awards range from $3,000 to $18,000 per year.

Faculty

The personal attention students receive from faculty both in and out of class, and the quality of faculty as experts in their fields are key strengths of the UNE experience. Students appreciate their faculty members as mentors, and trust them as accomplished scholars who impact their fields. From designing coastal trails and restoring wetlands on the UNE campus to caring for patients in need at the Biddeford Free Clinic, UNE faculty members not only work side-by-side with their students, but are recognized by their peers and other leaders for their expertise. UNE faculty members are national award recipients, Fulbright scholars, authors, and world-class researchers, and they share their knowledge unselfishly with their students.

Admission Requirements

Students applying for admission should submit a completed application, a $40 nonrefundable application fee, transcripts of all academic work (high school and college), and scores on either the ACT or SAT. Students who do not use English as their primary language must submit TOEFL scores. Students applying for admission should have completed a curriculum that includes English, mathematics, science, and social sciences. International students must also complete the International Student Supplemental Application. All prospective students are strongly encouraged to visit the campuses of the University of New England for an information session and tour. Information sessions and tours are held daily Monday through Friday; Saturday tours are also available. Prospective students can register for a tour at www.une.edu/admissions/undergrad/visits.

Application and Information

The undergraduate freshman admission application deadline is February 15; applications received after that date are reviewed on a space-available basis. There is a nonbinding December 1 early action application deadline with a December 31 notification date. Applications for the spring term are accepted through December 1.

For application information, students should contact:

University of New England
Office of Undergraduate Admissions
Hills Beach Road
Biddeford, Maine 04005
Phone: 207-283-0171
        800-477-4863 (toll-free)
Fax: 207-602-5900
E-mail: admissions@une.edu
Website: www.une.edu

UNE's 540-acre Biddeford Campus is situated on a beautiful coastal site where the Saco River flows into the Atlantic Ocean. The campus offers more than 4,000 feet of water frontage.

UNIVERSITY OF NEW HAMPSHIRE
DURHAM, NEW HAMPSHIRE

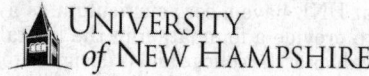

The University

The University of New Hampshire (UNH) is a rising star among American research universities, a community of exceptional faculty members and talented and energetic students from nearly fifty states and thirty countries. The University has a sizeable undergraduate population of approximately 12,800 but still feels cozy and intimate. This is due in part to a campus layout that is manageable and beautiful—with college greens, water, and a pleasing mix of classic and modern buildings that gradually give way to 2,600 acres of woods, fields, and farms. It is also due to the school's traditions of strong student-faculty interaction and active student culture. As one student put it, "It's easy to meet people and get involved in campus activities here. You need to have some initiative, but student leaders, residence hall staff, and others also seek you out."

The University offers students a variety of housing options, including halls of 100 to 600 students and two on-campus apartment complexes. Themed housing, such as honors, first-year experience, or international, is offered by dorm or floor. Holloway Commons, a spectacular dining and conference facility with seating for 850 and an after-hours café, opened in 2003, and Southeast Residential Community (SERC) Buildings A & B, 326- and 227-bed residence halls, opened in 2006. Parsons Hall, a chemistry teaching and research facility, underwent a $50-million renovation in 2009. Construction of the new Peter T. Paul College of Business and Economics building was completed in 2013.

The Memorial Union Building (MUB) is the University's community center. Housed in the MUB are two movie theaters, the UNH Copy Center, the UNH Bookstore, the Ticket Office, specific lounge/study space for both nontraditional and graduate students, and Granite Square Station, the undergraduate mail center. Computing and Information Services provides a computer cluster and a help desk with walk-in service. The MUB Food Court offers expanded dining options, and food service is also available in the Coffee Office. The Student Senate Office; Office of Multicultural Student Affairs; WUNH-radio; The New Hampshire, the student newspaper; and nearly 200 other student organizations originate in the MUB. Students at the University can participate in a rich cultural life. Numerous lectures, films, concerts, exhibitions, meet-the-artist receptions, master classes, dance performances, and theatrical productions are offered throughout the year. The UNH Celebrity Series, the Art Gallery, and the Departments of Music, Theater and Dance, and Art and Art History bring artists of international stature to campus. Most events are free for students.

Many opportunities for athletics and recreation, regardless of skill or ability, are offered through Campus Recreation. The Hamel Student Recreation Center is available to all full-time matriculating students. The center offers participants two multipurpose courts, a group exercise studio, a club/martial art studio, an 8,000-square-foot fitness center with more than 100 exercise stations, three basketball/volleyball courts, an indoor track, a lounge, several classrooms, locker rooms, towel and lock service at the equipment room, and saunas. Campus Recreation offers a variety of activities designed to make it easier to reach personal fitness goals and have fun. Participants may take part in one of the many group exercise classes, such as step aerobics, cycling, or cardio kickboxing. Other opportunities include Pilates, yoga, tai chi, a climbing wall, racquetball, personal training, or massage therapy. Noncredit courses are also offered, including CPR and first aid. The intramural sports

program consists of more than twenty different sports and activities offered to men's, women's, and co-rec teams. Campus Recreation forms and assists special interest groups or sport club teams to reflect the varied recreation and cultural preferences of campus community members. Some clubs are intensely competitive, requiring a daily commitment to workouts and conditioning. They compete either on an intercollegiate basis with New England teams or sponsor University tournaments. Other clubs meet on a casual come-when-you-can basis. In addition, Campus Recreation offers ice skating, manages a large outdoor recreation facility with its own sailing and canoe center, runs a children's camp (Camp Wildcat) in the summer, and supports the men's and women's sport club crew boat house. UNH also has twenty different men's and women's Division I sports teams, including football, which is Division I-FCS.

Location

Nestled in New Hampshire's seacoast region, the town of Durham is an outdoor-lover's dream, with ocean, ski and hiking mountains, and charming working-port cities nearby. Popular road trips for students include Boston (about an hour), Portsmouth (about 20 minutes), and the White Mountains (about an hour). With a nonstudent population of 8,000, Durham is a classic college town that caters to the student clientele. Durham's Main Street includes restaurants, coffeehouses, a bookstore, pizza shops, and other student hangouts.

Majors and Degrees

The University of New Hampshire comprises seven colleges and schools: College of Liberal Arts, College of Engineering and Physical Sciences, College of Health and Human Services, College of Life Sciences and Agriculture, Peter T. Paul College of Business and Economics, Thompson School of Applied Science (which offers two-year associate degree programs), and the University of New Hampshire at Manchester, the University's urban campus. The University offers more than 100 majors through these fully accredited academic divisions. New Hampshire enjoys a strong reputation in a wide range of academic fields, with biology, business administration, English, communication, engineering, environmental studies, history, hospitality management, kinesiology, marine and animal sciences, performing arts, political science, and psychology among those topping the list. The business school offers several options under the business administration major that include accounting, entrepreneurial venture creation, information systems, international business and economics, management, and a student-designed track.

Academic Programs

The Discovery Program, which encompasses the University's general education requirements, provides students with a broad foundation in the liberal arts and an introduction to the methods of inquiry needed for academic success. All students must complete ten courses which include writing skills; quantitative reasoning; biological and physical sciences; historical perspectives; world cultures; fine and performing arts; social science; humanities; and environment, technology, and society. A senior year Capstone Experience as well as inquiry courses allow students to reflect on their education and synthesize knowledge and skills gained from the Discovery Program. Depending on their academic program, students may begin course work in their major as early as their first year.

A major research university, UNH prides itself on producing students who have had meaningful research experiences with a world-class faculty. Programs such as the Undergraduate Research Opportunities Program and International Research Opportunities Program provide research grants each year for undergraduates to work closely with faculty members, on campus or abroad, on original projects. Over 1,000 students participated in the Undergraduate Research Conference in 2012. Students majoring in a wide range of subjects can access a wealth of research centers and facilities, some on the campus itself, others in surrounding towns. As New Hampshire's major public institution, the University is involved in a wide range of outreach programs with state and industry groups. These partnerships provide abundant opportunities for students interested in internships.

Academic Facilities

The Dimond Library is the state's only public university research library. The library offers three grand reading rooms, seating for 1,200 students, and state-of-the-art technology, including wireless and Internet. The Parker Adaptive Technology Room provides an array of technological options for patrons who have learning, mobility, or vision disabilities. Through ResNet, students who live on-campus have high-speed Internet access to UNH library resources, class software and information, e-mail, and other services. The Environmental Technology Building is a multidisciplinary science and engineering research facility with a focus on environmental technology development. Most of the University's cultural events take place in the Paul Creative Arts Center, which houses two theaters, dressing rooms, a well-equipped scene shop, a costume shop, a green room, storage facilities, classrooms, and the faculty and staff offices. New Hampshire Hall contains the Newman Dance Studio and a smaller stage studio.

Costs

The 2012–13 tuition and fees for undergraduate in-state students were $16,422. For out-of-state students, tuition and fees were $28,882. Room (double) and board (unlimited meal plan) cost $9,764.

Financial Aid

Approximately 65 percent of students receive some form of need-based financial assistance from UNH. University scholarships ranging from $1,000 to $10,000 are awarded automatically to qualified first-year students who apply for admission. Amounts are subject to change. Other scholarships are awarded by individual academic departments. The average financial aid package, including gift, loan, and employment assistance, was $13,252 for New Hampshire residents and $18,630 for nonresidents. The University participates in the Federal Pell Grant program, the Federal Supplemental Educational Opportunity Grant program, the Federal Perkins Loan program, the Federal Work-Study Program, and the Federal Stafford Student Loan program. Students are required to submit the Free Application for Federal Student Aid (FAFSA) by March 1.

Faculty

The University of New Hampshire has 596 full-time and 389 part-time faculty members. The student-faculty ratio is 20:1. The UNH faculty includes winners of the Pulitzer Prize, Guggenheim awards, and many other prestigious awards and honors, while the University ranks among the top campuses in the nation in the percentage of faculty members who have won Fulbright scholarships. This research productivity has a powerful effect on students, who can share the experience of discovery.

Student Government

The Student Senate comprises a governing body of student officers and senators. They are the voice of the student body, representing student opinion to members of the faculty, staff, and administration as well as the University community and the state legislature. The Senate believes that all students have the right to participate in University decisions and policy making. Committees of the Senate include areas in academics, residential life, commuters, health and human services, judicial affairs, and community change. They also approve and monitor the rates and uses of all mandatory student fees.

Admission Requirements

Admission to a bachelor's degree program is based upon successful completion of a strong secondary school program of college-preparatory course work. Primary consideration is given to the academic record, as demonstrated by the quality of the candidate's secondary school course selection and achievement. Consideration is also given to the student's recommendation, personal essay, additional information, character, initiative, leadership, special talents, and SAT or ACT with writing component results. Most successful candidates present at least 4 years of English and mathematics and 3 or more years of laboratory science, social science, and foreign language. Recommended mathematics preparation includes the equivalent of algebra I, geometry, algebra II, and trigonometry or advanced math. Students who plan to specialize in health, physical sciences, life sciences, engineering, or mathematics should present at least 4 years of mathematics, including trigonometry as well as laboratory course work in chemistry and/or physics. Students pursuing business-related studies should also have completed 4 years of mathematics, including trigonometry.

All candidates for admission to bachelor's degree programs are required to submit SAT or ACT scores with writing component results. SAT Subject Tests are not required. A foreign language SAT Subject Test may satisfy the foreign language requirement of the Bachelor of Arts degree programs. Required scores vary by test. International students whose primary language is not English must submit TOEFL or IELTS results. The recommended minimum TOEFL score is 213 (computer-based) or 550 (paper-based) or 80 (Internet-based). The minimum IELTS score is 6.5.

Candidates applying for programs in the Department of Music must make arrangements with the department chairperson for an audition (603-862-2404).

Application and Information

High school students who seek fall-semester admission may apply anytime after the start of the senior year and before the February 1 regular decision deadline. Admission notifications are provided on a continuous basis through April. Admitted first-year students have until May 1 to confirm their intent to enroll at the University. The review of candidates begins with the receipt of all required application materials. The Early Action (EA) Program allows candidates to receive a response by mid-January of their senior year; EA candidates must submit admission applications by November 15. In some cases, the Admission Committee requests senior mid-year grade reports in order to make a final admission decision. All positive admission decisions made prior to the completion of a candidate's course work in progress are considered provisional and are subject to the verification of satisfactory senior-year achievement when final high school transcripts are reviewed.

Office of Admissions
University of New Hampshire
3 Garrison Avenue
Durham, New Hampshire 03824-3501
Phone: 603-862-1360
Fax: 603-862-0077
Website: http://www.unh.edu/admissions
         http://www.facebook.com/universityofnewhampshire

UNIVERSITY OF NEW HAVEN
WEST HAVEN, CONNECTICUT

UNIVERSITY OF
NEW HAVEN

The University

The University of New Haven's (UNH) mission is to prepare career-ready graduates for meaningful roles in today's global economy and to nurture the pursuit of lifelong learning. Founded in 1920, the University of New Haven is a private, independent institution focused on combining professional education with liberal arts and sciences. UNH is committed to educational innovation, continuous improvement in career and professional education, and support of scholarship and professional development. UNH became a four-year college in 1958. Moving to its present location in West Haven in 1960, UNH rapidly expanded its programs, facilities, and faculty, attracting a student body that now stands at over 6,300—including the current enrollment of 4,267 full-time day students among its undergraduates.

The University is fully accredited by the New England Association of Schools and Colleges (NEASC). Individual programs, departments, and schools hold various forms of national professional accreditation. Four of the University of New Haven's bachelor's degree programs—chemical, civil, electrical, and mechanical engineering—are fully accredited by the Engineering Accreditation Commission of the Accreditation Board for Engineering and Technology, Inc. (EAC/ABET). The computer science program is fully accredited by the Computing Accreditation Commission of the Accreditation Board for Engineering and Technology, Inc. (CAC/ABET).

Despite a broad academic program, UNH is small enough to accommodate individualized educational needs. Programs evolve and adapt to meet changing career interests as well as the requirements of business, industry, and professional fields. Small classes foster close student-faculty relationships. Accelerated weekend and evening programs in business and convenient evening hours provide access for part-time students in engineering, computers, public safety, and the arts and sciences.

The main campus is in West Haven, Connecticut, on a hillside close to Long Island Sound. UNH also operates a satellite branch, the Southeastern Center in New London, Connecticut. Main campus administrative and classroom buildings support the University's four academic colleges: the College of Arts and Sciences, the College of Business, the Tagliatela College of Engineering, and the Henry C. Lee College of Criminal Justice and Forensic Sciences. Following the addition of the Graduate School in 1969, New Haven College was designated a university. Thirty master's degree programs attract full- and part-time graduate students, while nearly 100 associate and bachelor's degree programs are available to entering freshmen and transfer students in a great variety of academic disciplines.

Other main campus buildings include the Marvin K. Peterson Library, Echlin Hall, the Bayer Hall admissions building, the Campus Bookstore, new residence halls and apartments, and Bartels Hall, the campus center, which houses dining facilities and student activities. The Charger Gymnasium and athletic fields are located on the North Campus, just two short blocks from Maxcy Hall, the main administration building. The David A. Beckerman Recreational Center, a state-of-the-art athletic facility for the benefit of all students, opened in fall 2007.

The University of New Haven has one of the most respected and successful NCAA Division II athletics programs in the country, with Charger teams combining to make over 120 post-season tournament appearances. UNH is a member of the Northeast-10 Conference, one of the most prestigious and celebrated conferences in the nation. UNH and its student athletes have won numerous conference, regional, and national awards, both athletically and academically. The University offers sixteen varsity sports: men's baseball, basketball, cross-country, football, soccer, indoor and outdoor track and field; and women's basketball, cross-country, lacrosse, soccer, softball, tennis, indoor and outdoor track and field, and volleyball.

Approximately two thirds of the full-time undergraduate day students live on campus in the fourteen residence halls. More than 150 clubs and organizations are open to students. Included are student chapters of professional societies, religious organizations, social groups, special-interest clubs, student councils, cultural groups, and fraternities and sororities.

Location

West Haven is contiguous to New Haven. There are theaters that attract star performers from the entertainment world, a deepwater harbor and beaches, fine restaurants, museums, and galleries in the area. Numerous social and cultural programs are presented by the many colleges and universities in the area. New Haven is served by a local airport and major railroads, and its location at the junction of two interstate highways places the University of New Haven within easy driving distance of New York, Boston, Cape Cod, and the ski areas of New England.

Majors and Degrees

The College of Arts and Sciences offers a Bachelor of Arts degree in art, chemistry, communication, English, global studies, graphic design, history, interior design, liberal studies, mathematics, music, music and sound recording, music industry, political science, and psychology; and a Bachelor of Science degree in biology, biotechnology, dental hygiene, environmental science, marine biology, mathematics, music and sound recording, and nutrition and dietetics.

The College of Business offers the Bachelor of Science degree in accounting, finance, hospitality and tourism management, management, management of sport industries, and marketing. In addition, the College of Business has launched a fast-track study program allowing academically strong students the opportunity to earn a Bachelor of Science degree in business and a Master of Business Administration (M.B.A.) in just four years.

The Tagliatela College of Engineering offers a Bachelor of Science degree in chemical engineering, chemistry, civil engineering, computer engineering, computer science, electrical engineering, general engineering, information technology, mechanical engineering, sustainability studies, and system engineering.

The Henry C. Lee College of Criminal Justice and Forensic Sciences offers a Bachelor of Science degree in criminal justice, fire protection engineering, fire science, forensic science, legal studies, and national security.

Academic Programs

The University of New Haven offers a broad range of programs in both liberal arts and professional areas. Experiential learning is emphasized, and there are diverse and numerous opportunities for career-oriented internships, cooperative education, independent study, and industrial projects. Certain types of professional experience are required in a number of degree programs. The Center for Learning Resources offers a tutoring service open to all students.

The undergraduate division operates on a 4-1-4 calendar. Credit is given for successful scores on the CLEP and Advanced Placement examinations. A University honors program provides outstanding study opportunities in most undergraduate disciplines. The residence requirement for all degrees is 30 credit hours.

UNH believes that all students pursuing a bachelor's degree should develop a common set of skills; the University's goal is to prepare all graduates for the complex lives they will lead in a changing world. This can best be done through the University Core Curriculum, which consists of a minimum of 40 credit hours in six basic competencies.

Academic Facilities

The Marvin K. Peterson Library contains more than 400,000 volumes in hard copy and provides access to about 20,000 electronic books and 20,000 e-journals from the library website and Voyager online catalog. Databases are available on a wide variety of subjects, with a focus on business, criminal justice/forensic science, engineering, and psychology, as well as general arts and sciences. Through interlibrary loan services, the University community has access to the holdings of more than 8,650 libraries.

Communication majors participate in workshops along with studying sound, film, and television production and radio broadcasting techniques in well-equipped radio/television studios and laboratories. The Tagliatela College of Engineering has modern laboratories and equipment to support its programs. The College of Arts and Sciences maintains art studios, state-of-the-art recording studios, music practice rooms, and science, psychology, and language labs. Hands-on instruction and demonstrations are available in kitchen facilities for students in the hospitality and tourism and the nutrition and dietetics programs. Dental hygiene students gain experience in the Dental Hygiene Clinic.

There are more than a dozen computer labs for student use and teaching on campus. One of these is devoted to forensic computing instruction for the Henry C. Lee College of Criminal Justice and Forensic Sciences.

Costs

Estimated full-time undergraduate tuition for the 2013–14 academic year, including all fees, is $33,740; room and board cost $14,110.

Financial Aid

UNH offers a comprehensive financial aid program that includes University resources as well as state, federal, and private-aid programs. Approximately 85 percent of full-time undergraduate students receive some form of assistance. Students receive federal aid through the Federal Pell Grant, Federal Supplemental Educational Opportunity Grant, Federal Work-Study, Federal Perkins Loan, Federal Direct Student Loan, and Federal Direct PLUS loan programs. The University also administers programs sponsored by the state of Connecticut for Connecticut residents attending the University. Some students also qualify for financial aid from other states and from private companies, organizations, and foundations.

Faculty

It is a long-standing University policy that the faculty members teach a mix of undergraduate and graduate courses in order to preserve academic quality at all levels. Faculty members are selected and promoted primarily on the basis of teaching effectiveness, professional qualifications and performance, and contributions to the academic community. No classes are taught by teaching assistants. Some faculty members hold administrative positions and continue to teach. There are over 200 full-time and 400 part-time faculty members, making the student-faculty ratio 16:1. The majority of full-time faculty members (more than 80 percent) hold terminal degrees in their disciplines.

Student Government

The Undergraduate Student Government Association supervises annual expenditures by undergraduate clubs and organizations, directs liaison committees, supports student publications and the student-operated FM radio station, and schedules cultural and social events. Student representatives are elected annually to the University's Board of Governors.

Admission Requirements

To be eligible for admission, one must be a high school graduate or present evidence of equivalent preparation and have submitted all necessary application documents for consideration. The admissions decision is based on an applicant's high school record, SAT or ACT results, letter(s) of recommendation, and personal essay. Out-of-state residents are considered for admission on the same basis as in-state residents. The University of New Haven does not discriminate on the basis of age, color, sex, religion, race, sexual orientation, national origin, or disability in admission or treatment of students, administration or distribution of financial aid, or recruitment of employees.

Application and Information

To apply to the University of New Haven, one must submit a completed application (with $25 fee for electronic submission or $75 fee for paper submission), official records of all academic enrollment, SAT or ACT results, a letter of recommendation (from an academic source), and a personal statement (250–500 words). International students are required to demonstrate proficiency in English and provide documentation of financial support. The University of New Haven is authorized under federal law to enroll nonimmigrant alien students who meet the university's academic and English proficiency standards. Application documents are considered on a rolling admissions basis with the opportunity to apply for early action.

For more information, contact:

Undergraduate Admissions
University of New Haven
300 Boston Post Road
West Haven, Connecticut 06516
Phone: 203-932-7319
      800-DIAL-UNH (342-5864) Ext. 7319 (toll-free)
E-mail: adminfo@newhaven.edu
Website: http://www.newhaven.edu

Maxcy Hall on the main campus of the University of New Haven.

UNIVERSITY OF OREGON
EUGENE, OREGON

The University

At the University of Oregon (UO), students belong to a community dedicated to making a difference in the world. Whether changing a community, a law, or one person's mind, UO gives students the inspiration and resources needed to succeed. Potential students interested in exploring the UO online are invited to visit both the University's admissions website at http://admissions.uoregon.edu and Facebook page at http://www.facebook.com/UOAdmissions.

Many of UO's academic programs are internationally recognized for academic excellence. In 2012, the UO was listed among the top 8 percent of national universities according to *U.S. News & World Report* and was named one of *Forbes* magazine's 100 best research universities.

With a student-teacher ratio of 20:1 and an average class size of 20, students connect easily with faculty members and peers. Students have access to all the resources of a major research university, with 269 comprehensive academic programs and more than 250 student organizations.

Set in a 295-acre arboretum, the University of Oregon is aesthetically and environmentally green. Academic programs and student activities bring students to the forests, mountains, and rivers of Oregon's wilderness areas. The world's first green chemistry teaching methods were developed by UO students and faculty. The Lillis Business Complex was the first certified-green business school facility in the United States. Students have access to nationally recognized programs in sustainable business, architecture, and technology.

Students learn to see the world differently at UO, attending classes alongside peers from all fifty states, three U.S. territories, and ninety-five countries, and learning from faculty members of diverse religious, cultural, and ethnic heritages. The UO offers 170 study programs in ninety-five countries, giving students the opportunity to experience new cultures while earning credit toward their degree. More information can be found at http://studyabroad.uoregon.edu.

With eighteen NCAA Division I teams, as well as forty-five club sports, students have a variety of sports to play and teams to cheer for. Students root for the Ducks' football team at Autzen Stadium, the men's and women's basketball teams at the state-of-the-art Matthew Knight Arena, and track stars at the world-famous Hayward Field, often the site for U.S. Olympic team trials in track and field. Additional information regarding UO athletic programs is available at http://www.goducks.com.

Location

The UO is located in the center of Eugene (population 156,929), a classic college town that's small enough to bike across but large enough to offer diverse art, music, and social venues. The Hult Center for Performing Arts and the Grammy-winning Oregon Bach Festival lure a variety of acclaimed musical acts each year. Rolling Stone magazine included Eugene in its list of top 10 College Towns that Rock.

Eugene embraces the outdoors, with more than 100 city parks, 250 miles of bicycle trails, rock climbing areas, and beautiful public gardens, all within the city limits. Getting there is easy; the city is served by several major airlines and is on the main north-south Amtrak artery connecting Seattle and San Diego. More information is available at http://admissions.uoregon.edu/original.

Majors and Degrees

A complete list of undergraduate academic majors, minors, certificates, and preparatory programs is located at http://admissions.uoregon.edu/majors.

The School of Architecture and Allied Arts offers programs in architecture; art; art history; ceramics; community arts; digital arts; fibers; historic preservation; interior architecture; landscape architecture; material and product studies; metalsmithing and jewelry; multimedia; nonprofit administration; painting; photography; planning, public policy, and management; printmaking; product design; and sculpture.

The College of Arts and Sciences offers programs in African studies; anthropology; Asian studies; biochemistry; biology; chemistry; Chinese; cinema studies; classics; clinical laboratory science–medical technology*; comic and cartoon studies; comparative literature; computer and information science; computer information technology; creative writing; dentistry*; East Asian studies; economics; engineering*; English; environmental science; environmental studies; ethnic studies; European studies; folklore; forensic science*; French; general science; general social science; geography; geological sciences; German; German studies; Greek; health sciences*; history; humanities; human physiology; international studies; Italian; Japanese; Judaic studies; Latin; Latin American studies; law*; linguistics; marine biology; mathematics; mathematics and computer science; medicine*; medieval studies; nursing*; occupational therapy*; optometry*; peace studies; pharmacy*; philosophy; physical therapy*; physician assistant studies*; physics; podiatry*; political science; psychology; queer studies; religious studies; Romance languages; Russian and East European studies; Scandinavian; second-language acquisition and teaching; social work*; sociology; South Asian studies; Southeast Asian studies; Spanish; theater arts; veterinary medicine*; women's and gender studies; and writing, speaking, and critical reasoning.

The Charles H. Lundquist College of Business offers programs in accounting; business administration with concentrations in entrepreneurship, finance, information systems and operations management, marketing, and sports business.

The College of Education offers programs in communication disorders and sciences, educational foundations, family and human services, special education, and teacher education.*

The School of Journalism and Communication offers programs in communication studies, journalism, journalism: advertising, journalism: communication studies, and journalism: public relations.

The School of Music and Dance offers programs in dance, music, music composition, music education, music: jazz studies, and music performance.

An * denotes preparatory programs.

Academic Programs

The UO operates on a quarter system, and students spend about one third of their education on each of three areas: the general education requirements, major requirements, and elective credit. General education requirements include courses in the natural sciences, social sciences, humanities, and multicultural course work.

Freshman Interest Groups (FIGs) bring together a small group of first-year students interested in the same academic area in three related interdisciplinary courses. Freshman Seminars are small-group discussion courses taught by some of the UO's most outstanding faculty members. These academically rigorous programs provide a transition to college-level work. Details are available at http://firstyear.uoregon.edu. The Professional Distinctions Program gives students a competitive edge in the job market by complementing course work with a practical area of concentration. Skills are built through career workshops, internships, and other professional experiences. Learn more at http://uodistinctions.uoregon.edu.

The Robert D. Clark Honors College (CHC) offers the academic rigor of an outstanding small liberal arts college with the resources of a major research university. High-achieving students prepare for participation and leadership in society and come to understand the role of knowledge in their lives as global citizens. CHC classes are limited to 19 or fewer students and complement any UO major. The CHC application process is competitive, with an average of more than 1,500 applications for the 200 openings each year. Additional information about CHC can be found at http://honors.uoregon.edu.

Upon acceptance, qualified students will be invited to join the College Scholars program, which provides access to specialized courses, internship opportunities, and special scholarships. Faculty members help students develop their plans to achieve department honors or professional distinctions upon graduation. More details are available at http://csch.uoregon.edu.

Off-Campus Programs

The Career Center offers off-campus internships in fields related to students' academic majors or extracurricular interests. The IE3 Global Internships Program provides academic credit while students gain career experience through overseas internships. Additional information can be found at http://career.uoregon.edu and http://ie3global.ous.edu.

The Oregon Institute of Marine Biology on the Pacific coast offers access to deep sea, coastal watershed, and estuary habitats. Pine Mountain Observatory, near Bend, Oregon, offers study options in physics and astronomy. Students can participate in the annual Archaeology Field School in central Oregon's Northern Great Basin. More details are available at http://admissions.uoregon.edu/beyondeugene.

Cooperatively run by students, the Outdoor Program takes students beyond campus to Oregon's great outdoors. Activities available include snowboarding, skiing, rock climbing, hiking, surfing, and white-water rafting. Interested students can visit http://outdoorprogram.uoregon.edu for more information.

Academic Facilities

The University of Oregon Libraries, an Association of Research Libraries member, houses the second-largest research collection in the Northwest, including 3 million volumes and 90,000 journal subscriptions, both print and electronic. More information can be found at http://libweb.uoregon.edu.

Campus museums are valuable resources in the sciences and visual arts. The Jordan Schnitzer Museum of Art offers exhibitions of classical and contemporary art. The Museum of Natural and Cultural History features Native American artifacts, archaeological finds, and historically and scientifically significant items. Students appear in music, dance, and theater performances in newly refurbished facilities, including proscenium and black box performance spaces. Films, lectures, and cultural events are an everyday part of campus life. Additional details regarding arts and culture at UO are available at http://www.uoregon.edu/arts-and-culture.

Science facilities are among the best in the nation. Cutting-edge equipment is housed in the underground Lokey Laboratories, designed to minimize vibrations and stray electric fields. The UO is a pioneer in integrative science, and the new Lewis Integrative Science Building encourages interdisciplinary research and studies in areas such as nanotechnology, neuroscience, and solar energy. More information can be found at http://isci.uoregon.edu. Wireless Internet access is available in all buildings, and computer labs are available in the library, residence halls, and academic facilities across campus.

Costs

Resident undergraduate tuition and fees for the 2012–13 academic year were $9,258. Room and board in on-campus residence halls cost $10,260 per academic year for double occupancy. Books and supplies were estimated at $1,050 and personal expenses $2,430. The total was $22,998.

Nonresident undergraduate tuition and fees for the 2012–13 academic year were $28,653. Room and board in on-campus residence halls cost $10,260 per academic year for double occupancy. Books and supplies were estimated at $1,050 and personal expenses $2,430. The total cost for nonresidents was $42,393. Additional cost details are available at http://financialaid.uoregon.edu/cost_of_attendance.

Financial Aid

The UO makes a concerted effort to enable students to attend, regardless of family income. Financial aid in the form of grants, loans, and employment is available to qualifying students. The majority of students receive scholarships and financial aid that are awarded through the federal government, the University, and academic departments. To apply for financial aid, students must file the Free Application for Federal Student Aid (FAFSA) in early February. The UO's federal school code is 003223.

Incoming freshmen will be considered automatically for Summit, Apex, and General University scholarships by completing the UO admission application by January 15. Presidential and Diversity Excellence scholarships require separate applications due January 15. The Stamps scholarship also requires a separate application due November 1.

Summit and Apex scholarships are awarded to academically successful entering freshmen and range from $3,000 to $8,000 per year. General University and National Merit scholarships range from $1,500 to $2,700 per year. Presidential Scholarships, awarded each year to Oregon's brightest incoming freshmen, amount to approximately $9,000 per year. Diversity Excellence Scholarships range from partial to full tuition and fee waivers. Stamps scholarships, awarded to Oregon residents graduating from an Oregon high school, grant students full tuition, room, and board. Staton Scholarships in the amount of $5,750 are awarded each year to incoming Oregon students with extraordinary financial need.

More information regarding financial aid and scholarships can be found at http://financialaid.uoregon.edu.

Student Government

The Associated Students of the University of Oregon (ASUO) offers more than 250 student organizations, including cultural organizations, fraternities and sororities, student government, campus ministries, political groups, performing arts groups, international student clubs, and honor societies. The UO Student Vote Coalition led the nation in registering student voters in each of the past three presidential elections. The UO also ranks eighth in the nation for current Peace Corps volunteers. Additional details regarding the ASUO are available at http://asuo.uoregon.edu.

Admission Requirements

The early notification deadline for fall admission is November 1. The regular admission deadline for fall is January 15. To be eligible for freshman admission, an applicant must have a high school GPA of at least 3.0 on a 4.0 scale, be a graduate of a standard or accredited high school, submit SAT or ACT scores, and complete an application essay.

The UO requires the following college-preparatory courses: 4 years of English in preparatory composition and literature; 3 years of mathematics, including 1 year of algebra and 2 additional years of college-preparatory mathematics; 3 years of science in such areas as biology, chemistry, or physics; and 3 years of social science that could include 1 year of U.S. history, 1 year of global studies such as world history or geography, and one elective. Two years of the same second language in high school or two college terms of the same second language are also required.

Other factors considered for admission include the strength of high school course work, grade trend, essay, and senior-year course load. Academic potential and special talents also are considered. Additional admissions information is available at http://admissions.uoregon.edu/freshmen.

Application and Information

To apply, candidates should submit a completed application for admission, transcripts, SAT or ACT scores, essay, and a nonrefundable $50 application fee to the Office of Admissions.

For information and an application, students should contact:

Office of Admissions
1217 University of Oregon
Eugene, Oregon 97403-1217
Phone: 541-346-3201
　　　 800-BE-A-DUCK (toll-free)
Website: http://admissions.uoregon.edu
　　　 http://www.facebook.com/UOAdmissions
　　　 http://twitter.com/BeAnOregonDuck

UNIVERSITY OF PITTSBURGH AT BRADFORD

BRADFORD, PENNSYLVANIA

University of Pittsburgh Bradford

The University

The University of Pittsburgh at Bradford (Pitt-Bradford) can take students beyond—beyond the classroom by offering internships and research opportunities; beyond the degree by providing a robust Career Services Office and an informal alumni network; beyond 9-to-5 by offering an active student life, a friendly residence-life environment, excellent athletic and cultural facilities, and a wide range of recreational opportunities; beyond place by exposing students to the world and offering many study-abroad opportunities; and beyond students' expectations by giving them a college experience that can transform them.

At Pitt-Bradford, students live and learn on a safe, intimate campus, where they receive individual and personalized attention from committed professors who work at their side. In addition, students earn a degree from the University of Pittsburgh, which commands respect around the world.

Students can work out in a state-of-the-art fitness center or swim in the six-lane swimming pool in the Sport and Fitness Center. The building also houses facilities for intercollegiate and intramural athletic events.

The Frame-Westerberg Commons offers a place to eat, gather, and participate in campus life. The building houses the dining hall, where students can help themselves to a wide assortment of meals; a bookstore, which features an after-hours convenience store; offices for many student clubs and organizations; and areas to read or relax.

There are more than fifty clubs and organizations, varying from the campus radio station and newspaper to academic clubs, honor societies, and fraternities and sororities. Pitt-Bradford competes in Division III of the NCAA and fields seven men's teams in baseball, basketball, cross-country, golf, soccer, swimming, and tennis and seven women's teams in basketball, cross-country, soccer, softball, swimming, tennis, and volleyball.

Location

Pitt-Bradford encompasses 317 acres in the foothills of the Allegheny Mountains, only steps from the Allegheny National Forest. Pitt-Bradford also is a short drive from larger cities such as Buffalo, New York (80 miles north); Pittsburgh (160 miles southeast); and Erie, Pennsylvania (90 miles west). Pitt-Bradford can also be reached easily by car and plane.

At Pitt-Bradford, students have many opportunities to participate in cocurricular opportunities in the region, including cross-country and downhill skiing, snowboarding, snowshoeing, ice skating, biking, fishing, hiking, and hunting.

Majors and Degrees

Students may pursue four-year degrees in accounting, applied mathematics, athletic training, biology, biology education 7–12, broadcast communications, business, computer and information technology K–12, business management, chemistry, chemistry education 7–12, computer information systems and technology, criminal justice, early level education preK–4, economics, English, English education 7–12, environmental studies, environmental education K–12, general studies, health and physical education K–12, history/political science, hospitality management, human relations, interdisciplinary arts, mathematics education 7–12, nursing, physical sciences, psychology, public relations, radiological science, social sciences, social studies education 7–12, sociology, sport and recreation management, sports medicine, and writing.

Pitt-Bradford also offers associate degrees in engineering science, information systems, liberal studies, nursing (RN), and petroleum technology.

Students may also study engineering for up to two years at Pitt-Bradford and then complete a program at the Oakland campus in bioengineering, chemical and petroleum engineering, civil and environmental engineering, electrical and computer engineering, industrial engineering, materials science and engineering, or mechanical engineering.

Pitt-Bradford also provides programs offered in conjunction with the University of Pittsburgh School of Dental Medicine and the Pennsylvania College of Optometry. Students begin their studies at Pitt-Bradford and, after three years, transfer to the appropriate graduate school to complete four more years of study.

Pitt-Bradford also offers the first two years of study leading to the doctorate in pharmacy. Students must complete the program at the Oakland campus, where admission is competitive. The Pittsburgh School of Pharmacy pre-admits some qualified high school seniors, pending completion of the first two years of the pre-professional program at Pitt-Bradford.

The University also has an agreement with Lake Erie College of Osteopathic Medicine (LECOM), which allows qualifying students to continue their education in medicine at LECOM after their third year at Pitt-Bradford. Students who have successfully completed their first year of medical school classes at LECOM will receive their bachelor's degree from Pitt-Bradford. They will then continue at LECOM to finish their medical studies.

Academic Programs

The academic programs stress critical-thinking and communication skills and encourage hands-on learning through field experience, internships, and faculty-student collaboration on research. A Pitt-Bradford bachelor's degree requires 120–128 credit hours (requirements differ slightly among programs). Students need to complete between 60 and 70 credit hours to earn an associate degree.

The accounting major prepares students for the workplace, which has a growing need for accountants. The major also prepares students to earn a master's degree in either professional accountancy or business administration.

The biology program prepares students for careers in health-related professions, education, and research; technical positions in governmental agencies; and careers with food, pharmaceutical, chemical, and biotechnology companies. Most students interested in medicine, dentistry, optometry, pharmacy, osteopathy, physical therapy, occupational therapy, podiatry, chiropractic medicine, veterinary medicine, preclinical dietetics and nutrition, and a variety of careers in health and rehabilitation sciences are biology majors.

Students who choose to major in broadcast communications, English, public relations, or writing are able to work on the award-winning student newspaper, The Source; broadcast over the college radio station, WDRQ; and publish original works in the award-winning student literary magazine, Baily's Beads. Students also have access to an all-digital television studio and two digital radio facilities.

The business management program places a strong emphasis on teaching practical applications; courses often focus on cases taken from real business situations. Students may concentrate in accounting, finance, international business, or management information systems.

In the criminal justice program, students are able to intern with local and regional police departments, county court and probation offices, and a federal prison. State-of-the-art crime-scene investigatory tools enable students to work a crime scene using many of the same tools as professional law enforcement agents. In 2008, the University opened a Crime Scene Investigation (CSI) House, which enables students to process simulated crime scenes and collect evidence just like the pros.

An education major prepares a student for a career as a teacher in a world of rapid political, economic, scientific, and cultural change. The Education Department seeks to graduate students who have general knowledge and specific content knowledge, as well as sound theory and practice.

Students who graduate from the hospitality management program are prepared to work in a large hotel or resort, in a convention bureau or center, in the areas of event or banquet management, or on a cruise ship. As part of the program, students complete 800 hours of field work at such places as the ski resort in nearby Ellicottville, New York, and Glendorn, a luxurious mountain resort in Bradford.

The nursing program at Pitt-Bradford offers an Associate of Science degree that can be completed in two years and a Bachelor of Science in Nursing degree that requires two additional years. Students may commence this program upon completion of the associate degree.

In psychology, students gain knowledge in the scientific and theoretical aspects of psychology as well as the application of this knowledge. The major prepares students for graduate work in psychology and related disciplines and for employment in social service agencies, mental health centers, industries, and not-for-profit and governmental agencies.

Students may relocate to another University of Pittsburgh campus to complete academic programs not offered at Pitt-Bradford, but they may earn no more than 70 credits before transferring. All students in the arts and sciences may relocate, provided they are in good standing. Engineering students may relocate if they maintain a grade point average of at least 2.5.

Academic Facilities

In addition to the T. Edward and Tullah Hanley Library on campus, Pitt-Bradford students have online access to the entire University of Pittsburgh library system.

Blaisdell Hall, the fine arts and communication arts building, houses the art, communication arts, theater, and music programs and features state-of-the-art equipment. Students can find a computer graphics lab, two art studios, a music/theater rehearsal hall, and a radio and television studio. The building also houses a multipurpose theater and serves as the cultural center for the region by housing plays, concerts, lectures, and other arts-related events.

Fisher Hall houses the science programs, such as biology, chemistry, engineering, petroleum technology, and physics. The science labs, which were updated during the summer of 2010, are filled with up-to-date scientific equipment, enabling students to perform a variety of experiments. The building also has two computer-aided learning centers and, on the roof, a campus greenhouse.

In Swarts Hall, students take courses in business, education, sociology, anthropology, psychology, history/political science, languages, English, writing, and criminal justice. The building also houses a new nursing suite and multimedia classrooms that can turn a typical class into an audio and visual experience.

There is more to the Sport and Fitness Center than sports. The building also houses the athletic training, sports medicine, and sport and recreation management programs. The building houses a human performance lab and an athletic training room.

In the Ceramic Studio, students get their hands dirty—literally. Students have sixteen motorized pottery wheels, a manual kick wheel, a work table, and a kiln to help turn slabs of clay into art.

Costs

For 2012–13, tuition for full-time students was $5,985 per fifteen-week term for Pennsylvania residents and $11,183 for nonresidents. Nursing tuition was $7,667 per term for Pennsylvania residents and $14,261 for nonresidents. Room and board expenses were $4,044 per term. Other costs include an activity fee of $85 per term, a health fee of $50 per term, and a computer fee of $175 per term. Books and supplies cost approximately $500 per term.

Financial Aid

Pitt-Bradford believes that the cost of a college education should not be a deterrent to any student regardless of family financial circumstances. A variety of grants, scholarships, loans, and work-study opportunities are administered through the Financial Aid Office. All aid applicants must submit the Free Application for Federal Student Aid (FAFSA) by March 1 to receive priority consideration. Pennsylvania residents who complete the FAFSA by March 1 are also eligible for Pennsylvania Higher Education Assistance Agency (PHEAA) grants. Students who live outside of Pennsylvania should contact their state agency to learn more about the prerequisites for grants.

The University awards merit-based scholarships to those who demonstrate exceptional academic achievement. The University ROTC program is another possible source of aid. The University encourages veterans to contact the VA about educational benefits.

To learn more about financial assistance, students should contact the Financial Aid Office or visit the financial aid website at http://www.upb.pitt.edu/financialaid.

Faculty

Pitt-Bradford's 70 full-time faculty members hold doctorates and master's degrees from some of the most prestigious universities in the nation, including Cornell, Harvard, Stanford, and the University of Pittsburgh. Teaching is the primary activity of the faculty, and personal attention is emphasized in the classroom. Faculty members welcome the chance to meet with their students and know them by name. The student-faculty ratio is 19:1.

Student Government

Because Pitt-Bradford is a personalized campus, opportunities for leadership abound. Many students become campus leaders as early as their sophomore year. Regardless of students' background or interests, most find many places to become involved at Pitt-Bradford.

The Student Activities Council schedules comedy performances, lectures, art exhibits, movies, and trips to such cities as Toronto, Niagara Falls, Cooperstown, and New York City.

Admission Requirements

The Admissions Committee considers three primary factors in evaluating an applicant's ability to succeed in college work: the high school record, the results of standardized tests (SAT or ACT), and the high school's recommendations. In addition, personal qualifications, extracurricular activities, and potential to contribute to the college community may be taken into consideration.

Application and Information

Pitt-Bradford has a rolling admissions program, and students may apply at any time. All candidates are notified as soon as action is taken on their application.

Candidates for admission should complete and return the application with a nonrefundable $45 fee. Students must also submit an official copy of their high school record and scores from either the SAT or ACT. In addition to fulfilling the above requirements, transfer applicants must submit all official college transcripts and must have a minimum cumulative grade point average of 2.0.

The Office of Admissions welcomes campus visits by students and their families; such visits help students arrive at a final decision about Pitt-Bradford. Interviews and tours are scheduled Monday through Friday, 9 a.m. to 3 p.m., and on selected Saturdays. Arrangements can be made by contacting the Office of Admissions or by going online to http://www.upb.pitt.edu/visit.

For application forms, catalogs, and further information, students should contact:

Office of Admissions
University of Pittsburgh at Bradford
300 Campus Drive
Bradford, Pennsylvania 16701-2898
Phone: 814-362-7555
    800-872-1787 (toll-free)
Website: http://www.upb.pitt.edu
    http://www.facebook.com/PittBradford
    https://twitter.com/PittBradford

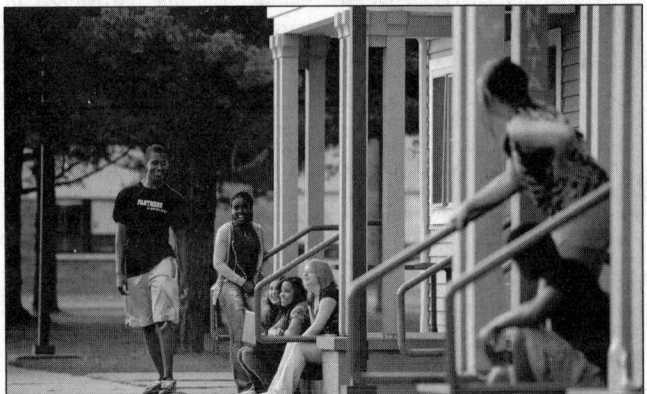

Students at the University of Pittsburgh at Bradford enjoy themselves after class.

UNIVERSITY OF PUGET SOUND

TACOMA, WASHINGTON

The College

Founded in 1888, University of Puget Sound is an independent college committed to the liberal arts and sciences, superb teaching, and the recognition of each student as an individual. A nationally acclaimed teaching faculty, well-planned facilities, and a limited enrollment ensure excellence in education.

Puget Sound, the only national liberal arts college in western Washington, is one of only two independent colleges in Washington State to be granted a chapter by Phi Beta Kappa. It leads small colleges in Washington State (and ranks in the top 5 on the West Coast) in terms of alumni who earn doctorate degrees. Many graduates have received undergraduate and postgraduate honors, including Rhodes, National Science Foundation, Fulbright, Rotary, Watson, Phi Kappa Phi, Truman, Goldwater, Hertz, and National Endowment for the Humanities fellowships and scholarships. Equally impressive, among national colleges and universities with fewer than 5,000 undergraduate students, Puget Sound is consistently named among the top colleges for number of alumni serving as Peace Corps volunteers worldwide.

Puget Sound enrolls 2,600 students, with more than 75 percent coming from outside Washington State. In addition, forty-four states and sixteen countries are represented in the student body. The student-to-faculty ratio is 12:1, the average class size is 19, and all courses are taught by professors.

Puget Sound is a vibrant residential community. Special theme houses and halls are available for students with common interests. In the fall of 2013, Puget Sound is scheduled to open its newest residence hall. It features themed residence options with areas of emphasis such as humanities, entrepreneurship, environmental outdoor leadership, international and global education, and honors. The neighboring residential community provides many facilities for those who wish to live off campus. Athletic facilities include Memorial Fieldhouse and Pamplin Fitness Center (which includes an indoor tennis pavilion), Wallace Pool, Peyton Field at Baker Stadium, an indoor climbing wall, and numerous varsity and intramural athletic fields.

Students find that participating in activities sponsored by the student government is an excellent way to learn outside the classroom and improve leadership abilities. Athletics include twenty-three varsity teams, various club teams, and numerous intramural teams. In addition, students are involved in a variety of clubs and associations, such as forensics, theater, music, radio station (which received an award from mtvU for best college radio station in the nation), art and literary magazines, weekly newspaper, yearbook, Student Senate, religious groups, Black Student Union, Hui-O-Hawaii, Earth Activists, Queer Alliance, Asian Pacific American Student Union, Community for Hispanic Awareness, and Habitat for Humanity. Seventy-five percent of students participate in community service activities.

Location

The campus is located in a residential neighborhood in the historic North End of Tacoma, 35 miles south of Seattle and easily accessible from Interstate 5 and SEA-TAC International Airport. Tacoma is a dynamic city of 200,000 people located close to the shores of Puget Sound and a short distance from ski slopes and the Pacific Ocean. It was ranked by *Money* magazine as one of the most livable medium-sized cities in the country. Tacoma also features Point Defiance Zoo and Aquarium, many parks, museums, a new convention center, and hospitals. The college occupies thirty-nine buildings on a 97-acre campus. The architecture is Tudor Gothic, with its distinctive red-brick pattern arches and porticoes.

Majors and Degrees

Puget Sound offers academic programs in more than fifty areas of study leading to the Bachelor of Arts, Bachelor of Science, and Bachelor of Music degrees. Academic programs include art, Asian languages and culture (majors are offered in Chinese, Japanese, and East Asian languages), biochemistry, biology, business, chemistry, classics, communication, comparative sociology, computer science, computer science in business, economics, English, exercise science, foreign languages and literature (majors relating to language and literature and language and culture are available through the study of French, German, and Spanish), geology, history, international political economy, mathematics, molecular and cellular biology, music, natural science, philosophy, physics, politics and government, psychology, religion, and theatre arts. Minors are offered in Latin American studies, African-American studies, environmental policy and decision-making, gender studies, humanities, neuroscience, and many other areas. The special interdisciplinary major allows exceptional students the opportunity to pursue a degree in a recognized interdisciplinary or emergent field.

Puget Sound offers a dual-degree program in engineering, leading to a joint Bachelor of Arts/Bachelor of Science degree in engineering. Students in this program complete prerequisites in chemistry, mathematics/computer science, and physics, then transfer to an accredited engineering school for course work in chemical, civil, electrical, environmental, mechanical, or petroleum engineering, among others. Affiliated schools are Washington University in St. Louis, Columbia University, and the University of Southern California.

Graduate degrees offered include the Master of Occupational Therapy, Doctor of Physical Therapy, Master of Arts in Teaching, and Master of Education.

Academic Programs

Academic rigor, freedom to take courses from across the curriculum, and opportunities for interdisciplinary study characterize the academic experience. At the heart of the academic program is the core curriculum—eight course groupings around which major and elective studies are arranged over a four-year period. The emphasis throughout a student's undergraduate education is on the acquisition of intellectual skills: the ability to express oneself clearly, orally and in writing; the ability to reason quantitatively; and the ability to think logically, critically, and independently. By mastering the literature and techniques of a specific academic major, the student learns to cultivate the unique power of his or her own mind and to respond vigorously, but humanely, to important social, moral, and intellectual challenges.

A particularly well-designed curriculum for the freshman year and a model program of academic advising and career counseling enable each student to develop his or her own skills and interests in preparation for a lifetime of creative work and leisure. Puget Sound's highly successful and award-winning student orientation process—Prelude, Passages and Perspectives—is a nine-day program that allows new students to become involved in writing and thinking seminars, academic workshops, community service, and a three-day adventure to the nearby Olympic Peninsula.

The academic year is divided into two semesters, beginning in late August and mid-January. A normal academic load is 4 units (typically four courses) per semester. Each unit of credit is equivalent to 6 quarter hours or 4 semester hours. Thirty-two units are required for graduation.

Off-Campus Programs

Puget Sound offers an outstanding selection of international opportunities for its students, with over 100 study-abroad programs in dozens of countries, including Australia, England, Scotland, Spain, France, Germany, Italy, Ghana, Austria, China, Japan, Madagascar, Taiwan, Argentina, Tanzania, and Chile, among others. The Pacific Rim/Asia Study-Travel Program offers students an intense year of study and travel in six to eight Asian countries.

Puget Sound's location in one of the fastest-growing regions of the country places its internship program at the forefront of national liberal arts colleges. Opportunities for undergraduate research abound, as students may apply for summer research grants in the sciences, social sciences, humanities, and the arts.

Academic Facilities

Collins Memorial Library contains more than 550,000 volumes of books and periodicals plus a sizable collection of federal and Washington State government publications, maps, microforms, videotapes, cassettes, compact discs, and other media materials. These resources are strengthened through participation in the Orbis Cascade Alliance, a consortium of twenty-seven public and private institutions of higher education in Oregon and Washington, with combined holdings of more than 22 million volumes. Other major academic facilities include Thompson Science Complex, Kittredge Art Gallery, Schneebeck Concert Hall, Norton Clapp Theatre, Lowry Wyatt Hall, and Slater Museum of Natural History. The new Weyerhaeuser Center for Health Sciences opened in 2011, housing undergraduate programs in psychology, neuroscience, and exercise Science along with the Graduate School of Occupational Therapy and Physical Therapy.

Puget Sound provides students of environmental science and marine biology with a superb outdoor laboratory. Equipment and facilities in the Thompson Science Complex include a modern greenhouse; an observatory; an aquarium with a tidal cycle; a state-of-the-art genetics laboratory; a scanning electron microscope and a transmission electron microscope; ultraviolet, visible, fluorescence, infrared, and nuclear magnetic resonance spectrophotometric equipment; and a seismograph. Students also have access to human cadavers. Special facilities are available for students of occupational and physical therapy, education, counseling, foreign languages, and psychology. The music building houses Schneebeck Concert Hall and provides a keyboard and music lab and twenty-two individual practice rooms, including a "V-Room," a unique facility in which the musician can change the acoustic properties of the room.

Wireless Internet access is available throughout campus. In addition, students have access to computer labs and state-of-the-art video editing facilities.

Costs

Tuition and student government fees are $41,640 and $228, respectively, for the 2013–14 academic year. Room and board cost $10,780.

Financial Aid

More than 90 percent of Puget Sound students receive financial aid in one or a combination of the following forms: scholarships, grants, low-interest loans, and part-time employment. Applicants are automatically considered for renewable merit scholarships that range in amount from $5,000 to $19,000 per year. In addition, Puget Sound offers many other scholarships by application or audition in music, theater, art, selected academic areas, forensics/debate, and leadership.

Faculty

Members of the faculty work closely with individual students both in the classroom and in student-originated research projects within and across the disciplines. Eighty-nine percent of the faculty members teach full-time; 98 percent of tenured faculty members hold a Ph.D. or an equivalent terminal degree. In agreement with Ted Taranovski, Professor Emeritus of History, faculty members feel that the University of Puget Sound is "an institution geared to human beings—small enough to give one a sense of community and yet large enough to provide an excellent academic curriculum; it is not an impersonal machine where people become cogs." In recent years, professors at Puget Sound have been recognized for their academic and teaching achievements through awards and distinctions, including the Graves Award in the Humanities and fellowships from various organizations, including the National Endowment for the Humanities, the American Council of Learned Societies, and the Danforth Foundation. Seven Puget Sound professors have been named Washington State Professor of the Year by the Carnegie Foundation for the Advancement of Teaching. Puget Sound has received more of these awards than any other college or university in the state.

Admission Requirements

Each applicant to University of Puget Sound is considered individually and is admitted on the basis of his or her qualifications and achievements. In considering applicants for freshman admission, the Admission Committee evaluates the following: high school course selection, high school grade point average, rank in graduating class (if available), SAT or ACT scores, a counselor's and an academic teacher's recommendations, an essay, a recommended interview, and extracurricular activities. College credit is awarded to students who have earned scores of 4 or higher on Advanced Placement examinations. Credit for a score of 3 is available for selected examinations only. Credit is also available for a score of 5, 6, or 7 on the International Baccalaureate higher-level examinations.

Application and Information

Prospective freshmen may apply for admission anytime after the beginning of the senior year in high school using the Common Application for freshmen. Admission decisions are mailed on or before April 1. The application deadline is January 15. Students who have decided that Puget Sound is their first-choice college may choose one of two early decision plans. Early Decision I has a November 15 application deadline, with admission and tentative financial aid notification by December 15. Early Decision II has a January 2 application deadline, with admission and tentative financial aid notification by February 15. Transfer students are admitted in both semesters. Students applying for transfer admission should submit the Common Application for transfers.

For more information about Puget Sound, students should contact:

Office of Admission
University of Puget Sound
1500 North Warner Street, #1062
Tacoma, Washington 98416-1062
Phone: 253-879-3211
        800-396-7191 (toll-free)
E-mail: admission@pugetsound.edu
Website: www.pugetsound.edu

Jones Hall, built in 1924.

UNIVERSITY OF REDLANDS
REDLANDS, CALIFORNIA

The University

The University of Redlands has, for more than 100 years, offered its students a tradition of superior liberal arts education. While students may select from a variety of programs that prepare them for professional or graduate school, the heart and foundation of Redlands is in liberal studies. Its outstanding faculty, educated in the world's finest colleges and universities, provides students with extraordinary opportunities for learning and growth through excellent teaching and close, informal interaction. Intense intellectual activity is balanced by opportunities for quiet reflection, fun, and recreation.

The University College of Arts and Sciences enrolls more than 2,500 students. Sixty percent of the freshman class comes from California and the remainder from forty-three other states and eleven countries. In addition to a strong academic program in the liberal arts, the sciences, pre-professional programs, and the arts, many extracurricular programs are available to the student, including music, drama, dance, and athletics. Internships are available for students in many academic programs. The School of Music and the Department of Theatre Arts provide a rich selection of cultural events throughout the year. Prominent speakers are invited to the campus each year to give major addresses and participate in classes and public discussion groups, and many social functions are organized by the Office of Student Life and individual residence halls. Additional social opportunities are provided for interested students by local nonresidential fraternities and sororities. The student services center provides assistance in the areas of career and personal counseling and academic support.

Seventy percent of the students live on campus in residence halls that offer a variety of accommodations, including single gender, coed by separate wings, and coed by alternate suites.

The University of Redlands is one of a select number of schools that have a chapter of Phi Beta Kappa, the nation's oldest and most prestigious academic honor society. In addition, 12 Redlands students have been awarded Fulbright awards within the past five years.

The University of Redlands offers master's programs in the fields of business, communicative disorders, education, geographic information systems, and music. The School of Education offers a Doctorate in Leadership for Educational Justice Ed.D. program.

Location

The University is located in the city of Redlands within the San Bernardino Valley. Overlooking the 160-acre campus are the two highest mountains in southern California, Mt. San Gorgonio and Mt. San Bernardino, each more than 10,000 feet high. Redlands has a population of 70,000 and is situated at an elevation of 1,500 feet. Metropolitan Los Angeles to the west and Palm Springs to the east are both about an hour's drive away by freeway.

Majors and Degrees

The B.A. degree is offered in the academic areas of Asian studies, biology, business administration, communicative disorders, creative writing, economics, English literature, environmental business, environmental studies, French, German, government, history, international relations, liberal studies, managerial studies, music, philosophy, psychology, race and ethnic studies, religion, sociology/anthropology, Spanish, studio art, theater arts, women's and gender studies, and visual and media studies. The B.S. degree is offered in accounting, biochemistry and molecular biology, biology, business administration, chemistry, economics, environmental policy and management, environmental science, mathematics, and physics. The professional degree of Bachelor of Music (B.M.) is offered by the School of Music. Primary and secondary credentials are granted by the School of Education. Strong interdisciplinary programs in Latin American studies, pre-law, and pre-medicine are also available.

Academic Programs

Academic majors are offered in the spirit of a liberal arts program, with emphasis on developing the whole student. In addition to the standard academic program, international-study programs, independent study, and an honors program are offered to provide greater diversity.

A liberal arts education, by definition, is an exposure to a wide variety of academic disciplines. Typically, such exposure carries no underlying theme but is distributed among broad categories such as the humanities, arts, social sciences, and natural sciences. The University of Redlands has never considered itself typical and, as a result, has developed an unusual approach to the implementation of its liberal arts philosophy by restructuring the general education requirements to provide a contemporary curriculum. This common experience emphasizes competence in writing, computing, problem solving, and creative skills, all of which are fundamental to a lifetime of learning and career development. In addition, the requirements include a first-year seminar that integrates the academic program and close personal relationships between students and faculty members. The overriding emphasis of this innovative curriculum is on a thorough investigation of human values as they affect the individual and society. An examination of the worth of the individual, respect for nature and life, free inquiry, and the understanding of other cultures are a few of the topics covered through various courses. The University hopes that this experience will broaden each student's understanding and better equip them to deal with today's dynamic society.

The Johnston Center for Integrative Studies provides a nontraditional approach for a select group of highly motivated students. Johnston Center students are exempted from most of the academic structure of Redlands and instead negotiate their entire course of study with a faculty/peer committee. Drawing from the Redlands curriculum as well as from courses created each semester by the Johnston community, each student proposes an individually designed general studies program and an area of concentration. Course performance is evaluated in a narrative format rather than with letter grades. These students live in the Johnston Center Complex, a living/learning community that includes student rooms, faculty offices, classrooms, and space for weekly community meetings. Students who are enrolled in the Johnston Center are expected to contribute to the life of the center's community.

The academic calendar divides the school year into a 4-4-1 plan, providing a fall semester, a spring semester, and a May term. The four classes taken in the fall semester are completed prior to the third Friday in December. The spring semester begins in January and runs through April. The four-week May term offers students the chance to pursue one subject in depth. Extensive off-campus opportunities, including internships, international study, and on-campus independent study, are available.

Academic Facilities

The institution has facilities with a mix of Greek, Spanish, and modern California architecture. The newly renovated ground floor of the Armacost Library includes rooms for collaboration and learning, the Fletcher Jones Computing Center, a student study area, the Bulldog café, and an Internet lounge. Other facilities include the Stauffer Complex for Science, Mathematics, and Environmental Studies; and a brand-new Center for the Arts, featuring the Glen Wallichs Theatre, Frederick Loewe Performance Hall, and an art gallery. The library houses 400,000 publications and online databases such as Dialog, ABI/INFORM, PsychLIT, ERIC, Wilson Indexes, and the Music Index. These facilities and surrounding common spaces also have access to a wireless network.

Costs

Tuition for 2013–14 is $40,990, and room and board costs are $12,314.

Financial Aid

Recognizing that many worthy and capable students find it impossible to obtain a college education without financial assistance, the University has established a program of aid. Most aid is need-based, but no-need scholarships based on academic achievement in high school and/or college are available. Presidential Scholarships are also available, based on grades and test scores, as are Achievement Awards. Talent Awards, ranging from $500 to $10,000 each, are available in art, creative writing, music, and theater.

Students seeking financial assistance should inquire through the Office of Admissions when applying for admission. The Free Application for Federal Student Aid (FAFSA) should be submitted by March 2. FAFSA forms received after this date are evaluated subject to the availability of funding. Forms may be obtained online at http://www.fafsa.gov.

Faculty

The highly qualified full-time faculty numbers 167 men and women, 80 percent of whom hold doctorates or other terminal degrees in their field. The wide variety of academic backgrounds represented in the faculty provides students with an excellent opportunity to live and work in an atmosphere of intellectual inquiry. Academic advising is handled by faculty members, and all students are assigned an adviser in the area of their major interest.

Student Government

Authority and responsibility for student government is delegated to the Associated Students of the University of Redlands by the president and the faculty to make possible genuine participation by students in the governance of the University. The organization is composed of all students in the college, and its officers are chosen by the student body. More than sixty positions of representation are open to students on faculty, administrative, trustee, and alumni committees. Among other activities and responsibilities, the student government finances and operates a student-union complex, on-campus shuttle, information center, vending program, convocation series, Internet radio station, and weekly newspaper.

Admission Requirements

Graduation from an accredited high school or the equivalent is necessary for admission. No set pattern of courses in high school is required, but applicants should have had 4 years of work in English and should have completed an academic program strongly emphasizing such studies as foreign language, science, mathematics (including algebra II), and social science. An average grade of at least B should have been maintained in the high school program. Applicants are requested to submit the results of the SAT or the ACT. The writing portion is used for placement in English classes but not admission. SAT Subject Tests are not required. Standardized test scores are not required of transfers who bring at least 24 transferable units to the University. International students, for whom English is not their first language, must submit the results from any of the following exams: TOEFL, IELTS, APIEL, PTE-A, iTEP, University of Cambridge ESOL examinations, or the International Baccalaureate Higher Level English exam.

Transfer students should have maintained a minimum 2.8 grade point average and may transfer up to 66 units of credit from a community college and 96 units from a four-year institution.

Application and Information

Applications are processed on a rolling basis. Those wishing to be considered for an academic or merit scholarship should apply by November 15. Those applying for need-based financial aid should apply by January 15. Transfer applicants should apply by March 1. Applications made after this date are considered on a space-available basis.

Further inquiries should be addressed to:

Office of Admissions
University of Redlands
P.O. Box 3080
Redlands, California 92373-0999
Phone: 800-455-5064 (toll-free)
Fax: 909-335-4089
E-mail: admissions@redlands.edu
Web site: http://www.redlands.edu

The University of Redlands stands out brilliantly against the majestic San Bernardino Mountains.

UNIVERSITY OF RHODE ISLAND
KINGSTON, RHODE ISLAND

The University

The University of Rhode Island (URI) is the largest university in the nation's smallest state. That means it offers the research and experiences typically found at larger universities, alongside the friendly, student-centered atmosphere of smaller institutions. Outreach is at the core of the University's role as a land-, sea-, and urban-grant institution. Whether tutoring inner-city children, monitoring water quality, building homes for Habitat, or offering medication review and counseling, students and faculty are always sharing their knowledge with people around the state, nation, and world.

The campus community represents diverse cultures, lifestyles, beliefs, religions, political affiliations, and philosophies. The University's 13,000 undergraduates come from forty-five U.S. states and territories and fifty-eight nations; 18 percent identify themselves as students of color. To ensure graduates are able to succeed and lead in the twenty-first-century world, one of the University's strategic priorities is to help all members of the campus community feel welcomed and valued and develop the ability to communicate, understand, and engage productively with people different than themselves.

About 6,200 students live on campus in twenty-three residence halls ranging from traditional corridor style to apartment style. In Freshman Village, more than a dozen residence halls are conveniently clustered together between the campus's academic, athletic, and recreational areas. To the east are most of the handsome granite academic buildings surrounding the spacious Quad—students' favorite place to hang out, study, and picnic during spring, summer, and fall. To the west are gymnasiums, athletic fields, indoor track and aquatics center, tennis courts, ice hockey arena, and a large event venue that's hosted such performers as Bob Dylan, Wiz Khalifa, and The Fray.

About 1,000 fraternity and sorority members live on campus in nationally affiliated houses. Other students commute from home, or rent houses and apartments in nearby beach communities. Meal plans are offered to all students, who enjoy home-style favorites, regional and ethnic specialties, vegan and vegetarian selections, and healthy options in award-winning dining halls.

The Memorial Union is the heart and hub of campus activity—home to more than 100 student clubs, bookstore, dining facilities, convenience store, hair salon, computer store, wireless "airport lounge," campus radio station and newspaper, game room, coffee shop, and more.

Location

The University's 1,200-acre campus is perfectly located in the historic village of Kingston, just 30 miles south of Providence, a 90-minute drive or quick train ride to Boston, and a few hours from New York City. It's also just 6 miles from Rhode Island's coastal beaches and nearest ski and snow park. Bus transportation is available from the campus to most areas of the state. The Kingston Amtrak train station is 1 mile from campus, and the T. F. Green International Airport is 25 miles away in Warwick, Rhode Island.

Majors and Degrees

The University of Rhode Island offers more than 100 undergraduate degree programs to spark students' creativity. To respond to the world's changing needs, the University often creates new degree programs, such as Forensic Chemistry, Supply Chain Management, and Chinese, and blends such disciplines as languages with textiles and pharmaceuticals, business with the environment, and underwater archaeology with engineering for various dual-degree and interdisciplinary programs. Specifically, URI offers the following degree programs:

Bachelor of Arts: Africana Studies, Anthropology, Art, Art History, Chemistry, Chinese, Classical Studies (with an option in classical civilization and culture), Communication Studies, Computer Science, Economics, English, Film Media, French, Gender and Women's Studies, German, History, Italian, Journalism, Mathematics, Music (options in jazz studies and music history and literature), Philosophy, Physics, Political Science, Psychology, Public Relations, Sociology, Spanish, and Writing and Rhetoric.

Bachelor of Science: Accounting, Animal Science and Technology (options in animal science, animal management, and pre–veterinary science), Aquaculture and Fishery Technology, Biological Sciences, Biology, Biomedical Engineering, Cell and Molecular Biology, Chemical Engineering (options in biology track and pharmaceutical track), Chemistry, Chemistry and Forensic Chemistry, Civil and Environmental Engineering, Communicative Disorders, Computer Engineering, Computer Science (with options in 3-D graphics and digital forensics), Economics, Education (with options in early childhood education, elementary education, music education, physical education, and secondary education), Electrical Engineering, Entrepreneurial Management, Environmental and Natural Resources Economics, Environmental Science and Management, Finance, General Business Administration, Geology and Geological Oceanography, Global Business Management, Industrial and Systems Engineering, Health Studies, Human Development and Family Studies, Kinesiology (with options in exercise science, health studies, and early contingent physical therapy), Landscape Architecture, Marine Affairs, Marine Biology, Mathematics, Marketing, Mechanical Engineering, Medical Laboratory Science and Biotechnology Manufacturing, Nursing, Nutrition and Dietetics, Ocean Engineering, Pharmaceutical Sciences, Physics (five-year Medical Physics), Physics and Physical Oceanography, Plant Sciences, Sociology (criminology and criminal justice), Supply Chain Management, Textiles, Fashion Merchandising and Design (with options in apparel studies, fashion merchandising, interior furnishings and design, and textile science), Textile Marketing, and Wildlife and Conservation Biology.

Other degree program options: Bachelor of Fine Arts in Art and Theater (options in acting, design and theater technology, directing, and stage management); Bachelor of Landscape Architecture; Bachelor of Music in Music Education, Music Composition, and Music Performance; dual-degree programs in International Business (B.S. in one of seven business disciplines and a B.A. in Chinese, French, German, or Spanish), and International Engineering (B.S. in one of the eight engineering disciplines and a B.A. in Chinese, French, German, or Spanish); accelerated five-year programs in Industrial Systems Engineering and Mechanical Engineering with both a B.S. and Master's of Business Administration; bachelor's–master's degree program in Speech–Language Pathology; a six-year Doctor of Pharmacy degree; and pre-professional preparation in dentistry, law, medicine, physical therapy, and veterinary studies.

Academic Programs

Among the University's strategic priorities is the integration of research, scholarship, and creative work into the undergraduate experience, whether students are majoring in the sciences or the humanities. Creative endeavors, experiential learning opportunities, internships, and research alongside faculty and graduate students are key to fostering a propensity for inquiry among graduates that will contribute ideas to global marketplace. URI strives to prepare its graduates to live and work in an increasingly globalized economy, by expanding the scope of international education partnerships, language programs, and study abroad, and by growing its international student population. Cross-discipline work is encouraged.

Freshmen are enrolled in University College for its strong support of a successful first-year experience—academically and socially. University College advisers help students choose majors, minors, and concentrations and appropriate courses for admittance into the desired degree-granting college. The University Honors Program offers academically talented students opportunities to broaden their intellectual development and strengthen their preparation in their major fields of study. Generally, 120 credits are required for a B.A. degree and 130 for a B.S. The University of Rhode Island operates on a two-semester calendar, with semesters beginning in September and January, and offers optional accelerated summer sessions. The University grants credit to scores of 3 or better on most College Board Advanced Placement exams, and may give credit for satisfactory scores on departmental proficiency examinations, College-Level Examination Program (CLEP) examinations, and International Baccalaureate Program exams.

Off-Campus Programs

The Office of Experiential Learning and Community Engagement offers more than 400 full- and part-time internships for academic credit, including one-semester and one-year programs in and outside the state. The Office of International Education and National Student Exchange offers more than 200 affiliated study-abroad programs in sixty countries. Students in the International Engineering program and the International Business program enjoy a full-year abroad, taking courses at partner universities and engaging in paid internships with leading international companies.

Academic Facilities

The University library has more than 1 million bound volumes and 1.5 million titles available electronically. Active research programs are carried on in all seven academic colleges. The Graduate School of Oceanography, located on the Narragansett Bay Campus, provides undergraduates with a living research lab for science-related courses. The University houses a large collection of American historic textiles, a center for robotics research, a planetarium, a Center of Excellence for Explosives Detection, Mitigation and Response, an Inner Space Center, a Digital Forensics and Cyber Security Center, Confucius Institute, two animal science farms, and the state Crime Lab for forensic study.

Costs

The comprehensive cost for 2012–13 was estimated at $39,814 for out-of-state students and $23,726 for Rhode Islanders. This covers tuition, fees, and room and board. Books, travel, laboratory fees, and personal expenses are not included in these figures. The University participates in the cooperative plan of the New England Board of Higher Education, whereby students from other New England states are able to enroll in certain degree programs not offered at their own state colleges for reduced tuition.

Financial Aid

To be considered for financial aid students must submit the Free Application for Federal Student Aid (FAFSA); priority is given to applications received by March 1. Merit scholarships are available to incoming freshmen with superior academic credentials with priority consideration given to those who apply by the December 1 early action deadline. For 2011–12, 75 percent of new students who completed applications were awarded some form of aid. Opportunities for employment through work-study programs are also available.

Faculty

The faculty consists of 684 full-time equivalent members, or 1 professor for every 15.5 students. Approximately 86 percent of the full-time faculty members hold doctoral degrees. Faculty members serve both the graduate and undergraduate populations and have wide-ranging interests and responsibilities. In addition to teaching and research, they serve as student advisers.

Student Government

The Student Senate represents the students to the administration and faculty, supervises extracurricular activities, and distributes activities funds among the various student organizations. Individual residence halls form their own governments. The Interfraternity Council supervises fraternity affairs, and the Panhellenic Association governs sorority life. The Commuter Association provides social activities and other assistance for commuter students.

Admission Requirements

Admission is competitive. Freshman candidates must submit a high school transcript and scores on SAT or ACT exams taken no later than January 1 of the senior year. International students for whom English is not the primary language must take the Test of English as a Foreign Language (TOEFL) or other approved English language tests (see Admission website). Admission counselors evaluate each applicant individually, and expect that all have completed at least 18 units of college-preparatory work, although specific unit requirements vary for some of the seven colleges of the University. Academic achievement in a challenging high school program receives the strongest consideration. An audition is required for the Bachelor of Music degree. Scores on equivalency exams may be presented by applicants who have not completed formal high school studies. Transfer students may enter in either semester (although some degree programs admit students only in the fall) and must submit transcripts of all previous work at both the high school and college levels. Early admission is available to high school juniors with superior records.

Students are selected primarily on the basis of academic competence and without regard to age, race, religion, color, sex, creed, national origin, disability, or sexual orientation.

Application and Information

Students often say that their campus visit is what made them decide to attend URI. Information sessions and tours are scheduled daily during the week and on many Saturdays throughout the year. Tour details, information about open house programs, and directions to campus can all be found at the URI admission website (http://www.uri.edu/admission). Students can also find URI admission representatives at college fairs in Rhode Island and throughout the Northeast and beyond during the academic year.

Students are encouraged to submit applications early in their final year of high school. The early action deadline is December 1, and students receive notification by January 31. The regular deadline for fall term freshman applications is February 1, and student receive notification by March 31. The deadline for transfer applications for fall is June 1. The closing date for spring-term applications is November 1. The University of Rhode Island is a Common Application School.

Requests for information should be directed to:

Office of Admission
University of Rhode Island
14 Upper College Road
Kingston, Rhode Island 02881
Phone: 401-874-7000
E-mail: admission@uri.edu
Website: http://www.uri.edu/admission

That Ram Marching Band became known as the Pride of New England in the 1960s. Today, these 100-plus spirited musicians from all majors greet new students every year on Welcome Day and still delight fans on the football field.

UNIVERSITY OF SAINT JOSEPH
WEST HARTFORD, CONNECTICUT

The University

The University of Saint Joseph (USJ) helps students focus on success and get the most from their college experience. USJ graduates are prepared for the future. Through career-focused, academically challenging programs, students explore their greatest potential and receive personalized attention and individual mentorship by expert faculty. Internships and field experience are available in all USJ programs, preparing students for a career, graduate school, entry to law school or medical school—the sky's the limit!

There are 1,052 talented undergraduates at USJ. Faculty members and students emphasize leadership in academics, career, and community. Drawing on its Mercy heritage, the University is a community that promotes the growth of the whole person. This is accomplished in a caring environment that encourages strong ethical values, personal integrity, and a sense of responsibility to the needs of society. Women lead every organization on campus, from the Business Society and Student Government to honors societies. Students shine in artistic performances, as coordinators of community service projects, and on the athletic fields. Students also serve with faculty members and administrators on University-wide committees. In the field of athletics, the University's women compete in eight NCAA Division III sports: basketball, cross-country, lacrosse, softball, soccer, swimming/diving, tennis, and volleyball. The O'Connell Athletic Center features a six-lane pool, gymnasium, suspended jogging track, dance studio, fitness center, outdoor track, softball field, and tennis courts for all students' recreational purposes.

The University of Saint Joseph has a beautiful residential campus in the bustling town of West Hartford. Approximately 70 percent of the first-year students live on campus. Student support services include career planning, alumni mentoring, internship placement, counseling, health services, academic advisement, and campus ministry.

USJ alumni have considerable impact on the welfare of their communities. They are leaders in many fields, including aerospace research, business, education, environmental science, law, medicine, and politics. Recent graduates enjoy successful careers as accountants, teachers, dieticians, nurses, government leaders, social workers, biologists, and managers of nonprofit organizations.

The University of Saint Joseph is accredited by the New England Association of Schools and Colleges. Program accreditors include: Accreditation Council for Pharmacy Education, Commission on Accreditation of the American Dietetic Association, American Chemical Society, Commission on Collegiate Nursing Education, American Association for Marriage and Family Therapy, National Council for the Accreditation of Teacher Education, Council on Social Work Education, Council for Accreditation of Counseling and Related Educational Programs.

Location

The University of Saint Joseph is located in suburban West Hartford, 4 miles from the state capitol and the city of Hartford's arts and entertainment district. Among the nearby attractions are the XL Center and Coliseum; Bushnell Performing Arts Center, where the latest Broadway musicals are performed; and the Wadsworth Atheneum, the oldest public art gallery in the United States. Hartford is a cosmopolitan city with diverse ethnic flavors. It is also the home of the Tony Award–winning Hartford Stage Company, the Hartford Symphony Orchestra, the Connecticut Opera Company, the Hartford Ballet, and the Dodge Music Center, which features indoor and outdoor concerts. West Hartford—which was named one of the ten best cities for the next decade by *Kilpinger's* magazine—has a thriving downtown. The Center, just minutes from campus, offers an array of coffee bars, boutiques, restaurants, and movie theaters in downtown's trendy Blue Back Square.

Majors and Degrees

The University of Saint Joseph has always enjoyed a strong academic reputation based on career-focused professional majors and is continuing to grow the list of major offerings. USJ recently included undergraduate majors in public health and public policy and advocacy that add to already renowned programs in accounting, art history, biochemistry, biology, chemistry, child study, English, family studies, history, international studies, management, mathematics, nursing, nutrition and dietetics, philosophy, psychology, religious studies, social work, Spanish, special education, and women's studies. Pre-professional programs are offered in conjunction with an academic major and include pre-pharmacy, pre-dentistry, pre-law, pre-medicine, pre–physical therapy, and pre–veterinary studies.

Teaching certification is offered in elementary education, secondary education, and special education. Research, clinical, and work placements are important components of all academic programs.

Academic Programs

Each student must complete a minimum of 120 credits to obtain a baccalaureate degree, and 47 of those credits must be distributed among the general education/liberal arts courses at the University. Students must take courses in the humanities, social sciences, natural sciences, philosophy, religious studies, and physical education. An academic advisement counselor assists each student in planning her program of study.

Many unique facets of the academic programs increase students' propensity for success. An honors program and several dual degree programs are offered. The Center for Academic Excellence (CAE) manages the University's award-winning Writing Portfolio Program, which enhances students' writing skills. The CAE also provides tutoring and other academic support services. An exciting component of most majors at USJ is the internship. USJ faculty members have myriad connections that allow students to get the most desirable internships in the area. Students earn credit for internships at a variety of sites, including the state capitol, the Bushnell Performing Arts Center, Aetna, legislative offices, the Connecticut Department of Economic Development, WVIT-TV, Connecticut Children's Medical Center, the Science Center of Connecticut, and numerous other businesses.

Off-Campus Programs

Students at the University of Saint Joseph may take courses at cooperating institutions through the Hartford Consortium for Higher Education. This is a special arrangement among five Hartford-area colleges—USJ, Trinity College, University of Connecticut Greater Hartford Branch, Central Connecticut State University, and the University of Hartford—through which students are able to cross register for courses as part of their full-time credit load. No additional tuition is charged, and all credits are transferable.

Students at USJ have countless opportunities for global study experiences through many study-abroad programs. Assisted by the Director of International Studies and Programs, students can plan for an international-study experience during a semester, winter recess, or even over spring break. USJ also offers specialized programs in Guyana, South America, and in the Netherlands. In Guyana, students in the education and health science fields participate at the University's sister hospital to gain valuable work experience abroad during their junior or senior years. The University also hosts an embedded course in the Netherlands, where students in psychology, social work, education, nutrition, and nursing travel to HAN University.

Students majoring in nursing, social work, and nutrition, and those in the graduate counseling program, may gain practical experience providing community-based, accessible health screenings and referrals; health and nutrition education; counseling services; and social work case management services at the Wellness Center on Church Street in Hartford. The University has also established a partnership with the Franciscan Center for Urban Ministry in order to reach out to its neighboring city and enhance the quality of life of its residents in need.

Academic Facilities

The Pope Pius XII Library has a collection of more than 134,000 volumes, including computer databases, periodicals, microforms, audiovisuals, a Sirsi online catalog, and OCLC interlibrary loans. A collection of materials used in elementary and secondary education is featured in the Curriculum Materials Center.

The University uses laboratory schools with several of its academic programs. The renowned School for Young Children, located one block from campus, is an operating preschool that provides child study majors with training and experience. The Gengras Center, located right on campus, is a special education school serving children and young adults (ages 4–21) from approximately fifty-three area cities and towns in Connecticut and Massachusetts. It provides for special education needs and also helps to prepare special education teachers.

The University's primary technology centers are located in McDonough Hall; Internet/Wi-Fi access is available throughout campus. Additional facilities and services include a media center that provides production materials, expertise, and equipment for making and using a number of media instructional aids; science and nursing labs; and the Carol Autorino Center for the Arts and Humanities. The center includes Lynch Hall, which houses the School of Humanities and Social Sciences, faculty offices, and classrooms; the Bruyette Athenaeum, featuring the 365-seat Hoffman Auditorium; the USJ Art Gallery; a print study room; large lecture hall; reception room; and music practice rooms. The building also houses the University's archives.

Costs

The tuition and fees for full-time freshmen entering in 2013 are $33,477. Room and board cost is approximately $12,642. The cost per credit for part-time students is $722.

Financial Aid

The goal of the University of Saint Joseph financial aid program is to place a high-quality, private education within the reach of as many qualified students as possible. This goal is achieved by offering need- and merit-based financial aid that includes a combination of scholarships, grants, loans, and on-campus employment opportunities. Approximately 95 percent of full-time undergraduate students receive some form of financial assistance. Merit-based scholarship awards are available to all eligible first-year, transfer, and international students.

Faculty

University of Saint Joseph faculty consists of 108 full-time faculty members and 4 librarians. Of the total faculty, 71 percent are women. Of the full-time faculty, over 80 percent hold the highest possible degrees in their fields. Small classes benefit both students and professors. The student-faculty ratio is 12:1. The faculty and all members of the University community promote the welfare of students and help them attain the objectives set forth by the University's mission. Faculty members also act as mentors before and after graduation; involve students in scholarly research; serve as advisers to many extracurricular activities, including sports, campus ministry, and community service; and direct students in independent study.

Student Government

The Student Government Association works for effective communication among students, faculty members, and administrators. Students are encouraged to voice their opinions and concerns to the association for consideration and action. In addition, student representatives sit as voting members with faculty members and administrators on major University-wide committees. The Student Government Association encourages the development of leadership skills and provides funds annually for several of its members to attend leadership workshops and conferences.

Admission Requirements

The University of Saint Joseph seeks women who are ready and willing to accept the challenge of rigorous academic programs while pursuing the interests that will help them achieve their professional goals. Applications are encouraged from interested students of every race, age, and religious affiliation. The University of Saint Joseph is committed to the goal of achieving equal educational opportunities and full participation for people with disabilities in higher education.

Candidates for first-year admission should complete a four-year course of study in a regionally accredited secondary school or have equivalent homeschooling preparation. The program should include 16 academic units in college-preparatory courses distributed among the areas of English, mathematics, natural sciences, social studies, and foreign languages. Applicants are required to submit a personal essay, SAT or ACT scores, official high school transcripts, and an academic letter of recommendation. A personal interview is a highly recommended part of the admission process, since it offers a mutual opportunity for the student and Admissions Counselors to discuss educational and professional goals.

The Office of Admissions operates on the principle that a student's ability, motivation, and maturity should be determined by a careful individual review of all the applicant's credentials, including the academic record, standardized test scores, written personal statement, and letter(s) of recommendation. Special consideration may be given to some applicants whose preparation varies from the recommended pattern but whose record gives evidence of genuine intellectual ability and interest. International students should contact the Office of Admissions for further information. Additional information is available online at usj.edu/admissions.

Application and Information

The University of Saint Joseph operates using a rolling admission, which means students can apply at any time during their senior year in high school. A nonrefundable $50 fee must be sent with paper applications; the application fee is waived for students who apply online via the University's website at usj.edu/apply or by using the Common Application. Students are encouraged to begin the financial aid process by completing the FAFSA form online at www.fafsa.ed.gov as soon as possible after January 1 of the year they are applying for admission. The priority deadline for completing the FAFSA is February 15. Students should complete the FAFSA using estimated income information if they or their families will not have completed their tax returns prior to February 15. Financial aid counselors are available to assist prospective students and families with the financial aid process.

For further information about admission to the University of Saint Joseph, students should contact:

Eileen Hocking
Director of Admissions
University of Saint Joseph
1678 Asylum Avenue
West Hartford, Connecticut 06117
United States
Phone: 860-231-5216
866-442-8752 (toll-free)
Fax: 860-231-5744
E-mail: admissions@usj.edu
Website: http://www.usj.edu/admissions

UNIVERSITY OF SAN FRANCISCO
SAN FRANCISCO, CALIFORNIA

UNIVERSITY OF
SAN FRANCISCO
CHANGE THE WORLD FROM HERE

The University

From its beginnings as a one-room schoolhouse, founded in 1855 by the Jesuits, the University of San Francisco (USF) has developed into one of the premier Jesuit Catholic universities on the West Coast. Throughout its history, USF has been committed to preparing students to improve the world in which they live. With more than 10,000 undergraduate and graduate students, the University has remained faithful to the Jesuit tradition and has maintained its small class size and low student-faculty ratio. Its programs in the arts, the sciences, business, education, nursing, and law foster a love of learning grounded by the challenge to serve society. The University's foundation encompasses academic excellence; the Jesuit, Catholic learning tradition; a multicultural, diverse community; and a global perspective that begins in San Francisco, which offers unparalleled opportunities for internships, service, and connections.

USF is one of the most diverse university campuses in the United States. Living and learning with a student body that consists of students from forty-seven states and seventy-five other countries is a unique opportunity. All new incoming freshmen under the age of 21 are required to live on the campus, unless they live within 40 miles of the University. More than 90 percent of the incoming freshmen and 35 percent of all undergraduates live on-campus.

The University offers five on-campus residence halls, two on-campus apartment-style residences, and one off-campus traditional residence hall. Gillson, Hayes-Healy, and Phelan house freshmen, while Lone Mountain houses sophomores and upper-division students. Fromm Hall is the only all-female residence hall for first- and second-year students. Located just twelve blocks from the USF campus, Pedro Arrupe Hall is the off-campus traditional residence hall offered to upper-division students. Loyola Village is a residential community that features apartment-style living for third-year, fourth-year, and graduate students. Most rooms in residence halls are doubles, with some single rooms available for upper-division students. Each residence hall has laundry facilities, study rooms, community kitchens, television lounges, and 24-hour front desk staff.

On the campus, students have access to various University facilities. The Koret Health and Recreation Center is an exciting complex that provides facilities for exercise, racquetball, court games, weight training, massage, personal training, and various aquatic activities in an Olympic-size pool. Tai Chi, yoga, hip-hop, and spinning are just some of the classes offered at Koret. Outdoor adventures include horseback riding, camping, sailing, and sea kayaking. Intramural and club sports are offered in the fall and spring semesters and include basketball, boxing, flag football, fencing, karate, soccer, lacrosse, rugby, and co-ed volleyball. Special aquatic sports include a Masters swim team and a water polo club. NCAA Division I sports include baseball, basketball, cross-country, golf, soccer, tennis, track and field, and women's volleyball.

Dining facilities are located all over campus and are within walking distance of the residence halls and classrooms. Located on the main campus, The Market Café offers a food court experience with a variety of choices, including global, vegan, homestyle classics, and vegetarian options. Other dining options include Outtakes Café, Outtahere Café, Crossroads Café, Club Ed in the School of Education, and Kendrick Café at the Law School.

Undergraduates keep busy by participating in over 100 on-campus, student-run associations, fraternities and sororities, honor societies, and clubs, such as the USF Rugby Club and Los Locos, a club that supports USF athletics. Among these clubs are the oldest continuously performing theater group west of the Mississippi River, an award-winning weekly newspaper, and a literary magazine.

For students interested in giving back to the community, the Office of Service-Learning and Community Action forms a partnership between the local community and USF. Students may participate in community service activities that include preparing meals for the homeless, tutoring underprivileged children, habitat restoration, and annual events such as AIDS Walk San Francisco.

Location

The University of San Francisco is located on a stunning 58-acre campus in a residential neighborhood just minutes from downtown San Francisco, the Financial District, Fisherman's Wharf, and the Pacific Ocean. The hilltop campus, renowned for its beautiful landscaping, borders the 1,000-acre Golden Gate Park and offers spectacular panoramic views of the city. The dynamic city of San Francisco keeps students entertained with concerts, the ballet, opera, museum exhibits, theater, and sporting events. Because of the diversity and geographical compactness of San Francisco, students find research facilities, opportunities for community involvement, and employment experiences that cannot be matched by most cities.

Majors and Degrees

The College of Arts and Sciences offers both B.A. and B.S. degrees. Popular majors include advertising, architecture and community design, art history/arts management, biology, chemistry, communication studies, comparative literature and culture, computer science, design, economics, economics 4+1, education (dual-degree in teacher preparation), English, environmental science, environmental studies, exercise and sports science, fine arts, French studies, history, international and development economics 4+1, Japanese studies, Latin American studies, mathematics, media studies, performing arts and social justice, philosophy, physics, physics/engineering (dual-degree, 3+2 program), politics, psychology, sociology, Spanish, theology and religious studies, undeclared arts, and undeclared science. The School of Management offers Bachelor of Science degrees in accounting, advanced global entrepreneurship management, business administration, entrepreneurship, finance, hospitality industry management, international business, and marketing with a concentration in multicultural marketing. The School of Nursing and Health Professions offers a four-year Bachelor of Science in Nursing for qualified high school graduates and for second-baccalaureate candidates.

USF has seventy-two minors and offers unique programs that enhance the learning experience at USF. Special programs include astronomy; African and African-American studies; Asia Pacific studies; Catholic studies and social thought; ethnic studies; film studies; honors program in the humanities; journalism; Judaic studies; Latino/a and Chicano/a Studies; Middle Eastern studies; neuroscience; 4+3 dual degrees in law, military science, premedical, and other pre-professional health studies; public relations; Saint Ignatius Institute program; a five-year dual-degree teacher preparation program that results in teacher certification at the elementary or secondary level; and the School of Management honors cohort program.

Academic Programs

The University of San Francisco is committed to providing students with the essentials of a well-rounded education. A baccalaureate degree is issued upon the successful completion of a 128-unit curriculum. The curriculum consists of 44 units of core courses chosen from six specified categories in addition to 80–85 units that are divided among departmental major requirements and electives. An honors program is available for selected superior students seeking a strong academic challenge. The academic year is based on the two-semester system, with summer sessions and a winter intersession also available.

In an effort to encourage high school students to move rapidly into the study of subjects now customarily reserved for colleges, the University of San Francisco honors advanced placement credits, as certified by the College Board's Advanced Placement Program tests and the International Baccalaureate program. The University also cooperates with the College-Level Examination Program (CLEP). Students intending to earn such credit must take the

CLEP examinations prior to registering at the University for their freshman courses.

The USF Pre-Professional Health Committee serves to guide and recommend students to medical and dental professional health schools as well as to schools for pharmacy, optometry, veterinary medicine, and podiatry. A student may complete the premedical or other pre–health science requirements as part of, or in addition to, the requirements of an academic major. The Pre-Professional Health Committee assists students with the application process, develops a professional file for each student, collects and mails recommendations to professional schools, conducts interviews in preparation for application, and endorses approved candidates via a committee letter of recommendation sent to all professional schools selected by the student.

The St. Ignatius Institute has an integrated core curriculum based on the great books of Western civilization and an emphasis upon the great works of Christianity. Any undergraduate student at the University, regardless of major, may take courses through the Institute to meet general education requirements. The University also offers Army ROTC. ROTC scholarships are available for qualified applicants and continuing students.

Off-Campus Programs

The University of San Francisco's Center for Global Education has numerous study-abroad programs available to students with junior standing and a cumulative minimum GPA of 3.0. Exchanges with Jesuit universities include locations in Japan, Mexico, China, Spain, Philippines, El Salvador, and Chile. USF's St. Ignatius Institute program includes an exchange with Oxford University in England. Affiliations with other Jesuit universities make travel to other countries possible, e.g., Gonzaga University's study-abroad program in Florence, Italy, and Loyola University of Chicago's program in Rome. USF is also an associate member of the Institute of European and Asian Studies, which offers programs in Durham and London, England; Paris, Dijon, and Nantes, France; Berlin and Freiburg, Germany; Vienna, Austria; Madrid and Salamanca, Spain; Milan, Italy; Tokyo and Nagoya, Japan; Moscow, Russia; Adelaide and Canberra, Australia; Beijing, China; and Singapore. Numerous other study-abroad opportunities are also available. USF assists students in selecting a location, applying to programs, making financial arrangements, registering for academic credit, securing a passport and visa, and making travel plans.

Academic Facilities

University of San Francisco students have access to Gleeson Library's more than 1.7 million holdings and Harney Science Center, which houses the Computer Center, Applied Math Laboratory, the Institute of Chemical Biology, and the Physics Research Laboratories. Cowell Hall, the base for nursing classes and the Nursing Skills Laboratory, also includes the Instructional Media Center. Students also have access to Phelan Hall, the home of *The Foghorn,* the official campus newspaper. Malloy Hall, headquarters for the School of Management, houses an additional computer laboratory and special seminar rooms. Kalmanovitz Hall houses all programs in the humanities and social sciences and features state-of-the-art classrooms, a rooftop sculpture garden, and seventeen laboratories for language, writing, media, and psychology.

Costs

Tuition for the 2012–13 school year was $38,490. Room and board were $12,640 for the academic year. Books, travel, and other expenses are about $5,100 per year.

Financial Aid

A variety of financial aid programs are available at the University, including scholarships, merit awards, grants, loans, and campus employment opportunities. Domestic students who wish to be considered for financial aid must file the Free Application for Federal Student Aid (FAFSA) by February 1. More than two thirds of all USF students receive some type of financial aid.

The University Scholars Program is available to new domestic freshmen applicants who have an exceptional cumulative GPA, SAT combined score, or ACT composite score. Scholars are awarded a non-need-based scholarship that pays a significant percentage of the cost of tuition for four years of undergraduate study. To remain eligible, University Scholars are expected to maintain a minimum GPA of 3.25. Eligible students are identified during the admission process and must apply under early action by the November 15 deadline.

Faculty

The University has 962 full- and part-time faculty members; 91 percent of them hold doctoral or terminal degrees in the field they teach. The University of San Francisco fosters a close relationship between students and faculty members. This is reflected in the small size of classes, the low student-faculty ratio, and the faculty members' availability for advising. Classes are not taught by student teachers or teachers' assistants.

Student Government

All undergraduates are members of the Associated Students of the University of San Francisco (ASUSF). ASUSF is the official representative body of undergraduate students at USF. The ASUSF government has three functions: to represent the official student viewpoint, to recommend policies, and to fund activities and services. ASUSF consists of three branches: the executive branch, the Student Senate, and the Student Court. The Senate comprises an executive board and student senators.

Admission Requirements

The University seeks students who are sincerely interested in pursuing a well-rounded education. The admission process is selective, and each application is reviewed individually. To enhance the quality and diversity of its student body, the University of San Francisco encourages men and women of all races, nationalities, and religious beliefs to apply. Eligibility is based on high school course work and GPA, the application essay, an academic and personal recommendation, and satisfactory test scores. Domestic applicants are required to submit SAT or ACT test scores with writing. International applicants are required to submit TOEFL or IELTS test scores; however, if an international applicant submits sufficient SAT or ACT test scores, the TOEFL or IELTS may be waived.

Application and Information

A completed application includes the application form, the application fee, a personal essay, all academic transcripts, standardized test scores, and up to two letters of recommendation. For the fall semester, the application deadlines are November 15 for early action (freshmen only) and January 15 for regular action (freshmen and transfers).

Inquiries should be addressed to:

Office of Admission
University of San Francisco
2130 Fulton Street
San Francisco, California 94117-1080
Phone: 415-422-6563
        800-CALL-USF (toll-free outside California)
Fax: 415-422-2217
E-mail: admission@usfca.edu
Website: http://www.usfca.edu
        http://www.facebook.com/University.of.San.Francisco
        http://twitter.com/USFCA
        http://www.youtube.com/usfcalifornia

The University of San Francisco—where students are invited to change the world.

UNIVERSITY OF SOUTH FLORIDA
TAMPA, FLORIDA

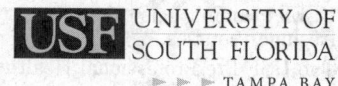

The University

The University of South Florida (USF) is among America's largest and most dynamic national research universities. Founded in 1956, USF opened in 1960 with an enrollment of nearly 2,000 and now has more than 47,000 students in more than 230 degree programs at the undergraduate, graduate, specialist, and doctoral levels.

USF's national stature as an academic institution was acknowledged by the Carnegie Foundation for the Advancement of Teaching, which ranked the University in the top tier of American colleges and universities as Research University (Very High Research Activity). USF is one of three universities in the state of Florida in the top tier. The University receives more than $344 million in external funding to support research and development projects. USF's libraries include more than 2.2 million titles and provide access to hundreds of databases worldwide.

USF's student body is as diverse as its academic program profile. African Americans, Hispanics, and students from other minority groups comprise 36 percent of the undergraduate student body. Approximately 58 percent of the students are women. Geographically, students come to the USF from all fifty states and more than 125 countries.

USF is accredited by the Commission on Colleges of the Southern Association of Colleges and Schools. In addition, a number of scientific, professional, and academic bodies confer accreditation in specific disciplines and groups of disciplines.

The Office of Career Services works with hundreds of companies to provide internships and cooperative education programs for students. The office also provides an online and on-campus referral service and interview program. Classes for students are available in resume writing, interviewing, and etiquette. The University hosts both full- and part-time career fairs each semester.

Traditional-style housing units, suites, apartments, fraternities and sororities, and married and family student housing units accommodate 16 percent of the students on the Tampa campus. Several thousand more students live in apartments located within walking distance of the campus. All residence halls are wired and furnished and include all utilities. Special-interest and honors housing is also available to students who qualify. Freshmen are required to live on campus their first year.

There are more than 500 student clubs and organizations at USF. The University also has over forty national fraternities and sororities. In addition, USF schedules a wide array of extracurricular programs, including concerts, movies, and a lecture series. USF is a member of the NCAA and the Big East Conference. All teams compete on the NCAA Division I level. USF's men's teams compete in intercollegiate baseball, basketball, cross-country, football, golf, soccer, tennis, and track. The USF women's teams compete in intercollegiate basketball, cross-country, golf, sailing, soccer, softball, tennis, track, and volleyball. Campus Recreation also offers club sports, intramural sports, and outdoor adventures. On the Tampa campus, there is an eighteen-hole championship golf course, four swimming pools, sand volleyball courts, tennis courts, a state-of-the-art recreation center, indoor and outdoor racquetball courts, and a private riverfront park.

Location

USF is located on 1,700 acres in north Tampa, across the street from the Busch Gardens Theme Park. Regional campuses are located in St. Petersburg and Sarasota/Manatee.

Majors and Degrees

At the undergraduate level, USF offers the following degree programs: accounting, advertising, Africana studies, American studies, anthropology, applied sciences, art studio and art history, behavioral healthcare, business administration, biology and microbiology, biomedical science, chemical engineering, chemistry, civil and environmental engineering, classics, communication, communication sciences and disorders, computer science and engineering, criminology, dance, dance studies, early childhood education, economics, electrical engineering, elementary education, English, environmental science and policy, finance, foreign languages, geography, geology, gerontology, government and international affairs, health professions (pre-health), health sciences, history, honors college research, hospitality management, industrial engineering, interdisciplinary classical civilizations, interdisciplinary natural science, interdisciplinary social sciences, international business, international studies, management, management information systems, marketing, mass communications, mathematics, mechanical engineering, medical technology, music, music education, music studies, nursing, philosophy, physical education, physics, political science, pre-law, psychology, public health, religious studies, secondary education, social work, sociology, special education, theater, and women's studies.

Academic Programs

USF offers students a well-rounded education through a core curriculum of general education and liberal arts requirements. In addition to fulfilling the general education requirements, each student must complete the necessary major and/or minor requirements to reach the minimum of 120 hours for graduation. USF also requires students to complete 9 hours of exit requirements; these courses complement the overall curriculum of all degree programs.

The University Honors College and University Experience are programs that help students broaden their horizons and expand their critical thinking skills. The University also offers Army, Air Force, and Naval ROTC leadership courses and off-campus courses for those students who prefer to study independently.

Off-Campus Programs

A cooperative education program is offered through the Office of Career Services. Students may either alternate semesters between school and work experience or choose to do a parallel program. Education Abroad offers a variety of study abroad opportunities in more than 25 countries including USF faculty-led summer and short-term programs, semester exchanges, dual-degree programs, international internships, independent research, and service learning.

Costs

For 2012–13, tuition costs were as follows: $6,330 for state residents attending full-time ($16,260 for nonresidents). Full- and part-time tuition and fees vary according to class time, course load, and location. Room and board costs were $8,960 and vary according to board plan, housing facility, and location. Costs are subject to change each academic year.

Financial Aid

The University of South Florida awards $292 million in aid to help students reach their educational goals. Financial aid is awarded according to each student's need, academic standing, and/or talents in relation to college costs and may include grants, loans, scholarships, and/or part-time employment. The priority application deadline is January 2 for academic scholarships and March 1 for federal and institutional aid. Need-based programs include federal monetary awards such as Federal Pell Grants, Federal Work-Study Program awards, Federal Stafford Student Loans, and Federal Perkins Loans. State aid includes programs such as the Florida Student Assistance Grant program, Florida Work Experience Program, and the Florida Bright Futures Scholarship program. To qualify for federal and state aid, students should submit the Free Application for Federal Student Aid (FAFSA).

Faculty

The University has 1,765 instructional faculty members, including 53 endowed chairs. Approximately 93 percent are full-time and more than 86 percent of faculty members hold a terminal degree in their field. Each student is assigned to an academic adviser and all faculty members are required to hold office hours to meet with students in groups or on an individual basis. The student-faculty ratio is 25:1.

Student Government

USF's Student Government is open to all students. Each college within the University and each regional campus elects its own Student Government representatives. The Student Government is divided into three branches: the executive, the legislative, and the judicial. Student Government is responsible for the allocation of all activity and service fees paid by student tuition. Student Government–sponsored events and services are free to students.

Admission Requirements

For admissions purposes, USF computes a high school GPA based on grades earned in all college-prep academic courses. In computing a GPA, USF assigns additional weight to grades earned in honors, dual enrollment, Advanced Placement (AP), Advanced Certificate of Education (AICE), and International Baccalaureate (IB) courses. The most important factors in determining admission to USF are the quality of the high school record, rigor of curriculum, and performance on either the SAT or ACT with writing.

To be considered for admission, freshman applicants must submit an application for admission, a nonrefundable $30 application fee, an official high school transcript, official SAT or ACT scores, and official GED or IETLS/TOEFL scores (if applicable).

Transfer applicants with fewer than 60 transferable semester credit hours are considered lower-level transfer students. These students must meet all freshman and transfer requirements and submit an application for admission, a nonrefundable $30 application fee, an official transcript from each college or university they have attended, an official high school transcript, SAT or ACT scores, and official GED or IETLS/TOEFL scores (if applicable). In addition, students with 12–23 transferrable credits are required to submit a personal statement that outlines the reasons why they wish to transfer to USF.

Upper-level transfer students are those with 60 or more transferable semester credit hours. These students must submit an application for admissions, a nonrefundable $30 application fee, an official transcript from each college or university they have attended, and IELTS/TOEFL scores (if applicable). In addition, upper-level transfer applicants with 102 or more transferrable credits must submit a personal statement indicating the reasons why they wish to transfer to USF.

Some students who show potential, but who do not meet the criteria for admission, may be placed on a waiting list or may be considered for the Student Support Services/Freshman Summer Institute held during the summer.

USF accepts transfer credits from institutions that are accredited by one of the regional accrediting agencies/commissions recognized by USF at the time the credits are earned. To be considered for admission, transfer applicants must have at least a 2.50 GPA (2.00 for students from select public community colleges in Florida), a 67 percent course completion ratio, and be in good academic standing from the last college or university they attended.

Application and Information

Students are encouraged to visit USF and experience the campus for themselves. Campus visit programs are offered Monday through Friday at 10 a.m. and 2 p.m. Tours are also offered on most Saturdays at 10 a.m. during the academic year (September through April). Reservations are strongly encouraged, and students may make reservations online at http://www.usf.edu/campusvisit.

For more information, students should contact:

David Lee Henry, Director of Admissions
University of South Florida
4202 East Fowler Avenue, SVC 1036
Tampa, Florida 33620-9951
Phone: 813-974-3350
Fax: 813-974-9689
Website: http://www.usf.edu/admissions

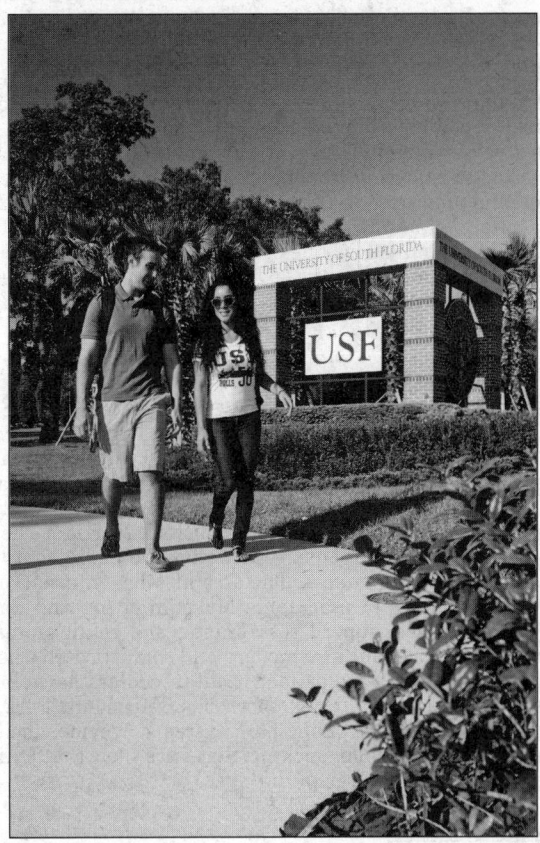

This is the place to be. Tampa not only has terrific weather, it has amazing cultural, recreational, internship, service-learning, and employment opportunities.

THE UNIVERSITY OF THE ARTS
Visual Arts, Design, Film, Music, Dance, Theater
PHILADELPHIA, PENNSYLVANIA

THE UNIVERSITY OF THE ARTS

The University

The University of the Arts (UArts) is located in the heart of Philadelphia's vibrant professional arts community. For more than 135 years, UArts has been a leader in educating artists, performers and creative individuals. More than 2,100 students from forty-three states and twenty-two countries are enrolled in undergraduate and graduate programs in the visual and performing arts, film and design. Comprised of the College of Media, Art and Design (CAMD), the College of Performing Arts (CPA), and the Division of Liberal Arts, the University offers intensive concentration within a major field as well as creative challenges in multidisciplinary exploration.

One quarter of students live in University housing, which provides coed apartment-style accommodations. Resident advisers live on each floor and there is 24-hour security. First-time students are guaranteed housing if their contracts are received by May 1. The University also assists students in finding off-campus residences. Dining Services operates several dining locations on campus, which are available to both residential and commuter students.

The graduate programs of the University of the Arts offer an impressive combination of strengths: an individualized and interactive learning environment, accomplished faculty members, access to outstanding facilities and resources, specialized studios, and programs of study that are both focused and flexible. UArts offers graduate degrees in art education; book arts/printmaking; industrial design; museum communication; museum education; museum exhibition, planning and design; jazz studies; and music education. A postbaccalaureate certificate in crafts is also offered.

Location

The University's campus spans the Avenue of the Arts from South Street to Walnut Street and is the cultural hub of Center City Philadelphia. Next door to the University's historic Hamilton Hall is the Kimmel Center for the Performing Arts; in adjacent blocks are the Academy of Music, Wilma Theater, Suzanne Roberts Theater, and the University's historic Merriam Theater, which books touring Broadway shows for the public and hosts UArts student performances. The area also has internationally renowned museums (Philadelphia Museum of Art and Barnes Museum), galleries, superb restaurants, and retail stores. Of historic importance, but also modern and sophisticated, the city is one of the nation's major metropolitan centers as well as a series of small, close-knit neighborhoods. Fairmount Park, one of the country's largest public park systems, provides facilities for sports activities and picnicking. Statistics show that UArts is one of the safest campuses in the city.

Majors and Degrees

The College of Art, Media, and Design confers degrees in three areas: film (B.F.A. in animation, film/video, and writing for film and television); art (B.F.A. in crafts, multidisciplinary fine arts, painting/drawing, photography, printmaking, and sculpture) and design (B.F.A. in graphic design and web development, and interaction design; B.S. in industrial design) as well as in college-wide programs (B.F.A. in illustration and design, art and technology). The college also offers the five-year B.F.A./M.A.T. program, which allows students to complete the requirements for a B.F.A. in studio art and Master of a Arts in Teaching in visual arts in five years. Undergraduate students in the college may also pursue a concentration in art therapy. The Division of Liberal Arts confers two degrees: a B.F.A. in creative writing and a B.A. in film and media studies. The School of Music confers B.M. degrees in composition, instrumental performance, and vocal performance, as well as a B.S. in music business, entrepreneurship, and technology. A four-year diploma in music is also available. The School of Dance offers a B.F.A. in dance. The School of Theater Arts offers B.F.A. degrees in acting; musical theater; theater design and technology; and directing, playwriting, and production.

Academic Programs

Students are attracted to the University of the Arts because of its dynamic, creative atmosphere, and opportunities for cross-discipline collaboration. Students are encouraged to take elective courses outside their chosen major, and many participate in collaborative projects with students from a range of other programs. All students take 42 credits in liberal arts, providing exposure to humanities, social sciences, and science, and giving students a historical and theoretical framework for their major fields.

Freshmen in the College of Art, Media, and Design spend their first year enrolling in courses in the College's Core Studies curriculum, which is designed to expose students to the skills, concepts, and techniques necessary for in-depth study of a specific field. Students are not required to declare a major until their sophomore year; the flexibility of the Core Studies curriculum allows highly focused students to begin concentrating on an area of study in their first year, while undecided students benefit from the breadth of topics explored in the curriculum. Core Studies includes courses exploring concepts of time, object, image, and environment, as well as introductory courses to the various majors within the schools.

Students who choose a concentration in the School of Film will focus on the sensory bases of moving-image art, cinematic art and storytelling; courses include documentary video, narrative video, screenwriting, film history, and video production. The School of Design curriculum challenges students to apply critical-thinking and problem-solving skills to design-oriented endeavors, including mobile web applications, product design, advertising and marketing, and typography. Programs within the School of Art are designed to allow students to pursue a highly focused study of one area, or offer the freedom to combine elements and techniques of various fine arts disciplines. All students within the school are encouraged to develop a well-rounded portfolio as well as their professional practice and research skills.

In the College of Performing Arts, the School of Music program stresses individualized training, with a performance emphasis. In this contemporary jazz–based program, students undergo intensive training in theory and musicianship, supplemented by master classes and ensemble work. Students in the School of Dance begin with two years of intensive studio training in the traditional study of ballet, jazz, and modern, as well as emerging and contemporary forms, before choosing an area of emphasis for their junior and senior years. In the Ira Brind School of Theater Arts, students can choose one of four majors: acting; musical theater; directing, playwriting, and production; and theater design and technology. All programs emphasize intensive training, with a goal of developing strong professional practices while giving students exposure to all elements of theatrical production.

In the Division of Liberal Arts, the creative writing program provides students the opportunity for immersive study in the craft of writing with small, workshop-style classes. Students will choose a concentration in either fiction or poetry, but are also able to sample other forms of writing such as creative nonfiction, playwriting, screenwriting, and graphic novels. Film and media studies is a theory-based program that allows students to explore the critical, historical, and aesthetic aspects of cinematic arts through a combination of studio classes and lecture-based seminars.

Academic Facilities

The University facilities are composed of numerous buildings along Philadelphia's Avenue of the Arts, including residence halls, academic and administrative buildings, studios, galleries, and performance venues.

College of Art, Media, and Design facilities include the typography lab; the Borowsky Center for Publication Arts; digital video editing suites; TV and video production studios; photo/film/animation labs and darkrooms; a scanner lab; an SGI lab; a bronze foundry and plaster workshop; and crafts studios and workshops for ceramics, metals, wood, glassblowing, papermaking, and fibers. Many programs offer individual workstations or studios for upperclassmen. Academic computing resources include more than twenty labs on Macintosh and PC platforms that can be used for animation, digital imaging, 3-D modeling, multimedia, music, CAD, web page design, and more. The University maintains several public galleries where students may exhibit their work along with curator-managed exhibitions of guest artists' work.

Performance spaces include the 1,800-seat Merriam Theater, the 239-seat Caplan Center for the Performing Arts black box theater and recital hall, the 200-seat Dance Theater, the Arts Bank main theater and cabaret theater, and the Gershman Hall black box theater. Other performing arts facilities include a recording studio; music technology (MIDI) studios; editing suites; practice rooms; dance and movement studios with barres, mirrors, and resilient floors; and acting studios.

Costs

Tuition for the 2013–14 academic year is $36,582. Accommodations in apartment-style dormitory units start at $8,610. The nineteen-meal-per-week board plan is $4,725.

Financial Aid

Last year, UArts provided nearly $10 million in scholarships and grants to new students alone. About one third went to those demonstrating financial need; the balance was awarded in talent- or merit-based scholarships. Overall, UArts students receive more than $50 million in scholarships, grants, loans, and part-time employment each year. Typically, more than 90 percent of the students enrolled on a full-time basis are eligible for some type of need-based aid. Where need exists, UArts assists in meeting costs within its available resources.

The University funds Trustees Scholarships, Presidential Scholarships, Promising Young Artist Awards, and Artist Grants based on artistic potential and academic achievement. Financial aid is also available on the applicant's demonstrated financial need. Applicants must submit the Free Application for Federal Student Aid (FAFSA). March 1 is the suggested filing date. The University administers a full range of Federal Aid programs. Applicants who wish to be considered for scholarships should complete applications for admission and financial aid prior to April 1. Families from many different income levels can qualify for some type of financial assistance. In addition, the University's location in a large, active city provides students with diverse opportunities for part-time employment.

Faculty

Faculty members are practicing professionals who are committed to the development of their students. As active participants in the arts, they have achieved recognition in their specific fields of study and real-world experience gives them the knowledge and understanding vital to the professional and personal growth of young, emerging artists. The faculty consists of 505 full- and part-time members; the majority hold advanced degrees. The faculty-student ratio is about 1:8.

Student Government

The student activities office sponsors a variety of on and off-campus activities to complement academic programs, as well as overseeing student organizations including Student Council, community service organizations, and a student-run gallery.

Admission Requirements

In addition to submitting a portfolio or auditioning, undergraduate applicants should submit their high school transcript, SAT or ACT scores, one letter of recommendation, and a personal statement of purpose.

The placement of transfer students is made after an evaluation of their portfolio or audition and a determination of their approved credits. Transfer students may be given advanced standing.

International applicants are required to submit scores on the Test of English as a Foreign Language (TOEFL) or the International English Language Testing System (IELTS). A minimum TOEFL score of 550pbt/80ibt, or an IELTS score of 6.0 is required for undergraduate programs. Students who do not meet these requirements may receive a conditional admittance pending completion of an ESL course.

The University of the Arts follows rolling admission system. Students are notified of their decisions as their applications are completed. Students are encouraged to submit applications by March 15 for fall admission and December 1 for spring admission.

For additional information, students should contact:

Office of Admission
The University of the Arts
320 South Broad Street
Philadelphia, Pennsylvania 19102
Phone: 215-717-6049
        800-616-ARTS (toll-free)
Fax: 215-717-6045
Website: http://www.uarts.edu

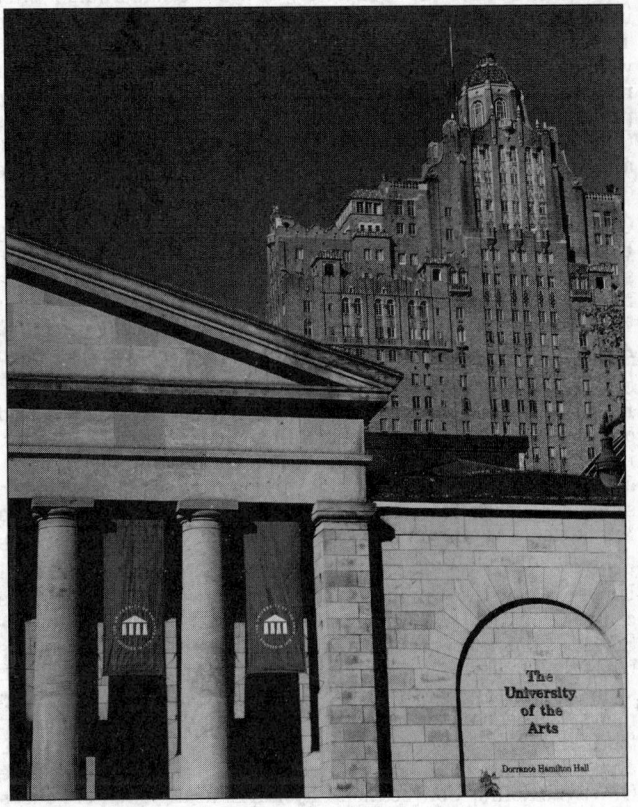

Hamilton Hall, located on the Avenue of the Arts in Center City Philadelphia.

UNIVERSITY OF THE CUMBERLANDS
WILLIAMSBURG, KENTUCKY

The University

Founded in 1889, Cumberland College became University of the Cumberlands on July 1, 2005, reflecting the diversity and excellence of options offered in high-quality education. The University is committed to providing a superior education within an exceptional Christian atmosphere at an affordable cost. Recognition by *U.S. News & World Report* in its list of America's Best Colleges and by the John Templeton Foundation as a member of its Honor Roll of Character Building Colleges signals that a University of the Cumberlands (UC) education is an exceptional value. Emphasizing the growth of the individual student, the University strives to instill in students the desire to be agents of change in the world and to use knowledge for the benefit of others as well as themselves.

UC is one of the few institutions where all students complete a leadership program. All students participate in community service as a component of this program.

University of the Cumberlands is a four-year, coed, liberal arts institution for higher education that offers a broad curriculum with more than thirty-five programs of undergraduate study, including eight preprofessional programs for professional and health science careers. Graduates enjoy a high acceptance rate to graduate and professional schools, particularly in science, business, and education. In fact, within five years of graduation, 66 percent of UC's alumni have completed or are pursuing a graduate or professional degree.

Graduate studies at University of the Cumberlands offer individual graduate courses as well as a Master of Arts in Teaching and a Master of Arts in Education degree programs with certification or concentration in various areas. Other master's programs include business administration (M.B.A.), professional counseling (M.A.P.C.), physician assistant studies (M.P.A.S.), Christian studies (M.A.C.S.), justice administration, and information systems security. Doctoral programs include educational leadership and clinical psychology.

One of the largest private institutions in the state of Kentucky, UC serves a diverse body of more than 1,800 undergraduate students from forty states and thirty countries. Primarily a residential campus, UC provides on-campus housing for about 75 percent of its students in the University's ten residence halls. A director, assisted by student staff members, supervises each hall.

Extracurricular activities abound. More than forty clubs and organizations provide students with a wide variety of activities, including a debate team, theater, musical performance groups, academic societies, an FM radio station, a student newspaper, student government, Baptist Campus Ministries, Appalachian Ministries, Mountain Outreach, Patriot Adventure Club, departmental clubs, and intramural sports.

University of the Cumberlands participates in intercollegiate competition. UC is a member of the NAIA Division I Mid-South Conference and offers opportunities in women's basketball, bowling, cross-country, golf, soccer, softball, swimming, tennis, track and field, volleyball, and wrestling; men's baseball, basketball, bowling, cross-country, football, golf, soccer, swimming, tennis, track and field, and wrestling; and coed archery and cheerleading. The O. Wayne Rollins Convocation/Physical Education Center houses a 2,700-seat athletic arena, the Dinah Taylor Aquatic Center, an indoor batting cage, a weight room, an indoor walking/jogging track, locker rooms, an intramural gymnasium, athletic training facilities, athletic offices, and classrooms.

The James H. Taylor II Stadium complex, which seats 2,400, includes a football field; an eight-lane, 400-meter all-weather track and field; the Patriot Pavilion; and a football practice field.

The Doyle Buhl Stadium and James Keelty Field are the home of Patriot baseball, with dugouts and locker rooms.

UC also has separate golf, soccer, softball, tennis, and wrestling facilities.

Location

One of the state's oldest cities, Williamsburg is located in southern Kentucky, 185 miles south of Cincinnati, Ohio, and 70 miles north of Knoxville, Tennessee. Williamsburg is known for its beautiful homes and the hospitality of its people. The University of the Cumberlands campus is situated on three hills above the town and, about 1 mile from exit 11, is easily accessed from I-75. UC has a well-kept campus that blends stately old buildings with new ones and has a panoramic view of the surrounding mountains and the Cumberland River Valley, an area known throughout the country for its lovely waterfalls, forests, and lakes. Famed Cumberland Falls State Resort Park is just 20 minutes from campus.

Majors and Degrees

University of the Cumberlands is accredited by the Commission on Colleges of the Southern Association of Colleges and Schools to award baccalaureate, master's, and doctoral degrees. It is approved by the Kentucky State Department of Education for teacher education and certification. Inquiries concerning the accreditation status of the University may be directed to the Commission on Colleges at 1866 Southern Lane, Decatur, Georgia 30033-4097 or by calling 404-676-4500.

Major fields of study are accounting, art, biology, business administration, chemistry, church music, communication arts, criminal justice, education, English, exercise and sport science, fitness and sport management, health, history, human services, journalism and public relations, management information systems, mathematics, music, philosophy, physics, political science, psychology, religion, Spanish, special education, and theater arts.

Minor fields can be chosen from the major fields or in biblical languages or French.

Preprofessional and special curricula are offered in military science, pre-dentistry, pre-engineering, pre-law, pre-medicine, pre-optometry, pre-pharmacy, pre–physical therapy, pre–physician assistant studies, pre–veterinary medicine, and religious vocations.

Academic Programs

University of the Cumberlands seeks to provide academic specialization within a broad framework of a liberal arts education. To supplement the in-depth knowledge acquired within each major, 37 semester hours of general studies from the areas of Christian faith and values, cultural and aesthetic values, the English language, humanities, leadership and community service, natural and mathematical sciences, physical education, and social sciences are required. Students must earn at least 128 semester hours to graduate with a bachelor's degree.

The academic year begins in late August, with the first semester ending in mid-December. The second semester runs from early January to early May. Two 4-week undergraduate summer sessions and two 4-week graduate summer sessions are also offered. Orientation, preregistration, and academic advising by faculty members begin in the summer preceding entrance.

Students may receive credit for successful scores on the Advanced Placement examinations of the College Board, the College-Level Examination Program (CLEP), and special departmental tests. Through the honors program, highly qualified students have the opportunity to undertake advanced independent study.

Students benefit from such special services as free tutorial assistance and those offered by the Career Services Center, the Center for Leadership Studies, and the Academic Resource Center.

Academic Facilities

The University of the Cumberlands campus contains thirty-five buildings reflecting antebellum architectural style. The new Correll Science Complex features state-of-the-art biology, chemistry, and physics labs providing graduate-level research opportunities.

The McGaw Music Building contains individual rehearsal and studio areas as well as a recital hall. The Norma Perkins Hagan Memorial Library houses thousands of book titles, periodical subscriptions, and microform titles. Sophisticated computer equipment provides access to millions of items from many of the nation's outstanding libraries. The instructional media center includes a children's library, a computerized language lab, and a listening library.

Other special academic features include a computer center, an art gallery, a word processing center for English composition, a theater, a 600-seat chapel, four large lecture halls, and the Distance Learning Laboratory.

Recent additions to the campus include the state-of-the-art Hutton School of Business, a 27,000-square-foot addition to the Science Building, and Harth Hall, a women's residence hall.

Costs

For 2013–14, the basic academic year expenses are $20,000 for tuition and fees and $7,500 for room and board, for a total of $27,500. There are no additional fees for out-of-state students. The average cost for books and supplies is approximately $500 per semester.

Financial Aid

University of the Cumberlands sponsors a large financial aid program that coordinates monies from federal, state, private, and University sources. Ninety-five percent of UC students share more than $30 million in aid.

To apply for financial aid, it is necessary to complete the Free Application for Federal Student Aid (FAFSA). For further information about financial aid opportunities, students should contact the Director of Financial Planning at 800-343-1609 (toll free). Applications made by March 1 are given priority for the fall semester.

Numerous scholarships and grants are available.

Faculty

There are 112 full-time and 33 part-time faculty members who are respected scholars and whose primary responsibility is to teach. Graduate assistants do not teach courses. The student-faculty ratio is 13:1, enabling students to receive ample attention and assistance from professors. Faculty members also serve as advisers to help students in planning their academic programs.

Admission Requirements

In compliance with federal law, including provisions of Title IX of the Educational Amendments of 1972 and Section 504 of the Rehabilitation Act of 1973, University of the Cumberlands does not illegally discriminate on the basis of race, sex, color, national or ethnic origin, age, disability, or military service in its administration of education policies, programs, or activities;

admissions policies; or employment. Under federal law, the University reserves the right to discriminate on the basis of sex in its undergraduate admissions programs. Further, the University reserves the right to deny admission to any applicant whose academic preparation, character, or personal conduct is determined to be inconsistent with the purpose and objectives of the University. Where possible, the University will seek to reasonably accommodate a student's disability. However, the University's obligation to reasonably accommodate a student's disability ends where the accommodation would pose an undue hardship on the University or where the accommodation in question would fundamentally alter the academic program. Inquiries or complaints should be directed to the Vice President for Academic Affairs.

The purpose of the admission process is to identify applicants who are likely to succeed academically at University of the Cumberlands and at the same time contribute positively to the campus community. The process considers such factors as high school records (including courses taken, grade trends, and rank in class), college records (if transferring from another institution), scores on the ACT or SAT, extracurricular activities and honors, and personal conduct.

Campus tours are available on weekdays by appointment and on selected Saturdays. Prospective students can take a tour of the beautiful campus; talk with students, professors, and coaches; spend the night in the residence halls; attend an athletic or extracurricular event; and get answers to questions during a session with an admissions counselor.

Application and Information

Applicants may apply online at http://www.ucumberlands.edu or may contact the Office of Admissions for an application form. Return the completed form to the University, along with the appropriate application fee, official transcripts of all high school and college work, and a copy of ACT or SAT scores. Each student is notified regarding official admission within ten working days after the application procedure has been completed.

Students accepted for admission must submit the required enrollment deposit.

Additional information can be obtained at:

Office of Admissions
University of the Cumberlands
816 Walnut Street
Williamsburg, Kentucky 40769
Phone: 606-539-4241
          800-343-1609 (toll-free)
E-mail: admiss@ucumberlands.edu
Website: http://www.ucumberlands.edu
          http://twitter.com/#!/UCumberlandsKy
          http://www.youtube.com/UCumberlandsMedia

University of the Cumberlands offers individualized learning and research opportunities.

UNIVERSITY OF THE SCIENCES
PHILADELPHIA, PENNSYLVANIA

USciences
University of the Sciences

Where healthcare and science converge.

The University

University of the Sciences (USciences) was founded in 1821 as Philadelphia College of Pharmacy, America's first college of pharmacy. University of the Sciences is located on a 35-acre campus in the University City section of Philadelphia, home to some of the nation's top universities, hospitals, and research facilities. Besides University of the Sciences, University of Pennsylvania and Drexel University also call University City home. The University currently enrolls approximately 2,500 undergraduate students in nineteen majors and over 300 students in twenty-one graduate programs. The campus consists of twenty-two buildings. The University offers a wide variety of cocurricular activities that include intercollegiate and intramural athletics; literary publications; social, professional, religious, and honors organizations; and musical and drama groups. University of the Sciences competes athletically at the NCAA Division II level and is a member of the Central Atlantic Collegiate Conference.

Location

The University's location in the University City section of Philadelphia offers considerable advantage and appeal. It not only offers a wide variety of educational opportunities, it also is a culturally, architecturally, and socially diverse community that caters to the local college student population. University of the Sciences is also actively involved with a number of local community organizations that are designed to foster improvement, development, and unity in the University City community. The Philadelphia metropolitan area is the home of more than forty other colleges and universities. University of the Sciences students realize that Philadelphia and its immediate region provide abundant off-campus clinical and scientific opportunities, which are required in a number of programs. Within a short 10-minute trolley ride to the Center City area are the vast cultural, historical, and shopping attractions of the fifth-largest city in the United States.

Majors and Degrees

University of the Sciences includes four undergraduate colleges: Philadelphia College of Pharmacy, which offers programs in pharmacy, pharmaceutical sciences, and pharmacology and toxicology; Samson College of Health Sciences, which offers programs in exercise science and wellness management, health science, medical laboratory science, occupational therapy, physical therapy, and physician assistant studies; Misher College of Arts and Sciences, which offers majors in biochemistry, biology, chemistry, environmental science, humanities and science, microbiology, pharmaceutical chemistry, physics, and psychology; and the newest college, Mayes College of Healthcare Business and Policy, which offers a number of graduate programs as well as a bachelor's degree in pharmaceutical and healthcare business. Students with strong academic interests in multiple areas may pursue double degrees, including two B.S. degrees or one B.S. degree and one entry-level professional degree.

Academic Programs

Three majors are offered in Philadelphia College of Pharmacy: a six-year Doctor of Pharmacy (Pharm.D.) program and four-year B.S. degree programs in pharmacology and toxicology and in pharmaceutical sciences. In the Doctor of Pharmacy program, students are guaranteed a seat in the professional phase (years 3–6) as long as the preprofessional phase (years 1–2) is successfully completed and an acceptable academic record is maintained. The pharmacy program at the University is recognized worldwide and prepares students for the increasingly clinical nature of pharmacy practice.

Pharmacology and toxicology, pharmaceutical sciences, and pharmaceutical and healthcare business are unique B.S. degree programs that provide excellent career opportunities and address specific manpower needs within the pharmaceutical and healthcare industries. Many graduates pursue postgraduate study as well as enter careers in research, manufacturing, and business.

Six programs of study are available in Samson College of Health Sciences: exercise science and wellness management, health science, medical laboratory science, occupational therapy, physical therapy, and physician assistant studies. Both physical therapy and occupational therapy programs are direct-entry, integrated undergraduate/professional degree programs that lead to the Doctor of Physical Therapy (D.P.T.) and Doctor of Occupational Therapy (Dr.O.T.), respectively. The physical therapy program was one of America's first programs to receive approval to offer the six-year, direct-entry D.P.T. In both the physical therapy and occupational therapy programs, students are admitted as first-year students and are guaranteed a professional-phase seat, provided an acceptable academic record is maintained. In the newest major in Samson College of Health Sciences, the B.S. degree in exercise science and wellness management, students learn about healthy lifestyles and living as well as how sports and leisure activities improve community well-being.

The physician assistant studies program at University of the Sciences leads to the Bachelor of Science in Health Science from USciences and Master of Science from either the Philadelphia College of Osteopathic Medicine (PCOM) or University of the Sciences. Students enrolled in the physician assistant studies program complete their preprofessional component (years 1–3) in the natural sciences, social sciences, and humanities at University of the Sciences. The professional component of the program can be completed at PCOM in twenty-seven months or at USciences in thirty-four months (with the summers off).

A four-year B.S. degree in health science for students who want to focus on general health care and community service is also available.

Medical laboratory science students at University of the Sciences receive an excellent three-year academic foundation in preparation for their fourth year, which is spent in a clinical setting at an approved hospital school of medical laboratory science.

Nine different four-year Bachelor of Science degree programs are offered in the Misher College of Arts and Sciences. They include biochemistry, biology, chemistry, environmental science, humanities and science, microbiology, physics, pharmaceutical chemistry, and psychology. Psychology students may elect to remain at the University for an additional year and qualify for the M.S. in health psychology program. Misher College of Arts and Sciences combines the expertise of an outstanding group of scientists, researchers, and educators with academic facilities that are not often found at an institution the size of University of the Sciences. This combination creates an academic atmosphere of especially high quality. Misher College also offers a popular advisory track in forensic science, which can stand alone as a minor. A forensic science certificate can be earned when paired with a major in biology, biochemistry, chemistry, environmental science, medical laboratory science, microbiology, or pharmaceutical chemistry.

The newest major in Misher College of Arts and Sciences is the B.S. in humanities and science. This major provides a unique combination of scientific and humanistic study, which is particularly attractive to students who want to pursue medical, dental, or veterinary studies.

University of the Sciences' strong tradition of excellence prepares graduates to enter postbaccalaureate degrees in medicine, dentistry, veterinary medicine, and other health professions. Traditionally, pre-med students choose to major in chemistry, biochemistry, biology, microbiology, pharmacology and toxicology, or psychology. The curricula in these and most of the other programs include the basic courses required for admission to medical school. Beginning with the first year, pre-med students receive individualized counseling by the preprofessional advisor and their faculty advisor in selecting courses to meet their career goals. Pre-med students may also elect to take advantage of the University's agreements with Philadelphia College of Osteopathic Medicine, the Commonwealth

Medical College, Pennsylvania College of Optometry at Salus University, Kornberg School of Dentistry at Temple University, or St. George University School of Veterinary Medicine, which reserve a number of seats each year for University of the Sciences students.

Students may enroll at University of the Sciences in the pre-professional program, and through a special orientation program, be introduced to the various academic disciplines and career opportunities available to them. Pre-professional students formally declare a major during the spring semester of the first year and choose from pre-medical, pre-dental, pre-veterinarian, and pre-health professional specializations.

Academic Facilities

Classes and laboratory course work are conducted in ten academic buildings on the University of the Sciences campus, while the remaining buildings serve as residence halls or support-service facilities. University of the Sciences houses more than 100 scientific laboratories and many computer terminals for student use. The Joseph W. England Library contains more than 84,000 volumes and 8,400 periodicals in addition to numerous electronic information programs.

Costs

Tuition for the 2012–13 academic year was $31,774; room and board were $13,054. Costs are subject to change.

Financial Aid

Types and sources of aid include Federal Perkins Loans; Health Professions Student Loans; Federal Work-Study Program; USciences Merit Scholarships; Athletic Grants; University need-based grants, deferred tuition payment plans; federal student loans; and scholarships received from states, municipalities, and service clubs or other organizations. All applicants who seek financial assistance must complete the Free Application for Federal Student Aid (FAFSA). The University's merit scholarship and grant program provides awards for both first-year and transfer candidates.

Faculty

There are 171 full-time faculty members. Of these, more than 100 have doctoral degrees. All full-time faculty members teach undergraduates, and many also teach graduate students and conduct research. Graduate assistants do not teach but serve as laboratory aides.

Student Government

Student government is comprised of representatives from all undergraduate classes and class officers. It takes an active part in governance through participation in faculty and administrative committees and sponsors a number of campus activities and functions.

Admission Requirements

University of the Sciences seeks students whose aptitudes and achievements are in the areas of science, mathematics, and humanities. Sixteen total high school credits are required and must include English (4 credits), mathematics (3 credits, including algebra I and II and plane geometry), and science (3 credits of laboratory science, including at least two of the following: biology, chemistry, and physics). Physical science, IPS, general science, or similar courses without a laboratory component do not fulfill the laboratory science requirement. Class rank, if provided by the applicant's high school, and grade point average are also considered in the admission decision process. Candidates are required to submit the results of their SAT and/or ACT examinations. Supplemental testing or an interview may be requested to clarify a specific aspect of a candidate's record. For students whose first language is not English, the Test of English as a Foreign Language (TOEFL) is suggested. Applications for transfer are welcome, although the number of seats available each year is less than that for first-year students, since all students admitted to University of the Sciences are admitted for the entire program length. Advanced standing may be achieved through the College Board's Advanced Placement Program, the International Baccalaureate program, or earned college credit.

University of the Sciences does not discriminate in the administration of its educational policies, admission policies, scholarship and loan programs, or athletic and other University-administered programs on the basis of sex, age, handicap, race, creed, color, or national origin. All students are entitled to all of the rights, privileges, programs, and activities generally accorded or made available to students at the University. This institutional policy complies with the requirements of Title IX of the Education Amendments of 1972 (45 CRF 86), Section 504 of the Rehabilitation Act of 1973, and other applicable statutes and regulations.

Application and Information

An admission application may be obtained by calling the Admission Office. Applicants may submit an online application at http://www.usciences.edu/applying. Each paper application must be accompanied by a nonrefundable $45 application fee. However, there is no fee for an online application. University of the Sciences is also a member of the Common Application. First-year applications for admission are considered until the entering class roster has been completed. University of the Sciences follows a rolling admission policy, and applicants are notified of the admission decision after the University has received all required data. Students accepted into any of the programs have until May 1 to submit a nonrefundable enrollment reservation deposit of $500 to hold a place in the class. Applicants accepted after May 1 have two weeks to submit a tuition deposit.

Applicants for transfer to the professional programs should submit completed applications no later than the following dates: physical therapy (February 1), pharmacy (March 1), occupational therapy (March 1), and physician assistant studies (March 15). All transfer applications are reviewed on a rolling basis except for physical therapy and pharmacy, which are reviewed during the spring semester.

Executive Director of Admission and Enrollment Services
University of the Sciences
600 South 43rd Street
Philadelphia, Pennsylvania 19104-4495
Phone: 215-596-8810
  888-996-8747 (toll-free)
Fax: 215-596-8821
E-mail: admit@usciences.edu
Website: http://www.usciences.edu

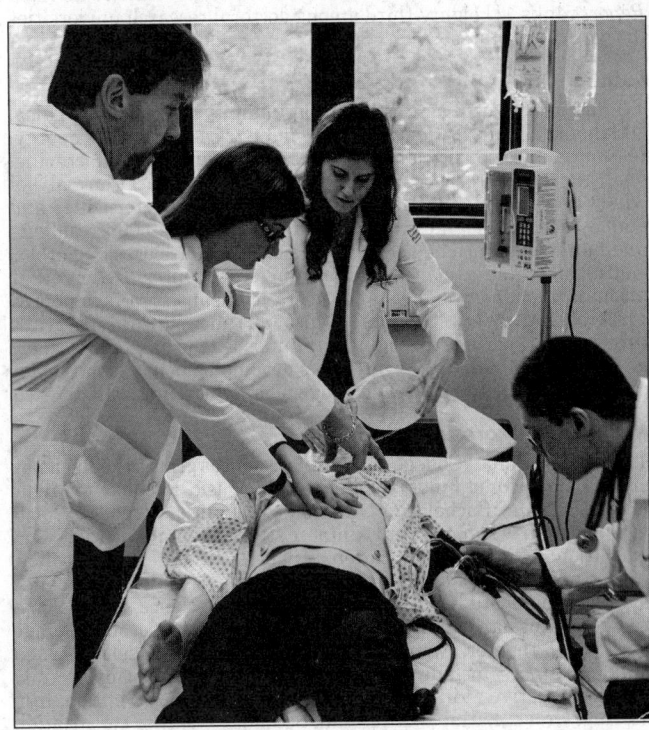

It all begins at University of the Sciences, where students embark on a challenging learning experience; where they get the education and training to be successful science and healthcare professionals; and where they go on to become pharmacists, occupational therapists, biologists, doctors, or health-policy specialists—just to name a few. USciences: where healthcare and science converge.

UNIVERSITY OF TULSA
TULSA, OKLAHOMA

The University

The University of Tulsa (TU) is a private, comprehensive degree-granting university that provides education of the highest quality in the arts, humanities, sciences, engineering, business, education, applied health sciences, and law. TU features three undergraduate colleges—the Henry Kendall College of Arts and Sciences, the Collins College of Business, and the College of Engineering and Natural Sciences—along with a College of Law and a Graduate School.

The University is fully accredited by the North Central Association of Colleges and Universities and is an NCAA Division IA participant in Conference USA. TU maintains a covenant relationship with the Presbyterian Church (U.S.A.).

TU's 11:1 student-faculty ratio, average class size of 19, and emphasis on individual attention anchor an educational culture where students receive both rigorous challenges and comprehensive support.

Extracurricular opportunities include intramural sports, special interest clubs, preprofessional organizations, national fraternities and sororities, community service organizations, student government, departmental honorary groups, and campus ministries.

Total fall 2011 enrollment was 4,187, with 3,084 undergraduates and 1,103 graduate and law students. The ratio of men to women is 54:46, and 18 percent of the students are multicultural. Over half the students are from out of state and international students make up 21 percent of the student population, with sixty-eight countries represented.

Based on academic reputation and other factors, *U.S. News & World Report* ranks TU eighty-third among doctoral/research universities in the United States.

Location

TU features a 216-acre residential campus in midtown Tulsa, Oklahoma. Tulsa's prominent industries include energy, telecommunications, technology, data processing, manufacturing, health care, aerospace, transportation, and education, all of which present TU students with opportunities for internships and employment after graduation. Tulsa has about 550,000 residents and has been named one of America's most livable cities by Forbes. Cultural assets include the Performing Arts Center, BOK Center (arena), acclaimed ballet and opera companies, a symphony, Philbrook Museum, Gilcrease Museum, and cultural festivals. Professional sports in Tulsa include minor league baseball, hockey, and arena football. The River Parks development has facilities for outdoor activities and extensive jogging and bicycling trails.

Majors and Degrees

The Henry Kendall College of Arts and Sciences grants the Bachelor of Arts, Bachelor of Fine Arts, Bachelor of Music, Bachelor of Music Education, and Bachelor of Science degrees in anthropology, art, art history, arts management, Chinese studies, communication, deaf education, economics, education, English, environmental policy, film studies, French, German, history, music, musical theater, organizational studies, philosophy, political science, psychology, religion, Russian studies, sociology, Spanish, speech/language pathology, theater, women's gender studies, and self-designed majors. Minors include most disciplines as well as advertising, classics, creative writing, dance, early childhood intervention, film scoring, Greek, Latin, and Russian. Secondary teacher certification is available in designated disciplines. Interdisciplinary certificate programs offer a way for students to focus their interests in advertising, African American studies, classics, creative writing, international studies, journalism studies, Judaic studies, legal thought, museum studies, and political philosophy.

The Collins College of Business awards the Bachelor of Science in Business Administration degree in accounting, economics, energy management, finance, management, management information systems, and marketing, and a Bachelor of Science in international business and language. Minors are available in most disciplines plus business administration (for nonmajors), coaching, health care informatics, and international business. Certificate programs are available in accounting, advertising, finance, management information systems, not-for-profit administration, and sports administration. Management majors may choose specializations in business law, entrepreneurship and family business management, or human resource management. The college is home to several specialized centers, including the Energy Management Program, Family Owned Business Institute, the Genave King Rogers Center for Business Law, and the Williams Risk Management Center. Within the college, the School of Nursing offers the Bachelor of Science degree in athletic training, exercise and sports science, and a Bachelor of Science in Nursing degree program.

The College of Engineering and Natural Sciences offers the Bachelor of Science degree in applied mathematics, biochemistry, biogeosciences, biological science (options in premedicine, predentistry, and preveterinary science), chemical engineering, chemistry, computer science, earth and environmental science, electrical engineering, engineering physics, geology, geophysics, information technology, mathematics, mechanical engineering, petroleum engineering, and physics. Minors are available in the science and computational science disciplines. The college features state-of-the-art research facilities, including the Center for Information Security and the Williams Communications Fiber Optic Networking Laboratory. Between 1995 and 2011, 48 TU engineering students were named recipients of the prestigious Barry M. Goldwater Scholarship, the nation's premier award for undergraduate students in engineering, math, or science.

Academic Programs

The Tulsa Curriculum links a broad, humanities-based core and writing-across-the-curriculum approach for all students with a highly flexible group of majors, minors, concentrations, and certificate programs. TU students can receive an education that is well-rounded, in-depth, and uniquely personalized. Candidates for graduation must complete at least 124 semester hours of course work, with more hours required of engineering and business administration majors.

The honors program engages students in a critical examination of the major epochs and ideas of Western thought and culture through careful study of primary texts. The acclaimed Tulsa Undergraduate Research Challenge (TURC) program combines advanced research in most disciplines, scholarship, and community service.

The TU Center for Information Security is developing defenses against cyber-terrorist attacks and information warfare. The center supports the University's National Security Agency (NSA)–accredited certificate program in information assurance, a curriculum that integrates information security with computer law and policy issues. TU has been designated a Center of Excellence in information assurance by the NSA and is one of six pioneer institutions selected by the National Science Foundation for the Federal Cyber Service Initiative (Cyber Corps).

Air Force ROTC is available through a satellite program.

Qualified students may receive credit through Advanced Placement testing. Students who complete the International Baccalaureate diploma can receive up to 30 college credit hours.

The University of Tulsa operates on a semester calendar. The fall term begins in late August and the spring term in early January.

Off-Campus Programs

The University is supportive of the study-abroad experience and the Office of Global Education helps students locate the perfect program, whether it is for TU credit or an intern/volunteer option. Students choose from hundreds of opportunities offered around the world through a direct exchange with an international university, an affiliate-sponsored program, or as part of a faculty-led course.

Academic Facilities

The University of Tulsa's libraries, historic McFarlin Library and Mabee Legal Information Center, house more than 4 million items. McFarlin holdings include over 920,000 volumes, 620,000 titles, 120,000 e-books, 40,000 electronic periodicals, 7,500 videos, and 10,000 recordings. McFarlin's special collections rare book holdings number over 125,000 volumes and are internationally recognized, particularly for holdings of Native American history and law, along with nineteenth- and twentieth-century Irish, English, and American literature. McFarlin is home to the papers of 2001 Nobel Laureate V. S. Naipaul. The 12,000-square-foot Academic Technology Center annex was dedicated in 2009, adding computer labs, a coffee shop, and restored reading rooms.

In 2012 the College of Engineering and Natural Sciences added to its existing Keplinger Hall, J. Newton Rayzor Hall, a $14-million home for the computer science and electrical engineering departments with twenty-four integrated classrooms and state-of-the-art teaching/research laboratories and Stephenson Hall, the new 38,600-square-foot home for the mechanical engineering department and McDougall School of Petroleum Engineering. Additional research facilities are housed at Tulsa's North Campus where government- and industry-funded research consortia explore innovations and solve problems faced by the petroleum industry while fostering student learning.

The Mary K. Chapman Center for Communicative Disorders serves the community with its clinical facility and is the learning center for the Department of Communication Disorders. The department has the latest equipment and instrumentation available for use in research, diagnostic, and therapy activities.

Helmerich Hall houses the Collins College of Business and was recently renovated inside and out with architectural elements to blend with the rest of campus and innovative learning spaces such as the Williams Students Services Center and Studio Blue. The Williams Risk Management Center, an advanced learning environment located in the Collins College of Business, combines the latest in trading-floor technology and advanced study in risk management theories and techniques. The Genave King Rogers Center for Business Law supports the business law specialization within the management major.

The Roxana Rózsa and Robert Eugene Lorton Performance Center opened in 2011. Home to the School of Music and the film studies department, the 77,000-square-foot facility includes a 700-seat concert hall, specialized rehearsal and practice rooms, and a film production suite with postproduction editing and scoring capabilities.

Kendall Hall is home to the department of theater and musical theater and features two fully equipped theaters, a scene shop, costume shop, and computer-design lab.

The Donald W. Reynolds Center is the campus arena and convocation center. This $28-million facility is the home for the intercollegiate basketball and volleyball programs and has cutting-edge facilities for video editing and training.

The Allen Chapman Activity Center features the University bookstore, student organization offices, the Great Hall for lectures and entertainment, a sports bar, food court, and fast-food venues.

Dedicated in 2007, the 29,000-square-foot Case Athletic Complex is home to the Golden Hurricane football program and adjoins the renovated H. A. Chapman Stadium where players enjoy one of the nation's elite college football training and playing environments.

The University's 34-acre sports and recreation complex features a 64,000-square-foot student fitness center, competition-grade tennis complex, track, NCAA soccer and softball fields, and intramural fields.

TU manages the acclaimed Gilcrease Museum and the two entities have embarked on an expansion into Tulsa's Brady Arts District to open the Zarrow Center for Art and Education, providing classes and studio space.

Costs

For 2013–14, the typical cost for students living on campus is $45,001, including $34,030 for tuition, $10,166 for room and board, and fees of $805. Expenses for books average about $1,200 per year.

Financial Aid

In 2012 nearly 90 percent of entering students received some form of financial aid (including grants, scholarships, work-study, and loans). TU offers a limited number of highly competitive Presidential Scholarships which cover full tuition, room, and board. All applicants may be considered for a range of University scholarships based on academic merit. Performance scholarships are available in music and theater by audition. The University of Tulsa participates in National Merit and National Achievement Scholarship Corporation's Finalist program and the National Hispanic Scholar Program. Applicants for aid should submit the Free Application for Federal Student Aid (FAFSA) by February 1 for priority consideration.

Faculty

The University has 309 full-time faculty members, with 96 percent having earned the highest degree in their field of study. The faculty is primarily a teaching faculty, although most of its members are also involved in funded research or publishing activities

Admission Requirements

The University of Tulsa seeks students whose academic background indicates potential for success in the university's rigorous academic environment. Performance in high school college-preparatory subjects and scores on the SAT or ACT are key factors in the admission evaluation, but each applicant is reviewed holistically. Each applicant's counselor recommendation; extracurricular activities; and indicators of leadership, creativity, and focus are all taken into consideration. Campus visits and interviews are highly recommended but not required.

Application and Information

TU has a nonbinding, early action freshman admission plan with an application deadline of November 1. Decisions are mailed within three weeks. Applications received after November 1 are reviewed under a rolling admission process with notifications made on an ongoing basis after mid-December.

An application, high school transcript, ACT or SAT score results, and a guidance counselor recommendation are required of freshman applicants. TU accepts the Common Application or its own online or paper application form. TU adheres to the national Candidate's Reply Date of May 1.

The University of Tulsa
Office of Undergraduate Admission
800 South Tucker Drive
Tulsa, Oklahoma 74104-3189
Phone: 918-631-2307 (in Tulsa)
     800-331-3050 (toll-free)
Fax: 918-631-5008
E-mail: admission@utulsa.edu
Website: http://www.utulsa.edu/admission
     http://www.utulsa.edu/admissionblog

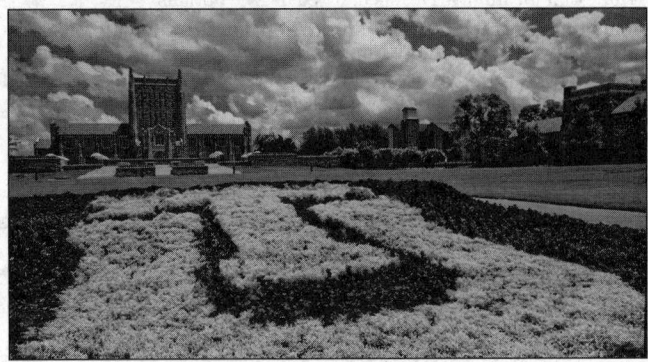

TU is among the top schools in *U.S. News & World Report's* 2013 America's Best Colleges.

UNIVERSITY OF WASHINGTON BOTHELL
BOTHELL, WASHINGTON

The University

The University of Washington Bothell (UW Bothell) opens the door to a nationally and internationally ranked university experience that inspires innovation and creativity. Faculty members are passionate about the knowledge they bring to the classroom and seek to provide a student-centered education in a collaborative learning environment. With 4,172 full-time students and approximately 290 faculty members, UW Bothell offers modest-sized classes, perfectly suited for meaningful interaction and critical thinking. Students take an active role in their educational experience, discover their own strengths and abilities, and ultimately learn how to fulfill their dreams, academic and otherwise.

The campus is located in the thriving, dynamic, and globally engaged greater Seattle area, home to some of the world's most iconic and entrepreneurial corporations, foundations, and arts organizations.

UW Bothell is one of three University of Washington campuses. Though providing distinctive offerings, its graduates earn a fully accredited UW degree.

The curriculum emphasizes close student-faculty interactions, collaboration among students, and hands-on learning. Outstanding regional connections present students with unique opportunities for projects, internships, and research with leading businesses and organizations. At UW Bothell, students earn a University of Washington degree while building a solid foundation of relevant knowledge, practical skills, and professional preparation.

In additional to its undergraduate degree programs, UW Bothell offers several graduate programs in disciplines including business, computing and software systems, cultural studies, education, nursing, policy studies, and fine arts.

Location

UW Bothell is located in Bothell, Washington, approximately 30 minutes northeast of Seattle. The campus sits atop a 128-acre plot of picturesque land overlooking protected wetlands and the Cascades beyond. The site was once home to the 500-acre, Boone-Truly purebred cattle ranch, which was sold in 1995 to the state of Washington.

Majors and Degrees

UW Bothell offers more than thirty degrees through a variety of programs as well as the School of Business; School of Science, Technology, Engineering, and Mathematics; and the School of Interdisciplinary Arts and Sciences. UW Bothell is proud of its reputation for innovative, specialized degree options.

Students can choose from an array of undergraduate degrees in disciplines including: American studies; applied computing; biology; business; business administration (with many options and concentrations); community psychology; computing and software systems; culture, literature, and the arts; electrical engineering; environmental science; environmental studies; global studies; interactive media design; interdisciplinary arts; interdisciplinary studies; mathematics; nursing; science, technology and society; and society, ethics and human behavior.

Postbaccalaureate courses include K–8 teacher certification as well as professional certification.

Off-Campus Programs

Students attending UW Bothell are able to take part in a variety of exceptional educational and technical programs made possible through collaborative efforts with a broad range of community partners. These opportunities are helpful in addressing workforce needs, as well as local and global challenges. Closer community ties will foster a better understanding of the skills and programs students and employers need, while enriching the education of the University's students by providing real-world experiences to learn from and the opportunity to give back to local communities.

UW Bothell takes advantage of the region's extraordinary capacity for creativity and innovation by connecting students to career-building experiences. Committed to the greater good, UW Bothell builds regional partnerships, inspires change, creates knowledge, shares discoveries, and prepares students for leadership in the state of Washington and beyond.

Academic Facilities

Although thoroughly modern, UW Bothell buildings were designed to complement the land's natural beauty; they are environmentally friendly and are equipped with advanced technology for faculty and student use. The UW Bothell campus is well known for its eco-friendly award-winning architecture, state-of-the-art technology, and breathtaking views. Its stunning architecture and landscaping garnered the American Institute of Architects 2002 Honor Award for Washington architecture.

UW Bothell takes its reputation as a green campus very seriously. Sustainability efforts are more than a concept to be studied. Instead, practicing consistent environmental caretaking is the norm. Examples abound, and include everything from LEED-certified buildings and solar panels to worm-assisted composting and pesticide-free landscape maintenance.

UW Bothell offers outstanding student support services: an award-winning on-campus library with access to the full UW library system, a career center, writing center, personal counseling, computer support, and mentoring available for first-generation students and English language learners (ELL).

Work continues on two exciting campus projects, the Sarah Simonds Green Conservatory and a science and academic building. The conservatory is designed to include education and exhibit space for historical displays and interpretive materials, as well as a greenhouse to support plant propagation. The 74,000-square-foot science and academic building, known as UW 3, will provide space for eleven science labs, several classrooms, gathering space and a 200-person lecture hall. More information, including a building rendering is available online at http://www.uwb.edu/about/neighbors/future/uw3. The recently completed Sports Field and Recreation Complex was a student-led and funded project that includes a multipurpose synthetic turf sports field, tennis courts, basketball court, and a sand volleyball court.

Costs

Tuition rates for 2012–13 for full-time (10 to 18 credits) undergraduate studies were $3,971 per quarter for Washington residents and $9,822 per quarter for nonresidents. Tuition rates for graduate and nondegree programs vary depending upon the individual program.

Financial Aid

As part of the University of Washington, UW Bothell participates in the Husky Promise Program, which is a vital part of the comprehensive financial aid program. The UW offers more than $160 million in financial aid each year, with nearly half of all undergraduates receiving aid. Each year, over 5,000 University of Washington students—both undergraduate and graduate—receive more than $20 million in scholarships alone through grants, gifts, or endowed funds.

Approximately one third of UW freshmen will be the first in their families to earn a bachelor's degree, and 30 percent of students come from families below the median income for the state of Washington. Beginning in fall quarter 2007, more than 5,000 UW students—nearly 20 percent of all undergraduates—are covered under the Husky Promise. Both the total number of students and the overall percentage covered by the Husky Promise are among the highest in the country when compared to similar programs at comparable institutions.

In addition to the Husky Promise Program, UW Bothell offers a variety of scholarship, fellowship, and financial aid opportunities.

The UW Bothell Purple and Gold Scholar Awards are available to U.S. residents from outside the state of Washington who have demonstrated extraordinary scholarship and aptitude. Detailed information about financial aid and scholarship opportunities are available in the web version of the UW Bothell Financial Aid and Scholarships Guide at http://www.uwb.edu/financialaid.

Faculty

At UW Bothell the educational relationship between faculty members and their students is paramount. Modest class sizes provide ample opportunity for students to engage with their professors in an environment that is inspiring yet challenging. Faculty members are encouraged to be innovative and creative in the classroom, and are supported in their desire to pursue research and other endeavors as well. They represent a wide variety of disciplines, and are all given the freedom and respect they deserve.

Above all, UW Bothell faculty members pay attention to the changing needs and interests of their students. Students are not only allowed a voice in the classroom, but are strongly encouraged to share their ideas and help shape classroom dynamics.

In today's technologically advanced world, adaptability is the key to ultimate success. With this in mind, UW Bothell faculty members utilize innovative teaching methods and interdisciplinary approaches, thus providing hands-on preparation for real life and career.

Campus Student Housing

More than 270 students live in UW Bothell student housing and enjoy all the conveniences of apartment-style living along with residence life programming, a vibrant community of learners, and a safe environment to student success.

This provides an opportunity for students to interact with diverse individuals, form study groups, and learn more about themselves. UW Bothell student residents socialize, thrive, and create lasting memories and friendships. On-campus student housing is located within a short distance from classrooms and services, as well as downtown Bothell shops, restaurants, and parks. Additional information is available online at http://www.uwb.edu/housing.

Student Government

Located within the Office of Student Life, the Associated Students of UW Bothell (ASUWB) serve as a voice for all students. The goal is to empower the student body through promoting clear communication between faculty members, administration, and students. ASUWB is the sole governing body for students, and its officers are elected.

ASUWB members strive to create an open, friendly campus atmosphere where students can get involved, make a difference, and have fun. There is a diverse selection of clubs and groups focusing on academic and recreational interests.

More information can be found online at http://www.uwb.edu/studentlife/asuwb/officers.

Admission Requirements

Admission requirements vary depending on specific program of interest. All freshman applicants must complete studies in the following minimum College Academic Distribution Requirements (advanced studies in each subject are encouraged): English, 4 years; mathematics, 3 years; social science, 3 years; lab science, 2 years (including one algebra-based lab); foreign language (includes American sign language), 2 years; fine, visual, or performing arts, ½ year; and academic electives, ½ year.

The UW Bothell admissions website (http://www.uwb.edu/admissions) provides additional details about these and other requirements.

Application and Information

Application deadlines vary depending on specific program of interest. A detailed list of these dates can be found at http://www.uwb.edu/admissions/application-dates.

For additional information, contact:
UW Bothell Enrollment Management
P.O. Box 358500
18115 Campus Way, NE
Bothell, Washington 98011-8246
Phone: 425-352-5000
          425-352-5303 (TDD)
E-mail: info@uwb.edu
Website: http://www.uwb.edu

University of Washington Bothell—inspiring innovation and creativity.

UNIVERSITY OF WYOMING
LARAMIE, WYOMING

The University

The University of Wyoming (UW) is a welcoming community of 13,000-plus students offering all the adventure, academic programs, research opportunities, advanced facilities, student life, and NCAA Division I athletics of a larger institution yet providing the individual attention, reasonable class sizes, and personalized instruction of a smaller school. The University offers the perfect environment for success complimented by endless outdoor activities. UW was founded in 1886 as a public land-grant institution and reflects the global community it serves, including hosting students from all fifty states and more than ninety countries.

Research done by UW professors and students pushes the boundaries of modern science and technology resulting in the University's classification as a Carnegie Doctoral/High Research institution. UW offers bachelor's degree programs through six undergraduate colleges and graduate and professional programs, including a Doctor of Pharmacy and the Juris Doctor. The average class size is 29 students, and the student-to-faculty ratio is 14:1.

Students can experience the camaraderie of 250-plus recognized student clubs and organizations, including fifteen national fraternities and sororities, honor and professional societies, political and faith-based organizations, and special interest groups. Students also have the opportunity to participate in more than sixty different intramural and club sports. UW is a NCAA Division I-A school with seventeen men's and women's sports competing in the Mountain West Conference.

UW has experienced tremendous growth in new academic, campus recreation, and student life facilities. UW's recently expanded $54-million College of Business building features behavioral and multimedia labs, and a state-of-the-art trading room where students manage a seven-figure portfolio. Students can engage their creative talents at UW's new visual arts center featuring 79,000 square feet of studio space for ceramics, drawing, painting, sculpting, and print making. Campus recreational facilities include the Wyoming Union, offering the UW bookstore, eating establishments, student computers, and study areas. Additional facilities on campus include Half Acre Gym, an indoor climbing wall, an eighteen-hole golf course, tennis and racquetball courts, weight rooms, and two swimming pools.

UW houses 2,400 students in six residence halls. First-year students are required to live on campus. While primarily coed, the residence halls offer unique living environments, including quiet/study floors, special-interest floors, honors floors, single-gender floors, and other academic living environments. UW also offers a variety of different Freshman Interest Groups (FIGS), which are living communities comprised of students who share common classes and academic interests. More information is available online at www.uwyo.edu/reslife-dining/.

Location

UW's 785-acre campus is located at the foot of the Rocky Mountains in Laramie, a scenic town of 30,000 people in southeastern Wyoming. No matter the time of year, UW students can be found outdoors. Many enjoy the easy access to skiing, boarding, snowmobiling, hiking, camping, hunting, fishing, rock climbing, and mountain biking. Laramie—with its blue skies, clean air, and 320 days of sunshine a year—is a friendly and supportive university town, located 45 miles west of Wyoming's capital, Cheyenne, and 130 miles northwest of Denver, Colorado.

Majors and Degrees

UW offers more than 200 areas of study within its six colleges, leading to B.A., B.S., B.F.A., and B.S.N. degrees.

The College of Agriculture and Natural Resources offers undergraduate majors in agricultural business (with options in agribusiness management, farm and ranch management, international agriculture, and livestock business management), agricultural communications, agroecology, animal and veterinary sciences (with options in animal biology, business, communication, equine science, meat science and food technology, pre–veterinary science, production, and range livestock), family and consumer science (with options in child development, dietetics, family and community services, human nutrition and food, premedicine, and textiles and merchandising), microbiology, molecular biology, organizational leadership, rangeland ecology, and watershed management.

The College of Arts and Sciences offers undergraduate majors in American Indian studies, American studies, anthropology, art, astronomy and astrophysics, biology, botany, chemistry, communication, criminal justice, English, French, gender and women's studies, geography, geology, geology and earth science, German, history, humanities/fine arts, international studies, journalism, mathematical sciences, mathematics, music (with options in education, performance, and theory and composition), philosophy, physics, physiology, political science, psychology, religious studies, Russian, social science, sociology, Spanish, statistics, theatre and dance, wildlife and fisheries biology and management, and zoology, as well as the option of a self-designed major.

The College of Business offers undergraduate majors in accounting, business administration, business economics, economics, finance, management, and marketing.

The College of Education offers undergraduate majors in elementary education (options in creative arts, international educational studies, American cultural diversity, environmental studies, interdisciplinary early childhood, or individual and society), and secondary education (options in agriculture education, art, English, mathematics, modern languages, sciences, social studies, and industrial technology education).

The College of Engineering and Applied Science offers undergraduate majors in architectural engineering (with structural systems or mechanical systems options), chemical engineering (with biomaterials and polymers, biomedical engineering, biotechnology, chemistry, environmental engineering, international, or mathematics options), civil engineering (with environmental, geotechnical, international, structural, transportation, or water resources options), computer engineering (with an international option), computer science (with business or international options), electrical engineering (with bioengineering, computer, or international options), energy systems engineering, mechanical engineering, and petroleum engineering.

The College of Health Sciences offers majors in dental hygiene, kinesiology and health promotion (with an athletic coaching option), nursing, pharmacy, physical education teaching, social work, dental hygiene, and speech-language and hearing sciences.

UW offers preprofessional programs in dentistry, law, medicine, nursing, occupational therapy, optometry, pharmacy, physical therapy, and veterinary medicine.

The School of Environment and Natural Resources also offers interdisciplinary studies that can be combined with course work in seven other fields of study, including the humanities, physical sciences, and social sciences.

Two interdisciplinary degrees are offered at UW. Energy resource management and development offers a diverse curriculum that combines engineering, science, business, law, and natural resources content to build a fundamental understanding of interaction and trade-offs between energy, environment, policy, and the economy. Earth system science, on the other hand, provides an integrated approach to issues of global environmental change. Students must choose one of the options of anthropology, atmospheric science, biology, botany, geography, geology and geophysics, secondary education, or soil science.

Academic Programs

The UW academic calendar consists of two semesters and a complete summer session. Depending on the degree program, students are required to complete 120 to 164 credit hours for graduation. Undergraduate programs for most majors can be completed in four years. Students may choose to double major within the same college, or they may pursue majors in separate colleges. Minors are also available in many areas. All students are required to complete the University Studies Program, a core curriculum that assists students in developing their knowledge of oral and written communication, mathematics, science, diversity, global awareness, government, and culture.

The University Honors Program provides academically ambitious undergraduates innovative and intellectual learning opportunities. Award-winning faculty members, unique and challenging course work, and senior research projects are the hallmarks of this program.

Off-Campus Programs

UW has over 700 international students and close to 100 international researchers/scholars representing over 90 countries. The International Students and Scholars Office provide support to this population through an extensive orientation program, the Friendship Families program, and the International Student Association, which arranges International Education Week and the weekly International Coffee Hour, along with other activities.

UW partners with over 400 exchange sites or study-abroad programs, allowing students to go almost anywhere in the world and study in English or a foreign language. International Programs also coordinates the National Student Exchange (NSE), which is a domestic student exchange consortium of U.S. colleges and universities.

The UW Outreach School extends the university learning experience to Wyoming and the nation through credit and noncredit programs. Courses are delivered via Internet/web-based instruction, compressed video, audio teleconferencing, flexible enrollment (correspondence study), and on-site instruction. Select programs are offered, and degree availability may be limited.

Academic Facilities

The University Libraries' collections number nearly 1.5 million volumes and offer links to a variety of library service collections. William Robertson Coe Library is the flagship library, housing the learning commons and materials from all academic disciplines outside of geology and law. Other library facilities include a geology library (Learning Resource Center), a plant research center (Rocky Mountain Herbarium Library), and a compact shelving facility (Library Annex) which houses the majority of UW Libraries' bound periodicals and government documents. Additional on-campus collections are housed in the American Heritage Center and the George W. Hopper Law Library.

Costs

UW annual tuition and fees for full-time undergraduates in the 2013–14 academic year are $4,404 for Wyoming residents and $14,124 for nonresidents (based on an average class load of 15 credit hours). Room and board (double occupancy, unlimited meal plan) costs are $9,451. Estimated expenses include $1,200 for books and supplies, $890 for travel costs, and $2,200 for personal expenses.

Financial Aid

Nearly 90 percent of all UW students receive financial assistance. More than $85 million is available in the form of scholarships, loans, grants, and work-study opportunities. The Free Application for Federal Student Aid (FAFSA) is required for need-based assistance (loans, grants, work-study) and for many scholarships. The priority deadline for FAFSA is March 1. Most scholarships at UW are based on academic merit. UW participates in the Western Undergraduate Exchange (WUE) program. The Rocky Mountain Scholars Award is available to nonresident students. Prospective students should visit www.uwyo.edu/admissions/scholarships for scholarship deadlines and additional application information.

Faculty

More than 700 professors from the world's most respected colleges and universities have come to teach at UW. Recognized nationally and internationally as experts, 85 percent of faculty members hold the highest degree in their field. UW professors are deeply committed to the success of their students. Ninety-two percent of undergraduate courses are taught by professors or professional lecturers, and many of the most distinguished and accomplished professors at UW teach first-year courses.

Admission Requirements

For assured admission, high school graduates and new first-year students with fewer than 30 transferable college credit hours should have a cumulative high school GPA of 3.0 or above. Students should also have a composite ACT score of 21 or greater or an SAT critical reading/math score of 980 or greater. In addition, all students need to complete 4 years of English, 4 years of mathematics, 4 years of science (including a physical science), 3 years of a social science, 2 years of the same foreign language, and 2 years of additional coursework (behavioral or social sciences, visual arts, performing arts, or humanities). Students who are unable to qualify for assured admission may be admissible with support. Freshman students admitted with support will be required to take part in Synergy, a national award-winning mentoring and support program that assists in the transition to college and increases the academic success rate for participants. Additional details can be found online at www.uwyo.edu/admissions. Transfer students with 30 or more transferable semester credit hours must have a minimum cumulative college GPA of 2.0.

Application and Information

Students must submit a completed UW Application for Admission, official high school or college transcripts, ACT or SAT scores, and a $40 nonrefundable application fee. Students may apply and pay the application fee online at www.uwyo.edu/apply. UW strongly encourages all prospective students and their parents to visit the campus. Explore www.uwyo.edu/visit to check out UW's various visit options and programs.

Admissions Office
Department 3435
University of Wyoming
1000 East University Avenue
Laramie, Wyoming 82071
United States
Phone: 307-766-5160
     800-DIAL-WYO (342-5996; toll-free)
E-mail: admissions@uwyo.edu
Website: http://www.uwyo.edu

UW Outdoor Program trip leader, Josh Fog, explains climbing-safety procedures to UW Honors students.

UTICA COLLEGE
UTICA, NEW YORK

The College

A private, independent college founded in 1946, Utica College (UC) is known for its excellent academic programs, outstanding faculty, personal attention, and diverse student population. The hallmarks of Utica College's academic programs are the integration of liberal and professional studies and a strong emphasis on internships, research, and other experiential learning opportunities, but UC is best known for the close, personal relationship students have with both faculty and staff members. Approximately 3,600 undergraduate and graduate students attend UC, including men and women from a wide variety of socioeconomic and cultural backgrounds as well as older students, veterans, and students with disabilities. While most students come from New York, New England, and the middle Atlantic states, students are drawn to UC from all parts of the United States, and there is a growing international student population.

Utica College offers thirty-seven majors, a broad selection of minors and special programs, and twenty-one graduate programs. UC also offers a robust selection of study-abroad opportunities as well as preprofessional programs and an honors program.

Utica College is located on a modern, 128-acre campus on the southwestern edge of Utica, New York. Its facilities include a recently completed science and technology complex comprised of state-of-the-art learning and research facilities for health professions and justice studies, the Frank E. Gannett Memorial Library, a fully equipped high-definition television studio and convergence media center, the Ralph F. Strebel Student Center, seven residence halls, an athletic center, a 1,200-seat stadium, and numerous athletic fields.

Half of UC's students live on campus in residence halls that feature a variety of housing options, modern amenities, and lounges for studying or relaxing with friends. Freshmen primarily live in North and South Halls, which offer mostly double-occupancy rooms. Campus dining services provide a wide variety of options, including American and international cuisines, vegetarian meals, a large salad bar, and lighter fare such as burgers and pizza. Students enjoy a range of dining venues, from the main dining commons in Strebel Student Center to a student-run coffeehouse, convenient cafés in the Library and academic buildings, and a Subway sandwich shop on campus.

Whether students live on or off campus, they can take advantage of more than eighty student organizations, focusing on community service, music, theater, and politics as well as fraternities, sororities, and major-related clubs that provide opportunities for students to organize career-related events. Students can write for the student newspaper, work at the College's radio station, submit entries for the literary magazine, or work on the yearbook. Students also have the opportunity to enjoy lectures, concerts, poetry readings, art exhibits, plays, and nationally recognized speakers.

Utica College offers twenty-five NCAA Division III varsity sports, including men's baseball, basketball, cross-country, football, ice hockey, lacrosse, soccer, swimming and diving, tennis, and track and field; women's basketball, cross-country, field hockey, ice hockey, lacrosse, soccer, softball, swimming and diving, tennis, track and field, volleyball, and water polo; and coed golf. UC also offers club sports and a wide variety of intramural opportunities. Utica College is a member of the Empire 8 Athletic Conference, the Eastern College Athletic Conference, and the New York State Women's Collegiate Athletic Association. Nearly a third of all UC students participate in at least one Division III intercollegiate sport, and more than 45 percent are active in intramural or nonvarsity club sports.

Athletic facilities include the 1,200-seat multisport Gaetano Stadium with a state-of-the-art field turf synthetic grass playing surface; the Clark Athletic Center, which contains a large gymnasium, racquetball courts, a swimming pool, saunas, a recently renovated 6,400-square-foot free-weight room and fully equipped fitness facility, and numerous outdoor fields and courts. Ice hockey games are played at the downtown Utica Memorial Auditorium, which features pro-style hockey locker rooms and training facilities.

Location

The city of Utica is located in the heart of the historic Mohawk Valley in the center of New York State. Just 90 miles west of Albany and 50 miles east of Syracuse, Utica has a thriving arts community, beautiful parks, and expanding shopping centers featuring national retailers. There are numerous recreational facilities, including a municipal ski slope and an excellent golf course less than a mile from the Utica College campus. Other nearby recreational opportunities include tennis, swimming, boating, fishing, hiking, and camping.

Majors and Degrees

Utica College offers undergraduate degree programs in accounting, aging studies, biochemistry, biology, business economics, chemistry, communication arts, computer science, construction management, criminal justice, criminal justice–economic crime investigation, cybersecurity and information assurance, economics, English, foreign language, geoscience, government and politics, health studies, health studies–human behavior, health studies–management, history, international studies, journalism studies, liberal studies, management, mathematics, nursing, occupational therapy, philosophy, physical therapy, physics, psychology, psychology–child life, public relations, public relations/journalism studies, risk management and insurance, sociology and anthropology, and therapeutic recreation.

Students interested in the occupational therapy or physical therapy major earn a bachelor's degree in health studies with direct entry into UC's graduate programs, as long as academic requirements are met. Utica College offers a master's degree in occupational therapy and a doctorate in physical therapy (D.P.T.).

Students may minor in aging studies, anthropology, chemistry, communication arts, computer science, creative writing, economics, English language, film studies, French, gender studies, geoscience, government, healthcare ethics, history, human rights advocacy, literature, management, mathematics, philosophy, philosophy of justice, psychology, recreation leadership, sociology, Spanish, theater, and writing.

Preprofessional programs include dentistry, law, medicine, optometry, podiatry, and veterinary medicine. Special programs are available in education, gerontology, engineering, and joint health professions.

Academic Programs

In addition to majors and minors, Utica College also offers a rapidly growing education program; students wishing to pursue a career in teaching choose either a liberal arts major (to teach elementary education) or a major in their intended field (to teach at the secondary level).

For those students who are undecided, the Academic Support Services Center provides academic advising and career counseling, and Career Services offers students opportunities to explore career options.

To earn a bachelor's degree, students must complete a minimum of 120 to 128 credits, satisfy major and major-related requirements, and complete any special program requirements. In addition, all Utica College students, regardless of their major, must complete a liberal arts core program as part of the degree requirements.

First-year seminar offers freshmen and transfer students opportunities to earn academic credit while learning how to make the transition to college. Utica College offers the Higher Education Opportunity Program (HEOP), the Collegiate Science and Technology Entry Program (CSTEP), and Summer Institute, which serves as an academic bridge between high school and college.

Off-Campus Programs

UC's study-abroad programs give students opportunities to widen their global perspectives through exchange programs with universities in Spain, Italy, Poland, Finland, Hungary, Peru, Scotland, and Wales, as well as American College in Dublin, Ireland, among other options. Special study-abroad opportunities include the College's annual forensic anthropology field school in Albania as well as learning experiences in London and elsewhere.

Students are encouraged to complete internships and field placements to gain professional experience with businesses and organizations while they are earning college credit. Utica College's cooperative education program allows students to earn money while gaining professional experience.

Academic Facilities

The Frank E. Gannett Memorial Library includes a collection of some 200,000 volumes, 1,200 serial subscriptions, hundreds of online journals, and a microform collection of more than 60,000 journals, newspapers, and books. Located on the lower level of the library are the Media Center, computer labs, the Edith Langley Barrett Fine Art Gallery, and a large concourse—the site of special events, such as musical recitals, receptions, and guest lectures.

Classes, laboratories, and faculty offices are located in the main academic complex and within UC's new science and technology complex. F. Eugene Romano Hall opened in summer 2007 and provides state-of-the-art classroom, laboratory, and clinical space, as well as learning technology for students in the health sciences. The innovative Economic Crime, Justice Studies, and Cybersecurity building opened in November 2008 and provides an appropriate platform for cutting-edge research and advanced learning at both the undergraduate and graduate levels.

Named in honor of one of UC's most celebrated faculty members, Professor Emeritus of Public Relations Raymond Simon, UC's state-of-the-art high-definition broadcast facility provides a hands-on learning environment for the next generation of media professionals.

Utica College maintains eleven computer laboratories with both IBM-compatible and Macintosh computers. Students have additional Internet access in the Pioneer Café and in all student residence hall rooms. Other resources include the Academic Support Services Center, the Math/Science Center, and the Writing Center.

Costs

For 2012–13, tuition was $30,890; room and board costs were $11,934. Student activity and technology fees totaled $520. Books and supplies average $1,284 per year.

Financial Aid

The College has been recognized as a best buy in education and works to control costs and keep its education affordable. The average financial aid package for freshmen in fall 2010 was $29,875—which exceeded the cost of tuition for the 2010–11 academic year. About two thirds of that aid came from grants and a third from loans and/or jobs. More than 90 percent of the freshmen received a financial aid package. At the same time, UC awarded numerous merit scholarships to students with outstanding grades and test scores.

Almost every federal and state financial aid program is available through Utica College. Students apply for institutional and governmental financial aid by filing the Free Application for Federal Student Aid (FAFSA) by February 15. UC offers three different deferred-payment programs that spread payments over the academic year.

Faculty

Utica College's faculty is diverse, energetic, accomplished, and devoted to their students. The vast majority of faculty members have earned their Ph.D. or other terminal degree, and while many are involved in research, the primary focus of faculty members is teaching. The typical class size is 20 students, the student-faculty ratio is 15:1, and all faculty members are involved in assisting students with their academic planning.

Student Government

One of Utica College's strongest traditions is student participation in the College's governance structure. Students may serve on a number of student governing bodies, and students also serve on all standing committees of the College.

Admission Requirements

Utica College admits students who can best benefit from the educational opportunities the College offers. The Admission Committee gives each application individual attention, and the potential for a student's success at UC is measured primarily by an evaluation of past academic performance, scholastic ability, and personal characteristics. Freshman applicants must have completed 16 academic units, including 4 years of English. Students should follow a college-preparatory program, including 3 units of mathematics, 3 units of science, 2 units of foreign language, and 3 units of social studies.

Application and Information

Students may apply for fall, spring, or summer admission. Materials required include a completed Utica College application form, official high school or college transcripts, and a $40 application fee. Utica College prefers, but does not require, SAT or ACT scores, with the exception of the programs listed below. A personal interview for all applications is strongly suggested.

Occupational therapy, physical therapy, nursing, and joint health professions program applicants must submit SAT or ACT scores, a preferred letter of clinical recommendation if applicable, and a personal statement. International students must complete the international student application form. The application fee is waived for students who apply to HEOP or CSTEP; however, SAT or ACT scores are required to be considered for either program.

The College conducts a rolling admissions program; however certain programs do have application deadlines. For students applying to the occupational therapy or physical therapy programs, the joint health professions program, or for academic achievement awards, the application deadline is January 15. For students applying to the nursing program, the preferred application deadline is February 1. The application deadline for the HEOP program is January 15. Students should note that a tuition deposit of $200 is required by April 1 to secure a place in the HEOP program.

Additional admissions information can be found online at http://www.utica.edu/admissions.

Inquiries should be sent to:

Director of Undergraduate Admissions
Utica College
1600 Burrstone Road
Utica, New York 13502-4892
Phone: 315-792-3006
      800-782-8884 (toll-free)
E-mail: admiss@utica.edu
Website: http://www.utica.edu
      http://www.facebook.com/UticaCollegeAdmissions
      http://twitter.com/uticacollege

F. Eugene Romano Hall at Utica College, a state-of-the-art center for learning and research in the health professions.

VANDERBILT UNIVERSITY
NASHVILLE, TENNESSEE

The University

In 1873, on the heels of the Civil War, Commodore Cornelius Vanderbilt gave $1 million to the university that now bears his name, with the hope that it would "contribute to strengthening the ties which should exist between all sections of our common country." Since then, Vanderbilt has enrolled America's most talented students and challenged them to expand their intellectual horizons in an inclusive environment based on open inquiry and respect. Vanderbilt's comprehensive interdisciplinary approach to education allows students to pursue a wide array of academic and curricular interests outside of their main focus of study and the University's progressive financial aid policies assure that it is often cited among the country's best values in national universities.

Consistently ranked among the top 20 universities in the country by *U.S. News & World Report*, Vanderbilt is a private research university that features four undergraduate schools and six graduate and professional schools. Each year, 1,600 first-year students join the University, bringing the total undergraduate population to approximately 6,800 students, many of whom collaborate with professors on cutting-edge research projects and present their findings at professional conferences. The 8:1 student-faculty ratio gives each student access to faculty members of prominence in every area of academic study. Full-time faculty members share their perspectives as instructors and advisers united by one goal: providing a challenging, comprehensive education that encourages broad perspectives and critical thinking.

Known for the rolling splendor of its 330-acre campus, which is classified as a national arboretum, Vanderbilt also offers a top-ranked residential experience for its undergraduates, nearly all of whom live on campus all four years. First-year students live and learn in The Martha Rivers Ingram Commons, a collection of ten residence halls, or Houses, clustered along one side of campus (seven of the Houses are LEED-certified). The Commons incorporates more than just bricks and mortar. Faculty members, including the Dean of The Ingram Commons and his family, live there, facilitating easy and meaningful interactions between students and professors. Frequent educational and social programming at The Ingram Commons invites students and faculty to explore current events and social issues.

Vanderbilt students take full advantage of student life in over 510 student organizations, a full range of study-abroad programs, Division I Athletics, and a variety of internship opportunities.

Location

Vanderbilt University is located in Nashville, the capital of Tennessee. Described by *Rolling Stone* (2011) as having the best music scene in the country, Nashville boasts a rich mosaic of cultures, vibrant arts, business, health and education sectors, and an array of recreational opportunities. Nashville hosts thousands of live concerts each year in every conceivable genre and is recognized as a top college city in America and an excellent location for businesses. Nashville's many personalities and striking natural beauty attract people from around the world.

Majors and Degrees

College of Arts and Science: African American and Diaspora Studies; American Studies; Anthropology; Art; Asian Studies; Biological Sciences; Chemistry; Classical Civilizations; Classical Languages; Classics; Communication of Science and Technology; Communication Studies; Earth and Environmental Sciences; Ecology, Evolution, and Organismal Biology; Economics; Economics and History; English; European Studies; Film Studies; French; French and European Studies; German; German and European Studies; History; History of Art; Italian and European Studies; Jewish Studies; Latin American Studies; Mathematics; Medicine, Health, and Society; Molecular and Cellular Biology; Neuroscience; Philosophy; Physics; Political Science; Psychology; Public Policy Studies; Religious Studies; Russian; Russian and European Studies; Sociology; Spanish; Spanish and European Studies; Spanish and

Portuguese; Spanish, Portuguese, and European Studies; Theater; Women's and Gender Studies; and individually designed majors.

Blair School of Music: Composition/Theory, Musical Arts, Musical Arts/Teacher Education, and Performance.

School of Engineering: Biomedical Engineering, Chemical Engineering, Civil Engineering, Computer Engineering, Computer Science, Electrical Engineering, Engineering Science, and Mechanical Engineering.

Peabody College of Education and Human Development: Child Development, Child Studies, Cognitive Studies, Early Childhood Education, Elementary Education, Human and Organizational Development, Secondary Education, and Special Education.

Graduate/Professional Schools: Divinity School, The Graduate School, Law School, Owen Graduate School of Management, School of Medicine, and School of Nursing.

Preprofessional advising is also available for students interested in pursuing graduate degrees in architecture, business, law, or health professions.

Academic Programs

Students apply directly to one of the four schools that offer undergraduate programs: the College of Arts and Science, the School of Engineering, Peabody College of Education and Human Development, or the Blair School of Music. In all four schools, honors programs and opportunities for independent study and internships are available. Roughly 40 percent of undergraduate students pursue double majors within and across all four undergraduate schools. This leads to some diverse combinations, such as pre-med students who study Spanish, engineers who study violin, math majors who study songwriting, or chemistry majors who study art history.

Vanderbilt operates on a two-semester calendar, and classes begin in late August. First-semester exams take place prior to the winter holidays, and the second semester ends in early May. A variety of courses are offered during Maymester and two summer sessions.

The College of Arts and Science provides many opportunities to experience a wide range of academic disciplines and subjects. Within the requirements of the AXLE (Achieving eXcellence in Liberal Education) curriculum, students refine their skills in writing, mathematics, foreign language, the humanities, natural sciences, social sciences, history, and culture.

The Blair School of Music offers the Bachelor of Music degree in composition and theory, musical arts, musical arts/teacher education, and performance. Instruction is available in every instrument of the orchestra as well as piano, organ, euphonium, multiple woodwinds, saxophone, classical guitar, and voice. Unlike many schools of music, Blair has no graduate students. The curriculum combines intensive musical training with liberal arts studies. Students take approximately one third of their courses outside of the music school. The Blair School also offers a music minor and a wide variety of courses, private instruction, and performing organizations for nonmajors.

For more than 125 years, the School of Engineering has educated engineers for practice in industry, government, consulting, teaching, and research careers. In addition to technical courses, each student's program includes a rich complement of course work in the humanities and social sciences, resulting in a balanced foundation for future achievement and the assumption of leadership roles in their chosen fields. All programs leading to a Bachelor of Engineering degree are ABET-accredited, and students can earn the Bachelor of Science degree while majoring in Computer Science or Engineering Science.

The top-ranked graduate school of education (according to *U.S. News & World Report*) for five years running, Peabody College offers degree programs leading to teacher certification and to careers in other areas of education, including child development, child studies, cognitive studies, and human and organizational development. The degree reflects a strong liberal arts foundation combined with a solid program of preprofessional courses and a multitude of internship and practicum opportunities. All undergraduates must complete requirements in communications, the humanities, mathematics, the natural sciences, and the social sciences. Moreover, students have an abundance of field experiences throughout their four years.

Off-Campus Programs

Study-abroad programs allow students to immerse themselves in languages and cultures around the world. More than 120 programs are offered in Argentina, Australia, Austria, Chile, China, Costa Rica, the Czech Republic, Denmark, the Dominican Republic, Egypt, England, France, Germany, Israel, Italy, Japan, Russia, Singapore, South Africa, and Spain, among others. Students receive direct credit for their courses, and the cost of tuition is usually the same as for study on campus in Nashville. In addition, any scholarships, grants, or loans a student has been awarded apply to Vanderbilt study-abroad programs. Students may also participate in programs sponsored by other universities by working with an adviser.

Academic Facilities

Students and faculty members take advantage of Vanderbilt's extensive library resources, obtaining easy access to books, periodicals, documents, microforms, and reference materials. The Jean and Alexander Heard Library is supported by ten major resource centers, including special collections, University Archives, and more than 8 million items.

Costs

The estimated costs for 2013–14 include: tuition, $41,928; housing, $9,208; meals, $4,890; books and supplies, $1,370; student activities and recreation fee, $1,054; personal expenses allowance, $2,662; first-year experience fee, $690; new student transcript fee, $30; engineering lab fee*, $650; and engineering laptop allowance*, $1,500. Travel allowances are variable. *The engineering laptop allowance and laboratory fee apply to engineering students only. First-year engineering students are required to either purchase a laptop from Vanderbilt or provide their own computer that meets published requirements.

Financial Aid

Through Opportunity Vanderbilt, the University makes three important commitments reflecting a strong dedication to making a Vanderbilt education possible: Vanderbilt is need-blind for all U.S. citizens and eligible non-citizens, Vanderbilt meets 100 percent of demonstrated need for all admitted students, and Vanderbilt's financial aid packages do not include loans. These three commitments combined place Vanderbilt among a small number of universities to adopt such progressive policies.

More than 60 percent of the University's undergraduate students received some type of financial aid in the 2012–13 school year. Need-based aid is awarded according to the evaluation of the FAFSA and the CSS/Financial Aid PROFILE.

Vanderbilt also awards merit-based scholarships to selected first-year applicants who demonstrate exceptional accomplishment and intellectual promise. Three signature scholarship programs comprise the majority of these honor scholarships: the Ingram Scholarship Program (for students who plan to combine a professional or business career with an exceptional commitment to community service), the Cornelius Vanderbilt Scholarship Program (for students who combine outstanding academic achievements with strong leadership and contributions outside the classroom), and the Chancellor's Scholarship Program (for students who have worked to build strong high school communities by bridging gaps among economically, socially, and racially diverse groups).

Faculty

Excluding the Schools of Medicine and Nursing, Vanderbilt has 1,041 full-time faculty members. All undergraduate faculty members, many of whom hold awards for distinguished scholarship, are required to teach undergraduates. A low student-faculty ratio of 8:1 provides for an intimate academic experience between students and professors who are recognized nationally and worldwide for their research. Ninety-one percent of classes have fewer than 50 students.

Student Government

The Vanderbilt Student Government provides students with an opportunity to participate actively in maintaining a high quality of life on campus. It works with many of the more than 510 student organizations to bring nationally prominent speakers to campus and provides an interesting and diverse array of programming throughout the year. A vital part of life at Vanderbilt is the honor system, which is governed entirely by students through representatives on the Honor Council. Each year, a senior is selected as a Young Alumni Trustee of the University's Board of Trust.

Admission Requirements

Vanderbilt seeks students with high standards of scholarship and character. Admission is based on a holistic review of academic and personal credentials.

The typical applicant will have completed 20 or more units in a challenging high school curriculum, including at least 2 years of foreign language study. Most applicants to the School of Engineering have completed at least 4 units of mathematics; calculus and physics are strongly recommended. The Admissions Committee evaluates each student's high school transcript, extracurricular involvement, counselor and teacher recommendations, and personal essay. Students must also submit scores (including the writing subscore) from either the SAT or the ACT. Applicants to the Blair School of Music are required to audition on their primary instrument. A personal audition is preferred, but applicants may audition by videotape with permission from the Blair School of Music.

Campus visits are highly recommended, though student interest is not used as a measure of admissibility. In addition to daily information sessions and campus tours, the Admissions Office offers various half-day and full-day visit programs for prospective students. All programs require reservations, so students are encouraged to call or visit admissions.vanderbilt.edu/visit in advance of their visit for information about group information sessions, campus tours, and opportunities to attend classes.

Application and Information

Students whose first choice is Vanderbilt may apply under one of Vanderbilt's early decision plans. Application materials must be postmarked by November 1 for Early Decision I and by January 1 for Early Decision II; notification is made by December 15 for Early Decision I and by February 15 for Early Decision II. Regular Decision applications are due January 1. Students are informed of the admission decision by April 1. Personal auditions are scheduled in December, January, and February for students applying to the Blair School of Music. Students seeking transfer admission should submit an application and all supporting materials by March 15 for fall semester entry.

Office of Undergraduate Admissions
Vanderbilt University
2305 West End Avenue
Nashville, Tennessee 37203-1727
Phone: 615-322-2561
       800-288-0432 (toll-free)
E-mail: admissions@vanderbilt.edu
Website: admissions.vanderbilt.edu
       facebook.com/vanderbiltadmissions
       twitter.com/vanderbiltu
       instagram.com/vanderbiltadmissions

Kirkland Hall, Vanderbilt's oldest and most historic building.

VAUGHN COLLEGE OF AERONAUTICS AND TECHNOLOGY

FLUSHING, NEW YORK

VaughnCollege
of aeronautics and technology

The College

Vaughn College of Aeronautics and Technology is a private, four-year college committed to providing its students with the excellent education and skills needed to achieve professional success in engineering, technology, management and aviation. Founded in 1932, the College, adjacent to LaGuardia Airport, is a small, high-quality institution where students can experience personal attention as they progress through academic course work. The College fosters a culture of excellence in which rigorous degree, professional, technical, and certification programs are offered. These programs, built upon the College's aeronautical heritage, incorporate the latest technology and meet the universal needs of the industries they serve. The result is well-educated graduates who are successful in their fields. The College's student body of more than 1,700 and its low, 15:1 student-faculty ratio ensure a highly personalized learning environment. More than 92 percent of Vaughn College graduates are employed or continue their educations within one year of obtaining their degrees, and they work in twenty countries and all fifty states.

On September 1, 2004, the College of Aeronautics became Vaughn College of Aeronautics and Technology. The name reflects the College's aviation heritage as well as its future as a greatly expanded academic institution, with new programs that include a bachelor's degree in mechatronic engineering and a master's-level management offering. The name change is part of the College's strategic plan that also includes plans for a new library, additional degree programs, and other improvements to the campus.

Location

Located in New York City, the College offers numerous internship opportunities with an array of technology, manufacturing, and aviation companies. The cultural, spiritual, and physical needs of the students are met by the outstanding facilities of New York City. Restaurants are easily accessible, and hospitals and other medical facilities are among the best in the world. New York City's legendary museums focus on arts, natural history, science, and world civilization.

Majors and Degrees

The College awards the Associate of Applied Science (A.A.S.) degree in aeronautical engineering technology, airport management, aviation maintenance, animation and digital technologies, electronic engineering technology–avionics, and flight.

The Bachelor of Science (B.S.) degree is available in general management, airline management, airport management, aviation maintenance, aviation maintenance management, electronic engineering technology–avionics, electronic engineering technology–general electronics, flight, mechatronics engineering, mechanical engineering technology–aeronautical option, and mechanical engineering technology–computer-aided design option. A nondegree course of study in air traffic control, a Federal Aviation Administration Collegiate Training Initiative program (AT-CTI), is also available. The College is one of thirty-six institutions nationwide to offer this program. There is also an aircraft dispatch program offered.

Academic Programs

All students in associate and baccalaureate degree programs complete a core curriculum as part of their degree requirements. The core curriculum is derived from the mission of the College and reflects what the institution believes is important and fundamental to students' education and development. In general, the core instills in students critical-thinking skills, values appropriate to an educated person, and the ability to communicate, and the curriculum provides context for advanced learning. The baccalaureate core consists of three components: academic seminars (2 credits, including the freshman year experience and information literacy), the liberal arts (21 credits, including a year of world and American literature), and math and science (16 credits).

Off-Campus Programs

Internships are an important part of a student's learning experience at Vaughn College, and they have led to job offers upon graduation. The department of career services and faculty chairs arrange for internships with top U.S. corporations. As a federally designated Hispanic-serving institution, the College participates with the Hispanic Association of Colleges and Universities (HACU) to place students in internships with various federal agencies year-round. Other active internships and cooperatives include the Boeing Company, Federal Aviation Administration (FAA), Federal Express, Global Air Dispatch, HACU, JetBlue, Lockheed Martin, the Metropolitan Transportation Authority (MTA), the National Broadcasting Company, the Northrop Grumman Corporation, Northwest Airlines, ORBIS, the Port Authority of New York and New Jersey, and Teterboro Airport.

Academic Facilities

Each laboratory provides the work/study environment suited to the requirements of each program. This practical, hands-on experience helps qualify students for immediate employment upon graduation. From the new mechatronics laboratory to the CATIA/NASTRAN computer center, the College is committed to providing students with the knowledge and tools they are likely to find in today's businesses. The College's $1-million flight simulator center features Frasca142 and 241 simulators, a Canadair regional jet trainer, and two Redbird simulators. In addition, a revolutionary educational partnership with Redbird Flight Simulations enables students to pursue FAA flight certifications and ratings at Redbird's innovative facility in San Marcos, Texas.

The College has substantially upgraded its technology environment over the past few years. Students have access to more than 200 computers in classrooms and labs, providing software applications for desktop publishing, word processing, spreadsheets, databases, and shared printing services. These computers also afford students the opportunity to interact with industry-leading applications used within their academic programs, including CATIA, SolidWorks, Nastran, and Patran. The College's recently created student portal provides online access to tools that enhance and support academic efforts. All of Vaughn's classrooms have updated instructional technologies, including projection, and Internet connectivity to classrooms and labs. Wireless access exists across campus, including within the residential facilities, and each student is provided a vaughn.edu e-mail address. Identification cards provide students with access to secured facilities, laundry payment, dining services, library access, vending and purchasing options, and more.

The College's library offers extensive general, technical, resource, and periodical material totaling more than 125,000 volumes. The real and virtual resources include books, periodicals, videos, and research databases. The video collection consists of subject videos to support the College's curriculum, general-interest videos, and movies. The library houses VHS tapes and DVDs and its research databases contain more than 8,000 full-text periodicals and newspapers. Ten personal computers are available for student use in the reference area. Vaughn is also nearing the construction phase of a new library that will provide students and faculty with a one-stop location for research materials, academic support services, and technology support. This new library, scheduled to open in 2013, triples the size of the current facility and is part of a more than $30-million renovation of Vaughn's campus planned over the next several years.

Costs

In 2012–13, full-time tuition (12 to 18 credits per semester) was $9,450. Students taking 11 credits or fewer paid $600 per credit. The semester fee, which covers the cost of orientation courses, Internet and computer usage, and student-support services, activities, and leadership programs, was $200.

For the 2012–13 academic year, rooms in Vaughn's four-year-old residence hall cost $4,515 for a double room and $5,200 for a single room, per semester. A $250 housing deposit is required. Residents live in either a two-person or a four-person suite with a semi-private bath. The residence hall has laundry, study, and kitchen facilities in a common area within the building. Residence hall rooms are supplied with a bed, dresser, closet, desk, chair, and wastebasket for each student. Each room is also equipped with phone and cable TV hookup and computer port.

Financial Aid

Vaughn College offers federal, state, and institutional funds to help students pay for their education. Ninety percent of students are eligible for some type of financial aid. The first step is to file the Free Application for Federal Student Aid (FAFSA) and, if appropriate, the New York State Tuition Assistance Program (TAP) application. Applications for the fall semester should be filed by March 1. The College recognizes academic excellence by awarding scholarships to high-achieving students pursuing Bachelor of Science degree programs. Applicants must file the FAFSA to be eligible.

Awards for new students include Founders' Scholarships, which are merit-based and range from $500 to $6,000 per year, and the need-based Vaughn College financial grants, which range from $250 to $2,200.

Faculty

What separates Vaughn College from other institutions is its uniquely committed faculty, whose members come to the classroom with extensive experience in such fields as engineering, manufacturing, management, and communications. Working closely with industry, the College has developed rigorous curricula that incorporate the latest technology and the knowledge students need for that all-important first professional position. The student-faculty ratio of 15:1 enables students to work closely with faculty members in classroom and laboratory settings.

Student Government

The Student Government Association (SGA) is primarily concerned with the quality of student life on campus. SGA carries the concerns of its constituency, the student body, to the administration and is the voice of the student body. Serving students as the liaison to the administration, SGA coordinates social programming and provides a system for cocurricular involvement through many clubs and organizations. SGA meets on a regular basis and encourages all students to attend meetings and become involved.

Admission Requirements

High school graduates must submit a completed application (available online at www.vaughn.edu); the $40 application fee; SAT or ACT scores; an official copy of the high school transcript and any college transcripts (if applicable); a copy of the high school diploma (or GED), complete with scores; and immunization records. Some students may need to take a placement exam, while flight operations applicants must pass the FAA Class III physical examination. An interview with an admissions counselor and a financial aid counselor is required for all flight operations applicants and recommended for all others.

Students who have lived in the United States for less than three years and for whom English is a second language, or international applicants from countries where English is not an official language, can substitute results of the TOEFL exam. Students who have completed 24 or more college credits are exempt from the SAT/ACT requirement.

Application and Information

The admissions office reviews applications on a rolling basis. All applicants are encouraged to file by March 1 for the fall semester and November 15 for the spring semester to best take advantage of scholarship opportunities.

Vaughn College of Aeronautics and Technology
86-01 23rd Avenue
Flushing, New York 11369
Phone: 718-429-6600
        866-6VAUGHN (toll-free)
Fax: 718-779-2231
E-mail: admitme@vaughn.edu
Website: http://www.vaughn.edu

Vaughn College is located in easy proximity of Manhattan.

VERMONT TECHNICAL COLLEGE
RANDOLPH CENTER AND WILLISTON, VERMONT

The College

Founded in 1866, Vermont Technical College's main campus is situated on a hilltop in Randolph Center, Vermont, in the heart of the Green Mountains. The College also has campuses in Williston, Bennington, and Brattleboro, Vermont, plus a network of extended nursing campuses statewide. Vermont Technical College is the only technical college in the Vermont State Colleges system. Most of the 1,650 students enrolled come from Vermont and the other New England states.

Through its bachelor's, associate, and certificate programs, the College provides students with a broad-based, practical education. As a result, Vermont Tech graduates are prepared to work effectively in a variety of positions, such as engineers, technicians, managers, and nurses. Degrees offered in the allied health fields of nursing, dental hygiene, and respiratory therapy prepare students to assume medical positions operating on the frontline of patient care.

The Randolph Campus has more than 544-acres including a Student Health and Physical Education (SHAPE) facility with a double-court gymnasium; a six-lane indoor pool; two racquetball courts; a brand-new, state-of-the-art fitness center; and a wireless café/lounge. The four residence halls can house more than 600 students, and additional housing is available at the College's Williston campus, just minutes from Burlington, Vermont. Every student room has connections for direct access to the campuswide computer network, telephone service, and cable TV lines.

Campus life at Vermont Tech includes sports, recreation, social events, and community service-learning opportunities. The Student Life Office arranges weekly activities and social events and provides students with support and counseling. There are many student clubs, from the student-run radio station WVTC-FM to student chapters of professional organizations. There is also an on-campus ski hill, where students can snowboard and ski after classes conclude for the day.

Students enthusiastically participate in the College's varsity and intramural sports clubs. Fall varsity sports include men's and women's cross-country and soccer. In the winter, the men's and women's basketball teams take the court. Varsity athletic programs are well-supported at Vermont Tech.

Vermont Tech maintains a national affiliation with the United States Collegiate Athletic Association (USCAA) Vermont Tech athletes compete in the Yankee Small College Conference (YSCC). The College has a rich history of athletic success, with many conference championships in various sports to its credit.

The College is accredited by the New England Association of Schools and Colleges. In addition, the following degree programs are accredited by the Technology Accreditation Commission of the Accreditation Board for Engineering and Technology, Inc. (TAC of ABET): architectural and building engineering technology, architectural engineering technology, civil and environmental engineering technology, computer engineering technology, electrical engineering technology, electromechanical engineering technology, and mechanical engineering technology. The veterinary technology program is accredited by the American Veterinary Medical Association as a program for educating veterinary technicians. Practical nursing programs are approved by the Vermont Board of Nursing and accredited by the National League for Nursing Accrediting Commission (NLNAC). The associate degree program in nursing is approved by the Vermont Board of Nursing. The dental hygiene program is accredited by the American Dental Association Commission on Dental Accreditation (CODA), and the respiratory therapy program is accredited by the Committee on Accreditation of Respiratory Care Programs (CoARC).

Location

Vermont Tech has two residential campuses in Randolph Center and Williston, Vermont. Each campus offers a wide variety of majors and lifestyle choices ranging from suburban to rural. Vermont Tech's

Randolph Center is rural but far from isolated—exit 4 off Interstate 89 is just 1 mile away. For day-to-day needs, the nearby village of Randolph offers a variety of shops and restaurants as well as a movie theater, a bowling alley, and the Chandler Music Hall. For special shopping and events, Burlington and Montpelier, Vermont, and Hanover, New Hampshire, are within an hour's drive. Boston and Montreal are just 3 hours away. In addition, there is convenient bus and train service in Randolph.

Vermont Tech's Williston campus is just minutes from downtown Burlington. More than 500 students take advantage of Williston's bachelor's, associate, and certificate programs. In addition to engineering and computer technology other majors offered on the Williston campus are dental hygiene, respiratory therapy, and professional pilot technology.

Students enjoy the variety of recreational activities available to them in Vermont. Some of the top ski resorts in the East are less than an hour from the campus. Students can also hike on the Appalachian Trail, canoe on numerous lakes and rivers, camp in the Green Mountain National Forest, and bike on the miles of country roads.

Majors and Degrees

Vermont Technical College offers a Bachelor of Science degree in architectural engineering technology, business technology and management, computer engineering technology, construction management, dental hygiene, diversified agriculture, electro-mechanical engineering technology, equine studies, fire and emergency services (proposed), information technology, software engineering, professional pilot technology, and sustainable design and technology.

Vermont Tech offers four programs leading to the Associate in Engineering degree: civil and environmental engineering technology, computer engineering technology, electrical engineering technology, and mechanical engineering technology.

Programs leading to the Associate in Applied Science degree include agribusiness management technology, architectural and building engineering technology, automotive technology, business technology and management, construction management, dairy farm management technology, diesel power technology, fire science, general engineering technology, landscape development and ornamental horticulture, and veterinary technology.

Programs leading to the Associate in Science degree include dental hygiene, information technology, nursing, respiratory therapy, and software engineering. The nursing programs (certificate, associate, and bachelor's degree) offered by Vermont Tech are located several locations throughout Vermont, including Bennington, Brattleboro, and Williston, as well as on the College's main campus in Randolph Center.

Academic Programs

Whether preparing for an associate or a bachelor's degree, Vermont Tech students receive a rigorous broad-based education centered on a core curriculum that includes both technical and general education electives. The number of credits required for graduation ranges from 65 to 72 for the associate degree and from 130 to 139 for the bachelor's degree, depending on the program. Honors courses are offered in all engineering technology programs. Most degree programs also offer project courses, in which students work as teams on real-world applications in their fields of study.

Academic Facilities

Vermont Tech students learn in modern laboratories with state-of-the-art equipment. Hartness Library is the on-campus library, serving about 3,000 on-campus, extended-campus, and distance education students of Vermont Tech and the Community College of Vermont. Open more than 80 hours per week during the academic year, Hartness houses an extensive collection of material and offers professional staff assistance with library research and information literacy skills. A library website (http://www.vctclib.org) gives access to thousands of full-text periodicals and reference databases. Students can request books 24 hours per day.

Facilities housed in the major academic buildings include four computer-aided drafting and design labs (one 13-station, one 19-station, and two 21-station); four 21-station general academic computing labs; an 8-station electrical/electronic lab; recently renovated mechanical labs that include computer numerically controlled equipment and computer-aided manufacturing software; state-of-the-art veterinary technology facilities, including a 12-station lab area, a radiography suite and darkroom, and a surgery suite; a biotechnology lab with instrumentation typical of the most modern research labs; a nursing lab with a dedicated computer room and nursing station; two civil engineering labs; architectural drafting studios; a campuswide microcomputer network with Internet access; four instrumented electronics labs; and a fully equipped automotive technology center with the latest in computerized diagnostics. Facilities at the College's Williston campus include an 8,400-square-foot dental hygiene clinic that features twenty-two dental operatories, four radiographic units, a dedicated classroom, faculty offices, and a patient reception area.

Agriculture students gain practical experience at the College's dairy facility, where a main free-stall barn houses a milking herd of 80 registered Holsteins. Students have the opportunity to participate in all aspects of the farm's management. Veterinary technology students work with several species of domestic animals in the livestock facility on the farm. Conant Hall houses most of the College's academic support services. Students visit the support services offices to sign up for tutoring, meet with counselors to discuss personal or academic issues, or visit the career/transfer center to update their resumes and explore career options and internship opportunities. Students with learning differences can find out about classroom accommodations and assistive technologies at the College's Center for Academic Success. The center offers drop-in and scheduled tutoring, supplemental instruction, study groups, and review sessions; the General Education Department's Writing and Communication Center is on the same floor and provides students with help in reading, writing, oral presentations, study skills, and assistive-technology training.

Costs

Tuition for 2012–13 was $11,088 per year for Vermont residents and $21,192 for out-of-state students. The yearly room rate was $5,232, and the annual meal plan was $3,554. Other required annual fees totaled $936. An additional $2,133 health insurance fee was required of students not covered by another medical plan. New students were assessed a $320 matriculation fee. Many of Vermont Tech's programs are available at reduced tuition to New England

students through the New England Regional Student Program, sponsored by the New England Board of Higher Education.

Financial Aid

About 80 percent of Vermont Tech students receive financial aid from federal, state, and campus-based sources. There are a growing number of institutional scholarships available, including the Vermont Technical College Scholars Program, as well as work-study opportunities. Prospective students seeking aid must file the Free Application for Federal Student Aid (FAFSA). Some state agencies may require additional information. Students are urged to apply for financial aid by the March 1 priority deadline so awards can be announced by May. However, applications are reviewed on a rolling basis after March 1 until available funds are exhausted. The Vermont Tech website provides more financial aid information.

Faculty

The College's excellence in instruction is a direct result of the quality of the faculty at Vermont Tech. More than 115 full- and part-time faculty members bring a special blend of industrial experience and teaching expertise to the College. Almost all have advanced degrees. Students are assured of individual attention as a result of the 11:1 student-faculty ratio.

Admission Requirements

Each applicant receives individual consideration for admission based on receipt and review of the official secondary school transcript, letters of recommendation, proof of high school graduation or a high school equivalency diploma, and SAT scores. A personal interview is strongly recommended for all applicants. Because of the technical nature of the curriculum, applicants should have a strong math and science aptitude.

Application and Information

Vermont Technical College follows a rolling admission policy, but timely application is recommended. Applicants are notified of their status within two weeks of receipt of their completed application and supporting documents. For more information on Vermont Technical College, students should contact:

Office of Admissions
Vermont Technical College
P.O. Box 500
Randolph Center, Vermont 05061
Phone: 802-728-1000
　　　　800-442-VTC-1 (admissions, toll-free)
Fax: 802-728-1321
E-mail: admissions@vtc.edu
Website: http://www.vtc.edu

The high-tech campus of Vermont Technical College is situated in a scenic New England village in the heart of Vermont.

VILLANOVA UNIVERSITY
VILLANOVA, PENNSYLVANIA

The University

Since 1842, Villanova University's Augustinian Catholic intellectual tradition has been the cornerstone of an academic community in which students learn to think critically, act compassionately, and succeed while serving others. There are more than 10,000 undergraduate, graduate, and law students in the College of Liberal Arts and Sciences, the Villanova School of Business, the College of Engineering, the College of Nursing, and the Villanova University School of Law. As students grow intellectually, Villanova prepares them to become ethical leaders who create positive change everywhere life takes them.

Villanova offers more than 50 rigorous academic programs, and there are 265 student organizations and 36 national honor societies on campus. Undergraduate full-time enrollment is 6,853; total University enrollment is 10,626.

Located just 12 miles (20 kilometers) west of Philadelphia, Villanova's picturesque campus has 65 buildings, including 26 residence halls. Award-winning dining services are available in 3 residence dining halls and 16 à la carte eateries, all with many culinary options. Students have access to several athletic and fitness facilities on campus; the newest is the Davis Center for Athletics, with state-of-the-art cardio machines, weight equipment, and free weights. Group exercise classes, including yoga and Pilates, are also offered regularly. Villanova has forty-four club and intramural sports on campus, and nearly 20 percent of the student body participates in varsity or club athletics.

To help facilitate the transition to college life, first-year students are encouraged to join a themed Learning Community. Community members live in the same residence halls, take their year-long Augustine and Culture Seminar together, and participate in co-curricular activities. These activities typically include lectures, plays, themed dinners, rich cultural events, and engaging trips. Through Learning Communities, students often form deeper, often lifelong, relationships with their classmates and professors, and become more fully engaged in their studies.

Location

Villanova students reap all the benefits of living within the beautiful and tranquil Philadelphia Main Line suburbs, while the University's convenient proximity to Philadelphia also provides endless opportunities to complement campus life with cultural, recreational, and social activities found only in a vibrant, major metropolitan area. Whether it's visiting world-class art and science museums, touring historic sites, sampling the impressive restaurant scene, browsing through countless stores and shops, or cheering on local professional sports teams, there is something for everyone to enjoy.

Majors and Degrees

Villanova's College of Liberal Arts and Sciences grants a Bachelor of Arts in Arab and Islamic Studies, Art History, Classical Studies, Communication, Criminal Justice, Cultural Studies, Economics, English, Environmental Studies, French and Francophone Studies, Gender and Women's Studies, Geography, Global Interdisciplinary Studies, History, Honors, Humanities, Italian, Latin American Studies, Philosophy, Political Science, Psychology, Secondary Education, Sociology, Spanish Studies, and Theology and Religious Studies. The college grants a Bachelor of Science in Astronomy and Astrophysics, Biochemistry, Biology, Chemistry, Comprehensive Science, Computer Science, Environmental Science, Honors, Mathematics and Statistics, and Physics.

Villanova School of Business (VSB) offers a Bachelor of Business Administration in Accountancy, Economics, Finance, Management,

Management Information Systems, and Marketing. VSB also offers co-majors in International Business and Real Estate.

Through the College of Engineering, Villanova grants a Bachelor of Science in Chemical Engineering, Civil Engineering, Computer Engineering, Electrical Engineering, and Mechanical Engineering.

Villanova offers a Bachelor of Science in Nursing through the College of Nursing and also offers the following Health Science Affiliation programs: Drexel University College of Medicine, Doctor of Medicine; University of Pennsylvania School of Dental Medicine, Doctor of Dental Medicine; Pennsylvania College of Optometry at Salus University, Doctor of Optometry; and Jefferson College of Health Professions of Thomas Jefferson University, Doctor of Physical Therapy, and a Master of Science in Occupational Therapy.

Accelerated bachelor's/master's degree programs are available in the following areas: Accountancy, Biology, Chemical Engineering, Chemistry, Civil Engineering, Classical Studies, Communication, Computer Engineering, Computer Science, Computer Science/Software Engineering, Electrical Engineering, Finance, Hispanic Studies, Liberal Studies, Mathematics, Mathematics/Applied Statistics, Mechanical Engineering, Nursing, Physics, Political Science, Psychology, Psychology and Human Resource Development, Secondary Education, Spanish Studies, and Theology and Religious Studies.

Academic Programs

Villanova, through the College of Liberal Arts and Sciences, is one of the few institutions in the country that offers an undergraduate program in Astronomy and Astrophysics, and one of only 18 Catholic colleges or universities in the nation to have a chapter of Phi Beta Kappa, the prestigious liberal arts and sciences honor society. It also is home to the Waterhouse Institute for the Study of Communication and Society—the only institute of its kind in the United States—which provides students with opportunities to explore the ethical dimensions of communication.

Highly ranked nationally, the Villanova School of Business is home to the Applied Finance Lab, where students have access to many of the real-time technologies available to Wall Street traders. The Clay Center at VSB assists students with important decisions regarding course selections, major and minors, and international experiences, and it helps coordinate internships and co-ops, which often lead to full-time job offers.

The College of Engineering, ranked among the best engineering programs in the nation, is home to three research units: the Center for Advanced Communications, the Center for Nonlinear Dynamics and Control, and the Center for the Advancement of Sustainability in Engineering. The Villanova Center for Engineering Education and Research houses state-of-the-art instructional and research labs, including the new Multidisciplinary Design Lab, and the 10,000-square-foot Structural Engineering Teaching and Research Laboratory offers additional engineering-related facilities.

The College of Nursing, designated a Center for Excellence in Nursing Education by the National League for Nursing, is housed in an advanced facility that features a 200-seat auditorium and a 200-seat lecture hall; future-oriented clinical simulation labs for health assessment, adult health, maternal/child health, anesthesia, and critical care; simulation labs for standardized patient observation and testing; a center for nursing research and scholarship; places for prayer and reflection; space for global health studies and international student activities; and areas for student, faculty, and alumni events and social interaction.

Naval and Marine Reserve Officers Training Corps (ROTC) programs are available on campus. Villanova has had an NROTC program for more than 50 years, and it is structured to complement a normal college lifestyle. Midshipmen are encouraged to participate fully in their academic programs as well as in extracurricular activities.

Off-Campus Programs

Villanova has a rich study-abroad program. Each year, approximately 750 students take advantage of international study opportunities in nearly 40 nations, including Ireland, Switzerland, Peru, England, France, Germany, Italy, China, Chile, Russia, Poland, Thailand, Spain, Australia, Rwanda, the West Indies, Madagascar, and Samoa.

Academic Facilities

Villanova's state-of-the-art classrooms and labs are complemented with a vast array of learning and career resources. Falvey Memorial Library contains more than 1,000,000 items and offers access to numerous databases. The Office of Learning Support Services assists students with learning disabilities, neurologically based disorders, and chronic illnesses. The Villanova Career Center helps students set and reach their professional development goals. Ninety-seven percent of the Villanova Class of 2012 was employed full-time or enrolled in graduate school within six months of degree completion. Approximately 5,000 jobs are posted on Villanova's job boards each year, and the average starting salary for recent graduates is $52,958.

Technology is widely available at Villanova. All residence halls are connected to the campus network. Students can participate in learning experiences across campus; receive curricular advising services; and access tests, webcasts, and library reserves online. Through Villanova's student portal, they can keep track of deadlines, class schedules, and financial aid information. Villanova's technology also provides easy access to meal plans, parking registration, laundry reservations, voting processes, ride sharing/carpooling, and basketball ticket lotteries. Students and parents can also sign up for NOVA Alert, the University's emergency notification system.

Costs

For the 2012–13 academic year, the average tuition was $42,150, and room and board were $11,393.

Financial Aid

For the 2012–13 freshman class, 73 percent of those who applied for need-based assistance were eligible to receive it, and 81 percent of those eligible for need-based assistance received Villanova Grants. More than $16.8 million in Villanova Grants were awarded, with an average award amount of $24,300. The average assistance package for students with demonstrated need (combining grants, scholarships, loans, and student employment) was $34,108.

Villanova offers a Presidential Scholarship program to attract academic, civic, and cultural leaders who represent diverse intellectual, social, racial, and economic backgrounds, including students from families in which few or no members have attended college. Successful candidates are awarded this renewable scholarship—which covers tuition, general fee, room and board, and books—for eight consecutive semesters.

Faculty

Villanova has 598 full-time faculty members; nearly 90 percent of them hold doctoral degrees. The student-to-faculty ratio is 12:1 and the average class size is 22.

Student Government

Empowering the Villanova student body since 1925, the Student Government Association (SGA) has three branches (administrative, community, and student relations) and twelve committees. The SGA provides opportunities for student leaders to serve the Villanova community as liaisons, representatives, and student senators.

Admission Requirements

Admission to Villanova is competitive. In addition to attracting academically talented, well-rounded students, Villanova seeks applicants who are compassionate and want to transform the world and make it a better place.

Villanova is a Common Application member institution. Prospective students are also required to complete the Villanova Supplement for Undergraduate Admission and submit an official high school transcript and Common Application School Report. Applicants must have their standardized test scores (SAT or ACT) reported directly by the College Board or ACT.

In the Villanova admissions process, high school performance is an extremely important selectivity factor. Each student's high school record, GPA, and class rank, along with each student's demonstration of character and personal abilities, are carefully considered. Extracurricular and volunteer activities are helpful to applicants in this regard. Another important factor is the personal essay. Since interviews are not part of the admission process, a well-crafted essay is essential for prospective students to explain who they are and why they should be selected to become Villanovans. (A recommendation from the secondary school counselor is also carefully considered.)

Prospective students who are not from the United States are encouraged to apply for admission to Villanova. Non-native English speakers must take the TOEFL or IELTS evaluations and have scores reported directly from the College Board. Villanova's International Student Services Office supports enrolled international students in areas including immigration rights and responsibilities; educational, social, and personal counseling; cultural adjustment issues; and campus and community activities.

Transferring to Villanova is possible, but selective. A completed transfer application, official transcripts from each postsecondary school attended, and a completed Dean of Students Transfer Evaluation form are required.

Application and Information

The deadline for early action and health affiliation program applications is November 1; regular decision deadline is January 7.

Villanova Office of University Admission
800 Lancaster Avenue
Villanova, Pennsylvania 19085-1672
Phone: 610-519-4000
Fax: 610-519-6450
E-mail: gotovu@villanova.edu
Website: http://www.villanova.edu

St. Thomas of Villanova Church, Villanova University.

WALSH UNIVERSITY
NORTH CANTON, OHIO

The University

Walsh University is a fully accredited, liberal arts and sciences Catholic university in North Canton, Ohio, offering fifty-five majors, seven graduate programs, and an accelerated-degree program for working adults. With 2,963 students and a 15:1 student-faculty ratio, the University offers a very friendly, supportive, and safe campus and a unique broad-based curriculum with close student-faculty interaction. Most residence halls and academic buildings on Walsh's 136-acre campus are new or have been renovated within the last several years, providing state-of-the-art facilities for students. Walsh also offers generous financial aid packages to 95 percent of full-time students.

Active and involved in campus and community life, more than 60 percent of Walsh students participate in extracurricular programs. Students also have the opportunity to participate in a variety of intramural sports. Walsh also offers seventeen intercollegiate sports including football, baseball, soccer, and volleyball. Walsh has been accepted into the NCAA Division II membership process and expects to have full standing before the end of the 2013 calendar year.

Walsh University welcomes students from around the world of all faiths and backgrounds. The University currently has students from numerous countries and looks forward to continued growth.

Walsh University was founded in 1960 by the Brothers of Christian Instruction and is accredited by the North Central Association/Higher Learning Commission, National League for Nursing Accrediting Commission, Ohio Department of Education, Ohio Board of Counseling and Social Work, American Physical Therapy Association, the Commission on Accreditation in Physical Therapy Education, Council for Accreditation of Counseling and Related Educational Programs, and the National Council for Accreditation of Teacher Education. Walsh is a member of the Ohio College Association, the National Association of Independent Colleges and Universities, and the Association of Catholic Colleges and Universities.

In addition to its undergraduate degree programs, Walsh offers seven graduate degree programs that include a twelve-month M.B.A., a Master of Science in Nursing, Master of Arts in Counseling and Human Development, Master of Arts in Education (M.A.Ed.), Master of Arts in Theology, Doctor of Nursing Practice (D.N.P.), and a Doctor of Physical Therapy.

Location

Walsh University has a beautiful, tree-lined campus located just 3 miles east of I-77 in North Canton, a safe, pleasant residential suburban community. Canton, which is about 5 miles south of the Walsh campus, is a city of 84,000 that offers a wide array of cultural, recreational, and athletic activities. Home of the Professional Football Hall of Fame, the President McKinley National Memorial, and the National First Ladies Library, the city also hosts a symphony orchestra, an art museum, and a civic opera, theater guild, and ballet. A number of major companies are headquartered in Stark County, including the Hoover Company, the Timken Company, and Diebold, Inc. Walsh also has satellite campuses in Medina, Canfield, and Akron, Ohio; Kisube, Uganda; and Castel Gandolfo, Italy just outside of Rome.

Majors and Degrees

Bachelor of Arts and Bachelor of Science degrees are offered in the following majors: accounting (general and specialized CPA tracks), bioinformatics, biology, chemistry, clinical laboratory science, communication, comprehensive science, computer science, corporate communication, criminal justice–sociology, education (early childhood, middle childhood, adolescence to young adulthood, integrated language arts, integrated mathematics teacher licensure, integrated science teacher licensure, integrated social studies teacher, intervention specialist, life science/biology teacher licensure, life science/biology and chemistry teacher licensure, multiage physical education, and physical education), English, environmental science, exercise science, family studies–sociology, finance, French, general business, general studies, global business, graphic design, history, international relations, management, management information systems, marketing, mathematics, museum studies, nursing, philosophy/theology, physical education, political science, psychology, psychology–community/clinical, research methods and data analysis–sociology, and Spanish.

Walsh offers preprofessional programs in dentistry, law, medicine, natural resources, occupational therapy, optometry, pharmacy, physical therapy, podiatry, and veterinary science. Each is developed within the context of a regular academic major. Walsh's physical therapy graduates have the option to continue their studies by entering Walsh's newly accredited Doctor of Physical Therapy degree program. Students enrolled in the University's B.A./M.A. program can earn a bachelor's degree in behavioral science and a master's degree in counseling and human development in 5½ years. An affiliation with Case Western Reserve University's (CWRU) program in dentistry leads to a B.S. from Walsh and ultimately a D.D.S. from CWRU.

In addition, Walsh offers the Associate of Arts degree in accounting, finance, human services, liberal arts, management, and marketing.

Academic Programs

The student's academic program comprises courses within the liberal arts, a major field of study, and elective courses. Major course work, constituting one fourth or more of a student's program of studies, is designed to help students prepare for their careers. Forty percent of a student's program of studies is within the liberal arts. Elective courses, which constitute the remaining portion of a student's program of studies, enable students to develop personal interests, take more courses within their major field, or enroll in additional core courses. The University encourages students to give careful thought to selecting a program of study and a major. While many students select double majors as a way to improve their career opportunities, the design of individual programs requires consultation with a faculty adviser and a division chair. To earn a bachelor's degree, students must successfully complete 130 semester hours.

Designed for the academically gifted, the honors program offers challenges that lead students to achieve academic excellence. Honors students take advantage of such offerings as special seminars, independent studies, internships, and research projects.

Students in Walsh's global learning program may choose to study for a semester or a summer at the University's Rome campus, Tanzania, Uganda, or many other international locations through Walsh's partnership with CCSA. The University's School for Professional Studies Program is for working adults who have earned college credits and who wish to earn their bachelor's degree in an accelerated format. Classes are scheduled on nights and weekends to accommodate busy schedules.

Academic Facilities

The Walsh Library contains 141,000 volumes, 270 current periodical subscriptions on paper, and 41,071 electronically. Databases bring many full-text articles immediately for download or print, and information technology systems enable online requests for physical delivery of material, often via rapid courier. Library staff members give introductory lectures on research techniques. The library has a quiet study room, a snack lounge, and a mini-theater. All library resources are available via the Internet.

Faculty

Walsh University fosters close working relationships between faculty members and students. Beyond classroom teaching, faculty members serve as student counselors and tutors and take on roles as advisers for student organizations. The Walsh faculty is composed of full-time, part-time, and adjunct members. The student-faculty ratio is 15:1. The majority of full-time faculty members hold Ph.D.'s or terminal degrees in their respective fields.

Student Government

Walsh University Student Government provides capable, responsible student governance. Through its executive, legislative, and judicial branches, it fosters student involvement in the governance of the University, serves as a forum for student opinion, and functions as a liaison between students, faculty and staff members, and the administration. Along with the Student Affairs staff, it plans student activities and community projects.

Costs

Tuition for the 2012–13 academic year was $23,550. Tuition, fees, and room and board charges total approximately $33,980 per year and vary by residence hall. Books and personal expenses cost an estimated $700–$900 for the year. The University reserves the right to change the cost structure without notice.

Financial Aid

Walsh is dedicated to providing outstanding liberal arts education at an affordable price. The primary purpose of Walsh University's financial aid program is to assist deserving students who cannot otherwise meet the costs of a college education. Financial aid takes the form of scholarships, work-study awards, grants, or loans, depending upon the resources available. The University offers a number of scholarships in amounts from $1,500 to full tuition, in addition to institutional need-based grants. The Alumni Association offers scholarships as well. State and federal grants and loans are available to students along with the University's work-study program that provides work compatible with a student's academic schedule. Financial aid is awarded for one year and is renewable in subsequent years if the student shows a continuing need and maintains an appropriate academic record.

Applicants for admission may apply for financial aid by submitting the Free Application for Federal Student Aid (FAFSA) and the University's financial aid form. To allow for timely notification of financial awards, the University recommends that the FAFSA be mailed by March 15 in order to receive full analysis by May 1. Prospective students may obtain a FAFSA from their high school guidance counselor or from the University's financial aid office. The Walsh financial aid form is available from the financial aid and admissions offices of the University.

Admission Requirements

Every student seeking admission to Walsh University is reviewed individually to assess the student's ability to meet the rigors of the University's curriculum. The composition of high school classes, grades achieved, class rank, and standardized test scores are all taken into consideration before an admission decision is rendered. Essays and interviews are highly recommended but not required.

Walsh grants credit for college-level work completed in high school and for credits earned through the College Level Examination Program. Qualified high school juniors and seniors may enroll for college credit under the University's postsecondary enrollment program. The University seeks a diverse student body.

Application and Information

Early application is recommended. Walsh University operates under a rolling admissions policy. The completed admission application, $25 application fee, ACT or SAT scores, and a high school transcript are required for a student's application to be considered for admission. Transfer students must also submit transcripts from all colleges and universities attended.

Interested students are encouraged to contact:

Brett Freshour
Vice President for Enrollment Management
Walsh University
2020 East Maple Street NW
North Canton, Ohio 44720-3336
Phone: 330-492-7172
   800-362-9846 (toll-free)
Fax: 330-490-7165
E-mail: admissions@walsh.edu
Website: http://www.walsh.edu
   http://www.facebook.com/walshu
   http://www.twitter.com/walshuniversity
   http://www.youtube.com/ohiowalshuniversity

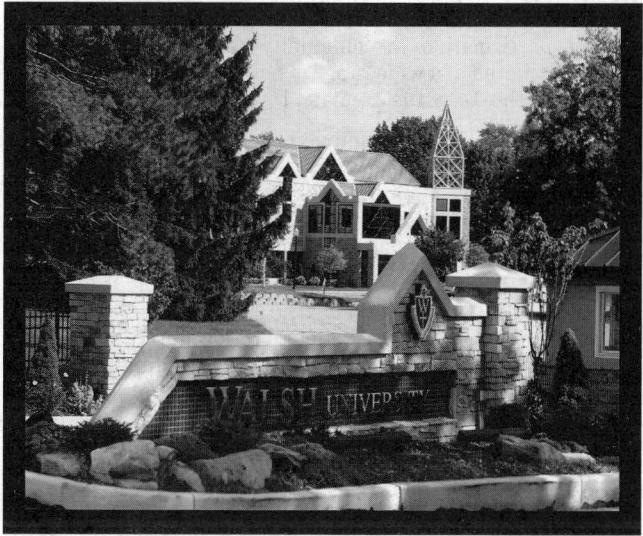

On the campus of Walsh University.

WARREN WILSON COLLEGE
ASHEVILLE, NORTH CAROLINA

The College

Warren Wilson College is distinctive among American colleges and universities. Strong environmental and international emphases enhance a learning triad of academics, work, and service. The College also is recognized as a campus leader in sustainable practices and facilities. As Samuel Schuman described Warren Wilson in his book Old Main: "Rather like Orwell's barnyard menagerie, all small colleges are unique, but some are more unique than others. [Warren Wilson's] program, emphases, population, and atmosphere are unmistakably its own."

Since its founding in 1894, Warren Wilson College has educated students with its unique blending of a strong liberal arts program, work for the College, and service to those in need—a triad that makes Warren Wilson unlike any other college. Its 900 undergraduate students come from forty-five states and twenty countries, creating a diverse and vibrant academic community.

The academic program features a first-rate faculty that does all of the teaching and frequently participates in research with students. About 85 percent of classes have fewer than 20 students, and discussion is an important part of teaching. Twenty-one majors are offered, with a commitment to quality in each program. Art, English, creative writing, biology, outdoor leadership, and the nationally recognized environmental studies program are the most popular majors.

Students at Warren Wilson are integral to the day-to-day operation of the College. Each student works 15 hours a week at a job that is essential to running the school. This experience helps build student confidence (students learn that there is no job they cannot learn to do) and a strong sense of community at the College. Many juniors and seniors have work assignments that coincide with their majors. Students receive a work stipend in the amount of $3,480 each year for the work they do.

Service is also integral to the College's way of thinking. Warren Wilson is one of only a few colleges in the country that require student participation in community service for graduation. Service is offered to a wide range of nonprofit organizations and agencies in the Asheville area and beyond.

The College's 1,100-acre campus includes a 300-acre working farm, 600 acres of managed forest, a 6-acre fruit and vegetable garden and 20 miles of hiking trails. The campus and surrounding area are havens for outdoor activities such as white-water sports, hiking, camping, mountain biking, and rock climbing.

About 90 percent of students and 30 percent of the faculty and staff members live on campus. The College offers men's and women's intercollegiate basketball, cross-country, soccer, and swimming, and its mountain bike team has finished in the top three nationally (Division II) for the past seven years. The College also offers intramural sports, a wellness program, and a wide range of outdoor programs among other activities.

Location

Warren Wilson, on the edge of the city of Asheville, North Carolina, is in the heart of the Blue Ridge Mountains. Asheville, a city of about 80,000 people, is considered one of the most livable cities in the United States and was selected by the National League of Cities as the All-America City for 1998.

Surrounded by more than 1 million acres of national forest, Asheville is located in an ideal setting, presenting views of outstanding beauty throughout all four seasons. In the spring and summer, variations in altitude together with warm southern sun favor native vegetation; dogwood, wildflowers, rhododendron, mountain laurel, and azaleas cover the mountains. The arresting beauty of the autumn colors attracts photographers, artists, and sports enthusiasts from the world over. During the winter, natural snow is enhanced by machine-made snow, producing excellent downhill skiing.

A short drive from the Warren Wilson campus are Great Smoky Mountains National Park, Pisgah National Forest, and the Blue Ridge Parkway, offering panoramic views, excellent camping facilities, and a perfect setting for class field trips.

Majors and Degrees

The bachelor's degree is awarded in art, biology, chemistry, creative writing, English, environmental studies, gender and women's studies, history and political science, global studies, integrative studies, mathematics, modern language, outdoor leadership, philosophy, psychology, religious studies, social work, and sociology/anthropology.

Academic Programs

The goal of the degree program at Warren Wilson College is the completion of three well-designed areas of study. First, students are expected to complete a core of required courses based on the theme "ways of knowing." A student earns 4 credits in each of the ten core areas. Second, students must develop a strength in one or more disciplines. A minimum of 128 semester hours is required for the baccalaureate degree, including the core plus major hours. Finally, a student must demonstrate the ability to work effectively with others by participation in the work and service programs.

There is a required freshman seminar designed to provide new students the opportunity to explore various fields. A senior seminar, designed as a capstone experience, is required, as is a senior letter to evaluate the student's college experiences.

All Warren Wilson students must demonstrate competence in writing and mathematics either through testing or by completing core courses.

Each semester in the academic calendar is broken into two 8-week terms. A student typically takes four courses per semester (3 or 4 credit hours per course).

Off-Campus Programs

In addition to academics, work, and service, all qualified students are afforded the opportunity to study abroad. The College heavily subsidizes the cost for a cross-cultural international experience taken during the junior year or summer.

Academic Facilities

The Martha Ellison Library houses a collection of 120,000 books and 450 periodicals. It provides written records in all areas of the College curriculum and contributes to the cultural enrichment of students. The library is open and served by librarians and student assistants 75 hours each week. The building provides open access to books and periodicals during these hours. Individual carrels, lounge areas, and microfilm readers and printers are available, and there are Windows and Macintosh computers that students may use as word processors or for other prescribed purposes, including access to the Internet.

Computerized literature searching is available. The Martha Ellison Library is a teaching library, providing extensive and continuing bibliographic services, including courses, for the entire student body. Any resource materials not owned by the library may be acquired through interlibrary loan.

The campus arts complex includes the modern Kittredge Theater; the Kittredge Music Wing, housing classrooms, studios, and a performance area; the Holden Arts Center, with a gallery, classrooms, studios, and a lecture hall; and an outdoor amphitheater. Instruction and performance events also take place in the chapel and the Craftshop/Ceramics Studio.

Costs

Total costs for the 2013–14 school year were $38,348. From this amount, the student's work program stipend of $3,480 is deducted, leaving an actual cost of $34,904 for each student before any other aid.

Financial Aid

Warren Wilson offers a comprehensive financial aid program that seeks to enroll students from all economic backgrounds. This is accomplished through a combination of work, loans, grants, entitlements, and scholarships to students who complete their file prior to May. Students and their families should file the FAFSA and the Warren Wilson Financial Aid Application to be considered for all possible funds.

Faculty

The teaching faculty consists of 70 full-time members. Of these, 93 percent hold doctoral degrees. All classes and labs are taught by faculty members, not graduate students. Faculty members—1 for every 12 students—are available after class, during regular office hours, and in their homes.

Student Government

The student body is involved in the democratic decision-making process of the College. A wide variety of leadership positions, elected and appointed, are open to students. Campuswide elections provide opportunities for student involvement in Student Caucus, Judicial Board and other College advisory committees. Student Caucus, the representative voice of the student body, is also responsible for appointing students to positions on approximately fifteen other campus committees ranging from Admission to Library to Buildings and Grounds.

Admission Requirements

Admission to Warren Wilson College is based on both the personal and the academic qualifications of the applicant.

The selection criteria are devised to choose a student body with high standards of scholarship and personal goals and a willingness to provide community service.

Each candidate for admission must present an academic transcript from a secondary school. The transcript must show at least 12 academic units (a unit is one year's study in one subject). At least 4 years of English, 2 years of algebra, 1 year of geometry, 2 years of laboratory science, and 2 years of history are recommended for admission. Performance during high school is the best predictor of success in college. Therefore, great emphasis is placed upon the high school record. Grade trends can be very important.

Applicants must submit a recommendation from their high school counselor and scores from the SAT or ACT. Students are also required to submit a personal essay. The College participates in the Common Application process.

Transfer students must present both high school and college transcripts. Transfer applicants must be in good standing with the college last attended and should also have a minimum 2.75 cumulative grade point average. At least one school year in residence at Warren Wilson is required for a transfer student to be eligible for a degree from Warren Wilson College.

There is no fee to apply for admission to Warren Wilson College.

Application and Information

An application form and further information may be obtained by contacting:

Office of Admission
Warren Wilson College
P.O. Box 9000
Asheville, North Carolina 28815-9000
Phone: 800-934-3536 (toll-free)
E-mail: admit@warren-wilson.edu
Website: http://www.warren-wilson.edu

In the heart of the Blue Ridge Mountains, the entrance to Warren Wilson College's valley is a sight that students long remember.

WEBB INSTITUTE
GLEN COVE, NEW YORK

The Institute

Webb Institute was founded in 1889 to provide an opportunity for worthy young students to obtain an education in the "art and science of designing ships and their propulsion systems." The Institute has followed this basic objective to the present, and its graduates are active throughout the United States in the ship design, ship construction, yacht design, and marine operations industries and in appropriate government offices.

The 26-acre campus is the former estate of Herbert L. Pratt and is located on Long Island Sound. Because of the Institute's small size and intensive academic program, varsity sports are limited. However, Webb participates in intercollegiate basketball, cross-country, sailing, soccer, tennis, and volleyball, for which ample facilities are provided. The campus has a gymnasium, tennis courts, playing fields, and a beach. Golf and swimming facilities are available nearby.

Webb Institute maintains an enrollment that ranges from 70 to 90 students who come from all over the world and all of whom live on campus.

Location

Glen Cove is a city of more than 25,000 residents and is located on Long Island's North Shore, which is nearly an hour from New York City. Convenient train service from Glen Cove to New York brings the variety of cultural, educational, and recreational activities available in the city within easy reach of Webb students.

Majors and Degrees

Webb Institute offers an engineering program in ship design, which involves both naval architecture and marine engineering. The undergraduate degree awarded is the Bachelor of Science in naval architecture and marine engineering.

Academic Programs

The engineering program in ship design consists of fundamental foundation courses in mathematics, science, and engineering sciences, capped by extensive professional design courses. A coherent program in humanities supplements the technical program to round out undergraduate education.

In addition, students have a two-month, cooperative job experience each year in the U.S. marine and maritime industry. During this period, freshmen work as helper mechanics in shipyards, sophomores obtain seagoing experience aboard ship, and juniors and seniors work as engineering assistants in design and technical offices of various marine firms. This important part of the program provides excellent articulation of the educational and career experiences. Innovative engineering ideas are encouraged in the thesis required during the last year. The program is fully accredited. Graduates are well equipped to pursue postgraduate studies.

Semesters run from late August to mid-December and from late February to late June. January and February are winter work periods, and the period from late June to late August is designated for vacation.

Academic Facilities

Full laboratory support is provided for chemistry, physics, metallurgy, and various engineering courses. A ship-model testing tank is available for ship and boat hull studies. Computer facilities are provided on campus. The Livingston Library contains extensive holdings in naval architecture, marine engineering, and general engineering, as well as collections in literature, arts, social sciences, and music.

Costs

All U.S. citizens and green card holders admitted to Webb are accepted on a tuition-and-fee-free basis (full scholarship). For non-citizens, the tuition fee for the 2013–14 year is

$42,750. Room and Board costs are $13,750. Nearly $800 per year is required for books and supplies. A $150 room deposit fee is payable on entry and refunded, less any breakage costs, on departure. The Student Organization requires a $100 deposit on entry, also refundable on departure.

Financial Aid

As stated, a full scholarship that covers tuition and fees is awarded to all accepted candidates who are U.S. citizens or green card holders. The winter work co-op in industry provides income for students that significantly assists in covering other expenses. Supplementary aid opportunities are available through the Federal Pell Grant, Federal Stafford Student Loans, and in-house grant programs. Students requiring financial assistance must submit the Free Application for Federal Student Aid (FAFSA) after March 31 but not later than July 1 of the year of entry.

Faculty

Webb Institute has a highly qualified faculty. Many members possess engineering licenses and engage in sponsored research programs, consult for commercial firms, and research and write technical papers. Classes are limited to 25 students, and the student-faculty ratio is 8:1. Each student is assigned a faculty adviser, and consultation with individual faculty members is encouraged.

Student Government

The Student Organization is highly active in student administrative, social, and educational affairs. It is supplemented by an Honor Council and honor system. Together, these entities provide students with a high degree of responsibility for ordering and conducting student life.

Admission Requirements

Admission to Webb is highly competitive. The qualifying requirements for admission are graduation from high school with a B+ (87) or better average in 16 credits of basic high school subjects. Admission selections are based on high school standing (generally in the upper 10 percent) and scores on the College Board's SAT and Subject Tests in Mathematics (Level 1 or 2), and Physics or Chemistry.

The final selection follows a personal interview conducted at Webb or at a location convenient to the applicant. The entering class is usually restricted to 25 freshmen.

All application papers must be submitted by February 15, and all required College Board tests must be taken before that date. Advanced placement is not given in any of the course offerings. Campus visits by interested students are strongly recommended; prior appointments must be made. An early decision plan is available for qualified candidates.

Webb Institute does not discriminate in admission in the areas of gender, race, or religion. Academic qualities and career motivation are the only criteria.

Application and Information

For a catalog and application forms, students may contact:

Office of Admissions
Webb Institute
Glen Cove, New York 11542
Phone: 516-671-2213, Ext. 107
E-mail: admissions@webb-institute.edu
Web site: http://www.webb-institute.edu

The academic facilities of Webb Institute are located on Long Island Sound in the former residence of Herbert L. Pratt.

WELLS COLLEGE
AURORA, NEW YORK

Wells College

The College

Wells College is ranked among the nation's top liberal arts colleges that offer high-quality education at an affordable price and has one of the most beautiful campuses in the United States. The College was established in 1868 by Henry Wells, who also founded the Wells Fargo and American Express companies.

At Wells, professors are dedicated to teaching, and because of the intimate nature of the campus community (the student body is 600), they get to know their students as individuals in and outside the classroom. Students frequently collaborate with their professors on original research and creative projects. At most other schools, these opportunities are only available to graduate students. Because faculty members at Wells know their students so well, they are especially effective advisers and mentors. Therefore, Wells students have a competitive edge entering careers and top graduate and professional schools.

Another aspect of the Wells tradition is hands-on learning. In addition to dynamic classroom teaching, Wells students have a variety of other experiential opportunities: internships, service, study abroad, and off-campus study. Professors encourage students to apply theory in practical settings and to discover what they want to do in life through involvement.

Wells currently fields intercollegiate teams at the NCAA Division III level in men's and women's cross-country, field hockey, men's and women's lacrosse, men's and women's soccer, softball, men's and women's swimming, men's and women's basketball, men's and women's golf, men's and women's volleyball, and women's tennis. There are also a number of intramural opportunities, including basketball, soccer, swimming, skiing, tennis, and volleyball. Athletic facilities include indoor and outdoor tennis courts, a gymnasium, a newly renovated fitness center, a nine-hole golf course, and a campus boathouse and dock used in teaching sailing, canoeing, and lifeguarding.

Wells has a full range of active student organizations, including a literary magazine and newspaper, music and drama groups, environmental and political organizations, and abundant opportunities for community service, among others. A busy calendar of cultural events, symposia, and lectures enhances the academic and social life of the College.

Location

Wells is located in the village of Aurora on the eastern shore of Cayuga Lake—part of New York's scenic Finger Lakes region. The area is well known for its high concentration of prestigious colleges and universities, including Cornell University, Ithaca College, Hobart and William Smith Colleges, Colgate University, Hamilton College, and Syracuse University. Aurora is 25 miles from Ithaca and 60 miles from both Rochester and Syracuse. Students have abundant opportunities for outdoor recreation and sports, including sailing, swimming, horseback riding, skiing, and hiking.

Majors and Degrees

Wells offers majors and concentrations in African American studies, American cultures, American studies, anthropology, art history, biochemistry and molecular biology, biology, chemistry, computer science, creative writing, dance, economics and management, English, environmental policies and values, environmental science, ethics and philosophy, government and politics, history, international studies, literature, management, mathematics, performing arts, physics, psychology, sociology, Spanish, studio art, theater and dance, visual arts, and women and gender studies. Students also have the option of a self-designed major. In addition, they can choose minors from a list of more than thirty programs.

Wells has also added an innovative Center for Business and Entrepreneurship, founded upon the tradition of liberal arts: learning that emphasizes critical thinking and problem solving. The role of the center is to help students build the skills and develop the discernment to know how and where they most want to serve society. As such, the center will offer students the opportunity to explore growing fields like arts administration, green businesses, not-for-profit organizations, and hospitality.

The College has pre-professional programs in dentistry, education, engineering, law, medicine, teaching, and veterinary medicine. Wells has a cross-registration agreement with nearby Ithaca College, Cayuga Community College, and Cornell University and affiliations with Cornell's engineering school.

Wells awards the Bachelor of Arts degree and has a number of programs through which students can earn their bachelor's degree at Wells and a graduate or professional degree from an affiliated university. Participating schools are Clarkson University, Columbia University, Cornell University (engineering), and the University of Rochester (business, community health, and education).

Academic Programs

All Wells students benefit from an academic environment similar to honors programs available to only a small number of students at other schools. The College has a tradition of preparing students for leadership in their chosen fields, and the breadth of knowledge they gain and the range of life experiences they encounter enable them to achieve their career goals and establish a foundation for a rich and fulfilling life.

All students entering Wells to pursue a four-year course of study leading to a bachelor's degree are required to take three themed seminars (12 semester hours) and the New Student Experience (WLLS 111). Distribution requirements are a foreign language (two courses or exemption by exam), formal reasoning (one course), arts and humanities (three courses), natural and social sciences (three courses), and physical education (four courses). Team sports and dance technique can partially satisfy requirements.

Approximately sixteen courses must be taken in the student's major, and at least six must be taken at Wells. Eighteen credit hours must be taken at the 300 level or above. A senior project or thesis and a comprehensive evaluation are required for graduation.

A student must successfully complete 120 semester hours (60 of which must be taken at Wells and through affiliated programs, such as study abroad) to be recommended by the faculty for a degree. To learn more about the academic program and requirements for transfer students, prospective students should visit the Wells College website.

Off-Campus Programs

Students can spend January term, a semester, or even a year in another college or university abroad or in the United States. Typically, Wells students choose to study off campus for a semester during the junior year, but many different possibilities are available depending on a student's academic program and interests.

The College offers affiliated study-abroad experiences in Belize, Denmark, France, Germany, Great Britain, Ireland, Italy, Japan, Mexico, Senegal, Spain, and Sweden. Currently, the three most popular programs are study abroad in Florence, Italy; Paris, France; and Seville, Spain. These off-campus study experiences are flexible as well as financially and academically accessible. After at least one semester at Wells, a student's financial aid applies to one semester of off-campus study.

Wells provides off-campus study options in the United States through its affiliations with American University, serving a wide range of academic and internship interests in Washington, D.C.; the Salt Center, offering documentary field studies in Portland, Maine; and the Public Leadership Education Network (PLEN), providing leadership development through seminars and internships in Washington, D.C. As part of the PLEN affiliation, students can spend a semester studying at the London School of Economics and Political Science and hold an internship in the British government. Through the School for Field Studies, Wells offers semester-long study-abroad experiences in Africa, Australia, the Caribbean, and other locations. The College also offers credit-bearing courses during the January term that take students to a single destination in the U.S. or abroad for intensive study that requires travel in a region or country with a faculty member.

Academic Facilities

From the contemporary elegance of Weld House to the nineteenth-century Glen Park mansion, the former home of College founder Henry Wells, the residence halls encompass enough variety to satisfy every taste. Students eat their meals together in the majestic Tudor-style dining hall in Main Building.

The Louis Jefferson Long Library has received numerous awards for its architectural design. Facilities include an online computer center, individual study carrels, seminar and group-study rooms, and an art gallery. There are department libraries in art, economics, English, mathematics, music, philosophy, and the sciences located across the campus.

The Barler Hall of Music houses a recital hall with superb acoustics, vocal and instrumental practice rooms, a music library, and a listening laboratory. Facilities for printmaking, painting, ceramics, sculpture, and photography are located in the Campbell Arts Building. The Cleveland Hall of Languages contains state-of-the-art equipment for learning foreign languages. Stratton Science Hall, completed in 2007, houses state-of-the-art laboratories for chemistry, biology, environmental science, and physics as well as a computer laboratory. Morgan Hall houses the Book Arts Center and the Wells College Press. Macmillan Hall has classrooms, faculty and administrative offices, several computer laboratories, and department libraries. The east wing of Macmillan contains the Margaret Phipps Auditorium, a theater facility used for teaching, concerts, lectures, and dramatic productions.

Costs

Wells has a long-term commitment to providing talented students with access to the best education, which requires offering excellence at an affordable price. Wells is ranked among the best liberal arts colleges in the nation, yet the cost of a Wells education is considerably less than the tuition charged by comparable schools.

The cost of a Wells education for the 2012–13 academic year was $33,200 for tuition, $11,900 for room and board, and $1,500 for fees.

Financial Aid

Approximately 90 percent of Wells students receive financial aid packaged in the form of grants, scholarships, loans, and work-study opportunities. The College works closely with students and their families to design a financial aid package that meets their needs and their budgets.

Award determinations are made on a rolling basis following acceptance. College financial aid is complex; however, Wells College's well-informed financial aid and admissions professionals are always pleased to answer questions and discuss methods of financing higher education with prospective students.

Applicants are considered for merit aid that is based largely on academic achievements and leadership abilities.

Faculty

At Wells, learning takes place in small, seminar-style classes where students are partners with faculty members in the learning process. Starting immediately in their first semester, students take classes with scholars who are recognized experts in their fields, not teaching assistants.

Nearly all Wells professors hold terminal degrees in their areas of expertise. They have been educated at the world's leading research universities, including Harvard, Yale, Columbia, Cornell, Brown, and Stanford. What students discover in Wells' classes is the importance of exploring ideas with others.

Wells is student centered, and academic programs focus on collaborative learning and teaching that meets the needs of students' different learning styles. As one would expect at a nationally recognized liberal arts college, professors are also engaged in research and a full range of scholarly activities. Their books are published by leading academic presses, their articles appear in top journals, and they are a presence at national and international conferences. Due to close faculty-student interaction, students have numerous opportunities to collaborate with faculty members on research, publications, and presentations.

Student Government

The student body is self-governing through the Collegiate Association. The three main governing bodies of the association are the Student-Faculty Administration Board, the Collegiate Council, and the Community Court. Students serve on faculty committees that make decisions concerning administrative and curricular matters.

Leadership development is an inherent part of the Wells experience, and students are encouraged to take an active role in student government and in the life of the campus community.

Admission Requirements

Wells admits students on the basis of the strength of their academic preparation. A student is expected to possess intellectual curiosity, motivation, and maturity to profit from the experience. In all cases, the College seeks students who have followed a solid college-preparatory program throughout high school.

Wells seeks students from varied backgrounds with diverse interests and talents in order to promote a stimulating learning community. Every admissions decision is made on an individual basis.

Wells students share an enthusiasm for academic pursuits and a serious intent to use their education in the future to enhance both their lives and the communities in which they choose to live.

Application and Information

Applications should be received early in the senior year of high school and not later than March 1 of the year in which entrance is desired. Applications from early decision and early action candidates must be received by December 15.

Transfer applications are reviewed on a rolling basis. Transfer students are eligible for merit scholarships and financial aid.

A campus visit is highly recommended for prospective students. For more information about Wells College or to schedule a campus visit, students should contact:

Admissions Office
Wells College
Aurora, New York 13026
Phone: 800-952-9355 (toll-free)
E-mail: admissions@wells.edu
Website: http://www.wells.edu
　　　http://www.facebook.com/wellscollege

Aerial view of Wells College.

WENTWORTH INSTITUTE OF TECHNOLOGY

BOSTON, MASSACHUSETTS

WENTWORTH
Institute of Technology

The Institute

Wentworth Institute of Technology was founded in 1904 to provide education in technology. Today, Wentworth has a current undergraduate day enrollment of approximately 3,800 men and women (3,400 full-time). The education acquired at Wentworth enables graduates to assume creative and responsible careers in business and industry. Wentworth is located on a 31-acre campus on Huntington Avenue in Boston.

Wentworth provides dormitory and suite-style residence halls on campus for men and women. Students in the residence halls are on a full meal plan with a full cafeteria, snack bar, and convenience store options on campus. Students living in a suite-style residence hall may prepare their own meals in their kitchen space.

Career counseling and placement assistance are available to all alumni and to students who have completed at least one semester of study at the Institute. While many graduates of Wentworth are employed in the Boston area, alumni have secured positions throughout the United States and abroad.

In addition to Wentworth's undergraduate programs, master's degree programs are awarded in architecture, construction management, and facility management.

Location

Boston is the educational center of New England. It is a city of charm, tradition, and elegance—a major center of art, science, music, history, medicine, and education. Wentworth is situated near the heart of Boston and is surrounded by institutions that provide the cultural advantages for which the city is famous. The Museum of Fine Arts, with its store of art treasures, is diagonally across the street, and admission is free to any student with a Wentworth ID card. Symphony Hall is just a few blocks away. The Harvard Medical School, the New England Conservatory of Music, Emmanuel College, Simmons College, Massachusetts College of Pharmacy and Health Sciences, Massachusetts College of Art and Design, Roxbury Community College, and Northeastern University are among the many educational institutions within a few blocks of the campus.

Majors and Degrees

Degree programs are offered in the fields of applied mathematics, architecture, computer science, construction management, design, engineering, engineering technology, and management. Bachelor of Science (B.S.) degrees are awarded in the following majors: applied mathematics, architecture, biomedical engineering, business management (optional concentrations in entrepreneurship or technology project management), civil engineering, computer engineering, computer engineering technology, computer information systems, computer networking, computer science, construction management, electromechanical engineering (optional concentration in biomedical systems engineering), electrical engineering, electronic engineering technology, engineering

(interdisciplinary), facility planning and management, industrial design, interior design, and mechanical engineering. Baccalaureate degrees in architecture and interior design are designated as first professional degrees. Completion of a Wentworth baccalaureate degree usually requires four years (five years for the electromechanical engineering degree, applied mathematics is a three-year program with a four-year option).

Academic Programs

At Wentworth, college-level study in technological fundamentals and principles is combined with appropriate laboratory, field, and studio experience. Students apply theory to practical problems, and they acquire skills and techniques by using, operating, and controlling equipment and instruments that are particular to their area of specialization. In addition, study in the social sciences and humanities provides a balanced understanding of the world in which graduates work. Wentworth's programs of study are more practical than theoretical in approach, and the Institute's academic requirements demand extensive time and effort.

During the first two years of study in a degree program at Wentworth, students lay the foundation for more advanced study in the third and fourth (and fifth, where applicable) years. While nearly all majors allow continuous study from the freshman through the senior year, the architecture major requires a petition for acceptance to the baccalaureate program during the sophomore year.

All bachelor's degree programs are conducted as cooperative (co-op) education programs: upon entering their third year, students alternate semesters of academic study at Wentworth with semester-long periods of employment in industry. Two semesters of co-op employment are required; one additional (summer) semester of co-op is optional. Both students and the companies that hire them are enthusiastic about the co-op program and agree that it is a mutually valuable experience.

Off-Campus Programs

Students have the option to study abroad in Wentworth's established programs in Germany and Ireland. As part of various programs and classes, Wentworth students have also traveled to many destinations, such as Nicaragua, the United Kingdom, Italy, Austria, the Czech Republic, Russia, and throughout Scandinavia.

Wentworth's membership in the Colleges of the Fenway (COF) gives students the intimacy of a small college community and the resources of a major university. The COF consortium members are Emmanuel College, Massachusetts College of Art and Design, Massachusetts College of Pharmacy and Health Sciences, Simmons College, Wentworth Institute of Technology, and Wheelock College. The consortium offers the benefits of cross-registration and access to social events, intramural teams, dance and theater troupes, a chorus and orchestra, professional activities, libraries, and campus facilities at five other colleges within walking distance of one another. The COF's Global Education Opportunities Center provides access to exchange programs and overseas institutions as well as cross-registration for faculty-led travel courses.

Academic Facilities

Wentworth's twenty-seven buildings house classrooms, studios, laboratories, administrative offices, and other facilities. Beatty Hall houses the Flanagan Campus Center, Schumann Fitness Center, Alumni Library, cafeteria, computer center, classrooms, recreation room, and office space. State-of-the-art laboratories, such as the Center for Sciences and Biomedical Engineering and the Manufacturing Center, are situated throughout the campus.

Costs

For 2013–14, tuition is $27,950, books and supplies are approximately $1,000, and the average room and board cost is about $12,550 (this figure varies according to accommodation). Tuition includes a brand new laptop that is outfitted with the complete suite of software used in the student's academic program.

Financial Aid

Scholarships are available to students who demonstrate need and academic promise. Merit-based scholarships are also available. Wentworth also provides federal and state financial assistance, such as Federal Pell and Federal Supplemental Educational Opportunity Grants, Federal Perkins Loans, Federal Work-Study Program awards, Gilbert Matching Grants, and Massachusetts No-Interest Loans, to students with financial need in accordance with federal and state guidelines.

Wentworth participates in the Federal Direct Lending program. As a result, students are eligible to borrow under the Federal Direct Stafford Student Loan program and parents may borrow under the Federal Direct PLUS program. Individuals participating in these programs borrow money directly from the federal government rather than through lending institutions.

In addition to these need-based programs, Wentworth also participates in the MEFA loan program sponsored by the Massachusetts Educational Financing Authority. Wentworth offers several payment options through payment plans and alternative loan financing.

To apply for financial aid, new students should complete the Free Application for Federal Student Aid (FAFSA) by March 1. Applications received after that date are considered as funds allow.

Faculty

Wentworth's faculty includes 145 full-time and 165 part-time members. The primary responsibility of every faculty member is teaching. Although professors may engage in some research and related work, student development remains the central mission of Wentworth's faculty. Upon entering Wentworth, every student is assigned a faculty adviser.

Student Government

Wentworth's Student Government performs an essential function as the official representative of the student body. Its purposes are to receive and express student opinion, to advance the best interests of the student body with the administration and faculty and with other institutions and associations, to support all extracurricular activities of the student body, and to serve as a bond between the student body and the faculty to foster cooperation and understanding. The Student Government is made up of elected representatives from each class section and the officers elected by the student body at large. The Student Government sponsors social functions and student organizations and serves as an advocate for student concerns.

Admission Requirements

Applicants must be graduates of secondary schools (or have passed the GED test) and must meet specific entrance requirements. All programs require four years of English, a laboratory science, and mathematics through algebra II in a college-preparatory program. Both the electromechanical engineering and the computer science programs require a background in precalculus or trigonometry. All programs require the submission of SAT or ACT scores. International students and transfers are welcome.

Application and Information

Students are admitted to Wentworth for September and January enrollment. Notification of admission is made on a rolling basis. The preferred method for applying is online at http://www.wit.edu/apply. The online application fee is $50. An application form, the application fee, transcripts from the secondary school and any colleges previously attended, SAT or ACT scores, a personal statement, and a letter of recommendation should be sent to:

Admissions Office
Wentworth Institute of Technology
550 Huntington Avenue
Boston, Massachusetts 02115
Phone: 617-989-4000
      800-556-0610 (toll-free)
Fax: 617-989-4010
E-mail: admissions@wit.edu
Website: http://www.wit.edu
      http://twitter.com/WITadmissions
      http://facebook.com/wentworthadmissions

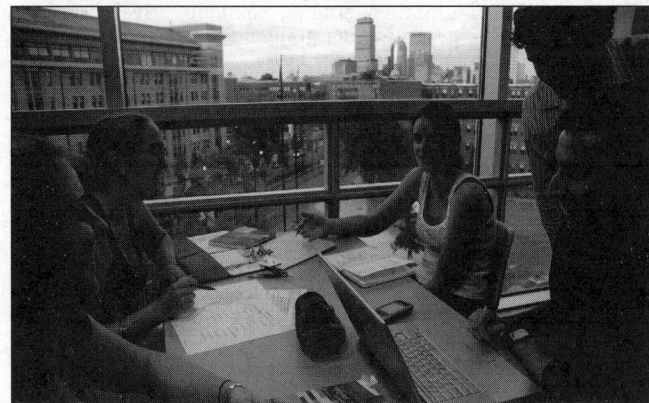

Wentworth residence hall study lounge.

WEST CHESTER UNIVERSITY OF PENNSYLVANIA
WEST CHESTER, PENNSYLVANIA

The University

West Chester University of Pennsylvania (WCU) is the second largest of the fourteen institutions in the Pennsylvania State System of Higher Education and the fourth-largest university in the Philadelphia metropolitan area. Officially founded in 1871, the University traces its heritage to the West Chester Academy, which existed from 1812 to 1869. The University's 402-acre campus has well-maintained facilities, including nine residence halls and two garden-style apartment complexes, plus a new performing arts center and a student recreation center. In keeping with West Chester's rich heritage, the University's Quadrangle buildings, part of the original campus, are on the National Register of Historic Places.

While the University attracts the majority of its students from Pennsylvania, New Jersey, and Delaware, it also enrolls many students from other areas across the United States and from more than fifty countries. The undergraduate enrollment includes approximately 12,834 women and men.

Each year, the University community schedules an impressive series of events, including programs with well-known musicians, authors, political figures, and others. More than 240 campus groups in music, theater, athletics, and other activities, as well as clubs, fraternities, sororities, service organizations, and honor societies, provide students with the opportunity to participate in a full range of programs. The University offers 30 intercollegiate sports and 24 club sports for men and women. In addition to the facilities in the health and physical education complex, the University has a field house and a gymnasium for varsity sports.

Location

The University is located in West Chester, a community in southeastern Pennsylvania that is strategically located at the center of the mid-Atlantic corridor. The seat of Chester County government for more than two centuries, West Chester retains much of its historical charm in its buildings and unspoiled countryside, yet it offers the twenty-first-century advantages of a town in the heart of a thriving suburban area. West Chester is just 25 miles west of Philadelphia and 17 miles north of Wilmington, Delaware, putting the libraries, museums, cultural resources, entertainment, and historical sites of both cities within easy reach. It is also only 2 hours from New York City and 3 hours from Washington, D.C.

Majors and Degrees

The Bachelor of Arts is offered in American studies, anthropology, art, biology, communication studies, communicative disorders, English, French, geography–geographic analysis, geography–urban/regional planning, German, history, Latin, liberal studies, literature, mathematics, philosophy, political science, political science–international relations, political science–applied public policy, psychology, Russian, sociology, Spanish, theater arts, and women's studies.

The Bachelor of Science is offered in accounting, athletic training, biochemistry, biology, biology–cell and molecular biology, biology–ecology, biology–medical technology, biology–microbiology, business management, chemistry, chemistry–biology (premed), computer science, criminal justice, economics, exercise science, finance, forensic and toxicological chemistry, geoscience–earth systems, geoscience–environmental, geosciences–geology, health and physical education, health science–general, health science–respiratory care, liberal studies–science and mathematics, liberal studies–professional studies, marketing, mathematics, nutrition and dietetics, pharmaceutical product development, physics, physics–engineering, public health–environmental, and public health–health promotion.

The Bachelor of Science in Nursing, the Bachelor of Fine Arts (studio arts), the Bachelor of Music (music education, performance, theory and composition, studies in an outside field), and the Bachelor of Social Work degrees are also offered.

The Bachelor of Science in Education degree is offered in biology, chemistry, communication–media, communication–speech, communication–theatre emphasis, early childhood education, earth-space science–astronomy, earth-space science–geology, elementary education, English, mathematics, physics, and special education.

Paraprofessional studies are available in medicine. Also available are early admission assurance programs with Drexel School of Medicine, Pennsylvania State University College of Medicine, Temple University School of Medicine, Temple University School of Dentistry, and Arcadia University Physician Assistant Program. In cooperation with Pennsylvania State University, West Chester University offers a 3-2 dual-degree program combining liberal arts, physics, and engineering. A similar, dual-degree cooperative physics/engineering program is available through affiliation with the School of Engineering and Textiles of Philadelphia University. As a member of the State System of Higher Education (PASSHE), special admission opportunities for scholarships to the Widener School of Law–Harrisburg Campus are also available.

Teacher certification programs are available in biology, chemistry, communications, early childhood education, elementary education, English, French, general science, German, health and physical education, Latin, mathematics, music education, physics, Russian, secondary education, social studies, Spanish, and special education. Certificates are also available in adapted physical education, athletic training, biology–medical technology, education for sustainability, and Russian studies.

Interdisciplinary areas of study include computer security certificate, ethnic studies, Honors College, Latin American studies, and Russian studies. Minors are available in most majors and in several interdisciplinary areas. The University also offers ROTC programs with cross-enrollment agreement with Widener University for Army ROTC and with St. Joseph's University for Air Force ROTC.

Academic Programs

West Chester University is a comprehensive institution now in its second century. The University comprises the College of Arts and Sciences, the College of Business and Public Affairs, the College of Education, the College of Health Sciences, and the College of Visual and Performing Arts. It operates on a two-semester basis; summer sessions are available.

An honors program is available to qualified students for both upper and lower division study; internships and field experiences, self-designed majors, and independent study are also offered. A variety of credit-by-examination programs are available.

Off-Campus Programs

Through the Study Abroad Program, students may spend one or more semesters in countries such as England, Italy, France, Australia, Spain, and Ireland. West Chester also sponsors a number of annual courses that include study abroad during spring, summer, and winter breaks.

West Chester University participates in the National Student Exchange Program, in which students spend up to a year at any one of more than 170 member schools across the United States, broadening their cultural and academic horizons. Automatic transfer of credit is arranged.

Academic Facilities

There are two libraries on campus: the Francis Harvey Green Library and the Presser Music Library. Library collections include more than 1,416,480 print and electronic volumes; 2,000 print journal subscriptions; 926,000 microforms; 52,500 sound recordings; 10,300 films, videos, and DVDs; 3,500 maps; Internet access to more than 130 databases (including 27,000 titles of streaming video and 67,700 albums of streaming audio); and the full-text from more than 67,700 journals. Unique digital collections include University graduate and undergraduate catalogs from 1874 to date; title pages and autographs from the Philips Autograph Library; the letters of

General Anthony Wayne; historic postcards, and other materials relating to the University and to local history. Services include free interlibrary loan, electronic and print reserves, more than one hundred public computer workstations, forty-six laptops for use in the library, and a Starbucks coffee shop.

The University's extensive computer facilities include more than 1000 PC and Macintosh workstations that are available to students in more than 72 portable/fixed computer labs. Majority of the buildings and the entire campus outdoors are wireless zones and Internet access is available in residence halls and computer labs. Students can use the computing facilities 16 hours a day during weekdays and open hours are available during the weekends.

The Merion Science Center, with modern multimedia lecture halls, extensive laboratories, and study areas where students can work together, connects to the Schmucker Science Center, which houses a fully equipped observatory and planetarium. The Center's extensive laboratories have a variety of advanced instruments such as a single-side band microscope—the world's second—as well as field inversion electrophoresis equipment for DNA analysis, and equipment for RFLP, PCR and DNA sequencing. The GIS computer lab has a first-order community base station and mobile GPS units to support coursework in geography, marketing and other subjects. Undergraduates have hands-on access to this equipment, as well as automated spectrophotometers, electron analytical equipment, atomic absorption spectrometers, and a variety of chromatographs, including gas chromatograph–mass spectrometers.

The campus includes a 100-acre natural area for environmental studies; speech and hearing and reading clinics; two theaters; music facilities with practice, rehearsal, and listening rooms; a large health and physical education complex that houses a gymnasium and a natatorium with two pool areas and a diving well; dance studios; research laboratories; physical therapy rooms; saunas; and a health resource center.

West Chester University is committed to providing barrier-free facilities for persons with impaired mobility.

Costs

West Chester University provides a high-quality education at an affordable cost. Full-time undergraduate students who are legal residents of Pennsylvania paid $6,428 for annual tuition for 12 to 18 semester hours in 2012–13. For more than 18 semester hours or fewer than 12, the cost was $268 per semester hour. Out-of-state students paid $16,070 per year for 12 to 18 semester hours and $670 per semester hour for more than 18 or fewer than 12. Room and board were $7,922 per year for on-campus residents in University-owned residence halls. Student fees for full-time students were $1,834 per year, plus a technology fee of $358 for in-state students and $542 for out-of-state students. Tuition is determined by the state.

Financial Aid

The financial aid available to students includes work-study programs, grants, loans, special awards, and scholarships. A limited number of merit scholarships are awarded based on the student's academic standing and accomplishments in high school. Students who qualify are invited to apply. About 70 percent of all full-time undergraduate students receive some form of aid.

Faculty

West Chester University has a faculty of over 750 members. The majority hold doctoral degrees, and many are engaged in research and serve as consultants in their field of expertise. The student-faculty ratio is 20:1.

Student Government

The Student Government Association represents all students on the West Chester campus. In addition, the Residence Hall Association represents resident students, and the Off Campus and Commuter Association represents commuting students.

Admission Requirements

Applicants to West Chester University are evaluated on the basis of scholarship, character, and potential for achievement in the programs to which they apply. The requirements for freshman admission consideration include graduation, with satisfactory scholarship, from an approved secondary school or approval by the Credentials Evaluation Division of the Pennsylvania Department of Education, or Pennsylvania Homeschoolers Accreditation

Agency; satisfactory scores on either the SAT, ACT, or TOEFL (for international applicants); and completion of a personal statement. The University offers other admissions options such as early admission and special admissions programs, including the Academic Development Program and a reduced course load program. Based on the scores received on Advanced Placement (AP) tests and subject examinations administered through the College-Level Examination Program (CLEP), students may receive advanced placement or credit.

Transfer applicants must have a minimum cumulative grade point average of 2.0 for admissions consideration. Certain academic programs require specific grade point averages above a 2.0 and may require an interview or specific course prerequisites.

Application and Information

Students are admitted for the fall or spring semester. Freshman applicants for the fall semester are encouraged to apply electronically and urged to begin the application process early in their senior year of high school. Transfers should begin the process beginning in January for the fall semester. Applicants for the spring semester should apply by November 1, however certain academic programs can close early. International students must apply by March 1 for the fall semester and September 1 for the spring semester. The Office of Admissions at West Chester University completes a preliminary evaluation of applicants once all information has been received and processed. The admissions committee reviews every application individually and each aspect of a student's file is considered. The admissions committee prioritizes applicants with the strongest academic credentials during the review process and notifies them of its decision as quickly as possible upon the completion of their file. Students are encouraged to visit WCU's campus. To arrange a visit or to attend an information session, or request additional information, students should visit www.wcupa.edu/admissions.

For additional information and required forms, students may contact:

Office of Admissions
Emil J. Messikomer Hall
West Chester University of Pennsylvania
100 West Rosedale Avenue
West Chester, Pennsylvania 19383
Phone: 610-436-3411
    877-315-2165 (toll-free)
E-mail: ugadmiss@wcupa.edu
Transfer: ugtransfer@wcupa.edu
International: uginternational@wcupa.edu
Website: http://www.wcupa.edu/admissions
        http://www.facebook.com/wcuadmissions
        http://twitter.com/AdmissionsWCUPA
        http://www.youtube.com/WCUofPA

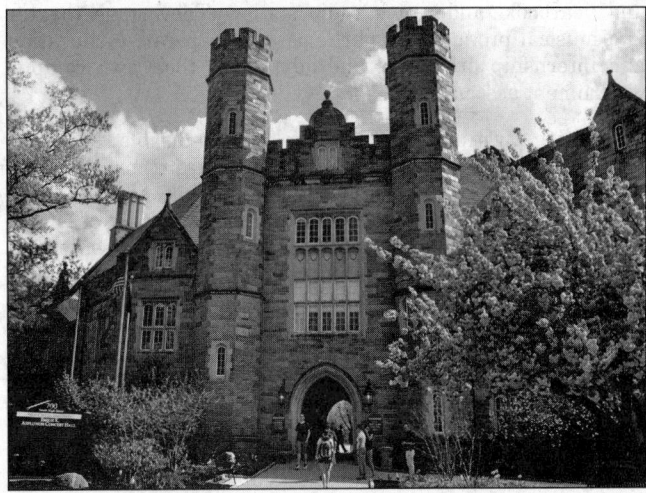

Philips Memorial Building is one of the historic Quadrangle buildings on the campus of West Chester University.

WESTERN CONNECTICUT STATE UNIVERSITY
DANBURY, CONNECTICUT

The University

Founded in 1903, Western Connecticut State University (Western) is dedicated to providing both a high-quality university education and a memorable campus experience at an affordable cost. With programs in the arts and sciences, business, and professional studies, Western takes pride in providing an outstanding education to more than 4,500 full-time undergraduates and nearly 2,000 graduate or part-time students.

Western offers excellent educational programs through five academic units: the Ancell School of Business, the School of Arts and Sciences, the School of Professional Studies, the School of Visual and Performing Arts, and the Division of Graduate Studies and External Programs. The most popular majors include communication, theater arts, education, business, justice and law administration, music, and nursing.

In addition to the University's full menu of undergraduate degrees, the Ancell School of Business offers the Master of Business Administration, Master of Health Administration, and Master of Science in justice administration. The School of Arts and Sciences offers the Master of Arts in biological and environmental sciences, earth and planetary sciences, English, history, and mathematics; the Master of Fine Arts is offered in professional writing. The School of Professional Studies offers the Master of Science in counselor education, elementary education, nursing, and secondary education; also offered is Western's Doctor of Education (Ed.D.) in instructional leadership. Prelaw and pre–health professions programs also are available. Western's newly formed School of Visual and Performing Arts offers the Master of Fine Arts in visual arts and the Master of Music Education.

The University is also rich with a number of learning and social activities beyond the classroom. Students run academic and fraternal organizations, publish an award-winning newspaper and yearbook, and run a radio station. They stage theater and musical productions, participate in cooperative education and internship programs, and administer their own campus government association.

The University provides services for learning-disabled students, study abroad, a University Scholars program, precollegiate and access initiatives, international student services, and community service learning opportunities. A variety of NCAA Division III men's and women's sports are represented on campus, and students enjoy intramural sports and a premier recreation center that includes a swimming pool, an indoor track, and weight-lifting machines. The campus also features a child-care center, a counseling center, a health services office, a career development center, and campus ministries.

Western is accredited by the New England Association of Schools and Colleges; the Board of Governors for Higher Education, State of Connecticut; the Connecticut State Department of Education; the American Chemical Society; the Commission on Collegiate Nursing Education; the Council on Social Work Education (baccalaureate level); the Council for Accreditation of Counseling and Related Educational Programs; and the National Association of Schools of Music.

Location

Western offers two campuses in Danbury, in the heart of western Connecticut, as well as a satellite campus in Waterbury. Danbury is a major city in Fairfield County in the foothills of the Berkshire Mountains, just 65 miles north of Manhattan and 50 miles west of Hartford.

In Danbury, the Midtown campus is a 34-acre, fifteen-building campus with an interesting mix of old and new architecture, and it offers easy access to downtown entertainment, restaurants, and shopping. The 364-acre Westside campus is ideal for hikers and nature buffs who want to discover its woodland wonders while enjoying state-of-the-art facilities. The Western-at-Waterbury campus offers a convenient location closer to the center of the state, with the same level of excellent service.

Majors and Degrees

The Ancell School of Business offers the Bachelor of Business Administration in accounting, finance, management, management information systems, and marketing, as well as the Bachelor of Science in justice and law administration.

The School of Arts and Sciences offers the Associate in Science, Bachelor of Arts, and Bachelor of Science degrees. The Associate in Science is offered in liberal arts. The Bachelor of Arts is offered in American studies, anthropology/sociology, biology, chemistry, communication, computer science, earth and planetary sciences–astronomy, economics, English, English–professional writing, history, mathematics, political science, psychology, social sciences, and Spanish. The Bachelor of Science is offered in medical technology and meteorology.

The School of Professional Studies offers the Bachelor of Arts and Bachelor of Science degrees. The Bachelor of Arts is offered in social work. The Bachelor of Science is offered in elementary education, health education, health promotion studies, nursing, and secondary education.

The School of Visual and Performing Arts offers the Bachelor of Arts, Bachelor of Science, and Bachelor of Music degrees. The Bachelor of Arts is offered in art, music, and theater arts. The Bachelor of Science is offered in music education, and the Bachelor of Music is offered with options in classical: voice or instrument or in jazz studies. Auditions are required for entrance into any of the music degree options.

Academic Programs

The University has developed a diverse mix of programs that are designed to inspire students. From the enlightening category of the arts to specialized fields of education, the emphasis is on the individual student's learning experience.

Special offerings at Western include the nation's first program in computer information security management and the only licensed meteorology program in Connecticut.

Academic Facilities

A number of facilities contribute to academic life on campus. The newly renovated and expanded library holds more than 200,000 volumes and over 400,000 bound periodicals, microforms, government documents, music scores, electronic resources, and audiovisual items. Western's extraordinary Science Building opened in 2005 to great acclaim for its ecology-friendly green design and cutting-edge lab and classroom equipment. Students are also encouraged to make use of Western's exceptional computer laboratory facilities and are invited to hone their craft in superior theater and musical facilities. Along with the rest of the greater Danbury community, they benefit from the offerings of the Western International Center; German Studies Center; Institute for Holistic Health Studies; Meteorological Studies and Weather Center; Jane Goodall Center for Excellence in Environmental Studies; Center for Collaboration; Center for Business Research; Center for Excellence in Learning and Teaching; Center for Excellence in the Study of Culture and Values; Center for Galactic Astronomy; Center for Graphics Research; Center for Professional Development; Center for Technology, Research, and Productivity; Westside Nature Preserve; and Westside Observatory and Planetarium.

Costs

As part of the Connecticut State System of Higher Education, Western provides a high-quality private university education at an exceptionally reasonable public school cost. It is estimated that a full-time, in-state undergraduate student who lives and has meals on campus will pay approximately $19,800 for 2013–14. A full-time, out-of-state undergraduate student who lives and has meals on campus will pay approximately $31,305 for 2013–14. This estimate of annual costs includes tuition, fees, and room and board. Books, laboratory fees, health insurance, and personal expenses were not included in the estimate.

Western participates in the New England Regional Student Program of the New England Board of Higher Education. This program offers residents of other New England states the opportunity to enroll at Western at Connecticut resident tuition rates, plus an additional fee, in programs that are not available in their home states. Details about the regional program can be obtained by contacting the Office of University Admissions.

Financial Aid

Any student who is matriculated at Western and registering for at least 6 credits per semester may apply for student aid, which includes federal, state, and institutional funding. Students must complete the Free Application for Federal Student Aid (FAFSA) and be sure to list Western's school code of 001380 in the college release section. If the student's file is selected for verification, appropriate signed copies of federal income tax returns must be submitted. Academic scholarships are available to students with superior academic credentials. Students with demonstrated financial need also have the opportunity to participate in work-study programs. For more information, students should contact the Financial Aid Office at 203-837-8580 or wcsufinancialaid@wcsu.edu.

Faculty

Nationally respected, Western's faculty members and administrators are continually cited for scholarly achievement. The faculty-student ratio is 1:15.6, and nearly 90 percent of the University's full-time faculty members have doctoral, terminal, or first professional degrees.

Admission Requirements

Western welcomes applications from all qualified individuals. Admission to the four undergraduate schools is competitive. University admissions criteria include grade point average, types of courses taken, extracurricular activities, and standardized test results. Applications are reviewed by admissions professionals. If an applicant feels that individual circumstances warrant special consideration, a personal letter explaining those circumstances may be submitted with the application.

Academic preparation is the most important factor in determining admission. Freshman candidates for admission must have a high school diploma from an accredited secondary school or an equivalency diploma. General Educational Development (GED) test scores must be converted into a State of Connecticut Equivalency Diploma.

Western applicants should present evidence of successful completion of the following academic units in high school with a cumulative grade average of B- (80) or higher: 4 years of English, including writing skills and literature; 3 years of mathematics, including algebra I, geometry, and algebra II; 2 years of social sciences, including U.S. history; 2 years of laboratory sciences; and 2 to 3 years of a single foreign language (3 years are recommended). Academic course work in computer science, visual arts, theater, music, or dance may be substituted for one of the areas above. Those applicants who do not meet these guidelines may be considered under the Educational Achievement and Access Program. For more information about the program, students should contact the Office of University Admissions.

For specific information about transfer student admission, early admission, freshman entrance with advanced standing, special transfer arrangements for associate degree recipients, guest student admission, readmit admission, fresh-start admission, and international student admission, students should contact the Office of University Admissions.

Interviews are not required, but candidates are encouraged to attend an information session before they enroll. These sessions provide information about the University and the admissions process and provide an important opportunity to assess how the University can help students meet their long-term educational goals. They also afford students the opportunity to meet with professors, other potential students, and current students. Student-guided tours are available. While on tour, students are able to visit the library, the residence halls, science and computer laboratories, the student center, and the recreation center. For information about appointments and campus visits, students should call the Office of University Admissions.

Application and Information

Western seeks to enroll students who will benefit from and contribute to the University. Rolling admissions for the fall semester begin December 1, with class spaces filled on a first-come basis. Rolling admissions for the spring semester begin October 1, with class spaces filled on a first-come basis. To apply, students should obtain an application from the Office of University Admissions or from a secondary school or community college guidance office. Western welcomes transfer and international student applications.

For application forms and more information, students should contact:

Office of University Admissions
Western Connecticut State University
181 White Street
Danbury, Connecticut 06810
Phone: 203-837-9000
        877-837-WCSU (toll-free)
E-mail: admissions@wcsu.edu
Website: http://www.wcsu.edu
         http://www.facebook.com/Western
         http://twitter.com/Western/

WESTMONT COLLEGE
SANTA BARBARA, CALIFORNIA

The College

Westmont College is a nationally ranked Christian liberal arts college in the evangelical tradition that remains focused on undergraduate education. One of the country's most dynamic interdenominational Christian colleges, Westmont combines a world-class education with an unbeatable coastal Southern California location to prepare students for fulfilling lives of leadership and service.

Residence life, athletics, off-campus programs, and opportunities for local and international outreach contribute to balanced personal and spiritual development. Alumni enter a wide variety of professions and vocations and pursue professional-, master's-, and doctoral-level programs at the world's finest research universities, including UCLA, Stanford, Harvard, Yale, Princeton, the University of Chicago, Cambridge, and many others. Westmont's 1,200 students come to Westmont from the majority of states and many countries throughout the world, the highest percentage come from California. Approximately 60 percent are women, 27 percent are students of color, and 2 percent are international students. Eight-five percent of the students live in the five residence halls on campus or the apartment complex off campus.

As a member of the National Association of Intercollegiate Athletics and the Golden State Athletic Conference, Westmont provides intercollegiate sports for men and women in basketball, cross-country, soccer, tennis, and track and field. Men also compete in intercollegiate baseball, club polo, club rugby, club soccer, club volleyball, club Ultimate (Frisbee), and club golf. Women also compete in intercollegiate volleyball, polo, club cheer, and club golf. The intramural program offers a wide variety of activities as well.

There are numerous clubs and organizations, including a student newspaper, literary magazine, yearbook, choral and music ensembles, multicultural club organizations, political organizations, theater productions, community service organizations, and Christian service, mission, and outreach programs. The Ruth Kerr Memorial Student Center houses the main campus dining facilities. An integral component of the Westmont experience is the Chapel Program, which students are required to attend three days a week. Chapel provides speakers and programs to inspire and challenge students to continue growing in their relationship with Christ.

Location

Westmont is located on a 111-acre campus, rich with pine, oak, and eucalyptus trees, in Montecito, an estate area of Santa Barbara between the Pacific Ocean and the Santa Ynez Mountains. Students enjoy the beach and mountain trails year-round. Santa Barbara has a wealth of history and culture, and theaters, libraries, community concerts, and other civic offerings are just minutes from the campus.

Majors and Degrees

Westmont awards Bachelor of Arts (B.A.) and Bachelor of Science (B.S.) degrees in twenty-nine liberal arts majors. These include alternative major, art, art history, biology, chemistry, communication studies, computer science, economics and business, education, engineering physics, English, English and modern languages, European studies, French, history, kinesiology, liberal studies mathematics, music, philosophy, physics, political science, psychology, religious studies, social science, sociology and anthropology, Spanish, and theater arts. The College offers a teacher-preparation program, which is approved by the California Commission for Teacher Preparation and Licensing, enabling students to qualify for either the single-subject or the multiple-subject credential. Pre-professional programs include athletic training, dentistry, engineering, law, medicine, ministry and missionary studies, pharmacy, physical therapy, and veterinary studies.

Academic Programs

All majors and programs of study feature thought-provoking and inspiring ways to integrate belief, thought, and action and to come to a deeper, more accurate understanding of the world. Westmont's commitment to academic freedom is clear, not only in courses that demand students' best critical thinking, but also through a wide range of opportunities and organizations that explore the world of ideas. Students consider issues of science and religion through the Pascal Society and attend lectures in the humanities sponsored by the Erasmus Society. As an exclusively undergraduate college, Westmont has a deep understanding of the ideas and issues that absorb students. From its faculty and staff members to its alumni, Westmont is committed to helping students grow through their questions toward an ever-deeper faith.

Off-Campus Programs

Off-campus programs include the Europe Semester, which is offered each fall and provides the broadest geographical scope, with extended stays in Athens, Florence, Jerusalem, London, Paris, and Rome. The England Semester, offered every other year, combines travel and residential study in the British Isles for students of literature. Westmont in Istanbul allows students to live in Constantinople, a city that is of the past and of the future, of grace and grit, of culture and politics, of faith and skepticism. Students attending the Westmont in Mexico Semester gain skills for effective cross-cultural living, experience incarnational ministry, and improve their Spanish language abilities. Semesters in France and Spain offer French and Spanish majors the opportunity to study these languages in their home countries, as does the Latin American Studies Program, which combines the study of Spanish culture and language in Belize, Chile, Costa Rica, and Honduras. Similar programs are offered at Jerusalem University College in Israel; the Middle East Studies Program at the American University in Cairo, Egypt; and in the Russian Studies Program in Moscow, Nizhni Novgorod, and St. Petersburg (through Westmont's membership in the Council for Christian Colleges and Universities). Participants in the International Business Institute program visit the major economic and political capitals of Europe and Asia. The Westmont Economics/Business Program in Asia introduces students to the diverse economic growth in the Pacific Rim. The East Asia Program addresses contemporary world issues in China, Japan, and Taiwan. An additional summer program in Asia offers students an opportunity to study life and culture in Sri Lanka. Domestic off-campus programs include the Westmont in San Francisco Program, which studies modern American urban society and offers internships; the Washington Semester, highlighting national political processes and incorporating internships in national, international, and economic policy, justice, and journalism; the Consortium Visitor Program, enabling students to study at any of the Christian College Consortium's twelve other member colleges; and other programs sponsored by the Council for Christian Colleges and Universities.

Academic Facilities

New buildings consist of the Adams Center for the Visual Arts, which includes a museum, studios, offices and classrooms; Winter Hall for Science and Mathematics; and the newly renovated observatory. The tri-level Roger John Voskuyl Library, named for Westmont's third president, provides access to information resources and services to support the research and information needs of faculty, staff, students and the surrounding community. The library collections include 237,000 books, media items, music scores, and microforms; 300 print periodical titles; and 105 online databases with access to 12,000 online periodicals. The Westmont community has access to additional resources through the Gold Coast Library Network, Camino and Interlibrary Loan Services. Westmont's network consists of both wired and wireless components. Wireless coverage extends through all campus buildings and most outdoor areas, with a total Internet bandwidth of 135 Mb/s. Students are provided Google Apps accounts through Westmont, providing e-mail, calendaring, document sharing, and 4 GB storage per student. The college provides a general access computer lab consisting of twenty-seven dual-platform iMacs located in the main floor of the library. Westmont's Learning Commons is also housed in the library. This twenty-first century space brings together library, technology, and other campus services in an environment designed to foster collaborative and creative work, and social interaction. Voskuyl Library is also home to other Westmont departments that provide student support services: the Office of Life Planning, Academic Advising and Disability Services, and Internship Programs are on the upper level; the Writer's Corner is on the main level; and the Information Technology offices are on the lower level. Porter Theatre contains state-of-the-art equipment for dramatic productions and concerts. The newly renovated George Carroll Observatory contains a 24-inch search-grade reflector telescope, the most powerful telescope between San Francisco and Los Angeles. The Mericos H. Whittier Science Building and Winter Hall for Science and Mathematics houses the College's science program and equipment, including an ultracentrifuge, a liquid scintillation counter for measuring radioactivity, physiographic units and other equipment for advanced physiological studies.

Costs

Tuition and fees for 2012–13 were $37,020, and room and board for the academic year were $11,740. The cost of books and personal expenses was estimated at $3,000.

Financial Aid

Westmont has a strong financial aid program, so no student should hesitate to apply for lack of financial resources. Eighty-five percent of Westmont's students receive some form of financial assistance. Westmont offers Monroe full-tuition scholarships, which are available only to first-year applicants who apply via the early action (nonbinding) process. A select group of these applicants are invited to the campus to participate in a formal competition process. Students should contact the Office of Admission for further details. Other merit awards in the financial aid program are the Dean's, Provost's, and President's Scholarships, which ranged from $10,000 to $15,000. These merit scholarships are awarded to students who have demonstrated impressive academic achievement. Westmont also gives awards to students who demonstrate strength in art, music, theater arts, dance, cultural diversity, and athletics. After submitting the Free Application for Federal Student Aid (FAFSA), students may be eligible for generous state grants, aid from federal programs, institutional grants, loans, and work-study programs.

Faculty

One of the highest priorities at Westmont is the attraction and retention of outstanding Christian teachers and scholars. The College's professors are dedicated to the integration of faith and learning, while also being actively involved in the lives of students. There are 95 full-time and 52 part-time faculty members. The student-faculty ratio is 11:1; the average class size is 18. Ninety-six percent of tenure-track faculty members hold a terminal degree. Westmont's faculty members are committed to teaching at the undergraduate level, and they have additional advising responsibilities with either incoming first-year students or students in their major. A director of first-year programs is responsible for the advising and orientation of new students. Although teaching is their primary scholarly activity, many faculty members engage in research, write books, and publish articles in leading journals and periodicals.

Student Government

The Westmont College Student Association (WCSA) is an entirely self-governing body. Students elect their own WCSA representatives, who are then responsible for organizing social, cultural, and educational activities. They actively participate in and are voting members on almost all faculty committees, while also allocating the student budget to various clubs and organizations. Westmont Student Ministries, another student-managed organization, is responsible for organizing on- and off-campus ministries and mission opportunities.

Admission Requirements

Westmont selects candidates for admission from those prospective students who produce evidence that they are prepared for the academic stimulation and spiritual vitality that are central to the character of Westmont. All applicants must submit one academic letter of recommendation, official high school or college transcripts, and official SAT or ACT scores. A pastoral/character reference is optional. An interview is strongly encouraged. For transfer students from an accredited two- or four-year college or university or a Bible college or university that is accredited by the American Association of Bible Colleges, the evaluation is based on achievement in solid, transferable course work; an assessment of the personal areas covered by the application (as stated above); and the quality of the written responses. High school records must be submitted if the applicant has completed fewer than 24 college-level credits at the time of application.

Application and Information

Entrance to Westmont is possible at the beginning of either the fall or spring semester. Westmont offers an early action plan. High school seniors interested in applying for early action must submit the application by November 1; notifications are mailed on January 1. The priority deadline for regular decision is February 10 for first-year applicants and March 15 for transfers; notifications are mailed on a rolling basis. Applications should be submitted online via Common Application with an application fee of $40. The Office of Admission encourages applicants to complete the application process as early as possible. Visitors are welcome at any time. Campus visitors can stay overnight in the residence halls, attend classes and chapel, speak with professors or coaches, have a music audition, share a portfolio with the art department, and have meals with Westmont students. Several Preview Day events are planned each semester. Westmont desires to enroll a well-rounded and balanced first-year class. One of Westmont's goals is to create a dynamic as well as culturally and traditionally diverse community of learners who bring with them a variety of attributes, accomplishments, backgrounds, and interests.

For further information regarding admissions students should contact:

Office of Admission
Westmont College
955 La Paz Road
Santa Barbara, California 93108
Phone: 800-777-9011 (toll-free)
Fax: 805-565-6234
E-mail: admissions@westmont.edu
Website: http://www.westmont.edu/
http://www.facebook.com/westmont
http://twitter.com/westmontnews

Nestled in the beautiful hills of Santa Barbara, California, Westmont is home to 1,200 undergraduate scholars, all seeking to engage the academy, church, and world.

WEST VIRGINIA WESLEYAN COLLEGE
BUCKHANNON, WEST VIRGINIA

The College

Founded in 1890, West Virginia Wesleyan College is a coeducational, residential, liberal arts college in Buckhannon, West Virginia. The College has an enrollment of 1,400 undergraduate students from thirty-five states and twenty-one countries. The average class size is 19 and the student-faculty ratio is 14:1. More than 75 percent of the faculty members hold the highest degree in their respective teaching field. Each fall, West Virginia Wesleyan enrolls approximately 400 freshmen and 50 transfers. Fifty-five percent of students originate from West Virginia, and the ratio of men to women is 1:1. Approximately 16 percent of the students are minority or international students. More than 85 percent of students live on campus, and housing is required for all four years of study. Housing options include residence halls, suites, on-campus apartments, and campus-adjacent residence units.

Among the many services available to students is the Academic and Career Center, which helps students with job placement, class scheduling, selection of a major program of study, internship opportunities, and international travel. The center also provides preparatory help for professional or graduate entrance exams such as the LSAT, GRE, or GMAT. The Health and Counseling Center allows students to receive personal and educational guidance, as well as health services. The Learning Center provides comprehensive learning resources for all students, as well as robust services for students with diagnosed learning differences.

In addition to challenging academic curriculum and innovative technology, Wesleyan offers a balanced and comprehensive student-life program. Cocurricular activities include twenty NCAA Division II varsity sports, intramurals, and outdoor recreation adventures. More than seventy campus organizations include vocal and instrumental musical ensembles, theatre arts, dance, community service, clubs, special interest groups, Greek life, and spiritual and religious life programming. On-campus media opportunities include a campus radio station, student newspaper, and yearbook. The student-run Bobcat Entertainment Board schedules cultural and social entertainment every week during the academic year.

Location

Situated in the foothills of the Allegheny Mountains, Wesleyan's picturesque 100-acre campus is located in the historic town of Buckhannon, West Virginia. Buckhannon is located two hours south of Pittsburgh, Pennsylvania, and 90 minutes north of Charleston, West Virginia. It is easily accessible by interstate highways. Buckhannon has been included in Norman Crampton's book, *The Top 100 Best Small Towns in America* and *The 120 Best College Towns in America*. Students are drawn to the attractive and friendly setting and the many restaurants, social events, and outdoor adventures available within a short distance from campus.

Majors and Degrees

The College awards Bachelor of Arts, Bachelor of Science, Bachelor of Science in Nursing, and Bachelor of Music Education degrees, in addition to a number of master's-level degrees. Majors include: accounting, art, arts administration, athletic training, biology, business administration, five-year bachelor's + master's in business administration, chemistry, Christian formation, communication studies, computer information science, computer science, criminal justice, economics, education (combined elementary/secondary, elementary, or secondary), engineering

3-2, English (literature, education, or writing), environmental science, environmental studies, exercise science, gender studies, graphic design, history, international business, international studies, management, marketing, mathematics, music (applied or theory), music education, musical theatre, nursing, painting and drawing, philosophy, photography, physics, political science, psychology, public relations, religion, sociology, sport business, and theatre arts.

Preprofessional study programs are offered in dentistry, law, medicine, optometry, pharmacy, physical therapy, and veterinary medicine. The degrees are determined by the content of the student's program.

West Virginia Wesleyan also offers the following master's degrees: Master of Science in Athletic Training, Master of Business Administration, Master of Fine Arts in Creative Writing, Master of Education, and Master of Science in Nursing.

Academic Programs

Students are required to complete 120 credit hours of course work to become eligible for graduation. Approximately one third of those hours are taken in a student's major, one third in the general studies curriculum requirement, and one third in electives. The general studies and elective courses are taken to develop and enhance a student's worldview.

Wesleyan operates on a traditional semester system. The optional May Term is a three-week intensive period of study giving students the opportunity to earn three credit hours. International travel opportunities are popular options during May Term.

The honors program is offered for superior students who meet the specific requirements and are willing to commit themselves to a rigorous and enriching curriculum that affirms the highest ideals of a liberal arts institution. Challenging classes and cultural outings are an integral part of the honors program and are offered throughout the academic year.

Advanced credit is available for students who achieve required scores on Advanced Placement exams, International Baccalaureate exams, and CLEP tests.

New students are assigned a faculty adviser who assists with course selection and student concerns. All first-year students are required to successfully complete a four-hour First Year Seminar course. In addition to helping students adapt to college life, the First Year Seminar courses are topical and apply credit toward a general studies requirement.

Off-Campus Programs

Study abroad is highly encouraged and is an important part of the Wesleyan student's experience. In the recent past, students have studied in such countries as Australia, Austria, Bolivia, Bulgaria, England, Ireland, Italy, Kenya, Korea, Spain, and Wales, but there are a number of other countries in which students may study. Internships are required for many majors and highly encouraged for others. They are available locally, as well as in cities such as Pittsburgh, New York, Washington, D.C., and others around the globe. These off-campus opportunities can be taken for a complete semester, during the May Term, or during the summer.

Academic Facilities

Wesleyan's twenty-four buildings, including eleven modern residence hall units, house some of the most impressive facilities in the region. Residence hall facilities include Fleming Hall, which was completely remodeled in 2008, and Dunn Hall, a new residence hall that opened to students in 2011. Other recent campus construction includes the Virginia Thomas Law Center for the Performing Arts and the Reemsnyder Research Center for the sciences. A brand-new wellness center with Nautilus equipment, full cardio theater, separate workout rooms, and locker room facilities opened in 2012.

The Annie Merner Pfeiffer Library houses more than 105,000 volumes, 700 periodicals, and 10,000 media materials. More than 220 million additional resources worldwide can be accessed through a number of online databases from students' own residence halls 24 hours a day. Located in the center of the campus is Wesley Chapel, the largest sanctuary in West Virginia, and the Martin Religious Center. The Benedum Campus and Community Center houses a convenience store, bookstore, swimming pool, the Cat's Claw restaurant, the campus radio station, and student services offices.

The Rockefeller Health and Physical Education Center includes a main gymnasium that seats 3,700, an intramural gymnasium, weight-training rooms, and an indoor Astroturf training and recreational area. Other key campus buildings include Christopher Hall of Science and the adjacent Reemsnyder Research Center, which houses state-of-the-art laboratories and classrooms to complement the Christopher's planetarium, herbarium, and greenhouse; Loar Hall, which includes a 165-seat recital hall and state-of-the-art computer music lab; Middleton Hall, which houses the admission offices and department of nursing; Haymond Hall of Science; and the Lynch-Raine Administration Building.

Costs

The 2013–14 costs at Wesleyan are $25,650 for tuition, $7,740 for room and board, and $1,144 for fees. Students should allow $700 for books per year. Wesleyan offers a 10-month interest-free monthly payment plan during the academic year.

Financial Aid

Wesleyan allocates nearly $15 million each year to help supplement the financial needs of students and their families. Merit scholarships are available for students who demonstrate excellence in the classroom, as well as those who demonstrate talent in the arts and athletics. Scholarship opportunities are available for students who have a strong commitment to community service and for those who have a comprehensive co-curricular resume. A variety of need-based programs are also available, including government grants and loans, institutional grants, and student employment. All students and their families should file the Free Application for Federal Student Aid by February 15. The institutional code for West Virginia Wesleyan is 003830.

Faculty

The faculty members at Wesleyan have a primary goal of teaching and advising. More than 75 percent of the full-time faculty members hold the highest degree in their respective fields. With a 14:1 student-faculty ratio, classes are small, and personal attention is evident in all departments. Not only are faculty members teachers and advisers, but they are also mentors and friends.

Student Government

The Student Senate is structured to encourage and promote student participation. The four peer-elected officers are elected by their respective classes or representative student organizations. Student Senate meets biweekly, along with faculty members, administration, and staff members, and is recognized as the driving force behind many initiatives and decisions on campus.

Admission Requirements

Wesleyan seeks students who have proven academic credentials, combined with achievements and talents that enhance the quality of life on campus. Students are selected by the Office of Admission on the basis of their high school transcripts, college entrance exam results, letters of recommendation, campus interviews, and other supportive information. All applicants must take the SAT or ACT and submit secondary school transcripts from all schools attended, along with the application for admission. Candidates are considered on an individual basis without regard to race, color, national origin, sex, sexual orientation, age, disability, or religious affiliation. Essays and campus interviews are strongly encouraged and may be required in some instances.

Transfer students from accredited institutions are considered for admission. All official college transcripts must be submitted, along with high school transcripts and college entrance exam results.

Applicants who complete their secondary education through an alternative program (e.g., home schooling) must present evidence that they have been adequately prepared for college work to be considered for admission. SAT or ACT results are also required.

Application and Information

Applicants must submit an application for admission, official transcripts, and ACT or SAT scores. The application review period opens each year on October 1. Applying online is free of charge at http://apply.wvwc.edu. A paper application is also available and can be submitted along with a $35 nonrefundable fee. Admission decisions are made on a rolling basis, and students are notified within three weeks of receipt of all required documents. The preferred application deadline is March 1 for the fall semester, and December 1 for the spring semester. Applicants who wish to be considered for merit scholarships must apply before March 1. Interviews, campus tours, faculty and staff appointments, and class visits are encouraged and may be arranged through the Office of Admission.

For additional information, students should contact:
Office of Admission
West Virginia Wesleyan College
59 College Avenue
Buckhannon, West Virginia 26201
Phone: 304-473-8510
          800-722-9933 (toll-free)
E-mail: admission@wvwc.edu
Website: http://www.wvwc.edu

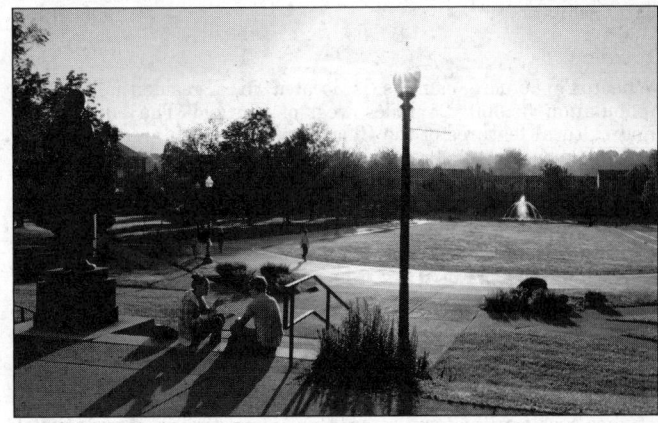

The Central Campus Green is one of many outdoor gathering spaces where students meet, study, and pass through on their way to classes and co-curricular activities.

WHEATON COLLEGE
WHEATON, ILLINOIS

Wheaton College
For Christ and His Kingdom

The College

Ranked by *U.S. News & World Report* as one of the nation's top liberal arts colleges, Wheaton College attracts exceptional students from all fifty states and more than forty countries. An interdenominational Christian liberal arts college, Wheaton takes the pursuit of faith and learning seriously. In addition to upholding an academically rigorous curriculum, Wheaton is committed to being a community that fearlessly pursues God's truth; invests in developing whole, well-rounded students; and prepares its graduates to lead lives that make a difference in the world.

Interdenominational and international in constituency, the student body at Wheaton College consists of approximately 2,400 undergraduates (including 200 students in the Conservatory of Music). Approximately 80 percent of the undergraduate students come from outside Illinois.

Wheaton College's 150-year history demonstrates the benefits of stable leadership in private Christian higher education—it has had only 8 presidents since it was founded in 1860. Wheaton has been faithful to its original precepts, and its legacy is shown in the lives of its graduates. Many distinguished graduate schools currently enroll Wheaton graduates in the dramatic arts, education, law, medicine, music, philosophy, science, and sociology. These include Notre Dame, Princeton, SMU, Yale, and the Universities of Chicago and Missouri–Kansas City; several of the Big Ten music schools; and the A.R.T./MXAT Institute for Advanced Theater Training at Harvard. Wheaton alumni also excel in a wealth of endeavors around the world, with many holding positions in business and finance, government and foreign service, teaching, ministry, law, medicine, and the arts. Wheaton graduates actively contribute to their communities and churches, and no matter what position they hold, they strive to make a difference in the world around them.

Wheaton offers a rich, life-changing education, with graduates trained for life, not just jobs. Students are taught to think, reason, and express themselves effectively. They should be able to attain knowledge and measure it against the truth of God's word, understand the importance of service, and value faith that embraces both right belief and right action. Developing strong, life-long relationships—with classmates, professors, and Jesus Christ—is a priority. Graduates are well-positioned for whatever they want to pursue and prepared to face the challenges of life. The Wheaton experience is distinctive and living and learning at Wheaton is extraordinary.

Location

Wheaton's 80-acre campus is located in a residential suburb (population 55,000) 25 miles west of Chicago. The educational and cultural features of the Chicago metropolitan area are easily accessible by train and regularly visited by students.

Majors and Degrees

Wheaton grants the Bachelor of Arts and Bachelor of Science degrees and, through the Wheaton Conservatory of Music, the Bachelor of Music and Bachelor of Music Education degrees.

The following majors are available in the arts and sciences: ancient languages, anthropology, applied health science, archaeology, art, biblical and theological studies, biology, business/economics, chemistry, Christian education and ministry, communication, computer science, economics, education, English, environmental studies, geology, history, interdisciplinary studies, international relations, mathematics, modern languages (French, German, and Spanish), music, philosophy, physics, political science, psychology, sociology, and urban studies. Also, 3-2 programs are offered in engineering and nursing, alongside a five-year cooperative engineering program with Illinois Institute of Technology and other engineering schools.

The Wheaton Conservatory of Music offers a full range of professional music majors, including composition, education, history/literature, performance, music with elective studies in an outside field, and music with an emphasis in a music-related field (such as media/film music, pedagogy, conducting, and collaborative piano). Students seeking these professional music degrees are accepted directly into the program by audition.

An on-campus program in military science leads to a commission in the U.S. Army at graduation. In addition to the majors offered, Wheaton has programs leading to teacher certification and to athletic training certification as well as programs preparing students for careers in business, health professions, law, and ministry.

Academic Programs

Wheaton is a distinctively Christian college where faculty members and students work together, both inside and outside the classroom, to apply Christian principles and values to the needs and problems of the individual and society. The vigorous search for knowledge and wisdom in any area of human activity is based on the belief that all truth is God's truth.

The academic curriculum combines with artistic, athletic, religious, service, and social activities to achieve a lively interaction of faith, learning, and living. Because of the College's strong commitment to developing effective servant/leaders for society worldwide and the church, there is a particularly strong integration of faith and learning in all degree programs.

A student's major is selected during the third semester of general education courses taken to meet competency and area requirements. Students must demonstrate competence (either by examination or by taking prescribed courses) in foreign language, mathematics, speech, and writing. All students must complete area requirements in applied health science, art, biblical studies, history, literature, music, natural science, philosophy, and social science. A student may be granted advanced placement or college credit on the basis of examination (SAT Subject Tests or AP). The number of credits granted and the level of placement are determined by the registrar and the chair of the department in which the course is taught.

Wheaton offers ten natural science majors—applied health science, biology, chemistry, computer science, environmental studies, geology, liberal arts engineering, liberal arts nursing, mathematics, and physics—in six academic departments. The Wheaton faculty members engage the study of science authoritatively, enthusiastically, and creatively in the classrooms and laboratories and beyond the campus. They are creative and offer more than two dozen general education courses in the natural sciences as well as the majors listed above. The programming includes the use of state-of-the-art technologies and techniques on the main Wheaton campus, cutting edge geological and biological studies in a large science station in the scientifically rich area of the Black Hills of South Dakota, and marine biology studies in Belize. In 2010, Wheaton's science departments moved into an $80-million science and mathematics facility with expanded teaching labs and research equipment.

Off-Campus Programs

Wheaton offers a variety of off-campus opportunities to enhance students' programs of study. The Wheaton Passage program is a popular camp experience available to new students at the College's Honey Rock Camp in northern Wisconsin. Another program, Human Needs and Global Resources (HNGR), combines classroom study with a six-month, field-based, service-learning internship in the Global South. A similar program in urban studies, Wheaton in Chicago, focuses on urban issues in U.S. cities and includes a semester living in College-owned housing in urban Chicago.

Other special summer programs for credit include field study at the Wheaton College Science Station in the Black Hills of South Dakota; working with youth at Honey Rock Camp; interdisciplinary study in East Asia; the study of English literature in England; language study in France, Germany, and Spain; the Wheaton in the Holy Lands program, involving biblical and archaeological studies; the Arts in London program, which includes course work in music, theater, and art; and an international study program based in England and the Netherlands, offering courses in economics, political science, and psychology.

Wheaton is a member of the Council of Christian Colleges and Universities, based in Washington, D.C. The council's activities increase students' learning opportunities by bringing special programs to campus and by providing off-campus study.

Off-campus programs include American Studies in Washington, D.C.; the Washington Journalism Center in Washington, D.C.; the Los Angeles Film Studies Center; the Contemporary Music Center in Martha's Vineyard; Latin American Studies in Costa Rica; Middle East Studies in Cairo; the Australia Studies Center; China Studies Program; the Scholar's Semester in Oxford; Russia Studies Program; and Uganda Studies Program. Wheaton has also recently affiliated with the International Sustainable Development Studies Institute in Thailand. In addition, Wheaton's membership in the Christian College Consortium allows students a semester of study at one of the other twelve consortium colleges.

Cooperative programs in social science are available at American and Drew Universities, and students may participate in a European seminar conducted by Gordon College.

Academic Facilities

An $80-million science and mathematics facility opened in fall 2010. The 128,000-square-feet of space includes eight teaching labs and research space designed to promote collaborative teacher-student research.

In 2009, an $11 million renovation of Adams Hall added art gallery and studio space. Edman Chapel, often the venue for concerts by world-class musicians, has undergone a $9 million renovation that added rehearsal space, including a large rehearsal room named for alum John Nelson, former conductor of Ensemble Orchestral de Paris.

In 2008, Wheaton's Memorial Student Center reopened after an extensive renovation to house the J. Dennis Hastert Center for Economics, Government, and Public Policy. The facility provides classroom, research, and public discussion space geared toward the study of economics, politics, and values in business, government, and ministry. Other recent additions to campus facilities include the Todd Beamer Student Center (2004); the Wade Center (2001), which houses the books and papers of seven British authors, including C. S. Lewis and J. R. R. Tolkien; and the Sports and Recreation Complex (2000).

Costs

Tuition for the 2013–14 year is $30,880; room and board for the year is $8,770.

Financial Aid

Realizing that a private college education is a sizable investment, Wheaton is committed to providing the necessary need-based financial aid so students can attend. Last year Wheaton awarded over $22 million in grants and scholarships.

The average need-based aid package for freshmen is about $20,000 and some merit aid is also available. The Career Development Center helps students to secure part-time jobs, as well as future employment.

Faculty

Over 94 percent of Wheaton's 198 full-time faculty members hold earned doctorates, and more than one third graduated from the top twenty-five graduate schools as designated in *U.S. News & World Report*. The professors' primary commitment as educators and advisers is enriched by their considerable research, publishing, and artistic activities. In addition, the professors are active Christians who strive to show how a profound commitment to God's word structures a vision of all of life, including intellectual life. They are dedicated to honoring a Christian perspective and to modeling Christ's love to their students.

All undergraduate courses are taught by faculty members.

To ensure a rich range of perspectives and expertise, every department at Wheaton has at least 3 full-time professors, and most have 5 to 10. The student-faculty ratio is 12:1.

Student Government

Student Government ensures a student voice in institutional affairs and provides a wide range of opportunities to develop leadership abilities. Student Government's vision is "To further the educational, spiritual, and relational development of the Wheaton College community as elected servant leaders representing student initiative, concern, creativity, and enthusiasm."

Besides Student Government, there are over forty academic, cultural, social justice, and entertainment student groups on campus. In addition, the Office of Christian Outreach provides opportunities for student ministry through student-run mission trips and ministries in urban and suburban Chicago.

Admission Requirements

Wheaton is a selective college that seeks to enroll students who evidence a vital Christian experience, high moral character, personal integrity, social concern, strong academic ability and motivation, and the desire to pursue Christian higher education as defined in the aims and objectives of the College. These qualities are evaluated by consideration of each applicant's academic record, autobiographical essays, test scores, recommendations, optional interview, and participation in extracurricular activities. For students applying to the Conservatory of Music, strong consideration is given to the evaluation of the required audition.

Applicants must have a high school diploma or the equivalent, and at the time of graduation should have completed a college-preparatory curriculum with a minimum of 18 acceptable units.

Satisfactory scores on the SAT or on the ACT examination are required of all applicants to the freshman class. The middle 50 percent range of scores for those admitted is 27–32 (ACT) and 1230–1400 (SAT composite math and verbal scores).

Application and Information

An application packet, complete with detailed instructions and requirements, can be obtained from the Admissions Office or online. For early action (nonbinding), students seeking admission in the fall term should apply to either the College of Arts and Sciences or the Conservatory of Music by November 1. The regular action deadline is January 10; the transfer application deadline is March 1. An admissions counselor can provide more information about Wheaton in general or the application process in particular.

Further information is available from:

Admissions Office
Wheaton College
501 College Avenue
Wheaton, Illinois 60187
Phone: 630-752-5005
        800-222-2419 (toll-free)
E-mail: admissions@wheaton.edu
Web site: http://www.wheaton.edu
        http://www.wheaton.edu/Admissions-and-Aid/Undergrad

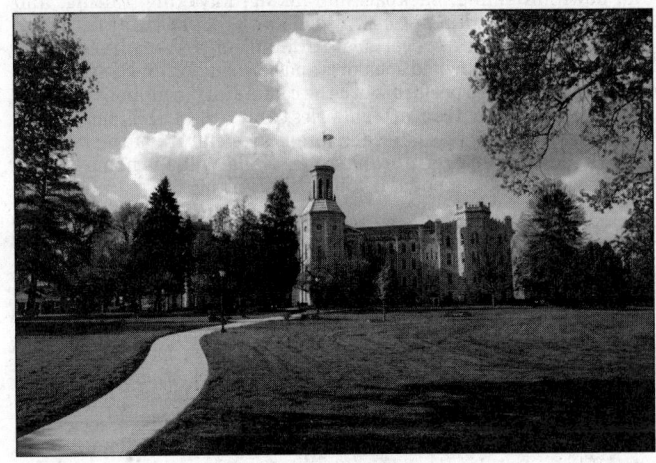

Historic Blanchard Hall overlooks Wheaton's front of campus.

WHITMAN COLLEGE
WALLA WALLA, WASHINGTON

The College

Challenging students to excel in the sciences, humanities, art, and social sciences, Whitman College is a nationally recognized liberal arts college. It combines the educational prestige of the best Eastern liberal arts colleges with the unpretentious values of the Pacific Northwest. Since 1882, students have chosen Whitman because of its commitment to undergraduate education. With 1,500 students and an average class size of 16, Whitman encourages students to be active participants in their education. In 1913, the College led the nation by requiring students to successfully complete comprehensive oral and written evaluations in their major field of study. The installation of a chapter of Phi Beta Kappa in 1919 marked the recognition of the high quality of Whitman's curriculum and the standards of teaching and learning that distinguish the College. Seventy percent of Whitman graduates enroll in graduate school within five years of earning their undergraduate degree.

Enrollment includes students from forty-eight states and thirty countries. As a residential college, approximately 70 percent of Whitman students live on campus. A variety of residence hall living options are available, including coeducational housing, apartment-style living, eleven special-interest houses, four fraternity houses, and an all-women's residence hall that houses, among others, the members of four national sororities. First-year students and sophomores are required to live on campus.

Whitman has an extremely engaged student body. "Whitties" participate in more than 130 interest groups, clubs, and organizations. The debate team ranked first in the country in parliamentary debate in 2010, 2011, and 2012. The highly ac-claimed theater department produces eight to ten shows each academic year, while the music department supports more than two dozen musical groups on campus. The College fields fourteen varsity teams and offers thirteen club sports and sixteen intramural activities. The Whitman club cycling team and men's and women's Ultimate (Frisbee) teams have won national championships in recent years. The varsity men's tennis and basketball and varsity women's basketball and cross-country teams have recently been nationally ranked.

Location

Whitman is located in Walla Walla, a historic community of 35,000 nestled in the foothills of the Blue Mountains of southeastern Washington. The Walla Walla Valley has four distinct seasons and enjoys 300 days of sunshine a year. With rich natural terrain at its doorstep, outdoor activities abound. These include cross-country and downhill skiing, backpacking, hiking, kayaking, rafting, and rock climbing. Whitman hosts a wide array of cultural activities on campus, including concerts, art exhibits, environmental forums, internationally renowned speakers and performers, and cinema arts films. Students also perform with the community symphony, browse in the area's seventeen art galleries, and act in the community theater. Parents appreciate the vibrant arts culture of the town as well as the wine and restaurant scene. Walla Walla is home to over 100 wineries and is a popular tourist destination.

Majors and Degrees

Whitman College confers the Bachelor of Arts (B.A.) degree, with departmental majors in anthropology; art (history, studio, and visual culture studies); Asian studies; biochemistry, biophysics, and molecular biology (BBMB); biology; chemistry; classics; economics; English; foreign languages and literatures (French, German studies, or Spanish); film and media studies; gender studies; geology; history; Latin American studies; mathematics; music; philosophy; physics; politics; psychology; religion; rhetoric studies; sociology; and theater. Combined or interdepartmental major study programs are offered in Asian studies, astronomy-geology, biology-geology, chemistry-geology, economics-mathematics, environmental studies (emphasis in biology, chemistry, economics, geology, physics, politics, or sociology), geology-physics, mathematics-physics, and

physics-astronomy. Minors are available in each of the departmental programs as well as Chinese, Japanese, Latin American and Caribbean literature, Latin American Studies, and world literature. Students with special interests may develop com-bined or interdepartmental major programs, subject to faculty approval. Whitman offers cooperative programs in engineering with Caltech, Columbia, Duke, the University of Washington, and Washington University in St. Louis; in environmental management or forestry with Duke; and oceanography with the University of Washington.

Academic Programs

Whitman's goal is to provide an atmosphere in which students can learn how to learn. At the heart of Whitman's academic curriculum is the general studies program. Through this program, students develop skills in intellectual reasoning, critical analysis of major works, effective writing, solid understanding of humanity's cultural and historic roots, valid bases for judgment of values, and confident abilities to ask tough questions. The general studies program consists of a first-year Encounters course and certain distribution requirements. Encounters is a two-semester course examining contact between peoples and cultures and the formation and transformation of dominant and competing worldviews. To satisfy distribution requirements, students complete at least 6 semester credits in fine arts, humanities, science, and social sciences; take 2 courses dealing with alternative voices; and take at least 1 course in quantitative analysis. Every candidate for graduation must complete at least 124 credits in appropriate course work with acceptable grades and a senior assessment. Whitman helps fund student research and internships, and approximately 200 students present professional-level research at the Annual Whitman Undergraduate Conference. Scores of 4 and 5 on the College Board's Advanced Placement tests are accepted for credit (the economics, English, and history departments accept only a score of 5). Whitman observes a two-semester calendar with a weeklong break for Thanksgiving, a month off over the winter holiday, and two weeks for spring break.

Off-Campus Programs

Whitman has strong study-abroad and domestic off-campus study programs. Each year, nearly half of the junior class studies off campus. There are 80 different programs available, spanning six of the seven continents (excluding Antarctica). In addition to academic course work, many students pursue internships and research opportunities. The College is formally affiliated with the Institute for the International Education of Students, with programs in Australia, Austria, China, England, France, Germany, and Italy. The school for field studies has opportunities in Australia, the Caribbean, Costa Rica, Kenya, and Mexico. Students may study at the Universities of East Anglia and York in England; St. Andrews University in Scotland; Doshisha University in Kyoto, Japan; and the University of Otago in Dunedin, New Zealand, and at programs in Argentina, Botswana, China, Costa Rica, Egypt, Greece, India, Ireland, Italy, Japan, Mexico, Spain, Sri Lanka, and Taiwan. Each year, 4 Whitman graduates are selected to teach English to university students in Kunming or Xi'an in the People's Republic of China. The College offers urban-semester programs in Chicago, Philadelphia, and Washington, D.C. Students may participate in one of more than 300 science research internships available through the College. Semester in the West, a signature program, is a semester-long, interdisciplinary traveling field-study program that investigates a myriad of issues throughout the intermountain West.

Academic Facilities

To enhance Whitman's learning environment, students have access to exceptional facilities and cultural resources. Penrose Memorial Library, open 24/7, houses more than 350,000 volumes and 2,000 subscriptions. In addition, the ORBIS Cascade Alliance provides access to approximately 3.5 million volumes that can be delivered to Whitman in less than 72 hours. Reid Campus Center, a 51,000-square-foot campus building, features a ballroom, cyber-lounge, coffeehouse performance space, and flexible dining and meeting facilities. Olin Hall of Humanities features an audiovisual center, a foreign-language learning lab, and the Donald Sheehan Art Gallery. A newer addition to Olin houses the computing equipment and is the center for the campus-wide fiber-optic network. Maxey Hall, expanded in 2011, houses the social sciences, includes a natural history and anthropology museum, a 350-seat auditorium, and animal demonstration labs. The Hall of Science houses a sophisticated physics lecture/demonstration hall and laboratory, expanded chemistry work stations, the Clise Planetarium, and support facilities for electron microscopes. It also contains laboratories for botany, ecology, vertebrate biology, physiology and developmental biology, and biochemistry and genetics; preparation and display cases for the herbarium and the preserved animal collections; a seismograph; and well-equipped student research laboratories. Some of the newest features include organic chemistry and geology labs, computer stations, and new greenhouse spaces. The 105,000-square-foot Hall of Science has more student-faculty research labs, and enhanced classroom space. Off campus, Whitman operates an observatory and the Johnston Wilderness Center—a 27-acre mountain property serving as an environmental studies field station. The Hall of Music houses an acoustically perfect performance hall and twenty-seven practice rooms that are open 24 hours a day. After a comprehensive renovation in 2011, Harper Joy Theater consists of two main stages, black box theaters, and new classrooms. Cordiner Hall is a 1,500-seat auditorium featuring a 3,000-pipe Holtkamp organ. The Fouts Center for the Arts, a 38,000-square-foot visual arts facility, opened in fall 2008.

Costs

Tuition for 2013–14 is $41,790. Room and board cost is $10,560. The estimated cost of books, supplies, and incidentals is $1,400. The associated student body fee is $336.

Financial Aid

Financial aid usually combines scholarships, student employment opportunities, and low-interest loans. In 2012–13, Whitman provided more than $25 million in scholarships. Forty-seven percent of Whitman students qualified for need-based aid. Roughly 50 percent of the students are employed on campus. Whitman also has an extensive merit scholarship program that rewards students who have demonstrated excellence in academics. These scholarships range from $4,000 to $13,000 and are renewable for four years. Scholarships are also available for students with exceptional talent in art, music, debate, theater, and leadership. To apply for financial aid, students must submit the Free Application for Federal Student Aid (FAFSA) and the CSS PROFILE. Early decision candidates should apply for financial aid by January 1; regular decision and transfer candidates must apply by February 1.

Faculty

Whitman College's faculty is comprised of individuals selected, retained, and promoted for demonstrated effectiveness as teachers as well as for leadership within their chosen fields. Ninety-eight percent of faculty members hold a doctoral degree or terminal degree in their field, and all serve as academic advisers. The student-faculty ratio is 10:1. Recognized nationally for faculty accessibility, Whitman offers personal attention outside the classroom, setting it apart from peer institutions. Students collaborate with professors on research projects, compete with them on athletic fields, serve with them on College committees, and dine in their homes. In the past five years, Whitman faculty members have distinguished themselves by receiving awards, honors, and fellowships from the National Institute of Mental Health, National Endowment for the Humanities, Battelle Research Institute, Washington State Arts Commission, Burlington Northern Foundation, Department of Health and Human Services, and Department of Energy.

Student Government

The College encourages students to participate and take leadership roles in self-governing campus organizations. The largest of these is the Associated Students of Whitman College (ASWC), in which every student is a member. ASWC acts through an elected student congress and executive council and is responsible for the *Whitman*

Pioneer (a weekly student newspaper), choral contest, Renaissance Faire, campus radio station KWCW (90.5 FM), and a multitude of all-campus concerts, speakers, films, and social events.

Admission Requirements

Whitman is a highly selective college that seeks academic excellence and diversity within its student body. Competition for admission is keen; about 70 percent of entering first-year students ranked in the top 10 percent of their high school class. Ninety-three percent were in the top quarter. The Admission Committee looks for evidence of intellectual achievement, motivation, creativity, responsibility, and maturity. The middle 50 percent of the class of 2016 scored in the following ranges on the SAT: 640–730 critical reading, 620–700 math, and 630–710 writing. The minimum TOEFL scores for international students are 85 on the Internet-based test and 560 on the paper test. The following pattern of high school subjects is highly recommended: 4 years of English, mathematics, science, and history or social sciences; at least 2 years of a foreign language; and 1 year of an art elective. Students who have decided early in their senior year that Whitman is their first-choice school are encouraged to apply for admission through early decision.

Application and Information

The application deadlines and notification dates for admission to Whitman are: early decision candidates apply by November 15 or January 1 and receive notification of admission by December 20 or February 1; regular decision applicants for the fall semester apply by January 15, and letters are postmarked by April 1; transfer students apply by March 1 and receive notification by April 20; and spring-semester candidates (if space is available) apply by November 15 and receive notification by December 15. First-year candidates are required to submit the following credentials: the Common Application, including the School Report Form; secondary school transcript; one teacher recommendation; and an application fee of $50. Whitman also requires test scores (SAT or ACT) and a personal supplement (a selection of writing prompts).

For more information, students should contact:

Office of Admission
Whitman College
345 Boyer Avenue
Walla Walla, Washington 99362-2046
Phone: 509-527-5176
       877-462-9448 (toll-free)
Fax: 509-527-4967
E-mail: admission@whitman.edu
Website: http://www.whitman.edu

Students on the Whitman College campus.

WILKES UNIVERSITY
WILKES-BARRE, PENNSYLVANIA

The University

Sitting in that first class at Wilkes University, students may notice something a little unexpected: professors and instructors genuinely interested in students' thoughts and aspirations.

A crucial part of personal engagement is hands-on learning. All Wilkes students can take advantage of numerous opportunities to get real-world experience in their field of interest, from starting a business to conducting research to actually using high-tech instruments that even graduate students at other institutions rarely touch.

Located at the foothills of the Pocono Mountains, along the shore of the Susquehanna River and within walking distance of downtown Wilkes-Barre, Pennsylvania, Wilkes University is a private, comprehensive institution with about 2,200 undergraduate students.

The University is structured into the College of Arts, Humanities, and Social Sciences; the College of Science and Engineering; the Nesbitt College of Pharmacy and Nursing; the Sidhu School of Business and Leadership; the School of Education; and University College (for undecided students). Wilkes offers a broad range of bachelor's and master's degree programs in the humanities, social and natural sciences, engineering, business administration, nursing, and education as well as the Master of Fine Arts, Doctor of Pharmacy, Doctor of Education, and Doctor of Nursing Practice degrees.

The Wilkes campus features a parklike quadrangle surrounded by modern classroom buildings and historic nineteenth-century mansions that have been restored as student residences and academic buildings. Campus facilities include the new Cohen Science Center (scheduled to open in fall 2013), a sports and conference center, an outdoor athletic complex and field house, a science classroom building, a modern academic classroom/office building, a performing arts center, an indoor recreation center, and a student center with a food court, café, entertainment rooms, post office, and ballroom.

Programs are designed to prepare students with a well-rounded liberal arts foundation that cultivates independent thinking and gives students the credentials necessary for entrance into graduate and professional schools and professional life. Academic advising integrated with career planning is stressed, and hands-on experiences are provided in laboratory, internship, and cooperative education settings. Free tutorial services are available to all students as well.

The University is accredited by the Middle States Association of Colleges and Schools and has specialized accreditation in the sciences, engineering, nursing, education, and business. More than 97 percent of students are employed or attending graduate/ professional school within one year of receiving their degrees.

First-year students enrolling prior to May 1 are guaranteed housing, and all students may have cars on campus. Campus housing is available for all four years. Architecturally, residence halls vary from modern, multifloor buildings to mansions listed on the National Register of Historic Places. Medical and dental care, department stores, specialty shops, and other services are available within three blocks of campus. A large number of nearby houses of religious worship welcome students' participation.

At Wilkes University, student activities complement academic life. Intercollegiate athletics encompass sixteen Division III sports, and an active and varied intramural program is offered. Nearly seventy clubs and organizations recognize student achievement and provide opportunities for leadership development, professional growth, and community service. The student-run Programming Board schedules movies and performances by comedians, musicians, and other entertainers, while other organizations sponsor dinner dances, block parties, and special events. The professionally run Student Development Office organizes various activities based on leadership, adventure, or cultural themes, as well as coordinates a unique e-mentor program that links current students with incoming freshmen to ease the transition to college life. Wilkes students are active

community volunteers, participating in numerous local and national service projects each year.

Master's degrees are awarded in bioengineering (new), business administration, creative writing, education, electrical engineering, engineering management, mechanical engineering, mathematics, and nursing. The University also offers terminal degrees in the fields of creative writing (M.F.A.), education (Ed.D.), nursing practice (D.N.P.), and pharmacy (Pharm.D.). In addition, Wilkes is the first school in Pennsylvania to offer a dual Doctor of Pharmacy and Master of Business Administration degree.

Location

The Luzerne County seat, Wilkes-Barre is a medium-sized city of 43,000 in the midst of a metropolitan area of 400,000. A wide range of recreational facilities are minutes away, including PNC Field (home of the Scranton/Wilkes-Barre RailRiders Triple A baseball team); the Mohegan Sun Arena, which serves as home for the Wilkes-Barre/Scranton Penguins hockey team; the Pocono Mountain ski resorts; numerous golf courses; state parks; outdoor tennis courts; and Pocono Downs harness racing.

The University is located in the historical district, between the entertainment and residential sections of the city. The entertainment district begins at the F. M. Kirby Center of Performing Arts, featuring symphony, ballet, theatrical, and musical performances, and encompasses the Wilkes University/King's College Barnes and Noble bookstore and café, a fourteen-screen movie complex, a nightclub, and numerous shops and restaurants. Other area cultural offerings include art galleries, ethnic and community festivals, and libraries and museums. The city is also approximately 2 hours from the cultural resources of both New York City and Philadelphia.

Wilkes-Barre is in proximity to the intersection of Interstates 80, 81, and 476 and within 3 to 6 hours of other major cities, such as Washington, D.C.; Baltimore; and Boston. The Wilkes-Barre/ Scranton International Airport enables travelers to arrive at most domestic destinations via one-stop or nonstop flights.

Majors and Degrees

Wilkes University offers Bachelor of Arts, Bachelor of Business Administration, and Bachelor of Science degrees. Majors include accounting; applied and engineering sciences; biochemistry; biology; chemistry; communications (concentrations in journalism, organizational communications, public relations, rhetoric and public communications, and telecommunications); computer information systems; computer science; criminology; earth and environmental sciences; electrical engineering; education: elementary and early childhood, middle-level, secondary (minor with a subject-area major), and special education (all with certification); engineering management; English (concentrations in literature and creative writing); entrepreneurship; environmental engineering; finance; history; integrative media; international studies; management; marketing; mathematics (new track in computational mathematics); mechanical engineering; medical laboratory sciences; musical theatre; nursing; philosophy; physics; political science; psychology; sociology; Spanish; and theatre arts. Wilkes also offers a guaranteed-seat first-professional program leading to the Doctor of Pharmacy degree.

The premedical and prelaw preparation programs are particularly strong. In addition to the University's prepharmacy program, other preprofessional programs are available in dentistry, occupational therapy, optometry, physical therapy, physician assistant, podiatry, and veterinary science. A full-time health sciences coordinator is dedicated to advising students who wish to continue study in a professional health-care field. The University offers affiliated programs in medicine with the Philadelphia College of Osteopathic Medicine and The Commonwealth Medical College; in optometry with the Pennsylvania College of Optometry and the State University of New York (SUNY) College of Optometry; in podiatry with Temple University School of Podiatric Medicine; in occupational therapy with Temple University;

in physical therapy with Drexel University, Temple University, and Widener University; in medical technology/medical laboratory sciences with Robert Packer Hospital; and in psychology with Widener University.

Academic Programs

Through a rigorous curriculum that emphasizes hands-on experience and training, Wilkes helps prepare students in all majors to adapt to a technologically and socially evolving world. To graduate, students are required to complete a core curriculum and must complete from 120 to 136 credits, depending upon their major field. Graduates demonstrate mastery of the fundamental intellectual skills as well as the essential concepts and techniques of their field. Wilkes also teaches students responsibility and independence by expecting and encouraging active participation in the classroom and laboratory.

The University operates on a dual-semester calendar, with optional summer sessions and a January intersession. Advanced Placement test credits, College Level Examination Program (CLEP) credits, and International Baccalaureate (I.B.) credits are accepted.

Off-Campus Programs

An extensive cooperative education program is available to all students, with credit applicable in most major fields. Many government offices and private businesses in northeastern Pennsylvania, as well as in New York City, Philadelphia, Harrisburg, and Washington, D.C., employ Wilkes students. The study-abroad adviser works with interested students, placing them in the situation best suited to their academic pursuits. Most recently, students have attended programs in Austria, England, the Dominican Republic, France, Germany, Italy, and Spain.

Academic Facilities

The 72,000-square-foot Cohen Science Center is slated to open in fall 2013. The Eugene S. Farley Library has more than 220,000 volumes of books and bound journals, 857 current print journal and newspaper subscriptions, hundreds of database searches, and 800,000 microforms. Complete laboratory facilities are available for biology, chemistry, earth and environmental sciences, engineering, nursing, pharmacy, and psychology. Student-produced programming is broadcast from WCLH-FM, the University's 2,000-watt radio station, and transmitted from a professional-quality television studio via a local cable provider. Technology-enhanced classrooms contain Intel-based Apple computers for student use. The Sordoni Art Gallery is professionally equipped and staffed and produces exhibits each year by regionally, nationally, and internationally known artists. The Dorothy Dickson Darte Center for the Performing Arts contains a fully equipped 500-seat main theater and a 45-seat black box theater for presentation of plays, concerts, ballet, and other performances and lectures. Adjoining the center are studios, practice and rehearsal rooms, and faculty offices for the Division of Performing Arts. Breiseth Hall accommodates extensive computer facilities, psychology research laboratories, an integrative media lab, and modern classrooms with the latest audiovisual equipment. The University also operates a state-of-the-art distance learning facility that allows global conferencing and study using Internet and videoconferencing technology.

Costs

For the 2012–13 academic year, tuition and fees were $29,326 per year, and room and board were $11,908. Books cost approximately $900 per year.

Financial Aid

Financial aid is available to those students who demonstrate quality academic ability and/or financial need, as verified by the Free Application for Federal Student Aid (FAFSA). Merit-based and need-based aid is available from Wilkes University for qualified students. Scholarships ranging from $6,000 to $13,000 per year are available to students solely on the basis of academic ability. Approximately 94 percent of the student body receive some type of financial assistance, including scholarships, grants, loans, and work-study awards.

Faculty

Wilkes University has a nationally recruited full-time faculty of 157 members, approximately 90 percent of whom have earned Ph.D.'s or terminal degrees in their chosen field. Faculty evaluation criteria emphasize teaching excellence and effective advising, while recognizing continued scholarly activities. The student-faculty ratio is 14:1.

Student Government

An active student government provides a structure for student participation in University governance and student discipline. The Inter-Residence Hall Council and Commuter Council coordinate extracurricular activities for on-campus and commuter students.

Admission Requirements

Admission to Wilkes University is traditional. SAT or ACT scores are required. In cases where a student has taken the examination more than once, scores from the highest testing in each category are used in the evaluation process. Applicants for the freshman class should either have completed or be in the process of completing a college-preparatory course of study, including 3 to 4 years of mathematics, social studies, science, and English. Additional courses should be elected in academic subjects according to individual interests. Acceptable electives include foreign language and computing, among others. Students who have not followed this pattern may still qualify for admission if there is other strong evidence of preparation for college work. Letters of recommendation are not required but may be submitted. Students intending to pursue a major in pharmacy or a major in the College of Pharmacy and Nursing should have completed algebra I and II, geometry, and trigonometry prior to enrollment. Students intending to major in nursing should have completed courses in biology and chemistry. An audition is required for all prospective musical theatre and theatre arts students. Transfer students must submit a transcript from every college previously attended. All students are admitted to the University and not to specific departments, with the exception of the professional Nesbitt College of Pharmacy and Nursing and the Division of Performing Arts. Students individually receive academic advisement at the time of registration and throughout their enrollment.

Wilkes University is an Equal Opportunity/Affirmative Action institution. No applicant shall be denied admission to the University because of race, color, gender, religion, national or ethnic origin, sexual orientation, or handicap.

Application and Information

Applications for admission should be completed early in the senior year of secondary school and sent to the Admissions Office. Applications are reviewed after all of the student's credentials have been received. The review of applications begins on September 15, and notification of the University's decision reaches the student two to four weeks after the application file is complete. The priority deadline for all applications is March 1; applications for the Guaranteed Seat Pharmacy Program must be received by February 1. Other health science programs may have additional deadlines; students should contact the Admissions Office for more information.

Admissions Office
Wilkes University
84 West South Street
Wilkes-Barre, Pennsylvania 18766
Phone: 570-408-4400
        800-945-5378 Ext. 4400 (toll-free)
Website: http://www.wilkes.edu

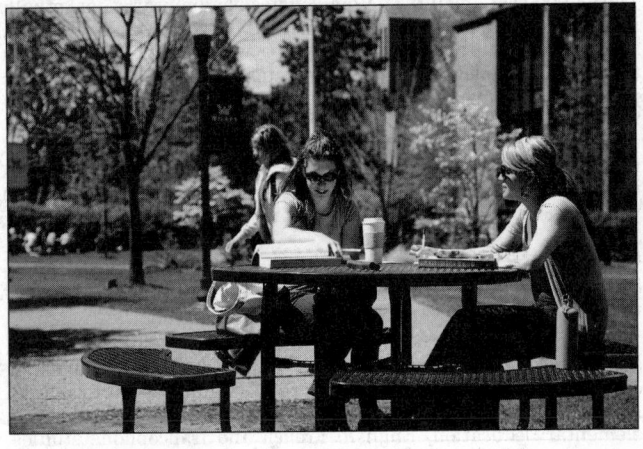

The campus of Wilkes University.

WILLIAM PATERSON UNIVERSITY OF NEW JERSEY

WAYNE, NEW JERSEY

The University

William Paterson University of New Jersey is a public university that offers an outstanding and affordable education to a diverse traditional and nontraditional student body through baccalaureate, graduate, and continuing education programs. Located in suburban Wayne, it serves nearly 11,500 full- and part-time students through five colleges: College of the Arts and Communication, Cotsakos College of Business, College of Education, College of Humanities and Social Sciences, and College of Science and Health.

The University is accredited by the Middle States Commission on Higher Education. Students can choose from 250 undergraduate and graduate academic programs on a beautiful campus with the facilities and equipment students need to succeed. Located on a 370-acre hilly, wooded site, William Paterson borders on High Mountain Preserve, which is nearly 1,200 acres of wetlands and woodlands; the campus is just three miles from Paterson's historic Great Falls and only 20 miles from the rich cultural, artistic, and commercial life of New York City.

William Paterson's small classes are taught by professors who are experts in their fields. Students enjoy individualized attention from faculty mentors who are committed to helping them develop strengths and uncover new ones. Financial aid is available to qualified students.

William Paterson offers students an active campus experience. Twenty-two percent of undergraduates reside on campus in ten residence halls or apartment-style facilities, which accommodate 2,600 students. Portions of the residence halls are dedicated to dynamic learning communities, as well as substance-free living.

Social, cultural, and recreational activities complement the academic programs. Cultural events take place throughout the year, featuring both William Paterson's own talent as well as renowned professional artists. Among events are concerts presenting jazz, classical, and contemporary music; theater productions; gallery exhibits; and the University's Distinguished Lecturer Series. The University Commons complex, including the John Victor Machuga Student Center, is the heart of the campus. This state-of-the-art campus center provides students with an exquisite setting for a vast array of social and extracurricular activities, dining venues, and student support services. There are more than eighty-five clubs and organizations to develop diverse activities for the entire student body. William Paterson has twenty-five social fraternities and sororities, and twenty-four honor societies. Students staff the award-winning campus radio station (WPSC) and the television station (WPC-TV), which develops a number of widely distributed television programs for local and statewide cable networks. The Recreation Center serves as the focal point for physical recreation. The 4,000-seat facility accommodates badminton, basketball, indoor tennis, volleyball, and racquetball courts, an exercise room, saunas, and Jacuzzis. "Pioneer spirit" is evident in the University's thirteen intercollegiate sports and numerous NCAA Division III post-season tournament appearances. In 2011, the Pioneers won first place in the All Girl Division college cheerleading and dance team national championship. Other club sports include the nationally ranked ice hockey, bowling, and rugby teams. Equestrian is also a club sport. The University has a competition-size indoor pool, outdoor tennis courts, and a lighted athletics field complex.

Majors and Degrees

Students can pursue B.A., B.S., B.F.A., B.M., and B.S.N. degrees through the University's five colleges.

Bachelor of Arts degrees are granted in Africana world studies, anthropology, art, art history, Asian studies, chemistry, communication, communication disorders, criminology and criminal justice, early childhood education, earth science, economics, elementary education, English, French and francophone studies, geography, history, Latin American and Latino studies, legal studies, liberal studies, mathematics, music, philosophy, political

science, psychology, secondary education, sociology, Spanish, sport management, and women's and gender studies.

Bachelor of Science degree programs include accounting, applied health, athletic training, biology, biotechnology, chemistry, computer science, environmental science, environmental sustainability, exercise science, global business, finance, financial planning, liberal studies with integrated math and science, management, marketing, mathematics, physical education, professional sales, and public health. The Bachelor of Science in Nursing is also offered.

The Bachelor of Fine Arts degree is awarded in fine arts. In the Bachelor of Music degree program, students can choose between performance, jazz, music education, and music management.

Courses leading to teacher certification are available in bilingual education, early childhood, elementary, secondary, special education, and teacher of students with disabilities (TSD).

For students planning a graduate education, degrees offered include a Master of Arts (M.A.), Master of Fine Arts (M.F.A.), Master of Science (M.S.), Master of Education (M.Ed.), Master of Business Administration (M.B.A.), Master of Arts in Teaching (M.A.T), Master of Music (M.M.), Master of Science in Nursing (M.S.N.), and Doctor of Nursing Practice (D.N.P.).

Academic Programs

The baccalaureate degree requires students to earn 120 credits in order to graduate. Approximately 31 to 40 of those credits are earned in University core curriculum (UCC) classes. Another 30 to 60 come from work in the student's major, and 20 to 40 can be earned in electives. UCC classes and major requirements will vary. The Career Development and Advisement Center counsels and advises students who are undecided as to their major, as well as their career choices.

Programs in the University Honors College offer students further challenges and include tracks in biopsychology, cognitive science, humanities, independent study, life science and environmental ethics, management, marketing, music, nursing, performing and literary arts, and social sciences. There are also preprofessional programs in dentistry, engineering, law, medicine (which includes dentistry, optometry, podiatry, and veterinary science), pharmacy, physical therapy, physician assistant studies, and speech-language pathology. Military experience may also be evaluated for credit.

Off-Campus Programs

William Paterson offers a special opportunity for off-campus study. Semester Abroad, a 15-credit program, is open to sophomores and juniors who wish to study for a semester at selected institutions in Australia, Denmark, Great Britain, Greece, Israel, Spain, and other countries around the world.

Academic Facilities

The new Science Complex features smart classrooms and sophisticated research laboratories designed to foster an interactive learning environment. The Nel Bolger R.N. Nursing Laboratory, located in Hunziker Wing, is a high-tech patient simulation laboratory suite that reflects actual hospital and clinical environments. The 1600 Valley Road facility houses the Cotsakos College of Business with its state-of-the-art Financial Learning Center, the Russ Berrie Institute, the Russ Berrie Professional Sales Lab, the College of Education, the Center for Continuing and Professional Education, and classrooms and computer laboratories. The Atrium contains computing support facilities, such as a writing center, multimedia language lab, and tutorial center. Among other academic resources are the nursing instructional facility, speech and hearing clinic, and child-care center. Hobart Hall, a state-of-the-art communication facility, houses television studios, computer labs, a film studio, an FCC-licensed FM radio station, and an uplink and four downlink satellite dishes. The site of the Allan and Michele Gorab Alumni House contains a pond, wetlands, woods, and a living laboratory for courses in biology and the environmental sciences. The David and Lorraine Cheng Library is open seven days a week when classes are in session and contains a collection of more than 360,000 volumes and 17,000 audiovisual items, with access to more than 50,000 electronic and print periodicals and journals. Cultural activities are supported by Shea Center for Performing Arts, which houses a 922-seat theater, as well as band, choral, and orchestral practice rooms and classrooms. The Ben Shahn Center for Visual Arts features extensive galleries, as well as art studios and classrooms, while the Power Art Center includes faculty offices and studios for three-dimensional design, photography, sculpture, ceramics, printmaking, woodworking, and painting.

Costs

Annual tuition (including fees) for the 2012–13 academic year was $11,694 for full-time (12 credits or more) students who are New Jersey residents and $19,094 for full-time nonresident students. Room and board cost approximately $10,310 per year. Total annual costs for a student living on campus were $22,004 for New Jersey residents and $29,404 for out-of-state students. These amounts are subject to change by the University's Board of Trustees.

Financial Aid

William Paterson provides a first-rate education at a reasonable cost. In accordance with the University's commitment to value in education, federal and state need-based financial aid programs are offered in the forms of grants, loans, scholarships, and work-study programs. In order to apply for financial aid, students should submit the Free Application for Federal Student Aid (FAFSA) to the United States Department of Education by April 1.

Each year, more than 1,600 scholarships totaling nearly $7 million are awarded for academic achievement, exceptional character qualities, leadership excellence, and financial need.

Faculty

William Paterson's faculty bring to the classroom a valuable blend of accomplished scholarship and practical, applied experience. Faculty members assist students with curriculum and career planning, which engenders open, personal communication between the students and faculty.

Through a formal reciprocal exchange relationship with various institutions worldwide, and through the Fulbright Scholarship Program, William Paterson University often hosts visiting international scholars. The University's faculty members have won thirty-eight Fulbright awards, one of the most prestigious academic distinctions in the world.

Student Government

The Student Government Association (SGA), of which all full-time and part-time students are automatically members, has become an influential voice in University decision making. Elected officers and various committees convey students' perspectives to the administration and advance their causes. The SGA is also responsible for chartering campus organizations and allocating student activity fees.

Admission Requirements

Admission is competitive. Admissions decisions for entering freshmen are based on a complete review of each student's academic record (course of study, grades, and rank) as well as the results of the SAT or ACT. Applicants are considered eligible if they have taken a minimum of 16 Carnegie units and have demonstrated strong academic ability. The students' secondary school record must show the following courses: English, 4 years (composition and literature); mathematics, 3 years (algebra I and II and geometry); laboratory science, 2 years (biology, chemistry, or physics); social science, 2 years (American history, world history, or political science);

and additional college-preparatory subjects, 5 units (advanced mathematics, literature, foreign language, or social sciences). In addition, students selecting a major in art or music (except musical studies) must submit a portfolio for review by the Art Department or must audition for the Music Department.

Transfer students must present at least 12 college-level credits with a minimum 2.0 GPA; science and nursing majors must have a recommended GPA of 3.0, and teacher certification program applicants must have a minimum 2.75 GPA. Applicants with fewer than 12 college credits must submit a high school transcript. Communication disorders majors must have a GPA of 3.5 and maintain a GPA of 3.3 once admitted to the graduate portion of the program. There are some limitations on the number of credits accepted; for example, a maximum of 70 credits from a two-year institution or 90 credits from a four-year college or university. Application review is completed only upon receipt of official transcripts from high schools, colleges, and universities. Unofficial transcripts or transcripts sent by students will not be used for admissions.

Application and Information

Application forms and transcripts from candidates for freshman status must be received by June 1 for fall admission and December 1 for spring admission. Freshmen scholarship candidates must submit completed application and supporting materials by February 15 for fall scholarship consideration; transfer students by May 1. Transfer students, readmitted students, and students seeking a second bachelor's degree must submit their materials by June 1 and December 1 for fall and spring entry, respectively. However, the University closes the application process earlier when the number of new and continuing students strains its ability to provide effective programs and services. A $50 application fee is required. Applications are reviewed on a rolling basis.

Campus tours are available during the fall and spring semesters on weekdays by appointment when classes are in session. Prospective student can sign up for a campus tour at www.wpunj.edu/campusvisit or take a virtual tour at www.wpunj.edu/virtualtour.

Office of Admissions
William Paterson University of New Jersey
Wayne, New Jersey 07470
Phone: 973-720-2125
E-mail: admissions@wpunj.edu
Website: http://www.wpunj.edu
 http://apps.facebook.com/WPAdmissions
 http://twitter.com/wpunj_admission

William Paterson University's hilltop suburban campus offers an environment where students may discover their unique strengths and find the power to achieve greatness.

WILLIAM PEACE UNIVERSITY
RALEIGH, NORTH CAROLINA

The University

William Peace University (WPU), located in downtown Raleigh, North Carolina, offers countless clubs and activities as well as innovative academic programs rooted in the liberal arts tradition. Its students develop an appreciation for lifelong learning, pursue meaningful careers, and build skills for ethical citizenship. The institution was founded in 1857 and named for founding benefactor William Peace, an elder of the First Presbyterian Church of Raleigh.

On average, more than 90 percent of William Peace University graduates find jobs or are enrolled in graduate school within a year of graduation.

William Peace University has been ranked among the nation's best in value-added gains in three of the four categories from the Collegiate Learning Assessment. This national assessment measures the improvement in critical thinking and analytical writing test scores of individual students between their freshman and senior years to determine how much they have learned while enrolled. WPU students also rank the University's academic programs among the best in the nation, according to the National Survey of Student Engagement.

Location

William Peace University offers the comfort of a small school with all the possibilities of a big city. Surrounded by beautiful oak trees and a large front lawn, the historic campus has carved out its own niche in downtown Raleigh. The University is just a short walk from the state capitol, museum, music halls, restaurants, theaters, and nightlife.

Students can observe the state legislature in session, dine downtown in popular cafes, attend concerts at the Raleigh Amphitheater and enjoy live theatre at the REP and North Carolina State University without ever needing a car.

Majors and Degrees

William Peace University offers Bachelor of Arts degrees in biology, communication, education, English, liberal studies, political science, pre-law, psychology, simulation and game design, and theater.

Bachelor of Science degrees are offered in biology (pre-med, pre-dental, pre–veterinary science) and business administration. A Bachelor of Fine Arts degree in musical theater is also offered.

A new core curriculum focuses on ethical decision making and emphasizes basic knowledge needed beyond graduation. In addition, there are mandatory courses in personal financial management, media literacy, and four years of writing courses within the English department. Students are also required to take a series of three classes focusing on career and professional development.

William Peace University also offers four evening, online, and/or classes-on-Saturday-only degrees through its School of Professional Studies. Students can earn a Bachelor of Arts degree in education, liberal studies, or psychology or a Bachelor of Science degree in business administration. Courses are taught by experienced faculty members in seven-week accelerated formats and include many opportunities for individualized academic advising. Classes are geared toward the unique needs of nontraditional students and working professionals.

Academic Programs

An academic internship related to the student's major is required in order to combine educational theory with job experience. Students are required to complete internships within their field of study during their junior or senior years. Internships are offered in conjunction with classes that include biweekly meetings with the faculty. Recent student internships sites include Duke University Medical Center, Mothers Against Drunk Driving, and the North Carolina General Assembly. In the past five years, an average of 60 percent of WPU graduates reported that their internship experience resulted in a job offer.

Eligible WPU students have the opportunity to join several national honor societies such as Sigma Tau Delta, Alpha Chi, Psi Chi, and TriBeta.

Students can also join the University's honors program that includes academic challenges, enriching experiences outside of the classroom, and opportunities to work on undergraduate research. The program allows academically talented and motivated students to study, conduct research, and exchange ideas in a challenging and supportive academic environment. It brings outstanding students and dynamic faculty together in courses that arouse curiosity and promote intellectual discovery and development. Program members can choose from a variety of courses that fulfill liberal education requirements, such as psychology, biology, cultural and physical anthropology, literature, and public speaking.

Students also have access to the Career Services Office, which provides career counseling, listings of internship options, workshops, and a resource library.

International study programs are offered in several parts of the world, and opportunities are available annually in a variety of other locations for short-term work or internships, or for a semester abroad.

Academic Facilities

William Peace University is a wireless campus. Students have access to courses and library facilities and online databases of other Raleigh colleges and universities through the Cooperating Raleigh Colleges consortium.

Computer laboratories, the library, and the student publications area are equipped with state-of-the-art computer hardware and software. There are specialized computer laboratories in the biology, media, theatre, and visual communication departments.

Student laboratories in the chemistry, general biology, and molecular and cellular biology departments are also available. A recital hall, the Leggett Theatre and a studio are available for students in the fine arts department.

Costs

Tuition and fees at William Peace University for the 2012–13 academic year were as follows: tuition, $23,700; room, $6,186; board, $2,814; and an annual student activity fee of $200. Costs are the same for both in-state and out-of-state students.

Financial Aid

William Peace University strongly believes that everyone should have access to a college education; therefore, the University is committed to making it as affordable as possible. At a time where colleges across the country are raising prices, WPU has actually lowered its costs.

Every accepted student is automatically considered for merit- and need-based aid (with a submitted FAFSA). Academic awards are available for the performing arts, community service, leadership, extracurricular activities, and more.

Through a combination of financial aid packaging, pursuit of scholarship and grant opportunities, and on-campus work-study groups, WPU works to make its educational program available to all qualified students, regardless of financial need. Information about payment options and the necessary forms are available online. Prospective students may call 919-508-2394 or e-mail finaid@peace.edu for more information on how to pay for college.

Faculty

William Peace University maintains a student-faculty ratio of 11:1.

Student Organizations and Activities

William Peace University offers more than thirty student clubs and organizations, including publications, performance groups and academic honor societies. Some of them include: Anthropology Club, cheer/drill collaboration, Campus Activities Board (CAB), Commuter Student Association, Helping Hands, MOSAIC (multicultural association), *Peace Times* (student newspaper), Student Government Association (SGA), Student Recreation Association, Society for Human Resource Management, Spectrum (LGBTQ), Student Athlete Advisory Committee, and William Peace University Singers.

Admission Requirements

William Peace University seeks to enroll individuals who will benefit from the academic programs and who will contribute to university life—a community upheld by the honor system, which requires students to maintain academic and personal integrity. The University encourages individuals with varied talents and interests representative of all social, economic, ethnic, and racial backgrounds to apply. Admission decisions are made on a rolling basis. The University does not discriminate in its recruitment and admission of students, regardless of gender, race, creed, color, religion, age, national and ethnic origin, sexual orientation, disability, or veteran status.

Admission requirements/procedures for students are defined by five categories: traditional first-year student (high school senior or graduate), high school student applying as a junior for early entrance, transfer student, international student, or former student (readmission).

Applications are reviewed individually and decisions are based on the following credentials: GPA in academic courses, SAT (verbal and math only) or ACT scores, course selection, rank in class, and an interview with an admissions representative, if requested. Further consideration will be given to an applicant's personal qualifications, co-curricular activities, community involvement, and overall potential for success. Consideration of a students' acceptance will also be granted upon the discretion of the Vice President for Enrollment.

Application and Information

Admissions decisions are made on a rolling basis. The Admissions Committee begins reviewing applications in July for the following fall. Applications received after April 1 for the fall semester and after November 1 for the spring semester are reviewed on a space-available basis.

The University requires each first-year applicant to submit an application, a nonrefundable $25 fee, SAT or ACT scores (senior-year scores are preferred), and an official transcript of all courses taken in high school. Transfer applicants must also submit official transcripts from all colleges and/or universities attended.

Inquiry cards and application forms may be completed online at www.peace.edu. Application forms and additional information may be obtained by contacting:

Office of Admissions
William Peace University
15 East Peace Street
Raleigh, North Carolina 27604
Phone: 919-508-2214
          800-PEACE-47
Fax: 919-508-2306
Website: http://www.peace.edu

William Peace University takes a different approach to higher education, going beyond lecture-based instruction and involving students more directly in their learning. William Peace students don't graduate college looking for any job; they graduate ready to enter the fields they went to college for in the first place.

WORCESTER POLYTECHNIC INSTITUTE
WORCESTER, MASSACHUSETTS

The University

Worcester Polytechnic Institute (WPI) believes in the power of its students to make an impact. They may want to be on the first Mars mission, find alternative energy sources, or work on cancer research. To prepare them for leadership and achievement after college, students do much more than study science and technology in the classroom and lab. They complete projects on campus and around the globe where they connect what they have learned in the classroom with pressing real-life challenges, from human health and the environment to business and engineering as well as the arts and humanities. Students grow personally, professionally, and intellectually as they discover how to apply their talents and turn ideas into tangible solutions.

WPI's aim is to educate students broadly so they can achieve greatly. Though WPI has a more than 145-year history, the curriculum, like its students, is both innovative and practical. Small classes, a flexible curriculum, and one-on-one interaction with professors at the top of their field make learning at WPI an experience unlike any other.

WPI has been widely recognized for its academic program. WPI was the only technological university out of sixteen national Leadership Institutions selected by the Association of American Colleges and Universities to serve as models of outstanding practices in liberal education. WPI is consistently ranked among the top national universities by *U.S. News & World Report*. In the National Survey of Student Engagement, WPI ranked number one for student-faculty interactions, which is a measure of the quality and quantity of time faculty members spend with undergraduates.

More than thirty areas of study in engineering, science, business management, and the liberal arts allow many academic options, from molecular biology to music. Exciting new interdisciplinary programs are driven by real-world demand, such as interactive media and game development, robotics engineering, architectural engineering, and environmental studies and engineering. The school also offers preprofessional programs and a five-year B.S./M.S. program.

With so many offerings, it is not surprising that more than 40 percent of students change their major at least once. At WPI, a comprehensive academic advising program and a wide array of academic support services help students make the right choices and reach their goals.

WPI students have received some of the nation's highest academic honors: the prestigious Marshall Scholarship, the NIH–Oxford/Cambridge Biomedical Research Scholarship, the Fulbright Scholarship, the Goldwater Scholarship, the Rotary Ambassadorial Scholarship, and the Society of Women Engineers Award. In addition, 2 students were recently named to the *USA Today* All-USA College Academic Team.

WPI is a member of the Colleges of Worcester Consortium, through which WPI students may register for courses at other colleges within the consortium and may take advantage of a wide range of cultural programming offered by consortium members. A consortium shuttle provides free transportation between campuses.

WPI has twenty varsity (NCAA Division III) athletics teams and thirty-four club and intramural sports. WPI won the Worcester Cup for six of the last seven years for the highest overall winning percentage in all sports in Worcester County. There are thirteen fraternities and five sororities, more than fifteen music or theater ensembles, and dozens of academic clubs, international organizations, religious groups, and other organizations. Overall there are more than 200 student clubs and activities.

Location

With its beautiful architecture, grassy quad, and ivy-covered walls, WPI has a traditional New England campus. Students stop and chat with their friends and professors on tree-lined paths, play pool between classes at the Campus Center, or get a coffee with friends. They study in the sun by the fountain in Reunion Plaza, go cosmic bowling, stop and smell the roses in the formal English garden behind Higgins House, or see a student play at the Little Theatre.

Home to twelve other colleges and universities and more than 35,000 college students, Worcester is a great college town. Late-night diners, clubs, museums, concert venues, and theaters are right down the hill from WPI in Worcester's vibrant downtown. Boston is less than an hour away by commuter rail, and there are great skiing and snowboarding at nearby Wachusett Mountain. Worcester is centrally located, with easy access to Providence, New York City, the Berkshires, the White Mountains, and Cape Cod.

Majors and Degrees

WPI offers the Bachelor of Science and the Bachelor of Arts degrees. Degree programs are offered in a wide variety of engineering and science: disciplines: actuarial mathematics, aerospace engineering, architectural engineering, biochemistry, biology and biotechnology, biomedical engineering, chemical engineering, chemistry, civil engineering, computer science, electrical and computer engineering, environmental engineering, environmental science, fire protection engineering, industrial engineering, interactive media and game development, mathematical sciences, mechanical engineering, physics, and robotics engineering.

In addition, there are programs in the areas of business and liberal arts: business/management; economics; environmental and sustainability studies; history; humanities and arts; international studies; literature; management engineering; management information systems; music; philosophy and religion; professional writing; psychology; society, technology, and policy; system dynamics; and theatre.

Four new interdisciplinary majors have been added to the curriculum in recent years: interactive media and game development, environmental engineering, bioinformatics and computational biology, and robotics engineering, which was the first undergraduate program in robotics in the nation. WPI offers several preprofessional programs, including dentistry, law, medicine, and veterinary medicine. Students may also design their own majors by combining courses offered in various WPI departments. Undergraduates who wish to continue their studies toward a master's degree at WPI may enroll in a combined, continuous B.S./M.S. program.

Academic Programs

Students take the equivalent of three courses (as either traditional courses or project work) during each of four 7-week terms (two in the fall and two in the spring). At WPI, learning is about more than just theories and ideas. Students learn how to put ideas into practice through the project-enriched curriculum. WPI undergraduates complete two projects before graduation: one directly related to their major and one working with a team of students to solve a problem at the intersection of society and technology—helping to bring electricity to remote villages in Thailand or studying the bioethics of cloning, for example. Students gain valuable professional skills, a talent for teamwork, and the confidence to dive right in no matter what the challenge.

WPI's academic program encourages collaboration, not competition. Students work closely together in project-oriented classes. Learning how to work in teams prepares students to achieve results and become leaders in life after college, no matter what path they take. Sixty-five percent of the classes have fewer than 20 students.

Top-tier employers seek out WPI graduates for their real-world experience and ability to work collaboratively. With a placement rate of more than 90 percent, students are recruited by leading organizations such as Pfizer, General Electric, Fidelity Investments, and IBM. Each year, WPI graduates are accepted at many prestigious graduate schools, including MIT, Yale, Princeton, Johns Hopkins, and Tufts University Medical School.

WPI graduates' starting salaries are higher than those of many other college graduates, according to the National Association of Colleges and Employers. In addition, WPI was recently recognized by Payscale.com for having the fourth highest average starting salaries among national universities.

Off-Campus Programs

WPI has sent more engineering and science students abroad than any other university as part of its hands-on, project-enriched curriculum. About half of WPI students complete projects outside the United States and two-thirds do projects off campus. With WPI's Global Perspective Program, students experience the challenge of solving real-world problems with their fellow students and immerse themselves in another culture. Students complete projects on campus or at any of the more than thirty project centers located on five continents around the globe, including Thailand, Australia, South Africa, Costa Rica, Switzerland, and the United States. Recent project sponsors include City of Venice, Italy; Desert Research Foundation, Namibia; Johnson & Johnson; Morgan Stanley; Environmental Protection Agency; and UNESCO. Through their seven-week project experience, students learn valuable professional skills, including communication, teamwork, and problem solving.

Academic Facilities

Among the many teaching, research, and project facilities available to undergraduates at WPI are a 71,000-square-foot campus center and a new Life Sciences and Bioengineering Center at Gateway Park, which is a state-of-the-art 130,000-square-foot facility at the life sciences-based campus that houses research in regenerative medicine, molecular nanotechnology, biosensors, plant systems, tissue engineering, and untethered health care. An $11-million renovation created the undergraduate Life Sciences Laboratory Center, which opened in 2009. The center has become WPI's main facility for undergraduate teaching and research in biology and biotechnology, biomedical engineering, chemistry and biochemistry, and chemical engineering. WPI's other state-of-the-art research facilities include two atomic-force microscopes, medical imaging laboratories, a fire science laboratory, a new team-based chemistry lab, a laser holography lab, a computer music lab, a satellite navigation lab, thirty multimedia classrooms and lecture halls, and a research library with thousands of electronic journals, books, databases, and nearly 300,000 volumes.

The university also has an exceptional computer and networking infrastructure. The facilities include nearly 600 computers in open-access, 24/7 labs; powerful UNIX workstations; a Web-based student information system; a high-speed data network that reaches every building and residence hall; and wireless access across the entire campus.

In addition to these existing facilities, a new state-of-the-art apartment-style residence hall, Faraday Hall, with over 200 beds, is slated to open in fall 2013. The building features recreation and fitness space, technology suites on the each floor, meeting rooms on the ground floor for group projects, and wireless access.

WPI opened a brand-new sports and recreation center in August 2012. It includes a four-court gymnasium, indoor jogging track, 14,000 square feet of fitness space, racquetball and squash courts, competition pool, workout studios, and rowing tanks.

Costs

For 2013–14, full-time tuition will be $42,178. Room and board charges are $13,082.

Financial Aid

For families with established financial need, aid, including financial aid packages, on-campus jobs, and loan programs, is available. In addition, all applicants are considered for merit scholarships. More information is available from WPI's Office of Financial Aid website at http://www.wpi.edu/+finaid.

Faculty

Besides being passionate about teaching, WPI's 460 full- and part-time faculty members are committed researchers and scholars with world-class credentials. They are leading contributors to the fields of bioengineering, cryptography, energy, fuel cells, information technology, and more. Thirteen members of the current faculty are Fulbright Scholars, one is a member of the National Academy of Engineering, and more than 50 are fellows of top national and international societies. In addition, 18 WPI professors have won the National Science Foundation's CAREER Award, which is its most prestigious award for young faculty members. WPI has a 14:1 student-faculty ratio. According to *U.S. News & World Report*, WPI faculty resources, which include salary, class size, and student-faculty ratio, rank forty-second among national universities.

Student Government

Through the Student Government Association, the Interfraternity Council, the Panhellenic Association, and the International Student Council, students self-govern and develop their own social programs. WPI prides itself on being a caring community that respects the contributions of individuals, appreciates the diversity of the student body, and emphasizes the importance of cooperation and teamwork.

Admission Requirements

Applicants for admission must have completed 4 years of English, 4 years of mathematics (including precalculus), and 2 years of lab science. Admission requirements include a school transcript, SAT or ACT scores or alternative materials through WPI's Flex Path, recommendations from a science or math teacher and a counselor, and a personal essay. For international students whose first language is not English, a TOEFL, IELTS, or Pearson's score is required.

The university has high standards for applicants but also looks for more than just outstanding academic performance. WPI takes care to admit students who will likely thrive at the university. They tend to be creative and curious; like to work in teams to get things done; are comfortable making their own decisions and setting their own courses; love math and science but feel just as passionate about literature, music, movies, and the arts; prefer to be leaders, not followers; and are ready to make a positive impact on the world around them.

Students are encouraged to visit the WPI campus to learn more about the university, see its facilities, and hear firsthand about the WPI experience from students and faculty members. WPI is open most school holidays and offers a wide range of options for tours, group information sessions, open houses, personal interviews, and Saturday visits. Details and schedules may be obtained from the Admissions Office website.

The deadline for early action round 1 is November 10, with notification by December 20. The deadline for early action round 2 is January 1, with notification by February 10. The regular decision deadline is February 1, with notification by April 1. For transfer admissions, the priority deadline is April 15; students are notified of admission decisions on a rolling basis.

Application and Information

To schedule a visit or request more information, students should contact:

Office of Admissions
Bartlett Center
Worcester Polytechnic Institute
100 Institute Road
Worcester, Massachusetts 01609-2280
Phone: 508-831-5286
Fax: 508-831-5875
E-mail: admissions@wpi.edu
Website: http://admissions.wpi.edu
　　　　http://www.facebook.com/WPIAdmissions
　　　　http://twitter.com/WPIAdmissions

Indexes

Majors

ACCOUNTING

Abilene Christian U (TX)
Adams State U (CO)
Adelphi U (NY)
AIB Coll of Business (IA)
Alabama State U (AL)
Albertus Magnus Coll (CT)
Albion Coll (MI)
Albright Coll (PA)
Alcorn State U (MS)
Alderson-Broaddus Coll (WV)
Alfred U (NY)
Alma Coll (MI)
Alvernia U (PA)
American Public U System (WV)
American U (DC)
The American U in Cairo (Egypt)
American U of Puerto Rico (PR)
Anderson U (IN)
Andrews U (MI)
Angelo State U (TX)
Appalachian State U (NC)
Arizona State U (AZ)
Arkansas State U (AR)
Arkansas Tech U (AR)
Asbury U (KY)
Ashland U (OH)
Assumption Coll (MA)
Athabasca U (AB, Canada)
Athens State U (AL)
Auburn U (AL)
Auburn U at Montgomery (AL)
Augsburg Coll (MN)
Augustana Coll (IL)
Augustana Coll (SD)
Aurora U (IL)
Avila U (MO)
Azusa Pacific U (CA)
Babson Coll (MA)
Baker U (KS)
Baldwin Wallace U (OH)
Ball State U (IN)
Barry U (FL)
Barton Coll (NC)
Baylor U (TX)
Bay Path Coll (MA)
Belhaven U (MS)
Bellarmine U (KY)
Belmont Abbey Coll (NC)
Belmont U (TN)
Bemidji State U (MN)
Benedictine Coll (KS)
Benedictine U (IL)
Bentley U (MA)
Berry Coll (GA)
Bethany Coll (WV)
Bethel Coll (IN)
Bethune-Cookman U (FL)
Binghamton U, State U of New York (NY)
Blackburn Coll (IL)
Bloomfield Coll (NJ)
Bloomsburg U of Pennsylvania (PA)
Bluefield Coll (VA)
Bluefield State Coll (WV)
Bluffton U (OH)
Bob Jones U (SC)
Boise State U (ID)
Boston Coll (MA)
Boston U (MA)
Bowie State U (MD)
Bowling Green State U (OH)
Bradley U (IL)
Bridgewater State U (MA)
Brock U (ON, Canada)
Bryant U (RI)
Buena Vista U (IA)
Butler U (IN)
Cabrini Coll (PA)
Caldwell Coll (NJ)
California Baptist U (CA)
California Lutheran U (CA)
California State U, Chico (CA)
California State U, Dominguez Hills (CA)
California State U, East Bay (CA)
California State U, Fresno (CA)
California State U, Fullerton (CA)
California State U, Long Beach (CA)

California State U, Northridge (CA)
California State U, San Bernardino (CA)
California State U, San Marcos (CA)
California State U, Stanislaus (CA)
Calumet Coll of Saint Joseph (IN)
Calvin Coll (MI)
Cameron U (OK)
Campbellsville U (KY)
Canisius Coll (NY)
Capital U (OH)
Cardinal Stritch U (WI)
Caribbean U (PR)
Carlow U (PA)
Carroll Coll (MT)
Carson-Newman U (TN)
Case Western Reserve U (OH)
Castleton State Coll (VT)
The Catholic U of America (DC)
Cedar Crest Coll (PA)
Cedarville U (OH)
Central Baptist Coll (AR)
Central Coll (IA)
Central Connecticut State U (CT)
Central Methodist U (MO)
Central Michigan U (MI)
Central Penn Coll (PA)
Central State U (OH)
Champlain Coll (VT)
Chapman U (CA)
Chatham U (PA)
Chestnut Hill Coll (PA)
Chowan U (NC)
Christian Brothers U (TN)
Christopher Newport U (VA)
City U of Seattle (WA)
Claremont McKenna Coll (CA)
Clark Atlanta U (GA)
Clarke U (IA)
Clayton State U (GA)
Clearwater Christian Coll (FL)
Cleary U (MI)
Clemson U (SC)
Cleveland State U (OH)
Coastal Carolina U (SC)
Coe Coll (IA)
The Coll at Brockport, State U of New York (NY)
Coll of Charleston (SC)
The Coll of Idaho (ID)
Coll of Mount St. Joseph (OH)
The Coll of New Jersey (NJ)
Coll of Saint Benedict (MN)
The Coll of Saint Rose (NY)
The Coll of St. Scholastica (MN)
Coll of Staten Island of the City U of New York (NY)
Coll of the Holy Cross (MA)
Coll of the Ozarks (MO)
The Coll of William and Mary (VA)
Colorado Mesa U (CO)
Colorado State U (CO)
Columbia Coll (MO)
Columbia Coll (SC)
Columbus State U (GA)
Concordia Coll (MN)
Concordia Coll–New York (NY)
Concordia U (QC, Canada)
Concordia U Chicago (IL)
Concordia U, Nebraska (NE)
Concordia U, St. Paul (MN)
Concordia U Wisconsin (WI)
Concord U (WV)
Converse Coll (SC)
Corban U (OR)
Cornerstone U (MI)
Creighton U (NE)
Culver-Stockton Coll (MO)
Dakota State U (SD)
Dakota Wesleyan U (SD)
Dalhousie U (NS, Canada)
Dallas Baptist U (TX)
Dalton State Coll (GA)
Davenport U, Grand Rapids (MI)
Defiance Coll (OH)
Delta State U (MS)
DePaul U (IL)
DeSales U (PA)
DeVry U, Phoenix (AZ)
DeVry U, Pomona (CA)

DeVry U, Westminster (CO)
DeVry U, Miramar (FL)
DeVry U, Orlando (FL)
DeVry U, Decatur (GA)
Dillard U (LA)
Doane Coll (NE)
Dominican Coll (NY)
Dominican U (IL)
Dordt Coll (IA)
Drake U (IA)
Drury U (MO)
Duquesne U (PA)
East Carolina U (NC)
East Central U (OK)
Eastern Illinois U (IL)
Eastern Mennonite U (VA)
Eastern Michigan U (MI)
Eastern New Mexico U (NM)
Eastern Washington U (WA)
East Tennessee State U (TN)
Edgewood Coll (WI)
Elizabeth City State U (NC)
Elizabethtown Coll (PA)
Elmira Coll (NY)
Elon U (NC)
Emmanuel Coll (MA)
Emporia State U (KS)
Endicott Coll (MA)
Excelsior Coll (NY)
Fairfield U (CT)
Fairleigh Dickinson U, Coll at Florham (NJ)
Fairleigh Dickinson U, Metropolitan Campus (NJ)
Fairmont State U (WV)
Faulkner U (AL)
Fayetteville State U (NC)
Felician Coll (NJ)
Ferris State U (MI)
Ferrum Coll (VA)
Flagler Coll (FL)
Florida Ag and Mech U (FL)
Florida Atlantic U (FL)
Florida Gulf Coast U (FL)
Florida Intl U (FL)
Florida National U (FL)
Florida Southern Coll (FL)
Florida State U (FL)
Fort Lewis Coll (CO)
Francis Marion U (SC)
Franklin Coll (IN)
Franklin Pierce U (NH)
Franklin U (OH)
Friends U (KS)
Frostburg State U (MD)
Furman U (SC)
Gallaudet U (DC)
Gannon U (PA)
Gardner-Webb U (NC)
Geneva Coll (PA)
George Fox U (OR)
George Mason U (VA)
Georgetown Coll (KY)
Georgetown U (DC)
Georgia Coll & State U (GA)
Georgia Regents U (GA)
Georgia Southern U (GA)
Georgia Southwestern State U (GA)
Georgia State U (GA)
Goldey-Beacom Coll (DE)
Gonzaga U (WA)
Gordon Coll (MA)
Goshen Coll (IN)
Governors State U (IL)
Graceland U (IA)
Grace U (NE)
Grambling State U (LA)
Grand Valley State U (MI)
Grand View U (IA)
Grantham U (MO)
Greenville Coll (IL)
Grove City Coll (PA)
Guilford Coll (NC)
Gustavus Adolphus Coll (MN)
Hamline U (MN)
Hampton U (VA)
Harding U (AR)
Hardin-Simmons U (TX)
Harris-Stowe State U (MO)
Hartwick Coll (NY)
Hawai`i Pacific U (HI)

HEC Montreal (QC, Canada)
Henderson State U (AR)
Hendrix Coll (AR)
High Point U (NC)
Hilbert Coll (NY)
Hillsdale Coll (MI)
Hofstra U (NY)
Holy Family U (PA)
Holy Names U (CA)
Hope Coll (MI)
Houghton Coll (NY)
Howard Payne U (TX)
Hunter Coll of the City U of New York (NY)
Huntingdon Coll (AL)
Huntington U (IN)
Husson U (ME)
Illinois Coll (IL)
Illinois State U (IL)
Illinois Wesleyan U (IL)
Immaculata U (PA)
Indiana State U (IN)
Indiana Tech (IN)
Indiana U of Pennsylvania (PA)
Indiana U–Purdue U Fort Wayne (IN)
Indiana Wesleyan U (IN)
Inter American U of Puerto Rico, Aguadilla Campus (PR)
Inter American U of Puerto Rico, Bayamón Campus (PR)
Inter American U of Puerto Rico, Fajardo Campus (PR)
Inter American U of Puerto Rico, Ponce Campus (PR)
Inter American U of Puerto Rico, San Germán Campus (PR)
Iona Coll (NY)
Iowa State U of Science and Technology (IA)
Ithaca Coll (NY)
Jacksonville State U (AL)
James Madison U (VA)
Jamestown Coll (ND)
John Brown U (AR)
John Carroll U (OH)
Johnson State Coll (VT)
Judson U (IL)
Juniata Coll (PA)
Kansas State U (KS)
Kansas Wesleyan U (KS)
Kean U (NJ)
Kennesaw State U (GA)
Kent State U (OH)
Kentucky Wesleyan Coll (KY)
Keuka Coll (NY)
Keystone Coll (PA)
King Coll (TN)
King's Coll (PA)
Kutztown U of Pennsylvania (PA)
Kuyper Coll (MI)
LaGrange Coll (GA)
Lake Erie Coll (OH)
Lakeland Coll (WI)
Lake Superior State U (MI)
Lamar U (TX)
Langston U (OK)
La Roche Coll (PA)
La Salle U (PA)
Lasell Coll (MA)
La Sierra U (CA)
Lebanon Valley Coll (PA)
Lee U (TN)
Lehigh U (PA)
Lehman Coll of the City U of New York (NY)
Le Moyne Coll (NY)
LeTourneau U (TX)
Lewis U (IL)
Liberty U (VA)
Limestone Coll (SC)
Lincoln Memorial U (TN)
Lincoln U (MO)
Lindenwood U (MO)
Linfield Coll (OR)
Lipscomb U (TN)
Lock Haven U of Pennsylvania (PA)
Long Island U–Brooklyn Campus (NY)
Long Island U–C. W. Post Campus (NY)

Louisiana Coll (LA)
Louisiana State U and Ag and Mech Coll (LA)
Louisiana State U in Shreveport (LA)
Lourdes U (OH)
Loyola Marymount U (CA)
Loyola U Chicago (IL)
Loyola U Maryland (MD)
Loyola U New Orleans (LA)
Lubbock Christian U (TX)
Luther Coll (IA)
Lynchburg Coll (VA)
Lyon Coll (AR)
Madonna U (MI)
Malone U (OH)
Manchester U (IN)
Manhattan Coll (NY)
Mansfield U of Pennsylvania (PA)
Maranatha Baptist Bible Coll (WI)
Marian U (WI)
Marietta Coll (OH)
Marist Coll (NY)
Marquette U (WI)
Marshall U (WV)
Mars Hill Coll (NC)
Marymount Manhattan Coll (NY)
Maryville U of Saint Louis (MO)
Marywood U (PA)
Massachusetts Coll of Liberal Arts (MA)
The Master's Coll and Sem (CA)
McKendree U (IL)
McMurry U (TX)
McNeese State U (LA)
Medaille Coll (NY)
Menlo Coll (CA)
Mercer U (GA)
Mercy Coll (NY)
Mercyhurst U (PA)
Merrimack Coll (MA)
Messiah Coll (PA)
Metropolitan State U of Denver (CO)
Miami U (OH)
Michigan State U (MI)
Middle Tennessee State U (TN)
Midwestern State U (TX)
Millikin U (IL)
Millsaps Coll (MS)
Minnesota State U Mankato (MN)
Minnesota State U Moorhead (MN)
Minot State U (ND)
Misericordia U (PA)
Mississippi Coll (MS)
Mississippi State U (MS)
Mississippi U for Women (MS)
Mississippi Valley State U (MS)
Missouri Baptist U (MO)
Missouri State U (MO)
Missouri Western State U (MO)
Molloy Coll (NY)
Monmouth Coll (IL)
Moravian Coll (PA)
Morehead State U (KY)
Mount Allison U (NB, Canada)
Mount Aloysius Coll (PA)
Mount Marty Coll (SD)
Mount Mary Coll (WI)
Mount Mercy U (IA)
Mount Saint Mary Coll (NY)
Mount St. Mary's Coll (CA)
Mount St. Mary's U (MD)
Mount Vernon Nazarene U (OH)
Muhlenberg Coll (PA)
Murray State U (KY)
National U (CA)
Nazareth Coll of Rochester (NY)
Neumann U (PA)
Newberry Coll (SC)
Newbury Coll (MA)
New England Coll (NH)
Newman U (KS)
New Mexico Highlands U (NM)
New Mexico State U (NM)
New York Inst of Technology (NY)
New York U (NY)
Niagara U (NY)
Norfolk State U (VA)
North Carolina Central U (NC)
North Carolina State U (NC)

North Carolina Wesleyan Coll (NC)
North Central Coll (IL)
North Dakota State U (ND)
Northeastern Illinois U (IL)
Northeastern U (MA)
Northern Arizona U (AZ)
Northern Illinois U (IL)
Northern Michigan U (MI)
Northern State U (SD)
North Greenville U (SC)
Northwest Christian U (OR)
Northwestern Coll (IA)
Northwestern Coll (MN)
Northwestern Oklahoma State U (OK)
Northwestern State U of Louisiana (LA)
Northwest Missouri State U (MO)
Northwest Nazarene U (ID)
Northwest U (WA)
Northwood U, Florida Campus (FL)
Northwood U, Michigan Campus (MI)
Northwood U, Texas Campus (TX)
Norwich U (VT)
Nova Southeastern U (FL)
Nyack Coll (NY)
Oakland U (MI)
Oglethorpe U (GA)
Ohio Dominican U (OH)
The Ohio State U (OH)
Ohio U (OH)
Ohio Valley U (WV)
Ohio Wesleyan U (OH)
Oklahoma Baptist U (OK)
Oklahoma Christian U (OK)
Oklahoma City U (OK)
Oklahoma State U (OK)
Old Dominion U (VA)
Oral Roberts U (OK)
Oregon State U (OR)
Ouachita Baptist U (AR)
Pace U (NY)
Pacific U (OR)
Palm Beach Atlantic U (FL)
Park U (MO)
Peirce Coll (PA)
Penn State Abington (PA)
Penn State Altoona (PA)
Penn State Beaver (PA)
Penn State Berks (PA)
Penn State Brandywine (PA)
Penn State DuBois (PA)
Penn State Erie, The Behrend Coll (PA)
Penn State Fayette, The Eberly Campus (PA)
Penn State Greater Allegheny (PA)
Penn State Hazleton (PA)
Penn State Lehigh Valley (PA)
Penn State Mont Alto (PA)
Penn State New Kensington (PA)
Penn State Schuylkill (PA)
Penn State Shenango (PA)
Penn State U Park (PA)
Penn State Wilkes-Barre (PA)
Penn State Worthington Scranton (PA)
Penn State York (PA)
Pennsylvania Coll of Technology (PA)
Pepperdine U, Malibu (CA)
Philadelphia U (PA)
Pittsburg State U (KS)
Plymouth State U (NH)
Point Loma Nazarene U (CA)
Point Park U (PA)
Portland State U (OR)
Post U (CT)
Potomac Coll (DC)
Providence Coll (RI)
Purdue U (IN)
Purdue U Calumet (IN)
Quincy U (IL)
Quinnipiac U (CT)
Radford U (VA)
Ramapo Coll of New Jersey (NJ)
Randolph-Macon Coll (VA)
Rasmussen Coll Bloomington (MN)
Rasmussen Coll Brooklyn Park (MN)
Rasmussen Coll Eagan (MN)
Rasmussen Coll Fargo (ND)
Rasmussen Coll Fort Myers (FL)
Rasmussen Coll Lake Elmo/ Woodbury (MN)

Rasmussen Coll Land O' Lakes (FL)
Rasmussen Coll Mankato (MN)
Rasmussen Coll Moorhead (MN)
Rasmussen Coll New Port Richey (FL)
Rasmussen Coll Ocala (FL)
Rasmussen Coll Rockford (IL)
Rasmussen Coll St. Cloud (MN)
Rasmussen Coll Tampa/Brandon (FL)
Regent U (VA)
Regis U (CO)
Rhode Island Coll (RI)
Rider U (NJ)
Robert Morris U (PA)
Roberts Wesleyan Coll (NY)
Rochester Inst of Technology (NY)
Rockford Coll (IL)
Roger Williams U (RI)
Roosevelt U (IL)
Rosemont Coll (PA)
Rutgers, The State U of New Jersey, Camden (NJ)
Rutgers, The State U of New Jersey, Newark (NJ)
Rutgers, The State U of New Jersey, New Brunswick (NJ)
Sacred Heart U (CT)
Sage Coll of Albany (NY)
Saginaw Valley State U (MI)
St. Ambrose U (IA)
Saint Anselm Coll (NH)
St. Bonaventure U (NY)
St. Edward's U (TX)
St. Francis Coll (NY)
St. Gregory's U, Shawnee (OK)
St. John Fisher Coll (NY)
Saint John's U (MN)
St. John's U (NY)
Saint Joseph's Coll (IN)
St. Joseph's Coll, Long Island Campus (NY)
St. Joseph's Coll, New York (NY)
Saint Joseph's U (PA)
Saint Leo U (FL)
Saint Louis U (MO)
Saint Martin's U (WA)
Saint Mary-of-the-Woods Coll (IN)
Saint Mary's Coll (IN)
Saint Mary's Coll of California (CA)
St. Mary's U (TX)
Saint Mary's U of Minnesota (MN)
Saint Michael's Coll (VT)
St. Norbert Coll (WI)
St. Thomas Aquinas Coll (NY)
St. Thomas U (FL)
Saint Vincent Coll (PA)
Salem State U (MA)
Salisbury U (MD)
Salve Regina U (RI)
Samford U (AL)
Sam Houston State U (TX)
San Diego State U (CA)
San Francisco State U (CA)
San Jose State U (CA)
Schreiner U (TX)
Scripps Coll (CA)
Seattle Pacific U (WA)
Seattle U (WA)
Seton Hill U (PA)
Shaw U (NC)
Shepherd U (WV)
Shippensburg U of Pennsylvania (PA)
Siena Coll (NY)
Siena Heights U (MI)
Simpson Coll (IA)
Simpson U (CA)
Slippery Rock U of Pennsylvania (PA)
Southeastern Louisiana U (LA)
Southeastern Oklahoma State U (OK)
Southeastern U (FL)
Southeast Missouri State U (MO)
Southern Arkansas U–Magnolia (AR)
Southern California Inst of Technology (CA)
Southern Connecticut State U (CT)
Southern Illinois U Carbondale (IL)
Southern Illinois U Edwardsville (IL)
Southern Methodist U (TX)
Southern Nazarene U (OK)
Southern New Hampshire U (NH)

Southern Oregon U (OR)
Southern Polytechnic State U (GA)
Southern Utah U (UT)
Southwest Baptist U (MO)
Southwestern Adventist U (TX)
Southwestern Coll (KS)
Southwestern U (TX)
Spalding U (KY)
Spring Arbor U (MI)
Spring Hill Coll (AL)
State U of New York at Fredonia (NY)
State U of New York at New Paltz (NY)
State U of New York at Oswego (NY)
State U of New York at Plattsburgh (NY)
State U of New York Coll at Geneseo (NY)
State U of New York Coll at Old Westbury (NY)
State U of New York Inst of Technology (NY)
Stephen F. Austin State U (TX)
Stetson U (FL)
Stevenson U (MD)
Stonehill Coll (MA)
Stratford U, Woodbridge (VA)
Suffolk U (MA)
Sullivan U (KY)
Sul Ross State U (TX)
Susquehanna U (PA)
Syracuse U (NY)
Tarleton State U (TX)
Taylor U (IN)
Temple U (PA)
Tennessee State U (TN)
Tennessee Wesleyan Coll (TN)
Texas A&M Intl U (TX)
Texas A&M U (TX)
Texas A&M U–Commerce (TX)
Texas A&M U–Kingsville (TX)
Texas Christian U (TX)
Texas Lutheran U (TX)
Texas Southern U (TX)
Texas State U–San Marcos (TX)
Texas Wesleyan U (TX)
Texas Woman's U (TX)
Thomas Edison State Coll (NJ)
Thomas More Coll (KY)
Thomas U (GA)
Thompson Rivers U (BC, Canada)
Tiffin U (OH)
Transylvania U (KY)
Trevecca Nazarene U (TN)
Trine U (IN)
Trinity Christian Coll (IL)
Trinity U (TX)
Troy U (AL)
Truman State U (MO)
Tulane U (LA)
Tuskegee U (AL)
Union Coll (KY)
Union Coll (NE)
Union U (TN)
Universidad Adventista de las Antillas (PR)
Université de Sherbrooke (QC, Canada)
Université du Québec en Outaouais (QC, Canada)
U at Albany, State U of New York (NY)
U at Buffalo, the State U of New York (NY)
The U of Akron (OH)
The U of Alabama (AL)
The U of Alabama at Birmingham (AL)
U of Alaska Anchorage (AK)
U of Alaska Fairbanks (AK)
The U of Arizona (AZ)
U of Arkansas at Little Rock (AR)
U of Bridgeport (CT)
The U of British Columbia (BC, Canada)
The U of British Columbia–Okanagan (BC, Canada)
U of Central Arkansas (AR)
U of Central Florida (FL)
U of Central Oklahoma (OK)
U of Charleston (WV)
U of Cincinnati (OH)
U of Colorado Boulder (CO)
U of Delaware (DE)
U of Denver (CO)

U of Evansville (IN)
The U of Findlay (OH)
U of Florida (FL)
U of Georgia (GA)
U of Great Falls (MT)
U of Guam (GU)
U of Guelph (ON, Canada)
U of Hartford (CT)
U of Hawaii at Manoa (HI)
U of Hawaii–West Oahu (HI)
U of Houston (TX)
U of Houston–Clear Lake (TX)
U of Houston–Downtown (TX)
U of Houston–Victoria (TX)
U of Idaho (ID)
U of Illinois at Chicago (IL)
U of Illinois at Springfield (IL)
U of Illinois at Urbana–Champaign (IL)
The U of Iowa (IA)
The U of Kansas (KS)
U of Kentucky (KY)
U of La Verne (CA)
U of Louisiana at Lafayette (LA)
U of Louisiana at Monroe (LA)
U of Louisville (KY)
U of Maine at Machias (ME)
U of Maryland, Coll Park (MD)
U of Maryland Eastern Shore (MD)
U of Maryland U Coll (MD)
U of Massachusetts Amherst (MA)
U of Massachusetts Dartmouth (MA)
U of Memphis (TN)
U of Miami (FL)
U of Michigan–Dearborn (MI)
U of Michigan–Flint (MI)
U of Minnesota, Crookston (MN)
U of Minnesota, Duluth (MN)
U of Minnesota, Twin Cities Campus (MN)
U of Mississippi (MS)
U of Missouri (MO)
U of Missouri–Kansas City (MO)
U of Missouri–St. Louis (MO)
U of Mobile (AL)
U of Montevallo (AL)
U of Mount Union (OH)
U of Nebraska at Omaha (NE)
U of Nebraska–Lincoln (NE)
U of Nevada, Las Vegas (NV)
U of Nevada, Reno (NV)
U of New Brunswick Fredericton (NB, Canada)
U of New Brunswick Saint John (NB, Canada)
U of New Haven (CT)
U of New Orleans (LA)
U of North Alabama (AL)
U of North Carolina at Asheville (NC)
The U of North Carolina at Charlotte (NC)
The U of North Carolina at Greensboro (NC)
The U of North Carolina at Pembroke (NC)
The U of North Carolina Wilmington (NC)
U of North Dakota (ND)
U of Northern Iowa (IA)
U of North Florida (FL)
U of North Georgia (GA)
U of North Texas (TX)
U of Notre Dame (IN)
U of Oklahoma (OK)
U of Oregon (OR)
U of Ottawa (ON, Canada)
U of Pennsylvania (PA)
U of Pittsburgh (PA)
U of Pittsburgh at Bradford (PA)
U of Pittsburgh at Greensburg (PA)
U of Portland (OR)
U of Puerto Rico at Bayamón (PR)
U of Puerto Rico at Ponce (PR)
U of Redlands (CA)
U of Regina (SK, Canada)
U of Rhode Island (RI)
U of Richmond (VA)
U of St. Francis (IL)
U of Saint Joseph (CT)
U of Saint Mary (KS)
U of St. Thomas (MN)
U of St. Thomas (TX)
U of San Diego (CA)
The U of Scranton (PA)
U of South Alabama (AL)

U of South Carolina (SC)
The U of South Dakota (SD)
U of Southern California (CA)
U of Southern Indiana (IN)
U of Southern Maine (ME)
U of Southern Mississippi (MS)
U of South Florida (FL)
The U of Tampa (FL)
The U of Tennessee (TN)
The U of Tennessee at Martin (TN)
The U of Texas at Arlington (TX)
The U of Texas at Austin (TX)
The U of Texas at Brownsville (TX)
The U of Texas at Dallas (TX)
The U of Texas at El Paso (TX)
The U of Texas at San Antonio (TX)
The U of Texas of the Permian Basin (TX)
The U of Texas–Pan American (TX)
U of the Cumberlands (KY)
U of the District of Columbia (DC)
U of the Incarnate Word (TX)
U of the Ozarks (AR)
U of the Virgin Islands (VI)
The U of Toledo (OH)
U of Tulsa (OK)
U of Utah (UT)
U of Washington, Bothell (WA)
U of Washington, Tacoma (WA)
U of Waterloo (ON, Canada)
The U of West Alabama (AL)
The U of Western Ontario (ON, Canada)
U of West Florida (FL)
U of West Georgia (GA)
U of Windsor (ON, Canada)
U of Wisconsin–Eau Claire (WI)
U of Wisconsin–Green Bay (WI)
U of Wisconsin–La Crosse (WI)
U of Wisconsin–Madison (WI)
U of Wisconsin–Milwaukee (WI)
U of Wisconsin–Parkside (WI)
U of Wisconsin–Platteville (WI)
U of Wisconsin–Stevens Point (WI)
U of Wisconsin–Superior (WI)
U of Wyoming (WY)
Upper Iowa U (IA)
Ursuline Coll (OH)
Utah State U (UT)
Utica Coll (NY)
Valdosta State U (GA)
Valparaiso U (IN)
Villanova U (PA)
Virginia Commonwealth U (VA)
Virginia Polytechnic Inst and State U (VA)
Virginia State U (VA)
Virginia Union U (VA)
Viterbo U (WI)
Wagner Coll (NY)
Wake Forest U (NC)
Walden U (MN)
Walla Walla U (WA)
Walsh U (OH)
Wartburg Coll (IA)
Washburn U (KS)
Washington & Jefferson Coll (PA)
Washington State U (WA)
Washington U in St. Louis (MO)
Waynesburg U (PA)
Wayne State U (MI)
Webber Intl U (FL)
Weber State U (UT)
Webster U (MO)
Wesley Coll (DE)
West Chester U of Pennsylvania (PA)
Western Carolina U (NC)
Western Connecticut State U (CT)
Western Illinois U (IL)
Western Kentucky U (KY)
Western Michigan U (MI)
Western State Colorado U (CO)
West Liberty U (WV)
Westminster Coll (MO)
Westminster Coll (UT)
West Texas A&M U (TX)
West Virginia State U (WV)
West Virginia U (WV)
West Virginia U Inst of Technology (WV)
West Virginia Wesleyan Coll (WV)
Wheeling Jesuit U (WV)
Whitworth U (WA)
Wichita State U (KS)
Widener U (PA)
Wilberforce U (OH)

(partial text at top left, obscured by black banner)

...jors
...nting

...ew Jersey

...OH)

...ouisiana (LA)
...ennsylvania (PA)
...the City U of New York

...wn State U (OH)

**...UNTING AND
...NESS/MANAGEMENT**
...ka Pacific U (AK)
...bson Coll (MA)
...nisius Coll (NY)
...hestnut Hill Coll (PA)
East Carolina U (NC)
EDP Coll of Puerto Rico, Inc. (PR)
Illinois State U (IL)
Keystone Coll (PA)
Maranatha Baptist Bible Coll (WI)
Mercy Coll (NY)
National U (CA)
Northcentral U (AZ)
Rasmussen Coll Appleton (WI)
Rasmussen Coll Fort Myers (FL)
Rasmussen Coll Green Bay (WI)
Rasmussen Coll Land O' Lakes (FL)
Rasmussen Coll New Port Richey (FL)
Rasmussen Coll Ocala (FL)
Rasmussen Coll Tampa/Brandon (FL)
Rasmussen Coll Wausau (WI)
Rocky Mountain Coll (MT)
St. Francis Coll (NY)
Sierra Nevada Coll (NV)
Spalding U (KY)
U of Great Falls (MT)
U of Illinois at Urbana–Champaign (IL)
The U of Western Ontario (ON, Canada)
Walla Walla U (WA)
Washington and Lee U (VA)
Western State Colorado U (CO)
Young Harris Coll (GA)

**ACCOUNTING AND
COMPUTER SCIENCE**
California State U, Chico (CA)
Goldey-Beacom Coll (DE)
Husson U (ME)
Saint Mary-of-the-Woods Coll (IN)
San Jose State U (CA)
Southern New Hampshire U (NH)

ACCOUNTING AND FINANCE
Babson Coll (MA)
Bentley U (MA)
Bethel U (MN)
Boise State U (ID)
Bridgewater State U (MA)
Clarkson U (NY)
DEREE—The American Coll of Greece (Greece)
Drake U (IA)
Ferris State U (MI)
Granite State Coll (NH)
Hiram Coll (OH)
Lourdes U (OH)
Northern Michigan U (MI)
Salem State U (MA)
Tabor Coll (KS)
U of North Dakota (ND)
U of Southern Maine (ME)
U of Waterloo (ON, Canada)
The U of Western Ontario (ON, Canada)
U of Windsor (ON, Canada)
Western State Colorado U (CO)

ACCOUNTING RELATED
Bentley U (MA)
Brigham Young U (UT)
Central Michigan U (MI)
Franklin U (OH)
Maryville U of Saint Louis (MO)
McDaniel Coll (MD)
North Dakota State U (ND)
Northern Michigan U (MI)
Rocky Mountain Coll (MT)

Saint Mary's Coll of California (CA)
State U of New York at Oswego (NY)

**ACCOUNTING TECHNOLOGY
AND BOOKKEEPING**
Ferris State U (MI)
Florida National U (FL)
Lewis-Clark State Coll (ID)
Post U (CT)
Rowan U (NJ)
St. Edward's U (TX)
U of Hawaii at Manoa (HI)
U of Miami (FL)

ACOUSTICS
American U (DC)

ACTING
Baldwin Wallace U (OH)
Bard Coll (NY)
Barry U (FL)
Baylor U (TX)
Belmont U (TN)
Bennington Coll (VT)
Boston U (MA)
Bradley U (IL)
Brigham Young U (UT)
California State U, Long Beach (CA)
Central Michigan U (MI)
Chapman U (CA)
Coe Coll (IA)
The Coll at Brockport, State U of New York (NY)
Columbia Coll Chicago (IL)
Dalhousie U (NS, Canada)
DePaul U (IL)
Drake U (IA)
Elon U (NC)
Emerson Coll (MA)
Florida State U (FL)
Hofstra U (NY)
Illinois Wesleyan U (IL)
Ithaca Coll (NY)
Johnson State Coll (VT)
Kean U (NJ)
Keene State Coll (NH)
Lindenwood U (MO)
Lipscomb U (TN)
Long Island U–C. W. Post Campus (NY)
Marymount Manhattan Coll (NY)
Nazareth Coll of Rochester (NY)
Northwest Missouri State U (MO)
Oakland U (MI)
Ohio U (OH)
Oklahoma City U (OK)
Old Dominion U (VA)
Oral Roberts U (OK)
Pace U (NY)
Penn State Abington (PA)
Penn State Altoona (PA)
Penn State Beaver (PA)
Penn State Berks (PA)
Penn State Brandywine (PA)
Penn State DuBois (PA)
Penn State Erie, The Behrend Coll (PA)
Penn State Fayette, The Eberly Campus (PA)
Penn State Greater Allegheny (PA)
Penn State Hazleton (PA)
Penn State Lehigh Valley (PA)
Penn State Mont Alto (PA)
Penn State New Kensington (PA)
Penn State Schuylkill (PA)
Penn State Shenango (PA)
Penn State U Park (PA)
Penn State Wilkes-Barre (PA)
Penn State Worthington Scranton (PA)
Penn State York (PA)
Pepperdine U, Malibu (CA)
Roosevelt U (IL)
St. Edward's U (TX)
Salem State U (MA)
Seton Hill U (PA)
Shenandoah U (VA)
Slippery Rock U of Pennsylvania (PA)
Suffolk U (MA)
Tabor Coll (KS)
Temple U (PA)
Texas Christian U (TX)
Trinity U (TX)
U of Hartford (CT)

U of Maryland, Baltimore County (MD)
U of Miami (FL)
U of Northern Iowa (IA)
U of Regina (SK, Canada)
U of Southern California (CA)
The U of the Arts (PA)
U of Windsor (ON, Canada)
Virginia Intermont Coll (VA)
Webster U (MO)
Western Michigan U (MI)
Wright State U (OH)

ACTUARIAL SCIENCE
Appalachian State U (NC)
Ashland U (OH)
Aurora U (IL)
Ball State U (IN)
Bellarmine U (KY)
Binghamton U, State U of New York (NY)
Bob Jones U (SC)
Bowling Green State U (OH)
Bradley U (IL)
Brigham Young U (UT)
Bryant U (RI)
Butler U (IN)
Central Coll (IA)
Central Michigan U (MI)
Concordia U (QC, Canada)
Concordia U Wisconsin (WI)
Dakota Wesleyan U (SD)
Drake U (IA)
Eastern Michigan U (MI)
Georgia State U (GA)
High Point U (NC)
Indiana U Northwest (IN)
Indiana U South Bend (IN)
Lebanon Valley Coll (PA)
Maryville U of Saint Louis (MO)
The Master's Coll and Sem (CA)
Michigan State U (MI)
Milwaukee School of Eng (WI)
North Central Coll (IL)
Northwestern Coll (IA)
Oakland U (MI)
The Ohio State U (OH)
Ohio U (OH)
Olivet Coll (MI)
Penn State Abington (PA)
Penn State Altoona (PA)
Penn State Beaver (PA)
Penn State Berks (PA)
Penn State Brandywine (PA)
Penn State DuBois (PA)
Penn State Erie, The Behrend Coll (PA)
Penn State Fayette, The Eberly Campus (PA)
Penn State Greater Allegheny (PA)
Penn State Hazleton (PA)
Penn State Lehigh Valley (PA)
Penn State Mont Alto (PA)
Penn State New Kensington (PA)
Penn State Schuylkill (PA)
Penn State Shenango (PA)
Penn State Wilkes-Barre (PA)
Penn State Worthington Scranton (PA)
Penn State York (PA)
Pittsburg State U (KS)
Purdue U (IN)
Quinnipiac U (CT)
Rider U (NJ)
Robert Morris U (PA)
Roosevelt U (IL)
St. John's U (NY)
Saint Joseph's U (PA)
Saint Mary's U of Minnesota (MN)
Siena Coll (NY)
Simon Fraser U (BC, Canada)
Simpson Coll (IA)
Slippery Rock U of Pennsylvania (PA)
Spring Arbor U (MI)
Temple U (PA)
Texas Christian U (TX)
U at Albany, State U of New York (NY)
U of Central Oklahoma (OK)
U of Illinois at Urbana–Champaign (IL)
The U of Iowa (IA)
U of Michigan–Flint (MI)
U of Minnesota, Twin Cities Campus (MN)
U of Nebraska–Lincoln (NE)

U of Pennsylvania (PA)
U of Regina (SK, Canada)
U of St. Thomas (MN)
The U of Texas at Dallas (TX)
The U of Texas at San Antonio (TX)
U of Waterloo (ON, Canada)
The U of Western Ontario (ON, Canada)
U of Wisconsin–Madison (WI)
U of Wisconsin–Milwaukee (WI)
Valparaiso U (IN)
Worcester Polytechnic Inst (MA)
Xavier U (OH)

**ADMINISTRATIVE ASSISTANT
AND SECRETARIAL SCIENCE**
Campbellsville U (KY)
EDP Coll of Puerto Rico, Inc. (PR)
Faith Baptist Bible Coll and Theological Sem (IA)
Inter American U of Puerto Rico, Bayamón Campus (PR)
Lamar U (TX)
Langston U (OK)
Lewis-Clark State Coll (ID)
Mount Vernon Nazarene U (OH)
Northwest Missouri State U (MO)
Sul Ross State U (TX)
Tennessee State U (TN)
Universidad Adventista de las Antillas (PR)
Valdosta State U (GA)

**ADULT AND CONTINUING
EDUCATION**
Auburn U (AL)
Brock U (ON, Canada)
Dakota Wesleyan U (SD)
Eastern Washington U (WA)
Fisher Coll (MA)
Louisiana Coll (LA)
Louisiana State U and Ag and Mech Coll (LA)
Mars Hill Coll (NC)
Tennessee State U (TN)
Texas A&M U–Commerce (TX)
U of Central Oklahoma (OK)
U of Georgia (GA)
U of Minnesota, Twin Cities Campus (MN)
U of Nevada, Las Vegas (NV)
U of New Brunswick Fredericton (NB, Canada)
U of Regina (SK, Canada)

**ADULT AND CONTINUING
EDUCATION
ADMINISTRATION**
Concordia Coll–New York (NY)
Marshall U (WV)
Penn State Abington (PA)
Penn State Altoona (PA)
Penn State Beaver (PA)
Penn State Berks (PA)
Penn State Brandywine (PA)
Penn State DuBois (PA)
Penn State Erie, The Behrend Coll (PA)
Penn State Fayette, The Eberly Campus (PA)
Penn State Greater Allegheny (PA)
Penn State Hazleton (PA)
Penn State Lehigh Valley (PA)
Penn State Mont Alto (PA)
Penn State New Kensington (PA)
Penn State Schuylkill (PA)
Penn State Shenango (PA)
Penn State U Park (PA)
Penn State Wilkes-Barre (PA)
Penn State Worthington Scranton (PA)
Penn State York (PA)

**ADULT DEVELOPMENT AND
AGING**
Bowling Green State U (OH)
Madonna U (MI)
St. Thomas U (NB, Canada)
U of Guelph (ON, Canada)
York Coll of the City U of New York (NY)

ADULT HEALTH NURSING
Concordia Coll–New York (NY)
Pennsylvania Coll of Technology (PA)
U of Rochester (NY)
Worcester State U (MA)

ADVERTISING
Acad of Art U (CA)
Adams State U (CO)
American Acad of Art (IL)
Appalachian State U (NC)
Art Center Coll of Design (CA)
Barry U (FL)
Bowling Green State U (OH)
Bradley U (IL)
Brigham Young U (UT)
California State U, East Bay (CA)
California State U, Fullerton (CA)
Central Michigan U (MI)
Columbia Coll Chicago (IL)
Drake U (IA)
Drury U (MO)
Emerson Coll (MA)
Fashion Inst of Technology (NY)
Ferris State U (MI)
Franklin Pierce U (NH)
Gannon U (PA)
Grand Valley State U (MI)
Hampton U (VA)
Harding U (AR)
Hawai'i Pacific U (HI)
Intl Acad of Design & Technology (FL)
Iona Coll (NY)
Iowa State U of Science and Technology (IA)
Kent State U (OH)
Lindenwood U (MO)
Louisiana Coll (LA)
Loyola U Chicago (IL)
Marquette U (WI)
Michigan State U (MI)
Murray State U (KY)
New York Inst of Technology (NY)
Northwest Missouri State U (MO)
Northwood U, Florida Campus (FL)
Oklahoma Christian U (OK)
Oklahoma City U (OK)
Pace U (NY)
Penn State Abington (PA)
Penn State Altoona (PA)
Penn State Beaver (PA)
Penn State Berks (PA)
Penn State Brandywine (PA)
Penn State DuBois (PA)
Penn State Erie, The Behrend Coll (PA)
Penn State Fayette, The Eberly Campus (PA)
Penn State Greater Allegheny (PA)
Penn State Hazleton (PA)
Penn State Lehigh Valley (PA)
Penn State Mont Alto (PA)
Penn State New Kensington (PA)
Penn State Schuylkill (PA)
Penn State Shenango (PA)
Penn State U Park (PA)
Penn State Wilkes-Barre (PA)
Penn State Worthington Scranton (PA)
Penn State York (PA)
Pepperdine U, Malibu (CA)
Pittsburg State U (KS)
Point Park U (PA)
Portland State U (OR)
Quinnipiac U (CT)
Rider U (NJ)
Rochester Inst of Technology (NY)
Rowan U (NJ)
St. Ambrose U (IA)
St. John's U (NY)
Salem State U (MA)
San Diego State U (CA)
San Jose State U (CA)
South Dakota State U (SD)
Southern Methodist U (TX)
Southern New Hampshire U (NH)
Spring Arbor U (MI)
Suffolk U (MA)
Syracuse U (NY)
Temple U (PA)
Texas State U–San Marcos (TX)
Texas Wesleyan U (TX)
Union U (TN)
The U of Alabama (AL)
U of Central Florida (FL)
U of Central Oklahoma (OK)
U of Colorado Boulder (CO)
U of Florida (FL)
U of Georgia (GA)
U of Houston (TX)
U of Idaho (ID)

U of Illinois at Urbana–Champaign (IL)
U of Miami (FL)
U of Missouri (MO)
U of Oklahoma (OK)
U of Oregon (OR)
U of South Carolina (SC)
U of Southern Indiana (IN)
U of Southern Mississippi (MS)
The U of Tennessee (TN)
The U of Texas at Arlington (TX)
The U of Texas at Austin (TX)
Washington State U (WA)
Washington U in St. Louis (MO)
Waynesburg U (PA)
Webster U (MO)
Wesleyan Coll (GA)
Western Kentucky U (KY)
Western Michigan U (MI)
West Texas A&M U (TX)
Widener U (PA)
Xavier U (OH)
Youngstown State U (OH)

AERONAUTICAL/AEROSPACE ENGINEERING TECHNOLOGY
Bowling Green State U (OH)
New York Inst of Technology (NY)
Saint Louis U (MO)
Utah State U (UT)

AERONAUTICS/AVIATION/AEROSPACE SCIENCE AND TECHNOLOGY
American Public U System (WV)
Arizona State U (AZ)
Augsburg Coll (MN)
Bridgewater State U (MA)
Delta State U (MS)
Elizabeth City State U (NC)
Embry-Riddle Aeronautical U–Daytona (FL)
Embry-Riddle Aeronautical U–Prescott (AZ)
Embry-Riddle Aeronautical U–Worldwide (FL)
Florida Inst of Technology (FL)
Inter American U of Puerto Rico, Bayamón Campus (PR)
Kent State U (OH)
Liberty U (VA)
Metropolitan State U of Denver (CO)
Middle Tennessee State U (TN)
The Ohio State U (OH)
Ohio U (OH)
Oklahoma State U (OK)
Pacific Union Coll (CA)
Purdue U (IN)
San Diego Christian Coll (CA)
San Jose State U (CA)
South Dakota State U (SD)
Southern Nazarene U (OK)
Texas Lutheran U (TX)
Texas Southern U (TX)
U of Alaska Anchorage (AK)
U of Minnesota, Crookston (MN)
U of Nebraska at Omaha (NE)
U of Oklahoma (OK)
U of the District of Columbia (DC)
Vaughn Coll of Aeronautics and Technology (NY)
Walla Walla U (WA)

AEROSPACE, AERONAUTICAL AND ASTRONAUTICAL/SPACE ENGINEERING
Arizona State U (AZ)
Auburn U (AL)
Boston U (MA)
California Polytechnic State U, San Luis Obispo (CA)
California State Polytechnic U, Pomona (CA)
California State U, Long Beach (CA)
Case Western Reserve U (OH)
Clarkson U (NY)
Daniel Webster Coll (NH)
Embry-Riddle Aeronautical U–Daytona (FL)
Embry-Riddle Aeronautical U–Prescott (AZ)
Florida Inst of Technology (FL)
Illinois Inst of Technology (IL)
Inter American U of Puerto Rico, Bayamón Campus (PR)

Iowa State U of Science and Technology (IA)
Massachusetts Inst of Technology (MA)
Mississippi State U (MS)
Missouri U of Science and Technology (MO)
New Mexico State U (NM)
North Carolina State U (NC)
The Ohio State U (OH)
Oklahoma State U (OK)
Penn State Abington (PA)
Penn State Altoona (PA)
Penn State Beaver (PA)
Penn State Berks (PA)
Penn State Brandywine (PA)
Penn State DuBois (PA)
Penn State Erie, The Behrend Coll (PA)
Penn State Fayette, The Eberly Campus (PA)
Penn State Greater Allegheny (PA)
Penn State Hazleton (PA)
Penn State Lehigh Valley (PA)
Penn State Mont Alto (PA)
Penn State New Kensington (PA)
Penn State Schuylkill (PA)
Penn State Shenango (PA)
Penn State U Park (PA)
Penn State Wilkes-Barre (PA)
Penn State Worthington Scranton (PA)
Penn State York (PA)
Purdue U (IN)
Rensselaer Polytechnic Inst (NY)
Rochester Inst of Technology (NY)
Saint Louis U (MO)
San Diego State U (CA)
San Jose State U (CA)
Stanford U (CA)
Syracuse U (NY)
Texas A&M U (TX)
Tuskegee U (AL)
United States Air Force Acad (CO)
United States Naval Acad (MD)
U at Buffalo, the State U of New York (NY)
The U of Akron (OH)
The U of Alabama (AL)
The U of Arizona (AZ)
U of California, Davis (CA)
U of California, Irvine (CA)
U of California, Los Angeles (CA)
U of Central Florida (FL)
U of Cincinnati (OH)
U of Colorado Boulder (CO)
U of Florida (FL)
U of Illinois at Urbana–Champaign (IL)
The U of Kansas (KS)
U of Maryland, Coll Park (MD)
U of Miami (FL)
U of Michigan (MI)
U of Minnesota, Twin Cities Campus (MN)
U of Notre Dame (IN)
U of Oklahoma (OK)
U of Southern California (CA)
The U of Tennessee (TN)
The U of Texas at Arlington (TX)
The U of Texas at Austin (TX)
U of Virginia (VA)
Utah State U (UT)
Virginia Polytechnic Inst and State U (VA)
Western Michigan U (MI)
West Virginia U (WV)
Wichita State U (KS)
Worcester Polytechnic Inst (MA)

AFRICAN AMERICAN/BLACK STUDIES
Amherst Coll (MA)
Arizona State U (AZ)
Bates Coll (ME)
Berea Coll (KY)
Binghamton U, State U of New York (NY)
Bowling Green State U (OH)
Brown U (RI)
California State U, Dominguez Hills (CA)
California State U, East Bay (CA)
California State U, Fresno (CA)
California State U, Fullerton (CA)
California State U, Long Beach (CA)

California State U, Los Angeles (CA)
California State U, Northridge (CA)
Chicago State U (IL)
City Coll of the City U of New York (NY)
Claflin U (SC)
Claremont McKenna Coll (CA)
Cleveland State U (OH)
Coe Coll (IA)
Colby Coll (ME)
Colgate U (NY)
The Coll at Brockport, State U of New York (NY)
Coll of Staten Island of the City U of New York (NY)
The Coll of William and Mary (VA)
The Coll of Wooster (OH)
Columbia U (NY)
Columbia U, School of General Studies (NY)
Dartmouth Coll (NH)
DePaul U (IL)
DePauw U (IN)
Dillard U (LA)
Dominican U (IL)
Earlham Coll (IN)
East Carolina U (NC)
Eastern Illinois U (IL)
Eastern Michigan U (MI)
Florida Ag and Mech U (FL)
Georgia State U (GA)
Gettysburg Coll (PA)
Guilford Coll (NC)
Hamilton Coll (NY)
Hampshire Coll (MA)
Hobart and William Smith Colls (NY)
Hunter Coll of the City U of New York (NY)
Indiana State U (IN)
Indiana U Bloomington (IN)
Indiana U Northwest (IN)
Indiana–Purdue U Indianapolis (IN)
The Johns Hopkins U (MD)
Kent State U (OH)
Knox Coll (IL)
Lehman Coll of the City U of New York (NY)
Loyola Marymount U (CA)
Loyola U Chicago (IL)
Luther Coll (IA)
Mercer U (GA)
Metropolitan State U of Denver (CO)
Miami U (OH)
Morehouse Coll (GA)
Mount Holyoke Coll (MA)
New York U (NY)
North Carolina State U (NC)
Northeastern U (MA)
The Ohio State U (OH)
Ohio U (OH)
Ohio Wesleyan U (OH)
Old Dominion U (VA)
Penn State Abington (PA)
Penn State Altoona (PA)
Penn State Beaver (PA)
Penn State Berks (PA)
Penn State Brandywine (PA)
Penn State DuBois (PA)
Penn State Erie, The Behrend Coll (PA)
Penn State Fayette, The Eberly Campus (PA)
Penn State Greater Allegheny (PA)
Penn State Hazleton (PA)
Penn State Lehigh Valley (PA)
Penn State Mont Alto (PA)
Penn State New Kensington (PA)
Penn State Schuylkill (PA)
Penn State Shenango (PA)
Penn State U Park (PA)
Penn State Wilkes-Barre (PA)
Penn State Worthington Scranton (PA)
Penn State York (PA)
Pitzer Coll (CA)
Pomona Coll (CA)
Portland State U (OR)
Purdue U (IN)
Ramapo Coll of New Jersey (NJ)
Rhode Island Coll (RI)
Rhodes Coll (TN)
Roosevelt U (IL)

Rutgers, The State U of New Jersey, Camden (NJ)
Rutgers, The State U of New Jersey, Newark (NJ)
Saint Louis U (MO)
San Diego State U (CA)
San Francisco State U (CA)
San Jose State U (CA)
Scripps Coll (CA)
Smith Coll (MA)
Sonoma State U (CA)
Southern Illinois U Carbondale (IL)
Southern Methodist U (TX)
Stanford U (CA)
State U of New York at New Paltz (NY)
State U of New York Coll at Cortland (NY)
State U of New York Coll at Geneseo (NY)
Stony Brook U, State U of New York (NY)
Suffolk U (MA)
Swarthmore Coll (PA)
Syracuse U (NY)
Temple U (PA)
Tufts U (MA)
U at Albany, State U of New York (NY)
U at Buffalo, the State U of New York (NY)
The U of Alabama (AL)
The U of Alabama at Birmingham (AL)
The U of Arizona (AZ)
U of California, Berkeley (CA)
U of California, Davis (CA)
U of California, Irvine (CA)
U of California, Los Angeles (CA)
U of California, Riverside (CA)
U of California, Santa Barbara (CA)
U of Central Arkansas (AR)
U of Cincinnati (OH)
U of Delaware (DE)
U of Georgia (GA)
U of Illinois at Chicago (IL)
The U of Iowa (IA)
The U of Kansas (KS)
U of Louisville (KY)
U of Maryland, Baltimore County (MD)
U of Maryland, Coll Park (MD)
U of Massachusetts Amherst (MA)
U of Massachusetts Boston (MA)
U of Memphis (TN)
U of Miami (FL)
U of Michigan (MI)
U of Michigan–Flint (MI)
U of Minnesota, Twin Cities Campus (MN)
U of Mississippi (MS)
U of Nebraska at Omaha (NE)
U of Nevada, Las Vegas (NV)
U of New Mexico (NM)
The U of North Carolina at Chapel Hill (NC)
The U of North Carolina at Charlotte (NC)
The U of North Carolina at Greensboro (NC)
U of Northern Colorado (CO)
U of Notre Dame (IN)
U of Oklahoma (OK)
U of Pennsylvania (PA)
U of Pittsburgh (PA)
U of Rhode Island (RI)
U of Rochester (NY)
U of South Carolina (SC)
U of Southern California (CA)
U of South Florida (FL)
The U of Texas at Austin (TX)
The U of Toledo (OH)
U of Virginia (VA)
U of Wisconsin–Madison (WI)
U of Wisconsin–Milwaukee (WI)
Vanderbilt U (TN)
Virginia Commonwealth U (VA)
Washington U in St. Louis (MO)
Wayne State U (MI)
Wellesley Coll (MA)
Wells Coll (NY)
Wesleyan U (CT)
Western Illinois U (IL)
Western Michigan U (MI)
Wheaton Coll (MA)
William Paterson U of New Jersey (NJ)

Wright State U (OH)
Yale U (CT)
York Coll of the City U of New York (NY)
Youngstown State U (OH)

AFRICAN LANGUAGES
U of California, Los Angeles (CA)
U of Wisconsin–Madison (WI)

AFRICAN STUDIES
Agnes Scott Coll (GA)
Augustana Coll (IL)
Bard Coll (NY)
Bowdoin Coll (ME)
Bowling Green State U (OH)
Carleton Coll (MN)
Colgate U (NY)
The Coll at Brockport, State U of New York (NY)
Columbia U, School of General Studies (NY)
Connecticut Coll (CT)
Dartmouth Coll (NH)
Dickinson Coll (PA)
Drew U (NJ)
Franklin & Marshall Coll (PA)
Hampshire Coll (MA)
Haverford Coll (PA)
Hobart and William Smith Colls (NY)
Hofstra U (NY)
Illinois Wesleyan U (IL)
Kennesaw State U (GA)
Kentucky State U (KY)
Lehigh U (PA)
Middlebury Coll (VT)
Oakland U (MI)
The Ohio State U (OH)
Ohio U (OH)
Portland State U (OR)
Rowan U (NJ)
Rutgers, The State U of New Jersey, New Brunswick (NJ)
St. Lawrence U (NY)
Simmons Coll (MA)
Tennessee State U (TN)
Tulane U (LA)
United States Military Acad (NY)
U of Chicago (IL)
The U of Iowa (IA)
The U of Kansas (KS)
U of Minnesota, Twin Cities Campus (MN)
U of Pennsylvania (PA)
U of Richmond (VA)
Vassar Coll (NY)
Washington U in St. Louis (MO)
Wellesley Coll (MA)
William Paterson U of New Jersey (NJ)
Yale U (CT)

AGRIBUSINESS
Abilene Christian U (TX)
Adams State U (CO)
American U of Beirut (Lebanon)
Andrews U (MI)
Angelo State U (TX)
Arkansas State U (AR)
Arkansas Tech U (AR)
Brigham Young U (UT)
Colorado State U (CO)
Eastern New Mexico U (NM)
Florida Ag and Mech U (FL)
Middle Tennessee State U (TN)
Mississippi State U (MS)
Missouri State U (MO)
New Mexico State U (NM)
North Carolina State U (NC)
North Dakota State U (ND)
Northwest Missouri State U (MO)
Penn State Abington (PA)
Penn State Altoona (PA)
Penn State Beaver (PA)
Penn State Berks (PA)
Penn State Brandywine (PA)
Penn State DuBois (PA)
Penn State Erie, The Behrend Coll (PA)
Penn State Fayette, The Eberly Campus (PA)
Penn State Greater Allegheny (PA)
Penn State Hazleton (PA)
Penn State Lehigh Valley (PA)
Penn State Mont Alto (PA)
Penn State New Kensington (PA)
Penn State Schuylkill (PA)

Penn State Shenango (PA)
Penn State U Park (PA)
Penn State Wilkes-Barre (PA)
Penn State Worthington Scranton (PA)
Penn State York (PA)
Purdue U (IN)
South Dakota State U (SD)
Southeast Missouri State U (MO)
Stephen F. Austin State U (TX)
Texas A&M U (TX)
Texas A&M U–Commerce (TX)
Texas State U–San Marcos (TX)
U of Delaware (DE)
U of Georgia (GA)
U of Minnesota, Crookston (MN)
U of Minnesota, Twin Cities Campus (MN)
U of Wyoming (WY)
Vermont Tech Coll (VT)
West Texas A&M U (TX)

AGRICULTURAL AND DOMESTIC ANIMAL SERVICES RELATED
Saint Mary-of-the-Woods Coll (IN)
Tarleton State U (TX)

AGRICULTURAL AND EXTENSION EDUCATION
New Mexico State U (NM)
North Carolina State U (NC)
Northwestern Oklahoma State U (OK)
Penn State Abington (PA)
Penn State Altoona (PA)
Penn State Beaver (PA)
Penn State Berks (PA)
Penn State Brandywine (PA)
Penn State DuBois (PA)
Penn State Erie, The Behrend Coll (PA)
Penn State Fayette, The Eberly Campus (PA)
Penn State Greater Allegheny (PA)
Penn State Hazleton (PA)
Penn State Lehigh Valley (PA)
Penn State Mont Alto (PA)
Penn State New Kensington (PA)
Penn State Schuylkill (PA)
Penn State Shenango (PA)
Penn State Wilkes-Barre (PA)
Penn State Worthington Scranton (PA)
Penn State York (PA)
Purdue U (IN)
U of Georgia (GA)
U of Illinois at Urbana–Champaign (IL)
The U of Tennessee (TN)

AGRICULTURAL AND FOOD PRODUCTS PROCESSING
Angelo State U (TX)
Dalhousie U (NS, Canada)
Kansas State U (KS)
The Ohio State U (OH)
Texas A&M U (TX)
The U of British Columbia (BC, Canada)
U of Florida (FL)
U of Nebraska–Lincoln (NE)
Washington State U (WA)

AGRICULTURAL ANIMAL BREEDING
U of Nevada, Reno (NV)

AGRICULTURAL BUSINESS AND MANAGEMENT
Alcorn State U (MS)
Arizona State U (AZ)
Brigham Young U (UT)
California Polytechnic State U, San Luis Obispo (CA)
California State Polytechnic U, Pomona (CA)
California State U, Chico (CA)
California State U, Fresno (CA)
Clemson U (SC)
Coll of the Ozarks (MO)
Fort Lewis Coll (CO)
Grace U (NE)
Hardin-Simmons U (TX)
Iowa State U of Science and Technology (IA)
Kansas State U (KS)
Lincoln U (MO)

Louisiana State U and Ag and Mech Coll (LA)
Michigan State U (MI)
Montana State U (MT)
Morrisville State Coll (NY)
The Ohio State U (OH)
Oklahoma State U (OK)
Oregon State U (OR)
Rocky Mountain Coll (MT)
Southern Arkansas U–Magnolia (AR)
State U of New York Coll of Agriculture and Technology at Cobleskill (NY)
Sul Ross State U (TX)
Tabor Coll (KS)
Texas A&M U (TX)
Texas A&M U–Kingsville (TX)
Tuskegee U (AL)
The U of Arizona (AZ)
U of Delaware (DE)
U of Guelph (ON, Canada)
U of Hawaii at Hilo (HI)
U of Idaho (ID)
U of Illinois at Urbana–Champaign (IL)
U of Louisiana at Monroe (LA)
U of Maryland Eastern Shore (MD)
U of Minnesota, Twin Cities Campus (MN)
U of Missouri (MO)
U of Nebraska at Kearney (NE)
U of Nebraska–Lincoln (NE)
U of Wisconsin–Madison (WI)
Upper Iowa U (IA)
Utah State U (UT)
Washington State U (WA)
West Texas A&M U (TX)

AGRICULTURAL BUSINESS AND MANAGEMENT RELATED
Penn State New Kensington (PA)
Purdue U (IN)
U of California, Davis (CA)
U of Minnesota, Twin Cities Campus (MN)
Utah State U (UT)

AGRICULTURAL BUSINESS TECHNOLOGY
The U of Arizona (AZ)
U of Minnesota, Crookston (MN)
Washington State U (WA)

AGRICULTURAL COMMUNICATION/ JOURNALISM
Auburn U (AL)
California Polytechnic State U, San Luis Obispo (CA)
Kansas State U (KS)
North Dakota State U (ND)
The Ohio State U (OH)
Oklahoma State U (OK)
Purdue U (IN)
South Dakota State U (SD)
Texas A&M U (TX)
U of Georgia (GA)
U of Idaho (ID)
U of Illinois at Urbana–Champaign (IL)
U of Nebraska–Lincoln (NE)
U of Wisconsin–Madison (WI)
U of Wyoming (WY)
Washington State U (WA)
West Texas A&M U (TX)

AGRICULTURAL ECONOMICS
Alcorn State U (MS)
Auburn U (AL)
Brigham Young U (UT)
Clemson U (SC)
Colorado State U (CO)
Kansas State U (KS)
Langston U (OK)
Mississippi State U (MS)
North Dakota State U (ND)
Northwest Missouri State U (MO)
The Ohio State U (OH)
Oklahoma State U (OK)
Oregon State U (OR)
Purdue U (IN)
South Dakota State U (SD)
Southern Illinois U Carbondale (IL)
Tarleton State U (TX)
Texas A&M U (TX)

AGRICULTURAL/FARM SUPPLIES RETAILING AND WHOLESALING
Texas A&M U (TX)

AGRICULTURAL MECHANIZATION
California Polytechnic State U, San Luis Obispo (CA)
Iowa State U of Science and Technology (IA)
Kansas State U (KS)
Montana State U (MT)
North Carolina State U (NC)
North Dakota State U (ND)
Penn State Abington (PA)
Penn State Altoona (PA)

U of Florida (FL)
U of Georgia (GA)
U of Guelph (ON, Canada)
U of Idaho (ID)
U of Illinois at Urbana–Champaign (IL)
U of Kentucky (KY)
U of Maryland, Coll Park (MD)
U of Massachusetts Amherst (MA)
U of Minnesota, Twin Cities Campus (MN)
U of Missouri (MO)
U of Nebraska–Lincoln (NE)
U of Nevada, Reno (NV)
U of Wisconsin–Madison (WI)
Utah State U (UT)
Virginia Polytechnic Inst and State U (VA)
Washington State U (WA)
West Virginia U (WV)

AGRICULTURAL ENGINEERING
Auburn U (AL)
California Polytechnic State U, San Luis Obispo (CA)
Clemson U (SC)
Dalhousie U (NS, Canada)
Dordt Coll (IA)
Florida Ag and Mech U (FL)
Iowa State U of Science and Technology (IA)
Kansas State U (KS)
Michigan State U (MI)
Missouri U of Science and Technology (MO)
North Carolina State U (NC)
North Dakota State U (ND)
The Ohio State U (OH)
Oklahoma State U (OK)
Oregon State U (OR)
Penn State Abington (PA)
Penn State Beaver (PA)
Penn State Brandywine (PA)
Penn State DuBois (PA)
Penn State Erie, The Behrend Coll (PA)
Penn State Fayette, The Eberly Campus (PA)
Penn State Greater Allegheny (PA)
Penn State Hazleton (PA)
Penn State Lehigh Valley (PA)
Penn State Mont Alto (PA)
Penn State New Kensington (PA)
Penn State Schuylkill (PA)
Penn State Shenango (PA)
Penn State U Park (PA)
Penn State Wilkes-Barre (PA)
Penn State Worthington Scranton (PA)
Penn State York (PA)
Purdue U (IN)
Rutgers, The State U of New Jersey, New Brunswick (NJ)
South Dakota State U (SD)
Texas A&M U (TX)
U of California, Los Angeles (CA)
U of Georgia (GA)
U of Hawaii at Manoa (HI)
U of Illinois at Urbana–Champaign (IL)
U of Kentucky (KY)
U of Maryland, Coll Park (MD)
U of Minnesota, Twin Cities Campus (MN)
U of Nebraska–Lincoln (NE)
The U of Tennessee (TN)
U of Wisconsin–Madison (WI)
Utah State U (UT)
Walla Walla U (WA)

Penn State Beaver (PA)
Penn State Berks (PA)
Penn State Brandywine (PA)
Penn State DuBois (PA)
Penn State Erie, The Behrend Coll (PA)
Penn State Fayette, The Eberly Campus (PA)
Penn State Greater Allegheny (PA)
Penn State Hazleton (PA)
Penn State Lehigh Valley (PA)
Penn State Mont Alto (PA)
Penn State New Kensington (PA)
Penn State Schuylkill (PA)
Penn State Shenango (PA)
Penn State U Park (PA)
Penn State Wilkes-Barre (PA)
Penn State Worthington Scranton (PA)
Penn State York (PA)
Purdue U (IN)
South Dakota State U (SD)
Stephen F. Austin State U (TX)
U of Idaho (ID)
U of Illinois at Urbana–Champaign (IL)
U of Minnesota, Crookston (MN)
U of Missouri (MO)
U of Nebraska–Lincoln (NE)
Washington State U (WA)

AGRICULTURAL MECHANIZATION RELATED
U of Minnesota, Twin Cities Campus (MN)

AGRICULTURAL POWER MACHINERY OPERATION
U of Minnesota, Crookston (MN)

AGRICULTURAL PRODUCTION
Stephen F. Austin State U (TX)

AGRICULTURAL PRODUCTION RELATED
Tarleton State U (TX)

AGRICULTURAL PUBLIC SERVICES RELATED
Oklahoma State U (OK)
U of Illinois at Urbana–Champaign (IL)
U of Kentucky (KY)

AGRICULTURAL TEACHER EDUCATION
Arkansas State U (AR)
Arkansas Tech U (AR)
Auburn U (AL)
California Polytechnic State U, San Luis Obispo (CA)
California State Polytechnic U, Pomona (CA)
California State U, Chico (CA)
California State U, Fresno (CA)
Clemson U (SC)
Coll of the Ozarks (MO)
Colorado State U (CO)
Dordt Coll (IA)
Eastern New Mexico U (NM)
Iowa State U of Science and Technology (IA)
Kansas State U (KS)
Langston U (OK)
Louisiana State U and Ag and Mech Coll (LA)
Mississippi State U (MS)
Missouri State U (MO)
Montana State U (MT)
New Mexico State U (NM)
North Carolina State U (NC)
North Dakota State U (ND)
Northwest Missouri State U (MO)
The Ohio State U (OH)
Oklahoma State U (OK)
Penn State U Park (PA)
Purdue U (IN)
South Dakota State U (SD)
Southeast Missouri State U (MO)
Southern Arkansas U–Magnolia (AR)
State U of New York at Oswego (NY)
Tarleton State U (TX)
U of Delaware (DE)
U of Florida (FL)
U of Georgia (GA)
U of Idaho (ID)

U of Illinois at Urbana–Champaign (IL)
U of Maryland Eastern Shore (MD)
U of Minnesota, Twin Cities Campus (MN)
U of Missouri (MO)
U of Nebraska–Lincoln (NE)
The U of Tennessee at Martin (TN)
U of Wisconsin–Platteville (WI)
U of Wyoming (WY)
Utah State U (UT)
Washington State U (WA)
West Virginia U (WV)

AGRICULTURE
Alcorn State U (MS)
American U of Beirut (Lebanon)
Angelo State U (TX)
Auburn U (AL)
Austin Peay State U (TN)
Berea Coll (KY)
California State U, Stanislaus (CA)
Cameron U (OK)
Dalhousie U (NS, Canada)
Dordt Coll (IA)
Ferrum Coll (VA)
Florida Ag and Mech U (FL)
Hampshire Coll (MA)
Illinois State U (IL)
Iowa State U of Science and Technology (IA)
Lincoln U (MO)
McNeese State U (LA)
Mississippi State U (MS)
Missouri State U (MO)
Montana State U (MT)
New Mexico State U (NM)
North Carolina State U (NC)
North Dakota State U (ND)
Northwestern Oklahoma State U (OK)
Northwest Missouri State U (MO)
Oregon State U (OR)
Penn State Abington (PA)
Penn State Altoona (PA)
Penn State Beaver (PA)
Penn State Berks (PA)
Penn State Brandywine (PA)
Penn State DuBois (PA)
Penn State Erie, The Behrend Coll (PA)
Penn State Fayette, The Eberly Campus (PA)
Penn State Greater Allegheny (PA)
Penn State Hazleton (PA)
Penn State Lehigh Valley (PA)
Penn State Mont Alto (PA)
Penn State New Kensington (PA)
Penn State Schuylkill (PA)
Penn State Shenango (PA)
Penn State U Park (PA)
Penn State Wilkes-Barre (PA)
Penn State Worthington Scranton (PA)
Penn State York (PA)
Purdue U (IN)
Rutgers, The State U of New Jersey, New Brunswick (NJ)
Sam Houston State U (TX)
South Dakota State U (SD)
Southern Arkansas U–Magnolia (AR)
Southern Illinois U Carbondale (IL)
Southern Utah U (UT)
Stephen F. Austin State U (TX)
Sterling Coll (VT)
Tennessee State U (TN)
Texas A&M U (TX)
Texas A&M U–Commerce (TX)
Texas A&M U–Kingsville (TX)
Texas State U–San Marcos (TX)
Truman State U (MO)
Tuskegee U (AL)
The U of British Columbia (BC, Canada)
U of Delaware (DE)
U of Georgia (GA)
U of Guam (GU)
U of Hawaii at Hilo (HI)
U of Maryland, Coll Park (MD)
U of Maryland Eastern Shore (MD)
U of Minnesota, Twin Cities Campus (MN)
U of Missouri (MO)
U of Nebraska–Lincoln (NE)
The U of Tennessee at Martin (TN)
U of Vermont (VT)

Utah State U (UT)
Virginia State U (VA)
Washington State U (WA)
Western Illinois U (IL)
Western Kentucky U (KY)
West Texas A&M U (TX)

AGRICULTURE AND AGRICULTURE OPERATIONS RELATED
California State U, Stanislaus (CA)
Coll of the Atlantic (ME)
Murray State U (KY)
The Ohio State U (OH)
Tarleton State U (TX)
The U of Arizona (AZ)
U of California, Davis (CA)
U of Kentucky (KY)
U of Minnesota, Twin Cities Campus (MN)

AGROECOLOGY AND SUSTAINABLE AGRICULTURE
Columbia U, School of General Studies (NY)
Dalhousie U (NS, Canada)
The Evergreen State Coll (WA)
Unity Coll (ME)
U of Minnesota, Crookston (MN)
U of New Hampshire (NH)
U of Wyoming (WY)

AGRONOMY AND CROP SCIENCE
Auburn U (AL)
California Polytechnic State U, San Luis Obispo (CA)
California State U, Chico (CA)
California State U, Fresno (CA)
Coll of the Ozarks (MO)
Colorado State U (CO)
Dalhousie U (NS, Canada)
Iowa State U of Science and Technology (IA)
Kansas State U (KS)
Mississippi State U (MS)
Missouri State U (MO)
New Mexico State U (NM)
North Carolina State U (NC)
Northwest Missouri State U (MO)
The Ohio State U (OH)
Oregon State U (OR)
Penn State Abington (PA)
Penn State Altoona (PA)
Penn State Beaver (PA)
Penn State Berks (PA)
Penn State Brandywine (PA)
Penn State DuBois (PA)
Penn State Erie, The Behrend Coll (PA)
Penn State Fayette, The Eberly Campus (PA)
Penn State Greater Allegheny (PA)
Penn State Hazleton (PA)
Penn State Mont Alto (PA)
Penn State New Kensington (PA)
Penn State Shenango (PA)
Penn State Wilkes-Barre (PA)
Penn State Worthington Scranton (PA)
Penn State York (PA)
Purdue U (IN)
South Dakota State U (SD)
State U of New York Coll of Agriculture and Technology at Cobleskill (NY)
Tarleton State U (TX)
Texas A&M U (TX)
Texas A&M U–Commerce (TX)
Texas A&M U–Kingsville (TX)
Tuskegee U (AL)
U of Guelph (ON, Canada)
U of Illinois at Urbana–Champaign (IL)
U of Kentucky (KY)
U of Minnesota, Crookston (MN)
U of Minnesota, Twin Cities Campus (MN)
U of Nebraska–Lincoln (NE)
The U of Tennessee at Martin (TN)
U of Vermont (VT)
U of Wisconsin–Madison (WI)
U of Wisconsin–Platteville (WI)
Utah State U (UT)
Virginia Polytechnic Inst and State U (VA)
Washington State U (WA)
West Texas A&M U (TX)

AIRCRAFT POWERPLANT TECHNOLOGY
Embry-Riddle Aeronautical U–Daytona (FL)
Embry-Riddle Aeronautical U–Worldwide (FL)
Thomas Edison State Coll (NJ)

AIR FORCE ROTC/AIR SCIENCE
La Salle U (PA)
The U of Iowa (IA)
Weber State U (UT)

AIRFRAME MECHANICS AND AIRCRAFT MAINTENANCE TECHNOLOGY
Kansas State U (KS)
LeTourneau U (TX)
Purdue U (IN)
Southeastern Oklahoma State U (OK)
Thomas Edison State Coll (NJ)
Vaughn Coll of Aeronautics and Technology (NY)
Wilmington U (DE)

AIRLINE PILOT AND FLIGHT CREW
Auburn U (AL)
Averett U (VA)
Baylor U (TX)
Bridgewater State U (MA)
Delta State U (MS)
Eastern Michigan U (MI)
Embry-Riddle Aeronautical U–Daytona (FL)
Embry-Riddle Aeronautical U–Prescott (AZ)
Farmingdale State Coll (NY)
Henderson State U (AR)
Indiana State U (IN)
Inter American U of Puerto Rico, Bayamón Campus (PR)
Kansas State U (KS)
LeTourneau U (TX)
Quincy U (IL)
Rocky Mountain Coll (MT)
Saint Louis U (MO)
Southeastern Oklahoma State U (OK)
U of Illinois at Urbana–Champaign (IL)
U of Louisiana at Monroe (LA)
U of Minnesota, Crookston (MN)
U of North Dakota (ND)
Western Michigan U (MI)
Westminster Coll (UT)

AIR TRAFFIC CONTROL
Arizona State U (AZ)
Daniel Webster Coll (NH)
Embry-Riddle Aeronautical U–Daytona (FL)
Embry-Riddle Aeronautical U–Prescott (AZ)
Hampton U (VA)
Inter American U of Puerto Rico, Bayamón Campus (PR)
LeTourneau U (TX)
Lewis U (IL)
Thomas Edison State Coll (NJ)
U of Maryland Eastern Shore (MD)
U of North Dakota (ND)

AIR TRANSPORTATION RELATED
Florida Inst of Technology (FL)
Thomas Edison State Coll (NJ)
U of North Dakota (ND)

ALGEBRA AND NUMBER THEORY
U of New Brunswick Saint John (NB, Canada)

ALLIED HEALTH AND MEDICAL ASSISTING SERVICES RELATED
Bowling Green State U-Firelands Coll (OH)
Cedarville U (OH)
Coll of Saint Elizabeth (NJ)
Jones Coll, Jacksonville (FL)
The Ohio State U (OH)
The Ohio State U at Lima (OH)
Queens U of Charlotte (NC)
Ramapo Coll of New Jersey (NJ)
Widener U (PA)

ALLIED HEALTH DIAGNOSTIC, INTERVENTION, AND TREATMENT PROFESSIONS RELATED
Fairleigh Dickinson U, Coll at Florham (NJ)
Fairleigh Dickinson U, Metropolitan Campus (NJ)
Hofstra U (NY)
Immaculata U (PA)
Lewis U (IL)
Millersville U of Pennsylvania (PA)
Northern Michigan U (MI)
Rutgers, The State U of New Jersey, Newark (NJ)
Tennessee Wesleyan Coll (TN)
Thomas Edison State Coll (NJ)
U of Arkansas for Medical Sciences (AR)
U of Medicine and Dentistry of New Jersey (NJ)
U of Nebraska at Kearney (NE)
The U of Toledo (OH)

ALTERNATIVE AND COMPLEMENTARY MEDICINE RELATED
Johnson State Coll (VT)

AMERICAN GOVERNMENT AND POLITICS
American Jewish U (CA)
Arizona Christian U (AZ)
Bard Coll (NY)
Bennington Coll (VT)
Bridgewater State U (MA)
Drury U (MO)
Emory & Henry Coll (VA)
Gallaudet U (DC)
Lynn U (FL)
The Master's Coll and Sem (CA)
Misericordia U (PA)
Oklahoma Christian U (OK)
Oklahoma City U (OK)
Southern Nazarene U (OK)
Suffolk U (MA)
United States Military Acad (NY)
Wayland Baptist U (TX)
Western Michigan U (MI)

AMERICAN HISTORY
Bard Coll (NY)
Bennington Coll (VT)
The Coll of Saint Rose (NY)
Florida Coll (FL)
Gettysburg Coll (PA)
Howard Payne U (TX)
Keene State Coll (NH)
Morningside Coll (IA)
Salem State U (MA)
Suffolk U (MA)
United States Military Acad (NY)
U of Regina (SK, Canada)
The U of Western Ontario (ON, Canada)

AMERICAN INDIAN/NATIVE AMERICAN STUDIES
Arizona State U (AZ)
Bemidji State U (MN)
California State U, East Bay (CA)
Colgate U (NY)
Concordia U (QC, Canada)
Creighton U (NE)
Dartmouth Coll (NH)
East Central U (OK)
The Evergreen State Coll (WA)
Fort Lewis Coll (CO)
Hampshire Coll (MA)
Humboldt State U (CA)
Inst of American Indian Arts (NM)
Northern Arizona U (AZ)
Northland Coll (WI)
Portland State U (OR)
St. Thomas U (NB, Canada)
San Diego State U (CA)
San Francisco State U (CA)
Sonoma State U (CA)
Stanford U (CA)
Trent U (ON, Canada)
U of Alaska Fairbanks (AK)
U of California, Berkeley (CA)
U of California, Davis (CA)
U of California, Los Angeles (CA)
U of California, Riverside (CA)
U of Hawaii at Manoa (HI)
The U of Iowa (IA)
U of Minnesota, Duluth (MN)

U of Minnesota, Twin Cities Campus (MN)
U of Nebraska at Omaha (NE)
U of New Mexico (NM)
The U of North Carolina at Pembroke (NC)
U of North Dakota (ND)
U of Oklahoma (OK)
U of Ottawa (ON, Canada)
U of Regina (SK, Canada)
U of Science and Arts of Oklahoma (OK)
The U of South Dakota (SD)
The U of Western Ontario (ON, Canada)
U of Wisconsin–Eau Claire (WI)
U of Wisconsin–Green Bay (WI)
U of Wyoming (WY)

AMERICAN LITERATURE
Bard Coll (NY)
Bennington Coll (VT)
Castleton State Coll (VT)
The Coll at Brockport, State U of New York (NY)
Oklahoma City U (OK)
Purdue U Calumet (IN)
Queens U of Charlotte (NC)
St. Lawrence U (NY)
U of California, Los Angeles (CA)
Washington U in St. Louis (MO)
Wheeling Jesuit U (WV)

AMERICAN NATIVE/NATIVE AMERICAN EDUCATION
The Coll of St. Scholastica (MN)
U of Minnesota, Duluth (MN)
U of Regina (SK, Canada)

AMERICAN NATIVE/NATIVE AMERICAN LANGUAGES
Bemidji State U (MN)
U of Alaska Fairbanks (AK)
U of Hawaii at Manoa (HI)
U of Regina (SK, Canada)

AMERICAN SIGN LANGUAGE (ASL)
Augustana Coll (SD)
Gardner-Webb U (NC)
Liberty U (VA)
Madonna U (MI)
Maryville Coll (TN)
Northeastern U (MA)
Rochester Inst of Technology (NY)
U of Houston (TX)
U of Rochester (NY)

AMERICAN STUDIES
Albright Coll (PA)
American U (DC)
Amherst Coll (MA)
Arizona State U (AZ)
Ashland U (OH)
Bard Coll (NY)
Bates Coll (ME)
Baylor U (TX)
Bennington Coll (VT)
Boston U (MA)
Bowling Green State U (OH)
Brown U (RI)
Bryant U (RI)
Cabrini Coll (PA)
California State U, Chico (CA)
California State U, Fullerton (CA)
California State U, Long Beach (CA)
California State U, San Bernardino (CA)
Carleton Coll (MN)
Case Western Reserve U (OH)
Cedarville U (OH)
Chowan U (NC)
Christopher Newport U (VA)
Claflin U (SC)
Claremont McKenna Coll (CA)
Clarkson U (NY)
Coe Coll (IA)
Colby Coll (ME)
Coll of Saint Elizabeth (NJ)
The Coll of Saint Rose (NY)
Coll of Staten Island of the City U of New York (NY)
The Coll of William and Mary (VA)
Columbia Coll (MO)
Columbia U (NY)
Columbia U, School of General Studies (NY)
Connecticut Coll (CT)

Creighton U (NE)
DePaul U (IL)
Dickinson Coll (PA)
Dominican U (IL)
Drew U (NJ)
Eckerd Coll (FL)
Elmira Coll (NY)
Emmanuel Coll (MA)
Fairfield U (CT)
Franklin & Marshall Coll (PA)
Franklin Coll (IN)
Franklin Pierce U (NH)
George Fox U (OR)
Georgetown Coll (KY)
Georgetown U (DC)
Gettysburg Coll (PA)
Goucher Coll (MD)
Hamilton Coll (NY)
Hampshire Coll (MA)
Hawai`i Pacific U (HI)
Hendrix Coll (AR)
High Point U (NC)
Hillsdale Coll (MI)
Hobart and William Smith Colls (NY)
Hofstra U (NY)
Illinois Wesleyan U (IL)
Indiana U Bloomington (IN)
Kansas State U (KS)
Keene State Coll (NH)
Kent State U (OH)
King Coll (TN)
Knox Coll (IL)
Lafayette Coll (PA)
Lehman Coll of the City U of New York (NY)
Lesley U (MA)
Lindenwood U (MO)
Lindsey Wilson Coll (KY)
Lipscomb U (TN)
Long Island U–C. W. Post Campus (NY)
Manhattanville Coll (NY)
Marist Coll (NY)
Mary Baldwin Coll (VA)
Miami U (OH)
Middlebury Coll (VT)
Mills Coll (CA)
Montreat Coll, Montreat (NC)
Mount Allison U (NB, Canada)
Mount St. Mary's Coll (CA)
Muhlenberg Coll (PA)
Nazareth Coll of Rochester (NY)
Nova Southeastern U (FL)
Oglethorpe U (GA)
Oklahoma City U (OK)
Oklahoma State U (OK)
Oregon State U (OR)
Pace U (NY)
Penn State Abington (PA)
Penn State Berks (PA)
Penn State Brandywine (PA)
Penn State Erie, The Behrend Coll (PA)
Penn State Harrisburg (PA)
Penn State Lehigh Valley (PA)
Penn State Schuylkill (PA)
Penn State Worthington Scranton (PA)
Penn State York (PA)
Pitzer Coll (CA)
Pomona Coll (CA)
Providence Coll (RI)
Purdue U (IN)
Ramapo Coll of New Jersey (NJ)
Reed Coll (OR)
Rider U (NJ)
Roger Williams U (RI)
Russell Sage Coll (NY)
Rutgers, The State U of New Jersey, Newark (NJ)
Rutgers, The State U of New Jersey, New Brunswick (NJ)
St. John Fisher Coll (NY)
Saint Louis U (MO)
Saint Mary's Coll of California (CA)
Saint Michael's Coll (VT)
St. Olaf Coll (MN)
Salve Regina U (RI)
San Francisco State U (CA)
San Jose State U (CA)
Scripps Coll (CA)
Sewanee: The U of the South (TN)
Siena Coll (NY)
Skidmore Coll (NY)
Smith Coll (MA)
Sonoma State U (CA)

Southern Nazarene U (OK)
Stanford U (CA)
State U of New York at Fredonia (NY)
State U of New York at Oswego (NY)
State U of New York Coll at Geneseo (NY)
State U of New York Coll at Old Westbury (NY)
Stetson U (FL)
Stonehill Coll (MA)
Stony Brook U, State U of New York (NY)
Syracuse U (NY)
Temple U (PA)
Tennessee Wesleyan Coll (TN)
Texas A&M U (TX)
Texas State U–San Marcos (TX)
Trinity Coll (CT)
Tufts U (MA)
Tulane U (LA)
U at Buffalo, the State U of New York (NY)
The U of Alabama (AL)
U of California, Berkeley (CA)
U of California, Davis (CA)
U of California, Santa Cruz (CA)
U of Hawaii at Manoa (HI)
U of Idaho (ID)
The U of Iowa (IA)
The U of Kansas (KS)
U of Maryland, Baltimore County (MD)
U of Maryland, Coll Park (MD)
U of Mary Washington (VA)
U of Massachusetts Boston (MA)
U of Miami (FL)
U of Michigan (MI)
U of Michigan–Dearborn (MI)
U of Minnesota, Twin Cities Campus (MN)
U of Missouri–Kansas City (MO)
U of Mount Union (OH)
U of New England (ME)
U of New Mexico (NM)
The U of North Carolina at Chapel Hill (NC)
The U of North Carolina at Pembroke (NC)
U of Notre Dame (IN)
U of Pennsylvania (PA)
U of Pittsburgh at Greensburg (PA)
U of Richmond (VA)
U of Rochester (NY)
U of Southern California (CA)
U of Southern Mississippi (MS)
U of South Florida (FL)
The U of Texas at Austin (TX)
The U of Texas at Dallas (TX)
The U of Texas at San Antonio (TX)
The U of Texas–Pan American (TX)
The U of Toledo (OH)
U of Washington, Bothell (WA)
U of Washington, Tacoma (WA)
The U of Western Ontario (ON, Canada)
U of Wyoming (WY)
Utah State U (UT)
Valparaiso U (IN)
Vanderbilt U (TN)
Vassar Coll (NY)
Virginia Wesleyan Coll (VA)
Warner Pacific Coll (OR)
Washington Coll (MD)
Washington U in St. Louis (MO)
Webster U (MO)
Wellesley Coll (MA)
Wells Coll (NY)
Wesleyan Coll (GA)
Wesleyan U (CT)
Wesley Coll (DE)
West Chester U of Pennsylvania (PA)
Western Connecticut State U (CT)
Western Washington U (WA)
Wheaton Coll (MA)
Whitworth U (WA)
Willamette U (OR)
Williams Coll (MA)
Wittenberg U (OH)
Yale U (CT)
Youngstown State U (OH)

ANALYTICAL CHEMISTRY
North Central Coll (IL)

The U of Western Ontario (ON, Canada)
West Chester U of Pennsylvania (PA)

ANATOMY
Andrews U (MI)
Minnesota State U Mankato (MN)
Tulane U (LA)
The U of Western Ontario (ON, Canada)

ANCIENT/CLASSICAL GREEK
Amherst Coll (MA)
Augustana Coll (IL)
Bard Coll (NY)
Baylor U (TX)
Boston Coll (MA)
Boston U (MA)
Brigham Young U (UT)
Brock U (ON, Canada)
California State U, Long Beach (CA)
Canisius Coll (NY)
Carleton Coll (MN)
Columbia U (NY)
Creighton U (NE)
Dartmouth Coll (NH)
DePauw U (IN)
Duquesne U (PA)
Franklin & Marshall Coll (PA)
Gettysburg Coll (PA)
Hampden-Sydney Coll (VA)
Hobart and William Smith Colls (NY)
Howard Payne U (TX)
Hunter Coll of the City U of New York (NY)
Indiana U Bloomington (IN)
Lawrence U (WI)
Loyola U Chicago (IL)
Loyola U New Orleans (LA)
Monmouth Coll (IL)
Mount Allison U (NB, Canada)
Mount Holyoke Coll (MA)
Multnomah U (OR)
Randolph Coll (VA)
Randolph-Macon Coll (VA)
Rice U (TX)
Rockford Coll (IL)
Rutgers, The State U of New Jersey, New Brunswick (NJ)
St. Olaf Coll (MN)
Samford U (AL)
Sewanee: The U of the South (TN)
Smith Coll (MA)
Southwestern U (TX)
Stanford U (CA)
Swarthmore Coll (PA)
U of California, Berkeley (CA)
U of California, Los Angeles (CA)
U of Georgia (GA)
The U of Iowa (IA)
U of Miami (FL)
U of Michigan (MI)
U of Minnesota, Twin Cities Campus (MN)
U of Nebraska–Lincoln (NE)
U of New Hampshire (NH)
U of Notre Dame (IN)
U of Richmond (VA)
The U of Scranton (PA)
The U of Texas at Austin (TX)
U of Vermont (VT)
The U of Western Ontario (ON, Canada)
Wake Forest U (NC)
Washington U in St. Louis (MO)
Wellesley Coll (MA)
Yale U (CT)

ANCIENT NEAR EASTERN AND BIBLICAL LANGUAGES
Baylor U (TX)
Belmont U (TN)
Carson-Newman U (TN)
Columbia Intl U (SC)
Concordia U (CA)
Concordia U Chicago (IL)
Concordia U Wisconsin (WI)
Geneva Coll (PA)
Howard Payne U (TX)
Lipscomb U (TN)
Luther Coll (IA)
The Master's Coll and Sem (CA)
Northwest Nazarene U (ID)
Northwest U (WA)
Oklahoma Baptist U (OK)

Union U (TN)
U of Chicago (IL)
Walla Walla U (WA)

ANCIENT STUDIES
Bates Coll (ME)
Boston U (MA)
Bowdoin Coll (ME)
Colby Coll (ME)
Columbia U (NY)
Columbia U, School of General Studies (NY)
Concordia U (QC, Canada)
Lehigh U (PA)
Loyola Marymount U (CA)
Mount Holyoke Coll (MA)
Ohio Wesleyan U (OH)
Rockford Coll (IL)
St. Olaf Coll (MN)
Stanford U (CA)
The U of Iowa (IA)
The U of Kansas (KS)
U of Maryland, Baltimore County (MD)
U of Miami (FL)
U of Michigan (MI)
U of Minnesota, Twin Cities Campus (MN)
U of Nebraska–Lincoln (NE)
U of Richmond (VA)
The U of Texas at Austin (TX)
Washington U in St. Louis (MO)
Wheaton Coll (MA)

ANIMAL-ASSISTED THERAPY
Carroll Coll (MT)

ANIMAL BEHAVIOR AND ETHOLOGY
Bucknell U (PA)
Canisius Coll (NY)
Franklin & Marshall Coll (PA)
Hampshire Coll (MA)
Southwestern U (TX)

ANIMAL GENETICS
Dartmouth Coll (NH)
Jacksonville State U (AL)
Ohio Wesleyan U (OH)
Rutgers, The State U of New Jersey, New Brunswick (NJ)
The U of British Columbia (BC, Canada)
Worcester Polytechnic Inst (MA)

ANIMAL HEALTH
Dalhousie U (NS, Canada)
Sul Ross State U (TX)
U of Georgia (GA)

ANIMAL/LIVESTOCK HUSBANDRY AND PRODUCTION
Dalhousie U (NS, Canada)
Dordt Coll (IA)
Purdue U (IN)
Rutgers, The State U of New Jersey, New Brunswick (NJ)
Tarleton State U (TX)
Texas A&M U (TX)
The U of British Columbia (BC, Canada)
U of Illinois at Urbana–Champaign (IL)
U of Minnesota, Twin Cities Campus (MN)

ANIMAL NUTRITION
Dalhousie U (NS, Canada)

ANIMAL PHYSIOLOGY
California State U, Fresno (CA)
Minnesota State U Mankato (MN)
Rutgers, The State U of New Jersey, New Brunswick (NJ)
Sonoma State U (CA)
U of Minnesota, Twin Cities Campus (MN)
U of New Brunswick Fredericton (NB, Canada)
Utah State U (UT)

ANIMAL SCIENCES
Abilene Christian U (TX)
Angelo State U (TX)
Arkansas State U (AR)
Auburn U (AL)
Berry Coll (GA)
California Polytechnic State U, San Luis Obispo (CA)

California State Polytechnic U, Pomona (CA)
California State U, Chico (CA)
California State U, Fresno (CA)
Clemson U (SC)
Coll of the Ozarks (MO)
Colorado State U (CO)
Dordt Coll (IA)
Hardin-Simmons U (TX)
Iowa State U of Science and Technology (IA)
Kansas State U (KS)
Langston U (OK)
Louisiana State U and Ag and Mech Coll (LA)
Lubbock Christian U (TX)
Mercy Coll (NY)
Michigan State U (MI)
Middle Tennessee State U (TN)
Mississippi State U (MS)
Missouri State U (MO)
Montana State U (MT)
New Mexico State U (NM)
North Carolina State U (NC)
North Dakota State U (ND)
Northwest Missouri State U (MO)
The Ohio State U (OH)
Oklahoma State U (OK)
Oregon State U (OR)
Penn State Abington (PA)
Penn State Altoona (PA)
Penn State Beaver (PA)
Penn State Berks (PA)
Penn State Brandywine (PA)
Penn State DuBois (PA)
Penn State Erie, The Behrend Coll (PA)
Penn State Fayette, The Eberly Campus (PA)
Penn State Greater Allegheny (PA)
Penn State Hazleton (PA)
Penn State Lehigh Valley (PA)
Penn State Mont Alto (PA)
Penn State New Kensington (PA)
Penn State Schuylkill (PA)
Penn State Shenango (PA)
Penn State U Park (PA)
Penn State Wilkes-Barre (PA)
Penn State Worthington Scranton (PA)
Penn State York (PA)
Purdue U (IN)
Rutgers, The State U of New Jersey, New Brunswick (NJ)
South Dakota State U (SD)
Southeast Missouri State U (MO)
Southern Illinois U Carbondale (IL)
Stephen F. Austin State U (TX)
Sul Ross State U (TX)
Tarleton State U (TX)
Tennessee State U (TN)
Texas A&M U (TX)
Texas A&M U–Commerce (TX)
Texas A&M U–Kingsville (TX)
Texas State U–San Marcos (TX)
Tuskegee U (AL)
The U of Arizona (AZ)
The U of British Columbia (BC, Canada)
U of California, Davis (CA)
U of Delaware (DE)
U of Denver (CO)
The U of Findlay (OH)
U of Florida (FL)
U of Georgia (GA)
U of Guelph (ON, Canada)
U of Hawaii at Hilo (HI)
U of Hawaii at Manoa (HI)
U of Idaho (ID)
U of Illinois at Urbana–Champaign (IL)
U of Kentucky (KY)
U of Maryland, Coll Park (MD)
U of Massachusetts Amherst (MA)
U of Minnesota, Crookston (MN)
U of Minnesota, Twin Cities Campus (MN)
U of Missouri (MO)
U of Nebraska–Lincoln (NE)
U of Nevada, Reno (NV)
U of New Hampshire (NH)
U of Rhode Island (RI)
The U of Tennessee (TN)
The U of Tennessee at Martin (TN)
U of Vermont (VT)
U of Wisconsin–Madison (WI)
U of Wisconsin–Platteville (WI)

U of Wyoming (WY)
Utah State U (UT)
Virginia Polytechnic Inst and State U (VA)
Washington State U (WA)
West Texas A&M U (TX)
West Virginia U (WV)

ANIMAL SCIENCES RELATED
Dalhousie U (NS, Canada)
Penn State Abington (PA)
Penn State Beaver (PA)
Penn State Brandywine (PA)
Penn State DuBois (PA)
Penn State Erie, The Behrend Coll (PA)
Penn State Fayette, The Eberly Campus (PA)
Penn State Greater Allegheny (PA)
Penn State Hazleton (PA)
Penn State Lehigh Valley (PA)
Penn State Mont Alto (PA)
Penn State New Kensington (PA)
Penn State Schuylkill (PA)
Penn State Shenango (PA)
Penn State Wilkes-Barre (PA)
Penn State Worthington Scranton (PA)
Penn State York (PA)
Purdue U (IN)
U of California, Davis (CA)
U of Illinois at Urbana–Champaign (IL)

ANIMATION, INTERACTIVE TECHNOLOGY, VIDEO GRAPHICS AND SPECIAL EFFECTS
Acad of Art U (CA)
American Acad of Art (IL)
Art Center Coll of Design (CA)
Bay State Coll (MA)
Becker Coll (MA)
Bennington Coll (VT)
Bradley U (IL)
Brigham Young U (UT)
Cleveland Inst of Art (OH)
Cogswell Polytechnical Coll (CA)
Coll for Creative Studies (MI)
Coll of the Atlantic (ME)
Concordia U (QC, Canada)
Davenport U, Grand Rapids (MI)
DePaul U (IL)
DigiPen Inst of Technology (WA)
Eastern Michigan U (MI)
East Tennessee State U (TN)
Fashion Inst of Technology (NY)
Ferris State U (MI)
George Mason U (VA)
Huntington U (IN)
Intl Acad of Design & Technology (FL)
Loyola Marymount U (CA)
Massachusetts Coll of Art and Design (MA)
Missouri Western State U (MO)
Montclair State U (NJ)
Northeastern U (MA)
Northwestern Coll (MN)
Pacific Northwest Coll of Art (OR)
Regent U (VA)
Ringling Coll of Art and Design (FL)
Rochester Inst of Technology (NY)
Rocky Mountain Coll of Art + Design (CO)
Sam Houston State U (TX)
Savannah Coll of Art and Design (GA)
School of the Art Inst of Chicago (IL)
Sullivan Coll of Technology and Design (KY)
U of Arkansas–Fort Smith (AR)
The U of the Arts (PA)
U of the Incarnate Word (TX)
Villa Maria Coll of Buffalo (NY)
Webster U (MO)

ANTHROPOLOGY
Adelphi U (NY)
Agnes Scott Coll (GA)
Albion Coll (MI)
Alma Coll (MI)
American U (DC)
The American U in Cairo (Egypt)
Amherst Coll (MA)
Appalachian State U (NC)
Arizona State U (AZ)

Athabasca U (AB, Canada)
Auburn U (AL)
Augustana Coll (IL)
Augustana Coll (SD)
Ball State U (IN)
Bard Coll (NY)
Bates Coll (ME)
Baylor U (TX)
Bennington Coll (VT)
Binghamton U, State U of New York (NY)
Bloomsburg U of Pennsylvania (PA)
Boise State U (ID)
Boston U (MA)
Bowdoin Coll (ME)
Bridgewater State U (MA)
Brown U (RI)
Bucknell U (PA)
Buffalo State Coll, State U of New York (NY)
Butler U (IN)
California Baptist U (CA)
California State Polytechnic U, Pomona (CA)
California State U, Chico (CA)
California State U, Dominguez Hills (CA)
California State U, East Bay (CA)
California State U, Fresno (CA)
California State U, Fullerton (CA)
California State U, Long Beach (CA)
California State U, Los Angeles (CA)
California State U, Northridge (CA)
California State U, San Bernardino (CA)
California State U, Stanislaus (CA)
Canisius Coll (NY)
Carleton Coll (MN)
Case Western Reserve U (OH)
The Catholic U of America (DC)
Central Coll (IA)
Central Connecticut State U (CT)
Central Michigan U (MI)
Centre Coll (KY)
City Coll of the City U of New York (NY)
Clarion U of Pennsylvania (PA)
Cleveland State U (OH)
Colby Coll (ME)
Colgate U (NY)
Coll of Charleston (SC)
The Coll of Idaho (ID)
Coll of the Holy Cross (MA)
The Coll of William and Mary (VA)
The Coll of Wooster (OH)
The Colorado Coll (CO)
Colorado State U (CO)
Columbia U (NY)
Columbia U, School of General Studies (NY)
Concordia U (QC, Canada)
Connecticut Coll (CT)
Cornell Coll (IA)
Creighton U (NE)
Dalhousie U (NS, Canada)
Dartmouth Coll (NH)
Davidson Coll (NC)
DePaul U (IL)
DePauw U (IN)
Dickinson Coll (PA)
Drake U (IA)
Drew U (NJ)
Earlham Coll (IN)
East Carolina U (NC)
Eastern Michigan U (MI)
Eastern New Mexico U (NM)
Eastern Washington U (WA)
East Tennessee State U (TN)
Eckerd Coll (FL)
Edinboro U of Pennsylvania (PA)
Elmira Coll (NY)
Elon U (NC)
Emory & Henry Coll (VA)
Florida Atlantic U (FL)
Florida Gulf Coast U (FL)
Fort Lewis Coll (CO)
Franklin & Marshall Coll (PA)
Franklin Pierce U (NH)
Furman U (SC)
George Mason U (VA)
Georgetown U (DC)
Georgia Southern U (GA)
Georgia State U (GA)
Gettysburg Coll (PA)
Goucher Coll (MD)

Grand Valley State U (MI)
Grinnell Coll (IA)
Gustavus Adolphus Coll (MN)
Hamilton Coll (NY)
Hamline U (MN)
Hampshire Coll (MA)
Hanover Coll (IN)
Hartwick Coll (NY)
Haverford Coll (PA)
Hawai`i Pacific U (HI)
Hendrix Coll (AR)
Hobart and William Smith Colls (NY)
Hofstra U (NY)
Humboldt State U (CA)
Hunter Coll of the City U of New York (NY)
Illinois State U (IL)
Illinois Wesleyan U (IL)
Indiana U Bloomington (IN)
Indiana U Northwest (IN)
Indiana U of Pennsylvania (PA)
Indiana U–Purdue U Fort Wayne (IN)
Indiana U–Purdue U Indianapolis (IN)
Indiana U South Bend (IN)
Iowa State U of Science and Technology (IA)
Ithaca Coll (NY)
Jacksonville State U (AL)
James Madison U (VA)
The Johns Hopkins U (MD)
Johnson State Coll (VT)
Juniata Coll (PA)
Kansas State U (KS)
Kennesaw State U (GA)
Kent State U (OH)
Kenyon Coll (OH)
Knox Coll (IL)
Kutztown U of Pennsylvania (PA)
Lafayette Coll (PA)
Lawrence U (WI)
Lee U (TN)
Lehigh U (PA)
Lehman Coll of the City U of New York (NY)
Linfield Coll (OR)
Long Island U–C. W. Post Campus (NY)
Longwood U (VA)
Louisiana State U and Ag and Mech Coll (LA)
Loyola U Chicago (IL)
Luther Coll (IA)
Macalester Coll (MN)
Mansfield U of Pennsylvania (PA)
Marquette U (WI)
Massachusetts Inst of Technology (MA)
Mercyhurst U (PA)
Metropolitan State U of Denver (CO)
Miami U (OH)
Michigan State U (MI)
Middle Tennessee State U (TN)
Millersville U of Pennsylvania (PA)
Mills Coll (CA)
Minnesota State U Mankato (MN)
Minnesota State U Moorhead (MN)
Mississippi State U (MS)
Missouri State U (MO)
Monmouth Coll (IL)
Monmouth U (NJ)
Montana State U (MT)
Montclair State U (NJ)
Mount Allison U (NB, Canada)
Mount Holyoke Coll (MA)
Muhlenberg Coll (PA)
Nazareth Coll of Rochester (NY)
New Coll of Florida (FL)
New Mexico State U (NM)
New York U (NY)
North Carolina State U (NC)
North Dakota State U (ND)
Northeastern Illinois U (IL)
Northern Arizona U (AZ)
Northern Illinois U (IL)
Oakland U (MI)
The Ohio State U (OH)
Ohio U (OH)
Ohio Wesleyan U (OH)
Oklahoma Baptist U (OK)
Oregon State U (OR)
Pacific Lutheran U (WA)
Penn State Abington (PA)
Penn State Altoona (PA)

Penn State Beaver (PA)
Penn State Berks (PA)
Penn State Brandywine (PA)
Penn State DuBois (PA)
Penn State Erie, The Behrend Coll (PA)
Penn State Fayette, The Eberly Campus (PA)
Penn State Greater Allegheny (PA)
Penn State Hazleton (PA)
Penn State Lehigh Valley (PA)
Penn State Mont Alto (PA)
Penn State New Kensington (PA)
Penn State Schuylkill (PA)
Penn State Shenango (PA)
Penn State U Park (PA)
Penn State Wilkes-Barre (PA)
Penn State Worthington Scranton (PA)
Penn State York (PA)
Pitzer Coll (CA)
Plymouth State U (NH)
Pomona Coll (CA)
Portland State U (OR)
Princeton U (NJ)
Principia Coll (IL)
Purchase Coll, State U of New York (NY)
Purdue U (IN)
Radford U (VA)
Reed Coll (OR)
Rhode Island Coll (RI)
Rhodes Coll (TN)
Rice U (TX)
Ripon Coll (WI)
Rockford Coll (IL)
Roger Williams U (RI)
Rollins Coll (FL)
Rutgers, The State U of New Jersey, Newark (NJ)
Rutgers, The State U of New Jersey, New Brunswick (NJ)
St. John Fisher Coll (NY)
St. John's U (NY)
St. Lawrence U (NY)
Saint Louis U (MO)
Saint Martin's U (WA)
Saint Mary's Coll of California (CA)
St. Mary's Coll of Maryland (MD)
St. Thomas U (NB, Canada)
Saint Vincent Coll (PA)
San Diego State U (CA)
San Francisco State U (CA)
San Jose State U (CA)
Scripps Coll (CA)
Sonoma State U (CA)
Southern Connecticut State U (CT)
Southern Illinois U Carbondale (IL)
Southern Illinois U Edwardsville (IL)
Southern Methodist U (TX)
Southern Oregon U (OR)
Southwestern U (TX)
Spelman Coll (GA)
Stanford U (CA)
State U of New York at New Paltz (NY)
State U of New York at Oswego (NY)
State U of New York at Plattsburgh (NY)
State U of New York Coll at Cortland (NY)
State U of New York Coll at Geneseo (NY)
State U of New York Coll at Potsdam (NY)
Stony Brook U, State U of New York (NY)
Susquehanna U (PA)
Sweet Briar Coll (VA)
Syracuse U (NY)
Temple U (PA)
Texas A&M U (TX)
Texas Christian U (TX)
Texas State U–San Marcos (TX)
Thomas Edison State Coll (NJ)
Transylvania U (KY)
Trent U (ON, Canada)
Trinity Coll (CT)
Trinity U (TX)
Tufts U (MA)
Tulane U (LA)

U at Albany, State U of New York (NY)
U at Buffalo, the State U of New York (NY)
The U of Akron (OH)
The U of Alabama (AL)
The U of Alabama at Birmingham (AL)
U of Alaska Anchorage (AK)
U of Alaska Fairbanks (AK)
The U of Arizona (AZ)
U of Arkansas at Little Rock (AR)
The U of British Columbia (BC, Canada)
The U of British Columbia–Okanagan (BC, Canada)
U of California, Berkeley (CA)
U of California, Davis (CA)
U of California, Irvine (CA)
U of California, Los Angeles (CA)
U of California, Merced (CA)
U of California, Riverside (CA)
U of California, Santa Barbara (CA)
U of California, Santa Cruz (CA)
U of Central Florida (FL)
U of Chicago (IL)
U of Cincinnati (OH)
U of Colorado Boulder (CO)
U of Colorado Colorado Springs (CO)
U of Colorado Denver (CO)
U of Delaware (DE)
U of Denver (CO)
U of Florida (FL)
U of Georgia (GA)
U of Guam (GU)
U of Guelph (ON, Canada)
U of Hawaii at Hilo (HI)
U of Hawaii at Manoa (HI)
U of Hawaii–West Oahu (HI)
U of Houston (TX)
U of Houston–Clear Lake (TX)
U of Idaho (ID)
U of Illinois at Chicago (IL)
U of Illinois at Urbana–Champaign (IL)
The U of Iowa (IA)
The U of Kansas (KS)
U of Kentucky (KY)
U of La Verne (CA)
U of Louisiana at Lafayette (LA)
U of Louisville (KY)
U of Maine at Farmington (ME)
U of Maryland, Baltimore County (MD)
U of Maryland, Coll Park (MD)
U of Mary Washington (VA)
U of Massachusetts Amherst (MA)
U of Massachusetts Boston (MA)
U of Memphis (TN)
U of Miami (FL)
U of Michigan (MI)
U of Michigan–Dearborn (MI)
U of Michigan–Flint (MI)
U of Minnesota, Duluth (MN)
U of Minnesota, Twin Cities Campus (MN)
U of Mississippi (MS)
U of Missouri (MO)
U of Missouri–St. Louis (MO)
The U of Montana Western (MT)
U of Nebraska–Lincoln (NE)
U of Nevada, Las Vegas (NV)
U of Nevada, Reno (NV)
U of New Brunswick Fredericton (NB, Canada)
U of New Hampshire (NH)
U of New Mexico (NM)
U of New Orleans (LA)
The U of North Carolina at Chapel Hill (NC)
The U of North Carolina at Charlotte (NC)
The U of North Carolina at Greensboro (NC)
The U of North Carolina Wilmington (NC)
U of North Dakota (ND)
U of Northern Colorado (CO)
U of Northern Iowa (IA)
U of North Florida (FL)
U of North Texas (TX)
U of Notre Dame (IN)
U of Oklahoma (OK)
U of Oregon (OR)
U of Ottawa (ON, Canada)
U of Pennsylvania (PA)

U of Pittsburgh (PA)
U of Pittsburgh at Greensburg (PA)
U of Redlands (CA)
U of Regina (SK, Canada)
U of Rhode Island (RI)
U of Richmond (VA)
U of Rochester (NY)
U of San Diego (CA)
U of South Alabama (AL)
U of South Carolina (SC)
The U of South Dakota (SD)
U of Southern California (CA)
U of Southern Mississippi (MS)
U of South Florida (FL)
The U of Tennessee (TN)
The U of Texas at Arlington (TX)
The U of Texas at Austin (TX)
The U of Texas at El Paso (TX)
The U of Texas at San Antonio (TX)
The U of Texas–Pan American (TX)
U of the District of Columbia (DC)
The U of Toledo (OH)
U of Tulsa (OK)
U of Utah (UT)
U of Vermont (VT)
U of Virginia (VA)
U of Waterloo (ON, Canada)
The U of Western Ontario (ON, Canada)
U of West Florida (FL)
U of West Georgia (GA)
U of Windsor (ON, Canada)
U of Wisconsin–Madison (WI)
U of Wisconsin–Milwaukee (WI)
U of Wyoming (WY)
Utah State U (UT)
Vanderbilt U (TN)
Vassar Coll (NY)
Virginia Commonwealth U (VA)
Wagner Coll (NY)
Wake Forest U (NC)
Washburn U (KS)
Washington and Lee U (VA)
Washington Coll (MD)
Washington State U (WA)
Washington U in St. Louis (MO)
Wayne State U (MI)
Weber State U (UT)
Wellesley Coll (MA)
Wells Coll (NY)
Wesleyan U (CT)
West Chester U of Pennsylvania (PA)
Western Carolina U (NC)
Western Connecticut State U (CT)
Western Kentucky U (KY)
Western Michigan U (MI)
Western Oregon U (OR)
Western State Colorado U (CO)
Western Washington U (WA)
Westminster Coll (MO)
Wheaton Coll (IL)
Wheaton Coll (MA)
Whitman Coll (WA)
Wichita State U (KS)
Widener U (PA)
Willamette U (OR)
William Paterson U of New Jersey (NJ)
Williams Coll (MA)
Wright State U (OH)
Yale U (CT)
York Coll of the City U of New York (NY)
Youngstown State U (OH)

ANTHROPOLOGY RELATED
Bridgewater State U (MA)
Howard Payne U (TX)
Mary Baldwin Coll (VA)
U of Delaware (DE)
U of Michigan (MI)
The U of Western Ontario (ON, Canada)
Western Washington U (WA)

APPAREL AND ACCESSORIES MARKETING
Philadelphia U (PA)
Stephens Coll (MO)
U of Rhode Island (RI)

APPAREL AND TEXTILE MANUFACTURING
Fashion Inst of Technology (NY)
Michigan State U (MI)
Purdue U (IN)

APPAREL AND TEXTILE MARKETING MANAGEMENT
Auburn U (AL)
Colorado State U (CO)
Indiana Tech (IN)
Northwest Missouri State U (MO)
Purdue U (IN)
Savannah Coll of Art and Design (GA)
South Dakota State U (SD)
U of Nebraska–Lincoln (NE)
U of the Incarnate Word (TX)
Wayne State U (MI)

APPAREL AND TEXTILES
Appalachian State U (NC)
Auburn U (AL)
Bob Jones U (SC)
Bowling Green State U (OH)
California State Polytechnic U, Pomona (CA)
California State U, Long Beach (CA)
Cheyney U of Pennsylvania (PA)
East Carolina U (NC)
Framingham State U (MA)
Georgia Southern U (GA)
Indiana State U (IN)
Indiana U Bloomington (IN)
Iowa State U of Science and Technology (IA)
Jacksonville State U (AL)
Kansas State U (KS)
Liberty U (VA)
Lipscomb U (TN)
Michigan State U (MI)
Middle Tennessee State U (TN)
Missouri State U (MO)
New Mexico State U (NM)
North Dakota State U (ND)
Northern Illinois U (IL)
The Ohio State U (OH)
Ohio U (OH)
Oregon State U (OR)
Philadelphia U (PA)
Purdue U (IN)
Rhode Island School of Design (RI)
Seattle Pacific U (WA)
Southern Illinois U Carbondale (IL)
Texas A&M U–Kingsville (TX)
The U of Akron (OH)
The U of Alabama (AL)
U of California, Davis (CA)
U of Central Oklahoma (OK)
U of Delaware (DE)
U of Hawaii at Manoa (HI)
U of Idaho (ID)
U of Kentucky (KY)
U of Minnesota, Twin Cities Campus (MN)
U of Missouri (MO)
U of Nebraska–Lincoln (NE)
The U of North Carolina at Greensboro (NC)
U of Northern Iowa (IA)
U of Southern Mississippi (MS)
The U of Texas at Austin (TX)
U of Wisconsin–Madison (WI)
U of Wisconsin–Stout (WI)
Virginia Polytechnic Inst and State U (VA)
Washington State U (WA)
Western Kentucky U (KY)
Western Michigan U (MI)

APPAREL AND TEXTILES RELATED
Purdue U (IN)
Savannah Coll of Art and Design (GA)
Stephens Coll (MO)

APPLIED AND PROFESSIONAL ETHICS
Carnegie Mellon U (PA)
Simpson Coll (IA)
Western Michigan U (MI)

APPLIED BEHAVIOR ANALYSIS
Western Michigan U (MI)

APPLIED ECONOMICS
Binghamton U, State U of New York (NY)
Brigham Young U (UT)
Bryant U (RI)
The Coll of St. Scholastica (MN)
Concordia U (QC, Canada)

Farmingdale State Coll (NY)
Flagler Coll (FL)
HEC Montreal (QC, Canada)
Ithaca Coll (NY)
Penn State Abington (PA)
Penn State Beaver (PA)
Penn State Brandywine (PA)
Penn State DuBois (PA)
Penn State Erie, The Behrend Coll (PA)
Penn State Fayette, The Eberly Campus (PA)
Penn State Greater Allegheny (PA)
Penn State Hazleton (PA)
Penn State Lehigh Valley (PA)
Penn State Mont Alto (PA)
Penn State New Kensington (PA)
Penn State Schuylkill (PA)
Penn State Shenango (PA)
Penn State Wilkes-Barre (PA)
Penn State Worthington Scranton (PA)
Penn State York (PA)
Purdue U (IN)
The U of Akron (OH)
The U of Arizona (AZ)
U of Minnesota, Twin Cities Campus (MN)
U of Northern Iowa (IA)
U of Rhode Island (RI)
U of Waterloo (ON, Canada)

APPLIED HORTICULTURE/ HORTICULTURAL BUSINESS SERVICES RELATED
Morrisville State Coll (NY)
U of Rhode Island (RI)

APPLIED HORTICULTURE/ HORTICULTURE OPERATIONS
Colorado State U (CO)
Farmingdale State Coll (NY)
Ferrum Coll (VA)
Iowa State U of Science and Technology (IA)
Kent State U (OH)
Kent State U at Salem (OH)
Roger Williams U (RI)
South Dakota State U (SD)
Texas A&M U (TX)
U of Georgia (GA)
U of Illinois at Urbana–Champaign (IL)

APPLIED LINGUISTICS
Mid-Atlantic Christian U (NC)
Portland State U (OR)

APPLIED MATHEMATICS
Alderson-Broaddus Coll (WV)
American U (DC)
American U of Beirut (Lebanon)
Arizona State U (AZ)
Auburn U (AL)
Baylor U (TX)
Belmont U (TN)
Bloomfield Coll (NJ)
Boise State U (ID)
Bowie State U (MD)
Brock U (ON, Canada)
Brown U (RI)
Bryant U (RI)
California State U, Chico (CA)
California State U, East Bay (CA)
California State U, Fullerton (CA)
California State U, Long Beach (CA)
Carnegie Mellon U (PA)
Carroll Coll (MT)
Case Western Reserve U (OH)
Christopher Newport U (VA)
Clarkson U (NY)
Coastal Carolina U (SC)
The Coll of Idaho (ID)
Columbia U (NY)
Columbia U, School of General Studies (NY)
Creighton U (NE)
East Central U (OK)
Farmingdale State Coll (NY)
Ferris State U (MI)
Florida Inst of Technology (FL)
Geneva Coll (PA)
Grand View U (IA)
Hampden-Sydney Coll (VA)
Hawai`i Pacific U (HI)
Humboldt State U (CA)
Illinois Inst of Technology (IL)

Indiana U of Pennsylvania (PA)
Indiana U South Bend (IN)
Inter American U of Puerto Rico, Bayamón Campus (PR)
Inter American U of Puerto Rico, San Germán Campus (PR)
Iona Coll (NY)
Jamestown Coll (ND)
The Johns Hopkins U (MD)
Kent State U (OH)
King Coll (TN)
Lamar U (TX)
La Salle U (PA)
Lasell Coll (MA)
Lipscomb U (TN)
Long Island U–C. W. Post Campus (NY)
Loyola Marymount U (CA)
Loyola U Maryland (MD)
Marist Coll (NY)
Mary Baldwin Coll (VA)
Maryville U of Saint Louis (MO)
The Master's Coll and Sem (CA)
Millsaps Coll (MS)
Missouri U of Science and Technology (MO)
Mount Allison U (NB, Canada)
New Coll of Florida (FL)
New Jersey Inst of Technology (NJ)
New York City Coll of Technology of the City U of New York (NY)
North Carolina State U (NC)
North Central Coll (IL)
Northern Illinois U (IL)
Oakland City U (IN)
Ohio U (OH)
Penn State Harrisburg (PA)
Polytechnic Inst of New York U (NY)
Purdue U (IN)
Purdue U Calumet (IN)
Queens U of Charlotte (NC)
Quinnipiac U (CT)
Rice U (TX)
Robert Morris U (PA)
Rutgers, The State U of New Jersey, Newark (NJ)
Saginaw Valley State U (MI)
St. Thomas Aquinas Coll (NY)
San Diego State U (CA)
San Francisco State U (CA)
San Jose State U (CA)
Seattle U (WA)
Siena Heights U (MI)
Simon Fraser U (BC, Canada)
Sonoma State U (CA)
State U of New York at Oswego (NY)
State U of New York Inst of Technology (NY)
Stony Brook U, State U of New York (NY)
Texas A&M U (TX)
Texas State U–San Marcos (TX)
Thompson Rivers U (BC, Canada)
Trent U (ON, Canada)
Trevecca Nazarene U (TN)
Tufts U (MA)
United States Naval Acad (MD)
U at Albany, State U of New York (NY)
U at Buffalo, the State U of New York (NY)
The U of Akron (OH)
U of Alaska Fairbanks (AK)
The U of British Columbia (BC, Canada)
U of California, Berkeley (CA)
U of California, Davis (CA)
U of California, Los Angeles (CA)
U of California, Merced (CA)
U of Central Oklahoma (OK)
U of Colorado Boulder (CO)
U of Colorado Colorado Springs (CO)
U of Houston–Downtown (TX)
U of Idaho (ID)
U of Miami (FL)
U of Nevada, Las Vegas (NV)
U of New Brunswick Fredericton (NB, Canada)
U of New Haven (CT)
The U of North Carolina at Chapel Hill (NC)
U of Northern Iowa (IA)
U of North Florida (FL)
U of Pittsburgh (PA)

U of Pittsburgh at Bradford (PA)
U of Pittsburgh at Greensburg (PA)
U of Rochester (NY)
U of South Carolina Aiken (SC)
The U of Tennessee at Chattanooga (TN)
The U of Texas at El Paso (TX)
U of the Virgin Islands (VI)
U of Tulsa (OK)
U of Utah (UT)
U of Waterloo (ON, Canada)
The U of Western Ontario (ON, Canada)
U of Windsor (ON, Canada)
U of Wisconsin–Madison (WI)
U of Wisconsin–Milwaukee (WI)
U of Wisconsin–Stout (WI)
Valdosta State U (GA)
Washington State U (WA)
Washington U in St. Louis (MO)
Weber State U (UT)
Wentworth Inst of Technology (MA)
Western Michigan U (MI)
Western Washington U (WA)
West Virginia State U (WV)
William Paterson U of New Jersey (NJ)
Worcester Polytechnic Inst (MA)
Yale U (CT)

APPLIED MATHEMATICS RELATED
Arizona State U (AZ)
Averett U (VA)
Belmont U (TN)
Berea Coll (KY)
DePaul U (IL)
Elizabethtown Coll (PA)
Keene State Coll (NH)
Purdue U (IN)
Temple U (PA)
U of California, Santa Barbara (CA)
U of Waterloo (ON, Canada)
U of Wisconsin–Milwaukee (WI)
Willamette U (OR)

APPLIED PSYCHOLOGY
Arizona State U (AZ)
Bryant U (RI)
Christian Brothers U (TN)
Farmingdale State Coll (NY)
Morrisville State Coll (NY)
Mount St. Mary's Coll (CA)
Pace U (NY)
U of Michigan–Flint (MI)

AQUACULTURE
Auburn U (AL)
Dalhousie U (NS, Canada)
Texas A&M U (TX)
U of New England (ME)

AQUATIC BIOLOGY/ LIMNOLOGY
Florida Inst of Technology (FL)
Stetson U (FL)
Texas State U–San Marcos (TX)
U of California, Santa Barbara (CA)
U of South Carolina (SC)

ARABIC
American U (DC)
American U of Beirut (Lebanon)
Bard Coll (NY)
Binghamton U, State U of New York (NY)
California State U, San Bernardino (CA)
Dartmouth Coll (NH)
DePaul U (IL)
Drew U (NJ)
Georgetown U (DC)
Hope Coll (MI)
Michigan State U (MI)
Middlebury Coll (VT)
National U (CA)
The Ohio State U (OH)
Tufts U (MA)
United States Military Acad (NY)
United States Naval Acad (MD)
U of California, Los Angeles (CA)
U of Georgia (GA)
U of Maryland, Coll Park (MD)
U of Minnesota, Twin Cities Campus (MN)
U of Notre Dame (IN)
U of Oklahoma (OK)
U of Ottawa (ON, Canada)
The U of Texas at Austin (TX)

U of Utah (UT)
Washington U in St. Louis (MO)

ARCHEOLOGY
The American U in Cairo (Egypt)
American U of Beirut (Lebanon)
The American U of Rome (Italy)
Bard Coll (NY)
Boston U (MA)
Bowdoin Coll (ME)
Bridgewater State U (MA)
Brock U (ON, Canada)
Brown U (RI)
The Coll of Wooster (OH)
Columbia U (NY)
Columbia U, School of General Studies (NY)
Cornell Coll (IA)
Dartmouth Coll (NH)
Dickinson Coll (PA)
Franklin Pierce U (NH)
Hamilton Coll (NY)
Haverford Coll (PA)
Hunter Coll of the City U of New York (NY)
The Johns Hopkins U (MD)
Lawrence U (WI)
Mercyhurst U (PA)
New York U (NY)
Penn State Abington (PA)
Penn State Altoona (PA)
Penn State Beaver (PA)
Penn State Berks (PA)
Penn State Brandywine (PA)
Penn State DuBois (PA)
Penn State Erie, The Behrend Coll (PA)
Penn State Fayette, The Eberly Campus (PA)
Penn State Greater Allegheny (PA)
Penn State Hazleton (PA)
Penn State Lehigh Valley (PA)
Penn State Mont Alto (PA)
Penn State New Kensington (PA)
Penn State Schuylkill (PA)
Penn State Shenango (PA)
Penn State U Park (PA)
Penn State Wilkes-Barre (PA)
Penn State Worthington Scranton (PA)
Penn State York (PA)
Prescott Coll (AZ)
Saint Mary's Coll of California (CA)
Simon Fraser U (BC, Canada)
Stanford U (CA)
State U of New York Coll at Potsdam (NY)
Sweet Briar Coll (VA)
Tufts U (MA)
The U of British Columbia (BC, Canada)
U of Cincinnati (OH)
U of Evansville (IN)
U of Missouri (MO)
The U of North Carolina at Chapel Hill (NC)
U of Southern California (CA)
The U of Texas at Austin (TX)
The U of Western Ontario (ON, Canada)
U of Wisconsin–La Crosse (WI)
Washington State U (WA)
Washington U in St. Louis (MO)
Wesleyan U (CT)
Western Washington U (WA)
Wheaton Coll (IL)
Yale U (CT)

ARCHITECTURAL AND BUILDING SCIENCES
Pennsylvania Coll of Technology (PA)

ARCHITECTURAL ENGINEERING
Andrews U (MI)
Auburn U (AL)
California Polytechnic State U, San Luis Obispo (CA)
Illinois Inst of Technology (IL)
Kansas State U (KS)
Lawrence Technological U (MI)
Milwaukee School of Eng (WI)
Missouri U of Science and Technology (MO)
Oklahoma State U (OK)
Penn State Abington (PA)
Penn State Altoona (PA)

Penn State Beaver (PA)
Penn State Berks (PA)
Penn State Brandywine (PA)
Penn State DuBois (PA)
Penn State Erie, The Behrend Coll (PA)
Penn State Fayette, The Eberly Campus (PA)
Penn State Greater Allegheny (PA)
Penn State Hazleton (PA)
Penn State Lehigh Valley (PA)
Penn State Mont Alto (PA)
Penn State New Kensington (PA)
Penn State Schuylkill (PA)
Penn State Shenango (PA)
Penn State U Park (PA)
Penn State Wilkes-Barre (PA)
Penn State Worthington Scranton (PA)
Penn State York (PA)
Purdue U (IN)
Tennessee State U (TN)
Texas A&M U–Kingsville (TX)
Tufts U (MA)
U of Cincinnati (OH)
U of Colorado Boulder (CO)
The U of Kansas (KS)
U of Miami (FL)
U of Nebraska–Lincoln (NE)
U of Oklahoma (OK)
The U of Texas at Austin (TX)
U of Wyoming (WY)
Worcester Polytechnic Inst (MA)

ARCHITECTURAL ENGINEERING TECHNOLOGY
Bluefield State Coll (WV)
Farmingdale State Coll (NY)
Ferris State U (MI)
Indiana U–Purdue U Indianapolis (IN)
Keene State Coll (NH)
New England Inst of Technology (RI)
Purdue U (IN)
Seminole State Coll of Florida (FL)
State U of New York Coll of Technology at Alfred (NY)
U of Hartford (CT)
U of Southern Mississippi (MS)
Vermont Tech Coll (VT)
Washington U in St. Louis (MO)

ARCHITECTURAL HISTORY AND CRITICISM
Brown U (RI)
Columbia U, School of General Studies (NY)
DePaul U (IL)
Lawrence Technological U (MI)
Savannah Coll of Art and Design (GA)
Syracuse U (NY)
The U of Kansas (KS)
U of San Diego (CA)
U of Virginia (VA)

ARCHITECTURAL TECHNOLOGY
Lawrence Technological U (MI)
New York City Coll of Technology of the City U of New York (NY)
Washington U in St. Louis (MO)
Western Kentucky U (KY)

ARCHITECTURE
Acad of Art U (CA)
Agnes Scott Coll (GA)
American U of Beirut (Lebanon)
Andrews U (MI)
Arizona State U (AZ)
Auburn U (AL)
Ball State U (IN)
Bennington Coll (VT)
Boston Architectural Coll (MA)
California Polytechnic State U, San Luis Obispo (CA)
California State Polytechnic U, Pomona (CA)
Carnegie Mellon U (PA)
The Catholic U of America (DC)
City Coll of the City U of New York (NY)
Clemson U (SC)
Coe Coll (IA)
Columbia U (NY)
Columbia U, School of General Studies (NY)

Connecticut Coll (CT)
Cooper Union for the Advancement of Science and Art (NY)
Cornell Coll (IA)
Dalhousie U (NS, Canada)
Drury U (MO)
Florida Ag and Mech U (FL)
Florida Atlantic U (FL)
Hampshire Coll (MA)
Hampton U (VA)
Hobart and William Smith Colls (NY)
Illinois Inst of Technology (IL)
Inter American U of Puerto Rico, San Germán Campus (PR)
Iowa State U of Science and Technology (IA)
Ithaca Coll (NY)
Judson U (IL)
Keene State Coll (NH)
Kent State U (OH)
Lawrence Technological U (MI)
Lebanese American U (Lebanon)
Lehigh U (PA)
Louisiana State U and Ag and Mech Coll (LA)
Marywood U (PA)
Massachusetts Coll of Art and Design (MA)
Massachusetts Inst of Technology (MA)
Miami U (OH)
Mississippi State U (MS)
New Jersey Inst of Technology (NJ)
North Carolina State U (NC)
Northeastern U (MA)
Norwich U (VT)
The Ohio State U (OH)
Oklahoma State U (OK)
Parsons The New School for Design (NY)
Penn State U Park (PA)
Philadelphia U (PA)
Polytechnic U of Puerto Rico (PR)
Portland State U (OR)
Princeton U (NJ)
Rensselaer Polytechnic Inst (NY)
Rhode Island School of Design (RI)
Rice U (TX)
Roger Williams U (RI)
Savannah Coll of Art and Design (GA)
Smith Coll (MA)
South Dakota State U (SD)
Southern California Inst of Architecture (CA)
Southern Illinois U Carbondale (IL)
Southern Polytechnic State U (GA)
Syracuse U (NY)
Temple U (PA)
Texas A&M U (TX)
Tulane U (LA)
Tuskegee U (AL)
U at Buffalo, the State U of New York (NY)
The U of Arizona (AZ)
U of California, Berkeley (CA)
U of California, Los Angeles (CA)
U of Central Florida (FL)
U of Cincinnati (OH)
U of Colorado Denver (CO)
U of Florida (FL)
U of Houston (TX)
U of Idaho (ID)
U of Illinois at Chicago (IL)
U of Illinois at Urbana–Champaign (IL)
The U of Kansas (KS)
U of Kentucky (KY)
U of Louisiana at Lafayette (LA)
U of Maryland, Coll Park (MD)
U of Massachusetts Amherst (MA)
U of Memphis (TN)
U of Miami (FL)
U of Michigan (MI)
U of Minnesota, Twin Cities Campus (MN)
U of Missouri–Kansas City (MO)
U of Nebraska–Lincoln (NE)
U of Nevada, Las Vegas (NV)
U of New Mexico (NM)
The U of North Carolina at Charlotte (NC)
U of Notre Dame (IN)
U of Oklahoma (OK)
U of Oregon (OR)

U of Pennsylvania (PA)
U of Southern California (CA)
The U of Tennessee (TN)
The U of Texas at Arlington (TX)
The U of Texas at Austin (TX)
The U of Texas at San Antonio (TX)
U of the District of Columbia (DC)
U of Utah (UT)
U of Virginia (VA)
U of Waterloo (ON, Canada)
U of Wisconsin–Milwaukee (WI)
Virginia Polytechnic Inst and State U (VA)
Washington State U (WA)
Washington U in St. Louis (MO)
Wellesley Coll (MA)
Wentworth Inst of Technology (MA)
Woodbury U (CA)
Yale U (CT)

ARCHITECTURE RELATED
Case Western Reserve U (OH)
Coll of the Holy Cross (MA)
Columbia U (NY)
Lipscomb U (TN)
Mount Holyoke Coll (MA)
New Jersey Inst of Technology (NJ)
New York Inst of Technology (NY)
Northern Michigan U (MI)
School of the Art Inst of Chicago (IL)
The U of Arizona (AZ)
U of Cincinnati (OH)
U of Illinois at Chicago (IL)
U of Illinois at Urbana–Champaign (IL)
U of Louisiana at Lafayette (LA)
U of Minnesota, Twin Cities Campus (MN)
U of Utah (UT)
Washington U in St. Louis (MO)

ARCHIVES/ARCHIVAL ADMINISTRATION
Emory & Henry Coll (VA)

AREA STUDIES RELATED
Appalachian State U (NC)
Bridgewater State U (MA)
Castleton State Coll (VT)
Eastern Michigan U (MI)
Gannon U (PA)
Gettysburg Coll (PA)
Hofstra U (NY)
Illinois Wesleyan U (IL)
Millersville U of Pennsylvania (PA)
Ramapo Coll of New Jersey (NJ)
St. Francis Coll (NY)
Stanford U (CA)
U of Alaska Fairbanks (AK)
U of California, Los Angeles (CA)
U of California, Santa Barbara (CA)
U of Illinois at Urbana–Champaign (IL)
U of Michigan–Dearborn (MI)
U of Minnesota, Twin Cities Campus (MN)
U of Pittsburgh (PA)
U of Virginia (VA)
U of Washington, Tacoma (WA)
Utah State U (UT)
Virginia Commonwealth U (VA)
Washington U in St. Louis (MO)
Williams Coll (MA)

ARMY ROTC/MILITARY SCIENCE
Hampton U (VA)
Jacksonville State U (AL)
La Salle U (PA)
Minnesota State U Mankato (MN)
Roger Williams U (RI)
The U of Iowa (IA)
U of Minnesota, Twin Cities Campus (MN)

ART
Agnes Scott Coll (GA)
Alabama State U (AL)
Alberta Coll of Art & Design (AB, Canada)
Albertus Magnus Coll (CT)
Albion Coll (MI)
Albright Coll (PA)
Alfred U (NY)
Alma Coll (MI)
Alverno Coll (WI)
American Acad of Art (IL)
American U (DC)

The American U in Cairo (Egypt)
Amherst Coll (MA)
Anderson U (SC)
Andrews U (MI)
Appalachian State U (NC)
Arizona State U (AZ)
Arkansas State U (AR)
Arkansas Tech U (AR)
Armstrong Atlantic State U (GA)
Art Center Coll of Design (CA)
Athens State U (AL)
Auburn U at Montgomery (AL)
Augsburg Coll (MN)
Augustana Coll (IL)
Augustana Coll (SD)
Aurora U (IL)
Austin Peay State U (TN)
Averett U (VA)
Avila U (MO)
Baldwin Wallace U (OH)
Ball State U (IN)
Bard Coll (NY)
Bates Coll (ME)
Baylor U (TX)
Belhaven U (MS)
Belmont U (TN)
Bemidji State U (MN)
Benedictine Coll (KS)
Berea Coll (KY)
Berry Coll (GA)
Bethany Coll (WV)
Bethany Lutheran Coll (MN)
Bethel Coll (IN)
Bethel U (MN)
Binghamton U, State U of New York (NY)
Blackburn Coll (IL)
Bluefield Coll (VA)
Bluffton U (OH)
Bob Jones U (SC)
Bowie State U (MD)
Bowling Green State U (OH)
Bradley U (IL)
Brock U (ON, Canada)
Brown U (RI)
Bucknell U (PA)
Buena Vista U (IA)
Buffalo State Coll, State U of New York (NY)
Caldwell Coll (NJ)
California Baptist U (CA)
California Lutheran U (CA)
California State Polytechnic U, Pomona (CA)
California State U, Chico (CA)
California State U, Dominguez Hills (CA)
California State U, Fresno (CA)
California State U, Fullerton (CA)
California State U, Long Beach (CA)
California State U, Los Angeles (CA)
California State U, Monterey Bay (CA)
California State U, Northridge (CA)
California State U, San Bernardino (CA)
California State U, Stanislaus (CA)
Calvin Coll (MI)
Cameron U (OK)
Campbellsville U (KY)
Capital U (OH)
Cardinal Stritch U (WI)
Carnegie Mellon U (PA)
Carson-Newman U (TN)
Castleton State Coll (VT)
The Catholic U of America (DC)
Cedar Crest Coll (PA)
Centenary Coll of Louisiana (LA)
Central Coll (IA)
Central Connecticut State U (CT)
Central Michigan U (MI)
Central State U (OH)
Centre Coll (KY)
Chapman U (CA)
Cheyney U of Pennsylvania (PA)
Chicago State U (IL)
City Coll of the City U of New York (NY)
Claflin U (SC)
Clarion U of Pennsylvania (PA)
Clark Atlanta U (GA)
Clarke U (IA)
Cleveland State U (OH)
Coe Coll (IA)
Colby Coll (ME)

Colgate U (NY)
The Coll at Brockport, State U of New York (NY)
The Coll of Idaho (ID)
Coll of Mount St. Joseph (OH)
The Coll of New Jersey (NJ)
Coll of Saint Benedict (MN)
Coll of Saint Elizabeth (NJ)
Coll of Saint Mary (NE)
The Coll of St. Scholastica (MN)
Coll of the Atlantic (ME)
Coll of the Ozarks (MO)
The Coll of William and Mary (VA)
Colorado Mesa U (CO)
Columbia Coll (MO)
Columbia Coll Chicago (IL)
Concordia Coll (MN)
Concordia Coll–New York (NY)
Concordia U (CA)
Concordia U Chicago (IL)
Concordia U, Nebraska (NE)
Concordia U, St. Paul (MN)
Concordia U Wisconsin (WI)
Connecticut Coll (CT)
Converse Coll (SC)
Corcoran Coll of Art and Design (DC)
Cornell Coll (IA)
Creighton U (NE)
Culver-Stockton Coll (MO)
Dallas Baptist U (TX)
Davidson Coll (NC)
DePaul U (IL)
Dillard U (LA)
Doane Coll (NE)
Drake U (IA)
Drew U (NJ)
Earlham Coll (IN)
East Carolina U (NC)
East Central U (OK)
Eastern Illinois U (IL)
Eastern Mennonite U (VA)
Eastern Michigan U (MI)
Eastern New Mexico U (NM)
East Tennessee State U (TN)
Edgewood Coll (WI)
Edinboro U of Pennsylvania (PA)
Elmira Coll (NY)
Elon U (NC)
Emmanuel Coll (MA)
Emporia State U (KS)
Evangel U (MO)
The Evergreen State Coll (WA)
Fairfield U (CT)
Fayetteville State U (NC)
Felician Coll (NJ)
Ferrum Coll (VA)
Florida Atlantic U (FL)
Florida Gulf Coast U (FL)
Florida Intl U (FL)
Fort Lewis Coll (CO)
Framingham State U (MA)
Francis Marion U (SC)
Franklin Pierce U (NH)
Friends U (KS)
Furman U (SC)
Gardner-Webb U (NC)
George Fox U (OR)
Georgia Coll & State U (GA)
Georgia Southern U (GA)
Georgia Southwestern State U (GA)
Gettysburg Coll (PA)
Gonzaga U (WA)
Gordon Coll (MA)
Goshen Coll (IN)
Goucher Coll (MD)
Governors State U (IL)
Graceland U (IA)
Grambling State U (LA)
Grand View U (IA)
Greenville Coll (IL)
Grinnell Coll (IA)
Guilford Coll (NC)
Gustavus Adolphus Coll (MN)
Hampton U (VA)
Hanover Coll (IN)
Hartwick Coll (NY)
Haverford Coll (PA)
Henderson State U (AR)
Hendrix Coll (AR)
Hillsdale Coll (MI)
Hiram Coll (OH)
Hobart and William Smith Colls (NY)
Hollins U (VA)
Holy Cross Coll (IN)

Houghton Coll (NY)
Howard Payne U (TX)
Humboldt State U (CA)
Hunter Coll of the City U of New York (NY)
Huntington U (IN)
Illinois Coll (IL)
Illinois State U (IL)
Illinois Wesleyan U (IL)
Indiana State U (IN)
Indiana U Bloomington (IN)
Indiana U East (IN)
Indiana U Kokomo (IN)
Indiana U of Pennsylvania (PA)
Indiana U–Purdue U Fort Wayne (IN)
Indiana U South Bend (IN)
Indiana U Southeast (IN)
Indiana Wesleyan U (IN)
Inter American U of Puerto Rico, San Germán Campus (PR)
Iowa State U of Science and Technology (IA)
Iowa Wesleyan Coll (IA)
Ithaca Coll (NY)
Jacksonville State U (AL)
James Madison U (VA)
Jamestown Coll (ND)
Johnson State Coll (VT)
Judson Coll (AL)
Judson U (IL)
Juniata Coll (PA)
Kalamazoo Coll (MI)
Kansas State U (KS)
Kansas Wesleyan U (KS)
Kean U (NJ)
Kennesaw State U (GA)
Keystone Coll (PA)
Knox Coll (IL)
Kutztown U of Pennsylvania (PA)
Lafayette Coll (PA)
Lakeland Coll (WI)
Lamar U (TX)
Lander U (SC)
Langston U (OK)
La Sierra U (CA)
Lebanon Valley Coll (PA)
Lehigh U (PA)
Lehman Coll of the City U of New York (NY)
Lesley U (MA)
Lewis U (IL)
Lincoln Memorial U (TN)
Lindenwood U (MO)
Linfield Coll (OR)
Lock Haven U of Pennsylvania (PA)
Long Island U–Brooklyn Campus (NY)
Louisiana Coll (LA)
Louisiana State U in Shreveport (LA)
Lourdes U (OH)
Loyola U Maryland (MD)
Loyola U New Orleans (LA)
Lubbock Christian U (TX)
Luther Coll (IA)
Lynchburg Coll (VA)
Lyon Coll (AR)
Macalester Coll (MN)
Manchester U (IN)
Mansfield U of Pennsylvania (PA)
Marietta Coll (OH)
Marist Coll (NY)
Marshall U (WV)
Mars Hill Coll (NC)
Mary Baldwin Coll (VA)
Maryland Inst Coll of Art (MD)
Marymount Manhattan Coll (NY)
Massachusetts Coll of Liberal Arts (MA)
McDaniel Coll (MD)
McKendree U (IL)
McNeese State U (LA)
Mercer U (GA)
Mercyhurst U (PA)
Metropolitan State U of Denver (CO)
Miami U (OH)
Michigan State U (MI)
Middle Tennessee State U (TN)
Midwestern State U (TX)
Millersville U of Pennsylvania (PA)
Mills Coll (CA)
Minnesota State U Mankato (MN)
Minnesota State U Moorhead (MN)
Minot State U (ND)
Mississippi Valley State U (MS)

Missouri State U (MO)
Missouri Western State U (MO)
Monmouth Coll (IL)
Monmouth U (NJ)
Montana State U (MT)
Moore Coll of Art & Design (PA)
Moravian Coll (PA)
Morehouse Coll (GA)
Mount Mary U (WI)
Mount Mercy U (IA)
Mount St. Mary's Coll (CA)
Mount St. Mary's U (MD)
Mount Vernon Nazarene U (OH)
Muhlenberg Coll (PA)
National U (CA)
Nazareth Coll of Rochester (NY)
Newberry Coll (SC)
New England Coll (NH)
New Jersey City U (NJ)
New Jersey Inst of Technology (NJ)
Newman U (KS)
New Mexico Highlands U (NM)
Nicholls State U (LA)
Norfolk State U (VA)
North Carolina Central U (NC)
North Central Coll (IL)
North Dakota State U (ND)
Northeastern Illinois U (IL)
Northeastern U (MA)
Northern Illinois U (IL)
Northern State U (SD)
Northland Coll (WI)
Northwestern Coll (IA)
Northwest Nazarene U (ID)
Notre Dame de Namur U (CA)
Oakland City U (IN)
Oglethorpe U (GA)
The Ohio State U (OH)
Ohio U (OH)
Oklahoma Baptist U (OK)
Oklahoma Christian U (OK)
Oklahoma City U (OK)
Oklahoma State U (OK)
Old Dominion U (VA)
Olivet Coll (MI)
Oral Roberts U (OK)
Oregon State U (OR)
Otis Coll of Art and Design (CA)
Pace U (NY)
Pacific Lutheran U (WA)
Pacific U (OR)
Parsons The New School for Design (NY)
Penn State Abington (PA)
Penn State Altoona (PA)
Penn State Beaver (PA)
Penn State Berks (PA)
Penn State Brandywine (PA)
Penn State DuBois (PA)
Penn State Erie, The Behrend Coll (PA)
Penn State Fayette, The Eberly Campus (PA)
Penn State Greater Allegheny (PA)
Penn State Hazleton (PA)
Penn State Lehigh Valley (PA)
Penn State Mont Alto (PA)
Penn State New Kensington (PA)
Penn State Schuylkill (PA)
Penn State Shenango (PA)
Penn State U Park (PA)
Penn State Wilkes-Barre (PA)
Penn State Worthington Scranton (PA)
Penn State York (PA)
Pepperdine U, Malibu (CA)
Piedmont Coll (GA)
Pittsburg State U (KS)
Pitzer Coll (CA)
Plymouth State U (NH)
Pomona Coll (CA)
Portland State U (OR)
Presbyterian Coll (SC)
Prescott Coll (AZ)
Purchase Coll, State U of New York (NY)
Purdue U (IN)
Queens U of Charlotte (NC)
Radford U (VA)
Randolph Coll (VA)
Reed Coll (OR)
Rhodes Coll (TN)
Rice U (TX)
Rider U (NJ)
Ripon Coll (WI)
Rivier U (NH)
Roanoke Coll (VA)

Roberts Wesleyan Coll (NY)
Rocky Mountain Coll (MT)
Roger Williams U (RI)
Rollins Coll (FL)
Rowan U (NJ)
Rutgers, The State U of New Jersey, Camden (NJ)
Rutgers, The State U of New Jersey, Newark (NJ)
Rutgers, The State U of New Jersey, New Brunswick (NJ)
Saginaw Valley State U (MI)
St. Ambrose U (IA)
St. Andrews U (NC)
Saint Anselm Coll (NH)
St. Edward's U (TX)
Saint John's U (MN)
St. Lawrence U (NY)
Saint Mary-of-the-Woods Coll (IN)
Saint Mary's Coll (IN)
Saint Mary's Coll of California (CA)
St. Mary's Coll of Maryland (MD)
Saint Michael's Coll (VT)
St. Norbert Coll (WI)
St. Olaf Coll (MN)
St. Thomas Aquinas Coll (NY)
Salem State U (MA)
Salisbury U (MD)
Samford U (AL)
Sam Houston State U (TX)
San Diego State U (CA)
San Francisco State U (CA)
San Jose State U (CA)
School of the Art Inst of Chicago (IL)
School of the Museum of Fine Arts, Boston (MA)
Scripps Coll (CA)
Seattle Pacific U (WA)
Seattle U (WA)
Sewanee: The U of the South (TN)
Shepherd U (WV)
Shippensburg U of Pennsylvania (PA)
Siena Heights U (MI)
Sierra Nevada Coll (NV)
Simmons Coll (MA)
Simon Fraser U (BC, Canada)
Simpson Coll (IA)
Skidmore Coll (NY)
Slippery Rock U of Pennsylvania (PA)
Smith Coll (MA)
Sonoma State U (CA)
Southeastern Louisiana U (LA)
Southeastern Oklahoma State U (OK)
Southeast Missouri State U (MO)
Southern Arkansas U–Magnolia (AR)
Southern Illinois U Carbondale (IL)
Southern Illinois U Edwardsville (IL)
Southern Oregon U (OR)
Southern Utah U (UT)
Southwest Baptist U (MO)
Southwestern U (TX)
Spelman Coll (GA)
Spring Arbor U (MI)
Stanford U (CA)
State U of New York at Fredonia (NY)
State U of New York at New Paltz (NY)
State U of New York at Oswego (NY)
State U of New York at Plattsburgh (NY)
State U of New York Coll at Old Westbury (NY)
State U of New York Coll at Potsdam (NY)
State U of New York Empire State Coll (NY)
Stephen F. Austin State U (TX)
Sterling Coll (KS)
Stetson U (FL)
Suffolk U (MA)
Sul Ross State U (TX)
Tarleton State U (TX)
Taylor U (IN)
Temple U (PA)
Tennessee State U (TN)
Texas Lutheran U (TX)
Texas State U–San Marcos (TX)
Texas Woman's U (TX)
Thomas Edison State Coll (NJ)

Tiffin U (OH)
Transylvania U (KY)
Trinity Coll (CT)
Trinity U (TX)
Troy U (AL)
Truman State U (MO)
Tulane U (LA)
Union U (TN)
Université du Québec en Outaouais (QC, Canada)
U at Albany, State U of New York (NY)
U at Buffalo, the State U of New York (NY)
The U of Alabama at Birmingham (AL)
U of Alaska Anchorage (AK)
U of Alaska Fairbanks (AK)
U of Arkansas at Little Rock (AR)
U of Arkansas–Fort Smith (AR)
U of California, Berkeley (CA)
U of California, Los Angeles (CA)
U of California, Riverside (CA)
U of California, Santa Cruz (CA)
U of Central Arkansas (AR)
U of Central Florida (FL)
U of Central Oklahoma (OK)
U of Charleston (WV)
U of Dallas (TX)
U of Delaware (DE)
U of Denver (CO)
U of Evansville (IN)
The U of Findlay (OH)
U of Georgia (GA)
U of Great Falls (MT)
U of Guam (GU)
U of Hawaii at Hilo (HI)
U of Hawaii at Manoa (HI)
U of Houston (TX)
U of Idaho (ID)
The U of Iowa (IA)
U of La Verne (CA)
U of Louisiana at Lafayette (LA)
U of Maine at Farmington (ME)
U of Maine at Machias (ME)
U of Massachusetts Boston (MA)
U of Memphis (TN)
U of Miami (FL)
U of Michigan (MI)
U of Minnesota, Duluth (MN)
U of Minnesota, Twin Cities Campus (MN)
U of Missouri (MO)
U of Missouri–Kansas City (MO)
U of Missouri–St. Louis (MO)
U of Mobile (AL)
U of Montevallo (AL)
U of Nebraska at Kearney (NE)
U of Nebraska at Omaha (NE)
U of Nevada, Las Vegas (NV)
U of Nevada, Reno (NV)
U of New Hampshire (NH)
U of New Mexico (NM)
U of North Alabama (AL)
U of North Carolina at Asheville (NC)
The U of North Carolina at Charlotte (NC)
The U of North Carolina at Greensboro (NC)
U of North Dakota (ND)
U of Northern Iowa (IA)
U of North Florida (FL)
U of North Georgia (GA)
U of North Texas (TX)
U of Oregon (OR)
U of Pikeville (KY)
U of Puget Sound (WA)
U of Rhode Island (RI)
U of Saint Mary (KS)
U of San Diego (CA)
U of Science and Arts of Oklahoma (OK)
U of South Alabama (AL)
U of Southern California (CA)
U of Southern Indiana (IN)
U of South Florida (FL)
The U of Tampa (FL)
The U of Tennessee at Chattanooga (TN)
The U of Texas at Arlington (TX)
The U of Texas at Austin (TX)
The U of Texas at Brownsville (TX)
The U of Texas at San Antonio (TX)
The U of Texas of the Permian Basin (TX)
U of the District of Columbia (DC)

U of the Incarnate Word (TX)
The U of Toledo (OH)
U of Utah (UT)
U of Virginia (VA)
U of Washington, Bothell (WA)
The U of Western Ontario (ON, Canada)
U of West Florida (FL)
U of West Georgia (GA)
U of Windsor (ON, Canada)
U of Wisconsin–Eau Claire (WI)
U of Wisconsin–Green Bay (WI)
U of Wisconsin–La Crosse (WI)
U of Wisconsin–Madison (WI)
U of Wisconsin–Milwaukee (WI)
U of Wisconsin–Parkside (WI)
U of Wisconsin–Platteville (WI)
U of Wyoming (WY)
Upper Iowa U (IA)
Utah State U (UT)
Valdosta State U (GA)
Valley City State U (ND)
Valparaiso U (IN)
Villa Maria Coll of Buffalo (NY)
Virginia Intermont Coll (VA)
Virginia Polytechnic Inst and State U (VA)
Virginia Wesleyan Coll (VA)
Viterbo U (WI)
Wabash Coll (IN)
Wagner Coll (NY)
Walla Walla U (WA)
Wartburg Coll (IA)
Washburn U (KS)
Washington & Jefferson Coll (PA)
Washington Coll (MD)
Washington U in St. Louis (MO)
Watkins Coll of Art, Design, & Film (TN)
Wayland Baptist U (TX)
Waynesburg U (PA)
Wayne State Coll (NE)
Wayne State U (MI)
Weber State U (UT)
Webster U (MO)
Wells Coll (NY)
Wesleyan U (CT)
West Chester U of Pennsylvania (PA)
Western Carolina U (NC)
Western Connecticut State U (CT)
Western Illinois U (IL)
Western Michigan U (MI)
Western Oregon U (OR)
Western State Colorado U (CO)
Western Washington U (WA)
Westfield State U (MA)
Westminster Coll (UT)
West Texas A&M U (TX)
West Virginia State U (WV)
West Virginia U (WV)
West Virginia Wesleyan Coll (WV)
Wheaton Coll (IL)
Whitman Coll (WA)
Whitworth U (WA)
Wichita State U (KS)
Willamette U (OR)
William Jewell Coll (MO)
William Paterson U of New Jersey (NJ)
Winthrop U (SC)
Wittenberg U (OH)
Wright State U (OH)
Xavier U (OH)
Xavier U of Louisiana (LA)
Yale U (CT)
York Coll of the City U of New York (NY)
Young Harris Coll (GA)
Youngstown State U (OH)

ART HISTORY, CRITICISM AND CONSERVATION

Acad of Art U (CA)
Adams State U (CO)
Adelphi U (NY)
Albertus Magnus Coll (CT)
Albion Coll (MI)
American U (DC)
American U of Beirut (Lebanon)
The American U of Paris (France)
The American U of Rome (Italy)
Augsburg Coll (MN)
Augustana Coll (IL)
Baker U (KS)
Baldwin Wallace U (OH)
Bard Coll (NY)

Baylor U (TX)
Belmont U (TN)
Bennington Coll (VT)
Binghamton U, State U of New York (NY)
Bloomsburg U of Pennsylvania (PA)
Boise State U (ID)
Boston Coll (MA)
Bowdoin Coll (ME)
Bowling Green State U (OH)
Bradley U (IL)
Bridgewater State U (MA)
Brown U (RI)
Bucknell U (PA)
Buffalo State Coll, State U of New York (NY)
California State U, Chico (CA)
California State U, Dominguez Hills (CA)
California State U, East Bay (CA)
California State U, Fullerton (CA)
California State U, Long Beach (CA)
California State U, San Bernardino (CA)
California State U, Stanislaus (CA)
Calvin Coll (MI)
Canisius Coll (NY)
Carleton Coll (MN)
Case Western Reserve U (OH)
The Catholic U of America (DC)
Centre Coll (KY)
Chapman U (CA)
Chatham U (PA)
City Coll of the City U of New York (NY)
Clarke U (IA)
Clark U (MA)
Colby Coll (ME)
Colgate U (NY)
Coll of Charleston (SC)
The Coll of New Rochelle (NY)
Coll of the Holy Cross (MA)
The Coll of William and Mary (VA)
The Coll of Wooster (OH)
The Colorado Coll (CO)
Colorado State U (CO)
Columbia U (NY)
Columbia U, School of General Studies (NY)
Concordia U (QC, Canada)
Connecticut Coll (CT)
Converse Coll (SC)
Cornell Coll (IA)
Dartmouth Coll (NH)
DePaul U (IL)
DePauw U (IN)
DEREE—The American Coll of Greece (Greece)
Dominican U (IL)
Drake U (IA)
Drew U (NJ)
Drury U (MO)
Duquesne U (PA)
East Carolina U (NC)
Eastern Michigan U (MI)
Eastern Washington U (WA)
Edinboro U of Pennsylvania (PA)
Elizabethtown Coll (PA)
Elon U (NC)
Eugene Lang Coll The New School for Liberal Arts (NY)
Fairfield U (CT)
Ferris State U (MI)
Flagler Coll (FL)
Florida Intl U (FL)
Florida Southern Coll (FL)
Florida State U (FL)
Franklin & Marshall Coll (PA)
Franklin U Switzerland (Switzerland)
Furman U (SC)
Gallaudet U (DC)
George Mason U (VA)
Georgetown U (DC)
Gettysburg Coll (PA)
Goucher Coll (MD)
Grand Valley State U (MI)
Gustavus Adolphus Coll (MN)
Hamilton Coll (NY)
Hamline U (MN)
Hampshire Coll (MA)
Hanover Coll (IN)
Hartwick Coll (NY)
Haverford Coll (PA)
Hiram Coll (OH)

Hobart and William Smith Colls (NY)
Hofstra U (NY)
Hollins U (VA)
Hope Coll (MI)
Humboldt State U (CA)
Hunter Coll of the City U of New York (NY)
Indiana U Bloomington (IN)
Indiana U–Purdue U Indianapolis (IN)
Ithaca Coll (NY)
James Madison U (VA)
John Cabot U (Italy)
John Carroll U (OH)
The Johns Hopkins U (MD)
Juniata Coll (PA)
Kalamazoo Coll (MI)
Kean U (NJ)
Kennesaw State U (GA)
Kent State U (OH)
Kenyon Coll (OH)
Knox Coll (IL)
Lafayette Coll (PA)
La Salle U (PA)
Lawrence U (WI)
Lehigh U (PA)
Lehman Coll of the City U of New York (NY)
Lindenwood U (MO)
Long Island U–C. W. Post Campus (NY)
Lourdes U (OH)
Loyola Marymount U (CA)
Loyola U Chicago (IL)
Loyola U Maryland (MD)
Manhattanville Coll (NY)
Marist Coll (NY)
Mars Hill Coll (NC)
Maryland Inst Coll of Art (MD)
Marymount Manhattan Coll (NY)
Massachusetts Coll of Art and Design (MA)
McDaniel Coll (MD)
Merrimack Coll (MA)
Messiah Coll (PA)
Miami U (OH)
Michigan State U (MI)
Middlebury Coll (VT)
Millsaps Coll (MS)
Mills Coll (CA)
Minnesota State U Mankato (MN)
Missouri State U (MO)
Moore Coll of Art & Design (PA)
Moravian Coll (PA)
Mount Allison U (NB, Canada)
Mount Holyoke Coll (MA)
Nazareth Coll of Rochester (NY)
New Coll of Florida (FL)
New England Coll (NH)
North Carolina State U (NC)
North Central Coll (IL)
Northern Illinois U (IL)
Northern Michigan U (MI)
Oakland U (MI)
Oglethorpe U (GA)
The Ohio State U (OH)
Ohio U (OH)
Ohio Wesleyan U (OH)
Oklahoma City U (OK)
Old Dominion U (VA)
Pace U (NY)
Penn State Abington (PA)
Penn State Altoona (PA)
Penn State Beaver (PA)
Penn State Berks (PA)
Penn State Brandywine (PA)
Penn State DuBois (PA)
Penn State Erie, The Behrend Coll (PA)
Penn State Fayette, The Eberly Campus (PA)
Penn State Greater Allegheny (PA)
Penn State Hazleton (PA)
Penn State Lehigh Valley (PA)
Penn State Mont Alto (PA)
Penn State New Kensington (PA)
Penn State Schuylkill (PA)
Penn State Shenango (PA)
Penn State U Park (PA)
Penn State Wilkes-Barre (PA)
Penn State Worthington Scranton (PA)
Penn State York (PA)
Pepperdine U, Malibu (CA)
Pitzer Coll (CA)
Plymouth State U (NH)

Pomona Coll (CA)
Portland State U (OR)
Presbyterian Coll (SC)
Princeton U (NJ)
Principia Coll (IL)
Providence Coll (RI)
Purchase Coll, State U of New York (NY)
Purdue U (IN)
Randolph Coll (VA)
Randolph-Macon Coll (VA)
Rhode Island Coll (RI)
Rice U (TX)
Roanoke Coll (VA)
Rockford Coll (IL)
Roger Williams U (RI)
Rollins Coll (FL)
Rosemont Coll (PA)
Rutgers, The State U of New Jersey, New Brunswick (NJ)
St. Bonaventure U (NY)
St. Lawrence U (NY)
Saint Louis U (MO)
Saint Mary's Coll of California (CA)
St. Olaf Coll (MN)
Saint Vincent Coll (PA)
Salem State U (MA)
Salve Regina U (RI)
San Diego State U (CA)
San Francisco Art Inst (CA)
San Jose State U (CA)
Savannah Coll of Art and Design (GA)
School of the Art Inst of Chicago (IL)
Scripps Coll (CA)
Seattle U (WA)
Seton Hill U (PA)
Sewanee: The U of the South (TN)
Siena Heights U (MI)
Skidmore Coll (NY)
Smith Coll (MA)
Sonoma State U (CA)
Southern Connecticut State U (CT)
Southern Methodist U (TX)
Southern Utah U (UT)
Southwestern U (TX)
Stanford U (CA)
State U of New York at Fredonia (NY)
State U of New York at New Paltz (NY)
State U of New York Coll at Cortland (NY)
State U of New York Coll at Geneseo (NY)
State U of New York Coll at Potsdam (NY)
Stephen F. Austin State U (TX)
Stonehill Coll (MA)
Stony Brook U, State U of New York (NY)
Suffolk U (MA)
Susquehanna U (PA)
Swarthmore Coll (PA)
Sweet Briar Coll (VA)
Syracuse U (NY)
Temple U (PA)
Texas Christian U (TX)
Thomas More Coll (KY)
Transylvania U (KY)
Trinity Coll (CT)
Trinity U (TX)
Truman State U (MO)
Tufts U (MA)
Tulane U (LA)
U at Albany, State U of New York (NY)
U at Buffalo, the State U of New York (NY)
The U of Akron (OH)
The U of Alabama (AL)
The U of Arizona (AZ)
The U of British Columbia (BC, Canada)
The U of British Columbia–Okanagan (BC, Canada)
U of California, Berkeley (CA)
U of California, Davis (CA)
U of California, Irvine (CA)
U of California, Los Angeles (CA)
U of California, Riverside (CA)
U of California, Santa Barbara (CA)
U of California, Santa Cruz (CA)
U of Chicago (IL)
U of Cincinnati (OH)
U of Colorado Boulder (CO)

U of Dallas (TX)
U of Delaware (DE)
U of Denver (CO)
U of Evansville (IN)
U of Florida (FL)
U of Georgia (GA)
U of Guelph (ON, Canada)
U of Hartford (CT)
U of Houston (TX)
U of Illinois at Chicago (IL)
U of Illinois at Urbana–Champaign (IL)
The U of Iowa (IA)
The U of Kansas (KS)
U of Kentucky (KY)
U of La Verne (CA)
U of Louisville (KY)
U of Maryland, Coll Park (MD)
U of Mary Washington (VA)
U of Massachusetts Amherst (MA)
U of Massachusetts Dartmouth (MA)
U of Memphis (TN)
U of Miami (FL)
U of Michigan (MI)
U of Michigan–Dearborn (MI)
U of Minnesota, Duluth (MN)
U of Minnesota, Twin Cities Campus (MN)
U of Mississippi (MS)
U of Missouri (MO)
U of Missouri–Kansas City (MO)
U of Missouri–St. Louis (MO)
U of Nebraska at Omaha (NE)
U of Nebraska–Lincoln (NE)
U of Nevada, Las Vegas (NV)
U of Nevada, Reno (NV)
U of New Mexico (NM)
U of New Orleans (LA)
The U of North Carolina at Chapel Hill (NC)
The U of North Carolina at Charlotte (NC)
The U of North Carolina Wilmington (NC)
U of Northern Iowa (IA)
U of North Texas (TX)
U of Notre Dame (IN)
U of Oklahoma (OK)
U of Oregon (OR)
U of Ottawa (ON, Canada)
U of Pennsylvania (PA)
U of Pittsburgh (PA)
U of Redlands (CA)
U of Regina (SK, Canada)
U of Rhode Island (RI)
U of Richmond (VA)
U of Rochester (NY)
U of Saint Joseph (CT)
U of St. Thomas (MN)
U of San Diego (CA)
U of South Carolina (SC)
U of Southern California (CA)
U of South Florida (FL)
The U of Tennessee (TN)
The U of Texas at Arlington (TX)
The U of Texas at Austin (TX)
The U of Texas at San Antonio (TX)
U of the Incarnate Word (TX)
The U of Toledo (OH)
U of Tulsa (OK)
U of Utah (UT)
U of Vermont (VT)
U of Waterloo (ON, Canada)
The U of Western Ontario (ON, Canada)
U of West Florida (FL)
U of Windsor (ON, Canada)
U of Wisconsin–Madison (WI)
U of Wisconsin–Milwaukee (WI)
U of Wisconsin–Superior (WI)
Ursuline Coll (OH)
Vassar Coll (NY)
Villanova U (PA)
Virginia Commonwealth U (VA)
Wake Forest U (NC)
Washburn U (KS)
Washington and Lee U (VA)
Washington U in St. Louis (MO)
Wayne State U (MI)
Webster U (MO)
Wellesley Coll (MA)
Wells Coll (NY)
Wesleyan Coll (GA)
Wesleyan U (CT)
Western Kentucky U (KY)
Western Michigan U (MI)

Western Washington U (WA)
West Virginia U (WV)
Wheaton Coll (MA)
Whitman Coll (WA)
Willamette U (OR)
William Paterson U of New Jersey (NJ)
Williams Coll (MA)
Winthrop U (SC)
Wright State U (OH)
Yale U (CT)
York Coll of the City U of New York (NY)
Youngstown State U (OH)

ARTIFICIAL INTELLIGENCE
Sullivan Coll of Technology and Design (KY)
U of Windsor (ON, Canada)
Worcester Polytechnic Inst (MA)

ARTS, ENTERTAINMENT, AND MEDIA MANAGEMENT
Belmont U (TN)
Champlain Coll (VT)
Drury U (MO)
St. Edward's U (TX)
Shenandoah U (VA)
State U of New York at Fredonia (NY)
U of Kentucky (KY)
U of North Alabama (AL)
U of Wisconsin–Green Bay (WI)

ARTS, ENTERTAINMENT, AND MEDIA MANAGEMENT RELATED
Belmont U (TN)
Delta State U (MS)
Hope Coll (MI)

ART TEACHER EDUCATION
Abilene Christian U (TX)
Acad of Art U (CA)
Adams State U (CO)
Adelphi U (NY)
Albright Coll (PA)
Alfred U (NY)
Alma Coll (MI)
Alverno Coll (WI)
Anderson U (SC)
Andrews U (MI)
Appalachian State U (NC)
Arkansas Tech U (AR)
Armstrong Atlantic State U (GA)
Asbury U (KY)
Ashland U (OH)
Assumption Coll (MA)
Augsburg Coll (MN)
Augustana Coll (IL)
Augustana Coll (SD)
Averett U (VA)
Baker U (KS)
Barton Coll (NC)
Baylor U (TX)
Belmont U (TN)
Bemidji State U (MN)
Berea Coll (KY)
Bethel Coll (IN)
Bethel U (MN)
Blackburn Coll (IL)
Boise State U (ID)
Boston U (MA)
Bowling Green State U (OH)
Bradley U (IL)
Bridgewater State U (MA)
Buena Vista U (IA)
Buffalo State Coll, State U of New York (NY)
California Lutheran U (CA)
California State U, Chico (CA)
California State U, Long Beach (CA)
Calvin Coll (MI)
Campbellsville U (KY)
Capital U (OH)
Cardinal Stritch U (WI)
Carlow U (PA)
Carson-Newman U (TN)
Case Western Reserve U (OH)
Central Connecticut State U (CT)
Central Michigan U (MI)
Central State U (OH)
City Coll of the City U of New York (NY)
Claflin U (SC)
Clarke U (IA)
Coe Coll (IA)

Coll for Creative Studies (MI)
Coll of Mount St. Joseph (OH)
The Coll of New Jersey (NJ)
The Coll of New Rochelle (NY)
The Coll of Saint Rose (NY)
Coll of the Ozarks (MO)
Colorado State U (CO)
Columbus State U (GA)
Concordia Coll (MN)
Concordia U (QC, Canada)
Concordia U Chicago (IL)
Concordia U, Nebraska (NE)
Concordia U, St. Paul (MN)
Concordia U Wisconsin (WI)
Concord U (WV)
Converse Coll (SC)
Culver-Stockton Coll (MO)
Dakota Wesleyan U (SD)
Defiance Coll (OH)
DePaul U (IL)
East Carolina U (NC)
East Central U (OK)
Eastern Michigan U (MI)
Eastern Washington U (WA)
Edgewood Coll (WI)
Elizabeth City State U (NC)
Elmira Coll (NY)
Evangel U (MO)
Fairmont State U (WV)
Fayetteville State U (NC)
Ferris State U (MI)
Flagler Coll (FL)
Florida Intl U (FL)
Florida Southern Coll (FL)
Francis Marion U (SC)
Franklin Pierce U (NH)
Friends U (KS)
Gallaudet U (DC)
Georgia State U (GA)
Goddard Coll (VT)
Graceland U (IA)
Grand Valley State U (MI)
Gustavus Adolphus Coll (MN)
Hampton U (VA)
Harding U (AR)
Hardin-Simmons U (TX)
Henderson State U (AR)
Hofstra U (NY)
Holy Family U (PA)
Hope Coll (MI)
Howard Payne U (TX)
Humboldt State U (CA)
Huntington U (IN)
Indiana State U (IN)
Indiana U Bloomington (IN)
Indiana U–Purdue U Fort Wayne (IN)
Indiana U–Purdue U Indianapolis (IN)
Indiana Wesleyan U (IN)
Inter American U of Puerto Rico, San Germán Campus (PR)
Iowa Wesleyan Coll (IA)
Ithaca Coll (NY)
Johnson State Coll (VT)
Kansas Wesleyan U (KS)
Kennesaw State U (GA)
Kent State U (OH)
Kentucky Wesleyan Coll (KY)
Keystone Coll (PA)
Lamar U (TX)
Langston U (OK)
Lawrence U (WI)
Lehman Coll of the City U of New York (NY)
Lincoln Memorial U (TN)
Lincoln U (MO)
Lindenwood U (MO)
Lindsey Wilson Coll (KY)
Lipscomb U (TN)
Long Island U–Brooklyn Campus (NY)
Long Island U–C. W. Post Campus (NY)
Louisiana Coll (LA)
Louisiana State U in Shreveport (LA)
Lubbock Christian U (TX)
Malone U (OH)
Manchester U (IN)
Manhattanville Coll (NY)
Mansfield U of Pennsylvania (PA)
Marian U (WI)
Mars Hill Coll (NC)
Maryland Inst Coll of Art (MD)
Maryville U of Saint Louis (MO)
Marywood U (PA)

Massachusetts Coll of Art and Design (MA)
McKendree U (IL)
McMurry U (TX)
Mercyhurst U (PA)
Messiah Coll (PA)
Miami U (OH)
Michigan State U (MI)
Middle Tennessee State U (TN)
Millikin U (IL)
Minnesota State U Mankato (MN)
Minnesota State U Moorhead (MN)
Minot State U (ND)
Mississippi Coll (MS)
Mississippi U for Women (MS)
Missouri State U (MO)
Missouri Western State U (MO)
Moore Coll of Art & Design (PA)
Moravian Coll (PA)
Morningside Coll (IA)
Mount Mary Coll (WI)
Mount Mercy U (IA)
Mount Vernon Nazarene U (OH)
Nazareth Coll of Rochester (NY)
New Jersey City U (NJ)
Nicholls State U (LA)
North Carolina Central U (NC)
North Central Coll (IL)
Northern Illinois U (IL)
Northern Michigan U (MI)
Northern State U (SD)
Northwestern Coll (IA)
Northwestern Coll (MN)
Northwest Missouri State U (MO)
Northwest Nazarene U (ID)
Oakland City U (IN)
Ohio Dominican U (OH)
The Ohio State U (OH)
Ohio Wesleyan U (OH)
Oklahoma Baptist U (OK)
Oklahoma City U (OK)
Olivet Coll (MI)
Oral Roberts U (OK)
Ouachita Baptist U (AR)
Pacific U (OR)
Palm Beach Atlantic U (FL)
Penn State Abington (PA)
Penn State Altoona (PA)
Penn State Beaver (PA)
Penn State Berks (PA)
Penn State Brandywine (PA)
Penn State DuBois (PA)
Penn State Erie, The Behrend Coll (PA)
Penn State Fayette, The Eberly Campus (PA)
Penn State Greater Allegheny (PA)
Penn State Hazleton (PA)
Penn State Lehigh Valley (PA)
Penn State Mont Alto (PA)
Penn State New Kensington (PA)
Penn State Schuylkill (PA)
Penn State Shenango (PA)
Penn State U Park (PA)
Penn State Wilkes-Barre (PA)
Penn State Worthington Scranton (PA)
Penn State York (PA)
Pittsburg State U (KS)
Plymouth State U (NH)
Point Loma Nazarene U (CA)
Purdue U (IN)
Rhode Island Coll (RI)
Rocky Mountain Coll (MT)
Rocky Mountain Coll of Art + Design (CO)
Saginaw Valley State U (MI)
St. Ambrose U (IA)
St. Edward's U (TX)
Saint Joseph's U (PA)
Saint Mary-of-the-Woods Coll (IN)
Saint Mary's Coll (IN)
Saint Michael's Coll (VT)
Saint Vincent Coll (PA)
Salem State U (MA)
School of the Art Inst of Chicago (IL)
Seton Hill U (PA)
Shawnee State U (OH)
Siena Heights U (MI)
Simpson Coll (IA)
Slippery Rock U of Pennsylvania (PA)
South Dakota State U (SD)
Southeastern Oklahoma State U (OK)
Southeast Missouri State U (MO)

Southern Arkansas U–Magnolia (AR)
Southern Connecticut State U (CT)
Southern Utah U (UT)
Southwest Baptist U (MO)
Spring Arbor U (MI)
State U of New York at New Paltz (NY)
Syracuse U (NY)
Taylor U (IN)
Temple U (PA)
Texas Christian U (TX)
Texas Lutheran U (TX)
Thomas More Coll (KY)
Transylvania U (KY)
Trinity Christian Coll (IL)
Union Coll (NE)
Union U (TN)
The U of Akron (OH)
The U of Arizona (AZ)
The U of British Columbia (BC, Canada)
U of Central Florida (FL)
U of Central Oklahoma (OK)
U of Denver (CO)
U of Evansville (IN)
The U of Findlay (OH)
U of Florida (FL)
U of Great Falls (MT)
U of Idaho (ID)
U of Illinois at Chicago (IL)
U of Illinois at Urbana–Champaign (IL)
The U of Iowa (IA)
The U of Kansas (KS)
U of Kentucky (KY)
U of Maryland, Coll Park (MD)
U of Maryland Eastern Shore (MD)
U of Massachusetts Dartmouth (MA)
U of Michigan–Flint (MI)
U of Minnesota, Duluth (MN)
U of Minnesota, Twin Cities Campus (MN)
U of Missouri (MO)
The U of Montana Western (MT)
U of Nebraska at Omaha (NE)
U of New Brunswick Fredericton (NB, Canada)
U of New Mexico (NM)
The U of North Carolina at Charlotte (NC)
The U of North Carolina at Greensboro (NC)
The U of North Carolina at Pembroke (NC)
U of Northern Iowa (IA)
U of North Florida (FL)
U of North Georgia (GA)
U of Regina (SK, Canada)
U of St. Francis (IL)
U of South Carolina (SC)
U of South Carolina Upstate (SC)
The U of South Dakota (SD)
U of Southern Maine (ME)
The U of Tennessee at Chattanooga (TN)
The U of Texas at El Paso (TX)
U of the Cumberlands (KY)
U of the District of Columbia (DC)
The U of Toledo (OH)
U of Vermont (VT)
U of Windsor (ON, Canada)
U of Wisconsin–La Crosse (WI)
U of Wisconsin–Madison (WI)
U of Wisconsin–Milwaukee (WI)
U of Wisconsin–Stout (WI)
U of Wisconsin–Superior (WI)
Upper Iowa U (IA)
Ursuline Coll (OH)
Valdosta State U (GA)
Valley City State U (ND)
Valparaiso U (IN)
Viterbo U (WI)
Walla Walla U (WA)
Wartburg Coll (IA)
Washburn U (KS)
Washington & Jefferson Coll (PA)
Washington U in St. Louis (MO)
Wayne State Coll (NE)
Wayne State U (MI)
Weber State U (UT)
Western Carolina U (NC)
Western Michigan U (MI)

Western State Colorado U (CO)
Western Washington U (WA)
West Liberty U (WV)
West Virginia State U (WV)
West Virginia Wesleyan Coll (WV)
Whitworth U (WA)
William Jewell Coll (MO)
William Paterson U of New Jersey (NJ)
Xavier U of Louisiana (LA)
Youngstown State U (OH)

ART THERAPY
Albertus Magnus Coll (CT)
Alverno Coll (WI)
Capital U (OH)
Carlow U (PA)
Cedar Crest Coll (PA)
Chowan U (NC)
The Coll of New Rochelle (NY)
Converse Coll (SC)
DePaul U (IL)
Edgewood Coll (WI)
Emmanuel Coll (MA)
Harding U (AR)
Indiana Wesleyan U (IN)
Lesley U (MA)
Lipscomb U (TN)
Long Island U–C. W. Post Campus (NY)
Marywood U (PA)
Mercyhurst U (PA)
Millikin U (IL)
Mount Mary Coll (WI)
Nazareth Coll of Rochester (NY)
Ohio Wesleyan U (OH)
Prescott Coll (AZ)
Russell Sage Coll (NY)
St. Thomas Aquinas Coll (NY)
Seton Hill U (PA)
Sierra Nevada Coll (NV)
U of Wisconsin–Superior (WI)
West Virginia Wesleyan Coll (WV)

ASIAN AMERICAN STUDIES
Arizona State U (AZ)
Binghamton U, State U of New York (NY)
California State U, East Bay (CA)
California State U, Fullerton (CA)
California State U, Long Beach (CA)
California State U, Los Angeles (CA)
California State U, Northridge (CA)
Columbia U (NY)
Columbia U, School of General Studies (NY)
Pitzer Coll (CA)
Pomona Coll (CA)
San Francisco State U (CA)
Scripps Coll (CA)
Stanford U (CA)
Stony Brook U, State U of New York (NY)
U of California, Berkeley (CA)
U of California, Davis (CA)
U of California, Irvine (CA)
U of California, Los Angeles (CA)
U of California, Riverside (CA)
U of California, Santa Barbara (CA)
U of Denver (CO)
U of Southern California (CA)

ASIAN HISTORY
Bard Coll (NY)
Gettysburg Coll (PA)
U of Regina (SK, Canada)

ASIAN STUDIES
Amherst Coll (MA)
Arizona State U (AZ)
Augustana Coll (IL)
Bard Coll (NY)
Baylor U (TX)
Belmont U (TN)
Bennington Coll (VT)
Berea Coll (KY)
Binghamton U, State U of New York (NY)
Bowdoin Coll (ME)
Bowling Green State U (OH)
California State U, Chico (CA)
California State U, Long Beach (CA)
California State U, Los Angeles (CA)
Calvin Coll (MI)

Carleton Coll (MN)
Case Western Reserve U (OH)
City Coll of the City U of New York (NY)
Claremont McKenna Coll (CA)
Clark U (MA)
Coe Coll (IA)
Colgate U (NY)
The Coll at Brockport, State U of New York (NY)
Coll of the Holy Cross (MA)
The Colorado Coll (CO)
Dartmouth Coll (NH)
Drew U (NJ)
Florida Intl U (FL)
Fort Lewis Coll (CO)
Furman U (SC)
Gonzaga U (WA)
Hamilton Coll (NY)
Hawai`i Pacific U (HI)
Hobart and William Smith Colls (NY)
Illinois Wesleyan U (IL)
Indiana U of Pennsylvania (PA)
John Carroll U (OH)
Kean U (NJ)
Knox Coll (IL)
Lehigh U (PA)
Loyola Marymount U (CA)
Macalester Coll (MN)
Manhattanville Coll (NY)
Marietta Coll (OH)
McDaniel Coll (MD)
Mount Holyoke Coll (MA)
Nazareth Coll of Rochester (NY)
Northeastern U (MA)
Ohio U (OH)
Old Dominion U (VA)
Penn State U Park (PA)
Pitzer Coll (CA)
Pomona Coll (CA)
Purdue U (IN)
Randolph-Macon Coll (VA)
Rice U (TX)
St. John's U (NY)
Saint Joseph's U (PA)
St. Lawrence U (NY)
St. Mary's Coll of Maryland (MD)
St. Olaf Coll (MN)
Samford U (AL)
San Diego State U (CA)
Scripps Coll (CA)
Sewanee: The U of the South (TN)
Skidmore Coll (NY)
Stanford U (CA)
State U of New York at New Paltz (NY)
Swarthmore Coll (PA)
Temple U (PA)
Texas State U–San Marcos (TX)
Trinity U (TX)
Tufts U (MA)
Tulane U (LA)
U at Albany, State U of New York (NY)
U at Buffalo, the State U of New York (NY)
The U of British Columbia (BC, Canada)
U of California, Berkeley (CA)
U of California, Los Angeles (CA)
U of California, Riverside (CA)
U of California, Santa Barbara (CA)
U of Cincinnati (OH)
U of Colorado Boulder (CO)
U of Delaware (DE)
U of Florida (FL)
U of Hawaii at Manoa (HI)
The U of Iowa (IA)
U of Maryland, Baltimore County (MD)
U of Maryland U Coll (MD)
U of Massachusetts Boston (MA)
U of Michigan (MI)
U of Mount Union (OH)
U of New Mexico (NM)
The U of North Carolina at Chapel Hill (NC)
U of Northern Colorado (CO)
U of Oregon (OR)
U of Puget Sound (WA)
U of Redlands (CA)
The U of Texas at Austin (TX)
The U of Toledo (OH)
U of Utah (UT)
U of Vermont (VT)
U of Washington, Tacoma (WA)

The U of Western Ontario (ON, Canada)
U of Wisconsin–Madison (WI)
Utah State U (UT)
Vanderbilt U (TN)
Vassar Coll (NY)
Washington State U (WA)
Washington U in St. Louis (MO)
Western Kentucky U (KY)
Wheaton Coll (MA)
Whitman Coll (WA)
Willamette U (OR)
William Paterson U of New Jersey (NJ)
Williams Coll (MA)

ASIAN STUDIES (EAST)
Augsburg Coll (MN)
Bates Coll (ME)
Binghamton U, State U of New York (NY)
Boston U (MA)
Brown U (RI)
Bucknell U (PA)
Colby Coll (ME)
Colgate U (NY)
Columbia U (NY)
Columbia U, School of General Studies (NY)
Connecticut Coll (CT)
DePaul U (IL)
DePauw U (IN)
Dickinson Coll (PA)
Gettysburg Coll (PA)
Grand Valley State U (MI)
Hamline U (MN)
Hampshire Coll (MA)
Haverford Coll (PA)
Hofstra U (NY)
Indiana U Bloomington (IN)
John Carroll U (OH)
The Johns Hopkins U (MD)
Lawrence U (WI)
Miami U (OH)
Middlebury Coll (VT)
Minnesota State U Moorhead (MN)
Mount Holyoke Coll (MA)
New York U (NY)
North Central Coll (IL)
Oakland U (MI)
Ohio Wesleyan U (OH)
Penn State Abington (PA)
Penn State Altoona (PA)
Penn State Beaver (PA)
Penn State Berks (PA)
Penn State Brandywine (PA)
Penn State DuBois (PA)
Penn State Erie, The Behrend Coll (PA)
Penn State Fayette, The Eberly Campus (PA)
Penn State Greater Allegheny (PA)
Penn State Hazleton (PA)
Penn State Lehigh Valley (PA)
Penn State Mont Alto (PA)
Penn State New Kensington (PA)
Penn State Schuylkill (PA)
Penn State Shenango (PA)
Penn State Worthington Scranton (PA)
Penn State York (PA)
Pomona Coll (CA)
Portland State U (OR)
Princeton U (NJ)
Rutgers, The State U of New Jersey, New Brunswick (NJ)
Seattle U (WA)
Simmons Coll (MA)
Smith Coll (MA)
Stanford U (CA)
United States Military Acad (NY)
U at Albany, State U of New York (NY)
The U of Arizona (AZ)
U of Bridgeport (CT)
U of California, Davis (CA)
U of California, Irvine (CA)
U of California, Los Angeles (CA)
U of Illinois at Urbana–Champaign (IL)
U of Minnesota, Twin Cities Campus (MN)
U of Missouri (MO)
U of Pennsylvania (PA)
U of Southern California (CA)
The U of Western Ontario (ON, Canada)

Valparaiso U (IN)
Washington U in St. Louis (MO)
Wayne State U (MI)
Wellesley Coll (MA)
Wesleyan U (CT)
Western Washington U (WA)
Wittenberg U (OH)
Yale U (CT)

ASIAN STUDIES (SOUTH)
Binghamton U, State U of New York (NY)
Brown U (RI)
Concordia U (QC, Canada)
Gettysburg Coll (PA)
Hampshire Coll (MA)
Indiana U Bloomington (IN)
Middlebury Coll (VT)
Mount Holyoke Coll (MA)
The U of British Columbia (BC, Canada)
U of Minnesota, Twin Cities Campus (MN)
U of Missouri (MO)
U of Pennsylvania (PA)
U of Wisconsin–Madison (WI)

ASIAN STUDIES (SOUTHEAST)
Tufts U (MA)
U of California, Berkeley (CA)
U of California, Los Angeles (CA)

ASTRONOMY
Amherst Coll (MA)
Baylor U (TX)
Benedictine Coll (KS)
Bennington Coll (VT)
Boston U (MA)
Brigham Young U (UT)
Case Western Reserve U (OH)
Central Michigan U (MI)
Colgate U (NY)
The Coll at Brockport, State U of New York (NY)
Columbia U (NY)
Columbia U, School of General Studies (NY)
Dartmouth Coll (NH)
Drake U (IA)
Franklin & Marshall Coll (PA)
George Mason U (VA)
Hampshire Coll (MA)
Haverford Coll (PA)
Indiana U Bloomington (IN)
Lehigh U (PA)
Minnesota State U Mankato (MN)
Mount Holyoke Coll (MA)
Northern Arizona U (AZ)
The Ohio State U (OH)
Ohio Wesleyan U (OH)
Penn State Abington (PA)
Penn State Altoona (PA)
Penn State Beaver (PA)
Penn State Berks (PA)
Penn State Brandywine (PA)
Penn State DuBois (PA)
Penn State Erie, The Behrend Coll (PA)
Penn State Fayette, The Eberly Campus (PA)
Penn State Greater Allegheny (PA)
Penn State Hazleton (PA)
Penn State Lehigh Valley (PA)
Penn State Mont Alto (PA)
Penn State New Kensington (PA)
Penn State Schuylkill (PA)
Penn State Shenango (PA)
Penn State U Park (PA)
Penn State Wilkes-Barre (PA)
Penn State Worthington Scranton (PA)
Penn State York (PA)
Pomona Coll (CA)
Rice U (TX)
San Diego State U (CA)
San Francisco State U (CA)
Smith Coll (MA)
Stony Brook U, State U of New York (NY)
Swarthmore Coll (PA)
Tufts U (MA)
The U of Arizona (AZ)
The U of British Columbia (BC, Canada)
U of California, Santa Cruz (CA)
U of Colorado Boulder (CO)
U of Florida (FL)
U of Georgia (GA)

U of Illinois at Urbana–Champaign (IL)
The U of Iowa (IA)
The U of Kansas (KS)
U of Maryland, Coll Park (MD)
U of Massachusetts Amherst (MA)
U of Michigan (MI)
U of Minnesota, Twin Cities Campus (MN)
U of Oklahoma (OK)
U of Southern California (CA)
The U of Texas at Austin (TX)
U of Toledo (OH)
U of Virginia (VA)
The U of Western Ontario (ON, Canada)
Valdosta State U (GA)
Valparaiso U (IN)
Vassar Coll (NY)
Villanova U (PA)
Washington State U (WA)
Wayne State U (MI)
Wellesley Coll (MA)
Wesleyan U (CT)
Whitman Coll (WA)
Williams Coll (MA)
Yale U (CT)
Youngstown State U (OH)

ASTRONOMY AND ASTROPHYSICS RELATED
Coll of Charleston (SC)
Florida Inst of Technology (FL)
Texas Christian U (TX)
U of Wyoming (WY)

ASTROPHYSICS
Agnes Scott Coll (GA)
Augsburg Coll (MN)
Baylor U (TX)
Boston U (MA)
Carnegie Mellon U (PA)
Colgate U (NY)
Columbia U (NY)
Columbia U, School of General Studies (NY)
Connecticut Coll (CT)
Franklin & Marshall Coll (PA)
Haverford Coll (PA)
Lehigh U (PA)
Michigan State U (MI)
Ohio U (OH)
Ohio Wesleyan U (OH)
Princeton U (NJ)
Rice U (TX)
Rutgers, The State U of New Jersey, New Brunswick (NJ)
San Francisco State U (CA)
Swarthmore Coll (PA)
Tufts U (MA)
U of California, Berkeley (CA)
U of California, Los Angeles (CA)
U of California, Santa Cruz (CA)
U of Cincinnati (OH)
U of Minnesota, Twin Cities Campus (MN)
U of New Mexico (NM)
U of Oklahoma (OK)
The U of Western Ontario (ON, Canada)
U of Wisconsin–Madison (WI)
Villanova U (PA)
Wellesley Coll (MA)
Whitman Coll (WA)
Williams Coll (MA)
Yale U (CT)

ATHLETIC TRAINING
Albion Coll (MI)
Alderson-Broaddus Coll (WV)
Alfred U (NY)
Alvernia U (PA)
Anderson U (IN)
Appalachian State U (NC)
Arkansas State U (AR)
Ashland U (OH)
Augsburg Coll (MN)
Augustana Coll (SD)
Aurora U (IL)
Averett U (VA)
Azusa Pacific U (CA)
Baldwin Wallace U (OH)
Barton Coll (NC)
Baylor U (TX)
Benedictine Coll (KS)
Bethel Coll (KS)
Bethel U (MN)
Boston U (MA)

Bowling Green State U (OH)
Bridgewater Coll (VA)
Bridgewater State U (MA)
Brigham Young U (UT)
Buena Vista U (IA)
California State U, East Bay (CA)
California State U, Fullerton (CA)
California State U, Long Beach (CA)
California State U, Northridge (CA)
Campbellsville U (KY)
Canisius Coll (NY)
Capital U (OH)
Castleton State Coll (VT)
Catawba Coll (NC)
Cedarville U (OH)
Central Coll (IA)
Central Connecticut State U (CT)
Central Methodist U (MO)
Central Michigan U (MI)
Chapman U (CA)
Clarke U (IA)
Coe Coll (IA)
The Coll at Brockport, State U of New York (NY)
Coll of Charleston (SC)
Coll of Mount St. Joseph (OH)
The Coll of William and Mary (VA)
Colorado Mesa U (CO)
Colorado State U (CO)
Concordia U (CA)
Concordia U Wisconsin (WI)
Concord U (WV)
Culver-Stockton Coll (MO)
Dakota Wesleyan U (SD)
Defiance Coll (OH)
Delta State U (MS)
DePauw U (IN)
Dominican Coll (NY)
Duquesne U (PA)
East Carolina U (NC)
East Central U (OK)
Eastern Illinois U (IL)
Eastern Michigan U (MI)
Eastern Washington U (WA)
East Texas Baptist U (TX)
Emory & Henry Coll (VA)
Emporia State U (KS)
Endicott Coll (MA)
Florida Gulf Coast U (FL)
Florida Southern Coll (FL)
Florida State U (FL)
Fort Lewis Coll (CO)
Franklin Coll (IN)
Frostburg State U (MD)
Gardner-Webb U (NC)
George Fox U (OR)
George Mason U (VA)
Georgetown Coll (KY)
Georgia Coll & State U (GA)
Georgia Southern U (GA)
Graceland U (IA)
Grand Valley State U (MI)
Guilford Coll (NC)
Gustavus Adolphus Coll (MN)
Harding U (AR)
Hardin-Simmons U (TX)
Henderson State U (AR)
High Point U (NC)
Hofstra U (NY)
Hope Coll (MI)
Howard Payne U (TX)
Huntingdon Coll (AL)
Huntington U (IN)
Illinois State U (IL)
Indiana State U (IN)
Indiana U Bloomington (IN)
Indiana U of Pennsylvania (PA)
Indiana Wesleyan U (IN)
Ithaca Coll (NY)
James Madison U (VA)
Johnson State Coll (VT)
Kansas State U (KS)
Kean U (NJ)
Keene State Coll (NH)
Kent State U (OH)
King U (TN)
King's Coll (PA)
Lake Superior State U (MI)
Lander U (SC)
Lasell Coll (MA)
Lees-McRae Coll (NC)
Lee U (TN)
Lewis U (IL)
Liberty U (VA)
Limestone Coll (SC)
Lincoln Memorial U (TN)

Lindenwood U (MO)
Linfield Coll (OR)
Lock Haven U of Pennsylvania (PA)
Long Island U–Brooklyn Campus (NY)
Longwood U (VA)
Louisiana Coll (LA)
Louisiana State U and Ag and Mech Coll (LA)
Lubbock Christian U (TX)
Luther Coll (IA)
Lynchburg Coll (VA)
Manchester U (IN)
Marietta Coll (OH)
Marist Coll (NY)
Marquette U (WI)
Marshall U (WV)
Mars Hill Coll (NC)
Marywood U (PA)
Massachusetts Coll of Liberal Arts (MA)
McKendree U (IL)
McMurry U (TX)
McNeese State U (LA)
Merrimack Coll (MA)
Messiah Coll (PA)
Miami U (OH)
Michigan State U (MI)
Middle Tennessee State U (TN)
Midwestern State U (TX)
Millikin U (IL)
Minnesota State U Mankato (MN)
Minnesota State U Moorhead (MN)
Minot State U (ND)
Missouri State U (MO)
Murray State U (KY)
New Mexico State U (NM)
North Carolina Central U (NC)
North Central Coll (IL)
Northern Arizona U (AZ)
Northern Illinois U (IL)
Northern Michigan U (MI)
Northwestern Coll (IA)
Northwest Nazarene U (ID)
Norwich U (VT)
Nova Southeastern U (FL)
The Ohio State U (OH)
Ohio U (OH)
Oklahoma Baptist U (OK)
Oklahoma State U (OK)
Olivet Coll (MI)
Oregon State U (OR)
Pacific U (OR)
Palm Beach Atlantic U (FL)
Park U (MO)
Penn State U Park (PA)
Pepperdine U, Malibu (CA)
Plymouth State U (NH)
Point Loma Nazarene U (CA)
Presentation Coll (SD)
Purdue U (IN)
Quinnipiac U (CT)
Radford U (VA)
Roanoke Coll (VA)
Rocky Mountain Coll (MT)
Rowan U (NJ)
Sacred Heart U (CT)
Saginaw Valley State U (MI)
Saint Joseph's Coll (IN)
Saint Louis U (MO)
Salem State U (MA)
Salisbury U (MD)
Samford U (AL)
Shawnee State U (OH)
Shaw U (NC)
Simpson Coll (IA)
Slippery Rock U of Pennsylvania (PA)
South Dakota State U (SD)
Southeastern Louisiana U (LA)
Southeast Missouri State U (MO)
Southern Arkansas U–Magnolia (AR)
Southern Connecticut State U (CT)
Southern Nazarene U (OK)
Southern Utah U (UT)
Southwest Baptist U (MO)
Southwestern Coll (KS)
State U of New York Coll at Cortland (NY)
Sterling Coll (KS)
Stony Brook U, State U of New York (NY)
Tabor Coll (KS)
Temple U (PA)
Texas A&M U–Commerce (TX)
Texas Christian U (TX)

Texas Lutheran U (TX)
Texas State U–San Marcos (TX)
Texas Wesleyan U (TX)
Troy U (AL)
Truman State U (MO)
Union Coll (KY)
Union U (TN)
Université de Sherbrooke (QC, Canada)
The U of Akron (OH)
The U of Alabama (AL)
U of Central Arkansas (AR)
U of Central Florida (FL)
U of Charleston (WV)
U of Cincinnati (OH)
U of Delaware (DE)
U of Evansville (IN)
U of Florida (FL)
U of Georgia (GA)
U of Idaho (ID)
U of Illinois at Urbana–Champaign (IL)
The U of Iowa (IA)
The U of Kansas (KS)
U of La Verne (CA)
U of Louisiana at Lafayette (LA)
U of Miami (FL)
U of Michigan (MI)
U of Minnesota, Duluth (MN)
U of Mobile (AL)
U of Mount Union (OH)
U of Nebraska at Omaha (NE)
U of Nebraska–Lincoln (NE)
U of Nevada, Las Vegas (NV)
U of New England (ME)
U of New Hampshire (NH)
The U of North Carolina at Charlotte (NC)
The U of North Carolina at Pembroke (NC)
The U of North Carolina Wilmington (NC)
U of North Dakota (ND)
U of Northern Iowa (IA)
U of North Florida (FL)
U of North Georgia (GA)
U of Pittsburgh at Bradford (PA)
U of Puerto Rico at Ponce (PR)
U of Southern Maine (ME)
U of Southern Mississippi (MS)
U of South Florida (FL)
The U of Tampa (FL)
The U of Tennessee at Martin (TN)
The U of Texas at Arlington (TX)
The U of Texas at Austin (TX)
The U of Texas of the Permian Basin (TX)
U of the Incarnate Word (TX)
U of Tulsa (OK)
U of Utah (UT)
U of Vermont (VT)
The U of West Alabama (AL)
U of Wisconsin–Eau Claire (WI)
U of Wisconsin–La Crosse (WI)
U of Wisconsin–Madison (WI)
U of Wisconsin–Milwaukee (WI)
U of Wisconsin–Stevens Point (WI)
Upper Iowa U (IA)
Valdosta State U (GA)
Washburn U (KS)
Washington State U (WA)
Waynesburg U (PA)
Wayne State Coll (NE)
Weber State U (UT)
West Chester U of Pennsylvania (PA)
Western Carolina U (NC)
Western Illinois U (IL)
Western Michigan U (MI)
Westfield State U (MA)
West Texas A&M U (TX)
West Virginia Wesleyan Coll (WV)
Wheeling Jesuit U (WV)
Whitworth U (WA)
Wichita State U (KS)
William Paterson U of New Jersey (NJ)
Xavier U (OH)
Youngstown State U (OH)

ATMOSPHERIC CHEMISTRY AND CLIMATOLOGY
Purdue U (IN)

ATMOSPHERIC PHYSICS AND DYNAMICS
Purdue U (IN)

ATMOSPHERIC SCIENCES AND METEOROLOGY
The Coll at Brockport, State U of New York (NY)
Creighton U (NE)
Dalhousie U (NS, Canada)
Embry-Riddle Aeronautical U–Daytona (FL)
Embry-Riddle Aeronautical U–Prescott (AZ)
Florida State U (FL)
Iowa State U of Science and Technology (IA)
Millersville U of Pennsylvania (PA)
North Carolina State U (NC)
Northern Illinois U (IL)
Ohio U (OH)
Penn State Abington (PA)
Penn State Altoona (PA)
Penn State Beaver (PA)
Penn State Berks (PA)
Penn State Brandywine (PA)
Penn State DuBois (PA)
Penn State Erie, The Behrend Coll (PA)
Penn State Fayette, The Eberly Campus (PA)
Penn State Greater Allegheny (PA)
Penn State Hazleton (PA)
Penn State Lehigh Valley (PA)
Penn State Mont Alto (PA)
Penn State New Kensington (PA)
Penn State Schuylkill (PA)
Penn State Shenango (PA)
Penn State York Park (PA)
Penn State Wilkes-Barre (PA)
Penn State Worthington Scranton (PA)
Penn State York (PA)
Plymouth State U (NH)
Purdue U (IN)
Rutgers, The State U of New Jersey, New Brunswick (NJ)
Saint Louis U (MO)
San Francisco State U (CA)
San Jose State U (CA)
State U of New York at Oswego (NY)
Stony Brook U, State U of New York (NY)
Texas A&M U (TX)
United States Air Force Acad (CO)
U at Albany, State U of New York (NY)
The U of British Columbia (BC, Canada)
U of California, Berkeley (CA)
U of California, Davis (CA)
U of Illinois at Urbana–Champaign (IL)
The U of Kansas (KS)
U of Louisiana at Monroe (LA)
U of Louisville (KY)
U of Maryland, Coll Park (MD)
U of Miami (FL)
U of Michigan (MI)
U of Missouri (MO)
U of Nebraska–Lincoln (NE)
U of Nevada, Reno (NV)
U of North Carolina at Asheville (NC)
U of North Dakota (ND)
U of South Alabama (AL)
U of Utah (UT)
U of Waterloo (ON, Canada)
U of Wisconsin–Madison (WI)
Valparaiso U (IN)
Western Connecticut State U (CT)

ATMOSPHERIC SCIENCES AND METEOROLOGY RELATED
East Carolina U (NC)
Purdue U (IN)
U of California, Los Angeles (CA)
U of the Incarnate Word (TX)

ATOMIC/MOLECULAR PHYSICS
Columbia U (NY)
San Diego State U (CA)
U of Waterloo (ON, Canada)

AUDIOLOGY
California State U, Long Beach (CA)
Cleveland State U (OH)
The Ohio State U (OH)

Purdue U (IN)
Stephen F. Austin State U (TX)
U of Illinois at Urbana–Champaign (IL)
U of Montevallo (AL)
U of Oklahoma Health Sciences Center (OK)
The U of Western Ontario (ON, Canada)

AUDIOLOGY AND SPEECH-LANGUAGE PATHOLOGY
Adelphi U (NY)
Andrews U (MI)
Arkansas State U (AR)
Auburn U (AL)
Augustana Coll (SD)
Ball State U (IN)
Bloomsburg U of Pennsylvania (PA)
Boston U (MA)
Bowling Green State U (OH)
Buffalo State Coll, State U of New York (NY)
California State U, East Bay (CA)
California State U, Fresno (CA)
California State U, Long Beach (CA)
Calvin Coll (MI)
Central Michigan U (MI)
The Coll of Idaho (ID)
Delta State U (MS)
East Carolina U (NC)
Eastern New Mexico U (NM)
Elmira Coll (NY)
Emerson Coll (MA)
Hardin-Simmons U (TX)
Hofstra U (NY)
Hunter Coll of the City U of New York (NY)
Illinois State U (IL)
Indiana State U (IN)
Indiana U Bloomington (IN)
Indiana U of Pennsylvania (PA)
Indiana U–Purdue U Fort Wayne (IN)
Iona Coll (NY)
Ithaca Coll (NY)
Kent State U (OH)
Lamar U (TX)
La Salle U (PA)
Lehman Coll of the City U of New York (NY)
Longwood U (VA)
Louisiana State U and Ag and Mech Coll (LA)
Marquette U (WI)
Marywood U (PA)
Mercy Coll (NY)
Minnesota State U Mankato (MN)
Missouri State U (MO)
Molloy Coll (NY)
Murray State U (KY)
Nazareth Coll of Rochester (NY)
New York U (NY)
Nicholls State U (LA)
Northeastern U (MA)
The Ohio State U (OH)
Ohio U (OH)
Old Dominion U (VA)
Purdue U (IN)
The Richard Stockton Coll of New Jersey (NJ)
St. John's U (NY)
Saint Louis U (MO)
Shaw U (NC)
Southeastern Louisiana U (LA)
Southern Connecticut State U (CT)
Southern Illinois U Edwardsville (IL)
State U of New York at Fredonia (NY)
State U of New York at Plattsburgh (NY)
State U of New York Coll at Cortland (NY)
Temple U (PA)
Tennessee State U (TN)
Texas A&M U–Kingsville (TX)
Texas Woman's U (TX)
U at Buffalo, the State U of New York (NY)
The U of Akron (OH)
The U of Alabama (AL)
U of Arkansas at Little Rock (AR)
U of Central Arkansas (AR)
U of Central Florida (FL)

U of Central Oklahoma (OK)
U of Florida (FL)
U of Hawaii at Manoa (HI)
U of Illinois at Urbana–Champaign (IL)
The U of Iowa (IA)
U of Kentucky (KY)
U of Louisiana at Lafayette (LA)
U of Louisiana at Monroe (LA)
U of Minnesota, Twin Cities Campus (MN)
U of Mississippi (MS)
U of New Mexico (NM)
The U of North Carolina at Greensboro (NC)
U of Northern Colorado (CO)
U of North Texas (TX)
U of Oklahoma Health Sciences Center (OK)
U of Pittsburgh (PA)
U of Redlands (CA)
U of South Alabama (AL)
U of Southern Mississippi (MS)
U of South Florida (FL)
The U of Texas at Dallas (TX)
The U of Texas at El Paso (TX)
U of the District of Columbia (DC)
The U of Toledo (OH)
U of Tulsa (OK)
U of Utah (UT)
U of Virginia (VA)
The U of Western Ontario (ON, Canada)
U of Wisconsin–Madison (WI)
U of Wisconsin–Milwaukee (WI)
U of Wisconsin–Stevens Point (WI)
U of Wyoming (WY)
Utah State U (UT)
Washington State U (WA)
West Chester U of Pennsylvania (PA)
Western Michigan U (MI)
Western Washington U (WA)
West Virginia U (WV)

AUDIOVISUAL COMMUNICATIONS TECHNOLOGIES RELATED
Greenville Coll (IL)
Webster U (MO)

AUDITING
Babson Coll (MA)
Carlow U (PA)
U of Illinois at Urbana–Champaign (IL)

AUSTRALIAN/OCEANIC/PACIFIC LANGUAGES
U of Hawaii–West Oahu (HI)

AUTOBODY/COLLISION AND REPAIR TECHNOLOGY
Lewis-Clark State Coll (ID)
Pennsylvania Coll of Technology (PA)

AUTOMOBILE/AUTOMOTIVE MECHANICS TECHNOLOGY
Lewis-Clark State Coll (ID)
Morrisville State Coll (NY)
New England Inst of Technology (RI)
Pittsburg State U (KS)
Walla Walla U (WA)

AUTOMOTIVE ENGINEERING TECHNOLOGY
Central Michigan U (MI)
Ferris State U (MI)
Indiana State U (IN)
Minnesota State U Mankato (MN)
Pennsylvania Coll of Technology (PA)
Southern Illinois U Carbondale (IL)
State U of New York Coll of Technology at Alfred (NY)
Weber State U (UT)
Western Washington U (WA)

AVIATION/AIRWAY MANAGEMENT
Auburn U (AL)
Averett U (VA)
Bridgewater State U (MA)
California State U, Los Angeles (CA)
Daniel Webster Coll (NH)
Eastern Michigan U (MI)
Eastern New Mexico U (NM)

Embry-Riddle Aeronautical U–Daytona (FL)
Embry-Riddle Aeronautical U–Worldwide (FL)
Fairmont State U (WV)
Farmingdale State Coll (NY)
Florida Inst of Technology (FL)
Hallmark Coll of Technology (TX)
Hampton U (VA)
Indiana State U (IN)
Inter American U of Puerto Rico, Bayamón Campus (PR)
Lewis U (IL)
Lynn U (FL)
Marywood U (PA)
Metropolitan State U of Denver (CO)
Minnesota State U Mankato (MN)
The Ohio State U (OH)
Ohio U (OH)
Purdue U (IN)
Quincy U (IL)
Rocky Mountain Coll (MT)
Saint Louis U (MO)
Salem State U (MA)
Southern Illinois U Carbondale (IL)
Tarleton State U (TX)
Texas Southern U (TX)
U of Illinois at Urbana–Champaign (IL)
U of North Dakota (ND)
U of North Texas (TX)
The U of Western Ontario (ON, Canada)
Vaughn Coll of Aeronautics and Technology (NY)
Western Michigan U (MI)
Westminster Coll (UT)
Wilmington U (DE)

AVIONICS MAINTENANCE TECHNOLOGY
Fairmont State U (WV)
LeTourneau U (TX)
Pennsylvania Coll of Technology (PA)
Purdue U (IN)
Southern Illinois U Carbondale (IL)
Vaughn Coll of Aeronautics and Technology (NY)
Western Michigan U (MI)
Wilmington U (DE)

AYURVEDIC MEDICINE
Maharishi U of Management (IA)

BAKING AND PASTRY ARTS
Stratford U (MD)

BALLET
Brigham Young U (UT)
Friends U (KS)
Indiana U Bloomington (IN)
Texas Christian U (TX)
U of Utah (UT)

BANKING AND FINANCIAL SUPPORT SERVICES
Buena Vista U (IA)
Husson U (ME)
Northwood U, Michigan Campus (MI)
Sam Houston State U (TX)
Texas Southern U (TX)
U of Illinois at Urbana–Champaign (IL)
U of Nebraska at Omaha (NE)
U of Nebraska–Lincoln (NE)
U of North Florida (FL)
U of North Texas (TX)
The U of Texas at Arlington (TX)
U of the Incarnate Word (TX)
West Liberty U (WV)

BEHAVIORAL SCIENCES
Andrews U (MI)
Athens State U (AL)
Augsburg Coll (MN)
Bemidji State U (MN)
Brown U (RI)
California Baptist U (CA)
California State U, Dominguez Hills (CA)
Carnegie Mellon U (PA)
Columbia Coll (SC)
Concordia Coll–New York (NY)
Concordia U (CA)
Concordia U, Nebraska (NE)
Dakota Wesleyan U (SD)

Duquesne U (PA)
East-West U (IL)
Evangel U (MO)
George Fox U (OR)
Goddard Coll (VT)
Inter American U of Puerto Rico, San Germán Campus (PR)
The Johns Hopkins U (MD)
Mars Hill Coll (NC)
Metropolitan State U of Denver (CO)
Minnesota State U Mankato (MN)
Missouri Baptist U (MO)
Mount Mary Coll (WI)
Northeastern U (MA)
Northern Michigan U (MI)
Point Park U (PA)
Purdue U (IN)
Purdue U North Central (IN)
Rocky Mountain Coll (AB, Canada)
San Jose State U (CA)
Sterling Coll (KS)
Tennessee Wesleyan Coll (TN)
Trevecca Nazarene U (TN)
Tufts U (MA)
United States Air Force Acad (CO)
U of Houston–Clear Lake (TX)
The U of Kansas (KS)
U of La Verne (CA)
U of Maine at Fort Kent (ME)
U of Maine at Machias (ME)
U of Missouri (MO)
U of Nebraska at Omaha (NE)
U of North Texas (TX)
U of Wisconsin–Green Bay (WI)
Walsh U (OH)
Widener U (PA)
William Paterson U of New Jersey (NJ)
Wilmington U (DE)
York Coll of Pennsylvania (PA)

BIBLICAL STUDIES

Abilene Christian U (TX)
Alaska Bible Coll (AK)
Amridge U (AL)
Anderson U (IN)
Andrews U (MI)
Appalachian Bible Coll (WV)
Arizona Christian U (AZ)
Asbury U (KY)
Azusa Pacific U (CA)
The Baptist Coll of Florida (FL)
Baptist U of the Americas (TX)
Barclay Coll (KS)
Belhaven U (MS)
Belmont U (TN)
Bethel Coll (IN)
Bethel U (MN)
Bluefield Coll (VA)
Blue Mountain Coll (MS)
Bob Jones U (SC)
Briercrest Coll (SK, Canada)
Cairn U (PA)
California Baptist U (CA)
Calvin Coll (MI)
Campbellsville U (KY)
Canisius Coll (NY)
Carson-Newman U (TN)
Cedarville U (OH)
Central Baptist Coll (AR)
Cincinnati Christian U (OH)
Clearwater Christian Coll (FL)
Coll of Biblical Studies–Houston (TX)
Columbia Bible Coll (BC, Canada)
Columbia Intl U (SC)
Corban U (OR)
Cornerstone U (MI)
Covenant Coll (GA)
Crossroads Coll (MN)
Dallas Baptist U (TX)
Eastern Mennonite U (VA)
East Texas Baptist U (TX)
Evangel U (MO)
Faith Baptist Bible Coll and Theological Sem (IA)
Faulkner U (AL)
Florida Christian Coll (FL)
Florida Coll (FL)
Gardner-Webb U (NC)
Geneva Coll (PA)
George Fox U (OR)
Global U (MO)
Grace U (NE)
Harding U (AR)
Hardin-Simmons U (TX)

Hope Intl U (CA)
Houghton Coll (NY)
Howard Payne U (TX)
Huntington U (IN)
Indiana Wesleyan U (IN)
John Brown U (AR)
Judson U (IL)
Kentucky Christian U (KY)
King Coll (TN)
Kingswood U (NB, Canada)
Kuyper Coll (MI)
Laurel U (NC)
Lee U (TN)
LeTourneau U (TX)
Liberty U (VA)
Lincoln Christian U (IL)
Lipscomb U (TN)
Lubbock Christian U (TX)
Luther Rice U (GA)
Malone U (OH)
Maple Springs Baptist Bible Coll and Sem (MD)
Maranatha Baptist Bible Coll (WI)
The Master's Coll and Sem (CA)
Master's Coll and Sem (ON, Canada)
Messiah Coll (PA)
Mid-Atlantic Christian U (NC)
Mid-Continent U (KY)
Montreat Coll, Montreat (NC)
Mount Vernon Nazarene U (OH)
Multnomah U (OR)
North Greenville U (SC)
Northwest Christian U (OR)
Northwestern Coll (MN)
Northwest Nazarene U (ID)
Northwest U (WA)
Nyack Coll (NY)
Oakland City U (IN)
Ohio Valley U (WV)
Oklahoma Baptist U (OK)
Oklahoma Christian U (OK)
Oklahoma City U (OK)
Oral Roberts U (OK)
Ouachita Baptist U (AR)
Palm Beach Atlantic U (FL)
Point Loma Nazarene U (CA)
Point U (GA)
Roberts Wesleyan Coll (NY)
Rocky Mountain Coll (AB, Canada)
Saint Louis Christian Coll (MO)
San Diego Christian Coll (CA)
Simpson U (CA)
Southeastern Bible Coll (AL)
Southern Methodist Coll (SC)
Southwest Baptist U (MO)
Spring Arbor U (MI)
Taylor U (IN)
Union U (TN)
Universidad Teolgica del Caribe (PR)
U of Evansville (IN)
The U of Western Ontario (ON, Canada)
Wheaton Coll (IL)

BILINGUAL AND MULTILINGUAL EDUCATION

Boise State U (ID)
Boston U (MA)
California State U, Stanislaus (CA)
Calvin Coll (MI)
Canisius Coll (NY)
Chicago State U (IL)
Goddard Coll (VT)
Long Island U–Brooklyn Campus (NY)
Loyola U Chicago (IL)
Midwestern State U (TX)
Mount Mary Coll (WI)
Northeastern Illinois U (IL)
State U of New York Coll at Old Westbury (NY)
Texas A&M Intl U (TX)
Texas Christian U (TX)
Texas Wesleyan U (TX)
U of Delaware (DE)
The U of Findlay (OH)
U of Maine at Fort Kent (ME)
U of Nebraska at Omaha (NE)
U of Regina (SK, Canada)
Washington State U (WA)
Western Illinois U (IL)
York Coll of the City U of New York (NY)

BILINGUAL, MULTILINGUAL, AND MULTICULTURAL EDUCATION RELATED

The Coll at Brockport, State U of New York (NY)

BIOCHEMICAL ENGINEERING

Hope Coll (MI)
U of Colorado Boulder (CO)
U of Georgia (GA)

BIOCHEMISTRY

Abilene Christian U (TX)
Adams State U (CO)
Adelphi U (NY)
Agnes Scott Coll (GA)
Albright Coll (PA)
Alma Coll (MI)
Alvernia U (PA)
American U (DC)
Anderson U (IN)
Andrews U (MI)
Arizona State U (AZ)
Asbury U (KY)
Auburn U (AL)
Augustana Coll (IL)
Augustana Coll (SD)
Azusa Pacific U (CA)
Bates Coll (ME)
Baylor U (TX)
Bay Path Coll (MA)
Belmont U (TN)
Benedictine Coll (KS)
Berry Coll (GA)
Binghamton U, State U of New York (NY)
Boston Coll (MA)
Bowdoin Coll (ME)
Bowling Green State U (OH)
Bradley U (IL)
Bridgewater State U (MA)
Brock U (ON, Canada)
Brown U (RI)
Bucknell U (PA)
California Lutheran U (CA)
California Polytechnic State U, San Luis Obispo (CA)
California State U, Chico (CA)
California State U, Dominguez Hills (CA)
California State U, East Bay (CA)
California State U, Fullerton (CA)
California State U, Long Beach (CA)
California State U, Los Angeles (CA)
California State U, Northridge (CA)
California State U, San Bernardino (CA)
California State U, San Marcos (CA)
Calvin Coll (MI)
Canisius Coll (NY)
Capital U (OH)
Case Western Reserve U (OH)
The Catholic U of America (DC)
Cedar Crest Coll (PA)
Central Coll (IA)
Central Connecticut State U (CT)
Central Michigan U (MI)
Centre Coll (KY)
Chapman U (CA)
Chatham U (PA)
Chestnut Hill Coll (PA)
Christian Brothers U (TN)
Christopher Newport U (VA)
City Coll of the City U of New York (NY)
Claflin U (SC)
Claremont McKenna Coll (CA)
Clarke U (IA)
Clark U (MA)
Clemson U (SC)
Coastal Carolina U (SC)
Coe Coll (IA)
Colby Coll (ME)
Colgate U (NY)
The Coll at Brockport, State U of New York (NY)
Coll of Mount St. Joseph (OH)
Coll of Saint Benedict (MN)
Coll of Saint Elizabeth (NJ)
The Coll of Saint Rose (NY)
The Coll of St. Scholastica (MN)
Coll of Staten Island of the City U of New York (NY)
The Coll of Wooster (OH)
The Colorado Coll (CO)

Colorado State U (CO)
Columbia U (NY)
Columbia U, School of General Studies (NY)
Connecticut Coll (CT)
Converse Coll (SC)
Cornell Coll (IA)
Dakota Wesleyan U (SD)
Dartmouth Coll (NH)
DePauw U (IN)
DeSales U (PA)
Dickinson Coll (PA)
Dominican U (IL)
Drake U (IA)
Drew U (NJ)
Duquesne U (PA)
Earlham Coll (IN)
East Carolina U (NC)
Eastern Mennonite U (VA)
Eastern Michigan U (MI)
Eastern New Mexico U (NM)
Eckerd Coll (FL)
Elizabethtown Coll (PA)
Elmira Coll (NY)
Emmanuel Coll (MA)
Fairfield U (CT)
Fairleigh Dickinson U, Coll at Florham (NJ)
Fairleigh Dickinson U, Metropolitan Campus (NJ)
Ferris State U (MI)
Florida Inst of Technology (FL)
Florida State U (FL)
Fort Lewis Coll (CO)
Franklin & Marshall Coll (PA)
Furman U (SC)
Geneva Coll (PA)
George Fox U (OR)
Georgetown U (DC)
Gettysburg Coll (PA)
Gonzaga U (WA)
Goucher Coll (MD)
Grand View U (IA)
Grinnell Coll (IA)
Grove City Coll (PA)
Gustavus Adolphus Coll (MN)
Hamilton Coll (NY)
Hamline U (MN)
Hampden-Sydney Coll (VA)
Harding U (AR)
Hartwick Coll (NY)
Haverford Coll (PA)
Hawai`i Pacific U (HI)
High Point U (NC)
Hiram Coll (OH)
Hobart and William Smith Colls (NY)
Hofstra U (NY)
Holy Family U (PA)
Hood Coll (MD)
Houghton Coll (NY)
Humboldt State U (CA)
Huntingdon Coll (AL)
Illinois Inst of Technology (IL)
Illinois State U (IL)
Indiana U Bloomington (IN)
Indiana U East (IN)
Indiana U Kokomo (IN)
Indiana U of Pennsylvania (PA)
Indiana U South Bend (IN)
Indiana Wesleyan U (IN)
Inter American U of Puerto Rico, Bayamón Campus (PR)
Iona Coll (NY)
Iowa State U of Science and Technology (IA)
Ithaca Coll (NY)
Jamestown Coll (ND)
John Brown U (AR)
Judson U (IL)
Juniata Coll (PA)
Kansas State U (KS)
Kennesaw State U (GA)
Kenyon Coll (OH)
Keuka Coll (NY)
King Coll (TN)
Knox Coll (IL)
Kutztown U of Pennsylvania (PA)
Lafayette Coll (PA)
LaGrange Coll (GA)
Lakeland Coll (WI)
La Salle U (PA)
La Sierra U (CA)
Lawrence Technological U (MI)
Lawrence U (WI)
Lee U (TN)
Lehigh U (PA)

Lehman Coll of the City U of New York (NY)
Le Moyne Coll (NY)
Lewis U (IL)
Liberty U (VA)
Lipscomb U (TN)
Louisiana State U and Ag and Mech Coll (LA)
Loyola Marymount U (CA)
Loyola U Chicago (IL)
Madonna U (MI)
Manchester U (IN)
Manhattan Coll (NY)
Manhattanville Coll (NY)
Mansfield U of Pennsylvania (PA)
Marietta Coll (OH)
Marist Coll (NY)
Maryville Coll (TN)
Maryville U of Saint Louis (MO)
McMurry U (TX)
Mercer U (GA)
Mercyhurst U (PA)
Merrimack Coll (MA)
Messiah Coll (PA)
Miami U (OH)
Michigan State U (MI)
Middlebury Coll (VT)
Millsaps Coll (MS)
Mills Coll (CA)
Minnesota State U Mankato (MN)
Misericordia U (PA)
Mississippi Coll (MS)
Mississippi State U (MS)
Missouri Baptist U (MO)
Missouri Western State U (MO)
Monmouth Coll (IL)
Montclair State U (NJ)
Moravian Coll (PA)
Mount Allison U (NB, Canada)
Mount Holyoke Coll (MA)
Mount St. Mary's Coll (CA)
Mount St. Mary's U (MD)
Muhlenberg Coll (PA)
Nazareth Coll of Rochester (NY)
New Coll of Florida (FL)
New Jersey Inst of Technology (NJ)
Newman U (KS)
New Mexico State U (NM)
New York U (NY)
Niagara U (NY)
North Carolina State U (NC)
North Central Coll (IL)
Northeastern U (MA)
Northern Michigan U (MI)
Northwestern Coll (MN)
Northwest Nazarene U (ID)
Notre Dame de Namur U (CA)
Oakland U (MI)
The Ohio State U (OH)
Oklahoma Baptist U (OK)
Oklahoma Christian U (OK)
Oklahoma City U (OK)
Oklahoma State U (OK)
Old Dominion U (VA)
Olivet Coll (MI)
Oral Roberts U (OK)
Pace U (NY)
Pacific Union Coll (CA)
Penn State Abington (PA)
Penn State Altoona (PA)
Penn State Beaver (PA)
Penn State Berks (PA)
Penn State Brandywine (PA)
Penn State DuBois (PA)
Penn State Erie, The Behrend Coll (PA)
Penn State Fayette, The Eberly Campus (PA)
Penn State Greater Allegheny (PA)
Penn State Hazleton (PA)
Penn State Lehigh Valley (PA)
Penn State Mont Alto (PA)
Penn State New Kensington (PA)
Penn State Schuylkill (PA)
Penn State Shenango (PA)
Penn State U Park (PA)
Penn State Wilkes-Barre (PA)
Penn State Worthington Scranton (PA)
Penn State York (PA)
Philadelphia U (PA)
Pittsburg State U (KS)
Pitzer Coll (CA)
Point Loma Nazarene U (CA)
Pomona Coll (CA)
Portland State U (OR)
Presbyterian Coll (SC)

Providence Coll (RI)
Purchase Coll, State U of New York (NY)
Purdue U (IN)
Queens U of Charlotte (NC)
Quinnipiac U (CT)
Ramapo Coll of New Jersey (NJ)
Reed Coll (OR)
Regis Coll (MA)
Regis U (CO)
Rice U (TX)
The Richard Stockton Coll of New Jersey (NJ)
Rider U (NJ)
Ripon Coll (WI)
Roanoke Coll (VA)
Roberts Wesleyan Coll (NY)
Rochester Inst of Technology (NY)
Rockford Coll (IL)
Rockhurst U (MO)
Roger Williams U (RI)
Rollins Coll (FL)
Roosevelt U (IL)
Rosemont Coll (PA)
Rowan U (NJ)
Russell Sage Coll (NY)
Rutgers, The State U of New Jersey, New Brunswick (NJ)
Saginaw Valley State U (MI)
Saint Anselm Coll (NH)
St. Bonaventure U (NY)
St. Edward's U (TX)
Saint John's U (MN)
Saint Joseph's Coll (IN)
Saint Joseph's U (PA)
St. Lawrence U (NY)
Saint Louis U (MO)
Saint Mary's Coll of California (CA)
St. Mary's Coll of Maryland (MD)
St. Mary's U (TX)
Saint Mary's U of Minnesota (MN)
Saint Michael's Coll (VT)
Salem State U (MA)
Samford U (AL)
San Francisco State U (CA)
San Jose State U (CA)
Schreiner U (TX)
Scripps Coll (CA)
Seattle Pacific U (WA)
Seattle U (WA)
Seton Hill U (PA)
Sewanee: The U of the South (TN)
Siena Coll (NY)
Simon Fraser U (BC, Canada)
Simpson Coll (IA)
Slippery Rock U of Pennsylvania (PA)
Smith Coll (MA)
South Dakota State U (SD)
Southern Methodist U (TX)
Southern Nazarene U (OK)
Southern Oregon U (OR)
Southwestern Coll (KS)
Southwestern U (TX)
Spelman Coll (GA)
Spring Arbor U (MI)
Spring Hill Coll (AL)
State U of New York at Fredonia (NY)
State U of New York at Plattsburgh (NY)
State U of New York Coll at Geneseo (NY)
State U of New York Coll at Old Westbury (NY)
State U of New York Coll at Potsdam (NY)
Stephen F. Austin State U (TX)
Stetson U (FL)
Stonehill Coll (MA)
Stony Brook U, State U of New York (NY)
Suffolk U (MA)
Susquehanna U (PA)
Swarthmore Coll (PA)
Syracuse U (NY)
Tabor Coll (KS)
Temple U (PA)
Texas A&M U (TX)
Texas Christian U (TX)
Texas State U–San Marcos (TX)
Texas Wesleyan U (TX)
Texas Woman's U (TX)
Thompson Rivers U (BC, Canada)
Trent U (ON, Canada)
Trinity Coll (CT)

Trinity U (TX)
Tufts U (MA)
Tulane U (LA)
Union Coll (NE)
United States Air Force Acad (CO)
Université de Sherbrooke (QC, Canada)
U at Albany, State U of New York (NY)
U at Buffalo, the State U of New York (NY)
The U of Akron (OH)
The U of Arizona (AZ)
The U of British Columbia (BC, Canada)
The U of British Columbia–Okanagan (BC, Canada)
U of California, Los Angeles (CA)
U of California, Riverside (CA)
U of California, Santa Barbara (CA)
U of California, Santa Cruz (CA)
U of Charleston (WV)
U of Cincinnati (OH)
U of Colorado Boulder (CO)
U of Colorado Colorado Springs (CO)
U of Dallas (TX)
U of Delaware (DE)
U of Denver (CO)
U of Evansville (IN)
U of Guelph (ON, Canada)
U of Houston (TX)
U of Idaho (ID)
U of Illinois at Chicago (IL)
U of Illinois at Urbana–Champaign (IL)
The U of Iowa (IA)
The U of Kansas (KS)
U of Maryland, Coll Park (MD)
U of Massachusetts Boston (MA)
U of Miami (FL)
U of Michigan (MI)
U of Michigan–Dearborn (MI)
U of Michigan–Flint (MI)
U of Minnesota, Duluth (MN)
U of Minnesota, Twin Cities Campus (MN)
U of Mississippi (MS)
U of Missouri (MO)
U of Missouri–St. Louis (MO)
U of Mount Union (OH)
U of Nebraska–Lincoln (NE)
U of Nevada, Las Vegas (NV)
U of Nevada, Reno (NV)
U of New Brunswick Fredericton (NB, Canada)
U of New England (ME)
U of New Mexico (NM)
The U of North Carolina at Greensboro (NC)
U of Northern Iowa (IA)
U of North Texas (TX)
U of Notre Dame (IN)
U of Oklahoma (OK)
U of Oregon (OR)
U of Ottawa (ON, Canada)
U of Pennsylvania (PA)
U of Puget Sound (WA)
U of Regina (SK, Canada)
U of Saint Joseph (CT)
U of St. Thomas (MN)
U of St. Thomas (TX)
U of San Diego (CA)
The U of Scranton (PA)
U of Southern California (CA)
U of Southern Indiana (IN)
The U of Tampa (FL)
The U of Texas at Arlington (TX)
The U of Texas at Austin (TX)
The U of Texas at Dallas (TX)
U of the Incarnate Word (TX)
U of the Sciences (PA)
The U of Toledo (OH)
U of Tulsa (OK)
U of Vermont (VT)
U of Waterloo (ON, Canada)
The U of Western Ontario (ON, Canada)
U of Windsor (ON, Canada)
U of Wisconsin–La Crosse (WI)
U of Wisconsin–Madison (WI)
U of Wisconsin–Milwaukee (WI)
U of Wisconsin–Stevens Point (WI)
Valparaiso U (IN)
Vassar Coll (NY)
Villanova U (PA)

Virginia Polytechnic Inst and State U (VA)
Viterbo U (WI)
Wabash Coll (IN)
Walla Walla U (WA)
Wartburg Coll (IA)
Washburn U (KS)
Washington & Jefferson Coll (PA)
Washington and Lee U (VA)
Washington State U (WA)
Washington U in St. Louis (MO)
Wellesley Coll (MA)
Wells Coll (NY)
Wesleyan U (CT)
West Chester U of Pennsylvania (PA)
Western Kentucky U (KY)
Western Michigan U (MI)
Western State Colorado U (CO)
Western Washington U (WA)
Westminster Coll (MO)
Wheaton Coll (MA)
Whitman Coll (WA)
Widener U (PA)
Wilkes U (PA)
William Jewell Coll (MO)
Worcester Polytechnic Inst (MA)
Xavier U of Louisiana (LA)

BIOCHEMISTRY AND MOLECULAR BIOLOGY

Bellarmine U (KY)
Belmont U (TN)
Benedictine U (IL)
Boston U (MA)
California State U, Long Beach (CA)
Carroll Coll (MT)
Culver-Stockton Coll (MO)
Dalhousie U (NS, Canada)
Florida Southern Coll (FL)
Harding U (AR)
Hardin-Simmons U (TX)
Hendrix Coll (AR)
Lebanon Valley Coll (PA)
Linfield Coll (OR)
Marquette U (WI)
Michigan State U (MI)
Minnesota State U Moorhead (MN)
North Dakota State U (ND)
Oklahoma City U (OK)
Oregon State U (OR)
Polytechnic Inst of New York U (NY)
Purdue U (IN)
Rhodes Coll (TN)
Simmons Coll (MA)
The U of British Columbia (BC, Canada)
U of California, Irvine (CA)
U of Georgia (GA)
U of Maryland, Baltimore County (MD)
U of Massachusetts Amherst (MA)
U of Minnesota, Duluth (MN)
U of New Hampshire (NH)
U of Regina (SK, Canada)
U of Waterloo (ON, Canada)
The U of Western Ontario (ON, Canada)
Whitman Coll (WA)
Wittenberg U (OH)

BIOCHEMISTRY, BIOPHYSICS AND MOLECULAR BIOLOGY RELATED

Amherst Coll (MA)
Blackburn Coll (IL)
California Baptist U (CA)
Indiana U Kokomo (IN)
Purdue U (IN)
Rensselaer Polytechnic Inst (NY)
Sweet Briar Coll (VA)
U of California, Santa Barbara (CA)
U of Miami (FL)
U of Waterloo (ON, Canada)
Xavier U (OH)

BIOENGINEERING AND BIOMEDICAL ENGINEERING

Alfred U (NY)
Arizona State U (AZ)
Binghamton U, State U of New York (NY)
Boston U (MA)
Brown U (RI)
Bucknell U (PA)
California Lutheran U (CA)

California Polytechnic State U, San Luis Obispo (CA)
California State U, Long Beach (CA)
Carnegie Mellon U (PA)
Case Western Reserve U (OH)
The Catholic U of America (DC)
City Coll of the City U of New York (NY)
Clemson U (SC)
The Coll of New Jersey (NJ)
Colorado School of Mines (CO)
Colorado State U (CO)
Columbia U (NY)
Dalhousie U (NS, Canada)
Florida Gulf Coast U (FL)
Florida Intl U (FL)
Gannon U (PA)
George Mason U (VA)
Harding U (AR)
Hofstra U (NY)
Illinois Inst of Technology (IL)
Indiana Tech (IN)
Indiana U–Purdue U Indianapolis (IN)
The Johns Hopkins U (MD)
Lawrence Technological U (MI)
Lehigh U (PA)
LeTourneau U (TX)
Louisiana State U and Ag and Mech Coll (LA)
Marquette U (WI)
Massachusetts Inst of Technology (MA)
Milwaukee School of Eng (WI)
Mississippi State U (MS)
National U (CA)
New Jersey Inst of Technology (NJ)
North Carolina State U (NC)
The Ohio State U (OH)
Oral Roberts U (OK)
Oregon State U (OR)
Penn State Abington (PA)
Penn State Altoona (PA)
Penn State Beaver (PA)
Penn State Berks (PA)
Penn State Brandywine (PA)
Penn State DuBois (PA)
Penn State Erie, The Behrend Coll (PA)
Penn State Fayette, The Eberly Campus (PA)
Penn State Greater Allegheny (PA)
Penn State Hazleton (PA)
Penn State Lehigh Valley (PA)
Penn State Mont Alto (PA)
Penn State New Kensington (PA)
Penn State Schuylkill (PA)
Penn State Shenango (PA)
Penn State U Park (PA)
Penn State Wilkes-Barre (PA)
Penn State Worthington Scranton (PA)
Penn State York (PA)
Purdue U (IN)
Rensselaer Polytechnic Inst (NY)
Rice U (TX)
Rochester Inst of Technology (NY)
Rutgers, The State U of New Jersey, New Brunswick (NJ)
Saint Louis U (MO)
Southern California Inst of Technology (CA)
Stanford U (CA)
Stony Brook U, State U of New York (NY)
Syracuse U (NY)
Temple U (PA)
Texas A&M U (TX)
Trinity Coll (CT)
Tufts U (MA)
Tulane U (LA)
U at Buffalo, the State U of New York (NY)
The U of Akron (OH)
The U of Alabama at Birmingham (AL)
The U of Arizona (AZ)
The U of British Columbia (BC, Canada)
U of California, Berkeley (CA)
U of California, Davis (CA)
U of California, Irvine (CA)
U of California, Merced (CA)
U of California, Riverside (CA)
U of California, Santa Cruz (CA)
U of Central Oklahoma (OK)

U of Cincinnati (OH)
U of Colorado Denver (CO)
U of Delaware (DE)
U of Florida (FL)
U of Guelph (ON, Canada)
U of Houston (TX)
U of Illinois at Chicago (IL)
U of Illinois at Urbana–Champaign (IL)
The U of Iowa (IA)
U of Louisville (KY)
U of Massachusetts Dartmouth (MA)
U of Memphis (TN)
U of Miami (FL)
U of Michigan (MI)
U of Ottawa (ON, Canada)
U of Pennsylvania (PA)
U of Pittsburgh (PA)
U of Rhode Island (RI)
U of Rochester (NY)
U of South Carolina (SC)
U of Southern California (CA)
The U of Tennessee (TN)
The U of Texas at Arlington (TX)
The U of Texas at Austin (TX)
The U of Texas at Dallas (TX)
The U of Toledo (OH)
U of Utah (UT)
U of Virginia (VA)
U of Wisconsin–Madison (WI)
Vanderbilt U (TN)
Virginia Commonwealth U (VA)
Walla Walla U (WA)
Washington State U (WA)
Washington U in St. Louis (MO)
Wayne State U (MI)
Wentworth Inst of Technology (MA)
Widener U (PA)
Worcester Polytechnic Inst (MA)
Wright State U (OH)
Yale U (CT)

BIOETHICS/MEDICAL ETHICS

American Jewish U (CA)
U of Miami (FL)
U of Rochester (NY)

BIOINFORMATICS

Baylor U (TX)
Canisius Coll (NY)
Claflin U (SC)
The Coll of Saint Rose (NY)
Dalhousie U (NS, Canada)
Davenport U, Grand Rapids (MI)
Gannon U (PA)
Indiana U Bloomington (IN)
Iowa State U of Science and Technology (IA)
Loyola U Chicago (IL)
New Jersey Inst of Technology (NJ)
New York City Coll of Technology of the City U of New York (NY)
Pacific Union Coll (CA)
Portland State U (OR)
Purdue U (IN)
Ramapo Coll of New Jersey (NJ)
Rensselaer Polytechnic Inst (NY)
Rochester Inst of Technology (NY)
St. Bonaventure U (NY)
St. Edward's U (TX)
Saint Vincent Coll (PA)
U at Buffalo, the State U of New York (NY)
U of California, Irvine (CA)
U of California, Santa Cruz (CA)
U of Denver (CO)
U of Maryland, Baltimore County (MD)
U of Nebraska at Omaha (NE)
U of Northern Iowa (IA)
U of Pennsylvania (PA)
U of Pittsburgh (PA)
U of St. Thomas (TX)
U of Waterloo (ON, Canada)
The U of Western Ontario (ON, Canada)
U of Windsor (ON, Canada)
Virginia Commonwealth U (VA)
Wheaton Coll (MA)
Whitworth U (WA)
Worcester State U (MA)

BIOLOGICAL AND BIOMEDICAL SCIENCES RELATED

Alderson-Broaddus Coll (WV)
Alvernia U (PA)

Bethel U (MN)
Boston U (MA)
Christopher Newport U (VA)
Dakota State U (SD)
The Evergreen State Coll (WA)
Farmingdale State Coll (NY)
Gordon State Coll (GA)
Grand Valley State U (MI)
Guilford Coll (NC)
Hiram Coll (OH)
Holy Names U (CA)
Indiana U Bloomington (IN)
Indiana U East (IN)
Inter American U of Puerto Rico, Bayamón Campus (PR)
Kent State U (OH)
Kent State U at Ashtabula (OH)
Kent State U at East Liverpool (OH)
Kent State U at Geauga (OH)
Kent State U at Salem (OH)
Kent State U at Stark (OH)
Kent State U at Trumbull (OH)
Kent State U at Tuscarawas (OH)
King U (TN)
Logan U–Coll of Chiropractic (MO)
Louisiana State U in Shreveport (LA)
Lynchburg Coll (VA)
Messiah Coll (PA)
Mount Aloysius Coll (PA)
Oklahoma City U (OK)
Park U (MO)
Penn State Abington (PA)
Penn State Altoona (PA)
Penn State Beaver (PA)
Penn State Berks (PA)
Penn State Brandywine (PA)
Penn State DuBois (PA)
Penn State Erie, The Behrend Coll (PA)
Penn State Fayette, The Eberly Campus (PA)
Penn State Greater Allegheny (PA)
Penn State Hazleton (PA)
Penn State Lehigh Valley (PA)
Penn State Mont Alto (PA)
Penn State New Kensington (PA)
Penn State Schuylkill (PA)
Penn State Shenango (PA)
Penn State U Park (PA)
Penn St. Wilkes-Barre (PA)
Penn State Worthington Scranton (PA)
Penn State York (PA)
Rochester Inst of Technology (NY)
Roger Williams U (RI)
Rutgers, The State U of New Jersey, Newark (NJ)
Sage Coll of Albany (NY)
Saint Mary's Coll of California (CA)
San Jose State U (CA)
Swarthmore Coll (PA)
Trevecca Nazarene U (TN)
U of Illinois at Urbana–Champaign (IL)
U of Maryland U Coll (MD)
U of Michigan (MI)
U of Minnesota, Twin Cities Campus (MN)
U of New Hampshire (NH)
U of North Dakota (ND)
U of Ottawa (ON, Canada)
U of Puerto Rico at Bayamón (PR)
U of Puerto Rico at Ponce (PR)
U of Wisconsin–Parkside (WI)
Ursuline Coll (OH)
Utah State U (UT)
Washington U in St. Louis (MO)
Western State Colorado U (CO)

BIOLOGICAL AND PHYSICAL SCIENCES
Adelphi U (NY)
Alfred U (NY)
Alice Lloyd Coll (KY)
Alvernia U (PA)
Athabasca U (AB, Canada)
Augsburg Coll (MN)
Averett U (VA)
Baldwin Wallace U (OH)
Bemidji State U (MN)
Bennington Coll (VT)
Bluefield State Coll (WV)
Brevard Coll (NC)
Brock U (ON, Canada)
Buena Vista U (IA)
California State U, Fresno (CA)

Calvin Coll (MI)
Castleton State Coll (VT)
Cheyney U of Pennsylvania (PA)
Clarion U of Pennsylvania (PA)
Coe Coll (IA)
Coll of Saint Benedict (MN)
Coll of the Atlantic (ME)
Concordia U (OR)
Covenant Coll (GA)
Dakota Wesleyan U (SD)
Delta State U (MS)
DePaul U (IL)
Dominican U (IL)
Eastern Michigan U (MI)
Edinboro U of Pennsylvania (PA)
The Evergreen State Coll (WA)
Fairleigh Dickinson U, Metropolitan Campus (NJ)
Gettysburg Coll (PA)
Grand Valley State U (MI)
Houghton Coll (NY)
Huntington U (IN)
Indiana U Kokomo (IN)
Indiana U of Pennsylvania (PA)
Indiana U–Purdue U Indianapolis (IN)
Iowa Wesleyan Coll (IA)
John Brown U (AR)
John Carroll U (OH)
The Johns Hopkins U (MD)
Johnson C. Smith U (NC)
Keene State Coll (NH)
Keystone Coll (PA)
King Coll (TN)
King's Coll (PA)
Kutztown U of Pennsylvania (PA)
Le Moyne Coll (NY)
Lock Haven U of Pennsylvania (PA)
Louisiana State U in Shreveport (LA)
Mansfield U of Pennsylvania (PA)
Mars Hill Coll (NC)
Maryville U of Saint Louis (MO)
The Master's Coll and Sem (CA)
Michigan State U (MI)
Middle Tennessee State U (TN)
Minnesota State U Mankato (MN)
Mississippi State U (MS)
Mount Allison U (NB, Canada)
National U (CA)
North Central Coll (IL)
Northwest Missouri State U (MO)
Oakland City U (IN)
Oklahoma City U (OK)
Olivet Coll (MI)
Penn State Abington (PA)
Penn State Altoona (PA)
Penn State Beaver (PA)
Penn State Berks (PA)
Penn State Brandywine (PA)
Penn State DuBois (PA)
Penn State Erie, The Behrend Coll (PA)
Penn State Fayette, The Eberly Campus (PA)
Penn State Greater Allegheny (PA)
Penn State Hazleton (PA)
Penn State Lehigh Valley (PA)
Penn State Mont Alto (PA)
Penn State New Kensington (PA)
Penn State Schuylkill (PA)
Penn State Shenango (PA)
Penn State U Park (PA)
Penn State Wilkes-Barre (PA)
Penn State Worthington Scranton (PA)
Penn State York (PA)
Portland State U (OR)
Purdue U (IN)
Quinnipiac U (CT)
Ramapo Coll of New Jersey (NJ)
Roberts Wesleyan Coll (NY)
Rockford Coll (IL)
Saint Anselm Coll (NH)
St. Gregory's U, Shawnee (OK)
Saint John's U (MN)
St. Mary's Coll of Maryland (MD)
St. Norbert Coll (WI)
San Francisco State U (CA)
Scripps Coll (CA)
Seattle U (WA)
Sierra Nevada Coll (NV)
Simon Fraser U (BC, Canada)
Southern Arkansas U–Magnolia (AR)
Spalding U (KY)

State U of New York at Fredonia (NY)
State U of New York Empire State Coll (NY)
Stony Brook U, State U of New York (NY)
Texas A&M U–Commerce (TX)
Trent U (ON, Canada)
Troy U (AL)
Union U (TN)
United States Air Force Acad (CO)
The U of Alabama at Birmingham (AL)
U of Alaska Anchorage (AK)
U of Alaska Fairbanks (AK)
U of Central Arkansas (AR)
U of Denver (CO)
The U of Findlay (OH)
U of Georgia (GA)
U of Houston–Downtown (TX)
U of Massachusetts Amherst (MA)
U of New Brunswick Fredericton (NB, Canada)
U of Northern Iowa (IA)
U of Oregon (OR)
U of Pittsburgh (PA)
U of Puget Sound (WA)
U of Regina (SK, Canada)
U of Southern Indiana (IN)
U of Southern Mississippi (MS)
U of South Florida (FL)
The U of Texas at San Antonio (TX)
The U of Toledo (OH)
U of Waterloo (ON, Canada)
The U of West Alabama (AL)
The U of Western Ontario (ON, Canada)
U of West Florida (FL)
U of Windsor (ON, Canada)
U of Wisconsin–Platteville (WI)
U of Wisconsin–Stevens Point (WI)
U of Wisconsin–Superior (WI)
Upper Iowa U (IA)
Virginia Commonwealth U (VA)
Walsh U (OH)
Warner Pacific Coll (OR)
Washington State U (WA)
Washington U in St. Louis (MO)
Western Washington U (WA)
Xavier U (OH)
Young Harris Coll (GA)

BIOLOGICAL/BIOSYSTEMS ENGINEERING
The U of Arizona (AZ)
U of Florida (FL)
U of Georgia (GA)
U of Guelph (ON, Canada)
U of Idaho (ID)
U of Nebraska–Lincoln (NE)

BIOLOGY/BIOLOGICAL SCIENCES
Abilene Christian U (TX)
Acadia U (NS, Canada)
Adams State U (CO)
Adelphi U (NY)
Agnes Scott Coll (GA)
Alabama State U (AL)
Albertus Magnus Coll (CT)
Albion Coll (MI)
Albright Coll (PA)
Alcorn State U (MS)
Alderson-Broaddus Coll (WV)
Alfred U (NY)
Alice Lloyd Coll (KY)
Alma Coll (MI)
Alvernia U (PA)
Alverno Coll (WI)
American U (DC)
The American U in Cairo (Egypt)
American U of Beirut (Lebanon)
Amherst Coll (MA)
Anderson U (IN)
Anderson U (SC)
Andrews U (MI)
Angelo State U (TX)
Appalachian State U (NC)
Arizona Christian U (AZ)
Arizona State U (AZ)
Arkansas State U (AR)
Arkansas Tech U (AR)
Armstrong Atlantic State U (GA)
Asbury U (KY)
Ashland U (OH)
Assumption Coll (MA)
Athens State U (AL)
Auburn U (AL)

Auburn U at Montgomery (AL)
Augsburg Coll (MN)
Augustana Coll (IL)
Augustana Coll (SD)
Aurora U (IL)
Austin Peay State U (TN)
Avila U (MO)
Azusa Pacific U (CA)
Baker U (KS)
Baldwin Wallace U (OH)
Ball State U (IN)
Bard Coll (NY)
Barry U (FL)
Barton Coll (NC)
Bastyr U (WA)
Bates Coll (ME)
Baylor U (TX)
Bay Path Coll (MA)
Belhaven U (MS)
Bellarmine U (KY)
Belmont Abbey Coll (NC)
Belmont U (TN)
Bemidji State U (MN)
Benedictine Coll (KS)
Benedictine U (IL)
Bennington Coll (VT)
Berea Coll (KY)
Berry Coll (GA)
Bethany Coll (WV)
Bethany Lutheran Coll (MN)
Bethel Coll (IN)
Bethel Coll (KS)
Bethel U (MN)
Bethune-Cookman U (FL)
Binghamton U, State U of New York (NY)
Blackburn Coll (IL)
Bloomfield Coll (NJ)
Bloomsburg U of Pennsylvania (PA)
Bluefield Coll (VA)
Blue Mountain Coll (MS)
Bluffton U (OH)
Bob Jones U (SC)
Boise State U (ID)
Boston Coll (MA)
Boston U (MA)
Bowdoin Coll (ME)
Bowie State U (MD)
Bowling Green State U (OH)
Bradley U (IL)
Brevard Coll (NC)
Bridgewater Coll (VA)
Bridgewater State U (MA)
Brock U (ON, Canada)
Brown U (RI)
Bryant U (RI)
Bryn Athyn Coll of the New Church (PA)
Bucknell U (PA)
Buena Vista U (IA)
Buffalo State Coll, State U of New York (NY)
Butler U (IN)
Cabrini Coll (PA)
Caldwell Coll (NJ)
California Baptist U (CA)
California Lutheran U (CA)
California Polytechnic State U, San Luis Obispo (CA)
California State Polytechnic U, Pomona (CA)
California State U, Chico (CA)
California State U, Dominguez Hills (CA)
California State U, East Bay (CA)
California State U, Fresno (CA)
California State U, Fullerton (CA)
California State U, Long Beach (CA)
California State U, Los Angeles (CA)
California State U, Monterey Bay (CA)
California State U, Northridge (CA)
California State U, San Bernardino (CA)
California State U, San Marcos (CA)
California State U, Stanislaus (CA)
Calvin Coll (MI)
Cameron U (OK)
Campbellsville U (KY)
Canisius Coll (NY)
Capital U (OH)
Cardinal Stritch U (WI)
Carleton Coll (MN)
Carlow U (PA)

Carnegie Mellon U (PA)
Carroll Coll (MT)
Carson-Newman U (TN)
Case Western Reserve U (OH)
Castleton State Coll (VT)
Catawba Coll (NC)
The Catholic U of America (DC)
Cedar Crest Coll (PA)
Cedarville U (OH)
Centenary Coll of Louisiana (LA)
Central Coll (IA)
Central Connecticut State U (CT)
Central Methodist U (MO)
Central State U (OH)
Centre Coll (KY)
Chapman U (CA)
Chatham U (PA)
Chestnut Hill Coll (PA)
Cheyney U of Pennsylvania (PA)
Chicago State U (IL)
Chowan U (NC)
Christian Brothers U (TN)
Christopher Newport U (VA)
The Citadel, The Military Coll of South Carolina (SC)
City Coll of the City U of New York (NY)
Claflin U (SC)
Claremont McKenna Coll (CA)
Clarion U of Pennsylvania (PA)
Clark Atlanta U (GA)
Clarke U (IA)
Clarkson U (NY)
Clark U (MA)
Clayton State U (GA)
Clearwater Christian Coll (FL)
Clemson U (SC)
Cleveland Chiropractic Coll–Kansas City Campus (KS)
Cleveland State U (OH)
Coastal Carolina U (SC)
Coe Coll (IA)
Colby Coll (ME)
Colgate U (NY)
The Coll at Brockport, State U of New York (NY)
Coll of Charleston (SC)
Coll of Coastal Georgia (GA)
The Coll of Idaho (ID)
Coll of Mount St. Joseph (OH)
The Coll of New Jersey (NJ)
The Coll of New Rochelle (NY)
Coll of Saint Benedict (MN)
Coll of Saint Elizabeth (NJ)
Coll of Saint Mary (NE)
The Coll of Saint Rose (NY)
The Coll of St. Scholastica (MN)
Coll of Staten Island of the City U of New York (NY)
Coll of the Atlantic (ME)
Coll of the Holy Cross (MA)
Coll of the Ozarks (MO)
The Coll of William and Mary (VA)
The Coll of Wooster (OH)
The Colorado Coll (CO)
Colorado Mesa U (CO)
Colorado State U (CO)
Columbia Coll (MO)
Columbia Coll (SC)
Columbia U (NY)
Columbia U, School of General Studies (NY)
Columbus State U (GA)
Concordia Coll (MN)
Concordia Coll–New York (NY)
Concordia U (CA)
Concordia U (OR)
Concordia U (QC, Canada)
Concordia U Chicago (IL)
Concordia U, Nebraska (NE)
Concordia U, St. Paul (MN)
Concordia U Texas (TX)
Concordia U Wisconsin (WI)
Concord U (WV)
Connecticut Coll (CT)
Converse Coll (SC)
Cornell Coll (IA)
Cornerstone U (MI)
Covenant Coll (GA)
Creighton U (NE)
Crown Coll (MN)
Culver-Stockton Coll (MO)
Curry Coll (MA)
Dakota Wesleyan U (SD)
Dalhousie U (NS, Canada)
Dallas Baptist U (TX)

Dalton State Coll (GA)
Dartmouth Coll (NH)
Davidson Coll (NC)
Defiance Coll (OH)
Delta State U (MS)
DePaul U (IL)
DePauw U (IN)
DeSales U (PA)
Dickinson Coll (PA)
Dillard U (LA)
Doane Coll (NE)
Dominican Coll (NY)
Dominican U (IL)
Dordt Coll (IA)
Drake U (IA)
Drew U (NJ)
Drury U (MO)
Duquesne U (PA)
Earlham Coll (IN)
East Carolina U (NC)
East Central U (OK)
Eastern Illinois U (IL)
Eastern Mennonite U (VA)
Eastern Michigan U (MI)
Eastern New Mexico U (NM)
Eastern Washington U (WA)
East Tennessee State U (TN)
East Texas Baptist U (TX)
Eckerd Coll (FL)
Edgewood Coll (WI)
Edinboro U of Pennsylvania (PA)
Elizabeth City State U (NC)
Elizabethtown Coll (PA)
Elmira Coll (NY)
Elon U (NC)
Emmanuel Coll (GA)
Emmanuel Coll (MA)
Emory & Henry Coll (VA)
Emporia State U (KS)
Evangel U (MO)
Excelsior Coll (NY)
Fairfield U (CT)
Fairleigh Dickinson U, Coll at
   Florham (NJ)
Fairleigh Dickinson U, Metropolitan
   Campus (NJ)
Fairmont State U (WV)
Farmingdale State Coll (NY)
Faulkner U (AL)
Fayetteville State U (NC)
Felician Coll (NJ)
Ferris State U (MI)
Ferrum Coll (VA)
Florida Ag and Mech U (FL)
Florida Atlantic U (FL)
Florida Gulf Coast U (FL)
Florida Inst of Technology (FL)
Florida Intl U (FL)
Florida Southern Coll (FL)
Framingham State U (MA)
Francis Marion U (SC)
Franklin & Marshall Coll (PA)
Franklin Coll (IN)
Franklin Pierce U (NH)
Friends U (KS)
Frostburg State U (MD)
Furman U (SC)
Gallaudet U (DC)
Gannon U (PA)
Gardner-Webb U (NC)
Geneva Coll (PA)
George Fox U (OR)
George Mason U (VA)
Georgetown Coll (KY)
Georgetown U (DC)
Georgia Coll & State U (GA)
Georgia Gwinnett Coll (GA)
Georgia Regents U (GA)
Georgia Southern U (GA)
Georgia Southwestern State U
   (GA)
Georgia State U (GA)
Gettysburg Coll (PA)
Gonzaga U (WA)
Gordon Coll (MA)
Goshen Coll (IN)
Goucher Coll (MD)
Governors State U (IL)
Graceland U (IA)
Grambling State U (LA)
Grand Valley State U (MI)
Grand View U (IA)
Greenville Coll (IL)
Grinnell Coll (IA)
Grove City Coll (PA)
Guilford Coll (NC)
Gustavus Adolphus Coll (MN)

Hamilton Coll (NY)
Hamline U (MN)
Hampden-Sydney Coll (VA)
Hampshire Coll (MA)
Hampton U (VA)
Hanover Coll (IN)
Harding U (AR)
Hardin-Simmons U (TX)
Hartwick Coll (NY)
Harvey Mudd Coll (CA)
Haverford Coll (PA)
Hawai`i Pacific U (HI)
Henderson State U (AR)
Hendrix Coll (AR)
High Point U (NC)
Hillsdale Coll (MI)
Hiram Coll (OH)
Hobart and William Smith Colls
   (NY)
Hofstra U (NY)
Hollins U (VA)
Holy Family U (PA)
Holy Names U (CA)
Hood Coll (MD)
Hope Coll (MI)
Houghton Coll (NY)
Howard Payne U (TX)
Humboldt State U (CA)
Hunter Coll of the City U of New
   York (NY)
Huntingdon Coll (AL)
Huntington U (IN)
Husson U (ME)
Illinois Coll (IL)
Illinois Inst of Technology (IL)
Illinois State U (IL)
Illinois Wesleyan U (IL)
Immaculata U (PA)
Indiana State U (IN)
Indiana U Bloomington (IN)
Indiana U East (IN)
Indiana U Kokomo (IN)
Indiana U Northwest (IN)
Indiana U of Pennsylvania (PA)
Indiana U–Purdue U Fort Wayne
   (IN)
Indiana U–Purdue U Indianapolis
   (IN)
Indiana U South Bend (IN)
Indiana U Southeast (IN)
Indiana Wesleyan U (IN)
Inter American U of Puerto Rico,
   Aguadilla Campus (PR)
Inter American U of Puerto Rico,
   Bayamón Campus (PR)
Inter American U of Puerto Rico,
   Fajardo Campus (PR)
Inter American U of Puerto Rico,
   Ponce Campus (PR)
Inter American U of Puerto Rico,
   San Germán Campus (PR)
Iona Coll (NY)
Iowa State U of Science and
   Technology (IA)
Iowa Wesleyan Coll (IA)
Ithaca Coll (NY)
Jacksonville State U (AL)
James Madison U (VA)
Jamestown Coll (ND)
Jarvis Christian Coll (TX)
John Brown U (AR)
John Carroll U (OH)
The Johns Hopkins U (MD)
Johnson C. Smith U (NC)
Johnson State Coll (VT)
Judson Coll (AL)
Judson U (IL)
Juniata Coll (PA)
Kalamazoo Coll (MI)
Kansas State U (KS)
Kansas Wesleyan U (KS)
Kean U (NJ)
Keene State Coll (NH)
Kennesaw State U (GA)
Kent State U (OH)
Kent State U at Stark (OH)
Kentucky Christian U (KY)
Kentucky State U (KY)
Kentucky Wesleyan Coll (KY)
Kenyon Coll (OH)
Keuka Coll (NY)
Keystone Coll (PA)
King Coll (TN)
King's Coll (PA)
The King's U Coll (AB, Canada)
Knox Coll (IL)
Kutztown U of Pennsylvania (PA)

Lafayette Coll (PA)
LaGrange Coll (GA)
Lake Erie Coll (OH)
Lakeland Coll (WI)
Lamar U (TX)
Lander U (SC)
Lane Coll (TN)
Langston U (OK)
La Roche Coll (PA)
La Salle U (PA)
La Sierra U (CA)
Lawrence U (WI)
Lebanese American U (Lebanon)
Lebanon Valley Coll (PA)
Lees-McRae Coll (NC)
Lee U (TN)
Lehigh U (PA)
Lehman Coll of the City U of New
   York (NY)
Le Moyne Coll (NY)
LeTourneau U (TX)
Lewis-Clark State Coll (ID)
Lewis U (IL)
Liberty U (VA)
Life U (GA)
Limestone Coll (SC)
Lincoln Memorial U (TN)
Lincoln U (MO)
Lindenwood U (MO)
Lindsey Wilson Coll (KY)
Linfield Coll (OR)
Lipscomb U (TN)
Lock Haven U of Pennsylvania (PA)
Logan U–Coll of Chiropractic (MO)
Long Island U–Brooklyn Campus
   (NY)
Long Island U–C. W. Post Campus
   (NY)
Longwood U (VA)
Louisiana Coll (LA)
Louisiana State U and Ag and
   Mech Coll (LA)
Louisiana State U at Alexandria
   (LA)
Louisiana State U in Shreveport
   (LA)
Lourdes U (OH)
Loyola Marymount U (CA)
Loyola U Chicago (IL)
Loyola U Maryland (MD)
Loyola U New Orleans (LA)
Lubbock Christian U (TX)
Luther Coll (IA)
Lynchburg Coll (VA)
Lynn U (FL)
Lyon Coll (AR)
Macalester Coll (MN)
Madonna U (MI)
Malone U (OH)
Manchester U (IN)
Manhattan Coll (NY)
Manhattanville Coll (NY)
Mansfield U of Pennsylvania (PA)
Maranatha Baptist Bible Coll (WI)
Marian U (WI)
Marietta Coll (OH)
Marist Coll (NY)
Marquette U (WI)
Marshall U (WV)
Mars Hill Coll (NC)
Mary Baldwin Coll (VA)
Marymount Manhattan Coll (NY)
Marymount U (VA)
Maryville Coll (TN)
Maryville U of Saint Louis (MO)
Marywood U (PA)
Massachusetts Coll of Liberal Arts
   (MA)
Massachusetts Inst of Technology
   (MA)
The Master's Coll and Sem (CA)
Mayville State U (ND)
McDaniel Coll (MD)
McKendree U (IL)
McMurry U (TX)
McNeese State U (LA)
Medaille Coll (NY)
Mercer U (GA)
Mercy Coll (NY)
Mercy Coll of Ohio (OH)
Mercyhurst U (PA)
Merrimack Coll (MA)
Messiah Coll (PA)
Metropolitan State U of Denver
   (CO)
Miami Dade Coll (FL)
Michigan State U (MI)

Middlebury Coll (VT)
Middle Tennessee State U (TN)
Midwestern State U (TX)
Millersville U of Pennsylvania (PA)
Millikin U (IL)
Millsaps Coll (MS)
Mills Coll (CA)
Minnesota State U Mankato (MN)
Minnesota State U Moorhead (MN)
Minot State U (ND)
Misericordia U (PA)
Mississippi Coll (MS)
Mississippi State U (MS)
Mississippi U for Women (MS)
Mississippi Valley State U (MS)
Missouri Baptist U (MO)
Missouri State U (MO)
Missouri U of Science and
   Technology (MO)
Missouri Western State U (MO)
Molloy Coll (NY)
Monmouth Coll (IL)
Monmouth U (NJ)
Montana State U (MT)
Montana Tech of The U of Montana
   (MT)
Montclair State U (NJ)
Montreat Coll, Montreat (NC)
Moravian Coll (PA)
Morehead State U (KY)
Morehouse Coll (GA)
Morningside Coll (IA)
Morris Coll (SC)
Mount Allison U (NB, Canada)
Mount Aloysius Coll (PA)
Mount Holyoke Coll (MA)
Mount Marty Coll (SD)
Mount Mary Coll (WI)
Mount Mercy U (IA)
Mount Saint Mary Coll (NY)
Mount St. Mary's Coll (CA)
Mount St. Mary's U (MD)
Mount Vernon Nazarene U (OH)
Muhlenberg Coll (PA)
Murray State U (KY)
National U (CA)
Nazareth Coll of Rochester (NY)
Neumann U (PA)
Newberry Coll (SC)
New Coll of Florida (FL)
New England Coll (NH)
New Jersey City U (NJ)
Newman U (KS)
New Mexico Highlands U (NM)
New Mexico Inst of Mining and
   Technology (NM)
New Mexico State U (NM)
New York Inst of Technology (NY)
New York U (NY)
Niagara U (NY)
Nicholls State U (LA)
Norfolk State U (VA)
North Carolina Central U (NC)
North Carolina State U (NC)
North Carolina Wesleyan Coll (NC)
North Central Coll (IL)
North Dakota State U (ND)
Northeastern Illinois U (IL)
Northeastern U (MA)
Northern Arizona U (AZ)
Northern Illinois U (IL)
Northern Michigan U (MI)
Northern State U (SD)
North Greenville U (SC)
Northland Coll (WI)
Northwest Christian U (OR)
Northwestern Coll (IA)
Northwestern Coll (MN)
Northwestern Oklahoma State U
   (OK)
Northwestern State U of Louisiana
   (LA)
Northwest Missouri State U (MO)
Northwest Nazarene U (ID)
Norwich U (VT)
Notre Dame de Namur U (CA)
Nova Southeastern U (FL)
Oakland City U (IN)
Oakland U (MI)
Oglethorpe U (GA)
Ohio Dominican U (OH)
The Ohio State U (OH)
The Ohio State U at Lima (OH)
Ohio U (OH)
Ohio Wesleyan U (OH)
Oklahoma Baptist U (OK)

Oklahoma Christian U (OK)
Oklahoma City U (OK)
Oklahoma State U (OK)
Old Dominion U (VA)
Olivet Coll (MI)
Oral Roberts U (OK)
Oregon State U (OR)
Ouachita Baptist U (AR)
Pace U (NY)
Pacific Lutheran U (WA)
Pacific Union Coll (CA)
Pacific U (OR)
Paine Coll (GA)
Palm Beach Atlantic U (FL)
Park U (MO)
Paul Quinn Coll (TX)
Penn State Abington (PA)
Penn State Altoona (PA)
Penn State Beaver (PA)
Penn State Berks (PA)
Penn State Brandywine (PA)
Penn State DuBois (PA)
Penn State Erie, The Behrend Coll
   (PA)
Penn State Fayette, The Eberly
   Campus (PA)
Penn State Greater Allegheny (PA)
Penn State Hazleton (PA)
Penn State Lehigh Valley (PA)
Penn State Mont Alto (PA)
Penn State New Kensington (PA)
Penn State Schuylkill (PA)
Penn State Shenango (PA)
Penn State U Park (PA)
Penn State Wilkes-Barre (PA)
Penn State Worthington Scranton
   (PA)
Penn State York (PA)
Pepperdine U, Malibu (CA)
Philadelphia U (PA)
Piedmont Coll (GA)
Pine Manor Coll (MA)
Pittsburg State U (KS)
Pitzer Coll (CA)
Plymouth State U (NH)
Point Loma Nazarene U (CA)
Point Park U (PA)
Point U (GA)
Pomona Coll (CA)
Portland State U (OR)
Post U (CT)
Presbyterian Coll (SC)
Presentation Coll (SD)
Principia Coll (IL)
Providence Coll (RI)
Purchase Coll, State U of New York
   (NY)
Purdue U (IN)
Purdue U Calumet (IN)
Purdue U North Central (IN)
Queens U of Charlotte (NC)
Quincy U (IL)
Quinnipiac U (CT)
Radford U (VA)
Ramapo Coll of New Jersey (NJ)
Randolph Coll (VA)
Randolph-Macon Coll (VA)
Reed Coll (OR)
Regis Coll (MA)
Regis U (CO)
Rensselaer Polytechnic Inst (NY)
Rhode Island Coll (RI)
Rhodes Coll (TN)
Rice U (TX)
The Richard Stockton Coll of New
   Jersey (NJ)
Rider U (NJ)
Ripon Coll (WI)
Rivier U (NH)
Roanoke Coll (VA)
Robert Morris U (PA)
Roberts Wesleyan Coll (NY)
Rochester Inst of Technology (NY)
Rockford Coll (IL)
Rockhurst U (MO)
Rocky Mountain Coll (MT)
Rogers State U (OK)
Roger Williams U (RI)
Rollins Coll (FL)
Roosevelt U (IL)
Rosemont Coll (PA)
Rowan U (NJ)
Russell Sage Coll (NY)
Rutgers, The State U of New
   Jersey, Camden (NJ)
Rutgers, The State U of New
   Jersey, Newark (NJ)

Rutgers, The State U of New Jersey, New Brunswick (NJ)
Sacred Heart U (CT)
Saginaw Valley State U (MI)
St. Ambrose U (IA)
St. Andrews U (NC)
Saint Anselm Coll (NH)
St. Bonaventure U (NY)
St. Edward's U (TX)
St. Francis Coll (NY)
St. Gregory's U, Shawnee (OK)
St. John Fisher Coll (NY)
Saint John's U (MN)
St. John's U (NY)
Saint Joseph's Coll (IN)
St. Joseph's Coll, Long Island Campus (NY)
St. Joseph's Coll, New York (NY)
Saint Joseph's U (PA)
St. Lawrence U (NY)
Saint Leo U (FL)
Saint Louis U (MO)
Saint Martin's U (WA)
Saint Mary-of-the-Woods Coll (IN)
Saint Mary's Coll (IN)
Saint Mary's Coll of California (CA)
St. Mary's Coll of Maryland (MD)
St. Mary's U (TX)
Saint Mary's U of Minnesota (MN)
Saint Michael's Coll (VT)
St. Norbert Coll (WI)
St. Olaf Coll (MN)
St. Thomas Aquinas Coll (NY)
St. Thomas U (FL)
Saint Vincent Coll (PA)
Salem Intl U (WV)
Salem State U (MA)
Salisbury U (MD)
Salve Regina U (RI)
Samford U (AL)
Sam Houston State U (TX)
San Diego Christian Coll (CA)
San Diego State U (CA)
San Francisco State U (CA)
San Jose State U (CA)
Schreiner U (TX)
Scripps Coll (CA)
Seattle Pacific U (WA)
Seattle U (WA)
Seton Hill U (PA)
Sewanee: The U of the South (TN)
Shawnee State U (OH)
Shaw U (NC)
Shenandoah U (VA)
Shepherd U (WV)
Shippensburg U of Pennsylvania (PA)
Siena Coll (NY)
Siena Heights U (MI)
Simmons Coll (MA)
Simon Fraser U (BC, Canada)
Simpson Coll (IA)
Simpson U (CA)
Skidmore Coll (NY)
Slippery Rock U of Pennsylvania (PA)
Smith Coll (MA)
Sonoma State U (CA)
South Dakota State U (SD)
Southeastern Louisiana U (LA)
Southeastern Oklahoma State U (OK)
Southeastern U (FL)
Southeast Missouri State U (MO)
Southern Arkansas U–Magnolia (AR)
Southern Connecticut State U (CT)
Southern Illinois U Carbondale (IL)
Southern Illinois U Edwardsville (IL)
Southern Methodist U (TX)
Southern Nazarene U (OK)
Southern Oregon U (OR)
Southern Polytechnic State U (GA)
Southern Utah U (UT)
Southwest Baptist U (MO)
Southwestern Adventist U (TX)
Southwestern Coll (KS)
Southwestern U (TX)
Spelman Coll (GA)
Spring Arbor U (MI)
Spring Hill Coll (AL)
Stanford U (CA)
State U of New York at Fredonia (NY)
State U of New York at New Paltz (NY)

State U of New York at Oswego (NY)
State U of New York at Plattsburgh (NY)
State U of New York Coll at Cortland (NY)
State U of New York Coll at Geneseo (NY)
State U of New York Coll at Old Westbury (NY)
State U of New York Coll at Potsdam (NY)
Stephen F. Austin State U (TX)
Stephens Coll (MO)
Sterling Coll (KS)
Stetson U (FL)
Stevenson U (MD)
Stonehill Coll (MA)
Stony Brook U, State U of New York (NY)
Suffolk U (MA)
Sul Ross State U (TX)
Susquehanna U (PA)
Swarthmore Coll (PA)
Sweet Briar Coll (VA)
Syracuse U (NY)
Tabor Coll (KS)
Tarleton State U (TX)
Taylor U (IN)
Temple U (PA)
Tennessee State U (TN)
Tennessee Wesleyan Coll (TN)
Texas A&M Intl U (TX)
Texas A&M U (TX)
Texas A&M U–Commerce (TX)
Texas A&M U–Kingsville (TX)
Texas Christian U (TX)
Texas Lutheran U (TX)
Texas Southern U (TX)
Texas State U–San Marcos (TX)
Texas Wesleyan U (TX)
Texas Woman's U (TX)
Thomas Edison State Coll (NJ)
Thomas More Coll (KY)
Thomas U (GA)
Thompson Rivers U (BC, Canada)
Transylvania U (KY)
Trent U (ON, Canada)
Trevecca Nazarene U (TN)
Trine U (IN)
Trinity Christian Coll (IL)
Trinity Coll (CT)
Trinity U (TX)
Troy U (AL)
Truman State U (MO)
Tufts U (MA)
Tulane U (LA)
Tuskegee U (AL)
Union Coll (KY)
Union Coll (NE)
Union U (TN)
United States Air Force Acad (CO)
United States Military Acad (NY)
Universidad Adventista de las Antillas (PR)
Université de Sherbrooke (QC, Canada)
U at Albany, State U of New York (NY)
U at Buffalo, the State U of New York (NY)
The U of Akron (OH)
The U of Alabama (AL)
The U of Alabama at Birmingham (AL)
U of Alaska Anchorage (AK)
U of Alaska Fairbanks (AK)
The U of Arizona (AZ)
U of Arkansas at Little Rock (AR)
U of Arkansas–Fort Smith (AR)
U of Bridgeport (CT)
The U of British Columbia (BC, Canada)
The U of British Columbia–Okanagan (BC, Canada)
U of California, Berkeley (CA)
U of California, Davis (CA)
U of California, Irvine (CA)
U of California, Los Angeles (CA)
U of California, Merced (CA)
U of California, Riverside (CA)
U of California, Santa Barbara (CA)
U of California, Santa Cruz (CA)
U of Central Arkansas (AR)
U of Central Florida (FL)
U of Central Oklahoma (OK)
U of Charleston (WV)

U of Chicago (IL)
U of Cincinnati (OH)
U of Colorado Colorado Springs (CO)
U of Colorado Denver (CO)
U of Dallas (TX)
U of Delaware (DE)
U of Denver (CO)
U of Evansville (IN)
The U of Findlay (OH)
U of Florida (FL)
U of Georgia (GA)
U of Great Falls (MT)
U of Guam (GU)
U of Guelph (ON, Canada)
U of Hartford (CT)
U of Hawaii at Hilo (HI)
U of Hawaii at Manoa (HI)
U of Houston (TX)
U of Houston–Clear Lake (TX)
U of Houston–Downtown (TX)
U of Houston–Victoria (TX)
U of Idaho (ID)
U of Illinois at Chicago (IL)
U of Illinois at Springfield (IL)
U of Illinois at Urbana–Champaign (IL)
The U of Iowa (IA)
The U of Kansas (KS)
U of Kentucky (KY)
U of La Verne (CA)
U of Louisiana at Lafayette (LA)
U of Louisiana at Monroe (LA)
U of Louisville (KY)
U of Maine at Farmington (ME)
U of Maine at Fort Kent (ME)
U of Maine at Machias (ME)
U of Maryland, Baltimore County (MD)
U of Maryland, Coll Park (MD)
U of Maryland Eastern Shore (MD)
U of Mary Washington (VA)
U of Massachusetts Amherst (MA)
U of Massachusetts Boston (MA)
U of Massachusetts Dartmouth (MA)
U of Memphis (TN)
U of Miami (FL)
U of Michigan (MI)
U of Michigan–Dearborn (MI)
U of Michigan–Flint (MI)
U of Minnesota, Crookston (MN)
U of Minnesota, Duluth (MN)
U of Minnesota, Twin Cities Campus (MN)
U of Mississippi (MS)
U of Missouri (MO)
U of Missouri–Kansas City (MO)
U of Missouri–St. Louis (MO)
U of Mobile (AL)
The U of Montana Western (MT)
U of Montevallo (AL)
U of Mount Union (OH)
U of Nebraska at Kearney (NE)
U of Nebraska at Omaha (NE)
U of Nebraska–Lincoln (NE)
U of Nevada, Las Vegas (NV)
U of Nevada, Reno (NV)
U of New Brunswick Fredericton (NB, Canada)
U of New Brunswick Saint John (NB, Canada)
U of New England (ME)
U of New Hampshire (NH)
U of New Haven (CT)
U of New Mexico (NM)
U of New Orleans (LA)
U of North Alabama (AL)
U of North Carolina at Asheville (NC)
The U of North Carolina at Chapel Hill (NC)
The U of North Carolina at Charlotte (NC)
The U of North Carolina at Greensboro (NC)
The U of North Carolina at Pembroke (NC)
The U of North Carolina Wilmington (NC)
U of North Dakota (ND)
U of Northern Colorado (CO)
U of Northern Iowa (IA)
U of North Florida (FL)
U of North Georgia (GA)
U of North Texas (TX)
U of Notre Dame (IN)

U of Oregon (OR)
U of Ottawa (ON, Canada)
U of Pennsylvania (PA)
U of Pikeville (KY)
U of Pittsburgh (PA)
U of Pittsburgh at Bradford (PA)
U of Pittsburgh at Greensburg (PA)
U of Portland (OR)
U of Puerto Rico at Bayamón (PR)
U of Puget Sound (WA)
U of Redlands (CA)
U of Regina (SK, Canada)
U of Rhode Island (RI)
U of Richmond (VA)
U of Rochester (NY)
U of St. Francis (IL)
U of Saint Joseph (CT)
U of Saint Mary (KS)
U of St. Thomas (MN)
U of St. Thomas (TX)
U of San Diego (CA)
U of Science and Arts of Oklahoma (OK)
The U of Scranton (PA)
U of South Alabama (AL)
U of South Carolina (SC)
U of South Carolina Aiken (SC)
U of South Carolina Upstate (SC)
U of Southern California (CA)
U of Southern Indiana (IN)
U of Southern Maine (ME)
U of Southern Mississippi (MS)
U of South Florida (FL)
The U of Tampa (FL)
The U of Tennessee (TN)
The U of Tennessee at Chattanooga (TN)
The U of Tennessee at Martin (TN)
The U of Texas at Arlington (TX)
The U of Texas at Austin (TX)
The U of Texas at Brownsville (TX)
The U of Texas at Dallas (TX)
The U of Texas at El Paso (TX)
The U of Texas at San Antonio (TX)
The U of Texas of the Permian Basin (TX)
The U of Texas–Pan American (TX)
U of the Cumberlands (KY)
U of the District of Columbia (DC)
U of the Incarnate Word (TX)
U of the Ozarks (AR)
U of the Sciences (PA)
U of the Virgin Islands (VI)
The U of Toledo (OH)
U of Tulsa (OK)
U of Utah (UT)
U of Vermont (VT)
U of Virginia (VA)
U of Washington, Bothell (WA)
U of Waterloo (ON, Canada)
The U of West Alabama (AL)
The U of Western Ontario (ON, Canada)
U of West Florida (FL)
U of West Georgia (GA)
U of Windsor (ON, Canada)
U of Wisconsin–Eau Claire (WI)
U of Wisconsin–Green Bay (WI)
U of Wisconsin–La Crosse (WI)
U of Wisconsin–Madison (WI)
U of Wisconsin–Milwaukee (WI)
U of Wisconsin–Platteville (WI)
U of Wisconsin–Stevens Point (WI)
U of Wisconsin–Superior (WI)
U of Wyoming (WY)
Upper Iowa U (IA)
Ursuline Coll (OH)
Utah State U (UT)
Utica Coll (NY)
Valdosta State U (GA)
Valley City State U (ND)
Valparaiso U (IN)
Vanderbilt U (TN)
Vassar Coll (NY)
Villanova U (PA)
Virginia Commonwealth U (VA)
Virginia Intermont Coll (VA)
Virginia Polytechnic Inst and State U (VA)
Virginia State U (VA)
Virginia Union U (VA)
Virginia Wesleyan Coll (VA)
Viterbo U (WI)
Wabash Coll (IN)
Wagner Coll (NY)
Wake Forest U (NC)
Waldorf Coll (IA)

Walla Walla U (WA)
Walsh U (OH)
Warner Pacific Coll (OR)
Wartburg Coll (IA)
Washburn U (KS)
Washington & Jefferson Coll (PA)
Washington and Lee U (VA)
Washington Coll (MD)
Washington State U (WA)
Washington U in St. Louis (MO)
Wayland Baptist U (TX)
Waynesburg U (PA)
Wayne State Coll (NE)
Wayne State U (MI)
Webster U (MO)
Wellesley Coll (MA)
Wells Coll (NY)
Wesleyan Coll (GA)
Wesleyan U (CT)
Wesley Coll (DE)
West Chester U of Pennsylvania (PA)
Western Carolina U (NC)
Western Connecticut State U (CT)
Western Illinois U (IL)
Western Kentucky U (KY)
Western Michigan U (MI)
Western Oregon U (OR)
Western State Colorado U (CO)
Western Washington U (WA)
Westfield State U (MA)
West Liberty U (WV)
Westminster Coll (MO)
Westminster Coll (UT)
West Texas A&M U (TX)
West Virginia State U (WV)
West Virginia U (WV)
West Virginia U Inst of Technology (WV)
West Virginia Wesleyan Coll (WV)
Wheaton Coll (IL)
Wheaton Coll (MA)
Wheeling Jesuit U (WV)
Whitman Coll (WA)
Whitworth U (WA)
Wichita State U (KS)
Widener U (PA)
Wilberforce U (OH)
Wilkes U (PA)
Willamette U (OR)
William Jewell Coll (MO)
William Paterson U of New Jersey (NJ)
William Peace U (NC)
William Penn U (IA)
Williams Coll (MA)
Winthrop U (SC)
Wittenberg U (OH)
Worcester Polytechnic Inst (MA)
Worcester State U (MA)
Wright State U (OH)
Xavier U (OH)
Xavier U of Louisiana (LA)
Yale U (CT)
York Coll of Pennsylvania (PA)
York Coll of the City U of New York (NY)
Young Harris Coll (GA)
Youngstown State U (OH)

BIOLOGY/BIOTECHNOLOGY LABORATORY TECHNICIAN
Cleveland State U (OH)
The Coll at Brockport, State U of New York (NY)
Gannon U (PA)
Niagara U (NY)
Penn State Abington (PA)
Penn State Altoona (PA)
Penn State Beaver (PA)
Penn State Berks (PA)
Penn State Brandywine (PA)
Penn State DuBois (PA)
Penn State Erie, The Behrend Coll (PA)
Penn State Fayette, The Eberly Campus (PA)
Penn State Greater Allegheny (PA)
Penn State Hazleton (PA)
Penn State Lehigh Valley (PA)
Penn State Mont Alto (PA)
Penn State New Kensington (PA)
Penn State Schuylkill (PA)
Penn State Shenango (PA)
Penn State U Park (PA)
Penn State Wilkes-Barre (PA)

Penn State Worthington Scranton (PA)
Penn State York (PA)
Point Park U (PA)
State U of New York at Fredonia (NY)
U of New Haven (CT)
Washburn U (KS)
Worcester Polytechnic Inst (MA)
York Coll of the City U of New York (NY)

BIOLOGY TEACHER EDUCATION
Abilene Christian U (TX)
Adams State U (CO)
Albion Coll (MI)
Alma Coll (MI)
Alvernia U (PA)
Anderson U (IN)
Appalachian State U (NC)
Arizona Christian U (AZ)
Arkansas State U (AR)
Arkansas Tech U (AR)
Ashland U (OH)
Assumption Coll (MA)
Augustana Coll (IL)
Averett U (VA)
Bethel U (MN)
Bethune-Cookman U (FL)
Blackburn Coll (IL)
Bluefield Coll (VA)
Blue Mountain Coll (MS)
Boise State U (ID)
Bowling Green State U (OH)
Bradley U (IL)
Bridgewater State U (MA)
Buena Vista U (IA)
Cabrini Coll (PA)
California State U, Chico (CA)
California State U, Long Beach (CA)
Calvin Coll (MI)
Campbellsville U (KY)
Canisius Coll (NY)
Carroll Coll (MT)
Cedarville U (OH)
Central Methodist U (MO)
Central Michigan U (MI)
Christian Brothers U (TN)
City Coll of the City U of New York (NY)
Clearwater Christian Coll (FL)
The Coll at Brockport, State U of New York (NY)
The Coll of New Jersey (NJ)
The Coll of Saint Rose (NY)
Coll of Staten Island of the City U of New York (NY)
Coll of the Ozarks (MO)
Colorado State U (CO)
Concordia Coll (MN)
Concordia U Chicago (IL)
Concordia U, Nebraska (NE)
Concordia U, St. Paul (MN)
Corban U (OR)
Cornerstone U (MI)
Culver-Stockton Coll (MO)
Dakota State U (SD)
Dakota Wesleyan U (SD)
Dallas Baptist U (TX)
Daytona State Coll (FL)
Dominican Coll (NY)
Dordt Coll (IA)
East Central U (OK)
Eastern Michigan U (MI)
Eastern Washington U (WA)
East Texas Baptist U (TX)
Edgewood Coll (WI)
Elizabeth City State U (NC)
Elmira Coll (NY)
Evangel U (MO)
Fayetteville State U (NC)
Ferris State U (MI)
Florida Inst of Technology (FL)
Fort Lewis Coll (CO)
Franklin Coll (IN)
Friends U (KS)
Gordon State Coll (GA)
Grand Valley State U (MI)
Greenville Coll (IL)
Gustavus Adolphus Coll (MN)
Harding U (AR)
Hofstra U (NY)
Hope Coll (MI)
Howard Payne U (TX)

Hunter Coll of the City U of New York (NY)
Huntingdon Coll (AL)
Huntington U (IN)
Husson U (ME)
Indiana U Bloomington (IN)
Indiana U Northwest (IN)
Indiana U–Purdue U Fort Wayne (IN)
Indiana U South Bend (IN)
Indiana U Southeast (IN)
Indiana Wesleyan U (IN)
Indian River State Coll (FL)
Inter American U of Puerto Rico, Aguadilla Campus (PR)
Inter American U of Puerto Rico, Fajardo Campus (PR)
Inter American U of Puerto Rico, Ponce Campus (PR)
Inter American U of Puerto Rico, San Germán Campus (PR)
Iona Coll (NY)
Iowa Wesleyan Coll (IA)
Ithaca Coll (NY)
Jamestown Coll (ND)
Johnson State Coll (VT)
Juniata Coll (PA)
Keene State Coll (NH)
Kennesaw State U (GA)
Kentucky Wesleyan Coll (KY)
Keuka Coll (NY)
King Coll (TN)
Le Moyne Coll (NY)
Lincoln Memorial U (TN)
Lincoln U (MO)
Lindenwood U (MO)
Lindsey Wilson Coll (KY)
Lipscomb U (TN)
Long Island U–C. W. Post Campus (NY)
Louisiana State U in Shreveport (LA)
Lubbock Christian U (TX)
Madonna U (MI)
Manchester U (IN)
Manhattanville Coll (NY)
Mansfield U of Pennsylvania (PA)
Maranatha Baptist Bible Coll (WI)
Marist Coll (NY)
Maryville Coll (TN)
Marywood U (PA)
Mayville State U (ND)
McKendree U (IL)
McMurry U (TX)
Mercyhurst U (PA)
Merrimack Coll (MA)
Messiah Coll (PA)
Miami Dade Coll (FL)
Miami U (OH)
Michigan State U (MI)
Millikin U (IL)
Minnesota State U Moorhead (MN)
Minot State U (ND)
Misericordia U (PA)
Mississippi Coll (MS)
Missouri State U (MO)
Molloy Coll (NY)
Moravian Coll (PA)
Morningside Coll (IA)
Morris Coll (SC)
Mount Mary Coll (WI)
Mount Vernon Nazarene U (OH)
Nazareth Coll of Rochester (NY)
Niagara U (NY)
North Carolina Central U (NC)
North Dakota State U (ND)
Northern Michigan U (MI)
Northwestern Coll (IA)
Northwest Missouri State U (MO)
Northwest Nazarene U (ID)
Northwest U (WA)
Oakland City U (IN)
Ohio Wesleyan U (OH)
Oklahoma City U (OK)
Pace U (NY)
Paine Coll (GA)
Palm Beach Atlantic U (FL)
Pittsburg State U (KS)
Point Park U (PA)
Purdue U Calumet (IN)
Rhode Island Coll (RI)
Rivier U (NH)
Roberts Wesleyan Coll (NY)
Rocky Mountain Coll (MT)
Saginaw Valley State U (MI)
St. Ambrose U (IA)
St. Edward's U (TX)

St. Francis Coll (NY)
St. Gregory's U, Shawnee (OK)
St. John Fisher Coll (NY)
St. John's U (NY)
St. Joseph's Coll, Long Island Campus (NY)
St. Joseph's Coll, New York (NY)
Saint Mary's U of Minnesota (MN)
Salve Regina U (RI)
Schreiner U (TX)
Seton Hill U (PA)
Southeastern U (FL)
Southern Polytechnic State U (GA)
Southern Utah U (UT)
Southwest Baptist U (MO)
Spring Arbor U (MI)
State U of New York at New Paltz (NY)
State U of New York at Plattsburgh (NY)
State U of New York Coll at Cortland (NY)
State U of New York Coll at Old Westbury (NY)
Stony Brook U, State U of New York (NY)
Texas A&M Intl U (TX)
Texas Wesleyan U (TX)
Trevecca Nazarene U (TN)
Trinity Christian Coll (IL)
Union Coll (NE)
Universidad Adventista de las Antillas (PR)
U of Arkansas–Fort Smith (AR)
U of California, Irvine (CA)
U of Charleston (WV)
U of Delaware (DE)
U of Evansville (IN)
U of Great Falls (MT)
U of Illinois at Chicago (IL)
The U of Iowa (IA)
U of Louisiana at Monroe (LA)
U of Maine at Farmington (ME)
U of Maine at Machias (ME)
U of Minnesota, Duluth (MN)
U of Minnesota, Twin Cities Campus (MN)
U of Missouri (MO)
U of Missouri–St. Louis (MO)
The U of Montana Western (MT)
U of Nebraska–Lincoln (NE)
The U of North Carolina at Greensboro (NC)
The U of North Carolina Wilmington (NC)
U of Regina (SK, Canada)
The U of South Dakota (SD)
The U of Tennessee at Martin (TN)
U of Waterloo (ON, Canada)
U of Windsor (ON, Canada)
U of Wisconsin–Superior (WI)
Utah State U (UT)
Utica Coll (NY)
Valley City State U (ND)
Valparaiso U (IN)
Virginia Intermont Coll (VA)
Viterbo U (WI)
Washburn U (KS)
Washington State U (WA)
Washington U in St. Louis (MO)
Waynesburg U (PA)
Wayne State Coll (NE)
Weber State U (UT)
Western Michigan U (MI)
Western State Colorado U (CO)
Western Washington U (WA)
Wheeling Jesuit U (WV)
Widener U (PA)
William Jewell Coll (MO)
Xavier U (OH)
Xavier U of Louisiana (LA)
York Coll of Pennsylvania (PA)
Youngstown State U (OH)

BIOMATHEMATICS, BIOINFORMATICS, AND COMPUTATIONAL BIOLOGY RELATED
Cedar Crest Coll (PA)
Florida Inst of Technology (FL)
Florida State U (FL)
Harvey Mudd Coll (CA)
U of California, Los Angeles (CA)
Walsh U (OH)
Washington U in St. Louis (MO)
Worcester Polytechnic Inst (MA)

BIOMEDICAL SCIENCES
Adventist U of Health Sciences (FL)
Auburn U (AL)
Bridgewater State U (MA)
Brigham Young U (UT)
Brock U (ON, Canada)
Brown U (RI)
Central Michigan U (MI)
Christian Brothers U (TN)
City Coll of the City U of New York (NY)
Colorado State U (CO)
Concordia Coll–New York (NY)
Concordia U Wisconsin (WI)
Florida Inst of Technology (FL)
Inter American U of Puerto Rico, Ponce Campus (PR)
Keuka Coll (NY)
Liberty U (VA)
Lynchburg Coll (VA)
Marist Coll (NY)
Marquette U (WI)
Maryville U of Saint Louis (MO)
McMurry U (TX)
Mississippi Coll (MS)
North Carolina Central U (NC)
North Carolina Wesleyan Coll (NC)
Northern Arizona U (AZ)
The Ohio State U (OH)
Oklahoma City U (OK)
Purdue U (IN)
Rochester Inst of Technology (NY)
Rutgers, The State U of New Jersey, New Brunswick (NJ)
St. Francis Coll (NY)
St. Gregory's U, Shawnee (OK)
Slippery Rock U of Pennsylvania (PA)
State U of New York at Fredonia (NY)
Suffolk U (MA)
Texas A&M U (TX)
Texas A&M U–Kingsville (TX)
U at Buffalo, the State U of New York (NY)
U of California, Riverside (CA)
U of Central Florida (FL)
U of Colorado Denver (CO)
U of Guelph (ON, Canada)
U of Michigan–Flint (MI)
U of Minnesota, Duluth (MN)
U of New England (ME)
U of New Hampshire (NH)
U of Ottawa (ON, Canada)
U of Pennsylvania (PA)
U of South Alabama (AL)
U of South Florida (FL)
Washington State U (WA)
Western Michigan U (MI)
Worcester Polytechnic Inst (MA)

BIOMEDICAL TECHNOLOGY
Andrews U (MI)
California State U, East Bay (CA)
Cleveland State U (OH)
DeVry Coll of New York (NY)
DeVry U, Phoenix (AZ)
DeVry U, Miramar (FL)
DeVry U, Orlando (FL)
DeVry U, Decatur (GA)
DeVry U, Chicago (IL)
DeVry U, North Brunswick (NJ)
DeVry U, Columbus (OH)
DeVry U, Fort Washington (PA)
DeVry U, Irving (TX)
Indiana U–Purdue U Indianapolis (IN)
Lawrence Technological U (MI)
New York Inst of Technology (NY)
Rutgers, The State U of New Jersey, Camden (NJ)
Suffolk U (MA)
Thomas Edison State Coll (NJ)
Wright State U (OH)

BIOMETRY/BIOMETRICS
Carnegie Mellon U (PA)
Rutgers, The State U of New Jersey, New Brunswick (NJ)
Stanford U (CA)
U of Delaware (DE)
U of Minnesota, Twin Cities Campus (MN)

BIOPHYSICS
Andrews U (MI)
Brigham Young U (UT)

Brown U (RI)
Carnegie Mellon U (PA)
Centenary Coll of Louisiana (LA)
Claremont McKenna Coll (CA)
Columbia U (NY)
Columbia U, School of General Studies (NY)
Hampden-Sydney Coll (VA)
Haverford Coll (PA)
Illinois Inst of Technology (IL)
Iowa State U of Science and Technology (IA)
The Johns Hopkins U (MD)
King Coll (TN)
La Sierra U (CA)
Lipscomb U (TN)
Loyola U Chicago (IL)
New Jersey Inst of Technology (NJ)
Oakland U (MI)
Oklahoma City U (OK)
Pacific Union Coll (CA)
St. Bonaventure U (NY)
St. Lawrence U (NY)
Southern Nazarene U (OK)
State U of New York Coll at Geneseo (NY)
Suffolk U (MA)
Syracuse U (NY)
Temple U (PA)
U at Buffalo, the State U of New York (NY)
The U of British Columbia (BC, Canada)
U of California, Los Angeles (CA)
U of Illinois at Urbana–Champaign (IL)
U of Michigan (MI)
U of New Brunswick Fredericton (NB, Canada)
U of Pennsylvania (PA)
U of San Diego (CA)
The U of Scranton (PA)
U of Southern California (CA)
U of Southern Indiana (IN)
The U of Western Ontario (ON, Canada)
Walla Walla U (WA)
Washington & Jefferson Coll (PA)
Washington U in St. Louis (MO)
Whitman Coll (WA)

BIOPSYCHOLOGY
Bucknell U (PA)
Carnegie Mellon U (PA)
Columbia U (NY)
Geneva Coll (PA)
Grand Valley State U (MI)
Immaculata U (PA)
Messiah Coll (PA)
Monmouth Coll (IL)
Morningside Coll (IA)
Mount Allison U (NB, Canada)
Northwest Missouri State U (MO)
Oglethorpe U (GA)
Philadelphia U (PA)
Rider U (NJ)
Simmons Coll (MA)
Spring Hill Coll (AL)
Tufts U (MA)
U of California, Santa Barbara (CA)
U of Guelph (ON, Canada)
Viterbo U (WI)
Wagner Coll (NY)
Washington U in St. Louis (MO)

BIOSTATISTICS
Emmanuel Coll (MA)
Simmons Coll (MA)
Tulane U (LA)
U at Buffalo, the State U of New York (NY)
U of Minnesota, Twin Cities Campus (MN)
The U of North Carolina at Chapel Hill (NC)
The U of Western Ontario (ON, Canada)

BIOTECHNOLOGY
Ashland U (OH)
Bay Path Coll (MA)
Brock U (ON, Canada)
California State Polytechnic U, Pomona (CA)
Calvin Coll (MI)
Central Baptist Coll (AR)
Claflin U (SC)

The Coll at Brockport, State U of New York (NY)
Elizabethtown Coll (PA)
Endicott Coll (MA)
Fayetteville State U (NC)
Ferris State U (MI)
Florida Gulf Coast U (FL)
Grand View U (IA)
Hunter Coll of the City U of New York (NY)
Indiana U Bloomington (IN)
Indiana U East (IN)
Indiana U–Purdue U Indianapolis (IN)
Inter American U of Puerto Rico, Aguadilla Campus (PR)
Inter American U of Puerto Rico, Ponce Campus (PR)
James Madison U (VA)
Kennesaw State U (GA)
Kent State U (OH)
Manhattan Coll (NY)
Marywood U (PA)
Massachusetts Coll of Liberal Arts (MA)
Missouri Baptist U (MO)
Missouri Western State U (MO)
Montana State U (MT)
North Carolina State U (NC)
North Dakota State U (ND)
Oregon State U (OR)
Plymouth State U (NH)
Rochester Inst of Technology (NY)
Roosevelt U (IL)
Rutgers, The State U of New Jersey, New Brunswick (NJ)
South Dakota State U (SD)
Southeastern Oklahoma State U (OK)
State U of New York at New Paltz (NY)
State U of New York Coll of Agriculture and Technology at Cobleskill (NY)
Stevenson U (MD)
Tufts U (MA)
U at Buffalo, the State U of New York (NY)
The U of British Columbia (BC, Canada)
U of California, Davis (CA)
U of Central Florida (FL)
U of Georgia (GA)
U of Houston (TX)
U of Houston–Downtown (TX)
U of Illinois at Urbana–Champaign (IL)
U of Kentucky (KY)
U of Nebraska at Omaha (NE)
U of Nevada, Reno (NV)
The U of North Carolina at Pembroke (NC)
U of Northern Iowa (IA)
U of Puerto Rico at Ponce (PR)
U of Waterloo (ON, Canada)
U of Windsor (ON, Canada)
Ursuline Coll (OH)
West Texas A&M U (TX)
Worcester State U (MA)
York Coll of the City U of New York (NY)

BLOOD BANK TECHNOLOGY
Rasmussen Coll St. Cloud (MN)

BOTANY/PLANT BIOLOGY
Andrews U (MI)
Auburn U (AL)
Bennington Coll (VT)
California State U, Long Beach (CA)
Coll of the Atlantic (ME)
Colorado State U (CO)
Connecticut Coll (CT)
Dalhousie U (NS, Canada)
Goddard Coll (VT)
Humboldt State U (CA)
Iowa State U of Science and Technology (IA)
Kent State U (OH)
Miami U (OH)
Michigan State U (MI)
North Carolina State U (NC)
North Dakota State U (ND)
The Ohio State U (OH)
Ohio U (OH)
Ohio Wesleyan U (OH)

Oklahoma State U (OK)
Oregon State U (OR)
Prescott Coll (AZ)
Purdue U (IN)
Rutgers, The State U of New Jersey, Newark (NJ)
San Francisco State U (CA)
Sonoma State U (CA)
Southern Illinois U Carbondale (IL)
U of California, Berkeley (CA)
U of California, Davis (CA)
U of California, Irvine (CA)
U of California, Riverside (CA)
U of Florida (FL)
U of Georgia (GA)
U of Great Falls (MT)
U of Hawaii at Manoa (HI)
U of Illinois at Urbana–Champaign (IL)
U of Minnesota, Twin Cities Campus (MN)
U of Nebraska–Lincoln (NE)
U of New Brunswick Fredericton (NB, Canada)
U of New Hampshire (NH)
U of Oklahoma (OK)
The U of Texas at El Paso (TX)
U of Vermont (VT)
U of Wisconsin–Madison (WI)
U of Wisconsin–Superior (WI)
U of Wyoming (WY)
Utah State U (UT)
Weber State U (UT)

BOTANY/PLANT BIOLOGY RELATED
Dalhousie U (NS, Canada)
Frostburg State U (MD)
Purdue U (IN)
U of Hawaii at Manoa (HI)
U of Minnesota, Twin Cities Campus (MN)

BRASS INSTRUMENTS
Houghton Coll (NY)
McNally Smith Coll of Music (MN)
The U of Kansas (KS)
Vanderbilt U (TN)

BROADCAST JOURNALISM
Auburn U (AL)
Barry U (FL)
Belmont U (TN)
Bemidji State U (MN)
Bluffton U (OH)
Bowie State U (MD)
Bowling Green State U (OH)
Brigham Young U (UT)
Buffalo State Coll, State U of New York (NY)
California State U, East Bay (CA)
California State U, Long Beach (CA)
Central State U (OH)
Chapman U (CA)
Chatham U (PA)
The Coll at Brockport, State U of New York (NY)
The Coll of New Rochelle (NY)
Coll of the Ozarks (MO)
Columbia Coll Chicago (IL)
Columbia Coll Hollywood (CA)
Drake U (IA)
Drury U (MO)
East Carolina U (NC)
Elon U (NC)
Emerson Coll (MA)
Evangel U (MO)
Five Towns Coll (NY)
Gettysburg Coll (PA)
Gonzaga U (WA)
Grace U (NE)
Grand View U (IA)
Hampton U (VA)
Harding U (AR)
Hardin-Simmons U (TX)
Hawai'i Pacific U (HI)
Humboldt State U (CA)
Huntington U (IN)
Ithaca Coll (NY)
John Brown U (AR)
Kuyper Coll (MI)
Lamar U (TX)
Langston U (OK)
La Salle U (PA)
Lindenwood U (MO)
Long Island U–C. W. Post Campus (NY)

Louisiana Coll (LA)
Manchester U (IN)
Massachusetts Coll of Liberal Arts (MA)
Mount Vernon Nazarene U (OH)
New England School of Communications (ME)
North Greenville U (SC)
Ohio U (OH)
Ohio Wesleyan U (OH)
Oklahoma Christian U (OK)
Oklahoma City U (OK)
Pacific U (OR)
Point Loma Nazarene U (CA)
Point Park U (PA)
Purdue U Calumet (IN)
Quinnipiac U (CT)
Southwestern Adventist U (TX)
State U of New York at New Paltz (NY)
State U of New York at Oswego (NY)
State U of New York at Plattsburgh (NY)
Suffolk U (MA)
Syracuse U (NY)
Troy U (AL)
Union U (TN)
U of Central Oklahoma (OK)
U of Colorado Boulder (CO)
The U of Findlay (OH)
U of Georgia (GA)
U of Illinois at Urbana–Champaign (IL)
U of La Verne (CA)
U of Miami (FL)
U of Missouri (MO)
U of Nebraska at Omaha (NE)
U of Nebraska–Lincoln (NE)
U of North Texas (TX)
U of Oklahoma (OK)
U of South Carolina (SC)
U of Southern California (CA)
The U of Texas at El Paso (TX)
U of the Ozarks (AR)
U of Wisconsin–Superior (WI)
Wartburg Coll (IA)
Washington State U (WA)
Western Kentucky U (KY)
West Texas A&M U (TX)

BUILDING/CONSTRUCTION FINISHING, MANAGEMENT, AND INSPECTION RELATED
California State U, Long Beach (CA)
John Brown U (AR)
Minnesota State U Mankato (MN)
Purdue U (IN)
U of Maryland Eastern Shore (MD)
U of the District of Columbia (DC)
U of Wisconsin–Platteville (WI)

BUILDING/CONSTRUCTION SITE MANAGEMENT
Pennsylvania Coll of Technology (PA)
Purdue U (IN)
Southern Utah U (UT)

BUILDING CONSTRUCTION TECHNOLOGY
Purdue U (IN)
U of Massachusetts Amherst (MA)

BUILDING/HOME/ CONSTRUCTION INSPECTION
Purdue U (IN)
Tuskegee U (AL)

BUILDING/PROPERTY MAINTENANCE
Purdue U (IN)

BUSINESS ADMINISTRATION AND MANAGEMENT
Abilene Christian U (TX)
Acadia U (NS, Canada)
Adams State U (CO)
Adelphi U (NY)
AIB Coll of Business (IA)
Alabama State U (AL)
Alaska Pacific U (AK)
Albertus Magnus Coll (CT)
Albion Coll (MI)
Albright Coll (PA)
Alcorn State U (MS)
Alderson-Broaddus Coll (WV)
Alfred U (NY)
Alice Lloyd Coll (KY)

Alliant Intl U (CA)
Alliant Intl U–México City (Mexico)
Alma Coll (MI)
Alvernia U (PA)
Alverno Coll (WI)
American Public U System (WV)
American U (DC)
American U in Bulgaria (Bulgaria)
The American U in Cairo (Egypt)
American U of Beirut (Lebanon)
American U of Puerto Rico (PR)
The American U of Rome (Italy)
Amridge U (AL)
Anderson U (IN)
Anderson U (SC)
Angelo State U (TX)
Antioch U Midwest (OH)
Appalachian State U (NC)
Arizona Christian U (AZ)
Arizona State U (AZ)
Arkansas State U (AR)
Arkansas Tech U (AR)
Ashland U (OH)
Assumption Coll (MA)
Athabasca U (AB, Canada)
Athens State U (AL)
Auburn U (AL)
Auburn U at Montgomery (AL)
Augsburg Coll (MN)
Augustana Coll (IL)
Augustana Coll (SD)
Aurora U (IL)
Avila U (MO)
Azusa Pacific U (CA)
Babson Coll (MA)
Baldwin Wallace U (OH)
Ball State U (IN)
The Baptist Coll of Florida (FL)
Baptist U of the Americas (TX)
Barclay Coll (KS)
Barry U (FL)
Barton Coll (NC)
Baylor U (TX)
Bay Path Coll (MA)
Beacon Coll (FL)
Becker Coll (MA)
Belhaven U (MS)
Belmont Abbey Coll (NC)
Belmont U (TN)
Bemidji State U (MN)
Benedictine Coll (KS)
Bentley U (MA)
Berea Coll (KY)
Berry Coll (GA)
Bethany Lutheran Coll (MN)
Bethel Coll (IN)
Bethel U (MN)
Bethune-Cookman U (FL)
Binghamton U, State U of New York (NY)
Blackburn Coll (IL)
Bloomfield Coll (NJ)
Bloomsburg U of Pennsylvania (PA)
Bluefield Coll (VA)
Bluefield State Coll (WV)
Blue Mountain Coll (MS)
Bluffton U (OH)
Bob Jones U (SC)
Boise State U (ID)
Boston Coll (MA)
Boston U (MA)
Bowie State U (MD)
Bowling Green State U (OH)
Bowling Green State U-Firelands Coll (OH)
Bradley U (IL)
Brevard Coll (NC)
Bridgewater Coll (VA)
Bridgewater State U (MA)
Briercrest Coll (SK, Canada)
Brock U (ON, Canada)
Bryant U (RI)
Bucknell U (PA)
Buena Vista U (IA)
Buffalo State Coll, State U of New York (NY)
Cabrini Coll (PA)
Cairn U (PA)
Caldwell Coll (NJ)
California Baptist U (CA)
California Lutheran U (CA)
California Polytechnic State U, San Luis Obispo (CA)
California State Polytechnic U, Pomona (CA)
California State U, Chico (CA)

California State U, Dominguez Hills (CA)
California State U, East Bay (CA)
California State U, Fresno (CA)
California State U, Fullerton (CA)
California State U, Long Beach (CA)
California State U, Los Angeles (CA)
California State U, Monterey Bay (CA)
California State U, Northridge (CA)
California State U, San Bernardino (CA)
California State U, San Marcos (CA)
California State U, Stanislaus (CA)
Calumet Coll of Saint Joseph (IN)
Calvin Coll (MI)
Cameron U (OK)
Campbellsville U (KY)
Canisius Coll (NY)
Capital U (OH)
Cardinal Stritch U (WI)
Caribbean U (PR)
Carlos Albizu U, Miami Campus (FL)
Carlow U (PA)
Carnegie Mellon U (PA)
Carroll Coll (MT)
Carson-Newman U (TN)
Case Western Reserve U (OH)
Castleton State Coll (VT)
Catawba Coll (NC)
Cedar Crest Coll (PA)
Cedarville U (OH)
Centenary Coll of Louisiana (LA)
Central Baptist Coll (AR)
Central Coll (IA)
Central Connecticut State U (CT)
Central Methodist U (MO)
Champlain Coll (VT)
Chapman U (CA)
Chatham U (PA)
Chestnut Hill Coll (PA)
Cheyney U of Pennsylvania (PA)
Chicago State U (IL)
Chipola Coll (FL)
Chowan U (NC)
Christian Brothers U (TN)
Christopher Newport U (VA)
The Citadel, The Military Coll of South Carolina (SC)
City Coll of the City U of New York (NY)
City U of Seattle (WA)
Claflin U (SC)
Clarion U of Pennsylvania (PA)
Clark Atlanta U (GA)
Clarke U (IA)
Clarkson U (NY)
Clark U (MA)
Clayton State U (GA)
Clearwater Christian Coll (FL)
Cleary U (MI)
Clemson U (SC)
Cleveland State U (OH)
Coastal Carolina U (SC)
Coe Coll (IA)
The Coll at Brockport, State U of New York (NY)
Coll of Charleston (SC)
Coll of Coastal Georgia (GA)
The Coll of Idaho (ID)
Coll of Mount St. Joseph (OH)
The Coll of New Jersey (NJ)
The Coll of New Rochelle (NY)
Coll of Saint Benedict (MN)
Coll of Saint Elizabeth (NJ)
Coll of Saint Mary (NE)
The Coll of Saint Rose (NY)
The Coll of St. Scholastica (MN)
Coll of the Ozarks (MO)
The Coll of William and Mary (VA)
Colorado Mountain Coll (CO)
Colorado Mountain Coll, Alpine Campus (CO)
Colorado Mountain Coll, Timberline Campus (CO)
Colorado State U (CO)
Columbia Centro Universitario, Yauco (PR)
Columbia Coll (MO)
Columbia Coll (SC)
Columbia Coll Chicago (IL)
Columbus State U (GA)
Concordia Coll (MN)

Concordia Coll Alabama (AL)
Concordia Coll–New York (NY)
Concordia U (CA)
Concordia U (OR)
Concordia U (QC, Canada)
Concordia U Chicago (IL)
Concordia U, Nebraska (NE)
Concordia U, St. Paul (MN)
Concordia U Texas (TX)
Concordia U Wisconsin (WI)
Concord U (WV)
Converse Coll (SC)
Corban U (OR)
Cornerstone U (MI)
Crossroads Coll (MN)
Crown Coll (MN)
Culver-Stockton Coll (MO)
Curry Coll (MA)
Dakota State U (SD)
Dakota Wesleyan U (SD)
Dalhousie U (NS, Canada)
Dallas Baptist U (TX)
Dalton State Coll (GA)
Daniel Webster Coll (NH)
Davenport U, Grand Rapids (MI)
Daytona State Coll (FL)
Delta State U (MS)
DePaul U (IL)
DEREE—The American Coll of
  Greece (Greece)
DeSales U (PA)
DeVry Coll of New York (NY)
DeVry U, Phoenix (AZ)
DeVry U, Pomona (CA)
DeVry U, Westminster (CO)
DeVry U, Miramar (FL)
DeVry U, Orlando (FL)
DeVry U, Decatur (GA)
DeVry U, Chicago (IL)
DeVry U, Kansas City (MO)
DeVry U, North Brunswick (NJ)
DeVry U, Columbus (OH)
DeVry U, Fort Washington (PA)
DeVry U, Houston (TX)
DeVry U, Irving (TX)
DeVry U, Arlington (VA)
DeVry U, Federal Way (WA)
DeVry U Online (IL)
Dillard U (LA)
Doane Coll (NE)
Dominican Coll (NY)
Dominican U (IL)
Dordt Coll (IA)
Drake U (IA)
Drew U (NJ)
Drury U (MO)
Dunwoody Coll of Technology (MN)
East Carolina U (NC)
East Central U (OK)
Eastern Illinois U (IL)
Eastern Mennonite U (VA)
Eastern Michigan U (MI)
Eastern New Mexico U (NM)
Eastern Washington U (WA)
East Tennessee State U (TN)
East-West U (IL)
Eckerd Coll (FL)
Edgewood Coll (WI)
Edinboro U of Pennsylvania (PA)
EDP Coll of Puerto Rico, Inc. (PR)
Elizabeth City State U (NC)
Elizabethtown Coll (PA)
Elmira Coll (NY)
Elon U (NC)
Emmanuel Coll (MA)
Emporia State U (KS)
Endicott Coll (MA)
Evangel U (MO)
Excelsior Coll (NY)
Fairfield U (CT)
Fairleigh Dickinson U, Coll at
  Florham (NJ)
Fairleigh Dickinson U, Metropolitan
  Campus (NJ)
Fairmont State U (WV)
Farmingdale State Coll (NY)
Faulkner U (AL)
Fayetteville State U (NC)
Felician Coll (NJ)
Ferris State U (MI)
Ferrum Coll (VA)
FIDM/The Fashion Inst of Design &
  Merchandising, Los Angeles
  Campus (CA)
Fisher Coll (MA)
Five Towns Coll (NY)
Flagler Coll (FL)

Florida Ag and Mech U (FL)
Florida Atlantic U (FL)
Florida Coll (FL)
Florida Intl U (FL)
Florida National U (FL)
Florida Southern Coll (FL)
Florida State U (FL)
Fort Lewis Coll (CO)
Francis Marion U (SC)
Franklin & Marshall Coll (PA)
Franklin Pierce U (NH)
Franklin U (OH)
Friends U (KS)
Frostburg State U (MD)
Furman U (SC)
Gallaudet U (DC)
Gannon U (PA)
Gardner-Webb U (NC)
Geneva Coll (PA)
George Fox U (OR)
George Mason U (VA)
Georgetown Coll (KY)
Georgetown U (DC)
Georgia Coll & State U (GA)
Georgia Southern U (GA)
Georgia Southwestern State U
  (GA)
Georgia State U (GA)
Gettysburg Coll (PA)
Goldey-Beacom Coll (DE)
Gonzaga U (WA)
Gordon Coll (MA)
Goshen Coll (IN)
Goucher Coll (MD)
Governors State U (IL)
Graceland U (IA)
Grace U (NE)
Grambling State U (LA)
Grand View U (IA)
Granite State Coll (NH)
Grantham U (MO)
Greenville Coll (IL)
Guilford Coll (NC)
Gustavus Adolphus Coll (MN)
Hamline U (MN)
Hampton U (VA)
Harding U (AR)
Hardin-Simmons U (TX)
Harris-Stowe State U (MO)
Hartwick Coll (NY)
Hawai'i Pacific U (HI)
HEC Montreal (QC, Canada)
Hickey Coll (MO)
High Point U (NC)
Hilbert Coll (NY)
Hillsdale Coll (MI)
Hiram Coll (OH)
Hofstra U (NY)
Holy Cross Coll (IN)
Holy Family U (PA)
Holy Names U (CA)
Hood Coll (MD)
Hope Coll (MI)
Hope Intl U (CA)
Houghton Coll (NY)
Howard Payne U (TX)
Humboldt State U (CA)
Huntingdon Coll (AL)
Huntington U (IN)
Husson U (ME)
Illinois Coll (IL)
Illinois Inst of Technology (IL)
Illinois State U (IL)
Illinois Wesleyan U (IL)
Immaculata U (PA)
Indiana State U (IN)
Indiana Tech (IN)
Indiana U of Pennsylvania (PA)
Indiana U–Purdue U Fort Wayne
  (IN)
Indiana Wesleyan U (IN)
Inter American U of Puerto Rico,
  Bayamón Campus (PR)
Inter American U of Puerto Rico,
  Fajardo Campus (PR)
Inter American U of Puerto Rico,
  Ponce Campus (PR)
Inter American U of Puerto Rico,
  San Germán Campus (PR)
Intl Business Coll, Fort Wayne (IN)
Intl U in Geneva (Switzerland)
Iona Coll (NY)
Iowa State U of Science and
  Technology (IA)
Iowa Wesleyan Coll (IA)
Ithaca Coll (NY)
Jacksonville State U (AL)

James Madison U (VA)
Jamestown Business Coll (NY)
Jamestown Coll (ND)
Jarvis Christian Coll (TX)
John Brown U (AR)
John Cabot U (Italy)
John Carroll U (OH)
Johnson C. Smith U (NC)
Johnson State Coll (VT)
Jones Coll, Jacksonville (FL)
Jones Intl U (CO)
Judson U (IL)
Juniata Coll (PA)
Kansas State U (KS)
Kansas Wesleyan U (KS)
Kean U (NJ)
Keene State Coll (NH)
Kennesaw State U (GA)
Kent State U (OH)
Kent State U at Ashtabula (OH)
Kent State U at Geauga (OH)
Kent State U at Salem (OH)
Kent State U at Stark (OH)
Kent State U at Trumbull (OH)
Kent State U at Tuscarawas (OH)
Kentucky Christian U (KY)
Kentucky Wesleyan Coll (KY)
Keuka Coll (NY)
Keystone Coll (PA)
King Coll (TN)
The King's Coll (NY)
King's Coll (PA)
The King's U Coll (AB, Canada)
Kutztown U of Pennsylvania (PA)
Kuyper Coll (MI)
LaGrange Coll (GA)
Lake Erie Coll (OH)
Lakeland Coll (WI)
Lake Superior State U (MI)
Lamar U (TX)
Lander U (SC)
Lane Coll (TN)
Langston U (OK)
La Salle U (PA)
Lasell Coll (MA)
La Sierra U (CA)
Laurel U (NC)
Lawrence Technological U (MI)
Lebanese American U (Lebanon)
Lebanon Valley Coll (PA)
Lees-McRae Coll (NC)
Lee U (TN)
Lehman Coll of the City U of New
  York (NY)
Le Moyne Coll (NY)
Lesley U (MA)
LeTourneau U (TX)
Lewis-Clark State Coll (ID)
Lewis U (IL)
Liberty U (VA)
Life U (GA)
Limestone Coll (SC)
Lincoln Memorial U (TN)
Lincoln U (PA)
Lindenwood U (MO)
Lindsey Wilson Coll (KY)
Lipscomb U (TN)
Lock Haven U of Pennsylvania (PA)
Long Island U–Brooklyn Campus
  (NY)
Long Island U–C. W. Post Campus
  (NY)
Longwood U (VA)
Louisiana Coll (LA)
Louisiana State U and Ag and
  Mech Coll (LA)
Louisiana State U at Alexandria
  (LA)
Louisiana State U in Shreveport
  (LA)
Lourdes U (OH)
Loyola Marymount U (CA)
Loyola U New Orleans (LA)
Lubbock Christian U (TX)
Luther Coll (IA)
Lynchburg Coll (VA)
Lynn U (FL)
Lyon Coll (AR)
Madonna U (MI)
Maharishi U of Management (IA)
Maine Maritime Acad (ME)
Malone U (OH)
Manchester U (IN)
Manhattanville Coll (NY)
Mansfield U of Pennsylvania (PA)
Maranatha Baptist Bible Coll (WI)
Marian U (WI)

Marietta Coll (OH)
Marist Coll (NY)
Marquette U (WI)
Marshall U (WV)
Mars Hill Coll (NC)
Mary Baldwin Coll (VA)
Marymount Coll, Palos Verdes,
  California (CA)
Marymount Manhattan Coll (NY)
Marymount U (VA)
Maryville Coll (TN)
Maryville U of Saint Louis (MO)
Marywood U (PA)
Massachusetts Coll of Liberal Arts
  (MA)
The Master's Coll and Sem (CA)
Mayville State U (ND)
McDaniel Coll (MD)
McKendree U (IL)
McMurry U (TX)
McNeese State U (LA)
Medaille Coll (NY)
Menlo Coll (CA)
Mercy Coll (NY)
Mercyhurst U (PA)
Merrimack Coll (MA)
Messiah Coll (PA)
Metropolitan State U of Denver
  (CO)
Miami U (OH)
Michigan State U (MI)
Mid-Continent U (KY)
Middle Tennessee State U (TN)
Midland U (TX)
Millersville U of Pennsylvania (PA)
Millikin U (IL)
Millsaps Coll (MS)
Milwaukee School of Eng (WI)
Minnesota State U Mankato (MN)
Minnesota State U Moorhead (MN)
Minot State U (ND)
Misericordia U (PA)
Mississippi Coll (MS)
Mississippi State U (MS)
Mississippi U for Women (MS)
Mississippi Valley State U (MS)
Missouri Baptist U (MO)
Missouri State U (MO)
Missouri U of Science and
  Technology (MO)
Missouri Western State U (MO)
Mitchell Coll (CT)
Molloy Coll (NY)
Monmouth Coll (IL)
Monmouth U (NJ)
Montclair State U (NJ)
Montreat Coll, Montreat (NC)
Moravian Coll (PA)
Morehead State U (KY)
Morehouse Coll (GA)
Morningside Coll (IA)
Morris Coll (SC)
Morrisville State Coll (NY)
Mount Allison U (NB, Canada)
Mount Aloysius Coll (PA)
Mount Marty Coll (SD)
Mount Mary Coll (WI)
Mount Mercy U (IA)
Mount Saint Mary Coll (NY)
Mount St. Mary's Coll (CA)
Mount Vernon Nazarene U (OH)
Muhlenberg Coll (PA)
Murray State U (KY)
National U (CA)
Nazareth Coll of Rochester (NY)
Neumann U (PA)
Newberry Coll (SC)
Newbury Coll (MA)
New England Coll (NH)
New England Inst of Technology
  (RI)
New Jersey City U (NJ)
New Jersey Inst of Technology (NJ)
Newman U (KS)
New Mexico Highlands U (NM)
New Mexico Inst of Mining and
  Technology (NM)
New Mexico State U (NM)
Niagara U (NY)
Nicholls State U (LA)
North Carolina Central U (NC)
North Carolina State U (NC)
North Carolina Wesleyan Coll (NC)
North Central Coll (IL)
Northcentral U (AZ)
North Dakota State U (ND)
Northeastern Illinois U (IL)

Northeastern U (MA)
Northern Arizona U (AZ)
Northern Illinois U (IL)
Northern Michigan U (MI)
North Greenville U (SC)
Northland Coll (WI)
Northwestern Coll (IA)
Northwestern Coll (MN)
Northwestern Oklahoma State U
  (OK)
Northwestern State U of Louisiana
  (LA)
Northwest Missouri State U (MO)
Northwest Nazarene U (ID)
Northwest U (WA)
Northwood U, Florida Campus (FL)
Northwood U, Michigan Campus
  (MI)
Northwood U, Texas Campus (TX)
Norwich U (VT)
Notre Dame de Namur U (CA)
Nova Southeastern U (FL)
Nyack Coll (NY)
Oakland City U (IN)
Oglethorpe U (GA)
Ohio Dominican U (OH)
The Ohio State U (OH)
The Ohio State U at Lima (OH)
The Ohio State U at Marion (OH)
The Ohio State U–Mansfield
  Campus (OH)
The Ohio State U–Newark Campus
  (OH)
Ohio U (OH)
Ohio Valley U (WV)
Ohio Wesleyan U (OH)
Okanagan Coll (BC, Canada)
Oklahoma Christian U (OK)
Oklahoma City U (OK)
Oklahoma State U (OK)
Old Dominion U (VA)
Olivet Coll (MI)
Oral Roberts U (OK)
Oregon State U (OR)
Ouachita Baptist U (AR)
Pace U (NY)
Pacific Lutheran U (WA)
Pacific States U (CA)
Pacific U (OR)
Paine Coll (GA)
Palm Beach Atlantic U (FL)
Palm Beach State Coll (FL)
Park U (MO)
Paul Quinn Coll (TX)
Peirce Coll (PA)
Penn State Beaver (PA)
Penn State Brandywine (PA)
Penn State DuBois (PA)
Penn State Erie, The Behrend Coll
  (PA)
Penn State Fayette, The Eberly
  Campus (PA)
Penn State Greater Allegheny (PA)
Penn State Harrisburg (PA)
Penn State Hazleton (PA)
Penn State Mont Alto (PA)
Penn State New Kensington (PA)
Penn State Shenango (PA)
Penn State Wilkes-Barre (PA)
Penn State Worthington Scranton
  (PA)
Penn State York (PA)
Pennsylvania Coll of Technology
  (PA)
Pepperdine U, Malibu (CA)
Philadelphia U (PA)
Piedmont Coll (GA)
Pittsburg State U (KS)
Plymouth State U (NH)
Point Loma Nazarene U (CA)
Point Park U (PA)
Point U (GA)
Polytechnic U of Puerto Rico (PR)
Portland State U (OR)
Post U (CT)
Potomac Coll (DC)
Potomac State Coll of West Virginia
  U (WV)
Presbyterian Coll (SC)
Prescott Coll (AZ)
Principia Coll (IL)
Providence Coll (RI)
Purdue U (IN)
Purdue U Calumet (IN)
Queens U of Charlotte (NC)
Quincy U (IL)
Quinnipiac U (CT)

Radford U (VA)
Ramapo Coll of New Jersey (NJ)
Rasmussen Coll Bismarck (ND)
Rasmussen Coll Bloomington (MN)
Rasmussen Coll Brooklyn Park (MN)
Rasmussen Coll Eagan (MN)
Rasmussen Coll Fargo (ND)
Rasmussen Coll Fort Myers (FL)
Rasmussen Coll Lake Elmo/Woodbury (MN)
Rasmussen Coll Land O' Lakes (FL)
Rasmussen Coll Mankato (MN)
Rasmussen Coll Moorhead (MN)
Rasmussen Coll New Port Richey (FL)
Rasmussen Coll Ocala (FL)
Rasmussen Coll Rockford (IL)
Rasmussen Coll St. Cloud (MN)
Rasmussen Coll Tampa/Brandon (FL)
Regent U (VA)
Regis U (CO)
Rensselaer Polytechnic Inst (NY)
Rhode Island Coll (RI)
Rhodes Coll (TN)
Rice U (TX)
The Richard Stockton Coll of New Jersey (NJ)
Ripon Coll (WI)
Rivier U (NH)
Roanoke Coll (VA)
Robert Morris U (PA)
Robert Morris U Illinois (IL)
Roberts Wesleyan Coll (NY)
Rochester Inst of Technology (NY)
Rockford Coll (IL)
Rockhurst U (MO)
Rocky Mountain Coll (MT)
Rogers State U (OK)
Roger Williams U (RI)
Rosemont Coll (PA)
Rowan U (NJ)
Rutgers, The State U of New Jersey, Camden (NJ)
Rutgers, The State U of New Jersey, Newark (NJ)
Rutgers, The State U of New Jersey, New Brunswick (NJ)
Sage Coll of Albany (NY)
Saginaw Valley State U (MI)
St. Ambrose U (IA)
St. Andrews U (NC)
St. Bonaventure U (NY)
St. Edward's U (TX)
St. Francis Coll (NY)
St. Gregory's U, Shawnee (OK)
St. John Fisher Coll (NY)
Saint John's U (MN)
St. John's U (NY)
St. Joseph's Coll, Long Island Campus (NY)
St. Joseph's Coll, New York (NY)
Saint Joseph's U (PA)
Saint Leo U (FL)
Saint Louis U (MO)
Saint Martin's U (WA)
Saint Mary-of-the-Woods Coll (IN)
Saint Mary's Coll (IN)
Saint Mary's Coll of California (CA)
St. Mary's U (TX)
Saint Michael's Coll (VT)
St. Norbert Coll (WI)
St. Thomas Aquinas Coll (NY)
St. Thomas U (FL)
Saint Vincent Coll (PA)
Salem Intl U (WV)
Salem State U (MA)
Salisbury U (MD)
Salve Regina U (RI)
Samford U (AL)
Sam Houston State U (TX)
San Diego Christian Coll (CA)
San Diego State U (CA)
San Francisco State U (CA)
San Jose State U (CA)
Santa Fe U of Art and Design (NM)
Schreiner U (TX)
Seattle Pacific U (WA)
Seattle U (WA)
Seminole State Coll of Florida (FL)
Seton Hill U (PA)
Shawnee State U (OH)
Shaw U (NC)
Shenandoah U (VA)
Shepherd U (WV)

Shippensburg U of Pennsylvania (PA)
Siena Heights U (MI)
Sierra Nevada Coll (NV)
Simmons Coll (MA)
Simon Fraser U (BC, Canada)
Simpson Coll (IA)
Simpson U (CA)
Slippery Rock U of Pennsylvania (PA)
Sonoma State U (CA)
Southeastern Louisiana U (LA)
Southeastern Oklahoma State U (OK)
Southeastern U (FL)
Southeast Missouri State U (MO)
Southern Arkansas U–Magnolia (AR)
Southern Connecticut State U (CT)
Southern Illinois U Carbondale (IL)
Southern Illinois U Edwardsville (IL)
Southern Methodist U (TX)
Southern Nazarene U (OK)
Southern New Hampshire U (NH)
Southern Oregon U (OR)
Southern Utah U (UT)
Southwest Baptist U (MO)
Southwestern Adventist U (TX)
Southwestern Coll (KS)
Spring Arbor U (MI)
Spring Hill Coll (AL)
State U of New York at Fredonia (NY)
State U of New York at New Paltz (NY)
State U of New York at Oswego (NY)
State U of New York at Plattsburgh (NY)
State U of New York Coll at Geneseo (NY)
State U of New York Coll at Old Westbury (NY)
State U of New York Coll at Potsdam (NY)
State U of New York Empire State Coll (NY)
State U of New York Inst of Technology (NY)
Stephen F. Austin State U (TX)
Stephens Coll (MO)
Sterling Coll (KS)
Stetson U (FL)
Stevenson U (MD)
Stonehill Coll (MA)
Stony Brook U, State U of New York (NY)
Stratford U, Falls Church (VA)
Stratford U, Woodbridge (VA)
Suffolk U (MA)
Sullivan U (KY)
Sul Ross State U (TX)
Susquehanna U (PA)
Syracuse U (NY)
Tabor Coll (KS)
Tarleton State U (TX)
Taylor U (IN)
Temple U (PA)
Tennessee State U (TN)
Tennessee Wesleyan Coll (TN)
Texas A&M Intl U (TX)
Texas A&M U (TX)
Texas A&M U–Commerce (TX)
Texas A&M U–Kingsville (TX)
Texas Lutheran U (TX)
Texas Southern U (TX)
Texas State U–San Marcos (TX)
Texas Wesleyan U (TX)
Texas Woman's U (TX)
Thomas Edison State Coll (NJ)
Thomas More Coll (KY)
Thomas U (GA)
Thompson Rivers U (BC, Canada)
Tiffin U (OH)
Trent U (ON, Canada)
Trevecca Nazarene U (TN)
Trident U Intl (CA)
Trine U (IN)
Trinity Christian Coll (IL)
Trinity U (TX)
Troy U (AL)
Truman State U (MO)
Tulane U (LA)
Tuskegee U (AL)
Union Coll (KY)
Union Coll (NE)

Union U (TN)
United States Air Force Acad (CO)
United States Military Acad (NY)
Universidad Adventista de las Antillas (PR)
Université de Sherbrooke (QC, Canada)
Université du Québec en Outaouais (QC, Canada)
Université Sainte-Anne (NS, Canada)
U at Albany, State U of New York (NY)
U at Buffalo, the State U of New York (NY)
The U of Akron (OH)
The U of Alabama (AL)
The U of Alabama at Birmingham (AL)
U of Alaska Anchorage (AK)
U of Alaska Fairbanks (AK)
U of Arkansas at Little Rock (AR)
U of Arkansas–Fort Smith (AR)
The U of British Columbia (BC, Canada)
U of California, Berkeley (CA)
U of California, Irvine (CA)
U of California, Merced (CA)
U of California, Riverside (CA)
U of Central Arkansas (AR)
U of Central Florida (FL)
U of Central Oklahoma (OK)
U of Charleston (WV)
U of Cincinnati (OH)
U of Colorado Boulder (CO)
U of Colorado Colorado Springs (CO)
U of Colorado Denver (CO)
U of Dallas (TX)
U of Denver (CO)
U of Evansville (IN)
The U of Findlay (OH)
U of Florida (FL)
U of Georgia (GA)
U of Great Falls (MT)
U of Guam (GU)
U of Hartford (CT)
U of Hawaii at Hilo (HI)
U of Hawaii at Manoa (HI)
U of Hawaii–West Oahu (HI)
U of Houston (TX)
U of Houston–Clear Lake (TX)
U of Houston–Downtown (TX)
U of Houston–Victoria (TX)
U of Idaho (ID)
U of Illinois at Chicago (IL)
U of Illinois at Springfield (IL)
U of Illinois at Urbana–Champaign (IL)
The U of Iowa (IA)
The U of Kansas (KS)
U of La Verne (CA)
U of Louisiana at Lafayette (LA)
U of Louisiana at Monroe (LA)
U of Maine at Fort Kent (ME)
U of Maine at Machias (ME)
U of Maryland Eastern Shore (MD)
U of Maryland U Coll (MD)
U of Mary Washington (VA)
U of Massachusetts Amherst (MA)
U of Massachusetts Boston (MA)
U of Memphis (TN)
U of Miami (FL)
U of Michigan (MI)
U of Michigan–Dearborn (MI)
U of Michigan–Flint (MI)
U of Minnesota, Crookston (MN)
U of Minnesota, Duluth (MN)
U of Minnesota, Twin Cities Campus (MN)
U of Mississippi (MS)
U of Missouri (MO)
U of Missouri–Kansas City (MO)
U of Missouri–St. Louis (MO)
U of Mobile (AL)
The U of Montana Western (MT)
U of Montevallo (AL)
U of Mount Union (OH)
U of Nebraska at Kearney (NE)
U of Nebraska at Omaha (NE)
U of Nebraska–Lincoln (NE)
U of Nevada, Las Vegas (NV)
U of Nevada, Reno (NV)
U of New Brunswick Fredericton (NB, Canada)
U of New Brunswick Saint John (NB, Canada)

U of New England (ME)
U of New Hampshire (NH)
U of New Hampshire at Manchester (NH)
U of New Haven (CT)
U of New Mexico (NM)
U of New Orleans (LA)
U of North Alabama (AL)
U of North Carolina at Asheville (NC)
The U of North Carolina at Chapel Hill (NC)
The U of North Carolina at Charlotte (NC)
The U of North Carolina at Greensboro (NC)
The U of North Carolina at Pembroke (NC)
The U of North Carolina Wilmington (NC)
U of North Dakota (ND)
U of Northern Colorado (CO)
U of Northern Iowa (IA)
U of North Florida (FL)
U of North Georgia (GA)
U of Oklahoma (OK)
U of Pennsylvania (PA)
U of Pikeville (KY)
U of Pittsburgh at Bradford (PA)
U of Pittsburgh at Greensburg (PA)
U of Portland (OR)
U of Puget Sound (WA)
U of Redlands (CA)
U of Regina (SK, Canada)
U of Rhode Island (RI)
U of Richmond (VA)
U of St. Francis (IL)
U of Saint Joseph (CT)
U of Saint Mary (KS)
U of St. Thomas (MN)
U of St. Thomas (TX)
U of San Diego (CA)
The U of Scranton (PA)
U of South Alabama (AL)
U of South Carolina (SC)
U of South Carolina Aiken (SC)
U of South Carolina Upstate (SC)
U of Southern California (CA)
U of Southern Indiana (IN)
U of Southern Maine (ME)
U of Southern Mississippi (MS)
The U of Tampa (FL)
The U of Tennessee (TN)
The U of Tennessee at Chattanooga (TN)
The U of Tennessee at Martin (TN)
The U of Texas at Arlington (TX)
The U of Texas at Austin (TX)
The U of Texas at Brownsville (TX)
The U of Texas at El Paso (TX)
The U of Texas at San Antonio (TX)
The U of Texas of the Permian Basin (TX)
The U of Texas–Pan American (TX)
U of the District of Columbia (DC)
U of the Incarnate Word (TX)
U of the Ozarks (AR)
U of the Virgin Islands (VI)
The U of Toledo (OH)
U of Tulsa (OK)
U of Utah (UT)
U of Vermont (VT)
U of Washington, Bothell (WA)
U of Washington, Tacoma (WA)
U of Waterloo (ON, Canada)
The U of West Alabama (AL)
The U of Western Ontario (ON, Canada)
U of West Florida (FL)
U of West Georgia (GA)
U of Windsor (ON, Canada)
U of Wisconsin–Eau Claire (WI)
U of Wisconsin–Green Bay (WI)
U of Wisconsin–La Crosse (WI)
U of Wisconsin–Madison (WI)
U of Wisconsin–Parkside (WI)
U of Wisconsin–Platteville (WI)
U of Wisconsin–Stevens Point (WI)
U of Wisconsin–Stout (WI)
U of Wisconsin–Superior (WI)
U of Wyoming (WY)
Upper Iowa U (IA)
Ursuline Coll (OH)
Utah State U (UT)
Utica Coll (NY)
Valdosta State U (GA)
Valley City State U (ND)

Vermont Tech Coll (VT)
Villanova U (PA)
Virginia Commonwealth U (VA)
Virginia Intermont Coll (VA)
Virginia Polytechnic Inst and State U (VA)
Virginia State U (VA)
Virginia Wesleyan Coll (VA)
Viterbo U (WI)
Wagner Coll (NY)
Walden U (MN)
Waldorf Coll (IA)
Walla Walla U (WA)
Walsh U (OH)
Warner Pacific Coll (OR)
Wartburg Coll (IA)
Washburn U (KS)
Washington and Lee U (VA)
Washington Coll (MD)
Washington State U (WA)
Washington U in St. Louis (MO)
Wayland Baptist U (TX)
Waynesburg U (PA)
Wayne State Coll (NE)
Webber Intl U (FL)
Weber State U (UT)
Webster U (MO)
Wells Coll (NY)
Wentworth Inst of Technology (MA)
Wesleyan Coll (GA)
Wesley Coll (DE)
West Chester U of Pennsylvania (PA)
Western Carolina U (NC)
Western Connecticut State U (CT)
Western Illinois U (IL)
Western Kentucky U (KY)
Western Michigan U (MI)
Western State Colorado U (CO)
Western Washington U (WA)
Westfield State U (MA)
West Liberty U (WV)
Westminster Coll (MO)
West Texas A&M U (TX)
West Virginia State U (WV)
West Virginia U (WV)
West Virginia U Inst of Technology (WV)
West Virginia Wesleyan Coll (WV)
Wheeling Jesuit U (WV)
Whitworth U (WA)
Wichita State U (KS)
Widener U (PA)
Wilberforce U (OH)
Wilkes U (PA)
William Jewell Coll (MO)
William Paterson U of New Jersey (NJ)
William Peace U (NC)
William Penn U (IA)
Wilmington U (DE)
Winthrop U (SC)
Wittenberg U (OH)
Woodbury U (CA)
Worcester Polytechnic Inst (MA)
Worcester State U (MA)
Wright State U (OH)
Xavier U (OH)
Xavier U of Louisiana (LA)
York Coll of Pennsylvania (PA)
York Coll of the City U of New York (NY)
Young Harris Coll (GA)
Youngstown State U (OH)

BUSINESS ADMINISTRATION, MANAGEMENT AND OPERATIONS RELATED
Adams State U (CO)
Alverno Coll (WI)
Babson Coll (MA)
Becker Coll (MA)
Benedictine U (IL)
Blackburn Coll (IL)
Bowling Green State U (OH)
Bradley U (IL)
California Polytechnic State U, San Luis Obispo (CA)
California State U, Chico (CA)
Capital U (OH)
Carlos Albizu U, Miami Campus (FL)
Clayton State U (GA)
Colorado Mesa U (CO)
Cornerstone U (MI)
Crossroads Coll (MN)
Crown Coll (MN)

DePaul U (IL)
DeVry Coll of New York (NY)
DeVry U, Phoenix (AZ)
DeVry U, Pomona (CA)
DeVry U, Westminster (CO)
DeVry U, Miramar (FL)
DeVry U, Orlando (FL)
DeVry U, Decatur (GA)
DeVry U, Chicago (IL)
DeVry U, Kansas City (MO)
DeVry U, North Brunswick (NJ)
DeVry U, Columbus (OH)
DeVry U, Fort Washington (PA)
DeVry U, Houston (TX)
DeVry U, Irving (TX)
DeVry U, Arlington (VA)
DeVry U, Federal Way (WA)
DeVry U Online (IL)
Eastern New Mexico U (NM)
Elizabethtown Coll (PA)
Embry-Riddle Aeronautical U–
    Daytona (FL)
Embry-Riddle Aeronautical U–
    Prescott (AZ)
Embry-Riddle Aeronautical U–
    Worldwide (FL)
Florida Inst of Technology (FL)
Franklin U (OH)
Gettysburg Coll (PA)
Hodges U (FL)
Hofstra U (NY)
Howard Payne U (TX)
Huntingdon Coll (AL)
Illinois Inst of Technology (IL)
Indiana Tech (IN)
John Brown U (AR)
Judson U (IL)
La Roche Coll (PA)
Le Moyne Coll (NY)
Limestone Coll (SC)
Lincoln Christian U (IL)
Lincoln Memorial U (TN)
Loyola U Chicago (IL)
Malone U (OH)
Marquette U (WI)
Mayville State U (ND)
Mercer U (GA)
Miami Dade Coll (FL)
Millikin U (IL)
Missouri Baptist U (MO)
Missouri State U (MO)
Morris Coll (SC)
Mount Mary Coll (WI)
North Dakota State U (ND)
Northwest Christian U (OR)
Oakland City U (IN)
Pennsylvania Coll of Technology
    (PA)
Pensacola State Coll (FL)
Pepperdine U, Malibu (CA)
Polk State Coll (FL)
Purdue U (IN)
Rider U (NJ)
Roosevelt U (IL)
Saint Leo U (FL)
Samford U (AL)
San Jose State U (CA)
Shenandoah U (VA)
Southern Nazarene U (OK)
Stony Brook U, State U of New York
    (NY)
Texas A&M U–Kingsville (TX)
Texas Christian U (TX)
The U of Alabama at Birmingham
    (AL)
U of Charleston (WV)
U of Houston–Clear Lake (TX)
U of Illinois at Springfield (IL)
U of Louisville (KY)
U of Maryland, Baltimore County
    (MD)
U of Maryland U Coll (MD)
U of Michigan–Dearborn (MI)
U of Ottawa (ON, Canada)
U of Pennsylvania (PA)
U of Puerto Rico at Bayamón (PR)
U of Puerto Rico at Ponce (PR)
U of St. Thomas (MN)
The U of Scranton (PA)
U of Southern Maine (ME)
U of the Incarnate Word (TX)
The U of Toledo (OH)
U of Waterloo (ON, Canada)
The U of Western Ontario (ON,
    Canada)
U of Wyoming (WY)
Ursuline Coll (OH)

Valdosta State U (GA)
Viterbo U (WI)
Washington U in St. Louis (MO)
Widener U (PA)
Woodbury U (CA)

BUSINESS AND PERSONAL/ FINANCIAL SERVICES MARKETING
DeSales U (PA)
Lindenwood U (MO)
Oklahoma City U (OK)
Purdue U (IN)
Walla Walla U (WA)

BUSINESS AUTOMATION/ TECHNOLOGY/DATA ENTRY
East Carolina U (NC)
Inter American U of Puerto Rico,
    Bayamón Campus (PR)
Mount Vernon Nazarene U (OH)
Purdue U (IN)
Suffolk U (MA)

BUSINESS/COMMERCE
Adams State U (CO)
Alice Lloyd Coll (KY)
Alvernia U (PA)
American Coll of Thessaloniki
    (Greece)
American Jewish U (CA)
Anderson U (SC)
Asbury U (KY)
Auburn U at Montgomery (AL)
Aurora U (IL)
Austin Peay State U (TN)
Avila U (MO)
Baker U (KS)
Ball State U (IN)
Baylor U (TX)
Bellarmine U (KY)
Belmont U (TN)
Bentley U (MA)
Bethel Coll (KS)
Bloomsburg U of Pennsylvania (PA)
Boise State U (ID)
Bowling Green State U (OH)
Brock U (ON, Canada)
California Baptist U (CA)
California State U, Dominguez Hills
    (CA)
Cambridge Coll (MA)
Canisius Coll (NY)
Caribbean U (PR)
The Catholic U of America (DC)
Central State U (OH)
Champlain Coll (VT)
Clayton State U (GA)
The Coll of New Rochelle (NY)
Coll of Staten Island of the City U of
    New York (NY)
Colorado Mesa U (CO)
Columbia Centro Universitario,
    Caguas (PR)
Columbia Coll (MO)
Columbus State U (GA)
Concordia U, Nebraska (NE)
Concordia U Texas (TX)
Covenant Coll (GA)
Dalhousie U (NS, Canada)
Davenport U, Grand Rapids (MI)
Delta State U (MS)
DeSales U (PA)
DeVry U, Phoenix (AZ)
DeVry U, Pomona (CA)
DeVry U, Westminster (CO)
DeVry U, Miramar (FL)
DeVry U, Orlando (FL)
DeVry U, Decatur (GA)
DeVry U, Chicago (IL)
DeVry U, Kansas City (MO)
DeVry U, Fort Washington (PA)
DeVry U, Houston (TX)
DeVry U, Irving (TX)
DeVry U, Arlington (VA)
DeVry U, Federal Way (WA)
DeVry U Online (IL)
Drake U (IA)
Earlham Coll (IN)
East Central U (OK)
Eastern Michigan U (MI)
East Texas Baptist U (TX)
Edgewood Coll (WI)
Florida State U (FL)
Framingham State U (MA)
Franklin Coll (IN)
Georgia Coll & State U (GA)
Georgia Gwinnett Coll (GA)

Goshen Coll (IN)
Grand Valley State U (MI)
Hawai`i Pacific U (HI)
HEC Montreal (QC, Canada)
Henderson State U (AR)
Hillsdale Free Will Baptist Coll (OK)
Hofstra U (NY)
Hollins U (VA)
Howard Payne U (TX)
Huntingdon Coll (AL)
Indiana U Bloomington (IN)
Indiana U East (IN)
Indiana U Kokomo (IN)
Indiana U Northwest (IN)
Indiana U of Pennsylvania (PA)
Indiana U–Purdue U Fort Wayne
    (IN)
Indiana U–Purdue U Indianapolis
    (IN)
Indiana U South Bend (IN)
Indiana U Southeast (IN)
Iowa Wesleyan Coll (IA)
Ithaca Coll (NY)
The Johns Hopkins U (MD)
Johnson State Coll (VT)
Judson Coll (AL)
Juniata Coll (PA)
Kalamazoo Coll (MI)
Kansas State U (KS)
Kentucky State U (KY)
La Sierra U (CA)
Lewis U (IL)
Limestone Coll (SC)
Linfield Coll (OR)
Lourdes U (OH)
Loyola Marymount U (CA)
Loyola U Maryland (MD)
Manchester U (IN)
Maryville Coll (TN)
Maryville U of Saint Louis (MO)
Massachusetts Inst of Technology
    (MA)
McMurry U (TX)
Mercer U (GA)
Midwestern State U (TX)
Milwaukee School of Eng (WI)
Mississippi U for Women (MS)
Missouri State U (MO)
Molloy Coll (NY)
Montana State U (MT)
Montana Tech of The U of Montana
    (MT)
Morehead State U (KY)
Mount Allison U (NB, Canada)
Mount Mary Coll (WI)
Mount Mercy U (IA)
Mount St. Mary's U (MD)
Mount Vernon Nazarene U (OH)
Murray State U (KY)
New England Inst of Technology
    (RI)
New Mexico State U (NM)
Niagara U (NY)
Norfolk State U (VA)
Northeastern Illinois U (IL)
Northeastern U (MA)
Northern Illinois U (IL)
Northern Michigan U (MI)
Oakland U (MI)
The Ohio State U at Lima (OH)
The Ohio State U at Marion (OH)
The Ohio State U–Mansfield
    Campus (OH)
The Ohio State U–Newark Campus
    (OH)
Ohio Valley U (WV)
Oklahoma Christian U (OK)
Oklahoma City U (OK)
Pace U (NY)
Pacific Union Coll (CA)
Penn State Abington (PA)
Penn State Altoona (PA)
Penn State Berks (PA)
Penn State Lehigh Valley (PA)
Penn State Schuylkill (PA)
Plymouth State U (NH)
Purdue U (IN)
Purdue U Calumet (IN)
Randolph Coll (VA)
Regis Coll (MA)
Rhode Island Coll (RI)
Rochester Inst of Technology (NY)
Roosevelt U (IL)
Saginaw Valley State U (MI)
St. Ambrose U (IA)
Saint Anselm Coll (NH)
Saint Joseph's Coll (IN)

Saint Leo U (FL)
Saint Mary's Coll of California (CA)
St. Thomas U (FL)
Saint Vincent Coll (PA)
Schreiner U (TX)
Seattle Pacific U (WA)
Skidmore Coll (NY)
Southern Arkansas U–Magnolia
    (AR)
Southern Methodist U (TX)
Southwestern U (TX)
Spalding U (KY)
Stephen F. Austin State U (TX)
Suffolk U (MA)
Sweet Briar Coll (VA)
Tabor Coll (KS)
Tarleton State U (TX)
Texas A&M U–Commerce (TX)
Texas A&M U–Kingsville (TX)
Thompson Rivers U (BC, Canada)
Transylvania U (KY)
Trident U Intl (CA)
Trinity Coll of Florida (FL)
Troy U (AL)
The U of Akron (OH)
The U of Arizona (AZ)
U of Arkansas at Little Rock (AR)
U of Bridgeport (CT)
The U of British Columbia (BC,
    Canada)
U of Central Arkansas (AR)
U of Central Florida (FL)
U of Central Oklahoma (OK)
U of Delaware (DE)
U of Denver (CO)
U of Georgia (GA)
U of Hawaii at Manoa (HI)
U of Houston–Clear Lake (TX)
U of Houston–Downtown (TX)
U of Illinois at Urbana–Champaign
    (IL)
The U of Kansas (KS)
U of Kentucky (KY)
U of Maryland, Coll Park (MD)
U of Massachusetts Dartmouth
    (MA)
U of Minnesota, Duluth (MN)
U of Minnesota, Twin Cities
    Campus (MN)
U of Missouri–St. Louis (MO)
U of Nebraska at Omaha (NE)
U of Nevada, Reno (NV)
U of North Texas (TX)
U of Notre Dame (IN)
U of Oregon (OR)
U of Pittsburgh (PA)
U of Redlands (CA)
U of Regina (SK, Canada)
U of Rhode Island (RI)
U of Rochester (NY)
U of Science and Arts of Oklahoma
    (OK)
U of South Alabama (AL)
The U of South Dakota (SD)
U of Southern Indiana (IN)
U of South Florida (FL)
The U of Texas at Austin (TX)
The U of Texas at Dallas (TX)
The U of Texas at San Antonio (TX)
U of the Cumberlands (KY)
The U of Toledo (OH)
U of Tulsa (OK)
U of Utah (UT)
U of Virginia (VA)
The U of Western Ontario (ON,
    Canada)
U of West Florida (FL)
U of Windsor (ON, Canada)
U of Wisconsin–Milwaukee (WI)
Utah State U (UT)
Virginia Commonwealth U (VA)
Wake Forest U (NC)
Waldorf Coll (IA)
Washburn U (KS)
Washington & Jefferson Coll (PA)
Washington State U (WA)
Washington U in St. Louis (MO)
Webber Intl U (FL)
West Chester U of Pennsylvania
    (PA)
Western Michigan U (MI)
Western Oregon U (OR)
Western Washington U (WA)
West Texas A&M U (TX)
West Virginia U (WV)
Wheaton Coll (MA)
Wright State U (OH)

Youngstown State U (OH)

BUSINESS/CORPORATE COMMUNICATIONS
AIB Coll of Business (IA)
Augustana Coll (SD)
Babson Coll (MA)
Bentley U (MA)
Brock U (ON, Canada)
Calvin Coll (MI)
Chestnut Hill Coll (PA)
Cleary U (MI)
Concordia U Chicago (IL)
Duquesne U (PA)
Elon U (NC)
Hawai`i Pacific U (HI)
Holy Names U (CA)
Jones Intl U (CO)
Marietta Coll (OH)
Morningside Coll (IA)
Mount Mary Coll (WI)
North Dakota State U (ND)
Ohio Dominican U (OH)
Penn State Abington (PA)
Point Loma Nazarene U (CA)
Purdue U (IN)
Rockhurst U (MO)
Roosevelt U (IL)
Saint Leo U (FL)
Stevenson U (MD)
Trinity Christian Coll (IL)
The U of Findlay (OH)
U of Houston (TX)
The U of Western Ontario (ON,
    Canada)
Walden U (MN)
Walsh U (OH)

BUSINESS FAMILY AND CONSUMER SCIENCES/ HUMAN SCIENCES
Brigham Young U (UT)
The Ohio State U (OH)
Purdue U (IN)
U of Houston (TX)
Virginia Polytechnic Inst and State
    U (VA)

BUSINESS, MANAGEMENT, AND MARKETING RELATED
Adelphi U (NY)
American U (DC)
Arizona State U (AZ)
Athens State U (AL)
Baylor U (TX)
Benedictine U (IL)
Bentley U (MA)
Bowling Green State U (OH)
Bridgewater State U (MA)
California State U, Dominguez Hills
    (CA)
Central Baptist Coll (AR)
Claflin U (SC)
Clemson U (SC)
Concordia Coll–New York (NY)
Corban U (OR)
Duquesne U (PA)
The Evergreen State Coll (WA)
Farmingdale State Coll (NY)
Franklin Coll Switzerland
    (Switzerland)
Greenville Coll (IL)
Grove City Coll (PA)
Hofstra U (NY)
Howard Payne U (TX)
Inter American U of Puerto Rico,
    Bayamón Campus (PR)
Lehigh U (PA)
Loyola U Chicago (IL)
Mercy Coll (NY)
Mercyhurst U (PA)
Messiah Coll (PA)
Missouri U of Science and
    Technology (MO)
New York U (NY)
Old Dominion U (VA)
Park U (MO)
Penn State U Park (PA)
Point Park U (PA)
Prescott Coll (AZ)
Presentation Coll (SD)
Purdue U (IN)
Purdue U North Central (IN)
Queens U of Charlotte (NC)
Roger Williams U (RI)
Sacred Heart U (CT)
Saint Mary's U of Minnesota (MN)
Seton Hill U (PA)

Sierra Nevada Coll (NV)
Skidmore Coll (NY)
Southeastern U (FL)
Southern California Inst of Technology (CA)
Southern New Hampshire U (NH)
State U of New York at Plattsburgh (NY)
State U of New York Coll of Agriculture and Technology at Cobleskill (NY)
State U of New York Coll of Technology at Alfred (NY)
State U of New York Coll of Technology at Canton (NY)
State U of New York Maritime Coll (NY)
Trevecca Nazarene U (TN)
Troy U (AL)
U of Louisiana at Lafayette (LA)
U of Minnesota, Crookston (MN)
The U of Toledo (OH)
The U of Western Ontario (ON, Canada)
U of Wisconsin–Stout (WI)
Utica Coll (NY)
Walla Walla U (WA)
Wentworth Inst of Technology (MA)
Western State Colorado U (CO)
Young Harris Coll (GA)

BUSINESS/MANAGERIAL ECONOMICS
Anderson U (IN)
Andrews U (MI)
Arkansas State U (AR)
Arkansas Tech U (AR)
Auburn U (AL)
Auburn U at Montgomery (AL)
Augsburg Coll (MN)
Ball State U (IN)
Bard Coll (NY)
Baylor U (TX)
Belmont U (TN)
Benedictine U (IL)
Bentley U (MA)
Bethany Coll (WV)
Boise State U (ID)
Boston Coll (MA)
Bradley U (IL)
Brock U (ON, Canada)
Buena Vista U (IA)
California State U, East Bay (CA)
California State U, Fullerton (CA)
California State U, Long Beach (CA)
California State U, San Bernardino (CA)
Campbellsville U (KY)
Canisius Coll (NY)
Capital U (OH)
Cardinal Stritch U (WI)
Carnegie Mellon U (PA)
Carson-Newman U (TN)
Catawba Coll (NC)
Chapman U (CA)
Chatham U (PA)
Clarion U of Pennsylvania (PA)
Clark Atlanta U (GA)
Cleveland State U (OH)
Coastal Carolina U (SC)
Coll of the Ozarks (MO)
The Coll of Wooster (OH)
Converse Coll (SC)
DePaul U (IL)
Duquesne U (PA)
Eastern Michigan U (MI)
Eastern Washington U (WA)
East Tennessee State U (TN)
Elizabethtown Coll (PA)
Elmira Coll (NY)
Fort Lewis Coll (CO)
Georgia Coll & State U (GA)
Georgia Southern U (GA)
Georgia State U (GA)
Gonzaga U (WA)
Grambling State U (LA)
Grand Valley State U (MI)
Grove City Coll (PA)
Gustavus Adolphus Coll (MN)
Hampden-Sydney Coll (VA)
HEC Montreal (QC, Canada)
Hofstra U (NY)
Hope Coll (MI)
Huntington U (IN)
Illinois Coll (IL)

Indiana U–Purdue U Fort Wayne (IN)
Inter American U of Puerto Rico, Bayamón Campus (PR)
Inter American U of Puerto Rico, San Germán Campus (PR)
Ithaca Coll (NY)
James Madison U (VA)
Kennesaw State U (GA)
Kent State U (OH)
Lafayette Coll (PA)
Lake Superior State U (MI)
La Salle U (PA)
Lehigh U (PA)
Lewis U (IL)
Limestone Coll (SC)
Lincoln Memorial U (TN)
Lipscomb U (TN)
Louisiana State U and Ag and Mech Coll (LA)
Louisiana State U in Shreveport (LA)
Loyola U Chicago (IL)
Loyola U New Orleans (LA)
Marquette U (WI)
Marshall U (WV)
Mars Hill Coll (NC)
Mercyhurst U (PA)
Messiah Coll (PA)
Miami U (OH)
Middle Tennessee State U (TN)
Midwestern State U (TX)
Mills Coll (CA)
Mississippi State U (MS)
Morehead State U (KY)
Mount Allison U (NB, Canada)
New York U (NY)
Niagara U (NY)
North Carolina State U (NC)
Northern Arizona U (AZ)
Northern State U (SD)
Northwest Missouri State U (MO)
Northwood U, Florida Campus (FL)
Oakland U (MI)
Oglethorpe U (GA)
The Ohio State U (OH)
The Ohio State U at Lima (OH)
The Ohio State U at Marion (OH)
The Ohio State U–Mansfield Campus (OH)
The Ohio State U–Newark Campus (OH)
Ohio U (OH)
Ohio Wesleyan U (OH)
Oklahoma City U (OK)
Oklahoma State U (OK)
Old Dominion U (VA)
Olivet Coll (MI)
Park U (MO)
Penn State Abington (PA)
Penn State Altoona (PA)
Penn State Beaver (PA)
Penn State Berks (PA)
Penn State Brandywine (PA)
Penn State DuBois (PA)
Penn State Erie, The Behrend Coll (PA)
Penn State Fayette, The Eberly Campus (PA)
Penn State Greater Allegheny (PA)
Penn State Hazleton (PA)
Penn State Lehigh Valley (PA)
Penn State Mont Alto (PA)
Penn State New Kensington (PA)
Penn State Schuylkill (PA)
Penn State Shenango (PA)
Penn State Wilkes-Barre (PA)
Penn State Worthington Scranton (PA)
Penn State York (PA)
Presbyterian Coll (SC)
Purdue U (IN)
Quinnipiac U (CT)
Randolph-Macon Coll (VA)
Rhode Island Coll (RI)
Rider U (NJ)
Sacred Heart U (CT)
Saginaw Valley State U (MI)
Saint Anselm Coll (NH)
Saint Louis U (MO)
Samford U (AL)
Seattle U (WA)
Sonoma State U (CA)
Southern Connecticut State U (CT)
Southern Illinois U Carbondale (IL)
Southern Illinois U Edwardsville (IL)

Spring Hill Coll (AL)
State U of New York at Plattsburgh (NY)
State U of New York Coll at Potsdam (NY)
Stephen F. Austin State U (TX)
Stetson U (FL)
Tennessee State U (TN)
Texas A&M Intl U (TX)
Texas State U–San Marcos (TX)
Union U (TN)
The U of Alabama (AL)
The U of Alabama at Birmingham (AL)
U of Alaska Anchorage (AK)
The U of Arizona (AZ)
U of California, Irvine (CA)
U of California, Los Angeles (CA)
U of California, Riverside (CA)
U of California, Santa Cruz (CA)
U of Central Florida (FL)
U of Central Oklahoma (OK)
U of Denver (CO)
U of Georgia (GA)
U of Guelph (ON, Canada)
U of Hawaii at Manoa (HI)
U of Idaho (ID)
The U of Iowa (IA)
U of Kentucky (KY)
U of Louisiana at Lafayette (LA)
U of Louisville (KY)
U of Maine at Farmington (ME)
U of Memphis (TN)
U of Miami (FL)
U of Mississippi (MS)
U of Missouri (MO)
U of Nebraska at Omaha (NE)
U of Nebraska–Lincoln (NE)
U of Nevada, Reno (NV)
U of New Brunswick Fredericton (NB, Canada)
U of New Haven (CT)
U of North Alabama (AL)
The U of North Carolina at Charlotte (NC)
The U of North Carolina at Greensboro (NC)
The U of North Carolina Wilmington (NC)
U of North Dakota (ND)
U of North Florida (FL)
U of North Texas (TX)
U of Oklahoma (OK)
U of Rochester (NY)
U of San Diego (CA)
U of South Carolina (SC)
U of Southern Mississippi (MS)
The U of Tennessee (TN)
The U of Tennessee at Martin (TN)
The U of Texas at Arlington (TX)
The U of Texas at San Antonio (TX)
The U of Texas of the Permian Basin (TX)
U of the Incarnate Word (TX)
The U of Toledo (OH)
The U of Western Ontario (ON, Canada)
U of West Florida (FL)
U of West Georgia (GA)
U of Windsor (ON, Canada)
U of Wisconsin–Platteville (WI)
U of Wisconsin–Superior (WI)
U of Wyoming (WY)
Utica Coll (NY)
Valdosta State U (GA)
Villanova U (PA)
Virginia Commonwealth U (VA)
Virginia Polytechnic Inst and State U (VA)
Virginia State U (VA)
Washburn U (KS)
Washington U in St. Louis (MO)
Weber State U (UT)
West Chester U of Pennsylvania (PA)
Western Illinois U (IL)
Western Kentucky U (KY)
Western Michigan U (MI)
Western State Colorado U (CO)
West Liberty U (WV)
Westminster Coll (UT)
West Texas A&M U (TX)
West Virginia U (WV)
West Virginia Wesleyan Coll (WV)
Wheaton Coll (IL)
Widener U (PA)

William Paterson U of New Jersey (NJ)
Wright State U (OH)
Xavier U (OH)
Youngstown State U (OH)

BUSINESS STATISTICS
Baylor U (TX)
HEC Montreal (QC, Canada)
Purdue U (IN)
Southern Oregon U (OR)
U of Denver (CO)
The U of Tennessee (TN)

BUSINESS TEACHER EDUCATION
Adams State U (CO)
Alabama State U (AL)
Alfred U (NY)
Appalachian State U (NC)
Arizona Christian U (AZ)
Arkansas State U (AR)
Arkansas Tech U (AR)
Armstrong Atlantic State U (GA)
Auburn U (AL)
Ball State U (IN)
Baylor U (TX)
Bethune-Cookman U (FL)
Bluefield Coll (VA)
Bowling Green State U (OH)
Buena Vista U (IA)
Buffalo State Coll, State U of New York (NY)
California State U, Dominguez Hills (CA)
Campbellsville U (KY)
Canisius Coll (NY)
Caribbean U (PR)
Carson-Newman U (TN)
Colorado State U (CO)
Concordia Coll (MN)
Concordia U, Nebraska (NE)
Concordia U Wisconsin (WI)
Concord U (WV)
Corban U (OR)
Dakota State U (SD)
Dakota Wesleyan U (SD)
Doane Coll (NE)
Dordt Coll (IA)
East Carolina U (NC)
Eastern Michigan U (MI)
Eastern New Mexico U (NM)
Eastern Washington U (WA)
Edgewood Coll (WI)
Emmanuel Coll (GA)
Evangel U (MO)
Fairmont State U (WV)
Fayetteville State U (NC)
Friends U (KS)
Grace U (NE)
Hampton U (VA)
Hardin-Simmons U (TX)
Henderson State U (AR)
Hofstra U (NY)
Howard Payne U (TX)
Illinois State U (IL)
Immaculata U (PA)
Indiana State U (IN)
Jarvis Christian Coll (TX)
John Brown U (AR)
La Salle U (PA)
Lee U (TN)
Lehman Coll of the City U of New York (NY)
Liberty U (VA)
Lincoln U (MO)
Lindenwood U (MO)
Louisiana Coll (LA)
Maranatha Baptist Bible Coll (WI)
McKendree U (IL)
Mercyhurst U (PA)
Middle Tennessee State U (TN)
Minot State U (ND)
Mississippi Coll (MS)
Mississippi State U (MS)
Missouri Baptist U (MO)
Missouri State U (MO)
Morehead State U (KY)
Mount Mary Coll (WI)
Mount Vernon Nazarene U (OH)
Nazareth Coll of Rochester (NY)
Niagara U (NY)
Nicholls State U (LA)
Norfolk State U (VA)
Northwestern Coll (IA)
Northwest Missouri State U (MO)
Oakland City U (IN)
Ohio Wesleyan U (OH)

Oklahoma City U (OK)
Oral Roberts U (OK)
Purdue U (IN)
Rider U (NJ)
Robert Morris U (PA)
St. Ambrose U (IA)
Saint Mary's Coll (IN)
Saint Vincent Coll (PA)
Southeast Missouri State U (MO)
Southern Arkansas U–Magnolia (AR)
Southern New Hampshire U (NH)
Southern Utah U (UT)
Tabor Coll (KS)
Temple U (PA)
Tennessee State U (TN)
Thomas More Coll (KY)
Trevecca Nazarene U (TN)
Trinity Christian Coll (IL)
Union Coll (NE)
Union U (TN)
The U of British Columbia (BC, Canada)
U of Central Arkansas (AR)
U of Central Oklahoma (OK)
The U of Findlay (OH)
U of Illinois at Urbana–Champaign (IL)
U of Maine at Fort Kent (ME)
U of Maine at Machias (ME)
U of Maryland Eastern Shore (MD)
U of Minnesota, Twin Cities Campus (MN)
U of Missouri (MO)
The U of Montana Western (MT)
U of Nebraska at Kearney (NE)
U of Nebraska–Lincoln (NE)
U of New Brunswick Fredericton (NB, Canada)
U of North Dakota (ND)
U of Northern Iowa (IA)
U of Regina (SK, Canada)
U of Southern Indiana (IN)
U of Southern Mississippi (MS)
U of South Florida (FL)
The U of Tennessee at Martin (TN)
The U of Toledo (OH)
U of West Georgia (GA)
U of Wisconsin–Superior (WI)
Upper Iowa U (IA)
Utah State U (UT)
Utica Coll (NY)
Valley City State U (ND)
Virginia Intermont Coll (VA)
Virginia State U (VA)
Virginia Union U (VA)
Viterbo U (WI)
Walla Walla U (WA)
Wayland Baptist U (TX)
Wayne State Coll (NE)
Weber State U (UT)
Western Kentucky U (KY)
Western Michigan U (MI)
West Virginia State U (WV)
William Penn U (IA)
Wright State U (OH)

CABINETMAKING AND MILLWORK
Pittsburg State U (KS)

CAD/CADD DRAFTING/ DESIGN TECHNOLOGY
Eastern Michigan U (MI)
Murray State U (KY)

CANADIAN GOVERNMENT AND POLITICS
The U of British Columbia (BC, Canada)

CANADIAN HISTORY
U of Regina (SK, Canada)

CANADIAN STUDIES
Acadia U (NS, Canada)
Athabasca U (AB, Canada)
Brock U (ON, Canada)
Dalhousie U (NS, Canada)
Franklin Coll (IN)
Mount Allison U (NB, Canada)
St. Lawrence U
Thompson Rivers U (BC, Canada)
Trent U (ON, Canada)
Université Sainte-Anne (NS, Canada)
The U of British Columbia (BC, Canada)

U of New Brunswick Fredericton (NB, Canada)
U of Ottawa (ON, Canada)
U of Regina (SK, Canada)
U of Vermont (VT)
U of Waterloo (ON, Canada)
The U of Western Ontario (ON, Canada)
Western Washington U (WA)

CARDIOVASCULAR TECHNOLOGY
Nebraska Methodist Coll (NE)
Pennsylvania Coll of Technology (PA)
U of Medicine and Dentistry of New Jersey (NJ)

CARIBBEAN STUDIES
Columbia U, School of General Studies (NY)
Hofstra U (NY)

CASINO MANAGEMENT
Central Michigan U (MI)

CELL AND MOLECULAR BIOLOGY
Adams State U (CO)
Bennington Coll (VT)
Binghamton U, State U of New York (NY)
Bradley U (IL)
Bridgewater State U (MA)
Bucknell U (PA)
Canisius Coll (NY)
Cedarville U (OH)
Christopher Newport U (VA)
The Coll at Brockport, State U of New York (NY)
The Colorado Coll (CO)
Concordia U (QC, Canada)
Connecticut Coll (CT)
Florida State U (FL)
Fort Lewis Coll (CO)
Grand Valley State U (MI)
The Johns Hopkins U (MD)
Liberty U (VA)
Marymount U (VA)
Missouri State U (MO)
Northwest Nazarene U (ID)
Ohio U (OH)
Oklahoma City U (OK)
Pittsburg State U (KS)
Purdue U (IN)
Salem State U (MA)
Seattle Pacific U (WA)
Seattle U (WA)
Texas A&M U (TX)
The U of Arizona (AZ)
U of California, Berkeley (CA)
U of California, Irvine (CA)
U of California, Los Angeles (CA)
U of Colorado Boulder (CO)
U of Illinois at Urbana–Champaign (IL)
U of Michigan (MI)
U of Minnesota, Duluth (MN)
The U of Tennessee at Martin (TN)
U of Wisconsin–Superior (WI)
Western Washington U (WA)

CELL BIOLOGY AND ANATOMICAL SCIENCES RELATED
Purdue U (IN)
Rutgers, The State U of New Jersey, New Brunswick (NJ)
Tulane U (LA)
Washington & Jefferson Coll (PA)
Yale U (CT)

CELL BIOLOGY AND ANATOMY
Dallas Baptist U (TX)
Huntingdon Coll (AL)
Purdue U (IN)
The U of Western Ontario (ON, Canada)
Western State Colorado U (CO)

CELL BIOLOGY AND HISTOLOGY
California State U, Dominguez Hills (CA)
California State U, Fresno (CA)
California State U, Long Beach (CA)
California State U, San Marcos (CA)

The Coll at Brockport, State U of New York (NY)
The Coll of Saint Rose (NY)
Humboldt State U (CA)
The Johns Hopkins U (MD)
Mansfield U of Pennsylvania (PA)
Montana State U (MT)
Purdue U (IN)
Rutgers, The State U of New Jersey, New Brunswick (NJ)
San Francisco State U (CA)
Sonoma State U (CA)
Tulane U (LA)
The U of British Columbia (BC, Canada)
U of California, Davis (CA)
U of California, Santa Barbara (CA)
U of California, Santa Cruz (CA)
U of Georgia (GA)
U of Illinois at Urbana–Champaign (IL)
U of Minnesota, Duluth (MN)
U of Minnesota, Twin Cities Campus (MN)
U of Utah (UT)
Western Washington U (WA)
Worcester Polytechnic Inst (MA)

CELL PHYSIOLOGY
Purdue U (IN)

CELTIC LANGUAGES
U of California, Berkeley (CA)

CERAMIC ARTS AND CERAMICS
Adams State U (CO)
Alberta Coll of Art & Design (AB, Canada)
Alfred U (NY)
Bennington Coll (VT)
Bowling Green State U (OH)
Bradley U (IL)
Brigham Young U (UT)
California State U, East Bay (CA)
California State U, Long Beach (CA)
Cleveland Inst of Art (OH)
Coe Coll (IA)
The Coll at Brockport, State U of New York (NY)
Coll of the Atlantic (ME)
Columbia Coll (MO)
Concordia U (QC, Canada)
Concord U (WV)
Franklin Pierce U (NH)
Hofstra U (NY)
Indiana Wesleyan U (IN)
Inter American U of Puerto Rico, San Germán Campus (PR)
Maryland Inst Coll of Art (MD)
Marywood U (PA)
Massachusetts Coll of Art and Design (MA)
Minnesota State U Mankato (MN)
Mississippi Coll (MS)
Northern Michigan U (MI)
Northwest Nazarene U (ID)
Ohio U (OH)
Pittsburg State U (KS)
Providence Coll (RI)
Rhode Island School of Design (RI)
Rochester Inst of Technology (NY)
Rutgers, The State U of New Jersey, New Brunswick (NJ)
Salve Regina U (RI)
School of the Art Inst of Chicago (IL)
School of the Museum of Fine Arts, Boston (MA)
Seton Hill U (PA)
State U of New York at New Paltz (NY)
Syracuse U (NY)
Temple U (PA)
Texas Christian U (TX)
The U of Akron (OH)
U of Dallas (TX)
U of Hartford (CT)
The U of Iowa (IA)
The U of Kansas (KS)
U of Massachusetts Dartmouth (MA)
U of Miami (FL)
U of Michigan (MI)
U of Oregon (OR)
U of Regina (SK, Canada)

The U of Texas at El Paso (TX)
U of the District of Columbia (DC)
Virginia Intermont Coll (VA)
Washington U in St. Louis (MO)
Western State Colorado U (CO)
Western Washington U (WA)
West Virginia Wesleyan Coll (WV)

CERAMIC SCIENCES AND ENGINEERING
Alfred U (NY)
Clemson U (SC)
Missouri U of Science and Technology (MO)
Rutgers, The State U of New Jersey, New Brunswick (NJ)
U of Illinois at Urbana–Champaign (IL)

CHEMICAL AND BIOMOLECULAR ENGINEERING
Massachusetts Inst of Technology (MA)
Milwaukee School of Eng (WI)
Purdue U (IN)

CHEMICAL ENGINEERING
American U of Beirut (Lebanon)
Arizona State U (AZ)
Auburn U (AL)
Brown U (RI)
Bucknell U (PA)
California State Polytechnic U, Pomona (CA)
California State U, Long Beach (CA)
Calvin Coll (MI)
Carnegie Mellon U (PA)
Case Western Reserve U (OH)
Christian Brothers U (TN)
City Coll of the City U of New York (NY)
Clarkson U (NY)
Clemson U (SC)
Cleveland State U (OH)
Colorado School of Mines (CO)
Colorado State U (CO)
Columbia U (NY)
Cooper Union for the Advancement of Science and Art (NY)
Dalhousie U (NS, Canada)
Elon U (NC)
Florida Ag and Mech U (FL)
Florida Inst of Technology (FL)
Gannon U (PA)
Hampton U (VA)
Hope Coll (MI)
Illinois Inst of Technology (IL)
Iowa State U of Science and Technology (IA)
The Johns Hopkins U (MD)
Kansas State U (KS)
Lafayette Coll (PA)
Lamar U (TX)
Lehigh U (PA)
Louisiana State U and Ag and Mech Coll (LA)
Manhattan Coll (NY)
Massachusetts Inst of Technology (MA)
Miami U (OH)
Michigan State U (MI)
Mississippi State U (MS)
Missouri U of Science and Technology (MO)
Montana State U (MT)
New Jersey Inst of Technology (NJ)
New Mexico Inst of Mining and Technology (NM)
New Mexico State U (NM)
North Carolina State U (NC)
Northeastern U (MA)
The Ohio State U (OH)
Ohio U (OH)
Oklahoma State U (OK)
Oregon State U (OR)
Penn State Abington (PA)
Penn State Altoona (PA)
Penn State Beaver (PA)
Penn State Berks (PA)
Penn State Brandywine (PA)
Penn State DuBois (PA)
Penn State Erie, The Behrend Coll (PA)
Penn State Fayette, The Eberly Campus (PA)
Penn State Greater Allegheny (PA)

Penn State Hazleton (PA)
Penn State Lehigh Valley (PA)
Penn State Mont Alto (PA)
Penn State New Kensington (PA)
Penn State Schuylkill (PA)
Penn State Shenango (PA)
Penn State U Park (PA)
Penn State Wilkes-Barre (PA)
Penn State Worthington Scranton (PA)
Penn State York (PA)
Polytechnic Inst of New York U (NY)
Polytechnic U of Puerto Rico (PR)
Princeton U (NJ)
Purdue U (IN)
Rensselaer Polytechnic Inst (NY)
Rice U (TX)
Rochester Inst of Technology (NY)
Rowan U (NJ)
Rutgers, The State U of New Jersey, New Brunswick (NJ)
San Jose State U (CA)
Stanford U (CA)
Stony Brook U, State U of New York (NY)
Syracuse U (NY)
Texas A&M U (TX)
Trine U (IN)
Tufts U (MA)
Tulane U (LA)
Tuskegee U (AL)
United States Military Acad (NY)
Université de Sherbrooke (QC, Canada)
U at Buffalo, the State U of New York (NY)
The U of Akron (OH)
The U of Alabama (AL)
The U of Arizona (AZ)
The U of British Columbia (BC, Canada)
U of California, Berkeley (CA)
U of California, Davis (CA)
U of California, Irvine (CA)
U of California, Los Angeles (CA)
U of California, Riverside (CA)
U of California, Santa Barbara (CA)
U of Cincinnati (OH)
U of Colorado Boulder (CO)
U of Delaware (DE)
U of Florida (FL)
U of Houston (TX)
U of Idaho (ID)
U of Illinois at Chicago (IL)
U of Illinois at Urbana–Champaign (IL)
The U of Iowa (IA)
The U of Kansas (KS)
U of Kentucky (KY)
U of Louisiana at Lafayette (LA)
U of Louisville (KY)
U of Maryland, Baltimore County (MD)
U of Maryland, Coll Park (MD)
U of Massachusetts Amherst (MA)
U of Michigan (MI)
U of Minnesota, Duluth (MN)
U of Minnesota, Twin Cities Campus (MN)
U of Mississippi (MS)
U of Missouri (MO)
U of Nebraska–Lincoln (NE)
U of Nevada, Reno (NV)
U of New Brunswick Fredericton (NB, Canada)
U of New Hampshire (NH)
U of New Haven (CT)
U of New Mexico (NM)
U of North Dakota (ND)
U of Notre Dame (IN)
U of Oklahoma (OK)
U of Ottawa (ON, Canada)
U of Pennsylvania (PA)
U of Pittsburgh (PA)
U of Rhode Island (RI)
U of Rochester (NY)
U of South Alabama (AL)
U of South Carolina (SC)
U of Southern California (CA)
U of South Florida (FL)
The U of Tennessee (TN)
The U of Tennessee at Chattanooga (TN)
The U of Texas at Austin (TX)
The U of Toledo (OH)
U of Tulsa (OK)

U of Utah (UT)
U of Virginia (VA)
U of Waterloo (ON, Canada)
The U of Western Ontario (ON, Canada)
U of Wisconsin–Madison (WI)
U of Wyoming (WY)
Vanderbilt U (TN)
Villanova U (PA)
Virginia Commonwealth U (VA)
Virginia Polytechnic Inst and State U (VA)
Washington State U (WA)
Washington U in St. Louis (MO)
Wayne State U (MI)
Western Michigan U (MI)
West Virginia U (WV)
West Virginia U Inst of Technology (WV)
Widener U (PA)
Worcester Polytechnic Inst (MA)
Xavier U (OH)
Yale U (CT)
Youngstown State U (OH)

CHEMICAL ENGINEERING RELATED
Purdue U (IN)

CHEMICAL ENGINEERING TECHNOLOGY
Purdue U (IN)

CHEMICAL PHYSICS
Adams State U (CO)
Augustana Coll (SD)
Bowdoin Coll (ME)
Carnegie Mellon U (PA)
Columbia U, School of General Studies (NY)
Hamilton Coll (NY)
Hendrix Coll (AR)
Lewis U (IL)
Michigan State U (MI)
Mississippi Coll (MS)
Saginaw Valley State U (MI)
Simon Fraser U (BC, Canada)
Swarthmore Coll (PA)
U of Guelph (ON, Canada)
U of Waterloo (ON, Canada)

CHEMICAL TECHNOLOGY
Inter American U of Puerto Rico, Bayamón Campus (PR)
Norwich U (VT)
U of Regina (SK, Canada)

CHEMISTRY
Abilene Christian U (TX)
Acadia U (NS, Canada)
Adams State U (CO)
Adelphi U (NY)
Agnes Scott Coll (GA)
Alabama State U (AL)
Albany Coll of Pharmacy and Health Sciences (NY)
Albertus Magnus Coll (CT)
Albion Coll (MI)
Albright Coll (PA)
Alcorn State U (MS)
Alderson-Broaddus Coll (WV)
Alfred U (NY)
Alma Coll (MI)
Alvernia U (PA)
Alverno Coll (WI)
American U (DC)
The American U in Cairo (Egypt)
American U of Beirut (Lebanon)
Amherst Coll (MA)
Anderson U (IN)
Andrews U (MI)
Angelo State U (TX)
Appalachian State U (NC)
Arizona State U (AZ)
Arkansas State U (AR)
Arkansas Tech U (AR)
Armstrong Atlantic State U (GA)
Asbury U (KY)
Ashland U (OH)
Assumption Coll (MA)
Athens State U (AL)
Auburn U (AL)
Augsburg Coll (MN)
Augustana Coll (IL)
Augustana Coll (SD)
Austin Peay State U (TN)
Azusa Pacific U (CA)
Baker U (KS)
Baldwin Wallace U (OH)

Ball State U (IN)
Bard Coll (NY)
Barry U (FL)
Barton Coll (NC)
Bates Coll (ME)
Baylor U (TX)
Belhaven U (MS)
Bellarmine U (KY)
Belmont U (TN)
Bemidji State U (MN)
Benedictine Coll (KS)
Benedictine U (IL)
Bennington Coll (VT)
Berea Coll (KY)
Berry Coll (GA)
Bethany Coll (WV)
Bethany Lutheran Coll (MN)
Bethel Coll (IN)
Bethel Coll (KS)
Bethel U (MN)
Bethune-Cookman U (FL)
Binghamton U, State U of New York (NY)
Blackburn Coll (IL)
Bloomfield Coll (NJ)
Bloomsburg U of Pennsylvania (PA)
Bluefield Coll (VA)
Bluffton U (OH)
Bob Jones U (SC)
Boise State U (ID)
Boston Coll (MA)
Boston U (MA)
Bowdoin Coll (ME)
Bowling Green State U (OH)
Bradley U (IL)
Bridgewater Coll (VA)
Bridgewater State U (MA)
Brock U (ON, Canada)
Brown U (RI)
Bucknell U (PA)
Buena Vista U (IA)
Buffalo State Coll, State U of New York (NY)
Butler U (IN)
Cabrini Coll (PA)
California Baptist U (CA)
California Lutheran U (CA)
California Polytechnic State U, San Luis Obispo (CA)
California State Polytechnic U, Pomona (CA)
California State U, Chico (CA)
California State U, Dominguez Hills (CA)
California State U, East Bay (CA)
California State U, Fresno (CA)
California State U, Fullerton (CA)
California State U; Long Beach (CA)
California State U, Los Angeles (CA)
California State U, Northridge (CA)
California State U, San Bernardino (CA)
California State U, San Marcos (CA)
California State U, Stanislaus (CA)
Calvin Coll (MI)
Cameron U (OK)
Campbellsville U (KY)
Canisius Coll (NY)
Capital U (OH)
Cardinal Stritch U (WI)
Carleton Coll (MN)
Carlow U (PA)
Carnegie Mellon U (PA)
Carroll Coll (MT)
Carson-Newman U (TN)
Case Western Reserve U (OH)
The Catholic U of America (DC)
Cedar Crest Coll (PA)
Cedarville U (OH)
Centenary Coll of Louisiana (LA)
Central Coll (IA)
Central Connecticut State U (CT)
Central Methodist U (MO)
Central Michigan U (MI)
Central State U (OH)
Centre Coll (KY)
Chapman U (CA)
Chatham U (PA)
Chestnut Hill Coll (PA)
Cheyney U of Pennsylvania (PA)
Chicago State U (IL)
Chowan U (NC)
Christian Brothers U (TN)

Christopher Newport U (VA)
The Citadel, The Military Coll of South Carolina (SC)
City Coll of the City U of New York (NY)
Claflin U (SC)
Claremont McKenna Coll (CA)
Clarion U of Pennsylvania (PA)
Clark Atlanta U (GA)
Clarke U (IA)
Clarkson U (NY)
Clark U (MA)
Clayton State U (GA)
Clemson U (SC)
Cleveland State U (OH)
Coastal Carolina U (SC)
Coe Coll (IA)
Colby Coll (ME)
Colgate U (NY)
The Coll at Brockport, State U of New York (NY)
Coll of Charleston (SC)
The Coll of Idaho (ID)
Coll of Mount St. Joseph (OH)
The Coll of New Jersey (NJ)
The Coll of New Rochelle (NY)
Coll of Saint Benedict (MN)
Coll of Saint Elizabeth (NJ)
Coll of Saint Mary (NE)
The Coll of Saint Rose (NY)
The Coll of St. Scholastica (MN)
Coll of Staten Island of the City U of New York (NY)
Coll of the Holy Cross (MA)
Coll of the Ozarks (MO)
The Coll of William and Mary (VA)
The Coll of Wooster (OH)
The Colorado Coll (CO)
Colorado School of Mines (CO)
Colorado State U (CO)
Columbia Coll (MO)
Columbia Coll (SC)
Columbia U (NY)
Columbia U, School of General Studies (NY)
Columbus State U (GA)
Concordia Coll (MN)
Concordia U (CA)
Concordia U (OR)
Concordia U (QC, Canada)
Concordia U Chicago (IL)
Concordia U, Nebraska (NE)
Concord U (WV)
Connecticut Coll (CT)
Converse Coll (SC)
Cornell Coll (IA)
Covenant Coll (GA)
Creighton U (NE)
Dalhousie U (NS, Canada)
Dalton State Coll (GA)
Dartmouth Coll (NH)
Davidson Coll (NC)
Delta State U (MS)
DePaul U (IL)
DePauw U (IN)
DeSales U (PA)
Dickinson Coll (PA)
Dillard U (LA)
Doane Coll (NE)
Dominican U (IL)
Dordt Coll (IA)
Drake U (IA)
Drew U (NJ)
Drury U (MO)
Duquesne U (PA)
Earlham Coll (IN)
East Carolina U (NC)
East Central U (OK)
Eastern Illinois U (IL)
Eastern Mennonite U (VA)
Eastern Michigan U (MI)
Eastern New Mexico U (NM)
Eastern Washington U (WA)
East Tennessee State U (TN)
East Texas Baptist U (TX)
Eckerd Coll (FL)
Edgewood Coll (WI)
Edinboro U of Pennsylvania (PA)
Elizabeth City State U (NC)
Elizabethtown Coll (PA)
Elmira Coll (NY)
Elon U (NC)
Emmanuel Coll (MA)
Emory & Henry Coll (VA)
Emporia State U (KS)
Evangel U (MO)
Excelsior Coll (NY)

Fairfield U (CT)
Fairleigh Dickinson U, Coll at Florham (NJ)
Fairleigh Dickinson U, Metropolitan Campus (NJ)
Fairmont State U (WV)
Fayetteville State U (NC)
Ferris State U (MI)
Ferrum Coll (VA)
Florida Ag and Mech U (FL)
Florida Atlantic U (FL)
Florida Gulf Coast U (FL)
Florida Inst of Technology (FL)
Florida Intl U (FL)
Florida Southern Coll (FL)
Florida State U (FL)
Fort Lewis Coll (CO)
Framingham State U (MA)
Francis Marion U (SC)
Franklin & Marshall Coll (PA)
Franklin Coll (IN)
Friends U (KS)
Frostburg State U (MD)
Furman U (SC)
Gallaudet U (DC)
Gannon U (PA)
Gardner-Webb U (NC)
Geneva Coll (PA)
George Fox U (OR)
George Mason U (VA)
Georgetown Coll (KY)
Georgetown U (DC)
Georgia Coll & State U (GA)
Georgia Regents U (GA)
Georgia Southern U (GA)
Georgia Southwestern State U (GA)
Georgia State U (GA)
Gettysburg Coll (PA)
Gonzaga U (WA)
Gordon Coll (MA)
Goshen Coll (IN)
Goucher Coll (MD)
Governors State U (IL)
Graceland U (IA)
Grambling State U (LA)
Grand Valley State U (MI)
Greenville Coll (IL)
Grinnell Coll (IA)
Grove City Coll (PA)
Guilford Coll (NC)
Gustavus Adolphus Coll (MN)
Hamilton Coll (NY)
Hamline U (MN)
Hampden-Sydney Coll (VA)
Hampshire Coll (MA)
Hampton U (VA)
Hanover Coll (IN)
Harding U (AR)
Hardin-Simmons U (TX)
Hartwick Coll (NY)
Harvey Mudd Coll (CA)
Haverford Coll (PA)
Hawai`i Pacific U (HI)
Henderson State U (AR)
Hendrix Coll (AR)
High Point U (NC)
Hillsdale Coll (MI)
Hiram Coll (OH)
Hobart and William Smith Colls (NY)
Hofstra U (NY)
Hollins U (VA)
Hood Coll (MD)
Hope Coll (MI)
Houghton Coll (NY)
Howard Payne U (TX)
Humboldt State U (CA)
Hunter Coll of the City U of New York (NY)
Huntingdon Coll (AL)
Huntington U (IN)
Husson U (ME)
Illinois Coll (IL)
Illinois Inst of Technology (IL)
Illinois State U (IL)
Illinois Wesleyan U (IL)
Immaculata U (PA)
Indiana State U (IN)
Indiana U Bloomington (IN)
Indiana U Kokomo (IN)
Indiana U Northwest (IN)
Indiana U of Pennsylvania (PA)
Indiana U–Purdue U Fort Wayne (IN)
Indiana U–Purdue U Indianapolis (IN)

Indiana U South Bend (IN)
Indiana U Southeast (IN)
Indiana Wesleyan U (IN)
Inter American U of Puerto Rico, Bayamón Campus (PR)
Inter American U of Puerto Rico, San Germán Campus (PR)
Iona Coll (NY)
Iowa State U of Science and Technology (IA)
Ithaca Coll (NY)
Jacksonville State U (AL)
James Madison U (VA)
Jamestown Coll (ND)
Jarvis Christian Coll (TX)
John Brown U (AR)
John Carroll U (OH)
The Johns Hopkins U (MD)
Johnson C. Smith U (NC)
Judson Coll (AL)
Judson U (IL)
Juniata Coll (PA)
Kalamazoo Coll (MI)
Kansas State U (KS)
Kansas Wesleyan U (KS)
Kean U (NJ)
Keene State Coll (NH)
Kennesaw State U (GA)
Kent State U (OH)
Kentucky State U (KY)
Kentucky Wesleyan Coll (KY)
Kenyon Coll (OH)
King Coll (TN)
King's Coll (PA)
The King's U Coll (AB, Canada)
Knox Coll (IL)
Kutztown U of Pennsylvania (PA)
Lafayette Coll (PA)
LaGrange Coll (GA)
Lake Erie Coll (OH)
Lakeland Coll (WI)
Lake Superior State U (MI)
Lamar U (TX)
Lander U (SC)
Lane Coll (TN)
Langston U (OK)
La Roche Coll (PA)
La Salle U (PA)
La Sierra U (CA)
Lawrence Technological U (MI)
Lawrence U (WI)
Lebanese American U (Lebanon)
Lebanon Valley Coll (PA)
Lee U (TN)
Lehigh U (PA)
Lehman Coll of the City U of New York (NY)
Le Moyne Coll (NY)
LeTourneau U (TX)
Lewis-Clark State Coll (ID)
Lewis U (IL)
Limestone Coll (SC)
Lincoln Memorial U (TN)
Lincoln U (MO)
Lindenwood U (MO)
Linfield Coll (OR)
Lipscomb U (TN)
Lock Haven U of Pennsylvania (PA)
Long Island U–Brooklyn Campus (NY)
Long Island U–C. W. Post Campus (NY)
Longwood U (VA)
Louisiana Coll (LA)
Louisiana State U and Ag and Mech Coll (LA)
Louisiana State U in Shreveport (LA)
Loyola Marymount U (CA)
Loyola U Chicago (IL)
Loyola U Maryland (MD)
Loyola U New Orleans (LA)
Lubbock Christian U (TX)
Luther Coll (IA)
Lynchburg Coll (VA)
Lyon Coll (AR)
Macalester Coll (MN)
Madonna U (MI)
Malone U (OH)
Manchester U (IN)
Manhattan Coll (NY)
Manhattanville Coll (NY)
Mansfield U of Pennsylvania (PA)
Marian U (WI)
Marietta Coll (OH)
Marist Coll (NY)
Marquette U (WI)

Marshall U (WV)
Mars Hill Coll (NC)
Mary Baldwin Coll (VA)
Maryville Coll (TN)
Maryville U of Saint Louis (MO)
Massachusetts Coll of Liberal Arts (MA)
Massachusetts Coll of Pharmacy and Health Sciences (MA)
Massachusetts Inst of Technology (MA)
Mayville State U (ND)
McDaniel Coll (MD)
McKendree U (IL)
McMurry U (TX)
McNeese State U (LA)
Mercer U (GA)
Mercyhurst U (PA)
Merrimack Coll (MA)
Messiah Coll (PA)
Metropolitan State U of Denver (CO)
Miami U (OH)
Michigan State U (MI)
Middlebury Coll (VT)
Middle Tennessee State U (TN)
Midwestern State U (TX)
Millersville U of Pennsylvania (PA)
Millikin U (IL)
Millsaps Coll (MS)
Mills Coll (CA)
Minnesota State U Mankato (MN)
Minnesota State U Moorhead (MN)
Minot State U (ND)
Misericordia U (PA)
Mississippi Coll (MS)
Mississippi State U (MS)
Mississippi U for Women (MS)
Mississippi Valley State U (MS)
Missouri Baptist U (MO)
Missouri State U (MO)
Missouri U of Science and Technology (MO)
Missouri Western State U (MO)
Monmouth Coll (IL)
Monmouth U (NJ)
Montana State U (MT)
Montana Tech of The U of Montana (MT)
Montclair State U (NJ)
Moravian Coll (PA)
Morehead State U (KY)
Morehouse Coll (GA)
Morningside Coll (IA)
Mount Allison U (NB, Canada)
Mount Holyoke Coll (MA)
Mount Marty Coll (SD)
Mount Mary Coll (WI)
Mount Saint Mary Coll (NY)
Mount St. Mary's Coll (CA)
Mount St. Mary's U (MD)
Mount Vernon Nazarene U (OH)
Muhlenberg Coll (PA)
Murray State U (KY)
Nazareth Coll of Rochester (NY)
Newberry Coll (SC)
New Coll of Florida (FL)
New Jersey City U (NJ)
New Jersey Inst of Technology (NJ)
Newman U (KS)
New Mexico Highlands U (NM)
New Mexico Inst of Mining and Technology (NM)
New Mexico State U (NM)
New York Inst of Technology (NY)
New York U (NY)
Niagara U (NY)
Nicholls State U (LA)
Norfolk State U (VA)
North Carolina Central U (NC)
North Carolina State U (NC)
North Carolina Wesleyan Coll (NC)
North Central Coll (IL)
North Dakota State U (ND)
Northeastern Illinois U (IL)
Northeastern U (MA)
Northern Arizona U (AZ)
Northern Illinois U (IL)
Northern Michigan U (MI)
Northern State U (SD)
Northland Coll (WI)
Northwestern Coll (IA)
Northwestern Oklahoma State U (OK)
Northwest Missouri State U (MO)
Northwest Nazarene U (ID)
Norwich U (VT)

Nova Southeastern U (FL)
Oakland City U (IN)
Oakland U (MI)
Oglethorpe U (GA)
Ohio Dominican U (OH)
The Ohio State U (OH)
Ohio U (OH)
Ohio Wesleyan U (OH)
Oklahoma Baptist U (OK)
Oklahoma Christian U (OK)
Oklahoma City U (OK)
Oklahoma State U (OK)
Old Dominion U (VA)
Olivet Coll (MI)
Oral Roberts U (OK)
Oregon State U (OR)
Ouachita Baptist U (AR)
Pace U (NY)
Pacific Lutheran U (WA)
Pacific Union Coll (CA)
Pacific U (OR)
Paine Coll (GA)
Park U (MO)
Penn State Abington (PA)
Penn State Altoona (PA)
Penn State Beaver (PA)
Penn State Berks (PA)
Penn State Brandywine (PA)
Penn State DuBois (PA)
Penn State Erie, The Behrend Coll (PA)
Penn State Fayette, The Eberly Campus (PA)
Penn State Greater Allegheny (PA)
Penn State Hazleton (PA)
Penn State Lehigh Valley (PA)
Penn State Mont Alto (PA)
Penn State New Kensington (PA)
Penn State Schuylkill (PA)
Penn State Shenango (PA)
Penn State U Park (PA)
Penn State Wilkes-Barre (PA)
Penn State Worthington Scranton (PA)
Penn State York (PA)
Pepperdine U, Malibu (CA)
Philadelphia U (PA)
Piedmont Coll (GA)
Pittsburg State U (KS)
Pitzer Coll (CA)
Plymouth State U (NH)
Point Loma Nazarene U (CA)
Pomona Coll (CA)
Portland State U (OR)
Presbyterian Coll (SC)
Princeton U (NJ)
Principia Coll (IL)
Providence Coll (RI)
Purchase Coll, State U of New York (NY)
Purdue U (IN)
Purdue U Calumet (IN)
Queens U of Charlotte (NC)
Quincy U (IL)
Quinnipiac U (CT)
Radford U (VA)
Ramapo Coll of New Jersey (NJ)
Randolph Coll (VA)
Randolph-Macon Coll (VA)
Reed Coll (OR)
Regis Coll (MA)
Regis U (CO)
Rensselaer Polytechnic Inst (NY)
Rhode Island Coll (RI)
Rhodes Coll (TN)
Rice U (TX)
The Richard Stockton Coll of New Jersey (NJ)
Rider U (NJ)
Ripon Coll (WI)
Roanoke Coll (VA)
Roberts Wesleyan Coll (NY)
Rochester Inst of Technology (NY)
Rockford Coll (IL)
Rockhurst U (MO)
Rocky Mountain Coll (MT)
Roger Williams U (RI)
Rollins Coll (FL)
Roosevelt U (IL)
Rosemont Coll (PA)
Rowan U (NJ)
Russell Sage Coll (NY)
Rutgers, The State U of New Jersey, Camden (NJ)
Rutgers, The State U of New Jersey, Newark (NJ)

Rutgers, The State U of New Jersey, New Brunswick (NJ)
Sacred Heart U (CT)
Saginaw Valley State U (MI)
St. Ambrose U (IA)
Saint Anselm Coll (NH)
St. Bonaventure U (NY)
St. Edward's U (TX)
St. Francis Coll (NY)
St. John Fisher Coll (NY)
Saint John's U (MN)
St. John's U (NY)
Saint Joseph's Coll (IN)
St. Joseph's Coll, Long Island Campus (NY)
St. Joseph's Coll, New York (NY)
Saint Joseph's U (PA)
St. Lawrence U (NY)
Saint Louis U (MO)
Saint Martin's U (WA)
Saint Mary's Coll (IN)
Saint Mary's Coll of California (CA)
St. Mary's Coll of Maryland (MD)
St. Mary's U (TX)
Saint Mary's U of Minnesota (MN)
Saint Michael's Coll (VT)
St. Norbert Coll (WI)
St. Olaf Coll (MN)
St. Thomas U (FL)
Saint Vincent Coll (PA)
Salem State U (MA)
Salisbury U (MD)
Salve Regina U (RI)
Samford U (AL)
Sam Houston State U (TX)
San Diego State U (CA)
San Francisco State U (CA)
San Jose State U (CA)
Schreiner U (TX)
Scripps Coll (CA)
Seattle Pacific U (WA)
Seattle U (WA)
Seton Hill U (PA)
Sewanee: The U of the South (TN)
Shawnee State U (OH)
Shaw U (NC)
Shenandoah U (VA)
Shepherd U (WV)
Shippensburg U of Pennsylvania (PA)
Siena Coll (NY)
Siena Heights U (MI)
Simmons Coll (MA)
Simon Fraser U (BC, Canada)
Simpson Coll (IA)
Skidmore Coll (NY)
Slippery Rock U of Pennsylvania (PA)
Smith Coll (MA)
Sonoma State U (CA)
South Dakota State U (SD)
Southeastern Louisiana U (LA)
Southeastern Oklahoma State U (OK)
Southeast Missouri State U (MO)
Southern Arkansas U–Magnolia (AR)
Southern Connecticut State U (CT)
Southern Illinois U Carbondale (IL)
Southern Illinois U Edwardsville (IL)
Southern Methodist U (TX)
Southern Nazarene U (OK)
Southern Oregon U (OR)
Southern Polytechnic State U (GA)
Southern Utah U (UT)
Southwest Baptist U (MO)
Southwestern Adventist U (TX)
Southwestern Coll (KS)
Southwestern U (TX)
Spelman Coll (GA)
Spring Arbor U (MI)
Spring Hill Coll (AL)
Stanford U (CA)
State U of New York at Fredonia (NY)
State U of New York at New Paltz (NY)
State U of New York at Oswego (NY)
State U of New York at Plattsburgh (NY)
State U of New York Coll at Cortland (NY)
State U of New York Coll at Geneseo (NY)

State U of New York Coll at Old Westbury (NY)
State U of New York Coll at Potsdam (NY)
Stephen F. Austin State U (TX)
Stetson U (FL)
Stevenson U (MD)
Stonehill Coll (MA)
Stony Brook U, State U of New York (NY)
Suffolk U (MA)
Sul Ross State U (TX)
Susquehanna U (PA)
Swarthmore Coll (PA)
Sweet Briar Coll (VA)
Syracuse U (NY)
Tabor Coll (KS)
Tarleton State U (TX)
Taylor U (IN)
Temple U (PA)
Tennessee State U (TN)
Tennessee Wesleyan Coll (TN)
Texas A&M Intl U (TX)
Texas A&M U (TX)
Texas A&M U–Commerce (TX)
Texas A&M U–Kingsville (TX)
Texas Christian U (TX)
Texas Lutheran U (TX)
Texas Southern U (TX)
Texas State U–San Marcos (TX)
Texas Wesleyan U (TX)
Texas Woman's U (TX)
Thomas More Coll (KY)
Thompson Rivers U (BC, Canada)
Transylvania U (KY)
Trent U (ON, Canada)
Trevecca Nazarene U (TN)
Trine U (IN)
Trinity Christian Coll (IL)
Trinity Coll (CT)
Trinity U (TX)
Troy U (AL)
Truman State U (MO)
Tufts U (MA)
Tulane U (LA)
Tuskegee U (AL)
Union Coll (KY)
Union Coll (NE)
Union U (TN)
United States Air Force Acad (CO)
United States Military Acad (NY)
United States Naval Acad (MD)
Université de Sherbrooke (QC, Canada)
U at Albany, State U of New York (NY)
U at Buffalo, the State U of New York (NY)
The U of Akron (OH)
The U of Alabama (AL)
The U of Alabama at Birmingham (AL)
U of Alaska Anchorage (AK)
U of Alaska Fairbanks (AK)
The U of Arizona (AZ)
U of Arkansas at Little Rock (AR)
U of Arkansas–Fort Smith (AR)
The U of British Columbia (BC, Canada)
The U of British Columbia–Okanagan (BC, Canada)
U of California, Berkeley (CA)
U of California, Davis (CA)
U of California, Irvine (CA)
U of California, Los Angeles (CA)
U of California, Merced (CA)
U of California, Riverside (CA)
U of California, Santa Barbara (CA)
U of California, Santa Cruz (CA)
U of Central Arkansas (AR)
U of Central Florida (FL)
U of Central Oklahoma (OK)
U of Charleston (WV)
U of Chicago (IL)
U of Cincinnati (OH)
U of Colorado Boulder (CO)
U of Colorado Colorado Springs (CO)
U of Colorado Denver (CO)
U of Dallas (TX)
U of Delaware (DE)
U of Denver (CO)
U of Evansville (IN)
The U of Findlay (OH)
U of Florida (FL)
U of Georgia (GA)
U of Great Falls (MT)

U of Guam (GU)
U of Guelph (ON, Canada)
U of Hartford (CT)
U of Hawaii at Hilo (HI)
U of Hawaii at Manoa (HI)
U of Houston (TX)
U of Houston–Clear Lake (TX)
U of Houston–Downtown (TX)
U of Idaho (ID)
U of Illinois at Chicago (IL)
U of Illinois at Springfield (IL)
U of Illinois at Urbana–Champaign (IL)
The U of Iowa (IA)
The U of Kansas (KS)
U of Kentucky (KY)
U of La Verne (CA)
U of Louisiana at Lafayette (LA)
U of Louisville (KY)
U of Maryland, Baltimore County (MD)
U of Maryland, Coll Park (MD)
U of Maryland Eastern Shore (MD)
U of Mary Washington (VA)
U of Massachusetts Amherst (MA)
U of Massachusetts Boston (MA)
U of Massachusetts Dartmouth (MA)
U of Memphis (TN)
U of Miami (FL)
U of Michigan (MI)
U of Michigan–Dearborn (MI)
U of Michigan–Flint (MI)
U of Minnesota, Duluth (MN)
U of Minnesota, Twin Cities Campus (MN)
U of Mississippi (MS)
U of Missouri (MO)
U of Missouri–Kansas City (MO)
U of Missouri–St. Louis (MO)
U of Montevallo (AL)
U of Mount Union (OH)
U of Nebraska at Kearney (NE)
U of Nebraska at Omaha (NE)
U of Nebraska–Lincoln (NE)
U of Nevada, Las Vegas (NV)
U of Nevada, Reno (NV)
U of New Brunswick Fredericton (NB, Canada)
U of New Brunswick Saint John (NB, Canada)
U of New England (ME)
U of New Hampshire (NH)
U of New Haven (CT)
U of New Mexico (NM)
U of New Orleans (LA)
U of North Alabama (AL)
U of North Carolina at Asheville (NC)
The U of North Carolina at Chapel Hill (NC)
The U of North Carolina at Charlotte (NC)
The U of North Carolina at Greensboro (NC)
The U of North Carolina at Pembroke (NC)
The U of North Carolina Wilmington (NC)
U of North Dakota (ND)
U of Northern Colorado (CO)
U of Northern Iowa (IA)
U of North Florida (FL)
U of North Georgia (GA)
U of North Texas (TX)
U of Notre Dame (IN)
U of Oklahoma (OK)
U of Oregon (OR)
U of Ottawa (ON, Canada)
U of Pennsylvania (PA)
U of Pikeville (KY)
U of Pittsburgh (PA)
U of Pittsburgh at Bradford (PA)
U of Pittsburgh at Greensburg (PA)
U of Portland (OR)
U of Puget Sound (WA)
U of Redlands (CA)
U of Regina (SK, Canada)
U of Rhode Island (RI)
U of Richmond (VA)
U of Rochester (NY)
U of Saint Joseph (CT)
U of Saint Mary (KS)
U of St. Thomas (MN)
U of St. Thomas (TX)
U of San Diego (CA)

U of Science and Arts of Oklahoma (OK)
The U of Scranton (PA)
U of South Alabama (AL)
U of South Carolina (SC)
U of South Carolina Aiken (SC)
U of South Carolina Upstate (SC)
The U of South Dakota (SD)
U of Southern California (CA)
U of Southern Indiana (IN)
U of Southern Maine (ME)
U of Southern Mississippi (MS)
U of South Florida (FL)
The U of Tampa (FL)
The U of Tennessee (TN)
The U of Tennessee at Chattanooga (TN)
The U of Tennessee at Martin (TN)
The U of Texas at Arlington (TX)
The U of Texas at Austin (TX)
The U of Texas at Brownsville (TX)
The U of Texas at Dallas (TX)
The U of Texas at El Paso (TX)
The U of Texas at San Antonio (TX)
The U of Texas of the Permian Basin (TX)
The U of Texas–Pan American (TX)
U of the Cumberlands (KY)
U of the District of Columbia (DC)
U of the Incarnate Word (TX)
U of the Ozarks (AR)
U of the Sciences (PA)
U of the Virgin Islands (VI)
The U of Toledo (OH)
U of Tulsa (OK)
U of Utah (UT)
U of Vermont (VT)
U of Virginia (VA)
U of Waterloo (ON, Canada)
The U of West Alabama (AL)
The U of Western Ontario (ON, Canada)
U of West Florida (FL)
U of West Georgia (GA)
U of Windsor (ON, Canada)
U of Wisconsin–Eau Claire (WI)
U of Wisconsin–Green Bay (WI)
U of Wisconsin–La Crosse (WI)
U of Wisconsin–Madison (WI)
U of Wisconsin–Milwaukee (WI)
U of Wisconsin–Parkside (WI)
U of Wisconsin–Platteville (WI)
U of Wisconsin–Stevens Point (WI)
U of Wisconsin–Superior (WI)
U of Wyoming (WY)
Upper Iowa U (IA)
Utah State U (UT)
Utica Coll (NY)
Valdosta State U (GA)
Valley City State U (ND)
Valparaiso U (IN)
Vanderbilt U (TN)
Vassar Coll (NY)
Villanova U (PA)
Virginia Commonwealth U (VA)
Virginia Polytechnic Inst and State U (VA)
Virginia State U (VA)
Virginia Union U (VA)
Virginia Wesleyan Coll (VA)
Viterbo U (WI)
Wabash Coll (IN)
Wagner Coll (NY)
Wake Forest U (NC)
Walla Walla U (WA)
Walsh U (OH)
Wartburg Coll (IA)
Washburn U (KS)
Washington & Jefferson Coll (PA)
Washington and Lee U (VA)
Washington Coll (MD)
Washington State U (WA)
Washington U in St. Louis (MO)
Wayland Baptist U (TX)
Waynesburg U (PA)
Wayne State Coll (NE)
Wayne State U (MI)
Weber State U (UT)
Wellesley Coll (MA)
Wells Coll (NY)
Wesleyan Coll (GA)
Wesleyan U (CT)
West Chester U of Pennsylvania (PA)
Western Carolina U (NC)
Western Connecticut State U (CT)
Western Illinois U (IL)

Western Kentucky U (KY)
Western Michigan U (MI)
Western Oregon U (OR)
Western State Colorado U (CO)
Western Washington U (WA)
Westfield State U (MA)
West Liberty U (WV)
Westminster Coll (MO)
Westminster Coll (UT)
West Texas A&M U (TX)
West Virginia State U (WV)
West Virginia U (WV)
West Virginia U Inst of Technology (WV)
West Virginia Wesleyan Coll (WV)
Wheaton Coll (IL)
Wheaton Coll (MA)
Wheeling Jesuit U (WV)
Whitman Coll (WA)
Whitworth U (WA)
Wichita State U (KS)
Widener U (PA)
Wilkes U (PA)
Willamette U (OR)
William Jewell Coll (MO)
William Paterson U of New Jersey (NJ)
Williams Coll (MA)
Winthrop U (SC)
Wittenberg U (OH)
Worcester Polytechnic Inst (MA)
Worcester State U (MA)
Wright State U (OH)
Xavier U (OH)
Xavier U of Louisiana (LA)
Yale U (CT)
York Coll of Pennsylvania (PA)
York Coll of the City U of New York (NY)
Youngstown State U (OH)

CHEMISTRY RELATED
Alvernia U (PA)
Belmont U (TN)
Boston U (MA)
Bridgewater Coll (VA)
Bridgewater State U (MA)
California State U, Chico (CA)
Case Western Reserve U (OH)
Coll of Charleston (SC)
Connecticut Coll (CT)
Dartmouth Coll (NH)
Duquesne U (PA)
Florida Inst of Technology (FL)
Florida State U (FL)
Keene State Coll (NH)
Loyola U New Orleans (LA)
Northern Michigan U (MI)
Palm Beach Atlantic U (FL)
Purdue U (IN)
Roger Williams U (RI)
Saginaw Valley State U (MI)
Saint Anselm Coll (NH)
Saint Mary's Coll of California (CA)
Saint Vincent Coll (PA)
Stony Brook U, State U of New York (NY)
Taylor U (IN)
Thompson Rivers U (BC, Canada)
U at Buffalo, the State U of New York (NY)
U of California, Berkeley (CA)
U of California, Santa Barbara (CA)
U of Chicago (IL)
U of Denver (CO)
U of Houston–Downtown (TX)
U of Northern Iowa (IA)
U of Notre Dame (IN)
The U of Scranton (PA)
U of Southern Mississippi (MS)
U of Wisconsin–Eau Claire (WI)
U of Wisconsin–Madison (WI)
U of Wisconsin–Milwaukee (WI)
Washington U in St. Louis (MO)
Wayne State U (MI)
Western Illinois U (IL)
Western Michigan U (MI)
Western State Colorado U (CO)
West Virginia Wesleyan Coll (WV)
Whitman Coll (WA)

CHEMISTRY TEACHER EDUCATION
Adams State U (CO)
Alma Coll (MI)
Alvernia U (PA)
Anderson U (IN)
Appalachian State U (NC)

Arkansas State U (AR)
Ashland U (OH)
Assumption Coll (MA)
Augustana Coll (IL)
Bethel U (MN)
Bethune-Cookman U (FL)
Bluefield Coll (VA)
Boston U (MA)
Bowling Green State U (OH)
Bradley U (IL)
Buena Vista U (IA)
Cabrini Coll (PA)
California State U, Chico (CA)
Calvin Coll (MI)
Campbellsville U (KY)
Canisius Coll (NY)
Carroll Coll (MT)
Cedarville U (OH)
Central Methodist U (MO)
Christian Brothers U (TN)
City Coll of the City U of New York (NY)
The Coll at Brockport, State U of New York (NY)
The Coll of New Jersey (NJ)
The Coll of Saint Rose (NY)
Coll of the Ozarks (MO)
Colorado State U (CO)
Concordia Coll (MN)
Concordia U Chicago (IL)
Concordia U, Nebraska (NE)
Concordia U, St. Paul (MN)
Creighton U (NE)
Dordt Coll (IA)
East Central U (OK)
Eastern Michigan U (MI)
Eastern Washington U (WA)
East Texas Baptist U (TX)
Edgewood Coll (WI)
Elizabeth City State U (NC)
Elmira Coll (NY)
Evangel U (MO)
Ferris State U (MI)
Florida Inst of Technology (FL)
Fort Lewis Coll (CO)
Franklin Coll (IN)
Grambling State U (LA)
Grand Valley State U (MI)
Greenville Coll (IL)
Grove City Coll (PA)
Gustavus Adolphus Coll (MN)
Hofstra U (NY)
Hope Coll (MI)
Huntingdon Coll (AL)
Huntington U (IN)
Husson U (ME)
Indiana U Bloomington (IN)
Indiana U Northwest (IN)
Indiana U–Purdue U Fort Wayne (IN)
Indiana U South Bend (IN)
Indiana Wesleyan U (IN)
Inter American U of Puerto Rico, San Germán Campus (PR)
Iowa Wesleyan Coll (IA)
Ithaca Coll (NY)
Jamestown Coll (ND)
Juniata Coll (PA)
Keene State Coll (NH)
Kent State U (OH)
Kentucky Wesleyan Coll (KY)
King Coll (TN)
Lee U (TN)
Le Moyne Coll (NY)
Lincoln Memorial U (TN)
Lincoln U (MO)
Lindenwood U (MO)
Lipscomb U (TN)
Long Island U–Brooklyn Campus (NY)
Long Island U–C. W. Post Campus (NY)
Louisiana State U in Shreveport (LA)
Lubbock Christian U (TX)
Madonna U (MI)
Manchester U (IN)
Manhattanville Coll (NY)
Mansfield U of Pennsylvania (PA)
Marist Coll (NY)
Maryville Coll (TN)
Mayville State U (ND)
McMurry U (TX)
Mercyhurst U (PA)
Merrimack Coll (MA)
Messiah Coll (PA)
Miami Dade Coll (FL)

Miami U (OH)
Michigan State U (MI)
Millikin U (IL)
Minnesota State U Moorhead (MN)
Minot State U (ND)
Misericordia U (PA)
Mississippi Coll (MS)
Missouri State U (MO)
Moravian Coll (PA)
Morningside Coll (IA)
Mount Marty Coll (SD)
Mount Mary Coll (WI)
Mount Vernon Nazarene U (OH)
Nazareth Coll of Rochester (NY)
Niagara U (NY)
North Carolina Central U (NC)
North Dakota State U (ND)
Northern Michigan U (MI)
Northwest Missouri State U (MO)
Northwest Nazarene U (ID)
Ohio Dominican U (OH)
Ohio Wesleyan U (OH)
Olivet Coll (MI)
Pace U (NY)
Pepperdine U, Malibu (CA)
Pittsburg State U (KS)
Purdue U (IN)
Purdue U Calumet (IN)
Rhode Island Coll (RI)
Roberts Wesleyan Coll (NY)
Saginaw Valley State U (MI)
St. Ambrose U (IA)
St. Edward's U (TX)
St. Francis Coll (NY)
St. John Fisher Coll (NY)
St. Joseph's Coll, Long Island Campus (NY)
St. Joseph's Coll, New York (NY)
Saint Mary's U of Minnesota (MN)
Schreiner U (TX)
Seton Hill U (PA)
Southern Polytechnic State U (GA)
Southern Utah U (UT)
Southwest Baptist U (MO)
Spring Arbor U (MI)
State U of New York at New Paltz (NY)
State U of New York at Plattsburgh (NY)
State U of New York Coll at Cortland (NY)
State U of New York Coll at Old Westbury (NY)
Stony Brook U, State U of New York (NY)
Syracuse U (NY)
Tabor Coll (KS)
Transylvania U (KY)
Trevecca Nazarene U (TN)
Trinity Christian Coll (IL)
Union Coll (NE)
U of Arkansas–Fort Smith (AR)
U of Delaware (DE)
U of Evansville (IN)
U of Great Falls (MT)
U of Illinois at Chicago (IL)
U of Illinois at Urbana–Champaign (IL)
The U of Iowa (IA)
U of Louisiana at Monroe (LA)
U of Maryland, Baltimore County (MD)
U of Michigan–Dearborn (MI)
U of Minnesota, Duluth (MN)
U of Missouri (MO)
U of Missouri–St. Louis (MO)
U of Nebraska–Lincoln (NE)
The U of North Carolina Wilmington (NC)
U of Regina (SK, Canada)
U of St. Thomas (MN)
The U of Tennessee at Martin (TN)
U of Waterloo (ON, Canada)
U of West Georgia (GA)
U of Windsor (ON, Canada)
U of Wisconsin–Superior (WI)
Utah State U (UT)
Utica Coll (NY)
Valley City State U (ND)
Valparaiso U (IN)
Viterbo U (WI)
Washburn U (KS)
Washington State U (WA)
Washington U in St. Louis (MO)
Waynesburg U (PA)
Wayne State Coll (NE)
Weber State U (UT)

Western Michigan U (MI)
Western State Colorado U (CO)
Western Washington U (WA)
Wheeling Jesuit U (WV)
Widener U (PA)
William Jewell Coll (MO)
Xavier U (OH)
Xavier U of Louisiana (LA)

CHILD-CARE AND SUPPORT SERVICES MANAGEMENT
Brigham Young U (UT)
Chestnut Hill Coll (PA)
Ferris State U (MI)
Messiah Coll (PA)
Seton Hill U (PA)
Siena Heights U (MI)
State U of New York Coll of Agriculture and Technology at Cobleskill (NY)
U of Minnesota, Twin Cities Campus (MN)
The U of Texas–Pan American (TX)

CHILD-CARE PROVISION
Brigham Young U (UT)
Wayne State Coll (NE)

CHILD DEVELOPMENT
Albertus Magnus Coll (CT)
Alcorn State U (MS)
Alliant Intl U (CA)
Appalachian State U (NC)
Auburn U (AL)
Bennington Coll (VT)
Bowling Green State U (OH)
Brigham Young U (UT)
California State U, East Bay (CA)
California State U, Fresno (CA)
California State U, Long Beach (CA)
California State U, Los Angeles (CA)
California State U, Northridge (CA)
Carson-Newman U (TN)
Central Michigan U (MI)
Coll of the Ozarks (MO)
Concordia U, St. Paul (MN)
East Carolina U (NC)
Eastern Washington U (WA)
East Tennessee State U (TN)
Gallaudet U (DC)
Goddard Coll (VT)
Goodwin Coll (CT)
Hampton U (VA)
Harding U (AR)
Henderson State U (AR)
Humboldt State U (CA)
Kansas State U (KS)
Kuyper Coll (MI)
Lesley U (MA)
Lewis-Clark State Coll (ID)
Madonna U (MI)
Michigan State U (MI)
Minnesota State U Mankato (MN)
Missouri Baptist U (MO)
Mount St. Mary's Coll (CA)
National U (CA)
Nova Southeastern U (FL)
Oklahoma Christian U (OK)
Pittsburg State U (KS)
Point Loma Nazarene U (CA)
Point U (GA)
Portland State U (OR)
Post U (CT)
Quinnipiac U (CT)
San Diego State U (CA)
Seton Hill U (PA)
Southern New Hampshire U (NH)
Texas Southern U (TX)
Texas Woman's U (TX)
Tufts U (MA)
The U of Akron (OH)
U of Alaska Fairbanks (AK)
U of Central Oklahoma (OK)
U of Guelph (ON, Canada)
U of Illinois at Urbana–Champaign (IL)
U of La Verne (CA)
U of Maryland Eastern Shore (MD)
U of Nevada, Reno (NV)
The U of North Carolina at Greensboro (NC)
U of Saint Joseph (CT)
U of Saint Mary (KS)
The U of Tennessee at Martin (TN)
The U of Texas at Arlington (TX)
U of the Incarnate Word (TX)

The U of Western Ontario (ON, Canada)
Vanderbilt U (TN)
Weber State U (UT)
Western Michigan U (MI)
West Virginia U (WV)
Youngstown State U (OH)

CHILDREN'S AND ADOLESCENT LITERATURE
Castleton State Coll (VT)

CHINESE
Bard Coll (NY)
Bates Coll (ME)
Bennington Coll (VT)
Boston U (MA)
Bryant U (RI)
California State U, Long Beach (CA)
California State U, Los Angeles (CA)
Calvin Coll (MI)
Carnegie Mellon U (PA)
Colgate U (NY)
Coll of the Holy Cross (MA)
Concordia Coll (MN)
Connecticut Coll (CT)
Dartmouth Coll (NH)
Georgetown U (DC)
Grinnell Coll (IA)
Hamilton Coll (NY)
Hobart and William Smith Colls (NY)
Hofstra U (NY)
Hope Coll (MI)
Hunter Coll of the City U of New York (NY)
Lawrence U (WI)
Lehigh U (PA)
Macalester Coll (MN)
Messiah Coll (PA)
Michigan State U (MI)
Middlebury Coll (VT)
National U (CA)
Nazareth Coll of Rochester (NY)
New Coll of Florida (FL)
North Central Coll (IL)
The Ohio State U (OH)
Oklahoma City U (OK)
Pacific Lutheran U (WA)
Pacific U (OR)
Penn State U Park (PA)
Pomona Coll (CA)
Portland State U (OR)
Reed Coll (OR)
Rutgers, The State U of New Jersey, New Brunswick (NJ)
San Francisco State U (CA)
San Jose State U (CA)
Scripps Coll (CA)
Stanford U (CA)
Swarthmore Coll (PA)
Trinity Coll (CT)
Trinity U (TX)
Tufts U (MA)
United States Military Acad (NY)
The U of British Columbia (BC, Canada)
U of California, Berkeley (CA)
U of California, Davis (CA)
U of California, Irvine (CA)
U of California, Los Angeles (CA)
U of California, Santa Barbara (CA)
U of Colorado Boulder (CO)
U of Georgia (GA)
U of Hawaii at Manoa (HI)
U of Houston (TX)
The U of Iowa (IA)
U of Kentucky (KY)
U of Maryland, Coll Park (MD)
U of Massachusetts Amherst (MA)
U of Minnesota, Twin Cities Campus (MN)
U of Mississippi (MS)
U of North Georgia (GA)
U of Notre Dame (IN)
U of Oklahoma (OK)
U of Oregon (OR)
U of Pittsburgh (PA)
U of Puget Sound (WA)
U of Regina (SK, Canada)
U of Utah (UT)
U of Vermont (VT)
U of Wisconsin–Madison (WI)
Vassar Coll (NY)
Wake Forest U (NC)
Washington U in St. Louis (MO)

Wellesley Coll (MA)
Williams Coll (MA)
Yale U (CT)

CHINESE STUDIES
The Coll of William and Mary (VA)
DePaul U (IL)
Drew U (NJ)
Gettysburg Coll (PA)
Pacific Lutheran U (WA)
U at Albany, State U of New York (NY)
U of California, Irvine (CA)
U of North Dakota (ND)
U of Richmond (VA)
The U of Western Ontario (ON, Canada)
Washington State U (WA)

CHIROPRACTIC ASSISTANT
Hawai`i Pacific U (HI)

CHRISTIAN STUDIES
Alderson-Broaddus Coll (WV)
Anderson U (SC)
Bethany Lutheran Coll (MN)
Bethel Coll (IN)
Bluefield Coll (VA)
California Baptist U (CA)
Canisius Coll (NY)
Coll of Biblical Studies–Houston (TX)
The Coll of St. Scholastica (MN)
Concordia U Wisconsin (WI)
Crown Coll (MN)
Gordon Coll (MA)
Hardin-Simmons U (TX)
Hillsdale Coll (MI)
Howard Payne U (TX)
Iowa Wesleyan Coll (IA)
Lee U (TN)
Liberty U (VA)
Lindenwood U (MO)
Loyola U New Orleans (LA)
Luther Rice U (GA)
McMurry U (TX)
Mercer U (GA)
Mid-Continent U (KY)
Mississippi Coll (MS)
Missouri Baptist U (MO)
Ouachita Baptist U (AR)
Roanoke Coll (VA)
Saint Mary's U of Minnesota (MN)
St. Thomas U (NB, Canada)
Simpson U (CA)
Stonehill Coll (MA)
Tabor Coll (KS)
Tennessee Wesleyan Coll (TN)
Texas Wesleyan U (TX)
Ursuline Coll (OH)
Wayland Baptist U (TX)

CINEMATOGRAPHY AND FILM/VIDEO PRODUCTION
Acad of Art U (CA)
American U (DC)
Art Center Coll of Design (CA)
Bard Coll (NY)
Belmont U (TN)
Bennington Coll (VT)
Binghamton U, State U of New York (NY)
Bob Jones U (SC)
Brigham Young U (UT)
California State U, Long Beach (CA)
California State U, Northridge (CA)
Calvin Coll (MI)
Chapman U (CA)
City Coll of the City U of New York (NY)
Cleveland State U (OH)
Columbia Coll Chicago (IL)
Columbia Coll Hollywood (CA)
Concordia U (QC, Canada)
DePaul U (IL)
Eastern New Mexico U (NM)
Eastern Washington U (WA)
Emerson Coll (MA)
The Evergreen State Coll (WA)
Fairleigh Dickinson U, Coll at Florham (NJ)
Five Towns Coll (NY)
George Fox U (OR)
George Mason U (VA)
Hawai`i Pacific U (HI)
Hunter Coll of the City U of New York (NY)

Ithaca Coll (NY)
John Brown U (AR)
Keene State Coll (NH)
La Sierra U (CA)
Liberty U (VA)
Long Island U–C. W. Post Campus (NY)
Loyola Marymount U (CA)
Maharishi U of Management (IA)
Massachusetts Coll of Art and Design (MA)
Mercy Coll (NY)
Miami Dade Coll (FL)
Middlebury Coll (VT)
Missouri Western State U (MO)
Montana State U (MT)
Montclair State U (NJ)
New England Inst of Technology (RI)
New England School of Communications (ME)
New Mexico Highlands U (NM)
New Mexico State U (NM)
New York U (NY)
Northern Michigan U (MI)
Ohio U (OH)
Oklahoma City U (OK)
Pacific Union Coll (CA)
Palm Beach Atlantic U (FL)
Point Park U (PA)
Purchase Coll, State U of New York (NY)
Quinnipiac U (CT)
Regent U (VA)
Rochester Inst of Technology (NY)
San Francisco Art Inst (CA)
Savannah Coll of Art and Design (GA)
School of the Art Inst of Chicago (IL)
School of the Museum of Fine Arts, Boston (MA)
Southern Illinois U Carbondale (IL)
Stanford U (CA)
Syracuse U (NY)
Taylor U (IN)
U of Central Arkansas (AR)
U of Central Florida (FL)
U of Illinois at Chicago (IL)
The U of Iowa (IA)
U of Miami (FL)
U of New Mexico (NM)
U of North Carolina School of the Arts (NC)
The U of North Carolina Wilmington (NC)
U of Oregon (OR)
U of Regina (SK, Canada)
U of Rhode Island (RI)
U of Southern California (CA)
The U of the Arts (PA)
Virginia Commonwealth U (VA)
Walla Walla U (WA)
Wayne State U (MI)
Webster U (MO)
Wheeling Jesuit U (WV)

CITY/URBAN, COMMUNITY AND REGIONAL PLANNING
Appalachian State U (NC)
Arizona State U (AZ)
Ball State U (IN)
Bridgewater State U (MA)
Buffalo State Coll, State U of New York (NY)
California Polytechnic State U, San Luis Obispo (CA)
California State Polytechnic U, Pomona (CA)
California State U, Chico (CA)
Concordia U (QC, Canada)
Dalhousie U (NS, Canada)
East Carolina U (NC)
Eastern Washington U (WA)
Florida Atlantic U (FL)
Frostburg State U (MD)
Indiana U of Pennsylvania (PA)
Iowa State U of Science and Technology (IA)
Mansfield U of Pennsylvania (PA)
Massachusetts Inst of Technology (MA)
Miami U (OH)
Michigan State U (MI)
Minnesota State U Mankato (MN)
Missouri State U (MO)
The Ohio State U (OH)

Plymouth State U (NH)
Portland State U (OR)
Rowan U (NJ)
Temple U (PA)
Texas A&M U (TX)
Texas State U–San Marcos (TX)
The U of Akron (OH)
The U of Arizona (AZ)
U of California, Davis (CA)
U of Cincinnati (OH)
U of Illinois at Urbana–Champaign (IL)
U of Missouri–Kansas City (MO)
U of Nevada, Las Vegas (NV)
U of New Hampshire (NH)
U of Virginia (VA)
U of Waterloo (ON, Canada)
The U of Western Ontario (ON, Canada)
Western Michigan U (MI)
Westfield State U (MA)

CIVIL ENGINEERING
American U of Beirut (Lebanon)
Arizona State U (AZ)
Arkansas State U (AR)
Auburn U (AL)
Boise State U (ID)
Bradley U (IL)
Brown U (RI)
Bucknell U (PA)
California Baptist U (CA)
California Polytechnic State U, San Luis Obispo (CA)
California State Polytechnic U, Pomona (CA)
California State U, Chico (CA)
California State U, Fresno (CA)
California State U, Fullerton (CA)
California State U, Long Beach (CA)
California State U, Los Angeles (CA)
California State U, Northridge (CA)
Calvin Coll (MI)
Caribbean U (PR)
Carnegie Mellon U (PA)
Carroll Coll (MT)
Case Western Reserve U (OH)
The Catholic U of America (DC)
Central Connecticut State U (CT)
Christian Brothers U (TN)
The Citadel, The Military Coll of South Carolina (SC)
City Coll of the City U of New York (NY)
Clarkson U (NY)
Clemson U (SC)
Cleveland State U (OH)
Colorado School of Mines (CO)
Colorado State U (CO)
Columbia U (NY)
Concordia U (QC, Canada)
Cooper Union for the Advancement of Science and Art (NY)
Dordt Coll (IA)
Florida Ag and Mech U (FL)
Florida Atlantic U (FL)
Florida Gulf Coast U (FL)
Florida Inst of Technology (FL)
Florida Intl U (FL)
George Fox U (OR)
George Mason U (VA)
Georgia Southern U (GA)
Gonzaga U (WA)
Hofstra U (NY)
Hope Coll (MI)
Illinois Inst of Technology (IL)
Indiana U–Purdue U Fort Wayne (IN)
Iowa State U of Science and Technology (IA)
The Johns Hopkins U (MD)
Kansas State U (KS)
Lafayette Coll (PA)
Lamar U (TX)
Lawrence Technological U (MI)
Lebanese American U (Lebanon)
Lehigh U (PA)
Lipscomb U (TN)
Louisiana State U and Ag and Mech Coll (LA)
Loyola Marymount U (CA)
Manhattan Coll (NY)
Marquette U (WI)

Massachusetts Inst of Technology (MA)
Merrimack Coll (MA)
Michigan State U (MI)
Milwaukee School of Eng (WI)
Minnesota State U Mankato (MN)
Mississippi State U (MS)
Missouri U of Science and Technology (MO)
Montana State U (MT)
New Jersey Inst of Technology (NJ)
New Mexico Inst of Mining and Technology (NM)
New Mexico State U (NM)
North Carolina State U (NC)
North Dakota State U (ND)
Northeastern U (MA)
Northern Arizona U (AZ)
Norwich U (VT)
The Ohio State U (OH)
Ohio U (OH)
Oklahoma State U (OK)
Old Dominion U (VA)
Oregon State U (OR)
Penn State Abington (PA)
Penn State Altoona (PA)
Penn State Beaver (PA)
Penn State Berks (PA)
Penn State Brandywine (PA)
Penn State DuBois (PA)
Penn State Erie, The Behrend Coll (PA)
Penn State Fayette, The Eberly Campus (PA)
Penn State Greater Allegheny (PA)
Penn State Harrisburg (PA)
Penn State Hazleton (PA)
Penn State Lehigh Valley (PA)
Penn State Mont Alto (PA)
Penn State New Kensington (PA)
Penn State Schuylkill (PA)
Penn State Shenango (PA)
Penn State U Park (PA)
Penn State Wilkes-Barre (PA)
Penn State Worthington Scranton (PA)
Penn State York (PA)
Polytechnic Inst of New York U (NY)
Polytechnic U of Puerto Rico (PR)
Portland State U (OR)
Princeton U (NJ)
Purdue U (IN)
Quinnipiac U (CT)
Rensselaer Polytechnic Inst (NY)
Rice U (TX)
Rockhurst U (MO)
Rowan U (NJ)
Rutgers, The State U of New Jersey, New Brunswick (NJ)
Saint Louis U (MO)
Saint Martin's U (WA)
San Diego State U (CA)
San Francisco State U (CA)
San Jose State U (CA)
Seattle U (WA)
South Dakota State U (SD)
Southern Illinois U Carbondale (IL)
Southern Illinois U Edwardsville (IL)
Southern Methodist U (TX)
Southern Polytechnic State U (GA)
Stanford U (CA)
Stony Brook U, State U of New York (NY)
Syracuse U (NY)
Temple U (PA)
Tennessee State U (TN)
Texas A&M U (TX)
Texas A&M U–Kingsville (TX)
Trine U (IN)
Tufts U (MA)
United States Air Force Acad (CO)
United States Coast Guard Acad (CT)
United States Military Acad (NY)
Université de Sherbrooke (QC, Canada)
U at Buffalo, the State U of New York (NY)
The U of Akron (OH)
The U of Alabama (AL)
The U of Alabama at Birmingham (AL)
U of Alaska Anchorage (AK)
U of Alaska Fairbanks (AK)
The U of Arizona (AZ)

The U of British Columbia (BC, Canada)
The U of British Columbia–Okanagan (BC, Canada)
U of California, Berkeley (CA)
U of California, Davis (CA)
U of California, Irvine (CA)
U of California, Los Angeles (CA)
U of Central Florida (FL)
U of Cincinnati (OH)
U of Colorado Boulder (CO)
U of Colorado Denver (CO)
U of Delaware (DE)
U of Evansville (IN)
U of Florida (FL)
U of Georgia (GA)
U of Hartford (CT)
U of Hawaii at Manoa (HI)
U of Houston (TX)
U of Idaho (ID)
U of Illinois at Chicago (IL)
U of Illinois at Urbana–Champaign (IL)
The U of Iowa (IA)
The U of Kansas (KS)
U of Kentucky (KY)
U of Louisiana at Lafayette (LA)
U of Louisville (KY)
U of Maryland, Coll Park (MD)
U of Massachusetts Amherst (MA)
U of Massachusetts Dartmouth (MA)
U of Memphis (TN)
U of Miami (FL)
U of Michigan (MI)
U of Minnesota, Duluth (MN)
U of Minnesota, Twin Cities Campus (MN)
U of Mississippi (MS)
U of Missouri (MO)
U of Missouri–Kansas City (MO)
U of Missouri–St. Louis (MO)
U of Mount Union (OH)
U of Nebraska–Lincoln (NE)
U of Nevada, Las Vegas (NV)
U of Nevada, Reno (NV)
U of New Brunswick Fredericton (NB, Canada)
U of New Hampshire (NH)
U of New Haven (CT)
U of New Mexico (NM)
U of New Orleans (LA)
The U of North Carolina at Charlotte (NC)
U of North Dakota (ND)
U of North Florida (FL)
U of Notre Dame (IN)
U of Oklahoma (OK)
U of Ottawa (ON, Canada)
U of Pittsburgh (PA)
U of Portland (OR)
U of Rhode Island (RI)
U of South Alabama (AL)
U of South Carolina (SC)
U of Southern California (CA)
U of South Florida (FL)
The U of Tennessee (TN)
The U of Tennessee at Chattanooga (TN)
The U of Texas at Arlington (TX)
The U of Texas at Austin (TX)
The U of Texas at El Paso (TX)
The U of Texas at San Antonio (TX)
U of the District of Columbia (DC)
The U of Toledo (OH)
U of Utah (UT)
U of Vermont (VT)
U of Virginia (VA)
U of Waterloo (ON, Canada)
The U of Western Ontario (ON, Canada)
U of Windsor (ON, Canada)
U of Wisconsin–Madison (WI)
U of Wisconsin–Milwaukee (WI)
U of Wisconsin–Platteville (WI)
U of Wyoming (WY)
Utah State U (UT)
Valparaiso U (IN)
Vanderbilt U (TN)
Villanova U (PA)
Virginia Polytechnic Inst and State U (VA)
Walla Walla U (WA)
Washington State U (WA)
Wayne State U (MI)
Wentworth Inst of Technology (MA)
Western Kentucky U (KY)

Western Michigan U (MI)
West Texas A&M U (TX)
West Virginia U (WV)
West Virginia U Inst of Technology (WV)
Widener U (PA)
Worcester Polytechnic Inst (MA)
Youngstown State U (OH)

CIVIL ENGINEERING RELATED
Bradley U (IL)
California Polytechnic State U, San Luis Obispo (CA)
Embry-Riddle Aeronautical U–Daytona (FL)
Oregon State U (OR)
Purdue U (IN)

CIVIL ENGINEERING TECHNOLOGY
Bluefield State Coll (WV)
Central Connecticut State U (CT)
Fairleigh Dickinson U, Metropolitan Campus (NJ)
Fairmont State U (WV)
Georgia Southern U (GA)
Indiana State U (IN)
Lincoln U (MO)
Metropolitan State U of Denver (CO)
Murray State U (KY)
Pennsylvania Coll of Technology (PA)
Point Park U (PA)
Purdue U (IN)
Rochester Inst of Technology (NY)
Roger Williams U (RI)
Southern Polytechnic State U (GA)
State U of New York Inst of Technology (NY)
Temple U (PA)
Texas Southern U (TX)
United States Military Acad (NY)
U of Houston–Downtown (TX)
The U of North Carolina at Charlotte (NC)
U of North Texas (TX)
The U of Toledo (OH)
Wentworth Inst of Technology (MA)
West Virginia U Inst of Technology (WV)
Youngstown State U (OH)

CLASSICAL, ANCIENT MEDITERRANEAN AND NEAR EASTERN STUDIES AND ARCHAEOLOGY
Bowdoin Coll (ME)
Columbia U (NY)
Creighton U (NE)
Hampshire Coll (MA)
Kalamazoo Coll (MI)
Purdue U (IN)
Saint Anselm Coll (NH)
Swarthmore Coll (PA)
Syracuse U (NY)
U of California, Berkeley (CA)
U of California, Davis (CA)
U of California, Irvine (CA)
U of California, Los Angeles (CA)
U of Illinois at Chicago (IL)
U of Michigan (MI)
U of Ottawa (ON, Canada)
U of Richmond (VA)

CLASSICS AND CLASSICAL LANGUAGES
Acadia U (NS, Canada)
Agnes Scott Coll (GA)
Amherst Coll (MA)
Asbury U (KY)
Assumption Coll (MA)
Augustana Coll (IL)
Augustana Coll (SD)
Ball State U (IN)
Baylor U (TX)
Belmont U (TN)
Binghamton U, State U of New York (NY)
Boston Coll (MA)
Boston U (MA)
Bowdoin Coll (ME)
Bowling Green State U (OH)
Brown U (RI)
Bucknell U (PA)
Calvin Coll (MI)
Carleton Coll (MN)
Carroll Coll (MT)
Case Western Reserve U (OH)

The Catholic U of America (DC)
Centre Coll (KY)
Christendom Coll (VA)
Christopher Newport U (VA)
Claremont McKenna Coll (CA)
Clark U (MA)
Coe Coll (IA)
Colby Coll (ME)
Colgate U (NY)
Coll of Charleston (SC)
The Coll of New Rochelle (NY)
Coll of Saint Benedict (MN)
Coll of the Holy Cross (MA)
The Coll of William and Mary (VA)
The Coll of Wooster (OH)
The Colorado Coll (CO)
Columbia U (NY)
Columbia U, School of General Studies (NY)
Concordia Coll (MN)
Concordia U (QC, Canada)
Connecticut Coll (CT)
Cornell Coll (IA)
Creighton U (NE)
Dalhousie U (NS, Canada)
Dartmouth Coll (NH)
Davidson Coll (NC)
DePauw U (IN)
Dickinson Coll (PA)
Drew U (NJ)
Duquesne U (PA)
Earlham Coll (IN)
Elmira Coll (NY)
The Evergreen State Coll (WA)
Franklin & Marshall Coll (PA)
Furman U (SC)
Georgetown U (DC)
Gettysburg Coll (PA)
Gonzaga U (WA)
Grand Valley State U (MI)
Grinnell Coll (IA)
Gustavus Adolphus Coll (MN)
Hamilton Coll (NY)
Hampden-Sydney Coll (VA)
Hanover Coll (IN)
Haverford Coll (PA)
Hendrix Coll (AR)
Hillsdale Coll (MI)
Hobart and William Smith Colls (NY)
Hofstra U (NY)
Hollins U (VA)
Hope Coll (MI)
Hunter Coll of the City U of New York (NY)
Illinois Wesleyan U (IL)
Indiana U Bloomington (IN)
John Carroll U (OH)
The Johns Hopkins U (MD)
Kenyon Coll (OH)
Knox Coll (IL)
La Salle U (PA)
Lawrence U (WI)
Lehigh U (PA)
Lehman Coll of the City U of New York (NY)
Loyola U Chicago (IL)
Loyola U Maryland (MD)
Loyola U New Orleans (LA)
Luther Coll (IA)
Macalester Coll (MN)
Manhattan Coll (NY)
Manhattanville Coll (NY)
Marquette U (WI)
Mercer U (GA)
Miami U (OH)
Middlebury Coll (VT)
Millsaps Coll (MS)
Monmouth Coll (IL)
Montclair State U (NJ)
Moravian Coll (PA)
Mount Allison U (NB, Canada)
Mount Holyoke Coll (MA)
New York U (NY)
North Central Coll (IL)
The Ohio State U (OH)
Ohio U (OH)
Ohio Wesleyan U (OH)
Pacific Lutheran U (WA)
Penn State Abington (PA)
Penn State Altoona (PA)
Penn State Beaver (PA)
Penn State Berks (PA)
Penn State Brandywine (PA)
Penn State DuBois (PA)
Penn State Erie, The Behrend Coll (PA)

Penn State Fayette, The Eberly Campus (PA)
Penn State Greater Allegheny (PA)
Penn State Hazleton (PA)
Penn State Lehigh Valley (PA)
Penn State Mont Alto (PA)
Penn State New Kensington (PA)
Penn State Schuylkill (PA)
Penn State Shenango (PA)
Penn State U Park (PA)
Penn State Wilkes-Barre (PA)
Penn State Worthington Scranton (PA)
Penn State York (PA)
Pitzer Coll (CA)
Pomona Coll (CA)
Princeton U (NJ)
Randolph Coll (VA)
Randolph-Macon Coll (VA)
Reed Coll (OR)
Rhodes Coll (TN)
Rice U (TX)
Rockford Coll (IL)
Rollins Coll (FL)
Rutgers, The State U of New Jersey, Newark (NJ)
Rutgers, The State U of New Jersey, New Brunswick (NJ)
Saint Anselm Coll (NH)
St. Bonaventure U (NY)
Saint John's U (MN)
Saint Louis U (MO)
Saint Michael's Coll (VT)
St. Olaf Coll (MN)
Samford U (AL)
San Diego State U (CA)
San Francisco State U (CA)
Scripps Coll (CA)
Sewanee: The U of the South (TN)
Siena Coll (NY)
Skidmore Coll (NY)
Smith Coll (MA)
Southern Illinois U Carbondale (IL)
Southwestern U (TX)
Stanford U (CA)
Swarthmore Coll (PA)
Sweet Briar Coll (VA)
Syracuse U (NY)
Temple U (PA)
Texas A&M U (TX)
Transylvania U (KY)
Trent U (ON, Canada)
Trinity Coll (CT)
Trinity U (TX)
Truman State U (MO)
Tufts U (MA)
Tulane U (LA)
U at Buffalo, the State U of New York (NY)
The U of Akron (OH)
The U of Arizona (AZ)
The U of British Columbia (BC, Canada)
U of California, Berkeley (CA)
U of California, Irvine (CA)
U of California, Santa Barbara (CA)
U of California, Santa Cruz (CA)
U of Chicago (IL)
U of Colorado Boulder (CO)
U of Dallas (TX)
U of Evansville (IN)
U of Florida (FL)
U of Georgia (GA)
U of Guelph (ON, Canada)
U of Hawaii at Manoa (HI)
U of Illinois at Chicago (IL)
U of Illinois at Urbana–Champaign (IL)
The U of Iowa (IA)
The U of Kansas (KS)
U of Kentucky (KY)
U of Maryland, Coll Park (MD)
U of Mary Washington (VA)
U of Massachusetts Amherst (MA)
U of Massachusetts Boston (MA)
U of Miami (FL)
U of Michigan (MI)
U of Minnesota, Twin Cities Campus (MN)
U of Mississippi (MS)
U of Missouri (MO)
U of Nebraska–Lincoln (NE)
U of New Brunswick Fredericton (NB, Canada)
U of New Brunswick Saint John (NB, Canada)
U of New Hampshire (NH)

U of New Mexico (NM)
U of North Carolina at Asheville (NC)
The U of North Carolina at Chapel Hill (NC)
The U of North Carolina at Greensboro (NC)
U of North Dakota (ND)
U of Notre Dame (IN)
U of Oklahoma (OK)
U of Oregon (OR)
U of Ottawa (ON, Canada)
U of Pennsylvania (PA)
U of Pittsburgh (PA)
U of Puget Sound (WA)
U of Regina (SK, Canada)
U of Rhode Island (RI)
U of Rochester (NY)
U of St. Thomas (MN)
The U of Scranton (PA)
U of South Carolina (SC)
U of Southern California (CA)
U of South Florida (FL)
The U of Tennessee (TN)
The U of Texas at Austin (TX)
The U of Texas at San Antonio (TX)
U of Utah (UT)
U of Vermont (VT)
U of Virginia (VA)
U of Waterloo (ON, Canada)
The U of Western Ontario (ON, Canada)
U of Windsor (ON, Canada)
U of Wisconsin–Madison (WI)
U of Wisconsin–Milwaukee (WI)
Valparaiso U (IN)
Vanderbilt U (TN)
Vassar Coll (NY)
Villanova U (PA)
Virginia Wesleyan Coll (VA)
Wabash Coll (IN)
Wake Forest U (NC)
Washington and Lee U (VA)
Washington U in St. Louis (MO)
Wayne State U (MI)
Wellesley Coll (MA)
Wesleyan U (CT)
Wheaton Coll (MA)
Whitman Coll (WA)
Willamette U (OR)
Williams Coll (MA)
Wright State U (OH)
Xavier U (OH)
Yale U (CT)

CLASSICS AND CLASSICAL LANGUAGES RELATED
California State U, Long Beach (CA)
Columbia U, School of General Studies (NY)
Eckerd Coll (FL)
Lawrence U (WI)
Marquette U (WI)
New Coll of Florida (FL)
Ohio U (OH)
Rutgers, The State U of New Jersey, Newark (NJ)
Saint Louis U (MO)
Tulane U (LA)
U of California, Los Angeles (CA)
Wheaton Coll (IL)
Wheaton Coll (MA)
Xavier U (OH)

CLINICAL, COUNSELING AND APPLIED PSYCHOLOGY RELATED
St. Francis Coll (NY)

CLINICAL LABORATORY SCIENCE/MEDICAL TECHNOLOGY
Abilene Christian U (TX)
Albany Coll of Pharmacy and Health Sciences (NY)
American U of Beirut (Lebanon)
Anderson U (IN)
Andrews U (MI)
Arizona State U (AZ)
Arkansas State U (AR)
Arkansas Tech U (AR)
Armstrong Atlantic State U (GA)
Auburn U (AL)
Augustana Coll (SD)
Austin Peay State U (TN)
Ball State U (IN)
Barry U (FL)

Baylor U (TX)
Bellarmine U (KY)
Belmont U (TN)
Bemidji State U (MN)
Benedictine U (IL)
Bethune-Cookman U (FL)
Blackburn Coll (IL)
Blue Mountain Coll (MS)
Bowling Green State U (OH)
Bradley U (IL)
Brigham Young U (UT)
Caldwell Coll (NJ)
California State U, Chico (CA)
California State U, Dominguez Hills (CA)
Cameron U (OK)
Campbellsville U (KY)
Canisius Coll (NY)
Carson-Newman U (TN)
Catawba Coll (NC)
The Catholic U of America (DC)
Cheyney U of Pennsylvania (PA)
The Coll at Brockport, State U of New York (NY)
Coll of Saint Elizabeth (NJ)
Coll of Saint Mary (NE)
The Coll of Saint Rose (NY)
Coll of Staten Island of the City U of New York (NY)
Concord U (WV)
Defiance Coll (OH)
DePaul U (IL)
DeVry U, Phoenix (AZ)
Dordt Coll (IA)
East Carolina U (NC)
East Central U (OK)
Eastern Illinois U (IL)
Eastern Mennonite U (VA)
Eastern Michigan U (MI)
Eastern New Mexico U (NM)
Edinboro U of Pennsylvania (PA)
Elmira Coll (NY)
Evangel U (MO)
Fairleigh Dickinson U, Coll at Florham (NJ)
Fairleigh Dickinson U, Metropolitan Campus (NJ)
Ferris State U (MI)
Florida Gulf Coast U (FL)
Gannon U (PA)
George Mason U (VA)
Georgia Regents U (GA)
Graceland U (IA)
Grand Valley State U (MI)
Hartwick Coll (NY)
Henderson State U (AR)
Holy Family U (PA)
Houghton Coll (NY)
Illinois Coll (IL)
Illinois State U (IL)
Indiana State U (IN)
Indiana U of Pennsylvania (PA)
Indiana U–Purdue U Fort Wayne (IN)
Indiana U–Purdue U Indianapolis (IN)
Indiana U Southeast (IN)
Indiana Wesleyan U (IN)
Inter American U of Puerto Rico, San Germán Campus (PR)
Jamestown Coll (ND)
Kansas State U (KS)
Kean U (NJ)
Kent State U (OH)
Kentucky Wesleyan Coll (KY)
Keuka Coll (NY)
King Coll (TN)
King's Coll (PA)
Lamar U (TX)
Langston U (OK)
Lebanon Valley Coll (PA)
Lincoln Memorial U (TN)
Lincoln U (MO)
Long Island U–Brooklyn Campus (NY)
Long Island U–C. W. Post Campus (NY)
Louisiana Coll (LA)
Louisiana State U at Alexandria (LA)
Loyola U Chicago (IL)
Madonna U (MI)
Malone U (OH)
Manchester U (IN)
Mansfield U of Pennsylvania (PA)
Marist Coll (NY)
Marquette U (WI)

Marshall U (WV)
Mary Baldwin Coll (VA)
Maryville U of Saint Louis (MO)
Marywood U (PA)
Mayville State U (ND)
McKendree U (IL)
McNeese State U (LA)
Mercy Coll (NY)
Miami U (OH)
Michigan State U (MI)
Midwestern State U (TX)
Minnesota State U Mankato (MN)
Minnesota State U Moorhead (MN)
Minot State U (ND)
Misericordia U (PA)
Mississippi State U (MS)
Missouri State U (MO)
Missouri Western State U (MO)
Monmouth U (NJ)
Morningside Coll (IA)
Mount Marty Coll (SD)
Mount Mercy U (IA)
Mount Saint Mary Coll (NY)
Mount Vernon Nazarene U (OH)
Norfolk State U (VA)
North Dakota State U (ND)
Northern Illinois U (IL)
Northern Michigan U (MI)
Northern State U (SD)
Northwestern Coll (IA)
Northwest Missouri State U (MO)
Oakland U (MI)
The Ohio State U (OH)
Oklahoma Christian U (OK)
Old Dominion U (VA)
Oral Roberts U (OK)
Pittsburg State U (KS)
Purdue U (IN)
Purdue U Calumet (IN)
Quincy U (IL)
Ramapo Coll of New Jersey (NJ)
Rhode Island Coll (RI)
Rochester Inst of Technology (NY)
Rockhurst U (MO)
Roosevelt U (IL)
Rutgers, The State U of New
    Jersey, Camden (NJ)
Rutgers, The State U of New
    Jersey, Newark (NJ)
Rutgers, The State U of New
    Jersey, New Brunswick (NJ)
Sage Coll of Albany (NY)
Saginaw Valley State U (MI)
St. Edward's U (TX)
St. Francis Coll (NY)
St. John's U (NY)
Saint Joseph's Coll (IN)
St. Joseph's Coll, Long Island
    Campus (NY)
St. Joseph's Coll, New York (NY)
Saint Leo U (FL)
Saint Louis U (MO)
Saint Mary-of-the-Woods Coll (IN)
Saint Mary's U of Minnesota (MN)
St. Thomas Aquinas Coll (NY)
Salem State U (MA)
Salisbury U (MD)
Salve Regina U (RI)
Seton Hill U (PA)
South Dakota State U (SD)
Southeast Missouri State U (MO)
Southern Arkansas U–Magnolia
    (AR)
Southwest Baptist U (MO)
Southwestern Adventist U (TX)
State U of New York at Fredonia
    (NY)
State U of New York at Plattsburgh
    (NY)
Stony Brook U, State U of New York
    (NY)
Tabor Coll (KS)
Tarleton State U (TX)
Tennessee State U (TN)
Texas Southern U (TX)
Texas State U–San Marcos (TX)
Texas Woman's U (TX)
Thomas Edison State Coll (NJ)
Thomas More Coll (KY)
Tuskegee U (AL)
Union Coll (NE)
Union U (TN)
U at Buffalo, the State U of New
    York (NY)
The U of Alabama at Birmingham
    (AL)
U of Alaska Anchorage (AK)

U of Arkansas for Medical Sciences
    (AR)
U of Bridgeport (CT)
U of Central Arkansas (AR)
U of Central Florida (FL)
U of Central Oklahoma (OK)
U of Cincinnati (OH)
U of Delaware (DE)
U of Evansville (IN)
The U of Findlay (OH)
U of Hartford (CT)
U of Hawaii at Manoa (HI)
U of Idaho (ID)
U of Illinois at Springfield (IL)
The U of Iowa (IA)
The U of Kansas (KS)
U of Kentucky (KY)
U of Louisiana at Monroe (LA)
U of Maryland Eastern Shore (MD)
U of Massachusetts Dartmouth
    (MA)
U of Medicine and Dentistry of New
    Jersey (NJ)
U of Michigan–Flint (MI)
U of Minnesota, Twin Cities
    Campus (MN)
U of Mississippi (MS)
U of Missouri–Kansas City (MO)
U of Mount Union (OH)
U of Nevada, Las Vegas (NV)
U of New England (ME)
U of New Hampshire (NH)
The U of North Carolina at Chapel
    Hill (NC)
The U of North Carolina at
    Charlotte (NC)
The U of North Carolina at
    Greensboro (NC)
U of North Dakota (ND)
U of North Texas (TX)
U of Rhode Island (RI)
U of St. Francis (IL)
The U of Scranton (PA)
U of Southern Mississippi (MS)
U of South Florida (FL)
The U of Tennessee (TN)
The U of Texas at Arlington (TX)
The U of Texas at Austin (TX)
The U of Texas at El Paso (TX)
The U of Texas at San Antonio (TX)
The U of Texas–Pan American (TX)
U of the District of Columbia (DC)
U of the Sciences (PA)
The U of Toledo (OH)
U of Utah (UT)
U of Vermont (VT)
U of West Florida (FL)
U of Wisconsin–La Crosse (WI)
U of Wisconsin–Milwaukee (WI)
U of Wisconsin–Stevens Point (WI)
Utah State U (UT)
Virginia Commonwealth U (VA)
Wake Forest U (NC)
Walla Walla U (WA)
Walsh U (OH)
Wartburg Coll (IA)
Washburn U (KS)
Wayne State U (MI)
Weber State U (UT)
Wesley Coll (DE)
Western Connecticut State U (CT)
Western Illinois U (IL)
Western Kentucky U (KY)
West Liberty U (WV)
West Texas A&M U (TX)
West Virginia U (WV)
Wichita State U (KS)
Wilkes U (PA)
Wright State U (OH)
Xavier U (OH)
York Coll of Pennsylvania (PA)
York Coll of the City U of New York
    (NY)
Youngstown State U (OH)

CLINICAL/MEDICAL LABORATORY ASSISTANT
National U (CA)

CLINICAL/MEDICAL LABORATORY SCIENCE AND ALLIED PROFESSIONS RELATED
Allen Coll (IA)
Auburn U (AL)
Bloomfield Coll (NJ)
The Coll of Idaho (ID)

Hunter Coll of the City U of New
    York (NY)
Roosevelt U (IL)
Saint Louis U (MO)

CLINICAL/MEDICAL LABORATORY TECHNOLOGY
Auburn U (AL)
Barry U (FL)
California State U, East Bay (CA)
Clarion U of Pennsylvania (PA)
Farmingdale State Coll (NY)
Indiana U–Purdue U Fort Wayne
    (IN)
Long Island U–C. W. Post Campus
    (NY)
Northern State U (SD)
Penn State DuBois (PA)
St. Thomas Aquinas Coll (NY)
Sonoma State U (CA)
The U of British Columbia (BC,
    Canada)
U of Maryland Eastern Shore (MD)
U of Missouri–Kansas City (MO)
U of New Mexico (NM)
U of Science and Arts of Oklahoma
    (OK)
Viterbo U (WI)
Washburn U (KS)
York Coll of the City U of New York
    (NY)

CLINICAL/MEDICAL SOCIAL WORK
Eastern New Mexico U (NM)
New Mexico Highlands U (NM)

CLINICAL NUTRITION
Kent State U (OH)
Messiah Coll (PA)
U of North Dakota (ND)

CLINICAL PASTORAL COUNSELING/PATIENT COUNSELING
Luther Rice U (GA)

CLINICAL PSYCHOLOGY
Husson U (ME)
Keene State Coll (NH)
Lamar U (TX)
Mansfield U of Pennsylvania (PA)
Simon Fraser U (BC, Canada)
Tennessee State U (TN)
Tufts U (MA)
The U of British Columbia (BC,
    Canada)
U of New Brunswick Fredericton
    (NB, Canada)
U of Windsor (ON, Canada)
Western State Colorado U (CO)

COGNITIVE PSYCHOLOGY AND PSYCHOLINGUISTICS
Averett U (VA)
Brown U (RI)
Dartmouth Coll (NH)
Lawrence U (WI)
Scripps Coll (CA)
State U of New York at Oswego
    (NY)
Tulane U (LA)
U of California, Santa Cruz (CA)
Vassar Coll (NY)
Washington U in St. Louis (MO)
Wellesley Coll (MA)
Yale U (CT)

COGNITIVE SCIENCE
California State U, Fresno (CA)
California State U, Stanislaus (CA)
Canisius Coll (NY)
Carnegie Mellon U (PA)
Case Western Reserve U (OH)
Central Michigan U (MI)
George Fox U (OR)
Hampshire Coll (MA)
Indiana U Bloomington (IN)
The Johns Hopkins U (MD)
Lawrence U (WI)
Lehigh U (PA)
Massachusetts Inst of Technology
    (MA)
Millsaps Coll (MS)
Pomona Coll (CA)
Rensselaer Polytechnic Inst (NY)
Simon Fraser U (BC, Canada)
State U of New York at Oswego
    (NY)
United States Military Acad (NY)

The U of British Columbia (BC,
    Canada)
U of California, Berkeley (CA)
U of California, Los Angeles (CA)
U of California, Merced (CA)
U of Delaware (DE)
U of Evansville (IN)
U of Georgia (GA)
U of Pennsylvania (PA)
U of Richmond (VA)
U of Southern California (CA)
The U of Texas at Dallas (TX)
U of Wisconsin–Stout (WI)
Vanderbilt U (TN)

COLLEGE STUDENT COUNSELING AND PERSONNEL SERVICES
Bowling Green State U (OH)
Lee U (TN)
The U of North Carolina at
    Pembroke (NC)

COMMERCIAL AND ADVERTISING ART
Acad of Art U (CA)
Alberta Coll of Art & Design (AB,
    Canada)
American Acad of Art (IL)
Arkansas State U (AR)
Art Center Coll of Design (CA)
Ashland U (OH)
Bemidji State U (MN)
Bob Jones U (SC)
Boise State U (ID)
Bowling Green State U (OH)
Buena Vista U (IA)
Buffalo State Coll, State U of New
    York (NY)
California State U, East Bay (CA)
California State U, Fresno (CA)
California State U, Long Beach
    (CA)
Cardinal Stritch U (WI)
Carson-Newman U (TN)
Clark U (MA)
Coll for Creative Studies (MI)
The Coll of New Jersey (NJ)
The Coll of Saint Rose (NY)
Columbia Coll Chicago (IL)
Columbus Coll of Art & Design
    (OH)
Concordia U Chicago (IL)
Concordia U, Nebraska (NE)
Concordia U Wisconsin (WI)
Curry Coll (MA)
Dominican U (IL)
Dordt Coll (IA)
Drake U (IA)
Fairmont State U (WV)
Fashion Inst of Technology (NY)
Franklin Pierce U (NH)
Graceland U (IA)
Hampton U (VA)
Indiana U–Purdue U Fort Wayne
    (IN)
Iowa State U of Science and
    Technology (IA)
Keene State Coll (NH)
Kent State U (OH)
Kutztown U of Pennsylvania (PA)
Lamar U (TX)
Lewis U (IL)
Lipscomb U (TN)
Louisiana Coll (LA)
Loyola U New Orleans (LA)
Marietta Coll (OH)
Marymount Manhattan Coll (NY)
Massachusetts Coll of Art and
    Design (MA)
Mercy Coll (NY)
Miami U (OH)
Millikin U (IL)
Minnesota State U Mankato (MN)
Mount Mary Coll (WI)
New York City Coll of Technology of
    the City U of New York (NY)
New York Inst of Technology (NY)
Northwest Nazarene U (ID)
Oklahoma Christian U (OK)
Oklahoma City U (OK)
O'More Coll of Design (TN)
Oral Roberts U (OK)
Otis Coll of Art and Design (CA)
Pennsylvania Coll of Technology
    (PA)
Philadelphia U (PA)
Pittsburg State U (KS)

Portland State U (OR)
Purchase Coll, State U of New York
    (NY)
Ringling Coll of Art and Design (FL)
Rochester Inst of Technology (NY)
Rutgers, The State U of New
    Jersey, New Brunswick (NJ)
Sage Coll of Albany (NY)
St. Norbert Coll (WI)
St. Thomas Aquinas Coll (NY)
Salem State U (MA)
Savannah Coll of Art and Design
    (GA)
Seton Hill U (PA)
Southwest Baptist U (MO)
State U of New York at Fredonia
    (NY)
State U of New York at New Paltz
    (NY)
State U of New York at Oswego
    (NY)
Suffolk U (MA)
Syracuse U (NY)
U of Central Oklahoma (OK)
U of Cincinnati (OH)
U of Denver (CO)
U of Massachusetts Dartmouth
    (MA)
U of Minnesota, Duluth (MN)
U of New Haven (CT)
U of North Georgia (GA)
U of North Texas (TX)
The U of Tennessee (TN)
The U of Texas at El Paso (TX)
U of Wisconsin–Stevens Point (WI)
Upper Iowa U (IA)
Villa Maria Coll of Buffalo (NY)
Walla Walla U (WA)
Wartburg Coll (IA)
Washington U in St. Louis (MO)
Waynesburg U (PA)
Weber State U (UT)
West Liberty U (WV)
William Paterson U of New Jersey
    (NJ)
Woodbury U (CA)
York Coll of Pennsylvania (PA)

COMMERCIAL PHOTOGRAPHY
Acad of Art U (CA)
Appalachian State U (NC)
Fashion Inst of Technology (NY)
Rochester Inst of Technology (NY)

COMMUNICATION
Alvernia U (PA)
American U of Puerto Rico (PR)
Arizona Christian U (AZ)
Arkansas State U (AR)
Asbury U (KY)
Bethany Lutheran Coll (MN)
Bethel U (MN)
Boston U (MA)
California State U, Northridge (CA)
Cleveland State U (OH)
The Coll of New Jersey (NJ)
Concordia Coll (MN)
Concordia U (CA)
DEREE—The American Coll of
    Greece (Greece)
DeSales U (PA)
DeVry U, Pomona (CA)
DeVry U, Westminster (CO)
DeVry U, Miramar (FL)
DeVry U, Orlando (FL)
DeVry U, Decatur (GA)
DeVry U, Chicago (IL)
DeVry U, Kansas City (MO)
DeVry U, Fort Washington (PA)
DeVry U, Houston (TX)
DeVry U, Irving (TX)
DeVry U Online (IL)
Eastern Illinois U (IL)
Eastern New Mexico U (NM)
Edgewood Coll (WI)
Fairfield U (CT)
Florida Coll (FL)
Florida Inst of Technology (FL)
Frostburg State U (MD)
Geneva Coll (PA)
Granite State Coll (NH)
Hamilton Coll (NY)
Henderson State U (AR)
High Point U (NC)
Holy Cross Coll (IN)
Huntingdon Coll (AL)
Huntington U (IN)

Indiana Wesleyan U (IN)
Lebanese American U (Lebanon)
Le Moyne Coll (NY)
Marymount U (VA)
Massachusetts Coll of Liberal Arts (MA)
Merrimack Coll (MA)
Misericordia U (PA)
Mississippi Coll (MS)
Neumann U (PA)
New Mexico State U (NM)
Nyack Coll (NY)
Oakland U (MI)
Oklahoma City U (OK)
Pacific Union Coll (CA)
Paine Coll (GA)
Portland State U (OR)
Purdue U (IN)
Randolph-Macon Coll (VA)
Roanoke Coll (VA)
Rowan U (NJ)
Saint Anselm Coll (NH)
St. John Fisher Coll (NY)
Saint Joseph's U (PA)
Simpson Coll (IA)
Southwestern Coll (KS)
Spalding U (KY)
Stephen F. Austin State U (TX)
Stetson U (FL)
Texas A&M U (TX)
Thomas More Coll (KY)
U of Arkansas–Fort Smith (AR)
U of Delaware (DE)
U of Evansville (IN)
U of Houston–Clear Lake (TX)
U of Houston–Downtown (TX)
U of Houston–Victoria (TX)
U of Illinois at Chicago (IL)
U of Illinois at Springfield (IL)
U of Michigan–Flint (MI)
U of Minnesota, Crookston (MN)
U of Minnesota, Duluth (MN)
U of Mount Union (OH)
U of North Dakota (ND)
U of San Diego (CA)
The U of Tampa (FL)
The U of Texas of the Permian Basin (TX)
U of Wisconsin–Eau Claire (WI)
U of Wisconsin–Green Bay (WI)
U of Wisconsin–Stevens Point (WI)
Walden U (MN)
Wheeling Jesuit U (WV)
William Peace U (NC)
Xavier U (OH)

COMMUNICATION AND JOURNALISM RELATED
The American U of Paris (France)
Arizona State U (AZ)
Arkansas State U (AR)
Auburn U (AL)
Benedictine U (IL)
Berry Coll (GA)
Bowling Green State U (OH)
Brigham Young U (UT)
California Lutheran U (CA)
California State U, Chico (CA)
Carlow U (PA)
Centenary Coll of Louisiana (LA)
Chestnut Hill Coll (PA)
Clarke U (IA)
Clemson U (SC)
The Coll at Brockport, State U of New York (NY)
Columbia Coll (SC)
Concordia U (QC, Canada)
Dalhousie U (NS, Canada)
The Evergreen State Coll (WA)
Farmingdale State Coll (NY)
Flagler Coll (FL)
Florida Inst of Technology (FL)
Florida Southern Coll (FL)
Friends U (KS)
Hawai`i Pacific U (HI)
Hope Coll (MI)
Immaculata U (PA)
Indiana U Kokomo (IN)
Judson U (IL)
Lake Erie Coll (OH)
Lehman Coll of the City U of New York (NY)
Madonna U (MI)
Malone U (OH)
Marquette U (WI)
Mary Baldwin Coll (VA)
Mercer U (GA)

Mercy Coll (NY)
Milwaukee School of Eng (WI)
Minot State U (ND)
National U (CA)
Newberry Coll (SC)
Newbury Coll (MA)
New England School of Communications (ME)
New York U (NY)
Norfolk State U (VA)
Northwest Christian U (OR)
Notre Dame de Namur U (CA)
The Ohio State U (OH)
Oklahoma Christian U (OK)
Oklahoma City U (OK)
Pace U (NY)
Penn State Abington (PA)
Penn State Altoona (PA)
Penn State Beaver (PA)
Penn State Berks (PA)
Penn State Brandywine (PA)
Penn State DuBois (PA)
Penn State Erie, The Behrend Coll (PA)
Penn State Fayette, The Eberly Campus (PA)
Penn State Greater Allegheny (PA)
Penn State Hazleton (PA)
Penn State Lehigh Valley (PA)
Penn State Mont Alto (PA)
Penn State New Kensington (PA)
Penn State Schuylkill (PA)
Penn State Shenango (PA)
Penn State U Park (PA)
Penn State Wilkes-Barre (PA)
Penn State Worthington Scranton (PA)
Penn State York (PA)
Point Park U (PA)
Quincy U (IL)
Quinnipiac U (CT)
Saint Mary's Coll of California (CA)
Siena Heights U (MI)
Southeastern Oklahoma State U (OK)
State U of New York Inst of Technology (NY)
Sterling Coll (KS)
Tiffin U (OH)
Trevecca Nazarene U (TN)
U of Guam (GU)
U of Illinois at Urbana–Champaign (IL)
U of Minnesota, Duluth (MN)
U of Minnesota, Twin Cities Campus (MN)
U of Wisconsin–Green Bay (WI)
Washington U in St. Louis (MO)
Webster U (MO)
West Virginia U (WV)
Wheeling Jesuit U (WV)
Young Harris Coll (GA)

COMMUNICATION AND MEDIA RELATED
Adelphi U (NY)
Alma Coll (MI)
Athabasca U (AB, Canada)
Belmont U (TN)
Bennington Coll (VT)
Calumet Coll of Saint Joseph (IN)
Cameron U (OK)
Canisius Coll (NY)
Cedarville U (OH)
The Coll at Brockport, State U of New York (NY)
Concordia U (QC, Canada)
Crown Coll (MN)
DePaul U (IL)
DeSales U (PA)
Eastern Mennonite U (VA)
Elizabethtown Coll (PA)
Elon U (NC)
Eugene Lang Coll The New School for Liberal Arts (NY)
Fairleigh Dickinson U, Metropolitan Campus (NJ)
Florida State U (FL)
Franklin Coll Switzerland (Switzerland)
Gardner-Webb U (NC)
Georgetown Coll (KY)
Greenville Coll (IL)
Hood Coll (MD)
Houghton Coll (NY)
Judson U (IL)
King's Coll (PA)

Lane Coll (TN)
La Roche Coll (PA)
Lasell Coll (MA)
Loyola U Chicago (IL)
Lynn U (FL)
Marquette U (WI)
Missouri Baptist U (MO)
Mitchell Coll (CT)
Montreat Coll, Montreat (NC)
New Jersey Inst of Technology (NJ)
New York U (NY)
Oklahoma City U (OK)
Penn State Erie, The Behrend Coll (PA)
Rochester Inst of Technology (NY)
Roger Williams U (RI)
Rollins Coll (FL)
St. Edward's U (TX)
St. Thomas U (FL)
Salve Regina U (RI)
Southern New Hampshire U (NH)
Southern Polytechnic State U (GA)
Southwestern Coll (KS)
Spring Arbor U (MI)
Stanford U (CA)
Taylor U (IN)
Unity Coll (ME)
Université de Sherbrooke (QC, Canada)
U of Colorado Boulder (CO)
U of Mobile (AL)
U of the Incarnate Word (TX)
The U of Western Ontario (ON, Canada)
U of Wisconsin–Superior (WI)
Virginia Wesleyan Coll (VA)
Walsh U (OH)
Wesley Coll (DE)
Wilmington U (DE)
Young Harris Coll (GA)

COMMUNICATION DISORDERS SCIENCES AND SERVICES RELATED
Long Island U–Brooklyn Campus (NY)
Ouachita Baptist U (AR)
U of Missouri (MO)
U of New Hampshire (NH)
U of Oklahoma Health Sciences Center (OK)
The U of Western Ontario (ON, Canada)

COMMUNICATION SCIENCES AND DISORDERS
Appalachian State U (NC)
Arizona State U (AZ)
Auburn U (AL)
Augustana Coll (IL)
Baldwin Wallace U (OH)
Baylor U (TX)
Bob Jones U (SC)
Bowling Green State U (OH)
Bridgewater State U (MA)
Brock U (ON, Canada)
Butler U (IN)
California Baptist U (CA)
California State U, Chico (CA)
California State U, Fresno (CA)
California State U, Fullerton (CA)
California State U, Long Beach (CA)
California State U, Los Angeles (CA)
California State U, Northridge (CA)
Carlos Albizu U (PR)
Case Western Reserve U (OH)
Central Michigan U (MI)
Eastern Illinois U (IL)
Emerson Coll (MA)
Governors State U (IL)
Hampton U (VA)
Harding U (AR)
Kansas State U (KS)
Lamar U (TX)
Minnesota State U Mankato (MN)
Minot State U (ND)
Northern Illinois U (IL)
Pace U (NY)
Penn State Abington (PA)
Penn State Altoona (PA)
Penn State Beaver (PA)
Penn State Berks (PA)
Penn State Brandywine (PA)
Penn State DuBois (PA)
Penn State Erie, The Behrend Coll (PA)

Penn State Fayette, The Eberly Campus (PA)
Penn State Greater Allegheny (PA)
Penn State Hazleton (PA)
Penn State Lehigh Valley (PA)
Penn State Mont Alto (PA)
Penn State New Kensington (PA)
Penn State Schuylkill (PA)
Penn State Shenango (PA)
Penn State U Park (PA)
Penn State Wilkes-Barre (PA)
Penn State Worthington Scranton (PA)
Penn State York (PA)
Portland State U (OR)
Radford U (VA)
Saint Mary's Coll (IN)
San Diego State U (CA)
San Francisco State U (CA)
San Jose State U (CA)
Southeast Missouri State U (MO)
Southern Illinois U Carbondale (IL)
State U of New York at Fredonia (NY)
State U of New York at New Paltz (NY)
Syracuse U (NY)
Texas State U–San Marcos (TX)
Truman State U (MO)
The U of Akron (OH)
The U of Arizona (AZ)
The U of British Columbia (BC, Canada)
U of Cincinnati (OH)
U of Colorado Boulder (CO)
U of Georgia (GA)
U of Houston (TX)
The U of Kansas (KS)
U of Maryland, Coll Park (MD)
U of Massachusetts Amherst (MA)
U of Minnesota, Duluth (MN)
U of Minnesota, Twin Cities Campus (MN)
U of Mississippi (MS)
U of Nebraska at Kearney (NE)
U of North Dakota (ND)
U of Oklahoma Health Sciences Center (OK)
U of Oregon (OR)
U of Redlands (CA)
U of Rhode Island (RI)
U of South Alabama (AL)
The U of South Dakota (SD)
The U of Texas at Austin (TX)
The U of Texas–Pan American (TX)
The U of Toledo (OH)
U of Vermont (VT)
The U of Western Ontario (ON, Canada)
U of Wisconsin–Eau Claire (WI)
U of Wisconsin–Stevens Point (WI)
Wayne State U (MI)
Western Carolina U (NC)
Western Illinois U (IL)
Western Kentucky U (KY)
West Texas A&M U (TX)
Wichita State U (KS)
William Paterson U of New Jersey (NJ)
Winthrop U (SC)
Worcester State U (MA)
Xavier U of Louisiana (LA)

COMMUNICATIONS TECHNOLOGIES AND SUPPORT SERVICES RELATED
Alverno Coll (WI)
Chestnut Hill Coll (PA)
Framingham State U (MA)
Lesley U (MA)
Minot State U (ND)
Salve Regina U (RI)
U of Windsor (ON, Canada)

COMMUNICATIONS TECHNOLOGY
Eastern Michigan U (MI)
Inter American U of Puerto Rico, Bayamón Campus (PR)
Lawrence Technological U (MI)
Sacred Heart U (CT)
Salve Regina U (RI)
Suffolk U (MA)
York Coll of the City U of New York (NY)

COMMUNITY HEALTH AND PREVENTIVE MEDICINE
Canisius Coll (NY)
Carroll Coll (MT)
Florida Gulf Coast U (FL)
George Mason U (VA)
Georgia Coll & State U (GA)
Governors State U (IL)
Hofstra U (NY)
Indiana U Bloomington (IN)
Minnesota State U Moorhead (MN)
Pine Manor Coll (MA)
Portland State U (OR)
Texas A&M U–Kingsville (TX)
Tufts U (MA)
U of Florida (FL)
U of Illinois at Urbana–Champaign (IL)
U of Wisconsin–Eau Claire (WI)
U of Wisconsin–La Crosse (WI)
Western Kentucky U (KY)

COMMUNITY HEALTH SERVICES COUNSELING
Canisius Coll (NY)
Carroll Coll (MT)
Eastern Washington U (WA)
Indiana State U (IN)
Indiana U–Purdue U Fort Wayne (IN)
James Madison U (VA)
Johnson C. Smith U (NC)
Longwood U (VA)
Morris Coll (SC)
Northeastern Illinois U (IL)
Northern Illinois U (IL)
Northern Michigan U (MI)
Ohio U (OH)
Texas A&M U (TX)
The U of Arizona (AZ)
U of Central Arkansas (AR)
The U of Kansas (KS)
U of Nebraska at Omaha (NE)
U of Northern Iowa (IA)
U of Pennsylvania (PA)
U of the Cumberlands (KY)
U of West Florida (FL)
Western Connecticut State U (CT)
Western Washington U (WA)
Worcester State U (MA)
Youngstown State U (OH)

COMMUNITY ORGANIZATION AND ADVOCACY
Alverno Coll (WI)
Bemidji State U (MN)
Bryant U (RI)
Central Michigan U (MI)
DePaul U (IL)
Emory & Henry Coll (VA)
Goddard Coll (VT)
Indiana Wesleyan U (IN)
Missouri Baptist U (MO)
New Mexico State U (NM)
New York U (NY)
Northern State U (SD)
Northland Coll (WI)
Prescott Coll (AZ)
Providence Coll (RI)
Rockhurst U (MO)
St. Joseph's Coll, New York (NY)
Saint Martin's U (WA)
Siena Heights U (MI)
Southern Arkansas U–Magnolia (AR)
State U of New York Empire State Coll (NY)
U of Alaska Fairbanks (AK)
U of Hartford (CT)
U of Massachusetts Boston (MA)
U of Saint Mary (KS)
The U of Texas at El Paso (TX)
The U of Toledo (OH)

COMMUNITY PSYCHOLOGY
Clayton State U (GA)
Goddard Coll (VT)
New York Inst of Technology (NY)
Rogers State U (OK)
U of Miami (FL)
U of Saint Mary (KS)
U of Washington, Bothell (WA)

COMPARATIVE LITERATURE
Agnes Scott Coll (GA)
The American U in Cairo (Egypt)
The American U of Paris (France)
Bard Coll (NY)
Barry U (FL)

Binghamton U, State U of New York (NY)
Blackburn Coll (IL)
Boston U (MA)
Brock U (ON, Canada)
Brown U (RI)
California State U, Fullerton (CA)
California State U, Long Beach (CA)
Carson-Newman U (TN)
Case Western Reserve U (OH)
Castleton State Coll (VT)
Chowan U (NC)
Christendom Coll (VA)
City Coll of the City U of New York (NY)
Clark U (MA)
Coe Coll (IA)
The Coll at Brockport, State U of New York (NY)
Coll of the Atlantic (ME)
Coll of the Holy Cross (MA)
The Coll of Wooster (OH)
The Colorado Coll (CO)
Columbia U (NY)
Columbia U, School of General Studies (NY)
Dalhousie U (NS, Canada)
Dartmouth Coll (NH)
Earlham Coll (IN)
Eckerd Coll (FL)
Eugene Lang Coll The New School for Liberal Arts (NY)
Franklin Coll Switzerland (Switzerland)
Franklin Pierce U (NH)
Georgetown U (DC)
Gettysburg Coll (PA)
Gonzaga U (WA)
Graceland U (IA)
Hamilton Coll (NY)
Harrison Middleton U (AZ)
Haverford Coll (PA)
High Point U (NC)
Hillsdale Coll (MI)
Hobart and William Smith Colls (NY)
Hofstra U (NY)
Houghton Coll (NY)
Hunter Coll of the City U of New York (NY)
Indiana U Bloomington (IN)
Inter American U of Puerto Rico, San Germán Campus (PR)
John Cabot U (Italy)
John Carroll U (OH)
Johnson State Coll (VT)
Kansas Wesleyan U (KS)
Lake Superior State U (MI)
Manchester U (IN)
Middlebury Coll (VT)
Mills Coll (CA)
Minnesota State U Mankato (MN)
Mount Allison U (NB, Canada)
New Coll of Florida (FL)
New England Coll (NH)
New York U (NY)
Northwest U (WA)
The Ohio State U (OH)
Ohio Wesleyan U (OH)
Pacific U (OR)
Penn State Abington (PA)
Penn State Altoona (PA)
Penn State Beaver (PA)
Penn State Berks (PA)
Penn State Brandywine (PA)
Penn State DuBois (PA)
Penn State Erie, The Behrend Coll (PA)
Penn State Fayette, The Eberly Campus (PA)
Penn State Greater Allegheny (PA)
Penn State Hazleton (PA)
Penn State Lehigh Valley (PA)
Penn State Mont Alto (PA)
Penn State New Kensington (PA)
Penn State Schuylkill (PA)
Penn State Shenango (PA)
Penn State U Park (PA)
Penn State Wilkes-Barre (PA)
Penn State Worthington Scranton (PA)
Penn State York (PA)
Princeton U (NJ)
Purchase Coll, State U of New York (NY)
Purdue U (IN)

Quinnipiac U (CT)
Ramapo Coll of New Jersey (NJ)
Reed Coll (OR)
Rockford Coll (IL)
Rutgers, The State U of New Jersey, New Brunswick (NJ)
Saint Mary's Coll of California (CA)
San Diego State U (CA)
San Francisco State U (CA)
Sewanee: The U of the South (TN)
Shimer Coll (IL)
Smith Coll (MA)
Sonoma State U (CA)
Stanford U (CA)
State U of New York Coll at Geneseo (NY)
State U of New York Coll at Old Westbury (NY)
Stony Brook U, State U of New York (NY)
Swarthmore Coll (PA)
Syracuse U (NY)
Trent U (ON, Canada)
Trinity Coll (CT)
United States Military Acad (NY)
U of California, Berkeley (CA)
U of California, Davis (CA)
U of California, Irvine (CA)
U of California, Los Angeles (CA)
U of California, Merced (CA)
U of California, Santa Barbara (CA)
U of California, Santa Cruz (CA)
U of Chicago (IL)
U of Delaware (DE)
U of Georgia (GA)
U of Illinois at Urbana–Champaign (IL)
The U of Iowa (IA)
U of La Verne (CA)
U of Massachusetts Amherst (MA)
U of Michigan (MI)
U of Minnesota, Twin Cities Campus (MN)
U of Nevada, Las Vegas (NV)
U of New Brunswick Fredericton (NB, Canada)
U of New Mexico (NM)
The U of North Carolina at Chapel Hill (NC)
U of Oregon (OR)
U of Pennsylvania (PA)
U of Pittsburgh at Greensburg (PA)
U of Redlands (CA)
U of Rochester (NY)
U of South Carolina (SC)
U of Southern California (CA)
The U of Texas at Dallas (TX)
The U of Toledo (OH)
U of Utah (UT)
U of Virginia (VA)
The U of Western Ontario (ON, Canada)
U of Wisconsin–Madison (WI)
U of Wisconsin–Milwaukee (WI)
Washington U in St. Louis (MO)
Wellesley Coll (MA)
Willamette U (OR)
William Paterson U of New Jersey (NJ)
Williams Coll (MA)
Yale U (CT)

COMPUTATIONAL AND APPLIED MATHEMATICS
Bryant U (RI)
Mary Baldwin Coll (VA)
U of Notre Dame (IN)
U of Southern California (CA)

COMPUTATIONAL BIOLOGY
Case Western Reserve U (OH)
Colby Coll (ME)
Purdue U (IN)

COMPUTATIONAL MATHEMATICS
Arizona State U (AZ)
Asbury U (KY)
Carnegie Mellon U (PA)
Coll of Saint Benedict (MN)
Embry-Riddle Aeronautical U–Daytona (FL)
Indiana U–Purdue U Fort Wayne (IN)
Marist Coll (NY)
Marquette U (WI)
Michigan State U (MI)
Rochester Inst of Technology (NY)

Saint John's U (MN)
Siena Coll (NY)
Southwestern U (TX)
U of California, Davis (CA)
U of California, Los Angeles (CA)
U of Illinois at Urbana–Champaign (IL)
U of Southern California (CA)
U of Waterloo (ON, Canada)

COMPUTATIONAL SCIENCE
Canisius Coll (NY)
Purdue U (IN)
The Richard Stockton Coll of New Jersey (NJ)
Texas A&M U–Commerce (TX)

COMPUTER AND INFORMATION SCIENCES
Adelphi U (NY)
Alcorn State U (MS)
Alverno Coll (WI)
American U (DC)
American U in Bulgaria (Bulgaria)
The American U of Paris (France)
American U of Puerto Rico (PR)
Andrews U (MI)
Angelo State U (TX)
Arizona State U (AZ)
Arkansas State U (AR)
Arkansas Tech U (AR)
Armstrong Atlantic State U (GA)
Assumption Coll (MA)
Athabasca U (AB, Canada)
Athens State U (AL)
Auburn U (AL)
Austin Peay State U (TN)
Avila U (MO)
Ball State U (IN)
Barton Coll (NC)
Bellarmine U (KY)
Belmont U (TN)
Bennington Coll (VT)
Bentley U (MA)
Berea Coll (KY)
Bethel U (MN)
Binghamton U, State U of New York (NY)
Bloomfield Coll (NJ)
Bluefield State Coll (WV)
Boston Coll (MA)
Bowie State U (MD)
Bowling Green State U (OH)
Bryant U (RI)
Bucknell U (PA)
Butler U (IN)
Caldwell Coll (NJ)
California Lutheran U (CA)
California State U, Fresno (CA)
California State U, Los Angeles (CA)
California State U, San Bernardino (CA)
Cameron U (OK)
Caribbean U (PR)
Carroll Coll (MT)
Castleton State Coll (VT)
The Catholic U of America (DC)
Cedar Crest Coll (PA)
Central Connecticut State U (CT)
Central State U (OH)
Chapman U (CA)
Chestnut Hill Coll (PA)
Chowan U (NC)
The Citadel, The Military Coll of South Carolina (SC)
Clarion U of Pennsylvania (PA)
Clark Atlanta U (GA)
Clarke U (IA)
Clemson U (SC)
Cleveland State U (OH)
Coastal Carolina U (SC)
Coll of Charleston (SC)
Coll of Mount St. Joseph (OH)
The Coll of New Jersey (NJ)
Coll of Saint Elizabeth (NJ)
The Coll of Saint Rose (NY)
The Coll of St. Scholastica (MN)
The Coll of William and Mary (VA)
Colorado Mesa U (CO)
Colorado State U (CO)
Columbia Coll (MO)
Columbus State U (GA)
Concordia U Chicago (IL)
Concordia U, Nebraska (NE)
Covenant Coll (GA)
Dakota State U (SD)
Dallas Baptist U (TX)

DEREE—The American Coll of Greece (Greece)
Dickinson Coll (PA)
Doane Coll (NE)
Dominican Coll (NY)
Earlham Coll (IN)
East Central U (OK)
Eastern Michigan U (MI)
Eastern New Mexico U (NM)
Eastern Washington U (WA)
East Tennessee State U (TN)
Edgewood Coll (WI)
Edinboro U of Pennsylvania (PA)
Elizabethtown Coll (PA)
Elon U (NC)
Emmanuel Coll (GA)
Emporia State U (KS)
Excelsior Coll (NY)
Fairfield U (CT)
Fairleigh Dickinson U, Coll at Florham (NJ)
Felician Coll (NJ)
Fisher Coll (MA)
Florida Ag and Mech U (FL)
Florida Atlantic U (FL)
Florida Gulf Coast U (FL)
Florida Intl U (FL)
Fort Lewis Coll (CO)
Framingham State U (MA)
Francis Marion U (SC)
Franklin & Marshall Coll (PA)
Franklin Coll (IN)
Friends U (KS)
Gallaudet U (DC)
Gannon U (PA)
Gardner-Webb U (NC)
Geneva Coll (PA)
George Fox U (OR)
George Mason U (VA)
Georgetown Coll (KY)
Georgia Coll & State U (GA)
Georgia Regents U (GA)
Georgia Southern U (GA)
Georgia State U (GA)
Goshen Coll (IN)
Governors State U (IL)
Grace U (NE)
Grand Valley State U (MI)
Greenville Coll (IL)
Grove City Coll (PA)
Guilford Coll (NC)
Hamilton Coll (NY)
Hartwick Coll (NY)
Hawai`i Pacific U (HI)
Henderson State U (AR)
Hope Coll (MI)
Howard Payne U (TX)
Illinois Inst of Technology (IL)
Indiana State U (IN)
Indiana U of Pennsylvania (PA)
Indiana U–Purdue U Fort Wayne (IN)
Indiana Wesleyan U (IN)
Inter American U of Puerto Rico, Fajardo Campus (PR)
Ithaca Coll (NY)
Jacksonville State U (AL)
James Madison U (VA)
John Jay Coll of Criminal Justice of the City U of New York (NY)
The Johns Hopkins U (MD)
Johnson C. Smith U (NC)
Jones Coll, Jacksonville (FL)
Juniata Coll (PA)
Kalamazoo Coll (MI)
Kansas State U (KS)
Kean U (NJ)
Keene State Coll (NH)
Kennesaw State U (GA)
Kent State U (OH)
Kentucky State U (KY)
Kentucky Wesleyan Coll (KY)
King's Coll (PA)
Knox Coll (IL)
Kuyper Coll (MI)
LaGrange Coll (GA)
Lander U (SC)
Lane Coll (TN)
La Roche Coll (PA)
La Salle U (PA)
Lee U (TN)
Lehman Coll of the City U of New York (NY)
Le Moyne Coll (NY)
Lewis-Clark State Coll (ID)
Liberty U (VA)
Lincoln Memorial U (TN)

Lindenwood U (MO)
Lock Haven U of Pennsylvania (PA)
Long Island U–Brooklyn Campus (NY)
Long Island U–C. W. Post Campus (NY)
Loyola Marymount U (CA)
Loyola U Chicago (IL)
Lubbock Christian U (TX)
Mansfield U of Pennsylvania (PA)
Marist Coll (NY)
Marquette U (WI)
Marshall U (WV)
Mars Hill Coll (NC)
Maryville Coll (TN)
Massachusetts Coll of Liberal Arts (MA)
The Master's Coll and Sem (CA)
Mayville State U (ND)
McDaniel Coll (MD)
McMurry U (TX)
Mercy Coll (NY)
Mercyhurst U (PA)
Merrimack Coll (MA)
Metropolitan State U of Denver (CO)
Miami U (OH)
Michigan State U (MI)
Midwestern State U (TX)
Millersville U of Pennsylvania (PA)
Minot State U (ND)
Misericordia U (PA)
Mississippi Coll (MS)
Mississippi State U (MS)
Missouri Western State U (MO)
Molloy Coll (NY)
Monmouth U (NJ)
Montreat Coll, Montreat (NC)
Morehead State U (KY)
Morehouse Coll (GA)
Morrisville State Coll (NY)
Mount St. Mary's U (MD)
National U (CA)
Neumann U (PA)
Neumont U (UT)
New England Coll (NH)
New England Inst of Technology (RI)
New Jersey City U (NJ)
New Jersey Inst of Technology (NJ)
New Mexico Highlands U (NM)
New Mexico State U (NM)
New York Inst of Technology (NY)
New York U (NY)
Norfolk State U (VA)
North Carolina Wesleyan Coll (NC)
Northeastern Illinois U (IL)
Northeastern U (MA)
Northern Michigan U (MI)
Northwest Missouri State U (MO)
Northwood U, Florida Campus (FL)
Northwood U, Michigan Campus (MI)
Notre Dame de Namur U (CA)
Nova Southeastern U (FL)
Oakland U (MI)
The Ohio State U (OH)
Ohio U (OH)
Okanagan Coll (BC, Canada)
Oklahoma Baptist U (OK)
Oklahoma City U (OK)
Oklahoma State U (OK)
Old Dominion U (VA)
Olivet Coll (MI)
Oral Roberts U (OK)
Pace U (NY)
Park U (MO)
Penn State Abington (PA)
Penn State Altoona (PA)
Penn State Beaver (PA)
Penn State Berks (PA)
Penn State Brandywine (PA)
Penn State DuBois (PA)
Penn State Erie, The Behrend Coll (PA)
Penn State Fayette, The Eberly Campus (PA)
Penn State Greater Allegheny (PA)
Penn State Harrisburg (PA)
Penn State Hazleton (PA)
Penn State Lehigh Valley (PA)
Penn State Mont Alto (PA)
Penn State New Kensington (PA)
Penn State Schuylkill (PA)
Penn State Shenango (PA)
Penn State U Park (PA)
Penn State Wilkes-Barre (PA)

Penn State Worthington Scranton (PA)
Penn State York (PA)
Philadelphia U (PA)
Portland State U (OR)
Principia Coll (IL)
Purdue U (IN)
Purdue U Calumet (IN)
Ramapo Coll of New Jersey (NJ)
Rhode Island Coll (RI)
Rice U (TX)
Rider U (NJ)
Roanoke Coll (VA)
Rochester Inst of Technology (NY)
Rollins Coll (FL)
Rowan U (NJ)
Rutgers, The State U of New Jersey, Camden (NJ)
Rutgers, The State U of New Jersey, Newark (NJ)
Sacred Heart U (CT)
Saginaw Valley State U (MI)
St. Bonaventure U (NY)
St. Edward's U (TX)
St. John Fisher Coll (NY)
St. John's U (NY)
Saint Joseph's Coll (IN)
Saint Joseph's U (PA)
Saint Leo U (FL)
Saint Louis U (MO)
Saint Mary-of-the-Woods Coll (IN)
St. Mary's Coll of Maryland (MD)
St. Norbert Coll (WI)
Saint Vincent Coll (PA)
Salem Intl U (WV)
Salem State U (MA)
Salisbury U (MD)
Sam Houston State U (TX)
Shaw U (NC)
Shepherd U (WV)
Shippensburg U of Pennsylvania (PA)
Siena Coll (NY)
Siena Heights U (MI)
Sierra Nevada Coll (NV)
Simmons Coll (MA)
Simpson Coll (IA)
Skidmore Coll (NY)
South Dakota State U (SD)
Southeastern Oklahoma State U (OK)
Southeast Missouri State U (MO)
Southern Arkansas U–Magnolia (AR)
Southern Nazarene U (OK)
Southern New Hampshire U (NH)
Southern Utah U (UT)
Southwest Baptist U (MO)
Southwestern U (TX)
Spring Hill Coll (AL)
State U of New York at New Paltz (NY)
State U of New York at Plattsburgh (NY)
State U of New York Coll at Old Westbury (NY)
State U of New York Coll at Potsdam (NY)
State U of New York Inst of Technology (NY)
Stephen F. Austin State U (TX)
Sterling Coll (KS)
Stetson U (FL)
Stevenson U (MD)
Stony Brook U, State U of New York (NY)
Suffolk U (MA)
Swarthmore Coll (PA)
Syracuse U (NY)
Tarleton State U (TX)
Taylor U (IN)
Temple U (PA)
Tennessee Wesleyan Coll (TN)
Texas A&M U–Commerce (TX)
Texas A&M U–Kingsville (TX)
Texas Christian U (TX)
Texas Southern U (TX)
Texas State U–San Marcos (TX)
Texas Woman's U (TX)
Thompson Rivers U (BC, Canada)
Tiffin U (OH)
Transylvania U (KY)
Trinity U (TX)
Troy U (AL)
Truman State U (MO)
Tulane U (LA)
United States Military Acad (NY)

United States Naval Acad (MD)
U at Albany, State U of New York (NY)
The U of Alabama (AL)
The U of Alabama at Birmingham (AL)
U of Alaska Fairbanks (AK)
The U of Arizona (AZ)
U of Arkansas–Fort Smith (AR)
U of California, Irvine (CA)
U of California, Los Angeles (CA)
U of Central Arkansas (AR)
U of Central Florida (FL)
U of Cincinnati (OH)
U of Colorado Colorado Springs (CO)
U of Colorado Denver (CO)
U of Delaware (DE)
U of Florida (FL)
U of Great Falls (MT)
U of Hartford (CT)
U of Hawaii at Manoa (HI)
U of Houston (TX)
U of Houston–Clear Lake (TX)
U of Houston–Downtown (TX)
U of Illinois at Urbana–Champaign (IL)
The U of Kansas (KS)
U of Kentucky (KY)
U of Louisiana at Lafayette (LA)
U of Maryland, Coll Park (MD)
U of Maryland U Coll (MD)
U of Mary Washington (VA)
U of Massachusetts Boston (MA)
U of Massachusetts Dartmouth (MA)
U of Michigan (MI)
U of Michigan–Dearborn (MI)
U of Michigan–Flint (MI)
U of Mississippi (MS)
U of Missouri (MO)
U of Mobile (AL)
U of Nebraska at Kearney (NE)
U of Nebraska–Lincoln (NE)
U of Nevada, Reno (NV)
U of New Hampshire (NH)
U of New Haven (CT)
U of New Mexico (NM)
U of North Alabama (AL)
U of North Dakota (ND)
U of North Florida (FL)
U of North Georgia (GA)
U of North Texas (TX)
U of Notre Dame (IN)
U of Oregon (OR)
U of Ottawa (ON, Canada)
U of Pikeville (KY)
U of Pittsburgh at Greensburg (PA)
U of Puerto Rico at Bayamón (PR)
U of Puerto Rico at Ponce (PR)
U of Rhode Island (RI)
U of Richmond (VA)
U of Saint Mary (KS)
U of South Alabama (AL)
U of South Carolina (SC)
U of South Carolina Upstate (SC)
The U of South Dakota (SD)
U of Southern California (CA)
U of Southern Indiana (IN)
U of Southern Mississippi (MS)
U of South Florida (FL)
The U of Tampa (FL)
The U of Texas at Austin (TX)
The U of Texas at Brownsville (TX)
The U of Texas at Dallas (TX)
The U of Texas of the Permian Basin (TX)
The U of Texas–Pan American (TX)
U of the Incarnate Word (TX)
U of Vermont (VT)
U of Virginia (VA)
U of Washington, Bothell (WA)
U of Washington, Tacoma (WA)
The U of Western Ontario (ON, Canada)
U of West Florida (FL)
U of West Georgia (GA)
U of Windsor (ON, Canada)
U of Wisconsin–Eau Claire (WI)
U of Wisconsin–La Crosse (WI)
U of Wisconsin–Madison (WI)
U of Wisconsin–Stevens Point (WI)
U of Wisconsin–Superior (WI)
Utah State U (UT)
Utica Coll (NY)
Valdosta State U (GA)
Valley City State U (ND)

Vassar Coll (NY)
Virginia Commonwealth U (VA)
Virginia Polytechnic Inst and State U (VA)
Wake Forest U (NC)
Walden U (MN)
Wartburg Coll (IA)
Washburn U (KS)
Washington State U (WA)
Washington U in St. Louis (MO)
Waynesburg U (PA)
Wayne State Coll (NE)
Wayne State U (MI)
Webber Intl U (FL)
Weber State U (UT)
Webster U (MO)
Wentworth Inst of Technology (MA)
West Chester U of Pennsylvania (PA)
Western Illinois U (IL)
Western Kentucky U (KY)
Western Michigan U (MI)
Western Washington U (WA)
Westminster Coll (UT)
West Texas A&M U (TX)
West Virginia Wesleyan Coll (WV)
Wheeling Jesuit U (WV)
Wichita State U (KS)
Widener U (PA)
Wilkes U (PA)
Worcester Polytechnic Inst (MA)
Worcester State U (MA)
Wright State U (OH)
Xavier U of Louisiana (LA)
Yale U (CT)

COMPUTER AND INFORMATION SCIENCES AND SUPPORT SERVICES RELATED
Amridge U (AL)
Arizona State U (AZ)
Bloomsburg U of Pennsylvania (PA)
Cabrini Coll (PA)
California State U, Chico (CA)
California State U, Los Angeles (CA)
Champlain Coll (VT)
City U of Seattle (WA)
Coll of Staten Island of the City U of New York (NY)
Columbia Coll (SC)
Columbia Coll Chicago (IL)
DePaul U (IL)
The Evergreen State Coll (WA)
Farmingdale State Coll (NY)
Ferris State U (MI)
Hofstra U (NY)
Husson U (ME)
Indiana Tech (IN)
Indiana U–Purdue U Indianapolis (IN)
Inter American U of Puerto Rico, Bayamón Campus (PR)
John Jay Coll of Criminal Justice of the City U of New York (NY)
Keene State Coll (NH)
Lehigh U (PA)
Limestone Coll (SC)
Long Island U–C. W. Post Campus (NY)
Mayville State U (ND)
Missouri U of Science and Technology (MO)
Morrisville State Coll (NY)
National U (CA)
New York U (NY)
Park U (MO)
Potomac Coll (DC)
Purdue U (IN)
Purdue U North Central (IN)
Roberts Wesleyan Coll (NY)
State U of New York Coll of Agriculture and Technology at Cobleskill (NY)
State U of New York Coll of Technology at Alfred (NY)
Taylor U (IN)
Tiffin U (OH)
U of Evansville (IN)
U of Great Falls (MT)
U of Michigan–Flint (MI)
U of Mount Union (OH)
U of Northern Iowa (IA)
U of Notre Dame (IN)
U of Pittsburgh (PA)
U of Washington, Bothell (WA)
Utah State U (UT)

Valley City State U (ND)
Washington U in St. Louis (MO)

COMPUTER AND INFORMATION SCIENCES RELATED
California State U, Dominguez Hills (CA)
California State U, Monterey Bay (CA)
Carnegie Mellon U (PA)
Coll of Charleston (SC)
The Colorado Coll (CO)
Columbia U, School of General Studies (NY)
Dakota Wesleyan U (SD)
DigiPen Inst of Technology (WA)
Eastern Illinois U (IL)
Grace U (NE)
Limestone Coll (SC)
Maryville Coll (TN)
Missouri State U (MO)
Neumont U (UT)
Taylor U (IN)
Université de Sherbrooke (QC, Canada)
U of Great Falls (MT)
U of Nebraska at Omaha (NE)
U of Windsor (ON, Canada)
U of Wisconsin–Stout (WI)
Wagner Coll (NY)
West Virginia U (WV)

COMPUTER AND INFORMATION SYSTEMS SECURITY
American Public U System (WV)
Auburn U at Montgomery (AL)
Dakota State U (SD)
Davenport U, Grand Rapids (MI)
DePaul U (IL)
Ferris State U (MI)
Fountainhead Coll of Technology (TN)
Franklin U (OH)
Frostburg State U (MD)
Hilbert Coll (NY)
Indiana Tech (IN)
Kennesaw State U (GA)
Lewis U (IL)
Limestone Coll (SC)
Lipscomb U (TN)
Loyola U Chicago (IL)
Mercy Coll (NY)
Pennsylvania Coll of Technology (PA)
Pittsburg State U (KS)
Potomac Coll (DC)
Rasmussen Coll Appleton (WI)
Rasmussen Coll Bismarck (ND)
Rasmussen Coll Blaine (MN)
Rasmussen Coll Bloomington (MN)
Rasmussen Coll Brooklyn Park (MN)
Rasmussen Coll Eagan (MN)
Rasmussen Coll Fargo (ND)
Rasmussen Coll Fort Myers (FL)
Rasmussen Coll Green Bay (WI)
Rasmussen Coll Lake Elmo/Woodbury (MN)
Rasmussen Coll Land O' Lakes (FL)
Rasmussen Coll Mankato (MN)
Rasmussen Coll Moorhead (MN)
Rasmussen Coll New Port Richey (FL)
Rasmussen Coll Ocala (FL)
Rasmussen Coll St. Cloud (MN)
Rasmussen Coll Tampa/Brandon (FL)
Rasmussen Coll Wausau (WI)
Rochester Inst of Technology (NY)
St. John's U (NY)
Southeast Missouri State U (MO)
State U of New York Coll of Technology at Alfred (NY)
Stratford U, Woodbridge (VA)
Sullivan Coll of Technology and Design (KY)
U of Colorado Colorado Springs (CO)
U of Great Falls (MT)
U of Illinois at Urbana–Champaign (IL)
U of Maryland U Coll (MD)
U of Miami (FL)
U of Nebraska at Omaha (NE)
U of Washington, Tacoma (WA)

Valley City State U (ND)
Washington U in St. Louis (MO)
Walla Walla U (WA)
Weber State U (UT)

COMPUTER ENGINEERING
American U of Beirut (Lebanon)
Arizona State U (AZ)
Auburn U (AL)
Bellarmine U (KY)
Bethune-Cookman U (FL)
Binghamton U, State U of New York (NY)
Boston U (MA)
Bradley U (IL)
Brown U (RI)
Bucknell U (PA)
California Baptist U (CA)
California Polytechnic State U, San Luis Obispo (CA)
California State Polytechnic U, Pomona (CA)
California State U, Chico (CA)
California State U, Fresno (CA)
California State U, Fullerton (CA)
California State U, Long Beach (CA)
California State U, Northridge (CA)
Capital U (OH)
Carnegie Mellon U (PA)
Case Western Reserve U (OH)
Cedarville U (OH)
Christopher Newport U (VA)
Claflin U (SC)
Clarkson U (NY)
Clemson U (SC)
Cleveland State U (OH)
The Coll of New Jersey (NJ)
Colorado State U (CO)
Columbia U (NY)
Concordia U (QC, Canada)
DigiPen Inst of Technology (WA)
Dordt Coll (IA)
Elizabethtown Coll (PA)
Embry-Riddle Aeronautical U–Daytona (FL)
Embry-Riddle Aeronautical U–Prescott (AZ)
Fairfield U (CT)
Florida Ag and Mech U (FL)
Florida Atlantic U (FL)
Florida Inst of Technology (FL)
Florida Intl U (FL)
George Fox U (OR)
George Mason U (VA)
Gonzaga U (WA)
Harding U (AR)
Hofstra U (NY)
Hope Coll (MI)
Illinois Inst of Technology (IL)
Indiana Tech (IN)
Indiana U–Purdue U Fort Wayne (IN)
Indiana U–Purdue U Indianapolis (IN)
Iowa State U of Science and Technology (IA)
The Johns Hopkins U (MD)
Johnson C. Smith U (NC)
Kansas State U (KS)
Lawrence Technological U (MI)
Lebanese American U (Lebanon)
Lehigh U (PA)
LeTourneau U (TX)
Liberty U (VA)
Lipscomb U (TN)
Louisiana State U and Ag and Mech Coll (LA)
Manhattan Coll (NY)
Marquette U (WI)
Miami U (OH)
Michigan State U (MI)
Midwestern State U (TX)
Milwaukee School of Eng (WI)
Minnesota State U Mankato (MN)
Mississippi State U (MS)
Missouri U of Science and Technology (MO)
Montana State U (MT)
New Jersey Inst of Technology (NJ)
North Carolina State U (NC)
North Dakota State U (ND)
Northeastern U (MA)
Norwich U (VT)
Oakland U (MI)
The Ohio State U (OH)
Oklahoma Christian U (OK)
Oklahoma State U (OK)
Old Dominion U (VA)

Oral Roberts U (OK)
Penn State Abington (PA)
Penn State Altoona (PA)
Penn State Beaver (PA)
Penn State Berks (PA)
Penn State Brandywine (PA)
Penn State DuBois (PA)
Penn State Erie, The Behrend Coll (PA)
Penn State Fayette, The Eberly Campus (PA)
Penn State Greater Allegheny (PA)
Penn State Hazleton (PA)
Penn State Lehigh Valley (PA)
Penn State Mont Alto (PA)
Penn State New Kensington (PA)
Penn State Schuylkill (PA)
Penn State Shenango (PA)
Penn State U Park (PA)
Penn State Wilkes-Barre (PA)
Penn State Worthington Scranton (PA)
Penn State York (PA)
Polytechnic Inst of New York U (NY)
Polytechnic U of Puerto Rico (PR)
Portland State U (OR)
Princeton U (NJ)
Purdue U (IN)
Purdue U Calumet (IN)
Rice U (TX)
Rochester Inst of Technology (NY)
Roger Williams U (RI)
Rutgers, The State U of New Jersey, New Brunswick (NJ)
Saint Louis U (MO)
St. Mary's U (TX)
San Diego State U (CA)
San Francisco State U (CA)
San Jose State U (CA)
Shepherd U (WV)
Southern Illinois U Carbondale (IL)
Southern Illinois U Edwardsville (IL)
Southern Methodist U (TX)
Stanford U (CA)
State U of New York at New Paltz (NY)
Stony Brook U, State U of New York (NY)
Suffolk U (MA)
Syracuse U (NY)
Taylor U (IN)
Texas A&M U (TX)
Trine U (IN)
Trinity Coll (CT)
Tufts U (MA)
Université de Sherbrooke (QC, Canada)
Université du Québec en Outaouais (QC, Canada)
U at Buffalo, the State U of New York (NY)
The U of Akron (OH)
U of Alaska Fairbanks (AK)
U of Bridgeport (CT)
The U of British Columbia (BC, Canada)
U of California, Irvine (CA)
U of California, Los Angeles (CA)
U of California, Merced (CA)
U of California, Riverside (CA)
U of California, Santa Barbara (CA)
U of California, Santa Cruz (CA)
U of Central Florida (FL)
U of Cincinnati (OH)
U of Colorado Boulder (CO)
U of Colorado Colorado Springs (CO)
U of Delaware (DE)
U of Denver (CO)
U of Evansville (IN)
U of Florida (FL)
U of Georgia (GA)
U of Guelph (ON, Canada)
U of Hartford (CT)
U of Houston (TX)
U of Houston–Clear Lake (TX)
U of Idaho (ID)
U of Illinois at Chicago (IL)
U of Illinois at Urbana–Champaign (IL)
The U of Kansas (KS)
U of Kentucky (KY)
U of La Verne (CA)
U of Louisiana at Lafayette (LA)
U of Louisville (KY)

U of Maryland, Baltimore County (MD)
U of Maryland, Coll Park (MD)
U of Massachusetts Amherst (MA)
U of Massachusetts Dartmouth (MA)
U of Memphis (TN)
U of Miami (FL)
U of Michigan (MI)
U of Minnesota, Twin Cities Campus (MN)
U of Missouri (MO)
U of Nebraska–Lincoln (NE)
U of Nevada, Las Vegas (NV)
U of Nevada, Reno (NV)
U of New Brunswick Fredericton (NB, Canada)
U of New Hampshire (NH)
U of New Haven (CT)
U of New Mexico (NM)
The U of North Carolina at Charlotte (NC)
U of North Texas (TX)
U of Notre Dame (IN)
U of Oklahoma (OK)
U of Ottawa (ON, Canada)
U of Pennsylvania (PA)
U of Pittsburgh (PA)
U of Portland (OR)
U of Rhode Island (RI)
The U of Scranton (PA)
U of South Alabama (AL)
U of South Carolina (SC)
U of Southern California (CA)
U of South Florida (FL)
The U of Tennessee (TN)
The U of Texas at Arlington (TX)
The U of Texas at Dallas (TX)
The U of Texas at San Antonio (TX)
The U of Texas–Pan American (TX)
The U of Toledo (OH)
U of Utah (UT)
U of Virginia (VA)
U of Waterloo (ON, Canada)
The U of Western Ontario (ON, Canada)
U of West Florida (FL)
U of Wisconsin–Madison (WI)
U of Wisconsin–Milwaukee (WI)
U of Wisconsin–Stout (WI)
U of Wyoming (WY)
Utah State U (UT)
Valparaiso U (IN)
Vanderbilt U (TN)
Villanova U (PA)
Virginia Commonwealth U (VA)
Virginia Polytechnic Inst and State U (VA)
Virginia State U (VA)
Walla Walla U (WA)
Washington State U (WA)
Washington U in St. Louis (MO)
Wentworth Inst of Technology (MA)
Western Michigan U (MI)
West Virginia U (WV)
West Virginia U Inst of Technology (WV)
Wichita State U (KS)
Wilberforce U (OH)
Worcester Polytechnic Inst (MA)
Wright State U (OH)
Xavier U of Louisiana (LA)
York Coll of Pennsylvania (PA)

COMPUTER ENGINEERING RELATED
Auburn U (AL)

COMPUTER ENGINEERING TECHNOLOGIES RELATED
U of Guelph (ON, Canada)

COMPUTER ENGINEERING TECHNOLOGY
Arizona State U (AZ)
Brock U (ON, Canada)
California State U, Long Beach (CA)
Central Connecticut State U (CT)
DeVry Coll of New York (NY)
DeVry U, Phoenix (AZ)
DeVry U, Pomona (CA)
DeVry U, Westminster (CO)
DeVry U, Miramar (FL)
DeVry U, Orlando (FL)
DeVry U, Decatur (GA)
DeVry U, Chicago (IL)
DeVry U, Kansas City (MO)

DeVry U, Columbus (OH)
DeVry U, Fort Washington (PA)
DeVry U, Houston (TX)
DeVry U, Irving (TX)
DeVry U, Arlington (VA)
DeVry U, Federal Way (WA)
DeVry U Online (IL)
Eastern Michigan U (MI)
Farmingdale State Coll (NY)
Georgia Southwestern State U (GA)
Grantham U (MO)
Indiana State U (IN)
Indiana U–Purdue U Fort Wayne (IN)
Indiana U–Purdue U Indianapolis (IN)
Lake Superior State U (MI)
LeTourneau U (TX)
Minnesota State U Mankato (MN)
Missouri Western State U (MO)
New York City Coll of Technology of the City U of New York (NY)
Norfolk State U (VA)
Rochester Inst of Technology (NY)
Seattle U (WA)
Shawnee State U (OH)
Southern Polytechnic State U (GA)
State U of New York Coll of Technology at Alfred (NY)
State U of New York Inst of Technology (NY)
Texas Southern U (TX)
U of Arkansas at Little Rock (AR)
U of Cincinnati (OH)
U of Hartford (CT)
U of Houston (TX)
U of Houston–Downtown (TX)
U of Memphis (TN)
U of Southern Mississippi (MS)
Utah State U (UT)
Vermont Tech Coll (VT)
Wentworth Inst of Technology (MA)

COMPUTER GRAPHICS
Alberta Coll of Art & Design (AB, Canada)
American Acad of Art (IL)
American U (DC)
Becker Coll (MA)
Bowie State U (MD)
California State U, Chico (CA)
California State U, East Bay (CA)
Champlain Coll (VT)
Cogswell Polytechnical Coll (CA)
Coll of the Atlantic (ME)
Concordia U (QC, Canada)
Creative Center (NE)
Dakota State U (SD)
DePaul U (IL)
Indiana Wesleyan U (IN)
John Brown U (AR)
Lindenwood U (MO)
Oakland City U (IN)
Polytechnic Inst of New York U (NY)
Purdue U (IN)
Purdue U Calumet (IN)
Rochester Inst of Technology (NY)
Rocky Mountain Coll of Art + Design (CO)
Rogers State U (OK)
School of the Art Inst of Chicago (IL)
School of the Museum of Fine Arts, Boston (MA)
State U of New York at Fredonia (NY)
Sullivan Coll of Technology and Design (KY)
Texas A&M U (TX)
U of California, Santa Cruz (CA)
U of Great Falls (MT)
U of Houston (TX)
U of Miami (FL)
U of Pennsylvania (PA)

COMPUTER HARDWARE ENGINEERING
Auburn U (AL)
Purdue U (IN)
United States Naval Acad (MD)

COMPUTER HARDWARE TECHNOLOGY
Purdue U (IN)
Temple U (PA)

COMPUTER/INFORMATION TECHNOLOGY SERVICES ADMINISTRATION RELATED
Bloomsburg U of Pennsylvania (PA)
Champlain Coll (VT)
Chestnut Hill Coll (PA)
Concordia U, St. Paul (MN)
Dalhousie U (NS, Canada)
Dordt Coll (IA)
Friends U (KS)
Frostburg State U (MD)
Granite State Coll (NH)
Hodges U (FL)
Holy Names U (CA)
Kent State U at Trumbull (OH)
Limestone Coll (SC)
Marywood U (PA)
Missouri State U (MO)
National U (CA)
Point Park U (PA)
Robert Morris U (PA)
St. Francis Coll (NY)
Southern Methodist U (TX)
State U of New York Coll of Technology at Delhi (NY)
Thompson Rivers U (BC, Canada)
U of Great Falls (MT)
U of Guam (GU)
U of Maryland, Baltimore County (MD)
Washington U in St. Louis (MO)

COMPUTER INSTALLATION AND REPAIR TECHNOLOGY
Inter American U of Puerto Rico, Bayamón Campus (PR)

COMPUTER PROGRAMMING
Andrews U (MI)
Belmont U (TN)
Brock U (ON, Canada)
Caribbean U (PR)
Champlain Coll (VT)
City U of Seattle (WA)
Clemson U (SC)
The Coll of Saint Rose (NY)
Creighton U (NE)
DePaul U (IL)
Dordt Coll (IA)
EDP Coll of Puerto Rico, Inc. (PR)
Farmingdale State Coll (NY)
Franklin Pierce U (NH)
Gannon U (PA)
Grace U (NE)
Hardin-Simmons U (TX)
Inter American U of Puerto Rico, Bayamón Campus (PR)
Inter American U of Puerto Rico, San Germán Campus (PR)
Lamar U (TX)
La Salle U (PA)
Limestone Coll (SC)
Marist Coll (NY)
Neumont U (UT)
Purdue U (IN)
Purdue U Calumet (IN)
Union Coll (KY)
Université de Sherbrooke (QC, Canada)
U of Great Falls (MT)
U of Illinois at Urbana–Champaign (IL)
U of Michigan–Dearborn (MI)
U of Mount Union (OH)
The U of Toledo (OH)
The U of Western Ontario (ON, Canada)
Walla Walla U (WA)
Youngstown State U (OH)

COMPUTER PROGRAMMING RELATED
Farmingdale State Coll (NY)
Neumont U (UT)
Purdue U (IN)

COMPUTER PROGRAMMING (SPECIFIC APPLICATIONS)
DePaul U (IL)
Marist Coll (NY)
Neumont U (UT)
Purdue U (IN)
Southern Polytechnic State U (GA)
U of Washington, Bothell (WA)
U of Windsor (ON, Canada)

COMPUTER PROGRAMMING (VENDOR/PRODUCT CERTIFICATION)
Marist Coll (NY)
Neumont U (UT)
Purdue U (IN)

COMPUTER SCIENCE
Abilene Christian U (TX)
Acadia U (NS, Canada)
Adams State U (CO)
Alabama State U (AL)
Albright Coll (PA)
Alderson-Broaddus Coll (WV)
Alma Coll (MI)
American Coll of Thessaloniki (Greece)
American U (DC)
The American U in Cairo (Egypt)
American U of Beirut (Lebanon)
Amherst Coll (MA)
Anderson U (IN)
Andrews U (MI)
Appalachian State U (NC)
Arizona State U (AZ)
Armstrong Atlantic State U (GA)
Ashland U (OH)
Athens State U (AL)
Augsburg Coll (MN)
Augustana Coll (IL)
Augustana Coll (SD)
Aurora U (IL)
Azusa Pacific U (CA)
Baker U (KS)
Baldwin Wallace U (OH)
Bard Coll (NY)
Barry U (FL)
Baylor U (TX)
Belmont U (TN)
Bemidji State U (MN)
Benedictine Coll (KS)
Benedictine U (IL)
Bennington Coll (VT)
Bethany Coll (WV)
Bethune-Cookman U (FL)
Binghamton U, State U of New York (NY)
Blackburn Coll (IL)
Bloomsburg U of Pennsylvania (PA)
Bob Jones U (SC)
Boise State U (ID)
Boston Coll (MA)
Bowdoin Coll (ME)
Bradley U (IL)
Bridgewater Coll (VA)
Bridgewater State U (MA)
Brock U (ON, Canada)
Brown U (RI)
Buena Vista U (IA)
California Lutheran U (CA)
California Polytechnic State U, San Luis Obispo (CA)
California State Polytechnic U, Pomona (CA)
California State U, Chico (CA)
California State U, Dominguez Hills (CA)
California State U, East Bay (CA)
California State U, Fresno (CA)
California State U, Fullerton (CA)
California State U, Long Beach (CA)
California State U, Los Angeles (CA)
California State U, Northridge (CA)
California State U, San Bernardino (CA)
California State U, San Marcos (CA)
California State U, Stanislaus (CA)
Calumet Coll of Saint Joseph (IN)
Calvin Coll (MI)
Cameron U (OK)
Canisius Coll (NY)
Capital U (OH)
Cardinal Stritch U (WI)
Carleton Coll (MN)
Carnegie Mellon U (PA)
Carroll Coll (MT)
Carson-Newman U (TN)
Case Western Reserve U (OH)
Catawba Coll (NC)
The Catholic U of America (DC)
Cedarville U (OH)
Central Coll (IA)
Central Methodist U (MO)
Central Michigan U (MI)
Central Penn Coll (PA)

Central State U (OH)
Centre Coll (KY)
Champlain Coll (VT)
Chapman U (CA)
Cheyney U of Pennsylvania (PA)
Chicago State U (IL)
Christian Brothers U (TN)
Christopher Newport U (VA)
City Coll of the City U of New York (NY)
Claflin U (SC)
Clark Atlanta U (GA)
Clarkson U (NY)
Clark U (MA)
Clayton State U (GA)
Clemson U (SC)
Coe Coll (IA)
Colby Coll (ME)
The Coll at Brockport, State U of New York (NY)
Coll of Saint Benedict (MN)
Coll of Saint Elizabeth (NJ)
Coll of Staten Island of the City U of New York (NY)
Coll of the Holy Cross (MA)
Coll of the Ozarks (MO)
The Coll of Wooster (OH)
Colorado School of Mines (CO)
Columbia Coll (MO)
Columbia U (NY)
Columbia U, School of General Studies (NY)
Concordia U (QC, Canada)
Concordia U, Nebraska (NE)
Concordia U Texas (TX)
Concordia U Wisconsin (WI)
Concord U (WV)
Connecticut Coll (CT)
Cornell U (IA)
Creighton U (NE)
Dalhousie U (NS, Canada)
Dallas Baptist U (TX)
Daniel Webster Coll (NH)
Dartmouth Coll (NH)
DePaul U (IL)
DePauw U (IN)
DeSales U (PA)
Dillard U (LA)
Doane Coll (NE)
Dominican U (IL)
Dordt Coll (IA)
Drake U (IA)
Drew U (NJ)
Drury U (MO)
Duquesne U (PA)
East Carolina U (NC)
Eastern Mennonite U (VA)
Eastern Michigan U (MI)
East-West U (IL)
Eckerd Coll (FL)
Elizabeth City State U (NC)
Elon U (NC)
Embry-Riddle Aeronautical U–Daytona (FL)
Embry-Riddle Aeronautical U–Prescott (AZ)
Endicott Coll (MA)
Evangel U (MO)
Fairleigh Dickinson U, Metropolitan Campus (NJ)
Fairmont State U (WV)
Fayetteville State U (NC)
Felician Coll (NJ)
Florida Inst of Technology (FL)
Florida Southern Coll (FL)
Fort Lewis Coll (CO)
Franklin Coll (IN)
Franklin Pierce U (NH)
Franklin U (OH)
Frostburg State U (MD)
Furman U (SC)
Gardner-Webb U (NC)
George Mason U (VA)
Georgetown Coll (KY)
Georgetown U (DC)
Georgia Southwestern State U (GA)
Georgia State U (GA)
Gettysburg Coll (PA)
Gonzaga U (WA)
Gordon Coll (MA)
Goucher Coll (MD)
Governors State U (IL)
Graceland U (IA)
Grace U (NE)
Grambling State U (LA)
Grand View U (IA)

Grantham U (MO)
Grinnell Coll (IA)
Gustavus Adolphus Coll (MN)
Hampden-Sydney Coll (VA)
Hampshire Coll (MA)
Hampton U (VA)
Hanover Coll (IN)
Harding U (AR)
Hartwick Coll (NY)
Harvey Mudd Coll (CA)
Haverford Coll (PA)
Hawai`i Pacific U (HI)
Hendrix Coll (AR)
High Point U (NC)
Hillsdale Coll (MI)
Hiram Coll (OH)
Hobart and William Smith Colls (NY)
Hofstra U (NY)
Hood Coll (MD)
Houghton Coll (NY)
Howard Payne U (TX)
Humboldt State U (CA)
Hunter Coll of the City U of New York (NY)
Huntington U (IN)
Illinois Coll (IL)
Illinois Inst of Technology (IL)
Illinois State U (IL)
Illinois Wesleyan U (IL)
Indiana Tech (IN)
Indiana U Bloomington (IN)
Indiana U Kokomo (IN)
Indiana U Northwest (IN)
Indiana–Purdue U Indianapolis (IN)
Indiana U South Bend (IN)
Indiana U Southeast (IN)
Inter American U of Puerto Rico, Aguadilla Campus (PR)
Inter American U of Puerto Rico, Bayamón Campus (PR)
Inter American U of Puerto Rico, Ponce Campus (PR)
Inter American U of Puerto Rico, San Germán Campus (PR)
Iona Coll (NY)
Ithaca Coll (NY)
Jamestown Coll (ND)
John Carroll U (OH)
Kansas Wesleyan U (KS)
Kentucky Wesleyan Coll (KY)
King Coll (TN)
King's Coll (PA)
The King's U Coll (AB, Canada)
Knox Coll (IL)
Lafayette Coll (PA)
Lakeland Coll (WI)
Lake Superior State U (MI)
Lamar U (TX)
Langston U (OK)
La Roche Coll (PA)
La Salle U (PA)
La Sierra U (CA)
Lawrence Technological U (MI)
Lawrence U (WI)
Lebanese American U (Lebanon)
Lebanon Valley Coll (PA)
Lehigh U (PA)
Lehman Coll of the City U of New York (NY)
LeTourneau U (TX)
Lewis-Clark State Coll (ID)
Lewis U (IL)
Limestone Coll (SC)
Lindenwood U (MO)
Linfield Coll (OR)
Lipscomb U (TN)
Lock Haven U of Pennsylvania (PA)
Long Island U–Brooklyn Campus (NY)
Long Island U–C. W. Post Campus (NY)
Longwood U (VA)
Louisiana State U and Ag and Mech Coll (LA)
Louisiana State U in Shreveport (LA)
Loyola U Maryland (MD)
Luther Coll (IA)
Lynchburg Coll (VA)
Madonna U (MI)
Maharishi U of Management (IA)
Malone U (OH)
Manchester U (IN)
Manhattan Coll (NY)
Manhattanville Coll (NY)

Mansfield U of Pennsylvania (PA)
Marietta Coll (OH)
Marist Coll (NY)
Mars Hill Coll (NC)
Massachusetts Coll of Liberal Arts (MA)
Massachusetts Inst of Technology (MA)
McKendree U (IL)
McNeese State U (LA)
Mercer U (GA)
Mercyhurst U (PA)
Merrimack Coll (MA)
Messiah Coll (PA)
Metropolitan State U of Denver (CO)
Middlebury Coll (VT)
Middle Tennessee State U (TN)
Millsaps Coll (MS)
Mills Coll (CA)
Minnesota State U Moorhead (MN)
Minot State U (ND)
Mississippi Coll (MS)
Mississippi Valley State U (MS)
Missouri State U (MO)
Missouri U of Science and Technology (MO)
Monmouth Coll (IL)
Montana State U (MT)
Montana Tech of The U of Montana (MT)
Moravian Coll (PA)
Mount Allison U (NB, Canada)
Mount Holyoke Coll (MA)
Mount Marty Coll (SD)
Mount Vernon Nazarene U (OH)
Murray State U (KY)
National U (CA)
Neumont U (UT)
Newbury Coll (MA)
New England Inst of Technology (RI)
New Jersey Inst of Technology (NJ)
New Mexico Inst of Mining and Technology (NM)
Niagara U (NY)
North Carolina Central U (NC)
North Carolina State U (NC)
Northcentral U (AZ)
North Dakota State U (ND)
Northeastern Illinois U (IL)
Northeastern U (MA)
Northern Arizona U (AZ)
Northern Illinois U (IL)
Northwestern Coll (IA)
Northwestern Oklahoma State U (OK)
Northwest Nazarene U (ID)
Norwich U (VT)
Nova Southeastern U (FL)
Nyack Coll (NY)
The Ohio State U (OH)
Ohio U (OH)
Ohio Wesleyan U (OH)
Oklahoma Baptist U (OK)
Oklahoma Christian U (OK)
Oklahoma City U (OK)
Oral Roberts U (OK)
Oregon State U (OR)
Ouachita Baptist U (AR)
Pace U (NY)
Pacific Lutheran U (WA)
Pacific States U (CA)
Pacific Union Coll (CA)
Pacific U (OR)
Palm Beach Atlantic U (FL)
Park U (MO)
Penn State Erie, The Behrend Coll (PA)
Pepperdine U, Malibu (CA)
Philadelphia U (PA)
Piedmont Coll (GA)
Plymouth State U (NH)
Point Loma Nazarene U (CA)
Polytechnic Inst of New York U (NY)
Polytechnic U of Puerto Rico (PR)
Pomona Coll (CA)
Portland State U (OR)
Providence Coll (RI)
Purdue U (IN)
Purdue U Calumet (IN)
Quincy U (IL)
Quinnipiac U (CT)
Radford U (VA)
Randolph-Macon Coll (VA)
Rasmussen Coll Appleton (WI)

Rasmussen Coll Bismarck (ND)
Rasmussen Coll Blaine (MN)
Rasmussen Coll Bloomington (MN)
Rasmussen Coll Brooklyn Park (MN)
Rasmussen Coll Eagan (MN)
Rasmussen Coll Fargo (ND)
Rasmussen Coll Fort Myers (FL)
Rasmussen Coll Green Bay (WI)
Rasmussen Coll Lake Elmo/Woodbury (MN)
Rasmussen Coll Land O' Lakes (FL)
Rasmussen Coll Mankato (MN)
Rasmussen Coll Moorhead (MN)
Rasmussen Coll New Port Richey (FL)
Rasmussen Coll Ocala (FL)
Rasmussen Coll St. Cloud (MN)
Rasmussen Coll Tampa/Brandon (FL)
Rasmussen Coll Wausau (WI)
Regis U (CO)
Rensselaer Polytechnic Inst (NY)
Rhodes Coll (TN)
Ripon Coll (WI)
Roanoke Coll (VA)
Roberts Wesleyan Coll (NY)
Rochester Inst of Technology (NY)
Rockford Coll (IL)
Rocky Mountain Coll (MT)
Roger Williams U (RI)
Roosevelt U (IL)
Rutgers, The State U of New Jersey, New Brunswick (NJ)
Saginaw Valley State U (MI)
St. Ambrose U (IA)
Saint Anselm Coll (NH)
St. Bonaventure U (NY)
St. Edward's U (TX)
Saint John's U (MN)
St. Lawrence U (NY)
Saint Martin's U (WA)
St. Mary's U (TX)
Saint Mary's U of Minnesota (MN)
Saint Michael's Coll (VT)
St. Olaf Coll (MN)
St. Thomas U (FL)
Samford U (AL)
San Diego State U (CA)
San Francisco State U (CA)
San Jose State U (CA)
Scripps Coll (CA)
Seattle U (WA)
Seton Hill U (PA)
Sewanee: The U of the South (TN)
Shaw U (NC)
Simon Fraser U (BC, Canada)
Simpson Coll (IA)
Slippery Rock U of Pennsylvania (PA)
Smith Coll (MA)
Sonoma State U (CA)
Southeastern Louisiana U (LA)
Southern California Inst of Technology (CA)
Southern Connecticut State U (CT)
Southern Illinois U Carbondale (IL)
Southern Illinois U Edwardsville (IL)
Southern Methodist U (TX)
Southern Oregon U (OR)
Southern Polytechnic State U (GA)
Southern Utah U (UT)
Southwest Baptist U (MO)
Southwestern Adventist U (TX)
Southwestern Coll (KS)
Spelman Coll (GA)
Spring Arbor U (MI)
Stanford U (CA)
State U of New York at Fredonia (NY)
State U of New York at Oswego (NY)
State U of New York at Plattsburgh (NY)
State U of New York Coll at Old Westbury (NY)
State U of New York Coll at Potsdam (NY)
Stetson U (FL)
Stonehill Coll (MA)
Stony Brook U, State U of New York (NY)
Suffolk U (MA)
Susquehanna U (PA)
Taylor U (IN)

Tennessee State U (TN)
Texas A&M U (TX)
Texas A&M U–Commerce (TX)
Texas Lutheran U (TX)
Texas Wesleyan U (TX)
Thomas Edison State Coll (NJ)
Thompson Rivers U (BC, Canada)
Trent U (ON, Canada)
Trine U (IN)
Trinity Christian Coll (IL)
Trinity Coll (CT)
Tufts U (MA)
Tulane U (LA)
Tuskegee U (AL)
Union U (TN)
United States Air Force Acad (CO)
United States Naval Acad (MD)
Universidad Adventista de las Antillas (PR)
Université de Sherbrooke (QC, Canada)
Université du Québec en Outaouais (QC, Canada)
U at Albany, State U of New York (NY)
U at Buffalo, the State U of New York (NY)
The U of Akron (OH)
U of Alaska Anchorage (AK)
U of Alaska Fairbanks (AK)
The U of Arizona (AZ)
U of Arkansas at Little Rock (AR)
U of Bridgeport (CT)
The U of British Columbia (BC, Canada)
The U of British Columbia–Okanagan (BC, Canada)
U of California, Berkeley (CA)
U of California, Irvine (CA)
U of California, Riverside (CA)
U of California, Santa Barbara (CA)
U of California, Santa Cruz (CA)
U of Central Oklahoma (OK)
U of Chicago (IL)
U of Colorado Boulder (CO)
U of Delaware (DE)
U of Denver (CO)
U of Evansville (IN)
The U of Findlay (OH)
U of Georgia (GA)
U of Great Falls (MT)
U of Guam (GU)
U of Guelph (ON, Canada)
U of Hawaii at Hilo (HI)
U of Hawaii at Manoa (HI)
U of Houston–Clear Lake (TX)
U of Houston–Victoria (TX)
U of Idaho (ID)
U of Illinois at Chicago (IL)
U of Illinois at Springfield (IL)
U of Illinois at Urbana–Champaign (IL)
The U of Iowa (IA)
U of La Verne (CA)
U of Louisiana at Monroe (LA)
U of Maine at Farmington (ME)
U of Maine at Fort Kent (ME)
U of Maryland, Baltimore County (MD)
U of Maryland Eastern Shore (MD)
U of Massachusetts Amherst (MA)
U of Memphis (TN)
U of Miami (FL)
U of Michigan–Flint (MI)
U of Minnesota, Duluth (MN)
U of Minnesota, Twin Cities Campus (MN)
U of Missouri (MO)
U of Missouri–Kansas City (MO)
U of Missouri–St. Louis (MO)
U of Nebraska at Omaha (NE)
U of Nevada, Las Vegas (NV)
U of Nevada, Reno (NV)
U of New Brunswick Fredericton (NB, Canada)
U of New Brunswick Saint John (NB, Canada)
U of New Haven (CT)
U of New Orleans (LA)
U of North Carolina at Asheville (NC)
The U of North Carolina at Chapel Hill (NC)
The U of North Carolina at Charlotte (NC)
The U of North Carolina at Greensboro (NC)

The U of North Carolina at Pembroke (NC)
The U of North Carolina Wilmington (NC)
U of Northern Iowa (IA)
U of Oklahoma (OK)
U of Pittsburgh (PA)
U of Pittsburgh at Bradford (PA)
U of Portland (OR)
U of Puget Sound (WA)
U of Redlands (CA)
U of Regina (SK, Canada)
U of Richmond (VA)
U of Rochester (NY)
U of St. Francis (IL)
U of San Diego (CA)
The U of Scranton (PA)
U of South Alabama (AL)
U of Southern California (CA)
U of Southern Indiana (IN)
U of Southern Maine (ME)
The U of Tennessee (TN)
The U of Tennessee at Chattanooga (TN)
The U of Tennessee at Martin (TN)
The U of Texas at Arlington (TX)
The U of Texas at El Paso (TX)
The U of Texas–Pan American (TX)
U of the District of Columbia (DC)
U of the Virgin Islands (VI)
The U of Toledo (OH)
U of Tulsa (OK)
U of Utah (UT)
U of Vermont (VT)
U of Waterloo (ON, Canada)
The U of Western Ontario (ON, Canada)
U of Windsor (ON, Canada)
U of Wisconsin–Green Bay (WI)
U of Wisconsin–Milwaukee (WI)
U of Wisconsin–Parkside (WI)
U of Wisconsin–Platteville (WI)
U of Wisconsin–Superior (WI)
U of Wyoming (WY)
Valdosta State U (GA)
Valparaiso U (IN)
Vanderbilt U (TN)
Villanova U (PA)
Virginia Polytechnic Inst and State U (VA)
Virginia State U (VA)
Virginia Wesleyan Coll (VA)
Wagner Coll (NY)
Walla Walla U (WA)
Walsh U (OH)
Wartburg Coll (IA)
Washington and Lee U (VA)
Washington Coll (MD)
Washington State U (WA)
Washington U in St. Louis (MO)
Waynesburg U (PA)
Weber State U (UT)
Webster U (MO)
Wellesley Coll (MA)
Wells Coll (NY)
Wentworth Inst of Technology (MA)
Wesleyan U (CT)
Western Carolina U (NC)
Western Connecticut State U (CT)
Western Michigan U (MI)
Western Oregon U (OR)
Western State Colorado U (CO)
Westfield State U (MA)
Westminster Coll (MO)
Westminster Coll (UT)
West Texas A&M U (TX)
West Virginia U (WV)
West Virginia U Inst of Technology (WV)
West Virginia Wesleyan Coll (WV)
Wheaton Coll (IL)
Wheaton Coll (MA)
Wheeling Jesuit U (WV)
Whitworth U (WA)
Widener U (PA)
Wilberforce U (OH)
Willamette U (OR)
William Paterson U of New Jersey (NJ)
William Penn U (IA)
Williams Coll (MA)
Wittenberg U (OH)
Worcester Polytechnic Inst (MA)
Xavier U (OH)
Xavier U of Louisiana (LA)
York Coll of Pennsylvania (PA)

York Coll of the City U of New York (NY)
Youngstown State U (OH)

COMPUTER SOFTWARE AND MEDIA APPLICATIONS RELATED
Champlain Coll (VT)
Coll of Charleston (SC)
Dakota Wesleyan U (SD)
DePaul U (IL)
Duquesne U (PA)
Florida State U (FL)
Holy Names U (CA)
Intl Acad of Design & Technology (FL)
Loyola U Chicago (IL)
Morrisville State Coll (NY)
Neumont U (UT)
U of Denver (CO)
U of Great Falls (MT)
The U of Western Ontario (ON, Canada)
U of Wisconsin–Stout (WI)

COMPUTER SOFTWARE ENGINEERING
Arizona State U (AZ)
Auburn U (AL)
Baldwin Wallace U (OH)
Brock U (ON, Canada)
Centennial Coll (ON, Canada)
Clarkson U (NY)
Cogswell Polytechnical Coll (CA)
Concordia U (QC, Canada)
Dalhousie U (NS, Canada)
DeVry U, Phoenix (AZ)
DeVry U, Pomona (CA)
DeVry U, Westminster (CO)
DeVry U, Orlando (FL)
DeVry U, Decatur (GA)
DeVry U, Fort Washington (PA)
DeVry U, Irving (TX)
DeVry U, Arlington (VA)
DeVry U, Federal Way (WA)
DeVry U Online (IL)
Embry-Riddle Aeronautical U–Daytona (FL)
Fairfield U (CT)
Florida Inst of Technology (FL)
Indiana Tech (IN)
Indiana Wesleyan U (IN)
Liberty U (VA)
Milwaukee School of Eng (WI)
Monmouth U (NJ)
Montana Tech of The U of Montana (MT)
National U (CA)
Penn State Erie, The Behrend Coll (PA)
Purdue U (IN)
Purdue U Calumet (IN)
Quinnipiac U (CT)
Robert Morris U (PA)
Rochester Inst of Technology (NY)
Shippensburg U of Pennsylvania (PA)
Southern Polytechnic State U (GA)
State U of New York at Oswego (NY)
Stratford U, Woodbridge (VA)
United States Coast Guard Acad (CT)
U of California, Irvine (CA)
U of Guelph (ON, Canada)
U of Illinois at Urbana–Champaign (IL)
U of Miami (FL)
U of Minnesota, Crookston (MN)
U of Northern Colorado (CO)
U of Ottawa (ON, Canada)
U of Regina (SK, Canada)
The U of Scranton (PA)
The U of Texas at Arlington (TX)
The U of Texas at Dallas (TX)
U of Waterloo (ON, Canada)
The U of Western Ontario (ON, Canada)
U of Wisconsin–Platteville (WI)
Vermont Tech Coll (VT)

COMPUTER SOFTWARE TECHNOLOGY
Purdue U (IN)
U of Regina (SK, Canada)

COMPUTER SUPPORT SPECIALIST
Purdue U (IN)

COMPUTER SYSTEMS ANALYSIS
Arizona State U (AZ)
Arkansas Tech U (AR)
Baldwin Wallace U (OH)
California Polytechnic State U, San Luis Obispo (CA)
Caribbean U (PR)
Clayton State U (GA)
Concordia U (QC, Canada)
DeVry Coll of New York (NY)
DeVry U, Phoenix (AZ)
DeVry U, Pomona (CA)
DeVry U, Westminster (CO)
DeVry U, Miramar (FL)
DeVry U, Orlando (FL)
DeVry U, Decatur (GA)
DeVry U, Chicago (IL)
DeVry U, Kansas City (MO)
DeVry U, North Brunswick (NJ)
DeVry U, Columbus (OH)
DeVry U, Fort Washington (PA)
DeVry U, Houston (TX)
DeVry U, Irving (TX)
DeVry U, Arlington (VA)
DeVry U, Federal Way (WA)
DeVry U Online (IL)
HEC Montreal (QC, Canada)
Inter American U of Puerto Rico, Bayamón Campus (PR)
Kent State U (OH)
New England Inst of Technology (RI)
Northern Arizona U (AZ)
Northwest Missouri State U (MO)
Purdue U (IN)
Rochester Inst of Technology (NY)
Saginaw Valley State U (MI)
St. Ambrose U (IA)
Seattle Pacific U (WA)
Shippensburg U of Pennsylvania (PA)
Sullivan U (KY)
Taylor U (IN)
Texas Christian U (TX)
Thompson Rivers U (BC, Canada)
U of Denver (CO)
U of Great Falls (MT)
U of Houston (TX)
U of Louisiana at Lafayette (LA)
U of North Dakota (ND)
U of Vermont (VT)
U of Washington, Bothell (WA)
U of Washington, Tacoma (WA)
West Virginia U Inst of Technology (WV)

COMPUTER SYSTEMS NETWORKING AND TELECOMMUNICATIONS
Baldwin Wallace U (OH)
Bloomfield Coll (NJ)
Boise State U (ID)
California State U, East Bay (CA)
Centennial Coll (ON, Canada)
Chowan U (NC)
Concordia U (QC, Canada)
Davenport U, Grand Rapids (MI)
DePaul U (IL)
DeVry Coll of New York (NY)
DeVry U, Phoenix (AZ)
DeVry U, Pomona (CA)
DeVry U, Westminster (CO)
DeVry U, Miramar (FL)
DeVry U, Orlando (FL)
DeVry U, Decatur (GA)
DeVry U, Chicago (IL)
DeVry U, Kansas City (MO)
DeVry U, North Brunswick (NJ)
DeVry U, Columbus (OH)
DeVry U, Fort Washington (PA)
DeVry U, Houston (TX)
DeVry U, Irving (TX)
DeVry U, Arlington (VA)
DeVry U, Federal Way (WA)
DeVry U Online (IL)
EDP Coll of Puerto Rico, Inc. (PR)
Ferris State U (MI)
Grantham U (MO)
Illinois State U (IL)
Indiana Tech (IN)
Inter American U of Puerto Rico, Aguadilla Campus (PR)
Inter American U of Puerto Rico, Ponce Campus (PR)
Iona Coll (NY)
The Johns Hopkins U (MD)
Kansas State U (KS)

Kean U (NJ)
Montana Tech of The U of Montana (MT)
Morrisville State Coll (NY)
Mount Vernon Nazarene U (OH)
Northern Michigan U (MI)
Northwestern Oklahoma State U (OK)
Ohio U (OH)
Pennsylvania Coll of Technology (PA)
Purdue U (IN)
Purdue U Calumet (IN)
Regis U (CO)
Rochester Inst of Technology (NY)
Roosevelt U (IL)
St. Ambrose U (IA)
State U of New York Coll of Technology at Alfred (NY)
Stevenson U (MD)
Thompson Rivers U (BC, Canada)
The U of Akron (OH)
The U of Findlay (OH)
U of Great Falls (MT)
U of Minnesota, Duluth (MN)
U of Minnesota, Twin Cities Campus (MN)
The U of North Carolina at Greensboro (NC)
U of Pennsylvania (PA)
U of the Incarnate Word (TX)
U of Wisconsin–Stout (WI)
Virginia Union U (VA)
Weber State U (UT)
Wentworth Inst of Technology (MA)
Western Illinois U (IL)
Western State Colorado U (CO)

COMPUTER TEACHER EDUCATION
Abilene Christian U (TX)
Alma Coll (MI)
Baylor U (TX)
Bowling Green State U (OH)
Buena Vista U (IA)
Colorado State U (CO)
Concordia U Chicago (IL)
Concordia U, Nebraska (NE)
Dakota State U (SD)
Dallas Baptist U (TX)
Dordt Coll (IA)
Duquesne U (PA)
Eastern Michigan U (MI)
Edgewood Coll (WI)
Hardin-Simmons U (TX)
Howard Payne U (TX)
Keene State Coll (NH)
Long Island U–Brooklyn Campus (NY)
Lubbock Christian U (TX)
McMurry U (TX)
Michigan State U (MI)
Olivet Coll (MI)
Southeastern Louisiana U (LA)
Union Coll (NE)
U of Nebraska–Lincoln (NE)
U of the Cumberlands (KY)
Utica Coll (NY)
Western Washington U (WA)
Wright State U (OH)

COMPUTER TECHNOLOGY/COMPUTER SYSTEMS TECHNOLOGY
Central Michigan U (MI)
Colorado State U (CO)
Daytona State Coll (FL)
Florida Atlantic U (FL)
Purdue U (IN)
Rensselaer Polytechnic Inst (NY)
Sullivan U (KY)
Wayne State U (MI)

CONDENSED MATTER AND MATERIALS PHYSICS
Rowan U (NJ)

CONDUCTING
Bard Coll (NY)
Chapman U (CA)
Lee U (TN)
Mannes Coll The New School for Music (NY)
McMurry U (TX)

CONSERVATION BIOLOGY
Boston U (MA)
Florida Inst of Technology (FL)
Philadelphia U (PA)

Prescott Coll (AZ)
Seattle U (WA)
Sterling Coll (VT)
U of Idaho (ID)
U of Maine at Machias (ME)
The U of Western Ontario (ON, Canada)
U of Wisconsin–Madison (WI)

CONSTRUCTION ENGINEERING
The American U in Cairo (Egypt)
American U of Beirut (Lebanon)
Arizona State U (AZ)
Bradley U (IL)
California State U, Long Beach (CA)
Concordia U (QC, Canada)
John Brown U (AR)
Marquette U (WI)
National U (CA)
North Carolina State U (NC)
North Dakota State U (ND)
Oregon State U (OR)
Polytechnic Inst of New York U (NY)
Purdue U (IN)
Southern Polytechnic State U (GA)
Texas A&M U–Commerce (TX)
The U of Alabama (AL)
U of Arkansas at Little Rock (AR)
U of Illinois at Urbana–Champaign (IL)
U of Nebraska–Lincoln (NE)
U of Nevada, Las Vegas (NV)
U of New Brunswick Fredericton (NB, Canada)

CONSTRUCTION ENGINEERING TECHNOLOGY
Bemidji State U (MN)
Bowling Green State U (OH)
California Baptist U (CA)
California State Polytechnic U, Pomona (CA)
California State U, Chico (CA)
California State U, Fresno (CA)
California State U, Long Beach (CA)
Central Michigan U (MI)
Colorado Mesa U (CO)
Colorado State U (CO)
Fairleigh Dickinson U, Metropolitan Campus (NJ)
Farmingdale State Coll (NY)
Florida Ag and Mech U (FL)
Florida Inst of Technology (FL)
Florida Intl U (FL)
Georgia Southern U (GA)
Indiana U–Purdue U Fort Wayne (IN)
John Brown U (AR)
Kansas State U (KS)
Michigan State U (MI)
Missouri Western State U (MO)
Montana State U (MT)
Norfolk State U (VA)
Northern Michigan U (MI)
The Ohio State U (OH)
Oklahoma State U (OK)
Pittsburg State U (KS)
Purdue U (IN)
Purdue U Calumet (IN)
Roger Williams U (RI)
San Diego State U (CA)
Seminole State Coll of Florida (FL)
South Dakota State U (SD)
Southern Illinois U Edwardsville (IL)
Texas A&M U (TX)
Texas A&M U–Commerce (TX)
Texas State U–San Marcos (TX)
Thomas Edison State Coll (NJ)
Tuskegee U (AL)
The U of Akron (OH)
U of Arkansas at Little Rock (AR)
U of Florida (FL)
U of Houston (TX)
U of Maryland Eastern Shore (MD)
U of Nebraska–Lincoln (NE)
U of North Florida (FL)
U of North Texas (TX)
The U of Toledo (OH)
Wayne State U (MI)
Western Carolina U (NC)
Western Kentucky U (KY)

CONSTRUCTION MANAGEMENT
Appalachian State U (NC)
Arizona State U (AZ)
Boise State U (ID)
California State U, Fresno (CA)
California State U, Northridge (CA)
Central Connecticut State U (CT)
Clemson U (SC)
Colorado State U (CO)
Eastern Michigan U (MI)
Ferris State U (MI)
Illinois State U (IL)
Indiana State U (IN)
John Brown U (AR)
Lawrence Technological U (MI)
Louisiana State U and Ag and Mech Coll (LA)
Michigan State U (MI)
Milwaukee School of Eng (WI)
Minnesota State U Moorhead (MN)
Mississippi State U (MS)
Missouri State U (MO)
North Dakota State U (ND)
Northern Arizona U (AZ)
The Ohio State U (OH)
Pittsburg State U (KS)
Purdue U (IN)
Sam Houston State U (TX)
Southern Polytechnic State U (GA)
Thompson Rivers U (BC, Canada)
U of Alaska Anchorage (AK)
U of Denver (CO)
U of Louisiana at Monroe (LA)
U of Northern Iowa (IA)
U of Oklahoma (OK)
U of Wisconsin–Stout (WI)
Vermont Tech Coll (VT)
Virginia Polytechnic Inst and State U (VA)
Washington State U (WA)
Wentworth Inst of Technology (MA)
Western Carolina U (NC)
Western Illinois U (IL)

CONSTRUCTION TRADES
Purdue U (IN)

CONSTRUCTION TRADES RELATED
John Brown U (AR)
Purdue U (IN)
State U of New York Coll of Technology at Alfred (NY)

CONSUMER ECONOMICS
South Dakota State U (SD)
U of Georgia (GA)
U of Illinois at Urbana–Champaign (IL)
The U of Tennessee (TN)
U of Utah (UT)

CONSUMER MERCHANDISING/ RETAILING MANAGEMENT
Bradley U (IL)
HEC Montreal (QC, Canada)
Madonna U (MI)
Newbury Coll (MA)
Oregon State U (OR)
Purdue U (IN)
San Francisco State U (CA)
Savannah Coll of Art and Design (GA)
Simmons Coll (MA)
U of Central Oklahoma (OK)
U of Memphis (TN)
U of Nebraska–Lincoln (NE)

CONSUMER SERVICES AND ADVOCACY
Carson-Newman U (TN)
Purdue U (IN)
Tennessee State U (TN)

CORRECTIONS
Adams State U (CO)
Asbury U (KY)
Bowling Green State U (OH)
California State U, East Bay (CA)
California State U, Stanislaus (CA)
The Coll at Brockport, State U of New York (NY)
Coll of the Ozarks (MO)
Excelsior Coll (NY)
Jacksonville State U (AL)
Lake Superior State U (MI)
Lamar U (TX)
Langston U (OK)

Lewis-Clark State Coll (ID)
Mercyhurst U (PA)
Minnesota State U Mankato (MN)
Oklahoma City U (OK)
Saint Louis U (MO)
Southeast Missouri State U (MO)
Spring Arbor U (MI)
Stephen F. Austin State U (TX)
Texas State U–San Marcos (TX)
Tiffin U (OH)
Tulane U (LA)
U of Great Falls (MT)
U of Minnesota, Crookston (MN)
U of New Mexico (NM)
U of Pittsburgh (PA)
The U of Texas at Brownsville (TX)
Washburn U (KS)
Weber State U (UT)
Western Oregon U (OR)

CORRECTIONS ADMINISTRATION
Inter American U of Puerto Rico, Fajardo Campus (PR)
Inter American U of Puerto Rico, Ponce Campus (PR)
U of Great Falls (MT)

CORRECTIONS AND CRIMINAL JUSTICE RELATED
Averett U (VA)
Bethune-Cookman U (FL)
Bob Jones U (SC)
Cameron U (OK)
Caribbean U (PR)
Cedarville U (OH)
The Coll at Brockport, State U of New York (NY)
Corban U (OR)
DeVry U, Phoenix (AZ)
DeVry U, Pomona (CA)
DeVry U, Miramar (FL)
DeVry U, Orlando (FL)
DeVry U, Decatur (GA)
DeVry U, Chicago (IL)
DeVry U, Kansas City (MO)
DeVry U, Houston (TX)
DeVry U, Arlington (VA)
DeVry U, Federal Way (WA)
DeVry U Online (IL)
Emporia State U (KS)
Goldey-Beacom Coll (DE)
Indiana Tech (IN)
La Roche Coll (PA)
Limestone Coll (SC)
Rasmussen Coll Bloomington (MN)
Rasmussen Coll Brooklyn Park (MN)
Rasmussen Coll Eagan (MN)
Rasmussen Coll Fargo (ND)
Rasmussen Coll Fort Myers (FL)
Rasmussen Coll Lake Elmo/ Woodbury (MN)
Rasmussen Coll Land O' Lakes (FL)
Rasmussen Coll Mankato (MN)
Rasmussen Coll Moorhead (MN)
Rasmussen Coll New Port Richey (FL)
Rasmussen Coll Ocala (FL)
Rasmussen Coll St. Cloud (MN)
Rasmussen Coll Tampa/Brandon (FL)
Roger Williams U (RI)
Saint Mary's U of Minnesota (MN)
Sam Houston State U (TX)
Southern New Hampshire U (NH)
The U of Alabama at Birmingham (AL)
U of Alaska Fairbanks (AK)
U of Great Falls (MT)
U of Michigan–Flint (MI)
Vincennes U (IN)
Weber State U (UT)

COSTUME DESIGN
Shenandoah U (VA)
Stephens Coll (MO)

COUNSELING PSYCHOLOGY
Arizona Christian U (AZ)
Bob Jones U (SC)
Crossroads Coll (MN)
Crown Coll (MN)
Eastern New Mexico U (NM)
Eastern Washington U (WA)
Emmanuel Coll (MA)
Fort Lewis Coll (CO)

Hope Intl U (CA)
Jamestown Coll (ND)
Lesley U (MA)
Maryville Coll (TN)
Mid-Atlantic Christian U (NC)
Mid-Continent U (KY)
Midwestern State U (TX)
Morningside Coll (IA)
Mount St. Mary's Coll (CA)
Newman U (KS)
Pittsburg State U (KS)
Point U (GA)
Prescott Coll (AZ)
San Diego Christian Coll (CA)
U of Chicago (IL)
Wayne State Coll (NE)

COUNSELOR EDUCATION/ SCHOOL COUNSELING AND GUIDANCE
Auburn U at Montgomery (AL)
Bowling Green State U (OH)
Buena Vista U (IA)
Clemson U (SC)
East Central U (OK)
Eastern New Mexico U (NM)
Florida Gulf Coast U (FL)
Goddard Coll (VT)
John Brown U (AR)
Lamar U (TX)
Marshall U (WV)
Midwestern State U (TX)
Tarleton State U (TX)
Texas A&M U–Commerce (TX)
Université de Sherbrooke (QC, Canada)
U of Central Oklahoma (OK)
U of Hawaii at Manoa (HI)
U of New Brunswick Fredericton (NB, Canada)
The U of North Carolina at Pembroke (NC)
The U of South Dakota (SD)
U of Windsor (ON, Canada)
Wright State U (OH)

CRAFTS, FOLK ART AND ARTISANRY
Bowling Green State U (OH)
Bridgewater State U (MA)
Brigham Young U (UT)
Cleveland Inst of Art (OH)
Coll for Creative Studies (MI)
Indiana U–Purdue U Fort Wayne (IN)
Kent State U (OH)
Kutztown U of Pennsylvania (PA)
Oregon Coll of Art & Craft (OR)
Rochester Inst of Technology (NY)
U of Illinois at Urbana–Champaign (IL)
The U of the Arts (PA)
Virginia Commonwealth U (VA)

CREATIVE WRITING
Adams State U (CO)
Agnes Scott Coll (GA)
Albion Coll (MI)
Arkansas Tech U (AR)
Asbury U (KY)
Ashland U (OH)
Augustana Coll (IL)
Baldwin Wallace U (OH)
Bard Coll (NY)
Belhaven U (MS)
Bennington Coll (VT)
Binghamton U, State U of New York (NY)
Bluffton U (OH)
Bob Jones U (SC)
Bowie State U (MD)
Bowling Green State U (OH)
Bridgewater State U (MA)
Brown U (RI)
Bucknell U (PA)
Butler U (IN)
California State U, East Bay (CA)
California State U, Long Beach (CA)
California State U, San Bernardino (CA)
Canisius Coll (NY)
Capital U (OH)
Cardinal Stritch U (WI)
Carlow U (PA)
Carnegie Mellon U (PA)
Carson-Newman U (TN)
Chapman U (CA)

Chatham U (PA)
Christian Brothers U (TN)
City Coll of the City U of New York (NY)
Coe Coll (IA)
Colby Coll (ME)
The Coll at Brockport, State U of New York (NY)
The Coll of Idaho (ID)
Coll of the Atlantic (ME)
The Colorado Coll (CO)
Colorado State U (CO)
Columbia Coll Chicago (IL)
Columbia U (NY)
Columbia U, School of General Studies (NY)
Concordia U (QC, Canada)
Converse Coll (SC)
Corban U (OR)
Cornell Coll (IA)
Creighton U (NE)
Dartmouth Coll (NH)
Eastern Michigan U (MI)
Eckerd Coll (FL)
Emerson Coll (MA)
Fairleigh Dickinson U, Coll at Florham (NJ)
Florida State U (FL)
Franklin & Marshall Coll (PA)
Franklin Coll Switzerland (Switzerland)
Franklin Pierce U (NH)
Gettysburg Coll (PA)
Goddard Coll (VT)
Hamilton Coll (NY)
Hamline U (MN)
Hampshire Coll (MA)
High Point U (NC)
Hiram Coll (OH)
Hofstra U (NY)
Hope Coll (MI)
Houghton Coll (NY)
Indiana Wesleyan U (IN)
Inst of American Indian Arts (NM)
Ithaca Coll (NY)
The Johns Hopkins U (MD)
Johnson State Coll (VT)
Knox Coll (IL)
Lehman Coll of the City U of New York (NY)
Lewis-Clark State Coll (ID)
Linfield Coll (OR)
Loyola U Maryland (MD)
Massachusetts Coll of Liberal Arts (MA)
Massachusetts Inst of Technology (MA)
McMurry U (TX)
Mercer U (GA)
Mills Coll (CA)
Minnesota State U Mankato (MN)
Morehead State U (KY)
Murray State U (KY)
New England Coll (NH)
North Central Coll (IL)
Northern Michigan U (MI)
Northland Coll (WI)
Oakland U (MI)
Ohio U (OH)
Ohio Wesleyan U (OH)
Oklahoma Christian U (OK)
Pacific U (OR)
Pepperdine U, Malibu (CA)
Pittsburg State U (KS)
Point Loma Nazarene U (CA)
Prescott Coll (AZ)
Purchase Coll, State U of New York (NY)
Purdue U (IN)
Randolph Coll (VA)
Rhode Island Coll (RI)
Roanoke Coll (VA)
Rocky Mountain Coll (MT)
Saint Joseph's Coll (IN)
St. Lawrence U (NY)
Saint Mary-of-the-Woods Coll (IN)
Saint Mary's Coll (IN)
San Francisco State U (CA)
Santa Fe U of Art and Design (NM)
School of the Art Inst of Chicago (IL)
Seattle U (WA)
Seton Hill U (PA)
Sewanee: The U of the South (TN)
Siena Heights U (MI)
Sierra Nevada Coll (NV)

Slippery Rock U of Pennsylvania (PA)
Southern Methodist U (TX)
Southern New Hampshire U (NH)
Southwestern Coll (KS)
Spalding U (KY)
State U of New York at Oswego (NY)
Stephen F. Austin State U (TX)
Stephens Coll (MO)
Suffolk U (MA)
Susquehanna U (PA)
Sweet Briar Coll (VA)
Texas Christian U (TX)
Trinity Coll (CT)
Truman State U (MO)
The U of Arizona (AZ)
The U of British Columbia (BC, Canada)
The U of British Columbia– Okanagan (BC, Canada)
U of California, Riverside (CA)
U of Cincinnati (OH)
U of Denver (CO)
U of Evansville (IN)
The U of Findlay (OH)
U of Great Falls (MT)
U of Houston (TX)
U of Idaho (ID)
U of Maine at Farmington (ME)
U of Maine at Machias (ME)
U of Miami (FL)
U of Michigan (MI)
U of Mount Union (OH)
U of Nebraska at Omaha (NE)
U of New Mexico (NM)
The U of North Carolina Wilmington (NC)
U of Pittsburgh (PA)
U of Pittsburgh at Bradford (PA)
U of Pittsburgh at Greensburg (PA)
U of Redlands (CA)
U of St. Thomas (MN)
U of Southern California (CA)
The U of Texas at El Paso (TX)
The U of the Arts (PA)
The U of Western Ontario (ON, Canada)
U of Windsor (ON, Canada)
Valparaiso U (IN)
Virginia Intermont Coll (VA)
Waldorf U (IA)
Washington U in St. Louis (MO)
Waynesburg U (PA)
Wells Coll (NY)
Western Michigan U (MI)
Western State Colorado U (CO)
Western Washington U (WA)
West Virginia Wesleyan Coll (WV)
Wheaton Coll (MA)
Wheeling Jesuit U (WV)
Wichita State U (KS)

CRIMINALISTICS AND CRIMINAL SCIENCE
Florida Gulf Coast U (FL)
Indiana Tech (IN)
Inter American U of Puerto Rico, Ponce Campus (PR)
Saint Leo U (FL)

CRIMINAL JUSTICE/LAW ENFORCEMENT ADMINISTRATION
Abilene Christian U (TX)
Adams State U (CO)
Albertus Magnus Coll (CT)
Alfred U (NY)
Alliant Intl U (CA)
Alvernia U (PA)
American Public U System (WV)
American U (DC)
Anderson U (IN)
Anderson U (SC)
Arizona State U (AZ)
Athens State U (AL)
Austin Peay State U (TN)
Averett U (VA)
Barton Coll (NC)
Bay Path Coll (MA)
Becker Coll (MA)
Bemidji State U (MN)
Blackburn Coll (IL)
Bluefield Coll (VA)
Boise State U (ID)
Bowie State U (MD)
Bowling Green State U (OH)
Bradley U (IL)

Brevard Coll (NC)
Buffalo State Coll, State U of New York (NY)
California Baptist U (CA)
California Lutheran U (CA)
California State U, East Bay (CA)
California State U, Long Beach (CA)
California State U, San Bernardino (CA)
Calumet Coll of Saint Joseph (IN)
Campbellsville U (KY)
Canisius Coll (NY)
Castleton State Coll (VT)
Catawba Coll (NC)
Chestnut Hill Coll (PA)
The Citadel, The Military Coll of South Carolina (SC)
Claflin U (SC)
The Coll at Brockport, State U of New York (NY)
The Coll of New Jersey (NJ)
The Coll of Saint Rose (NY)
Columbia Coll (MO)
Concordia U Texas (TX)
Concordia U Wisconsin (WI)
Culver-Stockton Coll (MO)
Curry Coll (MA)
Dalton State Coll (GA)
Dordt Coll (IA)
East Central U (OK)
East Tennessee State U (TN)
East Texas Baptist U (TX)
Elmira Coll (NY)
Evangel U (MO)
Excelsior Coll (NY)
Fairleigh Dickinson U, Metropolitan Campus (NJ)
Farmingdale State Coll (NY)
Faulkner U (AL)
Fayetteville State U (NC)
Felician Coll (NJ)
Ferris State U (MI)
Florida National U (FL)
Franklin Pierce U (NH)
Franklin U (OH)
Frostburg State U (MD)
Georgia Coll & State U (GA)
Gonzaga U (WA)
Graceland U (IA)
Grand Valley State U (MI)
Grand View U (IA)
Granite State Coll (NH)
Grantham U (MO)
Greenville Coll (IL)
Gustavus Adolphus Coll (MN)
Hampton U (VA)
Harris-Stowe State U (MO)
Hawai'i Pacific U (HI)
Indiana Tech (IN)
Indiana U East (IN)
Iona Coll (NY)
Jacksonville State U (AL)
John Jay Coll of Criminal Justice of the City U of New York (NY)
Judson Coll (AL)
Kansas Wesleyan U (KS)
Kean U (NJ)
Keuka Coll (NY)
Keystone Coll (PA)
Lake Erie Coll (OH)
Lake Superior State U (MI)
Lamar U (TX)
Langston U (OK)
Limestone Coll (SC)
Lincoln Memorial U (TN)
Lincoln U (MO)
Lindsey Wilson Coll (KY)
Lock Haven U of Pennsylvania (PA)
Lubbock Christian U (TX)
Lynn U (FL)
Mansfield U of Pennsylvania (PA)
Marist Coll (NY)
Mars Hill Coll (NC)
Marymount U (VA)
McKendree U (IL)
Mercy Coll (NY)
Merrimack Coll (MA)
Michigan State U (MI)
Middle Tennessee State U (TN)
Midwestern State U (TX)
Mississippi Coll (MS)
Mississippi Valley State U (MS)
Molloy Coll (NY)
Morris Coll (SC)
Morrisville State Coll (NY)
Mount Aloysius Coll (PA)

Mount Mary Coll (WI)
Mount Mercy U (IA)
Mount Vernon Nazarene U (OH)
National U (CA)
New England Coll (NH)
New England Inst of Technology (RI)
Newman U (KS)
New York Inst of Technology (NY)
Niagara U (NY)
North Carolina Wesleyan Coll (NC)
Northwest Nazarene U (ID)
Norwich U (VT)
Oakland City U (IN)
Ohio Dominican U (OH)
Ohio U–Zanesville (OH)
Oklahoma City U (OK)
Pace U (NY)
Paul Quinn Coll (TX)
Penn State Abington (PA)
Penn State Altoona (PA)
Penn State Beaver (PA)
Penn State Berks (PA)
Penn State Brandywine (PA)
Penn State DuBois (PA)
Penn State Erie, The Behrend Coll (PA)
Penn State Fayette, The Eberly Campus (PA)
Penn State Greater Allegheny (PA)
Penn State Hazleton (PA)
Penn State Lehigh Valley (PA)
Penn State Mont Alto (PA)
Penn State New Kensington (PA)
Penn State Schuylkill (PA)
Penn State Shenango (PA)
Penn State U Park (PA)
Penn State Wilkes-Barre (PA)
Penn State Worthington Scranton (PA)
Penn State York (PA)
Piedmont Coll (GA)
Pittsburg State U (KS)
Polk State Coll (FL)
Portland State U (OR)
Post U (CT)
Purdue U Calumet (IN)
Radford U (VA)
Regent U (VA)
Regis U (CO)
Roberts Wesleyan Coll (NY)
Rochester Inst of Technology (NY)
Rockhurst U (MO)
Rogers State U (OK)
Roger Williams U (RI)
Russell Sage Coll (NY)
Rutgers, The State U of New Jersey, New Brunswick (NJ)
Sacred Heart U (CT)
St. John's U (NY)
St. Joseph's Coll, Long Island Campus (NY)
St. Joseph's Coll, New York (NY)
Saint Louis U (MO)
St. Mary's U (TX)
St. Thomas Aquinas Coll (NY)
St. Thomas U (FL)
Salem Intl U (WV)
Salem State U (MA)
Salve Regina U (RI)
San Diego State U (CA)
San Francisco State U (CA)
Seattle U (WA)
Shenandoah U (VA)
Simpson Coll (IA)
Sonoma State U (CA)
Southeastern U (FL)
Southern Illinois U Carbondale (IL)
Southwest Baptist U (MO)
State U of New York at Fredonia (NY)
State U of New York at Oswego (NY)
State U of New York Coll of Technology at Canton (NY)
Suffolk U (MA)
Sul Ross State U (TX)
Tennessee State U (TN)
Texas Southern U (TX)
Thomas Edison State Coll (NJ)
Thomas U (GA)
Thompson Rivers U (BC, Canada)
Tiffin U (OH)
Trevecca Nazarene U (TN)
Trine U (IN)
Trinity Christian Coll (IL)
Union Coll (KY)

U at Albany, State U of New York (NY)
U of Arkansas–Fort Smith (AR)
U of Central Oklahoma (OK)
U of Colorado Colorado Springs (CO)
U of Colorado Denver (CO)
The U of Findlay (OH)
U of Georgia (GA)
U of Great Falls (MT)
U of Guam (GU)
U of Guelph (ON, Canada)
U of Hawaii–West Oahu (HI)
U of Louisville (KY)
U of Maryland Eastern Shore (MD)
U of Memphis (TN)
U of Minnesota, Crookston (MN)
U of Mississippi (MS)
U of Missouri–Kansas City (MO)
U of Nevada, Las Vegas (NV)
U of New Brunswick Saint John (NB, Canada)
U of New Haven (CT)
U of North Alabama (AL)
U of Oklahoma (OK)
U of Pittsburgh at Bradford (PA)
U of Pittsburgh at Greensburg (PA)
U of Regina (SK, Canada)
U of St. Francis (IL)
U of South Alabama (AL)
U of South Carolina (SC)
U of South Carolina Upstate (SC)
The U of South Dakota (SD)
The U of Tennessee at Chattanooga (TN)
The U of Tennessee at Martin (TN)
The U of Texas at Brownsville (TX)
The U of Texas at El Paso (TX)
The U of Texas–Pan American (TX)
U of the Incarnate Word (TX)
U of Wisconsin–Parkside (WI)
U of Wisconsin–Platteville (WI)
Utica Coll (NY)
Villanova U (PA)
Virginia Commonwealth U (VA)
Walden U (MN)
Waldorf Coll (IA)
Washburn U (KS)
Washington State U (WA)
Wayland Baptist U (TX)
Waynesburg U (PA)
Western Illinois U (IL)
Western Oregon U (OR)
West Liberty U (WV)
West Texas A&M U (TX)
West Virginia State U (WV)
West Virginia U Inst of Technology (WV)
West Virginia Wesleyan Coll (WV)
Widener U (PA)
Wilmington U (DE)
York Coll of Pennsylvania (PA)

CRIMINAL JUSTICE/POLICE SCIENCE
American U (DC)
Athabasca U (AB, Canada)
Bemidji State U (MN)
Bowling Green State U (OH)
California State U, East Bay (CA)
Caribbean U (PR)
Coll of the Ozarks (MO)
East Central U (OK)
Fairmont State U (WV)
George Mason U (VA)
Hilbert Coll (NY)
Husson U (ME)
Jacksonville State U (AL)
Kent State U at Tuscarawas (OH)
Lake Superior State U (MI)
Lamar U (TX)
Langston U (OK)
Louisiana Coll (LA)
Marian U (WI)
Middle Tennessee State U (TN)
Minnesota State U Mankato (MN)
Newbury Coll (MA)
Northern State U (SD)
Northwestern Oklahoma State U (OK)
Oklahoma City U (OK)
Rowan U (NJ)
St. Gregory's U, Shawnee (OK)
Southern Utah U (UT)
Stephen F. Austin State U (TX)
Texas State U–San Marcos (TX)
U of Great Falls (MT)

U of Hartford (CT)
U of Pittsburgh at Greensburg (PA)
U of Regina (SK, Canada)
U of the Virgin Islands (VI)
U of Washington, Tacoma (WA)
U of Wisconsin–Superior (WI)
Weber State U (UT)
Western Connecticut State U (CT)
Western Oregon U (OR)

CRIMINAL JUSTICE/SAFETY
Adelphi U (NY)
Alabama State U (AL)
Alcorn State U (MS)
American U (DC)
American U of Puerto Rico (PR)
Angelo State U (TX)
Appalachian State U (NC)
Athens State U (AL)
Auburn U at Montgomery (AL)
Augsburg Coll (MN)
Aurora U (IL)
Baldwin Wallace U (OH)
Ball State U (IN)
Becker Coll (MA)
Bellarmine U (KY)
Benedictine U (IL)
Bethel Coll (IN)
Bloomsburg U of Pennsylvania (PA)
Bluefield State Coll (WV)
Bluffton U (OH)
Bowling Green State U (OH)
Bowling Green State U-Firelands Coll (OH)
Bridgewater State U (MA)
Buena Vista U (IA)
Caldwell Coll (NJ)
California State U, Chico (CA)
California State U, Dominguez Hills (CA)
California State U, Fresno (CA)
California State U, Fullerton (CA)
California State U, Los Angeles (CA)
California State U, Stanislaus (CA)
Central Methodist U (MO)
Central Penn Coll (PA)
Central State U (OH)
Champlain Coll (VT)
Chicago State U (IL)
Chowan U (NC)
Clark Atlanta U (GA)
Clayton State U (GA)
Colorado Mesa U (CO)
Columbus State U (GA)
Concordia U, St. Paul (MN)
Dakota Wesleyan U (SD)
Dallas Baptist U (TX)
Delta State U (MS)
DeSales U (PA)
Dominican Coll (NY)
East Carolina U (NC)
Eastern New Mexico U (NM)
Edgewood Coll (WI)
Edinboro U of Pennsylvania (PA)
Elizabeth City State U (NC)
Endicott Coll (MA)
Excelsior Coll (NY)
Ferrum Coll (VA)
Florida Ag and Mech U (FL)
Florida Atlantic U (FL)
Florida Gulf Coast U (FL)
Florida Intl U (FL)
Florida National U (FL)
Friends U (KS)
Frostburg State U (MD)
Gannon U (PA)
Georgia Gwinnett Coll (GA)
Georgia Regents U (GA)
Georgia Southern U (GA)
Georgia State U (GA)
Governors State U (IL)
Grambling State U (LA)
Granite State Coll (NH)
Guilford Coll (NC)
Hamline U (MN)
Harding U (AR)
Hardin-Simmons U (TX)
Harris-Stowe State U (MO)
High Point U (NC)
Holy Family U (PA)
Howard Payne U (TX)
Husson U (ME)
Illinois State U (IL)
Immaculata U (PA)
Indiana U Bloomington (IN)
Indiana U Kokomo (IN)

Indiana U Northwest (IN)
Indiana U–Purdue U Indianapolis (IN)
Indiana U South Bend (IN)
Indiana U Southeast (IN)
Indiana Wesleyan U (IN)
Indian River State Coll (FL)
Inter American U of Puerto Rico, Aguadilla Campus (PR)
Inter American U of Puerto Rico, Fajardo Campus (PR)
Inter American U of Puerto Rico, Ponce Campus (PR)
Iowa Wesleyan Coll (IA)
Jamestown Coll (ND)
Judson U (IL)
Kennesaw State U (GA)
Kent State U (OH)
Kent State U at Ashtabula (OH)
Kent State U at East Liverpool (OH)
Kent State U at Salem (OH)
Kent State U at Stark (OH)
Kent State U at Trumbull (OH)
Kent State U at Tuscarawas (OH)
Kentucky State U (KY)
Kentucky Wesleyan Coll (KY)
King's Coll (PA)
Kutztown U of Pennsylvania (PA)
Lakeland Coll (WI)
Lane Coll (TN)
La Roche Coll (PA)
La Salle U (PA)
Lasell Coll (MA)
La Sierra U (CA)
Lewis U (IL)
Liberty U (VA)
Limestone Coll (SC)
Lindenwood U (MO)
Long Island U–C. W. Post Campus (NY)
Longwood U (VA)
Louisiana State U at Alexandria (LA)
Louisiana State U in Shreveport (LA)
Lourdes U (OH)
Loyola U Chicago (IL)
Lynn U (FL)
Madonna U (MI)
Marshall U (WV)
Marywood U (PA)
McNeese State U (LA)
Medaille Coll (NY)
Mercer U (GA)
Mercyhurst U (PA)
Messiah Coll (PA)
Metropolitan State U of Denver (CO)
Michigan State U (MI)
Minnesota State U Moorhead (MN)
Minot State U (ND)
Missouri Baptist U (MO)
Missouri Western State U (MO)
Mitchell Coll (CT)
Monmouth U (NJ)
Mount Marty Coll (SD)
Mount Vernon Nazarene U (OH)
Murray State U (KY)
National U (CA)
Neumann U (PA)
New Jersey City U (NJ)
New Mexico Highlands U (NM)
New Mexico State U (NM)
North Carolina Central U (NC)
North Dakota State U (ND)
Northeastern Illinois U (IL)
Northeastern U (MA)
Northern Michigan U (MI)
Northwestern Coll (MN)
Northwestern State U of Louisiana (LA)
Nova Southeastern U (FL)
Nyack Coll (NY)
Olivet Coll (MI)
Penn State Abington (PA)
Penn State Altoona (PA)
Penn State Erie, The Behrend Coll (PA)
Penn State Fayette, The Eberly Campus (PA)
Penn State Harrisburg (PA)
Penn State Schuylkill (PA)
Penn State Wilkes-Barre (PA)
Plymouth State U (NH)
Point Park U (PA)
Point U (GA)
Post U (CT)

Potomac State Coll of West Virginia U (WV)
Quincy U (IL)
Quinnipiac U (CT)
Rhode Island Coll (RI)
Roanoke Coll (VA)
Rochester Inst of Technology (NY)
Roosevelt U (IL)
Rosemont Coll (PA)
Rowan U (NJ)
Rutgers, The State U of New Jersey, Camden (NJ)
Rutgers, The State U of New Jersey, Newark (NJ)
Saginaw Valley State U (MI)
St. Ambrose U (IA)
Saint Anselm Coll (NH)
St. Edward's U (TX)
St. Francis Coll (NY)
Saint Joseph's Coll (IN)
Saint Leo U (FL)
Saint Martin's U (WA)
Sam Houston State U (TX)
San Diego State U (CA)
San Jose State U (CA)
Seattle U (WA)
Seton Hill U (PA)
Shaw U (NC)
Shippensburg U of Pennsylvania (PA)
Siena Heights U (MI)
Southeastern Louisiana U (LA)
Southeastern Oklahoma State U (OK)
Southern Arkansas U–Magnolia (AR)
Southern Illinois U Edwardsville (IL)
State U of New York at Plattsburgh (NY)
State U of New York Coll at Potsdam (NY)
Sullivan U (KY)
Tarleton State U (TX)
Temple U (PA)
Tennessee Wesleyan Coll (TN)
Texas A&M Intl U (TX)
Texas A&M U–Commerce (TX)
Texas Christian U (TX)
Texas State U–San Marcos (TX)
Texas Wesleyan U (TX)
Texas Woman's U (TX)
Thomas Edison State Coll (NJ)
Thomas More Coll (KY)
Thompson Rivers U (BC, Canada)
Troy U (AL)
Truman State U (MO)
The U of Akron (OH)
The U of Alabama (AL)
U of Arkansas at Little Rock (AR)
U of Bridgeport (CT)
U of Central Florida (FL)
U of Central Oklahoma (OK)
U of Cincinnati (OH)
U of Evansville (IN)
U of Great Falls (MT)
U of Houston–Downtown (TX)
U of Houston–Victoria (TX)
U of Illinois at Chicago (IL)
U of Illinois at Springfield (IL)
U of Louisiana at Lafayette (LA)
U of Louisiana at Monroe (LA)
U of Maryland U Coll (MD)
U of Massachusetts Boston (MA)
U of Michigan–Dearborn (MI)
U of Mount Union (OH)
U of Nebraska at Kearney (NE)
U of Nebraska at Omaha (NE)
The U of North Carolina at Charlotte (NC)
The U of North Carolina at Pembroke (NC)
The U of North Carolina Wilmington (NC)
U of North Dakota (ND)
U of Northern Colorado (CO)
U of North Florida (FL)
U of North Georgia (GA)
U of North Texas (TX)
U of Pikeville (KY)
U of Portland (OR)
U of Regina (SK, Canada)
U of Richmond (VA)
The U of Scranton (PA)
U of Southern Indiana (IN)
U of Southern Mississippi (MS)
The U of Texas at Arlington (TX)

The U of Texas at Brownsville (TX)
The U of Texas at San Antonio (TX)
The U of Texas of the Permian Basin (TX)
U of the Cumberlands (KY)
U of the Incarnate Word (TX)
The U of Toledo (OH)
U of West Florida (FL)
U of Wisconsin–Eau Claire (WI)
U of Wisconsin–Milwaukee (WI)
U of Wisconsin–Superior (WI)
U of Wyoming (WY)
Valdosta State U (GA)
Virginia State U (VA)
Virginia Wesleyan Coll (VA)
Viterbo U (WI)
Wayne State Coll (NE)
Wayne State U (MI)
Weber State U (UT)
West Chester U of Pennsylvania (PA)
Western Carolina U (NC)
Western Michigan U (MI)
Westfield State U (MA)
Westminster Coll (UT)
West Texas A&M U (TX)
Wichita State U (KS)
Wilkes U (PA)
William Paterson U of New Jersey (NJ)
Worcester State U (MA)
Xavier U (OH)
Youngstown State U (OH)

CRIMINOLOGY
Adams State U (CO)
Albright Coll (PA)
Alderson-Broaddus Coll (WV)
Arkansas State U (AR)
Auburn U (AL)
Barry U (FL)
Benedictine Coll (KS)
Butler U (IN)
Cabrini Coll (PA)
California State U, Fresno (CA)
California State U, Stanislaus (CA)
Capital U (OH)
Castleton State Coll (VT)
Cedar Crest Coll (PA)
Central Connecticut State U (CT)
Chatham U (PA)
Cleveland State U (OH)
Coll of Mount St. Joseph (OH)
Dominican U (IL)
Drury U (MO)
Eastern Michigan U (MI)
Eastern Washington U (WA)
Elizabethtown Coll (PA)
Emmanuel Coll (MA)
Fairleigh Dickinson U, Coll at Florham (NJ)
Florida Southern Coll (FL)
Florida State U (FL)
Framingham State U (MA)
Hofstra U (NY)
Howard Payne U (TX)
Husson U (ME)
Indiana State U (IN)
Indiana U of Pennsylvania (PA)
John Jay Coll of Criminal Justice of the City U of New York (NY)
Johnson C. Smith U (NC)
Lebanon Valley Coll (PA)
Lees-McRae Coll (NC)
Le Moyne Coll (NY)
Lindenwood U (MO)
Loyola U New Orleans (LA)
Lynchburg Coll (VA)
Marquette U (WI)
Mary Baldwin Coll (VA)
Maryville U of Saint Louis (MO)
Mississippi State U (MS)
Missouri State U (MO)
Mount St. Mary's Coll (CA)
Mount St. Mary's U (MD)
Niagara U (NY)
North Carolina State U (NC)
Northern Arizona U (AZ)
The Ohio State U (OH)
Ohio U (OH)
Ohio U–Chillicothe (OH)
Old Dominion U (VA)
Regis U (CO)
The Richard Stockton Coll of New Jersey (NJ)
Rivier U (NH)
Sage Coll of Albany (NY)

St. Edward's U (TX)
Saint Joseph's U (PA)
St. Mary's U (TX)
St. Thomas U (NB, Canada)
Simon Fraser U (BC, Canada)
Slippery Rock U of Pennsylvania (PA)
Southern Oregon U (OR)
Spring Hill Coll (AL)
State U of New York Coll at Cortland (NY)
State U of New York Coll at Old Westbury (NY)
Stonehill Coll (MA)
Suffolk U (MA)
Texas A&M U–Commerce (TX)
Texas A&M U–Kingsville (TX)
Thomas U (GA)
Thompson Rivers U (BC, Canada)
The U of Akron (OH)
U of California, Irvine (CA)
U of Delaware (DE)
U of Denver (CO)
U of Florida (FL)
U of Houston–Clear Lake (TX)
U of La Verne (CA)
U of Maryland, Coll Park (MD)
U of Massachusetts Dartmouth (MA)
U of Memphis (TN)
U of Miami (FL)
U of Minnesota, Duluth (MN)
U of Minnesota, Twin Cities Campus (MN)
U of Missouri–Kansas City (MO)
U of Missouri–St. Louis (MO)
U of Mount Union (OH)
U of Nevada, Reno (NV)
U of New Hampshire (NH)
U of Northern Iowa (IA)
U of Ottawa (ON, Canada)
U of Saint Mary (KS)
U of St. Thomas (MN)
U of Southern Maine (ME)
U of South Florida (FL)
The U of Tampa (FL)
The U of Texas at Dallas (TX)
The U of Texas of the Permian Basin (TX)
The U of Western Ontario (ON, Canada)
U of West Georgia (GA)
U of Windsor (ON, Canada)
Upper Iowa U (IA)
Valparaiso U (IN)
Virginia Union U (VA)
Virginia Wesleyan Coll (VA)
Western State Colorado U (CO)
Wheeling Jesuit U (WV)
William Penn U (IA)
Wright State U (OH)

CRISIS/EMERGENCY/DISASTER MANAGEMENT
Adelphi U (NY)
American Public U System (WV)
Arkansas State U (AR)
Arkansas Tech U (AR)
Kansas Wesleyan U (KS)
U of Alaska Fairbanks (AK)
U of Nebraska at Omaha (NE)

CROP PRODUCTION
North Dakota State U (ND)
U of Minnesota, Crookston (MN)
U of Minnesota, Twin Cities Campus (MN)
Washington State U (WA)

CULINARY ARTS
Coll of the Ozarks (MO)
Newbury Coll (MA)
Nicholls State U (LA)
Southern New Hampshire U (NH)
Stratford U (MD)
U of Charleston (WV)
U of Nevada, Las Vegas (NV)

CULINARY ARTS RELATED
Mississippi U for Women (MS)
Newbury Coll (MA)
U of Nevada, Las Vegas (NV)

CULINARY SCIENCE
The Culinary Inst of America (NY)
Mississippi State U (MS)

CULTURAL ANTHROPOLOGY
Prescott Coll (AZ)

Seattle U (WA)
Webster U (MO)

CULTURAL RESOURCE MANAGEMENT AND POLICY ANALYSIS
California State U, Dominguez Hills (CA)
U of Waterloo (ON, Canada)

CULTURAL STUDIES/ CRITICAL THEORY AND ANALYSIS
American Public U System (WV)
Bryant U (RI)
Goddard Coll (VT)
Howard Payne U (TX)
Northern Arizona U (AZ)
The U of Tampa (FL)
Western Kentucky U (KY)

CURRICULUM AND INSTRUCTION
Albertus Magnus Coll (CT)
Eastern Washington U (WA)
Franklin Pierce U (NH)
Midwestern State U (TX)
Northwest Missouri State U (MO)
Randolph Coll (VA)
Tarleton State U (TX)
Texas A&M U–Commerce (TX)
U of Minnesota, Twin Cities Campus (MN)
U of Regina (SK, Canada)
The U of South Dakota (SD)
The U of Western Ontario (ON, Canada)
Utah State U (UT)
Walden U (MN)
Wright State U (OH)

CUSTOMER SERVICE MANAGEMENT
Southwest Baptist U (MO)

CYBER/COMPUTER FORENSICS AND COUNTERTERRORISM
Champlain Coll (VT)

CYBER/ELECTRONIC OPERATIONS AND WARFARE
United States Naval Acad (MD)

CYTOGENETICS/GENETICS/ CLINICAL GENETICS TECHNOLOGY
Northern Michigan U (MI)

CYTOTECHNOLOGY
Albany Coll of Pharmacy and Health Sciences (NY)
Barry U (FL)
Edgewood Coll (WI)
Illinois Coll (IL)
Indiana U–Purdue U Indianapolis (IN)
Long Island U–Brooklyn Campus (NY)
Long Island U–C. W. Post Campus (NY)
Marian U (WI)
Marshall U (WV)
Massachusetts Coll of Liberal Arts (MA)
Oakland U (MI)
Saint Louis U (MO)
Saint Mary's U of Minnesota (MN)
Slippery Rock U of Pennsylvania (PA)
State U of New York at Plattsburgh (NY)
Stony Brook U, State U of New York (NY)
U of Arkansas for Medical Sciences (AR)
The U of Kansas (KS)
U of North Dakota (ND)
U of North Texas (TX)

DAIRY HUSBANDRY AND PRODUCTION
U of Vermont (VT)

DAIRY SCIENCE
California Polytechnic State U, San Luis Obispo (CA)
Eastern New Mexico U (NM)
Iowa State U of Science and Technology (IA)
Morrisville State Coll (NY)

South Dakota State U (SD)
Texas A&M U (TX)
U of Georgia (GA)
U of Minnesota, Twin Cities Campus (MN)
U of New Hampshire (NH)
U of Wisconsin–Madison (WI)
Utah State U (UT)
Virginia Polytechnic Inst and State U (VA)

DANCE
Adelphi U (NY)
Agnes Scott Coll (GA)
Alma Coll (MI)
Amherst Coll (MA)
Anderson U (IN)
Appalachian State U (NC)
Arizona State U (AZ)
Ball State U (IN)
Bard Coll (NY)
Bates Coll (ME)
Belhaven U (MS)
Bennington Coll (VT)
The Boston Conservatory (MA)
Butler U (IN)
California State U, East Bay (CA)
California State U, Fresno (CA)
California State U, Fullerton (CA)
California State U, Long Beach (CA)
California State U, Los Angeles (CA)
Case Western Reserve U (OH)
Cedar Crest Coll (PA)
Chapman U (CA)
The Coll at Brockport, State U of New York (NY)
The Colorado Coll (CO)
Colorado State U (CO)
Columbia Coll (SC)
Columbia Coll Chicago (IL)
Columbia U (NY)
Columbia U, School of General Studies (NY)
Concordia U (QC, Canada)
Connecticut Coll (CT)
DeSales U (PA)
Dickinson Coll (PA)
East Carolina U (NC)
Eastern Michigan U (MI)
Elon U (NC)
Eugene Lang Coll The New School for Liberal Arts (NY)
Florida State U (FL)
Franklin & Marshall Coll (PA)
George Mason U (VA)
Goucher Coll (MD)
Grand Valley State U (MI)
Gustavus Adolphus Coll (MN)
Hamilton Coll (NY)
Hampshire Coll (MA)
Hobart and William Smith Colls (NY)
Hofstra U (NY)
Hollins U (VA)
Hope Coll (MI)
Hunter Coll of the City U of New York (NY)
Johnson State Coll (VT)
The Juilliard School (NY)
Keene State Coll (NH)
Kennesaw State U (GA)
Kent State U (OH)
Kenyon Coll (OH)
Lamar U (TX)
La Roche Coll (PA)
Lehman Coll of the City U of New York (NY)
Lindenwood U (MO)
Long Island U–Brooklyn Campus (NY)
Long Island U–C. W. Post Campus (NY)
Loyola Marymount U (CA)
Loyola U Chicago (IL)
Manhattanville Coll (NY)
Marymount Manhattan Coll (NY)
Mercyhurst U (PA)
Messiah Coll (PA)
Middlebury Coll (VT)
Mills Coll (CA)
Montclair State U (NJ)
Mount Holyoke Coll (MA)
Muhlenberg Coll (PA)
New Mexico State U (NM)
New York U (NY)

Nova Southeastern U (FL)
Oakland U (MI)
The Ohio State U (OH)
Ohio U (OH)
Oklahoma City U (OK)
Oral Roberts U (OK)
Pace U (NY)
Palm Beach Atlantic U (FL)
Pitzer Coll (CA)
Point Park U (PA)
Pomona Coll (CA)
Prescott Coll (AZ)
Purchase Coll, State U of New York (NY)
Radford U (VA)
Randolph Coll (VA)
Reed Coll (OR)
Rhode Island Coll (RI)
Rider U (NJ)
Roger Williams U (RI)
Rutgers, The State U of New Jersey, New Brunswick (NJ)
St. Gregory's U, Shawnee (OK)
Saint Mary's Coll of California (CA)
St. Olaf Coll (MN)
Sam Houston State U (TX)
San Diego State U (CA)
San Francisco State U (CA)
San Jose State U (CA)
Scripps Coll (CA)
Seton Hill U (PA)
Shenandoah U (VA)
Simon Fraser U (BC, Canada)
Skidmore Coll (NY)
Slippery Rock U of Pennsylvania (PA)
Smith Coll (MA)
Southern Methodist U (TX)
State U of New York at Fredonia (NY)
State U of New York Coll at Potsdam (NY)
Stephen F. Austin State U (TX)
Stephens Coll (MO)
Swarthmore Coll (PA)
Sweet Briar Coll (VA)
Temple U (PA)
Texas Christian U (TX)
Texas State U–San Marcos (TX)
Texas Woman's U (TX)
Trinity Coll (CT)
Troy U (AL)
Tulane U (LA)
U at Buffalo, the State U of New York (NY)
The U of Akron (OH)
The U of Alabama (AL)
The U of Arizona (AZ)
U of Arkansas at Little Rock (AR)
U of California, Berkeley (CA)
U of California, Irvine (CA)
U of California, Santa Barbara (CA)
U of Central Oklahoma (OK)
U of Cincinnati (OH)
U of Colorado Boulder (CO)
U of Florida (FL)
U of Georgia (GA)
U of Hartford (CT)
U of Hawaii at Manoa (HI)
U of Houston (TX)
U of Idaho (ID)
U of Illinois at Urbana–Champaign (IL)
The U of Iowa (IA)
The U of Kansas (KS)
U of Maryland, Baltimore County (MD)
U of Maryland, Coll Park (MD)
U of Massachusetts Amherst (MA)
U of Michigan (MI)
U of Minnesota, Twin Cities Campus (MN)
U of Missouri–Kansas City (MO)
U of Nebraska–Lincoln (NE)
U of Nevada, Las Vegas (NV)
U of New Mexico (NM)
The U of North Carolina at Charlotte (NC)
The U of North Carolina at Greensboro (NC)
U of North Carolina School of the Arts (NC)
U of North Texas (TX)
U of Oklahoma (OK)
U of Oregon (OR)
U of Richmond (VA)
U of South Carolina (SC)

U of Southern Mississippi (MS)
U of South Florida (FL)
The U of Texas at Austin (TX)
The U of Texas–Pan American (TX)
The U of the Arts (PA)
U of Utah (UT)
U of Wisconsin–Madison (WI)
U of Wisconsin–Milwaukee (WI)
U of Wisconsin–Stevens Point (WI)
Utah State U (UT)
Valdosta State U (GA)
Virginia Commonwealth U (VA)
Washington U in St. Louis (MO)
Wayne State U (MI)
Weber State U (UT)
Webster U (MO)
Wells Coll (NY)
Wesleyan U (CT)
West Chester U of Pennsylvania (PA)
Western Kentucky U (KY)
Western Michigan U (MI)
Western Oregon U (OR)
Western Washington U (WA)
West Texas A&M U (TX)
Winthrop U (SC)
Wright State U (OH)

DANCE RELATED
Anderson U (IN)
Brigham Young U (UT)
California State U, Long Beach (CA)
Western Michigan U (MI)
Youngstown State U (OH)

DANCE THERAPY
Columbia Coll Chicago (IL)

DATA MODELING/ WAREHOUSING AND DATABASE ADMINISTRATION
Neumont U (UT)
Pennsylvania Coll of Technology (PA)
Purdue U (IN)
Purdue U Calumet (IN)
Rochester Inst of Technology (NY)

DATA PROCESSING AND DATA PROCESSING TECHNOLOGY
Arkansas State U (AR)
Bemidji State U (MN)
Central Baptist Coll (AR)
The Coll of Saint Rose (NY)
Farmingdale State Coll (NY)
U of New Brunswick Fredericton (NB, Canada)
U of Southern Mississippi (MS)

DEAF STUDIES
California State U, Northridge (CA)

DEMOGRAPHY AND POPULATION
The U of Western Ontario (ON, Canada)

DENTAL HYGIENE
Clayton State U (GA)
Dalhousie U (NS, Canada)
Eastern Washington U (WA)
East Tennessee State U (TN)
Farmingdale State Coll (NY)
Georgia Regents U (GA)
Indiana U South Bend (IN)
Lewis U (IL)
Massachusetts Coll of Pharmacy and Health Sciences (MA)
Midwestern State U (TX)
Minnesota State U Mankato (MN)
New York U (NY)
Northern Arizona U (AZ)
The Ohio State U (OH)
The Ohio State U at Lima (OH)
Old Dominion U (VA)
Pennsylvania Coll of Technology (PA)
Southern Illinois U Carbondale (IL)
State U of New York Coll of Technology at Canton (NY)
Tennessee State U (TN)
Texas Woman's U (TX)
Thomas Edison State Coll (NJ)
U of Arkansas for Medical Sciences (AR)
U of Arkansas–Fort Smith (AR)
U of Bridgeport (CT)

The U of British Columbia (BC, Canada)
U of Hawaii at Manoa (HI)
U of Louisiana at Monroe (LA)
U of Louisville (KY)
U of Michigan (MI)
U of Minnesota, Twin Cities Campus (MN)
U of Missouri–Kansas City (MO)
U of New England (ME)
U of New Haven (CT)
The U of North Carolina at Chapel Hill (NC)
U of Oklahoma Health Sciences Center (OK)
U of Pittsburgh (PA)
The U of South Dakota (SD)
U of Southern California (CA)
U of Southern Indiana (IN)
The U of Tennessee (TN)
U of Wyoming (WY)
Vermont Tech Coll (VT)
Virginia Commonwealth U (VA)
Weber State U (UT)
Western Kentucky U (KY)
West Liberty U (WV)
West Virginia U (WV)
Wichita State U (KS)
Youngstown State U (OH)

DENTAL SERVICES AND ALLIED PROFESSIONS RELATED
Clayton State U (GA)
Indiana U–Purdue U Indianapolis (IN)
U of Minnesota, Twin Cities Campus (MN)

DESIGN AND APPLIED ARTS RELATED
Alverno Coll (WI)
Arizona State U (AZ)
Art Center Coll of Design (CA)
Athabasca U (AB, Canada)
Azusa Pacific U (CA)
Bemidji State U (MN)
Buffalo State Coll, State U of New York (NY)
Columbia U, School of General Studies (NY)
Concordia U (QC, Canada)
Converse Coll (SC)
Ferris State U (MI)
Franklin Pierce U (NH)
Hampshire Coll (MA)
Harding U (AR)
Hofstra U (NY)
Inter American U of Puerto Rico, San Germán Campus (PR)
Lamar U (TX)
Mansfield U of Pennsylvania (PA)
Maryland Inst Coll of Art (MD)
McMurry U (TX)
Midwestern State U (TX)
Minnesota State U Mankato (MN)
New York Inst of Technology (NY)
Otis Coll of Art and Design (CA)
Parsons The New School for Design (NY)
Penn State Altoona (PA)
Penn State Berks (PA)
Penn State U Park (PA)
Point Park U (PA)
Portland State U (OR)
Purdue U (IN)
Roberts Wesleyan Coll (NY)
Salem State U (MA)
Savannah Coll of Art and Design (GA)
School of the Art Inst of Chicago (IL)
School of the Museum of Fine Arts, Boston (MA)
Schreiner U (TX)
Shawnee State U (OH)
State U of New York at Fredonia (NY)
Taylor U (IN)
U of California, Los Angeles (CA)
U of Illinois at Chicago (IL)
U of Massachusetts Dartmouth (MA)
U of Nebraska at Omaha (NE)
U of Oregon (OR)
The U of Toledo (OH)
U of Wisconsin–Stout (WI)
Washington U in St. Louis (MO)

Western Washington U (WA)
William Paterson U of New Jersey (NJ)

DESIGN AND VISUAL COMMUNICATIONS
Acad of Art U (CA)
Alberta Coll of Art & Design (AB, Canada)
Albright Coll (PA)
Alma Coll (MI)
American Acad of Art (IL)
American U (DC)
Anderson U (IN)
Auburn U (AL)
Belmont U (TN)
Bennington Coll (VT)
Bethel Coll (IN)
Boise State U (ID)
Bowling Green State U (OH)
Bowling Green State U–Firelands Coll (OH)
Buffalo State Coll, State U of New York (NY)
California State U, Chico (CA)
California State U, Monterey Bay (CA)
Carnegie Mellon U (PA)
Central Connecticut State U (CT)
Coll of Mount St. Joseph
Columbia Coll Chicago (IL)
Concordia U, St. Paul (MN)
Creative Center (NE)
Drury U (MO)
EDP Coll of Puerto Rico, Inc. (PR)
Endicott Coll (MA)
Farmingdale State Coll (NY)
Franklin Coll Switzerland (Switzerland)
Holy Cross Coll (IN)
Houghton Coll (NY)
Inst of American Indian Arts (NM)
Iowa State U of Science and Technology (IA)
Iowa Wesleyan Coll (IA)
Kean U (NJ)
La Roche Coll (PA)
Lawrence Technological U (MI)
Lees-McRae Coll (NC)
Lehigh U (PA)
Lewis U (IL)
Linfield Coll (OR)
Loyola U Chicago (IL)
Lubbock Christian U (TX)
Madonna U (MI)
Maryville Coll (TN)
Missouri State U (MO)
Nazareth Coll of Rochester (NY)
New Mexico Highlands U (NM)
New York City Coll of Technology of the City U of New York (NY)
North Carolina State U (NC)
Northern Arizona U (AZ)
The Ohio State U (OH)
Oral Roberts U (OK)
Pacific Northwest Coll of Art (OR)
Parsons The New School for Design (NY)
Purdue U (IN)
Radford U (VA)
Rensselaer Polytechnic Inst (NY)
Robert Morris U (PA)
Rochester Inst of Technology (NY)
Saginaw Valley State U (MI)
St. Ambrose U (IA)
Saint Mary-of-the-Woods Coll (IN)
San Francisco Art Inst (CA)
San Francisco State U (CA)
Savannah Coll of Art and Design (GA)
School of the Art Inst of Chicago (IL)
Seattle Pacific U (WA)
Southern Illinois U Carbondale (IL)
Spring Arbor U (MI)
Syracuse U (NY)
Texas State U–San Marcos (TX)
Thompson Rivers U (BC, Canada)
Université du Québec en Outaouais (QC, Canada)
U of Evansville (IN)
U of Hartford (CT)
The U of Kansas (KS)
U of Maryland, Baltimore County (MD)
U of Massachusetts Dartmouth (MA)

U of Miami (FL)
U of Michigan–Flint (MI)
U of Minnesota, Twin Cities Campus (MN)
U of Notre Dame (IN)
The U of Tennessee at Martin (TN)
The U of Texas at Austin (TX)
U of Wisconsin–Green Bay (WI)
U of Wisconsin–Stevens Point (WI)
Viterbo U (WI)
Washington U in St. Louis (MO)
Watkins Coll of Art, Design, & Film (TN)
Weber State U (UT)
Western Washington U (WA)
West Virginia U (WV)

DESKTOP PUBLISHING AND DIGITAL IMAGING DESIGN
Acad of Art U (CA)
California Baptist U (CA)
Chowan U (NC)
EDP Coll of Puerto Rico, Inc. (PR)
Purdue U (IN)
Rochester Inst of Technology (NY)
Saint Mary's U of Minnesota (MN)
Sullivan Coll of Technology and Design (KY)
Texas State U–San Marcos (TX)

DEVELOPMENTAL AND CHILD PSYCHOLOGY
Antioch U Midwest (OH)
Bay Path Coll (MA)
Bridgewater State U (MA)
California State U, East Bay (CA)
California State U, San Bernardino (CA)
California State U, Stanislaus (CA)
Carson-Newman U (TN)
Castleton State Coll (VT)
Eastern Washington U (WA)
East Texas Baptist U (TX)
Emmanuel Coll (MA)
Hampton U (VA)
Humboldt State U (CA)
Keene State Coll (NH)
Langston U (OK)
Lee U (TN)
Maryville Coll (TN)
Mills Coll (CA)
Minnesota State U Mankato (MN)
Mount St. Mary's Coll (CA)
Northern Michigan U (MI)
Purdue U (IN)
Quinnipiac U (CT)
St. Joseph's Coll, Long Island Campus (NY)
St. Joseph's Coll, New York (NY)
Sonoma State U (CA)
Spelman Coll (GA)
Suffolk U (MA)
Texas Christian U (TX)
Tufts U (MA)
The U of British Columbia (BC, Canada)
U of California, Santa Cruz (CA)
The U of Kansas (KS)
U of Minnesota, Twin Cities Campus (MN)
U of New Brunswick Fredericton (NB, Canada)
The U of Texas at Dallas (TX)
U of the District of Columbia (DC)
The U of Toledo (OH)
U of Windsor (ON, Canada)
U of Wisconsin–Green Bay (WI)
Utica Coll (NY)
Western Washington U (WA)

DEVELOPMENTAL BIOLOGY AND EMBRYOLOGY
Purdue U (IN)

DEVELOPMENT ECONOMICS AND INTERNATIONAL DEVELOPMENT
Brown U (RI)
Calvin Coll (MI)
Clark U (MA)
Dalhousie U (NS, Canada)
Georgia Southern U (GA)
Hope Intl U (CA)
Houghton Coll (NY)
John Brown U (AR)
Penn State Altoona (PA)
Penn State Berks (PA)
Point Loma Nazarene U (CA)
Seattle Pacific U (WA)

Taylor U (IN)
U of California, Los Angeles (CA)
U of Guelph (ON, Canada)
U of New Brunswick Saint John (NB, Canada)
U of Ottawa (ON, Canada)
U of St. Thomas (TX)
U of Vermont (VT)

DIAGNOSTIC MEDICAL SONOGRAPHY AND ULTRASOUND TECHNOLOGY
Adventist U of Health Sciences (FL)
Baptist Coll of Health Sciences (TN)
Benedictine U (IL)
Dalhousie U (NS, Canada)
Georgia Regents U (GA)
Lewis U (IL)
Misericordia U (PA)
Nebraska Methodist Coll (NE)
Newman U (KS)
Rochester Inst of Technology (NY)
Seattle U (WA)
U of Arkansas for Medical Sciences (AR)
U of Charleston (WV)
U of Medicine and Dentistry of New Jersey (NJ)
U of Missouri (MO)
Washburn U (KS)
Weber State U (UT)

DIESEL MECHANICS TECHNOLOGY
Lewis-Clark State Coll (ID)

DIETETICS
Abilene Christian U (TX)
Acadia U (NS, Canada)
American U of Beirut (Lebanon)
Andrews U (MI)
Appalachian State U (NC)
Arkansas State U (AR)
Ashland U (OH)
Ball State U (IN)
Bastyr U (WA)
Bowling Green State U (OH)
Bradley U (IL)
Buffalo State Coll, State U of New York (NY)
California Baptist U (CA)
California Polytechnic State U, San Luis Obispo (CA)
California State Polytechnic U, Pomona (CA)
California State U, Chico (CA)
California State U, Fresno (CA)
California State U, Long Beach (CA)
California State U, Los Angeles (CA)
California State U, San Bernardino (CA)
Carson-Newman U (TN)
Case Western Reserve U (OH)
Central Michigan U (MI)
Coll of Saint Elizabeth (NJ)
Coll of the Ozarks (MO)
Dominican U (IL)
East Carolina U (NC)
Eastern Michigan U (MI)
Edinboro U of Pennsylvania (PA)
Florida Intl U (FL)
Georgia State U (GA)
Harding U (AR)
Immaculata U (PA)
Iowa State U of Science and Technology (IA)
Jacksonville State U (AL)
Kansas State U (KS)
Keene State Coll (NH)
Lamar U (TX)
Langston U (OK)
Lehman Coll of the City U of New York (NY)
Life U (GA)
Lipscomb U (TN)
Mansfield U of Pennsylvania (PA)
Marshall U (WV)
Marywood U (PA)
Miami U (OH)
Michigan State U (MI)
Minnesota State U Mankato (MN)
Missouri State U (MO)
Mount Mary Coll (WI)
Nicholls State U (LA)

North Dakota State U (ND)
Northern Illinois U (IL)
Northwest Missouri State U (MO)
The Ohio State U (OH)
Ohio U (OH)
Ouachita Baptist U (AR)
Point Loma Nazarene U (CA)
Purdue U (IN)
San Diego State U (CA)
San Francisco State U (CA)
San Jose State U (CA)
Seton Hill U (PA)
Simmons Coll (MA)
Texas Christian U (TX)
Texas Southern U (TX)
Tuskegee U (AL)
The U of Akron (OH)
The U of Alabama (AL)
The U of British Columbia (BC, Canada)
U of Central Oklahoma (OK)
U of Cincinnati (OH)
U of Delaware (DE)
U of Georgia (GA)
U of Illinois at Chicago (IL)
U of Illinois at Urbana–Champaign (IL)
U of Louisiana at Lafayette (LA)
U of Maryland Eastern Shore (MD)
U of Medicine and Dentistry of New Jersey (NJ)
U of Minnesota, Twin Cities Campus (MN)
U of Missouri (MO)
U of New Haven (CT)
U of North Dakota (ND)
U of Northern Colorado (CO)
U of Oklahoma Health Sciences Center (OK)
U of Pittsburgh (PA)
U of Rhode Island (RI)
U of Southern Mississippi (MS)
The U of Tennessee at Martin (TN)
The U of Texas–Pan American (TX)
U of Vermont (VT)
The U of Western Ontario (ON, Canada)
U of Wisconsin–Stevens Point (WI)
U of Wisconsin–Stout (WI)
Viterbo U (WI)
Wayne State U (MI)
West Chester U of Pennsylvania (PA)
Western Carolina U (NC)
Youngstown State U (OH)

DIETETICS AND CLINICAL NUTRITION SERVICES RELATED
Coll of Saint Benedict (MN)
Madonna U (MI)
Purdue U (IN)
Saint John's U (MN)
Texas Christian U (TX)
Western Michigan U (MI)

DIETETIC TECHNOLOGY
Purdue U (IN)

DIGITAL ARTS
Acad of Art U (CA)
Bethany Lutheran Coll (MN)
Concordia U (QC, Canada)
Corcoran Coll of Art and Design (DC)
DeSales U (PA)
Hamline U (MN)
Lake Erie Coll (OH)
Lawrence Technological U (MI)
Marymount Coll, Palos Verdes, California (CA)
Merrimack Coll (MA)
Moore Coll of Art & Design (PA)
Point Park U (PA)
Seattle U (WA)
Southwestern Coll (KS)
State U of New York Coll of Technology at Alfred (NY)
Stetson U (FL)
Syracuse U (NY)
U of Central Florida (FL)
U of Florida (FL)
U of Massachusetts Dartmouth (MA)
U of Oregon (OR)
U of Southern California (CA)
The U of Tampa (FL)
The U of Toledo (OH)

DIGITAL COMMUNICATION AND MEDIA/MULTIMEDIA
Abilene Christian U (TX)
Ashland U (OH)
Baldwin Wallace U (OH)
Baylor U (TX)
Bennington Coll (VT)
Bradley U (IL)
Butler U (IN)
California Baptist U (CA)
California Lutheran U (CA)
California State U, Dominguez Hills (CA)
Calvin Coll (MI)
Canisius Coll (NY)
Cedar Crest Coll (PA)
Cedarville U (OH)
Clarkson U (NY)
Cleveland State U (OH)
Cogswell Polytechnical Coll (CA)
Concordia Coll–New York (NY)
Concordia U Wisconsin (WI)
Dallas Baptist U (TX)
Dordt Coll (IA)
Eastern Mennonite U (VA)
Florida Atlantic U (FL)
Franklin U (OH)
Georgia Southern U (GA)
Harding U (AR)
Hilbert Coll (NY)
Howard Payne U (TX)
Huntington U (IN)
Indiana U Bloomington (IN)
Indiana U Kokomo (IN)
Indiana U–Purdue U Indianapolis (IN)
John Brown U (AR)
Juniata Coll (PA)
Kutztown U of Pennsylvania (PA)
Lebanon Valley Coll (PA)
Lee U (TN)
Lewis U (IL)
Limestone Coll (SC)
Lindenwood U (MO)
Loyola U Chicago (IL)
Marywood U (PA)
Messiah Coll (PA)
Miami U (OH)
Mount Marty Coll (SD)
Mount Mercy U (IA)
Northern Michigan U (MI)
Ohio U (OH)
Point Park U (PA)
Queens U of Charlotte (NC)
Rensselaer Polytechnic Inst (NY)
Rochester Inst of Technology (NY)
Saginaw Valley State U (MI)
St. Bonaventure U (NY)
St. Edward's U (TX)
St. John Fisher Coll (NY)
San Diego State U (CA)
Savannah Coll of Art and Design (GA)
School of the Art Inst of Chicago (IL)
Simpson Coll (IA)
Slippery Rock U of Pennsylvania (PA)
Southern New Hampshire U (NH)
Southwestern Coll (KS)
State U of New York Coll of Technology at Alfred (NY)
Sullivan Coll of Technology and Design (KY)
Texas A&M U (TX)
Tiffin U (OH)
Trevecca Nazarene U (TN)
U of Denver (CO)
U of Georgia (GA)
U of Idaho (ID)
U of Miami (FL)
U of Mississippi (MS)
U of Northern Iowa (IA)
U of Rochester (NY)
The U of Scranton (PA)
The U of Tampa (FL)
The U of Texas at Arlington (TX)
The U of Texas at Dallas (TX)
U of the Incarnate Word (TX)
U of Waterloo (ON, Canada)
The U of Western Ontario (ON, Canada)
Valparaiso U (IN)
Washington State U (WA)
Webster U (MO)
Wellesley Coll (MA)
Wheeling Jesuit U (WV)

Wilkes U (PA)

DIRECTING AND THEATRICAL PRODUCTION
Baldwin Wallace U (OH)
Bard Coll (NY)
Belmont U (TN)
Bennington Coll (VT)
Binghamton U, State U of New York (NY)
Boston U (MA)
Bradley U (IL)
Brigham Young U (UT)
California State U, Long Beach (CA)
Coe Coll (IA)
Drake U (IA)
Hofstra U (NY)
Juniata Coll (PA)
Keene State Coll (NH)
Lindenwood U (MO)
Lipscomb U (TN)
Pace U (NY)
Pepperdine U, Malibu (CA)
Purdue U (IN)
Rider U (NJ)
Saint Joseph's Coll (IN)
Temple U (PA)
Texas Christian U (TX)
U of Chicago (IL)
U of Illinois at Urbana–Champaign (IL)
U of Miami (FL)
The U of the Arts (PA)
Webster U (MO)

DIVINITY/MINISTRY
Azusa Pacific U (CA)
Barclay Coll (KS)
Belmont U (TN)
Bethel Coll (IN)
Bluefield Coll (VA)
Briercrest Coll (SK, Canada)
Campbellsville U (KY)
Cardinal Stritch U (WI)
Cincinnati Christian U (OH)
Corban U (OR)
Faith Baptist Bible Coll and Theological Sem (IA)
Faulkner U (AL)
Florida Christian Coll (FL)
Global U (MO)
Grace U (NE)
Hope Coll (MI)
Huntington U (IN)
Indiana Wesleyan U (IN)
John Brown U (AR)
Kingswood U (NB, Canada)
Kuyper Coll (MI)
Laurel U (NC)
Luther Rice U (GA)
The Master's Coll and Sem (CA)
Master's Coll and Sem (ON, Canada)
Northwest Nazarene U (ID)
Northwest U (WA)
Oakland City U (IN)
Oklahoma Baptist U (OK)
Providence Coll (RI)
Regent U (VA)
Roberts Wesleyan Coll (NY)
Rocky Mountain Coll (AB, Canada)
San Diego Christian Coll (CA)
Trevecca Nazarene U (TN)
The U of Western Ontario (ON, Canada)
Viterbo U (WI)

DOCUMENTARY PRODUCTION
Ithaca Coll (NY)
Texas A&M U–Commerce (TX)
U at Albany, State U of New York (NY)

DRAFTING AND DESIGN TECHNOLOGY
East Carolina U (NC)
East Central U (OK)
Lewis-Clark State Coll (ID)
Northern Michigan U (MI)
Purdue U (IN)
Texas Southern U (TX)
Trine U (IN)
Western Michigan U (MI)

DRAFTING/DESIGN ENGINEERING TECHNOLOGIES RELATED
Murray State U (KY)
National U (CA)
Purdue U (IN)
Thomas Edison State Coll (NJ)

DRAMA AND DANCE TEACHER EDUCATION
Adams State U (CO)
Appalachian State U (NC)
Belmont U (TN)
Boise State U (ID)
Boston U (MA)
Bowling Green State U (OH)
Bradley U (IL)
Bridgewater State U (MA)
Columbia Coll (SC)
Columbus State U (GA)
Concordia U, Nebraska (NE)
Dordt Coll (IA)
East Carolina U (NC)
East Central U (OK)
East Texas Baptist U (TX)
Edgewood Coll (WI)
Emerson Coll (MA)
Hardin-Simmons U (TX)
Hofstra U (NY)
Hope Coll (MI)
Howard Payne U (TX)
Johnson State Coll (VT)
Keene State Coll (NH)
Lees-McRae Coll (NC)
Lee U (TN)
Lipscomb U (TN)
Maryville Coll (TN)
Missouri Baptist U (MO)
Montclair State U (NJ)
North Carolina Central U (NC)
Ohio Wesleyan U (OH)
Oklahoma City U (OK)
Point Park U (PA)
St. Edward's U (TX)
Shenandoah U (VA)
Southern Utah U (UT)
Trevecca Nazarene U (TN)
The U of Akron (OH)
U of Evansville (IN)
The U of Iowa (IA)
The U of Montana Western (MT)
The U of North Carolina at Charlotte (NC)
The U of North Carolina at Greensboro (NC)
U of Regina (SK, Canada)
The U of South Dakota (SD)
The U of the Arts (PA)
U of Windsor (ON, Canada)
Valparaiso U (IN)
Virginia Intermont Coll (VA)
Viterbo U (WI)
Washington U in St. Louis (MO)
Wayne State Coll (NE)
Weber State U (UT)
Western Washington U (WA)
William Jewell Coll (MO)

DRAMA THERAPY
Virginia Union U (VA)

DRAMATIC/THEATER ARTS
Abilene Christian U (TX)
Acadia U (NS, Canada)
Adelphi U (NY)
Agnes Scott Coll (GA)
Alabama State U (AL)
Albertus Magnus Coll (CT)
Albion Coll (MI)
Albright Coll (PA)
Alfred U (NY)
Alma Coll (MI)
Alvernia U (PA)
American U (DC)
The American U in Cairo (Egypt)
Amherst Coll (MA)
Anderson U (IN)
Anderson U (SC)
Angelo State U (TX)
Appalachian State U (NC)
Arizona State U (AZ)
Arkansas State U (AR)
Armstrong Atlantic State U (GA)
Asbury U (KY)
Ashland U (OH)
Auburn U (AL)
Augsburg Coll (MN)
Augustana Coll (IL)

Augustana Coll (SD)
Aurora U (IL)
Averett U (VA)
Avila U (MO)
Baker U (KS)
Ball State U (IN)
Bard Coll (NY)
Barry U (FL)
Barton Coll (NC)
Bates Coll (ME)
Baylor U (TX)
Belhaven U (MS)
Belmont U (TN)
Bemidji State U (MN)
Benedictine Coll (KS)
Bennington Coll (VT)
Berea Coll (KY)
Bethany Coll (WV)
Bethany Lutheran Coll (MN)
Bethel Coll (IN)
Bethel U (MN)
Binghamton U, State U of New York (NY)
Bloomsburg U of Pennsylvania (PA)
Bluefield Coll (VA)
Bob Jones U (SC)
Boise State U (ID)
Boston Coll (MA)
The Boston Conservatory (MA)
Boston U (MA)
Bowling Green State U (OH)
Bradley U (IL)
Brevard Coll (NC)
Bridgewater State U (MA)
Brock U (ON, Canada)
Brown U (RI)
Bucknell U (PA)
Buffalo State Coll, State U of New York (NY)
Butler U (IN)
California Baptist U (CA)
California Lutheran U (CA)
California Polytechnic State U, San Luis Obispo (CA)
California State Polytechnic U, Pomona (CA)
California State U, Chico (CA)
California State U, Dominguez Hills (CA)
California State U, East Bay (CA)
California State U, Fresno (CA)
California State U, Fullerton (CA)
California State U, Long Beach (CA)
California State U, Los Angeles (CA)
California State U, Northridge (CA)
California State U, San Bernardino (CA)
California State U, Stanislaus (CA)
Calvin Coll (MI)
Capital U (OH)
Cardinal Stritch U (WI)
Carleton Coll (MN)
Carnegie Mellon U (PA)
Carroll Coll (MT)
Carson-Newman U (TN)
Case Western Reserve U (OH)
Castleton State Coll (VT)
Catawba Coll (NC)
The Catholic U of America (DC)
Cedar Crest Coll (PA)
Cedarville U (OH)
Centenary Coll of Louisiana (LA)
Central Coll (IA)
Central Methodist U (MO)
Centre Coll (KY)
Chapman U (CA)
Cheyney U of Pennsylvania (PA)
Chowan U (NC)
Christopher Newport U (VA)
City Coll of the City U of New York (NY)
Claremont McKenna Coll (CA)
Clarion U of Pennsylvania (PA)
Clarke U (IA)
Clark U (MA)
Clayton State U (GA)
Cleveland State U (OH)
Coastal Carolina U (SC)
Coe Coll (IA)
Colby Coll (ME)
Colgate U (NY)
The Coll at Brockport, State U of New York (NY)
Coll of Charleston (SC)
The Coll of Idaho (ID)

Coll of Saint Benedict (MN)
Coll of Staten Island of the City U of New York (NY)
Coll of the Holy Cross (MA)
Coll of the Ozarks (MO)
The Coll of William and Mary (VA)
The Coll of Wooster (OH)
The Colorado Coll (CO)
Colorado Mesa U (CO)
Colorado State U (CO)
Columbia Coll Chicago (IL)
Columbia U (NY)
Columbia U, School of General Studies (NY)
Columbus State U (GA)
Concordia Coll (MN)
Concordia U (CA)
Concordia U (OR)
Concordia U (QC, Canada)
Concordia U Chicago (IL)
Concordia U, Nebraska (NE)
Concordia U, St. Paul (MN)
Connecticut Coll (CT)
Converse Coll (SC)
Cornell Coll (IA)
Covenant Coll (GA)
Creighton U (NE)
Culver-Stockton Coll (MO)
Dakota Wesleyan U (SD)
Dalhousie U (NS, Canada)
Dartmouth Coll (NH)
Davidson Coll (NC)
DePaul U (IL)
DePauw U (IN)
DeSales U (PA)
Dickinson Coll (PA)
Dillard U (LA)
Doane Coll (NE)
Dominican U (IL)
Dordt Coll (IA)
Drake U (IA)
Drew U (NJ)
Drury U (MO)
Duquesne U (PA)
Earlham Coll (IN)
East Carolina U (NC)
East Central U (OK)
Eastern Illinois U (IL)
Eastern Mennonite U (VA)
Eastern Michigan U (MI)
Eastern New Mexico U (NM)
Eastern Washington U (WA)
East Tennessee State U (TN)
East Texas Baptist U (TX)
Eckerd Coll (FL)
Edgewood Coll (WI)
Edinboro U of Pennsylvania (PA)
Elizabethtown Coll (PA)
Elmira Coll (NY)
Elon U (NC)
Emerson Coll (MA)
Emporia State U (KS)
Eugene Lang Coll The New School for Liberal Arts (NY)
The Evergreen State Coll (WA)
Fairfield U (CT)
Fairleigh Dickinson U, Coll at Florham (NJ)
Fairmont State U (WV)
Faulkner U (AL)
Ferrum Coll (VA)
Five Towns Coll (NY)
Flagler Coll (FL)
Florida Ag and Mech U (FL)
Florida Atlantic U (FL)
Florida Gulf Coast U (FL)
Florida Intl U (FL)
Florida Southern Coll (FL)
Florida State U (FL)
Fort Lewis Coll (CO)
Francis Marion U (SC)
Franklin & Marshall Coll (PA)
Franklin Coll (IN)
Franklin Pierce U (NH)
Friends U (KS)
Frostburg State U (MD)
Furman U (SC)
Gannon U (PA)
Gardner-Webb U (NC)
George Fox U (OR)
George Mason U (VA)
Georgetown Coll (KY)
Georgia Coll & State U (GA)
Georgia Southern U (GA)
Georgia Southwestern State U (GA)
Gettysburg Coll (PA)

Gonzaga U (WA)
Goshen Coll (IN)
Goucher Coll (MD)
Graceland U (IA)
Grand Valley State U (MI)
Grand View U (IA)
Greenville Coll (IL)
Grinnell Coll (IA)
Guilford Coll (NC)
Gustavus Adolphus Coll (MN)
Hamilton Coll (NY)
Hamline U (MN)
Hampshire Coll (MA)
Hampton U (VA)
Hanover Coll (IN)
Harding U (AR)
Hardin-Simmons U (TX)
Hartwick Coll (NY)
Henderson State U (AR)
Hendrix Coll (AR)
High Point U (NC)
Hillsdale Coll (MI)
Hiram Coll (OH)
Hofstra U (NY)
Hollins U (VA)
Hope Coll (MI)
Howard Payne U (TX)
Humboldt State U (CA)
Hunter Coll of the City U of New York (NY)
Huntington U (IN)
Illinois Coll (IL)
Illinois State U (IL)
Illinois Wesleyan U (IL)
Indiana State U (IN)
Indiana U Bloomington (IN)
Indiana U Northwest (IN)
Indiana U of Pennsylvania (PA)
Indiana U–Purdue U Fort Wayne (IN)
Indiana U South Bend (IN)
Iowa State U of Science and Technology (IA)
Ithaca Coll (NY)
Jacksonville State U (AL)
James Madison U (VA)
Jamestown Coll (ND)
Johnson State Coll (VT)
The Juilliard School (NY)
Juniata Coll (PA)
Kalamazoo Coll (MI)
Kansas State U (KS)
Kansas Wesleyan U (KS)
Kean U (NJ)
Kennesaw State U (GA)
Kent State U (OH)
Kenyon Coll (OH)
King's Coll (PA)
Knox Coll (IL)
Kuyper Coll (MI)
Lafayette Coll (PA)
LaGrange Coll (GA)
Lamar U (TX)
Langston U (OK)
Lawrence U (WI)
Lees-McRae Coll (NC)
Lehigh U (PA)
Lehman Coll of the City U of New York (NY)
Le Moyne Coll (NY)
Lewis U (IL)
Liberty U (VA)
Limestone Coll (SC)
Lindenwood U (MO)
Linfield Coll (OR)
Lipscomb U (TN)
Lock Haven U of Pennsylvania (PA)
Long Island U–C. W. Post Campus (NY)
Louisiana Coll (LA)
Louisiana State U and Ag and Mech Coll (LA)
Loyola Marymount U (CA)
Loyola U Chicago (IL)
Loyola U New Orleans (LA)
Lubbock Christian U (TX)
Luther Coll (IA)
Lynchburg Coll (VA)
Lynn U (FL)
Lyon Coll (AR)
Macalester Coll (MN)
Manchester U (IN)
Marietta Coll (OH)
Marquette U (WI)
Mars Hill Coll (NC)
Mary Baldwin Coll (VA)
Marymount Manhattan Coll (NY)

Maryville Coll (TN)
Marywood U (PA)
McDaniel Coll (MD)
McMurry U (TX)
Mercer U (GA)
Merrimack Coll (MA)
Messiah Coll (PA)
Metropolitan State U of Denver (CO)
Miami U (OH)
Michigan State U (MI)
Middlebury Coll (VT)
Middle Tennessee State U (TN)
Millikin U (IL)
Minnesota State U Mankato (MN)
Minnesota State U Moorhead (MN)
Mississippi Coll (MS)
Missouri Baptist U (MO)
Missouri State U (MO)
Missouri Western State U (MO)
Molloy Coll (NY)
Monmouth Coll (IL)
Monmouth U (NJ)
Montclair State U (NJ)
Morehead State U (KY)
Morehouse Coll (GA)
Morningside Coll (IA)
Mount Allison U (NB, Canada)
Mount Holyoke Coll (MA)
Mount Marty Coll (SD)
Mount Vernon Nazarene U (OH)
Muhlenberg Coll (PA)
Murray State U (KY)
Naropa U (CO)
Nazareth Coll of Rochester (NY)
Neumann U (PA)
Newberry Coll (SC)
New England Coll (NH)
New Mexico State U (NM)
The New School for Public Engagement (NY)
New York U (NY)
Niagara U (NY)
North Carolina Central U (NC)
North Carolina Wesleyan Coll (NC)
North Central Coll (IL)
North Dakota State U (ND)
Northeastern U (MA)
Northern Arizona U (AZ)
Northern Illinois U (IL)
Northern Michigan U (MI)
Northern State U (SD)
North Greenville U (SC)
Northwestern Coll (IA)
Northwestern Coll (MN)
Northwestern State U of Louisiana (LA)
Northwest Missouri State U (MO)
Northwest U (WA)
Notre Dame de Namur U (CA)
Nova Southeastern U (FL)
Oakland U (MI)
The Ohio State U (OH)
Ohio U (OH)
Ohio Wesleyan U (OH)
Oklahoma Baptist U (OK)
Oklahoma Christian U (OK)
Oklahoma City U (OK)
Oklahoma State U (OK)
Old Dominion U (VA)
Olivet Coll (MI)
Oral Roberts U (OK)
Ouachita Baptist U (AR)
Pacific U (OR)
Palm Beach Atlantic U (FL)
Park U (MO)
Pepperdine U, Malibu (CA)
Piedmont Coll (GA)
Pittsburg State U (KS)
Pitzer Coll (CA)
Plymouth State U (NH)
Point Loma Nazarene U (CA)
Point Park U (PA)
Pomona Coll (CA)
Portland State U (OR)
Presbyterian Coll (SC)
Prescott Coll (AZ)
Principia Coll (IL)
Purchase Coll, State U of New York (NY)
Purdue U (IN)
Queens U of Charlotte (NC)
Quinnipiac U (CT)
Radford U (VA)
Ramapo Coll of New Jersey (NJ)
Randolph Coll (VA)
Randolph-Macon Coll (VA)

Reed Coll (OR)
Rhode Island Coll (RI)
Rhodes Coll (TN)
Ripon Coll (WI)
Roanoke Coll (VA)
Rockford Coll (IL)
Rocky Mountain Coll (MT)
Rocky Mountain Coll (AB, Canada)
Roger Williams U (RI)
Rollins Coll (FL)
Roosevelt U (IL)
Rowan U (NJ)
Russell Sage Coll (NY)
Rutgers, The State U of New Jersey, Camden (NJ)
Rutgers, The State U of New Jersey, Newark (NJ)
Rutgers, The State U of New Jersey, New Brunswick (NJ)
Saginaw Valley State U (MI)
St. Ambrose U (IA)
St. Bonaventure U (NY)
St. Edward's U (TX)
St. Gregory's U, Shawnee (OK)
Saint John's U (MN)
St. John's U (NY)
St. Lawrence U (NY)
Saint Louis U (MO)
Saint Martin's U (WA)
Saint Mary's Coll (IN)
Saint Mary's Coll of California (CA)
St. Mary's Coll of Maryland (MD)
Saint Mary's U of Minnesota (MN)
Saint Michael's Coll (VT)
St. Norbert Coll (WI)
St. Olaf Coll (MN)
Saint Vincent Coll (PA)
Salem State U (MA)
Salisbury U (MD)
Salve Regina U (RI)
Samford U (AL)
San Diego State U (CA)
San Francisco State U (CA)
San Jose State U (CA)
Santa Fe U of Art and Design (NM)
Savannah Coll of Art and Design (GA)
Schreiner U (TX)
Scripps Coll (CA)
Seattle Pacific U (WA)
Seattle U (WA)
Seton Hill U (PA)
Sewanee: The U of the South (TN)
Shaw U (NC)
Shenandoah U (VA)
Siena Heights U (MI)
Simon Fraser U (BC, Canada)
Simpson Coll (IA)
Skidmore Coll (NY)
Slippery Rock U of Pennsylvania (PA)
Smith Coll (MA)
Sonoma State U (CA)
South Dakota State U (SD)
Southeastern Oklahoma State U (OK)
Southeastern U (FL)
Southeast Missouri State U (MO)
Southern Arkansas U–Magnolia (AR)
Southern Connecticut State U (CT)
Southern Illinois U Carbondale (IL)
Southern Illinois U Edwardsville (IL)
Southern Methodist U (TX)
Southern Oregon U (OR)
Southern Utah U (UT)
Southwest Baptist U (MO)
Southwestern Coll (KS)
Southwestern U (TX)
Spelman Coll (GA)
Spring Arbor U (MI)
Spring Hill Coll (AL)
Stanford U (CA)
State U of New York at Fredonia (NY)
State U of New York at New Paltz (NY)
State U of New York at Oswego (NY)
State U of New York at Plattsburgh (NY)
State U of New York Coll at Geneseo (NY)
State U of New York Coll at Potsdam (NY)
Stephen F. Austin State U (TX)

Stephens Coll (MO)
Sterling Coll (KS)
Stetson U (FL)
Stevenson U (MD)
Stony Brook U, State U of New York (NY)
Suffolk U (MA)
Sul Ross State U (TX)
Susquehanna U (PA)
Swarthmore Coll (PA)
Sweet Briar Coll (VA)
Syracuse U (NY)
Tarleton State U (TX)
Taylor U (IN)
Temple U (PA)
Tennessee Wesleyan Coll (TN)
Texas A&M U (TX)
Texas A&M U–Commerce (TX)
Texas A&M U–Kingsville (TX)
Texas Christian U (TX)
Texas Lutheran U (TX)
Texas Southern U (TX)
Texas State U–San Marcos (TX)
Texas Woman's U (TX)
Thomas Edison State Coll (NJ)
Thomas More Coll (KY)
Thompson Rivers U (BC, Canada)
Transylvania U (KY)
Trevecca Nazarene U (TN)
Trinity Coll (CT)
Trinity U (TX)
Truman State U (MO)
Tufts U (MA)
Tulane U (LA)
Union Coll (KY)
Union U (TN)
U at Buffalo, the State U of New York (NY)
The U of Akron (OH)
The U of Alabama (AL)
The U of Alabama at Birmingham (AL)
U of Alaska Anchorage (AK)
The U of Arizona (AZ)
U of Arkansas at Little Rock (AR)
U of Arkansas–Fort Smith (AR)
The U of British Columbia (BC, Canada)
The U of British Columbia–Okanagan (BC, Canada)
U of California, Berkeley (CA)
U of California, Irvine (CA)
U of California, Los Angeles (CA)
U of California, Riverside (CA)
U of California, Santa Barbara (CA)
U of California, Santa Cruz (CA)
U of Central Arkansas (AR)
U of Central Florida (FL)
U of Central Oklahoma (OK)
U of Cincinnati (OH)
U of Colorado Boulder (CO)
U of Colorado Denver (CO)
U of Dallas (TX)
U of Denver (CO)
U of Evansville (IN)
The U of Findlay (OH)
U of Florida (FL)
U of Georgia (GA)
U of Guelph (ON, Canada)
U of Hawaii at Manoa (HI)
U of Houston (TX)
U of Idaho (ID)
U of Illinois at Chicago (IL)
U of Illinois at Urbana–Champaign (IL)
The U of Iowa (IA)
The U of Kansas (KS)
U of Kentucky (KY)
U of La Verne (CA)
U of Louisville (KY)
U of Maine at Farmington (ME)
U of Maine at Machias (ME)
U of Maryland, Baltimore County (MD)
U of Maryland, Coll Park (MD)
U of Massachusetts Amherst (MA)
U of Memphis (TN)
U of Miami (FL)
U of Michigan (MI)
U of Michigan–Flint (MI)
U of Minnesota, Duluth (MN)
U of Minnesota, Twin Cities Campus (MN)
U of Mississippi (MS)
U of Missouri (MO)
U of Missouri–Kansas City (MO)
U of Missouri–St. Louis (MO)

U of Mobile (AL)
U of Montevallo (AL)
U of Mount Union (OH)
U of Nebraska at Kearney (NE)
U of Nebraska at Omaha (NE)
U of Nebraska–Lincoln (NE)
U of Nevada, Las Vegas (NV)
U of Nevada, Reno (NV)
U of New Brunswick Fredericton (NB, Canada)
U of New Hampshire (NH)
U of New Mexico (NM)
U of New Orleans (LA)
U of North Carolina at Asheville (NC)
The U of North Carolina at Chapel Hill (NC)
The U of North Carolina at Charlotte (NC)
The U of North Carolina at Greensboro (NC)
The U of North Carolina at Pembroke (NC)
U of North Carolina School of the Arts (NC)
The U of North Carolina Wilmington (NC)
U of North Dakota (ND)
U of Northern Colorado (CO)
U of Northern Iowa (IA)
U of North Texas (TX)
U of Notre Dame (IN)
U of Oklahoma (OK)
U of Oregon (OR)
U of Ottawa (ON, Canada)
U of Pennsylvania (PA)
U of Pittsburgh (PA)
U of Portland (OR)
U of Puget Sound (WA)
U of Regina (SK, Canada)
U of Rhode Island (RI)
U of Richmond (VA)
U of Saint Mary (KS)
U of St. Thomas (TX)
U of San Diego (CA)
U of Science and Arts of Oklahoma (OK)
The U of Scranton (PA)
U of South Alabama (AL)
U of South Carolina (SC)
The U of South Dakota (SD)
U of Southern California (CA)
U of Southern Indiana (IN)
U of Southern Maine (ME)
U of Southern Mississippi (MS)
U of South Florida (FL)
The U of Tampa (FL)
The U of Tennessee (TN)
The U of Tennessee at Chattanooga (TN)
The U of Tennessee at Martin (TN)
The U of Texas at Arlington (TX)
The U of Texas at El Paso (TX)
The U of Texas–Pan American (TX)
U of the Cumberlands (KY)
U of the District of Columbia (DC)
U of the Incarnate Word (TX)
U of the Ozarks (AR)
The U of Toledo (OH)
U of Tulsa (OK)
U of Utah (UT)
U of Vermont (VT)
U of Virginia (VA)
U of Waterloo (ON, Canada)
U of West Florida (FL)
U of West Georgia (GA)
U of Windsor (ON, Canada)
U of Wisconsin–Eau Claire (WI)
U of Wisconsin–Green Bay (WI)
U of Wisconsin–La Crosse (WI)
U of Wisconsin–Madison (WI)
U of Wisconsin–Milwaukee (WI)
U of Wisconsin–Parkside (WI)
U of Wisconsin–Stevens Point (WI)
U of Wisconsin–Superior (WI)
U of Wyoming (WY)
Utah State U (UT)
Valparaiso U (IN)
Vanderbilt U (TN)
Vassar Coll (NY)
Virginia Commonwealth U (VA)
Virginia Intermont Coll (VA)
Virginia Polytechnic Inst and State U (VA)
Virginia Wesleyan Coll (VA)
Viterbo U (WI)
Wabash Coll (IN)

Wagner Coll (NY)
Wake Forest U (NC)
Waldorf Coll (IA)
Wartburg Coll (IA)
Washburn U (KS)
Washington and Lee U (VA)
Washington Coll (MD)
Washington U in St. Louis (MO)
Wayland Baptist U (TX)
Wayne State Coll (NE)
Wayne State U (MI)
Weber State U (UT)
Webster U (MO)
Wellesley Coll (MA)
Wells Coll (NY)
Wesleyan U (CT)
West Chester U of Pennsylvania (PA)
Western Carolina U (NC)
Western Connecticut State U (CT)
Western Illinois U (IL)
Western Kentucky U (KY)
Western Oregon U (OR)
Western State Colorado U (CO)
Western Washington U (WA)
Westfield State U (MA)
Westminster Coll (UT)
West Texas A&M U (TX)
West Virginia U (WV)
West Virginia Wesleyan Coll (WV)
Wheeling Jesuit U (WV)
Whitman Coll (WA)
Whitworth U (WA)
Wichita State U (KS)
Wilkes U (PA)
Willamette U (OR)
William Jewell Coll (MO)
William Paterson U of New Jersey (NJ)
William Peace U (NC)
Williams Coll (MA)
Winthrop U (SC)
Wittenberg U (OH)
Wright State U (OH)
York Coll of Pennsylvania (PA)
York Coll of the City U of New York (NY)
Young Harris Coll (GA)
Youngstown State U (OH)

DRAMATIC/THEATER ARTS AND STAGECRAFT RELATED
Adams State U (CO)
Brigham Young U (UT)
California State U, Chico (CA)
Clarke U (IA)
Coastal Carolina U (SC)
Dalhousie U (NS, Canada)
DePaul U (IL)
Drake U (IA)
Fayetteville State U (NC)
Indiana U South Bend (IN)
Lee U (TN)
Lindenwood U (MO)
North Central Coll (IL)
Palm Beach Atlantic U (FL)
Pepperdine U, Malibu (CA)
Purdue U (IN)
Seton Hill U (PA)
Southern Illinois U Carbondale (IL)
Southern Utah U (UT)
Southwestern Coll (KS)
U at Buffalo, the State U of New York (NY)
U of Miami (FL)
U of Michigan–Flint (MI)
U of Nevada, Las Vegas (NV)
U of Northern Colorado (CO)
U of Regina (SK, Canada)
U of Southern California (CA)
Webster U (MO)
Western Kentucky U (KY)
Western Michigan U (MI)
Wheaton Coll (MA)

DRAWING
Acad of Art U (CA)
Adams State U (CO)
Alberta Coll of Art & Design (AB, Canada)
American Acad of Art (IL)
Bennington Coll (VT)
Bowling Green State U (OH)
Bradley U (IL)
Brigham Young U (UT)
Buffalo State Coll, State U of New York (NY)
California State U, East Bay (CA)

California State U, Long Beach (CA)
Carson-Newman U (TN)
Cleveland Inst of Art (OH)
The Coll at Brockport, State U of New York (NY)
Coll of the Atlantic (ME)
Colorado State U (CO)
Columbus State U (GA)
Drake U (IA)
Ferris State U (MI)
Georgia State U (GA)
Indiana U–Purdue U Fort Wayne (IN)
Inter American U of Puerto Rico, San Germán Campus (PR)
Lewis U (IL)
Lindenwood U (MO)
Maryland Inst Coll of Art (MD)
Minnesota State U Mankato (MN)
Mount Allison U (NB, Canada)
New England Coll (NH)
Northern Michigan U (MI)
Oakland U (MI)
Otis Coll of Art and Design (CA)
Pittsburg State U (KS)
Portland State U (OR)
Providence Coll (RI)
Rutgers, The State U of New Jersey, New Brunswick (NJ)
School of the Art Inst of Chicago (IL)
School of the Museum of Fine Arts, Boston (MA)
Seton Hill U (PA)
Sonoma State U (CA)
State U of New York at Fredonia (NY)
U of Hartford (CT)
The U of Iowa (IA)
U of Michigan (MI)
U of Missouri–St. Louis (MO)
U of Regina (SK, Canada)
The U of Texas at El Paso (TX)
The U of Toledo (OH)
U of Windsor (ON, Canada)
Virginia Intermont Coll (VA)
Washington U in St. Louis (MO)
Western Washington U (WA)
West Virginia Wesleyan Coll (WV)

DRIVER AND SAFETY TEACHER EDUCATION
William Penn U (IA)

DUTCH/FLEMISH
U of California, Berkeley (CA)

EARLY CHILDHOOD EDUCATION
Adams State & Coll (CO)
Alabama State U (AL)
Alma Coll (MI)
Alvernia U (PA)
Anderson U (SC)
Antioch U Midwest (OH)
Arizona State U (AZ)
Arkansas State U (AR)
Arkansas Tech U (AR)
Auburn U (AL)
Baldwin Wallace U (OH)
Baylor U (TX)
Bay Path U (MA)
Becker Coll (MA)
Belmont U (TN)
Bennington Coll (VT)
Berry Coll (GA)
Bethel Coll (IN)
Bloomsburg U of Pennsylvania (PA)
Bob Jones U (SC)
Boise State U (ID)
Boston U (MA)
Bradley U (IL)
Bridgewater State U (MA)
Brigham Young U (UT)
Bucknell U (PA)
Butler U (IN)
California Baptist U (CA)
California State U, Chico (CA)
California State U, Dominguez Hills (CA)
California State U, Fullerton (CA)
California State U, Los Angeles (CA)
California State U, Stanislaus (CA)
Calvin Coll (MI)
Cameron U (OK)
Canisius Coll (NY)

Capital U (OH)
Carlow U (PA)
The Catholic U of America (DC)
Cedar Crest Coll (PA)
Cedarville U (OH)
Central Methodist U (MO)
Central State U (OH)
Chatham U (PA)
Chestnut Hill Coll (PA)
Chicago State U (IL)
Christian Brothers U (TN)
City Coll of the City U of New York (NY)
City U of Seattle (WA)
Claflin U (SC)
Clarion U of Pennsylvania (PA)
Clark Atlanta U (GA)
Clemson U (SC)
Cleveland State U (OH)
Coastal Carolina U (SC)
The Coll at Brockport, State U of New York (NY)
Coll of Charleston (SC)
Coll of Mount St. Joseph (OH)
The Coll of New Jersey (NJ)
Coll of Saint Mary (NE)
Coll of the Ozarks (MO)
Colorado State U (CO)
Columbia Coll (SC)
Columbia Coll Chicago (IL)
Columbus State U (GA)
Concordia Coll Alabama (AL)
Concordia Coll–New York (NY)
Concordia U Chicago (IL)
Concordia U, Nebraska (NE)
Concordia U, St. Paul (MN)
DePaul U (IL)
DeSales U (PA)
Dominican U (IL)
Duquesne U (PA)
East Central U (OK)
Eastern New Mexico U (NM)
Eastern Washington U (WA)
Edgewood Coll (WI)
Edinboro U of Pennsylvania (PA)
Elizabethtown Coll (PA)
Endicott Coll (MA)
Evangel U (MO)
Fayetteville State U (NC)
Felician Coll (NJ)
Florida Ag and Mech U (FL)
Florida Atlantic U (FL)
Florida Gulf Coast U (FL)
Florida Intl U (FL)
Florida State U (FL)
Fort Lewis Coll (CO)
Francis Marion U (SC)
Frostburg State U (MD)
Gannon U (PA)
Georgia Coll & State U (GA)
Georgia Gwinnett Coll (GA)
Georgia Regents U (GA)
Gordon State Coll (GA)
Governors State U (IL)
Grambling State U (LA)
Granite State Coll (NH)
Greenville Coll (IL)
Grove City Coll (PA)
Harding U (AR)
Hardin-Simmons U (TX)
Harris-Stowe State U (MO)
Henderson State U (AR)
Hillsdale Coll (MI)
Hofstra U (NY)
Holy Family U (PA)
Hood Coll (MD)
Illinois Coll (IL)
Illinois State U (IL)
Indiana U Bloomington (IN)
Indiana U Kokomo (IN)
Indiana U–Purdue U Indianapolis (IN)
Inter American U of Puerto Rico, San Germán Campus (PR)
Iona Coll (NY)
Iowa Wesleyan Coll (IA)
John Brown U (AR)
Judson U (IL)
Juniata Coll (PA)
Keene State Coll (NH)
Kennesaw State U (GA)
Kent State U (OH)
Kent State U at Salem (OH)
Kent State U at Tuscarawas (OH)
Keystone Coll (PA)
King's Coll (PA)
Kutztown U of Pennsylvania (PA)

MAJORS LISTING

LaGrange Coll (GA)
Lake Erie Coll (OH)
Lake Superior State U (MI)
Lander U (SC)
La Roche Coll (PA)
Lasell Coll (MA)
Lebanon Valley Coll (PA)
Lee U (TN)
Lewis U (IL)
Lindenwood U (MO)
Louisiana State U and Ag and
    Mech Coll (LA)
Lourdes U (OH)
Loyola U Chicago (IL)
Lubbock Christian U (TX)
Lyon Coll (AR)
Madonna U (MI)
Malone U (OH)
Maranatha Baptist Bible Coll (WI)
Marian U (WI)
Marywood U (PA)
Mayville State U (ND)
McMurry U (TX)
McNeese State U (LA)
Merrimack Coll (MA)
Messiah Coll (PA)
Miami U (OH)
Michigan State U (MI)
Midwestern State U (TX)
Millersville U of Pennsylvania (PA)
Millikin U (IL)
Minnesota State U Moorhead (MN)
Misericordia U (PA)
Missouri Baptist U (MO)
Missouri State U (MO)
Missouri Western State U (MO)
Mitchell Coll (CT)
Morehead State U (KY)
Morehouse Coll (GA)
Morris Coll (SC)
Mount Aloysius Coll (PA)
Mount Saint Mary Coll (NY)
Mount Vernon Nazarene U (OH)
Murray State U (KY)
Naropa U (CO)
National U (CA)
Neumann U (PA)
Newberry Coll (SC)
Newman U (KS)
New Mexico State U (NM)
New York U (NY)
Nicholls State U (LA)
Northeastern Illinois U (IL)
Northern Arizona U (AZ)
Northern Illinois U (IL)
North Greenville U (SC)
Northwestern Coll (MN)
Northwestern Oklahoma State U
    (OK)
Northwestern State U of Louisiana
    (LA)
Nyack Coll (NY)
Ohio Dominican U (OH)
Ohio U (OH)
Ohio U–Chillicothe (OH)
Ohio Wesleyan U (OH)
Oklahoma Baptist U (OK)
Oklahoma Christian U (OK)
Oklahoma City U (OK)
Oral Roberts U (OK)
Ouachita Baptist U (AR)
Pacific Union Coll (CA)
Park U (MO)
Penn State U Park (PA)
Pine Manor Coll (MA)
Pittsburg State U (KS)
Plymouth State U (NH)
Point Park U (PA)
Point U (GA)
Presbyterian Coll (SC)
Prescott Coll (AZ)
Purdue U (IN)
Purdue U Calumet (IN)
Purdue U North Central (IN)
Rhode Island Coll (RI)
Ripon Coll (WI)
Rivier U (NH)
Roberts Wesleyan Coll (NY)
Roosevelt U (IL)
Rowan U (NJ)
St. Ambrose U (IA)
Salem State U (MA)
Salisbury U (MD)
Salve Regina U (RI)
San Francisco State U (CA)
San Jose State U (CA)
Schreiner U (TX)

Shawnee State U (OH)
Shippensburg U of Pennsylvania
    (PA)
Simmons Coll (MA)
South Dakota State U (SD)
Southeastern Louisiana U (LA)
Southeast Missouri State U (MO)
Southern Arkansas U–Magnolia
    (AR)
Southern Connecticut State U (CT)
Southern Illinois U Carbondale (IL)
Southern Illinois U Edwardsville
    (IL)
Southern Nazarene U (OK)
Southern New Hampshire U (NH)
Southwest Baptist U (MO)
Southwestern Coll (KS)
Spring Hill Coll (AL)
State U of New York Coll at
    Geneseo (NY)
State U of New York Coll at Old
    Westbury (NY)
Stephens Coll (MO)
Tennessee Wesleyan Coll (TN)
Texas A&M U–Commerce (TX)
Texas Christian U (TX)
Thomas U (GA)
Trevecca Nazarene U (TN)
Troy U (AL)
The U of Akron (OH)
The U of Alabama (AL)
The U of Alabama at Birmingham
    (AL)
U of Arkansas at Little Rock (AR)
U of Arkansas–Fort Smith (AR)
U of Central Florida (FL)
U of Delaware (DE)
U of Georgia (GA)
U of Guam (GU)
U of Hartford (CT)
U of Hawaii–West Oahu (HI)
U of Illinois at Urbana–Champaign
    (IL)
The U of Kansas (KS)
U of Kentucky (KY)
U of Louisiana at Lafayette (LA)
U of Maine at Farmington (ME)
U of Michigan–Dearborn (MI)
U of Michigan–Flint (MI)
U of Minnesota, Crookston (MN)
U of Missouri (MO)
U of Missouri–Kansas City (MO)
U of Missouri–St. Louis (MO)
U of Mobile (AL)
The U of Montana Western (MT)
U of Mount Union (OH)
U of New Mexico (NM)
U of New Orleans (LA)
The U of North Carolina at Chapel
    Hill (NC)
The U of North Carolina at
    Greensboro (NC)
U of North Dakota (ND)
U of North Florida (FL)
U of North Georgia (GA)
U of Oklahoma (OK)
U of Regina (SK, Canada)
U of Science and Arts of Oklahoma
    (OK)
The U of Scranton (PA)
U of South Carolina Aiken (SC)
U of Southern Indiana (IN)
U of South Florida (FL)
The U of Tennessee at
    Chattanooga (TN)
U of the Virgin Islands (VI)
U of Tulsa (OK)
U of Vermont (VT)
The U of West Alabama (AL)
U of West Florida (FL)
U of Wisconsin–Stevens Point (WI)
U of Wisconsin–Stout (WI)
Ursuline Coll (OH)
Valdosta State U (GA)
Vanderbilt U (TN)
Virginia Intermont Coll (VA)
Walsh U (OH)
Warner Pacific Coll (OR)
Washington State U (WA)
Wayland Baptist U (TX)
Wayne State Coll (NE)
Weber State U (UT)
Webster U (MO)
Wesleyan Coll (GA)
West Chester U of Pennsylvania
    (PA)
Western Kentucky U (KY)

Western Michigan U (MI)
Western Washington U (WA)
Wheeling Jesuit U (WV)
Widener U (PA)
Wilmington U (DE)
Worcester State U (MA)
Wright State U (OH)
Xavier U (OH)
Xavier U of Louisiana (LA)
York Coll of Pennsylvania (PA)
Young Harris Coll (GA)
Youngstown State U (OH)

EARTH SCIENCE EDUCATION
Boise State U (ID)
Calvin Coll (MI)
Central Michigan U (MI)
Florida Inst of Technology (FL)
Pace U (NY)
Purdue U (IN)
Syracuse U (NY)
U of Minnesota, Duluth (MN)
The U of Montana Western (MT)
Western Michigan U (MI)

EAST ASIAN LANGUAGES
Arizona State U (AZ)
Columbia U (NY)
Eckerd Coll (FL)
Grinnell Coll (IA)
Indiana U Bloomington (IN)
Michigan State U (MI)
Smith Coll (MA)
U of Illinois at Urbana–Champaign
    (IL)
The U of Kansas (KS)
U of Pennsylvania (PA)
U of Puget Sound (WA)
U of Southern California (CA)
The U of Texas at Austin (TX)
The U of Western Ontario (ON,
    Canada)
Washington and Lee U (VA)

EAST ASIAN LANGUAGES RELATED
Columbia U, School of General
    Studies (NY)
Dartmouth Coll (NH)
Michigan State U (MI)
U of Chicago (IL)
U of Florida (FL)
U of Minnesota, Twin Cities
    Campus (MN)
Washington U in St. Louis (MO)

ECOLOGY
Appalachian State U (NC)
Averett U (VA)
Barry U (FL)
Bemidji State U (MN)
Bennington Coll (VT)
California State U, Chico (CA)
California State U, Dominguez Hills
    (CA)
California State U, East Bay (CA)
California State U, Fresno (CA)
California State U, Long Beach
    (CA)
California State U, San Marcos
    (CA)
Castleton State Coll (VT)
Clark U (MA)
Colorado State U (CO)
Columbia U, School of General
    Studies (NY)
Concordia Coll–New York (NY)
Concordia U (QC, Canada)
Dartmouth Coll (NH)
Defiance Coll (OH)
Fort Lewis Coll (CO)
Georgetown Coll (KY)
Iowa State U of Science and
    Technology (IA)
Jacksonville State U (AL)
Lawrence U (WI)
Le Moyne Coll (NY)
Manchester U (IN)
Minnesota State U Mankato (MN)
Molloy Coll (NY)
New Mexico State U (NM)
New York U (NY)
Northern Michigan U (MI)
Ohio U (OH)
Oklahoma City U (OK)
Pittsburg State U (KS)
Pomona Coll (CA)
Prescott Coll (AZ)

Princeton U (NJ)
Rice U (TX)
Rocky Mountain Coll (MT)
Russell Sage Coll (NY)
Rutgers, The State U of New
    Jersey, New Brunswick (NJ)
San Francisco State U (CA)
Seattle Pacific U (WA)
Sierra Nevada Coll (NV)
Sonoma State U (CA)
State U of New York at Plattsburgh
    (NY)
Sterling Coll (VT)
Stony Brook U, State U of New York
    (NY)
Susquehanna U (PA)
Tulane U (LA)
Université de Sherbrooke (QC,
    Canada)
U at Buffalo, the State U of New
    York (NY)
The U of Akron (OH)
U of California, Los Angeles (CA)
U of California, Santa Cruz (CA)
U of Delaware (DE)
U of Denver (CO)
U of Georgia (GA)
U of Guelph (ON, Canada)
U of Illinois at Urbana–Champaign
    (IL)
U of Maine at Machias (ME)
U of Maryland, Coll Park (MD)
U of Maryland Eastern Shore (MD)
U of Michigan–Flint (MI)
U of Minnesota, Twin Cities
    Campus (MN)
U of New Brunswick Fredericton
    (NB, Canada)
U of New Haven (CT)
U of Northern Iowa (IA)
U of Pittsburgh (PA)
U of Waterloo (ON, Canada)
The U of Western Ontario (ON,
    Canada)
Utah State U (UT)
Washington Coll (MD)
Washington U in St. Louis (MO)
William Paterson U of New Jersey
    (NJ)
Yale U (CT)

ECOLOGY AND EVOLUTIONARY BIOLOGY
Angelo State U (TX)
Bradley U (IL)
Colby Coll (ME)
The Colorado Coll (CO)
Purdue U (IN)
The U of Arizona (AZ)
U of California, Irvine (CA)
U of Michigan (MI)
U of Pittsburgh (PA)
Vanderbilt U (TN)

ECOLOGY, EVOLUTION, SYSTEMATICS AND POPULATION BIOLOGY RELATED
Hofstra U (NY)
The Ohio State U (OH)
The U of British Columbia–
    Okanagan (BC, Canada)
U of California, Davis (CA)
U of California, Santa Barbara (CA)
U of Colorado Boulder (CO)
U of Guelph (ON, Canada)

E-COMMERCE
Bloomfield Coll (NJ)
DePaul U (IL)
King Coll (TN)
Lewis U (IL)
Maryville U of Saint Louis (MO)
Philadelphia U (PA)
Tiffin U (OH)
Trevecca Nazarene U (TN)
U of La Verne (CA)
U of North Texas (TX)
U of Ottawa (ON, Canada)
U of Pennsylvania (PA)
The U of Scranton (PA)
The U of Toledo (OH)
Western Michigan U (MI)
Winthrop U (SC)

ECONOMETRICS AND QUANTITATIVE ECONOMICS
Baldwin Wallace U (OH)
Bowdoin Coll (ME)

Bucknell U (PA)
Carnegie Mellon U (PA)
The Colorado Coll (CO)
Hampden-Sydney Coll (VA)
High Point U (NC)
Hofstra U (NY)
Scripps Coll (CA)
State U of New York at Oswego
    (NY)
Thompson Rivers U (BC, Canada)
United States Naval Acad (MD)
U of California, Irvine (CA)
U of California, Santa Barbara (CA)
U of Guelph (ON, Canada)
U of Minnesota, Twin Cities
    Campus (MN)
U of Rhode Island (RI)
Wake Forest U (NC)
Weber State U (UT)
Western Kentucky U (KY)

ECONOMICS
Acadia U (NS, Canada)
Adams State U (CO)
Adelphi U (NY)
Agnes Scott Coll (GA)
Albion Coll (MI)
Albright Coll (PA)
Alma Coll (MI)
American U (DC)
American U in Bulgaria (Bulgaria)
The American U in Cairo (Egypt)
American U of Beirut (Lebanon)
The American U of Paris (France)
Amherst Coll (MA)
Andrews U (MI)
Appalachian State U (NC)
Arizona State U (AZ)
Arkansas State U (AR)
Armstrong Atlantic State U (GA)
Ashland U (OH)
Assumption Coll (MA)
Auburn U (AL)
Augsburg Coll (MN)
Augustana Coll (IL)
Augustana Coll (SD)
Babson Coll (MA)
Baker U (KS)
Baldwin Wallace U (OH)
Ball State U (IN)
Bard Coll (NY)
Barry U (FL)
Barton Coll (NC)
Bates Coll (ME)
Baylor U (TX)
Bellarmine U (KY)
Bemidji State U (MN)
Benedictine Coll (KS)
Benedictine U (IL)
Berea Coll (KY)
Berry Coll (GA)
Bethany Coll (WV)
Bethel U (MN)
Binghamton U, State U of New York
    (NY)
Bloomsburg U of Pennsylvania (PA)
Bluffton U (OH)
Boise State U (ID)
Boston Coll (MA)
Boston U (MA)
Bowdoin Coll (ME)
Bowie State U (MD)
Bowling Green State U (OH)
Bradley U (IL)
Bridgewater Coll (VA)
Bridgewater State U (MA)
Brock U (ON, Canada)
Brown U (RI)
Bryant U (RI)
Bucknell U (PA)
Buffalo State Coll, State U of New
    York (NY)
Butler U (IN)
Caldwell Coll (NJ)
California Lutheran U (CA)
California Polytechnic State U, San
    Luis Obispo (CA)
California State Polytechnic U,
    Pomona (CA)
California State U, Chico (CA)
California State U, East Bay (CA)
California State U, Fresno (CA)
California State U, Fullerton (CA)
California State U, Long Beach
    (CA)
California State U, Los Angeles
    (CA)

California State U, Northridge (CA)
California State U, San Bernardino (CA)
California State U, San Marcos (CA)
California State U, Stanislaus (CA)
Calvin Coll (MI)
Campbellsville U (KY)
Canisius Coll (NY)
Capital U (OH)
Carleton Coll (MN)
Carnegie Mellon U (PA)
Case Western Reserve U (OH)
The Catholic U of America (DC)
Centenary Coll of Louisiana (LA)
Central Coll (IA)
Central Connecticut State U (CT)
Central Methodist U (MO)
Central Michigan U (MI)
Central State U (OH)
Centre Coll (KY)
Cheyney U of Pennsylvania (PA)
Chicago State U (IL)
Chowan U (NC)
Christopher Newport U (VA)
City Coll of the City U of New York (NY)
Claremont McKenna Coll (CA)
Clarion U of Pennsylvania (PA)
Clark U (MA)
Clemson U (SC)
Cleveland State U (OH)
Coastal Carolina U (SC)
Coe Coll (IA)
Colgate U (NY)
The Coll at Brockport, State U of New York (NY)
Coll of Charleston (SC)
The Coll of New Jersey (NJ)
The Coll of New Rochelle (NY)
Coll of Saint Benedict (MN)
Coll of Saint Elizabeth (NJ)
Coll of Staten Island of the City U of New York (NY)
Coll of the Atlantic (ME)
Coll of the Holy Cross (MA)
The Coll of William and Mary (VA)
The Coll of Wooster (OH)
The Colorado Coll (CO)
Colorado School of Mines (CO)
Colorado State U (CO)
Columbia U (NY)
Columbia U, School of General Studies (NY)
Concordia U (CA)
Concordia U (QC, Canada)
Concordia U Wisconsin (WI)
Connecticut Coll (CT)
Converse Coll (SC)
Cornell Coll (IA)
Creighton U (NE)
Dalhousie U (NS, Canada)
Dartmouth Coll (NH)
Davidson Coll (NC)
DePaul U (IL)
DePauw U (IN)
DEREE—The American Coll of Greece (Greece)
Dickinson Coll (PA)
Dillard U (LA)
Doane Coll (NE)
Dominican Coll (NY)
Dominican U (IL)
Drew U (NJ)
Drury U (MO)
Duquesne U (PA)
Earlham Coll (IN)
East Carolina U (NC)
Eastern Illinois U (IL)
Eastern Mennonite U (VA)
Eastern Michigan U (MI)
Eastern Washington U (WA)
East Tennessee State U (TN)
Eckerd Coll (FL)
Edgewood Coll (WI)
Edinboro U of Pennsylvania (PA)
Elizabethtown Coll (PA)
Elmira Coll (NY)
Elon U (NC)
Emmanuel Coll (MA)
Emory & Henry Coll (VA)
Emporia State U (KS)
Eugene Lang Coll The New School for Liberal Arts (NY)
Excelsior Coll (NY)
Fairfield U (CT)

Fairleigh Dickinson U, Coll at Florham (NJ)
Fairleigh Dickinson U, Metropolitan Campus (NJ)
Fairmont State U (WV)
Florida Ag and Mech U (FL)
Florida Atlantic U (FL)
Florida Gulf Coast U (FL)
Florida Intl U (FL)
Florida Southern Coll (FL)
Florida State U (FL)
Fort Lewis Coll (CO)
Framingham State U (MA)
Francis Marion U (SC)
Franklin & Marshall Coll (PA)
Franklin Coll (IN)
Franklin U (OH)
Frostburg State U (MD)
Furman U (SC)
Gardner-Webb U (NC)
George Fox U (OR)
George Mason U (VA)
Georgetown Coll (KY)
Georgetown U (DC)
Georgia Southern U (GA)
Georgia State U (GA)
Gettysburg Coll (PA)
Goldey-Beacom Coll (DE)
Gonzaga U (WA)
Gordon Coll (MA)
Goucher Coll (MD)
Graceland U (IA)
Grand Valley State U (MI)
Grinnell Coll (IA)
Grove City Coll (PA)
Guilford Coll (NC)
Gustavus Adolphus Coll (MN)
Hamilton Coll (NY)
Hamline U (MN)
Hampden-Sydney Coll (VA)
Hampshire Coll (MA)
Hampton U (VA)
Hanover Coll (IN)
Harding U (AR)
Hardin-Simmons U (TX)
Hartwick Coll (NY)
Haverford Coll (PA)
Hawai`i Pacific U (HI)
Hendrix Coll (AR)
Hillsdale Coll (MI)
Hiram Coll (OH)
Hobart and William Smith Colls (NY)
Hofstra U (NY)
Hollins U (VA)
Hood Coll (MD)
Hope Coll (MI)
Humboldt State U (CA)
Hunter Coll of the City U of New York (NY)
Huntington U (IN)
Illinois Coll (IL)
Illinois State U (IL)
Illinois Wesleyan U (IL)
Immaculata U (PA)
Indiana State U (IN)
Indiana U Bloomington (IN)
Indiana U Northwest (IN)
Indiana U of Pennsylvania (PA)
Indiana U–Purdue U Fort Wayne (IN)
Indiana U–Purdue U Indianapolis (IN)
Indiana U South Bend (IN)
Indiana U Southeast (IN)
Indiana Wesleyan U (IN)
Inter American U of Puerto Rico, San Germán Campus (PR)
Iona Coll (NY)
Iowa State U of Science and Technology (IA)
Ithaca Coll (NY)
Jacksonville State U (AL)
James Madison U (VA)
John Brown U (AR)
John Cabot U (Italy)
John Carroll U (OH)
John Jay Coll of Criminal Justice of the City U of New York (NY)
The Johns Hopkins U (MD)
Johnson C. Smith U (NC)
Juniata Coll (PA)
Kalamazoo Coll (MI)
Kansas State U (KS)
Kean U (NJ)
Keene State Coll (NH)
Kenyon Coll (OH)

King Coll (TN)
King's Coll (PA)
Knox Coll (IL)
Lafayette Coll (PA)
Lamar U (TX)
Langston U (OK)
La Salle U (PA)
La Sierra U (CA)
Lawrence U (WI)
Lebanese American U (Lebanon)
Lebanon Valley Coll (PA)
Lehman Coll of the City U of New York (NY)
Le Moyne Coll (NY)
Lincoln Memorial U (TN)
Lindenwood U (MO)
Linfield Coll (OR)
Long Island U–Brooklyn Campus (NY)
Long Island U–C. W. Post Campus (NY)
Longwood U (VA)
Louisiana Coll (LA)
Louisiana State U and Ag and Mech Coll (LA)
Loyola Marymount U (CA)
Loyola U Maryland (MD)
Loyola U New Orleans (LA)
Lubbock Christian U (TX)
Luther Coll (IA)
Lynchburg Coll (VA)
Lyon Coll (AR)
Macalester Coll (MN)
Manchester U (IN)
Manhattan Coll (NY)
Manhattanville Coll (NY)
Mansfield U of Pennsylvania (PA)
Marietta Coll (OH)
Marist Coll (NY)
Marquette U (WI)
Marshall U (WV)
Mars Hill Coll (NC)
Mary Baldwin Coll (VA)
Marymount U (VA)
Maryville Coll (TN)
Massachusetts Inst of Technology (MA)
McDaniel Coll (MD)
McKendree U (IL)
Mercer U (GA)
Merrimack Coll (MA)
Messiah Coll (PA)
Metropolitan State U of Denver (CO)
Miami U (OH)
Michigan State U (MI)
Middlebury Coll (VT)
Middle Tennessee State U (TN)
Midwestern State U (TX)
Millersville U of Pennsylvania (PA)
Millsaps Coll (MS)
Mills Coll (CA)
Minnesota State U Mankato (MN)
Minnesota State U Moorhead (MN)
Mississippi State U (MS)
Missouri State U (MO)
Missouri U of Science and Technology (MO)
Missouri Western State U (MO)
Monmouth Coll (IL)
Montana State U (MT)
Montclair State U (NJ)
Moravian Coll (PA)
Morehouse Coll (GA)
Mount Allison U (NB, Canada)
Mount Holyoke Coll (MA)
Mount St. Mary's U (MD)
Muhlenberg Coll (PA)
Murray State U (KY)
Nazareth Coll of Rochester (NY)
New Coll of Florida (FL)
New Jersey City U (NJ)
New Mexico State U (NM)
New York Inst of Technology (NY)
New York U (NY)
Niagara U (NY)
North Central Coll (IL)
North Dakota State U (ND)
Northeastern Illinois U (IL)
Northeastern U (MA)
Northern Illinois U (IL)
Northern Michigan U (MI)
Northern State U (SD)
Northwestern Coll (IA)
Northwest Missouri State U (MO)
Norwich U (VT)
Oakland U (MI)

Oglethorpe U (GA)
Ohio Dominican U (OH)
The Ohio State U (OH)
Ohio U (OH)
Ohio Wesleyan U (OH)
Oklahoma City U (OK)
Oklahoma State U (OK)
Old Dominion U (VA)
Oregon State U (OR)
Pace U (NY)
Pacific Lutheran U (WA)
Pacific U (OR)
Park U (MO)
Penn State Abington (PA)
Penn State Altoona (PA)
Penn State Beaver (PA)
Penn State Berks (PA)
Penn State Brandywine (PA)
Penn State DuBois (PA)
Penn State Erie, The Behrend Coll (PA)
Penn State Fayette, The Eberly Campus (PA)
Penn State Greater Allegheny (PA)
Penn State Hazleton (PA)
Penn State Lehigh Valley (PA)
Penn State Mont Alto (PA)
Penn State New Kensington (PA)
Penn State Schuylkill (PA)
Penn State Shenango (PA)
Penn State U Park (PA)
Penn State Wilkes-Barre (PA)
Penn State Worthington Scranton (PA)
Penn State York (PA)
Pepperdine U, Malibu (CA)
Pittsburg State U (KS)
Pitzer Coll (CA)
Point Park U (PA)
Pomona Coll (CA)
Portland State U (OR)
Princeton U (NJ)
Principia Coll (IL)
Providence Coll (RI)
Purchase Coll, State U of New York (NY)
Purdue U (IN)
Quinnipiac U (CT)
Radford U (VA)
Ramapo Coll of New Jersey (NJ)
Randolph Coll (VA)
Randolph-Macon Coll (VA)
Reed Coll (OR)
Regis U (CO)
Rensselaer Polytechnic Inst (NY)
Rhode Island Coll (RI)
Rhodes Coll (TN)
Rice U (TX)
The Richard Stockton Coll of New Jersey (NJ)
Rider U (NJ)
Ripon Coll (WI)
Roanoke Coll (VA)
Robert Morris U (PA)
Rochester Inst of Technology (NY)
Rockford Coll (IL)
Rockhurst U (MO)
Roger Williams U (RI)
Rollins Coll (FL)
Roosevelt U (IL)
Rosemont Coll (PA)
Rowan U (NJ)
Rutgers, The State U of New Jersey, Camden (NJ)
Rutgers, The State U of New Jersey, Newark (NJ)
Rutgers, The State U of New Jersey, New Brunswick (NJ)
Saginaw Valley State U (MI)
St. Ambrose U (IA)
Saint Anselm Coll (NH)
St. Edward's U (TX)
St. Francis Coll (NY)
St. John Fisher Coll (NY)
Saint John's U (MN)
St. John's U (NY)
Saint Joseph's Coll (IN)
Saint Joseph's U (PA)
St. Lawrence U (NY)
Saint Mary's Coll (IN)
Saint Mary's Coll of California (CA)
St. Mary's Coll of Maryland (MD)
St. Mary's U (TX)
Saint Michael's Coll (VT)
St. Norbert Coll (WI)
St. Olaf Coll (MN)
St. Thomas U (FL)

St. Thomas U (NB, Canada)
Saint Vincent Coll (PA)
Salem State U (MA)
Salisbury U (MD)
Salve Regina U (RI)
Sam Houston State U (TX)
San Diego State U (CA)
San Francisco State U (CA)
San Jose State U (CA)
Scripps Coll (CA)
Seattle Pacific U (WA)
Seattle U (WA)
Seton Hill U (PA)
Sewanee: The U of the South (TN)
Shepherd U (WV)
Shippensburg U of Pennsylvania (PA)
Siena Coll (NY)
Simmons Coll (MA)
Simon Fraser U (BC, Canada)
Simpson Coll (IA)
Skidmore Coll (NY)
Slippery Rock U of Pennsylvania (PA)
Smith Coll (MA)
Sonoma State U (CA)
South Dakota State U (SD)
Southeast Missouri State U (MO)
Southern Connecticut State U (CT)
Southern Illinois U Carbondale (IL)
Southern Illinois U Edwardsville (IL)
Southern Methodist U (TX)
Southern New Hampshire U (NH)
Southern Oregon U (OR)
Southern Utah U (UT)
Southwestern U (TX)
Spelman Coll (GA)
Stanford U (CA)
State U of New York at Fredonia (NY)
State U of New York at New Paltz (NY)
State U of New York at Oswego (NY)
State U of New York at Plattsburgh (NY)
State U of New York Coll at Cortland (NY)
State U of New York Coll at Geneseo (NY)
State U of New York Coll at Potsdam (NY)
State U of New York Empire State Coll (NY)
Stephen F. Austin State U (TX)
Stetson U (FL)
Stonehill Coll (MA)
Stony Brook U, State U of New York (NY)
Suffolk U (MA)
Susquehanna U (PA)
Swarthmore Coll (PA)
Sweet Briar Coll (VA)
Syracuse U (NY)
Tarleton State U (TX)
Taylor U (IN)
Temple U (PA)
Texas A&M U (TX)
Texas A&M U–Commerce (TX)
Texas Christian U (TX)
Texas Lutheran U (TX)
Texas Southern U (TX)
Texas State U–San Marcos (TX)
Thomas Edison State Coll (NJ)
Thomas More Coll (KY)
Thompson Rivers U (BC, Canada)
Transylvania U (KY)
Trent U (ON, Canada)
Trinity Coll (CT)
Trinity U (TX)
Truman State U (MO)
Tufts U (MA)
Tulane U (LA)
Tuskegee U (AL)
Union U (TN)
United States Air Force Acad (CO)
United States Military Acad (NY)
United States Naval Acad (MD)
U at Albany, State U of New York (NY)
U at Buffalo, the State U of New York (NY)
The U of Akron (OH)
U of Alaska Anchorage (AK)
U of Alaska Fairbanks (AK)
The U of Arizona (AZ)

The U of British Columbia (BC, Canada)
The U of British Columbia–Okanagan (BC, Canada)
U of California, Berkeley (CA)
U of California, Davis (CA)
U of California, Irvine (CA)
U of California, Los Angeles (CA)
U of California, Merced (CA)
U of California, Riverside (CA)
U of California, Santa Barbara (CA)
U of California, Santa Cruz (CA)
U of Central Arkansas (AR)
U of Central Florida (FL)
U of Central Oklahoma (OK)
U of Chicago (IL)
U of Cincinnati (OH)
U of Colorado Boulder (CO)
U of Colorado Colorado Springs (CO)
U of Colorado Denver (CO)
U of Dallas (TX)
U of Delaware (DE)
U of Denver (CO)
U of Evansville (IN)
The U of Findlay (OH)
U of Florida (FL)
U of Guelph (ON, Canada)
U of Hartford (CT)
U of Hawaii at Hilo (HI)
U of Hawaii at Manoa (HI)
U of Hawaii–West Oahu (HI)
U of Houston (TX)
U of Idaho (ID)
U of Illinois at Chicago (IL)
U of Illinois at Springfield (IL)
U of Illinois at Urbana–Champaign (IL)
The U of Iowa (IA)
The U of Kansas (KS)
U of Kentucky (KY)
U of La Verne (CA)
U of Louisville (KY)
U of Maryland, Baltimore County (MD)
U of Maryland, Coll Park (MD)
U of Mary Washington (VA)
U of Massachusetts Amherst (MA)
U of Massachusetts Boston (MA)
U of Massachusetts Dartmouth (MA)
U of Memphis (TN)
U of Miami (FL)
U of Michigan (MI)
U of Michigan–Dearborn (MI)
U of Michigan–Flint (MI)
U of Minnesota, Duluth (MN)
U of Minnesota, Twin Cities Campus (MN)
U of Mississippi (MS)
U of Missouri (MO)
U of Missouri–Kansas City (MO)
U of Missouri–St. Louis (MO)
U of Mount Union (OH)
U of Nebraska at Kearney (NE)
U of Nebraska at Omaha (NE)
U of Nebraska–Lincoln (NE)
U of Nevada, Las Vegas (NV)
U of New Brunswick Fredericton (NB, Canada)
U of New Brunswick Saint John (NB, Canada)
U of New Hampshire (NH)
U of New Mexico (NM)
U of North Carolina at Asheville (NC)
The U of North Carolina at Chapel Hill (NC)
The U of North Carolina at Charlotte (NC)
The U of North Carolina at Greensboro (NC)
The U of North Carolina Wilmington (NC)
U of North Dakota (ND)
U of Northern Colorado (CO)
U of Northern Iowa (IA)
U of North Florida (FL)
U of North Texas (TX)
U of Notre Dame (IN)
U of Oklahoma (OK)
U of Oregon (OR)
U of Ottawa (ON, Canada)
U of Pennsylvania (PA)
U of Pittsburgh (PA)
U of Pittsburgh at Bradford (PA)
U of Portland (OR)

U of Puget Sound (WA)
U of Redlands (CA)
U of Regina (SK, Canada)
U of Rhode Island (RI)
U of Richmond (VA)
U of Rochester (NY)
U of St. Thomas (MN)
U of San Diego (CA)
U of Science and Arts of Oklahoma (OK)
The U of Scranton (PA)
U of South Alabama (AL)
U of South Carolina (SC)
The U of South Dakota (SD)
U of Southern California (CA)
U of Southern Indiana (IN)
U of Southern Maine (ME)
U of South Florida (FL)
The U of Tampa (FL)
The U of Tennessee (TN)
The U of Tennessee at Chattanooga (TN)
The U of Tennessee at Martin (TN)
The U of Texas at Arlington (TX)
The U of Texas at Austin (TX)
The U of Texas at Dallas (TX)
The U of Texas at El Paso (TX)
The U of Texas–Pan American (TX)
The U of the District of Columbia (DC)
U of the Ozarks (AR)
The U of Toledo (OH)
U of Tulsa (OK)
U of Utah (UT)
U of Vermont (VT)
U of Virginia (VA)
U of Waterloo (ON, Canada)
The U of Western Ontario (ON, Canada)
U of West Florida (FL)
U of West Georgia (GA)
U of Windsor (ON, Canada)
U of Wisconsin–Eau Claire (WI)
U of Wisconsin–Green Bay (WI)
U of Wisconsin–La Crosse (WI)
U of Wisconsin–Madison (WI)
U of Wisconsin–Milwaukee (WI)
U of Wisconsin–Parkside (WI)
U of Wisconsin–Platteville (WI)
U of Wisconsin–Stevens Point (WI)
U of Wisconsin–Superior (WI)
Utah State U (UT)
Utica Coll (NY)
Valparaiso U (IN)
Vanderbilt U (TN)
Vassar Coll (NY)
Villanova U (PA)
Virginia Polytechnic Inst and State U (VA)
Wabash Coll (IN)
Wagner Coll (NY)
Wake Forest U (NC)
Walla Walla U (WA)
Wartburg Coll (IA)
Washburn U (KS)
Washington & Jefferson Coll (PA)
Washington and Lee U (VA)
Washington Coll (MD)
Washington State U (WA)
Washington U in St. Louis (MO)
Wayne State U (MI)
Weber State U (UT)
Webster U (MO)
Wellesley Coll (MA)
Wells Coll (NY)
Wesleyan Coll (GA)
Wesleyan U (CT)
Western Connecticut State U (CT)
Western Illinois U (IL)
Western Kentucky U (KY)
Western Michigan U (MI)
Western Oregon U (OR)
Western State Colorado U (CO)
Western Washington U (WA)
Westfield State U (MA)
Westminster Coll (MO)
West Virginia State U (WV)
West Virginia U (WV)
West Virginia Wesleyan Coll (WV)
Wheaton Coll (IL)
Wheaton Coll (MA)
Whitman Coll (WA)
Whitworth U (WA)
Wichita State U (KS)
Widener U (PA)
Willamette U (OR)
William Jewell Coll (MO)
Williams Coll (MA)

Wittenberg U (OH)
Worcester Polytechnic Inst (MA)
Worcester State U (MA)
Wright State U (OH)
Xavier U (OH)
Yale U (CT)
York Coll of Pennsylvania (PA)
York Coll of the City U of New York (NY)
Youngstown State U (OH)

ECONOMICS RELATED
Agnes Scott Coll (GA)
California State U, Chico (CA)
Carnegie Mellon U (PA)
The Colorado Coll (CO)
Columbia U, School of General Studies (NY)
Muhlenberg Coll (PA)
Purdue U (IN)
Thompson Rivers U (BC, Canada)
U of Delaware (DE)
U of Illinois at Urbana–Champaign (IL)
U of Regina (SK, Canada)
U of West Georgia (GA)
Valparaiso U (IN)
Washington & Jefferson Coll (PA)
Western Washington U (WA)
Wheeling Jesuit U (WV)

EDUCATION
Acadia U (NS, Canada)
Alabama State U (AL)
Albertus Magnus Coll (CT)
Alma Coll (MI)
Alverno Coll (WI)
Anderson U (IN)
Andrews U (MI)
Ashland U (OH)
Auburn U (AL)
Augsburg Coll (MN)
Ball State U (IN)
The Baptist Coll of Florida (FL)
Barry U (FL)
Baylor U (TX)
Becker Coll (MA)
Belmont Abbey Coll (NC)
Belmont U (TN)
Bemidji State U (MN)
Bennington Coll (VT)
Berea Coll (KY)
Bethany Coll (WV)
Bethel Coll (IN)
Bethune-Cookman U (FL)
Bloomfield Coll (NJ)
Bluefield Coll (VA)
Bowie State U (MD)
Bowling Green State U (OH)
Bowling Green State U-Firelands Coll (OH)
Brock U (ON, Canada)
Brown U (RI)
Bucknell U (PA)
Cabrini Coll (PA)
California Baptist U (CA)
Canisius Coll (NY)
Cardinal Stritch U (WI)
Carson-Newman U (TN)
Catawba Coll (NC)
The Catholic U of America (DC)
Cedar Crest Coll (PA)
Central Methodist U (MO)
Chapman U (CA)
Cheyney U of Pennsylvania (PA)
Chipola Coll (FL)
Chowan U (NC)
Christian Brothers U (TN)
Cincinnati Christian U (OH)
City Coll of the City U of New York (NY)
Clark Atlanta U (GA)
Clarke U (IA)
Clark U (MA)
Coe Coll (IA)
Colgate U (NY)
The Coll at Brockport, State U of New York (NY)
The Coll of New Rochelle (NY)
Coll of Saint Mary (NE)
Coll of the Atlantic (ME)
Colorado State U (CO)
Concordia Coll (MN)
Concordia Coll–New York (NY)
Concordia U (OR)
Concordia U (QC, Canada)
Concordia U Chicago (IL)

Concordia U, Nebraska (NE)
Concordia U, St. Paul (MN)
Concordia U Wisconsin (WI)
Concord U (WV)
Converse Coll (SC)
Corban U (OR)
Cornerstone U (MI)
Crown Coll (MN)
Curry Coll (MA)
Dakota Wesleyan U (SD)
Defiance Coll (OH)
Dominican Coll (NY)
Dordt Coll (IA)
Duquesne U (PA)
Eastern New Mexico U (NM)
Eastern Washington U (WA)
East Texas Baptist U (TX)
Elmira Coll (NY)
Elon U (NC)
Emmanuel Coll (MA)
Eugene Lang Coll The New School for Liberal Arts (NY)
Fairmont State U (WV)
Faulkner U (AL)
Felician Coll (NJ)
Ferrum Coll (VA)
Florida Gulf Coast U (FL)
Framingham State U (MA)
Franklin Pierce U (NH)
Furman U (SC)
Gallaudet U (DC)
Gardner-Webb U (NC)
Georgia Southern U (GA)
Gettysburg Coll (PA)
Goddard Coll (VT)
Goshen Coll (IN)
Goucher Coll (MD)
Graceland U (IA)
Gustavus Adolphus Coll (MN)
Hamline U (MN)
Hampshire Coll (MA)
Hampton U (VA)
Hardin-Simmons U (TX)
Harrison Middleton U (AZ)
Haverford Coll (PA)
High Point U (NC)
Hillsdale Coll (MI)
Hiram Coll (OH)
Humboldt State U (CA)
Huntington U (IN)
Illinois Coll (IL)
Illinois Wesleyan U (IL)
Indiana U–Purdue U Fort Wayne (IN)
Indiana Wesleyan U (IN)
Inter American U of Puerto Rico, San Germán Campus (PR)
Iowa State U of Science and Technology (IA)
Iowa Wesleyan Coll (IA)
Jacksonville State U (AL)
John Brown U (AR)
John Carroll U (OH)
Johnson State Coll (VT)
Juniata Coll (PA)
Kansas Wesleyan U (KS)
Kent State U (OH)
King Coll (TN)
Knox Coll (IL)
Lake Superior State U (MI)
Lamar U (TX)
Langston U (OK)
La Salle U (PA)
Lasell Coll (MA)
Lebanese American U (Lebanon)
Lee U (TN)
Lesley U (MA)
Limestone Coll (SC)
Lincoln Memorial U (TN)
Lindenwood U (MO)
Lindsey Wilson Coll (KY)
Lipscomb U (TN)
Long Island U–Brooklyn Campus (NY)
Long Island U–C. W. Post Campus (NY)
Loyola U Maryland (MD)
Macalester Coll (MN)
Manchester U (IN)
Manhattan Coll (NY)
Manhattanville Coll (NY)
Mansfield U of Pennsylvania (PA)
Marietta Coll (OH)
Mars Hill Coll (NC)
Maryville Coll (TN)
Massachusetts Coll of Liberal Arts (MA)

The Master's Coll and Sem (CA)
Mayville State U (ND)
Mercyhurst U (PA)
Merrimack Coll (MA)
Miami Dade Coll (FL)
Michigan State U (MI)
Millsaps Coll (MS)
Minnesota State U Mankato (MN)
Mississippi Valley State U (MS)
Missouri Baptist U (MO)
Monmouth U (NJ)
Moravian Coll (PA)
Morehouse Coll (GA)
Mount Marty Coll (SD)
Mount Mary Coll (WI)
Mount St. Mary's Coll (CA)
Mount Vernon Nazarene U (OH)
National U (CA)
Nazareth Coll of Rochester (NY)
New England Coll (NH)
Newman U (KS)
New Mexico State U (NM)
Niagara U (NY)
North Carolina State U (NC)
North Carolina Wesleyan Coll (NC)
North Central Coll (IL)
Northern Illinois U (IL)
Northern State U (SD)
Northwest U (WA)
Nova Southeastern U (FL)
Oakland City U (IN)
Ohio Wesleyan U (OH)
Oklahoma Baptist U (OK)
Oklahoma City U (OK)
Oklahoma State U (OK)
Oregon State U (OR)
Ouachita Baptist U (AR)
Pacific Lutheran U (WA)
Pacific U (OR)
Paul Quinn Coll (TX)
Pepperdine U, Malibu (CA)
Purdue U (IN)
Purdue U Calumet (IN)
Queens U of Charlotte (NC)
Quinnipiac U (CT)
Regent U (VA)
Regis U (CO)
Ripon Coll (WI)
Rivier U (NH)
Rockford Coll (IL)
Roger Williams U (RI)
Rowan U (NJ)
Sacred Heart U (CT)
St. Ambrose U (IA)
Saint Louis U (MO)
Saint Mary's Coll (IN)
St. Mary's U (TX)
Saint Michael's Coll (VT)
St. Thomas Aquinas Coll (NY)
St. Thomas U (NB, Canada)
Salem Intl U (WV)
Salem State U (MA)
San Diego Christian Coll (CA)
Schreiner U (TX)
Seattle Pacific U (WA)
Shawnee State U (OH)
Simmons Coll (MA)
Simon Fraser U (BC, Canada)
Simpson Coll (IA)
Skidmore Coll (NY)
Smith Coll (MA)
Southern Nazarene U (OK)
Southern New Hampshire U (NH)
Southwestern U (TX)
Spalding U (KY)
State U of New York at Fredonia (NY)
State U of New York at New Paltz (NY)
State U of New York at Oswego (NY)
State U of New York at Plattsburgh (NY)
State U of New York Coll at Geneseo (NY)
State U of New York Empire State Coll (NY)
Stetson U (FL)
Suffolk U (MA)
Tarleton State U (TX)
Tennessee State U (TN)
Tennessee Wesleyan Coll (TN)
Texas A&M U–Commerce (TX)
Texas Lutheran U (TX)
Texas Wesleyan U (TX)
Thompson Rivers U (BC, Canada)
Trent U (ON, Canada)

Trine U (IN)
Trinity Coll (CT)
Union Coll (KY)
Union U (TN)
Université de Sherbrooke (QC, Canada)
Université du Québec en Outaouais (QC, Canada)
Université Sainte-Anne (NS, Canada)
U of Alaska Anchorage (AK)
U of Alaska Fairbanks (AK)
U of Arkansas at Little Rock (AR)
The U of British Columbia (BC, Canada)
The U of British Columbia–Okanagan (BC, Canada)
U of California, Santa Cruz (CA)
U of Charleston (WV)
U of Cincinnati (OH)
U of Dallas (TX)
The U of Findlay (OH)
U of Hawaii at Manoa (HI)
U of Houston–Victoria (TX)
U of Maine at Fort Kent (ME)
U of Maine at Machias (ME)
U of Maryland Eastern Shore (MD)
U of Massachusetts Amherst (MA)
U of Massachusetts Boston (MA)
U of Michigan–Dearborn (MI)
U of Minnesota, Duluth (MN)
U of Minnesota, Twin Cities Campus (MN)
U of Missouri (MO)
U of Missouri–St. Louis (MO)
The U of Montana Western (MT)
U of Nevada, Las Vegas (NV)
U of New Brunswick Fredericton (NB, Canada)
U of New Brunswick Saint John (NB, Canada)
U of Oregon (OR)
U of Pittsburgh at Greensburg (PA)
U of Portland (OR)
U of Redlands (CA)
U of Regina (SK, Canada)
U of Saint Mary (KS)
U of St. Thomas (TX)
The U of South Dakota (SD)
U of Southern California (CA)
The U of Toledo (OH)
U of Tulsa (OK)
U of Utah (UT)
U of Vermont (VT)
U of Washington, Bothell (WA)
The U of Western Ontario (ON, Canada)
U of Windsor (ON, Canada)
U of Wisconsin–Green Bay (WI)
U of Wisconsin–Milwaukee (WI)
U of Wisconsin–Platteville (WI)
U of Wisconsin–Stevens Point (WI)
U of Wisconsin–Superior (WI)
Upper Iowa U (IA)
Valley City State U (ND)
Vanderbilt U (TN)
Villanova U (PA)
Virginia Intermont Coll (VA)
Viterbo U (WI)
Wagner Coll (NY)
Walden U (MN)
Walsh U (OH)
Washburn U (KS)
Washington & Jefferson Coll (PA)
Washington State U (WA)
Washington U in St. Louis (MO)
Webster U (MO)
Wells Coll (NY)
Wesley Coll (DE)
Westfield State U (MA)
West Liberty U (WV)
West Virginia State U (WV)
West Virginia Wesleyan Coll (WV)
Wheeling Jesuit U (WV)
Wilkes U (PA)
William Paterson U of New Jersey (NJ)
William Peace U (NC)
William Penn U (IA)
Wittenberg U (OH)
Xavier U (OH)
Xavier U of Louisiana (LA)
Young Harris Coll (GA)
Youngstown State U (OH)

EDUCATIONAL ADMINISTRATION AND SUPERVISION RELATED
Canisius Coll (NY)
Purdue U (IN)
The U of Western Ontario (ON, Canada)

EDUCATIONAL ASSESSMENT, EVALUATION, AND RESEARCH RELATED
Penn State Altoona (PA)
Penn State Berks (PA)
Penn State U Park (PA)
Purdue U (IN)

EDUCATIONAL ASSESSMENT, TESTING, AND MEASUREMENT
Purdue U (IN)

EDUCATIONAL EVALUATION AND RESEARCH
Purdue U (IN)

EDUCATIONAL, INSTRUCTIONAL, AND CURRICULUM SUPERVISION
Canisius Coll (NY)
Purdue U (IN)
Wright State U (OH)

EDUCATIONAL/ INSTRUCTIONAL TECHNOLOGY
Bowling Green State U (OH)
Bridgewater State U (MA)
California State U, Chico (CA)
Cameron U (OK)
Canisius Coll (NY)
Eastern Washington U (WA)
Jacksonville State U (AL)
Midwestern State U (TX)
Purdue U (IN)
Texas A&M U–Commerce (TX)
U of Central Oklahoma (OK)
The U of Toledo (OH)
The U of Western Ontario (ON, Canada)
Wayne State U (MI)
Western Illinois U (IL)
Western Oregon U (OR)
Widener U (PA)

EDUCATIONAL LEADERSHIP AND ADMINISTRATION
Auburn U at Montgomery (AL)
Canisius Coll (NY)
DePaul U (IL)
Eastern Washington U (WA)
Lamar U (TX)
Lee U (TN)
Midwestern State U (TX)
Purdue U (IN)
Tarleton State U (TX)
Tennessee State U (TN)
Texas A&M U–Commerce (TX)
U of Central Oklahoma (OK)
U of Minnesota, Crookston (MN)
U of Regina (SK, Canada)
U of the Incarnate Word (TX)
Wright State U (OH)

EDUCATIONAL PSYCHOLOGY
DePaul U (IL)
Jacksonville State U (AL)
Mississippi State U (MS)
Purdue U (IN)
Saint Vincent Coll (PA)
Texas A&M U–Commerce (TX)
U of Pittsburgh (PA)
U of Regina (SK, Canada)

EDUCATIONAL STATISTICS AND RESEARCH METHODS
Bucknell U (PA)
Purdue U (IN)

EDUCATIONAL SYSTEM ADMINISTRATION AND SUPERINTENDENCY
Dordt Coll (IA)
Purdue U (IN)

EDUCATION (MULTIPLE LEVELS)
Adams State U (CO)
Augustana Coll (SD)
Austin Peay State U (TN)
Averett U (VA)
Bowling Green State U (OH)
Canisius Coll (NY)

Central State U (OH)
Coll of Coastal Georgia (GA)
Coll of Saint Elizabeth (NJ)
Coll of Saint Mary (NE)
The Coll of St. Scholastica (MN)
Columbia Intl U (SC)
Columbia U (NY)
Concordia U Chicago (IL)
Concordia U Wisconsin (WI)
Dakota Wesleyan U (SD)
DePaul U (IL)
Dominican U (IL)
Dordt Coll (IA)
Eastern Washington U (WA)
Felician Coll (NJ)
Gannon U (PA)
Gardner-Webb U (NC)
Geneva Coll (PA)
Goddard Coll (VT)
Grace U (NE)
Hamline U (MN)
Harding U (AR)
Hillsdale Coll (MI)
Hofstra U (NY)
Illinois Coll (IL)
Indiana U Bloomington (IN)
Indiana Wesleyan U (IN)
Ithaca Coll (NY)
John Carroll U (OH)
Juniata Coll (PA)
Keystone Coll (PA)
Lake Superior State U (MI)
Lindenwood U (MO)
Lubbock Christian U (TX)
Manchester U (IN)
Manhattan Coll (NY)
Martin Luther Coll (MN)
McKendree U (IL)
Merrimack Coll (MA)
Mount Mary Coll (WI)
Mount Saint Mary Coll (NY)
New England Coll (NH)
Northland Coll (WI)
Northwest Christian U (OR)
Northwestern Coll (IA)
Nyack Coll (NY)
Ohio Dominican U (OH)
Ohio Wesleyan U (OH)
Purdue U (IN)
Purdue U Calumet (IN)
Quincy U (IL)
Rhode Island Coll (RI)
The Richard Stockton Coll of New Jersey (NJ)
Roger Williams U (RI)
St. Ambrose U (IA)
Saint Mary-of-the-Woods Coll (IN)
Samford U (AL)
San Diego Christian Coll (CA)
Shawnee State U (OH)
Tarleton State U (TX)
Tennessee Wesleyan Coll (TN)
Texas Lutheran U (TX)
Troy U (AL)
U of Great Falls (MT)
U of Illinois at Urbana–Champaign (IL)
U of Louisiana at Lafayette (LA)
U of Louisville (KY)
U of Maine at Fort Kent (ME)
U of Memphis (TN)
U of Minnesota, Duluth (MN)
The U of Montana Western (MT)
U of Nebraska–Lincoln (NE)
U of North Alabama (AL)
U of Puerto Rico at Bayamón (PR)
U of South Florida (FL)
The U of Tennessee at Martin (TN)
The U of Toledo (OH)
The U of West Alabama (AL)
U of Windsor (ON, Canada)
Utah State U (UT)
Virginia Wesleyan Coll (VA)
Wake Forest U (NC)
Walla Walla U (WA)
Washington State U (WA)
Washington U in St. Louis (MO)
Wayland Baptist U (TX)
Western Kentucky U (KY)
West Virginia Wesleyan Coll (WV)
William Jewell Coll (MO)
Wright State U (OH)

EDUCATION POLICY ANALYSIS
Purdue U (IN)

EDUCATION RELATED
Arizona State U (AZ)
Bowling Green State U (OH)
Brigham Young U (UT)
Cedarville U (OH)
Central State U (OH)
Concordia U, St. Paul (MN)
DePaul U (IL)
Edgewood Coll (WI)
The Evergreen State Coll (WA)
Lee U (TN)
Lindsey Wilson Coll (KY)
Mercer U (GA)
Midwestern State U (TX)
Mount Holyoke Coll (MA)
Mount Mary Coll (WI)
Northwest Missouri State U (MO)
Northwest Nazarene U (ID)
Park U (MO)
Point Park U (PA)
Prescott Coll (AZ)
Purdue U (IN)
Quincy U (IL)
Saginaw Valley State U (MI)
Saint Mary-of-the-Woods Coll (IN)
Saint Mary's U of Minnesota (MN)
State U of New York Coll at Potsdam (NY)
Sterling Coll (VT)
Swarthmore Coll (PA)
Thomas More Coll (KY)
Thompson Rivers U (BC, Canada)
U of Minnesota, Duluth (MN)
U of Minnesota, Twin Cities Campus (MN)
U of Nevada, Reno (NV)
U of Waterloo (ON, Canada)
Vanderbilt U (TN)
Waldorf U (IA)
Wayne State U (MI)
Wright State U (OH)

EDUCATION (SPECIFIC LEVELS AND METHODS) RELATED
Anderson U (SC)
Boston U (MA)
Brigham Young U (UT)
Colorado State U (CO)
Columbia Coll Chicago (IL)
Concordia Coll–New York (NY)
Immaculata U (PA)
Inter American U of Puerto Rico, San Germán Campus (PR)
John Brown U (AR)
Lynchburg Coll (VA)
Purdue U (IN)
Roger Williams U (RI)
Rowan U (NJ)
The U of Toledo (OH)
Washington U in St. Louis (MO)
Weber State U (UT)
Western Washington U (WA)
Wright State U (OH)
Xavier U (OH)

EDUCATION (SPECIFIC SUBJECT AREAS) RELATED
Appalachian State U (NC)
Averett U (VA)
Avila U (MO)
Baylor U (TX)
Bowling Green State U (OH)
Brigham Young U (UT)
Central Michigan U (MI)
The Coll of Saint Rose (NY)
Columbia Coll Chicago (IL)
Eastern Michigan U (MI)
Gardner-Webb U (NC)
Graceland U (IA)
Hope Coll (MI)
Indiana U Bloomington (IN)
Madonna U (MI)
Marywood U (PA)
Minot State U (ND)
Mississippi State U (MS)
Missouri State U (MO)
Missouri Western State U (MO)
Molloy Coll (NY)
Murray State U (KY)
Northern Michigan U (MI)
Old Dominion U (VA)
Plymouth State U (NH)
Point Park U (PA)
Purdue U (IN)
Regent U (VA)
St. Edward's U (TX)
Taylor U (IN)

U of Central Oklahoma (OK)
U of Kentucky (KY)
U of Michigan–Flint (MI)
U of Nebraska–Lincoln (NE)
U of New Hampshire (NH)
The U of North Carolina Wilmington (NC)
U of Ottawa (ON, Canada)
U of Regina (SK, Canada)
The U of Toledo (OH)
U of Wisconsin–Eau Claire (WI)
U of Wisconsin–Stout (WI)
Utah State U (UT)
Wayne State Coll (NE)
Weber State U (UT)
Western Washington U (WA)
Wright State U (OH)

ELECTRICAL AND ELECTRONIC ENGINEERING TECHNOLOGIES RELATED
Penn State Berks (PA)
Pennsylvania Coll of Technology (PA)
Pittsburg State U (KS)
Point Park U (PA)
Purdue U (IN)
Rochester Inst of Technology (NY)
Southern Illinois U Carbondale (IL)
Vaughn Coll of Aeronautics and Technology (NY)
Virginia State U (VA)
Wayne State U (MI)
West Virginia U Inst of Technology (WV)

ELECTRICAL AND ELECTRONICS ENGINEERING
The American U in Cairo (Egypt)
American U of Beirut (Lebanon)
Arizona State U (AZ)
Arkansas State U (AR)
Arkansas Tech U (AR)
Auburn U (AL)
Baylor U (TX)
Binghamton U, State U of New York (NY)
Bloomsburg U of Pennsylvania (PA)
Boise State U (ID)
Boston U (MA)
Bradley U (IL)
Brown U (RI)
Bucknell U (PA)
California Polytechnic State U, San Luis Obispo (CA)
California State Polytechnic U, Pomona (CA)
California State U, Chico (CA)
California State U, Fresno (CA)
California State U, Fullerton (CA)
California State U, Long Beach (CA)
California State U, Los Angeles (CA)
California State U, Northridge (CA)
Calvin Coll (MI)
Caribbean U (PR)
Carnegie Mellon U (PA)
Case Western Reserve U (OH)
The Catholic U of America (DC)
Cedarville U (OH)
Central Connecticut State U (CT)
Central Michigan U (MI)
Christian Brothers U (TN)
The Citadel, The Military Coll of South Carolina (SC)
City Coll of the City U of New York (NY)
Clarkson U (NY)
Clemson U (SC)
Cleveland State U (OH)
The Coll of New Jersey (NJ)
Colorado School of Mines (CO)
Colorado State U (CO)
Columbia U (NY)
Concordia U (QC, Canada)
Cooper Union for the Advancement of Science and Art (NY)
Dalhousie U (NS, Canada)
Dominican U (IL)
Dordt Coll (IA)
Eastern Washington U (WA)
Embry-Riddle Aeronautical U–Daytona (FL)
Embry-Riddle Aeronautical U–Prescott (AZ)
Fairfield U (CT)

Fairleigh Dickinson U, Metropolitan Campus (NJ)
Florida Ag and Mech U (FL)
Florida Atlantic U (FL)
Florida Inst of Technology (FL)
Florida Intl U (FL)
Franklin W. Olin Coll of Eng (MA)
Gannon U (PA)
George Fox U (OR)
George Mason U (VA)
Georgia Southern U (GA)
Gonzaga U (WA)
Grove City Coll (PA)
Hampton U (VA)
Harding U (AR)
Hofstra U (NY)
Hope Coll (MI)
Illinois Inst of Technology (IL)
Indiana Tech (IN)
Indiana U–Purdue U Fort Wayne (IN)
Indiana U–Purdue U Indianapolis (IN)
Inter American U of Puerto Rico, Bayamón Campus (PR)
Iowa State U of Science and Technology (IA)
John Brown U (AR)
The Johns Hopkins U (MD)
Kansas State U (KS)
Lafayette Coll (PA)
Lake Superior State U (MI)
Lamar U (TX)
Lawrence Technological U (MI)
Lebanese American U (Lebanon)
Lehigh U (PA)
LeTourneau U (TX)
Liberty U (VA)
Louisiana State U and Ag and Mech Coll (LA)
Loyola Marymount U (CA)
Manhattan Coll (NY)
Marquette U (WI)
Massachusetts Inst of Technology (MA)
Merrimack Coll (MA)
Miami U (OH)
Michigan State U (MI)
Milwaukee School of Eng (WI)
Minnesota State U Mankato (MN)
Mississippi State U (MS)
Missouri U of Science and Technology (MO)
Montana State U (MT)
Montana Tech of The U of Montana (MT)
New England Inst of Technology (RI)
New Jersey Inst of Technology (NJ)
New Mexico Highlands U (NM)
New Mexico Inst of Mining and Technology (NM)
New Mexico State U (NM)
New York Inst of Technology (NY)
Norfolk State U (VA)
North Carolina State U (NC)
North Dakota State U (ND)
Northeastern U (MA)
Northern Arizona U (AZ)
Northern Illinois U (IL)
Norwich U (VT)
Oakland U (MI)
The Ohio State U (OH)
Ohio U (OH)
Oklahoma Christian U (OK)
Oklahoma State U (OK)
Old Dominion U (VA)
Oral Roberts U (OK)
Oregon State U (OR)
Penn State Abington (PA)
Penn State Altoona (PA)
Penn State Beaver (PA)
Penn State Berks (PA)
Penn State Brandywine (PA)
Penn State DuBois (PA)
Penn State Erie, The Behrend Coll (PA)
Penn State Fayette, The Eberly Campus (PA)
Penn State Greater Allegheny (PA)
Penn State Harrisburg (PA)
Penn State Hazleton (PA)
Penn State Lehigh Valley (PA)
Penn State Mont Alto (PA)
Penn State New Kensington (PA)
Penn State Schuylkill (PA)
Penn State Shenango (PA)

Penn State U Park (PA)
Penn State Wilkes-Barre (PA)
Penn State Worthington Scranton (PA)
Penn State York (PA)
Polytechnic Inst of New York U (NY)
Polytechnic U of Puerto Rico (PR)
Portland State U (OR)
Princeton U (NJ)
Purdue U (IN)
Purdue U Calumet (IN)
Purdue U North Central (IN)
Rensselaer Polytechnic Inst (NY)
Rice U (TX)
Rochester Inst of Technology (NY)
Rockhurst U (MO)
Rowan U (NJ)
Rutgers, The State U of New Jersey, New Brunswick (NJ)
Saginaw Valley State U (MI)
Saint Louis U (MO)
St. Mary's U (TX)
San Diego State U (CA)
San Francisco State U (CA)
San Jose State U (CA)
Seattle Pacific U (WA)
Seattle U (WA)
South Dakota State U (SD)
Southern California Inst of Technology (CA)
Southern Illinois U Carbondale (IL)
Southern Illinois U Edwardsville (IL)
Southern Methodist U (TX)
Southern Polytechnic State U (GA)
Stanford U (CA)
State U of New York at New Paltz (NY)
State U of New York Inst of Technology (NY)
State U of New York Maritime Coll (NY)
Stony Brook U, State U of New York (NY)
Suffolk U (MA)
Syracuse U (NY)
Temple U (PA)
Tennessee State U (TN)
Texas A&M U (TX)
Texas A&M U–Kingsville (TX)
Texas State U–San Marcos (TX)
Trine U (IN)
Trinity Coll (CT)
Tufts U (MA)
Tulane U (LA)
Tuskegee U (AL)
United States Air Force Acad (CO)
United States Coast Guard Acad (CT)
United States Military Acad (NY)
United States Naval Acad (MD)
Université de Sherbrooke (QC, Canada)
U at Buffalo, the State U of New York (NY)
The U of Akron (OH)
The U of Alabama (AL)
The U of Alabama at Birmingham (AL)
U of Alaska Fairbanks (AK)
The U of British Columbia (BC, Canada)
The U of British Columbia–Okanagan (BC, Canada)
U of California, Berkeley (CA)
U of California, Davis (CA)
U of California, Irvine (CA)
U of California, Los Angeles (CA)
U of California, Riverside (CA)
U of California, Santa Barbara (CA)
U of California, Santa Cruz (CA)
U of Central Florida (FL)
U of Cincinnati (OH)
U of Colorado Boulder (CO)
U of Colorado Colorado Springs (CO)
U of Colorado Denver (CO)
U of Delaware (DE)
U of Denver (CO)
U of Evansville (IN)
U of Florida (FL)
U of Hartford (CT)
U of Hawaii at Manoa (HI)
U of Houston (TX)
U of Idaho (ID)
U of Illinois at Chicago (IL)

U of Illinois at Urbana–Champaign (IL)
The U of Iowa (IA)
The U of Kansas (KS)
U of Kentucky (KY)
U of Louisiana at Lafayette (LA)
U of Louisville (KY)
U of Maryland, Coll Park (MD)
U of Massachusetts Amherst (MA)
U of Massachusetts Dartmouth (MA)
U of Memphis (TN)
U of Miami (FL)
U of Michigan (MI)
U of Michigan–Dearborn (MI)
U of Minnesota, Duluth (MN)
U of Minnesota, Twin Cities Campus (MN)
U of Mississippi (MS)
U of Missouri (MO)
U of Missouri–Kansas City (MO)
U of Missouri–St. Louis (MO)
U of Nebraska–Lincoln (NE)
U of Nevada, Las Vegas (NV)
U of Nevada, Reno (NV)
U of New Brunswick Fredericton (NB, Canada)
U of New Hampshire (NH)
U of New Haven (CT)
U of New Mexico (NM)
U of New Orleans (LA)
The U of North Carolina at Charlotte (NC)
U of North Dakota (ND)
U of North Florida (FL)
U of North Texas (TX)
U of Notre Dame (IN)
U of Oklahoma (OK)
U of Ottawa (ON, Canada)
U of Pennsylvania (PA)
U of Pittsburgh (PA)
U of Portland (OR)
U of Regina (SK, Canada)
U of Rhode Island (RI)
U of Rochester (NY)
U of St. Thomas (MN)
The U of Scranton (PA)
U of South Alabama (AL)
U of South Carolina (SC)
U of Southern California (CA)
U of Southern Maine (ME)
U of South Florida (FL)
The U of Tennessee (TN)
The U of Tennessee at Chattanooga (TN)
The U of Texas at Arlington (TX)
The U of Texas at Austin (TX)
The U of Texas at Dallas (TX)
The U of Texas at El Paso (TX)
The U of Texas at San Antonio (TX)
The U of Texas–Pan American (TX)
U of the District of Columbia (DC)
The U of Toledo (OH)
U of Tulsa (OK)
U of Utah (UT)
U of Vermont (VT)
U of Virginia (VA)
U of Washington, Bothell (WA)
U of Waterloo (ON, Canada)
The U of Western Ontario (ON, Canada)
U of West Florida (FL)
U of Windsor (ON, Canada)
U of Wisconsin–Madison (WI)
U of Wisconsin–Milwaukee (WI)
U of Wisconsin–Platteville (WI)
U of Wyoming (WY)
Utah State U (UT)
Valparaiso U (IN)
Vanderbilt U (TN)
Villanova U (PA)
Virginia Commonwealth U (VA)
Virginia Polytechnic Inst and State U (VA)
Walla Walla U (WA)
Washington State U (WA)
Washington U in St. Louis (MO)
Wayne State U (MI)
Wentworth Inst of Technology (MA)
Western Carolina U (NC)
Western Kentucky U (KY)
Western Michigan U (MI)
West Virginia U (WV)
West Virginia U Inst of Technology (WV)
Wichita State U (KS)

Widener U (PA)
Wilberforce U (OH)
Wilkes U (PA)
Worcester Polytechnic Inst (MA)
Wright State U (OH)
Yale U (CT)
York Coll of Pennsylvania (PA)
Youngstown State U (OH)

ELECTRICAL, ELECTRONIC AND COMMUNICATIONS ENGINEERING TECHNOLOGY
Arizona State U (AZ)
Bluefield State Coll (WV)
Bowling Green State U (OH)
Buffalo State Coll, State U of New York (NY)
California State Polytechnic U, Pomona (CA)
California State U, Long Beach (CA)
Caribbean U (PR)
Cleveland State U (OH)
Daytona State Coll (FL)
DeVry Coll of New York (NY)
DeVry U, Phoenix (AZ)
DeVry U, Pomona (CA)
DeVry U, Westminster (CO)
DeVry U, Miramar (FL)
DeVry U, Orlando (FL)
DeVry U, Decatur (GA)
DeVry U, Chicago (IL)
DeVry U, Kansas City (MO)
DeVry U, North Brunswick (NJ)
DeVry U, Columbus (OH)
DeVry U, Fort Washington (PA)
DeVry U, Houston (TX)
DeVry U, Irving (TX)
DeVry U, Arlington (VA)
DeVry U, Federal Way (WA)
DeVry U Online (IL)
Eastern Michigan U (MI)
Fairleigh Dickinson U, Metropolitan Campus (NJ)
Fairmont State U (WV)
Farmingdale State Coll (NY)
Ferris State U (MI)
Florida Ag and Mech U (FL)
Georgia Southern U (GA)
Grantham U (MO)
Hampton U (VA)
Indiana State U (IN)
Indiana U–Purdue U Fort Wayne (IN)
Indiana U–Purdue U Indianapolis (IN)
Inter American U of Puerto Rico, Aguadilla Campus (PR)
Inter American U of Puerto Rico, Bayamón Campus (PR)
Inter American U of Puerto Rico, San Germán Campus (PR)
Jacksonville State U (AL)
Kansas State U (KS)
Lake Superior State U (MI)
LeTourneau U (TX)
Metropolitan State U of Denver (CO)
Miami Dade Coll (FL)
Milwaukee School of Eng (WI)
Minnesota State U Mankato (MN)
Missouri Western State U (MO)
Morehead State U (KY)
New England Inst of Technology (RI)
New York Inst of Technology (NY)
Norfolk State U (VA)
Northwestern State U of Louisiana (LA)
Oklahoma State U (OK)
Penn State Erie, The Behrend Coll (PA)
Purdue U (IN)
Purdue U Calumet (IN)
Roger Williams U (RI)
South Dakota State U (SD)
Southern Polytechnic State U (GA)
State U of New York Coll of Technology at Alfred (NY)
State U of New York Inst of Technology (NY)
Texas A&M U (TX)
Texas Southern U (TX)
Thomas Edison State Coll (NJ)
Troy U (AL)
The U of Akron (OH)
U of Arkansas at Little Rock (AR)

U of Hartford (CT)
U of Houston (TX)
U of Maryland Eastern Shore (MD)
U of Memphis (TN)
U of New Hampshire (NH)
U of New Hampshire at Manchester (NH)
The U of North Carolina at Charlotte (NC)
U of North Texas (TX)
U of Puerto Rico at Bayamón (PR)
U of Regina (SK, Canada)
U of Southern Mississippi (MS)
The U of Texas at Brownsville (TX)
The U of Toledo (OH)
Valencia Coll (FL)
Vaughn Coll of Aeronautics and Technology (NY)
Vermont Tech Coll (VT)
Wayne State U (MI)
Wentworth Inst of Technology (MA)
Western Carolina U (NC)
Western Washington U (WA)
Youngstown State U (OH)

ELECTRICAL, ELECTRONICS AND COMMUNICATIONS ENGINEERING RELATED
The U of Arizona (AZ)

ELECTRICAL/ELECTRONICS EQUIPMENT INSTALLATION AND REPAIR
Lewis-Clark State Coll (ID)

ELECTRICAL/ELECTRONICS MAINTENANCE AND REPAIR TECHNOLOGY RELATED
Sullivan Coll of Technology and Design (KY)

ELECTROMECHANICAL AND INSTRUMENTATION AND MAINTENANCE TECHNOLOGIES RELATED
Sullivan Coll of Technology and Design (KY)

ELECTROMECHANICAL ENGINEERING
Wentworth Inst of Technology (MA)

ELECTROMECHANICAL TECHNOLOGY
Bowling Green State U (OH)
Buffalo State Coll, State U of New York (NY)
Excelsior Coll (NY)
John Brown U (AR)
Murray State U (KY)
Rochester Inst of Technology (NY)
State U of New York Coll of Technology at Alfred (NY)
Temple U (PA)
U of Northern Iowa (IA)
The U of Toledo (OH)
Vermont Tech Coll (VT)
Wayne State U (MI)

ELEMENTARY AND MIDDLE SCHOOL ADMINISTRATION/ PRINCIPALSHIP
Berea Coll (KY)
Piedmont Coll (GA)
Purdue U (IN)

ELEMENTARY EDUCATION
Abilene Christian U (TX)
Acadia U (NS, Canada)
Alabama State U (AL)
Alaska Pacific U (AK)
Albright Coll (PA)
Alcorn State U (MS)
Alderson-Broaddus Coll (WV)
Alfred U (NY)
Alice Lloyd Coll (KY)
Alma Coll (MI)
Alverno Coll (WI)
American U (DC)
American U of Beirut (Lebanon)
American U of Puerto Rico (PR)
Anderson U (IN)
Anderson U (SC)
Andrews U (MI)
Appalachian State U (NC)
Arizona Christian U (AZ)
Arizona State U (AZ)
Asbury U (KY)
Ashland U (OH)
Assumption Coll (MA)
Athens State U (AL)

Auburn U (AL)
Auburn U at Montgomery (AL)
Augsburg Coll (MN)
Augustana Coll (IL)
Augustana Coll (SD)
Aurora U (IL)
Avila U (MO)
Baker U (KS)
Ball State U (IN)
The Baptist Coll of Florida (FL)
Barclay Coll (KS)
Barry U (FL)
Barton Coll (NC)
Baylor U (TX)
Bay Path Coll (MA)
Becker Coll (MA)
Belhaven U (MS)
Bellarmine U (KY)
Belmont Abbey Coll (NC)
Belmont U (TN)
Bemidji State U (MN)
Benedictine Coll (KS)
Benedictine U (IL)
Bennington Coll (VT)
Bethany Lutheran Coll (MN)
Bethel Coll (IN)
Bethel Coll (KS)
Bethel U (MN)
Bethune-Cookman U (FL)
Blackburn Coll (IL)
Bluefield Coll (VA)
Bluefield State Coll (WV)
Blue Mountain Coll (MS)
Bluffton U (OH)
Bob Jones U (SC)
Boise State U (ID)
Boston Coll (MA)
Boston U (MA)
Bowie State U (MD)
Bowling Green State U (OH)
Bradley U (IL)
Bridgewater State U (MA)
Brock U (ON, Canada)
Bryn Athyn Coll of the New Church (PA)
Bucknell U (PA)
Buena Vista U (IA)
Buffalo State Coll, State U of New York (NY)
Butler U (IN)
Cabrini Coll (PA)
Cairn U (PA)
Caldwell Coll (NJ)
Calumet Coll of Saint Joseph (IN)
Calvin Coll (MI)
Cameron U (OK)
Campbellsville U (KY)
Canisius Coll (NY)
Cardinal Stritch U (WI)
Caribbean U (PR)
Carlos Albizu U, Miami Campus (FL)
Carroll Coll (MT)
Carson-Newman U (TN)
Castleton State Coll (VT)
Catawba Coll (NC)
The Catholic U of America (DC)
Cedar Crest Coll (PA)
Central Coll (IA)
Central Connecticut State U (CT)
Central Methodist U (MO)
Centre Coll (KY)
Champlain Coll (VT)
Chatham U (PA)
Chestnut Hill Coll (PA)
Cheyney U of Pennsylvania (PA)
Chicago State U (IL)
Chowan U (NC)
Christian Brothers U (TN)
City Coll of the City U of New York (NY)
City U of Seattle (WA)
Claflin U (SC)
Clarion U of Pennsylvania (PA)
Clark U (MA)
Clearwater Christian Coll (FL)
Clemson U (SC)
Coastal Carolina U (SC)
Coe Coll (IA)
The Coll at Brockport, State U of New York (NY)
Coll of Charleston (SC)
The Coll of New Jersey (NJ)
The Coll of New Rochelle (NY)
Coll of Saint Benedict (MN)
Coll of Saint Mary (NE)
The Coll of Saint Rose (NY)

The Coll of St. Scholastica (MN)
Coll of Staten Island of the City U of New York (NY)
Coll of the Atlantic (ME)
Coll of the Ozarks (MO)
Columbia Coll (SC)
Columbia Intl U (SC)
Concordia Coll (MN)
Concordia Coll Alabama (AL)
Concordia Coll–New York (NY)
Concordia U (OR)
Concordia U (QC, Canada)
Concordia U Chicago (IL)
Concordia U, Nebraska (NE)
Concordia U, St. Paul (MN)
Concordia U Texas (TX)
Concordia U Wisconsin (WI)
Concord U (WV)
Converse Coll (SC)
Corban U (OR)
Cornell Coll (IA)
Cornerstone U (MI)
Covenant Coll (GA)
Creighton U (NE)
Crown Coll (MN)
Culver-Stockton Coll (MO)
Curry Coll (MA)
Dakota State U (SD)
Dakota Wesleyan U (SD)
Dallas Baptist U (TX)
Dalton State Coll (GA)
Daytona State Coll (FL)
Defiance Coll (OH)
Delta State U (MS)
DePaul U (IL)
DePauw U (IN)
DeSales U (PA)
Doane Coll (NE)
Dominican Coll (NY)
Dominican U (IL)
Dordt Coll (IA)
Drake U (IA)
Drury U (MO)
East Carolina U (NC)
East Central U (OK)
Eastern Illinois U (IL)
Eastern Michigan U (MI)
Eastern New Mexico U (NM)
East Texas Baptist U (TX)
Edgewood Coll (WI)
Edinboro U of Pennsylvania (PA)
Elizabeth City State U (NC)
Elmira Coll (NY)
Elon U (NC)
Emmanuel Coll (GA)
Emmanuel Coll (MA)
Emporia State U (KS)
Endicott Coll (MA)
Evangel U (MO)
Fairmont State U (WV)
Faith Baptist Bible Coll and Theological Sem (IA)
Faulkner U (AL)
Fayetteville State U (NC)
Felician Coll (NJ)
Five Towns Coll (NY)
Flagler Coll (FL)
Florida Ag and Mech U (FL)
Florida Atlantic U (FL)
Florida Coll (FL)
Florida Gulf Coast U (FL)
Florida Intl U (FL)
Florida Southern Coll (FL)
Fort Lewis Coll (CO)
Francis Marion U (SC)
Franklin Coll (IN)
Franklin Pierce U (NH)
Friends U (KS)
Frostburg State U (MD)
Furman U (SC)
Gannon U (PA)
Gardner-Webb U (NC)
Geneva Coll (PA)
George Fox U (OR)
Georgetown Coll (KY)
Georgia Southern U (GA)
Georgia Southwestern State U (GA)
Gettysburg Coll (PA)
Goddard Coll (VT)
Gonzaga U (WA)
Gordon Coll (MA)
Gordon State Coll (GA)
Goshen Coll (IN)
Governors State U (IL)
Graceland U (IA)
Grace U (NE)

Grambling State U (LA)
Grand Valley State U (MI)
Grand View U (IA)
Granite State Coll (NH)
Greenville Coll (IL)
Grove City Coll (PA)
Guilford Coll (NC)
Gustavus Adolphus Coll (MN)
Hamline U (MN)
Hampton U (VA)
Hanover Coll (IN)
Harding U (AR)
Harris-Stowe State U (MO)
Hawai`i Pacific U (HI)
High Point U (NC)
Hillsdale Coll (MI)
Hillsdale Free Will Baptist Coll (OK)
Hofstra U (NY)
Holy Cross Coll (IN)
Holy Family U (PA)
Hope Intl U (CA)
Houghton Coll (NY)
Howard Payne U (TX)
Hunter Coll of the City U of New York (NY)
Huntingdon Coll (AL)
Huntington U (IN)
Husson U (ME)
Illinois Coll (IL)
Illinois State U (IL)
Illinois Wesleyan U (IL)
Immaculata U (PA)
Indiana State U (IN)
Indiana Tech (IN)
Indiana U Bloomington (IN)
Indiana U East (IN)
Indiana U Kokomo (IN)
Indiana U Northwest (IN)
Indiana U of Pennsylvania (PA)
Indiana U–Purdue U Fort Wayne (IN)
Indiana U–Purdue U Indianapolis (IN)
Indiana U South Bend (IN)
Indiana U Southeast (IN)
Indiana Wesleyan U (IN)
Inter American U of Puerto Rico, Aguadilla Campus (PR)
Inter American U of Puerto Rico, Fajardo Campus (PR)
Inter American U of Puerto Rico, Ponce Campus (PR)
Inter American U of Puerto Rico, San Germán Campus (PR)
Iona Coll (NY)
Iowa State U of Science and Technology (IA)
Iowa Wesleyan Coll (IA)
Jacksonville State U (AL)
Jamestown Coll (ND)
Jarvis Christian Coll (TX)
John Brown U (AR)
John Carroll U (OH)
Johnson State Coll (VT)
Jones Coll, Jacksonville (FL)
Judson Coll (AL)
Judson U (IL)
Juniata Coll (PA)
Kansas State U (KS)
Kansas Wesleyan U (KS)
Kean U (NJ)
Keene State Coll (NH)
Kennesaw State U (GA)
Kentucky Christian U (KY)
Kentucky State U (KY)
Kentucky Wesleyan Coll (KY)
Keuka Coll (NY)
King's Coll (PA)
The King's U Coll (AB, Canada)
Kingswood U (NB, Canada)
Knox Coll (IL)
Kutztown U of Pennsylvania (PA)
Kuyper Coll (MI)
Lakeland Coll (WI)
Lake Superior State U (MI)
Lamar U (TX)
Lander U (SC)
Langston U (OK)
La Roche Coll (PA)
La Salle U (PA)
Lasell Coll (MA)
Laurel U (NC)
Lees-McRae Coll (NC)
Le Moyne Coll (NY)
Lesley U (MA)
LeTourneau U (TX)

Lewis-Clark State Coll (ID)
Lewis U (IL)
Limestone Coll (SC)
Lincoln Memorial U (TN)
Lincoln U (MO)
Lindenwood U (MO)
Lindsey Wilson Coll (KY)
Linfield Coll (OR)
Lipscomb U (TN)
Lock Haven U of Pennsylvania (PA)
Long Island U–Brooklyn Campus (NY)
Long Island U–C. W. Post Campus (NY)
Louisiana Coll (LA)
Louisiana State U and Ag and Mech Coll (LA)
Louisiana State U at Alexandria (LA)
Louisiana State U in Shreveport (LA)
Loyola U Chicago (IL)
Loyola U Maryland (MD)
Lubbock Christian U (TX)
Luther Coll (IA)
Lynchburg Coll (VA)
Lynn U (FL)
Madonna U (MI)
Maharishi U of Management (IA)
Manchester U (IN)
Manhattan Coll (NY)
Manhattanville Coll (NY)
Mansfield U of Pennsylvania (PA)
Maranatha Baptist Bible Coll (WI)
Marian U (WI)
Marietta Coll (OH)
Marquette U (WI)
Marshall U (WV)
Mars Hill Coll (NC)
Martin Luther Coll (MN)
Marymount U (VA)
Maryville U of Saint Louis (MO)
Marywood U (PA)
The Master's Coll and Sem (CA)
Mayville State U (ND)
McKendree U (IL)
McMurry U (TX)
McNeese State U (LA)
Medaille Coll (NY)
Mercer U (GA)
Mercyhurst U (PA)
Merrimack Coll (MA)
Messiah Coll (PA)
Michigan State U (MI)
Mid-Atlantic Christian U (NC)
Mid-Continent U (KY)
Millersville U of Pennsylvania (PA)
Millikin U (IL)
Minnesota State U Mankato (MN)
Minnesota State U Moorhead (MN)
Minot State U (ND)
Misericordia U (PA)
Mississippi Coll (MS)
Mississippi State U (MS)
Mississippi U for Women (MS)
Mississippi Valley State U (MS)
Missouri Baptist U (MO)
Missouri State U (MO)
Missouri Western State U (MO)
Mitchell Coll (CT)
Molloy Coll (NY)
Monmouth Coll (NJ)
Montana State U (MT)
Montreat Coll, Montreat (NC)
Moravian Coll (PA)
Morehead State U (KY)
Morningside Coll (IA)
Morris Coll (SC)
Mount Marty Coll (SD)
Mount Mary Coll (WI)
Mount Mercy U (IA)
Mount St. Mary's Coll (CA)
Mount St. Mary's U (MD)
Multnomah U (OR)
Murray State U (KY)
National U (CA)
Nazareth Coll of Rochester (NY)
Neumann U (PA)
Newberry Coll (SC)
New England Coll (NH)
New Jersey City U (NJ)
Newman U (KS)
New Mexico Highlands U (NM)
New Mexico State U (NM)
New York U (NY)
Niagara U (NY)
Nicholls State U (LA)

North Carolina Central U (NC)
North Carolina State U (NC)
North Carolina Wesleyan Coll (NC)
North Central Coll (IL)
Northeastern Illinois U (IL)
Northern Arizona U (AZ)
Northern Illinois U (IL)
Northern Michigan U (MI)
Northern State U (SD)
North Greenville U (SC)
Northwestern Coll (IA)
Northwestern Coll (MN)
Northwestern Oklahoma State U (OK)
Northwestern State U of Louisiana (LA)
Northwest Missouri State U (MO)
Northwest Nazarene U (ID)
Northwest U (WA)
Nova Southeastern U (FL)
Nyack Coll (NY)
Oakland City U (IN)
Oakland U (MI)
The Ohio State U at Lima (OH)
The Ohio State U at Marion (OH)
The Ohio State U–Mansfield Campus (OH)
The Ohio State U–Newark Campus (OH)
Ohio U–Zanesville (OH)
Ohio Valley U (WV)
Ohio Wesleyan U (OH)
Oklahoma Baptist U (OK)
Oklahoma Christian U (OK)
Oklahoma City U (OK)
Oklahoma State U (OK)
Oral Roberts U (OK)
Pace U (NY)
Pacific Union Coll (CA)
Pacific U (OR)
Paine Coll (GA)
Palm Beach Atlantic U (FL)
Park U (MO)
Penn State Abington (PA)
Penn State Altoona (PA)
Penn State Beaver (PA)
Penn State Berks (PA)
Penn State Brandywine (PA)
Penn State DuBois (PA)
Penn State Erie, The Behrend Coll (PA)
Penn State Fayette, The Eberly Campus (PA)
Penn State Greater Allegheny (PA)
Penn State Harrisburg (PA)
Penn State Hazleton (PA)
Penn State Lehigh Valley (PA)
Penn State Mont Alto (PA)
Penn State New Kensington (PA)
Penn State Schuylkill (PA)
Penn State Shenango (PA)
Penn State U Park (PA)
Penn State Wilkes-Barre (PA)
Penn State Worthington Scranton (PA)
Penn State York (PA)
Pepperdine U, Malibu (CA)
Pittsburg State U (KS)
Plymouth State U (NH)
Point Park U (PA)
Presbyterian Coll (SC)
Prescott Coll (AZ)
Principia Coll (IL)
Purdue U (IN)
Purdue U Calumet (IN)
Purdue U North Central (IN)
Queens U of Charlotte (NC)
Quincy U (IL)
Regis U (CO)
Rhode Island Coll (RI)
Rider U (NJ)
Ripon Coll (WI)
Rivier U (NH)
Robert Morris U (IL)
Rockford Coll (IL)
Rockhurst U (MO)
Rocky Mountain Coll (MT)
Roger Williams U (RI)
Rollins Coll (FL)
Roosevelt U (IL)
Rosemont Coll (PA)
Rowan U (NJ)
Russell Sage Coll (NY)
Sacred Heart U (CT)
Saginaw Valley State U (MI)
St. Ambrose U (IA)
St. Andrews U (NC)

Saint Anselm Coll (NH)
St. Bonaventure U (NY)
St. Gregory's U, Shawnee (OK)
St. John Fisher Coll (NY)
Saint John's U (MN)
St. John's U (NY)
Saint Joseph's Coll (IN)
St. Joseph's Coll, Long Island Campus (NY)
St. Joseph's Coll, New York (NY)
Saint Joseph's U (PA)
Saint Leo U (FL)
Saint Louis U (MO)
Saint Martin's U (WA)
Saint Mary-of-the-Woods Coll (IN)
Saint Mary's Coll (IN)
Saint Mary's U of Minnesota (MN)
Saint Michael's Coll (VT)
St. Norbert Coll (WI)
St. Thomas Aquinas Coll (NY)
St. Thomas U (FL)
Saint Vincent Coll (PA)
Salem State U (MA)
Salisbury U (MD)
Salve Regina U (RI)
San Diego Christian Coll (CA)
Schreiner U (TX)
Seton Hill U (PA)
Shaw U (NC)
Shepherd U (WV)
Siena Heights U (MI)
Simmons Coll (MA)
Simpson Coll (IA)
Skidmore Coll (NY)
Slippery Rock U of Pennsylvania (PA)
Southeastern Louisiana U (LA)
Southeastern Oklahoma State U (OK)
Southeastern U (FL)
Southeast Missouri State U (MO)
Southern Connecticut State U (CT)
Southern Illinois U Carbondale (IL)
Southern Illinois U Edwardsville (IL)
Southern Nazarene U (OK)
Southern New Hampshire U (NH)
Southern Utah U (UT)
Southwest Baptist U (MO)
Southwestern Adventist U (TX)
Southwestern Coll (KS)
Spalding U (KY)
Spring Arbor U (MI)
Spring Hill Coll (AL)
State U of New York at Fredonia (NY)
State U of New York at New Paltz (NY)
State U of New York at Oswego (NY)
State U of New York at Plattsburgh (NY)
State U of New York Coll at Cortland (NY)
State U of New York Coll at Geneseo (NY)
State U of New York Coll at Old Westbury (NY)
State U of New York Coll at Potsdam (NY)
Sterling Coll (KS)
Stetson U (FL)
Stevenson U (MD)
Sul Ross State U (TX)
Susquehanna U (PA)
Tabor Coll (KS)
Tarleton State U (TX)
Taylor U (IN)
Temple U (PA)
Tennessee State U (TN)
Tennessee Wesleyan Coll (TN)
Texas A&M U–Commerce (TX)
Texas Christian U (TX)
Texas Lutheran U (TX)
Thomas More Coll (KY)
Thompson Rivers U (BC, Canada)
Transylvania U (KY)
Trent U (ON, Canada)
Trevecca Nazarene U (TN)
Trine U (IN)
Trinity Christian Coll (IL)
Trinity Coll of Florida (FL)
Troy U (AL)
Tufts U (MA)
Tuskegee U (AL)
Union Coll (KY)
Union Coll (NE)

Union U (TN)
Universidad Adventista de las Antillas (PR)
Université de Sherbrooke (QC, Canada)
Université du Québec en Outaouais (QC, Canada)
Université Sainte-Anne (NS, Canada)
The U of Alabama (AL)
The U of Alabama at Birmingham (AL)
U of Alaska Anchorage (AK)
U of Alaska Anchorage, Kenai Peninsula Coll (AK)
U of Alaska Fairbanks (AK)
The U of Arizona (AZ)
U of Arkansas at Little Rock (AR)
The U of British Columbia (BC, Canada)
U of Central Florida (FL)
U of Central Oklahoma (OK)
U of Charleston (WV)
U of Cincinnati (OH)
U of Dallas (TX)
U of Delaware (DE)
U of Evansville (IN)
The U of Findlay (OH)
U of Florida (FL)
U of Great Falls (MT)
U of Guam (GU)
U of Hartford (CT)
U of Hawaii at Hilo (HI)
U of Hawaii at Manoa (HI)
U of Hawaii–West Oahu (HI)
U of Idaho (ID)
U of Illinois at Chicago (IL)
U of Illinois at Urbana–Champaign (IL)
The U of Iowa (IA)
The U of Kansas (KS)
U of Kentucky (KY)
U of Louisiana at Lafayette (LA)
U of Louisiana at Monroe (LA)
U of Louisville (KY)
U of Maine at Farmington (ME)
U of Maine at Fort Kent (ME)
U of Maine at Machias (ME)
U of Maryland, Coll Park (MD)
U of Maryland Eastern Shore (MD)
U of Miami (FL)
U of Michigan (MI)
U of Michigan–Dearborn (MI)
U of Michigan–Flint (MI)
U of Minnesota, Twin Cities Campus (MN)
U of Mississippi (MS)
U of Missouri (MO)
U of Missouri–Kansas City (MO)
U of Missouri–St. Louis (MO)
U of Mobile (AL)
The U of Montana Western (MT)
U of Montevallo (AL)
U of Nebraska at Kearney (NE)
U of Nebraska at Omaha (NE)
U of Nebraska–Lincoln (NE)
U of Nevada, Las Vegas (NV)
U of Nevada, Reno (NV)
U of New Brunswick Fredericton (NB, Canada)
U of New England (ME)
U of New Mexico (NM)
U of New Orleans (LA)
U of North Alabama (AL)
The U of North Carolina at Chapel Hill (NC)
The U of North Carolina at Charlotte (NC)
The U of North Carolina at Greensboro (NC)
The U of North Carolina at Pembroke (NC)
The U of North Carolina Wilmington (NC)
U of North Dakota (ND)
U of Northern Iowa (IA)
U of North Florida (FL)
U of Oklahoma (OK)
U of Pennsylvania (PA)
U of Pikeville (KY)
U of Pittsburgh at Bradford (PA)
U of Portland (OR)
U of Puerto Rico at Ponce (PR)
U of Redlands (CA)
U of Regina (SK, Canada)
U of Rhode Island (RI)
U of St. Francis (IL)

U of Saint Mary (KS)
U of St. Thomas (TX)
U of Science and Arts of Oklahoma (OK)
The U of Scranton (PA)
U of South Alabama (AL)
U of South Carolina (SC)
U of South Carolina Aiken (SC)
U of South Carolina Upstate (SC)
The U of South Dakota (SD)
U of Southern Indiana (IN)
U of Southern Mississippi (MS)
U of South Florida (FL)
The U of Tampa (FL)
The U of Tennessee at Martin (TN)
U of the Cumberlands (KY)
U of the District of Columbia (DC)
U of the Incarnate Word (TX)
U of the Ozarks (AR)
U of the Virgin Islands (VI)
The U of Toledo (OH)
U of Tulsa (OK)
U of Utah (UT)
U of Vermont (VT)
The U of West Alabama (AL)
The U of Western Ontario (ON, Canada)
U of West Florida (FL)
U of West Georgia (GA)
U of Windsor (ON, Canada)
U of Wisconsin–Eau Claire (WI)
U of Wisconsin–La Crosse (WI)
U of Wisconsin–Madison (WI)
U of Wisconsin–Platteville (WI)
U of Wisconsin–Stevens Point (WI)
U of Wisconsin–Superior (WI)
U of Wyoming (WY)
Upper Iowa U (IA)
Utah State U (UT)
Utica Coll (NY)
Valley City State U (ND)
Valparaiso U (IN)
Vanderbilt U (TN)
Virginia Intermont Coll (VA)
Virginia Union U (VA)
Virginia Wesleyan Coll (VA)
Viterbo U (WI)
Wagner Coll (NY)
Waldorf Coll (IA)
Walla Walla U (WA)
Warner Pacific Coll (OR)
Wartburg Coll (IA)
Washburn U (KS)
Washington State U (WA)
Washington U in St. Louis (MO)
Wayland Baptist U (TX)
Waynesburg U (PA)
Wayne State Coll (NE)
Wayne State U (MI)
Weber State U (UT)
Webster U (MO)
Wells Coll (NY)
West Chester U of Pennsylvania (PA)
Western Carolina U (NC)
Western Connecticut State U (CT)
Western Illinois U (IL)
Western Kentucky U (KY)
Western Michigan U (MI)
Western Washington U (WA)
Westfield State U (MA)
West Liberty U (WV)
Westminster Coll (MO)
Westminster Coll (UT)
West Texas A&M U (TX)
West Virginia State U (WV)
West Virginia U (WV)
West Virginia Wesleyan Coll (WV)
Wheaton Coll (IL)
Wheeling Jesuit U (WV)
Whitworth U (WA)
Wichita State U (KS)
Widener U (PA)
Wilkes U (PA)
William Jewell Coll (MO)
William Paterson U of New Jersey (NJ)
William Penn U (IA)
Winthrop U (SC)
Worcester State U (MA)
Wright State U (OH)
Xavier U (OH)
Xavier U of Louisiana (LA)
York Coll of the City U of New York (NY)
Youngstown State U (OH)

ELEMENTARY PARTICLE PHYSICS
Purdue U (IN)

EMERGENCY MEDICAL TECHNOLOGY (EMT PARAMEDIC)
Colorado Mesa U (CO)
Concordia U Chicago (IL)
Creighton U (NE)
Loyola U Chicago (IL)
U of Maryland, Baltimore County (MD)
U of New Mexico (NM)
Western Carolina U (NC)

ENERGY MANAGEMENT AND SYSTEMS TECHNOLOGY
Creighton U (NE)
Ferris State U (MI)
Illinois State U (IL)
Lamar U (TX)
State U of New York Coll of Technology at Canton (NY)
Unity Coll (ME)
Vermont Tech Coll (VT)

ENGINEERING
Abilene Christian U (TX)
Albion Coll (MI)
Arizona State U (AZ)
Arkansas State U (AR)
Auburn U (AL)
Ball State U (IN)
Barry U (FL)
Bates Coll (ME)
Baylor U (TX)
Benedictine Coll (KS)
Bethany Lutheran Coll (MN)
Bethel Coll (IN)
Binghamton U, State U of New York (NY)
Boston U (MA)
Brown U (RI)
Buffalo State Coll, State U of New York (NY)
California Baptist U (CA)
California State Polytechnic U, Pomona (CA)
California State U, Long Beach (CA)
California State U, Los Angeles (CA)
Calvin Coll (MI)
Carnegie Mellon U (PA)
Case Western Reserve U (OH)
The Catholic U of America (DC)
Clarkson U (NY)
Clark U (MA)
Coll of Staten Island of the City U of New York (NY)
Colorado School of Mines (CO)
Cooper Union for the Advancement of Science and Art (NY)
Dalhousie U (NS, Canada)
Dartmouth Coll (NH)
Daytona State Coll (FL)
Dominican U (IL)
Dordt Coll (IA)
East Carolina U (NC)
Elizabethtown Coll (PA)
Elon U (NC)
Florida Inst of Technology (FL)
Franklin W. Olin Coll of Eng (MA)
Frostburg State U (MD)
Geneva Coll (PA)
George Fox U (OR)
Gonzaga U (WA)
Grand Valley State U (MI)
Harvey Mudd Coll (CA)
Hiram Coll (OH)
Hope Coll (MI)
Indiana U–Purdue U Indianapolis (IN)
Inter American U of Puerto Rico, Bayamón Campus (PR)
Inter American U of Puerto Rico, San Germán Campus (PR)
Iowa State U of Science and Technology (IA)
James Madison U (VA)
John Brown U (AR)
The Johns Hopkins U (MD)
Kansas Wesleyan U (KS)
Kent State U (OH)
Kent State U at Tuscarawas (OH)
King Coll (TN)
Lafayette Coll (PA)

LaGrange Coll (GA)
LeTourneau U (TX)
Liberty U (VA)
Loyola U Maryland (MD)
Lubbock Christian U (TX)
Maine Maritime Acad (ME)
Manchester U (IN)
Manhattan Coll (NY)
Marshall U (WV)
Maryville Coll (TN)
Massachusetts Maritime Acad (MA)
McKendree U (IL)
McNeese State U (LA)
Mercer U (GA)
Messiah Coll (PA)
Miami U (OH)
Michigan State U (MI)
Mills Coll (CA)
Milwaukee School of Eng (WI)
Missouri U of Science and Technology (MO)
Montana State U (MT)
Montana Tech of The U of Montana (MT)
New Mexico Highlands U (NM)
North Carolina State U (NC)
Northeastern U (MA)
Northland Coll (WI)
Northwestern Coll (MN)
Oglethorpe U (GA)
The Ohio State U (OH)
Oklahoma Christian U (OK)
Old Dominion U (VA)
Oral Roberts U (OK)
Pacific Lutheran U (WA)
Purdue U (IN)
Purdue U Calumet (IN)
Quinnipiac U (CT)
Rensselaer Polytechnic Inst (NY)
Robert Morris U (PA)
Rochester Inst of Technology (NY)
Roger Williams U (RI)
Rutgers, The State U of New Jersey, Camden (NJ)
Rutgers, The State U of New Jersey, Newark (NJ)
Saint Anselm Coll (NH)
Saint Louis U (MO)
Saint Mary's Coll of California (CA)
St. Thomas U (FL)
Saint Vincent Coll (PA)
San Jose State U (CA)
Schreiner U (TX)
Seattle Pacific U (WA)
Spelman Coll (GA)
Stanford U (CA)
Stony Brook U, State U of New York (NY)
Swarthmore Coll (PA)
Syracuse U (NY)
Tennessee State U (TN)
Texas Christian U (TX)
Trinity Coll (CT)
Tufts U (MA)
United States Air Force Acad (CO)
United States Naval Acad (MD)
U at Buffalo, the State U of New York (NY)
The U of Akron (OH)
U of Alaska Anchorage (AK)
U of Alaska Fairbanks (AK)
U of California, Irvine (CA)
U of Cincinnati (OH)
U of Delaware (DE)
U of Denver (CO)
U of Hartford (CT)
U of Illinois at Urbana–Champaign (IL)
The U of Iowa (IA)
U of Louisville (KY)
U of Maryland, Baltimore County (MD)
U of Michigan (MI)
U of Minnesota, Duluth (MN)
U of Minnesota, Twin Cities Campus (MN)
U of Mississippi (MS)
U of Missouri–Kansas City (MO)
U of Nebraska–Lincoln (NE)
U of New Brunswick Fredericton (NB, Canada)
U of New Brunswick Saint John (NB, Canada)
U of New Haven (CT)
U of North Carolina at Asheville (NC)

MAJORS LISTING

U of Oklahoma (OK)
U of Portland (OR)
U of Regina (SK, Canada)
U of Rochester (NY)
U of Southern Indiana (IN)
U of South Florida (FL)
The U of Tennessee at
Chattanooga (TN)
The U of Tennessee at Martin (TN)
The U of Toledo (OH)
U of Utah (UT)
U of Virginia (VA)
The U of Western Ontario (ON,
Canada)
U of Windsor (ON, Canada)
Vaughn Coll of Aeronautics and
Technology (NY)
Wake Forest U (NC)
Walla Walla U (WA)
Wartburg Coll (IA)
Washington U in St. Louis (MO)
Weber State U (UT)
Wells Coll (NY)
Wentworth Inst of Technology (MA)
Western Illinois U (IL)
Widener U (PA)
Wilkes U (PA)
Youngstown State U (OH)

ENGINEERING ACOUSTICS
Purdue U (IN)

ENGINEERING CHEMISTRY
Oakland U (MI)
Purdue U (IN)

ENGINEERING DESIGN
Purdue U (IN)

ENGINEERING FIELDS RELATED
California State U, Chico (CA)
Purdue U (IN)

ENGINEERING/INDUSTRIAL MANAGEMENT
Arizona State U (AZ)
California State U, Chico (CA)
California State U, Long Beach
(CA)
Claremont McKenna Coll (CA)
Clarkson U (NY)
Clemson U (SC)
Columbia U (NY)
Eastern Michigan U (MI)
Farmingdale State Coll (NY)
Fort Lewis Coll (CO)
Grantham U (MO)
Grove City Coll (PA)
Illinois Inst of Technology (IL)
John Brown U (AR)
Lake Superior State U (MI)
Lawrence Technological U (MI)
Massachusetts Maritime Acad
(MA)
Miami U (OH)
Middle Tennessee State U (TN)
Missouri State U (MO)
Missouri U of Science and
Technology (MO)
Morehead State U (KY)
National U (CA)
Polytechnic Inst of New York U
(NY)
Purdue U (IN)
Purdue U Calumet (IN)
Saginaw Valley State U (MI)
South Dakota State U (SD)
Stanford U (CA)
State U of New York Coll of
Technology at Canton (NY)
Sweet Briar Coll (VA)
United States Merchant Marine
Acad (NY)
United States Military Acad (NY)
The U of Arizona (AZ)
U of Illinois at Chicago (IL)
U of Michigan–Flint (MI)
U of Portland (OR)
The U of Scranton (PA)
The U of Tennessee at
Chattanooga (TN)
U of the Incarnate Word (TX)
U of Vermont (VT)
Washburn U (KS)
Western Michigan U (MI)
Widener U (PA)
Wilkes U (PA)
Worcester Polytechnic Inst (MA)

ENGINEERING MECHANICS
Carroll Coll (MT)
Clemson U (SC)
Columbia U (NY)
Dordt Coll (IA)
Fairfield U (CT)
The Johns Hopkins U (MD)
Lehigh U (PA)
Lipscomb U (TN)
Purdue U (IN)
United States Air Force Acad (CO)
U of Illinois at Urbana–Champaign
(IL)
U of Windsor (ON, Canada)
U of Wisconsin–Madison (WI)
Virginia Polytechnic Inst and State
U (VA)
Worcester Polytechnic Inst (MA)

ENGINEERING PHYSICS/ APPLIED PHYSICS
Adams State U (CO)
Arkansas Tech U (AR)
Augustana Coll (IL)
Augustana Coll (SD)
Belmont U (TN)
Bemidji State U (MN)
Bradley U (IL)
Brown U (RI)
Case Western Reserve U (OH)
Christian Brothers U (TN)
Colorado School of Mines (CO)
Colorado State U (CO)
Columbia U (NY)
Dartmouth Coll (NH)
Eastern Michigan U (MI)
Embry-Riddle Aeronautical U–
Daytona (FL)
Fairfield U (CT)
Fort Lewis Coll (CO)
Illinois Inst of Technology (IL)
John Carroll U (OH)
Juniata Coll (PA)
Kutztown U of Pennsylvania (PA)
Lehigh U (PA)
Loyola Marymount U (CA)
Miami U (OH)
Mississippi Coll (MS)
Morehouse Coll (GA)
Morningside Coll (IA)
Murray State U (KY)
New Mexico State U (NM)
Northwest Nazarene U (ID)
Oakland U (MI)
The Ohio State U (OH)
Oral Roberts U (OK)
Oregon State U (OR)
Point Loma Nazarene U (CA)
Providence Coll (RI)
Purdue U (IN)
Randolph Coll (VA)
Rensselaer Polytechnic Inst (NY)
St. Ambrose U (IA)
Saint Louis U (MO)
Saint Mary's U of Minnesota (MN)
Samford U (AL)
Southeast Missouri State U (MO)
Tarleton State U (TX)
Taylor U (IN)
Trevecca Nazarene U (TN)
Tufts U (MA)
U at Buffalo, the State U of New
York (NY)
The U of British Columbia (BC,
Canada)
U of California, Berkeley (CA)
U of Colorado Boulder (CO)
U of Illinois at Chicago (IL)
U of Illinois at Urbana–Champaign
(IL)
The U of Kansas (KS)
U of Massachusetts Boston (MA)
U of Michigan (MI)
U of Nevada, Reno (NV)
U of Northern Iowa (IA)
U of Oklahoma (OK)
U of Pittsburgh (PA)
The U of Texas at Brownsville (TX)
The U of Toledo (OH)
U of Tulsa (OK)
The U of Western Ontario (ON,
Canada)
U of Wisconsin–Madison (WI)
U of Wisconsin–Platteville (WI)
Washington and Lee U (VA)
Worcester Polytechnic Inst (MA)
Wright State U (OH)

Yale U (CT)

ENGINEERING RELATED
Agnes Scott Coll (GA)
Alfred U (NY)
Anderson U (SC)
Arizona State U (AZ)
Auburn U (AL)
Boston U (MA)
California State U, Chico (CA)
California State U, Long Beach
(CA)
Carnegie Mellon U (PA)
The Coll of Idaho (ID)
Eastern Illinois U (IL)
Gettysburg Coll (PA)
Hawai'i Pacific U (HI)
Indiana Tech (IN)
Indiana U–Purdue U Indianapolis
(IN)
Iowa State U of Science and
Technology (IA)
Kentucky Wesleyan Coll (KY)
Lehigh U (PA)
Maryville U of Saint Louis (MO)
Milwaukee School of Eng (WI)
Mississippi State U (MS)
Norfolk State U (VA)
Northern Michigan U (MI)
Oakland U (MI)
The Ohio State U (OH)
Ohio Wesleyan U (OH)
Park U (MO)
Penn State Altoona (PA)
Penn State Berks (PA)
Penn State U Park (PA)
Principia Coll (IL)
Purdue U (IN)
Rochester Inst of Technology (NY)
State U of New York at Oswego
(NY)
Transylvania U (KY)
Tufts U (MA)
U of California, Davis (CA)
U of Delaware (DE)
U of Maryland, Coll Park (MD)
U of Michigan–Dearborn (MI)
U of Pennsylvania (PA)
U of the Cumberlands (KY)
U of Waterloo (ON, Canada)
U of Wisconsin–Platteville (WI)
Waynesburg U (PA)
Wentworth Inst of Technology (MA)
Western Michigan U (MI)
Wheaton Coll (IL)
Worcester Polytechnic Inst (MA)
Wright State U (OH)
York Coll of Pennsylvania (PA)

ENGINEERING-RELATED TECHNOLOGIES
Purdue U (IN)
Rochester Inst of Technology (NY)
United States Merchant Marine
Acad (NY)

ENGINEERING SCIENCE
Abilene Christian U (TX)
Belmont U (TN)
Benedictine U (IL)
Bethel U (MN)
Bob Jones U (SC)
California Polytechnic State U, San
Luis Obispo (CA)
The Coll of New Jersey (NJ)
Colorado State U (CO)
Hofstra U (NY)
Iowa State U of Science and
Technology (IA)
Lamar U (TX)
Lipscomb U (TN)
Morehouse Coll (GA)
New Jersey Inst of Technology (NJ)
Ohio Wesleyan U (OH)
Penn State Abington (PA)
Penn State Altoona (PA)
Penn State Beaver (PA)
Penn State Berks (PA)
Penn State Brandywine (PA)
Penn State DuBois (PA)
Penn State Erie, The Behrend Coll
(PA)
Penn State Fayette, The Eberly
Campus (PA)
Penn State Greater Allegheny (PA)
Penn State Hazleton (PA)
Penn State Lehigh Valley (PA)
Penn State Mont Alto (PA)

Penn State New Kensington (PA)
Penn State Schuylkill (PA)
Penn State Shenango (PA)
Penn State U Park (PA)
Penn State Wilkes-Barre (PA)
Penn State Worthington Scranton
(PA)
Penn State York (PA)
Purdue U (IN)
Rensselaer Polytechnic Inst (NY)
Rutgers, The State U of New
Jersey, New Brunswick (NJ)
St. Mary's U (TX)
St. Thomas Aquinas Coll (NY)
Simon Fraser U (BC, Canada)
Smith Coll (MA)
Sonoma State U (CA)
Southern Utah U (UT)
Sweet Briar Coll (VA)
Trinity U (TX)
Tufts U (MA)
Tulane U (LA)
United States Air Force Acad (CO)
U of California, Berkeley (CA)
U of Miami (FL)
U of Michigan (MI)
U of Michigan–Flint (MI)
U of New Mexico (NM)
U of Pittsburgh (PA)
U of Portland (OR)
U of Rochester (NY)
U of South Carolina (SC)
U of the Cumberlands (KY)
The U of Western Ontario (ON,
Canada)
Vanderbilt U (TN)
Wartburg Coll (IA)
Wheeling Jesuit U (WV)
Wright State U (OH)
Yale U (CT)

ENGINEERING TECHNOLOGIES AND ENGINEERING RELATED
Arkansas State U (AR)
Ball State U (IN)
Bowling Green State U (OH)
Cameron U (OK)
East Carolina U (NC)
Eastern Washington U (WA)
Elizabeth City State U (NC)
Keene State Coll (NH)
Northwest Missouri State U (MO)
Old Dominion U (VA)
Pennsylvania Coll of Technology
(PA)
Purdue U (IN)
Rogers State U (OK)
Shawnee State U (OH)
Thomas Edison State Coll (NJ)
United States Military Acad (NY)
The U of British Columbia (BC,
Canada)
U of Hartford (CT)
U of Minnesota, Twin Cities
Campus (MN)
The U of North Carolina at
Charlotte (NC)
The U of West Alabama (AL)

ENGINEERING TECHNOLOGY
Austin Peay State U (TN)
Berry Coll (GA)
Buffalo State Coll, State U of New
York (NY)
California State Polytechnic U,
Pomona (CA)
California State U, Long Beach
(CA)
Dordt Coll (IA)
Eastern New Mexico U (NM)
East Tennessee State U (TN)
Fairmont State U (WV)
Grambling State U (LA)
Indiana State U (IN)
Kent State U (OH)
Kent State U at Tuscarawas (OH)
Lawrence Technological U (MI)
LeTourneau U (TX)
Maine Maritime Acad (ME)
McNeese State U (LA)
Miami U (OH)
Middle Tennessee State U (TN)
Midwestern State U (TX)
New Jersey Inst of Technology (NJ)
New Mexico State U (NM)
Northern Illinois U (IL)
Pittsburg State U (KS)

Purdue U (IN)
Southeastern Louisiana U (LA)
Southeast Missouri State U (MO)
Southern Illinois U Carbondale (IL)
Southern Polytechnic State U (GA)
Southern Utah U (UT)
Temple U (PA)
Texas A&M U (TX)
Texas State U–San Marcos (TX)
Tuskegee U (AL)
U of Delaware (DE)
U of Hartford (CT)
U of Maryland Eastern Shore (MD)
U of Memphis (TN)
U of South Carolina Upstate (SC)
The U of West Alabama (AL)
U of West Florida (FL)
U of Wisconsin–Stout (WI)
Walla Walla U (WA)
Western Carolina U (NC)
Western Illinois U (IL)
West Texas A&M U (TX)
West Virginia U Inst of Technology
(WV)
William Penn U (IA)
Youngstown State U (OH)

ENGLISH
Abilene Christian U (TX)
Acadia U (NS, Canada)
Adams State U (CO)
Adelphi U (NY)
Agnes Scott Coll (GA)
Alabama State U (AL)
Albertus Magnus Coll (CT)
Albion Coll (MI)
Albright Coll (PA)
Alcorn State U (MS)
Alderson-Broaddus Coll (WV)
Alfred U (NY)
Alice Lloyd Coll (KY)
Alma Coll (MI)
Alvernia U (PA)
Alverno Coll (WI)
American Public U System (WV)
American U (DC)
The American U in Cairo (Egypt)
American U of Beirut (Lebanon)
Amherst Coll (MA)
Anderson U (IN)
Anderson U (SC)
Andrews U (MI)
Angelo State U (TX)
Appalachian State U (NC)
Arizona State U (AZ)
Arkansas State U (AR)
Arkansas Tech U (AR)
Armstrong Atlantic State U (GA)
Asbury U (KY)
Ashland U (OH)
Assumption Coll (MA)
Athabasca U (AB, Canada)
Athens State U (AL)
Auburn U (AL)
Auburn U at Montgomery (AL)
Augsburg Coll (MN)
Augustana Coll (IL)
Augustana Coll (SD)
Aurora U (IL)
Austin Peay State U (TN)
Averett U (VA)
Avila U (MO)
Azusa Pacific U (CA)
Baker U (KS)
Baldwin Wallace U (OH)
Ball State U (IN)
Bard Coll (NY)
Barry U (FL)
Barton Coll (NC)
Bates Coll (ME)
Baylor U (TX)
Belhaven U (MS)
Bellarmine U (KY)
Belmont Abbey Coll (NC)
Belmont U (TN)
Bemidji State U (MN)
Benedictine Coll (KS)
Benedictine U (IL)
Bennington Coll (VT)
Bentley U (MA)
Berea Coll (KY)
Berry Coll (GA)
Bethany Coll (WV)
Bethany Lutheran Coll (MN)
Bethel Coll (IN)
Bethel Coll (KS)
Bethel U (MN)

Bethune-Cookman U (FL)
Binghamton U, State U of New York (NY)
Blackburn Coll (IL)
Bloomfield Coll (NJ)
Bloomsburg U of Pennsylvania (PA)
Bluefield Coll (VA)
Blue Mountain Coll (MS)
Bluffton U (OH)
Bob Jones U (SC)
Boise State U (ID)
Boston Coll (MA)
Boston U (MA)
Bowdoin Coll (ME)
Bowie State U (MD)
Bowling Green State U (OH)
Bradley U (IL)
Brevard Coll (NC)
Bridgewater Coll (VA)
Bridgewater State U (MA)
Brock U (ON, Canada)
Brown U (RI)
Bryant U (RI)
Bryn Athyn Coll of the New Church (PA)
Bucknell U (PA)
Buena Vista U (IA)
Buffalo State Coll, State U of New York (NY)
Butler U (IN)
Cabrini Coll (PA)
Caldwell Coll (NJ)
California Baptist U (CA)
California Lutheran U (CA)
California Polytechnic State U, San Luis Obispo (CA)
California State Polytechnic U, Pomona (CA)
California State U, Chico (CA)
California State U, Dominguez Hills (CA)
California State U, East Bay (CA)
California State U, Fresno (CA)
California State U, Fullerton (CA)
California State U, Long Beach (CA)
California State U, Los Angeles (CA)
California State U, Northridge (CA)
California State U, San Bernardino (CA)
California State U, San Marcos (CA)
California State U, Stanislaus (CA)
Calumet Coll of Saint Joseph (IN)
Calvin Coll (MI)
Cameron U (OK)
Campbellsville U (KY)
Canisius Coll (NY)
Capital U (OH)
Cardinal Stritch U (WI)
Carleton Coll (MN)
Carlow U (PA)
Carnegie Mellon U (PA)
Carroll Coll (MT)
Carson-Newman U (TN)
Case Western Reserve U (OH)
Catawba Coll (NC)
The Catholic U of America (DC)
Cedar Crest Coll (PA)
Cedarville U (OH)
Centenary Coll of Louisiana (LA)
Central Coll (IA)
Central Connecticut State U (CT)
Central Methodist U (MO)
Central Michigan U (MI)
Central State U (OH)
Centre Coll (KY)
Chapman U (CA)
Chatham U (PA)
Chestnut Hill Coll (PA)
Cheyney U of Pennsylvania (PA)
Chicago State U (IL)
Chowan U (NC)
Christian Brothers U (TN)
Christopher Newport U (VA)
The Citadel, The Military Coll of South Carolina (SC)
City Coll of the City U of New York (NY)
Claflin U (SC)
Claremont McKenna Coll (CA)
Clarion U of Pennsylvania (PA)
Clark Atlanta U (GA)
Clarke U (IA)
Clark U (MA)
Clayton State U (GA)

Clearwater Christian Coll (FL)
Clemson U (SC)
Cleveland State U (OH)
Coastal Carolina U (SC)
Coe Coll (IA)
Colby Coll (ME)
Colgate U (NY)
The Coll at Brockport, State U of New York (NY)
Coll of Charleston (SC)
The Coll of Idaho (ID)
Coll of Mount St. Joseph (OH)
The Coll of New Jersey (NJ)
The Coll of New Rochelle (NY)
Coll of Saint Benedict (MN)
Coll of Saint Elizabeth (NJ)
Coll of Saint Mary (NE)
The Coll of Saint Rose (NY)
The Coll of St. Scholastica (MN)
Coll of Staten Island of the City U of New York (NY)
Coll of the Atlantic (ME)
Coll of the Holy Cross (MA)
Coll of the Ozarks (MO)
The Coll of William and Mary (VA)
The Coll of Wooster (OH)
The Colorado Coll (CO)
Colorado Mesa U (CO)
Colorado State U (CO)
Columbia Coll (MO)
Columbia Coll (SC)
Columbia Intl U (SC)
Columbia U (NY)
Columbia U, School of General Studies (NY)
Columbus State U (GA)
Concordia Coll (MN)
Concordia Coll–New York (NY)
Concordia U (CA)
Concordia U (OR)
Concordia U (QC, Canada)
Concordia U Chicago (IL)
Concordia U, Nebraska (NE)
Concordia U, St. Paul (MN)
Concordia U Texas (TX)
Concordia U Wisconsin (WI)
Concord U (WV)
Connecticut Coll (CT)
Converse Coll (SC)
Corban U (OR)
Cornell Coll (IA)
Cornerstone U (MI)
Covenant Coll (GA)
Creighton U (NE)
Crown Coll (MN)
Culver-Stockton Coll (MO)
Curry Coll (MA)
Dakota Wesleyan U (SD)
Dalhousie U (NS, Canada)
Dallas Baptist U (TX)
Dalton State Coll (GA)
Dartmouth Coll (NH)
Davidson Coll (NC)
Defiance Coll (OH)
Delta State U (MS)
DePaul U (IL)
DePauw U (IN)
DEREE—The American Coll of Greece (Greece)
DeSales U (PA)
Dickinson Coll (PA)
Dillard U (LA)
Doane Coll (NE)
Dominican Coll (NY)
Dominican U (IL)
Dordt Coll (IA)
Drake U (IA)
Drew U (NJ)
Drury U (MO)
Duquesne U (PA)
Earlham Coll (IN)
East Carolina U (NC)
East Central U (OK)
Eastern Illinois U (IL)
Eastern Mennonite U (VA)
Eastern Michigan U (MI)
Eastern New Mexico U (NM)
Eastern Washington U (WA)
East Tennessee State U (TN)
East Texas Baptist U (TX)
East-West U (IL)
Eckerd Coll (FL)
Edgewood Coll (WI)
Edinboro U of Pennsylvania (PA)
Elizabeth City State U (NC)
Elizabethtown Coll (PA)
Elmira Coll (NY)

Elon U (NC)
Emmanuel Coll (GA)
Emmanuel Coll (MA)
Emporia State U (KS)
Endicott Coll (MA)
Eugene Lang Coll The New School for Liberal Arts (NY)
Evangel U (MO)
The Evergreen State Coll (WA)
Fairfield U (CT)
Fairleigh Dickinson U, Coll at Florham (NJ)
Fairleigh Dickinson U, Metropolitan Campus (NJ)
Fairmont State U (WV)
Faulkner U (AL)
Fayetteville State U (NC)
Felician Coll (NJ)
Ferrum Coll (VA)
Flagler Coll (FL)
Florida Ag and Mech U (FL)
Florida Atlantic U (FL)
Florida Gulf Coast U (FL)
Florida Intl U (FL)
Florida Southern Coll (FL)
Florida State U (FL)
Fort Lewis Coll (CO)
Framingham State U (MA)
Francis Marion U (SC)
Franklin & Marshall Coll (PA)
Franklin Coll (IN)
Franklin Pierce U (NH)
Friends U (KS)
Frostburg State U (MD)
Furman U (SC)
Gallaudet U (DC)
Gardner-Webb U (NC)
Geneva Coll (PA)
George Fox U (OR)
George Mason U (VA)
Georgetown Coll (KY)
Georgetown U (DC)
Georgia Coll & State U (GA)
Georgia Gwinnett Coll (GA)
Georgia Regents U (GA)
Georgia Southern U (GA)
Georgia Southwestern State U (GA)
Georgia State U (GA)
Gettysburg Coll (PA)
Goldey-Beacom Coll (DE)
Gonzaga U (WA)
Gordon Coll (MA)
Gordon State Coll (GA)
Goshen Coll (IN)
Goucher Coll (MD)
Governors State U (IL)
Graceland U (IA)
Grambling State U (LA)
Grand Valley State U (MI)
Grand View U (IA)
Greenville Coll (IL)
Grinnell Coll (IA)
Grove City Coll (PA)
Guilford Coll (NC)
Gustavus Adolphus Coll (MN)
Hamilton Coll (NY)
Hamline U (MN)
Hampden-Sydney Coll (VA)
Hampshire Coll (MA)
Hampton U (VA)
Hanover Coll (IN)
Harding U (AR)
Hardin-Simmons U (TX)
Hartwick Coll (NY)
Haverford Coll (PA)
Hawai'i Pacific U (HI)
Henderson State U (AR)
Hendrix Coll (AR)
High Point U (NC)
Hilbert Coll (NY)
Hillsdale Coll (MI)
Hiram Coll (OH)
Hobart and William Smith Colls (NY)
Hofstra U (NY)
Hollins U (VA)
Holy Cross Coll (IN)
Holy Family U (PA)
Holy Names U (CA)
Hood Coll (MD)
Hope Coll (MI)
Hope Intl U (CA)
Houghton Coll (NY)
Howard Payne U (TX)
Humboldt State U (CA)

Hunter Coll of the City U of New York (NY)
Huntingdon Coll (AL)
Huntington U (IN)
Husson U (ME)
Illinois Coll (IL)
Illinois State U (IL)
Immaculata U (PA)
Indiana State U (IN)
Indiana U Bloomington (IN)
Indiana U East (IN)
Indiana U Kokomo (IN)
Indiana U Northwest (IN)
Indiana U of Pennsylvania (PA)
Indiana U–Purdue U Fort Wayne (IN)
Indiana U–Purdue U Indianapolis (IN)
Indiana U South Bend (IN)
Indiana U Southeast (IN)
Indiana Wesleyan U (IN)
Inter American U of Puerto Rico, San Germán Campus (PR)
Iona Coll (NY)
Iowa State U of Science and Technology (IA)
Iowa Wesleyan Coll (IA)
Ithaca Coll (NY)
Jacksonville State U (AL)
James Madison U (VA)
Jamestown Coll (ND)
Jarvis Christian Coll (TX)
John Brown U (AR)
John Carroll U (OH)
John Jay Coll of Criminal Justice of the City U of New York (NY)
The Johns Hopkins U (MD)
Johnson C. Smith U (NC)
Johnson State Coll (VT)
Judson Coll (AL)
Judson U (IL)
Juniata Coll (PA)
Kalamazoo Coll (MI)
Kansas State U (KS)
Kansas Wesleyan U (KS)
Kean U (NJ)
Keene State Coll (NH)
Kennesaw State U (GA)
Kent State U (OH)
Kent State U at Ashtabula (OH)
Kent State U at East Liverpool (OH)
Kent State U at Geauga (OH)
Kent State U at Salem (OH)
Kent State U at Stark (OH)
Kent State U at Trumbull (OH)
Kent State U at Tuscarawas (OH)
Kentucky State U (KY)
Kentucky Wesleyan Coll (KY)
Kenyon Coll (OH)
Keuka Coll (NY)
King Coll (TN)
King's Coll (PA)
The King's U Coll (AB, Canada)
Knox Coll (IL)
Kutztown U of Pennsylvania (PA)
Lafayette Coll (PA)
LaGrange Coll (GA)
Lake Erie Coll (OH)
Lakeland Coll (WI)
Lake Superior State U (MI)
Lamar U (TX)
Lander U (SC)
Lane Coll (TN)
Langston U (OK)
La Roche Coll (PA)
La Salle U (PA)
Lasell Coll (MA)
La Sierra U (CA)
Lawrence Technological U (MI)
Lawrence U (WI)
Lebanese American U (Lebanon)
Lebanon Valley Coll (PA)
Lees-McRae Coll (NC)
Lee U (TN)
Lehigh U (PA)
Lehman Coll of the City U of New York (NY)
Le Moyne Coll (NY)
Lesley U (MA)
LeTourneau U (TX)
Lewis-Clark State Coll (ID)
Lewis U (IL)
Liberty U (VA)
Limestone Coll (SC)
Lincoln Memorial U (TN)
Lincoln U (MO)
Lindenwood U (MO)

Lindsey Wilson Coll (KY)
Linfield Coll (OR)
Lipscomb U (TN)
Lock Haven U of Pennsylvania (PA)
Long Island U–Brooklyn Campus (NY)
Long Island U–C. W. Post Campus (NY)
Longwood U (VA)
Louisiana Coll (LA)
Louisiana State U and Ag and Mech Coll (LA)
Louisiana State U at Alexandria (LA)
Louisiana State U in Shreveport (LA)
Lourdes U (OH)
Loyola Marymount U (CA)
Loyola U Chicago (IL)
Loyola U Maryland (MD)
Loyola U New Orleans (LA)
Lubbock Christian U (TX)
Luther Coll (IA)
Lynchburg Coll (VA)
Lynn U (FL)
Lyon Coll (AR)
Macalester Coll (MN)
Madonna U (MI)
Maharishi U of Management (IA)
Malone U (OH)
Manchester U (IN)
Manhattan Coll (NY)
Manhattanville Coll (NY)
Mansfield U of Pennsylvania (PA)
Maranatha Baptist Bible Coll (WI)
Marian U (WI)
Marietta Coll (OH)
Marist Coll (NY)
Marquette U (WI)
Marshall U (WV)
Mars Hill Coll (NC)
Mary Baldwin Coll (VA)
Marymount Manhattan Coll (NY)
Marymount U (VA)
Maryville Coll (TN)
Maryville U of Saint Louis (MO)
Marywood U (PA)
Massachusetts Coll of Liberal Arts (MA)
Massachusetts Inst of Technology (MA)
The Master's Coll and Sem (CA)
Mayville State U (ND)
McDaniel Coll (MD)
McKendree U (IL)
McMurry U (TX)
McNeese State U (LA)
Medaille Coll (NY)
Mercer U (GA)
Mercy Coll (NY)
Mercyhurst U (PA)
Merrimack Coll (MA)
Messiah Coll (PA)
Metropolitan State U of Denver (CO)
Miami U (OH)
Michigan State U (MI)
Mid-Continent U (KY)
Middle Tennessee State U (TN)
Midwestern State U (TX)
Millersville U of Pennsylvania (PA)
Millikin U (IL)
Millsaps Coll (MS)
Mills Coll (CA)
Minnesota State U Mankato (MN)
Minot State U (ND)
Misericordia U (PA)
Mississippi Coll (MS)
Mississippi State U (MS)
Mississippi U for Women (MS)
Mississippi Valley State U (MS)
Missouri Baptist U (MO)
Missouri State U (MO)
Missouri U of Science and Technology (MO)
Missouri Western State U (MO)
Molloy Coll (NY)
Monmouth Coll (IL)
Monmouth U (NJ)
Montana State U (MT)
Montclair State U (NJ)
Montreat Coll, Montreat (NC)
Moravian Coll (PA)
Morehead State U (KY)
Morehouse Coll (GA)
Morningside Coll (IA)
Morris Coll (SC)

Mount Allison U (NB, Canada)
Mount Aloysius Coll (PA)
Mount Holyoke Coll (MA)
Mount Marty Coll (SD)
Mount Mary Coll (WI)
Mount Mercy U (IA)
Mount Saint Mary Coll (NY)
Mount St. Mary's Coll (CA)
Mount St. Mary's U (MD)
Mount Vernon Nazarene U (OH)
Muhlenberg Coll (PA)
Multnomah U (OR)
Murray State U (KY)
Naropa U (CO)
National U (CA)
Nazareth Coll of Rochester (NY)
Neumann U (PA)
Newberry Coll (SC)
New Coll of Florida (FL)
New England Coll (NH)
New Jersey City U (NJ)
Newman U (KS)
New Mexico Highlands U (NM)
New Mexico State U (NM)
New York U (NY)
Niagara U (NY)
Nicholls State U (LA)
Norfolk State U (VA)
North Carolina Central U (NC)
North Carolina State U (NC)
North Carolina Wesleyan Coll (NC)
North Central Coll (IL)
North Dakota State U (ND)
Northeastern Illinois U (IL)
Northeastern U (MA)
Northern Arizona U (AZ)
Northern Illinois U (IL)
Northern Michigan U (MI)
Northern State U (SD)
North Greenville U (SC)
Northland Coll (WI)
Northwest Christian U (OR)
Northwestern Coll (IA)
Northwestern Coll (MN)
Northwestern Oklahoma State U (OK)
Northwestern State U of Louisiana (LA)
Northwest Missouri State U (MO)
Northwest Nazarene U (ID)
Northwest U (WA)
Norwich U (VT)
Notre Dame de Namur U (CA)
Nova Southeastern U (FL)
Nyack Coll (NY)
Oakland U (MI)
Oglethorpe U (GA)
Ohio Dominican U (OH)
The Ohio State U (OH)
The Ohio State U at Lima (OH)
The Ohio State U at Marion (OH)
The Ohio State U–Mansfield Campus (OH)
The Ohio State U–Newark Campus (OH)
Ohio U (OH)
Ohio Wesleyan U (OH)
Oklahoma Christian U (OK)
Oklahoma City U (OK)
Oklahoma State U (OK)
Old Dominion U (VA)
Olivet Coll (MI)
Oral Roberts U (OK)
Oregon State U (OR)
Ouachita Baptist U (AR)
Pace U (NY)
Pacific Lutheran U (WA)
Pacific Union Coll (CA)
Pacific U (OR)
Paine Coll (GA)
Palm Beach Atlantic U (FL)
Park U (MO)
Penn State Abington (PA)
Penn State Altoona (PA)
Penn State Beaver (PA)
Penn State Berks (PA)
Penn State Brandywine (PA)
Penn State DuBois (PA)
Penn State Erie, The Behrend Coll (PA)
Penn State Fayette, The Eberly Campus (PA)
Penn State Greater Allegheny (PA)
Penn State Harrisburg (PA)
Penn State Hazleton (PA)
Penn State Lehigh Valley (PA)
Penn State Mont Alto (PA)

Penn State New Kensington (PA)
Penn State Schuylkill (PA)
Penn State Shenango (PA)
Penn State U Park (PA)
Penn State Wilkes-Barre (PA)
Penn State Worthington Scranton (PA)
Penn State York (PA)
Pepperdine U, Malibu (CA)
Piedmont Coll (GA)
Pine Manor Coll (MA)
Pittsburg State U (KS)
Pitzer Coll (CA)
Plymouth State U (NH)
Point Loma Nazarene U (CA)
Point Park U (PA)
Point U (GA)
Pomona Coll (CA)
Portland State U (OR)
Presbyterian Coll (SC)
Princeton U (NJ)
Principia Coll (IL)
Providence Coll (RI)
Purdue U (IN)
Purdue U Calumet (IN)
Purdue U North Central (IN)
Queens U of Charlotte (NC)
Quincy U (IL)
Quinnipiac U (CT)
Radford U (VA)
Randolph Coll (VA)
Randolph-Macon Coll (VA)
Reed Coll (OR)
Regent U (VA)
Regis Coll (MA)
Regis U (CO)
Rhode Island Coll (RI)
Rhodes Coll (TN)
Rice U (TX)
The Richard Stockton Coll of New Jersey (NJ)
Rider U (NJ)
Ripon Coll (WI)
Rivier U (NH)
Roanoke Coll (VA)
Robert Morris U (PA)
Roberts Wesleyan Coll (NY)
Rockford Coll (IL)
Rockhurst U (MO)
Rocky Mountain Coll (MT)
Roger Williams U (RI)
Rollins Coll (FL)
Roosevelt U (IL)
Rosemont Coll (PA)
Rowan U (NJ)
Russell Sage Coll (NY)
Rutgers, The State U of New Jersey, Camden (NJ)
Rutgers, The State U of New Jersey, Newark (NJ)
Rutgers, The State U of New Jersey, New Brunswick (NJ)
Sacred Heart U (CT)
Saginaw Valley State U (MI)
St. Ambrose U (IA)
St. Andrews U (NC)
Saint Anselm Coll (NH)
St. Bonaventure U (NY)
St. Edward's U (TX)
St. Francis Coll (NY)
St. Gregory's U, Shawnee (OK)
St. John Fisher Coll (NY)
Saint John's U (MN)
St. John's U (NY)
Saint Joseph's Coll (IN)
St. Joseph's Coll, Long Island Campus (NY)
St. Joseph's Coll, New York (NY)
Saint Joseph's U (PA)
St. Lawrence U (NY)
Saint Leo U (FL)
Saint Louis U (MO)
Saint Martin's U (WA)
Saint Mary-of-the-Woods Coll (IN)
Saint Mary's Coll (IN)
Saint Mary's Coll of California (CA)
St. Mary's Coll of Maryland (MD)
St. Mary's U (TX)
Saint Michael's Coll (VT)
St. Norbert Coll (WI)
St. Olaf Coll (MN)
St. Thomas Aquinas Coll (NY)
St. Thomas U (FL)
St. Thomas U (NB, Canada)
Saint Vincent Coll (PA)
Salem State U (MA)
Salisbury U (MD)

Salve Regina U (RI)
Samford U (AL)
Sam Houston State U (TX)
San Diego Christian Coll (CA)
San Diego State U (CA)
San Francisco State U (CA)
San Jose State U (CA)
Schreiner U (TX)
Scripps Coll (CA)
Seattle Pacific U (WA)
Seattle U (WA)
Seton Hill U (PA)
Sewanee: The U of the South (TN)
Shawnee State U (OH)
Shaw U (NC)
Shenandoah U (VA)
Shepherd U (WV)
Shippensburg U of Pennsylvania (PA)
Siena Coll (NY)
Siena Heights U (MI)
Sierra Nevada Coll (NV)
Simmons Coll (MA)
Simon Fraser U (BC, Canada)
Simpson Coll (IA)
Simpson U (CA)
Skidmore Coll (NY)
Slippery Rock U of Pennsylvania (PA)
Smith Coll (MA)
Sonoma State U (CA)
South Dakota State U (SD)
Southeastern Louisiana U (LA)
Southeastern Oklahoma State U (OK)
Southeastern U (FL)
Southeast Missouri State U (MO)
Southern Arkansas U–Magnolia (AR)
Southern Connecticut State U (CT)
Southern Illinois U Carbondale (IL)
Southern Illinois U Edwardsville (IL)
Southern Methodist U (TX)
Southern Nazarene U (OK)
Southern New Hampshire U (NH)
Southern Oregon U (OR)
Southern Utah U (UT)
Southwest Baptist U (MO)
Southwestern Adventist U (TX)
Southwestern Coll (KS)
Southwestern U (TX)
Spelman Coll (GA)
Spring Arbor U (MI)
Spring Hill Coll (AL)
Stanford U (CA)
State U of New York at Fredonia (NY)
State U of New York at New Paltz (NY)
State U of New York at Oswego (NY)
State U of New York at Plattsburgh (NY)
State U of New York Coll at Cortland (NY)
State U of New York Coll at Geneseo (NY)
State U of New York Coll at Potsdam (NY)
Stephen F. Austin State U (TX)
Stephens Coll (MO)
Sterling Coll (KS)
Stetson U (FL)
Stevenson U (MD)
Stonehill Coll (MA)
Stony Brook U, State U of New York (NY)
Suffolk U (MA)
Sul Ross State U (TX)
Susquehanna U (PA)
Swarthmore Coll (PA)
Sweet Briar Coll (VA)
Syracuse U (NY)
Tabor Coll (KS)
Tarleton State U (TX)
Taylor U (IN)
Temple U (PA)
Tennessee State U (TN)
Tennessee Wesleyan Coll (TN)
Texas A&M Intl U (TX)
Texas A&M U (TX)
Texas A&M U–Commerce (TX)
Texas A&M U–Kingsville (TX)
Texas Christian U (TX)
Texas Lutheran U (TX)
Texas Southern U (TX)

Texas State U–San Marcos (TX)
Texas Wesleyan U (TX)
Texas Woman's U (TX)
Thomas Edison State Coll (NJ)
Thomas More Coll (KY)
Thomas U (GA)
Thompson Rivers U (BC, Canada)
Tiffin U (OH)
Transylvania U (KY)
Trent U (ON, Canada)
Trevecca Nazarene U (TN)
Trinity Christian Coll (IL)
Trinity Coll (CT)
Trinity U (TX)
Troy U (AL)
Truman State U (MO)
Tufts U (MA)
Tulane U (LA)
Tuskegee U (AL)
Union Coll (KY)
Union Coll (NE)
Union U (TN)
United States Air Force Acad (CO)
United States Naval Acad (MD)
Université de Sherbrooke (QC, Canada)
Université Sainte-Anne (NS, Canada)
U at Albany, State U of New York (NY)
U at Buffalo, the State U of New York (NY)
The U of Akron (OH)
The U of Alabama (AL)
The U of Alabama at Birmingham (AL)
U of Alaska Anchorage (AK)
U of Alaska Fairbanks (AK)
The U of Arizona (AZ)
U of Arkansas at Little Rock (AR)
U of Arkansas–Fort Smith (AR)
U of Bridgeport (CT)
The U of British Columbia (BC, Canada)
The U of British Columbia–Okanagan (BC, Canada)
U of California, Berkeley (CA)
U of California, Davis (CA)
U of California, Irvine (CA)
U of California, Los Angeles (CA)
U of California, Riverside (CA)
U of California, Santa Barbara (CA)
U of Central Arkansas (AR)
U of Central Florida (FL)
U of Central Oklahoma (OK)
U of Charleston (WV)
U of Chicago (IL)
U of Cincinnati (OH)
U of Colorado Boulder (CO)
U of Colorado Colorado Springs (CO)
U of Colorado Denver (CO)
U of Dallas (TX)
U of Delaware (DE)
U of Denver (CO)
U of Evansville (IN)
The U of Findlay (OH)
U of Florida (FL)
U of Georgia (GA)
U of Great Falls (MT)
U of Guam (GU)
U of Guelph (ON, Canada)
U of Hartford (CT)
U of Hawaii at Hilo (HI)
U of Hawaii at Manoa (HI)
U of Hawaii–West Oahu (HI)
U of Houston (TX)
U of Houston–Clear Lake (TX)
U of Houston–Downtown (TX)
U of Houston–Victoria (TX)
U of Idaho (ID)
U of Illinois at Chicago (IL)
U of Illinois at Springfield (IL)
U of Illinois at Urbana–Champaign (IL)
The U of Iowa (IA)
The U of Kansas (KS)
U of Kentucky (KY)
U of La Verne (CA)
U of Louisiana at Lafayette (LA)
U of Louisiana at Monroe (LA)
U of Louisville (KY)
U of Maine at Farmington (ME)
U of Maine at Fort Kent (ME)
U of Maine at Machias (ME)
U of Maryland, Baltimore County (MD)

U of Maryland, Coll Park (MD)
U of Maryland Eastern Shore (MD)
U of Maryland U Coll (MD)
U of Mary Washington (VA)
U of Massachusetts Amherst (MA)
U of Massachusetts Boston (MA)
U of Massachusetts Dartmouth (MA)
U of Memphis (TN)
U of Miami (FL)
U of Michigan (MI)
U of Michigan–Dearborn (MI)
U of Michigan–Flint (MI)
U of Minnesota, Duluth (MN)
U of Minnesota, Twin Cities Campus (MN)
U of Mississippi (MS)
U of Missouri (MO)
U of Missouri–Kansas City (MO)
U of Missouri–St. Louis (MO)
U of Mobile (AL)
The U of Montana Western (MT)
U of Montevallo (AL)
U of Mount Union (OH)
U of Nebraska at Kearney (NE)
U of Nebraska at Omaha (NE)
U of Nebraska–Lincoln (NE)
U of Nevada, Las Vegas (NV)
U of Nevada, Reno (NV)
U of New Brunswick Fredericton (NB, Canada)
U of New Brunswick Saint John (NB, Canada)
U of New England (ME)
U of New Hampshire (NH)
U of New Hampshire at Manchester (NH)
U of New Haven (CT)
U of New Mexico (NM)
U of New Orleans (LA)
U of North Alabama (AL)
U of North Carolina at Asheville (NC)
The U of North Carolina at Chapel Hill (NC)
The U of North Carolina at Charlotte (NC)
The U of North Carolina at Greensboro (NC)
The U of North Carolina at Pembroke (NC)
The U of North Carolina Wilmington (NC)
U of North Dakota (ND)
U of Northern Colorado (CO)
U of Northern Iowa (IA)
U of North Florida (FL)
U of North Georgia (GA)
U of North Texas (TX)
U of Notre Dame (IN)
U of Oklahoma (OK)
U of Oregon (OR)
U of Ottawa (ON, Canada)
U of Pennsylvania (PA)
U of Pikeville (KY)
U of Pittsburgh at Bradford (PA)
U of Pittsburgh at Greensburg (PA)
U of Portland (OR)
U of Puget Sound (WA)
U of Redlands (CA)
U of Regina (SK, Canada)
U of Rhode Island (RI)
U of Richmond (VA)
U of Rochester (NY)
U of St. Francis (IL)
U of Saint Joseph (CT)
U of Saint Mary (KS)
U of St. Thomas (MN)
U of St. Thomas (TX)
U of San Diego (CA)
U of Science and Arts of Oklahoma (OK)
The U of Scranton (PA)
U of South Alabama (AL)
U of South Carolina (SC)
U of South Carolina Aiken (SC)
U of South Carolina Upstate (SC)
The U of South Dakota (SD)
U of Southern California (CA)
U of Southern Indiana (IN)
U of Southern Maine (ME)
U of Southern Mississippi (MS)
U of South Florida (FL)
The U of Tampa (FL)
The U of Tennessee (TN)
The U of Tennessee at Chattanooga (TN)

The U of Tennessee at Martin (TN)
The U of Texas at Arlington (TX)
The U of Texas at Austin (TX)
The U of Texas at Brownsville (TX)
The U of Texas at El Paso (TX)
The U of Texas at San Antonio (TX)
The U of Texas of the Permian Basin (TX)
The U of Texas–Pan American (TX)
U of the Cumberlands (KY)
U of the District of Columbia (DC)
U of the Incarnate Word (TX)
U of the Ozarks (AR)
U of the Virgin Islands (VI)
The U of Toledo (OH)
U of Tulsa (OK)
U of Utah (UT)
U of Vermont (VT)
U of Virginia (VA)
U of Waterloo (ON, Canada)
The U of West Alabama (AL)
The U of Western Ontario (ON, Canada)
U of West Florida (FL)
U of West Georgia (GA)
U of Windsor (ON, Canada)
U of Wisconsin–Eau Claire (WI)
U of Wisconsin–Green Bay (WI)
U of Wisconsin–La Crosse (WI)
U of Wisconsin–Madison (WI)
U of Wisconsin–Milwaukee (WI)
U of Wisconsin–Parkside (WI)
U of Wisconsin–Platteville (WI)
U of Wisconsin–Stevens Point (WI)
U of Wisconsin–Superior (WI)
U of Wyoming (WY)
Upper Iowa U (IA)
Ursuline Coll (OH)
Utah State U (UT)
Utica Coll (NY)
Valdosta State U (GA)
Valley City State U (ND)
Valparaiso U (IN)
Vanderbilt U (TN)
Vassar Coll (NY)
Villanova U (PA)
Virginia Commonwealth U (VA)
Virginia Intermont Coll (VA)
Virginia Polytechnic Inst and State U (VA)
Virginia State U (VA)
Virginia Union U (VA)
Virginia Wesleyan Coll (VA)
Viterbo U (WI)
Wabash Coll (IN)
Wagner Coll (NY)
Wake Forest U (NC)
Waldorf Coll (IA)
Walla Walla U (WA)
Walsh U (OH)
Warner Pacific Coll (OR)
Wartburg Coll (IA)
Washburn U (KS)
Washington & Jefferson Coll (PA)
Washington and Lee U (VA)
Washington Coll (MD)
Washington State U (WA)
Washington U in St. Louis (MO)
Wayland Baptist U (TX)
Waynesburg U (PA)
Wayne State Coll (NE)
Wayne State U (MI)
Weber State U (UT)
Webster U (MO)
Wellesley Coll (MA)
Wells Coll (NY)
Wesleyan Coll (GA)
Wesleyan U (CT)
Wesley Coll (DE)
West Chester U of Pennsylvania (PA)
Western Carolina U (NC)
Western Connecticut State U (CT)
Western Illinois U (IL)
Western Kentucky U (KY)
Western Michigan U (MI)
Western Oregon U (OR)
Western State Colorado U (CO)
Western Washington U (WA)
Westfield State U (MA)
West Liberty U (WV)
Westminster Coll (MO)
Westminster Coll (UT)
West Texas A&M U (TX)
West Virginia State U (WV)
West Virginia U (WV)
West Virginia Wesleyan Coll (WV)

Wheaton Coll (IL)
Wheaton Coll (MA)
Wheeling Jesuit U (WV)
Whitman Coll (WA)
Whitworth U (WA)
Wichita State U (KS)
Widener U (PA)
Wilkes U (PA)
Willamette U (OR)
William Jewell Coll (MO)
William Paterson U of New Jersey (NJ)
William Peace U (NC)
Williams Coll (MA)
Winthrop U (SC)
Wittenberg U (OH)
Worcester State U (MA)
Wright State U (OH)
Xavier U (OH)
Xavier U of Louisiana (LA)
Yale U (CT)
York Coll of Pennsylvania (PA)
York Coll of the City U of New York (NY)
Young Harris Coll (GA)
Youngstown State U (OH)

ENGLISH AS A SECOND/FOREIGN LANGUAGE (TEACHING)
American U (DC)
Bethel U (MN)
Briercrest Coll (SK, Canada)
Brigham Young U (UT)
Brock U (ON, Canada)
California State U, Stanislaus (CA)
Calvin Coll (MI)
Carroll Coll (MT)
The Catholic U of America (DC)
Concordia U (QC, Canada)
Concordia U, Nebraska (NE)
Concordia U, St. Paul (MN)
Concordia U Wisconsin (WI)
Crown Coll (MN)
Doane Coll (NE)
Eastern Washington U (WA)
Gardner-Webb U (NC)
Goshen Coll (IN)
Granite State Coll (NH)
Hawai'i Pacific U (HI)
Houghton Coll (NY)
Howard Payne U (TX)
Huntington U (IN)
Indiana Wesleyan U (IN)
Inter American U of Puerto Rico, Aguadilla Campus (PR)
Inter American U of Puerto Rico, Fajardo Campus (PR)
Inter American U of Puerto Rico, Ponce Campus (PR)
Inter American U of Puerto Rico, San Germán Campus (PR)
Kent State U (OH)
Langston U (OK)
Lebanese American U (Lebanon)
Le Moyne Coll (NY)
Liberty U (VA)
Lipscomb U (TN)
Maryville Coll (TN)
Multnomah U (OR)
Niagara U (NY)
Northwestern Coll (MN)
Northwest U (WA)
Nyack Coll (NY)
Oklahoma Christian U (OK)
Oklahoma City U (OK)
Salisbury U (MD)
Simmons Coll (MA)
Stony Brook U, State U of New York (NY)
Tarleton State U (TX)
Union U (TN)
The U of British Columbia (BC, Canada)
The U of Findlay (OH)
U of Guam (GU)
U of Minnesota, Twin Cities Campus (MN)
U of New Brunswick Fredericton (NB, Canada)
U of New Brunswick Saint John (NB, Canada)
U of Northern Iowa (IA)
Washington State U (WA)
Wichita State U (KS)
William Penn U (IA)
Wright State U (OH)

ENGLISH/FRENCH AS A SECOND/FOREIGN LANGUAGE (TEACHING) RELATED
U of Ottawa (ON, Canada)

ENGLISH LANGUAGE AND LITERATURE RELATED
Binghamton U, State U of New York (NY)
Columbia Coll (SC)
Columbia U, School of General Studies (NY)
Concordia Coll–New York (NY)
Dakota State U (SD)
Doane Coll (NE)
Emmanuel Coll (MA)
Fort Lewis Coll (CO)
Hofstra U (NY)
Middlebury Coll (VT)
Moravian Coll (PA)
Mount Mary Coll (WI)
Oklahoma City U (OK)
Olivet Coll (MI)
Patrick Henry Coll (VA)
Point Loma Nazarene U (CA)
Purdue U (IN)
Rowan U (NJ)
Saint Leo U (FL)
Saint Mary's Coll of California (CA)
Saint Mary's U of Minnesota (MN)
Tabor Coll (KS)
U of Great Falls (MT)
U of Michigan (MI)
U of Pennsylvania (PA)
The U of Western Ontario (ON, Canada)
Viterbo U (WI)
Washington U in St. Louis (MO)
Webster U (MO)
Western Kentucky U (KY)

ENGLISH/LANGUAGE ARTS TEACHER EDUCATION
Abilene Christian U (TX)
Adams State U (CO)
Albion Coll (MI)
Alice Lloyd Coll (KY)
Alma Coll (MI)
Alvernia U (PA)
Alverno Coll (WI)
Anderson U (IN)
Anderson U (SC)
Appalachian State U (NC)
Arizona Christian U (AZ)
Arkansas State U (AR)
Arkansas Tech U (AR)
Assumption Coll (MA)
Auburn U (AL)
Augustana Coll (IL)
The Baptist Coll of Florida (FL)
Barry U (FL)
Baylor U (TX)
Bethel Coll (IN)
Bethel U (MN)
Bethune-Cookman U (FL)
Blackburn Coll (IL)
Bluefield Coll (VA)
Blue Mountain Coll (MS)
Bob Jones U (SC)
Boise State U (ID)
Boston U (MA)
Bowling Green State U (OH)
Bradley U (IL)
Bridgewater State U (MA)
Buena Vista U (IA)
Buffalo State Coll, State U of New York (NY)
Cabrini Coll (PA)
Cairn U (PA)
California State U, Chico (CA)
California State U, Long Beach (CA)
Calumet Coll of Saint Joseph (IN)
Cameron U (OK)
Campbellsville U (KY)
Canisius Coll (NY)
Capital U (OH)
Caribbean U (PR)
Carroll Coll (MT)
The Catholic U of America (DC)
Cedarville U (OH)
Christian Brothers U (TN)
Claflin U (SC)
Clearwater Christian Coll (FL)
The Coll at Brockport, State U of New York (NY)
The Coll of New Jersey (NJ)

The Coll of Saint Rose (NY)
Coll of Staten Island of the City of New York (NY)
Coll of the Ozarks (MO)
Colorado State U (CO)
Columbus State U (GA)
Concordia U (OR)
Concordia U Chicago (IL)
Concordia U, Nebraska (NE)
Corban U (OR)
Cornerstone U (MI)
Covenant Coll (GA)
Crown Coll (MN)
Culver-Stockton Coll (MO)
Dakota State U (SD)
Dakota Wesleyan U (SD)
Dallas Baptist U (TX)
Delta State U (MS)
Dominican Coll (NY)
Duquesne U (PA)
East Carolina U (NC)
East Central U (OK)
Eastern Michigan U (MI)
Eastern Washington U (WA)
East Texas Baptist U (TX)
Edgewood Coll (WI)
Elizabeth City State U (NC)
Elmira Coll (NY)
Emmanuel Coll (GA)
Faith Baptist Bible Coll and Theological Sem (IA)
Fayetteville State U (NC)
Ferris State U (MI)
Florida Ag and Mech U (FL)
Florida Atlantic U (FL)
Fort Lewis Coll (CO)
Franklin Coll (IN)
Friends U (KS)
Gardner-Webb U (NC)
Goddard Coll (VT)
Gordon State Coll (GA)
Grambling State U (LA)
Grand Valley State U (MI)
Greenville Coll (IL)
Harding U (AR)
Hardin-Simmons U (TX)
Hofstra U (NY)
Holy Family U (PA)
Hope Coll (MI)
Howard Payne U (TX)
Huntingdon Coll (AL)
Huntington U (IN)
Indiana U Bloomington (IN)
Indiana U Northwest (IN)
Indiana U–Purdue U Fort Wayne (IN)
Indiana U–Purdue U Indianapolis (IN)
Indiana U South Bend (IN)
Indiana U Southeast (IN)
Indiana Wesleyan U (IN)
Inter American U of Puerto Rico, San Germán Campus (PR)
Iona Coll (NY)
Iowa Wesleyan Coll (IA)
Ithaca Coll (NY)
Jamestown Coll (ND)
Johnson State Coll (VT)
Judson Coll (AL)
Juniata Coll (PA)
Keene State Coll (NH)
Kennesaw State U (GA)
Kentucky Christian U (KY)
Kentucky Wesleyan Coll (KY)
Keuka Coll (NY)
King Coll (TN)
La Roche Coll (PA)
Lee U (TN)
Le Moyne Coll (NY)
Lewis-Clark State Coll (ID)
Limestone Coll (SC)
Lincoln U (MO)
Lipscomb U (TN)
Long Island U–Brooklyn Campus (NY)
Long Island U–C. W. Post Campus (NY)
Louisiana State U in Shreveport (LA)
Loyola U Chicago (IL)
Madonna U (MI)
Malone U (OH)
Manchester U (IN)
Manhattanville Coll (NY)
Mansfield U of Pennsylvania (PA)
Maranatha Baptist Bible Coll (WI)
Marian U (WI)

Marist Coll (NY)
Maryville Coll (TN)
Marywood U (PA)
Mayville State U (ND)
McKendree U (IL)
McMurry U (TX)
Medaille Coll (NY)
Mercyhurst U (PA)
Merrimack Coll (MA)
Messiah Coll (PA)
Miami U (OH)
Midwestern State U (TX)
Millikin U (IL)
Minnesota State U Moorhead (MN)
Minot State U (ND)
Misericordia U (PA)
Mississippi Coll (MS)
Mississippi Valley State U (MS)
Missouri State U (MO)
Missouri Western State U (MO)
Molloy Coll (NY)
Morningside Coll (IA)
Morris Coll (SC)
Mount Marty Coll (SD)
Mount Mary Coll (WI)
Mount Vernon Nazarene U (OH)
National U (CA)
Nazareth Coll of Rochester (NY)
Nicholls State U (LA)
North Carolina Central U (NC)
North Carolina State U (NC)
North Dakota State U (ND)
Northern Michigan U (MI)
North Greenville U (SC)
Northwestern Coll (IA)
Northwestern Coll (MN)
Northwestern Oklahoma State U (OK)
Northwest Missouri State U (MO)
Northwest Nazarene U (ID)
Northwest U (WA)
Nyack Coll (NY)
The Ohio State U at Lima (OH)
The Ohio State U at Marion (OH)
The Ohio State U–Mansfield Campus (OH)
The Ohio State U–Newark Campus (OH)
Oklahoma Baptist U (OK)
Oklahoma Christian U (OK)
Oklahoma City U (OK)
Oral Roberts U (OK)
Pace U (NY)
Paine Coll (GA)
Palm Beach Atlantic U (FL)
Pepperdine U, Malibu (CA)
Pittsburg State U (KS)
Point Park U (PA)
Purdue U Calumet (IN)
Queens U of Charlotte (NC)
Rhode Island Coll (RI)
Rivier U (NH)
Roberts Wesleyan Coll (NY)
Rocky Mountain Coll (MT)
Saginaw Valley State U (MI)
St. Ambrose U (IA)
St. Francis Coll (NY)
St. Gregory's U, Shawnee (OK)
St. John Fisher Coll (NY)
St. John's U (NY)
St. Joseph's Coll, Long Island Campus (NY)
St. Joseph's Coll, New York (NY)
Saint Mary's U of Minnesota (MN)
Salve Regina U (RI)
Samford U (AL)
Schreiner U (TX)
Seattle Pacific U (WA)
Seton Hill U (PA)
Shaw U (NC)
Simpson U (CA)
Southeastern Louisiana U (LA)
Southeastern Oklahoma State U (OK)
Southeastern U (FL)
Southeast Missouri State U (MO)
Southern Nazarene U (OK)
Southern New Hampshire U (NH)
Southern Utah U (UT)
Southwest Baptist U (MO)
Southwestern Coll (KS)
Spring Arbor U (MI)
State U of New York at New Paltz (NY)
State U of New York at Plattsburgh (NY)

Stony Brook U, State U of New York (NY)
Syracuse U (NY)
Taylor U (IN)
Temple U (PA)
Texas A&M Intl U (TX)
Texas Christian U (TX)
Texas Wesleyan U (TX)
Tiffin U (OH)
Trevecca Nazarene U (TN)
Trinity Christian Coll (IL)
Union Coll (NE)
The U of Akron (OH)
U of Arkansas–Fort Smith (AR)
U of Central Florida (FL)
U of Central Oklahoma (OK)
U of Delaware (DE)
U of Evansville (IN)
U of Georgia (GA)
U of Great Falls (MT)
U of Idaho (ID)
U of Illinois at Chicago (IL)
U of Illinois at Urbana–Champaign (IL)
U of Louisiana at Monroe (LA)
U of Maine at Farmington (ME)
U of Maine at Fort Kent (ME)
U of Maine at Machias (ME)
U of Michigan–Flint (MI)
U of Minnesota, Twin Cities Campus (MN)
U of Mississippi (MS)
U of Missouri–St. Louis (MO)
The U of Montana Western (MT)
U of Nebraska–Lincoln (NE)
The U of North Carolina at Greensboro (NC)
The U of North Carolina at Pembroke (NC)
The U of North Carolina Wilmington (NC)
U of Oklahoma (OK)
U of Regina (SK, Canada)
U of St. Francis (IL)
U of St. Thomas (MN)
The U of South Dakota (SD)
U of South Florida (FL)
The U of Tennessee at Chattanooga (TN)
The U of Tennessee at Martin (TN)
The U of Toledo (OH)
U of Vermont (VT)
U of Windsor (ON, Canada)
U of Wisconsin–Superior (WI)
Ursuline Coll (OH)
Utica Coll (NY)
Valley City State U (ND)
Valparaiso U (IN)
Virginia Intermont Coll (VA)
Viterbo U (WI)
Washburn U (KS)
Washington State U (WA)
Washington U in St. Louis (MO)
Wayland Baptist U (TX)
Waynesburg U (PA)
Wayne State Coll (NE)
Wayne State U (MI)
Weber State U (UT)
Webster U (MO)
Western Carolina U (NC)
Western Michigan U (MI)
Western State Colorado U (CO)
Western Washington U (WA)
West Virginia Wesleyan Coll (WV)
Wheeling Jesuit U (WV)
Widener U (PA)
William Jewell Coll (MO)
William Penn U (IA)
York Coll of Pennsylvania (PA)
Youngstown State U (OH)

ENGLISH LITERATURE (BRITISH AND COMMONWEALTH)
American U of Beirut (Lebanon)
Bard Coll (NY)
Bennington Coll (VT)
Concordia U (QC, Canada)
Gannon U (PA)
Hofstra U (NY)
Hunter Coll of the City U of New York (NY)
Indiana U–Purdue U Fort Wayne (IN)
Marian U (WI)
New York U (NY)
Pace U (NY)

St. Lawrence U (NY)
Saint Mary's Coll (IN)
U of Pittsburgh (PA)
Washington U in St. Louis (MO)
Wheeling Jesuit U (WV)

ENTOMOLOGY
Iowa State U of Science and Technology (IA)
Michigan State U (MI)
The Ohio State U (OH)
Oklahoma State U (OK)
Purdue U (IN)
Texas A&M U (TX)
U of California, Davis (CA)
U of California, Riverside (CA)
U of Delaware (DE)
U of Florida (FL)
U of Georgia (GA)
U of Illinois at Urbana–Champaign (IL)
U of Minnesota, Twin Cities Campus (MN)
U of Nebraska–Lincoln (NE)
U of New Brunswick Fredericton (NB, Canada)
U of New Hampshire (NH)
U of Wisconsin–Madison (WI)
Utah State U (UT)

ENTREPRENEURIAL AND SMALL BUSINESS RELATED
Babson Coll (MA)
Crown Coll (MN)
Fairleigh Dickinson U, Coll at Florham (NJ)
Fairleigh Dickinson U, Metropolitan Campus (NJ)
Fashion Inst of Technology (NY)
Florida State U (FL)
Lipscomb U (TN)
Loyola U Chicago (IL)
Purdue U (IN)

ENTREPRENEURSHIP
The American U of Paris (France)
Anderson U (IN)
Ashland U (OH)
Avila U (MO)
Babson Coll (MA)
Baldwin Wallace U (OH)
Ball State U (IN)
Baylor U (TX)
Belmont U (TN)
Binghamton U, State U of New York (NY)
Bradley U (IL)
Brigham Young U (UT)
Bryant U (RI)
Buena Vista U (IA)
California State U, Dominguez Hills (CA)
California State U, Fullerton (CA)
Canisius Coll (NY)
Clarkson U (NY)
Cleary U (MI)
Cogswell Polytechnical Coll (CA)
Coll of the Atlantic (ME)
Crown Coll (MN)
Dalhousie U (NS, Canada)
Duquesne U (PA)
Eastern Michigan U (MI)
Elon U (NC)
Fairleigh Dickinson U, Coll at Florham (NJ)
Gannon U (PA)
George Fox U (OR)
Grove City Coll (PA)
Hampshire Coll (MA)
Hawai'i Pacific U (HI)
HEC Montreal (QC, Canada)
Hofstra U (NY)
Indiana Wesleyan U (IN)
Inter American U of Puerto Rico, Aguadilla Campus (PR)
Inter American U of Puerto Rico, Bayamón Campus (PR)
Inter American U of Puerto Rico, Ponce Campus (PR)
Inter American U of Puerto Rico, San Germán Campus (PR)
Iowa State U of Science and Technology (IA)
Juniata Coll (PA)
Kent State U (OH)
Lake Erie Coll (OH)
Lasell Coll (MA)
Lindenwood U (MO)

Lipscomb U (TN)
Lynn U (FL)
Marquette U (WI)
Mars Hill Coll (NC)
Menlo Coll (CA)
Millikin U (IL)
Missouri State U (MO)
Morrisville State Coll (NY)
Northeastern U (MA)
Northern Michigan U (MI)
Northwood U, Florida Campus (FL)
Northwood U, Michigan Campus (MI)
Oklahoma State U (OK)
Pace U (NY)
Purdue U (IN)
Purdue U Calumet (IN)
Quinnipiac U (CT)
Rider U (NJ)
Rowan U (NJ)
St. Edward's U (TX)
Saint Louis U (MO)
St. Mary's U (TX)
Saint Mary's U of Minnesota (MN)
Salem State U (MA)
Samford U (AL)
Seton Hill U (PA)
Shenandoah U (VA)
Sierra Nevada Coll (NV)
South Dakota State U (SD)
Southern Methodist U (TX)
Southern Polytechnic State U (GA)
State U of New York at Plattsburgh (NY)
Stetson U (FL)
Suffolk U (MA)
Syracuse U (NY)
Temple U (PA)
Thomas Edison State Coll (NJ)
Trine U (IN)
U of Alaska Anchorage (AK)
The U of Arizona (AZ)
The U of British Columbia–Okanagan (BC, Canada)
U of Central Arkansas (AR)
U of Hartford (CT)
U of Houston (TX)
U of Illinois at Chicago (IL)
U of Illinois at Urbana–Champaign (IL)
U of Maine at Machias (ME)
U of Miami (FL)
U of Minnesota, Crookston (MN)
U of Nevada, Las Vegas (NV)
U of North Dakota (ND)
U of Notre Dame (IN)
U of Ottawa (ON, Canada)
U of Pittsburgh at Bradford (PA)
U of Regina (SK, Canada)
U of St. Francis (IL)
U of St. Thomas (MN)
U of Southern Indiana (IN)
The U of Tampa (FL)
The U of Texas at San Antonio (TX)
The U of Toledo (OH)
U of Utah (UT)
U of Vermont (VT)
The U of Western Ontario (ON, Canada)
Virginia Intermont Coll (VA)
Virginia Union U (VA)
Washington State U (WA)
Washington U in St. Louis (MO)
Western Carolina U (NC)
Western Kentucky U (KY)
Western State Colorado U (CO)
Wichita State U (KS)
Wilkes U (PA)
Xavier U (OH)
York Coll of Pennsylvania (PA)

ENVIRONMENTAL BIOLOGY
American U (DC)
Bennington Coll (VT)
Bethel U (IN)
Blackburn Coll (IL)
Boston U (MA)
Bridgewater State U (MA)
California State Polytechnic U, Pomona (CA)
Cedar Crest Coll (PA)
Central Methodist U (MO)
Chowan U (NC)
Christopher Newport U (VA)
Colby Coll (ME)
Colgate U (NY)

The Coll at Brockport, State U of New York (NY)
Coll of the Atlantic (ME)
Columbia U (NY)
Columbia U, School of General Studies (NY)
Cornerstone U (MI)
Elizabethtown Coll (PA)
Ferris State U (MI)
Fort Lewis Coll (CO)
Franklin Pierce U (NH)
Friends U (KS)
Greenville Coll (IL)
Houghton Coll (NY)
Humboldt State U (CA)
Inter American U of Puerto Rico, Bayamón Campus (PR)
Iona Coll (NY)
Jacksonville State U (AL)
Keystone Coll (PA)
Liberty U (VA)
Lindenwood U (MO)
Manchester U (IN)
The Master's Coll and Sem (CA)
McDaniel Coll (MD)
Michigan State U (MI)
Minnesota State U Mankato (MN)
Monmouth U (NJ)
Philadelphia U (PA)
Pittsburg State U (KS)
Plymouth State U (NH)
St. Lawrence U (NY)
Saint Mary's U of Minnesota (MN)
Salem State U (MA)
Sewanee: The U of the South (TN)
Southern Nazarene U (OK)
State U of New York Coll at Cortland (NY)
Suffolk U (MA)
Texas A&M U (TX)
Tulane U (LA)
Unity Coll (ME)
The U of British Columbia (BC, Canada)
U of Guelph (ON, Canada)
U of La Verne (CA)
U of Mount Union (OH)
U of New Brunswick Saint John (NB, Canada)
U of Regina (SK, Canada)
The U of Tennessee at Martin (TN)
U of Windsor (ON, Canada)
Washington U in St. Louis (MO)
Western State Colorado U (CO)
Westfield State U (MA)
William Penn U (IA)

ENVIRONMENTAL CHEMISTRY
Colby Coll (ME)
Columbia U, School of General Studies (NY)
Lawrence Technological U (MI)
Oakland U (MI)
Pittsburg State U (KS)
Purdue U (IN)
St. Edward's U (TX)
U of Georgia (GA)

ENVIRONMENTAL CONTROL TECHNOLOGIES RELATED
Inter American U of Puerto Rico, Bayamón Campus (PR)
New York Inst of Technology (NY)
Purdue U (IN)
Thomas Edison State Coll (NJ)

ENVIRONMENTAL DESIGN/ARCHITECTURE
Art Center Coll of Design (CA)
Auburn U (AL)
Ball State U (IN)
Bennington Coll (VT)
Boston Architectural Coll (MA)
Bowling Green State U (OH)
Coll of the Atlantic (ME)
Dalhousie U (NS, Canada)
Lawrence Technological U (MI)
Montana State U (MT)
North Carolina State U (NC)
North Dakota State U (ND)
Otis Coll of Art and Design (CA)
Purdue U (IN)
Rutgers, The State U of New Jersey, New Brunswick (NJ)
Stony Brook U, State U of New York (NY)

Texas A&M U (TX)
U at Buffalo, the State U of New York (NY)
U of Colorado Boulder (CO)
U of Houston (TX)
U of Massachusetts Amherst (MA)
U of Memphis (TN)
U of Minnesota, Twin Cities Campus (MN)
U of Missouri–Kansas City (MO)
U of New Mexico (NM)
U of Oklahoma (OK)
U of Pennsylvania (PA)

ENVIRONMENTAL EDUCATION
Coll of the Atlantic (ME)
Johnson State Coll (VT)
Prescott Coll (AZ)
Purdue U (IN)
Sonoma State U (CA)
U of Maine at Machias (ME)

ENVIRONMENTAL ENGINEERING TECHNOLOGY
Bowling Green State U (OH)
California State U, Long Beach (CA)
City Coll of the City U of New York (NY)
Middle Tennessee State U (TN)
North Carolina State U (NC)
Purdue U (IN)
Shawnee State U (OH)
Temple U (PA)
United States Military Acad (NY)
The U of British Columbia (BC, Canada)
U of Guelph (ON, Canada)
West Virginia U Inst of Technology (WV)

ENVIRONMENTAL/ENVIRONMENTAL HEALTH ENGINEERING
Arizona State U (AZ)
California Polytechnic State U, San Luis Obispo (CA)
Central State U (OH)
Christian Brothers U (TN)
Clarkson U (NY)
Colorado School of Mines (CO)
Colorado State U (CO)
Columbia U (NY)
Dalhousie U (NS, Canada)
Florida Gulf Coast U (FL)
Florida Intl U (FL)
Gannon U (PA)
Hope Coll (MI)
Humboldt State U (CA)
Indiana Tech (IN)
The Johns Hopkins U (MD)
Lafayette Coll (PA)
Lehigh U (PA)
Louisiana State U and Ag and Mech Coll (LA)
Manhattan Coll (NY)
Marquette U (WI)
Massachusetts Inst of Technology (MA)
Massachusetts Maritime Acad (MA)
Missouri U of Science and Technology (MO)
Montana Tech of The U of Montana (MT)
New Mexico Inst of Mining and Technology (NM)
North Carolina State U (NC)
Northern Arizona U (AZ)
The Ohio State U (OH)
Old Dominion U (VA)
Oral Roberts U (OK)
Oregon State U (OR)
Penn State Abington (PA)
Penn State Altoona (PA)
Penn State Beaver (PA)
Penn State Berks (PA)
Penn State Brandywine (PA)
Penn State DuBois (PA)
Penn State Erie, The Behrend Coll (PA)
Penn State Fayette, The Eberly Campus (PA)
Penn State Greater Allegheny (PA)
Penn State Harrisburg (PA)
Penn State Hazleton (PA)
Penn State Lehigh Valley (PA)

Penn State Mont Alto (PA)
Penn State New Kensington (PA)
Penn State Schuylkill (PA)
Penn State Shenango (PA)
Penn State Park (PA)
Penn State Wilkes-Barre (PA)
Penn State Worthington Scranton (PA)
Penn State York (PA)
Polytechnic U of Puerto Rico (PR)
Rensselaer Polytechnic Inst (NY)
Rice U (TX)
Roger Williams U (RI)
San Diego State U (CA)
Seattle U (WA)
Southern Methodist U (TX)
Stanford U (CA)
Syracuse U (NY)
Taylor U (IN)
Tufts U (MA)
Tulane U (LA)
United States Air Force Acad (CO)
United States Military Acad (NY)
U at Buffalo, the State U of New York (NY)
U of California, Berkeley (CA)
U of California, Irvine (CA)
U of California, Merced (CA)
U of California, Riverside (CA)
U of Central Florida (FL)
U of Cincinnati (OH)
U of Colorado Boulder (CO)
U of Delaware (DE)
U of Florida (FL)
U of Georgia (GA)
U of Illinois at Urbana–Champaign (IL)
U of Miami (FL)
U of Nevada, Reno (NV)
U of New Hampshire (NH)
U of North Dakota (ND)
U of Notre Dame (IN)
U of Oklahoma (OK)
U of Pennsylvania (PA)
U of Regina (SK, Canada)
U of Southern California (CA)
U of Vermont (VT)
U of Waterloo (ON, Canada)
The U of Western Ontario (ON, Canada)
U of Windsor (ON, Canada)
U of Wisconsin–Platteville (WI)
Utah State U (UT)
Wilkes U (PA)
Worcester Polytechnic Inst (MA)
Yale U (CT)

ENVIRONMENTAL HEALTH
American U of Beirut (Lebanon)
Baylor U (TX)
Boise State U (ID)
Bowling Green State U (OH)
California State U, Northridge (CA)
Colorado State U (CO)
Drury U (MO)
East Carolina U (NC)
East Central U (OK)
East Tennessee State U (TN)
Illinois State U (IL)
Mississippi Valley State U (MS)
Oakland U (MI)
Ohio U (OH)
Purdue U (IN)
Roger Williams U (RI)
Texas Southern U (TX)
U of Arkansas at Little Rock (AR)
U of Georgia (GA)
U of Illinois at Urbana–Champaign (IL)
The U of North Carolina at Chapel Hill (NC)
U of Regina (SK, Canada)
Western Carolina U (NC)
Western Kentucky U (KY)
Wright State U (OH)
York Coll of the City U of New York (NY)

ENVIRONMENTAL PSYCHOLOGY
Embry-Riddle Aeronautical U–Daytona (FL)
Purdue U (IN)

ENVIRONMENTAL SCIENCE
Abilene Christian U (TX)
Alaska Pacific U (AK)
Albright Coll (PA)

Alderson-Broaddus Coll (WV)
Alverno Coll (WI)
American Public U System (WV)
Appalachian State U (NC)
Ashland U (OH)
Assumption Coll (MA)
Auburn U (AL)
Baylor U (TX)
Bellarmine U (KY)
Belmont U (TN)
Benedictine U (IL)
Bennington Coll (VT)
Berry Coll (GA)
Bethel U (MN)
Bethune-Cookman U (FL)
Blackburn Coll (IL)
Bradley U (IL)
Brevard Coll (NC)
Bridgewater Coll (VA)
Brigham Young U (UT)
Brown U (RI)
Bryant U (RI)
Buena Vista U (IA)
California Baptist U (CA)
California Lutheran U (CA)
California State U, Fresno (CA)
California State U, Long Beach (CA)
California State U, Monterey Bay (CA)
Calvin Coll (MI)
Canisius Coll (NY)
Capital U (OH)
Cedarville U (OH)
Central Methodist U (MO)
Central Michigan U (MI)
Chatham U (PA)
Chestnut Hill Coll (PA)
Claflin U (SC)
Clarion U of Pennsylvania (PA)
Clarkson U (NY)
Cleveland State U (OH)
Coe Coll (IA)
Colby Coll (ME)
The Colorado Coll (CO)
Colorado Mesa U (CO)
Columbia Coll (MO)
Columbia U, School of General Studies (NY)
Concordia U (QC, Canada)
Concordia U Chicago (IL)
Concordia U Texas (TX)
Concord U (WV)
Dalhousie U (NS, Canada)
Dallas Baptist U (TX)
DePaul U (IL)
DEREE—The American Coll of Greece (Greece)
Dickinson Coll (PA)
Dominican U (IL)
Drake U (IA)
Drury U (MO)
Duquesne U (PA)
Earlham Coll (IN)
Eastern New Mexico U (NM)
Eastern Washington U (WA)
Edinboro U of Pennsylvania (PA)
Elon U (NC)
Endicott Coll (MA)
The Evergreen State Coll (WA)
Fairleigh Dickinson U, Metropolitan Campus (NJ)
Florida Ag and Mech U (FL)
Florida Inst of Technology (FL)
Franklin & Marshall Coll (PA)
Frostburg State U (MD)
Gannon U (PA)
Gardner-Webb U (NC)
Geneva Coll (PA)
George Mason U (VA)
Georgia Coll & State U (GA)
Gettysburg Coll (PA)
Gonzaga U (WA)
Goshen Coll (IA)
Hardin-Simmons U (TX)
Hartwick Coll (NY)
Hawai`i Pacific U (HI)
Hood Coll (MD)
Humboldt State U (CA)
Hunter Coll of the City U of New York (NY)
Husson U (ME)
Indiana U Bloomington (IN)
Indiana U–Purdue U Indianapolis (IN)
Inter American U of Puerto Rico, Ponce Campus (PR)

Inter American U of Puerto Rico, San Germán Campus (PR)
John Brown U (AR)
The Johns Hopkins U (MD)
Juniata Coll (PA)
Keuka Coll (NY)
King's Coll (PA)
Kutztown U of Pennsylvania (PA)
Lander U (SC)
Lewis U (IL)
Lincoln U (MO)
Lindenwood U (MO)
Lipscomb U (TN)
Long Island U–C. W. Post Campus (NY)
Louisiana State U and Ag and Mech Coll (LA)
Lourdes U (OH)
Loyola Marymount U (CA)
Loyola U Chicago (IL)
Lynchburg Coll (VA)
Madonna U (MI)
Marietta Coll (OH)
Marist Coll (NY)
Marshall U (WV)
Maryville U of Saint Louis (MO)
Marywood U (PA)
Massachusetts Coll of Liberal Arts (MA)
Massachusetts Maritime Acad (MA)
McDaniel Coll (MD)
Mercer U (GA)
Messiah Coll (PA)
Metropolitan State U of Denver (CO)
Miami U (OH)
Michigan State U (MI)
Midwestern State U (TX)
Mills Coll (CA)
Monmouth Coll (IL)
Montana State U (MT)
Muhlenberg Coll (PA)
National U (CA)
Nazareth Coll of Rochester (NY)
New England Coll (NH)
New Mexico State U (NM)
North Carolina Central U (NC)
North Carolina State U (NC)
Northern Arizona U (AZ)
Northern Michigan U (MI)
Northwest U (WA)
Oakland U (MI)
The Ohio State U (OH)
Oklahoma State U (OK)
Oregon State U (OR)
Pace U (NY)
Piedmont Coll (GA)
Pitzer Coll (CA)
Point Loma Nazarene U (CA)
Point Park U (PA)
Post U (CT)
Queens U of Charlotte (NC)
Ramapo Coll of New Jersey (NJ)
Randolph Coll (VA)
Rensselaer Polytechnic Inst (NY)
Rhodes Coll (TN)
Rochester Inst of Technology (NY)
Rocky Mountain Coll (MT)
Roger Williams U (RI)
St. Bonaventure U (NY)
Saint Louis U (MO)
St. Norbert Coll (WI)
Saint Vincent Coll (PA)
Salisbury U (MD)
Samford U (AL)
Sam Houston State U (TX)
Scripps Coll (CA)
Seattle U (WA)
Siena Heights U (MI)
Sierra Nevada Coll (NV)
Simmons Coll (MA)
Simon Fraser U (BC, Canada)
Simpson Coll (IA)
Skidmore Coll (NY)
Southeast Missouri State U (MO)
Southern Methodist U (TX)
State U of New York Coll at Cortland (NY)
Stephen F. Austin State U (TX)
Stetson U (FL)
Suffolk U (MA)
Sweet Briar Coll (VA)
Taylor U (IN)
Temple U (PA)
Texas A&M U (TX)
Texas A&M U–Commerce (TX)

Texas Christian U (TX)
Texas State U–San Marcos (TX)
Thomas Edison State Coll (NJ)
Thomas More Coll (KY)
Thompson Rivers U (BC, Canada)
Trinity Coll (CT)
Troy U (AL)
United States Military Acad (NY)
Unity Coll (ME)
U at Albany, State U of New York (NY)
The U of Alabama (AL)
The U of Arizona (AZ)
U of California, Irvine (CA)
U of California, Los Angeles (CA)
U of California, Riverside (CA)
U of Delaware (DE)
U of Denver (CO)
U of Evansville (IN)
U of Florida (FL)
U of Georgia (GA)
U of Guelph (ON, Canada)
U of Hawaii at Manoa (HI)
U of Houston (TX)
U of Houston–Clear Lake (TX)
U of Idaho (ID)
U of Illinois at Chicago (IL)
U of Illinois at Urbana–Champaign (IL)
U of Louisiana at Lafayette (LA)
U of Maryland, Baltimore County (MD)
U of Maryland, Coll Park (MD)
U of Massachusetts Amherst (MA)
U of Michigan–Dearborn (MI)
U of Michigan–Flint (MI)
U of Minnesota, Duluth (MN)
U of Mobile (AL)
The U of Montana Western (MT)
U of Mount Union (OH)
U of Nebraska at Omaha (NE)
U of New England (ME)
U of New Hampshire (NH)
U of New Mexico (NM)
The U of North Carolina at Chapel Hill (NC)
The U of North Carolina at Pembroke (NC)
The U of North Carolina Wilmington (NC)
U of Northern Iowa (IA)
U of Notre Dame (IN)
U of Oklahoma (OK)
U of Oregon (OR)
U of Ottawa (ON, Canada)
U of Rochester (NY)
U of St. Francis (IL)
U of St. Thomas (TX)
The U of Scranton (PA)
U of South Carolina (SC)
U of Southern Maine (ME)
U of South Florida (FL)
The U of Tennessee at Chattanooga (TN)
The U of Texas at Arlington (TX)
The U of Texas at Brownsville (TX)
The U of Texas at San Antonio (TX)
The U of Texas–Pan American (TX)
U of the Incarnate Word (TX)
U of the Sciences (PA)
The U of Toledo (OH)
U of Utah (UT)
U of Vermont (VT)
U of Virginia (VA)
U of Washington, Bothell (WA)
U of Washington, Tacoma (WA)
U of Waterloo (ON, Canada)
The U of Western Ontario (ON, Canada)
U of West Florida (FL)
U of West Georgia (GA)
U of Windsor (ON, Canada)
U of Wisconsin–Green Bay (WI)
U of Wisconsin–Madison (WI)
U of Wisconsin–Milwaukee (WI)
Upper Iowa U (IA)
Valdosta State U (GA)
Valparaiso U (IN)
Vassar Coll (NY)
Villanova U (PA)
Virginia Intermont Coll (VA)
Walla Walla U (WA)
Washington State U (WA)
Washington U in St. Louis (MO)
Wayland Baptist U (TX)
Wayne State U (MI)
Wesleyan Coll (GA)

Western Carolina U (NC)
Western Washington U (WA)
Westfield State U (MA)
Westminster Coll (MO)
West Texas A&M U (TX)
West Virginia Wesleyan Coll (WV)
Wheaton Coll (MA)
Wheeling Jesuit U (WV)
Willamette U (OR)
Williams Coll (MA)
Winthrop U (SC)
Wittenberg U (OH)
Youngstown State U (OH)

ENVIRONMENTAL STUDIES
Acadia U (NS, Canada)
Adelphi U (NY)
Alaska Pacific U (AK)
Albion Coll (MI)
Alfred U (NY)
American U (DC)
Amherst Coll (MA)
Appalachian State U (NC)
Augustana Coll (IL)
Bard Coll (NY)
Barton Coll (NC)
Bates Coll (ME)
Baylor U (TX)
Bellarmine U (KY)
Bemidji State U (MN)
Bennington Coll (VT)
Bethany Coll (WV)
Bethel U (MN)
Binghamton U, State U of New York (NY)
Boise State U (ID)
Boston Coll (MA)
Bowdoin Coll (ME)
Bowling Green State U (OH)
Brevard Coll (NC)
Brown U (RI)
Bucknell U (PA)
California State U, East Bay (CA)
California State U, Monterey Bay (CA)
California State U, San Bernardino (CA)
Calvin Coll (MI)
Canisius Coll (NY)
Carleton Coll (MN)
Carroll Coll (MT)
Case Western Reserve U (OH)
Castleton State Coll (VT)
Catawba Coll (NC)
Central Coll (IA)
Champlain Coll (VT)
Chatham U (PA)
City Coll of the City U of New York (NY)
Claremont McKenna Coll (CA)
Cleveland State U (OH)
Coe Coll (IA)
Colby Coll (ME)
Colgate U (NY)
The Coll at Brockport, State U of New York (NY)
The Coll of Idaho (ID)
The Coll of New Rochelle (NY)
Coll of Saint Benedict (MN)
Coll of the Atlantic (ME)
Coll of the Holy Cross (MA)
The Coll of William and Mary (VA)
The Colorado Coll (CO)
Colorado Mountain Coll, Timberline Campus (CO)
Columbia U (NY)
Concordia Coll (MN)
Concordia U Texas (TX)
Concordia U Wisconsin (WI)
Connecticut Coll (CT)
Cornell Coll (IA)
Creighton U (NE)
Curry Coll (MA)
Dalhousie U (NS, Canada)
Dartmouth Coll (NH)
Davidson Coll (NC)
DePauw U (IN)
Dickinson Coll (PA)
Doane Coll (NE)
Dordt Coll (IA)
Drake U (IA)
Drury U (MO)
Earlham Coll (IN)
Eastern Mennonite U (VA)
Eckerd Coll (FL)
Elmira Coll (NY)
Elon U (NC)

Emory & Henry Coll (VA)
Eugene Lang Coll The New School for Liberal Arts (NY)
The Evergreen State Coll (WA)
Ferrum Coll (VA)
Florida Intl U (FL)
Florida Southern Coll (FL)
Fort Lewis Coll (CO)
Framingham State U (MA)
Franklin & Marshall Coll (PA)
Franklin Coll Switzerland (Switzerland)
Franklin Pierce U (NH)
Furman U (SC)
Georgetown U (DC)
Georgia Coll & State U (GA)
Gettysburg Coll (PA)
Goddard Coll (VT)
Goodwin Coll (CT)
Goucher Coll (MD)
Guilford Coll (NC)
Gustavus Adolphus Coll (MN)
Hamilton Coll (NY)
Hamline U (MN)
Hampshire Coll (MA)
Hampton U (VA)
Hawai`i Pacific U (HI)
Hendrix Coll (AR)
Hiram Coll (OH)
Hobart and William Smith Colls (NY)
Hofstra U (NY)
Hollins U (VA)
Humboldt State U (CA)
Illinois Coll (IL)
Illinois Wesleyan U (IL)
Immaculata U (PA)
Inter American U of Puerto Rico, San Germán Campus (PR)
Iowa State U of Science and Technology (IA)
Ithaca Coll (NY)
John Brown U (AR)
John Carroll U (OH)
The Johns Hopkins U (MD)
Johnson State Coll (VT)
Judson U (IL)
Juniata Coll (PA)
Keene State Coll (NH)
Keystone Coll (PA)
King's Coll (PA)
The King's U Coll (AB, Canada)
Knox Coll (IL)
Lake Superior State U (MI)
Lamar U (TX)
La Salle U (PA)
Lasell Coll (MA)
Lawrence U (WI)
Lehigh U (PA)
Le Moyne Coll (NY)
Lesley U (MA)
Lincoln Memorial U (TN)
Linfield Coll (OR)
Long Island U–C. W. Post Campus (NY)
Luther Coll (IA)
Lynchburg Coll (VA)
Lynn U (FL)
Macalester Coll (MN)
Maharishi U of Management (IA)
Manchester U (IN)
Mansfield U of Pennsylvania (PA)
Marietta Coll (OH)
Marist Coll (NY)
Maryville Coll (TN)
Maryville U of Saint Louis (MO)
Massachusetts Coll of Liberal Arts (MA)
Massachusetts Maritime Acad (MA)
McDaniel Coll (MD)
McKendree U (IL)
Mercer U (GA)
Merrimack Coll (MA)
Michigan State U (MI)
Middlebury Coll (VT)
Mills Coll (CA)
Minnesota State U Mankato (MN)
Minnesota State U Moorhead (MN)
Mitchell Coll (CT)
Montreat Coll, Montreat (NC)
Moravian Coll (PA)
Mount Allison U (NB, Canada)
Mount Holyoke Coll (MA)
Mount St. Mary's U (MD)
Naropa U (CO)
National U (CA)

Neumann U (PA)
New Coll of Florida (FL)
New England Coll (NH)
New Mexico Highlands U (NM)
New Mexico Inst of Mining and Technology (NM)
North Carolina Wesleyan Coll (NC)
Northeastern Illinois U (IL)
Northeastern U (MA)
Northern Arizona U (AZ)
Northern Illinois U (IL)
Northern State U (SD)
Northland Coll (WI)
Norwich U (VT)
Nova Southeastern U (FL)
The Ohio State U (OH)
Ohio U (OH)
Ohio Wesleyan U (OH)
Oklahoma City U (OK)
Olivet Coll (MI)
Pace U (NY)
Pacific Lutheran U (WA)
Pacific Union Coll (CA)
Pacific U (OR)
Penn State Altoona (PA)
Penn State U Park (PA)
Piedmont Coll (GA)
Plymouth State U (NH)
Pomona Coll (CA)
Portland State U (OR)
Post U (CT)
Prescott Coll (AZ)
Principia Coll (IL)
Purchase Coll, State U of New York (NY)
Queens U of Charlotte (NC)
Ramapo Coll of New Jersey (NJ)
Randolph Coll (VA)
Randolph-Macon Coll (VA)
Reed Coll (OR)
Regis U (CO)
The Richard Stockton Coll of New Jersey (NJ)
Rider U (NJ)
Ripon Coll (WI)
Roanoke Coll (VA)
Robert Morris U (PA)
Rocky Mountain Coll (MT)
Rollins Coll (FL)
Rosemont Coll (PA)
Rowan U (NJ)
Rutgers, The State U of New Jersey, Newark (NJ)
Rutgers, The State U of New Jersey, New Brunswick (NJ)
Saint Anselm Coll (NH)
St. Edward's U (TX)
Saint John's U (MN)
St. John's U (NY)
Saint Joseph's U (PA)
St. Lawrence U (NY)
Saint Leo U (FL)
Saint Michael's Coll (VT)
St. Olaf Coll (MN)
St. Thomas U (FL)
St. Thomas U (NB, Canada)
Saint Vincent Coll (PA)
Salve Regina U (RI)
San Diego State U (CA)
San Francisco State U (CA)
San Jose State U (CA)
Seattle U (WA)
Sewanee: The U of the South (TN)
Shenandoah U (VA)
Shepherd U (WV)
Shippensburg U of Pennsylvania (PA)
Siena Coll (NY)
Skidmore Coll (NY)
Smith Coll (MA)
Sonoma State U (CA)
South Dakota State U (SD)
Southern Methodist U (TX)
Southern New Hampshire U (NH)
Southern Oregon U (OR)
Southwestern U (TX)
Spelman Coll (GA)
Stanford U (CA)
State U of New York at Fredonia (NY)
State U of New York at Plattsburgh (NY)
State U of New York Coll at Cortland (NY)
State U of New York Coll at Potsdam (NY)

State U of New York Coll of Agriculture and Technology at Cobleskill (NY)
Sterling Coll (VT)
Stonehill Coll (MA)
Stony Brook U, State U of New York (NY)
Sul Ross State U (TX)
Sweet Briar Coll (VA)
Tarleton State U (TX)
Taylor U (IN)
Temple U (PA)
Tennessee Wesleyan Coll (TN)
Texas A&M U (TX)
Texas Southern U (TX)
Thomas Edison State Coll (NJ)
Trent U (ON, Canada)
Trine U (IN)
Tufts U (MA)
Tulane U (LA)
Tuskegee U (AL)
United States Military Acad (NY)
Université de Sherbrooke (QC, Canada)
U of Alaska Anchorage (AK)
The U of Arizona (AZ)
The U of British Columbia (BC, Canada)
The U of British Columbia–Okanagan (BC, Canada)
U of California, Davis (CA)
U of California, Irvine (CA)
U of California, Santa Barbara (CA)
U of California, Santa Cruz (CA)
U of Central Arkansas (AR)
U of Chicago (IL)
U of Cincinnati (OH)
U of Colorado Boulder (CO)
U of Delaware (DE)
U of Evansville (IN)
The U of Findlay (OH)
U of Georgia (GA)
U of Guelph (ON, Canada)
The U of Iowa (IA)
The U of Kansas (KS)
U of Maine at Farmington (ME)
U of Maine at Fort Kent (ME)
U of Maine at Machias (ME)
U of Maryland, Baltimore County (MD)
U of Maryland Eastern Shore (MD)
U of Michigan (MI)
U of Michigan–Dearborn (MI)
U of Minnesota, Duluth (MN)
U of Minnesota, Twin Cities Campus (MN)
U of Missouri (MO)
U of Missouri–Kansas City (MO)
The U of Montana Western (MT)
U of Nebraska–Lincoln (NE)
U of Nevada, Las Vegas (NV)
U of New England (ME)
U of North Carolina at Asheville (NC)
The U of North Carolina at Chapel Hill (NC)
The U of North Carolina Wilmington (NC)
U of North Dakota (ND)
U of Oklahoma (OK)
U of Oregon (OR)
U of Ottawa (ON, Canada)
U of Pennsylvania (PA)
U of Pittsburgh at Bradford (PA)
U of Portland (OR)
U of Redlands (CA)
U of Rhode Island (RI)
U of Richmond (VA)
U of Rochester (NY)
U of St. Thomas (TX)
U of San Diego (CA)
U of Southern California (CA)
U of Southern Maine (ME)
The U of Tampa (FL)
The U of Tennessee at Martin (TN)
U of the District of Columbia (DC)
U of the Ozarks (AR)
The U of Toledo (OH)
U of Tulsa (OK)
U of Utah (UT)
U of Vermont (VT)
U of Washington, Bothell (WA)
U of Washington, Tacoma (WA)
U of Waterloo (ON, Canada)
The U of Western Ontario (ON, Canada)
U of West Georgia (GA)

U of Windsor (ON, Canada)
U of Wisconsin–Green Bay (WI)
U of Wisconsin–Madison (WI)
U of Wyoming (WY)
Vassar Coll (NY)
Villanova U (PA)
Virginia Commonwealth U (VA)
Virginia Polytechnic Inst and State U (VA)
Virginia Wesleyan Coll (VA)
Walla Walla U (WA)
Washington & Jefferson Coll (PA)
Washington and Lee U (VA)
Washington Coll (MD)
Washington U in St. Louis (MO)
Waynesburg U (PA)
Wellesley Coll (MA)
Wells Coll (NY)
Wesleyan U (CT)
Wesley Coll (DE)
Western Michigan U (MI)
Western State Colorado U (CO)
Western Washington U (WA)
Westminster Coll (MO)
Westminster Coll (UT)
Wheaton Coll (IL)
Wheeling Jesuit U (WV)
Widener U (PA)
William Paterson U of New Jersey (NJ)
Williams Coll (MA)
Worcester Polytechnic Inst (MA)
Yale U (CT)

ENVIRONMENTAL TOXICOLOGY
Clarkson U (NY)
U of California, Davis (CA)

EPIDEMIOLOGY
U of Rochester (NY)
The U of Western Ontario (ON, Canada)

EQUESTRIAN STUDIES
Asbury U (KY)
Averett U (VA)
Becker Coll (MA)
Colorado State U (CO)
Houghton Coll (NY)
Judson Coll (AL)
Lake Erie Coll (OH)
North Dakota State U (ND)
Post U (CT)
Rocky Mountain Coll (MT)
Rutgers, The State U of New Jersey, New Brunswick (NJ)
Saint Mary-of-the-Woods Coll (IN)
Stephens Coll (MO)
Sul Ross State U (TX)
The U of Findlay (OH)
The U of Montana Western (MT)
Virginia Intermont Coll (VA)
West Texas A&M U (TX)

ETHICS
Bridgewater State U (MA)
Carroll Coll (MT)
Drake U (IA)
Southern Methodist Coll (SC)
Syracuse U (NY)
U of Michigan–Flint (MI)
U of Ottawa (ON, Canada)
U of Southern California (CA)
U of Washington, Bothell (WA)
The U of Western Ontario (ON, Canada)

ETHNIC, CULTURAL MINORITY, GENDER, AND GROUP STUDIES RELATED
Albion Coll (MI)
American U (DC)
Bethel U (MN)
Boise State U (ID)
Bowling Green State U (OH)
California Polytechnic State U, San Luis Obispo (CA)
California State Polytechnic U, Pomona (CA)
California State U, Chico (CA)
California State U, Stanislaus (CA)
Chatham U (PA)
The Colorado Coll (CO)
Columbia U, School of General Studies (NY)
Connecticut Coll (CT)
Cornell Coll (IA)
Dakota Wesleyan U (SD)

Davidson Coll (NC)
Eugene Lang Coll The New School for Liberal Arts (NY)
The Evergreen State Coll (WA)
Grinnell Coll (IA)
Hampshire Coll (MA)
Hawai`i Pacific U (HI)
Indiana U Bloomington (IN)
Indiana U South Bend (IN)
Lawrence U (WI)
Mills Coll (CA)
Mount Holyoke Coll (MA)
Northeastern Illinois U (IL)
Oregon State U (OR)
St. Francis Coll (NY)
Saint Michael's Coll (VT)
Skidmore Coll (NY)
Stanford U (CA)
Stonehill Coll (MA)
U at Buffalo, the State U of New York (NY)
U of California, Berkeley (CA)
U of Chicago (IL)
U of Colorado Boulder (CO)
U of Colorado Colorado Springs (CO)
U of Denver (CO)
U of Hawaii at Manoa (HI)
U of Illinois at Chicago (IL)
U of Kentucky (KY)
U of Nebraska at Omaha (NE)
U of Nebraska–Lincoln (NE)
U of New Brunswick Saint John (NB, Canada)
U of Pittsburgh (PA)
U of Regina (SK, Canada)
U of Southern California (CA)
U of Utah (UT)
U of Washington, Tacoma (WA)
The U of Western Ontario (ON, Canada)
Washington State U (WA)
Washington U in St. Louis (MO)
Wayne State U (MI)
Wellesley Coll (MA)
Westfield State U (MA)
Whitman Coll (WA)
Wichita State U (KS)
Williams Coll (MA)
Yale U (CT)

ETHNIC STUDIES
Arizona State U (AZ)
Colorado State U (CO)
Edgewood Coll (WI)
Goddard Coll (VT)
Messiah Coll (PA)
Minnesota State U Moorhead (MN)
St. Olaf Coll (MN)
U of Colorado Denver (CO)
U of San Diego (CA)
The U of Texas at Austin (TX)

EUROPEAN HISTORY
Bard Coll (NY)
Bennington Coll (VT)
Gettysburg Coll (PA)
Howard Payne U (TX)
Keene State Coll (NH)
Salem State U (MA)
Suffolk U (MA)
U of Regina (SK, Canada)

EUROPEAN STUDIES
American U in Bulgaria (Bulgaria)
The American U of Paris (France)
Amherst Coll (MA)
Bard Coll (NY)
Belmont U (TN)
Bennington Coll (VT)
Bowling Green State U (OH)
California State U, Fullerton (CA)
Canisius Coll (NY)
Carnegie Mellon U (PA)
Central Michigan U (MI)
The Coll at Brockport, State U of New York (NY)
Dalhousie U (NS, Canada)
Drew U (NJ)
Fort Lewis Coll (CO)
Georgetown Coll (KY)
Gettysburg Coll (PA)
Hampshire Coll (MA)
Hillsdale Coll (MI)
Hobart and William Smith Colls (NY)
Loyola Marymount U (CA)
Middlebury Coll (VT)

Millsaps Coll (MS)
New Coll of Florida (FL)
New York U (NY)
Ohio U (OH)
Portland State U (OR)
Sacred Heart U (CT)
Saint Joseph's U (PA)
Saint Mary's Coll of California (CA)
San Diego State U (CA)
Scripps Coll (CA)
Seattle Pacific U (WA)
Sewanee: The U of the South (TN)
Stony Brook U, State U of New York (NY)
Texas State U–San Marcos (TX)
Trinity U (TX)
United States Military Acad (NY)
The U of British Columbia (BC, Canada)
U of California, Irvine (CA)
U of California, Los Angeles (CA)
U of Delaware (DE)
U of Guelph (ON, Canada)
The U of Kansas (KS)
U of Minnesota, Twin Cities Campus (MN)
U of Missouri (MO)
U of New Hampshire (NH)
U of New Mexico (NM)
The U of North Carolina at Chapel Hill (NC)
U of Richmond (VA)
U of South Carolina (SC)
The U of Texas at Austin (TX)
The U of Toledo (OH)
U of Vermont (VT)
Vanderbilt U (TN)
Washington U in St. Louis (MO)
Webster U (MO)

EUROPEAN STUDIES (WESTERN)
Illinois Wesleyan U (IL)
Seattle U (WA)
U of Nebraska–Lincoln (NE)

EVOLUTIONARY BIOLOGY
Bennington Coll (VT)
Case Western Reserve U (OH)
Coll of the Atlantic (ME)
Columbia U, School of General Studies (NY)
Dartmouth Coll (NH)
Rice U (TX)
Rutgers, The State U of New Jersey, New Brunswick (NJ)
Tulane U (LA)
Yale U (CT)

EXECUTIVE ASSISTANT/ EXECUTIVE SECRETARY
Bowling Green State U (OH)
Caribbean U (PR)
Inter American U of Puerto Rico, Bayamón Campus (PR)
U of Puerto Rico at Bayamón (PR)
U of Puerto Rico at Ponce (PR)

EXERCISE PHYSIOLOGY
Baldwin Wallace U (OH)
Baylor U (TX)
Bethany Lutheran Coll (MN)
The Coll at Brockport, State U of New York (NY)
The Coll of St. Scholastica (MN)
Concordia U Wisconsin (WI)
East Carolina U (NC)
Lynchburg Coll (VA)
Mercyhurst U (PA)
Merrimack Coll (MA)
Syracuse U (NY)
U at Buffalo, the State U of New York (NY)
U of California, Davis (CA)
U of Delaware (DE)
U of Florida (FL)
U of Massachusetts Amherst (MA)
U of Miami (FL)
U of Southern Maine (ME)
West Virginia U (WV)

EXPERIMENTAL PSYCHOLOGY
Keene State Coll (NH)
Moravian Coll (PA)
Northern Michigan U (MI)
Tiffin U (OH)
Tufts U (MA)

The U of British Columbia (BC, Canada)
U of Rochester (NY)
U of South Carolina (SC)
The U of Toledo (OH)

FACILITIES PLANNING AND MANAGEMENT
Eastern Michigan U (MI)
Missouri State U (MO)
New York City Coll of Technology of the City U of New York (NY)

FAMILY AND COMMUNITY SERVICES
Alderson-Broaddus Coll (WV)
Andrews U (MI)
Bowling Green State U (OH)
Curry Coll (MA)
East Carolina U (NC)
Harding U (AR)
Iowa State U of Science and Technology (IA)
John Brown U (AR)
Keystone Coll (PA)
La Roche Coll (PA)
Messiah Coll (PA)
Michigan State U (MI)
Oklahoma Baptist U (OK)
Oklahoma Christian U (OK)
Stevenson U (MD)
Union U (TN)
U of California, Santa Cruz (CA)
U of Florida (FL)
U of Maine at Machias (ME)
U of Maryland, Coll Park (MD)
U of Miami (FL)
U of Minnesota, Twin Cities Campus (MN)
U of Northern Iowa (IA)
U of Wisconsin–Madison (WI)
Youngstown State U (OH)

FAMILY AND CONSUMER ECONOMICS RELATED
Andrews U (MI)
Bowling Green State U (OH)
Brigham Young U (UT)
California State U, Fresno (CA)
Carson-Newman U (TN)
Fairmont State U (WV)
Iowa State U of Science and Technology (IA)
Louisiana Coll (LA)
Minnesota State U Mankato (MN)
Tennessee State U (TN)
The U of Akron (OH)
U of Hawaii at Manoa (HI)
U of Maryland Eastern Shore (MD)
U of Minnesota, Twin Cities Campus (MN)
U of Missouri (MO)
U of Nebraska at Kearney (NE)
U of Nebraska–Lincoln (NE)
U of Northern Iowa (IA)
U of Wisconsin–Stevens Point (WI)
Utah State U (UT)
Virginia State U (VA)

FAMILY AND CONSUMER SCIENCES/HOME ECONOMICS TEACHER EDUCATION
Appalachian State U (NC)
Baylor U (TX)
Bowling Green State U (OH)
Bradley U (IL)
Bridgewater Coll (VA)
Carson-Newman U (TN)
Cheyney U of Pennsylvania (PA)
Colorado State U (CO)
Concordia U, Nebraska (NE)
East Carolina U (NC)
Fairmont State U (WV)
Georgia Southern U (GA)
Hampton U (VA)
Harding U (AR)
Immaculata U (PA)
Iowa State U of Science and Technology (IA)
Jacksonville State U (AL)
Lamar U (TX)
Langston U (OK)
Marywood U (PA)
Mercyhurst U (PA)
Messiah Coll (PA)
Michigan State U (MI)
Minnesota State U Mankato (MN)
Missouri State U (MO)
Mount Vernon Nazarene U (OH)

New Mexico State U (NM)
North Dakota State U (ND)
Northern Illinois U (IL)
Northwest Missouri State U (MO)
The Ohio State U (OH)
The Ohio State U at Lima (OH)
Ohio U (OH)
Pittsburg State U (KS)
Seton Hill U (PA)
Southeast Missouri State U (MO)
The U of Akron (OH)
U of Central Arkansas (AR)
U of Central Oklahoma (OK)
U of Georgia (GA)
U of Guam (GU)
U of Maryland Eastern Shore (MD)
U of Minnesota, Twin Cities Campus (MN)
U of New Brunswick Fredericton (NB, Canada)
The U of Tennessee at Martin (TN)
U of the District of Columbia (DC)
U of Wisconsin–Stevens Point (WI)
U of Wisconsin–Stout (WI)
Utah State U (UT)
Virginia Polytechnic Inst and State U (VA)
Washington State U (WA)
Wayne State Coll (NE)
Western Kentucky U (KY)
Western Michigan U (MI)
Winthrop U (SC)
Youngstown State U (OH)

FAMILY AND CONSUMER SCIENCES/HUMAN SCIENCES
Auburn U (AL)
Ball State U (IN)
Baylor U (TX)
Berea Coll (KY)
Bowling Green State U (OH)
Bradley U (IL)
Bridgewater Coll (VA)
Brigham Young U (UT)
California State U, East Bay (CA)
California State U, Long Beach (CA)
California State U, Northridge (CA)
Carson-Newman U (TN)
Coll of the Atlantic (ME)
Coll of the Ozarks (MO)
Colorado State U (CO)
Delta State U (MS)
East Central U (OK)
Eastern Illinois U (IL)
Eastern New Mexico U (NM)
East Tennessee State U (TN)
Fairmont State U (WV)
Framingham State U (MA)
Harding U (AR)
Henderson State U (AR)
Illinois State U (IL)
Indiana State U (IN)
Indiana U of Pennsylvania (PA)
Iowa State U of Science and Technology (IA)
Jacksonville State U (AL)
Lamar U (TX)
Langston U (OK)
Liberty U (VA)
Lipscomb U (TN)
Louisiana State U and Ag and Mech Coll (LA)
Madonna U (MI)
Marshall U (WV)
The Master's Coll and Sem (CA)
Michigan State U (MI)
Minnesota State U Mankato (MN)
Mississippi State U (MS)
Montana State U (MT)
Montclair State U (NJ)
Mount Vernon Nazarene U (OH)
New Mexico Highlands U (NM)
Nicholls State U (LA)
North Carolina Central U (NC)
Northwestern State U of Louisiana (LA)
Pittsburg State U (KS)
Point Loma Nazarene U (CA)
Purdue U (IN)
Regis U (CO)
Rutgers, The State U of New Jersey, New Brunswick (NJ)
Sam Houston State U (TX)
San Francisco State U (CA)
Seattle Pacific U (WA)
Seton Hill U (PA)

Shepherd U (WV)
Southeastern Louisiana U (LA)
Southeast Missouri State U (MO)
Southern Utah U (UT)
Stephen F. Austin State U (TX)
Tarleton State U (TX)
Texas A&M U–Kingsville (TX)
Texas Southern U (TX)
Texas State U–San Marcos (TX)
Texas Woman's U (TX)
The U of Alabama (AL)
The U of British Columbia (BC, Canada)
U of Central Arkansas (AR)
U of Central Oklahoma (OK)
U of Kentucky (KY)
U of Maryland Eastern Shore (MD)
U of Minnesota, Twin Cities Campus (MN)
U of Montevallo (AL)
U of New Mexico (NM)
U of North Alabama (AL)
U of Saint Joseph (CT)
The U of Tennessee at Martin (TN)
The U of Texas at Austin (TX)
The U of Western Ontario (ON, Canada)
U of Wyoming (WY)
Washington State U (WA)
Wayne State Coll (NE)
Western Illinois U (IL)
Youngstown State U (OH)

FAMILY AND CONSUMER SCIENCES/HUMAN SCIENCES BUSINESS SERVICES RELATED
Brigham Young U (UT)
U of Illinois at Urbana–Champaign (IL)

FAMILY AND CONSUMER SCIENCES/HUMAN SCIENCES COMMUNICATION
U of Georgia (GA)

FAMILY AND CONSUMER SCIENCES/HUMAN SCIENCES RELATED
California State U, Long Beach (CA)
Norfolk State U (VA)
U of Minnesota, Twin Cities Campus (MN)
The U of Western Ontario (ON, Canada)

FAMILY PRACTICE NURSING
Grand Valley State U (MI)
Michigan State U (MI)
South Dakota State U (SD)
The U of Western Ontario (ON, Canada)
U of Windsor (ON, Canada)

FAMILY PSYCHOLOGY
Arizona Christian U (AZ)
Corban U (OR)
Lee U (TN)

FAMILY RESOURCE MANAGEMENT
Arizona State U (AZ)
Brigham Young U (UT)
Iowa State U of Science and Technology (IA)
Middle Tennessee State U (TN)
The Ohio State U (OH)
The Ohio State U at Lima (OH)
Ohio U (OH)
Pittsburg State U (KS)
South Dakota State U (SD)
The U of Alabama (AL)
U of Georgia (GA)

FAMILY SYSTEMS
Anderson U (IN)
Bowling Green State U (OH)
Central Michigan U (MI)
John Brown U (AR)
Lipscomb U (TN)
Lubbock Christian U (TX)
Mid-Atlantic Christian U (NC)
Mississippi U for Women (MS)
Spring Arbor U (MI)
The U of Akron (OH)
U of Minnesota, Twin Cities Campus (MN)
U of Southern Mississippi (MS)
Weber State U (UT)
Western Michigan U (MI)

FARM AND RANCH MANAGEMENT
Iowa State U of Science and Technology (IA)
Lake Erie Coll (OH)
Tarleton State U (TX)
Texas A&M U (TX)
Texas Christian U (TX)
The U of Findlay (OH)
U of Illinois at Urbana–Champaign (IL)
U of Minnesota, Crookston (MN)

FASHION/APPAREL DESIGN
Acad of Art U (CA)
Baylor U (TX)
Bennington Coll (VT)
Bowling Green State U (OH)
Buffalo State Coll, State U of New York (NY)
Clark Atlanta U (GA)
Columbia Coll Chicago (IL)
Columbus Coll of Art & Design (OH)
Dalhousie U (NS, Canada)
Dominican U (IL)
EDP Coll of Puerto Rico, Inc. (PR)
Fashion Inst of Technology (NY)
Ferris State U (MI)
Hampton U (VA)
Indiana U Bloomington (IN)
Intl Acad of Design & Technology (FL)
Iowa State U of Science and Technology (IA)
Kent State U (OH)
Lamar U (TX)
Lasell Coll (MA)
Lindenwood U (MO)
Marist Coll (NY)
Marymount U (VA)
Massachusetts Coll of Art and Design (MA)
Michigan State U (MI)
Montclair State U (NJ)
Moore Coll of Art & Design (PA)
Mount Mary Coll (WI)
O'More Coll of Design (TN)
Otis Coll of Art and Design (CA)
Parsons The New School for Design (NY)
Philadelphia U (PA)
Point Loma Nazarene U (CA)
Rhode Island School of Design (RI)
Sacred Heart U (CT)
Savannah Coll of Art and Design (GA)
School of the Art Inst of Chicago (IL)
Stephens Coll (MO)
Syracuse U (NY)
Texas Woman's U (TX)
U of Cincinnati (OH)
U of Delaware (DE)
U of Maryland Eastern Shore (MD)
U of Minnesota, Twin Cities Campus (MN)
U of North Texas (TX)
U of the Incarnate Word (TX)
Ursuline Coll (OH)
Villa Maria Coll of Buffalo (NY)
Virginia Commonwealth U (VA)
Washington U in St. Louis (MO)
Woodbury U (CA)

FASHION MERCHANDISING
Ashland U (OH)
Baylor U (TX)
Bay State Coll (MA)
Bowling Green State U (OH)
Bradley U (IL)
Buffalo State Coll, State U of New York (NY)
California State U, Long Beach (CA)
Carson-Newman U (TN)
Dominican U (IL)
East Central U (OK)
Eastern Michigan U (MI)
Fashion Inst of Technology (NY)
Fisher Coll (MA)
Hampton U (VA)
Harding U (AR)
Immaculata U (PA)
Indiana U of Pennsylvania (PA)
Intl Acad of Design & Technology (FL)

Kent State U (OH)
Lamar U (TX)
Lasell Coll (MA)
Lindenwood U (MO)
Lipscomb U (TN)
Louisiana State U and Ag and
  Mech Coll (LA)
Lynn U (FL)
Marist Coll (NY)
Mars Hill Coll (NC)
Marymount U (VA)
Mercyhurst U (NY)
Mount Mary Coll (WI)
Newbury Coll (MA)
Northwood U, Michigan Campus
  (MI)
Parsons The New School for
  Design (NY)
Philadelphia U (PA)
Pittsburg State U (KS)
Sacred Heart U (CT)
Sam Houston State U (TX)
Stephen F. Austin State U (TX)
Texas Christian U (TX)
Texas State U–San Marcos (TX)
Texas Woman's U (TX)
U of Bridgeport (CT)
U of Central Oklahoma (OK)
U of Georgia (GA)
U of Illinois at Urbana–Champaign
  (IL)
U of Maryland Eastern Shore (MD)
U of Minnesota, Twin Cities
  Campus (MN)
U of North Texas (TX)
The U of Tennessee at Martin (TN)
Ursuline Coll (OH)
Utah State U (UT)
Woodbury U (CA)
Youngstown State U (OH)

**FIBER, TEXTILE AND
WEAVING ARTS**
Acad of Art U (CA)
Adams State U (CO)
Alberta Coll of Art & Design (AB,
  Canada)
Bowling Green State U (OH)
California State U, Long Beach
  (CA)
Colorado State U (CO)
Maryland Inst Coll of Art (MD)
Massachusetts Coll of Art and
  Design (MA)
Philadelphia U (PA)
Rhode Island School of Design
  (RI)
Savannah Coll of Art and Design
  (GA)
School of the Art Inst of Chicago
  (IL)
Temple U (PA)
The U of Kansas (KS)
U of Massachusetts Dartmouth
  (MA)
U of Michigan (MI)
U of Oregon (OR)
Western Washington U (WA)

FILIPINO/TAGALOG
U of Hawaii at Manoa (HI)

FILM/CINEMA/VIDEO STUDIES
American U (DC)
The American U of Paris (France)
The American U of Rome (Italy)
Baldwin Wallace U (OH)
Bard Coll (NY)
Bennington Coll (VT)
Boston Coll (MA)
Bowling Green State U (OH)
Brigham Young U (UT)
Brock U (ON, Canada)
Brown U (RI)
California Baptist U (CA)
California State U, Long Beach
  (CA)
California State U, Northridge (CA)
Calvin Coll (MI)
Carleton Coll (MN)
Carson-Newman U (TN)
Centenary Coll of Louisiana (LA)
Champlain Coll (VT)
Chapman U (CA)
Claremont McKenna Coll (CA)
Clark U (MA)
Coe Coll (IA)

Coll of Staten Island of the City U of
  New York (NY)
The Colorado Coll (CO)
Columbia Coll Chicago (IL)
Columbia Coll Hollywood (CA)
Columbia U (NY)
Columbia U, School of General
  Studies (NY)
Concordia U (QC, Canada)
Connecticut Coll (CT)
Curry Coll (MA)
Dartmouth Coll (NH)
DeSales U (PA)
Dominican U (IL)
Eastern Michigan U (MI)
Eastern Washington U (WA)
Emerson Coll (MA)
The Evergreen State Coll (WA)
Florida State U (FL)
Georgia State U (GA)
Grand Valley State U (MI)
Hunter Coll of the City U of New
  York (NY)
Huntington U (IN)
Ithaca Coll (NY)
John Brown U (AR)
The Johns Hopkins U (MD)
Kean U (NJ)
Keene State Coll (NH)
Lafayette Coll (PA)
La Salle U (PA)
La Sierra U (CA)
Long Island U–C. W. Post Campus
  (NY)
Lynn U (FL)
McDaniel Coll (MD)
Minnesota State U Moorhead (MN)
Mount Holyoke Coll (MA)
Northeastern U (MA)
Northwest U (WA)
Oakland U (MI)
The Ohio State U (OH)
Pace U (NY)
Penn State Abington (PA)
Penn State Altoona (PA)
Penn State Beaver (PA)
Penn State Berks (PA)
Penn State Brandywine (PA)
Penn State DuBois (PA)
Penn State Erie, The Behrend Coll
  (PA)
Penn State Fayette, The Eberly
  Campus (PA)
Penn State Greater Allegheny (PA)
Penn State Hazleton (PA)
Penn State Lehigh Valley (PA)
Penn State Mont Alto (PA)
Penn State New Kensington (PA)
Penn State Schuylkill (PA)
Penn State Shenango (PA)
Penn State U Park (PA)
Penn State Wilkes-Barre (PA)
Penn State Worthington Scranton
  (PA)
Penn State York (PA)
Pepperdine U, Malibu (CA)
Pitzer Coll (CA)
Pomona Coll (CA)
Purchase Coll, State U of New York
  (NY)
Quinnipiac U (CT)
Rhode Island Coll (RI)
Rhode Island School of Design
  (RI)
Roger Williams U (RI)
Rutgers, The State U of New
  Jersey, New Brunswick (NJ)
San Francisco State U (CA)
Santa Fe U of Art and Design (NM)
School of the Art Inst of Chicago
  (IL)
School of the Museum of Fine Arts,
  Boston (MA)
Seattle U (WA)
Simon Fraser U (BC, Canada)
Smith Coll (MA)
Southeastern U (FL)
Southern Methodist U (TX)
Southwestern Coll (KS)
Stanford U (CA)
State U of New York at Fredonia
  (NY)
Stephens Coll (MO)
Stevenson U (MD)
Suffolk U (MA)
Temple U (PA)

U at Buffalo, the State U of New
  York (NY)
U of Alaska Fairbanks (AK)
The U of Arizona (AZ)
U of Arkansas at Little Rock (AR)
The U of British Columbia (BC,
  Canada)
U of California, Berkeley (CA)
U of California, Davis (CA)
U of California, Irvine (CA)
U of California, Los Angeles (CA)
U of California, Santa Barbara (CA)
U of California, Santa Cruz (CA)
U of Chicago (IL)
U of Colorado Boulder (CO)
U of Georgia (GA)
U of Hartford (CT)
U of Illinois at Urbana–Champaign
  (IL)
The U of Iowa (IA)
The U of Kansas (KS)
U of Louisiana at Lafayette (LA)
U of Maryland, Coll Park (MD)
U of Michigan (MI)
U of Minnesota, Twin Cities
  Campus (MN)
U of Nebraska–Lincoln (NE)
U of Nevada, Las Vegas (NV)
U of New Mexico (NM)
U of North Carolina School of the
  Arts (NC)
U of Oklahoma (OK)
U of Pennsylvania (PA)
U of Pittsburgh (PA)
U of Regina (SK, Canada)
U of Richmond (VA)
U of Rochester (NY)
U of Southern California (CA)
The U of Tampa (FL)
The U of the Arts (PA)
The U of Toledo (OH)
U of Tulsa (OK)
U of Utah (UT)
U of Vermont (VT)
U of Waterloo (ON, Canada)
The U of Western Ontario (ON,
  Canada)
U of Windsor (ON, Canada)
U of Wisconsin–Milwaukee (WI)
Vanderbilt U (TN)
Vassar Coll (NY)
Washington U in St. Louis (MO)
Watkins Coll of Art, Design, & Film
  (TN)
Wayne State U (MI)
Webster U (MO)
Wellesley Coll (MA)
Wells Coll (NY)
Wesleyan U (CT)
Wheaton Coll (MA)
Whitman Coll (WA)
Wright State U (OH)
Yale U (CT)

**FILM/VIDEO AND
PHOTOGRAPHIC ARTS
RELATED**
Arizona State U (AZ)
Art Center Coll of Design (CA)
Brigham Young U (UT)
Chatham U (PA)
Cleveland State U (OH)
Coe Coll (IA)
Coll of the Atlantic (ME)
Columbus Coll of Art & Design
  (OH)
Fairfield U (CT)
Five Towns Coll (NY)
Hampshire Coll (MA)
Hollins U (VA)
La Roche Coll (PA)
Maryland Inst Coll of Art (MD)
Mount St. Mary's Coll (CA)
New England School of
  Communications (ME)
Northern Michigan U (MI)
Oklahoma City U (OK)
Ringling Coll of Art and Design (FL)
Saint Joseph's U (PA)
School of the Art Inst of Chicago
  (IL)
School of the Museum of Fine Arts,
  Boston (MA)
Scripps Coll (CA)
Spring Arbor U (MI)
Swarthmore Coll (PA)
U of Illinois at Chicago (IL)

U of Minnesota, Twin Cities
  Campus (MN)
U of Regina (SK, Canada)
U of Southern California (CA)
The U of the Arts (PA)
Wellesley Coll (MA)
Western Michigan U (MI)
Woodbury U (CA)

FINANCE
Abilene Christian U (TX)
Adams State U (CO)
Adelphi U (NY)
Alabama State U (AL)
Albertus Magnus Coll (CT)
Albion Coll (MI)
Albright Coll (PA)
Alfred U (NY)
American U (DC)
The American U of Paris (France)
Anderson U (IN)
Angelo State U (TX)
Appalachian State U (NC)
Arizona State U (AZ)
Arkansas State U (AR)
Ashland U (OH)
Auburn U (AL)
Auburn U at Montgomery (AL)
Augsburg Coll (MN)
Aurora U (IL)
Averett U (VA)
Avila U (MO)
Babson Coll (MA)
Baldwin Wallace U (OH)
Ball State U (IN)
Barry U (FL)
Baylor U (TX)
Bellarmine U (KY)
Belmont U (TN)
Benedictine U (IL)
Bentley U (MA)
Berry Coll (GA)
Binghamton U, State of New York
  (NY)
Boise State U (ID)
Boston Coll (MA)
Boston U (MA)
Bowling Green State U (OH)
Bradley U (IL)
Bridgewater State U (MA)
Brock U (ON, Canada)
Bryant U (RI)
Butler U (IN)
Cabrini Coll (PA)
California State U, Chico (CA)
California State U, Dominguez Hills
  (CA)
California State U, East Bay (CA)
California State U, Fresno (CA)
California State U, Fullerton (CA)
California State U, Long Beach
  (CA)
California State U, Northridge (CA)
California State U, San Bernardino
  (CA)
California State U, Stanislaus (CA)
Canisius Coll (NY)
Carroll Coll (MT)
Castleton State Coll (VT)
The Catholic U of America (DC)
Cedarville U (OH)
Central Connecticut State U (CT)
Central Michigan U (MI)
Christopher Newport U (VA)
Clarion U of Pennsylvania (PA)
Cleary U (MI)
Clemson U (SC)
Cleveland State U (OH)
Coastal Carolina U (SC)
The Coll at Brockport, State U of
  New York (NY)
The Coll of St. Scholastica (MN)
The Coll of William and Mary (VA)
Colorado State U (CO)
Columbia Coll (MO)
Columbus State U (GA)
Concordia U (QC, Canada)
Concordia U, St. Paul (MN)
Converse Coll (SC)
Corban U (OR)
Cornerstone U (MI)
Creighton U (NE)
Culver-Stockton Coll (MO)
Dakota State U (SD)
Dalhousie U (NS, Canada)
Dallas Baptist U (TX)
Davenport U, Grand Rapids (MI)

Delta State U (MS)
DePaul U (IL)
DeSales U (PA)
Dominican Coll (NY)
Dominican U (IL)
Drake U (IA)
Drury U (MO)
Duquesne U (PA)
East Carolina U (NC)
East Central U (OK)
Eastern Illinois U (IL)
Eastern Michigan U (MI)
Eastern Washington U (WA)
East Tennessee State U (TN)
Elon U (NC)
Emporia State U (KS)
Excelsior Coll (NY)
Fairfield U (CT)
Fairleigh Dickinson U, Coll at
  Florham (NJ)
Fairleigh Dickinson U, Metropolitan
  Campus (NJ)
Fairmont State U (WV)
Fayetteville State U (NC)
Ferris State U (MI)
Florida Atlantic U (FL)
Florida Gulf Coast U (FL)
Florida Intl U (FL)
Florida State U (FL)
Fort Lewis Coll (CO)
Francis Marion U (SC)
Franklin Pierce U (NH)
Franklin U (OH)
Friends U (KS)
Gannon U (PA)
Gardner-Webb U (NC)
George Fox U (OR)
George Mason U (VA)
Georgetown U (DC)
Georgia Regents U (GA)
Georgia Southern U (GA)
Georgia State U (GA)
Goldey-Beacom Coll (DE)
Gonzaga U (WA)
Grand Valley State U (MI)
Hamline U (MN)
Hampton U (VA)
Harding U (AR)
Hardin-Simmons U (TX)
Hawai'i Pacific U (HI)
HEC Montreal (QC, Canada)
Hillsdale Coll (MI)
Hofstra U (NY)
Howard Payne U (TX)
Husson U (ME)
Illinois Coll (IL)
Illinois State U (IL)
Immaculata U (PA)
Indiana State U (IN)
Indiana U of Pennsylvania (PA)
Indiana U–Purdue U Fort Wayne
  (IN)
Indiana Wesleyan U (IN)
Inter American U of Puerto Rico,
  Bayamón Campus (PR)
Inter American U of Puerto Rico,
  Ponce Campus (PR)
Inter American U of Puerto Rico,
  San Germán Campus (PR)
Iona Coll (NY)
Iowa State U of Science and
  Technology (IA)
Ithaca Coll (NY)
Jacksonville State U (AL)
James Madison U (VA)
John Carroll U (OH)
Juniata Coll (PA)
Kansas State U (KS)
Kean U (NJ)
Kennesaw State U (GA)
Kent State U (OH)
King Coll (TN)
King's Coll (PA)
Kutztown U of Pennsylvania (PA)
Lake Erie Coll (OH)
Lake Superior State U (MI)
Lamar U (TX)
La Roche Coll (PA)
La Salle U (PA)
Lasell Coll (MA)
La Sierra U (CA)
Lehigh U (PA)
Le Moyne Coll (NY)
LeTourneau U (TX)
Lewis U (IL)
Lincoln Memorial U (TN)
Lindenwood U (MO)

Linfield Coll (OR)
Long Island U–Brooklyn Campus (NY)
Long Island U–C. W. Post Campus (NY)
Louisiana Coll (LA)
Louisiana State U and Ag and Mech Coll (LA)
Louisiana State U in Shreveport (LA)
Loyola U Chicago (IL)
Loyola U Maryland (MD)
Loyola U New Orleans (LA)
Lubbock Christian U (TX)
Manchester U (IN)
Manhattan Coll (NY)
Manhattanville Coll (NY)
Marian (WI)
Marietta Coll (OH)
Marquette U (WI)
Marshall U (WV)
Mars Hill Coll (NC)
Maryville Coll (TN)
The Master's Coll and Sem (CA)
McKendree U (IL)
McMurry U (TX)
McNeese State U (LA)
Menlo Coll (CA)
Mercer U (GA)
Mercyhurst U (PA)
Merrimack Coll (MA)
Metropolitan State U of Denver (CO)
Miami U (OH)
Michigan State U (MI)
Middle Tennessee State U (TN)
Midwestern State U (TX)
Millikin U (IL)
Minnesota State U Mankato (MN)
Minnesota State U Moorhead (MN)
Minot State U (ND)
Mississippi Coll (MS)
Mississippi State U (MS)
Missouri State U (MO)
Missouri Western State U (MO)
Molloy Coll (NY)
Morehead State U (KY)
Mount Mercy U (IA)
Mount Vernon Nazarene U (OH)
Murray State U (KY)
New England Coll (NH)
New Mexico Highlands U (NM)
New Mexico State U (NM)
New York Inst of Technology (NY)
Nicholls State U (LA)
North Central Coll (IL)
North Dakota State U (ND)
Northeastern Illinois U (IL)
Northeastern U (MA)
Northern Arizona U (AZ)
Northern Illinois U (IL)
Northern Michigan U (MI)
Northern State U (SD)
Northwestern Coll (MN)
Northwest Missouri State U (MO)
Northwest Nazarene U (ID)
Northwood U, Florida Campus (FL)
Northwood U, Michigan Campus (MI)
Nova Southeastern U (FL)
Oakland U (MI)
Ohio Dominican U (OH)
The Ohio State U (OH)
Ohio U (OH)
Oklahoma Baptist U (OK)
Oklahoma Christian U (OK)
Oklahoma City U (OK)
Oklahoma State U (OK)
Old Dominion U (VA)
Olivet Coll (MI)
Oral Roberts U (OK)
Oregon State U (OR)
Pace U (NY)
Pacific U (OR)
Palm Beach Atlantic U (FL)
Penn State Abington (PA)
Penn State Altoona (PA)
Penn State Beaver (PA)
Penn State Berks (PA)
Penn State Brandywine (PA)
Penn State DuBois (PA)
Penn State Erie, The Behrend Coll (PA)
Penn State Fayette, The Eberly Campus (PA)
Penn State Greater Allegheny (PA)

Penn State Harrisburg (PA)
Penn State Hazleton (PA)
Penn State Lehigh Valley (PA)
Penn State Mont Alto (PA)
Penn State New Kensington (PA)
Penn State Schuylkill (PA)
Penn State Shenango (PA)
Penn State U Park (PA)
Penn State Wilkes-Barre (PA)
Penn State Worthington Scranton (PA)
Penn State York (PA)
Pepperdine U, Malibu (CA)
Philadelphia U (PA)
Pittsburg State U (KS)
Plymouth State U (NH)
Polytechnic U of Puerto Rico (PR)
Portland State U (OR)
Post U (CT)
Providence Coll (RI)
Purdue U Calumet (IN)
Queens U of Charlotte (NC)
Quincy U (IL)
Quinnipiac U (CT)
Radford U (VA)
Regis U (CO)
Rhode Island Coll (RI)
Rider U (NJ)
Rivier U (NH)
Robert Morris U (PA)
Rochester Inst of Technology (NY)
Rockford Coll (IL)
Roger Williams U (RI)
Roosevelt U (IL)
Rowan U (NJ)
Rutgers, The State U of New Jersey, Camden (NJ)
Rutgers, The State U of New Jersey, Newark (NJ)
Rutgers, The State U of New Jersey, New Brunswick (NJ)
Sacred Heart U (CT)
Saginaw Valley State U (MI)
St. Ambrose U (IA)
Saint Anselm Coll (NH)
St. Bonaventure U (NY)
St. Edward's U (TX)
St. Gregory's U, Shawnee (OK)
St. John Fisher Coll (NY)
St. John's U (NY)
Saint Joseph's U (PA)
Saint Louis U (MO)
St. Mary's U (TX)
Saint Mary's U of Minnesota (MN)
St. Thomas Aquinas Coll (NY)
St. Thomas U (FL)
Saint Vincent Coll (PA)
Salem State U (MA)
Salisbury U (MD)
Salve Regina U (RI)
Samford U (AL)
Sam Houston State U (TX)
San Diego State U (CA)
San Francisco State U (CA)
San Jose State U (CA)
Schreiner U (TX)
Seattle U (WA)
Shippensburg U of Pennsylvania (PA)
Siena Coll (NY)
Sierra Nevada Coll (NV)
Simmons Coll (MA)
Slippery Rock U of Pennsylvania (PA)
Southeastern Louisiana U (LA)
Southeastern Oklahoma State U (OK)
Southeastern U (FL)
Southeast Missouri State U (MO)
Southern Connecticut State U (CT)
Southern Illinois U Carbondale (IL)
Southern Methodist U (TX)
Southern Nazarene U (OK)
Southern Utah U (UT)
Southwest Baptist U (MO)
Southwestern Coll (KS)
Spring Arbor U (MI)
State U of New York at Fredonia (NY)
State U of New York at New Paltz (NY)
State U of New York at Oswego (NY)
State U of New York at Plattsburgh (NY)
State U of New York Coll at Old Westbury (NY)

State U of New York Coll of Technology at Canton (NY)
Stephen F. Austin State U (TX)
Stetson U (FL)
Stonehill Coll (MA)
Suffolk U (MA)
Sullivan U (KY)
Syracuse U (NY)
Tarleton State U (TX)
Taylor U (IN)
Temple U (PA)
Tennessee Wesleyan Coll (TN)
Texas A&M Intl U (TX)
Texas A&M U (TX)
Texas A&M U–Commerce (TX)
Texas A&M U–Kingsville (TX)
Texas Christian U (TX)
Texas Lutheran U (TX)
Texas State U–San Marcos (TX)
Texas Wesleyan U (TX)
Texas Woman's U (TX)
Thomas Edison State Coll (NJ)
Thompson Rivers U (BC, Canada)
Tiffin U (OH)
Trinity U (TX)
Troy U (AL)
Tulane U (LA)
Tuskegee U (AL)
Union U (TN)
Université de Sherbrooke (QC, Canada)
The U of Akron (OH)
The U of Alabama (AL)
The U of Alabama at Birmingham (AL)
U of Alaska Anchorage (AK)
The U of Arizona (AZ)
U of Arkansas at Little Rock (AR)
U of Bridgeport (CT)
The U of British Columbia (BC, Canada)
The U of British Columbia–Okanagan (BC, Canada)
U of Central Arkansas (AR)
U of Central Florida (FL)
U of Central Oklahoma (OK)
U of Charleston (WV)
U of Cincinnati (OH)
U of Colorado Boulder (CO)
U of Delaware (DE)
U of Denver (CO)
U of Evansville (IN)
The U of Findlay (OH)
U of Florida (FL)
U of Georgia (GA)
U of Guelph (ON, Canada)
U of Hartford (CT)
U of Hawaii at Manoa (HI)
U of Houston (TX)
U of Houston–Clear Lake (TX)
U of Houston–Downtown (TX)
U of Houston–Victoria (TX)
U of Idaho (ID)
U of Illinois at Chicago (IL)
U of Illinois at Urbana–Champaign (IL)
The U of Iowa (IA)
The U of Kansas (KS)
U of Kentucky (KY)
U of Louisiana at Lafayette (LA)
U of Louisiana at Monroe (LA)
U of Louisville (KY)
U of Maryland, Coll Park (MD)
U of Maryland U Coll (MD)
U of Massachusetts Amherst (MA)
U of Massachusetts Dartmouth (MA)
U of Memphis (TN)
U of Miami (FL)
U of Michigan–Dearborn (MI)
U of Michigan–Flint (MI)
U of Minnesota, Duluth (MN)
U of Minnesota, Twin Cities Campus (MN)
U of Mississippi (MS)
U of Missouri (MO)
U of Missouri–St. Louis (MO)
U of Montevallo (AL)
U of Mount Union (OH)
U of Nebraska at Omaha (NE)
U of Nebraska–Lincoln (NE)
U of Nevada, Las Vegas (NV)
U of Nevada, Reno (NV)
U of New Brunswick Fredericton (NB, Canada)
U of New Haven (CT)
U of New Orleans (LA)

U of North Alabama (AL)
The U of North Carolina at Charlotte (NC)
The U of North Carolina at Greensboro (NC)
The U of North Carolina Wilmington (NC)
U of North Dakota (ND)
U of Northern Iowa (IA)
U of North Florida (FL)
U of North Georgia (GA)
U of North Texas (TX)
U of Notre Dame (IN)
U of Oklahoma (OK)
U of Ottawa (ON, Canada)
U of Pennsylvania (PA)
U of Pittsburgh (PA)
U of Portland (OR)
U of Puerto Rico at Bayamón (PR)
U of Puerto Rico at Ponce (PR)
U of Regina (SK, Canada)
U of Rhode Island (RI)
U of St. Francis (IL)
U of St. Thomas (MN)
U of St. Thomas (TX)
U of San Diego (CA)
The U of Scranton (PA)
U of South Alabama (AL)
U of South Carolina (SC)
The U of South Dakota (SD)
U of Southern Indiana (IN)
U of Southern Maine (ME)
U of Southern Mississippi (MS)
U of South Florida (FL)
The U of Tampa (FL)
The U of Tennessee (TN)
The U of Tennessee at Martin (TN)
The U of Texas at Austin (TX)
The U of Texas at Brownsville (TX)
The U of Texas at Dallas (TX)
The U of Texas at El Paso (TX)
The U of Texas at San Antonio (TX)
The U of Texas of the Permian Basin (TX)
The U of Texas–Pan American (TX)
U of the District of Columbia (DC)
The U of Toledo (OH)
U of Tulsa (OK)
U of Utah (UT)
U of Washington, Tacoma (WA)
The U of Western Ontario (ON, Canada)
U of West Florida (FL)
U of West Georgia (GA)
U of Windsor (ON, Canada)
U of Wisconsin–Eau Claire (WI)
U of Wisconsin–La Crosse (WI)
U of Wisconsin–Madison (WI)
U of Wisconsin–Milwaukee (WI)
U of Wisconsin–Parkside (WI)
U of Wisconsin–Superior (WI)
U of Wyoming (WY)
Utah State U (UT)
Valdosta State U (GA)
Valparaiso U (IN)
Villanova U (PA)
Virginia Polytechnic Inst and State U (VA)
Virginia Union U (VA)
Wagner Coll (NY)
Wake Forest U (NC)
Walla Walla U (WA)
Wartburg Coll (IA)
Washburn U (KS)
Washington State U (WA)
Washington U in St. Louis (MO)
Waynesburg U (PA)
Wayne State U (MI)
Webber Intl U (FL)
Weber State U (UT)
Webster U (MO)
West Chester U of Pennsylvania (PA)
Western Carolina U (NC)
Western Connecticut State U (CT)
Western Illinois U (IL)
Western Kentucky U (KY)
Western Michigan U (MI)
Western Washington U (WA)
Westminster Coll (UT)
West Texas A&M U (TX)
West Virginia U (WV)
Wichita State U (KS)
Wilkes U (PA)
William Paterson U of New Jersey (NJ)
Wilmington U (DE)

Wright State U (OH)
Xavier U (OH)
York Coll of Pennsylvania (PA)
Youngstown State U (OH)

FINANCE AND FINANCIAL MANAGEMENT SERVICES RELATED
Babson Coll (MA)
Columbia U, School of General Studies (NY)
Goldey-Beacom Coll (DE)
Grove City Coll (PA)
Hofstra U (NY)
Immaculata U (PA)
James Madison U (VA)
Minot State U (ND)
National U (CA)
Olivet Coll (MI)
Saint Mary's Coll of California (CA)
San Jose State U (CA)
State U of New York Coll of Technology at Alfred (NY)
The U of Tampa (FL)
Virginia Commonwealth U (VA)
Westminster Coll (UT)

FINANCIAL FORENSICS AND FRAUD INVESTIGATION
Canisius Coll (NY)
Champlain Coll (VT)

FINANCIAL MATHEMATICS
American U (DC)
Asbury U (KY)
Carnegie Mellon U (PA)
Trevecca Nazarene U (TN)
U of Cincinnati (OH)
U of Kentucky (KY)

FINANCIAL PLANNING AND SERVICES
Baylor U (TX)
Brigham Young U (UT)
Bryant U (RI)
Central Michigan U (MI)
Franklin U (OH)
Jamestown Coll (ND)
Lubbock Christian U (TX)
Marywood U (PA)
Northern Michigan U (MI)
Olivet Coll (MI)
Saint Joseph's U (PA)
Southern Methodist U (TX)
State U of New York Coll of Technology at Alfred (NY)
The U of Akron (OH)
U of Illinois at Urbana–Champaign (IL)
U of North Texas (TX)
U of Wisconsin–Madison (WI)
Western Michigan U (MI)
Widener U (PA)
William Paterson U of New Jersey (NJ)

FINE AND STUDIO ARTS MANAGEMENT
Appalachian State U (NC)
Belhaven U (MS)
Bellarmine U (KY)
Buena Vista U (IA)
California State U, East Bay (CA)
Chatham U (PA)
Coll of Charleston (SC)
The Coll of Idaho (ID)
Columbia Coll Chicago (IL)
Culver-Stockton Coll (MO)
DePaul U (IL)
Eastern Michigan U (MI)
Fashion Inst of Technology (NY)
Fort Lewis Coll (CO)
Indiana U Bloomington (IN)
Ithaca Coll (NY)
Kansas Wesleyan U (KS)
Lake Erie Coll (OH)
Lipscomb U (TN)
Long Island U–C. W. Post Campus (NY)
Mary Baldwin Coll (VA)
Maryland Inst Coll of Art (MD)
Marywood U (PA)
Massachusetts Coll of Liberal Arts (MA)
Mercyhurst U (PA)
Messiah Coll (PA)
Minot State U (ND)
North Carolina State U (NC)
Nova Southeastern U (FL)

Oklahoma City U (OK)
Parsons The New School for Design (NY)
Purchase Coll, State U of New York (NY)
Randolph-Macon Coll (VA)
Rider U (NJ)
Ringling Coll of Art and Design (FL)
Saint Vincent Coll (PA)
Seton Hill U (PA)
Simmons Coll (MA)
Spring Hill Coll (AL)
State U of New York at Fredonia (NY)
Suffolk U (MA)
Tiffin U (OH)
The U of Iowa (IA)
U of Tulsa (OK)
U of Waterloo (ON, Canada)
U of Wisconsin–Stevens Point (WI)
Upper Iowa U (IA)
Viterbo U (WI)
Wagner Coll (NY)
Wartburg Coll (IA)
Waynesburg U (PA)
Westminster Coll (UT)
Whitworth U (WA)

FINE ARTS RELATED
Acad of Art U (CA)
Adelphi U (NY)
Art Center Coll of Design (CA)
Ball State U (IN)
Benedictine U (IL)
Bowdoin Coll (ME)
Bowling Green State U (OH)
California State U, Long Beach (CA)
The Coll of Saint Rose (NY)
Coll of Staten Island of the City U of New York (NY)
Columbus Coll of Art & Design (OH)
Covenant Coll (GA)
Ferris State U (MI)
Grand Valley State U (MI)
Hampshire Coll (MA)
Hood Coll (MD)
Huntingdon Coll (AL)
Indiana Wesleyan U (IN)
Kentucky Wesleyan Coll (KY)
Kenyon Coll (OH)
Lake Erie Coll (OH)
Lindenwood U (MO)
Long Island U–Brooklyn Campus (NY)
Long Island U–C. W. Post Campus (NY)
Loyola U Maryland (MD)
Loyola U New Orleans (LA)
Madonna U (MI)
Maryland Inst Coll of Art (MD)
Molloy Coll (NY)
Monmouth U (NJ)
New York U (NY)
Northern Michigan U (MI)
Oakland U (MI)
Oklahoma City U (OK)
Oregon Coll of Art & Craft (OR)
Point Loma Nazarene U (CA)
Purchase Coll, State U of New York (NY)
Rhode Island School of Design (RI)
Rutgers, The State U of New Jersey, Newark (NJ)
St. John's U (NY)
School of the Art Inst of Chicago (IL)
School of the Museum of Fine Arts, Boston (MA)
Seton Hill U (PA)
Skidmore Coll (NY)
Thompson Rivers U (BC, Canada)
The U of Akron (OH)
U of California, Los Angeles (CA)
U of Denver (CO)
U of Hartford (CT)
U of Maryland, Baltimore County (MD)
U of Mary Washington (VA)
U of Massachusetts Dartmouth (MA)
U of Michigan (MI)
U of Regina (SK, Canada)
The U of the Arts (PA)

The U of Western Ontario (ON, Canada)
Widener U (PA)

FINE/STUDIO ARTS
Abilene Christian U (TX)
Acad of Art U (CA)
Alberta Coll of Art & Design (AB, Canada)
Albertus Magnus Coll (CT)
Albion Coll (MI)
Alderson-Broaddus Coll (WV)
Alfred U (NY)
American Acad of Art (IL)
American U (DC)
American U of Beirut (Lebanon)
Amherst Coll (MA)
Anderson U (IN)
Angelo State U (TX)
Appalachian State U (NC)
Art Center Coll of Design (CA)
Asbury U (KY)
Ashland U (OH)
Auburn U (AL)
Augsburg Coll (MN)
Baker U (KS)
Baldwin Wallace U (OH)
Bard Coll (NY)
Barton Coll (NC)
Baylor U (TX)
Bellarmine U (KY)
Belmont U (TN)
Bemidji State U (MN)
Benedictine U (IL)
Bennington Coll (VT)
Bethany Coll (WV)
Bethany Lutheran Coll (MN)
Bethel Coll (KS)
Bethel U (MN)
Bloomsburg U of Pennsylvania (PA)
Boston Coll (MA)
Bowdoin Coll (ME)
Bowling Green State U (OH)
Bradley U (IL)
Brevard Coll (NC)
Bridgewater Coll (VA)
Bridgewater State U (MA)
Brigham Young U (UT)
Brock U (ON, Canada)
Brown U (RI)
Bucknell U (PA)
Buffalo State Coll, State U of New York (NY)
Caldwell Coll (NJ)
California Polytechnic State U, San Luis Obispo (CA)
California State U, Chico (CA)
California State U, East Bay (CA)
California State U, Fullerton (CA)
California State U, Long Beach (CA)
California State U, Stanislaus (CA)
Calvin Coll (MI)
Canisius Coll (NY)
Cardinal Stritch U (WI)
Carleton Coll (MN)
Carlow U (PA)
Cedarville U (OH)
Centenary Coll of Louisiana (LA)
Central Michigan U (MI)
Chapman U (CA)
Chatham U (PA)
Chowan U (NC)
Christian Brothers U (TN)
Christopher Newport U (VA)
Claflin U (SC)
Clark U (MA)
Coastal Carolina U (SC)
Coe Coll (IA)
Colby Coll (ME)
The Coll at Brockport, State U of New York (NY)
Coll for Creative Studies (MI)
Coll of Charleston (SC)
The Coll of Idaho (ID)
The Coll of New Jersey (NJ)
The Coll of New Rochelle (NY)
Coll of Saint Benedict (MN)
Coll of Staten Island of the City U of New York (NY)
Coll of the Holy Cross (MA)
Coll of the Ozarks (MO)
The Coll of Wooster (OH)
The Colorado Coll (CO)
Colorado State U (CO)
Columbia Coll (SC)
Columbia Coll Chicago (IL)

Concordia U (QC, Canada)
Concordia U, Nebraska (NE)
Concordia U, St. Paul (MN)
Concord U (WV)
Converse Coll (SC)
Cooper Union for the Advancement of Science and Art (NY)
Corcoran Coll of Art and Design (DC)
Creighton U (NE)
Culver-Stockton Coll (MO)
Dakota Wesleyan U (SD)
Dartmouth Coll (NH)
DePauw U (IN)
Dickinson Coll (PA)
Dominican U (IL)
Drake U (IA)
Drury U (MO)
East Carolina U (NC)
Eastern Washington U (WA)
Edinboro U of Pennsylvania (PA)
Elizabeth City State U (NC)
Elizabethtown Coll (PA)
Elmira Coll (NY)
Emmanuel Coll (MA)
Endicott Coll (MA)
The Evergreen State Coll (WA)
Fairfield U (CT)
Fashion Inst of Technology (NY)
Ferris State U (MI)
Flagler Coll (FL)
Florida Ag and Mech U (FL)
Florida Intl U (FL)
Florida Southern Coll (FL)
Florida State U (FL)
Franklin & Marshall Coll (PA)
Franklin Pierce U (NH)
Frostburg State U (MD)
Furman U (SC)
Gallaudet U (DC)
Gardner-Webb U (NC)
Georgetown Coll (KY)
Georgetown U (DC)
Gettysburg Coll (PA)
Graceland U (IA)
Grand View U (IA)
Hamilton Coll (NY)
Hamline U (MN)
Hampden-Sydney Coll (VA)
Harding U (AR)
Hardin-Simmons U (TX)
High Point U (NC)
Hiram Coll (OH)
Hobart and William Smith Colls (NY)
Hofstra U (NY)
Holy Family U (PA)
Hope Coll (MI)
Howard Payne U (TX)
Humboldt State U (CA)
Hunter Coll of the City U of New York (NY)
Huntingdon Coll (AL)
Huntington U (IN)
Illinois State U (IL)
Indiana State U (IN)
Indiana U Bloomington (IN)
Indiana U Kokomo (IN)
Indiana U Northwest (IN)
Indiana U of Pennsylvania (PA)
Indiana U–Purdue U Fort Wayne (IN)
Indiana U–Purdue U Indianapolis (IN)
Indiana U South Bend (IN)
Indiana U Southeast (IN)
Inst of American Indian Arts (NM)
Iowa Wesleyan Coll (IA)
Ithaca Coll (NY)
Jamestown Coll (ND)
Johnson State Coll (VT)
Judson U (IL)
Juniata Coll (PA)
Kean U (NJ)
Keene State Coll (NH)
Kentucky State U (KY)
Keystone Coll (PA)
Knox Coll (IL)
Kutztown U of Pennsylvania (PA)
Lafayette Coll (PA)
Lamar U (TX)
La Sierra U (CA)
Lawrence U (WI)
Lebanese American U (Lebanon)
Lee U (TN)
Liberty U (VA)
Limestone Coll (SC)

Lincoln U (MO)
Lindenwood U (MO)
Lindsey Wilson Coll (KY)
Linfield Coll (OR)
Lipscomb U (TN)
Lock Haven U of Pennsylvania (PA)
Long Island U–C. W. Post Campus (NY)
Louisiana Coll (LA)
Louisiana State U and Ag and Mech Coll (LA)
Loyola Marymount U (CA)
Loyola U Chicago (IL)
Madonna U (MI)
Maharishi U of Management (IA)
Malone U (OH)
Manchester U (IN)
Manhattanville Coll (NY)
Marian U (WI)
Marietta Coll (OH)
Marist Coll (NY)
Mars Hill Coll (NC)
Maryland Inst Coll of Art (MD)
Marymount Manhattan Coll (NY)
Marymount U (VA)
Maryville Coll (TN)
Maryville U of Saint Louis (MO)
Massachusetts Coll of Art and Design (MA)
McMurry U (TX)
Mercyhurst U (PA)
Merrimack Coll (MA)
Messiah Coll (PA)
Middlebury Coll (VT)
Millikin U (IL)
Millsaps Coll (MS)
Mills Coll (CA)
Minnesota State U Mankato (MN)
Minnesota State U Moorhead (MN)
Mississippi Coll (MS)
Missouri Western State U (MO)
Montana State U (MT)
Montclair State U (NJ)
Moore Coll of Art & Design (PA)
Moravian Coll (PA)
Morehead State U (KY)
Morningside Coll (IA)
Mount Allison U (NB, Canada)
Mount Holyoke Coll (MA)
Mount Mary Coll (WI)
Murray State U (KY)
Naropa U (CO)
Nazareth Coll of Rochester (NY)
New Coll of Florida (FL)
New England Coll (NH)
New Mexico State U (NM)
New York Inst of Technology (NY)
New York U (NY)
Northeastern U (MA)
Northern Arizona U (AZ)
Northern Illinois U (IL)
North Greenville U (SC)
Northwestern Coll (MN)
Northwestern State U of Louisiana (LA)
Northwest Missouri State U (MO)
Notre Dame de Namur U (CA)
Nova Southeastern U (FL)
Oakland U (MI)
Ohio Dominican U (OH)
The Ohio State U (OH)
Ohio U (OH)
Ohio Wesleyan U (OH)
Oklahoma Baptist U (OK)
Oklahoma City U (OK)
Oral Roberts U (OK)
Otis Coll of Art and Design (CA)
Ouachita Baptist U (AR)
Pace U (NY)
Pacific Lutheran U (WA)
Pacific Northwest Coll of Art (OR)
Pacific Union Coll (CA)
Paier Coll of Art, Inc. (CT)
Palm Beach Atlantic U (FL)
Park U (MO)
Parsons The New School for Design (NY)
Pennsylvania Coll of Art & Design (PA)
Piedmont Coll (GA)
Pitzer Coll (CA)
Plymouth State U (NH)
Point Loma Nazarene U (CA)
Pomona Coll (CA)
Presbyterian Coll (SC)
Prescott Coll (AZ)
Principia Coll (IL)

Providence Coll (RI)
Queens U of Charlotte (NC)
Randolph Coll (VA)
Randolph-Macon Coll (VA)
Reed Coll (OR)
Rhode Island Coll (RI)
Rice U (TX)
The Richard Stockton Coll of New Jersey (NJ)
Ringling Coll of Art and Design (FL)
Rivier U (NH)
Rochester Inst of Technology (NY)
Rocky Mountain Coll of Art + Design (CO)
Rosemont Coll (PA)
Sage Coll of Albany (NY)
Saginaw Valley State U (MI)
St. Ambrose U (IA)
Saint John's U (MN)
Saint Joseph's Coll (IN)
St. Lawrence U (NY)
Saint Louis U (MO)
Saint Mary's U of Minnesota (MN)
St. Thomas Aquinas Coll (NY)
Saint Vincent Coll (PA)
Salisbury U (MD)
Salve Regina U (RI)
San Jose State U (CA)
Santa Fe U of Art and Design (NM)
School of the Art Inst of Chicago (IL)
School of the Museum of Fine Arts, Boston (MA)
Scripps Coll (CA)
Seton Hill U (PA)
Sewanee: The U of the South (TN)
Shawnee State U (OH)
Siena Coll (NY)
Sierra Nevada Coll (NV)
Simpson Coll (IA)
Slippery Rock U of Pennsylvania (PA)
Smith Coll (MA)
Sonoma State U (CA)
Southern Arkansas U–Magnolia (AR)
Southern Connecticut State U (CT)
Southern Illinois U Carbondale (IL)
Southern Illinois U Edwardsville (IL)
Southern Methodist U (TX)
Southern Utah U (UT)
Spring Hill Coll (AL)
Stanford U (CA)
State U of New York at Fredonia (NY)
State U of New York at New Paltz (NY)
State U of New York at Plattsburgh (NY)
State U of New York Coll at Cortland (NY)
Stonehill Coll (MA)
Suffolk U (MA)
Susquehanna U (PA)
Swarthmore Coll (PA)
Sweet Briar Coll (VA)
Syracuse U (NY)
Tarleton State U (TX)
Texas A&M–Commerce (TX)
Texas A&M U–Kingsville (TX)
Texas Southern U (TX)
Texas State U–San Marcos (TX)
Thomas More Coll (KY)
Thompson Rivers U (BC, Canada)
Trinity Christian Coll (IL)
Trinity Coll (CT)
Truman State U (MO)
Tulane U (LA)
Union Coll (NE)
Unity Coll (ME)
Université du Québec en Outaouais (QC, Canada)
U at Buffalo, the State U of New York (NY)
The U of Akron (OH)
The U of Alabama (AL)
U of Alaska Anchorage (AK)
The U of Arizona (AZ)
U of Arkansas at Little Rock (AR)
The U of British Columbia (BC, Canada)
U of California, Davis (CA)
U of California, Irvine (CA)
U of California, Riverside (CA)
U of California, Santa Barbara (CA)
U of Central Florida (FL)

U of Cincinnati (OH)
U of Colorado Boulder (CO)
U of Colorado Denver (CO)
U of Dallas (TX)
U of Delaware (DE)
U of Florida (FL)
U of Georgia (GA)
U of Great Falls (MT)
U of Guelph (ON, Canada)
U of Houston–Clear Lake (TX)
U of Idaho (ID)
U of Illinois at Chicago (IL)
U of Illinois at Springfield (IL)
The U of Kansas (KS)
U of Kentucky (KY)
U of Louisiana at Monroe (LA)
U of Louisville (KY)
U of Maryland, Baltimore County (MD)
U of Maryland, Coll Park (MD)
U of Massachusetts Amherst (MA)
U of Miami (FL)
U of Michigan–Flint (MI)
U of Minnesota, Duluth (MN)
U of Minnesota, Twin Cities Campus (MN)
U of Mississippi (MS)
U of Missouri–Kansas City (MO)
U of Missouri–St. Louis (MO)
U of Mount Union (OH)
U of Nebraska at Omaha (NE)
U of Nebraska–Lincoln (NE)
U of Nevada, Las Vegas (NV)
U of New Hampshire (NH)
U of New Haven (CT)
U of New Orleans (LA)
U of North Carolina at Asheville (NC)
The U of North Carolina at Chapel Hill (NC)
The U of North Carolina at Charlotte (NC)
The U of North Carolina at Greensboro (NC)
The U of North Carolina at Pembroke (NC)
The U of North Carolina Wilmington (NC)
U of Northern Colorado (CO)
U of Northern Iowa (IA)
U of North Florida (FL)
U of North Georgia (GA)
U of North Texas (TX)
U of Notre Dame (IN)
U of Oklahoma (OK)
U of Oregon (OR)
U of Ottawa (ON, Canada)
U of Pennsylvania (PA)
U of Pittsburgh (PA)
U of Redlands (CA)
U of Regina (SK, Canada)
U of Rhode Island (RI)
U of Richmond (VA)
U of Rochester (NY)
U of St. Thomas (TX)
U of Science and Arts of Oklahoma (OK)
U of South Carolina (SC)
U of South Carolina Aiken (SC)
U of South Carolina Upstate (SC)
U of Southern California (CA)
U of Southern Maine (ME)
U of South Florida (FL)
The U of Tennessee (TN)
The U of Texas at Arlington (TX)
The U of Texas at Austin (TX)
The U of Texas at El Paso (TX)
The U of Texas–Pan American (TX)
The U of the Arts (PA)
U of the Cumberlands (KY)
U of the District of Columbia (DC)
U of the Incarnate Word (TX)
U of the Ozarks (AR)
The U of Toledo (OH)
U of Tulsa (OK)
U of Vermont (VT)
U of Waterloo (ON, Canada)
The U of Western Ontario (ON, Canada)
U of West Florida (FL)
U of Windsor (ON, Canada)
U of Wisconsin–Stevens Point (WI)
U of Wisconsin–Superior (WI)
Ursuline Coll (OH)
Vanderbilt U (TN)
Vassar Coll (NY)
Virginia Intermont Coll (VA)

Virginia Union U (VA)
Viterbo U (WI)
Wake Forest U (NC)
Walla Walla U (WA)
Washington and Lee U (VA)
Washington State U (WA)
Washington U in St. Louis (MO)
Watkins Coll of Art, Design, & Film (TN)
Webster U (MO)
Wellesley Coll (MA)
Wells Coll (NY)
Wesleyan Coll (GA)
Wesleyan U (CT)
West Chester U of Pennsylvania (PA)
Western Carolina U (NC)
Western Illinois U (IL)
Western Kentucky U (KY)
Western Michigan U (MI)
Western State Colorado U (CO)
Westminster Coll (UT)
West Texas A&M U (TX)
West Virginia Wesleyan Coll (WV)
Wheeling Jesuit U (WV)
Whitworth U (WA)
Willamette U (OR)
William Paterson U of New Jersey (NJ)
Williams Coll (MA)
Xavier U (OH)
York Coll of Pennsylvania (PA)
Youngstown State U (OH)

FIRE PREVENTION AND SAFETY TECHNOLOGY
Athens State U (AL)
Cogswell Polytechnical Coll (CA)
Oklahoma State U (OK)
Thomas Edison State Coll (NJ)
U of New Haven (CT)
West Texas A&M U (TX)

FIRE PROTECTION RELATED
The U of Akron (OH)
U of New Haven (CT)

FIRE SCIENCE/FIREFIGHTING
Hampton U (VA)
John Jay Coll of Criminal Justice of the City U of New York (NY)
Lake Superior State U (MI)
Lewis-Clark State Coll (ID)
Madonna U (MI)
New Jersey City U (NJ)
Providence Coll (RI)
U of Florida (FL)
U of New Brunswick Fredericton (NB, Canada)

FIRE SERVICES ADMINISTRATION
American Public U System (WV)
Bowling Green State U (OH)
California State U, Los Angeles (CA)
Cogswell Polytechnical Coll (CA)
Colorado State U (CO)
Fayetteville State U (NC)
Holy Family U (PA)
John Jay Coll of Criminal Justice of the City U of New York (NY)
Lewis U (IL)
Lindenwood U (MO)
St. Thomas U (FL)
Salem State U (MA)
Southern Illinois U Carbondale (IL)
U of Cincinnati (OH)
U of Maryland U Coll (MD)
U of Nebraska at Omaha (NE)
The U of North Carolina at Charlotte (NC)
Waldorf Coll (IA)
Western Oregon U (OR)

FISHING AND FISHERIES SCIENCES AND MANAGEMENT
Albion Coll (MI)
Clemson U (SC)
Colorado State U (CO)
Humboldt State U (CA)
Iowa State U of Science and Technology (IA)
Lake Superior State U (MI)
Mansfield U of Pennsylvania (PA)
Michigan State U (MI)
The Ohio State U (OH)
Oregon State U (OR)

Texas A&M U (TX)
U of Alaska Fairbanks (AK)
The U of British Columbia (BC, Canada)
U of Idaho (ID)
U of Minnesota, Twin Cities Campus (MN)
U of Missouri (MO)
U of New Brunswick Fredericton (NB, Canada)
U of Rhode Island (RI)
The U of Tennessee at Martin (TN)

FLIGHT INSTRUCTION
South Dakota State U (SD)
U of North Dakota (ND)

FOLKLORE
Indiana U Bloomington (IN)
U of Oregon (OR)

FOODS AND NUTRITION RELATED
California State U, Long Beach (CA)
Samford U (AL)
The U of British Columbia (BC, Canada)
Utah State U (UT)

FOOD SCIENCE
Acadia U (NS, Canada)
American U of Beirut (Lebanon)
Auburn U (AL)
California Polytechnic State U, San Luis Obispo (CA)
California State Polytechnic U, Pomona (CA)
Clemson U (SC)
Dalhousie U (NS, Canada)
Dominican U (IL)
Framingham State U (MA)
Kansas State U (KS)
Lamar U (TX)
Michigan State U (MI)
Mississippi State U (MS)
North Carolina State U (NC)
North Dakota State U (ND)
The Ohio State U (OH)
Oklahoma State U (OK)
Oregon State U (OR)
Penn State Abington (PA)
Penn State Altoona (PA)
Penn State Beaver (PA)
Penn State Berks (PA)
Penn State Brandywine (PA)
Penn State DuBois (PA)
Penn State Erie, The Behrend Coll (PA)
Penn State Fayette, The Eberly Campus (PA)
Penn State Greater Allegheny (PA)
Penn State Hazleton (PA)
Penn State Lehigh Valley (PA)
Penn State Mont Alto (PA)
Penn State New Kensington (PA)
Penn State Schuylkill (PA)
Penn State Shenango (PA)
Penn State U Park (PA)
Penn State Wilkes-Barre (PA)
Penn State Worthington Scranton (PA)
Penn State York (PA)
Purdue U (IN)
Rutgers, The State U of New Jersey, New Brunswick (NJ)
San Jose State U (CA)
Texas A&M U (TX)
Tuskegee U (AL)
The U of British Columbia (BC, Canada)
U of California, Davis (CA)
U of Delaware (DE)
U of Florida (FL)
U of Georgia (GA)
U of Guelph (ON, Canada)
U of Idaho (ID)
U of Illinois at Urbana–Champaign (IL)
U of Kentucky (KY)
U of Maryland, Coll Park (MD)
U of Massachusetts Amherst (MA)
U of Minnesota, Twin Cities Campus (MN)
U of Missouri (MO)
U of Nebraska–Lincoln (NE)
The U of Tennessee (TN)
U of the District of Columbia (DC)

U of Wisconsin–Madison (WI)
Virginia Polytechnic Inst and State U (VA)
Washington State U (WA)

FOOD SCIENCE AND TECHNOLOGY RELATED
Appalachian State U (NC)
North Dakota State U (ND)
The U of British Columbia (BC, Canada)
U of Illinois at Urbana–Champaign (IL)

FOOD SERVICE AND DINING ROOM MANAGEMENT
Sam Houston State U (TX)

FOOD SERVICE SYSTEMS ADMINISTRATION
Dominican U (IL)
Iowa State U of Science and Technology (IA)
Lipscomb U (TN)
Northwest Missouri State U (MO)
Ohio U (OH)
Rochester Inst of Technology (NY)
Simmons Coll (MA)
U of Wisconsin–Stout (WI)
Western Michigan U (MI)

FOODS, NUTRITION, AND WELLNESS
Acadia U (NS, Canada)
Alcorn State U (MS)
Andrews U (MI)
Arizona State U (AZ)
Auburn U (AL)
Bastyr U (WA)
Benedictine U (IL)
Bluffton U (OH)
Bowling Green State U (OH)
Bradley U (IL)
Bridgewater Coll (VA)
California State U, Fresno (CA)
California State U, Los Angeles (CA)
California State U, San Bernardino (CA)
Carson-Newman U (TN)
Cedar Crest Coll (PA)
Coll of the Ozarks (MO)
Dominican U (IL)
Georgia Southern U (GA)
Goddard Coll (VT)
Hunter Coll of the City U of New York (NY)
Indiana State U (IN)
Indiana U of Pennsylvania (PA)
Iowa State U of Science and Technology (IA)
Ithaca Coll (NY)
Jacksonville State U (AL)
James Madison U (VA)
Langston U (OK)
Lehman Coll of the City U of New York (NY)
Lincoln U (MO)
Madonna U (MI)
The Master's Coll and Sem (CA)
Middle Tennessee State U (TN)
Minnesota State U Mankato (MN)
Montclair State U (NJ)
Morrisville State Coll (NY)
Murray State U (KY)
New Mexico State U (NM)
New York U (NY)
Northern Illinois U (IL)
The Ohio State U (OH)
Ohio U (OH)
Oklahoma State U (OK)
Pepperdine U, Malibu (CA)
Point Loma Nazarene U (CA)
Purdue U (IN)
Radford U (VA)
Saint Louis U (MO)
Samford U (AL)
Sam Houston State U (TX)
Seattle Pacific U (WA)
South Dakota State U (SD)
State U of New York at Plattsburgh (NY)
Stephen F. Austin State U (TX)
Texas A&M U (TX)
Texas Southern U (TX)
Texas State U–San Marcos (TX)
Texas Woman's U (TX)
Trevecca Nazarene U (TN)
Tuskegee U (AL)

The U of Akron (OH)
U of Alaska Anchorage (AK)
The U of British Columbia (BC, Canada)
U of Central Arkansas (AR)
U of Central Oklahoma (OK)
U of Delaware (DE)
U of Georgia (GA)
U of Idaho (ID)
U of Kentucky (KY)
U of Minnesota, Twin Cities Campus (MN)
U of Missouri (MO)
U of Nebraska–Lincoln (NE)
U of Nevada, Reno (NV)
U of New Mexico (NM)
The U of North Carolina at Chapel Hill (NC)
U of Northern Iowa (IA)
U of Ottawa (ON, Canada)
U of Rhode Island (RI)
The U of Tennessee (TN)
The U of Texas at Austin (TX)
The U of Western Ontario (ON, Canada)
Virginia Polytechnic Inst and State U (VA)
Waldorf Coll (IA)
Washington State U (WA)
Wayne State U (MI)
Youngstown State U (OH)

FOOD TECHNOLOGY AND PROCESSING
Brigham Young U (UT)
Iowa State U of Science and Technology (IA)
New Mexico State U (NM)
Tennessee State U (TN)
U of Illinois at Urbana–Champaign (IL)

FOREIGN LANGUAGES AND LITERATURES
Arkansas State U (AR)
Arkansas Tech U (AR)
Assumption Coll (MA)
Auburn U (AL)
Auburn U at Montgomery (AL)
Augustana Coll (SD)
Austin Peay State U (TN)
Benedictine Coll (KS)
Bennington Coll (VT)
Bloomsburg U of Pennsylvania (PA)
Boston U (MA)
California Polytechnic State U, San Luis Obispo (CA)
Cameron U (OK)
Central Methodist U (MO)
The Citadel, The Military Coll of South Carolina (SC)
Colorado State U (CO)
Covenant Coll (GA)
Delta State U (MS)
Duquesne U (PA)
Eastern Illinois U (IL)
East Tennessee State U (TN)
Edinboro U of Pennsylvania (PA)
Elmira Coll (NY)
Elon U (NC)
Emporia State U (KS)
Eugene Lang Coll The New School for Liberal Arts (NY)
Excelsior Coll (NY)
Framingham State U (MA)
Francis Marion U (SC)
Frostburg State U (MD)
Gannon U (PA)
George Mason U (VA)
Gordon Coll (MA)
Hamilton Coll (NY)
James Madison U (VA)
Juniata Coll (PA)
Kansas State U (KS)
Kenyon Coll (OH)
Knox Coll (IL)
Lake Erie Coll (OH)
Long Island U–Brooklyn Campus (NY)
Long Island U–C. W. Post Campus (NY)
Longwood U (VA)
Loyola U New Orleans (LA)
Manchester U (IN)
Marshall U (WV)
Massachusetts Inst of Technology (MA)
McNeese State U (LA)

Mercyhurst U (PA)
Middle Tennessee State U (TN)
Mississippi State U (MS)
Monmouth U (NJ)
Montana State U (MT)
New Mexico State U (NM)
New York U (NY)
Northern Arizona U (AZ)
Oakland U (MI)
Old Dominion U (VA)
Pace U (NY)
Penn State Berks (PA)
Penn State Lehigh Valley (PA)
Pitzer Coll (CA)
Presbyterian Coll (SC)
Principia Coll (IL)
Purdue U (IN)
Purdue U Calumet (IN)
Queens U of Charlotte (NC)
Radford U (VA)
The Richard Stockton Coll of New
  Jersey (NJ)
Roger Williams U (RI)
Rutgers, The State U of New
  Jersey, New Brunswick (NJ)
St. Lawrence U (NY)
St. Mary's Coll of Maryland (MD)
Samford U (AL)
Scripps Coll (CA)
Southern Illinois U Edwardsville
  (IL)
Stanford U (CA)
State U of New York Coll at Old
  Westbury (NY)
Stephen F. Austin State U (TX)
Stonehill Coll (MA)
Suffolk U (MA)
Sweet Briar Coll (VA)
Syracuse U (NY)
Thomas Edison State Coll (NJ)
Tulane U (LA)
Union U (TN)
The U of Alabama (AL)
The U of Alabama at Birmingham
  (AL)
U of Alaska Anchorage (AK)
U of Alaska Fairbanks (AK)
U of Arkansas at Little Rock (AR)
U of California, Riverside (CA)
U of California, Santa Cruz (CA)
U of Delaware (DE)
U of Hartford (CT)
U of Idaho (ID)
U of Louisiana at Lafayette (LA)
U of Louisiana at Monroe (LA)
U of Maryland, Baltimore County
  (MD)
U of Mary Washington (VA)
U of Memphis (TN)
U of Minnesota, Twin Cities
  Campus (MN)
U of Montevallo (AL)
U of Nebraska at Omaha (NE)
U of New Mexico (NM)
U of New Orleans (LA)
U of North Alabama (AL)
The U of North Carolina at Chapel
  Hill (NC)
U of North Dakota (ND)
U of Northern Colorado (CO)
U of Ottawa (ON, Canada)
U of Puget Sound (WA)
The U of Scranton (PA)
U of South Alabama (AL)
U of Southern Mississippi (MS)
The U of Tennessee at
  Chattanooga (TN)
The U of Texas at Arlington (TX)
Utica Coll (NY)
Virginia Commonwealth U (VA)
Washington Coll (MD)
Washington State U (WA)
Wayne State Coll (NE)
Wayne State U (MI)
Western Washington U (WA)
West Virginia U (WV)
Wichita State U (KS)
Widener U (PA)
Winthrop U (SC)
Wright State U (OH)
Youngstown State U (OH)

FOREIGN LANGUAGES RELATED
Arizona State U (AZ)
Augustana Coll (SD)
Averett U (VA)

Bennington Coll (VT)
Binghamton U, State U of New York
  (NY)
The Evergreen State Coll (WA)
Excelsior Coll (NY)
Georgia Regents U (GA)
Georgia Southern U (GA)
Hood Coll (MD)
Indiana State U (IN)
Indiana U of Pennsylvania (PA)
Kennesaw State U (GA)
Mississippi Coll (MS)
New York U (NY)
Purchase Coll, State U of New York
  (NY)
Saint Mary's Coll of California (CA)
Southern Illinois U Carbondale (IL)
U of Alaska Fairbanks (AK)
U of California, Berkeley (CA)
U of California, Los Angeles (CA)
U of Michigan–Flint (MI)
U of West Georgia (GA)
Western Washington U (WA)
Yale U (CT)

FOREIGN LANGUAGE TEACHER EDUCATION
Arkansas State U (AR)
Arkansas Tech U (AR)
Ashland U (OH)
Auburn U (AL)
Baylor U (TX)
Boston U (MA)
Bowling Green State U (OH)
Buffalo State Coll, State U of New
  York (NY)
Cameron U (OK)
Central Methodist U (MO)
The Coll at Brockport, State U of
  New York (NY)
Concordia Coll (MN)
Eastern Michigan U (MI)
Elmira Coll (NY)
Gannon U (PA)
Gardner-Webb U (NC)
Grand Valley State U (MI)
Hofstra U (NY)
Indiana U Bloomington (IN)
Iona Coll (NY)
Long Island U–C. W. Post Campus
  (NY)
Manchester U (IN)
Mercyhurst U (PA)
Miami U (OH)
Moravian Coll (PA)
Nazareth Coll of Rochester (NY)
New York U (NY)
Ohio Dominican U (OH)
Ohio Wesleyan U (OH)
Oral Roberts U (OK)
Penn State Abington (PA)
Penn State Altoona (PA)
Penn State Beaver (PA)
Penn State Berks (PA)
Penn State Brandywine (PA)
Penn State DuBois (PA)
Penn State Erie, The Behrend Coll
  (PA)
Penn State Fayette, The Eberly
  Campus (PA)
Penn State Greater Allegheny (PA)
Penn State Mont Alto (PA)
Penn State Shenango (PA)
Penn State U Park (PA)
Penn State Worthington Scranton
  (PA)
Penn State York (PA)
Rhode Island Coll (RI)
Seton Hill U (PA)
Southeast Missouri State U (MO)
State U of New York at New Paltz
  (NY)
State U of New York Coll at Old
  Westbury (NY)
Stony Brook U, State U of New York
  (NY)
Temple U (PA)
U of Central Florida (FL)
U of Georgia (GA)
U of Illinois at Urbana–Champaign
  (IL)
U of Minnesota, Duluth (MN)
U of Nebraska–Lincoln (NE)
U of Nevada, Reno (NV)
U of Northern Iowa (IA)
U of Oklahoma (OK)
The U of South Dakota (SD)

U of South Florida (FL)
The U of Tennessee at
  Chattanooga (TN)
U of Vermont (VT)
U of Windsor (ON, Canada)
Valdosta State U (GA)
Valparaiso U (IN)
Virginia Wesleyan Coll (VA)
Washington State U (WA)
Wayne State Coll (NE)
Wheeling Jesuit U (WV)
William Jewell Coll (MO)
Youngstown State U (OH)

FORENSIC CHEMISTRY
Ashland U (OH)
Chestnut Hill Coll (PA)
Emmanuel Coll (MA)
Maryville U of Saint Louis (MO)
Missouri Baptist U (MO)
Palm Beach Atlantic U (FL)
St. Edward's U (TX)
Sam Houston State U (TX)
Slippery Rock U of Pennsylvania
  (PA)
U of Rhode Island (RI)
Western Carolina U (NC)

FORENSIC PSYCHOLOGY
Bay Path Coll (MA)
Canisius Coll (NY)
Castleton State Coll (VT)
The Coll of Saint Rose (NY)
Florida Inst of Technology (FL)
John Jay Coll of Criminal Justice of
  the City U of New York (NY)
St. Ambrose U (IA)
Seattle U (WA)
Tiffin U (OH)
Walden U (MN)
Walla Walla U (WA)
Western State Colorado U (CO)

FORENSIC SCIENCE AND TECHNOLOGY
Alvernia U (PA)
American Public U System (WV)
Bay Path Coll (MA)
Becker Coll (MA)
Bluefield Coll (VA)
Bryant U (RI)
Buffalo State Coll, State U of New
  York (NY)
Cedar Crest Coll (PA)
Cedarville U (OH)
Chestnut Hill Coll (PA)
The Coll of Saint Rose (NY)
Columbia Coll (MO)
Defiance Coll (OH)
Eastern New Mexico U (NM)
Farmingdale State Coll (NY)
Fayetteville State U (NC)
Friends U (KS)
George Mason U (VA)
Hilbert Coll (NY)
Hofstra U (NY)
Indiana U–Purdue U Indianapolis
  (IN)
Inter American U of Puerto Rico,
  Aguadilla Campus (PR)
Inter American U of Puerto Rico,
  Bayamón Campus (PR)
Jacksonville State U (AL)
John Jay Coll of Criminal Justice of
  the City U of New York (NY)
Keystone Coll (PA)
King Coll (TN)
Lewis U (IL)
Long Island U–C. W. Post Campus
  (NY)
Loyola U Chicago (IL)
Lynn U (FL)
Madonna U (MI)
Marian U (WI)
Marymount U (VA)
Mercyhurst U (PA)
Mount Marty Coll (SD)
Newman U (KS)
New Mexico Highlands U (NM)
Northwest Nazarene U (ID)
Olivet Coll (MI)
Pace U (NY)
Penn State Altoona (PA)
Penn State Berks (PA)
Penn State U Park (PA)
Point Park U (PA)
Roberts Wesleyan Coll (NY)
Russell Sage Coll (NY)

St. Andrews U (NC)
St. Edward's U (TX)
Seattle U (WA)
Seton Hill U (PA)
Simpson Coll (IA)
State U of New York Coll of
  Technology at Alfred (NY)
Syracuse U (NY)
Texas A&M U (TX)
Thomas More Coll (KY)
Tiffin U (OH)
Trine U (IN)
U of Central Florida (FL)
U of Central Oklahoma (OK)
The U of Findlay (OH)
U of Great Falls (MT)
U of Maryland U Coll (MD)
U of Nebraska–Lincoln (NE)
U of New Haven (CT)
U of North Dakota (ND)
The U of Scranton (PA)
The U of Tampa (FL)
U of Windsor (ON, Canada)
U of Wisconsin–Platteville (WI)
Virginia Commonwealth U (VA)
Washburn U (KS)
Waynesburg U (PA)
Weber State U (UT)
West Virginia U (WV)
Wichita State U (KS)
York Coll of Pennsylvania (PA)
Youngstown State U (OH)

FOREST ENGINEERING
Oregon State U (OR)
U of New Brunswick Fredericton
  (NB, Canada)

FOREST/FOREST RESOURCES MANAGEMENT
Clemson U (SC)
Elizabethtown Coll (PA)
Louisiana State U and Ag and
  Mech Coll (LA)
North Carolina State U (NC)
Oregon State U (OR)
Stephen F. Austin State U (TX)
Texas A&M U (TX)
The U of British Columbia (BC,
  Canada)
U of California, Berkeley (CA)
U of Idaho (ID)
West Virginia U (WV)

FORESTRY
Albion Coll (MI)
Albright Coll (PA)
Baylor U (TX)
California Polytechnic State U, San
  Luis Obispo (CA)
Coll of Saint Benedict (MN)
Georgia Southern U (GA)
Humboldt State U (CA)
Iowa State U of Science and
  Technology (IA)
Michigan State U (MI)
Mississippi State U (MS)
New Mexico Highlands U (NM)
Northland Coll (WI)
The Ohio State U (OH)
Oklahoma State U (OK)
Purdue U (IN)
Saint John's U (MN)
Sewanee: The U of the South (TN)
Southern Illinois U Carbondale (IL)
Stephen F. Austin State U (TX)
Texas A&M U (TX)
The U of British Columbia (BC,
  Canada)
U of California, Berkeley (CA)
U of Florida (FL)
U of Georgia (GA)
U of Illinois at Urbana–Champaign
  (IL)
U of Minnesota, Twin Cities
  Campus (MN)
U of Missouri (MO)
U of Nevada, Reno (NV)
U of New Brunswick Fredericton
  (NB, Canada)
U of New Hampshire (NH)
The U of Tennessee (TN)
U of the District of Columbia (DC)
U of Vermont (VT)
U of Wisconsin–Stevens Point (WI)
Utah State U (UT)
Virginia Polytechnic Inst and State
  U (VA)

FORESTRY RELATED
Roger Williams U (RI)
Sterling Coll (VT)
U of Minnesota, Twin Cities
  Campus (MN)
Utah State U (UT)

FOREST SCIENCES AND BIOLOGY
Auburn U (AL)
Colorado State U (CO)
Northern Arizona U (AZ)
Penn State Abington (PA)
Penn State Altoona (PA)
Penn State Beaver (PA)
Penn State Berks (PA)
Penn State Brandywine (PA)
Penn State DuBois (PA)
Penn State Erie, The Behrend Coll
  (PA)
Penn State Fayette, The Eberly
  Campus (PA)
Penn State Greater Allegheny (PA)
Penn State Hazleton (PA)
Penn State Lehigh Valley (PA)
Penn State Mont Alto (PA)
Penn State New Kensington (PA)
Penn State Schuylkill (PA)
Penn State Shenango (PA)
Penn State U Park (PA)
Penn State Wilkes-Barre (PA)
Penn State Worthington Scranton
  (PA)
Penn State York (PA)
U of Idaho (ID)
U of Illinois at Urbana–Champaign
  (IL)
U of Kentucky (KY)
U of Wisconsin–Madison (WI)

FOREST TECHNOLOGY
Penn State Abington (PA)
Penn State Altoona (PA)
Penn State Beaver (PA)
Penn State Berks (PA)
Penn State Brandywine (PA)
Penn State DuBois (PA)
Penn State Erie, The Behrend Coll
  (PA)
Penn State Fayette, The Eberly
  Campus (PA)
Penn State Greater Allegheny (PA)
Penn State Hazleton (PA)
Penn State Lehigh Valley (PA)
Penn State Mont Alto (PA)
Penn State New Kensington (PA)
Penn State Schuylkill (PA)
Penn State Shenango (PA)
Penn State U Park (PA)
Penn State Wilkes-Barre (PA)
Penn State Worthington Scranton
  (PA)
Penn State York (PA)

FRENCH
Acadia U (NS, Canada)
Adelphi U (NY)
Agnes Scott Coll (GA)
Albion Coll (MI)
Albright Coll (PA)
Alma Coll (MI)
American U (DC)
The American U of Paris (France)
Amherst Coll (MA)
Anderson U (IN)
Andrews U (MI)
Appalachian State U (NC)
Arizona State U (AZ)
Asbury U (KY)
Ashland U (OH)
Assumption Coll (MA)
Athabasca U (AB, Canada)
Auburn U (AL)
Augsburg Coll (MN)
Augustana Coll (IL)
Augustana Coll (SD)
Baker U (KS)
Baldwin Wallace U (OH)
Ball State U (IN)
Bard Coll (NY)
Barry U (FL)
Bates Coll (ME)
Baylor U (TX)
Belmont U (TN)
Benedictine Coll (KS)
Bennington Coll (VT)
Berea Coll (KY)
Berry Coll (GA)

MAJORS LISTING

Binghamton U, State U of New York (NY)
Boise State U (ID)
Boston Coll (MA)
Boston U (MA)
Bowdoin Coll (ME)
Bowling Green State U (OH)
Bradley U (IL)
Bridgewater Coll (VA)
Brock U (ON, Canada)
Brown U (RI)
Bryant U (RI)
Bucknell U (PA)
Buffalo State Coll, State U of New York (NY)
Butler U (IN)
Cabrini Coll (PA)
California Lutheran U (CA)
California State U, Chico (CA)
California State U, East Bay (CA)
California State U, Fresno (CA)
California State U, Fullerton (CA)
California State U, Long Beach (CA)
California State U, Los Angeles (CA)
California State U, Northridge (CA)
California State U, San Bernardino (CA)
Calvin Coll (MI)
Canisius Coll (NY)
Capital U (OH)
Cardinal Stritch U (WI)
Carleton Coll (MN)
Carnegie Mellon U (PA)
Carroll Coll (MT)
Case Western Reserve U (OH)
The Catholic U of America (DC)
Centenary Coll of Louisiana (LA)
Central Coll (IA)
Central Connecticut State U (CT)
Central Methodist U (MO)
Central Michigan U (MI)
Centre Coll (KY)
Chapman U (CA)
Chestnut Hill Coll (PA)
Cheyney U of Pennsylvania (PA)
Chowan U (NC)
Christopher Newport U (VA)
City Coll of the City U of New York (NY)
Claremont McKenna Coll (CA)
Clarion U of Pennsylvania (PA)
Clark Atlanta U (GA)
Clark U (MA)
Cleveland State U (OH)
Coe Coll (IA)
Colby Coll (ME)
Colgate U (NY)
The Coll at Brockport, State U of New York (NY)
Coll of Charleston (SC)
The Coll of New Rochelle (NY)
Coll of Saint Benedict (MN)
Coll of the Holy Cross (MA)
The Coll of William and Mary (VA)
The Coll of Wooster (OH)
The Colorado Coll (CO)
Colorado State U (CO)
Columbia U (NY)
Columbia U, School of General Studies (NY)
Columbus State U (GA)
Concordia Coll (MN)
Concordia U (QC, Canada)
Connecticut Coll (CT)
Cornell Coll (IA)
Creighton U (NE)
Dalhousie U (NS, Canada)
Dartmouth Coll (NH)
Davidson Coll (NC)
DePaul U (IL)
DePauw U (IN)
Dickinson Coll (PA)
Doane Coll (NE)
Dominican U (IL)
Drew U (NJ)
Drury U (MO)
Earlham Coll (IN)
East Carolina U (NC)
Eastern Michigan U (MI)
Eastern Washington U (WA)
Eckerd Coll (FL)
Edgewood Coll (WI)
Elizabethtown Coll (PA)
Elmira Coll (NY)
Elon U (NC)

Fairfield U (CT)
Fairleigh Dickinson U, Coll at Florham (NJ)
Fairleigh Dickinson U, Metropolitan Campus (NJ)
Fairmont State U (WV)
Florida Atlantic U (FL)
Florida Intl U (FL)
Francis Marion U (SC)
Franklin & Marshall Coll (PA)
Franklin Coll (IN)
Furman U (SC)
Gardner-Webb U (NC)
Georgetown Coll (KY)
Georgetown U (DC)
Georgia Coll & State U (GA)
Georgia Southern U (GA)
Georgia State U (GA)
Gettysburg Coll (PA)
Gonzaga U (WA)
Gordon Coll (MA)
Goucher Coll (MD)
Grand Valley State U (MI)
Grinnell Coll (IA)
Grove City Coll (PA)
Guilford Coll (NC)
Gustavus Adolphus Coll (MN)
Hamilton Coll (NY)
Hampden-Sydney Coll (VA)
Hanover Coll (IN)
Harding U (AR)
Hartwick Coll (NY)
Haverford Coll (PA)
Hendrix Coll (AR)
High Point U (NC)
Hillsdale Coll (MI)
Hiram Coll (OH)
Hobart and William Smith Colls (NY)
Hofstra U (NY)
Hollins U (VA)
Hood Coll (MD)
Hope Coll (MI)
Humboldt State U (CA)
Hunter Coll of the City U of New York (NY)
Illinois Coll (IL)
Illinois State U (IL)
Illinois Wesleyan U (IL)
Immaculata U (PA)
Indiana U Bloomington (IN)
Indiana U Northwest (IN)
Indiana U of Pennsylvania (PA)
Indiana U–Purdue U Fort Wayne (IN)
Indiana U–Purdue U Indianapolis (IN)
Indiana U South Bend (IN)
Indiana U Southeast (IN)
Iona Coll (NY)
Iowa State U of Science and Technology (IA)
Ithaca Coll (NY)
Jacksonville State U (AL)
Jamestown Coll (ND)
John Carroll U (OH)
The Johns Hopkins U (MD)
Johnson C. Smith U (NC)
Juniata Coll (PA)
Kalamazoo Coll (MI)
Keene State Coll (NH)
Kent State U (OH)
Kenyon Coll (OH)
King Coll (TN)
King's Coll (PA)
Knox Coll (IL)
Lafayette Coll (PA)
Lake Erie Coll (OH)
Lamar U (TX)
Lane Coll (TN)
La Salle U (PA)
Lawrence U (WI)
Lebanon Valley Coll (PA)
Lee U (TN)
Lehigh U (PA)
Lehman Coll of the City U of New York (NY)
Le Moyne Coll (NY)
Lindenwood U (MO)
Linfield Coll (OR)
Lipscomb U (TN)
Lock Haven U of Pennsylvania (PA)
Long Island U–C. W. Post Campus (NY)
Louisiana Coll (LA)
Louisiana State U and Ag and Mech Coll (LA)

Loyola Marymount U (CA)
Loyola U Chicago (IL)
Loyola U Maryland (MD)
Loyola U New Orleans (LA)
Luther Coll (IA)
Lynchburg Coll (VA)
Macalester Coll (MN)
Manchester U (IN)
Manhattan Coll (NY)
Manhattanville Coll (NY)
Marist Coll (NY)
Marquette U (WI)
Mary Baldwin Coll (VA)
Marywood U (PA)
McDaniel Coll (MD)
Mercer U (GA)
Merrimack Coll (MA)
Messiah Coll (PA)
Miami U (OH)
Michigan State U (MI)
Middlebury Coll (VT)
Millersville U of Pennsylvania (PA)
Mills Coll (CA)
Minnesota State U Mankato (MN)
Mississippi Coll (MS)
Missouri State U (MO)
Missouri Western State U (MO)
Monmouth Coll (IL)
Montclair State U (NJ)
Moravian Coll (PA)
Morehead State U (KY)
Morehouse Coll (GA)
Mount Allison U (NB, Canada)
Mount Holyoke Coll (MA)
Mount Mary Coll (WI)
Mount St. Mary's Coll (CA)
Mount St. Mary's U (MD)
Muhlenberg Coll (PA)
Murray State U (KY)
Nazareth Coll of Rochester (NY)
New Coll of Florida (FL)
New York U (NY)
Niagara U (NY)
North Carolina Central U (NC)
North Carolina State U (NC)
North Central Coll (IL)
North Dakota State U (ND)
Northeastern Illinois U (IL)
Northern Illinois U (IL)
Northern Michigan U (MI)
Northern State U (SD)
Oakland U (MI)
Oglethorpe U (GA)
The Ohio State U (OH)
Ohio U (OH)
Ohio Wesleyan U (OH)
Oklahoma City U (OK)
Oklahoma State U (OK)
Oral Roberts U (OK)
Oregon State U (OR)
Pacific Lutheran U (WA)
Pacific U (OR)
Penn State Abington (PA)
Penn State Altoona (PA)
Penn State Beaver (PA)
Penn State Berks (PA)
Penn State Brandywine (PA)
Penn State DuBois (PA)
Penn State Erie, The Behrend Coll (PA)
Penn State Fayette, The Eberly Campus (PA)
Penn State Greater Allegheny (PA)
Penn State Hazleton (PA)
Penn State Lehigh Valley (PA)
Penn State Mont Alto (PA)
Penn State New Kensington (PA)
Penn State Schuylkill (PA)
Penn State Shenango (PA)
Penn State U Park (PA)
Penn State Wilkes-Barre (PA)
Penn State Worthington Scranton (PA)
Penn State York (PA)
Pepperdine U, Malibu (CA)
Pittsburg State U (KS)
Plymouth State U (NH)
Pomona Coll (CA)
Portland State U (OR)
Presbyterian Coll (SC)
Princeton U (NJ)
Principia Coll (IL)
Providence Coll (RI)
Purchase Coll, State U of New York (NY)
Purdue U Calumet (IN)
Randolph Coll (VA)

Randolph-Macon Coll (VA)
Reed Coll (OR)
Regis U (CO)
Rhode Island Coll (RI)
Rhodes Coll (TN)
Rice U (TX)
Rider U (NJ)
Ripon Coll (WI)
Roanoke Coll (VA)
Rockford Coll (IL)
Rockhurst U (MO)
Rollins Coll (FL)
Rosemont Coll (PA)
Rutgers, The State U of New Jersey, Camden (NJ)
Rutgers, The State U of New Jersey, Newark (NJ)
Rutgers, The State U of New Jersey, New Brunswick (NJ)
Sacred Heart U (CT)
Saginaw Valley State U (MI)
St. Ambrose U (IA)
Saint Anselm Coll (NH)
St. Bonaventure U (NY)
St. Edward's U (TX)
St. John Fisher Coll (NY)
Saint John's U (MN)
St. John's U (NY)
Saint Joseph's U (PA)
St. Lawrence U (NY)
Saint Louis U (MO)
Saint Mary's Coll (IN)
Saint Mary's Coll of California (CA)
St. Mary's U (TX)
Saint Michael's Coll (VT)
St. Norbert Coll (WI)
St. Olaf Coll (MN)
St. Thomas U (NB, Canada)
Saint Vincent Coll (PA)
Salisbury U (MD)
Salve Regina U (RI)
Samford U (AL)
San Diego State U (CA)
San Francisco State U (CA)
San Jose State U (CA)
Scripps Coll (CA)
Seattle U (WA)
Sewanee: The U of the South (TN)
Shippensburg U of Pennsylvania (PA)
Siena Coll (NY)
Simmons Coll (MA)
Simon Fraser U (BC, Canada)
Simpson Coll (IA)
Skidmore Coll (NY)
Slippery Rock U of Pennsylvania (PA)
Smith Coll (MA)
Sonoma State U (CA)
South Dakota State U (SD)
Southern Connecticut State U (CT)
Southern Illinois U Carbondale (IL)
Southern Methodist U (TX)
Southern Oregon U (OR)
Southern Utah U (UT)
Southwestern U (TX)
Spelman Coll (GA)
Stanford U (CA)
State U of New York at Fredonia (NY)
State U of New York at New Paltz (NY)
State U of New York at Oswego (NY)
State U of New York at Plattsburgh (NY)
State U of New York Coll at Cortland (NY)
State U of New York Coll at Geneseo (NY)
State U of New York Coll at Potsdam (NY)
Stetson U (FL)
Stonehill Coll (MA)
Stony Brook U, State U of New York (NY)
Suffolk U (MA)
Susquehanna U (PA)
Swarthmore Coll (PA)
Sweet Briar Coll (VA)
Syracuse U (NY)
Temple U (PA)
Tennessee State U (TN)
Tennessee Wesleyan Coll (TN)
Texas A&M U (TX)
Texas Christian U (TX)
Texas Southern U (TX)

Texas State U–San Marcos (TX)
Transylvania U (KY)
Trent U (ON, Canada)
Trinity Coll (CT)
Trinity U (TX)
Truman State U (MO)
Tufts U (MA)
Tulane U (LA)
Union Coll (NE)
Union U (TN)
United States Military Acad (NY)
Université de Sherbrooke (QC, Canada)
Université Sainte-Anne (NS, Canada)
U at Buffalo, the State U of New York (NY)
The U of Akron (OH)
U of Alaska Anchorage (AK)
The U of Arizona (AZ)
U of Arkansas at Little Rock (AR)
The U of British Columbia (BC, Canada)
The U of British Columbia–Okanagan (BC, Canada)
U of California, Berkeley (CA)
U of California, Davis (CA)
U of California, Irvine (CA)
U of California, Los Angeles (CA)
U of California, Riverside (CA)
U of California, Santa Barbara (CA)
U of Central Arkansas (AR)
U of Central Florida (FL)
U of Central Oklahoma (OK)
U of Cincinnati (OH)
U of Colorado Boulder (CO)
U of Colorado Denver (CO)
U of Dallas (TX)
U of Denver (CO)
U of Evansville (IN)
U of Florida (FL)
U of Georgia (GA)
U of Hawaii at Manoa (HI)
U of Houston (TX)
U of Idaho (ID)
U of Illinois at Chicago (IL)
U of Illinois at Urbana–Champaign (IL)
The U of Iowa (IA)
The U of Kansas (KS)
U of Kentucky (KY)
U of La Verne (CA)
U of Louisville (KY)
U of Maine at Fort Kent (ME)
U of Maryland, Coll Park (MD)
U of Massachusetts Amherst (MA)
U of Massachusetts Boston (MA)
U of Massachusetts Dartmouth (MA)
U of Miami (FL)
U of Michigan (MI)
U of Michigan–Dearborn (MI)
U of Michigan–Flint (MI)
U of Minnesota, Duluth (MN)
U of Minnesota, Twin Cities Campus (MN)
U of Mississippi (MS)
U of Missouri (MO)
U of Missouri–Kansas City (MO)
U of Missouri–St. Louis (MO)
U of Mount Union (OH)
U of Nebraska at Kearney (NE)
U of Nebraska–Lincoln (NE)
U of Nevada, Las Vegas (NV)
U of Nevada, Reno (NV)
U of New Brunswick Fredericton (NB, Canada)
U of New Brunswick Saint John (NB, Canada)
U of New Hampshire (NH)
U of New Mexico (NM)
U of North Carolina at Asheville (NC)
The U of North Carolina at Charlotte (NC)
The U of North Carolina at Greensboro (NC)
The U of North Carolina Wilmington (NC)
U of North Dakota (ND)
U of Northern Colorado (CO)
U of North Georgia (GA)
U of North Texas (TX)
U of Notre Dame (IN)
U of Oklahoma (OK)
U of Oregon (OR)
U of Ottawa (ON, Canada)

U of Pennsylvania (PA)
U of Pittsburgh (PA)
U of Puget Sound (WA)
U of Redlands (CA)
U of Regina (SK, Canada)
U of Rhode Island (RI)
U of Richmond (VA)
U of Rochester (NY)
U of St. Thomas (MN)
U of St. Thomas (TX)
U of San Diego (CA)
The U of Scranton (PA)
U of South Carolina (SC)
The U of South Dakota (SD)
U of Southern California (CA)
U of Southern Indiana (IN)
U of Southern Maine (ME)
U of South Florida (FL)
The U of Tennessee (TN)
The U of Tennessee at Martin (TN)
The U of Texas at Arlington (TX)
The U of Texas at Austin (TX)
The U of Texas at El Paso (TX)
The U of Texas at San Antonio (TX)
The U of Texas–Pan American (TX)
U of the Cumberlands (KY)
The U of Toledo (OH)
U of Tulsa (OK)
U of Utah (UT)
U of Vermont (VT)
U of Virginia (VA)
U of Waterloo (ON, Canada)
The U of Western Ontario (ON, Canada)
U of West Florida (FL)
U of Windsor (ON, Canada)
U of Wisconsin–Eau Claire (WI)
U of Wisconsin–Green Bay (WI)
U of Wisconsin–La Crosse (WI)
U of Wisconsin–Madison (WI)
U of Wisconsin–Milwaukee (WI)
U of Wisconsin–Stevens Point (WI)
U of Wyoming (WY)
Utah State U (UT)
Valdosta State U (GA)
Valparaiso U (IN)
Vanderbilt U (TN)
Vassar Coll (NY)
Villanova U (PA)
Virginia Polytechnic Inst and State U (VA)
Virginia Wesleyan Coll (VA)
Wabash Coll (IN)
Wake Forest U (NC)
Walla Walla U (WA)
Walsh U (OH)
Wartburg Coll (IA)
Washburn U (KS)
Washington & Jefferson Coll (PA)
Washington and Lee U (VA)
Washington Coll (MD)
Washington State U (WA)
Washington U in St. Louis (MO)
Weber State U (UT)
Webster U (MO)
Wellesley Coll (MA)
Wesleyan Coll (GA)
Wesleyan U (CT)
West Chester U of Pennsylvania (PA)
Western Carolina U (NC)
Western Illinois U (IL)
Western Kentucky U (KY)
Western Michigan U (MI)
Western Washington U (WA)
Westminster Coll (MO)
Wheaton Coll (IL)
Wheeling Jesuit U (WV)
Whitman Coll (WA)
Whitworth U (WA)
Wichita State U (KS)
Widener U (PA)
Willamette U (OR)
William Jewell Coll (MO)
Williams Coll (MA)
Wittenberg U (OH)
Wright State U (OH)
Xavier U (OH)
Xavier U of Louisiana (LA)
Yale U (CT)
York Coll of the City U of New York (NY)
Youngstown State U (OH)

FRENCH AS A SECOND/ FOREIGN LANGUAGE (TEACHING)
Saginaw Valley State U (MI)
U of Windsor (ON, Canada)

FRENCH LANGUAGE TEACHER EDUCATION
Albion Coll (MI)
Alma Coll (MI)
Anderson U (IN)
Appalachian State U (NC)
Ashland U (OH)
Assumption Coll (MA)
Auburn U (AL)
Augustana Coll (IL)
Bethel U (MN)
Boise State U (ID)
California Lutheran U (CA)
California State U, Chico (CA)
Calvin Coll (MI)
Canisius Coll (NY)
The Catholic U of America (DC)
Central Michigan U (MI)
The Coll at Brockport, State U of New York (NY)
Colorado State U (CO)
Concordia Coll (MN)
East Carolina U (NC)
Eastern Michigan U (MI)
Eastern Washington U (WA)
Edgewood Coll (WI)
Elmira Coll (NY)
Franklin Coll (IN)
Gardner-Webb U (NC)
Grand Valley State U (MI)
Harding U (AR)
Hofstra U (NY)
Hope Coll (MI)
Indiana U Bloomington (IN)
Indiana U Northwest (IN)
Indiana U–Purdue U Fort Wayne (IN)
Indiana U–Purdue U Indianapolis (IN)
Indiana U South Bend (IN)
Iona Coll (NY)
Ithaca Coll (NY)
Juniata Coll (PA)
Keene State Coll (NH)
King Coll (TN)
Lee U (TN)
Le Moyne Coll (NY)
Lindenwood U (MO)
Lipscomb U (TN)
Long Island U–C. W. Post Campus (NY)
Louisiana State U in Shreveport (LA)
Manchester U (IN)
Manhattanville Coll (NY)
Marist Coll (NY)
Marywood U (PA)
Messiah Coll (PA)
Miami U (OH)
Michigan State U (MI)
Missouri State U (MO)
Missouri Western State U (MO)
Moravian Coll (PA)
Niagara U (NY)
North Carolina Central U (NC)
North Carolina State U (NC)
North Dakota State U (ND)
Northern Michigan U (MI)
Ohio U (OH)
Ohio Wesleyan U (OH)
Pittsburg State U (KS)
Purdue U Calumet (IN)
Rhode Island Coll (RI)
St. Ambrose U (IA)
St. John Fisher Coll (NY)
Salve Regina U (RI)
Southern Utah U (UT)
State U of New York at New Paltz (NY)
State U of New York at Plattsburgh (NY)
State U of New York Coll at Cortland (NY)
Stony Brook U, State U of New York (NY)
Université Sainte-Anne (NS, Canada)
The U of Akron (OH)
U of Delaware (DE)
U of Evansville (IN)
U of Illinois at Chicago (IL)

U of Illinois at Urbana–Champaign (IL)
The U of Iowa (IA)
U of Maine at Fort Kent (ME)
U of Michigan–Flint (MI)
U of Minnesota, Duluth (MN)
U of Missouri–St. Louis (MO)
U of Nebraska–Lincoln (NE)
The U of North Carolina at Greensboro (NC)
The U of North Carolina Wilmington (NC)
U of Regina (SK, Canada)
The U of South Dakota (SD)
The U of Tennessee at Martin (TN)
U of the Cumberlands (KY)
The U of Toledo (OH)
U of Waterloo (ON, Canada)
U of Windsor (ON, Canada)
Valparaiso U (IN)
Washburn U (KS)
Washington State U (WA)
Washington U in St. Louis (MO)
Weber State U (UT)
Western Michigan U (MI)
Western Washington U (WA)
Wheeling Jesuit U (WV)
Widener U (PA)
Xavier U of Louisiana (LA)
Youngstown State U (OH)

FRENCH STUDIES
American U (DC)
Bard Coll (NY)
Brock U (ON, Canada)
Brown U (RI)
Carleton Coll (MN)
Case Western Reserve U (OH)
Coe Coll (IA)
The Colorado Coll (CO)
Columbia U (NY)
Columbia U, School of General Studies (NY)
Franklin Coll Switzerland (Switzerland)
Lake Superior State U (MI)
Mills Coll (CA)
New Coll of Florida (FL)
Rhode Island Coll (RI)
Saint Joseph's U (PA)
Skidmore Coll (NY)
Smith Coll (MA)
Suffolk U (MA)
U of Guelph (ON, Canada)
U of New Hampshire (NH)
U of North Florida (FL)
The U of Scranton (PA)
U of Waterloo (ON, Canada)
The U of Western Ontario (ON, Canada)
U of Windsor (ON, Canada)
Wagner Coll (NY)
Wellesley Coll (MA)
Wheaton Coll (MA)

FUNERAL DIRECTION/ SERVICE
Wayne State U (MI)

FUNERAL SERVICE AND MORTUARY SCIENCE
Gannon U (PA)
Lindenwood U (MO)
Point Park U (PA)
St. John's U (NY)
Southern Illinois U Carbondale (IL)
U of Central Oklahoma (OK)
U of Minnesota, Twin Cities Campus (MN)

FURNITURE DESIGN AND MANUFACTURING
Rhode Island School of Design (RI)

GAME AND INTERACTIVE MEDIA DESIGN
Abilene Christian U (TX)
Acad of Art U (CA)
Champlain Coll (VT)
Cleveland Inst of Art (OH)
Dakota State U (SD)
Daniel Webster Coll (NH)
DeSales U (PA)
DigiPen Inst of Technology (WA)
Franklin U (OH)
Indiana Wesleyan U (IN)
Neumont U (UT)
Oklahoma Christian U (OK)

Quinnipiac U (CT)
Ringling Coll of Art and Design (FL)
Rochester Inst of Technology (NY)
Rocky Mountain Coll of Art + Design (CO)
St. Edward's U (TX)
Savannah Coll of Art and Design (GA)
Shawnee State U (OH)
Southwestern Coll (KS)
U of California, Irvine (CA)
U of Nebraska at Omaha (NE)
U of Southern California (CA)
The U of Texas at Dallas (TX)
William Peace U (NC)

GAY/LESBIAN STUDIES
Bennington Coll (VT)
Hampshire Coll (MA)
Mills Coll (CA)
Trinity Coll (CT)
The U of Western Ontario (ON, Canada)

GENERAL STUDIES
Albertus Magnus Coll (CT)
Alfred U (NY)
American Public U System (WV)
Anderson U (IN)
Antioch U Midwest (OH)
Antioch U Santa Barbara (CA)
Arkansas State U (AR)
Athabasca U (AB, Canada)
Austin Peay State U (TN)
Ball State U (IN)
Bluefield State Coll (WV)
Bob Jones U (SC)
Boise State U (ID)
Buffalo State Coll, State U of New York (NY)
Calumet Coll of Saint Joseph (IN)
Cameron U (OK)
Caribbean U (PR)
The Catholic U of America (DC)
Champlain Coll (VT)
Chicago State U (IL)
City U of Seattle (WA)
Clearwater Christian Coll (FL)
Coll of Mount St. Joseph (OH)
Columbia Coll (MO)
Columbia Intl U (SC)
Concordia U, St. Paul (MN)
Concordia U Wisconsin (WI)
Crown Coll (MN)
Delta State U (MS)
DePaul U (IL)
Dordt Coll (IA)
East Central U (OK)
Eastern New Mexico U (NM)
East Tennessee State U (TN)
Emporia State U (KS)
Fairfield U (CT)
Fairleigh Dickinson U, Coll at Florham (NJ)
Fairleigh Dickinson U, Metropolitan Campus (NJ)
Ferris State U (MI)
Florida Inst of Technology (FL)
Fort Lewis Coll (CO)
George Mason U (VA)
Georgia Southern U (GA)
Grantham U (MO)
Hampton U (VA)
Harding U (AR)
Henderson State U (AR)
Howard Payne U (TX)
Illinois State U (IL)
Indiana U Bloomington (IN)
Indiana U East (IN)
Indiana U Kokomo (IN)
Indiana U Northwest (IN)
Indiana U of Pennsylvania (PA)
Indiana U–Purdue U Fort Wayne (IN)
Indiana U–Purdue U Indianapolis (IN)
Indiana U South Bend (IN)
Indiana U Southeast (IN)
Indiana Wesleyan U (IN)
John Brown U (AR)
Kent State U (OH)
Kent State U at East Liverpool (OH)
Kent State U at Geauga (OH)
Kent State U at Salem (OH)
Kent State U at Stark (OH)
Kent State U at Trumbull (OH)
Kent State U at Tuscarawas (OH)

Kentucky Wesleyan Coll (KY)
Kutztown U of Pennsylvania (PA)
LaGrange Coll (GA)
La Roche Coll (PA)
La Salle U (PA)
Lee U (TN)
Liberty U (VA)
Lincoln Christian U (IL)
Lindenwood U (MO)
Lipscomb U (TN)
Louisiana State U in Shreveport (LA)
Loyola U Chicago (IL)
Loyola U New Orleans (LA)
Madonna U (MI)
Marist Coll (NY)
Marshall U (WV)
Mayville State U (ND)
McNeese State U (LA)
Mid-Continent U (KY)
Minot State U (ND)
Misericordia U (PA)
Montana Tech of The U of Montana (MT)
Morehead State U (KY)
Mount Marty Coll (SD)
Mount Mary Coll (WI)
Murray State U (KY)
National U (CA)
New Coll of Florida (FL)
New Mexico Inst of Mining and Technology (NM)
New Mexico State U (NM)
Nicholls State U (LA)
Northwestern Oklahoma State U (OK)
Northwestern State U of Louisiana (LA)
Northwest U (WA)
Nova Southeastern U (FL)
Ohio Dominican U (OH)
Ohio Wesleyan U (OH)
Oklahoma State U (OK)
Pace U (NY)
Pacific Union Coll (CA)
Palm Beach Atlantic U (FL)
Pittsburg State U (KS)
Point Park U (PA)
Providence Coll (RI)
Quincy U (IL)
Roberts Wesleyan Coll (NY)
Saginaw Valley State U (MI)
St. John's Coll (NM)
St. Joseph's Coll, New York (NY)
Saint Louis U (MO)
Salem State U (MA)
Samford U (AL)
Sam Houston State U (TX)
Seattle Pacific U (WA)
Seton Hill U (PA)
Shawnee State U (OH)
Shepherd U (WV)
Shimer Coll (IL)
Shippensburg U of Pennsylvania (PA)
Siena Heights U (MI)
Simon Fraser U (BC, Canada)
Southeastern Louisiana U (LA)
Southeastern Oklahoma State U (OK)
Southeast Missouri State U (MO)
Southern Arkansas U–Magnolia (AR)
Southern Methodist U (TX)
Southern New Hampshire U (NH)
Southern Utah U (UT)
Southwestern Adventist U (TX)
Southwestern Coll (KS)
Spring Hill Coll (AL)
State U of New York Inst of Technology (NY)
Temple U (PA)
Texas A&M U–Commerce (TX)
Texas Christian U (TX)
Texas Southern U (TX)
Texas State U–San Marcos (TX)
Texas Woman's U (TX)
Thompson Rivers U (BC, Canada)
Tiffin U (OH)
Trinity Coll of Florida (FL)
U of Alaska Fairbanks (AK)
U of Bridgeport (CT)
The U of British Columbia–Okanagan (BC, Canada)
U of Central Florida (FL)
U of Charleston (WV)
U of Delaware (DE)

U of Hartford (CT)
U of Idaho (ID)
U of Illinois at Urbana–Champaign (IL)
U of Louisiana at Lafayette (LA)
U of Louisiana at Monroe (LA)
U of Maine at Farmington (ME)
U of Maine at Machias (ME)
U of Massachusetts Amherst (MA)
U of Memphis (TN)
U of Miami (FL)
U of Michigan (MI)
U of Michigan–Dearborn (MI)
U of Mississippi (MS)
U of Missouri (MO)
U of Missouri–Kansas City (MO)
U of Mobile (AL)
U of Nebraska at Kearney (NE)
U of Nebraska at Omaha (NE)
U of Nevada, Reno (NV)
U of New Haven (CT)
U of New Mexico (NM)
U of New Orleans (LA)
U of North Dakota (ND)
U of North Georgia (GA)
U of North Texas (TX)
U of St. Thomas (TX)
U of South Florida (FL)
The U of Tennessee at Martin (TN)
The U of Texas at Arlington (TX)
The U of Texas–Pan American (TX)
U of the Cumberlands (KY)
U of the Ozarks (AR)
The U of Toledo (OH)
U of Utah (UT)
U of Washington, Bothell (WA)
U of Wisconsin–Stevens Point (WI)
Virginia Intermont Coll (VA)
Western Illinois U (IL)
Western Kentucky U (KY)
Western Washington U (WA)
West Texas A&M U (TX)
West Virginia U (WV)
Wichita State U (KS)
Widener U (PA)
Youngstown State U (OH)

GENETICS
Cedar Crest Coll (PA)
Clemson U (SC)
Iowa State U of Science and Technology (IA)
New Mexico State U (NM)
North Carolina State U (NC)
Ohio Wesleyan U (OH)
Thompson Rivers U (BC, Canada)
U of California, Davis (CA)
U of California, Irvine (CA)
U of Georgia (GA)
U of New Hampshire (NH)
The U of Western Ontario (ON, Canada)
U of Wisconsin–Madison (WI)
Washington State U (WA)

GEOCHEMISTRY
Bowling Green State U (OH)
Bridgewater State U (MA)
Brown U (RI)
The Coll of Saint Rose (NY)
Columbia U (NY)
Grand Valley State U (MI)
Hope Coll (MI)
State U of New York at Fredonia (NY)
State U of New York at New Paltz (NY)
State U of New York at Oswego (NY)
State U of New York Coll at Cortland (NY)
State U of New York Coll at Geneseo (NY)
U of Maine at Farmington (ME)
U of New Brunswick Fredericton (NB, Canada)
U of Waterloo (ON, Canada)
Western Michigan U (MI)

GEOGRAPHIC INFORMATION SCIENCE AND CARTOGRAPHY
Binghamton U, State U of New York (NY)
Brigham Young U (UT)
East Central U (OK)
Kennesaw State U (GA)
Michigan State U (MI)
Northern Michigan U (MI)

Radford U (VA)
Rowan U (NJ)
Salem State U (MA)
Stephen F. Austin State U (TX)
Texas A&M U (TX)
Texas State U–San Marcos (TX)
The U of Akron (OH)
U of Minnesota, Duluth (MN)
U of Oklahoma (OK)
U of Ottawa (ON, Canada)
The U of Texas at Dallas (TX)
U of Wisconsin–Madison (WI)
U of Wisconsin–Platteville (WI)
Western Kentucky U (KY)
Western Michigan U (MI)

GEOGRAPHY
Adams State U (CO)
Appalachian State U (NC)
Arizona State U (AZ)
Arkansas State U (AR)
Auburn U (AL)
Augustana Coll (IL)
Ball State U (IN)
Bemidji State U (MN)
Binghamton U, State U of New York (NY)
Boston U (MA)
Bowling Green State U (OH)
Bridgewater State U (MA)
Brock U (ON, Canada)
Bucknell U (PA)
Buffalo State Coll, State U of New York (NY)
California State Polytechnic U, Pomona (CA)
California State U, Chico (CA)
California State U, Dominguez Hills (CA)
California State U, East Bay (CA)
California State U, Fresno (CA)
California State U, Fullerton (CA)
California State U, Long Beach (CA)
California State U, Los Angeles (CA)
California State U, Northridge (CA)
California State U, San Bernardino (CA)
California State U, Stanislaus (CA)
Calvin Coll (MI)
Central Connecticut State U (CT)
Central State U (OH)
Chicago State U (IL)
Chowan U (NC)
City Coll of the City U of New York (NY)
Clark U (MA)
Colgate U (NY)
Concordia U (QC, Canada)
Concordia U Chicago (IL)
Concordia U, Nebraska (NE)
Concord U (WV)
Dartmouth Coll (NH)
DePaul U (IL)
East Carolina U (NC)
Eastern Illinois U (IL)
Eastern Michigan U (MI)
Eastern Washington U (WA)
East Tennessee State U (TN)
Edinboro U of Pennsylvania (PA)
Emory & Henry Coll (VA)
Excelsior Coll (NY)
Fayetteville State U (NC)
Florida Atlantic U (FL)
Florida Intl U (FL)
Florida State U (FL)
Framingham State U (MA)
Francis Marion U (SC)
Frostburg State U (MD)
George Mason U (VA)
Georgia Coll & State U (GA)
Georgia Southern U (GA)
Georgia State U (GA)
Grand Valley State U (MI)
Gustavus Adolphus Coll (MN)
Hofstra U (NY)
Humboldt State U (CA)
Hunter Coll of the City U of New York (NY)
Illinois State U (IL)
Indiana State U (IN)
Indiana U Bloomington (IN)
Indiana U of Pennsylvania (PA)
Indiana U–Purdue U Indianapolis (IN)
Indiana U Southeast (IN)

Jacksonville State U (AL)
James Madison U (VA)
The Johns Hopkins U (MD)
Kansas State U (KS)
Keene State Coll (NH)
Kennesaw State U (GA)
Kent State U (OH)
Kutztown U of Pennsylvania (PA)
Lehman Coll of the City U of New York (NY)
Long Island U–C. W. Post Campus (NY)
Louisiana State U and Ag and Mech Coll (LA)
Macalester Coll (MN)
Mansfield U of Pennsylvania (PA)
Marshall U (WV)
Miami U (OH)
Michigan State U (MI)
Middlebury Coll (VT)
Millersville U of Pennsylvania (PA)
Minnesota State U Mankato (MN)
Missouri State U (MO)
Montclair State U (NJ)
Morehead State U (KY)
Mount Allison U (NB, Canada)
Mount Holyoke Coll (MA)
New Mexico State U (NM)
North Carolina Central U (NC)
Northeastern Illinois U (IL)
Northern Arizona U (AZ)
Northern Illinois U (IL)
Northern Michigan U (MI)
Northwest Missouri State U (MO)
The Ohio State U (OH)
Ohio U (OH)
Ohio Wesleyan U (OH)
Oklahoma State U (OK)
Old Dominion U (VA)
Oregon State U (OR)
Park U (MO)
Penn State Abington (PA)
Penn State Altoona (PA)
Penn State Beaver (PA)
Penn State Berks (PA)
Penn State Brandywine (PA)
Penn State DuBois (PA)
Penn State Erie, The Behrend Coll (PA)
Penn State Fayette, The Eberly Campus (PA)
Penn State Greater Allegheny (PA)
Penn State Hazleton (PA)
Penn State Lehigh Valley (PA)
Penn State Mont Alto (PA)
Penn State New Kensington (PA)
Penn State Schuylkill (PA)
Penn State Shenango (PA)
Penn State U Park (PA)
Penn State Wilkes-Barre (PA)
Penn State Worthington Scranton (PA)
Penn State York (PA)
Pittsburg State U (KS)
Plymouth State U (NH)
Portland State U (OR)
Radford U (VA)
Rhode Island Coll (RI)
Rowan U (NJ)
Rutgers, The State U of New Jersey, New Brunswick (NJ)
Salem State U (MA)
Salisbury U (MD)
Samford U (AL)
Sam Houston State U (TX)
San Diego State U (CA)
San Francisco State U (CA)
San Jose State U (CA)
Shippensburg U of Pennsylvania (PA)
Simon Fraser U (BC, Canada)
Slippery Rock U of Pennsylvania (PA)
Sonoma State U (CA)
South Dakota State U (SD)
Southern Connecticut State U (CT)
Southern Illinois U Carbondale (IL)
Southern Illinois U Edwardsville (IL)
State U of New York at New Paltz (NY)
State U of New York at Plattsburgh (NY)
State U of New York Coll at Cortland (NY)
State U of New York Coll at Geneseo (NY)

Stephen F. Austin State U (TX)
Stetson U (FL)
Syracuse U (NY)
Taylor U (IN)
Texas A&M U (TX)
Texas A&M U–Kingsville (TX)
Texas Christian U (TX)
Texas State U–San Marcos (TX)
Thompson Rivers U (BC, Canada)
Trent U (ON, Canada)
United States Air Force Acad (CO)
United States Military Acad (NY)
U at Albany, State U of New York (NY)
U at Buffalo, the State U of New York (NY)
The U of Akron (OH)
The U of Alabama (AL)
U of Alaska Fairbanks (AK)
The U of Arizona (AZ)
The U of British Columbia (BC, Canada)
The U of British Columbia–Okanagan (BC, Canada)
U of California, Berkeley (CA)
U of California, Los Angeles (CA)
U of California, Santa Barbara (CA)
U of Central Arkansas (AR)
U of Central Oklahoma (OK)
U of Chicago (IL)
U of Cincinnati (OH)
U of Colorado Boulder (CO)
U of Colorado Colorado Springs (CO)
U of Colorado Denver (CO)
U of Delaware (DE)
U of Denver (CO)
U of Florida (FL)
U of Georgia (GA)
U of Guelph (ON, Canada)
U of Hawaii at Hilo (HI)
U of Hawaii at Manoa (HI)
U of Houston–Clear Lake (TX)
U of Idaho (ID)
U of Illinois at Urbana–Champaign (IL)
The U of Iowa (IA)
The U of Kansas (KS)
U of Kentucky (KY)
U of Louisville (KY)
U of Maine at Farmington (ME)
U of Maryland, Baltimore County (MD)
U of Maryland, Coll Park (MD)
U of Mary Washington (VA)
U of Massachusetts Amherst (MA)
U of Memphis (TN)
U of Miami (FL)
U of Minnesota, Duluth (MN)
U of Minnesota, Twin Cities Campus (MN)
U of Missouri (MO)
U of Missouri–Kansas City (MO)
U of Nebraska at Kearney (NE)
U of Nebraska at Omaha (NE)
U of Nebraska–Lincoln (NE)
U of Nevada, Reno (NV)
U of New Hampshire (NH)
U of New Mexico (NM)
U of North Alabama (AL)
The U of North Carolina at Chapel Hill (NC)
The U of North Carolina at Charlotte (NC)
The U of North Carolina at Greensboro (NC)
The U of North Carolina Wilmington (NC)
U of North Dakota (ND)
U of Northern Colorado (CO)
U of Northern Iowa (IA)
U of North Texas (TX)
U of Oklahoma (OK)
U of Oregon (OR)
U of Ottawa (ON, Canada)
U of Regina (SK, Canada)
U of Richmond (VA)
U of St. Thomas (MN)
U of South Alabama (AL)
U of South Carolina (SC)
U of Southern California (CA)
U of Southern Mississippi (MS)
U of South Florida (FL)
The U of Tennessee (TN)
The U of Tennessee at Martin (TN)
The U of Texas at Austin (TX)
The U of Texas at El Paso (TX)

The U of Texas at San Antonio (TX)
The U of Toledo (OH)
U of Utah (UT)
U of Vermont (VT)
U of Waterloo (ON, Canada)
The U of Western Ontario (ON, Canada)
U of West Georgia (GA)
U of Wisconsin–Eau Claire (WI)
U of Wisconsin–La Crosse (WI)
U of Wisconsin–Madison (WI)
U of Wisconsin–Milwaukee (WI)
U of Wisconsin–Parkside (WI)
U of Wisconsin–Platteville (WI)
U of Wisconsin–Stevens Point (WI)
U of Wyoming (WY)
Utah State U (UT)
Valparaiso U (IN)
Vassar Coll (NY)
Villanova U (PA)
Virginia Polytechnic Inst and State U (VA)
Wayne State Coll (NE)
Weber State U (UT)
West Chester U of Pennsylvania (PA)
Western Carolina U (NC)
Western Illinois U (IL)
Western Kentucky U (KY)
Western Michigan U (MI)
Western Oregon U (OR)
Western Washington U (WA)
West Texas A&M U (TX)
West Virginia U (WV)
William Paterson U of New Jersey (NJ)
Wittenberg U (OH)
Worcester State U (MA)
Wright State U (OH)
Youngstown State U (OH)

GEOGRAPHY RELATED
Bridgewater State U (MA)
Brigham Young U (UT)
Northern Michigan U (MI)
Ohio U (OH)
South Dakota State U (SD)
Temple U (PA)
U of California, Los Angeles (CA)
U of Mary Washington (VA)
U of Miami (FL)

GEOGRAPHY TEACHER EDUCATION
Central Michigan U (MI)
Concordia U, Nebraska (NE)
Grand Valley State U (MI)
Mayville State U (ND)
Michigan State U (MI)
Northern Michigan U (MI)
Rhode Island Coll (RI)
U of Delaware (DE)
The U of Tennessee at Martin (TN)
U of Windsor (ON, Canada)
Valparaiso U (IN)
Wayne State Coll (NE)
Western Michigan U (MI)

GEOLOGICAL AND EARTH SCIENCES/GEOSCIENCES RELATED
Baylor U (TX)
Boston U (MA)
Bridgewater State U (MA)
Brigham Young U (UT)
California State U, Chico (CA)
California State U, Fullerton (CA)
Cedarville U (OH)
The Coll at Brockport, State U of New York (NY)
Earlham Coll (IN)
Eckerd Coll (FL)
Hamilton Coll (NY)
Lehigh U (PA)
Murray State U (KY)
Old Dominion U (VA)
Oregon State U (OR)
Pacific Lutheran U (WA)
Penn State Abington (PA)
Penn State Altoona (PA)
Penn State Beaver (PA)
Penn State Berks (PA)
Penn State Brandywine (PA)
Penn State DuBois (PA)
Penn State Erie, The Behrend Coll (PA)
Penn State Fayette, The Eberly Campus (PA)

Penn State Greater Allegheny (PA)
Penn State Hazleton (PA)
Penn State Lehigh Valley (PA)
Penn State Mont Alto (PA)
Penn State New Kensington (PA)
Penn State Schuylkill (PA)
Penn State Shenango (PA)
Penn State U Park (PA)
Penn State Wilkes-Barre (PA)
Penn State Worthington Scranton (PA)
Penn State York (PA)
Princeton U (NJ)
Salisbury U (MD)
San Jose State U (CA)
Stanford U (CA)
Texas A&M U (TX)
U of California, Los Angeles (CA)
U of Guelph (ON, Canada)
U of Illinois at Urbana–Champaign (IL)
U of Miami (FL)
U of Nevada, Las Vegas (NV)
U of Northern Iowa (IA)
U of Oklahoma (OK)
U of Pittsburgh (PA)
The U of Texas at Arlington (TX)
U of Utah (UT)
U of West Georgia (GA)
U of Wyoming (WY)
Utica Coll (NY)
Western State Colorado U (CO)
Western Washington U (WA)
Whitman Coll (WA)
Wittenberg U (OH)
Yale U (CT)

GEOLOGICAL/GEOPHYSICAL ENGINEERING
Colorado School of Mines (CO)
Missouri U of Science and Technology (MO)
Montana Tech of The U of Montana (MT)
Rutgers, The State U of New Jersey, Newark (NJ)
Tufts U (MA)
U of Alaska Fairbanks (AK)
The U of British Columbia (BC, Canada)
U of California, Berkeley (CA)
U of California, Los Angeles (CA)
U of Michigan (MI)
U of Minnesota, Twin Cities Campus (MN)
U of Mississippi (MS)
U of Nevada, Reno (NV)
U of New Brunswick Fredericton (NB, Canada)
U of North Dakota (ND)
U of Rochester (NY)
U of Utah (UT)
U of Waterloo (ON, Canada)
U of Wisconsin–Madison (WI)

GEOLOGY/EARTH SCIENCE
Acadia U (NS, Canada)
Adams State U (CO)
Alaska Pacific U (AK)
Albion Coll (MI)
Alfred U (NY)
American U of Beirut (Lebanon)
Amherst Coll (MA)
Angelo State U (TX)
Appalachian State U (NC)
Arizona State U (AZ)
Arkansas Tech U (AR)
Ashland U (OH)
Auburn U (AL)
Augustana Coll (IL)
Austin Peay State U (TN)
Ball State U (IN)
Bates Coll (ME)
Baylor U (TX)
Bemidji State U (MN)
Binghamton U, State U of New York (NY)
Bloomsburg U of Pennsylvania (PA)
Boise State U (ID)
Boston Coll (MA)
Boston U (MA)
Bowdoin Coll (ME)
Bowling Green State U (OH)
Bridgewater State U (MA)
Brock U (ON, Canada)
Brown U (RI)
Bucknell U (PA)

Buffalo State Coll, State U of New York (NY)
California Lutheran U (CA)
California Polytechnic State U, San Luis Obispo (CA)
California State Polytechnic U, Pomona (CA)
California State U, Chico (CA)
California State U, Dominguez Hills (CA)
California State U, East Bay (CA)
California State U, Fresno (CA)
California State U, Fullerton (CA)
California State U, Long Beach (CA)
California State U, Los Angeles (CA)
California State U, Northridge (CA)
California State U, San Bernardino (CA)
California State U, Stanislaus (CA)
Calvin Coll (MI)
Carleton Coll (MN)
Case Western Reserve U (OH)
Castleton State Coll (VT)
Cedarville U (OH)
Centenary Coll of Louisiana (LA)
Central Connecticut State U (CT)
Central Michigan U (MI)
Central State U (OH)
City Coll of the City U of New York (NY)
Clarion U of Pennsylvania (PA)
Clark U (MA)
Clemson U (SC)
Cleveland State U (OH)
Colby Coll (ME)
Colgate U (NY)
The Coll at Brockport, State U of New York (NY)
Coll of Charleston (SC)
The Coll of William and Mary (VA)
The Coll of Wooster (OH)
The Colorado Coll (CO)
Colorado State U (CO)
Columbia U (NY)
Columbia U, School of General Studies (NY)
Columbus State U (GA)
Concordia U Chicago (IL)
Cornell Coll (IA)
Dalhousie U (NS, Canada)
Dartmouth Coll (NH)
DePauw U (IN)
Dickinson Coll (PA)
East Carolina U (NC)
Eastern Illinois U (IL)
Eastern Michigan U (MI)
Eastern Washington U (WA)
East Tennessee State U (TN)
Edinboro U of Pennsylvania (PA)
Elizabeth City State U (NC)
Emporia State U (KS)
Excelsior Coll (NY)
Florida Atlantic U (FL)
Florida Intl U (FL)
Florida State U (FL)
Fort Lewis Coll (CO)
Franklin & Marshall Coll (PA)
Frostburg State U (MD)
Furman U (SC)
George Mason U (VA)
Georgia Southern U (GA)
Georgia Southwestern State U (GA)
Georgia State U (GA)
Grand Valley State U (MI)
Guilford Coll (NC)
Gustavus Adolphus Coll (MN)
Hamilton Coll (NY)
Hanover Coll (IN)
Hardin-Simmons U (TX)
Hartwick Coll (NY)
Haverford Coll (PA)
Hobart and William Smith Colls (NY)
Hofstra U (NY)
Hope Coll (MI)
Humboldt State U (CA)
Illinois State U (IL)
Indiana State U (IN)
Indiana U Bloomington (IN)
Indiana U Northwest (IN)
Indiana U of Pennsylvania (PA)
Indiana U–Purdue U Fort Wayne (IN)

Indiana U–Purdue U Indianapolis (IN)
Iowa State U of Science and Technology (IA)
Jacksonville State U (AL)
James Madison U (VA)
The Johns Hopkins U (MD)
Juniata Coll (PA)
Kansas State U (KS)
Kean U (NJ)
Keene State Coll (NH)
Kent State U (OH)
Keystone Coll (PA)
Kutztown U of Pennsylvania (PA)
Lafayette Coll (PA)
Lake Superior State U (MI)
Lamar U (TX)
La Salle U (PA)
Lawrence U (WI)
Lehman Coll of the City U of New York (NY)
Lock Haven U of Pennsylvania (PA)
Long Island U–C. W. Post Campus (NY)
Louisiana State U and Ag and Mech Coll (LA)
Macalester Coll (MN)
Mansfield U of Pennsylvania (PA)
Marietta Coll (OH)
Marshall U (WV)
Massachusetts Inst of Technology (MA)
Mercyhurst U (PA)
Miami U (OH)
Michigan State U (MI)
Middlebury Coll (VT)
Middle Tennessee State U (TN)
Midwestern State U (TX)
Millersville U of Pennsylvania (PA)
Millsaps Coll (MS)
Minnesota State U Mankato (MN)
Minnesota State U Moorhead (MN)
Minot State U (ND)
Mississippi State U (MS)
Missouri State U (MO)
Missouri U of Science and Technology (MO)
Montana State U (MT)
Montclair State U (NJ)
Moravian Coll (PA)
Morehead State U (KY)
Mount Allison U (NB, Canada)
Mount Holyoke Coll (MA)
National U (CA)
New Jersey City U (NJ)
New Mexico Highlands U (NM)
New Mexico Inst of Mining and Technology (NM)
New Mexico State U (NM)
North Carolina State U (NC)
North Dakota State U (ND)
Northeastern Illinois U (IL)
Northeastern U (MA)
Northern Arizona U (AZ)
Northern Illinois U (IL)
Northern Michigan U (MI)
Northland Coll (WI)
Northwest Missouri State U (MO)
Norwich U (VT)
The Ohio State U (OH)
Ohio U (OH)
Ohio Wesleyan U (OH)
Oklahoma State U (OK)
Oregon State U (OR)
Pace U (NY)
Pacific Lutheran U (WA)
Penn State Abington (PA)
Penn State Altoona (PA)
Penn State Beaver (PA)
Penn State Berks (PA)
Penn State Brandywine (PA)
Penn State DuBois (PA)
Penn State Erie, The Behrend Coll (PA)
Penn State Fayette, The Eberly Campus (PA)
Penn State Greater Allegheny (PA)
Penn State Hazleton (PA)
Penn State Lehigh Valley (PA)
Penn State Mont Alto (PA)
Penn State New Kensington (PA)
Penn State Schuylkill (PA)
Penn State Shenango (PA)
Penn State U Park (PA)
Penn State Wilkes-Barre (PA)
Penn State Worthington Scranton (PA)

Penn State York (PA)
Piedmont Coll (GA)
Pomona Coll (CA)
Portland State U (OR)
Purdue U (IN)
Radford U (VA)
Rensselaer Polytechnic Inst (NY)
Rice U (TX)
The Richard Stockton Coll of New Jersey (NJ)
Rider U (NJ)
Rocky Mountain Coll (MT)
Rutgers, The State U of New Jersey, Newark (NJ)
Rutgers, The State U of New Jersey, New Brunswick (NJ)
St. Lawrence U (NY)
Saint Louis U (MO)
St. Mary's U (TX)
St. Norbert Coll (WI)
Salem State U (MA)
Sam Houston State U (TX)
San Diego State U (CA)
San Francisco State U (CA)
San Jose State U (CA)
Scripps Coll (CA)
Sewanee: The U of the South (TN)
Shawnee State U (OH)
Shippensburg U of Pennsylvania (PA)
Simon Fraser U (BC, Canada)
Skidmore Coll (NY)
Slippery Rock U of Pennsylvania (PA)
Smith Coll (MA)
Sonoma State U (CA)
Southern Connecticut State U (CT)
Southern Illinois U Carbondale (IL)
Southern Methodist U (TX)
Southern Oregon U (OR)
Southern Utah U (UT)
Stanford U (CA)
State U of New York at Fredonia (NY)
State U of New York at New Paltz (NY)
State U of New York at Oswego (NY)
State U of New York at Plattsburgh (NY)
State U of New York Coll at Cortland (NY)
State U of New York Coll at Geneseo (NY)
State U of New York Coll at Potsdam (NY)
Stephen F. Austin State U (TX)
Stony Brook U, State U of New York (NY)
Sul Ross State U (TX)
Susquehanna U (PA)
Syracuse U (NY)
Tarleton State U (TX)
Taylor U (IN)
Temple U (PA)
Texas A&M U (TX)
Texas A&M U–Kingsville (TX)
Texas Christian U (TX)
Trinity U (TX)
Tufts U (MA)
Tulane U (LA)
U at Buffalo, the State U of New York (NY)
The U of Akron (OH)
The U of Alabama (AL)
U of Alaska Anchorage (AK)
U of Alaska Fairbanks (AK)
The U of Arizona (AZ)
U of Arkansas at Little Rock (AR)
The U of British Columbia (BC, Canada)
U of California, Berkeley (CA)
U of California, Davis (CA)
U of California, Irvine (CA)
U of California, Los Angeles (CA)
U of California, Merced (CA)
U of California, Riverside (CA)
U of California, Santa Barbara (CA)
U of California, Santa Cruz (CA)
U of Cincinnati (OH)
U of Colorado Boulder (CO)
U of Delaware (DE)
U of Florida (FL)
U of Georgia (GA)
U of Hawaii at Hilo (HI)
U of Hawaii at Manoa (HI)
U of Houston (TX)

U of Idaho (ID)
U of Illinois at Chicago (IL)
U of Illinois at Urbana–Champaign (IL)
The U of Iowa (IA)
The U of Kansas (KS)
U of Kentucky (KY)
U of Louisiana at Lafayette (LA)
U of Maine at Farmington (ME)
U of Maryland, Coll Park (MD)
U of Massachusetts Amherst (MA)
U of Massachusetts Boston (MA)
U of Memphis (TN)
U of Miami (FL)
U of Michigan (MI)
U of Michigan–Dearborn (MI)
U of Minnesota, Duluth (MN)
U of Minnesota, Twin Cities Campus (MN)
U of Mississippi (MS)
U of Missouri (MO)
U of Missouri–Kansas City (MO)
U of Mount Union (OH)
U of Nebraska at Omaha (NE)
U of Nebraska–Lincoln (NE)
U of Nevada, Las Vegas (NV)
U of Nevada, Reno (NV)
U of New Brunswick Fredericton (NB, Canada)
U of New Brunswick Saint John (NB, Canada)
U of New Hampshire (NH)
U of New Mexico (NM)
U of New Orleans (LA)
The U of North Carolina at Chapel Hill (NC)
The U of North Carolina Wilmington (NC)
U of North Dakota (ND)
U of Northern Colorado (CO)
U of Northern Iowa (IA)
U of Oklahoma (OK)
U of Oregon (OR)
U of Ottawa (ON, Canada)
U of Pennsylvania (PA)
U of Pittsburgh (PA)
U of Puget Sound (WA)
U of Regina (SK, Canada)
U of Rhode Island (RI)
U of Rochester (NY)
U of St. Thomas (MN)
U of South Alabama (AL)
U of South Carolina (SC)
The U of South Dakota (SD)
U of Southern California (CA)
U of Southern Indiana (IN)
U of Southern Maine (ME)
U of Southern Mississippi (MS)
U of South Florida (FL)
The U of Tennessee (TN)
The U of Tennessee at Chattanooga (TN)
The U of Tennessee at Martin (TN)
The U of Texas at Arlington (TX)
The U of Texas at Austin (TX)
The U of Texas at Dallas (TX)
The U of Texas at El Paso (TX)
The U of Texas at San Antonio (TX)
The U of Texas of the Permian Basin (TX)
The U of Toledo (OH)
U of Tulsa (OK)
U of Utah (UT)
U of Vermont (VT)
U of Waterloo (ON, Canada)
The U of Western Ontario (ON, Canada)
U of West Georgia (GA)
U of Windsor (ON, Canada)
U of Wisconsin–Eau Claire (WI)
U of Wisconsin–Green Bay (WI)
U of Wisconsin–Madison (WI)
U of Wisconsin–Milwaukee (WI)
U of Wisconsin–Parkside (WI)
U of Wisconsin–Platteville (WI)
U of Wisconsin–Stevens Point (WI)
U of Wyoming (WY)
Utah State U (UT)
Valparaiso U (IN)
Vanderbilt U (TN)
Vassar Coll (NY)
Virginia Polytechnic Inst and State U (VA)
Virginia Wesleyan Coll (VA)
Washington and Lee U (VA)
Washington State U (WA)
Washington U in St. Louis (MO)

Wayland Baptist U (TX)
Wayne State U (MI)
Weber State U (UT)
Wellesley Coll (MA)
Wesleyan U (CT)
West Chester U of Pennsylvania (PA)
Western Carolina U (NC)
Western Connecticut State U (CT)
Western Illinois U (IL)
Western Kentucky U (KY)
Western Michigan U (MI)
Western State Colorado U (CO)
Western Washington U (WA)
West Texas A&M U (TX)
West Virginia U (WV)
Wheaton Coll (IL)
Whitman Coll (WA)
Wichita State U (KS)
Wilkes U (PA)
William Paterson U of New Jersey (NJ)
Williams Coll (MA)
Wittenberg U (OH)
Wright State U (OH)
York Coll of the City U of New York (NY)
Youngstown State U (OH)

GEOPHYSICS AND SEISMOLOGY
Baylor U (TX)
Boise State U (ID)
Boston Coll (MA)
Boston U (MA)
Bowling Green State U (OH)
Brown U (RI)
Eastern Michigan U (MI)
Michigan State U (MI)
Missouri U of Science and Technology (MO)
New Mexico Inst of Mining and Technology (NM)
Rice U (TX)
St. Lawrence U (NY)
Saint Louis U (MO)
Southern Methodist U (TX)
Stanford U (CA)
State U of New York at Fredonia (NY)
State U of New York Coll at Geneseo (NY)
Texas A&M U (TX)
The U of Akron (OH)
The U of British Columbia (BC, Canada)
U of California, Los Angeles (CA)
U of California, Riverside (CA)
U of California, Santa Barbara (CA)
U of Chicago (IL)
U of Houston (TX)
U of Minnesota, Twin Cities Campus (MN)
U of Nevada, Reno (NV)
U of New Brunswick Fredericton (NB, Canada)
U of Oklahoma (OK)
U of Ottawa (ON, Canada)
U of South Carolina (SC)
The U of Texas at Austin (TX)
The U of Texas at El Paso (TX)
U of Tulsa (OK)
U of Utah (UT)
U of Waterloo (ON, Canada)
Western Michigan U (MI)
Western Washington U (WA)

GEOTECHNICAL AND GEOENVIRONMENTAL ENGINEERING
U of Illinois at Urbana–Champaign (IL)

GERMAN
Agnes Scott Coll (GA)
Albion Coll (MI)
Alfred U (NY)
Alma Coll (MI)
American U (DC)
Amherst Coll (MA)
Arizona State U (AZ)
Auburn U (AL)
Augsburg Coll (MN)
Augustana Coll (IL)
Augustana Coll (SD)
Baker U (KS)
Baldwin Wallace U (OH)
Ball State U (IN)

Bard Coll (NY)
Bates Coll (ME)
Baylor U (TX)
Belmont U (TN)
Bemidji State U (MN)
Berea Coll (KY)
Berry Coll (GA)
Binghamton U, State U of New York (NY)
Boise State U (ID)
Boston Coll (MA)
Boston U (MA)
Bowdoin Coll (ME)
Bowling Green State U (OH)
Brock U (ON, Canada)
Brown U (RI)
Bucknell U (PA)
Butler U (IN)
California Lutheran U (CA)
California State U, Chico (CA)
California State U, Long Beach (CA)
Calvin Coll (MI)
Canisius Coll (NY)
Carleton Coll (MN)
Carnegie Mellon U (PA)
Case Western Reserve U (OH)
The Catholic U of America (DC)
Central Connecticut State U (CT)
Central Michigan U (MI)
Centre Coll (KY)
Christopher Newport U (VA)
Coe Coll (IA)
Colby Coll (ME)
Colgate U (NY)
Coll of Charleston (SC)
Coll of Saint Benedict (MN)
Coll of the Holy Cross (MA)
The Coll of William and Mary (VA)
The Coll of Wooster (OH)
The Colorado Coll (CO)
Colorado State U (CO)
Columbia U (NY)
Columbia U, School of General Studies (NY)
Concordia Coll (MN)
Concordia U Wisconsin (WI)
Converse Coll (SC)
Cornell Coll (IA)
Creighton U (NE)
Dalhousie U (NS, Canada)
Dartmouth Coll (NH)
Davidson Coll (NC)
DePaul U (IL)
DePauw U (IN)
Dickinson Coll (PA)
Doane Coll (NE)
Drew U (NJ)
Drury U (MO)
Earlham Coll (IN)
East Carolina U (NC)
Eastern Michigan U (MI)
Edinboro U of Pennsylvania (PA)
Elizabethtown Coll (PA)
Fairfield U (CT)
Franklin & Marshall Coll (PA)
Furman U (SC)
Georgetown Coll (KY)
Georgetown U (DC)
Georgia Southern U (GA)
Georgia State U (GA)
Gettysburg Coll (PA)
Gonzaga U (WA)
Gordon Coll (MA)
Grinnell Coll (IA)
Guilford Coll (NC)
Gustavus Adolphus Coll (MN)
Hamline U (MN)
Hampden-Sydney Coll (VA)
Hanover Coll (IN)
Hartwick Coll (NY)
Haverford Coll (PA)
Hendrix Coll (AR)
Hillsdale Coll (MI)
Hofstra U (NY)
Hood Coll (MD)
Hope Coll (MI)
Hunter Coll of the City U of New York (NY)
Illinois Coll (IL)
Illinois State U (IL)
Illinois Wesleyan U (IL)
Immaculata U (PA)
Indiana U–Purdue U Fort Wayne (IN)
Indiana U–Purdue U Indianapolis (IN)

Indiana U South Bend (IN)
Indiana U Southeast (IN)
Iowa State U of Science and Technology (IA)
Ithaca Coll (NY)
Jacksonville State U (AL)
Jamestown Coll (ND)
John Carroll U (OH)
The Johns Hopkins U (MD)
Juniata Coll (PA)
Kalamazoo Coll (MI)
Kent State U (OH)
Kenyon Coll (OH)
Knox Coll (IL)
Lafayette Coll (PA)
Lake Erie Coll (OH)
Lakeland Coll (WI)
La Salle U (PA)
Lawrence U (WI)
Lebanon Valley Coll (PA)
Lehigh U (PA)
Linfield Coll (OR)
Lipscomb U (TN)
Lock Haven U of Pennsylvania (PA)
Loyola U Maryland (MD)
Luther Coll (IA)
Macalester Coll (MN)
Marquette U (WI)
McDaniel Coll (MD)
Mercer U (GA)
Messiah Coll (PA)
Miami U (OH)
Michigan State U (MI)
Middlebury Coll (VT)
Millersville U of Pennsylvania (PA)
Minnesota State U Mankato (MN)
Minot State U (ND)
Missouri State U (MO)
Moravian Coll (PA)
Mount Allison U (NB, Canada)
Mount St. Mary's U (MD)
Muhlenberg Coll (PA)
Murray State U (KY)
Nazareth Coll of Rochester (NY)
New Coll of Florida (FL)
New York U (NY)
North Central Coll (IL)
Northern Illinois U (IL)
Northern State U (SD)
Oakland U (MI)
The Ohio State U (OH)
Ohio U (OH)
Ohio Wesleyan U (OH)
Oklahoma City U (OK)
Oklahoma State U (OK)
Oregon State U (OR)
Pacific Lutheran U (WA)
Pacific U (OR)
Penn State Abington (PA)
Penn State Altoona (PA)
Penn State Beaver (PA)
Penn State Berks (PA)
Penn State Brandywine (PA)
Penn State DuBois (PA)
Penn State Erie, The Behrend Coll (PA)
Penn State Fayette, The Eberly Campus (PA)
Penn State Greater Allegheny (PA)
Penn State Hazleton (PA)
Penn State Lehigh Valley (PA)
Penn State Mont Alto (PA)
Penn State New Kensington (PA)
Penn State Schuylkill (PA)
Penn State Shenango (PA)
Penn State U Park (PA)
Penn State Wilkes-Barre (PA)
Penn State Worthington Scranton (PA)
Penn State York (PA)
Pepperdine U, Malibu (CA)
Pomona Coll (CA)
Portland State U (OR)
Princeton U (NJ)
Principia Coll (IL)
Randolph-Macon Coll (VA)
Reed Coll (OR)
Rhodes Coll (TN)
Rice U (TX)
Rider U (NJ)
Ripon Coll (WI)
Rosemont Coll (PA)
Rutgers, The State U of New Jersey, Camden (NJ)
Rutgers, The State U of New Jersey, Newark (NJ)

Rutgers, The State U of New Jersey, New Brunswick (NJ)
St. Ambrose U (IA)
Saint John's U (MN)
Saint Joseph's U (PA)
St. Lawrence U (NY)
Saint Louis U (MO)
Saint Mary's Coll of California (CA)
St. Norbert Coll (WI)
St. Olaf Coll (MN)
Samford U (AL)
San Diego State U (CA)
San Francisco State U (CA)
San Jose State U (CA)
Scripps Coll (CA)
Sewanee: The U of the South (TN)
Simpson Coll (IA)
Skidmore Coll (NY)
Smith Coll (MA)
South Dakota State U (SD)
Southern Connecticut State U (CT)
Southern Illinois U Carbondale (IL)
Southern Methodist U (TX)
Southern Oregon U (OR)
Southern Utah U (UT)
Southwestern U (TX)
Stanford U (CA)
State U of New York at New Paltz (NY)
State U of New York at Oswego (NY)
State U of New York Coll at Cortland (NY)
Stetson U (FL)
Stony Brook U, State U of New York (NY)
Suffolk U (MA)
Susquehanna U (PA)
Swarthmore Coll (PA)
Sweet Briar Coll (VA)
Syracuse U (NY)
Temple U (PA)
Texas A&M U (TX)
Texas Christian U (TX)
Texas State U–San Marcos (TX)
Transylvania U (KY)
Trent U (ON, Canada)
Trinity Coll (CT)
Trinity U (TX)
Truman State U (MO)
Tufts U (MA)
Tulane U (LA)
Union Coll (NE)
United States Military Acad (NY)
U at Buffalo, the State U of New York (NY)
U of Alaska Anchorage (AK)
The U of Arizona (AZ)
The U of British Columbia (BC, Canada)
U of California, Berkeley (CA)
U of California, Davis (CA)
U of California, Los Angeles (CA)
U of California, Santa Barbara (CA)
U of California, Santa Cruz (CA)
U of Central Oklahoma (OK)
U of Chicago (IL)
U of Cincinnati (OH)
U of Dallas (TX)
U of Denver (CO)
U of Evansville (IN)
U of Florida (FL)
U of Georgia (GA)
U of Hawaii at Manoa (HI)
U of Illinois at Urbana–Champaign (IL)
The U of Iowa (IA)
U of Kentucky (KY)
U of Maryland, Coll Park (MD)
U of Miami (FL)
U of Michigan (MI)
U of Minnesota, Duluth (MN)
U of Minnesota, Twin Cities Campus (MN)
U of Mississippi (MS)
U of Missouri (MO)
U of Missouri–Kansas City (MO)
U of Missouri–St. Louis (MO)
U of Mount Union (OH)
U of Nebraska at Kearney (NE)
U of Nebraska–Lincoln (NE)
U of Nevada, Las Vegas (NV)
U of New Brunswick Fredericton (NB, Canada)
U of New Brunswick Saint John (NB, Canada)
U of New Hampshire (NH)

U of New Mexico (NM)
U of North Carolina at Asheville (NC)
The U of North Carolina at Charlotte (NC)
The U of North Carolina at Greensboro (NC)
The U of North Carolina Wilmington (NC)
U of North Dakota (ND)
U of North Texas (TX)
U of Notre Dame (IN)
U of Oregon (OR)
U of Ottawa (ON, Canada)
U of Pennsylvania (PA)
U of Pittsburgh (PA)
U of Puget Sound (WA)
U of Redlands (CA)
U of Regina (SK, Canada)
U of Rhode Island (RI)
U of Rochester (NY)
U of St. Thomas (MN)
The U of Scranton (PA)
U of South Carolina (SC)
The U of South Dakota (SD)
U of Southern California (CA)
U of Southern Indiana (IN)
U of South Florida (FL)
The U of Tennessee (TN)
The U of Texas at Arlington (TX)
The U of Texas at Austin (TX)
The U of Texas at El Paso (TX)
The U of Toledo (OH)
U of Tulsa (OK)
U of Utah (UT)
U of Virginia (VA)
U of Waterloo (ON, Canada)
The U of Western Ontario (ON, Canada)
U of Windsor (ON, Canada)
U of Wisconsin–La Crosse (WI)
U of Wisconsin–Platteville (WI)
U of Wisconsin–Stevens Point (WI)
U of Wyoming (WY)
Utah State U (UT)
Valparaiso U (IN)
Vanderbilt U (TN)
Vassar Coll (NY)
Virginia Polytechnic Inst and State U (VA)
Virginia Wesleyan Coll (VA)
Wabash Coll (IN)
Wake Forest U (NC)
Wartburg Coll (IA)
Washburn U (KS)
Washington & Jefferson Coll (PA)
Washington and Lee U (VA)
Washington Coll (MD)
Washington U in St. Louis (MO)
Wayne State U (MI)
Weber State U (UT)
Webster U (MO)
Wellesley Coll (MA)
Wesleyan U (CT)
West Chester U of Pennsylvania (PA)
Western Carolina U (NC)
Western Kentucky U (KY)
Western Michigan U (MI)
Western Oregon U (OR)
Western Washington U (WA)
Wheaton Coll (IL)
Wheaton Coll (MA)
Whitman Coll (WA)
Willamette U (OR)
Williams Coll (MA)
Wittenberg U (OH)
Wright State U (OH)
Xavier U (OH)
Yale U (CT)

GERMANIC LANGUAGES
Bennington Coll (VT)
Eastern Michigan U (MI)
Grand Valley State U (MI)
Indiana U Bloomington (IN)
New Coll of Florida (FL)
U of Colorado Boulder (CO)
The U of Kansas (KS)
U of Oklahoma (OK)
The U of Texas at San Antonio (TX)
U of Wisconsin–Eau Claire (WI)
U of Wisconsin–Green Bay (WI)
U of Wisconsin–Madison (WI)
U of Wisconsin–Milwaukee (WI)
Washington U in St. Louis (MO)

GERMANIC LANGUAGES RELATED
Calvin Coll (MI)
Columbia U, School of General Studies (NY)

GERMAN LANGUAGE TEACHER EDUCATION
Albion Coll (MI)
Alma Coll (MI)
Auburn U (AL)
Augustana Coll (IL)
Boise State U (ID)
California Lutheran U (CA)
California State U, Chico (CA)
Calvin Coll (MI)
Canisius Coll (NY)
The Catholic U of America (DC)
Central Michigan U (MI)
Colorado State U (CO)
Concordia Coll (MN)
Concordia U Wisconsin (WI)
East Carolina U (NC)
Eastern Michigan U (MI)
Grand Valley State U (MI)
Hofstra U (NY)
Hope Coll (MI)
Hunter Coll of the City U of New York (NY)
Indiana U Bloomington (IN)
Indiana U–Purdue U Fort Wayne (IN)
Indiana U–Purdue U Indianapolis (IN)
Indiana U South Bend (IN)
Ithaca Coll (NY)
Juniata Coll (PA)
Messiah Coll (PA)
Miami U (OH)
Michigan State U (MI)
Minot State U (ND)
Missouri State U (MO)
Moravian Coll (PA)
Ohio U (OH)
Ohio Wesleyan U (OH)
St. Ambrose U (IA)
Southern Utah U (UT)
State U of New York at New Paltz (NY)
U of Delaware (DE)
U of Evansville (IN)
U of Illinois at Chicago (IL)
U of Illinois at Urbana–Champaign (IL)
The U of Iowa (IA)
U of Minnesota, Duluth (MN)
U of Missouri–St. Louis (MO)
U of Nebraska–Lincoln (NE)
The U of South Dakota (SD)
The U of Tennessee at Martin (TN)
The U of Toledo (OH)
U of Windsor (ON, Canada)
Valparaiso U (IN)
Washburn U (KS)
Washington U in St. Louis (MO)
Weber State U (UT)
Western Michigan U (MI)
Western Washington U (WA)

GERMAN STUDIES
American U (DC)
Bard Coll (NY)
Brock U (ON, Canada)
Brown U (RI)
Case Western Reserve U (OH)
Central Coll (IA)
Coe Coll (IA)
Coll of the Holy Cross (MA)
The Coll of Wooster (OH)
Columbia U (NY)
Connecticut Coll (CT)
Franklin & Marshall Coll (PA)
Georgetown U (KY)
Hamilton Coll (NY)
Ithaca Coll (NY)
Kutztown U of Pennsylvania (PA)
Linfield Coll (OR)
Manhattanville Coll (NY)
Moravian Coll (PA)
Mount Holyoke Coll (MA)
North Carolina State U (NC)
Northern Michigan U (MI)
Smith Coll (MA)
Stanford U (CA)
Suffolk U (MA)
Sweet Briar Coll (VA)
U of California, Irvine (CA)
U of California, Riverside (CA)
U of Illinois at Chicago (IL)
U of Massachusetts Amherst (MA)
U of Richmond (VA)
The U of Scranton (PA)
The U of Western Ontario (ON, Canada)
U of Windsor (ON, Canada)
Wellesley Coll (MA)
Wheaton Coll (MA)

GERONTOLOGY
Alfred U (NY)
Barton Coll (NC)
Bethune-Cookman U (FL)
Bowling Green State U (OH)
California State U, Chico (CA)
California State U, East Bay (CA)
Canisius U (NY)
Case Western Reserve U (OH)
Ithaca Coll (NY)
John Carroll U (OH)
Langston U (OK)
Lindenwood U (MO)
Madonna U (MI)
Miami U (OH)
Minnesota State U Moorhead (MN)
Missouri State U (MO)
Mount St. Mary's Coll (CA)
Purdue U Calumet (IN)
Quinnipiac U (CT)
St. Bonaventure U (NY)
St. Thomas U (NB, Canada)
San Diego State U (CA)
Thomas Edison State Coll (NJ)
U of Maryland U Coll (MD)
U of Nebraska at Omaha (NE)
U of Nevada, Las Vegas (NV)
U of Northern Iowa (IA)
U of North Texas (TX)
U of Regina (SK, Canada)
U of Southern California (CA)
U of South Florida (FL)
Weber State U (UT)
Wichita State U (KS)
York Coll of the City U of New York (NY)
Youngstown State U (OH)

GRAPHIC AND PRINTING EQUIPMENT OPERATION/ PRODUCTION
Chowan U (NC)
Fairmont State U (WV)
Ferris State U (MI)
Georgia Southern U (GA)
Lewis-Clark State Coll (ID)
Western Illinois U (IL)

GRAPHIC COMMUNICATIONS
Arizona State U (AZ)
California Polytechnic State U, San Luis Obispo (CA)
Chowan U (NC)
Clemson U (SC)
Eastern Washington U (WA)
Grand View U (IA)
Illinois State U (IL)
Lynn U (FL)
Murray State U (KY)
Point Loma Nazarene U (CA)
Rochester Inst of Technology (NY)
Roger Williams U (RI)
School of the Art Inst of Chicago (IL)
Southern Nazarene U (OK)
State U of New York Coll of Technology at Canton (NY)
U of Maryland U Coll (MD)
U of New Brunswick Saint John (NB, Canada)
U of North Dakota (ND)
U of Northern Iowa (IA)
Walla Walla U (WA)

GRAPHIC COMMUNICATIONS RELATED
Castleton State Coll (VT)
Rasmussen Coll Appleton (WI)
Rasmussen Coll Aurora (IL)
Rasmussen Coll Bismarck (ND)
Rasmussen Coll Blaine (MN)
Rasmussen Coll Bloomington (MN)
Rasmussen Coll Brooklyn Park (MN)
Rasmussen Coll Eagan (MN)
Rasmussen Coll Fargo (ND)
Rasmussen Coll Fort Myers (FL)
Rasmussen Coll Green Bay (WI)
Rasmussen Coll Lake Elmo/ Woodbury (MN)
Rasmussen Coll Land O' Lakes (FL)
Rasmussen Coll Mankato (MN)
Rasmussen Coll Mokena/Tinley Park (IL)
Rasmussen Coll New Port Richey (FL)
Rasmussen Coll Ocala (FL)
Rasmussen Coll Rockford (IL)
Rasmussen Coll Romeoville/Joliet (IL)
Rasmussen Coll St. Cloud (MN)
Rasmussen Coll Tampa/Brandon (FL)
Rasmussen Coll Wausau (WI)
Sullivan Coll of Technology and Design (KY)
U of Wisconsin–Stout (WI)

GRAPHIC DESIGN
Abilene Christian U (TX)
Acad of Art U (CA)
Adams State U (CO)
Alberta Coll of Art & Design (AB, Canada)
Albertus Magnus Coll (CT)
Alma Coll (MI)
American U (DC)
American U of Beirut (Lebanon)
Appalachian State U (NC)
Arizona State U (AZ)
Art Center Coll of Design (CA)
Assumption Coll (MA)
Auburn U (AL)
Augustana Coll (IL)
Becker Coll (MA)
Belhaven U (MS)
Benedictine U (IL)
Bluffton U (OH)
Boise State U (ID)
Boston U (MA)
Bradley U (IL)
Bridgewater State U (MA)
Brigham Young U (UT)
Cabrini Coll (PA)
Caldwell Coll (NJ)
California State Polytechnic U, Pomona (CA)
California State U, Chico (CA)
California State U, Dominguez Hills (CA)
California State U, Fresno (CA)
California State U, Long Beach (CA)
Cedarville U (OH)
Chapman U (CA)
Chatham U (PA)
Chowan U (NC)
City Coll of the City U of New York (NY)
Cleveland Inst of Art (OH)
Coastal Carolina U (SC)
Coll for Creative Studies (MI)
Coll of Mount St. Joseph (OH)
Colorado Mesa U (CO)
Colorado State U (CO)
Columbia Coll (MO)
Concordia U (CA)
Concordia U Wisconsin (WI)
Concord U (WV)
Corcoran Coll of Art and Design (DC)
Creighton U (NE)
Culver-Stockton Coll (MO)
Curry Coll (MA)
DePaul U (IL)
Dordt Coll (IA)
Drake U (IA)
East Central U (OK)
Eastern Washington U (WA)
Edgewood Coll (WI)
Elizabeth City State U (NC)
Emmanuel Coll (MA)
Fashion Inst of Technology (NY)
Ferris State U (MI)
Flagler Coll (FL)
Florida Ag and Mech U (FL)
Florida Southern Coll (FL)
Florida State U (FL)
Georgia Southern U (GA)
Grand View U (IA)
Harding U (AR)
Hardin-Simmons U (TX)
High Point U (NC)
Huntington U (IN)

Indiana U–Purdue U Fort Wayne (IN)
Intl Acad of Design & Technology (FL)
Iowa State U of Science and Technology (IA)
John Brown U (AR)
Judson U (IL)
Lasell Coll (MA)
Lebanese American U (Lebanon)
Liberty U (VA)
Limestone Coll (SC)
Madonna U (MI)
Mansfield U of Pennsylvania (PA)
Marian U (WI)
Marietta Coll (OH)
Mars Hill Coll (NC)
Maryland Inst Coll of Art (MD)
Marymount U (VA)
Maryville U of Saint Louis (MO)
Marywood U (PA)
Mercer U (GA)
Mercyhurst U (PA)
Mississippi Coll (MS)
Missouri Western State U (MO)
Montclair State U (NJ)
Moore Coll of Art & Design (PA)
Moravian Coll (PA)
Morningside Coll (IA)
Mount Mary Coll (WI)
Mount Mercy U (IA)
Mount Vernon Nazarene U (OH)
Newbury Coll (MA)
North Carolina State U (NC)
North Central Coll (IL)
Northeastern U (MA)
Northern Michigan U (MI)
Northwestern Coll (IA)
Northwestern Coll (MN)
Northwest Nazarene U (ID)
Ohio Dominican U (OH)
Ohio U (OH)
Oklahoma Baptist U (OK)
Oklahoma City U (OK)
Oral Roberts U (OK)
Ouachita Baptist U (AR)
Pacific Northwest Coll of Art (OR)
Pacific Union Coll (CA)
Paier Coll of Art, Inc. (CT)
Palm Beach Atlantic U (FL)
Park U (MO)
Penn State Abington (PA)
Penn State Altoona (PA)
Penn State Beaver (PA)
Penn State Berks (PA)
Penn State Brandywine (PA)
Penn State DuBois (PA)
Penn State Erie, The Behrend Coll (PA)
Penn State Fayette, The Eberly Campus (PA)
Penn State Greater Allegheny (PA)
Penn State Hazleton (PA)
Penn State Lehigh Valley (PA)
Penn State Mont Alto (PA)
Penn State New Kensington (PA)
Penn State Schuylkill (PA)
Penn State Shenango (PA)
Penn State U Park (PA)
Penn State Wilkes-Barre (PA)
Penn State Worthington Scranton (PA)
Penn State York (PA)
Pennsylvania Coll of Art & Design (PA)
Philadelphia U (PA)
Plymouth State U (NH)
Point Loma Nazarene U (CA)
Portland State U (OR)
Queens U of Charlotte (NC)
Quincy U (IL)
Rhode Island School of Design (RI)
Rider U (NJ)
Ringling Coll of Art and Design (FL)
Rivier U (NH)
Robert Morris U Illinois (IL)
Rochester Inst of Technology (NY)
Rocky Mountain Coll of Art + Design (CO)
Sacred Heart U (CT)
Sage Coll of Albany (NY)
St. Ambrose U (IA)
St. Edward's U (TX)
St. John's U (NY)
Saint Mary's U of Minnesota (MN)
St. Norbert Coll (WI)

Saint Vincent Coll (PA)
Salve Regina U (RI)
Samford U (AL)
San Diego State U (CA)
San Jose State U (CA)
Santa Fe U of Art and Design (NM)
Savannah Coll of Art and Design (GA)
School of the Art Inst of Chicago (IL)
School of the Museum of Fine Arts, Boston (MA)
Schreiner U (TX)
Simpson Coll (IA)
South Dakota State U (SD)
Southern New Hampshire U (NH)
Southern Utah U (UT)
Spring Arbor U (MI)
Spring Hill Coll (AL)
Stephens Coll (MO)
Stonehill Coll (MA)
Sullivan Coll of Technology and Design (KY)
Susquehanna U (PA)
Tabor Coll (KS)
Temple U (PA)
Texas A&M U–Commerce (TX)
Texas Christian U (TX)
Union Coll (NE)
The U of Akron (OH)
U of Arkansas–Fort Smith (AR)
U of Bridgeport (CT)
U of Denver (CO)
U of Florida (FL)
U of Hartford (CT)
U of Houston (TX)
U of Illinois at Chicago (IL)
U of Illinois at Urbana–Champaign (IL)
The U of Kansas (KS)
U of Miami (FL)
U of Michigan (MI)
U of Minnesota, Duluth (MN)
U of Missouri–St. Louis (MO)
U of Nebraska at Omaha (NE)
U of North Dakota (ND)
U of South Florida (FL)
The U of Tampa (FL)
The U of Tennessee at Martin (TN)
The U of the Arts (PA)
U of the District of Columbia (DC)
U of the Incarnate Word (TX)
Ursuline Coll (OH)
Villa Maria Coll of Buffalo (NY)
Virginia Commonwealth U (VA)
Viterbo U (WI)
Walla Walla U (WA)
Washington U in St. Louis (MO)
Wayland Baptist U (TX)
Waynesburg U (PA)
Wayne State Coll (NE)
Western Michigan U (MI)
Western State Colorado U (CO)
West Texas A&M U (TX)
Wichita State U (KS)
Xavier U (OH)
Youngstown State U (OH)

GREENHOUSE MANAGEMENT
U of Minnesota, Crookston (MN)

HAZARDOUS MATERIALS MANAGEMENT AND WASTE TECHNOLOGY
Rochester Inst of Technology (NY)

HEALTH AND MEDICAL ADMINISTRATIVE SERVICES RELATED
Clayton State U (GA)
Concordia Coll–New York (NY)
Mount Mercy U (IA)
Pennsylvania Coll of Technology (PA)
Ursuline Coll (OH)
Washburn U (KS)
Weber State U (UT)
Western Michigan U (MI)

HEALTH AND PHYSICAL EDUCATION/FITNESS
American U (DC)
Arkansas State U (AR)
Asbury U (KY)
Austin Peay State U (TN)
Averett U (VA)
Baker U (KS)
Baldwin Wallace U (OH)
Baylor U (TX)

Belmont U (TN)
Berea Coll (KY)
Bethel Coll (IN)
Bethel Coll (KS)
Blackburn Coll (IL)
Bluffton U (OH)
Bob Jones U (SC)
Boise State U (ID)
Brevard Coll (NC)
Bridgewater Coll (VA)
California Polytechnic State U, San Luis Obispo (CA)
California State Polytechnic U, Pomona (CA)
California State U, Chico (CA)
California State U, Dominguez Hills (CA)
California State U, Fullerton (CA)
California State U, Monterey Bay (CA)
California State U, Stanislaus (CA)
Cameron U (OK)
Capital U (OH)
Carroll Coll (MT)
Castleton State Coll (VT)
Cedarville U (OH)
Central Michigan U (MI)
Claflin U (SC)
Cleveland State U (OH)
The Coll at Brockport, State U of New York (NY)
Coll of the Ozarks (MO)
Concordia Coll (MN)
Concordia U (CA)
Concordia U, Nebraska (NE)
Concordia U Texas (TX)
Concordia U Wisconsin (WI)
Dallas Baptist U (TX)
DePaul U (IL)
Doane Coll (NE)
Dordt Coll (IA)
East Central U (OK)
Eastern Michigan U (MI)
Eastern Washington U (WA)
East Tennessee State U (TN)
East Texas Baptist U (TX)
Emory & Henry Coll (VA)
Evangel U (MO)
Ferrum Coll (VA)
Friends U (KS)
Gardner-Webb U (NC)
George Fox U (OR)
Georgia Southern U (GA)
Guilford Coll (NC)
Hanover Coll (IN)
Hardin-Simmons U (TX)
Houghton Coll (NY)
Howard Payne U (TX)
Indiana U of Pennsylvania (PA)
Iowa State U of Science and Technology (IA)
Iowa Wesleyan Coll (IA)
Ithaca Coll (NY)
Jacksonville State U (AL)
James Madison U (VA)
Jarvis Christian Coll (TX)
John Brown U (AR)
Johnson State Coll (VT)
Keene State Coll (NH)
La Sierra U (CA)
Lee U (TN)
Liberty U (VA)
Lincoln Memorial U (TN)
Linfield Coll (OR)
Longwood U (VA)
Lubbock Christian U (TX)
Luther Coll (IA)
Lynchburg Coll (VA)
Maryville Coll (TN)
Marywood U (PA)
The Master's Coll and Sem (CA)
Mayville State U (ND)
McDaniel Coll (MD)
Miami U (OH)
Middle Tennessee State U (TN)
Mississippi U for Women (MS)
Missouri Western State U (MO)
Monmouth Coll (IL)
Monmouth U (NJ)
Morehead State U (KY)
Morehouse Coll (GA)
New England Coll (NH)
North Carolina Central U (NC)
Northern Illinois U (IL)
Northern Michigan U (MI)
Northwestern Coll (MN)

Northwestern State U of Louisiana (LA)
Northwest Nazarene U (ID)
The Ohio State U (OH)
Ohio U (OH)
Oklahoma Baptist U (OK)
Olivet Coll (MI)
Oral Roberts U (OK)
Oregon State U (OR)
Pacific Union Coll (CA)
Pittsburg State U (KS)
Plymouth State U (NH)
Point Loma Nazarene U (CA)
Quincy U (IL)
Randolph Coll (VA)
Rocky Mountain Coll (MT)
Rowan U (NJ)
St. Ambrose U (IA)
St. Gregory's U, Shawnee (OK)
Saint Joseph's Coll (IN)
Saint Mary's Coll of California (CA)
St. Mary's U (TX)
Salem State U (MA)
Samford U (AL)
San Diego State U (CA)
San Jose State U (CA)
Shawnee State U (OH)
Slippery Rock U of Pennsylvania (PA)
South Dakota State U (SD)
Southeast Missouri State U (MO)
Southwest Baptist U (MO)
Southwestern Adventist U (TX)
Spring Arbor U (MI)
Sterling Coll (KS)
Syracuse U (NY)
Tabor Coll (KS)
Tennessee Wesleyan Coll (TN)
Texas A&M Intl U (TX)
Texas A&M U (TX)
Texas A&M U–Kingsville (TX)
Texas Christian U (TX)
Texas Southern U (TX)
U of Alaska Anchorage (AK)
U of Delaware (DE)
The U of Findlay (OH)
U of Georgia (GA)
U of Great Falls (MT)
U of Guam (GU)
The U of Kansas (KS)
U of Louisville (KY)
U of Massachusetts Boston (MA)
U of Mobile (AL)
The U of Montana Western (MT)
U of Montevallo (AL)
U of New Orleans (LA)
The U of North Carolina at Chapel Hill (NC)
The U of North Carolina at Charlotte (NC)
The U of North Carolina at Pembroke (NC)
The U of North Carolina Wilmington (NC)
U of Northern Iowa (IA)
U of North Texas (TX)
U of Ottawa (ON, Canada)
U of Regina (SK, Canada)
U of Science and Arts of Oklahoma (OK)
U of Southern Maine (ME)
U of Southern Mississippi (MS)
The U of Tampa (FL)
The U of Tennessee at Martin (TN)
The U of Texas at Austin (TX)
The U of Texas at Brownsville (TX)
The U of Texas at San Antonio (TX)
U of the Cumberlands (KY)
U of Utah (UT)
U of West Florida (FL)
U of Windsor (ON, Canada)
U of Wisconsin–La Crosse (WI)
U of Wisconsin–Stevens Point (WI)
U of Wisconsin–Superior (WI)
Valdosta State U (GA)
Valley City State U (ND)
Valparaiso U (IN)
Virginia Intermont Coll (VA)
Walla Walla U (WA)
Walsh U (OH)
Weber State U (UT)
Wesleyan U (CT)
West Chester U of Pennsylvania (PA)
Western Washington U (WA)
West Virginia U (WV)
West Virginia Wesleyan Coll (WV)

William Penn U (IA)
Wright State U (OH)
Youngstown State U (OH)

HEALTH AND PHYSICAL EDUCATION RELATED
Adelphi U (NY)
Arizona State U (AZ)
Averett U (VA)
Avila U (MO)
Bloomsburg U of Pennsylvania (PA)
Bowling Green State U (OH)
Bridgewater State U (MA)
California State U, Long Beach (CA)
Coe Coll (IA)
The Coll at Brockport, State U of New York (NY)
Concordia Coll (MN)
Concordia U Wisconsin (WI)
Cornell Coll (IA)
East Carolina U (NC)
John Brown U (AR)
Limestone Coll (SC)
Lock Haven U of Pennsylvania (PA)
Mayville State U (ND)
Midwestern State U (TX)
Mount Vernon Nazarene U (OH)
Naropa U (CO)
North Greenville U (SC)
Regis Coll (MA)
Rocky Mountain Coll (MT)
Saint Mary's Coll of California (CA)
South Dakota State U (SD)
Southern Nazarene U (OK)
Texas Lutheran U (TX)
U of Central Oklahoma (OK)
The U of Iowa (IA)
U of New England (ME)
U of Utah (UT)
U of Wisconsin–Superior (WI)
Valdosta State U (GA)
Virginia Intermont Coll (VA)
Wayne State Coll (NE)

HEALTH AND WELLNESS
Antioch U Midwest (OH)
Canisius Coll (NY)
Indiana U Kokomo (IN)
Indiana Wesleyan U (IN)
Johnson C. Smith U (NC)
Keene State Coll (NH)
Missouri Baptist U (MO)
Oklahoma City U (OK)
Presentation Coll (SD)
Sam Houston State U (TX)
Texas A&M U (TX)
Texas A&M U–Commerce (TX)
Texas Woman's U (TX)
Trevecca Nazarene U (TN)
U of Houston (TX)
The U of Texas–Pan American (TX)
U of Wisconsin–La Crosse (WI)
U of Wisconsin–Stout (WI)
U of Wisconsin–Superior (WI)
Viterbo U (WI)

HEALTH COMMUNICATION
Grand Valley State U (MI)
Juniata Coll (PA)
North Dakota State U (ND)
U of Houston (TX)

HEALTH/HEALTH-CARE ADMINISTRATION
Adams State U (CO)
Alaska Pacific U (AK)
Appalachian State U (NC)
Auburn U (AL)
Augustana Coll (SD)
Baker Coll of Port Huron (MI)
Baldwin Wallace U (OH)
Baptist Coll of Health Sciences (TN)
Belhaven U (MS)
Benedictine U (IL)
Bowling Green State U (OH)
Brock U (ON, Canada)
California Baptist U (CA)
California State U, Dominguez Hills (CA)
California State U, Long Beach (CA)
California State U, San Bernardino (CA)

Carlow U (PA)
Chestnut Hill Coll (PA)
Cleary U (MI)
Coastal Carolina U (SC)
The Coll at Brockport, State U of New York (NY)
Columbia Coll (MO)
Concordia U (CA)
Concordia U (OR)
Concordia U, St. Paul (MN)
Concordia U Wisconsin (WI)
Corban U (OR)
Creighton U (NE)
Dallas Baptist U (TX)
Davenport U, Grand Rapids (MI)
DeVry U, Pomona (CA)
DeVry U, Westminster (CO)
DeVry U, Miramar (FL)
DeVry U, Orlando (FL)
DeVry U, Decatur (GA)
DeVry U, Houston (TX)
DeVry U Online (IL)
Dillard U (LA)
Dominican Coll (NY)
East Carolina U (NC)
Eastern Michigan U (MI)
Eastern Washington U (WA)
Ferris State U (MI)
Florida Ag and Mech U (FL)
Florida Atlantic U (FL)
Florida Intl U (FL)
Florida Southern Coll (FL)
Franklin U (OH)
Frostburg State U (MD)
Gardner-Webb U (NC)
Goldey-Beacom Coll (DE)
Granite State Coll (NH)
Harding U (AR)
Harris-Stowe State U (MO)
Hodges U (FL)
Howard Payne U (TX)
Husson U (ME)
Immaculata U (PA)
Indiana U–Purdue U Fort Wayne (IN)
Indiana U–Purdue U Indianapolis (IN)
Indian River State Coll (FL)
Iona Coll (NY)
Ithaca Coll (NY)
James Madison U (VA)
Lancaster General Coll of Nursing & Health Sciences (PA)
Langston U (OK)
Lebanon Valley Coll (PA)
Lee U (TN)
Lehman Coll of the City U of New York (NY)
Lewis U (IL)
Limestone Coll (SC)
Lindenwood U (MO)
Lourdes U (OH)
Loyola U Chicago (IL)
Madonna U (MI)
Malone U (OH)
Marian U (WI)
Mary Baldwin Coll (VA)
Marywood U (PA)
Mercy Coll of Health Sciences (IA)
Mercy Coll of Ohio (OH)
Metropolitan State U of Denver (CO)
Misericordia U (PA)
Missouri Baptist U (MO)
Mount Mercy U (IA)
National U (CA)
Newbury Coll (MA)
New England Coll (NH)
Norfolk State U (VA)
Ohio U (OH)
Oregon State U (OR)
Peirce Coll (PA)
Penn State Abington (PA)
Penn State Altoona (PA)
Penn State Beaver (PA)
Penn State Berks (PA)
Penn State Brandywine (PA)
Penn State DuBois (PA)
Penn State Erie, The Behrend Coll (PA)
Penn State Fayette, The Eberly Campus (PA)
Penn State Greater Allegheny (PA)
Penn State Hazleton (PA)
Penn State Lehigh Valley (PA)
Penn State Mont Alto (PA)
Penn State New Kensington (PA)

Penn State Schuylkill (PA)
Penn State Shenango (PA)
Penn State U Park (PA)
Penn State Wilkes-Barre (PA)
Penn State Worthington Scranton (PA)
Penn State York (PA)
Potomac Coll (DC)
Providence Coll (RI)
Rasmussen Coll Appleton (WI)
Rasmussen Coll Aurora (IL)
Rasmussen Coll Bismarck (ND)
Rasmussen Coll Blaine (MN)
Rasmussen Coll Bloomington (MN)
Rasmussen Coll Brooklyn Park (MN)
Rasmussen Coll Eagan (MN)
Rasmussen Coll Fargo (ND)
Rasmussen Coll Fort Myers (FL)
Rasmussen Coll Green Bay (WI)
Rasmussen Coll Lake Elmo/Woodbury (MN)
Rasmussen Coll Land O' Lakes (FL)
Rasmussen Coll Mankato (MN)
Rasmussen Coll Mokena/Tinley Park (IL)
Rasmussen Coll Moorhead (MN)
Rasmussen Coll New Port Richey (FL)
Rasmussen Coll Ocala (FL)
Rasmussen Coll Rockford (IL)
Rasmussen Coll Romeoville/Joliet (IL)
Rasmussen Coll St. Cloud (MN)
Rasmussen Coll Tampa/Brandon (FL)
Rasmussen Coll Wausau (WI)
Rhode Island Coll (RI)
Roberts Wesleyan Coll (NY)
Roger Williams U (RI)
St. John's U (NY)
St. Joseph's Coll, Long Island Campus (NY)
St. Joseph's Coll, New York (NY)
Saint Leo U (FL)
St. Thomas U (FL)
San Jose State U (CA)
Shippensburg U of Pennsylvania (PA)
Simpson U (CA)
Southern Illinois U Carbondale (IL)
Southwestern Adventist U (TX)
Spring Arbor U (MI)
State U of New York Coll of Technology at Canton (NY)
Stonehill Coll (MA)
Tennessee State U (TN)
Texas Southern U (TX)
Texas State U–San Marcos (TX)
Thomas More Coll (KY)
Trident U Intl (CA)
The U of Alabama at Birmingham (AL)
U of Central Florida (FL)
U of Evansville (IN)
U of Great Falls (MT)
U of Hawaii–West Oahu (HI)
U of Houston–Clear Lake (TX)
U of Kentucky (KY)
U of La Verne (CA)
U of Louisiana at Lafayette (LA)
U of Medicine and Dentistry of New Jersey (NJ)
U of Miami (FL)
U of Michigan–Dearborn (MI)
U of Michigan–Flint (MI)
U of Minnesota, Crookston (MN)
U of Minnesota, Duluth (MN)
U of Nebraska at Omaha (NE)
U of Nevada, Las Vegas (NV)
U of New England (ME)
U of New Hampshire (NH)
The U of North Carolina at Chapel Hill (NC)
U of North Florida (FL)
U of Pennsylvania (PA)
U of Rhode Island (RI)
U of St. Francis (IL)
The U of Scranton (PA)
U of Southern Indiana (IN)
U of South Florida (FL)
The U of Texas at El Paso (TX)
U of Wisconsin–Eau Claire (WI)
Upper Iowa U (IA)
Ursuline Coll (OH)
Valparaiso U (IN)

Viterbo U (WI)
Walden U (MN)
Washington U in St. Louis (MO)
Waynesburg U (PA)
Webster U (MO)
West Chester U of Pennsylvania (PA)
Western Carolina U (NC)
Western Illinois U (IL)
Western Kentucky U (KY)
West Virginia U Inst of Technology (WV)
Wichita State U (KS)
Wilberforce U (OH)

HEALTH INFORMATION/MEDICAL RECORDS ADMINISTRATION
Alabama State U (AL)
Arkansas Tech U (AR)
Boise State U (ID)
Bowling Green State U (OH)
Charter Oak State Coll (CT)
Chicago State U (IL)
Coll of Coastal Georgia (GA)
The Coll of St. Scholastica (MN)
Dakota State U (SD)
Dalhousie U (NS, Canada)
Davenport U, Grand Rapids (MI)
Duquesne U (PA)
East Carolina U (NC)
Eastern Washington U (WA)
Fairleigh Dickinson U, Metropolitan Campus (NJ)
Ferris State U (MI)
Florida Ag and Mech U (FL)
Georgia Regents U (GA)
Illinois State U (IL)
Indiana U–Purdue U Indianapolis (IN)
Indiana U Southeast (IN)
Kean U (NJ)
Long Island U–C. W. Post Campus (NY)
Missouri Western State U (MO)
The Ohio State U (OH)
The Ohio State U at Lima (OH)
Peirce Coll (PA)
Pennsylvania Coll of Technology (PA)
Rasmussen Coll Appleton (WI)
Rasmussen Coll Aurora (IL)
Rasmussen Coll Bismarck (ND)
Rasmussen Coll Blaine (MN)
Rasmussen Coll Bloomington (MN)
Rasmussen Coll Brooklyn Park (MN)
Rasmussen Coll Eagan (MN)
Rasmussen Coll Fargo (ND)
Rasmussen Coll Fort Myers (FL)
Rasmussen Coll Green Bay (WI)
Rasmussen Coll Lake Elmo/Woodbury (MN)
Rasmussen Coll Land O' Lakes (FL)
Rasmussen Coll Mankato (MN)
Rasmussen Coll Mokena/Tinley Park (IL)
Rasmussen Coll Moorhead (MN)
Rasmussen Coll New Port Richey (FL)
Rasmussen Coll Ocala (FL)
Rasmussen Coll Rockford (IL)
Rasmussen Coll Romeoville/Joliet (IL)
Rasmussen Coll St. Cloud (MN)
Rasmussen Coll Tampa/Brandon (FL)
Rasmussen Coll Wausau (WI)
Regis U (CO)
Saint Louis U (MO)
State U of New York Inst of Technology (NY)
Stephens Coll (MO)
Temple U (PA)
Tennessee State U (TN)
Texas Southern U (TX)
Texas State U–San Marcos (TX)
Trevecca Nazarene U (TN)
The U of Alabama at Birmingham (AL)
U of Central Florida (FL)
U of Cincinnati (OH)
U of Illinois at Chicago (IL)
The U of Kansas (KS)
U of Louisiana at Lafayette (LA)

U of Medicine and Dentistry of New Jersey (NJ)
U of Pittsburgh (PA)
The U of Tennessee (TN)
The U of Toledo (OH)
U of Wisconsin–Green Bay (WI)
Weber State U (UT)
Western Carolina U (NC)
Western Kentucky U (KY)

HEALTH INFORMATION/MEDICAL RECORDS TECHNOLOGY
Fisher Coll (MA)
Franklin U (OH)
Resurrection U (IL)
St. John's U (NY)

HEALTH/MEDICAL PHYSICS
Belmont U (TN)
Bloomsburg U of Pennsylvania (PA)
California State U, Dominguez Hills (CA)
California State U, Northridge (CA)
Oregon State U (OR)
U of Guelph (ON, Canada)
U of Nevada, Las Vegas (NV)

HEALTH/MEDICAL PREPARATORY PROGRAMS RELATED
Abilene Christian U (TX)
Arizona State U (AZ)
Asbury U (KY)
Aurora U (IL)
Avila U (MO)
Baylor U (TX)
Benedictine U (IL)
Binghamton U, State U of New York (NY)
Bloomsburg U of Pennsylvania (PA)
Bob Jones U (SC)
Cleveland State U (OH)
Concordia U, Nebraska (NE)
Duquesne U (PA)
Emory & Henry Coll (VA)
Gannon U (PA)
Guilford Coll (NC)
Hodges U (FL)
Hofstra U (NY)
Ithaca Coll (NY)
Juniata Coll (PA)
Kent State U (OH)
Kent State U at Ashtabula (OH)
Lee U (TN)
Le Moyne Coll (NY)
Lipscomb U (TN)
Lock Haven U of Pennsylvania (PA)
Lubbock Christian U (TX)
Madonna U (MI)
Maryville U of Saint Louis (MO)
Mercer U (GA)
Mercyhurst U (PA)
Northern Illinois U (IL)
Northern Michigan U (MI)
Point Park U (PA)
Seattle Pacific U (WA)
Southern Nazarene U (OK)
The U of Findlay (OH)
U of Minnesota, Twin Cities Campus (MN)
U of Missouri (MO)
U of Regina (SK, Canada)
U of South Alabama (AL)
U of Waterloo (ON, Canada)
Utica Coll (NY)
Valley City State U (ND)
Virginia Intermont Coll (VA)
Western Washington U (WA)

HEALTH/MEDICAL PSYCHOLOGY
Bridgewater State U (MA)
Castleton State Coll (VT)
Massachusetts Coll of Pharmacy and Health Sciences (MA)

HEALTH OCCUPATIONS TEACHER EDUCATION
Baylor U (TX)
Midwestern State U (TX)
Northwest U (WA)
U of Central Oklahoma (OK)
U of Maine at Farmington (ME)

HEALTH PROFESSIONS RELATED
Alma Coll (MI)
Alvernia U (PA)
Armstrong Atlantic State U (GA)

Athens State U (AL)
Azusa Pacific U (CA)
Baldwin Wallace U (OH)
Bastyr U (WA)
Boise State U (ID)
Boston U (MA)
Bowling Green State U (OH)
Bradley U (IL)
Brock U (ON, Canada)
California State U, East Bay (CA)
California State U, Fresno (CA)
California State U, Long Beach (CA)
California State U, Los Angeles (CA)
California State U, San Bernardino (CA)
Caribbean U (PR)
Castleton State Coll (VT)
Clemson U (SC)
Cleveland State U (OH)
The Coll at Brockport, State U of New York (NY)
Concordia Coll–New York (NY)
Corban U (OR)
Dalhousie U (NS, Canada)
DePaul U (IL)
DeSales U (PA)
East Tennessee State U (TN)
Elizabethtown Coll (PA)
The Evergreen State Coll (WA)
Excelsior Coll (NY)
Fairmont State U (WV)
Ferris State U (MI)
Florida Atlantic U (FL)
Furman U (SC)
George Mason U (VA)
Georgetown U (DC)
Gettysburg Coll (PA)
Inter American U of Puerto Rico, Ponce Campus (PR)
Inter American U of Puerto Rico, San Germán Campus (PR)
Johnson State Coll (VT)
King Coll (TN)
King's Coll (PA)
Lamar U (TX)
Lock Haven U of Pennsylvania (PA)
Long Island U–Brooklyn Campus (NY)
Long Island U–C. W. Post Campus (NY)
Manchester U (IN)
Marquette U (WI)
Maryville U of Saint Louis (MO)
Massachusetts Coll of Pharmacy and Health Sciences (MA)
Mercy Coll (NY)
Minnesota State U Mankato (MN)
Molloy Coll (NY)
Morrisville State Coll (NY)
New Jersey City U (NJ)
Newman U (KS)
Northern Illinois U (IL)
Norwich U (VT)
Oakland U (MI)
The Ohio State U (OH)
Old Dominion U (VA)
Pacific U (OR)
Point Park U (PA)
Purdue U (IN)
Randolph Coll (VA)
Russell Sage Coll (NY)
St. Francis Coll (NY)
St. John's U (NY)
St. Joseph's Coll, Long Island Campus (NY)
St. Joseph's Coll, New York (NY)
Saint Joseph's U (PA)
Saint Louis U (MO)
Saint Mary-of-the-Woods Coll (IN)
San Francisco State U (CA)
Sonoma State U (CA)
State U of New York Coll at Cortland (NY)
Stony Brook U, State U of New York (NY)
Syracuse U (NY)
Tennessee Wesleyan Coll (TN)
Thomas Edison State Coll (NJ)
The U of Alabama (AL)
U of Alaska Anchorage (AK)
U of Arkansas at Little Rock (AR)
U of Bridgeport (CT)
The U of British Columbia–Okanagan (BC, Canada)
U of California, Santa Cruz (CA)

U of Central Arkansas (AR)
U of Charleston (WV)
U of Cincinnati (OH)
U of Colorado Colorado Springs (CO)
U of Delaware (DE)
U of Hartford (CT)
U of Louisiana at Monroe (LA)
U of Maryland, Baltimore County (MD)
U of Nevada, Reno (NV)
U of New Brunswick Saint John (NB, Canada)
U of New England (ME)
The U of North Carolina Wilmington (NC)
U of Northern Iowa (IA)
U of Pennsylvania (PA)
U of Pittsburgh (PA)
The U of Tennessee at Martin (TN)
The U of Texas at El Paso (TX)
U of Waterloo (ON, Canada)
The U of Western Ontario (ON, Canada)
U of Wisconsin–Parkside (WI)
U of Wisconsin–Stevens Point (WI)
Walla Walla U (WA)
Washington U in St. Louis (MO)
Wayne State U (MI)
West Liberty U (WV)
William Paterson U of New Jersey (NJ)
Worcester State U (MA)
Youngstown State U (OH)

HEALTH SERVICES ADMINISTRATION
Chapman U (CA)
Florida National U (FL)
Indiana U Northwest (IN)
Indiana U–Purdue U Fort Wayne (IN)
Indiana U–Purdue U Indianapolis (IN)
Inter American U of Puerto Rico, Ponce Campus (PR)
Minnesota State U Moorhead (MN)
Robert Morris U (IL)
Saint Louis U (MO)
Slippery Rock U of Pennsylvania (PA)
Sullivan U (KY)
U of Illinois at Urbana–Champaign (IL)
U of Washington, Tacoma (WA)
Ursuline Coll (OH)

HEALTH SERVICES/ALLIED HEALTH/HEALTH SCIENCES
Adventist U of Health Sciences (FL)
Albany Coll of Pharmacy and Health Sciences (NY)
Alderson-Broaddus Coll (WV)
Alvernia U (PA)
Boston U (MA)
Brevard Coll (NC)
California Baptist U (CA)
California State U, Chico (CA)
California State U, Dominguez Hills (CA)
California State U, Fullerton (CA)
California State U, Northridge (CA)
Canisius Coll (NY)
Carroll Coll (MT)
Central Baptist Coll (AR)
Chicago State U (IL)
Chowan U (NC)
The Coll of Idaho (ID)
The Coll of St. Scholastica (MN)
Coll of the Ozarks (MO)
Columbus State U (GA)
Corban U (OR)
Dalhousie U (NS, Canada)
DePaul U (IL)
Fairleigh Dickinson U, Coll at Florham (NJ)
Ferrum Coll (VA)
Florida Ag and Mech U (FL)
Florida Atlantic U (FL)
Florida Gulf Coast U (FL)
Friends U (KS)
Goodwin Coll (CT)
Graceland U (IA)
Hendrix Coll (AR)
Hofstra U (NY)
Lancaster General Coll of Nursing & Health Sciences (PA)

Lebanon Valley Coll (PA)
Lee U (TN)
Marywood U (PA)
Mercy Coll (NY)
Mercy Coll of Health Sciences (IA)
Mercy Coll of Ohio (OH)
Mercyhurst U (PA)
Merrimack Coll (MA)
Miami Dade Coll (FL)
Misericordia U (PA)
Monmouth U (NJ)
National U (CA)
Nicholls State U (LA)
Northwestern State U of Louisiana (LA)
Nova Southeastern U (FL)
Olivet Coll (MI)
Queens U of Charlotte (NC)
Quinnipiac U (CT)
The Richard Stockton Coll of New Jersey (NJ)
Sacred Heart U (CT)
Saginaw Valley State U (MI)
Saint Joseph's U (PA)
San Diego State U (CA)
San Jose State U (CA)
Spalding U (KY)
Stephen F. Austin State U (TX)
Stetson U (FL)
Stony Brook U, State U of New York (NY)
Texas A&M U (TX)
Texas A&M U–Kingsville (TX)
Texas Southern U (TX)
Texas Woman's U (TX)
Thompson Rivers U (BC, Canada)
Trident U Intl (CA)
U of Alaska Anchorage (AK)
U of Central Florida (FL)
U of Florida (FL)
U of Hartford (CT)
U of Kentucky (KY)
U of Medicine and Dentistry of New Jersey (NJ)
U of Miami (FL)
U of Michigan–Flint (MI)
U of Minnesota, Crookston (MN)
U of Missouri–Kansas City (MO)
U of Northern Colorado (CO)
U of North Florida (FL)
U of North Texas (TX)
U of Ottawa (ON, Canada)
U of Southern Mississippi (MS)
The U of Texas at Brownsville (TX)
The U of Texas at Dallas (TX)
The U of Texas at San Antonio (TX)
U of the Incarnate Word (TX)
U of the Sciences (PA)
U of Utah (UT)
U of Washington, Bothell (WA)
The U of Western Ontario (ON, Canada)
U of West Florida (FL)
Ursuline Coll (OH)
Walden U (MN)
Washington U in St. Louis (MO)
Western Kentucky U (KY)
Westminster Coll (UT)
West Texas A&M U (TX)
Wheaton Coll (IL)
Wheeling Jesuit U (WV)
Widener U (PA)

HEALTH TEACHER EDUCATION
Alma Coll (MI)
Appalachian State U (NC)
Armstrong Atlantic State U (GA)
Auburn U (AL)
Augsburg Coll (MN)
Austin Peay State U (TN)
Averett U (VA)
Ball State U (IN)
Baylor U (TX)
Bemidji State U (MN)
Bethel U (MN)
Bluefield Coll (VA)
Bowling Green State U (OH)
Bridgewater State U (MA)
California State U, Chico (CA)
California State U, San Bernardino (CA)
California State U, Stanislaus (CA)
Campbellsville U (KY)
Capital U (OH)
Central Michigan U (MI)

The Coll at Brockport, State U of New York (NY)
Concordia Coll (MN)
Concordia U, Nebraska (NE)
Concordia U, St. Paul (MN)
Concord U (WV)
Curry Coll (MA)
Defiance Coll (OH)
DePaul U (IL)
East Carolina U (NC)
Eastern Illinois U (IL)
Eastern Washington U (WA)
Elon U (NC)
Fayetteville State U (NC)
Gardner-Webb U (NC)
George Mason U (VA)
Graceland U (IA)
Grand Valley State U (MI)
Gustavus Adolphus Coll (MN)
Hampton U (VA)
Harding U (AR)
Hofstra U (NY)
Houghton Coll (NY)
Hunter Coll of the City U of New York (NY)
Illinois State U (IL)
Indiana U Bloomington (IN)
Inter American U of Puerto Rico, San Germán Campus (PR)
Iowa State U of Science and Technology (IA)
Iowa Wesleyan Coll (IA)
Ithaca Coll (NY)
Jacksonville State U (AL)
John Brown U (AR)
Kansas Wesleyan U (KS)
Kent State U (OH)
Lamar U (TX)
Lee U (TN)
Lehman Coll of the City U of New York (NY)
Lincoln Memorial U (TN)
Long Island U–C. W. Post Campus (NY)
Louisiana Coll (LA)
Malone U (OH)
Maryville Coll (TN)
Mayville State U (ND)
Michigan State U (MI)
Middle Tennessee State U (TN)
Minnesota State U Mankato (MN)
Minnesota State U Moorhead (MN)
Missouri Baptist U (MO)
Montclair State U (NJ)
Morehead State U (KY)
Murray State U (KY)
National U (CA)
New Mexico Highlands U (NM)
North Carolina Central U (NC)
North Dakota State U (ND)
Northern Illinois U (IL)
Northern Michigan U (MI)
Northern State U (SD)
Northwestern Oklahoma State U (OK)
Ohio Wesleyan U (OH)
Olivet Coll (MI)
Oral Roberts U (OK)
Portland State U (OR)
Rhode Island Coll (RI)
Rocky Mountain Coll (MT)
Roger Williams U (RI)
St. Ambrose U (IA)
Salisbury U (MD)
South Dakota State U (SD)
Southern Illinois U Carbondale (IL)
Southern Illinois U Edwardsville (IL)
Southern Oregon U (OR)
Southwest Baptist U (MO)
State U of New York at Oswego (NY)
State U of New York Coll at Cortland (NY)
Tennessee State U (TN)
Texas A&M U–Commerce (TX)
Trident U Intl (CA)
Troy U (AL)
Union Coll (KY)
The U of Alabama at Birmingham (AL)
U of Charleston (WV)
U of Cincinnati (OH)
U of Great Falls (MT)
U of Kentucky (KY)
U of Maine at Farmington (ME)
U of Maryland, Coll Park (MD)

U of Minnesota, Duluth (MN)
U of Minnesota, Twin Cities Campus (MN)
The U of Montana Western (MT)
U of Mount Union (OH)
U of Nevada, Las Vegas (NV)
U of New Brunswick Fredericton (NB, Canada)
U of New Mexico (NM)
U of Northern Iowa (IA)
U of Regina (SK, Canada)
U of St. Thomas (MN)
The U of South Dakota (SD)
U of the Cumberlands (KY)
U of the District of Columbia (DC)
The U of Toledo (OH)
U of Windsor (ON, Canada)
U of Wisconsin–La Crosse (WI)
Utah State U (UT)
Valley City State U (ND)
Virginia Commonwealth U (VA)
Washington State U (WA)
Wayne State U (MI)
Western Connecticut State U (CT)
Western Illinois U (IL)
Western Michigan U (MI)
West Liberty U (WV)
West Virginia State U (WV)
West Virginia Wesleyan Coll (WV)
William Paterson U of New Jersey (NJ)
William Penn U (IA)
York Coll of the City U of New York (NY)
Youngstown State U (OH)

HEATING, AIR CONDITIONING, VENTILATION AND REFRIGERATION MAINTENANCE TECHNOLOGY
Lewis-Clark State Coll (ID)

HEAVY EQUIPMENT MAINTENANCE TECHNOLOGY
Ferris State U (MI)

HEBREW
Bard Coll (NY)
Binghamton U, State U of New York (NY)
Brigham Young U (UT)
Columbia U, School of General Studies (NY)
Concordia U Wisconsin (WI)
Dartmouth Coll (NH)
Hofstra U (NY)
Hunter Coll of the City U of New York (NY)
Lehman Coll of the City U of New York (NY)
Multnomah U (OR)
New York U (NY)
The Ohio State U (OH)
Temple U (PA)
U of California, Los Angeles (CA)
U of Cincinnati (OH)
U of Illinois at Urbana–Champaign (IL)
U of Michigan (MI)
U of Minnesota, Twin Cities Campus (MN)
U of Utah (UT)
U of Wisconsin–Madison (WI)
Washington U in St. Louis (MO)

HERBALISM
Bastyr U (WA)

HIGHER EDUCATION/HIGHER EDUCATION ADMINISTRATION
Texas A&M U–Commerce (TX)

HISPANIC-AMERICAN, PUERTO RICAN, AND MEXICAN-AMERICAN/CHICANO STUDIES
Arizona State U (AZ)
Boston Coll (MA)
Bowling Green State U (OH)
Brown U (RI)
California State U, Dominguez Hills (CA)
California State U, East Bay (CA)
California State U, Fresno (CA)
California State U, Fullerton (CA)

California State U, Long Beach (CA)
California State U, Los Angeles (CA)
California State U, Northridge (CA)
Cedar Crest Coll (PA)
Claremont McKenna Coll (CA)
The Colorado Coll (CO)
Columbia U (NY)
Columbia U, School of General Studies (NY)
Connecticut Coll (CT)
Dartmouth Coll (NH)
Fort Lewis Coll (CO)
Gettysburg Coll (PA)
Hofstra U (NY)
Hunter Coll of the City U of New York (NY)
Loyola Marymount U (CA)
Metropolitan State U of Denver (CO)
Mills Coll (CA)
Pitzer Coll (CA)
Pomona Coll (CA)
Rutgers, The State U of New Jersey, Newark (NJ)
Rutgers, The State U of New Jersey, New Brunswick (NJ)
San Diego State U (CA)
San Francisco State U (CA)
Scripps Coll (CA)
Sonoma State U (CA)
Southern Methodist U (TX)
Stanford U (CA)
Sul Ross State U (TX)
Trent U (ON, Canada)
Tulane U (LA)
U at Albany, State U of New York (NY)
The U of Arizona (AZ)
U of California, Berkeley (CA)
U of California, Davis (CA)
U of California, Irvine (CA)
U of California, Los Angeles (CA)
U of California, Riverside (CA)
U of California, Santa Barbara (CA)
U of California, Santa Cruz (CA)
U of Michigan (MI)
U of Minnesota, Twin Cities Campus (MN)
U of Northern Colorado (CO)
The U of Scranton (PA)
U of Southern California (CA)
The U of Texas at El Paso (TX)
The U of Texas at San Antonio (TX)
The U of Texas–Pan American (TX)
U of Washington, Tacoma (WA)

HISPANIC AND LATIN AMERICAN LANGUAGES
Hamilton Coll (NY)

HISTOLOGIC TECHNOLOGY/HISTOTECHNOLOGIST
Oakland U (MI)

HISTORIC PRESERVATION AND CONSERVATION
Coll of Charleston (SC)
Roger Williams U (RI)
Saint Mary's Coll of California (CA)
Salve Regina U (RI)
Savannah Coll of Art and Design (GA)
Southeast Missouri State U (MO)
U of Delaware (DE)
U of Mary Washington (VA)
Ursuline Coll (OH)

HISTORY
Abilene Christian U (TX)
Acadia U (NS, Canada)
Adams State U (CO)
Adelphi U (NY)
Agnes Scott Coll (GA)
Alabama State U (AL)
Albertus Magnus Coll (CT)
Albion Coll (MI)
Albright Coll (PA)
Alcorn State U (MS)
Alderson-Broaddus Coll (WV)
Alfred U (NY)
Alice Lloyd Coll (KY)
Alma Coll (MI)
Alvernia U (PA)
Alverno Coll (WI)
American Public U System (WV)
American U (DC)

American U in Bulgaria (Bulgaria)
The American U in Cairo (Egypt)
American U of Beirut (Lebanon)
The American U of Paris (France)
Amherst Coll (MA)
Anderson U (IN)
Anderson U (SC)
Andrews U (MI)
Angelo State U (TX)
Appalachian State U (NC)
Arizona State U (AZ)
Arkansas State U (AR)
Arkansas Tech U (AR)
Armstrong Atlantic State U (GA)
Asbury U (KY)
Ashland U (OH)
Assumption Coll (MA)
Athabasca U (AB, Canada)
Athens State U (AL)
Auburn U (AL)
Auburn U at Montgomery (AL)
Augsburg Coll (MN)
Augustana Coll (IL)
Augustana Coll (SD)
Aurora U (IL)
Austin Peay State U (TN)
Averett U (VA)
Avila U (MO)
Azusa Pacific U (CA)
Baker U (KS)
Baldwin Wallace U (OH)
Ball State U (IN)
Bard Coll (NY)
Barry U (FL)
Barton Coll (NC)
Bates Coll (ME)
Baylor U (TX)
Belhaven U (MS)
Bellarmine U (KY)
Belmont Abbey Coll (NC)
Belmont U (TN)
Bemidji State U (MN)
Benedictine Coll (KS)
Benedictine U (IL)
Bennington Coll (VT)
Bentley U (MA)
Berea Coll (KY)
Berry Coll (GA)
Bethany Coll (WV)
Bethany Lutheran Coll (MN)
Bethel Coll (IN)
Bethel Coll (KS)
Bethel U (MN)
Binghamton U, State U of New York (NY)
Blackburn Coll (IL)
Bloomfield Coll (NJ)
Bloomsburg U of Pennsylvania (PA)
Bluefield Coll (VA)
Blue Mountain Coll (MS)
Bluffton U (OH)
Bob Jones U (SC)
Boise State U (ID)
Boston Coll (MA)
Boston U (MA)
Bowdoin Coll (ME)
Bowie State U (MD)
Bowling Green State U (OH)
Bradley U (IL)
Brevard Coll (NC)
Bridgewater Coll (VA)
Bridgewater State U (MA)
Brock U (ON, Canada)
Brown U (RI)
Bryant U (RI)
Bryn Athyn Coll of the New Church (PA)
Bucknell U (PA)
Buena Vista U (IA)
Buffalo State Coll, State U of New York (NY)
Butler U (IN)
Cabrini Coll (PA)
Caldwell Coll (NJ)
California Baptist U (CA)
California Lutheran U (CA)
California Polytechnic State U, San Luis Obispo (CA)
California State Polytechnic U, Pomona (CA)
California State U, Chico (CA)
California State U, Dominguez Hills (CA)
California State U, East Bay (CA)
California State U, Fresno (CA)
California State U, Fullerton (CA)

California State U, Long Beach (CA)
California State U, Los Angeles (CA)
California State U, Northridge (CA)
California State U, San Bernardino (CA)
California State U, San Marcos (CA)
California State U, Stanislaus (CA)
Calvin Coll (MI)
Cameron U (OK)
Campbellsville U (KY)
Canisius Coll (NY)
Capital U (OH)
Cardinal Stritch U (WI)
Carleton Coll (MN)
Carlow U (PA)
Carroll Coll (MT)
Carson-Newman U (TN)
Case Western Reserve U (OH)
Castleton State Coll (VT)
Catawba Coll (NC)
The Catholic U of America (DC)
Cedar Crest Coll (PA)
Cedarville U (OH)
Centenary Coll of Louisiana (LA)
Central Coll (IA)
Central Connecticut State U (CT)
Central Methodist U (MO)
Central State U (OH)
Centre Coll (KY)
Chapman U (CA)
Chatham U (PA)
Chestnut Hill Coll (PA)
Chicago State U (IL)
Chowan U (NC)
Christendom Coll (VA)
Christian Brothers U (TN)
Christopher Newport U (VA)
The Citadel, The Military Coll of South Carolina (SC)
City Coll of the City U of New York (NY)
Claflin U (SC)
Claremont McKenna Coll (CA)
Clarion U of Pennsylvania (PA)
Clark Atlanta U (GA)
Clarke U (IA)
Clarkson U (NY)
Clark U (MA)
Clayton State U (GA)
Clearwater Christian Coll (FL)
Clemson U (SC)
Cleveland State U (OH)
Coastal Carolina U (SC)
Coe Coll (IA)
Colby Coll (ME)
Colgate U (NY)
The Coll at Brockport, State U of New York (NY)
Coll of Charleston (SC)
The Coll of Idaho (ID)
Coll of Mount St. Joseph (OH)
The Coll of New Jersey (NJ)
The Coll of New Rochelle (NY)
Coll of Saint Benedict (MN)
Coll of Saint Elizabeth (NJ)
The Coll of St. Scholastica (MN)
Coll of Staten Island of the City U of New York (NY)
Coll of the Holy Cross (MA)
Coll of the Ozarks (MO)
The Coll of William and Mary (VA)
The Coll of Wooster (OH)
The Colorado Coll (CO)
Colorado Mesa U (CO)
Colorado State U (CO)
Columbia Coll (MO)
Columbia Coll (SC)
Columbia U (NY)
Columbia U, School of General Studies (NY)
Columbus State U (GA)
Concordia Coll (MN)
Concordia Coll–New York (NY)
Concordia U (CA)
Concordia U (QC, Canada)
Concordia U Chicago (IL)
Concordia U, Nebraska (NE)
Concordia U, St. Paul (MN)
Concordia U Texas (TX)
Concordia U Wisconsin (WI)
Concord U (WV)
Connecticut Coll (CT)
Converse Coll (SC)
Corban U (OR)

Cornell Coll (IA)
Cornerstone U (MI)
Covenant Coll (GA)
Creighton U (NE)
Crown Coll (MN)
Culver-Stockton Coll (MO)
Curry Coll (MA)
Dakota Wesleyan U (SD)
Dalhousie U (NS, Canada)
Dallas Baptist U (TX)
Dalton State Coll (GA)
Dartmouth Coll (NH)
Davidson Coll (NC)
Defiance Coll (OH)
Delta State U (MS)
DePaul U (IL)
DePauw U (IN)
DEREE—The American Coll of Greece (Greece)
DeSales U (PA)
Dickinson Coll (PA)
Dillard U (LA)
Doane Coll (NE)
Dominican Coll (NY)
Dominican U (IL)
Dordt Coll (IA)
Drake U (IA)
Drew U (NJ)
Drury U (MO)
Duquesne U (PA)
Earlham Coll (IN)
East Carolina U (NC)
East Central U (OK)
Eastern Illinois U (IL)
Eastern Mennonite U (VA)
Eastern Michigan U (MI)
Eastern New Mexico U (NM)
Eastern Washington U (WA)
East Tennessee State U (TN)
East Texas Baptist U (TX)
Eckerd Coll (FL)
Edgewood Coll (WI)
Edinboro U of Pennsylvania (PA)
Elizabeth City State U (NC)
Elizabethtown Coll (PA)
Elmira Coll (NY)
Elon U (NC)
Emmanuel Coll (MA)
Emory & Henry Coll (VA)
Emporia State U (KS)
Endicott Coll (MA)
Eugene Lang Coll The New School for Liberal Arts (NY)
Evangel U (MO)
Excelsior Coll (NY)
Fairfield U (CT)
Fairleigh Dickinson U, Coll at Florham (NJ)
Fairleigh Dickinson U, Metropolitan Campus (NJ)
Fairmont State U (WV)
Faulkner U (AL)
Fayetteville State U (NC)
Felician Coll (NJ)
Ferris State U (MI)
Ferrum Coll (VA)
Flagler Coll (FL)
Florida Ag and Mech U (FL)
Florida Atlantic U (FL)
Florida Coll (FL)
Florida Gulf Coast U (FL)
Florida Intl U (FL)
Florida Southern Coll (FL)
Florida State U (FL)
Fort Lewis Coll (CO)
Framingham State U (MA)
Francis Marion U (SC)
Franklin & Marshall Coll (PA)
Franklin Coll (IN)
Franklin Coll Switzerland (Switzerland)
Franklin Pierce U (NH)
Friends U (KS)
Frostburg State U (MD)
Furman U (SC)
Gannon U (PA)
Gardner-Webb U (NC)
Geneva Coll (PA)
George Fox U (OR)
George Mason U (VA)
Georgetown Coll (KY)
Georgetown U (DC)
Georgia Coll & State U (GA)
Georgia Gwinnett Coll (GA)
Georgia Regents U (GA)
Georgia Southern U (GA)

Georgia Southwestern State U (GA)
Georgia State U (GA)
Gettysburg Coll (PA)
Gonzaga U (WA)
Gordon Coll (MA)
Gordon State Coll (GA)
Goshen Coll (IN)
Goucher Coll (MD)
Graceland U (IA)
Grambling State U (LA)
Grand Valley State U (MI)
Grand View U (IA)
Granite State Coll (NH)
Greenville Coll (IL)
Grinnell Coll (IA)
Grove City Coll (PA)
Guilford Coll (NC)
Gustavus Adolphus Coll (MN)
Hamilton Coll (NY)
Hamline U (MN)
Hampden-Sydney Coll (VA)
Hampshire Coll (MA)
Hampton U (VA)
Hanover Coll (IN)
Harding U (AR)
Hardin-Simmons U (TX)
Hartwick Coll (NY)
Haverford Coll (PA)
Hawai`i Pacific U (HI)
Henderson State U (AR)
Hendrix Coll (AR)
High Point U (NC)
Hillsdale Coll (MI)
Hiram Coll (OH)
Hobart and William Smith Colls (NY)
Hofstra U (NY)
Hollins U (VA)
Holy Cross Coll (IN)
Holy Family U (PA)
Holy Names U (CA)
Hood Coll (MD)
Hope Coll (MI)
Houghton Coll (NY)
Howard Payne U (TX)
Humboldt State U (CA)
Hunter Coll of the City U of New York (NY)
Huntingdon Coll (AL)
Huntington U (IN)
Illinois Coll (IL)
Illinois State U (IL)
Illinois Wesleyan U (IL)
Immaculata U (PA)
Indiana State U (IN)
Indiana U Bloomington (IN)
Indiana U East (IN)
Indiana U Northwest (IN)
Indiana U of Pennsylvania (PA)
Indiana U–Purdue U Fort Wayne (IN)
Indiana U–Purdue U Indianapolis (IN)
Indiana U South Bend (IN)
Indiana U Southeast (IN)
Indiana Wesleyan U (IN)
Iona Coll (NY)
Iowa State U of Science and Technology (IA)
Iowa Wesleyan Coll (IA)
Ithaca Coll (NY)
Jacksonville State U (AL)
James Madison U (VA)
Jamestown Coll (ND)
Jarvis Christian Coll (TX)
John Brown U (AR)
John Carroll U (OH)
The Johns Hopkins U (MD)
Johnson C. Smith U (NC)
Johnson State Coll (VT)
Judson Coll (AL)
Judson U (IL)
Juniata Coll (PA)
Kalamazoo Coll (MI)
Kansas State U (KS)
Kansas Wesleyan U (KS)
Kean U (NJ)
Keene State Coll (NH)
Kennesaw State U (GA)
Kent State U (OH)
Kent State U at Stark (OH)
Kentucky Christian U (KY)
Kentucky Wesleyan Coll (KY)
Kenyon Coll (OH)
Keuka Coll (NY)
King Coll (TN)

King's Coll (PA)
The King's U Coll (AB, Canada)
Knox Coll (IL)
Kutztown U of Pennsylvania (PA)
Lafayette Coll (PA)
LaGrange Coll (GA)
Lake Erie Coll (OH)
Lakeland Coll (WI)
Lake Superior State U (MI)
Lamar U (TX)
Lander U (SC)
Lane Coll (TN)
Langston U (OK)
La Roche Coll (PA)
La Salle U (PA)
Lasell Coll (MA)
La Sierra U (CA)
Lawrence U (WI)
Lebanese American U (Lebanon)
Lebanon Valley Coll (PA)
Lee U (TN)
Lehigh U (PA)
Lehman Coll of the City U of New York (NY)
Le Moyne Coll (NY)
LeTourneau U (TX)
Lewis U (IL)
Liberty U (VA)
Limestone Coll (SC)
Lincoln Memorial U (TN)
Lincoln U (MO)
Lindenwood U (MO)
Lindsey Wilson Coll (KY)
Linfield Coll (OR)
Lipscomb U (TN)
Lock Haven U of Pennsylvania (PA)
Long Island U–Brooklyn Campus (NY)
Long Island U–C. W. Post Campus (NY)
Longwood U (VA)
Louisiana Coll (LA)
Louisiana State U and Ag and Mech Coll (LA)
Louisiana State U at Alexandria (LA)
Louisiana State U in Shreveport (LA)
Lourdes U (OH)
Loyola Marymount U (CA)
Loyola U Chicago (IL)
Loyola U Maryland (MD)
Loyola U New Orleans (LA)
Lubbock Christian U (TX)
Luther Coll (IA)
Lynchburg Coll (VA)
Lyon Coll (AR)
Macalester Coll (MN)
Madonna U (MI)
Malone U (OH)
Manchester U (IN)
Manhattan Coll (NY)
Manhattanville Coll (NY)
Mansfield U of Pennsylvania (PA)
Marian U (WI)
Marietta Coll (OH)
Marist Coll (NY)
Marquette U (WI)
Marshall U (WV)
Mars Hill Coll (NC)
Mary Baldwin Coll (VA)
Marymount Manhattan Coll (NY)
Marymount U (VA)
Maryville Coll (TN)
Maryville U of Saint Louis (MO)
Marywood U (PA)
Massachusetts Coll of Liberal Arts (MA)
Massachusetts Inst of Technology (MA)
The Master's Coll and Sem (CA)
McDaniel Coll (MD)
McKendree U (IL)
McMurry U (TX)
McNeese State U (LA)
Mercer U (GA)
Mercy Coll (NY)
Mercyhurst U (PA)
Merrimack Coll (MA)
Messiah Coll (PA)
Metropolitan State U of Denver (CO)
Miami U (OH)
Michigan State U (MI)
Middlebury Coll (VT)
Middle Tennessee State U (TN)
Midwestern State U (TX)

Millersville U of Pennsylvania (PA)
Millikin U (IL)
Millsaps Coll (MS)
Mills Coll (CA)
Minnesota State U Mankato (MN)
Minnesota State U Moorhead (MN)
Minot State U (ND)
Misericordia U (PA)
Mississippi Coll (MS)
Mississippi State U (MS)
Mississippi U for Women (MS)
Mississippi Valley State U (MS)
Missouri Baptist U (MO)
Missouri State U (MO)
Missouri U of Science and Technology (MO)
Missouri Western State U (MO)
Molloy Coll (NY)
Monmouth Coll (IL)
Monmouth U (NJ)
Montana State U (MT)
Montclair State U (NJ)
Montreat Coll, Montreat (NC)
Moravian Coll (PA)
Morehead State U (KY)
Morehouse Coll (GA)
Morningside Coll (IA)
Morris Coll (SC)
Mount Allison U (NB, Canada)
Mount Holyoke Coll (MA)
Mount Marty Coll (SD)
Mount Mary Coll (WI)
Mount Mercy U (IA)
Mount Saint Mary Coll (NY)
Mount St. Mary's Coll (CA)
Mount St. Mary's U (MD)
Mount Vernon Nazarene U (OH)
Muhlenberg Coll (PA)
Multnomah U (OR)
Murray State U (KY)
Nazareth Coll of Rochester (NY)
Newberry Coll (SC)
New Coll of Florida (FL)
New England Coll (NH)
New Jersey City U (NJ)
New Jersey Inst of Technology (NJ)
Newman U (KS)
New Mexico Highlands U (NM)
New Mexico State U (NM)
New York U (NY)
Niagara U (NY)
Nicholls State U (LA)
Norfolk State U (VA)
North Carolina Central U (NC)
North Carolina State U (NC)
North Carolina Wesleyan Coll (NC)
North Central Coll (IL)
North Dakota State U (ND)
Northeastern Illinois U (IL)
Northeastern U (MA)
Northern Arizona U (AZ)
Northern Illinois U (IL)
Northern Michigan U (MI)
Northern State U (SD)
North Greenville U (SC)
Northland Coll (WI)
Northwest Christian U (OR)
Northwestern Coll (IA)
Northwestern Coll (MN)
Northwestern Oklahoma State U (OK)
Northwestern State U of Louisiana (LA)
Northwest Missouri State U (MO)
Northwest Nazarene U (ID)
Northwest U (WA)
Norwich U (VT)
Notre Dame de Namur U (CA)
Nova Southeastern U (FL)
Nyack Coll (NY)
Oakland U (MI)
Oglethorpe U (GA)
Ohio Dominican U (OH)
The Ohio State U (OH)
The Ohio State U at Lima (OH)
The Ohio State U at Marion (OH)
The Ohio State U–Mansfield Campus (OH)
The Ohio State U–Newark Campus (OH)
Ohio U (OH)
Ohio U–Chillicothe (OH)
Ohio Valley U (WV)
Ohio Wesleyan U (OH)
Oklahoma Baptist U (OK)
Oklahoma Christian U (OK)
Oklahoma City U (OK)

Oklahoma State U (OK)
Old Dominion U (VA)
Olivet Coll (MI)
Oral Roberts U (OK)
Oregon State U (OR)
Ouachita Baptist U (AR)
Pace U (NY)
Pacific Lutheran U (WA)
Pacific Union Coll (CA)
Pacific U (OR)
Paine Coll (GA)
Palm Beach Atlantic U (FL)
Park U (MO)
Patrick Henry Coll (VA)
Paul Quinn Coll (TX)
Penn State Abington (PA)
Penn State Altoona (PA)
Penn State Beaver (PA)
Penn State Berks (PA)
Penn State Brandywine (PA)
Penn State DuBois (PA)
Penn State Erie, The Behrend Coll (PA)
Penn State Fayette, The Eberly Campus (PA)
Penn State Greater Allegheny (PA)
Penn State Hazleton (PA)
Penn State Lehigh Valley (PA)
Penn State Mont Alto (PA)
Penn State New Kensington (PA)
Penn State Schuylkill (PA)
Penn State Shenango (PA)
Penn State U Park (PA)
Penn State Wilkes-Barre (PA)
Penn State Worthington Scranton (PA)
Penn State York (PA)
Pepperdine U, Malibu (CA)
Piedmont Coll (GA)
Pine Manor Coll (MA)
Pittsburg State U (KS)
Pitzer Coll (CA)
Plymouth State U (NH)
Point Loma Nazarene U (CA)
Point Park U (PA)
Pomona Coll (CA)
Portland State U (OR)
Presbyterian Coll (SC)
Princeton U (NJ)
Principia Coll (IL)
Providence Coll (RI)
Purchase Coll, State U of New York (NY)
Purdue U (IN)
Purdue U Calumet (IN)
Queens U of Charlotte (NC)
Quincy U (IL)
Quinnipiac U (CT)
Radford U (VA)
Ramapo Coll of New Jersey (NJ)
Randolph Coll (VA)
Randolph-Macon Coll (VA)
Reed Coll (OR)
Regent U (VA)
Regis Coll (MA)
Regis U (CO)
Rhode Island Coll (RI)
Rhodes Coll (TN)
Rice U (TX)
The Richard Stockton Coll of New Jersey (NJ)
Rider U (NJ)
Ripon Coll (WI)
Rivier U (NH)
Roanoke Coll (VA)
Roberts Wesleyan Coll (NY)
Rockford Coll (IL)
Rockhurst U (MO)
Rocky Mountain Coll (MT)
Roger Williams U (RI)
Rollins Coll (FL)
Roosevelt U (IL)
Rosemont Coll (PA)
Rowan U (NJ)
Russell Sage Coll (NY)
Rutgers, The State U of New Jersey, Camden (NJ)
Rutgers, The State U of New Jersey, Newark (NJ)
Rutgers, The State U of New Jersey, New Brunswick (NJ)
Sacred Heart U (CT)
Saginaw Valley State U (MI)
St. Ambrose U (IA)
Saint Anselm Coll (NH)
St. Bonaventure U (NY)
St. Edward's U (TX)

MAJORS LISTING

St. Francis Coll (NY)
St. Gregory's U, Shawnee (OK)
St. John Fisher Coll (NY)
Saint John's U (MN)
St. John's U (NY)
Saint Joseph's Coll (IN)
St. Joseph's Coll, Long Island Campus (NY)
St. Joseph's Coll, New York (NY)
Saint Joseph's U (PA)
St. Lawrence U (NY)
Saint Leo U (FL)
Saint Louis U (MO)
Saint Mary's Coll (IN)
Saint Mary's Coll of California (CA)
St. Mary's Coll of Maryland (MD)
St. Mary's U (TX)
Saint Mary's U of Minnesota (MN)
Saint Michael's Coll (VT)
St. Norbert Coll (WI)
St. Olaf Coll (MN)
St. Thomas Aquinas Coll (NY)
St. Thomas U (FL)
St. Thomas U (NB, Canada)
Saint Vincent Coll (PA)
Salem State U (MA)
Salisbury U (MD)
Salve Regina U (RI)
Samford U (AL)
Sam Houston State U (TX)
San Diego Christian Coll (CA)
San Diego State U (CA)
San Francisco State U (CA)
San Jose State U (CA)
Schreiner U (TX)
Scripps Coll (CA)
Seattle Pacific U (WA)
Seattle U (WA)
Seton Hill U (PA)
Sewanee: The U of the South (TN)
Shawnee State U (OH)
Shenandoah U (VA)
Shepherd U (WV)
Shippensburg U of Pennsylvania (PA)
Siena Coll (NY)
Siena Heights U (MI)
Simmons Coll (MA)
Simon Fraser U (BC, Canada)
Simpson Coll (IA)
Simpson U (CA)
Skidmore Coll (NY)
Slippery Rock U of Pennsylvania (PA)
Smith Coll (MA)
Sonoma State U (CA)
South Dakota State U (SD)
Southeastern Louisiana U (LA)
Southeastern Oklahoma State U (OK)
Southeastern U (FL)
Southeast Missouri State U (MO)
Southern Arkansas U–Magnolia (AR)
Southern Connecticut State U (CT)
Southern Illinois U Carbondale (IL)
Southern Illinois U Edwardsville (IL)
Southern Methodist U (TX)
Southern Nazarene U (OK)
Southern New Hampshire U (NH)
Southern Oregon U (OR)
Southern Utah U (UT)
Southwest Baptist U (MO)
Southwestern Adventist U (TX)
Southwestern Coll (KS)
Southwestern U (TX)
Spelman Coll (GA)
Spring Arbor U (MI)
Spring Hill Coll (AL)
Stanford U (CA)
State U of New York at Fredonia (NY)
State U of New York at New Paltz (NY)
State U of New York at Oswego (NY)
State U of New York at Plattsburgh (NY)
State U of New York Coll at Cortland (NY)
State U of New York Coll at Geneseo (NY)
State U of New York Coll at Old Westbury (NY)
State U of New York Coll at Potsdam (NY)

State U of New York Empire State Coll (NY)
Stephen F. Austin State U (TX)
Sterling Coll (KS)
Stetson U (FL)
Stevenson U (MD)
Stonehill Coll (MA)
Stony Brook U, State U of New York (NY)
Suffolk U (MA)
Sul Ross State U (TX)
Susquehanna U (PA)
Swarthmore Coll (PA)
Sweet Briar Coll (VA)
Syracuse U (NY)
Tabor Coll (KS)
Tarleton State U (TX)
Taylor U (IN)
Temple U (PA)
Tennessee State U (TN)
Tennessee Wesleyan Coll (TN)
Texas A&M Intl U (TX)
Texas A&M U (TX)
Texas A&M U–Commerce (TX)
Texas A&M U–Kingsville (TX)
Texas Christian U (TX)
Texas Lutheran U (TX)
Texas Southern U (TX)
Texas State U–San Marcos (TX)
Texas Wesleyan U (TX)
Texas Woman's U (TX)
Thomas Edison State Coll (NJ)
Thomas More Coll (KY)
Thompson Rivers U (BC, Canada)
Tiffin U (OH)
Transylvania U (KY)
Trent U (ON, Canada)
Trevecca Nazarene U (TN)
Trinity Christian Coll (IL)
Trinity Coll (CT)
Trinity U (TX)
Troy U (AL)
Truman State U (MO)
Tufts U (MA)
Tulane U (LA)
Tuskegee U (AL)
Union Coll (KY)
Union Coll (NE)
Union U (TN)
United States Air Force Acad (CO)
United States Naval Acad (MD)
Universidad Adventista de las Antillas (PR)
Université de Sherbrooke (QC, Canada)
Université Sainte-Anne (NS, Canada)
U at Albany, State U of New York (NY)
U at Buffalo, the State U of New York (NY)
The U of Akron (OH)
The U of Alabama (AL)
The U of Alabama at Birmingham (AL)
U of Alaska Anchorage (AK)
U of Alaska Fairbanks (AK)
The U of Arizona (AZ)
U of Arkansas at Little Rock (AR)
U of Arkansas–Fort Smith (AR)
The U of British Columbia (BC, Canada)
The U of British Columbia–Okanagan (BC, Canada)
U of California, Berkeley (CA)
U of California, Davis (CA)
U of California, Irvine (CA)
U of California, Los Angeles (CA)
U of California, Merced (CA)
U of California, Riverside (CA)
U of California, Santa Barbara (CA)
U of California, Santa Cruz (CA)
U of Central Arkansas (AR)
U of Central Florida (FL)
U of Central Oklahoma (OK)
U of Charleston (WV)
U of Chicago (IL)
U of Cincinnati (OH)
U of Colorado Boulder (CO)
U of Colorado Colorado Springs (CO)
U of Colorado Denver (CO)
U of Dallas (TX)
U of Delaware (DE)
U of Denver (CO)
U of Evansville (IN)
The U of Findlay (OH)

U of Florida (FL)
U of Georgia (GA)
U of Great Falls (MT)
U of Guam (GU)
U of Guelph (ON, Canada)
U of Hartford (CT)
U of Hawaii at Hilo (HI)
U of Hawaii at Manoa (HI)
U of Hawaii–West Oahu (HI)
U of Houston (TX)
U of Houston–Clear Lake (TX)
U of Houston–Downtown (TX)
U of Houston–Victoria (TX)
U of Idaho (ID)
U of Illinois at Chicago (IL)
U of Illinois at Springfield (IL)
U of Illinois at Urbana–Champaign (IL)
The U of Iowa (IA)
The U of Kansas (KS)
U of Kentucky (KY)
U of La Verne (CA)
U of Louisiana at Lafayette (LA)
U of Louisiana at Monroe (LA)
U of Louisville (KY)
U of Maine at Farmington (ME)
U of Maine at Machias (ME)
U of Maryland, Baltimore County (MD)
U of Maryland, Coll Park (MD)
U of Maryland Eastern Shore (MD)
U of Maryland U Coll (MD)
U of Mary Washington (VA)
U of Massachusetts Amherst (MA)
U of Massachusetts Boston (MA)
U of Massachusetts Dartmouth (MA)
U of Memphis (TN)
U of Miami (FL)
U of Michigan (MI)
U of Michigan–Dearborn (MI)
U of Michigan–Flint (MI)
U of Minnesota, Twin Cities Campus (MN)
U of Mississippi (MS)
U of Missouri (MO)
U of Missouri–Kansas City (MO)
U of Missouri–St. Louis (MO)
U of Mobile (AL)
The U of Montana Western (MT)
U of Montevallo (AL)
U of Mount Union (OH)
U of Nebraska at Kearney (NE)
U of Nebraska at Omaha (NE)
U of Nebraska–Lincoln (NE)
U of Nevada, Las Vegas (NV)
U of Nevada, Reno (NV)
U of New Brunswick Fredericton (NB, Canada)
U of New Brunswick Saint John (NB, Canada)
U of New England (ME)
U of New Hampshire (NH)
U of New Hampshire at Manchester (NH)
U of New Haven (CT)
U of New Mexico (NM)
U of New Orleans (LA)
U of North Alabama (AL)
U of North Carolina at Asheville (NC)
The U of North Carolina at Chapel Hill (NC)
The U of North Carolina at Charlotte (NC)
The U of North Carolina at Greensboro (NC)
The U of North Carolina at Pembroke (NC)
The U of North Carolina Wilmington (NC)
U of North Dakota (ND)
U of Northern Colorado (CO)
U of Northern Iowa (IA)
U of North Florida (FL)
U of North Georgia (GA)
U of North Texas (TX)
U of Notre Dame (IN)
U of Oklahoma (OK)
U of Oregon (OR)
U of Ottawa (ON, Canada)
U of Pennsylvania (PA)
U of Pikeville (KY)
U of Pittsburgh (PA)
U of Pittsburgh at Bradford (PA)
U of Portland (OR)
U of Puget Sound (WA)

U of Redlands (CA)
U of Regina (SK, Canada)
U of Rhode Island (RI)
U of Richmond (VA)
U of Rochester (NY)
U of St. Francis (IL)
U of Saint Joseph (CT)
U of Saint Mary (KS)
U of St. Thomas (MN)
U of St. Thomas (TX)
U of San Diego (CA)
U of Science and Arts of Oklahoma (OK)
The U of Scranton (PA)
U of South Alabama (AL)
U of South Carolina (SC)
U of South Carolina Aiken (SC)
U of South Carolina Upstate (SC)
The U of South Dakota (SD)
U of Southern California (CA)
U of Southern Indiana (IN)
U of Southern Maine (ME)
U of Southern Mississippi (MS)
U of South Florida (FL)
The U of Tampa (FL)
The U of Tennessee (TN)
The U of Tennessee at Chattanooga (TN)
The U of Tennessee at Martin (TN)
The U of Texas at Arlington (TX)
The U of Texas at Austin (TX)
The U of Texas at Brownsville (TX)
The U of Texas at Dallas (TX)
The U of Texas at El Paso (TX)
The U of Texas at San Antonio (TX)
The U of Texas of the Permian Basin (TX)
The U of Texas–Pan American (TX)
U of the Cumberlands (KY)
U of the District of Columbia (DC)
U of the Incarnate Word (TX)
U of the Ozarks (AR)
The U of Toledo (OH)
U of Tulsa (OK)
U of Utah (UT)
U of Vermont (VT)
U of Virginia (VA)
U of Waterloo (ON, Canada)
The U of West Alabama (AL)
The U of Western Ontario (ON, Canada)
U of West Florida (FL)
U of West Georgia (GA)
U of Windsor (ON, Canada)
U of Wisconsin–Eau Claire (WI)
U of Wisconsin–Green Bay (WI)
U of Wisconsin–La Crosse (WI)
U of Wisconsin–Madison (WI)
U of Wisconsin–Milwaukee (WI)
U of Wisconsin–Parkside (WI)
U of Wisconsin–Platteville (WI)
U of Wisconsin–Stevens Point (WI)
U of Wisconsin–Superior (WI)
U of Wyoming (WY)
Ursuline Coll (OH)
Utah State U (UT)
Utica Coll (NY)
Valdosta State U (GA)
Valley City State U (ND)
Valparaiso U (IN)
Vanderbilt U (TN)
Vassar Coll (NY)
Villanova U (PA)
Virginia Commonwealth U (VA)
Virginia Intermont Coll (VA)
Virginia Polytechnic Inst and State U (VA)
Virginia State U (VA)
Virginia Union U (VA)
Virginia Wesleyan Coll (VA)
Wabash Coll (IN)
Wagner Coll (NY)
Wake Forest U (NC)
Waldorf Coll (IA)
Walla Walla U (WA)
Walsh U (OH)
Warner Pacific Coll (OR)
Wartburg Coll (IA)
Washburn U (KS)
Washington & Jefferson Coll (PA)
Washington and Lee U (VA)
Washington Coll (MD)
Washington State U (WA)
Washington U in St. Louis (MO)
Wayland Baptist U (TX)
Waynesburg U (PA)
Wayne State Coll (NE)

Wayne State U (MI)
Weber State U (UT)
Webster U (MO)
Wellesley Coll (MA)
Wells Coll (NY)
Wesleyan Coll (GA)
Wesleyan U (CT)
Wesley Coll (DE)
West Chester U of Pennsylvania (PA)
Western Carolina U (NC)
Western Connecticut State U (CT)
Western Illinois U (IL)
Western Kentucky U (KY)
Western Michigan U (MI)
Western Oregon U (OR)
Western State Colorado U (CO)
Western Washington U (WA)
Westfield State U (MA)
West Liberty U (WV)
Westminster Coll (MO)
Westminster Coll (UT)
West Texas A&M U (TX)
West Virginia State U (WV)
West Virginia U (WV)
West Virginia U Inst of Technology (WV)
West Virginia Wesleyan Coll (WV)
Wheaton Coll (IL)
Wheaton Coll (MA)
Wheeling Jesuit U (WV)
Whitman Coll (WA)
Whitworth U (WA)
Wichita State U (KS)
Widener U (PA)
Wilkes U (PA)
Willamette U (OR)
William Jewell Coll (MO)
William Paterson U of New Jersey (NJ)
William Penn U (IA)
Williams Coll (MA)
Winthrop U (SC)
Wittenberg U (OH)
Woodbury U (CA)
Worcester Polytechnic Inst (MA)
Worcester State U (MA)
Wright State U (OH)
Xavier U (OH)
Xavier U of Louisiana (LA)
Yale U (CT)
York Coll of Pennsylvania (PA)
York Coll of the City U of New York (NY)
Young Harris Coll (GA)
Youngstown State U (OH)

HISTORY AND PHILOSOPHY OF SCIENCE AND TECHNOLOGY
Bard Coll (NY)
Case Western Reserve U (OH)
Dalhousie U (NS, Canada)
Farmingdale State Coll (NY)
The Johns Hopkins U (MD)
Polytechnic Inst of New York U (NY)
U of Chicago (IL)
U of Oklahoma (OK)
U of Pennsylvania (PA)
U of Pittsburgh (PA)
U of Wisconsin–Madison (WI)
Worcester Polytechnic Inst (MA)

HISTORY RELATED
Arizona State U (AZ)
Bridgewater Coll (VA)
Bridgewater State U (MA)
Carnegie Mellon U (PA)
Indiana U Kokomo (IN)
Marquette U (WI)
Mercyhurst U (PA)
National U (CA)
The Ohio State U (OH)
The Ohio State U at Lima (OH)
The Ohio State U at Marion (OH)
The Ohio State U–Mansfield Campus (OH)
The Ohio State U–Newark Campus (OH)
Point U (GA)
Purdue U North Central (IN)
Saint Mary's U of Minnesota (MN)
United States Military Acad (NY)
U at Albany, State U of New York (NY)
U of Regina (SK, Canada)
U of Southern California (CA)

Vanderbilt U (TN)
Viterbo U (WI)

HISTORY TEACHER EDUCATION
Abilene Christian U (TX)
Albion Coll (MI)
Alma Coll (MI)
Anderson U (SC)
Appalachian State U (NC)
Assumption Coll (MA)
Auburn U (AL)
Augustana Coll (IL)
Averett U (VA)
Bluefield Coll (VA)
Boise State U (ID)
Bowling Green State U (OH)
Bradley U (IL)
Buena Vista U (IA)
Calvin Coll (MI)
Campbellsville U (KY)
Carroll Coll (MT)
The Catholic U of America (DC)
Central Michigan U (MI)
Christian Brothers U (TN)
The Coll at Brockport, State U of New York (NY)
The Coll of New Jersey (NJ)
Coll of Staten Island of the City U of New York (NY)
Coll of the Ozarks (MO)
Concordia U Chicago (IL)
Concordia U, Nebraska (NE)
Concordia U Wisconsin (WI)
Cornerstone U (MI)
Covenant Coll (GA)
Culver-Stockton Coll (MO)
Dakota Wesleyan U (SD)
Dallas Baptist U (TX)
Dominican Coll (NY)
Dominican U (IL)
Dordt Coll (IA)
East Central U (OK)
Eastern Michigan U (MI)
East Texas Baptist U (TX)
Elizabeth City State U (NC)
Elmira Coll (NY)
Evangel U (MO)
Ferris State U (MI)
Friends U (KS)
Gardner-Webb U (NC)
Gordon State Coll (GA)
Grand Valley State U (MI)
Greenville Coll (IL)
Hardin-Simmons U (TX)
Holy Family U (PA)
Hope Coll (MI)
Howard Payne U (TX)
Huntingdon Coll (AL)
Indiana U–Purdue U Fort Wayne (IN)
Inter American U of Puerto Rico, San Germán Campus (PR)
Iowa Wesleyan Coll (IA)
Ithaca Coll (NY)
Jamestown Coll (ND)
Johnson State Coll (VT)
King Coll (TN)
Lee U (TN)
Lincoln Memorial U (TN)
Lindenwood U (MO)
Lipscomb U (TN)
Lubbock Christian U (TX)
Manchester U (IN)
Maranatha Baptist Bible Coll (WI)
Maryville Coll (TN)
Mayville State U (ND)
McKendree U (IL)
McMurry U (TX)
Merrimack Coll (MA)
Michigan State U (MI)
Minot State U (ND)
Missouri State U (MO)
Moravian Coll (PA)
Morningside Coll (IA)
Mount Marty Coll (SD)
Mount Mary Coll (WI)
Mount Vernon Nazarene U (OH)
Nazareth Coll of Rochester (NY)
North Carolina Central U (NC)
North Dakota State U (ND)
Northern Michigan U (MI)
Northwest Nazarene U (ID)
Ohio Wesleyan U (OH)
Paine Coll (GA)
Rhode Island Coll (RI)
Rocky Mountain Coll (MT)
Saginaw Valley State U (MI)
St. Ambrose U (IA)
St. Edward's U (TX)
St. John Fisher Coll (NY)
Salve Regina U (RI)
Samford U (AL)
Schreiner U (TX)
Southern Utah U (UT)
Spring Arbor U (MI)
State U of New York at New Paltz (NY)
Stony Brook U, State U of New York (NY)
Texas A&M Intl U (TX)
Texas Lutheran U (TX)
Texas Wesleyan U (TX)
Tiffin U (OH)
Trevecca Nazarene U (TN)
Trinity Christian Coll (IL)
Union Coll (NE)
Universidad Adventista de las Antillas (PR)
U of Arkansas–Fort Smith (AR)
U of Central Oklahoma (OK)
U of Delaware (DE)
U of Great Falls (MT)
U of Illinois at Chicago (IL)
U of Illinois at Urbana–Champaign (IL)
The U of Iowa (IA)
U of Maine at Machias (ME)
U of Michigan–Flint (MI)
The U of Montana Western (MT)
The U of South Dakota (SD)
The U of Tennessee at Martin (TN)
U of Windsor (ON, Canada)
U of Wisconsin–Superior (WI)
Utica Coll (NY)
Valley City State U (ND)
Valparaiso U (IN)
Virginia Intermont Coll (VA)
Wartburg Coll (IA)
Washburn U (KS)
Washington State U (WA)
Washington U in St. Louis (MO)
Wayne State Coll (NE)
Weber State U (UT)
Western Michigan U (MI)
Western State Colorado U (CO)
Western Washington U (WA)
Wheeling Jesuit U (WV)
Widener U (PA)
Xavier U of Louisiana (LA)

HOLISTIC HEALTH
Prescott Coll (AZ)

HOLOCAUST AND RELATED STUDIES
Drew U (NJ)
Keene State Coll (NH)

HOME FURNISHINGS AND EQUIPMENT INSTALLATION
Brigham Young U (UT)

HOMELAND SECURITY
American Public U System (WV)
Angelo State U (TX)
Concordia U (OR)
Dakota Wesleyan U (SD)
Daniel Webster Coll (NH)
Embry-Riddle Aeronautical U–Daytona (FL)
Mississippi Coll (MS)
Monmouth U (NJ)
National U (CA)
Northcentral U (AZ)
Saint Leo U (FL)
Tulane U (LA)
The U of Arizona (AZ)

HOMELAND SECURITY, LAW ENFORCEMENT, FIREFIGHTING AND PROTECTIVE SERVICES RELATED
Clayton State U (GA)
Eastern Michigan U (MI)
Florida Atlantic U (FL)
Lewis U (IL)
Madonna U (MI)
Marian U (WI)
Massachusetts Maritime Acad (MA)
Miami Dade Coll (FL)
Mitchell Coll (CT)
North Dakota State U (ND)
Northwestern Oklahoma State U (OK)
Penn State Altoona (PA)
Penn State Berks (PA)
Penn State U Park (PA)
Point Park U (PA)
Roberts Wesleyan Coll (NY)
St. Ambrose U (IA)
Thomas Edison State Coll (NJ)
Tiffin U (OH)
Virginia Commonwealth U (VA)
Washburn U (KS)
Western Illinois U (IL)

HORSE HUSBANDRY/EQUINE SCIENCE AND MANAGEMENT
Becker Coll (MA)
Bethany Coll (WV)
Morrisville State Coll (NY)
Saint Mary-of-the-Woods Coll (IN)
Tiffin U (OH)
U of Kentucky (KY)
U of Minnesota, Crookston (MN)
Vermont Tech Coll (VT)

HORTICULTURAL SCIENCE
Auburn U (AL)
California State U, Fresno (CA)
Clemson U (SC)
Coll of the Ozarks (MO)
Colorado State U (CO)
Ferrum Coll (VA)
Iowa State U of Science and Technology (IA)
Kansas State U (KS)
Michigan State U (MI)
Mississippi State U (MS)
Missouri State U (MO)
Montana State U (MT)
New Mexico State U (NM)
North Carolina State U (NC)
Northwest Missouri State U (MO)
Oklahoma State U (OK)
Oregon State U (OR)
Penn State Abington (PA)
Penn State Altoona (PA)
Penn State Beaver (PA)
Penn State Berks (PA)
Penn State Brandywine (PA)
Penn State DuBois (PA)
Penn State Erie, The Behrend Coll (PA)
Penn State Fayette, The Eberly Campus (PA)
Penn State Greater Allegheny (PA)
Penn State Hazleton (PA)
Penn State Lehigh Valley (PA)
Penn State Mont Alto (PA)
Penn State New Kensington (PA)
Penn State Schuylkill (PA)
Penn State Shenango (PA)
Penn State U Park (PA)
Penn State Wilkes-Barre (PA)
Penn State Worthington Scranton (PA)
Penn State York (PA)
Purdue U (IN)
Southeast Missouri State U (MO)
Stephen F. Austin State U (TX)
Tarleton State U (TX)
Temple U (PA)
The U of British Columbia (BC, Canada)
U of Cincinnati (OH)
U of Florida (FL)
U of Hawaii at Hilo (HI)
U of Idaho (ID)
U of Illinois at Urbana–Champaign (IL)
U of Minnesota, Crookston (MN)
U of Minnesota, Twin Cities Campus (MN)
U of Nebraska–Lincoln (NE)
U of New Hampshire (NH)
U of Vermont (VT)
U of Wisconsin–Madison (WI)
Utah State U (UT)
Virginia Polytechnic Inst and State U (VA)
Washington State U (WA)

HOSPITAL AND HEALTH-CARE FACILITIES ADMINISTRATION
Avila U (MO)
Champlain Coll (VT)
Clayton State U (GA)
Governors State U (IL)
Indiana Tech (IN)
Ithaca Coll (NY)
Long Island U–C. W. Post Campus (NY)
Newman U (KS)
New York City Coll of Technology of the City U of New York (NY)
St. Joseph's Coll, Long Island Campus (NY)
St. Joseph's Coll, New York (NY)
Saint Joseph's U (PA)
State U of New York Coll of Technology at Canton (NY)
Thomas Edison State Coll (NJ)
The U of Alabama (AL)
U of St. Francis (IL)
The U of South Dakota (SD)
The U of Toledo (OH)
U of Wisconsin–Milwaukee (WI)
Ursuline Coll (OH)
Youngstown State U (OH)

HOSPITALITY ADMINISTRATION
American Public U System (WV)
Appalachian State U (NC)
Arkansas Tech U (AR)
Belmont U (TN)
Boston U (MA)
Bowling Green State U (OH)
Bradley U (IL)
Buffalo State Coll, State U of New York (NY)
California State Polytechnic U, Pomona (CA)
Central Michigan U (MI)
Coll of Charleston (SC)
Coll of the Ozarks (MO)
Colorado Mesa U (CO)
Concord U (WV)
Dallas Baptist U (TX)
Delta State U (MS)
DePaul U (IL)
East Carolina U (NC)
Eastern Michigan U (MI)
Endicott Coll (MA)
Fairleigh Dickinson U, Coll at Florham (NJ)
Fairleigh Dickinson U, Metropolitan Campus (NJ)
Ferris State U (MI)
Fisher Coll (MA)
Florida Atlantic U (FL)
Florida Intl U (FL)
Florida State U (FL)
Georgia State U (GA)
Grand Valley State U (MI)
Husson U (ME)
Indiana U Kokomo (IN)
Indiana U of Pennsylvania (PA)
Indiana U–Purdue U Fort Wayne (IN)
James Madison U (VA)
Johnson State Coll (VT)
Kent State U (OH)
Kent State U at Ashtabula (OH)
Lasell Coll (MA)
Lebanese American U (Lebanon)
Lewis-Clark State Coll (ID)
Lynn U (FL)
Madonna U (MI)
Marywood U (PA)
Mercyhurst U (PA)
Metropolitan State U of Denver (CO)
Michigan State U (MI)
Missouri State U (MO)
Mitchell Coll (CT)
Morrisville State Coll (NY)
New Mexico State U (NM)
New York City Coll of Technology of the City U of New York (NY)
North Carolina Central U (NC)
North Dakota State U (ND)
Northern Arizona U (AZ)
Northern Michigan U (MI)
Northwestern State U of Louisiana (LA)
The Ohio State U (OH)
Oklahoma State U (OK)
The Richard Stockton Coll of New Jersey (NJ)
Robert Morris U (PA)
Rochester Inst of Technology (NY)
Roosevelt U (IL)
Rutgers, The State U of New Jersey, Camden (NJ)
St. John's U (NY)
Saint Leo U (FL)
Saint Louis U (MO)
Salem State U (MA)
San Diego State U (CA)
San Francisco State U (CA)
San Jose State U (CA)
Seton Hill U (PA)
Southeast Missouri State U (MO)
Southern New Hampshire U (NH)
Southern Utah U (UT)
Stephen F. Austin State U (TX)
Stratford U (MD)
Stratford U, Falls Church (VA)
Stratford U, Woodbridge (VA)
Sullivan U (KY)
Temple U (PA)
Thomas Edison State Coll (NJ)
Tiffin U (OH)
Trident U Intl (CA)
Tuskegee U (AL)
U of Central Florida (FL)
U of Cincinnati (OH)
U of Delaware (DE)
U of Denver (CO)
U of Illinois at Urbana–Champaign (IL)
U of Kentucky (KY)
U of Louisiana at Lafayette (LA)
U of Massachusetts Amherst (MA)
U of Memphis (TN)
U of Mississippi (MS)
U of Nebraska–Lincoln (NE)
U of Nevada, Las Vegas (NV)
U of New Brunswick Saint John (NB, Canada)
U of New Hampshire (NH)
U of New Haven (CT)
U of New Orleans (LA)
The U of North Carolina at Greensboro (NC)
U of North Texas (TX)
U of Pittsburgh at Bradford (PA)
U of South Carolina (SC)
U of South Florida (FL)
U of the Virgin Islands (VI)
U of West Florida (FL)
U of Wisconsin–Stout (WI)
Virginia State U (VA)
Washington State U (WA)
Webber Intl U (FL)
Western Carolina U (NC)
Western Kentucky U (KY)
Youngstown State U (OH)

HOSPITALITY ADMINISTRATION RELATED
Auburn U (AL)
California State U, Dominguez Hills (CA)
California State U, Fullerton (CA)
DEREE—The American Coll of Greece (Greece)
Harris-Stowe State U (MO)
Lynn U (FL)
Morrisville State Coll (NY)
Niagara U (NY)
Penn State Abington (PA)
Penn State Altoona (PA)
Penn State Beaver (PA)
Penn State Berks (PA)
Penn State Brandywine (PA)
Penn State DuBois (PA)
Penn State Erie, The Behrend Coll (PA)
Penn State Fayette, The Eberly Campus (PA)
Penn State Greater Allegheny (PA)
Penn State Hazleton (PA)
Penn State Lehigh Valley (PA)
Penn State Mont Alto (PA)
Penn State New Kensington (PA)
Penn State Schuylkill (PA)
Penn State Shenango (PA)
Penn State U Park (PA)
Penn State Wilkes-Barre (PA)
Penn State Worthington Scranton (PA)
Penn State York (PA)
Southern Illinois U Carbondale (IL)
U of Nevada, Las Vegas (NV)
U of Southern Mississippi (MS)
Widener U (PA)

HOSPITALITY AND RECREATION MARKETING
Ferris State U (MI)
Rochester Inst of Technology (NY)

Tuskegee U (AL)
U of Minnesota, Twin Cities Campus (MN)

HOTEL/MOTEL ADMINISTRATION
Ashland U (OH)
Auburn U (AL)
Bethune-Cookman U (FL)
Buffalo State Coll, State U of New York (NY)
California State U, Long Beach (CA)
Central Michigan U (MI)
Cheyney U of Pennsylvania (PA)
Concord U (WV)
Ferris State U (MI)
Georgia Southern U (GA)
Grand Valley State U (MI)
Hampton U (VA)
Indiana U–Purdue U Fort Wayne (IN)
Inter American U of Puerto Rico, Aguadilla Campus (PR)
Inter American U of Puerto Rico, Fajardo Campus (PR)
Inter American U of Puerto Rico, Ponce Campus (PR)
Iowa State U of Science and Technology (IA)
Kansas State U (KS)
Keuka Coll (NY)
Langston U (OK)
Newbury Coll (MA)
New York Inst of Technology (NY)
New York U (NY)
Niagara U (NY)
Northwood U, Florida Campus (FL)
Northwood U, Michigan Campus (MI)
The Ohio State U (OH)
Pace U (NY)
Rochester Inst of Technology (NY)
St. Thomas U (FL)
South Dakota State U (SD)
Southern Oregon U (OR)
State U of New York at Plattsburgh (NY)
State U of New York Coll of Technology at Delhi (NY)
U of Central Oklahoma (OK)
U of Delaware (DE)
U of Denver (CO)
The U of Findlay (OH)
U of Guelph (ON, Canada)
U of Houston (TX)
U of Maine at Machias (ME)
U of Maryland Eastern Shore (MD)
U of Memphis (TN)
U of Missouri (MO)
U of Nevada, Las Vegas (NV)
U of New Haven (CT)
U of Southern Mississippi (MS)
The U of Tennessee (TN)
Virginia Polytechnic Inst and State U (VA)
Widener U (PA)

HOTEL, MOTEL, AND RESTAURANT MANAGEMENT
Endicott Coll (MA)

HOUSING AND HUMAN ENVIRONMENTS
Harding U (AR)
Missouri State U (MO)
Ohio U (OH)
Oklahoma State U (OK)
Oregon State U (OR)
The U of Akron (OH)
U of Georgia (GA)
U of Minnesota, Twin Cities Campus (MN)
U of Missouri (MO)
U of Northern Iowa (IA)
Utah State U (UT)

HOUSING AND HUMAN ENVIRONMENTS RELATED
Bob Jones U (SC)
U of Nevada, Reno (NV)

HUMAN BIOLOGY
Hamline U (MN)
Scripps Coll (CA)
The U of Kansas (KS)
U of Wisconsin–Green Bay (WI)

HUMAN COMPUTER INTERACTION
U of Guelph (ON, Canada)

HUMAN DEVELOPMENT AND FAMILY STUDIES
Abilene Christian U (TX)
Antioch U Midwest (OH)
Auburn U (AL)
Baylor U (TX)
Boston Coll (MA)
Bowling Green State U (OH)
Brigham Young U (UT)
California State U, East Bay (CA)
California State U, Long Beach (CA)
California State U, San Bernardino (CA)
Colorado State U (CO)
Concordia U, St. Paul (MN)
Connecticut Coll (CT)
Eckerd Coll (FL)
Florida State U (FL)
Georgia Southern U (GA)
Hope Intl U (CA)
Howard Payne U (TX)
Indiana State U (IN)
Indiana U of Pennsylvania (PA)
Kansas State U (KS)
Kent State U (OH)
Kent State U at Salem (OH)
Kent State U at Stark (OH)
Kentucky State U (KY)
Lesley U (MA)
Liberty U (VA)
Miami U (OH)
Missouri State U (MO)
Mitchell Coll (CT)
New Mexico State U (NM)
North Dakota State U (ND)
Northern Illinois U (IL)
Northwest Missouri State U (MO)
The Ohio State U (OH)
Ohio U (OH)
Oklahoma State U (OK)
Oregon State U (OR)
Penn State Abington (PA)
Penn State Altoona (PA)
Penn State Beaver (PA)
Penn State Berks (PA)
Penn State Brandywine (PA)
Penn State DuBois (PA)
Penn State Erie, The Behrend Coll (PA)
Penn State Fayette, The Eberly Campus (PA)
Penn State Greater Allegheny (PA)
Penn State Harrisburg (PA)
Penn State Hazleton (PA)
Penn State Lehigh Valley (PA)
Penn State Mont Alto (PA)
Penn State New Kensington (PA)
Penn State Schuylkill (PA)
Penn State Shenango (PA)
Penn State U Park (PA)
Penn State Wilkes-Barre (PA)
Penn State Worthington Scranton (PA)
Penn State York (PA)
Purdue U (IN)
Rockford Coll (IL)
St. Joseph's Coll, Long Island Campus (NY)
St. Joseph's Coll, New York (NY)
Samford U (AL)
San Diego Christian Coll (CA)
Seattle Pacific U (WA)
South Dakota State U (SD)
State U of New York at Oswego (NY)
State U of New York at Plattsburgh (NY)
State U of New York Empire State Coll (NY)
Stephen F. Austin State U (TX)
Stephens Coll (MO)
Syracuse U (NY)
Texas State U–San Marcos (TX)
Texas Woman's U (TX)
The U of Alabama (AL)
The U of Arizona (AZ)
U of California, Davis (CA)
U of Georgia (GA)
U of Guelph (ON, Canada)
U of Houston (TX)
U of Idaho (ID)
U of Illinois at Urbana–Champaign (IL)

U of Louisiana at Lafayette (LA)
U of Memphis (TN)
U of Missouri (MO)
U of Nevada, Reno (NV)
U of New Hampshire (NH)
U of New Mexico (NM)
The U of North Carolina at Greensboro (NC)
U of North Texas (TX)
U of Rhode Island (RI)
The U of Tennessee (TN)
The U of Texas at Austin (TX)
The U of Texas of the Permian Basin (TX)
U of the District of Columbia (DC)
U of Utah (UT)
U of Vermont (VT)
U of Waterloo (ON, Canada)
U of Wisconsin–Madison (WI)
U of Wisconsin–Stout (WI)
Utah State U (UT)
Virginia Polytechnic Inst and State U (VA)
Walden U (MN)
Warner Pacific Coll (OR)
Washington State U (WA)
Youngstown State U (OH)

HUMAN DEVELOPMENT AND FAMILY STUDIES RELATED
American Public U System (WV)
Auburn U (AL)
Ball State U (IN)
Binghamton U, State U of New York (NY)
Bowling Green State U (OH)
Columbia Coll (SC)
Harding U (AR)
Hope Intl U (CA)
LaGrange Coll (GA)
Merrimack Coll (MA)
The U of Alabama (AL)

HUMANITIES
Adelphi U (NY)
Albertus Magnus Coll (CT)
Antioch U Midwest (OH)
Athens State U (AL)
Augsburg Coll (MN)
Baylor U (TX)
Belhaven U (MS)
Bemidji State U (MN)
Benedictine U (IL)
Bennington Coll (VT)
Bluefield State Coll (WV)
Bob Jones U (SC)
Bradley U (IL)
Briercrest Coll (SK, Canada)
Brock U (ON, Canada)
Bucknell U (PA)
Buffalo State Coll, State U of New York (NY)
California State U, Chico (CA)
California State U, Monterey Bay (CA)
California State U, Northridge (CA)
California State U, San Bernardino (CA)
Catawba Coll (NC)
Chowan U (NC)
Clarkson U (NY)
Clearwater Christian Coll (FL)
Colgate U (NY)
Coll of Saint Benedict (MN)
Coll of Saint Mary (NE)
The Coll of Saint Rose (NY)
The Coll of St. Scholastica (MN)
Columbia Intl U (SC)
Concordia Coll (MN)
Concordia U (CA)
Concordia U (OR)
Concordia U (QC, Canada)
Concordia U Wisconsin (WI)
Corban U (OR)
DePaul U (IL)
Dominican Coll (NY)
Eastern Washington U (WA)
Eckerd Coll (FL)
Edinboro U of Pennsylvania (PA)
Elmira Coll (NY)
The Evergreen State Coll (WA)
Fairleigh Dickinson U, Coll at Florham (NJ)
Fairleigh Dickinson U, Metropolitan Campus (NJ)
Faulkner U (AL)
Felician Coll (NJ)
Florida Christian Coll (FL)

Florida Inst of Technology (FL)
Florida Southern Coll (FL)
Florida State U (FL)
Fort Lewis Coll (CO)
Hampden-Sydney Coll (VA)
Harding U (AR)
Harrison Middleton U (AZ)
Hawai`i Pacific U (HI)
Hillsdale Free Will Baptist Coll (OK)
Holy Apostles Coll and Sem (CT)
Holy Family U (PA)
Holy Names U (CA)
Houghton Coll (NY)
Howard Payne U (TX)
Hunter Coll of the City U of New York (NY)
Indiana U East (IN)
Indiana U Kokomo (IN)
John Cabot U (Italy)
John Carroll U (OH)
Johnson State Coll (VT)
Juniata Coll (PA)
Kansas State U (KS)
Kent State U (OH)
Kentucky Christian U (KY)
The King's Coll (NY)
Lasell Coll (MA)
Lawrence Technological U (MI)
Lee U (TN)
Lesley U (MA)
Lincoln Memorial U (TN)
Long Island U–Brooklyn Campus (NY)
Loyola Marymount U (CA)
Lubbock Christian U (TX)
Maranatha Baptist Bible Coll (WI)
Marshall U (WV)
Messiah Coll (PA)
Michigan State U (MI)
Midwestern State U (TX)
Minnesota State U Mankato (MN)
Montclair State U (NJ)
Mount Allison U (NB, Canada)
New Coll of Florida (FL)
New York U (NY)
North Central Coll (IL)
Northland Coll (WI)
Northwestern Coll (IA)
Northwest Missouri State U (MO)
Northwest Nazarene U (ID)
Nova Southeastern U (FL)
Oakland City U (IN)
The Ohio State U (OH)
Ohio Wesleyan U (OH)
Oklahoma Baptist U (OK)
Oklahoma City U (OK)
Pacific U (OR)
Penn State Harrisburg (PA)
Pepperdine U, Malibu (CA)
Plymouth State U (NH)
Point U (GA)
Pomona Coll (CA)
Portland State U (OR)
Prescott Coll (AZ)
Principia Coll (IL)
Providence Coll (RI)
Purchase Coll, State U of New York (NY)
Purdue U (IN)
Quincy U (IL)
Regis U (CO)
Roberts Wesleyan Coll (NY)
Rockford Coll (IL)
Rollins Coll (FL)
Rosemont Coll (PA)
Sage Coll of Albany (NY)
St. Andrews U (NC)
Saint John's U (MN)
Saint Louis U (MO)
Saint Mary-of-the-Woods Coll (IN)
Saint Mary's Coll (IN)
St. Norbert Coll (WI)
St. Thomas Aquinas Coll (NY)
San Diego State U (CA)
San Francisco State U (CA)
San Jose State U (CA)
Scripps Coll (CA)
Seattle U (WA)
Shimer Coll (IL)
Siena Heights U (MI)
Sierra Nevada Coll (NV)
Simon Fraser U (BC, Canada)
Spring Hill Coll (AL)
State U of New York Coll at Old Westbury (NY)
State U of New York Empire State Coll (NY)

Stetson U (FL)
Stony Brook U, State U of New York (NY)
Suffolk U (MA)
Tennessee State U (TN)
Thomas Edison State Coll (NJ)
Thomas More Coll (KY)
Thomas U (GA)
Trent U (ON, Canada)
Trinity U (TX)
United States Air Force Acad (CO)
United States Military Acad (NY)
The U of Akron (OH)
U of Arkansas at Little Rock (AR)
U of Bridgeport (CT)
U of California, Irvine (CA)
U of California, Riverside (CA)
U of Central Florida (FL)
U of Chicago (IL)
U of Colorado Boulder (CO)
U of Hawaii–West Oahu (HI)
U of Houston–Clear Lake (TX)
U of Houston–Downtown (TX)
U of Houston–Victoria (TX)
U of Illinois at Urbana–Champaign (IL)
The U of Kansas (KS)
U of Louisville (KY)
U of Massachusetts Amherst (MA)
U of Michigan (MI)
U of Michigan–Dearborn (MI)
U of Minnesota, Twin Cities Campus (MN)
U of Mobile (AL)
U of New Hampshire (NH)
U of New Hampshire at Manchester (NH)
U of New Mexico (NM)
U of Northern Iowa (IA)
U of Oklahoma (OK)
U of Oregon (OR)
U of Ottawa (ON, Canada)
U of Pennsylvania (PA)
U of Pittsburgh (PA)
U of Pittsburgh at Bradford (PA)
U of Pittsburgh at Greensburg (PA)
U of Regina (SK, Canada)
U of San Diego (CA)
U of Southern Maine (ME)
U of South Florida (FL)
The U of Tennessee at Chattanooga (TN)
The U of Texas at Austin (TX)
The U of Texas at San Antonio (TX)
The U of Texas of the Permian Basin (TX)
U of the Ozarks (AR)
U of the Virgin Islands (VI)
The U of Toledo (OH)
U of Utah (UT)
U of Washington, Bothell (WA)
U of Washington, Tacoma (WA)
U of West Florida (FL)
U of Wisconsin–Green Bay (WI)
U of Wisconsin–Parkside (WI)
U of Wyoming (WY)
Ursuline Coll (OH)
Valparaiso U (IN)
Villanova U (PA)
Virginia Wesleyan Coll (VA)
Waldorf Coll (IA)
Walla Walla U (WA)
Washington Coll (MD)
Washington State U (WA)
Washington U in St. Louis (MO)
Webster U (MO)
Wesleyan Coll (GA)
Wesleyan U (CT)
Western Oregon U (OR)
Western Washington U (WA)
Widener U (PA)
Willamette U (OR)
William Paterson U of New Jersey (NJ)
Worcester Polytechnic Inst (MA)
Yale U (CT)

HUMAN NUTRITION
Baylor U (TX)
Case Western Reserve U (OH)
Colorado State U (CO)
Kansas State U (KS)
Life U (GA)
Metropolitan State U of Denver (CO)
The Ohio State U (OH)
Penn State Abington (PA)

Penn State Altoona (PA)
Penn State Beaver (PA)
Penn State Berks (PA)
Penn State Brandywine (PA)
Penn State DuBois (PA)
Penn State Erie, The Behrend Coll (PA)
Penn State Fayette, The Eberly Campus (PA)
Penn State Greater Allegheny (PA)
Penn State Hazleton (PA)
Penn State Lehigh Valley (PA)
Penn State Mont Alto (PA)
Penn State New Kensington (PA)
Penn State Schuylkill (PA)
Penn State Shenango (PA)
Penn State U Park (PA)
Penn State Wilkes-Barre (PA)
Penn State Worthington Scranton (PA)
Penn State York (PA)
Rochester Inst of Technology (NY)
Southern Utah U (UT)
Syracuse U (NY)
Tarleton State U (TX)
The U of British Columbia (BC, Canada)
U of Guelph (ON, Canada)
U of Houston (TX)
U of Illinois at Urbana–Champaign (IL)
U of Kentucky (KY)
Washington State U (WA)

HUMAN RESOURCES DEVELOPMENT
Clemson U (SC)
Concordia U Texas (TX)
Grantham U (MO)
Hawai‘i Pacific U (HI)
Limestone Coll (SC)
Midwestern State U (TX)
Oakland U (MI)
The Ohio State U (OH)
Park U (MO)
Pittsburg State U (KS)
Texas A&M U (TX)
U of Houston (TX)
U of Regina (SK, Canada)
U of Wisconsin–Milwaukee (WI)

HUMAN RESOURCES MANAGEMENT
Albion Coll (MI)
Alvernia U (PA)
American U of Puerto Rico (PR)
Anderson U (SC)
Antioch U Midwest (OH)
Athabasca U (AB, Canada)
Athens State U (AL)
Auburn U (AL)
Auburn U at Montgomery (AL)
Avila U (MO)
Baldwin Wallace U (OH)
Ball State U (IN)
Barton Coll (NC)
Baylor U (TX)
Boston Coll (MA)
Bowling Green State U (OH)
Bradley U (IL)
Brigham Young U (UT)
Brock U (ON, Canada)
Bryant U (RI)
Buena Vista U (IA)
Cabrini Coll (PA)
California State U, Chico (CA)
California State U, East Bay (CA)
California State U, Fresno (CA)
California State U, Long Beach (CA)
Canisius Coll (NY)
The Catholic U of America (DC)
Central Michigan U (MI)
Chestnut Hill Coll (PA)
Cleary U (MI)
Coll of Saint Elizabeth (NJ)
Columbia Coll (MO)
Concordia U (QC, Canada)
Concordia U, St. Paul (MN)
Concordia U Texas (TX)
Converse Coll (SC)
Davenport U, Grand Rapids (MI)
DePaul U (IL)
Dominican Coll (NY)
East Central U (OK)
Eastern Washington U (WA)
Excelsior Coll (NY)
Faulkner U (AL)

Ferris State U (MI)
Florida Atlantic U (FL)
Florida Intl U (FL)
Franklin U (OH)
Friends U (KS)
Georgia Southwestern State U (GA)
Goldey-Beacom Coll (DE)
Hawai‘i Pacific U (HI)
HEC Montreal (QC, Canada)
Holy Names U (CA)
Huntington U (IN)
Indiana State U (IN)
Indiana U of Pennsylvania (PA)
Inter American U of Puerto Rico, Aguadilla Campus (PR)
Inter American U of Puerto Rico, Bayamón Campus (PR)
Inter American U of Puerto Rico, Fajardo Campus (PR)
Inter American U of Puerto Rico, Ponce Campus (PR)
Inter American U of Puerto Rico, San Germán Campus (PR)
John Carroll U (OH)
Judson U (IL)
Juniata Coll (PA)
King's Coll (PA)
Kutztown U of Pennsylvania (PA)
Lake Erie Coll (OH)
La Salle U (PA)
La Sierra U (CA)
Lewis U (IL)
Lindenwood U (MO)
Lipscomb U (TN)
Lourdes U (OH)
Loyola U Chicago (IL)
Lynchburg Coll (VA)
Madonna U (MI)
Mansfield U of Pennsylvania (PA)
Marian U (WI)
Marietta Coll (OH)
Marquette U (WI)
Maryville Coll (TN)
Mercyhurst U (PA)
Michigan State U (MI)
Mount Mercy U (IA)
Nazareth Coll of Rochester (NY)
Neumann U (PA)
New York Inst of Technology (NY)
Niagara U (NY)
North Central Coll (IL)
Northcentral U (AZ)
Northeastern Illinois U (IL)
Northeastern U (MA)
Oakland City U (IN)
Oakland U (MI)
The Ohio State U (OH)
Ohio U (OH)
Ohio U–Chillicothe (OH)
Ohio Valley U (WV)
Pace U (NY)
Peirce Coll (PA)
Point Park U (PA)
Portland State U (OR)
Purdue U Calumet (IN)
Purdue U North Central (IN)
Quinnipiac U (CT)
Rasmussen Coll Bismarck (ND)
Rasmussen Coll Bloomington (MN)
Rasmussen Coll Brooklyn Park (MN)
Rasmussen Coll Eagan (MN)
Rasmussen Coll Fort Myers (FL)
Rasmussen Coll Lake Elmo/ Woodbury (MN)
Rasmussen Coll Land O' Lakes (FL)
Rasmussen Coll Mankato (MN)
Rasmussen Coll Moorhead (MN)
Rasmussen Coll New Port Richey (FL)
Rasmussen Coll Ocala (FL)
Rasmussen Coll Tampa/Brandon (FL)
Regent U (VA)
Regis U (CO)
Roberts Wesleyan Coll (NY)
Roger Williams U (RI)
Roosevelt U (IL)
Rowan U (NJ)
Saint Joseph's U (PA)
Saint Leo U (FL)
Saint Mary-of-the-Woods Coll (IN)
St. Mary's U (TX)
Saint Mary's U of Minnesota (MN)
Salem State U (MA)

Sam Houston State U (TX)
San Jose State U (CA)
Seton Hill U (PA)
Simpson U (CA)
Spring Arbor U (MI)
State U of New York at Oswego (NY)
State U of New York Coll of Technology at Alfred (NY)
Sullivan U (KY)
Tarleton State U (TX)
Tennessee Wesleyan Coll (TN)
Texas A&M U–Commerce (TX)
Texas Woman's U (TX)
Thomas Edison State Coll (NJ)
Thompson Rivers U (BC, Canada)
Tiffin U (OH)
The U of Akron (OH)
U of Alaska Fairbanks (AK)
The U of Arizona (AZ)
The U of British Columbia–Okanagan (BC, Canada)
U of Central Oklahoma (OK)
The U of Findlay (OH)
U of Guelph (ON, Canada)
U of Hawaii at Manoa (HI)
U of Idaho (ID)
U of Illinois at Urbana–Champaign (IL)
The U of Iowa (IA)
U of Maryland U Coll (MD)
U of Massachusetts Dartmouth (MA)
U of Miami (FL)
U of Michigan–Dearborn (MI)
U of Minnesota, Duluth (MN)
U of Minnesota, Twin Cities Campus (MN)
U of Nebraska at Omaha (NE)
U of Nevada, Las Vegas (NV)
U of New Brunswick Fredericton (NB, Canada)
The U of North Carolina at Chapel Hill (NC)
U of North Dakota (ND)
U of Ottawa (ON, Canada)
U of Pennsylvania (PA)
U of Regina (SK, Canada)
U of St. Francis (IL)
U of St. Thomas (MN)
The U of Scranton (PA)
U of Southern Mississippi (MS)
The U of Tennessee (TN)
The U of Tennessee at Martin (TN)
The U of Texas at San Antonio (TX)
U of the Incarnate Word (TX)
U of Toledo (OH)
U of Waterloo (ON, Canada)
The U of Western Ontario (ON, Canada)
U of Windsor (ON, Canada)
U of Wisconsin–Parkside (WI)
Ursuline Coll (OH)
Utah State U (UT)
Valley City State U (ND)
Washington U in St. Louis (MO)
Weber State U (UT)
Webster U (MO)
Western Illinois U (IL)
Western Washington U (WA)
Wichita State U (KS)
Wilmington U (DE)
Wright State U (OH)
Xavier U (OH)
Youngstown State U (OH)

HUMAN RESOURCES MANAGEMENT AND SERVICES RELATED
Albertus Magnus Coll (CT)
Becker Coll (MA)
Bradley U (IL)
Carlow U (PA)
Grand Valley State U (MI)
Immaculata U (PA)
Menlo Coll (CA)
Niagara U (NY)
Park U (MO)
Simpson U (CA)
Université du Québec en Outaouais (QC, Canada)
The U of British Columbia (BC, Canada)
U of Mount Union (OH)
U of Oklahoma (OK)
U of the District of Columbia (DC)
Western Michigan U (MI)

Widener U (PA)

HUMAN SERVICES
Alaska Pacific U (AK)
Albertus Magnus Coll (CT)
Antioch U Midwest (OH)
Beacon Coll (FL)
Bethel Coll (IN)
California State U, Dominguez Hills (CA)
California State U, Fullerton (CA)
California State U, Monterey Bay (CA)
California State U, San Bernardino (CA)
Calumet Coll of Saint Joseph (IN)
Carson-Newman U (TN)
Chestnut Hill Coll (PA)
City U of Seattle (WA)
Columbia Coll (MO)
Concordia U, St. Paul (MN)
Dakota Wesleyan U (SD)
Doane Coll (NE)
East Central U (OK)
East Tennessee State U (TN)
Elmira Coll (NY)
Elon U (NC)
Fairmont State U (WV)
Fisher Coll (MA)
Geneva Coll (PA)
Graceland U (IA)
Grand View U (IA)
High Point U (NC)
Hilbert Coll (NY)
Holy Names U (CA)
Indiana Tech (IN)
Inter American U of Puerto Rico, Aguadilla Campus (PR)
Iowa Wesleyan Coll (IA)
Judson U (IL)
Kennesaw State U (GA)
Kentucky Wesleyan Coll (KY)
Lake Superior State U (MI)
Lasell Coll (MA)
Lesley U (MA)
Lincoln Christian U (IL)
Lindenwood U (MO)
Lindsey Wilson Coll (KY)
Loyola U Chicago (IL)
Lynn U (FL)
Marian U (WI)
Mercer U (GA)
Merrimack Coll (MA)
Metropolitan State U of Denver (CO)
Missouri Baptist U (MO)
Montreat Coll, Montreat (NC)
Mount Marty Coll (SD)
Mount Saint Mary Coll (NY)
New York City Coll of Technology of the City U of New York (NY)
Northeastern U (MA)
Notre Dame de Namur U (CA)
Park U (MO)
Post U (CT)
Prescott Coll (AZ)
Quincy U (IL)
Quinnipiac U (CT)
Rocky Mountain Coll (AB, Canada)
St. John's U (NY)
Saint Leo U (FL)
Saint Mary-of-the-Woods Coll (IN)
Saint Mary's U of Minnesota (MN)
St. Thomas U (FL)
Samford U (AL)
Seton Hill U (PA)
Siena Heights U (MI)
Southeastern U (FL)
Southwest Baptist U (MO)
State U of New York Coll at Cortland (NY)
State U of New York Empire State Coll (NY)
Tennessee Wesleyan Coll (TN)
Texas A&M U–Kingsville (TX)
Thomas Edison State Coll (NJ)
Tiffin U (OH)
Troy U (AL)
U of Bridgeport (CT)
U of Delaware (DE)
U of Great Falls (MT)
U of Hartford (CT)
U of Maine at Machias (ME)
U of Nevada, Las Vegas (NV)
U of North Texas (TX)
U of Oregon (OR)
The U of Scranton (PA)

U of the Cumberlands (KY)
U of Utah (UT)
Upper Iowa U (IA)
Villanova U (PA)
Virginia Wesleyan Coll (VA)
Walden U (MN)
Wayland Baptist U (TX)
Wesleyan Coll (GA)
Western Washington U (WA)
William Penn U (IA)

HYDROLOGY AND WATER RESOURCES SCIENCE
California State U, Chico (CA)
The Coll at Brockport, State U of New York (NY)
Humboldt State U (CA)
Northland Coll (WI)
Rensselaer Polytechnic Inst (NY)
Tarleton State U (TX)
The U of Arizona (AZ)
U of California, Davis (CA)
U of California, Santa Barbara (CA)
U of New Hampshire (NH)
The U of Texas at Austin (TX)
U of Wisconsin–Stevens Point (WI)
Western Michigan U (MI)

ILLUSTRATION
Acad of Art U (CA)
Alberta Coll of Art & Design (AB, Canada)
American Acad of Art (IL)
Art Center Coll of Design (CA)
Boise State U (ID)
Brigham Young U (UT)
California State U, Long Beach (CA)
Cleveland Inst of Art (OH)
Coll for Creative Studies (MI)
Columbus Coll of Art & Design (OH)
Fashion Inst of Technology (NY)
Ferris State U (MI)
Indiana Wesleyan U (IN)
John Brown U (AR)
Lawrence Technological U (MI)
Maryland Inst Coll of Art (MD)
Marywood U (PA)
Moore Coll of Art & Design (PA)
Northern Michigan U (MI)
Pacific Northwest Coll of Art (OR)
Paier Coll of Art, Inc. (CT)
Parsons The New School for Design (NY)
Pennsylvania Coll of Art & Design (PA)
Rhode Island School of Design (RI)
Ringling Coll of Art and Design (FL)
Rochester Inst of Technology (NY)
Rocky Mountain Coll of Art + Design (CO)
St. John's U (NY)
Savannah Coll of Art and Design (GA)
School of the Art Inst of Chicago (IL)
School of the Museum of Fine Arts, Boston (MA)
Syracuse U (NY)
U of Bridgeport (CT)
U of Hartford (CT)
The U of Kansas (KS)
U of Michigan (MI)
The U of the Arts (PA)
Virginia Commonwealth U (VA)
Washington U in St. Louis (MO)

IMMUNOLOGY
The U of Western Ontario (ON, Canada)

INDUSTRIAL AND ORGANIZATIONAL PSYCHOLOGY
Albright Coll (PA)
Baldwin Wallace U (OH)
Bridgewater State U (MA)
California State U, East Bay (CA)
Canisius Coll (NY)
Concordia U (CA)
Corban U (OR)
Farmingdale State Coll (NY)
Fort Lewis Coll (CO)
Franklin U (OH)
Goldey-Beacom Coll (DE)
Holy Family U (PA)

Ithaca Coll (NY)
Maryville U of Saint Louis (MO)
Marywood U (PA)
Middle Tennessee State U (TN)
Morningside Coll (IA)
Northwest Missouri State U (MO)
Point Loma Nazarene U (CA)
Saint Mary's Coll of California (CA)
U of Illinois at Urbana–Champaign (IL)
The U of Tennessee at Martin (TN)
Washington U in St. Louis (MO)

INDUSTRIAL AND PRODUCT DESIGN

Acad of Art U (CA)
Appalachian State U (NC)
Arizona State U (AZ)
Art Center Coll of Design (CA)
Auburn U (AL)
California State U, Long Beach (CA)
Carnegie Mellon U (PA)
Cedarville U (OH)
Clemson U (SC)
Cleveland Inst of Art (OH)
Coll for Creative Studies (MI)
Columbia Coll Chicago (IL)
Columbus Coll of Art & Design (OH)
Fashion Inst of Technology (NY)
Ferris State U (MI)
Iowa State U of Science and Technology (IA)
Kean U (NJ)
Lawrence Technological U (MI)
Massachusetts Coll of Art and Design (MA)
Metropolitan State U of Denver (CO)
New Jersey Inst of Technology (NJ)
North Carolina State U (NC)
The Ohio State U (OH)
Parsons The New School for Design (NY)
Pennsylvania Coll of Technology (PA)
Philadelphia U (PA)
Rhode Island School of Design (RI)
Rochester Inst of Technology (NY)
Sam Houston State U (TX)
San Francisco State U (CA)
San Jose State U (CA)
Savannah Coll of Art and Design (GA)
Stanford U (CA)
Syracuse U (NY)
U of Bridgeport (CT)
U of Cincinnati (OH)
U of Houston (TX)
U of Illinois at Chicago (IL)
U of Illinois at Urbana–Champaign (IL)
The U of Kansas (KS)
U of Louisiana at Lafayette (LA)
U of Michigan (MI)
The U of the Arts (PA)
U of Wisconsin–Platteville (WI)
Virginia Polytechnic Inst and State U (VA)
Walla Walla U (WA)
Wentworth Inst of Technology (MA)
Western Washington U (WA)

INDUSTRIAL ELECTRONICS TECHNOLOGY

Lewis-Clark State Coll (ID)
Sam Houston State U (TX)
Sullivan Coll of Technology and Design (KY)

INDUSTRIAL ENGINEERING

Arizona State U (AZ)
Auburn U (AL)
Binghamton U, State U of New York (NY)
Bradley U (IL)
California Polytechnic State U, San Luis Obispo (CA)
California State Polytechnic U, Pomona (CA)
California State U, East Bay (CA)
California State U, Long Beach (CA)
Caribbean U (PR)
Clemson U (SC)
Columbia U (NY)

Concordia U (QC, Canada)
Dalhousie U (NS, Canada)
Elizabethtown Coll (PA)
Florida Ag and Mech U (FL)
Hofstra U (NY)
Indiana Tech (IN)
Inter American U of Puerto Rico, Bayamón Campus (PR)
Iowa State U of Science and Technology (IA)
Kansas State U (KS)
Kent State U (OH)
Lamar U (TX)
Lawrence Technological U (MI)
Lebanese American U (Lebanon)
Lehigh U (PA)
Liberty U (VA)
Louisiana State U and Ag and Mech Coll (LA)
Milwaukee School of Eng (WI)
Mississippi State U (MS)
Missouri U of Science and Technology (MO)
Montana State U (MT)
New Jersey Inst of Technology (NJ)
New Mexico State U (NM)
New York Inst of Technology (NY)
North Carolina State U (NC)
North Dakota State U (ND)
Northeastern U (MA)
Northern Illinois U (IL)
Oakland U (MI)
The Ohio State U (OH)
Ohio U (OH)
Oklahoma State U (OK)
Oregon State U (OR)
Penn State Abington (PA)
Penn State Altoona (PA)
Penn State Beaver (PA)
Penn State Berks (PA)
Penn State Brandywine (PA)
Penn State DuBois (PA)
Penn State Erie, The Behrend Coll (PA)
Penn State Fayette, The Eberly Campus (PA)
Penn State Greater Allegheny (PA)
Penn State Hazleton (PA)
Penn State Lehigh Valley (PA)
Penn State Mont Alto (PA)
Penn State New Kensington (PA)
Penn State Schuylkill (PA)
Penn State Shenango (PA)
Penn State U Park (PA)
Penn State Wilkes-Barre (PA)
Penn State Worthington Scranton (PA)
Penn State York (PA)
Polytechnic U of Puerto Rico (PR)
Purdue U (IN)
Quinnipiac U (CT)
Rensselaer Polytechnic Inst (NY)
Rochester Inst of Technology (NY)
Rutgers, The State U of New Jersey, New Brunswick (NJ)
St. Ambrose U (IA)
St. Mary's U (TX)
San Jose State U (CA)
Southern Illinois U Edwardsville (IL)
Stanford U (CA)
State U of New York Maritime Coll (NY)
Tennessee State U (TN)
Texas A&M U (TX)
Texas A&M U–Commerce (TX)
Texas A&M U–Kingsville (TX)
Texas State U–San Marcos (TX)
United States Coast Guard Acad (CT)
U at Buffalo, the State U of New York (NY)
U of Alaska Fairbanks (AK)
The U of Arizona (AZ)
U of Central Florida (FL)
U of Houston (TX)
U of Illinois at Chicago (IL)
U of Illinois at Urbana–Champaign (IL)
The U of Iowa (IA)
U of Louisville (KY)
U of Massachusetts Amherst (MA)
U of Miami (FL)
U of Michigan (MI)
U of Michigan–Dearborn (MI)
U of Minnesota, Duluth (MN)

U of Minnesota, Twin Cities Campus (MN)
U of Missouri (MO)
U of Oklahoma (OK)
U of Pittsburgh (PA)
U of Regina (SK, Canada)
U of Rhode Island (RI)
U of San Diego (CA)
U of Southern California (CA)
U of South Florida (FL)
The U of Tennessee (TN)
The U of Texas at Arlington (TX)
The U of Texas at El Paso (TX)
The U of Texas–Pan American (TX)
The U of Toledo (OH)
U of Vermont (VT)
U of Windsor (ON, Canada)
U of Wisconsin–Madison (WI)
U of Wisconsin–Milwaukee (WI)
U of Wisconsin–Platteville (WI)
Virginia Polytechnic Inst and State U (VA)
Wayne State U (MI)
Western Michigan U (MI)
West Virginia U (WV)
Wichita State U (KS)
Worcester Polytechnic Inst (MA)
Youngstown State U (OH)

INDUSTRIAL MECHANICS AND MAINTENANCE TECHNOLOGY

Sullivan Coll of Technology and Design (KY)
The U of West Alabama (AL)

INDUSTRIAL PRODUCTION TECHNOLOGIES RELATED

Bowling Green State U (OH)
Central Michigan U (MI)
Ferris State U (MI)
Georgia Southern U (GA)
Millersville U of Pennsylvania (PA)
Mississippi State U (MS)
Missouri State U (MO)
Pennsylvania Coll of Technology (PA)
Purdue U North Central (IN)
Tarleton State U (TX)
The U of West Alabama (AL)
Valdosta State U (GA)
Wayne State Coll (NE)

INDUSTRIAL RADIOLOGIC TECHNOLOGY

Concordia U Wisconsin (WI)
U of Maryland Eastern Shore (MD)

INDUSTRIAL SAFETY TECHNOLOGY

Rochester Inst of Technology (NY)
U of Houston–Downtown (TX)

INDUSTRIAL TECHNOLOGY

Ball State U (IN)
Bemidji State U (MN)
Bowling Green State U (OH)
Buffalo State Coll, State U of New York (NY)
California State U, Fresno (CA)
California State U, Long Beach (CA)
California State U, Los Angeles (CA)
Central Connecticut State U (CT)
Central State U (OH)
Dunwoody Coll of Technology (MN)
East Carolina U (NC)
Eastern Illinois U (IL)
Eastern Michigan U (MI)
Elizabeth City State U (NC)
Fairmont State U (WV)
Farmingdale State Coll (NY)
Ferris State U (MI)
Illinois State U (IL)
Indiana State U (IN)
Indiana U–Purdue U Fort Wayne (IN)
Jacksonville State U (AL)
Lake Superior State U (MI)
Lamar U (TX)
Langston U (OK)
Lawrence Technological U (MI)
Middle Tennessee State U (TN)
Millersville U of Pennsylvania (PA)
Mississippi State U (MS)
Mississippi Valley State U (MS)
Northern Illinois U (IL)
Northern Michigan U (MI)

Northwestern State U of Louisiana (LA)
Ohio U (OH)
Sam Houston State U (TX)
Southeastern Louisiana U (LA)
Southeast Missouri State U (MO)
Southern Arkansas U–Magnolia (AR)
Southern Illinois U Carbondale (IL)
State U of New York Coll of Technology at Alfred (NY)
Tennessee State U (TN)
Texas A&M U–Commerce (TX)
Texas A&M U–Kingsville (TX)
Texas Southern U (TX)
Texas State U–San Marcos (TX)
U of Idaho (ID)
U of Louisiana at Lafayette (LA)
U of North Dakota (ND)
U of Northern Iowa (IA)
U of Southern Maine (ME)
U of Southern Mississippi (MS)
The U of Texas of the Permian Basin (TX)
The U of Toledo (OH)
The U of West Alabama (AL)
U of Wisconsin–Platteville (WI)
Vincennes U (IN)
Western Kentucky U (KY)
Western Washington U (WA)
West Virginia U Inst of Technology (WV)
William Penn U (IA)

INFORMATICS

Arizona State U (AZ)
Coll of Mount St. Joseph (OH)
Indiana U Bloomington (IN)
Indiana U East (IN)
Indiana U Kokomo (IN)
Indiana U Northwest (IN)
Indiana U–Purdue U Indianapolis (IN)
Indiana U South Bend (IN)
Indiana U Southeast (IN)
U of California, Irvine (CA)
U of Louisiana at Lafayette (LA)
U of Michigan (MI)

INFORMATION RESOURCES MANAGEMENT

Abilene Christian U (TX)
Athens State U (AL)
Grantham U (MO)
Juniata Coll (PA)
Lewis U (IL)
Lipscomb U (TN)
Lubbock Christian U (TX)
Michigan State U (MI)
Mount St. Mary's U (MD)
Rasmussen Coll Land O' Lakes (FL)
Rasmussen Coll New Port Richey (FL)
Rasmussen Coll Ocala (FL)
Rasmussen Coll Tampa/Brandon (FL)
Salve Regina U (RI)
U of California, Irvine (CA)
U of Wisconsin–Eau Claire (WI)
Western Michigan U (MI)

INFORMATION SCIENCE/ STUDIES

Adelphi U (NY)
Alabama State U (AL)
Albertus Magnus Coll (CT)
Albright Coll (PA)
Anderson U (IN)
Andrews U (MI)
Armstrong Atlantic State U (GA)
Ashland U (OH)
Athabasca U (AB, Canada)
Averett U (VA)
Barry U (FL)
Beacon Coll (FL)
Belmont U (TN)
Bemidji State U (MN)
Benedictine U (IL)
Bethune-Cookman U (FL)
Boise State U (ID)
Bradley U (IL)
Brock U (ON, Canada)
Buffalo State Coll, State U of New York (NY)
California Lutheran U (CA)
California State U, East Bay (CA)
California State U, Northridge (CA)

California State U, Stanislaus (CA)
Campbellsville U (KY)
Carnegie Mellon U (PA)
Carson-Newman U (TN)
Catawba Coll (NC)
Central Coll (IA)
Chowan U (NC)
Christopher Newport U (VA)
Clarion U of Pennsylvania (PA)
Clayton State U (GA)
Clemson U (SC)
Coastal Carolina U (SC)
Coll of Charleston (SC)
Colorado State U (CO)
Columbia U, School of General Studies (NY)
Concord U (WV)
Dakota State U (SD)
DePaul U (IL)
Doane Coll (NE)
East Carolina U (NC)
Elizabethtown Coll (PA)
Emporia State U (KS)
Excelsior Coll (NY)
Faulkner U (AL)
Ferrum Coll (VA)
Fort Lewis Coll (CO)
Friends U (KS)
Frostburg State U (MD)
Gallaudet U (DC)
George Fox U (OR)
Georgia Southern U (GA)
Goldey-Beacom Coll (DE)
Gonzaga U (WA)
Grambling State U (LA)
Grand Valley State U (MI)
Grand View U (IA)
Guilford Coll (NC)
Hampton U (VA)
Harris-Stowe State U (MO)
HEC Montreal (QC, Canada)
Husson U (ME)
Illinois Coll (IL)
Illinois State U (IL)
Immaculata U (PA)
Indiana U–Purdue U Fort Wayne (IN)
Inter American U of Puerto Rico, Ponce Campus (PR)
Inter American U of Puerto Rico, San Germán Campus (PR)
James Madison U (VA)
Johnson State Coll (VT)
Kansas State U (KS)
Kansas Wesleyan U (KS)
Kennesaw State U (GA)
King Coll (TN)
Lamar U (TX)
La Salle U (PA)
La Sierra U (CA)
Lehigh U (PA)
LeTourneau U (TX)
Limestone Coll (SC)
Lincoln U (MO)
Lipscomb U (TN)
Long Island U–C. W. Post Campus (NY)
Louisiana State U in Shreveport (LA)
Mansfield U of Pennsylvania (PA)
Marietta Coll (OH)
Marist Coll (NY)
McKendree U (IL)
Mercer U (GA)
Mercy Coll (NY)
Mercyhurst U (PA)
Messiah Coll (PA)
Michigan State U (MI)
Midwestern State U (TX)
Minnesota State U Mankato (MN)
Minnesota State U Moorhead (MN)
Missouri U of Science and Technology (MO)
Missouri Western State U (MO)
Molloy Coll (NY)
Murray State U (KY)
National U (CA)
New Jersey Inst of Technology (NJ)
Newman U (KS)
New Mexico Highlands U (NM)
New Mexico State U (NM)
New York City Coll of Technology of the City U of New York (NY)
New York Inst of Technology (NY)
New York U (NY)
Niagara U (NY)
North Carolina Central U (NC)

Northeastern U (MA)
Northwestern Coll (IA)
Northwestern Oklahoma State U (OK)
Northwestern State U of Louisiana (LA)
Oakland City U (IN)
Ohio Dominican U (OH)
The Ohio State U (OH)
Oklahoma Baptist U (OK)
Oklahoma Christian U (OK)
Pace U (NY)
Penn State Abington (PA)
Penn State Altoona (PA)
Penn State Beaver (PA)
Penn State Berks (PA)
Penn State Brandywine (PA)
Penn State DuBois (PA)
Penn State Erie, The Behrend Coll (PA)
Penn State Fayette, The Eberly Campus (PA)
Penn State Greater Allegheny (PA)
Penn State Harrisburg (PA)
Penn State Lehigh Valley (PA)
Penn State Mont Alto (PA)
Penn State New Kensington (PA)
Penn State Schuylkill (PA)
Penn State Shenango (PA)
Penn State U Park (PA)
Penn State Wilkes-Barre (PA)
Penn State Worthington Scranton (PA)
Penn State York (PA)
Philadelphia U (PA)
Portland State U (OR)
Purdue U Calumet (IN)
Quincy U (IL)
Quinnipiac U (CT)
Radford U (VA)
Ramapo Coll of New Jersey (NJ)
The Richard Stockton Coll of New Jersey (NJ)
Robert Morris U (PA)
Rutgers, The State U of New Jersey, Newark (NJ)
Rutgers, The State U of New Jersey, New Brunswick (NJ)
Sage Coll of Albany (NY)
St. Ambrose U (IA)
St. Joseph's Coll, Long Island Campus (NY)
St. Joseph's Coll, New York (NY)
Saint Joseph's U (PA)
St. Mary's U (TX)
Saint Michael's Coll (VT)
St. Thomas Aquinas Coll (NY)
St. Thomas U (FL)
Salisbury U (MD)
San Francisco State U (CA)
Slippery Rock U of Pennsylvania (PA)
Southeastern Oklahoma State U (OK)
Southern Illinois U Carbondale (IL)
Southern Nazarene U (OK)
Southwestern Adventist U (TX)
State U of New York at Fredonia (NY)
State U of New York at Oswego (NY)
State U of New York Coll at Old Westbury (NY)
State U of New York Inst of Technology (NY)
Stevenson U (MD)
Stony Brook U, State U of New York (NY)
Stratford U, Woodbridge (VA)
Suffolk U (MA)
Susquehanna U (PA)
Syracuse U (NY)
Texas A&M Intl U (TX)
Texas A&M U–Commerce (TX)
Texas Lutheran U (TX)
Thompson Rivers U (BC, Canada)
Tulane U (LA)
Union U (TN)
United States Military Acad (NY)
Université de Sherbrooke (QC, Canada)
U at Albany, State U of New York (NY)
U at Buffalo, the State U of New York (NY)
U of Arkansas at Little Rock (AR)
U of Bridgeport (CT)

U of California, Santa Cruz (CA)
U of Cincinnati (OH)
U of Great Falls (MT)
U of Hartford (CT)
U of Houston (TX)
U of Illinois at Chicago (IL)
The U of Iowa (IA)
U of Maryland, Baltimore County (MD)
U of Maryland, Coll Park (MD)
U of Maryland U Coll (MD)
U of Miami (FL)
U of Michigan–Flint (MI)
U of Nebraska at Omaha (NE)
U of New Brunswick Fredericton (NB, Canada)
U of New Haven (CT)
The U of North Carolina at Chapel Hill (NC)
U of North Georgia (GA)
U of North Texas (TX)
U of Oklahoma (OK)
U of Pittsburgh (PA)
The U of Scranton (PA)
U of South Alabama (AL)
U of South Carolina (SC)
U of South Carolina Upstate (SC)
U of South Florida (FL)
The U of Texas at Brownsville (TX)
The U of Texas at El Paso (TX)
The U of Texas of the Permian Basin (TX)
U of the District of Columbia (DC)
The U of Toledo (OH)
U of Tulsa (OK)
U of Vermont (VT)
U of Washington, Bothell (WA)
The U of Western Ontario (ON, Canada)
U of Wisconsin–Green Bay (WI)
U of Wisconsin–Milwaukee (WI)
U of Wisconsin–Superior (WI)
Utah State U (UT)
Valdosta State U (GA)
Virginia Commonwealth U (VA)
Virginia Polytechnic Inst and State U (VA)
Washington U in St. Louis (MO)
Wayne State Coll (NE)
Wayne State U (MI)
Weber State U (UT)
Wentworth Inst of Technology (MA)
Westfield State U (MA)
West Liberty U (WV)
West Virginia Wesleyan Coll (WV)
Wheeling Jesuit U (WV)
Widener U (PA)
Wilkes U (PA)
Woodbury U (CA)
Worcester Polytechnic Inst (MA)
York Coll of the City U of New York (NY)

INFORMATION TECHNOLOGY
Abilene Christian U (TX)
American Public U System (WV)
Arkansas Tech U (AR)
Armstrong Atlantic State U (GA)
Baylor U (TX)
Bluefield Coll (VA)
Bluffton U (OH)
Bob Jones U (SC)
Boise State U (ID)
Brigham Young U (UT)
Bryant U (RI)
Cabrini Coll (PA)
Caldwell Coll (NJ)
California Baptist U (CA)
California State U, Chico (CA)
California State U, Dominguez Hills (CA)
California State U, Fullerton (CA)
California State U, Los Angeles (CA)
California State U, Stanislaus (CA)
Cameron U (OK)
Carnegie Mellon U (PA)
Central Michigan U (MI)
Christopher Newport U (VA)
Clayton State U (GA)
Coll of the Ozarks (MO)
Columbus State U (GA)
Creighton U (NE)
Curry Coll (MA)
DePaul U (IL)

DEREE—The American Coll of Greece (Greece)
DeSales U (PA)
East Carolina U (NC)
Fairleigh Dickinson U, Metropolitan Campus (NJ)
Ferris State U (MI)
Florida Ag and Mech U (FL)
Florida Intl U (FL)
Franklin U (OH)
Frostburg State U (MD)
Furman U (SC)
George Mason U (VA)
Georgia Gwinnett Coll (GA)
Georgia Southwestern State U (GA)
Granite State Coll (NH)
Harding U (AR)
Houghton Coll (NY)
Humboldt State U (CA)
Illinois Inst of Technology (IL)
Illinois State U (IL)
Indiana State U (IN)
Indiana–Purdue U Fort Wayne (IN)
Jamestown Coll (ND)
Johnson C. Smith U (NC)
Juniata Coll (PA)
Kentucky State U (KY)
Keystone Coll (PA)
Kutztown U of Pennsylvania (PA)
La Roche Coll (PA)
Lawrence Technological U (MI)
Liberty U (VA)
Lindenwood U (MO)
Lipscomb U (TN)
Long Island U–C. W. Post Campus (NY)
Loyola U Chicago (IL)
Marian U (WI)
Marist Coll (NY)
Marquette U (WI)
Marymount U (VA)
McKendree U (IL)
McMurry U (TX)
Merrimack Coll (MA)
Missouri Baptist U (MO)
Montclair State U (NJ)
Morrisville State Coll (NY)
Mount Aloysius Coll (PA)
Mount Marty Coll (SD)
Mount Saint Mary Coll (NY)
Murray State U (KY)
Nazareth Coll of Rochester (NY)
Neumont U (UT)
Newbury Coll (MA)
New England Inst of Technology (RI)
New Jersey Inst of Technology (NJ)
New Mexico Inst of Mining and Technology (NM)
New Mexico State U (NM)
Oakland U (MI)
Ohio U (OH)
Ohio U–Chillicothe (OH)
Oklahoma City U (OK)
Olivet Coll (MI)
Peirce Coll (PA)
Plymouth State U (NH)
Point Park U (PA)
Regent U (VA)
Rensselaer Polytechnic Inst (NY)
Rivier U (NH)
Robert Morris U Illinois (IL)
Rochester Inst of Technology (NY)
Sacred Heart U (CT)
San Diego State U (CA)
San Jose State U (CA)
Seminole State Coll of Florida (FL)
Simmons Coll (MA)
Slippery Rock U of Pennsylvania (PA)
Southern New Hampshire U (NH)
Southern Polytechnic State U (GA)
State U of New York Coll of Technology at Alfred (NY)
State U of New York Coll of Technology at Canton (NY)
Stephen F. Austin State U (TX)
Stratford U, Falls Church (VA)
Sullivan Coll of Technology and Design (KY)
Temple U (PA)
Texas Christian U (TX)
Thomas More Coll (KY)
Tiffin U (OH)
Trevecca Nazarene U (TN)

Trident U Intl (CA)
United States Military Acad (NY)
Université de Sherbrooke (QC, Canada)
The U of British Columbia–Okanagan (BC, Canada)
U of Central Florida (FL)
U of Cincinnati (OH)
U of Denver (CO)
U of Great Falls (MT)
U of Houston–Clear Lake (TX)
The U of Kansas (KS)
U of Massachusetts Boston (MA)
U of Missouri–Kansas City (MO)
U of Nebraska at Omaha (NE)
U of New Hampshire (NH)
The U of North Carolina at Pembroke (NC)
U of St. Francis (IL)
U of Saint Mary (KS)
U of South Alabama (AL)
U of South Florida (FL)
The U of Toledo (OH)
U of Tulsa (OK)
U of Washington, Tacoma (WA)
The U of Western Ontario (ON, Canada)
U of West Florida (FL)
U of Wisconsin–Stevens Point (WI)
Vermont Tech Coll (VT)
Virginia State U (VA)
Washington & Jefferson Coll (PA)
Webster U (MO)
Western Illinois U (IL)
Western Kentucky U (KY)
Wilmington U (DE)
Youngstown State U (OH)

INFORMATION TECHNOLOGY PROJECT MANAGEMENT
Pace U (NY)

INORGANIC CHEMISTRY
The U of Western Ontario (ON, Canada)

INSTITUTIONAL FOOD WORKERS
Immaculata U (PA)

INSTRUMENTATION TECHNOLOGY
Northern Michigan U (MI)

INSURANCE
Appalachian State U (NC)
Baylor U (TX)
Bowling Green State U (OH)
Bradley U (IL)
Delta State U (MS)
Excelsior Coll (NY)
Gannon U (PA)
Georgia State U (GA)
Illinois State U (IL)
Illinois Wesleyan U (IL)
Indiana State U (IN)
Kent State U at Salem (OH)
Mississippi State U (MS)
Missouri State U (MO)
Northern Michigan U (MI)
The Ohio State U (OH)
Olivet Coll (MI)
St. John's U (NY)
Saint Joseph's U (PA)
Southern Methodist U (TX)
Temple U (PA)
U of Central Arkansas (AR)
U of Georgia (GA)
U of Hartford (CT)
U of Houston–Downtown (TX)
U of Illinois at Urbana–Champaign (IL)
U of Louisiana at Lafayette (LA)
U of Louisiana at Monroe (LA)
U of Minnesota, Twin Cities Campus (MN)
U of Mississippi (MS)
U of Nebraska–Lincoln (NE)
U of North Texas (TX)
U of Pennsylvania (PA)
U of South Carolina (SC)
U of Wisconsin–La Crosse (WI)
U of Wisconsin–Madison (WI)

INTELLIGENCE
Coastal Carolina U (SC)
Henley-Putnam U (CA)

INTERCULTURAL/ MULTICULTURAL AND DIVERSITY STUDIES
Columbia Bible Coll (BC, Canada)
Columbia Intl U (SC)
Concordia U (QC, Canada)
Evangel U (MO)
The Evergreen State Coll (WA)
Goddard Coll (VT)
Indiana Wesleyan U (IN)
Judson U (IL)
Macalester Coll (MN)
Northwest U (WA)
Rocky Mountain Coll (AB, Canada)
Trevecca Nazarene U (TN)
U of Regina (SK, Canada)
U of the Incarnate Word (TX)
U of Washington, Tacoma (WA)
Villanova U (PA)
Western Oregon U (OR)

INTERDISCIPLINARY STUDIES
Agnes Scott Coll (GA)
Albright Coll (PA)
Alfred U (NY)
Alice Lloyd Coll (KY)
The American U of Rome (Italy)
Amherst Coll (MA)
Augsburg Coll (MN)
Bard Coll (NY)
Bay Path Coll (MA)
Bethany Coll (WV)
Blackburn Coll (IL)
Bloomfield Coll (NJ)
Bluefield Coll (VA)
Boston Coll (MA)
Boston U (MA)
Brock U (ON, Canada)
Bryn Athyn Coll of the New Church (PA)
Bucknell U (PA)
California Lutheran U (CA)
California State U, East Bay (CA)
California State U, Long Beach (CA)
California State U, Los Angeles (CA)
California State U, San Bernardino (CA)
Calvin Coll (MI)
Carleton Coll (MN)
Carson-Newman U (TN)
Castleton State Coll (VT)
Catawba Coll (NC)
Centenary Coll of Louisiana (LA)
Central Methodist U (MO)
Chowan U (NC)
Clark U (MA)
Coe Coll (IA)
The Coll at Brockport, State U of New York (NY)
Coll of the Atlantic (ME)
The Coll of William and Mary (VA)
The Coll of Wooster (OH)
Columbia Coll Chicago (IL)
Concordia U (OR)
Connecticut Coll (CT)
Corban U (OR)
Cornell Coll (IA)
Cornerstone U (MI)
DePauw U (IN)
Earlham Coll (IN)
Eckerd Coll (FL)
Elmira Coll (NY)
Emerson Coll (MA)
Eugene Lang Coll The New School for Liberal Arts (NY)
Fairleigh Dickinson U, Metropolitan Campus (NJ)
Florida Inst of Technology (FL)
Geneva Coll (PA)
George Fox U (OR)
Georgetown U (DC)
Gettysburg Coll (PA)
Goddard Coll (VT)
Grinnell Coll (IA)
Guilford Coll (NC)
Gustavus Adolphus Coll (MN)
Hamilton Coll (NY)
Harris-Stowe State U (MO)
Hendrix Coll (AR)
Hillsdale Coll (MI)
Hillsdale Free Will Baptist Coll (OK)
Hollins U (VA)
Houghton Coll (NY)
Illinois Coll (IL)
Indiana U Bloomington (IN)
Indiana U Southeast (IN)

Iowa State U of Science and Technology (IA)
Ithaca Coll (NY)
John Brown U (AR)
John Carroll U (OH)
The Johns Hopkins U (MD)
Jones Coll, Jacksonville (FL)
Judson Coll (AL)
Kalamazoo Coll (MI)
Kentucky Wesleyan Coll (KY)
Keuka Coll (NY)
King Coll (TN)
Kuyper Coll (MI)
Lake Superior State U (MI)
Lamar U (TX)
Lasell Coll (MA)
Lees-McRae Coll (NC)
Lehman Coll of the City U of New York (NY)
LeTourneau U (TX)
Lewis-Clark State Coll (ID)
Lipscomb U (TN)
Long Island U–Brooklyn Campus (NY)
Long Island U–C. W. Post Campus (NY)
Louisiana Coll (LA)
Maranatha Baptist Bible Coll (WI)
Marist Coll (NY)
Mars Hill Coll (NC)
Martin Luther Coll (MN)
Massachusetts Coll of Liberal Arts (MA)
Middle Tennessee State U (TN)
Midwestern State U (TX)
Mills Coll (CA)
Minnesota State U Moorhead (MN)
Mount Allison U (NB, Canada)
Mount Saint Mary Coll (NY)
Newbury Coll (MA)
North Dakota State U (ND)
Northern Arizona U (AZ)
North Greenville U (SC)
Northland Coll (WI)
Northwest U (WA)
Nyack Coll (NY)
Oakland City U (IN)
Oglethorpe U (GA)
Oklahoma Baptist U (OK)
Olivet Coll (MI)
Pepperdine U, Malibu (CA)
Piedmont Coll (GA)
Pittsburg State U (KS)
Pomona Coll (CA)
Rhodes Coll (TN)
Ripon Coll (WI)
Rochester Inst of Technology (NY)
Rocky Mountain Coll (MT)
Russell Sage Coll (NY)
Rutgers, The State U of New Jersey, New Brunswick (NJ)
St. Andrews U (NC)
Saint Mary's Coll (IN)
Saint Mary's Coll of California (CA)
St. Thomas U (NB, Canada)
San Diego Christian Coll (CA)
Sierra Nevada Coll (NV)
Simpson Coll (IA)
Smith Coll (MA)
Sonoma State U (CA)
Southern Oregon U (OR)
Southwestern Coll (KS)
Stanford U (CA)
State U of New York at Fredonia (NY)
State U of New York Empire State Coll (NY)
Sterling Coll (KS)
Stevenson U (MD)
Suffolk U (MA)
Sweet Briar Coll (VA)
Syracuse U (NY)
Tarleton State U (TX)
Tennessee Wesleyan Coll (TN)
Texas A&M U–Commerce (TX)
Texas Southern U (TX)
Trent U (ON, Canada)
Trevecca Nazarene U (TN)
Trinity Coll (CT)
United States Air Force Acad (CO)
Université de Sherbrooke (QC, Canada)
U at Albany, State U of New York (NY)
The U of Alabama (AL)
U of Alaska Anchorage (AK)
The U of Arizona (AZ)

U of Bridgeport (CT)
The U of British Columbia (BC, Canada)
U of California, Santa Barbara (CA)
U of Central Florida (FL)
U of Evansville (IN)
U of Guam (GU)
U of Hartford (CT)
U of Hawaii at Hilo (HI)
The U of Iowa (IA)
U of Maine at Farmington (ME)
U of Massachusetts Dartmouth (MA)
U of Memphis (TN)
U of Michigan–Flint (MI)
U of Missouri (MO)
U of Nevada, Las Vegas (NV)
U of North Alabama (AL)
U of North Dakota (ND)
U of North Florida (FL)
U of North Texas (TX)
U of Oklahoma (OK)
U of Portland (OR)
U of Puget Sound (WA)
U of Redlands (CA)
U of Richmond (VA)
U of Saint Mary (KS)
U of St. Thomas (MN)
U of South Carolina Upstate (SC)
The U of Tennessee at Martin (TN)
The U of Texas at Dallas (TX)
The U of Texas at El Paso (TX)
The U of Toledo (OH)
U of Vermont (VT)
U of Waterloo (ON, Canada)
The U of Western Ontario (ON, Canada)
U of Wisconsin–Parkside (WI)
Vassar Coll (NY)
Virginia Polytechnic Inst and State U (VA)
Virginia State U (VA)
Virginia Wesleyan Coll (VA)
Walden U (MN)
Wayne State Coll (NE)
Wesleyan Coll (GA)
Wesleyan U (CT)
Western Oregon U (OR)
Western State Colorado U (CO)
West Liberty U (WV)
Woodbury U (CA)
Worcester Polytechnic Inst (MA)

INTERIOR ARCHITECTURE
Arizona State U (AZ)
Auburn U (AL)
Boston Architectural Coll (MA)
Bowling Green State U (OH)
Central Michigan U (MI)
Chatham U (PA)
Coll of Mount St. Joseph (OH)
Indiana State U (IN)
La Roche Coll (PA)
Lawrence Technological U (MI)
Lebanese American U (Lebanon)
Louisiana State U and Ag and Mech Coll (LA)
Miami U (OH)
Mississippi State U (MS)
Philadelphia U (PA)
Rhode Island School of Design (RI)
School of the Art Inst of Chicago (IL)
Stephen F. Austin State U (TX)
U of Houston (TX)
U of Louisiana at Lafayette (LA)
U of Missouri (MO)
U of Nebraska–Lincoln (NE)
U of Nevada, Las Vegas (NV)
U of New Haven (CT)
U of Oregon (OR)
U of Southern Mississippi (MS)
The U of Texas at Arlington (TX)
The U of Texas at San Antonio (TX)
Villa Maria Coll of Buffalo (NY)
Woodbury U (CA)

INTERIOR DESIGN
Abilene Christian U (TX)
Acad of Art U (CA)
Anderson U (SC)
Appalachian State U (NC)
Art Center Coll of Design (CA)
Auburn U (AL)
Baylor U (TX)
Bay Path Coll (MA)

California State U, Chico (CA)
California State U, Fresno (CA)
California State U, Long Beach (CA)
Carson-Newman U (TN)
Cleveland Inst of Art (OH)
Coll for Creative Studies (MI)
Colorado State U (CO)
Columbia Coll Chicago (IL)
Columbus Coll of Art & Design (OH)
Concordia U Wisconsin (WI)
Converse Coll (SC)
Corcoran Coll of Art and Design (DC)
Dunwoody Coll of Technology (MN)
East Carolina U (NC)
Eastern Michigan U (MI)
East Tennessee State U (TN)
EDP Coll of Puerto Rico, Inc. (PR)
Endicott Coll (MA)
Fashion Inst of Technology (NY)
Ferris State U (MI)
Florida Intl U (FL)
Florida State U (FL)
Georgia Southern U (GA)
Hampton U (VA)
Harding U (AR)
High Point U (NC)
Indiana U Bloomington (IN)
Indiana U of Pennsylvania (PA)
Indiana U–Purdue U Fort Wayne (IN)
Indiana U–Purdue U Indianapolis (IN)
Indiana Wesleyan U (IN)
Intl Acad of Design & Technology (FL)
Iowa State U of Science and Technology (IA)
Kansas State U (KS)
Kean U (NJ)
Kent State U (OH)
Lamar U (TX)
Lebanese American U (Lebanon)
Maryland Inst Coll of Art (MD)
Marymount U (VA)
Maryville U of Saint Louis (MO)
Marywood U (PA)
Mercyhurst U (PA)
Michigan State U (MI)
Middle Tennessee State U (TN)
Mississippi Coll (MS)
Moore Coll of Art & Design (PA)
Mount Mary Coll (WI)
Newbury Coll (MA)
New England Inst of Technology (RI)
New Jersey Inst of Technology (NJ)
New York Inst of Technology (NY)
New York School of Interior Design (NY)
North Dakota State U (ND)
Northern Arizona U (AZ)
The Ohio State U (OH)
Oklahoma Christian U (OK)
O'More Coll of Design (TN)
Oregon State U (OR)
Otis Coll of Art and Design (CA)
Paier Coll of Art, Inc. (CT)
Park U (MO)
Parsons The New School for Design (NY)
Philadelphia U (PA)
Pittsburg State U (KS)
Point Loma Nazarene U (CA)
Queens U of Charlotte (NC)
Ringling Coll of Art and Design (FL)
Rochester Inst of Technology (NY)
Rocky Mountain Coll of Art + Design (CO)
Samford U (AL)
Sam Houston State U (TX)
San Diego State U (CA)
San Francisco State U (CA)
San Jose State U (CA)
Savannah Coll of Art and Design (GA)
Seattle Pacific U (WA)
Seminole State Coll of Florida (FL)
South Dakota State U (SD)
Southern Illinois U Carbondale (IL)
Stephens Coll (MO)
Suffolk U (MA)
Sullivan Coll of Technology and Design (KY)
Texas Christian U (TX)

Texas State U–San Marcos (TX)
Thompson Rivers U (BC, Canada)
The U of Alabama (AL)
U of Bridgeport (CT)
U of Central Arkansas (AR)
U of Central Oklahoma (OK)
U of Charleston (WV)
U of Cincinnati (OH)
U of Florida (FL)
U of Idaho (ID)
The U of Kansas (KS)
U of Kentucky (KY)
U of Minnesota, Twin Cities Campus (MN)
The U of North Carolina at Greensboro (NC)
U of Northern Iowa (IA)
U of North Texas (TX)
U of Oklahoma (OK)
The U of Tennessee (TN)
The U of Tennessee at Chattanooga (TN)
The U of Tennessee at Martin (TN)
The U of Texas at Austin (TX)
The U of Texas at San Antonio (TX)
U of the Incarnate Word (TX)
U of Wisconsin–Madison (WI)
U of Wisconsin–Stevens Point (WI)
Utah State U (UT)
Valdosta State U (GA)
Virginia Commonwealth U (VA)
Virginia Polytechnic Inst and State U (VA)
Washington State U (WA)
Watkins Coll of Art, Design, & Film (TN)
Wentworth Inst of Technology (MA)
Western Carolina U (NC)
Western Michigan U (MI)

INTERMEDIA/MULTIMEDIA
Acad of Art U (CA)
Alberta Coll of Art & Design (AB, Canada)
American U (DC)
Art Center Coll of Design (CA)
Bennington Coll (VT)
Calumet Coll of Saint Joseph (IN)
Champlain Coll (VT)
City Coll of the City U of New York (NY)
The Coll of New Jersey (NJ)
Columbia Coll Chicago (IL)
Concordia U (QC, Canada)
Emerson Coll (MA)
The Evergreen State Coll (WA)
Georgia Regents U (GA)
Hawai`i Pacific U (HI)
Indiana U of Pennsylvania (PA)
Long Island U–C. W. Post Campus (NY)
Lynn U (FL)
Maryland Inst Coll of Art (MD)
Massachusetts Coll of Art and Design (MA)
Mills Coll (CA)
Missouri State U (MO)
Northeastern U (MA)
Pacific Northwest Coll of Art (OR)
Purchase Coll, State U of New York (NY)
Ramapo Coll of New Jersey (NJ)
Rochester Inst of Technology (NY)
School of the Art Inst of Chicago (IL)
School of the Museum of Fine Arts, Boston (MA)
State U of New York at Fredonia (NY)
U of Hartford (CT)
U of Regina (SK, Canada)
The U of the Arts (PA)
Weber State U (UT)
Western Washington U (WA)
Worcester Polytechnic Inst (MA)

INTERNATIONAL AGRICULTURE
Dalhousie U (NS, Canada)
Iowa State U of Science and Technology (IA)
Tarleton State U (TX)
U of California, Davis (CA)
U of Illinois at Urbana–Champaign (IL)
U of Missouri (MO)
Utah State U (UT)

INTERNATIONAL AND COMPARATIVE EDUCATION
Stony Brook U, State U of New York (NY)

INTERNATIONAL AND INTERCULTURAL COMMUNICATION
Linfield Coll (OR)
Pacific Union Coll (CA)

INTERNATIONAL BUSINESS/TRADE/COMMERCE
Adams State U (CO)
Albertus Magnus Coll (CT)
Albright Coll (PA)
Alliant Intl U–México City (Mexico)
Alverno Coll (WI)
The American U of Paris (France)
The American U of Rome (Italy)
Anderson U (IN)
Angelo State U (TX)
Appalachian State U (NC)
Arkansas State U (AR)
Assumption Coll (MA)
Auburn U (AL)
Augsburg Coll (MN)
Augustana Coll (IL)
Avila U (MO)
Babson Coll (MA)
Baker U (KS)
Baldwin Wallace U (OH)
Barry U (FL)
Baylor U (TX)
Belmont U (TN)
Benedictine U (IL)
Bentley U (MA)
Bethel Coll (IN)
Bethune-Cookman U (FL)
Binghamton U, State U of New York (NY)
Bob Jones U (SC)
Boise State U (ID)
Boston U (MA)
Bowling Green State U (OH)
Bradley U (IL)
Bridgewater State U (MA)
Brock U (ON, Canada)
Bryant U (RI)
Buena Vista U (IA)
Butler U (IN)
Caldwell Coll (NJ)
California State U, Dominguez Hills (CA)
California State U, Fresno (CA)
California State U, Fullerton (CA)
California State U, Long Beach (CA)
Canisius Coll (NY)
Cardinal Stritch U (WI)
The Catholic U of America (DC)
Cedarville U (OH)
Central Coll (IA)
Central Michigan U (MI)
Champlain Coll (VT)
Chatham U (PA)
Chestnut Hill Coll (PA)
City U of Seattle (WA)
Clarion U of Pennsylvania (PA)
Clemson U (SC)
Cleveland State U (OH)
The Coll at Brockport, State U of New York (NY)
Coll of Charleston (SC)
The Coll of Idaho (ID)
Coll of the Ozarks (MO)
Columbia Coll (MO)
Concordia Coll (MN)
Concordia Coll–New York (NY)
Concordia U (QC, Canada)
Concordia U Wisconsin (WI)
Converse Coll (SC)
Cornell Coll (IA)
Creighton U (NE)
Dalhousie U (NS, Canada)
Davenport U, Grand Rapids (MI)
DEREE—The American Coll of Greece (Greece)
DeSales U (PA)
Dickinson Coll (PA)
Dillard U (LA)
Dominican Coll (NY)
Dominican U (IL)
Drake U (IA)
Duquesne U (PA)
Eastern Mennonite U (VA)
Eastern Michigan U (MI)
Eckerd Coll (FL)

Elizabethtown Coll (PA)
Elmira Coll (NY)
Elon U (NC)
Excelsior Coll (NY)
Fairfield U (CT)
Felician Coll (NJ)
Florida Atlantic U (FL)
Florida Inst of Technology (FL)
Florida Intl U (FL)
Fort Lewis Coll (CO)
Franklin Coll Switzerland
   (Switzerland)
Friends U (KS)
Gannon U (PA)
Gardner-Webb U (NC)
George Fox U (OR)
Georgetown U (DC)
Georgia Southern U (GA)
Gettysburg Coll (PA)
Goldey-Beacom Coll (DE)
Gonzaga U (WA)
Graceland U (IA)
Grand Valley State U (MI)
Grove City Coll (PA)
Gustavus Adolphus Coll (MN)
Hamline U (MN)
Harding U (AR)
Hawai`i Pacific U (HI)
HEC Montreal (QC, Canada)
High Point U (NC)
Hilbert Coll (NY)
Hofstra U (NY)
Holy Family U (PA)
Husson U (ME)
Illinois State U (IL)
Illinois Wesleyan U (IL)
Indiana U of Pennsylvania (PA)
Inter American U of Puerto Rico,
   Ponce Campus (PR)
Iona Coll (NY)
Iowa State U of Science and
   Technology (IA)
Ithaca Coll (NY)
James Madison U (VA)
Jamestown Coll (ND)
John Brown U (AR)
John Carroll U (OH)
Juniata Coll (PA)
Kennesaw State U (GA)
King Coll (TN)
King's Coll (PA)
Kuyper Coll (MI)
Lake Erie Coll (OH)
Lakeland Coll (WI)
La Roche Coll (PA)
La Salle U (PA)
Lasell Coll (MA)
Lawrence Technological U (MI)
LeTourneau U (TX)
Lewis U (IL)
Lindenwood U (MO)
Linfield Coll (OR)
Lipscomb U (TN)
Louisiana State U and Ag and
   Mech Coll (LA)
Loyola U Chicago (IL)
Loyola U New Orleans (LA)
Lynn U (FL)
Madonna U (MI)
Maine Maritime Acad (ME)
Mansfield U of Pennsylvania (PA)
Marietta Coll (OH)
Marshall U (WV)
Maryville Coll (TN)
Maryville U of Saint Louis (MO)
Marywood U (PA)
Massachusetts Coll of Liberal Arts
   (MA)
Massachusetts Maritime Acad
   (MA)
Menlo Coll (CA)
Mercer U (GA)
Merrimack Coll (MA)
Messiah Coll (PA)
Midwestern State U (TX)
Millikin U (IL)
Milwaukee School of Eng (WI)
Minnesota State U Mankato (MN)
Minot State U (ND)
Monmouth Coll (IL)
Monmouth U (NJ)
Moravian Coll (PA)
Mount Allison U (NB, Canada)
Mount St. Mary's Coll (CA)
Mount Vernon Nazarene U (OH)
Murray State U (KY)
Nazareth Coll of Rochester (NY)

Neumann U (PA)
Newbury Coll (MA)
New Jersey Inst of Technology (NJ)
New Mexico State U (NM)
New York Inst of Technology (NY)
New York U (NY)
Niagara U (NY)
North Central Coll (IL)
Northeastern U (MA)
Northern State U (SD)
North Greenville U (SC)
Northwestern Coll (MN)
Northwest Missouri State U (MO)
Northwest Nazarene U (ID)
Northwood U, Florida Campus (FL)
Northwood U, Michigan Campus
   (MI)
Ohio Dominican U (OH)
The Ohio State U (OH)
Ohio U (OH)
Ohio Wesleyan U (OH)
Oklahoma Baptist U (OK)
Oklahoma City U (OK)
Oklahoma State U (OK)
Oral Roberts U (OK)
Pace U (NY)
Palm Beach Atlantic U (FL)
Penn State DuBois (PA)
Penn State Erie, The Behrend Coll
   (PA)
Penn State Harrisburg (PA)
Penn State Lehigh Valley (PA)
Penn State Schuylkill (PA)
Pepperdine U, Malibu (CA)
Philadelphia U (PA)
Pittsburg State U (KS)
Potomac Coll (DC)
Quinnipiac U (CT)
Ramapo Coll of New Jersey (NJ)
Rhodes Coll (TN)
Rider U (NJ)
Rochester Inst of Technology (NY)
Roger Williams U (RI)
Rollins Coll (FL)
Saginaw Valley State U (MI)
St. Ambrose U (IA)
Saint Anselm Coll (NH)
St. Edward's U (TX)
Saint Joseph's U (PA)
Saint Louis U (MO)
Saint Mary's Coll of California (CA)
St. Mary's U (TX)
Saint Mary's U of Minnesota (MN)
St. Norbert Coll (WI)
St. Thomas U (FL)
Saint Vincent Coll (PA)
Salem Intl U (WV)
Salem State U (MA)
Samford U (AL)
Sam Houston State U (TX)
San Diego State U (CA)
San Francisco State U (CA)
San Jose State U (CA)
Schreiner U (TX)
Seattle U (WA)
Seton Hill U (PA)
Sierra Nevada Coll (NV)
Simpson Coll (IA)
Southeastern U (FL)
Southeast Missouri State U (MO)
Southern New Hampshire U (NH)
Southwestern Adventist U (TX)
Spring Hill Coll (AL)
State U of New York at New Paltz
   (NY)
State U of New York at Plattsburgh
   (NY)
Stephen F. Austin State U (TX)
Stetson U (FL)
Stonehill Coll (MA)
Suffolk U (MA)
Tarleton State U (TX)
Taylor U (IN)
Temple U (PA)
Texas A&M U–Kingsville (TX)
Texas Christian U (TX)
Thomas Edison State Coll (NJ)
Tiffin U (OH)
Trinity U (TX)
Union Coll (KY)
Université du Québec en
   Outaouais (QC, Canada)
U at Buffalo, the State U of New
   York (NY)
The U of Akron (OH)
U of Arkansas at Little Rock (AR)
U of Bridgeport (CT)

The U of British Columbia (BC,
   Canada)
U of Cincinnati (OH)
U of Delaware (DE)
U of Denver (CO)
U of Evansville (IN)
The U of Findlay (OH)
U of Georgia (GA)
U of Hawaii at Manoa (HI)
U of Houston–Downtown (TX)
U of La Verne (CA)
U of Maryland, Coll Park (MD)
U of Memphis (TN)
U of Miami (FL)
U of Michigan–Flint (MI)
U of Minnesota, Twin Cities
   Campus (MN)
U of Missouri (MO)
U of Missouri–St. Louis (MO)
U of Mount Union (OH)
U of Nebraska–Lincoln (NE)
U of Nevada, Las Vegas (NV)
U of Nevada, Reno (NV)
U of New Brunswick Fredericton
   (NB, Canada)
U of New Haven (CT)
The U of North Carolina at
   Charlotte (NC)
The U of North Carolina at
   Greensboro (NC)
U of North Florida (FL)
U of Ottawa (ON, Canada)
U of Pennsylvania (PA)
U of Pittsburgh (PA)
U of Portland (OR)
U of Regina (SK, Canada)
U of Rhode Island (RI)
U of St. Francis (IL)
U of St. Thomas (MN)
U of San Diego (CA)
The U of Scranton (PA)
U of South Carolina (SC)
U of Southern Mississippi (MS)
U of South Florida (FL)
The U of Tampa (FL)
The U of Tennessee at Martin (TN)
The U of Texas at Arlington (TX)
The U of Texas at Dallas (TX)
The U of Texas at San Antonio (TX)
The U of Texas–Pan American (TX)
U of the Incarnate Word (TX)
The U of Toledo (OH)
U of Tulsa (OK)
U of Washington, Tacoma (WA)
U of Waterloo (ON, Canada)
The U of Western Ontario (ON,
   Canada)
U of Wisconsin–Eau Claire (WI)
U of Wisconsin–La Crosse (WI)
U of Wisconsin–Madison (WI)
Utica Coll (NY)
Valdosta State U (GA)
Valparaiso U (IN)
Villanova U (PA)
Waldorf Coll (IA)
Walla Walla U (WA)
Wartburg Coll (IA)
Washington & Jefferson Coll (PA)
Washington State U (WA)
Washington U in St. Louis (MO)
Waynesburg U (PA)
Wayne State U (MI)
Wesleyan Coll (GA)
Western Kentucky U (KY)
Western Washington U (WA)
Westminster Coll (MO)
Westminster Coll (UT)
Whitworth U (WA)
Wichita State U (KS)
Widener U (PA)
William Paterson U of New Jersey
   (NJ)
Wright State U (OH)
Xavier U (OH)

**INTERNATIONAL
ECONOMICS**
Albion Coll (MI)
The American U of Paris (France)
Belmont U (TN)
Brock U (ON, Canada)
California State U, Chico (CA)
Carson-Newman U (TN)
The Coll of Idaho (ID)
The Colorado Coll (CO)
Elon U (NC)

Franklin Coll Switzerland
   (Switzerland)
Georgetown U (DC)
Georgia State U (GA)
Gettysburg Coll (PA)
HEC Montreal (QC, Canada)
John Carroll U (OH)
Lawrence U (WI)
Mary Baldwin Coll (VA)
Rhodes Coll (TN)
Rockford Coll (IL)
St. Lawrence U (NY)
Salve Regina U (RI)
Seattle U (WA)
State U of New York at Oswego
   (NY)
Suffolk U (MA)
Texas Christian U (TX)
U of California, Los Angeles (CA)
U of California, Santa Cruz (CA)
U of Puget Sound (WA)
U of Richmond (VA)
U of St. Thomas (MN)
U of West Georgia (GA)
Valparaiso U (IN)
Washington U in St. Louis (MO)
Weber State U (UT)

INTERNATIONAL FINANCE
Babson Coll (MA)
Brigham Young U (UT)
The Catholic U of America (DC)
Franklin Coll Switzerland
   (Switzerland)
HEC Montreal (QC, Canada)
Texas Christian U (TX)
The U of Western Ontario (ON,
   Canada)
Washington U in St. Louis (MO)

**INTERNATIONAL/GLOBAL
STUDIES**
Abilene Christian U (TX)
Adelphi U (NY)
Albertus Magnus Coll (CT)
Albion Coll (MI)
Alfred U (NY)
Alverno Coll (WI)
American Public U System (WV)
American U (DC)
The American U of Rome (Italy)
Appalachian State U (NC)
Arizona State U (AZ)
Arkansas Tech U (AR)
Assumption Coll (MA)
Baker U (KS)
Baldwin Wallace U (OH)
Belhaven U (MS)
Benedictine U (IL)
Bennington Coll (VT)
Bentley U (MA)
Briercrest Coll (SK, Canada)
Bryant U (RI)
California Baptist U (CA)
Carnegie Mellon U (PA)
Case Western Reserve U (OH)
Cedar Crest Coll (PA)
Cedarville U (OH)
Central Coll (IA)
Central Connecticut State U (CT)
Chatham U (PA)
Chicago State U (IL)
City Coll of the City U of New York
   (NY)
Colby Coll (ME)
Coll of Charleston (SC)
The Coll of New Rochelle (NY)
Coll of Saint Elizabeth (NJ)
The Coll of St. Scholastica (MN)
Coll of Staten Island of the City U of
   New York (NY)
Colorado State U (CO)
Concordia Coll (MN)
Concordia Coll–New York (NY)
Concordia U (CA)
Doane Coll (NE)
East Texas Baptist U (TX)
Emmanuel Coll (MA)
Endicott Coll (MA)
The Evergreen State Coll (WA)
Frostburg State U (MD)
Gannon U (PA)
George Fox U (OR)
Greenville Coll (IL)
Hamline U (MN)
Hampshire Coll (MA)
Hanover Coll (IN)
Harding U (AR)

Hawai`i Pacific U (HI)
Hofstra U (NY)
Hope Coll (MI)
Illinois Wesleyan U (IL)
John Brown U (AR)
Juniata Coll (PA)
Kenyon Coll (OH)
Knox Coll (IL)
La Sierra U (CA)
Lebanon Valley Coll (PA)
Lehigh U (PA)
Le Moyne Coll (NY)
Louisiana State U and Ag and
   Mech Coll (LA)
Luther Coll (IA)
Macalester Coll (MN)
Manchester U (IN)
Maryville U of Saint Louis (MO)
McKendree U (IL)
Mercyhurst U (PA)
Michigan State U (MI)
Midwestern State U (TX)
Minnesota State U Moorhead (MN)
Mississippi Coll (MS)
Missouri State U (MO)
Monmouth Coll (IL)
Morningside Coll (IA)
Mount Mary Coll (WI)
New Coll of Florida (FL)
North Carolina State U (NC)
North Dakota State U (ND)
The Ohio State U (OH)
Oregon State U (OR)
Pacific Lutheran U (WA)
Pepperdine U, Malibu (CA)
Pittsburg State U (KS)
Pitzer Coll (CA)
Point Loma Nazarene U (CA)
Point Park U (PA)
Presbyterian Coll (SC)
Providence Coll (RI)
Randolph Coll (VA)
Randolph-Macon Coll (VA)
Rockford Coll (IL)
Roger Williams U (RI)
Russell Sage Coll (NY)
Sacred Heart U (CT)
St. Bonaventure U (NY)
St. Edward's U (TX)
St. Lawrence U (NY)
Saint Leo U (FL)
Saint Mary's Coll (IN)
Saint Mary's U of Minnesota (MN)
Salisbury U (MD)
Salve Regina U (RI)
Samford U (AL)
Scripps Coll (CA)
Sierra Nevada Coll (NV)
South Dakota State U (SD)
Southeast Missouri State U (MO)
Southern Illinois U Carbondale (IL)
Southern Methodist U (TX)
Spring Arbor U (MI)
State U of New York Coll at
   Cortland (NY)
Tabor Coll (KS)
Tennessee Wesleyan Coll (TN)
Texas A&M U (TX)
Texas State U–San Marcos (TX)
Thomas More Coll (KY)
U at Albany, State U of New York
   (NY)
U of Alaska Anchorage (AK)
The U of Arizona (AZ)
U of California, Irvine (CA)
U of California, Los Angeles (CA)
U of California, Riverside (CA)
U of California, Santa Barbara (CA)
U of Central Arkansas (AR)
U of Central Florida (FL)
U of Colorado Boulder (CO)
U of Colorado Denver (CO)
U of Florida (FL)
U of Hartford (CT)
U of Illinois at Springfield (IL)
U of Illinois at Urbana–Champaign
   (IL)
The U of Iowa (IA)
The U of Kansas (KS)
U of Kentucky (KY)
U of La Verne (CA)
U of Maine at Farmington (ME)
U of Michigan (MI)
U of Minnesota, Duluth (MN)
U of Nebraska at Omaha (NE)
U of Nebraska–Lincoln (NE)
U of New Mexico (NM)

U of New Orleans (LA)
The U of North Carolina at Chapel Hill (NC)
The U of North Carolina at Charlotte (NC)
U of North Dakota (ND)
U of Northern Colorado (CO)
U of North Florida (FL)
U of North Texas (TX)
U of Oklahoma (OK)
U of Oregon (OR)
U of Ottawa (ON, Canada)
U of Pennsylvania (PA)
U of Regina (SK, Canada)
U of Saint Joseph (CT)
The U of South Dakota (SD)
The U of Texas at Arlington (TX)
The U of Texas at Austin (TX)
U of Utah (UT)
U of Washington, Bothell (WA)
U of Washington, Tacoma (WA)
U of Waterloo (ON, Canada)
The U of Western Ontario (ON, Canada)
U of Wisconsin–Madison (WI)
U of Wisconsin–Milwaukee (WI)
U of Wisconsin–Stevens Point (WI)
U of Wyoming (WY)
Valparaiso U (IN)
Villanova U (PA)
Washington & Jefferson Coll (PA)
Webster U (MO)
Western Carolina U (NC)
Western Michigan U (MI)
Westminster Coll (MO)
Wheeling Jesuit U (WV)
Willamette U (OR)

INTERNATIONAL MARKETING
Fashion Inst of Technology (NY)
Oklahoma Baptist U (OK)
Oral Roberts U (OK)
Pace U (NY)
Texas Christian U (TX)

INTERNATIONAL POLICY ANALYSIS
Southern Methodist U (TX)

INTERNATIONAL PUBLIC HEALTH
California Baptist U (CA)
Clemson U (SC)
Mercer U (GA)
The U of Iowa (IA)

INTERNATIONAL RELATIONS AND AFFAIRS
Agnes Scott Coll (GA)
Albion Coll (MI)
Alliant Intl U–México City (Mexico)
Alverno Coll (WI)
American Coll of Thessaloniki (Greece)
American Public U System (WV)
American U (DC)
American U in Bulgaria (Bulgaria)
The American U of Rome (Italy)
Augsburg Coll (MN)
Augustana Coll (SD)
Azusa Pacific U (CA)
Bard Coll (NY)
Barry U (FL)
Baylor U (TX)
Belmont U (TN)
Benedictine U (IL)
Bennington Coll (VT)
Berry Coll (GA)
Bethany Coll (WV)
Bethel U (MN)
Bethune-Cookman U (FL)
Binghamton U, State U of New York (NY)
Bob Jones U (SC)
Boston U (MA)
Bowling Green State U (OH)
Bradley U (IL)
Bridgewater Coll (VA)
Bridgewater State U (MA)
Brown U (RI)
Bucknell U (PA)
Butler U (IN)
California Baptist U (CA)
California Lutheran U (CA)
California State U, Chico (CA)
California State U, East Bay (CA)
California State U, Long Beach (CA)

California State U, Monterey Bay (CA)
Calvin Coll (MI)
Canisius Coll (NY)
Capital U (OH)
Carleton Coll (MN)
Carnegie Mellon U (PA)
Carroll Coll (MT)
Case Western Reserve U (OH)
Catawba Coll (NC)
Central Michigan U (MI)
Centre Coll (KY)
Chatham U (PA)
City Coll of the City U of New York (NY)
Claremont McKenna Coll (CA)
Clark U (MA)
Cleveland State U (OH)
Colgate U (NY)
The Coll at Brockport, State U of New York (NY)
The Coll of Idaho (ID)
The Coll of New Jersey (NJ)
Coll of Staten Island of the City U of New York (NY)
The Coll of William and Mary (VA)
The Coll of Wooster (OH)
Concordia Coll–New York (NY)
Connecticut Coll (CT)
Cornell Coll (IA)
Creighton U (NE)
Dalhousie U (NS, Canada)
DePaul U (IL)
Dickinson Coll (PA)
Dominican U (IL)
Drake U (IA)
Drury U (MO)
Duquesne U (PA)
Eastern Michigan U (MI)
Eastern Washington U (WA)
East Tennessee State U (TN)
Eckerd Coll (FL)
Edgewood Coll (WI)
Elmira Coll (NY)
Elon U (NC)
Embry-Riddle Aeronautical U–Prescott (AZ)
Fairfield U (CT)
Fairleigh Dickinson U, Metropolitan Campus (NJ)
Ferrum Coll (VA)
Florida Intl U (FL)
Florida State U (FL)
Francis Marion U (SC)
Franklin Coll Switzerland (Switzerland)
George Mason U (VA)
Georgetown U (DC)
Georgia Southern U (GA)
Gettysburg Coll (PA)
Gonzaga U (WA)
Gordon Coll (MA)
Goucher Coll (MD)
Graceland U (IA)
Grand Valley State U (MI)
Guilford Coll (NC)
Hamilton Coll (NY)
Hampden-Sydney Coll (VA)
Hampshire Coll (MA)
Hawai`i Pacific U (HI)
Hendrix Coll (AR)
High Point U (NC)
Hillsdale Coll (MI)
Hobart and William Smith Colls (NY)
Hollins U (VA)
Holy Names U (CA)
Howard Payne U (TX)
Illinois Coll (IL)
Illinois Wesleyan U (IL)
Immaculata U (PA)
Indiana U Bloomington (IN)
Indiana U of Pennsylvania (PA)
Indiana U–Purdue U Indianapolis (IN)
Indiana U Southeast (IN)
Indiana Wesleyan U (IN)
Intl U in Geneva (Switzerland)
Iona Coll (NY)
Iowa State U of Science and Technology (IA)
James Madison U (VA)
John Brown U (AR)
John Cabot U (Italy)
John Carroll U (OH)
The Johns Hopkins U (MD)
Juniata Coll (PA)

Kennesaw State U (GA)
Kent State U (OH)
Knox Coll (IL)
Lafayette Coll (PA)
La Roche Coll (PA)
Lawrence U (WI)
Lebanese American U (Lebanon)
Lehigh U (PA)
Liberty U (VA)
Lindenwood U (MO)
Linfield Coll (OR)
Lock Haven U of Pennsylvania (PA)
Long Island U–C. W. Post Campus (NY)
Loyola U Chicago (IL)
Lynchburg Coll (VA)
Lynn U (FL)
Manhattan Coll (NY)
Manhattanville Coll (NY)
Mansfield U of Pennsylvania (PA)
Marshall U (WV)
Mary Baldwin Coll (VA)
Marymount Manhattan Coll (NY)
Maryville Coll (TN)
McKendree U (IL)
Mercer U (GA)
Miami U (OH)
Michigan State U (MI)
Middlebury Coll (VT)
Middle Tennessee State U (TN)
Mills Coll (CA)
Minnesota State U Mankato (MN)
Morehouse Coll (GA)
Morningside Coll (IA)
Mount Allison U (NB, Canada)
Mount Holyoke Coll (MA)
Mount Mercy U (IA)
Mount St. Mary's U (MD)
Muhlenberg Coll (PA)
Murray State U (KY)
Nazareth Coll of Rochester (NY)
Newberry Coll (SC)
New York U (NY)
Niagara U (NY)
Northeastern U (MA)
Northern Arizona U (AZ)
Northern Michigan U (MI)
Northwest Nazarene U (ID)
Norwich U (VT)
Nova Southeastern U (FL)
Oakland U (MI)
Oglethorpe U (GA)
The Ohio State U (OH)
Ohio U (OH)
Ohio Wesleyan U (OH)
Oklahoma Baptist U (OK)
Old Dominion U (VA)
Oral Roberts U (OK)
Pacific U (OR)
Penn State Abington (PA)
Penn State Altoona (PA)
Penn State Beaver (PA)
Penn State Berks (PA)
Penn State Brandywine (PA)
Penn State DuBois (PA)
Penn State Erie, The Behrend Coll (PA)
Penn State Fayette, The Eberly Campus (PA)
Penn State Greater Allegheny (PA)
Penn State Hazleton (PA)
Penn State Lehigh Valley (PA)
Penn State Mont Alto (PA)
Penn State New Kensington (PA)
Penn State Schuylkill (PA)
Penn State Shenango (PA)
Penn State U Park (PA)
Penn State Wilkes-Barre (PA)
Penn State Worthington Scranton (PA)
Penn State York (PA)
Pepperdine U, Malibu (CA)
Point Park U (PA)
Pomona Coll (CA)
Portland State U (OR)
Queens U of Charlotte (NC)
Quinnipiac U (CT)
Reed Coll (OR)
Regis Coll (MA)
Rhodes Coll (TN)
Rider U (NJ)
Roanoke Coll (VA)
Rochester Inst of Technology (NY)
Rockhurst U (MO)
Rollins Coll (FL)
Roosevelt U (IL)
Saginaw Valley State U (MI)

Saint Anselm Coll (NH)
St. John Fisher Coll (NY)
Saint Joseph's Coll (IN)
Saint Joseph's U (PA)
Saint Louis U (MO)
Saint Mary's Coll of California (CA)
St. Mary's U (TX)
St. Norbert Coll (WI)
Samford U (AL)
San Diego State U (CA)
San Francisco State U (CA)
Seattle U (WA)
Seton Hill U (PA)
Sewanee: The U of the South (TN)
Shawnee State U (OH)
Shaw U (NC)
Simmons Coll (MA)
Simpson Coll (IA)
Skidmore Coll (NY)
Sonoma State U (CA)
Southern Nazarene U (OK)
Southern Oregon U (OR)
Southern Polytechnic State U (GA)
Southwestern Adventist U (TX)
Southwestern U (TX)
Spring Hill Coll (AL)
Stanford U (CA)
State U of New York at New Paltz (NY)
State U of New York at Oswego (NY)
State U of New York Coll at Cortland (NY)
State U of New York Coll at Geneseo (NY)
Stetson U (FL)
Suffolk U (MA)
Susquehanna U (PA)
Sweet Briar Coll (VA)
Syracuse U (NY)
Taylor U (IN)
Temple U (PA)
Texas Christian U (TX)
Texas State U–San Marcos (TX)
Tiffin U (OH)
Trent U (ON, Canada)
Trinity Coll (CT)
Tufts U (MA)
Tulane U (LA)
United States Military Acad (NY)
The U of Alabama (AL)
U of Bridgeport (CT)
The U of British Columbia (BC, Canada)
The U of British Columbia–Okanagan (BC, Canada)
U of California, Davis (CA)
U of Chicago (IL)
U of Cincinnati (OH)
U of Delaware (DE)
U of Denver (CO)
U of Evansville (IN)
U of Georgia (GA)
U of Hartford (CT)
U of Idaho (ID)
U of La Verne (CA)
U of Mary Washington (VA)
U of Memphis (TN)
U of Miami (FL)
U of Minnesota, Duluth (MN)
U of Minnesota, Twin Cities Campus (MN)
U of Mississippi (MS)
U of Mount Union (OH)
U of Nebraska at Kearney (NE)
U of Nebraska–Lincoln (NE)
U of Nevada, Reno (NV)
U of New Brunswick Fredericton (NB, Canada)
U of New Brunswick Saint John (NB, Canada)
U of North Georgia (GA)
U of Ottawa (ON, Canada)
U of Pennsylvania (PA)
U of Redlands (CA)
U of Rochester (NY)
U of St. Thomas (TX)
U of San Diego (CA)
The U of Scranton (PA)
U of South Carolina (SC)
U of Southern California (CA)
U of Southern Indiana (IN)
U of Southern Mississippi (MS)
U of South Florida (FL)
The U of Tennessee at Martin (TN)
U of the Incarnate Word (TX)
The U of Toledo (OH)

U of Virginia (VA)
U of Washington, Tacoma (WA)
U of Waterloo (ON, Canada)
The U of Western Ontario (ON, Canada)
U of West Florida (FL)
U of West Georgia (GA)
U of Windsor (ON, Canada)
U of Wisconsin–Parkside (WI)
U of Wisconsin–Platteville (WI)
U of Wisconsin–Stevens Point (WI)
U of Wisconsin–Superior (WI)
Utica Coll (NY)
Valparaiso U (IN)
Vassar Coll (NY)
Virginia Polytechnic Inst and State U (VA)
Virginia Wesleyan Coll (VA)
Wagner Coll (NY)
Walsh U (OH)
Wartburg Coll (IA)
Washington Coll (MD)
Washington U in St. Louis (MO)
Webster U (MO)
Wellesley Coll (MA)
Wells Coll (NY)
Wesleyan Coll (GA)
Western Kentucky U (KY)
Western Oregon U (OR)
Westminster Coll (MO)
West Virginia Wesleyan Coll (WV)
Wheaton Coll (IL)
Wheaton Coll (MA)
Whitworth U (WA)
Widener U (PA)
Wilkes U (PA)
William Jewell Coll (MO)
Wittenberg U (OH)
Wright State U (OH)
Xavier U (OH)
York Coll of Pennsylvania (PA)

INVESTMENTS AND SECURITIES
Babson Coll (MA)
Central Michigan U (MI)
Lynn U (FL)
U of Nebraska at Omaha (NE)
U of Nebraska–Lincoln (NE)
U of North Dakota (ND)

IRANIAN LANGUAGES
National U (CA)
U of Maryland, Coll Park (MD)
U of Utah (UT)
Washington U in St. Louis (MO)

IRISH STUDIES
Canisius Coll (NY)
Sacred Heart U (CT)

ISLAMIC STUDIES
Boston Coll (MA)
DePaul U (IL)
The Ohio State U (OH)
Swarthmore Coll (PA)
U of Minnesota, Twin Cities Campus (MN)
The U of Texas at Austin (TX)
The U of Western Ontario (ON, Canada)
Villanova U (PA)
Washington U in St. Louis (MO)
Wellesley Coll (MA)

ITALIAN
The American U of Rome (Italy)
Arizona State U (AZ)
Bard Coll (NY)
Bennington Coll (VT)
Binghamton U, State U of New York (NY)
Boston Coll (MA)
Boston U (MA)
Brock U (ON, Canada)
Brown U (RI)
California State U, Long Beach (CA)
Central Connecticut State U (CT)
Coll of Staten Island of the City U of New York (NY)
Coll of the Holy Cross (MA)
The Colorado Coll (CO)
Columbia U (NY)
Columbia U, School of General Studies (NY)
Concordia U (QC, Canada)
Connecticut Coll (CT)

Dartmouth Coll (NH)
DePaul U (IL)
Dominican U (IL)
Drew U (NJ)
Fairfield U (CT)
Florida Intl U (FL)
Georgetown U (DC)
Gettysburg Coll (PA)
Gonzaga U (WA)
Haverford Coll (PA)
Hofstra U (NY)
Hunter Coll of the City U of New York (NY)
Indiana U Bloomington (IN)
Iona Coll (NY)
Ithaca Coll (NY)
The Johns Hopkins U (MD)
Lake Erie Coll (OH)
La Salle U (PA)
Lehman Coll of the City U of New York (NY)
Long Island U–C. W. Post Campus (NY)
Loyola U Chicago (IL)
Middlebury Coll (VT)
Montclair State U (NJ)
Mount Holyoke Coll (MA)
Nazareth Coll of Rochester (NY)
New York U (NY)
The Ohio State U (OH)
Penn State Abington (PA)
Penn State Altoona (PA)
Penn State Beaver (PA)
Penn State Berks (PA)
Penn State Brandywine (PA)
Penn State DuBois (PA)
Penn State Erie, The Behrend Coll (PA)
Penn State Fayette, The Eberly Campus (PA)
Penn State Greater Allegheny (PA)
Penn State Hazleton (PA)
Penn State Lehigh Valley (PA)
Penn State Mont Alto (PA)
Penn State New Kensington (PA)
Penn State Schuylkill (PA)
Penn State Shenango (PA)
Penn State U Park (PA)
Penn State Wilkes-Barre (PA)
Penn State Worthington Scranton (PA)
Penn State York (PA)
Pepperdine U, Malibu (CA)
Providence Coll (RI)
Rosemont Coll (PA)
Rutgers, The State U of New Jersey, Newark (NJ)
Rutgers, The State U of New Jersey, New Brunswick (NJ)
St. John's U (NY)
Saint Joseph's U (PA)
Saint Louis U (MO)
Saint Mary's Coll (IN)
Saint Mary's Coll of California (CA)
San Francisco State U (CA)
Scripps Coll (CA)
Smith Coll (MA)
Southern Connecticut State U (CT)
Southern Methodist U (TX)
Stanford U (CA)
Stony Brook U, State U of New York (NY)
Susquehanna U (PA)
Syracuse U (NY)
Temple U (PA)
Trinity Coll (CT)
Tulane U (LA)
U at Buffalo, the State U of New York (NY)
The U of Arizona (AZ)
The U of British Columbia (BC, Canada)
U of California, Berkeley (CA)
U of California, Davis (CA)
U of California, Los Angeles (CA)
U of California, Santa Barbara (CA)
U of Colorado Boulder (CO)
U of Delaware (DE)
U of Denver (CO)
U of Georgia (GA)
U of Houston (TX)
U of Illinois at Chicago (IL)
U of Illinois at Urbana–Champaign (IL)
The U of Iowa (IA)
U of Maryland, Coll Park (MD)
U of Massachusetts Amherst (MA)

U of Massachusetts Boston (MA)
U of Michigan (MI)
U of Minnesota, Twin Cities Campus (MN)
U of Notre Dame (IN)
U of Oklahoma (OK)
U of Oregon (OR)
U of Ottawa (ON, Canada)
U of Pennsylvania (PA)
U of Pittsburgh (PA)
U of Rhode Island (RI)
The U of Scranton (PA)
U of Southern California (CA)
U of South Florida (FL)
The U of Tennessee (TN)
The U of Texas at Austin (TX)
U of Virginia (VA)
The U of Western Ontario (ON, Canada)
U of Windsor (ON, Canada)
U of Wisconsin–Madison (WI)
U of Wisconsin–Milwaukee (WI)
Vassar Coll (NY)
Villanova U (PA)
Washington U in St. Louis (MO)
Wellesley Coll (MA)
Wesleyan U (CT)
Yale U (CT)
York Coll of the City U of New York (NY)
Youngstown State U (OH)

ITALIAN STUDIES
Assumption Coll (MA)
Boston U (MA)
Brock U (ON, Canada)
Brown U (RI)
Coll of the Holy Cross (MA)
The Colorado Coll (CO)
Columbia U (NY)
Columbia U, School of General Studies (NY)
Dalhousie U (NS, Canada)
Dickinson Coll (PA)
Franklin Coll Switzerland (Switzerland)
John Cabot U (Italy)
Merrimack Coll (MA)
Miami U (OH)
Scripps Coll (CA)
Southern Methodist U (TX)
Tufts U (MA)
Tulane U (LA)
U of California, Santa Cruz (CA)
U of Richmond (VA)
U of San Diego (CA)
The U of Scranton (PA)
U of Vermont (VT)
The U of Western Ontario (ON, Canada)
U of Windsor (ON, Canada)
Wellesley Coll (MA)
Wheaton Coll (MA)

JAPANESE
Ball State U (IN)
Bates Coll (ME)
Bennington Coll (VT)
Boston U (MA)
California State U, Fullerton (CA)
California State U, Long Beach (CA)
California State U, Los Angeles (CA)
California State U, Monterey Bay (CA)
Calvin Coll (MI)
Carnegie Mellon U (PA)
Colgate U (NY)
Connecticut Coll (CT)
Dartmouth Coll (NH)
Eastern Michigan U (MI)
Elizabethtown Coll (PA)
Georgetown U (DC)
Gettysburg Coll (PA)
Gustavus Adolphus Coll (MN)
Hobart and William Smith Colls (NY)
Lawrence U (WI)
Linfield Coll (OR)
Macalester Coll (MN)
Michigan State U (MI)
Middlebury Coll (VT)
Murray State U (KY)
North Central Coll (IL)
Oakland U (MI)
The Ohio State U (OH)

Pacific U (OR)
Penn State Abington (PA)
Penn State Altoona (PA)
Penn State Beaver (PA)
Penn State Berks (PA)
Penn State Brandywine (PA)
Penn State DuBois (PA)
Penn State Erie, The Behrend Coll (PA)
Penn State Fayette, The Eberly Campus (PA)
Penn State Greater Allegheny (PA)
Penn State Hazleton (PA)
Penn State Lehigh Valley (PA)
Penn State Mont Alto (PA)
Penn State New Kensington (PA)
Penn State Schuylkill (PA)
Penn State Shenango (PA)
Penn State U Park (PA)
Penn State Wilkes-Barre (PA)
Penn State Worthington Scranton (PA)
Penn State York (PA)
Pomona Coll (CA)
Portland State U (OR)
San Diego State U (CA)
San Francisco State U (CA)
San Jose State U (CA)
Scripps Coll (CA)
Stanford U (CA)
Swarthmore Coll (PA)
Trinity Coll (CT)
Tufts U (MA)
U of Alaska Anchorage (AK)
U of Alaska Fairbanks (AK)
U of California, Berkeley (CA)
U of California, Davis (CA)
U of California, Irvine (CA)
U of California, Los Angeles (CA)
U of California, Santa Barbara (CA)
U of Colorado Boulder (CO)
The U of Findlay (OH)
U of Georgia (GA)
U of Hawaii at Hilo (HI)
U of Hawaii at Manoa (HI)
The U of Iowa (IA)
U of Kentucky (KY)
U of Maryland, Coll Park (MD)
U of Massachusetts Amherst (MA)
U of Minnesota, Twin Cities Campus (MN)
U of Mount Union (OH)
The U of North Carolina at Charlotte (NC)
U of Notre Dame (IN)
U of Oregon (OR)
U of Pittsburgh (PA)
U of Puget Sound (WA)
U of Regina (SK, Canada)
U of Rochester (NY)
U of Utah (UT)
U of Vermont (VT)
The U of Western Ontario (ON, Canada)
U of Wisconsin–Madison (WI)
Vassar Coll (NY)
Wake Forest U (NC)
Washington U in St. Louis (MO)
Wellesley Coll (MA)
Western Michigan U (MI)
Western Washington U (WA)
Williams Coll (MA)
Yale U (CT)

JAPANESE STUDIES
Case Western Reserve U (OH)
Earlham Coll (IN)
Gettysburg Coll (PA)
Gustavus Adolphus Coll (MN)
Hope Coll (MI)
U at Albany, State U of New York (NY)
Willamette U (OR)

JAZZ/JAZZ STUDIES
Bard Coll (NY)
Bennington Coll (VT)
Berklee Coll of Music (MA)
Bowling Green State U (OH)
Brigham Young U (UT)
Capital U (OH)
Central State U (OH)
City Coll of the City U of New York (NY)
Concordia U (QC, Canada)
DePaul U (IL)
Drake U (IA)

Five Towns Coll (NY)
Florida State U (FL)
Hampton U (VA)
Hofstra U (NY)
Hope Coll (MI)
Ithaca Coll (NY)
Johnson State Coll (VT)
Lamar U (TX)
Limestone Coll (SC)
Long Island U–Brooklyn Campus (NY)
Loyola U New Orleans (LA)
Michigan State U (MI)
New England Conservatory of Music (MA)
The New School for Jazz and Contemporary Music (NY)
North Carolina Central U (NC)
North Central Coll (IL)
The Ohio State U (OH)
Peabody Conservatory of The Johns Hopkins U (MD)
Roosevelt U (IL)
Rutgers, The State U of New Jersey, New Brunswick (NJ)
Shenandoah U (VA)
Temple U (PA)
Texas State U–San Marcos (TX)
Thompson Rivers U (BC, Canada)
The U of Akron (OH)
U of Hartford (CT)
U of Illinois at Urbana–Champaign (IL)
The U of Iowa (IA)
U of Miami (FL)
U of Michigan (MI)
U of Minnesota, Duluth (MN)
U of Nevada, Las Vegas (NV)
The U of North Carolina at Greensboro (NC)
U of North Florida (FL)
U of North Texas (TX)
U of Oregon (OR)
U of Rochester (NY)
U of Southern California (CA)
The U of Texas at Austin (TX)
Villa Maria Coll of Buffalo (NY)
Webster U (MO)
Western Michigan U (MI)
William Paterson U of New Jersey (NJ)

JEWISH/JUDAIC STUDIES
American Jewish U (CA)
American U (DC)
Arizona State U (AZ)
Bard Coll (NY)
Bennington Coll (VT)
Binghamton U, State U of New York (NY)
Brown U (RI)
California State U, Chico (CA)
California State U, Northridge (CA)
City Coll of the City U of New York (NY)
Clark U (MA)
Coll of Charleston (SC)
Concordia U (QC, Canada)
DePaul U (IL)
Dickinson Coll (PA)
Drew U (NJ)
Eugene Lang Coll The New School for Liberal Arts (NY)
Florida Atlantic U (FL)
Gettysburg Coll (PA)
Hofstra U (NY)
Hunter Coll of the City U of New York (NY)
Indiana U Bloomington (IN)
Lehman Coll of the City U of New York (NY)
Northeastern U (MA)
The Ohio State U (OH)
Penn State Abington (PA)
Penn State Altoona (PA)
Penn State Beaver (PA)
Penn State Berks (PA)
Penn State Brandywine (PA)
Penn State DuBois (PA)
Penn State Erie, The Behrend Coll (PA)
Penn State Fayette, The Eberly Campus (PA)
Penn State Greater Allegheny (PA)
Penn State Hazleton (PA)
Penn State Lehigh Valley (PA)
Penn State Mont Alto (PA)

Penn State New Kensington (PA)
Penn State Schuylkill (PA)
Penn State Shenango (PA)
Penn State U Park (PA)
Penn State Wilkes-Barre (PA)
Penn State Worthington Scranton (PA)
Penn State York (PA)
Rutgers, The State U of New Jersey, New Brunswick (NJ)
San Diego State U (CA)
San Francisco State U (CA)
Scripps Coll (CA)
Syracuse U (NY)
Temple U (PA)
Trinity Coll (CT)
Tufts U (MA)
Tulane U (LA)
U at Buffalo, the State U of New York (NY)
The U of Arizona (AZ)
U of California, Los Angeles (CA)
U of Chicago (IL)
U of Colorado Boulder (CO)
U of Florida (FL)
U of Hartford (CT)
U of Maryland, Coll Park (MD)
U of Massachusetts Amherst (MA)
U of Miami (FL)
U of Michigan (MI)
U of Minnesota, Twin Cities Campus (MN)
U of Oklahoma (OK)
U of Oregon (OR)
U of Pennsylvania (PA)
U of Southern California (CA)
The U of Texas at Austin (TX)
The U of Western Ontario (ON, Canada)
U of Wisconsin–Madison (WI)
U of Wisconsin–Milwaukee (WI)
Vanderbilt U (TN)
Vassar Coll (NY)
Washington U in St. Louis (MO)
Wellesley Coll (MA)
Yale U (CT)

JOURNALISM
Abilene Christian U (TX)
American U (DC)
American U in Bulgaria (Bulgaria)
The American U in Cairo (Egypt)
Andrews U (MI)
Angelo State U (TX)
Appalachian State U (NC)
Arkansas State U (AR)
Arkansas Tech U (AR)
Asbury U (KY)
Ashland U (OH)
Auburn U (AL)
Augustana Coll (SD)
Averett U (VA)
Ball State U (IN)
Barry U (FL)
Baylor U (TX)
Belmont U (TN)
Bemidji State U (MN)
Benedictine Coll (KS)
Bennington Coll (VT)
Bethel U (MN)
Bob Jones U (SC)
Boston U (MA)
Bowling Green State U (OH)
Bradley U (IL)
Brigham Young U (UT)
Buffalo State Coll, State U of New York (NY)
Butler U (IN)
California Baptist U (CA)
California Lutheran U (CA)
California Polytechnic State U, San Luis Obispo (CA)
California State U, Chico (CA)
California State U, Dominguez Hills (CA)
California State U, East Bay (CA)
California State U, Fresno (CA)
California State U, Fullerton (CA)
California State U, Long Beach (CA)
California State U, Northridge (CA)
Campbellsville U (KY)
Canisius Coll (NY)
Carson-Newman U (TN)
Castleton State Coll (VT)
Cedarville U (OH)
Central Connecticut State U (CT)

Central Michigan U (MI)
Central State U (OH)
Chatham U (PA)
Cincinnati Christian U (OH)
Cleveland State U (OH)
The Coll at Brockport, State U of New York (NY)
The Coll of St. Scholastica (MN)
Coll of the Ozarks (MO)
Colorado State U (CO)
Columbia Coll Chicago (IL)
Concordia U (QC, Canada)
Concordia U Chicago (IL)
Concordia U, St. Paul (MN)
Corban U (OR)
Creighton U (NE)
Curry Coll (MA)
Delta State U (MS)
DePaul U (IL)
Doane Coll (NE)
Dominican U (IL)
Dordt Coll (IA)
Drake U (IA)
Drury U (MO)
Duquesne U (PA)
East Central U (OK)
Eastern Illinois U (IL)
Eastern Michigan U (MI)
Eastern Washington U (WA)
Elon U (NC)
Emerson Coll (MA)
Florida Ag and Mech U (FL)
Franklin Coll (IN)
Franklin Pierce U (NH)
Gannon U (PA)
Gardner-Webb U (NC)
George Fox U (OR)
Georgia Coll & State U (GA)
Georgia Southern U (GA)
Georgia State U (GA)
Gettysburg Coll (PA)
Gonzaga U (WA)
Grand Valley State U (MI)
Grand View U (IA)
Hampton U (VA)
Harding U (AR)
Hawai`i Pacific U (HI)
Henderson State U (AR)
Hofstra U (NY)
Humboldt State U (CA)
Huntington U (IN)
Illinois Inst of Technology (IL)
Illinois State U (IL)
Indiana U Bloomington (IN)
Indiana U of Pennsylvania (PA)
Indiana U–Purdue U Indianapolis (IN)
Indiana U Southeast (IN)
Indiana Wesleyan U (IN)
Inter American U of Puerto Rico, Ponce Campus (PR)
Iona Coll (NY)
Iowa State U of Science and Technology (IA)
Ithaca Coll (NY)
John Brown U (AR)
Johnson State Coll (VT)
Kansas State U (KS)
Keene State Coll (NH)
Kent State U (OH)
Lamar U (TX)
Langston U (OK)
La Salle U (PA)
Lasell Coll (MA)
Lebanese American U (Lebanon)
Lehigh U (PA)
Lewis U (IL)
Liberty U (VA)
Lincoln U (MO)
Lindenwood U (MO)
Lipscomb U (TN)
Lock Haven U of Pennsylvania (PA)
Long Island U–Brooklyn Campus (NY)
Long Island U–C. W. Post Campus (NY)
Louisiana Coll (LA)
Loyola U Chicago (IL)
Lynn U (FL)
Madonna U (MI)
Mansfield U of Pennsylvania (PA)
Marietta Coll (OH)
Marquette U (WI)
Marshall U (WV)
Massachusetts Coll of Liberal Arts (MA)
Mercer U (GA)

Messiah Coll (PA)
Metropolitan State U of Denver (CO)
Miami U (OH)
Michigan State U (MI)
Minnesota State U Mankato (MN)
Mississippi Coll (MS)
Missouri State U (MO)
Morrisville State Coll (NY)
Mount Mercy U (IA)
Mount Vernon Nazarene U (OH)
Murray State U (KY)
New England Coll (NH)
New Mexico State U (NM)
New York U (NY)
Norfolk State U (VA)
North Central Coll (IL)
Northeastern U (MA)
Northern Arizona U (AZ)
Northern Illinois U (IL)
North Greenville U (SC)
Northwestern Coll (IA)
Northwestern Coll (MN)
Northwest Missouri State U (MO)
Oakland U (MI)
The Ohio State U (OH)
Ohio U (OH)
Ohio Wesleyan U (OH)
Oklahoma Baptist U (OK)
Oklahoma Christian U (OK)
Oklahoma City U (OK)
Oklahoma State U (OK)
Olivet Coll (MI)
Pacific U (OR)
Palm Beach Atlantic U (FL)
Patrick Henry Coll (VA)
Penn State Abington (PA)
Penn State Altoona (PA)
Penn State Beaver (PA)
Penn State Berks (PA)
Penn State Brandywine (PA)
Penn State DuBois (PA)
Penn State Erie, The Behrend Coll (PA)
Penn State Fayette, The Eberly Campus (PA)
Penn State Greater Allegheny (PA)
Penn State Hazleton (PA)
Penn State Lehigh Valley (PA)
Penn State Mont Alto (PA)
Penn State New Kensington (PA)
Penn State Schuylkill (PA)
Penn State Shenango (PA)
Penn State U Park (PA)
Penn State Wilkes-Barre (PA)
Penn State Worthington Scranton (PA)
Penn State York (PA)
Pepperdine U, Malibu (CA)
Pittsburg State U (KS)
Point Loma Nazarene U (CA)
Point Park U (PA)
Purchase Coll, State U of New York (NY)
Purdue U Calumet (IN)
Queens U of Charlotte (NC)
Quinnipiac U (CT)
Radford U (VA)
Rider U (NJ)
Rochester Inst of Technology (NY)
Roosevelt U (IL)
Rowan U (NJ)
Rutgers, The State U of New Jersey, Newark (NJ)
Rutgers, The State U of New Jersey, New Brunswick (NJ)
St. Ambrose U (IA)
St. Bonaventure U (NY)
St. John's U (NY)
Saint Mary's U of Minnesota (MN)
St. Thomas Aquinas Coll (NY)
St. Thomas U (NB, Canada)
Salem State U (MA)
Samford U (AL)
San Diego State U (CA)
San Francisco State U (CA)
San Jose State U (CA)
Seattle U (WA)
Seton Hill U (PA)
Shippensburg U of Pennsylvania (PA)
Slippery Rock U of Pennsylvania (PA)
South Dakota State U (SD)
Southeastern U (FL)
Southern Arkansas U–Magnolia (AR)

Southern Connecticut State U (CT)
Southern Illinois U Carbondale (IL)
Southern Methodist U (TX)
Southwestern Adventist U (TX)
Southwestern Coll (KS)
Spring Hill Coll (AL)
State U of New York at New Paltz (NY)
State U of New York at Oswego (NY)
State U of New York at Plattsburgh (NY)
Stony Brook U, State U of New York (NY)
Suffolk U (MA)
Syracuse U (NY)
Tabor Coll (KS)
Temple U (PA)
Texas A&M U–Commerce (TX)
Texas Christian U (TX)
Texas Southern U (TX)
Texas State U–San Marcos (TX)
Texas Wesleyan U (TX)
Thomas Edison State Coll (NJ)
Thompson Rivers U (BC, Canada)
Tiffin U (OH)
Trent U (ON, Canada)
Trevecca Nazarene U (TN)
Troy U (AL)
Union Coll (NE)
Union U (TN)
U at Albany, State U of New York (NY)
The U of Alabama (AL)
U of Alaska Anchorage (AK)
U of Alaska Fairbanks (AK)
The U of Arizona (AZ)
U of Arkansas at Little Rock (AR)
U of Bridgeport (CT)
U of Central Arkansas (AR)
U of Central Florida (FL)
U of Central Oklahoma (OK)
U of Cincinnati (OH)
U of Colorado Boulder (CO)
U of Denver (CO)
The U of Findlay (OH)
U of Florida (FL)
U of Georgia (GA)
U of Hawaii at Manoa (HI)
U of Houston (TX)
U of Idaho (ID)
U of Illinois at Urbana–Champaign (IL)
The U of Iowa (IA)
The U of Kansas (KS)
U of Kentucky (KY)
U of La Verne (CA)
U of Maryland, Coll Park (MD)
U of Massachusetts Amherst (MA)
U of Memphis (TN)
U of Miami (FL)
U of Minnesota, Twin Cities Campus (MN)
U of Mississippi (MS)
U of Missouri (MO)
U of Nebraska at Kearney (NE)
U of Nebraska at Omaha (NE)
U of Nevada, Reno (NV)
U of New Mexico (NM)
The U of North Carolina at Chapel Hill (NC)
U of Northern Colorado (CO)
U of North Texas (TX)
U of Oklahoma (OK)
U of Oregon (OR)
U of Ottawa (ON, Canada)
U of Pittsburgh at Greensburg (PA)
U of Portland (OR)
U of Regina (SK, Canada)
U of Rhode Island (RI)
U of Richmond (VA)
U of South Carolina (SC)
U of Southern California (CA)
U of Southern Indiana (IN)
U of Southern Mississippi (MS)
The U of Tennessee (TN)
The U of Texas at Arlington (TX)
The U of Texas at Austin (TX)
The U of Texas at El Paso (TX)
The U of Texas–Pan American (TX)
U of the Cumberlands (KY)
U of the Incarnate Word (TX)
The U of Toledo (OH)
U of West Georgia (GA)
U of Wisconsin–Eau Claire (WI)
U of Wisconsin–Madison (WI)
U of Wisconsin–Superior (WI)

U of Wyoming (WY)
Utah State U (UT)
Utica Coll (NY)
Virginia Union U (VA)
Walla Walla U (WA)
Wartburg Coll (IA)
Washington and Lee U (VA)
Washington State U (WA)
Waynesburg U (PA)
Wayne State U (MI)
Weber State U (UT)
Webster U (MO)
Western Illinois U (IL)
Western Kentucky U (KY)
Western Michigan U (MI)
Western Washington U (WA)
West Texas A&M U (TX)
West Virginia U (WV)
Whitworth U (WA)
William Penn U (IA)
Youngstown State U (OH)

JOURNALISM RELATED
Arizona State U (AZ)
Benedictine U (IL)
Bowling Green State U (OH)
California State U, Long Beach (CA)
Central Michigan U (MI)
Columbia Coll (SC)
Concordia Coll (MN)
Cornerstone U (MI)
Edinboro U of Pennsylvania (PA)
Kentucky State U (KY)
Missouri Baptist U (MO)
National U (CA)
Oklahoma State U (OK)
Roosevelt U (IL)
Simpson Coll (IA)
Southern Nazarene U (OK)
Syracuse U (NY)
The U of Akron (OH)
U of California, Irvine (CA)
U of Nebraska at Omaha (NE)
U of Nebraska–Lincoln (NE)
U of Oregon (OR)
U of St. Thomas (MN)
The U of Western Ontario (ON, Canada)
Webster U (MO)
Western Washington U (WA)

JUVENILE CORRECTIONS
Harris-Stowe State U (MO)

KEYBOARD INSTRUMENTS
Abilene Christian U (TX)
Acadia U (NS, Canada)
Andrews U (MI)
Baldwin Wallace U (OH)
Bard Coll (NY)
Barry U (FL)
Bennington Coll (VT)
Berklee Coll of Music (MA)
Bob Jones U (SC)
Bowling Green State U (OH)
Brigham Young U (UT)
Butler U (IN)
California Baptist U (CA)
California State U, Chico (CA)
Campbellsville U (KY)
Capital U (OH)
Carnegie Mellon U (PA)
Carson-Newman U (TN)
Catawba Coll (NC)
The Catholic U of America (DC)
Chapman U (CA)
Cincinnati Christian U (OH)
Columbia Coll (SC)
Concordia U, Nebraska (NE)
Converse Coll (SC)
Dallas Baptist U (TX)
Dordt Coll (IA)
Drake U (IA)
East Central U (OK)
East Texas Baptist U (TX)
Furman U (SC)
Grace U (NE)
Hardin-Simmons U (TX)
Hillsdale Free Will Baptist Coll (OK)
Hope Coll (MI)
Houghton Coll (NY)
Howard Payne U (TX)
Illinois Wesleyan U (IL)
Indiana U–Purdue U Fort Wayne (IN)
Inter American U of Puerto Rico, San Germán Campus (PR)

Ithaca Coll (NY)
Lamar U (TX)
Lawrence U (WI)
Lipscomb U (TN)
Louisiana Coll (LA)
Madonna U (MI)
Mannes Coll The New School for Music (NY)
Maryville Coll (TN)
The Master's Coll and Sem (CA)
McNally Smith Coll of Music (MN)
Mississippi Coll (MS)
Mount Allison U (NB, Canada)
New England Conservatory of Music (MA)
The New School for Jazz and Contemporary Music (NY)
Northwestern Coll (MN)
Nyack Coll (NY)
Oakland U (MI)
The Ohio State U (OH)
Ohio U (OH)
Oklahoma City U (OK)
Oral Roberts U (OK)
Ouachita Baptist U (AR)
Palm Beach Atlantic U (FL)
Peabody Conservatory of The Johns Hopkins U (MD)
Point Loma Nazarene U (CA)
Rider U (NJ)
Roberts Wesleyan Coll (NY)
Roosevelt U (IL)
Samford U (AL)
San Francisco Conservatory of Music (CA)
Shenandoah U (VA)
Southeastern U (FL)
Southern Methodist U (TX)
Spring Arbor U (MI)
State U of New York at Fredonia (NY)
State U of New York at New Paltz (NY)
Stetson U (FL)
Syracuse U (NY)
Tabor Coll (KS)
Texas Christian U (TX)
Union U (TN)
The U of Akron (OH)
The U of British Columbia (BC, Canada)
U of Central Oklahoma (OK)
U of Cincinnati (OH)
U of Delaware (DE)
The U of Iowa (IA)
The U of Kansas (KS)
U of Miami (FL)
U of Nebraska at Omaha (NE)
U of Redlands (CA)
U of Southern California (CA)
The U of Tennessee at Martin (TN)
U of Tulsa (OK)
The U of Western Ontario (ON, Canada)
Valparaiso U (IN)
Vanderbilt U (TN)
Walla Walla U (WA)
Weber State U (UT)
Western Michigan U (MI)
Whitworth U (WA)
Willamette U (OR)
Xavier U of Louisiana (LA)

KINDERGARTEN/PRESCHOOL EDUCATION
Albright Coll (PA)
Alma Coll (MI)
Appalachian State U (NC)
Armstrong Atlantic State U (GA)
Ashland U (OH)
Athens State U (AL)
Augsburg Coll (MN)
Ball State U (IN)
Barry U (FL)
Baylor U (TX)
Becker Coll (MA)
Bluefield Coll (VA)
Bluffton U (OH)
Boston Coll (MA)
Bowie State U (MD)
Bowling Green State U (OH)
Bowling Green State U-Firelands Coll (OH)
Bucknell U (PA)
Buffalo State Coll, State U of New York (NY)
Butler U (IN)

Cabrini Coll (PA)
Cairn U (PA)
California Polytechnic State U, San Luis Obispo (CA)
Cardinal Stritch U (WI)
Carson-Newman U (TN)
Central Methodist U (MO)
Cheyney U of Pennsylvania (PA)
Cincinnati Christian U (OH)
The Coll of Saint Rose (NY)
Columbia Coll Chicago (IL)
Concordia U (OR)
Concordia U (QC, Canada)
Concordia U, Nebraska (NE)
Concordia U Wisconsin (WI)
Concord U (WV)
Converse Coll (SC)
Curry Coll (MA)
East Carolina U (NC)
Eastern Illinois U (IL)
Elizabeth City State U (NC)
Evangel U (MO)
Faulkner U (AL)
Furman U (SC)
Georgia State U (GA)
Hampton U (VA)
Hillsdale Coll (MI)
Humboldt State U (CA)
Hunter Coll of the City U of New York (NY)
Inter American U of Puerto Rico, Aguadilla Campus (PR)
Inter American U of Puerto Rico, Ponce Campus (PR)
Inter American U of Puerto Rico, San Germán Campus (PR)
Jacksonville State U (AL)
Jarvis Christian Coll (TX)
John Brown U (AR)
John Carroll U (OH)
Kean U (NJ)
King Coll (TN)
Lakeland Coll (WI)
Lamar U (TX)
Langston U (OK)
Lasell Coll (MA)
Lees-McRae Coll (NC)
Lesley U (MA)
Lincoln Memorial U (TN)
Lock Haven U of Pennsylvania (PA)
Long Island U–C. W. Post Campus (NY)
Louisiana Coll (LA)
Mansfield U of Pennsylvania (PA)
Marshall U (WV)
Martin Luther Coll (MN)
Michigan State U (MI)
Middle Tennessee State U (TN)
Minnesota State U Mankato (MN)
Mississippi Valley State U (MS)
Mount Vernon Nazarene U (OH)
New Jersey City U (NJ)
New Mexico Highlands U (NM)
Norfolk State U (VA)
North Carolina Central U (NC)
Northeastern Illinois U (IL)
Northern Illinois U (IL)
Northwestern Oklahoma State U (OK)
Nova Southeastern U (FL)
Ohio Dominican U (OH)
Ohio Wesleyan U (OH)
Oklahoma Baptist U (OK)
Oklahoma Christian U (OK)
Oklahoma City U (OK)
Pacific U (OR)
Piedmont Coll (GA)
Post U (CT)
St. Thomas Aquinas Coll (NY)
Shaw U (NC)
Siena Heights U (MI)
Southeastern Oklahoma State U (OK)
State U of New York at Fredonia (NY)
State U of New York Coll at Cortland (NY)
State U of New York Coll at Potsdam (NY)
Susquehanna U (PA)
Tennessee State U (TN)
Texas A&M Intl U (TX)
Thomas U (GA)
Tufts U (MA)
Union U (TN)
Université de Sherbrooke (QC, Canada)

Université du Québec en Outaouais (QC, Canada)
U of Alaska Anchorage (AK)
The U of Arizona (AZ)
The U of British Columbia (BC, Canada)
U of Central Arkansas (AR)
U of Central Oklahoma (OK)
U of Cincinnati (OH)
U of Georgia (GA)
U of Great Falls (MT)
U of Illinois at Urbana–Champaign (IL)
U of Maryland, Coll Park (MD)
U of Maryland Eastern Shore (MD)
U of Minnesota, Crookston (MN)
U of Minnesota, Duluth (MN)
U of Minnesota, Twin Cities Campus (MN)
U of Missouri (MO)
U of Nevada, Las Vegas (NV)
U of New Brunswick Fredericton (NB, Canada)
The U of North Carolina at Charlotte (NC)
The U of North Carolina at Pembroke (NC)
The U of North Carolina Wilmington (NC)
U of Northern Iowa (IA)
U of Regina (SK, Canada)
U of South Carolina Upstate (SC)
The U of Tennessee at Martin (TN)
U of the District of Columbia (DC)
The U of Toledo (OH)
U of Vermont (VT)
U of Windsor (ON, Canada)
U of Wisconsin–Platteville (WI)
U of Wisconsin–Stevens Point (WI)
Utah State U (UT)
Valdosta State U (GA)
Virginia Union U (VA)
Wagner Coll (NY)
Walsh U (OH)
Wartburg Coll (IA)
Washington State U (WA)
Western Carolina U (NC)
Westfield State U (MA)
West Liberty U (WV)
West Virginia State U (WV)
West Virginia Wesleyan Coll (WV)
Widener U (PA)

KINESIOLOGY AND EXERCISE SCIENCE
Acadia U (NS, Canada)
Adams State U (CO)
Albion Coll (MI)
Alma Coll (MI)
American Public U System (WV)
Anderson U (SC)
Angelo State U (TX)
Appalachian State U (NC)
Arizona State U (AZ)
Arkansas State U (AR)
Augustana Coll (SD)
Baker U (KS)
Barry U (FL)
Bastyr U (WA)
Becker Coll (MA)
Belhaven U (MS)
Bellarmine U (KY)
Belmont U (TN)
Berea Coll (KY)
Berry Coll (GA)
Bethany Lutheran Coll (MN)
Bethel Coll (IN)
Bethel U (MN)
Bluefield Coll (VA)
Blue Mountain Coll (MS)
Boise State U (ID)
Brevard Coll (NC)
Bridgewater State U (MA)
Brigham Young U (UT)
Brock U (ON, Canada)
Buffalo State Coll, State U of New York (NY)
Cabrini Coll (PA)
California Baptist U (CA)
California Lutheran U (CA)
California State U, Chico (CA)
California State U, East Bay (CA)
California State U, Long Beach (CA)
California State U, Los Angeles (CA)
California State U, Northridge (CA)

Calvin Coll (MI)
Capital U (OH)
Carson-Newman U (TN)
Castleton State Coll (VT)
Cedarville U (OH)
Central Coll (IA)
Chatham U (PA)
Chowan U (NC)
Clearwater Christian Coll (FL)
Coastal Carolina U (SC)
The Coll at Brockport, State U of New York (NY)
The Coll of Idaho (ID)
Colorado Mesa U (CO)
Colorado State U (CO)
Columbus State U (GA)
Concordia U (QC, Canada)
Concordia U Chicago (IL)
Concordia U, Nebraska (NE)
Concordia U, St. Paul (MN)
Concordia U Texas (TX)
Corban U (OR)
Cornell Coll (IA)
Cornerstone U (MI)
Creighton U (NE)
Dakota State U (SD)
Dakota Wesleyan U (SD)
Dalhousie U (NS, Canada)
Defiance Coll (OH)
DePauw U (IN)
DeSales U (PA)
Dordt Coll (IA)
Drury U (MO)
East Central U (OK)
Eastern Illinois U (IL)
Eastern Mennonite U (VA)
Eastern Michigan U (MI)
Eastern Washington U (WA)
Elon U (NC)
Emmanuel Coll (GA)
Florida Atlantic U (FL)
Florida Gulf Coast U (FL)
Florida Southern Coll (FL)
Florida State U (FL)
Frostburg State U (MD)
Gannon U (PA)
Georgetown Coll (KY)
Georgia Coll & State U (GA)
Georgia Gwinnett Coll (GA)
Georgia Regents U (GA)
Georgia Southern U (GA)
Gonzaga U (WA)
Gordon Coll (MA)
Greenville Coll (IL)
Grove City Coll (PA)
Guilford Coll (NC)
Hanover Coll (IN)
Harding U (AR)
Hardin-Simmons U (TX)
Hendrix Coll (AR)
High Point U (NC)
Hillsdale Free Will Baptist Coll (OK)
Hope Coll (MI)
Humboldt State U (CA)
Huntingdon Coll (AL)
Huntington U (IN)
Illinois State U (IL)
Immaculata U (PA)
Indiana State U (IN)
Indiana U Bloomington (IN)
Indiana U–Purdue U Indianapolis (IN)
Indiana Wesleyan U (IN)
Iowa Wesleyan Coll (IA)
Ithaca Coll (NY)
Jacksonville State U (AL)
Jamestown Coll (ND)
John Brown U (AR)
Johnson State Coll (VT)
Kansas State U (KS)
Keene State Coll (NH)
Kennesaw State U (GA)
Kent State U (OH)
Kentucky Wesleyan Coll (KY)
Kuyper Coll (MI)
LaGrange Coll (GA)
Lakeland Coll (WI)
Lake Superior State U (MI)
Lander U (SC)
Lasell Coll (MA)
La Sierra U (CA)
Lewis-Clark State Coll (ID)
Liberty U (VA)
Lincoln Memorial U (TN)
Lindenwood U (MO)
Linfield Coll (OR)
Lipscomb U (TN)

Louisiana Coll (LA)
Lubbock Christian U (TX)
Malone U (OH)
Manchester U (IN)
Marshall U (WV)
Mars Hill Coll (NC)
Maryville Coll (TN)
The Master's Coll and Sem (CA)
McDaniel Coll (MD)
McMurry U (TX)
McNeese State U (LA)
Messiah Coll (PA)
Miami U (OH)
Michigan State U (MI)
Minnesota State U Moorhead (MN)
Mississippi Coll (MS)
Missouri Baptist U (MO)
Missouri State U (MO)
Monmouth Coll (IL)
Morehead State U (KY)
Morehouse Coll (GA)
Mount Vernon Nazarene U (OH)
Murray State U (KY)
Norfolk State U (VA)
North Carolina Wesleyan Coll (NC)
North Central Coll (IL)
Northern Arizona U (AZ)
Northern Michigan U (MI)
Northwest Christian U (OR)
Northwestern Coll (IA)
Northwestern Coll (MN)
Northwest Nazarene U (ID)
Notre Dame de Namur U (CA)
Nova Southeastern U (FL)
The Ohio State U (OH)
Ohio U (OH)
Oklahoma Baptist U (OK)
Oklahoma City U (OK)
Oral Roberts U (OK)
Ouachita Baptist U (AR)
Pacific Union Coll (CA)
Pacific U (OH)
Penn State Abington (PA)
Penn State Altoona (PA)
Penn State Beaver (PA)
Penn State Berks (PA)
Penn State Brandywine (PA)
Penn State DuBois (PA)
Penn State Erie, The Behrend Coll (PA)
Penn State Fayette, The Eberly Campus (PA)
Penn State Greater Allegheny (PA)
Penn State Hazleton (PA)
Penn State Lehigh Valley (PA)
Penn State Mont Alto (PA)
Penn State New Kensington (PA)
Penn State Schuylkill (PA)
Penn State Shenango (PA)
Penn State U Park (PA)
Penn State Wilkes-Barre (PA)
Penn State Worthington Scranton (PA)
Penn State York (PA)
Pepperdine U, Malibu (CA)
Pittsburg State U (KS)
Point Loma Nazarene U (CA)
Point U (GA)
Queens U of Charlotte (NC)
Rice U (TX)
Roanoke Coll (VA)
Rocky Mountain Coll (MT)
Rutgers, The State U of New Jersey, New Brunswick (NJ)
Sacred Heart U (CT)
Saginaw Valley State U (MI)
St. Edward's U (TX)
St. Gregory's U, Shawnee (OK)
Saint Louis U (MO)
Saint Mary's Coll of California (CA)
St. Mary's U (TX)
St. Olaf Coll (MN)
Salem State U (MA)
Salisbury U (MD)
Samford U (AL)
Sam Houston State U (TX)
San Diego Christian Coll (CA)
San Francisco State U (CA)
Schreiner U (TX)
Seattle Pacific U (WA)
Seattle U (WA)
Shaw U (NC)
Shippensburg U of Pennsylvania (PA)
Simmons Coll (MA)
Simon Fraser U (BC, Canada)
Simpson Coll (IA)

Skidmore Coll (NY)
Slippery Rock U of Pennsylvania (PA)
Sonoma State U (CA)
Southern Arkansas U–Magnolia (AR)
Southern Illinois U Carbondale (IL)
Southern Illinois U Edwardsville (IL)
Southern Nazarene U (OK)
Southwest Baptist U (MO)
Southwestern Adventist U (TX)
Southwestern U (TX)
Spring Arbor U (MI)
State U of New York Coll at Cortland (NY)
Tarleton State U (TX)
Taylor U (IN)
Temple U (PA)
Tennessee Wesleyan Coll (TN)
Texas A&M U–Commerce (TX)
Texas Lutheran U (TX)
Texas Southern U (TX)
Texas Wesleyan U (TX)
Texas Woman's U (TX)
Transylvania U (KY)
Trinity Christian Coll (IL)
Truman State U (MO)
Union Coll (NE)
Union U (TN)
United States Military Acad (NY)
Université de Sherbrooke (QC, Canada)
The U of British Columbia (BC, Canada)
The U of British Columbia–Okanagan (BC, Canada)
U of Central Arkansas (AR)
U of Delaware (DE)
U of Evansville (IN)
U of Guelph (ON, Canada)
U of Hawaii at Manoa (HI)
U of Houston (TX)
U of Houston–Clear Lake (TX)
U of Idaho (ID)
U of Illinois at Chicago (IL)
U of Illinois at Urbana–Champaign (IL)
The U of Iowa (IA)
U of La Verne (CA)
U of Louisiana at Monroe (LA)
U of Maryland, Coll Park (MD)
U of Memphis (TN)
U of Michigan (MI)
U of Minnesota, Duluth (MN)
U of Minnesota, Twin Cities Campus (MN)
U of Mississippi (MS)
U of Mount Union (OH)
U of Nebraska at Omaha (NE)
U of Nevada, Las Vegas (NV)
U of New Brunswick Fredericton (NB, Canada)
U of New Brunswick Saint John (NB, Canada)
U of New England (ME)
U of New Hampshire (NH)
The U of North Carolina at Greensboro (NC)
U of Northern Colorado (CO)
U of Oklahoma (OK)
U of Ottawa (ON, Canada)
U of Puget Sound (WA)
U of Regina (SK, Canada)
U of Rhode Island (RI)
The U of Scranton (PA)
U of South Carolina (SC)
U of South Carolina Aiken (SC)
U of Southern California (CA)
U of Southern Indiana (IN)
The U of Tennessee (TN)
The U of Tennessee at Chattanooga (TN)
The U of Texas at Arlington (TX)
The U of Texas of the Permian Basin (TX)
The U of Texas–Pan American (TX)
U of the Incarnate Word (TX)
U of the Sciences (PA)
The U of Toledo (OH)
U of Tulsa (OK)
U of Utah (UT)
U of Vermont (VT)
U of Virginia (VA)
U of Waterloo (ON, Canada)
The U of Western Ontario (ON, Canada)

U of Windsor (ON, Canada)
U of Wisconsin–Eau Claire (WI)
U of Wisconsin–La Crosse (WI)
U of Wisconsin–Madison (WI)
U of Wisconsin–Milwaukee (WI)
U of Wisconsin–Superior (WI)
U of Wyoming (WY)
Upper Iowa U (IA)
Valparaiso U (IN)
Viterbo U (WI)
Wake Forest U (NC)
Walla Walla U (WA)
Warner Pacific Coll (OR)
Washington State U (WA)
Waynesburg U (PA)
Western Illinois U (IL)
Western Kentucky U (KY)
Western Michigan U (MI)
Western Oregon U (OR)
Western State Colorado U (CO)
West Liberty U (WV)
West Texas A&M U (TX)
West Virginia Wesleyan Coll (WV)
Wichita State U (KS)
Willamette U (OR)
William Paterson U of New Jersey (NJ)
Youngstown State U (OH)

KINESIOTHERAPY
Boston U (MA)
Bridgewater State U (MA)
California State U, Long Beach (CA)
Loyola Marymount U (CA)
U of Regina (SK, Canada)

KNOWLEDGE MANAGEMENT
Framingham State U (MA)
Saint Joseph's U (PA)
Saint Louis U (MO)

KOREAN
Brigham Young U (UT)
The Ohio State U (OH)
U of California, Irvine (CA)
U of California, Los Angeles (CA)
U of Hawaii at Manoa (HI)

LABOR AND INDUSTRIAL RELATIONS
Athabasca U (AB, Canada)
Bowling Green State U (OH)
Brock U (ON, Canada)
Clarion U of Pennsylvania (PA)
Cleveland State U (OH)
Indiana U–Purdue U Fort Wayne (IN)
Ithaca Coll (NY)
New York U (NY)
Penn State Abington (PA)
Penn State Altoona (PA)
Penn State Beaver (PA)
Penn State Berks (PA)
Penn State Brandywine (PA)
Penn State DuBois (PA)
Penn State Erie, The Behrend Coll (PA)
Penn State Fayette, The Eberly Campus (PA)
Penn State Greater Allegheny (PA)
Penn State Hazleton (PA)
Penn State Lehigh Valley (PA)
Penn State Mont Alto (PA)
Penn State New Kensington (PA)
Penn State Schuylkill (PA)
Penn State Shenango (PA)
Penn State U Park (PA)
Penn State Wilkes-Barre (PA)
Penn State Worthington Scranton (PA)
Penn State York (PA)
Rider U (NJ)
Rutgers, The State U of New Jersey, New Brunswick (NJ)
San Francisco State U (CA)
State U of New York at Fredonia (NY)
State U of New York Coll at Old Westbury (NY)
State U of New York Coll at Potsdam (NY)
State U of New York Empire State Coll (NY)
Temple U (PA)
Université du Québec en Outaouais (QC, Canada)
U of Bridgeport (CT)

The U of Iowa (IA)
U of Minnesota, Twin Cities Campus (MN)

LABOR STUDIES
California State U, Dominguez Hills (CA)
Eastern Michigan U (MI)
Hofstra U (NY)
Indiana U Bloomington (IN)
Indiana U Kokomo (IN)
Indiana U Northwest (IN)
Indiana U–Purdue U Indianapolis (IN)
Indiana U South Bend (IN)
U of Windsor (ON, Canada)
Wayne State U (MI)

LANDSCAPE ARCHITECTURE
Acad of Art U (CA)
American U of Beirut (Lebanon)
Arizona State U (AZ)
Ball State U (IN)
Boston Architectural Coll (MA)
California Polytechnic State U, San Luis Obispo (CA)
California State Polytechnic U, Pomona (CA)
Clemson U (SC)
Coll of the Atlantic (ME)
Colorado State U (CO)
Iowa State U of Science and Technology (IA)
Louisiana State U and Ag and Mech Coll (LA)
Michigan State U (MI)
Mississippi State U (MS)
North Carolina State U (NC)
North Dakota State U (ND)
The Ohio State U (OH)
Oklahoma State U (OK)
Penn State Brandywine (PA)
Penn State Lehigh Valley (PA)
Penn State Schuylkill (PA)
Penn State U Park (PA)
Penn State Wilkes-Barre (PA)
Philadelphia U (PA)
Purdue U (IN)
Temple U (PA)
Texas A&M U (TX)
The U of British Columbia (BC, Canada)
U of California, Berkeley (CA)
U of California, Davis (CA)
U of Delaware (DE)
U of Florida (FL)
U of Georgia (GA)
U of Idaho (ID)
U of Illinois at Urbana–Champaign (IL)
U of Kentucky (KY)
U of Maryland, Coll Park (MD)
U of Massachusetts Amherst (MA)
U of Minnesota, Twin Cities Campus (MN)
U of Nebraska–Lincoln (NE)
U of Nevada, Las Vegas (NV)
U of Oregon (OR)
U of Rhode Island (RI)
U of Wisconsin–Madison (WI)
Utah State U (UT)
Virginia Polytechnic Inst and State U (VA)
Washington State U (WA)
West Virginia U (WV)

LANDSCAPING AND GROUNDSKEEPING
Andrews U (MI)
Florida Southern Coll (FL)
Mississippi State U (MS)
Oklahoma State U (OK)
Penn State Abington (PA)
Penn State Altoona (PA)
Penn State Beaver (PA)
Penn State Berks (PA)
Penn State Brandywine (PA)
Penn State DuBois (PA)
Penn State Erie, The Behrend Coll (PA)
Penn State Fayette, The Eberly Campus (PA)
Penn State Greater Allegheny (PA)
Penn State Hazleton (PA)
Penn State Lehigh Valley (PA)
Penn State Mont Alto (PA)
Penn State New Kensington (PA)
Penn State Schuylkill (PA)

Penn State Shenango (PA)
Penn State U Park (PA)
Penn State Wilkes-Barre (PA)
Penn State Worthington Scranton (PA)
Penn State York (PA)
South Dakota State U (SD)
U of Minnesota, Crookston (MN)
U of Nebraska–Lincoln (NE)

LAND USE PLANNING AND MANAGEMENT
Central Michigan U (MI)
Metropolitan State U of Denver (CO)
Montana State U (MT)
The U of Western Ontario (ON, Canada)

LANGUAGE INTERPRETATION AND TRANSLATION
Bard Coll (NY)
Brigham Young U (UT)
Concordia U (QC, Canada)
Mississippi Coll (MS)
Southern Nazarene U (OK)
Université du Québec en Outaouais (QC, Canada)
U of Ottawa (ON, Canada)

LASER AND OPTICAL ENGINEERING
U of Rochester (NY)

LATIN
Acadia U (NS, Canada)
Amherst Coll (MA)
Augustana Coll (IL)
Ball State U (IN)
Bard Coll (NY)
Baylor U (TX)
Binghamton U, State U of New York (NY)
Boston Coll (MA)
Boston U (MA)
Bowling Green State U (OH)
Butler U (IN)
Calvin Coll (MI)
Canisius Coll (NY)
Carleton Coll (MN)
The Catholic U of America (DC)
Colgate U (NY)
The Coll of Wooster (OH)
Concordia Coll (MN)
Creighton U (NE)
Dartmouth Coll (NH)
DePauw U (IN)
Duquesne U (PA)
Franklin & Marshall Coll (PA)
Furman U (SC)
Gettysburg Coll (PA)
Hampden-Sydney Coll (VA)
Haverford Coll (PA)
Hobart and William Smith Colls (NY)
Hofstra U (NY)
Hunter Coll of the City U of New York (NY)
John Carroll U (OH)
Kent State U (OH)
Lawrence U (WI)
Lehman Coll of the City U of New York (NY)
Loyola U Chicago (IL)
Loyola U Maryland (MD)
Mercer U (GA)
Missouri State U (MO)
Monmouth Coll (IL)
Montclair State U (NJ)
Mount Allison U (NB, Canada)
Mount Holyoke Coll (MA)
Randolph Coll (VA)
Randolph-Macon Coll (VA)
Rice U (TX)
Rockford Coll (IL)
Rutgers, The State U of New Jersey, New Brunswick (NJ)
Saint Joseph's U (PA)
Saint Mary's Coll of California (CA)
St. Olaf Coll (MN)
Samford U (AL)
Sewanee: The U of the South (TN)
Smith Coll (MA)
Southwestern U (TX)
Stanford U (CA)
Swarthmore Coll (PA)
Tufts U (MA)
Tulane U (LA)

The U of British Columbia (BC, Canada)
U of California, Berkeley (CA)
U of California, Irvine (CA)
U of Georgia (GA)
The U of Iowa (IA)
U of Miami (FL)
U of Michigan (MI)
U of Minnesota, Twin Cities Campus (MN)
U of Missouri (MO)
U of Nebraska–Lincoln (NE)
U of New Brunswick Fredericton (NB, Canada)
U of New Hampshire (NH)
U of Ottawa (ON, Canada)
U of Richmond (VA)
U of St. Thomas (MN)
The U of Scranton (PA)
The U of Texas at Austin (TX)
U of Vermont (VT)
The U of Western Ontario (ON, Canada)
U of Windsor (ON, Canada)
U of Wisconsin–Madison (WI)
Virginia Wesleyan Coll (VA)
Wabash Coll (IN)
Wake Forest U (NC)
Washington U in St. Louis (MO)
Wellesley Coll (MA)
West Chester U of Pennsylvania (PA)
Western Michigan U (MI)
Wheaton Coll (MA)
Wright State U (OH)
Yale U (CT)

LATIN AMERICAN AND CARIBBEAN STUDIES
Coll of Charleston (SC)
Mount Holyoke Coll (MA)
Rollins Coll (FL)
U of Georgia (GA)
U of Michigan (MI)
U of Wisconsin–Madison (WI)
U of Wisconsin–Milwaukee (WI)

LATIN AMERICAN STUDIES
Adelphi U (NY)
Albion Coll (MI)
Albright Coll (PA)
American U (DC)
Assumption Coll (MA)
Bard Coll (NY)
Baylor U (TX)
Bennington Coll (VT)
Binghamton U, State U of New York (NY)
Blackburn Coll (IL)
Boston U (MA)
Bowdoin Coll (ME)
Bowling Green State U (OH)
Brown U (RI)
Bucknell U (PA)
California State U, Chico (CA)
California State U, East Bay (CA)
California State U, Fullerton (CA)
California State U, Los Angeles (CA)
California State U, Northridge (CA)
Canisius Coll (NY)
Carleton Coll (MN)
Carnegie Mellon U (PA)
City Coll of the City U of New York (NY)
Colby Coll (ME)
Colgate U (NY)
The Coll at Brockport, State U of New York (NY)
The Coll of William and Mary (VA)
Columbia U (NY)
Columbia U, School of General Studies (NY)
Connecticut Coll (CT)
Cornell Coll (IA)
Dartmouth Coll (NH)
Davidson Coll (NC)
DePaul U (IL)
Dickinson Coll (PA)
Earlham Coll (IN)
Flagler Coll (FL)
Fort Lewis Coll (CO)
George Mason U (VA)
Gettysburg Coll (PA)
Gustavus Adolphus Coll (MN)
Hamline U (MN)
Hampshire Coll (MA)
Haverford Coll (PA)

Hobart and William Smith Colls (NY)
Hofstra U (NY)
Hood Coll (MD)
Hunter Coll of the City U of New York (NY)
Illinois Wesleyan U (IL)
The Johns Hopkins U (MD)
Kent State U (OH)
Lehman Coll of the City U of New York (NY)
Macalester Coll (MN)
Miami U (OH)
Middlebury Coll (VT)
Millsaps Coll (MS)
New Coll of Florida (FL)
New York U (NY)
Oakland U (MI)
Ohio U (OH)
Ohio Wesleyan U (OH)
Pace U (NY)
Penn State Abington (PA)
Penn State Altoona (PA)
Penn State Beaver (PA)
Penn State Berks (PA)
Penn State Brandywine (PA)
Penn State DuBois (PA)
Penn State Erie, The Behrend Coll (PA)
Penn State Fayette, The Eberly Campus (PA)
Penn State Greater Allegheny (PA)
Penn State Hazleton (PA)
Penn State Lehigh Valley (PA)
Penn State Mont Alto (PA)
Penn State New Kensington (PA)
Penn State Schuylkill (PA)
Penn State Shenango (PA)
Penn State U Park (PA)
Penn State Wilkes-Barre (PA)
Penn State Worthington Scranton (PA)
Penn State York (PA)
Pomona Coll (CA)
Portland State U (OR)
Prescott Coll (AZ)
Rhode Island Coll (RI)
Rhodes Coll (TN)
Rice U (TX)
Ripon Coll (WI)
Rutgers, The State U of New Jersey, New Brunswick (NJ)
St. Edward's U (TX)
Saint Louis U (MO)
Saint Mary's Coll of California (CA)
St. Olaf Coll (MN)
Samford U (AL)
San Diego State U (CA)
Scripps Coll (CA)
Seattle Pacific U (WA)
Skidmore Coll (NY)
Smith Coll (MA)
Southern Methodist U (TX)
Southwestern U (TX)
Stanford U (CA)
State U of New York at New Paltz (NY)
State U of New York at Plattsburgh (NY)
Swarthmore Coll (PA)
Syracuse U (NY)
Temple U (PA)
Trinity U (TX)
Tufts U (MA)
Tulane U (LA)
Union Coll (KY)
United States Military Acad (NY)
U at Albany, State U of New York (NY)
The U of Alabama (AL)
The U of Arizona (AZ)
The U of British Columbia (BC, Canada)
U of California, Berkeley (CA)
U of California, Los Angeles (CA)
U of California, Riverside (CA)
U of California, Santa Cruz (CA)
U of Central Florida (FL)
U of Chicago (IL)
U of Delaware (DE)
U of Denver (CO)
U of Idaho (ID)
U of Illinois at Chicago (IL)
U of Illinois at Urbana–Champaign (IL)
The U of Iowa (IA)
The U of Kansas (KS)

U of Kentucky (KY)
U of Miami (FL)
U of Minnesota, Twin Cities Campus (MN)
U of Missouri (MO)
U of Nebraska at Omaha (NE)
U of Nebraska–Lincoln (NE)
U of New Mexico (NM)
The U of North Carolina at Chapel Hill (NC)
The U of North Carolina at Charlotte (NC)
U of Oregon (OR)
U of Pennsylvania (PA)
U of Richmond (VA)
U of South Carolina (SC)
The U of Texas at Austin (TX)
The U of Texas at El Paso (TX)
The U of Toledo (OH)
U of Utah (UT)
U of Vermont (VT)
The U of Western Ontario (ON, Canada)
U of Wisconsin–Eau Claire (WI)
Vanderbilt U (TN)
Vassar Coll (NY)
Villanova U (PA)
Washington Coll (MD)
Washington U in St. Louis (MO)
Wellesley Coll (MA)
Wesleyan U (CT)
Westminster Coll (UT)
Willamette U (OR)
William Paterson U of New Jersey (NJ)
Yale U (CT)

LATIN TEACHER EDUCATION
Assumption Coll (MA)
Boston U (MA)
Brigham Young U (UT)
Concordia Coll (MN)
Duquesne U (PA)
Indiana U Bloomington (IN)
Miami U (OH)
Missouri State U (MO)
Ohio Wesleyan U (OH)
U of Delaware (DE)
U of Illinois at Urbana–Champaign (IL)
Western Michigan U (MI)

LAY MINISTRY
Abilene Christian U (TX)
Arizona Christian U (AZ)
Saint Mary's U of Minnesota (MN)
Southeastern Bible Coll (AL)
Trevecca Nazarene U (TN)

LEARNING SCIENCES
The U of Arizona (AZ)

LEGAL ADMINISTRATIVE ASSISTANT/SECRETARY
Lewis-Clark State Coll (ID)
Texas A&M U–Commerce (TX)

LEGAL ASSISTANT/PARALEGAL
Boston U (MA)
California State U, Chico (CA)
Calumet Coll of Saint Joseph (IN)
Champlain Coll (VT)
Clayton State U (GA)
Coll of Mount St. Joseph (OH)
Coll of Saint Mary (NE)
Concordia U Wisconsin (WI)
Davenport U, Grand Rapids (MI)
East Central U (OK)
Eastern Michigan U (MI)
Faulkner U (AL)
Florida Gulf Coast U (FL)
Gannon U (PA)
Grand Valley State U (MI)
Hampton U (VA)
Hilbert Coll (NY)
Husson U (ME)
Indiana Tech (IN)
Jones Coll, Jacksonville (FL)
Kent State U (OH)
Lake Erie Coll (OH)
Lewis-Clark State Coll (ID)
Lewis U (IL)
Madonna U (MI)
Marymount U (VA)
Maryville U of Saint Louis (MO)
Minnesota State U Moorhead (MN)
Mississippi Coll (MS)
Mississippi U for Women (MS)

Morehead State U (KY)
National U (CA)
New York City Coll of Technology of the City U of New York (NY)
Nova Southeastern U (FL)
Peirce Coll (PA)
Pennsylvania Coll of Technology (PA)
Post U (CT)
Quinnipiac U (CT)
Roger Williams U (RI)
Roosevelt U (IL)
Saint Mary-of-the-Woods Coll (IN)
Southern Illinois U Carbondale (IL)
State U of New York Coll of Technology at Canton (NY)
Stevenson U (MD)
Suffolk U (MA)
Sullivan U (KY)
Texas A&M U–Commerce (TX)
Texas Wesleyan U (TX)
Texas Woman's U (TX)
U of Central Florida (FL)
U of Cincinnati (OH)
U of Evansville (IN)
U of Great Falls (MT)
U of Hartford (CT)
U of Houston–Clear Lake (TX)
U of La Verne (CA)
U of Mississippi (MS)
U of Southern Mississippi (MS)
The U of Tennessee at Chattanooga (TN)
The U of Toledo (OH)
U of West Florida (FL)
Ursuline Coll (OH)
Valdosta State U (GA)
Washburn U (KS)
Wesley Coll (DE)

LEGAL PROFESSIONS AND STUDIES RELATED
Armstrong Atlantic State U (GA)
Ball State U (IN)
Central Penn Coll (PA)
Hamline U (MN)
Hodges U (FL)
Maryville U of Saint Louis (MO)
National U (CA)
New Jersey Inst of Technology (NJ)
Ramapo Coll of New Jersey (NJ)
Roger Williams U (RI)
St. John's U (NY)
Temple U (PA)
Tulane U (LA)
U of Illinois at Springfield (IL)
U of Nebraska at Omaha (NE)
U of Nebraska–Lincoln (NE)
U of Pennsylvania (PA)
U of Tulsa (OK)

LEGAL STUDIES
Adams State U (CO)
American Public U System (WV)
American U (DC)
Amherst Coll (MA)
Arizona State U (AZ)
Bay Path Coll (MA)
Bridgewater State U (MA)
California State U, Chico (CA)
Central Michigan U (MI)
Claremont McKenna Coll (CA)
Coll of the Atlantic (ME)
DeSales U (PA)
Dickinson Coll (PA)
Dominican U (IL)
Emory & Henry Coll (VA)
Florida National U (FL)
Goldey-Beacom Coll (DE)
Hampshire Coll (MA)
Harding U (AR)
Hood Coll (MD)
James Madison U (VA)
John Jay Coll of Criminal Justice of the City U of New York (NY)
Lasell Coll (MA)
Lipscomb U (TN)
Manhattanville Coll (NY)
Nazareth Coll of Rochester (NY)
Newbury Coll (MA)
North Carolina Wesleyan Coll (NC)
Northwest U (WA)
Park U (MO)
Point Park U (PA)
Quinnipiac U (CT)
St. John's U (NY)
Saint Joseph's U (PA)
Saint Louis U (MO)

Scripps Coll (CA)
State U of New York at Fredonia (NY)
Stevenson U (MD)
Suffolk U (MA)
Tiffin U (OH)
United States Air Force Acad (CO)
Université de Sherbrooke (QC, Canada)
U of California, Berkeley (CA)
U of California, Santa Barbara (CA)
U of California, Santa Cruz (CA)
U of Hartford (CT)
U of Maryland U Coll (MD)
U of Massachusetts Amherst (MA)
U of Miami (FL)
U of New Brunswick Fredericton (NB, Canada)
U of New Haven (CT)
U of Pittsburgh (PA)
The U of Western Ontario (ON, Canada)
U of Windsor (ON, Canada)
U of Wisconsin–Madison (WI)
U of Wisconsin–Superior (WI)
Virginia Intermont Coll (VA)
Webster U (MO)
Wilmington U (DE)

LIBERAL ARTS AND SCIENCES AND HUMANITIES RELATED
Auburn U (AL)
Barton Coll (NC)
Belhaven U (MS)
Bennington Coll (VT)
Brigham Young U (UT)
California Polytechnic State U, San Luis Obispo (CA)
California State U, Dominguez Hills (CA)
Carnegie Mellon U (PA)
The Colorado Coll (CO)
Concordia Coll (MN)
Crown Coll (MN)
Duquesne U (PA)
Fairfield U (CT)
Florida Atlantic U (FL)
George Mason U (VA)
Georgia Coll & State U (GA)
Goddard Coll (VT)
Hampshire Coll (MA)
Howard Payne U (TX)
The Johns Hopkins U (MD)
Kent State U at Ashtabula (OH)
Kent State U at East Liverpool (OH)
Kent State U at Geauga (OH)
Kent State U at Salem (OH)
Kent State U at Stark (OH)
Kent State U at Trumbull (OH)
Kent State U at Tuscarawas (OH)
Loyola U New Orleans (LA)
Malone U (OH)
Marshall U (WV)
Marymount Coll, Palos Verdes, California (CA)
Missouri Baptist U (MO)
Mount Aloysius Coll (PA)
National U (CA)
North Carolina State U (NC)
Oakland U (MI)
Ohio U (OH)
Ohio U–Chillicothe (OH)
Pepperdine U, Malibu (CA)
Prescott Coll (AZ)
Purdue U (IN)
Roger Williams U (RI)
Sacred Heart U (CT)
Saint Anselm Coll (NH)
St. John's Coll (NM)
Saint Louis U (MO)
Saint Mary's Coll of California (CA)
Salem State U (MA)
Shimer Coll (IL)
Southern Methodist U (TX)
Tulane U (LA)
The U of Akron (OH)
U of California, Los Angeles (CA)
U of California, Santa Barbara (CA)
U of Illinois at Urbana–Champaign (IL)
U of Maryland U Coll (MD)
U of Mary Washington (VA)
U of Massachusetts Amherst (MA)
U of Minnesota, Twin Cities Campus (MN)
U of Oklahoma (OK)
U of Rhode Island (RI)

U of Wisconsin–Milwaukee (WI)
U of Wisconsin–Platteville (WI)
Valdosta State U (GA)
Vassar Coll (NY)
Walsh U (OH)
Wayland Baptist U (TX)
Western Illinois U (IL)

LIBERAL ARTS AND SCIENCES/LIBERAL STUDIES
Abilene Christian U (TX)
Adams State U (CO)
Alaska Pacific U (AK)
Albion Coll (MI)
Alcorn State U (MS)
Alderson-Broaddus Coll (WV)
Alliant Intl U–México City (Mexico)
Alvernia U (PA)
Alverno Coll (WI)
American Jewish U (CA)
American U (DC)
Amridge U (AL)
Antioch U Midwest (OH)
Antioch U Santa Barbara (CA)
Appalachian State U (NC)
Arizona State U (AZ)
Armstrong Atlantic State U (GA)
Ashland U (OH)
Athabasca U (AB, Canada)
Athens State U (AL)
Auburn U at Montgomery (AL)
Augsburg Coll (MN)
Augustana Coll (IL)
Augustana Coll (SD)
Austin Peay State U (TN)
Averett U (VA)
Azusa Pacific U (CA)
Ball State U (IN)
Barry U (FL)
Bay Path Coll (MA)
Beacon Coll (FL)
Becker Coll (MA)
Bellarmine U (KY)
Belmont U (TN)
Bemidji State U (MN)
Benedictine Coll (KS)
Bennington Coll (VT)
Bentley U (MA)
Bethany Lutheran Coll (MN)
Bethel Coll (IN)
Bethune-Cookman U (FL)
Bluefield Coll (VA)
Bowling Green State U (OH)
Bowling Green State U-Firelands Coll (OH)
Bridgewater Coll (VA)
Brigham Young U (UT)
Brock U (ON, Canada)
Buffalo State Coll, State U of New York (NY)
Butler U (IN)
Cabrini Coll (PA)
California Lutheran U (CA)
California Polytechnic State U, San Luis Obispo (CA)
California State Polytechnic U, Pomona (CA)
California State U, Chico (CA)
California State U, Dominguez Hills (CA)
California State U, East Bay (CA)
California State U, Fresno (CA)
California State U, Fullerton (CA)
California State U, Long Beach (CA)
California State U, Los Angeles (CA)
California State U, Monterey Bay (CA)
California State U, Northridge (CA)
California State U, San Bernardino (CA)
California State U, San Marcos (CA)
California State U, Stanislaus (CA)
Calumet Coll of Saint Joseph (IN)
Cambridge Coll (MA)
Canisius Coll (NY)
Cardinal Stritch U (WI)
Carlow U (PA)
Carnegie Mellon U (PA)
Carson-Newman U (TN)
The Catholic U of America (DC)
Cedar Crest Coll (PA)
Cedarville U (OH)
Central Michigan U (MI)

Champlain Coll (VT)
Chapman U (CA)
Charter Oak State Coll (CT)
Chatham U (PA)
Chestnut Hill Coll (PA)
Chicago State U (IL)
Christian Brothers U (TN)
Clarkson U (NY)
Clayton State U (GA)
Cleveland State U (OH)
Coastal Carolina U (SC)
Coe Coll (IA)
Coll of Mount St. Joseph (OH)
The Coll of New Rochelle (NY)
Coll of Saint Benedict (MN)
The Coll of Saint Rose (NY)
The Coll of Saints John Fisher & Thomas More (TX)
Coll of the Atlantic (ME)
Colorado Mesa U (CO)
Colorado State U (CO)
Columbia Coll (SC)
Columbia Coll Chicago (IL)
Columbus State U (GA)
Concordia Coll–New York (NY)
Concordia U (CA)
Concordia U (OR)
Concordia U Texas (TX)
Concordia U Wisconsin (WI)
Corban U (OR)
Cornell Coll (IA)
Crossroads Coll (MN)
Culver-Stockton Coll (MO)
Dakota State U (SD)
Dakota Wesleyan U (SD)
Dallas Baptist U (TX)
Defiance Coll (OH)
DEREE—The American Coll of Greece (Greece)
DeSales U (PA)
Duquesne U (PA)
East Carolina U (NC)
Eastern Illinois U (IL)
Eastern Mennonite U (VA)
Eastern New Mexico U (NM)
East Tennessee State U (TN)
Edinboro U of Pennsylvania (PA)
Elmira Coll (NY)
Emmanuel Coll (MA)
Endicott Coll (MA)
Eugene Lang Coll The New School for Liberal Arts (NY)
The Evergreen State Coll (WA)
Excelsior Coll (NY)
Faulkner U (AL)
Felician Coll (NJ)
Ferrum Coll (VA)
Flagler Coll (FL)
Florida Atlantic U (FL)
Florida Coll (FL)
Florida Gulf Coast U (FL)
Florida Intl U (FL)
Fort Lewis Coll (CO)
Framingham State U (MA)
Francis Marion U (SC)
Franklin Pierce U (NH)
Friends U (KS)
Frostburg State U (MD)
Gannon U (PA)
George Mason U (VA)
Georgetown U (DC)
Gettysburg Coll (PA)
Gonzaga U (WA)
Governors State U (IL)
Graceland U (IA)
Grace U (NE)
Grand Valley State U (MI)
Grand View U (IA)
Granite State Coll (NH)
Greenville Coll (IL)
Harris-Stowe State U (MO)
Hillsdale Free Will Baptist Coll (OK)
Hofstra U (NY)
Holy Cross Coll (IN)
Holy Names U (CA)
Hope Intl U (CA)
Houghton Coll (NY)
Howard Payne U (TX)
Humboldt State U (CA)
Huntington U (IN)
Husson U (ME)
Illinois Coll (IL)
Illinois Inst of Technology (IL)
Illinois Wesleyan U (IL)
Immaculata U (PA)
Indiana State U (IN)
Indiana U Bloomington (IN)

Iona Coll (NY)
Iowa State U of Science and Technology (IA)
Iowa Wesleyan Coll (IA)
Ithaca Coll (NY)
James Madison U (VA)
The Johns Hopkins U (MD)
Johnson C. Smith U (NC)
Johnson State Coll (VT)
Juniata Coll (PA)
Kansas Wesleyan U (KS)
Kent State U (OH)
Kent State U at Tuscarawas (OH)
Kentucky State U (KY)
Keuka Coll (NY)
Lake Superior State U (MI)
Lamar U (TX)
Lander U (SC)
Langston U (OK)
La Roche Coll (PA)
Lasell Coll (MA)
La Sierra U (CA)
Lesley U (MA)
Lewis U (IL)
Liberty U (VA)
Limestone Coll (SC)
Lincoln Memorial U (TN)
Lincoln U (MO)
Lindenwood U (MO)
Lock Haven U of Pennsylvania (PA)
Long Island U–Brooklyn Campus (NY)
Long Island U–C. W. Post Campus (NY)
Longwood U (VA)
Louisiana Coll (LA)
Louisiana State U and Ag and Mech Coll (LA)
Louisiana State U at Alexandria (LA)
Loyola Marymount U (CA)
Lynn U (FL)
Manchester U (IN)
Manhattan Coll (NY)
Mansfield U of Pennsylvania (PA)
Marian U (WI)
Marietta Coll (OH)
Mars Hill Coll (NC)
Marymount Coll, Palos Verdes, California (CA)
Marymount Manhattan Coll (NY)
Marymount U (VA)
Maryville U of Saint Louis (MO)
Massachusetts Coll of Liberal Arts (MA)
Massachusetts Inst of Technology (MA)
The Master's Coll and Sem (CA)
McNeese State U (LA)
Medaille Coll (NY)
Mercy Coll (NY)
Merrimack Coll (MA)
Miami U (OH)
Middlebury Coll (VT)
Middle Tennessee State U (TN)
Midwestern State U (TX)
Mississippi State U (MS)
Mississippi U for Women (MS)
Mitchell Coll (CT)
Molloy Coll (NY)
Monmouth Coll (IL)
Montana State U (MT)
Montana Tech of The U of Montana (MT)
Morris Coll (SC)
Mount Allison U (NB, Canada)
Mount Aloysius Coll (PA)
Mount Marty Coll (SD)
Mount Mary Coll (WI)
Mount St. Mary's Coll (CA)
Murray State U (KY)
National U (CA)
Neumann U (PA)
New Coll of Florida (FL)
Newman U (KS)
New Mexico Highlands U (NM)
New Saint Andrews Coll (ID)
The New School for Public Engagement (NY)
New York City Coll of Technology of the City U of New York (NY)
New York U (NY)
Niagara U (NY)
North Carolina State U (NC)
North Central Coll (IL)
Northeastern Illinois U (IL)
Northern Arizona U (AZ)

Northern Illinois U (IL)
Northern Michigan U (MI)
North Greenville U (SC)
Northwestern Coll (IA)
Northwestern State U of Louisiana (LA)
Northwest Nazarene U (ID)
Notre Dame de Namur U (CA)
Oakland U (MI)
Ohio Dominican U (OH)
Ohio Valley U (WV)
Oklahoma Christian U (OK)
Oklahoma City U (OK)
Oklahoma State U (OK)
Olivet Coll (MI)
Oral Roberts U (OK)
Oregon State U (OR)
Pacific U (OR)
Park U (MO)
Patrick Henry Coll (VA)
Penn State Abington (PA)
Penn State Altoona (PA)
Penn State Beaver (PA)
Penn State Berks (PA)
Penn State Brandywine (PA)
Penn State DuBois (PA)
Penn State Erie, The Behrend Coll (PA)
Penn State Fayette, The Eberly Campus (PA)
Penn State Greater Allegheny (PA)
Penn State Lehigh Valley (PA)
Penn State Mont Alto (PA)
Penn State New Kensington (PA)
Penn State Schuylkill (PA)
Penn State Shenango (PA)
Penn State U Park (PA)
Penn State Wilkes-Barre (PA)
Penn State Worthington Scranton (PA)
Penn State York (PA)
Pepperdine U, Malibu (CA)
Point Loma Nazarene U (CA)
Point Park U (PA)
Pomona Coll (CA)
Portland State U (OR)
Providence Coll (RI)
Purchase Coll, State U of New York (NY)
Purdue U North Central (IN)
Quincy U (IL)
Quinnipiac U (CT)
Ramapo Coll of New Jersey (NJ)
Randolph Coll (VA)
Regis Coll (MA)
Regis U (CO)
Rhode Island Coll (RI)
The Richard Stockton Coll of New Jersey (NJ)
Rider U (NJ)
Rivier U (NH)
Roberts Wesleyan Coll (NY)
Rogers State U (OK)
Roger Williams U (RI)
Roosevelt U (IL)
Rowan U (NJ)
Rutgers, The State U of New Jersey, Camden (NJ)
Rutgers, The State U of New Jersey, New Brunswick (NJ)
St. Edward's U (TX)
St. Francis Coll (NY)
St. Gregory's U, Shawnee (OK)
St. John Fisher Coll (NY)
St. John's Coll (MD)
St. John's Coll (NM)
Saint John's U (MN)
St. John's U (NY)
St. Joseph's Coll, Long Island Campus (NY)
St. Joseph's Coll, New York (NY)
Saint Joseph Sem Coll (LA)
Saint Joseph's U (PA)
Saint Leo U (FL)
Saint Mary-of-the-Woods Coll (IN)
Saint Mary's Coll of California (CA)
St. Olaf Coll (MN)
St. Thomas U (FL)
Saint Vincent Coll (PA)
Salisbury U (MD)
Salve Regina U (RI)
San Diego Christian Coll (CA)
San Diego State U (CA)
San Francisco State U (CA)
San Jose State U (CA)
Schreiner U (TX)
Seattle Pacific U (WA)

Seattle U (WA)
Shaw U (NC)
Shenandoah U (VA)
Shimer Coll (IL)
Simon Fraser U (BC, Canada)
Simpson U (CA)
Skidmore Coll (NY)
Soka U of America (CA)
Sonoma State U (CA)
South Dakota State U (SD)
Southern Connecticut State U (CT)
Southern Illinois U Carbondale (IL)
Southern Illinois U Edwardsville (IL)
Southern Oregon U (OR)
Southwestern Coll (KS)
Spalding U (KY)
State U of New York at Fredonia (NY)
State U of New York at New Paltz (NY)
State U of New York at Plattsburgh (NY)
Stephens Coll (MO)
Suffolk U (MA)
Sullivan U (KY)
Susquehanna U (PA)
Sweet Briar Coll (VA)
Syracuse U (NY)
Tabor Coll (KS)
Tarleton State U (TX)
Tennessee State U (TN)
Texas A&M U–Commerce (TX)
Thomas Aquinas Coll (CA)
Thomas Edison State Coll (NJ)
Thomas More Coll (KY)
Thomas U (GA)
Thompson Rivers U (BC, Canada)
Transylvania U (KY)
Trent U (ON, Canada)
Trine U (IN)
Troy U (AL)
Tulane U (LA)
U at Buffalo, the State U of New York (NY)
The U of Akron (OH)
U of Alaska Anchorage (AK)
U of Alaska Anchorage, Kenai Peninsula Coll (AK)
U of Alaska Fairbanks (AK)
U of Arkansas at Little Rock (AR)
The U of British Columbia (BC, Canada)
U of California, Riverside (CA)
U of California, Santa Barbara (CA)
U of Central Arkansas (AR)
U of Central Oklahoma (OK)
U of Chicago (IL)
U of Cincinnati (OH)
U of Delaware (DE)
U of Evansville (IN)
U of Georgia (GA)
U of Hawaii at Manoa (HI)
U of Houston (TX)
U of Houston–Victoria (TX)
U of Illinois at Springfield (IL)
U of Illinois at Urbana–Champaign (IL)
The U of Iowa (IA)
The U of Kansas (KS)
U of La Verne (CA)
U of Louisville (KY)
U of Maine at Farmington (ME)
U of Maine at Fort Kent (ME)
U of Maryland Eastern Shore (MD)
U of Mary Washington (VA)
U of Massachusetts Dartmouth (MA)
U of Memphis (TN)
U of Michigan–Dearborn (MI)
U of Michigan–Flint (MI)
U of Minnesota, Twin Cities Campus (MN)
U of Mississippi (MS)
U of Missouri–St. Louis (MO)
U of Nebraska–Lincoln (NE)
U of New Brunswick Fredericton (NB, Canada)
U of New Brunswick Saint John (NB, Canada)
U of New England (ME)
U of New Haven (CT)
U of New Mexico (NM)
U of North Carolina at Asheville (NC)
The U of North Carolina at Chapel Hill (NC)

The U of North Carolina at Greensboro (NC)
U of Northern Iowa (IA)
U of North Florida (FL)
U of Notre Dame (IN)
U of Oklahoma (OK)
U of Pennsylvania (PA)
U of Pittsburgh (PA)
U of Pittsburgh at Bradford (PA)
U of Redlands (CA)
U of Regina (SK, Canada)
U of Rochester (NY)
U of St. Francis (IL)
U of Saint Mary (KS)
U of St. Thomas (TX)
U of San Diego (CA)
The U of Scranton (PA)
U of South Carolina (SC)
U of South Carolina Aiken (SC)
The U of South Dakota (SD)
U of Southern Indiana (IN)
U of Southern Maine (ME)
The U of Tampa (FL)
The U of Texas at Austin (TX)
U of the Incarnate Word (TX)
The U of Toledo (OH)
U of Tulsa (OK)
U of Vermont (VT)
U of Virginia (VA)
U of Washington, Tacoma (WA)
U of Waterloo (ON, Canada)
The U of Western Ontario (ON, Canada)
U of Wisconsin–Eau Claire (WI)
U of Wisconsin–Green Bay (WI)
U of Wisconsin–Platteville (WI)
Utah State U (UT)
Utica Coll (NY)
Valdosta State U (GA)
Villanova U (PA)
Virginia State U (VA)
Viterbo U (WI)
Walsh U (OH)
Warner Pacific Coll (OR)
Washburn U (KS)
Washington Coll (MD)
Washington State U (WA)
Washington U in St. Louis (MO)
Weber State U (UT)
Wesley Coll (DE)
West Chester U of Pennsylvania (PA)
Western Carolina U (NC)
Western Connecticut State U (CT)
Western Illinois U (IL)
Western Washington U (WA)
Westfield State U (MA)
West Virginia U (WV)
Wheeling Jesuit U (WV)
Wilkes U (PA)
William Jewell Coll (MO)
William Paterson U of New Jersey (NJ)
William Peace U (NC)
Wittenberg U (OH)
Wright State U (OH)
Xavier U (OH)
York Coll of the City U of New York (NY)
Youngstown State U (OH)

LIBRARY AND INFORMATION SCIENCE
Ball State U (IN)
Clarion U of Pennsylvania (PA)
Kutztown U of Pennsylvania (PA)
Southern Connecticut State U (CT)
Texas A&M U–Commerce (TX)
U of Minnesota, Twin Cities Campus (MN)
U of Nebraska at Omaha (NE)
U of Southern Mississippi (MS)

LIBRARY SCIENCE RELATED
U of Great Falls (MT)

LICENSED PRACTICAL/ VOCATIONAL NURSE TRAINING
Crown Coll (MN)
The U of Western Ontario (ON, Canada)
York Coll of Pennsylvania (PA)

LINGUISTIC AND COMPARATIVE LANGUAGE STUDIES RELATED
Brigham Young U (UT)

Iowa State U of Science and Technology (IA)
U of California, Los Angeles (CA)
U of California, Santa Barbara (CA)

LINGUISTICS
Baylor U (TX)
Bethel U (MN)
Binghamton U, State U of New York (NY)
Boston U (MA)
Brock U (ON, Canada)
Brown U (RI)
California State U, Chico (CA)
California State U, Dominguez Hills (CA)
California State U, Fresno (CA)
California State U, Fullerton (CA)
California State U, Monterey Bay (CA)
California State U, Northridge (CA)
Calvin Coll (MI)
Carleton Coll (MN)
Carnegie Mellon U (PA)
Central Coll (IA)
City Coll of the City U of New York (NY)
Cleveland State U (OH)
The Coll of William and Mary (VA)
Columbia U (NY)
Concordia U (QC, Canada)
Dartmouth Coll (NH)
Eastern Michigan U (MI)
Florida Atlantic U (FL)
Georgetown U (DC)
Georgia State U (GA)
Gordon Coll (MA)
Hampshire Coll (MA)
Hofstra U (NY)
Indiana U Bloomington (IN)
Iowa State U of Science and Technology (IA)
Lawrence U (WI)
Lehman Coll of the City U of New York (NY)
Macalester Coll (MN)
Massachusetts Inst of Technology (MA)
Miami U (OH)
Michigan State U (MI)
Mid-Atlantic Christian U (NC)
Montclair State U (NJ)
New York U (NY)
Northeastern Illinois U (IL)
Northeastern U (MA)
Oakland U (MI)
The Ohio State U (OH)
Ohio U (OH)
Pitzer Coll (CA)
Pomona Coll (CA)
Portland State U (OR)
Purdue U (IN)
Reed Coll (OR)
Rice U (TX)
Rutgers, The State U of New Jersey, New Brunswick (NJ)
San Diego State U (CA)
San Jose State U (CA)
Scripps Coll (CA)
Seattle Pacific U (WA)
Simon Fraser U (BC, Canada)
Southern Illinois U Carbondale (IL)
Stanford U (CA)
State U of New York at Oswego (NY)
Stony Brook U, State U of New York (NY)
Swarthmore Coll (PA)
Syracuse U (NY)
Temple U (PA)
Truman State U (MO)
Tulane U (LA)
U at Albany, State U of New York (NY)
U at Buffalo, the State U of New York (NY)
U of Alaska Fairbanks (AK)
The U of Arizona (AZ)
The U of British Columbia (BC, Canada)
U of California, Berkeley (CA)
U of California, Davis (CA)
U of California, Los Angeles (CA)
U of California, Riverside (CA)
U of California, Santa Barbara (CA)
U of California, Santa Cruz (CA)
U of Chicago (IL)

U of Cincinnati (OH)
U of Colorado Boulder (CO)
U of Delaware (DE)
U of Florida (FL)
U of Georgia (GA)
U of Hawaii at Hilo (HI)
U of Houston (TX)
U of Illinois at Urbana–Champaign (IL)
The U of Iowa (IA)
The U of Kansas (KS)
U of Kentucky (KY)
U of Maryland, Coll Park (MD)
U of Massachusetts Amherst (MA)
U of Michigan (MI)
U of Minnesota, Twin Cities Campus (MN)
U of Mississippi (MS)
U of Missouri (MO)
U of New Brunswick Fredericton (NB, Canada)
U of New Brunswick Saint John (NB, Canada)
U of New Hampshire (NH)
U of New Mexico (NM)
The U of North Carolina at Chapel Hill (NC)
U of Oklahoma (OK)
U of Oregon (OR)
U of Ottawa (ON, Canada)
U of Pennsylvania (PA)
U of Pittsburgh (PA)
U of Regina (SK, Canada)
U of Rochester (NY)
U of Southern California (CA)
U of Southern Maine (ME)
The U of Texas at Arlington (TX)
The U of Texas at Austin (TX)
The U of Texas at El Paso (TX)
The U of Toledo (OH)
U of Utah (UT)
The U of Western Ontario (ON, Canada)
U of Wisconsin–Madison (WI)
U of Wisconsin–Milwaukee (WI)
Washington State U (WA)
Washington U in St. Louis (MO)
Wayne State U (MI)
Wellesley Coll (MA)
Western Washington U (WA)
Yale U (CT)

LITERATURE
American U (DC)
Bryant U (RI)
Calvin Coll (MI)
Castleton State Coll (VT)
Concordia U, St. Paul (MN)
Duquesne U (PA)
Franklin Coll Switzerland (Switzerland)
Huntington U (IN)
Lipscomb U (TN)
Massachusetts Coll of Liberal Arts (MA)
Mississippi Coll (MS)
Saint Mary's U of Minnesota (MN)
Southwestern Coll (KS)
Washington U in St. Louis (MO)
Williams Coll (MA)

LITERATURE RELATED
The American U of Paris (France)

LOGIC
Carnegie Mellon U (PA)
U of Pennsylvania (PA)

LOGISTICS, MATERIALS, AND SUPPLY CHAIN MANAGEMENT
American Public U System (WV)
Arkansas State U (AR)
Athens State U (AL)
Auburn U (AL)
Baylor U (TX)
Binghamton U, State U of New York (NY)
Boise State U (ID)
Bowling Green State U (OH)
Brigham Young U (UT)
Bryant U (RI)
California State U, Dominguez Hills (CA)
Central Michigan U (MI)
Clarkson U (NY)
Clayton State U (GA)
Concordia U (QC, Canada)

Duquesne U (PA)
Eastern Michigan U (MI)
Georgia Southern U (GA)
Hofstra U (NY)
Iowa State U of Science and Technology (IA)
Lehigh U (PA)
Maine Maritime Acad (ME)
Michigan State U (MI)
Missouri State U (MO)
Niagara U (NY)
Northeastern U (MA)
The Ohio State U (OH)
Park U (MO)
Penn State Beaver (PA)
Penn State Brandywine (PA)
Penn State Fayette, The Eberly Campus (PA)
Penn State Greater Allegheny (PA)
Penn State Hazleton (PA)
Penn State Lehigh Valley (PA)
Penn State New Kensington (PA)
Penn State Schuylkill (PA)
Penn State Shenango (PA)
Penn State York (PA)
Portland State U (OR)
Shippensburg U of Pennsylvania (PA)
Southeastern Louisiana U (LA)
State U of New York at New Paltz (NY)
Sullivan U (KY)
Syracuse U (NY)
U of Alaska Anchorage (AK)
The U of Findlay (OH)
U of Illinois at Urbana–Champaign (IL)
The U of Kansas (KS)
U of Maryland, Coll Park (MD)
U of Memphis (TN)
U of Nebraska–Lincoln (NE)
U of North Texas (TX)
U of Puerto Rico at Bayamón (PR)
U of St. Francis (IL)
The U of Tennessee (TN)
The U of Texas at Austin (TX)
The U of Toledo (OH)
U of Wisconsin–Stout (WI)
Weber State U (UT)
Western Illinois U (IL)
Western Michigan U (MI)
Wright State U (OH)
York Coll of Pennsylvania (PA)

MAGNETIC RESONANCE IMAGING (MRI) TECHNOLOGY
Saint Louis U (MO)

MANAGEMENT INFORMATION SYSTEMS
Adams State U (CO)
American U (DC)
Angelo State U (TX)
Appalachian State U (NC)
Auburn U (AL)
Auburn U at Montgomery (AL)
Augsburg Coll (MN)
Augustana Coll (SD)
Aurora U (IL)
Avila U (MO)
Azusa Pacific U (CA)
Babson Coll (MA)
Ball State U (IN)
Barry U (FL)
Baylor U (TX)
Belmont U (TN)
Binghamton U, State U of New York (NY)
Boston Coll (MA)
Boston U (MA)
Bowling Green State U (OH)
Bradley U (IL)
Bridgewater Coll (VA)
Bridgewater State U (MA)
Buena Vista U (IA)
California State U, Chico (CA)
California State U, East Bay (CA)
California State U, Fresno (CA)
California State U, Long Beach (CA)
California State U, San Bernardino (CA)
Calvin Coll (MI)
Canisius Coll (NY)
Carson-Newman U (TN)
Cedarville U (OH)
Central Connecticut State U (CT)
Central Michigan U (MI)

Claflin U (SC)
Clarkson U (NY)
Cleary U (MI)
Clemson U (SC)
Cleveland State U (OH)
Colorado Mesa U (CO)
Colorado State U (CO)
Columbia Coll (MO)
Columbus State U (GA)
Concordia U (QC, Canada)
Concordia U, Nebraska (NE)
Concordia U, St. Paul (MN)
Corban U (OR)
Cornerstone U (MI)
Creighton U (NE)
Dallas Baptist U (TX)
Dalton State Coll (GA)
Daniel Webster Coll (NH)
Delta State U (MS)
DePaul U (IL)
DeSales U (PA)
Dominican Coll (NY)
Dordt Coll (IA)
Drury U (MO)
Duquesne U (PA)
East Carolina U (NC)
Eastern Michigan U (MI)
Eastern New Mexico U (NM)
Eastern Washington U (WA)
Edgewood Coll (WI)
Excelsior Coll (NY)
Fairfield U (CT)
Fayetteville State U (NC)
Felician Coll (NJ)
Ferrum Coll (VA)
Florida Atlantic U (FL)
Florida Intl U (FL)
Francis Marion U (SC)
Franklin U (OH)
Gannon U (PA)
Gardner-Webb U (NC)
George Fox U (OR)
Georgia Regents U (GA)
Georgia Southern U (GA)
Goldey-Beacom Coll (DE)
Graceland U (IA)
Grand View U (IA)
Greenville Coll (IL)
Hardin-Simmons U (TX)
HEC Montreal (QC, Canada)
Henderson State U (AR)
Hofstra U (NY)
Holy Family U (PA)
Howard Payne U (TX)
Husson U (ME)
Illinois Coll (IL)
Immaculata U (PA)
Indiana State U (IN)
Indiana U of Pennsylvania (PA)
Inter American U of Puerto Rico, Aguadilla Campus (PR)
Inter American U of Puerto Rico, Bayamón Campus (PR)
Inter American U of Puerto Rico, Fajardo Campus (PR)
Inter American U of Puerto Rico, Ponce Campus (PR)
Iona Coll (NY)
Iowa State U of Science and Technology (IA)
Jamestown Coll (ND)
John Brown U (AR)
Johnson State Coll (VT)
Judson U (IL)
King Coll (TN)
La Salle U (PA)
Lehigh U (PA)
Le Moyne Coll (NY)
LeTourneau U (TX)
Lewis U (IL)
Liberty U (VA)
Lindenwood U (MO)
Loyola U Chicago (IL)
Lubbock Christian U (TX)
Luther Coll (IA)
Madonna U (MI)
Marshall U (WV)
Maryville U of Saint Louis (MO)
Massachusetts Coll of Liberal Arts (MA)
The Master's Coll and Sem (CA)
McMurry U (TX)
Menlo Coll (CA)
Mercer U (GA)
Miami U (OH)
Middle Tennessee State U (TN)
Millikin U (IL)

Milwaukee School of Eng (WI)
Minot State U (ND)
Misericordia U (PA)
Mississippi State U (MS)
Missouri State U (MO)
Morehead State U (KY)
Mount Mercy U (IA)
Mount Vernon Nazarene U (OH)
Newman U (KS)
New Mexico Highlands U (NM)
New York Inst of Technology (NY)
Nicholls State U (LA)
North Central Coll (IL)
North Dakota State U (ND)
Northeastern U (MA)
Northern Arizona U (AZ)
Northern Illinois U (IL)
Northern Michigan U (MI)
Northern State U (SD)
Northwestern Coll (MN)
Northwest Missouri State U (MO)
Northwood U, Michigan Campus (MI)
Oakland U (MI)
The Ohio State U (OH)
Ohio U (OH)
Oklahoma Baptist U (OK)
Oklahoma City U (OK)
Oklahoma State U (OK)
Old Dominion U (VA)
Oral Roberts U (OK)
Oregon State U (OR)
Park U (MO)
Penn State Abington (PA)
Penn State Altoona (PA)
Penn State Beaver (PA)
Penn State Berks (PA)
Penn State Brandywine (PA)
Penn State DuBois (PA)
Penn State Erie, The Behrend Coll (PA)
Penn State Fayette, The Eberly Campus (PA)
Penn State Greater Allegheny (PA)
Penn State Harrisburg (PA)
Penn State Hazleton (PA)
Penn State Lehigh Valley (PA)
Penn State Mont Alto (PA)
Penn State New Kensington (PA)
Penn State Schuylkill (PA)
Penn State Shenango (PA)
Penn State U Park (PA)
Penn State Wilkes-Barre (PA)
Penn State Worthington Scranton (PA)
Penn State York (PA)
Philadelphia U (PA)
Point Loma Nazarene U (CA)
Post U (CT)
Regis U (CO)
Rhode Island Coll (RI)
Robert Morris U (PA)
Rochester Inst of Technology (NY)
Rockford Coll (IL)
Rocky Mountain Coll (MT)
Roger Williams U (RI)
Rowan U (NJ)
St. Gregory's U, Shawnee (OK)
St. John's U (NY)
Saint Joseph's U (PA)
Saint Louis U (MO)
Saint Mary's Coll (IN)
Salem State U (MA)
Schreiner U (TX)
Seattle Pacific U (WA)
Seattle U (WA)
Seton Hill U (PA)
Shawnee State U (OH)
Simmons Coll (MA)
Simon Fraser U (BC, Canada)
Southeastern U (FL)
Southern Illinois U Edwardsville (IL)
Southwestern Coll (KS)
Spring Arbor U (MI)
State U of New York at Plattsburgh (NY)
State U of New York Coll at Old Westbury (NY)
State U of New York Coll of Technology at Canton (NY)
Stetson U (FL)
Suffolk U (MA)
Tarleton State U (TX)
Temple U (PA)
Texas A&M U–Commerce (TX)
Texas A&M U–Kingsville (TX)

Texas Southern U (TX)
Texas State U–San Marcos (TX)
Thompson Rivers U (BC, Canada)
Trident U Intl (CA)
Troy U (AL)
Université du Québec en Outaouais (QC, Canada)
The U of Akron (OH)
The U of Alabama (AL)
The U of Alabama at Birmingham (AL)
U of Alaska Anchorage (AK)
The U of Arizona (AZ)
U of Arkansas at Little Rock (AR)
U of Bridgeport (CT)
The U of British Columbia (BC, Canada)
U of Central Arkansas (AR)
U of Colorado Boulder (CO)
U of Delaware (DE)
U of Denver (CO)
U of Evansville (IN)
U of Georgia (GA)
U of Hawaii at Manoa (HI)
U of Houston (TX)
U of Houston–Downtown (TX)
U of Idaho (ID)
U of Illinois at Springfield (IL)
U of Illinois at Urbana–Champaign (IL)
The U of Iowa (IA)
The U of Kansas (KS)
U of Louisiana at Monroe (LA)
U of Louisville (KY)
U of Massachusetts Dartmouth (MA)
U of Memphis (TN)
U of Michigan–Dearborn (MI)
U of Minnesota, Duluth (MN)
U of Minnesota, Twin Cities Campus (MN)
U of Mississippi (MS)
U of Missouri (MO)
U of Missouri–St. Louis (MO)
U of Nevada, Las Vegas (NV)
U of New Orleans (LA)
U of North Alabama (AL)
The U of North Carolina at Charlotte (NC)
The U of North Carolina Wilmington (NC)
U of Northern Iowa (IA)
U of North Texas (TX)
U of Notre Dame (IN)
U of Oklahoma (OK)
U of Ottawa (ON, Canada)
U of Pennsylvania (PA)
U of Puget Sound (WA)
U of Redlands (CA)
U of Southern Mississippi (MS)
U of South Florida (FL)
The U of Tennessee at Martin (TN)
The U of Texas at Arlington (TX)
The U of Texas at Austin (TX)
The U of Texas at Dallas (TX)
The U of Texas at San Antonio (TX)
The U of Texas–Pan American (TX)
U of the Cumberlands (KY)
U of the District of Columbia (DC)
U of the Incarnate Word (TX)
The U of Toledo (OH)
U of Tulsa (OK)
U of Utah (UT)
The U of West Alabama (AL)
The U of Western Ontario (ON, Canada)
U of West Florida (FL)
U of West Georgia (GA)
U of Wisconsin–Green Bay (WI)
U of Wisconsin–La Crosse (WI)
U of Wisconsin–Madison (WI)
U of Wisconsin–Milwaukee (WI)
Upper Iowa U (IA)
Ursuline Coll (OH)
Villanova U (PA)
Virginia Union U (VA)
Viterbo U (WI)
Wake Forest U (NC)
Walla Walla U (WA)
Washington State U (WA)
Wayne State U (MI)
Weber State U (UT)
Webster U (MO)
Western Carolina U (NC)
Western Connecticut State U (CT)
Western Kentucky U (KY)
Western State Colorado U (CO)

Western Washington U (WA)
Westminster Coll (MO)
West Texas A&M U (TX)
West Virginia U (WV)
Wichita State U (KS)
Worcester Polytechnic Inst (MA)
Wright State U (OH)
Xavier U (OH)
York Coll of Pennsylvania (PA)
York Coll of the City U of New York (NY)
Youngstown State U (OH)

MANAGEMENT INFORMATION SYSTEMS AND SERVICES RELATED
Arkansas Tech U (AR)
Buena Vista U (IA)
California State U, Chico (CA)
DeSales U (PA)
Franklin U (OH)
Midwestern State U (TX)
Montana Tech of The U of Montana (MT)
Newberry Coll (SC)
Northern Michigan U (MI)
Rogers State U (OK)
St. Bonaventure U (NY)
Sam Houston State U (TX)
Thomas Edison State Coll (NJ)
Westminster Coll (UT)
Widener U (PA)

MANAGEMENT SCIENCE
Aurora U (IL)
Belmont U (TN)
Bridgewater State U (MA)
California State U, Northridge (CA)
Cambridge U (MA)
The Catholic U of America (DC)
Central Methodist U (MO)
Dalhousie U (NS, Canada)
DePaul U (IL)
DEREE—The American Coll of Greece (Greece)
Duquesne U (PA)
Eastern Illinois U (IL)
Elon U (NC)
Grand Valley State U (MI)
Granite State Coll (NH)
Hardin-Simmons U (TX)
Hawai`i Pacific U (HI)
HEC Montreal (QC, Canada)
Inter American U of Puerto Rico, Bayamón Campus (PR)
John Brown U (AR)
La Roche Coll (PA)
Lehigh U (PA)
Louisiana State U and Ag and Mech Coll (LA)
Lourdes U (OH)
Manhattan Coll (NY)
Northeastern U (MA)
Northern Illinois U (IL)
Oakland City U (IN)
Oklahoma Baptist U (OK)
Oklahoma City U (OK)
Oral Roberts U (OK)
Pine Manor Coll (MA)
Portland State U (OR)
Quincy U (IL)
Rider U (NJ)
Rocky Mountain Coll (MT)
Roosevelt U (IL)
Rutgers, The State U of New Jersey, New Brunswick (NJ)
St. Ambrose U (IA)
St. Gregory's U, Shawnee (OK)
Saint Leo U (FL)
Salve Regina U (RI)
Shippensburg U of Pennsylvania (PA)
Siena Coll (NY)
Simon Fraser U (BC, Canada)
Southeastern Oklahoma State U (OK)
Southern Illinois U Carbondale (IL)
State U of New York at Oswego (NY)
Texas A&M U (TX)
Texas Christian U (TX)
Texas Wesleyan U (TX)
Trinity U (TX)
Tuskegee U (AL)
United States Coast Guard Acad (CT)
The U of Alabama (AL)
U of California, Merced (CA)

U of Delaware (DE)
U of Florida (FL)
U of Great Falls (MT)
U of Illinois at Chicago (IL)
U of Illinois at Urbana–Champaign (IL)
The U of Iowa (IA)
U of Kentucky (KY)
U of Maryland, Coll Park (MD)
U of Memphis (TN)
U of Miami (FL)
U of Missouri–St. Louis (MO)
U of St. Francis (IL)
U of South Carolina (SC)
The U of Tennessee at Martin (TN)
The U of Texas at San Antonio (TX)
The U of Toledo (OH)
U of Washington, Tacoma (WA)
The U of Western Ontario (ON, Canada)
U of Wyoming (WY)
Valparaiso U (IN)
Vaughn Coll of Aeronautics and Technology (NY)
Virginia Polytechnic Inst and State U (VA)
Wake Forest U (NC)
Western Kentucky U (KY)
Wheeling Jesuit U (WV)
William Paterson U of New Jersey (NJ)

MANAGEMENT SCIENCES AND QUANTITATIVE METHODS RELATED
Canisius Coll (NY)
George Mason U (VA)
Indiana State U (IN)
Inter American U of Puerto Rico, Fajardo Campus (PR)
Pace U (NY)
Penn State Lehigh Valley (PA)
Penn State Schuylkill (PA)
Rutgers, The State U of New Jersey, New Brunswick (NJ)
The U of Iowa (IA)
U of Pennsylvania (PA)
The U of Toledo (OH)

MANUFACTURING ENGINEERING
Boston U (MA)
Bradley U (IL)
Brigham Young U (UT)
California Polytechnic State U, San Luis Obispo (CA)
California State Polytechnic U, Pomona (CA)
California State U, Northridge (CA)
Central Michigan U (MI)
Central State U (OH)
Fairfield U (CT)
Hofstra U (NY)
Miami U (OH)
National U (CA)
New England Inst of Technology (RI)
North Dakota State U (ND)
Oregon State U (OR)
Robert Morris U (PA)
Southern Illinois U Edwardsville (IL)
Texas State U–San Marcos (TX)
U of California, Berkeley (CA)
U of Illinois at Urbana–Champaign (IL)
U of Michigan–Dearborn (MI)
U of Wisconsin–Stout (WI)
Virginia State U (VA)
Washington State U (WA)
Western Michigan U (MI)
Wichita State U (KS)

MANUFACTURING ENGINEERING TECHNOLOGY
Arizona State U (AZ)
Berea Coll (KY)
Bradley U (IL)
California State U, Long Beach (CA)
Central Connecticut State U (CT)
Central Michigan U (MI)
East Carolina U (NC)
Eastern Michigan U (MI)
Farmingdale State Coll (NY)
Ferris State U (MI)
Indiana State U (IN)
Lewis-Clark State Coll (ID)

Midwestern State U (TX)
Missouri Western State U (MO)
Morehead State U (KY)
Murray State U (KY)
New England Inst of Technology (RI)
Pennsylvania Coll of Technology (PA)
Pittsburg State U (KS)
Rochester Inst of Technology (NY)
Roger Williams U (RI)
State U of New York Coll of Technology at Alfred (NY)
Sullivan Coll of Technology and Design (KY)
Tarleton State U (TX)
Temple U (PA)
Texas A&M U (TX)
Texas State U–San Marcos (TX)
Thomas Edison State Coll (NJ)
The U of Akron (OH)
U of Memphis (TN)
U of Northern Iowa (IA)
U of North Texas (TX)
U of Regina (SK, Canada)
U of Southern Indiana (IN)
Wayne State U (MI)
Western Carolina U (NC)
Western Kentucky U (KY)
Western Washington U (WA)

MARINE BIOLOGY AND BIOLOGICAL OCEANOGRAPHY
Alabama State U (AL)
Alaska Pacific U (AK)
Auburn U (AL)
Barry U (FL)
Bemidji State U (MN)
Boston U (MA)
Brown U (RI)
California State U, Long Beach (CA)
Coastal Carolina U (SC)
Coll of Charleston (SC)
Coll of the Atlantic (ME)
Dalhousie U (NS, Canada)
Eckerd Coll (FL)
Fairleigh Dickinson U, Coll at Florham (NJ)
Fairleigh Dickinson U, Metropolitan Campus (NJ)
Florida Inst of Technology (FL)
Florida Intl U (FL)
Florida Southern Coll (FL)
Gettysburg Coll (PA)
Hampton U (VA)
Hawai`i Pacific U (HI)
Humboldt State U (CA)
Jacksonville State U (AL)
Maine Maritime Acad (ME)
Monmouth U (NJ)
New Coll of Florida (FL)
Northeastern U (MA)
Northwest Missouri State U (MO)
Nova Southeastern U (FL)
Prescott Coll (AZ)
The Richard Stockton Coll of New Jersey (NJ)
Roger Williams U (RI)
Rollins Coll (FL)
Rutgers, The State U of New Jersey, New Brunswick (NJ)
Salem State U (MA)
Samford U (AL)
San Francisco State U (CA)
San Jose State U (CA)
Sonoma State U (CA)
Southwestern Coll (KS)
Spring Hill Coll (AL)
Stony Brook U, State U of New York (NY)
Suffolk U (MA)
Troy U (AL)
Unity Coll (ME)
The U of Alabama (AL)
The U of British Columbia (BC, Canada)
U of California, Los Angeles (CA)
U of California, Santa Barbara (CA)
U of California, Santa Cruz (CA)
U of Guelph (ON, Canada)
U of Hawaii at Hilo (HI)
U of Hawaii at Manoa (HI)
U of Maine at Machias (ME)
U of Maryland Eastern Shore (MD)
U of Miami (FL)

U of Mobile (AL)
U of New England (ME)
U of New Haven (CT)
U of North Alabama (AL)
The U of North Carolina Wilmington (NC)
U of Oregon (OR)
U of Puerto Rico at Ponce (PR)
U of Rhode Island (RI)
U of San Diego (CA)
U of South Carolina (SC)
U of Southern Mississippi (MS)
The U of Tampa (FL)
U of the Virgin Islands (VI)
The U of West Alabama (AL)
U of West Florida (FL)
Waynesburg U (PA)
Western Washington U (WA)

MARINE MAINTENANCE AND SHIP REPAIR TECHNOLOGY
Lamar U (TX)

MARINE SCIENCE/MERCHANT MARINE OFFICER
Hampton U (VA)
Maine Maritime Acad (ME)
Massachusetts Maritime Acad (MA)
United States Merchant Marine Acad (NY)
U of Delaware (DE)
U of South Carolina (SC)

MARINE SCIENCES
California State U, Monterey Bay (CA)

MARINE TRANSPORTATION RELATED
United States Merchant Marine Acad (NY)

MARITIME STUDIES
Coll of the Atlantic (ME)
United States Merchant Marine Acad (NY)

MARKETING/MARKETING MANAGEMENT
Abilene Christian U (TX)
Adams State U (CO)
Adelphi U (NY)
Alabama State U (AL)
Albertus Magnus Coll (CT)
Albright Coll (PA)
Alderson-Broaddus Coll (WV)
Alfred U (NY)
Alvernia U (PA)
Alverno Coll (WI)
American Public U System (WV)
Anderson U (IN)
Andrews U (MI)
Angelo State U (TX)
Appalachian State U (NC)
Arizona State U (AZ)
Arkansas State U (AR)
Ashland U (OH)
Assumption Coll (MA)
Athabasca U (AB, Canada)
Auburn U (AL)
Auburn U at Montgomery (AL)
Augsburg Coll (MN)
Aurora U (IL)
Averett U (VA)
Avila U (MO)
Azusa Pacific U (CA)
Babson Coll (MA)
Baldwin Wallace U (OH)
Ball State U (IN)
Barry U (FL)
Barton Coll (NC)
Baylor U (TX)
Bay Path Coll (MA)
Becker Coll (MA)
Belmont U (TN)
Benedictine U (IL)
Bentley U (MA)
Berry Coll (GA)
Binghamton U, State U of New York (NY)
Blackburn Coll (IL)
Bluffton U (OH)
Boise State U (ID)
Boston Coll (MA)
Boston U (MA)
Bowie State U (MD)
Bradley U (IL)
Bridgewater State U (MA)

Brock U (ON, Canada)
Bryant U (RI)
Buena Vista U (IA)
Butler U (IN)
Cabrini Coll (PA)
Caldwell Coll (NJ)
California Baptist U (CA)
California Lutheran U (CA)
California State U, Chico (CA)
California State U, Dominguez Hills (CA)
California State U, East Bay (CA)
California State U, Fresno (CA)
California State U, Fullerton (CA)
California State U, Long Beach (CA)
California State U, Northridge (CA)
California State U, San Bernardino (CA)
California State U, Stanislaus (CA)
Campbellsville U (KY)
Canisius Coll (NY)
Capital U (OH)
Caribbean U (PR)
Carson-Newman U (TN)
Castleton State Coll (VT)
Catawba Coll (NC)
Cedarville U (OH)
Central Baptist Coll (AR)
Central Connecticut State U (CT)
Central Michigan U (MI)
Champlain Coll (VT)
Chatham U (PA)
Chestnut Hill Coll (PA)
Chowan U (NC)
Christopher Newport U (VA)
Claflin U (SC)
Clarion U of Pennsylvania (PA)
Clayton State U (GA)
Cleary U (MI)
Clemson U (SC)
Cleveland State U (OH)
Coastal Carolina U (SC)
The Coll at Brockport, State U of New York (NY)
The Coll of St. Scholastica (MN)
Coll of the Ozarks (MO)
The Coll of William and Mary (VA)
Colorado State U (CO)
Columbia Coll (MO)
Columbia Coll Chicago (IL)
Columbus State U (GA)
Concordia U (OR)
Concordia U (QC, Canada)
Concordia U Chicago (IL)
Concordia U, St. Paul (MN)
Concordia U Wisconsin (WI)
Converse Coll (SC)
Cornerstone U (MI)
Creighton U (NE)
Dakota State U (SD)
Dalhousie U (NS, Canada)
Dallas Baptist U (TX)
Dalton State Coll (GA)
Daniel Webster Coll (NH)
Davenport U, Grand Rapids (MI)
Delta State U (MS)
DePaul U (IL)
DEREE—The American Coll of Greece (Greece)
DeSales U (PA)
Dominican Coll (NY)
Dominican U (IL)
Drake U (IA)
Drury U (MO)
Duquesne U (PA)
East Carolina U (NC)
Eastern Illinois U (IL)
Eastern Michigan U (MI)
Eastern Washington U (WA)
East Tennessee State U (TN)
Elizabethtown Coll (PA)
Elmira Coll (NY)
Elon U (NC)
Emerson Coll (MA)
Emporia State U (KS)
Evangel U (MO)
Excelsior Coll (NY)
Fairfield U (CT)
Fairleigh Dickinson U, Coll at Florham (NJ)
Fairleigh Dickinson U, Metropolitan Campus (NJ)
Faulkner U (AL)
Fayetteville State U (NC)
Felician Coll (NJ)
Ferris State U (MI)

Fisher Coll (MA)
Florida Atlantic U (FL)
Florida Gulf Coast U (FL)
Florida Intl U (FL)
Fort Lewis Coll (CO)
Francis Marion U (SC)
Franklin Pierce U (NH)
Franklin U (OH)
Friends U (KS)
Gannon U (PA)
Gardner-Webb U (NC)
George Fox U (OR)
George Mason U (VA)
Georgetown U (DC)
Georgia Coll & State U (GA)
Georgia Southern U (GA)
Georgia Southwestern State U (GA)
Georgia State U (GA)
Goldey-Beacom Coll (DE)
Gonzaga U (WA)
Grambling State U (LA)
Grand Valley State U (MI)
Greenville Coll (IL)
Grove City Coll (PA)
Hamline U (MN)
Hampton U (VA)
Harding U (AR)
Hardin-Simmons U (TX)
Hawai`i Pacific U (HI)
HEC Montreal (QC, Canada)
High Point U (NC)
Hillsdale Coll (MI)
Hofstra U (NY)
Holy Names U (CA)
Howard Payne U (TX)
Huntington U (IN)
Husson U (ME)
Illinois State U (IL)
Immaculata U (PA)
Indiana State U (IN)
Indiana U of Pennsylvania (PA)
Indiana U–Purdue U Fort Wayne (IN)
Indiana Wesleyan U (IN)
Inter American U of Puerto Rico, Aguadilla Campus (PR)
Inter American U of Puerto Rico, Bayamón Campus (PR)
Inter American U of Puerto Rico, Fajardo Campus (PR)
Inter American U of Puerto Rico, Ponce Campus (PR)
Inter American U of Puerto Rico, San Germán Campus (PR)
Iona Coll (NY)
Iowa State U of Science and Technology (IA)
Ithaca Coll (NY)
Jacksonville State U (AL)
James Madison U (VA)
Jamestown Coll (ND)
John Brown U (AR)
John Carroll U (OH)
Johnson State Coll (VT)
Judson U (IL)
Juniata Coll (PA)
Kansas State U (KS)
Kean U (NJ)
Kennesaw State U (GA)
Kent State U (OH)
Kent State U at Stark (OH)
Keuka Coll (NY)
King's Coll (PA)
Kutztown U of Pennsylvania (PA)
Lake Erie Coll (OH)
Lakeland Coll (WI)
Lamar U (TX)
La Roche Coll (PA)
La Salle U (PA)
Lasell Coll (MA)
La Sierra U (CA)
Lehigh U (PA)
Le Moyne Coll (NY)
LeTourneau U (TX)
Lewis U (IL)
Limestone Coll (SC)
Lincoln Memorial U (TN)
Lindenwood U (MO)
Linfield Coll (OR)
Lipscomb U (TN)
Long Island U–Brooklyn Campus (NY)
Long Island U–C. W. Post Campus (NY)
Louisiana Coll (LA)

Louisiana State U and Ag and Mech Coll (LA)
Louisiana State U in Shreveport (LA)
Loyola U Chicago (IL)
Loyola U New Orleans (LA)
Lubbock Christian U (TX)
Lynchburg Coll (VA)
Lynn U (FL)
Madonna U (MI)
Malone U (OH)
Manchester U (IN)
Manhattan Coll (NY)
Mansfield U of Pennsylvania (PA)
Maranatha Baptist Bible Coll (WI)
Marian U (WI)
Marietta Coll (OH)
Marquette U (WI)
Marshall U (WV)
Mars Hill Coll (NC)
Maryville Coll (TN)
Maryville U of Saint Louis (MO)
Marywood U (PA)
Massachusetts Coll of Liberal Arts (MA)
McKendree U (IL)
McMurry U (TX)
McNeese State U (LA)
Menlo Coll (CA)
Mercer U (GA)
Mercyhurst U (PA)
Merrimack Coll (MA)
Messiah Coll (PA)
Metropolitan State U of Denver (CO)
Miami U (OH)
Michigan State U (MI)
Middle Tennessee State U (TN)
Midwestern State U (TX)
Millikin U (IL)
Minnesota State U Mankato (MN)
Minot State U (ND)
Misericordia U (PA)
Mississippi Coll (MS)
Mississippi State U (MS)
Missouri Baptist U (MO)
Missouri State U (MO)
Missouri Western State U (MO)
Montana State U (MT)
Morehead State U (KY)
Mount Mary Coll (WI)
Mount Mercy U (IA)
Mount St. Mary's Coll (CA)
Mount Vernon Nazarene U (OH)
Murray State U (KY)
Nazareth Coll of Rochester (NY)
Neumann U (PA)
New England Coll (NH)
New England School of Communications (ME)
New Mexico Highlands U (NM)
New Mexico State U (NM)
New York Inst of Technology (NY)
Niagara U (NY)
Nicholls State U (LA)
North Carolina Wesleyan Coll (NC)
North Central Coll (IL)
Northcentral U (AZ)
North Dakota State U (ND)
Northeastern Illinois U (IL)
Northeastern U (MA)
Northern Arizona U (AZ)
Northern Illinois U (IL)
Northern Michigan U (MI)
Northern State U (SD)
North Greenville U (SC)
Northwestern Coll (MN)
Northwest Missouri State U (MO)
Northwest Nazarene U (ID)
Northwest U (WA)
Northwood U, Florida Campus (FL)
Northwood U, Michigan Campus (MI)
Northwood U, Texas Campus (TX)
Nova Southeastern U (FL)
Oakland U (MI)
The Ohio State U (OH)
Ohio U (OH)
Ohio Valley U (WV)
Oklahoma Baptist U (OK)
Oklahoma Christian U (OK)
Oklahoma City U (OK)
Oklahoma State U (OK)
Old Dominion U (VA)
Olivet Coll (MI)
Oral Roberts U (OK)
Oregon State U (OR)

Pace U (NY)
Pacific U (OR)
Palm Beach Atlantic U (FL)
Park U (MO)
Penn State Abington (PA)
Penn State Altoona (PA)
Penn State Beaver (PA)
Penn State Berks (PA)
Penn State Brandywine (PA)
Penn State DuBois (PA)
Penn State Erie, The Behrend Coll (PA)
Penn State Fayette, The Eberly Campus (PA)
Penn State Greater Allegheny (PA)
Penn State Harrisburg (PA)
Penn State Hazleton (PA)
Penn State Lehigh Valley (PA)
Penn State Mont Alto (PA)
Penn State New Kensington (PA)
Penn State Schuylkill (PA)
Penn State Shenango (PA)
Penn State U Park (PA)
Penn State Wilkes-Barre (PA)
Penn State Worthington Scranton (PA)
Penn State York (PA)
Philadelphia U (PA)
Pittsburg State U (KS)
Plymouth State U (NH)
Polytechnic U of Puerto Rico (PR)
Portland State U (OR)
Post U (CT)
Providence Coll (RI)
Quincy U (IL)
Quinnipiac U (CT)
Radford U (VA)
Rasmussen Coll Bloomington (MN)
Rasmussen Coll Brooklyn Park (MN)
Rasmussen Coll Eagan (MN)
Rasmussen Coll Fort Myers (FL)
Rasmussen Coll Lake Elmo/ Woodbury (MN)
Rasmussen Coll Land O' Lakes (FL)
Rasmussen Coll Mankato (MN)
Rasmussen Coll Moorhead (MN)
Rasmussen Coll New Port Richey (FL)
Rasmussen Coll Ocala (FL)
Rasmussen Coll St. Cloud (MN)
Rasmussen Coll Tampa/Brandon (FL)
Regent U (VA)
Regis U (CO)
Rhode Island Coll (RI)
Rider U (NJ)
Rivier U (NH)
Robert Morris U (PA)
Roberts Wesleyan Coll (NY)
Rochester Inst of Technology (NY)
Rockford Coll (IL)
Roger Williams U (RI)
Roosevelt U (IL)
Rowan U (NJ)
Rutgers, The State U of New Jersey, Camden (NJ)
Rutgers, The State U of New Jersey, Newark (NJ)
Rutgers, The State U of New Jersey, New Brunswick (NJ)
Sacred Heart U (CT)
Saginaw Valley State U (MI)
St. Ambrose U (IA)
St. Bonaventure U (NY)
St. Edward's U (TX)
St. Gregory's U, Shawnee (OK)
St. John's U (NY)
St. Joseph's Coll, Long Island Campus (NY)
St. Joseph's Coll, New York (NY)
Saint Joseph's U (PA)
Saint Leo U (FL)
Saint Louis U (MO)
Saint Mary-of-the-Woods Coll (IN)
Saint Mary's Coll (IN)
St. Mary's U (TX)
Saint Mary's U of Minnesota (MN)
St. Thomas Aquinas Coll (NY)
St. Thomas U (FL)
Saint Vincent Coll (PA)
Salem State U (MA)
Salisbury U (MD)
Salve Regina U (RI)
Samford U (AL)
Sam Houston State U (TX)

San Diego State U (CA)
San Francisco State U (CA)
San Jose State U (CA)
Schreiner U (TX)
Seattle U (WA)
Seton Hill U (PA)
Shippensburg U of Pennsylvania (PA)
Siena Coll (NY)
Simmons Coll (MA)
Simpson Coll (IA)
Slippery Rock U of Pennsylvania (PA)
Southeastern Louisiana U (LA)
Southeastern Oklahoma State U (OK)
Southeastern U (FL)
Southeast Missouri State U (MO)
Southern Connecticut State U (CT)
Southern Illinois U Carbondale (IL)
Southern Methodist U (TX)
Southern Nazarene U (OK)
Southern New Hampshire U (NH)
Southern Oregon U (OR)
Southern Utah U (UT)
Southwest Baptist U (MO)
Southwestern Coll (KS)
Spring Hill Coll (AL)
State U of New York at Fredonia (NY)
State U of New York at Oswego (NY)
State U of New York at Plattsburgh (NY)
State U of New York Coll at Old Westbury (NY)
Stephen F. Austin State U (TX)
Stetson U (FL)
Stonehill Coll (MA)
Suffolk U (MA)
Syracuse U (NY)
Taylor U (IN)
Temple U (PA)
Tennessee Wesleyan Coll (TN)
Texas A&M Intl U (TX)
Texas A&M U (TX)
Texas A&M U–Commerce (TX)
Texas A&M U–Kingsville (TX)
Texas Christian U (TX)
Texas Southern U (TX)
Texas State U–San Marcos (TX)
Texas Wesleyan U (TX)
Texas Woman's U (TX)
Thomas Edison State Coll (NJ)
Tiffin U (OH)
Trevecca Nazarene U (TN)
Trine U (IN)
Trinity U (TX)
Tulane U (LA)
Tuskegee U (AL)
Union Coll (KY)
Union U (TN)
Université de Sherbrooke (QC, Canada)
The U of Akron (OH)
The U of Alabama (AL)
The U of Alabama at Birmingham (AL)
U of Alaska Anchorage (AK)
The U of Arizona (AZ)
U of Arkansas at Little Rock (AR)
U of Bridgeport (CT)
The U of British Columbia (BC, Canada)
The U of British Columbia– Okanagan (BC, Canada)
U of Central Arkansas (AR)
U of Central Florida (FL)
U of Central Oklahoma (OK)
U of Charleston (WV)
U of Cincinnati (OH)
U of Colorado Boulder (CO)
U of Delaware (DE)
U of Denver (CO)
U of Evansville (IN)
The U of Findlay (OH)
U of Florida (FL)
U of Georgia (GA)
U of Great Falls (MT)
U of Guelph (ON, Canada)
U of Hartford (CT)
U of Hawaii at Manoa (HI)
U of Houston (TX)
U of Houston–Clear Lake (TX)
U of Houston–Downtown (TX)
U of Houston–Victoria (TX)
U of Idaho (ID)

U of Illinois at Chicago (IL)
U of Illinois at Urbana–Champaign (IL)
The U of Iowa (IA)
The U of Kansas (KS)
U of Kentucky (KY)
U of La Verne (CA)
U of Louisiana at Lafayette (LA)
U of Louisiana at Monroe (LA)
U of Louisville (KY)
U of Maine at Machias (ME)
U of Maryland, Coll Park (MD)
U of Maryland U Coll (MD)
U of Massachusetts Amherst (MA)
U of Massachusetts Dartmouth (MA)
U of Memphis (TN)
U of Miami (FL)
U of Michigan–Dearborn (MI)
U of Michigan–Flint (MI)
U of Minnesota, Crookston (MN)
U of Minnesota, Duluth (MN)
U of Minnesota, Twin Cities Campus (MN)
U of Mississippi (MS)
U of Missouri (MO)
U of Missouri–St. Louis (MO)
U of Montevallo (AL)
U of Mount Union (OH)
U of Nebraska at Omaha (NE)
U of Nebraska–Lincoln (NE)
U of Nevada, Las Vegas (NV)
U of Nevada, Reno (NV)
U of New Brunswick Fredericton (NB, Canada)
U of New Haven (CT)
U of New Orleans (LA)
U of North Alabama (AL)
The U of North Carolina at Charlotte (NC)
The U of North Carolina Wilmington (NC)
U of North Dakota (ND)
U of Northern Iowa (IA)
U of North Florida (FL)
U of North Georgia (GA)
U of North Texas (TX)
U of Notre Dame (IN)
U of Oklahoma (OK)
U of Ottawa (ON, Canada)
U of Pennsylvania (PA)
U of Pittsburgh (PA)
U of Portland (OR)
U of Puerto Rico at Bayamón (PR)
U of Puerto Rico at Ponce (PR)
U of Regina (SK, Canada)
U of Rhode Island (RI)
U of St. Francis (IL)
U of St. Thomas (MN)
U of St. Thomas (TX)
U of San Diego (CA)
The U of Scranton (PA)
U of South Alabama (AL)
U of South Carolina (SC)
The U of South Dakota (SD)
U of Southern Indiana (IN)
U of Southern Maine (ME)
U of Southern Mississippi (MS)
U of South Florida (FL)
The U of Tampa (FL)
The U of Tennessee (TN)
The U of Tennessee at Martin (TN)
The U of Texas at Arlington (TX)
The U of Texas at Austin (TX)
The U of Texas at Brownsville (TX)
The U of Texas at Dallas (TX)
The U of Texas at El Paso (TX)
The U of Texas at San Antonio (TX)
The U of Texas of the Permian Basin (TX)
The U of Texas–Pan American (TX)
U of the Incarnate Word (TX)
U of the Ozarks (AR)
The U of Toledo (OH)
U of Tulsa (OK)
U of Utah (UT)
U of Washington, Tacoma (WA)
The U of West Alabama (AL)
The U of Western Ontario (ON, Canada)
U of West Florida (FL)
U of West Georgia (GA)
U of Windsor (ON, Canada)
U of Wisconsin–Eau Claire (WI)
U of Wisconsin–La Crosse (WI)
U of Wisconsin–Madison (WI)
U of Wisconsin–Milwaukee (WI)

U of Wisconsin–Parkside (WI)
U of Wisconsin–Superior (WI)
U of Wyoming (WY)
Upper Iowa U (IA)
Ursuline Coll (OH)
Utah State U (UT)
Valdosta State U (GA)
Valparaiso U (IN)
Villanova U (PA)
Virginia Commonwealth U (VA)
Virginia Intermont Coll (VA)
Virginia Polytechnic Inst and State U (VA)
Virginia State U (VA)
Virginia Union U (VA)
Viterbo U (WI)
Walla Walla U (WA)
Walsh U (OH)
Wartburg Coll (IA)
Washburn U (KS)
Washington State U (WA)
Washington U in St. Louis (MO)
Waynesburg U (PA)
Wayne State U (MI)
Webber Intl U (FL)
Weber State U (UT)
Webster U (MO)
Wesley Coll (DE)
Western Carolina U (NC)
Western Connecticut State U (CT)
Western Illinois U (IL)
Western Kentucky U (KY)
Western Michigan U (MI)
Western State Colorado U (CO)
Western Washington U (WA)
West Liberty U (WV)
Westminster Coll (UT)
West Texas A&M U (TX)
West Virginia U (WV)
West Virginia Wesleyan Coll (WV)
Wheeling Jesuit U (WV)
Wichita State U (KS)
Widener U (PA)
Wilberforce U (OH)
Wilkes U (PA)
Wilmington U (DE)
Woodbury U (CA)
Wright State U (OH)
Xavier U (OH)
Xavier U of Louisiana (LA)
York Coll of Pennsylvania (PA)
York Coll of the City U of New York (NY)
Youngstown State U (OH)

MARKETING RELATED
Babson Coll (MA)
Bowling Green State U (OH)
Duquesne U (PA)
Franklin U (OH)
Lourdes U (OH)
Mary Baldwin Coll (VA)
Newbury Coll (MA)
Oklahoma City U (OK)
Pace U (NY)
Saginaw Valley State U (MI)
Stephens Coll (MO)
Sullivan U (KY)
Troy U (AL)
The U of Iowa (IA)
U of Minnesota, Duluth (MN)
U of Mississippi (MS)
U of South Florida (FL)
Washington U in St. Louis (MO)
Western Carolina U (NC)
Western Michigan U (MI)
Wheeling Jesuit U (WV)

MARKETING RESEARCH
Ashland U (OH)
Boston U (MA)
Bowling Green State U (OH)
Fashion Inst of Technology (NY)
Inter American U of Puerto Rico, Bayamón Campus (PR)
Ithaca Coll (NY)
Mercyhurst U (PA)
National U (CA)
Newbury Coll (MA)
U of Illinois at Urbana–Champaign (IL)
The U of Toledo (OH)

MARRIAGE AND FAMILY THERAPY/COUNSELING
DeSales U (PA)
Grace U (NE)
John Brown U (AR)

Oklahoma Baptist U (OK)
U of Nevada, Las Vegas (NV)

MASS COMMUNICATION/ MEDIA
Abilene Christian U (TX)
Acad of Art U (CA)
Adams State U (CO)
Albion Coll (MI)
Alcorn State U (MS)
American Jewish U (CA)
American U (DC)
American U in Bulgaria (Bulgaria)
The American U in Cairo (Egypt)
The American U of Paris (France)
Anderson U (IN)
Andrews U (MI)
Ashland U (OH)
Auburn U (AL)
Augsburg Coll (MN)
Augustana Coll (IL)
Austin Peay State U (TN)
Baker U (KS)
Baldwin Wallace U (OH)
Barry U (FL)
Barton Coll (NC)
Belmont U (TN)
Bemidji State U (MN)
Benedictine Coll (KS)
Bentley U (MA)
Berea Coll (KY)
Bethel Coll (KS)
Bethel U (MN)
Bethune-Cookman U (FL)
Bloomsburg U of Pennsylvania (PA)
Bluefield Coll (VA)
Bob Jones U (SC)
Boise State U (ID)
Bowie State U (MD)
Bridgewater Coll (VA)
Brock U (ON, Canada)
Buena Vista U (IA)
Buffalo State Coll, State U of New York (NY)
California Lutheran U (CA)
California State U, Chico (CA)
California State U, East Bay (CA)
California State U, Fresno (CA)
California State U, Long Beach (CA)
Calvin Coll (MI)
Campbellsville U (KY)
Carlow U (PA)
Carson-Newman U (TN)
Castleton State Coll (VT)
Catawba Coll (NC)
Cedar Crest Coll (PA)
Central Penn Coll (PA)
Chestnut Hill Coll (PA)
Cheyney U of Pennsylvania (PA)
City Coll of the City U of New York (NY)
City U of Seattle (WA)
Claflin U (SC)
Clark U (MA)
Clemson U (SC)
The Coll at Brockport, State U of New York (NY)
The Coll of New Rochelle (NY)
The Coll of Wooster (OH)
Colorado Mesa U (CO)
Columbia Intl U (SC)
Concordia U (QC, Canada)
Concordia U, Nebraska (NE)
Concordia U, St. Paul (MN)
Concordia U Texas (TX)
Concordia U Wisconsin (WI)
Concord U (WV)
Cornerstone U (MI)
Culver-Stockton Coll (MO)
Curry Coll (MA)
Defiance Coll (OH)
DePaul U (IL)
DePauw U (IN)
Dillard U (LA)
Dordt Coll (IA)
Drake U (IA)
East Central U (OK)
East Tennessee State U (TN)
East Texas Baptist U (TX)
Edinboro U of Pennsylvania (PA)
Emerson Coll (MA)
Emmanuel Coll (GA)
Endicott Coll (MA)
Excelsior Coll (NY)
Felician Coll (NJ)
Fisher Coll (MA)

Five Towns Coll (NY)
Florida Gulf Coast U (FL)
Florida Intl U (FL)
Francis Marion U (SC)
Franklin Pierce U (NH)
Frostburg State U (MD)
Gardner-Webb U (NC)
Gonzaga U (WA)
Goucher Coll (MD)
Governors State U (IL)
Grambling State U (LA)
Grand View U (IA)
Greenville Coll (IL)
Gustavus Adolphus Coll (MN)
Hampton U (VA)
Hanover Coll (IN)
Hardin-Simmons U (TX)
Hawai'i Pacific U (HI)
High Point U (NC)
Hiram Coll (OH)
Hobart and William Smith Colls (NY)
Hofstra U (NY)
Hollins U (VA)
Holy Family U (PA)
Howard Payne U (TX)
Hunter Coll of the City U of New York (NY)
Huntington U (IN)
Illinois Coll (IL)
Illinois State U (IL)
Indiana U–Purdue U Fort Wayne (IN)
Indiana U South Bend (IN)
Indiana Wesleyan U (IN)
Inter American U of Puerto Rico, Bayamón Campus (PR)
Intl U in Geneva (Switzerland)
Iona Coll (NY)
Iowa State U of Science and Technology (IA)
Ithaca Coll (NY)
Jamestown Coll (ND)
John Brown U (AR)
John Cabot U (Italy)
John Carroll U (OH)
Johnson C. Smith U (NC)
Kansas Wesleyan U (KS)
Kuyper Coll (MI)
Lamar U (TX)
Langston U (OK)
La Salle U (PA)
Lehman Coll of the City U of New York (NY)
Lewis U (IL)
Lincoln Memorial U (TN)
Lindenwood U (MO)
Lindsey Wilson Coll (KY)
Linfield Coll (OR)
Lipscomb U (TN)
Louisiana Coll (LA)
Louisiana State U and Ag and Mech Coll (LA)
Louisiana State U at Alexandria (LA)
Louisiana State U in Shreveport (LA)
Lubbock Christian U (TX)
Lynn U (FL)
Macalester Coll (MN)
Manchester U (IN)
Mansfield U of Pennsylvania (PA)
Marquette U (WI)
Marymount Coll, Palos Verdes, California (CA)
Maryville U of Saint Louis (MO)
Massachusetts Inst of Technology (MA)
The Master's Coll and Sem (CA)
McNeese State U (LA)
Medaille Coll (NY)
Mercer U (GA)
Mercy Coll (NY)
Miami U (OH)
Michigan State U (MI)
Middle Tennessee State U (TN)
Midwestern State U (TX)
Minnesota State U Mankato (MN)
Minnesota State U Moorhead (MN)
Mississippi Coll (MS)
Mississippi Valley State U (MS)
Missouri State U (MO)
Morris Coll (SC)
Mount Saint Mary Coll (NY)
New England Coll (NH)
Newman U (KS)
Niagara U (NY)

Nicholls State U (LA)
North Carolina Central U (NC)
North Greenville U (SC)
Northwestern Oklahoma State U (OK)
Northwest Nazarene U (ID)
Oklahoma Baptist U (OK)
Oklahoma Christian U (OK)
Oklahoma City U (OK)
Ouachita Baptist U (AR)
Pace U (NY)
Pacific U (OR)
Paul Quinn Coll (TX)
Piedmont Coll (GA)
Point Loma Nazarene U (CA)
Point Park U (PA)
Principia Coll (IL)
Quinnipiac U (CT)
Robert Morris U (PA)
Rutgers, The State U of New Jersey, New Brunswick (NJ)
Sacred Heart U (CT)
St. Ambrose U (IA)
Saint Joseph's Coll (IN)
Saint Mary-of-the-Woods Coll (IN)
St. Mary's U (TX)
Saint Michael's Coll (VT)
St. Thomas Aquinas Coll (NY)
St. Thomas U (FL)
St. Thomas U (NB, Canada)
Sam Houston State U (TX)
Scripps Coll (CA)
Shaw U (NC)
Sonoma State U (CA)
Southern Illinois U Edwardsville (IL)
Southwestern Adventist U (TX)
Spalding U (KY)
State U of New York at Fredonia (NY)
State U of New York at Oswego (NY)
Stephen F. Austin State U (TX)
Stephens Coll (MO)
Suffolk U (MA)
Sul Ross State U (TX)
Tennessee State U (TN)
Texas State U–San Marcos (TX)
Tiffin U (OH)
Trevecca Nazarene U (TN)
Tulane U (LA)
Union Coll (KY)
Union U (TN)
U at Albany, State U of New York (NY)
U of Alaska Anchorage (AK)
U of Bridgeport (CT)
U of California, Berkeley (CA)
U of Charleston (WV)
U of Denver (CO)
U of Hawaii at Manoa (HI)
U of Houston (TX)
U of Illinois at Urbana–Champaign (IL)
The U of Iowa (IA)
U of Louisiana at Lafayette (LA)
U of Louisiana at Monroe (LA)
U of Maryland, Baltimore County (MD)
U of Maryland Eastern Shore (MD)
U of Memphis (TN)
U of Miami (FL)
U of Minnesota, Twin Cities Campus (MN)
U of Missouri (MO)
U of Missouri–Kansas City (MO)
U of Missouri–St. Louis (MO)
U of Nebraska at Kearney (NE)
U of Nevada, Las Vegas (NV)
U of New Hampshire at Manchester (NH)
U of New Mexico (NM)
U of North Alabama (AL)
U of North Carolina at Asheville (NC)
The U of North Carolina at Chapel Hill (NC)
The U of North Carolina at Greensboro (NC)
The U of North Carolina at Pembroke (NC)
U of North Florida (FL)
U of Oregon (OR)
U of Pittsburgh (PA)
U of Pittsburgh at Greensburg (PA)
U of Portland (OR)
U of St. Francis (IL)

U of Southern Indiana (IN)
U of Southern Maine (ME)
U of South Florida (FL)
The U of Tennessee at Chattanooga (TN)
The U of Texas at El Paso (TX)
The U of Texas at San Antonio (TX)
The U of Texas of the Permian Basin (TX)
The U of Texas–Pan American (TX)
U of the District of Columbia (DC)
U of the Incarnate Word (TX)
U of the Ozarks (AR)
The U of Toledo (OH)
U of Utah (UT)
U of Washington, Bothell (WA)
The U of Western Ontario (ON, Canada)
U of West Florida (FL)
U of Wisconsin–Eau Claire (WI)
U of Wisconsin–Milwaukee (WI)
U of Wisconsin–Platteville (WI)
U of Wisconsin–Superior (WI)
Upper Iowa U (IA)
Valdosta State U (GA)
Valley City State U (ND)
Vassar Coll (NY)
Villanova U (PA)
Virginia Commonwealth U (VA)
Virginia State U (VA)
Virginia Wesleyan Coll (VA)
Walla Walla U (WA)
Wartburg Coll (IA)
Washburn U (KS)
Washington State U (WA)
Wayland Baptist U (TX)
Wayne State Coll (NE)
Webster U (MO)
Wesley Coll (DE)
Western Kentucky U (KY)
West Liberty U (WV)
West Texas A&M U (TX)
Wheeling Jesuit U (WV)
Whitworth U (WA)
Widener U (PA)
Wilberforce U (OH)
William Paterson U of New Jersey (NJ)
William Penn U (IA)
Winthrop U (SC)
Worcester State U (MA)
Wright State U (OH)
Xavier U of Louisiana (LA)
York Coll of Pennsylvania (PA)

MATERIALS ENGINEERING
Alfred U (NY)
Arizona State U (AZ)
Auburn U (AL)
Boise State U (ID)
Brown U (RI)
California Polytechnic State U, San Luis Obispo (CA)
California State U, Long Beach (CA)
Case Western Reserve U (OH)
Clemson U (SC)
Illinois Inst of Technology (IL)
Iowa State U of Science and Technology (IA)
The Johns Hopkins U (MD)
Lehigh U (PA)
Massachusetts Inst of Technology (MA)
Michigan State U (MI)
New Mexico Inst of Mining and Technology (NM)
North Carolina State U (NC)
The Ohio State U (OH)
Purdue U (IN)
Rensselaer Polytechnic Inst (NY)
Rice U (TX)
San Jose State U (CA)
U at Albany, State U of New York (NY)
The U of Alabama at Birmingham (AL)
The U of British Columbia (BC, Canada)
U of California, Davis (CA)
U of California, Irvine (CA)
U of California, Los Angeles (CA)
U of California, Merced (CA)
U of Cincinnati (OH)
U of Florida (FL)
U of Idaho (ID)

U of Illinois at Urbana–Champaign (IL)
U of Kentucky (KY)
U of Maryland, Coll Park (MD)
U of Michigan (MI)
U of Minnesota, Twin Cities Campus (MN)
U of Pennsylvania (PA)
U of Pittsburgh (PA)
The U of Tennessee (TN)
U of Utah (UT)
The U of Western Ontario (ON, Canada)
U of Windsor (ON, Canada)
U of Wisconsin–Madison (WI)
U of Wisconsin–Milwaukee (WI)
Virginia Polytechnic Inst and State U (VA)
Washington State U (WA)
Worcester Polytechnic Inst (MA)
Wright State U (OH)

MATERIALS SCIENCE
Carnegie Mellon U (PA)
Case Western Reserve U (OH)
Columbia U (NY)
The Johns Hopkins U (MD)
Michigan State U (MI)
The Ohio State U (OH)
Penn State Abington (PA)
Penn State Altoona (PA)
Penn State Beaver (PA)
Penn State Berks (PA)
Penn State Brandywine (PA)
Penn State DuBois (PA)
Penn State Erie, The Behrend Coll (PA)
Penn State Fayette, The Eberly Campus (PA)
Penn State Greater Allegheny (PA)
Penn State Hazleton (PA)
Penn State Lehigh Valley (PA)
Penn State Mont Alto (PA)
Penn State New Kensington (PA)
Penn State Schuylkill (PA)
Penn State Shenango (PA)
Penn State U Park (PA)
Penn State Wilkes-Barre (PA)
Penn State Worthington Scranton (PA)
Penn State York (PA)
Rice U (TX)
Stanford U (CA)
United States Air Force Acad (CO)
The U of Arizona (AZ)
U of California, Berkeley (CA)
U of California, Los Angeles (CA)
U of California, Riverside (CA)
U of Illinois at Urbana–Champaign (IL)
U of North Texas (TX)
U of Pennsylvania (PA)
U of Wisconsin–Eau Claire (WI)
Worcester Polytechnic Inst (MA)

MATHEMATICAL BIOLOGY
Trevecca Nazarene U (TN)
U of Houston (TX)
U of Pittsburgh (PA)

MATHEMATICAL STATISTICS AND PROBABILITY
Carnegie Mellon U (PA)
Concordia Coll–New York (NY)
Concordia U (QC, Canada)
U of Miami (FL)
The U of Western Ontario (ON, Canada)

MATHEMATICS
Abilene Christian U (TX)
Acadia U (NS, Canada)
Adams State U (CO)
Adelphi U (NY)
Agnes Scott Coll (GA)
Alabama State U (AL)
Albertus Magnus Coll (CT)
Albion Coll (MI)
Albright Coll (PA)
Alcorn State U (MS)
Alfred U (NY)
Alma Coll (MI)
Alvernia U (PA)
Alverno Coll (WI)
American U (DC)
American U in Bulgaria (Bulgaria)
The American U in Cairo (Egypt)
American U of Beirut (Lebanon)

Amherst Coll (MA)
Anderson U (IN)
Anderson U (SC)
Andrews U (MI)
Angelo State U (TX)
Antioch U Midwest (OH)
Appalachian State U (NC)
Arizona State U (AZ)
Arkansas State U (AR)
Arkansas Tech U (AR)
Armstrong Atlantic State U (GA)
Asbury U (KY)
Ashland U (OH)
Assumption Coll (MA)
Athens State U (AL)
Auburn U (AL)
Auburn U at Montgomery (AL)
Augsburg Coll (MN)
Augustana Coll (IL)
Augustana Coll (SD)
Aurora U (IL)
Austin Peay State U (TN)
Averett U (VA)
Avila U (MO)
Azusa Pacific U (CA)
Baker U (KS)
Baldwin Wallace U (OH)
Ball State U (IN)
Bard Coll (NY)
Barry U (FL)
Barton Coll (NC)
Bates Coll (ME)
Baylor U (TX)
Belhaven U (MS)
Bellarmine U (KY)
Belmont Abbey Coll (NC)
Belmont U (TN)
Bemidji State U (MN)
Benedictine Coll (KS)
Benedictine U (IL)
Bennington Coll (VT)
Bentley U (MA)
Berea Coll (KY)
Berry Coll (GA)
Bethany Coll (WV)
Bethany Lutheran Coll (MN)
Bethel Coll (IN)
Bethel Coll (KS)
Bethel U (MN)
Bethune-Cookman U (FL)
Binghamton U, State U of New York (NY)
Blackburn Coll (IL)
Bloomsburg U of Pennsylvania (PA)
Bluefield Coll (VA)
Blue Mountain Coll (MS)
Bluffton U (OH)
Bob Jones U (SC)
Boise State U (ID)
Boston Coll (MA)
Boston U (MA)
Bowdoin Coll (ME)
Bowie State U (MD)
Bowling Green State U (OH)
Bradley U (IL)
Brevard Coll (NC)
Bridgewater Coll (VA)
Bridgewater State U (MA)
Brock U (ON, Canada)
Brown U (RI)
Bucknell U (PA)
Buena Vista U (IA)
Buffalo State Coll, State U of New York (NY)
Butler U (IN)
Cabrini Coll (PA)
Caldwell Coll (NJ)
California Baptist U (CA)
California Lutheran U (CA)
California Polytechnic State U, San Luis Obispo (CA)
California State Polytechnic U, Pomona (CA)
California State U, Chico (CA)
California State U, Dominguez Hills (CA)
California State U, East Bay (CA)
California State U, Fresno (CA)
California State U, Fullerton (CA)
California State U, Long Beach (CA)
California State U, Los Angeles (CA)
California State U, Monterey Bay (CA)
California State U, Northridge (CA)

California State U, San Bernardino (CA)
California State U, San Marcos (CA)
California State U, Stanislaus (CA)
Calvin Coll (MI)
Cameron U (OK)
Campbellsville U (KY)
Capital U (OH)
Cardinal Stritch U (WI)
Carleton Coll (MN)
Carlow U (PA)
Carnegie Mellon U (PA)
Carroll Coll (MT)
Carson-Newman U (TN)
Case Western Reserve U (OH)
Castleton State Coll (VT)
Catawba Coll (NC)
The Catholic U of America (DC)
Cedar Crest Coll (PA)
Cedarville U (OH)
Centenary Coll of Louisiana (LA)
Central Coll (IA)
Central Connecticut State U (CT)
Central Methodist U (MO)
Central State U (OH)
Centre Coll (KY)
Chapman U (CA)
Chatham U (PA)
Chestnut Hill Coll (PA)
Cheyney U of Pennsylvania (PA)
Chicago State U (IL)
Chowan U (NC)
Christian Brothers U (TN)
Christopher Newport U (VA)
The Citadel, The Military Coll of South Carolina (SC)
City Coll of the City U of New York (NY)
Claflin U (SC)
Claremont McKenna Coll (CA)
Clarion U of Pennsylvania (PA)
Clark Atlanta U (GA)
Clarke U (IA)
Clarkson U (NY)
Clark U (MA)
Clayton State U (GA)
Clearwater Christian Coll (FL)
Clemson U (SC)
Cleveland State U (OH)
Coe Coll (IA)
Colby Coll (ME)
Colgate U (NY)
The Coll at Brockport, State U of New York (NY)
Coll of Charleston (SC)
Coll of Coastal Georgia (GA)
The Coll of Idaho (ID)
Coll of Mount St. Joseph (OH)
The Coll of New Jersey (NJ)
The Coll of New Rochelle (NY)
Coll of Saint Benedict (MN)
Coll of Saint Elizabeth (NJ)
Coll of Saint Mary (NE)
The Coll of Saint Rose (NY)
The Coll of St. Scholastica (MN)
Coll of Staten Island of the City U of New York (NY)
Coll of the Holy Cross (MA)
Coll of the Ozarks (MO)
The Coll of William and Mary (VA)
The Coll of Wooster (OH)
The Colorado Coll (CO)
Colorado Mesa U (CO)
Colorado School of Mines (CO)
Colorado State U (CO)
Columbia Coll (MO)
Columbia Coll (SC)
Columbia U (NY)
Columbia U, School of General Studies (NY)
Columbus State U (GA)
Concordia Coll (MN)
Concordia Coll–New York (NY)
Concordia U (CA)
Concordia U (QC, Canada)
Concordia U Chicago (IL)
Concordia U, Nebraska (NE)
Concordia U, St. Paul (MN)
Concordia U Texas (TX)
Concordia U Wisconsin (WI)
Concord U (WV)
Connecticut Coll (CT)
Converse Coll (SC)
Corban U (OR)
Cornell Coll (IA)
Covenant Coll (GA)

Creighton U (NE)
Culver-Stockton Coll (MO)
Dakota Wesleyan U (SD)
Dalhousie U (NS, Canada)
Dallas Baptist U (TX)
Dalton State Coll (GA)
Dartmouth Coll (NH)
Davidson Coll (NC)
Defiance Coll (OH)
Delta State U (MS)
DePaul U (IL)
DePauw U (IN)
DeSales U (PA)
Dickinson Coll (PA)
Dillard U (LA)
Doane Coll (NE)
Dominican Coll (NY)
Dominican U (IL)
Dordt Coll (IA)
Drake U (IA)
Drew U (NJ)
Drury U (MO)
Duquesne U (PA)
Earlham Coll (IN)
East Carolina U (NC)
East Central U (OK)
Eastern Illinois U (IL)
Eastern Mennonite U (VA)
Eastern Michigan U (MI)
Eastern New Mexico U (NM)
Eastern Washington U (WA)
East Tennessee State U (TN)
East Texas Baptist U (TX)
East-West U (IL)
Eckerd Coll (FL)
Edgewood Coll (WI)
Edinboro U of Pennsylvania (PA)
Elizabeth City State U (NC)
Elizabethtown Coll (PA)
Elmira Coll (NY)
Elon U (NC)
Emmanuel Coll (GA)
Emmanuel Coll (MA)
Emory & Henry Coll (VA)
Emporia State U (KS)
Evangel U (MO)
Excelsior Coll (NY)
Fairfield U (CT)
Fairleigh Dickinson U, Coll at Florham (NJ)
Fairleigh Dickinson U, Metropolitan Campus (NJ)
Fairmont State U (WV)
Fayetteville State U (NC)
Felician Coll (NJ)
Ferris State U (MI)
Ferrum Coll (VA)
Florida Ag and Mech U (FL)
Florida Atlantic U (FL)
Florida Gulf Coast U (FL)
Florida Inst of Technology (FL)
Florida Intl U (FL)
Florida Southern Coll (FL)
Florida State U (FL)
Fort Lewis Coll (CO)
Framingham State U (MA)
Francis Marion U (SC)
Franklin & Marshall Coll (PA)
Franklin Coll (IN)
Franklin Pierce U (NH)
Friends U (KS)
Frostburg State U (MD)
Furman U (SC)
Gallaudet U (DC)
Gannon U (PA)
Gardner-Webb U (NC)
George Fox U (OR)
George Mason U (VA)
Georgetown Coll (KY)
Georgetown U (DC)
Georgia Coll & State U (GA)
Georgia Gwinnett Coll (GA)
Georgia Regents U (GA)
Georgia Southern U (GA)
Georgia Southwestern State U (GA)
Georgia State U (GA)
Gettysburg Coll (PA)
Gonzaga U (WA)
Gordon Coll (MA)
Gordon State Coll (GA)
Goshen Coll (IN)
Goucher Coll (MD)
Governors State U (IL)
Graceland U (IA)
Grand Valley State U (MI)
Greenville Coll (IL)

Grinnell Coll (IA)
Grove City Coll (PA)
Guilford Coll (NC)
Gustavus Adolphus Coll (MN)
Hamilton Coll (NY)
Hamline U (MN)
Hampden-Sydney Coll (VA)
Hampshire Coll (MA)
Hampton U (VA)
Hanover Coll (IN)
Harding U (AR)
Hardin-Simmons U (TX)
Harris-Stowe State U (MO)
Hartwick Coll (NY)
Harvey Mudd Coll (CA)
Haverford Coll (PA)
Henderson State U (AR)
Hendrix Coll (AR)
High Point U (NC)
Hillsdale Coll (MI)
Hiram Coll (OH)
Hobart and William Smith Colls (NY)
Hofstra U (NY)
Hollins U (VA)
Holy Family U (PA)
Hood Coll (MD)
Hope Coll (MI)
Houghton Coll (NY)
Howard Payne U (TX)
Humboldt State U (CA)
Hunter Coll of the City U of New York (NY)
Huntingdon Coll (AL)
Huntington U (IN)
Illinois Coll (IL)
Illinois State U (IL)
Illinois Wesleyan U (IL)
Immaculata U (PA)
Indiana State U (IN)
Indiana U Bloomington (IN)
Indiana U East (IN)
Indiana U Kokomo (IN)
Indiana U Northwest (IN)
Indiana U of Pennsylvania (PA)
Indiana U–Purdue U Fort Wayne (IN)
Indiana U–Purdue U Indianapolis (IN)
Indiana U South Bend (IN)
Indiana U Southeast (IN)
Indiana Wesleyan U (IN)
Inter American U of Puerto Rico, Bayamón Campus (PR)
Inter American U of Puerto Rico, San Germán Campus (PR)
Iona Coll (NY)
Iowa State U of Science and Technology (IA)
Ithaca Coll (NY)
Jacksonville State U (AL)
James Madison U (VA)
Jamestown Coll (ND)
Jarvis Christian Coll (TX)
John Brown U (AR)
John Carroll U (OH)
The Johns Hopkins U (MD)
Johnson C. Smith U (NC)
Johnson State Coll (VT)
Judson Coll (AL)
Judson U (IL)
Juniata Coll (PA)
Kalamazoo Coll (MI)
Kansas State U (KS)
Kansas Wesleyan U (KS)
Kean U (NJ)
Keene State Coll (NH)
Kennesaw State U (GA)
Kent State U (OH)
Kent State U at Stark (OH)
Kentucky State U (KY)
Kentucky Wesleyan Coll (KY)
Kenyon Coll (OH)
Keuka Coll (NY)
King Coll (TN)
King's Coll (PA)
Knox Coll (IL)
Kutztown U of Pennsylvania (PA)
Lafayette Coll (PA)
LaGrange Coll (GA)
Lake Erie Coll (OH)
Lakeland Coll (WI)
Lake Superior State U (MI)
Lamar U (TX)
Lander U (SC)
Lane Coll (TN)
Langston U (OK)

La Roche Coll (PA)
La Salle U (PA)
La Sierra U (CA)
Lawrence Technological U (MI)
Lawrence U (WI)
Lebanese American U (Lebanon)
Lebanon Valley Coll (PA)
Lee U (TN)
Lehigh U (PA)
Lehman Coll of the City U of New York (NY)
Le Moyne Coll (NY)
LeTourneau U (TX)
Lewis-Clark State Coll (ID)
Lewis U (IL)
Liberty U (VA)
Limestone Coll (SC)
Lincoln Memorial U (TN)
Lincoln U (MO)
Lindenwood U (MO)
Linfield Coll (OR)
Lipscomb U (TN)
Lock Haven U of Pennsylvania (PA)
Long Island U–Brooklyn Campus (NY)
Long Island U–C. W. Post Campus (NY)
Longwood U (VA)
Louisiana Coll (LA)
Louisiana State U and Ag and Mech Coll (LA)
Louisiana State U at Alexandria (LA)
Louisiana State U in Shreveport (LA)
Loyola Marymount U (CA)
Loyola U Chicago (IL)
Loyola U Maryland (MD)
Loyola U New Orleans (LA)
Lubbock Christian U (TX)
Luther Coll (IA)
Lynchburg Coll (VA)
Lyon Coll (AR)
Macalester Coll (MN)
Madonna U (MI)
Maharishi U of Management (IA)
Malone U (OH)
Manchester U (IN)
Manhattan Coll (NY)
Manhattanville Coll (NY)
Mansfield U of Pennsylvania (PA)
Marian U (WI)
Marietta Coll (OH)
Marist Coll (NY)
Marquette U (WI)
Marshall U (WV)
Mars Hill Coll (NC)
Mary Baldwin Coll (VA)
Marymount U (VA)
Maryville Coll (TN)
Maryville U of Saint Louis (MO)
Marywood U (PA)
Massachusetts Coll of Liberal Arts (MA)
Massachusetts Inst of Technology (MA)
The Master's Coll and Sem (CA)
Mayville State U (ND)
McDaniel Coll (MD)
McKendree U (IL)
McMurry U (TX)
McNeese State U (LA)
Medaille Coll (NY)
Mercer U (GA)
Mercy Coll (NY)
Mercyhurst U (PA)
Merrimack Coll (MA)
Messiah Coll (PA)
Metropolitan State U of Denver (CO)
Miami U (OH)
Michigan State U (MI)
Mid-Continent U (KY)
Middlebury Coll (VT)
Middle Tennessee State U (TN)
Midwestern State U (TX)
Millersville U of Pennsylvania (PA)
Millikin U (IL)
Millsaps Coll (MS)
Mills Coll (CA)
Minnesota State U Mankato (MN)
Minnesota State U Moorhead (MN)
Minot State U (ND)
Misericordia U (PA)
Mississippi Coll (MS)
Mississippi State U (MS)
Mississippi U for Women (MS)

Mississippi Valley State U (MS)
Missouri Baptist U (MO)
Missouri State U (MO)
Missouri Western State U (MO)
Molloy Coll (NY)
Monmouth Coll (IL)
Monmouth U (NJ)
Montana State U (MT)
Montana Tech of The U of Montana (MT)
Montclair State U (NJ)
Moravian Coll (PA)
Morehead State U (KY)
Morehouse Coll (GA)
Morningside Coll (IA)
Morris Coll (SC)
Mount Allison U (NB, Canada)
Mount Holyoke Coll (MA)
Mount Marty Coll (SD)
Mount Mary Coll (WI)
Mount Mercy U (IA)
Mount Saint Mary Coll (NY)
Mount St. Mary's Coll (CA)
Mount St. Mary's U (MD)
Mount Vernon Nazarene U (OH)
Muhlenberg Coll (PA)
Murray State U (KY)
National U (CA)
Nazareth Coll of Rochester (NY)
Newberry Coll (SC)
New Coll of Florida (FL)
New Jersey City U (NJ)
New Jersey Inst of Technology (NJ)
Newman U (KS)
New Mexico Highlands U (NM)
New Mexico Inst of Mining and Technology (NM)
New Mexico State U (NM)
New York U (NY)
Niagara U (NY)
Nicholls State U (LA)
Norfolk State U (VA)
North Carolina Central U (NC)
North Carolina State U (NC)
North Carolina Wesleyan Coll (NC)
North Central Coll (IL)
North Dakota State U (ND)
Northeastern Illinois U (IL)
Northeastern U (MA)
Northern Arizona U (AZ)
Northern Illinois U (IL)
Northern Michigan U (MI)
Northern State U (SD)
North Greenville U (SC)
Northland Coll (WI)
Northwest Christian U (OR)
Northwestern Coll (IA)
Northwestern Coll (MN)
Northwestern Oklahoma State U (OK)
Northwestern State U of Louisiana (LA)
Northwest Missouri State U (MO)
Northwest Nazarene U (ID)
Northwest U (WA)
Norwich U (VT)
Nyack Coll (NY)
Oakland City U (IN)
Oakland U (MI)
Oglethorpe U (GA)
Ohio Dominican U (OH)
The Ohio State U (OH)
Ohio U (OH)
Ohio Wesleyan U (OH)
Oklahoma Baptist U (OK)
Oklahoma Christian U (OK)
Oklahoma City U (OK)
Oklahoma State U (OK)
Old Dominion U (VA)
Olivet Coll (MI)
Oral Roberts U (OK)
Oregon State U (OR)
Ouachita Baptist U (AR)
Pace U (NY)
Pacific Lutheran U (WA)
Pacific Union Coll (CA)
Pacific U (OR)
Paine Coll (GA)
Palm Beach Atlantic U (FL)
Park U (MO)
Paul Quinn Coll (TX)
Penn State Abington (PA)
Penn State Altoona (PA)
Penn State Beaver (PA)
Penn State Berks (PA)
Penn State Brandywine (PA)
Penn State DuBois (PA)

Penn State Erie, The Behrend Coll (PA)
Penn State Fayette, The Eberly Campus (PA)
Penn State Greater Allegheny (PA)
Penn State Hazleton (PA)
Penn State Lehigh Valley (PA)
Penn State Mont Alto (PA)
Penn State New Kensington (PA)
Penn State Schuylkill (PA)
Penn State Shenango (PA)
Penn State U Park (PA)
Penn State Wilkes-Barre (PA)
Penn State Worthington Scranton (PA)
Penn State York (PA)
Pepperdine U, Malibu (CA)
Piedmont Coll (GA)
Pittsburg State U (KS)
Pitzer Coll (CA)
Plymouth State U (NH)
Point Loma Nazarene U (CA)
Pomona Coll (CA)
Portland State U (OR)
Presbyterian Coll (SC)
Princeton U (NJ)
Principia Coll (IL)
Providence Coll (RI)
Purchase Coll, State U of New York (NY)
Purdue U (IN)
Purdue U Calumet (IN)
Queens U of Charlotte (NC)
Quincy U (IL)
Quinnipiac U (CT)
Radford U (VA)
Ramapo Coll of New Jersey (NJ)
Randolph Coll (VA)
Randolph-Macon Coll (VA)
Reed Coll (OR)
Regent U (VA)
Regis U (CO)
Rensselaer Polytechnic Inst (NY)
Rhode Island Coll (RI)
Rhodes Coll (TN)
Rice U (TX)
The Richard Stockton Coll of New Jersey (NJ)
Rider U (NJ)
Ripon Coll (WI)
Rivier U (NH)
Roanoke Coll (VA)
Roberts Wesleyan Coll (NY)
Rochester Inst of Technology (NY)
Rockford Coll (IL)
Rockhurst U (MO)
Rocky Mountain Coll (MT)
Roger Williams U (RI)
Rollins Coll (FL)
Roosevelt U (IL)
Rosemont Coll (PA)
Rowan U (NJ)
Russell Sage Coll (NY)
Rutgers, The State U of New Jersey, Camden (NJ)
Rutgers, The State U of New Jersey, Newark (NJ)
Rutgers, The State U of New Jersey, New Brunswick (NJ)
Sacred Heart U (CT)
Saginaw Valley State U (MI)
St. Ambrose U (IA)
Saint Anselm Coll (NH)
St. Bonaventure U (NY)
St. Edward's U (TX)
St. Francis Coll (NY)
St. Gregory's U, Shawnee (OK)
St. John Fisher Coll (NY)
Saint John's U (MN)
St. John's U (NY)
Saint Joseph's Coll (IN)
St. Joseph's Coll, Long Island Campus (NY)
St. Joseph's Coll, New York (NY)
Saint Joseph's U (PA)
St. Lawrence U (NY)
Saint Leo U (FL)
Saint Louis U (MO)
Saint Martin's U (WA)
Saint Mary-of-the-Woods Coll (IN)
Saint Mary's Coll (IN)
Saint Mary's Coll of California (CA)
St. Mary's Coll of Maryland (MD)
St. Mary's U (TX)
Saint Mary's U of Minnesota (MN)
Saint Michael's Coll (VT)
St. Norbert Coll (WI)

St. Olaf Coll (MN)
St. Thomas Aquinas Coll (NY)
St. Thomas U (FL)
St. Thomas U (NB, Canada)
Saint Vincent Coll (PA)
Salem State U (MA)
Salisbury U (MD)
Salve Regina U (RI)
Samford U (AL)
Sam Houston State U (TX)
San Diego State U (CA)
San Francisco State U (CA)
San Jose State U (CA)
Schreiner U (TX)
Scripps Coll (CA)
Seattle Pacific U (WA)
Seattle U (WA)
Seton Hill U (PA)
Sewanee: The U of the South (TN)
Shawnee State U (OH)
Shaw U (NC)
Shenandoah U (VA)
Shepherd U (WV)
Shippensburg U of Pennsylvania (PA)
Siena Coll (NY)
Siena Heights U (MI)
Simmons Coll (MA)
Simon Fraser U (BC, Canada)
Simpson Coll (IA)
Simpson U (CA)
Skidmore Coll (NY)
Slippery Rock U of Pennsylvania (PA)
Smith Coll (MA)
Sonoma State U (CA)
South Dakota State U (SD)
Southeastern Louisiana U (LA)
Southeastern Oklahoma State U (OK)
Southeastern U (FL)
Southeast Missouri State U (MO)
Southern Arkansas U–Magnolia (AR)
Southern Connecticut State U (CT)
Southern Illinois U Carbondale (IL)
Southern Illinois U Edwardsville (IL)
Southern Methodist U (TX)
Southern Nazarene U (OK)
Southern New Hampshire U (NH)
Southern Oregon U (OR)
Southern Polytechnic State U (GA)
Southern Utah U (UT)
Southwest Baptist U (MO)
Southwestern Adventist U (TX)
Southwestern Coll (KS)
Southwestern U (TX)
Spelman Coll (GA)
Spring Arbor U (MI)
Spring Hill Coll (AL)
Stanford U (CA)
State U of New York at Fredonia (NY)
State U of New York at New Paltz (NY)
State U of New York at Oswego (NY)
State U of New York at Plattsburgh (NY)
State U of New York Coll at Cortland (NY)
State U of New York Coll at Geneseo (NY)
State U of New York Coll at Old Westbury (NY)
State U of New York Coll at Potsdam (NY)
State U of New York Empire State Coll (NY)
Stephen F. Austin State U (TX)
Sterling Coll (KS)
Stetson U (FL)
Stonehill Coll (MA)
Stony Brook U, State U of New York (NY)
Suffolk U (MA)
Sul Ross State U (TX)
Susquehanna U (PA)
Swarthmore Coll (PA)
Sweet Briar Coll (VA)
Syracuse U (NY)
Tabor Coll (KS)
Tarleton State U (TX)
Taylor U (IN)
Temple U (PA)
Tennessee State U (TN)

Tennessee Wesleyan Coll (TN)
Texas A&M Intl U (TX)
Texas A&M U (TX)
Texas A&M U–Commerce (TX)
Texas A&M U–Kingsville (TX)
Texas Christian U (TX)
Texas Lutheran U (TX)
Texas Southern U (TX)
Texas State U–San Marcos (TX)
Texas Wesleyan U (TX)
Texas Woman's U (TX)
Thomas Edison State Coll (NJ)
Thomas More Coll (KY)
Thompson Rivers U (BC, Canada)
Transylvania U (KY)
Trent U (ON, Canada)
Trevecca Nazarene U (TN)
Trine U (IN)
Trinity Christian Coll (IL)
Trinity Coll (CT)
Trinity U (TX)
Troy U (AL)
Truman State U (MO)
Tufts U (MA)
Tulane U (LA)
Tuskegee U (AL)
Union Coll (KY)
Union Coll (NE)
Union U (TN)
United States Air Force Acad (CO)
United States Military Acad (NY)
United States Naval Acad (MD)
Université de Sherbrooke (QC, Canada)
U at Albany, State U of New York (NY)
U at Buffalo, the State U of New York (NY)
The U of Akron (OH)
The U of Alabama (AL)
The U of Alabama at Birmingham (AL)
U of Alaska Anchorage (AK)
U of Alaska Fairbanks (AK)
The U of Arizona (AZ)
U of Arkansas at Little Rock (AR)
U of Arkansas–Fort Smith (AR)
U of Bridgeport (CT)
The U of British Columbia (BC, Canada)
The U of British Columbia–Okanagan (BC, Canada)
U of California, Berkeley (CA)
U of California, Davis (CA)
U of California, Irvine (CA)
U of California, Los Angeles (CA)
U of California, Riverside (CA)
U of California, Santa Barbara (CA)
U of California, Santa Cruz (CA)
U of Central Arkansas (AR)
U of Central Florida (FL)
U of Central Oklahoma (OK)
U of Chicago (IL)
U of Cincinnati (OH)
U of Colorado Boulder (CO)
U of Colorado Colorado Springs (CO)
U of Colorado Denver (CO)
U of Dallas (TX)
U of Delaware (DE)
U of Denver (CO)
U of Evansville (IN)
The U of Findlay (OH)
U of Florida (FL)
U of Georgia (GA)
U of Great Falls (MT)
U of Guam (GU)
U of Hartford (CT)
U of Hawaii at Hilo (HI)
U of Hawaii at Manoa (HI)
U of Houston (TX)
U of Houston–Clear Lake (TX)
U of Houston–Downtown (TX)
U of Houston–Victoria (TX)
U of Idaho (ID)
U of Illinois at Chicago (IL)
U of Illinois at Springfield (IL)
U of Illinois at Urbana–Champaign (IL)
The U of Iowa (IA)
The U of Kansas (KS)
U of Kentucky (KY)
U of La Verne (CA)
U of Louisiana at Lafayette (LA)
U of Louisiana at Monroe (LA)
U of Louisville (KY)
U of Maine at Farmington (ME)

U of Maryland, Baltimore County (MD)
U of Maryland, Coll Park (MD)
U of Maryland Eastern Shore (MD)
U of Mary Washington (VA)
U of Massachusetts Amherst (MA)
U of Massachusetts Boston (MA)
U of Massachusetts Dartmouth (MA)
U of Memphis (TN)
U of Miami (FL)
U of Michigan (MI)
U of Michigan–Dearborn (MI)
U of Michigan–Flint (MI)
U of Minnesota, Duluth (MN)
U of Minnesota, Twin Cities Campus (MN)
U of Mississippi (MS)
U of Missouri (MO)
U of Missouri–Kansas City (MO)
U of Missouri–St. Louis (MO)
U of Mobile (AL)
The U of Montana Western (MT)
U of Montevallo (AL)
U of Mount Union (OH)
U of Nebraska at Kearney (NE)
U of Nebraska at Omaha (NE)
U of Nebraska–Lincoln (NE)
U of Nevada, Las Vegas (NV)
U of Nevada, Reno (NV)
U of New Brunswick Fredericton (NB, Canada)
U of New Brunswick Saint John (NB, Canada)
U of New England (ME)
U of New Hampshire (NH)
U of New Haven (CT)
U of New Mexico (NM)
U of New Orleans (LA)
U of North Alabama (AL)
U of North Carolina at Asheville (NC)
The U of North Carolina at Chapel Hill (NC)
The U of North Carolina at Charlotte (NC)
The U of North Carolina at Greensboro (NC)
The U of North Carolina at Pembroke (NC)
The U of North Carolina Wilmington (NC)
U of North Dakota (ND)
U of Northern Colorado (CO)
U of Northern Iowa (IA)
U of North Florida (FL)
U of North Georgia (GA)
U of North Texas (TX)
U of Notre Dame (IN)
U of Oklahoma (OK)
U of Oregon (OR)
U of Ottawa (ON, Canada)
U of Pennsylvania (PA)
U of Pikeville (KY)
U of Pittsburgh (PA)
U of Portland (OR)
U of Puget Sound (WA)
U of Redlands (CA)
U of Regina (SK, Canada)
U of Rhode Island (RI)
U of Richmond (VA)
U of Rochester (NY)
U of St. Francis (IL)
U of Saint Joseph (CT)
U of Saint Mary (KS)
U of St. Thomas (MN)
U of St. Thomas (TX)
U of San Diego (CA)
U of Science and Arts of Oklahoma (OK)
The U of Scranton (PA)
U of South Alabama (AL)
U of South Carolina (SC)
U of South Carolina Upstate (SC)
The U of South Dakota (SD)
U of Southern California (CA)
U of Southern Indiana (IN)
U of Southern Maine (ME)
U of Southern Mississippi (MS)
U of South Florida (FL)
The U of Tampa (FL)
The U of Tennessee (TN)
The U of Tennessee at Chattanooga (TN)
The U of Tennessee at Martin (TN)
The U of Texas at Arlington (TX)
The U of Texas at Austin (TX)

The U of Texas at Brownsville (TX)
The U of Texas at Dallas (TX)
The U of Texas at El Paso (TX)
The U of Texas at San Antonio (TX)
The U of Texas of the Permian Basin (TX)
The U of Texas–Pan American (TX)
U of the Cumberlands (KY)
U of the District of Columbia (DC)
U of the Incarnate Word (TX)
U of the Ozarks (AR)
U of the Virgin Islands (VI)
The U of Toledo (OH)
U of Tulsa (OK)
U of Utah (UT)
U of Vermont (VT)
U of Virginia (VA)
U of Washington, Bothell (WA)
U of Waterloo (ON, Canada)
The U of West Alabama (AL)
The U of Western Ontario (ON, Canada)
U of West Florida (FL)
U of West Georgia (GA)
U of Windsor (ON, Canada)
U of Wisconsin–Eau Claire (WI)
U of Wisconsin–Green Bay (WI)
U of Wisconsin–La Crosse (WI)
U of Wisconsin–Madison (WI)
U of Wisconsin–Milwaukee (WI)
U of Wisconsin–Parkside (WI)
U of Wisconsin–Platteville (WI)
U of Wisconsin–Stevens Point (WI)
U of Wisconsin–Superior (WI)
U of Wyoming (WY)
Upper Iowa U (IA)
Ursuline Coll (OH)
Utah State U (UT)
Utica Coll (NY)
Valdosta State U (GA)
Valley City State U (ND)
Valparaiso U (IN)
Vanderbilt U (TN)
Vassar Coll (NY)
Villanova U (PA)
Virginia Commonwealth U (VA)
Virginia Polytechnic Inst and State U (VA)
Virginia State U (VA)
Virginia Union U (VA)
Virginia Wesleyan Coll (VA)
Viterbo U (WI)
Wabash Coll (IN)
Wagner Coll (NY)
Wake Forest U (NC)
Walla Walla U (WA)
Walsh U (OH)
Wartburg Coll (IA)
Washburn U (KS)
Washington & Jefferson Coll (PA)
Washington and Lee U (VA)
Washington Coll (MD)
Washington State U (WA)
Washington U in St. Louis (MO)
Wayland Baptist U (TX)
Waynesburg U (PA)
Wayne State Coll (NE)
Wayne State U (MI)
Weber State U (UT)
Webster U (MO)
Wellesley Coll (MA)
Wells Coll (NY)
Wesleyan Coll (GA)
Wesleyan U (CT)
West Chester U of Pennsylvania (PA)
Western Carolina U (NC)
Western Connecticut State U (CT)
Western Illinois U (IL)
Western Kentucky U (KY)
Western Michigan U (MI)
Western Oregon U (OR)
Western State Colorado U (CO)
Western Washington U (WA)
Westfield State U (MA)
West Liberty U (WV)
Westminster Coll (MO)
Westminster Coll (UT)
West Texas A&M U (TX)
West Virginia State U (WV)
West Virginia U (WV)
West Virginia U Inst of Technology (WV)
West Virginia Wesleyan Coll (WV)
Wheaton Coll (IL)
Wheaton Coll (MA)
Wheeling Jesuit U (WV)

Whitman Coll (WA)
Whitworth U (WA)
Wichita State U (KS)
Widener U (PA)
Wilkes U (PA)
Willamette U (OR)
William Jewell Coll (MO)
William Paterson U of New Jersey (NJ)
Williams Coll (MA)
Winthrop U (SC)
Wittenberg U (OH)
Worcester Polytechnic Inst (MA)
Worcester State U (MA)
Wright State U (OH)
Xavier U (OH)
Xavier U of Louisiana (LA)
Yale U (CT)
York Coll of Pennsylvania (PA)
York Coll of the City U of New York (NY)
Young Harris Coll (GA)
Youngstown State U (OH)

MATHEMATICS AND COMPUTER SCIENCE

Anderson U (IN)
Bennington Coll (VT)
Bowdoin Coll (ME)
Brown U (RI)
Cardinal Stritch U (WI)
Chestnut Hill Coll (PA)
The Colorado Coll (CO)
DePaul U (IL)
Dominican U (IL)
Drew U (NJ)
Eastern Illinois U (IL)
Florida Southern Coll (FL)
George Mason U (VA)
Hampden-Sydney Coll (VA)
Hofstra U (NY)
Immaculata U (PA)
Indiana U–Purdue U Fort Wayne (IN)
Ithaca Coll (NY)
Lake Superior State U (MI)
Lawrence Technological U (MI)
Lawrence U (WI)
Long Island U–C. W. Post Campus (NY)
Loyola U Chicago (IL)
Manchester U (IN)
Massachusetts Inst of Technology (MA)
Mount Allison U (NB, Canada)
Palm Beach Atlantic U (FL)
Pepperdine U, Malibu (CA)
Piedmont Coll (GA)
Purdue U Calumet (IN)
Rochester Inst of Technology (NY)
St. Joseph's Coll, Long Island Campus (NY)
St. Joseph's Coll, New York (NY)
St. Lawrence U (NY)
Saint Mary's Coll (IN)
Saint Mary's Coll of California (CA)
Salem State U (MA)
Southern Oregon U (OR)
Stanford U (CA)
Temple U (PA)
U at Albany, State U of New York (NY)
The U of Akron (OH)
U of Alaska Anchorage (AK)
U of Illinois at Chicago (IL)
U of Illinois at Urbana–Champaign (IL)
U of Oregon (OR)
U of Regina (SK, Canada)
U of St. Francis (IL)
The U of Tampa (FL)
The U of Texas at Austin (TX)
U of Waterloo (ON, Canada)
U of Windsor (ON, Canada)
Washington U in St. Louis (MO)
Western Washington U (WA)
Wheaton Coll (MA)
Whitman Coll (WA)

MATHEMATICS AND STATISTICS

Canisius Coll (NY)
Colby Coll (ME)
Dakota State U (SD)
Luther Coll (IA)
U of South Alabama (AL)

MATHEMATICS AND STATISTICS RELATED

The American U of Paris (France)
Anderson U (IN)
Carnegie Mellon U (PA)
Columbia U, School of General Studies (NY)
The Evergreen State Coll (WA)
Georgia Regents U (GA)
Hofstra U (NY)
Indiana U of Pennsylvania (PA)
New York U (NY)
Ohio U (OH)
Oregon State U (OR)
Purchase Coll, State U of New York (NY)
St. Joseph's Coll, Long Island Campus (NY)
St. Joseph's Coll, New York (NY)
Saint Mary's Coll of California (CA)
Seattle Pacific U (WA)
Tulane U (LA)
The U of British Columbia–Okanagan (BC, Canada)
U of Minnesota, Duluth (MN)
U of Missouri–Kansas City (MO)
U of New Hampshire (NH)
The U of North Carolina at Charlotte (NC)
U of Pittsburgh (PA)
U of Regina (SK, Canada)
U of Rochester (NY)
Wesley Coll (DE)
Western State Colorado U (CO)

MATHEMATICS RELATED

California Baptist U (CA)
Carnegie Mellon U (PA)
Grambling State U (LA)
Hillsdale Coll (MI)
Seton Hill U (PA)
Sweet Briar Coll (VA)
United States Military Acad (NY)
U of California, Los Angeles (CA)
U of Miami (FL)
U of Pittsburgh (PA)
U of Waterloo (ON, Canada)

MATHEMATICS TEACHER EDUCATION

Abilene Christian U (TX)
Adams State U (CO)
Albion Coll (MI)
Alice Lloyd Coll (KY)
Alma Coll (MI)
Alvernia U (PA)
Anderson U (IN)
Anderson U (SC)
Appalachian State U (NC)
Arizona Christian U (AZ)
Arkansas State U (AR)
Arkansas Tech U (AR)
Assumption Coll (MA)
Auburn U (AL)
Augustana Coll (IL)
Averett U (VA)
Baylor U (TX)
Bennington Coll (VT)
Berry Coll (GA)
Bethel Coll (IN)
Bethel U (MN)
Blackburn Coll (IL)
Bluefield Coll (VA)
Blue Mountain Coll (MS)
Bob Jones U (SC)
Boise State U (ID)
Boston U (MA)
Bowdoin Coll (ME)
Bowie State U (MD)
Bowling Green State U (OH)
Bradley U (IL)
Brock U (ON, Canada)
Buena Vista U (IA)
Buffalo State Coll, State U of New York (NY)
Cabrini Coll (PA)
Cairn U (PA)
California Baptist U (CA)
California Lutheran U (CA)
California State U, Chico (CA)
California State U, Long Beach (CA)
Calvin Coll (MI)
Cameron U (OK)
Campbellsville U (KY)
Canisius Coll (NY)
Capital U (OH)
Carroll Coll (MT)

Castleton State Coll (VT)
Cedarville U (OH)
Central Michigan U (MI)
Chipola Coll (FL)
Christian Brothers U (TN)
City Coll of the City U of New York (NY)
Claflin U (SC)
Clearwater Christian Coll (FL)
Clemson U (SC)
The Coll at Brockport, State U of New York (NY)
The Coll of New Jersey (NJ)
The Coll of Saint Rose (NY)
Coll of Staten Island of the City U of New York (NY)
Coll of the Ozarks (MO)
Colorado State U (CO)
Columbus State U (GA)
Concordia Coll (MN)
Concordia U (OR)
Concordia U Chicago (IL)
Concordia U, Nebraska (NE)
Concordia U, St. Paul (MN)
Corban U (OR)
Cornerstone U (MI)
Covenant Coll (GA)
Culver-Stockton Coll (MO)
Dakota State U (SD)
Dakota Wesleyan U (SD)
Dallas Baptist U (TX)
Daytona State Coll (FL)
Delta State U (MS)
Dominican Coll (NY)
Duquesne U (PA)
East Carolina U (NC)
East Central U (OK)
Eastern Michigan U (MI)
Eastern Washington U (WA)
East Texas Baptist U (TX)
Edgewood Coll (WI)
Elizabeth City State U (NC)
Elmira Coll (NY)
Emmanuel Coll (GA)
Fayetteville State U (NC)
Felician Coll (NJ)
Ferris State U (MI)
Florida Ag and Mech U (FL)
Florida Atlantic U (FL)
Florida Inst of Technology (FL)
Franklin Coll (IN)
Friends U (KS)
Gardner-Webb U (NC)
Geneva Coll (PA)
Gordon State Coll (GA)
Grambling State U (LA)
Grand Valley State U (MI)
Greenville Coll (IL)
Gustavus Adolphus Coll (MN)
Harding U (AR)
Hardin-Simmons U (TX)
Hawai'i Pacific U (HI)
Hofstra U (NY)
Hope Coll (MI)
Howard Payne U (TX)
Hunter Coll of the City U of New York (NY)
Huntingdon Coll (AL)
Huntington U (IN)
Indiana U Bloomington (IN)
Indiana U Northwest (IN)
Indiana U–Purdue U Fort Wayne (IN)
Indiana U South Bend (IN)
Indiana U Southeast (IN)
Indiana Wesleyan U (IN)
Indian River State Coll (FL)
Inter American U of Puerto Rico, San Germán Campus (PR)
Iona Coll (NY)
Iowa Wesleyan Coll (IA)
Ithaca Coll (NY)
Jamestown Coll (ND)
John Brown U (AR)
Johnson State Coll (VT)
Judson Coll (AL)
Juniata Coll (PA)
Keene State Coll (NH)
Kennesaw State U (GA)
Kent State U (OH)
Kentucky Christian U (KY)
Kentucky Wesleyan Coll (KY)
Keuka Coll (NY)
Keystone Coll (PA)
King Coll (TN)
Lee U (TN)
Le Moyne Coll (NY)

Lewis-Clark State Coll (ID)
Limestone Coll (SC)
Lincoln Memorial U (TN)
Lincoln U (MO)
Lindenwood U (MO)
Lindsey Wilson Coll (KY)
Lipscomb U (TN)
Long Island U–Brooklyn Campus (NY)
Long Island U–C. W. Post Campus (NY)
Louisiana State U in Shreveport (LA)
Loyola U Chicago (IL)
Madonna U (MI)
Manchester U (IN)
Manhattanville Coll (NY)
Mansfield U of Pennsylvania (PA)
Maranatha Baptist Bible Coll (WI)
Marist Coll (NY)
Marquette U (WI)
Maryville Coll (TN)
Marywood U (PA)
Mayville State U (ND)
McKendree U (IL)
McMurry U (TX)
Medaille Coll (NY)
Mercyhurst U (PA)
Merrimack Coll (MA)
Messiah Coll (PA)
Miami Dade Coll (FL)
Miami U (OH)
Michigan State U (MI)
Midwestern State U (TX)
Millikin U (IL)
Minnesota State U Moorhead (MN)
Minot State U (ND)
Misericordia U (PA)
Mississippi Valley State U (MS)
Missouri State U (MO)
Molloy Coll (NY)
Moravian Coll (PA)
Morningside Coll (IA)
Morris Coll (SC)
Mount Marty Coll (SD)
Mount Mary Coll (WI)
Mount Vernon Nazarene U (OH)
National U (CA)
Nazareth Coll of Rochester (NY)
New York City Coll of Technology of the City U of New York (NY)
New York U (NY)
Niagara U (NY)
Nicholls State U (LA)
North Carolina Central U (NC)
North Carolina State U (NC)
North Dakota State U (ND)
Northern Michigan U (MI)
North Greenville U (SC)
Northwestern Coll (MN)
Northwestern Oklahoma State U (OK)
Northwest Missouri State U (MO)
Northwest Nazarene U (ID)
Northwest U (WA)
Nyack Coll (NY)
Oakland City U (IN)
Ohio Dominican U (OH)
Ohio Valley U (WV)
Ohio Wesleyan U (OH)
Oklahoma Baptist U (OK)
Oklahoma Christian U (OK)
Oklahoma City U (OK)
Olivet Coll (MI)
Oral Roberts U (OK)
Pace U (NY)
Paine Coll (GA)
Palm Beach Atlantic U (FL)
Pepperdine U, Malibu (CA)
Pittsburg State U (KS)
Plymouth State U (NH)
Point Park U (PA)
Queens U of Charlotte (NC)
Regis Coll (MA)
Rhode Island Coll (RI)
Rivier U (NH)
Roberts Wesleyan Coll (NY)
Rocky Mountain Coll (MT)
Saginaw Valley State U (MI)
St. Ambrose U (IA)
St. Edward's U (TX)
St. Francis Coll (NY)
St. Gregory's U, Shawnee (OK)
St. John Fisher Coll (NY)
St. John's U (NY)
St. Joseph's Coll, Long Island Campus (NY)

St. Joseph's Coll, New York (NY)
Saint Mary's U of Minnesota (MN)
Salve Regina U (RI)
Schreiner U (TX)
Seton Hill U (PA)
Shawnee State U (OH)
Shaw U (NC)
Simpson U (CA)
Southeastern Oklahoma State U (OK)
Southeastern U (FL)
Southeast Missouri State U (MO)
Southern Nazarene U (OK)
Southern New Hampshire U (NH)
Southern Polytechnic State U (GA)
Southern Utah U (UT)
Southwest Baptist U (MO)
Southwestern Coll (KS)
Spring Arbor U (MI)
State U of New York at New Paltz (NY)
State U of New York Coll at Cortland (NY)
State U of New York Coll at Old Westbury (NY)
State U of New York Coll at Potsdam (NY)
Stony Brook U, State U of New York (NY)
Syracuse U (NY)
Taylor U (IN)
Temple U (PA)
Texas A&M Intl U (TX)
Texas Christian U (TX)
Texas Lutheran U (TX)
Texas Wesleyan U (TX)
Trevecca Nazarene U (TN)
Trine U (IN)
Trinity Christian Coll (IL)
Union Coll (NE)
Universidad Adventista de las Antillas (PR)
The U of Akron (OH)
U of Arkansas–Fort Smith (AR)
U of Central Arkansas (AR)
U of Central Florida (FL)
U of Central Oklahoma (OK)
U of Cincinnati (OH)
U of Delaware (DE)
U of Evansville (IN)
U of Georgia (GA)
U of Great Falls (MT)
U of Hartford (CT)
U of Illinois at Chicago (IL)
U of Illinois at Urbana–Champaign (IL)
The U of Iowa (IA)
U of Louisiana at Monroe (LA)
U of Maine at Farmington (ME)
U of Maine at Fort Kent (ME)
U of Maine at Machias (ME)
U of Michigan–Dearborn (MI)
U of Michigan–Flint (MI)
U of Minnesota, Duluth (MN)
U of Mississippi (MS)
U of Missouri (MO)
U of Missouri–St. Louis (MO)
The U of Montana Western (MT)
U of Nebraska–Lincoln (NE)
U of New Hampshire (NH)
The U of North Carolina at Greensboro (NC)
The U of North Carolina at Pembroke (NC)
The U of North Carolina Wilmington (NC)
U of North Dakota (ND)
U of Northern Iowa (IA)
U of North Florida (FL)
U of Oklahoma (OK)
U of Regina (SK, Canada)
U of St. Francis (IL)
U of St. Thomas (MN)
The U of South Dakota (SD)
U of Southern Maine (ME)
U of South Florida (FL)
The U of Tennessee at Chattanooga (TN)
The U of Tennessee at Martin (TN)
The U of Toledo (OH)
U of Tulsa (OK)
U of Vermont (VT)
U of Waterloo (ON, Canada)
U of Windsor (ON, Canada)
U of Wisconsin–Superior (WI)
Ursuline Coll (OH)
Utah State U (UT)

Utica Coll (NY)
Valley City State U (ND)
Valparaiso U (IN)
Vincennes U (IN)
Viterbo U (WI)
Walsh U (OH)
Wartburg Coll (IA)
Washburn U (KS)
Washington State U (WA)
Washington U in St. Louis (MO)
Waynesburg U (PA)
Wayne State Coll (NE)
Wayne State U (MI)
Weber State U (UT)
Western Carolina U (NC)
Western Michigan U (MI)
Western State Colorado U (CO)
Western Washington U (WA)
West Virginia Wesleyan Coll (WV)
Wheeling Jesuit U (WV)
Widener U (PA)
William Penn U (IA)
York Coll of Pennsylvania (PA)
Youngstown State U (OH)

MECHANICAL DRAFTING AND CAD/CADD
Eastern Michigan U (MI)
Indiana U–Purdue U Indianapolis (IN)
Purdue U (IN)

MECHANICAL ENGINEERING
Alfred U (NY)
The American U in Cairo (Egypt)
American U of Beirut (Lebanon)
Andrews U (MI)
Arizona State U (AZ)
Arkansas State U (AR)
Arkansas Tech U (AR)
Auburn U (AL)
Baylor U (TX)
Binghamton U, State U of New York (NY)
Boise State U (ID)
Boston U (MA)
Bradley U (IL)
Brown U (RI)
Bucknell U (PA)
California Baptist U (CA)
California Polytechnic State U, San Luis Obispo (CA)
California State Polytechnic U, Pomona (CA)
California State U, Chico (CA)
California State U, Fresno (CA)
California State U, Fullerton (CA)
California State U, Long Beach (CA)
California State U, Los Angeles (CA)
California State U, Northridge (CA)
Calvin Coll (MI)
Carnegie Mellon U (PA)
Case Western Reserve U (OH)
Cedarville U (OH)
Central Michigan U (MI)
Christian Brothers U (TN)
City Coll of the City U of New York (NY)
Clarkson U (NY)
Clemson U (SC)
Cleveland State U (OH)
The Coll of New Jersey (NJ)
Colorado School of Mines (CO)
Colorado State U (CO)
Columbia U (NY)
Concordia U (QC, Canada)
Cooper Union for the Advancement of Science and Art (NY)
Daniel Webster Coll (NH)
Dordt Coll (IA)
Eastern Washington U (WA)
Embry-Riddle Aeronautical U–Daytona (FL)
Embry-Riddle Aeronautical U–Prescott (AZ)
Fairfield U (CT)
Florida Ag and Mech U (FL)
Florida Atlantic U (FL)
Florida Inst of Technology (FL)
Florida Intl U (FL)
Franklin W. Olin Coll of Eng (MA)
Gannon U (PA)
George Fox U (OR)
Georgia Southern U (GA)
Gonzaga U (WA)

Grove City Coll (PA)
Harding U (AR)
Hofstra U (NY)
Hope Coll (MI)
Illinois Inst of Technology (IL)
Indiana Tech (IN)
Indiana U–Purdue U Fort Wayne (IN)
Indiana U–Purdue U Indianapolis (IN)
Inter American U of Puerto Rico, Bayamón Campus (PR)
Iowa State U of Science and Technology (IA)
John Brown U (AR)
The Johns Hopkins U (MD)
Kansas State U (KS)
Lafayette Coll (PA)
Lake Superior State U (MI)
Lamar U (TX)
Lawrence Technological U (MI)
Lebanese American U (Lebanon)
Lehigh U (PA)
LeTourneau U (TX)
Lipscomb U (TN)
Louisiana State U and Ag and Mech Coll (LA)
Loyola Marymount U (CA)
Manhattan Coll (NY)
Marquette U (WI)
Massachusetts Inst of Technology (MA)
Merrimack Coll (MA)
Miami U (OH)
Michigan State U (MI)
Milwaukee School of Eng (WI)
Minnesota State U Mankato (MN)
Mississippi State U (MS)
Missouri U of Science and Technology (MO)
Montana State U (MT)
New England Inst of Technology (RI)
New Jersey Inst of Technology (NJ)
New Mexico Inst of Mining and Technology (NM)
New Mexico State U (NM)
New York Inst of Technology (NY)
North Carolina State U (NC)
North Dakota State U (ND)
Northeastern U (MA)
Northern Arizona U (AZ)
Northern Illinois U (IL)
Norwich U (VT)
Oakland U (MI)
The Ohio State U (OH)
Ohio U (OH)
Oklahoma Christian U (OK)
Oklahoma State U (OK)
Old Dominion U (VA)
Oral Roberts U (OK)
Oregon State U (OR)
Penn State Abington (PA)
Penn State Altoona (PA)
Penn State Beaver (PA)
Penn State Berks (PA)
Penn State Brandywine (PA)
Penn State DuBois (PA)
Penn State Erie, The Behrend Coll (PA)
Penn State Fayette, The Eberly Campus (PA)
Penn State Greater Allegheny (PA)
Penn State Harrisburg (PA)
Penn State Hazleton (PA)
Penn State Lehigh Valley (PA)
Penn State Mont Alto (PA)
Penn State New Kensington (PA)
Penn State Schuylkill (PA)
Penn State Shenango (PA)
Penn State U Park (PA)
Penn State Wilkes-Barre (PA)
Penn State Worthington Scranton (PA)
Penn State York (PA)
Polytechnic Inst of New York U (NY)
Polytechnic U of Puerto Rico (PR)
Portland State U (OR)
Princeton U (NJ)
Purdue U (IN)
Purdue U Calumet (IN)
Purdue U North Central (IN)
Quinnipiac U (CT)
Rensselaer Polytechnic Inst (NY)
Rice U (TX)
Rochester Inst of Technology (NY)

Rockhurst U (MO)
Rowan U (NJ)
Rutgers, The State U of New Jersey, New Brunswick (NJ)
Saginaw Valley State U (MI)
Saint Louis U (MO)
Saint Martin's U (WA)
San Diego State U (CA)
San Francisco State U (CA)
San Jose State U (CA)
Seattle U (WA)
South Dakota State U (SD)
Southern Illinois U Carbondale (IL)
Southern Illinois U Edwardsville (IL)
Southern Methodist U (TX)
Southern Polytechnic State U (GA)
Stanford U (CA)
State U of New York Maritime Coll (NY)
Stony Brook U, State U of New York (NY)
Syracuse U (NY)
Temple U (PA)
Tennessee State U (TN)
Texas A&M U (TX)
Texas A&M U–Kingsville (TX)
Texas Christian U (TX)
Trine U (IN)
Trinity Coll (CT)
Tufts U (MA)
Tuskegee U (AL)
United States Air Force Acad (CO)
United States Coast Guard Acad (CT)
United States Military Acad (NY)
United States Naval Acad (MD)
Université de Sherbrooke (QC, Canada)
U at Buffalo, the State U of New York (NY)
The U of Akron (OH)
The U of Alabama (AL)
The U of Alabama at Birmingham (AL)
U of Alaska Fairbanks (AK)
The U of Arizona (AZ)
The U of British Columbia (BC, Canada)
The U of British Columbia–Okanagan (BC, Canada)
U of California, Berkeley (CA)
U of California, Davis (CA)
U of California, Irvine (CA)
U of California, Los Angeles (CA)
U of California, Merced (CA)
U of California, Riverside (CA)
U of California, Santa Barbara (CA)
U of Central Florida (FL)
U of Cincinnati (OH)
U of Colorado Boulder (CO)
U of Colorado Colorado Springs (CO)
U of Colorado Denver (CO)
U of Delaware (DE)
U of Denver (CO)
U of Evansville (IN)
U of Florida (FL)
U of Guelph (ON, Canada)
U of Hartford (CT)
U of Hawaii at Manoa (HI)
U of Houston (TX)
U of Idaho (ID)
U of Illinois at Chicago (IL)
U of Illinois at Urbana–Champaign (IL)
The U of Iowa (IA)
The U of Kansas (KS)
U of Kentucky (KY)
U of Louisiana at Lafayette (LA)
U of Louisville (KY)
U of Maryland, Baltimore County (MD)
U of Maryland, Coll Park (MD)
U of Massachusetts Amherst (MA)
U of Massachusetts Dartmouth (MA)
U of Memphis (TN)
U of Miami (FL)
U of Michigan (MI)
U of Michigan–Dearborn (MI)
U of Michigan–Flint (MI)
U of Minnesota, Duluth (MN)
U of Minnesota, Twin Cities Campus (MN)
U of Mississippi (MS)
U of Missouri (MO)

U of Missouri–Kansas City (MO)
U of Missouri–St. Louis (MO)
U of Mount Union (OH)
U of Nebraska–Lincoln (NE)
U of Nevada, Las Vegas (NV)
U of Nevada, Reno (NV)
U of New Brunswick Fredericton (NB, Canada)
U of New Hampshire (NH)
U of New Haven (CT)
U of New Mexico (NM)
U of New Orleans (LA)
The U of North Carolina at Charlotte (NC)
U of North Dakota (ND)
U of North Florida (FL)
U of North Texas (TX)
U of Notre Dame (IN)
U of Oklahoma (OK)
U of Ottawa (ON, Canada)
U of Pennsylvania (PA)
U of Pittsburgh (PA)
U of Portland (OR)
U of Rhode Island (RI)
U of Rochester (NY)
U of St. Thomas (MN)
U of San Diego (CA)
U of South Alabama (AL)
U of South Carolina (SC)
U of Southern California (CA)
U of Southern Maine (ME)
U of South Florida (FL)
The U of Tennessee (TN)
The U of Tennessee at Chattanooga (TN)
The U of Texas at Arlington (TX)
The U of Texas at Austin (TX)
The U of Texas at Dallas (TX)
The U of Texas at El Paso (TX)
The U of Texas at San Antonio (TX)
The U of Texas of the Permian Basin (TX)
The U of Texas–Pan American (TX)
U of the District of Columbia (DC)
The U of Toledo (OH)
U of Tulsa (OK)
U of Utah (UT)
U of Vermont (VT)
U of Virginia (VA)
U of Waterloo (ON, Canada)
The U of Western Ontario (ON, Canada)
U of Windsor (ON, Canada)
U of Wisconsin–Madison (WI)
U of Wisconsin–Milwaukee (WI)
U of Wisconsin–Platteville (WI)
U of Wyoming (WY)
Utah State U (UT)
Valparaiso U (IN)
Vanderbilt U (TN)
Villanova U (PA)
Virginia Commonwealth U (VA)
Virginia Polytechnic Inst and State U (VA)
Walla Walla U (WA)
Washington State U (WA)
Washington U in St. Louis (MO)
Wayne State U (MI)
Wentworth Inst of Technology (MA)
Western Kentucky U (KY)
Western Michigan U (MI)
West Texas A&M U (TX)
West Virginia U (WV)
West Virginia Inst of Technology (WV)
Wichita State U (KS)
Widener U (PA)
Wilkes U (PA)
William Penn U (IA)
Worcester Polytechnic Inst (MA)
Wright State U (OH)
Yale U (CT)
York Coll of Pennsylvania (PA)
Youngstown State U (OH)

MECHANICAL ENGINEERING/ MECHANICAL TECHNOLOGY
Arizona State U (AZ)
Bluefield State Coll (WV)
Bowling Green State U (OH)
Buffalo State Coll, State U of New York (NY)
California State U, Long Beach (CA)
Central Connecticut State U (CT)
Central Michigan U (MI)
Colorado Mesa U (CO)

Eastern Michigan U (MI)
Eastern Washington U (WA)
Fairleigh Dickinson U, Metropolitan Campus (NJ)
Fairmont State U (WV)
Farmingdale State Coll (NY)
Ferris State U (MI)
Georgia Southern U (GA)
Indiana U–Purdue U Fort Wayne (IN)
Lake Superior State U (MI)
LeTourneau U (TX)
Metropolitan State U of Denver (CO)
Midwestern State U (TX)
Milwaukee School of Eng (WI)
Montana State U (MT)
Nicholls State U (LA)
Northern Michigan U (MI)
Oklahoma State U (OK)
Penn State Erie, The Behrend Coll (PA)
Pennsylvania Coll of Technology (PA)
Pittsburg State U (KS)
Point Park U (PA)
Roger Williams U (RI)
Southern Polytechnic State U (GA)
State U of New York Coll of Technology at Alfred (NY)
State U of New York Inst of Technology (NY)
Sullivan Coll of Technology and Design (KY)
United States Military Acad (NY)
The U of Akron (OH)
U of Arkansas at Little Rock (AR)
The U of British Columbia (BC, Canada)
U of Hartford (CT)
U of Houston (TX)
U of New Hampshire (NH)
U of New Hampshire at Manchester (NH)
The U of North Carolina at Charlotte (NC)
U of North Texas (TX)
The U of Texas at Brownsville (TX)
U of the District of Columbia (DC)
The U of Toledo (OH)
Virginia State U (VA)
Wayne State U (MI)
Wentworth Inst of Technology (MA)
Youngstown State U (OH)

MECHANICAL ENGINEERING TECHNOLOGIES RELATED
Cleveland State U (OH)
Indiana State U (IN)
Indiana U–Purdue U Indianapolis (IN)
New York Inst of Technology (NY)
Pennsylvania Coll of Technology (PA)
Purdue U (IN)
Purdue U North Central (IN)
U of Hartford (CT)
Vaughn Coll of Aeronautics and Technology (NY)

MECHANICS AND REPAIR
Lewis-Clark State Coll (ID)

MECHATRONICS, ROBOTICS, AND AUTOMATION ENGINEERING
Lawrence Technological U (MI)

MEDICAL ANTHROPOLOGY
Creighton U (NE)

MEDICAL/HEALTH MANAGEMENT AND CLINICAL ASSISTANT
Davenport U, Grand Rapids (MI)
Lewis-Clark State Coll (ID)
Stratford U, Woodbridge (VA)

MEDICAL ILLUSTRATION
Cleveland Inst of Art (OH)
Iowa State U of Science and Technology (IA)
Rochester Inst of Technology (NY)

MEDICAL INFORMATICS
Champlain Coll (VT)
Coll of Mount St. Joseph (OH)
Misericordia U (PA)
Montana Tech of The U of Montana (MT)

U of Waterloo (ON, Canada)
Western Michigan U (MI)

MEDICAL MICROBIOLOGY AND BACTERIOLOGY
Adams State U (CO)
Auburn U (AL)
Bowling Green State U (OH)
California Polytechnic State U, San Luis Obispo (CA)
Dalhousie U (NS, Canada)
Humboldt State U (CA)
Inter American U of Puerto Rico, Bayamón Campus (PR)
Minnesota State U Mankato (MN)
Mississippi State U (MS)
Montana State U (MT)
New Mexico State U (NM)
Ohio Wesleyan U (OH)
Penn State Abington (PA)
Penn State Altoona (PA)
Penn State Beaver (PA)
Penn State Berks (PA)
Penn State Brandywine (PA)
Penn State DuBois (PA)
Penn State Erie, The Behrend Coll (PA)
Penn State Fayette, The Eberly Campus (PA)
Penn State Greater Allegheny (PA)
Penn State Hazleton (PA)
Penn State Lehigh Valley (PA)
Penn State Mont Alto (PA)
Penn State New Kensington (PA)
Penn State Schuylkill (PA)
Penn State Shenango (PA)
Penn State U Park (PA)
Penn State Wilkes-Barre (PA)
Penn State Worthington Scranton (PA)
Penn State York (PA)
Pomona Coll (CA)
Quinnipiac U (CT)
Rutgers, The State U of New Jersey, New Brunswick (NJ)
San Francisco State U (CA)
Sonoma State U (CA)
Université de Sherbrooke (QC, Canada)
The U of British Columbia (BC, Canada)
U of California, Los Angeles (CA)
U of California, Santa Barbara (CA)
U of Delaware (DE)
U of Florida (FL)
U of Minnesota, Twin Cities Campus (MN)
U of New Brunswick Fredericton (NB, Canada)
U of South Florida (FL)
The U of Texas at El Paso (TX)
U of Vermont (VT)
U of Wisconsin–La Crosse (WI)
Utah State U (UT)
Wagner Coll (NY)
Worcester Polytechnic Inst (MA)
Xavier U of Louisiana (LA)

MEDICAL OFFICE ASSISTANT
Concordia U Wisconsin (WI)
Lewis-Clark State Coll (ID)

MEDICAL RADIOLOGIC TECHNOLOGY
Alderson-Broaddus Coll (WV)
Arkansas State U (AR)
Avila U (MO)
Ball State U (IN)
Baptist Coll of Health Sciences (TN)
Belmont U (TN)
Bloomsburg U of Pennsylvania (PA)
Boise State U (ID)
California State U, Long Beach (CA)
Clarion U of Pennsylvania (PA)
Concordia U Wisconsin (WI)
Fairleigh Dickinson U, Coll at Florham (NJ)
Georgia Regents U (GA)
Grand Valley State U (MI)
Indiana U Kokomo (IN)
Indiana U–Purdue U Indianapolis (IN)
Indiana U South Bend (IN)
Kent State U at Salem (OH)
La Roche Coll (PA)

Long Island U–C. W. Post Campus (NY)
Massachusetts Coll of Pharmacy and Health Sciences (MA)
Minot State U (ND)
Misericordia U (PA)
Morehead State U (KY)
Mount Aloysius Coll (PA)
Mount Marty Coll (SD)
New York City Coll of Technology of the City U of New York (NY)
North Central Coll (IL)
Oakland U (MI)
The Ohio State U (OH)
Oregon Health & Science U (OR)
Roosevelt U (IL)
St. Francis Coll (NY)
Saint Louis U (MO)
Texas State U–San Marcos (TX)
Thomas Edison State Coll (NJ)
Thompson Rivers U (BC, Canada)
U of Arkansas for Medical Sciences (AR)
U of Central Arkansas (AR)
U of Cincinnati (OH)
The U of Findlay (OH)
U of Hartford (CT)
U of Michigan–Flint (MI)
U of Missouri (MO)
U of Nevada, Las Vegas (NV)
U of New Mexico (NM)
The U of North Carolina at Chapel Hill (NC)
U of St. Francis (IL)
U of Southern Indiana (IN)
U of Vermont (VT)
U of Wisconsin–La Crosse (WI)
Valencia Coll (FL)
Wayne State U (MI)
Weber State U (UT)

MEDICAL STAFF SERVICES TECHNOLOGY
Converse Coll (SC)
Mount Vernon Nazarene U (OH)

MEDICINAL AND PHARMACEUTICAL CHEMISTRY
King Coll (TN)
Pittsburg State U (KS)
U of Guelph (ON, Canada)
U of Michigan (MI)
U of the Sciences (PA)
Worcester Polytechnic Inst (MA)

MEDIEVAL AND RENAISSANCE STUDIES
Bard Coll (NY)
Binghamton U, State U of New York (NY)
Brown U (RI)
The Catholic U of America (DC)
Cleveland State U (OH)
Coll of the Holy Cross (MA)
The Coll of William and Mary (VA)
Columbia U (NY)
Cornell Coll (IA)
Dickinson Coll (PA)
Drew U (NJ)
Georgetown U (DC)
Hanover Coll (IN)
Mount Allison U (NB, Canada)
Mount Holyoke Coll (MA)
New Coll of Florida (FL)
The Ohio State U (OH)
Ohio Wesleyan U (OH)
Penn State Abington (PA)
Penn State Altoona (PA)
Penn State Beaver (PA)
Penn State Berks (PA)
Penn State Brandywine (PA)
Penn State DuBois (PA)
Penn State Erie, The Behrend Coll (PA)
Penn State Fayette, The Eberly Campus (PA)
Penn State Greater Allegheny (PA)
Penn State Hazleton (PA)
Penn State Lehigh Valley (PA)
Penn State Mont Alto (PA)
Penn State New Kensington (PA)
Penn State Schuylkill (PA)
Penn State Shenango (PA)
Penn State U Park (PA)
Penn State Wilkes-Barre (PA)
Penn State Worthington Scranton (PA)

Penn State York (PA)
Rutgers, The State U of New Jersey, New Brunswick (NJ)
St. Olaf Coll (MN)
Sewanee: The U of the South (TN)
Smith Coll (MA)
Southern Methodist U (TX)
Swarthmore Coll (PA)
Tulane U (LA)
U at Albany, State U of New York (NY)
U of California, Santa Barbara (CA)
U of Chicago (IL)
The U of Iowa (IA)
U of Michigan (MI)
U of Nebraska–Lincoln (NE)
U of Notre Dame (IN)
U of Oregon (OR)
U of Ottawa (ON, Canada)
U of Regina (SK, Canada)
The U of Toledo (OH)
U of Waterloo (ON, Canada)
Vassar Coll (NY)
Washington and Lee U (VA)
Wellesley Coll (MA)
Wesleyan U (CT)

MEETING AND EVENT PLANNING
Lasell Coll (MA)
Lynn U (FL)
U of Central Florida (FL)

MENTAL AND SOCIAL HEALTH SERVICES AND ALLIED PROFESSIONS RELATED
Clarion U of Pennsylvania (PA)
Old Dominion U (VA)
Pennsylvania Coll of Technology (PA)
Roger Williams U (RI)
U of Puerto Rico at Ponce (PR)
The U of Toledo (OH)
Washburn U (KS)

MENTAL HEALTH COUNSELING
Canisius Coll (NY)
Iona Coll (NY)
Kansas Wesleyan U (KS)
Lee U (TN)
U of Maine at Farmington (ME)

MERCHANDISING, SALES, AND MARKETING OPERATIONS RELATED (GENERAL)
Dalhousie U (NS, Canada)
Eastern Michigan U (MI)
Georgia State U (GA)
Lincoln U (MO)
Post U (CT)
U of Hartford (CT)
Washington U in St. Louis (MO)

MERCHANDISING, SALES, AND MARKETING OPERATIONS RELATED (SPECIALIZED)
Baylor U (TX)
Carlow U (PA)
Fashion Inst of Technology (NY)
Gannon U (PA)
Saint Joseph's U (PA)

METAL AND JEWELRY ARTS
Acad of Art U (CA)
Adams State U (CO)
Alberta Coll of Art & Design (AB, Canada)
Bowling Green State U (OH)
California State U, Long Beach (CA)
Cleveland Inst of Art (OH)
The Coll at Brockport, State U of New York (NY)
Colorado State U (CO)
Ferris State U (MI)
Hofstra U (NY)
Massachusetts Coll of Art and Design (MA)
Northern Michigan U (MI)
Pittsburg State U (KS)
Rhode Island School of Design (RI)
Rochester Inst of Technology (NY)
Savannah Coll of Art and Design (GA)

School of the Art Inst of Chicago (IL)
School of the Museum of Fine Arts, Boston (MA)
Seton Hill U (PA)
State U of New York at New Paltz (NY)
Syracuse U (NY)
Temple U (PA)
The U of Akron (OH)
The U of Iowa (IA)
The U of Kansas (KS)
U of Massachusetts Dartmouth (MA)
U of Michigan (MI)
U of Oregon (OR)
Western State Colorado U (CO)

METALLURGICAL ENGINEERING
Colorado School of Mines (CO)
Missouri U of Science and Technology (MO)
Montana Tech of The U of Montana (MT)
The U of Alabama (AL)
The U of British Columbia (BC, Canada)
U of Illinois at Urbana–Champaign (IL)
U of Minnesota, Twin Cities Campus (MN)
U of Nevada, Reno (NV)
The U of Texas at El Paso (TX)
U of Utah (UT)

METEOROLOGY
Central Michigan U (MI)
The Coll at Brockport, State U of New York (NY)
Dalhousie U (NS, Canada)
Florida Inst of Technology (FL)
Florida State U (FL)
Metropolitan State U of Denver (CO)
Northland Coll (WI)
U of Hawaii at Manoa (HI)
U of Miami (FL)
The U of North Carolina at Charlotte (NC)
U of Oklahoma (OK)
U of the Incarnate Word (TX)
U of Utah (UT)
U of Wisconsin–Milwaukee (WI)
Virginia Polytechnic Inst and State U (VA)
Western Illinois U (IL)
Western Kentucky U (KY)

MICROBIOLOGICAL SCIENCES AND IMMUNOLOGY RELATED
Dalhousie U (NS, Canada)
The U of Western Ontario (ON, Canada)

MICROBIOLOGY
Albany Coll of Pharmacy and Health Sciences (NY)
Arizona State U (AZ)
Auburn U (AL)
Brigham Young U (UT)
California State U, Chico (CA)
California State U, Dominguez Hills (CA)
California State U, Long Beach (CA)
California State U, Los Angeles (CA)
Clemson U (SC)
Colorado State U (CO)
Indiana U Bloomington (IN)
Inter American U of Puerto Rico, Aguadilla Campus (PR)
Inter American U of Puerto Rico, Ponce Campus (PR)
Inter American U of Puerto Rico, San Germán Campus (PR)
Iowa State U of Science and Technology (IA)
Kansas State U (KS)
Louisiana State U and Ag and Mech Coll (LA)
Miami U (OH)
Michigan State U (MI)
North Carolina State U (NC)
North Dakota State U (ND)
Northern Arizona U (AZ)
Northern Michigan U (MI)

The Ohio State U (OH)
Ohio U (OH)
Oklahoma State U (OK)
Oregon State U (OR)
San Diego State U (CA)
South Dakota State U (SD)
Southern Illinois U Carbondale (IL)
Texas A&M U (TX)
Texas State U–San Marcos (TX)
The U of Alabama (AL)
The U of Arizona (AZ)
The U of British Columbia–Okanagan (BC, Canada)
U of California, Berkeley (CA)
U of California, Davis (CA)
U of California, Santa Barbara (CA)
U of Georgia (GA)
U of Guelph (ON, Canada)
U of Hawaii at Manoa (HI)
U of Idaho (ID)
U of Illinois at Urbana–Champaign (IL)
The U of Iowa (IA)
The U of Kansas (KS)
U of Maryland, Coll Park (MD)
U of Massachusetts Amherst (MA)
U of Michigan (MI)
U of Michigan–Dearborn (MI)
U of Nebraska–Lincoln (NE)
U of Northern Iowa (IA)
U of Oklahoma (OK)
U of Pittsburgh (PA)
U of Rhode Island (RI)
The U of Texas at Arlington (TX)
U of the Sciences (PA)
U of Vermont (VT)
The U of Western Ontario (ON, Canada)
U of Wisconsin–La Crosse (WI)
U of Wisconsin–Madison (WI)
U of Wisconsin–Milwaukee (WI)
U of Wyoming (WY)
Washington State U (WA)
Weber State U (UT)

MICROBIOLOGY AND IMMUNOLOGY
U of California, Irvine (CA)
U of Miami (FL)

MIDDLE/NEAR EASTERN AND SEMITIC LANGUAGES
Indiana U Bloomington (IN)
U of Pennsylvania (PA)
The U of Texas at Austin (TX)

MIDDLE/NEAR EASTERN AND SEMITIC LANGUAGES RELATED
Columbia U, School of General Studies (NY)
Pomona Coll (CA)
U of Michigan (MI)
Wayne State U (MI)

MIDDLE SCHOOL EDUCATION
Abilene Christian U (TX)
Alaska Pacific U (AK)
Albertus Magnus Coll (CT)
Alice Lloyd Coll (KY)
Alvernia U (PA)
Alverno Coll (WI)
Appalachian State U (NC)
Arkansas State U (AR)
Arkansas Tech U (AR)
Armstrong Atlantic State U (GA)
Asbury U (KY)
Ashland U (OH)
Assumption Coll (MA)
Avila U (MO)
Baker U (KS)
Baldwin Wallace U (OH)
Barton Coll (NC)
Bellarmine U (KY)
Belmont U (TN)
Bennington Coll (VT)
Berea Coll (KY)
Berry Coll (GA)
Bethel Coll (IN)
Bloomsburg U of Pennsylvania (PA)
Bluefield Coll (VA)
Bluffton U (OH)
Bob Jones U (SC)
Bowling Green State U (OH)
Butler U (IN)
Capital U (OH)
Carlow U (PA)
Catawba Coll (NC)
Cedarville U (OH)

Central Methodist U (MO)
Central State U (OH)
Champlain Coll (VT)
Claflin U (SC)
Clarion U of Pennsylvania (PA)
Clark U (MA)
Clayton State U (GA)
Cleveland State U (OH)
Coastal Carolina U (SC)
The Coll at Brockport, State U of New York (NY)
Coll of Charleston (SC)
Coll of Mount St. Joseph (OH)
Coll of the Atlantic (ME)
Coll of the Ozarks (MO)
Columbia Coll (SC)
Columbus State U (GA)
Concordia Coll–New York (NY)
Concordia U, Nebraska (NE)
Concordia U, St. Paul (MN)
Concordia U Texas (TX)
Concordia U Wisconsin (WI)
Dakota Wesleyan U (SD)
Duquesne U (PA)
East Carolina U (NC)
Edinboro U of Pennsylvania (PA)
Elizabeth City State U (NC)
Elizabethtown Coll (PA)
Elmira Coll (NY)
Elon U (NC)
Emmanuel Coll (GA)
Evangel U (MO)
Fayetteville State U (NC)
Florida Inst of Technology (FL)
Gardner-Webb U (NC)
Geneva Coll (PA)
Georgetown Coll (KY)
Georgia Coll & State U (GA)
Georgia Regents U (GA)
Georgia Southern U (GA)
Georgia Southwestern State U (GA)
Gettysburg Coll (PA)
Gordon Coll (MA)
Grace U (NE)
Grand Valley State U (MI)
Granite State Coll (NH)
Grove City Coll (PA)
Hampton U (VA)
Harding U (AR)
Harris-Stowe State U (MO)
Henderson State U (AR)
High Point U (NC)
Howard Payne U (TX)
Huntington U (IN)
Indiana Wesleyan U (IN)
Iowa Wesleyan Coll (IA)
Ithaca Coll (NY)
Jacksonville State U (AL)
Johnson State Coll (VT)
Kennesaw State U (GA)
Kent State U (OH)
Kent State U at Geauga (OH)
Kent State U at Stark (OH)
Kentucky Christian U (KY)
Kentucky Wesleyan Coll (KY)
Keystone Coll (PA)
King Coll (TN)
Kutztown U of Pennsylvania (PA)
Lake Erie Coll (OH)
Lakeland Coll (WI)
Lake Superior State U (MI)
Lesley U (MA)
Lincoln U (MO)
Lindenwood U (MO)
Lindsey Wilson Coll (KY)
Lipscomb U (TN)
Lourdes U (OH)
Lubbock Christian U (TX)
Malone U (OH)
Manchester U (IN)
Manhattan Coll (NY)
Marian U (WI)
Mars Hill Coll (NC)
Maryville U of Saint Louis (MO)
The Master's Coll and Sem (CA)
McKendree U (IL)
McMurry U (TX)
Medaille Coll (NY)
Mercer U (GA)
Mercyhurst U (PA)
Merrimack Coll (MA)
Messiah Coll (PA)
Miami U (OH)
Michigan State U (MI)
Millersville U of Pennsylvania (PA)
Misericordia U (PA)

Missouri Baptist U (MO)
Missouri State U (MO)
Morehead State U (KY)
Mount Aloysius Coll (PA)
Mount Mary Coll (WI)
Mount Mercy U (IA)
Mount Vernon Nazarene U (OH)
Murray State U (KY)
Newberry Coll (SC)
Nicholls State U (LA)
North Carolina Central U (NC)
North Carolina State U (NC)
North Carolina Wesleyan Coll (NC)
Northwest Missouri State U (MO)
Nova Southeastern U (FL)
Oakland City U (IN)
Ohio Dominican U (OH)
The Ohio State U (OH)
The Ohio State U at Lima (OH)
The Ohio State U at Marion (OH)
The Ohio State U–Mansfield Campus (OH)
The Ohio State U–Newark Campus (OH)
Ohio Wesleyan U (OH)
Ouachita Baptist U (AR)
Paine Coll (GA)
Piedmont Coll (GA)
Point U (GA)
Presbyterian Coll (SC)
Rockhurst U (MO)
Roger Williams U (RI)
Saint Leo U (FL)
Saint Louis U (MO)
Salem State U (MA)
Schreiner U (TX)
Shippensburg U of Pennsylvania (PA)
Southeastern Louisiana U (LA)
Southeast Missouri State U (MO)
Southern Arkansas U–Magnolia (AR)
Southwest Baptist U (MO)
State U of New York Coll at Cortland (NY)
State U of New York Coll at Old Westbury (NY)
Stevenson U (MD)
Tarleton State U (TX)
Texas Lutheran U (TX)
Thomas More Coll (KY)
Thomas U (GA)
Transylvania U (KY)
Union Coll (KY)
The U of Akron (OH)
U of Arkansas–Fort Smith (AR)
U of Central Arkansas (AR)
U of Cincinnati (OH)
U of Georgia (GA)
U of Great Falls (MT)
The U of Kansas (KS)
U of Kentucky (KY)
U of Louisiana at Lafayette (LA)
U of Maryland, Coll Park (MD)
U of Missouri (MO)
U of Missouri–Kansas City (MO)
U of Mount Union (OH)
The U of North Carolina at Chapel Hill (NC)
The U of North Carolina at Charlotte (NC)
The U of North Carolina at Greensboro (NC)
The U of North Carolina at Pembroke (NC)
The U of North Carolina Wilmington (NC)
U of North Dakota (ND)
U of Northern Iowa (IA)
U of North Florida (FL)
U of North Georgia (GA)
U of Pikeville (KY)
U of Regina (SK, Canada)
U of St. Thomas (MN)
The U of Scranton (PA)
U of South Carolina (SC)
U of South Carolina Aiken (SC)
U of South Carolina Upstate (SC)
The U of Tennessee at Chattanooga (TN)
U of the Cumberlands (KY)
U of the Ozarks (AR)
U of Vermont (VT)
The U of Western Ontario (ON, Canada)
U of West Florida (FL)
U of Wisconsin–Platteville (WI)

Ursuline Coll (OH)
Valdosta State U (GA)
Virginia Wesleyan Coll (VA)
Walsh U (OH)
Warner Pacific Coll (OR)
Washington U in St. Louis (MO)
Wayland Baptist U (TX)
Wayne State Coll (NE)
Webster U (MO)
West Chester U of Pennsylvania (PA)
Western Carolina U (NC)
Western Kentucky U (KY)
Westminster Coll (MO)
West Virginia Wesleyan Coll (WV)
Wheeling Jesuit U (WV)
Wilkes U (PA)
William Jewell Coll (MO)
Wilmington U (DE)
Wright State U (OH)
Xavier U (OH)
Xavier U of Louisiana (LA)
Young Harris Coll (GA)
Youngstown State U (OH)

MILITARY APPLIED SCIENCES RELATED
United States Military Acad (NY)

MILITARY HISTORY
American Public U System (WV)
Rogers State U (OK)

MILITARY INSTALLATION MANAGEMENT
American Public U System (WV)

MILITARY STUDIES
Hawai`i Pacific U (HI)
Pacific Lutheran U (WA)
United States Air Force Acad (CO)

MILITARY TECHNOLOGIES AND APPLIED SCIENCES RELATED
Alcorn State U (MS)

MINING AND MINERAL ENGINEERING
Colorado School of Mines (CO)
Missouri U of Science and Technology (MO)
Montana Tech of The U of Montana (MT)
New Mexico Inst of Mining and Technology (NM)
Penn State Abington (PA)
Penn State Altoona (PA)
Penn State Beaver (PA)
Penn State Berks (PA)
Penn State Brandywine (PA)
Penn State DuBois (PA)
Penn State Erie, The Behrend Coll (PA)
Penn State Fayette, The Eberly Campus (PA)
Penn State Greater Allegheny (PA)
Penn State Hazleton (PA)
Penn State Lehigh Valley (PA)
Penn State Mont Alto (PA)
Penn State New Kensington (PA)
Penn State Schuylkill (PA)
Penn State Shenango (PA)
Penn State York Park (PA)
Penn State Wilkes-Barre (PA)
Penn State Worthington Scranton (PA)
Penn State York (PA)
Southern Illinois U Carbondale (IL)
U of Alaska Fairbanks (AK)
The U of Arizona (AZ)
The U of British Columbia (BC, Canada)
U of Kentucky (KY)
U of Minnesota, Twin Cities Campus (MN)
U of Nevada, Reno (NV)
U of Utah (UT)
Virginia Polytechnic Inst and State U (VA)
West Virginia U (WV)

MINING AND PETROLEUM TECHNOLOGIES RELATED
U of Alaska Fairbanks (AK)

MINING TECHNOLOGY
Bluefield State Coll (WV)

MISSIONARY STUDIES AND MISSIOLOGY
Asbury U (KY)
Bethel Coll (IN)
Bob Jones U (SC)
Briercrest Coll (SK, Canada)
California Baptist U (CA)
Central Baptist Coll (AR)
City Vision Coll (MO)
Columbia Bible Coll (BC, Canada)
Concordia U, St. Paul (MN)
Concordia U Wisconsin (WI)
Corban U (OR)
Crossroads Coll (MN)
Crown Coll (MN)
Dordt Coll (IA)
East Texas Baptist U (TX)
Faith Baptist Bible Coll and Theological Sem (IA)
Gardner-Webb U (NC)
Global U (MO)
Grace U (NE)
Harding U (AR)
Hardin-Simmons U (TX)
Hillsdale Free Will Baptist Coll (OK)
Hope Intl U (CA)
Howard Payne U (TX)
Huntington U (IN)
Indiana Wesleyan U (IN)
Kuyper Coll (MI)
Lee U (TN)
LeTourneau U (TX)
Liberty U (VA)
Lincoln Christian U (IL)
Lipscomb U (TN)
Lubbock Christian U (TX)
Maranatha Baptist Bible Coll (WI)
Mid-Atlantic Christian U (NC)
Mount Vernon Nazarene U (OH)
Multnomah U (OR)
North Greenville U (SC)
Northwestern Coll (MN)
Northwest Nazarene U (ID)
Northwest U (WA)
Nyack Coll (NY)
Oklahoma Christian U (OK)
Oral Roberts U (OK)
Ouachita Baptist U (AR)
Palm Beach Atlantic U (FL)
Simpson U (CA)
Southeastern U (FL)
Southern Nazarene U (OK)
Southwest Baptist U (MO)
Tabor Coll (KS)
Trinity Coll of Florida (FL)
Wayland Baptist U (TX)

MODELING, VIRTUAL ENVIRONMENTS AND SIMULATION
Daniel Webster Coll (NH)
DigiPen Inst of Technology (WA)
Pennsylvania Coll of Technology (PA)
U of Colorado Colorado Springs (CO)
U of Idaho (ID)

MODERN GREEK
Butler U (IN)
Calvin Coll (MI)
Colgate U (NY)
Columbia U (NY)
Concordia U Wisconsin (WI)
Furman U (SC)
John Carroll U (OH)
Lehman Coll of the City U of New York (NY)
The Ohio State U (OH)
Saint Mary's Coll of California (CA)
Trent U (ON, Canada)
Tufts U (MA)
Tulane U (LA)
U of Michigan (MI)
U of New Brunswick Fredericton (NB, Canada)
Wabash Coll (IN)
Wright State U (OH)

MODERN LANGUAGES
Alma Coll (MI)
Bemidji State U (MN)
Clark U (MA)
Clemson U (SC)
The Coll of William and Mary (VA)
Cornell Coll (IA)
Franklin Coll Switzerland (Switzerland)

Gettysburg Coll (PA)
Hampton U (VA)
King Coll (TN)
La Salle U (PA)
Long Island U–Brooklyn Campus (NY)
Louisiana Coll (LA)
Metropolitan State U of Denver (CO)
Middlebury Coll (VT)
Minnesota State U Mankato (MN)
Mount Allison U (NB, Canada)
Nazareth Coll of Rochester (NY)
Pacific U (OR)
Pomona Coll (CA)
Presbyterian Coll (SC)
Purchase Coll, State U of New York (NY)
Rivier U (NH)
St. Bonaventure U (NY)
St. Lawrence U (NY)
Saint Mary's Coll of California (CA)
Saint Michael's Coll (VT)
St. Thomas Aquinas Coll (NY)
Suffolk U (MA)
Trent U (ON, Canada)
Trinity Coll (CT)
U of New Brunswick Fredericton (NB, Canada)
U of Ottawa (ON, Canada)
The U of Western Ontario (ON, Canada)
U of Windsor (ON, Canada)
Walla Walla U (WA)
Walsh U (OH)
Washington U in St. Louis (MO)
Widener U (PA)
Wright State U (OH)

MOLECULAR BIOCHEMISTRY
Clarkson U (NY)
Simon Fraser U (BC, Canada)
U of California, Davis (CA)
U of Richmond (VA)

MOLECULAR BIOLOGY
Alverno Coll (WI)
Arizona State U (AZ)
Assumption Coll (MA)
Auburn U (AL)
Blackburn Coll (IL)
Boston U (MA)
Brown U (RI)
California Lutheran U (CA)
California State U, Fresno (CA)
California State U, San Marcos (CA)
Central Connecticut State U (CT)
Centre Coll (KY)
Chestnut Hill Coll (PA)
Claremont McKenna Coll (CA)
Clarion U of Pennsylvania (PA)
Clark U (MA)
Coe Coll (IA)
Colby Coll (ME)
Colgate U (NY)
The Coll at Brockport, State U of New York (NY)
The Coll of Wooster (OH)
Connecticut Coll (CT)
Dartmouth Coll (NH)
Florida Inst of Technology (FL)
Gettysburg Coll (PA)
Goshen Coll (IN)
Hampton U (VA)
Humboldt State U (CA)
The Johns Hopkins U (MD)
Kenyon Coll (OH)
Lawrence Technological U (MI)
Lehigh U (PA)
Messiah Coll (PA)
Middlebury Coll (VT)
Millikin U (IL)
Montclair State U (NJ)
Pitzer Coll (CA)
Pomona Coll (CA)
Princeton U (NJ)
Rollins Coll (FL)
Rutgers, The State U of New Jersey, New Brunswick (NJ)
San Francisco State U (CA)
San Jose State U (CA)
Scripps Coll (CA)
Simon Fraser U (BC, Canada)
Stetson U (FL)
Tulane U (LA)

U at Albany, State U of New York (NY)
The U of British Columbia–Okanagan (BC, Canada)
U of California, Santa Barbara (CA)
U of California, Santa Cruz (CA)
U of Denver (CO)
U of Guelph (ON, Canada)
U of Idaho (ID)
The U of Kansas (KS)
U of Michigan–Flint (MI)
U of Minnesota, Duluth (MN)
U of New Brunswick Fredericton (NB, Canada)
U of Pittsburgh (PA)
U of Puget Sound (WA)
The U of Scranton (PA)
The U of Texas at Dallas (TX)
U of Vermont (VT)
U of Wisconsin–Eau Claire (WI)
U of Wisconsin–Madison (WI)
U of Wisconsin–Parkside (WI)
U of Wyoming (WY)
Vanderbilt U (TN)
Wayland Baptist U (TX)
Wells Coll (NY)
Wesleyan U (CT)
Whitman Coll (WA)
William Jewell Coll (MO)
Worcester Polytechnic Inst (MA)
Yale U (CT)

MOLECULAR GENETICS
Michigan State U (MI)
The Ohio State U (OH)
Texas A&M U (TX)
U of Guelph (ON, Canada)
U of Vermont (VT)
Washington State U (WA)

MOLECULAR PHARMACOLOGY
The U of Scranton (PA)

MONTESSORI TEACHER EDUCATION
Canisius Coll (NY)
Oklahoma City U (OK)
Siena Heights U (MI)
Xavier U (OH)

MOVEMENT THERAPY AND MOVEMENT EDUCATION
Brock U (ON, Canada)
Pacific Lutheran U (WA)
Texas Christian U (TX)
U of Vermont (VT)

MULTICULTURAL EDUCATION
Carnegie Mellon U (PA)
Fort Lewis Coll (CO)
Goddard Coll (VT)
Indiana Wesleyan U (IN)

MULTI/INTERDISCIPLINARY STUDIES RELATED
Abilene Christian U (TX)
Adams State U (CO)
Adelphi U (NY)
Agnes Scott Coll (GA)
Albright Coll (PA)
American U (DC)
Anderson U (IN)
Angelo State U (TX)
Arizona State U (AZ)
Arkansas State U (AR)
Arkansas Tech U (AR)
Athens State U (AL)
Baldwin Wallace U (OH)
Bates Coll (ME)
Baylor U (TX)
Bellarmine U (KY)
Belmont U (TN)
Bennington Coll (VT)
Bentley U (MA)
Berea Coll (KY)
Berry Coll (GA)
Bethel U (MN)
Binghamton U, State U of New York (NY)
Bluffton U (OH)
Boise State U (ID)
Boston U (MA)
Bowdoin Coll (ME)
Bowling Green State U (OH)
Brevard Coll (NC)
Bryn Athyn Coll of the New Church (PA)

Bucknell U (PA)
Buena Vista U (IA)
Buffalo State Coll, State U of New York (NY)
California Baptist U (CA)
California Lutheran U (CA)
California Polytechnic State U, San Luis Obispo (CA)
California State U, Chico (CA)
California State U, Dominguez Hills (CA)
California State U, Long Beach (CA)
California State U, Los Angeles (CA)
California State U, Monterey Bay (CA)
California State U, Stanislaus (CA)
Cameron U (OK)
Capital U (OH)
Carroll Coll (MT)
Cedarville U (OH)
Central Coll (IA)
Central Connecticut State U (CT)
Chestnut Hill Coll (PA)
Christopher Newport U (VA)
Claremont McKenna Coll (CA)
Clarkson U (NY)
Cleveland State U (OH)
Colby Coll (ME)
The Coll of Idaho (ID)
The Coll of New Jersey (NJ)
The Coll of New Rochelle (NY)
Coll of Saint Benedict (MN)
Coll of Saint Elizabeth (NJ)
The Coll of Saint Rose (NY)
The Coll of William and Mary (VA)
The Coll of Wooster (OH)
The Colorado Coll (CO)
Columbia Coll Chicago (IL)
Cornell Coll (IA)
Cornerstone U (MI)
Covenant Coll (GA)
Dalhousie U (NS, Canada)
Dallas Baptist U (TX)
Dartmouth Coll (NH)
Davidson Coll (NC)
Delta State U (MS)
DePauw U (IN)
Earlham Coll (IN)
East Central U (OK)
Eastern Illinois U (IL)
Eastern Mennonite U (VA)
Eastern Michigan U (MI)
Eastern New Mexico U (NM)
Eastern Washington U (WA)
East Tennessee State U (TN)
East Texas Baptist U (TX)
Edgewood Coll (WI)
Embry-Riddle Aeronautical U–Daytona (FL)
Embry-Riddle Aeronautical U–Prescott (AZ)
Emmanuel Coll (MA)
Emporia State U (KS)
The Evergreen State Coll (WA)
Farmingdale State Coll (NY)
Florida Inst of Technology (FL)
Florida Southern Coll (FL)
Franklin & Marshall Coll (PA)
Franklin U (OH)
Gannon U (PA)
Georgetown Coll (KY)
Georgetown U (DC)
Georgia State U (GA)
Goshen Coll (IN)
Goucher Coll (MD)
Granite State Coll (NH)
Grantham U (MO)
Greenville Coll (IL)
Guilford Coll (NC)
Hamline U (MN)
Hampshire Coll (MA)
Harris-Stowe State U (MO)
Hillsdale Free Will Baptist Coll (OK)
Hood Coll (MD)
Hope Coll (MI)
Howard Payne U (TX)
Humboldt State U (CA)
Illinois Wesleyan U (IL)
Immaculata U (PA)
Indiana U–Purdue U Indianapolis (IN)
Iowa State U of Science and Technology (IA)
Ithaca Coll (NY)
John Brown U (AR)

Judson U (IL)
Juniata Coll (PA)
Kalamazoo Coll (MI)
Keene State Coll (NH)
Kennesaw State U (GA)
Kentucky Christian U (KY)
Kentucky Wesleyan Coll (KY)
Kenyon Coll (OH)
Knox Coll (IL)
Lake Erie Coll (OH)
Lane Coll (TN)
Lasell Coll (MA)
Lebanon Valley Coll (PA)
Lee U (TN)
Lewis-Clark State Coll (ID)
Lewis U (IL)
Liberty U (VA)
Long Island U–Brooklyn Campus (NY)
Louisiana State U and Ag and Mech Coll (LA)
Lourdes U (OH)
Loyola Marymount U (CA)
Loyola U Chicago (IL)
Loyola U Maryland (MD)
Luther Coll (IA)
Manchester U (IN)
Manhattan Coll (NY)
Marian U (WI)
Marquette U (WI)
Maryville Coll (TN)
McDaniel Coll (MD)
McMurry U (TX)
Mercer U (GA)
Mercyhurst U (PA)
Messiah Coll (PA)
Michigan State U (MI)
Mid-Continent U (KY)
Middle Tennessee State U (TN)
Millikin U (IL)
Millsaps Coll (MS)
Minnesota State U Moorhead (MN)
Mississippi State U (MS)
Mississippi U for Women (MS)
Missouri Baptist U (MO)
Missouri Western State U (MO)
Monmouth U (NJ)
Montclair State U (NJ)
Mount Holyoke Coll (MA)
Mount Mary Coll (WI)
Mount Mercy U (IA)
Mount St. Mary's U (MD)
Naropa U (CO)
National U (CA)
Newman U (KS)
New York Inst of Technology (NY)
Norfolk State U (VA)
North Central Coll (IL)
Northern Illinois U (IL)
Northwest Christian U (OR)
Northwestern Coll (MN)
Northwestern Oklahoma State U (OK)
Northwestern State U of Louisiana (LA)
Northwest Missouri State U (MO)
The Ohio State U (OH)
Ohio Wesleyan U (OH)
Old Dominion U (VA)
Oregon State U (OR)
Pace U (NY)
Palm Beach Atlantic U (FL)
Park U (MO)
Penn State Erie, The Behrend Coll (PA)
Penn State Harrisburg (PA)
Pepperdine U, Malibu (CA)
Plymouth State U (NH)
Point Park U (PA)
Princeton U (NJ)
Radford U (VA)
Regis Coll (MA)
Rice U (TX)
Robert Morris U (PA)
Robert Morris U Illinois (IL)
Rocky Mountain Coll (MT)
Rogers State U (OK)
Roger Williams U (RI)
Rollins Coll (FL)
Rowan U (NJ)
Rutgers, The State U of New Jersey, Camden (NJ)
Rutgers, The State U of New Jersey, Newark (NJ)
Sage Coll of Albany (NY)
St. Ambrose U (IA)
Saint Anselm Coll (NH)

Saint John's U (MN)
Saint Martin's U (WA)
Saint Mary's Coll of California (CA)
St. Mary's Coll of Maryland (MD)
Sam Houston State U (TX)
San Diego Christian Coll (CA)
San Diego State U (CA)
San Francisco State U (CA)
San Jose State U (CA)
Scripps Coll (CA)
Sewanee: The U of the South (TN)
Shippensburg U of Pennsylvania (PA)
Simmons Coll (MA)
Sonoma State U (CA)
South Dakota State U (SD)
Southeastern Oklahoma State U (OK)
Southeast Missouri State U (MO)
Southern Arkansas U–Magnolia (AR)
Southern Illinois U Carbondale (IL)
Southern Methodist U (TX)
Southern Utah U (UT)
State U of New York Coll at Potsdam (NY)
Stephen F. Austin State U (TX)
Stephens Coll (MO)
Stonehill Coll (MA)
Stony Brook U, State U of New York (NY)
Tarleton State U (TX)
Temple U (PA)
Tennessee Wesleyan Coll (TN)
Texas A&M U (TX)
Texas A&M U–Commerce (TX)
Texas A&M U–Kingsville (TX)
Texas State U–San Marcos (TX)
Texas Wesleyan U (TX)
Texas Woman's U (TX)
Thomas Edison State Coll (NJ)
Thomas More Coll (KY)
Thompson Rivers U (BC, Canada)
Truman State U (MO)
Tulane U (LA)
U at Albany, State U of New York (NY)
U at Buffalo, the State U of New York (NY)
The U of Akron (OH)
U of Alaska Fairbanks (AK)
The U of Arizona (AZ)
U of Arkansas at Little Rock (AR)
U of Arkansas–Fort Smith (AR)
U of California, Berkeley (CA)
U of California, Davis (CA)
U of California, Irvine (CA)
U of California, Los Angeles (CA)
U of California, Santa Barbara (CA)
U of Central Arkansas (AR)
U of Cincinnati (OH)
U of Colorado Colorado Springs (CO)
U of Colorado Denver (CO)
U of Denver (CO)
U of Evansville (IN)
U of Florida (FL)
U of Houston (TX)
U of Houston–Clear Lake (TX)
U of Houston–Downtown (TX)
U of Houston–Victoria (TX)
U of Idaho (ID)
U of Kentucky (KY)
U of Maryland, Baltimore County (MD)
U of Maryland, Coll Park (MD)
U of Maryland U Coll (MD)
U of Mary Washington (VA)
U of Massachusetts Amherst (MA)
U of Massachusetts Boston (MA)
U of Massachusetts Dartmouth (MA)
U of Memphis (TN)
U of Michigan (MI)
U of Michigan–Dearborn (MI)
U of Michigan–Flint (MI)
U of Minnesota, Crookston (MN)
U of Minnesota, Twin Cities Campus (MN)
U of Missouri–St. Louis (MO)
U of Mobile (AL)
U of Montevallo (AL)
U of Nebraska at Omaha (NE)
U of New Hampshire (NH)
U of New Orleans (LA)
The U of North Carolina at Pembroke (NC)

U of North Dakota (ND)
U of Northern Colorado (CO)
U of North Texas (TX)
U of Pikeville (KY)
U of Pittsburgh (PA)
U of Richmond (VA)
U of St. Francis (IL)
U of Saint Mary (KS)
U of St. Thomas (MN)
The U of South Dakota (SD)
U of Southern California (CA)
U of South Florida (FL)
The U of Tennessee (TN)
The U of Texas at Arlington (TX)
The U of Texas at Austin (TX)
The U of Texas at Brownsville (TX)
The U of Texas of the Permian Basin (TX)
The U of Texas–Pan American (TX)
The U of Toledo (OH)
U of Virginia (VA)
U of Washington, Bothell (WA)
U of Washington, Tacoma (WA)
U of Waterloo (ON, Canada)
The U of West Alabama (AL)
The U of Western Ontario (ON, Canada)
U of Wisconsin–Green Bay (WI)
U of Wisconsin–Milwaukee (WI)
U of Wisconsin–Stevens Point (WI)
U of Wisconsin–Superior (WI)
U of Wyoming (WY)
Utah State U (UT)
Valparaiso U (IN)
Vanderbilt U (TN)
Vassar Coll (NY)
Villanova U (PA)
Virginia Commonwealth U (VA)
Virginia Intermont Coll (VA)
Virginia Wesleyan Coll (VA)
Viterbo U (WI)
Waldorf Coll (IA)
Washburn U (KS)
Washington & Jefferson Coll (PA)
Washington and Lee U (VA)
Washington Coll (MD)
Washington State U (WA)
Washington U in St. Louis (MO)
Western Kentucky U (KY)
Western Michigan U (MI)
Western Washington U (WA)
West Texas A&M U (TX)
Wheaton Coll (IL)
Wheaton Coll (MA)
Wichita State U (KS)
Wilkes U (PA)
Xavier U (OH)
Yale U (CT)

MUSEUM STUDIES
Centenary Coll of Louisiana (LA)
Coll of the Atlantic (ME)
Drew U (NJ)
Inst of American Indian Arts (NM)
Juniata Coll (PA)
Moore Coll of Art & Design (PA)
Randolph Coll (VA)
The U of Iowa (IA)
The U of Western Ontario (ON, Canada)
Walsh U (OH)

MUSIC
Abilene Christian U (TX)
Acadia U (NS, Canada)
Adams State U (CO)
Adelphi U (NY)
Agnes Scott Coll (GA)
Alabama State U (AL)
Albion Coll (MI)
Albright Coll (PA)
Alderson-Broaddus Coll (WV)
Alma Coll (MI)
Alverno Coll (WI)
American U (DC)
Andrews U (MI)
Angelo State U (TX)
Arizona State U (AZ)
Arkansas State U (AR)
Arkansas Tech U (AR)
Armstrong Atlantic State U (GA)
Asbury U (KY)
Ashland U (OH)
Assumption Coll (MA)
Auburn U (AL)

Augsburg Coll (MN)
Augustana Coll (IL)
Augustana Coll (SD)
Aurora U (IL)
Austin Peay State U (TN)
Averett U (VA)
Avila U (MO)
Azusa Pacific U (CA)
Baker U (KS)
Baldwin Wallace U (OH)
Ball State U (IN)
Bard Coll (NY)
Bates Coll (ME)
Baylor U (TX)
Belhaven U (MS)
Bellarmine U (KY)
Belmont U (TN)
Bemidji State U (MN)
Benedictine Coll (KS)
Benedictine U (IL)
Bennington Coll (VT)
Berea Coll (KY)
Berklee Coll of Music (MA)
Berry Coll (GA)
Bethany Coll (WV)
Bethany Lutheran Coll (MN)
Bethel Coll (IN)
Bethel U (MN)
Binghamton U, State U of New York (NY)
Blackburn Coll (IL)
Bloomsburg U of Pennsylvania (PA)
Bluefield Coll (VA)
Blue Mountain Coll (MS)
Bluffton U (OH)
Boise State U (ID)
Boston Coll (MA)
The Boston Conservatory (MA)
Boston U (MA)
Bowdoin Coll (ME)
Bowling Green State U (OH)
Bradley U (IL)
Brevard Coll (NC)
Bridgewater State U (MA)
Brock U (ON, Canada)
Brown U (RI)
Bucknell U (PA)
Buffalo State Coll, State U of New York (NY)
Butler U (IN)
Cairn U (PA)
Caldwell Coll (NJ)
California Baptist U (CA)
California Lutheran U (CA)
California Polytechnic State U, San Luis Obispo (CA)
California State Polytechnic U, Pomona (CA)
California State U, Chico (CA)
California State U, Dominguez Hills (CA)
California State U, East Bay (CA)
California State U, Fresno (CA)
California State U, Fullerton (CA)
California State U, Long Beach (CA)
California State U, Los Angeles (CA)
California State U, Monterey Bay (CA)
California State U, Northridge (CA)
California State U, San Bernardino (CA)
California State U, Stanislaus (CA)
Calvin Coll (MI)
Cameron U (OK)
Campbellsville U (KY)
Capital U (OH)
Cardinal Stritch U (WI)
Carleton Coll (MN)
Carnegie Mellon U (PA)
Carson-Newman U (TN)
Case Western Reserve U (OH)
Castleton State Coll (VT)
Catawba Coll (NC)
The Catholic U of America (DC)
Cedar Crest Coll (PA)
Cedarville U (OH)
Centenary Coll of Louisiana (LA)
Central Baptist Coll (AR)
Central Coll (IA)
Central Connecticut State U (CT)
Central Methodist U (MO)
Central Michigan U (MI)
Centre Coll (KY)
Chapman U (CA)
Chatham U (PA)

Chestnut Hill Coll (PA)
Cheyney U of Pennsylvania (PA)
Chicago State U (IL)
Chowan U (NC)
City Coll of the City U of New York (NY)
Claflin U (SC)
Clark Atlanta U (GA)
Clarke U (IA)
Clark U (MA)
Clayton State U (GA)
Cleveland State U (OH)
Coastal Carolina U (SC)
Coe Coll (IA)
Colby Coll (ME)
Colgate U (NY)
Coll of Charleston (SC)
The Coll of Idaho (ID)
Coll of Mount St. Joseph (OH)
The Coll of New Jersey (NJ)
Coll of Saint Benedict (MN)
Coll of Saint Elizabeth (NJ)
The Coll of Saint Rose (NY)
Coll of Staten Island of the City U of New York (NY)
Coll of the Atlantic (ME)
Coll of the Holy Cross (MA)
Coll of the Ozarks (MO)
The Coll of William and Mary (VA)
The Coll of Wooster (OH)
The Colorado Coll (CO)
Colorado Mesa U (CO)
Colorado State U (CO)
Columbia Coll (SC)
Columbia Coll Chicago (IL)
Columbia U (NY)
Columbia U, School of General Studies (NY)
Columbus State U (GA)
Concordia Coll (MN)
Concordia Coll–New York (NY)
Concordia U (OR)
Concordia U (QC, Canada)
Concordia U Chicago (IL)
Concordia U, Nebraska (NE)
Concordia U, St. Paul (MN)
Concordia U Wisconsin (WI)
Connecticut Coll (CT)
Converse Coll (SC)
Corban U (OR)
Cornell Coll (IA)
Cornerstone U (MI)
Covenant Coll (GA)
Creighton U (NE)
Crossroads Coll (MN)
Crown Coll (MN)
Culver-Stockton Coll (MO)
Dakota Wesleyan U (SD)
Dalhousie U (NS, Canada)
Dallas Baptist U (TX)
Dartmouth Coll (NH)
Davidson Coll (NC)
Delta State U (MS)
DePaul U (IL)
DePauw U (IN)
DEREE—The American Coll of Greece (Greece)
Dickinson Coll (PA)
Dillard U (LA)
Doane Coll (NE)
Dominican U (IL)
Dordt Coll (IA)
Drake U (IA)
Drew U (NJ)
Drury U (MO)
Earlham Coll (IN)
East Central U (OK)
Eastern Illinois U (IL)
Eastern Mennonite U (VA)
Eastern Michigan U (MI)
Eastern New Mexico U (NM)
Eastern Washington U (WA)
East Tennessee State U (TN)
East Texas Baptist U (TX)
Eckerd Coll (FL)
Edgewood Coll (WI)
Edinboro U of Pennsylvania (PA)
Elizabeth City State U (NC)
Elizabethtown Coll (PA)
Elmira Coll (NY)
Elon U (NC)
Emmanuel Coll (GA)
Emporia State U (KS)
Evangel U (MO)
Excelsior Coll (NY)
Fairfield U (CT)
Fayetteville State U (NC)

Felician Coll (NJ)
Five Towns Coll (NY)
Florida Ag and Mech U (FL)
Florida Atlantic U (FL)
Florida Coll (FL)
Florida Intl U (FL)
Florida Southern Coll (FL)
Florida State U (FL)
Fort Lewis Coll (CO)
Francis Marion U (SC)
Franklin & Marshall Coll (PA)
Franklin Pierce U (NH)
Friends U (KS)
Frostburg State U (MD)
Furman U (SC)
Gardner-Webb U (NC)
Geneva Coll (PA)
George Fox U (OR)
Georgetown Coll (KY)
Georgia Coll & State U (GA)
Georgia Regents U (GA)
Georgia Southern U (GA)
Georgia Southwestern State U (GA)
Gettysburg Coll (PA)
Gonzaga U (WA)
Gordon Coll (MA)
Goshen Coll (IN)
Goucher Coll (MD)
Graceland U (IA)
Grace U (NE)
Grambling State U (LA)
Grand Valley State U (MI)
Grand View U (IA)
Greenville Coll (IL)
Grinnell Coll (IA)
Grove City Coll (PA)
Guilford Coll (NC)
Gustavus Adolphus Coll (MN)
Hamilton Coll (NY)
Hamline U (MN)
Hampshire Coll (MA)
Hampton U (VA)
Hanover Coll (IN)
Harding U (AR)
Hardin-Simmons U (TX)
Hartwick Coll (NY)
Haverford Coll (PA)
Henderson State U (AR)
Hendrix Coll (AR)
High Point U (NC)
Hillsdale Coll (MI)
Hiram Coll (OH)
Hobart and William Smith Colls (NY)
Hofstra U (NY)
Hollins U (VA)
Holy Names U (CA)
Hood Coll (MD)
Hope Coll (MI)
Houghton Coll (NY)
Humboldt State U (CA)
Hunter Coll of the City U of New York (NY)
Huntington U (IN)
Illinois Coll (IL)
Illinois State U (IL)
Illinois Wesleyan U (IL)
Immaculata U (PA)
Indiana State U (IN)
Indiana U of Pennsylvania (PA)
Indiana U–Purdue U Fort Wayne (IN)
Indiana U South Bend (IN)
Indiana U Southeast (IN)
Inter American U of Puerto Rico, San Germán Campus (PR)
Iowa State U of Science and Technology (IA)
Iowa Wesleyan Coll (IA)
Ithaca Coll (NY)
Jacksonville State U (AL)
Jamestown Coll (ND)
John Brown U (AR)
The Johns Hopkins U (MD)
Johnson C. Smith U (NC)
Johnson State Coll (VT)
Judson Coll (AL)
The Juilliard School (NY)
Kalamazoo Coll (MI)
Kansas State U (KS)
Kean U (NJ)
Kennesaw State U (GA)
Kent State U (OH)
Kentucky State U (KY)
Kenyon Coll (OH)
King Coll (TN)

The King's U Coll (AB, Canada)
Kingswood U (NB, Canada)
Knox Coll (IL)
Kutztown U of Pennsylvania (PA)
Lafayette Coll (PA)
LaGrange Coll (GA)
Lakeland Coll (WI)
Lamar U (TX)
Lander U (SC)
Lane Coll (TN)
Langston U (OK)
La Sierra U (CA)
Lawrence U (WI)
Lee U (TN)
Lehigh U (PA)
Lehman Coll of the City U of New
    York (NY)
Lewis U (IL)
Liberty U (VA)
Limestone Coll (SC)
Lindenwood U (MO)
Linfield Coll (OR)
Lipscomb U (TN)
Lock Haven U of Pennsylvania (PA)
Long Island U–C. W. Post Campus
    (NY)
Louisiana Coll (LA)
Louisiana State U and Ag and
    Mech Coll (LA)
Loyola Marymount U (CA)
Loyola U Chicago (IL)
Loyola U New Orleans (LA)
Lubbock Christian U (TX)
Luther Coll (IA)
Lynchburg Coll (VA)
Lynn U (FL)
Lyon Coll (AR)
Macalester Coll (MN)
Madonna U (MI)
Malone U (OH)
Manchester U (IN)
Manhattanville Coll (NY)
Mannes Coll The New School for
    Music (NY)
Mansfield U of Pennsylvania (PA)
Marian U (WI)
Marietta Coll (OH)
Mars Hill Coll (NC)
Mary Baldwin Coll (VA)
Maryville Coll (TN)
Massachusetts Coll of Liberal Arts
    (MA)
Massachusetts Inst of Technology
    (MA)
The Master's Coll and Sem (CA)
McDaniel Coll (MD)
McKendree U (IL)
McMurry U (TX)
Mercer U (GA)
Mercyhurst U (PA)
Messiah Coll (PA)
Metropolitan State U of Denver
    (CO)
Miami U (OH)
Michigan State U (MI)
Middlebury Coll (VT)
Middle Tennessee State U (TN)
Midwestern State U (TX)
Millersville U of Pennsylvania (PA)
Millikin U (IL)
Millsaps Coll (MS)
Mills Coll (CA)
Minnesota State U Mankato (MN)
Minnesota State U Moorhead (MN)
Minot State U (ND)
Mississippi Coll (MS)
Mississippi State U (MS)
Mississippi U for Women (MS)
Mississippi Valley State U (MS)
Missouri Baptist U (MO)
Missouri State U (MO)
Missouri Western State U (MO)
Molloy Coll (NY)
Monmouth Coll (IL)
Monmouth U (NJ)
Montana State U (MT)
Montclair State U (NJ)
Moravian Coll (PA)
Morehead State U (KY)
Morehouse Coll (GA)
Morningside Coll (IA)
Mount Allison U (NB, Canada)
Mount Holyoke Coll (MA)
Mount Marty Coll (SD)
Mount Mercy U (IA)
Mount St. Mary's Coll (CA)
Mount Vernon Nazarene U (OH)

Muhlenberg Coll (PA)
Murray State U (KY)
Naropa U (CO)
Nazareth Coll of Rochester (NY)
Newberry Coll (SC)
New Coll of Florida (FL)
New Jersey City U (NJ)
New Mexico Highlands U (NM)
The New School for Jazz and
    Contemporary Music (NY)
Nicholls State U (LA)
Norfolk State U (VA)
North Carolina Central U (NC)
North Central Coll (IL)
North Dakota State U (ND)
Northeastern Illinois U (IL)
Northeastern U (MA)
Northern Arizona U (AZ)
Northern Illinois U (IL)
Northern Michigan U (MI)
Northern State U (SD)
Northwest Christian U (OR)
Northwestern Coll (IA)
Northwestern Coll (MN)
Northwestern Oklahoma State U
    (OK)
Northwest Missouri State U (MO)
Northwest Nazarene U (ID)
Northwest U (WA)
Notre Dame de Namur U (CA)
Nova Southeastern U (FL)
Nyack Coll (NY)
Oakland City U (IN)
Oakland U (MI)
The Ohio State U (OH)
Ohio Wesleyan U (OH)
Oklahoma Baptist U (OK)
Oklahoma Christian U (OK)
Oklahoma City U (OK)
Oklahoma State U (OK)
Olivet Coll (MI)
Oral Roberts U (OK)
Oregon State U (OR)
Ouachita Baptist U (AR)
Pacific Lutheran U (WA)
Pacific Union Coll (CA)
Pacific U (OR)
Palm Beach Atlantic U (FL)
Park U (MO)
Peabody Conservatory of The
    Johns Hopkins U (MD)
Penn State Altoona (PA)
Penn State Beaver (PA)
Penn State Berks (PA)
Penn State Brandywine (PA)
Penn State DuBois (PA)
Penn State Greater Allegheny (PA)
Penn State Hazleton (PA)
Penn State Mont Alto (PA)
Penn State New Kensington (PA)
Penn State Shenango (PA)
Penn State U Park (PA)
Penn State Wilkes-Barre (PA)
Penn State Worthington Scranton
    (PA)
Penn State York (PA)
Pepperdine U, Malibu (CA)
Piedmont Coll (GA)
Pittsburg State U (KS)
Pitzer Coll (CA)
Plymouth State U (NH)
Point Loma Nazarene U (CA)
Point U (GA)
Pomona Coll (CA)
Portland State U (OR)
Presbyterian Coll (SC)
Princeton U (NJ)
Principia Coll (IL)
Providence Coll (RI)
Queens U of Charlotte (NC)
Quincy U (IL)
Radford U (VA)
Ramapo Coll of New Jersey (NJ)
Randolph-Macon Coll (VA)
Reed Coll (OR)
Rhode Island Coll (RI)
Rhodes Coll (TN)
Rice U (TX)
Ripon Coll (WI)
Roanoke Coll (VA)
Roberts Wesleyan Coll (NY)
Rockford Coll (IL)
Rocky Mountain Coll (AB, Canada)
Roger Williams U (RI)
Rollins Coll (FL)
Rowan U (NJ)

Rutgers, The State U of New
    Jersey, Camden (NJ)
Rutgers, The State U of New
    Jersey, Newark (NJ)
Rutgers, The State U of New
    Jersey, New Brunswick (NJ)
Saginaw Valley State U (MI)
St. Ambrose U (IA)
Saint John's U (MN)
Saint Joseph's U (PA)
St. Lawrence U (NY)
Saint Louis U (MO)
Saint Martin's U (WA)
Saint Mary-of-the-Woods Coll (IN)
Saint Mary's Coll (IN)
Saint Mary's Coll of California (CA)
St. Mary's Coll of Maryland (MD)
St. Mary's U (TX)
Saint Mary's U of Minnesota (MN)
Saint Michael's Coll (VT)
St. Norbert Coll (WI)
St. Olaf Coll (MN)
Saint Vincent Coll (PA)
Salem State U (MA)
Salisbury U (MD)
Salve Regina U (RI)
Sam Houston State U (TX)
San Diego Christian Coll (CA)
San Francisco Conservatory of
    Music (CA)
San Francisco State U (CA)
San Jose State U (CA)
Santa Fe U of Art and Design (NM)
Schreiner U (TX)
Scripps Coll (CA)
Seattle Pacific U (WA)
Seton Hill U (PA)
Sewanee: The U of the South (TN)
Shaw U (NC)
Shenandoah U (VA)
Shepherd U (WV)
Simmons Coll (MA)
Simon Fraser U (BC, Canada)
Simpson Coll (IA)
Simpson U (CA)
Slippery Rock U of Pennsylvania
    (PA)
Smith Coll (MA)
Sonoma State U (CA)
South Dakota State U (SD)
Southeastern Oklahoma State U
    (OK)
Southeastern U (FL)
Southeast Missouri State U (MO)
Southern Arkansas U–Magnolia
    (AR)
Southern Connecticut State U (CT)
Southern Illinois U Carbondale (IL)
Southern Illinois U Edwardsville
    (IL)
Southern Methodist U (TX)
Southern Nazarene U (OK)
Southern Oregon U (OR)
Southern Utah U (UT)
Southwest Baptist U (MO)
Southwestern Adventist U (TX)
Southwestern Coll (KS)
Southwestern U (TX)
Spelman Coll (GA)
Spring Arbor U (MI)
Stanford U (CA)
State U of New York at Fredonia
    (NY)
State U of New York at New Paltz
    (NY)
State U of New York at Oswego
    (NY)
State U of New York at Plattsburgh
    (NY)
State U of New York Coll at
    Geneseo (NY)
State U of New York Coll at
    Potsdam (NY)
Stephen F. Austin State U (TX)
Sterling Coll (KS)
Stetson U (FL)
Stony Brook U, State U of New York
    (NY)
Sul Ross State U (TX)
Susquehanna U (PA)
Swarthmore Coll (PA)
Sweet Briar Coll (VA)
Syracuse U (NY)
Tabor Coll (KS)
Tarleton State U (TX)
Taylor U (IN)
Temple U (PA)

Tennessee State U (TN)
Tennessee Wesleyan Coll (TN)
Texas A&M U (TX)
Texas A&M U–Commerce (TX)
Texas A&M U–Kingsville (TX)
Texas Christian U (TX)
Texas Lutheran U (TX)
Texas Southern U (TX)
Texas State U–San Marcos (TX)
Texas Wesleyan U (TX)
Texas Woman's U (TX)
Thomas Edison State Coll (NJ)
Thompson Rivers U (BC, Canada)
Tiffin U (OH)
Trinity Christian Coll (IL)
Trinity Coll (CT)
Trinity U (TX)
Troy U (AL)
Truman State U (MO)
Tufts U (MA)
Tulane U (LA)
Union Coll (NE)
Union U (TN)
U of Albany, State U of New York
    (NY)
U at Buffalo, the State U of New
    York (NY)
The U of Akron (OH)
The U of Alabama (AL)
The U of Alabama at Birmingham
    (AL)
U of Alaska Anchorage (AK)
U of Alaska Fairbanks (AK)
The U of Arizona (AZ)
U of Arkansas at Little Rock (AR)
U of Arkansas–Fort Smith (AR)
U of Bridgeport (CT)
The U of British Columbia (BC,
    Canada)
U of California, Berkeley (CA)
U of California, Davis (CA)
U of California, Irvine (CA)
U of California, Los Angeles (CA)
U of California, Riverside (CA)
U of California, Santa Barbara (CA)
U of California, Santa Cruz (CA)
U of Central Arkansas (AR)
U of Central Oklahoma (OK)
U of Chicago (IL)
U of Cincinnati (OH)
U of Colorado Boulder (CO)
U of Colorado Denver (CO)
U of Delaware (DE)
U of Denver (CO)
U of Evansville (IN)
U of Florida (FL)
U of Georgia (GA)
U of Guelph (ON, Canada)
U of Hartford (CT)
U of Hawaii at Hilo (HI)
U of Hawaii at Manoa (HI)
U of Houston (TX)
U of Idaho (ID)
U of Illinois at Chicago (IL)
U of Illinois at Urbana–Champaign
    (IL)
The U of Iowa (IA)
The U of Kansas (KS)
U of La Verne (CA)
U of Louisiana at Lafayette (LA)
U of Louisville (KY)
U of Maine at Farmington (ME)
U of Maine at Machias (ME)
U of Maryland, Baltimore County
    (MD)
U of Maryland, Coll Park (MD)
U of Mary Washington (VA)
U of Massachusetts Amherst (MA)
U of Massachusetts Boston (MA)
U of Massachusetts Dartmouth
    (MA)
U of Memphis (TN)
U of Miami (FL)
U of Michigan (MI)
U of Michigan–Flint (MI)
U of Minnesota, Duluth (MN)
U of Minnesota, Twin Cities
    Campus (MN)
U of Mississippi (MS)
U of Missouri (MO)
U of Missouri–Kansas City (MO)
U of Missouri–St. Louis (MO)
U of Mobile (AL)
U of Montevallo (AL)
U of Mount Union (OH)
U of Nebraska at Kearney (NE)
U of Nebraska at Omaha (NE)

U of Nebraska–Lincoln (NE)
U of Nevada, Las Vegas (NV)
U of Nevada, Reno (NV)
U of New Hampshire (NH)
U of New Haven (CT)
U of New Orleans (LA)
U of North Alabama (AL)
U of North Carolina at Asheville
    (NC)
The U of North Carolina at Chapel
    Hill (NC)
The U of North Carolina at
    Charlotte (NC)
The U of North Carolina at
    Greensboro (NC)
The U of North Carolina at
    Pembroke (NC)
The U of North Carolina
    Wilmington (NC)
U of North Dakota (ND)
U of Northern Colorado (CO)
U of Northern Iowa (IA)
U of North Florida (FL)
U of North Georgia (GA)
U of North Texas (TX)
U of Notre Dame (IN)
U of Oklahoma (OK)
U of Oregon (OR)
U of Ottawa (ON, Canada)
U of Pennsylvania (PA)
U of Pittsburgh (PA)
U of Portland (OR)
U of Puget Sound (WA)
U of Redlands (CA)
U of Regina (SK, Canada)
U of Rhode Island (RI)
U of Richmond (VA)
U of Rochester (NY)
U of St. Francis (IL)
U of St. Thomas (MN)
U of St. Thomas (TX)
U of San Diego (CA)
U of Science and Arts of Oklahoma
    (OK)
U of South Alabama (AL)
U of South Carolina (SC)
U of South Carolina Upstate (SC)
U of Southern California (CA)
U of Southern Maine (ME)
U of Southern Mississippi (MS)
The U of Tampa (FL)
The U of Tennessee (TN)
The U of Tennessee at
    Chattanooga (TN)
The U of Tennessee at Martin (TN)
The U of Texas at Arlington (TX)
The U of Texas at Austin (TX)
The U of Texas at Brownsville (TX)
The U of Texas at El Paso (TX)
The U of Texas at San Antonio (TX)
The U of Texas–Pan American (TX)
U of the Cumberlands (KY)
U of the Incarnate Word (TX)
U of the Ozarks (AR)
The U of Toledo (OH)
U of Tulsa (OK)
U of Utah (UT)
U of Vermont (VT)
U of Virginia (VA)
U of Waterloo (ON, Canada)
The U of Western Ontario (ON,
    Canada)
U of Windsor (ON, Canada)
U of Wisconsin–Eau Claire (WI)
U of Wisconsin–Green Bay (WI)
U of Wisconsin–La Crosse (WI)
U of Wisconsin–Madison (WI)
U of Wisconsin–Milwaukee (WI)
U of Wisconsin–Parkside (WI)
U of Wisconsin–Platteville (WI)
U of Wisconsin–Stevens Point (WI)
U of Wisconsin–Superior (WI)
U of Wyoming (WY)
Utah State U (UT)
Valdosta State U (GA)
Valley City State U (ND)
Valparaiso U (IN)
Vassar Coll (NY)
Villa Maria Coll of Buffalo (NY)
Virginia Polytechnic Inst and State
    U (VA)
Virginia State U (VA)
Virginia Union U (VA)
Virginia Wesleyan Coll (VA)
Viterbo U (WI)
Wabash Coll (IN)
Wagner Coll (NY)

Wake Forest U (NC)
Waldorf Coll (IA)
Walla Walla U (WA)
Warner Pacific Coll (OR)
Wartburg Coll (IA)
Washburn U (KS)
Washington & Jefferson Coll (PA)
Washington and Lee U (VA)
Washington Coll (MD)
Washington State U (WA)
Washington U in St. Louis (MO)
Wayland Baptist U (TX)
Wayne State Coll (NE)
Wayne State U (MI)
Weber State U (UT)
Webster U (MO)
Wellesley Coll (MA)
Wesleyan Coll (GA)
Wesleyan U (CT)
West Chester U of Pennsylvania (PA)
Western Carolina U (NC)
Western Connecticut State U (CT)
Western Illinois U (IL)
Western Michigan U (MI)
Western Oregon U (OR)
Western State Colorado U (CO)
Western Washington U (WA)
Westfield State U (MA)
Westminster Coll (UT)
West Texas A&M U (TX)
West Virginia U (WV)
West Virginia Wesleyan Coll (WV)
Wheaton Coll (IL)
Wheaton Coll (MA)
Wheeling Jesuit U (WV)
Whitman Coll (WA)
Whitworth U (WA)
Wichita State U (KS)
Wilberforce U (OH)
Willamette U (OR)
William Jewell Coll (MO)
William Paterson U of New Jersey (NJ)
William Penn U (IA)
Williams Coll (MA)
Winthrop U (SC)
Wittenberg U (OH)
Worcester Polytechnic Inst (MA)
Wright State U (OH)
Xavier U (OH)
Xavier U of Louisiana (LA)
Yale U (CT)
York Coll of Pennsylvania (PA)
York Coll of the City U of New York (NY)
Young Harris Coll (GA)
Youngstown State U (OH)

MUSICAL INSTRUMENT FABRICATION AND REPAIR
Barton Coll (NC)

MUSICAL THEATER
Central Michigan U (MI)
Converse Coll (SC)
Creighton U (NE)
Culver-Stockton Coll (MO)
Elon U (NC)
Florida Southern Coll (FL)
Indiana U Bloomington (IN)
Lees-McRae Coll (NC)
Lindenwood U (MO)
Messiah Coll (PA)
Millikin U (IL)
Mississippi Coll (MS)
Missouri Baptist U (MO)
Oakland U (MI)
Pace U (NY)
Roosevelt U (IL)
Sam Houston State U (TX)
San Diego Christian Coll (CA)
Santa Fe U of Art and Design (NM)
Shenandoah U (VA)
Southwestern Coll (KS)
Texas Christian U (TX)
The U of Arizona (AZ)
U of California, Irvine (CA)
U of Idaho (ID)
U of Michigan (MI)
U of North Dakota (ND)
U of Oklahoma (OK)
The U of Tampa (FL)
The U of the Arts (PA)
Virginia Intermont Coll (VA)
Western Michigan U (MI)
West Texas A&M U (TX)
William Peace U (NC)

Young Harris Coll (GA)

MUSIC HISTORY, LITERATURE, AND THEORY
American U (DC)
Baldwin Wallace U (OH)
Bard Coll (NY)
Baylor U (TX)
Bennington Coll (VT)
Bowling Green State U (OH)
Bridgewater Coll (VA)
Brigham Young U (UT)
Bucknell U (PA)
California State U, Long Beach (CA)
Calvin Coll (MI)
The Catholic U of America (DC)
The Coll of Wooster (OH)
Concordia Coll–New York (NY)
Converse Coll (SC)
Dalhousie U (NS, Canada)
Eugene Lang Coll The New School for Liberal Arts (NY)
Hardin-Simmons U (TX)
Hofstra U (NY)
Keene State Coll (NH)
Lafayette Coll (PA)
Lehigh U (PA)
Loyola Marymount U (CA)
Mount Allison U (NB, Canada)
Nazareth Coll of Rochester (NY)
New Coll of Florida (FL)
New England Conservatory of Music (MA)
The Ohio State U (OH)
Ohio U (OH)
Ouachita Baptist U (AR)
Randolph Coll (VA)
Rice U (TX)
Rider U (NJ)
St. Bonaventure U (NY)
Saint Joseph's Coll (IN)
Skidmore Coll (NY)
State U of New York at Fredonia (NY)
Syracuse U (NY)
Temple U (PA)
The U of Akron (OH)
The U of British Columbia (BC, Canada)
U of California, Los Angeles (CA)
U of Cincinnati (OH)
U of Delaware (DE)
U of Hartford (CT)
U of Idaho (ID)
U of Illinois at Urbana–Champaign (IL)
U of Kentucky (KY)
U of Michigan (MI)
U of Minnesota, Twin Cities Campus (MN)
U of North Texas (TX)
U of Redlands (CA)
U of Regina (SK, Canada)
U of Vermont (VT)
The U of Western Ontario (ON, Canada)
U of Windsor (ON, Canada)
Washington U in St. Louis (MO)
Western Washington U (WA)
Wheaton Coll (IL)
Whitman Coll (WA)
Wright State U (OH)
Youngstown State U (OH)

MUSIC MANAGEMENT
Anderson U (IN)
Appalachian State U (NC)
Belmont U (TN)
Berklee Coll of Music (MA)
Berry Coll (GA)
Boise State U (ID)
Bradley U (IL)
Butler U (IN)
Capital U (OH)
Chowan U (NC)
Columbia Coll Chicago (IL)
Dallas Baptist U (TX)
DePaul U (IL)
DePauw U (IN)
Drake U (IA)
Elizabeth City State U (NC)
Five Towns Coll (NY)
Florida Atlantic U (FL)
Florida Southern Coll (FL)
Gardner-Webb U (NC)
Geneva Coll (PA)
Greenville Coll (IL)

Grove City Coll (PA)
Hardin-Simmons U (TX)
Hofstra U (NY)
Huntington U (IN)
Johnson State Coll (VT)
Judson U (IL)
Kentucky Christian U (KY)
Lebanon Valley Coll (PA)
Lewis U (IL)
Lindenwood U (MO)
Loyola U New Orleans (LA)
Lubbock Christian U (TX)
Mansfield U of Pennsylvania (PA)
Marian U (WI)
The Master's Coll and Sem (CA)
McNally Smith Coll of Music (MN)
Middle Tennessee State U (TN)
Minnesota State U Mankato (MN)
Minnesota State U Moorhead (MN)
Missouri Baptist U (MO)
Montreat Coll, Montreat (NC)
Nazareth Coll of Rochester (NY)
Northwest Christian U (OR)
Northwest U (WA)
Oklahoma City U (OK)
Saint Joseph's Coll (IN)
Southeastern U (FL)
Southern Oregon U (OR)
State U of New York at Fredonia (NY)
Syracuse U (NY)
Trevecca Nazarene U (TN)
Union U (TN)
U of Evansville (IN)
U of Hartford (CT)
U of Idaho (ID)
U of Memphis (TN)
U of New Haven (CT)
U of Puget Sound (WA)
U of Southern California (CA)
The U of Texas at San Antonio (TX)
The U of the Arts (PA)
U of the Incarnate Word (TX)
Villa Maria Coll of Buffalo (NY)
Warner Pacific Coll (OR)
Western State Colorado U (CO)
William Paterson U of New Jersey (NJ)

MUSICOLOGY AND ETHNOMUSICOLOGY
Bennington Coll (VT)
Bowling Green State U (OH)
Brown U (RI)
Converse Coll (SC)
East Tennessee State U (TN)
The New School for Jazz and Contemporary Music (NY)
Roger Williams U (RI)
U of California, Los Angeles (CA)
U of Denver (CO)
The U of Kansas (KS)
U of Regina (SK, Canada)

MUSIC PEDAGOGY
Baylor U (TX)
Brigham Young U (UT)
Cedarville U (OH)
Holy Names U (CA)
Huntington U (IN)
Lawrence U (WI)
Maranatha Baptist Bible Coll (WI)
Michigan State U (MI)
Oklahoma City U (OK)
Samford U (AL)
Spring Arbor U (MI)
Temple U (PA)
U of Minnesota, Duluth (MN)
U of Oklahoma (OK)
The U of Tennessee at Martin (TN)
The U of Western Ontario (ON, Canada)
Viterbo U (WI)

MUSIC PERFORMANCE
Adams State U (CO)
Albion Coll (MI)
Alcorn State U (MS)
Alderson-Broaddus Coll (WV)
American U (DC)
Anderson U (IN)
Anderson U (SC)
Appalachian State U (NC)
Arizona State U (AZ)
Arkansas State U (AR)
Augustana Coll (IL)
Avila U (MO)
Baldwin Wallace U (OH)

Bard Coll (NY)
Baylor U (TX)
Bennington Coll (VT)
Berklee Coll of Music (MA)
Bethel Coll (IN)
Bethel U (MN)
Bethune-Cookman U (FL)
Binghamton U, State U of New York (NY)
Bob Jones U (SC)
Boise State U (ID)
The Boston Conservatory (MA)
Boston U (MA)
Bowling Green State U (OH)
Bradley U (IL)
Brevard Coll (NC)
Bucknell U (PA)
Buena Vista U (IA)
Butler U (IN)
California Baptist U (CA)
California State U, Chico (CA)
California State U, Fullerton (CA)
California State U, Long Beach (CA)
California State U, Los Angeles (CA)
California State U, Stanislaus (CA)
Calvin Coll (MI)
Canisius Coll (NY)
Capital U (OH)
Carnegie Mellon U (PA)
The Catholic U of America (DC)
Cedarville U (OH)
Central Methodist U (MO)
Central State U (OH)
Chapman U (CA)
Christopher Newport U (VA)
City Coll of the City U of New York (NY)
Coe Coll (IA)
The Coll of Saint Rose (NY)
The Coll of St. Scholastica (MN)
The Coll of Wooster (OH)
Colorado State U (CO)
Columbia Coll (SC)
Columbia Coll Chicago (IL)
Columbus State U (GA)
Concordia Coll (MN)
Concordia Coll–New York (NY)
Concordia U (QC, Canada)
Concordia U Chicago (IL)
Converse Coll (SC)
Corban U (OR)
Cornerstone U (MI)
Covenant Coll (GA)
Dalhousie U (NS, Canada)
DePaul U (IL)
DePauw U (IN)
Dillard U (LA)
Dordt Coll (IA)
Drake U (IA)
Duquesne U (PA)
East Carolina U (NC)
East Central U (OK)
Eastern Michigan U (MI)
Elon U (NC)
Florida Gulf Coast U (FL)
Fort Lewis Coll (CO)
Friends U (KS)
Gardner-Webb U (NC)
Geneva Coll (PA)
George Mason U (VA)
Georgia Regents U (GA)
Georgia Southern U (GA)
Georgia State U (GA)
Gordon Coll (MA)
Grove City Coll (PA)
Gustavus Adolphus Coll (MN)
Hamline U (MN)
Hardin-Simmons U (TX)
Henderson State U (AR)
Hillsdale Free Will Baptist Coll (OK)
Hofstra U (NY)
Holy Names U (CA)
Hope Coll (MI)
Houghton Coll (NY)
Howard Payne U (TX)
Huntingdon Coll (AL)
Huntington U (IN)
Illinois State U (IL)
Illinois Wesleyan U (IL)
Immaculata U (PA)
Indiana State U (IN)
Indiana U Bloomington (IN)
Indiana U of Pennsylvania (PA)
Indiana U–Purdue U Fort Wayne (IN)

Indiana U South Bend (IN)
Indiana Wesleyan U (IN)
Inter American U of Puerto Rico, San Germán Campus (PR)
Ithaca Coll (NY)
James Madison U (VA)
Jamestown Coll (ND)
John Brown U (AR)
Johnson State Coll (VT)
Judson U (IL)
The Juilliard School (NY)
Kean U (NJ)
Keene State Coll (NH)
Kennesaw State U (GA)
Kentucky Christian U (KY)
Lawrence U (WI)
Lebanon Valley Coll (PA)
Limestone Coll (SC)
Lipscomb U (TN)
Long Island U–Brooklyn Campus (NY)
Long Island U–C. W. Post Campus (NY)
Louisiana State U and Ag and Mech Coll (LA)
Loyola U New Orleans (LA)
Lynn U (FL)
Madonna U (MI)
Manchester U (IN)
Mannes Coll The New School for Music (NY)
Mansfield U of Pennsylvania (PA)
Maranatha Baptist Bible Coll (WI)
Mars Hill Coll (NC)
Maryville Coll (TN)
Marywood U (PA)
McNeese State U (LA)
Mercer U (GA)
Mercyhurst U (PA)
Messiah Coll (PA)
Miami U (OH)
Michigan State U (MI)
Midwestern State U (TX)
Millikin U (IL)
Minnesota State U Moorhead (MN)
Missouri Baptist U (MO)
Missouri State U (MO)
Molloy Coll (NY)
Montreat Coll, Montreat (NC)
Moravian Coll (PA)
Morningside Coll (IA)
Mount Allison U (NB, Canada)
Mount Vernon Nazarene U (OH)
Naropa U (CO)
Nazareth Coll of Rochester (NY)
Newberry Coll (SC)
New England Conservatory of Music (MA)
New Mexico State U (NM)
The New School for Jazz and Contemporary Music (NY)
New York U (NY)
Northern Arizona U (AZ)
North Greenville U (SC)
Northwestern Coll (MN)
Northwestern State U of Louisiana (LA)
Northwest Nazarene U (ID)
Notre Dame de Namur U (CA)
Nyack Coll (NY)
Oakland City U (IN)
Oakland U (MI)
The Ohio State U (OH)
Ohio U (OH)
Ohio Wesleyan U (OH)
Oklahoma Baptist U (OK)
Oklahoma City U (OK)
Old Dominion U (VA)
Oral Roberts U (OK)
Ouachita Baptist U (AR)
Pacific Union Coll (CA)
Pacific U (OR)
Palm Beach Atlantic U (FL)
Penn State U Park (PA)
Piedmont Coll (GA)
Pittsburg State U (KS)
Point Loma Nazarene U (CA)
Portland State U (OR)
Randolph Coll (VA)
Rhode Island Coll (RI)
Rice U (TX)
Rockford Coll (IL)
Rocky Mountain Coll (MT)
Roosevelt U (IL)
Rowan U (NJ)
Saint Mary's U of Minnesota (MN)
St. Olaf Coll (MN)

Saint Vincent Coll (PA)
Samford U (AL)
San Diego Christian Coll (CA)
San Diego State U (CA)
San Francisco Conservatory of Music (CA)
San Francisco State U (CA)
San Jose State U (CA)
Seton Hill U (PA)
Shenandoah U (VA)
Simpson Coll (IA)
Slippery Rock U of Pennsylvania (PA)
Southeastern Louisiana U (LA)
Southeastern Oklahoma State U (OK)
Southeastern U (FL)
Southern Methodist U (TX)
Southern Nazarene U (OK)
Southwestern Coll (KS)
State U of New York Coll at Potsdam (NY)
Stetson U (FL)
Susquehanna U (PA)
Syracuse U (NY)
Tabor Coll (KS)
Temple U (PA)
Texas A&M U–Commerce (TX)
Texas A&M U–Kingsville (TX)
Texas Christian U (TX)
Texas State U–San Marcos (TX)
Thompson Rivers U (BC, Canada)
Transylvania U (KY)
Trevecca Nazarene U (TN)
Trinity U (TX)
Truman State U (MO)
Tulane U (LA)
Union Coll (NE)
Union U (TN)
U at Buffalo, the State U of New York (NY)
The U of Akron (OH)
U of Alaska Anchorage (AK)
The U of Arizona (AZ)
U of California, Irvine (CA)
U of Central Arkansas (AR)
U of Central Florida (FL)
U of Cincinnati (OH)
U of Colorado Boulder (CO)
U of Delaware (DE)
U of Denver (CO)
U of Evansville (IN)
U of Georgia (GA)
U of Hartford (CT)
U of Houston (TX)
U of Idaho (ID)
U of Illinois at Urbana–Champaign (IL)
The U of Kansas (KS)
U of Kentucky (KY)
U of Louisiana at Lafayette (LA)
U of Louisiana at Monroe (LA)
U of Maryland, Coll Park (MD)
U of Massachusetts Amherst (MA)
U of Miami (FL)
U of Michigan (MI)
U of Michigan–Flint (MI)
U of Minnesota, Duluth (MN)
U of Missouri–Kansas City (MO)
U of Missouri–St. Louis (MO)
U of Mount Union (OH)
U of Nebraska at Omaha (NE)
U of Nevada, Reno (NV)
U of New Mexico (NM)
The U of North Carolina at Chapel Hill (NC)
The U of North Carolina at Greensboro (NC)
The U of North Carolina at Pembroke (NC)
U of North Carolina School of the Arts (NC)
The U of North Carolina Wilmington (NC)
U of North Dakota (ND)
U of Northern Iowa (IA)
U of North Florida (FL)
U of North Georgia (GA)
U of North Texas (TX)
U of Oregon (OR)
U of Puget Sound (WA)
U of Redlands (CA)
U of Rhode Island (RI)
U of Rochester (NY)
U of St. Francis (IL)
The U of South Dakota (SD)
U of Southern California (CA)

U of Southern Maine (ME)
U of South Florida (FL)
The U of Tampa (FL)
The U of Tennessee at Martin (TN)
The U of Texas at Arlington (TX)
The U of Texas at Austin (TX)
The U of Texas at San Antonio (TX)
The U of Texas–Pan American (TX)
The U of the Arts (PA)
U of the Incarnate Word (TX)
U of Tulsa (OK)
U of Vermont (VT)
The U of Western Ontario (ON, Canada)
U of West Florida (FL)
U of West Georgia (GA)
U of Windsor (ON, Canada)
U of Wisconsin–Madison (WI)
U of Wisconsin–Stevens Point (WI)
U of Wisconsin–Superior (WI)
U of Wyoming (WY)
Valdosta State U (GA)
Valparaiso U (IN)
Villa Maria Coll of Buffalo (NY)
Virginia Commonwealth U (VA)
Viterbo U (WI)
Walla Walla U (WA)
Wartburg Coll (IA)
Washburn U (KS)
Washington State U (WA)
Wayland Baptist U (TX)
Weber State U (UT)
Webster U (MO)
West Chester U of Pennsylvania (PA)
Western Carolina U (NC)
Western Connecticut State U (CT)
Western Illinois U (IL)
Western Kentucky U (KY)
Western Michigan U (MI)
Western Washington U (WA)
West Texas A&M U (TX)
Wheaton Coll (IL)
Whitman Coll (WA)
Willamette U (OR)
William Jewell Coll (MO)
William Peace U (NC)
Wright State U (OH)
Xavier U of Louisiana (LA)
Youngstown State U (OH)

MUSIC RELATED
Acad of Art U (CA)
Alverno Coll (WI)
Ball State U (IN)
Bellarmine U (KY)
Belmont U (TN)
Bethel Coll (KS)
Brigham Young U (UT)
Brown U (RI)
California State U, Chico (CA)
Capital U (OH)
Concordia U (CA)
Connecticut Coll (CT)
DePaul U (IL)
Duquesne U (PA)
Friends U (KS)
Greenville Coll (IL)
Hampton U (VA)
Huntingdon Coll (AL)
Illinois Wesleyan U (IL)
Indiana U Bloomington (IN)
Indiana U South Bend (IN)
Keene State Coll (NH)
Kent State U (OH)
Kent State U at Stark (OH)
Lee U (TN)
Long Island U–Brooklyn Campus (NY)
Loyola U New Orleans (LA)
Marian U (WI)
McNally Smith Coll of Music (MN)
Mercer U (GA)
Messiah Coll (PA)
Mississippi Coll (MS)
Missouri Western State U (MO)
Murray State U (KY)
Palm Beach Atlantic U (FL)
Roosevelt U (IL)
Saint Mary's U of Minnesota (MN)
School of the Art Inst of Chicago (IL)
Tabor Coll (KS)
Trevecca Nazarene U (TN)
U of Delaware (DE)
U of Denver (CO)
U of Hartford (CT)

U of Memphis (TN)
U of Miami (FL)
U of Michigan (MI)
U of North Carolina at Asheville (NC)
U of Tulsa (OK)
The U of Western Ontario (ON, Canada)
Valparaiso U (IN)
Vanderbilt U (TN)
Western Illinois U (IL)
Western Kentucky U (KY)
West Virginia U (WV)
Wheaton Coll (IL)
Wichita State U (KS)

MUSIC TEACHER EDUCATION
Abilene Christian U (TX)
Acadia U (NS, Canada)
Adams State U (CO)
Adelphi U (NY)
Alabama State U (AL)
Albion Coll (MI)
Alderson-Broaddus Coll (WV)
Alma Coll (MI)
Alverno Coll (WI)
Anderson U (IN)
Anderson U (SC)
Andrews U (MI)
Appalachian State U (NC)
Arizona State U (AZ)
Arkansas State U (AR)
Arkansas Tech U (AR)
Armstrong Atlantic State U (GA)
Asbury U (KY)
Ashland U (OH)
Auburn U (AL)
Augsburg Coll (MN)
Augustana Coll (IL)
Augustana Coll (SD)
Baker U (KS)
Baldwin Wallace U (OH)
The Baptist Coll of Florida (FL)
Baylor U (TX)
Belmont U (TN)
Bemidji State U (MN)
Benedictine Coll (KS)
Benedictine U (IL)
Berea Coll (KY)
Berklee Coll of Music (MA)
Berry Coll (GA)
Bethel Coll (IN)
Bethel U (MN)
Bethune-Cookman U (FL)
Bluefield Coll (VA)
Blue Mountain Coll (MS)
Bluffton U (OH)
Bob Jones U (SC)
Boise State U (ID)
The Boston Conservatory (MA)
Boston U (MA)
Bowling Green State U (OH)
Bradley U (IL)
Brevard Coll (NC)
Bridgewater State U (MA)
Brock U (ON, Canada)
Bucknell U (PA)
Buena Vista U (IA)
Buffalo State Coll, State U of New York (NY)
Butler U (IN)
California Baptist U (CA)
California Lutheran U (CA)
California State U, Chico (CA)
California State U, Fresno (CA)
California State U, Fullerton (CA)
Calvin Coll (MI)
Cameron U (OK)
Campbellsville U (KY)
Capital U (OH)
Carson-Newman U (TN)
Case Western Reserve U (OH)
Castleton State Coll (VT)
Catawba Coll (NC)
Cedarville U (OH)
Central Coll (IA)
Central Connecticut State U (CT)
Central Methodist U (MO)
Central State U (OH)
Chapman U (CA)
Chestnut Hill Coll (PA)
Chicago State U (IL)
Chowan U (NC)
City Coll of the City U of New York (NY)
Claflin U (SC)
Clarion U of Pennsylvania (PA)

Clarke U (IA)
Clearwater Christian Coll (FL)
Coe Coll (IA)
The Coll of New Jersey (NJ)
The Coll of Saint Rose (NY)
Coll of the Ozarks (MO)
The Coll of Wooster (OH)
Colorado State U (CO)
Columbia Coll (SC)
Columbus State U (GA)
Concordia Coll (MN)
Concordia U Chicago (IL)
Concordia U, Nebraska (NE)
Concordia U, St. Paul (MN)
Concordia U Wisconsin (WI)
Concord U (WV)
Converse Coll (SC)
Corban U (OR)
Cornell Coll (IA)
Cornerstone U (MI)
Crown Coll (MN)
Culver-Stockton Coll (MO)
Dakota Wesleyan U (SD)
Dallas Baptist U (TX)
Delta State U (MS)
DePaul U (IL)
DePauw U (IN)
Dordt Coll (IA)
Drake U (IA)
Duquesne U (PA)
East Carolina U (NC)
East Central U (OK)
Eastern Michigan U (MI)
Eastern Washington U (WA)
East Texas Baptist U (TX)
Edgewood Coll (WI)
Elon U (NC)
Emmanuel Coll (GA)
Emporia State U (KS)
Evangel U (MO)
Fairmont State U (WV)
Faith Baptist Bible Coll and Theological Sem (IA)
Fayetteville State U (NC)
Five Towns Coll (NY)
Florida Ag and Mech U (FL)
Florida Atlantic U (FL)
Florida Southern Coll (FL)
Fort Lewis Coll (CO)
Friends U (KS)
Furman U (SC)
Gardner-Webb U (NC)
Geneva Coll (PA)
George Fox U (OR)
Georgetown Coll (KY)
Georgia Coll & State U (GA)
Georgia Regents U (GA)
Georgia Southern U (GA)
Gettysburg Coll (PA)
Gonzaga U (WA)
Gordon Coll (MA)
Graceland U (IA)
Grace U (NE)
Grand Valley State U (MI)
Greenville Coll (IL)
Grove City Coll (PA)
Gustavus Adolphus Coll (MN)
Hampton U (VA)
Harding U (AR)
Hardin-Simmons U (TX)
Hartwick Coll (NY)
Hofstra U (NY)
Hope Coll (MI)
Houghton Coll (NY)
Howard Payne U (TX)
Humboldt State U (CA)
Huntingdon Coll (AL)
Huntington U (IN)
Illinois State U (IL)
Illinois Wesleyan U (IL)
Immaculata U (PA)
Indiana U Bloomington (IN)
Indiana U–Purdue U Fort Wayne (IN)
Indiana U South Bend (IN)
Indiana Wesleyan U (IN)
Inter American U of Puerto Rico, San Germán Campus (PR)
Iowa State U of Science and Technology (IA)
Iowa Wesleyan Coll (IA)
Ithaca Coll (NY)
Jacksonville State U (AL)
Jamestown Coll (ND)
Jarvis Christian Coll (TX)
John Brown U (AR)
Johnson State Coll (VT)

Judson Coll (AL)
Judson U (IL)
Kansas State U (KS)
Kean U (NJ)
Keene State Coll (NH)
Kennesaw State U (GA)
Kent State U (OH)
Lakeland Coll (WI)
Lamar U (TX)
Langston U (OK)
La Sierra U (CA)
Lawrence U (WI)
Lebanon Valley Coll (PA)
Lee U (TN)
Limestone Coll (SC)
Lincoln U (MO)
Lindenwood U (MO)
Lipscomb U (TN)
Long Island U–Brooklyn Campus (NY)
Long Island U–C. W. Post Campus (NY)
Louisiana Coll (LA)
Louisiana State U and Ag and Mech Coll (LA)
Loyola U New Orleans (LA)
Lubbock Christian U (TX)
Madonna U (MI)
Malone U (OH)
Manchester U (IN)
Manhattanville Coll (NY)
Mansfield of Pennsylvania (PA)
Maranatha Baptist Bible Coll (WI)
Marian U (WI)
Marietta Coll (OH)
Mars Hill Coll (NC)
Maryville Coll (TN)
Marywood U (PA)
The Master's Coll and Sem (CA)
McKendree U (IL)
Mercer U (GA)
Mercyhurst U (PA)
Messiah Coll (PA)
Metropolitan State U of Denver (CO)
Miami U (OH)
Michigan State U (MI)
Midwestern State U (TX)
Millikin U (IL)
Minnesota State U Mankato (MN)
Minnesota State U Moorhead (MN)
Minot State U (ND)
Mississippi Coll (MS)
Mississippi State U (MS)
Mississippi Valley State U (MS)
Missouri Baptist U (MO)
Missouri State U (MO)
Missouri Western State U (MO)
Montana State U (MT)
Moravian Coll (PA)
Morningside Coll (IA)
Mount Marty Coll (SD)
Mount Mary Coll (WI)
Mount Mercy U (IA)
Mount Vernon Nazarene U (OH)
Nazareth Coll of Rochester (NY)
Newberry Coll (SC)
New Jersey City U (NJ)
New Mexico State U (NM)
New York U (NY)
Nicholls State U (LA)
North Carolina Central U (NC)
North Central Coll (IL)
North Dakota State U (ND)
Northern Arizona U (AZ)
Northern Illinois U (IL)
Northern Michigan U (MI)
Northern State U (SD)
North Greenville U (SC)
Northwestern Coll (IA)
Northwestern Coll (MN)
Northwestern Oklahoma State U (OK)
Northwestern State U of Louisiana (LA)
Northwest Missouri State U (MO)
Northwest Nazarene U (ID)
Northwest U (WA)
Nyack Coll (NY)
Oakland City U (IN)
Oakland U (MI)
The Ohio State U (OH)
Ohio Wesleyan U (OH)
Oklahoma Baptist U (OK)
Oklahoma Christian U (OK)
Oklahoma City U (OK)
Oklahoma State U (OK)

Olivet Coll (MI)
Oral Roberts U (OK)
Ouachita Baptist U (AR)
Pacific Lutheran U (WA)
Pacific Union Coll (CA)
Pacific U (OR)
Palm Beach Atlantic U (FL)
Peabody Conservatory of The Johns Hopkins U (MD)
Penn State U Park (PA)
Pepperdine U, Malibu (CA)
Pittsburg State U (KS)
Plymouth State U (NH)
Point Loma Nazarene U (CA)
Presbyterian Coll (SC)
Providence Coll (RI)
Quincy U (IL)
Rhode Island Coll (RI)
Rider U (NJ)
Ripon Coll (WI)
Roberts Wesleyan Coll (NY)
Rocky Mountain Coll (MT)
Roosevelt U (IL)
Rowan U (NJ)
Rutgers, The State U of New Jersey, New Brunswick (NJ)
Saginaw Valley State U (MI)
St. Ambrose U (IA)
Saint Mary's Coll (IN)
Saint Mary's U of Minnesota (MN)
St. Norbert Coll (WI)
St. Olaf Coll (MN)
Salve Regina U (RI)
Samford U (AL)
San Diego State U (CA)
Schreiner U (TX)
Seton Hill U (PA)
Shenandoah U (VA)
Simpson Coll (IA)
Simpson U (CA)
Sonoma State U (CA)
South Dakota State U (SD)
Southeastern Oklahoma State U (OK)
Southeastern U (FL)
Southeast Missouri State U (MO)
Southern Arkansas U–Magnolia (AR)
Southern Methodist U (TX)
Southern Nazarene U (OK)
Southern New Hampshire U (NH)
Southern Utah U (UT)
Southwest Baptist U (MO)
Southwestern Coll (KS)
Spring Arbor U (MI)
State U of New York at Fredonia (NY)
State U of New York Coll at Potsdam (NY)
Sterling Coll (KS)
Stetson U (FL)
Susquehanna U (PA)
Syracuse U (NY)
Tabor Coll (KS)
Tarleton State U (TX)
Taylor U (IN)
Temple U (PA)
Texas A&M U–Commerce (TX)
Texas Christian U (TX)
Texas Lutheran U (TX)
Texas Wesleyan U (TX)
Transylvania U (KY)
Trevecca Nazarene U (TN)
Trinity Christian Coll (IL)
Union Coll (NE)
Union U (TN)
The U of Akron (OH)
The U of Alabama (AL)
U of Alaska Anchorage (AK)
The U of Arizona (AZ)
U of Arkansas–Fort Smith (AR)
The U of British Columbia (BC, Canada)
U of Central Florida (FL)
U of Central Oklahoma (OK)
U of Cincinnati (OH)
U of Colorado Boulder (CO)
U of Delaware (DE)
U of Evansville (IN)
U of Florida (FL)
U of Georgia (GA)
U of Hartford (CT)
U of Idaho (ID)
U of Illinois at Urbana–Champaign (IL)
The U of Iowa (IA)
The U of Kansas (KS)

U of Kentucky (KY)
U of Louisville (KY)
U of Maryland, Coll Park (MD)
U of Maryland Eastern Shore (MD)
U of Miami (FL)
U of Michigan (MI)
U of Michigan–Flint (MI)
U of Minnesota, Duluth (MN)
U of Minnesota, Twin Cities Campus (MN)
U of Missouri (MO)
U of Missouri–Kansas City (MO)
U of Missouri–St. Louis (MO)
The U of Montana Western (MT)
U of Mount Union (OH)
U of Nebraska at Omaha (NE)
U of Nebraska–Lincoln (NE)
U of Nevada, Reno (NV)
U of New Brunswick Fredericton (NB, Canada)
U of New Mexico (NM)
The U of North Carolina at Charlotte (NC)
The U of North Carolina at Greensboro (NC)
The U of North Carolina at Pembroke (NC)
The U of North Carolina Wilmington (NC)
U of North Dakota (ND)
U of Northern Colorado (CO)
U of Northern Iowa (IA)
U of North Florida (FL)
U of North Georgia (GA)
U of Oklahoma (OK)
U of Oregon (OR)
U of Portland (OR)
U of Puget Sound (WA)
U of Redlands (CA)
U of Regina (SK, Canada)
U of Rochester (NY)
U of St. Francis (IL)
U of St. Thomas (MN)
U of South Carolina (SC)
U of South Carolina Aiken (SC)
The U of South Dakota (SD)
U of Southern California (CA)
U of Southern Maine (ME)
U of Southern Mississippi (MS)
U of South Florida (FL)
The U of Tampa (FL)
The U of Tennessee at Chattanooga (TN)
The U of Tennessee at Martin (TN)
U of the Cumberlands (KY)
U of the District of Columbia (DC)
U of the Incarnate Word (TX)
U of the Virgin Islands (VI)
The U of Toledo (OH)
U of Tulsa (OK)
U of Vermont (VT)
U of West Florida (FL)
U of West Georgia (GA)
U of Windsor (ON, Canada)
U of Wisconsin–Green Bay (WI)
U of Wisconsin–Madison (WI)
U of Wisconsin–Milwaukee (WI)
U of Wisconsin–Stevens Point (WI)
U of Wisconsin–Superior (WI)
U of Wyoming (WY)
Utah State U (UT)
Valdosta State U (GA)
Valley City State U (ND)
Valparaiso U (IN)
Vanderbilt U (TN)
VanderCook Coll of Music (IL)
Viterbo U (WI)
Walla Walla U (WA)
Warner Pacific Coll (OR)
Wartburg Coll (IA)
Washburn U (KS)
Washington State U (WA)
Wayland Baptist U (TX)
Wayne State Coll (NE)
Weber State U (UT)
Webster U (MO)
Western Carolina U (NC)
Western Connecticut State U (CT)
Western Michigan U (MI)
Western State Colorado U (CO)
Western Washington U (WA)
West Liberty U (WV)
West Virginia State U (WV)
West Virginia Wesleyan Coll (WV)
Wheaton Coll (IL)
Whitworth U (WA)
Wichita State U (KS)

William Jewell Coll (MO)
William Paterson U of New Jersey (NJ)
Winthrop U (SC)
Wright State U (OH)
Xavier U (OH)
Xavier U of Louisiana (LA)
York Coll of Pennsylvania (PA)
Young Harris Coll (GA)
Youngstown State U (OH)

MUSIC TECHNOLOGY

Bethune-Cookman U (FL)
Cogswell Polytechnical Coll (CA)
Indiana U–Purdue U Indianapolis (IN)
McNally Smith Coll of Music (MN)
Shenandoah U (VA)
Stetson U (FL)
Transylvania U (KY)
U of Michigan (MI)
The U of Texas at Austin (TX)

MUSIC THEORY AND COMPOSITION

Adams State U (CO)
American U (DC)
Arizona State U (AZ)
Augustana Coll (IL)
Baldwin Wallace U (OH)
Bard Coll (NY)
Baylor U (TX)
Belmont U (TN)
Bennington Coll (VT)
Berklee Coll of Music (MA)
Boise State U (ID)
The Boston Conservatory (MA)
Boston U (MA)
Bowling Green State U (OH)
Bradley U (IL)
Bucknell U (PA)
Butler U (IN)
California Baptist U (CA)
California State U, Chico (CA)
California State U, Long Beach (CA)
Calvin Coll (MI)
Capital U (OH)
Carnegie Mellon U (PA)
Carson-Newman U (TN)
The Catholic U of America (DC)
Central Michigan U (MI)
Chapman U (CA)
City Coll of the City U of New York (NY)
Coe Coll (IA)
The Coll of Wooster (OH)
Colorado State U (CO)
Concordia Coll (MN)
Concordia U (QC, Canada)
Concordia U Chicago (IL)
Dalhousie U (NS, Canada)
Dallas Baptist U (TX)
DePaul U (IL)
DePauw U (IN)
East Carolina U (NC)
Florida Southern Coll (FL)
Florida State U (FL)
Gardner-Webb U (NC)
Georgia Southern U (GA)
Grace U (NE)
Hardin-Simmons U (TX)
Hofstra U (NY)
Hope Coll (MI)
Houghton Coll (NY)
Illinois Wesleyan U (IL)
Indiana Wesleyan U (IN)
Ithaca Coll (NY)
Keene State Coll (NH)
Lawrence U (WI)
Lipscomb U (TN)
Long Island U–Brooklyn Campus (NY)
Loyola U New Orleans (LA)
Lynn U (FL)
Madonna U (MI)
Manchester U (IN)
Mannes Coll The New School for Music (NY)
Maryville Coll (TN)
McNally Smith Coll of Music (MN)
Michigan State U (MI)
Minnesota State U Moorhead (MN)
Moravian Coll (PA)
Newberry Coll (SC)
New England Conservatory of Music (MA)

The New School for Jazz and Contemporary Music (NY)
Northwestern Coll (MN)
Northwest Nazarene U (ID)
Nyack Coll (NY)
The Ohio State U (OH)
Ohio U (OH)
Oklahoma Baptist U (OK)
Oklahoma City U (OK)
Oral Roberts U (OK)
Ouachita Baptist U (AR)
Palm Beach Atlantic U (FL)
Pepperdine U, Malibu (CA)
Point Loma Nazarene U (CA)
Randolph Coll (VA)
Rice U (TX)
Rider U (NJ)
Roosevelt U (IL)
Rowan U (NJ)
St. Olaf Coll (MN)
Samford U (AL)
San Francisco Conservatory of Music (CA)
Shenandoah U (VA)
Southern Methodist U (TX)
Stetson U (FL)
Susquehanna U (PA)
Syracuse U (NY)
Temple U (PA)
Texas Christian U (TX)
Trinity U (TX)
Tulane U (LA)
The U of Akron (OH)
The U of British Columbia (BC, Canada)
U of Cincinnati (OH)
U of Delaware (DE)
U of Georgia (GA)
U of Idaho (ID)
U of Illinois at Urbana–Champaign (IL)
The U of Kansas (KS)
U of Miami (FL)
U of Michigan (MI)
U of Minnesota, Duluth (MN)
U of Missouri–Kansas City (MO)
U of Nebraska at Omaha (NE)
U of Nevada, Las Vegas (NV)
The U of North Carolina at Greensboro (NC)
U of Northern Iowa (IA)
U of North Texas (TX)
U of Oregon (OR)
U of Redlands (CA)
U of Regina (SK, Canada)
U of Rhode Island (RI)
U of Rochester (NY)
U of Southern California (CA)
The U of Texas at Austin (TX)
The U of Texas at San Antonio (TX)
The U of the Arts (PA)
U of Tulsa (OK)
The U of Western Ontario (ON, Canada)
U of West Georgia (GA)
U of Windsor (ON, Canada)
Valparaiso U (IN)
Vanderbilt U (TN)
Wartburg Coll (IA)
Washington State U (WA)
Washington U in St. Louis (MO)
Webster U (MO)
Western Connecticut State U (CT)
Western Michigan U (MI)
Western Washington U (WA)
West Texas A&M U (TX)
Wheaton Coll (IL)
Whitman Coll (WA)
Willamette U (OR)
William Jewell Coll (MO)
Youngstown State U (OH)

MUSIC THERAPY

Alverno Coll (WI)
Appalachian State U (NC)
Arizona State U (AZ)
Augsburg Coll (MN)
Baldwin Wallace U (OH)
Berklee Coll of Music (MA)
The Coll of Wooster (OH)
Colorado State U (CO)
Concordia U Wisconsin (WI)
Converse Coll (SC)
Drury U (MO)
Duquesne U (PA)
East Carolina U (NC)
Eastern Michigan U (MI)

Elizabethtown Coll (PA)
Florida State U (FL)
Georgia Coll & State U (GA)
Immaculata U (PA)
Indiana U–Purdue U Fort Wayne (IN)
Loyola U New Orleans (LA)
Lubbock Christian U (TX)
Maryville U of Saint Louis (MO)
Marywood U (PA)
Mercyhurst U (PA)
Montclair State U (NJ)
Nazareth Coll of Rochester (NY)
Queens U of Charlotte (NC)
Saint Mary-of-the-Woods Coll (IN)
Sam Houston State U (TX)
Seattle Pacific U (WA)
Seton Hill U (PA)
Shenandoah U (VA)
Slippery Rock U of Pennsylvania (PA)
Southern Methodist U (TX)
State U of New York at Fredonia (NY)
State U of New York at New Paltz (NY)
Temple U (PA)
Thompson Rivers U (BC, Canada)
U of Evansville (IN)
U of Georgia (GA)
The U of Iowa (IA)
The U of Kansas (KS)
U of Louisville (KY)
U of Miami (FL)
U of Minnesota, Twin Cities Campus (MN)
U of Missouri–Kansas City (MO)
U of North Dakota (ND)
U of the Incarnate Word (TX)
Utah State U (UT)
Wartburg Coll (IA)
Western Michigan U (MI)
West Texas A&M U (TX)

NANOTECHNOLOGY

U at Albany, State U of New York (NY)
U of Guelph (ON, Canada)

NATIONAL SECURITY POLICY

Angelo State U (TX)
Baldwin Wallace U (OH)

NATURAL RESOURCE ECONOMICS

Baldwin Wallace U (OH)
Colorado State U (CO)
Juniata Coll (PA)
Malone U (OH)
Michigan State U (MI)
New Mexico State U (NM)
U of Guelph (ON, Canada)
U of New Hampshire (NH)
U of Rhode Island (RI)
The U of Tennessee (TN)

NATURAL RESOURCE RECREATION AND TOURISM

Unity Coll (ME)
U of Georgia (GA)
U of Idaho (ID)

NATURAL RESOURCES AND CONSERVATION RELATED

Bowling Green State U (OH)
California Polytechnic State U, San Luis Obispo (CA)
Mount Mercy U (IA)
Northwest Missouri State U (MO)
Penn State Abington (PA)
Penn State Altoona (PA)
Penn State Beaver (PA)
Penn State Berks (PA)
Penn State Brandywine (PA)
Penn State DuBois (PA)
Penn State Erie, The Behrend Coll (PA)
Penn State Fayette, The Eberly Campus (PA)
Penn State Greater Allegheny (PA)
Penn State Hazleton (PA)
Penn State Lehigh Valley (PA)
Penn State Mont Alto (PA)
Penn State New Kensington (PA)
Penn State Schuylkill (PA)
Penn State Shenango (PA)
Penn State U Park (PA)
Penn State Wilkes-Barre (PA)

Penn State Worthington Scranton (PA)
Penn State York (PA)
Prescott Coll (AZ)
Sterling Coll (VT)
Texas A&M U–Kingsville (TX)
U of Alaska Fairbanks (AK)
The U of British Columbia (BC, Canada)
U of California, Davis (CA)
U of Louisiana at Lafayette (LA)
U of New Hampshire (NH)
U of Wisconsin–Stevens Point (WI)
Utah State U (UT)

NATURAL RESOURCES/ CONSERVATION
Ball State U (IN)
Clemson U (SC)
Colorado State U (CO)
The Evergreen State Coll (WA)
Grand Valley State U (MI)
Gustavus Adolphus Coll (MN)
Humboldt State U (CA)
Kent State U (OH)
Manchester U (IN)
Montana State U (MT)
Morrisville State Coll (NY)
North Carolina State U (NC)
Northern Michigan U (MI)
Northland Coll (WI)
The Ohio State U (OH)
Penn State Abington (PA)
Penn State Altoona (PA)
Penn State Beaver (PA)
Penn State Berks (PA)
Penn State Brandywine (PA)
Penn State DuBois (PA)
Penn State Erie, The Behrend Coll (PA)
Penn State Fayette, The Eberly Campus (PA)
Penn State Greater Allegheny (PA)
Penn State Hazleton (PA)
Penn State Lehigh Valley (PA)
Penn State Mont Alto (PA)
Penn State New Kensington (PA)
Penn State Schuylkill (PA)
Penn State Shenango (PA)
Penn State U Park (PA)
Penn State Wilkes-Barre (PA)
Penn State Worthington Scranton (PA)
Penn State York (PA)
Purdue U (IN)
Rutgers, The State U of New Jersey, New Brunswick (NJ)
Southeastern Oklahoma State U (OK)
State U of New York at Plattsburgh (NY)
State U of New York Coll of Agriculture and Technology at Cobleskill (NY)
Stony Brook U, State U of New York (NY)
Suffolk U (MA)
Texas A&M U (TX)
The U of Arizona (AZ)
The U of British Columbia (BC, Canada)
U of California, Berkeley (CA)
U of California, Davis (CA)
U of Illinois at Urbana–Champaign (IL)
U of Kentucky (KY)
U of Maryland, Coll Park (MD)
U of Maryland U Coll (MD)
U of Massachusetts Amherst (MA)
U of Michigan–Flint (MI)
U of Minnesota, Crookston (MN)
U of Minnesota, Twin Cities Campus (MN)
U of Missouri (MO)
U of Nebraska–Lincoln (NE)
U of Nevada, Reno (NV)
U of New Hampshire (NH)
U of Vermont (VT)
U of Wisconsin–Stevens Point (WI)
Upper Iowa U (IA)
Washington State U (WA)
Washington U in St. Louis (MO)

NATURAL RESOURCES/ CONSERVATION RELATED
Colby Coll (ME)
Sierra Nevada Coll (NV)
Stanford U (CA)

U of Illinois at Urbana–Champaign (IL)

NATURAL RESOURCES LAW ENFORCEMENT AND PROTECTIVE SERVICES
Unity Coll (ME)
U of Minnesota, Crookston (MN)

NATURAL RESOURCES MANAGEMENT AND POLICY
Alaska Pacific U (AK)
Angelo State U (TX)
Bowling Green State U (OH)
California State U, Chico (CA)
Clark U (MA)
Colorado State U (CO)
Humboldt State U (CA)
Iowa State U of Science and Technology (IA)
Johnson State Coll (VT)
Louisiana State U and Ag and Mech Coll (LA)
New Mexico Highlands U (NM)
North Carolina State U (NC)
North Dakota State U (ND)
Oregon State U (OR)
Rochester Inst of Technology (NY)
Sewanee: The U of the South (TN)
South Dakota State U (SD)
Tabor Coll (KS)
Texas A&M U (TX)
Tuskegee U (AL)
The U of British Columbia (BC, Canada)
U of California, Berkeley (CA)
U of Delaware (DE)
U of Guelph (ON, Canada)
U of Hawaii at Manoa (HI)
U of Idaho (ID)
U of Illinois at Urbana–Champaign (IL)
U of La Verne (CA)
U of Miami (FL)
U of Minnesota, Crookston (MN)
U of Minnesota, Twin Cities Campus (MN)
U of Nebraska–Lincoln (NE)
U of Nevada, Reno (NV)
U of Rhode Island (RI)
The U of Tennessee at Martin (TN)
U of Wisconsin–Stevens Point (WI)
Western Carolina U (NC)
Xavier U (OH)

NATURAL RESOURCES MANAGEMENT AND POLICY RELATED
Humboldt State U (CA)
Keystone Coll (PA)
Massachusetts Maritime Acad (MA)
Moravian Coll (PA)
Morrisville State Coll (NY)
The Ohio State U (OH)
Rutgers, The State U of New Jersey, New Brunswick (NJ)
Sterling Coll (VT)
The U of British Columbia (BC, Canada)
U of Illinois at Urbana–Champaign (IL)
U of Minnesota, Twin Cities Campus (MN)
The U of Tennessee at Martin (TN)
The U of Western Ontario (ON, Canada)

NATURAL SCIENCES
Athens State U (AL)
Augsburg Coll (MN)
Azusa Pacific U (CA)
Bemidji State U (MN)
Benedictine Coll (KS)
Bethel Coll (KS)
Blue Mountain Coll (MS)
California State U, Dominguez Hills (CA)
California State U, Fresno (CA)
California State U, Los Angeles (CA)
California State U, San Bernardino (CA)
Calvin Coll (MI)
Case Western Reserve U (OH)
Castleton State Coll (VT)
Central Coll (IA)
Christian Brothers U (TN)
Colgate U (NY)

Coll of Saint Benedict (MN)
Coll of Saint Mary (NE)
The Coll of St. Scholastica (MN)
Coll of the Atlantic (ME)
Colorado State U (CO)
Concordia Coll (MN)
Concordia U (OR)
Concordia U Chicago (IL)
Concordia U, Nebraska (NE)
Dallas Baptist U (TX)
Defiance Coll (OH)
Doane Coll (NE)
Dominican U (IL)
Dordt Coll (IA)
Edgewood Coll (WI)
The Evergreen State Coll (WA)
Felician Coll (NJ)
Harrison Middleton U (AZ)
Hofstra U (NY)
Houghton Coll (NY)
Humboldt State U (CA)
Indiana U East (IN)
Inter American U of Puerto Rico, San Germán Campus (PR)
The Johns Hopkins U (MD)
Juniata Coll (PA)
Kansas State U (KS)
Lesley U (MA)
LeTourneau U (TX)
Lewis-Clark State Coll (ID)
Loyola Marymount U (CA)
Madonna U (MI)
The Master's Coll and Sem (CA)
Minnesota State U Mankato (MN)
Mount Allison U (NB, Canada)
Mount Saint Mary Coll (NY)
Muhlenberg Coll (PA)
National U (CA)
New Coll of Florida (FL)
Oklahoma Baptist U (OK)
Oregon State U (OR)
Pacific Union Coll (CA)
Park U (MO)
Pepperdine U, Malibu (CA)
Saint John's U (MN)
Shimer Coll (IL)
Siena Heights U (MI)
Spelman Coll (GA)
State U of New York Coll at Geneseo (NY)
Taylor U (IN)
Thomas Edison State Coll (NJ)
Trent U (ON, Canada)
U of Alaska Anchorage (AK)
The U of Arizona (AZ)
U of Hawaii at Hilo (HI)
U of La Verne (CA)
U of Nebraska at Omaha (NE)
U of Pennsylvania (PA)
U of Pittsburgh at Greensburg (PA)
U of Puget Sound (WA)
U of Science and Arts of Oklahoma (OK)
The U of Toledo (OH)
U of Wisconsin–Stevens Point (WI)
Virginia Wesleyan Coll (VA)
Viterbo U (WI)
Washington U in St. Louis (MO)
Western Oregon U (OR)
Xavier U (OH)

NAVAL ARCHITECTURE AND MARINE ENGINEERING
Maine Maritime Acad (ME)
Massachusetts Maritime Acad (MA)
State U of New York Maritime Coll (NY)
United States Coast Guard Acad (CT)
United States Merchant Marine Acad (NY)
United States Naval Acad (MD)
U of Michigan (MI)
U of Minnesota, Twin Cities Campus (MN)
U of New Orleans (LA)
Webb Inst (NY)

NAVAL SCIENCE AND OPERATIONAL STUDIES
U of Wisconsin–Madison (WI)

NAVY/MARINE CORPS ROTC/ NAVAL SCIENCE
Hampton U (VA)

NEAR AND MIDDLE EASTERN STUDIES
The American U in Cairo (Egypt)
Bard Coll (NY)
Brown U (RI)
Claremont McKenna Coll (CA)
Columbia Intl U (SC)
Columbia U (NY)
Columbia U, School of General Studies (NY)
Dartmouth Coll (NH)
Dickinson Coll (PA)
Drew U (NJ)
Hampshire Coll (MA)
Hood Coll (MD)
The Johns Hopkins U (MD)
McDaniel Coll (MD)
Mount Holyoke Coll (MA)
New York U (NY)
Portland State U (OR)
Princeton U (NJ)
Rutgers, The State U of New Jersey, New Brunswick (NJ)
Scripps Coll (CA)
Smith Coll (MA)
Swarthmore Coll (PA)
Syracuse U (NY)
Texas State U–San Marcos (TX)
Tufts U (MA)
United States Military Acad (NY)
The U of Arizona (AZ)
U of California, Berkeley (CA)
U of California, Santa Barbara (CA)
U of Massachusetts Amherst (MA)
U of Michigan (MI)
U of Minnesota, Twin Cities Campus (MN)
U of Richmond (VA)
The U of Texas at Austin (TX)
The U of Toledo (OH)
U of Utah (UT)
The U of Western Ontario (ON, Canada)
Washington U in St. Louis (MO)
Wellesley Coll (MA)

NETWORK AND SYSTEM ADMINISTRATION
Champlain Coll (VT)
Dordt Coll (IA)
Rochester Inst of Technology (NY)
State U of New York Coll of Technology at Alfred (NY)
Sullivan Coll of Technology and Design (KY)
U of Great Falls (MT)

NEUROBIOLOGY AND ANATOMY
Andrews U (MI)
Georgetown U (DC)
New Coll of Florida (FL)
St. Lawrence U (NY)
U of California, Davis (CA)
U of California, Irvine (CA)

NEUROBIOLOGY AND BEHAVIOR
Assumption Coll (MA)

NEUROSCIENCE
Agnes Scott Coll (GA)
Amherst Coll (MA)
Augustana Coll (IL)
Baldwin Wallace U (OH)
Bard Coll (NY)
Bates Coll (ME)
Baylor U (TX)
Belmont U (TN)
Boston U (MA)
Bowdoin Coll (ME)
Bowling Green State U (OH)
Brock U (ON, Canada)
Brown U (RI)
Bucknell U (PA)
Carnegie Mellon U (PA)
Cedar Crest Coll (PA)
Centenary Coll of Louisiana (LA)
Central Michigan U (MI)
Christopher Newport U (VA)
Claremont McKenna Coll (CA)
Clark U (MA)
Colby Coll (ME)
Colgate U (NY)
Coll of Mount St. Joseph (OH)
The Coll of William and Mary (VA)
The Coll of Wooster (OH)
The Colorado Coll (CO)

Columbia U, School of General Studies (NY)
Concordia U (QC, Canada)
Connecticut Coll (CT)
Dalhousie U (NS, Canada)
Dickinson Coll (PA)
Dominican U (IL)
Drake U (IA)
Drew U (NJ)
Earlham Coll (IN)
Emmanuel Coll (MA)
Franklin & Marshall Coll (PA)
Furman U (SC)
George Mason U (VA)
Georgia State U (GA)
Hamilton Coll (NY)
Hampshire Coll (MA)
Hiram Coll (OH)
Hope Coll (MI)
Indiana U Bloomington (IN)
Indiana U–Purdue U Indianapolis (IN)
John Carroll U (OH)
The Johns Hopkins U (MD)
Kenyon Coll (OH)
King Coll (TN)
King's Coll (PA)
Knox Coll (IL)
Lawrence U (WI)
Lehigh U (PA)
Macalester Coll (MN)
Maryville Coll (TN)
Massachusetts Inst of Technology (MA)
Middlebury Coll (VT)
Mount Holyoke Coll (MA)
Muhlenberg Coll (PA)
New York U (NY)
Northeastern U (MA)
Northwest Nazarene U (ID)
Ohio U (OH)
Ohio Wesleyan U (OH)
Pitzer Coll (CA)
Pomona Coll (CA)
Regis U (CO)
Rhodes Coll (TN)
Rice U (TX)
St. Lawrence U (NY)
Scripps Coll (CA)
Skidmore Coll (NY)
Smith Coll (MA)
Stonehill Coll (MA)
Syracuse U (NY)
Temple U (PA)
Texas Christian U (TX)
Trinity Coll (CT)
Trinity U (TX)
Tulane U (LA)
The U of Alabama at Birmingham (AL)
The U of Arizona (AZ)
U of California, Los Angeles (CA)
U of California, Riverside (CA)
U of California, Santa Cruz (CA)
U of Cincinnati (OH)
U of Delaware (DE)
U of Evansville (IN)
U of Illinois at Chicago (IL)
U of Miami (FL)
U of Michigan (MI)
U of Minnesota, Twin Cities Campus (MN)
U of Mount Union (OH)
U of Nebraska at Omaha (NE)
U of New Hampshire (NH)
U of Pennsylvania (PA)
U of Pittsburgh (PA)
U of Rochester (NY)
U of San Diego (CA)
The U of Scranton (PA)
U of Southern California (CA)
The U of Texas at Dallas (TX)
The U of Western Ontario (ON, Canada)
U of Windsor (ON, Canada)
Vanderbilt U (TN)
Washington and Lee U (VA)
Washington State U (WA)
Washington U in St. Louis (MO)
Wellesley Coll (MA)
Western Washington U (WA)
Westminster Coll (UT)
Wheaton Coll (MA)

NONPROFIT MANAGEMENT
Alaska Pacific U (AK)
Arizona State U (AZ)

Austin Peay State U (TN)
Bryant U (RI)
City Vision Coll (MO)
Cleveland State U (OH)
Columbia Intl U (SC)
Concordia U Chicago (IL)
Dalhousie U (NS, Canada)
Duquesne U (PA)
Fairleigh Dickinson U, Metropolitan
Campus (NJ)
Franklin U (OH)
Friends U (KS)
Gettysburg Coll (PA)
Hardin-Simmons U (TX)
Hawai`i Pacific U (HI)
High Point U (NC)
Hope Intl U (CA)
Huntington U (IN)
Lakeland Coll (WI)
Prescott Coll (AZ)
Rogers State U (OK)
St. Joseph's Coll, Long Island
Campus (NY)
St. Joseph's Coll, New York (NY)
Thompson Rivers U (BC, Canada)
Tiffin U (OH)
Trevecca Nazarene U (TN)
U of Minnesota, Twin Cities
Campus (MN)
U of South Carolina Upstate (SC)
William Jewell Coll (MO)

NORWEGIAN
Brigham Young U (UT)
Pacific Lutheran U (WA)
St. Olaf Coll (MN)
U of North Dakota (ND)

**NUCLEAR AND INDUSTRIAL
RADIOLOGIC TECHNOLOGIES
RELATED**
Mount Mary Coll (WI)

NUCLEAR ENGINEERING
Kansas State U (KS)
Massachusetts Inst of Technology
(MA)
Missouri U of Science and
Technology (MO)
North Carolina State U (NC)
Oregon State U (OR)
Penn State Abington (PA)
Penn State Altoona (PA)
Penn State Beaver (PA)
Penn State Berks (PA)
Penn State Brandywine (PA)
Penn State DuBois (PA)
Penn State Erie, The Behrend Coll
(PA)
Penn State Fayette, The Eberly
Campus (PA)
Penn State Greater Allegheny (PA)
Penn State Hazleton (PA)
Penn State Lehigh Valley (PA)
Penn State Mont Alto (PA)
Penn State New Kensington (PA)
Penn State Schuylkill (PA)
Penn State Shenango (PA)
Penn State U Park (PA)
Penn State Wilkes-Barre (PA)
Penn State Worthington Scranton
(PA)
Penn State York (PA)
Purdue U (IN)
Rensselaer Polytechnic Inst (NY)
Texas A&M U (TX)
United States Military Acad (NY)
U of California, Berkeley (CA)
U of Florida (FL)
U of Illinois at Urbana–Champaign
(IL)
U of Michigan (MI)
U of New Mexico (NM)
The U of Tennessee (TN)
U of Wisconsin–Madison (WI)
Worcester Polytechnic Inst (MA)

**NUCLEAR ENGINEERING
TECHNOLOGY**
Thomas Edison State Coll (NJ)
United States Merchant Marine
Acad (NY)
United States Military Acad (NY)

**NUCLEAR MEDICAL
TECHNOLOGY**
Allen Coll (IA)
Baptist Coll of Health Sciences
(TN)

Barry U (FL)
Benedictine U (IL)
Cedar Crest Coll (PA)
Dalhousie U (NS, Canada)
Edinboro U of Pennsylvania (PA)
Ferris State U (MI)
Georgia Regents U (GA)
Indiana U of Pennsylvania (PA)
Indiana U–Purdue U Indianapolis
(IN)
Lewis U (IL)
Long Island U–Brooklyn Campus
(NY)
Long Island U–C. W. Post Campus
(NY)
Manhattan Coll (NY)
Massachusetts Coll of Pharmacy
and Health Sciences (MA)
North Central Coll (IL)
Oakland U (MI)
Old Dominion U (VA)
Robert Morris U (PA)
Roosevelt U (IL)
Saint Louis U (MO)
Saint Mary's U of Minnesota (MN)
Salem State U (MA)
Thomas Edison State Coll (NJ)
U at Buffalo, the State U of New
York (NY)
The U of Alabama at Birmingham
(AL)
U of Arkansas for Medical Sciences
(AR)
U of Central Arkansas (AR)
U of Cincinnati (OH)
The U of Iowa (IA)
U of Medicine and Dentistry of New
Jersey (NJ)
U of Missouri (MO)
U of Nevada, Las Vegas (NV)
U of Oklahoma Health Sciences
Center (OK)
U of St. Francis (IL)
U of the Incarnate Word (TX)
U of Vermont (VT)
U of Wisconsin–La Crosse (WI)
Weber State U (UT)
Wheeling Jesuit U (WV)
York Coll of Pennsylvania (PA)

**NUCLEAR/NUCLEAR POWER
TECHNOLOGY**
U of North Texas (TX)

NUCLEAR PHYSICS
Arkansas Tech U (AR)

NURSING ADMINISTRATION
Central Methodist U (MO)
Huntington U (IN)
Midwestern State U (TX)
Nova Southeastern U (FL)
The U of Toledo (OH)
U of Washington, Tacoma (WA)
The U of Western Ontario (ON,
Canada)
Wheeling Jesuit U (WV)

NURSING EDUCATION
U of the District of Columbia (DC)

NURSING PRACTICE
Benedictine Coll (KS)
Bluefield Coll (VA)
Christian Brothers U (TN)
Concordia Coll–New York (NY)
Florida National U (FL)
Lebanese American U (Lebanon)
Misericordia U (PA)
Siena Heights U (MI)
Stratford U, Falls Church (VA)

NURSING SCIENCE
Brock U (ON, Canada)
Cedar Crest Coll (PA)
Coll of Saint Elizabeth (NJ)
EDP Coll of Puerto Rico, Inc. (PR)
Holy Names U (CA)
Kean U (NJ)
Kent State U at Geauga (OH)
Kent State U at Trumbull (OH)
Lander U (SC)
Millersville U of Pennsylvania (PA)
Monmouth U (NJ)
New Jersey City U (NJ)
The Ohio State U (OH)
Oklahoma City U (OK)
Pensacola State Coll (FL)
Queens U of Charlotte (NC)

Sam Houston State U (TX)
Siena Heights U (MI)
Trinity Coll of Nursing and Health
Sciences (IL)
U of Alaska Anchorage (AK)
U of California, Irvine (CA)
U of Illinois at Chicago (IL)
U of New Hampshire at Manchester
(NH)
Wayne State U (MI)
Xavier U (OH)

NUTRITION SCIENCES
Auburn U (AL)
Boston U (MA)
California State U, Los Angeles
(CA)
Canisius Coll (NY)
Case Western Reserve U (OH)
Coll of Saint Benedict (MN)
Concordia Coll (MN)
Goddard Coll (VT)
La Salle U (PA)
Lebanese American U (Lebanon)
Louisiana State U and Ag and
Mech Coll (LA)
McNeese State U (LA)
Messiah Coll (PA)
Michigan State U (MI)
New York Inst of Technology (NY)
North Carolina State U (NC)
The Ohio State U (OH)
Pepperdine U, Malibu (CA)
Russell Sage Coll (NY)
Rutgers, The State U of New
Jersey, New Brunswick (NJ)
Saint John's U (MN)
Southern Illinois U Carbondale (IL)
Syracuse U (NY)
Texas Woman's U (TX)
The U of Arizona (AZ)
U of California, Berkeley (CA)
U of California, Davis (CA)
U of Delaware (DE)
U of Georgia (GA)
U of Guelph (ON, Canada)
U of Hawaii at Manoa (HI)
U of Illinois at Chicago (IL)
U of Massachusetts Amherst (MA)
U of Minnesota, Twin Cities
Campus (MN)
U of Nevada, Las Vegas (NV)
U of Nevada, Reno (NV)
U of New Hampshire (NH)
The U of North Carolina at
Greensboro (NC)
U of Northern Colorado (CO)
U of Saint Joseph (CT)
U of Southern Indiana (IN)
U of the District of Columbia (DC)
U of the Incarnate Word (TX)
U of Vermont (VT)
U of Wisconsin–Madison (WI)
U of Wisconsin–Milwaukee (WI)
Washington State U (WA)

**OCCUPATIONAL HEALTH
AND INDUSTRIAL HYGIENE**
California State U, Fresno (CA)
Grand Valley State U (MI)
Montana Tech of The U of Montana
(MT)
Oakland U (MI)
Ohio U (OH)
Roger Williams U (RI)

**OCCUPATIONAL SAFETY
AND HEALTH TECHNOLOGY**
California State U, Fresno (CA)
Embry-Riddle Aeronautical U–
Daytona (FL)
Embry-Riddle Aeronautical U–
Prescott (AZ)
Fairmont State U (WV)
Grand Valley State U (MI)
Indiana State U (IN)
Indiana U of Pennsylvania (PA)
Jacksonville State U (AL)
Keene State Coll (NH)
Marshall U (WV)
Millersville U of Pennsylvania (PA)
Murray State U (KY)
Rochester Inst of Technology (NY)
Slippery Rock U of Pennsylvania
(PA)
Southeastern Louisiana U (LA)
Southeastern Oklahoma State U
(OK)

Southwest Baptist U (MO)
U of Central Oklahoma (OK)
U of Houston–Downtown (TX)
U of North Dakota (ND)
U of Regina (SK, Canada)

OCCUPATIONAL THERAPY
Alabama State U (AL)
Bay Path Coll (MA)
Calvin Coll (MI)
Coll of Saint Benedict (MN)
Concordia U Wisconsin (WI)
Dalhousie U (NS, Canada)
Dominican Coll (NY)
Dominican U (IL)
Duquesne U (PA)
Eastern Michigan U (MI)
Eastern Washington U (WA)
Elizabethtown Coll (PA)
Grand Valley State U (MI)
Hawai`i Pacific U (HI)
Husson U (ME)
Illinois Coll (IL)
Ithaca Coll (NY)
Keuka Coll (NY)
Long Island U–Brooklyn Campus
(NY)
McKendree U (IL)
Mount Mary Coll (WI)
Nazareth Coll of Rochester (NY)
New York Inst of Technology (NY)
Penn State Mont Alto (PA)
Quinnipiac U (CT)
Sacred Heart U (CT)
Saint John's U (MN)
Saint Louis U (MO)
Saint Vincent Coll (PA)
San Jose State U (CA)
Spalding U (KY)
Stony Brook U, State U of New York
(NY)
Tuskegee U (AL)
U at Buffalo, the State U of New
York (NY)
The U of Findlay (OH)
The U of Kansas (KS)
U of Minnesota, Twin Cities
Campus (MN)
U of Missouri (MO)
U of New England (ME)
U of New Hampshire (NH)
U of Ottawa (ON, Canada)
U of Pittsburgh (PA)
The U of Scranton (PA)
U of Southern California (CA)
U of Southern Indiana (IN)
U of the Sciences (PA)
U of Utah (UT)
The U of Western Ontario (ON,
Canada)
U of Wisconsin–Milwaukee (WI)
Wartburg Coll (IA)
Western Michigan U (MI)
Worcester State U (MA)
Xavier U (OH)
York Coll of the City U of New York
(NY)

OCEAN ENGINEERING
California State U, Long Beach
(CA)
Florida Atlantic U (FL)
Florida Inst of Technology (FL)
Texas A&M U (TX)
United States Naval Acad (MD)
U of Rhode Island (RI)
Virginia Polytechnic Inst and State
U (VA)

**OCEANOGRAPHY (CHEMICAL
AND PHYSICAL)**
Central Michigan U (MI)
Coll of the Atlantic (ME)
Dalhousie U (NS, Canada)
Elizabeth City State U (NC)
Florida Inst of Technology (FL)
Hawai`i Pacific U (HI)
Humboldt State U (CA)
Kutztown U of Pennsylvania (PA)
Lamar U (TX)
Louisiana State U and Ag and
Mech Coll (LA)
Maine Maritime Acad (ME)
Millersville U of Pennsylvania (PA)
North Carolina State U (NC)
Rider U (NJ)
United States Coast Guard Acad
(CT)

United States Naval Acad (MD)
The U of British Columbia (BC,
Canada)
U of Miami (FL)
U of Michigan (MI)
U of South Carolina (SC)
U of West Florida (FL)

OFFICE MANAGEMENT
Adams State U (CO)
American U of Puerto Rico (PR)
Babson Coll (MA)
Ball State U (IN)
Bowling Green State U (OH)
Clayton State U (GA)
East Central U (OK)
Indiana State U (IN)
Indiana U of Pennsylvania (PA)
Inter American U of Puerto Rico,
Aguadilla Campus (PR)
Inter American U of Puerto Rico,
Fajardo Campus (PR)
Inter American U of Puerto Rico,
Ponce Campus (PR)
Inter American U of Puerto Rico,
San Germán Campus (PR)
Loyola U Chicago (IL)
Maranatha Baptist Bible Coll (WI)
Middle Tennessee State U (TN)
Mississippi Valley State U (MS)
National U (CA)
Rider U (NJ)
Roosevelt U (IL)
Southwest Baptist U (MO)
Tabor Coll (KS)
Tarleton State U (TX)
The U of Akron–Wayne Coll (OH)
U of South Carolina (SC)
U of Southern Indiana (IN)
The U of Toledo (OH)
Valley City State U (ND)

OPERATIONS MANAGEMENT
Arizona State U (AZ)
Auburn U (AL)
Babson Coll (MA)
Ball State U (IN)
Bismarck State Coll (ND)
Boise State U (ID)
Boston Coll (MA)
Boston U (MA)
Bowling Green State U (OH)
California State U, Chico (CA)
California State U, Dominguez Hills
(CA)
California State U, Long Beach
(CA)
California State U, Stanislaus (CA)
Central Michigan U (MI)
Cleveland State U (OH)
Concordia U (QC, Canada)
Dalton State Coll (GA)
Edinboro U of Pennsylvania (PA)
Excelsior Coll (NY)
Farmingdale State Coll (NY)
Ferris State U (MI)
Fort Lewis Coll (CO)
Franklin U (OH)
Governors State U (IL)
Indiana U–Purdue U Fort Wayne
(IN)
Indiana U–Purdue U Indianapolis
(IN)
Inter American U of Puerto Rico,
Ponce Campus (PR)
Iowa State U of Science and
Technology (IA)
Le Moyne Coll (NY)
Loyola U Chicago (IL)
Marian U (WI)
Miami U (OH)
Minnesota State U Moorhead (MN)
Missouri Baptist U (MO)
Northern Illinois U (IL)
Oakland U (MI)
The Ohio State U (OH)
Oregon State U (OR)
Purdue U (IN)
Purdue U North Central (IN)
Roger Williams U (RI)
Saginaw Valley State U (MI)
South Dakota State U (SD)
Southern New Hampshire U (NH)
State U of New York Coll of
Technology at Canton (NY)
Texas A&M U–Commerce (TX)
Texas Southern U (TX)

Thomas Edison State Coll (NJ)
Thompson Rivers U (BC, Canada)
Trine U (IN)
The U of Akron (OH)
The U of Arizona (AZ)
U of Cincinnati (OH)
U of Delaware (DE)
U of Houston (TX)
U of Idaho (ID)
U of Illinois at Urbana–Champaign (IL)
U of Massachusetts Amherst (MA)
U of Massachusetts Dartmouth (MA)
U of Michigan–Flint (MI)
U of Minnesota, Crookston (MN)
U of Minnesota, Twin Cities Campus (MN)
U of Nebraska at Kearney (NE)
U of North Carolina at Asheville (NC)
The U of North Carolina at Charlotte (NC)
U of North Dakota (ND)
U of North Texas (TX)
U of Pennsylvania (PA)
U of St. Thomas (MN)
The U of Scranton (PA)
U of Southern Indiana (IN)
The U of Texas at San Antonio (TX)
The U of Toledo (OH)
U of Utah (UT)
U of Wisconsin–Madison (WI)
U of Wisconsin–Milwaukee (WI)
U of Wisconsin–Stout (WI)
Utah State U (UT)
Washington State U (WA)
Washington U in St. Louis (MO)
Wentworth Inst of Technology (MA)
Western Washington U (WA)
Widener U (PA)

OPERATIONS RESEARCH
Babson Coll (MA)
Bowling Green State U (OH)
California State U, Fullerton (CA)
Canisius Coll (NY)
Carnegie Mellon U (PA)
Columbia U (NY)
Long Island U–Brooklyn Campus (NY)
Milwaukee School of Eng (WI)
New York U (NY)
Princeton U (NJ)
Southern Methodist U (TX)
United States Air Force Acad (CO)
United States Coast Guard Acad (CT)
United States Military Acad (NY)
United States Naval Acad (MD)
U of California, Berkeley (CA)
U of Illinois at Urbana–Champaign (IL)
U of New Brunswick Fredericton (NB, Canada)
U of Waterloo (ON, Canada)

OPHTHALMIC AND OPTOMETRIC SUPPORT SERVICES AND ALLIED PROFESSIONS RELATED
Tennessee Wesleyan Coll (TN)

OPHTHALMIC LABORATORY TECHNOLOGY
Abilene Christian U (TX)
U of Ottawa (ON, Canada)

OPHTHALMIC TECHNOLOGY
U of Arkansas for Medical Sciences (AR)

OPTICAL SCIENCES
The Ohio State U (OH)
Saginaw Valley State U (MI)
The U of Arizona (AZ)
U of Rochester (NY)
Western Washington U (WA)

ORGANIC CHEMISTRY
Concordia U (QC, Canada)
The U of Western Ontario (ON, Canada)

ORGANIZATIONAL BEHAVIOR
Anderson U (IN)
Anderson U (SC)
Athabasca U (AB, Canada)
Benedictine U (IL)

Bluffton U (OH)
Bowling Green State U (OH)
Brown U (RI)
Central Baptist Coll (AR)
Central Michigan U (MI)
Claflin U (SC)
Coll of Mount St. Joseph (OH)
The Coll of St. Scholastica (MN)
DePaul U (IL)
Eastern Mennonite U (VA)
Edgewood Coll (WI)
Goodwin Coll (CT)
Greenville Coll (IL)
Indian River State Coll (FL)
John Brown U (AR)
Lewis U (IL)
Loyola U Chicago (IL)
Manhattan Coll (NY)
Mid-Continent U (KY)
National U (CA)
Neumann U (PA)
Oakland City U (IN)
Oral Roberts U (OK)
Palm Beach Atlantic U (FL)
Penn State Abington (PA)
Penn State Altoona (PA)
Penn State Beaver (PA)
Penn State Berks (PA)
Penn State Brandywine (PA)
Penn State DuBois (PA)
Penn State Erie, The Behrend Coll (PA)
Penn State Fayette, The Eberly Campus (PA)
Penn State Greater Allegheny (PA)
Penn State Harrisburg (PA)
Penn State Hazleton (PA)
Penn State Lehigh Valley (PA)
Penn State Mont Alto (PA)
Penn State New Kensington (PA)
Penn State Schuylkill (PA)
Penn State Shenango (PA)
Penn State U Park (PA)
Penn State Wilkes-Barre (PA)
Penn State Worthington Scranton (PA)
Penn State York (PA)
Pitzer Coll (CA)
Regent U (VA)
Rider U (NJ)
Robert Morris U (PA)
Roosevelt U (IL)
St. Ambrose U (IA)
Saint Joseph's U (PA)
Saint Louis U (MO)
Scripps Coll (CA)
Simpson U (CA)
Temple U (PA)
United States Military Acad (NY)
U of Cincinnati (OH)
U of Illinois at Urbana–Champaign (IL)
U of Michigan (MI)
U of Mobile (AL)
U of Nebraska at Omaha (NE)
U of North Texas (TX)
U of Oklahoma (OK)
U of St. Francis (IL)
U of the Incarnate Word (TX)
The U of Toledo (OH)
U of Tulsa (OK)
The U of Western Ontario (ON, Canada)
Waldorf Coll (IA)
Wayne State U (MI)
Woodbury U (CA)

ORGANIZATIONAL COMMUNICATION
Assumption Coll (MA)
Bloomsburg U of Pennsylvania (PA)
Bradley U (IL)
Brigham Young U (UT)
Buena Vista U (IA)
California State U, Chico (CA)
Calvin Coll (MI)
Capital U (OH)
Cedarville U (OH)
Cleveland State U (OH)
Emmanuel Coll (GA)
Fairleigh Dickinson U, Metropolitan Campus (NJ)
Florida Coll (FL)
Franklin U (OH)
George Fox U (OR)

Howard Payne U (TX)
Indiana U–Purdue U Fort Wayne (IN)
Judson U (IL)
Lindenwood U (MO)
Lipscomb U (TN)
Lubbock Christian U (TX)
Marian U (WI)
McKendree U (IL)
Missouri State U (MO)
Murray State U (KY)
North Central Coll (IL)
Northwest Missouri State U (MO)
Northwest U (WA)
Pace U (NY)
Roosevelt U (IL)
St. Francis Coll (NY)
Southeastern U (FL)
Southeast Missouri State U (MO)
Suffolk U (MA)
Tabor Coll (KS)
Temple U (PA)
Trevecca Nazarene U (TN)
The U of Akron (OH)
U of Idaho (ID)
U of Illinois at Urbana–Champaign (IL)
U of Mount Union (OH)
U of Northern Iowa (IA)
Viterbo U (WI)
Washington State U (WA)
Western Kentucky U (KY)
Western Michigan U (MI)
William Jewell Coll (MO)

ORGANIZATIONAL LEADERSHIP
Auburn U at Montgomery (AL)
California Baptist U (CA)
Central Penn Coll (PA)
Cleveland State U (OH)
Gannon U (PA)
Indiana Tech (IN)
Indiana Wesleyan U (IN)
LaGrange Coll (GA)
Lincoln Christian U (IL)
Marquette U (WI)
McNeese State U (LA)
Mid-Atlantic Christian U (NC)
Northwestern State U of Louisiana (LA)
Oral Roberts U (OK)
Point U (GA)
St. Thomas U (FL)
Southeastern Louisiana U (LA)
Spring Hill Coll (AL)
U of Evansville (IN)
U of Houston (TX)
U of Louisiana at Lafayette (LA)
U of Louisiana at Monroe (LA)
U of New Orleans (LA)
U of Wisconsin–Eau Claire (WI)
Western Kentucky U (KY)
Wheeling Jesuit U (WV)

ORNAMENTAL HORTICULTURE
California State U, Fresno (CA)
Iowa State U of Science and Technology (IA)
The Ohio State U (OH)
Tarleton State U (TX)
Texas A&M U (TX)
U of Florida (FL)
U of Illinois at Urbana–Champaign (IL)
U of the District of Columbia (DC)
U of Wisconsin–Platteville (WI)

OUTDOOR EDUCATION
Huntington U (IN)
Murray State U (KY)
Northland Coll (WI)
Sierra Nevada Coll (NV)
Unity Coll (ME)
Young Harris Coll (GA)

PACIFIC AREA/PACIFIC RIM STUDIES
Hawai'i Pacific U (HI)
U of Guam (GU)
U of Hawaii–West Oahu (HI)

PACKAGING SCIENCE
Indiana State U (IN)
Michigan State U (MI)
U of Wisconsin–Stout (WI)

PAINTING
Acad of Art U (CA)
Adams State U (CO)
Alberta Coll of Art & Design (AB, Canada)
American Acad of Art (IL)
Art Center Coll of Design (CA)
Bennington Coll (VT)
Boston U (MA)
Bowling Green State U (OH)
Bradley U (IL)
Brigham Young U (UT)
Buffalo State Coll, State U of New York (NY)
California State U, East Bay (CA)
California State U, Long Beach (CA)
Cleveland Inst of Art (OH)
Coe Coll (IA)
The Coll at Brockport, State U of New York (NY)
Colorado State U (CO)
Columbia Coll (MO)
Concordia U (QC, Canada)
Drake U (IA)
Ferris State U (MI)
Harding U (AR)
Hofstra U (NY)
Indiana U–Purdue U Fort Wayne (IN)
Indiana Wesleyan U (IN)
Inter American U of Puerto Rico, San Germán Campus (PR)
Kent State U (OH)
Lewis U (IL)
Maryland Inst Coll of Art (MD)
Marywood U (PA)
Massachusetts Coll of Art and Design (MA)
Mississippi Coll (MS)
Northern Michigan U (MI)
Northwest Nazarene U (ID)
Oakland U (MI)
Pacific Northwest Coll of Art (OR)
Pittsburg State U (KS)
Providence Coll (RI)
Rhode Island School of Design (RI)
Ringling Coll of Art and Design (FL)
Rochester Inst of Technology (NY)
Rutgers, The State U of New Jersey, New Brunswick (NJ)
Salem State U (MA)
Salve Regina U (RI)
San Francisco Art Inst (CA)
Savannah Coll of Art and Design (GA)
School of the Art Inst of Chicago (IL)
School of the Museum of Fine Arts, Boston (MA)
Seton Hill U (PA)
State U of New York at New Paltz (NY)
Syracuse U (NY)
Temple U (PA)
Texas Christian U (TX)
U of Dallas (TX)
U of Hartford (CT)
U of Houston (TX)
U of Illinois at Chicago (IL)
U of Illinois at Urbana–Champaign (IL)
The U of Iowa (IA)
The U of Kansas (KS)
U of Massachusetts Dartmouth (MA)
U of Miami (FL)
U of Missouri–St. Louis (MO)
U of Oregon (OR)
U of Regina (SK, Canada)
The U of the Arts (PA)
U of Windsor (ON, Canada)
Virginia Commonwealth U (VA)
Virginia Intermont Coll (VA)
Washington U in St. Louis (MO)
Western State Colorado U (CO)
Western Washington U (WA)
West Virginia Wesleyan Coll (WV)

PALEONTOLOGY
Bowling Green State U (OH)
Mercyhurst U (PA)

PALLIATIVE CARE NURSING
Madonna U (MI)

PAPER SCIENCE AND ENGINEERING
U of Wisconsin–Stevens Point (WI)
Western Michigan U (MI)

PARASITOLOGY
Bowling Green State U (OH)

PARKS, RECREATION AND LEISURE
Alabama State U (AL)
Alaska Pacific U (AK)
Alcorn State U (MS)
Arizona State U (AZ)
Aurora U (IL)
Bemidji State U (MN)
Bethune-Cookman U (FL)
Brevard Coll (NC)
Bridgewater State U (MA)
Brock U (ON, Canada)
California Polytechnic State U, San Luis Obispo (CA)
California State U, Chico (CA)
California State U, East Bay (CA)
California State U, Fresno (CA)
California State U, Long Beach (CA)
California State U, Northridge (CA)
Calvin Coll (MI)
Campbellsville U (KY)
Carson-Newman U (TN)
Catawba Coll (NC)
Central State U (OH)
Cheyney U of Pennsylvania (PA)
The Coll at Brockport, State U of New York (NY)
Concordia U (QC, Canada)
Dalhousie U (NS, Canada)
Dordt Coll (IA)
East Central U (OK)
Eastern Washington U (WA)
Elon U (NC)
Emporia State U (KS)
Evangel U (MO)
Ferrum Coll (VA)
Fort Lewis Coll (CO)
Frostburg State U (MD)
Georgia Coll & State U (GA)
Georgia Southern U (GA)
Gordon Coll (MA)
Graceland U (IA)
Grambling State U (LA)
Greenville Coll (IL)
Houghton Coll (NY)
Humboldt State U (CA)
Huntington U (IN)
Indiana U Bloomington (IN)
Ithaca Coll (NY)
Jacksonville State U (AL)
Johnson State Coll (VT)
Kutztown U of Pennsylvania (PA)
Lake Superior State U (MI)
Limestone Coll (SC)
Lindenwood U (MO)
Lindsey Wilson Coll (KY)
Lock Haven U of Pennsylvania (PA)
Manchester U (IN)
Mars Hill Coll (NC)
Maryville Coll (TN)
Messiah Coll (PA)
Metropolitan State U of Denver (CO)
Michigan State U (MI)
Minnesota State U Mankato (MN)
Missouri State U (MO)
Montreat Coll, Montreat (NC)
Morris Coll (SC)
Newberry Coll (SC)
New England Coll (NH)
New Mexico Highlands U (NM)
Northern Arizona U (AZ)
Northern Michigan U (MI)
North Greenville U (SC)
Northwest Nazarene U (ID)
The Ohio State U (OH)
Ohio U (OH)
Oklahoma Baptist U (OK)
Oklahoma State U (OK)
Oregon State U (OR)
Radford U (VA)
St. Andrews U (NC)
St. Thomas Aquinas Coll (NY)
Salem State U (MA)
San Diego State U (CA)
San Francisco State U (CA)
San Jose State U (CA)
Shaw U (NC)
Shepherd U (WV)

Simpson U (CA)
Southeastern Oklahoma State U (OK)
Southeast Missouri State U (MO)
Southern Connecticut State U (CT)
Southern Illinois U Carbondale (IL)
Southern Utah U (UT)
Southwest Baptist U (MO)
Spring Arbor U (MI)
State U of New York at Plattsburgh (NY)
State U of New York Coll at Cortland (NY)
Sterling Coll (VT)
Temple U (PA)
Tennessee State U (TN)
Texas A&M U (TX)
U of Georgia (GA)
U of Illinois at Urbana–Champaign (IL)
The U of Iowa (IA)
U of Maine at Machias (ME)
U of Minnesota, Duluth (MN)
U of Minnesota, Twin Cities Campus (MN)
U of Missouri (MO)
U of Nebraska at Kearney (NE)
U of Nebraska at Omaha (NE)
U of Nevada, Las Vegas (NV)
U of New Brunswick Fredericton (NB, Canada)
The U of North Carolina at Greensboro (NC)
U of Northern Iowa (IA)
U of Ottawa (ON, Canada)
U of South Alabama (AL)
The U of South Dakota (SD)
U of Southern Mississippi (MS)
The U of Toledo (OH)
U of Utah (UT)
U of Waterloo (ON, Canada)
Upper Iowa U (IA)
Utah State U (UT)
Virginia Commonwealth U (VA)
Virginia Wesleyan Coll (VA)
Wesley Coll (DE)
Western Michigan U (MI)
Western State Colorado U (CO)
Western Washington U (WA)
Westfield State U (MA)
West Virginia State U (WV)
William Jewell Coll (MO)
William Paterson U of New Jersey (NJ)
William Penn U (IA)
York Coll of Pennsylvania (PA)

PARKS, RECREATION AND LEISURE FACILITIES MANAGEMENT
Appalachian State U (NC)
Arkansas Tech U (AR)
Asbury U (KY)
Bluffton U (OH)
California State U, Chico (CA)
California State U, Fresno (CA)
Chicago State U (IL)
Clemson U (SC)
Coll of the Ozarks (MO)
Colorado State U (CO)
Concord U (WV)
East Carolina U (NC)
Eastern Illinois U (IL)
Eastern Michigan U (MI)
Eastern Washington U (WA)
Ferris State U (MI)
Florida Intl U (FL)
Franklin Pierce U (NH)
Georgia Southwestern State U (GA)
Henderson State U (AR)
Humboldt State U (CA)
Illinois State U (IL)
Indiana State U (IN)
Indiana Tech (IN)
Indiana Wesleyan U (IN)
John Brown U (AR)
Kansas State U (KS)
Kean U (NJ)
Kent State U (OH)
Keystone Coll (PA)
Lake Superior State U (MI)
Marshall U (WV)
Middle Tennessee State U (TN)
Minnesota State U Mankato (MN)
Missouri Western State U (MO)
Mount Marty Coll (SD)

New England Coll (NH)
New Mexico Highlands U (NM)
New York U (NY)
North Carolina Central U (NC)
North Carolina State U (NC)
Northwest Missouri State U (MO)
Old Dominion U (VA)
Oral Roberts U (OK)
Penn State Abington (PA)
Penn State Altoona (PA)
Penn State Beaver (PA)
Penn State Berks (PA)
Penn State Brandywine (PA)
Penn State DuBois (PA)
Penn State Erie, The Behrend Coll (PA)
Penn State Fayette, The Eberly Campus (PA)
Penn State Greater Allegheny (PA)
Penn State Hazleton (PA)
Penn State Lehigh Valley (PA)
Penn State Mont Alto (PA)
Penn State New Kensington (PA)
Penn State Schuylkill (PA)
Penn State Shenango (PA)
Penn State U Park (PA)
Penn State Wilkes-Barre (PA)
Penn State Worthington Scranton (PA)
Penn State York (PA)
Pittsburg State U (KS)
St. Joseph's Coll, Long Island Campus (NY)
St. Joseph's Coll, New York (NY)
Slippery Rock U of Pennsylvania (PA)
South Dakota State U (SD)
State U of New York Coll at Cortland (NY)
State U of New York Coll of Technology at Delhi (NY)
Texas A&M U (TX)
Texas State U–San Marcos (TX)
Thomas U (GA)
Trine U (IN)
Union Coll (KY)
Union U (TN)
The U of British Columbia (BC, Canada)
U of Delaware (DE)
U of Florida (FL)
U of Idaho (ID)
U of Maine at Machias (ME)
U of Minnesota, Crookston (MN)
U of Minnesota, Twin Cities Campus (MN)
U of Mississippi (MS)
U of New Hampshire (NH)
The U of North Carolina Wilmington (NC)
U of North Dakota (ND)
U of Northern Colorado (CO)
U of North Texas (TX)
U of St. Francis (IL)
U of Vermont (VT)
U of Waterloo (ON, Canada)
U of West Georgia (GA)
U of Wisconsin–La Crosse (WI)
Wayland Baptist U (TX)
Webber Intl U (FL)
Western Carolina U (NC)
Western Illinois U (IL)
Western Kentucky U (KY)
Western State Colorado U (CO)
West Virginia U (WV)

PARKS, RECREATION, LEISURE, AND FITNESS STUDIES RELATED
Belhaven U (MS)
Brigham Young U (UT)
The Coll at Brockport, State U of New York (NY)
Franklin Coll (IN)
Lee U (TN)
New England Coll (NH)
Plymouth State U (NH)
St. Edward's U (TX)
Trinity Christian Coll (IL)
U of North Alabama (AL)
The U of Toledo (OH)
U of Waterloo (ON, Canada)
Utah State U (UT)
Western State Colorado U (CO)

PASTORAL COUNSELING AND SPECIALIZED MINISTRIES RELATED
Greenville Coll (IL)
John Brown U (AR)
Lee U (TN)
Lipscomb U (TN)
Madonna U (MI)
Malone U (OH)
Maranatha Baptist Bible Coll (WI)
Multnomah U (OR)
Northwestern Coll (MN)
Ouachita Baptist U (AR)

PASTORAL STUDIES/ COUNSELING
The Baptist Coll of Florida (FL)
Barclay Coll (KS)
Bethel Coll (IN)
California Baptist U (CA)
Campbellsville U (KY)
Clearwater Christian Coll (FL)
Coll of Mount St. Joseph (OH)
Columbia Bible Coll (BC, Canada)
Columbia Intl U (SC)
Concordia U, Nebraska (NE)
Concordia U Wisconsin (WI)
Corban U (OR)
Cornerstone U (MI)
Crown Coll (MN)
Dominican U (IL)
East Texas Baptist U (TX)
Emmanuel Coll (GA)
Faith Baptist Bible Coll and Theological Sem (IA)
Faulkner U (AL)
Gardner-Webb U (NC)
George Fox U (OR)
Grace U (NE)
Greenville Coll (IL)
Hillsdale Free Will Baptist Coll (OK)
Houghton Coll (NY)
Indiana Wesleyan U (IN)
John Brown U (AR)
Kentucky Christian U (KY)
Kuyper Coll (MI)
Laurel U (NC)
Lee U (TN)
Lindenwood U (MO)
Loyola U Chicago (IL)
Maple Springs Baptist Bible Coll and Sem (MD)
Maranatha Baptist Bible Coll (WI)
The Master's Coll and Sem (CA)
Mount Vernon Nazarene U (OH)
Multnomah U (OR)
Newman U (KS)
Northwest Nazarene U (ID)
Northwest U (WA)
Oral Roberts U (OK)
Ouachita Baptist U (AR)
Rocky Mountain Coll (AB, Canada)
St. Gregory's U, Shawnee (OK)
Saint Joseph's Coll (IN)
St. Thomas U (FL)
San Diego Christian Coll (CA)
Simpson U (CA)
Southwest Baptist U (MO)
Spring Arbor U (MI)
Trinity Coll of Florida (FL)
Union Coll (NE)
Universidad Teolgica del Caribe (PR)
U of Saint Mary (KS)
U of St. Thomas (TX)
Walsh U (OH)
Warner Pacific Coll (OR)

PATHOLOGIST ASSISTANT
St. John's U (NY)
Wayne State U (MI)

PATHOLOGY/EXPERIMENTAL PATHOLOGY
Penn State Berks (PA)
The U of North Carolina at Chapel Hill (NC)

PEACE STUDIES AND CONFLICT RESOLUTION
Bennington Coll (VT)
Bethel U (MN)
California State U, Dominguez Hills (CA)
Chapman U (CA)
Clark U (MA)
Colgate U (NY)
Coll of Saint Benedict (MN)
Creighton U (NE)

DePaul U (IL)
DePauw U (IN)
Earlham Coll (IN)
Eastern Mennonite U (VA)
George Mason U (VA)
Gettysburg Coll (PA)
Goshen Coll (IN)
Goucher Coll (MD)
Guilford Coll (NC)
Hamline U (MN)
Hampshire Coll (MA)
Haverford Coll (PA)
John Carroll U (OH)
Juniata Coll (PA)
Kent State U (OH)
Manchester U (IN)
Manhattan Coll (NY)
Marquette U (WI)
Messiah Coll (PA)
Naropa U (CO)
Nazareth Coll of Rochester (NY)
Norwich U (VT)
Ohio Dominican U (OH)
Saint Anselm Coll (NH)
Saint John's U (MN)
Salisbury U (MD)
Swarthmore Coll (PA)
Tufts U (MA)
U of California, Berkeley (CA)
U of Missouri (MO)
The U of North Carolina at Chapel Hill (NC)
U of Ottawa (ON, Canada)
U of St. Thomas (MN)
The U of Western Ontario (ON, Canada)
U of Wisconsin–Superior (WI)
Wartburg Coll (IA)
Wellesley Coll (MA)
Whitworth U (WA)

PEDIATRIC NURSING
Youngstown State U (OH)

PERCUSSION INSTRUMENTS
Acadia U (NS, Canada)
Berklee Coll of Music (MA)
The Boston Conservatory (MA)
Five Towns Coll (NY)
Houghton Coll (NY)
Inter American U of Puerto Rico, San Germán Campus (PR)
Lawrence U (WI)
Maryville Coll (TN)
McNally Smith Coll of Music (MN)
Mount Allison U (NB, Canada)
New England Conservatory of Music (MA)
Oklahoma Christian U (OK)
Oklahoma City U (OK)
Peabody Conservatory of The Johns Hopkins U (MD)
San Francisco Conservatory of Music (CA)
State U of New York at Fredonia (NY)
Syracuse U (NY)
U of Central Oklahoma (OK)
The U of Iowa (IA)
The U of Kansas (KS)
Vanderbilt U (TN)
Xavier U of Louisiana (LA)

PERIOPERATIVE/OPERATING ROOM AND SURGICAL NURSING
Purdue U Calumet (IN)
Texas A&M Intl U (TX)

PERSONALITY PSYCHOLOGY
Pace U (NY)

PETROLEUM ENGINEERING
Colorado School of Mines (CO)
Louisiana State U and Ag and Mech Coll (LA)
Marietta Coll (OH)
Missouri U of Science and Technology (MO)
Montana Tech of The U of Montana (MT)
New Mexico Inst of Mining and Technology (NM)
Penn State Abington (PA)
Penn State Altoona (PA)
Penn State Beaver (PA)
Penn State Berks (PA)
Penn State Brandywine (PA)
Penn State DuBois (PA)

Penn State Erie, The Behrend Coll (PA)
Penn State Fayette, The Eberly Campus (PA)
Penn State Greater Allegheny (PA)
Penn State Hazleton (PA)
Penn State Lehigh Valley (PA)
Penn State Mont Alto (PA)
Penn State New Kensington (PA)
Penn State Schuylkill (PA)
Penn State Shenango (PA)
Penn State U Park (PA)
Penn State Wilkes-Barre (PA)
Penn State Worthington Scranton (PA)
Penn State York (PA)
Stanford U (CA)
Texas A&M U (TX)
Texas A&M U–Kingsville (TX)
U of Alaska Fairbanks (AK)
U of Houston (TX)
The U of Kansas (KS)
U of Louisiana at Lafayette (LA)
U of North Dakota (ND)
U of Oklahoma (OK)
U of Regina (SK, Canada)
U of Southern California (CA)
The U of Texas at Austin (TX)
The U of Texas of the Permian Basin (TX)
U of Tulsa (OK)
U of Wyoming (WY)
West Virginia U (WV)

PETROLEUM TECHNOLOGY
American U of Beirut (Lebanon)
Mercyhurst U (PA)
Nicholls State U (LA)

PHARMACEUTICAL MARKETING AND MANAGEMENT
DeSales U (PA)

PHARMACEUTICAL SCIENCES
Albany Coll of Pharmacy and Health Sciences (NY)
Belmont U (TN)
Cleveland State U (OH)
Duquesne U (PA)
U at Buffalo, the State U of New York (NY)
U of California, Irvine (CA)
U of Georgia (GA)
U of Houston (TX)
U of Michigan (MI)
U of Pittsburgh (PA)
West Virginia Wesleyan Coll (WV)

PHARMACEUTICS AND DRUG DESIGN
The Ohio State U (OH)
South Dakota State U (SD)
U of Rhode Island (RI)
The U of Toledo (OH)
West Chester U of Pennsylvania (PA)

PHARMACOLOGY
Georgia Southern U (GA)
Maryville Coll (TN)
Stony Brook U, State U of New York (NY)
The U of British Columbia (BC, Canada)
U of California, Santa Barbara (CA)
U of Ottawa (ON, Canada)
The U of Western Ontario (ON, Canada)

PHARMACOLOGY AND TOXICOLOGY
U at Buffalo, the State U of New York (NY)
U of the Sciences (PA)
The U of Western Ontario (ON, Canada)
U of Wisconsin–Madison (WI)

PHARMACOLOGY AND TOXICOLOGY RELATED
Massachusetts Coll of Pharmacy and Health Sciences (MA)

PHARMACY
Butler U (IN)
Cedarville U (OH)
The Coll of Idaho (ID)
Dalhousie U (NS, Canada)
Drake U (IA)

Illinois Inst of Technology (IL)
Lebanese American U (Lebanon)
Lipscomb U (TN)
Long Island U–Brooklyn Campus (NY)
Manchester U (IN)
Massachusetts Coll of Pharmacy and Health Sciences (MA)
Northeastern U (MA)
The Ohio State U (OH)
Presbyterian Coll (SC)
Purdue U (IN)
Rutgers, The State U of New Jersey, New Brunswick (NJ)
St. John's U (NY)
St. Louis Coll of Pharmacy (MO)
Saint Vincent Coll (PA)
South Dakota State U (SD)
The U of British Columbia (BC, Canada)
U of Delaware (DE)
The U of Iowa (IA)
The U of Kansas (KS)
U of Louisiana at Monroe (LA)
U of Minnesota, Twin Cities Campus (MN)
U of Missouri–Kansas City (MO)
U of the Sciences (PA)
The U of Toledo (OH)
U of Utah (UT)

PHARMACY ADMINISTRATION AND PHARMACY POLICY AND REGULATORY AFFAIRS
Drake U (IA)
U of Michigan (MI)

PHARMACY, PHARMACEUTICAL SCIENCES, AND ADMINISTRATION RELATED
Albany Coll of Pharmacy and Health Sciences (NY)
Dalhousie U (NS, Canada)
Duquesne U (PA)
Florida Ag and Mech U (FL)
Massachusetts Coll of Pharmacy and Health Sciences (MA)
North Dakota State U (ND)
U of Mississippi (MS)
U of Missouri–Kansas City (MO)
The U of North Carolina at Chapel Hill (NC)
U of the Sciences (PA)
The U of Toledo (OH)

PHILOSOPHY
Acadia U (NS, Canada)
Adelphi U (NY)
Agnes Scott Coll (GA)
Albertus Magnus Coll (CT)
Albion Coll (MI)
Albright Coll (PA)
Alfred U (NY)
Alma Coll (MI)
Alvernia U (PA)
Alverno Coll (WI)
American Public U System (WV)
American U (DC)
The American U in Cairo (Egypt)
American U of Beirut (Lebanon)
Amherst Coll (MA)
Anderson U (IN)
Angelo State U (TX)
Appalachian State U (NC)
Arizona State U (AZ)
Arkansas State U (AR)
Asbury U (KY)
Ashland U (OH)
Assumption Coll (MA)
Auburn U (AL)
Augsburg Coll (MN)
Augustana Coll (IL)
Augustana Coll (SD)
Austin Peay State U (TN)
Azusa Pacific U (CA)
Baker U (KS)
Baldwin Wallace U (OH)
Ball State U (IN)
Bard Coll (NY)
Barry U (FL)
Bates Coll (ME)
Baylor U (TX)
Belhaven U (MS)
Bellarmine U (KY)
Belmont U (TN)
Bemidji State U (MN)
Benedictine Coll (KS)

Benedictine U (IL)
Bennington Coll (VT)
Bentley U (MA)
Berea Coll (KY)
Bethel Coll (IN)
Bethel U (MN)
Binghamton U, State U of New York (NY)
Bloomfield Coll (NJ)
Bloomsburg U of Pennsylvania (PA)
Boise State U (ID)
Boston Coll (MA)
Boston U (MA)
Bowdoin Coll (ME)
Bowling Green State U (OH)
Bradley U (IL)
Bridgewater State U (MA)
Brock U (ON, Canada)
Brown U (RI)
Bucknell U (PA)
Buffalo State Coll, State U of New York (NY)
Butler U (IN)
Cabrini Coll (PA)
California Baptist U (CA)
California Lutheran U (CA)
California Polytechnic State U, San Luis Obispo (CA)
California State Polytechnic U, Pomona (CA)
California State U, Chico (CA)
California State U, Dominguez Hills (CA)
California State U, East Bay (CA)
California State U, Fresno (CA)
California State U, Fullerton (CA)
California State U, Long Beach (CA)
California State U, Los Angeles (CA)
California State U, Northridge (CA)
California State U, San Bernardino (CA)
California State U, Stanislaus (CA)
Calvin Coll (MI)
Canisius Coll (NY)
Capital U (OH)
Carleton Coll (MN)
Carlow U (PA)
Carnegie Mellon U (PA)
Carroll Coll (MT)
Carson-Newman U (TN)
Case Western Reserve U (OH)
Castleton State Coll (VT)
Catawba Coll (NC)
The Catholic U of America (DC)
Cedarville U (OH)
Centenary Coll of Louisiana (LA)
Central Coll (IA)
Central Connecticut State U (CT)
Central Methodist U (MO)
Central Michigan U (MI)
Centre Coll (KY)
Chapman U (CA)
Chowan U (NC)
Christendom Coll (VA)
Christian Brothers U (TN)
Christopher Newport U (VA)
City Coll of the City U of New York (NY)
Claremont McKenna Coll (CA)
Clarion U of Pennsylvania (PA)
Clark Atlanta U (GA)
Clarke U (IA)
Clark U (MA)
Clayton State U (GA)
Clemson U (SC)
Cleveland State U (OH)
Coastal Carolina U (SC)
Coe Coll (IA)
Colby Coll (ME)
Colgate U (NY)
The Coll at Brockport, State U of New York (NY)
Coll of Charleston (SC)
The Coll of Idaho (ID)
The Coll of New Jersey (NJ)
The Coll of New Rochelle (NY)
Coll of Saint Benedict (MN)
Coll of Saint Elizabeth (NJ)
The Coll of Saint Rose (NY)
Coll of Staten Island of the City U of New York (NY)
Coll of the Atlantic (ME)
Coll of the Holy Cross (MA)
The Coll of William and Mary (VA)
The Coll of Wooster (OH)

The Colorado Coll (CO)
Colorado State U (CO)
Columbia Coll (MO)
Columbia U (NY)
Columbia U, School of General Studies (NY)
Concordia Coll (MN)
Concordia Coll–New York (NY)
Concordia U (QC, Canada)
Concordia U Chicago (IL)
Connecticut Coll (CT)
Converse Coll (SC)
Cornell Coll (IA)
Covenant Coll (GA)
Creighton U (NE)
Curry Coll (MA)
Dakota Wesleyan U (SD)
Dalhousie U (NS, Canada)
Dallas Baptist U (TX)
Dartmouth Coll (NH)
Davidson Coll (NC)
DePaul U (IL)
DePauw U (IN)
DEREE—The American Coll of Greece (Greece)
DeSales U (PA)
Dickinson Coll (PA)
Doane Coll (NE)
Dominican U (IL)
Dordt Coll (IA)
Drake U (IA)
Drew U (NJ)
Drury U (MO)
Duquesne U (PA)
Earlham Coll (IN)
East Carolina U (NC)
Eastern Illinois U (IL)
Eastern Michigan U (MI)
Eastern Washington U (WA)
East Tennessee State U (TN)
Eckerd Coll (FL)
Edinboro U of Pennsylvania (PA)
Elizabethtown Coll (PA)
Elmira Coll (NY)
Elon U (NC)
Emmanuel Coll (MA)
Emory & Henry Coll (VA)
Eugene Lang Coll The New School for Liberal Arts (NY)
Excelsior Coll (NY)
Fairfield U (CT)
Fairleigh Dickinson U, Coll at Florham (NJ)
Fairleigh Dickinson U, Metropolitan Campus (NJ)
Felician Coll (NJ)
Ferrum Coll (VA)
Flagler Coll (FL)
Florida Atlantic U (FL)
Florida Gulf Coast U (FL)
Florida Intl U (FL)
Florida Southern Coll (FL)
Florida State U (FL)
Fort Lewis Coll (CO)
Franklin & Marshall Coll (PA)
Franklin Coll (IN)
Frostburg State U (MD)
Furman U (SC)
Gallaudet U (DC)
Gannon U (PA)
Geneva Coll (PA)
George Fox U (OR)
George Mason U (VA)
Georgetown Coll (KY)
Georgetown U (DC)
Georgia Coll & State U (GA)
Georgia Southern U (GA)
Georgia State U (GA)
Gettysburg Coll (PA)
Gonzaga U (WA)
Gordon Coll (MA)
Goucher Coll (MD)
Grand Valley State U (MI)
Greenville Coll (IL)
Grinnell Coll (IA)
Grove City Coll (PA)
Guilford Coll (NC)
Gustavus Adolphus Coll (MN)
Hamilton Coll (NY)
Hamline U (MN)
Hampden-Sydney Coll (VA)
Hampshire Coll (MA)
Hanover Coll (IN)
Hardin-Simmons U (TX)
Hartwick Coll (NY)
Haverford Coll (PA)
Hendrix Coll (AR)

High Point U (NC)
Hillsdale Coll (MI)
Hiram Coll (OH)
Hobart and William Smith Colls (NY)
Hofstra U (NY)
Hollins U (VA)
Holy Apostles Coll and Sem (CT)
Holy Names U (CA)
Hood Coll (MD)
Hope Coll (MI)
Houghton Coll (NY)
Howard Payne U (TX)
Humboldt State U (CA)
Hunter Coll of the City U of New York (NY)
Huntington U (IN)
Illinois Coll (IL)
Illinois State U (IL)
Illinois Wesleyan U (IL)
Indiana State U (IN)
Indiana U Bloomington (IN)
Indiana U Northwest (IN)
Indiana U of Pennsylvania (PA)
Indiana U–Purdue U Fort Wayne (IN)
Indiana U–Purdue U Indianapolis (IN)
Indiana U South Bend (IN)
Indiana U Southeast (IN)
Indiana Wesleyan U (IN)
Iona Coll (NY)
Iowa State U of Science and Technology (IA)
Ithaca Coll (NY)
John Carroll U (OH)
The Johns Hopkins U (MD)
Juniata Coll (PA)
Kalamazoo Coll (MI)
Kansas State U (KS)
Kennesaw State U (GA)
Kent State U (OH)
Kenyon Coll (OH)
King Coll (TN)
King's Coll (PA)
The King's U Coll (AB, Canada)
Knox Coll (IL)
Kutztown U of Pennsylvania (PA)
Lafayette Coll (PA)
La Salle U (PA)
Lawrence U (WI)
Lebanese American U (Lebanon)
Lebanon Valley Coll (PA)
Lee U (TN)
Lehigh U (PA)
Lehman Coll of the City U of New York (NY)
Le Moyne Coll (NY)
Lewis U (IL)
Liberty U (VA)
Lincoln Christian U (IL)
Lindenwood U (MO)
Linfield Coll (OR)
Lipscomb U (TN)
Lock Haven U of Pennsylvania (PA)
Long Island U–Brooklyn Campus (NY)
Long Island U–C. W. Post Campus (NY)
Louisiana Coll (LA)
Louisiana State U and Ag and Mech Coll (LA)
Loyola Marymount U (CA)
Loyola U Chicago (IL)
Loyola U Maryland (MD)
Loyola U New Orleans (LA)
Luther Coll (IA)
Lynchburg Coll (VA)
Macalester Coll (MN)
Malone U (OH)
Manchester U (IN)
Manhattan Coll (NY)
Manhattanville Coll (NY)
Mansfield U of Pennsylvania (PA)
Marietta Coll (OH)
Marist Coll (NY)
Marquette U (WI)
Mary Baldwin Coll (VA)
Marymount U (VA)
Maryville Coll (TN)
Marywood U (PA)
Massachusetts Coll of Liberal Arts (MA)
Massachusetts Inst of Technology (MA)
McDaniel Coll (MD)
McKendree U (IL)

Mercer U (GA)
Mercyhurst U (PA)
Merrimack Coll (MA)
Messiah Coll (PA)
Metropolitan State U of Denver (CO)
Miami U (OH)
Michigan State U (MI)
Middlebury Coll (VT)
Middle Tennessee State U (TN)
Millersville U of Pennsylvania (PA)
Millikin U (IL)
Millsaps Coll (MS)
Mills Coll (CA)
Minnesota State U Mankato (MN)
Minnesota State U Moorhead (MN)
Misericordia U (PA)
Mississippi State U (MS)
Missouri State U (MO)
Missouri U of Science and Technology (MO)
Missouri Western State U (MO)
Molloy Coll (NY)
Monmouth Coll (IL)
Montana State U (MT)
Montclair State U (NJ)
Moravian Coll (PA)
Morehead State U (KY)
Morehouse Coll (GA)
Morningside Coll (IA)
Mount Allison U (NB, Canada)
Mount Holyoke Coll (MA)
Mount Mary Coll (WI)
Mount Mercy U (IA)
Mount St. Mary's Coll (CA)
Mount St. Mary's U (MD)
Mount Vernon Nazarene U (OH)
Muhlenberg Coll (PA)
Murray State U (KY)
Nazareth Coll of Rochester (NY)
New Coll of Florida (FL)
New England Coll (NH)
New Jersey City U (NJ)
Newman U (KS)
New Mexico State U (NM)
New York U (NY)
Niagara U (NY)
North Carolina State U (NC)
North Central Coll (IL)
North Dakota State U (ND)
Northeastern Illinois U (IL)
Northeastern U (MA)
Northern Arizona U (AZ)
Northern Illinois U (IL)
Northern Michigan U (MI)
Northwestern Coll (IA)
Northwest Missouri State U (MO)
Northwest Nazarene U (ID)
Northwest U (WA)
Notre Dame de Namur U (CA)
Nova Southeastern U (FL)
Nyack Coll (NY)
Oakland U (MI)
Oglethorpe U (GA)
Ohio Dominican U (OH)
The Ohio State U (OH)
Ohio U (OH)
Ohio Wesleyan U (OH)
Oklahoma Baptist U (OK)
Oklahoma City U (OK)
Oklahoma State U (OK)
Old Dominion U (VA)
Oregon State U (OR)
Ouachita Baptist U (AR)
Pacific Lutheran U (WA)
Pacific U (OR)
Palm Beach Atlantic U (FL)
Penn State Abington (PA)
Penn State Altoona (PA)
Penn State Beaver (PA)
Penn State Berks (PA)
Penn State Brandywine (PA)
Penn State DuBois (PA)
Penn State Erie, The Behrend Coll (PA)
Penn State Fayette, The Eberly Campus (PA)
Penn State Greater Allegheny (PA)
Penn State Hazleton (PA)
Penn State Lehigh Valley (PA)
Penn State Mont Alto (PA)
Penn State New Kensington (PA)
Penn State Schuylkill (PA)
Penn State Shenango (PA)
Penn State U Park (PA)
Penn State Wilkes-Barre (PA)

Penn State Worthington Scranton (PA)
Penn State York (PA)
Pepperdine U, Malibu (CA)
Piedmont Coll (GA)
Pitzer Coll (CA)
Plymouth State U (NH)
Point Loma Nazarene U (CA)
Pomona Coll (CA)
Portland State U (OR)
Presbyterian Coll (SC)
Princeton U (NJ)
Principia Coll (IL)
Providence Coll (RI)
Purchase Coll, State U of New York (NY)
Purdue U (IN)
Purdue U Calumet (IN)
Queens U of Charlotte (NC)
Quinnipiac U (CT)
Randolph Coll (VA)
Randolph-Macon Coll (VA)
Reed Coll (OR)
Regis U (CO)
Rensselaer Polytechnic Inst (NY)
Rhode Island Coll (RI)
Rhodes Coll (TN)
Rice U (TX)
Rider U (NJ)
Ripon Coll (WI)
Roanoke Coll (VA)
Rochester Inst of Technology (NY)
Rockford Coll (IL)
Rockhurst U (MO)
Rocky Mountain Coll (MT)
Roger Williams U (RI)
Rollins Coll (FL)
Roosevelt U (IL)
Rosemont Coll (PA)
Rutgers, The State U of New Jersey, Camden (NJ)
Rutgers, The State U of New Jersey, Newark (NJ)
Rutgers, The State U of New Jersey, New Brunswick (NJ)
Sacred Heart U (CT)
St. Ambrose U (IA)
Saint Anselm Coll (NH)
St. Bonaventure U (NY)
Saint Charles Borromeo Sem, Overbrook (PA)
St. Edward's U (TX)
St. Francis Coll (NY)
St. Gregory's U, Shawnee (OK)
St. John Fisher Coll (NY)
Saint John's U (MN)
St. John's U (NY)
Saint Joseph's Coll (IN)
Saint Joseph's U (PA)
St. Lawrence U (NY)
Saint Louis U (MO)
Saint Mary's Coll (IN)
Saint Mary's Coll of California (CA)
St. Mary's Coll of Maryland (MD)
St. Mary's U (TX)
Saint Mary's U of Minnesota (MN)
Saint Michael's Coll (VT)
St. Norbert Coll (WI)
St. Olaf Coll (MN)
St. Thomas Aquinas Coll (NY)
St. Thomas U (NB, Canada)
Saint Vincent Coll (PA)
Salisbury U (MD)
Salve Regina U (RI)
Samford U (AL)
Sam Houston State U (TX)
San Diego State U (CA)
San Francisco State U (CA)
San Jose State U (CA)
Scripps Coll (CA)
Seattle Pacific U (WA)
Seattle U (WA)
Sewanee: The U of the South (TN)
Shaw U (NC)
Siena Coll (NY)
Siena Heights U (MI)
Simmons Coll (MA)
Simon Fraser U (BC, Canada)
Simpson Coll (IA)
Skidmore Coll (NY)
Slippery Rock U of Pennsylvania (PA)
Smith Coll (MA)
Sonoma State U (CA)
Southeast Missouri State U (MO)
Southern Connecticut State U (CT)
Southern Illinois U Carbondale (IL)

Southern Illinois U Edwardsville (IL)
Southern Methodist U (TX)
Southern Nazarene U (OK)
Southern Utah U (UT)
Southwestern U (TX)
Spelman Coll (GA)
Spring Arbor U (MI)
Spring Hill Coll (AL)
Stanford U (CA)
State U of New York at Fredonia (NY)
State U of New York at New Paltz (NY)
State U of New York at Oswego (NY)
State U of New York at Plattsburgh (NY)
State U of New York Coll at Cortland (NY)
State U of New York Coll at Geneseo (NY)
State U of New York Coll at Old Westbury (NY)
State U of New York Coll at Potsdam (NY)
Stephen F. Austin State U (TX)
Stetson U (FL)
Stonehill Coll (MA)
Stony Brook U, State U of New York (NY)
Suffolk U (MA)
Susquehanna U (PA)
Swarthmore Coll (PA)
Sweet Briar Coll (VA)
Syracuse U (NY)
Tabor Coll (KS)
Taylor U (IN)
Temple U (PA)
Texas A&M U (TX)
Texas Christian U (TX)
Texas Lutheran U (TX)
Texas State U–San Marcos (TX)
Thomas Edison State Coll (NJ)
Thomas More Coll (KY)
Thompson Rivers U (BC, Canada)
Transylvania U (KY)
Trent U (ON, Canada)
Trinity Christian Coll (IL)
Trinity Coll (CT)
Trinity U (TX)
Tufts U (MA)
Tulane U (LA)
Union U (TN)
Université de Sherbrooke (QC, Canada)
U at Albany, State U of New York (NY)
U at Buffalo, the State U of New York (NY)
The U of Akron (OH)
The U of Alabama (AL)
The U of Alabama at Birmingham (AL)
U of Alaska Anchorage (AK)
U of Alaska Fairbanks (AK)
The U of Arizona (AZ)
U of Arkansas at Little Rock (AR)
The U of British Columbia (BC, Canada)
The U of British Columbia–Okanagan (BC, Canada)
U of California, Berkeley (CA)
U of California, Davis (CA)
U of California, Irvine (CA)
U of California, Los Angeles (CA)
U of California, Riverside (CA)
U of California, Santa Barbara (CA)
U of California, Santa Cruz (CA)
U of Central Arkansas (AR)
U of Central Florida (FL)
U of Central Oklahoma (OK)
U of Chicago (IL)
U of Cincinnati (OH)
U of Colorado Boulder (CO)
U of Colorado Colorado Springs (CO)
U of Colorado Denver (CO)
U of Dallas (TX)
U of Delaware (DE)
U of Denver (CO)
U of Evansville (IN)
The U of Findlay (OH)
U of Florida (FL)
U of Georgia (GA)
U of Guam (GU)
U of Guelph (ON, Canada)

U of Hartford (CT)
U of Hawaii at Hilo (HI)
U of Hawaii at Manoa (HI)
U of Hawaii–West Oahu (HI)
U of Houston (TX)
U of Houston–Downtown (TX)
U of Idaho (ID)
U of Illinois at Chicago (IL)
U of Illinois at Springfield (IL)
U of Illinois at Urbana–Champaign (IL)
The U of Iowa (IA)
The U of Kansas (KS)
U of Kentucky (KY)
U of La Verne (CA)
U of Louisville (KY)
U of Maryland, Baltimore County (MD)
U of Maryland, Coll Park (MD)
U of Massachusetts Amherst (MA)
U of Massachusetts Boston (MA)
U of Massachusetts Dartmouth (MA)
U of Memphis (TN)
U of Miami (FL)
U of Michigan (MI)
U of Michigan–Dearborn (MI)
U of Michigan–Flint (MI)
U of Minnesota, Duluth (MN)
U of Minnesota, Twin Cities Campus (MN)
U of Mississippi (MS)
U of Missouri (MO)
U of Missouri–Kansas City (MO)
U of Missouri–St. Louis (MO)
U of Mount Union (OH)
U of Nebraska at Kearney (NE)
U of Nebraska at Omaha (NE)
U of Nebraska–Lincoln (NE)
U of Nevada, Las Vegas (NV)
U of Nevada, Reno (NV)
U of New Brunswick Fredericton (NB, Canada)
U of New Brunswick Saint John (NB, Canada)
U of New Hampshire (NH)
U of New Mexico (NM)
U of New Orleans (LA)
U of North Carolina at Asheville (NC)
The U of North Carolina at Chapel Hill (NC)
The U of North Carolina at Charlotte (NC)
The U of North Carolina at Greensboro (NC)
U of North Dakota (ND)
U of Northern Colorado (CO)
U of Northern Iowa (IA)
U of North Florida (FL)
U of North Texas (TX)
U of Notre Dame (IN)
U of Oklahoma (OK)
U of Oregon (OR)
U of Ottawa (ON, Canada)
U of Pennsylvania (PA)
U of Pittsburgh (PA)
U of Portland (OR)
U of Puget Sound (WA)
U of Redlands (CA)
U of Regina (SK, Canada)
U of Rhode Island (RI)
U of Richmond (VA)
U of Rochester (NY)
U of Saint Joseph (CT)
U of St. Thomas (MN)
U of St. Thomas (TX)
U of San Diego (CA)
The U of Scranton (PA)
U of South Alabama (AL)
U of South Carolina (SC)
The U of South Dakota (SD)
U of Southern California (CA)
U of Southern Indiana (IN)
U of Southern Maine (ME)
U of Southern Mississippi (MS)
U of South Florida (FL)
The U of Tampa (FL)
The U of Tennessee (TN)
The U of Tennessee at Martin (TN)
The U of Texas at Arlington (TX)
The U of Texas at Austin (TX)
The U of Texas at El Paso (TX)
The U of Texas at San Antonio (TX)
The U of Texas–Pan American (TX)
U of the Incarnate Word (TX)
U of the Ozarks (AR)

The U of Toledo (OH)
U of Tulsa (OK)
U of Utah (UT)
U of Vermont (VT)
U of Virginia (VA)
U of Waterloo (ON, Canada)
The U of Western Ontario (ON, Canada)
U of West Florida (FL)
U of West Georgia (GA)
U of Windsor (ON, Canada)
U of Wisconsin–Eau Claire (WI)
U of Wisconsin–Green Bay (WI)
U of Wisconsin–La Crosse (WI)
U of Wisconsin–Madison (WI)
U of Wisconsin–Milwaukee (WI)
U of Wisconsin–Parkside (WI)
U of Wisconsin–Platteville (WI)
U of Wisconsin–Stevens Point (WI)
U of Wyoming (WY)
Ursuline Coll (OH)
Utah State U (UT)
Utica Coll (NY)
Valdosta State U (GA)
Valparaiso U (IN)
Vanderbilt U (TN)
Vassar Coll (NY)
Villanova U (PA)
Virginia Commonwealth U (VA)
Virginia Polytechnic Inst and State U (VA)
Virginia Wesleyan Coll (VA)
Wabash Coll (IN)
Wagner Coll (NY)
Wake Forest U (NC)
Walla Walla U (WA)
Walsh U (OH)
Wartburg Coll (IA)
Washburn U (KS)
Washington & Jefferson Coll (PA)
Washington and Lee U (VA)
Washington Coll (MD)
Washington State U (WA)
Washington U in St. Louis (MO)
Wayne State U (MI)
Weber State U (UT)
Webster U (MO)
Wellesley Coll (MA)
Wells Coll (NY)
Wesleyan Coll (GA)
Wesleyan U (CT)
West Chester U of Pennsylvania (PA)
Western Carolina U (NC)
Western Illinois U (IL)
Western Michigan U (MI)
Western Oregon U (OR)
Western Washington U (WA)
Westminster Coll (MO)
Westminster Coll (UT)
West Virginia U (WV)
West Virginia Wesleyan Coll (WV)
Wheaton Coll (IL)
Wheaton Coll (MA)
Wheeling Jesuit U (WV)
Whitman Coll (WA)
Whitworth U (WA)
Wichita State U (KS)
Wilkes U (PA)
Willamette U (OR)
William Jewell Coll (MO)
William Paterson U of New Jersey (NJ)
Williams Coll (MA)
Wittenberg U (OH)
Worcester Polytechnic Inst (MA)
Wright State U (OH)
Xavier U (OH)
Xavier U of Louisiana (LA)
Yale U (CT)
York Coll of Pennsylvania (PA)
York Coll of the City U of New York (NY)
Youngstown State U (OH)

PHILOSOPHY AND RELIGIOUS STUDIES

Arizona State U (AZ)
Bethune-Cookman U (FL)
Coll of the Ozarks (MO)
Concordia Coll–New York (NY)
Dakota Wesleyan U (SD)
LaGrange Coll (GA)
Montreat Coll, Montreat (NC)
Oklahoma City U (OK)
Pace U (NY)
Paine Coll (GA)

The Richard Stockton Coll of New Jersey (NJ)
St. Andrews U (NC)
St. Joseph's Coll, Long Island Campus (NY)
St. Joseph's Coll, New York (NY)
Southwestern Coll (KS)

PHILOSOPHY AND RELIGIOUS STUDIES RELATED

Barton Coll (NC)
Berry Coll (GA)
Bethune-Cookman U (FL)
Bridgewater Coll (VA)
Buena Vista U (IA)
Claflin U (SC)
Covenant Coll (GA)
Eastern Mennonite U (VA)
The Evergreen State Coll (WA)
Florida Ag and Mech U (FL)
Friends U (KS)
Graceland U (IA)
Harrison Middleton U (AZ)
Hendrix Coll (AR)
Holy Names U (CA)
Iowa Wesleyan Coll (IA)
James Madison U (VA)
John Brown U (AR)
Juniata Coll (PA)
Lyon Coll (AR)
Mary Baldwin Coll (VA)
Marymount Manhattan Coll (NY)
Millsaps Coll (MS)
Newberry Coll (SC)
Ouachita Baptist U (AR)
Point Loma Nazarene U (CA)
Quincy U (IL)
Radford U (VA)
Roberts Wesleyan Coll (NY)
Rocky Mountain Coll (MT)
Rowan U (NJ)
Saint Joseph's Coll (IN)
Samford U (AL)
San Francisco State U (CA)
Shawnee State U (OH)
Shaw U (NC)
State U of New York at Oswego (NY)
Sterling Coll (KS)
Syracuse U (NY)
Union U (TN)
U of Maine at Farmington (ME)
U of Mary Washington (VA)
The U of North Carolina at Pembroke (NC)
The U of North Carolina Wilmington (NC)
U of Notre Dame (IN)
The U of Tennessee at Chattanooga (TN)
U of the Ozarks (AR)
Viterbo U (WI)
Washington U in St. Louis (MO)
West Virginia Wesleyan Coll (WV)
Winthrop U (SC)

PHILOSOPHY RELATED

Lewis U (IL)
Mount Vernon Nazarene U (OH)
The U of Arizona (AZ)
U of Massachusetts Boston (MA)
U of Pennsylvania (PA)
U of Regina (SK, Canada)
U of Southern California (CA)
Washington U in St. Louis (MO)
Wheeling Jesuit U (WV)

PHOTOGRAPHIC AND FILM/ VIDEO TECHNOLOGY

New England School of Communications (ME)
Rochester Inst of Technology (NY)
St. John's U (NY)
Villa Maria Coll of Buffalo (NY)

PHOTOGRAPHY

Acad of Art U (CA)
Adams State U (CO)
Alberta Coll of Art & Design (AB, Canada)
Albertus Magnus Coll (CT)
American Acad of Art (IL)
Art Center Coll of Design (CA)
Bard Coll (NY)
Barry U (FL)
Bennington Coll (VT)
Bowling Green State U (OH)
Bradley U (IL)

Bridgewater State U (MA)
Buffalo State Coll, State U of New York (NY)
California State U, East Bay (CA)
California State U, Long Beach (CA)
Carson-Newman U (TN)
Chatham U (PA)
Cleveland Inst of Art (OH)
Coe Coll (IA)
Colorado State U (CO)
Columbia Coll (MO)
Columbia Coll Chicago (IL)
Concordia U (QC, Canada)
Concordia U Wisconsin (WI)
Corcoran Coll of Art and Design (DC)
Dominican U (IL)
Eastern Mennonite U (VA)
Ferris State U (MI)
Gallaudet U (DC)
Grand Valley State U (MI)
Hampton U (VA)
Hofstra U (NY)
Indiana U–Purdue U Fort Wayne (IN)
Indiana Wesleyan U (IN)
Inter American U of Puerto Rico, San Germán Campus (PR)
Intl Acad of Design & Technology (FL)
Ithaca Coll (NY)
John Brown U (AR)
King Coll (TN)
Long Island U–C. W. Post Campus (NY)
Maryland Inst Coll of Art (MD)
Marymount Manhattan Coll (NY)
Marywood U (PA)
Massachusetts Coll of Art and Design (MA)
Moore Coll of Art & Design (PA)
Morningside Coll (IA)
Mount Allison U (NB, Canada)
New England Coll (NH)
New York U (NY)
Northern Arizona U (AZ)
Northern Michigan U (MI)
Oakland U (MI)
Ohio U (OH)
Otis Coll of Art and Design (CA)
Pacific Northwest Coll of Art (OR)
Pacific Union Coll (CA)
Paier Coll of Art, Inc. (CT)
Parsons The New School for Design (NY)
Pennsylvania Coll of Art & Design (PA)
Point Park U (PA)
Prescott Coll (AZ)
Purchase Coll, State U of New York (NY)
Rhode Island School of Design (RI)
Ringling Coll of Art and Design (FL)
Rivier U (NH)
Rutgers, The State U of New Jersey, New Brunswick (NJ)
Sage Coll of Albany (NY)
St. Edward's U (TX)
St. John's U (NY)
Salem State U (MA)
Salve Regina U (RI)
Sam Houston State U (TX)
San Francisco Art Inst (CA)
Santa Fe U of Art and Design (NM)
Savannah Coll of Art and Design (GA)
School of the Art Inst of Chicago (IL)
School of the Museum of Fine Arts, Boston (MA)
Seattle U (WA)
State U of New York at New Paltz (NY)
Syracuse U (NY)
Temple U (PA)
Texas A&M U–Commerce (TX)
Texas Christian U (TX)
Texas State U–San Marcos (TX)
Thomas Edison State Coll (NJ)
The U of Akron (OH)
U of Central Florida (FL)
U of Central Oklahoma (OK)
U of Hartford (CT)
U of Houston (TX)

U of Illinois at Chicago (IL)
U of Illinois at Urbana–Champaign (IL)
The U of Iowa (IA)
U of La Verne (CA)
U of Massachusetts Dartmouth (MA)
U of Miami (FL)
U of Missouri–St. Louis (MO)
U of Nebraska at Omaha (NE)
U of Oregon (OR)
The U of the Arts (PA)
Virginia Commonwealth U (VA)
Virginia Intermont Coll (VA)
Washington U in St. Louis (MO)
Watkins Coll of Art, Design, & Film (TN)
Weber State U (UT)
Webster U (MO)
Western State Colorado U (CO)
Western Washington U (WA)
Youngstown State U (OH)

PHOTOJOURNALISM
Bradley U (IL)
Central Michigan U (MI)
Corcoran Coll of Art and Design (DC)
Hawai'i Pacific U (HI)
Kent State U (OH)
Ohio U (OH)
Pittsburg State U (KS)
Point Park U (PA)
Rochester Inst of Technology (NY)
St. John's U (NY)
Sierra Nevada Coll (NV)
U of Miami (FL)
U of Missouri (MO)
Walla Walla U (WA)
Western Kentucky U (KY)

PHYSICAL AND BIOLOGICAL ANTHROPOLOGY
The U of Western Ontario (ON, Canada)

PHYSICAL CHEMISTRY
Rice U (TX)
The U of Western Ontario (ON, Canada)

PHYSICAL EDUCATION TEACHING AND COACHING
Adams State U (CO)
Adelphi U (NY)
Alabama State U (AL)
Alderson-Broaddus Coll (WV)
Alice Lloyd Coll (KY)
Alma Coll (MI)
American U of Puerto Rico (PR)
Anderson U (IN)
Anderson U (SC)
Appalachian State U (NC)
Arkansas State U (AR)
Arkansas Tech U (AR)
Armstrong Atlantic State U (GA)
Asbury U (KY)
Athens State U (AL)
Auburn U (AL)
Augsburg Coll (MN)
Augustana Coll (SD)
Aurora U (IL)
Averett U (VA)
Azusa Pacific U (CA)
Ball State U (IN)
Barry U (FL)
Barton Coll (NC)
Baylor U (TX)
Belmont U (TN)
Bemidji State U (MN)
Benedictine Coll (KS)
Benedictine U (IL)
Berry Coll (GA)
Bethany Coll (WV)
Bethel Coll (IN)
Bethel U (MN)
Bethune-Cookman U (FL)
Blackburn Coll (IL)
Bluefield Coll (VA)
Blue Mountain Coll (MS)
Boise State U (ID)
Boston U (MA)
Bowling Green State U (OH)
Bridgewater Coll (VA)
Bridgewater State U (MA)
Brock U (ON, Canada)
Buena Vista U (IA)
Cairn U (PA)

California Lutheran U (CA)
California State U, Chico (CA)
California State U, East Bay (CA)
California State U, Fresno (CA)
California State U, Long Beach (CA)
California State U, San Bernardino (CA)
California State U, Stanislaus (CA)
Calvin Coll (MI)
Cameron U (OK)
Campbellsville U (KY)
Canisius Coll (NY)
Capital U (OH)
Caribbean U (PR)
Carroll Coll (MT)
Carson-Newman U (TN)
Castleton State Coll (VT)
Catawba Coll (NC)
Cedarville U (OH)
Central Connecticut State U (CT)
Central Methodist U (MO)
Chicago State U (IL)
Chowan U (NC)
The Citadel, The Military Coll of South Carolina (SC)
Clarke U (IA)
Clearwater Christian Coll (FL)
Coastal Carolina U (SC)
Coe Coll (IA)
The Coll at Brockport, State U of New York (NY)
Coll of Charleston (SC)
The Coll of Idaho (ID)
The Coll of New Jersey (NJ)
Coll of the Ozarks (MO)
Columbus State U (GA)
Concordia Coll (MN)
Concordia U (OR)
Concordia U Chicago (IL)
Concordia U, Nebraska (NE)
Concordia U, St. Paul (MN)
Concordia U Wisconsin (WI)
Concord U (WV)
Corban U (OR)
Cornell Coll (IA)
Cornerstone U (MI)
Crown Coll (MN)
Culver-Stockton Coll (MO)
Dakota State U (SD)
Dakota Wesleyan U (SD)
Dallas Baptist U (TX)
Defiance Coll (OH)
Delta State U (MS)
DePaul U (IL)
DePauw U (IN)
Doane Coll (NE)
Dordt Coll (IA)
Drury U (MO)
East Carolina U (NC)
East Central U (OK)
Eastern Mennonite U (VA)
Eastern Michigan U (MI)
Eastern New Mexico U (NM)
East Texas Baptist U (TX)
Elizabeth City State U (NC)
Elon U (NC)
Endicott Coll (MA)
Evangel U (MO)
Fairmont State U (WV)
Faulkner U (AL)
Fayetteville State U (NC)
Florida Ag and Mech U (FL)
Florida Intl U (FL)
Florida Southern Coll (FL)
Fort Lewis Coll (CO)
Franklin Coll (IN)
Friends U (KS)
Frostburg State U (MD)
Gallaudet U (DC)
Gardner-Webb U (NC)
George Mason U (VA)
Georgia Regents U (GA)
Georgia Southern U (GA)
Georgia Southwestern State U (GA)
Georgia State U (GA)
Gettysburg Coll (PA)
Gonzaga U (WA)
Goshen Coll (IN)
Graceland U (IA)
Grambling State U (LA)
Grand Valley State U (MI)
Grand View U (IA)
Greenville Coll (IL)
Gustavus Adolphus Coll (MN)
Hampton U (VA)

Hardin-Simmons U (TX)
Henderson State U (AR)
High Point U (NC)
Hillsdale Coll (MI)
Hofstra U (NY)
Hope Coll (MI)
Houghton Coll (NY)
Howard Payne U (TX)
Humboldt State U (CA)
Hunter Coll of the City U of New York (NY)
Huntingdon Coll (AL)
Huntington U (IN)
Husson U (ME)
Illinois Coll (IL)
Illinois State U (IL)
Indiana State U (IN)
Indiana Tech (IN)
Indiana Wesleyan U (IN)
Inter American U of Puerto Rico, Aguadilla Campus (PR)
Inter American U of Puerto Rico, San Germán Campus (PR)
Iowa Wesleyan Coll (IA)
Ithaca Coll (NY)
Jacksonville State U (AL)
Jamestown Coll (ND)
Jarvis Christian Coll (TX)
John Carroll U (OH)
Johnson State Coll (VT)
Judson U (IL)
Kansas Wesleyan U (KS)
Kean U (NJ)
Keene State Coll (NH)
Kennesaw State U (GA)
Kent State U (OH)
Kentucky State U (KY)
Kentucky Wesleyan Coll (KY)
King Coll (TN)
Lamar U (TX)
Lander U (SC)
Lane Coll (TN)
Langston U (OK)
Lees-McRae Coll (NC)
LeTourneau U (TX)
Lewis-Clark State Coll (ID)
Limestone Coll (SC)
Lincoln Memorial U (TN)
Lincoln U (PA)
Lindenwood U (MO)
Lindsey Wilson Coll (KY)
Lipscomb U (TN)
Lock Haven U of Pennsylvania (PA)
Long Island U–Brooklyn Campus (NY)
Long Island U–C. W. Post Campus (NY)
Louisiana Coll (LA)
Louisiana State U and Ag and Mech Coll (LA)
Lubbock Christian U (TX)
Madonna U (MI)
Malone U (OH)
Manchester U (IN)
Manhattan Coll (NY)
Maranatha Baptist Bible Coll (WI)
Marshall U (WV)
Mars Hill Coll (NC)
Maryville Coll (TN)
The Master's Coll and Sem (CA)
Mayville State U (ND)
McKendree U (IL)
McMurry U (TX)
McNeese State U (LA)
Messiah Coll (PA)
Michigan State U (MI)
Millikin U (IL)
Minnesota State U Mankato (MN)
Minnesota State U Moorhead (MN)
Minot State U (ND)
Mississippi Coll (MS)
Mississippi State U (MS)
Mississippi Valley State U (MS)
Missouri Baptist U (MO)
Missouri State U (MO)
Monmouth Coll (IL)
Montclair State U (NJ)
Morehead State U (KY)
National U (CA)
New England Coll (NH)
New Mexico Highlands U (NM)
New Mexico State U (NM)
Nicholls State U (LA)
North Carolina Central U (NC)
North Central Coll (IL)
North Dakota State U (ND)
Northeastern Illinois U (IL)

Northern Illinois U (IL)
Northern Michigan U (MI)
Northern State U (SD)
Northwestern Coll (IA)
Northwestern Coll (MN)
Northwestern Oklahoma State U (OK)
Northwestern State U of Louisiana (LA)
Northwest Missouri State U (MO)
Northwest Nazarene U (ID)
Norwich U (VT)
Oakland City U (IN)
The Ohio State U (OH)
Ohio U (OH)
Ohio Valley U (WV)
Ohio Wesleyan U (OH)
Oklahoma Baptist U (OK)
Oklahoma Christian U (OK)
Oklahoma City U (OK)
Oklahoma State U (OK)
Old Dominion U (VA)
Oral Roberts U (OK)
Ouachita Baptist U (AR)
Pacific Union Coll (CA)
Palm Beach Atlantic U (FL)
Paul Quinn Coll (TX)
Pepperdine U, Malibu (CA)
Pittsburg State U (KS)
Purdue U (IN)
Quincy U (IL)
Radford U (VA)
Rhode Island Coll (RI)
Ripon Coll (WI)
Roanoke Coll (VA)
Roberts Wesleyan Coll (NY)
Rockford Coll (IL)
Rocky Mountain Coll (MT)
Rowan U (NJ)
Sage Coll of Albany (NY)
Saginaw Valley State U (MI)
St. Ambrose U (IA)
St. Andrews U (NC)
St. Bonaventure U (NY)
St. Edward's U (TX)
St. Francis Coll (NY)
Salem Intl U (WV)
Salem State U (MA)
Salisbury U (MD)
Samford U (AL)
San Diego Christian Coll (CA)
San Francisco State U (CA)
Schreiner U (TX)
Shenandoah U (VA)
Simpson Coll (IA)
Slippery Rock U of Pennsylvania (PA)
Sonoma State U (CA)
Southeastern Louisiana U (LA)
Southeastern Oklahoma State U (OK)
Southeast Missouri State U (MO)
Southern Arkansas U–Magnolia (AR)
Southern Illinois U Carbondale (IL)
Southern Illinois U Edwardsville (IL)
Southern Nazarene U (OK)
Southern Oregon U (OR)
Southwest Baptist U (MO)
Southwestern Coll (KS)
Spring Arbor U (MI)
State U of New York Coll at Cortland (NY)
Sterling Coll (KS)
Sul Ross State U (TX)
Syracuse U (NY)
Tabor Coll (KS)
Tarleton State U (TX)
Tennessee State U (TN)
Texas A&M Intl U (TX)
Texas Christian U (TX)
Texas Lutheran U (TX)
Transylvania U (KY)
Trevecca Nazarene U (TN)
Trine U (IN)
Trinity Christian Coll (IL)
Union Coll (KY)
Union Coll (NE)
Union U (TN)
Université de Sherbrooke (QC, Canada)
The U of Akron (OH)
The U of Alabama (AL)
The U of Alabama at Birmingham (AL)
U of Alaska Anchorage (AK)

U of Central Arkansas (AR)
U of Central Florida (FL)
U of Central Oklahoma (OK)
The U of Findlay (OH)
U of Great Falls (MT)
U of Guam (GU)
U of Idaho (ID)
U of Illinois at Urbana–Champaign (IL)
The U of Kansas (KS)
U of Kentucky (KY)
U of Louisiana at Lafayette (LA)
U of Louisiana at Monroe (LA)
U of Maryland, Coll Park (MD)
U of Maryland Eastern Shore (MD)
U of Memphis (TN)
U of Michigan (MI)
U of Minnesota, Duluth (MN)
U of Minnesota, Twin Cities Campus (MN)
U of Missouri–St. Louis (MO)
The U of Montana Western (MT)
U of Mount Union (OH)
U of Nebraska at Kearney (NE)
U of Nebraska–Lincoln (NE)
U of Nevada, Las Vegas (NV)
U of New Brunswick Fredericton (NB, Canada)
U of New Mexico (NM)
The U of North Carolina at Greensboro (NC)
The U of North Carolina at Pembroke (NC)
The U of North Carolina Wilmington (NC)
U of North Dakota (ND)
U of Northern Iowa (IA)
U of North Florida (FL)
U of North Georgia (GA)
U of Pittsburgh (PA)
U of Pittsburgh at Bradford (PA)
U of Regina (SK, Canada)
U of St. Thomas (MN)
U of South Alabama (AL)
U of South Carolina (SC)
U of South Carolina Upstate (SC)
The U of South Dakota (SD)
U of Southern Indiana (IN)
U of Southern Mississippi (MS)
U of South Florida (FL)
U of the Cumberlands (KY)
U of the District of Columbia (DC)
U of the Incarnate Word (TX)
U of the Ozarks (AR)
The U of Toledo (OH)
U of Vermont (VT)
The U of West Alabama (AL)
U of West Georgia (GA)
U of Windsor (ON, Canada)
U of Wisconsin–Platteville (WI)
U of Wisconsin–Stevens Point (WI)
U of Wisconsin–Superior (WI)
U of Wyoming (WY)
Upper Iowa U (IA)
Utah State U (UT)
Valdosta State U (GA)
Valley City State U (ND)
Valparaiso U (IN)
Virginia Intermont Coll (VA)
Virginia State U (VA)
Walla Walla U (WA)
Walsh U (OH)
Warner Pacific Coll (OR)
Wartburg Coll (IA)
Washburn U (KS)
Washington State U (WA)
Wayland Baptist U (TX)
Wayne State Coll (NE)
Wayne State U (MI)
Weber State U (UT)
Wesley Coll (DE)
Western Carolina U (NC)
Western Illinois U (IL)
Western Kentucky U (KY)
Western Michigan U (MI)
Western State Colorado U (CO)
Western Washington U (WA)
West Liberty U (WV)
Westminster Coll (MO)
West Virginia State U (WV)
West Virginia U (WV)
West Virginia U Inst of Technology (WV)
West Virginia Wesleyan Coll (WV)
Whitworth U (WA)
William Jewell Coll (MO)

William Paterson U of New Jersey (NJ)
William Penn U (IA)
Winthrop U (SC)
Wright State U (OH)
Xavier U of Louisiana (LA)
York Coll of the City U of New York (NY)
Youngstown State U (OH)

PHYSICAL FITNESS TECHNICIAN
Trevecca Nazarene U (TN)

PHYSICAL SCIENCES
Anderson U (IN)
Arizona State U (AZ)
Arkansas Tech U (AR)
Auburn U at Montgomery (AL)
Bemidji State U (MN)
Bennington Coll (VT)
Bethany Lutheran Coll (MN)
Brock U (ON, Canada)
California State U, East Bay (CA)
California State U, Stanislaus (CA)
Calvin Coll (MI)
Chowan U (NC)
Christian Brothers U (TN)
Coe Coll (IA)
Colgate U (NY)
Colorado Mesa U (CO)
Concordia U Chicago (IL)
Concordia U, Nebraska (NE)
Dakota State U (SD)
Defiance Coll (OH)
Doane Coll (NE)
Emporia State U (KS)
The Evergreen State Coll (WA)
Florida Inst of Technology (FL)
Graceland U (IA)
Hampshire Coll (MA)
Hampton U (VA)
Juniata Coll (PA)
Kansas State U (KS)
Keene State Coll (NH)
La Sierra U (CA)
Linfield Coll (OR)
Long Island U–Brooklyn Campus (NY)
The Master's Coll and Sem (CA)
Michigan State U (MI)
Midwestern State U (TX)
Minnesota State U Mankato (MN)
Minot State U (ND)
Mississippi U for Women (MS)
Montana Tech of The U of Montana (MT)
Mount Vernon Nazarene U (OH)
Muhlenberg Coll (PA)
New Mexico Inst of Mining and Technology (NM)
Northwestern State U of Louisiana (LA)
Penn State Erie, The Behrend Coll (PA)
Ripon Coll (WI)
Roger Williams U (RI)
Rowan U (NJ)
St. John's U (NY)
Saint Michael's Coll (VT)
Saint Vincent Coll (PA)
San Diego State U (CA)
San Francisco State U (CA)
Seattle Pacific U (WA)
Southern Nazarene U (OK)
Southern Utah U (UT)
Southwestern U (TX)
Suffolk U (MA)
Texas A&M Intl U (TX)
Trent U (ON, Canada)
Trine U (IN)
Troy U (AL)
United States Military Acad (NY)
United States Naval Acad (MD)
U of California, Berkeley (CA)
U of California, Riverside (CA)
U of Chicago (IL)
U of Guelph (ON, Canada)
U of Houston–Clear Lake (TX)
U of Maryland, Coll Park (MD)
U of Minnesota, Twin Cities Campus (MN)
U of North Dakota (ND)
U of Ottawa (ON, Canada)
U of Pittsburgh (PA)
U of Pittsburgh at Bradford (PA)
U of Southern California (CA)
U of Southern Maine (ME)

The U of Toledo (OH)
U of Utah (UT)
U of Wisconsin–Superior (WI)
U of Wyoming (WY)
Villanova U (PA)
Warner Pacific Coll (OR)
Washburn U (KS)
Washington State U (WA)
Wesleyan Coll (GA)
Western Kentucky U (KY)
Westfield State U (MA)
William Paterson U of New Jersey (NJ)
Worcester State U (MA)

PHYSICAL SCIENCES RELATED
Bowling Green State U (OH)
Cedar Crest Coll (PA)
Central Connecticut State U (CT)
The Coll of St. Scholastica (MN)
Covenant Coll (GA)
Eastern Michigan U (MI)
George Mason U (VA)
John Brown U (AR)
Morehouse Coll (GA)
Rochester Inst of Technology (NY)
Stony Brook U, State U of New York (NY)
U of California, Davis (CA)
U of Mary Washington (VA)
U of North Alabama (AL)
The U of North Carolina at Chapel Hill (NC)
U of the Ozarks (AR)
U of Utah (UT)
Wayne State U (MI)
Worcester Polytechnic Inst (MA)
Xavier U (OH)

PHYSICAL THERAPY
Andrews U (MI)
Armstrong Atlantic State U (GA)
Bellarmine U (KY)
Bowling Green State U (OH)
California State U, Fresno (CA)
Chicago State U (IL)
Coll of Saint Benedict (MN)
Concordia U (QC, Canada)
Concordia U Wisconsin (WI)
Dalhousie U (NS, Canada)
Dominican U (IL)
Duquesne U (PA)
Grand Valley State U (MI)
Gustavus Adolphus Coll (MN)
Hampton U (VA)
Hawai`i Pacific U (HI)
Husson U (ME)
Ithaca Coll (NY)
Keystone Coll (PA)
Langston U (OK)
Long Island U–Brooklyn Campus (NY)
Loyola U Chicago (IL)
Maryville U of Saint Louis (MO)
Mount Saint Mary Coll (NY)
Mount Vernon Nazarene U (OH)
Nazareth Coll of Rochester (NY)
Neumann U (PA)
New York Inst of Technology (NY)
Northeastern U (MA)
Northern Illinois U (IL)
Northwest Nazarene U (ID)
Quinnipiac U (CT)
Sacred Heart U (CT)
Saint John's U (MN)
Saint Vincent Coll (PA)
Simmons Coll (MA)
Tarleton State U (TX)
Tennessee State U (TN)
Thompson Rivers U (BC, Canada)
The U of Akron (OH)
The U of Findlay (OH)
U of Hartford (CT)
U of Maryland Eastern Shore (MD)
U of Minnesota, Twin Cities Campus (MN)
U of North Dakota (ND)
U of Ottawa (ON, Canada)
The U of Scranton (PA)
The U of Tennessee at Chattanooga (TN)
U of the Sciences (PA)
The U of Toledo (OH)
U of Utah (UT)
The U of Western Ontario (ON, Canada)
Wichita State U (KS)

PHYSICIAN ASSISTANT
Augsburg Coll (MN)
Butler U (IN)
City Coll of the City U of New York (NY)
Cleveland State U (OH)
DeSales U (PA)
Duquesne U (PA)
Gannon U (PA)
Grand Valley State U (MI)
Hofstra U (NY)
Long Island U–Brooklyn Campus (NY)
New York Inst of Technology (NY)
Pennsylvania Coll of Technology (PA)
Philadelphia U (PA)
Quinnipiac U (CT)
Rochester Inst of Technology (NY)
St. Francis Coll (NY)
St. John's U (NY)
Saint Vincent Coll (PA)
Seton Hill U (PA)
Southern Illinois U Carbondale (IL)
Union Coll (NE)
U of Kentucky (KY)
The U of South Dakota (SD)
U of the Sciences (PA)
U of Wisconsin–Parkside (WI)
Wagner Coll (NY)
York Coll of the City U of New York (NY)

PHYSICS
Abilene Christian U (TX)
Acadia U (NS, Canada)
Adams State U (CO)
Adelphi U (NY)
Agnes Scott Coll (GA)
Albion Coll (MI)
Albright Coll (PA)
Alfred U (NY)
Alma Coll (MI)
American U (DC)
The American U in Cairo (Egypt)
American U of Beirut (Lebanon)
Amherst Coll (MA)
Anderson U (IN)
Andrews U (MI)
Angelo State U (TX)
Appalachian State U (NC)
Arizona State U (AZ)
Arkansas State U (AR)
Arkansas Tech U (AR)
Armstrong Atlantic State U (GA)
Ashland U (OH)
Auburn U (AL)
Augsburg Coll (MN)
Augustana Coll (IL)
Augustana Coll (SD)
Austin Peay State U (TN)
Azusa Pacific U (CA)
Baker U (KS)
Baldwin Wallace U (OH)
Ball State U (IN)
Bard Coll (NY)
Bates Coll (ME)
Baylor U (TX)
Bellarmine U (KY)
Belmont U (TN)
Bemidji State U (MN)
Benedictine Coll (KS)
Benedictine U (IL)
Bennington Coll (VT)
Berea Coll (KY)
Berry Coll (GA)
Bethel U (MN)
Binghamton U, State U of New York (NY)
Bloomsburg U of Pennsylvania (PA)
Bluffton U (OH)
Bob Jones U (SC)
Boise State U (ID)
Boston Coll (MA)
Boston U (MA)
Bowdoin Coll (ME)
Bowling Green State U (OH)
Bradley U (IL)
Bridgewater Coll (VA)
Bridgewater State U (MA)
Brock U (ON, Canada)
Brown U (RI)
Bucknell U (PA)
Buena Vista U (IA)
Buffalo State Coll, State U of New York (NY)
Butler U (IN)

California Lutheran U (CA)
California Polytechnic State U, San Luis Obispo (CA)
California State Polytechnic U, Pomona (CA)
California State U, Chico (CA)
California State U, Dominguez Hills (CA)
California State U, East Bay (CA)
California State U, Fresno (CA)
California State U, Fullerton (CA)
California State U, Long Beach (CA)
California State U, Los Angeles (CA)
California State U, Northridge (CA)
California State U, San Bernardino (CA)
California State U, Stanislaus (CA)
Calvin Coll (MI)
Cameron U (OK)
Canisius Coll (NY)
Carleton Coll (MN)
Carnegie Mellon U (PA)
Carroll Coll (MT)
Carson-Newman U (TN)
The Catholic U of America (DC)
Cedarville U (OH)
Central Coll (IA)
Central Connecticut State U (CT)
Central Methodist U (MO)
Central Michigan U (MI)
Centre Coll (KY)
Chatham U (PA)
Chicago State U (IL)
Christian Brothers U (TN)
The Citadel, The Military Coll of South Carolina (SC)
City Coll of the City U of New York (NY)
Claremont McKenna Coll (CA)
Clarion U of Pennsylvania (PA)
Clark Atlanta U (GA)
Clarkson U (NY)
Clark U (MA)
Clemson U (SC)
Cleveland State U (OH)
Coastal Carolina U (SC)
Coe Coll (IA)
Colby Coll (ME)
Colgate U (NY)
The Coll at Brockport, State U of New York (NY)
Coll of Charleston (SC)
The Coll of Idaho (ID)
The Coll of New Jersey (NJ)
Coll of Saint Benedict (MN)
Coll of Staten Island of the City U of New York (NY)
Coll of the Holy Cross (MA)
The Coll of William and Mary (VA)
The Coll of Wooster (OH)
The Colorado Coll (CO)
Colorado State U (CO)
Columbia U (NY)
Columbia U, School of General Studies (NY)
Concordia Coll (MN)
Concordia U (QC, Canada)
Cornell Coll (IA)
Covenant Coll (GA)
Creighton U (NE)
Curry Coll (MA)
Dalhousie U (NS, Canada)
Dartmouth Coll (NH)
Davidson Coll (NC)
DePaul U (IL)
DePauw U (IN)
Dickinson Coll (PA)
Dillard U (LA)
Doane Coll (NE)
Dordt Coll (IA)
Drake U (IA)
Drew U (NJ)
Drury U (MO)
Duquesne U (PA)
Earlham Coll (IN)
East Carolina U (NC)
East Central U (OK)
Eastern Illinois U (IL)
Eastern Michigan U (MI)
Eastern Washington U (WA)
East Tennessee State U (TN)
Eckerd Coll (FL)
Edinboro U of Pennsylvania (PA)
Elizabeth City State U (NC)
Elizabethtown Coll (PA)

Elon U (NC)
Emory & Henry Coll (VA)
Emporia State U (KS)
Excelsior Coll (NY)
Fairfield U (CT)
Fairleigh Dickinson U, Metropolitan Campus (NJ)
Florida Ag and Mech U (FL)
Florida Atlantic U (FL)
Florida Inst of Technology (FL)
Florida Intl U (FL)
Florida State U (FL)
Francis Marion U (SC)
Franklin & Marshall Coll (PA)
Frostburg State U (MD)
Furman U (SC)
Geneva Coll (PA)
George Mason U (VA)
Georgetown Coll (KY)
Georgetown U (DC)
Georgia Coll & State U (GA)
Georgia Regents U (GA)
Georgia Southern U (GA)
Georgia State U (GA)
Gettysburg Coll (PA)
Gonzaga U (WA)
Gordon Coll (MA)
Goshen Coll (IN)
Goucher Coll (MD)
Grambling State U (LA)
Grand Valley State U (MI)
Greenville Coll (IL)
Grinnell Coll (IA)
Grove City Coll (PA)
Guilford Coll (NC)
Gustavus Adolphus Coll (MN)
Hamilton Coll (NY)
Hamline U (MN)
Hampden-Sydney Coll (VA)
Hampshire Coll (MA)
Hampton U (VA)
Hanover Coll (IN)
Harding U (AR)
Hardin-Simmons U (TX)
Hartwick Coll (NY)
Harvey Mudd Coll (CA)
Haverford Coll (PA)
Henderson State U (AR)
Hendrix Coll (AR)
High Point U (NC)
Hillsdale Coll (MI)
Hiram Coll (OH)
Hobart and William Smith Colls (NY)
Hofstra U (NY)
Hollins U (VA)
Hope Coll (MI)
Houghton Coll (NY)
Humboldt State U (CA)
Hunter Coll of the City U of New York (NY)
Illinois Coll (IL)
Illinois Inst of Technology (IL)
Illinois State U (IL)
Illinois Wesleyan U (IL)
Indiana State U (IN)
Indiana U Bloomington (IN)
Indiana U of Pennsylvania (PA)
Indiana U–Purdue U Fort Wayne (IN)
Indiana U–Purdue U Indianapolis (IN)
Indiana U South Bend (IN)
Iona Coll (NY)
Iowa State U of Science and Technology (IA)
Ithaca Coll (NY)
Jacksonville State U (AL)
James Madison U (VA)
John Carroll U (OH)
The Johns Hopkins U (MD)
Juniata Coll (PA)
Kalamazoo Coll (MI)
Kansas State U (KS)
Kansas Wesleyan U (KS)
Kent State U (OH)
Kentucky Wesleyan Coll (KY)
Kenyon Coll (OH)
King Coll (TN)
King's Coll (PA)
Knox Coll (IL)
Kutztown U of Pennsylvania (PA)
Lafayette Coll (PA)
Lamar U (TX)
Lane Coll (TN)
Lawrence Technological U (MI)
Lawrence U (WI)

Lebanon Valley Coll (PA)
Lehigh U (PA)
Lehman Coll of the City U of New York (NY)
Le Moyne Coll (NY)
Lewis U (IL)
Lincoln U (MO)
Linfield Coll (OR)
Lipscomb U (TN)
Lock Haven U of Pennsylvania (PA)
Long Island U–Brooklyn Campus (NY)
Long Island U–C. W. Post Campus (NY)
Longwood U (VA)
Louisiana Coll (LA)
Louisiana State U and Ag and Mech Coll (LA)
Louisiana State U in Shreveport (LA)
Loyola Marymount U (CA)
Loyola U Chicago (IL)
Loyola U Maryland (MD)
Loyola U New Orleans (LA)
Luther Coll (IA)
Lynchburg Coll (VA)
Macalester Coll (MN)
Manchester U (IN)
Manhattan Coll (NY)
Manhattanville Coll (NY)
Mansfield U of Pennsylvania (PA)
Marietta Coll (OH)
Marquette U (WI)
Marshall U (WV)
Mary Baldwin Coll (VA)
Massachusetts Coll of Liberal Arts (MA)
Massachusetts Inst of Technology (MA)
McDaniel Coll (MD)
McMurry U (TX)
Mercer U (GA)
Merrimack Coll (MA)
Messiah Coll (PA)
Metropolitan State U of Denver (CO)
Miami U (OH)
Michigan State U (MI)
Middlebury Coll (VT)
Middle Tennessee State U (TN)
Midwestern State U (TX)
Millersville U of Pennsylvania (PA)
Millikin U (IL)
Millsaps Coll (MS)
Minnesota State U Mankato (MN)
Minnesota State U Moorhead (MN)
Minot State U (ND)
Mississippi Coll (MS)
Mississippi State U (MS)
Missouri State U (MO)
Missouri U of Science and Technology (MO)
Monmouth Coll (IL)
Montana State U (MT)
Montclair State U (NJ)
Moravian Coll (PA)
Morehead State U (KY)
Morehouse Coll (GA)
Morningside Coll (IA)
Mount Allison U (NB, Canada)
Mount Holyoke Coll (MA)
Mount Vernon Nazarene U (OH)
Muhlenberg Coll (PA)
Murray State U (KY)
New Coll of Florida (FL)
New Jersey City U (NJ)
New Jersey Inst of Technology (NJ)
New Mexico Highlands U (NM)
New Mexico Inst of Mining and Technology (NM)
New Mexico State U (NM)
New York Inst of Technology (NY)
New York U (NY)
Norfolk State U (VA)
North Carolina Central U (NC)
North Carolina State U (NC)
North Central Coll (IL)
North Dakota State U (ND)
Northeastern Illinois U (IL)
Northeastern U (MA)
Northern Arizona U (AZ)
Northern Illinois U (IL)
Northern Michigan U (MI)
Northwest Missouri State U (MO)
Northwest Nazarene U (ID)
Norwich U (VT)
Oakland U (MI)

Oglethorpe U (GA)
The Ohio State U (OH)
Ohio U (OH)
Ohio Wesleyan U (OH)
Oklahoma Baptist U (OK)
Oklahoma City U (OK)
Oklahoma State U (OK)
Old Dominion U (VA)
Oral Roberts U (OK)
Oregon State U (OR)
Ouachita Baptist U (AR)
Pacific Lutheran U (WA)
Pacific Union Coll (CA)
Pacific U (OR)
Penn State Abington (PA)
Penn State Altoona (PA)
Penn State Beaver (PA)
Penn State Berks (PA)
Penn State Brandywine (PA)
Penn State DuBois (PA)
Penn State Erie, The Behrend Coll (PA)
Penn State Fayette, The Eberly Campus (PA)
Penn State Greater Allegheny (PA)
Penn State Hazleton (PA)
Penn State Lehigh Valley (PA)
Penn State Mont Alto (PA)
Penn State New Kensington (PA)
Penn State Schuylkill (PA)
Penn State Shenango (PA)
Penn State U Park (PA)
Penn State Wilkes-Barre (PA)
Penn State Worthington Scranton (PA)
Penn State York (PA)
Pepperdine U, Malibu (CA)
Piedmont Coll (GA)
Pittsburg State U (KS)
Pitzer Coll (CA)
Point Loma Nazarene U (CA)
Polytechnic Inst of New York U (NY)
Pomona Coll (CA)
Portland State U (OR)
Presbyterian Coll (SC)
Princeton U (NJ)
Principia Coll (IL)
Purchase Coll, State U of New York (NY)
Purdue U (IN)
Purdue U Calumet (IN)
Radford U (VA)
Randolph Coll (VA)
Ramapo Coll of New Jersey (NJ)
Randolph-Macon Coll (VA)
Reed Coll (OR)
Rensselaer Polytechnic Inst (NY)
Rhode Island Coll (RI)
Rhodes Coll (TN)
Rice U (TX)
The Richard Stockton Coll of New Jersey (NJ)
Rider U (NJ)
Roanoke Coll (VA)
Roberts Wesleyan Coll (NY)
Rockhurst U (MO)
Rollins Coll (FL)
Rowan U (NJ)
Rutgers, The State U of New Jersey, Camden (NJ)
Rutgers, The State U of New Jersey, Newark (NJ)
Rutgers, The State U of New Jersey, New Brunswick (NJ)
Saginaw Valley State U (MI)
St. Ambrose U (IA)
Saint Anselm Coll (NH)
St. Bonaventure U (NY)
St. John Fisher Coll (NY)
Saint John's U (MN)
St. John's U (NY)
Saint Joseph's U (PA)
St. Lawrence U (NY)
Saint Louis U (MO)
Saint Mary's Coll of California (CA)
St. Mary's Coll of Maryland (MD)
St. Mary's U (TX)
Saint Mary's U of Minnesota (MN)
Saint Michael's Coll (VT)
St. Norbert Coll (WI)
St. Olaf Coll (MN)
Saint Vincent Coll (PA)
Salisbury U (MD)
Samford U (AL)
Sam Houston State U (TX)
San Diego State U (CA)

San Francisco State U (CA)
San Jose State U (CA)
Scripps Coll (CA)
Seattle Pacific U (WA)
Seattle U (WA)
Sewanee: The U of the South (TN)
Shippensburg U of Pennsylvania (PA)
Siena Coll (NY)
Simmons Coll (MA)
Simon Fraser U (BC, Canada)
Simpson Coll (IA)
Skidmore Coll (NY)
Slippery Rock U of Pennsylvania (PA)
Smith Coll (MA)
Sonoma State U (CA)
South Dakota State U (SD)
Southeastern Louisiana U (LA)
Southeast Missouri State U (MO)
Southern Arkansas U–Magnolia (AR)
Southern Connecticut State U (CT)
Southern Illinois U Carbondale (IL)
Southern Illinois U Edwardsville (IL)
Southern Methodist U (TX)
Southern Nazarene U (OK)
Southern Oregon U (OR)
Southern Polytechnic State U (GA)
Southwestern U (TX)
Spelman Coll (GA)
Spring Arbor U (MI)
Stanford U (CA)
State U of New York at Fredonia (NY)
State U of New York at New Paltz (NY)
State U of New York at Oswego (NY)
State U of New York at Plattsburgh (NY)
State U of New York Coll at Cortland (NY)
State U of New York Coll at Geneseo (NY)
State U of New York Coll at Potsdam (NY)
Stephen F. Austin State U (TX)
Stetson U (FL)
Stonehill Coll (MA)
Stony Brook U, State U of New York (NY)
Suffolk U (MA)
Susquehanna U (PA)
Swarthmore Coll (PA)
Sweet Briar Coll (VA)
Syracuse U (NY)
Tarleton State U (TX)
Taylor U (IN)
Temple U (PA)
Tennessee State U (TN)
Texas A&M U (TX)
Texas A&M U–Commerce (TX)
Texas A&M U–Kingsville (TX)
Texas Christian U (TX)
Texas Lutheran U (TX)
Texas Southern U (TX)
Texas State U–San Marcos (TX)
Thomas More Coll (KY)
Thompson Rivers U (BC, Canada)
Transylvania U (KY)
Trent U (ON, Canada)
Trevecca Nazarene U (TN)
Trinity Coll (CT)
Trinity U (TX)
Truman State U (MO)
Tufts U (MA)
Tulane U (LA)
Tuskegee U (AL)
Union Coll (NE)
Union U (TN)
United States Air Force Acad (CO)
United States Military Acad (NY)
United States Naval Acad (MD)
Université de Sherbrooke (QC, Canada)
U at Albany, State U of New York (NY)
U at Buffalo, the State U of New York (NY)
The U of Akron (OH)
The U of Alabama (AL)
The U of Alabama at Birmingham (AL)
U of Alaska Fairbanks (AK)
The U of Arizona (AZ)

U of Arkansas at Little Rock (AR)
The U of British Columbia (BC, Canada)
The U of British Columbia–Okanagan (BC, Canada)
U of California, Berkeley (CA)
U of California, Davis (CA)
U of California, Irvine (CA)
U of California, Los Angeles (CA)
U of California, Merced (CA)
U of California, Riverside (CA)
U of California, Santa Barbara (CA)
U of California, Santa Cruz (CA)
U of Central Arkansas (AR)
U of Central Florida (FL)
U of Central Oklahoma (OK)
U of Chicago (IL)
U of Cincinnati (OH)
U of Colorado Boulder (CO)
U of Colorado Colorado Springs (CO)
U of Colorado Denver (CO)
U of Dallas (TX)
U of Delaware (DE)
U of Denver (CO)
U of Evansville (IN)
U of Florida (FL)
U of Georgia (GA)
U of Guelph (ON, Canada)
U of Hartford (CT)
U of Hawaii at Hilo (HI)
U of Hawaii at Manoa (HI)
U of Houston (TX)
U of Houston–Clear Lake (TX)
U of Idaho (ID)
U of Illinois at Chicago (IL)
U of Illinois at Urbana–Champaign (IL)
The U of Iowa (IA)
The U of Kansas (KS)
U of Kentucky (KY)
U of La Verne (CA)
U of Louisiana at Lafayette (LA)
U of Louisville (KY)
U of Maryland, Baltimore County (MD)
U of Maryland, Coll Park (MD)
U of Mary Washington (VA)
U of Massachusetts Amherst (MA)
U of Massachusetts Boston (MA)
U of Massachusetts Dartmouth (MA)
U of Memphis (TN)
U of Miami (FL)
U of Michigan (MI)
U of Michigan–Dearborn (MI)
U of Michigan–Flint (MI)
U of Minnesota, Duluth (MN)
U of Minnesota, Twin Cities Campus (MN)
U of Mississippi (MS)
U of Missouri (MO)
U of Missouri–Kansas City (MO)
U of Missouri–St. Louis (MO)
U of Mount Union (OH)
U of Nebraska at Kearney (NE)
U of Nebraska at Omaha (NE)
U of Nebraska–Lincoln (NE)
U of Nevada, Las Vegas (NV)
U of Nevada, Reno (NV)
U of New Brunswick Fredericton (NB, Canada)
U of New Brunswick Saint John (NB, Canada)
U of New Hampshire (NH)
U of New Mexico (NM)
U of New Orleans (LA)
U of North Alabama (AL)
U of North Carolina at Asheville (NC)
The U of North Carolina at Chapel Hill (NC)
The U of North Carolina at Charlotte (NC)
The U of North Carolina at Greensboro (NC)
The U of North Carolina at Pembroke (NC)
The U of North Carolina Wilmington (NC)
U of North Dakota (ND)
U of Northern Colorado (CO)
U of North Florida (FL)
U of North Georgia (GA)
U of North Texas (TX)
U of Notre Dame (IN)
U of Oklahoma (OK)

U of Oregon (OR)
U of Ottawa (ON, Canada)
U of Pennsylvania (PA)
U of Pittsburgh (PA)
U of Portland (OR)
U of Puget Sound (WA)
U of Redlands (CA)
U of Regina (SK, Canada)
U of Rhode Island (RI)
U of Richmond (VA)
U of Rochester (NY)
U of St. Thomas (MN)
U of San Diego (CA)
U of Science and Arts of Oklahoma (OK)
The U of Scranton (PA)
U of South Alabama (AL)
U of South Carolina (SC)
The U of South Dakota (SD)
U of Southern California (CA)
U of Southern Maine (ME)
U of Southern Mississippi (MS)
U of South Florida (FL)
The U of Tennessee (TN)
The U of Tennessee at Chattanooga (TN)
The U of Texas at Arlington (TX)
The U of Texas at Austin (TX)
The U of Texas at Brownsville (TX)
The U of Texas at Dallas (TX)
The U of Texas at El Paso (TX)
The U of Texas at San Antonio (TX)
The U of Texas–Pan American (TX)
U of the Cumberlands (KY)
U of the District of Columbia (DC)
U of the Sciences (PA)
The U of Toledo (OH)
U of Tulsa (OK)
U of Utah (UT)
U of Vermont (VT)
U of Virginia (VA)
U of Waterloo (ON, Canada)
The U of Western Ontario (ON, Canada)
U of West Florida (FL)
U of West Georgia (GA)
U of Windsor (ON, Canada)
U of Wisconsin–Eau Claire (WI)
U of Wisconsin–La Crosse (WI)
U of Wisconsin–Madison (WI)
U of Wisconsin–Milwaukee (WI)
U of Wisconsin–Parkside (WI)
U of Wisconsin–Stevens Point (WI)
U of Wyoming (WY)
Utah State U (UT)
Utica Coll (NY)
Valdosta State U (GA)
Valparaiso U (IN)
Vanderbilt U (TN)
Vassar Coll (NY)
Villanova U (PA)
Virginia Commonwealth U (VA)
Virginia Polytechnic Inst and State U (VA)
Virginia State U (VA)
Wabash Coll (IN)
Wagner Coll (NY)
Wake Forest U (NC)
Walla Walla U (WA)
Wartburg Coll (IA)
Washburn U (KS)
Washington & Jefferson Coll (PA)
Washington and Lee U (VA)
Washington Coll (MD)
Washington State U (WA)
Washington U in St. Louis (MO)
Wayne State U (MI)
Weber State U (UT)
Wellesley Coll (MA)
Wells Coll (NY)
Wesleyan U (CT)
West Chester U of Pennsylvania (PA)
Western Illinois U (IL)
Western Kentucky U (KY)
Western Michigan U (MI)
Western State Colorado U (CO)
Western Washington U (WA)
Westminster Coll (MO)
Westminster Coll (UT)
West Texas A&M U (TX)
West Virginia U (WV)
West Virginia Wesleyan Coll (WV)
Wheaton Coll (IL)
Wheaton Coll (MA)
Wheeling Jesuit U (WV)
Whitman Coll (WA)

Whitworth U (WA)
Wichita State U (KS)
Widener U (PA)
Willamette U (OR)
William Jewell Coll (MO)
Williams Coll (MA)
Wittenberg U (OH)
Worcester Polytechnic Inst (MA)
Wright State U (OH)
Xavier U (OH)
Xavier U of Louisiana (LA)
Yale U (CT)
York Coll of the City U of New York (NY)
Youngstown State U (OH)

PHYSICS RELATED
Bridgewater Coll (VA)
Bridgewater State U (MA)
Brigham Young U (UT)
California State U, Chico (CA)
Carson-Newman U (TN)
Christopher Newport U (VA)
The Coll at Brockport, State U of New York (NY)
Coll of Saint Benedict (MN)
The Coll of Wooster (OH)
Embry-Riddle Aeronautical U–Daytona (FL)
Embry-Riddle Aeronautical U–Prescott (AZ)
Florida Inst of Technology (FL)
Fort Lewis Coll (CO)
Hampden-Sydney Coll (VA)
Illinois Inst of Technology (IL)
Indiana U of Pennsylvania (PA)
Lawrence Technological U (MI)
Linfield Coll (OR)
Morehouse Coll (GA)
Pittsburg State U (KS)
Presbyterian Coll (SC)
Rensselaer Polytechnic Inst (NY)
Rutgers, The State U of New Jersey, Newark (NJ)
Saint John's U (MN)
Saint Mary's U of Minnesota (MN)
Southern Arkansas U–Magnolia (AR)
Spring Arbor U (MI)
U of Alaska Fairbanks (AK)
U of California, Davis (CA)
U of Nevada, Las Vegas (NV)
U of Northern Iowa (IA)
U of North Texas (TX)
U of Notre Dame (IN)
U of Regina (SK, Canada)
U of Rochester (NY)
The U of Western Ontario (ON, Canada)
Whitman Coll (WA)

PHYSICS TEACHER EDUCATION
Abilene Christian U (TX)
Alma Coll (MI)
Anderson U (IN)
Appalachian State U (NC)
Arkansas State U (AR)
Auburn U (AL)
Bethel U (MN)
Bowling Green State U (OH)
Bradley U (IL)
Buena Vista U (IA)
Canisius Coll (NY)
Cedarville U (OH)
Central Methodist U (MO)
Central Michigan U (MI)
Christian Brothers U (TN)
City Coll of the City U of New York (NY)
The Coll at Brockport, State U of New York (NY)
The Coll of New Jersey (NJ)
Colorado State U (CO)
Concordia Coll (MN)
Concordia U, Nebraska (NE)
East Central U (OK)
Eastern Michigan U (MI)
Eastern Washington U (WA)
Florida Inst of Technology (FL)
Grand Valley State U (MI)
Greenville Coll (IL)
Grove City Coll (PA)
Gustavus Adolphus Coll (MN)
Hofstra U (NY)
Hope Coll (MI)
Husson U (ME)
Indiana U Bloomington (IN)

Indiana U–Purdue U Fort Wayne (IN)
Indiana U South Bend (IN)
Ithaca Coll (NY)
Juniata Coll (PA)
King Coll (TN)
Le Moyne Coll (NY)
Lincoln U (MO)
Lipscomb U (TN)
Louisiana State U in Shreveport (LA)
Madonna U (MI)
Manchester U (IN)
Mansfield U of Pennsylvania (PA)
Messiah Coll (PA)
Miami Dade Coll (FL)
Michigan State U (MI)
Minnesota State U Moorhead (MN)
Minot State U (ND)
Missouri State U (MO)
Moravian Coll (PA)
Morningside Coll (IA)
Mount Vernon Nazarene U (OH)
North Carolina Central U (NC)
North Dakota State U (ND)
Northern Michigan U (MI)
Northwest Missouri State U (MO)
Ohio Dominican U (OH)
Ohio Wesleyan U (OH)
Pittsburg State U (KS)
Purdue U Calumet (IN)
Rhode Island Coll (RI)
Roberts Wesleyan Coll (NY)
Saginaw Valley State U (MI)
St. Ambrose U (IA)
St. John Fisher Coll (NY)
St. John's U (NY)
Saint Mary's U of Minnesota (MN)
Saint Vincent Coll (PA)
Southern Polytechnic State U (GA)
State U of New York at New Paltz (NY)
State U of New York Coll at Cortland (NY)
Stony Brook U, State U of New York (NY)
Syracuse U (NY)
Trevecca Nazarene U (TN)
Union Coll (NE)
U of Delaware (DE)
U of Evansville (IN)
U of Illinois at Chicago (IL)
U of Illinois at Urbana–Champaign (IL)
U of Maryland, Baltimore County (MD)
U of Minnesota, Duluth (MN)
U of Missouri (MO)
U of Missouri–St. Louis (MO)
U of Nebraska–Lincoln (NE)
U of Regina (SK, Canada)
U of St. Thomas (MN)
The U of South Dakota (SD)
U of Waterloo (ON, Canada)
U of West Georgia (GA)
U of Windsor (ON, Canada)
Utah State U (UT)
Utica Coll (NY)
Valparaiso U (IN)
Washington State U (WA)
Washington U in St. Louis (MO)
Weber State U (UT)
Western Michigan U (MI)
Wheeling Jesuit U (WV)
William Jewell Coll (MO)
Xavier U (OH)

PHYSIOLOGICAL PSYCHOLOGY/PSYCHOBIOLOGY
Albright Coll (PA)
Binghamton U, State U of New York (NY)
Centre Coll (KY)
Florida Atlantic U (FL)
Holy Family U (PA)
Holy Names U (CA)
Houghton Coll (NY)
La Sierra U (CA)
Lebanon Valley Coll (PA)
Mills Coll (CA)
Mount Allison U (NB, Canada)
Pace U (NY)
Quinnipiac U (CT)
Ripon Coll (WI)
Saint Mary's Coll of California (CA)

Simmons Coll (MA)
Swarthmore Coll (PA)
U of California, Los Angeles (CA)
U of Colorado Denver (CO)
U of Michigan (MI)
U of New Brunswick Fredericton (NB, Canada)
U of New England (ME)
The U of Western Ontario (ON, Canada)
Vassar Coll (NY)
Washington Coll (MD)

PHYSIOLOGY
Brigham Young U (UT)
California State U, Long Beach (CA)
Marquette U (WI)
Michigan State U (MI)
Northern Michigan U (MI)
Oklahoma Baptist U (OK)
Oklahoma State U (OK)
San Jose State U (CA)
Seattle Pacific U (WA)
Southern Illinois U Carbondale (IL)
The U of Arizona (AZ)
The U of British Columbia (BC, Canada)
U of California, Los Angeles (CA)
U of California, Santa Barbara (CA)
U of Colorado Boulder (CO)
U of Illinois at Urbana–Champaign (IL)
U of Oregon (OR)
U of Ottawa (ON, Canada)
The U of Western Ontario (ON, Canada)
U of Wyoming (WY)

PLANETARY ASTRONOMY AND SCIENCE
Florida Inst of Technology (FL)
U of Waterloo (ON, Canada)
The U of Western Ontario (ON, Canada)

PLANT MOLECULAR BIOLOGY
Pittsburg State U (KS)
U of Illinois at Urbana–Champaign (IL)

PLANT NURSERY MANAGEMENT
Colorado State U (CO)

PLANT PATHOLOGY/PHYTOPATHOLOGY
New Mexico State U (NM)
The Ohio State U (OH)
U of Georgia (GA)
U of Wisconsin–Madison (WI)

PLANT PHYSIOLOGY
Pittsburg State U (KS)

PLANT PROTECTION AND INTEGRATED PEST MANAGEMENT
California State Polytechnic U, Pomona (CA)
Iowa State U of Science and Technology (IA)
Penn State U Park (PA)
U of Delaware (DE)
U of Hawaii at Manoa (HI)
U of Illinois at Urbana–Champaign (IL)
U of Minnesota, Twin Cities Campus (MN)
Washington State U (WA)
West Texas A&M U (TX)

PLANT SCIENCES
Arkansas State U (AR)
Auburn U (AL)
California State U, Fresno (CA)
Dalhousie U (NS, Canada)
Louisiana State U and Ag and Mech Coll (LA)
Middle Tennessee State U (TN)
Montana State U (MT)
The Ohio State U (OH)
Rutgers, The State U of New Jersey, New Brunswick (NJ)
Southeast Missouri State U (MO)
Southern Illinois U Carbondale (IL)
State U of New York Coll of Agriculture and Technology at Cobleskill (NY)
Tuskegee U (AL)

The U of Arizona (AZ)
U of California, Santa Cruz (CA)
U of Delaware (DE)
U of Florida (FL)
U of Guelph (ON, Canada)
U of Massachusetts Amherst (MA)
U of Minnesota, Crookston (MN)
U of Minnesota, Twin Cities Campus (MN)
U of Missouri (MO)
The U of Tennessee (TN)
U of Vermont (VT)
The U of Western Ontario (ON, Canada)
Utah State U (UT)
Washington State U (WA)

PLANT SCIENCES RELATED
Auburn U (AL)
Sterling Coll (VT)
U of Hawaii at Manoa (HI)
Utah State U (UT)
West Virginia U (WV)

PLASTICS AND POLYMER ENGINEERING TECHNOLOGY
Eastern Michigan U (MI)
Ferris State U (MI)
Pennsylvania Coll of Technology (PA)
Pittsburg State U (KS)
Shawnee State U (OH)
Weber State U (UT)
Western Washington U (WA)

PLAYWRITING AND SCREENWRITING
Bard Coll (NY)
Bennington Coll (VT)
Brigham Young U (UT)
Chapman U (CA)
Columbia Coll Chicago (IL)
Concordia U (QC, Canada)
DePaul U (IL)
Emerson Coll (MA)
Loyola Marymount U (CA)
Ohio U (OH)
Point Park U (PA)
Purchase Coll, State U of New York (NY)
Savannah Coll of Art and Design (GA)
Slippery Rock U of Pennsylvania (PA)
U of Southern California (CA)
The U of the Arts (PA)

POLISH
U of Illinois at Chicago (IL)
U of Michigan (MI)
U of Pittsburgh (PA)
U of Wisconsin–Madison (WI)

POLITICAL COMMUNICATION
Cedarville U (OH)
Emerson Coll (MA)
Suffolk U (MA)
Weber State U (UT)

POLITICAL ECONOMY
The Evergreen State Coll (WA)
U of Southern California (CA)
U of Washington, Bothell (WA)
U of Washington, Tacoma (WA)
Williams Coll (MA)

POLITICAL SCIENCE AND GOVERNMENT
Abilene Christian U (TX)
Acadia U (NS, Canada)
Adelphi U (NY)
Agnes Scott Coll (GA)
Alabama State U (AL)
Albertus Magnus Coll (CT)
Albion Coll (MI)
Albright Coll (PA)
Alcorn State U (MS)
Alderson-Broaddus Coll (WV)
Alfred U (NY)
Alma Coll (MI)
Alvernia U (PA)
Alverno Coll (WI)
American Jewish U (CA)
American Public U System (WV)
American U (DC)
The American U in Cairo (Egypt)
American U of Beirut (Lebanon)
Amherst Coll (MA)
Anderson U (IN)

Andrews U (MI)
Angelo State U (TX)
Appalachian State U (NC)
Arizona State U (AZ)
Arkansas State U (AR)
Arkansas Tech U (AR)
Armstrong Atlantic State U (GA)
Asbury U (KY)
Ashland U (OH)
Assumption Coll (MA)
Athabasca U (AB, Canada)
Athens State U (AL)
Auburn U (AL)
Auburn U at Montgomery (AL)
Augsburg Coll (MN)
Augustana Coll (IL)
Augustana Coll (SD)
Aurora U (IL)
Austin Peay State U (TN)
Averett U (VA)
Avila U (MO)
Azusa Pacific U (CA)
Baldwin Wallace U (OH)
Ball State U (IN)
Bard Coll (NY)
Barry U (FL)
Barton Coll (NC)
Bates Coll (ME)
Baylor U (TX)
Belhaven U (MS)
Bellarmine U (KY)
Belmont U (TN)
Bemidji State U (MN)
Benedictine Coll (KS)
Benedictine U (IL)
Bennington Coll (VT)
Berea Coll (KY)
Berry Coll (GA)
Bethany Coll (WV)
Bethel U (MN)
Bethune-Cookman U (FL)
Binghamton U, State U of New York (NY)
Blackburn Coll (IL)
Bloomfield Coll (NJ)
Bloomsburg U of Pennsylvania (PA)
Boise State U (ID)
Boston Coll (MA)
Boston U (MA)
Bowdoin Coll (ME)
Bowie State U (MD)
Bowling Green State U (OH)
Bradley U (IL)
Bridgewater Coll (VA)
Bridgewater State U (MA)
Brock U (ON, Canada)
Brown U (RI)
Bryant U (RI)
Bucknell U (PA)
Buena Vista U (IA)
Buffalo State Coll, State U of New York (NY)
Butler U (IN)
Cabrini U (PA)
Caldwell Coll (NJ)
California Baptist U (CA)
California Lutheran U (CA)
California Polytechnic State U, San Luis Obispo (CA)
California State Polytechnic U, Pomona (CA)
California State U, Chico (CA)
California State U, Dominguez Hills (CA)
California State U, East Bay (CA)
California State U, Fresno (CA)
California State U, Fullerton (CA)
California State U, Long Beach (CA)
California State U, Los Angeles (CA)
California State U, Northridge (CA)
California State U, San Bernardino (CA)
California State U, San Marcos (CA)
California State U, Stanislaus (CA)
Calvin U (MI)
Cameron U (OK)
Campbellsville U (KY)
Canisius U (NY)
Capital U (OH)
Cardinal Stritch U (WI)
Carleton Coll (MN)
Carlow U (PA)
Carroll Coll (MT)
Carson-Newman U (TN)

Case Western Reserve U (OH)
Catawba Coll (NC)
The Catholic U of America (DC)
Cedar Crest Coll (PA)
Cedarville U (OH)
Centenary Coll of Louisiana (LA)
Central Coll (IA)
Central Connecticut State U (CT)
Central Methodist U (MO)
Central Michigan U (MI)
Central State U (OH)
Centre Coll (KY)
Chapman U (CA)
Chatham U (PA)
Chestnut Hill Coll (PA)
Cheyney U of Pennsylvania (PA)
Chicago State U (IL)
Chowan U (NC)
Christendom Coll (VA)
Christopher Newport U (VA)
The Citadel, The Military Coll of South Carolina (SC)
City Coll of the City U of New York (NY)
Claremont McKenna Coll (CA)
Clarion U of Pennsylvania (PA)
Clark Atlanta U (GA)
Clarkson U (NY)
Clark U (MA)
Clayton State U (GA)
Clemson U (SC)
Cleveland State U (OH)
Coastal Carolina U (SC)
Coe Coll (IA)
Colby Coll (ME)
Colgate U (NY)
The Coll at Brockport, State U of New York (NY)
Coll of Charleston (SC)
The Coll of Idaho (ID)
The Coll of New Jersey (NJ)
The Coll of New Rochelle (NY)
Coll of Saint Benedict (MN)
The Coll of Saint Rose (NY)
Coll of Staten Island of the City U of New York (NY)
Coll of the Holy Cross (MA)
The Coll of William and Mary (VA)
The Coll of Wooster (OH)
The Colorado Coll (CO)
Colorado Mesa U (CO)
Colorado State U (CO)
Columbia Coll (MO)
Columbia Coll (SC)
Columbia U (NY)
Columbia U, School of General Studies (NY)
Columbus State U (GA)
Concordia Coll (MN)
Concordia U (CA)
Concordia U (QC, Canada)
Concordia U Chicago (IL)
Concordia U Wisconsin (WI)
Concord U (WV)
Connecticut Coll (CT)
Converse Coll (SC)
Cornell Coll (IA)
Creighton U (NE)
Culver-Stockton Coll (MO)
Curry Coll (MA)
Dalhousie U (NS, Canada)
Dallas Baptist U (TX)
Dartmouth Coll (NH)
Davidson Coll (NC)
Delta State U (MS)
DePaul U (IL)
DePauw U (IN)
DeSales U (PA)
Dickinson Coll (PA)
Dillard U (LA)
Doane Coll (NE)
Dominican U (IL)
Dordt Coll (IA)
Drake U (IA)
Drew U (NJ)
Drury U (MO)
Duquesne U (PA)
Earlham Coll (IN)
East Carolina U (NC)
East Central U (OK)
Eastern Illinois U (IL)
Eastern Michigan U (MI)
Eastern New Mexico U (NM)
Eastern Washington U (WA)
East Tennessee State U (TN)
East Texas Baptist U (TX)
Eckerd Coll (FL)

Edgewood Coll (WI)
Edinboro U of Pennsylvania (PA)
Elizabeth City State U (NC)
Elizabethtown Coll (PA)
Elmira Coll (NY)
Elon U (NC)
Emmanuel Coll (MA)
Emory & Henry Coll (VA)
Emporia State U (KS)
Endicott Coll (MA)
Evangel U (MO)
The Evergreen State Coll (WA)
Excelsior Coll (NY)
Fairfield U (CT)
Fairleigh Dickinson U, Coll at Florham (NJ)
Fairleigh Dickinson U, Metropolitan Campus (NJ)
Fairmont State U (WV)
Faulkner U (AL)
Fayetteville State U (NC)
Felician Coll (NJ)
Ferris State U (MI)
Ferrum Coll (VA)
Flagler Coll (FL)
Florida Ag and Mech U (FL)
Florida Atlantic U (FL)
Florida Gulf Coast U (FL)
Florida Intl U (FL)
Florida Southern Coll (FL)
Florida State U (FL)
Fort Lewis Coll (CO)
Framingham State U (MA)
Francis Marion U (SC)
Franklin & Marshall Coll (PA)
Franklin Coll (IN)
Franklin Pierce U (NH)
Friends U (KS)
Frostburg State U (MD)
Furman U (SC)
Gannon U (PA)
Gardner-Webb U (NC)
Geneva Coll (PA)
George Fox U (OR)
Georgetown Coll (KY)
Georgetown U (DC)
Georgia Coll & State U (GA)
Georgia Gwinnett Coll (GA)
Georgia Regents U (GA)
Georgia Southern U (GA)
Georgia Southwestern State U (GA)
Georgia State U (GA)
Gettysburg Coll (PA)
Gonzaga U (WA)
Gordon Coll (MA)
Goucher Coll (MD)
Grambling State U (LA)
Grand Valley State U (MI)
Grand View U (IA)
Greenville Coll (IL)
Grinnell Coll (IA)
Grove City Coll (PA)
Guilford Coll (NC)
Gustavus Adolphus Coll (MN)
Hamilton Coll (NY)
Hamline U (MN)
Hampden-Sydney Coll (VA)
Hampshire Coll (MA)
Hampton U (VA)
Hanover Coll (IN)
Harding U (AR)
Hardin-Simmons U (TX)
Hartwick Coll (NY)
Haverford Coll (PA)
Hawai`i Pacific U (HI)
Henderson State U (AR)
Hendrix Coll (AR)
High Point U (NC)
Hilbert Coll (NY)
Hillsdale Coll (MI)
Hiram Coll (OH)
Hobart and William Smith Colls (NY)
Hofstra U (NY)
Hollins U (VA)
Holy Family U (PA)
Hood Coll (MD)
Hope Coll (MI)
Houghton Coll (NY)
Howard Payne U (TX)
Humboldt State U (CA)
Hunter Coll of the City U of New York (NY)
Huntingdon Coll (AL)
Huntington U (IN)
Illinois Coll (IL)

Illinois Inst of Technology (IL)
Illinois State U (IL)
Illinois Wesleyan U (IL)
Immaculata U (PA)
Indiana State U (IN)
Indiana U Bloomington (IN)
Indiana U East (IN)
Indiana U Northwest (IN)
Indiana U of Pennsylvania (PA)
Indiana U–Purdue U Fort Wayne (IN)
Indiana U–Purdue U Indianapolis (IN)
Indiana U South Bend (IN)
Indiana U Southeast (IN)
Indiana Wesleyan U (IN)
Inter American U of Puerto Rico, San Germán Campus (PR)
Iona Coll (NY)
Iowa State U of Science and Technology (IA)
Ithaca Coll (NY)
Jacksonville State U (AL)
James Madison U (VA)
Jamestown Coll (ND)
John Brown U (AR)
John Cabot U (Italy)
John Carroll U (OH)
John Jay Coll of Criminal Justice of the City U of New York (NY)
The Johns Hopkins U (MD)
Johnson C. Smith U (NC)
Johnson State Coll (VT)
Juniata Coll (PA)
Kalamazoo Coll (MI)
Kansas State U (KS)
Kean U (NJ)
Keene State Coll (NH)
Kennesaw State U (GA)
Kent State U (OH)
Kentucky State U (KY)
Kentucky Wesleyan Coll (KY)
Kenyon Coll (OH)
King Coll (TN)
King's Coll (PA)
Knox Coll (IL)
Kutztown U of Pennsylvania (PA)
Lafayette Coll (PA)
LaGrange Coll (GA)
Lake Erie Coll (OH)
Lake Superior State U (MI)
Lamar U (TX)
Lander U (SC)
La Roche Coll (PA)
La Salle U (PA)
Lawrence U (WI)
Lebanese American U (Lebanon)
Lebanon Valley Coll (PA)
Lee U (TN)
Lehigh U (PA)
Lehman Coll of the City U of New York (NY)
Le Moyne Coll (NY)
Lewis U (IL)
Liberty U (VA)
Lincoln U (MO)
Lindenwood U (MO)
Linfield Coll (OR)
Lipscomb U (TN)
Lock Haven U of Pennsylvania (PA)
Long Island U–Brooklyn Campus (NY)
Long Island U–C. W. Post Campus (NY)
Longwood U (VA)
Louisiana State U and Ag and Mech Coll (LA)
Louisiana State U in Shreveport (LA)
Loyola Marymount U (CA)
Loyola U Chicago (IL)
Loyola U Maryland (MD)
Loyola U New Orleans (LA)
Luther Coll (IA)
Lynchburg Coll (VA)
Lynn U (FL)
Lyon Coll (AR)
Macalester Coll (MN)
Malone U (OH)
Manchester U (IN)
Manhattan Coll (NY)
Manhattanville Coll (NY)
Mansfield U of Pennsylvania (PA)
Marietta Coll (OH)
Marist Coll (NY)
Marquette U (WI)
Marshall U (WV)

Mars Hill Coll (NC)
Mary Baldwin Coll (VA)
Marymount Manhattan Coll (NY)
Marymount U (VA)
Maryville Coll (TN)
Massachusetts Coll of Liberal Arts (MA)
Massachusetts Inst of Technology (MA)
The Master's Coll and Sem (CA)
McDaniel Coll (MD)
McKendree U (IL)
McMurry U (TX)
McNeese State U (LA)
Mercer U (GA)
Mercy Coll (NY)
Mercyhurst U (PA)
Merrimack Coll (MA)
Messiah Coll (PA)
Metropolitan State U of Denver (CO)
Miami U (OH)
Michigan State U (MI)
Middlebury Coll (VT)
Middle Tennessee State U (TN)
Midwestern State U (TX)
Millersville U of Pennsylvania (PA)
Millikin U (IL)
Millsaps Coll (MS)
Mills Coll (CA)
Minnesota State U Mankato (MN)
Minnesota State U Moorhead (MN)
Mississippi Coll (MS)
Mississippi State U (MS)
Mississippi U for Women (MS)
Mississippi Valley State U (MS)
Missouri State U (MO)
Missouri Western State U (MO)
Molloy Coll (NY)
Monmouth Coll (IL)
Monmouth U (NJ)
Montana State U (MT)
Montclair State U (NJ)
Moravian Coll (PA)
Morehead State U (KY)
Morehouse Coll (GA)
Morningside Coll (IA)
Morris Coll (SC)
Mount Allison U (NB, Canada)
Mount Holyoke Coll (MA)
Mount Mercy U (IA)
Mount Saint Mary Coll (NY)
Mount St. Mary's Coll (CA)
Mount St. Mary's U (MD)
Mount Vernon Nazarene U (OH)
Muhlenberg Coll (PA)
Murray State U (KY)
Nazareth Coll of Rochester (NY)
Neumann U (PA)
Newberry Coll (SC)
New Coll of Florida (FL)
New England Coll (NH)
New Jersey City U (NJ)
New Mexico Highlands U (NM)
New Mexico State U (NM)
New York Inst of Technology (NY)
New York U (NY)
Niagara U (NY)
Nicholls State U (LA)
Norfolk State U (VA)
North Carolina Central U (NC)
North Carolina State U (NC)
North Carolina Wesleyan Coll (NC)
North Central Coll (IL)
North Dakota State U (ND)
Northeastern Illinois U (IL)
Northeastern U (MA)
Northern Arizona U (AZ)
Northern Illinois U (IL)
Northern Michigan U (MI)
Northern State U (SD)
Northwestern Coll (IA)
Northwestern Oklahoma State U (OK)
Northwest Missouri State U (MO)
Northwest Nazarene U (ID)
Northwest U (WA)
Norwich U (VT)
Notre Dame de Namur U (CA)
Oakland U (MI)
Oglethorpe U (GA)
Ohio Dominican U (OH)
The Ohio State U (OH)
Ohio U (OH)
Ohio Wesleyan U (OH)
Oklahoma Baptist U (OK)
Oklahoma City U (OK)

Oklahoma State U (OK)
Old Dominion U (VA)
Oral Roberts U (OK)
Oregon State U (OR)
Ouachita Baptist U (AR)
Pace U (NY)
Pacific Lutheran U (WA)
Pacific U (OR)
Palm Beach Atlantic U (FL)
Park U (MO)
Patrick Henry Coll (VA)
Penn State Abington (PA)
Penn State Altoona (PA)
Penn State Beaver (PA)
Penn State Berks (PA)
Penn State Brandywine (PA)
Penn State DuBois (PA)
Penn State Erie, The Behrend Coll (PA)
Penn State Fayette, The Eberly Campus (PA)
Penn State Greater Allegheny (PA)
Penn State Hazleton (PA)
Penn State Lehigh Valley (PA)
Penn State Mont Alto (PA)
Penn State New Kensington (PA)
Penn State Schuylkill (PA)
Penn State Shenango (PA)
Penn State U Park (PA)
Penn State Wilkes-Barre (PA)
Penn State Worthington Scranton (PA)
Penn State York (PA)
Pepperdine U, Malibu (CA)
Piedmont Coll (GA)
Pine Manor Coll (MA)
Pittsburg State U (KS)
Pitzer Coll (CA)
Plymouth State U (NH)
Point Loma Nazarene U (CA)
Point Park U (PA)
Pomona Coll (CA)
Portland State U (OR)
Presbyterian Coll (SC)
Prescott Coll (AZ)
Princeton U (NJ)
Principia Coll (IL)
Providence Coll (RI)
Purchase Coll, State U of New York (NY)
Purdue U (IN)
Purdue U Calumet (IN)
Queens U of Charlotte (NC)
Quincy U (IL)
Quinnipiac U (CT)
Radford U (VA)
Ramapo Coll of New Jersey (NJ)
Randolph Coll (VA)
Randolph-Macon Coll (VA)
Reed Coll (OR)
Regis Coll (MA)
Regis U (CO)
Rhode Island Coll (RI)
Rhodes Coll (TN)
Rice U (TX)
The Richard Stockton Coll of New Jersey (NJ)
Rider U (NJ)
Ripon Coll (WI)
Rivier U (NH)
Roanoke Coll (VA)
Rochester Inst of Technology (NY)
Rockford Coll (IL)
Rockhurst U (MO)
Rocky Mountain Coll (MT)
Roger Williams U (RI)
Rollins Coll (FL)
Roosevelt U (IL)
Rosemont Coll (PA)
Rowan U (NJ)
Russell Sage Coll (NY)
Rutgers, The State U of New Jersey, Camden (NJ)
Rutgers, The State U of New Jersey, Newark (NJ)
Rutgers, The State U of New Jersey, New Brunswick (NJ)
Saginaw Valley State U (MI)
St. Ambrose U (IA)
Saint Anselm Coll (NH)
St. Bonaventure U (NY)
St. Edward's U (TX)
St. Francis Coll (NY)
St. Gregory's U, Shawnee (OK)
St. John Fisher Coll (NY)
Saint John's U (MN)
St. John's U (NY)

Saint Joseph's Coll (IN)
St. Joseph's Coll, New York (NY)
Saint Joseph's U (PA)
St. Lawrence U (NY)
Saint Leo U (FL)
Saint Louis U (MO)
Saint Martin's U (WA)
Saint Mary's Coll (IN)
Saint Mary's Coll of California (CA)
St. Mary's Coll of Maryland (MD)
St. Mary's U (TX)
Saint Michael's Coll (VT)
St. Norbert Coll (WI)
St. Olaf Coll (MN)
St. Thomas U (FL)
St. Thomas U (NB, Canada)
Saint Vincent Coll (PA)
Salem State U (MA)
Salisbury U (MD)
Salve Regina U (RI)
Samford U (AL)
Sam Houston State U (TX)
San Diego State U (CA)
San Francisco State U (CA)
San Jose State U (CA)
Schreiner U (TX)
Scripps Coll (CA)
Seattle Pacific U (WA)
Seattle U (WA)
Seton Hill U (PA)
Sewanee: The U of the South (TN)
Shaw U (NC)
Shenandoah U (VA)
Shepherd U (WV)
Shippensburg U of Pennsylvania (PA)
Siena Coll (NY)
Simmons Coll (MA)
Simon Fraser U (BC, Canada)
Simpson Coll (IA)
Skidmore Coll (NY)
Slippery Rock U of Pennsylvania (PA)
Smith Coll (MA)
Sonoma State U (CA)
South Dakota State U (SD)
Southeastern Louisiana U (LA)
Southeastern Oklahoma State U (OK)
Southeast Missouri State U (MO)
Southern Arkansas U–Magnolia (AR)
Southern Connecticut State U (CT)
Southern Illinois U Carbondale (IL)
Southern Illinois U Edwardsville (IL)
Southern Methodist U (TX)
Southern New Hampshire U (NH)
Southern Oregon U (OR)
Southern Polytechnic State U (GA)
Southern Utah U (UT)
Southwest Baptist U (MO)
Southwestern U (TX)
Spelman Coll (GA)
Spring Arbor U (MI)
Spring Hill Coll (AL)
Stanford U (CA)
State U of New York at Fredonia (NY)
State U of New York at New Paltz (NY)
State U of New York at Oswego (NY)
State U of New York at Plattsburgh (NY)
State U of New York Coll at Cortland (NY)
State U of New York Coll at Geneseo (NY)
State U of New York Coll at Potsdam (NY)
Stephen F. Austin State U (TX)
Stetson U (FL)
Stonehill Coll (MA)
Stony Brook U, State U of New York (NY)
Suffolk U (MA)
Sul Ross State U (TX)
Susquehanna U (PA)
Swarthmore Coll (PA)
Sweet Briar Coll (VA)
Syracuse U (NY)
Tarleton State U (TX)
Taylor U (IN)
Temple U (PA)
Tennessee State U (TN)
Texas A&M Intl U (TX)

Texas A&M U (TX)
Texas A&M U–Commerce (TX)
Texas A&M U–Kingsville (TX)
Texas Christian U (TX)
Texas Lutheran U (TX)
Texas Southern U (TX)
Texas State U–San Marcos (TX)
Texas Wesleyan U (TX)
Texas Woman's U (TX)
Thomas Edison State Coll (NJ)
Thomas More Coll (KY)
Thomas U (GA)
Thompson Rivers U (BC, Canada)
Transylvania U (KY)
Trent U (ON, Canada)
Trinity Christian Coll (IL)
Trinity Coll (CT)
Trinity U (TX)
Troy U (AL)
Truman State U (MO)
Tufts U (MA)
Tulane U (LA)
Tuskegee U (AL)
Union U (TN)
United States Air Force Acad (CO)
United States Coast Guard Acad (CT)
United States Military Acad (NY)
United States Naval Acad (MD)
U at Albany, State U of New York (NY)
U at Buffalo, the State U of New York (NY)
The U of Akron (OH)
The U of Alabama (AL)
The U of Alabama at Birmingham (AL)
U of Alaska Anchorage (AK)
U of Alaska Fairbanks (AK)
The U of Arizona (AZ)
U of Arkansas at Little Rock (AR)
The U of British Columbia (BC, Canada)
The U of British Columbia–Okanagan (BC, Canada)
U of California, Berkeley (CA)
U of California, Davis (CA)
U of California, Irvine (CA)
U of California, Los Angeles (CA)
U of California, Merced (CA)
U of California, Riverside (CA)
U of California, Santa Barbara (CA)
U of California, Santa Cruz (CA)
U of Central Arkansas (AR)
U of Central Florida (FL)
U of Central Oklahoma (OK)
U of Charleston (WV)
U of Chicago (IL)
U of Cincinnati (OH)
U of Colorado Boulder (CO)
U of Colorado Colorado Springs (CO)
U of Colorado Denver (CO)
U of Dallas (TX)
U of Delaware (DE)
U of Denver (CO)
U of Evansville (IN)
The U of Findlay (OH)
U of Florida (FL)
U of Georgia (GA)
U of Great Falls (MT)
U of Guam (GU)
U of Hartford (CT)
U of Hawaii at Hilo (HI)
U of Hawaii at Manoa (HI)
U of Hawaii–West Oahu (HI)
U of Houston (TX)
U of Houston–Downtown (TX)
U of Idaho (ID)
U of Illinois at Chicago (IL)
U of Illinois at Springfield (IL)
U of Illinois at Urbana–Champaign (IL)
The U of Iowa (IA)
The U of Kansas (KS)
U of Kentucky (KY)
U of La Verne (CA)
U of Louisiana at Lafayette (LA)
U of Louisiana at Monroe (LA)
U of Louisville (KY)
U of Maine at Farmington (ME)
U of Maryland, Baltimore County (MD)
U of Maryland, Coll Park (MD)
U of Maryland U Coll (MD)
U of Mary Washington (VA)
U of Massachusetts Amherst (MA)

U of Massachusetts Boston (MA)
U of Massachusetts Dartmouth (MA)
U of Memphis (TN)
U of Miami (FL)
U of Michigan (MI)
U of Michigan–Dearborn (MI)
U of Michigan–Flint (MI)
U of Minnesota, Duluth (MN)
U of Minnesota, Twin Cities Campus (MN)
U of Mississippi (MS)
U of Missouri (MO)
U of Missouri–Kansas City (MO)
U of Missouri–St. Louis (MO)
U of Mobile (AL)
The U of Montana Western (MT)
U of Montevallo (AL)
U of Mount Union (OH)
U of Nebraska at Kearney (NE)
U of Nebraska at Omaha (NE)
U of Nebraska–Lincoln (NE)
U of Nevada, Las Vegas (NV)
U of Nevada, Reno (NV)
U of New Brunswick Fredericton (NB, Canada)
U of New Brunswick Saint John (NB, Canada)
U of New England (ME)
U of New Hampshire (NH)
U of New Haven (CT)
U of New Mexico (NM)
U of New Orleans (LA)
U of North Alabama (AL)
U of North Carolina at Asheville (NC)
The U of North Carolina at Chapel Hill (NC)
The U of North Carolina at Greensboro (NC)
The U of North Carolina at Pembroke (NC)
The U of North Carolina Wilmington (NC)
U of North Dakota (ND)
U of Northern Colorado (CO)
U of Northern Iowa (IA)
U of North Florida (FL)
U of North Georgia (GA)
U of North Texas (TX)
U of Notre Dame (IN)
U of Oklahoma (OK)
U of Oregon (OR)
U of Ottawa (ON, Canada)
U of Pennsylvania (PA)
U of Pittsburgh (PA)
U of Pittsburgh at Bradford (PA)
U of Pittsburgh at Greensburg (PA)
U of Portland (OR)
U of Puget Sound (WA)
U of Redlands (CA)
U of Regina (SK, Canada)
U of Rhode Island (RI)
U of Richmond (VA)
U of Rochester (NY)
U of St. Francis (IL)
U of Saint Mary (KS)
U of St. Thomas (MN)
U of St. Thomas (TX)
U of San Diego (CA)
U of Science and Arts of Oklahoma (OK)
The U of Scranton (PA)
U of South Alabama (AL)
U of South Carolina (SC)
U of South Carolina Aiken (SC)
U of South Carolina Upstate (SC)
The U of South Dakota (SD)
U of Southern California (CA)
U of Southern Indiana (IN)
U of Southern Maine (ME)
U of Southern Mississippi (MS)
U of South Florida (FL)
The U of Tampa (FL)
The U of Tennessee (TN)
The U of Tennessee at Chattanooga (TN)
The U of Tennessee at Martin (TN)
The U of Texas at Arlington (TX)
The U of Texas at Austin (TX)
The U of Texas at Brownsville (TX)
The U of Texas at Dallas (TX)
The U of Texas at El Paso (TX)
The U of Texas at San Antonio (TX)
The U of Texas of the Permian Basin (TX)
The U of Texas–Pan American (TX)

U of the Cumberlands (KY)
U of the District of Columbia (DC)
U of the Incarnate Word (TX)
The U of Toledo (OH)
U of Tulsa (OK)
U of Utah (UT)
U of Vermont (VT)
U of Virginia (VA)
U of Washington, Tacoma (WA)
U of Waterloo (ON, Canada)
The U of Western Ontario (ON, Canada)
U of West Florida (FL)
U of West Georgia (GA)
U of Windsor (ON, Canada)
U of Wisconsin–Eau Claire (WI)
U of Wisconsin–Green Bay (WI)
U of Wisconsin–La Crosse (WI)
U of Wisconsin–Madison (WI)
U of Wisconsin–Milwaukee (WI)
U of Wisconsin–Parkside (WI)
U of Wisconsin–Platteville (WI)
U of Wisconsin–Stevens Point (WI)
U of Wisconsin–Superior (WI)
U of Wyoming (WY)
Utah State U (UT)
Utica Coll (NY)
Valdosta State U (GA)
Valparaiso U (IN)
Vanderbilt U (TN)
Vassar Coll (NY)
Villanova U (PA)
Virginia Commonwealth U (VA)
Virginia Polytechnic Inst and State U (VA)
Virginia State U (VA)
Virginia Union U (VA)
Virginia Wesleyan Coll (VA)
Wabash Coll (IN)
Wagner Coll (NY)
Wake Forest U (NC)
Walsh U (OH)
Wartburg Coll (IA)
Washburn U (KS)
Washington & Jefferson Coll (PA)
Washington and Lee U (VA)
Washington Coll (MD)
Washington State U (WA)
Washington U in St. Louis (MO)
Wayne State Coll (NE)
Wayne State U (MI)
Weber State U (UT)
Webster U (MO)
Wellesley Coll (MA)
Wells Coll (NY)
Wesleyan Coll (GA)
Wesleyan U (CT)
Wesley Coll (DE)
West Chester U of Pennsylvania (PA)
Western Carolina U (NC)
Western Connecticut State U (CT)
Western Illinois U (IL)
Western Kentucky U (KY)
Western Michigan U (MI)
Western Oregon U (OR)
Western State Colorado U (CO)
Western Washington U (WA)
Westfield State U (MA)
West Liberty U (WV)
Westminster Coll (MO)
Westminster Coll (UT)
West Texas A&M U (TX)
West Virginia State U (WV)
West Virginia U (WV)
West Virginia Wesleyan Coll (WV)
Wheaton Coll (IL)
Wheaton Coll (MA)
Wheeling Jesuit U (WV)
Whitman Coll (WA)
Whitworth U (WA)
Wichita State U (KS)
Widener U (PA)
Wilberforce U (OH)
Wilkes U (PA)
Willamette U (OR)
William Jewell Coll (MO)
William Paterson U of New Jersey (NJ)
William Penn U (IA)
Williams Coll (MA)
Winthrop U (SC)
Wittenberg U (OH)
Woodbury U (CA)
Wright State U (OH)
Xavier U (OH)

Xavier U of Louisiana (LA)
Yale U (CT)
York Coll of Pennsylvania (PA)
York Coll of the City U of New York (NY)
Young Harris Coll (GA)
Youngstown State U (OH)

POLITICAL SCIENCE AND GOVERNMENT RELATED
American Jewish U (CA)
American U in Bulgaria (Bulgaria)
Belmont U (TN)
Bennington Coll (VT)
Buena Vista U (IA)
Capital U (OH)
Claflin U (SC)
Clarion U of Pennsylvania (PA)
Columbia U, School of General Studies (NY)
George Mason U (VA)
Georgetown Coll (KY)
Lebanese American U (Lebanon)
McDaniel Coll (MD)
Muhlenberg Coll (PA)
National U (CA)
Regis Coll (MA)
Sacred Heart U (CT)
Saint Mary's Coll of California (CA)
Saint Mary's U of Minnesota (MN)
Trevecca Nazarene U (TN)
U of California, Davis (CA)
U of Guelph (ON, Canada)
U of Hartford (CT)
U of Northern Iowa (IA)
Virginia Intermont Coll (VA)
Western Michigan U (MI)
Whitman Coll (WA)
William Peace U (NC)

POLYMER CHEMISTRY
Clemson U (SC)
Pittsburg State U (KS)
The U of Akron (OH)
U of Wisconsin–Stevens Point (WI)

POLYMER/PLASTICS ENGINEERING
Case Western Reserve U (OH)
Penn State Erie, The Behrend Coll (PA)
The U of Akron (OH)
U of Illinois at Urbana–Champaign (IL)
U of Southern California (CA)
U of Wisconsin–Stout (WI)

PORTUGUESE
Florida Intl U (FL)
Georgetown U (DC)
Indiana U Bloomington (IN)
The Ohio State U (OH)
Rhode Island Coll (RI)
Rutgers, The State U of New Jersey, New Brunswick (NJ)
Smith Coll (MA)
Tulane U (LA)
United States Military Acad (NY)
U of California, Los Angeles (CA)
U of California, Santa Barbara (CA)
U of Florida (FL)
U of Illinois at Urbana–Champaign (IL)
The U of Iowa (IA)
U of Massachusetts Amherst (MA)
U of Massachusetts Dartmouth (MA)
U of New Mexico (NM)
The U of Texas at Austin (TX)
U of Wisconsin–Madison (WI)
Yale U (CT)

POULTRY SCIENCE
Auburn U (AL)
Mississippi State U (MS)
North Carolina State U (NC)
Stephen F. Austin State U (TX)
Texas A&M U (TX)
Tuskegee U (AL)
U of Georgia (GA)
U of Maryland Eastern Shore (MD)
U of Wisconsin–Madison (WI)
Virginia Polytechnic Inst and State U (VA)

PRACTICAL NURSING, VOCATIONAL NURSING AND

NURSING ASSISTANTS RELATED
St. Joseph's Coll, Long Island Campus (NY)
St. Joseph's Coll, New York (NY)

PRE-CHIROPRACTIC
Augustana Coll (SD)
Millikin U (IL)
Oklahoma City U (OK)

PRE-DENTISTRY STUDIES
Abilene Christian U (TX)
Acadia U (NS, Canada)
Albertus Magnus Coll (CT)
Alma Coll (MI)
American U (DC)
Anderson U (IN)
Ashland U (OH)
Auburn U (AL)
Augsburg Coll (MN)
Augustana Coll (SD)
Baldwin Wallace U (OH)
Ball State U (IN)
Barry U (FL)
Bethany Coll (WV)
Blackburn Coll (IL)
Boise State U (ID)
Boston U (MA)
Bowling Green State U (OH)
Buffalo State Coll, State U of New York (NY)
California State U, Chico (CA)
California State U, East Bay (CA)
Calvin Coll (MI)
Campbellsville U (KY)
Cardinal Stritch U (WI)
Cedar Crest Coll (PA)
Centenary Coll of Louisiana (LA)
Chapman U (CA)
City Coll of the City U of New York (NY)
Clark U (MA)
Coe Coll (IA)
The Coll at Brockport, State U of New York (NY)
Coll of Saint Benedict (MN)
Concordia U Chicago (IL)
Concordia U, Nebraska (NE)
Cornerstone U (MI)
Dalhousie U (NS, Canada)
Defiance Coll (OH)
Dordt Coll (IA)
Drake U (IA)
Elmira Coll (NY)
Evangel U (MO)
Florida Southern Coll (FL)
Franklin Pierce U (NH)
Furman U (SC)
Gardner-Webb U (NC)
Georgia Southern U (GA)
Gettysburg Coll (PA)
Graceland U (IA)
Grand Valley State U (MI)
Gustavus Adolphus Coll (MN)
Hamline U (MN)
Hampton U (VA)
Hillsdale Coll (MI)
Hobart and William Smith Colls (NY)
Hofstra U (NY)
Houghton Coll (NY)
Illinois Coll (IL)
Indiana U–Purdue U Fort Wayne (IN)
Indiana Wesleyan U (IN)
Iowa State U of Science and Technology (IA)
Iowa Wesleyan Coll (IA)
John Carroll U (OH)
Juniata Coll (PA)
Kansas Wesleyan U (KS)
Kentucky Wesleyan Coll (KY)
Keuka Coll (NY)
King's Coll (PA)
Lake Superior State U (MI)
Lamar U (TX)
Langston U (OK)
La Salle U (PA)
Lawrence U (WI)
Lehigh U (PA)
Le Moyne Coll (NY)
LeTourneau U (TX)
Limestone Coll (SC)
Lindenwood U (MO)
Lindsey Wilson Coll (KY)
Lipscomb U (TN)
Lock Haven U of Pennsylvania (PA)

Loyola U New Orleans (LA)
Madonna U (MI)
Manchester U (IN)
Maryville U of Saint Louis (MO)
Mayville State U (ND)
McKendree U (IL)
Mercer U (GA)
Mercyhurst U (PA)
Midwestern State U (TX)
Millikin U (IL)
Minnesota State U Mankato (MN)
Mount Allison U (NB, Canada)
Mount Mercy U (IA)
Mount Vernon Nazarene U (OH)
Nazareth Coll of Rochester (NY)
Newman U (KS)
Niagara U (NY)
North Central Coll (IL)
Northern Michigan U (MI)
Northern State U (SD)
Northwestern Oklahoma State U (OK)
Northwest Nazarene U (ID)
Oglethorpe U (GA)
The Ohio State U (OH)
Ohio Wesleyan U (OH)
Oklahoma City U (OK)
Ouachita Baptist U (AR)
Pacific U (OR)
Pepperdine U, Malibu (CA)
Pittsburg State U (KS)
Queens U of Charlotte (NC)
Quinnipiac U (CT)
Regis U (CO)
Rhode Island Coll (RI)
Ripon Coll (WI)
Rivier U (NH)
Roberts Wesleyan Coll (NY)
Rochester Inst of Technology (NY)
Rockford Coll (IL)
Rutgers, The State U of New Jersey, New Brunswick (NJ)
Sacred Heart U (CT)
Saint Anselm Coll (NH)
Saint John's U (MN)
Saint Michael's Coll (VT)
St. Thomas U (FL)
Simpson Coll (IA)
Sonoma State U (CA)
Spring Hill Coll (AL)
State U of New York at Oswego (NY)
State U of New York Coll at Cortland (NY)
State U of New York Coll at Geneseo (NY)
Stetson U (FL)
Sul Ross State U (TX)
Susquehanna U (PA)
Syracuse U (NY)
Tarleton State U (TX)
Texas Wesleyan U (TX)
Trinity U (TX)
Union U (TN)
U of Bridgeport (CT)
U of Dallas (TX)
U of Evansville (IN)
U of Hartford (CT)
U of Illinois at Chicago (IL)
The U of Iowa (IA)
U of Maryland, Coll Park (MD)
U of Maryland Eastern Shore (MD)
U of Massachusetts Amherst (MA)
U of Minnesota, Twin Cities Campus (MN)
U of Nebraska–Lincoln (NE)
U of New Brunswick Fredericton (NB, Canada)
U of New England (ME)
U of Portland (OR)
U of Regina (SK, Canada)
U of St. Francis (IL)
The U of Tennessee at Martin (TN)
The U of Toledo (OH)
U of Windsor (ON, Canada)
U of Wisconsin–Parkside (WI)
Upper Iowa U (IA)
Utah State U (UT)
Utica Coll (NY)
Valley City State U (ND)
Virginia Wesleyan Coll (VA)
Wagner Coll (NY)
Walla Walla U (WA)
Walsh U (OH)
Washburn U (KS)
Washington Coll (MD)
Washington U in St. Louis (MO)

Waynesburg U (PA)
Wells Coll (NY)
West Liberty U (WV)
West Virginia State U (WV)
West Virginia Wesleyan Coll (WV)
Whitworth U (WA)
Widener U (PA)
William Paterson U of New Jersey (NJ)
William Penn U (IA)
Young Harris Coll (GA)
Youngstown State U (OH)

PRE-ENGINEERING
Asbury U (KY)
Augustana Coll (SD)
Azusa Pacific U (CA)
Baldwin Wallace U (OH)
Canisius Coll (NY)
Drake U (IA)
Faulkner U (AL)
Houghton Coll (NY)
Le Moyne Coll (NY)
Midwestern State U (TX)
Northwest Nazarene U (ID)
Ouachita Baptist U (AR)
Pittsburg State U (KS)
Roberts Wesleyan Coll (NY)
Scripps Coll (CA)
Simpson Coll (IA)
Slippery Rock U of Pennsylvania (PA)
Spring Hill Coll (AL)
The U of Scranton (PA)
Valley City State U (ND)
Wagner Coll (NY)
Waynesburg U (PA)
West Texas A&M U (TX)
Wheeling Jesuit U (WV)

PRE-LAW STUDIES
Abilene Christian U (TX)
Acadia U (NS, Canada)
Albertus Magnus Coll (CT)
Albright Coll (PA)
Alma Coll (MI)
American U (DC)
Anderson U (IN)
Andrews U (MI)
Ashland U (OH)
Auburn U (AL)
Augsburg Coll (MN)
Augustana Coll (SD)
Azusa Pacific U (CA)
Babson Coll (MA)
Bard Coll (NY)
Barry U (FL)
Baylor U (TX)
Bemidji State U (MN)
Bennington Coll (VT)
Bethany Coll (WV)
Bethel Coll (IN)
Binghamton U, State U of New York (NY)
Blackburn Coll (IL)
Bowling Green State U (OH)
Bryant U (RI)
Buffalo State Coll, State U of New York (NY)
California State U, Dominguez Hills (CA)
California State U, Fresno (CA)
Calumet Coll of Saint Joseph (IN)
Calvin Coll (MI)
Campbellsville U (KY)
Cardinal Stritch U (WI)
Cedar Crest Coll (PA)
Cedarville U (OH)
Centenary Coll of Louisiana (LA)
Chowan U (NC)
City Coll of the City U of New York (NY)
Clark U (MA)
Clearwater Christian Coll (FL)
Coe Coll (IA)
The Coll at Brockport, State U of New York (NY)
The Coll of New Rochelle (NY)
Coll of Saint Benedict (MN)
The Coll of Saint Rose (NY)
Concordia Coll–New York (NY)
Concordia U Chicago (IL)
Concordia U, Nebraska (NE)
Concordia U Wisconsin (WI)
Corban U (OR)
Crown Coll (MN)
Curry Coll (MA)

Dalhousie U (NS, Canada)
Defiance Coll (OH)
DeSales U (PA)
Dominican Coll (NY)
Dominican U (IL)
Dordt Coll (IA)
Drake U (IA)
Elmira Coll (NY)
Emmanuel Coll (GA)
Emory & Henry Coll (VA)
Evangel U (MO)
Faulkner U (AL)
Florida Inst of Technology (FL)
Francis Marion U (SC)
Franklin Pierce U (NH)
Furman U (SC)
Gannon U (PA)
Gardner-Webb U (NC)
Gettysburg Coll (PA)
Grand View U (IA)
Gustavus Adolphus Coll (MN)
Hamline U (MN)
Hampton U (VA)
Hartwick Coll (NY)
Hawai`i Pacific U (HI)
Hiram Coll (OH)
Hobart and William Smith Colls (NY)
Hofstra U (NY)
Houghton Coll (NY)
Howard Payne U (TX)
Huntington U (IN)
Illinois Coll (IL)
Indiana Tech (IN)
Indiana Wesleyan U (IN)
Iowa State U of Science and Technology (IA)
Iowa Wesleyan Coll (IA)
Ithaca Coll (NY)
John Carroll U (OH)
Juniata Coll (PA)
Kansas Wesleyan U (KS)
Kentucky Wesleyan Coll (KY)
Keuka Coll (NY)
Keystone Coll (PA)
King Coll (TN)
King's Coll (PA)
Lake Superior State U (MI)
Langston U (OK)
Lawrence U (WI)
Le Moyne Coll (NY)
LeTourneau U (TX)
Limestone Coll (SC)
Lincoln Memorial U (TN)
Lindenwood U (MO)
Lindsey Wilson Coll (KY)
Lipscomb U (TN)
Louisiana Coll (LA)
Lubbock Christian U (TX)
Madonna U (MI)
Manchester U (IN)
Mansfield U of Pennsylvania (PA)
Mars Hill Coll (NC)
Massachusetts Coll of Liberal Arts (MA)
The Master's Coll and Sem (CA)
Mayville State U (ND)
McKendree U (IL)
Michigan State U (MI)
Midwestern State U (TX)
Millikin U (IL)
Minnesota State U Mankato (MN)
Mount Allison U (NB, Canada)
Mount Mercy U (IA)
Mount Vernon Nazarene U (OH)
Nazareth Coll of Rochester (NY)
New England Coll (NH)
Newman U (KS)
Niagara U (NY)
North Central Coll (IL)
Northern Arizona U (AZ)
Northern Michigan U (MI)
Northern State U (SD)
Northwestern Oklahoma State U (OK)
Northwest Nazarene U (ID)
Notre Dame de Namur U (CA)
Nova Southeastern U (FL)
Oakland City U (IN)
Oglethorpe U (GA)
Ohio Wesleyan U (OH)
Oklahoma Christian U (OK)
Oklahoma City U (OK)
Ouachita Baptist U (AR)
Pacific Lutheran U (WA)
Pacific Union Coll (CA)
Palm Beach Atlantic U (FL)

Pepperdine U, Malibu (CA)
Pittsburg State U (KS)
Purdue U Calumet (IN)
Queens U of Charlotte (NC)
Quinnipiac U (CT)
Regis U (CO)
Rensselaer Polytechnic Inst (NY)
Rhode Island Coll (RI)
Ripon Coll (WI)
Rivier U (NH)
Roberts Wesleyan Coll (NY)
Rochester Inst of Technology (NY)
Rockford Coll (IL)
Rutgers, The State U of New Jersey, New Brunswick (NJ)
Saint Anselm Coll (NH)
Saint John's U (MN)
Saint Mary-of-the-Woods Coll (IN)
Saint Michael's Coll (VT)
St. Thomas U (FL)
Seton Hill U (PA)
Siena Heights U (MI)
Simpson Coll (IA)
Smith Coll (MA)
Sonoma State U (CA)
Southern Oregon U (OR)
State U of New York at Fredonia (NY)
State U of New York at New Paltz (NY)
State U of New York at Oswego (NY)
State U of New York Coll at Cortland (NY)
State U of New York Coll at Geneseo (NY)
Stephens Coll (MO)
Stetson U (FL)
Suffolk U (MA)
Sul Ross State U (TX)
Susquehanna U (PA)
Syracuse U (NY)
Texas Wesleyan U (TX)
Trine U (IN)
Trinity U (TX)
Union U (TN)
United States Military Acad (NY)
U of Bridgeport (CT)
U of California, Santa Barbara (CA)
U of California, Santa Cruz (CA)
U of Dallas (TX)
The U of Findlay (OH)
U of Illinois at Urbana–Champaign (IL)
The U of Iowa (IA)
U of Maryland, Coll Park (MD)
U of Maryland Eastern Shore (MD)
U of Minnesota, Twin Cities Campus (MN)
U of New Brunswick Fredericton (NB, Canada)
U of Pittsburgh at Greensburg (PA)
U of Portland (OR)
U of Regina (SK, Canada)
U of St. Francis (IL)
The U of Toledo (OH)
U of Windsor (ON, Canada)
U of Wisconsin–Superior (WI)
Utah State U (UT)
Valley City State U (ND)
Wabash Coll (IN)
Wagner Coll (NY)
Walla Walla U (WA)
Warner Pacific Coll (OR)
Washburn U (KS)
Washington Coll (MD)
Wayland Baptist U (TX)
Waynesburg U (PA)
Webber Intl U (FL)
Wells Coll (NY)
Western State Colorado U (CO)
West Liberty U (WV)
Westminster Coll (MO)
West Texas A&M U (TX)
West Virginia Wesleyan Coll (WV)
Whitworth U (WA)
William Paterson U of New Jersey (NJ)
William Peace U (NC)
William Penn U (IA)
Xavier U of Louisiana (LA)
Young Harris Coll (GA)
Youngstown State U (OH)

PREMEDICAL STUDIES
Abilene Christian U (TX)

Acadia U (NS, Canada)
Albertus Magnus Coll (CT)
Alma Coll (MI)
American U (DC)
Anderson U (IN)
Andrews U (MI)
Ashland U (OH)
Auburn U (AL)
Augsburg Coll (MN)
Augustana Coll (IL)
Augustana Coll (SD)
Averett U (VA)
Baldwin Wallace U (OH)
Ball State U (IN)
Bard Coll (NY)
Barry U (FL)
Bemidji State U (MN)
Bennington Coll (VT)
Bethany Coll (WV)
Bethel U (IN)
Binghamton U, State U of New York (NY)
Blackburn Coll (IL)
Bluffton U (OH)
Bob Jones U (SC)
Boise State U (ID)
Bowling Green State U (OH)
Buffalo State Coll, State U of New York (NY)
California State U, Chico (CA)
California State U, East Bay (CA)
Calvin Coll (MI)
Campbellsville U (KY)
Cardinal Stritch U (WI)
Caribbean U (PR)
Cedar Crest Coll (PA)
Centenary Coll of Louisiana (LA)
Chapman U (CA)
Chowan U (NC)
City Coll of the City U of New York (NY)
Clark U (MA)
Clearwater Christian Coll (FL)
Coe Coll (IA)
The Coll at Brockport, State U of New York (NY)
The Coll of New Rochelle (NY)
Coll of Saint Benedict (MN)
Concordia U (OR)
Concordia U Chicago (IL)
Concordia U, Nebraska (NE)
Concord U (WV)
Cornerstone U (MI)
Dalhousie U (NS, Canada)
Defiance Coll (OH)
Dominican U (IL)
Dordt Coll (IA)
Drake U (IA)
Earlham Coll (IN)
Elmira Coll (NY)
Evangel U (MO)
Florida Southern Coll (FL)
Franklin Pierce U (NH)
Furman U (SC)
Gannon U (PA)
Gardner-Webb U (NC)
Georgia Southern U (GA)
Gettysburg Coll (PA)
Graceland U (IA)
Grand Valley State U (MI)
Gustavus Adolphus Coll (MN)
Hamline U (MN)
Hampton U (VA)
Hartwick Coll (NY)
Hawai`i Pacific U (HI)
Hillsdale Coll (MI)
Hobart and William Smith Colls (NY)
Hofstra U (NY)
Houghton Coll (NY)
Huntington U (IN)
Illinois Coll (IL)
Immaculata U (PA)
Indiana U–Purdue U Fort Wayne (IN)
Indiana U–Purdue U Indianapolis (IN)
Indiana Wesleyan U (IN)
Inter American U of Puerto Rico, Bayamón Campus (PR)
Iowa State U of Science and Technology (IA)
Iowa Wesleyan Coll (IA)
Ithaca Coll (NY)
John Carroll U (OH)
Johnson State Coll (VT)
Juniata Coll (PA)

Kansas Wesleyan U (KS)
Kentucky Wesleyan Coll (KY)
Keuka Coll (NY)
Keystone Coll (PA)
King Coll (TN)
King's Coll (PA)
Langston U (OK)
La Salle U (PA)
Lawrence U (WI)
Lehigh U (PA)
Le Moyne Coll (NY)
LeTourneau U (TX)
Limestone Coll (SC)
Lincoln Memorial U (TN)
Lindenwood U (MO)
Lindsey Wilson Coll (KY)
Lipscomb U (TN)
Lock Haven U of Pennsylvania (PA)
Loyola U New Orleans (LA)
Madonna U (MI)
Manchester U (IN)
Mars Hill Coll (NC)
Maryville U of Saint Louis (MO)
Massachusetts Coll of Liberal Arts (MA)
Massachusetts Coll of Pharmacy and Health Sciences (MA)
The Master's Coll and Sem (CA)
Mayville State U (ND)
McKendree U (IL)
Mercer U (GA)
Mercy Coll of Health Sciences (IA)
Michigan State U (MI)
Midwestern State U (TX)
Millikin U (IL)
Minnesota State U Mankato (MN)
Mount Allison U (NB, Canada)
Mount Mercy U (IA)
Mount Vernon Nazarene U (OH)
Nazareth Coll of Rochester (NY)
Newman U (KS)
New York Inst of Technology (NY)
Niagara U (NY)
North Carolina Wesleyan Coll (NC)
North Central Coll (IL)
Northern Michigan U (MI)
Northern State U (SD)
Northwestern Oklahoma State U (OK)
Northwest Nazarene U (ID)
Notre Dame de Namur U (CA)
Nova Southeastern U (FL)
Oakland City U (IN)
Oglethorpe U (GA)
Ohio Wesleyan U (OH)
Oklahoma City U (OK)
Ouachita Baptist U (AR)
Pacific Lutheran U (WA)
Pacific U (OR)
Penn State Abington (PA)
Penn State Altoona (PA)
Penn State Beaver (PA)
Penn State Berks (PA)
Penn State Brandywine (PA)
Penn State DuBois (PA)
Penn State Erie, The Behrend Coll (PA)
Penn State Fayette, The Eberly Campus (PA)
Penn State Greater Allegheny (PA)
Penn State Hazleton (PA)
Penn State Lehigh Valley (PA)
Penn State Mont Alto (PA)
Penn State New Kensington (PA)
Penn State Schuylkill (PA)
Penn State Shenango (PA)
Penn State U Park (PA)
Penn State Wilkes-Barre (PA)
Penn State Worthington Scranton (PA)
Penn State York (PA)
Pepperdine U, Malibu (CA)
Philadelphia U (PA)
Pittsburg State U (KS)
Pomona Coll (CA)
Purdue U Calumet (IN)
Queens U of Charlotte (NC)
Quinnipiac U (CT)
Regis U (CO)
Rensselaer Polytechnic Inst (NY)
Rhode Island Coll (RI)
Ripon Coll (WI)
Rivier U (NH)
Roberts Wesleyan Coll (NY)
Rochester Inst of Technology (NY)
Rockford Coll (IL)

Rutgers, The State U of New Jersey, New Brunswick (NJ)
Sacred Heart U (CT)
St. Andrews U (NC)
Saint Anselm Coll (NH)
Saint John's U (MN)
Saint Michael's Coll (VT)
St. Thomas Aquinas Coll (NY)
St. Thomas U (FL)
Samford U (AL)
Simpson Coll (IA)
Slippery Rock U of Pennsylvania (PA)
Smith Coll (MA)
Sonoma State U (CA)
Southeastern U (FL)
Southern Oregon U (OR)
Spring Hill Coll (AL)
State U of New York at Fredonia (NY)
State U of New York at Oswego (NY)
State U of New York Coll at Cortland (NY)
State U of New York Coll at Geneseo (NY)
Stetson U (FL)
Sul Ross State U (TX)
Susquehanna U (PA)
Syracuse U (NY)
Tarleton State U (TX)
Texas Lutheran U (TX)
Trine U (IN)
Trinity U (TX)
Union U (TN)
Université de Sherbrooke (QC, Canada)
The U of Akron (OH)
U of Bridgeport (CT)
U of California, Santa Cruz (CA)
U of Dallas (TX)
U of Evansville (IN)
The U of Findlay (OH)
U of Hartford (CT)
The U of Iowa (IA)
U of Maine at Machias (ME)
U of Maryland Eastern Shore (MD)
U of Massachusetts Amherst (MA)
U of Minnesota, Twin Cities Campus (MN)
U of Nebraska–Lincoln (NE)
U of New Brunswick Fredericton (NB, Canada)
U of New England (ME)
U of Notre Dame (IN)
U of Portland (OR)
U of Regina (SK, Canada)
U of St. Francis (IL)
The U of Tennessee at Martin (TN)
The U of Toledo (OH)
U of Windsor (ON, Canada)
U of Wisconsin–Madison (WI)
U of Wisconsin–Milwaukee (WI)
U of Wisconsin–Parkside (WI)
Upper Iowa U (IA)
Utah State U (UT)
Utica Coll (NY)
Valley City State U (ND)
Virginia Intermont Coll (VA)
Virginia Wesleyan Coll (VA)
Wabash Coll (IN)
Wagner Coll (NY)
Walla Walla U (WA)
Walsh U (OH)
Warner Pacific Coll (OR)
Washburn U (KS)
Washington Coll (MD)
Washington State U (WA)
Washington U in St. Louis (MO)
Waynesburg U (PA)
Wells Coll (NY)
West Chester U of Pennsylvania (PA)
West Liberty U (WV)
West Virginia State U (WV)
West Virginia Wesleyan Coll (WV)
Wheeling Jesuit U (WV)
Whitworth U (WA)
Widener U (PA)
William Paterson U of New Jersey (NJ)
William Penn U (IA)
Xavier U of Louisiana (LA)
Young Harris Coll (GA)
Youngstown State U (OH)

PRENURSING STUDIES
American U (DC)
Baylor U (TX)
Brigham Young U (UT)
California State U, Fullerton (CA)
Cleveland State U (OH)
The Coll of Idaho (ID)
Concordia U, Nebraska (NE)
Gettysburg Coll (PA)
Hardin-Simmons U (TX)
Houghton Coll (NY)
Juniata Coll (PA)
Limestone Coll (SC)
Lindenwood U (MO)
Lipscomb U (TN)
Madonna U (MI)
McMurry U (TX)
Missouri Baptist U (MO)
Northwestern Coll (MN)
Oklahoma City U (OK)
Ouachita Baptist U (AR)
St. Thomas U (FL)
San Diego State U (CA)
Simpson Coll (IA)
State U of New York Coll at Geneseo (NY)
Tennessee Wesleyan Coll (TN)
Wright State U (OH)

PRE-OCCUPATIONAL THERAPY
Augustana Coll (SD)
Millikin U (IL)
Trevecca Nazarene U (TN)

PRE-OPTOMETRY
Augustana Coll (SD)
Calvin Coll (MI)
Lehigh U (PA)
Le Moyne Coll (NY)
Millikin U (IL)
Oklahoma City U (OK)
Simpson Coll (IA)
U of Evansville (IN)
Young Harris Coll (GA)

PRE-PHARMACY STUDIES
Abilene Christian U (TX)
American U (DC)
Ashland U (OH)
Auburn U (AL)
Augustana Coll (SD)
Baldwin Wallace U (OH)
Barry U (FL)
Benedictine U (IL)
Calvin Coll (MI)
Coll of Saint Benedict (MN)
Concordia U, Nebraska (NE)
Dalhousie U (NS, Canada)
Dominican U (IL)
Dordt Coll (IA)
Emmanuel Coll (GA)
Emory & Henry Coll (VA)
Gardner-Webb U (NC)
Georgia Southern U (GA)
Gettysburg Coll (PA)
Hamline U (MN)
Houghton Coll (NY)
Huntington U (IN)
Iowa Wesleyan Coll (IA)
Juniata Coll (PA)
King Coll (TN)
King's Coll (PA)
Le Moyne Coll (NY)
Limestone Coll (SC)
Lindsey Wilson Coll (KY)
Lipscomb U (TN)
Long Island U–C. W. Post Campus (NY)
Mayville State U (ND)
Midwestern State U (TX)
Millikin U (IL)
Mount Allison U (NB, Canada)
Mount Vernon Nazarene U (OH)
Northern Michigan U (MI)
Northwest Nazarene U (ID)
Oklahoma City U (OK)
Ouachita Baptist U (AR)
Pittsburg State U (KS)
Purdue U Calumet (IN)
Roberts Wesleyan Coll (NY)
Saint John's U (MN)
Simpson Coll (IA)
Slippery Rock U of Pennsylvania (PA)
Tarleton State U (TX)
Texas Southern U (TX)
Union U (TN)

U of Charleston (WV)
U of Evansville (IN)
The U of Iowa (IA)
U of Minnesota, Twin Cities Campus (MN)
U of Nebraska–Lincoln (NE)
U of Regina (SK, Canada)
U of St. Francis (IL)
The U of Tennessee at Martin (TN)
U of Windsor (ON, Canada)
U of Wisconsin–Parkside (WI)
Valley City State U (ND)
Walsh U (OH)
Washburn U (KS)
Washington U in St. Louis (MO)
West Virginia Wesleyan Coll (WV)
Wheeling Jesuit U (WV)
Young Harris Coll (GA)
Youngstown State U (OH)

PRE-PHYSICAL THERAPY
Asbury U (KY)
Augustana Coll (SD)
California Baptist U (CA)
Calvin Coll (MI)
Iowa Wesleyan Coll (IA)
Massachusetts Coll of Liberal Arts (MA)
Midwestern State U (TX)
Millikin U (IL)
Oklahoma City U (OK)
Pittsburg State U (KS)
Saint Mary's U of Minnesota (MN)
Simpson Coll (IA)
Trevecca Nazarene U (TN)
U of Kentucky (KY)
Walsh U (OH)

PRE-THEOLOGY/PRE-MINISTERIAL STUDIES
Alma Coll (MI)
Ashland U (OH)
Augustana Coll (SD)
California Baptist U (CA)
Calvin Coll (MI)
Cedarville U (OH)
Coll of Saint Benedict (MN)
Columbia Bible Coll (BC, Canada)
Columbia Intl U (SC)
Concordia Coll–New York (NY)
Concordia U (OR)
Concordia U Chicago (IL)
Concordia U, Nebraska (NE)
Corban U (OR)
Cornerstone U (MI)
Crossroads Coll (MN)
Grace U (NE)
John Brown U (AR)
Kuyper Coll (MI)
Lee U (TN)
Manchester U (IN)
Martin Luther Coll (MN)
Mid-Atlantic Christian U (NC)
Mount Allison U (NB, Canada)
Northwestern Coll (MN)
Nyack Coll (NY)
Ohio Wesleyan U (OH)
Oral Roberts U (OK)
Point Loma Nazarene U (CA)
Point U (GA)
Saint John's U (MN)
Simpson Coll (IA)
Southeastern U (FL)
Tennessee Wesleyan Coll (TN)
Trinity Coll of Florida (FL)
U of Dallas (TX)
Washburn U (KS)
Waynesburg U (PA)

PRE-VETERINARY STUDIES
Abilene Christian U (TX)
Acadia U (NS, Canada)
Albertus Magnus Coll (CT)
Alma Coll (MI)
American U (DC)
Anderson U (IN)
Andrews U (MI)
Ashland U (OH)
Auburn U (AL)
Augsburg Coll (MN)
Augustana Coll (SD)
Baldwin Wallace U (OH)
Barry U (FL)
Becker Coll (MA)
Bemidji State U (MN)
Bethany Coll (WV)
Binghamton U, State U of New York (NY)

Blackburn Coll (IL)
Boise State U (ID)
Buffalo State Coll, State U of New York (NY)
California State U, Chico (CA)
California State U, East Bay (CA)
Calvin Coll (MI)
Campbellsville U (KY)
Cardinal Stritch U (WI)
Cedar Crest Coll (PA)
Centenary Coll of Louisiana (LA)
Chapman U (CA)
City Coll of the City U of New York (NY)
Clark U (MA)
Coe Coll (IA)
The Coll at Brockport, State U of New York (NY)
Coll of Saint Benedict (MN)
Coll of the Atlantic (ME)
Concordia Coll–New York (NY)
Concordia U, Nebraska (NE)
Concord U (WV)
Cornerstone U (MI)
Dalhousie U (NS, Canada)
Defiance Coll (OH)
Dordt Coll (IA)
Drake U (IA)
Elmira Coll (NY)
Emory & Henry Coll (VA)
Evangel U (MO)
Florida Southern Coll (FL)
Franklin Pierce U (NH)
Furman U (SC)
Gardner-Webb U (NC)
Georgia Southern U (GA)
Gettysburg Coll (PA)
Grand Valley State U (MI)
Gustavus Adolphus Coll (MN)
Hamline U (MN)
Hampton U (VA)
Hartwick Coll (NY)
Hillsdale Coll (MI)
Hobart and William Smith Colls (NY)
Hofstra U (NY)
Houghton Coll (NY)
Illinois Coll (IL)
Indiana U–Purdue U Fort Wayne (IN)
Indiana Wesleyan U (IN)
Iowa State U of Science and Technology (IA)
Iowa Wesleyan Coll (IA)
John Carroll U (OH)
Juniata Coll (PA)
Kansas Wesleyan U (KS)
Kentucky Wesleyan Coll (KY)
Keuka Coll (NY)
King Coll (TN)
King's Coll (PA)
Langston U (OK)
La Salle U (PA)
Lawrence U (WI)
Le Moyne Coll (NY)
LeTourneau U (TX)
Limestone Coll (SC)
Lincoln Memorial U (TN)
Lindenwood U (MO)
Lindsey Wilson Coll (KY)
Lipscomb U (TN)
Lock Haven U of Pennsylvania (PA)
Loyola U New Orleans (LA)
Manchester U (IN)
Mars Hill Coll (NC)
Mayville State U (ND)
McKendree U (IL)
Mercyhurst U (PA)
Midwestern State U (TX)
Millikin U (IL)
Minnesota State U Mankato (MN)
Montana State U (MT)
Mount Allison U (NB, Canada)
Mount Mercy U (IA)
Mount Vernon Nazarene U (OH)
Nazareth Coll of Rochester (NY)
Newman U (KS)
Niagara U (NY)
North Central Coll (IL)
Northern Michigan U (MI)
Northwest Missouri State U (MO)
Northwest Nazarene U (ID)
Oakland City U (IN)
Oglethorpe U (GA)
Ohio Wesleyan U (OH)
Oklahoma City U (OK)
Ouachita Baptist U (AR)

Pacific U (OR)
Penn State U Park (PA)
Pittsburg State U (KS)
Purdue U (IN)
Purdue U Calumet (IN)
Queens U of Charlotte (NC)
Quinnipiac U (CT)
Regis U (CO)
Rhode Island Coll (RI)
Ripon Coll (WI)
Rivier U (NH)
Roberts Wesleyan Coll (NY)
Rochester Inst of Technology (NY)
Rockford Coll (IL)
Sacred Heart U (CT)
St. Andrews U (NC)
Saint John's U (MN)
Saint Michael's Coll (VT)
Simpson Coll (IA)
Sonoma State U (CA)
Spring Hill Coll (AL)
State U of New York at Fredonia (NY)
State U of New York at Oswego (NY)
State U of New York Coll at Geneseo (NY)
Stetson U (FL)
Sul Ross State U (TX)
Susquehanna U (PA)
Syracuse U (NY)
Tarleton State U (TX)
Texas A&M U (TX)
Trinity U (TX)
The U of Arizona (AZ)
U of Bridgeport (CT)
The U of British Columbia (BC, Canada)
U of Delaware (DE)
U of Evansville (IN)
The U of Findlay (OH)
U of Illinois at Chicago (IL)
U of Illinois at Urbana–Champaign (IL)
The U of Iowa (IA)
U of Maryland, Coll Park (MD)
U of Massachusetts Amherst (MA)
U of Minnesota, Crookston (MN)
U of Minnesota, Twin Cities Campus (MN)
U of Nebraska–Lincoln (NE)
U of Nevada, Reno (NV)
U of New Brunswick Fredericton (NB, Canada)
U of Regina (SK, Canada)
U of St. Francis (IL)
The U of Tennessee at Martin (TN)
The U of Toledo (OH)
U of Wisconsin–Parkside (WI)
Upper Iowa U (IA)
Utah State U (UT)
Utica Coll (NY)
Valley City State U (ND)
Virginia Intermont Coll (VA)
Virginia Wesleyan Coll (VA)
Wabash Coll (IN)
Walla Walla U (WA)
Walsh U (OH)
Warner Pacific Coll (OR)
Washburn U (KS)
Washington Coll (MD)
Washington U in St. Louis (MO)
Waynesburg U (PA)
Wells Coll (NY)
West Virginia State U (WV)
West Virginia Wesleyan Coll (WV)
Whitworth U (WA)
Widener U (PA)
Young Harris Coll (GA)
Youngstown State U (OH)

PRINTING MANAGEMENT
Coll of the Ozarks (MO)
Ferris State U (MI)
Kean U (NJ)
Pittsburg State U (KS)
Rochester Inst of Technology (NY)
West Virginia U Inst of Technology (WV)

PRINTMAKING
Acad of Art U (CA)
Adams State U (CO)
Alberta Coll of Art & Design (AB, Canada)
Bennington Coll (VT)
Bowling Green State U (OH)

Bradley U (IL)
Brigham Young U (UT)
Buffalo State Coll, State U of New York (NY)
California State U, East Bay (CA)
California State U, Long Beach (CA)
Central Michigan U (MI)
Cleveland Inst of Art (OH)
Columbia Coll (MO)
Concordia U (QC, Canada)
Drake U (IA)
Indiana U–Purdue U Fort Wayne (IN)
Indiana Wesleyan U (IN)
Inter American U of Puerto Rico, San Germán Campus (PR)
Maryland Inst Coll of Art (MD)
Massachusetts Coll of Art and Design (MA)
Mount Allison U (NB, Canada)
Northern Michigan U (MI)
Northwest Nazarene U (ID)
Ohio U (OH)
Pacific Northwest Coll of Art (OR)
Purchase Coll, State U of New York (NY)
Rhode Island School of Design (RI)
Ringling Coll of Art and Design (FL)
Rutgers, The State U of New Jersey, New Brunswick (NJ)
Salem State U (MA)
San Francisco Art Inst (CA)
Savannah Coll of Art and Design (GA)
School of the Art Inst of Chicago (IL)
School of the Museum of Fine Arts, Boston (MA)
Seton Hill U (PA)
Sonoma State U (CA)
State U of New York at New Paltz (NY)
Syracuse U (NY)
Temple U (PA)
Texas Christian U (TX)
The U of Akron (OH)
U of Dallas (TX)
U of Hartford (CT)
The U of Iowa (IA)
The U of Kansas (KS)
U of Miami (FL)
U of Michigan (MI)
U of Missouri–St. Louis (MO)
U of Oregon (OR)
U of Regina (SK, Canada)
The U of Texas at El Paso (TX)
The U of the Arts (PA)
U of Windsor (ON, Canada)
Virginia Intermont Coll (VA)
Washington U in St. Louis (MO)
Western State Colorado U (CO)
Western Washington U (WA)

PROFESSIONAL, TECHNICAL, BUSINESS, AND SCIENTIFIC WRITING
Arizona State U (AZ)
Boise State U (ID)
Bowling Green State U (OH)
Carnegie Mellon U (PA)
Cedarville U (OH)
Chatham U (PA)
Concordia U, St. Paul (MN)
Dakota State U (SD)
Eastern Michigan U (MI)
Eastern Washington U (WA)
Elizabethtown Coll (PA)
Farmingdale State Coll (NY)
Ferris State U (MI)
Indiana U–Purdue U Fort Wayne (IN)
Iowa State U of Science and Technology (IA)
James Madison U (VA)
Juniata Coll (PA)
King Coll (TN)
Kutztown U of Pennsylvania (PA)
Madonna U (MI)
Maryville Coll (TN)
Massachusetts Coll of Liberal Arts (MA)
Michigan State U (MI)
Missouri State U (MO)
Montana Tech of The U of Montana (MT)

Mount Mary Coll (WI)
New Jersey Inst of Technology (NJ)
New Mexico Inst of Mining and Technology (NM)
New York Inst of Technology (NY)
Penn State Berks (PA)
Penn State Lehigh Valley (PA)
Pittsburg State U (KS)
Saint Leo U (FL)
Salem State U (MA)
San Francisco State U (CA)
Savannah Coll of Art and Design (GA)
Slippery Rock U of Pennsylvania (PA)
Spring Arbor U (MI)
Tarleton State U (TX)
Taylor U (IN)
U of Arkansas at Little Rock (AR)
U of Arkansas–Fort Smith (AR)
U of Hartford (CT)
U of Houston–Downtown (TX)
U of Idaho (ID)
U of Wisconsin–Stout (WI)
Valparaiso U (IN)
Winthrop U (SC)
Worcester Polytechnic Inst (MA)
York Coll of Pennsylvania (PA)
Youngstown State U (OH)

PROJECT MANAGEMENT
Huntington U (IN)
Malone U (OH)
Northcentral U (AZ)
Wentworth Inst of Technology (MA)

PSYCHIATRIC/MENTAL HEALTH SERVICES TECHNOLOGY
Indiana U–Purdue U Fort Wayne (IN)
U of Alaska Anchorage (AK)

PSYCHOLOGY
Abilene Christian U (TX)
Acadia U (NS, Canada)
Adams State U (CO)
Adelphi U (NY)
Agnes Scott Coll (GA)
Alabama State U (AL)
Alaska Pacific U (AK)
Albertus Magnus Coll (CT)
Albion Coll (MI)
Albright Coll (PA)
Alcorn State U (MS)
Alderson-Broaddus Coll (WV)
Alfred U (NY)
Alliant Intl U (CA)
Alliant Intl U–México City (Mexico)
Alma Coll (MI)
Alvernia U (PA)
Alverno Coll (WI)
American Jewish U (CA)
American Public U System (WV)
American U (DC)
The American U in Cairo (Egypt)
American U of Beirut (Lebanon)
The American U of Paris (France)
Amherst Coll (MA)
Anderson U (IN)
Anderson U (SC)
Andrews U (MI)
Angelo State U (TX)
Appalachian State U (NC)
Arizona State U (AZ)
Arkansas State U (AR)
Arkansas Tech U (AR)
Armstrong Atlantic State U (GA)
Asbury U (KY)
Ashland U (OH)
Assumption Coll (MA)
Athabasca U (AB, Canada)
Athens State U (AL)
Auburn U (AL)
Auburn U at Montgomery (AL)
Augsburg Coll (MN)
Augustana Coll (IL)
Augustana Coll (SD)
Aurora U (IL)
Austin Peay State U (TN)
Averett U (VA)
Avila U (MO)
Azusa Pacific U (CA)
Baker U (KS)
Baldwin Wallace U (OH)
Ball State U (IN)
Barclay Coll (KS)
Bard Coll (NY)

Barry U (FL)
Barton Coll (NC)
Bastyr U (WA)
Bates Coll (ME)
Baylor U (TX)
Bay Path Coll (MA)
Beacon Coll (FL)
Becker Coll (MA)
Belhaven U (MS)
Bellarmine U (KY)
Belmont Abbey Coll (NC)
Belmont U (TN)
Bemidji State U (MN)
Benedictine Coll (KS)
Benedictine U (IL)
Bennington Coll (VT)
Berea Coll (KY)
Berry Coll (GA)
Bethany Coll (WV)
Bethany Lutheran Coll (MN)
Bethel Coll (IN)
Bethel Coll (KS)
Bethel U (MN)
Bethune-Cookman U (FL)
Binghamton U, State U of New York (NY)
Blackburn Coll (IL)
Bloomfield Coll (NJ)
Bloomsburg U of Pennsylvania (PA)
Bluefield Coll (VA)
Blue Mountain Coll (MS)
Bluffton U (OH)
Boise State U (ID)
Boston Coll (MA)
Boston U (MA)
Bowdoin Coll (ME)
Bowie State U (MD)
Bowling Green State U (OH)
Brevard Coll (NC)
Bridgewater Coll (VA)
Bridgewater State U (MA)
Brock U (ON, Canada)
Brown U (RI)
Bryant U (RI)
Bryn Athyn Coll of the New Church (PA)
Bucknell U (PA)
Buena Vista U (IA)
Buffalo State Coll, State U of New York (NY)
Butler U (IN)
Cabrini Coll (PA)
Caldwell Coll (NJ)
California Baptist U (CA)
California Lutheran U (CA)
California Polytechnic State U, San Luis Obispo (CA)
California State Polytechnic U, Pomona (CA)
California State U, Chico (CA)
California State U, Dominguez Hills (CA)
California State U, East Bay (CA)
California State U, Fresno (CA)
California State U, Fullerton (CA)
California State U, Long Beach (CA)
California State U, Los Angeles (CA)
California State U, Monterey Bay (CA)
California State U, Northridge (CA)
California State U, San Bernardino (CA)
California State U, San Marcos (CA)
California State U, Stanislaus (CA)
Calumet Coll of Saint Joseph (IN)
Calvin Coll (MI)
Cambridge Coll (MA)
Cameron U (OK)
Campbellsville U (KY)
Canisius Coll (NY)
Capital U (OH)
Cardinal Stritch U (WI)
Carleton Coll (MN)
Carlos Albizu U (PR)
Carlos Albizu U, Miami Campus (FL)
Carlow U (PA)
Carnegie Mellon U (PA)
Carroll Coll (MT)
Carson-Newman U (TN)
Case Western Reserve U (OH)
Castleton State Coll (VT)
Catawba Coll (NC)
The Catholic U of America (DC)

Cedar Crest Coll (PA)
Cedarville U (OH)
Centenary Coll of Louisiana (LA)
Central Baptist Coll (AR)
Central Coll (IA)
Central Connecticut State U (CT)
Central Methodist U (MO)
Central Michigan U (MI)
Central State U (OH)
Centre Coll (KY)
Chapman U (CA)
Chatham U (PA)
Chestnut Hill Coll (PA)
Cheyney U of Pennsylvania (PA)
Chicago State U (IL)
Chowan U (NC)
Christian Brothers U (TN)
Christopher Newport U (VA)
Cincinnati Christian U (OH)
The Citadel, The Military Coll of South Carolina (SC)
City Coll of the City U of New York (NY)
City U of Seattle (WA)
Claremont McKenna Coll (CA)
Clarion U of Pennsylvania (PA)
Clark Atlanta U (GA)
Clarke U (IA)
Clarkson U (NY)
Clark U (MA)
Clearwater Christian Coll (FL)
Clemson U (SC)
Cleveland State U (OH)
Coastal Carolina U (SC)
Coe Coll (IA)
Colby Coll (ME)
Colgate U (NY)
Coll of Charleston (SC)
Coll of Coastal Georgia (GA)
The Coll of Idaho (ID)
Coll of Mount St. Joseph (OH)
The Coll of New Jersey (NJ)
The Coll of New Rochelle (NY)
Coll of Saint Benedict (MN)
Coll of Saint Elizabeth (NJ)
Coll of Saint Mary (NE)
The Coll of Saint Rose (NY)
The Coll of St. Scholastica (MN)
Coll of Staten Island of the City U of New York (NY)
Coll of the Atlantic (ME)
Coll of the Holy Cross (MA)
Coll of the Ozarks (MO)
The Coll of William and Mary (VA)
The Coll of Wooster (OH)
The Colorado Coll (CO)
Colorado Mesa U (CO)
Colorado State U (CO)
Columbia Coll (MO)
Columbia Coll (SC)
Columbia Intl U (SC)
Columbia U (NY)
Columbia U, School of General Studies (NY)
Columbus State U (GA)
Concordia Coll (MN)
Concordia Coll–New York (NY)
Concordia U (CA)
Concordia U (OR)
Concordia U (QC, Canada)
Concordia U Chicago (IL)
Concordia U, Nebraska (NE)
Concordia U, St. Paul (MN)
Concordia U Wisconsin (WI)
Concord U (WV)
Connecticut Coll (CT)
Converse Coll (SC)
Corban U (OR)
Cornell Coll (IA)
Cornerstone U (MI)
Covenant Coll (GA)
Creighton U (NE)
Crown Coll (MN)
Culver-Stockton Coll (MO)
Curry Coll (MA)
Dakota Wesleyan U (SD)
Dalhousie U (NS, Canada)
Dallas Baptist U (TX)
Daniel Webster Coll (NH)
Dartmouth Coll (NH)
Davidson Coll (NC)
Defiance Coll (OH)
Delta State U (MS)
DePaul U (IL)
DePauw U (IN)
DEREE—The American Coll of Greece (Greece)

DeSales U (PA)
Dickinson Coll (PA)
Dillard U (LA)
Doane Coll (NE)
Dominican Coll (NY)
Dominican U (IL)
Dordt Coll (IA)
Drake U (IA)
Drew U (NJ)
Drury U (MO)
Duquesne U (PA)
Earlham Coll (IN)
East Carolina U (NC)
East Central U (OK)
Eastern Illinois U (IL)
Eastern Mennonite U (VA)
Eastern Michigan U (MI)
Eastern New Mexico U (NM)
Eastern Washington U (WA)
East Tennessee State U (TN)
East Texas Baptist U (TX)
Eckerd Coll (FL)
Edgewood Coll (WI)
Edinboro U of Pennsylvania (PA)
Elizabeth City State U (NC)
Elizabethtown Coll (PA)
Elmira Coll (NY)
Elon U (NC)
Emmanuel Coll (GA)
Emmanuel Coll (MA)
Emory & Henry Coll (VA)
Emporia State U (KS)
Endicott Coll (MA)
Eugene Lang Coll The New School for Liberal Arts (NY)
Evangel U (MO)
Excelsior Coll (NY)
Fairfield U (CT)
Fairleigh Dickinson U, Coll at Florham (NJ)
Fairleigh Dickinson U, Metropolitan Campus (NJ)
Fairmont State U (WV)
Faulkner U (AL)
Fayetteville State U (NC)
Felician Coll (NJ)
Ferris State U (MI)
Ferrum Coll (VA)
Fisher Coll (MA)
Flagler Coll (FL)
Florida Ag and Mech U (FL)
Florida Atlantic U (FL)
Florida Gulf Coast U (FL)
Florida Inst of Technology (FL)
Florida Intl U (FL)
Florida Southern Coll (FL)
Florida State U (FL)
Fort Lewis Coll (CO)
Framingham State U (MA)
Francis Marion U (SC)
Franklin & Marshall Coll (PA)
Franklin Coll (IN)
Franklin Pierce U (NH)
Friends U (KS)
Frostburg State U (MD)
Furman U (SC)
Gallaudet U (DC)
Gannon U (PA)
Gardner-Webb U (NC)
Geneva Coll (PA)
George Fox U (OR)
George Mason U (VA)
Georgetown Coll (KY)
Georgetown U (DC)
Georgia Coll & State U (GA)
Georgia Gwinnett Coll (GA)
Georgia Regents U (GA)
Georgia Southern U (GA)
Georgia Southwestern State U (GA)
Georgia State U (GA)
Gettysburg Coll (PA)
Goldey-Beacom Coll (DE)
Gonzaga U (WA)
Gordon Coll (MA)
Goshen Coll (IN)
Goucher Coll (MD)
Governors State U (IL)
Graceland U (IA)
Grace Coll (IN)
Grambling State U (LA)
Grand Valley State U (MI)
Grand View U (IA)
Granite State Coll (NH)
Greenville Coll (IL)
Grinnell Coll (IA)
Grove City Coll (PA)

Guilford Coll (NC)
Gustavus Adolphus Coll (MN)
Hamilton Coll (NY)
Hamline U (MN)
Hampden-Sydney Coll (VA)
Hampshire Coll (MA)
Hampton U (VA)
Hanover Coll (IN)
Harding U (AR)
Hardin-Simmons U (TX)
Hartwick Coll (NY)
Haverford Coll (PA)
Hawai'i Pacific U (HI)
Henderson State U (AR)
Hendrix Coll (AR)
High Point U (NC)
Hilbert Coll (NY)
Hillsdale Coll (MI)
Hillsdale Free Will Baptist Coll (OK)
Hiram Coll (OH)
Hobart and William Smith Colls (NY)
Hofstra U (NY)
Hollins U (VA)
Holy Cross Coll (IN)
Holy Family U (PA)
Holy Names U (CA)
Hood Coll (MD)
Hope Coll (MI)
Hope Intl U (CA)
Houghton Coll (NY)
Howard Payne U (TX)
Humboldt State U (CA)
Hunter Coll of the City U of New York (NY)
Huntingdon Coll (AL)
Huntington U (IN)
Husson U (ME)
Illinois Coll (IL)
Illinois Inst of Technology (IL)
Illinois State U (IL)
Illinois Wesleyan U (IL)
Immaculata U (PA)
Indiana State U (IN)
Indiana Tech (IN)
Indiana U Bloomington (IN)
Indiana U East (IN)
Indiana U Kokomo (IN)
Indiana U Northwest (IN)
Indiana U of Pennsylvania (PA)
Indiana U–Purdue U Fort Wayne (IN)
Indiana U–Purdue U Indianapolis (IN)
Indiana U South Bend (IN)
Indiana U Southeast (IN)
Indiana Wesleyan U (IN)
Inter American U of Puerto Rico, Aguadilla Campus (PR)
Inter American U of Puerto Rico, Fajardo Campus (PR)
Inter American U of Puerto Rico, Ponce Campus (PR)
Inter American U of Puerto Rico, San Germán Campus (PR)
Iona Coll (NY)
Iowa State U of Science and Technology (IA)
Iowa Wesleyan Coll (IA)
Ithaca Coll (NY)
Jacksonville State U (AL)
James Madison U (VA)
Jamestown Coll (ND)
John Brown U (AR)
John Carroll U (OH)
The Johns Hopkins U (MD)
Johnson C. Smith U (NC)
Johnson State Coll (VT)
Judson Coll (AL)
Judson U (IL)
Juniata Coll (PA)
Kalamazoo Coll (MI)
Kansas State U (KS)
Kansas Wesleyan U (KS)
Kean U (NJ)
Keene State Coll (NH)
Kennesaw State U (GA)
Kent State U (OH)
Kent State U at Ashtabula (OH)
Kent State U at East Liverpool (OH)
Kent State U at Geauga (OH)
Kent State U at Salem (OH)
Kent State U at Stark (OH)
Kent State U at Trumbull (OH)
Kent State U at Tuscarawas (OH)
Kentucky Christian U (KY)
Kentucky State U (KY)

Kentucky Wesleyan Coll (KY)
Kenyon Coll (OH)
Keuka Coll (NY)
Keystone Coll (PA)
King Coll (TN)
King's Coll (PA)
The King's U Coll (AB, Canada)
Knox Coll (IL)
Kutztown U of Pennsylvania (PA)
Lafayette Coll (PA)
LaGrange Coll (GA)
Lake Erie Coll (OH)
Lakeland Coll (WI)
Lake Superior State U (MI)
Lamar U (TX)
Lander U (SC)
Langston U (OK)
La Roche Coll (PA)
La Salle U (PA)
Lasell Coll (MA)
La Sierra U (CA)
Laurel U (NC)
Lawrence Technological U (MI)
Lawrence U (WI)
Lebanese American U (Lebanon)
Lebanon Valley Coll (PA)
Lees-McRae Coll (NC)
Lee U (TN)
Lehigh U (PA)
Lehman Coll of the City U of New York (NY)
Le Moyne Coll (NY)
LeTourneau U (TX)
Lewis-Clark State Coll (ID)
Lewis U (IL)
Liberty U (VA)
Life U (GA)
Limestone Coll (SC)
Lincoln Christian U (IL)
Lincoln Memorial U (TN)
Lincoln U (MO)
Lindenwood U (MO)
Lindsey Wilson Coll (KY)
Linfield Coll (OR)
Lipscomb U (TN)
Lock Haven U of Pennsylvania (PA)
Long Island U–Brooklyn Campus (NY)
Long Island U–C. W. Post Campus (NY)
Longwood U (VA)
Louisiana Coll (LA)
Louisiana State U and Ag and Mech Coll (LA)
Louisiana State U at Alexandria (LA)
Louisiana State U in Shreveport (LA)
Lourdes U (OH)
Loyola Marymount U (CA)
Loyola U Chicago (IL)
Loyola U Maryland (MD)
Loyola U New Orleans (LA)
Lubbock Christian U (TX)
Luther Coll (IA)
Lynchburg Coll (VA)
Lynn U (FL)
Lyon Coll (AR)
Macalester Coll (MN)
Madonna U (MI)
Malone U (OH)
Manchester U (IN)
Manhattan Coll (NY)
Manhattanville Coll (NY)
Mansfield U of Pennsylvania (PA)
Marian U (WI)
Marietta Coll (OH)
Marist Coll (NY)
Marquette U (WI)
Marshall U (WV)
Mars Hill Coll (NC)
Mary Baldwin Coll (VA)
Marymount Coll, Palos Verdes, California (CA)
Marymount Manhattan Coll (NY)
Marymount U (VA)
Maryville Coll (TN)
Maryville U of Saint Louis (MO)
Marywood U (PA)
Massachusetts Coll of Liberal Arts (MA)
McDaniel Coll (MD)
McKendree U (IL)
McMurry U (TX)
McNeese State U (LA)
Medaille Coll (NY)
Menlo Coll (CA)

Mercer U (GA)
Mercy Coll (NY)
Mercyhurst U (PA)
Merrimack Coll (MA)
Messiah Coll (PA)
Metropolitan State U of Denver (CO)
Miami U (OH)
Michigan State U (MI)
Mid-Continent U (KY)
Middlebury Coll (VT)
Middle Tennessee State U (TN)
Midwestern State U (TX)
Millersville U of Pennsylvania (PA)
Millikin U (IL)
Millsaps Coll (MS)
Mills Coll (CA)
Minnesota State U Mankato (MN)
Minnesota State U Moorhead (MN)
Minot State U (ND)
Misericordia U (PA)
Mississippi Coll (MS)
Mississippi State U (MS)
Mississippi U for Women (MS)
Missouri Baptist U (MO)
Missouri State U (MO)
Missouri U of Science and Technology (MO)
Missouri Western State U (MO)
Mitchell Coll (CT)
Molloy Coll (NY)
Monmouth Coll (IL)
Monmouth U (NJ)
Montana State U (MT)
Montclair State U (NJ)
Moravian Coll (PA)
Morehead State U (KY)
Morehouse Coll (GA)
Morningside Coll (IA)
Mount Allison U (NB, Canada)
Mount Aloysius Coll (PA)
Mount Holyoke Coll (MA)
Mount Marty Coll (SD)
Mount Mary Coll (WI)
Mount Mercy U (IA)
Mount Saint Mary Coll (NY)
Mount St. Mary's Coll (CA)
Mount St. Mary's U (MD)
Mount Vernon Nazarene U (OH)
Muhlenberg Coll (PA)
Multnomah U (OR)
Murray State U (KY)
Naropa U (CO)
National U (CA)
Nazareth Coll of Rochester (NY)
Neumann U (PA)
Newberry Coll (SC)
Newbury Coll (MA)
New Coll of Florida (FL)
New England Coll (NH)
New Jersey City U (NJ)
Newman U (KS)
New Mexico Highlands U (NM)
New Mexico Inst of Mining and Technology (NM)
New Mexico State U (NM)
New York Inst of Technology (NY)
New York U (NY)
Niagara U (NY)
Nicholls State U (LA)
Norfolk State U (VA)
North Carolina Central U (NC)
North Carolina State U (NC)
North Carolina Wesleyan Coll (NC)
North Central Coll (IL)
Northcentral U (AZ)
North Dakota State U (ND)
Northeastern Illinois U (IL)
Northeastern U (MA)
Northern Arizona U (AZ)
Northern Illinois U (IL)
Northern Michigan U (MI)
Northern State U (SD)
North Greenville U (SC)
Northwestern Coll (IA)
Northwestern Coll (MN)
Northwestern Oklahoma State U (OK)
Northwestern State U of Louisiana (LA)
Northwest Missouri State U (MO)
Northwest Nazarene U (ID)
Northwest U (WA)
Norwich U (VT)
Notre Dame de Namur U (CA)
Nova Southeastern U (FL)
Nyack Coll (NY)

Oakland U (MI)
Oglethorpe U (GA)
Ohio Dominican U (OH)
The Ohio State U (OH)
The Ohio State U at Lima (OH)
The Ohio State U at Marion (OH)
The Ohio State U–Mansfield Campus (OH)
Ohio U (OH)
Ohio Valley U (WV)
Ohio Wesleyan U (OH)
Oklahoma Baptist U (OK)
Oklahoma Christian U (OK)
Oklahoma City U (OK)
Oklahoma State U (OK)
Old Dominion U (VA)
Olivet Coll (MI)
Oral Roberts U (OK)
Oregon State U (OR)
Ouachita Baptist U (AR)
Pace U (NY)
Pacific Lutheran U (WA)
Pacific Union Coll (CA)
Pacific U (OR)
Paine Coll (GA)
Palm Beach Atlantic U (FL)
Park U (MO)
Penn State Abington (PA)
Penn State Altoona (PA)
Penn State Beaver (PA)
Penn State Berks (PA)
Penn State Brandywine (PA)
Penn State DuBois (PA)
Penn State Erie, The Behrend Coll (PA)
Penn State Fayette, The Eberly Campus (PA)
Penn State Greater Allegheny (PA)
Penn State Harrisburg (PA)
Penn State Hazleton (PA)
Penn State Lehigh Valley (PA)
Penn State Mont Alto (PA)
Penn State New Kensington (PA)
Penn State Schuylkill (PA)
Penn State Shenango (PA)
Penn State U Park (PA)
Penn State Wilkes-Barre (PA)
Penn State Worthington Scranton (PA)
Penn State York (PA)
Pepperdine U, Malibu (CA)
Philadelphia U (PA)
Piedmont Coll (GA)
Pine Manor Coll (MA)
Pittsburg State U (KS)
Pitzer Coll (CA)
Plymouth State U (NH)
Point Loma Nazarene U (CA)
Point Park U (PA)
Point U (GA)
Pomona Coll (CA)
Portland State U (OR)
Post U (CT)
Presbyterian Coll (SC)
Prescott Coll (AZ)
Presentation Coll (SD)
Princeton U (NJ)
Providence Coll (RI)
Purchase Coll, State U of New York (NY)
Purdue U (IN)
Purdue U Calumet (IN)
Purdue U North Central (IN)
Queens U of Charlotte (NC)
Quincy U (IL)
Quinnipiac U (CT)
Radford U (VA)
Ramapo Coll of New Jersey (NJ)
Randolph Coll (VA)
Randolph-Macon Coll (VA)
Reed Coll (OR)
Regent U (VA)
Regis Coll (MA)
Regis U (CO)
Rensselaer Polytechnic Inst (NY)
Rhode Island Coll (RI)
Rhodes Coll (TN)
Rice U (TX)
The Richard Stockton Coll of New Jersey (NJ)
Rider U (NJ)
Ripon Coll (WI)
Rivier U (NH)
Roanoke Coll (VA)
Robert Morris U (PA)
Roberts Wesleyan Coll (NY)
Rochester Inst of Technology (NY)

Rockford Coll (IL)
Rockhurst U (MO)
Rocky Mountain Coll (MT)
Roger Williams U (RI)
Rollins Coll (FL)
Roosevelt U (IL)
Rosemont Coll (PA)
Rowan U (NJ)
Russell Sage Coll (NY)
Rutgers, The State U of New Jersey, Camden (NJ)
Rutgers, The State U of New Jersey, Newark (NJ)
Rutgers, The State U of New Jersey, New Brunswick (NJ)
Sacred Heart U (CT)
Sage Coll of Albany (NY)
Saginaw Valley State U (MI)
St. Ambrose U (IA)
St. Andrews U (NC)
Saint Anselm Coll (NH)
St. Bonaventure U (NY)
St. Edward's U (TX)
St. Francis Coll (NY)
St. Gregory's U, Shawnee (OK)
St. John Fisher Coll (NY)
Saint John's U (MN)
St. John's U (NY)
Saint Joseph's Coll (IN)
St. Joseph's Coll, Long Island Campus (NY)
St. Joseph's Coll, New York (NY)
Saint Joseph's U (PA)
St. Lawrence U (NY)
Saint Leo U (FL)
Saint Louis U (MO)
Saint Martin's U (WA)
Saint Mary-of-the-Woods Coll (IN)
Saint Mary's Coll (IN)
Saint Mary's Coll of California (CA)
St. Mary's Coll of Maryland (MD)
St. Mary's U (TX)
Saint Mary's U of Minnesota (MN)
Saint Michael's Coll (VT)
St. Norbert Coll (WI)
St. Olaf Coll (MN)
St. Thomas Aquinas Coll (NY)
St. Thomas U (FL)
St. Thomas U (NB, Canada)
Saint Vincent Coll (PA)
Salem State U (MA)
Salisbury U (MD)
Salve Regina U (RI)
Samford U (AL)
Sam Houston State U (TX)
San Diego Christian Coll (CA)
San Diego State U (CA)
San Francisco State U (CA)
San Jose State U (CA)
Schreiner U (TX)
Scripps Coll (CA)
Seattle Pacific U (WA)
Seattle U (WA)
Seton Hill U (PA)
Sewanee: The U of the South (TN)
Shawnee State U (OH)
Shaw U (NC)
Shenandoah U (VA)
Shepherd U (WV)
Shippensburg U of Pennsylvania (PA)
Siena Coll (NY)
Siena Heights U (MI)
Sierra Nevada Coll (NV)
Simmons Coll (MA)
Simon Fraser U (BC, Canada)
Simpson Coll (IA)
Simpson U (CA)
Skidmore Coll (NY)
Slippery Rock U of Pennsylvania (PA)
Smith Coll (MA)
Sonoma State U (CA)
South Dakota State U (SD)
Southeastern Louisiana U (LA)
Southeastern Oklahoma State U (OK)
Southeastern U (FL)
Southeast Missouri State U (MO)
Southern Arkansas U–Magnolia (AR)
Southern Connecticut State U (CT)
Southern Illinois U Carbondale (IL)
Southern Illinois U Edwardsville (IL)
Southern Methodist U (TX)
Southern Nazarene U (OK)

Southern New Hampshire U (NH)
Southern Oregon U (OR)
Southern Polytechnic State U (GA)
Southern Utah U (UT)
Southwest Baptist U (MO)
Southwestern Adventist U (TX)
Southwestern Coll (KS)
Southwestern U (TX)
Spalding U (KY)
Spelman Coll (GA)
Spring Arbor U (MI)
Spring Hill Coll (AL)
Stanford U (CA)
State U of New York at Fredonia (NY)
State U of New York at New Paltz (NY)
State U of New York at Oswego (NY)
State U of New York at Plattsburgh (NY)
State U of New York Coll at Cortland (NY)
State U of New York Coll at Geneseo (NY)
State U of New York Coll at Old Westbury (NY)
State U of New York Coll at Potsdam (NY)
State U of New York Inst of Technology (NY)
Stephen F. Austin State U (TX)
Stephens Coll (MO)
Stetson U (FL)
Stevenson U (MD)
Stonehill Coll (MA)
Stony Brook U, State U of New York (NY)
Suffolk U (MA)
Sul Ross State U (TX)
Susquehanna U (PA)
Swarthmore Coll (PA)
Sweet Briar Coll (VA)
Syracuse U (NY)
Tabor Coll (KS)
Tarleton State U (TX)
Taylor U (IN)
Temple U (PA)
Tennessee State U (TN)
Tennessee Wesleyan Coll (TN)
Texas A&M Intl U (TX)
Texas A&M U (TX)
Texas A&M U–Commerce (TX)
Texas A&M U–Kingsville (TX)
Texas Christian U (TX)
Texas Lutheran U (TX)
Texas Southern U (TX)
Texas State U–San Marcos (TX)
Texas Wesleyan U (TX)
Texas Woman's U (TX)
Thomas Edison State Coll (NJ)
Thomas More Coll (KY)
Thomas U (GA)
Thompson Rivers U (BC, Canada)
Tiffin U (OH)
Transylvania U (KY)
Trent U (ON, Canada)
Trevecca Nazarene U (TN)
Trine U (IN)
Trinity Christian Coll (IL)
Trinity Coll (CT)
Trinity Coll of Florida (FL)
Trinity U (TX)
Troy U (AL)
Truman State U (MO)
Tufts U (MA)
Tulane U (LA)
Tuskegee U (AL)
Union Coll (KY)
Union Coll (NE)
Union U (TN)
United States Military Acad (NY)
Universidad Adventista de las Antillas (PR)
Université de Sherbrooke (QC, Canada)
Université du Québec en Outaouais (QC, Canada)
U at Albany, State U of New York (NY)
U at Buffalo, the State U of New York (NY)
The U of Akron (OH)
The U of Alabama (AL)
The U of Alabama at Birmingham (AL)
U of Alaska Anchorage (AK)

U of Alaska Anchorage, Kenai Peninsula Coll (AK)
U of Alaska Fairbanks (AK)
The U of Arizona (AZ)
U of Arkansas at Little Rock (AR)
U of Arkansas–Fort Smith (AR)
U of Bridgeport (CT)
The U of British Columbia (BC, Canada)
The U of British Columbia–Okanagan (BC, Canada)
U of California, Berkeley (CA)
U of California, Davis (CA)
U of California, Irvine (CA)
U of California, Los Angeles (CA)
U of California, Merced (CA)
U of California, Riverside (CA)
U of California, Santa Barbara (CA)
U of California, Santa Cruz (CA)
U of Central Arkansas (AR)
U of Central Florida (FL)
U of Central Oklahoma (OK)
U of Charleston (WV)
U of Chicago (IL)
U of Cincinnati (OH)
U of Colorado Boulder (CO)
U of Colorado Colorado Springs (CO)
U of Colorado Denver (CO)
U of Dallas (TX)
U of Delaware (DE)
U of Denver (CO)
U of Evansville (IN)
The U of Findlay (OH)
U of Florida (FL)
U of Georgia (GA)
U of Great Falls (MT)
U of Guam (GU)
U of Guelph (ON, Canada)
U of Hartford (CT)
U of Hawaii at Hilo (HI)
U of Hawaii at Manoa (HI)
U of Hawaii–West Oahu (HI)
U of Houston (TX)
U of Houston–Clear Lake (TX)
U of Houston–Downtown (TX)
U of Houston–Victoria (TX)
U of Idaho (ID)
U of Illinois at Chicago (IL)
U of Illinois at Springfield (IL)
U of Illinois at Urbana–Champaign (IL)
The U of Iowa (IA)
The U of Kansas (KS)
U of Kentucky (KY)
U of La Verne (CA)
U of Louisiana at Lafayette (LA)
U of Louisiana at Monroe (LA)
U of Louisville (KY)
U of Maine at Farmington (ME)
U of Maine at Machias (ME)
U of Maryland, Baltimore County (MD)
U of Maryland, Coll Park (MD)
U of Maryland U Coll (MD)
U of Mary Washington (VA)
U of Massachusetts Amherst (MA)
U of Massachusetts Boston (MA)
U of Massachusetts Dartmouth (MA)
U of Memphis (TN)
U of Miami (FL)
U of Michigan (MI)
U of Michigan–Dearborn (MI)
U of Michigan–Flint (MI)
U of Minnesota, Duluth (MN)
U of Minnesota, Twin Cities Campus (MN)
U of Mississippi (MS)
U of Missouri (MO)
U of Missouri–Kansas City (MO)
U of Missouri–St. Louis (MO)
U of Mobile (AL)
The U of Montana Western (MT)
U of Montevallo (AL)
U of Mount Union (OH)
U of Nebraska at Kearney (NE)
U of Nebraska at Omaha (NE)
U of Nebraska–Lincoln (NE)
U of Nevada, Las Vegas (NV)
U of Nevada, Reno (NV)
U of New Brunswick Fredericton (NB, Canada)
U of New Brunswick Saint John (NB, Canada)
U of New England (ME)
U of New Hampshire (NH)

U of New Hampshire at Manchester (NH)
U of New Haven (CT)
U of New Mexico (NM)
U of New Orleans (LA)
U of North Alabama (AL)
U of North Carolina at Asheville (NC)
The U of North Carolina at Chapel Hill (NC)
The U of North Carolina at Charlotte (NC)
The U of North Carolina at Greensboro (NC)
The U of North Carolina at Pembroke (NC)
The U of North Carolina Wilmington (NC)
U of North Dakota (ND)
U of Northern Colorado (CO)
U of Northern Iowa (IA)
U of North Florida (FL)
U of North Georgia (GA)
U of North Texas (TX)
U of Notre Dame (IN)
U of Oklahoma (OK)
U of Oregon (OR)
U of Ottawa (ON, Canada)
U of Pennsylvania (PA)
U of Pikeville (KY)
U of Pittsburgh (PA)
U of Pittsburgh at Bradford (PA)
U of Pittsburgh at Greensburg (PA)
U of Portland (OR)
U of Puerto Rico at Ponce (PR)
U of Puget Sound (WA)
U of Redlands (CA)
U of Regina (SK, Canada)
U of Rhode Island (RI)
U of Richmond (VA)
U of Rochester (NY)
U of St. Francis (IL)
U of Saint Joseph (CT)
U of Saint Mary (KS)
U of St. Thomas (MN)
U of St. Thomas (TX)
U of San Diego (CA)
U of Science and Arts of Oklahoma (OK)
The U of Scranton (PA)
U of South Alabama (AL)
U of South Carolina Aiken (SC)
U of South Carolina Upstate (SC)
The U of South Dakota (SD)
U of Southern California (CA)
U of Southern Indiana (IN)
U of Southern Maine (ME)
U of Southern Mississippi (MS)
U of South Florida (FL)
The U of Tampa (FL)
The U of Tennessee (TN)
The U of Tennessee at Chattanooga (TN)
The U of Tennessee at Martin (TN)
The U of Texas at Arlington (TX)
The U of Texas at Austin (TX)
The U of Texas at Brownsville (TX)
The U of Texas at Dallas (TX)
The U of Texas at El Paso (TX)
The U of Texas at San Antonio (TX)
The U of Texas of the Permian Basin (TX)
The U of Texas–Pan American (TX)
U of the Cumberlands (KY)
U of the District of Columbia (DC)
U of the Incarnate Word (TX)
U of the Ozarks (AR)
U of the Sciences (PA)
U of the Virgin Islands (VI)
The U of Toledo (OH)
U of Tulsa (OK)
U of Utah (UT)
U of Vermont (VT)
U of Virginia (VA)
U of Washington, Tacoma (WA)
U of Waterloo (ON, Canada)
The U of West Alabama (AL)
The U of Western Ontario (ON, Canada)
U of West Florida (FL)
U of West Georgia (GA)
U of Windsor (ON, Canada)
U of Wisconsin–Eau Claire (WI)
U of Wisconsin–Green Bay (WI)
U of Wisconsin–La Crosse (WI)
U of Wisconsin–Madison (WI)
U of Wisconsin–Milwaukee (WI)

U of Wisconsin–Parkside (WI)
U of Wisconsin–Platteville (WI)
U of Wisconsin–Stevens Point (WI)
U of Wisconsin–Stout (WI)
U of Wisconsin–Superior (WI)
U of Wyoming (WY)
Upper Iowa U (IA)
Ursuline Coll (OH)
Utah State U (UT)
Utica Coll (NY)
Valdosta State U (GA)
Valley City State U (ND)
Valparaiso U (IN)
Vanderbilt U (TN)
Vassar Coll (NY)
Villanova U (PA)
Virginia Commonwealth U (VA)
Virginia Intermont Coll (VA)
Virginia Polytechnic Inst and State U (VA)
Virginia State U (VA)
Virginia Union U (VA)
Virginia Wesleyan Coll (VA)
Viterbo U (WI)
Wabash Coll (IN)
Wagner Coll (NY)
Wake Forest U (NC)
Walden U (MN)
Waldorf Coll (IA)
Walla Walla U (WA)
Walsh U (OH)
Warner Pacific Coll (OR)
Wartburg Coll (IA)
Washburn U (KS)
Washington & Jefferson Coll (PA)
Washington and Lee U (VA)
Washington Coll (MD)
Washington State U (WA)
Washington U in St. Louis (MO)
Wayland Baptist U (TX)
Waynesburg U (PA)
Wayne State Coll (NE)
Wayne State U (MI)
Weber State U (UT)
Webster U (MO)
Wellesley Coll (MA)
Wells Coll (NY)
Wesleyan Coll (GA)
Wesleyan U (CT)
Wesley Coll (DE)
West Chester U of Pennsylvania (PA)
Western Carolina U (NC)
Western Connecticut State U (CT)
Western Illinois U (IL)
Western Kentucky U (KY)
Western Michigan U (MI)
Western Oregon U (OR)
Western State Colorado U (CO)
Western Washington U (WA)
Westfield State U (MA)
West Liberty U (WV)
Westminster Coll (MO)
Westminster Coll (UT)
West Texas A&M U (TX)
West Virginia State U (WV)
West Virginia U (WV)
West Virginia U Inst of Technology (WV)
West Virginia Wesleyan Coll (WV)
Wheaton Coll (IL)
Wheaton Coll (MA)
Wheeling Jesuit U (WV)
Whitman Coll (WA)
Whitworth U (WA)
Wichita State U (KS)
Widener U (PA)
Wilberforce U (OH)
Wilkes U (PA)
Willamette U (OR)
William Jewell Coll (MO)
William Paterson U of New Jersey (NJ)
William Peace U (NC)
William Penn U (IA)
Williams Coll (MA)
Wilmington U (DE)
Winthrop U (SC)
Wittenberg U (OH)
Woodbury U (CA)
Worcester State U (MA)
Wright State U (OH)
Xavier U (OH)
Xavier U of Louisiana (LA)
Yale U (CT)
York Coll of Pennsylvania (PA)

York Coll of the City U of New York (NY)
Young Harris Coll (GA)
Youngstown State U (OH)

PSYCHOLOGY RELATED
Adams State U (CO)
American Jewish U (CA)
Buena Vista U (IA)
California Baptist U (CA)
Canisius Coll (NY)
Cedarville U (OH)
Central Baptist Coll (AR)
Champlain Coll (VT)
East Central U (OK)
The Evergreen State Coll (WA)
Kean U (NJ)
Loyola U Chicago (IL)
Loyola U New Orleans (LA)
Madonna U (MI)
Marist Coll (NY)
Mary Baldwin Coll (VA)
Mayville State U (ND)
National U (CA)
Northwest Christian U (OR)
Pittsburg State U (KS)
Quincy U (IL)
Saint Mary's Coll of California (CA)
St. Mary's Coll of Maryland (MD)
State U of New York at Oswego (NY)
Swarthmore Coll (PA)
U of Michigan–Flint (MI)
U of New England (ME)
U of St. Thomas (MN)
The U of Toledo (OH)
The U of Western Ontario (ON, Canada)
Western State Colorado U (CO)

PSYCHOLOGY TEACHER EDUCATION
Albion Coll (MI)
Alma Coll (MI)
Boise State U (ID)
Bradley U (IL)
Brigham Young U (UT)
California Lutheran U (CA)
Campbellsville U (KY)
Lee U (TN)
Ohio Wesleyan U (OH)
Pittsburg State U (KS)
Rocky Mountain Coll (MT)
St. Ambrose U (IA)
U of Delaware (DE)
Valparaiso U (IN)
Wayne State Coll (NE)
Widener U (PA)

PUBLIC ADMINISTRATION
Alfred U (NY)
American U of Beirut (Lebanon)
Athabasca U (AB, Canada)
Auburn U (AL)
Auburn U at Montgomery (AL)
Augustana Coll (IL)
Baylor U (TX)
Blackburn Coll (IL)
Bowling Green State U (OH)
Brock U (ON, Canada)
Buena Vista U (IA)
California Lutheran U (CA)
California State U, Chico (CA)
California State U, Dominguez Hills (CA)
California State U, East Bay (CA)
California State U, Fresno (CA)
California State U, Fullerton (CA)
California State U, San Bernardino (CA)
Calvin Coll (MI)
Capital U (OH)
Central Methodist U (MO)
Cleveland State U (OH)
Colorado Mesa U (CO)
Concordia U (QC, Canada)
Creighton U (NE)
Doane Coll (NE)
Eastern Michigan U (MI)
Eastern Washington U (WA)
Elon U (NC)
Evangel U (MO)
The Evergreen State Coll (WA)
Fisher Coll (MA)
Flagler Coll (FL)
Florida Atlantic U (FL)
Florida Intl U (FL)
Franklin U (OH)

George Mason U (VA)
Grand Valley State U (MI)
Harding U (AR)
Hawai`i Pacific U (HI)
Henderson State U (AR)
Indiana U Bloomington (IN)
Indiana U East (IN)
Indiana U Kokomo (IN)
Indiana U Northwest (IN)
Indiana U–Purdue U Fort Wayne (IN)
Indiana U–Purdue U Indianapolis (IN)
Indiana U South Bend (IN)
Inter American U of Puerto Rico, San Germán Campus (PR)
Iowa State U of Science and Technology (IA)
James Madison U (VA)
John Carroll U (OH)
John Jay Coll of Criminal Justice of the City U of New York (NY)
The Johns Hopkins U (MD)
Kean U (NJ)
Kentucky State U (KY)
Kutztown U of Pennsylvania (PA)
La Salle U (PA)
Lewis U (IL)
Lincoln U (MO)
Lindenwood U (MO)
Lipscomb U (TN)
Long Island U–C. W. Post Campus (NY)
Louisiana Coll (LA)
Miami U (OH)
Midwestern State U (TX)
Millsaps Coll (MS)
Minnesota State U Mankato (MN)
Mississippi U for Women (MS)
Mississippi Valley State U (MS)
Missouri State U (MO)
Murray State U (KY)
National U (CA)
New York U (NY)
Northern Michigan U (MI)
Northern State U (SD)
Northwest Missouri State U (MO)
Oakland U (MI)
Ohio Wesleyan U (OH)
Park U (MO)
Plymouth State U (NH)
Point Park U (PA)
Regent U (VA)
Regis U (CO)
Rhode Island Coll (RI)
Rogers State U (OK)
Roger Williams U (RI)
Roosevelt U (IL)
Saginaw Valley State U (MI)
St. Ambrose U (IA)
St. John's U (NY)
Saint Joseph's U (PA)
St. Thomas U (FL)
Samford U (AL)
San Diego State U (CA)
Seattle U (WA)
Shaw U (NC)
Shenandoah U (VA)
Shippensburg U of Pennsylvania (PA)
Siena Heights U (MI)
Southern New Hampshire U (NH)
Stephen F. Austin State U (TX)
Suffolk U (MA)
Syracuse U (NY)
Tennessee State U (TN)
Texas Southern U (TX)
Texas State U–San Marcos (TX)
Thomas Edison State Coll (NJ)
U at Albany, State U of New York (NY)
U of Alaska Anchorage (AK)
The U of Arizona (AZ)
U of Central Arkansas (AR)
U of Central Florida (FL)
U of Guam (GU)
U of Guelph (ON, Canada)
U of Hawaii–West Oahu (HI)
U of Houston–Clear Lake (TX)
The U of Kansas (KS)
U of La Verne (CA)
U of Maine at Fort Kent (ME)
U of Maine at Machias (ME)
U of Michigan–Flint (MI)
U of Missouri–St. Louis (MO)
U of Nebraska at Omaha (NE)
U of New Haven (CT)

The U of North Carolina at Pembroke (NC)
U of North Dakota (ND)
U of Northern Iowa (IA)
U of North Texas (TX)
U of Oklahoma (OK)
U of Oregon (OR)
U of Ottawa (ON, Canada)
U of Pittsburgh (PA)
U of Regina (SK, Canada)
U of St. Thomas (MN)
The U of Tennessee (TN)
The U of Tennessee at Martin (TN)
The U of Texas at Brownsville (TX)
The U of Texas at Dallas (TX)
The U of Western Ontario (ON, Canada)
U of Wisconsin–Green Bay (WI)
U of Wisconsin–La Crosse (WI)
U of Wisconsin–Stevens Point (WI)
Upper Iowa U (IA)
Virginia State U (VA)
Wagner Coll (NY)
Walden U (MN)
Washburn U (KS)
Waynesburg U (PA)
Wayne State U (MI)
Western Oregon U (OR)
West Texas A&M U (TX)
West Virginia U Inst of Technology (WV)

PUBLIC ADMINISTRATION AND SOCIAL SERVICE PROFESSIONS RELATED
Coll of Coastal Georgia (GA)
Columbia Coll (SC)
Dakota Wesleyan U (SD)
Emory & Henry Coll (VA)
The Evergreen State Coll (WA)
Lasell Coll (MA)
New York U (NY)
Northeastern Illinois U (IL)
State U of New York Empire State Coll (NY)
Trevecca Nazarene U (TN)
Troy U (AL)
U of Maryland U Coll (MD)
U of Minnesota, Twin Cities Campus (MN)

PUBLIC/APPLIED HISTORY
Arkansas Tech U (AR)
Concordia U (QC, Canada)
East Carolina U (NC)
McMurry U (TX)
North Dakota State U (ND)
Salem State U (MA)
U of California, Santa Barbara (CA)
Western Michigan U (MI)

PUBLIC HEALTH
Agnes Scott Coll (GA)
Alma Coll (MI)
American Public U System (WV)
Bluffton U (OH)
Bowling Green State U (OH)
Brock U (ON, Canada)
California State U, Long Beach (CA)
Calvin Coll (MI)
Dillard U (LA)
Drew U (NJ)
East Tennessee State U (TN)
Elon U (NC)
Fort Lewis Coll (CO)
Hunter Coll of the City U of New York (NY)
Indiana U–Purdue U Indianapolis (IN)
The Johns Hopkins U (MD)
Keystone Coll (PA)
LaGrange Coll (GA)
Marshall U (WV)
Mercyhurst U (PA)
Minnesota State U Mankato (MN)
National U (CA)
Northern Arizona U (AZ)
Oregon State U (OR)
Purdue U (IN)
Rutgers, The State U of New Jersey, New Brunswick (NJ)
Saint Louis U (MO)
Slippery Rock U of Pennsylvania (PA)
Southern Connecticut State U (CT)
State U of New York Coll at Old Westbury (NY)

Trident U Intl (CA)
Tufts U (MA)
U at Albany, State U of New York (NY)
U of Alaska Anchorage (AK)
The U of Arizona (AZ)
U of Colorado Denver (CO)
U of Evansville (IN)
U of Massachusetts Amherst (MA)
U of Nebraska at Omaha (NE)
U of Rochester (NY)
U of Southern Mississippi (MS)
The U of Tampa (FL)
The U of Texas at Austin (TX)
U of the Cumberlands (KY)
Walden U (MN)
Wayne State U (MI)
West Chester U of Pennsylvania (PA)
Westminster Coll (UT)
William Paterson U of New Jersey (NJ)

PUBLIC HEALTH/COMMUNITY NURSING
Capital U (OH)
Hawai`i Pacific U (HI)
Northern Illinois U (IL)
U of Miami (FL)
The U of Western Ontario (ON, Canada)
Walla Walla U (WA)
Wright State U (OH)

PUBLIC HEALTH EDUCATION AND PROMOTION
Appalachian State U (NC)
Baldwin Wallace (OH)
California Baptist U (CA)
California State U, Long Beach (CA)
Central Michigan U (MI)
Chicago State U (IL)
Coastal Carolina (SC)
Dalhousie U (NS, Canada)
East Carolina U (NC)
Eastern Washington U (WA)
Georgia Southern U (GA)
Inter American U of Puerto Rico, Ponce Campus (PR)
Ithaca Coll (NY)
Liberty U (VA)
Louisiana State U in Shreveport (LA)
Lynchburg Coll (VA)
Malone U (OH)
Marymount U (VA)
Mississippi U for Women (MS)
New Mexico State U (NM)
North Carolina Central U (NC)
Oklahoma State U (OK)
Oregon State U (OR)
Plymouth State U (NH)
Simmons Coll (MA)
Southeastern Louisiana U (LA)
State U of New York Coll at Potsdam (NY)
Temple U (PA)
Texas State U–San Marcos (TX)
Thomas Edison State Coll (NJ)
U of Georgia (GA)
The U of Iowa (IA)
U of Michigan–Flint (MI)
The U of North Carolina at Charlotte (NC)
The U of North Carolina at Greensboro (NC)
The U of North Carolina Wilmington (NC)
U of St. Thomas (MN)
The U of Scranton (PA)
U of Southern California (CA)
The U of Texas at Austin (TX)
The U of Toledo (OH)
U of Utah (UT)
U of Wisconsin–La Crosse (WI)
Walla Walla U (WA)

PUBLIC HEALTH RELATED
Franklin & Marshall Coll (PA)
Hampshire Coll (MA)
The Richard Stockton Coll of New Jersey (NJ)
Shenandoah U (VA)
U of California, Berkeley (CA)
U of California, Irvine (CA)
U of Illinois at Urbana–Champaign (IL)

U of Maryland, Coll Park (MD)
U of South Carolina (SC)
Utah State U (UT)

PUBLIC POLICY ANALYSIS
Albion Coll (MI)
Arizona State U (AZ)
Bennington Coll (VT)
Bentley U (MA)
Brigham Young U (UT)
Bryant U (RI)
Carnegie Mellon U (PA)
Chatham U (PA)
Coll of the Atlantic (ME)
The Coll of William and Mary (VA)
Dakota Wesleyan U (SD)
DePaul U (IL)
Dickinson Coll (PA)
Georgia State U (GA)
Hamilton Coll (NY)
Hampshire Coll (MA)
Hobart and William Smith Colls (NY)
Howard Payne U (TX)
Indiana U–Purdue U Fort Wayne (IN)
Indiana Wesleyan U (IN)
The Johns Hopkins U (MD)
Massachusetts Coll of Liberal Arts (MA)
Michigan State U (MI)
Mills Coll (CA)
New Coll of Florida (FL)
Penn State Harrisburg (PA)
Pomona Coll (CA)
Princeton U (NJ)
Regent U (VA)
Rice U (TX)
Rochester Inst of Technology (NY)
Sage Coll of Albany (NY)
St. Mary's Coll of Maryland (MD)
Saint Vincent Coll (PA)
Scripps Coll (CA)
Southeastern U (FL)
Southern Methodist U (TX)
Stanford U (CA)
Suffolk U (MA)
Trevecca Nazarene U (TN)
Trinity Coll (CT)
U at Albany, State U of New York (NY)
U of California, Riverside (CA)
U of Chicago (IL)
U of Delaware (DE)
U of Denver (CO)
U of Michigan (MI)
U of Mississippi (MS)
The U of North Carolina at Chapel Hill (NC)
U of Pennsylvania (PA)
U of Regina (SK, Canada)
U of Rhode Island (RI)
U of Southern California (CA)
The U of Texas at Dallas (TX)
The U of Toledo (OH)
U of Virginia (VA)
Vanderbilt U (TN)
Virginia Polytechnic Inst and State U (VA)
Wagner Coll (NY)
Washington State U (WA)
Wells Coll (NY)

PUBLIC POLICY ANALYSIS RELATED
U of Nebraska at Omaha (NE)

PUBLIC RELATIONS, ADVERTISING, AND APPLIED COMMUNICATION
Belmont U (TN)
Bluffton U (OH)
Butler U (IN)
California Baptist U (CA)
California State U, Dominguez Hills (CA)
Florida Southern Coll (FL)
Goshen Coll (IN)
Houghton Coll (NY)
Howard Payne U (TX)
Lake Erie Coll (OH)
Lasell Coll (MA)
Lynn U (FL)
Marist Coll (NY)
Massachusetts Coll of Liberal Arts (MA)
Messiah Coll (PA)
Oklahoma City U (OK)

Point Park U (PA)
Seattle U (WA)
Simpson Coll (IA)
Syracuse U (NY)
Taylor U (IN)
Texas Christian U (TX)
U of Kentucky (KY)
U of Nebraska–Lincoln (NE)

PUBLIC RELATIONS, ADVERTISING, AND APPLIED COMMUNICATION RELATED
Abilene Christian U (TX)
Belmont U (TN)
Bradley U (IL)
Brigham Young U (UT)
Buena Vista U (IA)
California Lutheran U (CA)
The Coll at Brockport, State U of New York (NY)
The Coll of St. Scholastica (MN)
Columbia Coll (MO)
DePaul U (IL)
Duquesne U (PA)
Hardin-Simmons U (TX)
Howard Payne U (TX)
John Brown U (AR)
Lipscomb U (TN)
Marietta Coll (OH)
Marywood U (PA)
Metropolitan State U of Denver (CO)
Missouri Western State U (MO)
Northern Arizona U (AZ)
Northern Michigan U (MI)
Oklahoma City U (OK)
Oklahoma State U (OK)
Rochester Inst of Technology (NY)
St. John's U (NY)
Saint Mary's U of Minnesota (MN)
Southern New Hampshire U (NH)
Spring Arbor U (MI)
Spring Hill Coll (AL)
State U of New York at Plattsburgh (NY)
Temple U (PA)
U of Central Arkansas (AR)
The U of Tampa (FL)
U of Vermont (VT)
Virginia State U (VA)
Washington State U (WA)
Weber State U (UT)
Western Michigan U (MI)

PUBLIC RELATIONS/IMAGE MANAGEMENT
American U (DC)
Andrews U (MI)
Appalachian State U (NC)
Auburn U (AL)
Avila U (MO)
Baldwin Wallace U (OH)
Barry U (FL)
Belmont U (TN)
Bowie State U (MD)
Bowling Green State U (OH)
Bradley U (IL)
Buffalo State Coll, State U of New York (NY)
California Lutheran U (CA)
California State U, Chico (CA)
California State U, Dominguez Hills (CA)
California State U, East Bay (CA)
California State U, Fresno (CA)
California State U, Fullerton (CA)
California State U, Long Beach (CA)
Capital U (OH)
Cardinal Stritch U (WI)
Carroll Coll (MT)
Castleton State Coll (VT)
Champlain Coll (VT)
Chapman U (CA)
Chatham U (PA)
Cleveland State U (OH)
Coe Coll (IA)
The Coll at Brockport, State U of New York (NY)
Coll of the Ozarks (MO)
Columbia Coll Chicago (IL)
Curry Coll (MA)
Dominican U (IL)
Drake U (IA)
Drury U (MO)
Eastern Michigan U (MI)
Emerson Coll (MA)
Ferris State U (MI)

Florida Ag and Mech U (FL)
Florida Southern Coll (FL)
Franklin U (OH)
Georgia Southern U (GA)
Gonzaga U (WA)
Greenville Coll (IL)
Hampton U (VA)
Harding U (AR)
Hawai`i Pacific U (HI)
Hofstra U (NY)
Huntington U (IN)
Illinois State U (IL)
Indiana Wesleyan U (IN)
Inter American U of Puerto Rico, Ponce Campus (PR)
Iona Coll (NY)
Ithaca Coll (NY)
John Brown U (AR)
Kent State U (OH)
La Salle U (PA)
Lasell Coll (MA)
Lee U (TN)
Lewis U (IL)
Lipscomb U (TN)
Long Island U–C. W. Post Campus (NY)
Mansfield U of Pennsylvania (PA)
Marist Coll (NY)
Marquette U (WI)
The Master's Coll and Sem (CA)
McKendree U (IL)
Miami U (OH)
Middle Tennessee State U (TN)
Minnesota State U Mankato (MN)
Mississippi Coll (MS)
Missouri Baptist U (MO)
Monmouth Coll (IL)
Mount Mary Coll (WI)
Mount Mercy U (IA)
Mount Saint Mary Coll (NY)
Mount Vernon Nazarene U (OH)
Murray State U (KY)
New England Coll (NH)
New England School of Communications (ME)
North Dakota State U (ND)
Northern Michigan U (MI)
Northwestern Coll (IA)
Northwestern Coll (MN)
Northwest Missouri State U (MO)
Ohio Dominican U (OH)
Ohio U–Zanesville (OH)
Oklahoma Christian U (OK)
Oklahoma City U (OK)
Palm Beach Atlantic U (FL)
Pepperdine U, Malibu (CA)
Point Park U (PA)
Purdue U Calumet (IN)
Quinnipiac U (CT)
Rider U (NJ)
Rochester Inst of Technology (NY)
Roosevelt U (IL)
Rowan U (NJ)
St. Ambrose U (IA)
Salem State U (MA)
San Diego State U (CA)
San Jose State U (CA)
Slippery Rock U of Pennsylvania (PA)
Southern Methodist U (TX)
State U of New York at New Paltz (NY)
State U of New York at Oswego (NY)
Stephens Coll (MO)
Suffolk U (MA)
Syracuse U (NY)
Taylor U (IN)
Temple U (PA)
Texas A&M U–Commerce (TX)
Texas State U–San Marcos (TX)
Tiffin U (OH)
Union Coll (NE)
Union U (TN)
The U of Akron (OH)
The U of Alabama (AL)
U of Central Oklahoma (OK)
The U of Findlay (OH)
U of Florida (FL)
U of Georgia (GA)
U of Houston (TX)
U of Idaho (ID)
U of Louisiana at Lafayette (LA)
U of Miami (FL)
U of Northern Iowa (IA)
U of Oregon (OR)
U of Ottawa (ON, Canada)

U of Pittsburgh at Bradford (PA)
U of Rhode Island (RI)
U of South Carolina (SC)
U of Southern California (CA)
The U of Tennessee (TN)
The U of Texas at Arlington (TX)
The U of Texas at Austin (TX)
Ursuline Coll (OH)
Utica Coll (NY)
Walla Walla U (WA)
Wartburg Coll (IA)
Washington State U (WA)
Wayne State U (MI)
Weber State U (UT)
Webster U (MO)
Western Kentucky U (KY)
West Virginia Wesleyan Coll (WV)
William Penn U (IA)
Xavier U (OH)
York Coll of Pennsylvania (PA)

PUBLISHING
California State U, Chico (CA)
Emerson Coll (MA)
Graceland U (IA)
Rochester Inst of Technology (NY)
U of Missouri (MO)

PURCHASING, PROCUREMENT/ ACQUISITIONS AND CONTRACTS MANAGEMENT
Arizona State U (AZ)
Athens State U (AL)
California State U, East Bay (CA)
Central Michigan U (MI)
Potomac Coll (DC)
U of Houston–Downtown (TX)
U of Illinois at Urbana–Champaign (IL)
U of the District of Columbia (DC)

QUALITY CONTROL AND SAFETY TECHNOLOGIES RELATED
Madonna U (MI)
Rochester Inst of Technology (NY)
U of Central Oklahoma (OK)

QUALITY CONTROL TECHNOLOGY
Bowling Green State U (OH)
California State U, Dominguez Hills (CA)
California State U, Long Beach (CA)
Ferris State U (MI)
San Jose State U (CA)

RADIATION BIOLOGY
Suffolk U (MA)

RADIATION PROTECTION/ HEALTH PHYSICS TECHNOLOGY
Indiana U–Purdue U Indianapolis (IN)
Lewis U (IL)
Thomas Edison State Coll (NJ)

RADIO AND TELEVISION
American U (DC)
Appalachian State U (NC)
Arkansas State U (AR)
Auburn U (AL)
Ball State U (IN)
Barry U (FL)
Bemidji State U (MN)
Bowling Green State U (OH)
Bradley U (IL)
Buffalo State Coll, State U of New York (NY)
Butler U (IN)
California State U, Fresno (CA)
California State U, Fullerton (CA)
California State U, Long Beach (CA)
California State U, Los Angeles (CA)
California State U, Monterey Bay (CA)
Castleton State Coll (VT)
Chicago State U (IL)
The Coll at Brockport, State U of New York (NY)
Columbia Coll Chicago (IL)
Columbia Coll Hollywood (CA)
Curry Coll (MA)
Drake U (IA)
Emerson Coll (MA)

Evangel U (MO)
Franklin Pierce U (NH)
Georgia Southern U (GA)
Grand Valley State U (MI)
Hardin-Simmons U (TX)
Hofstra U (NY)
Iona Coll (NY)
Ithaca Coll (NY)
John Brown U (AR)
Kent State U (OH)
Lamar U (TX)
Langston U (OK)
La Salle U (PA)
Lasell Coll (MA)
Lebanese American U (Lebanon)
Lewis U (IL)
Loyola Marymount U (CA)
Marietta Coll (OH)
The Master's Coll and Sem (CA)
Messiah Coll (PA)
Minot State U (ND)
Missouri Baptist U (MO)
Murray State U (KY)
New York Inst of Technology (NY)
North Central Coll (IL)
Northern Arizona U (AZ)
Northwestern Coll (MN)
Northwest Missouri State U (MO)
Ohio U (OH)
Oklahoma Christian U (OK)
Oklahoma City U (OK)
Pacific U (OR)
Pittsburg State U (KS)
Point Park U (PA)
Rider U (NJ)
St. Ambrose U (IA)
St. Francis Coll (NY)
San Diego State U (CA)
San Francisco State U (CA)
San Jose State U (CA)
Savannah Coll of Art and Design (GA)
Southeastern U (FL)
Southern Illinois U Carbondale (IL)
Southwestern Coll (KS)
State U of New York at Fredonia (NY)
State U of New York at Plattsburgh (NY)
Stephens Coll (MO)
Syracuse U (NY)
Temple U (PA)
Texas A&M U–Commerce (TX)
Texas Southern U (TX)
Texas State U–San Marcos (TX)
Texas Wesleyan U (TX)
Troy U (AL)
Union U (TN)
The U of Akron (OH)
The U of Alabama (AL)
U of Arkansas at Little Rock (AR)
U of Central Florida (FL)
U of Central Oklahoma (OK)
U of Florida (FL)
U of Houston (TX)
U of Kentucky (KY)
U of Miami (FL)
U of Missouri (MO)
U of Montevallo (AL)
U of North Texas (TX)
U of Pittsburgh at Bradford (PA)
U of Southern California (CA)
U of Southern Indiana (IN)
The U of Texas at Arlington (TX)
The U of Texas at Austin (TX)
U of the Incarnate Word (TX)
The U of Western Ontario (ON, Canada)
U of Wisconsin–Superior (WI)
Walla Walla U (WA)
Wartburg Coll (IA)
Waynesburg U (PA)
Wayne State U (MI)
Western Illinois U (IL)
Western Kentucky U (KY)
Xavier U (OH)
Youngstown State U (OH)

RADIO AND TELEVISION BROADCASTING TECHNOLOGY
Asbury U (KY)
Coll of the Ozarks (MO)
Emerson Coll (MA)
Ferris State U (MI)
Gannon U (PA)
Gardner-Webb U (NC)

Goshen Coll (IN)
New England School of Communications (ME)
New York U (NY)
Northwest Nazarene U (ID)
Point Park U (PA)
Rowan U (NJ)
Suffolk U (MA)
Trevecca Nazarene U (TN)

RADIOLOGIC TECHNOLOGY/ SCIENCE
Adventist U of Health Sciences (FL)
Austin Peay State U (TN)
Baptist Coll of Health Sciences (TN)
Bluefield State Coll (WV)
Colorado Mesa U (CO)
Dalhousie U (NS, Canada)
Friends U (KS)
Henderson State U (AR)
Holy Family U (PA)
Indiana U Northwest (IN)
Inter American U of Puerto Rico, Aguadilla Campus (PR)
Inter American U of Puerto Rico, Ponce Campus (PR)
Inter American U of Puerto Rico, San Germán Campus (PR)
Jamestown Coll (ND)
Lewis U (IL)
Manhattan Coll (NY)
Marian U (WI)
Marshall U (WV)
Massachusetts Coll of Pharmacy and Health Sciences (MA)
McNeese State U (LA)
Missouri State U (MO)
National U (CA)
Nebraska Methodist Coll (NE)
North Dakota State U (ND)
Northern Michigan U (MI)
Northwestern State U of Louisiana (LA)
Oakland U (MI)
The Ohio State U (OH)
Presentation Coll (SD)
Quinnipiac U (CT)
Rhode Island Coll (RI)
St. John's U (NY)
Southeastern Louisiana U (LA)
U of Arkansas–Fort Smith (AR)
U of Charleston (WV)
U of Louisiana at Monroe (LA)
U of Missouri (MO)
U of Oklahoma Health Sciences Center (OK)
U of Pittsburgh at Bradford (PA)
U of St. Francis (IL)
U of South Alabama (AL)
Virginia Commonwealth U (VA)
Widener U (PA)
York Coll of Pennsylvania (PA)

RADIO, TELEVISION, AND DIGITAL COMMUNICATION RELATED
Brigham Young U (UT)
Champlain Coll (VT)
Clark Atlanta U (GA)
The Coll at Brockport, State U of New York (NY)
Drake U (IA)
Drury U (MO)
Emerson Coll (MA)
Hofstra U (NY)
John Brown U (AR)
Keystone Coll (PA)
Madonna U (MI)
Marquette U (WI)
Neumann U (PA)
North Dakota State U (ND)
Rogers State U (OK)
Sacred Heart U (CT)
San Francisco State U (CA)
Spring Hill Coll (AL)
Texas Christian U (TX)
The U of Akron (OH)
Washington State U (WA)
Western Carolina U (NC)

RANGE SCIENCE AND MANAGEMENT
Colorado State U (CO)
Humboldt State U (CA)
New Mexico State U (NM)
North Dakota State U (ND)

Oregon State U (OR)
South Dakota State U (SD)
Sul Ross State U (TX)
Tarleton State U (TX)
Texas A&M U (TX)
U of Idaho (ID)
U of Nebraska–Lincoln (NE)
U of Wyoming (WY)
Utah State U (UT)

READING TEACHER EDUCATION
Baylor U (TX)
Canisius Coll (NY)
Catawba Coll (NC)
Clarion U of Pennsylvania (PA)
Concordia U Chicago (IL)
Dordt Coll (IA)
East Central U (OK)
Eastern Michigan U (MI)
Eastern Washington U (WA)
Grand Valley State U (MI)
Granite State Coll (NH)
Harding U (AR)
Hardin-Simmons U (TX)
Iowa Wesleyan Coll (IA)
Michigan State U (MI)
Midwestern State U (TX)
Roger Williams U (RI)
State U of New York Coll at Cortland (NY)
Tennessee State U (TN)
Texas A&M Intl U (TX)
Texas A&M U–Commerce (TX)
Texas Wesleyan U (TX)
U of Central Oklahoma (OK)
U of Great Falls (MT)
The U of North Carolina at Pembroke (NC)
U of Northern Iowa (IA)
Upper Iowa U (IA)
Washington State U (WA)
William Penn U (IA)
Wright State U (OH)

REAL ESTATE
Arizona State U (AZ)
Baylor U (TX)
Bowling Green State U (OH)
California State U, Dominguez Hills (CA)
California State U, East Bay (CA)
California State U, Fresno (CA)
Central Michigan U (MI)
Clarion U of Pennsylvania (PA)
Colorado State U (CO)
DePaul U (IL)
Florida Atlantic U (FL)
Florida Intl U (FL)
Georgia State U (GA)
Marquette U (WI)
Menlo Coll (CA)
Minnesota State U Mankato (MN)
Mississippi State U (MS)
New York U (NY)
The Ohio State U (OH)
Portland State U (OR)
San Diego State U (CA)
Southern Methodist U (TX)
Syracuse U (NY)
Temple U (PA)
Texas Christian U (TX)
Thomas Edison State Coll (NJ)
The U of Akron (OH)
The U of British Columbia (BC, Canada)
U of Central Florida (FL)
U of Central Oklahoma (OK)
U of Cincinnati (OH)
U of Denver (CO)
U of Florida (FL)
U of Georgia (GA)
U of Guelph (ON, Canada)
U of Illinois at Urbana–Champaign (IL)
U of Miami (FL)
U of Mississippi (MS)
U of Missouri (MO)
U of Nebraska at Omaha (NE)
U of Nevada, Las Vegas (NV)
U of Northern Iowa (IA)
U of North Texas (TX)
U of Pennsylvania (PA)
U of St. Thomas (MN)
U of San Diego (CA)
U of South Carolina (SC)
The U of Texas at Arlington (TX)
The U of Texas at El Paso (TX)

U of West Georgia (GA)
U of Wisconsin–Madison (WI)
U of Wisconsin–Stout (WI)
Villanova U (PA)
Virginia Commonwealth U (VA)
Washington State U (WA)

RECORDING ARTS TECHNOLOGY
American U (DC)
Belmont U (TN)
Berklee Coll of Music (MA)
Butler U (IN)
Columbia Coll Chicago (IL)
Five Towns Coll (NY)
Greenville Coll (IL)
Indiana U Bloomington (IN)
Intl Acad of Design & Technology (FL)
Ithaca Coll (NY)
Lebanon Valley Coll (PA)
Loyola Marymount U (CA)
Malone U (OH)
New England Inst of Technology (RI)
New England School of Communications (ME)
Peabody Conservatory of The Johns Hopkins U (MD)
Savannah Coll of Art and Design (GA)
State U of New York at Fredonia (NY)
Texas Southern U (TX)
Texas State U–San Marcos (TX)
U of Hartford (CT)
York Coll of Pennsylvania (PA)

REGIONAL STUDIES
The U of Colorado (CO)
Columbia U, School of General Studies (NY)
Houghton Coll (NY)
Mercer U (GA)
Prescott Coll (AZ)
United States Military Acad (NY)
U of Mississippi (MS)
U of Regina (SK, Canada)
Washington U in St. Louis (MO)

REGISTERED NURSING, NURSING ADMINISTRATION, NURSING RESEARCH AND CLINICAL NURSING RELATED
Cleveland State U (OH)
Columbia Centro Universitario, Caguas (PR)
Molloy Coll (NY)
Rowan U (NJ)
Tabor Coll (KS)
Thompson Rivers U (BC, Canada)
Union Coll (KY)

REGISTERED NURSING/ REGISTERED NURSE
Abilene Christian U (TX)
Adams State U (CO)
Adelphi U (NY)
Adventist U of Health Sciences (FL)
Alcorn State U (MS)
Alderson-Broaddus Coll (WV)
Allen Coll (IA)
Alvernia U (PA)
Alverno Coll (WI)
American Public U System (WV)
American U of Beirut (Lebanon)
Anderson U (IN)
Andrews U (MI)
Angelo State U (TX)
Appalachian State U (NC)
Arizona State U (AZ)
Arkansas State U (AR)
Arkansas Tech U (AR)
Armstrong Atlantic State U (GA)
Athabasca U (AB, Canada)
Auburn U (AL)
Auburn U at Montgomery (AL)
Augsburg Coll (MN)
Augustana Coll (SD)
Aurora U (IL)
Austin Peay State U (TN)
Azusa Pacific U (CA)
Baker U (KS)
Baldwin Wallace U (OH)
Ball State U (IN)
Baptist Coll of Health Sciences (TN)
Barry U (FL)

Barton Coll (NC)
Baylor U (TX)
Becker Coll (MA)
Bellarmine U (KY)
Belmont U (TN)
Bemidji State U (MN)
Benedictine U (IL)
Berea Coll (KY)
Berry Coll (GA)
Bethel Coll (IN)
Bethel Coll (KS)
Bethel U (MN)
Bethune-Cookman U (FL)
Binghamton U, State U of New York (NY)
Bloomfield Coll (NJ)
Bloomsburg U of Pennsylvania (PA)
Bob Jones U (SC)
Boise State U (ID)
Boston Coll (MA)
Bowie State U (MD)
Bowling Green State U (OH)
Bowling Green State U-Firelands Coll (OH)
Bradley U (IL)
Caldwell Coll (NJ)
California Baptist U (CA)
California State U, Chico (CA)
California State U, Dominguez Hills (CA)
California State U, East Bay (CA)
California State U, Fresno (CA)
California State U, Fullerton (CA)
California State U, Long Beach (CA)
California State U, Los Angeles (CA)
California State U, Monterey Bay (CA)
California State U, Northridge (CA)
California State U, San Bernardino (CA)
California State U, Stanislaus (CA)
Calvin Coll (MI)
Campbellsville U (KY)
Capital U (OH)
Cardinal Stritch U (WI)
Carlow U (PA)
Carroll Coll (MT)
Carson-Newman U (TN)
Case Western Reserve U (OH)
Castleton State Coll (VT)
The Catholic U of America (DC)
Cedarville U (OH)
Central Connecticut State U (CT)
Central Methodist U (MO)
Chamberlain Coll of Nursing, Miramar (FL)
Chamberlain Coll of Nursing (GA)
Chamberlain Coll of Nursing (IN)
Chamberlain Coll of Nursing (MO)
Chamberlain Coll of Nursing, Cleveland (OH)
Chamberlain Coll of Nursing (TX)
Chatham U (PA)
Chicago State U (IL)
Chipola Coll (FL)
Clarion U of Pennsylvania (PA)
Clarke U (IA)
Clayton State U (GA)
Clemson U (SC)
Cleveland State U (OH)
Coastal Carolina U (SC)
Coe Coll (IA)
The Coll at Brockport, State U of New York (NY)
Coll of Coastal Georgia (GA)
Coll of Mount St. Joseph (OH)
The Coll of New Jersey (NJ)
The Coll of New Rochelle (NY)
Coll of Saint Benedict (MN)
Coll of Saint Mary (NE)
The Coll of St. Scholastica (MN)
Coll of Staten Island of the City U of New York (NY)
Coll of the Ozarks (MO)
Colorado Mesa U (CO)
Columbia Centro Universitario, Yauco (PR)
Columbia Intl U (SC)
Columbus State U (GA)
Concordia Coll (MN)
Concordia U (IL)
Concordia U (OR)
Concordia U Texas (TX)
Concordia U Wisconsin (WI)
Creighton U (NE)

Crown Coll (MN)
Culver-Stockton Coll (MO)
Curry Coll (MA)
Dakota Wesleyan U (SD)
Dalhousie U (NS, Canada)
Dalton State Coll (GA)
Davenport U, Grand Rapids (MI)
Defiance Coll (OH)
Delta State U (MS)
DePaul U (IL)
DeSales U (PA)
Dillard U (LA)
Dominican Coll (NY)
Dominican U (IL)
Dordt Coll (IA)
Duquesne U (PA)
East Carolina U (NC)
East Central U (OK)
Eastern Illinois U (IL)
Eastern Mennonite U (VA)
Eastern Michigan U (MI)
Eastern New Mexico U (NM)
Eastern Washington U (WA)
East Tennessee State U (TN)
East Texas Baptist U (TX)
Edgewood Coll (WI)
Edinboro U of Pennsylvania (PA)
Elmira Coll (NY)
Emporia State U (KS)
Endicott Coll (MA)
Fairfield U (CT)
Fairleigh Dickinson U, Metropolitan
  Campus (NJ)
Fairmont State U (WV)
Farmingdale State Coll (NY)
Fayetteville State U (NC)
Felician Coll (NJ)
Ferris State U (MI)
Florida Ag and Mech U (FL)
Florida Atlantic U (FL)
Florida Gateway Coll (FL)
Florida Intl U (FL)
Florida National U (FL)
Florida Southern Coll (FL)
Framingham State U (MA)
Francis Marion U (SC)
Frostburg State U (MD)
Gannon U (PA)
Gardner-Webb U (NC)
George Fox U (OR)
George Mason U (VA)
Georgetown U (DC)
Georgia Coll & State U (GA)
Georgia Regents U (GA)
Georgia Southern U (GA)
Georgia Southwestern State U
  (GA)
Georgia State U (GA)
Goldfarb School of Nursing at
  Barnes-Jewish Coll (MO)
Gonzaga U (WA)
Goodwin Coll (CT)
Goshen Coll (IN)
Governors State U (IL)
Graceland U (IA)
Grambling State U (LA)
Grand Valley State U (MI)
Grand View U (IA)
Granite State Coll (NH)
Gustavus Adolphus Coll (MN)
Hampton U (VA)
Harding U (AR)
Hardin-Simmons U (TX)
Hartwick Coll (NY)
Hawai`i Pacific U (HI)
Henderson State U (AR)
Hiram Coll (OH)
Holy Family U (PA)
Holy Names U (CA)
Hope Coll (MI)
Hunter Coll of the City U of New
  York (NY)
Husson U (ME)
Illinois State U (IL)
Illinois Wesleyan U (IL)
Immaculata U (PA)
Indiana State U (IN)
Indiana U Bloomington (IN)
Indiana U East (IN)
Indiana U Kokomo (IN)
Indiana U Northwest (IN)
Indiana U of Pennsylvania (PA)
Indiana U–Purdue U Fort Wayne
  (IN)
Indiana U–Purdue U Indianapolis
  (IN)

Indiana U South Bend (IN)
Indiana U Southeast (IN)
Indiana Wesleyan U (IN)
Indian River State Coll (FL)
Inter American U of Puerto Rico,
  Aguadilla Campus (PR)
Inter American U of Puerto Rico,
  San Germán Campus (PR)
Iowa Wesleyan Coll (IA)
Jacksonville State U (AL)
James Madison U (VA)
Jamestown Coll (ND)
The Johns Hopkins U (MD)
Kansas Wesleyan U (KS)
Keene State Coll (NH)
Kennesaw State U (GA)
Kent State U (OH)
Kent State U at East Liverpool (OH)
Kent State U at Geauga (OH)
Kent State U at Salem (OH)
Kent State U at Stark (OH)
Kent State U at Trumbull (OH)
Kentucky Christian U (KY)
Kentucky State U (KY)
Keuka Coll (NY)
King Coll (TN)
Kuyper Coll (MI)
LaGrange Coll (GA)
Lake Superior State U (MI)
Lamar U (TX)
Lancaster General Coll of Nursing
  & Health Sciences (PA)
Lander U (SC)
Langston U (OK)
La Roche Coll (PA)
La Salle U (PA)
Lees-McRae Coll (NC)
Lehman Coll of the City U of New
  York (NY)
Le Moyne Coll (NY)
Lewis-Clark State Coll (ID)
Lewis U (IL)
Liberty U (VA)
Lincoln Memorial U (TN)
Lincoln U (MO)
Lindsey Wilson Coll (KY)
Linfield Coll (OR)
Lipscomb U (TN)
Lock Haven U of Pennsylvania (PA)
Long Island U–Brooklyn Campus
  (NY)
Long Island U–C. W. Post Campus
  (NY)
Longwood U (VA)
Louisiana Coll (LA)
Louisiana State U at Alexandria
  (LA)
Lourdes U (OH)
Loyola U Chicago (IL)
Lubbock Christian U (TX)
Luther Coll (IA)
Lynchburg Coll (VA)
Madonna U (MI)
Malone U (OH)
Mansfield U of Pennsylvania (PA)
Maranatha Baptist Bible Coll (WI)
Marian U (WI)
Marquette U (WI)
Marshall U (WV)
Marymount U (VA)
Maryville Coll (TN)
Maryville U of Saint Louis (MO)
Marywood U (PA)
Massachusetts Coll of Pharmacy
  and Health Sciences (MA)
McKendree U (IL)
McMurry U (TX)
McNeese State U (LA)
Mercy Coll (NY)
Mercy Coll of Health Sciences (IA)
Mercy Coll of Ohio (OH)
Mercyhurst U (PA)
Messiah Coll (PA)
Metropolitan State U of Denver
  (CO)
Miami Dade Coll (FL)
Miami U (OH)
Michigan State U (MI)
Middle Tennessee State U (TN)
Midwestern State U (TX)
Millikin U (IL)
Milwaukee School of Eng (WI)
Minnesota State U Mankato (MN)
Minnesota State U Moorhead (MN)
Minot State U (ND)
Misericordia U (PA)
Mississippi Coll (MS)

Mississippi U for Women (MS)
Missouri State U (MO)
Missouri Western State U (MO)
Molloy Coll (NY)
Montana State U (MT)
Montana Tech of The U of Montana
  (MT)
Montreat Coll, Montreat (NC)
Moravian Coll (PA)
Morehead State U (KY)
Morningside Coll (IA)
Morrisville State Coll (NY)
Mount Aloysius Coll (PA)
Mount Marty Coll (SD)
Mount Mercy U (IA)
Mount Saint Mary Coll (NY)
Mount St. Mary's Coll (CA)
Mount Vernon Nazarene U (OH)
Murray State U (KY)
Nazareth Coll of Rochester (NY)
Nebraska Methodist Coll (NE)
Neumann U (PA)
Newberry Coll (SC)
Newman U (KS)
New Mexico Highlands U (NM)
New Mexico State U (NM)
New York City Coll of Technology of
  the City U of New York (NY)
New York Inst of Technology (NY)
New York U (NY)
Niagara U (NY)
Nicholls State U (LA)
Norfolk State U (VA)
North Carolina Central U (NC)
North Dakota State U (ND)
Northeastern U (MA)
Northern Arizona U (AZ)
Northern Illinois U (IL)
Northern Michigan U (MI)
Northwestern Coll (IA)
Northwestern Coll (MN)
Northwestern Oklahoma State U
  (OK)
Northwestern State U of Louisiana
  (LA)
Northwest Missouri State U (MO)
Northwest Nazarene U (ID)
Northwest U (WA)
Norwich U (VT)
Nova Southeastern U (FL)
Nyack Coll (NY)
Oakland U (MI)
The Ohio State U (OH)
The Ohio State U at Lima (OH)
The Ohio State U at Marion (OH)
The Ohio State U–Mansfield
  Campus (OH)
Ohio U (OH)
Ohio U–Chillicothe (OH)
Oklahoma Baptist U (OK)
Oklahoma Christian U (OK)
Oklahoma City U (OK)
Old Dominion U (VA)
Olympic Coll (WA)
Oral Roberts U (OK)
Oregon Health & Science U (OR)
Pace U (NY)
Pacific Lutheran U (WA)
Pacific Union Coll (CA)
Palm Beach Atlantic U (FL)
Penn State Abington (PA)
Penn State Altoona (PA)
Penn State Beaver (PA)
Penn State Berks (PA)
Penn State Brandywine (PA)
Penn State DuBois (PA)
Penn State Erie, The Behrend Coll
  (PA)
Penn State Fayette, The Eberly
  Campus (PA)
Penn State Greater Allegheny (PA)
Penn State Harrisburg (PA)
Penn State Hazleton (PA)
Penn State Lehigh Valley (PA)
Penn State Mont Alto (PA)
Penn State New Kensington (PA)
Penn State Schuylkill (PA)
Penn State Shenango (PA)
Penn State U Park (PA)
Penn State Wilkes-Barre (PA)
Penn State Worthington Scranton
  (PA)
Penn State York (PA)
Piedmont Coll (GA)
Pittsburg State U (KS)
Plymouth State U (NH)
Point Loma Nazarene U (CA)

Polk State Coll (FL)
Presentation Coll (SD)
Purdue U (IN)
Purdue U Calumet (IN)
Purdue U North Central (IN)
Quincy U (IL)
Quinnipiac U (CT)
Radford U (VA)
Ramapo Coll of New Jersey (NJ)
Rasmussen Coll Fort Myers (FL)
Rasmussen Coll Land O' Lakes
  (FL)
Rasmussen Coll New Port Richey
  (FL)
Rasmussen Coll Tampa/Brandon
  (FL)
Regis Coll (MA)
Regis U (CO)
Research Coll of Nursing (MO)
Resurrection U (IL)
Rhode Island Coll (RI)
The Richard Stockton Coll of New
  Jersey (NJ)
Rivier U (NH)
Robert Morris U (PA)
Roberts Wesleyan Coll (NY)
Rockford Coll (IL)
Rockhurst U (MO)
Rogers State U (OK)
Rowan U (NJ)
Russell Sage Coll (NY)
Rutgers, The State U of New
  Jersey, Camden (NJ)
Rutgers, The State U of New
  Jersey, Newark (NJ)
Rutgers, The State U of New
  Jersey, New Brunswick (NJ)
Sacred Heart U (CT)
Sage Coll of Albany (NY)
Saginaw Valley State U (MI)
St. Ambrose U (IA)
Saint Francis Medical Center Coll
  of Nursing (IL)
St. John Fisher Coll (NY)
Saint John's U (MN)
Saint Joseph's Coll (IN)
Saint Louis U (MO)
Saint Martin's U (WA)
Saint Mary's Coll (IN)
Saint Mary's Coll of California (CA)
St. Olaf Coll (MN)
Salem State U (MA)
Salisbury U (MD)
Salve Regina U (RI)
Samford U (AL)
Samuel Merritt U (CA)
San Diego State U (CA)
Sanford Coll of Nursing (ND)
San Francisco State U (CA)
San Jose State U (CA)
Seattle Pacific U (WA)
Seattle U (WA)
Shawnee State U (OH)
Shenandoah U (VA)
Shepherd U (WV)
Siena Heights U (MI)
Simmons Coll (MA)
Simpson U (CA)
Slippery Rock U of Pennsylvania
  (PA)
Sonoma State U (CA)
South Dakota State U (SD)
Southeast Missouri State U (MO)
Southern Arkansas U–Magnolia
  (AR)
Southern Connecticut State U (CT)
Southern Illinois U Edwardsville
  (IL)
Southern Nazarene U (OK)
Southern Oregon U (OR)
Southern Utah U (UT)
Southwest Baptist U (MO)
Southwestern Adventist U (TX)
Spalding U (KY)
Spring Hill Coll (AL)
State Coll of Florida Manatee-
  Sarasota (FL)
State U of New York at New Paltz
  (NY)
State U of New York at Plattsburgh
  (NY)
State U of New York Coll of
  Technology at Canton (NY)
State U of New York Empire State
  Coll (NY)
State U of New York Inst of
  Technology (NY)

Stephen F. Austin State U (TX)
Stevenson U (MD)
Stratford U, Woodbridge (VA)
Sullivan U (KY)
Tarleton State U (TX)
Temple U (PA)
Tennessee State U (TN)
Tennessee Wesleyan Coll (TN)
Texas A&M Intl U (TX)
Texas A&M U–Commerce (TX)
Texas Christian U (TX)
Texas State U–San Marcos (TX)
Texas Woman's U (TX)
Thomas Edison State Coll (NJ)
Thomas More Coll (KY)
Thomas U (GA)
Thompson Rivers U (BC, Canada)
Trent U (ON, Canada)
Trevecca Nazarene U (TN)
Trinity Christian Coll (IL)
Trinity Coll of Nursing and Health
  Sciences (IL)
Troy U (AL)
Truman State U (MO)
Tuskegee U (AL)
Union Coll (NE)
Union U (TN)
Universidad Adventista de las
  Antillas (PR)
Université de Sherbrooke (QC,
  Canada)
Université du Québec en
  Outaouais (QC, Canada)
U at Buffalo, the State U of New
  York (NY)
The U of Akron (OH)
The U of Alabama (AL)
The U of Alabama at Birmingham
  (AL)
U of Alaska Anchorage (AK)
The U of Arizona (AZ)
U of Arkansas at Little Rock (AR)
U of Arkansas for Medical
  Sciences (AR)
U of Arkansas–Fort Smith (AR)
The U of British Columbia (BC,
  Canada)
The U of British Columbia–
  Okanagan (BC, Canada)
U of Central Arkansas (AR)
U of Central Florida (FL)
U of Central Oklahoma (OK)
U of Charleston (WV)
U of Cincinnati (OH)
U of Colorado Colorado Springs
  (CO)
U of Colorado Denver (CO)
U of Delaware (DE)
U of Evansville (IN)
U of Florida (FL)
U of Guam (GU)
U of Hartford (CT)
U of Hawaii at Hilo (HI)
U of Hawaii at Manoa (HI)
U of Houston–Victoria (TX)
U of Illinois at Chicago (IL)
The U of Iowa (IA)
The U of Kansas (KS)
U of Kentucky (KY)
U of Louisiana at Lafayette (LA)
U of Louisiana at Monroe (LA)
U of Louisville (KY)
U of Maine at Fort Kent (ME)
U of Massachusetts Amherst (MA)
U of Massachusetts Boston (MA)
U of Massachusetts Dartmouth
  (MA)
U of Memphis (TN)
U of Miami (FL)
U of Michigan (MI)
U of Michigan–Flint (MI)
U of Missouri (MO)
U of Missouri–Kansas City (MO)
U of Missouri–St. Louis (MO)
U of Mobile (AL)
U of Nevada, Las Vegas (NV)
U of Nevada, Reno (NV)
U of New Brunswick Fredericton
  (NB, Canada)
U of New Brunswick Saint John
  (NB, Canada)
U of New England (ME)
U of New Hampshire (NH)
U of New Mexico (NM)
U of North Alabama (AL)
The U of North Carolina at Chapel
  Hill (NC)

The U of North Carolina at Charlotte (NC)
The U of North Carolina at Greensboro (NC)
The U of North Carolina at Pembroke (NC)
The U of North Carolina Wilmington (NC)
U of North Dakota (ND)
U of Northern Colorado (CO)
U of North Florida (FL)
U of North Georgia (GA)
U of Oklahoma Health Sciences Center (OK)
U of Ottawa (ON, Canada)
U of Pennsylvania (PA)
U of Pikeville (KY)
U of Pittsburgh (PA)
U of Pittsburgh at Bradford (PA)
U of Portland (OR)
U of Regina (SK, Canada)
U of Rhode Island (RI)
U of Rochester (NY)
U of St. Francis (IL)
U of Saint Joseph (CT)
U of Saint Mary (KS)
The U of Scranton (PA)
U of South Alabama (AL)
U of South Carolina (SC)
U of South Carolina Aiken (SC)
U of South Carolina Upstate (SC)
The U of South Dakota (SD)
U of Southern Indiana (IN)
U of Southern Maine (ME)
U of Southern Mississippi (MS)
U of South Florida (FL)
The U of Tampa (FL)
The U of Tennessee (TN)
The U of Tennessee at Chattanooga (TN)
The U of Tennessee at Martin (TN)
The U of Texas at Arlington (TX)
The U of Texas at Austin (TX)
The U of Texas at Brownsville (TX)
The U of Texas at El Paso (TX)
The U of Texas–Pan American (TX)
U of the Incarnate Word (TX)
U of the Virgin Islands (VI)
The U of Toledo (OH)
U of Tulsa (OK)
U of Utah (UT)
U of Vermont (VT)
U of Virginia (VA)
U of Washington, Bothell (WA)
U of Washington, Tacoma (WA)
The U of Western Ontario (ON, Canada)
U of West Florida (FL)
U of West Georgia (GA)
U of Windsor (ON, Canada)
U of Wisconsin–Eau Claire (WI)
U of Wisconsin–Green Bay (WI)
U of Wisconsin–Madison (WI)
U of Wisconsin–Milwaukee (WI)
U of Wisconsin–Parkside (WI)
U of Wyoming (WY)
Ursuline Coll (OH)
Utica Coll (NY)
Valdosta State U (GA)
Valparaiso U (IN)
Villanova U (PA)
Vincennes U (IN)
Virginia Commonwealth U (VA)
Viterbo U (WI)
Wagner Coll (NY)
Walden U (MN)
Walla Walla U (WA)
Walsh U (OH)
Washburn U (KS)
Washington State U (WA)
Wayland Baptist U (TX)
Waynesburg U (PA)
Webster U (MO)
Wesley Coll (DE)
West Chester U of Pennsylvania (PA)
Western Carolina U (NC)
Western Connecticut State U (CT)
Western Illinois U (IL)
Western Kentucky U (KY)
Western Michigan U (MI)
Westfield State U (MA)
West Liberty U (WV)
Westminster Coll (UT)
West Texas A&M U (TX)
West Virginia U (WV)

West Virginia U Inst of Technology (WV)
West Virginia Wesleyan Coll (WV)
Wheeling Jesuit U (WV)
Whitworth U (WA)
Wichita State U (KS)
Widener U (PA)
Wilkes U (PA)
William Jewell Coll (MO)
William Paterson U of New Jersey (NJ)
Wilmington U (DE)
Worcester State U (MA)
Wright State U (OH)
York Coll of Pennsylvania (PA)
York Coll of the City U of New York (NY)
Youngstown State U (OH)

REHABILITATION AND THERAPEUTIC PROFESSIONS RELATED
Assumption Coll (MA)
Boston U (MA)
California State U, Los Angeles (CA)
Coll of Saint Mary (NE)
Hilbert Coll (NY)
Indiana U of Pennsylvania (PA)
Ithaca Coll (NY)
Penn State Abington (PA)
Penn State Altoona (PA)
Penn State Beaver (PA)
Penn State Berks (PA)
Penn State Brandywine (PA)
Penn State DuBois (PA)
Penn State Erie, The Behrend Coll (PA)
Penn State Fayette, The Eberly Campus (PA)
Penn State Greater Allegheny (PA)
Penn State Hazleton (PA)
Penn State Lehigh Valley (PA)
Penn State Mont Alto (PA)
Penn State New Kensington (PA)
Penn State Schuylkill (PA)
Penn State Shenango (PA)
Penn State U Park (PA)
Penn State Wilkes-Barre (PA)
Penn State Worthington Scranton (PA)
Penn State York (PA)
Prescott Coll (AZ)
Southern Illinois U Carbondale (IL)
Thomas U (GA)
Troy U (AL)
U of Maine at Farmington (ME)
U of Maryland Eastern Shore (MD)
U of Medicine and Dentistry of New Jersey (NJ)
U of North Texas (TX)
U of Waterloo (ON, Canada)
The U of Western Ontario (ON, Canada)
Wilberforce U (OH)

REHABILITATION SCIENCE
Arkansas Tech U (AR)
Stephen F. Austin State U (TX)
U of North Dakota (ND)
U of Pittsburgh (PA)
The U of Texas–Pan American (TX)
U of the Incarnate Word (TX)

RELIGIOUS EDUCATION
Andrews U (MI)
Asbury U (KY)
Ashland U (OH)
Barclay Coll (KS)
Bob Jones U (SC)
Campbellsville U (KY)
Cardinal Stritch U (WI)
Cedarville U (OH)
Cincinnati Christian U (OH)
Coll of Mount St. Joseph (OH)
Columbia Coll (SC)
Columbia Intl U (SC)
Concordia Coll–New York (NY)
Concordia U (CA)
Concordia U (OR)
Concordia U Chicago (IL)
Concordia U, Nebraska (NE)
Concordia U, St. Paul (MN)
Concordia U Texas (TX)
Concordia U Wisconsin (WI)
Corban U (OR)
Crossroads Coll (MN)
Crown Coll (MN)
Dallas Baptist U (TX)

Defiance Coll (OH)
Edgewood Coll (WI)
Faith Baptist Bible Coll and Theological Sem (IA)
Florida Christian Coll (FL)
Florida Coll (FL)
Florida Southern Coll (FL)
Gardner-Webb U (NC)
Global U (MO)
Grace U (NE)
Harding U (AR)
Hillsdale Free Will Baptist Coll (OK)
Houghton Coll (NY)
Howard Payne U (TX)
Huntingdon Coll (AL)
Indiana Wesleyan U (IN)
Inter American U of Puerto Rico, Fajardo Campus (PR)
John Carroll U (OH)
Kansas Wesleyan U (KS)
Kingswood U (NB, Canada)
Kuyper Coll (MI)
La Salle U (PA)
Laurel U (NC)
Lee U (TN)
Lincoln Christian U (IL)
Lindsey Wilson Coll (KY)
Louisiana Coll (LA)
Loyola U Chicago (IL)
Loyola U New Orleans (LA)
Malone U (OH)
The Master's Coll and Sem (CA)
Master's Coll and Sem (ON, Canada)
Messiah Coll (PA)
Morris Coll (SC)
Mount Vernon Nazarene U (OH)
Multnomah U (OR)
Northwestern Coll (IA)
Northwest Nazarene U (ID)
Northwest U (WA)
Oakland City U (IN)
Oklahoma Christian U (OK)
Oklahoma City U (OK)
Oral Roberts U (OK)
Pepperdine U, Malibu (CA)
Presbyterian Coll (SC)
Saint Louis Christian Coll (MO)
Saint Mary's U of Minnesota (MN)
Saint Vincent Coll (PA)
Seattle Pacific U (WA)
Simpson U (CA)
Southern Nazarene U (OK)
Southwest Baptist U (MO)
Sterling Coll (KS)
Taylor U (IN)
Universidad Adventista de las Antillas (PR)
Universidad Teolgica del Caribe (PR)
U of the Cumberlands (KY)
Wayland Baptist U (TX)
West Virginia Wesleyan Coll (WV)
Wheaton Coll (IL)

RELIGIOUS/SACRED MUSIC
Anderson U (IN)
Anderson U (SC)
Arizona Christian U (AZ)
Asbury U (KY)
Barclay Coll (KS)
Baylor U (TX)
Bethany Lutheran Coll (MN)
Bethel U (MN)
Bluefield Coll (VA)
Blue Mountain Coll (MS)
Bowling Green State U (OH)
Briercrest Coll (SK, Canada)
Calvin Coll (MI)
Campbellsville U (KY)
Cedarville U (OH)
Central Baptist Coll (AR)
Cincinnati Christian U (OH)
Clarke U (IA)
Clearwater Christian Coll (FL)
Coll of the Ozarks (MO)
Columbia Intl U (SC)
Concordia Coll–New York (NY)
Concordia U Chicago (IL)
Concordia U, Nebraska (NE)
Concordia U, St. Paul (MN)
Concordia U Texas (TX)
Concordia U Wisconsin (WI)
Corban U (OR)
Crossroads Coll (MN)
Crown Coll (MN)
Dallas Baptist U (TX)

Drake U (IA)
East Central U (OK)
East Texas Baptist U (TX)
Emmanuel Coll (GA)
Evangel U (MO)
Faith Baptist Bible Coll and Theological Sem (IA)
Furman U (SC)
Gardner-Webb U (NC)
Grace U (NE)
Gustavus Adolphus Coll (MN)
Hardin-Simmons U (TX)
Hillsdale Free Will Baptist Coll (OK)
Hope Intl U (CA)
Howard Payne U (TX)
Huntington U (IN)
Indiana Wesleyan U (IN)
John Brown U (AR)
Judson U (IL)
Kentucky Christian U (KY)
Kuyper Coll (MI)
Lee U (TN)
Liberty U (VA)
Lincoln Christian U (IL)
Lincoln U (MO)
Louisiana Coll (LA)
Madonna U (MI)
Malone U (OH)
Maranatha Baptist Bible Coll (WI)
The Master's Coll and Sem (CA)
Mississippi Coll (MS)
Missouri Baptist U (MO)
Moravian Coll (PA)
Mount Vernon Nazarene U (OH)
Multnomah U (OR)
North Greenville U (SC)
Northwest Nazarene U (ID)
Northwest U (WA)
Nyack Coll (NY)
Oklahoma Baptist U (OK)
Oklahoma City U (OK)
Oral Roberts U (OK)
Ouachita Baptist U (AR)
Point Loma Nazarene U (CA)
Quincy U (IL)
Rider U (NJ)
Saint Louis Christian Coll (MO)
St. Olaf Coll (MN)
Samford U (AL)
San Diego Christian Coll (CA)
Seton Hill U (PA)
Shenandoah U (VA)
Southeastern U (FL)
Southern Nazarene U (OK)
Texas Christian U (TX)
Trevecca Nazarene U (TN)
Union U (TN)
U of Hartford (CT)
U of Mobile (AL)
U of the Cumberlands (KY)
Wartburg Coll (IA)
Wayland Baptist U (TX)
William Jewell Coll (MO)

RELIGIOUS STUDIES
Agnes Scott Coll (GA)
Albertus Magnus Coll (CT)
Albion Coll (MI)
Albright Coll (PA)
Alma Coll (MI)
Alvernia U (PA)
Alverno Coll (WI)
American Public U System (WV)
American U (DC)
Amherst Coll (MA)
Anderson U (IN)
Anderson U (SC)
Andrews U (MI)
Appalachian State U (NC)
Arizona State U (AZ)
Ashland U (OH)
Athens State U (AL)
Augsburg Coll (MN)
Augustana Coll (IL)
Augustana Coll (SD)
Aurora U (IL)
Averett U (VA)
Avila U (MO)
Azusa Pacific U (CA)
Baker U (KS)
Baldwin Wallace U (OH)
Ball State U (IN)
Bard Coll (NY)
Bates Coll (ME)
Baylor U (TX)
Belmont U (TN)
Bemidji State U (MN)

Berea Coll (KY)
Bethany Coll (WV)
Bethany Lutheran Coll (MN)
Bethel Coll (KS)
Bloomfield Coll (NJ)
Bluefield Coll (VA)
Bluffton U (OH)
Boston U (MA)
Bowdoin Coll (ME)
Bradley U (IL)
Brevard Coll (NC)
Briercrest Coll (SK, Canada)
Brown U (RI)
Bucknell U (PA)
Butler U (IN)
Cabrini Coll (PA)
Cairn U (PA)
California Lutheran U (CA)
California State U, East Bay (CA)
California State U, Fresno (CA)
California State U, Fullerton (CA)
California State U, Long Beach (CA)
California State U, Northridge (CA)
Calumet Coll of Saint Joseph (IN)
Calvin Coll (MI)
Campbellsville U (KY)
Canisius Coll (NY)
Capital U (OH)
Cardinal Stritch U (WI)
Carleton Coll (MN)
Carson-Newman U (TN)
Case Western Reserve U (OH)
Catawba Coll (NC)
The Catholic U of America (DC)
Centenary Coll of Louisiana (LA)
Central Coll (IA)
Central Methodist U (MO)
Central Michigan U (MI)
Centre Coll (KY)
Chapman U (CA)
Chowan U (NC)
Christian Brothers U (TN)
Claremont McKenna Coll (CA)
Clark Atlanta U (GA)
Clarke U (IA)
Cleveland State U (OH)
Coe Coll (IA)
Colby Coll (ME)
Colgate U (NY)
Coll of Charleston (SC)
The Coll of Idaho (ID)
Coll of Mount St. Joseph (OH)
The Coll of New Rochelle (NY)
The Coll of Saint Rose (NY)
The Coll of St. Scholastica (MN)
Coll of the Holy Cross (MA)
The Coll of William and Mary (VA)
The Coll of Wooster (OH)
The Colorado Coll (CO)
Columbia Bible Coll (BC, Canada)
Columbia Coll (SC)
Columbia U (NY)
Columbia U, School of General Studies (NY)
Concordia Coll (MN)
Concordia Coll–New York (NY)
Concordia U (CA)
Concordia U (OR)
Concordia U (QC, Canada)
Concordia U Chicago (IL)
Concordia U Wisconsin (WI)
Connecticut Coll (CT)
Converse Coll (SC)
Corban U (OR)
Cornell Coll (IA)
Culver-Stockton Coll (MO)
Dalhousie U (NS, Canada)
Dartmouth Coll (NH)
Davidson Coll (NC)
Defiance Coll (OH)
DePaul U (IL)
DePauw U (IN)
Dickinson Coll (PA)
Doane Coll (NE)
Dordt Coll (IA)
Drake U (IA)
Drew U (NJ)
Drury U (MO)
Earlham Coll (IN)
Eastern New Mexico U (NM)
East Texas Baptist U (TX)
Eckerd Coll (FL)
Edgewood Coll (WI)
Elizabethtown Coll (PA)
Elmira Coll (NY)
Elon U (NC)

Emmanuel Coll (MA)
Emory & Henry Coll (VA)
Eugene Lang Coll The New School
  for Liberal Arts (NY)
Fairfield U (CT)
Faulkner U (AL)
Felician Coll (NJ)
Ferrum Coll (VA)
Florida Intl U (FL)
Florida Southern Coll (FL)
Franklin & Marshall Coll (PA)
Franklin Coll (IN)
Furman U (SC)
Gardner-Webb U (NC)
George Mason U (VA)
Georgetown Coll (KY)
Georgia State U (GA)
Gettysburg Coll (PA)
Gonzaga U (WA)
Goshen Coll (IN)
Goucher Coll (MD)
Graceland U (IA)
Grand View U (IA)
Greenville Coll (IL)
Grinnell Coll (IA)
Grove City Coll (PA)
Guilford Coll (NC)
Gustavus Adolphus Coll (MN)
Hamilton Coll (NY)
Hamline U (MN)
Hampden-Sydney Coll (VA)
Hampshire Coll (MA)
Hampton U (VA)
Hartwick Coll (NY)
Haverford Coll (PA)
Hendrix Coll (AR)
High Point U (NC)
Hillsdale Coll (MI)
Hiram Coll (OH)
Hobart and William Smith Colls
  (NY)
Hofstra U (NY)
Hollins U (VA)
Holy Apostles Coll and Sem (CT)
Holy Family U (PA)
Holy Names U (CA)
Hood Coll (MD)
Hope Coll (MI)
Hope Intl U (CA)
Houghton Coll (NY)
Humboldt State U (CA)
Hunter Coll of the City U of New
  York (NY)
Huntingdon Coll (AL)
Huntington U (IN)
Illinois Coll (IL)
Illinois Wesleyan U (IL)
Indiana U Bloomington (IN)
Indiana U of Pennsylvania (PA)
Indiana U–Purdue U Indianapolis
  (IN)
Iona Coll (NY)
Iowa State U of Science and
  Technology (IA)
Jamestown Coll (ND)
Jarvis Christian Coll (TX)
John Brown U (AR)
John Carroll U (OH)
Judson Coll (AL)
Juniata Coll (PA)
Kalamazoo Coll (MI)
Kansas Wesleyan U (KS)
Kenyon Coll (OH)
King Coll (TN)
Kingswood U (NB, Canada)
Lafayette Coll (PA)
LaGrange Coll (GA)
Lakeland Coll (WI)
Lane Coll (TN)
La Roche Coll (PA)
La Salle U (PA)
La Sierra U (CA)
Laurel U (NC)
Lawrence U (WI)
Lebanon Valley Coll (PA)
Lees-McRae Coll (NC)
Lehigh U (PA)
Le Moyne Coll (NY)
LeTourneau U (TX)
Lewis U (IL)
Liberty U (VA)
Lindenwood U (MO)
Linfield Coll (OR)
Louisiana Coll (LA)
Lourdes U (OH)
Loyola U Maryland (MD)
Loyola U New Orleans (LA)

Luther Coll (IA)
Lynchburg Coll (VA)
Macalester Coll (MN)
Madonna U (MI)
Manchester U (IN)
Manhattan Coll (NY)
Manhattanville Coll (NY)
Marian U (WI)
Mars Hill Coll (NC)
Mary Baldwin Coll (VA)
Marymount U (VA)
Maryville Coll (TN)
Marywood U (PA)
The Master's Coll and Sem (CA)
McDaniel Coll (MD)
McKendree U (IL)
Mercyhurst U (PA)
Merrimack Coll (MA)
Miami U (OH)
Michigan State U (MI)
Middlebury Coll (VT)
Millsaps Coll (MS)
Missouri State U (MO)
Molloy Coll (NY)
Monmouth Coll (IL)
Montclair State U (NJ)
Moravian Coll (PA)
Morehouse Coll (GA)
Morningside Coll (IA)
Mount Allison U (NB, Canada)
Mount Holyoke Coll (MA)
Mount Marty Coll (SD)
Mount Mary Coll (WI)
Mount Mercy U (IA)
Mount St. Mary's Coll (CA)
Mount Vernon Nazarene U (OH)
Muhlenberg Coll (PA)
Naropa U (CO)
Nazareth Coll of Rochester (NY)
New Coll of Florida (FL)
New York U (NY)
Niagara U (NY)
North Carolina State U (NC)
North Carolina Wesleyan Coll (NC)
North Central Coll (IL)
Northeastern U (MA)
Northwestern Coll (IA)
Northwest Nazarene U (ID)
Northwest U (WA)
Notre Dame de Namur U (CA)
Nyack Coll (NY)
Oakland City U (IN)
Ohio U (OH)
Ohio Valley U (WV)
Ohio Wesleyan U (OH)
Oklahoma Baptist U (OK)
Oklahoma Christian U (OK)
Oklahoma City U (OK)
Pacific Lutheran U (WA)
Pacific Union Coll (CA)
Paul Quinn Coll (TX)
Penn State Abington (PA)
Penn State Altoona (PA)
Penn State Beaver (PA)
Penn State Berks (PA)
Penn State Brandywine (PA)
Penn State DuBois (PA)
Penn State Erie, The Behrend Coll
  (PA)
Penn State Fayette, The Eberly
  Campus (PA)
Penn State Greater Allegheny (PA)
Penn State Hazleton (PA)
Penn State Lehigh Valley (PA)
Penn State Mont Alto (PA)
Penn State New Kensington (PA)
Penn State Schuylkill (PA)
Penn State Shenango (PA)
Penn State Wilkes-Barre (PA)
Penn State Worthington Scranton
  (PA)
Penn State York (PA)
Pepperdine U, Malibu (CA)
Piedmont Coll (GA)
Pitzer Coll (CA)
Pomona Coll (CA)
Portland State U (OR)
Presbyterian Coll (SC)
Princeton U (NJ)
Principia Coll (IL)
Queens U of Charlotte (NC)
Randolph Coll (VA)
Randolph-Macon Coll (VA)
Reed Coll (OR)
Regis U (CO)
Rhodes Coll (TN)
Rice U (TX)

Ripon Coll (WI)
Roanoke Coll (VA)
Roberts Wesleyan Coll (NY)
Rocky Mountain Coll (MT)
Rollins Coll (FL)
Rosemont Coll (PA)
Rutgers, The State U of New
  Jersey, New Brunswick (NJ)
Sacred Heart U (CT)
St. Francis Coll (NY)
St. John Fisher Coll (NY)
Saint Joseph's U (PA)
St. Lawrence U (NY)
Saint Leo U (FL)
Saint Martin's U (WA)
Saint Mary's Coll (IN)
Saint Mary's Coll of California (CA)
St. Mary's Coll of Maryland (MD)
Saint Michael's Coll (VT)
St. Norbert Coll (WI)
St. Olaf Coll (MN)
St. Thomas Aquinas Coll (NY)
St. Thomas U (FL)
St. Thomas U (NB, Canada)
Salve Regina U (RI)
Samford U (AL)
San Diego State U (CA)
San Jose State U (CA)
Schreiner U (TX)
Scripps Coll (CA)
Seattle U (WA)
Seton Hill U (PA)
Sewanee: The U of the South (TN)
Shenandoah U (VA)
Siena Coll (NY)
Siena Heights U (MI)
Simpson Coll (IA)
Skidmore Coll (NY)
Smith Coll (MA)
Southern Methodist U (TX)
Southwest Baptist U (MO)
Southwestern Adventist U (TX)
Southwestern U (TX)
Spelman Coll (GA)
Spring Arbor U (MI)
Spring Hill Coll (AL)
Stanford U (CA)
State U of New York Coll at Old
  Westbury (NY)
Stetson U (FL)
Stonehill Coll (MA)
Stony Brook U, State U of New York
  (NY)
Susquehanna U (PA)
Swarthmore Coll (PA)
Sweet Briar Coll (VA)
Syracuse U (NY)
Temple U (PA)
Tennessee Wesleyan Coll (TN)
Texas Christian U (TX)
Texas Wesleyan U (TX)
Thomas Edison State Coll (NJ)
Thomas More Coll (KY)
Transylvania U (KY)
Trevecca Nazarene U (TN)
Trinity Coll (CT)
Trinity U (TX)
Tufts U (MA)
Tulane U (LA)
Union Coll (KY)
Union U (TN)
U at Albany, State U of New York
  (NY)
The U of Alabama (AL)
The U of Arizona (AZ)
U of Bridgeport (CT)
The U of British Columbia (BC,
  Canada)
U of California, Berkeley (CA)
U of California, Davis (CA)
U of California, Irvine (CA)
U of California, Los Angeles (CA)
U of California, Riverside (CA)
U of California, Santa Barbara (CA)
U of Central Arkansas (AR)
U of Central Florida (FL)
U of Colorado Boulder (CO)
U of Denver (CO)
The U of Findlay (OH)
U of Florida (FL)
U of Georgia (GA)
U of Great Falls (MT)
U of Hawaii at Manoa (HI)
U of Illinois at Urbana–Champaign
  (IL)
The U of Iowa (IA)
The U of Kansas (KS)

U of La Verne (CA)
U of Miami (FL)
U of Michigan (MI)
U of Minnesota, Twin Cities
  Campus (MN)
U of Mississippi (MS)
U of Missouri (MO)
U of Mobile (AL)
U of Mount Union (OH)
U of Nebraska at Omaha (NE)
U of New Mexico (NM)
U of North Carolina at Asheville
  (NC)
The U of North Carolina at Chapel
  Hill (NC)
The U of North Carolina at
  Charlotte (NC)
The U of North Carolina at
  Greensboro (NC)
U of North Dakota (ND)
U of Northern Iowa (IA)
U of Oklahoma (OK)
U of Oregon (OR)
U of Ottawa (ON, Canada)
U of Pennsylvania (PA)
U of Pikeville (KY)
U of Pittsburgh (PA)
U of Puget Sound (WA)
U of Redlands (CA)
U of Regina (SK, Canada)
U of Richmond (VA)
U of Rochester (NY)
U of Saint Joseph (CT)
U of St. Thomas (MN)
U of San Diego (CA)
The U of Scranton (PA)
U of South Carolina (SC)
U of Southern California (CA)
U of Southern Mississippi (MS)
U of South Florida (FL)
The U of Tennessee (TN)
The U of Texas at Austin (TX)
U of the Incarnate Word (TX)
U of the Ozarks (AR)
The U of Toledo (OH)
U of Tulsa (OK)
U of Vermont (VT)
U of Virginia (VA)
U of Waterloo (ON, Canada)
The U of Western Ontario (ON,
  Canada)
U of Wisconsin–Eau Claire (WI)
U of Wisconsin–Madison (WI)
U of Wisconsin–Milwaukee (WI)
U of Wyoming (WY)
Vanderbilt U (TN)
Vassar Coll (NY)
Villanova U (PA)
Virginia Commonwealth U (VA)
Virginia Intermont Coll (VA)
Virginia Wesleyan Coll (VA)
Viterbo U (WI)
Wabash Coll (IN)
Wake Forest U (NC)
Walla Walla U (WA)
Warner Pacific Coll (OR)
Wartburg Coll (IA)
Washburn U (KS)
Washington and Lee U (VA)
Washington State U (WA)
Washington U in St. Louis (MO)
Webster U (MO)
Wellesley Coll (MA)
Wesleyan Coll (GA)
Wesleyan U (CT)
Western Illinois U (IL)
Western Kentucky U (KY)
Western Michigan U (MI)
Westminster Coll (MO)
West Virginia Wesleyan Coll (WV)
Wheaton Coll (MA)
Wheeling Jesuit U (WV)
Whitman Coll (WA)
Whitworth U (WA)
Willamette U (OR)
William Jewell Coll (MO)
Williams Coll (MA)
Wittenberg U (OH)
Wright State U (OH)
Xavier U (OH)
Yale U (CT)
Young Harris Coll (GA)
Youngstown State U (OH)

RELIGIOUS STUDIES RELATED
Belmont U (TN)

Bryn Athyn Coll of the New Church
  (PA)
Drew U (NJ)
Newberry Coll (SC)
St. Edward's U (TX)
U of Regina (SK, Canada)
The U of Western Ontario (ON,
  Canada)
Ursuline Coll (OH)

REPRODUCTIVE BIOLOGY
Bradley U (IL)

**RESEARCH AND
EXPERIMENTAL
PSYCHOLOGY RELATED**
Mount St. Mary's Coll (CA)
St. Edward's U (TX)
U of Michigan–Flint (MI)

RESORT MANAGEMENT
California State U, Chico (CA)
Coastal Carolina U (SC)
Florida Gulf Coast U (FL)
Lakeland Coll (WI)
Rochester Inst of Technology (NY)
Sierra Nevada Coll (NV)

RESPIRATORY CARE THERAPY
Armstrong Atlantic State U (GA)
Ball State U (IN)
Baptist Coll of Health Sciences
  (TN)
Bellarmine U (KY)
Boise State U (ID)
Bowling Green State U-Firelands
  Coll (OH)
Canisius Coll (NY)
Dakota State U (SD)
Dalhousie U (NS, Canada)
Fairleigh Dickinson U, Coll at
  Florham (NJ)
Florida Ag and Mech U (FL)
Gannon U (PA)
Georgia Regents U (GA)
Georgia State U (GA)
Indiana U of Pennsylvania (PA)
Indiana U–Purdue U Indianapolis
  (IN)
Long Island U–Brooklyn Campus
  (NY)
Marshall U (WV)
Midwestern State U (TX)
Missouri State U (MO)
Nebraska Methodist Coll (NE)
North Dakota State U (ND)
Northern Michigan U (MI)
The Ohio State U (OH)
Salisbury U (MD)
Shenandoah U (VA)
Stony Brook U, State U of New York
  (NY)
Tennessee State U (TN)
Texas Southern U (TX)
Texas State U–San Marcos (TX)
Thomas Edison State Coll (NJ)
Thompson Rivers U (BC, Canada)
Universidad Adventista de las
  Antillas (PR)
The U of Akron (OH)
The U of Alabama at Birmingham
  (AL)
U of Hartford (CT)
The U of Kansas (KS)
U of Medicine and Dentistry of New
  Jersey (NJ)
U of Missouri (MO)
The U of North Carolina at
  Charlotte (NC)
U of South Alabama (AL)
The U of Toledo (OH)
U of Waterloo (ON, Canada)
Weber State U (UT)
Wheeling Jesuit U (WV)
York Coll of Pennsylvania (PA)
Youngstown State U (OH)

**RESPIRATORY THERAPY
TECHNICIAN**
Dalhousie U (NS, Canada)

**RESTAURANT, CULINARY,
AND CATERING
MANAGEMENT**
Bowling Green State U (OH)
Coll of the Ozarks (MO)
Pennsylvania Coll of Technology
  (PA)

State U of New York Coll of Technology at Delhi (NY)
U of Hawaii–West Oahu (HI)
U of Illinois at Urbana–Champaign (IL)

RESTAURANT/FOOD SERVICES MANAGEMENT
Coll of the Ozarks (MO)
Colorado State U (CO)
The Culinary Inst of America (NY)
Lindenwood U (MO)
Messiah Coll (PA)
Morrisville State Coll (NY)
Niagara U (NY)
The Ohio State U (OH)
Rochester Inst of Technology (NY)
The U of Alabama (AL)
U of Alaska Anchorage (AK)
U of Central Florida (FL)
U of Missouri (MO)

RETAILING
American Public U System (WV)
Bowling Green State U (OH)
Central Michigan U (MI)
Purdue U Calumet (IN)
Southern New Hampshire U (NH)
U of Central Oklahoma (OK)
U of Minnesota, Twin Cities Campus (MN)
U of South Carolina (SC)
U of Wisconsin–Madison (WI)

RETAIL MANAGEMENT
The U of Arizona (AZ)

RHETORIC AND COMPOSITION
Ashland U (OH)
Auburn U (AL)
Augsburg Coll (MN)
Bates Coll (ME)
Bemidji State U (MN)
Bowling Green State U (OH)
Brigham Young U (UT)
California Polytechnic State U, San Luis Obispo (CA)
California State U, East Bay (CA)
California State U, Fresno (CA)
California State U, Fullerton (CA)
California State U, Long Beach (CA)
California State U, Los Angeles (CA)
Calvin Coll (MI)
Carson-Newman U (TN)
Clark Atlanta U (GA)
Clemson U (SC)
Coe Coll (IA)
The Coll at Brockport, State U of New York (NY)
Coll of Saint Benedict (MN)
Columbus State U (GA)
Concordia U, Nebraska (NE)
Cornell Coll (IA)
Cornerstone U (MI)
Creighton U (NE)
DePaul U (IL)
Drake U (IA)
Duquesne U (PA)
East Central U (OK)
East Tennessee State U (TN)
East Texas Baptist U (TX)
Emerson Coll (MA)
Evangel U (MO)
Fairmont State U (WV)
Ferris State U (MI)
George Mason U (VA)
Georgia Coll & State U (GA)
Georgia Southern U (GA)
Gonzaga U (WA)
Graceland U (IA)
Greenville Coll (IL)
Gustavus Adolphus Coll (MN)
Hardin-Simmons U (TX)
Humboldt State U (CA)
Illinois Coll (IL)
Indiana U South Bend (IN)
Iowa State U of Science and Technology (IA)
Ithaca Coll (NY)
Kansas Wesleyan U (KS)
Kutztown U of Pennsylvania (PA)
Lehman Coll of the City U of New York (NY)
Lipscomb U (TN)
Lock Haven U of Pennsylvania (PA)

Long Island U–Brooklyn Campus (NY)
Louisiana Coll (LA)
Louisiana State U in Shreveport (LA)
Manchester U (IN)
Marietta Coll (OH)
Marshall U (WV)
The Master's Coll and Sem (CA)
McKendree U (IL)
Metropolitan State U of Denver (CO)
Miami U (OH)
Minnesota State U Mankato (MN)
Mississippi Valley State U (MS)
North Central Coll (IL)
Northeastern Illinois U (IL)
Northern Arizona U (AZ)
Northern State U (SD)
Northwestern Coll (IA)
Northwestern Oklahoma State U (OK)
Northwest Missouri State U (MO)
Oglethorpe U (GA)
Oklahoma Baptist U (OK)
Oklahoma Christian U (OK)
Oklahoma City U (OK)
Old Dominion U (VA)
Ouachita Baptist U (AR)
Pepperdine U, Malibu (CA)
Portland State U (OR)
Rider U (NJ)
Saint John's U (MN)
St. John's U (NY)
St. Joseph's Coll, Long Island Campus (NY)
St. Joseph's Coll, New York (NY)
San Jose State U (CA)
Shippensburg U of Pennsylvania (PA)
Southern Illinois U Carbondale (IL)
Southern Illinois U Edwardsville (IL)
State U of New York at New Paltz (NY)
State U of New York Coll at Cortland (NY)
Stephen F. Austin State U (TX)
Tarleton State U (TX)
Temple U (PA)
Texas A&M U–Commerce (TX)
Texas Southern U (TX)
Texas State U–San Marcos (TX)
Texas Wesleyan U (TX)
Trinity U (TX)
Troy U (AL)
Union U (TN)
U at Albany, State U of New York (NY)
U of Arkansas at Little Rock (AR)
U of California, Berkeley (CA)
U of Cincinnati (OH)
U of Illinois at Urbana–Champaign (IL)
The U of Iowa (IA)
U of Minnesota, Twin Cities Campus (MN)
U of Montevallo (AL)
U of Nebraska at Kearney (NE)
U of New Mexico (NM)
The U of North Carolina at Greensboro (NC)
U of North Texas (TX)
U of Pittsburgh (PA)
U of Rhode Island (RI)
U of Richmond (VA)
The U of South Dakota (SD)
U of South Florida (FL)
The U of Texas at Arlington (TX)
The U of Texas at El Paso (TX)
U of Washington, Tacoma (WA)
U of Waterloo (ON, Canada)
U of Wisconsin–Platteville (WI)
U of Wisconsin–Superior (WI)
Utah State U (UT)
Valdosta State U (GA)
Wabash Coll (IN)
Walla Walla U (WA)
West Chester U of Pennsylvania (PA)
West Virginia Wesleyan Coll (WV)
Whitworth U (WA)
Willamette U (OR)
York Coll of the City U of New York (NY)
Youngstown State U (OH)

RHETORIC AND COMPOSITION/WRITING RELATED
Pepperdine U, Malibu (CA)
Syracuse U (NY)

ROBOTICS TECHNOLOGY
Alcorn State U (MS)
Indiana State U (IN)
Indiana U–Purdue U Indianapolis (IN)
Lake Superior State U (MI)
Purdue U (IN)
Sullivan Coll of Technology and Design (KY)

ROMANCE LANGUAGES
Bard Coll (NY)
Bowdoin Coll (ME)
Carleton Coll (MN)
City Coll of the City U of New York (NY)
Colgate U (NY)
Dartmouth Coll (NH)
DePauw U (IN)
Elmira Coll (NY)
Franklin Coll Switzerland (Switzerland)
Gettysburg Coll (PA)
Haverford Coll (PA)
Hunter Coll of the City U of New York (NY)
The Johns Hopkins U (MD)
Merrimack Coll (MA)
Mount Allison U (NB, Canada)
Mount Holyoke Coll (MA)
Point Loma Nazarene U (CA)
Pomona Coll (CA)
Ripon Coll (WI)
Rockford Coll (IL)
St. Thomas Aquinas Coll (NY)
Stanford U (CA)
Truman State U (MO)
Tufts U (MA)
The U of British Columbia (BC, Canada)
U of Georgia (GA)
U of Hawaii at Manoa (HI)
U of Illinois at Chicago (IL)
U of Maryland, Coll Park (MD)
U of Michigan (MI)
U of Nevada, Las Vegas (NV)
U of New Brunswick Fredericton (NB, Canada)
U of Notre Dame (IN)
U of Oregon (OR)
Vanderbilt U (TN)
Washington and Lee U (VA)
Washington U in St. Louis (MO)
Wesleyan U (CT)
Wheeling Jesuit U (WV)

ROMANCE LANGUAGES RELATED
Hood Coll (MD)
U of Chicago (IL)
U of Michigan–Flint (MI)
The U of North Carolina at Chapel Hill (NC)
U of Pennsylvania (PA)

RURAL SOCIOLOGY
U of Wisconsin–Madison (WI)

RUSSIAN
American U (DC)
Amherst Coll (MA)
Arizona State U (AZ)
Bard Coll (NY)
Bates Coll (ME)
Baylor U (TX)
Boston Coll (MA)
Boston U (MA)
Bowdoin Coll (ME)
Bowling Green State U (OH)
Bucknell U (PA)
Carleton Coll (MN)
Colgate U (NY)
Coll of the Holy Cross (MA)
Columbia U (NY)
Columbia U, School of General Studies (NY)
Cornell Coll (IA)
Dalhousie U (NS, Canada)
Dartmouth Coll (NH)
Dickinson Coll (PA)
Drew U (NJ)
Georgetown U (DC)
Goucher Coll (MD)

Grinnell Coll (IA)
Gustavus Adolphus Coll (MN)
Haverford Coll (PA)
Hofstra U (NY)
Hope Coll (MI)
Hunter Coll of the City U of New York (NY)
Juniata Coll (PA)
Kent State U (OH)
La Salle U (PA)
Lawrence U (WI)
Lehman Coll of the City U of New York (NY)
Luther Coll (IA)
Macalester Coll (MN)
Michigan State U (MI)
Middlebury Coll (VT)
New Coll of Florida (FL)
New York U (NY)
Northern Illinois U (IL)
The Ohio State U (OH)
Ohio U (OH)
Oklahoma State U (OK)
Penn State Abington (PA)
Penn State Altoona (PA)
Penn State Beaver (PA)
Penn State Berks (PA)
Penn State Brandywine (PA)
Penn State DuBois (PA)
Penn State Erie, The Behrend Coll (PA)
Penn State Fayette, The Eberly Campus (PA)
Penn State Greater Allegheny (PA)
Penn State Hazleton (PA)
Penn State Lehigh Valley (PA)
Penn State Mont Alto (PA)
Penn State New Kensington (PA)
Penn State Schuylkill (PA)
Penn State Shenango (PA)
Penn State U Park (PA)
Penn State Wilkes-Barre (PA)
Penn State Worthington Scranton (PA)
Penn State York (PA)
Pomona Coll (CA)
Portland State U (OR)
Reed Coll (OR)
Rider U (NJ)
Rutgers, The State U of New Jersey, New Brunswick (NJ)
Saint Louis U (MO)
St. Olaf Coll (MN)
San Diego State U (CA)
Scripps Coll (CA)
Seattle Pacific U (WA)
Sewanee: The U of the South (TN)
Smith Coll (MA)
Swarthmore Coll (PA)
Syracuse U (NY)
Temple U (PA)
Texas A&M U (TX)
Trinity Coll (CT)
Trinity U (TX)
Truman State U (MO)
Tufts U (MA)
Tulane U (LA)
United States Military Acad (NY)
U of Alaska Anchorage (AK)
The U of Arizona (AZ)
The U of British Columbia (BC, Canada)
U of California, Davis (CA)
U of California, Los Angeles (CA)
U of Denver (CO)
U of Florida (FL)
U of Georgia (GA)
U of Hawaii at Manoa (HI)
U of Illinois at Chicago (IL)
U of Illinois at Urbana–Champaign (IL)
The U of Iowa (IA)
U of Kentucky (KY)
U of Maryland, Coll Park (MD)
U of Michigan (MI)
U of Minnesota, Twin Cities Campus (MN)
U of Missouri (MO)
U of Nebraska–Lincoln (NE)
U of New Brunswick Fredericton (NB, Canada)
U of New Hampshire (NH)
U of Notre Dame (IN)
U of Oklahoma (OK)
U of Ottawa (ON, Canada)
U of Pennsylvania (PA)
U of Pittsburgh (PA)

U of Rochester (NY)
U of South Carolina (SC)
U of Southern California (CA)
U of South Florida (FL)
The U of Tennessee (TN)
The U of Texas at Arlington (TX)
The U of Texas at Austin (TX)
U of Utah (UT)
U of Vermont (VT)
U of Waterloo (ON, Canada)
U of Wisconsin–Madison (WI)
U of Wisconsin–Milwaukee (WI)
U of Wyoming (WY)
Vanderbilt U (TN)
Vassar Coll (NY)
Wake Forest U (NC)
Wellesley Coll (MA)
Wesleyan U (CT)
West Chester U of Pennsylvania (PA)
Wheaton Coll (MA)
Williams Coll (MA)
Yale U (CT)

RUSSIAN, CENTRAL EUROPEAN, EAST EUROPEAN AND EURASIAN STUDIES
Bowdoin Coll (ME)
Hawai`i Pacific U (HI)
Michigan State U (MI)
Middlebury Coll (VT)
Portland State U (OR)
Rutgers, The State U of New Jersey, New Brunswick (NJ)
The U of British Columbia (BC, Canada)
U of Missouri (MO)
Wayne State U (MI)
Wesleyan U (CT)

RUSSIAN STUDIES
American U (DC)
Bard Coll (NY)
Boston Coll (MA)
Bowling Green State U (OH)
Brown U (RI)
Carleton Coll (MN)
Carnegie Mellon U (PA)
Colby Coll (ME)
Colgate U (NY)
Coll of the Holy Cross (MA)
The Coll of Wooster (OH)
The Colorado Coll (CO)
Columbia U (NY)
Columbia U, School of General Studies (NY)
Cornell Coll (IA)
Dalhousie U (NS, Canada)
Dartmouth Coll (NH)
DePauw U (IN)
George Mason U (VA)
Grand Valley State U (MI)
Gustavus Adolphus Coll (MN)
Hamilton Coll (NY)
Hobart and William Smith Colls (NY)
Kent State U (OH)
Lafayette Coll (PA)
La Salle U (PA)
Lawrence U (WI)
Middlebury Coll (VT)
Mount Holyoke Coll (MA)
Muhlenberg Coll (PA)
Rhodes Coll (TN)
Rutgers, The State U of New Jersey, New Brunswick (NJ)
St. Olaf Coll (MN)
San Diego State U (CA)
Scripps Coll (CA)
Smith Coll (MA)
Stetson U (FL)
Syracuse U (NY)
Tufts U (MA)
Tulane U (LA)
United States Military Acad (NY)
U of Alaska Fairbanks (AK)
The U of British Columbia (BC, Canada)
U of California, Los Angeles (CA)
U of California, Riverside (CA)
U of California, Santa Cruz (CA)
U of Chicago (IL)
U of Colorado Boulder (CO)
U of Delaware (DE)
U of Illinois at Urbana–Champaign (IL)
The U of Kansas (KS)
U of Maryland, Coll Park (MD)

U of Massachusetts Amherst (MA)
U of Michigan (MI)
U of Minnesota, Twin Cities Campus (MN)
U of Missouri (MO)
U of Oregon (OR)
U of Richmond (VA)
U of Rochester (NY)
The U of Texas at Austin (TX)
U of Tulsa (OK)
U of Vermont (VT)
U of Waterloo (ON, Canada)
Vanderbilt U (TN)
Washington and Lee U (VA)
Washington U in St. Louis (MO)
Wellesley Coll (MA)
Wesleyan U (CT)
Wheaton Coll (MA)
Wittenberg U (OH)
Yale U (CT)

SALES AND MARKETING/MARKETING AND DISTRIBUTION TEACHER EDUCATION
Bowling Green State U (OH)
Colorado State U (CO)
East Carolina U (NC)
Eastern Michigan U (MI)
Eastern New Mexico U (NM)
Fayetteville State U (NC)
Middle Tennessee State U (TN)
North Carolina State U (NC)
Rider U (NJ)
State U of New York at Oswego (NY)
U of Minnesota, Twin Cities Campus (MN)
U of Wisconsin–Stout (WI)
Utah State U (UT)
Western Michigan U (MI)
Wright State U (OH)

SALES, DISTRIBUTION, AND MARKETING OPERATIONS
American U of Puerto Rico (PR)
Babson Coll (MA)
Baylor U (TX)
Bowling Green State U (OH)
Brock U (ON, Canada)
Concordia U, St. Paul (MN)
Dalton State Coll (GA)
Hampton U (VA)
Harding U (AR)
HEC Montreal (QC, Canada)
Husson U (ME)
Kennesaw State U (GA)
McKendree U (IL)
Middle Tennessee State U (TN)
New York U (NY)
Quinnipiac U (CT)
Seton Hill U (PA)
Texas A&M U (TX)
Tuskegee U (AL)
The U of Akron (OH)
U of Central Oklahoma (OK)
The U of Findlay (OH)
U of Houston (TX)
U of Illinois at Urbana–Champaign (IL)
U of Memphis (TN)
U of Minnesota, Twin Cities Campus (MN)
U of North Texas (TX)
U of Pennsylvania (PA)
U of the Incarnate Word (TX)
U of Wisconsin–Stout (WI)
U of Wisconsin–Superior (WI)
West Chester U of Pennsylvania (PA)

SANSKRIT AND CLASSICAL INDIAN LANGUAGES
Bard Coll (NY)

SCANDINAVIAN LANGUAGES
Augsburg Coll (MN)
Augustana Coll (IL)
Gustavus Adolphus Coll (MN)
Luther Coll (IA)
U of California, Berkeley (CA)
U of California, Los Angeles (CA)
U of Minnesota, Twin Cities Campus (MN)
The U of Texas at Austin (TX)

SCANDINAVIAN STUDIES
Concordia Coll (MN)
Gustavus Adolphus Coll (MN)

Pacific Lutheran U (WA)
U of Wisconsin–Madison (WI)

SCHOOL LIBRARIAN/SCHOOL LIBRARY MEDIA
The Coll of St. Scholastica (MN)
East Central U (OK)
U of Great Falls (MT)

SCHOOL PSYCHOLOGY
Eastern Washington U (WA)
Texas A&M U–Commerce (TX)

SCIENCE TEACHER EDUCATION
Abilene Christian U (TX)
Adams State U (CO)
Albion Coll (MI)
Alfred U (NY)
Alice Lloyd Coll (KY)
Alma Coll (MI)
Alverno Coll (WI)
Andrews U (MI)
Arizona Christian U (AZ)
Arkansas Tech U (AR)
Ashland U (OH)
Assumption Coll (MA)
Auburn U (AL)
Ball State U (IN)
Baylor U (TX)
Bemidji State U (MN)
Bethel Coll (IN)
Bluefield Coll (VA)
Bob Jones U (SC)
Boston U (MA)
Bowie State U (MD)
Bowling Green State U (OH)
Bradley U (IL)
Brigham Young U (UT)
Brock U (ON, Canada)
Buena Vista U (IA)
Buffalo State Coll, State U of New York (NY)
California Lutheran U (CA)
California State U, San Marcos (CA)
Calvin Coll (MI)
Cameron U (OK)
Campbellsville U (KY)
Canisius Coll (NY)
Capital U (OH)
Cardinal Stritch U (WI)
Castleton State Coll (VT)
Cedarville U (OH)
Central Methodist U (MO)
Central Michigan U (MI)
Chipola Coll (FL)
City Coll of the City U of New York (NY)
Clemson U (SC)
Coe Coll (IA)
The Coll at Brockport, State U of New York (NY)
Coll of Saint Mary (NE)
The Coll of Saint Rose (NY)
Coll of the Atlantic (ME)
Coll of the Ozarks (MO)
Colorado State U (CO)
Columbus State U (GA)
Concordia Coll–New York (NY)
Concordia U (OR)
Concordia U Chicago (IL)
Concordia U, Nebraska (NE)
Concordia U Wisconsin (WI)
Cornerstone U (MI)
Covenant Coll (GA)
Crown Coll (MN)
Dallas Baptist U (TX)
Defiance Coll (OH)
Doane Coll (NE)
Dordt Coll (IA)
East Carolina U (NC)
East Central U (OK)
Eastern Illinois U (IL)
Eastern Michigan U (MI)
Eastern Washington U (WA)
Edgewood Coll (WI)
Elizabethtown Coll (PA)
Elmira Coll (NY)
Elon U (NC)
Evangel U (MO)
Fairmont State U (WV)
Florida Ag and Mech U (FL)
Florida Atlantic U (FL)
Florida Inst of Technology (FL)
Gettysburg Coll (PA)
Graceland U (IA)
Grand Valley State U (MI)

Grove City Coll (PA)
Harding U (AR)
Hardin-Simmons U (TX)
Hofstra U (NY)
Hope Coll (MI)
Hunter Coll of the City U of New York (NY)
Huntington U (IN)
Indiana State U (IN)
Indiana U–Purdue U Fort Wayne (IN)
Indiana U South Bend (IN)
Indiana Wesleyan U (IN)
Indian River State Coll (FL)
Inter American U of Puerto Rico, San Germán Campus (PR)
Ithaca Coll (NY)
Judson Coll (AL)
Juniata Coll (PA)
Keene State Coll (NH)
Kent State U (OH)
Lakeland Coll (WI)
La Salle U (PA)
Le Moyne Coll (NY)
Lewis-Clark State Coll (ID)
Lincoln Memorial U (TN)
Lindenwood U (MO)
Louisiana Coll (LA)
Loyola U Chicago (IL)
Lubbock Christian U (TX)
Madonna U (MI)
Malone U (OH)
Manchester U (IN)
Mansfield U of Pennsylvania (PA)
Maranatha Baptist Bible Coll (WI)
Marian U (WI)
Mars Hill Coll (NC)
Marywood U (PA)
The Master's Coll and Sem (CA)
Mercyhurst U (PA)
Merrimack Coll (MA)
Miami Dade Coll (FL)
Miami U (OH)
Michigan State U (MI)
Midwestern State U (TX)
Minnesota State U Mankato (MN)
Minot State U (ND)
Mississippi Valley State U (MS)
Missouri Baptist U (MO)
Missouri State U (MO)
Montana State U (MT)
Moravian Coll (PA)
Morningside Coll (IA)
Mount Mary Coll (WI)
Mount Mercy U (IA)
Mount Vernon Nazarene U (OH)
New Mexico Highlands U (NM)
New York U (NY)
Niagara U (NY)
Nicholls State U (LA)
North Carolina State U (NC)
North Dakota State U (ND)
Northern Michigan U (MI)
Northland Coll (WI)
Northwestern Oklahoma State U (OK)
Northwest Missouri State U (MO)
Oakland City U (IN)
Ohio Dominican U (OH)
Oklahoma Baptist U (OK)
Oklahoma Christian U (OK)
Oklahoma City U (OK)
Olivet Coll (MI)
Oral Roberts U (OK)
Ouachita Baptist U (AR)
Purdue U Calumet (IN)
Rhode Island Coll (RI)
St. Ambrose U (IA)
Shawnee State U (OH)
Southeastern Oklahoma State U (OK)
Southeastern U (FL)
Southeast Missouri State U (MO)
Southern Illinois U Edwardsville (IL)
Southern Nazarene U (OK)
Southern New Hampshire U (NH)
Southern Utah U (UT)
Southwest Baptist U (MO)
State U of New York at Fredonia (NY)
State U of New York at New Paltz (NY)
State U of New York at Oswego (NY)
State U of New York Coll at Cortland (NY)

State U of New York Coll at Old Westbury (NY)
Stony Brook U, State U of New York (NY)
Tarleton State U (TX)
Taylor U (IN)
Temple U (PA)
Texas A&M Intl U (TX)
Texas Christian U (TX)
Trine U (IN)
Union U (TN)
The U of Akron (OH)
The U of Arizona (AZ)
The U of British Columbia (BC, Canada)
U of Central Arkansas (AR)
U of Central Florida (FL)
U of Central Oklahoma (OK)
U of Charleston (WV)
The U of Findlay (OH)
U of Georgia (GA)
U of Great Falls (MT)
U of Illinois at Urbana–Champaign (IL)
The U of Iowa (IA)
U of Kentucky (KY)
U of Maine at Farmington (ME)
U of Maine at Machias (ME)
U of Michigan–Dearborn (MI)
U of Minnesota, Duluth (MN)
U of Minnesota, Twin Cities Campus (MN)
U of Mississippi (MS)
U of Missouri (MO)
The U of Montana Western (MT)
U of Nebraska–Lincoln (NE)
U of New Brunswick Fredericton (NB, Canada)
The U of North Carolina at Pembroke (NC)
U of North Dakota (ND)
U of Northern Iowa (IA)
U of North Florida (FL)
U of Notre Dame (IN)
U of Oklahoma (OK)
U of Regina (SK, Canada)
U of St. Francis (IL)
U of St. Thomas (MN)
The U of South Dakota (SD)
U of South Florida (FL)
The U of Tennessee at Chattanooga (TN)
The U of Tennessee at Martin (TN)
The U of Toledo (OH)
U of Vermont (VT)
U of Windsor (ON, Canada)
U of Wisconsin–Eau Claire (WI)
U of Wisconsin–La Crosse (WI)
U of Wisconsin–Platteville (WI)
U of Wisconsin–Stout (WI)
U of Wisconsin–Superior (WI)
Upper Iowa U (IA)
Ursuline Coll (OH)
Utah State U (UT)
Valley City State U (ND)
Valparaiso U (IN)
Vincennes U (IN)
Viterbo U (WI)
Walsh U (OH)
Warner Pacific Coll (OR)
Washington State U (WA)
Washington U in St. Louis (MO)
Wayland Baptist U (TX)
Waynesburg U (PA)
Wayne State Coll (NE)
Wayne State U (MI)
Weber State U (UT)
Webster U (MO)
Western Carolina U (NC)
Western State Colorado U (CO)
Western Washington U (WA)
West Virginia State U (WV)
Widener U (PA)
William Penn U (IA)
Wilmington U (DE)
Wright State U (OH)
Xavier U (OH)
Xavier U of Louisiana (LA)
York Coll of Pennsylvania (PA)
Youngstown State U (OH)

SCIENCE TECHNOLOGIES RELATED
Arizona State U (AZ)
Bridgewater State U (MA)
Clemson U (SC)
Kean U (NJ)

Madonna U (MI)
North Carolina State U (NC)
Northern Arizona U (AZ)
The U of Arizona (AZ)
U of Wisconsin–Stout (WI)
Willamette U (OR)

SCIENCE, TECHNOLOGY AND SOCIETY
Arizona State U (AZ)
Butler U (IN)
California State Polytechnic U, Pomona (CA)
Claremont McKenna Coll (CA)
Colby Coll (ME)
Dalhousie U (NS, Canada)
Eastern Michigan U (MI)
Georgetown U (DC)
James Madison U (VA)
Lehigh U (PA)
Massachusetts Inst of Technology (MA)
Morrisville State Coll (NY)
New Jersey Inst of Technology (NJ)
North Carolina State U (NC)
Penn State U Park (PA)
Pitzer Coll (CA)
Rensselaer Polytechnic Inst (NY)
Rutgers, The State U of New Jersey, Newark (NJ)
Scripps Coll (CA)
Slippery Rock U of Pennsylvania (PA)
Stanford U (CA)
Stony Brook U, State U of New York (NY)
U of Alaska Anchorage (AK)
U of Puget Sound (WA)
U of Washington, Bothell (WA)
U of Windsor (ON, Canada)
Vanderbilt U (TN)
Vassar Coll (NY)
Washington U in St. Louis (MO)
Wesleyan U (CT)
Worcester Polytechnic Inst (MA)

SCULPTURE
Acad of Art U (CA)
Alberta Coll of Art & Design (AB, Canada)
Bennington Coll (VT)
Boston U (MA)
Bowling Green State U (OH)
Bradley U (IL)
Brigham Young U (UT)
Buffalo State Coll, State U of New York (NY)
California State U, East Bay (CA)
California State U, Long Beach (CA)
Cleveland Inst of Art (OH)
The Coll at Brockport, State U of New York (NY)
Colorado State U (CO)
Concordia U (QC, Canada)
Dominican U (IL)
Drake U (IA)
Ferris State U (MI)
Indiana U–Purdue U Fort Wayne (IN)
Inter American U of Puerto Rico, San Germán Campus (PR)
Maryland Inst Coll of Art (MD)
Marywood U (PA)
Massachusetts Coll of Art and Design (MA)
Minnesota State U Mankato (MN)
Mississippi Coll (MS)
Mount Allison U (NB, Canada)
Northern Michigan U (MI)
Northwest Nazarene U (ID)
Ohio U (OH)
Otis Coll of Art and Design (CA)
Pacific Northwest Coll of Art (OR)
Portland State U (OR)
Rhode Island School of Design (RI)
Ringling Coll of Art and Design (FL)
Rochester Inst of Technology (NY)
Rutgers, The State U of New Jersey, New Brunswick (NJ)
Salem State U (MA)
San Francisco Art Inst (CA)
Savannah Coll of Art and Design (GA)
School of the Art Inst of Chicago (IL)

School of the Museum of Fine Arts, Boston (MA)
Seton Hill U (PA)
Sonoma State U (CA)
State U of New York at New Paltz (NY)
Syracuse U (NY)
Temple U (PA)
Texas Christian U (TX)
The U of Akron (OH)
U of Dallas (TX)
U of Hartford (CT)
U of Houston (TX)
U of Illinois at Urbana–Champaign (IL)
The U of Iowa (IA)
The U of Kansas (KS)
U of Massachusetts Dartmouth (MA)
U of Miami (FL)
U of Michigan (MI)
U of Oregon (OR)
U of Regina (SK, Canada)
The U of Texas at El Paso (TX)
The U of the Arts (PA)
U of Windsor (ON, Canada)
Virginia Commonwealth U (VA)
Virginia Intermont Coll (VA)
Washington U in St. Louis (MO)
Western State Colorado U (CO)
Western Washington U (WA)

SECONDARY EDUCATION
Abilene Christian U (TX)
Acadia U (NS, Canada)
Alabama State U (AL)
Albertus Magnus Coll (CT)
Albright Coll (PA)
Alderson-Broaddus Coll (WV)
Alfred U (NY)
Alice Lloyd Coll (KY)
Alma Coll (MI)
American U (DC)
Andrews U (MI)
Arizona Christian U (AZ)
Arizona State U (AZ)
Ashland U (OH)
Assumption Coll (MA)
Auburn U (AL)
Auburn U at Montgomery (AL)
Augsburg Coll (MN)
Augustana Coll (SD)
Baker U (KS)
Baylor U (TX)
Belmont U (TN)
Bemidji State U (MN)
Benedictine Coll (KS)
Bennington Coll (VT)
Bethel Coll (IN)
Blackburn Coll (IL)
Bluefield Coll (VA)
Boston Coll (MA)
Bowie State U (MD)
Brock U (ON, Canada)
Bucknell U (PA)
Buffalo State Coll, State U of New York (NY)
Butler U (IN)
Caldwell Coll (NJ)
Calvin Coll (MI)
Campbellsville U (KY)
Canisius Coll (NY)
Cardinal Stritch U (WI)
Caribbean U (PR)
Carroll Coll (MT)
Carson-Newman U (TN)
Castleton State Coll (VT)
Catawba Coll (NC)
The Catholic U of America (DC)
Cedar Crest Coll (PA)
Central Methodist U (MO)
Central State U (OH)
Champlain Coll (VT)
Cheyney U of Pennsylvania (PA)
Chipola Coll (FL)
The Citadel, The Military Coll of South Carolina (SC)
City Coll of the City U of New York (NY)
Clarke U (IA)
Clark U (MA)
Clemson U (SC)
Coe Coll (IA)
The Coll at Brockport, State U of New York (NY)
Coll of Charleston (SC)
The Coll of New Jersey (NJ)

Coll of Saint Benedict (MN)
Coll of Saint Mary (NE)
Coll of the Atlantic (ME)
Coll of the Ozarks (MO)
Concordia U (OR)
Concordia U Chicago (IL)
Concordia U, Nebraska (NE)
Concordia U, St. Paul (MN)
Concordia U Texas (TX)
Concordia U Wisconsin (WI)
Concord U (WV)
Corban U (OR)
Cornell Coll (IA)
Cornerstone U (MI)
Daytona State Coll (FL)
Defiance Coll (OH)
DePaul U (IL)
Dominican Coll (NY)
Dominican U (IL)
Dordt Coll (IA)
Drake U (IA)
East Central U (OK)
Elmira Coll (NY)
Elon U (NC)
Emmanuel Coll (MA)
Emporia State U (KS)
Evangel U (MO)
Fairmont State U (WV)
Faulkner U (AL)
Felician Coll (NJ)
Flagler Coll (FL)
Florida Gulf Coast U (FL)
Florida Southern Coll (FL)
Fort Lewis Coll (CO)
Franklin Pierce U (NH)
Furman U (SC)
Gannon U (PA)
Gardner-Webb U (NC)
Gettysburg Coll (PA)
Gonzaga U (WA)
Graceland U (IA)
Grace U (NE)
Grambling State U (LA)
Grand Valley State U (MI)
Granite State Coll (NH)
Grove City Coll (PA)
Guilford Coll (NC)
Gustavus Adolphus Coll (MN)
Hamline U (MN)
Hampton U (VA)
Harding U (AR)
Harris-Stowe State U (MO)
High Point U (NC)
Hillsdale Coll (MI)
Hillsdale Free Will Baptist Coll (OK)
Hofstra U (NY)
Houghton Coll (NY)
Howard Payne U (TX)
Humboldt State U (CA)
Hunter Coll of the City U of New York (NY)
Huntington U (IN)
Illinois Coll (IL)
Indiana U Bloomington (IN)
Indiana U East (IN)
Indiana U Kokomo (IN)
Indiana U Northwest (IN)
Indiana U–Purdue U Fort Wayne (IN)
Indiana U–Purdue U Indianapolis (IN)
Indiana U South Bend (IN)
Indiana U Southeast (IN)
Indiana Wesleyan U (IN)
Inter American U of Puerto Rico, San Germán Campus (PR)
Iona Coll (NY)
Iowa State U of Science and Technology (IA)
Iowa Wesleyan Coll (IA)
Ithaca Coll (NY)
Jacksonville State U (AL)
Jarvis Christian Coll (TX)
John Brown U (AR)
John Carroll U (OH)
Johnson State Coll (VT)
Judson U (IL)
Kansas State U (KS)
Keene State Coll (NH)
Kentucky Wesleyan Coll (KY)
Keuka Coll (NY)
The King's U Coll (AB, Canada)
Knox Coll (IL)
Kuyper Coll (MI)
Lake Erie Coll (OH)
Lakeland Coll (WI)

Lake Superior State U (MI)
Lamar U (TX)
Lander U (SC)
Langston U (OK)
La Salle U (PA)
Lasell Coll (MA)
Lawrence U (WI)
Lee U (TN)
Le Moyne Coll (NY)
Lesley U (MA)
LeTourneau U (TX)
Lewis U (IL)
Lincoln Memorial U (TN)
Lindenwood U (MO)
Lindsey Wilson Coll (KY)
Lock Haven U of Pennsylvania (PA)
Long Island U–Brooklyn Campus (NY)
Long Island U–C. W. Post Campus (NY)
Louisiana Coll (LA)
Lourdes U (OH)
Loyola U Chicago (IL)
Lubbock Christian U (TX)
Maharishi U of Management (IA)
Manchester U (IN)
Manhattanville Coll (NY)
Mansfield U of Pennsylvania (PA)
Marian U (WI)
Marietta Coll (OH)
Marquette U (WI)
Marshall U (WV)
Mars Hill Coll (NC)
The Master's Coll and Sem (CA)
McKendree U (IL)
McMurry U (TX)
McNeese State U (LA)
Medaille Coll (NY)
Mercyhurst U (PA)
Merrimack Coll (MA)
Michigan State U (MI)
Midwestern State U (TX)
Minnesota State U Mankato (MN)
Mississippi State U (MS)
Missouri Baptist U (MO)
Missouri State U (MO)
Missouri U of Science and Technology (MO)
Monmouth U (NJ)
Moravian Coll (PA)
Mount Aloysius Coll (PA)
Mount Marty Coll (SD)
Mount Mercy U (IA)
Mount Saint Mary Coll (NY)
Mount St. Mary's Coll (CA)
National U (CA)
Nazareth Coll of Rochester (NY)
New England Coll (NH)
Newman U (KS)
New Mexico State U (NM)
Niagara U (NY)
North Carolina Wesleyan Coll (NC)
North Central Coll (IL)
Northern Michigan U (MI)
Northern State U (SD)
Northland Coll (WI)
Northwestern Coll (IA)
Northwestern Oklahoma State U (OK)
Northwestern State U of Louisiana (LA)
Northwest Nazarene U (ID)
Northwest U (WA)
Nova Southeastern U (FL)
Oakland City U (IN)
Ohio Dominican U (OH)
Ohio U (OH)
Ohio U–Chillicothe (OH)
Ohio Valley U (WV)
Ohio Wesleyan U (OH)
Oklahoma Christian U (OK)
Oklahoma City U (OK)
Oklahoma State U (OK)
Ouachita Baptist U (AR)
Pacific U (OR)
Penn State Abington (PA)
Penn State Altoona (PA)
Penn State Beaver (PA)
Penn State Berks (PA)
Penn State Brandywine (PA)
Penn State DuBois (PA)
Penn State Erie, The Behrend Coll (PA)
Penn State Fayette, The Eberly Campus (PA)
Penn State Greater Allegheny (PA)
Penn State Hazleton (PA)

Penn State Lehigh Valley (PA)
Penn State Mont Alto (PA)
Penn State New Kensington (PA)
Penn State Schuylkill (PA)
Penn State Shenango (PA)
Penn State U Park (PA)
Penn State Wilkes-Barre (PA)
Penn State Worthington Scranton (PA)
Penn State York (PA)
Pepperdine U, Malibu (CA)
Prescott Coll (AZ)
Presentation Coll (SD)
Providence Coll (RI)
Purdue U Calumet (IN)
Purdue U North Central (IN)
Queens U of Charlotte (NC)
Rhode Island Coll (RI)
Rider U (NJ)
Ripon Coll (WI)
Rivier U (NH)
Rockford Coll (IL)
Rockhurst U (MO)
Rocky Mountain Coll (MT)
Roger Williams U (RI)
Sacred Heart U (CT)
St. Ambrose U (IA)
Saint Anselm Coll (NH)
Saint John's U (MN)
Saint Leo U (FL)
Saint Michael's Coll (VT)
St. Thomas Aquinas Coll (NY)
St. Thomas U (FL)
Salem Intl U (WV)
Salem State U (MA)
Salve Regina U (RI)
San Diego Christian Coll (CA)
Shepherd U (WV)
Siena Coll (NY)
Siena Heights U (MI)
Simmons Coll (MA)
Simpson Coll (IA)
Slippery Rock U of Pennsylvania (PA)
Southern Connecticut State U (CT)
Spring Arbor U (MI)
Spring Hill Coll (AL)
State U of New York at Fredonia (NY)
State U of New York at New Paltz (NY)
State U of New York at Oswego (NY)
State U of New York Coll at Cortland (NY)
State U of New York Coll at Old Westbury (NY)
Stetson U (FL)
Susquehanna U (PA)
Tabor Coll (KS)
Tarleton State U (TX)
Tennessee Wesleyan Coll (TN)
Texas A&M U–Commerce (TX)
Texas Christian U (TX)
Thomas More Coll (KY)
Thomas U (GA)
Trent U (ON, Canada)
Trine U (IN)
Troy U (AL)
Union Coll (KY)
Union U (TN)
Unity Coll (ME)
Universidad Adventista de las Antillas (PR)
Université de Sherbrooke (QC, Canada)
Université du Québec en Outaouais (QC, Canada)
Université Sainte-Anne (NS, Canada)
The U of Alabama (AL)
The U of Alabama at Birmingham (AL)
U of Alaska Anchorage (AK)
The U of British Columbia (BC, Canada)
U of Central Oklahoma (OK)
U of Cincinnati (OH)
U of Dallas (TX)
The U of Findlay (OH)
U of Great Falls (MT)
U of Guam (GU)
U of Hartford (CT)
U of Hawaii at Hilo (HI)
U of Hawaii at Manoa (HI)
U of Idaho (ID)

U of Illinois at Urbana–Champaign (IL)
The U of Iowa (IA)
The U of Kansas (KS)
U of Louisiana at Lafayette (LA)
U of Louisiana at Monroe (LA)
U of Maine at Farmington (ME)
U of Maryland, Coll Park (MD)
U of Michigan (MI)
U of Michigan–Dearborn (MI)
U of Minnesota, Twin Cities Campus (MN)
U of Missouri (MO)
U of Missouri–Kansas City (MO)
U of Missouri–St. Louis (MO)
The U of Montana Western (MT)
U of Nebraska at Omaha (NE)
U of Nevada, Las Vegas (NV)
U of New Brunswick Fredericton (NB, Canada)
U of New Mexico (NM)
U of New Orleans (LA)
U of North Alabama (AL)
U of North Florida (FL)
U of Pittsburgh at Bradford (PA)
U of Portland (OR)
U of Redlands (CA)
U of Regina (SK, Canada)
U of Rhode Island (RI)
U of St. Thomas (TX)
The U of Scranton (PA)
U of South Alabama (AL)
U of South Carolina Aiken (SC)
U of South Carolina Upstate (SC)
The U of South Dakota (SD)
The U of Tampa (FL)
The U of Tennessee at Chattanooga (TN)
U of the Cumberlands (KY)
U of the Ozarks (AR)
The U of Toledo (OH)
U of Vermont (VT)
The U of Western Ontario (ON, Canada)
U of West Georgia (GA)
U of Windsor (ON, Canada)
U of Wisconsin–Platteville (WI)
U of Wisconsin–Stevens Point (WI)
U of Wyoming (WY)
Utah State U (UT)
Utica Coll (NY)
Valley City State U (ND)
Valparaiso U (IN)
Vanderbilt U (TN)
Villanova U (PA)
Virginia Intermont Coll (VA)
Virginia Polytechnic Inst and State U (VA)
Virginia Wesleyan Coll (VA)
Wagner Coll (NY)
Waldorf Coll (IA)
Walsh U (OH)
Warner Pacific Coll (OR)
Wartburg Coll (IA)
Washington State U (WA)
Washington U in St. Louis (MO)
Waynesburg U (PA)
Webster U (MO)
Wells Coll (NY)
Western Connecticut State U (CT)
Western Oregon U (OR)
West Liberty U (WV)
Westminster Coll (MO)
West Texas A&M U (TX)
West Virginia State U (WV)
West Virginia Wesleyan Coll (WV)
Wheaton Coll (IL)
Wheeling Jesuit U (WV)
Whitworth U (WA)
Wichita State U (KS)
William Jewell Coll (MO)
William Paterson U of New Jersey (NJ)
William Penn U (IA)
Wright State U (OH)
Xavier U of Louisiana (LA)
York Coll of the City U of New York (NY)
Young Harris Coll (GA)
Youngstown State U (OH)

SECONDARY SCHOOL ADMINISTRATION/ PRINCIPALSHIP
The U of North Carolina at Pembroke (NC)

SECURITIES SERVICES ADMINISTRATION
American Public U System (WV)
Central Penn Coll (PA)
The Coll at Brockport, State U of New York (NY)
Davenport U, Grand Rapids (MI)
Henley-Putnam U (CA)
St. John's U (NY)
Vincennes U (IN)
Washburn U (KS)
Webber Intl U (FL)

SECURITY AND LOSS PREVENTION
Farmingdale State Coll (NY)
Lewis U (IL)
National U (CA)
Northern Michigan U (MI)
Saint Louis U (MO)

SELLING SKILLS AND SALES
Bradley U (IL)
U of Memphis (TN)
Weber State U (UT)
William Paterson U of New Jersey (NJ)

SIGN LANGUAGE INTERPRETATION AND TRANSLATION
Augustana Coll (SD)
Bethel Coll (IN)
Bloomsburg U of Pennsylvania (PA)
Columbia Coll Chicago (IL)
Gallaudet U (DC)
Goshen Coll (IN)
Indiana U–Purdue U Indianapolis (IN)
Kent State U (OH)
Madonna U (MI)
Maryville Coll (TN)
Mount Aloysius Coll (PA)
Quincy U (IL)
Rochester Inst of Technology (NY)
Troy U (AL)
U of Arkansas at Little Rock (AR)
U of Louisville (KY)
U of New Hampshire at Manchester (NH)
U of New Mexico (NM)
U of Northern Colorado (CO)
U of North Florida (FL)
Valdosta State U (GA)
Western Oregon U (OR)
Wright State U (OH)

SLAVIC, BALTIC, AND ALBANIAN LANGUAGES RELATED
Rutgers, The State U of New Jersey, Newark (NJ)

SLAVIC LANGUAGES
Boston Coll (MA)
Columbia U (NY)
Columbia U, School of General Studies (NY)
Indiana U Bloomington (IN)
Princeton U (NJ)
Stanford U (CA)
The U of British Columbia (BC, Canada)
U of California, Berkeley (CA)
U of California, Los Angeles (CA)
U of California, Santa Barbara (CA)
U of Chicago (IL)
U of Illinois at Chicago (IL)
U of Illinois at Urbana–Champaign (IL)
The U of Kansas (KS)
U of Minnesota, Twin Cities Campus (MN)
U of Pittsburgh (PA)
U of Virginia (VA)
Wayne State U (MI)

SLAVIC STUDIES
Baylor U (TX)
Columbia U, School of General Studies (NY)
Connecticut Coll (CT)
Lawrence U (WI)
U of Ottawa (ON, Canada)
U of Waterloo (ON, Canada)

SMALL BUSINESS ADMINISTRATION
Adams State U (CO)
Avila U (MO)

Babson Coll (MA)
Bradley U (IL)
Carson-Newman U (TN)
Chowan U (NC)
Dalhousie U (NS, Canada)
Hilbert Coll (NY)
Huntington U (IN)
Husson U (ME)
Lewis-Clark State Coll (ID)
North Central Coll (IL)
Northern Michigan U (MI)
Purdue U Calumet (IN)
Saint Joseph's U (PA)
U of Nebraska at Omaha (NE)

SOCIAL AND PHILOSOPHICAL FOUNDATIONS OF EDUCATION
Eastern Washington U (WA)
Hope Intl U (CA)
Transylvania U (KY)
Washington U in St. Louis (MO)

SOCIAL PSYCHOLOGY
Bennington Coll (VT)
Brigham Young U (UT)
Clarion U of Pennsylvania (PA)
Florida Atlantic U (FL)
Grand Valley State U (MI)
Keene State Coll (NH)
Lawrence U (WI)
Maryville U of Saint Louis (MO)
Moravian Coll (PA)
Northwest Missouri State U (MO)
Penn State Abington (PA)
Prescott Coll (AZ)
U of California, Irvine (CA)
U of New England (ME)
U of Wisconsin–Superior (WI)
Western Michigan U (MI)

SOCIAL SCIENCES
Adelphi U (NY)
Albertus Magnus Coll (CT)
Albion Coll (MI)
Alice Lloyd Coll (KY)
Alverno Coll (WI)
American U (DC)
Andrews U (MI)
Arizona State U (AZ)
Asbury U (KY)
Ashland U (OH)
Athens State U (AL)
Augsburg Coll (MN)
Azusa Pacific U (CA)
Ball State U (IN)
Belhaven U (MS)
Bemidji State U (MN)
Benedictine Coll (KS)
Benedictine U (IL)
Bennington Coll (VT)
Berry Coll (GA)
Bethany Lutheran Coll (MN)
Bethel Coll (IN)
Bethel U (MN)
Binghamton U, State U of New York (NY)
Bluefield State Coll (WV)
Bluffton U (OH)
Boise State U (ID)
Bowling Green State U (OH)
Brock U (ON, Canada)
Caldwell Coll (NJ)
California Lutheran U (CA)
California State Polytechnic U, Pomona (CA)
California State U, Los Angeles (CA)
California State U, Monterey Bay (CA)
California State U, San Bernardino (CA)
California State U, San Marcos (CA)
California State U, Stanislaus (CA)
Calvin Coll (MI)
Campbellsville U (KY)
Canisius Coll (NY)
Cardinal Stritch U (WI)
Castleton State Coll (VT)
Central Coll (IA)
Central Connecticut State U (CT)
Central Michigan U (MI)
Cheyney U of Pennsylvania (PA)
Clarkson U (NY)
Cleveland State U (OH)
Colgate U (NY)
Coll of Saint Benedict (MN)

Coll of Saint Mary (NE)
The Coll of St. Scholastica (MN)
Colorado Mesa U (CO)
Colorado State U (CO)
Concordia Coll (MN)
Concordia Coll–New York (NY)
Concordia U (OR)
Concordia U, Nebraska (NE)
Corban U (OR)
Defiance Coll (OH)
Delta State U (MS)
DePaul U (IL)
Doane Coll (NE)
Dominican Coll (NY)
Dordt Coll (IA)
Eastern Mennonite U (VA)
Eastern Michigan U (MI)
Eastern New Mexico U (NM)
Edgewood Coll (WI)
Edinboro U of Pennsylvania (PA)
Elizabethtown Coll (PA)
Elmira Coll (NY)
Emporia State U (KS)
Eugene Lang Coll The New School for Liberal Arts (NY)
Faulkner U (AL)
Ferrum Coll (VA)
Florida Atlantic U (FL)
Florida Southern Coll (FL)
Florida State U (FL)
Frostburg State U (MD)
Gardner-Webb U (NC)
Gettysburg Coll (PA)
Governors State U (IL)
Grambling State U (LA)
Grand Valley State U (MI)
Gustavus Adolphus Coll (MN)
Hampton U (VA)
Harding U (AR)
Harrison Middleton U (AZ)
Hawai`i Pacific U (HI)
Holy Apostles Coll and Sem (CT)
Hope Intl U (CA)
Howard Payne U (TX)
Humboldt State U (CA)
Illinois Inst of Technology (IL)
Inter American U of Puerto Rico, San Germán Campus (PR)
Ithaca Coll (NY)
James Madison U (VA)
The Johns Hopkins U (MD)
Johnson C. Smith U (NC)
Juniata Coll (PA)
Kansas State U (KS)
Kansas Wesleyan U (KS)
Keene State Coll (NH)
Kentucky State U (KY)
Keuka Coll (NY)
Keystone Coll (PA)
The King's U Coll (AB, Canada)
Kutztown U of Pennsylvania (PA)
Lake Erie Coll (OH)
Lake Superior State U (MI)
La Salle U (PA)
Lesley U (MA)
Lewis-Clark State Coll (ID)
Liberty U (VA)
Lock Haven U of Pennsylvania (PA)
Long Island U–Brooklyn Campus (NY)
Loyola U New Orleans (LA)
Manchester U (IN)
Mansfield U of Pennsylvania (PA)
Mars Hill Coll (NC)
Marywood U (PA)
Mayville State U (ND)
McKendree U (IL)
Mercy Coll (NY)
Mercyhurst U (PA)
Michigan State U (MI)
Mid-Continent U (KY)
Minnesota State U Mankato (MN)
Minot State U (ND)
Misericordia U (PA)
Mississippi U for Women (MS)
Missouri Baptist U (MO)
Montreat Coll, Montreat (NC)
Moravian Coll (PA)
Morehead State U (KY)
Mount Mary Coll (WI)
Mount Saint Mary Coll (NY)
Muhlenberg Coll (PA)
Nazareth Coll of Rochester (NY)
New Coll of Florida (FL)
New York Inst of Technology (NY)
New York U (NY)
Niagara U (NY)

North Central Coll (IL)
North Dakota State U (ND)
Northwestern Oklahoma State U (OK)
Notre Dame de Namur U (CA)
Oakland City U (IN)
Oklahoma Baptist U (OK)
Olivet Coll (MI)
Pace U (NY)
Piedmont Coll (GA)
Plymouth State U (NH)
Point Loma Nazarene U (CA)
Point Park U (PA)
Point U (GA)
Portland State U (OR)
Providence Coll (RI)
Purdue U (IN)
Quinnipiac U (CT)
Radford U (VA)
Ramapo Coll of New Jersey (NJ)
Regis U (CO)
Rhode Island Coll (RI)
Robert Morris U (PA)
Rockford Coll (IL)
Rogers State U (OK)
Roger Williams U (RI)
Roosevelt U (IL)
Rosemont Coll (PA)
Sage Coll of Albany (NY)
St. Andrews U (NC)
St. Gregory's U, Shawnee (OK)
Saint John's U (MN)
St. John's U (NY)
St. Joseph's Coll, Long Island Campus (NY)
St. Joseph's Coll, New York (NY)
Saint Mary's Coll of California (CA)
Saint Mary's U of Minnesota (MN)
St. Thomas Aquinas Coll (NY)
San Diego State U (CA)
San Jose State U (CA)
Sewanee: The U of the South (TN)
Shawnee State U (OH)
Shimer Coll (IL)
Siena Heights U (MI)
Southern Arkansas U–Magnolia (AR)
Southern Illinois U Carbondale (IL)
Southern New Hampshire U (NH)
Southern Oregon U (OR)
Southwestern Adventist U (TX)
Spalding U (KY)
Spring Arbor U (MI)
Spring Hill Coll (AL)
State U of New York at New Paltz (NY)
State U of New York Coll at Old Westbury (NY)
State U of New York Empire State Coll (NY)
Stetson U (FL)
Suffolk U (MA)
Sul Ross State U (TX)
Tabor Coll (KS)
Texas A&M Intl U (TX)
Texas A&M U–Commerce (TX)
Thomas Edison State Coll (NJ)
Thomas U (GA)
Trent U (ON, Canada)
Trine U (IN)
Troy U (AL)
United States Air Force Acad (CO)
Université du Québec en Outaouais (QC, Canada)
U at Buffalo, the State U of New York (NY)
The U of Akron (OH)
U of Bridgeport (CT)
The U of British Columbia (BC, Canada)
U of California, Irvine (CA)
U of Central Florida (FL)
U of Chicago (IL)
U of Cincinnati (OH)
U of Dallas (TX)
U of Denver (CO)
U of Great Falls (MT)
U of Hawaii–West Oahu (HI)
U of Houston–Downtown (TX)
U of Houston–Victoria (TX)
U of La Verne (CA)
U of Maine at Fort Kent (ME)
U of Maryland Eastern Shore (MD)
U of Maryland U Coll (MD)
U of Massachusetts Boston (MA)
U of Michigan (MI)
U of Michigan–Dearborn (MI)

U of Mobile (AL)
The U of Montana Western (MT)
U of Montevallo (AL)
U of Nevada, Las Vegas (NV)
U of North Alabama (AL)
U of North Dakota (ND)
U of Northern Colorado (CO)
U of North Georgia (GA)
U of North Texas (TX)
U of Oregon (OR)
U of Ottawa (ON, Canada)
U of Pennsylvania (PA)
U of Pittsburgh (PA)
U of Pittsburgh at Bradford (PA)
U of Pittsburgh at Greensburg (PA)
U of Regina (SK, Canada)
U of St. Thomas (MN)
U of Southern Indiana (IN)
U of South Florida (FL)
The U of Texas–Pan American (TX)
U of the Virgin Islands (VI)
U of Utah (UT)
U of West Florida (FL)
U of Windsor (ON, Canada)
U of Wisconsin–Platteville (WI)
U of Wisconsin–Stevens Point (WI)
U of Wisconsin–Stout (WI)
U of Wisconsin–Superior (WI)
U of Wyoming (WY)
Upper Iowa U (IA)
Utica Coll (NY)
Valley City State U (ND)
Valparaiso U (IN)
Vanderbilt U (TN)
Virginia Wesleyan Coll (VA)
Viterbo U (WI)
Warner Pacific Coll (OR)
Washington State U (WA)
Washington U in St. Louis (MO)
Wayland Baptist U (TX)
Waynesburg U (PA)
Wayne State Coll (NE)
Webster U (MO)
Wesleyan Coll (GA)
Wesleyan U (CT)
Western Connecticut State U (CT)
Western Kentucky U (KY)
Western Oregon U (OR)
West Liberty U (WV)
Westminster Coll (UT)
West Texas A&M U (TX)
Widener U (PA)
William Paterson U of New Jersey (NJ)
Worcester Polytechnic Inst (MA)
Wright State U (OH)
Youngstown State U (OH)

SOCIAL SCIENCES RELATED
Abilene Christian U (TX)
Bennington Coll (VT)
Bloomsburg U of Pennsylvania (PA)
Boston U (MA)
Bowling Green State U (OH)
California Polytechnic State U, San Luis Obispo (CA)
Caribbean U (PR)
Cleveland State U (OH)
The Coll of Idaho (ID)
Coll of Staten Island of the City U of New York (NY)
Concordia U (QC, Canada)
Concordia U Texas (TX)
Covenant Coll (GA)
Elizabethtown Coll (PA)
The Evergreen State Coll (WA)
Georgetown U (DC)
Gettysburg Coll (PA)
Hamline U (MN)
Indiana U of Pennsylvania (PA)
John Jay Coll of Criminal Justice of the City U of New York (NY)
Kalamazoo Coll (MI)
Loyola U Maryland (MD)
Mary Baldwin Coll (VA)
Marywood U (PA)
Midwestern State U (TX)
Millersville U of Pennsylvania (PA)
Monmouth U (NJ)
Mount Aloysius Coll (PA)
Mount Holyoke Coll (MA)
Mount Mary Coll (WI)
New Mexico Highlands U (NM)
New York U (NY)
Northern Arizona U (AZ)
Northwest Missouri State U (MO)
Plymouth State U (NH)

Purchase Coll, State U of New York (NY)
Roger Williams U (RI)
Rutgers, The State U of New Jersey, New Brunswick (NJ)
Sage Coll of Albany (NY)
Saint Mary's Coll of California (CA)
Simon Fraser U (BC, Canada)
Skidmore Coll (NY)
United States Military Acad (NY)
The U of Alabama at Birmingham (AL)
U of California, Berkeley (CA)
U of Chicago (IL)
U of Denver (CO)
U of Massachusetts Amherst (MA)
U of New England (ME)
U of Pittsburgh (PA)
U of Regina (SK, Canada)
U of Rhode Island (RI)
U of Rochester (NY)
U of Southern Maine (ME)
The U of Tennessee at Chattanooga (TN)
U of Washington, Tacoma (WA)
U of Waterloo (ON, Canada)
The U of Western Ontario (ON, Canada)
U of West Florida (FL)
U of Wisconsin–Green Bay (WI)
Washington U in St. Louis (MO)
Whitman Coll (WA)

SOCIAL SCIENCE TEACHER EDUCATION

Arkansas State U (AR)
Auburn U (AL)
Averett U (VA)
Baylor U (TX)
Blackburn Coll (IL)
Blue Mountain Coll (MS)
Boise State U (ID)
Bowling Green State U (OH)
Bradley U (IL)
Brigham Young U (UT)
Buena Vista U (IA)
California Lutheran U (CA)
Campbellsville U (KY)
Carroll Coll (MT)
Central Methodist U (MO)
Central Michigan U (MI)
Chowan U (NC)
Concordia U Chicago (IL)
Concordia U, Nebraska (NE)
Corban U (OR)
Cornerstone U (MI)
Delta State U (MS)
Dominican Coll (NY)
Dordt Coll (IA)
Eastern Illinois U (IL)
Eastern Michigan U (MI)
Eastern Washington U (WA)
Elmira Coll (NY)
Emmanuel Coll (GA)
Emporia State U (KS)
Fayetteville State U (NC)
Ferris State U (MI)
Florida Ag and Mech U (FL)
Florida Atlantic U (FL)
Gardner-Webb U (NC)
Grace U (NE)
Henderson State U (AR)
Johnson State Coll (VT)
Judson Coll (AL)
Knox Coll (IL)
Lewis-Clark State Coll (ID)
Lincoln U (MO)
Lindenwood U (MO)
Lindsey Wilson Coll (KY)
Manchester U (IN)
Mansfield U of Pennsylvania (PA)
Marywood U (PA)
Mayville State U (ND)
McKendree U (IL)
Medaille Coll (NY)
Mercyhurst U (PA)
Michigan State U (MI)
Millikin U (IL)
Minot State U (ND)
Mississippi Valley State U (MS)
Montana State U (MT)
Mount St. Mary's U (MD)
Northern Michigan U (MI)
Northwest Missouri State U (MO)
Oakland City U (IN)
Pacific Union Coll (CA)
Purdue U Calumet (IN)

Rhode Island Coll (RI)
St. Ambrose U (IA)
Saint Mary's U of Minnesota (MN)
Shawnee State U (OH)
Simpson U (CA)
Southeastern U (FL)
Southern Utah U (UT)
Southwest Baptist U (MO)
State U of New York at New Paltz (NY)
Union Coll (NE)
U of Central Florida (FL)
U of Great Falls (MT)
U of Illinois at Urbana–Champaign (IL)
U of Maine at Farmington (ME)
U of Maine at Fort Kent (ME)
U of Maine at Machias (ME)
The U of Montana Western (MT)
U of Nebraska–Lincoln (NE)
The U of North Carolina at Greensboro (NC)
U of North Dakota (ND)
U of Northern Iowa (IA)
The U of South Dakota (SD)
U of South Florida (FL)
U of Utah (UT)
U of Wisconsin–Superior (WI)
Upper Iowa U (IA)
Utica Coll (NY)
Valley City State U (ND)
Valparaiso U (IN)
Wartburg Coll (IA)
Washington U in St. Louis (MO)
Wayne State Coll (NE)
Weber State U (UT)
Western Michigan U (MI)
Western State Colorado U (CO)
Western Washington U (WA)
William Penn U (IA)
Youngstown State U (OH)

SOCIAL STUDIES TEACHER EDUCATION

Abilene Christian U (TX)
Adams State U (CO)
Alice Lloyd Coll (KY)
Alma Coll (MI)
Alvernia U (PA)
Alverno Coll (WI)
Anderson U (IN)
Arizona Christian U (AZ)
Arkansas Tech U (AR)
Augustana Coll (SD)
Averett U (VA)
The Baptist Coll of Florida (FL)
Baylor U (TX)
Bethel Coll (IN)
Bethel U (MN)
Bethune-Cookman U (FL)
Bluefield Coll (VA)
Bob Jones U (SC)
Boston U (MA)
Bowling Green State U (OH)
Bradley U (IL)
Buffalo State Coll, State U of New York (NY)
Cabrini Coll (PA)
Cairn U (PA)
Calvin Coll (MI)
Cameron U (OK)
Campbellsville U (KY)
Canisius Coll (NY)
Capital U (OH)
Carroll Coll (MT)
Castleton State Coll (VT)
Cedarville U (OH)
Central Michigan U (MI)
City Coll of the City U of New York (NY)
Clearwater Christian Coll (FL)
Cleveland State U (OH)
The Coll at Brockport, State U of New York (NY)
The Coll of Saint Rose (NY)
Coll of the Ozarks (MO)
Colorado State U (CO)
Columbus State U (GA)
Concordia Coll (MN)
Concordia U (OR)
Concordia U, St. Paul (MN)
Corban U (OR)
Cornerstone U (MI)
Crown Coll (MN)
Dordt Coll (IA)
Duquesne U (PA)
East Carolina U (NC)

East Central U (OK)
Eastern Michigan U (MI)
Eastern Washington U (WA)
East Texas Baptist U (TX)
Elmira Coll (NY)
Ferris State U (MI)
Franklin Coll (IN)
Gannon U (PA)
Grambling State U (LA)
Grand Valley State U (MI)
Granite State Coll (NH)
Gustavus Adolphus Coll (MN)
Harding U (AR)
Hardin-Simmons U (TX)
Hofstra U (NY)
Holy Family U (PA)
Hope Coll (MI)
Howard Payne U (TX)
Huntington U (IN)
Illinois State U (IL)
Indiana State U (IN)
Indiana U Bloomington (IN)
Indiana U Northwest (IN)
Indiana U–Purdue U Fort Wayne (IN)
Indiana U–Purdue U Indianapolis (IN)
Indiana U South Bend (IN)
Indiana U Southeast (IN)
Indiana Wesleyan U (IN)
Inter American U of Puerto Rico, Fajardo Campus (PR)
Inter American U of Puerto Rico, San Germán Campus (PR)
Iona Coll (NY)
Iowa Wesleyan Coll (IA)
Ithaca Coll (NY)
John Brown U (AR)
Johnson State Coll (VT)
Juniata Coll (PA)
Keene State Coll (NH)
Kennesaw State U (GA)
Kent State U (OH)
Kentucky Christian U (KY)
Kentucky Wesleyan Coll (KY)
Keuka Coll (NY)
Keystone Coll (PA)
Le Moyne Coll (NY)
Long Island U–Brooklyn Campus (NY)
Long Island U–C. W. Post Campus (NY)
Louisiana State U in Shreveport (LA)
Lubbock Christian U (TX)
Madonna U (MI)
Malone U (OH)
Manchester U (IN)
Manhattanville Coll (NY)
Mansfield U of Pennsylvania (PA)
Maranatha Baptist Bible Coll (WI)
Marian U (WI)
Marist Coll (NY)
Maryville Coll (TN)
Merrimack Coll (MA)
Messiah Coll (PA)
Miami U (OH)
Michigan State U (MI)
Midwestern State U (TX)
Minnesota State U Mankato (MN)
Minnesota State U Moorhead (MN)
Mississippi Coll (MS)
Molloy Coll (NY)
Moravian Coll (PA)
Morris Coll (SC)
Mount Mary Coll (WI)
Mount Vernon Nazarene U (OH)
Nazareth Coll of Rochester (NY)
New York U (NY)
Niagara U (NY)
Nicholls State U (LA)
North Carolina State U (NC)
North Dakota State U (ND)
Northern Michigan U (MI)
North Greenville U (SC)
Northland Coll (WI)
Northwestern Coll (MN)
Northwest U (WA)
Nyack Coll (NY)
Oakland City U (IN)
Ohio Dominican U (OH)
Ohio Wesleyan U (OH)
Oklahoma Baptist U (OK)
Oklahoma Christian U (OK)
Oral Roberts U (OK)
Ouachita Baptist U (AR)
Pace U (NY)

Penn State Harrisburg (PA)
Pittsburg State U (KS)
Purdue U Calumet (IN)
Rhode Island Coll (RI)
Rivier U (NH)
Roberts Wesleyan Coll (NY)
Rocky Mountain Coll (MT)
St. Edward's U (TX)
St. Francis Coll (NY)
St. Gregory's U, Shawnee (OK)
St. John Fisher Coll (NY)
St. John's U (NY)
St. Joseph's Coll, Long Island Campus (NY)
St. Joseph's Coll, New York (NY)
Saint Mary-of-the-Woods Coll (IN)
St. Mary's U (TX)
St. Olaf Coll (MN)
St. Thomas U (FL)
Siena Heights U (MI)
Southeastern Louisiana U (LA)
Southeastern Oklahoma State U (OK)
Southeast Missouri State U (MO)
Southern Nazarene U (OK)
Southern New Hampshire U (NH)
Spring Arbor U (MI)
State U of New York at New Paltz (NY)
State U of New York Coll at Cortland (NY)
State U of New York Coll at Old Westbury (NY)
Stony Brook U, State U of New York (NY)
Syracuse U (NY)
Taylor U (IN)
Temple U (PA)
Texas A&M Intl U (TX)
Texas Christian U (TX)
Texas Lutheran U (TX)
Trine U (IN)
Universidad Adventista de las Antillas (PR)
The U of Akron (OH)
U of Central Arkansas (AR)
U of Central Oklahoma (OK)
U of Charleston (WV)
U of Evansville (IN)
U of Georgia (GA)
U of Great Falls (MT)
U of Illinois at Urbana–Champaign (IL)
The U of Iowa (IA)
U of Kentucky (KY)
U of Louisiana at Monroe (LA)
U of Michigan–Dearborn (MI)
U of Michigan–Flint (MI)
U of Minnesota, Duluth (MN)
U of Minnesota, Twin Cities Campus (MN)
U of Mississippi (MS)
U of Missouri (MO)
U of Missouri–St. Louis (MO)
The U of North Carolina at Greensboro (NC)
The U of North Carolina at Pembroke (NC)
U of Oklahoma (OK)
U of Regina (SK, Canada)
U of St. Francis (IL)
U of St. Thomas (MN)
The U of Tennessee at Chattanooga (TN)
U of the Cumberlands (KY)
The U of Toledo (OH)
U of Vermont (VT)
U of Wisconsin–Eau Claire (WI)
U of Wisconsin–La Crosse (WI)
U of Wisconsin–Superior (WI)
Ursuline Coll (OH)
Utah State U (UT)
Utica Coll (NY)
Virginia Intermont Coll (VA)
Virginia Wesleyan Coll (VA)
Viterbo U (WI)
Warner Pacific Coll (OR)
Washington State U (WA)
Washington U in St. Louis (MO)
Wayland Baptist U (TX)
Waynesburg U (PA)
Wayne State U (MI)
Weber State U (UT)
Webster U (MO)
Western Carolina U (NC)
Western Michigan U (MI)
Western Washington U (WA)

Wheeling Jesuit U (WV)
Widener U (PA)
William Jewell Coll (MO)
Xavier U of Louisiana (LA)
York Coll of Pennsylvania (PA)
Youngstown State U (OH)

SOCIAL WORK

Abilene Christian U (TX)
Adams State U (CO)
Adelphi U (NY)
Alabama State U (AL)
Albertus Magnus Coll (CT)
Alvernia U (PA)
Anderson U (IN)
Andrews U (MI)
Angelo State U (TX)
Appalachian State U (NC)
Arizona State U (AZ)
Arkansas State U (AR)
Asbury U (KY)
Ashland U (OH)
Auburn U (AL)
Augsburg Coll (MN)
Aurora U (IL)
Austin Peay State U (TN)
Avila U (MO)
Azusa Pacific U (CA)
Ball State U (IN)
Barton Coll (NC)
Baylor U (TX)
Belmont U (TN)
Bemidji State U (MN)
Bethany Coll (WV)
Bethel Coll (KS)
Bethel U (MN)
Bloomsburg U of Pennsylvania (PA)
Bluffton U (OH)
Boise State U (ID)
Bowie State U (MD)
Bowling Green State U (OH)
Bowling Green State U-Firelands Coll (OH)
Bradley U (IL)
Bridgewater State U (MA)
Buena Vista U (IA)
Buffalo State Coll, State U of New York (NY)
Cabrini Coll (PA)
Cairn U (PA)
California State U, East Bay (CA)
California State U, Fresno (CA)
California State U, Long Beach (CA)
California State U, Los Angeles (CA)
California State U, San Bernardino (CA)
Calvin Coll (MI)
Campbellsville U (KY)
Capital U (OH)
Caribbean U (PR)
Carlow U (PA)
Castleton State Coll (VT)
The Catholic U of America (DC)
Cedar Crest Coll (PA)
Cedarville U (OH)
Central Baptist Coll (AR)
Central Connecticut State U (CT)
Central Michigan U (MI)
Central State U (OH)
Champlain Coll (VT)
Chapman U (CA)
Chatham U (PA)
Christopher Newport U (VA)
Clark Atlanta U (GA)
Clarke U (IA)
Cleveland State U (OH)
Coll of Mount St. Joseph (OH)
The Coll of New Rochelle (NY)
The Coll of Saint Rose (NY)
The Coll of St. Scholastica (MN)
Coll of Staten Island of the City U of New York (NY)
Coll of the Ozarks (MO)
Colorado State U (CO)
Columbia Coll (SC)
Concordia Coll (MN)
Concordia Coll–New York (NY)
Concordia U (OR)
Concordia U Chicago (IL)
Concordia U Wisconsin (WI)
Concord U (WV)
Cornerstone U (MI)
Creighton U (NE)
Dalhousie U (NS, Canada)
Dalton State Coll (GA)

Defiance Coll (OH)
Delta State U (MS)
Dominican Coll (NY)
Dordt Coll (IA)
East Carolina U (NC)
East Central U (OK)
Eastern Mennonite U (VA)
Eastern Michigan U (MI)
Eastern Washington U (WA)
East Tennessee State U (TN)
Edinboro U of Pennsylvania (PA)
Elizabeth City State U (NC)
Elizabethtown Coll (PA)
Elmira Coll (NY)
Evangel U (MO)
Fayetteville State U (NC)
Ferrum Coll (VA)
Florida Ag and Mech U (FL)
Florida Atlantic U (FL)
Florida Gulf Coast U (FL)
Florida Intl U (FL)
Florida State U (FL)
Franklin Pierce U (NH)
Frostburg State U (MD)
Gannon U (PA)
George Fox U (OR)
George Mason U (VA)
Georgia Regents U (GA)
Georgia State U (GA)
Gordon Coll (MA)
Goshen Coll (IN)
Governors State U (IL)
Graceland U (IA)
Grambling State U (LA)
Grand Valley State U (MI)
Greenville Coll (IL)
Hampton U (VA)
Harding U (AR)
Hardin-Simmons U (TX)
Hawai`i Pacific U (HI)
Henderson State U (AR)
Hood Coll (MD)
Hope Coll (MI)
Howard Payne U (TX)
Humboldt State U (CA)
Huntington U (IN)
Illinois State U (IL)
Indiana State U (IN)
Indiana U Bloomington (IN)
Indiana U East (IN)
Indiana U Northwest (IN)
Indiana U–Purdue U Indianapolis (IN)
Indiana Wesleyan U (IN)
Inter American U of Puerto Rico, Aguadilla Campus (PR)
Inter American U of Puerto Rico, Fajardo Campus (PR)
Iona Coll (NY)
Jacksonville State U (AL)
James Madison U (VA)
Jarvis Christian Coll (TX)
Johnson C. Smith U (NC)
Judson Coll (AL)
Juniata Coll (PA)
Kansas State U (KS)
Kentucky Christian U (KY)
Kentucky State U (KY)
Keuka Coll (NY)
Kutztown U of Pennsylvania (PA)
Kuyper Coll (MI)
Lamar U (TX)
La Salle U (PA)
La Sierra U (CA)
Lebanese American U (Lebanon)
Lehman Coll of the City U of New York (NY)
Lewis-Clark State Coll (ID)
Lewis U (IL)
Limestone Coll (SC)
Lincoln Memorial U (TN)
Lincoln U (MO)
Lindenwood U (MO)
Lipscomb U (TN)
Lock Haven U of Pennsylvania (PA)
Long Island U–Brooklyn Campus (NY)
Long Island U–C. W. Post Campus (NY)
Longwood U (VA)
Louisiana Coll (LA)
Lourdes U (OH)
Loyola U Chicago (IL)
Lubbock Christian U (TX)
Luther Coll (IA)
Madonna U (MI)
Malone U (OH)

Manchester U (IN)
Mansfield U of Pennsylvania (PA)
Marian U (WI)
Marist Coll (NY)
Marshall U (WV)
Mars Hill Coll (NC)
Mary Baldwin Coll (VA)
Marywood U (PA)
McDaniel Coll (MD)
McKendree U (IL)
Mercy Coll (NY)
Mercyhurst U (PA)
Messiah Coll (PA)
Metropolitan State U of Denver (CO)
Miami U (OH)
Michigan State U (MI)
Middle Tennessee State U (TN)
Midwestern State U (TX)
Millersville U of Pennsylvania (PA)
Millikin U (IL)
Minnesota State U Mankato (MN)
Minnesota State U Moorhead (MN)
Minot State U (ND)
Misericordia U (PA)
Mississippi Coll (MS)
Mississippi State U (MS)
Mississippi Valley State U (MS)
Missouri State U (MO)
Missouri Western State U (MO)
Molloy Coll (NY)
Monmouth U (NJ)
Montclair State U (NJ)
Morehead State U (KY)
Mount Mary Coll (WI)
Mount Mercy U (IA)
Mount Saint Mary Coll (NY)
Mount St. Mary's Coll (CA)
Mount Vernon Nazarene U (OH)
Murray State U (KY)
Nazareth Coll of Rochester (NY)
New Mexico State U (NM)
New York U (NY)
Niagara U (NY)
Norfolk State U (VA)
North Carolina Central U (NC)
North Carolina State U (NC)
Northeastern Illinois U (IL)
Northern Arizona U (AZ)
Northern Michigan U (MI)
Northwestern Coll (IA)
Northwestern Oklahoma State U (OK)
Northwestern State U of Louisiana (LA)
Northwest Nazarene U (ID)
Nyack Coll (NY)
Oakland U (MI)
Oglethorpe U (GA)
Ohio Dominican U (OH)
The Ohio State U (OH)
Ohio U (OH)
Oral Roberts U (OK)
Pacific Lutheran U (WA)
Pacific Union Coll (CA)
Pacific U (OR)
Park U (MO)
Pittsburg State U (KS)
Plymouth State U (NH)
Point Loma Nazarene U (CA)
Portland State U (OR)
Post U (CT)
Presentation Coll (SD)
Providence Coll (RI)
Purdue U North Central (IN)
Radford U (VA)
Ramapo Coll of New Jersey (NJ)
Regis Coll (MA)
Rhode Island Coll (RI)
The Richard Stockton Coll of New Jersey (NJ)
Roberts Wesleyan Coll (NY)
Rockford Coll (IL)
Rutgers, The State U of New Jersey, Camden (NJ)
Rutgers, The State U of New Jersey, Newark (NJ)
Rutgers, The State U of New Jersey, New Brunswick (NJ)
Sacred Heart U (CT)
Saginaw Valley State U (MI)
St. Edward's U (TX)
Saint Leo U (FL)
Saint Louis U (MO)
Saint Martin's U (WA)
Saint Mary's Coll (IN)
St. Olaf Coll (MN)

St. Thomas U (NB, Canada)
Salem State U (MA)
Salisbury U (MD)
Salve Regina U (RI)
San Diego State U (CA)
San Francisco State U (CA)
San Jose State U (CA)
Seattle U (WA)
Seton Hill U (PA)
Shaw U (NC)
Shepherd U (WV)
Shippensburg U of Pennsylvania (PA)
Siena Coll (NY)
Siena Heights U (MI)
Skidmore Coll (NY)
Slippery Rock U of Pennsylvania (PA)
Southeastern Louisiana U (LA)
Southeastern U (FL)
Southeast Missouri State U (MO)
Southern Arkansas U–Magnolia (AR)
Southern Connecticut State U (CT)
Southern Illinois U Carbondale (IL)
Southern Illinois U Edwardsville (IL)
Southwest Baptist U (MO)
Southwestern Adventist U (TX)
Spalding U (KY)
Spring Arbor U (MI)
State U of New York at Fredonia (NY)
State U of New York at New Paltz (NY)
State U of New York at Plattsburgh (NY)
State U of New York Coll at Cortland (NY)
Stephen F. Austin State U (TX)
Stony Brook U, State U of New York (NY)
Suffolk U (MA)
Syracuse U (NY)
Tabor Coll (KS)
Tarleton State U (TX)
Taylor U (IN)
Temple U (PA)
Tennessee State U (TN)
Texas A&M U–Commerce (TX)
Texas A&M U–Kingsville (TX)
Texas Christian U (TX)
Texas Southern U (TX)
Texas State U–San Marcos (TX)
Texas Woman's U (TX)
Thomas U (GA)
Thompson Rivers U (BC, Canada)
Trevecca Nazarene U (TN)
Trinity Christian Coll (IL)
Troy U (AL)
Tuskegee U (AL)
Union Coll (KY)
Union Coll (NE)
Union U (TN)
Université de Sherbrooke (QC, Canada)
Université du Québec en Outaouais (QC, Canada)
U at Albany, State U of New York (NY)
The U of Akron (OH)
The U of Akron–Wayne Coll (OH)
The U of Alabama (AL)
The U of Alabama at Birmingham (AL)
U of Alaska Anchorage (AK)
U of Alaska Fairbanks (AK)
U of Arkansas at Little Rock (AR)
The U of British Columbia (BC, Canada)
The U of British Columbia–Okanagan (BC, Canada)
U of California, Berkeley (CA)
U of Central Florida (FL)
U of Charleston (WV)
U of Cincinnati (OH)
The U of Findlay (OH)
U of Georgia (GA)
U of Guam (GU)
U of Hawaii at Manoa (HI)
U of Houston–Clear Lake (TX)
U of Houston–Downtown (TX)
U of Illinois at Chicago (IL)
U of Illinois at Springfield (IL)
The U of Iowa (IA)
The U of Kansas (KS)
U of Kentucky (KY)

U of Louisiana at Monroe (LA)
U of Louisville (KY)
U of Maryland, Baltimore County (MD)
U of Maryland Eastern Shore (MD)
U of Memphis (TN)
U of Michigan–Flint (MI)
U of Minnesota, Twin Cities Campus (MN)
U of Mississippi (MS)
U of Missouri (MO)
U of Missouri–St. Louis (MO)
U of Montevallo (AL)
U of Nebraska at Kearney (NE)
U of Nebraska at Omaha (NE)
U of Nevada, Las Vegas (NV)
U of Nevada, Reno (NV)
U of New Hampshire (NH)
U of North Alabama (AL)
The U of North Carolina at Charlotte (NC)
The U of North Carolina at Greensboro (NC)
The U of North Carolina at Pembroke (NC)
The U of North Carolina Wilmington (NC)
U of North Dakota (ND)
U of Northern Iowa (IA)
U of North Texas (TX)
U of Oklahoma (OK)
U of Ottawa (ON, Canada)
U of Pikeville (KY)
U of Pittsburgh (PA)
U of Portland (OR)
U of Regina (SK, Canada)
U of St. Francis (IL)
U of Saint Joseph (CT)
U of St. Thomas (MN)
U of South Alabama (AL)
U of South Carolina (SC)
The U of South Dakota (SD)
U of Southern Indiana (IN)
U of Southern Maine (ME)
U of Southern Mississippi (MS)
U of South Florida (FL)
The U of Tennessee (TN)
The U of Tennessee at Chattanooga (TN)
The U of Tennessee at Martin (TN)
The U of Texas at Arlington (TX)
The U of Texas at Austin (TX)
The U of Texas at El Paso (TX)
The U of Texas of the Permian Basin (TX)
The U of Texas–Pan American (TX)
U of the Cumberlands (KY)
U of the District of Columbia (DC)
U of the Virgin Islands (VI)
The U of Toledo (OH)
U of Utah (UT)
U of Vermont (VT)
U of Washington, Tacoma (WA)
U of Waterloo (ON, Canada)
The U of Western Ontario (ON, Canada)
U of West Florida (FL)
U of Windsor (ON, Canada)
U of Wisconsin–Eau Claire (WI)
U of Wisconsin–Green Bay (WI)
U of Wisconsin–Madison (WI)
U of Wisconsin–Milwaukee (WI)
U of Wisconsin–Superior (WI)
U of Wyoming (WY)
Ursuline Coll (OH)
Utah State U (UT)
Valparaiso U (IN)
Virginia Commonwealth U (VA)
Virginia Intermont Coll (VA)
Virginia State U (VA)
Virginia Union U (VA)
Virginia Wesleyan Coll (VA)
Viterbo U (WI)
Walla Walla U (WA)
Warner Pacific Coll (OR)
Wartburg Coll (IA)
Washburn U (KS)
Wayne State U (MI)
Weber State U (UT)
West Chester U of Pennsylvania (PA)
Western Carolina U (NC)
Western Connecticut State U (CT)
Western Illinois U (IL)
Western Kentucky U (KY)
Western Michigan U (MI)
Westfield State U (MA)

West Liberty U (WV)
West Texas A&M U (TX)
West Virginia State U (WV)
West Virginia U (WV)
Wichita State U (KS)
Widener U (PA)
Wilberforce U (OH)
Winthrop U (SC)
Wright State U (OH)
Xavier U (OH)
York Coll of the City U of New York (NY)
Youngstown State U (OH)

SOCIAL WORK RELATED
Eastern Washington U (WA)
Marquette U (WI)
Tabor Coll (KS)
The U of Western Ontario (ON, Canada)

SOCIOLOGY
Abilene Christian U (TX)
Acadia U (NS, Canada)
Adelphi U (NY)
Agnes Scott Coll (GA)
Albertus Magnus Coll (CT)
Albion Coll (MI)
Albright Coll (PA)
Alcorn State U (MS)
Alfred U (NY)
Alma Coll (MI)
Alverno Coll (WI)
American Public U System (WV)
American U (DC)
The American U in Cairo (Egypt)
Amherst Coll (MA)
Anderson U (IN)
Andrews U (MI)
Angelo State U (TX)
Appalachian State U (NC)
Arizona State U (AZ)
Arkansas State U (AR)
Arkansas Tech U (AR)
Asbury U (KY)
Ashland U (OH)
Assumption Coll (MA)
Athabasca U (AB, Canada)
Athens State U (AL)
Auburn U (AL)
Auburn U at Montgomery (AL)
Augsburg Coll (MN)
Augustana Coll (IL)
Augustana Coll (SD)
Aurora U (IL)
Austin Peay State U (TN)
Averett U (VA)
Avila U (MO)
Azusa Pacific U (CA)
Baker U (KS)
Baldwin Wallace U (OH)
Ball State U (IN)
Bard Coll (NY)
Barry U (FL)
Bates Coll (ME)
Baylor U (TX)
Bellarmine U (KY)
Belmont U (TN)
Bemidji State U (MN)
Benedictine Coll (KS)
Benedictine U (IL)
Bennington Coll (VT)
Berea Coll (KY)
Bethany Lutheran Coll (MN)
Bethel Coll (IN)
Bethune-Cookman U (FL)
Binghamton U, State U of New York (NY)
Bloomfield Coll (NJ)
Bloomsburg U of Pennsylvania (PA)
Boise State U (ID)
Boston Coll (MA)
Boston U (MA)
Bowdoin Coll (ME)
Bowie State U (MD)
Bowling Green State U (OH)
Bradley U (IL)
Bridgewater Coll (VA)
Bridgewater State U (MA)
Brock U (ON, Canada)
Brown U (RI)
Bryant U (RI)
Bucknell U (PA)
Buena Vista U (IA)
Buffalo State Coll, State U of New York (NY)
Butler U (IN)

Cabrini Coll (PA)
Caldwell Coll (NJ)
California Baptist U (CA)
California Lutheran U (CA)
California Polytechnic State U, San Luis Obispo (CA)
California State Polytechnic U, Pomona (CA)
California State U, Dominguez Hills (CA)
California State U, East Bay (CA)
California State U, Fresno (CA)
California State U, Fullerton (CA)
California State U, Long Beach (CA)
California State U, Los Angeles (CA)
California State U, Northridge (CA)
California State U, San Bernardino (CA)
California State U, San Marcos (CA)
California State U, Stanislaus (CA)
Calvin Coll (MI)
Cameron U (OK)
Campbellsville U (KY)
Canisius Coll (NY)
Capital U (OH)
Cardinal Stritch U (WI)
Carleton Coll (MN)
Carlow U (PA)
Carroll Coll (MT)
Carson-Newman U (TN)
Case Western Reserve U (OH)
Castleton State Coll (VT)
Catawba Coll (NC)
The Catholic U of America (DC)
Cedarville U (OH)
Centenary Coll of Louisiana (LA)
Central Coll (IA)
Central Connecticut State U (CT)
Central Methodist U (MO)
Central Michigan U (MI)
Central State U (OH)
Centre Coll (KY)
Chapman U (CA)
Chestnut Hill Coll (PA)
Cheyney U of Pennsylvania (PA)
Chicago State U (IL)
Chowan U (NC)
Christopher Newport U (VA)
City Coll of the City U of New York (NY)
Claflin U (SC)
Clarion U of Pennsylvania (PA)
Clark Atlanta U (GA)
Clarkson U (NY)
Clark U (MA)
Clayton State U (GA)
Clemson U (SC)
Cleveland State U (OH)
Coastal Carolina U (SC)
Coe Coll (IA)
Colby Coll (ME)
Colgate U (NY)
The Coll at Brockport, State U of New York (NY)
Coll of Charleston (SC)
Coll of Mount St. Joseph (OH)
The Coll of New Jersey (NJ)
The Coll of New Rochelle (NY)
Coll of Saint Benedict (MN)
Coll of Saint Elizabeth (NJ)
The Coll of Saint Rose (NY)
Coll of the Holy Cross (MA)
Coll of the Ozarks (MO)
The Coll of William and Mary (VA)
The Coll of Wooster (OH)
The Colorado Coll (CO)
Colorado Mesa U (CO)
Colorado State U (CO)
Columbia Coll (MO)
Columbia U (NY)
Columbia U, School of General Studies (NY)
Columbus State U (GA)
Concordia Coll (MN)
Concordia Coll–New York (NY)
Concordia U (QC, Canada)
Concordia U Chicago (IL)
Concordia U, Nebraska (NE)
Concordia U, St. Paul (MN)
Concord U (WV)
Connecticut Coll (CT)
Converse Coll (SC)
Cornell Coll (IA)
Covenant Coll (GA)

Creighton U (NE)
Curry Coll (MA)
Dalhousie U (NS, Canada)
Dallas Baptist U (TX)
Dartmouth Coll (NH)
Davidson Coll (NC)
DePaul U (IL)
DePauw U (IN)
DEREE—The American Coll of Greece (Greece)
Dickinson Coll (PA)
Dillard U (LA)
Doane Coll (NE)
Dominican U (IL)
Dordt Coll (IA)
Drake U (IA)
Drew U (NJ)
Drury U (MO)
Duquesne U (PA)
Earlham Coll (IN)
East Carolina U (NC)
East Central U (OK)
Eastern Illinois U (IL)
Eastern Michigan U (MI)
Eastern New Mexico U (NM)
Eastern Washington U (WA)
East Tennessee State U (TN)
East Texas Baptist U (TX)
Eckerd Coll (FL)
Edgewood Coll (WI)
Edinboro U of Pennsylvania (PA)
Elizabeth City State U (NC)
Elmira Coll (NY)
Elon U (NC)
Emmanuel Coll (MA)
Emory & Henry Coll (VA)
Emporia State U (KS)
Evangel U (MO)
The Evergreen State Coll (WA)
Excelsior Coll (NY)
Fairfield U (CT)
Fairleigh Dickinson U, Coll at Florham (NJ)
Fairleigh Dickinson U, Metropolitan Campus (NJ)
Fairmont State U (WV)
Fayetteville State U (NC)
Ferris State U (MI)
Flagler Coll (FL)
Florida Ag and Mech U (FL)
Florida Atlantic U (FL)
Florida Gulf Coast U (FL)
Florida Intl U (FL)
Florida Southern Coll (FL)
Florida State U (FL)
Fort Lewis Coll (CO)
Framingham State U (MA)
Francis Marion U (SC)
Franklin & Marshall Coll (PA)
Franklin Coll (IN)
Franklin Pierce U (NH)
Friends U (KS)
Frostburg State U (MD)
Furman U (SC)
Gallaudet U (DC)
Gardner-Webb U (NC)
Geneva Coll (PA)
George Fox U (OR)
George Mason U (VA)
Georgetown Coll (KY)
Georgetown U (DC)
Georgia Coll & State U (GA)
Georgia Regents U (GA)
Georgia Southern U (GA)
Georgia Southwestern State U (GA)
Georgia State U (GA)
Gettysburg Coll (PA)
Gonzaga U (WA)
Gordon Coll (MA)
Goshen Coll (IN)
Goucher Coll (MD)
Grambling State U (LA)
Grand Valley State U (MI)
Greenville Coll (IL)
Grinnell Coll (IA)
Grove City Coll (PA)
Guilford Coll (NC)
Gustavus Adolphus Coll (MN)
Hamilton Coll (NY)
Hamline U (MN)
Hampshire Coll (MA)
Hampton U (VA)
Hanover Coll (IN)
Hardin-Simmons U (TX)
Hartwick Coll (NY)
Haverford Coll (PA)

Hawai'i Pacific U (HI)
Henderson State U (AR)
Hendrix Coll (AR)
High Point U (NC)
Hillsdale Coll (MI)
Hiram Coll (OH)
Hobart and William Smith Colls (NY)
Hofstra U (NY)
Hollins U (VA)
Holy Family U (PA)
Holy Names U (CA)
Hood Coll (MD)
Hope Coll (MI)
Houghton Coll (NY)
Howard Payne U (TX)
Humboldt State U (CA)
Hunter Coll of the City U of New York (NY)
Huntington U (IN)
Illinois Coll (IL)
Illinois Inst of Technology (IL)
Illinois State U (IL)
Illinois Wesleyan U (IL)
Immaculata U (PA)
Indiana U Bloomington (IN)
Indiana U East (IN)
Indiana U Kokomo (IN)
Indiana U Northwest (IN)
Indiana U of Pennsylvania (PA)
Indiana U–Purdue U Fort Wayne (IN)
Indiana U–Purdue U Indianapolis (IN)
Indiana U South Bend (IN)
Indiana U Southeast (IN)
Indiana Wesleyan U (IN)
Inter American U of Puerto Rico, Ponce Campus (PR)
Inter American U of Puerto Rico, San Germán Campus (PR)
Iona Coll (NY)
Iowa State U of Science and Technology (IA)
Iowa Wesleyan Coll (IA)
Ithaca Coll (NY)
Jacksonville State U (AL)
James Madison U (VA)
Jarvis Christian Coll (TX)
John Carroll U (OH)
The Johns Hopkins U (MD)
Johnson State Coll (VT)
Judson U (IL)
Juniata Coll (PA)
Kansas State U (KS)
Kansas Wesleyan U (KS)
Kean U (NJ)
Keene State Coll (NH)
Kennesaw State U (GA)
Kent State U (OH)
Kent State U at Ashtabula (OH)
Kent State U at Stark (OH)
Kenyon Coll (OH)
Keuka Coll (NY)
King's Coll (PA)
The King's U Coll (AB, Canada)
Knox Coll (IL)
Kutztown U of Pennsylvania (PA)
Lafayette Coll (PA)
LaGrange Coll (GA)
Lakeland Coll (WI)
Lake Superior State U (MI)
Lamar U (TX)
Lander U (SC)
Lane Coll (TN)
Langston U (OK)
La Roche Coll (PA)
La Salle U (PA)
Lasell Coll (MA)
La Sierra U (CA)
Lebanon Valley Coll (PA)
Lee U (TN)
Lehigh U (PA)
Lehman Coll of the City U of New York (NY)
Le Moyne Coll (NY)
Lewis U (IL)
Lincoln U (MO)
Lindenwood U (MO)
Linfield Coll (OR)
Lock Haven U of Pennsylvania (PA)
Long Island U–Brooklyn Campus (NY)
Long Island U–C. W. Post Campus (NY)
Longwood U (VA)
Louisiana Coll (LA)

Louisiana State U and Ag and Mech Coll (LA)
Louisiana State U in Shreveport (LA)
Lourdes U (OH)
Loyola Marymount U (CA)
Loyola U Chicago (IL)
Loyola U Maryland (MD)
Loyola U New Orleans (LA)
Luther Coll (IA)
Lynchburg Coll (VA)
Macalester Coll (MN)
Madonna U (MI)
Manchester U (IN)
Manhattan Coll (NY)
Manhattanville Coll (NY)
Mansfield U of Pennsylvania (PA)
Marquette U (WI)
Marshall U (WV)
Mars Hill Coll (NC)
Mary Baldwin Coll (VA)
Marymount Manhattan Coll (NY)
Marymount U (VA)
Maryville Coll (TN)
Maryville U of Saint Louis (MO)
Massachusetts Coll of Liberal Arts (MA)
McDaniel Coll (MD)
McKendree U (IL)
McMurry U (TX)
McNeese State U (LA)
Mercer U (GA)
Mercy Coll (NY)
Mercyhurst U (PA)
Merrimack Coll (MA)
Messiah Coll (PA)
Metropolitan State U of Denver (CO)
Miami U (OH)
Michigan State U (MI)
Middlebury Coll (VT)
Middle Tennessee State U (TN)
Midwestern State U (TX)
Millersville U of Pennsylvania (PA)
Millikin U (IL)
Mills Coll (CA)
Minnesota State U Mankato (MN)
Minnesota State U Moorhead (MN)
Minot State U (ND)
Mississippi Coll (MS)
Mississippi State U (MS)
Mississippi Valley State U (MS)
Missouri State U (MO)
Missouri Western State U (MO)
Molloy Coll (NY)
Monmouth Coll (IL)
Monmouth U (NJ)
Montana State U (MT)
Montclair State U (NJ)
Moravian Coll (PA)
Morehead State U (KY)
Morehouse Coll (GA)
Morris Coll (SC)
Mount Allison U (NB, Canada)
Mount Holyoke Coll (MA)
Mount Mercy U (IA)
Mount Saint Mary Coll (NY)
Mount St. Mary's Coll (CA)
Mount St. Mary's U (MD)
Mount Vernon Nazarene U (OH)
Muhlenberg Coll (PA)
Murray State U (KY)
National U (CA)
Nazareth Coll of Rochester (NY)
Newberry Coll (SC)
New Coll of Florida (FL)
New England Coll (NH)
New Jersey City U (NJ)
Newman U (KS)
New Mexico State U (NM)
New York Inst of Technology (NY)
New York U (NY)
Niagara U (NY)
Nicholls State U (LA)
Norfolk State U (VA)
North Carolina State U (NC)
North Carolina Wesleyan Coll (NC)
North Central Coll (IL)
North Dakota State U (ND)
Northeastern Illinois U (IL)
Northeastern U (MA)
Northern Arizona U (AZ)
Northern Illinois U (IL)
Northern Michigan U (MI)
Northern State U (SD)
Northland Coll (WI)
Northwestern Coll (IA)

Northwestern Oklahoma State U (OK)
Northwest Missouri State U (MO)
Notre Dame de Namur U (CA)
Nova Southeastern U (FL)
Nyack Coll (NY)
Oakland U (MI)
Oglethorpe U (GA)
Ohio Dominican U (OH)
The Ohio State U (OH)
Ohio U (OH)
Ohio Wesleyan U (OH)
Oklahoma Baptist U (OK)
Oklahoma City U (OK)
Oklahoma State U (OK)
Old Dominion U (VA)
Olivet Coll (MI)
Oregon State U (OR)
Ouachita Baptist U (AR)
Pacific Lutheran U (WA)
Pacific U (OR)
Paine Coll (GA)
Park U (MO)
Penn State Abington (PA)
Penn State Altoona (PA)
Penn State Beaver (PA)
Penn State Berks (PA)
Penn State Brandywine (PA)
Penn State DuBois (PA)
Penn State Erie, The Behrend Coll (PA)
Penn State Fayette, The Eberly Campus (PA)
Penn State Greater Allegheny (PA)
Penn State Harrisburg (PA)
Penn State Hazleton (PA)
Penn State Lehigh Valley (PA)
Penn State Mont Alto (PA)
Penn State New Kensington (PA)
Penn State Schuylkill (PA)
Penn State Shenango (PA)
Penn State U Park (PA)
Penn State Wilkes-Barre (PA)
Penn State Worthington Scranton (PA)
Penn State York (PA)
Pepperdine U, Malibu (CA)
Piedmont Coll (GA)
Pittsburg State U (KS)
Pitzer Coll (CA)
Plymouth State U (NH)
Point Loma Nazarene U (CA)
Pomona Coll (CA)
Portland State U (OR)
Post U (CT)
Presbyterian Coll (SC)
Prescott Coll (AZ)
Princeton U (NJ)
Principia Coll (IL)
Providence Coll (RI)
Purchase Coll, State U of New York (NY)
Purdue U (IN)
Purdue U Calumet (IN)
Queens U of Charlotte (NC)
Quinnipiac U (CT)
Radford U (VA)
Ramapo Coll of New Jersey (NJ)
Randolph Coll (VA)
Randolph-Macon Coll (VA)
Reed Coll (OR)
Regis Coll (MA)
Regis U (CO)
Rhode Island Coll (RI)
Rice U (TX)
The Richard Stockton Coll of New Jersey (NJ)
Rider U (NJ)
Ripon Coll (WI)
Rivier U (NH)
Roanoke Coll (VA)
Rockford Coll (IL)
Rocky Mountain Coll (MT)
Roger Williams U (RI)
Rollins Coll (FL)
Roosevelt U (IL)
Rosemont Coll (PA)
Rowan U (NJ)
Russell Sage Coll (NY)
Rutgers, The State U of New Jersey, Camden (NJ)
Rutgers, The State U of New Jersey, Newark (NJ)
Rutgers, The State U of New Jersey, New Brunswick (NJ)
Sacred Heart U (CT)
Saginaw Valley State U (MI)

St. Ambrose U (IA)
Saint Anselm Coll (NH)
St. Bonaventure U (NY)
St. Edward's U (TX)
St. Francis Coll (NY)
St. John Fisher Coll (NY)
Saint John's U (MN)
St. John's U (NY)
Saint Joseph's Coll (IN)
St. Joseph's Coll, Long Island Campus (NY)
St. Joseph's Coll, New York (NY)
Saint Joseph's U (PA)
St. Lawrence U (NY)
Saint Leo U (FL)
Saint Louis U (MO)
Saint Mary's Coll (IN)
Saint Mary's Coll of California (CA)
St. Mary's Coll of Maryland (MD)
St. Mary's U (TX)
Saint Mary's U of Minnesota (MN)
Saint Michael's Coll (VT)
St. Norbert Coll (WI)
St. Olaf Coll (MN)
St. Thomas U (NB, Canada)
Saint Vincent Coll (PA)
Salem State U (MA)
Salisbury U (MD)
Salve Regina U (RI)
Samford U (AL)
Sam Houston State U (TX)
San Diego State U (CA)
San Francisco State U (CA)
San Jose State U (CA)
Scripps Coll (CA)
Seattle Pacific U (WA)
Seattle U (WA)
Seton Hill U (PA)
Shawnee State U (OH)
Shaw U (NC)
Shenandoah U (VA)
Shepherd U (WV)
Shippensburg U of Pennsylvania (PA)
Siena Coll (NY)
Simmons Coll (MA)
Simon Fraser U (BC, Canada)
Simpson Coll (IA)
Skidmore Coll (NY)
Smith Coll (MA)
Sonoma State U (CA)
South Dakota State U (SD)
Southeastern Louisiana U (LA)
Southeastern Oklahoma State U (OK)
Southern Connecticut State U (CT)
Southern Illinois U Carbondale (IL)
Southern Illinois U Edwardsville (IL)
Southern Methodist U (TX)
Southern Nazarene U (OK)
Southern Oregon U (OR)
Southern Utah U (UT)
Southwest Baptist U (MO)
Southwestern U (TX)
Spelman Coll (GA)
Spring Arbor U (MI)
Spring Hill Coll (AL)
Stanford U (CA)
State U of New York at Fredonia (NY)
State U of New York at New Paltz (NY)
State U of New York at Oswego (NY)
State U of New York at Plattsburgh (NY)
State U of New York Coll at Cortland (NY)
State U of New York Coll at Geneseo (NY)
State U of New York Coll at Old Westbury (NY)
State U of New York Coll at Potsdam (NY)
State U of New York Inst of Technology (NY)
Stephen F. Austin State U (TX)
Stetson U (FL)
Stonehill Coll (MA)
Stony Brook U, State U of New York (NY)
Suffolk U (MA)
Susquehanna U (PA)
Sweet Briar Coll (VA)
Syracuse U (NY)
Tarleton State U (TX)

Taylor U (IN)
Temple U (PA)
Tennessee State U (TN)
Tennessee Wesleyan Coll (TN)
Texas A&M Intl U (TX)
Texas A&M U (TX)
Texas A&M U–Commerce (TX)
Texas A&M U–Kingsville (TX)
Texas Christian U (TX)
Texas Lutheran U (TX)
Texas Southern U (TX)
Texas State U–San Marcos (TX)
Texas Wesleyan U (TX)
Texas Woman's U (TX)
Thomas Edison State Coll (NJ)
Thomas More Coll (KY)
Thomas U (GA)
Thompson Rivers U (BC, Canada)
Transylvania U (KY)
Trent U (ON, Canada)
Trevecca Nazarene U (TN)
Trinity Christian Coll (IL)
Trinity Coll (CT)
Trinity U (TX)
Troy U (AL)
Truman State U (MO)
Tufts U (MA)
Tulane U (LA)
Tuskegee U (AL)
Union Coll (KY)
Union U (TN)
United States Military Acad (NY)
Université du Québec en Outaouais (QC, Canada)
U at Albany, State U of New York (NY)
U at Buffalo, the State U of New York (NY)
The U of Akron (OH)
The U of Alabama (AL)
The U of Alabama at Birmingham (AL)
U of Alaska Anchorage (AK)
U of Alaska Fairbanks (AK)
The U of Arizona (AZ)
U of Arkansas at Little Rock (AR)
The U of British Columbia (BC, Canada)
The U of British Columbia–Okanagan (BC, Canada)
U of California, Berkeley (CA)
U of California, Davis (CA)
U of California, Irvine (CA)
U of California, Los Angeles (CA)
U of California, Merced (CA)
U of California, Riverside (CA)
U of California, Santa Barbara (CA)
U of California, Santa Cruz (CA)
U of Central Arkansas (AR)
U of Central Florida (FL)
U of Central Oklahoma (OK)
U of Chicago (IL)
U of Cincinnati (OH)
U of Colorado Boulder (CO)
U of Colorado Colorado Springs (CO)
U of Colorado Denver (CO)
U of Delaware (DE)
U of Denver (CO)
U of Evansville (IN)
The U of Findlay (OH)
U of Florida (FL)
U of Georgia (GA)
U of Great Falls (MT)
U of Guam (GU)
U of Guelph (ON, Canada)
U of Hartford (CT)
U of Hawaii at Hilo (HI)
U of Hawaii at Manoa (HI)
U of Hawaii–West Oahu (HI)
U of Houston (TX)
U of Houston–Clear Lake (TX)
U of Houston–Downtown (TX)
U of Idaho (ID)
U of Illinois at Chicago (IL)
U of Illinois at Urbana–Champaign (IL)
The U of Iowa (IA)
The U of Kansas (KS)
U of Kentucky (KY)
U of La Verne (CA)
U of Louisiana at Lafayette (LA)
U of Louisiana at Monroe (LA)
U of Louisville (KY)
U of Maine at Farmington (ME)
U of Maryland, Baltimore County (MD)

U of Maryland, Coll Park (MD)
U of Maryland Eastern Shore (MD)
U of Mary Washington (VA)
U of Massachusetts Amherst (MA)
U of Massachusetts Boston (MA)
U of Massachusetts Dartmouth (MA)
U of Memphis (TN)
U of Miami (FL)
U of Michigan (MI)
U of Michigan–Dearborn (MI)
U of Michigan–Flint (MI)
U of Minnesota, Duluth (MN)
U of Minnesota, Twin Cities Campus (MN)
U of Mississippi (MS)
U of Missouri (MO)
U of Missouri–Kansas City (MO)
U of Missouri–St. Louis (MO)
U of Mobile (AL)
The U of Montana Western (MT)
U of Montevallo (AL)
U of Mount Union (OH)
U of Nebraska at Kearney (NE)
U of Nebraska at Omaha (NE)
U of Nebraska–Lincoln (NE)
U of Nevada, Las Vegas (NV)
U of Nevada, Reno (NV)
U of New Brunswick Fredericton (NB, Canada)
U of New Brunswick Saint John (NB, Canada)
U of New England (ME)
U of New Hampshire (NH)
U of New Mexico (NM)
U of New Orleans (LA)
U of North Alabama (AL)
U of North Carolina at Asheville (NC)
The U of North Carolina at Chapel Hill (NC)
The U of North Carolina at Greensboro (NC)
The U of North Carolina at Pembroke (NC)
The U of North Carolina Wilmington (NC)
U of North Dakota (ND)
U of Northern Colorado (CO)
U of Northern Iowa (IA)
U of North Florida (FL)
U of North Georgia (GA)
U of North Texas (TX)
U of Notre Dame (IN)
U of Oklahoma (OK)
U of Oregon (OR)
U of Ottawa (ON, Canada)
U of Pennsylvania (PA)
U of Pikeville (KY)
U of Pittsburgh (PA)
U of Pittsburgh at Bradford (PA)
U of Portland (OR)
U of Puget Sound (WA)
U of Redlands (CA)
U of Regina (SK, Canada)
U of Rhode Island (RI)
U of Richmond (VA)
U of St. Thomas (MN)
U of San Diego (CA)
U of Science and Arts of Oklahoma (OK)
The U of Scranton (PA)
U of South Alabama (AL)
U of South Carolina (SC)
U of South Carolina Aiken (SC)
U of South Carolina Upstate (SC)
The U of South Dakota (SD)
U of Southern California (CA)
U of Southern Indiana (IN)
U of Southern Maine (ME)
U of Southern Mississippi (MS)
U of South Florida (FL)
The U of Tampa (FL)
The U of Tennessee (TN)
The U of Tennessee at Martin (TN)
The U of Texas at Arlington (TX)
The U of Texas at Austin (TX)
The U of Texas at Brownsville (TX)
The U of Texas at Dallas (TX)
The U of Texas at El Paso (TX)
The U of Texas at San Antonio (TX)
The U of Texas of the Permian Basin (TX)
The U of Texas–Pan American (TX)
U of the District of Columbia (DC)
U of the Incarnate Word (TX)
U of the Ozarks (AR)

The U of Toledo (OH)
U of Tulsa (OK)
U of Utah (UT)
U of Vermont (VT)
U of Virginia (VA)
U of Waterloo (ON, Canada)
The U of West Alabama (AL)
The U of Western Ontario (ON, Canada)
U of West Florida (FL)
U of West Georgia (GA)
U of Windsor (ON, Canada)
U of Wisconsin–Eau Claire (WI)
U of Wisconsin–La Crosse (WI)
U of Wisconsin–Madison (WI)
U of Wisconsin–Milwaukee (WI)
U of Wisconsin–Parkside (WI)
U of Wisconsin–Stevens Point (WI)
U of Wisconsin–Superior (WI)
U of Wyoming (WY)
Upper Iowa U (IA)
Ursuline Coll (OH)
Utah State U (UT)
Utica Coll (NY)
Valdosta State U (GA)
Valparaiso U (IN)
Vanderbilt U (TN)
Vassar Coll (NY)
Villanova U (PA)
Virginia Commonwealth U (VA)
Virginia Polytechnic Inst and State U (VA)
Virginia State U (VA)
Virginia Wesleyan Coll (VA)
Viterbo U (WI)
Wagner Coll (NY)
Wake Forest U (NC)
Walla Walla U (WA)
Walsh U (OH)
Wartburg Coll (IA)
Washburn U (KS)
Washington & Jefferson Coll (PA)
Washington and Lee U (VA)
Washington Coll (MD)
Washington State U (WA)
Wayland Baptist U (TX)
Waynesburg U (PA)
Wayne State Coll (NE)
Wayne State U (MI)
Weber State U (UT)
Webster U (MO)
Wellesley Coll (MA)
Wells Coll (NY)
Wesleyan U (CT)
West Chester U of Pennsylvania (PA)
Western Carolina U (NC)
Western Connecticut State U (CT)
Western Illinois U (IL)
Western Kentucky U (KY)
Western Michigan U (MI)
Western Oregon U (OR)
Western State Colorado U (CO)
Western Washington U (WA)
Westfield State U (MA)
West Liberty U (WV)
Westminster Coll (MO)
Westminster Coll (UT)
West Texas A&M U (TX)
West Virginia State U (WV)
West Virginia U (WV)
West Virginia Wesleyan Coll (WV)
Wheaton Coll (IL)
Wheaton Coll (MA)
Whitman Coll (WA)
Whitworth U (WA)
Wichita State U (KS)
Widener U (PA)
Wilberforce U (OH)
Wilkes U (PA)
Willamette U (OR)
William Paterson U of New Jersey (NJ)
William Penn U (IA)
Williams Coll (MA)
Winthrop U (SC)
Wittenberg U (OH)
Worcester State U (MA)
Wright State U (OH)
Xavier U (OH)
Xavier U of Louisiana (LA)
Yale U (CT)
York Coll of Pennsylvania (PA)
York Coll of the City U of New York (NY)
Youngstown State U (OH)

SOCIOLOGY AND ANTHROPOLOGY
Albion Coll (MI)
Alma Coll (MI)
American U of Beirut (Lebanon)
Coll of Staten Island of the City U of New York (NY)
Goucher Coll (MD)
Governors State U (IL)
Millsaps Coll (MS)
Oakland U (MI)
Pace U (NY)
Rochester Inst of Technology (NY)
Swarthmore Coll (PA)
Transylvania U (KY)
U of Illinois at Springfield (IL)

SOIL CHEMISTRY AND PHYSICS
The U of Tennessee (TN)

SOIL SCIENCE AND AGRONOMY
California Polytechnic State U, San Luis Obispo (CA)
Colorado State U (CO)
Michigan State U (MI)
New Mexico State U (NM)
North Dakota State U (ND)
Oklahoma State U (OK)
Penn State Abington (PA)
Penn State Altoona (PA)
Penn State Beaver (PA)
Penn State Berks (PA)
Penn State Brandywine (PA)
Penn State DuBois (PA)
Penn State Erie, The Behrend Coll (PA)
Penn State Fayette, The Eberly Campus (PA)
Penn State Greater Allegheny (PA)
Penn State Hazleton (PA)
Penn State Lehigh Valley (PA)
Penn State Mont Alto (PA)
Penn State New Kensington (PA)
Penn State Schuylkill (PA)
Penn State Shenango (PA)
Penn State Wilkes-Barre (PA)
Penn State Worthington Scranton (PA)
Penn State York (PA)
The U of British Columbia (BC, Canada)
U of California, Davis (CA)
U of Florida (FL)
U of Georgia (GA)
U of Minnesota, Twin Cities Campus (MN)
U of Nebraska–Lincoln (NE)
U of New Hampshire (NH)
The U of Tennessee at Martin (TN)
U of Wisconsin–Madison (WI)
U of Wisconsin–Stevens Point (WI)
Utah State U (UT)
Washington State U (WA)

SOIL SCIENCES RELATED
Brigham Young U (UT)
North Carolina State U (NC)
U of Hawaii at Manoa (HI)

SOLAR ENERGY TECHNOLOGY
Appalachian State U (NC)

SOUTH ASIAN LANGUAGES
The U of British Columbia (BC, Canada)
U of Chicago (IL)
U of Minnesota, Twin Cities Campus (MN)
Yale U (CT)

SPANISH
Abilene Christian U (TX)
Adams State U (CO)
Adelphi U (NY)
Agnes Scott Coll (GA)
Albertus Magnus Coll (CT)
Albion Coll (MI)
Albright Coll (PA)
Alfred U (NY)
Alma Coll (MI)
American U (DC)
Amherst Coll (MA)
Anderson U (IN)
Anderson U (SC)
Andrews U (MI)
Angelo State U (TX)

Appalachian State U (NC)
Arizona State U (AZ)
Armstrong Atlantic State U (GA)
Asbury U (KY)
Ashland U (OH)
Assumption Coll (MA)
Auburn U (AL)
Auburn U at Montgomery (AL)
Augsburg Coll (MN)
Augustana Coll (IL)
Augustana Coll (SD)
Aurora U (IL)
Austin Peay State U (TN)
Azusa Pacific U (CA)
Baker U (KS)
Baldwin Wallace U (OH)
Ball State U (IN)
Baptist U of the Americas (TX)
Bard Coll (NY)
Barry U (FL)
Barton Coll (NC)
Bates Coll (ME)
Baylor U (TX)
Bellarmine U (KY)
Belmont U (TN)
Bemidji State U (MN)
Benedictine Coll (KS)
Benedictine U (IL)
Bennington Coll (VT)
Berea Coll (KY)
Berry Coll (GA)
Bethany Coll (WV)
Bethel Coll (IN)
Bethel U (MN)
Binghamton U, State U of New York (NY)
Blackburn Coll (IL)
Blue Mountain Coll (MS)
Bluffton U (OH)
Bob Jones U (SC)
Boise State U (ID)
Boston Coll (MA)
Boston U (MA)
Bowdoin Coll (ME)
Bowling Green State U (OH)
Bradley U (IL)
Bridgewater Coll (VA)
Bridgewater State U (MA)
Brock U (ON, Canada)
Brown U (RI)
Bryant U (RI)
Bucknell U (PA)
Buena Vista U (IA)
Buffalo State Coll, State U of New York (NY)
Butler U (IN)
Cabrini Coll (PA)
Caldwell Coll (NJ)
California Baptist U (CA)
California Lutheran U (CA)
California State Polytechnic U, Pomona (CA)
California State U, Dominguez Hills (CA)
California State U, East Bay (CA)
California State U, Fresno (CA)
California State U, Fullerton (CA)
California State U, Long Beach (CA)
California State U, Los Angeles (CA)
California State U, Monterey Bay (CA)
California State U, Northridge (CA)
California State U, San Bernardino (CA)
California State U, San Marcos (CA)
California State U, Stanislaus (CA)
Calvin Coll (MI)
Canisius Coll (NY)
Capital U (OH)
Cardinal Stritch U (WI)
Carleton Coll (MN)
Carnegie Mellon U (PA)
Carroll Coll (MT)
Carson-Newman U (TN)
Case Western Reserve U (OH)
Castleton State Coll (VT)
Catawba Coll (NC)
The Catholic U of America (DC)
Cedarville U (OH)
Central Coll (IA)
Central Connecticut State U (CT)
Central Methodist U (MO)
Central Michigan U (MI)
Centre Coll (KY)

Chapman U (CA)
Chestnut Hill Coll (PA)
Cheyney U of Pennsylvania (PA)
Chicago State U (IL)
Chowan U (NC)
Christopher Newport U (VA)
City Coll of the City U of New York (NY)
Claremont McKenna Coll (CA)
Clarion U of Pennsylvania (PA)
Clark Atlanta U (GA)
Clarke U (IA)
Clark U (MA)
Cleveland State U (OH)
Coastal Carolina U (SC)
Coe Coll (IA)
Colby Coll (ME)
Colgate U (NY)
The Coll at Brockport, State U of New York (NY)
Coll of Charleston (SC)
The Coll of Idaho (ID)
The Coll of New Jersey (NJ)
The Coll of New Rochelle (NY)
Coll of Saint Benedict (MN)
Coll of Saint Elizabeth (NJ)
The Coll of Saint Rose (NY)
The Coll of St. Scholastica (MN)
Coll of Staten Island of the City U of New York (NY)
Coll of the Holy Cross (MA)
Coll of the Ozarks (MO)
The Coll of Wooster (OH)
The Colorado Coll (CO)
Colorado Mesa U (CO)
Colorado State U (CO)
Columbia Coll (SC)
Columbia U (NY)
Columbus State U (GA)
Concordia Coll (MN)
Concordia U (QC, Canada)
Concordia U Chicago (IL)
Concordia U, Nebraska (NE)
Concordia U Wisconsin (WI)
Connecticut Coll (CT)
Converse Coll (SC)
Cornell Coll (IA)
Cornerstone U (MI)
Creighton U (NE)
Dalhousie U (NS, Canada)
Dartmouth Coll (NH)
Davidson Coll (NC)
DePaul U (IL)
DePauw U (IN)
DeSales U (PA)
Dickinson Coll (PA)
Doane Coll (NE)
Dominican Coll (NY)
Dominican U (IL)
Dordt Coll (IA)
Drew U (NJ)
Drury U (MO)
Duquesne U (PA)
Earlham Coll (IN)
East Carolina U (NC)
East Central U (OK)
Eastern Mennonite U (VA)
Eastern Michigan U (MI)
Eastern New Mexico U (NM)
Eastern Washington U (WA)
East Texas Baptist U (TX)
Eckerd Coll (FL)
Edgewood Coll (WI)
Edinboro U of Pennsylvania (PA)
Elizabethtown Coll (PA)
Elmira Coll (NY)
Elon U (NC)
Emmanuel Coll (MA)
Evangel U (MO)
Fairfield U (CT)
Fairleigh Dickinson U, Coll at Florham (NJ)
Fairleigh Dickinson U, Metropolitan Campus (NJ)
Fayetteville State U (NC)
Ferrum Coll (VA)
Flagler Coll (FL)
Florida Atlantic U (FL)
Florida Gulf Coast U (FL)
Florida Intl U (FL)
Florida Southern Coll (FL)
Fort Lewis Coll (CO)
Francis Marion U (SC)
Franklin & Marshall Coll (PA)
Franklin Coll (IN)
Friends U (KS)
Furman U (SC)

Gallaudet U (DC)
Gardner-Webb U (NC)
George Fox U (OR)
Georgetown Coll (KY)
Georgetown U (DC)
Georgia Coll & State U (GA)
Georgia State U (GA)
Gettysburg Coll (PA)
Gonzaga U (WA)
Gordon Coll (MA)
Goshen Coll (IN)
Goucher Coll (MD)
Grand Valley State U (MI)
Greenville Coll (IL)
Grinnell Coll (IA)
Grove City Coll (PA)
Guilford Coll (NC)
Gustavus Adolphus Coll (MN)
Hamline U (MN)
Hampden-Sydney Coll (VA)
Hanover Coll (IN)
Harding U (AR)
Hardin-Simmons U (TX)
Hartwick Coll (NY)
Haverford Coll (PA)
Henderson State U (AR)
Hendrix Coll (AR)
High Point U (NC)
Hillsdale Coll (MI)
Hiram Coll (OH)
Hobart and William Smith Colls (NY)
Hofstra U (NY)
Hollins U (VA)
Holy Names U (CA)
Hood Coll (MD)
Hope Coll (MI)
Houghton Coll (NY)
Howard Payne U (TX)
Humboldt State U (CA)
Hunter Coll of the City U of New York (NY)
Illinois Coll (IL)
Illinois State U (IL)
Illinois Wesleyan U (IL)
Immaculata U (PA)
Indiana U Bloomington (IN)
Indiana U Northwest (IN)
Indiana U of Pennsylvania (PA)
Indiana U–Purdue U Fort Wayne (IN)
Indiana U–Purdue U Indianapolis (IN)
Indiana U South Bend (IN)
Indiana U Southeast (IN)
Indiana Wesleyan U (IN)
Iona Coll (NY)
Iowa State U of Science and Technology (IA)
Ithaca Coll (NY)
Jacksonville State U (AL)
Jamestown Coll (ND)
John Brown U (AR)
John Carroll U (OH)
The Johns Hopkins U (MD)
Johnson C. Smith U (NC)
Judson U (AL)
Juniata Coll (PA)
Kalamazoo Coll (MI)
Kansas Wesleyan U (KS)
Kean U (NJ)
Keene State Coll (NH)
Kent State U (OH)
Kentucky State U (KY)
Kentucky Wesleyan Coll (KY)
Kenyon Coll (OH)
King Coll (TN)
King's Coll (PA)
Knox Coll (IL)
Kutztown U of Pennsylvania (PA)
Lafayette Coll (PA)
LaGrange Coll (GA)
Lake Erie Coll (OH)
Lakeland Coll (WI)
Lamar U (TX)
Lander U (SC)
La Salle U (PA)
La Sierra U (CA)
Lawrence U (WI)
Lebanon Valley Coll (PA)
Lee U (TN)
Lehigh U (PA)
Lehman Coll of the City U of New York (NY)
Le Moyne Coll (NY)
Liberty U (VA)
Lincoln U (MO)

Lindenwood U (MO)
Linfield Coll (OR)
Lipscomb U (TN)
Lock Haven U of Pennsylvania (PA)
Long Island U–C. W. Post Campus (NY)
Louisiana Coll (LA)
Louisiana State U and Ag and Mech Coll (LA)
Loyola Marymount U (CA)
Loyola U Chicago (IL)
Loyola U Maryland (MD)
Loyola U New Orleans (LA)
Luther Coll (IA)
Lynchburg Coll (VA)
Lyon Coll (AR)
Macalester Coll (MN)
Madonna U (MI)
Malone U (OH)
Manchester U (IN)
Manhattan Coll (NY)
Manhattanville Coll (NY)
Mansfield U of Pennsylvania (PA)
Marian U (WI)
Marietta Coll (OH)
Marist Coll (NY)
Marquette U (WI)
Mars Hill Coll (NC)
Mary Baldwin Coll (VA)
Maryville Coll (TN)
Marywood U (PA)
McDaniel Coll (MD)
McKendree U (IL)
McMurry U (TX)
Mercer U (GA)
Mercy Coll (NY)
Merrimack Coll (MA)
Messiah Coll (PA)
Miami U (OH)
Michigan State U (MI)
Middlebury Coll (VT)
Midwestern State U (TX)
Millersville U of Pennsylvania (PA)
Millikin U (IL)
Millsaps Coll (MS)
Mills Coll (CA)
Minnesota State U Mankato (MN)
Minnesota State U Moorhead (MN)
Minot State U (ND)
Mississippi Coll (MS)
Mississippi U for Women (MS)
Missouri State U (MO)
Missouri Western State U (MO)
Molloy Coll (NY)
Monmouth Coll (IL)
Montclair State U (NJ)
Moravian Coll (PA)
Morehead State U (KY)
Morehouse Coll (GA)
Morningside Coll (IA)
Mount Allison U (NB, Canada)
Mount Holyoke Coll (MA)
Mount Mary Coll (WI)
Mount Saint Mary Coll (NY)
Mount St. Mary's Coll (CA)
Mount St. Mary's U (MD)
Mount Vernon Nazarene U (OH)
Muhlenberg Coll (PA)
Murray State U (KY)
National U (CA)
Nazareth Coll of Rochester (NY)
Newberry Coll (SC)
New Coll of Florida (FL)
New Jersey City U (NJ)
New Mexico Highlands U (NM)
New York U (NY)
Niagara U (NY)
North Carolina Central U (NC)
North Carolina State U (NC)
North Central Coll (IL)
North Dakota State U (ND)
Northeastern Illinois U (IL)
Northeastern U (MA)
Northern Arizona U (AZ)
Northern Illinois U (IL)
Northern Michigan U (MI)
Northern State U (SD)
North Greenville U (SC)
Northwestern Coll (IA)
Northwestern U (MN)
Northwestern Oklahoma State U (OK)
Northwest Missouri State U (MO)
Northwest Nazarene U (ID)
Oakland U (MI)
Oglethorpe U (GA)
The Ohio State U (OH)

Ohio U (OH)
Ohio Wesleyan U (OH)
Oklahoma Baptist U (OK)
Oklahoma Christian U (OK)
Oklahoma City U (OK)
Oklahoma State U (OK)
Oral Roberts U (OK)
Oregon State U (OR)
Ouachita Baptist U (AR)
Pace U (NY)
Pacific Lutheran U (WA)
Pacific Union Coll (CA)
Pacific U (OR)
Park U (MO)
Penn State Abington (PA)
Penn State Altoona (PA)
Penn State Beaver (PA)
Penn State Berks (PA)
Penn State Brandywine (PA)
Penn State DuBois (PA)
Penn State Erie, The Behrend Coll (PA)
Penn State Fayette, The Eberly Campus (PA)
Penn State Greater Allegheny (PA)
Penn State Hazleton (PA)
Penn State Lehigh Valley (PA)
Penn State Mont Alto (PA)
Penn State New Kensington (PA)
Penn State Schuylkill (PA)
Penn State Shenango (PA)
Penn State U Park (PA)
Penn State Wilkes-Barre (PA)
Penn State Worthington Scranton (PA)
Penn State York (PA)
Pepperdine U, Malibu (CA)
Piedmont Coll (GA)
Pittsburg State U (KS)
Pitzer Coll (CA)
Plymouth State U (NH)
Point Loma Nazarene U (CA)
Pomona Coll (CA)
Portland State U (OR)
Presbyterian Coll (SC)
Princeton U (NJ)
Principia Coll (IL)
Providence Coll (RI)
Purchase Coll, State U of New York (NY)
Purdue U Calumet (IN)
Quinnipiac U (CT)
Ramapo Coll of New Jersey (NJ)
Randolph Coll (VA)
Randolph-Macon Coll (VA)
Reed Coll (OR)
Regis Coll (MA)
Regis U (CO)
Rhode Island Coll (RI)
Rhodes Coll (TN)
Rice U (TX)
Rider U (NJ)
Ripon Coll (WI)
Rivier U (NH)
Roanoke Coll (VA)
Roberts Wesleyan Coll (NY)
Rockford Coll (IL)
Rockhurst U (MO)
Rollins Coll (FL)
Rosemont Coll (PA)
Rowan U (NJ)
Rutgers, The State U of New Jersey, Camden (NJ)
Rutgers, The State U of New Jersey, Newark (NJ)
Rutgers, The State U of New Jersey, New Brunswick (NJ)
Sacred Heart U (CT)
Saginaw Valley State U (MI)
St. Ambrose U (IA)
Saint Anselm Coll (NH)
St. Bonaventure U (NY)
St. Edward's U (TX)
St. Francis Coll (NY)
St. John Fisher Coll (NY)
Saint John's U (MN)
St. John's U (NY)
St. Joseph's Coll, Long Island Campus (NY)
St. Joseph's Coll, New York (NY)
Saint Joseph's U (PA)
St. Lawrence U (NY)
Saint Louis U (MO)
Saint Mary's Coll (IN)
Saint Mary's Coll of California (CA)
St. Mary's U (TX)
Saint Mary's U of Minnesota (MN)

Saint Michael's Coll (VT)
St. Norbert Coll (WI)
St. Olaf Coll (MN)
St. Thomas Aquinas Coll (NY)
St. Thomas U (NB, Canada)
Saint Vincent Coll (PA)
Salem State U (MA)
Salisbury U (MD)
Salve Regina U (RI)
Samford U (AL)
Sam Houston State U (TX)
San Diego State U (CA)
San Francisco State U (CA)
San Jose State U (CA)
Scripps Coll (CA)
Seattle U (WA)
Seton Hill U (PA)
Sewanee: The U of the South (TN)
Shenandoah U (VA)
Shepherd U (WV)
Shippensburg U of Pennsylvania (PA)
Siena Coll (NY)
Siena Heights U (MI)
Simmons Coll (MA)
Simpson Coll (IA)
Skidmore Coll (NY)
Slippery Rock U of Pennsylvania (PA)
Smith Coll (MA)
Sonoma State U (CA)
South Dakota State U (SD)
Southeastern Louisiana U (LA)
Southeastern Oklahoma State U (OK)
Southern Arkansas U–Magnolia (AR)
Southern Connecticut State U (CT)
Southern Illinois U Carbondale (IL)
Southern Methodist U (TX)
Southern Nazarene U (OK)
Southern Oregon U (OR)
Southern Utah U (UT)
Southwest Baptist U (MO)
Southwestern U (TX)
Spelman Coll (GA)
Spring Arbor U (MI)
Spring Hill Coll (AL)
Stanford U (CA)
State U of New York at Fredonia (NY)
State U of New York at New Paltz (NY)
State U of New York at Oswego (NY)
State U of New York at Plattsburgh (NY)
State U of New York Coll at Cortland (NY)
State U of New York Coll at Geneseo (NY)
State U of New York Coll at Old Westbury (NY)
State U of New York Coll at Potsdam (NY)
Stetson U (FL)
Stonehill Coll (MA)
Stony Brook U, State U of New York (NY)
Suffolk U (MA)
Sul Ross State U (TX)
Susquehanna U (PA)
Swarthmore Coll (PA)
Sweet Briar Coll (VA)
Syracuse U (NY)
Tarleton State U (TX)
Taylor U (IN)
Temple U (PA)
Tennessee State U (TN)
Tennessee Wesleyan Coll (TN)
Texas A&M Intl U (TX)
Texas A&M U (TX)
Texas A&M U–Commerce (TX)
Texas A&M U–Kingsville (TX)
Texas Christian U (TX)
Texas Lutheran U (TX)
Texas Southern U (TX)
Texas State U–San Marcos (TX)
Texas Wesleyan U (TX)
Thomas More Coll (KY)
Transylvania U (KY)
Trinity Christian Coll (IL)
Trinity Coll (CT)
Trinity (TX)
Truman State U (MO)
Tufts U (MA)
Tulane U (LA)

Union Coll (NE)
Union U (TN)
United States Military Acad (NY)
Universidad Adventista de las Antillas (PR)
U at Albany, State U of New York (NY)
U at Buffalo, the State U of New York (NY)
The U of Akron (OH)
The U of Alabama (AL)
U of Alaska Anchorage (AK)
The U of Arizona (AZ)
U of Arkansas at Little Rock (AR)
U of Arkansas–Fort Smith (AR)
The U of British Columbia (BC, Canada)
The U of British Columbia–Okanagan (BC, Canada)
U of California, Berkeley (CA)
U of California, Davis (CA)
U of California, Irvine (CA)
U of California, Los Angeles (CA)
U of California, Riverside (CA)
U of California, Santa Barbara (CA)
U of Central Arkansas (AR)
U of Central Florida (FL)
U of Central Oklahoma (OK)
U of Cincinnati (OH)
U of Colorado Boulder (CO)
U of Colorado Colorado Springs (CO)
U of Colorado Denver (CO)
U of Dallas (TX)
U of Delaware (DE)
U of Denver (CO)
U of Evansville (IN)
The U of Findlay (OH)
U of Florida (FL)
U of Georgia (GA)
U of Guelph (ON, Canada)
U of Hawaii at Manoa (HI)
U of Houston (TX)
U of Houston–Downtown (TX)
U of Idaho (ID)
U of Illinois at Chicago (IL)
U of Illinois at Urbana–Champaign (IL)
The U of Iowa (IA)
The U of Kansas (KS)
U of Kentucky (KY)
U of La Verne (CA)
U of Louisville (KY)
U of Maryland, Coll Park (MD)
U of Massachusetts Amherst (MA)
U of Massachusetts Boston (MA)
U of Massachusetts Dartmouth (MA)
U of Miami (FL)
U of Michigan (MI)
U of Michigan–Dearborn (MI)
U of Michigan–Flint (MI)
U of Minnesota, Duluth (MN)
U of Minnesota, Twin Cities Campus (MN)
U of Mississippi (MS)
U of Missouri (MO)
U of Missouri–Kansas City (MO)
U of Missouri–St. Louis (MO)
U of Mount Union (OH)
U of Nebraska at Kearney (NE)
U of Nebraska–Lincoln (NE)
U of Nevada, Las Vegas (NV)
U of Nevada, Reno (NV)
U of New Brunswick Fredericton (NB, Canada)
U of New Brunswick Saint John (NB, Canada)
U of New Hampshire (NH)
U of New Mexico (NM)
U of North Carolina at Asheville (NC)
The U of North Carolina at Charlotte (NC)
The U of North Carolina at Greensboro (NC)
The U of North Carolina at Pembroke (NC)
The U of North Carolina Wilmington (NC)
U of North Dakota (ND)
U of Northern Colorado (CO)
U of Northern Iowa (IA)
U of North Florida (FL)
U of North Georgia (GA)
U of North Texas (TX)
U of Notre Dame (IN)

U of Oklahoma (OK)
U of Oregon (OR)
U of Ottawa (ON, Canada)
U of Pennsylvania (PA)
U of Pittsburgh (PA)
U of Pittsburgh at Greensburg (PA)
U of Portland (OR)
U of Puget Sound (WA)
U of Redlands (CA)
U of Regina (SK, Canada)
U of Rhode Island (RI)
U of Richmond (VA)
U of Rochester (NY)
U of Saint Joseph (CT)
U of St. Thomas (MN)
U of St. Thomas (TX)
U of San Diego (CA)
The U of Scranton (PA)
U of South Carolina (SC)
U of South Carolina Upstate (SC)
The U of South Dakota (SD)
U of Southern California (CA)
U of Southern Indiana (IN)
U of South Florida (FL)
The U of Tampa (FL)
The U of Tennessee (TN)
The U of Tennessee at Martin (TN)
The U of Texas at Arlington (TX)
The U of Texas at Austin (TX)
The U of Texas at Brownsville (TX)
The U of Texas at El Paso (TX)
The U of Texas at San Antonio (TX)
The U of Texas of the Permian Basin (TX)
The U of Texas–Pan American (TX)
U of the Cumberlands (KY)
U of the District of Columbia (DC)
U of the Incarnate Word (TX)
U of the Ozarks (AR)
The U of Toledo (OH)
U of Tulsa (OK)
U of Utah (UT)
U of Vermont (VT)
U of Virginia (VA)
U of Waterloo (ON, Canada)
The U of Western Ontario (ON, Canada)
U of West Florida (FL)
U of Windsor (ON, Canada)
U of Wisconsin–Eau Claire (WI)
U of Wisconsin–Green Bay (WI)
U of Wisconsin–La Crosse (WI)
U of Wisconsin–Madison (WI)
U of Wisconsin–Milwaukee (WI)
U of Wisconsin–Parkside (WI)
U of Wisconsin–Platteville (WI)
U of Wisconsin–Stevens Point (WI)
U of Wyoming (WY)
Utah State U (UT)
Valdosta State U (GA)
Valley City State U (ND)
Valparaiso U (IN)
Vanderbilt U (TN)
Vassar Coll (NY)
Villanova U (PA)
Virginia Polytechnic Inst and State U (VA)
Virginia Wesleyan Coll (VA)
Viterbo U (WI)
Wabash Coll (IN)
Wagner Coll (NY)
Wake Forest U (NC)
Walla Walla U (WA)
Walsh U (OH)
Wartburg Coll (IA)
Washburn U (KS)
Washington & Jefferson Coll (PA)
Washington and Lee U (VA)
Washington Coll (MD)
Washington State U (WA)
Washington U in St. Louis (MO)
Wayland Baptist U (TX)
Wayne State Coll (NE)
Weber State U (UT)
Webster U (MO)
Wellesley Coll (MA)
Wells Coll (NY)
Wesleyan Coll (GA)
Wesleyan U (CT)
West Chester U of Pennsylvania (PA)
Western Carolina U (NC)
Western Connecticut State U (CT)
Western Illinois U (IL)
Western Kentucky U (KY)
Western Michigan U (MI)
Western Oregon U (OR)

Western State Colorado U (CO)
Western Washington U (WA)
Westfield State U (MA)
Westminster Coll (MO)
West Texas A&M U (TX)
Wheaton Coll (IL)
Wheeling Jesuit U (WV)
Whitman Coll (WA)
Whitworth U (WA)
Widener U (PA)
Wilkes U (PA)
Willamette U (OR)
William Jewell Coll (MO)
William Paterson U of New Jersey (NJ)
Williams Coll (MA)
Wittenberg U (OH)
Worcester State U (MA)
Wright State U (OH)
Xavier U (OH)
Xavier U of Louisiana (LA)
Yale U (CT)
York Coll of Pennsylvania (PA)
York Coll of the City U of New York (NY)
Young Harris Coll (GA)
Youngstown State U (OH)

SPANISH AND IBERIAN STUDIES
Bard Coll (NY)
Coe Coll (IA)
The U of Western Ontario (ON, Canada)

SPANISH LANGUAGE TEACHER EDUCATION
Abilene Christian U (TX)
Adams State U (CO)
Albion Coll (MI)
Alma Coll (MI)
Anderson U (IN)
Appalachian State U (NC)
Ashland U (OH)
Assumption Coll (MA)
Auburn U (AL)
Augustana Coll (IL)
Baylor U (TX)
Bethel Coll (IN)
Bethel U (MN)
Blue Mountain Coll (MS)
Bob Jones U (SC)
Boise State U (ID)
Buena Vista U (IA)
California Lutheran U (CA)
Calvin Coll (MI)
Canisius Coll (NY)
Carroll Coll (MT)
The Catholic U of America (DC)
Cedarville U (OH)
Central Michigan U (MI)
The Coll at Brockport, State U of New York (NY)
Coll of Saint Mary (NE)
The Coll of Saint Rose (NY)
Colorado State U (CO)
Concordia Coll (MN)
Concordia U, Nebraska (NE)
Concordia U Wisconsin (WI)
Dordt Coll (IA)
Duquesne U (PA)
East Carolina U (NC)
Eastern Michigan U (MI)
Eastern Washington U (WA)
East Texas Baptist U (TX)
Edgewood Coll (WI)
Elmira Coll (NY)
Evangel U (MO)
Fayetteville State U (NC)
Franklin Coll (IN)
Friends U (KS)
Gardner-Webb U (NC)
Georgia Southern U (GA)
Grand Valley State U (MI)
Greenville Coll (IL)
Harding U (AR)
Hardin-Simmons U (TX)
Hofstra U (NY)
Holy Family U (PA)
Hope Coll (MI)
Howard Payne U (TX)
Indiana U Bloomington (IN)
Indiana U Northwest (IN)
Indiana U–Purdue U Fort Wayne (IN)
Indiana U–Purdue U Indianapolis (IN)
Indiana U South Bend (IN)

Indiana Wesleyan U (IN)
Inter American U of Puerto Rico, Aguadilla Campus (PR)
Inter American U of Puerto Rico, Fajardo Campus (PR)
Inter American U of Puerto Rico, San Germán Campus (PR)
Iona Coll (NY)
Ithaca Coll (NY)
Juniata Coll (PA)
Keene State Coll (NH)
Kentucky Wesleyan Coll (KY)
King Coll (TN)
Lee U (TN)
Le Moyne Coll (NY)
Lindenwood U (MO)
Lipscomb U (TN)
Long Island U–Brooklyn Campus (NY)
Long Island U–C. W. Post Campus (NY)
Lubbock Christian U (TX)
Malone U (OH)
Manchester U (IN)
Manhattanville Coll (NY)
Mansfield U of Pennsylvania (PA)
Marian U (WI)
Marist Coll (NY)
Maryville Coll (TN)
Marywood U (PA)
McMurry U (TX)
Messiah Coll (PA)
Miami U (OH)
Michigan State U (MI)
Minnesota State U Moorhead (MN)
Minot State U (ND)
Missouri Western State U (MO)
Molloy Coll (NY)
Moravian Coll (PA)
Morningside Coll (IA)
Mount Mary Coll (WI)
Mount Vernon Nazarene U (OH)
Niagara U (NY)
North Carolina Central U (NC)
North Carolina State U (NC)
North Dakota State U (ND)
Northern Michigan U (MI)
Northwest Missouri State U (MO)
Northwest Nazarene U (ID)
Ohio U (OH)
Ohio Wesleyan U (OH)
Oklahoma Baptist U (OK)
Oral Roberts U (OK)
Pace U (NY)
Pittsburg State U (KS)
Rhode Island Coll (RI)
Roberts Wesleyan Coll (NY)
Saginaw Valley State U (MI)
St. Ambrose U (IA)
St. Edward's U (TX)
St. John Fisher Coll (NY)
St. John's U (NY)
St. Joseph's Coll, Long Island Campus (NY)
St. Joseph's Coll, New York (NY)
Saint Mary's U of Minnesota (MN)
Salem State U (MA)
Salve Regina U (RI)
Southeastern Oklahoma State U (OK)
Southern Utah U (UT)
State U of New York at New Paltz (NY)
State U of New York at Plattsburgh (NY)
State U of New York Coll at Cortland (NY)
State U of New York Coll at Old Westbury (NY)
Stony Brook U, State U of New York (NY)
Taylor U (IN)
Texas A&M Intl U (TX)
Trinity Christian Coll (IL)
The U of Akron (OH)
U of Arkansas–Fort Smith (AR)
U of Delaware (DE)
U of Evansville (IN)
U of Illinois at Chicago (IL)
U of Illinois at Urbana–Champaign (IL)
The U of Iowa (IA)
U of Michigan–Flint (MI)
U of Minnesota, Duluth (MN)
U of Missouri–St. Louis (MO)
U of Nebraska–Lincoln (NE)

The U of North Carolina at Greensboro (NC)
The U of North Carolina Wilmington (NC)
The U of South Dakota (SD)
The U of Tennessee at Martin (TN)
U of the Cumberlands (KY)
The U of Toledo (OH)
Valley City State U (ND)
Valparaiso U (IN)
Viterbo U (WI)
Washburn U (KS)
Washington State U (WA)
Washington U in St. Louis (MO)
Weber State U (UT)
Western Carolina U (NC)
Western Michigan U (MI)
Western State Colorado U (CO)
Western Washington U (WA)
Wheeling Jesuit U (WV)
Widener U (PA)
William Jewell Coll (MO)
Xavier U of Louisiana (LA)
York Coll of Pennsylvania (PA)
Youngstown State U (OH)

SPECIAL EDUCATION
Abilene Christian U (TX)
Adams State U (CO)
Alabama State U (AL)
American U of Puerto Rico (PR)
Anderson U (SC)
Arizona State U (AZ)
Armstrong Atlantic State U (GA)
Asbury U (KY)
Ashland U (OH)
Athens State U (AL)
Auburn U (AL)
Augustana Coll (SD)
Aurora U (IL)
Austin Peay State U (TN)
Avila U (MO)
Barry U (FL)
Barton Coll (NC)
Baylor U (TX)
Bellarmine U (KY)
Benedictine Coll (KS)
Benedictine U (IL)
Bloomsburg U of Pennsylvania (PA)
Bluffton U (OH)
Boise State U (ID)
Boston U (MA)
Bowie State U (MD)
Bowling Green State U (OH)
Bridgewater State U (MA)
Brigham Young U (UT)
Buena Vista U (IA)
Buffalo State Coll, State U of New York (NY)
Cabrini Coll (PA)
Calvin Coll (MI)
Capital U (OH)
Cardinal Stritch U (WI)
Caribbean U (PR)
Carson-Newman U (TN)
Castleton State Coll (VT)
Cedarville U (OH)
Central State U (OH)
Cheyney U of Pennsylvania (PA)
Christian Brothers U (TN)
City U of Seattle (WA)
Clarion U of Pennsylvania (PA)
Clemson U (SC)
Cleveland State U (OH)
Coastal Carolina U (SC)
Coll of Charleston (SC)
Coll of Mount St. Joseph (OH)
The Coll of New Jersey (NJ)
The Coll of New Rochelle (NY)
The Coll of Saint Rose (NY)
Columbia Coll (SC)
Columbus State U (GA)
Concordia U Chicago (IL)
Concordia U, Nebraska (NE)
Concord U (WV)
Converse Coll (SC)
Curry Coll (MA)
Dakota Wesleyan U (SD)
DePaul U (IL)
Doane Coll (NE)
Dominican Coll (NY)
East Carolina U (NC)
East Central U (OK)
Eastern Illinois U (IL)
Eastern New Mexico U (NM)
Eastern Washington U (WA)
East Tennessee State U (TN)

Edinboro U of Pennsylvania (PA)
Elizabeth City State U (NC)
Elon U (NC)
Evangel U (MO)
Fairmont State U (WV)
Felician Coll (NJ)
Florida Atlantic U (FL)
Florida Gulf Coast U (FL)
Florida Intl U (FL)
Furman U (SC)
Gannon U (PA)
Geneva Coll (PA)
Georgia Coll & State U (GA)
Georgia Gwinnett Coll (GA)
Georgia Regents U (GA)
Georgia Southern U (GA)
Georgia Southwestern State U (GA)
Gonzaga U (WA)
Gordon Coll (MA)
Goshen Coll (IN)
Goucher Coll (MD)
Grand Valley State U (MI)
Greenville Coll (IL)
Grove City Coll (PA)
Hampton U (VA)
High Point U (NC)
Holy Family U (PA)
Houghton Coll (NY)
Huntington U (IN)
Illinois State U (IL)
Indiana State U (IN)
Indiana U Bloomington (IN)
Indiana U of Pennsylvania (PA)
Indiana U South Bend (IN)
Indiana U Southeast (IN)
Indiana Wesleyan U (IN)
Indian River State Coll (FL)
Inter American U of Puerto Rico, Fajardo Campus (PR)
Inter American U of Puerto Rico, Ponce Campus (PR)
Inter American U of Puerto Rico, San Germán Campus (PR)
Jacksonville State U (AL)
John Brown U (AR)
John Carroll U (OH)
Kansas Wesleyan U (KS)
Kean U (NJ)
Kent State U (OH)
Keuka Coll (NY)
Kutztown U of Pennsylvania (PA)
Lake Erie Coll (OH)
Lamar U (TX)
Lander U (SC)
Langston U (OK)
La Salle U (PA)
Lebanon Valley Coll (PA)
Lee U (TN)
Le Moyne Coll (NY)
Lesley U (MA)
Lewis U (IL)
Lindenwood U (MO)
Lock Haven U of Pennsylvania (PA)
Louisiana Coll (LA)
Loyola U Chicago (IL)
Loyola U Maryland (MD)
Lubbock Christian U (TX)
Manchester U (IN)
Manhattan Coll (NY)
Mansfield U of Pennsylvania (PA)
Mars Hill Coll (NC)
Marymount U (VA)
Marywood U (PA)
Medaille Coll (NY)
Mercyhurst U (PA)
Merrimack Coll (MA)
Metropolitan State U of Denver (CO)
Miami Dade Coll (FL)
Miami U (OH)
Michigan State U (MI)
Middle Tennessee State U (TN)
Midwestern State U (TX)
Millersville U of Pennsylvania (PA)
Minnesota State U Moorhead (MN)
Mississippi State U (MS)
Missouri State U (MO)
Monmouth U (NJ)
Morehead State U (KY)
Morningside Coll (IA)
Mount Marty Coll (SD)
Mount Vernon Nazarene U (OH)
Murray State U (KY)
Nazareth Coll of Rochester (NY)
New England Coll (NH)
New Jersey City U (NJ)

New Mexico Highlands U (NM)
New Mexico State U (NM)
Niagara U (NY)
Northeastern Illinois U (IL)
Northern Arizona U (AZ)
Northern Michigan U (MI)
Northern State U (SD)
Northwestern Oklahoma State U (OK)
Nova Southeastern U (FL)
Ohio Dominican U (OH)
The Ohio State U (OH)
Ohio U (OH)
Oklahoma Baptist U (OK)
Oklahoma City U (OK)
Oral Roberts U (OK)
Pace U (NY)
Penn State Abington (PA)
Penn State Altoona (PA)
Penn State Beaver (PA)
Penn State Berks (PA)
Penn State Brandywine (PA)
Penn State DuBois (PA)
Penn State Erie, The Behrend Coll (PA)
Penn State Fayette, The Eberly Campus (PA)
Penn State Greater Allegheny (PA)
Penn State Hazleton (PA)
Penn State Lehigh Valley (PA)
Penn State Mont Alto (PA)
Penn State New Kensington (PA)
Penn State Schuylkill (PA)
Penn State Shenango (PA)
Penn State U Park (PA)
Penn State Wilkes-Barre (PA)
Penn State Worthington Scranton (PA)
Penn State York (PA)
Piedmont Coll (GA)
Providence Coll (RI)
Quincy U (IL)
Rhode Island Coll (RI)
Rivier U (NH)
Roberts Wesleyan Coll (NY)
Rockford Coll (IL)
Roosevelt U (IL)
Rowan U (NJ)
Saginaw Valley State U (MI)
St. Bonaventure U (NY)
St. Edward's U (TX)
St. John Fisher Coll (NY)
St. John's U (NY)
St. Joseph's Coll, Long Island Campus (NY)
St. Joseph's Coll, New York (NY)
Saint Joseph's U (PA)
Saint Louis U (MO)
Saint Martin's U (WA)
Saint Mary-of-the-Woods Coll (IN)
St. Thomas Aquinas Coll (NY)
Salve Regina U (RI)
Seattle Pacific U (WA)
Shawnee State U (OH)
Slippery Rock U of Pennsylvania (PA)
Southeastern U (FL)
Southeast Missouri State U (MO)
Southern Connecticut State U (CT)
Southern Illinois U Carbondale (IL)
Southern Illinois U Edwardsville (IL)
Spalding U (KY)
Spring Arbor U (MI)
State U of New York at New Paltz (NY)
State U of New York at Plattsburgh (NY)
State U of New York Coll at Geneseo (NY)
State U of New York Coll at Old Westbury (NY)
Tabor Coll (KS)
Tennessee State U (TN)
Texas A&M Intl U (TX)
Texas A&M U–Commerce (TX)
Texas Christian U (TX)
Trevecca Nazarene U (TN)
Trinity Christian Coll (IL)
Union Coll (KY)
Union U (TN)
Université de Sherbrooke (QC, Canada)
Université du Québec en Outaouais (QC, Canada)
The U of Akron (OH)
The U of Alabama (AL)

The U of Arizona (AZ)
The U of British Columbia (BC, Canada)
U of Central Florida (FL)
U of Central Oklahoma (OK)
U of Cincinnati (OH)
U of Evansville (IN)
The U of Findlay (OH)
U of Florida (FL)
U of Georgia (GA)
U of Great Falls (MT)
U of Guam (GU)
U of Idaho (ID)
U of Illinois at Urbana–Champaign (IL)
U of Kentucky (KY)
U of Maine at Farmington (ME)
U of Maryland, Coll Park (MD)
U of Maryland Eastern Shore (MD)
U of Memphis (TN)
U of Mississippi (MS)
U of Missouri–St. Louis (MO)
U of Mount Union (OH)
U of Nebraska at Kearney (NE)
U of Nebraska at Omaha (NE)
U of Nevada, Las Vegas (NV)
U of Nevada, Reno (NV)
U of New Brunswick Fredericton (NB, Canada)
U of New Mexico (NM)
The U of North Carolina at Charlotte (NC)
The U of North Carolina at Greensboro (NC)
The U of North Carolina at Pembroke (NC)
The U of North Carolina Wilmington (NC)
U of Northern Colorado (CO)
U of Northern Iowa (IA)
U of North Florida (FL)
U of North Georgia (GA)
U of Oklahoma (OK)
U of St. Francis (IL)
U of Saint Joseph (CT)
U of South Alabama (AL)
U of South Carolina Aiken (SC)
The U of South Dakota (SD)
U of Southern Mississippi (MS)
U of South Florida (FL)
The U of Tennessee (TN)
The U of Tennessee at Chattanooga (TN)
The U of Tennessee at Martin (TN)
U of the Cumberlands (KY)
U of the District of Columbia (DC)
The U of Toledo (OH)
U of Utah (UT)
The U of West Alabama (AL)
U of West Florida (FL)
U of West Georgia (GA)
U of Windsor (ON, Canada)
U of Wisconsin–Eau Claire (WI)
U of Wisconsin–Madison (WI)
U of Wisconsin–Milwaukee (WI)
U of Wisconsin–Stevens Point (WI)
U of Wisconsin–Stout (WI)
U of Wisconsin–Superior (WI)
U of Wyoming (WY)
Ursuline Coll (OH)
Utah State U (UT)
Valdosta State U (GA)
Vanderbilt U (TN)
Vincennes U (IN)
Virginia Union U (VA)
Virginia Wesleyan Coll (VA)
Walsh U (OH)
Washington State U (WA)
Waynesburg U (PA)
Wayne State Coll (NE)
Wayne State U (MI)
Weber State U (UT)
Webster U (MO)
West Chester U of Pennsylvania (PA)
Western Carolina U (NC)
Western Illinois U (IL)
Western Kentucky U (KY)
Western Washington U (WA)
Westfield State U (MA)
Westminster Coll (UT)
West Virginia Wesleyan Coll (WV)
Whitworth U (WA)
Widener U (PA)
William Paterson U of New Jersey (NJ)
William Penn U (IA)

Winthrop U (SC)
Xavier U (OH)
Youngstown State U (OH)

SPECIAL EDUCATION–EARLY CHILDHOOD
California Baptist U (CA)
Canisius Coll (NY)
Clarion U of Pennsylvania (PA)
Daytona State Coll (FL)
Eastern Washington U (WA)
Edgewood Coll (WI)
Harding U (AR)
Indiana U of Pennsylvania (PA)
Inter American U of Puerto Rico, Aguadilla Campus (PR)
Inter American U of Puerto Rico, Ponce Campus (PR)
Judson U (IL)
Juniata Coll (PA)
Keuka Coll (NY)
Lindenwood U (MO)
Roberts Wesleyan Coll (NY)
State U of New York Coll at Geneseo (NY)
Syracuse U (NY)
U of Illinois at Urbana–Champaign (IL)
U of Vermont (VT)
York Coll of Pennsylvania (PA)

SPECIAL EDUCATION–ELEMENTARY SCHOOL
Alvernia U (PA)
Canisius Coll (NY)
Granite State Coll (NH)
Shawnee State U (OH)
Syracuse U (NY)
U of Wyoming (WY)
Virginia Intermont Coll (VA)

SPECIAL EDUCATION–GIFTED AND TALENTED
Canisius Coll (NY)
Flagler Coll (FL)
Grand Valley State U (MI)
U of Great Falls (MT)
Wright State U (OH)

SPECIAL EDUCATION–INDIVIDUALS WHO ARE DEVELOPMENTALLY DELAYED
Saint Mary-of-the-Woods Coll (IN)

SPECIAL EDUCATION–INDIVIDUALS WITH AUTISM
Inter American U of Puerto Rico, Ponce Campus (PR)

SPECIAL EDUCATION–INDIVIDUALS WITH EMOTIONAL DISTURBANCES
Augsburg Coll (MN)
Eastern Michigan U (MI)
Grand Valley State U (MI)
Hope Coll (MI)
Morningside Coll (IA)
Northern Michigan U (MI)
Olivet Coll (MI)
U of Maine at Farmington (ME)
U of South Florida (FL)
The U of Toledo (OH)
Western Michigan U (MI)

SPECIAL EDUCATION–INDIVIDUALS WITH HEARING IMPAIRMENTS
Augustana Coll (SD)
Barton Coll (NC)
Boston U (MA)
Bowling Green State U (OH)
Canisius Coll (NY)
The Coll of New Jersey (NJ)
Converse Coll (SC)
Eastern Michigan U (MI)
Flagler Coll (FL)
Grand Valley State U (MI)
Indiana U of Pennsylvania (PA)
Judson U (IL)
Michigan State U (MI)
Minot State U (ND)
Texas Christian U (TX)
U of Nebraska–Lincoln (NE)
The U of North Carolina at Greensboro (NC)
U of Science and Arts of Oklahoma (OK)
U of Southern Mississippi (MS)

The U of Toledo (OH)
U of Tulsa (OK)

**SPECIAL EDUCATION–
INDIVIDUALS WITH
INTELLECTUAL DISABILITIES**
Bowling Green State U (OH)
Eastern Michigan U (MI)
Grand Valley State U (MI)
Manchester U (IN)
Minot State U (ND)
Morningside Coll (IA)
Northern Michigan U (MI)
Oakland City U (IN)
Prescott Coll (AZ)
U of Maine at Farmington (ME)
U of South Florida (FL)
Valdosta State U (GA)
Walsh U (OH)
Western Michigan U (MI)

**SPECIAL EDUCATION–
INDIVIDUALS WITH
MULTIPLE DISABILITIES**
Ball State U (IN)
Bowling Green State U (OH)
Bradley U (IL)
Dominican Coll (NY)
Grand Valley State U (MI)
Northwest Missouri State U (MO)
U of Illinois at Urbana–Champaign
(IL)
The U of North Carolina
Wilmington (NC)
The U of Toledo (OH)
Walsh U (OH)
Wright State U (OH)

**SPECIAL EDUCATION–
INDIVIDUALS WITH
ORTHOPEDIC AND OTHER
PHYSICAL HEALTH
IMPAIRMENTS**
Eastern Michigan U (MI)
Grand Valley State U (MI)
U of Puerto Rico at Bayamón (PR)

**SPECIAL EDUCATION–
INDIVIDUALS WITH SPECIFIC
LEARNING DISABILITIES**
Appalachian State U (NC)
Baldwin Wallace U (OH)
Bethune-Cookman U (FL)
Bowling Green State U (OH)
Bradley U (IL)
Calvin Coll (MI)
Canisius Coll (NY)
Flagler Coll (FL)
Hope Coll (MI)
Judson U (IL)
Malone U (OH)
Michigan State U (MI)
Northern Michigan U (MI)
Prescott Coll (AZ)
State U of New York at New Paltz
(NY)
U of Maine at Farmington (ME)
U of South Carolina Upstate (SC)
U of South Florida (FL)
The U of Toledo (OH)
West Virginia Wesleyan Coll (WV)
Wheeling Jesuit U (WV)
Wright State U (OH)

**SPECIAL EDUCATION–
INDIVIDUALS WITH SPEECH/
LANGUAGE IMPAIRMENTS**
Baylor U (TX)
Buffalo State Coll, State U of New
York (NY)
Eastern Michigan U (MI)
Emerson Coll (MA)
Ithaca Coll (NY)
Long Island U–Brooklyn Campus
(NY)
Minot State U (ND)
New Mexico State U (NM)
Pace U (NY)
State U of New York Coll at
Cortland (NY)
U of Nebraska at Omaha (NE)
The U of Toledo (OH)
Wayne State U (MI)

**SPECIAL EDUCATION–
INDIVIDUALS WITH VISION
IMPAIRMENTS**
Eastern Michigan U (MI)
Kutztown U of Pennsylvania (PA)
St. Francis Coll (NY)
The U of Toledo (OH)

**SPECIAL EDUCATION–JUNIOR
HIGH/MIDDLE SCHOOL**
Clarion U of Pennsylvania (PA)
Virginia Intermont Coll (VA)

**SPECIAL EDUCATION
RELATED**
Auburn U (AL)
Bowling Green State U (OH)
Canisius Coll (NY)
Dakota State U (SD)
East Carolina U (NC)
Hood Coll (MD)
Inter American U of Puerto Rico,
San Germán Campus (PR)
Juniata Coll (PA)
Kean U (NJ)
Keene State Coll (NH)
Lee U (TN)
Lincoln U (MO)
Lock Haven U of Pennsylvania (PA)
Minot State U (ND)
Saint Mary-of-the-Woods Coll (IN)
Southeastern Oklahoma State U
(OK)
Southern New Hampshire U (NH)
U of Hartford (CT)
U of Missouri (MO)
U of Nebraska–Lincoln (NE)
The U of North Carolina at
Charlotte (NC)
U of Southern Indiana (IN)
The U of Toledo (OH)
Wright State U (OH)

**SPECIAL EDUCATION–
SECONDARY SCHOOL**
Canisius Coll (NY)
Oklahoma City U (OK)
Virginia Intermont Coll (VA)

**SPECIAL PRODUCTS
MARKETING**
Buffalo State Coll, State U of New
York (NY)
Concord U (WV)
Dominican U (IL)
Fashion Inst of Technology (NY)
Iowa State U of Science and
Technology (IA)
Rochester Inst of Technology (NY)
Saint Joseph's U (PA)
Stephen F. Austin State U (TX)
U of Maryland Eastern Shore (MD)
U of North Texas (TX)

**SPEECH COMMUNICATION
AND RHETORIC**
Abilene Christian U (TX)
Alabama State U (AL)
Albertus Magnus Coll (CT)
Albion Coll (MI)
Albright Coll (PA)
Alderson-Broaddus Coll (WV)
Alfred U (NY)
Alvernia U (PA)
Alverno Coll (WI)
American U (DC)
American U of Puerto Rico (PR)
The American U of Rome (Italy)
Anderson U (SC)
Appalachian State U (NC)
Arizona State U (AZ)
Arkansas Tech U (AR)
Auburn U at Montgomery (AL)
Augustana Coll (SD)
Aurora U (IL)
Avila U (MO)
Azusa Pacific U (CA)
Baldwin Wallace U (OH)
Ball State U (IN)
Barry U (FL)
Baylor U (TX)
Belhaven U (MS)
Bellarmine U (KY)
Belmont U (TN)
Benedictine U (IL)
Bethany Coll (WV)
Bethany Lutheran Coll (MN)
Bethel Coll (IN)
Bethune-Cookman U (FL)
Blackburn Coll (IL)
Bluffton U (OH)
Boise State U (ID)
Boston Coll (MA)
Bowling Green State U (OH)
Bridgewater State U (MA)
Brock U (ON, Canada)
Bryant U (RI)

Buena Vista U (IA)
Buffalo State Coll, State U of New
York (NY)
Butler U (IN)
Cabrini Coll (PA)
Caldwell Coll (NJ)
California Baptist U (CA)
California State Polytechnic U,
Pomona (CA)
California State U, Chico (CA)
California State U, Dominguez Hills
(CA)
California State U, Fresno (CA)
California State U, Fullerton (CA)
California State U, Los Angeles
(CA)
California State U, San Marcos
(CA)
California State U, Stanislaus (CA)
Calvin Coll (MI)
Capital U (OH)
Cardinal Stritch U (WI)
Carlos Albizu U (PR)
Carroll Coll (MT)
The Catholic U of America (DC)
Cedar Crest Coll (PA)
Cedarville U (OH)
Central Coll (IA)
Central Connecticut State U (CT)
Central Methodist U (MO)
Champlain Coll (VT)
Chapman U (CA)
Chowan U (NC)
Christopher Newport U (VA)
Clarkson U (NY)
Clayton State U (GA)
Cleveland State U (OH)
Coastal Carolina U (SC)
The Coll at Brockport, State U of
New York (NY)
Coll of Charleston (SC)
Coll of Mount St. Joseph (OH)
The Coll of New Rochelle (NY)
Coll of Saint Elizabeth (NJ)
The Coll of Saint Rose (NY)
The Coll of St. Scholastica (MN)
Coll of Staten Island of the City U of
New York (NY)
Coll of the Ozarks (MO)
The Coll of Wooster (OH)
Colorado State U (CO)
Columbia Coll (MO)
Columbia Coll (SC)
Columbia Intl U (SC)
Concordia Coll (MN)
Concordia U Chicago (IL)
Concordia U, Nebraska (NE)
Corban U (OR)
Creighton U (NE)
Culver-Stockton Coll (MO)
Dakota Wesleyan U (SD)
DePaul U (IL)
Dominican U (IL)
Drury U (MO)
Duquesne U (PA)
East Carolina U (NC)
East Central U (OK)
Eastern Michigan U (MI)
Eastern Washington U (WA)
Eckerd Coll (FL)
Elizabeth City State U (NC)
Embry-Riddle Aeronautical U–
Daytona (FL)
Emerson Coll (MA)
Emmanuel Coll (MA)
Emporia State U (KS)
The Evergreen State Coll (WA)
Fairfield U (CT)
Fairleigh Dickinson U, Coll at
Florham (NJ)
Fayetteville State U (NC)
Felician Coll (NJ)
Ferris State U (MI)
Florida Atlantic U (FL)
Florida Intl U (FL)
Florida Southern Coll (FL)
Furman U (SC)
Gallaudet U (DC)
George Fox U (OR)
George Mason U (VA)
Georgia Regents U (GA)
Georgia Southern U (GA)
Georgia State U (GA)
Gordon Coll (MA)
Goshen Coll (IN)
Governors State U (IL)
Grace U (NE)

Grand Valley State U (MI)
Grove City Coll (PA)
Hamline U (MN)
Hampshire Coll (MA)
Harding U (AR)
Hardin-Simmons U (TX)
Hawai'i Pacific U (HI)
Hillsdale Coll (MI)
Hillsdale Free Will Baptist Coll (OK)
Hofstra U (NY)
Hope Coll (MI)
Houghton Coll (NY)
Howard Payne U (TX)
Huntington U (IN)
Illinois State U (IL)
Indiana State U (IN)
Indiana Tech (IN)
Indiana U Bloomington (IN)
Indiana U East (IN)
Indiana U Kokomo (IN)
Indiana U Northwest (IN)
Indiana U of Pennsylvania (PA)
Indiana U–Purdue U Fort Wayne
(IN)
Indiana U–Purdue U Indianapolis
(IN)
Indiana U South Bend (IN)
Indiana U Southeast (IN)
Indiana Wesleyan U (IN)
Inter American U of Puerto Rico,
Bayamón Campus (PR)
Iona Coll (NY)
Iowa Wesleyan Coll (IA)
Jacksonville State U (AL)
James Madison U (VA)
Jamestown Coll (ND)
John Brown U (AR)
Judson U (IL)
Juniata Coll (PA)
Kansas State U (KS)
Kean U (NJ)
Keene State Coll (NH)
Kennesaw State U (GA)
Kent State U (OH)
Kent State U at Ashtabula (OH)
Kent State U at East Liverpool (OH)
Kent State U at Salem (OH)
Kent State U at Stark (OH)
Kent State U at Trumbull (OH)
Kent State U at Tuscarawas (OH)
Kentucky Wesleyan Coll (KY)
Keuka Coll (NY)
Kuyper Coll (MI)
La Sierra U (CA)
Lawrence Technological U (MI)
Lewis-Clark State Coll (ID)
Lewis U (IL)
Lindenwood U (MO)
Linfield Coll (OR)
Long Island U–Brooklyn Campus
(NY)
Long Island U–C. W. Post Campus
(NY)
Longwood U (VA)
Louisiana State U and Ag and
Mech Coll (LA)
Loyola Marymount U (CA)
Loyola U Chicago (IL)
Loyola U Maryland (MD)
Loyola U New Orleans (LA)
Luther Coll (IA)
Lynchburg Coll (VA)
Manchester U (IN)
Marian U (WI)
Marietta Coll (OH)
Marymount Manhattan Coll (NY)
Mayville State U (ND)
McDaniel Coll (MD)
McKendree U (IL)
Mercer U (GA)
Mercyhurst U (PA)
Merrimack Coll (MA)
Messiah Coll (PA)
Michigan State U (MI)
Millersville U of Pennsylvania (PA)
Millikin U (IL)
Millsaps Coll (MS)
Minnesota State U Moorhead (MN)
Mississippi Coll (MS)
Mississippi State U (MS)
Mississippi U for Women (MS)
Missouri State U (MO)
Missouri Western State U (MO)
Molloy Coll (NY)
Monmouth Coll (IL)
Monmouth U (NJ)
Montclair State U (NJ)

Morehead State U (KY)
Mount Mary Coll (WI)
Mount Mercy U (IA)
Mount St. Mary's U (MD)
Mount Vernon Nazarene U (OH)
Nazareth Coll of Rochester (NY)
New Jersey City U (NJ)
New Mexico Highlands U (NM)
New York U (NY)
North Carolina State U (NC)
Northern Illinois U (IL)
Northern Michigan U (MI)
Northwest Christian U (OR)
Northwestern Coll (MN)
Northwestern State U of Louisiana
(LA)
Northwest Nazarene U (ID)
Norwich U (VT)
Notre Dame de Namur U (CA)
Nova Southeastern U (FL)
Oglethorpe U (GA)
Ohio Dominican U (OH)
The Ohio State U (OH)
Ohio U (OH)
Oklahoma Baptist U (OK)
Oral Roberts U (OK)
Oregon State U (OR)
Ouachita Baptist U (AR)
Pace U (NY)
Palm Beach Atlantic U (FL)
Park U (MO)
Penn State Abington (PA)
Penn State Altoona (PA)
Penn State Beaver (PA)
Penn State Berks (PA)
Penn State Brandywine (PA)
Penn State DuBois (PA)
Penn State Erie, The Behrend Coll
(PA)
Penn State Fayette, The Eberly
Campus (PA)
Penn State Greater Allegheny (PA)
Penn State Harrisburg (PA)
Penn State Hazleton (PA)
Penn State Lehigh Valley (PA)
Penn State Mont Alto (PA)
Penn State New Kensington (PA)
Penn State Schuylkill (PA)
Penn State Shenango (PA)
Penn State U Park (PA)
Penn State Wilkes-Barre (PA)
Penn State Worthington Scranton
(PA)
Penn State York (PA)
Pepperdine U, Malibu (CA)
Pine Manor Coll (MA)
Plymouth State U (NH)
Point Loma Nazarene U (CA)
Purchase Coll, State U of New York
(NY)
Purdue U (IN)
Purdue U Calumet (IN)
Purdue U North Central (IN)
Radford U (VA)
Ramapo Coll of New Jersey (NJ)
Randolph Coll (VA)
Regent U (VA)
Regis Coll (MA)
Regis U (CO)
Rensselaer Polytechnic Inst (NY)
Rhode Island Coll (RI)
The Richard Stockton Coll of New
Jersey (NJ)
Rider U (NJ)
Ripon Coll (WI)
Robert Morris U (PA)
Roberts Wesleyan Coll (NY)
Rochester Inst of Technology (NY)
Rockhurst U (MO)
Rocky Mountain Coll (MT)
Roger Williams U (RI)
Roosevelt U (IL)
Rosemont Coll (PA)
Rutgers, The State U of New
Jersey, New Brunswick (NJ)
Saginaw Valley State U (MI)
Saint Anselm Coll (NH)
St. Francis Coll (NY)
St. Gregory's U, Shawnee (OK)
St. John's U (NY)
Saint Joseph's U (PA)
Saint Louis U (MO)
Saint Mary's Coll (IN)
Saint Mary's Coll of California (CA)
St. Mary's U (TX)
St. Norbert Coll (WI)
Saint Vincent Coll (PA)

Salem State U (MA)
Salisbury U (MD)
Samford U (AL)
Sam Houston State U (TX)
San Diego Christian Coll (CA)
San Francisco State U (CA)
Schreiner U (TX)
Seattle Pacific U (WA)
Seton Hill U (PA)
Shenandoah U (VA)
Shepherd U (WV)
Simmons Coll (MA)
Simon Fraser U (BC, Canada)
Simpson U (CA)
Slippery Rock U of Pennsylvania (PA)
Sonoma State U (CA)
South Dakota State U (SD)
Southeastern Louisiana U (LA)
Southeastern Oklahoma State U (OK)
Southeast Missouri State U (MO)
Southern Connecticut State U (CT)
Southern Oregon U (OR)
Southern Utah U (UT)
Southwest Baptist U (MO)
Southwestern Coll (KS)
Southwestern U (TX)
Spalding U (KY)
Spring Arbor U (MI)
State U of New York at New Paltz (NY)
State U of New York at Plattsburgh (NY)
State U of New York Coll at Cortland (NY)
State U of New York Coll at Old Westbury (NY)
Stonehill Coll (MA)
Suffolk U (MA)
Susquehanna U (PA)
Syracuse U (NY)
Texas A&M Intl U (TX)
Texas A&M U–Kingsville (TX)
Texas Christian U (TX)
Texas Lutheran U (TX)
Texas Southern U (TX)
Thomas Edison State Coll (NJ)
Thomas U (GA)
Tiffin U (OH)
Trevecca Nazarene U (TN)
Trine U (IN)
Trinity Christian Coll (IL)
Trinity U (TX)
Troy U (AL)
Truman State U (MO)
U at Albany, State U of New York (NY)
U at Buffalo, the State U of New York (NY)
The U of Akron (OH)
The U of Alabama (AL)
The U of Alabama at Birmingham (AL)
U of Alaska Fairbanks (AK)
The U of Arizona (AZ)
U of Arkansas at Little Rock (AR)
U of California, Davis (CA)
U of California, Santa Barbara (CA)
U of Central Florida (FL)
U of Central Oklahoma (OK)
U of Cincinnati (OH)
U of Colorado Boulder (CO)
U of Colorado Colorado Springs (CO)
U of Colorado Denver (CO)
U of Delaware (DE)
U of Denver (CO)
U of Georgia (GA)
U of Hartford (CT)
U of Hawaii at Manoa (HI)
U of Houston (TX)
U of Illinois at Chicago (IL)
U of Illinois at Urbana–Champaign (IL)
The U of Iowa (IA)
The U of Kansas (KS)
U of Kentucky (KY)
U of La Verne (CA)
U of Louisiana at Lafayette (LA)
U of Louisville (KY)
U of Maryland, Coll Park (MD)
U of Maryland U Coll (MD)
U of Massachusetts Amherst (MA)
U of Memphis (TN)
U of Miami (FL)
U of Michigan (MI)

U of Michigan–Dearborn (MI)
U of Minnesota, Twin Cities Campus (MN)
U of Missouri (MO)
U of Missouri–St. Louis (MO)
U of Mobile (AL)
U of Nebraska at Omaha (NE)
U of Nebraska–Lincoln (NE)
U of Nevada, Las Vegas (NV)
U of Nevada, Reno (NV)
U of New Brunswick Saint John (NB, Canada)
U of New Hampshire (NH)
U of New Haven (CT)
U of New Mexico (NM)
U of North Alabama (AL)
The U of North Carolina at Chapel Hill (NC)
The U of North Carolina at Charlotte (NC)
The U of North Carolina at Greensboro (NC)
The U of North Carolina Wilmington (NC)
U of Northern Colorado (CO)
U of Northern Iowa (IA)
U of Oklahoma (OK)
U of Ottawa (ON, Canada)
U of Pennsylvania (PA)
U of Pikeville (KY)
U of Puget Sound (WA)
U of Rhode Island (RI)
U of St. Thomas (TX)
U of Science and Arts of Oklahoma (OK)
The U of Scranton (PA)
U of South Alabama (AL)
U of South Carolina Aiken (SC)
U of South Carolina Upstate (SC)
U of Southern California (CA)
U of Southern Maine (ME)
U of Southern Mississippi (MS)
The U of Tennessee (TN)
The U of Tennessee at Chattanooga (TN)
The U of Texas at Austin (TX)
The U of Texas at Brownsville (TX)
The U of Texas at San Antonio (TX)
The U of Texas–Pan American (TX)
U of the Cumberlands (KY)
U of the Incarnate Word (TX)
U of the Virgin Islands (VI)
The U of Toledo (OH)
U of Tulsa (OK)
U of Utah (UT)
U of Washington, Tacoma (WA)
U of Waterloo (ON, Canada)
U of Wisconsin–La Crosse (WI)
U of Wisconsin–Madison (WI)
U of Wisconsin–Milwaukee (WI)
U of Wisconsin–Parkside (WI)
U of Wisconsin–Stevens Point (WI)
U of Wyoming (WY)
Utica Coll (NY)
Valparaiso U (IN)
Vanderbilt U (TN)
Virginia Polytechnic Inst and State U (VA)
Wake Forest U (NC)
Waldorf Coll (IA)
Wartburg Coll (IA)
Washburn U (KS)
Washington U in St. Louis (MO)
Wayland Baptist U (TX)
Waynesburg U (PA)
Wayne State Coll (NE)
Wayne State U (MI)
Webber Intl U (FL)
Weber State U (UT)
Webster U (MO)
Wesleyan Coll (GA)
Western Carolina U (NC)
Western Connecticut State U (CT)
Western Illinois U (IL)
Western Kentucky U (KY)
Western Michigan U (MI)
Western Washington U (WA)
Westfield State U (MA)
West Texas A&M U (TX)
West Virginia State U (WV)
West Virginia Wesleyan Coll (WV)
Wheaton Coll (IL)
Whitman Coll (WA)
Wichita State U (KS)
Wilkes U (PA)
William Jewell Coll (MO)
William Peace U (NC)

William Penn U (IA)
Wittenberg U (OH)
Woodbury U (CA)
Worcester State U (MA)
Wright State U (OH)
York Coll of Pennsylvania (PA)

SPEECH-LANGUAGE PATHOLOGY
Abilene Christian U (TX)
Caribbean U (PR)
Cleveland State U (OH)
Columbia Coll (SC)
Duquesne U (PA)
Eastern Michigan U (MI)
Eastern Washington U (WA)
Edinboro U of Pennsylvania (PA)
Emerson Coll (MA)
Geneva Coll (PA)
Harding U (AR)
Inter American U of Puerto Rico, Fajardo Campus (PR)
Inter American U of Puerto Rico, Ponce Campus (PR)
James Madison U (VA)
Lehman Coll of the City U of New York (NY)
Loyola U Maryland (MD)
Marshall U (WV)
Marymount Manhattan Coll (NY)
Minnesota State U Moorhead (MN)
Mississippi U for Women (MS)
Nazareth Coll of Rochester (NY)
Northern Michigan U (MI)
Oklahoma State U (OK)
Rockhurst U (MO)
Texas Christian U (TX)
Trinity Christian Coll (IL)
U of Montevallo (AL)
U of Nebraska–Lincoln (NE)
U of Nevada, Reno (NV)
U of Northern Iowa (IA)
U of Oklahoma Health Sciences Center (OK)
U of Science and Arts of Oklahoma (OK)
The U of Toledo (OH)
The U of Western Ontario (ON, Canada)
U of West Georgia (GA)
Valdosta State U (GA)
Xavier U of Louisiana (LA)

SPEECH-LANGUAGE PATHOLOGY ASSISTANT
Caribbean U (PR)

SPEECH TEACHER EDUCATION
Albion Coll (MI)
Anderson U (IN)
Arkansas Tech U (AR)
Augustana Coll (SD)
Bemidji State U (MN)
Boise State U (ID)
Bowling Green State U (OH)
Brigham Young U (UT)
Buena Vista U (IA)
Capital U (OH)
Carroll Coll (MT)
Colorado State U (CO)
Concordia U, Nebraska (NE)
Culver-Stockton Coll (MO)
Dordt Coll (IA)
East Central U (OK)
East Texas Baptist U (TX)
Elmira Coll (NY)
Evangel U (MO)
Friends U (KS)
Harding U (AR)
Hardin-Simmons U (TX)
Howard Payne U (TX)
Indiana U–Purdue U Fort Wayne (IN)
King Coll (TN)
McKendree U (IL)
Northwestern Coll (IA)
Northwest U (WA)
Oklahoma City U (OK)
Olivet Coll (MI)
Saginaw Valley State U (MI)
St. Ambrose U (IA)
Southern Nazarene U (OK)
Southern Utah U (UT)
Southwest Baptist U (MO)
Southwestern Coll (KS)
State U of New York at New Paltz (NY)

Trevecca Nazarene U (TN)
The U of Iowa (IA)
U of Michigan–Flint (MI)
U of Northern Iowa (IA)
U of St. Thomas (MN)
The U of South Dakota (SD)
U of the Cumberlands (KY)
U of Windsor (ON, Canada)
Wartburg Coll (IA)
Wayne State Coll (NE)
Western Washington U (WA)
William Jewell Coll (MO)

SPORT AND FITNESS ADMINISTRATION/MANAGEMENT
Abilene Christian U (TX)
Adelphi U (NY)
AIB Coll of Business (IA)
Albertus Magnus Coll (CT)
Alderson-Broaddus Coll (WV)
Alice Lloyd Coll (KY)
Alvernia U (PA)
American U (DC)
Arkansas State U (AR)
Asbury U (KY)
Athens State U (AL)
Augustana Coll (SD)
Averett U (VA)
Baker U (KS)
Baldwin Wallace U (OH)
Barry U (FL)
Barton Coll (NC)
Becker Coll (MA)
Belhaven U (MS)
Belmont Abbey Coll (NC)
Bemidji State U (MN)
Bethany Coll (WV)
Bethel Coll (IN)
Blackburn Coll (IL)
Bluffton U (OH)
Bowling Green State U (OH)
Bridgewater State U (MA)
Brock U (ON, Canada)
Buena Vista U (IA)
Calvin Coll (MI)
Canisius Coll (NY)
Castleton State Coll (VT)
Cedarville U (OH)
Central Methodist U (MO)
Chowan U (NC)
The Citadel, The Military Coll of South Carolina (SC)
Claflin U (SC)
Clarke U (IA)
Clayton State U (GA)
Cleveland State U (OH)
Coastal Carolina U (SC)
The Coll at Brockport, State U of New York (NY)
The Coll of Idaho (ID)
Coll of Mount St. Joseph (OH)
Colorado Mesa U (CO)
Columbia Coll (MO)
Concordia Coll–New York (NY)
Concordia U (OR)
Concordia U Chicago (IL)
Concordia U, Nebraska (NE)
Concordia U, St. Paul (MN)
Concordia U Wisconsin (WI)
Corban U (OR)
Cornerstone U (MI)
Crown Coll (MN)
Culver-Stockton Coll (MO)
Dakota Wesleyan U (SD)
Daniel Webster Coll (NH)
Davenport U, Grand Rapids (MI)
Defiance Coll (OH)
DeSales U (PA)
Dordt Coll (IA)
Eastern Mennonite U (VA)
Eastern Michigan U (MI)
East Tennessee State U (TN)
Elon U (NC)
Emmanuel Coll (GA)
Emory & Henry Coll (VA)
Endicott Coll (MA)
Farmingdale State Coll (NY)
Faulkner U (AL)
Ferrum Coll (VA)
Flagler Coll (FL)
Florida Inst of Technology (FL)
Fort Lewis Coll (CO)
Franklin Pierce U (NH)
Friends U (KS)
Gannon U (PA)
Gardner-Webb U (NC)

Geneva Coll (PA)
Georgia Southern U (GA)
Goldey-Beacom Coll (DE)
Gonzaga U (WA)
Greenville Coll (IL)
Guilford Coll (NC)
Hamline U (MN)
Hampton U (VA)
Harding U (AR)
Hilbert Coll (NY)
Holy Family U (PA)
Howard Payne U (TX)
Huntingdon Coll (AL)
Husson U (ME)
Indiana Tech (IN)
Indiana Wesleyan U (IN)
Inter American U of Puerto Rico, San Germán Campus (PR)
Ithaca Coll (NY)
Jamestown Coll (ND)
John Brown U (AR)
Johnson C. Smith U (NC)
Johnson State Coll (VT)
Judson U (IL)
Kennesaw State U (GA)
Kent State U (OH)
Kentucky Wesleyan Coll (KY)
Keystone Coll (PA)
King Coll (TN)
Lake Erie Coll (OH)
Lasell Coll (MA)
Lees-McRae Coll (NC)
LeTourneau U (TX)
Lewis U (IL)
Liberty U (VA)
Limestone Coll (SC)
Lindenwood U (MO)
Lock Haven U of Pennsylvania (PA)
Louisiana State U and Ag and Mech Coll (LA)
Lubbock Christian U (TX)
Lynchburg Coll (VA)
Lynn U (FL)
Madonna U (MI)
Malone U (OH)
Manchester U (IN)
Maranatha Baptist Bible Coll (WI)
Marian U (WI)
Marietta Coll (OH)
Mars Hill Coll (NC)
Maryville U of Saint Louis (MO)
McKendree U (IL)
Medaille Coll (NY)
Menlo Coll (CA)
Merrimack Coll (MA)
Messiah Coll (PA)
Miami U (OH)
Midwestern State U (TX)
Millikin U (IL)
Minnesota State U Mankato (MN)
Minot State U (ND)
Misericordia U (PA)
Mississippi Coll (MS)
Missouri Baptist U (MO)
Mitchell Coll (CT)
Montana State U (MT)
Morehead State U (KY)
Mount St. Mary's U (MD)
Mount Vernon Nazarene U (OH)
Neumann U (PA)
Newbury Coll (MA)
New England Coll (NH)
Niagara U (NY)
North Carolina State U (NC)
North Central Coll (IL)
North Dakota State U (ND)
Northern Michigan U (MI)
Northern State U (SD)
North Greenville U (SC)
Northwestern Coll (IA)
Northwood U, Florida Campus (FL)
Northwood U, Michigan Campus (MI)
Nova Southeastern U (FL)
Ohio Dominican U (OH)
The Ohio State U (OH)
Oklahoma Baptist U (OK)
Oklahoma Christian U (OK)
Oklahoma City U (OK)
Olivet Coll (MI)
Plymouth State U (NH)
Post U (CT)
Principia Coll (IL)
Quincy U (IL)
Rice U (TX)
Roanoke Coll (VA)
Robert Morris U (PA)

Rockhurst U (MO)
Rocky Mountain Coll (MT)
Rogers State U (OK)
Sacred Heart U (CT)
St. Ambrose U (IA)
St. Bonaventure U (NY)
St. John Fisher Coll (NY)
St. John's U (NY)
Saint Joseph's Coll (IN)
Saint Leo U (FL)
Saint Mary's Coll of California (CA)
St. Thomas Aquinas Coll (NY)
St. Thomas U (FL)
Salem Intl U (WV)
Salem State U (MA)
Samford U (AL)
Schreiner U (TX)
Seattle Pacific U (WA)
Seton Hill U (PA)
Shawnee State U (OH)
Siena Heights U (MI)
Simpson Coll (IA)
Slippery Rock U of Pennsylvania (PA)
Southeastern Louisiana U (LA)
Southeastern U (FL)
Southeast Missouri State U (MO)
Southern Illinois U Carbondale (IL)
Southern Nazarene U (OK)
Southern New Hampshire U (NH)
Southwest Baptist U (MO)
Southwestern Coll (KS)
Spring Arbor U (MI)
State U of New York at Oswego (NY)
Stetson U (FL)
Syracuse U (NY)
Tabor Coll (KS)
Taylor U (IN)
Tennessee Wesleyan Coll (TN)
Texas A&M U (TX)
Texas A&M U–Commerce (TX)
Texas Lutheran U (TX)
Texas Southern U (TX)
Texas State U–San Marcos (TX)
Thomas More Coll (KY)
Tiffin U (OH)
Trevecca Nazarene U (TN)
Trine U (IN)
Troy U (AL)
Union Coll (KY)
Union Coll (NE)
Union U (TN)
The U of Akron (OH)
U of Charleston (WV)
U of Cincinnati (OH)
U of Delaware (DE)
U of Evansville (IN)
The U of Findlay (OH)
U of Florida (FL)
U of Houston (TX)
U of Illinois at Urbana–Champaign (IL)
The U of Iowa (IA)
U of Louisville (KY)
U of Massachusetts Amherst (MA)
U of Memphis (TN)
U of Miami (FL)
U of Michigan (MI)
U of Minnesota, Crookston (MN)
U of Minnesota, Twin Cities Campus (MN)
U of Mount Union (OH)
U of Nebraska at Kearney (NE)
U of Nevada, Las Vegas (NV)
U of New England (ME)
U of North Florida (FL)
U of Pittsburgh at Bradford (PA)
U of Regina (SK, Canada)
U of Saint Mary (KS)
U of South Carolina (SC)
U of Southern Indiana (IN)
The U of Tampa (FL)
The U of Tennessee (TN)
The U of Texas at Austin (TX)
U of the Cumberlands (KY)
U of the Incarnate Word (TX)
U of Tulsa (OK)
The U of Western Ontario (ON, Canada)
U of Windsor (ON, Canada)
U of Wisconsin–Parkside (WI)
Valparaiso U (IN)
Virginia Intermont Coll (VA)
Viterbo U (WI)
Waldorf Coll (IA)
Walla Walla U (WA)

Wartburg Coll (IA)
Washington State U (WA)
Wayland Baptist U (TX)
Wayne State Coll (NE)
Western Carolina U (NC)
Western State Colorado U (CO)
West Virginia Wesleyan Coll (WV)
Widener U (PA)
William Paterson U of New Jersey (NJ)
William Penn U (IA)
Wilmington U (DE)
Winthrop U (SC)
Xavier U (OH)
York Coll of Pennsylvania (PA)

SPORTS COMMUNICATION
Bradley U (IL)
Lasell Coll (MA)
Oklahoma State U (OK)
Queens U of Charlotte (NC)
U of Evansville (IN)

SPORTS STUDIES
Bethel Coll (IN)
Bryant U (RI)
Canisius Coll (NY)
Central Michigan U (MI)
Huntington U (IN)
Lakeland Coll (WI)
St. Bonaventure U (NY)
Southwestern Coll (KS)
Texas Christian U (TX)
Trevecca Nazarene U (TN)
Washington State U (WA)
Western Kentucky U (KY)

STATISTICS
American U (DC)
American U of Beirut (Lebanon)
Appalachian State U (NC)
Arizona State U (AZ)
Baylor U (TX)
Bowling Green State U (OH)
Brock U (ON, Canada)
Bryant U (RI)
California Baptist U (CA)
California Polytechnic State U, San Luis Obispo (CA)
California State U, East Bay (CA)
California State U, Fullerton (CA)
California State U, Long Beach (CA)
Carnegie Mellon U (PA)
Case Western Reserve U (OH)
Central Michigan U (MI)
Colorado School of Mines (CO)
Columbia U (NY)
Columbia U, School of General Studies (NY)
Concordia U (QC, Canada)
Dalhousie U (NS, Canada)
Eastern Michigan U (MI)
Elon U (NC)
Florida Intl U (FL)
Florida State U (FL)
Grand Valley State U (MI)
Hunter Coll of the City U of New York (NY)
Indiana U Bloomington (IN)
Indiana U–Purdue U Fort Wayne (IN)
Iowa State U of Science and Technology (IA)
Kansas State U (KS)
Lehigh U (PA)
Loyola U Chicago (IL)
Loyola U Maryland (MD)
Miami U (OH)
Michigan State U (MI)
Montana State U (MT)
Montana Tech of The U of Montana (MT)
Mount Holyoke Coll (MA)
North Carolina State U (NC)
North Dakota State U (ND)
Northwest Missouri State U (MO)
Oakland U (MI)
Ohio Wesleyan U (OH)
Oklahoma State U (OK)
Penn State Abington (PA)
Penn State Altoona (PA)
Penn State Beaver (PA)
Penn State Berks (PA)
Penn State Brandywine (PA)
Penn State DuBois (PA)
Penn State Erie, The Behrend Coll (PA)

Penn State Fayette, The Eberly Campus (PA)
Penn State Greater Allegheny (PA)
Penn State Hazleton (PA)
Penn State Lehigh Valley (PA)
Penn State Mont Alto (PA)
Penn State New Kensington (PA)
Penn State Schuylkill (PA)
Penn State Shenango (PA)
Penn State U Park (PA)
Penn State Wilkes-Barre (PA)
Penn State Worthington Scranton (PA)
Penn State York (PA)
Purdue U (IN)
Rice U (TX)
Rochester Inst of Technology (NY)
Rutgers, The State U of New Jersey, New Brunswick (NJ)
St. John Fisher Coll (NY)
San Diego State U (CA)
San Francisco State U (CA)
Simon Fraser U (BC, Canada)
Slippery Rock U of Pennsylvania (PA)
Sonoma State U (CA)
Southern Methodist U (TX)
Stanford U (CA)
The U of Akron (OH)
The U of British Columbia (BC, Canada)
U of California, Berkeley (CA)
U of California, Davis (CA)
U of California, Los Angeles (CA)
U of California, Riverside (CA)
U of California, Santa Barbara (CA)
U of Central Florida (FL)
U of Chicago (IL)
U of Delaware (DE)
U of Florida (FL)
U of Georgia (GA)
U of Illinois at Chicago (IL)
U of Illinois at Urbana–Champaign (IL)
The U of Iowa (IA)
U of Maryland, Baltimore County (MD)
U of Michigan (MI)
U of Minnesota, Duluth (MN)
U of Minnesota, Twin Cities Campus (MN)
U of Missouri (MO)
U of Nevada, Las Vegas (NV)
U of New Brunswick Fredericton (NB, Canada)
U of New Brunswick Saint John (NB, Canada)
U of New Mexico (NM)
The U of North Carolina Wilmington (NC)
U of North Florida (FL)
U of Ottawa (ON, Canada)
U of Pennsylvania (PA)
U of Pittsburgh (PA)
U of Regina (SK, Canada)
U of Rochester (NY)
U of South Carolina (SC)
U of South Florida (FL)
The U of Tennessee (TN)
The U of Tennessee at Martin (TN)
The U of Texas at El Paso (TX)
The U of Texas at San Antonio (TX)
U of Vermont (VT)
U of Waterloo (ON, Canada)
The U of Western Ontario (ON, Canada)
U of Wisconsin–Madison (WI)
U of Wyoming (WY)
Utah State U (UT)
Virginia Polytechnic Inst and State U (VA)
Washington U in St. Louis (MO)
Western Michigan U (MI)
Wright State U (OH)
Xavier U of Louisiana (LA)

STATISTICS RELATED
Dordt Coll (IA)
Saint Mary's Coll (IN)
United States Military Acad (NY)

STRATEGIC STUDIES
Washington State U (WA)

STRINGED INSTRUMENTS
Acadia U (NS, Canada)
Bard Coll (NY)
Bennington Coll (VT)

Berklee Coll of Music (MA)
The Boston Conservatory (MA)
Brigham Young U (UT)
Butler U (IN)
Carnegie Mellon U (PA)
Converse Coll (SC)
Five Towns Coll (NY)
Hardin-Simmons U (TX)
Hope Coll (MI)
Houghton Coll (NY)
Inter American U of Puerto Rico, San Germán Campus (PR)
Lamar U (TX)
Lawrence U (WI)
Mannes Coll The New School for Music (NY)
McNally Smith Coll of Music (MN)
Mount Allison U (NB, Canada)
New England Conservatory of Music (MA)
The New School for Jazz and Contemporary Music (NY)
Northwestern Coll (MN)
Oklahoma City U (OK)
Peabody Conservatory of The Johns Hopkins U (MD)
Roosevelt U (IL)
San Francisco Conservatory of Music (CA)
Seattle U (WA)
State U of New York at Fredonia (NY)
Stetson U (FL)
Syracuse U (NY)
Texas Christian U (TX)
The U of Akron (OH)
The U of British Columbia (BC, Canada)
U of Central Oklahoma (OK)
The U of Iowa (IA)
The U of Kansas (KS)
U of Nebraska at Omaha (NE)
U of Southern California (CA)
The U of Western Ontario (ON, Canada)
Vanderbilt U (TN)
Willamette U (OR)
Xavier U of Louisiana (LA)

STRUCTURAL ENGINEERING
Penn State Harrisburg (PA)
U at Buffalo, the State U of New York (NY)
U of Central Florida (FL)
U of Illinois at Urbana–Champaign (IL)
U of Southern California (CA)
The U of Toledo (OH)
Western Michigan U (MI)

STUDENT COUNSELING AND PERSONNEL SERVICES RELATED
Samford U (AL)

SUBSTANCE ABUSE/ ADDICTION COUNSELING
Alvernia U (PA)
Chowan U (NC)
City Vision Coll (MO)
The Coll at Brockport, State U of New York (NY)
Indiana U–Purdue U Fort Wayne (IN)
Indiana Wesleyan U (IN)
Kansas Wesleyan U (KS)
Keene State Coll (NH)
Minot State U (ND)
Newman U (KS)
Northwestern State U of Louisiana (LA)
Pittsburg State U (KS)
Rhode Island Coll (RI)
Roger Williams U (RI)
Tiffin U (OH)
U of Central Arkansas (AR)
U of Cincinnati (OH)
U of Great Falls (MT)
The U of South Dakota (SD)
Washburn U (KS)

SURGICAL TECHNOLOGY
Nebraska Methodist Coll (NE)

SURVEYING ENGINEERING
Ferris State U (MI)
Florida Atlantic U (FL)

SURVEYING TECHNOLOGY
East Tennessee State U (TN)
Ferris State U (MI)
Metropolitan State U of Denver (CO)
New Mexico State U (NM)
Nicholls State U (LA)
The Ohio State U (OH)
Penn State Wilkes-Barre (PA)
Polytechnic U of Puerto Rico (PR)
Roger Williams U (RI)
Southern Polytechnic State U (GA)
State U of New York Coll of Technology at Alfred (NY)
Troy U (AL)
The U of Akron (OH)
U of Alaska Anchorage (AK)
U of Florida (FL)
U of New Brunswick Fredericton (NB, Canada)

SUSTAINABILITY STUDIES
Arizona State U (AZ)
Aurora U (IL)
Colorado Mountain Coll (CO)
Colorado Mountain Coll, Alpine Campus (CO)
Colorado Mountain Coll, Timberline Campus (CO)
Creighton U (NE)
The Evergreen State Coll (WA)
Furman U (SC)
George Mason U (VA)
Goddard Coll (VT)
Hofstra U (NY)
Judson U (IL)
Kean U (NJ)
Lipscomb U (TN)
Messiah Coll (PA)
Pittsburg State U (KS)
Rensselaer Polytechnic Inst (NY)
The Richard Stockton Coll of New Jersey (NJ)
Roosevelt U (IL)
Sierra Nevada Coll (NV)
Stephen F. Austin State U (TX)
Stony Brook U, State U of New York (NY)
Trent U (ON, Canada)
U of Florida (FL)
U of New Haven (CT)
U of Northern Colorado (CO)
The U of Western Ontario (ON, Canada)
U of Wisconsin–Platteville (WI)
U of Wisconsin–Stout (WI)
Viterbo U (WI)
Webster U (MO)
Wheeling Jesuit U (WV)

SWEDISH
Brigham Young U (UT)

SYSTEM, NETWORKING, AND LAN/WAN MANAGEMENT
Alcorn State U (MS)
Champlain Coll (VT)
Dakota State U (SD)
Hallmark Coll of Technology (TX)
Northern Michigan U (MI)
Rochester Inst of Technology (NY)
Southern Nazarene U (OK)
State U of New York Coll of Technology at Alfred (NY)
Texas A&M U (TX)
U of Great Falls (MT)
U of Hawaii–West Oahu (HI)

SYSTEMS ENGINEERING
Belmont U (TN)
Case Western Reserve U (OH)
Ferris State U (MI)
George Mason U (VA)
Maine Maritime Acad (ME)
Rochester Inst of Technology (NY)
Southern Polytechnic State U (GA)
Stanford U (CA)
United States Military Acad (NY)
United States Naval Acad (MD)
The U of Arizona (AZ)
U of Arkansas at Little Rock (AR)
U of Florida (FL)
The U of North Carolina at Charlotte (NC)
U of Pennsylvania (PA)
U of Southern California (CA)
U of Virginia (VA)
U of Waterloo (ON, Canada)

U of Wyoming (WY)
Washington U in St. Louis (MO)

SYSTEMS SCIENCE AND THEORY
Boston U (MA)
Carnegie Mellon U (PA)
James Madison U (VA)
Marshall U (WV)
Stanford U (CA)
United States Military Acad (NY)
U of Wyoming (WY)
Washington U in St. Louis (MO)
Yale U (CT)

TAXATION
Canisius Coll (NY)
Grand Valley State U (MI)

TECHNICAL AND SCIENTIFIC COMMUNICATION
Illinois Inst of Technology (IL)
Indiana U–Purdue U Indianapolis (IN)
Lehigh U (PA)

TECHNICAL TEACHER EDUCATION
Athens State U (AL)
Auburn U (AL)
Bowling Green State U (OH)
Eastern Illinois U (IL)
Ferris State U (MI)
Montana State U (MT)
The Ohio State U (OH)
Pittsburg State U (KS)
Rhode Island Coll (RI)
South Dakota State U (SD)
The U of Akron (OH)
U of Idaho (ID)
U of Illinois at Urbana–Champaign (IL)
U of Kentucky (KY)
U of Minnesota, Twin Cities Campus (MN)
U of Missouri (MO)
U of Wisconsin–Stout (WI)
Utah State U (UT)
Valley City State U (ND)
Wayne State U (MI)
Western Michigan U (MI)
Wright State U (OH)

TECHNOLOGY/INDUSTRIAL ARTS TEACHER EDUCATION
Appalachian State U (NC)
Ball State U (IN)
Bemidji State U (MN)
Berea Coll (KY)
Bowling Green State U (OH)
Buffalo State Coll, State U of New York (NY)
Central Connecticut State U (CT)
Central Michigan U (MI)
Chicago State U (IL)
The Coll of New Jersey (NJ)
Colorado State U (CO)
Concordia U, Nebraska (NE)
Eastern Michigan U (MI)
Georgia Southern U (GA)
Illinois State U (IL)
Indiana State U (IN)
Keene State Coll (NH)
Lindenwood U (MO)
Middle Tennessee State U (TN)
New Mexico Highlands U (NM)
New York City Coll of Technology of the City U of New York (NY)
North Carolina State U (NC)
The Ohio State U (OH)
Pittsburg State U (KS)
Purdue U (IN)
Rhode Island Coll (RI)
Southeast Missouri State U (MO)
Southern Utah U (UT)
State U of New York at Oswego (NY)
U of Minnesota, Twin Cities Campus (MN)
The U of Montana Western (MT)
U of New Mexico (NM)
U of Northern Iowa (IA)
U of the Ozarks (AR)
U of Wisconsin–Platteville (WI)
U of Wisconsin–Stout (WI)
U of Wyoming (WY)
Utah State U (UT)
Valley City State U (ND)
Viterbo U (WI)
Wayland Baptist U (TX)

Wayne State Coll (NE)
Western Michigan U (MI)
Western Washington U (WA)
Westfield State U (MA)

TELECOMMUNICATIONS ENGINEERING
The U of Texas at Dallas (TX)

TELECOMMUNICATIONS TECHNOLOGY
California State U, East Bay (CA)
Canisius Coll (NY)
Columbia Coll Hollywood (CA)
Farmingdale State Coll (NY)
Ferris State U (MI)
Inter American U of Puerto Rico, Bayamón Campus (PR)
Lawrence Technological U (MI)
New York City Coll of Technology of the City U of New York (NY)
New York Inst of Technology (NY)
Pace U (NY)
Pacific U (OR)
Pepperdine U, Malibu (CA)
Rochester Inst of Technology (NY)
St. John's U (NY)
Southern Polytechnic State U (GA)
U of Wisconsin–Platteville (WI)

TERRORISM AND COUNTERTERRORISM OPERATIONS
Henley-Putnam U (CA)

TEXTILE SCIENCE
Michigan State U (MI)
U of Nebraska–Lincoln (NE)

TEXTILE SCIENCES AND ENGINEERING
Auburn U (AL)
Clemson U (SC)
North Carolina State U (NC)
Philadelphia U (PA)
U of Massachusetts Dartmouth (MA)

THEATER DESIGN AND TECHNOLOGY
Baldwin Wallace U (OH)
Baylor U (TX)
Belmont U (TN)
Bennington Coll (VT)
Binghamton U, State U of New York (NY)
Boston U (MA)
Brigham Young U (UT)
Central Michigan U (MI)
Coe Coll (IA)
Coll of the Ozarks (MO)
Columbia Coll Chicago (IL)
Concordia U (QC, Canada)
DePaul U (IL)
Doane Coll (NE)
Elon U (NC)
Emerson Coll (MA)
Florida Southern Coll (FL)
Huntington U (IN)
Illinois Wesleyan U (IL)
Ithaca Coll (NY)
Kean U (NJ)
Keene State Coll (NH)
Lindenwood U (MO)
Lipscomb U (TN)
Millikin U (IL)
Nazareth Coll of Rochester (NY)
New Jersey Inst of Technology (NJ)
New York City Coll of Technology of the City U of New York (NY)
Northwest Missouri State U (MO)
Oakland U (MI)
Oklahoma City U (OK)
Oral Roberts U (OK)
Penn State Abington (PA)
Penn State Altoona (PA)
Penn State Beaver (PA)
Penn State Berks (PA)
Penn State Brandywine (PA)
Penn State DuBois (PA)
Penn State Erie, The Behrend Coll (PA)
Penn State Fayette, The Eberly Campus (PA)
Penn State Greater Allegheny (PA)
Penn State Hazleton (PA)
Penn State Lehigh Valley (PA)
Penn State Mont Alto (PA)
Penn State New Kensington (PA)
Penn State Schuylkill (PA)
Penn State Shenango (PA)

Penn State U Park (PA)
Penn State Wilkes-Barre (PA)
Penn State Worthington Scranton (PA)
Penn State York (PA)
Pepperdine U, Malibu (CA)
Purchase Coll, State U of New York (NY)
Rocky Mountain Coll (MT)
Salem State U (MA)
Santa Fe U of Art and Design (NM)
Savannah Coll of Art and Design (GA)
Seton Hill U (PA)
Shenandoah U (VA)
Slippery Rock U of Pennsylvania (PA)
Southwestern Coll (KS)
State U of New York at New Paltz (NY)
Stephens Coll (MO)
Texas Christian U (TX)
Trinity U (TX)
U of Alaska Anchorage (AK)
U of Alaska Fairbanks (AK)
The U of Arizona (AZ)
U of Cincinnati (OH)
The U of Kansas (KS)
U of Miami (FL)
U of Michigan (MI)
U of Michigan–Flint (MI)
U of New Mexico (NM)
U of North Carolina School of the Arts (NC)
U of Regina (SK, Canada)
U of Southern California (CA)
The U of the Arts (PA)
Virginia Intermont Coll (VA)
Webster U (MO)
Western Michigan U (MI)
Western State Colorado U (CO)
Wright State U (OH)

THEATER LITERATURE, HISTORY AND CRITICISM
Albertus Magnus Coll (CT)
Averett U (VA)
Bard Coll (NY)
Bennington Coll (VT)
Bowdoin Coll (ME)
Buena Vista U (IA)
Clark Atlanta U (GA)
Dalhousie U (NS, Canada)
DePaul U (IL)
Eugene Lang Coll The New School for Liberal Arts (NY)
Keene State Coll (NH)
Marymount Manhattan Coll (NY)
Moravian Coll (PA)
Saint Mary's Coll of California (CA)
Salem State U (MA)
State U of New York at New Paltz (NY)
Suffolk U (MA)
U of Illinois at Urbana–Champaign (IL)
Washington & Jefferson Coll (PA)
Washington U in St. Louis (MO)
Western Michigan U (MI)
West Virginia U (WV)

THEATER/THEATER ARTS MANAGEMENT
Berry Coll (GA)
Canisius Coll (NY)
DEREE—The American Coll of Greece (Greece)
Massachusetts Coll of Liberal Arts (MA)
Messiah Coll (PA)
Nazareth Coll of Rochester (NY)
Oglethorpe U (GA)
Ohio U (OH)
Oklahoma City U (OK)
Pace U (NY)
Quinnipiac U (CT)
Regent U (VA)
Sam Houston State U (TX)
Seton Hill U (PA)
Slippery Rock U of Pennsylvania (PA)
Texas Wesleyan U (TX)
The U of British Columbia (BC, Canada)
U of Evansville (IN)
U of Miami (FL)
U of Regina (SK, Canada)
U of Richmond (VA)

U of Southern California (CA)
William Peace U (NC)

THEOLOGICAL AND MINISTERIAL STUDIES RELATED
Concordia U (QC, Canada)
Concordia U, St. Paul (MN)
Hardin-Simmons U (TX)
Hope Intl U (CA)
Howard Payne U (TX)
Huntington U (IN)
John Brown U (AR)
Judson U (IL)
Lee U (TN)
Lincoln Christian U (IL)
Northwest Christian U (OR)
Northwestern Coll (MN)
Point Loma Nazarene U (CA)
Saint Mary-of-the-Woods Coll (IN)
Trinity Coll of Florida (FL)
Viterbo U (WI)

THEOLOGY
Alvernia U (PA)
Anderson U (IN)
Andrews U (MI)
Appalachian Bible Coll (WV)
Assumption Coll (MA)
Augsburg Coll (MN)
Azusa Pacific U (CA)
Baptist Missionary Association Theological Sem (TX)
Barry U (FL)
Bellarmine U (KY)
Belmont Abbey Coll (NC)
Benedictine Coll (KS)
Benedictine U (IL)
Bluefield Coll (VA)
Bob Jones U (SC)
Boston Coll (MA)
Briercrest Coll (SK, Canada)
Caldwell Coll (NJ)
Calumet Coll of Saint Joseph (IN)
Calvin Coll (MI)
Carlow U (PA)
Carroll Coll (MT)
Cedarville U (OH)
Christendom Coll (VA)
Coll of Saint Benedict (MN)
Coll of Saint Elizabeth (NJ)
Coll of Saint Mary (NE)
Concordia U (OR)
Concordia U (QC, Canada)
Concordia U Chicago (IL)
Concordia U, Nebraska (NE)
Concordia U, St. Paul (MN)
Concordia U Wisconsin (WI)
Creighton U (NE)
Crossroads Coll (MN)
Crown Coll (MN)
DeSales U (PA)
Dominican U (IL)
Dordt Coll (IA)
Duquesne U (PA)
Eastern Mennonite U (VA)
Gannon U (PA)
Georgetown U (DC)
Global U (MO)
Hanover Coll (IN)
Hardin-Simmons U (TX)
Hillsdale Free Will Baptist Coll (OK)
Holy Cross Coll (IN)
Holy Trinity Orthodox Sem (NY)
Houghton Coll (NY)
Howard Payne U (TX)
Huntington U (IN)
Immaculata U (PA)
Indiana Wesleyan U (IN)
John Brown U (AR)
King's Coll (PA)
The King's U Coll (AB, Canada)
Kuyper Coll (MI)
Laurel U (NC)
Lee U (TN)
Lincoln Christian U (IL)
Louisiana Coll (LA)
Loyola Marymount U (CA)
Loyola U Chicago (IL)
Lubbock Christian U (TX)
Marquette U (WI)
Martin Luther Coll (MN)
The Master's Coll and Sem (CA)
Master's Coll and Sem (ON, Canada)
Morris Coll (SC)
Mount Mary Coll (WI)
Mount St. Mary's U (MD)

Mount Vernon Nazarene U (OH)
Multnomah U (OR)
Newman U (KS)
Northwest Nazarene U (ID)
Oakland City U (IN)
Ohio Dominican U (OH)
Oral Roberts U (OK)
Ouachita Baptist U (AR)
Pacific Lutheran U (WA)
Pacific Union Coll (CA)
Palm Beach Atlantic U (FL)
Point U (GA)
Providence Coll (RI)
Rockhurst U (MO)
Rocky Mountain Coll (AB, Canada)
St. Ambrose U (IA)
Saint Anselm Coll (NH)
St. Bonaventure U (NY)
St. Gregory's U, Shawnee (OK)
Saint John's U (MN)
St. John's U (NY)
Saint Louis Christian Coll (MO)
Saint Louis U (MO)
Saint Mary's Coll of California (CA)
St. Mary's U (TX)
Saint Mary's U of Minnesota (MN)
Saint Vincent Coll (PA)
Seattle Pacific U (WA)
Southern Nazarene U (OK)
Southwest Baptist U (MO)
Southwestern Adventist U (TX)
Spring Arbor U (MI)
Texas Lutheran U (TX)
Trinity Christian Coll (IL)
Union Coll (NE)
Union U (TN)
Universidad Adventista de las Antillas (PR)
U of Chicago (IL)
U of Dallas (TX)
U of Evansville (IN)
U of Great Falls (MT)
U of Minnesota, Twin Cities Campus (MN)
U of Notre Dame (IN)
U of Portland (OR)
U of St. Francis (IL)
U of Saint Mary (KS)
U of St. Thomas (TX)
The U of Western Ontario (ON, Canada)
Valparaiso U (IN)
Walla Walla U (WA)
Walsh U (OH)
Warner Pacific Coll (OR)
Wheeling Jesuit U (WV)
Xavier U of Louisiana (LA)

THEOLOGY AND RELIGIOUS VOCATIONS RELATED
Belmont U (TN)
Cedarville U (OH)
Concordia Coll–New York (NY)
Crossroads Coll (MN)
Lee U (TN)
Master's Coll and Sem (ON, Canada)
Missouri Baptist U (MO)
Newman U (KS)
Ouachita Baptist U (AR)
St. Edward's U (TX)
Simpson U (CA)
Southeastern U (FL)
Southern Nazarene U (OK)
Trevecca Nazarene U (TN)
Trinity Christian Coll (IL)
Union U (TN)
U of St. Thomas (TX)

THEORETICAL AND MATHEMATICAL PHYSICS
Carnegie Mellon U (PA)
Chapman U (CA)
Oregon State U (OR)
Sweet Briar Coll (VA)
U at Buffalo, the State U of New York (NY)
U of Guelph (ON, Canada)
U of Ottawa (ON, Canada)
The U of Western Ontario (ON, Canada)
Viterbo U (WI)

THERAPEUTIC RECREATION
Alderson-Broaddus Coll (WV)
Brigham Young U (UT)
California State U, Chico (CA)
California State U, East Bay (CA)
Calvin Coll (MI)

Catawba Coll (NC)
The Coll at Brockport, State U of New York (NY)
Concordia U (QC, Canada)
Dalhousie U (NS, Canada)
East Carolina U (NC)
Eastern Michigan U (MI)
Eastern Washington U (WA)
Grand Valley State U (MI)
Hampton U (VA)
Indiana Tech (IN)
Ithaca Coll (NY)
Longwood U (VA)
Minnesota State U Mankato (MN)
Pittsburg State U (KS)
St. Andrews U (NC)
Shaw U (NC)
Slippery Rock U of Pennsylvania (PA)
State U of New York Coll at Cortland (NY)
Temple U (PA)
Unity Coll (ME)
The U of Iowa (IA)
The U of North Carolina Wilmington (NC)
U of Southern Maine (ME)
The U of Toledo (OH)
U of Waterloo (ON, Canada)
U of Wisconsin–La Crosse (WI)
U of Wisconsin–Milwaukee (WI)
Utica Coll (NY)
Western Carolina U (NC)
West Virginia State U (WV)

TOOL AND DIE TECHNOLOGY
Utah State U (UT)

TOURISM AND TRAVEL SERVICES MANAGEMENT
Arizona State U (AZ)
Brock U (ON, Canada)
California State U, Chico (CA)
Concord U (WV)
Fort Lewis Coll (CO)
George Mason U (VA)
Hawai`i Pacific U (HI)
Indiana U–Purdue U Indianapolis (IN)
Johnson State Coll (VT)
Mansfield U of Pennsylvania (PA)
Niagara U (NY)
Plymouth State U (NH)
St. Thomas U (FL)
Salem State U (MA)
Southern New Hampshire U (NH)
State U of New York Coll of Technology at Delhi (NY)
State U of New York Maritime Coll (NY)
Texas A&M U (TX)
Thompson Rivers U (BC, Canada)
U of Central Florida (FL)
U of Guelph (ON, Canada)
U of Hawaii at Manoa (HI)
U of Maine at Machias (ME)
U of Nevada, Las Vegas (NV)
U of South Carolina (SC)
The U of Texas at San Antonio (TX)

TOURISM AND TRAVEL SERVICES MARKETING
Rochester Inst of Technology (NY)
Western Michigan U (MI)

TOURISM PROMOTION
Bowling Green State U (OH)

TOXICOLOGY
Ashland U (OH)
Eastern Michigan U (MI)
Nazareth Coll of Rochester (NY)
Penn State Beaver (PA)
Penn State Berks (PA)
Penn State DuBois (PA)
Penn State Fayette, The Eberly Campus (PA)
Penn State Greater Allegheny (PA)
Penn State Hazleton (PA)
Penn State Mont Alto (PA)
Penn State New Kensington (PA)
Penn State Shenango (PA)
Penn State U Park (PA)
Penn State Wilkes-Barre (PA)
Penn State York (PA)
St. John's U (NY)
U of California, Berkeley (CA)
U of Guelph (ON, Canada)
U of Louisiana at Monroe (LA)

The U of Western Ontario (ON, Canada)

TRADE AND INDUSTRIAL TEACHER EDUCATION
Athens State U (AL)
Auburn U (AL)
Bemidji State U (MN)
Bowling Green State U (OH)
Buffalo State Coll, State U of New York (NY)
California State U, Long Beach (CA)
California State U, San Bernardino (CA)
Colorado State U (CO)
Concordia U, Nebraska (NE)
Eastern New Mexico U (NM)
Florida Ag and Mech U (FL)
Indiana State U (IN)
Indiana U of Pennsylvania (PA)
Iowa State U of Science and Technology (IA)
Kent State U (OH)
Lindenwood U (MO)
Norfolk State U (VA)
San Diego State U (CA)
Southern Illinois U Carbondale (IL)
State U of New York at Oswego (NY)
Temple U (PA)
U of Central Florida (FL)
U of Central Oklahoma (OK)
U of Louisville (KY)
U of Minnesota, Twin Cities Campus (MN)
U of Nebraska–Lincoln (NE)
U of Southern Maine (ME)
U of the District of Columbia (DC)
U of the Virgin Islands (VI)
The U of Toledo (OH)
U of West Florida (FL)
U of Wyoming (WY)
Upper Iowa U (IA)
Valdosta State U (GA)
Virginia State U (VA)
Wayland Baptist U (TX)
Western Kentucky U (KY)
Western Michigan U (MI)

TRANSPORTATION AND MATERIALS MOVING RELATED
Lewis U (IL)
Maine Maritime Acad (ME)
Niagara U (NY)
Tennessee State U (TN)
United States Merchant Marine Acad (NY)
The U of British Columbia (BC, Canada)

TRANSPORTATION/MOBILITY MANAGEMENT
Bridgewater State U (MA)
U of North Florida (FL)
U of Pennsylvania (PA)
U of Wisconsin–Superior (WI)

TURF AND TURFGRASS MANAGEMENT
Clemson U (SC)
Florida Southern Coll (FL)
New Mexico State U (NM)
North Carolina State U (NC)
North Dakota State U (ND)
The Ohio State U (OH)
Penn State Abington (PA)
Penn State Altoona (PA)
Penn State Beaver (PA)
Penn State Berks (PA)
Penn State Brandywine (PA)
Penn State DuBois (PA)
Penn State Erie, The Behrend Coll (PA)
Penn State Fayette, The Eberly Campus (PA)
Penn State Greater Allegheny (PA)
Penn State Hazleton (PA)
Penn State Lehigh Valley (PA)
Penn State Mont Alto (PA)
Penn State New Kensington (PA)
Penn State Schuylkill (PA)
Penn State Shenango (PA)
Penn State U Park (PA)
Penn State Wilkes-Barre (PA)
Penn State Worthington Scranton (PA)
Penn State York (PA)

Rutgers, The State U of New Jersey, New Brunswick (NJ)
Texas A&M U (TX)
U of Georgia (GA)
U of Minnesota, Crookston (MN)
U of Nebraska–Lincoln (NE)

TURKISH
U of Utah (UT)

URBAN EDUCATION AND LEADERSHIP
The Coll of New Jersey (NJ)
U of Delaware (DE)
U of Wisconsin–Milwaukee (WI)

URBAN FORESTRY
Texas A&M U (TX)
U of California, Davis (CA)
U of Illinois at Urbana–Champaign (IL)
U of Minnesota, Crookston (MN)

URBAN MINISTRY
Crown Coll (MN)

URBAN STUDIES/AFFAIRS
Albertus Magnus Coll (CT)
The American U of Paris (France)
Arizona State U (AZ)
Augsburg Coll (MN)
Ball State U (IN)
Boston U (MA)
Brown U (RI)
Buffalo State Coll, State U of New York (NY)
Butler U (IN)
California State U, Dominguez Hills (CA)
California State U, Northridge (CA)
California State U, Stanislaus (CA)
Canisius Coll (NY)
Cleveland State U (OH)
Coll of Charleston (SC)
The Coll of Wooster (OH)
Columbia U (NY)
Columbia U, School of General Studies (NY)
Concordia U (QC, Canada)
Connecticut Coll (CT)
DePaul U (IL)
Dillard U (LA)
Eugene Lang Coll The New School for Liberal Arts (NY)
Furman U (SC)
Hampshire Coll (MA)
Harris-Stowe State U (MO)
Haverford Coll (PA)
Hobart and William Smith Colls (NY)
Hunter Coll of the City U of New York (NY)
Langston U (OK)
Lipscomb U (TN)
Loyola Marymount U (CA)
Manhattan Coll (NY)
Minnesota State U Mankato (MN)
Morehouse Coll (GA)
New Coll of Florida (FL)
New Jersey City U (NJ)
New York U (NY)
Northeastern Illinois U (IL)
Oglethorpe U (GA)
Ohio U (OH)
Ohio Wesleyan U (OH)
Polytechnic Inst of New York U (NY)
Portland State U (OR)
Purchase Coll, State U of New York (NY)
Rhodes Coll (TN)
Rutgers, The State U of New Jersey, Camden (NJ)
Rutgers, The State U of New Jersey, New Brunswick (NJ)
Saint Louis U (MO)
San Diego State U (CA)
San Francisco Art Inst (CA)
San Francisco State U (CA)
Stanford U (CA)
Temple U (PA)
Trinity U (TX)
Tufts U (MA)
U at Albany, State U of New York (NY)
The U of British Columbia (BC, Canada)
U of California, Berkeley (CA)
U of California, Irvine (CA)
U of Cincinnati (OH)

U of Illinois at Chicago (IL)
U of Minnesota, Duluth (MN)
U of Minnesota, Twin Cities Campus (MN)
U of Missouri–Kansas City (MO)
U of Nebraska at Omaha (NE)
U of New Orleans (LA)
U of Pennsylvania (PA)
U of Pittsburgh (PA)
The U of Texas at Austin (TX)
The U of Toledo (OH)
U of Utah (UT)
U of Washington, Tacoma (WA)
The U of Western Ontario (ON, Canada)
U of Wisconsin–Green Bay (WI)
Vassar Coll (NY)
Virginia Commonwealth U (VA)
Warner Pacific Coll (OR)
Washington U in St. Louis (MO)
Wayne State U (MI)
Worcester State U (MA)
Wright State U (OH)

VEHICLE AND VEHICLE PARTS AND ACCESSORIES MARKETING
Northwood U, Florida Campus (FL)
Northwood U, Michigan Campus (MI)

VETERINARY/ANIMAL HEALTH TECHNOLOGY
Brigham Young U (UT)
Medaille Coll (NY)
Michigan State U (MI)
Mississippi State U (MS)
Murray State U (KY)
North Dakota State U (ND)
Purdue U (IN)
State U of New York Coll of Technology at Canton (NY)
State U of New York Coll of Technology at Delhi (NY)
Thomas Edison State Coll (NJ)
U of Nebraska–Lincoln (NE)

VISION SCIENCE/ PHYSIOLOGICAL OPTICS
U of the Incarnate Word (TX)

VISUAL AND PERFORMING ARTS
American U (DC)
The American U of Rome (Italy)
Arizona State U (AZ)
Armstrong Atlantic State U (GA)
Art Center Coll of Design (CA)
Assumption Coll (MA)
Bennington Coll (VT)
Blackburn Coll (IL)
Bloomfield Coll (NJ)
Blue Mountain Coll (MS)
Brown U (RI)
Bucknell U (PA)
California Baptist U (CA)
California State U, San Marcos (CA)
Centenary Coll of Louisiana (LA)
Champlain Coll (VT)
Chowan U (NC)
Clemson U (SC)
Columbia U (NY)
Columbia U, School of General Studies (NY)
Concordia U (QC, Canada)
Cooper Union for the Advancement of Science and Art (NY)
Delta State U (MS)
DEREE—The American Coll of Greece (Greece)
Eckerd Coll (FL)
Emerson Coll (MA)
Eugene Lang Coll The New School for Liberal Arts (NY)
The Evergreen State Coll (WA)
Fairleigh Dickinson U, Coll at Florham (NJ)
Fairleigh Dickinson U, Metropolitan Campus (NJ)
Fayetteville State U (NC)
Ferrum Coll (VA)
Gannon U (PA)
George Mason U (VA)
Gettysburg Coll (PA)
Indiana U of Pennsylvania (PA)
Inter American U of Puerto Rico, San Germán Campus (PR)
Iowa State U of Science and Technology (IA)

Ithaca Coll (NY)
Johnson C. Smith U (NC)
Johnson State Coll (VT)
Kent State U (OH)
King Coll (TN)
LaGrange Coll (GA)
Lindenwood U (MO)
Long Island U–C. W. Post Campus (NY)
Longwood U (VA)
Maryland Inst Coll of Art (MD)
Massachusetts Coll of Liberal Arts (MA)
Mississippi State U (MS)
Mississippi U for Women (MS)
Missouri State U (MO)
Naropa U (CO)
New Mexico Highlands U (NM)
New Mexico State U (NM)
Oklahoma City U (OK)
Oregon State U (OR)
Penn State Abington (PA)
Penn State Altoona (PA)
Penn State Beaver (PA)
Penn State Berks (PA)
Penn State Brandywine (PA)
Penn State DuBois (PA)
Penn State Erie, The Behrend Coll (PA)
Penn State Fayette, The Eberly Campus (PA)
Penn State Greater Allegheny (PA)
Penn State Hazleton (PA)
Penn State Lehigh Valley (PA)
Penn State Mont Alto (PA)
Penn State New Kensington (PA)
Penn State Schuylkill (PA)
Penn State Shenango (PA)
Penn State U Park (PA)
Penn State Wilkes-Barre (PA)
Penn State Worthington Scranton (PA)
Penn State York (PA)
Pine Manor Coll (MA)
Prescott Coll (AZ)
Providence Coll (RI)
Purchase Coll, State U of New York (NY)
Ramapo Coll of New Jersey (NJ)
Regis U (CO)
Rensselaer Polytechnic Inst (NY)
The Richard Stockton Coll of New Jersey (NJ)
Rogers State U (OK)
Roger Williams U (RI)
Rutgers, The State U of New Jersey, New Brunswick (NJ)
St. Bonaventure U (NY)
St. Gregory's U, Shawnee (OK)
Saint Joseph's U (PA)
San Jose State U (CA)
School of the Art Inst of Chicago (IL)
Seattle U (WA)
Shenandoah U (VA)
South Dakota State U (SD)
Southeast Missouri State U (MO)
Southern Polytechnic State U (GA)
State U of New York at New Paltz (NY)
State U of New York Coll at Old Westbury (NY)
State U of New York Coll at Potsdam (NY)
Stonehill Coll (MA)
Suffolk U (MA)
Tennessee Wesleyan Coll (TN)
Texas Southern U (TX)
The U of Arizona (AZ)
The U of British Columbia (BC, Canada)
The U of British Columbia–Okanagan (BC, Canada)
U of Colorado Colorado Springs (CO)
U of Houston–Downtown (TX)
U of Louisiana at Lafayette (LA)
U of Maine at Machias (ME)
U of Mary Washington (VA)
The U of Montana Western (MT)
U of Mount Union (OH)
U of North Carolina School of the Arts (NC)
U of Pennsylvania (PA)
U of Regina (SK, Canada)
U of St. Francis (IL)
U of Saint Mary (KS)
The U of South Dakota (SD)

U of Southern California (CA)
U of Southern Mississippi (MS)
The U of Tennessee at Martin (TN)
The U of Texas at Austin (TX)
The U of Texas at Dallas (TX)
U of Utah (UT)
U of Windsor (ON, Canada)
U of Wisconsin–Superior (WI)
Valdosta State U (GA)
Vassar Coll (NY)
Virginia State U (VA)
Viterbo U (WI)
Western Washington U (WA)
Wichita State U (KS)
Worcester State U (MA)

VISUAL AND PERFORMING ARTS RELATED
Adelphi U (NY)
Baldwin Wallace U (OH)
The Baptist Coll of Florida (FL)
Brigham Young U (UT)
Cameron U (OK)
Clemson U (SC)
Columbia U, School of General Studies (NY)
Grambling State U (LA)
Illinois State U (IL)
Illinois Wesleyan U (IL)
Marywood U (PA)
Millikin U (IL)
Molloy Coll (NY)
New York U (NY)
Oklahoma City U (OK)
Penn State Altoona (PA)
Prescott Coll (AZ)
Providence Coll (RI)
Purchase Coll, State U of New York (NY)
Rice U (TX)
Russell Sage Coll (NY)
Sacred Heart U (CT)
Saint Mary's Coll of California (CA)
Samford U (AL)
San Francisco Art Inst (CA)
School of the Art Inst of Chicago (IL)
School of the Museum of Fine Arts, Boston (MA)
Seton Hill U (PA)
Simon Fraser U (BC, Canada)
Spring Arbor U (MI)
State U of New York Coll at Geneseo (NY)
U of California, Davis (CA)
U of Chicago (IL)
U of Michigan (MI)
U of New Haven (CT)
U of South Florida (FL)
U of Washington, Bothell (WA)
U of Wisconsin–Green Bay (WI)
Webster U (MO)
Western State Colorado U (CO)

VITICULTURE AND ENOLOGY
Washington State U (WA)

VOCATIONAL REHABILITATION COUNSELING
Bowling Green State U (OH)
East Carolina U (NC)
East Central U (OK)
Emporia State U (KS)
Maryville U of Saint Louis (MO)
U of Illinois at Urbana–Champaign (IL)
U of Wisconsin–Madison (WI)
U of Wisconsin–Stout (WI)
Wright State U (OH)

VOICE AND OPERA
Abilene Christian U (TX)
Acadia U (NS, Canada)
Andrews U (MI)
Arizona Christian U (AZ)
Baldwin Wallace U (OH)
Bard Coll (NY)
Barry U (FL)
Belmont U (TN)
Bennington Coll (VT)
Berklee Coll of Music (MA)
The Boston Conservatory (MA)
Boston U (MA)
Bowling Green State U (OH)
Brigham Young U (UT)
Butler U (IN)
California Baptist U (CA)

California State U, Long Beach (CA)
Calvin Coll (MI)
Campbellsville U (KY)
Capital U (OH)
Carnegie Mellon U (PA)
Carson-Newman U (TN)
Catawba Coll (NC)
The Catholic U of America (DC)
Chapman U (CA)
Cincinnati Christian U (OH)
Concordia U, Nebraska (NE)
Converse Coll (SC)
Dallas Baptist U (TX)
Dordt Coll (IA)
Drake U (IA)
East Central U (OK)
East Texas Baptist U (TX)
Five Towns Coll (NY)
Furman U (SC)
Grace U (NE)
Hardin-Simmons U (TX)
Hope Coll (MI)
Houghton Coll (NY)
Howard Payne U (TX)
Illinois Wesleyan U (IL)
Indiana U–Purdue U Fort Wayne (IN)
Ithaca Coll (NY)
Lamar U (TX)
Langston U (OK)
Lawrence U (WI)
Lipscomb U (TN)
Long Island U–C. W. Post Campus (NY)
Louisiana Coll (LA)
Madonna U (MI)
Mannes Coll The New School for Music (NY)
Maryville Coll (TN)
The Master's Coll and Sem (CA)
McNally Smith Coll of Music (MN)
Minnesota State U Mankato (MN)
Mississippi Coll (MS)
Mount Allison U (NB, Canada)
New England Conservatory of Music (MA)
Northern State U (SD)
Northwestern Coll (MN)
Notre Dame de Namur U (CA)
Nyack Coll (NY)
Oakland U (MI)
The Ohio State U (OH)
Ohio U (OH)
Oklahoma Baptist U (OK)
Oklahoma Christian U (OK)
Oklahoma City U (OK)
Oral Roberts U (OK)
Ouachita Baptist U (AR)
Palm Beach Atlantic U (FL)
Peabody Conservatory of The Johns Hopkins U (MD)
Point Loma Nazarene U (CA)
Queens U of Charlotte (NC)
Roberts Wesleyan Coll (NY)
Roosevelt U (IL)
Samford U (AL)
San Francisco Conservatory of Music (CA)
Southeastern U (FL)
Southern Methodist U (TX)
State U of New York at Fredonia (NY)
State U of New York at New Paltz (NY)
Stetson U (FL)
Syracuse U (NY)
Temple U (PA)
Texas Christian U (TX)
Trinity U (TX)
Union U (TN)
The U of Akron (OH)
The U of British Columbia (BC, Canada)
U of Central Oklahoma (OK)
U of Cincinnati (OH)
U of Delaware (DE)
U of Idaho (ID)
U of Illinois at Urbana–Champaign (IL)
The U of Iowa (IA)
The U of Kansas (KS)
U of Miami (FL)
U of Mobile (AL)
U of Nebraska at Omaha (NE)
U of North Carolina School of the Arts (NC)
U of Redlands (CA)

U of Southern California (CA)
The U of Tennessee at Martin (TN)
U of Tulsa (OK)
The U of Western Ontario (ON, Canada)
Valparaiso U (IN)
Vanderbilt U (TN)
Washington U in St. Louis (MO)
Weber State U (UT)
Western Michigan U (MI)
Whitworth U (WA)
Willamette U (OR)
William Paterson U of New Jersey (NJ)

WATER RESOURCES ENGINEERING
Central State U (OH)
U of Guelph (ON, Canada)
U of Illinois at Urbana–Champaign (IL)
U of Nevada, Reno (NV)

WATER, WETLANDS, AND MARINE RESOURCES MANAGEMENT
Colorado State U (CO)
Florida Gulf Coast U (FL)
Stony Brook U, State U of New York (NY)
Texas State U–San Marcos (TX)
U of Minnesota, Crookston (MN)
U of New Hampshire (NH)
Western State Colorado U (CO)

WEB/MULTIMEDIA MANAGEMENT AND WEBMASTER
American Public U System (WV)
Georgia Coll & State U (GA)
Grace U (NE)
Hawai`i Pacific U (HI)
Indiana Tech (IN)
Lewis-Clark State Coll (ID)
Limestone Coll (SC)
Morrisville State Coll (NY)
Neumont U (UT)
New England School of Communications (ME)
Northern Michigan U (MI)
Pepperdine U, Malibu (CA)
Rochester Inst of Technology (NY)
State U of New York Coll of Technology at Alfred (NY)
Trevecca Nazarene U (TN)
U of Great Falls (MT)
U of St. Francis (IL)

WEB PAGE, DIGITAL/ MULTIMEDIA AND INFORMATION RESOURCES DESIGN
Acad of Art U (CA)
American Acad of Art (IL)
Azusa Pacific U (CA)
Bradley U (IL)
Columbia Coll Chicago (IL)
Concordia U (QC, Canada)
Creighton U (NE)
Dakota Wesleyan U (SD)
DePaul U (IL)
DeVry U, Phoenix (AZ)
DeVry U, Pomona (CA)
DeVry U, Westminster (CO)
DeVry U, Miramar (FL)
DeVry U, Orlando (FL)
DeVry U, Decatur (GA)
DeVry U, Chicago (IL)
DeVry U, Kansas City (MO)
DeVry U, North Brunswick (NJ)
DeVry U, Columbus (OH)
DeVry U, Fort Washington (PA)
DeVry U, Houston (TX)
DeVry U, Irving (TX)
DeVry U, Arlington (VA)
DeVry U, Federal Way (WA)
DeVry U Online (IL)
Duquesne U (PA)
Franklin U (OH)
Hampshire Coll (MA)
Harding U (AR)
Indiana Wesleyan U (IN)
Intl Acad of Design & Technology (FL)
Iona Coll (NY)
Iowa Wesleyan Coll (IA)
Lasell Coll (MA)
Lindenwood U (MO)
Lipscomb U (TN)
Mercyhurst U (PA)

National U (CA)
Neumont U (UT)
New York City Coll of Technology of the City U of New York (NY)
Northwest Missouri State U (MO)
Pennsylvania Coll of Technology (PA)
Quinnipiac U (CT)
Rasmussen Coll Bloomington (MN)
Rasmussen Coll Brooklyn Park (MN)
Rasmussen Coll Eagan (MN)
Rasmussen Coll Fort Myers (FL)
Rasmussen Coll Lake Elmo/ Woodbury (MN)
Rasmussen Coll Land O' Lakes (FL)
Rasmussen Coll Mankato (MN)
Rasmussen Coll Moorhead (MN)
Rasmussen Coll New Port Richey (FL)
Rasmussen Coll Ocala (FL)
Rasmussen Coll Rockford (IL)
Rasmussen Coll St. Cloud (MN)
Rasmussen Coll Tampa/Brandon (FL)
Rider U (NJ)
Rochester Inst of Technology (NY)
School of the Art Inst of Chicago (IL)
Sullivan Coll of Technology and Design (KY)
Trevecca Nazarene U (TN)
U of Great Falls (MT)
U of Mount Union (OH)
U of North Carolina at Asheville (NC)
The U of the Arts (PA)
U of Washington, Bothell (WA)
U of Wisconsin–Stevens Point (WI)
Walla Walla U (WA)
Webster U (MO)

WELDING TECHNOLOGY
LeTourneau U (TX)
Lewis-Clark State Coll (ID)
The Ohio State U (OH)

WILDLIFE BIOLOGY
Adams State U (CO)
Clemson U (SC)
Coll of the Atlantic (ME)
Colorado State U (CO)
Friends U (KS)
Frostburg State U (MD)
Kansas State U (KS)
Keystone Coll (PA)
Lees-McRae Coll (NC)
Ohio U (OH)
Texas State U–San Marcos (TX)
U of Guelph (ON, Canada)
U of Michigan–Flint (MI)
U of New Brunswick Fredericton (NB, Canada)
U of Vermont (VT)
U of Wyoming (WY)
West Texas A&M U (TX)

WILDLIFE, FISH AND WILDLANDS SCIENCE AND MANAGEMENT
Albion Coll (MI)
Arkansas State U (AR)
Arkansas Tech U (AR)
Auburn U (AL)
Coll of the Ozarks (MO)
Dakota Wesleyan U (SD)
Eastern New Mexico U (NM)
Frostburg State U (MD)
Humboldt State U (CA)
Juniata Coll (PA)
Lake Superior State U (MI)
Lincoln Memorial U (TN)
McNeese State U (LA)
Michigan State U (MI)
Mississippi State U (MS)
Missouri State U (MO)
Missouri Western State U (MO)
Montana State U (MT)
Murray State U (KY)
New Mexico State U (NM)
Northland Coll (WI)
Northwest Missouri State U (MO)
The Ohio State U (OH)
Oregon State U (OR)
Purdue U (IN)
South Dakota State U (SD)

State U of New York Coll of Agriculture and Technology at Cobleskill (NY)
Stephen F. Austin State U (TX)
Sterling Coll (VT)
Sul Ross State U (TX)
Tarleton State U (TX)
Texas A&M U (TX)
Texas A&M U–Commerce (TX)
Texas A&M U–Kingsville (TX)
Unity Coll (ME)
U of Alaska Fairbanks (AK)
The U of British Columbia (BC, Canada)
U of Delaware (DE)
U of Florida (FL)
U of Georgia (GA)
U of Idaho (ID)
U of Illinois at Urbana–Champaign (IL)
U of Minnesota, Twin Cities Campus (MN)
U of Missouri (MO)
U of Nevada, Reno (NV)
U of New Brunswick Fredericton (NB, Canada)
U of New Hampshire (NH)
U of Rhode Island (RI)
The U of Tennessee (TN)
The U of Tennessee at Martin (TN)
U of Wisconsin–Madison (WI)
U of Wisconsin–Stevens Point (WI)
Utah State U (UT)
Valley City State U (ND)
Washington State U (WA)
West Virginia U (WV)

WOMEN'S MINISTRY
Corban U (OR)

WOMEN'S STUDIES
Agnes Scott Coll (GA)
Albion Coll (MI)
Albright Coll (PA)
Alverno Coll (WI)
American U (DC)
Amherst Coll (MA)
Appalachian State U (NC)
Arizona State U (AZ)
Armstrong Atlantic State U (GA)
Athabasca U (AB, Canada)
Augsburg Coll (MN)
Augustana Coll (IL)
Ball State U (IN)
Bates Coll (ME)
Bennington Coll (VT)
Berea Coll (KY)
Bowdoin Coll (ME)
Bowling Green State U (OH)
Brock U (ON, Canada)
Brown U (RI)
Bucknell U (PA)
California State U, Fresno (CA)
California State U, Fullerton (CA)
California State U, Long Beach (CA)
California State U, Northridge (CA)
California State U, San Marcos (CA)
Canisius Coll (NY)
Carleton Coll (MN)
Case Western Reserve U (OH)
Central Michigan U (MI)
Chatham U (PA)
City Coll of the City U of New York (NY)
Clark U (MA)
Cleveland State U (OH)
Colby Coll (ME)
Colgate U (NY)
The Coll at Brockport, State U of New York (NY)
Coll of Charleston (SC)
The Coll of New Jersey (NJ)
The Coll of New Rochelle (NY)
Coll of Saint Benedict (MN)
Coll of Saint Elizabeth (NJ)
The Coll of Saint Rose (NY)
The Coll of William and Mary (VA)
The Coll of Wooster (OH)
The Colorado Coll (CO)
Columbia U (NY)
Columbia U, School of General Studies (NY)
Concordia U (QC, Canada)
Concordia U Chicago (IL)
Connecticut Coll (CT)
Cornell Coll (IA)

Curry Coll (MA)
Dalhousie U (NS, Canada)
Dartmouth Coll (NH)
DePaul U (IL)
DePauw U (IN)
Dickinson Coll (PA)
Dominican U (IL)
Drew U (NJ)
Duquesne U (PA)
Earlham Coll (IN)
East Carolina U (NC)
Eastern Michigan U (MI)
Eastern Washington U (WA)
East Tennessee State U (TN)
Eckerd Coll (FL)
Florida Intl U (FL)
Fort Lewis Coll (CO)
Georgetown U (DC)
Georgia State U (GA)
Gettysburg Coll (PA)
Goucher Coll (MD)
Grand Valley State U (MI)
Guilford Coll (NC)
Gustavus Adolphus Coll (MN)
Hamilton Coll (NY)
Hamline U (MN)
Hampshire Coll (MA)
Hobart and William Smith Colls (NY)
Hofstra U (NY)
Hollins U (VA)
Hope Coll (MI)
Hunter Coll of the City U of New York (NY)
Illinois Wesleyan U (IL)
Indiana U–Purdue U Fort Wayne (IN)
Iowa State U of Science and Technology (IA)
Kansas State U (KS)
Keene State Coll (NH)
Kenyon Coll (OH)
Knox Coll (IL)
Lafayette Coll (PA)
Lehigh U (PA)
Loyola Marymount U (CA)
Loyola U Chicago (IL)
Luther Coll (IA)
Macalester Coll (MN)
Manchester U (IN)
Merrimack Coll (MA)
Miami U (OH)
Michigan State U (MI)
Middlebury Coll (VT)
Mills Coll (CA)
Minnesota State U Mankato (MN)
Minnesota State U Moorhead (MN)
Montclair State U (NJ)
Nazareth Coll of Rochester (NY)
New Jersey City U (NJ)
New Mexico State U (NM)
North Carolina State U (NC)
North Dakota State U (ND)
Northeastern Illinois U (IL)
Northern Arizona U (AZ)
Northland Coll (WI)
Oakland U (MI)
The Ohio State U (OH)
Ohio U (OH)
Ohio Wesleyan U (OH)
Old Dominion U (VA)
Oregon State U (OR)
Pace U (NY)
Pacific Lutheran U (WA)
Penn State Abington (PA)
Penn State Altoona (PA)
Penn State Beaver (PA)
Penn State Berks (PA)
Penn State Brandywine (PA)
Penn State DuBois (PA)
Penn State Erie, The Behrend Coll (PA)
Penn State Fayette, The Eberly Campus (PA)
Penn State Greater Allegheny (PA)
Penn State Hazleton (PA)
Penn State Lehigh Valley (PA)
Penn State Mont Alto (PA)
Penn State New Kensington (PA)
Penn State Schuylkill (PA)
Penn State Shenango (PA)
Penn State Park (PA)
Penn State Wilkes-Barre (PA)
Penn State Worthington Scranton (PA)
Penn State York (PA)
Pitzer Coll (CA)
Pomona Coll (CA)

Portland State U (OR)
Providence Coll (RI)
Purchase Coll, State U of New York (NY)
Randolph-Macon Coll (VA)
Rhode Island Coll (RI)
Rice U (TX)
Rosemont Coll (PA)
Rutgers, The State U of New Jersey, Newark (NJ)
Rutgers, The State U of New Jersey, New Brunswick (NJ)
Sacred Heart U (CT)
St. Bonaventure U (NY)
Saint John's U (MN)
Saint Louis U (MO)
Saint Mary's Coll of California (CA)
St. Olaf Coll (MN)
St. Thomas U (NB, Canada)
San Diego State U (CA)
San Francisco State U (CA)
Scripps Coll (CA)
Seattle U (WA)
Simmons Coll (MA)
Simon Fraser U (BC, Canada)
Smith Coll (MA)
Sonoma State U (CA)
Southwestern U (TX)
Spelman Coll (GA)
Stanford U (CA)
State U of New York at Fredonia (NY)
State U of New York at New Paltz (NY)
State U of New York at Oswego (NY)
State U of New York at Plattsburgh (NY)
State U of New York Coll at Potsdam (NY)
Stony Brook U, State U of New York (NY)
Suffolk U (MA)
Swarthmore Coll (PA)
Syracuse U (NY)
Temple U (PA)
Texas A&M U (TX)
Trent U (ON, Canada)
Trinity Coll (CT)
Tufts U (MA)
Tulane U (LA)
U at Albany, State U of New York (NY)
The U of Arizona (AZ)
The U of British Columbia (BC, Canada)
U of California, Berkeley (CA)
U of California, Davis (CA)
U of California, Irvine (CA)
U of California, Los Angeles (CA)
U of California, Riverside (CA)
U of California, Santa Barbara (CA)
U of California, Santa Cruz (CA)
U of Cincinnati (OH)
U of Colorado Boulder (CO)
U of Delaware (DE)
U of Florida (FL)
U of Georgia (GA)
U of Hartford (CT)
U of Hawaii at Manoa (HI)
U of Houston–Clear Lake (TX)
U of Illinois at Chicago (IL)
U of Illinois at Urbana–Champaign (IL)
The U of Iowa (IA)
The U of Kansas (KS)
U of Louisville (KY)
U of Maryland, Baltimore County (MD)
U of Maryland, Coll Park (MD)
U of Massachusetts Amherst (MA)
U of Massachusetts Boston (MA)
U of Massachusetts Dartmouth (MA)
U of Miami (FL)
U of Michigan (MI)
U of Michigan–Dearborn (MI)
U of Minnesota, Duluth (MN)
U of Minnesota, Twin Cities Campus (MN)
U of Nebraska–Lincoln (NE)
U of Nevada, Las Vegas (NV)
U of Nevada, Reno (NV)
U of New Hampshire (NH)
U of New Mexico (NM)
U of North Carolina at Asheville (NC)

The U of North Carolina at Chapel Hill (NC)
The U of North Carolina at Greensboro (NC)
U of Oklahoma (OK)
U of Oregon (OR)
U of Ottawa (ON, Canada)
U of Pennsylvania (PA)
U of Regina (SK, Canada)
U of Rhode Island (RI)
U of Richmond (VA)
U of Rochester (NY)
U of Saint Joseph (CT)
U of St. Thomas (MN)
The U of Scranton (PA)
U of South Carolina (SC)
U of Southern Maine (ME)
U of South Florida (FL)
The U of Texas at Austin (TX)
The U of Toledo (OH)
U of Utah (UT)
U of Vermont (VT)
U of Waterloo (ON, Canada)
The U of Western Ontario (ON, Canada)
U of Windsor (ON, Canada)
U of Wisconsin–Eau Claire (WI)
U of Wisconsin–La Crosse (WI)
U of Wisconsin–Madison (WI)
U of Wisconsin–Milwaukee (WI)
U of Wyoming (WY)
Vanderbilt U (TN)
Vassar Coll (NY)
Villanova U (PA)
Virginia Commonwealth U (VA)
Virginia Wesleyan Coll (VA)
Washington State U (WA)
Washington U in St. Louis (MO)
Webster U (MO)
Wellesley Coll (MA)
Wells Coll (NY)
Wesleyan Coll (GA)
Wesleyan U (CT)
West Chester U of Pennsylvania (PA)
Western Illinois U (IL)
Western Michigan U (MI)
Wheaton Coll (MA)
Wichita State U (KS)
Willamette U (OR)
William Paterson U of New Jersey (NJ)
Wright State U (OH)
Yale U (CT)

WOOD SCIENCE AND WOOD PRODUCTS/PULP AND PAPER TECHNOLOGY
North Carolina State U (NC)
Oregon State U (OR)
The U of British Columbia (BC, Canada)
U of Idaho (ID)
U of Minnesota, Twin Cities Campus (MN)
U of Wisconsin–Stevens Point (WI)
West Virginia U (WV)

WOODWIND INSTRUMENTS
Acadia U (NS, Canada)
Berklee Coll of Music (MA)
The Boston Conservatory (MA)
Five Towns Coll (NY)
Houghton Coll (NY)
Lawrence U (WI)
Maryville Coll (TN)
Mount Allison U (NB, Canada)
New England Conservatory of Music (MA)
Oklahoma Christian U (OK)
Oklahoma City U (OK)
Peabody Conservatory of The Johns Hopkins U (MD)
San Francisco Conservatory of Music (CA)
State U of New York at Fredonia (NY)
U of Central Oklahoma (OK)
The U of Iowa (IA)
The U of Kansas (KS)
U of Michigan (MI)
Vanderbilt U (TN)
Xavier U of Louisiana (LA)

WOODWORKING
Pittsburg State U (KS)
Rochester Inst of Technology (NY)

WOODWORKING RELATED
Pittsburg State U (KS)

WORK AND FAMILY STUDIES
Brigham Young U (UT)

WRITING
Augustana Coll (IL)
Aurora U (IL)
Baylor U (TX)
Bennington Coll (VT)
Brigham Young U (UT)
Calvin Coll (MI)
Canisius Coll (NY)
Carroll Coll (MT)
Champlain Coll (VT)
Columbia U, School of General Studies (NY)
DePauw U (IN)
Drury U (MO)
Eastern Michigan U (MI)
Ferris State U (MI)
Florida Southern Coll (FL)
Geneva Coll (PA)
Georgia Southern U (GA)
Gettysburg Coll (PA)
Graceland U (IA)
Grand Valley State U (MI)
Huntington U (IN)
Indiana U–Purdue U Fort Wayne (IN)
Indiana Wesleyan U (IN)
Jamestown Coll (ND)
Lakeland Coll (WI)
La Roche Coll (PA)
Lipscomb U (TN)
Marian U (WI)
Marquette U (WI)
Massachusetts Coll of Liberal Arts (MA)
Mississippi Coll (MS)
Northwest U (WA)
Oakland U (MI)
Oral Roberts U (OK)
Prescott Coll (AZ)
Purdue U Calumet (IN)
St. Edward's U (TX)
Salem State U (MA)
Spring Hill Coll (AL)
U of Central Arkansas (AR)
U of Colorado Denver (CO)
U of Evansville (IN)
U of Great Falls (MT)
U of Illinois at Urbana–Champaign (IL)
U of Michigan–Flint (MI)
U of Minnesota, Twin Cities Campus (MN)
U of Mount Union (OH)
The U of Tampa (FL)
The U of Texas at Austin (TX)
The U of Western Ontario (ON, Canada)
Wartburg Coll (IA)
Western Michigan U (MI)

YOUTH MINISTRY
Anderson U (IN)
Andrews U (MI)
Arizona Christian U (AZ)
Asbury U (KY)
Benedictine Coll (KS)
Bethel Coll (IN)
Bethel U (MN)
Bluffton U (OH)
Briercrest Coll (SK, Canada)
Cedarville U (OH)
Columbia Intl U (SC)
Concordia U Wisconsin (WI)
Corban U (OR)
Crossroads Coll (MN)
Crown Coll (MN)
Dordt Coll (IA)
East Texas Baptist U (TX)
Florida Southern Coll (FL)
Geneva Coll (PA)
Gordon Coll (MA)
Grace U (NE)
Greenville Coll (IL)
Harding U (AR)
Hardin-Simmons U (TX)
Hillsdale Free Will Baptist Coll (OK)
Hope Intl U (CA)
Howard Payne U (TX)
Huntingdon Coll (AL)
Huntington U (IN)
Indiana Wesleyan U (IN)
John Brown U (AR)
Judson U (IL)

King Coll (TN)
Kuyper Coll (MI)
Lee U (TN)
Lincoln Christian U (IL)
Lipscomb U (TN)
Lubbock Christian U (TX)
Malone U (OH)
Maranatha Baptist Bible Coll (WI)
Master's Coll and Sem (ON, Canada)
Mid-Atlantic Christian U (NC)
Mount Vernon Nazarene U (OH)
Multnomah U (OR)
North Greenville U (SC)
Northwestern Coll (MN)
Northwest U (WA)
Nyack Coll (NY)
Rocky Mountain Coll (AB, Canada)
Simpson U (CA)
Southern Nazarene U (OK)
Spring Arbor U (MI)
Tabor Coll (KS)
Trevecca Nazarene U (TN)
Trinity Coll of Florida (FL)

YOUTH SERVICES
Murray State U (KY)
Roger Williams U (RI)
Thompson Rivers U (BC, Canada)
U of Hawaii at Manoa (HI)
The U of Western Ontario (ON, Canada)

ZOOLOGY/ANIMAL BIOLOGY
Andrews U (MI)
Auburn U (AL)
Bennington Coll (VT)
California State U, Long Beach (CA)
Canisius Coll (NY)
Coll of the Atlantic (ME)
Colorado State U (CO)
Dalhousie U (NS, Canada)
Humboldt State U (CA)
Kent State U (OH)
Liberty U (VA)
Malone U (OH)
Mars Hill Coll (NC)
Miami U (OH)
Michigan State U (MI)
North Carolina State U (NC)
North Dakota State U (ND)
Northern Michigan U (MI)
The Ohio State U (OH)
Ohio U (OH)
Ohio Wesleyan U (OH)
Oklahoma State U (OK)
Oregon State U (OR)
Rutgers, The State U of New Jersey, Newark (NJ)
San Francisco State U (CA)
Sonoma State U (CA)
Southern Illinois U Carbondale (IL)
State U of New York at Oswego (NY)
Tarleton State U (TX)
Texas A&M U (TX)
Texas State U–San Marcos (TX)
Thompson Rivers U (BC, Canada)
The U of British Columbia (BC, Canada)
The U of British Columbia–Okanagan (BC, Canada)
U of California, Davis (CA)
U of California, Santa Barbara (CA)
U of Florida (FL)
U of Guelph (ON, Canada)
U of Hawaii at Manoa (HI)
U of Minnesota, Twin Cities Campus (MN)
U of New Brunswick Fredericton (NB, Canada)
U of New Hampshire (NH)
U of Oklahoma (OK)
U of Rhode Island (RI)
The U of Texas at El Paso (TX)
U of Vermont (VT)
U of Wisconsin–Madison (WI)
U of Wyoming (WY)
Utah State U (UT)
Washington State U (WA)
Weber State U (UT)

ZOOLOGY/ANIMAL BIOLOGY RELATED
Canisius Coll (NY)

Entrance Difficulty

This index groups colleges by their own assessment of their entrance difficulty level. The colleges were asked to select the level that most closely corresponds to their entrance difficulty, according to the guidelines below. Institutions for which high school class rank and/or standardized test scores do not apply as admission criteria were asked to select the level that best indicates their entrance difficulty as compared to other institutions.

MOST DIFFICULT

More than 75 percent of the freshmen were in the top 10 percent of their high school class and scored over 1310 on the SAT (critical reading and mathematical combined) or over 29 on the ACT (composite); about 30 percent or fewer of the applicants were accepted.

Amherst Coll (MA)
Bates Coll (ME)
Bowdoin Coll (ME)
Brown U (RI)
Bucknell U (PA)
Carnegie Mellon U (PA)
Claremont McKenna Coll (CA)
Colby Coll (ME)
Colgate U (NY)
The Coll of William and Mary (VA)
Columbia U (NY)
Columbia U, School of General Studies (NY)
Cooper Union for the Advancement of Science and Art (NY)
Dartmouth Coll (NH)
Franklin W. Olin Coll of Eng (MA)
Georgetown U (DC)
Gettysburg Coll (PA)
Harvey Mudd Coll (CA)
Haverford Coll (PA)
The Johns Hopkins U (MD)
The Juilliard School (NY)
Lehigh U (PA)
Massachusetts Inst of Technology (MA)
Middlebury Coll (VT)
New York U (NY)
Pomona Coll (CA)
Princeton U (NJ)
Reed Coll (OR)
Rice U (TX)
Stanford U (CA)
Swarthmore Coll (PA)
Trinity Coll (CT)
Tufts U (MA)
United States Air Force Acad (CO)
United States Military Acad (NY)
U of Chicago (IL)
U of Notre Dame (IN)
U of Pennsylvania (PA)
U of Southern California (CA)
Vanderbilt U (TN)
Washington and Lee U (VA)
Washington U in St. Louis (MO)
Webb Inst (NY)
Wellesley Coll (MA)
Wesleyan U (CT)
Williams Coll (MA)
Yale U (CT)

VERY DIFFICULT

More than 50 percent of the freshmen were in the top 10 percent of their high school class and scored over 1230 on the SAT or over 26 on the ACT; about 60 percent or fewer applicants were accepted.

Agnes Scott Coll (GA)
American U (DC)
American U in Bulgaria (Bulgaria)
The American U in Cairo (Egypt)
Art Center Coll of Design (CA)
Babson Coll (MA)

Bard Coll (NY)
Bennington Coll (VT)
Bentley U (MA)
Binghamton U, State U of New York (NY)
Boston Coll (MA)
Boston U (MA)
Butler U (IN)
Carleton Coll (MN)
Case Western Reserve U (OH)
Centre Coll (KY)
Chapman U (CA)
Christopher Newport U (VA)
Clarkson U (NY)
The Coll of New Jersey (NJ)
The Coll of Saints John Fisher & Thomas More (TX)
Coll of the Atlantic (ME)
Coll of the Holy Cross (MA)
The Colorado Coll (CO)
Colorado School of Mines (CO)
Connecticut Coll (CT)
Davidson Coll (NC)
Dickinson Coll (PA)
Earlham Coll (IN)
Emerson Coll (MA)
Eugene Lang Coll The New School for Liberal Arts (NY)
Florida State U (FL)
Franklin & Marshall Coll (PA)
Grinnell Coll (IA)
Gustavus Adolphus Coll (MN)
Hamilton Coll (NY)
Hendrix Coll (AR)
Hillsdale Coll (MI)
Hobart and William Smith Colls (NY)
Illinois Wesleyan U (IL)
James Madison U (VA)
Kalamazoo Coll (MI)
Kenyon Coll (OH)
Knox Coll (IL)
Lawrence U (WI)
Loyola Marymount U (CA)
Macalester Coll (MN)
Mannes Coll The New School for Music (NY)
Marist Coll (NY)
Maryland Inst Coll of Art (MD)
Massachusetts Coll of Art and Design (MA)
Missouri U of Science and Technology (MO)
Mount Holyoke Coll (MA)
Muhlenberg Coll (PA)
New Coll of Florida (FL)
New England Conservatory of Music (MA)
The New School for Jazz and Contemporary Music (NY)
North Carolina State U (NC)
Northeastern U (MA)
Oglethorpe U (GA)
The Ohio State U (OH)
Ohio Wesleyan U (OH)
Parsons The New School for Design (NY)
Patrick Henry Coll (VA)
Peabody Conservatory of The Johns Hopkins U (MD)
Penn State Abington (PA)
Penn State Altoona (PA)
Penn State Berks (PA)
Penn State Erie, The Behrend Coll (PA)
Penn State Harrisburg (PA)
Penn State U Park (PA)
Pepperdine U, Malibu (CA)
Pitzer Coll (CA)
Polytechnic Inst of New York U (NY)
Presbyterian Coll (SC)
Rensselaer Polytechnic Inst (NY)
Rhode Island School of Design (RI)
Rhodes Coll (TN)
The Richard Stockton Coll of New Jersey (NJ)
St. John's Coll (NM)
St. Lawrence U (NY)
St. Mary's Coll of Maryland (MD)
St. Olaf Coll (MN)
San Jose State U (CA)
School of the Art Inst of Chicago (IL)

Scripps Coll (CA)
Sewanee: The U of the South (TN)
Skidmore Coll (NY)
Smith Coll (MA)
Soka U of America (CA)
Southwestern U (TX)
Spelman Coll (GA)
State U of New York at New Paltz (NY)
State U of New York Coll at Geneseo (NY)
State U of New York Maritime Coll (NY)
Stonehill Coll (MA)
Stony Brook U, State U of New York (NY)
Syracuse U (NY)
Texas Christian U (TX)
Thomas Aquinas Coll (CA)
Transylvania U (KY)
Trinity U (TX)
Tulane U (LA)
United States Coast Guard Acad (CT)
United States Merchant Marine Acad (NY)
United States Naval Acad (MD)
U at Albany, State U of New York (NY)
The U of British Columbia (BC, Canada)
U of California, Davis (CA)
U of California, Irvine (CA)
U of California, Los Angeles (CA)
U of California, Riverside (CA)
U of California, Santa Barbara (CA)
U of California, Santa Cruz (CA)
U of Florida (FL)
U of Illinois at Urbana–Champaign (IL)
U of Mary Washington (VA)
U of Miami (FL)
U of Michigan (MI)
The U of North Carolina at Chapel Hill (NC)
U of North Florida (FL)
U of Puerto Rico at Bayamón (PR)
U of Richmond (VA)
U of Rochester (NY)
U of San Diego (CA)
The U of Texas at Austin (TX)
The U of Texas at Dallas (TX)
U of Tulsa (OK)
U of Virginia (VA)
The U of Western Ontario (ON, Canada)
U of Wisconsin–Madison (WI)
Vassar Coll (NY)
Villanova U (PA)
Wake Forest U (NC)
Washington & Jefferson Coll (PA)
Wheaton Coll (IL)
Wheaton Coll (MA)
Whitman Coll (WA)
Willamette U (OR)
Worcester Polytechnic Inst (MA)

MODERATELY DIFFICULT

More than 75 percent of the freshmen were in the top half of their high school class and scored over 1010 on the SAT or over 18 on the ACT; about 85 percent or fewer of the applicants were accepted.

Abilene Christian U (TX)
Acadia U (NS, Canada)
Adams State U (CO)
Adelphi U (NY)
Alaska Pacific U (AK)
Albany Coll of Pharmacy and Health Sciences (NY)
Alberta Coll of Art & Design (AB, Canada)
Albertus Magnus Coll (CT)
Albion Coll (MI)
Albright Coll (PA)
Alcorn State U (MS)
Alderson-Broaddus Coll (WV)
Alfred U (NY)
Alice Lloyd Coll (KY)
Allen Coll (IA)

Alliant Intl U–México City (Mexico)
Alma Coll (MI)
Alvernia U (PA)
Alverno Coll (WI)
American Acad of Art (IL)
American Jewish U (CA)
The American U of Paris (France)
The American U of Rome (Italy)
Anderson U (IN)
Anderson U (SC)
Andrews U (MI)
Angelo State U (TX)
Antioch U Santa Barbara (CA)
Appalachian State U (NC)
Arizona State U (AZ)
Arkansas State U (AR)
Arkansas Tech U (AR)
Asbury U (KY)
Ashland U (OH)
Assumption Coll (MA)
Auburn U (AL)
Auburn U at Montgomery (AL)
Augsburg Coll (MN)
Augustana Coll (IL)
Augustana Coll (SD)
Aurora U (IL)
Austin Peay State U (TN)
Averett U (VA)
Azusa Pacific U (CA)
Baker U (KS)
Baldwin Wallace U (OH)
Ball State U (IN)
Baptist Coll of Health Sciences (TN)
Barry U (FL)
Baylor U (TX)
Bay Path Coll (MA)
Beacon Coll (FL)
Becker Coll (MA)
Belhaven U (MS)
Bellarmine U (KY)
Belmont Abbey Coll (NC)
Belmont U (TN)
Bemidji State U (MN)
Benedictine Coll (KS)
Benedictine U (IL)
Berea Coll (KY)
Berklee Coll of Music (MA)
Berry Coll (GA)
Bethany Coll (WV)
Bethany Lutheran Coll (MN)
Bethel Coll (KS)
Bethel U (MN)
Blackburn Coll (IL)
Bloomfield Coll (NJ)
Bloomsburg U of Pennsylvania (PA)
Blue Mountain Coll (MS)
Bluffton U (OH)
Boise State U (ID)
The Boston Conservatory (MA)
Bowling Green State U (OH)
Bradley U (IL)
Bridgewater Coll (VA)
Bridgewater State U (MA)
Brigham Young U (UT)
Bryant U (RI)
Buena Vista U (IA)
Buffalo State Coll, State U of New York (NY)
Cabrini Coll (PA)
Cairn U (PA)
Caldwell Coll (NJ)
California Lutheran U (CA)
California Polytechnic State U, San Luis Obispo (CA)
California State Polytechnic U, Pomona (CA)
California State U, Chico (CA)
California State U, Dominguez Hills (CA)
California State U, East Bay (CA)
California State U, Fullerton (CA)
California State U, Long Beach (CA)
California State U, Los Angeles (CA)
California State U, Monterey Bay (CA)
California State U, Northridge (CA)
California State U, San Bernardino (CA)
California State U, San Marcos (CA)
California State U, Stanislaus (CA)
Calvin Coll (MI)

Campbellsville U (KY)
Canisius Coll (NY)
Capital U (OH)
Cardinal Stritch U (WI)
Carlos Albizu U, Miami Campus (FL)
Carlow U (PA)
Carroll Coll (MT)
Carson-Newman U (TN)
Castleton State Coll (VT)
Catawba Coll (NC)
The Catholic U of America (DC)
Cedar Crest Coll (PA)
Cedarville U (OH)
Centenary Coll of Louisiana (LA)
Central Coll (IA)
Central Connecticut State U (CT)
Central Methodist U (MO)
Central Michigan U (MI)
Chamberlain Coll of Nursing, Miramar (FL)
Chamberlain Coll of Nursing (MO)
Chamberlain Coll of Nursing (TX)
Champlain Coll (VT)
Chatham U (PA)
Chestnut Hill Coll (PA)
Christendom Coll (VA)
Christian Brothers U (TN)
The Citadel, The Military Coll of South Carolina (SC)
City Coll of the City U of New York (NY)
Clark Atlanta U (GA)
Clarke U (IA)
Clark U (MA)
Cleary U (MI)
Clemson U (SC)
Cleveland Inst of Art (OH)
Cleveland State U (OH)
Coastal Carolina U (SC)
Coe Coll (IA)
Cogswell Polytechnical Coll (CA)
The Coll at Brockport, State U of New York (NY)
Coll for Creative Studies (MI)
Coll of Charleston (SC)
The Coll of Idaho (ID)
Coll of Mount St. Joseph (OH)
The Coll of New Rochelle (NY)
Coll of Saint Benedict (MN)
Coll of Saint Elizabeth (NJ)
The Coll of Saint Rose (NY)
The Coll of St. Scholastica (MN)
Coll of the Ozarks (MO)
The Coll of Wooster (OH)
Colorado State U (CO)
Columbia Coll (MO)
Columbia Coll (SC)
Columbia Coll Chicago (IL)
Columbus Coll of Art & Design (OH)
Concordia Coll (MN)
Concordia Coll Alabama (AL)
Concordia Coll–New York (NY)
Concordia U (CA)
Concordia U (OR)
Concordia U (QC, Canada)
Concordia U Chicago (IL)
Concordia U, Nebraska (NE)
Concordia U Texas (TX)
Concordia U Wisconsin (WI)
Converse Coll (SC)
Corban U (OR)
Corcoran Coll of Art and Design (DC)
Cornell Coll (IA)
Covenant Coll (GA)
Creighton U (NE)
The Culinary Inst of America (NY)
Culver-Stockton Coll (MO)
Curry Coll (MA)
Dakota Wesleyan U (SD)
Dalhousie U (NS, Canada)
Dallas Baptist U (TX)
Daniel Webster Coll (NH)
Defiance Coll (OH)
DePaul U (IL)
DePauw U (IN)
DEREE—The American Coll of Greece (Greece)
DeSales U (PA)
Dillard U (LA)
Doane Coll (NE)

Dominican U (IL)
Dordt Coll (IA)
Drake U (IA)
Drew U (NJ)
Drury U (MO)
Duquesne U (PA)
East Carolina U (NC)
Eastern Illinois U (IL)
Eastern Mennonite U (VA)
Eastern Michigan U (MI)
East Tennessee State U (TN)
East Texas Baptist U (TX)
Eckerd Coll (FL)
Edgewood Coll (WI)
Edinboro U of Pennsylvania (PA)
Elizabeth City State U (NC)
Elizabethtown Coll (PA)
Elmira Coll (NY)
Elon U (NC)
Embry-Riddle Aeronautical U–Daytona (FL)
Embry-Riddle Aeronautical U–Prescott (AZ)
Emmanuel Coll (GA)
Emmanuel Coll (MA)
Endicott Coll (MA)
Evangel U (MO)
The Evergreen State Coll (WA)
Fairfield U (CT)
Fairleigh Dickinson U, Coll at Florham (NJ)
Fairleigh Dickinson U, Metropolitan Campus (NJ)
Farmingdale State Coll (NY)
Fashion Inst of Technology (NY)
Felician Coll (NJ)
FIDM/The Fashion Inst of Design & Merchandising, Los Angeles Campus (CA)
Five Towns Coll (NY)
Flagler Coll (FL)
Florida Ag and Mech U (FL)
Florida Atlantic U (FL)
Florida Coll (FL)
Florida Gulf Coast U (FL)
Florida Inst of Technology (FL)
Florida Intl U (FL)
Florida National U (FL)
Florida Southern Coll (FL)
Fort Lewis Coll (CO)
Framingham State U (MA)
Francis Marion U (SC)
Franklin Coll (IN)
Franklin Coll Switzerland (Switzerland)
Friends U (KS)
Frostburg State U (MD)
Furman U (SC)
Gallaudet U (DC)
Gannon U (PA)
Gardner-Webb U (NC)
Geneva Coll (PA)
George Fox U (OR)
George Mason U (VA)
Georgetown Coll (KY)
Georgia Coll & State U (GA)
Georgia Southern U (GA)
Georgia Southwestern State U (GA)
Georgia State U (GA)
Goddard Coll (VT)
Goldfarb School of Nursing at Barnes-Jewish Coll (MO)
Gonzaga U (WA)
Gordon Coll (MA)
Goshen Coll (IN)
Goucher Coll (MD)
Graceland U (IA)
Grace U (NE)
Grand Valley State U (MI)
Greenville Coll (IL)
Grove City Coll (PA)
Guilford Coll (NC)
Hallmark Coll of Technology (TX)
Hamline U (MN)
Hampden-Sydney Coll (VA)
Hampshire Coll (MA)
Hampton U (VA)
Hanover Coll (IN)
Harding U (AR)
Hardin-Simmons U (TX)
Hartwick Coll (NY)
Hawai`i Pacific U (HI)

HEC Montreal (QC, Canada)
Henderson State U (AR)
High Point U (NC)
Hiram Coll (OH)
Hofstra U (NY)
Hollins U (VA)
Holy Cross Coll (IN)
Holy Names U (CA)
Hood Coll (MD)
Hope Coll (MI)
Hope Intl U (CA)
Houghton Coll (NY)
Howard Payne U (TX)
Humboldt State U (CA)
Hunter Coll of the City U of New York (NY)
Huntington U (IN)
Husson U (ME)
Illinois Coll (IL)
Illinois Inst of Technology (IL)
Illinois State U (IL)
Immaculata U (PA)
Indiana State U (IN)
Indiana Tech (IN)
Indiana U Bloomington (IN)
Indiana U East (IN)
Indiana U of Pennsylvania (PA)
Indiana U–Purdue U Indianapolis (IN)
Indiana U South Bend (IN)
Indiana Wesleyan U (IN)
Inter American U of Puerto Rico, Aguadilla Campus (PR)
Inter American U of Puerto Rico, Fajardo Campus (PR)
Inter American U of Puerto Rico, Ponce Campus (PR)
Inter American U of Puerto Rico, San Germán Campus (PR)
Intl U in Geneva (Switzerland)
Iona Coll (NY)
Iowa State U of Science and Technology (IA)
Iowa Wesleyan Coll (IA)
Ithaca Coll (NY)
John Brown U (AR)
John Carroll U (OH)
John Jay Coll of Criminal Justice of the City U of New York (NY)
Johnson C. Smith U (NC)
Johnson State Coll (VT)
Judson Coll (AL)
Judson U (IL)
Juniata Coll (PA)
Kansas Wesleyan U (KS)
Kean U (NJ)
Keene State Coll (NH)
Kennesaw State U (GA)
Kent State U (OH)
Kentucky Christian U (KY)
Kentucky Wesleyan Coll (KY)
Keuka Coll (NY)
King Coll (TN)
The King's Coll (NY)
King's Coll (PA)
The King's U Coll (AB, Canada)
Kingswood U (NB, Canada)
Kutztown U of Pennsylvania (PA)
Kuyper Coll (MI)
LaGrange Coll (GA)
Lake Erie Coll (OH)
Lake Superior State U (MI)
Lancaster General Coll of Nursing & Health Sciences (PA)
Lander U (SC)
La Salle U (PA)
Lasell Coll (MA)
Lawrence Technological U (MI)
Lebanese American U (Lebanon)
Lebanon Valley Coll (PA)
Lehman Coll of the City U of New York (NY)
Le Moyne Coll (NY)
LeTourneau U (TX)
Lewis U (IL)
Lincoln Christian U (IL)
Lincoln Memorial U (TN)
Lindenwood U (MO)
Linfield Coll (OR)
Lipscomb U (TN)
Lock Haven U of Pennsylvania (PA)
Logan U–Coll of Chiropractic (MO)
Long Island U–Brooklyn Campus (NY)
Long Island U–C. W. Post Campus (NY)
Longwood U (VA)

Louisiana Coll (LA)
Louisiana State U and Ag and Mech Coll (LA)
Louisiana State U at Alexandria (LA)
Louisiana State U in Shreveport (LA)
Loyola U Chicago (IL)
Loyola U Maryland (MD)
Loyola U New Orleans (LA)
Lubbock Christian U (TX)
Luther Coll (IA)
Lynchburg Coll (VA)
Lynn U (FL)
Lyon Coll (AR)
Madonna U (MI)
Maharishi U of Management (IA)
Maine Maritime Acad (ME)
Malone U (OH)
Manchester U (IN)
Manhattan Coll (NY)
Manhattanville Coll (NY)
Mansfield U of Pennsylvania (PA)
Marian U (WI)
Marietta Coll (OH)
Marquette U (WI)
Marshall U (WV)
Mars Hill Coll (NC)
Martin Luther Coll (MN)
Mary Baldwin Coll (VA)
Marymount Manhattan Coll (NY)
Marymount U (VA)
Maryville Coll (TN)
Maryville U of Saint Louis (MO)
Marywood U (PA)
Massachusetts Coll of Liberal Arts (MA)
Massachusetts Maritime Acad (MA)
The Master's Coll and Sem (CA)
McDaniel Coll (MD)
McKendree U (IL)
McMurry U (TX)
McNally Smith Coll of Music (MN)
McNeese State U (LA)
Medaille Coll (NY)
Menlo Coll (CA)
Mercer U (GA)
Mercy Coll (NY)
Mercy Coll of Ohio (OH)
Mercyhurst U (PA)
Merrimack Coll (MA)
Messiah Coll (PA)
Miami U (OH)
Michigan State U (MI)
Middle Tennessee State U (TN)
Midwestern State U (TX)
Millersville U of Pennsylvania (PA)
Millikin U (IL)
Millsaps Coll (MS)
Mills Coll (CA)
Milwaukee School of Eng (WI)
Minnesota State U Mankato (MN)
Minnesota State U Moorhead (MN)
Minot State U (ND)
Misericordia U (PA)
Mississippi Coll (MS)
Mississippi State U (MS)
Mississippi U for Women (MS)
Missouri Baptist U (MO)
Missouri State U (MO)
Mitchell Coll (CT)
Molloy Coll (NY)
Monmouth Coll (IL)
Monmouth U (NJ)
Montana State U (MT)
Montana Tech of The U of Montana (MT)
Montclair State U (NJ)
Montreat Coll, Montreat (NC)
Moore Coll of Art & Design (PA)
Moravian Coll (PA)
Morehouse Coll (GA)
Morningside Coll (IA)
Morrisville State Coll (NY)
Mount Allison U (NB, Canada)
Mount Mary Coll (WI)
Mount Mercy U (IA)
Mount Saint Mary Coll (NY)
Mount St. Mary's Coll (CA)
Mount St. Mary's U (MD)
Mount Vernon Nazarene U (OH)

Multnomah U (OR)
Murray State U (KY)
Naropa U (CO)
Nazareth Coll of Rochester (NY)
Nebraska Methodist Coll (NE)
Neumont U (UT)
Newberry Coll (SC)
New Jersey City U (NJ)
New Jersey Inst of Technology (NJ)
New Mexico Inst of Mining and Technology (NM)
New Mexico State U (NM)
New Saint Andrews Coll (ID)
The New School for Public Engagement (NY)
New York Inst of Technology (NY)
New York School of Interior Design (NY)
Niagara U (NY)
Norfolk State U (VA)
North Carolina Wesleyan Coll (NC)
North Central Coll (IL)
North Dakota State U (ND)
Northern Arizona U (AZ)
Northern Illinois U (IL)
Northland Coll (WI)
Northwest Christian U (OR)
Northwestern Coll (IA)
Northwestern Coll (MN)
Northwestern Oklahoma State U (OK)
Northwestern State U of Louisiana (LA)
Northwest Missouri State U (MO)
Northwest Nazarene U (ID)
Northwest U (WA)
Northwood U, Florida Campus (FL)
Northwood U, Michigan Campus (MI)
Northwood U, Texas Campus (TX)
Norwich U (VT)
Notre Dame de Namur U (CA)
Nova Southeastern U (FL)
Oakland U (MI)
Ohio Dominican U (OH)
Ohio U (OH)
Oklahoma Baptist U (OK)
Oklahoma State U (OK)
Old Dominion U (VA)
O'More Coll of Design (TN)
Oral Roberts U (OK)
Oregon Coll of Art & Craft (OR)
Oregon State U (OR)
Otis Coll of Art and Design (CA)
Ouachita Baptist U (AR)
Pace U (NY)
Pacific Lutheran U (WA)
Pacific Union Coll (CA)
Pacific U (OR)
Palm Beach Atlantic U (FL)
Park U (MO)
Paul Quinn Coll (TX)
Penn State Beaver (PA)
Penn State Brandywine (PA)
Penn State DuBois (PA)
Penn State Fayette, The Eberly Campus (PA)
Penn State Greater Allegheny (PA)
Penn State Hazleton (PA)
Penn State Lehigh Valley (PA)
Penn State Mont Alto (PA)
Penn State New Kensington (PA)
Penn State Schuylkill (PA)
Penn State Shenango (PA)
Penn State Wilkes-Barre (PA)
Penn State Worthington Scranton (PA)
Penn State York (PA)
Pennsylvania Coll of Art & Design (PA)
Philadelphia U (PA)
Piedmont Coll (GA)
Pine Manor Coll (MA)
Plymouth State U (NH)
Point Loma Nazarene U (CA)
Point Park U (PA)
Point U (GA)
Portland State U (OR)
Post U (CT)
Prescott Coll (AZ)
Principia Coll (IL)
Purchase Coll, State U of New York (NY)
Purdue U (IN)
Purdue U Calumet (IN)
Queens U of Charlotte (NC)

Quincy U (IL)
Quinnipiac U (CT)
Radford U (VA)
Ramapo Coll of New Jersey (NJ)
Randolph Coll (VA)
Randolph-Macon Coll (VA)
Regis Coll (MA)
Regis U (CO)
Research Coll of Nursing (MO)
Resurrection U (IL)
Rhode Island Coll (RI)
Rider U (NJ)
Ringling Coll of Art and Design (FL)
Ripon Coll (WI)
Rivier U (NH)
Roanoke Coll (VA)
Roberts Wesleyan Coll (NY)
Rochester Inst of Technology (NY)
Rockford Coll (IL)
Rockhurst U (MO)
Rocky Mountain Coll (MT)
Rocky Mountain Coll of Art + Design (CO)
Roger Williams U (RI)
Rollins Coll (FL)
Roosevelt U (IL)
Rosemont Coll (PA)
Rowan U (NJ)
Russell Sage Coll (NY)
Rutgers, The State U of New Jersey, Camden (NJ)
Rutgers, The State U of New Jersey, Newark (NJ)
Rutgers, The State U of New Jersey, New Brunswick (NJ)
Sacred Heart U (CT)
Saginaw Valley State U (MI)
St. Ambrose U (IA)
St. Andrews U (NC)
Saint Anselm Coll (NH)
St. Bonaventure U (NY)
Saint Charles Borromeo Sem, Overbrook (PA)
St. Edward's U (TX)
St. Francis Coll (NY)
St. John Fisher Coll (NY)
St. John's Coll (MD)
Saint John's U (MN)
St. John's U (NY)
Saint Joseph's Coll (IN)
St. Joseph's Coll, Long Island Campus (NY)
St. Joseph's Coll, New York (NY)
Saint Joseph's U (PA)
Saint Leo U (FL)
St. Louis Coll of Pharmacy (MO)
Saint Louis U (MO)
Saint Martin's U (WA)
Saint Mary-of-the-Woods Coll (IN)
Saint Mary's Coll (IN)
Saint Mary's Coll of California (CA)
St. Mary's U (TX)
Saint Mary's U of Minnesota (MN)
Saint Michael's Coll (VT)
St. Norbert Coll (WI)
St. Thomas Aquinas Coll (NY)
St. Thomas U (NB, Canada)
Saint Vincent Coll (PA)
Salisbury U (MD)
Salve Regina U (RI)
Samford U (AL)
Sam Houston State U (TX)
Samuel Merritt U (CA)
San Diego Christian Coll (CA)
San Diego State U (CA)
Sanford Coll of Nursing (ND)
San Francisco Art Inst (CA)
San Francisco State U (CA)
Santa Fe U of Art and Design (NM)
Savannah Coll of Art and Design (GA)
School of the Museum of Fine Arts, Boston (MA)
Schreiner U (TX)
Seattle Pacific U (WA)
Seattle U (WA)
Seton Hill U (PA)
Shenandoah U (VA)
Shepherd U (WV)
Shimer Coll (IL)
Shippensburg U of Pennsylvania (PA)
Siena Coll (NY)
Siena Heights U (MI)

Sierra Nevada Coll (NV)
Simmons Coll (MA)
Simon Fraser U (BC, Canada)
Simpson Coll (IA)
Simpson U (CA)
Slippery Rock U of Pennsylvania (PA)
Sonoma State U (CA)
Southeastern Louisiana U (LA)
Southeastern Oklahoma State U (OK)
Southeast Missouri State U (MO)
Southern Arkansas U–Magnolia (AR)
Southern California Inst of Architecture (CA)
Southern Connecticut State U (CT)
Southern Illinois U Carbondale (IL)
Southern Illinois U Edwardsville (IL)
Southern Methodist U (TX)
Southern New Hampshire U (NH)
Southern Oregon U (OR)
Southern Polytechnic State U (GA)
Southern Utah U (UT)
Southwest Baptist U (MO)
Spalding U (KY)
Spring Arbor U (MI)
Spring Hill Coll (AL)
State U of New York at Fredonia (NY)
State U of New York at Oswego (NY)
State U of New York at Plattsburgh (NY)
State U of New York Coll at Cortland (NY)
State U of New York Coll at Old Westbury (NY)
State U of New York Coll at Potsdam (NY)
State U of New York Coll of Technology at Alfred (NY)
State U of New York Coll of Technology at Delhi (NY)
State U of New York Inst of Technology (NY)
Stephen F. Austin State U (TX)
Stephens Coll (MO)
Sterling Coll (VT)
Stetson U (FL)
Stevenson U (MD)
Suffolk U (MA)
Sullivan Coll of Technology and Design (KY)
Susquehanna U (PA)
Sweet Briar Coll (VA)
Tabor Coll (KS)
Tarleton State U (TX)
Taylor U (IN)
Temple U (PA)
Texas A&M Intl U (TX)
Texas A&M U (TX)
Texas A&M U–Commerce (TX)
Texas A&M U–Kingsville (TX)
Texas Lutheran U (TX)
Texas State U–San Marcos (TX)
Texas Wesleyan U (TX)
Thomas More Coll (KY)
Tiffin U (OH)
Trent U (ON, Canada)
Trevecca Nazarene U (TN)
Trine U (IN)
Trinity Christian Coll (IL)
Trinity Coll of Nursing and Health Sciences (IL)
Troy U (AL)
Truman State U (MO)
Tuskegee U (AL)
Union Coll (KY)
Union Coll (NE)
Union U (TN)
Unity Coll (ME)
Université de Sherbrooke (QC, Canada)
U at Buffalo, the State U of New York (NY)
The U of Akron (OH)
The U of Alabama (AL)
The U of Alabama at Birmingham (AL)
The U of Arizona (AZ)
U of Bridgeport (CT)
The U of British Columbia–Okanagan (BC, Canada)
U of California, Merced (CA)
U of Central Arkansas (AR)
U of Central Florida (FL)
U of Charleston (WV)
U of Cincinnati (OH)
U of Colorado Boulder (CO)
U of Colorado Colorado Springs (CO)
U of Colorado Denver (CO)
U of Dallas (TX)
U of Delaware (DE)

U of Denver (CO)
U of Evansville (IN)
The U of Findlay (OH)
U of Georgia (GA)
U of Guelph (ON, Canada)
U of Hartford (CT)
U of Hawaii at Hilo (HI)
U of Hawaii at Manoa (HI)
U of Hawaii–West Oahu (HI)
U of Houston (TX)
U of Idaho (ID)
U of Illinois at Chicago (IL)
U of Illinois at Springfield (IL)
The U of Iowa (IA)
The U of Kansas (KS)
U of Kentucky (KY)
U of La Verne (CA)
U of Louisiana at Lafayette (LA)
U of Louisiana at Monroe (LA)
U of Louisville (KY)
U of Maine at Farmington (ME)
U of Maine at Machias (ME)
U of Maryland, Baltimore County (MD)
U of Maryland, Coll Park (MD)
U of Maryland Eastern Shore (MD)
U of Massachusetts Amherst (MA)
U of Massachusetts Boston (MA)
U of Massachusetts Dartmouth (MA)
U of Memphis (TN)
U of Michigan–Dearborn (MI)
U of Michigan–Flint (MI)
U of Minnesota, Crookston (MN)
U of Minnesota, Duluth (MN)
U of Minnesota, Twin Cities Campus (MN)
U of Mississippi (MS)
U of Missouri (MO)
U of Missouri–Kansas City (MO)
U of Missouri–St. Louis (MO)
U of Mobile (AL)
U of Montevallo (AL)
U of Mount Union (OH)
U of Nebraska at Kearney (NE)
U of Nebraska–Lincoln (NE)
U of Nevada, Las Vegas (NV)
U of Nevada, Reno (NV)
U of New Brunswick Fredericton (NB, Canada)
U of New Brunswick Saint John (NB, Canada)
U of New England (ME)
U of New Hampshire (NH)
U of New Hampshire at Manchester (NH)
U of New Haven (CT)
U of New Mexico (NM)
U of New Orleans (LA)
U of North Carolina at Asheville (NC)
The U of North Carolina at Charlotte (NC)
The U of North Carolina at Greensboro (NC)
The U of North Carolina at Pembroke (NC)
The U of North Carolina Wilmington (NC)
U of Northern Colorado (CO)
U of Northern Iowa (IA)
U of North Georgia (GA)
U of North Texas (TX)
U of Oklahoma (OK)
U of Oregon (OR)
U of Ottawa (ON, Canada)
U of Pittsburgh (PA)
U of Pittsburgh at Greensburg (PA)
U of Portland (OR)
U of Puerto Rico at Ponce (PR)
U of Puget Sound (WA)
U of Redlands (CA)
U of Rhode Island (RI)
U of St. Francis (IL)
U of Saint Joseph (CT)
U of Saint Mary (KS)
U of St. Thomas (MN)
U of St. Thomas (TX)
U of Science and Arts of Oklahoma (OK)
The U of Scranton (PA)
U of South Alabama (AL)
U of South Carolina (SC)
U of South Carolina Aiken (SC)
U of South Carolina Upstate (SC)
The U of South Dakota (SD)
U of Southern Indiana (IN)

INDEXES

U of Southern Maine (ME)
U of Southern Mississippi (MS)
U of South Florida (FL)
The U of Tampa (FL)
The U of Tennessee (TN)
The U of Tennessee at Chattanooga (TN)
The U of Tennessee at Martin (TN)
The U of Texas at Arlington (TX)
The U of Texas of the Permian Basin (TX)
The U of the Arts (PA)
U of the Cumberlands (KY)
U of the Incarnate Word (TX)
U of the Ozarks (AR)
U of the Sciences (PA)
U of Utah (UT)
U of Vermont (VT)
U of Washington, Bothell (WA)
U of Waterloo (ON, Canada)
U of West Florida (FL)
U of Windsor (ON, Canada)
U of Wisconsin–Eau Claire (WI)
U of Wisconsin–Green Bay (WI)
U of Wisconsin–La Crosse (WI)
U of Wisconsin–Milwaukee (WI)
U of Wisconsin–Parkside (WI)
U of Wisconsin–Stevens Point (WI)
U of Wisconsin–Stout (WI)
U of Wisconsin–Superior (WI)
U of Wyoming (WY)
Upper Iowa U (IA)
Utah State U (UT)
Utica Coll (NY)
Valdosta State U (GA)
Valparaiso U (IN)
Vaughn Coll of Aeronautics and Technology (NY)
Vermont Tech Coll (VT)
Virginia Polytechnic Inst and State U (VA)
Virginia Union U (VA)
Virginia Wesleyan Coll (VA)
Viterbo U (WI)
Wabash Coll (IN)
Waldorf Coll (IA)
Walla Walla U (WA)
Walsh U (OH)
Warner Pacific Coll (OR)
Wartburg Coll (IA)
Washington Coll (MD)
Washington State U (WA)
Watkins Coll of Art, Design, & Film (TN)
Waynesburg U (PA)
Webber Intl U (FL)
Webster U (MO)
Wells Coll (NY)
Wentworth Inst of Technology (MA)
Wesleyan Coll (GA)
Wesley Coll (DE)
West Chester U of Pennsylvania (PA)
Western Carolina U (NC)
Western Connecticut State U (CT)
Western Illinois U (IL)
Western Michigan U (MI)
Western Oregon U (OR)
Western State Colorado U (CO)
Western Washington U (WA)
Westfield State U (MA)
Westminster Coll (MO)
Westminster Coll (UT)
West Texas A&M U (TX)
West Virginia U (WV)
West Virginia Wesleyan Coll (WV)
Wheeling Jesuit U (WV)
Whitworth U (WA)
Widener U (PA)
Wilkes U (PA)
William Jewell Coll (MO)
William Paterson U of New Jersey (NJ)
William Peace U (NC)
William Penn U (IA)
Winthrop U (SC)
Wittenberg U (OH)
Woodbury U (CA)
Worcester State U (MA)
Xavier U (OH)
Xavier U of Louisiana (LA)
York Coll of Pennsylvania (PA)

York Coll of the City U of New York (NY)
Young Harris Coll (GA)

MINIMALLY DIFFICULT

Most freshmen were not in the top half of their high school class and scored somewhat below 1010 on the SAT or below 19 on the ACT; up to 95 percent of the applicants were accepted.

Adventist U of Health Sciences (FL)
AIB Coll of Business (IA)
Alabama State U (AL)
Alaska Bible Coll (AK)
American Coll of Thessaloniki (Greece)
Amridge U (AL)
Arizona Christian U (AZ)
Armstrong Atlantic State U (GA)
Avila U (MO)
Baker Coll of Clinton Township (MI)
Baker Coll of Port Huron (MI)
Barclay Coll (KS)
Barton Coll (NC)
Bay State Coll (MA)
Bethel Coll (IN)
Bethune-Cookman U (FL)
Bob Jones U (SC)
Bowie State U (MD)
Brevard Coll (NC)
Bryn Athyn Coll of the New Church (PA)
California Baptist U (CA)
California State U, Fresno (CA)
Caribbean U (PR)
Central Baptist Coll (AR)
Central Penn Coll (PA)
Central State U (OH)
Cheyney U of Pennsylvania (PA)
Chicago State U (IL)
Chowan U (NC)
Cincinnati Christian U (OH)
Claflin U (SC)
Clarion U of Pennsylvania (PA)
Clayton State U (GA)
Clearwater Christian Coll (FL)
Coll of Coastal Georgia (GA)
Coll of Saint Mary (NE)
Colorado Mesa U (CO)
Columbia Centro Universitario, Yauco (PR)
Columbia Coll Hollywood (CA)
Columbia Intl U (SC)
Columbus State U (GA)
Concordia U, St. Paul (MN)
Concord U (WV)
Cornerstone U (MI)
Crown Coll (MN)
Dakota State U (SD)
Darton State Coll (GA)
Davenport U, Grand Rapids (MI)
DeVry Coll of New York (NY)
DeVry U, Phoenix (AZ)
DeVry U, Pomona (CA)
DeVry U, Miramar (FL)
DeVry U, Orlando (FL)
DeVry U, Decatur (GA)
DeVry U, Chicago (IL)
DeVry U, Kansas City (MO)
DeVry U, North Brunswick (NJ)
DeVry U, Columbus (OH)
DeVry U, Fort Washington (PA)
DeVry U, Houston (TX)
DeVry U, Irving (TX)
DeVry U, Arlington (VA)
DeVry U, Federal Way (WA)
DeVry U Online (IL)
DigiPen Inst of Technology (WA)
Dunwoody Coll of Technology (MN)
East Central U (OK)
East-West U (IL)
EDP Coll of Puerto Rico, Inc. (PR)
Embry-Riddle Aeronautical U–Worldwide (FL)
Fairmont State U (WV)
Faith Baptist Bible Coll and Theological Sem (IA)
Faulkner U (AL)
Fayetteville State U (NC)
Ferris State U (MI)
Ferrum Coll (VA)

Fisher Coll (MA)
Florida Christian Coll (FL)
Franklin Pierce U (NH)
Goodwin Coll (CT)
Gordon State Coll (GA)
Grand View U (IA)
Hilbert Coll (NY)
Hodges U (FL)
Holy Family U (PA)
Indiana U Kokomo (IN)
Indiana U Northwest (IN)
Indiana U–Purdue U Fort Wayne (IN)
Indiana U Southeast (IN)
Jacksonville State U (AL)
Jamestown Business Coll (NY)
Jamestown Coll (ND)
Jarvis Christian Coll (TX)
Kentucky State U (KY)
Keystone Coll (PA)
Lakeland Coll (WI)
Lamar U (TX)
Lane Coll (TN)
Langston U (OK)
La Roche Coll (PA)
La Sierra U (CA)
Laurel U (NC)
Lees-McRae Coll (NC)
Lewis-Clark State Coll (ID)
Liberty U (VA)
Life U (GA)
Limestone Coll (SC)
Lindsey Wilson Coll (KY)
Lourdes U (OH)
Maple Springs Baptist Bible Coll and Sem (MD)
Marymount Coll, Palos Verdes, California (CA)
Metropolitan State U of Denver (CO)
Mid-Atlantic Christian U (NC)
Mid-Continent U (KY)
Mississippi Valley State U (MS)
Morehead State U (KY)
Mount Aloysius Coll (PA)
Mount Marty Coll (SD)
National U (CA)
Neumann U (PA)
Newbury Coll (MA)
New England Coll (NH)
New England School of Communications (ME)
Newman U (KS)
New Mexico Highlands U (NM)
North Carolina Central U (NC)
Northcentral U (AZ)
Northeastern Illinois U (IL)
Northern Michigan U (MI)
Northern State U (SD)
North Greenville U (SC)
Nyack Coll (NY)
Oakland City U (IN)
Ohio Valley U (WV)
Olivet Coll (MI)
Pacific Northwest Coll of Art (OR)
Paine Coll (GA)
Pittsburg State U (KS)
Polytechnic U of Puerto Rico (PR)
Purdue U North Central (IN)
Rasmussen Coll Appleton (WI)
Rasmussen Coll Aurora (IL)
Rasmussen Coll Bismarck (ND)
Rasmussen Coll Blaine (MN)
Rasmussen Coll Bloomington (MN)
Rasmussen Coll Brooklyn Park (MN)
Rasmussen Coll Eagan (MN)
Rasmussen Coll Fargo (ND)
Rasmussen Coll Fort Myers (FL)
Rasmussen Coll Green Bay (WI)
Rasmussen Coll Lake Elmo/Woodbury (MN)
Rasmussen Coll Land O' Lakes (FL)
Rasmussen Coll Mankato (MN)
Rasmussen Coll Mokena/Tinley Park (IL)
Rasmussen Coll Moorhead (MN)
Rasmussen Coll New Port Richey (FL)
Rasmussen Coll Ocala (FL)
Rasmussen Coll Ocala School of Nursing (FL)
Rasmussen Coll Rockford (IL)
Rasmussen Coll Romeoville/Joliet (IL)
Rasmussen Coll St. Cloud (MN)
Rasmussen Coll Tampa/Brandon (FL)

INDEXES

Rasmussen Coll Wausau (WI)
Regent U (VA)
Robert Morris U (PA)
Robert Morris U Illinois (IL)
Sage Coll of Albany (NY)
St. Gregory's U, Shawnee (OK)
Saint Joseph Sem Coll (LA)
Saint Louis Christian Coll (MO)
St. Thomas U (FL)
Salem State U (MA)
Shaw U (NC)
South Dakota State U (SD)
Southeastern U (FL)
Southern Methodist Coll (SC)
Southwestern Adventist U (TX)
Southwestern Coll (KS)
State U of New York Coll of Agriculture and Technology at
    Cobleskill (NY)
State U of New York Coll of Technology at Canton (NY)
State U of New York Empire State Coll (NY)
Sterling Coll (KS)
Stratford U (MD)
Sullivan U (KY)
Tennessee State U (TN)
Tennessee Wesleyan Coll (TN)
Texas Woman's U (TX)
Thomas U (GA)
Trident U Intl (CA)
Trinity Coll of Florida (FL)
Universidad Adventista de las Antillas (PR)
U of Alaska Fairbanks (AK)
U of Arkansas at Little Rock (AR)
U of Arkansas–Fort Smith (AR)
U of Central Oklahoma (OK)
U of Houston–Clear Lake (TX)
U of Houston–Victoria (TX)
U of Maine at Fort Kent (ME)
The U of Montana Western (MT)
U of Nebraska at Omaha (NE)
U of North Alabama (AL)
U of North Dakota (ND)
U of Pittsburgh at Bradford (PA)
U of Regina (SK, Canada)
The U of Texas at El Paso (TX)
U of the Virgin Islands (VI)
U of Washington, Tacoma (WA)
The U of West Alabama (AL)
U of West Georgia (GA)
Ursuline Coll (OH)
Villa Maria Coll of Buffalo (NY)
Virginia Intermont Coll (VA)
Virginia State U (VA)
Wayland Baptist U (TX)
Wayne State U (MI)
Western Kentucky U (KY)
West Liberty U (WV)
West Virginia State U (WV)
West Virginia U Inst of Technology (WV)
Wilberforce U (OH)
Wright State U (OH)

NONCOMPETITIVE

*Virtually all applicants were accepted regardless of high
school rank or test scores.*

Acad of Art U (CA)
American Baptist Coll of American Baptist Theological
    Sem (TN)
American Public U System (WV)
American U of Puerto Rico (PR)
Antioch U Midwest (OH)
Appalachian Bible Coll (WV)
Athabasca U (AB, Canada)
Athens State U (AL)
The Baptist Coll of Florida (FL)
Baptist Missionary Association Theological Sem (TX)
Baptist U of the Americas (TX)
Bismarck State Coll (ND)
Bluefield State Coll (WV)
Boston Architectural Coll (MA)
Bowling Green State U-Firelands Coll (OH)
Briercrest Coll (SK, Canada)
Calumet Coll of Saint Joseph (IN)
Cambridge Coll (MA)
Cameron U (OK)
Carlos Albizu U (PR)
Charter Oak State Coll (CT)
Chipola Coll (FL)
City U of Seattle (WA)
Cleveland Chiropractic Coll–Kansas City Campus (KS)
Coll of Biblical Studies–Houston (TX)
Coll of Staten Island of the City U of New York (NY)
Colorado Mountain Coll (CO)
Colorado Mountain Coll, Alpine Campus (CO)
Colorado Mountain Coll, Timberline Campus (CO)
Columbia Bible Coll (BC, Canada)
Columbia Centro Universitario, Caguas (PR)
Crossroads Coll (MN)
Dalton State Coll (GA)
Daytona State Coll (FL)
Delta State U (MS)
DeVry U, Westminster (CO)
Dominican Coll (NY)
Eastern New Mexico U (NM)
Emporia State U (KS)
Florida Gateway Coll (FL)
Fountainhead Coll of Technology (TN)
Franklin U (OH)
Global U (MO)
Grambling State U (LA)
Granite State Coll (NH)
Grantham U (MO)
Harris-Stowe State U (MO)
Hillsdale Free Will Baptist Coll (OK)
Holy Apostles Coll and Sem (CT)
Holy Trinity Orthodox Sem (NY)
Indian River State Coll (FL)
Intl Acad of Design & Technology (FL)
Jones Coll, Jacksonville (FL)
Jones Intl U (CO)
Kansas State U (KS)
Kent State U at Ashtabula (OH)
Kent State U at East Liverpool (OH)
Kent State U at Geauga (OH)
Kent State U at Salem (OH)
Kent State U at Stark (OH)

Kent State U at Trumbull (OH)
Kent State U at Tuscarawas (OH)
Lincoln U (MO)
Luther Rice U (GA)
Maranatha Baptist Bible Coll (WI)
Master's Coll and Sem (ON, Canada)
Mayville State U (ND)
Miami Dade Coll (FL)
Midland Coll (TX)
Missouri Western State U (MO)
Morris Coll (SC)
New England Inst of Technology (RI)
New York City Coll of Technology of the City U of New
    York (NY)
Nicholls State U (LA)
The Ohio State U at Lima (OH)
The Ohio State U at Marion (OH)
The Ohio State U–Mansfield Campus (OH)
The Ohio State U–Newark Campus (OH)
Ohio U–Chillicothe (OH)
Ohio U–Zanesville (OH)
Oklahoma Christian U (OK)
Oklahoma State U, Oklahoma City (OK)
Olympic Coll (WA)
Pacific States U (CA)
Palm Beach State Coll (FL)
Peirce Coll (PA)
Pennsylvania Coll of Technology (PA)
Pensacola State Coll (FL)
Polk State Coll (FL)
Potomac Coll (DC)
Potomac State Coll of West Virginia U (WV)
Presentation Coll (SD)
Rocky Mountain Coll (AB, Canada)
Rogers State U (OK)
Seminole State Coll of Florida (FL)
Shawnee State U (OH)
Southeastern Bible Coll (AL)
Southern Nazarene U (OK)
State Coll of Florida Manatee-Sarasota (FL)
Stratford U, Falls Church (VA)
Sul Ross State U (TX)
Texas Southern U (TX)
Thomas Edison State Coll (NJ)
Université du Québec en Outaouais (QC, Canada)
The U of Akron–Wayne Coll (OH)
U of Alaska Anchorage (AK)
U of Alaska Anchorage, Kenai Peninsula Coll (AK)
U of Great Falls (MT)
U of Guam (GU)
U of Houston–Downtown (TX)
U of Maryland U Coll (MD)
U of Pikeville (KY)
The U of Texas at Brownsville (TX)
The U of Texas–Pan American (TX)
U of the District of Columbia (DC)
The U of Toledo (OH)
Valley City State U (ND)
Vincennes U (IN)
Washburn U (KS)
Wayne State Coll (NE)
Weber State U (UT)
Wichita State U (KS)
Wilmington U (DE)
Youngstown State U (OH)

Cost Ranges

LESS THAN $2000

Colleges with Room and Board
United States Naval Acad (MD)

$2000–$3999

Colleges with No Room and Board or with Room Only
Global U (MO)
Seminole State Coll of Florida (FL)
State Coll of Florida Manatee-Sarasota (FL)
U of Puerto Rico at Bayamón (PR)
Valencia Coll (FL)

$4000–$5999

Colleges with No Room and Board or with Room Only
American U of Puerto Rico (PR)
Inter American U of Puerto Rico, Aguadilla Campus (PR)
Inter American U of Puerto Rico, Bayamón Campus (PR)
Inter American U of Puerto Rico, Fajardo Campus (PR)
Inter American U of Puerto Rico, Ponce Campus (PR)
Logan U–Coll of Chiropractic (MO)
Luther Rice U (GA)
New York City Coll of Technology of the City U of New York (NY)
U of Hawaii–West Oahu (HI)

$6000–$7999

Colleges with No Room and Board or with Room Only
American Public U System (WV)
Baker Coll of Clinton Township (MI)
Baker Coll of Port Huron (MI)
California State U, San Marcos (CA)
Carlos Albizu U (PR)
City Vision Coll (MO)
Cleveland Chiropractic Coll–Kansas City Campus (KS)
EDP Coll of Puerto Rico, Inc. (PR)
Embry-Riddle Aeronautical U–Worldwide (FL)
Harrison Middleton U (AZ)
Jones Coll, Jacksonville (FL)
Polytechnic U of Puerto Rico (PR)
U of Guam (GU) (room only)
U of Hawaii at Hilo (HI)
U of Medicine and Dentistry of New Jersey (NJ)
York Coll of the City U of New York (NY)

Colleges with Room and Board
Coll of the Ozarks (MO)
Midland Coll (TX)
Universidad Teol?a del Caribe (PR)

$8000–$9999

Colleges with No Room and Board or with Room Only
Columbia Centro Universitario, Caguas (PR)
Columbia Centro Universitario, Yauco (PR)
Northcentral U (AZ)
Northeastern Illinois U (IL)
U of Houston (TX)
Western Oregon U (OR)

Colleges with Room and Board
Baptist U of the Americas (TX)
Dalton State Coll (GA)
Inter American U of Puerto Rico, San Germán Campus (PR)

New Mexico Highlands U (NM)
Universidad Adventista de las Antillas (PR)

$10,000–$11,999

Colleges with No Room and Board or with Room Only
American Baptist Coll of American Baptist Theological Sem (TN) (room only)
Auburn U at Montgomery (AL) (room only)
Hunter Coll of the City U of New York (NY) (room only)
Jamestown Business Coll (NY)
New Saint Andrews Coll (ID)
Resurrection U (IL)
Sanford Coll of Nursing (ND)
U of Washington, Tacoma (WA)

Colleges with Room and Board
Alabama State U (AL)
American U in Bulgaria (Bulgaria)
Brigham Young U (UT)
The Coll of Saints John Fisher & Thomas More (TX)
Colorado Mountain Coll (CO)
Colorado Mountain Coll, Alpine Campus (CO)
Colorado Mountain Coll, Timberline Campus (CO)
Eastern New Mexico U (NM)
Elizabeth City State U (NC)
Minot State U (ND)
Mississippi U for Women (MS)
Rogers State U (OK)
The U of Montana Western (MT)
Utah State U (UT)
Valley City State U (ND)

$12,000–$13,999

Colleges with No Room and Board or with Room Only
Florida National U (FL)
Jones Intl U (CO)
Paier Coll of Art, Inc. (CT)
Potomac Coll (DC)

Colleges with Room and Board
Boise State U (ID)
Caribbean U (PR)
Concordia Coll Alabama (AL)
Concord U (WV)
Delta State U (MS)
Fairmont State U (WV)
Langston U (OK)
Midwestern State U (TX)
Mississippi Valley State U (MS)
Northern State U (SD)
Penn State Abington (PA)
Penn State Brandywine (PA)
Penn State DuBois (PA)
Penn State Fayette, The Eberly Campus (PA)
Penn State Lehigh Valley (PA)
Penn State Wilkes-Barre (PA)
Penn State Worthington Scranton (PA)
Penn State York (PA)
Saint Louis Christian Coll (MO)
Texas A&M U–Commerce (TX)
Texas Woman's U (TX)
U of Alaska Fairbanks (AK)
U of Arkansas–Fort Smith (AR)
U of Southern Indiana (IN)
U of Southern Mississippi (MS)
U of the District of Columbia (DC)
The U of West Alabama (AL)
U of Wisconsin–Platteville (WI)
Webb Inst (NY)
Western Carolina U (NC)

$14,000–$15,999

Colleges with No Room and Board or with Room Only
Baptist Coll of Health Sciences (TN) (room only)
Calumet Coll of Saint Joseph (IN)
Florida Christian Coll (FL) (room only)
National U (CA)
Rasmussen Coll Appleton (WI)
Rasmussen Coll Aurora (IL)
Rasmussen Coll Bismarck (ND)
Rasmussen Coll Fargo (ND)
Rasmussen Coll Fort Myers (FL)
Rasmussen Coll Green Bay (WI)
Rasmussen Coll Land O' Lakes (FL)
Rasmussen Coll Mokena/Tinley Park (IL)
Rasmussen Coll New Port Richey (FL)
Rasmussen Coll Ocala (FL)
Rasmussen Coll Rockford (IL)
Rasmussen Coll Romeoville/Joliet (IL)
Rasmussen Coll Tampa/Brandon (FL)
Rasmussen Coll Wausau (WI)
Stratford U, Newport News (VA)
U of California, Davis (CA)

Colleges with Room and Board
Alaska Bible Coll (AK)
California State U, Monterey Bay (CA)
Fort Lewis Coll (CO)
Frostburg State U (MD)
Minnesota State U Mankato (MN)
Mississippi State U (MS)
New Coll of Florida (FL)
Nicholls State U (LA)
Norfolk State U (VA)
Oklahoma State U (OK)
Texas A&M U–Kingsville (TX)
U of Arkansas at Little Rock (AR)
U of Maine at Fort Kent (ME)
U of Maine at Machias (ME)
U of Maryland Eastern Shore (MD)
U of Nebraska at Omaha (NE)
The U of North Carolina at Greensboro (NC)
U of North Georgia (GA)
U of South Alabama (AL)
U of South Florida (FL)
U of Wisconsin–Parkside (WI)
U of Wisconsin–Stevens Point (WI)
U of Wisconsin–Stout (WI)

$16,000–$17,999

Colleges with No Room and Board or with Room Only
Chamberlain Coll of Nursing, Miramar (FL)
Chamberlain Coll of Nursing (GA)
Chamberlain Coll of Nursing (IN)
Chamberlain Coll of Nursing (MO)
Chamberlain Coll of Nursing, Cleveland (OH)
Chamberlain Coll of Nursing (TX)
DeVry Coll of New York (NY)
DeVry U, Phoenix (AZ)
DeVry U, Pomona (CA)
DeVry U, Westminster (CO)
DeVry U, Miramar (FL)
DeVry U, Orlando (FL)
DeVry U, Decatur (GA)
DeVry U, Chicago (IL)
DeVry U, Kansas City (MO)
DeVry U, North Brunswick (NJ)
DeVry U, Columbus (OH)
DeVry U, Fort Washington (PA)
DeVry U, Houston (TX)
DeVry U, Irving (TX)
DeVry U, Arlington (VA)

DeVry U, Federal Way (WA)
DeVry U Online (IL)
Lourdes U (OH)
Rasmussen Coll Blaine (MN)
Rasmussen Coll Bloomington (MN)
Rasmussen Coll Brooklyn Park (MN)
Rasmussen Coll Eagan (MN)
Rasmussen Coll Lake Elmo/Woodbury (MN)
Rasmussen Coll Mankato (MN)
Rasmussen Coll Moorhead (MN)
Rasmussen Coll Ocala School of Nursing (FL)
Rasmussen Coll St. Cloud (MN)
Stratford U (MD)

Colleges with Room and Board

Ball State U (IN)
California State U, Dominguez Hills (CA)
California State U, Fresno (CA)
California State U, Long Beach (CA)
California State U, Los Angeles (CA)
Hillsdale Free Will Baptist Coll (OK)
James Madison U (VA)
Lamar U (TX)
Lock Haven U of Pennsylvania (PA)
Louisiana State U and Ag and Mech Coll (LA)
Mansfield U of Pennsylvania (PA)
Martin Luther Coll (MN)
Northern Michigan U (MI)
Park U (MO)
Saginaw Valley State U (MI)
Southern Oregon U (OR)
State U of New York Inst of Technology (NY)
U of Colorado Colorado Springs (CO)
U of Colorado Denver (CO)
The U of Iowa (IA)
U of Maine at Farmington (ME)
U of Michigan–Flint (MI)
U of Nevada, Las Vegas (NV)
U of North Carolina School of the Arts (NC)
U of North Texas (TX)
Western State Colorado U (CO)

$18,000–$19,999

Colleges with No Room and Board or with Room Only

AIB Coll of Business (IA) **(room only)**
Columbia Coll (MO)
Dunwoody Coll of Technology (MN)
Goodwin Coll (CT)
Villa Maria Coll of Buffalo (NY)

Colleges with Room and Board

Bob Jones U (SC)
Bridgewater State U (MA)
California Polytechnic State U, San Luis Obispo (CA)
California State Polytechnic U, Pomona (CA)
California State U, Fullerton (CA)
California State U, Northridge (CA)
Castleton State Coll (VT)
The Coll at Brockport, State U of New York (NY)
Humboldt State U (CA)
Jarvis Christian Coll (TX)
Louisiana Coll (LA)
Maranatha Baptist Bible Coll (WI)
Mid-Atlantic Christian U (NC)
Morrisville State Coll (NY)
Oakland U (MI)
Purchase Coll, State U of New York (NY)
State U of New York Coll at Cortland (NY)
State U of New York Coll of Technology at Alfred (NY)
Trinity Coll of Florida (FL)
U at Albany, State U of New York (NY)
The U of Arizona (AZ)
U of Hawaii at Manoa (HI)
U of Missouri–St. Louis (MO)
Western Connecticut State U (CT)

$20,000–$24,999

Colleges with No Room and Board or with Room Only

Central Methodist U (MO)
FIDM/The Fashion Inst of Design & Merchandising, Los Angeles Campus (CA)
Lancaster General Coll of Nursing & Health Sciences (PA)
Nebraska Methodist Coll (NE) **(room only)**
New England Inst of Technology (RI)
Pacific States U (CA) **(room only)**
Saint Francis Medical Center Coll of Nursing (IL) **(room only)**
Trinity Coll of Nursing and Health Sciences (IL)

Colleges with Room and Board

Bethune-Cookman U (FL)
Blackburn Coll (IL)
California State U, San Bernardino (CA)
Central Penn Coll (PA)
Cheyney U of Pennsylvania (PA)
Cincinnati Christian U (OH)
Cleveland State U (OH)
Dillard U (LA)
Grove City Coll (PA)
Husson U (ME)
Jamestown Coll (ND)
John Cabot U (Italy)
Judson Coll (AL)
Kentucky Christian U (KY)
Lee U (TN)
Michigan State U (MI)
Mississippi Coll (MS)
New England School of Communications (ME)
Oklahoma Christian U (OK)
Penn State Altoona (PA)
Penn State Beaver (PA)
Penn State Berks (PA)
Penn State Erie, The Behrend Coll (PA)
Penn State Greater Allegheny (PA)
Penn State Harrisburg (PA)
Penn State Hazleton (PA)
Penn State Mont Alto (PA)
Presentation Coll (SD)
Ramapo Coll of New Jersey (NJ)
Regent U (VA)
Rowan U (NJ)
Saint Leo U (FL)
Salem Intl U (WV)
San Diego State U (CA)
U of Delaware (DE)
U of Illinois at Chicago (IL)
U of Illinois at Springfield (IL)
U of Virginia (VA)
Vermont Tech Coll (VT)
Wilberforce U (OH)

$25,000–$29,999

Colleges with No Room and Board or with Room Only

Cabrini Coll (PA)
Cairn U (PA) **(room only)**
Cogswell Polytechnical Coll (CA) **(room only)**
East-West U (IL) **(room only)**
Goldey-Beacom Coll (DE) **(room only)**
Goldfarb School of Nursing at Barnes-Jewish Coll (MO)
Neumont U (UT) **(room only)**
O'More Coll of Design (TN)
Rocky Mountain Coll of Art + Design (CO)
Santa Fe U of Art and Design (NM)
Watkins Coll of Art, Design, & Film (TN) **(room only)**

Colleges with Room and Board

Alderson-Broaddus Coll (WV)
Allen Coll (IA)
Belhaven U (MS)
Bryn Athyn Coll of the New Church (PA)
Clearwater Christian Coll (FL)
Columbia Intl U (SC)
Concordia U, St. Paul (MN)
Crown Coll (MN)

Grand View U (IA)
Hampton U (VA)
Hilbert Coll (NY)
Kentucky Wesleyan Coll (KY)
Liberty U (VA)
Limestone Coll (SC)
Lincoln Memorial U (TN)
Oakland City U (IN)
Ohio Valley U (WV)
Ouachita Baptist U (AR)
Piedmont Coll (GA)
San Jose State U (CA)
Southern Nazarene U (OK)
Sterling Coll (KS)
Sullivan Coll of Technology and Design (KY)
Tuskegee U (AL)
Union Coll (NE)
U of California, Los Angeles (CA)
U of California, Merced (CA)
U of California, Riverside (CA)
U of California, Santa Barbara (CA)
U of California, Santa Cruz (CA)
U of Great Falls (MT)
U of Illinois at Urbana–Champaign (IL)
U of the Cumberlands (KY)
Waldorf Coll (IA)
Xavier U of Louisiana (LA)
York Coll of Pennsylvania (PA)

$30,000 AND OVER

Colleges with No Room and Board or with Room Only

Barry U (FL) **(room only)**
Beacon Coll (FL)
Creative Center (NE)
Illinois Inst of Technology (IL)
Moore Coll of Art & Design (PA) **(room only)**
New York School of Interior Design (NY) **(room only)**
Pacific Northwest Coll of Art (OR) **(room only)**
Samuel Merritt U (CA)
Southern California Inst of Architecture (CA)
Texas Christian U (TX)
U of Portland (OR) **(room only)**
Wartburg Coll (IA) **(room only)**

Colleges with Room and Board

Abilene Christian U (TX)
Acad of Art U (CA)
Agnes Scott Coll (GA)
Alaska Pacific U (AK)
Albright Coll (PA)
Alfred U (NY)
Alvernia U (PA)
American Jewish U (CA)
Anderson U (IN)
Anderson U (SC)
Asbury U (KY)
Augustana Coll (IL)
Aurora U (IL)
Avila U (MO)
Babson Coll (MA)
Bard Coll (NY)
Baylor U (TX)
Bellarmine U (KY)
Bethel Coll (IN)
Bethel Coll (KS)
Bradley U (IL)
Bridgewater Coll (VA)
Bryant U (RI)
Bucknell U (PA)
Butler U (IN)
Caldwell Coll (NJ)
Calvin Coll (MI)
Campbellsville U (KY)
Carnegie Mellon U (PA)
Catawba Coll (NC)
Central Coll (IA)
Centre Coll (KY)
Champlain Coll (VT)
Chapman U (CA)
Chatham U (PA)
Chestnut Hill Coll (PA)

Chowan U (NC)
Christendom Coll (VA)
Clarke U (IA)
Clarkson U (NY)
Clark U (MA)
Cleveland Inst of Art (OH)
Coe Coll (IA)
Coll for Creative Studies (MI)
The Coll of Idaho (ID)
Coll of Mount St. Joseph (OH)
The Coll of New Rochelle (NY)
The Coll of Saint Rose (NY)
The Coll of St. Scholastica (MN)
Coll of the Atlantic (ME)
Coll of the Holy Cross (MA)
Columbia Coll (SC)
Columbia Coll Hollywood (CA)
Concordia Coll (MN)
Concordia Coll–New York (NY)
Concordia U (CA)
Concordia U Chicago (IL)
Concordia U, Nebraska (NE)
Connecticut Coll (CT)
Corcoran Coll of Art and Design (DC)
Cornerstone U (MI)
Covenant Coll (GA)
Culver-Stockton Coll (MO)
Davidson Coll (NC)
DePauw U (IN)
DigiPen Inst of Technology (WA)
Dominican U (IL)
Drake U (IA)
Drew U (NJ)
Drury U (MO)
Duquesne U (PA)
Earlham Coll (IN)
Eastern Mennonite U (VA)
Eckerd Coll (FL)
Elizabethtown Coll (PA)
Elmira Coll (NY)
Embry-Riddle Aeronautical U–Daytona (FL)
Embry-Riddle Aeronautical U–Prescott (AZ)
Emerson Coll (MA)
Eugene Lang Coll The New School for Liberal Arts (NY)
Felician Coll (NJ)
Ferrum Coll (VA)
Fisher Coll (MA)
Franklin & Marshall Coll (PA)
Franklin Coll (IN)
Franklin Pierce U (NH)
Franklin W. Olin Coll of Eng (MA)
Gannon U (PA)
Geneva Coll (PA)
Gordon Coll (MA)
Goshen Coll (IN)
Goucher Coll (MD)
Graceland U (IA)
Guilford Coll (NC)
Hampshire Coll (MA)
Hardin-Simmons U (TX)
Hartwick Coll (NY)
Hawai`i Pacific U (HI)
Hendrix Coll (AR)
Hillsdale Coll (MI)
Holy Cross Coll (IN)
Hope Coll (MI)
Hope Intl U (CA)
Houghton Coll (NY)
Howard Payne U (TX)
Huntington U (IN)
Indiana Tech (IN)
Indiana Wesleyan U (IN)
Iona Coll (NY)
John Brown U (AR)
John Carroll U (OH)
The Johns Hopkins U (MD)

Judson U (IL)
The Juilliard School (NY)
Juniata Coll (PA)
Kansas Wesleyan U (KS)
Kenyon Coll (OH)
Keystone Coll (PA)
Knox Coll (IL)
Lafayette Coll (PA)
Lake Erie Coll (OH)
Le Moyne Coll (NY)
Lesley U (MA)
Lewis U (IL)
Lindsey Wilson Coll (KY)
Loyola U Chicago (IL)
Loyola U New Orleans (LA)
Luther Coll (IA)
Lynn U (FL)
Macalester Coll (MN)
Maharishi U of Management (IA)
Malone U (OH)
Manchester U (IN)
Manhattan Coll (NY)
Manhattanville Coll (NY)
Mannes Coll The New School for Music (NY)
Marietta Coll (OH)
Marquette U (WI)
Mars Hill Coll (NC)
Mary Baldwin Coll (VA)
Marymount Manhattan Coll (NY)
Marymount U (VA)
Maryville Coll (TN)
Marywood U (PA)
The Master's Coll and Sem (CA)
McDaniel Coll (MD)
McKendree U (IL)
Menlo Coll (CA)
Messiah Coll (PA)
Middlebury Coll (VT)
Mills Coll (CA)
Milwaukee School of Eng (WI)
Mitchell Coll (CT)
Monmouth Coll (IL)
Montreat Coll, Montreat (NC)
Mount Holyoke Coll (MA)
Mount Mary Coll (WI)
Mount Mercy U (IA)
Mount Saint Mary Coll (NY)
Mount St. Mary's Coll (CA)
Mount Vernon Nazarene U (OH)
Naropa U (CO)
Newberry Coll (SC)
Newbury Coll (MA)
New England Coll (NH)
The New School for Jazz and Contemporary Music (NY)
North Carolina Wesleyan Coll (NC)
Northland Coll (WI)
Northwest Christian U (OR)
Northwestern Coll (IA)
Northwestern Coll (MN)
Northwest Nazarene U (ID)
Northwood U, Florida Campus (FL)
Notre Dame de Namur U (CA)
Nova Southeastern U (FL)
Nyack Coll (NY)
Oglethorpe U (GA)
Oral Roberts U (OK)
Pacific Lutheran U (WA)
Pacific Union Coll (CA)
Palm Beach Atlantic U (FL)
Parsons The New School for Design (NY)
Patrick Henry Coll (VA)
Pine Manor Coll (MA)
Princeton U (NJ)
Principia Coll (IL)
Quincy U (IL)
Quinnipiac U (CT)

Regis U (CO)
Rhode Island School of Design (RI)
Rice U (TX)
Ripon Coll (WI)
Roanoke Coll (VA)
Robert Morris U Illinois (IL)
Roberts Wesleyan Coll (NY)
Rochester Inst of Technology (NY)
Rocky Mountain Coll (MT)
Rosemont Coll (PA)
St. Ambrose U (IA)
Saint Anselm Coll (NH)
St. Bonaventure U (NY)
St. Edward's U (TX)
St. John Fisher Coll (NY)
St. John's Coll (NM)
St. Louis Coll of Pharmacy (MO)
Saint Martin's U (WA)
Saint Mary's Coll of California (CA)
St. Mary's U (TX)
Saint Mary's U of Minnesota (MN)
Saint Michael's Coll (VT)
St. Thomas Aquinas Coll (NY)
San Diego Christian Coll (CA)
Sewanee: The U of the South (TN)
Shimer Coll (IL)
Siena Coll (NY)
Siena Heights U (MI)
Sierra Nevada Coll (NV)
Simmons Coll (MA)
Simpson Coll (IA)
Simpson U (CA)
Soka U of America (CA)
Southern Methodist U (TX)
Southern New Hampshire U (NH)
Southwestern Coll (KS)
Southwestern U (TX)
Stanford U (CA)
Stonehill Coll (MA)
Thomas Aquinas Coll (CA)
Thomas More Coll (KY)
Tiffin U (OH)
Trine U (IN)
Trinity Christian Coll (IL)
Tufts U (MA)
U of Denver (CO)
The U of Findlay (OH)
U of Hartford (CT)
U of La Verne (CA)
U of Puget Sound (WA)
U of Richmond (VA)
U of San Diego (CA)
U of Tulsa (OK)
Upper Iowa U (IA)
Ursuline Coll (OH)
Vaughn Coll of Aeronautics and Technology (NY)
Virginia Intermont Coll (VA)
Virginia Wesleyan Coll (VA)
Wabash Coll (IN)
Wagner Coll (NY)
Wake Forest U (NC)
Walla Walla U (WA)
Washington Coll (MD)
Washington U in St. Louis (MO)
Wellesley Coll (MA)
Wentworth Inst of Technology (MA)
Westminster Coll (UT)
West Virginia Wesleyan Coll (WV)
Wheaton Coll (MA)
William Jewell Coll (MO)
William Peace U (NC)
Wittenberg U (OH)
Worcester Polytechnic Inst (MA)
Xavier U (OH)
Yale U (CT)
Young Harris Coll (GA)

INDEXES

Advertisers Index

INDEXES

Alphabetical Listing of Colleges and Universities

INDEXES

INDEXES

INDEXES

INDEXES

INDEXES

Geographic Listing of Close-Ups

NOTES

NOTES

NOTES

NOTES

NOTES